Uncle John's
4-PLY BATHROOM READER

by
The Bathroom Readers' Institute

St. Martin's Press New York

The following permissions are from Uncle John's 1st Bathroom Reader.

"Flipper" originally appeared in *Animal Superstars*. Copyright © 1985, by John Javna. Reprinted by permission of the author.

"Politics of Oz" originally appeared in *The Utne Reader*, July/August 1988. Copyright © 1988, by Michael Dregni. Reprinted by permission of the author.

"Doo-Wop Sounds" originally appeared in *The Doo-Wop Sing-Along Notebook*. Copyright © 1985, by John Javna. Reprinted by permission of the author.

"Caveat Eater" Copyright © 1988, by David Goines. Reprinted by permission of the author.

"7 Cool Flicks," "10 Cool Books," and "The Hipster Saint" originally appeared in *The Catalog of Cool*. Copyright © 1982, by Gene Sculatti. Reprinted by permission of the author.

"Congressional Wit" and "Party Lines" originally appeared in *Will the Gentleman Yield?* Copyright © 1988, by Bill Hogan and Mike Hill. Reprinted by permission of the publisher.

"Riddles" originally appeared in *Riddles*. Copyright © 1983, by Mark Bryant. Reprinted by permission of the publisher.

 Printed in the United States of America. For information, address St. Martin's Press, 175 Fifth Avenue, New York, N.Y. 10010.

www.stmartins.com

Produced and packaged by Javnarama
Design by Javnarama

The Library of Congress has cataloged the hardcover edition as follows:

Bathroom Readers' Institute (N.Y.)
Uncle John's Bathroom Reader.
ISBN 978-0-312-31818-5 (hardcover)
ISBN 978-0-312-66841-9 (paper over board)
1. Wit and humor. I. Title.
PN6153.B28 1988
818'.5407

St. Martin's Press books may be purchased for educational, business, or promotional use. For information on bulk purchases, please contact Macmillan Corporate and Premium Sales Department at 1-800-221-7945, extension 5442, or write specialmarkets@macmillan.com.

10 9 8 7 6 5

"Our Anthem," "Louie, Louie," "Sounds of Silence," "Weird Inspirations," "One-Liners," "Rock Characters," "Five Beatles Songs," "Dead Man's Curve," and "The Magic Dragon" originally appeared in *Behind the Hits*, Copyright © 1985, by Bob Shannon and John Javna. Reprinted by permission of the authors.

"Elvis' Toothbrush" and "Celebrity Mania" originally appeared in *Meet the Stars*, Copyright © 1985, by Missy Laws. Reprinted by permission of Ross Books.

"M*A*S*H," "Andy Griffith Show," "Just the Facts," "I Love Lucy," "Star Trek," "Perry Mason," "Gilligan's Island," and "The Twilight Zone" originally appeared in *Cult TV*. Copyright © 1985, by John Javna. Reprinted by permission of the author.

"The Fabulous '60s," and "Birth of the Bikini" originally appeared in *60s!*. Copyright © 1983, by John Javna and Gordon Javna. Reprinted by permission of the authors.

THANK YOU

The Bathroom Readers' Institute sincerely thanks the people whose advice and assistance made this book possible.

John Javna
Gordon Javna
Bob Shannon
Stuart Moore
Rachel Blau
Andrea Sohn
Gordon Van Gelder
Co-op Type
Byron Brown
Donna McCrohan
Max Allan Collins
Eric Lefcowitz
Cynthia Robins
Peter Handel
Penelope Houston
Gene Sculatti
Michael Dregni
David Goines
Dr. Lisa Berlin
Jeff Abrahams
Steve Gorlick
Leslie Boies
Jack Mingo
Franz Ross
Sam Javna
Charlie Weimer
Stephen Louis
Carla Small
Lorrie Bodger
Gideon Javna
Dayna Macy
Reddy Kilowatt
Gene Novogrodsky
Bob Migdal
Betsy Joyce
Greg Small
Adrienne Levine
Jay Nitschke
Mike Goldfinger
Doug Burnet

[illegible]

[illegible]

[illegible]

[illegible]

THANK-YOU

[illegible]

[illegible]

Uncle John's

BATHROOM READER

INTRODUCTION

There are two kinds of people in the world—people who read in the bathroom, and people who don't.

People who *do,* share a few of the subtler joys and frustrations of life—e.g., the joy of discovering a really interesting article in the latest issue of a favorite magazine as you head to the head, or the frustration of trying to find something suitable to read...at the last minute. This isn't something we talk about, but it's understood.

People who *don't* read in the bathroom haven't got a clue about why people who do, do. This book isn't for them.

Uncle John's Bathroom Reader is the first book especially for people who love to read in the bathroom. It was conceived in 1987, when a group of socially active citizens in Berkeley, California realized that the publishing industry had plenty of books for every room of the house (bedside readers, cookbooks, coffee-table books, etc.) *except* the bathroom—where up to 60% of Americans read. It was clearly time for bathroom readers to come out of the water closet and "Say it loud, I read in there and I'm proud!"

Consequently, they formed The Bathroom Readers' Institute to fight for the rights of bathroom readers everywhere.

Under their sensitive guidance, *The Reader* has been specially designed with the needs of bathroom readers in mind: It's full of brief but interesting articles that can be read in a few seconds, or a few minutes. It covers a variety of subjects (so a reader never has to settle for the "same old thing"). And it's arranged so a reader can just flip it open to any page; no planning, no searching. We hope you enjoy it. As we say at the Bathroom Readers' Institute: "Go With the Flow."

CONTENTS

NOTE

Because the B.R.I. understands your reading needs, we've divided the contents by length as well as subject.

Short—a quick read

Medium—1 to 3 pages

Long—for those extended visits, when something a little more involved is required.

THE NAME GAME

Short

Medium

TOYLAND

Short

Medium

POP-POURRI

Short

Medium

Long

MOUTHING OFF

Short

STRANGE DEATHS

Medium

MYTH AMERICA

Short

Medium

FOOD FOR THOUGHT

Short

Medium

Long

WORDPLAY

Short

Medium

AMUSEMENTS

Short

SCIENCE

Short

Medium

Long

PRIME-TIME PROVERBS

Short

UNSUNG COOL

Short

Medium

THE PERSONAL COLUMNS

Short

BANNED IN THE USA

Short

Medium

BATHROOM NEWS

Medium

JUST FOR FUN

Short

ENTERTAINMENT

Short

Medium

Long

PRIVATE LIVES

Short

Medium

Long

WINNERS & LOSERS

Medium

Long

HEROES & VILLAINS

Medium

Long

MISCELLANEOUS

Short

Medium

Long

PLAYING AROUND

Medium

IT'S A CONSPIRACY

Medium

Long

OUR ANTHEM

Ever have people banging on the bathroom door, telling you to "hurry up and get out of there"? Then you'll be glad to know your response has already been immortalized in a classic soul tune. From Behind the Hits, *by Bob Shannon.*

In the '60s, Memphis' Stax Records had the most talented lineup of studio musicians and singers in the south. There was Otis Redding, Rufus Thomas, Booker T. and the M.G.'s, Carla Thomas, Eddie Floyd, and Sam and Dave.

Sam Moore and Dave Prater joined the Stax family in 1965. They were assigned to the writing/production team of Dave Porter and Isaac Hayes, and the partnership clicked big, producing a string of near-perfect Soul masterpieces. First to hit the charts was "You Don't Know Like I Know"; and their first big hit was "Soul Man." In between was a song that almost made the pop Top 20—a record that would have been a much bigger hit if it hadn't been for radio censorship.

White Top 40 stations were just getting used to playing black Soul records in 1966 when "Hold On, I'm Comin'" was released. Because of its suggestive title, many radio stations refused to air it at all. And those that did often made the situation worse as deejays drooled over the sexual implications of the song. In reality, the lyrics were simply about one lover giving the other support "when times are bad." "Coming" just meant "coming to the rescue." Sam and Dave's macho, boastful delivery and sly laughs throughout the song didn't help their case, although they helped to make it a great record. Stax changed the title to "Hold On, I'm A-Comin'" to placate the FCC, but the damage was already done.

If only the radio jocks had known the true story of its conception! You see, Hayes and Porter were in the studio, writing some songs. Porter left for a minute, and when he didn't come back, an impatient Hayes went looking for him. His room-to-room search finally ended up at—you guessed it—the men's room door. Porter was taking his time in there, and Hayes yelled at him to hurry up. Porter's irritated reply: "Hey man, hold on. I'm comin'." And a song was born.

The most valuable bathtub in the world is valued at $5 million. It is solid gold.

BATHROOM LORE

It seems appropriate to begin this volume with a little background on the room you're probably sitting in right now.

THE FIRST BATHROOM

The idea of a separate room for the disposal of "bodily waste" goes back at least 10,000 years (8,000 B.C.). On Orkney, an island off the coast of Scotland, the inhabitants combined stone huts with a drainage system that carried the waste directly into a nearby stream.

THE FIRST SOPHISTICATED PLUMBING

• Bathtubs dating back to 2000 B.C. have been found on the island of Crete (where there's also evidence of the first flush toilet). Considering they were built almost 4,000 years ago, the similarity to modern baths is startling.

• Around 1500 B.C., elite Egyptians had hot and cold running water; it came into their homes through a system of copper tubing or pipes.

THE FIRST SOCIAL BATHING

The ancient Romans took their bathing seriously, building public facilities wherever they settled—including London. The more elaborate of these included massage salons, food and wine, gardens, exercise rooms, and in at least one case, a public library. Co-ed bathing was not uncommon, nor frowned upon.

BACK TO FILTH

• As Christianity became increasingly powerful, techniques of plumbing and waste disposal—and cleanliness in general—were forgotten; only in monasteries was this knowledge preserved.

• For hundreds of years people in Europe basically stopped washing their bodies, in large part because nudity—even for reasons of health or hygiene—was regarded as sinful by the Church.

• In some cases a reverence for dirt arose in its place. St. Francis of Assisi, for example, believed "dirtiness was an insignia of holiness."

• Upper-class citizens tried to cover up the inevitable body odors with clothes and perfume, but the rest of the population suffered with the rank smells of filth.

CHAMBER POTS AND STREET ETIQUETTE

• Until the early 1800s, Europeans relieved themselves in chamber pots, outhouses, streets, alleys, and anywhere else they happened to feel like it.

• It was so common to relieve oneself in public that people were concerned about how to behave if they noticed acquaintances "urinating or defecating" on the street. Proper etiquette: Act like you don't see them.

• Chamber pots were used at night, or when it was too cold to go outside. Their contents were supposed to be picked up once a day by a "waste man," who carted the community's leavings to a public cesspool.

• But frequently, the chamber pot was surreptitiously dumped at night, which made it dangerous to go strolling in the evening.

DISEASE AND CHANGE

The lack of bathing took an enormous toll on the European population of the Middle Ages, as epidemics caused by unsanitary living conditions became matter-of-fact. But in the 1830s, a London outbreak of Cholera—a disease the English believed could only be contracted by inferior races—finally convinced the English government to put its power behind public sanitation. Over the next 50 years, the British constructed major new public facilities that set the pace for the rest of the world.

THE MODERN FLUSH TOILET

The modern flush toilet was invented by an Englishman named Alexander Cumming in 1775. Cumming's toilet emptied directly into a pipe which then carried the undesirable matter to a cesspool. Other toilets had done this, too; but Cumming's major improvement was the addition of a "stink trap" that kept water in the pipe, and thus blocked odor.

About 10 billion cigarettes are produced annually throughout the world.

THOMAS CRAPPER

It is widely believed that an Englishman named Thomas Crapper invented the toilet. Not true. That was a hoax.

HEAD FOR THE JOHN

• In the mid-1500s in England, a chamber pot was referred to as a *Jake*. A hundred years later, it became a *John*, or *Cousin John*. In the mid-1800s, it was also dubbed a *Joe*.
• That still may not be the source of the term *John* for the bathroom—it may date to the 1920s, when Men's and Ladies' rooms became common in public places. They were also referred to as *Johns* and *Janes*—presumably after John and Jane Doe.
• The term *potty* comes from the pint-sized chamber pot built for kids.

BATHROOMS

• The bathroom we know—with a combination toilet and bath—didn't exist until the 1850s. And then only for the rich.
• Until then, the term bathroom—which came into use in the 1820s or 1830s—meant, literally, a room with a bathtub in it.

A FEW AMERICAN FIRSTS

• First American hotel with indoor modern bathrooms: The Tremont House in Boston, 1880s.
• First toilet in the White House: 1825, installed for John Quincy Adams (leading to a new slang term for toilet—a *quincy*).
• First city with modern waterworks: Philadelphia, 1820.
• First city with a modern sewage system: Boston, 1823.

THE FIRST TOILET PAPER

• Toilet paper was introduced in America in 1857, as a package of loose sheets. But it was too much like the paper Americans already used—the Sears catalog. It flopped.
• In 1879, an Englishman named Walter Alcock created the first perforated rolls of toilet paper. He couldn't sell them.
• In 1880, things got rolling. Philadelphia's Scott Brothers saw the potential for a product that would constantly have to be replaced and introduced Waldorf Tissue (later ScotTissue), which was discreetly sold in plain brown wrappers. The timing was right—there were enough bathrooms to make them a success.

Every day, people around the world drink more than 300 million Cokes.

PRIME-TIME PROVERBS

TV's comments about everyday life in America. From Prime Time Proverbs, *a forthcoming book by Jack Mingo.*

ON FOOD:

"Why am I bothering to eat this chocolate? I might as well apply it directly to my thighs."

—Rhoda Morgenstern,
Mary Tyler Moore Show

Gracie: "The reason I put the salt in the pepper shaker and the pepper in the salt shaker is that people are always getting them mixed up. Now when they get mixed up, they'll be right.."

—Burns and Allen

"Six years, and you haven't learned *anything*—it's *white wine* with Hershey Bars."

—Harvey Barnes,
Making the Grade

ON THE BATTLE OF THE SEXES:

"Early to bed, early to rise, and your girl goes out with other guys."

—Bob Collins,
Love That Bob

"Carmine and I have an understanding. I'm allowed to date other men, and he's allowed to date ugly women."

—Shirley Feeney,
Laverne and Shirley

ON MARRIED LIFE:

Edith: "Do you like bein' alone with me?"
Archie: "Certainly I like being alone with you. What's on television?"

—All in the Family

ON MONEY:

"There are two things [I won't do for money]. I won't kill for it and I won't marry for it. Other than that, I'm open to about anything."

—Jim Rockford,
The Rockford Files

CURRENT EVENTS:

"What's this I hear about making Puerto Rico a steak? The next thing they'll be wanting is a salad, and then a baked potato."

—Emily Litella
(Gilda Radner)
Saturday Night Live

Only 1/4 of the American population lives in rural areas.

THE FABULOUS '60S

Odds and ends about America's favorite decade, from 60s!, by John and Gordon Javna.

CUT 'EM SOME SLACKS. It wasn't considered "ladylike" to wear pants in the '60s. In 1968, for example, *Women's Wear Daily* polled several employers about it. Some of the comments: Macy's, New York: "We don't allow it"; First National Bank of Boston: "We would allow our women employees to wear pants if they continue to act like women"; Citizens and Southern National Bank, Atlanta: "We would not want to be among the first...."

OFF WITH HER PANTS. In 1969 Judy Carne, a star of "Laugh-In," visited the posh "21" Club wearing a "tunic-topped pants suit." When the management refused to let her in because of its policy against women in pants, she took off her pants, checked them in the checkroom, and sailed off into the dining room wearing only her tunic—barely long enough to be called a micro-mini-skirt. The club changed its policy on pants the next day.

WHICH DOPE? Spiro Agnew's daughter was suspended from school while they investigated her for smoking dope.

FAST FOOD: A few '60s fast-food flops you never ate at: Johnny Carson's "Here's Johnny's!" restaurants; Mahalia Jackson's Glori-Fried Chicken; Mickey Mantle's Southern Cooking; Tony Bennett Spaghetti House; Alice's Restaurants.

TV OR NOT TV? In 1967, a lady went on "Let's Make a Deal" dressed as a little girl holding a baby bottle. Monty Hall took away her baby bottle and said, "All right, for two hundred dollars, show me another nipple."

WHY WE DON'T OWN THE MOON: The U.S. waived any claim to the moon by signing the Treaty on Exploration and Use of Outer Space in 1967. This established the lunar surface as the property of all mankind.

One slice to go: America's first pizzeria opened in New York City in 1895.

FAMOUS FOR 15 MINUTES

Andy Warhol was prophetic when he said, "In the future, everyone will be famous for 15 minutes." Here are a few examples of what we have to look forward to.

THE STAR: Annabella Battistella, a.k.a Fanne Foxe, "The Argentine Firecracker," voluptuous Latin "exotic dancer."

THE HEADLINE: "Stripper sinks political career."

WHAT HAPPENED: Late one night in October 1972, a suspicious Washington, D.C. cop pulled over an erratically moving vehicle. The inebriated driver turned out to be Congressman Wilbur Mills of Arkansas, a 36-year veteran of the House and chairman of its powerful Ways and Means Committee. In the car with him were his next-door neighbor, 38-year-old Annabella Battistella (a stripper known on stage as Fanne Foxe), and some friends—all headed home after a night of carousing. At some point during the confrontation—no one is sure exactly why—Annabella suddenly ran screaming from the car and jumped or slipped into the Tidal Basin, a shallow section of the Potomac river. The event became front page news, and it was revealed that the staid Mills—happily married for 40 years—had been having an affair with Fanne.

Shock waves rippled through Washington, but Fanne cashed in immediately, booking a tour of East Coast strip joints as "the Washington Tidal Basin Girl" ("You've read about her, now see her in person!"). She claimed to be making $3,000 a week, and that a "big toy company" was planning a Fanne doll. She even got the Harvard Republican Club's "Newcomer of the Year" award.

THE AFTERMATH: Mills' career was jeopardized, but it seemed as though he'd pull through—until two months later, when he suddenly appeared onstage in a seedy Boston strip joint, and gave Fanne a kiss. That was it. "I'm a sick man," he told colleagues when they challenged his authority. Mills was hospitalized, and Fanne continued to take it off, but faded into obscurity.

Walter Cavanaugh, "Mr. Plastic Fantastic," has 1,196 different valid credit cards.

THE STAR: Scott Halprin, a San Francisco teenager.

THE HEADLINE: "Rock Star for a Night: Kid From Audience Steps Forward."

WHAT HAPPENED: In 1973 the Who were in San Francisco playing the first show of what was to be a major U.S. tour. As the opening bars of "Won't Get Fooled Again" burst from the massive sound system at the Cow Palace, the group's unpredictable drummer, Keith Moon, suddenly slumped over, totally out of it, unable to hit another cymbal. Moon was escorted offstage and returned shortly after, seemingly revived. But a few minutes later, he collapsed again, this time completely unable to continue.

In a bizarre fantasy-come-true, the Who's leader, Pete Townsend, went to the edge of the stage and asked for volunteers. A 19-year-old named Scott Halprin bounded forward...and soon he found himself playing "Magic Bus" and "My Generation." "It happened really quick," said Halprin later. "I didn't have time to think about it and get nervous. I really admired their stamina...I only played three numbers and I was dead."

THE AFTERMATH: Keith Moon recovered (at least for a few more years). Halprin didn't become a star, but he was the subject of a small piece in *Rolling Stone*. "That drummer," said lead singer Roger Daltry, "was really good."

THE STAR: Peg Entwistle, aspiring actress.

THE HEADLINE: "Starlet Plunges to Death in Desperate Dive."

WHAT HAPPENED: Young Peg Entwistle had been a success on the Broadway stage, and she arrived in Hollywood expecting to build a career in motion pictures. Unfortunately, it didn't work out. So in September of 1932, she decided to end it all. She did it in the grand Cecil B. DeMille style: she climbed to the top of the 50-foot-high H in the "Hollywood" sign above the city, and leaped to her death. It made national news, although it was a little too late to do her career any good.

AFTERMATH: Hollywood, "the city of broken dreams," had a new fad. Disappointed would-be movie stars continued to take their own lives by jumping off the sign.

The biggest recorded bubble ever blown with bubble gum was 22 inches in diameter.

THE STAR: Sacheen Littlefeather, a Native American political activist, and an Oscar stand-in for Marlon Brando.

THE HEADLINE: "Brando Refuses Oscar, Sends Surrogate in Protest Over Indian Rights."

WHAT HAPPENED: In 1972, Marlon Brando was nominated for a Best Actor Oscar for his role in *The Godfather*. Brando was becoming increasingly politicized and at the time, the plight of the American Indians was his primary interest. So he arranged to have a young activist named Sacheen Littlefeather accept the award (if he won) in his place, handing her a three-page speech to read. When the time came, dressed in full Indian regalia, Ms. Littlefeather shocked the audience and TV network—and Roger Moore, the man trying to present it—by refusing the award for Brando and reading a short speech (the Academy refused to allow the long one) which decried the treatment of the Indian in Hollywood films.

AFTERMATH: Littlefeather had regularly played bit parts in films herself, but after the incident found herself blacklisted for several years. She was also harassed by both the FBI and unknown individuals. She is still an activist, but feels bitter about the experience.

THE STAR: Eddie Gaedel, a 3' 7" midget.

THE HEADLINE: "Small Man in Big Leagues: A Veeck Stunt."

WHAT HAPPENED: It was a Sunday doubleheader with the Detroit Tigers on August 19, 1951, and the St. Louis Browns were celebrating the 50th anniversary of the American League. Between games, Brown owner Bill Veeck wheeled a huge cake out onto the field, and out popped Eddie Gaedel, wearing a Browns uniform with the number 1/8 on it. During the first inning of the next game, Gaedel popped out of the dugout and informed the umpire he was pinch hitting. Challenged, Veeck produced a valid contract. Pitching is difficult as it is, but a 3'7" person has a strike zone of about 18 inches. Gaedel walked on four straight pitches. He then left for a pinch-runner.

AFTERMATH: Gaedel made a quick 100 bucks for his appearance, and American League president Will Harridge issued a solemn declaration barring midgets from baseball, and warning Veeck not to try any similar stunts.

Life span: The oldest known goldfish lived to 41 years of age. Its name was Fred.

WORDPLAY

Here are the origins of a few common phrases.

FALL GUY
Meaning: Someone who takes the blame.
Background: The first people to "fall" were Adam and Eve, who fell from grace and were booted out of Eden. In England, this gave rise to the term "take a fall," meaning "to be arrested," often in conjunction with taking the rap for someone else. Someone who took a fall was known as a "fall guy."

BETWEEN A ROCK AND A HARD PLACE
Meaning: In trouble, stuck with two undesirable choices.
Background: This is an updated version of an expression dating back to the Ancient Greeks, "between Scylla and Charybdis." The former was a large rock that endangered seamen in the Straits of Messina, the latter was a potentially fatal whirlpool on the opposite side. Sailors tried to avoid sailing between them. It is speculated that Charybdis is known as "a hard place" partly because it's so hard to pronounce.

KEEP YOUR SHIRT ON
Meaning: Stay calm.
Background: Probably from the age-old response to a challenge to fight. You rip your shirt off to fight, and you keep it on if you're avoiding one.

SWAN SONG
Meaning: A final, best performance.
Background: Though in actuality swans don't make many sounds, in legends the bird was believed to give a final, wonderful song just before it died.

STOOL PIGEON
Meaning: An informer, a traitor.
Background: To catch passenger pigeons (now extinct), hunters would nail a pigeon to a stool. Its alarmed cries would attract other birds, and the hunters would shoot them by the thousand. The poor creature that played the traitor was a "stool pigeon."

Weighty stuff: The heaviest dog on record was a St. Bernard that weighed 310 pounds.

THE TWILIGHT ZONE

Picture, if you will, a 5-foot, 5-inch ex-boxer who produced, created, and often wrote what may be the best television program in history.
From Cult TV, *by John Javna.*

"You're traveling through another dimension, a dimension not only of sight and sound, but of mind; a journey into a wondrous land whose boundaries are that of the imagination. That's the signpost up ahead! Your next stop...the Twilight Zone!"

HOW IT STARTED

In the mid-'50s, Rod Serling was an award-winning writer for the celebrated TV anthology series, "Playhouse 90." However, he became frustrated with the inane changes sponsors insisted on making to his scripts. One sponsor (an auto maker) demanded that the Chrysler building be painted out of a scene. Another (a tobacco company) deleted the word "lucky" from a script because Lucky Strikes weren't their brand. And when an insurance company refused to allow a central character to commit suicide, Serling quit. People were shocked that the outspoken playwright left a cushy job at one of TV's most prestigious programs to write and produce his own "fantasy" show. But Serling knew exactly what he was doing. By operating under the cover of fantasy, Serling could get his message across without getting it censored.

In 1957, he reworked a script that had aired years before on a local Cincinnati station, and presented it to CBS as the "Twilight Zone" pilot. CBS wasn't interested, but Desilu Productions aired it as an episode of "Desilu Playhouse." It generated more viewer response than any other show that season, and CBS decided to take another look. They requested a second script from Serling ("The Happy Place"), which was deemed too depressing. So he wrote a third, this time keeping the concept simple and straightforward. In February, 1959, "Where Is Everybody" was accepted by CBS as a pilot; in March, Gener-

According to *Guinness*, an Arkansas boy grew a 260-lb. watermelon in 1985.

al Foods bought it; and on October 2, 1959, living rooms across America entered "The Twilight Zone."

INSIDE FACTS

The Amazing Serling: In real life, Rod Serling was a nervous wreck in front of the camera. It was his idea to introduce and close the episodes himself, but he remained an uneasy, sweating mess right through the last show. "Only my laundress really knows how frightened I am," he said of his appearances.

He was incredibly productive. He worked 18-hour days, and could turn out a completed "Twilight Zone" script in around 35 hours—much of it dictated into a tape recorder while he sat by the swimming pool of his L.A. home. In the first season, he wrote a phenomenal 80% of the scripts; by the fifth season, he was still producing about 50% of them.

Sadly, Serling died during open heart surgery in 1975. He was 50 years old.

Calling All Writers. One of Serling's biggest complaints about network procedure was that new talent was constantly being smothered by the system. So he invited amateur writers to send in their manuscripts if they thought they were good enough. It was an interesting lesson—he received 14,000 scripts in five days. Of the 500 that Serling and his staff got around to reading, only two of those were of "professional quality." Did he use those two? He couldn't—they "didn't fit the show."

Name Game. Fans think that Rod Serling invented the term "Twilight Zone." So did Serling. He'd never heard anyone use it before, so he assumed he'd created it. He was in for a surprise: after the show debuted, he was informed that Air Force pilots used the phrase to describe "a moment when a plane is coming down on approach and it cannot see the horizon."

Belated Thanks. Although it was considered a "prestige" show, "The Twilight Zone" never had good enough ratings to excite advertisers. Sometimes, in fact, sponsors didn't even understand what the show was about. In the first season, one of the sponsors called up CBS every Monday to demand an explanation of Friday's show. "And then," said Serling, "he demanded an explanation of the explanation."

According to one survey, 2/3 of the men in America believe in love at first sight.

THE WRONG IDEA

Some words try their best to mislead you.

French Fries actually came from Belgium, not France.

Fairy tales are seldom about fairies.

One horsepower represents the amount of power it takes to move 550 pounds one foot in one second. Actually, it would take one-and-a-half horses to pull off this feat.

Your **funny bone** is a nerve, not a bone.

Fabric softeners grease and lubricate the fibers of material to make it feel soft—they do not actually soften them.

Great Danes hail from Germany, not Denmark.

Brazil nuts are seeds, not nuts (but they do come from Brazil).

Shooting stars are meteors, not exploding stars.

Hardwood comes from deciduous trees. **Softwood** comes from evergreen trees. But the terms "hard' and "soft" have nothing to do with how tough or weak the wood really is. Balsa wood, for example—which you can practically cut with fingernails—is technically a hardwood.

Your **backbone** is actually thirty-three different bones.

Rice Paper has absolutely no rice in it.

Moth-holes in sweaters are created by larvae before they become grown-up moths.

Mountain Goats do live in the hills, but they aren't goats—they're small antelopes.

Coconuts are really giant seeds, not nuts.

10-gallon hats are for oversize heads, but they only hold about a gallon of liquid.

Electric eels are capable of producing a whopping 650 volts—but they aren't eels.

Around 3/4 of all Americans say they are content with their lives.

BRAINTEASERS

We've included a few simple logic problems in the book. For obvious reasons, they don't require heavy math or pencil and paper. Answers are on p. 234.

My Uncle Gordon is quite absent-minded. One day I ran into him on the street. He was mumbling to himself, and seemed quite perplexed.

"What's the matter, Uncle Gordon?" I asked.

"Hmm? Oh, it's you, nephew. I was just trying to figure out what day today is."

"Well that's easy enough," I replied, a little relieved that it wasn't anything serious. "Today is—"

Uncle Gordon cut me off.

"Now, I now that the day before the day after tomorrow will be Saturday. And the day after the day before yesterday was Thursday. But what is today?"

Can you help him?

Uncle Gordon and I were sitting on a park bench together. I was reading a book, and Gordon was reading the newspaper.

"Well, well," he mused. "Here's a little poem I don't understand". And he recited it:

"*A box without hinges, key or lid.*
Yet golden treasure inside is hid."

"It's a riddle," I explained.

"But what's the answer?" he demanded.

Do you know?

Uncle Gordon was puzzled by a math problem: "If one car starts from New York at 11 A.M. and travels 55 m.p.h, and another car starts from Boston at 1.P.M. and travels 60 m.p.h., which car will be nearer New York when they meet?"

"But Uncle Gordon, " I chided him, "That's easy."

You know the answer, of course.

The first beer can was used by Kreuger Beer, and introduced in 1935.

A FOOD IS BORN

These foods are common, so you've probably never even wondered where they came from. Here are the answers anyway.

BAGELS. According to *The Bagels' Bagel Book:* "In 1683 in Vienna, Austria, a local Jewish baker wanted to thank the King of Poland for protecting his countrymen from Turkish invaders. He made a special hard roll in the shape of a riding stirrup—'Beugel' in Austrian—commemorating the king's favorite pastime, and giving the bagel its distinctive shape."

MAYONNAISE. Originally brought to France by Duke Richelieu, who tasted it while visiting Mahon, a city on the island of Minorca. It was eventually dubbed Mahonaisse by French chefs, and considered a delicacy in Europe. In America, it became known as mayonnaise, but for over a century was still regarded as suitable for only the most elegant meals. Finally, in 1912, Richard Hellman, a German immigrant, began packing it and selling it in jars from his New York deli. This transformed mayonnaise from a carefully-prepared treat for the select few, to a mass-merchandised condiment.

GATORADE. According to *60s!*, by John and Gordon Javna: "In 1965, Dr. Robert Cade was studying the effects of heat exhaustion on football players at the University of Florida (whose team name is the Gators). He analyzed the body liquids lost in sweating and within three minutes came up with the formula for Gatorade. Two years later, Cade sold the formula to Stokely-Van Camp. Soon, annual sales were well over $50 million and Gatorade could be found on the training tables of over three hundred college sports teams, a thousand high school squads, and all but two pro football teams."

7-UP. According to *Parade* magazine: "In October 1929, just before the stock market crash, St. Louis businessman Charles L. Grigg began marketing a beverage called Bib-Label Lithiated Lemon-Lime Soda. His slogan: 'Takes the "Ouch" out of grouch.' The drink was a huge success during the Depression, perhaps because it contained lithium, a powerful drug now prescribed for manic-depressives....The drink's unwieldy name was later changed to 7-UP. The '7' stood for its 7-ounce bottle, the 'UP' for 'bottoms up,' or for the bubbles rising from its heavy carbonation, which was later reduced. The lithium was listed on the label until the mid-'40s."

CHEWING GUM. American Indians chewed resin from freshly cut spruce bark, and colonial settlers occasionally chewed "a limp paraffin," but it wasn't until the late 1860s that chewing gum become a commercial success. A Staten Island inventor named Thomas Adams noticed that his visiting neighbor from Mexico—the deposed dictator Santa Ana—"seemed to enjoy chewing...lumps of gum from the sapodilla plant, now known as chicle"....Adams decided chicle was better than paraffin, and went to market with "Adams New York Gum—Snapping and Stretching." Later, he tried adding flavors and found that licorice tasted best. Still later, he invented a "gum-making machine" that made mass production possible.

POPSICLES. Eleven-year-old Frank Epperson accidentally left a mixture of powdered soda mix and water on his back porch one winter night in 1905. The next morning, Frank found the stuff frozen, with the stirring stick standing straight up in the jar. He pulled it out, and had the first "Epperson icicle"—or "Epsicle." He later renamed it "Popsicle," since he'd made it with soda pop. It was patented in 1923, eighteen years later.

THE ICE CREAM CONE. It happened at the 1904 World's Fair in Saint Louis (where the hot dog and the hamburger were also popularized). An ice cream vendor who was selling cups of the frozen dessert had so many customers in the hot weather that he ran out of cups. In desperation, he looked around to see if another nearby vendor might have some spare containers, but all he could find was a waffle concession. He quickly bought some waffles and began selling them wrapped around a scoop of ice cream. The substitute became even more popular than the original, and it spread around the country.

Patty Hearst's prison T-shirt: "Being kidnapped is always having to say you're sorry."

7 COOL FLICKS

7 unsung cool films recommended by Gene Sculatti, author of The Catalog of Cool.

CAGED MEN (1973). Wrestling great Abdullah the Butcher and his (real life) midget manager make screen debuts, playing desperate lifers trying to grow pot in a jail greenhouse. Hammerlocks and hopheads.

CHE! (1969). Unwatchable, even within its genre (bogus "revolutionary" films of the late sixties), but singularly brilliant for its perverse casting: Jack Palance as Fidel Castro. Arriba!

DECOY FOR TERROR (1970). Beatnik artist murders his models ("They always *move!*") by freezing them. Cool climax: a power outage causes one, frozen posed with a bow and arrow, to release the arrow, killing artist who's just finished his masterpiece. Neil Sedaka sings "Do the Waterbug" (Do the Cow/If you want to right now...").

HIT LADY (1964). Women's lib comes knocking in sharp threads: Yvette Mimeux as a bikini-clad mob assassin. Groovy.

KITTEN WITH A WHIP (1964). Ann-Margaret, as a delinquent-on-the-run, holes up with Senator John Forsythe and threatens to cry rape if he chucks her.

R.P.M. (1970). The only thing that could beat Ann-Margaret playing a campus radical is Anthony Quinn as a left-leaning, motorcycle-riding professor named Taco. R.P.M. offers both.

THUNDER ROAD (1958). Flickdom's granddaddy of cool, bad Bob Mitchum in a barbiturate-soaked performance....When some creep tries running moonshiner Mitch off the road, Mr. Heavylids cooly removes the old cig from his lip and flicks it across his car, out the window, and into the creep's car. It lands on his lap and he drives screaming to his death over an embankment. Mitchum never changes his expression.

In 1987, a 1,400-year-old lump of still-edible cheese was unearthed in Ireland.

TOY ORIGINS

You've loved them. You've played with them.
You've probably lost parts to them.
Now, here's where they came from.

SCRABBLE. Created in 1931 by an out-of-work architect named Alfred Botts. He hoped he could support his family by inventing a successful word game, but before the game was refined, he had his job back. That was just as well; when he finally showed his hand-made "Criss-Cross" to toy companies, they insisted it had no potential—it was too intellectual.

In 1948, Botts and a friend went into business manufacturing the game—now called Scrabble—in an old schoolhouse. It was an unsophisticated cottage industry that enabled the friend to barely eke out a living. But in the summer of 1952, for no apparent reason, Scrabble suddenly became a fad. In two years, the partners went from selling less than ten thousand games a year to selling more than four million. To meet the growing demand, the rights were sold to Selchow-Righter, and thirty years later, Scrabble ranks as the second-best selling game in history.

LINCOLN LOGS. In 1916, Frank Lloyd Wright went to Tokyo to supervise construction of the Imperial Palace Hotel, a magnificent building, assembled with an inner frame of wood so it would withstand earthquakes better. Wright brought his son John with him, and as John watched workers move the huge timbers required for the structure, he came up with an idea for a wooden construction toy. When he returned to America, John created Lincoln Logs.

SILLY PUTTY. In 1945, an engineer at a General Electric laboratory in New Haven, Connecticut, was assigned the task of trying to create synthetic rubber. One day he combined boric acid with silicone oil. The result: a bizarre substance with a variety of fascinating properties (it bounced, stretched, and could be broken with a hammer), but no practical use. It became a New Haven conversation piece.

#1 Dead entertainer: In 1988, Elvis earned an estimated $15 million.

Several years later, a marketing man named Peter Hodgson saw a group of adults playing with the stuff at a cocktail party. Hodgson was putting together a mail order catalog for a toy store at the time, and decided to include this "nutty putty" in it. The response was amazing. Even without a photo, the "putty" outsold everything in the catalog except crayons. Hodgson knew he had a winner—so he bought $147-worth of putty from G.E., and packaged it in little plastic eggs. In the first five years, over 32 million containers of the stuff were sold worldwide.

RUBIK'S CUBE. Devised by Hungarian mathematician Erno Rubik in 1974 as an aid for teaching math concepts to his students. Rubik realized the puzzle's possibilities as a toy, and ended up selling two million of the cubes in Hungary alone—a total of one cube for every five Hungarians. In 1980, the Ideal Toy Corporation bought the rights, and the puzzle became a world-wide craze. Rubik reportedly became "the first self-made millionaire in a Communist country."

SLINKY. Richard James, a marine engineer, was trying to invent a spring that could be used to offset the effects of a boat's movement on sensitive navigational instruments. One day he knocked a sample spring off a high shelf—but instead of simply falling, it uncoiled like a snake and "crawled" down to the floor. James realized he had a toy product, gave it a name, and formed the James Toy Company to manufacture it.

TINKER TOYS. Charles Pajeau, an Evanston, Illinois stone-worker, conceived of Tinker Toys in 1913 after observing some kids playing with "pencils, sticks, and empty spools of thread." He designed it in a garage in back of his house, and brought the finished toy—packed in its famous cannister—to the 1914 American Toy Fair. But the public wouldn't buy it. So Pajeau had to prove his marketing genius again; at Christmastime, he dressed some midgets in elf costumes and had them play with Tinker Toys in the windows of New York's Grand Central Station and Chicago's Marshall Field's department store. The publicity this stunt attracted made all the difference—a year later, over a million sets had been sold.

The first stereo record went on the market in 1958.

WILL ROGERS SAID...

A tiny piece of the rich legacy left by America's national humorist during the '20s and '30s.

"You can't say civilization don't advance, for in every war they kill you a new way."

"Half our life is spent trying to find something to do with the time we have rushed through life trying to save."

"Being a hero is about the shortest-lived profession on earth."

"I don't make jokes—I just watch the government and report the facts."

"Everybody is ignorant, only on different subjects."

"Everything is funny as long as it's happening to somebody else."

"The American people are generous and will forgive almost any weakness with the exception of stupidity."

"I guess the truth can hurt you worse in an election than about anything that could happen to you."

"American people like to have you repent; then they are generous."

"Income Tax has made more liars out of the American people than golf."

"Nobody wants to be called common people, especially common people."

"Lord, the money we do spend on Government and it's not one bit better than the government we got for one third the money twenty years ago."

"It must be nice to belong to some legislative body and just pick money out of the air."

"Half the people in the U.S. are living on interest paid by people who will never get the last mortgage paid."

"No man is great if he thinks he is."

"A remark generally hurts in proportion to its truth."

The first scheduled TV broadcast, in 1931, featured George Gershwin and Kate Smith.

MYTH AMERICA

You've believed these stories since you were a kid. Most Americans have, because they were taught to us as sacred truths. Well, sorry. Here's another look.

SAVAGES

The Myth: "Scalping" was a brutal tactic invented by the Indians to terrorize the settlers.

The Truth: Scalping was actually an old European tradition dating back hundreds of years. Dutch and English colonists were paid a "scalp bounty" by their leaders as a means of keeping the Indians scared and out of the way. Finally the Indians caught on and adopted the practice themselves. The settlers apparently forgot its origins and another falsehood about Indian cruelty was born.

MOTHER OF THE FLAG

The Myth: Betsy Ross, a Philadelphia seamstress, designed and sewed the first American flag at the behest of the Founding Fathers.

Background: This story first surfaced in 1870 when Betsy Ross's grandson told a meeting of the Pennsylvania Historical Society that his grandmother had been asked to make a flag for the new nation. The tale must have touched a nerve, because it quickly spread and soon was regarded as the truth.

The Truth: While Betsy Ross did in fact sew flags for the Pennsylvania Navy, there is no proof to back up her grandson's tale. Ironically, no one is sure who designed the flag. The best guess is that the flag's design is derived from a military banner carried during the American Revolution.

MIDNIGHT RAMBLER

The Myth: Paul Revere made a solitary, dramatic midnight ride to warn patriots in Lexington and Concord that the British were coming.

Background: Revere's effort was first glorified in Henry Wadsworth Longfellow's poem, "The Midnight Ride of Paul

Revere." Longfellow may have written the ode out of guilt—his grandfather had tried to court-martial Revere during the Revolutionary War. The charge: "Unsoldierly behavior tending toward cowardice." (Revere was not convicted.)

The Truth: Paul Revere was actually one of two men who attempted the famous ride...and it was the other one, William Dawes, who made it to Concord. Revere didn't make it—he was stopped by British troops. As for Revere's patriotic motives: According to Patricia Lee Holt, in *George Washington Had No Middle Name*, "Paul Revere billed the Massachusetts State House 10 pounds 4 shillings to cover his expenses for his ride."

INDIAN MADE

The Myth: Pochahontas and Captain John Smith were in love. When her father tried to chop Smith's head off, Pochahontas put her own neck on the line and begged her father to spare her beloved.

Background: John Smith told people this had occurred.

The Truth: Smith probably made it up. He did know Pochahontas in Jamestown, but they weren't an item. All that's known about her is that "she apparently entertained the colonists by performing cartwheels in the nude."

AMERICUS THE BEAUTIFUL

The Myth: Amerigo Vespucci, a Florentine navigator, made four trips to the New World from 1497 to 1502. The newly discovered land was named America in his honor.

Background: Vespucci wrote an account of his four voyages. An Italian mapmaker was so impressed by it that he put "Americus's" name on the first known map of the New World.

The Truth: America is named after a probable fraud. Scholars doubt Vespucci really made those trips at all.

THANKSGIVING

The Myth: The Pilgrims ate a Thanksgiving feast of turkey and pumpkin pie after their first year in the New World, and we've been doing it ever since.

The Truth: Thanksgiving didn't become a national holiday until Abraham Lincoln declared it in 1863, and the Pilgrims ate neither the bird we call turkey, nor pumpkin pie.

About 1/6 of the male population in America weighs over 200 lbs.

MOVIE OF DOOM

Getting a job in a movie can be hazardous to your health—in unexpected ways.

THE VICTIMS: More than 90 of the 220 people working on the film *The Conqueror*, including director Dick Powell, stars John Wayne, Agnes Moorhead, and Susan Hayward, and dozens of secondary players and crew members.

THE CIRCUMSTANCES

On May 19, 1953, the U.S. government tested a powerful A-bomb at Yucca Flats, Nevada. In St. George, Utah, 100 miles to the west, people were fascinated by the event. As *Macleans* magazine described it: "Some of the people went up on the hillside outside town to watch the blast, because nobody told them not to. A few hours later, grey ash began to sift over the Black Hill west of the city; it drifted across the lawns, clung to laundry on the lines, burned the skin of people in the streets....The town's citizens were merely instructed to wash the ash off their automobiles. They were urged not to worry."

A year later, the cast and crew of the film *The Conqueror*, a schlock version of the life of Genghis Khan (John Wayne was Genghis), arrived in St. George to film on location at a nearby desert. They—and the fulltime residents of St. George—were unaware that radiation levels were extraordinarily high in the area...and that, in fact, the entire perimeter may have been contaminated by fallout.

The result: Wayne and almost 100 others—about 45% of the people associated with the filming—died of cancer over the next 30 years. Residents of St. George also had an unusually high incidence of cancer.

UNANSWERED QUESTIONS

- Was the cancer caused by the cumulative, long-lasting effects of low-level radiation?
- Was the area contaminated?

The first city in history to boast a million inhabitants was London, in 1811.

• Did the government know about it, and intentionally conceal the information?

POSSIBLE CONCLUSIONS

• Government officials were as naive as the citizens of St. George, believing that it was adequate (as they told one St. George resident) to take a shower and change one's clothes when exposed to low-level radiation.

• The low-level radiation didn't cause the cancer that killed so many of the cast and crew of *The Conqueror*. Certainly, not all of them blamed atomic testing for it. (Wayne, a fervent anti-communist, never did. On the other hand, actress Jeanne Gerson, asserting she was the last of the film's stars still living, sued the government when she, too, contracted cancer at age 76.) Still, while no definite link has been (or can be) proven, the situation is highly suspicious; about 45% of the crew contracted cancer, a rate which far exceeds any reasonable statistical probability.

• The government knew it was endangering the lives of American citizens—it had essentially doomed the people working on the movie—but felt it was worth the sacrifice of a few lives to further their knowledge of nuclear power. Considerable evidence which points to this conclusion is coming to light. "Documents made public in 1979," says *Macleans*, "show a long-term pattern to confuse and mislead the public about the dangers of fallout."

For example: An official memo written in 1953—the year of the Yucca Flats test—insisted that "people have got to learn to live with the facts of life, and part of the facts of life is fallout." Another said, "We must not let anything interfere with these tests—nothing." And a subsequent study in 1963 which indicated serious health risks to people exposed to high levels of radiation was suppressed by the Atomic Energy Commission because, one official wrote, "The public would know they have not been told the truth."

So it may, in fact, be true that the U.S. government was responsible for the death of Duke Wayne. And the 1954 B-film, which he reluctantly took on, turned out to be a bomb in more ways than one.

The first heart transplant took place on December 3, 1967.

THE JAVA JIVE

This might well be the B.R.I. membership's favorite drink. But did you know...

• Americans drink about 400 million cups of coffee per day—or 146 billion cups every year.

• Coffee has absolutely no nutritional value.

• Legend has it that coffee was discovered over 1,000 years ago, when an Abyssinian goatherder noticed his goats prancing on their hind legs after sampling the fruit of a wild coffee tree. He tried the raw berries himself and began dancing wildly.

• Four out of five adults in the US drink coffee. They put away an average of two cups a day, which adds up to about a third of the world's supply.

• The coffee tree is really an evergreen shrub. It grows to about 25 feet high.

• Per capita, Finns drink the most coffee in the world.

• Hot Water Politics:
Tea was the most popular drink in the Colonies until 1773, when King George III levied a tax on it. After the Boston Tea Party, coffee became the drink of preference, and much of the Revolution was planned in the patriots' favorite new type of meeting place—the coffee house.

• Over 10,000 different studies have analyzed the medical effects of caffeine—and there still are no conclusive results.

• Caffeine is tasteless.

• An average cup of coffee contains 100 milligrams of caffeine; a cup of espresso has 200.

• Signs of caffeine overdose:
1) Cold Sweat
2) The Shakes
3) Heart Palpitations, plus a feeling of Impending Doom

• The symptoms of caffeine withdrawal:
1) Headaches
2) Nervousness
3) Irritability

• Researchers believe that heavy coffee drinkers use the drug to treat themselves for the most common psychiatric condition: depression.

2/3 of the books published in America are paperbacks.

PRESIDENTIAL AFFAIRS

Until details of John Kennedy's private life began to surface, Americans believed their presidents were above "playing around." Now we know better. Some samples:

THOMAS JEFFERSON

The egalitarian aristocrat of Virginia who theoretically opposed slavery, yet owned dozens of slaves, was quite fond of one in particular—the light-skinned Sally Hemings. Jefferson fathered five children with Hemings, four of whom survived. The children apparently passed into the white community with little trouble, and Jefferson's will directed that after his death they be "freed." They were. One son, Madison Heming, resembled Jefferson closely, and reportedly wrote about his life at Monticello in 1873.

WARREN HARDING

One of America's most inept chief executives, he was so indiscreet with his affairs that some historians speculate that his wife retaliated by poisoning him while he was in office.

Harding carried on long liaisons with at least two different women. One, a Mrs. Phillips, was the wife of a department store owner in Marion, Ohio. She tried to cash in on her relationship with Harding when he was nominated for president by the Republicans, and was probably sent to Japan with a huge chunk of cash in exchange for maintaining her silence.

Harding's romantic poetry to her was discovered after her death. An excerpt: "I love you more than all the world. Possession wholly imploring. Mid passion I am oftimes whirled, oftimes admire—adoring. Oh God! If fate would only give Us privilege to love and live!"

Another of Harding's lovers, Nan Britton, wrote a book in 1927 in which she claimed to have given birth to his daughter in 1919. Her story is less documented than Mrs. Phillips's, but is regarded by historians as probably true.

DWIGHT D. EISENHOWER

This paragon of middle-American virtue gave in to temptation during World War II. While his wife, Mamie, followed his career from the states, another woman—Kay Summersby—kept him company. Eisenhower was the head of the Allied forces in Europe; Kay was his driver for over three years. In her 1977 book, *Past Forgetting: My Love Affair with Dwight D. Eisenhower*, Summersby (a former British model) details what actually happened between the two during the war. Apparently, she and Eisenhower tried on several occasions to consummate their affection for each other—but Ike was unable to really "rise" to the moment. An unhappy marriage had apparently stripped the 5-star General of his libido and work was the substitute he used in its place.

LYNDON BAINES JOHNSON

LBJ had no such problem; as his former press secretary, George Reedy, commented in a Johnson biography: "[LBJ] had the instincts of a Turkish sultan in Istanbul." One tale: In 1950 one of his many sexual partners became pregnant. According to the woman, Madeline Brown, Johnson quietly took care of her—both before and after the birth of a son named Steven. For twenty-one years the two carried on, with Johnson setting her up in an apartment for discreet get-togethers.

JOHN KENNEDY

The stories about JFK's sexual exploits are too numerous to recount. He chased women like a man possessed, but his family name and connections helped keep that part of his personal life out of the news until years after his death. Movie stars, White House workers, "staff" members and gangsters' girlfriends were all the subject of Kennedy's penetrating lifestyle. Some reports now acknowledge that often two women were included in the fun.

FRANKLIN ROOSEVELT

The love of FDR's life apparently wasn't Eleanor, but a woman named Lucy Mercer, Eleanor's one-time social secretary. Their affair was discovered by Mrs. Roosevelt, who confronted FDR with the information. He promised to end the relationship, but it is reported that Mercer was with him when he died in 1945—almost 30 years after the relationship had begun.

Elvis collected statuettes of Joan of Arc and Venus de Milo.

BRAIN TEASERS

These simple logic problems have appeared in American game books in various forms for almost a century. We confess that they're not as hard as they first seem to be—we've stayed away from heavy math problems and—for obvious reasons—anything you'd need a pencil to solve.

A man needs something specific for his house, so he goes to a hardware store to purchase it. When he asks the clerk the price, the clerk answers that "the price of one is fifty cents, the price of thirty is one dollar, and the price of one hundred forty-four is one dollar and fifty cents." What is the man buying?

Two boys were playing on a tool shed roof when the roof collapsed with a crash. The boys fell uninjured to the floor below, but when they picked themselves up, the face of one boy was covered with dirt and the other boy's was still clean. Instantly, the boy with the clean face ran off to wash his face, while the one with the dirty face remained placidly behind. Why did the boy with the clean face act as he did?

A tree has one blossom on it at the beginning of June. The blossoms double in area every 24 hours. It takes the entire month for the tree to be covered completely with blossoms. On what date will the tree be half-covered?

You have one match. You enter a room that contains a wood-burning stove, a kerosene lamp and a fireplace. Which should you light first?

There is a town in Newfoundland, Canada called Dildo.

DEFINITIONS

While you're sitting there, you might like to improve your vocabulary a bit. Here are some obscure words and definitions to study.

Peccadillo: A slight or trifling sin; a fault
Sesamoid: Having the shape of a sesame seed
Anserine: Gooselike, as in goose bumps on skin
Wanion: Disaster or bad luck
Joad: A migratory worker
Pettifogger: An inferior lawyer
Feverwort: A weedy herb
Squamous: Covered with scales
Cachinnate: To laugh noisily
Erubescence: Process of turning red, blushing
Histoplasmosis: A respiratory illness caused by inhaling festered bat dung
Paraselene: A mock moon appearing on a lunar halo
Yerk: To tie with a jerk
Bilbo: A finely tempered Spanish sword
Verisimilitude: Appearance of truth
Salubrious: Wholesome
Fecund: Fruitful
Epistemology: A school of philosophy that includes the study of the nature of human knowledge
Yowie: A small ewe
Parsimony: Stinginess
Holm: An island in a river
Coriaceous: Tough, leathery texture
Mullion: A vertical dividing piece between window lights or panels
Sippet: A triangular piece of toasted or french bread used to garnish a dish of hash
Infrangible: Not breakable
Sudorific: Causing perspiration
Cerulean: Sky blue
Pomology: The study of fruit
Rusticate: To send into the country
Agnomen: An added name due to some special achievement
Saponification: Process of making soap
Motet: A sacred musical composition for several voices
Lycanthropy: The power of turning a human being into a wolf by magic or witchcraft. Wolfman science.

The most common bird in the world is the starling.

GILLIGAN'S ISLAND

Few TV shows have been both as reviled and beloved as "Gilligan's Island"—sometimes by the same people. Two unanswered questions remain about this program:
1) Where did they get all those clothes?
2) How did they last for three years without sex?

HOW IT STARTED

In 1963, veteran TV writer Sherwood Schwartz ("The Red Skelton Show", "I Married Joan") was ready to break away from writing other people's shows and create his own sitcom. A literate man with degrees in zoology and psychology, Schwartz had an idea for a meaningful show: He'd take representative members of American society, strand them on an island (this was inspired by Defoe's *Robinson Crusoe*), and their interaction would be a microcosm of life in the U.S.

How this idea turned into "Gilligan's Island" is anyone's guess. In the end, Sherwood's castaways were more caricatures than characters. He called them *clichés*: "The wealthy, the Hollywood glamour girl, the country girl, the professor, the misfit, and the resourceful bull of a man." He added, "Anybody who is watching can identify with someone." Yes, but would they want to?

Schwartz brought his concept to CBS and United Artists; both agreed to finance a pilot. But after the pilot was filmed, CBS started playing with the premise. Network president Jim Aubrey felt it should be a story about a charter boat that went out on a new adventure every week. "How would the audience know what those guys were doing on the island?" he wanted to know. It looked like Schwartz's original idea was sunk. Then he had a brainstorm—explain the premise in a theme song! He wrote his own tune and performed it at a meeting of CBS brass (probably a first). And on the basis of that song, CBS ok'd the castaways. Now do we thank them or what?

INSIDE FACTS

Even "Gilligan's Island" wasn't sanitized enough for the censors!

Never mind that there wasn't a hint of sex in three years on a deserted island. CBS censors still objected to Tina Louise's low-cut dresses and Dawn Wells' exposed navel.

• Believe it or not, some viewers took the show seriously. The U.S. Coast Guard received several telegrams from concerned citizens asking why they didn't rescue the *Minnow*'s crew.

• Schwartz picked the name "Gilligan" from out of the Los Angeles phone book.

• Schwartz originally wanted Jerry Van Dyke to play Gilligan. He turned it down in favor of the lead in a different TV series—"My Mother the Car." Another actor wanted to play the Skipper, but was rejected: Carroll "Archie Bunker" O'Connor.

EVERYONE'S A CRITIC

The public loved Gilligan, but most critics hated it. A sample:

• *L.A. Times:* "'Gilligan's Island' is a show that should never have reached the airwaves, this season or any other."

• *S.F. Chronicle:* "It is difficult to believe that this show was written, directed, and produced by adults. It marks a new low in the networks' estimation of public intelligence."

THE PILOT FILM

• It was shot in Hawaii, just a few miles from the spot where *South Pacific* was filmed.

• One of the major problems faced by the production crew during the pilot's filming: frogs. Inexplicably, they piled up by the hundreds outside the doors of the on-site cottages.

• Filming of the pilot was completed on November 22, 1963—the day J.F.K. was assassinated.

ABOUT THE ISLAND

• It was man-made, located in the middle of an artificial lake at CBS's Studio Center in Hollywood, and surrounded by painted landscapes, artificial palm trees, and wind machines.

• At one point, the concrete lake-bottom leaked. So it had to be completely drained, repaired, and filled again.

• It cost $75,000 to build.

Killer Ant: The black bulldog ant of Australia and Tasmania can kill a person.

CRYONICS

At one time or another, everyone has toyed with the idea of eternal life—or at least, of being able to put things on hold and come back, when cures for today's terminal diseases have been found. Enter the technology of cryonics, the attempt to preserve human life by storing bodies at subfreezing temperatures.

WHAT IT IS

Theoretically, cryonics is a way of putting nature on ice, of creating suspended animation in human beings by freezing them—a notion that can be traced back to 1964, when physics professor Robert Ettinger wrote and published a book called *The Prospect of Immortality*.

At death, the body is cooled to near freezing and the blood is removed and replaced with a synthetic solution. Then the body is placed in a stainless steel tank filled with liquid nitrogen. The reason: when living tissue is cooled at a controlled rate to the temperature of liquid nitrogen, all molecular and biological activity stops. Theoretically, with its biological clock stopped, the tissue stays viable via suspended animation.

The body is kept in the tank at subfreezing temperatures, until the anticipated day when technology makes "re-animation" possible.

When will that be? According to a committed cryonicist: "The technology of freezing is still very primitive, and will require advances in thawing and resuscitation that may not be available for two centuries, if ever."

IS IT STRICTLY FOR LUNATICS?

At first a lot of scientists thought it was a money-making scam (and many still do), a false hope for people who are unable to accept the inevitability of their own deaths. But recently theory has given way to practice as biologists at the University of California have been able to revive ice-cold hamsters and dogs.

Freezing, said one of the UC scientists, "is nature's way of saying 'time out.' It's a way of putting life on hold. For instance, some frogs go through the winter with 1/3-to-1/2 of their body's water turned into ice. They can go without breathing, eating or even without a heartbeat. In the spring, they thaw out and go on with their lives."

Throughout the years, the basic doctrine of cryonics has not varied: the dead are considered temporarily incurable.

WHAT IT IS NOT

Cryonics shouldn't be confused with cryobiology, a recognized branch of medical research that studies the effects of very low temperatures on living tissue. Cryobiology has enabled scientists and physicians to freeze blood, corneas, bone marrow, sperm and even human embryos for use at a future time. However, organs such as the pancreas, the kidney and the human heart (to be used in transplant surgery) have proven to be unusable if frozen (which makes the whole premise behind cryonics highly suspect).

FREEZER FACTS

• The American Cryonics Society says that its membership numbers 100 people who have committed themselves for freezing after death.

• In three cryonics centers in California and Michigan, the earthly remains of 15 people are on ice. There used to be 45, but 30 of the tanks leaked.

• Freezing doesn't come cheap. The price tag for return in the 21st century varies between $100,000 and $125,000.

• For a reduced price of $30,000 one may have his head frozen instead of his entire body. The head may or may not be grafted onto a healthy body at some future date; the guiding idea is that cloning will make other body parts easy to replicate in the future when the technology is available.

• Cryonicists do have a sense of humor. Their slogan is: "Freeze, Wait, Reanimate." The standard joke is "Many are cold, but few are frozen."

• "There's a poem we like to quote," says one cryonicist:

"I really think that I could freeze,
My mother-in-law with the greatest of ease.

The only thing that gives me pause,
Is what will happen when she thaws."

• **Whoops:** When Saul Kent's mother, Dora, died after years of suffering from arthritis and a degenerative brain disease, he hired Alcor Life Extension Foundation, a cryonics facility in Fullerton, California, to freeze her head until it could be revived and attached to a new body. There was one hitch, however: Dora Kent may not have been dead before her head was removed. Besides, the old woman may not have wanted to be turned into a human ice cube; she never signed the consent forms.

RECENT DEVELOPMENTS: Research physiologists at the University of California at Berkeley froze a three-year-old beagle named Miles and revived him.

•Miles was anaesthetized and placed on a bed of ice until his temperature fell from his normal 100.5 degrees (F) to 68 degrees.

•Next, the pooch, drained of his own blood (which was replaced with a clear, synthetic blood that wouldn't clot in the cold) was frozen.

•Legally "dead" for the hour his body spent at below 50 degrees, Miles was thawed, given back his blood and returned to perfect doggie health.

FOR NOW: While the Miles experiments may lead scientists to give ailing humans "the big chill" until cures for their diseases have been found, experiments with freezing a patient's own blood may alleviate a lot of problems right now. Surgery requires a lot of donated blood (which may or may not be contaminated); with freezing and the use of synthetic blood, a patient's own blood can be recycled.

WHAT ABOUT UNCLE WALT?

The most enticing rumor associated with cryonics is that Walt Disney had his body frozen and is planning to return some day. Is it true? In the book *Disney's World*, an associate reveals: "My information is that he *is* frozen down....[And] if he does come back, there's going to be hell to pay. He wouldn't approve of much that's gone on at the [Disney] Studios...."

Thomas Wedgwood took the world's first photograph in 1802.

FLIPPER

The most famous aquatic animal superstar is the dolphin who starred in her own TV series. Here's the inside scoop on Flipper, from Animal Superstars, *by John Javna.*

ORIGIN:

"Lassie in a wet suit," as one TV critic jokingly described "Flipper," was exactly what underwater stunt man Ricou Browning had in mind when he created Flipper in the early '60s.

"I was watching 'Lassie' on television with my kids one night," he says, "and I thought, 'Wouldn't it be great to do an animal show similar to "Lassie" with a kid and a dolphin?'" He envisioned the story as a book, but the idea was turned down by every publisher Browning sent it to.

So he tried movie producers instead. At the time, very little was known about dolphins, and no one knew if they could be trained to become film performers. But when Browning sent his ideas to producer Ivan Tors, Tors couldn't resist the challenge. "Let's make a movie of...that story of yours," he told Browning. The result: two films, a TV series, and the #1 aquatic superstar of all time.

ABOUT THE STAR

Species: Dolphin

- Length: seven feet
- Weight: 300 lb.
- Number of teeth: 84
- Speed: Up to 40 miles per hour
- Favorite foods: Mullets and butterfish
- Sex: Female
- Name: Mitzi was the star of two Flipper films. Suzy starred in the TV series—until she became too rough with the actors. Then Cathy replaced her.

INSIDE FACTS

- **Secrets of success:** Unlike previous dolphin trainers who worked on dry land, everyone connected with "Flipper" interacted with the animals in the water. This cut training time from six months per trick to three weeks.

• Flipper's most memorable trick—carrying a boy on her back—was really a "fetch." Browning threw his nine-year-old son in the water and ordered Flipper to retrieve him. She put her fin under his arm, and off they went.

TRICKS AND TRAINING

• **The Trainer:** Although Ivan Tors worked with the dolphins sometimes, Ricou Browning was their trainer. Browning had been a diver on "Sea Hunt," and (are you ready for this?) played the creature in *The Creature from the Black Lagoon*.

• The stars of "Flipper" could learn new tricks in one shot, as long as their human trainers were "smart enough" to communicate what they wanted.

• Each dolphin could learn the 35 basic maneuvers that the role of Flipper required in only six months.

• Essential tricks included "fetching" (Mitzi could fetch up to five things at once), towing a boat with a rope, shaking hands with her flipper, hitting the water with her tail, and letting a person hold her flipper while she swam.

STAR GOSSIP

Ivan Tors had a very special relationship with Suzy, the dolphin who played Flipper on TV—she'd saved his life.

• When Suzy was first being trained, Tors swam out into a lagoon to meet her. But she swam away, refusing to let him near her. Tors chased her until he was exhausted. Then he surfaced to get his breath—and was overwhelmed by a huge wave. As he desperately called for help, he suddenly felt Suzy's dorsal fin underneath him. He grabbed it, and she towed him to safety, winning his gratitude—and a starring role on the show.

SCREEN CREDITS

• 1963: *Flipper* (film). Co-stars: Chuck Connors, Luke Halpin.

• 1964: *Flipper's New Adventures* (film). Co-stars: Brian Kelly, Luke Halpin.

• 1964-67: "Flipper" (TV series). 88 episodes. Co-stars: Brian Kelly, Luke Halpin, Tommy Norden, Pete the Pelican, Spray the Retriever.

PRIME-TIME PROVERBS

TV comments about everyday life in America. From Prime Time Proverbs, *by Jack Mingo.*

ON MARRIAGE:
"Son, stay clear of weddings because one of them is liable to be your own."
—Pappy Maverick, *Maverick*

"Just because I've been married for twenty-five years is no reason to stop being sexy."
—Ralph Kramden, *The Honeymooners*

Groucho: "Are you married, Georgette?"
Contestant: "Yes, I've been married to the same man for thirty-one years."
Groucho: "Well if he's been married for thirty-one years, he's not the same man."
—You Bet Your Life

ON TELEVISION:
"Well, Beaver, this may be hard for you to believe, but life isn't exactly like television."
—Ward Cleaver, *Leave It to Beaver*

"It's just plain foolishness, squattin' all day in front of that little black box, starin' bleary-eyed at people who ain't more than two inches high. It's a passin' fancy, I tell you, like buggy whips and high button shoes."
—Grandpa Amos McCoy *The Real McCoys*

Maggie: "It's four o'clock in the morning and you're watching a test pattern."
Dave: "I know, but I want to see how it ends."
—My Mother the Car

ON RACE & RELIGION:
"Jesus was a Jew, yes, but only on his mother's side."
—Archie Bunker, *All In the Family*

"Have you always been a Negro, or are you just trying to be fashionable?"
—Dr. Morton Chesley, *Julia*

"You keep talking about minorities. Well mister, you're a psycho, and they're a minority, too."
—Sgt. Joe Friday, *Dragnet*

WHAT A DOLL!

Barbie is the product that toymakers dream of. She never goes out of style...and each succeeding generation loves to play with her. What a doll!

Children have been playing with dolls for thousands of years, but the most popular doll in the history of the world has only been in existence since 1959. It's Barbie, of course. Since Mattel's buxom fashionplate was first introduced, more than 400 million Barbie dolls have been sold. And the number is growing every day.

Some toys are just toys. But Barbie is a way of life.

From the outset, she encouraged little girls to be good consumers. "Barbie was important not for herself, but for all that could be added to her," explains Thomas Hine in *Populuxe*. "She had party dresses, and gowns for the prom, and a wedding ensemble....She had a boyfriend, Ken, a little sister, and a Corvette. There was always something new to buy for her—a more stylish outfit, a new kind of fashion, a different fantasy."

But Barbie carried other social messages besides the joys of consumerism. The joy of sex, for example. With her large breasts and hourglass figure, Barbie resembled a teenage Jayne Mansfield; she was clearly a traditional sex object. Yet you knew you'd never see Barbie stuck in anyone's kitchen, barefoot and pregnant. It's no coincidence that Barbie debuted at about the same time as The Pill. As much as any child's toy could in 1960, she represented an ideal of sexual freedom.

And how about Barbie's obsession with looks and possessions? Sure, they propagated a shallow set of values to the little girls who adored her. But they also implied independence. Prior to Barbie, every popular doll in America was a baby doll. Barbie signified a change. Girls didn't have to play "mommy" anymore. They had a new kind of role model—a career girl who could be a model, a nurse, a nightclub singer...even an astronaut. Sure, Barbie had expensive taste, but she didn't depend on her boyfriend for anything. In fact, Barbie was the boss in that relationship. It was *Barbie*'s Corvette, remember—Ken just went along for the ride.

BARBIE'S ROOTS

The real Barbie (yes, there was one) was the daughter of Ruth and Eliot Handler, who founded Mattel after World War II. The idea for the teenage fashion doll came to Ruth when she noticed that Barbie preferred playing with shapely paper dolls to playing with baby dolls. The Handlers gambled that other modern girls would feel the same way. The Handlers had a son, too, named Ken.

Barbie was introduced at the New York Toy Fair in February, 1959. The first Barbie dolls cost $3—today, in mint condition, they're worth over $1,000. And the figure keeps rising.

Barbie's creators based her appearance on the prevailing standards of beauty in 1959—Brigitte Bardot, with her perky pony tail and knock-out figure, and Grace Kelly's patrician blondness.

She was originally called a three-dimensional fashion drawing. Said Ruth Handler, "Barbie was originally created to project every little girl's dream of the future," and part of that future meant being grown up. Grown up to a little girl, was having breasts. It was no accident that a lingerie line was one of the first sets of Barbie clothes available.

Collectors seem certain that the design for Barbie was lifted from a German doll named "Lilli"—which was, in turn, based on a cartoon character created for the daily newspaper *Bild-Zeitung*. Ironically, the German Lilli was not a wholesome teenager, but a winsome, sexually loose gold-digger. Maybe that explains her body.

ALL DRESSED UP...

Barbie was sold as a teenage fashion model, but her wardrobe was definitely haute couture, or as close to Parisian fashion as one could come with a doll. Whenever new costumes were planned for the doll, Mattel designer Charlotte Johnson and her staff traveled to Europe to see the collections of Dior, Jacques Fath, Balenciaga, Givenchy, Mme. Gres, Balmain and Schiaparelli. Then they adapted what they saw.

Barbie has always been on the top of pop fashion trends. In

The longest-lived insects are queen termites, which live for up to 100 years.

the late'50s and early '60s, her wardrobe included white gloves and pillbox hats. By the '70s, she was the prototypical exercise nut in leotards and tights—so she'd look great in her hot pants outfits and fringed suede vests. By 1980, she was a disco singer wearing glitter togs and toting a microphone.

...AND NO PLACE TO GO

Overall, the most popular Barbie outfits are wedding gowns. But although she has all the necessary gear for a fancy wedding (and has for about 30 years), Barbie has never actually taken the plunge. She and Ken haven't even set a date.

• Mattel is the world's largest manufacturer of "women's" clothing. They produce 20 million Barbie outfits a year.

BARBIE FACTS

• In 1987, Mattel sold $450 million worth of Barbie merchandise—that's almost $1 billion on the retail level.

• Barbie's last name is Roberts.

• Barbie is a college graduate. She attended a generic educational institution called State College.

• The Barbie Fan Club has over 600,000 members worldwide.

• Not that you care, but...what would happen if you laid all the Barbie dolls that have been sold since 1959 in a line, head-to-toe? According to Mattel press releases, "that's enough dolls to circle the earth more than three-and-a-half times."

• Some Barbie features over the years: Fashion Queen Barbie had wigs in 1963; in 1966, Barbie's hair and clothes changed color "when swabbed with a special solution"; there was "a motorized stage in 1971, which, when activated, made Live Action Barbie dance"; 1980's Western Barbie winked. And the beat goes on.

BARBIE FLOPS

• Two Barbie flops: "Colored Francy," and "Kissing Barbie." "Kissing Barbie"'s lips moved, but Mattel didn't make a "Kissing Ken," so there was nobody for Barbie to pucker up with.

• In 1986, Mattel tried to introduce a Barbie clothing line for real girls from 7 to 14 years old. Their slogan: "We Girls Can Do Anything." Mattel marketed the clothes in stores like J.C. Penney and K-Mart; but it didn't work.

Ostriches measure up to nine feet from head to feet. They weigh as much as 350 pounds.

CUSTOMS

Where did they come from? A few random examples.

TIPPING

Some think it began in the 17th century, when restaurants had boxes labelled T.I.P.—To Insure Promptness—on the wall beside their entrances. Patrons who wanted their food in a hurry deposited a few coins in the box before they sat down.

AN APPLE FOR THE TEACHER

Now an outmoded custom, it stems from the days when public school teachers were paid with whatever the community they served could afford. Often they were given food or goods in lieu of cash.

THE TOOTH FAIRY

In Germany, where the idea apparently originated, the tooth was not placed under a pillow. Instead, it was put in a rat hole because it was thought that the new tooth growing in would take on the "dental quality" of the animal who found it.

STRIPED BARBER POLES

Barbers were once a lot more versatile than they are today. They not only cut hair, they performed surgery as well. When the barbers finished, the towels used to soak up excess blood were hung outside to dry on a pole. As the wind dried them they wrapped around the pole, making a design, so to speak, of red and white stripes.

ADVICE TO SINGLES

From the 1700s: "If you want to get married, stand on your head and chew a piece of gristle out of a beef neck and swallow it, and you will get anyone you want."

The zipper was invented in 1893, for use in shoes.

MARILYN SAID...

Marilyn Monroe was known for saying exactly what was on her mind. A fascinating collection of quotes is in Marilyn Monroe: A Never-Ending Dream, *by Guus Luijters.*

"I think femininity and beauty are ageless and can't be faked, and that true glamour—I know the manufacturers aren't going to like this—isn't a factory product. Not real glamour, in any case, which is based on femininity. Sexuality is only attractive when it's natural and spontaneous."

"Bobby Kennedy promised to marry me. What do you think of that?"

"A career is a wonderful thing, but you can't snuggle up to it on a cold night."

[*After JFK had surreptitiously slipped his hand under her dress*] "I bet he doesn't put his hand up Jacqueline's dress. I bet no one does. Is she ever stiff!"

"I've noticed that men generally leave married women alone and treat them with respect. It's too bad for married women. Men are always ready to respect someone who bores them. And if most married women, even the pretty ones, look so dull, it's because they're getting too much respect."

"My ass is way too big. They tell me men like it like that. Crazy, huh?"

"Blonde hair and breasts, that's how I got started. I couldn't act. All I had was my blonde hair and a body men liked. The reason I got ahead is that I was lucky and met the right men."

"People are always looking at me as if I were a kind of mirror instead of a person. They don't see me, they see their own hidden thoughts and then they whitewash themselves by claiming that I embody those secret thoughts."

Kotex was first manufactured as bandages, during World War I.

VALENTINE'S DAY

Beginning in kindergarten, we exchange cards with classmates and friends on Valentine's Day. Later, it's flowers and presents for loved ones. Here's why we do it.

VALENTINE'S DAY

This "lovers' holiday" is an anomaly. It was actually an effort by the Catholic Church to *keep* teenagers from becoming lovers.

Before Christ was born, it was a Roman tradition for teenage girls and boys to gather every February in the name of the god Lupercus, and randomly select a "mate" for a year. They were permitted to do anything they liked together (and what else would teenagers do?).

When Christians gained power in the Roman Empire, they wanted to bring this practice to an end. So they selected a substitute for Lupercus (to be the focus of a parallel holiday)—St. Valentine, a bishop who had reputedly been tortured and executed by Emperor Claudius II in 270 A.D, for performing marriages after Claudius had outlawed them in the Empire. This symbol of more "wholesome" love, was reluctantly accepted by the Romans. But just to be sure no one gave in to temptation, the Catholic Church made it a mortal sin to worship Lupercus. Eventually, Valentine's Day became a recognized holiday throughout Western Europe.

VALENTINE CARDS

If teens couldn't get together in February, what could they do? They could send each other respectful notes of affection. And they did, although it seems like a poor substitute. At any rate, sending lover's greetings became a part of the Valentine's day ritual, and when Christian influence grew, the practice of sending notes on February 14 spread with it.

The first greeting cards didn't appear until the 18th century. Printed cards were common in Germany by the 1780s; they were called *Freundschaftkarten*, or "friendship cards." The first American cards were manufactured in the 1870s, at an amazing cost of up to thirty-five dollars apiece.

If an orangutan belches at you, watch out. He's warning you to stay out of his territory.

ENQUIRING MINDS...

The National Enquirer, *"America's most popular newspaper," deals in gossip coupled with oddity. Celebrity "confessions" share space with miracle cures, religious wonders (Jesus's face in a taco), advice on relationships, psychic predictions, UFO/alien kidnap tales, weight loss schemes, interesting trivia and occasionally, a legit news scoop.*

VITAL STATS

Circulation: Over 4.5 million weekly

Weekly readership: 15-20 million

Founder: Generoso Pope, Jr., who died on September 25, 1988.

Earnings: Unknown, because the *Enquirer* is privately held.

Headquarters: Lantana, Florida (Pope moved the paper from New Jersey to Florida because he liked the weather.)

Staff: Largely British, Scottish and Australian—writers and editors steeped in the tradition of England's Fleet Street tabloid operations, where they essentially make the news up if it's not exciting enough.

Salaries: Staff is paid on a scale that far surpasses more traditional journalists. In 1981, it was revealed that beginning reporters made over $40,000 and editors could make as much as $80,000; presumably that salary base has risen drastically. However, story editors are paid according to how many of their staff's articles appear in print, so the competition for space in the *Enquirer* is stiff and the burn-out factor is very high. Reporters who last longer than 18 months are a rare breed.

Philosophy: To Pope's way of thinking, the *Enquirer* was not out to win prizes—it is mass entertainment, pure and simple.

In the *Enquirer*'s inner sanctum, the highest compliment Pope could pay an editor was that he had a "Hey Martha!" story—one "so astonishing and compelling" that the reader would stop mid-sentence and turn to his wife or someone nearby and say "Hey Martha, get a load of this!" The rest of the editors had to settle for "Gee-whiz" stories.

SCOOPS AND STORIES

Some memorable efforts by the Enquirer:

THE SCOOP: A photo of Elvis Presley in his coffin.

HOW THEY DID IT: When Elvis died on August 16, 1977, the *Enquirer* flew staff members to Memphis and set up headquarters in a boarding house. The reporters were instructed to find a "blockbuster" scoop, something to eclipse the emerging stories about the King's drug habit. One staffer came up with the idea of a photograph of Presley in his coffin, and that was it. The night before the funeral, reporters bought a number of cameras and handed them out to "mourners" along with a liberal sprinkling of cold, hard cash.

The day after the funeral, the command center was littered with snaps of the King lying in state. The next issue of the *Enquirer* went on sale with Elvis' corpse on the cover. It quickly became the newspaper's all-time biggest (at that time) seller.

THE SCOOP: A Photo of Bing Crosby in *his* coffin.

HOW THEY DID IT: This time a reporter dressed as a priest conned his way into the private ceremony held for Bing. As he left the service with his snapshot, the priest/reporter admonished ABC reporter Geraldo Rivera not to bother the Crosby family at such a sensitive moment.

THE SCOOP: Photographs of Democratic presidential candidate Gary Hart in Bimini with Miami model Donna Rice. The photos (snapped by Rice's friend Lynn Armandt) showed Rice sitting on Hart's lap and Hart, surrounded by Rice, Armandt and a male friend, standing on the stage of a Bimini bar holding a pair of maracas.

The story details the long, romantic weekend the two spent aboard the yacht, *Monkey Business*, and quotes Rice as saying to several unnamed friends that Hart had said he loved her, and that he would divorce his long-suffering wife, Lee, *after* he was elected president.

Quotes like this one: "When Gary has a few beers, he becomes a wild and crazy guy, nothing like the straight serious man you see on TV" sank Hart's campaign for good.

HOW THEY DID IT: More than 12 editors and researchers

Levi's were invented for the California gold miners in 1873.

were involved in tracking down people who had either seen Hart and friends in Bimini or knew Donna Rice and her friend Lynn. Most of the story was drawn from what the loose-lipped Rice later told friends about the weekend. The tab for the photos came to a reputed $25,000.

THE SCOOP: The last hours of John Belushi as told by Cathy Evelyn Smith....and a confession by Smith that it was she who gave Belushi his final "speedball," the injection of cocaine and heroin that killed him.
HOW THEY DID IT: *Enquirer* reporters actually uncovered more information on Belushi's death than the Los Angeles Police Department. Then they tracked Smith down and paid her $15,000 to talk to them. The tell-all interview led police to reopen the case and further investigate her role in the incident. Eight months later, a Los Angeles grand jury indicted Smith for murder along with 13 counts of administering a dangerous drug. The evidence against Smith included the *Enquirer*'s interview tapes.

THE SCOOP: Carol Burnett was seen acting "boisterous and disorderly" in a Washington, D.C. restaurant.
HOW THEY DID IT: By stretching the facts. At least, that's what Burnett said as she sued them for big bucks... and won. In a rare retraction, the *Enquirer* admitted the error of its ways, but not without a parting shot.

The Quote: "As far as we're concerned," said an editor, "the Carol Burnett decision essentially means that Carol Burnett is now the only woman in America officially adjudicated as 'not the life of the party.'"

THE SCOOP: The Three Mile Island disaster was sabotage.
HOW THEY DID IT: According to an ex-reporter, they took a statement by a local cop that an elderly couple at a nearby motel looked a little suspicious to him...combined it with a similar statement that the radio and can opener the old couple had could conceivably be called a "dangerous weapon" and "sophisticated communications equipment," and pieced the rest of the totally misleading story together from there.

The first transcontinental phone call: 1915, from New York to San Francsico.

ANCIENT RIDDLES

These old riddles—and hundreds more—have been reproduced in the book Riddles—Ancient and Modern, *by Mark Bryant, published by Peter Bedrick Books. They're more "what am I?" than traditional riddles. Some of them are pretty hard, but they're all very clever. And all are authentically old.*

1. "The beginning of eternity,
The end of time and space,
The beginning of every end,
And the end of every place."
Hint: *It's in front of you right now.*

2. "I never was, am always to be,
None ever saw me, nor ever will,
And yet I am the confidence of all
Who live and breathe on this terrestrial ball."
Hint: *It never comes.*

3. "Runs over fields and woods all day,
Under the bed at night sits not alone,
With long tongue hanging out,
A-waiting for a bone."
Hint: *It's something very close to you.*

4. "At night they come without being fetched, and by day they are lost without being stolen."
Hint: *They belong to the night.*

5. "Fatherless and motherless,
Born without a skin,
Spoke when it came into the world,
And never spoke again."
Hint: *If you had no nose, you'd never know this one.*

6. "What gets wet when drying?"
No hint.

7. "There was a green house.
Inside the green house there was a white house.
Inside the white house there was a red house.
Inside the red house there were lots of black babies.
Hint: *A fruit.*

BYPASS SURGERY

For a change of pace, here's some medical history. Written by Dr. Lisa Berlin.

Today open heart surgery is performed using a cardiopulmonary bypass pump, a mechanical device that pumps blood and performs gas exchange. It allows surgeons to enter the heart directly without risking damage to other organs through lack of blood and oxygen.

Before mechanical bypass systems were perfected, one of the pioneers in this area, Dr. Walton Lillehei, used the heart and lungs of another living person to perform these vital functions. The patients usually were young children with life-threatening congenital heart defects, and the donors were usually parents. Child and parent lay side by side on separate tables in the operating room, and tubes connected the circulatory systems of each. The tubing went from the superior and inferior vena cavae of the child, major veins draining oxygen-poor blood into the heart, to a large vein in the parent. The blood then went to the parent's heart and lungs, picked up oxygen and released carbon dioxide, and then traveled back to the infant's aorta, or major artery, through a second tube placed in the parent's aorta.

Although this technique allowed for the correction of otherwise inoperable heart defects at a relatively small risk to the child, there were some complications involving the donors. It was eventually replaced by the purely mechanical systems in use today.

TOTALLY UNRELATED NEWS REPORT

A few years ago, someone sent us this article.

Ironton, Ohio. "Church members burned records albums and cassettes, after hearing evangelist Jim Brown of Psalms 150 in South Point say the "Mr. Ed" television theme conveys a satanic message to unwary listeners.

"'A horse is a horse'—when played backwards—contains the message 'the source is Satan' and 'Someone sung this song for Satan,' Brown said."

The theme song to "Mr. Ed" was written by the composers who wrote "Que Sera, Sera."

THE POPE

It was a tragedy that the Pope passed away. But there was nothing anyone could have done about it...or was there?

THE VICTIM: Pope John Paul I, leader of the Roman Catholic Church for a scant thirty-three days.

THE CIRCUMSTANCES: On September 29, 1978, the deceased Pope was discovered in his own bed; he had apparently died during the night. The cause, according to his doctors, was a heart attack. This didn't come as a surprise, however. Vatican offcials explained that the Pope had been ailing for some time. Fourteen hours later, the Pontiff was embalmed...without an autopsy.

UNANSWERED QUESTIONS: An entire book—*In God's Name: An Investigation Into the Murder of Pope John Paul I*—has been written about them by author David Yallop. A few of the more interesting ones:

- Why would the Vatican doctors claim to know the cause of death without performing an autopsy? Why didn't they do an autopsy? And what was the hurry to get the body embalmed?
- Why did the Vatican claim they anticipated a heart attack when all available evidence indicates the opposite? Three months before his death, for example, the Pope had an EKG which indicated a healthy heart; and his blood pressure was low.
- Why was he reported to have been reading a Medieval religious text when he died, when he had actually been reading some "personal papers"? What were the papers? And why did the Vatican say the Rev. John Magee discovered the corpse when it was really a nun named Sister Vincenza? What did the Sister see?

POSSIBLE CONCLUSIONS:

- It's just another conspiracy theory with no basis in reality.
- The Pope was murdered by conservative elements within the

Church because he planned a liberalization of some important rules, particularly regarding birth control.

• He was murdered by forces connected to the Vatican Bank scandals. As it was later revealed, the Vatican Bank was mixed up in a number of shady transactions involving some equally shady characters at that time—including Michael Sindona, a banker whose Mafia connections were exposed after the Franklin National Bank (which he owned) failed.

Sindona was later convicted of hiring hit men to kill an official of the Italian government who was investigating him. Why wouldn't he repeat the approach if the Pope had decided to expose him? Sindona, by the way, died of poisoning in jail.

There were several other questionable characters dealing with the Vatican Bank. Any of them or their associates might have assassinated the Pope if they felt sufficiently threatened. But as one author points out, we'll probably never know what really happened.

DEATH BY WATER BED

Reported by The Realist *in the '60s.*

"Malcolm Coors, a University of Arizona grad student in economics, became the first fatality of the waterbed fad. He had been watching a late-night talk show on his tiny Sony television, which had frayed electrical connecting wires. The set fell into a puddle—the result of his cat clawing at the waterbed—and he was electrocuted. The electrically charged water seeped up and surrounded his body before he could reach safety. Coors would have been 23 years old two days later."

KILLER TALK SHOW

The Realist also reported the rather bizarre circumstances of the death of publisher and health-food advocate J. I. Rodale. Rodale, who created the popular *Prevention* magazine, made an appearance on "The Dick Cavett Show" in the late '60s, confidently discussing his physical well-being. "He said that doctors had given him 6 months to live 30 years ago, but because of the food he ate, he would live to be a hundred." A little later in the show he appeared to have fallen asleep, and Cavett and guest Pete Hamill chuckled about it...until they realized he was dead. The taped show did not air.

There are an average of around 700 tornadoes every year in the U.S.

CONFUCIUS SAY...

Yes, there really was a Confucius. He was a Chinese sage and philosopher who lived from 551 to 479 B.C. Here are a few of the things he actually said.

"They who know *the truth* are not equal to those who love it, and they who love it are not equal to those who delight in it."

"The superior man has neither anxiety nor fear."

"Without knowing the force of words it is impossible to know men."

"We don't know yet about life, how can we know about death?"

"Being true to oneself is the law of God. To try to be true to oneself is the law of man."

"To be fond of learning is to be near to knowledge."

"Silence is a true friend who never betrays."

"The superior man thinks always of virtue; the common man thinks of comfort."

"He does not preach what he practices till he has practiced what he preaches."

"He who learns but does not think, is lost! He who thinks but does not learn is in great danger!"

"It is only the wisest and the very stupidest who cannot change."

"To see what is right and not to do it is want of courage."

"Our greatest glory is not in never falling but in rising every time we fall."

"True goodness springs from a man's own heart. All men are born good."

"The superior man is firm in the right way, and not merely firm."

"Sincerity and truth are the basis of every virtue."

"The strength of a nation is derived from the integrity of its homes."

Big Bucks: In 1988, Michael Jackson earned an estimated $60 million.

FAMOUS OVERDUBS

Sometimes a few words can make a big difference in a film. Here are three examples of voices being added to movies without the public knowing about it.

GIANT

James Dean's last film was an adaptation of Edna Ferber's *Giant*. "The last big speech Jimmy, as Jett Rink, made [was] when he addressed all of the Texas crowd who had spurned him. It was a drunken soliloquy, and Dean, in his attempt at accurate excellence, had slurred some meaningful words so badly, they had to be re-recorded." Unfortunately, by this time Dean had had his fatal accident. So his friend Nick Adams stepped in and did the overdub. "Nick, a noted mimic, could imitate anybody from Cary Grant...to Robert Wagner. He was able to redo parts of Jimmy's last speech so perfectly, it was years before anyone knew all those words had not come directly from Dean's own lips."

DR. STRANGELOVE

At the end of Stanley Kubrick's masterpiece of black humor, a B-52 with a doomsday bomb is headed for Russia. "Inside the B-52 Kong [played by Slim Pickens] and his men are opening their survival kits while over the intercom the major itemizes the incongruous contents." Slim Pickens, with his heavy Southern accent, comments: "Shoot, a fellah could have a pretty good weekend in Vegas with all that." Actually, the original line was "a fellah could have a pretty good weekend in Dallas with all that." But Wills went in and overdubbed the name of the city after JFK was assassinated.

THE EXORCIST

One of the most potent scenes in *The Exorcist* is "the voice of the devil emanating from the on-screen mouth of fourteen-year-old Linda Blair." How did she do it? She didn't. The voice turned out to belong to actress Mercedes McCambridge, who commented: "If people had heard her saying some of those obscenities, they would have fallen over laughing."

CAMPAIGN SMEARS

Campaign smears are ugly, but they're a part of American politics, and have been since the first elections. A few notable examples:

THE 1828 PRESIDENTIAL CAMPAIGN

During his second try for the presidency, Andrew Jackson was subjected to vicious slander by incumbent John Quincy Adams.

Jackson was termed "a blood-thirsty wild man, the son of a black and a prostitute and a murderer who had put to death soldiers who offended him." And he was accused of being an adulterer. This hit home. Unfortunately, Jackson's wife Rachel had married him unaware that she was still legally married to someone else; her previous marriage hadn't been officially dissolved. It was merely a technicality, but Adams's supporters relentlessly pursued it, dragging Rachel's name through the mud throughout the country.

By the time the matter was straightened out, Jackson had won the election....But he went to the White House alone. Rachel Jackson died of a heart attack; Jackson and his supporters attributed it to the brutal attacks during the campaign.

THE 1884 PRESIDENTIAL CAMPAIGN

In 1884 the governor of New York, Grover Cleveland, was closing in on the Democratic nomination for president when a Buffalo newspaper accused him of fathering an illegitimate boy ten years earlier.

Had he? Cleveland, a bachelor at the time, had indeed dated the woman. And he had contributed to the support of a child. But Cleveland was never proven to be the child's father; in fact, the woman admitted it could have been any one of a number of men. Nonetheless, when the presidential campaign began, the child was a part of it. Cleveland had to live with the chant: "Ma, Ma, Where's my Pa? Gone to the White House, ha! ha! ha!"

Interestingly, Cleveland's opponent, James G. Blaine, had his own problems—political scandals in his home state of Maine, and anti-Catholic prejudice—and wasn't able to capitalize on Cleveland's vulnerable position. Cleveland won.

THE 1864 PRESIDENTIAL CAMPAIGN

Anticipating the next election, Abraham Lincoln's enemies tried to undermine his presidency. A whispering campaign in Washington suggested that Lincoln's wife, Mary Todd, was secretly aiding the Confederates. It was a spurious charge, but it gained enough credibility to force the president to appear before a secret congressional committee investigating the matter. His prestige was slightly tarnished, but Lincoln was still re-elected.

THE FLORIDA SENATORIAL CAMPAIGN OF 1950

This is a textbook case of a politician using rhetoric to pander to the fears of less-educated people. Congressman George Smathers was challenging incumbent Senator Claude Pepper in Florida's Democratic senatorial primary in 1950. Smathers, the underdog, circulated printed material in the rural towns of central and northern Florida accusing Pepper of the following "indecencies":

- That his brother was a "practicing Homosapien."
- That he had a sister in New York who was a "thespian."
- And that Pepper himself had "matriculated" with young women.

To top it off, Smathers jumped on the early McCarthy bandwagon and saddled Claude with the nickname "Red" Pepper. Smathers won.

THE PRESIDENTIAL CAMPAIGN OF 1988

It keeps coming back. Sounding every bit like Joseph McCarthy, George Bush accused his opponent, Michael Dukakis, of being "a card-carrying member" of the American Civil Liberties Union—an organization devoted to upholding the Constitution and, ironically, one defending Oliver North at the time. The motive: people who knew nothing about the ACLU would respond to the phrase "card-carrying," identifying it with "commie." It worked.

As a person ages, the first sense to go is the sense of smell.

REAGANISMS

Some of Ronald Reagan's choicest comments.

"I'm not medical. I'm not a lawyer and I'm not medical, either."

"I'm no linguist, but I have been told that in the Russian language there isn't even a word for freedom."

"The taxpayer—that's someone who works for the federal government but doesn't have to take a civil service examination."

"Imagine if people in our nation could see the Bolshoi Ballet again, while Soviet children could see American plays and hear groups like the Beach Boys. And how about Soviet children watching 'Sesame Street'?"

"I'm concentrating on dog heaven."

"Boy, after seeing *Rambo* last night, I know what to do the next time this happens."

[On South Africa] "They have eliminated the segregation that we had in our own country, the type of thing where hotels and restaurants and places of entertainment and so forth were segregated—that has all been eliminated."

"Nuclear war would be the greatest tragedy, I think, ever experienced by mankind in the history of mankind."

"I'm not a lawyer, and I don't intend to get into too many legal areas where I might be caught short."

"If you've seen one redwood, you've seen them all."

"Why should we subsidize intellectual curiosity?"

"Government exists to protect us from each other. Where Government has gone beyond its limits is in deciding to protect us from ourselves."

"The best minds are not in government. If any were, business would hire them away."

The "first electronic computer" was built in 1889 for the U.S. Census Bureau.

SUPERSTITIONS

Many of us secretly believe far fetched legends— that broken mirrors and black cats really do bring bad luck, for example. It's amusing to discover the sources of our silliness.

LADDERS: The belief that walking under a ladder propped up against a building will bring bad luck comes from the early Christians. They held that the leaning ladder formed a triangle, and that this symbol of the Holy Trinity shouldn't be violated by walking through it. Those who did were considered in league with the devil.

FRIDAY THE THIRTEENTH: Friday, in general, is considered an unlucky day. An old poem goes: "Now Friday came. Your old wives say / Of all the week's the unluckiest day."

Adam and Eve were supposed to have been kicked out of the Garden of Eden on a Friday; Noah's great flood started on a Friday; and Christ was crucified on a Friday. Couple this with the fact that 12 witches plus the Devil—totalling 13—are necessary for a Satanic meeting, and the resulting combination (of Friday plus 13) is a deadly one.

SNEEZES: The European/American tradition of saying "God bless you" when someone sneezes originated during the sixth century. It was already customary to congratulate someone when they sneezed (the prevalent idea being that a sneeze expelled evil from the body), but when a plague whose symptoms included violent sneezes began spreading around southern Europe, the Pope stepped in. He declared that since a sneeze could be a sign of imminent death, people should bless the sneezer. The phrase caught on and became commonplace.

BREAKING A MIRROR: At one time in the ancient world, mirrors were used to tell fortunes. If a mirror was broken during the reading, it meant the person was doomed. Later, this was amended; a person's image was interpreted as a symbol of health, and a cracked image in a mirror meant imminent ill-

Tarantula spiders have been known to live for over two years without eating.

ness. But ultimately, the superstition of seven years bad luck is common today because it was used to scare European servants in the 1400s and 1500s into using extra care when polishing their masters' expensive mirrors. No servant (or anyone, for that matter) wanted to court a lifetime of bad luck. The belief spread, and became ingrained in European culture.

SALT: The origin of this nearly worldwide superstition is hard to trace, but it logically stems from salt's historic importance as a spice and medicine. If you were the kind of person who could spill something as precious as salt, you were clearly headed for trouble. Some historians attribute the rituals surrounding salt to Judas spilling the stuff at the table during the Last Supper, but that's spurious. The antidote—throwing a few grains over your left shoulder—is a little puzzling. The best explanation: in some cultures, people believed that nasty spirits inhabited the left side, and tossing some salt over the shoulder hit them right in the eyes—thus preventing their evil deeds.

ST. CHRISTOPHER MEDALS: Supposedly the patron saint of travellers. But many authorities don't believe there ever was a Saint Christopher.

BLACK CATS: In ancient Egypt, cats were regarded as spiritual creatures, and among the most exalted Goddesses was Bast, a black female cat. But in European culture, the black cat became an animal to avoid. Apparently in the Middle Ages, when ignorant peasants were convinced that witches and evil demons were living among them, cats were singled out as suspicious creatures (perhaps because of their silent, fluid movements, or the way they stare, or even their occasionally unworldly wailing). The fact that some of the women who cared for the cats were old and grizzled—i.e., witch material—probably added to the legend. Ultimately, people came to believe that a black cat was the nighttime embodiment of a witch.

LADYBUGS: "Ladybird, ladybird, fly away home...." It's considered bad luck to kill one of these orange, spotted insects because it represents the Virgin Mary.

In 1986, the program "Wheel of Fortune" earned over $100 million.

FAMILIAR NAMES

Some people achieve immortality because their names become commonly associated with an item or activity. You know the names—now here are the people.

R. J. Lechmere Guppy. A clergyman living in Trinidad. He sent several species of tropical fish to the British Museum, including a tiny specimen which now bears his name.

Dr. J. I. Guillotin. A French physician. Moved by mercy, he endorsed what he thought was a more humane method of execution than hanging. Ironically, the guillotine—which he did not invent—"is now synonymous with needless and brutal slaughter."

Jules Leotard. A renowned French acrobat of the nineteenth century. Designed and introduced the tight-fitting oufit "that does not hide your best features."

Tom Collins. A nineteenth century English Bartender at Limmer's Old House in London.

Amelia Jenks Bloomer. An outspoken late-nineteenth century feminist. Did not invent bloomers, but advocated their use by women (instead of corsets and cumbersome hoop skirts).

Nicholas Chauvin. Fanatically loyal soldier in Napoleon's army. Inspired the word *chauvinism*.

Cesar Ritz. A Swiss hotelier. Founded a chain of fancy hotels, which he named after himself.

John Duns Scotus. A respected scholar and theologian of the thirteenth century. Two hundred years after his death in 1308, his followers were known as "Scotists, Dunsmen, and Dunses," and were reviled for their resistance to the new ideas of the Renaissance. More enlightened thinkers chided the Dunses for their ignorance. Eventually *Dunses* became *dunces*.

Jean Nicot. French ambassador to Portugal in the 1550s. First brought tobacco to France. When nicotine was found in tobacco leaves in 1818, it was named after him.

Henry Shrapnel. English inventor. Created the shell that helped beat Napoleon in 1815.

Helen Porter Mitchell. A celebrated opera singer whose professional name was Melba (taken from her hometown of Melbourne, Australia). When she was dieting, she ate thin, crisp slices of bread now called Melba Toast. When she wasn't, she ate a dessert called Peach Melba.

Sylvester Graham. A food faddist of the early 1800s. Advocated vegetarianism and high fiber; he was called "the poet of bran meal and pumpkins" by Ralph Waldo Emerson. His followers were called *Grahamites*, and food he recommended included *Graham crackers* and *Graham flour*.

Etienne de Silhouette. Louis XIV's unpopular controller-general in 1759. He made shadow portraits, "recommending them for their cheapness," and they were named after him.

Haile Selassie. The emperor of Ethiopia, known as "The Lion of Judah." His real name was "Ras Tafari"—which explains the origin of the term *Rastafarian*.

Charles Wenburg. A nineteenth century shipping mogul. He discovered a new recipe for lobster and passed it on to Lorenzo Delmonico, who named it after him—*Lobster Wenburg*. Shortly after, Wenburg was ejected from Delmonico's Restaurant for fighting. His punishment: the first three letters of the dish were transposed; *Lobster Wenburg* became *Lobster Newburg*.

Charles Cunningham Boycott. A tyrannical land agent for an absentee owner. The Englishman was overseer of the Earl of Erne's estate in Ireland. When, after two consecutive bad potato harvests, farmers demanded lower rents, Boycott tried to evict them. The result: the farmers banded together and harrassed Boycott until he fled Ireland.

Around 200 people die while watching football games every year.

MYTH AMERICA

Very little of what we are taught about the "taming of the West" is true, and the legend of George Armstrong Custer is a perfect example.

A BRAVE INDIAN FIGHTER?

The Myth: General George Armstrong Custer was one of the U. S. Army's great soldiers during the western expansion. His valiant battle at the Little Bighorn—fighting a horde of renegade Indians that outnumbered his small cavalry unit 1,000 to 1 (Custer's Last Stand)—was an example of the fearlessness that made the white man's victory over the red man inevitable.

At one time so many people believed it that Custer was the hero of several films, and the main character in a prime-time TV series. ("The Legend of Custer" ran for a few months in 1967 on ABC.) Custer was also the subject of a million-selling record, "Please Mr. Custer," in 1958.

The Truth:

- Custer was a lieutenant colonel, not a general. (He had briefly been a major general during the Civil War, but was immediately demoted to captain when the war ended.)
- Custer was far from an exemplary soldier. He finished last in his class at West Point in 1861. And in 1867, he left his command to visit his wife; when he was caught, he was court-martialed and kicked out of the service for a year. He was allowed to return only because the Army needed help fighting Indians.
- Custer's Last Stand wasn't heroism, it was stupidity. Custer's division was supposed to be a small part of a major attack, led by General Alfred Terry—who was planning to meet Custer in two days with his troops. Custer was instructed to wait for Terry. Instead, he led his 266 men into battle, where they were all slaughtered. Historians speculate that the foolishly ambitious Custer believed a victory would earn him a presidential nomination, or that he had unwarranted contempt for the Indians' fighting ability.

WHAT AM I?

In the late twenties, America's intellectual elite devised a word game called "What Am I?" The idea was to offer literate clues to the identity of a common object or phenomenon without giving the answer away. These four examples are from the 1920s book about the game. Answers are on page 234.

1. I wear the face of a leader of men. My financial worth is small and my appearance not impressive, yet my presence is a passport to any country and society. I have the entrée alike to the boudoir and the armed camp; I penetrate to royal palaces and to the far corners of the earth. In my youth I am bright and fresh-looking; later, my face is marred and disfigured and I am cast aside as nothing; but when I am very old I am eagerly sought, and a safe refuge is provided for me, where I am exhibited to admiring visitors. What am I?

2. Everything that is presented to me I return at once. Although helpless I can wound; although speechless I can encourage. People are afraid of my fabled revenge so I am seldom hurt. Children adore me. A widely known character once went through me and discovered an amazing country. What am I?

3. Changeless through uncounted centuries, I am still the symbol of inconstancy. I am dead and cold in death, yet I exercise irresistible power, renewed every day, over that which is thousands of miles distant from me. I cause strange sensations in dogs and lovers and once inspired athletic ambitions in the domestic cow. I am a symbol of mania and of a formidably rising nation. Though I have a well-rounded character nobody has ever seen more than one side of me. What am I?

4. I am positively the worst ever. I am absolutely the best on record. I am always surpassing myself. My past is negligible, my future a matter of universal concern and infinite conjecture. Most people profess a prophetic vision of me, but birds and animals know more about me than they do. Everybody complains of me, but nobody ever does anything to correct or improve me. What am I?

A Swiss scientist named A. E. Fick invented contact lenses in 1887.

NIXON SEZ

It's probably been a while since you've thought about Tricky Dick. Just in case you're beginning to wonder why you didn't trust him in the first place, here's a refresher.

"I'll speak for the man, or against him, whichever will do him most good."

"We cannot judge it before it is concluded, and we cannot judge it even after it has been concluded."

"I rate myself a deeply committed pacifist."

"You won't have Nixon to kick around any more, gentlemen. This is my last Press Conference."

"Let us begin by committing ourselves to the truth, to see it like it is and to tell it like it is, to find the truth, to speak the truth and live with the truth. That's what we'll do."

"You can say that this Administration will have the first complete, far-reaching attack on the problem of hunger in history. Use all the rhetoric, so long as it doesn't cost money."

"I never made the [football] team...I was not heavy enough to play the line, not fast enough to play halfback and not smart enough to be a quarterback."

"When the President does it, that means it is not illegal."

"I like the job I have now, but, if I had my life to live over again, I'd like to have ended up as a sports writer."

"I would have made a good pope."

"I hear that whenever anyone in the White House tells a lie, Nixon gets a royalty."

"I'm not a lovable man."

"Call it paranoia, but paranoia for peace isn't that bad."

"Once you get into this great stream of history, you can't get out."

The first stewardesses were on United Airlines, in 1930. They had to be registered nurses.

M*A*S*H

*"M*A*S*H" was the first comedy on television to deal directly with the ugly facts of war, as well as the funny ones. The American public responded by making it one of the most popular programs in the history of the medium.*

HOW IT STARTED: When Richard Hornberger [pen name: Richard Hooker] completed the memoirs of his days with the 8055th MASH unit in Korea, he hardly expected he'd have a best-seller on his hands. And for the next eight years, his expectations were borne out—by rejection slips. He couldn't even get it published.

Finally in 1968, after securing a partner to polish up the manuscript, *M*A*S*H* was published by William Morrow and Co. Initially the book was a flop. But it caught the eye of Ingo Preminger (Otto's brother), who bought the movie rights and commissioned a screenplay (adapted by Ring Lardner, Jr.). Directed by Robert Altman, and starring Eliot Gould and Donald Sutherland, *M*A*S*H* was a phenomenal success—which caused *M*A*S*H* (the book) to become a surprise best-seller. 20th Century Fox elected to further capitalize on the movie by creating a low-budget television pilot using sets and props from the film.

When CBS decided to give the series a shot (or at least finance a pilot), nothing had been written yet. So producer Gene Reynolds called his friend Larry Gelbart in England and asked for a script. Gelbart whipped one out in two days.

*M*A*S*H* (the TV show) premiered in September, 1972 to low ratings and poor reviews. But CBS didn't lose faith. It allowed the show to struggle through its first season and, in an unusual act of foresight, kept it going into the next season—when it became a hit.

INSIDE FACTS:

Just the facts. More than half of the *M*A*S*H* storylines were the product of painstaking research. Larry Gelbart worked with photocopies of '50s issues of *Time* magazine and kept a master list of Korean names, a map of Korea, and an Army handbook on his desk.

Ladies' man. Alan Alda's support of the feminist movement is a tribute to Sister Elizabeth Kenney, whose cure for infantile paralysis (discovered during World War I) wasn't recognized by the male-dominated medical profession for nearly 20 years. The application of her theories cured Alda's childhood case of polio.

The real thing. The model for the *M*A*S*H* 4077th was the 8055th. In real life, the 8055th had a staff of 10 doctors and 12 nurses, and treated roughly 200 patients at a time.

The last show. The final 2 1/2 hour episode, *Goodbye, Farewell, and Amen*, was broadcast on February 28, 1983. Commercial time for the episode sold briskly at $450,000 per 30 second spot ($50,000 more than for the Super Bowl telecast), and over 125 million viewers were on hand (35 million more than watched *Roots*).

Funnier than fiction. Many of the episodes were based on stories purchased from Korean War MASH unit veterans.

Right Flank. Richard Hornberger (author of *M*A*S*H*) is actually a conservative Republican who fashioned Hawkeye after himself (real hometown: Crabapple Cove, Maine)—and didn't like the way Alda portrayed him at all. In fact, he was offended by the anti-war message of the show.

Korea or Vietnam? Make no mistake—the apparent anti-Vietnam bent of the early *M*A*S*H* wasn't coincidental. It was specifically written that way. Reynolds and Gelbart managed to air a weekly vilification of U.S. involvement in Southeast Asia by pre-dating it 20 years. Neat trick.

The set. *M*A*S*H* outdoor scenes were shot at the 20th Century Fox Ranch (now Malibu Canyon State Park). But most of the footage was shot at Fox Studios, where the *M*A*S*H* compound measured only 45' x 90', and came complete with a Korean landscape backdrop and a **rubber** floor!

Bill Cosby made an estimated $50 million in 1988.

THE POLITICS OF OZ

This fascinating story of how The Wizard of Oz might really be a political allegory comes from the Utne Reader, *"The Best of the Alternative Press."*
Written by Michael Dregni.

Who would believe that the battle between the gold and the silver standard in turn-of-the-century U.S. politics would make a good plot for a children's fantasy book?

And who would believe that a story as delightful as *The Wizard of Oz* could also have meaning for adults?

In These Times (Feb. 18, 1987) exposes Oz as a parable of populism, the 1890s Midwestern political movement led by William Jennings Bryan. The populists challenged Eastern banks and railroads, which they charged with oppressing farmers and industrial workers. Bryan felt that farmers were being crucified on a cross of gold; a switch to silver-backed currency would make money plentiful for all.

Oz author L. Frank Baum was a populist—and also a bit of a fantasizer. As editor of a South Dakota newspaper, he advised poor farmers to feed wood shavings to starving livestock, after fitting the beasts with special green glasses so they would think they were eating grass.

After Bryan's 1896 bid for the presidency failed, Baum was so moved to write the first of his long-running Oz series.

The allegory begins with the title: Oz is short for ounce, the measure for gold. Dorothy, hailing from the populist stronghold of Kansas, represents the common person. The Tin Woodsman is the industrial worker who is rusted solid, referring to the factories shut down in the 1893 depression. The Scarecrow is the farmer who lacks the brains to realize his own political interests. And the Cowardly Lion is Bryan himself, with a loud orator's roar but little else.

After vanquishing the Wicked Witch of the East (the Eastern banker) Dorothy frees the Munchkins (the little people). With the witch's silver slippers (the silver standard), Dorothy starts down the Yellow Brick Road (the gold standard) to the Eme-

The LaCoste shirt is named after French tennis star Rene LaCoste, Davis Cup winner in 1927.

rald City (Washington). There the group meets the Wizard (the president), who, like all good politicians, appears as whatever people wish to see. When the Wizard is defrocked, the Scarecrow denounces him as a humbug, which is the core of Baum's message, writes Michael A. Genovese in the Minneapolis *Star Tribune* (March 22, 1988).

Dorothy saves the day by dousing the Wicked Witch of the West with water, evoking the drought that was plaguing Midwestern farms at the time. The Wizard flies away in a hot-air balloon, the Scarecrow is left in charge of Oz, the Tin Woodsman rules the East, and the Cowardly Lion returns to the forest—Bryan had lost the election.

In the 1939 movie starring Judy Garland, the populist parable lost out to Hollywood escapism, and Dorothy's silver slippers were inexplicably changed to ruby. However, Baum might have applauded the use of black and white film depicting the grim reality of Kansas farm fortunes and color stock for the fantasy world of Oz. And the song "Somewhere Over the Rainbow" suited well the populist dream.

TOTALLY UNRELATED GOSSIP

According to Ed Lucaire in *Celebrity Trivia*:

- Clark Gable had no teeth; he wore dentures—which bothered the actresses he worked with. "His false teeth were just too much," complained Grace Kelly. And Vivian Leigh swore she would quit doing love scenes with him in *Gone With the Wind* "unless he washed out his mouth."
- Hugh Hefner was still a virgin on his 22nd birthday.
- Charles Bronson got his first part in a movie, *You're In the Navy Now* (1951), because "he could belch on cue."
- Adolf Hitler owned about 9,000 acres of land in Colorado. Hitler's favorite film was *King Kong*. His favorite song was Walt Disney's "Who's Afraid of the Big, Bad Wolf?"
- Jerry Lewis never wears the same pair of socks twice.

In Los Angeles, there are fewer people than there are automobiles.

QUOTES FROM JFK

Some better-known remarks made by our 35th president.

"There is no city in the United States in which I get a warmer welcome and less votes than Columbus, Ohio."

[*To his brother in 1960, before the election*] "Do you realize the responsibility I carry? I'm the only person standing between Nixon and the White House."

"When we got into office, the thing that surprised me most was to find that things were just as bad as we'd been saying they were."

[*At a press conference prior to the 1960 election*] "I have just received the following telegram from my generous Daddy. It says, 'Dear Jack: Don't buy a single more vote than is necessary. I'll be damned if I'm going to pay for a landslide.'"

"When power corrupts, poetry cleanses."

Question: "The Republican National Committee recently adopted a resolution saying you were pretty much of a failure. How do you feel about that?"
Pres. Kennedy: "I assume it passed unanimously."

"When written in Chinese, the word "crisis" is composed of two characters: one represents danger, the other represents opportunity."

"In a free society, art is not a weapon."

"Failure has no friends."

"Conformity is the jailer of freedom and the enemy of growth."

"Let us never negotiate out of fear. But let us never fear to negotiate."

"We must use time as a tool not as a couch."

"The war against hunger is truly mankind's war of liberation."

"The blessings of liberty have too often stood for privilege, materialism and a life of ease."

The first bra was created by a French designer in 1902. But bras didn't catch on until 1913.

THE LOUIE, LOUIE STORY

"Louie, Louie" is arguably the most recorded rock 'n' roll song of all time. The following history is from Behind the Hits, *by Bob Shannon and John Javna. The authors credit the "extensive liner notes" written by Doc Pelzell for Rhino Records' "Louie, Louie" album—an album consisting completely of different versions of the song.*

Besides groupies and recording contracts, what do Frank Zappa, Julie London, Iggy Pop, Barry White, Tom Petty and the Heartbreakers, Blondie, the Beach Boys, David McCallum, Toots and the Maytals, and the Kinks have in common? You guessed it. They—and thousands of other artists—have all performed versions of "the most easily recognizable rock 'n' roll song of all time"—"Louie, Louie." This three-chord wonder has been singled out by many critics as *the* definitive rock 'n' roll song. Yet it wasn't until seven or eight years *after* it was originally recorded that most American teens heard it for the first time.

In 1955, Richard Berry, a young black musician, was playing in Los Angeles with a Mexican group called Ricky Rivera and the Rhythm Rockers. One of the band's songs, "El Loco Cha Cha Cha," had a contagious rhythm figure in it that Berry just couldn't get out of his mind. And while he was waiting backstage to perform at the Harmony Club Ballroom one night, the words "Louie, Louie" popped into his head and superimposed themselves around the persistent riff; "the rest just fell into place." His main lyrical influence: a composition called "One for My Baby," which was sung from the viewpoint of a customer who was speaking to a bartender named Joe. In it, the singer said: "One for my baby/One for the road/Set 'em up Joe." In Berry's composition, the bartender became Louie, and the customer was telling Louie how he intended to sail to Jamaica to find his true love. The speech patterns and the use of Jamaica in the song were inspired by Berry's exposure to Latin music, and by Chuck (no relation) Berry's "Havana Moon," a similarly styled song that was popular at the time.

When Berry wrote "Louie, Louie," he was under contract to

Modern Records. But because of a dispute over the royalties for the sixty-plus songs he had written for the label, he saved the tune until his contract expired and he could record it for Flip Records. Flip released it in 1956 and it became a respectable R&B hit, selling (according to Berry) around 130,000 copies. A year later, however, sales had tapered off, and Berry needed some money for his upcoming wedding. So he sold the record sales publishing rights to "Louie Louie," retaining only the radio and television performance rights. He philosophically chalks this sale up to "experience." After all, who could have predicted the bizarre set of circumstances that would, a few years later, turn this song into a monster hit?

About five years later in Seattle, Washington, an obscure singer by the name of Rockin' Robin Roberts discovered Berry's recording of "Louie Louie" while browsing through the bargain bin of a local record store. "Louie" soon became Roberts' signature song and he took it with him through a succession of local bands. Finally, he joined one of the area's more popular groups, the Wailers (no relation to Bob Marley's contingent), and they decided to cut the song for their own Etiquette Records label. It was a regional hit in the Northwest, but when Liberty Records released it nationally, it flopped.

Kids in most of America still didn't know the song, but in Portland, Oregon, "Louie, Louie" was hot. One night, a Portland Top 40 band called the Kingsmen were playing a local dance with friendly rivals Paul Revere and the Raiders. During one of their breaks, they happened to notice that a lot of their audience had gathered around a juke box, and were dancing enthusiastically to the Wailers' record. Since this reaction was exactly what the Kingsmen were looking for in their own performances, they decided to include the song in their act; each member agreed to learn the song by their next rehearsal. But the only one to follow through on the pact was lead singer Jack Ely. Consequently, he had to teach it to the rest of the group; when he remembered it incorrectly, no one knew it. He taught the band a 1-2-3, 1-2, 1-2-3, 1-2 version, rather than the Wailers' 1-2-3-4, 1-2-, 1-2-3-4, 1-2 rendition. The result: he made the tune faster. It's interesting to speculate: would the song have been as successful if Ely hadn't accidentally altered it?

Anyway, the group got the response they were looking for. They were asked to play it as much as eight or nine times a night. One Friday in May, 1963, the band decided, just for kicks, to do a marathon version of the song to see who could last longer, the dancers or the band. Even bass player Bob Norby, who didn't sing, warbled a few verses just to keep the song going for approximately forty-five minutes. Despite the band's boredom, audience response was so positive that arrangements were made that night to record "Louie, Louie" the next day.

Actually, the Kingsmen had been wanting to get into the studio for some time. Their reason: a summer job. "That's really what 'Louie, Louie' was intended for," members of the band admit now, "an audition tape for a job on a steamship line for the summer. To Australia. We never got there, though. We had this hit record instead and had to go play the White House. And Wyoming. And Iowa." After pooling their money to come up with the $50 they needed for the two-hour session, the group went to the only recording studio in Portland and made their demo. Facilities were, at best, primitive. Mikes were placed next to amps that had been muffled with coats and blankets. Jack Ely's lead vocal was yelled up to a mike that was suspended near the studio's fifteen-foot ceiling—which explains the garbled lyrics that ultimately helped make the Kingsmen's record so successful. Strange twist: the very next day, Paul Revere and the Raiders, with Mark Lindsay on Sax, went into the same studio to record *their* version of "Louie, Louie."

Both the Kingsmen and Paul Revere's versions got local airplay, and Revere's actually did much better at the outset.

THE KINGSMEN: "Radio stations in those days used to promote their own shows—dances, record hops, local supermarket openings...and the Kingsmen were the house band for a station called KISN—y'know, we'd go out and do all the shows with all the jocks. And so, as soon as we recorded 'Louie, Louie,' of course, they put it on the air...Paul Revere's version got instant play all up and down the West Coast as soon as it was released; ours was only played in the Portland area, basically. But after a few months, toward the end of '63, a copy of two of our records got back to Boston. A disc jockey named Early

In 1984, a New Jersey man opened a summer camp for Cabbage Patch dolls.

Bird on an FM R&B station started playing it, thinking that we were an East Coast Rhythm and blues group or something. There was no precedent for this type of sound east of the Rockies. Eventually, Arnie 'Woo-Woo' Ginsberg on WBZ started blasting it all over the Northeast. Then it spread out all over the East Coast, into New York City. And then it became a national hit."

Going back a few months: after "Louie, Louie" began getting airplay in Boston, it was picked up for pressing and distribution by Wand Records. It fared well; by September, the record had reached #94 on the *Billboard* charts, and was climbing rapidly. But the final shot-in-the-arm that boosted the record to the top of the charts for four months caught even the Kingsmen off-guard; someone, somewhere, decided that the words were dirty. Without warning, rumors spread that Ely's slurred vocals were laced with obscenities, and soon every teenager in America was trying to figure out what Ely was "really" saying. They even did it at the band's live performances.

THE KINGSMEN: "It was kind of disheartening at first. Before we knew that there was this 'dirty lyrics' controversy, we thought that something was wrong with the band because we'd be playing all night long and when we'd hit our closer, which was 'Louie, Louie'—at the time our only hit—everyone would stop watching us. No one would pay attention any longer; they'd all pull these pieces of paper out of their pockets and start reading along...and singing. And they're going, 'Y'know, which version is right?' It was weird, having all these people come up to you like that." J. Edgar Hoover certainly wasn't going to stand for obscenity on the airwaves (neither was the state of Indiana, which banned "Louie"). The FBI and FCC launched a "Louie, Louie" investigation, playing the record at every speed from 16 to 78 rpm. They called in both Jack Ely and Richard Berry to testify about the lyrics. And in the end: the FCC concluded that, "We found the record to be unintelligible at any speed we played it." They hadn't found what they were looking for, but the FCC's efforts weren't entirely fruitless—they helped create a rock 'n' roll classic. With all that "negative" publicity, the record took off. It sold over eight million copies. "Well, you know," a member of the Kingsmen laughs today, "when the FBI and Lyndon Baines Johnson say, 'You can't do this,' that really does wonders for record sales."

The average American eats about 1 1/2 tons of food every year.

MOST COMMON WORDS

How's your vocabulary? Not particularly good, according to one etymologist.

One of the most entertaining books to peruse in the bathroom is Stuart Flexner's *I Hear America Talking*, an examination of America's speech. According to Flexner, there are an estimated 600,000 words in our English language—but the average American only understands around 2%-3% of them...and actually uses only *half* that amount. "Of these," Flexner says, "just 10 basic words account for over 25% of all speech and 50 simple words for almost 60%, with between 1,500 and 2,000 words accounting for 99% of everything we say." The most commonly used word is *I*, followed by *you*, *the*, and *a*. Of our written language, Flexner says: "[It] is only a little more varied than our spoken one, 70 words making up 50% of it....We are more likely to qualify our words and to use *but*, *or*, *if*, *so*, *which*, and *who*. In general, too...we use shorter sentences, fewer auxiliary verbs, and more active verbs."

The 50 Most Common Words

I	A	About	Do
You	An	Now	Are
He	On	Just	Want
She	To	Not	Can
It	Of	That	Would
We	In	This	Go
They	For	Is	Think
Me	With	Get	Say
Him	Out	Was	Be
Her	From	Will	See
Them	Over	Have	Know
What	And	Don't	Tell
The			Thing

The first sound recording ever made was "Mary Had a Little Lamb," in 1877 by Tom Edison.

HULA HOOPS

The Hula Hoop was a pioneer, the first major fad created and fueled by the new power in America—TV ads.

The Hula Hoop originated in Australia, where it was simply a bamboo exercise ring used in gym classes. In 1957, an Australian company began selling the ring in retail stores—which attracted the attention of a small California toy manufacturer named Wham-O.

Wham-O's owners made a few wooden rings for their kids ("They just wouldn't put the hoop down"), took them to cocktail parties ("Folks had to have a couple of drinks in them to take a whack at it")...and then decided they had a hot item on their hands. They began producing a plastic version, naming it a Hula Hoop after the motion it resembled—the Hawaiian hula dance.

Wham-O introduced it to the American public in January 1958, and it quickly became the biggest toy craze in history (up to that time). During the year over 20 million—$30 million worth—were sold. The Hula Hoop was the quintessential fad item, though; by November 1958 the Wall Street Journal was already announcing: "Hoops Have Had It." A brief comeback occurred in 1965, when Wham-O introduced the "Shoop-Shoop" Hula Hoop, with a ball-bearing in it to make noise, but it just wasn't the same.

HOOP FACTS:

- According to the *British Medical Journal*, the Hula Hoop was responsible for an increase in back, neck, and abdominal injuries.
- Indonesia banned Hula Hoops because they "might stimulate passion." Japan forbade them on public streets.
- The official news agency in China called Hula Hoops "A nauseating craze." In the Soviet Union the hoop was seen as a "symbol of the emptiness of American Culture."
- Hula Hoop Endurance records: longest whirl—four hours (over 18,000 turns), by a 10 year old Boston boy; most hoops twirled simultaneously—14, by an 11-year-old in Michigan.

You're more likely to catch people's colds from shaking hands with them than their sneezes.

THE HUNTING ACCIDENT

To people who noticed it in the obituaries on November 10, 1977, it seemed like just another unfortunate accident. But it may have been something more....

THE VICTIM: William C. Sullivan, former third-in-command in the FBI under J. Edgar Hoover, "the only liberal Democrat ever to break into the top ranks of the Bureau." For a decade, he ran the FBI's Domestic Intelligence division (including the investigation following JFK's assassination). In 1971 he was summarily fired by Hoover. Sullivan subsequently emerged as an active—and effective—critic of the Bureau.

THE CIRCUMSTANCES:
On November 9, 1977, shortly after daybreak, Sullivan went to meet two hunting companions near his Sugar Hill, New Hampshire home. He never made it. On the way, he was shot to death by the eighteen-year-old son of a state policeman. The young man claimed that (despite the fact that his rifle was equipped with a telescopic sight) he had mistaken Sullivan for a deer.

Two months later, the killer received his sentence in court: a $500 fine and a ten-year suspension of his hunting license.

UNANSWERED QUESTIONS:
Was it an accident, or the elimination of an adversary who knew too much? Consider these coincidences:

• As the FBI's illegal activities came to light in the mid-'70s, Bureau men were being brought to trial. At the time of his death, Sullivan was scheduled to be the chief witness against ex-agent John Kearny, who had been indicted for illegal wiretapping.

• At the time of the accident, Sullivan was writing a tell-all book about his years in the FBI. The book was ultimately completed by his co-author and was published by W. W. Norton and Company. But it had no author to champion it to the media, and no one to do a sequel—the author was dead.

• In 1976, Congress voted to open its own investigation of the JFK and Martin Luther King assassinations. "Sullivan would have been questioned by the Assassinations Committe in 1978," says Anthony Summers in his book about the death of JFK (*Conspiracy*). He goes on: "Sullivan had been head of the FBI's Division Five, which handled much of the King and Kennedy investigations....In 1975, Sullivan responded in opaque fashion to a question from a Congressional committee about Oswald. Asked whether he had seen anything in the files to indicate a relationship between Oswald and the CIA, Sullivan replied, 'No, I think there may be something on that, but you asked me if I had seen anything. I don't recall ever having seen anything like that, but I think there is something on that point....It rings a bell in my head.' Sullivan's fatal accident occurred before the Assassinations Committee could ask him to be more specific about the source of that bell in his mind."

POSSIBLE CONCLUSIONS:

• *It was a hunting accident.* Sullivan's co-author on *The Bureau*, Bill Brown, says he flew to New Hampshire and checked it out—and was satisfied that the incident really was an accident.

• *It was an assassination.* We asked several hunting enthusiasts about the probability of the shooting being an accident, based on their experience. The conclusion: they're skeptical that an experienced hunter with a telescopic sight could confuse a man with a deer. Among other things, the hunter would have to look carefully to verify that the "deer" was old enough—and the right sex—to shoot legally. If it wasn't a hunting accident? Two possibilities: either people associated with the FBI who would be damaged by Sullivan's testimony/revelations decided to eliminate him; or someone associated with the Kennedy assassination wanted him silenced.

What's your guess?

CAR NAMES

They're a part of your life; you know them as well as you know your own name. But do you know where they come from?

SOME REAL PEOPLE

Chevrolet. Louis Chevrolet, a race car driver and designer who co-founded the company which later merged with GM.

Oldsmobile. Ransom Eli Olds, an auto pioneer who started the Olds Motor Vehicle company in 1897.

Rolls-Royce. A combination of Sir Henry Royce's and Charles Rolls's names. Royce founded the company in 1903, Rolls promoted the car.

Mercedes-Benz. The *Benz* is Karl Benz, believed by many to be the inventor of the automobile in 1879. *Mercedes* comes from a young girl named Mercedes Jellinek, whose father was a German diplomat and an investor in the company.

Dodge. John and Horace Dodge. Set up the Dodge Brothers Machine Shop in Detroit in 1901, and were immediately hired to make transmissions for Ransom Olds. In 1914, they started their own car company, building low-cost autos to compete with Ford.

Buick. David Dunbar Buick, a Scotsman. Gave up his failing Buick Motor Car Company to William Durant, who in 1908 turned it into the nation's most successful—and used it as the cornerstone of the General Motors empire. Buick died broke; he was "so poor he could afford neither a telephone nor a Buick."

Chrysler. Walter Chrysler. A huge man, all of his Chrysler cars were designed extra-large, so they'd be comfortable for him to sit in.

SOME INSTANT WORDS

Caravan. A car combined with a van—a Car-a-van!

Nissan Sentra. According to one of the men who named it: "It's the company's mainstream, or central, car, and they wanted consumers to understand that it was quite safe, even though it was small. The word *Sentra* sounds likes *central*, as well as *sentry*, which evokes images of safety."

Corvair. A combination of the sporty Corvette and the family-oriented Bel Air.

Volvo. Means *I roll* in Latin.

Camaro. According to GM in 1967, it meant pal in French, a fitting title because "the real mission of our automobile is to be a close companion to its owner." But a French auto executive corrected them: "It doesn't mean anything in English, and it doesn't mean anything in French, either."

Toronado. Literally means, in Spanish, *floating bull*. But that has nothing to do with the car; GM just thought it sounded classy and exciting.

SOME SECOND CHOICES

Mustang. Original name: Torino.

Ford expected to appeal exclusively to young sports car lovers with this vehicle. The name *Torino* was chosen because it sounded like an Italian sports car; the projected ad campaign called it "the new import...from Detroit." But last-minute market research showed that the car could appeal to all buyers, and a new name had to be chosen. Colt, Maverick, and Bronco (all used for later cars) were considered. But Mustang seemed best, bringing to mind cowboys, adventure, and the Wild West. As one Ford man put it, "It had the excitement of the wide-open spaces, and it was as American as all hell."

Pontiac Firebird. Original name: the Banshee.

The press releases were out, the initial announcement had been made, and then someone at Pontiac discovered that in Irish folklore, a Banshee is "a supernatural being whose wailing foretells death." That, of course, would have been a public relations disaster; it would have been like calling a car "the Grim Reaper." Who would dare buy it? The firebird, a creature of Native American legends, was chosen instead.

BIRTH OF THE BIKINI

Conservatives have long pointed to the bikini as an example of our moral decline; yet history shows that the bikini is related to the A-bomb and war, not simply sex.

The atomic bomb is responsible for many terrible things and at least one attractive thing—the bikini.

In July 1946, the American government announced that it would be exploding an atomic bomb. It was just a test, but this was the first *announced* atomic bomb blast, and people's imaginations ran wild. Rumors spread that it was going to be a "super bomb" that could easily get out of control, start a massive chain reaction, and blow up the world.

Party Time.

These rumors were especially prevalent in Paris, which had recently suffered through the trauma of German occupation in World War II. Parisians simply couldn't take any more pressure....So instead of protesting the impending explosion, they celebrated. Hostesses used the bomb threat as an excuse to hold "end-of-the-world" parties; young men used it as an excuse to convince reluctant girl friends to give in (if the world was going to end, why not break *all* the rules?). And when it was revealed that the test would take place in the then-unheard-of Bikini Atoll, the parties became "Bikini" parties.

A Publicity Stunt

Meanwhile, a fashion show was being planned for the Piscine Molitor in Paris on July 5, 1946 (note: *piscine* is French for swimming pool). Its promoters wanted to attract attention, and since people seemed to be throwing modesty to the wind, the promoters came up with the idea of a "Bikini" costume—one that would go as far as anyone dared go with a bathing suit. So in the middle of the fashion show, Paris model Micheline Bernardini suddenly stepped out before the audience wearing a scanty two-piece bathing suit—the world's first "bikini." Of course the scandalous suit got international publicity...and a new style was born.

Nothing new under the sun: Archaeologists have now found evidence that bikinis were worn in Sicily as early as 2000, B.C.

STAR TREK

This is the show that started the cult TV boom. It has now spawned an industry that includes movies, toys, videos, etc. Here are some facts about it, from Cult TV, *by John Javna.*

HOW STAR TREK BEGAN: Gene Roddenberry, the head writer for a popular western called *Have Gun, Will Travel*, was also a science fiction buff. He saw a lot of similarities between space exploration and the experiences of the American pioneers—so he conceived of a TV space fantasy that would be similar to a western series, complete with continuing characters (which hadn't ever been done). He based his idea on a popular show named *Wagon Train*. He called his idea a "wagon train to the stars." A star trek.

In 1964, while producing an MGM series *The Lieutenant*, Roddenberry created a workable format for his space show. MGM turned it down, but Desilu bought it and sold the idea to NBC. The network financed the pilot called "The Cage." This was filmed in November and December. It cost $630,000—an outrageous amount for the time—and featured only two members of the final cast—Majel Barret and Leonard Nimoy. The captain's name wasn't Kirk—it was Pike. he was played by Jeffrey Hunter.

The pilot was submitted to NBC in February, 1965. They rejected it. But the project wasn't canned; NBC still saw promise in the series and authorized an unprecedented second pilot—including an almost entirely new cast. The new film was entitled "Where No Man Has Gone Before." It featured Shatner as Kirk, Nimoy as Science Officer Spock, Doohan as Scotty, and Takei as Physicist Sulu. For the record, the doctor's name was Mark Piper. He was played by Paul Fix.

The second pilot was submitted in January, 1966. A month later NBC accepted it for their coming fall schedule.

INSIDE FACTS

Easier than landing. The Enterprise's "transporter" was developed as a cost-cutting measure. It provided an inexpensive means to transport characters from the ship to the next set (landings are expensive). The "glittering" effect (as the transporter dissolved and relocated the passengers' atoms) was provided by aluminum dust.

The Starship Enterprise. Three models of the Enterprise were used in filming: a 4-inch miniature, a 3-foot model, and a 14-foot plastic model that now hangs in the Smithsonian.

Those Ears. Spock's pointed ears were originally included as a throw-in when Roddenberry contracted with a special-effects house to produce three monster heads.
•The first pair were "gruesome," according to Nimoy. "They were rough and porous, like alligator skin." But two days before shooting, they were finally modified to everyone's satisfaction.
•Nimoy objected to wearing the ears, but Roddenberry offered a compromise—wear them for a while, and if they didn't work out, Spock could have "plastic surgery" and have them altered. Nimoy agreed.
•A typical pair of ears lasted from three to five days.

On the air. Believe it or not, the highest *Star Trek* ever ranked in a year's prime time rating was #52.

Logical thinking. One of Leonard Nimoy's contributions was the Vulcan nerve pinch. In one scene, he was supposed to sneak up behind a character and whack him on the head with a gun. But he objected that Vulcans wouldn't be so crude. As a substitute, he made up the legendary maneuver on the spot.

The Source. Incipient Trekkies who want a first-hand look at the inspiration for many of *Star Trek's* distinctive features should view the 1956 film *Forbidden Planet*, which starred Walter Pidgeon, Anne Francis, and Leslie Neilsen. Some of the "similarities" are amazing.

Fat City. Alert fans can tell in what part of the season an episode was filmed just by observing William Shatner's stomach. Always in top shape before shooting began, Shatner appeared trim and fit in early-season episodes. But as the season wore on, time to exercise became harder to find, and his waistline expanded.

In Germany more people have the last name of Schultz than any other name.

COMMON PHRASES

What do these familiar phrases really mean? Etymologists have researched them and come up with these explanations.

SMELL A RAT
Meaning: To sense that something is wrong.
Background: In earlier times, it was fairly common for people to have rats infesting their houses. And if a rat died in a place where it wasn't visible—inside a wall, for example—the person who lived in the house didn't know about it until he could literally smell the decaying rodent. That's how he could tell something was amiss.

HAM ACTOR (HAM)
Meaning: Someone who enjoys putting on a show, or who plays rather obviously to an audience (though not necessarily on stage).
Background: An American phrase originating in the 1880s. Minstrel shows, mass entertainment of the time, often featured less-than-talented performers who overacted. They frequently appeared in "blackface," and used ham fat to remove their make-up. Thus they were referred to as "ham fat men," later shortened to "ham."

WHIPPING BOY
Meaning: A scapegoat, or someone who is habitually picked on.
Background: Hundreds of years ago, it was normal practice for a European prince to be raised with a commoner of the same age. Since princes couldn't be disciplined like ordinary kids, the commoner would be beaten whenever the prince did something wrong. The commoner was called the prince's *whipping boy*.

RAINING CATS AND DOGS
Meaning: Torrential rain
Background: In the days before garbage collection, people tossed their trash in the gutter—including deceased house pets—and it just lay there. When it rained really hard, the garbage,

including the bodies of dead cats and dogs, went floating down the street. So there had to be a hell of a lot of water for it to rain cats and dogs.

HIT THE PANIC BUTTON

Meaning: "Speaking or acting in unnecessary haste."
Background: Coined during World War II, by men in the Air Force. According to Lt. Col. James Jackson, in *American Speech* magazine: "The actual source seems...to have been the bell system used in [B-17 and B-24] bombers for emergency procedures such as bailout and ditching. In case of fighter or flak damage so extensive that the bomber had to be abandoned, the pilot rang a 'prepare to abandon' ring, and then a ring meaning 'jump.' The bell system was used since the intercom was apt to be out if there was extensive damage. The implications of the phrase seem to have come from those few times when pilots hit the panic button too soon and rang for emergency procedures over minor damage, causing their crews to bail out unnecessarily."

HACK WRITER

Meaning: Writer who churns out words for money.
Background: In Victorian England, a hackney, or "hack," was a carriage for hire. (The term is still used in reference to taxi drivers, who need their "hack's licenses" to work.) It became a description of anyone who plies their trade strictly for cash.

PIE IN THE SKY

Meaning: An illusion, a dream, a fantasy. An unrealistic goal.
Background: Joe Hill, a famous labor organizer of the early 20th century, wrote a tune called "The Preacher and the Slave," in which he accused the clergy of promising a better life in Heaven while people starved on Earth. A few of the lines: "Work and pray, live on hay, you'll get pie in the sky when you die (That's a lie!)."

HARD AND FAST

Meaning: "Unalterable."
Background: "Refers to a vessel that is stuck on the bottom, which is hard, where it is held fast."

The animal with the largest eyes on earth: the giant squid, with eyes as big as pie plates.

ROCK CHARACTERS

Many pop songs are about real people, although most of the public never knows exactly who. Here are a few examples, from Behind the Hits, *by Bob Shannon and John Javna.*

DONNA, Ritchie Valens. 1959/Top 5. Donna Ludwig was Ritchie's high school girlfriend. Valens quit high school to go on tour when his record was released. It hit #2 in December, 1958, and Ritchie was killed a few months later in the February, 1959, plane crash with Buddy Holly and Big Bopper Richardson.

LET IT BE, the Beatles. 1969/#1. Who is "Mother Mary"? Paul McCartney: "My mother's name was Mary, so that was probably what that was about."

CATHY'S CLOWN, the Everly Brothers. 1960/#1. Cathy was Don Everly's high school girlfriend in Knoxville, Tennessee.

KILLING ME SOFTLY WITH HIS SONG, Roberta Flack. 1973/#1. The singer referred to in the song is Don McLean, composer of "American Pie." Songwriter Lori Lieberman saw him perform in Los Angeles, and was so knocked out that she wrote a ten-minute song about it. Roberta Flack rewrote the tune and had a hit with it.

DIANA, Paul Anka. 1957/#1. Diana Ayoub was an older girl with whom 15-year-old Paul Anka was infatuated. "She was a girl I saw at church and saw now and then at functions," he says. "She was a little out of my league. She was twenty and I was fifteen—and she really didn't want anything to do with me, which made it even worse." Worse still, Diana was babysitting for Anka's younger brother and sister, so it was hard to avoid her. Anka wrote a poem about her and set it to music. It became a #1 hit and a million-seller, and launched his show business career.

OH! CAROL, Neil Sedaka. 1959/Top 10. Carol was Carole Klein, whom singer Neil Sedaka described as "a scrawny girl, with dirty blonde hair, a long nose, and funny buck teeth." She was a fan of Sedaka's Brooklyn high school group, the Tokens, and used to hang around with Sedaka. After "Oh! Carol" hit, the real Carole put out an answer record called "Oh Neil," which flopped. Later she married Gerry Goffin and after changing her name to Carole King, she wrote classic pop songs like "Up on the Roof."

ROSANNA, Toto, 1982/#2. It's about actress Rosanna Arquette.

SEXY SADIE, the Beatles. 1968/"The White Album." Not a single, but worth mentioning. Sadie was the Maharishi Mahesh Yogi, father of "Transcendental Meditation" ("TM"), whom the Beatles followed to India in 1967. John Lennon dubbed him "sexy" after he found out the Maharishi had tried to make it with Mia Farrow, a disciple who was staying at the Maharishi's retreat at the same time the Beatles were.

WINDY, the Association. 1967/#1. Although the Association sang about a *girl* named Windy, the song was actually written about a man. The composer was Ruthann Friedman and Windy, her boyfriend, was an original hippie, living in San Francisco's Haight-Ashbury district. In that context the lyrics make a lot more sense. Example: he's "tripping" down the streets of the city. The song was originally written in waltz (3/4) time.

HEY JUDE, the Beatles. 1968/#1. Jude is Julian Lennon. In 1968, John Lennon had fallen in love with Yoko Ono and wanted to divorce his wife, Cynthia. It was messy at first—Cynthia retreated to Italy with her mother and son, Julian. But finally she returned to England to discuss terms of the divorce. "The only way I could get in touch with John was through Peter Brown at Apple," she says, "and when I finally did meet him, Yoko was there. He insisted she should stay." Julian was feeling the effects of the battle, and Paul McCartney, who was good friends with the boy, went to see him. As McCartney drove he began improvising a consoling melody. The words that went with it were "Hey Jules..." McCartney: "Then I thought a better name was Jude. A bit more country and western for me." Ironically, John Lennon thought that McCartney had written the song for *him*.

Americans spend $8 billion a year on pornography.

ST. LENNY SAYS...

No one explained the innate contradictions of society better than Lenny Bruce.

"All my humor is based on destruction and despair. If the whole world were tranquil, without disease and violence, I'd be standing in the breadline—right back of J. Edgar Hoover."

"Every day people are straying away from the church and going back to God. Really."

[About drugs] "I'll die young ...but it's like kissing God."

"[The Crucifixion] was just one of those parties that got out of hand."

"People should be taught what is, not what should be."

"There's nothing sadder than an old hipster."

"If the bedroom is dirty to you, then you are a true atheist, because...if anyone in this audience believes that God made his body, and your body is dirty, the fault lies with the manufacturer."

[*The dedication to his autobiography*] "I dedicate this book to all the followers of Christ and his teachings; in particular to a true Christian—Jimmy Hoffa—because he hired ex-convicts as, I assume, Christ would have."

"We're all the same people....And it discourages me that we try so desperately to be unique."

[*On his legal problems*] "What I need is a lawyer with enough juice to get Ray Charles a driver's license."

"I'm not original. The only way I could truly say I was original is if I created the English language. I did, man, but they don't believe me."

"Marijuana will be legal some day, because the many law students who now smoke pot will some day become Congressmen and legalize it in order to protect themselves."

According to one poll, nearly 3/4 of all American women wear a bra that is the wrong size.

CONGRESSIONAL WIT

Even congressmen can be funny—albeit sometimes unintentionally. Bill Hogan and Mike Hill scoured the Congressional Record and came up with Congress's most amusing moments for their book, Will the Gentleman Yield?, *published by* **Ten Speed** *Press.*

SHEA A LITTLE LONGER

Mr. *Domenici.* Will the Senator yield for a question without losing his right to the floor?
Mr. *D'Amato.* Certainly.
Mr. *Domenici.* If the Senator is going to stay here and talk until Saturday night, would he give me his ticket to the Mets game? He can stay here and I will go.

—Sens. Pete V. Domenici (R-N. Mex.) and
Alfonse M. D'Amato (R-N.Y.)
October 16, 1986

POTATO, GRENADA

Mr. Speaker, some 40 years ago, George Gershwin popularized a little ditty that went like this:

"You like po-ta-to and I like po-tah-to,
You like to-ma-to, and I like to-mah-to,
Po-ta-to, po-tah-to, To-ma-to, to-mah-to!
Let's call the whole thing off!"

At about the same time that Mr. Gershwin was writing his tune, Mr. Reagan was starring in the kind of movies that recent incidents in Grenada cannot help but remind one of. Think about it for a moment—a small Caribbean island, a band of bearded local militia, a lot of beautiful and confused residents, and throw in a few angry tourists for comic relief. Unfortunately, this is not a grade B movie, it is not even a very good script—two American marines have already lost their lives.

But if that is the way Mr. Reagan persists in looking at these issues maybe he will listen to a little advice from Mr. Gersh-

The flu was first described by Hippocrates, in 412 B.C.

win. If Gershwin were alive today, perhaps he would consider this rewrite:

You like po-ta-to, I like po-tah-to,
You say Gre-na-da, I say Gre-nah-da,
Po-ta-to, po-tah-to, Gre-na-da, Gre-nah-da,
Let's call the whole thing off.

—Rep. James M. Shannon (D-Mass.)
October 26, 1983

TEED OFF AT THE POST OFFICE? REMEMBER LARRY

Mr. Speaker, a recent item in the *Washington Star* told of one Larry Ryan who scored a hole-in-one while playing in the Pittsfield, Mass., Post Office Golf Tournament. But his was a dubious achievement. He drove from the third tee and the ball went 180 yards away—into the cup on the first green.

Some would find this an apt analogy to the operations of the Postal Service. So, whenever you receive mail intended for another—a not uncommon occurrence—it is a safe guess that our Postal Service is using the Larry Ryan method of delivery.

—Rep. Charles H. Wilson (D-Calif.)
June 10, 1975

OH GOD

I recall something that involved my good Baptist friend, Bill D. Moyers....

President Johnson called on Bill one day to open a Cabinet meeting with prayer. Bill was sitting at the end of the Cabinet table, and when he had finished the prayer, the President said, "Bill, we couldn't hear you up here."

Bill said, "I wasn't talking to you, Mr. President."

—Rep. Brooks Hays (D-Ark.)
May 19, 1977

CONE HEAD

Mr. Speaker, I have introduced a resolution declaring July Ice Cream Month and July 15 as Ice Cream Day....Ice cream is good for you.

If you feel dejected or frustrated, eat ice cream; if the legis-

***The African Queen* was originally supposed to star David Niven and Bette Davis.**

lative processes frustrate you, eat ice cream; if you are happy and want to celebrate, eat ice cream. Not only will you help an industry and American workers but it is good, it is just plain good.

—Rep. E de la Garza (D-Tex.)
June 7, 1984

GOLDEN OLDIE

I am reminded of the time when Emanuel Celler was in the House, and I served with him. Emanuel Celler was the oldest Member of that body at that time. He was...speaking in support of a measure I had introduced, and he forgot certain facts about which I reminded him.

He said, "Oh yes, yes. How clearly I recall that now. You know, there are three signs of aging. The first is that you tend to forget things rather easily—and for the life of me, I don't know what the other two things are."

[Laughter.]

—Sen. Spark M. Matsunaga (D-Hawaii)
March 12, 1980

STARK DIFFERENCES

Mr. Speaker, the *Washington Post* reports that the Army has granted a $139,000 contract to the University of Maryland to conduct a study of how to prepare healthy food that tastes good. I submit that the Army asking a college food service about healthy, tasty food is rather like Phyllis Diller asking Joan Rivers about beauty aids....

—Rep. Fortney H. (Pete) Stark (D-Calif.)
October 10, 1986

UPS AND DOWNS

Mr. Speaker, after careful and scholarly study I have concluded that the principal cause of congressional inefficiency is the elevator system in the Longworth Building.

—Rep. Andrew Jacobs, Jr. (D-Ind.)
June 15, 1976

The first all-talking movie was called *The Lights of New York*.

BUTCH AND SUNDANCE

Butch Cassidy and the Sundance Kid, *starring Paul Newman and Robert Redford, is the highest-grossing cowboy film of all-time. For those of you who assume that the pair's wild on-screen exploits were pure fantasy, here's a surprise.*

Of all the outlaws, desperadoes and personalities of the West, perhaps none have captured the fancy of Americans more than Butch Cassidy and the Sundance Kid. They were master bank and train robbers, outlaws who seldom used their guns, and among the very few who lived to spend and enjoy the enormous wealth they captured in the waning days of the Wild West.

Cassidy, whose real name was Robert Leroy Parker, was born in 1866 to Mormon parents in Utah. Harry Longabaugh, the Sundance Kid, probably hailed from New Jersey or Pennsylvania sometime in the late 1860s. Both Cassidy and Sundance were products of the times, when small ranchers and businessmen were often overwhelmed by the well-financed "robber barons" of the era. Some historians believe their robbery exploits were a reaction to the emerging monopoly capitalism mentality, while others feel it was simply a case of "bad company."

At any rate, Cassidy, Sundance, and their gang—known both as the Hole in the Wall Gang and the Wild Bunch—were masters of the big heist. They perfected the technique of the three-man robbery—one man to hold the horse, one to hold the gun, and of course, one to grab the cash. The gang was particularly famous for their stylish technique. When the boys took a train, they blew up the baggage cars with dynamite...but *never* hurt the passengers or crew. And the robberies were always well planned out from start to finish—which accounts for their long and lucrative careers.

In 1900, with the Wild Bunch's numbers diminishing (due to the steady pursuit of the famous Pinkerton Detective Agency), Cassidy, Sundance and a third man robbed a bank in a remote part of Nevada and netted over $32,000 in cash. They split up to meet again in Texas, where a wild spending spree ensued.

In 1901, the two discussed plans to go to South America, then pulled a final train robbery, demolishing a baggage car and making off with thousands in bank notes. After a brief visit to New York City, the pair and Sundance's lover went to Argentina and bought a ranch. There they apparently led a quiet life. But in 1906, probably because they were running out of money, they robbed a bank in a nearby town.

After a trip back to the United States by Sundance and his ailing mistress, the pair met up again, sometime around 1909 in Bolivia. A violent shoot out with the Bolivian cavalry (probably during a robbery) ensued, and it was from that point on that their legend began to really take shape. Accounts of what happened during and after the shootout vary: Some say both men died; some think Cassidy survived; but most are now convinced that both outlaws actually escaped, with Sundance rejoining his long-time lover and living quietly in Wyoming until 1956. As for Cassidy, he probably changed his name and died in a nursing home in Washington state in 1937.

Whatever the real story, it's clear that Butch Cassidy and the Sundance Kid were among the cleverest and shrewdest outlaws ever to emerge from the Old West.

FACTS ABOUT THE WEST

- Billy the Kid was from Brooklyn, New York.
- The most common causes of death for old-time cowboys: pneumonia and riding accidents.
- Most cowboys didn't like carrying guns—they got in the way when they were riding, and scared their horses or cattle.

TOP TEN BABY NAMES

What's in a name? Sugar and spice? Or the herd instinct? Here's what parents have been naming their kids for the last fifty years.

Most popular baby names in 1925:

For Girls:	For Boys:
1. Mary	Robert
2. Barbara	John
3. Dorothy	William
4. Betty	James
5. Ruth	Charles
6. Margaret	Richard
7. Helen	George
8. Elizabeth	Donald
9. Jean	Joseph
10. Ann	Edward

Most popular baby names in 1948:

For Girls:	For Boys:
1. Linda	Robert
2. Mary	John
3. Barbara	James
4. Patricia	Michael
5. Susan	William
6. Kathleen	Richard
7. Carol	Joseph
8. Nancy	Thomas
9. Margaret	Stephen
10. Diane	David

Most popular baby names in 1974:

For Girls:	For Boys:
1. Jennifer	Michael
2. Michelle	John
3. Christine	Robert
4. Lisa	David
5. Maria	Christopher
6. Melissa	Anthony
7. Nicole	Joseph
8. Elizabeth	Jason
9. Jessica	James
10. Erica	Jose

Most popular baby names in 1987:

For Girls:	For Boys:
1. Jessica	Michael
2. Jennifer	Christopher
3. Ashley	Matthew
4. Amanda	Daniel
5. Christine	Joseph
6. Sara(h)	David
7. Nicole	Andrew
8. Stephanie	Steven
9. Melissa	Brian
10. Danielle	Robert

The Statue of Liberty was originally built for the Suez Canal.

MONOPOLY

Monopoly is the best selling game in history. It has been published in twenty-eight countries and nineteen different languages and is more popular in the eighties than ever.

If there was ever a way to introduce the concept of capitalism to children, this game is it.

Background: In 1904, "The Landlord's Game," a board game which included the purchasing of property, utilities and a "public park" space, was patented. Apparently Charles Darrow, the father of Monopoly, "borrowed" much of this game.

The Origin. Following the stock market crash of 1929, Darrow—an engineer by trade—found himself unemployed and short of cash like the rest of the country. To kill time (and keep his spirits up), he began devising a game involving "plenty of money for the player to invest or speculate with." Because he was interested in real estate he made that the primary focus; and because he personally didn't believe in credit or borrowing money, he made the whole thing a cash proposition.

Darrow had visited Atlantic City shortly before the stock market crashed, so he transferred his fond memories of the town to the board—thus the Boardwalk, railroad lines and property of the New Jersey resort are represented there.

The original version of the game was crudely painted on a piece of linoleum. But that didn't stop family and friends from getting hooked on it—and demanding their own sets. "I hadn't anything better to do, so I began to make the games," Darrow explained. "I charged people $4.00 a copy." Although Darrow did no advertising, he soon began to receive orders from all over the country. He was shocked but excited. Looking for more distribution, he took the game to Parker Brothers...and was turned down cold. Says one writer: "George and Charles Parker thought Monopoly took much too long to play, the rules were hopelessly complicated, and there were at least fifty-two

The most common street name in America is "Park Street."

other weak points they believed ruled the game out as far as they were concerned."

Darrow was upset by the decision, but decided to distribute the games on his own. He took them to two major retailers—Wanamaker's Department Store in Philadelphia, and FAO Schwartz, New York's most prestigious toy store—and convinced them to stock Monopoly. When both quickly sold out their entire stock, the Parker brothers reconsidered. They purchased the rights to make the game...and watched, astounded, as Monopoly sold so fast that it kept the toy company—which was on the edge of insolvency—from going under.

Parker Brothers sold every Monopoly set they could manufacture for Christmas, 1934, and the demand didn't die down after the holidays. They were soon literally inundated with requests for more; orders were so plentiful they had to be stacked in laundry baskets and stored in hallways. The company had never even heard of a product being so much in demand.

By mid-February of the following year, Parker Brothers was selling more than twenty thousand sets of Monopoly per week. Darrow, as one would imagine, was financially set for life. And the reluctant toy company had its hands on the most lucrative game in the history of the toy industry.

GUINNESS ON MONOPOLY

- Largest Monopoly game in history: Took place on full-size sidewalks and streets in Huntington, Pennsylvania, on a board that was bigger than a square city block. Sponsored by students at Juniata College, who cast huge foam dice from a third-story fire escape and kept players informed of their moves by using walkie-talkie-equipped bicycle messengers. April, 1967.
- Longest Monopoly game underwater: 1,008 hours, by the Lodi, California, Diving School. That's forty-two days, one hundred forty players.
- Longest Monopoly game in a moving elevator: sixteen days.
- Longest Monopoly game ever: 1,416 hours. Players: McCluer North Games Club, Florissant, Missouri.
- Longest Monopoly game in a bathtub: 99 hours.
- Longest anti-gravitational Monopoly game: 36 hours.

In 1985, "The Cosby Show" was the highest-ranking TV program in South Africa.

10 COOL BOOKS

From Gene Sculatti, here's a list of ten obscure but hip books which may be suitable for future bathroom reading.

BEEN DOWN SO LONG IT LOOKS LIKE UP TO ME —*Richard Fariña*
The fact that he may inadvertently have invented Tom Robbins should not be held against this late great. This ...is *the* missed link between the beatbooks of Kerouac, Brossard, etc. and the great hippie novels that were never written. Maybe the flower kids took one look at *Been Down So Long* and gave up.

CONFESSIONS OF A HOAXER —*Alan Abel*
OK, there've been odder political candidates than Yetta Brosten, more ludicrous rock stars than Count Von Blitzstein, social protests every bit as ill-founded as the campaign to clothe nude animals. But they didn't all have a single mastermind behind them. Alan Abel got away with the above and more (including staging the debut of the world's first topless string quartet). *Confessions* makes it look easy, as well as eminently worthwhile.

A CONFEDERACY OF DUNCES
—*John Kennedy Toole*
The coolest American hero of recent years wore earflaps, caroused with b-girls in a Bourbon Street dive called the Night of Joy, and contended with a mad world and a mother who feared he'd become "a communiss." They don't make 'em like this anymore. A Pulitzer Prize winner.

FLASH AND FILIGREE
—*Terry Southern*
The brilliant comic writer's first novel, containing the boss TV game show "What's My Disease," a seduction scene comprised solely of grappling maneuvers, and "Ononono-pleaseno's." Surpassed only by his short story "Blood of a Wig" (in *Red Dirt Marijuana and Other Tastes*).

GORMENGHAST TRILOGY —*Mervyn Peake*
One critic described *Titus Groan*, *Gormenghast*, and *Titus Alone* as "Charles Dickens on opium." Psycho-

More Americans visit Tijuana than any other foreign city.

logically rich, koo-koo characters live in a huge crumbling castle located somewhere in Peake's brain. The first two novels are great, the third isn't. A companion novella *Boy in Darkness*, is even more unreal.

MINE ENEMY GROWS OLDER —*Alexander King*
By 1958, the man Lenny Bruce christened "the junkie Mark Twain" had seen it all and done most of it twice. Long before he became a high-watt fixture on Jack Paar's TV show, Alex the Great had painted covers for Mencken's *Smart Set* magazine, scrawled Chinese murals on the walls of kosher deli's and been photo editor of *Life*....He'd also been a morphine addict, submitted to bagel therapy at an asylum as batty as Kesey's cuckoo's nest, and played chess with A-bomb "spy" Alger Hiss. Bonus: King explains why, between 1917 and 1948 he only wore pink neckties.

OZZIE —*Ozzie Nelson*
Dedicated to Harriet. It takes 309 pages, but Daddy-O spills it all in this 1977 autobio: what he did for a living all those years on *Ozzie and Harriet*, his days on the road, that time at Rutgers when a young student presented him with a lit marijuana cigarette. (Oz put it in his pocket. It burned.)

THE SECRET LIFE OF SALVADOR DALI
A Forties autobiography from the twentieth century's most profound comedian. Mind-boggling anecdotes, opinions, and self-analysis spill out over the page, filtered through Dali's aristo-punk attitude. (He once shellacked his hair.) Always outrageous, *never* dull.

THE WANDERERS —*Richard Price*
The coolest, craziest juvenile delinquent trip ever put down. Noo Yawk at its most fearsome, funniest. Irish Ducky Boys roam their gang turf like midget dinosaurs, Chinese Wongs take no shit, and everybody listens to Dion.

WRITE IF YOU GET WORK: THE BEST OF BOB & RAY
Worth hunting for if you remember their insane commercials, *Mad* articles, or the deadpan dada of their radio comedy. Reprints classic bits—"Spelling Bee," "Lightbulb Collector," and more.

THE REAL ARTICLE

A random sampling of first-person articles, dialogue, correspondence. You are there.

SOUR GRAPES

In 1957, Frank Sinatra—a teen idol in the '40s—wrote this piece about rock 'n' roll in a magazine called Western World:

"My only deep sorrow is the unrelenting insistence of recording and motion picture companies upon purveying the most brutal, ugly, degenerate, vicious form of expression it has been my displeasure to hear and naturally I'm referring to the bulk of rock 'n' roll.

"It fosters almost totally negative and destructive reactions in young people," he said. "It smells phony and false. It is sung, played, and written for the most part by cretinous goons and by means of its almost imbecilic reiterations and sly, lewd—in plain fact—dirty lyrics, it manages to be the martial music of every sideburned delinquent on the face of the earth."

FORGETTABLE FIRST FILM

On September 15, 1937, Variety *reviewed a film called* Love Is On the Air*—which happened to be Ronald Reagan's first movie appearance. Ironically, Reagan starred as a citizen who exposed a corrupt link between businessmen and politicians.*

"In the lead, Ronald Reagan, whom Warners is trying to build up into a juvenile lead, is a spot-newscaster on a radio station. If he exceeds in authority and importance that role played in radio actually, the public probably won't notice. But they are bound to notice that the plot is the one about the newspaperman who, against the advice and even threats from higher-ups, does his community the good turn of dragging into the open the connections between racketeering gangsters and the businessmen and political job-holders who protect the lawless and share the booty....

"Reagan, before the camera all the way, gives rather an in-and-out performance. He's best when in fast physical action...."

FARTS IN SPACE

An official NASA transcript of a conversation between astronauts John Young and Charles Duke during the moon launch on April 21, 1972.

Young: "I got the farts again. I got 'em again, Charlie. I don't know what the hell gives 'em to me."

Duke: [unintelligible]

Young: "Certainly not—I think it's acid in the stomach. I really do."

Duke: "Probably is."

Young: "I mean, I haven't eaten this much citrus fruit in twenty years. And I'll tell you one thing—in another twelve...days, I ain't never eating any more. And if they offer to serve me potassium with my breakfast, I'm going to throw up. I like an occasional orange, I really do. But I'll be damned if I'm going to be buried in oranges."

ABE LINCOLN'S BEARD

A copy of the letter—written to Abraham Lincoln while he campaigned for president in 1860—which inspired Lincoln to grow a beard.

Westfield, Chautauqua Co., N.Y.
October 15, 1860

Dear Sir,
I am a little girl 11 years old, but want you should be President of the United States very much so I hope you won't think me very bold to write to such a great man as you are.

Have you any little girls about as large as I am if so give them my love and tell her to write me if you cannot answer this letter. I have got four brothers and part of them will vote for you any way and if you will let your whiskers grow. I will try to get the rest of them to vote for you. You would look a great deal better, for your face is so thin. All the ladies like whiskers and they would tease their husbands to vote for you and then you would be President.

Grace Bedell

Over 450 million copies of author Barbara Cartland's books have been sold—a record.

REAGAN'S RESOLUTION

In November, 1955, Ronald Reagan wrote an article for The Hollywood Reporter *about his work in TV, films, and politics. Among his comments:*

"I have for the past months been doubling, combining television and motion picture chores. This manifold job has taught me one thing for sure: never again will I allow myself to get into a position where I must make a choice between a seat in Congress and a comfortable position in the arms of my leading lady.

"Actors are citizens and should exert those rights by speaking their minds, but the actor's first duty is to his profession. Hence, you can rest assured that I will never again run for mayor or anything but head man in my own household...."

HANK WILLIAMS' LAST WORDS

Hank Williams died on December 31, 1952, sitting in the back of his Cadillac. When his body was discovered, a piece of paper was found clutched in his right hand. On it were Hank Williams's last words. They were:

"We met, we lived and dear we loved, then comes that fatal day, the love that felt so dear fades far away. Tonight love hath one alone and lonesome, all that I could sing, I you you [sic] still and always will, but that's the poison we have to pay."

MODEL CITIZEN

Twiggy was a hero to millions of girls in the '60s. Esquire *magazine quoted this encounter with a reporter who actually asked her a real question.*

Reporter: "Twiggy, do you know what happened at Hiroshima?"
Twiggy: "Where's that?"
Reporter: "In Japan."
Twiggy: "I've never heard of it. What happened there?"
Reporter: "A hundred thousand people died on the spot."
Twiggy: "Oh, God! When did you say it happened? Where? Hiroshima? But that's ghastly! A hundred thousand dead? It's frightful. Men are mad."

A beehive hairdo that stood 6 feet, 6 inches is the tallest recorded hairdo in the world.

MARK TWAIN SAYS...

No one in the history of American literature combined sardonic wit, warmth, and intelligence as Mark Twain did in his novels.

"Adam and Eve had many advantages, but the principal one was that they escaped teething."

"Reader, suppose you were an idiot. And suppose you were a member of Congress. But I repeat myself."

"Get your facts first, and then you can distort them as much as you please."

"It is better to keep your mouth shut and appear stupid than to open it and remove all doubt."

"It is by the goodness of God that we have in our country three unspeakably precious things: freedom of speech, freedom of conscience, and the prudence never to practice either."

"Truth is the most valuable thing we have. Let us economize it."

"A man pretty much always refuses another man's first offer, no matter what it is."

"Be good, and you will be lonesome."

"There are three kinds of lies—lies, damned lies and statistics."

"Noise proves nothing. Often a hen who has merely laid an egg cackles as if she has laid an asteroid."

"The principle difference between a cat and a lie is that a cat only has nine lives."

"Man is the only animal that blushes. Or needs to."

"I believe that our Heavenly Father invented man because he was disappointed in the monkey."

"War talk by men who have been in a war is always interesting, whereas moon talk by a poet who has not been in the moon is likely to be dull."

PLACES' NAMES

The fascinating history of place-naming in America is captured in the classic Names on the Land. *Author George R. Stewart demonstrates several of the main sources for common U.S. names.*

RIVERS. "On August 4, 1830, the inhabitants of an...undistinguished western village filed [to become a town]. They had previously been known as Fort Dearborn, but Dearborn (the man for whom it was named)...had merely been Secretary of War under Jefferson, and was no hero....So, in accordance with the fashion of the time, the town-founders took the name of the river, and wrote Chicago upon their [application]. It was a good example of a name adopted without knowledge of its meaning, for if the founders had known it to be Onion river, or allegedly Skunk or Smelling River, they would very likely have kept Dearborn."

HEROES. "At San Jacinto, on April 21, 1836, General Sam Houston waved his old campaign hat as a signal, and the Texans charged, shouting 'Remember the Alamo!' Within a few months a town was laid out near the battlefield; its promoters combined patriotism with advertisement, and called it Houston."

THE ANCIENT WORLD. "[John Charles] Fremont made his best stroke in California. The Spaniards had neglected to supply a name to the passage connecting San Francisco Bay with the ocean. Although Fremont had never been to Constantinople, he fancied a resemblance between that ancient harbor and the western strait;...He wrote accordingly: 'I give the name *Chrysoplaye*, or *Golden Gate*; for the same reasons that the harbor of Byzantium was called *Chrysoceras*, or *Golden Horn*.'"

LANDOWNERS. "One of the five boroughs of New York City...is always *The Bronx*, never just a naked *Bronx*....This dates from the 17th century, a time when a man named Jonas Bronck farmed...land north of Manhattan Island. When people back then said they were going to the Broncks, they really meant it."

GLOBAL VILLAGE

B.R.I. member Eric Lefcowitz contributed this batch of world statistics. Unfortunately, stats are generally buried in books that are too large and cumbersome for bathroom reading.

With the advent of computers and lasers, and both digital and satellite technology, Marshall McLuhan's late Sixties version of a "global village" is more relevant than ever. The media's ability to transmit information is just a small part of the development of global consciousness, however. The depletion of the earth's oxygen through the destruction of rain forests, the ozone layer and the "greenhouse effect" have become world issues. As we found out with Chernobyl, one country does not have a nuclear accident—they all do.

So maybe Uncle Walt was right: it's a small world, after all....Actually, if you want to be precise, it's not so small—the land area of the world is 135,841,000 kilometers, or 52,500,000 square miles.

Here are some other world statistics.

There are approximately

- 1.2 billion households
- 5 billion people
- 1.8 billion people working
- 1.5 billion children under 15
- 32 million teachers
- 4 million doctors
- 8,240 daily newspapers
- 72 million movie seats
- 527 million television sets
- 453 million telephones
- 300 million passenger cars
- 250,000 movie theaters

Here are some world averages:

- Approximate life expectancy at birth: 62 years
- Life expectancy, female: 59 years; male: 53 years
- Literacy rate: 70%
- Daily Calorie Supply per Capita: 2,607
- Size of a Household: 4.1
- Gross Global Product (GGP): $2,633

However, drastic differences come to light when you subject global averages to quantitative analysis. For example, in terms of male life expectancy, the country of Iceland ranks the highest with 73 years. On the low end of the scale are the African nations of Togo (31.50), Chad (29) and Gabon (25). Neither America nor England are in the top 10.

For female life expectancy, Iceland again ranks number one at 79.20 years. Upper Volta, however, brings up the rear with 31.10.

Other global highs and lows:

- Hottest place—Aroune, Mali. Highest recorded temperature: 130 degrees Fahrenheit (54.4 Centigrade).
- Coldest place—Eismitte, Greenland. Lowest recorded temperature: -85 degrees Fahrenheit (-64.8 Centigrade).
- Wettest place—Cherrapunji, India. Highest recorded rainfall (in 1983): 425 inches of rain.

The Media

TV: According to a 1980 poll, Canada has the most hours of TV broadcasting in the world—over 6 million per year. The U.S. is in second place with 5 1/2 million, followed by Japan and Brazil. England is tenth. If you lived in Cyprus , Norway, Pakistan, or about a dozen other countries, you could watch less than 3,000 hours...if you watched TV *every single minute* there was something on the air. Compare that with the viewing habits of (and influences on) the average American, who routinely watches me than 8 hours of television per day.

Movies: People in the U.S.S.R. watch more movies than anyone in the world—about a third of all movie attendance. Among the countries that average the most films seen per capita: Iceland, the Falkland Islands, Singapore, Hong Kong, and Grenada. The least: Uganda, Tanzania, and other African nations.

FIVE BEATLE SONGS

It's fun to learn the origin of any Beatles song; here is a random selection of five tunes to read about, from Behind the Hits, *by Bob Shannon and John Javna.*

PLEASE PLEASE ME, 1964

LENNON (in an interview with *Playboy*): "It was my attempt at writing a Roy Orbison song, would you believe it? I wrote it in the bedroom in my house at Menlove Avenue, which was my auntie's place...I heard Roy Orbison doing 'Only the Lonely' or something. And...I was intrigued by the words of 'Please lend your little ears to my pleas'—a Bing Crosby song. I was always intrigued by the double use of the word *please*. So it was a combination of Bing Crosby and Roy Orbison." The Beatles, by the way, were once the opening act for headliner Roy Orbison on a British tour.

MICHELLE, 1966

McCARTNEY (to Paul Gambaccini): "I just fancied writing some French words....I had a friend whose wife taught French...and I just asked her, you know, what we could figure out that was French. We got words that go together well. It was mainly because I always used to think the song sounded like a French thing...I can't speak French, really, so we sorted out some actual words."

ELEANOR RIGBY, 1966

McCARTNEY (in *Paul McCartney in His Own Words*): "I think it was 'Miss Daisy Hawkins' originally, picking up the rice in a church after a wedding....At first I thought it was a young Miss Daisy Hawkins...but then I saw I'd said she was picking up the rice in a church, so she had to be a cleaner, she'd missed the wedding and she was suddenly lonely. In fact, she had missed it all—she was the spinster type.

"[But] I didn't really like 'Daisy Hawkins'—I wanted a name that was more real. The thought just came, 'Eleanor Rigby picks up the rice and lives in a dream,' so there she was. The

One company manufactures an edible set of Monopoly, made of chocolate and butterscotch.

next thing was Father Mackenzie. It was going to be Father McCartney, but then I thought that was a bit of a hang-up for my dad, being in this lonely song. So we looked through the phone book. That's the beauty of working at random—it does come up perfectly, much better than if you try to think it with your intellect. Anyway, there was Father Mackenzie, just as I had imagined him, lonely, darning his socks."

NOWHERE MAN, 1966

LENNON: "I was just sitting, trying to think of a song, and I thought of myself sitting there, doing nothing and getting nowhere. Once I'd thought of that, it was easy. It all came out. No, I remember now, I'd actually stopped trying to think of something. Nothing would come. I was cheesed off and went for a lie-down, having given up. Then I thought of myself as a 'Nowhere Man,' sitting in his nowhere land."

DO YOU WANT TO KNOW A SECRET, 1964

LENNON (in *Playboy* again): "My mother...was a comedienne....She used to get up in pubs and things like that. She had a good voice....She used to do this little tune when I was just a one- or two-year-old. The tune was from a Disney movie—[singing] 'Want to know a secret? Promise not to tell. You are standing by a wishing well.'

"I wrote [the song] and gave it to George to sing. I thought it would be a good vehicle for him because it only had three notes and he wasn't the best singer in the world."

MISCELLANEOUS BEATLES STATS

- In less than a decade, they sold over 125 million singles and 85 million LPs.
- They had the most #1 records during the '60s—17—compared to the second-place Supremes, who had 12.
- They had the most Top 10 hits in the '60s—29.
- In one year—1964—they had 31 songs that hit the charts.
- On April 4, 1964, they had all of the top 5 songs on the Billboard charts: 1) "Can't Buy Me Love"; 2)"Twist and Shout"; 3)"She Loves You"; 4) "I Wanna Hold Your Hand"; 5) "Please Please Me."

THE FABULOUS '60s

If you were there, you remember the "topless" controversy of the mid-'60s. If you weren't, this might give you an idea of what it was like.

THE INSIDE STORY: The Origin of the Topless Bathing Suit

The topless suit began simply as a prediction. One day in 1963, in an interview, fashion designer Rudi Gernreich commented that "in five years every American woman will be wearing a bathing suit that is bare above the waist." After saying that, he realized that if *he* didn't make that topless suit immediately, someone else would. But should he?

Before he could decide, Hess Brothers department store in Allentown, Pennsylvania, ordered some. Then other stores across the United States did, too. Gernreich put the suit into production.

One of the things that focused national attention on the topless suit was that 1964 was an election year, and the Republican party seized on it as a symbol of the "decadence" in America.

This produced millions of dollars worth of publicity for Gernreich, who said in amazement: "I never dreamed it would go beyond the fashion business into sociology."

By the way, the topless suit was never popular to wear—only three thousand were sold.

'60s MADNESS

Topless Bathing

June 1964—New York City Commissioner of Parks Newbold Morris said women wearing topless bathing suits on N.Y.C. beaches would be issued summonses by police for indecent exposure. L.A. police issued the same warning.

July 1964—The Vatican newspaper *L'Osservatore Roma* headlined an article on topless bathing suits "The Ultimate Shame," and said it "negates moral sense."

June 1964—In an article entitled "Back to Barbarism," the Soviet newspaper *Izvestia* called the topless suits a sign of America's moral decay. "So the decay of the moneybags society continues," it said.

July 1964—The topless suit was modeled in the *San Francisco Chronicle*—by a four-year-old-girl.

THE REVEREND ED WATT

In Dallas, the Reverend Ed Watt and a group of protesters from the Carroll Avenue Baptist Mission picketed a department store that was displaying a topless bathing suit in its window. Their placards read: "We Protest these Suits in the Name of Christ." Watt said that church action was long overdue—topless shorts would be next.

The picketing continued until the department store removed the one topless suit it had from its display.

Were the protesters successful? Not exactly. They attracted so much attention to the suit that someone went into the store and bought it.

MORE '60S MADNESS:

Bottled Eggs

September 3, 1962: "Fresh eggs sold by the bottle are being test-marketed in National Tea Co. stores. The secret (which the developer, Chicago's David Cleaver Produce Co., won't reveal) is in the 'simple but patentable method' of getting the shell-less eggs into the bottle without breaking the yolks. The eggs readily pour out of the bottle one at a time, yolks cushioned by the whites. National Tea claims that refrigerated bottled eggs keep longer than eggs in the shell (six to eight weeks vs. four to six) because the capped bottle offers an airtight seal while the shell is porous. The bottles come in one-pound (about ten eggs) and two-pound (twenty eggs) sizes. Cost: About eight cents more per dozen than eggs in the carton."

Puppy Love.

1962: A fallout shelter for pets was put on the market, "to give pets an equal chance for survival."

1966: Upjohn introduced an oral contraceptive for dogs, for "Planned Puppyhood."

Elvis Presley had more records on the *Billboard* charts—107—than any other artist.

DOO-WOP SOUNDS

You've heard classic street-corner rock 'n' roll tunes before—"Why Do Fools Fall in Love," "Come Go With Me," etc. And you've probably noticed the crazy syllables the groups sing in the background. Ever wonder what they'd look like spelled out? Here are 20 great doo-wop syllables from The Doo-Wop Sing-Along Song Book.

1. **Hooodly-Papa-Kow, Papa-Kow, Papa-Kow (YEAH), Hooodly-Papa-Kow, Papa Kow, Papa Kow.** A gem from Frankie Lymon and the Teenagers.

2. **Pa-pa-pa-pa-pa-pa-pa-Oom-A-Mow-Mow, Papa-Oom Mow Mow.** One of the most famous rock syllable combos, from a group called the Rivingtons and a semi-doo-wop tune called—big surprise—"Papa Oom Mow Mow."

3. **Oop-Shoop, Shang-A-Lack-A-Cheek-A-Bock.** One of the all-time greats, a background section from the Earls' "Remember Then" (1961).

4. **Diddle-iddle-iddle-iddle-it (YEAH), Diddle-iddle-iddle-iddle-it.** Notable for its persistence, in a classic doo-wop tune by Herb Cox and the Cleftones, "Little Girl of Mine" (1956).

5. **Neh-neh-neh-neh, neh neh-neh-neh neh-neh-neh, Neh-neh-neh-neh-neh, neh-neh-neh-neh (repeat the whole thing two more times), Werp-A-Tul-Werp, Neh-Neh-Neh-Neh, Neh-Neh-Neh-Neh.** A perfect example of why you have to hear doo-wop to appreciate it. The opening of "The Closer You Are," by the Magnificent Four.

6. **I Su-mokem Boo-eye-ay, I sumokem boo.** Doo-wop's classic drug reference. From "Ling Ting Tong," by the Five Keys.

7. (Bom-bom) Cheer-Up, (Bom-bom) Cheer-up, (Bom-Bom) Cheer-Up, (Bom-bom) Cheer-Up. A favorite adaptation of a real word into a doo-wop. From the Pentagons' "To Be Loved."

8. Rama Lama-Lama-Lama-Lama Ding Dong, Rama Lama-Lama-Lama-Lama-Lama Ding. That's the Edsels playing homage to George Jones, Jr.'s girlfriend, "Rama Lama Ding Dong."

9. Rang Tang Ding Dong, Rankety Sing. Weird syllable combination from "Ring Tang Ding Dong (I am the Japanese Sandman)," by the Cellos.

10. Ka-Ding-Dong, Ding-Dong, Ka-Ding-Dong, Ding-Dong, Ding. The sound of the singer's heart in the G-Clefs' thriller, "Ka-Ding-Dong."

11. Yip, Yip, Yip, Yip Boom, Sha-Na-Na-Na, Sha-Na-Na-Na-Na. It's from "Get A Job" by the Silhouettes and it's not only a great doo-wop, it's the symbol of the '70s doo-wop revival. The quasi-greaser band from Columbia University got its name from this background.

12. Sho-Dot'n' Shoby-Doh, Sho-Dot'n' Shoby-Doh. From Fred Parris and the Five Satins' classic "In the Still of the Night." Strangely, although it's sold millions of records, the highest this song ever reached on the *Billboard* charts was #25.

13. Dom-Dooby-Dom Woh-oh, Dooby Dooby, Dom Dooby Dom, Woh-oh, Dooby Dooby, Dom Dooby Dom Woh-Oh, tonight I fell in love. Sort of a white bread doo-wop, but kind of catchy. From the Tokens' "Tonight I Fell In Love."

14. Tuh-tuh-tuh-tuh-tuh-tuh-tuh-aaa-ooo-ooo-ooo-ooo-ooo. A super doo-wop. This is the end of a line in "Unchained Melody," by Vito and the Salutations. The one that starts "Oh my love, my darling, I hunger for your...." Originally, the next word was "touch." In doo-wop it became this 13-syllable creature.

15. A-Wop-bop-A-Loo-bop-A-Bop--Bam-Boom. For sentimental reasons. From Little Richard's "Tutti Frutti."

The first sperm banks opened in 1964; they were located in Tokyo and Iowa City.

16. Iminni-ma-ma-ma-Iminni-ma-ma-ma-gin-A-tion. Imin-i-ni-ma-ima-ima-ma-gin-aaaa-tion. The doo-wop spelling for the word "imagination," as interpreted by the Quotations.

17. Shoh-Be-Doo-Wop-Wah-Da. The controversial last line in "What's Your Name," by Don and Juan. No one seems to agree on what they're saying. Here's my version.

18. Wah-Wah-OOO, Chop Chop Chop. An original from "Tell Me Why," by the Rob Roys.

19. Wop-wop-Doodly-wop-Wop-wop. Wop-wop, Doodly-wop-Wop-Wop. The El Doradoes lead into the instrumental break in "At My Front Door."

20. And of course: **Bomp-ba-ba-bomp, Ba-bom-ba-bom-bomp, Ba-ba-bomp-ba-ba-bomp, A-dang-a-dang-dang. A-ding-a-dong-ding, Bluuuue Moooon.**

From the Marcels' adaptation of the Rogers and Hart classic, "Blue Moon." Originally, this song was written for a '30s film—Jean Harlow was supposed to sing it! She never did.

The Marcels, from Pittsburgh, Pa., however, made it the #1 song in America in 1961.

SAD NEWS. *Variety*, March 6, 1968

"Frankie Lymon, 26, a click disk artist as a moppet blues singer back in 1956-58, died of an apparent overdose of narcotics in the New York apartment of a friend. A GI, Lymon had come to New York to start a disk comeback with Roulette Records.

"Lymon was among the original youngsters to ride in on the rock 'n' roll cycle early in the 1950s. His big hits included "Why Do Fools Fall In Love," "Goody, Goody," and "I'm Not a Juvenile Delinquent," recorded with a combo called the Teenagers. He clicked both in rhythm and blues and pop grooves for a few years.

"As the youngster grew up and lost his precocity, he also lost impact and faded into obscurity. He was arrested a few times on assorted charges, including narcotics raps. In the last year, he claimed to have rid himself of the dope habit and had written stories about how he had kicked the habit.

"His wife survives him."

California has had the most Miss Americas since the pageant began in 1921.

JUNK FOOD CONTROVERSY

As junk food has become an integral part of American life, it has also become the focal point in issues unrelated to eating.

FRITOS CORN CHIPS

Background: Invented 1932, by Elmer Doolin. Doolin, a Texan, bought the recipe—and the whole concept of the corn chip—from a cook at a Mexican border cafe. (He paid $100 for it.) Then he began turning out the chips by hand in his mother's kitchen, ten pounds per hour. When demand increased, Doolin invented a machine that would make the chips automatically. As the company grew, it moved into larger quarters in Dallas, Texas. In 1945, the Frito Company merged with H. W. Lay and Co., Atlanta-based maker of Lay's potato chips, and achieved national distribution.

The Controversy: In the '60s, Frito-Lay was accused of anti-Mexican racism (an ironic assertion, considering the origin of the product). The reason: it introduced the Frito Bandito, a mustachioed cartoon character who showed up on TV in 1967, ready to steal your Fritos Corn Chips.

In his prime, the Bandito devised some pretty sneaky ways of fleecing gringos. One commercial showed the Apollo astronauts landing on the moon. Who do you think they found there waiting for them? The Frito Bandito, standing next to a parking meter with his burro. "I ham the moon parking lot attendant," he announced. "Now if you will kindly deposit one bag of cronchy Fritos corn cheeps for the first hour..."

But after Frito-Lay decided to use him in all its commercials, the Mexican-American Anti-Defamation Committee protested publicly that the Bandito was spreading the "racist message that Mexicans are sneaky thieves." Frito vehemently denied any hidden meaning or racist intent. But several California TV stations quickly banned the commercials and the Anti-Defamation Committec announced its intention of asking the FCC for equal time.

Appoximately 50% of the area of the earth is covered by the Pacific Ocean.

Although he was an effective TV salesman, the Frito Bandito was ultimately withdrawn from Frito commercials.

HOSTESS TWINKIES

Background: Invented in 1931 by James Dewar, manager of Continental Bakeries' Chicago factory. He envisioned the product as a way of using the company's thousands of shortcake pans (which were otherwise employed only during the strawberry season) full-time...and as a way of having a low-priced snack to sell during the Depression. The cakes were originally called Little Shortcake Fingers, but during a business trip Dewar and a friend noticed a shoe factory sign that read "Home of Twinkle Toe Shoes." Dewar had been looking for a new name for his product; his friend suggested he call it "Twinkle Fingers," which was shortened to Twinkies. The five-cent snack soon became one of Continental's best-selling items.

The Controversy: In 1979, a San Francisco employee named Dan White went on a rampage and killed two important politicians—Mayor George Moscone and Supervisor Harvey Milk—in City Hall. His case seemed indefensible...but in the ensuing trial White's attorney, Douglas Schmidt, did come up with a palatable defense. He blamed his client's behavior on junk food—specifically Twinkies. Psychiatrist Martin Blinder testified that White had eaten too many Twinkies, and that their high sugar content had resulted in "diminished mental capacity." It sounded preposterous, but to the shock of the grieving city, the jury bought this explanation and convicted White of voluntary manslaughter instead of murder. In San Francisco, people still refer to it as the "Twinkie defense."

PRINGLE'S POTATO CHIPS

Background: The potato chip was invented in 1853 by a chef named George Crum in Saratoga Springs, New York. Apparently, a customer at the restaurant where Crum worked kept sending back French Fries, complaining that they were too thick. Finally, the exasperated Crum cut the potatoes paper-thin...and the customer loved them. "Saratoga Chips" became the specialty of the house, and ultimately a national snack.

For many years, large food companies avoided manufacturing

It takes up to two million flowers to make one pound of honey.

potato chips, despite their popularity. The reason: potato chips were hard to transport long distances without heavy breakage. And they got stale too quickly.

Then in 1969, General Mills and Proctor & Gamble each introduced "newfangled" kinds of potato chips. General Mills called theirs "Chipos." P & G called theirs "Pringle's Potato Chips."

This new product wasn't a sliced potato (as the traditional chip is), but a wafer made from "reconstituted potato granules." Each chip was made from scratch, so each could be formed in exactly the same shape and size—which meant the chips could now be designed to be stackable, and thus they could be packaged in break-proof cannisters, complete with preservatives. A food conglomerate's dream.

The Controversy: Would this mean the end of the potato chip as we knew it? Potato chip manufacturers were afraid it would—so in 1970, the Potato Chip Institute (the trade organization for potato chip makers around the U.S.) went on the offensive and sued General Mills for calling their Chipos "new fashioned potato chips." Chipos, the chipmakers asserted, were not "authentic" chips, and General Mills had no right to equate them with America's classic snack. "We don't like synthetics riding on the potato chip's reputation," said Francis X. Rice, the president of the organization.

By the time the suit gathered steam, however, it was clear that the new chips would never be as popular as the old ones. So the suit was quietly dropped.

Frito-Lay, the nation's largest potato chip manufacturer, straddled the issue. They joined as a party in the Potato Chip Institute's suit, but also came out with their own new-style chip—Munchos...just in case.

UNRELATED COMMENT

"Being in politics is like being a football coach. You have to be smart enough to understand the game, and dumb enough to think it's important."

—***Ex-Senator Eugene McCarthy***

ELVIS' TOOTHBRUSH

A bizarre—but true—tale of fan weirdness, from the book How to Meet the Stars, *by Missy Laws. Published by Ross Books, Berkeley, CA.*

THE SCENARIO: *A rabid Elvis fan called "Sir Mordrid" and two women were visiting Las Vegas. A celebrity they met in a casino invited them "to meet my good friend Elvis."*

"The four of them went to the Hilton Hotel, where Elvis was performing two shows nightly. They entered the backstage area and confronted a mob. Sir Mordrid could feel the pounding of his heart as he grew nearer to the superstar's private dressing room.

"Because he had an enormous collection of Elvis memorabilia and had attended a vast quantity of his concerts, Sir Mordrid considered himself to be the number one fan of the legendary performer.

"Upon seeing Elvis, Sir Mordrid began to feel dizzy and got sweaty palms. In order to hide his nervous behavior, he headed for a table of food in the corner. Nonstop, he crammed lobster, finger sandwiches and strawberries into his mouth. Between bites, he could see across the room where [the celebrity] was introducing the two girls to Elvis.

"'Where's Sir Mordrid?' [the celebrity] questioned. But upon noticing him hunched over the snack table, he continued, 'Sir Mordrid, come on over. I want to introduce you to Elvis.'

"Panic struck Sir Mordrid as he almost choked on an entire sandwich. Hesitantly he walked over to his idol.

"Sir Mordrid meekly said, 'Hi,' but then, without giving Elvis a chance to speak, he chattered on, attempting to cover his anxiety. The only thing he could think of to say was a joke that he had learned the previous day. Elvis quietly listened, certain that there must be some significance to the joke if this guy insisted on telling it at what seemed to be such an inappropriate time.

[Sir Mordrid told the joke and, staring at Elvis, asked him if he knew what the punchline was.]

"Smiling, the singer answered, 'What?'

"Suddenly, Sir Mordrid was so absorbed in his own feelings of anxiety that he couldn't remember the punchline. He panicked. He could feel the lobster, finger sandwiches and strawberries threatening to come up.

"He broke away from the singer and muttered, 'Excuse me.' He sprinted towards a gentleman standing near the doorway. He pleaded, 'Do you know where the rest room is? I feel really sick!'

"The man pointed to Elvis' private bathroom and said, 'I think it's in there.' Although it was obvious that this was designated as an exclusive chamber for only Elvis, Sir Mordrid ignored this minor detail as he hurled himself inside, slamming and locking the door.

"While Sir Mordrid expelled every bit of food from his stomach, there was a knock. A voice firmly called, 'I'm sorry, but you're not allowed in there.'

"Sir Mordrid ignored this remark. After several minutes of screaming and banging on the door, the man stopped trying to get Sir Mordrid out of the rest room.

"Sir Mordrid stood in silence and noticed a disgusting taste in his mouth. Glancing at the sink, he saw a clear, oblong box engraved with the initials 'E.P.' Inside was a toothbrush. A tube of toothpaste rested behind it.

"After checking to make sure the door was indeed locked, he brushed his teeth with his idol's personal toothbrush. Afterward, he dried it off and replaced it exactly as he had found it. He returned to the party, but kept his distance from Elvis for the rest of the evening."

ELVIS FACTS

• For one stretch of two years, the singer reportedly ate nothing but meat loaf, mashed potatoes, and tomatoes.

• His idol was General Douglas MacArthur.

• He memorized every line of dialogue from the George C. Scott film, *Patton*.

ON THE BALLOT

There's no easier way to get your name into print than to run for office...unless you try to get a laugh at the same time. Some notable politicians' names:

SISTER BOOM-BOOM. A transvestite who dresses as a nun, he/she ran for mayor of San Francsico in 1982...and received 23,121 votes.

JELLO BIAFRA. Lead singer of the Dead Kennedys, a San Francisco-based rock band. Ran for mayor of San Francisco in 1982.

NONE OF THE ABOVE. Never actually made it to the ballot, but his heart was in the right place. Luther Knox changed his name (legally) to *None of the Above* in order to give Louisianans a choice "to say no" to mainstream candidates in their 1979 gubernatorial election.

BANANAS THE CLOWN. Another almost-made-it...onto the ballot, that is. When Lester Johnson decided to run for a seat on the city council in Salt Lake City, he submitted this name. He was rejected, although he accurately protested that "it wouldn't be unprecedented for a clown to be in city government."

LOUIS ABALOFIA. It's not a weird name, and we're not even sure it's the right spelling, but Louis deserves some mention here. Running for president, he passed out leaflets bearing his official campaign photo—a picture of himself stark naked. His campaign slogan, emblazoned at the top: "I have nothing to hide."

TARQUIN FINTIMLINBINWHIMBINLIN BUS STOP-F'TANG-F'TANG-OLE-BISCUIT BARREL. In 1981, a new political party—the Raving Looney Society of Cambridge—nominated this candidate (a real person otherwise known as John Lewis) for a seat in the British Parliament. The media referred to him as "Mr. Tarquin Biscuit-Barrel," and more than two hundred people actually voted for him.

In 1980, the Yellow Pages accidentally listed a Texas funeral home under frozen foods.

CAVEAT EATER

By David Goines

The ten fundamental rules for selecting an eating place in an unfamiliar environment are simple to remember and easy to follow.

1. Never eat in anything that moves, i.e., trains, airplanes, and revolving restaurants. As a corollary, never eat any food that can be purchased and consumed without leaving your car.

2. Never eat on the top of anything, i.e., any restaurant situated at the top of any building or structure, such as "The Top of the Mark."

3. Never eat in anyplace with a theme: waitresses dressed as pirates, menus die-cut in the shape of a cowboy hat, cute incomprehensible names for ordinary beverages and dishes. As a corollary, shun foods allegedly prepared by animals, elves, or pixies: Granny Goose potato chips, etc.

4. Never eat anyplace that serves an infinite amount of food at a fixed price.

5. Never eat anyplace that has a name formatted "The (adjective) (noun)," i.e., "The Hungry Hunter," "The Velvet Turtle," etc.

6. Eat the local product. Beef in Kansas City and Chicago, Jewish delicatessens in New York. Seafood in New Orleans. Bread, wine, and salad in San Francisco. If there is no local product, as in Salt Lake City, don't eat. Or pack a lunch.

7. Never eat in an ethnic restaurant in which no people of that ethnicity are eating.

8. Never eat anyplace called "Mom's," or incorporating the concept of motherhood into the restaurant or food product. Doubly to be avoided is the concept of grandmotherhood.

9. Never drink anything with more than two ingredients: Ice is an ingredient.

10. The quality of a restaurant is in inverse proportion to the size of its pepper grinders.

According to *Billboard* magazine, the "Top Artist" of the '70s was Elton John.

JUST THE FACTS

"Dragnet" is the most popular cop show in TV history. It spanned two generations (running from 1951 to 1959, then returning in 1967 for three seasons). Its monotoned hero, Sgt. Joe Friday, became so familiar that thirty-five years after the show debuted, Dan Ayckroyd's film parody of Friday and his exploits was one of the biggest movie hits of 1987.

Dragnet" played an important role in television history. It was the first realistic crime show ever to air, and the first TV show to treat law enforcement as a day-to-day job—portraying the police as normal working stiffs. Other shows like "Gangbusters" glamorized police work—but Sgt. Joe Friday wasn't colorful, didn't wear a snappy costume, wasn't even particularly interesting. He was a guy with a job to do, and he plodded through it day after day ("12:14 PM. We approached the suspect's house. It looked deserted. We rang the doorbell."). "Dragnet"'s enormous popularity inspired other police shows to take the same approach. "We couldn't have shows like 'Hill Street Blues' if it hadn't been for 'Dragnet,'" comments one TV critic.

HOW IT STARTED: In 1948, after struggling to break into the movies, a radio performer named Jack Webb finally landed a small part in a police thriller called *He Walked By Night*. One day during the filming, Webb was hanging around with his friend, Sgt. Marty Wynn of the L.A.P.D. (the movie's technical adviser). Wynn made a suggestion: "Jack," he said, "I can arrange for you to have access to all the cases in the L.A. police files, and maybe you could do something with them."

Wynn went on to explain that he wanted to hear a radio drama that portrayed police work honestly. No "Gangbusters" stuff. Webb insisted that "Gangbusters" was what people wanted and declined the offer.

But the more he thought about Wynn's idea, the better he liked it. About ten months after the conversation, Webb began writing an outline for this "realistic" show. He did research by accompanying Wynn and his partner in their patrol car.

When Webb had a format, characters, and a title, he made a radio audition record of the show and brought it to NBC...which signed him as a summer replacement at $150 a week, starring and directing. *Dragnet* premiered on June 3, 1949; within two years, it was the top show on radio. The jump to TV was inevitable, but Webb held out until NBC gave him $38,000 to film a pilot (instead of doing it live). The pilot aired on December 16, 1951, and the series began its official run about four weeks later. It immediately became the #2 show on television (behind "I Love Lucy"), and remained popular for 11 years.

INSIDE FACTS

Smoky places. The early '50s shows were sponsored by Chesterfield cigarettes, and Webb and others in the cast often took time to elaborately light up and smoke, to plug the sponsor's product. The '60s shows are much less smoky.

Police Disguise. Each episode of *Dragnet* was based on an actual case. It was selected from the files provided to Webb by a special detail of three L.A.P.D. officers. After Webb picked the case, he adapted it to a script, altering enough details to make it unrecognizable—even to the criminal—but retaining the basic facts.

It's only TV, lady. Sgt. Friday was so real to the public that people often went to L.A.P.D. headquarters to meet him. At first the department was at a loss about how to deal with them. But later, they came up with a standard answer: "Sorry, it's Joe's day off."

Sgt. Everyman. Webb on the name: "Some (people) have said I was thinking of Robinson Crusoe and his man Friday. Or that I thought of it on Friday. I really didn't know where it came from, except that I wanted a name that had no connotations at all. He could be Jewish, or Greek, or English, or anything. He could be all men to all people in their living room."

Friday's return. "Dragnet" was going to return as a 1967 TV movie-of-the-week. But the film came off so well that it was used as a pilot for a new series instead. Retitled "Dragnet '67," it became a virtual parody of itself, with anti-drug preaching, and embarrassing Hollywood hippies. It was "camp" humor to much of its audience.

RUMORS

Why do people believe wild, unsubstantiated stories? According to some psychologists, "rumors make things simpler than they really are." And while people won't believe just anything, it's surprising what stories have flourished in the past. Many of these tales are still in circulation today....

RUMOR: McDonald's adds earthworms to its hamburger meat.
HOW IT SPREAD: Apparently the stories began in Atlanta in 1979 and were originally aimed at a competitor, Wendy's. "But," as a psychologist commented, "industrial rumors tend to gravitate to the industry leader." Another possibility: an article in *Reader's Digest* about worm farms mentioned that such farms tend to attract animals that like to eat worms, making the farm "a veritable McDonald's" for such animals.
WHAT HAPPENED: To fight it, McDonald's held a press conference in Atlanta and produced a letter from the U.S. Secretary of Agriculture stating that the burgers were, and always had been, 100% beef.

THE RUMOR: Sweaters at K-Mart are infested with hatching baby snakes.
HOW IT SPREAD: The story—that a shopper was trying on sweaters, felt something prick her skin, and discovered she'd been bitten by a rare poisonous snake from Taiwan—was probably started by a competitor.
WHAT HAPPENED: K-Mart has chosen to ignore it.

THE RUMOR: Mikey, the cute kid in the Life cereal commercials, died by exploding after ingesting a combination of "Pop Rocks" candy and soda pop.
HOW IT SPREAD: Unknown.
WHAT HAPPENED: This rumor was so prevalant that Life Cereal redesigned their box to include a photo of several kids

and Mikey, now grown up. The object was to identify Mikey, and of course, reassure us that he hadn't exploded after all.

THE RUMOR: A teenage girl was squeezed to death while sitting in the bathtub in cold water trying to shrink her new Levis.
HOW IT SPREAD: Unknown.
WHAT HAPPENED: No action taken, but a great story.

THE RUMOR: A woman attempted to dry her poodle in a microwave oven and the dog exploded.
HOW IT SPREAD: A classic example of how a rumor reflects fears, this one stemming from concerns about new technology.
WHAT HAPPENED: The public's awareness of microwave ovens was increased, and as people realized the story was just a rumor, they relaxed and accepted the product as safe.

THE RUMOR: Bubble Yum gum, made by Life Savers, had spider eggs in it.
HOW IT SPREAD: Apparently this story began in New York City, where kids began telling each other not to buy Bubble Yum because it contained the aforementioned additive.
WHAT HAPPENED: Life Savers at first paid little attention to the story, but a senior vice president wanted to find out how the story began, so he ordered a phone survey and asked consumers and their parents if they'd heard the rumors. He next checked with retailers to see what they knew....In fact, many were upset and wanted the company to reassure them. In the end, Life Savers published a full-page newspaper ad which said, "Somebody is telling your kids very bad lies about a very good gum." It worked, and the story died. Bubble Yum maintained its position as the #1 selling bubble gum.

THE RUMOR: Another Soviet nuclear accident—similar to the 1986 disaster at Chernobyl—occurred.
HOW IT SPREAD: Apparently it originated in either Stockholm or Moscow and reached world financial markets.
WHAT HAPPENED: The dollar surged in value, but only temporarily. The following day, February 4, 1988, the *Wall*

The largest airline in the world is Aeroflot, the official Soviet airline.

Street Journal reported that the "accident" was just a rumor. Nonetheless, its effect on world economic markets was undeniable. When the truth became known, the dollar then eased back to its relative value against other currencies.

THE RUMOR: A leper worked in the factory where Spud cigarettes—the first king size menthol filter brand—were manufactured in the 1940s.
HOW IT STARTED: Unknown.
WHAT HAPPENED: Within six months, the brand vanished from stores.

THE RUMOR: Procter & Gamble's company trademark is a satanic symbol signifying a pact with the devil.
HOW IT STARTED: Surfaced in 1980. Refers to the profile of a man-in-the-moon and 13 stars in the trademark, which was created in 1850.
WHAT HAPPENED: In June of 1982, P & G received 15,000 telephone inquiries. The company responded by filing lawsuits against individuals linked to the story and recruiting religious leaders, including Rev. Jerry Falwell, to refute the rumor and publicly declare the company "pure."

THE RUMOR: Xerox copy machine toner gives you cancer.
HOW IT STARTED: 1978, a research team found that extracts of a copier toner caused mutations in bacteria cells and another team reported mutations in mouse cells. The story was picked up by a newspaper which inflated the results from mutagenic to cancer-causing. Though the toner was not Xerox's, the company's name became associated with the findings. An Australian newspaper featured the headline, "Tens of Thousands at Risk."
WHAT HAPPENED: Thousands of customers called Xerox. Every query was answered by company representatives. Health records of 60,000 Xerox employees were reviewed for cancer. A Xerox Vice president presented facts in defense of his company to the Environmental Protection Agency, which resulted in an EPA news release assuring copier users not to be concerned.

ELVIS: WAR ON DRUGS

The secret life of "The King" included a secret visit to the FBI and a desire to meet "the greatest living American," J. Edgar Hoover. Totally bizarre.

After Elvis Presley's death in 1977 we learned about his tragic drug problems. Coroners found a veritable pharmacy in the King of Rock 'n' Roll's bloodstream.

The revelations of Elvis' drug abuse were shocking to his loyal fans but not to insiders. Presley's bodyguard, Red West, described him as a "walking pharmaceutical shop who took pills to get up, pills to go to sleep, and pills to go out on the job."

The supreme irony of his drug habit is that Presley, himself, was a dedicated antidrug crusader. According to Penny Stallings book, "Rock 'n' Roll Confidential": "At one time he'd even turned his home into an arsenal, with the idea of meting out backwoods justice to local drug pushers whose names he'd obtained from the Memphis narcs. He sometimes had to be physically restrained from carrying out his plan."

The most bizarre twist in this story is Presley's visit to Washington D.C. in late 1970. During his visit, Presley (who was already addicted to barbiturates and amphetamines) received a special agent's badge of the Bureau of Narcotics and Dangerous Drugs from then-President Richard Nixon.

After his meeting with Nixon, Presley requested a personal audience with the man he considered "the greatest living American": J. Edgar Hoover. Thanks to the Freedom of Information Act, the files of this event are now available.

From the available data it seems that the FBI—always conscious of its image—was quite concerned with Elvis' visit. In an official memorandum dated 12-30-70, the question of whether Presley should meet the Director was discussed. "During the height of his popularity," the memo stated, "during the latter part of the 1950s and early 1960s, his gyrations while performing were the subject of considerable criticism by the public and comment in the press."

An African ostrich egg weighs about 30 lbs. A 200-lb. man can stand on it without breaking it.

The memo concluded: "Presley's sincerity and good intentions notwithstanding, he is certainly not the type of individual whom the Director would wish to meet. It is noted at the present time he is wearing his hair down to his shoulders and indulges in wearing all sorts of exotic dress."

Although a meeting with Hoover was ruled out (Presley's entourage was told he was out of town), the FBI did arrange for a special tour of their facilities on December 31, 1970.

The following is an account of his tour from FBI files:

"Presley...and six individuals who provide security for Presley visited FBI Headquarters and were afforded a very special tour of our facilities in accordance with plans approved by the Director.

"Regrets were expressed to Presley and his party in connection with their request to meet the Director. Presley indicated that he has long been an admirer of Mr. Hoover, and has read material prepared by the Director including 'Masters of Deceit,' 'A Study of Communism' as well as 'J. Edgar Hoover on Communism.' Presley noted that in his opinion no one has ever done as much for his country as has Mr. Hoover, and that he, Presley, considers the Director 'the greatest living American.' He spoke most favorably of the Bureau.

"Despite his rather bizarre personal appearance, Presley seemed a serious minded individual who expressed concern over some of the problems confronting our country, particularly those involving young people. In this regard, in private comments made following his tour, he indicated that he, Presley, is the 'living proof that America is the land of opportunity' since he rose from truck driver to prominent entertainer almost overnight. He said that he spends as much time as his schedule permits informally talking to young people and discussing what they consider to be their problems with them. Presley said that his long hair and unusual apparel were merely tools of his trade and provided him access to and rapport with many people particularly on college campuses who considered themselves 'anti-establishment.' Presley said that while he has a limited education, he has been able to command a certain amount of respect and attention from this segment of the population and in an informal way point out the errors of their ways. He advised that he does not consider himself competent to address

Pogo sticks were first used by sacrificial dancers in Borneo.

large groups but much rather prefers small gatherings in community centers and the like, where he makes himself accessible for talks and discussions regarding the evils of narcotics and other problems of concern to teenagers and other young people.

"Following their tour, Presley privately advised that he has volunteered his services to the President in connection with the narcotics problem and that Mr. Nixon had responded by furnishing him with an Agent's badge of the Bureau of Narcotics and Dangerous Drugs. Presley was carrying this badge in his pocket and displayed it.

"Presley advised that he wished the Director to be aware that he, Presley, from time to time is approached by individuals and groups in and outside the entertainment business whose motives and goals he is convinced are not in the best interests of this country and who seek to have him lend his name to their questionable activities. In this regard, he volunteered to make such information available to the Bureau on a confidential basis whenever it came to his attention. He further indicated that he wanted the Director to know that should the Bureau ever have any need of his services in any way that he would be delighted to be of assistance.

"Presley indicated that he is of the opinion that the Beatles laid the groundwork for many of the problems we are having with young people by their filthy unkempt appearances and suggestive music while entertaining in this country during the early and middle 1960s. He advised that the Smothers Brothers, Jane Fonda, and other persons in the entertainment industry of their ilk have a lot to answer for in the hereafter for the way they have poisoned young minds by disparaging the United States in their public statements and unsavory activities...

"He noted that he can be contacted any time through his Memphis address and that because of problems he has had with people tampering with his mail, such correspondence should be addressed to him under the pseudonym, Colonel Jon Burrows."

The file concludes: "Presley did give the impression of being a sincere, young man who is conscious of the many problems confronting this country. In view of his unique position in the entertainment business, his favorable comments concerning the

A leopon is a cross between a leopard and a lion. Such creatures really exist.

Director and the Bureau, and his offer to be of assistance as well as the fact that he has been recognized by the Junior Chamber of Commerce and the President, it is felt that a letter from the Director would be in order."

LITTLE-KNOWN FACTS ABOUT J. EDGAR HOOVER

•Hoover wanted to be president, and believed he could unseat FDR in 1936.

•He had FBI agents conduct a top-secret, unofficial poll in the South and Southwest, where he thought he had the strongest support. "He's a great man," the agents were told to say. "Many people think we'd be better off if Hoover were president." Hoover was shocked to discover that many law enforcement chiefs didn't even want him to continue as director of the FBI.

•Hoover gave up chasing the presidency, and focused his sights on attorney general instead. He planned to use that position as a stepping-stone to become a justice of the Supreme Court. To achieve this goal, he surreptitiously backed and assisted Thomas Dewey in his presidential race against Harry Truman in 1948. Dewey lost.

•He assisted Richard Nixon in his race against JFK in 1960, supplying sensitive data to Nixon for the debates. Nixon lost.

•Hoover once told a top lieutenant that he'd never married "because God had made a woman like Eleanor Roosevelt."

•Whether that's true or not, he rarely fraternized with women, and he and his top aide, Clyde Tolson, went everywhere together.

•In his 48 years with the FBI, Hoover never made an arrest or conducted an investigation.

•Hoover never once left America while he was in charge of the FBI.

•According to a top aide, Hoover didn't even know how to use a gun.

GROUCHO SEZ...

A few choice words from the master.

"I must say I find television very educational. The minute somebody turns it on I go into the library and read a good book."

"Please accept my resignation. I don't want to belong to any club that will accept me as a member."

"I didn't like the play, but then I saw it under adverse conditions—the curtain was up."

"Dig trenches? With our men being killed off like flies? There isn't time to dig trenches. We'll have to buy them ready made."

"Do you suppose I could buy back my introduction to you?"

"I've worked myself up from nothing to a state of extreme poverty."

Mrs. Teasdale: "He's had a change of heart."
Firefly [Groucho]: "A lot of good that'll do him. He's still got the same face."

"Military intelligence is a contradiction in terms."

"Any man who says he can see through a woman is missing a lot."

"A man is as young as the woman he feels."

"She got her good looks from her father—he's a plastic surgeon."

"There's one way to find out if a man is honest—ask him. If he says 'Yes,' you know he is a crook."

[Feeling patient's pulse] "Either he's dead, or my watch has stopped."

"Age is not a particularly interesting subject. Anyone can get old. All you have to do is live long enough."

"Send two dozen roses to Room 424 and put 'Emily, I love you' on the back of the bill."

WORD PLAY

What do these familiar phrases really mean? Etymologists have researched them and come up with these explanations.

Fly Off the Handle
Meaning: To get irrationally angry.
Background: Refers to axe heads, which, in the days before mass merchandising, were sometimes fastened poorly to their handles. If one flew off while being used, it was a dangerous situation...with unpredictable results.

Get a Bad Break
Meaning: To be unlucky.
Background: Refers to the game of pool, which begins with a player hitting the cue ball into the rest of the balls and "breaking" them apart (separating them). If the player gets a good break, he pockets several balls. If it's a bad break, he gets nothing. Other terms: "Gets all the breaks," "them's the breaks," etc.

Peeping Tom
Meaning: Someone who looks in the windows of people's homes.
Background: From the legend of Lady Godiva, who rode naked through the streets of Coventry in order to get her husband, Lord Leofric, to reduce taxes. She requested that the citizens stay inside and close their shutters while she rode. Everyone did "except the town tailor, Tom, who peeped through the shutters."

High on the Hog
Meaning; Luxurious, prosperous.
Background: The tastiest parts of a hog are its upper parts. If you're living high on the hog, you've got the best it has to offer.

Pull the Wool Over Someone's Eyes
Meaning: Fool someone
Background: "Goes back to the days when all gentlemen wore powdered wigs like the ones still worn by the judges in British courts. The word wool was then a popular, joking term for hair....The expression 'Pull the wool over his eyes' came from

the practice of tilting a man's wig over his eyes, so that he'd be unable to see what was going on."

Hooker
Meaning: A prostitute.
Background: Although occasionally used before the Civil War, its widespread popularity can probably be traced to General Joseph Hooker, a Union soldier who was well-known for the liquor and whores in his camp. He was ultimately demoted, and Washington prostitutes were jokingly referred to as "Hooker's Division."

To Talk Turkey
Meaning: To speak frankly
Background: Derived from a popular, if demeaning, joke in Colonial America:
"A white man and an Indian went out hunting together, agreeing to divide whatever they bagged equally. At the end of the day, they had two crows and two turkeys. 'You can have whichever you like,' the white man told his companion—'Either I'll take the turkeys and you take the crows, or you take the crows and I'll take the turkeys.' The Indian demurred, saying, 'You talk all turkey for you, but you not talk turkey to me.'"

Rack Your Brain
Meaning: Think hard
Background: Refers to a Medieval instrument of torture, the rack, on which people were stretched until—in the worst cases—their limbs were pulled off. When you rack your brain, you subject yourself to a sort of mental torture, stretching it as far as it will go.

Let the Cat Out of the Bag
Meaning: Reveal the truth
Background: Refers to con game practiced at country fairs in old England. "A trickster would try to palm off on an unwary bumpkin a cat in a burlap bag, claiming it was a suckling pig." If the victim figured out the trick and insisted on seeing the merchandise, the cat had to be let out of the bag.

The earliest known board game was used around 3,000 B.C. It is an ancestor of backgammon.

MYTH AMERICA

All it takes to create a widely accepted myth is a popular "historical" movie or television show... or a damn good liar, like Davy Crockett

The Myth: Davy Crockett was an American hero, a clean-cut frontier superman who:

- "Killed him a b'ar when he was only three"
- Was the greatest Indian fighter of his day
- Could shoot a rifle better than any man alive
- Was a respected Congressman who considered running for president
- Was the last man to die at the Alamo

Background: Much of this "information" was taken from Crockett's autobiography and a series of Crockett *Almanacs* which were published between 1835 and 1856.

But it was Walt Disney who made the legend stick. In December, 1954 he unveiled a TV mini-series about Crockett with an episode called "Davy Crockett, Indian fighter." The folk hero became an instant national fad, surprising even Uncle Walt. In a matter of months, merchants sold millions of dollars worth of official Davy Crockett coonskin caps, bubblegum cards, toy guns, fringed jackets, etc. Fourteen-million copies of Crockett's life story were sold. The Davy Crockett theme song hit the national top 20 four times in one year, with four different versions. Sample verse: "Fought single-handed through the Injun War, Till the Creeks was whipped and peace was in store, And while he was handlin' this risky chore, Made hisself a legend forevermore."

The Truth: Crockett was:

- A drunk who deserted his wife and children
- A "scout" who avoided going into battle against the Indians by hiring a substitute
- A congressman with one of the worst absentee records in history.

In 1980, a secretary at Deere & Co. was fired "for making a Xerox copy of her bottom."

The only thing that seems to be consistent with the legend is that Crockett did die at the Alamo. But that, says author Paul Sann in *Fads, Follies, and Delusions*, was "more bungling and stupidity than heroism."

During the Crockett craze, several journalists researched the new American hero. Some sample comments:

"He was never king of anything, except maybe the Tennessee Tall Tales and Bourbon Samplers' Association. When he claimed that he had shot 105 bear in nine months, his fellow tipplers refused to believe a word of it, on the grounds that Davy couldn't count that high."

—John Fisher, *Harper's* magazine.

"He was out on the frontier only because it was an easier place to live than in a home with a growing brood. Davy had a flock of children and he left them and never bothered with any of them again. He set the cause of married life back about 200 years."

—Harry Golden, syndicated columnist

"Davy grew up to be a very brave young man, who would bear any hardship to escape a routine day's work."

—Murray Kempton, *New York Post*

Ironically Fess Parker, who played the lead in the Disney version of Crockett's life—and became a star as a result—was also a bit of a fraud. Says Leonard Mosley in *Disney's World*, "Parker hated Wild West roles. As in the case of most minor Hollywood actors, hunger had sometimes forced him to play in Western films, and he found he was allergic to horses and loathed the clothing cowboys wore. His...lip curled in derision and distaste when he saw the drawings of Davy Crockett's outfit.....But eventually hunger won out, and Parker signed up for the film. They had to teach him how to ride a horse, first, and do it without having him come down with a case of hives. His leather breeches were specially sprayed before he wore them, and when he was out of camera range he shied away from them as if they were a bunch of poison ivy, swearing they would give him "crotch rot." Parker later played TV's Daniel Boone for 6 years.

Grace Slick named her child "god" with a small "g" because "we've got to be humble."

DEAD MAN'S CURVE

This is one of rock's classic disaster songs. But it's the only one that was actually fulfilled by the man who wrote it.

Dead Man's Curve" was a top ten hit for Jan and Dean in 1964. But it became even more famous when Jan—who co-wrote the song with Los Angeles disc jockey Roger Christian—actually had an accident that paralleled the crash in the song. An eerie prediction? A simple coincidence? A cursed song? No one will ever know.

But we do know the story behind the song:

ROGER CHRISTIAN: "Dead Man's Curve is in Los Angeles, right near UCLA, on Sunset Boulevard. It's a downhill, winding turn that's bowed to the outside, so centrifugal force, comin' down the hill, will throw you into the opposite lane if you don't watch it. And that's just what happened. I was a deejay at KRLA in Los Angeles, and I was reading the news one night. I read that Mel Blanc had been seriously injured and he was on the verge of death, from an accident where he was struck at Dead Man's curve.

"Blanc was like my idol because he was a voiceover man and could do all kinds of voices [note: Blanc was the voice of Bugs Bunny, Porky Pig, etc.]. I watched the news copy every hour to see how he was doing; they didn't think he was gonna live—but he did. He was in the hospital for six months.

"I thought someone ought to write a song about Dead Man's Curve. I said, 'Well, we ought to make it into a race,' because Jan and I were really into racing. Every Saturday night we'd meet and go to Sunset and Vine...and we'd race. I had a Jaguar XKE, and Jan had a Stingray—the same cars that are in the song."

The weirdest part of the story is that Roger didn't intend for "Dead Man's Curve" to be a "disaster" song at all—he wanted the race to end in a tie.

But Jan *insisted* that the song end with a disastrous crash. And in real life, shortly after, Jan was paralyzed in a serious car accident...on Dead Man's Curve.

I LOVE LUCY

I Love Lucy ran from 1951 to 1957. It was the #1 show in America for 4 of those 6 years.

HOW IT STARTED: In 1948, Lucille Ball became a radio star in the CBS series, *My Favorite Husband.* It co-starred Richard Denning as her spouse, a Midwestern bank president.

Two years later, CBS decided to move the show to TV, with Denning continuing as her "husband." But to their surprise, Lucy refused. She insisted that the only way she'd do a TV series was if her real-life husband—Desi Arnaz—was her co-star. CBS balked. "Who," they asked, "would believe that a redheaded movie star and a Cuban bandleader were married?" But Lucy was determined; she thought it was the only way to save her marriage.

To prove to CBS that the public would accept them together, Lucy and Desi put together a vaudeville act and went on the road, performing live. They were billed as *Desi Arnaz and Band with Lucille Ball.* They got rave reviews in New York and Chicago—and interest from NBC.

CBS didn't want to let Lucy get away, so they capitulated and half-heartedly authorized a pilot. At first they couldn't find a sponsor for it, and had practically given up on the project when Phillip Morris cigarettes finally agreed to back it.

But there was still a problem. The sponsors wanted the show done live in New York, (where the biggest audience was), and the Arnazes refused to leave Hollywood. They came up with a unique (for the time) compromise: each program was filmed in front of a live audience in California, then edited and transported to the East Coast for a "live" broadcast. This made it the first TV series ever filmed, and gave us *I Love Lucy* reruns.

INSIDE FACTS:

Sorry about that, chief. On January 20, 1953, two important events were televised: Lucy's birth to Little Ricky in the "Lucy Goes to the Hospital" episode of *I Love Lucy*, and Dwight D.

Eisenhower's inauguration. Lucy outdrew Ike by 15 million viewers—44 million to 29 million.

Good timing. When *I Love Lucy* premiered, Lucy was 40, Desi was 35, Vivian Vance was 39 and William Frawley was 64.

Out of sight. After the success of *I Love Lucy*, Desi changed hats again, this time from actor to producer. One of his productions, *The Untouchables*, put mobster Al Capone in such a bad light that a contract was reportedly put out on his life. After selling his share of Desilu to Lucy for $2,552,975 in 1962 (she sold it for $17 million just five years later), he retired to a ranch east of Los Angeles to raise thoroughbred horses. He died in 1986.

Name Game. Coming up with a name for the program was a struggle. Sponsors wanted to call it The Lucille Ball Show, but Lucy wanted Desi's name on it, too. They finally agreed that *I Love Lucy* was acceptable, since the "I" referred to Desi, and it came first in the title. Clever solution to a potentially volatile problem.

Paley's folly. Bill Paley, president of CBS, thought there was absolutely no hope for a series about a dingbat redhead and her Cuban bandleader husband. So he cheerfully handed over all future rights for *I Love Lucy* to Desilu Productions.

Star Wars. While all appeared calm to viewers at home, squabbles on the set were common. Lucy and Desi's tiffs were the stuff of legends, while William Frawley and Vivian Vance really couldn't stand each other. Vance couldn't see why anyone would believe she was married to "that old man"; Frawley often referred to Vance as "that sack of doorknobs."

Red-dy Or Not: During the McCarthy "red scares" in the early '50s, Lucille Ball was accused of being a communist by columnist Walter Winchell, who discovered that she had once joined a leftist organization in the '30s. Believe it or not, this revelation actually threatened her career. Desi went to her defense: "The only thing red about Lucy," he responded, "is her hair. And that's not even real." Lucy is not a true redhead.

It's the Law: In Washington, D.C. no building can be taller than the Capitol.

THE 20-YEAR PRESIDENTIAL CURSE

From 1840 to 1980, every president elected in a year that ended in zero died while in office. Only Ronald Reagan managed to escape the presidential curse—and he barely survived an assassination attempt.

THE VICTIMS: Seven presidents of the United States: William Henry Harrison (the ninth president), Abraham Lincoln (the sixteenth president), James Garfield (the twentieth president), William McKinley (the twenty-fifth president), Warren G. Harding (the twenty-ninth president), Franklin D. Roosevelt (the thirty-second president), and John F. Kennedy (the thirty-fifth president).

THE CIRCUMSTANCES:

- Harrison was elected in 1840. He died of pneumonia on April 4, 1841, one month after taking office.
- Lincoln was elected in 1860. He was assassinated during his second term, in 1865.
- Garfield was elected in 1880. He was shot by a deranged man as he boarded a train in July, 1881. He died two months later.
- McKinley was elected to his second term in 1900. He was assassinated in 1901 by an anarchist who "wanted to kill a ruler."
- Harding was elected in 1920. He supposedly died of pneumonia in 1923, but it is suspected that he was poisoned.
- FDR was elected to his third term in 1940. He died of a cerebral hemorrhage, shortly after being elected to his 4th term.
- JFK was elected in 1960. He was assassinated in Dallas in 1963.

UNANSWERED QUESTIONS: How is it possible that for the last 120 years, *all* of the presidents elected during a year ending in zero died while in office?

POSSIBLE CONCLUSIONS:

No rational ones. A curse? A cosmic sick joke?

In 1977, a 13-year-old boy discovered a tooth growing on his left foot.

NAME THAT FOOD

We take these household names for granted, but they had to start somewhere. Here's where.

Aunt Jemima: Charles Rutt invented America's first pancake mix, but it bombed without a catchy name. One night in 1889, he saw a blackface vaudeville show featuring a tune called *Aunt Jemima*—which was sung by an actor in drag. Somehow, that inspired the image of Southern hospitality Rutt was looking for...and it worked. Instant success.

Spam Luncheon Meat: Combines the SP from spice and the AM from ham.

Baby Ruth candy bar: Most people think this was inspired by baseball's Babe Ruth. Not true. Originally called Kandy Kake, it was renamed in the 1920s to honor a contemporary celebrity—ex-President Grover Cleveland's daughter, Ruth, the first child born in the White House, and known to the public as "Baby Ruth" despite the fact she was in her late twenties. Within a few years, it was the best-selling candy in America. Footnote: N.Y. Yankee Babe Ruth once tried marketing his own brand of candy, *Babe Ruth's Home Run Candy*; the Curtiss Candy Co. took him to court and enjoined him from using his own name.

Tootsie Roll: Leo Hirschfield, an Austrian immigrant, originally hand-rolled the candies for his daughter, Tootsie.

Crackerjacks: This unnamed combination of peanuts, popcorn and sugar had been around since the 1870s, but was bulk-shipped in wooden crates; when it arrived in stores, it would be stuck together in massive lumps. In 1890, the company finally licked the problem with a new sugar-coating process. A salesman tasted it and exclaimed "That's cracker jack!" The phrase was slang at the time for something great or excellent.

Chef Boy-ar-dee Spaghetti & Meatballs: Boy-ar-dee is a phonetic spelling of the inventor's name—Hector Boiardi. An Italian immigrant and restauranteur, Boiardi devised the recipe in a small room above his Cleveland restaurant in 1929. His picture still appears on the label.

Oreo Cookies: Oreo means *hill* in Greek. The original version of the cookie was mound-shaped, not flat.

Fig Newtons: In 1895, a new machine was installed at a Massachusetts cookie company called the Kennedy Biscuit Works. Among the machine's capabilities: it could wrap cookie dough around jam. The first jam the company tried it with just happened to be "made from figs." And since their policy was to name their products after neighboring towns, Newton, Mass. was honored in the title. Hence *Fig Newtons*.

Wonder Bread: Introduced after W.W.I.; it was the successor to *Mary Maid*, a popular brand of bread manufactured by the Taggart Baking Company of Indianapolis, Indiana. They wanted to maintain the appeal of their previous product, and the name *Wonder* filled the bill—it was easy to remember, and implied "goodness." Footnote: the balloons on the wrapper were inspired by the International Balloon Race, held at the Indianapolis Speedway. A Taggart vice president saw the sky filled with multi-colored balloons and decided to incorporate them into a package design.

Coca Cola: Named for two of its original ingredients—coca leaves (yes, the ones that give us cocaine), and Kola nuts.

Budweiser Beer: In the 1870s, German-born Adolphus Busch and his partner produced a light-colored beer, inspired by a beer they'd seen brewed in Budweis, Czechoslovakia.

The geographical center of the North American continent: Rugby, North Dakota.

OFF TO SEE THE WIZARD

The original Wizard of Oz *is one of the most popular children's series ever. L. Frank Baum wrote the first one in 1901, perhaps as a political allegory (see "The Politics of Oz," elsewhere in this book). It was so popular that he wound up writing several more. In modern America, the book's long-term popularity is guaranteed by the lasting appeal of the 1939 film starring Judy Garland. These excerpts are from the original manuscript of* The Wizard of Oz.

ON THE ROAD THROUGH THE FOREST

"Tell me something about yourself and the country you came from," said the Scarecrow, when Dorothy had finished her dinner. So she told him all about Kansas, and how gray everything was there, and how the cyclone had carried her to this queer Land of Oz.

The Scarecrow listened carefully, and said, "I cannot understand why you should wish to leave this beautiful country and go back to the dry, gray place you call Kansas."

"That is because you have no brains," answered the girl. "No matter how dreary and gray our homes are, we people of flesh and blood would rather live there than in any other country, be it ever so beautiful. There is no place like home."

The Scarecrow sighed.

"Of course I cannot understand it," he said. "If your heads are stuffed with straw, like mine, you would probably all live in the beautiful places, and then Kansas would have no people at all. It is fortunate for Kansas that you have brains."...

THE SCARECROW

"It was a lonely life to lead, for I had nothing to think of, having been made only the day before. Many crows and other birds flew into the cornfield, but as soon as they saw me they flew away again, thinking I was a Munchkin; and this pleased me and made me feel that I was quite an important person. By and by an old crow flew near me, and after looking at me carefully he perched upon my shoulder and said:

"'I wonder if that farmer thought to fool me in this clumsy manner. Any crow of sense could see that you are only stuffed with straw.' Then he hopped down at my feet and ate all the corn he wanted. The other birds, seeing he was not harmed by me, came to eat the corn too, so in a short time there was a great flock of them about me.

"I felt sad at this, for it showed I was not such a good Scarecrow after all; but the old crow comforted me, saying, 'If you only had brains in your head you would be as good a man as any of them, and a better man than some of them. Brains are the only things worth having in this world, no matter whether one is a crow or a man.'

"After the crows had gone I thought this over, and decided I would try hard to get some brains. By good luck, you came along and pulled me off the stake, and from what you say I am sure the Great Oz will give me brains as soon as we get to the Emerald City."

"I hope so," said Dorothy earnestly, "since you seem anxious to have them."

"Oh, yes. I am anxious," returned the Scarecrow. "It is such an uncomfortable feeling to know one is a fool."...

THE TIN WOODMAN

"My head is quite empty," answered the Woodman. "But once I had brains, and a heart also. So, having tried them both, I should much rather have a heart."

"And why is that?" asked the Scarecrow.

"I will tell you my story, and then you will know."

So, while they were walking through the forest, the Tin Woodman told the following story:

"I was born the son of a woodman who chopped down trees in the forest and sold the wood for a living. When I grew up I too became a woodchopper, and after my father died I took care of my old mother as long as she lived. Then I made up my mind that instead of living alone I would marry, so that I might not become lonely.

"There was one of the Munchkin girls who was so beautiful that I soon grew to love her with all my heart. She, on her part, promised to marry me as soon as I could earn enough money to build a better house for her. So I set to work harder than ever. But the girl lived with an old woman who did not want her to marry anyone, for she was so lazy she wished the girl to remain with her and do the cooking and the housework. So the old woman went to the Wicked Witch of the East, and promised her two sheep and a cow if she would prevent the marriage. Thereupon the Wicked Witch enchanted my ax, and when I was chopping away at my best one day, for I was anxious to get the new house and my wife as soon as possible, the ax slipped all at once and cut off my left leg.

"This at first seemed a great misfortune, for I knew a one-legged man could not do very well as a wood-chopper. So I went to a tinsmith and had him make me a new leg out of tin. The leg worked very well, once I was used to it. But my action angered the Wicked Witch of the East, for she had promised the old woman I should not marry the pretty Munchkin girl. When I began chopping again, my ax slipped and cut off my right leg. Again I went to the tinner, and again he made me a leg out of tin. After this the enchanted ax cut off my arms, one after the other; but, nothing daunted me, I had them replaced with tin ones. The Wicked Witch then made the ax slip and cut off my head, and at first I thought that was the end of me. But the tinner happened to come along, and he made me a new head out of tin.

"I thought I had beaten the Wicked Witch then, and I worked harder than ever; but I little knew how cruel my enemy could be. She thought of a new way to kill my love for the beautiful Munchkin maiden, and made my ax slip again, so that it cut right through my body, splitting me into two halves. Once more the tinner came to my help and made me a body of tin, fastening my tin arms and legs and head to it, by means of joints, so that I could move around as well as ever. But alas! I had now no heart, so that I lost all my love for the Munchkin girl, and did not care whether I married her or not. I suppose she is still living with the old woman, waiting for me to come after her.

"My body shone so brightly in the sun that I felt very proud of it and it did not matter now if my ax slipped, for it could not cut me. There was only one danger—that my joints would rust. But I kept an oil-can in my cottage and took care to oil

The first known brothel opened its doors in 550 B.C. in Athens, Greece.

myself whenever I needed it. However, there came a day when I forgot to do this, and, being caught in a rainstorm, before I thought of the danger my joints had rusted, and I was left to stand in the woods until you came to help me. It was a terrible thing to undergo, but during the year I stood there I had time to think that the greatest loss I had ever known was the loss of my heart. While I was in love I was the happiest man on earth; but no one can love who has not a heart...."

THE COWARDLY LION

"You are nothing but a big coward."

"I know it," said the Lion, hanging his head in shame. "I've always known it. But how can I help it?"

"What makes you a coward?" asked Dorothy, looking at the great beast in wonder, for he was as big as a small horse.

"It's a mystery," replied the Lion. "I suppose I was born that way. All the other animals in the forest naturally expect me to be brave, for the Lion is everywhere thought to be the King of Beasts. I learned that if I roared very loudly every living thing was frightened and got out of my way. Whenever I've met a man I've been awfully scared. But I just roared at him, and he has always run away as fast as he could go. If the elephants and the tigers and the bears had ever tried to fight me, I should have run myself—I'm such a coward; but just as soon as they hear me roar they all try to get away from me, and of course I let them go."

"But that isn't right. The King of Beasts shouldn't be a coward," said the Scarecrow.

"I know it," returned the Lion, wiping a tear from his eye with the tip of his paw. "It is my great sorrow, and makes my life very unhappy. But whenever there is danger, my heart begins to beat fast."

"Perhaps you have heart disease," said the Tin Woodman.

"It may be," said the Lion.

"If you have," continued the Tin Woodman, "you ought to be glad, for it proves you have a heart. For my part, I have no heart, so I cannot have heart disease."

"Perhaps," said the Lion thoughtfully, "if I had no heart I should not be a coward."

"Have you brains?" asked the Scarecrow.

Canine Facts: The greyhound has the best eyesight of all breeds of dogs.

"I supposed so. I've never looked to see," replied the Lion.

"I am going to the Great Oz to ask him to give me some," remarked the Scarecrow, "for my head is stuffed with straw."...

"Do you think Oz could give me courage?" asked the Cowardly Lion.

"Just as easily as he could give me brains," said the Scarecrow.

"Or give me a heart," said the Tin Woodman.

"Or send me back to Kansas," said Dorothy.

"Then, if you don't mind, I'll go with you," said the Lion, "for my life is simply unbearable without a bit of courage."

"You will be very welcome," answered Dorothy, "for you will help to keep away the other wild beasts. It seems to me they must be more cowardly than you are if they allow you to scare them so easily."

"They really are," said the Lion, "but that doesn't make me any braver, and as long as I know myself to be a coward I shall be unhappy."

RANDOM GOSSIP:

- Author Margaret Mitchell's only casting suggestion for the film *Gone With the Wind*: She thought Groucho Marx should play Rhett Butler.
- Bob Newhart became a successful comedian without performing at clubs—while he was an accountant in the Illinois State Unemployment Office, he just recorded some wacky phone conversations he made to a friend...and sold them to a record company.
- Peter O'Toole is obsessed with green sox. He always wears them, even while sleeping. In fact, he once almost lost a movie role because he wouldn't take them off. In the end, he agreed to carry them in his pocket instead.
- Comedian Albert Brooks's real name is Albert Einstein.
- Ludwig von Beethoven never took a bath during the time he was writing his Ninth Symphony.
- Attila the Hun was probably a dwarf.
- Charlton Heston, a noted conservative, was once an artists' model who posed in the nude.

About 1 million Americans say they drink Coca Cola for breakfast.

CELEBRITY MANIA

This gets the Ed Wood, Jr. Award for Weirdness. Missy Laws, a professional celebrity-chaser, has written a book entitled How to Meet the Stars *(Ross Books, Berkeley, CA). The volume offers a glimpse into the mind of a Fan, and boy is it strange. In case you're scheming to meet the celeb of your dreams, here's a sample of Missy's advice to you. Used courtesy of Ross Books.*

PRETEND YOU'RE AN OLD FRIEND. To portray an old friend, you must inform your star that you have met him previously. All you need to know is a place he has visited and the approximate time he was there.

Your opening line would be, "Hi. I don't know if you remember, but I met you before at (name of place he has been before)."

You may wonder how you can say this if it isn't true. The well-known meet so many strangers that it is simply impossible to remember them all. Therefore, if you insist that the two of you have previously met, your celebrity has little reason to doubt you. Even if he questions your accuracy, it's likely he'll be polite and not dispute your claim.

Perhaps you are certain that your star frequented a particular restaurant in the month of June. You could claim to have met him there. Maybe you know he cut an album at a specific recording studio. You could say that you originally introduced yourself to him there.

However, do not blindly invent a place and circumstance, or your luminary may unravel the lie and label you a fool.

Why is it a good idea to pretend to be an "old friend" by saying that the two of you met before? Partly because it's a good icebreaker. You leave the lines of communication open. In an obscure way, it gives you both something in common.

Also, if your celebrity thinks he has previously met you, he may feel more comfortable in your presence. If the two of you really had come in contact and he doesn't remember, then it's

Life span: A gorilla lives to about 40 years of age.

obvious you didn't cause trouble. Your star wouldn't forget if he had a reason to dislike you.

PRETEND TO BE RICH

There are a couple of things to remember when portraying an important person. First, if you dress and act as if you're wealthy, not only will you be more believable in the role, but you may also make your celebrity less leery of you.

Famous people are often suspicious of strangers, and rightly so, for often outsiders have insincere reasons for wanting to know the renowned. Money, for example, may be their objective. Dressing as if you're rich may help alleviate your celebrity's worries.

People are generally more comfortable with those on the same monetary level as they are, and most stars fall into the category of upper-level income citizens. They may more readily accept you as their equal if you outfit yourself to look like you're from the same social class. This could ease you into either a personal or business relationship more rapidly.

It's easy to fake wealth. You could find a classy, expensive-looking outfit at a thrift shop or garage sale. Inexpensive baubles could dangle from your ears and drape around your neck. If someone has the nerve to ask you, "Are those jewels real?" you could skirt the issue by responding, "They were a gift." Perhaps they were a gift to yourself from yourself!

I used to borrow prestigious antique automobiles from my friends or relatives when I really wanted to impress a luminary. If a star was extremely important to me, I'd appear in a different car each time I visited him. On Monday night I might have a Mercedes. On Tuesday I might have a Corvette, and on Wednesday I might have a Ferrari. Some celebrities probably thought I was wealthier than they were!

Mary Tyler Moore: "I know a funny Carol Burnett story. Once a fan followed her into the bathroom. The fan poked her head under the stall and shoved a pen and a piece of paper at Carol [for an autograph]."

PERRY MASON

Lawyer shows have always been popular on TV, but without a doubt, this is the most popular of them all. It inspired an entire generation to become attorneys. From Cult TV.

HOW IT STARTED: In the early '20s, a lawyer named Erle Stanley Gardner decided to give up his practice and become a full-time mystery writer. He wrote like a madman. He wrote so much that his fingers started bleeding. But it didn't pay off—no one wanted to buy his stories, not even the lowly pulp magazines he was trying to write for.

Eventually, his style improved, and he began selling literally hundreds of short mystery stories to magazines every year. Then, in 1933, he wrote two novels. One featured a lawyer named Ed Stark. The other was about a detective named Samuel Keene (who doubled as an astrologer). No one bought them, but the head of the William Morrow Publishing Co. suggested that Gardner combine his two heroes into one, creating a lawyer/detective. Gardner obliged. He created *Perry Mason*, whose first adventure, *The Case of the Velvet Claw*, was published in 1934.

By 1955 there were 70 Perry Mason novels, and Perry had become a popular movie and radio character.

But Gardner never liked what movie studios did with his hero. So when he got an offer to sell the TV rights for $1 million, he turned it down. Instead, he and his former agent, Cornwell Jackson, formed Paisano Productions to do their own *Mason* TV show. Jackson's wife, Gail, became executive producer. It aired for the first time on September 21, 1957, and lasted on CBS until the end of the 1965-1966 season.

INSIDE FACTS:

Deja vu. Gardner was so prolific that he couldn't remember what he'd written previously. Sometimes he'd be halfway through a new Perry Mason story before he or his staff realized he'd already used the plot before.

Court is adjourned. In Perry's last case, "The Case of the Final

Lifespan: An average lion lives for 25 years.

Fade-Out," the judge was played by his creator, Erle Stanley Gardner. And the killer was...Dick Clark.

Win some, lose some. Surprise! Perry did NOT win every case. He lost at least three of them. But there were extenuating circumstances, of course. And the second was a trick:

1. In "The Case of the Terrified Typist," the killer was an imposter, pretending to be Perry's real client; the guilty verdict was thrown out.
2. "The Case of the Witless Witness" opened with Perry losing a civil suit to a judge he later defended for murder in the same episode. Doesn't really count, does it?
3. And in "The Case of the Deadly Verdict," his client was falsely convicted when she withheld key evidence. They got the *real* killer in the end.

Barbara Hale, 1963: "I occasionally attended meetings of legal secretaries, and the first thing they want to know is 'How do you arrange to go out with the boss every night?' The next is 'Why don't we ever see your typewriter?' "

He can dream, can't he? Erle Stanley Gardner liked Raymond Burr's performance but was particularly fond of Bill Talman as Hamilton Burger. "He actually looks like he expects to win a case," Gardner said, admiringly.

By the book. The *Perry Mason* radio show was more a romance than a detective series. It began with the emphasis on mysteries, but Gardner found that his courtroom dramas didn't adapt well to radio. As a soap opera, however, it was enormously successful. When it moved to television it remained a soap. The name was changed from *Perry Mason* to *Edge of Night*.

Book 'em, Perry. Gardner did not write the teleplays, but almost all of the 70+ Perry Mason novels were adapted for the series.

He's Back: Raymond Burr was so popular as Perry Mason that when he came back as the character in 1985, in a made-for-TV movie called *The Return of Perry Mason*, the show was higher-rated than any TV film of the season.

Liquid Assets: Water is heavier than ice.

THE MAGIC DRAGON

"Puff the Magic Dragon" is probably one of the best-known folk songs in the world. But is it really about drugs? Here's the answer, from Behind the Hits, *by Bob Shannon.*

Lenny Lipton's first year of college wasn't easy. Not because he was homesick—he was glad to finally be out of Brooklyn—but for some reason, he was having a hard time getting used to being on his own. There were so many things to think about: girls; money; a career. Growing up obviously wasn't going to be easy. Lenny secretly began to miss his childhood.

The fall of 1958 and winter of 1959 passed. So did Lenny, who managed to survive at Cornell in spite of his emotional turmoil. And then one evening in the spring of 1959, a few days after his nineteenth birthday, Lenny made one of the most important decisions of his life. He decided to go to the library.

He was supposed to have dinner that night with a friend who lived off-campus, but it was still early. So Lenny wandered over to the library in the Cornell Student Union. He scanned the shelves until he found a volume of poems by Ogden Nash, then pulled it from the shelves and retired to a chair with it. Lenny was struck by a simple rhyme about the "Really-o Truly-o Dragon." In fact, he was inspired by it. "If Ogden Nash can write that kind of stuff, so can I," he thought.

Lenny returned the book and left the library and headed for his friend's house. As he walked down the hill that led from Cornell into the town of Ithaca, he thought of Ogden Nash's dragon. And then he thought of his own dragon. As he approached his friend's house, Lenny incorporated his dragon into a little poem about a subject that was never far from his mind in those days—the end of childhood.

When Lenny got to 343 State Street, he knocked on the door. No answer. Apparently neither his friend nor his friend's roommate, Peter Yarrow, was home. But Lenny wanted to get this poem onto paper, so he went inside anyway. He headed straight for a typewriter—which happened be Yarrow's. Lenny

On the average, a working man spends 8 minutes a day cooking. A working woman spends 50.

sat down and began typing as fast as he could. In three minutes, he typed out his poem—and then he got up and left. He didn't bother taking "Puff the Magic Dragon" with him. He didn't care, he'd gotten it out of his system. He just left it sitting in the typewriter.

Folk music was popular at Cornell in the late '50s, and Peter Yarrow was a big man in the folk scene. Although he was still an undergraduate, he taught a class on folk music, performed, and often organized concerts. As Lipton tells it, Yarrow returned home that night, found the poem sitting in his typewriter, and wrote a melody for it. Eventually Yarrow became part of Peter, Paul, and Mary, and they included the song about "Puff" in their act.

Years went by. And Lipton forgot all about this three-minute poem. Until a friend from Cornell happened to mention that he'd seen Peter Yarrow perform "Puff" with his new group. Yarrow had told him that Lenny had written it. Was it true?

Suddenly, Lenny's little poem came back to him.

In the world of rock 'n' roll, one inevitably runs into stories about unscrupulous operators who've stolen songs from their rightful owners. So it's nice to be able to write about a case in which an honest man went out of his way to find a writer. That's what happened here. When it began to look as if "Puff" was really going to be worth something, Peter Yarrow tracked Lenny Lipton down to let him know about it. And he's always listed Lipton as co-writer—even when Lenny didn't remember having invented the world's most popular dragon.

For years, people have speculated about the meaning of "Puff." But Lenny is quite clear about what was on his mind when he wrote it: "Loss of innocence, and having to face an adult world," he says. "It's surely not about drugs. I can tell you that at Cornell in 1959, *no one* smoked grass." None of the "suggestive" names were thought out—they just popped into his head as he was walking along that night. "I find the fact that people interpret it as a drug song annoying," he says. "It would be insidious to propagandize about drugs in a song for little kids. I think it's a very sentimental tune."

It's had remarkable success for a poem that took three minutes to compose. It reached Number Two on the national charts in 1963, and in the '70s became the basis of a continuing series of children's cartoons.

In 1984, the National Coca Company of Peru introduced toothpaste with cocaine in it.

A-BOMB VS. YOUR CAR

This article first appeared in a 1957 car magazine which is now defunct. It revealed the "shocking truth" about a car's chance of surviving a nuclear blast. B.R. Institute member Steve Gorlick has been saving it for years, hoping for a chance to share it. "It's real Atomic Cafe *stuff," he says. "In retrospect, it's preposterous....But people ate it up in 1957. We were so naive back then."*

The story of "Your Car vs. The Bomb" began on the barren Nevada desert in the chill gray hours before dawn of March 17, 1953. At exactly 5:20 AM on that St. Patrick's Day, the rugged landscape suddenly became brighter than the sunniest day in June. The earth rocked and rolled and a king-sized shock wave swept across the sand as the awesome mushroom cloud of a nuclear explosion began its ascent into the stratosphere.

A split-second earlier, the desert near the site of the blast had appeared like a small parking lot with 51 automobiles—some old and some new—standing at various distances from the tall steel tower which supported the nuclear device. Some were within one-half mile of the structure—much too close to escape obliteration from a hydrogen bomb, but near enough to the atomic weapon to provide a good test of a car's sturdiness.

As the terrific roar reverberated through the Nevada mountain, these same cars stood almost as they had a few moments earlier, but there was a difference—a difference which can mean much to millions of American car owners.

A few cars had rolled over, some were on fire, broken glass was scattered throughout the area and almost all vehicles appeared to have been struck by a giant fist. Tops were dished in and sides and fenders were crumpled.

Experts Inspect Cars

When experts from the Federal Civil Defense Administration and the Society of Automotive Engineers inspected the cars, they found that:

Fabulous Flop: Former Yippie Jerry Rubin declared in 1980 that "My goal is at the age of

1. Cars which would run before the blast *would* run after the blast, if they had not burned.

2. All cars had survived the blast with *no appreciable structural damage* to frames, front and rear suspensions, and motor mounts.

3. Safety plate glass in cars near ground zero of the weapon was blown out in large pieces which were badly cracked, *but did not shatter*. In most cases, *all cars escaped damage to windows*. There were a number of instances where safety glass gave under the blast impact but did not blow entirely out of the frame.

In a few cars, only a relatively small hole was blown in the center of the caved-in glass!...Curved windshields and rear windows generally resisted the blast better than small or similar sized flat glass surfaces.

4. The percentage of cars lost to fire was very low. Where fire occurred it apparently began with smoldering seat covers, head liners and door panels. There was some scorching of paint, tire sidewalls and other exposed surfaces. There was no evidence that gasoline tanks or fuel systems had contributed to the initial fire hazard. There were no fuel tank explosions, even where the car was burned out.

5. There was no significant difference between makes or models of cars, with exception of wooden-bodied station wagons. These suffered more. No convertibles were tested.

6. The only tire failures were due to fire.

7. In cases where car windows were closed, the greatest damage was done to dished roofs and side panels.

What About Occupants?

All right—so much for the cars themselves. But what would have happened if you had been in one of these crates?

To answer this question, Civil Defense engineers placed

35 to act like I'm 15." Within a few years, he was running a "networking" service and

mannequins in many of the cars, all seated as if in driving position. Some of these mannequins showed a great deal of heat flash damage within three-quarters of a mile from the tower. Human skin at this distance would have been badly burned. In many instances the dished tops were pressed down hard on the mannequins' heads, indicating severe or fatal injury if it had been your head.

Thus it was found that while automobiles offered some protection from the bomb—if they were out of the area of complete destruction and if the occupants had had time to duck down below window level—basements and other permanent type shelters would be your best bet for protection from the bomb. However, a brick house standing a few hundred feet further away from the blast than were some of the cars was completely demolished.

One of the most important findings in the test was this:

Cars which could be operated before the blast still would run after the blast.

What does this mean to the average motorist?

The Federal Civil Defense Administration is vitally concerned with this question. Its experts point out that the nation has no guarantee that a potential enemy will not launch an attack against our cities and industries. Nor will we ever have assurance that natural disaster—flood, fire, tornado, hurricane, blizzard and earthquake—will spare us before, during and after attack, if the latter should come. Those who might escape the bombs still could face the threat of natural disaster at any time.

New Cars Would Be Out

If this country ever is hit with nuclear weapons, you can be certain that our automobile plants will be knocked out—if the enemy can do it—stopping production completely. If the plants escape the raids their output most certainly will be diverted to military demands. In any event, *you just won't be able to get a new car for no one knows how long.* Many cars would be destroyed in such raids and a lot of family jalopies would be damaged. It's the damaged cars which may mean the difference between survival for you and your family, and further disaster.

The surest way to escape any kind of trouble is:
Just don't be there when it happens.

The family car can play an important part in helping you obey this axiom because it provides three essential elements vital to escape from danger.

• **First**, if we are to put distance between ourselves and the source of danger, we must have dependable, speedy transportation from the trouble spot. The family car is a must on this.

• **Second**, no matter where we are the family must have shelter. Despite its relatively small size (but they're growing bigger every year), the American automobile is a sort of house on wheels. It provides a haven from sun, wind, rain, and snow. It can shelter you from insects and even wild animals. It can also shield, to some degree, against the deadly radioactive fallout from a nuclear bomb—the stuff Adlai Stevenson kicked about in the last presidential election campaign.

• **Third**, the family car provides storage for food, clothing and other items vital during an emergency. The roomy luggage compartment of your car can easily accommodate several days' supply of food, clothing and other gear.

However, the car will serve this purpose only if you equip it properly and keep it in good condition. Good luck.

Close shave: In the course of a decade, a man is likely to shave off a pound of whiskers.

GANDHI SPEAKS

The fact that Mahatma Gandhi was a man of compassion and peace makes him unique among the powerful politicians of the 20th century.

"Freedom is not worth having if it does not connote freedom to err."

[*Responding to an interviewer who asked what Gandhi thought of Western civilization*] "I think it would be a good idea."

"If non-violence is the law of our being, the future is with women."

"All fear is a sign of want of faith. Cultivate the quiet courage of dying without killing. For man lives freely only by his readiness to die."

"Non-violence is not a garment to be put on and off at will. Its seat is in the heart and it must be an inseparable part of our very being."

"I have known many meat-eaters to be far more non-violent than vegetarians."

"A non-violent revolution is not a program of seizure of power. It is a programme of transformation and relationships, ending in a peaceful transfer of power."

"The slave clings to his chains and he must have them struck from him."

"No sacrifice is worth the name unless it is a joy. Sacrifice and a long face go ill together."

"Honesty is incompatible with amassing a large fortune."

"There is enough for the needy but not for the greedy."

"To a man with an empty stomach food is God."

"Prayer is not an old woman's idle amusement. Properly understood and applied it is the most potent instrument of action."

"There is more to life than increasing its speed."

WEIRD INSPIRATIONS

You can find the inspiration for that great rock song you're trying to write in the oddest place. These are from Behind the Hits, *by John Javna and Bob Shannon.*

ALL SHOOK UP, Elvis Presley. 1957/#1

This story will probably come as a pleasant surprise to Pepsi Cola. They don't know that their product inspired one of the all-time great Elvis tunes.

1957: Otis Blackwell was sitting in his office at Shalimar Music, desperately trying to come up with a follow-up to his composition, "Don't Be Cruel." It wasn't going to be easy to match; recorded by Elvis, "Don't Be Cruel" had been #1 on the charts for *eleven* weeks, making it the top song of 1956. Now Presley wanted another song and Otis wanted to give him one. But nothing came. Then Al Stanton, one of the partners at Shalimar, happened to wander in.

Blackwell: "He walked in with a bottle of Pepsi, shaking it as they did at the time. Al said, 'Otis, I've got an idea. Why don't you write a song called "All Shook Up?"' A couple of days later I brought the song in and said, 'Look man, I did something with it!'" So did Presley. It hit #1 and stayed there for nine weeks, enough to make an Otis Blackwell song the most popular record of the year *again*! All from a fizzing bottle of Pepsi.

MONY, MONY — Tommy James and the Shondells.
1968/#3

People who work for the Mutual of New York Insurance Company—also known as M.O.N.Y—probably can't imagine that the staid, conservative company has something to do with rock 'n' roll. They think it's just a coincidence that the name of their company is also the title of this song....But it isn't.

M.O.N.Y.'s central office in New York City is a 40-story building located at 1740 Broadway. On top is a huge old sign that flashes the company's name in neon at night. This sign inspired Tommy James' 1968 hit.

50% of Americans ride bikes at least once in a while.

James: "The night we wrote the song, we were absolutely devastated because we couldn't come up with a 'Bony Moronie,' a 'Sloopy' kind of title, and we knew that's what it had to be. It had to be a girl's name that nobody had ever heard of before.

"We were going through the dictionary, but nothing was happening. We were just totally frustrated. I walked out onto my terrace—I lived in Manhattan at the time—and I was just sort of scanning around, looking for just any part of a name, anything. I was just kind of staring out into space, and all of a sudden, I looked up and I saw [what I was looking for]...I said [to my manager], 'Ritchie, c'mere.' He came over and I said, 'Look.'...And all of a sudden, here's this 'M.O.N.Y.' with a dollar sign in the middle of the 'O.' The song was kind of etched in stone in New York, I guess. We both just fell down laughing."

Other Weird Ones:

• Paul Simon was inspired to write **"Mother and Child Reunion"** by a chicken-and-egg dish in a Chinese restaurant.

• **"Heartbreak Hotel,"** Elvis's first #1 hit, was inspired by a highly publicized suicide note that was printed on the front page of the Miami Herald. It began with the line, "I walk a lonely street...."

• The Teddy Bears' 1958 #1 song, **"To Know Him Is to Love Him,"** was inspired by the epitaph on group-member Phil Spector's father's tombstone.

• Melanie's million-seller, **"Brand New Key,"** came to her after she'd broken a strict vegetarian diet by eating a McDonald's hamburger.

• **"Be-Bop-A-Lula"** was inspired by a Little Lulu comic book.

• Ray Davies of the Kinks got the idea for the chord changes in **"You Really Got Me"** from a performer he saw on TV who "played" half-filled glasses of water with spoons.

• **"Running on Empty"** came to Jackson Browne because, in a tough period of his life, he kept forgetting to fill up his car with gas.

If your body temperature was 86 degrees, you could live to be 200.

ANDY GRIFFITH SHOW

Although lots of city slickers don't care for the cornball world of Mayberry, U.S.A., this show is one of America's cult classics. Here's some info, from Cult TV, *by John Javna.*

HOW IT STARTED: While he was still riding high in the movies in the '50s, Andy Griffith avoided TV. But when his films started receiving less kind reviews and the quality of the scripts he was offered fell off, he figured it was time to make the jump to the small screen.

In 1960 he let his agents at William Morris know that he was looking for a TV series. They, in turn, contacted Sheldon Leonard, executive producer of *The Danny Thomas Show*, and asked him to devise a show specifically for their client.

Griffith's forte seemed to be playing "hillbillies" (as in *No Time For Sergeants*, where he played fresh-off-the-farm Will Stockdale). So Leonard came up with a rural sitcom featuring Andy as the sheriff, mayor, justice of the peace, and newspaper editor of a small North Carolina town. Andy didn't like the idea—but he liked Sheldon Leonard—so he agreed to give it a try. They decided to air the pilot as an episode of *The Danny Thomas Show*, to showcase it for potential sponsors.

Griffith took ten days off from *Destry*, a Broadway play in which he was starring, went to Hollywood, and shot the pilot (which featured Ronny Howard and Frances Bavier). Called *Danny Meets Andy Griffith*, it aired on February 15, 1960 as the final *Danny Thomas Show* episode of the 1959-60 season.

It was so well received that the sponsor for the *Thomas* show, General Foods, signed up for the *Griffith* show immediately. They were on the air six months later.

INSIDE FACTS:

Mayberry is loosely based on Andy Griffith's North Carolina hometown, Mount Airy. "Andy never left Mount Airy," a resident told *TV Guide* in 1966. "He plain took it to Hollywood with him."

Fatherly advice. Ronny Howard was only six when he was cast as Opie, so his father, actor Rance Howard, chaperoned him. The first time Ronny had a tantrum about cooperating with the director, his father came up and spanked him right on the set. He rarely complained after that, and developed a reputation with the cast as a great kid.

Going straight. Many of the comic attributes which were originally planned for Andy were shifted to Barney Fife; Andy then became Mayberry's straight man, and Barney its clown.

About Barney. Don Knotts described his interpretation of Barney Fife this way: "I thought of Barney as a childlike man who was funny mainly because he was never able to hide anything in his face. If he was sad, he really looked sad. If he was angry, he acted angry. Children do that—pout, get overjoyed, or whatever. Barney never hid anything. He wasn't able to. In my mind that was really the key to Barney's character."

Communications breakdown. Don Knotts left the show in 1965 because he understood that Andy Griffith didn't want to do the show for more than five years. Knotts had already negotiated a movie contract with Universal Pictures when Andy changed his mind, and couldn't stay on as a regular. He did return, though, to make five more appearances as Barney in the last three seasons.

The real Mayberry. *The Griffith Show* was shot in three locations. The interior scenes were shot at Desilu Studios (the jail, Andy's house, etc.). The exterior scenes of Mayberry were shot at a lot in Culver City (where the main street was constructed). And the bucolic shots (the opening scene, etc.) were shot at Franklin Canyon, a Los Angeles reservoir.

Now you see 'em...

- Jack Nicholson appeared in two episodes.
- Howard McNear (Floyd the Barber) was out of the series for over a year (including the whole 1963-64 season) after he had a stroke. He returned in 1964 and stayed until 1967.
- George Lindsay auditioned for the part of Gomer Pyle and was rejected. Later, he was offered Goober's role.

Phone Crazy: The Pentagon made almost $85 million worth of phone calls in 1986.

INVENTIONS IN THE NEWS

We thought it would be interesting to take a look at the 1st newspaper reports on various inventions that changed our lives. These are excerpts from the actual articles.

The Flashlight...

LIGHT FROM AN ELECTRIC CURRENT

October 22, 1877

"Electricity in a hand-lamp is the most recent fruit of inventive enterprise. Messrs. Voison and Drouier, of Paris, have just patented a new scheme for obtaining light from an electric current. The apparatus consists of a single cell enclosed in a light mahogany case....The whole operation is performed so quickly that it may be said to be almost simultaneous with the pressing of the finger on the plunger.

"The principle of the invention is, of course, well known, but the mode of applying it is altogether novel. The apparatus is very simple, and it is noiseless in its working."

Music over the wire...

MUSIC BY TELEGRAPH

July 23, 1876

"The *Boston Traveller* prints the following statement: A few nights ago Prof. Bell was in communication with a telegraph operator in New York, and commenced experimenting with one of his inventions pertaining to the transmission of musical sounds. He made use of his phonetic organ and played the tune of 'America,' and asked the operator in New York what he heard. 'I hear the tune of "America,"' replied New York; 'give us another.' Prof. Bell then played 'Auld Lang Syne.' 'What do you hear now?' 'I hear the tune of "Auld Lang Syne," with the full chords, distinctly,' replied New York. Thus the astounding discovery has been made that a man can play upon musical instruments in New York, New Orleans, or London, or Paris, and be heard distinctly in Boston! If this can be done, why cannot distinguished performers execute the most artistic and beautiful music in Paris and an audience assemble in Music Hall, Boston, to listen? Prof. Bell's other im-

There are 3 times as many astrologers as astronomers in America.

provement, viz., the transmission of the human voice, has become so far perfected that persons have conversed over one thousand miles of wire with perfect ease, although as yet the vocal sounds are not loud enough to be heard by more than one or two persons. But if the human voice can now be sent over the wire, and so distinctively that when two or three known parties are telegraphing the voices of each can be recognized, we may soon have distinguished men delivering speeches in Washington, New York, or London and audiences assembled in Music Hall or Faneuil Hall to listen."

Television...

BELIN SHOWS TELE-VISION

December 2, 1922

"Tele-vision or 'long-distance sight' by wireless, had a preliminary experimental demonstration at the Sorbonne today by Edward Belin, inventor of the transmission of photo-graphs by wire. Flashes of light were directed on a selenium element, which, through another instrument, produced sound waves. These waves were then taken up by a wireless apparatus that reproduced the flashes of light on a mirror.

"This was offered as proof that the general principle of projecting a stationary scene had been solved."

Radio...

TOPICS OF THE TIMES

May 26, 1897

"English electricians, particularly those connected with the army and navy, are much interested in the Marconi system of telegraphy without wires. Some remarkable work has already been done with this machine, and improvements being made are expected to add many miles to the two or three over which it is already effective.

The system, it is thought, will be of especial use to the commanders of fleets at sea by enabling them to communicate with their other vessels without the use of visible signals."

Movie projector...

REALITIES OF ANIMAL MOTION

November 18, 1882

"Prof. Eadweard Muybridge, whose success in instantly photographing the motion of the horse in running has overturned all previous ideas on the subject, lectured last evening in the Turf Club

About 96% of all American children can recognize Ronald McDonald.

Theatre under the auspices of the Turf Club....

"Prof. Muybridge's subject was 'The Romance and Reality of Animal Motion,' and he illustrated his lecture upon a large screen by means of a *zoopraxiscope*, which an eminent English writer describes as 'a magic lantern run mad.' With this instrument the Professor produced upon the canvas, first stationary figures of the horse in the different positions assumed in the walk, the pace, the rack, the canter, and the gallop, and afterward displayed the figure of the animal, first at a walk across the canvas, then pacing, cantering, galloping, and even jumping the hurdle... the spectator could almost believe that he saw miniature horses with their riders racing across the screen."

Pocket Calculator...

POCKET COMPUTER CAN HANDLE TASKS OF UNIT 150 TIMES ITS SIZE

October 20, 1961

"Texas Instruments, Inc., has developed a vest pocket computer.

The gadget isn't much bigger than a pack of cigarets and weighs only 10 ounces, but it will do the same tasks as a conventional transistorized computer 150 times its size and 48 times heavier, the company claims.

Texas Instruments built the compact computer for the Air Force, to show it could be done. But it is offering components for sale that could be used to build almost any electronic equipment now using vacuum tubes or transistors.

P.E. Haggerty, president, says the little parts will be competitively priced for 'high reliability, small-run military requirements in 1963.' But their initial offering price runs something like 50 times the equivalent weight in good diamonds. In lots of 1,000 the components will sell for $50 to $65; since it takes 587 components to make a computer, the parts would be priced at $29,350 or more.

Initial use of equipment made from the networks is expected to be in the missile and space field....Future price reductions and development will lead to industrial uses in a few years and perhaps eventual consumer uses, the company feels. At the moment the company can suggest no immediately practical industrial or consumer uses, but officials are in no way perturbed."

THE HIPSTER SAINT

Contributed by Gene Sculatti, one of America's hippest cultural observers, and author of The Catalog of Cool. *Gene believes that the late great Lord Buckley is one of the hippest cats ever to make the scene in America.*

Maybe we shouldn't be talking about Lord Buckley at all.

It's just that, having been a secret so long, could he stand the public acclaim? Besides, words were his axe, and when it comes to that instrument, nobody blew it better.

Richard "Lord" Buckley (1906-60) was the embodiment of life lived coolly. If the coolest one can be is fashioning an accurate expression of what's inside, then Buckley was easily, to borrow a phrase from him, one of "the wildest, grooviest, hippest, swingin'-est, double-frantic, maddest, most exquisite" cats that ever breathed.

It also helps if what's inside is good to start with. Like maybe a huge heart. Tons of compassion. A mind that spontaneously generates material to entertain itself even when there are no audiences around. Or a conviction that language itself is the headiest brew and that staying drunk is divine.

Lord Buckley had all this inside. You'll know that when you hear his records. They're all that survive a life and a "career" that was by all accounts unpredictable and gloriously insane.

Much of the material on albums like *Way Out Humor* and *A Most Immaculately Hip Aristocrat* takes the form of parables. The best known may be his life of Christ "The Nazz" ("The sweetest far-out cat that ever stomped on this Sweet Green Sphere!"). There are also routines on Gandhi ("The Hip Gahn"), Jonah and the whale, Poe's "Raven," and Marc Antony's oration at Caesar's funeral.

The two that made a believer of me are Buckley's profile of the Spanish explorer Alvar Nuñez de Vaca and—best of all—his interpretation of the life of Einstein called "The Hip Einie."

On the multicandle brainpower of this most eminent "sphere-gasser" and his continual job loot predicaments: "Now here was a cat who carried so much *wiggage*—he was gig-less! He *could* not find a wheel to turn! He sounded all the hubcaps within' reach but nathan shakin'. He could *not* connect." Buckley rolls on, in an extrapolation of black jazz-rap, to clue us in on Einstein's subsequent relocation to Switzerland: "Now, not digging the lick, you see, of these double-square kicks the cats were puttin' down, he saved his beans and finally he swung with a Swiss passport, *swooped* the scene and lit in the land of the Coool, to prove and groove with the Alpine-heads!"

Ultimately, the Hip Einie connects with a gig, a pad, a wife and kids. Writing down his scientific theories, he soon becomes "the king of all Spaceheads," flips the physics-chemistry community on its ear, ascends to top dog status at the U of Zurich, and wows the world. Buckley shouts, whispers, wails like an evangelist wired to a generator, stomps through the tale (there is no way to repeat or paraphrase his explication of Einstein's theory—you have to be there) and finally winds down.

Buckley's personal (and sometimes highly public) life was a true trip itself. Born of Indian extraction in California's Mother Lode gold country in '06, he gravitated to Frisco, then to the Texas oil fields. He spent the Thirties doing standup in Capone-style Chicago speakeasies, made it to New York and married "Lady" Buckley. By the mid-Fifties he was reigning hepcat to a circle of admirers that included Sinatra, Robert Mitchum and Stuart Whitman. Ed Sullivan put him on TV; Jonathan Winters, Redd Foxx, and every other comedian dug him. Ultimately, he suffered the Bruce-type fuzz busts—in New York City in '60, where he died in November.

Which is great and dramatic, and somebody should (and somebody else will) make a movie of it someday. But what really counts is first-person Buckley, his work. Here's a sample:

"Now you see in Hip Talk, they call William Shakespeare 'Willie the Shake!' You know why they call him 'Willie the Shake?' Because HE SHOOK EVERYBODY!! They gave this Cat five cents' worth of ink and a nickel's worth of paper and he sat down and wrote up such a breeze, WHAMMMMM!! Everybody got off! Period! He was a hard, tight, tough Cat. Pen in hand, he was a Mother Superior."

The average American consumes almost ten pounds of "chemical additives" annually.

FABULOUS FOOD FLOPS

Americans will eat almost anything. We consume billions of Twinkies, drink oceans of Kool-Aid, devour millions of pounds of processed cheese spread. But even we have our limits—some food products are so outrageous that no one will touch them. Like these.

CORN FLAKES WITH FREEZE-DRIED FRUIT. In the '60s, the lure of space-age food technology was too seductive for cereal giants Kellogg and Post to resist.

The year was 1964. Freeze-drying had been "perfected" by NASA, so Post decided to add freeze-dried strawberries to its cornflakes. Just add milk, they told wide-eyed consumers, and these dried-out berries miraculously turned back into real fruit.

"Corn Flakes with Strawberries" took off like a rocket; supermarkets couldn't keep the product on their shelves. Exulting, Post built a multi-million dollar plant to produce the cereal and added two new fruity varieties to their line: "Corn Flakes with Blueberies," and "Corn Flakes with Peaches."

Meanwhile, Kellogg's was test-marketing its own version of high-tech fruit 'n' cereal: "Corn Flakes with Instant Bananas." The Battle Creek cereal giant bought the rights to the song, "Yes We Have No Bananas," and hired Jimmy Durante to croak new lyrics at a piano: "Yes, we now have bananas...." But the prognosis wasn't good. One Kellogg's salesman described the product as "cardboard discs in a box."

It turned out that freeze-dried fruit got soft on the outside, but stayed crunchy on the inside. What's worse: by the time the fruit was soft enough to eat, the cereal was soggy. Millions of families bought "Corn Flakes with Strawberries" once, but never came back for a second helping—leaving both cereal giants stuck with a bountiful harvest of unwanted pseudo-fruit.

OTHER FREEZE-DRIED FLOPS: Freeze-dried mushrooms in a box, from Armour foods; freeze-dried cottage cheese ("with cultured sour cream dressing"), from Holland Dairies.

According to a reliable source, Sammy Davis, Jr. still owns 6 Nehru jackets.

WEIRD BEER

Here are two beer ideas that America refused to swallow:

- In 1965, Dr. Robert Cade came up with the formula for Gatorade. Two years later, he sold it to Stokely-Van Camp. What did he do with the profits? He developed "Hop 'n' Gator," a mixture of beer and Gatorade. The Pittsburgh Brewing Company actually produced it in 1969...but it was canned right away.
- Not to be outdone, the Lone Star Brewing Company retaliated with flavored beer in 1970. It was available in three exciting tastes: cola, grapefruit, and lemon-lime. But of course, it wasn't available too long. Cola-flavored beer?

McDONALD'S MISTAKE

In the '50s, Catholics still weren't permitted to eat meat on Friday's—a problem for McDonald's. Since the fast food giant only had hamburgers on its menu, sales slumped every week in Catholic areas. McDonald's needed a creative alternative...and Ray Kroc, Chairman of the Board, had one. Putting his marketing genius to work, he came up with the "Hula Burger."

Picture a toasted bun, covered with a piece of melted American cheese, mustard, ketchup, a pickle...and a slice of grilled pineapple. Sound appetizing?

The "Hula Burger" had no meat, so it was perfect for Fridays. But it had another problem—Kroc couldn't get anyone to buy it. Customers all said, "I love the Hula, but where's the burger?" McDonald's' vegetarian experiment was abandoned after a few months. It wasn't until 1962 that the religious crisis was solved with the "Filet-O-Fish" sandwich.

A QUICK ONE

In the mid-'60s, Hires developed a brand new product and rushed it out to supermarkets...where it went sour. The product: root beer-flavored milk.

GIMME A LIGHT

Believe it or not, "light beer"—a huge success today—was a dud in 1967. Two light beers were introduced that year.

The first was Gablinger's—also known as "the Edsel of

Research indicates that mosquitoes are attracted to people who have recently eaten bananas.

Beers." Brewed on the East Coast by Reingold, it was named after the Swiss chemist who'd formulated it—Hersch Gablinger. Reingold put his picture on the cans, trying to make him a celebrity, but it was no use. The "no carbohydrate" beer was so watery it wouldn't even hold a head. And the slogan, "It doesn't fill you up," didn't mean anything to beer-drinkers in 1967.

If that wasn't enough, the federal government seized a shipment of Gablinger's because of "misleading" statements on the label, and a Reingold competitor filed a lawsuit, charging that the product was falsely promoted. Reingold made all the necessary changes, but by that time Gablinger's was a lost cause.

The other "light" beer was called...Lite Beer. That's right—the same one that over-the-hill athletes have promoted on television for the last decade. In 1967, it was marketed by a Cincinnati brewery named Meister Brau. They called it "low calorie beer," and their ads featured "Miss Lite," a 21-year-old California blonde in a leotard. But Lite was ahead of its time, and people who were into low-cal foods weren't into drinking beer. Lite lasted for about a year, then disappeared.

IT AIN'T OVER TIL IT'S OVER: In the late '70s, the Miller Brewing Company purchased Meister Brau and its various assets—including the trade name *Lite*. Styles had changed in a decade, and the time was right for "diet beer." So in 1979, Miller launched its "new" beer with a memorable ad campaign featuring aging macho men fighting over whether Lite was more attractive because it tasted good or because it didn't make them feel full. The result: the beer that flopped in '67 was the second-leading beer in America (behind Bud) twenty years later.

BEER NOTES

• Legally, a beer doesn't actually have to be lower in calories to call itself "light" beer. All that's required is for the beer to be light in color.

• In 1986, Anheuser-Busch sold more beer than any brewery in history—72,300,000 barrels.

• Smoke and drink? Tastes good, but doubles your health risk.

About 7% of all working Americans have worked at McDonald's at some time.

ONE-LINERS

Occasionally a random phrase in a conversation inspires a hit record. Here are some examples.

MY BOYFRIEND'S BACK, the Angels. 1963/#1
Abraham Lincoln High School in Brooklyn was fertile ground for musicians and singers. Neil Sedaka and the Tokens went there. So did songwriter/producer Bob Feldman. Bob graduated in 1958 and moved across the East River to Manhattan, where he became a staff writer for April-Blackwood Music.

Five years later he heard that the Sweet Shoppe across the street from Lincoln High, his favorite hangout in the '50s, was being torn down. So he went back for a last look. "While I was there," Feldman recalls, "an altercation started between a young girl and a hoody-looking young man with a leather jacket and a great D.A. [duck's-ass hairstyle]. She was pointing a finger at him and screaming, "My boyfriend's back and you're gonna be in trouble. You've been spreading lies about me all over school and when he gets ahold of you, you're gonna be sorry you were ever born.'"

That night Bob told his writing partners, Jerry Goldstein and Richard Gotterher, about the incident and they sat down and wrote a song about it. The Angels recorded the tune a few weeks later, and it became a million-seller—one of the biggest hits of 1963.

OH PRETTY WOMAN, Roy Orbison. 1964/#1
Roy Orbison's wife, Claudette, was already a famous rock 'n' roll name by the '60s. Orbison wrote the flip side of the Everly Brothers' 1958 classic, "All I Have to Do Is Dream," as a tribute to her. But the tune she inspired in 1964 meant even more to Roy's career; he sang it himself.

It started with a shopping trip. Roy and Billy Dees, a songwriter Orbison collaborated with, were sitting in the Orbisons' house when Claudette announced she was going into town to

In 1647, New York became the first city in America with a paved street.

buy some groceries. "Do you need any money?" Roy asked. Dee said, "A pretty woman never needs any money." Then he turned to Roy and said, "Hey, how about that for a song title?" Orbison liked the idea of a "pretty woman," but not the part about the money. After Mrs. Orbison left, Roy and Billy began turning the phrase into a song. And when she returned, carrying her bags of food, she was greeted by the debut performance of Roy's second #1 tune.

In 1982, Van Halen remade the song.

OTHER ONE-LINERS

•Otis Redding and drummer Al Jackson were discussing the problems of going on tour, and Redding started complaining too much. Jackson said, "What are you griping about? You're on the road all the time. All you can look for is a little respect when you come home." Redding took the line and wrote **"Respect"** from it.

•**"He Ain't Heavy, He's My Brother"** was inspired by Father Flanagan's Boy's Town poster. The poster had a picture of a priest on one side, and a two kids facing him, one sitting on the other's shoulders. The caption read, "He ain't heavy Father, he's my brother."

•Marvin Gaye's biographer visited Gaye in Belgium, where the singer was living in 1982 after a bitter divorce. The biographer noticed sado-masochistic magazines in Gaye's apartment, and suggested that Gaye needed some "sexual healing." It inspired the tune **"Sexual Healing,"** Gaye's first top 10 hit in five years, and a Grammy-winner.

•"The Jack Benny Show" occasionally featured a used car salesman who swore that every car had been owned by "a little old lady from Pasadena." Jan Berry, of Jan and Dean, was studying geriatrics at the time; he based a million-selling song on the phrase—**"The Little Old Lady From Pasadena."**

•Lamont Dozier was having a fight with his girlfriend. He shouted at her, **"Stop in the name of love!"**

The first pay phone was installed in a Hartford, Connecticut bank in 1889. The price: 5¢.

EINSTEIN SAYS...

A few words of wisdom from the white-maned genius.

[Explaining the concept of relativity] "When you are courting a nice girl an hour seems like a second. When you sit on a red-hot cinder a second seems like an hour. That's relativity."

"The most beautiful thing we can experience is the mysterious. It is the source of all true art and science."

"Imagination is more important than knowledge."

"The hardest thing in the world to understand is the income tax."

"God is subtle, but he is not malicious."

"An empty stomach is not a good political adviser."

"Nothing is more destructive of respect for the government and the law of the land than passing laws which cannot be enforced."

"We should take care not to make the intellect our god; it has, of course, powerful muscles, but no personality."

"I don't believe in mathematics."

"The release of atom power has changed everything except our way of thinking, and thus we are being driven unarmed towards a catastrophe."

[When asked how he felt about seeing his ideas used in the atomic bomb] "If only I had known, I should have become a watchmaker."

"Art is the expression of the profoundest thoughts in the simplest way."

"Everything should be made as simple as possible, but not simpler."

"Science without religion is lame, religion without science is blind."

"Whoever is careless with the truth in small matters cannot be trusted with important matters."

Thomas Edison demonstrated the first practical electric lightbulb on December 20, 1879.

THE FBI: WATCHING TV

According to a former ranking agent, the FBI spends an extraordinary amount of time and money on p.r. ...and not nearly enough on solving crimes. A case in point:

In 1986, it was revealed that between 1959 and 1963 the FBI employed agents to watch, report on, and try to influence the content of the TV series "The Untouchables." The reason: Director J. Edgar Hoover was incensed that it portrayed Treasury Agent Eliot Ness as the major crimebuster of his era, ignoring the FBI completely.

"Hoover fumed when episodes showed Ness solving a crime that fell under the FBI's regular jurisdiction," wrote William Barret in *Rolling Stone*. "'We must find some way to prevent FBI cases from being used,' [he] wrote. His staff launched an immediate investigation into published reports—apparently false—that ex-FBI agents were writing scripts for the show."

Actually, J. Edgar Hoover's monitoring of "The Untouchables" barely scratched the surface of the FBI's elaborate surveillance of Hollywood scripts during his tenure as director (48 years). Hoover's obsession with Hollywood's depiction of the Bureau in films and on television led to some strange investigations. FBI files on Rock Hudson, Groucho Marx and Walt Disney reveal the paranoid scope of the Bureau's efforts to reshape its image for public consumption.

As an unelected government official at the whim of periodic presidential reappointments, Hoover—who served as director from 1924 until his death in 1972—had every reason to protect the G-Man's glorified position in popular culture. FBI-sanctioned projects, such as "The FBI" TV series (1965-73) starring Efrem Zimbalist, Jr., helped solidify the Bureau's pre-Watergate public standing and thus Hoover's stranglehold as director.

Hoover himself admitted in a posthumously published article written for *TV Guide* (May 20, 1972) that the Bureau had final approval rights over the scripts, sponsors and actors portraying FBI agents in "The FBI" TV series. The Director also collected a neat $500 per episode. "We know," Hoover wrote in *TV Guide* "that a less than first-rate program could cheapen the FBI's name and have an adverse effect on its image.... Perhaps we are inclined towards Puritanism in an increasingly permissive world."

Only after Hoover's death and the post-Nixon flurry of bureaucratic reform—such as the re-amended Freedom of Information Act of 1974 which subjected FBI documents to declassification—did the truth behind the FBI's Hollywood surveillance become known.

During his almost 50-year reign as Bureau chief, Hoover had been rumored to have amassed a Personal and Confidential file on every major player in both political and entertainment circles, including intimate (but often unsubstantiated) details of drinking, drugging and sexual peccadillos. Unfortunately, the contents of Hoover's P&C files will never be known, thanks to his private secretary Helen Gandy, who shredded every file upon Hoover's death, except one: the pedigree of his terriers, G-Boy and Cindy. (That file, incidentally, had been saved for Clyde Tolson, Hoover's right hand man—some say literally—and brief successor at the Bureau.)

Fortunately, various bits of Hooverana in the form of Official and Confidential files managed to survive the purge. These documents—available for public scrutiny (and cheap thrills) at the FBI's Freedom of Information Act Reading Room in Washington—have revealed the methods by which Hoover managed to meddle into any film production or television series that included a portrayal of an FBI agent.

The following are some examples:

WALT DISNEY

Not even Uncle Walt could escape the Bureau's dragnet. The movie in question was *Moon Pilot,* a harmless Disney pre-*I Dream of Jeannie* comedy about an astronaut who meets an alien before a space mission.

After learning that *Moon Pilot*'s script portrayed FBI agents as ineffectual bumblers, Hoover ordered the chief of the Bureau's Los Angeles division to contact Disney for a meeting, where he was asked to change the film's reference from FBI agents to Federal security agents. Despite Disney's protestations that the change was "unrealistic," dialogue changes were tailored to meet Hoover's specifications.

The real snafu started when Hoover was sent a newspaper review of *Moon Pilot* which referred to the bureau's portrayal "as a mass of dolts." On the margin of the review (which is included in Disney's FBI file), Hoover scrawled "I am amazed Disney would do this. He probably has been infiltrated."

Apparently, the squabble carried over to another Disney production, *That Darn Cat* (1964), which was also closely monitored by the Los Angeles division for references to the FBI. The matter was dropped—according to an FBI memorandum in Disney's file—after "an established source at the Disney studios" confirmed that the script depicted "the FBI in a most complimentary manner."

ROCK HUDSON

In 1982, Rock Hudson's FBI file was rush-released in the midst of the media circus surrounding his AIDS-related death. The most quoted part of the released documents was as follows: "Rock Hudson has not been the subject of an FBI investigation. During 1965, however, a confidential informant reported that several years ago while he was in New York he had an 'affair' with movie star Rock Hudson. The informant stated that from personal knowledge he knew that Rock Hudson was a homosexual. The belief was expressed that by 'personal knowledge' the informant meant he had personally indulged in homosexual acts with Hudson or had witnessed or received the information of individuals who had done so."

This document had been sent to Mildred Stegall, White House staff-member during LBJ's presidency.

Since Hoover himself had been rumored to be gay (never proven but he was a bachelor all his life), he had particular interest in major figures who were gay. For example, Tennessee Williams' FBI files include this: "Subsequently, in connection with the investigation for the Department in 1961 (expurged) the Bureau ascertained that Thomas Lanier Williams has the reputation of being a homosexual. (Expurged.) Further, the Office of Naval Intelligence, in a separate inquiry, secured statements from individuals who admitted participating in homosexual acts with Williams."

Only 10% of the athletes who sign pro baseball contracts ever make it into the major leagues.

Hoover, then, was particularly alarmed to find out that Rock Hudson might be playing an FBI agent in a movie. According to *Daily Variety* (9/5/67), Hudson had been signed to play "an FBI agent who becomes involved with a jewel thief." This revelation sent shockwaves through the Bureau. An investigation into the movie called *The Quiet Couple* (eventually released as *A Fine Pair*) proved that *Daily Variety's* information was erroneous—Hudson's role was that of an ex-police officer. Still, the Bureau made several follow-up reports (and wasted untold thousands of taxpayers' dollars) to make sure Hudson did not play an FBI agent.

GROUCHO MARX

Obviously, any Jewish celebrity with the name Marx was going to be under Hoover's intense scrutiny. Although Marx's FBI files include inconclusive investigations into his possible Communist affiliations, it is the references to his TV series, "You Bet Your Life," that show the Bureau's sensitivity to every mention of the FBI.

Included in Marx's files are the following entries:

"(Expurged) called on 2/29/60 to advise that he had been listening to the captioned program on last Thursday, 2/25/60, on NBC, Channel 4, and that one of the contestants was an individual described by (expurged) as a 'stumble bum' who admitted being a former pugilist and bootlegger. (Expurged) said that when this contestant, whose name he did not recall, stated he had been a bootlegger, Marx asked, 'You mean you were a bootlegger for the FBI?' in an apparent effort to be funny. (Expurged) said the contestant made some non-committal answer and there was little laughter from the audience. (Expurged) stated that he felt that Marx's question was in poor taste and simply wanted to call it to the Bureau's attention."

"We received a letter from (Expurged) Los Angeles 48, California, suggesting that the director see Romaine Rielding talk Russian to Groucho Marx on the Groucho Marx television show Thursday evening, January 29, 1959.

"The show was monitored and there was nothing on it concerning the Bureau or matters of any interest to us."

WORD PLAY

Common phrases and their origins

To Peter Out
Possibly comes from France, where peter means "fart." According to one expert: "'Peter out' would then be equivalent to 'fizzle out,' since...the original 'fizzle' was a noiseless fart."

A Wild Goose Chase
A game played in Elizabethan England—a crazy version of follow-the-leader, on horseback. People believed wild geese acted this way.

Red Tape
The stuff used by bureaucrats in the 19th century to tie together packets of official documents.

Different Drummer
Coined by Henry David Thoreau. In his own words: "If a man does not keep pace with his companions, perhaps it is because he marches to a different drummer."

To Quit Cold Turkey
"Typically, a person [who quits drugs or drinking] undergoes bouts of sweating and chills, with goosebumps. ....Anyone who has seen a plucked turkey prepared for the oven...will at once understand the image."

The Jig Is Up
"First heard during Shakespeare's time. Jig was then a slang word for *trick*, so the phrase simply meant, 'Your trick or deceit has been found out.'"

Toodle-oo
Derived from the French phrase, *Tout a l'heure*, which means "See you later."

Jerk
In Victorian times, masturbation was considered the road to insanity. People who showed the "results" of self-abuse—stupidity, dimwittedness, etc.—were referred to as *Jerk-offs*. Later, just calling someone a *jerk* was sufficent to get the point across.

Someone's Gone to Pot
Like food that's cooked and eaten....It's gone to (the) pot. It's done, finished, over.

Alexander Graham Bell was 29 years old when he invented the telephone.

FRANKS & DOGS

Some food is so much a part of our lives that we never stop to ask where it comes from. Here are some answers you can chew on.

THE SAUSAGE: ANCIENT HISTORY

• The Babylonians were the first to come up with the concept over 3,500 years ago by stuffing spiced meat into animal intestines.

• Other civilizations adopted and modified the sausage. The Greeks called it "orya." In the 9th Century B.C., the Greek poet Homer praised the sausage in his epic the *Odyssey*.

• The Romans, whose army marched on its stomach, loved the sausage. It is mentioned in the oldest known Roman cookbook, dated 228 A.D. They called it "salsus"—which ultimately became *sausage*.

THE WEINER. Over the next 1000 years, the popularity of sausages spread throughout Europe. By the Middle Ages, they began to take on regional characteristics; their shape and size varied from country to country, and local creations were named for the towns in which they originated. Austria gave birth to the "Vienna sausage" or *wienerwurst*, from which the term "weiner" is derived.

THE FRANKFURTER. The modern hot dog—the frankfurter—is descended from a spiced, smoked, slightly curved, thin sausage developed in Frankfurt, Germany.

• According to German lore, the shape of this "Frankfurter" was a tribute to a popular pet dachshund that belonged to a local butcher. The result: by the 1850s, it was commonly called a "dachshund sausage." It was customarily eaten with sauerkraut and mustard. But no bun.

• In the 1890s, a German immigrant named Charles Feltman began selling "dachshund sausages" on the street in Coney Island, NY. He became so successful that he was able to open a "frankfurter" restaurant—the first in the United States.

THE BUN. In 1904, at the St. Louis "Louisiana Purchase Exposition," another Frankfurt native sold "dachshund" sausages.

Americans' two favorite foods are steak and potatoes.

The effect was far-reaching: besides popularizing the food nationwide, this entrepreneur improved the package by introducing the bun. Here's how: Gloves were customarily supplied for customers to wear while eating their frankfurters. But at the fair, too many people walked away still wearing them; the vendor soon ran out of spare gloves. In desperation, he convinced a nearby baker to make frank-shaped rolls as a substitute for gloves. The rolls actually worked better; a new tradition was born.

THE HOT DOG. The name *Hot Dog* was coined in 1906. A syndicated cartoonist named Tad Dorgan was enjoying a baseball game at New York's Polo Grounds. Inspired by the vendors' call of "Get your red hot dachshund dogs!" he went back to his office and began sketching a cartoon based on the notion of a real dachshund in a bun, covered with mustard. When he couldn't come up with the correct spelling of dachshund, he supposedly just settled for "hot dog." The name stuck. Ironically, although Dorgan is clearly given credit for the name, the original cartoon has never been found.

THE HAMBURGER

- The hamburger originated with the warring Mongolian and Turkish tribes known as Tatars who shredded low-quality beef before cooking to make it taste better.

- The dish was introduced to Germany sometime before the 14th century where it was spiced and prepared cooked or raw. From the town of Hamburg the dish became known as "Hamburg steak."

- In the 1880's, German immigrants brought the Hamburg specialty to America where it became known as "hamburger steak." It was also known as "Salisbury Steak," named after the English Dr. J.H. Salisbury, who recommended to his patients that they eat beef three times a day.

- The "hamburg" began its ascent to unparalleled popularity when it was served as a sandwich at the 1904 St. Louis World's Fair. Unfortunately, no one knows exactly how its association with ketchup started, or who thought of serving it on a bun.

- Today, the hamburger is *the* most popular entrée in American restaurants.

PARTY LINES

People often ask if there's really any difference between the two major political parties. To answer the question, Rep. Andrew Jacobs of Indiana rose in the House of Representatives and offered this delineation. It was recorded in Will the Gentleman Yield?, *by Bill Hogan and Mike Hill, and is reprinted with permission of Ten Speed Press.*

TO BE READ ALOUD BY A DEMOCRAT TO A REPUBLICAN, OR A REPUBLICAN TO A DEMOCRAT:

Democrats seldom make good polo players.

The people you see coming out of white wooden churches are Republicans.

Democrats buy most of the books that have been banned somewhere. Republicans form censorship committees and read them as a group.

Republicans are likely to have fewer but larger debts that cause them no concern.

Democrats owe a lot of small bills. They don't worry either.

Republicans consume three-fourths of all the rutabaga produced in this country. The remainder is thrown out.

Republicans usually wear hats and almost always clean their paintbrushes.

Democrats give their worn-out clothes to those less fortunate. Republicans wear theirs.

Republicans post all the signs saying *No Trespassing* and *These Deer are Private Property* and so on. Democrats bring picnic baskets and start their bonfires with signs.

Republicans employ exterminators. Democrats step on bugs.

Republicans have governesses for their children. Democrats have grandmothers.

Democrats name their children after currently popular sports figures, politicians and entertainers. Republican children are named after their parents or grandparents according to where the most money is.

Large cities such as New York are filled with Republicans—up until 5 p.m. At this point there is a phenomenon much like

Olympic highjump: Penguins can jump as high as 6 feet in the air.

an automatic washer starting the spin cycle. People begin pouring out of every exit of the city. These are Republicans going home.

Democrats keep trying to cut down on smoking, but are not successful. Neither are Republicans.

Republicans tend to keep their shades drawn, though there isn't any reason why they should. Democrats ought to, but don't.

Republicans fish from the stern of a chartered boat. Democrats sit on the dock and let the fish come to them.

Republicans study the financial pages of the newspaper. Democrats put them in the bottom of the bird cage.

Most of the stuff you see alongside the road has been thrown out of car windows by Democrats.

On Saturday, Republicans head for the hunting lodge or the yacht club. Democrats wash the car and get a haircut.

Republicans raise dahlias, Dalmatians and eyebrows. Democrats raise Airedales, kids and taxes.

Democrats eat the fish they catch. Republicans hang them on the wall.

Democrats watch TV crime and Western shows that make them clench their fists and become red in the face. Republicans get the same effect from presidential press conferences.

Christmas cards that Democrats send are filled with reindeer and chimneys and long messages. Republicans select cards containing a spray of holly, or a single candle.

Democrats are continually saying, "This Christmas we're going to be sensible." Republicans consider this highly unlikely.

Republicans smoke cigars on weekdays.

Republicans have guest rooms. Democrats have spare rooms filled with old baby furniture.

Republican boys date Democratic girls. They plan to marry Republican girls, but feel they're entitled to a little fun first.

Democrats make up plans and then do something else. Republicans follow the plans their grandfathers made.

Democrats purchase all the tools—the power saws and mowers. A Republican probably wouldn't know how to use a screwdriver.

Democrats suffer from chapped hands and headaches. Republicans have tennis elbow and gout.

Republicans sleep in twin beds—some even in separate rooms. That is why there are more Democrats.

SOUNDS OF SILENCE

The unusual history of the record that made Simon and Garfunkel famous, from the book Behind the Hits, *by Bob Shannon and John Javna.*

As late as March 1965, Simon and Garfunkel were still just another unknown folk duo who played at Greenwich Village coffee houses. Their act consisted of a few folk standards, a few Dylan tunes, and a few originals.

Then they got a break; Paul Simon managed to interest Columbia producer Tom Wilson in his material. The result: Simon and Garfunkel's first album, a record called "Wednesday Morning, 3 AM." It featured Simon on acoustic guitar, and included "Sounds of Silence," which Paul had written the previous year.

It bombed, and Simon and Garfunkel broke up. Paul moved to England; Artie went back to college.

That could have been the end of the story. But unknown to the singers, a Boston radio station began playing "Sounds of Silence" regularly...and Columbia suddenly became interested. They'd had Top 40 success with the folk-rock music of the Byrds, so they decided it was worth trying to turn S&G into a folk-rock act, too.

The secret: All Columbia had to do was add electric instruments to the S&G tracks already on tape. That task fell to Tom Wilson. Without telling Simon and Garfunkel about it, he gathered a bunch of studio musicians at the Columbia recording studios in New York City and had them add their own music to S&G's. Vinnie Bell was the guitarist in that session.

Vinnie Bell: "We had no idea what we were going to work on that day—we were just doing a session. So we got there and there were no artists...and we had no music; they just played a ...record of these two guys singing....Well, everybody got out their own paper and we started jotting down music. We each made up our own parts because there was no arranger on it. And then we played along to this existing track."

So, thanks to a handful of anonymous New York sidemen, the acoustic version of "Sounds" became electrified. Then Columbia issued it as the new single from their latest "folk-rock discovery," Simon and Garfunkel. Top 40 stations, unaware that the duo no longer existed, immediately played it and soon it was shooting up the charts.

A few weeks later, Paul Simon got a call in England telling him that his record was the #1 song in America. You can imagine his shock—he didn't even know it existed! Of course, Simon flew back to the States, S&G reunited, and America had two new poet-heroes. Simon, however, apparently had no idea who'd played the electric instruments on his record—which proved embarrassing when he and Garfunkel appeared on NBC's prime time rock 'n' roll TV show, "Hullaballoo." Here's what happened:

Vinnie Bell: "I was working [in the house band] on 'Hullaballoo,' and of course we'd get all the big groups on the show. It was a lot of fun for me, because I would see all my friends. I recorded with all those people. The Stones used to come on—I worked with them. Dionne Warwick was a regular guest....All those people, y'know. Well, now Simon and Garfunkel have a big hit, 'Sounds of Silence,' so they came on the show. And during the rehearsal, Paul Simon talked to the musical conductor, Peter Matz. He said, 'I'd like to show the guitar player how to play this [part].' But Peter Matz knew I did the record; he said, 'I think he knows.' But Paul Simon insisted. He said, 'No, I did a special thing on the record that I want him to do with the sound.' And Peter Matz looked at me, and he said, 'All right, go ahead.' So Simon walked through the orchestra and when he got to me, he said, 'Hi, I'm Paul Simon.' I said, 'Hi, I'm Vinnie Bell.' He said, 'I'd like to show you, if you don't mind, how I did this thing on the record. We have a record out, I don't know if you know it, it's a big hit, "Sounds of Silence."' So I said to him, 'Yes, I know the record. To tell you the truth, I know just what to play.' He said, 'No, here, just watch my fingers,' and showed me with his guitar. 'Paul,' I said, '*I did the record.*' And of course there was silence. And he said, 'Well...okay....Are you sure you did the record?' I said, 'Yeah, it's *this*, right?' And I played [the part for him]. He said, 'Yeah, that's it.' I just told him, "Don't worry."'

The most money ever paid for a cow in an auction was $1.3 million.

PETER PAN

This is one of the most engaging works of fantasy you'll find anywhere. After seeing Walt Disney's sugary version, you'll be surprised how ironic and sophisticated the original is.

BACKGROUND

Peter Pan *was written by Sir James Matthew Barrie, one of England's most celebrated writers. It was first presented as a play in London in 1904, and was so well received that in 1906 Barrie wrote a sequel called* Peter Pan in Kensington Gardens. *In 1911, Barrie finally published* Peter Pan and Wendy, *the famous prose adaptation of the original play. The following is excerpted from that work.*

Mrs. Darling first heard of Peter when she was tidying up her children's minds. It is the nightly custom of every good mother after her children are asleep to rummage in their minds and put things straight for the next morning, repacking into their proper places the many articles that have wandered during the day. If you could keep awake (but of course you can't) you would see your own mother doing this, and you would find it very interesting to watch her. It is quite like tidying up drawers. You would see her on her knees, I expect, lingering humorously over some of your contents, wondering where on earth you had picked this thing up, making discoveries sweet and not so sweet, pressing this to her cheek as if it were as nice as a kitten, and hurriedly stowing that out of sight. When you wake in the morning, the naughtiness and evil passions with which you went to bed have been folded up small and placed at the bottom of your mind; and on the top, beautifully aired, are spread out your prettier thoughts, ready for you to put on.

I don't know whether you have ever seen a map of a person's mind. Doctors sometimes draw maps of other parts of you, and your own map can become intensely interesting, but catch them trying to draw a map of a child's mind, which is not only confused, but keeps going round all the time. There are zigzag lines on it, just like your temperature on a card, and these are probably roads in the island; for the Neverland is always more or less an island, with astonishing splashes of colour here and there, and coral reefs and rakish-looking craft in the offing, and savages and lonely lairs, and gnomes who are mostly tailors, and caves through which a river runs, and princes with six elder brothers, and a hut fast going to decay, and one very small old lady with a hooked nose. It would be an easy map if that were all; but there is also first day at school, religion, fathers, the round pond, needlework, murders, hangings, verbs that take the dative, chocolate pudding day, getting into braces, say ninety-nine, threepence for pulling out your tooth yourself, and so on; and either these are part of the island or they are another map showing through, and it is all rather confusing, especially as nothing will stand still.

Of course the Neverlands vary a good deal. John's, for instance, had a lagoon with flamingoes flying over it at which John was shooting, while Michael, who is very small, had a flamingo with lagoons flying over it. John lived in a boat turned upside down on the sands, Michael in a wigwam, Wendy in a house of leaves deftly sewn together. John had no friends, Michael had friends at night, Wendy had a pet wolf forsaken by its parents; but on the whole the Neverlands have a family resemblance, and if they stood in a row you could say of them that they have each other's nose, and so forth. On these magic shores children at play are forever beaching their coracles. We too have been there; we can still hear the sound of the surf, though we shall land no more.

Of all delectable lands the Neverland is snuggest and most compact; not large and sprawly, you know, with tedious distances between one adventure, but nicely crammed. When you play at it by day with the chairs and tablecloth, it is not in the least alarming, but in the two minutes before you go to sleep it becomes very nearly real. That is why there are night-lights.

Occasionally in her travels through her children's minds Mrs.

Life Span: Rattlesnakes live for about nineteen years.

Darling found things she could not understand, and of these quite the most perplexing was the word Peter. She knew of no Peter, and yet he was here and there in John and Michael's minds, while Wendy's began to be scrawled all over with him. The name stood out in bolder letters than any of the other words, and as Mrs. Darling gazed she felt that it had an oddly cocky appearance.

'Yes, he is rather cocky,' Wendy admitted with regret. Her mother had been questioning her.

'But who is he, my pet?'

'He is Peter Pan, you know, mother.'

At first Mrs. Darling did not know, but after thinking back into her childhood she just remembered a Peter Pan who was said to live with the fairies. There were odd stories about him; as that when children died he went part of the way with them, so that they should not be frightened. She had believed in him at the time, but now that she was married and full of sense she quite doubted whether there was any such person.

'Besides,' she said to Wendy, 'he would be grown up by this time.'

'Oh no, he isn't grown up,' Wendy assured her confidently, 'and he is just my size.' She meant that he was her size in both mind and body; she didn't know how she knew it, she just knew it.

Mrs. Darling consulted Mr. Darling, but he smiled pooh-pooh. 'Mark my words,' he said, 'it is some nonsense Nana has been putting into their heads; just the sort of idea a dog would have. Leave it alone, and it will blow over.'

But it would not blow over; soon the troublesome boy gave Mrs. Darling quite a shock.

Children have the strangest adventures without being troubled by them. For instance, they may remember to mention, a week after the event happened, that when they were in the wood they met their dead father and had a game with him. It was in this casual way that Wendy one morning made a disquieting revelation. Some leaves of a tree had been found on the nursery floor, which certainly were not there when the children went to bed, and Mrs. Darling was puzzling over them when Wendy said with a tolerant smile:

'I do believe it is that Peter again!'

'Whatever do you mean, Wendy?'

'It is so naughty of him not to wipe,' Wendy said, sighing. She was a tidy child.

She explained in quite a matter-of-fact way that she thought Peter sometimes came to the nursery in the night and sat on the foot of her bed and played his pipes to her. Unfortunately she never woke, so she didn't know how she knew, she just knew.

'What nonsense you talk, precious. No one can get into the house without knocking.'

'I think he comes in by the window,' she said.

'My love, it is three floors up.'

'Were not the leaves at the foot of the window, mother?'

It was quite true; the leaves had been found very near the window.

Mrs. Darling did not know what to think, for it all seemed so natural to Wendy that you could not dismiss it by saying she had been dreaming.

'My child,' the mother cried, 'why did you not tell me of this before?'

'I forgot,' said Wendy lightly. She was in a hurry to get her breakfast.

Oh, surely she must have been dreaming.

But, on the other hand, there were the leaves. Mrs. Darling examined them carefully; they were skeleton leaves, but she was sure they did not come from any tree that grew in England. She crawled about the floor, peering at it with a candle for marks of a strange foot. She rattled the poker up the chimney and tapped the walls. She let down a tape from the window to the pavement, and it was a sheer drop of thirty feet, without so much as a spout to climb up by.

Certainly Wendy had been dreaming.

Tall tale: The average person is about a quarter of an inch taller at night.

CARY GRANT, ACID-HEAD

We think of Timothy Leary, Jimi Hendrix , etc. as the quintessential LSD freaks. But Cary Grant—of all people—was into acid before those guys ever heard of it.

Before Timothy Leary and the counterculture discovered LSD—before it was even illegal—the unflappable, ultimately dignified Cary Grant was tripping out every Saturday.

It was 1957. Grant's wife, Betsy Drake, had been going to the Psychiatric Institute of Beverly Hills to undergo an unusual form of chemical therapy. The Institute's directors believed that the little-known drug LSD "acted as a psychic energizer, emptying the subconscious mind and intensifying emotions a hundred times." Drake had been taking it regularly, and it had done wonders for her. So when she realized that Grant was on the verge of a nervous breakdown, she convinced him to try it, too.

Working with Dr. Mortimer Hartman, whom the actor referred to as "My wise Mahatma," Cary began the sessions under strict medical supervision. First he was given a dose of LSD in the therapist's offices; he spent several hours in treatment. Then he was given a depressant to calm him down. Finally, he was driven home to rest and recover for a day. Grant found the effects of the drug astounding. "The first thing that happens to you," he told friends, "is you don't want to look at who you are. Then the light breaks through; to use the cliché, you are enlightened." Hallucinating under the drug gave the otherwise staid Briton a new freedom. Once, he admitted, "I imagined myself as a giant penis launching off from Earth like a spaceship."

Grant continued this treatment for two years; he took hundreds of acid trips. Previously he had been reluctant to talk about his personal life. (An instructive anecdote: a reporter once cabled this question to him: "How old Cary Grant?"

Grant's evasive reply: "Old Cary Grant fine.") Now at age 55, thrilled by the new outlook on life that the drug gave him, he spoke to friends, the media, college students—anyone who would listen—about the benefits of LSD therapy.

"I have been born again," he declared. I have been through a psychiatric experience which has completely changed me. It was horrendous. I had to face things about myself which I never admitted, which I didn't know were there. Now I know I hurt every woman I ever loved. I was an utter fake, a self-opinionated bore, a know-all who knew very little."

A Sampling of Grant's "Acid Revelations"

- "Respect women because they are wiser than men...(they) have an innate wisdom we men try to despoil from the time we're sixteen years old."
- "The only way to remain happy is to know nothing or everything. Unfortunately, it is impossible to know nothing for very long."
- "A man owes it to me—if I have to look at him—to keep his hair combed and his teeth cleaned."
- "Deplore your mistakes. Regret them as much as you like. But don't really expect to learn by them."
- "Don't expect to be rewarded if you...tell the truth. Hypocrisy no longer has any power to shock us. We encounter it every day. But we encounter the truth so seldom that it shocks and embarrasses us, and we run from it."

Unfortunately, Grant's acid-inspired statement that "My next marriage will be complete" wasn't accurate—although he did have the child he said he was now ready to "beget." When he and actress Dyan Cannon (who swore she had only taken acid once before their marriage—and never during) decided to divorce, it turned ugly. She accused him of being an "apostle of LSD," "an unfit father," and said he insisted that she trip out. "He told me the new me would be created through LSD," she declared in court.

In later years, Grant refused to discuss the remarkable drug. "My intention in taking LSD," he finally told a reporter, "was to make myself happy. A man would have to be a fool to take something that *didn't* make him happy."

According to one survey, nearly 3/4 of all Americans believe in vigilante justice.

PRESIDENTIAL QUIZ

Odds and Ends about American presidents.

1) In which state were the most presidents born?

2) The first president not born a British subject was:
a) Martin Van Buren
b) William Henry Harrison
c) Andrew Knox Polk

3) The only president who was never elected to any national office was...

4) Which president was into boxing and jujitsu?
a) Abe Lincoln
b) Teddy Roosevelt
c) John Kennedy

5) The first woman appointed to the cabinet was Frances Perkins. Who appointed her?

6) Who was the first president to weigh over 300 lbs.?

7) The first president to have documented nervous breakdowns (he had five before he became president) was...

8) The only president known to have ancestors who were American Indians was...

9) Which of these presidents was a bowling enthusiast?
a) Herbert Hoover
b) Harry Truman
c) Richard Nixon

10) What is the significance of the film, *Hellcats of the Navy* ?

11) Who was the first U.S. president to appear on national public TV?

12) Who was the first president to be inaugurated in Washington, D.C.?
a) George Washington
b) Thomas Jefferson
c) Andrew Jackson

13) The first bachelor president is considered likely to have been homosexual (his V.P., nicknamed "Miss Nancy," was thought to be his lover). Who was he?

14) More presidents were officially residents of this state when they were elected than any other. Which state?

15) How many presidents have there been?

One in ten truck drivers is a woman.

CAR BOMB: THE EDSEL

In the lore of American business, the name Edsel is synonomous with total failure. Yet hardly anyone knows anything about the Edsel. The story is almost too stupid to believe, but here it is. Judge for yourself.

The story of the Edsel sounds like a *Mad* magazine parody of the auto industry of the '50s: The people at Ford were so intent on using the latest novelty gadgets, super-sophisticated marketing techniques, and "personality surveys" to sell their new vehicle that they forgot to give their customers a car, too. Everything, from beginning to end, was done wrong ....And to top it off, Ford had the bad luck to unveil its upscale bomb during an economic slump that was responsible for the worst overall car sales in a decade. Things couldn't have gotten much worse.

"How much planning went into the Edsel? In a sense, it must be the most thoroughly planned product ever introduced."

—*Fortune* magazine, September, 1957.

THE PLAN: Ford, the #2 car manufacturer in the '50s, was losing too much business to GM in the "trade-up" field. Upwardly mobile consumers who started with an ordinary Ford or Chevrolet eventually wanted something a little more prestigious. Surveys showed that they "traded up" to either an Oldsmobile or a Buick—rarely a Mercury, which was all Ford had to offer in the upper range. So in the early '50s, Ford executives decided to create a whole new line of cars to attract "the young executive or the professional family on its way up." It was to be "the first new line of cars...started from scratch by a major manufacturer" since the Mercury was introduced in 1938. Ford committed $250 million to the project.

THE EXECUTION: Ford concentrated on three key elements: Design, Dealers, and "Personality."

DESIGN: Roy Brown, from the Lincoln division, was assigned the task of styling the Edsel. "His first move," reported one magazine, "was to take his stylists out to a busy intersection to look at cars. To no one's surprise, they decided all American cars looked pretty much alike."

"I wanted a car with strong identity, " Brown explained before the Edsel's unveiling, "one that could be recognized instantly from the front, the side, or rear." An example: Struck by the fact that front grilles on American cars were all "massive and horizontal," Brown decided a vertical grille would set the Edsel apart visually. His 1957 analysis of the result: "It is crisp and fresh-looking. That grille could become a classic." [It did, of course, but not exactly the way Brown foresaw it; the famous "toilet-seat" grille remains a classic example of tasteless excess in car design.]

The interior was next. Neil Blume was assigned the task of "loading it with exciting things for Edsel dealers to talk about." He came up with 23 selling points, most of which were simply cosmetic. Some examples: "A drum-like speedometer that glows a menacing red when the car exceeds a preset speed;" "a thermometer that registers the temperature both inside and outside the car;" "a single-dial heating and ventilating control;" and "gearshift buttons sensibly located in the steering wheel hub."

DEALERS: Ford wanted exclusive dealers for the Edsel—not salesmen who also handled Fords, Mercurys, or any other brand. The reason: they figured the car stood a better chance of succeeding if the Edsel was all a dealer had to offer. So beginning in 1955, they began trying to woo dealers away from their competition, offering the the chance of a lifetime to become the first Edsel dealers. The amazing thing is that it worked. Almost 200 GM dealers jumped to the Edsel; 150 Chrysler-Plymouth dealers took the bait; another 200 dealers from smaller manufacturers went for it. Each had to plunk down over $100,000 (1957 money), and in some cases, they hadn't even seen the car—they took it on faith that Ford was behind the project 100%...and how could Ford miss? It was like buying a ticket on the *Titanic*.

PERSONALITY: The Edsel may have been the first auto to rely on sophisticated marketing profiles to target its potential customers. Ford wanted to know what the car's "personality"

According to Gallup, the man most admired by America in 1974 was Henry Kissinger.

should be, so they hired a marketing expert named David Wallace to tell them. Begining in 1955, Wallace worked with the Bureau of Applied Social Research at Columbia University, doing market studies and polling consumers to find out how they *felt* about various makes of automobiles. It was he who determined that the Edsel should be positioned as "the smart car for young families."

But it was a crazy survey. They approached their new car strictly as a status symbol, asking questions about what *impressed* people, without asking what people would *buy*."The trouble here," commented one critic, "[is] that they didn't ask questions that elicited meaningful replies. Ford asked no questions at all about car prices, cost of upkeep, cost of operation, cars too long for garages, etc. In fact, the consumer research program...completely ignored automobiles as functioning machines of transportation."

In addition, Ford frequently ignored the research and reverted to its standard decision-making techniques..."If you ask how a policy was determined, like the choice of green as the Edsel's color" said one writer at the time, "you may still be told 'Well, So-and-so liked it, and he has the power. That's the way it is.'" The marketing men weren't particularly pleased with the choice of the name Edsel, either. [Edsel Ford was Henry Ford II's father—it's obvious who picked that one.] "Just look at the associations," complained one. "Edsel, diesel, pretzel—Good Lord! It's a wonderful name for a plow or a tractor, but a car? They can make it elegant, but it will take them two or three years and $50 million to do it." [An aside: Wallace corresponded with poet Marianne Moore about names for the new car. The ones she suggested included: Mongoose Cigique, Pastelogram, Pluma Piluma and Utopian Turtletop.]

In the end, Wallace shrugged it off. "All we can do is advise them how to merchandise the car," he said. "We can't tell them how to create it."

THE UNVEILING: "On September 4, 1957, after a year of intensive and elaborate build-up (in which no detail of the car was revealed) and better than a month before any of the 1958 models were out, the public was finally invited to see the dream made real." People couldn't resist the invitation; for the first week, Edsel showrooms were packed. But within a month, it was clear that customers had just come to look. No one was buying the car. Ford announced that "They're simply waiting to see what the other makes will offer; they'll be back," but Ford was dreaming. October's sales were worse than September's, and November's were so bad that dealers started going bankrupt. The main Edsel dealer in New York City quit, declaring that "The Ford Motor Company has laid an egg."

Ford used every trick it knew to lure people into the showrooms—it raised the Edsel ad budget to a record $20 million, offered the car to state highway officials at huge discounts to give the car some road respectability, offered rebates to dealers...But nothing worked.

In retrospect, perhaps the most amazing thing about this new product is the fact that Ford concentrated so much effort on the "sell" that the car itself was overlooked. Not only did it offer nothing new—it was even inadequately supplied with the basics. The brakes, for example, were the same as Ford used on its smaller cars, although the Edsel was considerably heavier than the rest of the Ford line.

TEST REPORTS: Here are a few of the comments *Consumer Reports* made when it test-drove the celebrated new auto:

- "The public expected the new name to be on a new-from-the-ground-up car. CU's answer: the Edsel has no...advantages over other brands. The car is almost entirely conventional in construction, utilizing components from the 1957 Ford...and Mercury."
- "Edsels offer nothing new in passenger accommodations—unless 'contour seats' feel different to you....The interior dimensions are, for the most part, those of the 1957 Ford Fairlane, one of the least roomy of last year's cars."
- "The amount of shake present...on rough roads—which wasn't long in making itself heard as squeaks and rattles—went well beyond any acceptable limit."
- "As a matter of simple fact, combined with the car's tendency to shake like jelly, Edsel's handling represents retrogression rather than progress in design and behavior."
- "The 'luxury-loaded' Edsel—as one magazine cover described it—will certainly please anyone who confuses gadgetry with true luxury."

A sneeze zooms out of your mouth at over 600 m.p.h.

• "The center of the steering wheel is not, in CU's opinion, a good pushbutton location.... To look at the Edsel buttons pulls the driver's eyes clear down off the road."
• "The Edsel instrument panel is a mismanaged dilly."
And so it went. Fundamentally, the magazine had nothing good to say about Ford's new product—except that it had great acceleration.

EVEN MORE REASONS IT FLOPPED:
• It was an effort to get into the mid-sized car market.... But in 1956 and 1957, the mid-sized car was in trouble. Anyone in the auto industry knew that. What Ford should have done was to bring out a low-priced, innovative economy model, a car to compete with the German Volkswagen. Instead, Ford produced an instant white elephant.
• Rotten timing. In September 1957, the stock market was in a downturn. In fact, the Edsel and the economic recession hit the market at exactly the same time.
• Ford introduced its new car with its 1958 prices at exactly the same time that the 1957 models were being discounted to clear them out. Consequently, the attention the company had sought for its new baby focused instead on its price. Consumers, dealers and bankers alike, balked at higher car prices in general—but because Edsel was the first car to announce them, the brunt of the public's displeasure landed right at Edsel's doorstep.
• The over-designed status symbol appeared a month before Russia successfully launched its Sputnik. In the wake of the U.S.S.R.'s feat, embarrassed Americans shunned opulent new cars as symbols of a misguided national priority. The emphasis in American culture temporarily shifted to academics and practicality.

THE AFTERMATH
The Edsel lasted for two years. Shortly after it bombed, the *Wall Street Journal* ran this little squib: "Ford Motor has called on the Institute of Motivational Research to find out why Americans buy foreign economy cars."

P.S.: Edsel Ford, the car's unfortunate namesake, was a progressive minded, artistic thinker whose death preceded that of his father. Neither he nor Henry Ford ever saw the Edsel.

Six hours after you brush your teeth, plaque starts forming again.

THE FABULOUS '60S

More odds and ends about America's favorite decade, from 60s!, by John and Gordon Javna

FLASH-IN-THE-PANTIES. In the summer of 1960, Macy's installed a men's underwear vending machine. It was national news; throngs of people swarmed into the store to get a look at the contraption—so many, in fact, that Macy's had to move it from the ground level to the fifth floor to avoid store traffic jams. But it died there; the bare facts were that nobody wanted to buy boxer shorts from a machine.

AUTO MANIPULATION. Ford's Thunderbird was so popular in the early '60s that when John F. Kennedy requested 25 of them for his inaugural parade, Ford had none to supply; they were all sold out, and none of the waiting buyers would relinquish his claim to a new T-Bird (not even for the President). After some desperate juggling, Ford finally decided to make a few of its customers wait until after the inauguration.

UNFRIENDLY SKIES. In 1967 in Ankara, Turkey, farmers marched to the American and Soviet embassies and demanded compensation for flood damages to their crops. The floods, they charged, were caused by Russian and American spaceships, which had torn "holes in the sky." The Russian ambassador suggested that if they really thought there was a hole in the sky, they ought to be trying to figure out how to fix it, not complaining to him about it.

POLITICAL IMAGE. After JFK's election in 1960, Robert J. Donovan's book *PT 109*—an account of the heroic rescue Kennedy pulled off during World War II—became a bestseller. A movie version wasn't far behind; but who would star? JFK, it turns out, wanted Warren Beatty to play him. But the director considered Beatty too unstable, and hired Cliff Robertson for the part instead. Kennedy sent his press secretary, Pierre Salinger, to protest the choice. The director's reply to the president: "Don't tell *me* how to make an exploitation movie."

The hair on your head grows about an inch every 2-3 months.

BRAINTEASERS

Still more logic puzzles. Remember—no heavy math or pencils needed.

You know," said my Uncle Gordon, "an eccentric friend of mine decided that one of his two sons should take over his horse-breeding business. Being a sporting man, he arranged a horse race between the two sons. But being eccentric, he decided that the son who owned the *slowest* horse would win the business. Naturally each son was worried that the other would cheat by holding his horse back and not letting it run freely. So they decided to ask me for advice. I don't mean to be immodest," he said, grinning, "but I solved their problem with two words."

What did Uncle Gordon say?

"You know," said my Uncle Gordon, "people on Wall Street say that 1987 dollars are worth more than 1985 dollars."

"Uncle Gordon, you old faker," I said, "everybody knows that."

Why is it true?

"I know a man," said Uncle Gordon, "who lives on the 25th floor of an apartment building. Every morning he rides the elevator down to the street level, gets out and goes to work. But when he comes home at night, he only rides the elevator to the 8th floor and then walks up the stairs the rest of the way. Know why?"

"I haven't the foggiest idea," I answered.

Do you?

"Once in Asia," said Uncle Gordon, "I was captured by bandits. They told me: 'Make a statement—if you speak the truth, we'll hang you...if you say something false, we'll shoot you.' I thought it over for a minute, and then uttered a phrase that confused the robbers so completely that they let me go."

What did he say?

Head-lines: Fine hair grows twice as fast as coarse hair.

HOLIDAYS

We celebrate them every year without having the slightest idea where they really came from... Here are a few enlightening tidbits.

EASTER

Although we know it as the Christian celebration of the Resurrection of Christ, the name "Easter" derives from Eostre, the dawn goddess of Anglo-Saxon myth—who was traditionally honored with an annual festival at the beginning of spring. This celebration happened to coincide with Christian holy days, and so was co-opted by that religion. In America, Easter was largely ignored until immediately after the Civil War. The war-torn country needed a holiday which stressed rebirth, so observance of Easter became important.

EASTER RABBIT

Take your pick: The rabbit is either a traditional symbol of fertility that represents spring, or the rabbit was the earthly symbol of the goddess Eostre.

EASTER EGG

The egg represents birth and resurrection. It was apparently an ancient pre-Christian tradition to give people decorated eggs as gifts in the spring.

APRIL FOOL'S DAY

Until 1564, it was a tradition to begin the New Year with a week of celebration, ending with a big party. But the calendar was different then, and the New Year began on March 25—which meant that the annual party was held on April 1. In 1564, a new calendar was instituted, making January 1 the New Year. People who forgot—or didn't realize—what had happened, and still showed up to celebrate on April 1, were called "April fools."

MOTHER'S DAY

Created in response to the prolific letter-writing campaign of a Miss Anna Jarvis, a West Virginia school teacher who wanted to honor her own deceased mother. How could anyone say no? In 1914, six years after Jarvis began her campaign, President Woodrow Wilson signed a bill proclaiming the second Sunday in May as America's official Mother's Day. Jarvis was named the head of the official Mother's Day committee, and greeting card, flower, and candy sellers—thrilled at the opportunity to sell more of their goods—supported the effort with advertising. (In 1986 it was reported that over 150 million cards and 8 million bouquets of flowers were sent on Mother's Day.)

By the mid-'30s, however, Anna Jarvis was so disgusted with the commercialization of the holiday that she disavowed it. This didn't faze American businesses one bit. They set up their own organization to support Mother's Day, and with the backing of the American public, the holiday continues to flourish.

CHRISTMAS

No one knows exactly when Christ was born, but according to accounts in the Bible, it might well not be December 25—the activities of the shepherds described in conjunction with the event are associated with spring, not winter. Nor did Christians celebrate Christ's birth when the religion was new. It wasn't until around the third century A.D. that December 25 was sanctioned as a holy day by the Church. The reason: It seems likely that Christian fathers were trying to compete with another growing religion, Mithraism—the worship of a sun god—whose big day was December 25.

THE CHRISTMAS TREE

Might have begun in pre-Christian Europe, where the Nordic people believed that fruit trees and evergreens were embodiments of powerful spirits, although there are several other equally plausible legends. German families in the 16th century began bringing evergreens into their homes during the holiday season. They were known as *Christbaume* or "Christ trees," and were decorated with fruit, candles, and cookies.

The *Christbaum* was taken to England by Queen Victoria's German husband, Prince Albert. The first American Christmas trees were brought by German immigrants in the 1820s, but it wasn't until the beginning of the 20th century that Christmas trees became a mainstream custom in the States.

Only about 5% of American men say they are satisfied with the way they look.

HANGING CHRISTMAS STOCKINGS

The custom of hanging stockings on the mantel to receive small gifts originated with St. Nicholas, the Turkish version of our own Santa Claus. Long ago, St. Nick was supposed to have provided dowries for the three daughters of a poor nobleman. He threw bags of money through their windows (in one version, down the chimney), where the gifts happened to fall into a stocking that was hung out to dry by the fire.

SANTA CLAUS

The first Santa was the bishop of Myra of Asia Minor, St. Nicholas—who today remains a principal saint of the Eastern Orthodox church. In the 4th Century, he distributed presents to good children on his feast day, December 6.

During the Protestant Reformation, St. Nicholas was replaced in many countries by the Christmas Man, known in England as Father Christmas and in France as Pere Noel. But in the Netherlands, where St. Nicholas was the patron saint of sailors, he remained popular. There he was known as Sint Nikolaas or Sinterclaas, and Dutch children expected him to leave goodies in their wooden clogs on his feast day. Both this tradition and the name were Americanized. Sinterclaas became Santa Claus.

Amazingly, most of the things American kids believe about Santa originated with the 1822 poem, "The Night Before Christmas," by Dr. Clement C. Moore; the image of the tubby, jolly man in the red suit can be attributed to some 1860s illustrations by celebrated political cartoonist, Thomas Nast.

WASHINGTON'S BIRTHDAY

Surprisingly, the Father of Our Country's birthday was first celebrated as a national holiday in 1780, during his lifetime. But it was his real birthday, February 11, they celebrated.

GROUNDHOG DAY

Originally, this was a European planting superstition—if hedgehogs saw their shadows when they emerged from hibernation, planting was put off a few weeks. American settlers adapted the day to the groundhog.

About 1/3 of all Americans ride bicycles.

MONKEE TALES

In 1987, the Monkees returned, spurred by exposure on MTV and books like A Monkees Tale, *by Eric Lefcowitz.*

HISTORY

On September 8, 1965, director Bob Rafelson and producer Bert Schneider (together as Raybert Productions) placed an ad in *Variety* magazine that read:

"Madness!! Auditions
Folk & Rock Musicians-Singers
For Acting Roles in New TV Series
Running Parts for 4 Insane Boys, Age 17-21
Want Spirited Ben Frank's Types
Have Courage To Work
Must Come Down For Interview"

The idea was to create an American TV version of the Beatles—a pre-fab four.

In all, 437 applicants showed up at Raybert's offices trying to become the four finalists for a "musical situation comedy" called "The Monkees." Among those rejected were Harry Nilsson, Paul Williams, Danny Hutton (Three Dog Night), Rodney Bingenheimer, Steven Stills and, according to legend, Charlie Manson. Eventually Rafelson and Schneider narrowed it down to four: Davy Jones, Micky Dolenz, Michael Nesmith and Peter Tork. NBC bought the pilot, RCA agreed to distribute the records and almost overnight, the Monkees were a pop phenomenon.

With corporate power and a crack creative team behind them (director Paul Mazursky co-wrote the pilot), the Monkees first single, "Last Train To Clarksville," sold 250,000 copies before the series even debuted—despite the fact that the group did little more than sing on cue. Later it hit number one—as did the group's first album...and the group's second single...and the group's second album...etc.

The show debuted in the 1966-67 season, and never rated

highly. One problem: Many NBC affiliates refused to carry a show that had long-haired "hippie" types as the heroes. But it was a respected program. Most people aren't aware that in addition to having hit records (including the #1 song of 1967, "I'm a Believer"), the Monkees won two Emmy awards for best sitcom.

At the end of the second season NBC cancelled the series, so the group concentrated its efforts on a movie called *Head* (now a cult classic) instead. It was released with little fanfare in 1968.

The group's last project with all four members was a bizarre TV special entitled "33 1/3 Revolutions Per Monkee," which featured Jerry Lee Lewis, Fats Domino and Little Richard as guests. NBC ran the show against the Oscars, dooming it to obscurity. The Monkees themselves soon disappeared, splitting in 1970.

MONKEE FACTS

• In 1965, Peter Tork was playing with Stephen Stills in the Buffalo Fish—an early incarnation of the Buffalo Springfield. It was Stills, in fact, who tipped off Tork—then washing dishes for $50 a week—that TV producers were still casting for the Monkees (Stills auditioned, but lost out due to bad teeth and a receding hairline). Tork was the last hired and the first to quit the group in 1968.

• Micky Dolenz wasn't a drummer. He agreed to play drums only after the other Monkees refused.

• Davy Jones' big break came with the stage musical "Oliver!" where he played the role of the Artful Dodger. When the musical moved from London to New York, Jones became an instant teen star, winning a Tony nomination for his role. Ironically, Jones—along with the rest of the cast of "Oliver!"—appeared on the Ed Sullivan Show which included the Beatles' first American TV appearance.

• In terms of fan mail, Jones was always the most popular Monkee.

• Michael Nesmith's mother, Bette Nesmith, was a commercial artist who invented Liquid Paper (i.e., typewriter correction fluid). Michael inherited millions of dollars from her.

• Jack Nicholson co-wrote *Head*. Nicholson also made a cameo appearance in the movie.

• Frank Zappa made a rare guest appearance on "The Monkees" TV series and in *Head*.

• Due to Davy Jones' popularity, another English singer named Jones was forced to change his real name to...David Bowie.

• Monkeeing Around: Davy Jones was due to be drafted for duty in Vietnam when suddenly (by coincidence?) someone broke into the local Army recruitment branch and stole the file cabinet with Jones' file.

• Jimi Hendrix was the Monkees' opening act on their 1967 summer tour of the States. Micky Dolenz had seen Hendrix perform in a New York club and later signed Hendrix following his historic show at Monterey Pop (where both Dolenz and Tork were stage announcers). Monkees fans, however, were unprepared for the overt sexuality and strange guitar work of the Jimi Hendrix Experience—they kept cheering, "We Want the Monkees." Finally, after the group's show at Forest Hills, New York, Hendrix and the Monkees amicably split company. The official excuse for Hendrix leaving the tour was the Daughters of The American Revolution had banned him for being too sexually suggestive.

• Bob Rafelson and Bert Schneider later went on to form BBS Productions, which produced films such as *Easy Rider*, *The Last Picture Show* and *Hearts and Minds*.

• In 1980, Michael Nesmith received the first video Grammy award for his one-hour video special, "Elephant Parts." Nesmith has produced such movies as *Tapeheads* and *Repo Man*.

• In 1986, Micky Dolenz, Peter Tork and Davy Jones reunited for a massively-successful 20th Anniversary Monkees Tour. Although Nesmith declined to tour, he did show up for the encore at the group's 9/6/86 appearance at Hollywood's Greek Theatre. Thanks to MTV exposure of the original series, the Monkees experienced a surge in popularity, culminating in the hit single, "That Was Then, This Is Now." In an unprecedented showing on the *Billboard* charts, the Monkees had seven albums in the Hot 200, six of which were reissues of original albums.

The condom—made originally of linen—was invented in the early 1500s.

BRAINTEASERS

A few more simple logic problems to entertain you.
Remember: no heavy math or pencils needed.

This is a true story," my uncle Gordon said. "When I was living in Vermont, the minister of a local church fell asleep during the services. He dreamed he was a French nobleman during the French Revolution, had been sentenced to die, and was waiting for the blade of the guillotine to fall. Right then, his wife noticed he was asleep and poked him on the back of the neck with a pencil to wake him up. It was a terrible thing—the shock was so great that he had a heart attack and fell over, dead."

"Come on, Uncle Gordon," I replied. "That can't possibly be true."

How could I be so sure that my uncle was kidding me?

One day, Uncle Gordon and I were walking down a busy street, and we noticed four workmen digging. "Hm-m-m," my uncle mused. "If it takes four men four days to dig four holes, how long would it take one man to dig half a hole?"

What's the answer?

Every summer my Uncle Gordon goes to his house in the country. One summer, he asked me to forward his mail to him. I assured him I would. A month went by, and one night he angrily called to ask where his mail was—he hadn't received any yet.

"I'm sorry Uncle Gordon," I replied, "but you forgot to give me your mailbox key."

He apologized profusely, and promised to mail me the key right away. Another month went by, and when he returned, he was fuming.

"I never got a bit of mail!" he screamed. "How could you be so irresponsible?!!"

"Sorry, unk, but it wasn't my fault," I replied.

What did I mean?

The first known contraceptive was crocodile dung, used by Egyptians in 2000 B.C.

THE LASER

Tired of reading about music and TV? Try this.

In a scant 30 years, the laser (short for Light Amplification by Stimulated Emission of Radiation) has become as indispensable to the fields of communication, medicine, industry, manufacturing and the military, as the wheel. The concentrated beam of a laser can bore a hole through a diamond or mend a detached retina. It can slice through a sheet of metal like a hot knife through aged Brie or it can read the price code on a can of creamed corn at your local supermarket check-out counter.

DEVELOPMENT

Lasers were developed in the late '50s and early '60s, growing out of earlier research studies of microwave amplifying devices called masers. Because of this parallel development, early lasers were called *optical masers* because they amplified light in the same manner that masers amplified microwaves. The first laser was produced by Theodore H. Maiman at Hughes Research Laboratory using a ruby crystal as the amplifying medium.

HOW THEY WORK

Simply put, lasers collect and harness light to produce an intense beam of radiation in a single, pure color.

To know something about how lasers work is to have a crash course in the basic nature of the atom. Every atom stores energy. The amount of energy in the atom depends on the motion of the electrons that circle the nucleus of the atom. When the atom absorbs energy, its own energy level increases and the atom becomes "excited."

To return to its normal unexcited state, the atom must release its extra energy in the form of light. This release is called "spontaneous emission." When the atom returns to its lower energy state, it emits a "photon," the basic unit of all radiation.

An ordinary light source, such as the common electric bulb, emits photons of light independently in a random manner. That light is called "incoherent." Wavelengths of light issuing from a laser, on the other hand, are organized or "coherent," and work in conjunction with one another, producing an amplified stream of photons which all have the same wavelength and move in the same direction.

Because of its highly directional beam (unlike radio waves, laser beams spread only slightly as they travel), lasers can transmit information with little interference. And because they operate on a higher frequency than conventional electronic transmitters, lasers can carry more information than radio waves, allowing them to transmit both telephone and television programs at the same time.

THREE DIFFERENT KINDS

The three major types of lasers, based on their light-amplifying medium are solid lasers, gas lasers and liquid lasers:

Solid Lasers: The light-amplifying substance may be a crystal, glass or a semiconductor. For instance, crystal lasers have a fluorescent crystal, such as a ruby. Ruby lasers produce intensely powerful bursts of light that can drill through solid steel. A garnet crystal laser which emits a continuous beam of light may be used as a drill or a range finder. Glass lasers are used by scientists in experiments with plasmas. And semiconductor lasers, which convert electricity into coherent light, are useful in the communications industry.

Gas lasers: The light-amplifying source, a mixture of gases, is contained in a glass or quartz tube. Unlike ruby or glass lasers, gas lasers can produce a continuous beam of light which has a narrow frequency range than the light from a solid laser. Gas lasers are used in communications and in measuring.

Liquid lasers: Chemical dyes dissolved in methanol and contained in a glass tube are the light-amplifying sources for liquid lasers. The only kind of laser that can have its light frequency adjusted, liquid lasers are used by scientists to study the properties of atomic and molecular systems.

The air that leaves your body when you exhale floats out at a rate of about 15 m.p.h.

THE LASER IN YOUR LIFE

In the '60s, people who understood lasers looked forward to the day when they would be a part our everyday lives. In 1963, for example, *Life* magazine reported of a laser test: "This dazzling demonstration only hints at the vast power and versatility of laser beams. Although lasers today are still laboratory tools, scientists foresee a variety of future uses."

Then, in the '70s, the laser came into its own—not only as those eerie green special effects projected during elaborate rock shows, but as technical medical marvels—"bloodless scalpels" used to treat certain types of cancers, to stop bleeding stomach ulcers and, more recently, to perform complicated microsurgeries.

Today, the dreams of scientists two decades ago have largely come true. The impact of laser technology encompasses everything from child care (pricking holes in baby-bottle nipples) and home entertainment (creating audio equipment systems that can reproduce sound with studio or live-performance accuracy) to cost-effective communications (lowering the cost of transoceanic telephone calls through the use of optical fibers) and "national defense" (creating space-based "Star Wars" weaponry).

TOTALLY UNRELATED INFORMATION

Weird Lawsuits: In 1985, a Budweiser radio commercial featured a recreation of the Bill Mazeroski home run that won the 1960 World Series for the Pittsburgh Pirates. It went: "Ditmar delivers...Mazeroski swings...It's going back, back...." The thing is, Ralph Terry was the pitcher who threw that ball for the Yankees, not Art Ditmar—and Ditmar was angry to hear his name mentioned. So he sued Anheuser-Busch for half-a-million dollars, charging "his reputation had been tarnished."

Meat takes longer than other foods to digest.

PRIME-TIME PROVERBS

More comments about everyday life in America. From Prime Time Proverbs, *a forthcoming book by Jack Mingo.*

ON TELEVISION:
"Television has done much for psychiatry by spreading information about it...as well as contributing to the need for it."

—Alfred Hitchcock,
Alfred Hitchcock Presents

George: "Gracie, what do you think of television?"
Gracie: "I think it's wonderful—I hardly ever watch radio anymore."

—*Burns and Allen*

ON GROWING UP:
"You don't need any brains to grow up. It just happens to ya."

—Gilbert Bates,
Leave It to Beaver

"I used to do a year in 365 days. Now they go by much faster."

—Dr. Graham,
Ben Casey

ON MONEY:
The Riddler: "This is my dream come true!...Nothing stands between me and the Lost Treasure of the Incas!...And it's worth millions...MILLIONS!!!
Batman: "Just remember, Riddler, you can't buy friends with money."

—*Batman*

"There's only one thing more important than money— and that's more money."

—"Pappy" Maverick,
Maverick

ON PHYSICS:
"A dog can't get struck by lightning. You know why? Cause he's too close to the ground. See, lightning strikes tall things. Now, if they were giraffes out there in that field, now then we'd be in trouble. But you sure don't have to worry about dogs."

—Barney Fife,
The Andy Griffith Show

ON EATING RIGHT:
John Burns: "I try to eat only natural things."
Louie DePalma: "How'd you like a sack of dirt?"

—*Taxi*

Your fingernails grow up to four times faster than your toenails.

ALICE TAKES A TRIP

The final selection in our Bathroom Reader*—and the longest—is from* Through the Looking Glass, *by Lewis Carroll. This is a particular favorite, because it is one of the few works of fiction you can pick up and begin anywhere (a bathroom reading requisite). In this passage, Alice meets Humpty Dumpty. Due to space limitations, we've cut out some of the poetry. But if you enjoy what's here, you can pick up an unabridged copy for your bathroom.*

A*lice finds herself in a grocery store, talking to a sheep.*

"I should like to buy an egg, please," she said timidly. "How do you sell them?"

"Fivepence...for one—twopence for two," the Sheep replied.

"Then two are cheaper than one?" Alice said in a surprised tone, taking out her purse.

"Only you *must* eat them both, if you buy two," said the Sheep.

"Then I'll have *one* please," said Alice, as she put the money down on the counter. For she thought to herself, "They mightn't be at all nice, you know."

The Sheep took the money and put it away in a box: then she said, "I never put things into people's hands—that would never do—you must get it for yourself." And so saying, she went off to the other end of the shop, and set the egg upright on the shelf.

"I wonder why it wouldn't do?" thought Alice, as she groped her way among the tables and chairs, for the shop was very dark towards the end. "The egg seems to get further away the more I walk towards it. Let me see, is this a chair? Why, it's got branches, I declare! How very odd to find trees growing here! And actually here's a little brook! Well, this is the very queerest shop I ever saw!"

So she went on, wondering more and more at every step, as everything turned into a tree the moment she came to it, and she quite expected the egg to do the same.

However, the egg only got larger and larger, and more and more human; when she had come within a few yards of it, she saw that it had eyes and a nose and mouth; and, when she had come close to it, she saw clearly that it was HUMPTY DUMPTY himself. "It can't be anybody else!" she said to herself. "I'm as certain of it, as if his name were written all over his face!"

It might have been written a hundred times, easily, on that enormous face. Humpty Dumpty was sitting, with his legs crossed like a Turk, on the top of a high wall—such a narrow one that Alice quite wondered how he could keep his balance—and, as his eyes were steadily fixed in the opposite direction, and he didn't take the least notice of her, she thought he must be a stuffed figure after all.

"And how exactly like an egg he is!" she said aloud, standing with her hands ready to catch him, for she was every moment expecting him to fall.

"It's *very* provoking," Humpty Dumpty said after a long silence, looking away from Alice as she spoke, "to be called an egg—*very*!"

"I said you *looked* like an egg, Sir," Alice gently explained. "And some eggs are very pretty, you know," she added, hoping to turn her remark into a sort of compliment.

"Some people," said Humpty Dumpty, looking away from her as usual, "have no more sense than a baby!"

Alice didn't know what to say to this: it wasn't at all like conversation, she thought, as he never said anything to *her*; in fact, his last remark was evidently addressed to a tree—so she stood and softly repeated to herself:

"Humpty Dumpty sat on a wall:
Humpty Dumpty had a great fall.
All the King's horses and all the King's men
Couldn't put Humpty Dumpty in his place again."

"That last line is much too long for the poetry," she added, almost out loud, forgetting that Humpty Dumpty would hear her.

"Don't stand chattering to yourself like that," Humpty Dumpty said, looking at her for the first time, "but tell me your name and your business."

"My *name* is Alice, but—"

A hard rain falls at the rate of about 20 m.p.h.

"It's a stupid name enough!" Humpty Dumpty interrupted impatiently. 'What does it mean?'

"*Must* a name mean something?" Alice asked doubtfully.

"Of course it must," Humpty Dumpty said with a short laugh: "*my* name means the shape I am—and a good handsome shape it is, too. With a name like yours, you might be any shape, almost."

"Why do you sit out here all alone?" said Alice, not wishing to begin an argument.

"Why, because there's nobody with me!" cried Humpty Dumpty. "Did you think I didn't know the answer to *that*? Ask another!"

"Don't you think you'd be safer down on the ground?" Alice went on, not with any idea of making another riddle, but simply in her good-natured anxiety for the queer creature. "That wall is so *very* narrow!"

"What tremendously easy riddles you ask!" Humpty Dumpty growled out. "Of course I don't think so! Why, if ever I *did* fall off—which there's no chance of—but *if* I did—"

Here he pursed his lips, and looked so solemn and grand that Alice could hardly help laughing. "*If* I *did* fall," he went on, "*the King has promised me*—ah, you may turn pale, if you like! You didn't think I was going to say that, did you? *The King has promised me—with his very own mouth*—to—to—"

"To send all his horses and all his men," Alice interrupted, rather unwisely.

"Now I declare that's too bad!" Humpty Dumpty cried, breaking into a sudden passion. "You've been listening at doors—and behind trees—and down chimneys—or you couldn't have known it!"

"I haven't indeed!" Alice said very gently. "It's in a book."

"Ah, well! They may write such things in a *book*," Humpty Dumpty said in a calmer tone. "That's what you call a History of England, that is. Now, take a good look at me! I'm one that has spoken to a King, *I* am: mayhap you'll never see such another: and, to show you I'm not proud, you may shake hands with me!" And he grinned almost from ear to ear, as he leant forwards (and as nearly as possible fell off the wall in doing so) and offered Alice his hand. She watched him a little anxiously as she took it. "If he smiled much more the ends of his mouth might meet behind," she thought: "And then I don't know *what* would happen to his head! I'm afraid it would come off!"

"Yes, all his horses and all his men," Humpty Dumpty went on. "They'd pick me up again in a minute, *they* would! However, this conversation is going a little too fast; let's go back to the last remark but one."

"I'm afraid I can't quite remember it," Alice said, very politely.

"In that case we start afresh," said Humpty Dumpty, "and it's my turn to choose a subject—" ("He talks about it just as if it was a game!" thought Alice.) "So here's a question for you. How old did you say you were?"

Alice made a short calculation, and said "Seven years and six months."

"Wrong!" Humpty Dumpty exclaimed triumphantly. "You never said a word like it!"

"I thought you meant 'How old *are* you?'" Alice explained.

"If I'd meant that, I'd have said it," said Humpty Dumpty.

Alice didn't want to begin another argument, so she said nothing.

"Seven years and six months!" Humpty Dumpty repeated thoughtfully. "An uncomfortable sort of age. Now if you'd asked my advice, I'd have said 'Leave off at seven'—but it's too late now."

"I never ask advice about growing," Alice said indignantly.

"Too proud?" the other enquired.

Alice felt even more indignant at this suggestion. "I mean," she said, "that one can't help growing older."

"*One* can't, perhaps," said Humpty Dumpty; "but *two* can. With proper assistance, you might have left off at seven."

"What a beautiful belt you've got on!" Alice suddenly remarked. (They had quite enough of the subject of age, she thought: and, if they really were to take turns in choosing subjects, it was her turn now.) "At least," she corrected herself on second thoughts, "a beautiful cravat, I should have said—no, a belt, I mean—I beg your pardon!" she added in dismay, for Humpty Dumpty looked thoroughly offended, and she began to wish she hadn't chosen that subject. "If only I knew," she thought to herself, "which was neck and which was waist!"

Estimate: By the year 2,000, there will be more than 100,000 people over the age of 100.

Evidently Humpty Dumpty was very angry, though he said nothing for a minute or two. When he *did* speak again, it was in a deep growl.

"It is a—most—provoking—thing," he said at last, "when a person doesn't know a cravat from a belt!"

"I know it's very ignorant of me," Alice said, in so humble a tone that Humpty Dumpty relented.

"It's a cravat, child, and a beautiful one, as you say. It's a present from the White King and Queen. There now!"

"Is it really?" said Alice, quite pleased to find that she *had* chosen a good subject after all.

"They gave it me," Humpty Dumpty continued thoughtfully as he crossed one knee over the other and clasped his hands round it, "they gave it me—for an un-birthday present."

"I beg your pardon," Alice said with a puzzled air.

"I'm not offended," said Humpty Dumpty.

"I mean, what *is* an un-birthday present?"

"A present given when it isn't your birthday, of course."

Alice considered a little. "I like birthday presents best," she said at last.

"You don't know what you're talking about!" cried Humpty Dumpty. "How many days are there in a year?"

"Three hundred and sixty-five," said Alice.

"And how many birthdays have you?"

"One."

"And if you take one from three hundred and sixty-five what remains?"

"Three hundred and sixty-four, of course."

Humpty Dumpty looked doubtful. "I'd rather see that one on paper," he said.

Alice couldn't help smiling as she took out her memorandum book, and worked the sum for him:

$$\begin{array}{r} 365 \\ \underline{-\ 1} \\ 364 \end{array}$$

Humpty Dumpty took the book and looked at it carefully. "That seems to be done right—" he began.

"You're holding it upside down!" Alice interrupted.

Ivan the Terrible built the Kremlin—then gouged the architect's eyes out to

"To be sure I was!" Humpty Dumpty said gaily as she turned it round for him. "I thought it looked a little queer. As I was saying, that *seems* to be done right—though I haven't time to look it over thoroughly just now—and that shows that there are three hundred and sixty-four days when you might get un-birth-birthday presents—"

"Certainly," said Alice.

"And only one for birthday presents, you know. There's glory for you!"

"I don't know what you mean by 'glory,'" Alice said.

Humpty Dumpty smiled contemptuously. "Of course you don't—till I tell you. I meant 'there's a nice knock-down argument for you!'"

"But 'glory' doesn't mean 'a nice knock-down argument,'" Alice objected.

"When *I* use a word," Humpty Dumpty said, in rather a scornful tone, "It means just what I choose it to mean—neither more nor less."

"The question is," said Alice, "whether you *can* make words mean so many different thing."

"The question is," said Humpty Dumpty, "which is to be master—that's all."

Alice was too much puzzled to say anything; so after a minute Humpty Dumpty began again. "They've a temper, some of them—particularly verbs: they're the proudest—adjectives you can do anything with, but not verbs—however, *I* can manage the whole lot of them! Impenetrability! That's what *I* say!

"Would you tell me please," said Alice, "what that means?" "Now you talk like a reasonable child," said Humpty Dumpty, looking very much pleased. "I meant by 'impenetrability' that we've had enough of that subject, and it would be just as well if you'd mention what you mean to do next, as I suppose you don't mean to stop here all the rest of your life."

"That's a great deal to make one word mean," Alice said in a thoughtful tone.

"When I make a word do a lot of work like that," said Humpty Dumpty, "I always pay it extra."

"Oh!" said Alice. She was too much puzzled to make any other remark.

"Ah, you should see 'em come round me of a Saturday night," Humpty Dumpty went on, wagging his head gravely from side

prevent him from ever designing another structure like it.

to side, "for to get their wages, you know."

(Alice didn't venture to ask what he paid them with; so you see I can't tell *you*.)

[*Humpty Dumpty explains Jabberwocky to Alice, and then recites his own poem...*]

"I sent a message to the fish:
I told them this is what I wish.

The little fishes of the sea,
They sent an answer back to me.

The little fishes' answer was,
'We cannot do it, Sir, because—'"

"I'm afraid I don't quite understand," said Alice.

"It gets easier further on," Humpty Dumpty replied.

"I sent to them again to say,
'It will be better to obey.'

The fishes answered, with a grin,
'Why, what a temper you are in!'

I told them once, I told them twice:
They would not listen to advice.

I took a kettle large and new,
Fit for the deed I had to do.

My heart went hop, my heart went thump:
I filled the kettle at the pump.

Then someone came to me and said,
'The little fishes are in bed.'

I said to him, I said it plain,
'Then you must wake them up again.'

I said it very loud and clear,
I went and shouted in his ear."

Humpty Dumpty raised his voice almost to a scream as he repeated this verse, and Alice thought with a shudder, "I wouldn't have been the messenger for anything!"

Holly has never grown in Hollywood—the town was named after an estate in Illinois.

"But he was very stiff and proud:
He said, 'you needn't shout so loud!'

And he was very proud and stiff:
He said, 'I'd go and wake them, if—'

I took a corkscrew from the shelf:
I went to wake them up myself!

And when I found the door was locked,
I pulled and pushed and kicked and knocked

And when I found the door was shut,
I tried to turn the handle, but—"

There was a long pause.

"Is that all?" Alice timidly asked.

"That's all," said Humpty Dumpty. "Good-bye."

This was rather sudden, Alice thought: but, after such a very strong hint that she ought to be going, she felt that it would hardly be civil to stay. So she got up and held out her hand. "Good-bye, till we meet again!" she said as cheerfully as she could.

"I shouldn't know you again if we did meet," Humpty Dumpty replied in a discontented tone, giving her one of his fingers to shake: "you're so exactly like other people."

"The face is what one goes by, generally," Alice remarked in a thoughtful tone.

"That's just what I complain of," said Humpty Dumpty. "Your face is the same as everybody has—the two eyes, so—" (marking their places in the air with his thumb) "nose in the middle, mouth under. It's always the same. Now if you have the two eyes on the same side of the nose, for instance—or the mouth at the top—that would be *some* help."

"It wouldn't look nice," Alice objected, but Humpty Dumpty only shut his eyes, and said, "Wait till you've tried."

Alice waited a minute to see if he would speak again, but, as he never opened his eyes or took any further notice of her, she said, "Good-bye!" once more, and, getting no answer to this, she quietly walked away: But she couldn't help saying to herself as she went, "Of all the unsatisfactory...people I ever met—" She never finished the sentence, for at this moment a heavy crash shook the forest from end to end.

Almost 1/10 of the garbage Americans produce is plastics.

SOLUTION PAGE

PAGE 32, BRAINTEASERS:

1. Friday; 2. An egg; the riddle is by J. R. R. Tolkien; 3. Neither—when they meet, they're the same distance from N.Y.

PAGE 46, BRAINTEASERS:

1. House numbers; 2. He saw the other boy's face and assumed his was just as dirty; 3. June 29, the next-to-last day of the month; 4. The match

PAGE 65, ANCIENT RIDDLES:

1. The Letter "E"; 2. Tomorrow; 3. A shoe; 4. The stars; 5. A fart; 6. A towel; 7. A watermelon

PAGE 79, WHAT AM I?

1. A postage stamp; 2. A mirror; 3. The moon; 4. The weather

PAGE 207, PRESIDENTIAL QUIZ:

1. Virginia; 2. a, Martin Van Buren; 3. Gerald Ford, who was appointed to the vice presidency before he became president; 4. b, Teddy Roosevelt; 5. Franklin D. Roosevelt; 6. William Howard Taft; 7. Warren G. Harding; 8. Calvin Coolidge; 9. c, Richard Nixon; 10. It is the first Hollywood film in which a future president (Ronald Reagan) and first lady (Nancy Davis) co-starred; 11. Dwight Eisenhower; 12. b, Thomas Jefferson; 13. James Buchanan; 14. New York; 15. 41 as of January, 1989.

PAGE 214, BRAINTEASERS:

1. "Trade horses"; 2. $1987 is worth more than $1985; 3. He's a midget, and the highest button he can reach is the one for 8th floor; "I will die by shooting." If they shot him, that would be true, so he would have to die by hanging—but that would make his statement false. Unable to reconcile the two, they gave up.

PAGE 221, BRAINTEASERS:

1. If the minister died without ever waking up, it would be impossible to know what he'd been dreaming; 2. You can't dig half a hole; 3. He mailed me the key, but I couldn't get into the mailbox to get it.

Uncle John's
SECOND BATHROOM READER

THANK YOU

The Bathroom Readers' Institute sincerely thanks the people whose advice and assistance made this book possible.

Michael Brunsfeld
Richard Kizu-Blair
John Javna
Gordon Javna
Bob Shannon
Stuart Moore
Rachel Blau
Andrea Sohn
Gordon Van Gelder
Fifth Street Computers
Eric Lefcowitz
Mike Wilkins
Jim Morton
Gene Brissie
Ivan Stang
Northwest EXTRA
Carol Schreiber
Penelope Houston
Fritz von Springmeyer
Gene Sculatti
Pat Mitchell
Steve Gorelick
Leslie Boies
Jack Mingo
Franz Ross
Sam Javna
Charlie Weimer
Stephen Louis
Carla Small
Lorrie Bodger
Gideon Javna
Reddy Kilowatt
Gene Novogrodsky
Bob Migdal
Betsy Joyce
Greg Small
Adrienne Levine
Jay Nitschke
Mike Goldfinger

And all the Bathroom Readers

INTRODUCTION

When the Bathroom Readers' Institute put together our first *Uncle John's Bathroom Reader* last year, we urged America's secret readers to come out of the water closet, to "sit down and be counted." And they did, pouring into bookstores around America by the tens of thousands.

Clearly, we've flushed out a new "silent majority"—which is great, because as you might imagine, we really love our work.

- First, it's a challenge to come up with interesting ideas for pieces in the book.
- Second, it's a pleasure to write for an audience we know is going to read every page at least once...and sometimes two or three times.
- And finally, *The Bathroom Reader* gives us a chance to do some throughly enjoyable research; rest assured that everything included here has been tested under actual Bathroom Readers' conditions.

What has the B.R.I. learned about bathroom reading?

- The ideal piece of lavatory lit is a unique blend of light reading and weighty subject matter.
- The topics should be heavy enough to provide food for thought, but avoid clogging the reader's mind wth details.
- The bits of information should be easy to absorb.
- Ideas should flow smoothly from one article to the next.
- A person's mind is more fluid when he or she is in the john, so the best bathroom reading is informative as well as entertaining.

We could go on and on (as we often do), but if you're a bathroom reader, you can already read the writing on the wall.

Go ahead and take the plunge into *Uncle John's Second Bathroom Reader*. And remember: "Go With the Flow."

UNCLE JOHN'S MAILBAG

Our first Uncle John's Bathroom Reader *brought in lots of mail with interesting comments...and suggestions for this second volume. Here's a random sample*

Dear Fellow Bathroom Connoisseurs:
I thoroughly enjoyed your first book....For many years I would search my house for something interesting to read before I would enter my asylum. I have even been known to do my homework while I was in the bathroom. In fact, when I was younger I once watched a whole quarter of the Super Bowl while in the bathroom. It's relaxing and quiet in there, and no one bothers you—except for the few who don't understand, and ask you every few minutes if you've fallen in.

—*Adam B., Richmond Heights, Missouri*

Dear Uncle John,
I am from a long line of Bathroom Readers. At first I thought it was an Italian thing to do crosswords and read for long periods of time in the head, because my father is Italian and my grandfather was straight off the boat....Now I know better.

—*Vinnie B.*

Uncle John,
It was a strain writing, but now that we've started, it's a relief. I'm sure the feeling will pass, so being brief, we'd like to "sit down and be counted"—It's the only way to get a-head in life. We've enjoyed the book—it has really bowled us over! We were unable to flush out any discrepancies....Well, that about wipes it up.

—*Mike and Dan M., Colora, Maryland*

Dear Sirs:
What about the possibility of inserting a picture of a wayside comfort station such as were common in the Roman Empire days? In case you are not familiar with this convenience, let me say that it would normally consist of a group of holes, perhaps 25 in number, in an open location in the main part of an ancient city or town. All

The character most often portrayed in films is Sherlock Holmes—193 times since 1900.

seats were side by side without any pretence or privacy. I can imagine that such a citizen convenience was a hub of gossip and activity for both men and women.

—R. Wilfed B., Totonto, Canada

Dear B.R.I.

We really enjoyed Volume I of your book and have a great idea for a few pages in Volume II: Elvis Presley sightings!! They've been rampant this year, most notably in Kalamazoo, Michigan, where the King reportedly frequents all-night grocery stores and Burger Kings.

—Ron and Lisa B., Des Moines, Iowa

Uncle John—

We always kept the Sears Catalog in our outhouse and used the paper. We had already bought what we wanted out of it, of course. Talk about rough—that stuff was worse than corn cobs!

—Dan R., Athens, Georgia

Dear B.R.I.—

All right, I confess! I read your book cover-to-cover on an airplane—not in the bathroom!

—Julie S., Merritt Island, Florida

Gentlemen:

I enjoyed the footnotes immensely. Maybe some of them can be questions next time, such as:

- Why are hot dog buns packed 8 to a package while the hot dogs themselves always come 10 to a package? To even things out, you have to buy 5 packs of buns, and 4 packs of weiners.
- Why are toilet papers and tissues scented? You shouldn't be able to smell tissues if your nose is stuffed up, and you shouldn't be putting toilet paper up to your nose....Should you?

—Andy D., Gainesville, Fla.

Dear Uncle John:

I laughed so hard while reading your book that I dropped it in the toilet. Don't worry—I bought another one.

—Bill D., Tenafly, N.J.

THOMAS CRAPPER: MYTH OR HERO?

If our mail was any gauge, the most controversial tidbit in the first Bathroom Reader *was our comment that the widely accepted notion that Thomas Crapper invented the toilet is a hoax. Readers sent all kinds of evidence "proving" that Crapper was real. But was he? Let's take a closer look.*

FLUSHED WITH PRIDE

The name Thomas Crapper appears to have been unknown among bathroom historians until 1969, when English writer Wallace Reyburn published a 99-page book entitled *Flushed With Pride—The Story of Thomas Crapper*.

This biography (which Reyburn's publisher calls "The Little Classic of the Smallest Room") begins this way:

"Never has the saying 'a prophet is without honor in his own land' been more true than in the case of Thomas Crapper. Here was a man whose foresight, ingenuity, and perseverence brought to perfection one of the great boons to mankind. But is his name revered in the same way as, for example, that of the Earl of Sandwich?"

Of course not. Not, anyway, until Reyburn's book was published.

CRAPPER, THE MAN

According to Reyburn:

- Tom Crapper was born in 1837, and died in 1910.
- He is responsible for many toilet innovations—including, as bathroom-ologist Pat Mitchell puts it, "the toilets that flush in a rush seen in public restrooms today, and the…trap in plumbing that keeps sewer gas from rising into our homes."
- But the most important of Crapper's alleged accomplishments was "Crapper's Valveless Water Waste Preventer," an apparatus that made flushing more efficient. *Cleaning Management* magazine calls it "the forerunner of our present-day flush system."
- For this contribution, Crapper was supposedly appointed the Royal Plumber by King Edward VII.

The squares you're most likely to land on in Monopoly: Illinois Ave. and B&O Railroad.

• Crapper's name was stenciled on all the cisterns—and later, toilets—his company manufactured: "T. Crapper & Co., Chelsea, London." American soldiers stationed in England during World War I began calling a toilet a "crapper."

FACT OR FICTION?

Beats us. But here are a few possibilities to consider:

• The premier bathroom history, an impressive tome called *Clean and Decent*, makes absolutely no mention of Thomas Crapper.

• Reyburn followed up *Flushed With Pride* with another social "history," entitled *Bust Up: The Uplifting Tale of Otto Titzling and the Development of the Bra.*

• Charles Panati, in *Extraordinary Origins of Everyday Things*, notes that "the acculmulation of toilet-humor puns, double-entendres, and astonishing coincidences eventually reveals...Reyburn's hoax." He offers some examples: "He moved to London and eventually settled on Fleet Street, where he perfected the 'Crapper W.C. Cistern after many dry runs.'...The installation of a flushing toilet at the Royal Palace was 'a high-water mark in Crapper's career.'... He was particularly close with his niece, 'Emma Crapper,' and had a friend named 'B.S.' "

• On the other hand, Pat Mitchell sent us this information: "It seems that in recent years, a certain Ken Grabowski, researcher at the Field Museum of Natural History in Chicago, has unselfishly, unswervingly, and unrelentingly sought to uncover the truth. His findings? Indeed, there was a Thomas Crapper (1836-1910). And Crapper founded a London plumbing fixture company in 1861. His efforts did produce many improvements in the fixtures he manufactured. His company's products (with his name upon them) were distributed all over Europe. Military barracks included. These were still there during World War I."

CONCLUSION

The Bathroom Readers Institute is stuck; we can't relieve the tension or wipe away the rumors. The legend of Crapper seems to have survived all the stink people have made about his life. Or, as Pat Mitchell puts it, "I'm not certain the legend can be killed, but if it could, does B.R.I. want to be the executioner?"

It's not polite to stare, but a butterfly probably can't help it—it has 12,000 eyes.

COMMON PHRASES

In the first Bathroom Reader *we supplied the origins of familiar phrases. Here are some more.*

STEAL SOMEONE'S THUNDER
Meaning: To pre-empt; to draw attention away from someone else's achievements in favor of your own.
Background: English dramatist John Dennis invented a gadget for imitating the sound of thunder and introduced it in a play in the early 1700s. The play flopped. Soon after, Dennis noted that another play in the same theater was using his sound-effects device. He angrily exclaimed, "That is my thunder, by God; the villains will play my thunder, but not my play." The story got around London, and the phrase grew out of it.

PAY THROUGH THE NOSE
Meaning: To pay a high price; to pay dearly.
Background: Comes from ninth-century Ireland. When the Danes conquered the Irish, they imposed an exorbitant Nose Tax on the island's inhabitants. "They took a census (by counting noses) and levied oppressive sums on their victims, forcing them to pay by threatening to have their noses actually slit." Paying the tax was "paying through the nose."

HAPPY AS A CLAM
Meaning; Blissfully happy; perfectly content.
Background: The original phrase was, "Happy as a clam at high tide." Why at high tide? Because people can't dig clams out then. They're "safe and happy" until low tide, when their breeding grounds are exposed. The saying was shortened through use.

TO LAY AN EGG
Meaning: To fail.
Background: From the British sport of cricket. When you fail to score, you get a zero—which looks like an egg. The term is also taken from baseball, where a zero is a "goose egg."

There are more cars in Southern California than there are cows in India.

SWEET NUTHIN'S

Interesting facts about American candies from B.R.I. member Jim Morton.

THREE MUSKETEERS. Most people today have no idea where the name for the Three Musketeers bar came from. Advertising in the fifties and sixties suggested the candy bar was so named because it was big enough for three people to share. The truth is, Three Musketeers bars were originally made of three separate nougat sections: vanilla, chocolate and strawberry. Eventually, the strawberry and vanilla nougat sections were eliminated, leaving only chocolate nougat in each Three Musketeers bar.

BLACK CROWS. The Mason Candy Company decided to introduce a new candy treat in 1890. The candy, a licorice-flavored gumdrop, was to be called Black Rose. But the printer misunderstood the instructions and printed the wrappers with the name "Black Crows." The printer refused to reprint the job, claiming it was Mason's mistake. Rather than pay to reprint the wrappers, the folks at Mason decided to change the name of the product. Today, one-hundred years later, Black Crows are still available by that name.

M&Ms. In 1930, Frank Mars, a candy-maker in Chicago, told his son Forrest to get out of the country and not come back. Forrest went to England with a few thousand dollars and the recipe for Milky Ways. He quickly set up shop and began selling his own versions of his father's candy bars. While in England, Forrest discovered "Smarties," a candy-coated chocolate treat that was popular with the Brits. He bought the rights to market "Smarties" in America, where he went into partnership with a business associate named Bruce Murrie. The candies were called M&Ms; short for Mars and Murrie.

HERSHEY'S. Milton Hershey, the inventor of the Hershey Bar, was an unusual man. As a child he was brought up in a strict Mennonite family. Unlike most entrepreneurs, he never sought the usual material wealth that accompanies success. In 1909 he took a large sum of the money he had earned making candy bars, and opened the

Milton Hershey School for orphaned boys. Nine years later he donated the candy company to a trust for the school. Today, the Milton Hershey School and School Trust still own 56% of the Hershey Company.

SPARKLERS. Wintergreen LifeSavers, when chewed in the dark, give off sparks. This is due to a chemical process known as triboluminescence.

SUGAR DADDY. Robert O. Welch, the inventor of the Sugar Daddy, is also the founder of the John Birch Society.

MEXICAN HATS. Heide's Mexican Hats candies were originally called "Wetem and Wearems." Kids were supposed to lick the candies and stick them to their foreheads. What possible reason for kids wanting to use the candies in this fashion is unknown.

CRACKER JACKS. The dog on the Cracker Jack package is named Bingo, after the folk song that generations of kids were forced to learn in grade school.

OH HENRY. Every day at about the same time, a young man named Henry would stop in at the Williamson Candy Company in Chicago, and flirt with the girls making the candy. Soon the girls were asking Henry to do things for them. Whenever he came into the store they would start, "Oh Henry, will you do this! Oh Henry, will you do that!" When Williamson introduced a new candy bar in 1920, one of the salesmen suggested that they call the bar "Oh Henry" in honor of the likeable young fellow.

CHARLESTON CHEW. Sometimes the names of candy bars come from fads that are popular when they are introduced. The Charleston Chew was introduced during the roaring twenties when the Charleston dance craze was in full swing.

CLARK BAR. Often candy manufacturers spend hours agonizing over what to call their confections. But David L. Clark wasn't one to waste time on such efforts. When he introduced his candy bar in 1917 he simply named it after himself.

THE LAST LAUGH: EPITAPHS

Who collects unusual epitaphs? Lots of people, we're discovering. Here are some authentic ones, supplied by B.R.I. members.

Seen in Falkirk, Scotland:
Solomon Pease
Here under this sod, and under these trees
Is buried the body of Solomon Pease
But here in his hole lies only the pod,
His soul is shelled out, and gone up to God.

Seen in Hatfield, Massachusetts:
Arabella Young, 1771
Here lies as silent clay,
Miss Arabella Young.
Who on the 21st of May,
Began to hold her tongue.

Seen in Bradford, Vermont:
Mary S. Hoyt, 1836
She lived—what more can then be said?
She died—and all we know she's dead.

Seen in Skaneatles, New York:
Sally Briggs
Underneath this pile of stones,
Lies all that's left of Sally Jones.
Her name was Briggs, it was not Jones,
But Jones was used to rhyme with stones.

Seen in Topsfield, Massachusetts:
Mary Lefavour, 1797
Reader pass on and ne'er waste your time
On bad biography and bitter rhyme.
For what I am this cum'brous clay insures
And what I was, is no affair of yours.

Seen in Lincoln, Maine:
Sacred to the memory of Jared Bates,
Who died Aug. the 6th, 1800.
His widow, aged 24, lives at 7 Elm Street,
Has every qualification for a good wife,
And longs to be comforted.

Seen in Kent, England:
Grim death took me without any warning.
I was well at night, and dead in the morning.

Seen in Tombstone, Arizona:
Lester Moore
Here lies
Lester Moore
Four slugs from a 44.
No Les
No more.

With the amount of fuel held in a jumbo jet, you could drive around the world in a car 4 times.

ELEMENTARY, MY DEAR STEVE

The famous sleuth, Leslie Boies, and her faithful companion, Steve, have a few simple mysteries for you to solve. *Answers on p. 454*

The celebrated detective, Leslie Boies, was home working on a case one day when Steve came wandering in.

"I just saw the strangest thing," he mused. "A man walked into Effie's Bar down on Carlotta Street and ordered a glass of water. Suddenly the bartender pulled out a gun and pointed it at him."

"What happened then, Steve?" Leslie looked up, interested.

"That's the strange part—the man said " 'Thank you,' and left"

"Well, I expect he would," Leslie chuckled. "The bartender did him a favor."

What had happened in the bar?

2. Steve was reading the newspaper, and Leslie was combing her hair.

"Here's a story about a guy named Moore," Steve told her, "whose life was saved by a *dream*. Apparently, he owns some sort of factory and commutes into the city every morning at 7:00 A.M.. Then he takes the 5:30 P.M. train home every night.

"One morning last week, he met the night watchman as he arrived at work. The night watchman told him that he'd had a dream the previous night that the 5:30 train would crash that day...and he warned Moore not to take his regular train. Would you believe it—Moore actually waited and took a later train. And afterwards, he heard that the 5:30 P.M. train *did* crash! Now, Moore is trying to figure out how to reward the night watchman. What do you think he should do, Les?"

Leslie looked up and thought for a second.

"Well, Moore should give the him a bonus...and then he should fire the guy."

Steve was startled. "Huh? Why do you say that, Les?"

"Why Steve, I'm surprised at you. It's elementary."

What was Leslie thinking?

Turtles don't have any teeth.

AD TRICKS

Former adman Terry Galanoy once wrote a book called Down the Tube, *in which he revealed many secrets of making TV ads, including these:*

BEER ADS
"For years, static pictures of a glass of beer have been made with a light-grade motor oil in the bottom of the glass and a foamy head of whipped-up detergent on top."

SHAMPOO ADS
The models "washing" their hair in shampoo commercials are often really using something else on their heads. According to Galanoy, they either use laundry detergent, because "it whips up creamy and frothy and rich-looking," or "beaten egg whites, which are carefully laid on the hair not by beauticians, but by home economists, who ice up the lady's head as if they were icing up a cake."

FOOD ADS
"There are a lot of everyday camera tricks for making food look better. Soap chips are sprinkled on cereal because they look more like sugar than sugar does. Lard is scooped out to make ice cream shapes in a sundae dish because ice cream melts under hot lights and lard doesn't. Small stones replace boiled rice because boiled rice goes out a sticky mess."

HAIR COLOR ADS
"You...can't be sure at whom you are looking. For example, one commercial for Clairol hair coloring used one girl for the front of the hair and another for the back. The back of the first girl's hair wasn't attractive enough, but they wanted her face, so they hired a back-of-the-head backup for her."

TESTIMONIALS
Those hidden camera commercials?..."Sometimes they have to shoot 100 women and enough film to make three features in order to get one 'spontaneous' endorsement."

Until 1796, the state of Tennessee was known as Franklin.

PRIME TIME PROVERBS

TV's comments about everyday life in America, collected by Jack Mingo and John Javna for their book, Prime Time Proverbs*—an excellent supplement for your bathroom library.*

ON REVENGE

Sam: "Let me give you some advice, Carla. I suggest you turn the other cheek."
Carla: "Mooning her isn't enough—I want to hurt her!"

—***Cheers***

ON RELIGION

"Let's leave religion to the televangelists. After all, they're the professionals."

—Cheviot,
Max Headroom

"Edith, Sunday's supposed to be the day of rest. How can I rest when I'm going to church?"

—Archie Bunker
All in the Family

"I thought I was on my way to Nirvana. All I ended up with was recurrent flashbacks of the original Mouseketeers."

—Reverend Jim Ignatowski,
Taxi

ON OPPORTUNITY

"How do you like my luck? Every time opportunity knocks, I ain't got enough money to open the door."

—Sgt. Ernie Bilko,
The Phil Silvers Show

ON SINGLE MOTHERS

Blanche: "It says here in this Spock book that it's important to have male role models during your formative years."
Rose: " Well, what does Spock know about raising babies? On Vulcan they're all in pods."

—*The Golden Girls*

ON LIFE

Coach Ernie Pantusso: "How's life, Norm?"
Norm Peterson: "It's a dog-eat-dog world, and I'm wearing Milkbone underwear."

—***Cheers***

Wednesday Addams: "Look, a black widow spider village."
Gomez Addams: "Amazing, just like a tiny human world."
Wednesday: "Yes, all they do is fight."
Morticia Addams: "Well, that's life."

The Addams Family

RUMORS

Here's the second installment of a feature we included in BR #1. Rumors are a special kind of gossip—outrageous stories that, one expert explains, "reveal the desires, fears, and obsessions of a society." They're also a lot of fun. Did you hear the one about...

RUMOR: Proctor & Gamble is secretly owned by the Moonies (Reverend Sun Myung Moon's Unification Church).
HOW IT STARTED: Apparently, it was originally fueled by widespread paranoia about Moon's flower-selling legions. (They're everywhere!) The secret tipoff was supposed to be P&G's logo—the man in the moon. It was "a signal" to other Moonies.
WHAT HAPPENED: Proctor & Gamble executives first got wind of the rumor in 1979 and ignored it...until they got over 1,000 phone inquiries about the matter in a single month. Alarmed, they sent a letter to newspaper editors around the country pointing out that neither the Unification Church nor Rev. Moon owned even one share of stock in the company. Despite this, P&G continued to get 300 inquiries about it every month for several years.

THE RUMOR: A few years ago, three white Midwestern women, visiting New York City for the first time, were on an elevator in their hotel. A large black man with a big dog got on and hissed, "Sit, Lady." The terrified women immediately slid to the floor—whereupon the man informed them he was actually talking to his dog, Lady. The embarrassed women got up and contritely began asking about restaurants. They got the gentleman's recommendation for a good one, went, and enjoyed it. And when it came time to pay the bill, they were informed it had already been taken care of...by Reggie Jackson, the man they'd "met" in the elevator.
HOW IT STARTED: Unknown, but the story was reported as fact all over the country, including stories in newspapers in New York, L.A., Detroit, and Salt Lake City.
WHAT HAPPENED: A New York reporter finally called Jackson and asked him to confirm it. Jackson's reply: "I've heard that story a million times and it's not true. I would never own a dog in New York. It would be cruel."

The word "girl" shows up in the Bible only once.

THE RUMOR: Green M&Ms are an aphrodisiac.
HOW IT STARTED: Unknown.
WHAT HAPPENED: M&M Mars, the company that makes the candy, gets frequent requests for custom-packed bags of green M&Ms. They always refuse.

THE RUMOR: While President Richard Nixon was visiting China, he tried to steal a priceless Chinese teacup by slipping it into his briefcase. The Chinese spotted him. But instead of confronting Nixon directly, they entertained him with a magician who—while performing—surreptitiously retrieved the cup and substituted a worthless replica. Nixon didn't realize it 'til he got back to the U.S.
HOW IT STARTED: The official Chinese news agency released the story.
WHAT HAPPENED: The American government ignored it. Experts explained that the Chinese used it as propaganda to reinforce their self-image: "It symbolized," said one expert, "the victory of the resourceful Chinese over the crafty foreigner, and the ability of the Chinese to know how to act without having anyone lose face."

THE RUMOR: McDonald's owner Ray Kroc contributed a big chunk of his company's profits to the Church of Satan, a devil-worshiping cult in San Francisco.
HOW IT STARTED: Unknown, but a McDonald's manager first heard it in a Georgia fundamentalist church in 1979.
WHAT HAPPENED: Not wanting to give it credibility, McDonald's ignored it until it spread so far that an Ohio minister claimed Kroc had actually admitted it was true on "The Phil Donahue Show," and a few religious groups began calling for a boycott of the food chain. The company's public relations director quickly obtained a transcript of the program to prove Kroc had said nothing of the kind, then made appearances before several fundamentalist groups to explain the situation. It worked—they retracted boycott calls and dropped the matter.

THE RUMOR: When Army brass was planning its 1983 invasion of Grenada, they decided they needed someone who could speak Spanish, to communicate with the Grenadian citizens. So they convinced a Spanish-speaking supply sergeant named Ontiveros to

land with the first paratroopers. He jumped, came under fire, and spent the entire invasion morning shouting 'Qué pasa?' at uncomprehending Grenadians. Finally, Sergeant Ontiveros realized that the Army had screwed up—Grenadians speak English, not Spanish.
HOW IT STARTED: It was a popular rumor in the Army, "reflecting," as one source put it, " the feelings of enlisted soldiers toward the officers who had planned the invasion."
WHAT HAPPENED: A reporter checked the names listed on the invasion force, and found there was no one named Ontiveros in it. An Army press officer added: "I don't doubt the story for a minute.... Except that it's not true."

THE RUMOR: Dr. Pepper's secret ingredient is prune juice.
HOW IT STARTED: Unknown, but it's been whispered for about 40 years. The company speculates that the combination of Dr. Pepper's unidentifiable "fruity taste" and their penchant for secrecy about the soft drink's formula stimulates kids' imaginations.
WHAT HAPPENED: The company prepared a pamphlet which they send out to people who ask about the ingredients. It says: "There are 23 flavors and other ingredients (none of which are prunes) that produce the inimitable taste of Dr. Pepper."

THE RUMOR: Mama Cass of the group, "the Mamas and Papas," died by choking on a ham sandwich.
HOW IT STARTED: When the 220-lb. Mama died suddenly in 1974, her doctor issued a quick statement speculating that "she probably choked on a sandwich."
WHAT HAPPENED: The bizarre report was picked up by newspapers, including *The New York Times* and *Rolling Stone* magazine, and presented as fact. Actually, when the coroner's report was issued a week later; it gave the cause of death as a heart attack "brought on by obesity." Too late—the rumor was already circulating.

THE RUMOR: Ex-president Jimmy Carter saw a UFO.
HOW IT STARTED: Carter is responsible. He told someone: "I don't laugh at people any more when they say they've seen UFOs, because I've seen one myself." He then described it in detail.
WHAT HAPPENED: The Air Force issued a statement explaining that Carter had mistaken the planet Venus for an alien spacecraft.

Census report: U.S. men live longest in the Pacific states (Ore., Cal., Hawaii, Alaska, Wash.).

TALES OF '60s TV

Weird things happened on TV during the '60s.
Here are a few examples.

THE SAGA OF ARNOLD ZENKER

On March 29, 1967, television actors went on strike. And Walter Cronkite—the most popular newscaster in America—decided to walk out with them. CBS was forced to fill his anchor spot with one of their executives—but who could take Cronkite's place? They auditioned seven men for the spot, and all of them seemed too tense.

Finally, in desperation, they picked their 28-year-old manager of programming, Arnold Zenker—without an audition—because he had looked calm on a local newscast that morning. And for no apparent reason, he was an overnight smash. He received 3,000 fan letters. In fact, he was so popular that when Cronkite returned a few weeks later, he opened his first show with, "Good evening. This is Walter Cronkite, sitting in for Arnold Zenker."

"Bring back Zenker" buttons could be seen in TV studios for a while, but the novelty gradually wore off. Zenker, however, was still in shock. "There's nothing like breaking in on the 'Cronkite Show,' " he said in a classic understatement.

LONG GREEN

On January 13, 1965, the irreverent TV host Soupy Sales was suspended from his New York children's program. Why? Because he told young viewers to reach in their fathers' billfolds and send him "those little green pieces of paper." The station manager announced he was afraid the joke might be "misinterpreted" by viewers.

THE WEDDING

One of the most-watched televison events of the decade (and certainly one of the most talked-about) was the marriage of Tiny Tim to Miss Vicky Budinger on "The Tonight Show."

Tiny Tim, the ukelele player who'd been catapulted to fame on "Laugh-In," had mentioned that he was getting married, within earshot of a "Tonight Show" publicist. The PR man suggested to

Census results: American women live longest in the South (Ken., Tenn., Miss., Ala.).

Johnny Carson that he offer to let Tim get married right on the program. Tim's response: "Oh, could we?"

NBC went all out. For the man who sang "Tiptoe Through the Tulips," they ordered ten thousand tulips directly from Holland and filled the stage with them. Miss Vicky wore a $2,500 Victorian gown, Tim a black silk frock coat with a top hat. They passed up Carson's champagne toast in favor of a milk-and-honey drink that Tim concocted, and when they were pronounced man and wife, they kissed. "The fifth kiss we ever had," said Tiny.

Then they flew off to their honeymoon and at least three days of celibacy. ("S-E-X is the least important part of marriage," explained Mr. Tim.)

THE NEW NIXON

In 1968 the Republican candidate for president, Richard Nixon, went on "Laugh-In" and said, "Sock It to Me." Believe it or not, this little event might have helped him squeak by Hubert Humphrey in the presidential election. Why? Nixon's image for two decades had been that of a humorless, colorless character. His appearance on a "hip" show lent credibility to his claim that he was a "new" Nixon. Ironically, Hubert Humphrey was also asked to appear, but declined. Rowan and Martin planned to have him say "Sock it to him, not me" right after Nixon went on. When Humphrey realized his mistake, he asked to appear also. But it was too late.

TOURIST BONANZA

"Bonanza" was the #1 TV show in America in 1964 and 1965. It seemed so real to people that they refused to believe the Ponderosa Ranch was an imaginary place. To accommodate them, a special tour was set up near Lake Tahoe, where outdoor scenes for "Bonanza" were filmed. Guides brought tourists to an anonymous old shack in the Lake Tahoe area and told them it was the "real" Ponderosa.

UH-H-H-H

Walter Cronkite was known for his ability to keep talking on the air, no matter what was going on. But one time—and only one time—he was left speechless.

What did it? The moon landing. "I just went blank," Cronkite explained afterward.

The only place you can see the sun rise on the Pacific and set on the Atlantic is Panama.

REVERSED

PHOBIAS

Are you struck with terror at the thought of wool? If someone mentions spiders, do you go limp? Maybe you've got a phobia. See if any of these rings a bell:

Aulophobia: Fear of flutes
Neophobia: Fear of anything new
Bogyphobia: Fear of demons and goblins
Triskaidekaphobia: Fear of the number 13
Gamophobia: Fear of marriage
Scopophobia: fear of being stared at
Aurophobia: Fear of gold
Chrematophobia: Fear of money
Astraphobia: Fear of thunder and lightning
Blennophobia: Fear of slime
Phasmophobia: Fear of ghosts
Arachnephobia: Fear of spiders
Hedonophobia: Fear of pleasure
Chaetophobia: Fear of hair
Catoptrophobia: Fear of mirrors
Ombrophobia: Fear of rain
Isopterpophobia: Fear of termites
Laliophobia: Fear of talking
Pogonophobia: Fear of beards
Theophobia: Fear of God
Ecclesiophobia: Fear of churches
Taurophobia: Fear of bulls
Teratophobia: Fear of monsters
Tapinophobia: Fear of small things
Homichlophobia: Fear of fog
Geumophobia: Fear of flavors
Hadephobia: Fear of hell
Gymnophobia: Fear of nudity
Levophobia: Fear of things on the left side of the body
Ichthyophobia: Fear of fish
Mechanophobia: Fear of machines
Pteronophobia: Fear of feathers
Politicophobia: Fear of politicians
Siderodromophobia: Fear of trains (or traveling on them)
Symmetrophobia: Fear of things that are symmetrical
Xenophobia: Fear of foreigners and unfamiliar things
Zoophobia: Fear of animals
Anthrophobia: Fear of people
Ophidiophobia: Fear of snakes
Graphophobia: Fear of writing in public
Linonophobia: Fear of string
Pantophobia: Fear of everything

Hear, hear: You'll find a snake's ears in its jaws.

FAMILIAR NAMES

Some people achieve immortality because their names become commonly associated with an item or activity. You already know the names—now here are the people.

Joel Roberts Poinsett. A lifelong American diplomat, secretary of war under Martin Van Buren. While ambassador to Mexico, he brought the first *poinsettia* back to the United States.

Patrick Hooligan. A notorious hoodlum who lived in London in the mid-1800s. His name became a generic term for "trouble-maker."

Leopold von Sacher-Masoch. An Austrian novelist. His books reflected his sexual disorder, a craving which was later dubbed *masochism*.

Frederick S. Duesenburg. An automobile manufacturer. His 1930 Duesenburg SJ was the most exquisite vehicle of its time, so impressive that its nickname—the Duesey—became a slang term for something really terrific. When someone says, "That's a real doozey," they're talking about Frederick.

Charles Mason / Jeremiah Dixon. English surveyors. In the 1760s, they were called in to settle a boundary dispute between two prominent Colonial families—the Penns of Pennsylvania, and the Calverts of Maryland. A hundred years later, the line they laid out became the North/South border.

Arnold Reuben. A New York deli owner in the '40s and '50s. He put corned beef, sauerkraut, and Russian dressing on a piece of rye bread and named the whole thing after himself—the Reuben sandwich.

Alexander Graham Bell. Inventor of the telephone (1876). The standard measurement of "sound intensity," the *decibel*, was named in his honor.

Sir Benjamin Hall. The "chief commissioner of works" for the British government in the 1850s, when the tower clock on the Houses of Parliament got its largest bell. Newspapers of the time dubbed it "Big Ben," after Hall.

Pierre Magnol. A French professor of botany in the 1600s. Gave us the flower name *magnolia.*

Alessandro Volta. A celebrated Italian physicist. His experiments with electricity in the late 1700s led to the invention of the dry-cell battery. The *volt* was named for him.

Belinda Blurb. A model portrayed on a book jacket by American illustrator Gelett Burgess. She inspired the common term for a publisher's comments on a book cover.

Samuel A. Maverick. Texas cattle baron in the mid-1800s. Had so many unbranded stray calves that they became known as *mavericks.* Eventually, the term came to include independent-minded people as well.

Franz Anton Mesmer. An Austrian physician. Popularized outrageous medical theories on animal magnetism in Paris in 1780s. He *mesmerized* the public.

Guy Fawkes. English political agitator who tried to blow up Parliament in 1605, but was caught and executed. The British began celebrating November 5 as Guy Fawkes Day, burning effigies of "the old Guy." Since the effigies were dressed in old clothes, the term *guy* came to mean *bum.* In America during Colonial times, its meaning was broadened to mean any male.

William Russell Frisbie. American pie maker. Founded the Frisbie Pie Company in Bridgeport, Connecticut, in 1871. In the early 1900s, students from Yale—located up the road in New Haven, Connecticut—found they could flip the Frisbie pie tins like flying saucers.

Madame de Pompadour. Mistress of King Louis XV of France in the mid-1700s. Popularized the hairstyle that reappeared, in modified form, on the heads of Elvis and James Dean.

Why do flamingoes hold their heads upside down? It's the only way they can eat.

CELLULOID HEROES

Popular films often inspire musicians to write their best songs. Here are a few examples.

THAT'LL BE THE DAY, by Buddy Holly and Jerry Allison (The Crickets).
INSPIRATION: *The Searchers*.
John Wayne's favorite—and maybe his best—cowboy film, *The Searchers*, was released in 1956.

Wayne's character in the movie was a defiant, macho loner, an anti-hero who fit right in with the James Dean/Marlon Brando image of the mid-'50s. Whenever anyone said something he disagreed with, he'd sneer, "That'll be the day." The phrase caught on among teenagers, and two high school musicians from Lubbock, Texas, Buddy Holly and Jerry Allison, used it in a song.

They recorded it with their band, the Crickets, in 1957, and it became the first hit in a series of records that made Holly a rock legend.

THE MIGHTY QUINN, by Bob Dylan.
INSPIRATION: *The Savage Innocents*.
Who—or what—inspired Bob Dylan to write "The Mighty Quinn (Quinn the Eskimo)"? He's not saying, but chances are it was a little-known 1960 film called *The Savage Innocents*.

What does the movie have to do with Quinn the Eskimo? Well, it starred Anthony Quinn. And he played an Eskimo.

NIGHT MOVES, by Bob Seger.
INSPIRATION: *American Graffiti*.
"The song was inspired by *American Graffiti*," Seger says. " I came out of the theater in 1972 thinking, 'Hey, I've got a story to tell, too! Nobody has ever told about how it was to grow up in my neck of the woods.' "

So Seger wrote "Night Moves" about the early '60s, when he and his teenage friends around Ann Arbor, Michigan would drive into farmers' fields to party. "Everybody had their headlights on, so there was light to dance," Seger recalls. "They'd play 45s, and we'd be blasting them out: Ronettes, Crystals...." Seger's personal

UNCLE JOHN'S LETTER OF THE YEAR

Of all the mail we received—and there was plenty—one stood out as our "Letter of the Year." Here it is.

BACKGROUND: In our previous volume, we included a comment from Mary Tyler Moore about how far fans will go to get autographs. She said:

"I know a funny Carol Burnett story. Once a fan followed her into the bathroom. The fan poked her head under the stall and shoved a pen and a piece of paper at Carol for an autograph."

Okay, got it? Now here's our Letter of the Year.

June 4, 1989

Dear Uncle John,

I am a third grade teacher...I teach a literature selection during the year...and this year I selected *The Wizard of Oz*, one of my personal favorites. My son suggested that I read the excerpts and comments about this story in *Uncle John's Bathroom Reader*. I did, and was fascinated by the political implications of this child's tale.

However, this is not why I write. I am astounded to tell you that as I thumbed through your pages, I found an article on page 152—"Celebrity Mania"—that was about ME! I am referring to a quote of Mary Tyler Moore's regarding Carol Burnett.

Here is the real scoop. *I* was the fan referred to in the story. However, it does my heart good to know that not only the common people, but also the rich and famous like to embellish a good story now and then.

Many years ago, sometime in the early sixties, my husband and I had gone to Las Vegas. We tried to get tickets to see Carol Burnett's show. I think it must have been one of her very first forays away from the world of television and Garry Moore. [*Uncle John's note: She got her start on daytime TV, in "The Garry Moore Show"*.]

We were told that she was sold out. The disappointment of my life! (So far—I was young then.) Trudging away from the desk, I happened to see Carol going into the ladies' room. On impulse, I followed her in. Now my recollections are just a little different from Miss Burnett's. Ever the lady, I waited outside the stall, just as I would to use the facilities. I had no intention of "peeking under the stall." When Carol came out, I zipped inside, shut the door and sat down. Oh!, be still my heart—the seat was still warm. (Isn't this gross? Remember, I was very young.) That would have been enough for me. To live to tell the tale. Yet, when I came out to wash my hands, SHE was still there by the sink. Gathering up my courage I said to her . . .

"Oh MissBurnett,I'msosorrythatIcan'tgetticketsto seeyour-show whileweare-here.It'sabigdisappointment.CanIhaveyourautograph? Yourshowisallsoldout!!!!"

Whereupon she grabbed her head as only Carol Burnett can do and said in that great voice, "I had no idea that so many people would want to see me!" She added, "Why don't you and your husband come in to watch the dress rehearsal" . . . or whatever it was they were doing. "Just tell them at the door that I said it's O.K."

Well, I got my autograph—went to find my husband—walking on air! He said, "Sure, sure, sure. Who did you *really* get to sign that envelope?" He wouldn't go with me because he thought I was making it up, and I was too frightened to go alone. I never did get to see Carol Burnett do a show, but I still have the autograph. I'll never part with it.

Addendum: Just a couple of weeks ago I was installing a new toilet seat in my bathroom and I thought of Carol. (I'm sure she would be *thrilled* to know that I think of her every time I sit there!) Anyway, I was thinking that I should probably box up the old one and send it to her. Maybe she would like to sit on one of mine for a change.

Anyway, she has given me years of pleasure, not only in watching her, but in the telling and re-telling of my story. I know fans can be a pain...but I'd do it all over again.

Sincerely,

Cynthia L.

THE PATENTED CAR

This is a bit of lost history. We take it for granted that anyone who wants to can build a car. Few people realize that that right actually had to be won in court at the beginning of this century, by Henry Ford.

CASHING IN

In the late 1870s George Selden, a lawyer/inventor specializing in patents, heard about the development of the automobile in Europe. He realized that it was a product of the future, and "set his mind to working out the precise legal definition and wording of a patent that would give him the sole right to license and charge royalties on future automobile development in America." Some twenty years later, with the auto industry beginning to show signs of life, he set up a partnership with a few wealthy Wall Street sharks and began asserting his "rights" with automakers. To his surprise, even the five biggest car manufacturers agreed to pay him royalties rather than go to court.

THE CARMAKERS' CARTEL

By 1903, this royalty-paying alliance of carmakers had officially become the Association of Licensed Automobile Manufacturers (ALAM). Henry Ford, then a fledgling automaker, applied for membership...and was refused. His reaction: "Let them try to put me out of business!" He took out ads telling his dealers that "the Selden patent does not cover any practicable machine," and dared Selden's group to take him to court. They did.

BATTLING IN COURT

Ford and the ALAM battled it out for six years. Then in 1909, a Federal judge determined that Selden's patent was valid; Selden and his allies legally owned *all rights* to the car. Immediately, carmakers that had held off on joining the ALAM —including the newly formed General Motors—fell in line to pay royalties.

The ALAM magnanimously offered to settle cheaply with Ford, but Henry fought on. "There will be no let up in this legal fight," he announced angrily. Finally, on January 9, 1911, a Federal Court of Appeals ruled in Ford's favor. Selden and his cronies were forced to give up; the ALAM was never heard from again.

Dirty snow melts quicker than clean snow.

YOU'RE PUTTING ME ON!

The history of some modern wearables.

WHAT A HEEL

In the 1600s, Louis XIV of France added a few inches to the heels of his boots because he was so short. To his annoyance, he started a fad in the Royal Court—soon everyone was wearing elevated heels. So he made his even higher. And so did everyone else. This went on until it got ridiculous. Eventually, men's heels got smaller—but women's stayed high. In the 1800s, American women copied the styles of Paris, and high heels—called "French heels" at first—became a part of American fashion.

TIES THAT BIND

The necktie fashion originated with a band of Croatian soldiers who showed up in France in the mid-1600s. Part of their uniforms were fancy scarves made of linen or muslin; and this looked so impressive to the French that they began wearing fancy linen scarves themselves. They called the scarves *cravats*. Meanwhile, King Charles II of England picked up on the fashion—and when cravats became part of *his* daily wear, the rest of England followed. Over the next century, the cravat evolved into the modern tie.

SNEAKING AROUND

The modern sneaker was introduced in 1917, when the National India Rubber Company came up with *Peds*. Or at least, that's what they wanted to call their new shoe. It turned out that the name *Peds* was already registered; so they quickly changed the name to *Keds* (with a *K* for "kids"). The original sneakers had black soles and brown tops, because those were the popular colors for traditional men's footwear.

TUX & ROLLS

Pierre Lorillard IV, scion of the tobacco company, lived in Tuxedo Park, N.Y. In 1886, he decided he was sick of the formalwear of the day, and had his tailor make suits without tails. In a daring move for Victorian high society gent, he planned to wear one of these scandalous suits to the annual Autumn Ball. But he chickened out at the last minute. Instead, his son and his son's friends wore the suits. No scandal here; since the Lorillards were rich, everyone copied them. The outrageous suit became a fashion. It was even named for its birthplace. And a century later, the tuxedo industry is grossing a half a billion dollars annually.

WRANGLING AROUND

The Blue Bell Overall company was the largest manufacturer of denim bib overalls in the world, but after World War II, they wanted to expand—and decided to add blue jeans to their line of clothing. The name they picked for their new product was Wrangler. At first, since Levi-Strauss had the better stores all sewn up, Blue Bell sold its Wranglers only to discount chains, like J. C. Penney's. But eventually they hired Hollywood stars to plug the jeans, and they became as fashionable as Levi's.

STRAIGHT-LACED

The shoelace was invented in England in 1790. Until then, shoes were always fastened with buckles.

MADE IN THE SHADES

According to Gene Sculatti, in *The Catalog of Cool*: "The first sunglasses were made in 1885 in Philadelphia. Seeking an alternative to costly amber and micalens glasses, a glazier simply put small circles of window glass out in the sun, exposing them to several summers' rays." Sunglasses were popular, but weren't faddish until the '20s, when a bankrupt French comb manufacturer began turning out an assortment of bizarre sunglass frames, trying to find something people would buy. They were shaped like "peacocks, butterflies, pistols, wings, masks, etc. These were gobbled up by the international pre-jet set of the '30s, and soon became true 'trinkets of the bourgeoisie.' " Since then, luminaries like Jackie O., Elton John, Marcello Mastroianni, Audrey Hepburn, and even Barry Goldwater have kept them stylish.

NEHRU WOULD BE PROUD

The Nehru jacket was popularized—briefly—by Johnny Carson, who wore it on TV in the '60s.

Just one part oil per million parts of water will make drinking water taste and smell funny.

MONSTER MOVIES

The inside dope on a few of the all-time great horror flicks.

FRANKENSTEIN (1931). The role that made Boris Karloff a star was originally offered to both Bela Lugosi and John Carradine; both turned it down. One of the factors: the monster costume weighed 62 pounds and the makeup took four hours to apply every day.

• Karloff had to wear 22-pound size 24 boots. He also donned two pairs of pants with steel struts shoved in them, and a double-thickness quilted suit.

• His facial makeup was one-sixteenth of an inch thick, and the bolts on the sides of his neck left long-term scars.

• The famous scene in which the monster carries Dr. Frankenstein was memorable for Karloff, too—he strained his back, and ultimately had to have an operation to fix it.

• Bette Davis wanted the part of Mrs. Frankenstein, but was turned down because she was "too aggressive."

DRACULA (1931). Bela Lugosi became the first great monster of the talkie era with his role in this film. He had been playing Count Dracula on Broadway since 1927, so he already knew the part. Unfortunately, he was only paid $500 for his classic film performance.

• Among the film's lighting tricks: "Twin pencil-spotlights" were shined in Lugosi's eyes to give Count Dracula his legendary hypnotic stare.

• The Castle Dracula and Carfax Abbey sets were so expensive to build that Universal Pictures kept and reused them. You can spot them in numerous Universal films of the '30s.

• The enormous spider web on Dracula's staircase was actually a string of rubber cement. And the mountains shown in the first scenes were really the Rockies—not the Alps or Carpathians.

THE MUMMY (1932) Boris Karloff's second big monster flick was inspired by the discovery of King Tut's tomb in 1922...and the widespread belief—because several men on the Tut expedition had died mysteriously—that there was a real-life curse connected to it.

• Karloff was wrapped every day in linen and gauze, and was covered with mud.

Survey results: 98% of American drivers think they drive better than anyone else.

• He had become so famous as Frankenstein's monster the previous year that he was billed simply as "Karloff." Only Greta Garbo could match that.

THE WOLF MAN (1941). Lon Chaney, Jr. starred; it was his favorite role. Based on a popular 1935 English film, *Werewolf of London*, it was a surprise hit. Universal released it two days after Pearl Harbor, and expected low box office receipts. But instead of being distracted *by* the news, Americans wanted to be distracted *from* it.
• Chaney's werewolf makeup took five hours to apply every day.
• The same makeup man who created the Mummy and Frankenstein's monster for Boris Karloff created Chaney's werewolf.
• The werewolf costume was actually made of yak hair.

THE THING (1951). Director Howard Hawks's flick about an alien discovered near an Arctic research station is notable for two reasons: First, it kicked off the whole "it came from outer space" genre in the '50s; and second, the actor playing the monster was James Arness—"Gunsmoke" 's Matt Dillon. Arness, who's 6 feet-5 inches tall, wore four-inch lifts. He was onscreen about 3 minutes.

THEM! (1954). Another B-film breakthough—the first of the "giant mutated insects" genre. In this one, huge killer ants were found in the desert. But again, it was one of the actors who made the film memorable—Fess Parker. In 1954 Walt Disney, planning a feature about Davy Crockett, couldn't find the right man to play the lead...until he saw *Them!* He immediately hired Parker, who became one of America's hottest actors as the King of the Wild Frontier—and later, as Dan'l Boone. Also featured in the film: Arness, who was a year away from TV stardom, and Leonard Nimoy.

THE CREATURE FROM THE BLACK LAGOON (1954). The star of this 3-D epic, the scaly creature who's become the symbol of all '50s cheapo monsters, was actually modeled after the Oscar statue given at the Academy Awards.
• Two different actors appeared inside the latex costume. On land, it was a big fellow named Ben Chapman. In water, it was champion swimmer Ricou Browning, whose main claim to fame was that a decade later, he created and trained TV's most famous aquatic hero—Flipper.

Michael Landon played the title role of *I Was a Teenage Werewolf* in 1957.

MYTH AMERICA

You've probably believed these stories since you were a kid. Most Americans have, because they were taught to us as sacred truths. Well, here's another look at them.

HILL OF BEANS

The Myth: The Battle of Bunker Hill—where the Americans first faced the Redcoats—was the colonists' initial triumph in the Revolutionary War.

The Truth: Not only did the British wallop the Americans in the encounter, the whole thing wasn't even fought on Bunker Hill. The American troops *had* actually been ordered to defend Bunker Hill, but there was an enormous foul-up and somehow, they wound up trying to protect nearby Breed's Hill, which was more vulnerable to attack. They paid for it—when the fighting was over, the Americans had been chased away by the British troops. Casualties were heavy for both sides; about 450 Americans were killed, and a staggering 1,000 (out of 2,100 soldiers) Redcoats bit the dust.

PILGRIMS ' PROGRESS

The Myth: The Pilgrims were headed for Massachusetts.

The Truth: They were headed for "Hudson's River." Because of poor navigation and unexpected winds, the first land they sighted was Cape Cod. They tried to sail south, but "dangerous shoales and roaring breakers" prevented it. So they reluctantly turned back. By this time, the crew of the *Mayflower* (no, the ship wasn't manned by Pilgrims) was sick of them and hustled them off the boat as fast as they could.

The Myth: The Pilgrims landed at Plymouth Rock.

Background: This tale originated in 1741, more than 100 years after the Pilgrims arrived. It has been attributed to a then-95-year-old man named Thomas Fraunce, who claimed his father had told him the story when he was a boy. However, his father hadn't landed with the pilgrims—he reached America 3 years after they did.

The Truth: The Pilgrims first landed in Provincetown, Massachusetts.

In 1989, gamblers lost a record $4.43 billion in Nevada casinos.

AND SO FOURTH...

The Myth: American independence was declared on July 4th.

Background: Because the Declaration of Independence is dated July 4th, people associate that date with American independence. In fact, independence was declared first...and was confirmed with the document a few days later.

The Truth: The Continental Congress declared independence on July 2nd. One of the Founding Fathers, John Adams, is quoted as having written his wife on July 3rd: "The 2nd day of July, 1776, will be the most memorable...in the history of America. I am apt to believe it will be celebrated by succeeding generations, as the great anniversary Festival."

• **Note:** Actually, the first Independence Day celebration—by the Continental Congress—was on July 8th, 1776.

A SIGN OF THE TIMES

The Myth: In a hushed hall in Philadelphia on July 4, 1776, each signer of the Declaration of Independence proudly and publicly took his turn affixing his signature to the document.

Background: This tale was apparently concocted by Thomas Jefferson and Benjamin Franklin, who wrote about it in letters after the event.

The Truth: Only 2 people—John Hancock and Charles Thomson —signed the Declaration of Independence on July 4th. It wasn't until about a month later, on August 2, that the majority of the delegates signed it. And it wasn't until 5 years later, in 1781, that the last signature was finally added.

• How public was the signing? The Continental Congress would only admit that Hancock's and Thomson's names were on the document. Everyone else signed in secrecy. It wasn't until the following January that the signers' names were made public.

YANKEE DOODLE

The Myth: "Yankee Doodle" was originally a patriotic song.

The Truth: It was composed in England as an anti-American tune. The phrase "stuck a feather in his cap and called it macaroni" referred to a foppish English group called the Macaroni Club, whose members wore ludicrous "continental" fashions they mistakenly believed to be elegant. The British laughed at "Yankee Doodle dandies," bumpkins who didn't know how silly they really were.

Texas is the most expensive place in the U.S. to get a divorce. Idaho is the cheapest.

BUSHSPEAK

President Bush has a unique way of presenting his ideas. Newspapers have dubbed it "Bushspeak."

"America's freedom is the example to which the world expires."

To a gathering of Hispanic high school students:
"You don't have to go to college to achieve success. We need the people who do the hard, physical work."

On his years with Ronald Reagan:
"For seven and a half years I have worked alongside him, and I am proud to be his partner. We have had triumphs, we have made mistakes, we have had sex..."

On a tour of a Nazi death camp:
"Boy, they were big on crematoriums, weren't they?"

"If this country...ever loses its interest in fishing, we got real trouble."

Political analysis while on the campaign trail:
"It's no exaggeration to say the undecideds could go one way or another."

To the head of the Jordanian Army:
"Tell me, General, how dead is the Dead Sea?"

"I can announce that our dog is pregnant. This happened yesterday. A beautiful experience. We expect to have puppies in the White House."

"This isn't a signal. It's a direct statement. If it's a signal, fine."

On his gun control position:
"And you know, you look at the amount of people committing crimes with a gun—I looked up the gun registration, which I oppose. I went down—I told you or you heard me say this: But I had the guy doing up a file today."

"When I ran for office in Texas, they said, 'This guy's from New England.' I said, 'Wait a minute. I couldn't help that, I wanted to be near my mother at the time.' "

"He would have been in deep doo-doo."

ADVICE TO SINGLES

Before self-help books like How to Pick Up Girls *and* How to Marry the Man of Your Choice *were available, people relied on aphrodisiacs and rituals to score with the opposite sex. These honest-to-goodness recipes were collected by love-starved historians.*

FOR THE MARRIAGE-MINDED:

"If you want to get married, stand on your head and chew a piece of gristle out of a beef neck and swallow it, and you will get anyone you want."

—American folklore

❤

"If you can walk around the block with your mouth full of water, you will be married within a year."

—American folklore

❤

" To win your beloved's affection: Take a piece of clothing into which you have freely perspired, and burn and powder it with some of your hair. Mix with your spit and blood and introduce it into the food and drink which your loved one will consume."

—English folklore

❤

APHRODISIACS:

"Take three pubic hairs and three from the left armpit. Burn them on a hot shovel. Pulverize and insert into a piece of bread. Dip bread in soup and feed to a lover."

—Albertus Magnus,
Medieval philosopher

❤

"Shed your clothes completely, and at the stroke of midnight beneath a cloudless moon, walk three times around a house. For each step you take, throw a handful of salt behind you. If no one has seen you by the time you have finished, the person you love will be mad for you."

— Dutch folklore

❤

Annual event: The U.S. uses more steel making bottle caps than car bodies.

BASEBALL NAMES

If you're a baseball fan, you know these names by heart. But you probably don't know where they came from. Here are the stories behind some famous names.

Los Angeles Dodgers. Formed in Brooklyn, New York, in 1890. Brooklyn had hundreds of trolleys zig-zagging through its streets, and pedestrians were constantly scurrying out of their way. That's why their baseball team was called the Brooklyn Trolley Dodgers (later shortened to Dodgers). The team moved to L.A. in 1958.

Houston Astros. Formed in 1961, they were originally called the Colt .45s, after the famous gun. But by 1965, when their new stadium opened, Houston had become famous as the home of NASA's Mission Control. Both the stadium (Astrodome) and the team were named in honor of America's astronauts.

Pittsburgh Pirates. In 1876, they were known as the Alleghenies (after the neighboring Allegheny River). But in the 1890s, they earned a new nickname—the Pirates—when they stole a few players from a rival Philadelphia baseball club.

San Francisco Giants. The New York Gothams baseball club were fighting for a National League championship in 1886. After one particularly stunning victory, their manager proudly addressed them as "My big fellows, my giants." The name stuck. The New York Giants moved to San Francisco in 1958.

Cleveland Indians. From 1869 to 1912, the Cleveland baseball team had five different names—including the Forest Citys, the Naps, and the Spiders. Then in 1913 a popular player named Luis Francis Sockalexis died. He had been the first American Indian ever to play pro baseball and the team was renamed in his honor.

Chicago Cubs. Apparently they had no official nickname at the turn of the century (although they were informally called the Colts and the Orphans). Then, in 1902, a sportswriter dubbed them "the

Cubs" because it was short enough to fit into a newspaper headline. The name caught on, and 5 years later the team officially adopted it.

Cincinnati Reds. Formed in 1869, the team was originally called the Red Stockings. Later, they were known as the Reds—until the early '50s, when McCarthyism was rampant. No one wanted to be called a "Red" then—it sounded too much like "Commie." So the team actually made an official name change, to Redlegs. When the patriotic panic died down, they quietly switched back to Reds.

Detroit Tigers. Legend says that the Detroit Creams (the cream of the baseball crop) became the Tigers in 1896, when their manager decided their black and brown striped socks reminded him of tiger stripes.

Montreal Expos. The Canadian city was awarded a baseball franchise in 1968, partly because its 1967 World's Fair—called Expo '67—had been successful. The team was named in honor of the event.

New York Yankees. They were first called the Highlanders or Hilltoppers, because their ballfield was located at the highest point in the city. Again, sportswriters got fed up trying to fit the names into headlines. So in 1909, a newsman arbitrarily called them Yankees—patriotic slang for "Americans." After World War I, when jingoistic fervor was rampant ("The Yanks are coming"), the team officially became the Yankees.

Baltimore Orioles. Were named for the Maryland state bird in the early 1900s.

Kansas City Royals, San Diego Padres, Seattle Mariners, Texas Rangers, Toronto Blue Jays. All 5 are expansion teams. All 5 got their names in public "name-our-new-team" conte
although formed in 1969, got their name in
contest was held to name a *minor league* team
er, San Diego was awarded a major league fra
ballclub adopted the old name.

WHICH STOOGE ARE YOU?

The B.R.I. is pleased to present this penetrating social analysis by Ivan Stang, the brains behind the Church of the Sub-Genius.

There are three kinds of people in this world. I know, you've heard that before. Everybody has their "three types of people," or their four types, or five types....

But there are three, and the models for these types come neither from psychology nor ancient religion. They come from Columbia Studios, and they are archetypally embodied in The Three Stooges.

The Stooges unwittingly—of course—left us a rich legacy of deft interpretations of the most primal human behavior patterns. Their short films, seen as a whole, form a tapestry in which the interactions of people as individuals, corporations, and nations are distilled to a microcosm, a pure essence of existential folly.

There are but a small percentage of Moes in any given population: perhaps five percent. There are even fewer Curlys. The vast bulk of humanity are Larrys. (Though represented by male characters, the three types also apply to women.)

THE MOE PERSONALITY

Moe is the active personality, and if not always dominant, always striving to be. Moe is the one who spurs the others into action. He devises plans to better their lot, but when his plans fail the other two suffer the consequences. But is Moe any less the fool because they follow his plans?

He is a natural manipulator, only partially because the others are waiting to be manipulated. He would want to manipulate them anyway, even if they weren't so willing.

THE LARRY PERSONALITY

Larry is a born follower, a blank slate that only reacts (and slowly at that) to external stimuli. He never initiates action. He is Moe's absolute tool, the truest "stooge." When Moe's abuse finally does make him angry, he lashes out not at Moe, but at Curly. No matter how he suffers under Moe's yoke, he never really rebels. He argues, t gives up easily.

re it not for the presence of his friends, Larry probably would live in peace—a dull, flat, mechanical peace. Though clumsy, he is still the most employable of the three—for the other two are incapable of following orders, although for different reasons.

THE CURLY PERSONALITY

Curly is the only likeable one, a truly rare human model. He is the holy man, the Divine Fool. He is as creative and active as Moe—but it is a spontaneous and joyous kind of creativity, no good for the kind of plotting and scheming required by a Moe-dominated society. He is a free spirit, but correspondingly unable to function well in a world of Moes and Larrys. He, like Larry, is perpetually abused, but he intuitively understands what is happening to him and reacts far more angrily—if equally ineffectually. He is everyone's favorite Stooge because he is the funniest; through his innate nobility and natural humility he constantly bests Moe, but it is in an unconscious way, and it is only apparent to the outside observer. Curly himself is hardly aware of his talents; his weakness is that he does not know his own strength, and cannot trust his own luck.

In real life, Curlys are usually branded by the Moes and Larrys around them as retarded, schizophrenic, maladjusted, or just plain stupid...whereas in reality, it is only Curly who understands the truth. Remaining cheerful through adversity, he wins battles not by fighting, but by "accidentally" unleashing "accidents" in which his enemies injure themselves.

STOOGE CO-EXISTENCE

Alien to feelings of avarice or ambition, Curly is the opposite of Moe. Yet the two are drawn together by some inexplicable balancing force of nature. The Larrys, though, are ever the in-betweeners, slug-like nonentities caught in the crossfire of cosmic dualities—yet remaining there by some herding instinct that makes being a casualty of the Moe-Curly battle preferable to life alone with other Larrys.

Only the existence of the blameless, bovine Larrys makes that of Moe or Curly possible. They are able to maintain their level of glandular brutality and senseless destruction only at the expense of the unquestioning, loyal worker drone whose income partially supports their excesses. Were he not there to diffuse Moe's anger by becoming another recipient of his blows, Curly would have been killed long ago, and Moe would have committed suicide out of

Americans owned 2.1 million computers in 1981. In 1989 we own 37.8 million of them.

loneliness.

The horror of it all is that the three types need each other to survive. Of all nature's cycles of parasitic symbiosis, the one involving the three human types is the most nightmarish. It rages around us all the time in real life, spreading death and madness, yet when we see it on the screen we call it "comedy."

NYUK NYUK NYUK: THE STOOGES IN ACTION

A doctor doubts the Stooges' qualifications as surgeons.
Doctor: "Why, you don't even know how to deliver an anesthetic."
The Stooges pull out wooden mallets.
Moe: "Give him some anethesia."
Larry and Curly clobber him on the head with their mallets.

The Stooges are about to operate on a patient, planning out their strategy by playing tic-tac-toe on the sheet covering him.
Moe: "Give him another anesthetic, boys. I think it's wearing off.
Patient (sitting up): "No it isn't."
Larry (roughly pushing him down): "Lay down. Are you trying to make a fool out of us doctors?"
Wham!

Moe: "Whaddya up to now?"
Curly (bowling): "I just got a poifect score!"
Moe: "No ya haven't. Ya need another strike."
Wham!

Curly is holding an unwrapped cigar up to his ear.
Moe: "What're ya doin'?"
Curly: "Listenin' to the band. Nyuk, nyuk, nyuk."
Moe: "Would you like to hear some birdies?"
Curly: "I'd love it!"
Moe: "Take off yer hat!"
Wham!

Secretary: "Mattie Herring is here to see you."
Moe: "Mattie Herring? Sounds fishy. Send her in."
Secretary: "Now?"
Moe: "No, marinate her first."
Curly: "And don't forget the onions. Nuyuk, nyuk, nyuk."

DEFINITIONS

In the first Bathroom Reader *we included some uncommon words, and their meanings, to help build anemic vocabularies. Here's another batch.*

Franch: To eat greedily
Rhotacism: Excessive use of the letter "R"
Manumission: The official act of freeing a slave
Netop: A friend
Gash-gabbit: Having a protruding chin
Girn: To bare your teeth in anger or in sadness
Wamfle: To walk around with flapping clothes
Charientism: An elegantly veiled insult
Juglandaceous: Pertaining to walnuts
Kakistocracy: Government of a state by its worst citizens
Ergophile: A person who loves to work
Lingible: Meant to be licked
Cicisbeo: A married woman's well-known lover
Moll-buzzer: A thief whose specialty is robbing women
Yerd: To beat with a stick
Mubblefubble: Mental depression
Nash-gob: An arrogant gossip
Zuber: The European breed of buffalo
Nazzard: A lowly or weak person
Alliaphage: A garlic eater
Nuddle: To push something with your nose
Glossolalia: Gibberish; babble
Ribazuba: Ivory from a walrus
Eristic: Argumentative
Roddikin: A cow or deer's fourth stomach
Mabble: To wrap your head
Scobberlotcher: An idle person
Irrefragable: Undeniable
Shench: To pour a drink for someone
Palilalia: Helplessly repeating a phrase faster and faster.
Shongable: A shoemaking tax
Slibbersauce: A disgusting substance
Walm: To bubble up
Cherubimical: Inebriated
Dendrofilous: Loving trees enough to live in them
Kinetosis: Travel sickness
Oligophrenia: Extreme mental retardation
Ranarium: A frog farm

American grow tomatoes at home more often than any other fruit or vegetable.

ONLY IN AMERICA

It started out as a social protest song, and wound up a boring patriotic anthem. Here is a fascinating true story of how politics can influence popular music.

BACKGROUND

The story of "Only in America," recorded by Jay and the Americans in 1963 for United Artists Records, reveals a lot about the racial consciousness of the music business—and about how political censorship takes place behind the scenes in the U.S.

THE SONG:

The year was 1963. American blacks were demonstrating for civil rights. One black leader, Medgar Evers, was shot and killed in Jackson, Mississippi and another, Martin Luther King, led a massive March on Washington, delivering his immortal "I have a dream" speech.

On the radio, a young white group called Jay and the Americans was following up its 1962 hit, "She Cried," with a seemingly patriotic pop tune, "Only in America." Lead singer Jay Black sang about the very American dream from which blacks were saying they were excluded. In "the land of opportunity," he sang, a poor boy could be parking cars one day and be a movie star the next, grow up to be President, or win the ultimate rock 'n' roll prize, a "classy girl."

But the irony of "Only in America" was that it was originally written for an all-black vocal quartet called the Drifters—one of the most popular groups in America—who had consistently scored with million-sellers like "Under the Boardwalk" and "On Broadway." And the original lyrics had a far different slant.

BEHIND THE SCENES

According to co-writer Barry Mann, the song was intended to deliver a strong message about black life in the United States. An original verse was: "Only in America / Land of opportunity / Can they save a seat in the back of the bus just for me./ Only in America / Where they preach the Golden Rule / Will they start to march when my kids want to go to school."

Arguing that the pop charts weren't ready for such strident social commentary, Atlantic Records asked for new lyrics.

"They said it would never get played," Mann recalls, "so we changed it to fit a WASP." But with the Drifters singing the revamped version, the song took on a different sort of irony. According to producer Mike Stoller, "They were afraid of it. They thought they'd get too much flak. It would be too controversial. We felt it would make a strong ironic statement—that it would be more effective—four black guys singing about what was obviously not taking place."

Stuck with an unreleasable song, the producers took their instrumental track over to the other label they worked with, United Artists, where Jay and the Americans recorded. The group loved the song, UA bought the music tracks from Atlantic, and a whitewashed "Only in America" wound up in the Top 25 in 1963.

Mike Stoller was disappointed. Because of the changes in the song and who sang it, people wouldn't have a clue about its original theme. "It was straight ahead. It didn't have any irony in it at all, as done by Jay and the Americans. The point behind the message in the lyrics was lost, as far as we were concerned. It had to have been done with a black group. With a white group, it was just a kind of patriotic song."

UNRELATED TRIVIA

According to *Celebrity Trivia,* by Edward Lucaire:

• "After his high school graduation, Johnny Carson hitchhiked to California, acquired a naval cadet's uniform, and managed to do three noteworthy things: He danced with Marlene Dietrich at the Stage Door Canteen; he was sawed in half by Orson Welles in a magic act (he volunteered from the audience); and he was arrested by the Military Police for impersonating a serviceman."

• Before she became an actress, Margaret Hamilton—who scared the daylights out of millions of children as the Wicked Witch of the West in the film version of *The Wizard of Oz*—taught nursery school and kindergarten.

• Once, while visiting Monte Carlo, Charlie Chaplin entered a "Charlie Chaplin look-alike contest." He not only didn't win...he came in *third.*

• Gary Cooper's real name was Frank. His agent renamed him "Gary" because her hometown was Gary, Indiana.

It takes 8 seconds to make a baseball bat in a bat factory.

THE FRISBEE STORY

Playing with a Frisbee is one of America's most popular outdoor activities. The story behind the product, from Charles Panati:

THE ORIGINAL FRISBIE

"In the 1870s, New England confectioner William Russell Frisbie opened a bakery that carried a line of homemade pies in circular tin pans embossed with the family surname. Bridgeport historians do not know if children in Frisbie's day tossed empty tins for amusement, but sailing the pans did become a popular diversion among students at Yale University in the mid-1940s. The school's New Haven campus was not far from the Bridgeport pie factory, which served stores throughout the region...."

THE INVENTOR

"The son of the inventor of the sealed-beam automobile headlight, [Walter Frederick] Morrison was intrigued with the possibility of alien visits from outer space, a topic that in the '50s captured the minds of Hollywood film makers and the American public. Hoping to capitalize on America's UFO mania, Morrison devised a lightweight metal toy disk (which he'd later construct of plastic) that in shape and airborne movements mimicked the flying saucers on movie screens across the country. He teamed up with the Wham-O Company of San Gabriel, California, and on January 13, 1957, the first toy 'Flyin' Saucers' debuted in selected West Coast stores."

THE FRISBEE IS BORN

"Within a year, UFOs in plastic were already something of a hazard on California beaches. But the items remained largely a Southern California phenomenon.To increase sales, Wham-O's president, Richard Knerr, undertook a promotional tour of Eastern college campuses, distributing free plastic UFOs. To his astonishment, he discovered students at two Ivy League schools, Yale and Harvard, playing a lawn game that involved tossing metal pie tins. They called the disks 'Frisbies' and the relaxation 'Frisbie-ing.' The name appealed to Knerr, and unaware of the existence of the Frisbie Pie Company, he trademarked the word "Frisbee" in 1959. And from the original pie tin in the sky, a national craze was launched."

DUMB PREDICTIONS

Elsewhere in The Bathroom Reader, *we've included amazingly accurate predictions. These are amazingly dumb ones.*

"The abolishment of pain in surgery is a chimera. It is absurd to go on seeking it today. Knife and pain are two words in surgery that must forever be associated in the consciousness of the patient. To this compulsory combination we shall have to adjust ourselves."

—Dr. Alfred Velpeau, 1839

Anesthesia was introduced 7 years later

"While theoretically and technically television may be feasible, commercially and financially I consider it an impossibility, a development of which we need waste little time dreaming."

—Lee De Forest,
"Father of the Radio," 1926

"At present, few scientists foresee any serious or practical use for atomic energy. They regard the atom-splitting experiments as useful steps in the attempt to describe the atom more accurately, not as the key to the unlocking of any new power."

—*Fortune* magazine, 1938

"What can be more palpably absurd than the prospect held out of locomotives traveling twice as fast as stagecoaches?"

—*The Quarterly Review*, 1825

"The ordinary 'horseless carriage' is at present a luxury for the wealthy; and although its price will probably fall in the future, it will never, of course, come into as common use as the bicycle."

—*The Literary Digest*, 1889

"The energy necessary to propel a ship would be many times greater than that required to drive a train of cars at the same speed; hence as a means of rapid transit, flying could not begin to compete with the railroad."

—*Popular Science* magazine, 1897

Sarah Bernhardt often slept in a coffin.

YOU ANIMAL!

They're as famous as most human stars, but what do we really know about them? Some gossip about America's favorite animals:

LASSIE

The most successful animal actor ever, starred in 7 feature films and a TV series that ran for 19 years—2nd on the all-time list behind "Gunsmoke." But there wasn't just 1 Lassie—there were 6 of them. And they were all female impersonators. Lassie was supposed to be a she-dog; in real life, "she" was always a he.

Lassie was created by writer Eric Knight in a 1938 *Saturday Evening Post* short story. But although the dog went on to make more money than any animal actor in history, Knight got no royalties—he'd already sold the rights to MGM in 1941 for a paltry $8,000.

SMOKEY THE BEAR

Smokey is the only celebrity in America with his own ZIP code—20252. He's also the only bear in the world with his own secretarial staff; the U.S. government employs 3 full-time secretaries to answer his mail. Smokey was named after "Smokey Joe" Martin, Assistant Fire Chief in New York City between 1919 and 1930.

CHEETAH

Tarzan's favorite chimp seemed angelic in the Tarzan movies, but was dangerous to work with. During one scene in 1932's *Tarzan the Ape Man*, a little of Jane's (Maureen O'Sullivan's) hair got in Cheetah's eyes, blinding the chimp. Cheetah went crazy on the set and bit O'Sullivan. Another time, Cheetah was supposed to kiss O'Sullivan during a scene. As their faces met, the chimp sneezed all over her.

One of the reasons Cheetah looked so convincing as a "thinking" animal was that many of the tricks the chimp already knew were written into the Tarzan scripts. For example, Cheetah was adept at crawling on his stomach. So in *Tarzan and His Mate* (1934), a scene was included in which the chimp escaped from an attacking rhinoceros by crawling through the tall grass.

The Dead Sea is really a lake.

RIN TIN TIN

Rinty was film's first bona fide animal superstar. He made his film debut in 1922, and his box office success over the next few years literally saved Warner Brothers' Studio from bankruptcy. During the '20s, when he made some 22 movies and was voted the #1 movie star in America (no kidding), Rinty was insured for $250,000. In the early '30s, he lived in a Hollywood mansion across the street from Jean Harlow. His sons and grandsons were among the dogs used in later films, and in the 1954-59 TV series.

ELSIE THE COW

The Borden milk symbol started as a cartoon in Borden's ads in 1938. But at the 1939 New York World's Fair, visitors to the Borden exhibit kept asking, "Where's Elsie?" Borden needed an answer, so they picked the most attractive cow in their milking exhibit—a 975 lb. Jersey named "You'll Do, Lobelia"—and renamed her Elsie. They built her a special display—a "bovine boudoir"—that was so successful she got a screen contract, playing Buttercup in the 1940 version of *Little Men*. Elsie became a national celebrity: She went on tour and raised $10 million in U.S. War Bonds; she gave birth to a calf in the window of Macy's department store (behind a modest curtain, of course); she was even awarded a "Doctorate of Bovinity" at Ohio State in 1948.

MORRIS THE CAT

America's best-known catfood salesman was originally named "Lucky" by his owner—because he was discovered at an animal shelter in Hinsdale, Illinois about 20 minutes before he was going to be "put to sleep." As Morris, he was the the first animal star ever featured on "Lifestyles of the Rich and Famous."

TOTO

Almost didn't make it into MGM's 1939 film *The Wizard of Oz*; the MGM prop department was using W. W. Denslow's original illustrations as a casting guide, but they couldn't identify the breed of dog in the pictures. Sketches were sent all over the world, but no one responded—until Hollywood trainer Carl Spitz happened to see the illustrations. He knew right away that they were looking for his Cairn Terrier, Terry. When Spitz took Terry to the studio, someone grabbed him and shouted "That's the dog we want!"

Cosmic coincidence? Both Elvis and his mom died when they were 42.

COOKING WITH POWER TOOLS

Here's a handy cooking idea from Jack Mingo, author of the Official Couch Potato Handbook.

Many of you have power tools sitting around your homes that you never use. Almost all of them, with a little imagination, can be adapted for food preparation. For example: Take a household power drill, poke the bit through the plastic lid of a 15 oz. styrofoam cup, and voilà! You've got a blender that's ideal for highspeed whipping. A jigsaw is great for slicing and dicing. A good belt sander will peel potatoes in a jiffy. And a butane torch is perfect for Pop Tarts flambé.

Caution: Power tool cooking should be attempted only if tools are properly shielded and grounded. Wear safety lenses. Some power tools will interfere with TV reception, so confine preparation to commercials. Power tool cookery is NOT recommended while bathing.

Here are three of our favorite power tool recipes:

THE CHEESE CHOC-DOG

Ingredients

- 1 Package hot dogs
- 1 Loaf generic white bread
- 1 Can aerosol cheese product
- Electric Drill with 1/4" bit
- 1 Squeeze-bottle of Hershey's Chocolate syrup
- Safety Lenses

Instructions

1. Put on safety lenses.
2. Hold unopened package of hot dogs with ends pointing toward you.
3. Using slow speed, carefully drill each hot dog lengthwise.
4. Open package and remove hot dogs. Each should now have a hole down the center.
5. Fill cavities with aerosol cheese product.
6. Place hot dog on slice of white bread. Pinch bread into a trough around the hot dog and squirt liberally with chocolate syrup. Pop

in toaster oven for 10-12 minutes, or until cheese is runny.

TUBE-STEAK PATÉ

This is the award-winning recipe in the 1982 Chef Aldo International Couch Potato Bake Off. I highly recommend it for its near-European sensibility.

Ingredients

- 1 Oscar Mayer all-meat hot dog
- 1 Tsp. sweet pickle relish
- 2 Green olives, pimentos left in
- 8 Saltine crackers
- Mayonnaise
- Pepper
- Power tool blender (or real blender)

Instructions

1. Rev blender up to full speed and drop in hot dog.
2. Add relish and olives. Let blend at high speed for 90 seconds.
3. Spread the saltine crackers generously with mayonnaise.
4. Spread paté on crackers; add pepper to taste. Makes 8 servings.

EXTRA SHARP CARROT CAKE

This extra-easy version of the old favorite is almost indistinguishable from traditional recipes (the cola and spices even turn the Bisquick a rich, golden brown color). You can double the recipe and use a regular size aluminum pie tin.

Ingredients

- 2-3 Skinny carrots
- 1/2 Handful brown sugar
- 1 Can generic cola
- 1 Pot pie tin
- 1 Handful Bisquick
- 1/2 Handful pumpkin pie spices
- Electric pencil sharpener

Instructions

1. Shred carrots in clean pencil sharpener.
2. Line bottom of pot pie tin with carrot shavings.
3. Add Bisquick, sugar, and spices.
4. Knead slowly with hands, adding a small amount of the cola. Continue to knead and add cola until batter is the consistency of fresh Play-Doh.
5. Adjust sugar and spices to taste.
6. Bake in toaster oven at 400° for 15-22 minutes.
7. Remove from oven. When cool, carrot cake can be frosted with canned or aerosol frosting. A real health treat.

Swedes drink more coffee than anyone else.

INVENTION IN THE NEWS:

While many B.R.I. members enjoy reading current newspapers on the seat of learning, the B.R.I.'s staff historian is particularly fond of old ones. "It's like reliving history," he says. For some time now, he's been searching through old issues of The New York Times, *looking for an account of the Wright Brothers' flight in 1903. He hasn't found it, and here's why: Only one newspaper, the* Norfolk Virginia Pilot, *published an account of the first airplane flight. Luckily, B.R.I. member Gene Brissie had a copy. Here's part of it.*

FLYING MACHINE SOARS 3 MILES IN TEETH OF HIGH WIND OVER SAND HILLS AND WAVES AT KITTY HAWK ON CAROLINA COAST

No Balloon Attached to Hold It!!

December 17, 1903

The problem of aerial navigation without the use of a balloon has been solved at last!

Over the sand hills of the North Carolina coast yesterday, near Kittyhawk, two Ohio men proved that they could soar through the air in a flying machine of their own construction, with the power to steer and speed it at will.

This, too, in the face of a wind blowing at the registered velocity of twenty-one miles an hour!

Like a monster bird, the invention hovered above the breakers and circled over the rolling sand hills at the command of its navigator and, after soaring for three miles, it gracefully descended to earth again, and rested lightly upon the spot selected by the man in the car as a suitable landing place.

While the United States government has been spending thousands of dollars in an effort to make practicable the ideas of Professor Langley, of the Smithsonian Institute, Wilbur and Orville Wright, two brothers, natives of Dayton, Ohio, have, quietly, even secretly, perfected their invention and put it to a successful test.

They are not yet ready that the world should know the methods they have adopted in conquering the air, but the *Virginian Pilot* is able to state authentically the nature of their invention, its principles and its chief dimensions. . . . [Ed. note: the flight began with the plane rolling down a track.]

Wilbur Wright, the chief inventor of the machine, sat in the operator's car, and when all was ready his brother unfastened the catch which held the invention at the top of the slope. The big box began to move slowly at first, acquiring velocity as it went, and when halfway down the hundred feet the engine was started. . . . When the end of the incline was reached the machine shot out into space without a perceptible fall.

Keeping its altitude, the machine slowly began to go higher and higher until it finally soared sixty feet above the ground.

Maintaining this height, the forward speed of the huge affair increased until a velocity of eight miles was attained.

All this time the machine headed into a twenty-one-mile wind.

The little crowd of fisherfolk and coast guards, who have been watching the construction of the machine with unconcealed curiosity since September, were amazed.

They endeavored to race over the sand and keep up with the thing in the air, but it soon distanced them and continued its flight alone.

Steadily it pursued its way, first tacking to port, then to starboard, and then driving straight ahead.

"It is a success," declared Orville Wright to the crowd on the beach after the first mile had been covered.

But the inventor waited. Not until he had accomplished three miles, putting the machine through all sorts of maneuvers en route, was he satisfied.

Then he selected a suitable place to land and, gracefully circling, drew his invention slowly to the earth, where it settled, like some big bird, in the chosen spot.

"Eureka!" he cried.

The success of the Wright brothers in their invention is the result of three years of hard work.

The spot selected for the building and perfecting of the machine is one of the most desolate upon the Atlantic seaboard; no better place could scarcely have been selected to maintain secrecy.

It is said the Wright brothers intend constructing a much larger machine, but before this they will go back to their homes for the holidays.

The real James Bond was an ornithologist, not a spy.

COMMON PHRASES

What do these familiar phrases really mean? Etymologists have researched them and come up with these explanations.

FEATHER IN YOUR CAP
Meaning: An achievement.
Background: Dates back to 1346, when, according to scholars, "the English Black Prince was awarded the crest of John, King of Bohemia—3 ostrich feathers—after distinguishing himself at the Battle of Crecy." It started a tradition; thereafter, any knight who fought well was allowed to wear a feather in his helmet.

PRIVATE EYE
Meaning: A private detective.
Background: The Pinkerton Detective Agency, founded in 1850, used the motto "We Never Sleep," and accompanied it with a picture of an open eye. It was commonly referred to as "The Eye," and Pinkerton agents, hired by private concerns, were called "Private Eyes."

LOCK, STOCK, AND BARREL
Meaning; The whole thing.
Background: Guns. The lock (firing mechanism), stock (wooden mount), and barrel constituted the main parts of an old rifle.

DOG DAYS
Meaning: The hottest days of summer.
Background: The Ancient Romans believed that there was a period during the summer when "the brightest star in the heavens, the dog star 'Sirius,' added its heat to the sun's, making these days a veritable inferno."

GREAT SCOTT!
Meaning: An exclamation of surprise or amazement.
Background: One of America's most admired soldiers during the 19th century was General Winfield Scott, hero of the Mexican War in 1847. He inspired the phrase in the mid-1800s.

When he's feeling amorous, the male sea otter grabs the female's nose with his teeth.

FAMOUS CHEATERS

You've heard the old adage, "Cheaters never win." But when they do win, we never find out about them. We only know about the ones who get caught. Like these folks:

THE CULPRIT: Rosie Ruiz, a 26-year-old New Yorker.

SCENARIO: Ms. Ruiz appeared to be the fastest woman runner in the 26-mile Boston Marathon in 1980, stumbling across the finish line with an impressive time of 2 hours, 31 minutes, and 56 seconds. The only thing was, no one remembered seeing her run the course. And she couldn't recall anything about the route she was supposed to have taken. Very suspicious. Then a friend revealed that Ruiz's impressive showing in the New York Marathon a few months earlier was a fraud. Rosie, claimed the friend, had skipped most of the race and taken the subway to the finish line. Was Boston a fraud, too? Ruiz denied it.

VERDICT: After an embarrassing public controversy, race officials determined that Rosie had only run the last two miles of the marathon, and stripped her of her title.

AFTERMATH: In 1984, Ruiz was arrested in Miami for trying to sell two kilos of cocaine to a cop. Police said she was a member of an all-woman cocaine ring.

THE CULPRIT: Dave Bresnahan, a catcher for the Williamsport (Pennsylvania) Bills.

SCENARIO: It was September, 1987, a minor league baseball game—Williamsport vs. Reading.

Reading was at bat, with two outs and a man on third. After a pitch, the catcher (Bresnahan) leaped to his feet and threw to the third baseman, apparently trying to catch the runner off base. He missed by a mile—the "ball" sailed into the outfield and the runner headed home...only to find the catcher waiting there with the ball in his hand, ready to tag him out. How did Bresnahan get the ball so fast? Answer: he never actually threw the ball—instead, he threw a potato he'd hidden in his uniform.

At any one time, there are 1800 thunderstorms taking place somewhere in the world.

VERDICT: Unfortunately, the authorities didn't appreciate this prank. Not only was the runner called safe and Bresnahan ejected from the game, but the following day the parent Cleveland Indians released Bresnahan from the team.
AFTERMATH: Bresnahan moved to Arizona and got a job selling real estate. But his stunt became so famous that a year later, the Williamsport Bills invited him back to recreate it...and to honor him by retiring his number!

THE CULPRIT: Janet Cooke, a reporter for the *Washington Post.*
SCENARIO: Cooke arrived at the Post with impressive credentials—she said she'd graduated from Vassar with honors and had gotten a master's degree at the University of Toledo. She was assigned to do local stories, and in 1980 told her editor that she'd heard of an 8-year-old who was addicted to heroin. "Find that kid," the editor reportedly told her, "and it's a front-page story." Cooke came back with a detailed account of how a ghetto woman had allowed her lover to inject—and addict—her young son. The tale was titled "Jimmy's World," and it caused an immediate furor in Washington. Cooke refused to reveal her sources, so the mayor put the full resources of the police behind an effort to find the child. The board of education was bombarded with questions and complaints. But the newspaper stood by Cooke. In fact, they nominated her for a Pulitzer Prize, journalism's most prestigious award. And she won. But as reporters gathered biographical information for their story about her, they discovered she had lied about her background. And the Post's executives discovered, to their horror, that Cooke had fabricated the entire story of "Jimmy's World."
VERDICT: Cooke, in tears, offered her resignation. The *Post* accepted it. The Pulitzer went to Teresa Carpenter of the *Village Voice*, instead.
AFTERMATH: The *Post* published a front-page story criticizing itself. On the legal front, several members of the Washington Board of Education sued Cooke and the *Post* to recover the money the city has spent trying to find "Jimmy," and for damages for being falsely accused of concealing "Jimmy" 's identity.

All gondolas in Venice must be painted black, unless they belong to high public officials.

FABULOUS FLOPS

Next time you read about some amazing overnight success, remember these equally fabulous stinkers.

THE GTO SHOE

In the '60s, Thom McAn Shoes cashed in on every fad. They marketed Beatle Boots, Monkee Boots, Chubby Checker Twister boots, and even Ravi Shankar "Bombay Buckles." But they lost their magic touch when they tried to ride the hot car fad of the mid-'60s with GTO shoes, "the world's first high-performance shoe." Promoted in conjunction with Pontiac's celebrated GTO, the footwear came equipped with "pointed toes, beveled accelerator heels, and double-beam eyelets."

The Pontiac GTO was a huge success, but most of Thom McAn's GTO shoes wound up being donated to charity.

INSTANT FISH.

In the early '60s, one of the owners of the Wham-O Mfg. Co.—makers of Hula Hoops and Frisbees—was on vacation in Africa. One evening, he camped beside a dry lake bed; during the night it rained, and the lake filled up. The next day he noticed there were fish in the lake. "How could that be?" he thought. "Fish don't grow overnight."

When he got back to California, he asked a biologist friend what had happened, and was told that there was indeed a fish in that part of the world whose eggs lay dormant until they were exposed to water. Then the eggs hatched and the fish emerged.

It sounded like an incredible idea for a product—"Instant Fish." At his urging, Wham-O hurriedly built huge fish tanks in their factory and imported thousands of fish so they could start collecting their eggs.

Meanwhile, the annual New York Toy Fair, where toy store owners from all over the U.S. buy merchandise, was taking place....And "Instant Fish" was the smash of the show. In one week, Wham-O took orders for $10 million worth of fish (an incredible amount in the mid-'60s). Even when the company refused to take any more orders, people sneaked to Wham-O's hotel rooms and slipped orders under the door. "Instant Fish" was a gold mine.

Except that nobody told the fish. They just couldn't lay eggs fast enough to supply all the excited toy store owners. Desperate, Wham-O owners tried everything they could think of: They tried covering the windows to darken the inside of their plant; they tried warmer room temperatures...and they tried cooler ones; they even tried piping romantic music into the tanks. But nothing worked. Wham-O finally had to admit that "Instant Fish" had laid its own enormous egg. And after shipping only a few of the fish, they canceled all the orders.

"TURN ON"

In 1968 and 1969, "Laugh-In" was TV's #1 show. Hoping to buy themselves a copycat hit, ABC hired "Laugh-In" executive producer George Schlatter to create an identical series. And by mid-1969, he'd put together "Turn-On," which ABC promoted as "the second coming of 'Laugh-In'," a "visual, comedic, sensory assault." "Turn-On" premiered on Feb. 5, 1969. It was so bad that the next day, phone calls poured in from ABC affiliates all over the U.S., saying that they refused ever to carry the show again. Embarrassed, the network cancelled it immediately, making it the shortest-lived primetime series in TV history.

THE ANIMAL OF THE MONTH CLUB

In the '50s and '60s, mail order "thing-of-the-month" clubs were big business—worth close to a billion dollars a year. Americans were buying a Fruit-of-the Month, a Candy-of-the-Month, a House-of-the-Month (architectural plans), a Cheese-of-the-Month, Flowers-of-the-Month, and so on. How far could the fad go? Creative Playthings took it to the limit when it introduced an "Animal of the Month Club" in the late '60s. Every month, the company promised, an exotic "pet," such as an Argentine toad snail, a musk turtle, a newt, a Mongolian gerbil, or others, would arrive in the mail at subscribers' houses.

But shipping exotic pets turned out to be a crazy—and cruel—idea. In 1968, for example, Creative Playthings had orders for 4,000 Argentine toads and couldn't find enough of them in the Argentine swamps to supply the demand. But that wasn't the worst of their problems. Ever try bulk-mailing animals? The creatures-of-the-month often arrived squashed, or dehydrated. Mercifully, Creative Playthings took its losses and gave up.

UNCLE WALT'S SECRETS

Everyone knows about Walt Disney—or do they? Check it out for yourself.

STRANGE LOVE AFFAIR

Walt once confessed, "I love Mickey Mouse more than any woman I've ever known."

HIS PASSION FOR TRAIN WRECKS

Like Gomez Addams, Walt relaxed with model trains—but Walt's were big enough to ride on: The Disney "ride 'em" scale model railroad was half a mile long; it circled his estate, and even wound through a tunnel under his wife's flower beds.

The Disneys spent a great deal of time riding the little train. If you were a really good friend, Uncle Walt made you an official "vice president" of his railroad.

But Disney was more like Gomez than met the eye. According to *Everybody's Business*: "Disney especially enjoyed planning wrecks because he had so much fun repairing the damage. Once, after buying two new engines, he told George Murphy (then an actor and one of the road's 'vice-presidents'; later a U.S. senator): 'Boy, we're sure going to have some wrecks now!' "

PEN-ULTIMATE SECRETS

• Most people believe that Walt was a cartooning genius. But according to author Richard Schickel in *The Disney Version*, he couldn't draw Donald Duck or any of his other famous characters! According to *Everybody's Business*:

• "Disney was known to ask his animators to show him how to turn out a quick sketch of Mickey Mouse to accompany autographs."

• "Walt grew up on a small farm in Missouri, where he picked up a feeling for what middle America wanted in their movies. He also picked up a bit of anti-Semitism, which he showed in a rather nasty caricature of a Jewish peddler in his first big cartoon success, *The Three Little Pigs*."

• "Disney's real signature bore no resemblance to the famous logo that appeared on all his products. Ironically, a number of people have thrown away authentically signed books and records under the impression that the autographs were fake."

More films are made in India each year than in any other country.

THE BIRTH OF A FLAKE

You probably think that corn flakes have always been with us. Not so. The cereal flake was accidentally born less than a century ago. Here's the tale.

BACKGROUND

It all started with a devoutly religious woman named Sister Ellen Harmon White, a Seventh Day Adventist who in 1844 decided it was time for her to ascend to heaven in a laundry basket. Along with others in her congregation, she stood for hours on a Maine hilltop, waiting to be carried away...but nothing happened. Sister Ellen wasn't disappointed, however. She took it as a sign that God still had important things for her to do in this world—and she set out to accomplish them.

In 1863, she and her husband traveled to Otsego, Michigan, where she had a vision: The Lord told her that people could only achieve "purity of mind and spirit" by eating properly—water, fruits, and vegetables, with a little bit of bread made from Graham flour. Another vision told her to open a sanitarium in nearby Battle Creek, where people could heal themselves with this diet.

THE BATTLE CREEK SANITARIUM

1866, the Western Health Reform Institute at Battle Creek was opened. It had no doctor on its staff for ten years. But in 1876, a 25-year-old Adventist who had just graduated from Bellevue Medical College—Dr. John Harvey Kellogg—was hired to run it. Kellogg's first official act was to hire his younger brother, William Keith (W. K.) as chief clerk.

Kellogg set out to turn the institution into an influential one. He changed the name to Battle Creek Sanitarium, and screened potential patients so that no one who was seriously ill was ever admitted. What he wanted were "tired businessmen, sufferers from dyspepsia...and neurotics." So people were invariably cured, and the San (as it was called) began attracting the wealthy and famous from all over the country. John D. Rockefeller, Henry Ford, Harvey Firestone, and others were among the guests. At the same time, Kellogg wrote voluminously, making his somewhat looney medical views influential with common Americans who would never make it to Battle Creek.

The first chain store was the A&P. It was founded in 1842.

KELLOGG GETS FLAKEY

The diet in this now world-famous institution was strictly vegetarian. But to make the food more palatable to non-vegetarians, the Kelloggs and their staff set up a special kitchen in which they experimented with new dishes. Among their creations: hamburger substitutes, a coffee substitute called Caramel Coffee, and cereal flakes.

The flakes were an accident. Kellogg originally required his patients to begin each meal by chewing a piece of hard zwieback bread. But when a patient broke a tooth on it, he started experimenting with substitutes. One experiment entailed running boiled wheat dough through rollers, turning it into thin sheets before it was toasted and ground into flour.

On one occasion in 1895, Kellogg left some pans full of dough sitting while he was called away on an emergency. When he returned (it's not clear exactly how much later), he ran the dough through the rollers—but instead of thin sheets, he got a bunch of flakes. He toasted them and served them to his patients... who loved them. The flake was born.

NOT A CORNY JOKE

Kellogg and his staff came up with two flake variations—rice and corn. The corn was a flop (too tough and tasteless) until someone got the idea to use only the heart of the corn, and to flavor it with malt. Then it instantly became the most requested variety.

Realizing that he was sitting on a commercial bonanza, Dr. Kellogg set up the Sanitarium Health Food Company with his brother (keeping it separate from the San and the Adventist Church) and began selling his flakes. In the first year, he sold over 100,000 pounds of them. Business kept growing, and Kellogg kept getting wealthier.

"CEREAL SODOM"

But then things suddenly got out of hand. Dozens of cereal entrepreneurs moved in on Kellogg's territory and cut his profits. Subtly capitalizing on the reputation of the San, 42 Battle Creek-based cereal companies sprang up, each making ludicrous health claims for its products...and each making a fortune. Sister Ellen Hanson White was furious; she felt Dr. Kellogg had desecrated the Divine vision that inspired the San, and Battle Creek had now become a

A minnow's teeth are in its throat.

"cereal Sodom." On the other side, Will Kellogg was pressuring his brother to cash in like all the other cereal companies—which Dr. Kellogg adamantly opposed. His practices were already attracting some unfavorable attention from the medical profession, and he didn't want to focus any more attention on himself.

DR. KELLOGG LOSES CONTROL

Here's what happened: Dr. Kellogg, a tight man with a dollar, had been giving out stock in his cereal company to employees in lieu of pay raises. But it backfired, because his brother Will quietly bought the stock up until, in 1906, he had control of the entire enterprise—which he renamed the Kellogg Toasted Corn Flakes Company. He immediately placed an advertisement in the *Ladies' Home Journal*, which brought in a flood of orders. Sales leapt from 33 cases a day to 2,900 cases a day. But Dr. Kellogg wasn't happy about it. He called William a traitor...and the two never spoke to each other again.

Meanwhile, the Kellogg's Corn Flake Company prospered. As *Everybody's Business* puts it: "By 1909 the company was selling more than 1 million cases a year. Two years later, the advertising budget had reached $1 million, part of which was used to erect the world's largest electric sign on the Mecca Building at Times Square in New York, with K in *Kellogg* 66 feet tall."

THE KELLOGGS' FATE

Both of the Kellogg brothers were expelled from the Seventh Day Adventist church. The San, even without religious affiliation, flourished under Dr. Kellogg's direction until 1933. Then the Depression deprived it of many wealthy clients, and its source of revenue. Deeply in debt, it was forced to close in 1938. John Harvey Kellogg lived until 1942 when, at the age of 91, he succumbed to pneumonia.

William (W. K.) Kellogg, whose signature is on every box of Kellogg's cereal, lived to be 92 years of age. He died in 1951. His legacy: a $5 billion dried breakfast cereal business.

BY THE WAY...

Remember these cereals? Rice Krinkles; King Vitaman; Frosty-Os; Crispy Critters; Apple Jacks; Puffa Puffa Rice; Wheat Honeys....

THE ADDAMS FAMILY

"They're creepy and they're kooky, mysterious and spooky...." You know the rest. But here are a few things you didn't know about TV's weirdest sitcom family.

HOW IT STARTED

Charles Addams' ghoulish cartoon characters first appeared in *The New Yorker* magazine and developed a cult following strong enough to warrant several volumes of cartoons. It was one of these collections that inspired the TV show. Early in 1963, TV executive David Levy noticed an Addams book in a N.Y. store window. "Eureka!" he thought. "There's an idea for a great TV show." Unaware that Addams had already rejected other TV offers, Levy called *The New Yorker* and made an appointment to meet him. They met at the Plaza Hotel.

"Addams was tall and young-looking for his age, with a twinkle in his eye," recalls Levy. "He spoke laconically, with a very dry wit. I remembered a famous quote of his: Emerging from a big screening of Liz Taylor's Cleopatra with actress Joan Fontaine on his arm, he was asked if he enjoyed the movie. He said 'Yes.' What part? 'I liked the asp.'

"I had all this in mind when I met him, but for two hours over drinks we talked of *nothing* but novelist John O'Hara!"

It was a strange way to discuss a TV series.

Addams and O'Hara, it turned out, had been drinking buddies since Prohibition. And Levy had worked with O'Hara on TV adaptations of his short stories. The O'Hara connection made all the difference. After two hours, Addams suggested that they meet the next day to finalize an agreement...and "The Addams Family" TV series was born.

INSIDE FACTS

Go, Gomez

After John Astin's first sitcom, "I'm Dickens, He's Fenster," was cancelled, he auditioned for "The Addams Family," and was turned down...for the part of *Lurch.* He didn't even try out for Gomez. But the producer spied John leaving the room, grabbed him, and

Before 1863, mail service in the U.S. was free.

offered him the lead role on the spot. The only condition: Astin had to grow a mustache. He grabbed the role.

Hair Today...

It took Carolyn Jones two hours every day to put on Morticia's makeup. The final touch: she wore a wig made of—what else?—human hair.

• Believe it or not, Jones was only the producer's *3rd* choice to play Morticia! ABC insisted that they needed a "name" actress, and Jones was the only well-known performer in the running (she had been nominated for an Oscar in 1956)—so she got the part.

Itt's Alive!

Cousin Itt's (you remember, the ball of fur with a hat on) voice was supplied by "Addams" producer Nat Perrin, who recited gibberish into a tape recorder and played it back at a higher speed.

Name Game

Addams, who'd never given his characters first names, had to come up with some for the TV show. (It was one of the few contributions he actually made to the sitcom; other than that, he did nothing except give his approval.) Within a week he'd decided on all of them—except for Mr. Addams, who almost wound up being called "Repelli" (for repellent) instead of Gomez.

True Fans

• When Ringo Starr met John Astin in 1965, he greeted Astin by grabbing his hand and kissing his way up his arm. And Astin hadn't said a word of French!

• In the early '80s, punk-rocker Siouxsie Sioux, of Siouxsie and the Banshees, wrote in a "portrait-of-the-artist" column, "My role model, inspiration, and heroine is Morticia Addams."

• Lurch got fan mail from teenage girls who thought he was cuter than the Beatles.

Home Sweet Home

The unique interior of the Addams house was inspired by the real-life Manhattan apartment of Charles Addams, which contained suits of armor, an antique cross-bow collection, and other odds-and-ends (with the emphasis on "odds").

Mosquitoes flap their wings 1,000 times every second.

ROAD KILL

One of the stranger studies in human behavior we've ever heard of was a recent experiment to find out how people react to animals on the highway. Here's what they found out.

THE TEST

David Shepherd, a biology professor at Southeastern Louisiana University, put rubber reptiles "on or near roads" and watched how 22,000 motorists reacted to them. His conclusion: "There are apparently very few animals hit accidentally on the highway."

WHAT THEY DID

To find out how drivers would respond to reptiles on the road, Shepherd and his crew put fake snakes and turtles in places where drivers would hit them if they kept driving straight; they also put the rubber reptiles where drivers had to go way out of their way to hit them. Shepherd's comment: "We found that while eighty-seven percent of drivers tried to avoid the animals, six percent went out of their way to hit them—with snakes getting squashed twice as often as turtles."

WEIRD REACTIONS

Apparently, there's something about a reptile on the road that makes some drivers bloodthirsty. A few examples Shepherd witnessed:

- "A truck driver crossed the center line, went into the opposite lane of traffic, and drove onto the shoulder of the road to run over a 'turtle.' "
- A normal housewife who saw what she thought was a snake in the road swerved to kill it, "then turned around to run over it five more times."
- "A policeman crushed a 'snake' with his tires, then stopped and pulled his gun. I quickly jumped from some bushes and explained it was a fake."

His conclusion: "Some people just have a mean streak toward animals."

The patent for the ball-point pen was awarded to John J. Loud of Weymouth, Mass. in 1888.

MANIAC

Believe it or not, the gruesome horror flick, The Texas Chainsaw Massacre, *inspired one of the best-selling dance tunes of the '80s.*

GOOFING AROUND

One night, musician/songwriter Michael Sembello and his writing partner rented a copy of *The Texas Chainsaw Massacre*, a particularly gruesome horror film. After watching it on Sembello's VCR, they decided—just for kicks, because they were sick of love songs—to write a tune about a mass-murderer. They did a rough version of the song, put it on cassette, then went back to working on other projects.

RUSHIN' ROULETTE

A few weeks later, record producer Phil Ramone asked Sembello to supply some music for an upcoming Paramount film—a dance movie called *Flashdance*. Michael came up with 2 or 3 songs he thought might work; then he asked his wife to copy them onto a tape and send them off to Paramount. She went into the studio and picked up a cassette, did the copying, and rushed it into the mail.

The next day his wife took a call from someone at Paramount. The guys at the studio had listened to all the songs, and there was one they were crazy about—they'd tested it with a specific dance scene, and it worked perfectly. They definitely wanted to use it in the film. "Which song?" she asked. The reply: "I don't know. It's the song at the very end of the tape that keeps repeating something about a maniac." Sembello's wife was horrified—it was the song about the mass murderer! She'd sent the tape without realizing it was at the very end of the cassette. "No, no, that's not supposed to be on the cassette!" she pleaded. But Paramount was adamant—they loved it and wanted it.

NEW CHARACTER

When Michael found out, he was so shocked that he didn't even believe his wife. But Ramone confirmed it, adding that Paramount wanted the lyrics changed to fit the dance scene. In this new version, the maniac was dance-crazy, not bloodthirsty.

"Maniac"—the song no one was ever supposed to hear—became Sembello's first hit—a million-seller, #1 song, and Oscar nominee.

WARHOLISMS

Andy Warhol understood modern America. Some comments:

"Try the Andy Warhol New York City Diet: When I order in a restaurant, I order everything I don't want, so I have a lot to play around with while everyone else eats."

"An artist is a person who produces things that people don't need to have but that he—for some reason—thinks it would be a good idea to give them."

"It's not what you are that counts, it's what they *think* you are."

"Employees make the best dates. You don't have to pick them up and they're always tax deductible."

"Sex is the biggest nothing of all time."

"Being born is like being kidnapped. And then sold into slavery."

"It's the movies that have really been running things in America ever since they were invented. They show you what to do, how to do it, when to do it, how to feel about it, and how to *look* when you feel about it."

"The most exciting attractions are between opposites that never meet."

"The nicer I am, the more people think I'm lying.'"

"I always run into strong women who are looking for weak men to dominate them."

"I never think that people die. They just go to department stores."

"After being alive, the next hardest work is having sex."

"Dying's the most embarrassing thing that can ever happen to you."

"I am a deeply superficial person."

"The more information you get, the less fantasy you have."

"Muscles are great. Everybody should have at least one that they can show off."

A Saudi Arabian woman can get a divorce if her husband doesn't give her coffee.

THE CONDENSED MAN

One of the most famous names in American food is Borden's. This tale of Gail Borden, an inventor and classic American eccentric, comes from Everybody's Business.

SMALL IS BEAUTIFUL

"Gail Borden was obsessed by the idea that food could be preserved by condensing, but his early experiments were unsuccessful....A condensed meat 'biscuit' he invented for Texans headed for California during the 1850s Gold Rush proved to be nutritious, but tasted awful....Undeterred, Borden continued his experiments with dehydrating and concentrating foods. 'I mean to put a potato into a pillbox, a pumpkin into a tablespoon, the biggest sort of watermelon into a saucer,' he declared."

THE PERFECT HOST

"He once subjected friends to a dinner party consisting entirely of the products of his experiments: condensed and concentrated soups, main course, fruits, and extracts. While Borden ate heartily and discoursed enthusiastically on the fine flavors of his concoctions, his guests toyed unhappily with their food. All firmly refused second helpings.

"Afterward, the unfortunate diners were lured onto another of Borden's inventions, the 'land schooner,' a contraption that used wind power to move on land. Its sails raised, the schooner moved down the beach, gaining speed at an alarming rate. Borden's passengers yelled for him to stop—at which point it was discovered that the braking mechanism was ineffective. As panic broke out, Borden swung the rudder the wrong way, and the schooner splashed into the waves, capsizing and dumping all hands into the sea. Unhurt, the group scrambled ashore. 'Where's Gail?' inquired one of Borden's dripping guests....'Drowned, I...hope!' "

CONDENSED FOR ETERNITY

"Neither drowned nor discouraged, Borden went on...to found what...became a giant corporation, built on his 1863 discovery of a process for making condensed milk. As he rode the train to work in New York City each day, he passed a cemetery where he had built his own tombstone—in the shape of a can of condensed milk."

The Neanderthal Man's brain was bigger than yours is.

THE FABULOUS '60s

Odds and ends about America's favorite decade, from the fabulous book 60s!, by John and Gordon Javna.

SOUP'S ON

Not everyone appreciated Pop Art. When Andy Warhol's first Campbell's Soup Can paintings went on display in an L.A. art gallery in 1961—for $100 apiece—another gallery down the street contemptuously stacked soup cans in its windows with the sign: "The real thing, 29¢."

WARHOL AGAIN

For a show at a gallery in Toronto in 1965, Warhol moved 80 of his Pop Art sculptures of Brillo boxes, cornflakes boxes, and the like across the Canadian border—only to discover that they were classified as "merchandise" instead of "art" by the Canadian government. That meant that the gallery owner had to pay an import duty, which he refused to do. He told newsmen that Canada had embarrassed itself and was now the "laughingstock of the art world." Government spokesmen countered that the boxes looked too much like their commercial counterparts, and "the only thing the artist adds is his signature."

"But," said Warhol, "I don't sign them."

MR. SPACEMAN

On April 12, 1961, one of man's impossible dreams was realized when Yuri Gagarin, a 27-year-old Russian test pilot, orbited the earth. He thus became the first man in history to actually see our planet. His 108-minute flight for the Soviet Union made him a worldwide hero. After the experience, he returned to testing new aircraft. Tragically, he was killed in a plane crash in 1968 and did not live to see man walk on the moon.

GIMME A BURGER, BABY

McDonald's menu in 1964:

- Hamburgers 15¢
- French fries 12¢
- Shakes 20¢.

FIVE REACTIONS TO THE MOON LANDING

In 1969, the whole world watched as Neil Armstrong and crew walked on the moon. Some unusual reactions.

1. In Ghana: Nagai Kassa VII, a tribal chief, listened to the Apollo 11 saga on his shortwave radio through the Voice of America. Reportedly, he was worried that the astronauts would fall off the moon, and was amazed that they were able to fit on it at all. "The moon is so small as I see it that I didn't think there would be enough room," he said.

2. In India: Astrologers wondered if the moon was "too tainted for use in soothsaying, now that a man has walked on it."

3. In Alaska: Unimpressed by the scientific aspects of the lunar escapade, an Eskimo interpreted the moon landing for a reporter as a way to predict the weather. He said it was a sure sign of a "hard winter next year."

4. Somewhere in the Arab World: Al Fatah, the terrorist organization, objected that Arab newspapers were giving more attention to the moon landing than to "terrorist missions against Israel."

5. In New York City: The lunar landing was celebrated with a "moon bash" in Central Park. The Department of Parks invited the millions of New Yorkers to enjoy huge screens with live TV coverage, searchlights, a film collage, synthetic Northern Lights, dancing to "moon music," inflatable sculpture, and a blue-cheese picnic.

MISS AVERAGE AMERICA

Our all-time favorite beauty contest is the National College Queen Pageant, a little-known pageant that awarded some lucky college girl a title and prizes for excelling in the most mundane activities imaginable. "We are idealizing the well-rounded average," explained the show's promoter in 1962. Some of the events in which contestants had to compete:

- Blouse-ironing
- Cooking hamburgers
- "Doodling designs with colored inks on electric blankets"
- Carrying coffee cups and pots across a room to the judges' table and pouring (to evaluate "skill and poise as a hostess")
- Sandal decoration
- A fierce debate on "right and wrong hairstyles."

TV's RULES TO LIVE BY

More words of wisdom from Prime Time Proverbs.

"Remember—the Eagle may soar but the weasel never gets sucked up into a jet engine."

—Rick Simon,
Simon and Simon

"The first thing to do when you're being stalked by an angry mob with raspberries, is to release a tiger."

—John Cleese,
Monty Python's Flying Circus

"Always enter a strange hotel room with extreme caution, especially one with a samurai warrior in it."

—Thomas Magnum,
Magnum P.I.

"If you can't fight 'em, and they won't let you join 'em, best get out of the county."

—Pappy Maverick,
Maverick

"Just keep laughin'."

—Bozo the Clown,
Bozo's Circus

"The older you get, the better you get—unless you're a banana."

— Rose,
The Golden Girls

"Like my old skleenball coach used to say, 'Find out what you don't do well, then don't do it.' "

— Alf,
ALF

"As we say in the sewer, if you're not prepared to go all the way, don't put your boots on in the first place."

—Ed Norton,
The Honeymooners

"An ounce of prevention is worth a pound of bandages and adhesive tape."

—Groucho Marx,
You Bet Your Life

"It's been the lesson of my life that nothing that sounds that good ever really happens."

—Alex Reiger,
Taxi

"Never wear polyester underwear if you're going to be hit by lightning."

—Roz,
Night Court

"A watched cauldron never bubbles."

Morticia Addams,
The Addams Family

Donald Duck comics were banned from libraries in Finland because he doesn't wear pants.

GIMME SOME SKIN

When you meet someone socially, what do you do? Shake hands? Tip your hat? Here's the background story on some traditional greetings.

THE HANDSHAKE

From *Extraordinary Origins of Everyday Things:*

"In its oldest recorded use, a handshake signified the conferring of power from a god to an earthly ruler....

"In Babylonia, around 1800 B.C., it was required that the king grasp the hands of a statue of Marduk, the civilization's chief deity. The act, which took place annually during the New Year's festival, served to transfer authority to the potentate for an additional year. So persuasive was the ceremony that when the Assyrians defeated and occupied Babylonia, subsequent Assyrian kings felt compelled to adopt the ritual, lest they offend a major heavenly being....

"Folklore offers an earlier, more speculative origin of the handshake: An ancient villager who chanced to meet a man he didn't recognize reacted automatically by reaching for his dagger. The stranger did likewise, and the two spent time cautiously circling each other. If both became satisfied that the situation called for a parley instead of a fight to the death, daggers were reinserted into their sheaths, and right hands—the weapon hands—were extended as a token of goodwill. This is also offered as the reason why women, who throughout history were never the bearers of weapons, never developed the custom of the handshake."

TIPPING YOUR HAT, BOWING, CURTSYING, ETC.

From *Extraordinary Origins of Everyday Things:*

"The gentlemanly practice of tipping one's hat goes back in principle to ancient Assyrian times, when captives were required to strip naked to demonstrate subjugation to their conquerors. The Greeks required new servants to strip from the waist up. Removing an article of clothing became a standard act of respect. Romans approached a holy shrine only after taking their sandals off. And a person of low rank removed his shoes before entering a superior's home—a custom the Japanese have brought, somewhat modified,

Each $1,000 raise in a wife's salary increases the chances for divorce or separation by 1%.

into modern times. In England, women took off their gloves when presented to royalty. In fact, two other gestures, one male, one female, are remnants of acts of subjugation or respect: the bow and the curtsy; the latter was at one time a full genuflection.

"By the Middle Ages in Europe, the symbol of serfdom to a feudal lord was restricted to baring the head. The implicit message was the same as in earlier days: 'I am your obedient servant.' So persuasive was the gesture that the Christian Church adopted it, requiring that men remove their hats on entering a church.

"Eventually, it became standard etiquette for a man to show respect for an equal by merely tipping his hat."

GIVING A MILITARY SALUTE.

The formal military salute seems to have started in medieval England, when soldiers were commonly clad in armor. Two possible explanations for its origin:

- At jousting tournaments, knights paraded past the queen with hands held over their eyes, a symbolic gesture suggesing they were protecting themselves from her "blinding beauty."
- When two knights in armor met on the road, they raised their visors to show respect...and to demonstrate that they had no violent intentions. This position—one hand held at the forehead—became a formal military greeting. It outlasted the practice of wearing armor.

BUSINESS CARDS

Today, business cards are a means of establishing credibility as a professional. But until the early part of this century, they were "calling cards," and they were used exclusively for social purposes. They were "upper class"; presenting a calling card when you met or visited someone indicated that you didn't have to work for a living. And there was an elaborate etiquette surrounding their use (e.g., should a single woman leave a calling card for a gentleman?). But as the middle classes got into the act, the calling card became another means of making a business contact. Today, that's all it is.

GOOD-BYE

Good-bye is probably a shortened version of the old term, "God be with you."

FAMOUS FOR 15 MINUTES

We included this feature—based on Andy Warhol's comment that "in the future, everyone will be famous for 15 minutes"—in the first Bathroom Reader. Here it is again, with new stars.

THE STAR: Robert Opel, a 33-year-old unemployed actor.
THE HEADLINE: "Streaker Steals Oscar Show."
WHAT HAPPENED: Near the end of the 1974 Academy Awards ceremony, host David Niven was introducing the woman who would present the Best Picture award—Elizabeth Taylor. "She is," he was saying fondly, "a very important contributor to world entertainment, and someone quite likely—"

Suddenly his speech was interrupted by screams and laughter as a naked man streaked across the stage in back of him. Niven stuttered for a second, then recovered and commented, "Ladies and gentlemen, that was bound to happen. Just think, the only laugh that man will probably ever get is for stripping and showing off his shortcomings." Then he gave the floor to Taylor, who quipped, "That's a pretty tough act to follow."

Meanwhile, the streaker had been caught backstage and was produced by security, fully clothed, for the press. "I have no official connection with the Academy," Robert Opel told reporters. But observers speculated that Oscar show producer Jack Haley, Jr. had created the whole incident as a publicity stunt. He denied it, declaring: "I would have used a pretty girl instead."

THE AFTERMATH: Opel made an appearance on "The Mike Douglas Show," debuted as a stand-up comedian in Hollywood, and was hired to streak at other Hollywood affairs (e.g., one honoring Rudolf Nureyev). Then he disappeared from public view. Five years later, he made the news again when was brutally murdered at a sex paraphernalia shop he owned in San Francisco.

THE STAR: Jimmy Nicol, a little-known English drummer.
THE HEADLINE: "Ringo Heads to Hospital as Beatles Tour with New Drummer."
WHAT HAPPENED: In June, 1964 the Fab Four were getting

publicity shots taken at a photographer's, when drummer Ringo Starr suddenly collapsed. He was rushed to a hospital, and was diagnosed as having tonsillitis. This was a huge problem—the Beatles were about to leave for a world tour. Their solution: They hired a local session drummer named Jimmy Nicol to play with them while Ringo recovered. Overnight, the bewildered Nicol became a member of the world's most popular band.

Nicol played with the Beatles for two weeks—in Holland, Hong Kong, and Australia. Ringo finally felt well enough to join the band Down Under, and after one last performance—with Ringo watching—Jimmy reluctantly returned to England.

THE AFTERMATH: Inspired, Nicol started his own band, called the Shubdubs. Unfortunately, they went nowhere.

THE STAR: Jackie Mitchell, 17-year-old lefthanded pitcher for the Chattanooga Lookouts, a minor league baseball team.

THE HEADLINE: "Female Hurler Fans Ruth and Gehrig."

WHAT HAPPENED: It was April 2, 1931. The mighty New York Yankees were "working their way north at the end of spring training," playing minor league teams along the way. Today, they were in Chattanooga, Tennessee. When the first two Yankee batters got hits, the manager decided to make a pitching change. He brought in his latest acquisition, a local player who had never pitched in a pro game before—Jackie Mitchell. She was, in fact, the first woman *ever* to play in a pro game. And the first batter she had to face was Babe Ruth. A tough situation; but she was tough. Jackie struck the Babe out in 5 pitches...and then proceeded to strike out "Larrupin' Lou" Gehrig in 3.

It was an impressive debut for a rookie, but it was a little suspect —Joe Engel, owner of the Lookouts, was known for publicity stunts, and this game had been planned for April 1 (the April Fools' Day game was rained out). Still, Jackie insisted to her dying day that it was on the level, and you can't argue with record books.

AFTERMATH: *The New York Times* praised Jackie in an editorial, hailing her feat as a blow for women's rights.

Mitchell never made it as a pro—she played ball around Chattanooga for 6 years, then quit to marry and to take over the family business (optometry). She died in 1987.

THE STAR: Harold Russell, a disabled World War II veteran.
THE HEADLINE: "Non-actor Wins Oscar for First Film Role."
WHAT HAPPENED: In 1946, director William Wyler made a film called *The Best Years of Our Lives*, depicting the personal struggles of several returning World War II vets. It was a hot topic, and the movie attracted a first-class cast: Frederic March, Myrna Loy, Virginia Mayo, Dana Andrews...and Harold Russell.

Russell had lost both his hands in an explosion at a Georgia training camp during the war. The Army asked him to appear in a short film about disabled veterans, and Wyler spotted him in it.

The director essentially cast Russell as himself—a severely disabled man trying to readjust to everyday life. Wyler wouldn't let him take acting lessons; and his performance was so powerful that it carried the film. *The Best Years of Our Lives* captured 7 Oscars—including best picture, best actor (Frederic March), best director, best screenplay, and best supporting actor—Russell.
AFTERMATH: Russell didn't appear in another film for 34 years. He can be seen in the 1980 feature, *Inside Moves*.

THE STAR: Valerie Solanas, founder of SCUM—the Society for Cutting Up Men.
THE HEADLINE: "Warhol Felled By SCUM."
WHAT HAPPENED: Valerie Solanas had hung around Andy Warhol's studio in the '60s. She'd even appeared in his movie, *I, a Man*. So the artist whom friends called "the ultimate voyeur" was shocked when Valerie pulled out a gun one day in June, 1968 and shot him. Solanas, it turned out, was irked that Warhol hadn't bothered commenting on the script of a play she'd left with him.

Andy was seriously wounded; doctors only gave him a 50-50 chance to survive. Meanwhile Valerie turned herself in, telling the patrolman to whom she surrendered, "He had too much control over my life." She was immediately sent for psychiatric observation, while she and her organization were splashed across the tabloid front pages.
AFTERMATH: Warhol lived, Solanas was imprisoned, and the whole incident stands as an ironic reminder that no one—not even the man who first articulated the idea—is immune when someone's 15 minutes arrive.

Painting accounts for almost half the cost of automobile assembly.

NEAR MISSES

A surprising amount of movie parts that turn lesser lights into stars are cast simply because bigger stars have turned the roles down. Take these, for example:

CASABLANCA (1942). The lead role was originally offered not to Humphrey Bogart, but to movie tough guy George Raft—who turned it down because he didn't like the script. Earlier, Raft also turned down the part of Sam Spade in *The Maltese Falcon* (1941) because he didn't trust the young director (John Huston), and the lead in *High Sierra* (1941) because he thought it was bad luck to die onscreen. Bogart took both of those roles, too, and built a career on them.

DRACULA (1931). The choice for the film was Universal's master of horror, Lon Chaney, Sr. But Chaney died in August, 1930, a few months before filming began. Second choice: Bela Lugosi, who'd played the vampire on Broadway. Lugosi was rushed to Hollywood, became a surprise star, and was typecast as a movie ghoul for the rest of his career.

THE WIZARD OF OZ (1939). This was supposed to star "Americas's Sweetheart," Shirley Temple. MGM was willing to trade the services of its two biggest stars—Clark Gable and Jean Harlow—to 20th Century Fox to get the little actress. But Darryl Zanuck, Fox's chief, refused—so the part of Dorothy went to little-known Judy Garland. Ironically, Miss Temple was cast in a similar movie the following year, called *The Blue Bird*. It bombed and ruined her film career.

More Shuffling:

- W. C. Fields was supposed to be the Wizard, but he was dropped when he held out for more money. His replacement was Frank Morgan.
- Ray Bolger was supposed to be the Tin Woodsman, and Buddy Ebsen was supposed to be the Scarecrow. But they traded parts. Then Ebsen's lungs got infected when he inhaled the metallic dust sprayed on his costume, and he spent the next six weeks in an iron lung. He was replaced by Jack Haley.

MIDNIGHT COWBOY (1969): Dustin Hoffman's intended co-star was Michael Sarazin. But Sarazin turned it down...and Jon Voight became an overnight star.

GONE WITH THE WIND (1939): The original Scarlett and Rhett were Bette Davis and Errol Flynn. That was Jack Warner's idea, anyway, when Warner Brothers still planned to finance the film. But Davis absolutely refused to have anything to do with Flynn, so Warner pulled out. When MGM got involved, producer David O. Selznick asked them for Gary Cooper to play Rhett—but he was refused. Finally he wound up with Clark Gable, who took the part simply because he wanted some quick money to finance an impending divorce.

• Despite the hoopla about finding *the* actress to play Scarlett at the last minute, Selznick apparently knew who he wanted quite early. When he saw Vivien Leigh in the British film *A Yank at Oxford*, his mind was made up. The rest was just p.r.

FRANKENSTEIN (1931): After the success of *Dracula*, Bela Lugosi was in line for all the good monster parts—including this one. But he turned *Frankenstein* down when he found out the monster wouldn't have any dialogue. Instead, an English actor named William Henry Pratt (Boris Karloff) got the role and became an international star.

ON THE WATERFRONT (1954): Marlon Brando won an Academy Award for his performance, but the producers originally wanted Montgomery Clift to star instead.

SOMEBODY UP THERE LIKES ME (1956): Young, little-known actor Paul Newman lost several choice parts to James Dean—including the role of Cal in *Giant*, and the lead in this biography of boxer Rocky Graziano. Then suddenly, before shooting on *Somebody Up There* started, Dean was dead. Newman was picked to step in, and the movie was his springboard to stardom.

TARZAN THE APE MAN (1932): Swimming star Johnny Weissmuller made a living with Tarzan pictures for decades, but only because Clark Gable turned the first one down.

You use up as many calories sitting in a sauna for 15 minutes as you do jogging for a mile.

MUSTANG: CAR OF THE '60s

The original Ford Mustang, a sporty car for "everyman," introduced in 1964, is now a symbol of the entire decade. Its early history is fascinating.

The Mustang was the most successful car ever introduced by the American auto industry. But in terms of the '60s, it was more than a car. Its popularity was an expression of the simple truth of the decade—that everyone wanted to look, feel, and act young.

ORIGIN OF THE CAR

• The Mustang was the pet project of Ford General Manager Lee Iacocca, who kept notes on new car ideas in a little black book. Because Ford kept getting letters from car buffs who wanted a car like the 1955 T-Bird, Iacocca felt there was a market for a new "personal sports car" waiting to be developed. Research also showed that the population was getting younger, and that young people bought more cars per capita than any other segment of the population.

• Based on these findings—and Iacocca's instinct—Ford decided to create a car that was sporty yet low-priced, so young people and middle-income groups could afford it. But it also had to be capable of taking enough options to make it a luxury car.

• The new project was dubbed "T-5." Ford engineers and designers worked under maximum security in a windowless room, known as "The Tomb"; even the wastepaper was burned under supervision.

• Over a three-year period they came up with many two-seat prototypes—XT-Bird, Allegro, Aventura, and Mustang I (loved by car enthusiasts, but considered too sporty by Iacocca)—but all were scrapped in favor of a four-seat model with a large trunk. It was completed in spring 1963.

• The Mustang was designed to be versatile. The buyer had options: two different engines, whitewalls, power disc brakes, racing hubcaps, sports console, and so on. As Dr. Seymour Marshak, Ford's market research manager, said admiringly, "This flexibility makes this car the greatest thing since the Erector Set."

• Since Ford figured the T-5's market was the young sports car

The most popular color for cars is white. 10% of all cars sold in the U.S. are white.

buyer, the name "Torino" was chosen because it sounded like an Italian sports car. The projected ad campaign called it "the new import . . . from Detroit."

• But last-minute market research showed that this car could appeal to all buyers, and a new name had to be chosen. Colt, Bronco, and Maverick (all used for later cars) were considered. But "Mustang" seemed best for T-5, bringing to mind cowboys, adventure, and the Wild West. As one Ford man put it, "It had the excitement of the wide-open spaces, and it was American as all hell."

• The Mustang was introduced on April 17, 1964. On that day, over 4 million people visited the 6,500 Ford dealers across the country to get a look at it...and they bought 22,542 of them.

• In the first three months of production, a record 100,000 Mustangs were sold. It was an instant status symbol, with people vying for the limited supply as though it was a contraband item.

MUSTANG FEVER

The introduction of the Mustang on April 17, 1964 was a big event. Here are 5 of the bizarre things that happened that day.

1. A Mustang was the pace car for a stock car race in Huntsville, Alabama. When it drove onto the track, thousands of people scaled the retaining wall to get a better look at it. The race was delayed for over an hour.

2. A cement truck crashed through the plate-glass window of a Seattle Ford dealer when the driver lost control of his vehicle. The reason: He was staring at the new Mustangs on display there. They looked "like some of them expensive Italian racers," he explained.

3. A Chicago Ford dealer was forced to lock the doors of his showroom models because too many people were trying to get into them at the same time.

4. A Texas dealer put a new Mustang on a lift to show a prospective customer the underside of the vehicle. By the time his demonstration was over, the showroom was filled with people, and he had to leave the Mustang up in the air for the rest of the day.

5. A New Jersey Ford dealer had only one Mustang and 15 eager buyers, so he auctioned it off. The winner of the auction insisted on sleeping in the car to be sure the dealer didn't sell it to someone else before his check cleared.

60% of the cost of food is in transporting it.

STRANGE LAWSUITS

These days, it seems like people will sue each other over practically anything. Here are a few real-life examples of unusual legal battles.

THE PLAINTIFF: An unidentified 40-year-old woman from Poughkeepsie, New York.

THE DEFENDANT: Her plastic surgeon.

THE LAWSUIT: The woman had an operation to tighten her stomach in 1979. When it was over, she discovered that her belly-button was now 2-1/2 inches off center. She claimed "the operation had left a large deformed hole in her stomach and had disrupted her business and her life." She sued the doctor for malpractice.

VERDICT: She was awarded $854,000 by the New York State Supreme Court, and ultimately settled with the doctor for $200,000. A year later, she had her bellybutton surgically corrected.

THE PLAINTIFF: An unidentified woman from San Francisco.

THE DEFENDANT: Her priest.

THE LAWSUIT: The woman embezzled around $30,000 from the Catholic Church, and was overcome by guilt. "I couldn't take the pressure anymore," she said. "I needed to talk with someone, and the only person I could talk with was my priest." So she went into the confessional and admitted what she'd done. She expected absolution and forgiveness; instead, the priest turned her in to the police. She spent 7 months in jail, and when she got out, she sued the priest for $5 million for "violation of confidentiality."

VERDICT: Settled out of court.

THE PLAINTIFFS: Bruce and Susan S., from Manitoba, Canada.

THE DEFENDANT: Winnipeg International Airport.

THE LAWSUIT: One day in 1988, the couple and their baby daughter, Anna, showed up at the Winnipeg Airport to catch a flight. At the gate, the airport security guard X-rayed their carry-on luggage—and then picked up Anna and sent her through the X-ray machine, too. The couple immediately took their daughter to a hospital to see if the X-rays had harmed her. She was okay, but they still sued the airport—"for the time lost while waiting for test results as well as the fare of the missed flight."

VERDICT: Settled out of court.

THE PLAINTIFF: Robert K., "a 36-year-old Philadelphia real estate manager."

THE DEFENDANT: The Transcendental Meditation Society and the guru Maharishi Mahesh Yogi.

THE LAWSUIT: Mr. K. worked with TM groups for 11 years, but he finally sued them because "he was never able to achieve the 'perfect state of life' they promised, and he suffered psychological disorders as a result. One broken agreement: he had been told he would be taught to 'fly' through self-levitation, but he learned only to 'hop with the legs folded in the lotus position.' "

VERDICT: "A U.S. district court jury in Washington, D.C. awarded him nearly $138,000 in damages."

THE PLAINTIFF: A 19-year-old man from New York City.

THE DEFENDANT: The City Transit Authority.

THE LAWSUIT: The 19-year-old decided to commit suicide by throwing himself off a subway platform into the path of an oncoming train. The train didn't stop in time to avoid hitting him, but it didn't kill him, either—he lost a leg, an arm, and part of the other arm. So he sued the Transit Authority, claiming "the motorman was negligent in not stopping the train quickly enough."

THE VERDICT: They settled out of court for $650,000—despite the fact that while they were negotiating the settlement, the man threw himself off a subway platform—and failed to kill himself—a second time.

AND LET'S NOT FORGET...

Two 1974 cases involving CBS-TV. The first one, a claim by studio technician Hamilton Morgan that "The Beverly Hillbillies" was originally his idea, was settled out of court (reportedly with a big cash settlement to Morgan). The second charged that CBS's Paladin character in "Have Gun, Will Travel" was pirated from a retired rodeo performer. The case went to court, and CBS lost.

The book most often read by high school English classes: Shakespeare's *Romeo and Juliet*.

"COME UP AND SEE ME..."

Comments from film actress Mae West.

"Marriage is a great institution, but I'm not ready for an institution yet."

"It's hard to be funny when you have to be clean."

"She's the kind of girl who climbed the ladder of success, wrong by wrong."

"Between two evils, I always pick the one I haven't tried before."

"I generally avoid temptation—unless I can't resist it."

"It's not the men in my life that counts—it's the life in my men."

"He who hesitates is last."

"When women go wrong, men go right after them."

"Too much of a good thing can be wonderful."

"I used to be Snow White...but I drifted."

"I only like two kinds of men—domestic and foreign."

"Is that a gun in your pocket, or are you glad to see me?"

"Give a man a free hand and he'll run it all over you."

"I've been in more laps than a napkin."

"A man in the house is worth two in the street."

"He's the kind of man a woman would have to marry to get rid of."

"Brains are an asset...if you hide them."

"I don't look down on men, but I certainly don't look up to them either. I never found a man I could love—or trust—the way I loved myself."

"When I'm good, I'm very good. But when I'm bad, I'm better."

"I always say, keep a diary and one day it will keep you."

"I've always had a weakness for foreign affairs."

The average bank teller loses about $250 every year.

WE'VE ONLY JUST BEGUN

Ads are so pervasive in society that we often don't even know one when we hear it. Like this one.

Some people think "We've Only Just Begun" is a great love song. Actually, it's a bank commercial.

BACKGROUND: In 1968, officials of the Crocker Bank in California approached a San Francisco ad agency about trying to attract young people to their institution. There was a strong anti-establishment feeling among college graduates at the time, and the bank felt it had to make an extra effort to reach them.

The ad executive in charge of the project came up with a basic approach. "The one thing that all young people have in common," he explained later, "is that they're starting out on new things—beginning careers, setting up a household for the first time, and so on. So the ad campaign was developed around that theme." The slogan: "We've only just begun."

THE BUCK STARTS HERE: The ad exec got an inspiration—he decided to pay a songwriter to create a *real* song called "We've Only Just Begun," instead of just a coming up with a jingle. That way, if the song made the charts, there would be extra benefits to his client whenever it was played on the radio. So he commissioned tunesmith Paul Williams to write a song with the phrase "We've Only Just Begun" in it.

As part of the deal, the bank used it on their commercials—but Williams was also free to do whatever he wanted with it.

What did he do with it? He sold it to the Carpenters, who recorded a saccharine version that sold millions of records, and became a wedding and elevator standard.

Meanwhile, the bank made its money back by licensing commercial right for the song to other banks around the country.

THE ULTIMATE IRONY: The bank realized it didn't *want* young people's business. Young adults flocked to the Crocker Bank to borrow money, but they didn't have any collateral. They turned out to be bad risks, and the ad campaign was stopped.

U.S. airports are busier on Thursdays than any other day.

NOTHING TO SNEEZE AT

Why do we say "God Bless You" when we sneeze? Charles Panati checked it out, and came up with the answer in his Extraordinary Origins of Everyday Things.

"Gesundheit,' say Germans; 'Felicita,' say Italians; Arabs clasp hands and reverently bow. Every culture believes in a benediction following a sneeze. The custom goes back to a time when a sneeze was regarded as a sign of great personal danger."

SNEEZING SUPERSTITIONS

"For centuries, man believed that life's essence, the soul, resided in the head and that a sneeze could accidentally expel the vital force. This suspicion was reinforced by the deathbed sneezing of the sick. Every effort was made to hold back a sneeze, and an inadvertent or unsuppressed sneeze was greeted with immediate good luck chants."

THE GREEK SNEEZE

"Enlightenment arrived in the fourth century B.C. witn the teachings of Aristotle and Hippocrates, the 'father of medicine.' Both Greek scholars explained sneezing as the head's reaction to a foreign or offensive substance that crept into the nostrils. They observed that sneezing, when associated with existing illness, often foretold death. For these ill-boding sneezes, they recommended such benedictions as 'Long may you live!' 'May you enjoy good health!' and 'Jupiter preserve you!' "

THE ROMAN SNEEZE

"About a hundred years later, Roman physicians extrapolated the lore and superstition surrounding a sneeze.

"The Romans preached the view that sneezing, by an otherwise healthy individual, was the body's attempt to expel the sinister spirits of later illnesses. Thus, to withhold a sneeze was to incubate disease, to invite debility and death. Consequently, a vogue of sneezing swept the Roman Empire and engendered a host of new post-sneeze benedictions: 'Congratulations' to a person having robustly executed a sneeze; and to a person quavering on the verge of an exhalation, the encouraging 'Good luck to you.' "

Howdy Doody had 48 freckles.

THE CHRISTIAN SNEEZE

"The Christian expression 'God bless you' has a still different origin. It began by papal fiat in the sixth century, during the reign of Pope Gregory the Great. A virulent pestilence raged throughout Italy, one foreboding symptom being severe, chronic sneezing. So deadly was the plague that people died shortly after manifesting its symptoms; thus, sneezing became synonymous with imminent death.

"Pope Gregory beseeched the healthy to pray for the sick. He also ordered that such well-intended though leisurely phrases as 'May you enjoy good health' be replaced with his own more urgent and pointed invocation, 'God bless you!' And if no well-wisher was around to invoke the blessing, the sneezer was advised to exclaim aloud, 'God help me!'

"Pope Gregory's post-sneeze supplications spread throughout Europe, hand in hand with the plague, and the seriousness with which a sneeze was regarded was captured in a new expression, which survives to this day: 'Not to be sneezed at.' "

WORLD-CLASS SNEEZING

- According to the *Guinness Book of World Records*, "The most chronic sneezing fit ever recorded is that of Donna Griffiths." On January 13, 1981, the 12-year-old from Pershore, England began sneezing and kept sneezing every day for 978 days. The previous record was 194 days.
- In the first year, she sneezed an estimated one million times.
- Her first "sneeze-free day" in almost three years was September 16, 1983.

The *Guinness Book* has somehow also come up with an account of the most powerful sneeze ever recorded:
"The highest speed at which expelled particles have been measured to travel," it says, is "103.6 miles per hour."

MISC. LAST THING ON THE PAGE

The phrase "Bring home the bacon" comes from the 1700s, when the term *bacon* was criminal slang for "booty" or "loot." If you brought home the *bacon*, you fulfilled your mission and returned with "the goods," which is how we use it today.

SO LONG, ROUTE 66

You may not know it, but America's most famous highway is slowly disappearing, a victim of progress.

Although many American highways have been celebrated, few can match the romance and lore of Route 66—the 2,200-mile-long highway that was once the primary route between Chicago and Los Angeles. Route 66 has been immortalized in song ("Get Your Kicks on Route 66") and on the screen (the hit 1960s TV series).

Although it has now been bypassed by superhighways, it's still cherished by an enthusiastic cult of motorists who venture off the new interstates in search of a piece of America's history—which they seem to find on the old Route 66 backroads that still exist.

ROUTE 66 FACTS

• Route 66 began as a series of cattle and wagon train trails. By the early 1900s, the route was known as the "National Old Trails Highway."

• It was first designated Route 66 in 1926, while it was still mostly dirt and gravel. At the time, East-West routes were given even numbers, North-South got odd numbers. Route 66's Midwest path landed it between Route 2 (the northernmost route running from Maine to Idaho) and Route 96 (on the southern Texas border).

• In 1937, paving was completed. The finished highway went through eight states (Illinois, Missouri, Mississippi, Oklahoma, Texas, New Mexico, Arizona, and California) and three time zones.

• Route 66 was the road of choice for "Dust Bowl" Okies fleeing to California during the Depression of the early 1930's. John Steinbeck included Route 66 in his classic *The Grapes Of Wrath*, calling it "the mother road" on which the Joad family travelled West.

• Route 66 nicknames: The Will Rogers Highway, the Postal Highway, and the Ozark Trail.

• The TV show "Route 66" was actually filmed in Oregon and Florida. The series ran from October 7, 1960 until September 18, 1964. It starred Martin Milner and George Maharis as Tod Stiles and Buz Murdock. They drove a '62 Corvette.

• **The beginning of the end:** President Eisenhower ordered the construction of 42,500 miles of interstate highways in 1956. New superhighways like Interstate 40—which runs parallel to Route 66 from Oklahoma City to L.A.—eventually replaced the country backroads. As a result, small businesses which once thrived by the highway began to disappear in favor of fast-food franchises and hotel chains. Three interstates—40, 44, and 55—eventually replaced Route 66, whose last original stretch of highway (Williams, AZ) closed in the mid-1980s.

THE SONG

• In 1946, Bobby Troupe was driving from his home in Pennsylvania to try and make it as a songwriter in Los Angeles. At one point in the trip, his wife, Cynthia, suggested that he try and write a song about Highway 40. Troupe didn't think much of the suggestion. "Then later, out of Chicago, when we realized that we'd be following the same highway all the way to California," Troup recalls. "She whispered, kind of hesitantly because of the put-down on the first suggestion, 'Get your kicks on Route 66.' " By the time Troupe and his wife hit L.A. the song was nearly complete. Nat King Cole was the first to record it—everyone from Nelson Riddle and the Rolling Stones to Depeche Mode have done their version of "Route 66."

ROUTE 66 LANDMARKS

• Route 66 officially began on Jackson Boulevard and Michigan Avenue in Chicago. It ended at Ocean Avenue and Santa Monica Boulevard in Santa Monica, California, where a plaque can still be found dedicated to the Will Rogers Highway. It reads: "This Main Street of America Highway 66 was the first road he travelled in a career that led him straight to the hearts of his countrymen."

• The state of Arizona has preserved 105 miles of Route 66 as a historic state highway—it contains the longest drivable stretch of the road that still exits, running from Seligman to Topock, Arizona.

• Clark Gable and Carole Lombard spent their first honeymoon night on Rte. 66, in the Beale Hotel in Kingman, Arizona in 1939.

• Route 66 crosses the Texas panhandle and goes through Amarillo, home of the Cadillac Ranch (immortalized by Bruce Springsteen).

• Major cities you can still see on Route 66: Chicago, St. Louis, Oklahoma City, Amarillo, Albuquerque, and L.A.

The leaders in per capita consumption of chocolate: #1, Switzerland; #2, Norway. #3, Britain.

HELLO, I'M MR. ED

A horse is a horse, of course, of course. Unless he's on TV. Then anything can happen. Mr. Ed is probably TV's first legitimate animal folk hero.

HOW IT STARTED.
Arthur Lubin couldn't understand it. His films about *Francis the Talking Mule* had made a small fortune, but he still couldn't interest the TV networks in a similar concept he'd created for the small screen. He envisioned a show about a talking horse named Mr. Ed. (The idea was inspired by a series of magazine stories about a horse that not only talked, but frequently got drunk.) But no one—not even his projected star, comedian Alan Young—would consider the series when Lubin proposed it in 1954.

Lubin kept trying, and three years later, in 1957, he finally found a backer who agreed to bankroll a pilot film—comedian George Burns, who along with his pal, Jack Benny, thought the concept of a talking horse was hilarious.

Now that Lubin had some money, he approached Young again with a concrete offer. But again Young turned him down. "It's not the kind of thing I want to do," said Alan, who'd had his own CBS variety show in the early '50s (but was now working in England). Lubin went ahead and made a pilot anyway, using a different actor; in fact, all the stars in the original pilot were different from the TV show—even Mr. Ed. But he still couldn't sell the show.

Lubin was nothing if not persistent. He offered the part to Young *again* a few years later. And this time Young decided it was his only chance to get back into American TV. So he accepted. Lubin wanted to call it "The Alan Young Show," but Young refused that. "Why should I take the rap if it bombs?" he asked. So it became "Mr. Ed."

When the networks didn't pick up the show, the Studebaker Company (a now-defunct auto maker) purchased it and put it into syndication in 1960. To everyone except Lubin's (and Burns's) surprise, it was an instant hit. A year later, CBS bought it, making it the first syndicated show ever to be picked up by a network. It aired until 1965 on Sunday nights.

There are 91 million households in the U.S.

INSIDE FACTS

Les Is More

• Mr. Ed, an 1100-lb. golden palomino, wouldn't respond to any of his co-stars. He only took orders from his trainer, Les Hilton—which meant that Hilton had to be on the set all the time, barking out commands or giving them with hand signals.

• Hilton was often hidden in the scene or lying on the floor just out of camera range. If you're watching Mr. Ed and you want to know where Hilton is, just watch Ed's eyes. Ed is always looking at him (even if it seems that he's involved in the action).

Vital Stats

Ed's real name was Bamboo Harvester. He was born in 1954, and supposedly died in 1979 at the age of 25. His daily diet was 20 lbs. of hay, washed down with a gallon of sweet tea.

Take Five

Like any star, Ed could be moody and difficult to work with. When he was tired of working, he'd just walk off the set. And when he was hungry, shooting stopped while he strolled over to his bale of hay and ate. When he was bored, he'd cross his hind legs and yawn.

Historic Preservation

The classic Mr. Ed theme was first recorded in Italy—by an opera singer! It was so bad that Arthur Lubin started looking for a new song to use. But Jay Livingstone, Oscar-winning ("Que Sera, Sera") co-writer of the tune, recorded his own version which Lubin liked enough to use on the show. Livingstone sings it on the air.

Stunt Horse

There was no stand-in while Ed performed his stunts. He could really open the barn door (left or right side) and answer the telephone. He couldn't really talk, though. His lips were moved by a nylon bit.

The Voice

The voice of Mr. Ed was kept a secret. It was actually Allen "Rocky" Lane, a former cowboy star. For obvious reasons, Lane billed himself as "an actor who prefers to remain anonymous."

In 1900 only 41% of all Americans lived to be 65. In 1989, 79% do.

FREUDIAN SLIPS

From the mind of Sigmund Freud...

"America is a mistake, a giant mistake!"

"When a man is freed of religion, he has a better chance to live a normal and wholesome life."

"Anatomy is destiny."

"What progress we are making. In the Middle Ages they would have burnt me; nowadays they are content with burning my books."

"Thought is action in rehearsal."

"The great question...which I have not been able to answer, despite my thirty years in research into the feminine soul, is 'What do women want?' "

"Sometimes a cigar is just a cigar."

"The more the fruits of knowledge become accessible to men, the more widespread is the decline of religious belief."

"Neurosis seems to be a human privilege."

"The goal of all life is death."

"The first human being who hurled an insult instead of a stone was the founder of civilization."

"When one of my family complains that he or she has bitten his tongue, bruised her finger, and so on, instead of the expected sympathy, I put the question, 'Why did you do that?' "

"We hate the criminal, and deal with him severely, because we view in his deed, as in a distorting mirror, our own criminal instincts."

"When making a decision of minor importance, I have always found it advantageous to consider all the pros and cons. In vital matters, however, such as the choice of a mate or profession, decisions should come from the unconscious, from somewhere within ourselves. In the important decisions of our personal lives we should be governed by the deep inner needs of our nature."

41% of all Americans say they want their child to be President of the United States.

PRESIDENTIAL CURIOSITIES

Nowadays, former presidents—even disgraced ones—are treated with respect and deference. So it's enlightening to find out that the presidential office wasn't always a royal one.

FACT: The government of the United States completely ignored the death of one former president because he was considered a traitor.

THE PRESIDENT: John Tyler (10th president, 1841-45).

BACKGROUND: A Virginia aristocrat, Tyler was William Henry Harrison's running mate in 1840. When Harrison died in 1841, he became president. But 20 years later, the 71-year-old joined the Confederacy. He died in 1861 while serving as a Virginia representative in the Confederate Congress, and was buried with full honors by the rebels. In Washington, however, his death was never publicly acknowledged.

FACT: One president had to borrow money to get to his own inauguration.

THE PRESIDENT: George Washington (1st president, 1789-97).

BACKGROUND: Washington wasn't poor—he was among America's largest landowners. But when it came time to travel to New York City for his inauguration in 1789, he didn't have any money. So "The Father of Our Country" had to borrow about $600 to get there. One consolation: his presidential salary was $25,000.

FACT: One ex-president was so destitute in his final years that circus impresario P. T. ("There's a sucker born every minute") Barnum actually offered him $100,000 to take a nationwide tour with his personal memorabilia.

THE PRESIDENT: Ulysses S. Grant (18th president, 1869-77).

BACKGROUND: In the early 1880s, Grant invested his life savings—about $100,000—in a banking firm in which one of his sons was a partner. The head of the company turned out to be a swindler, and the firm went broke in 1884. Grant was not only penniless, but had terminal cancer when Barnum wrote that year and suggested a quick money-making tour. Grant refused. Instead, in an effort to leave his wife something after his death, he wrote his memoirs. Mark Twain published them posthumously, and they earned over $500,000 for the Grant estate.

FACT: Another ex-president was so broke that friends created a lottery in his name and began selling raffle tickets in Washington.
PRESIDENT: Thomas Jefferson (3rd president, 1801-1809).
BACKGROUND: Brilliant in other fields, Jefferson apparently had no head for business. When he came close to bankruptcy in his final years, friends and political allies put together the "Thomas Jefferson Lottery" to benefit the ex-president. Fortunately, Jefferson was spared this embarrassment when enough money was raised privately to keep him financially afloat.

FACT: One president never voted in a presidential election until *he* was the one running for office.
THE PRESIDENT: Zachary Taylor (12th president, 1849-50).
BACKGROUND: "Old Rough and Ready," a national military hero in the Mexican War, was completely apolitical until he was bitten by the presidential bug. When an aide first suggested that he run for the office, he reputedly answered "Stop your nonsense and drink your whiskey!"

When he actually was nominated by the Whigs, he didn't find out about it until weeks after the convention. The Whig party's letter informing him of the news arrived collect, and Taylor refused to pay the postage due—so he never read it. The nominators had to send another letter—prepaid—to tell him. When Taylor voted in the national elections of 1848, it was the first time he'd ever voted for a president—and he probably wouldn't have bothered then either, if he hadn't been on the ballot.

FACT: One president was a licensed bartender.
THE PRESIDENT: Abraham Lincoln (16th president, 1861-65).
BACKGROUND: In 1833, Honest Abe was co-owner of a saloon in Springfield, Illinois, called *Berry and Lincoln*. He needed his license to sell booze.

MONEY TALK

What do you really know about your money?

THE GREENBACK DOLLAR

The Federal government didn't start printing paper money until 1861.

• When the Civil War broke out, people began hoarding coins—and soon there was virtually no U.S. money in circulation. So Congress was forced to authorize the Treasury Department to create paper currency.

• These bills were nicknamed "Greenbacks" after the color ink used on one side. Lincoln, then president, was pictured on them.

• Congress stipulated that paper money had to be signed either by the Treasurer of the United States or people designated by him. Today the signature is printed on the bills, but in 1862 money had to be signed by hand. So 6 people—2 men and 4 women—worked in the attic of the Treasury building every day, signing, sorting, and sealing our first $1 and $2 bills.

THE BUCKS START HERE

Today, paper money worth over $12 billion is printed every year—an average of more than $10 million a day.

• About 2/3 of the paper money printed is $1 bills.

• A $1 bill lasts for about 1-1/2 years in circulation.

• The average bill is exchanged 400 times in its lifetime.

• It costs the government about 2.5¢ to print a $1 bill. It costs the same amount to print a $100 bill.

• Modern U.S. currency is printed on special paper, a blend of rag bond, cotton, and linen, supplied by a single manufacturer, Crane and Company of Massachusetts.

• U.S. paper money is printed three separate times—once each for front and back, and then it's reprinted with an overlay of green ink.

• The current U.S. dollar is 1/3 smaller than it was in 1929.

VITAL STATS

Size of a bill: 2.61 inches x 6.14 inches.

Thickness: .0043 inches. (233 of them make a stack an inch high.)

Weight: 490 bills equals a pound. A million $1 bills weigh approximately a ton.

Laid end-to-end around the equator, it would take 257,588,120 dollar bills to circle the earth.

THE BIG BUCKS

• There are officially 12 different denominations of U.S. paper money, ranging from $1 to $100,000.

• The highest denomination printed in the last 45 years is a $100. In fact, everything over $100 has been officially "retired" from circulation for 30 years.

• The $100,000 bill has never been available to the public. It's only for transactions between the Treasury Department and the Federal Reserve.

• The $2 bill was resurrected in 1976—the only piece of new engraved currency in 60 years. It was a flop; the mint recently got rid of the last remaining bills in storage by burning them.

• Who's on what? $50—Ulysses S. Grant ; $100—Ben Franklin; $500—William McKinley; $1,000—Grover Cleveland; $5,000—James Madison; $10,000—Salmon P. Chase; $100,000—Woodrow Wilson.

COIN OF THE REALM

• The first U.S. coin to bear the words, "United States of America," was a penny piece made in 1727. It was also inscribed with the plain-spoken motto: "Mind your own business."

• All American coins struck since 1792, when the first United States mint was established in Philadelphia, have been stamped with the word, "Liberty."

• The average coin circulates for a minimum of 15-20 years.

• Originally, the dime, quarter, and half dollar were 90% silver, 10% copper. But in the early '60s, the price of silver began to climb, and government officials worried that people would melt coins down for the precious metals.

• The result: Congress passed the 1965 Coinage Act, eliminating all silver from the three coins. Instead, the composition was changed to "clad" metal—a combination of three strips of metal. The faces are made of 75% copper and 25% nickel; the core is pure copper, which you can see on the side.

• In 1965, anticipating the disappearance of old quarters due to the value of the silver, the government issued almost 2 billion new ones (compared to an average annual production of 225 million). That's why you find so many 1965 quarters in circulation.

• Nickels are now made of 75% copper, 25% nickel.

• Pennies are now bronze. They contain 95% copper, 5% zinc.

Although they had many million-sellers, Creedence Clearwater Revival never had a #1 song.

AROUND THE HOUSE

The origins of a few common items.

BAND-AIDS (1921).
In 1921 Earle Dickson, an employee of Johnson & Johnson, married a woman who kept injuring herself in the kitchen.
• As he carefully bandaged her cuts and burns with gauze and adhesive tape numerous times, he became frustrated; the clumsy bandages kept falling off. So he decided to create something "that would stay in place, be easily applied, and still retain its sterility." He stuck some gauze in the center of a piece of adhesive tape, and covered the whole thing with crinoline to keep it sterile. It worked.
• He made up a bunch for his wife, and took a few in to show his co-workers. The company's owner, James Johnson, heard about it and asked for a demonstration—which convinced him to begin manufacturing the product
• By the '80s, over 100 billion Band-Aids had been sold. Dickson, who became an exec at J & J, was amply rewarded for his efforts.

IVORY SOAP (1879).
Harley Procter and his cousin, chemist James Gamble, came up with a special new soap in 1878. It was smooth and fragrant, and produced a consistent lather...but it wasn't Ivory—it was called White Soap—and it didn't float.
• One day in 1879, the man operating P & G's soap-mixing machine forgot to turn it off when he went to lunch. On returning, he discovered that so much air had been whipped into the soap that it actually floated.
• For some reason, the batch wasn't discarded—it was made into bars and shipped out with the other White Soap. Soon, to their surprise, P&G was getting letters demanding more of "that soap that floats." So they started putting extra air in every bar
• Now that they had a unique product, they nedded a unique name. And they found it in the Bible. Procter was reading the 45th Psalm—which says: "All thy garments smell of myrrh, and aloes, and cassia, out of the ivory palaces..." —when it hit him that *Ivory* was just word he was looking for.
• In October, 1879 the first bar of Ivory Soap was sold.

That's huge: In the 4th century, the Romans had a stadium that held 380,000 spectators.

VELCRO (1957).

A young Swiss inventor named George De Mestral went for a hike one day in 1948. When he returned, he was annoyed to find burrs stuck to his clothes. But his annoyance turned to fascination. Why, he wondered, wouldn't it be possible to create synthetic burrs that could be used as fasteners?

• Most people scoffed at the idea; but a French weaver took him seriously. Using a small loom, the weaver hand-wove two cotton strips that stuck together when they touched. The secret: one strip had hooks, the other had loops.

• But De Mestral had to figure out how to mass-produce it...and he needed tougher material than cotton, which quickly wore out.

• Years passed; De Mestral experimented constantly. Finally he found a suitable material—nylon, which, it turned out, became very hard when treated with infrared light.

• Now he knew how to make the *loops* by machine—but he still couldn't figure out how to mass-produce the *hooks*.

• Finally a solution hit him. He bought a pair of barber's clippers and took them to a weaver. With the clippers, he demonstrated his idea—a loom that snipped loops as it wove them, creating little nylon hooks. He worked on the project for a year—and when it was finally completed, Velcro ("Vel" for velvet, "cro" for crochet) was born. The product had taken a decade to perfect.

THE ELECTRIC TOASTER (1919).

The first electric toasters, which appeared around 1900, were primitively constructed heating coils that were terrible fire hazards.

• However, they were a luxury—it was the first time in history that people didn't need to fire up a stove just to make a piece of toast.

• There was a built-in problem, though—the bread had to be constantly watched or it would burn to a crisp.

• In 1919, Charles Strite, a Minnesota factory worker, got sick of the burnt toast in the company cafeteria. So in his spare time, he designed and patented the first pop-up toaster. Then he went into business manufacturing them. It took years to work out the bugs, but by 1926, Strite's "Toastmasters" were relatively foolproof.

• A few years later, a New York businessman purchased Strite's company, and invested heavily in advertising—which proved to be the key ingredient in making the toaster a common household. appliance. Every home "had to have one"...and now they do.

That's a lotta nerve: You have 45 miles of nerves in your body.

ACCORDING TO JEFFERSON

Wisdom from Thomas Jefferson, one of our Founding Fathers.

"A little rebellion now and then is a good thing."

"The man who reads nothing at all is better educated than the man who reads nothing but newspapers."

"The tree of liberty must be refreshed for time to time with the blood of patriots and tyrants. It is its natural manure."

"I tremble for my country when I reflect that God is just."

"Never buy what you do not want, because it is cheap; it will be dear to you."

"Question with boldness even the very existence of a God; because, if there be one, he must more approve of the homage of reason than that of a blindfolded fear."

"Never spend money before you have it."

"The art of life is the avoiding of pain."

"The Earth belongs...to the living. The dead have neither rights nor powers over it."

"The tax which will be paid for education is not more than the thousandth part of what will be paid to kings, priests, and nobles who will rise up among us if we leave the people to ignorance."

"Resistance to tyrants is obedience to God."

"To the press alone, chequered as it is with abuses, the world is indebted for all the triumphs which have been gained by reason and humanity over error and oppresion."

"Do not bite at the bait of pleasure till you know there is no hook beneath it."

"The legitimate powers of government extend to such acts as are injurious to others. But it does me no injury for my neighbor to say there are twenty gods, or no God. It neither picks my pocket nor breaks my leg."

LIMERICKS

Limericks have been around since the 1700s. The authors of these silly ditties (except for the one by Edward Lear) are unknown.

There was a young fellow
named Clyde,
Who once at a funeral was
spied.
When asked who was dead,
He smilingly said,
"I don't know—I just came
for the ride."

There was a young man of
Calcutta
Who had a most terrible
stutta,
He said: "Pass the h. . .ham,
And the j . . .j . . .j . . .jam,
And the b.…b…b…b…b…
b…butta."

There was a young man from
Darjeeling,
Who got on a bus bound for
Ealing;
It said at the door:
"Don't spit on the floor,"
So he carefully spat on the
ceiling.

There was an old fellow named
Cager
Who, as the result of a wager,
Offered to fart
The whole oboe part
Of Mozart's *Quartet in F
Major*.

There was a young fellow of
Lyme
Who lived with three wives at
one time.
When asked: "Why the third?"
He replied: "One's absurd,
And bigamy, sir, is a crime."

There was a brave fellow
named Gere,
Who hadn't an atom of fear.
He indulged a desire
To touch a live wire,
And any last line will do
here.

An epicure, dining in Crewe,
Once found a large mouse in
his stew.
Said the waiter: "Don't shout,
Or wave it about,
Or the rest will be wanting
one, too."

A mouse in her room woke
Miss Dowd,
Who was frightened and
screamed very loud.
Then a happy thought hit
her—
To scare off the critter,
She sat up in bed and
meowed.

—Edward Lear

What color was Christopher Columbus's hair? Blonde.

INSIDE MOTHER GOOSE

We've sung and recited these rhymes since we were kids. Little did we know that they weren't just nonsense. Here's the inside scoop about what they really meant.

***Humpty Dumpty** sat on a wall, Humpty Dumpty had a great fall. All the King's horses and all the king's men, couldn't put Humpty together again.*

Background: According to Katherine Thomas in *The Real Personages of Mother Goose*, this rhyme is 500 years old and refers to King Richard III of England. In 1483 his reign ended when he fell from his mount during battle; he was slain as he stood shouting "My kingdom for a horse!"

• Richard's fall made him Humpty Dumpty. Originally the last line was "Could not set Humpty up again"—which can be interpreted as either putting him back on his horse, or back on the throne.

***Old King Cole** was a merry old soul, a merry old soul was he. He called for his pipe and he called for his bowl, and he called for his fiddlers three."*

Background: There was actually a King Cole in Britain during the third century. No one knows much about him, but historians agree that he's the subject of the poem. Of interest: There's a Roman amphitheater in Colchester, England which has been known as "King Cole's Kitchen" for centuries.

***Little Jack Horner** sat in a corner, eating his Christmas pie. He stuck in his thumb and he pulled out a plum, and said "What a good boy am I."*

Background: In the mid-1500s, when King Henry VIII was confiscating lands belonging to the Catholic church, the Abbot of Glastonbury—the richest abbey in the British kingdom—tried to bribe the monarch by sending him a special Christmas pie. Inside the pie, the abbot had enclosed the deeds to 12 manor houses.

The courier who delivered the pie to the king was the abbot's aide, Thomas Horner.(The name "Jack" was contemporary slang for any male, particularly a "knave"). On his way, Horner stopped, stuck in his hand, and pulled out one of the deeds from the pie—a plum called Mells Manor. Shortly after, Horner moved into Mells, and his family still lives there today (although they deny the story).

Ironically, the abbot was later put on trial for his life—and Horner was one of the judges who condemned him to death.

***Jack be nimble**, Jack be quick, Jack jump over the candlestick.*

Background: for centuries, jumping over a candlestick was a method of fortune-telling in England. According to *The Oxford Dictionary of Nursery Rhymes*: "A candlestick with a lighted candle was placed on the floor and if, when jumping over it, the light was nmot extinguished, good luck was supposed to follow during the coming year."

***Ring around the rosy**, a pocket full of posies.*
Ashes, ashes, we all fall down

Background: According to James Leasor in *The Plague and the Fire*, this "had its origin in the [London Plague of 1664]. Rosy refers to the rosy rash of plague....The posies were herbs and spices carried to ward off the disease; sneezing was a common symptom of those close to death. In the *Annotated Mother Goose*, the authors note that the third line is often given as a sneezing noise ("At-choo, at-choo"), and that " 'We all fall down' was, in a way, exactly what happened."

WHO WAS MOTHER GOOSE?

No one's quite sure. There are at least two possibilities, according to *The Annotated Mother Goose*:

• Charles Perrault, a French writer, "published a collection of fairy tales called *Tales of My Mother Goose* in 1697. The book contains eight stories: 'Little Red Riding Hood,' 'Bluebeard,' 'Puss In Boots,' " etc.

• But many scholars maintain that Mother Goose was actually one Elizabeth Foster Goose, of Boston, Mass. In 1692, when she was 27, Elizabeth married a widower named Isaac Goose and immediately inherited a family of 10 children. One of her step-daughters married a printer several years later and the printer enjoyed listening to "Mother Goose" recite old rhymes to the younger children. In 1719, he published a collection called *Songs for the Nursery, or Mother Goose's Melodies*.

In 1980, there was only one country in the world with no telephones—Bhutan.

BUT THEY'D NEVER BEEN THERE

Songs about places can be so convincing that it's hard to believe the people who wrote them haven't been there themselves. But that's often the case. Three prime examples:

TAKE ME HOME, COUNTRY ROADS; JOHN DENVER

John Denver sounds so sincere singing this song that it's hard to believe he wasn't born and raised in West Virginia. But he wasn't. Denver didn't even write it; two musicians named Bill Danoff and Taffy Nivert did.

And they didn't grow up in West Virginia either. In fact, they'd never even been there when the song was composed.

It was actually written while they were on their way to a Nivert family reunion in *Maryland*. As they drove through the countryside, along the winding, tree-lined roads, Bill passed the time by writing a little tune about their rural surroundings. Gradually, it became "Take Me Home, Country Roads."

How did West Virginia get into the song? A friend of Bill's kept sending him picture postcards from the Mountain State with notes like, "West Virginia's almost heaven." Bill was so impressed by the postcards that he incorporated them into the lyrics of the song.

John Denver discovered the tune in 1970, while he was performing at a Washington, D.C. folk club. Bill and Taffy were also performing there, and one evening they played Denver their half-finished "Country Roads." The three of them stayed up all night finishing it. Denver put it on his next RCA album; it made him a star, and made Bill and Taffy some hefty royalties. Presumably, they've been to West Virginia by now.

WOODSTOCK; CROSBY, STILLS, NASH, AND YOUNG

The most famous tribute to the most famous musical event in rock history was written by Joni Mitchell. Millions of young Americans have listened to the hit versions by Crosby, Stills, Nash, and Young and by Matthews' Southern Comfort (as well as an album cut featuring Joni herself) and imagined enviously what it was like to be at Woodstock.

But what they don't know is that Joni *wasn't at the festival.* She was watching it on TV, like most of America.

She'd been traveling with Crosby, Stills and Nash (who played one of their first gigs ever at the mammoth rock concert), and they were all staying in New York City before heading up to the festival. But Mitchell's managers, David Geffen and Elliot Roberts, decided she wouldn't be able to make her scheduled appearance on "The Dick Cavett Show" if she went to Woodstock—so they cancelled her appearance there; Joni was left behind in New York.

Mitchell says: "The deprivation of not being able to go provided me with an intense angle on Woodstock. I was one of the fans."

But in the song, she sounds like one of the eyewitnesses.

PROUD MARY;
CREEDENCE CLEARWATER REVIVAL

This million-selling single about an old Mississippi paddlewheeler established Creedence Clearwater Revival as America's chief exponent of "swamp rock."

They were quickly recognized as the most promising artists to emerge from New Orleans since Fats Domino.

There was only one catch: Creedence Clearwater Revival wasn't from New Orleans. They were from El Cerrito, California. And they had never even been to New Orleans. In fact, the farthest east that songwriter John Fogarty had ever gotten was to Montana. And the closest thing to a bayou that he'd ever seen was the swampland around Winters, California.

Actually, Proud Mary wasn't originally going to be a Mississippi riverboat at all. Fogarty initially envisioned her as a "washer woman." But the first few chords he played with reminded him of a paddle-wheel going around. That brought him to thoughts of the Mississippi River, and Mary became a boat.

How did Fogarty manage to pull it off so well? The best explanation he could come up with for his "authentic" sound was that he'd listened to a lot of New Orleans music (like Fats Domino) when he was young.

IRRELEVANT NOTE: Not even one of the 13 actors who played Charlie Chan in movies, radio, Broadway, or TV were Chinese or of Chinese ancestry.

The most extras ever used in a movie was 300,000, for the film *Gandhi* in 1981.

PRIME-TIME PROVERBS

TV's comments about everyday life in America
From Prime Time Proverbs, *by Jack Mingo and John Javna.*

ON AGING
Dorothy: "Age is just a state of mind."
Blanche: "Tell that to my thighs."

—*The Golden Girls*

Fred Sanford: "I still want to sow some wild oats!"
Lamont Sanford: "At your age, you don't have no wild oats—you got shredded wheat!"

—*Sanford and Son*

ON RELATIONSHIPS
"You can make a man eat shredded cardboard. . . . If you know the right tricks."

—Jeannie's sister,
I Dream of Jeannie

Sam Malone: "You've made my life a living hell."
Diane Chambers: "I didn't want you to think I was easy."

—*Cheers*

ON HUMAN NATURE
"I'm only human, Meathead... and to be human is to be violent."

—Archie Bunker,
All in the Family

"Everyone's a character—some of us just haven't met the right writer yet."

—Dash Goff,
Designing Women

"I think man is the most interesting insect, don't you?"

—Marvin Martian,
The Bugs Bunny Show

ON ANATOMY
Cosmetic Clerk: "You know what the fastest way to a man's heart is?"
Roseanne: "Yeah. Through his chest!"

—*Roseanne*

ON MARRIAGE
"Just because we're married to men doesn't mean we've got anything in common with them."

—Ethel Mertz,
I Love Lucy

"Why can't they invent something for us to marry instead of women?"

—Fred Flintstone,
The Flintstones

All wet: The average 150-lb. man should consume 2.9 quarts of water (in any form) each day.

MARK TWAIN & POLITICS

In 1912, Mark Twain declared he was running for the presidency. Here's what he told the press:

On His Reasons for Running: "A patriotic American must do something around election time, and...I see nothing else to do but become a candidate for President. Even the best among us will do the most repulsive things when smitten with a Presidential madness."

On His Position: "I am in favor of anything and everything anybody is in favor of."

On His Character: "The rumor that I buried a dead aunt under my grapevine was correct. The vine needed fertilizing; my aunt had to be buried, and I dedicated her to this high purpose. Does that unfit me for the Presidency? The Constitution of this country does not say so. No other citizen was ever considered unworthy of this office because he enriched his grapevine with his dead relatives. Why should I be selected as the first victim of an absurd prejudice?"

On Corruption: "We have humble God-fearing Christian men among us who will stoop to do things for a million dollars that they ought not to be willing to do for less than two million."

On the Arms Race: "The idea is that these formidable new war-inventions will make war impossible by and by—but I doubt it."

On Women's Rights: "Their wonderful campaign lasted a great many years, and is the most wonderful in history, for it achieved a revolution—the only one achieved in history for the emancipation of half a nation that cost not a drop of blood."

On Civil Rights: "It is a worthy thing to fight for one's freedom; it is another sight finer to fight for another man's."

On Liberty: "I believe we ought to retain all our liberties. We can't afford to throw them away. They didn't come to us in a night. The trouble with us in America is that we haven't learned to speak the truth. We have thrown away the most valuable asset we have—the individual right to oppose both flag and country when by one's self we believe them to be in the wrong."

GET SMART

The most popular satire in the history of TV was this spy takeoff starring Don Adams and Barbara Feldon.

HOW IT STARTED.

The spy craze began quietly in 1963 with the release of the first James Bond film, *Dr. No.* By the end of 1964, there were 2 more Bond epics and a hit TV spinoff ("The Man from UNCLE"). Spies were everywhere, and Dan Melnick, a packager at Talent Associates, decided to parody them on TV. He picked comedy writers Mel Brooks (still years away from his first film) and Buck Henry to create the satire. "No one had ever done a show about an idiot before," Brooks said in 1965. "I decided to be the first."

The appropriate name for a sitcom idiot, they figured, was Smart. And since every secret agent needed a number, they gave theirs 86—the code bartenders use to cut off service to a drunk ("86 that guy"). Smart also needed a beautiful companion, so they created a slightly daffy Mata Hari named "99" (instead of "69") to costar.

"We had no special comedian in mind for Smart," Henry said at the time. "We wrote dialogue suitable for any standup comedian. But we had our eyes on a definite Mata Hari—Barbara Feldon."

ABC loved the idea and commissioned a pilot script. But when they read what Brooks and Henry had written, they backed out of the deal. The story had the evil KAOS threatening to blow up the Statue of Liberty, which ABC called "dirty and un-American." Instead, the show was sold to NBC.

"Get Smart" became the highest-rated new show of the 1965–66 season, and the episode ABC rejected was nominated for an Emmy.

SIC 'EM

Barbara Feldon was the first of many models who became famous by starring in TV ads. Her big break: A commercial for a men's hair product called Top Brass. She stretched out on a rug and purred, "Sic 'em, tiger." That got her so much attention that she was offered TV guest roles as an actress. A spot as an industrial spy on a show called "East Side, West Side" earned her the role of 99.

No wonder they're confused: There are 68,000 miles of telephone lines in the Pentagon.

WOULD YOU BELIEVE...

Don Adams and comedian Bill "Jose Jimenez" Dana were old friends. So when Dana got his own sitcom in 1963 ("The Bill Dana Show"), he included Adams in the cast, playing a dumb house detective named Byron Glick—essentially the same role he played as Maxwell Smart. Dana's show was cancelled in 1965, leaving Adams free to take the starring role in "Get Smart" the same year.

THE VOICE

In the '50s, Adams' stand-up comedy routine included impersonations of famous personalities, including actor William Powell. For Max's voice, he just did his Powell imitation in a higher pitch.

THE OLD ONE-LINER TRICK

Max was famous for one-liners like "Sorry about that, Chief," and "Would you believe..." They became fads, with kids adopting them as hip slang. But it wasn't an accident. From the outset, Don Adams anticipated it and insisted the show's writers build them into the stories. Most of them were already part of Adams' comedy routine. He brought "Would you believe..." from "The Bill Dana Show" and borrowed "Sorry about that" from Ernie Kovacs' protege, Joe Mikalos. As the old lines got stale, writers began adding new ones, like "The old _____ trick."

THE BURGER KING

Here's a whopper. Which cast member had the most successful post-"Get Smart" acting career? King Moody, who played the semi-regular villain, Starker. He became Ronald McDonald on McDonald's TV commercials.

TRUE CONFESSIONS

Don Adams on the quality of the show: "At first, I wanted every show to be a classic. [But] I then came to the realization that when you do a show every week, you can't be a classic. If you can do 3 out of 5 which are good, you should be happy with that."

NAME GAME

According to Buck Henry, Agent 99's real name was never revealed. In one episode, she was introduced as "Susan Hilton." But in the end, she explained to Max that it was just a cover name.

Room to breathe: In 1610, the population of the American colonies was 350 people.

MORE EPITAPHS

More unusual epitaphs and tombstone rhymes from our wandering B.R.I. tombstone-ologists.

Seen in Enosburg, Vermont:
In memory of Anna
Here lies the body of our
Anna,
Done to death by a banana.
It wasn't the fruit that laid her
low,
But the skin of the thing that
made her go.

Seen in Burlington, Mass.:
Anthony Drake
Sacred to the memory of
Anthonly Drake,
Who died for peace and
quietness sake.
His wife was constantly
scoldin' and scoffin',
So he sought for repose in a
$12 coffin.

Seen in Winslow, Maine:
Beza Wood, 1792-1837
Here lies one Wood
enclosed in wood,
One within the other.
The outer wood is very good.
We cannot praise the other.

Seen in Boot Hill Cemetery, Dodge City, Kansas:
He played five Aces.
Now he's playing the harp.

Seen in the English countryside:
Mary Ford, 1790
Here lieth Mary—the wife of
John Ford.
We hope her soul is gone to
the Lord.
But if for Hell she has changed
this life,
She would rather be there
than be John Ford's wife.

Seen in Canaan, N.H.:
Sarah Shute, 1803-1840
Here lies, cut down like unripe
fruit,
The wife of Deacon Amos
Shute.
She died of drinking too much
coffee,
Anno Domini eighteen forty.

Seen in Burlington, N.J:
Mary Ann Lowder, 1798
Here lies the body of Mary
Ann Lowder,
Who burst while drinking a
Seidlitz powder.
Called from this world to her
Heavenly Rest
She should have waited till it
effervesced.

If a Turkish person is wearing violet, he or she might be in mourning.

THE ORIGIN OF LEVI'S

Blue jeans are as American as apple pie and bathroom reading. In fact, you might have a pair around your ankles right now.

CANVASING THE CUSTOMERS

In 1850—during the California gold rush—a 17-year-old named Levi Strauss moved from New York City to San Francisco to sell dry goods to the miners. • He tried to sell canvas to them for their tents, but found little interest in it. So he made pants out of the material instead.

• The miners loved them. Although the pants weren't particularly comfortable, they were the first pants durable enough to withstand the miners' rugged living conditions.

• People nicknamed the pants Levi's, after their creator.

A RIVETING EXPERIENCE

Some years later, Levi Strauss began using denim in his pants. It was still tough, but it was softer and more comfortable than canvas.

• He also found that when the denim pants were dyed blue, they wouldn't show soil and stains as much. Miners appreciated this, and Levi's became even more popular.

• Meanwhile, miners found that after heavy use, the pockets often ripped the pants at the seams.

• A Nevada tailor named Jacob Davis solved that problem for his customers by securing each pocket seam with a rivet. It worked so well, in fact, that Davis wrote to Levi Strauss offering to sell him the idea. Strauss took him up on it; copper rivets first appeared on Levis in 1873. They became a hallmark of the company's product.

LEVI'S' MIDDLE-AGE SPREAD

Levi's were working people's pants for their first 75 years. Then, in the '30s, an advertisement for jeans ran in *Vogue* magazine. The reaction was so great that jeans became the rage. Jitterbugging teenagers started wearing them with the cuffs rolled up, and they've been fashionable ever since.

• Meanwhile, the Levi Strauss Company branched out into manufacturing other items as well as blue jeans...and by 1970 it had become the largest clothing manufacturer in the world.

Breathe deep: Your right lung takes in more air than your left one does.

MYTH AMERICA

Here's a myth in reverse—a tale most people believe is fictional, but is actually true.

THE MYTH: Uncle Sam is a fictional character, created by cartoonists as a symbol of America's government and our "national character."

BACKGROUND: Ironically, while Americans routinely believe historical tales which are completely false, we're skeptical of some that are actually true. This is a case in point. For years, it was assumed there was no real Uncle Sam. Then, in 1961, a historian stumbled on proof that "Uncle Sam" had actually existed.

THE TRUTH: There's a detailed account of the Uncle Sam story in Charles Panati's book *Extraordinary Origins of Everyday Things*: Here are some excerpts:.

BACKGROUND

• "Uncle Sam was Samuel Wilson. He was born in Arlington, Massachusetts, on September 13, 1766....At age 14, [he] joined the army and fought in the American Revolution."

• "With independence from Britain won, Sam moved in 1789 to Troy, New York, and opened a meat-packing company. Because of his jovial manner and fair business practices, he was affectionately known to townsfolk as Uncle Sam."

OUR "UNCLE SAM" IS BORN

• "During the War of 1812, government troops were quartered near Troy. Sam Wilson's fair-dealing reputation won him a military contract to provide beef and pork to soldiers. To indicate that certain crates of meat produced at his warehouse were destined for military use, Sam stamped them with a large 'U.S.'—for 'United States,' though the abbreviation was not yet in the vernacular."

•"On October 1, 1812, government inspectors made a routine tour of the plant. They asked a meat packer what the ubiquitously stamped 'U.S.' stood for. The worker, himself uncertain, joked that the letters must represent the initials of his employer, Uncle Sam."

• "The error was perpetuated. Soon soldiers began referring to all military rations as bounty from Uncle Sam. Before long, they were calling all government-issued supplies property of Uncle Sam. They even saw themselves as Uncle Sam's men."

UNCLES SAM'S WARDROBE

"The...familiar and colorful image of Uncle Sam we know today arose piecemeal, almost one item at a time, each the contribution of an illustrator."

• "The first Uncle Sam illustrations appeared in New England newspapers in 1820."

• "Solid red pants were introduced during...Jackson's presidency."

• "The...beard first appeared during Abraham Lincoln's term, inspired by the President's own beard, which set a trend at the time."

• "By the late nineteenth century, Uncle Sam was such a popular national figure that cartoonists decided he should appear more patriotically attired. They adorned his red pants with white stripes and his top hat with both stars and stripes. His costume became an embodiment of the country's flag."

• "It was Thomas Nast, the famous...cartoonist of the Civil War and Reconstruction period, who made Uncle Sam tall, thin, and hollowcheeked. Coincidentally, Nast's Uncle Sam strongly resembles drawings of the real-life Sam Wilson. But Nast's model was actually Abraham Lincoln."

•"The most famous portrayal of Uncle Sam—the one most frequently reproduced and widely recognized—was painted in this century by American artist James Montgomery Flagg. The stern-faced, stiff-armed, finger-pointing figure appeared on World War I posters captioned: 'I Want You for U.S. Army.'...Flagg's Uncle Sam, though, is not an Abe Lincoln likeness, but a self-portrait."

A MYTH UNCOVERED

• "During these years ...the character of Uncle Sam was still only a myth. The identity of his prototype first came to light in early 1961. A historian, Thomas Gerson, discovered a May 12, 1830, issue of the *New York Gazette* newspaper in the archives of the New York Historical Society. In it, a detailed firsthand account explained how Pheodorus Bailey, postmaster of New York City, had witnessed the Uncle Sam legend take root in Troy, New York."

• Sam was officially acknowledged during JFK's administration, "by an act of the 87th Congress, which states that 'the Congress salutes 'Uncle Sam' Wilson of Troy, New York, as the progenitor of America's National symbol.' "

THE BIRTH OF G.I. JOE

G.I. Joe, the first successful doll for boys, seems to be going as strong today as he was the year he was introduced.

HIS BIRTH. By 1963 Mattel's Barbie doll was so popular that Don Levine, creative director of the Hasbro Toy Co., suggested manufacturing a boys' version. "But instead of fashion," he explained, "we'll make it a soldier, and we'll sell extra uniforms and weapons."

• But would boys buy dolls? Hedging its bets, Hasbro decided never to call it a "doll"—only an "action soldier." And they decided to give it a scarred face to make it seem more masculine.

HIS NAME. Hasbro planned to make different sets of uniforms for each branch of the service (Army, Navy, Air Force, Marines) and give each a different name—Salty the Sailor, Rocky the Marine, etc. But the marketing department insisted on one name. One night, Levine happened to see the 1945 film *The Story of G.I. Joe* on television, and realized that "G.I. Joe" was perfect.

HIS BODY. Unlike Barbie, the boy's doll had to be fully movable. But Hasbro wasn't sure if it could be done. One day Levine was walking past an art-supply store when he noticed a display of small wooden, jointed models that artists use to draw different body positions. He bought a dozen, and they copied the construction.

HIS LIFE.

1964: Joe is introduced to the toy industry; toy store owners avoid him, sure that American parents won't buy their sons dolls. But Hasbro sticks with it, and in the first year over $30 million worth of G.I. Joe and accessories are sold—including 2 million dolls.

1968: With the increasing unpopularity of the war in Vietnam, parents begin to reject war toys. Joe's sales plummet to less than a third of their previous level. He's almost wiped out, but Hasbro saves the day by changing him from a soldier to an adventurer.

1978: *Star Wars* action figures are hot, and no one wants a G.I. Joe anymore. He's dead meat. Hasbro drops him from their line.

1982: Joe returns. Raised from the dead with his "G.I. Joe Team," he storms the toy market and becomes the #1 seller again. From 1982-88, he racks up over $600 million in sales. Go Joe!

It must be love: women's hearts beat faster than men's.

POLITICAL DOUBLE-T

Every year, the Committee on Public Doublespeak of National Council of Teachers of English "honors" public figures (or organizations) who "use language that is grossly deceptive, evasive, confusing, and self-contradictory." Here are some examples, taken from their annual news releases.

In 1980:
• President Jimmy Carter declared that the failed effort to rescue American hostages in Iran was an "incomplete success."

In 1981:
• The Department of Agriculture decided that ketchup was a vegetable and could "be counted as one of the two vegetables required as part of the school lunch program."

In 1982:
• The Environmental Protection Agency prohibited its employees from using the term "acid rain." Instead, they were told to use the term "poorly buffered precipitation."
• Lewis Thurston, chief of staff for New Jersey's governor, Thomas Kean, insisted that "staff members do not have chauffeurs." Rather, they have "aides who drive."
• When it was pointed out that a commercial sponsored by the Republican National Committee misrepresented the facts, a Republican official declared: "Since when is a commercial supposed to be accurate?"

In 1984:
• When American troops in Lebanon were evacuated to ships offshore, Secretary of Defense Caspar Weinberger claimed this did not constitute a withdrawal. "We are not leaving Lebanon," he said. "The Marines are merely being deployed two or three miles to the west."
• Investigating an accident, the National Transportation Safety Board called an airplane crash "controlled flight into terrain."
• The Pentagon called peace "permanent pre-hostility."
• The CIA called mercenary soldiers hired to fight in Nicaragua "unilaterally controlled Latino assets."

Hard to Believe: Chemically speaking, your blood is very close to sea water.

In 1986:

•NASA referred to the *Challenger* astronauts' bodies as "recovered components," and their coffins as "crew transfer containers."

• Disregarding Due Process of Law, Attorney General Edwin Meese suggested that if a person is arrested, he's almost certainly guilty. "If a person is innocent of a crime," he explained, "he is not a suspect." Then he insisted to a reporter that "I...consider myself in the forefront of the civil rights movement in the country today."

• The Defense Department defined a hammer as a "manually powered fastener-driving impact device," a flashlight as an "Emergency Exit Light," and a tent as a "frame-supported tension structure."

• When a missile flew out of control and crashed, the Defense Dept. said it had merely "impacted with the ground prematurely."

In 1987

• Oliver North said he wasn't lying about his actions in Iran-Contra—he was "cleaning up the historical record," and creating "a different version from the facts." In discussing a false chronology of events which he helped to construct, North said he "was provided with additional input that was radically different from the truth," adding: "I assisted in furthering that version."

• The U.S. Army called killing "servicing the target."

• The U.S. Navy called a limited armed conflict "violent peace."

• South Africa's Deputy Minister for Information set the record straight, commenting that "We do not have censorship. What we have is a limitation of what newspapers can report."

In 1988:

• Senator Orrin Hatch of Utah explained that "Capital punishment is our society's recognition of the sanctity of human life."

• The Chrysler Corporation, on laying off 5,000 workers, said it had simply "initiated a career alternative enhancement program."

• In a report, the U.S. Department of Agriculture called cows, pigs, and chickens "grain-consuming animal units."

• General Motors announced, as it closed an entire plant, that it was making a "volume-related production schedule adjustment."

• The Massachusetts Department of Public Works called road signs "ground-mounted confirmatory route markers."

Dieter's secret: If you eat 11 pounds of potatoes, you only gain one pound of weight.

BATHROOM ECOLOGY

We all know and love the bathroom—but we still have a lot to learn about it. Believe it or not, the way we use it can affect the world around us in significant ways. Here's some valuable information from the great new book, 50 Simple Things You Can Do to Save the Earth, *by the Earthworks Group.*

THE TOILET

• Each time your toilet is flushed, it uses 5 to 7 gallons of water—in fact, 40% of the pure water you use in your house is flushed down the toilet.

Bathroom Ecology: You can save 1-2 gallons with each flush if you put something in the tank that reduces the amount of water the tank will hold. This is called a "displacement device."

• Don't use a brick. Small pieces can break off and damage your plumbing system.

• Small juice bottles, dishwashing soap bottles, or laundry soap bottles work well. Soak off the label, fill the bottle with water, put on the cap, and put it in the tank.

• Be careful that the bottle doesn't interfere with the flushing mechanism.

• You may need to experiment with bottle sizes—different toilets need different amounts of water to flush effectively. Option: put a few stones in the bottom of the bottle to weight it down.

Savings: 1-2 gallons per flush.

Results: If the average toilet is flushed about 8 times a day, that means a savings of 8-16 gallons every day, 56-112 gallons a week, 2900-5800 gallons a year. If only 10,000 people were to put a bottle in the tank, that would equal a savings of 29 to 58 million gallons a year! And if 100,000 people did it...well, use your own imagination.

THE SINK

• A running faucet puts 3-5 gallons of water down the drain every minute.

• You use 10-15 gallons of water if you leave the tap running while you brush your teeth.

• If you shave with the water on, you use 10-20 gallons each time.

Bathroom Ecology: If you just wet and rinse your brush when you brush your teeth, you use only 1/2 gallon of water. *Savings*: Up to 9 gallons each time you brush.

• If you fill the basin when you shave, you use only 1 gallon of water. *Savings*: Up to 14 gallons each time you shave.

• Install a Low-Flow Faucet Aerator. It's a simple device that screws onto the end of your faucet and cuts the flow *in half*. But don't worry—since it mixes air in with the water, the water comes out just as fast as before.

• Low-flow faucet aerators sell for less than $4 at hardware and plumbing stores everywhere.

THE SHOWER & BATH

• Showers account for a whopping 32% of home water use.

• A standard shower head has a flow rate of 5 to 10 gallons of water per minute. So a 5-minute shower uses around 25 gallons.

Bathroom Ecology: First of all, take showers instead of baths. Depending on the size of the tub, a bath will generally use around 50 gallons of water…or more—which is about double the water use of a shower.

• Try installing a "low-flow shower head." It can reduce your overall water use by 50% or more.

• With a low-flow shower head, a family of four accustomed to 5-minute showers will save nearly 22,000 gallons of water per year.

• For a family of four, the $ savings from a low-flow shower head can amount to $100 a year in water saved, plus $150 a year in energy costs-—for all that hot water you don't have to heat.

• So the cost of a low-flow shower head—generally, less than $15 at any plumbing supply or hardware store—can be recouped in a month.

AEROSOL CANS

• At one time, aerosol cans routinely used gases called CFCs as propellants. But it was discovered that CFCs were harmful to the Earth's ozone layer, and CFCs were banned. End of problem? No. Their replacements—gases like butane and propane—are also harmful to the environment. They mix with sunlight to create smog…which contributes to the acid rain problem.

Bathroom Ecology: Use non-aerosols whenever possible.

Around the world, more people eat herring than any other fish.

MODERN MYTHOLOGY

These characters are as famous in our culture as Pegasus or Hercules were in Greek myths. Where did they come from?

THE PLAYBOY BUNNY. When Hugh Hefner was a little boy, one of his prized possessions was "a blanket with bunnies all over it." Apparently, he never outgrew it—when he started *Playboy* magazine, he used the same bunny as his symbol.

THE JOLLY GREEN GIANT. In the early 1920s, the Minnesota Valley Canning Company introduced a new, large variety of peas to the American market. They called the peas "green giants," and because the law required it to protect their trademark, they put a picture of a Green Giant on the label. Where did they get the original art? They lifted it from *Grimm's Fairy Tales*. Oddly enough, the original giant was white, not green; he looked like a dwarf, not a giant; and he wasn't jolly—he was scowling. His image eventually softened, and he became such a powerful symbol that the company changed its name to the Green Giant Co.

BETTY CROCKER. The Washburn Crosby Company, a Minneapolis flour maker, got so many letters asking for baking advice that in 1921, they made up a character to write back to consumers. They picked the name "Betty" because it sounded "warm and friendly," and "Crocker" was picked to honor a former company director. To come up with a signature for Betty (so she could sign "her" letters), the company held a contest for its women employees. The winner—which is still used today—was submitted by a secretary.

THE QUAKER OATS MAN. In 1891, seven oatmeal millers combined to form the American Cereal Company. One of the seven was Quaker Mill of Ravenna, Ohio, which had trademarked the Quaker man 14 years earlier. So when the American Cereal Company changed its name to Quaker Oats in 1901, the Quaker man was revived as its symbol. The real Quakers weren't too happy about this, by the way. They tried to get Congress to prohibit manufacturers from using religions' names on their products.

The average American eats 10 lbs. of chocolate a year.

FAST FOOD FACTS

Fascinating factoids about fast food.

There are more than 55,000 fast food restaurants in the U.S.

When Colonel Sanders started selling chicken in the late '50s, he was 65 years old. His only goal was to make $1,000 a month.

Two-thirds of the eateries in the U.S. serve fast food. And two-thirds of the people who go out to eat get their meals at fast food restaurants.

Fast food fries are usually sprayed with sugar, which gives them their brown coloring when cooked.

Domino's offers 10 different toppings for its pizza. That means you can get 3.9 million different combinations of pizzas there.

Pepsico, Pepsi's parent company, is one of the world's largest fast food restaurateurs. Among its holdings: Kentucky Fried Chicken, Taco Bell, and Pizza Hut. All serve Pepsi, of course. Pepsico also owns Frito-Lay.

Every day, approximately 46 million Americans eat at fast food restaurants.

Colonel Sanders wasn't particularly fond of Kentucky Fried Chicken after he sold it. He called the "extra-crispy" chicken "a damn fried doughball stuck on some chicken," and he said the KFC gravy was "pure wallpaper paste."

Wendy's was named after the daughter of the company's founder, Dave Thomas.

Thomas claims his square burgers are designed for grill efficiency. Others say it's "a marketing ploy." The four corners hang out over the edge of the bun, making the burger look bigger.

Regional fast food numbers:
#1. The Midwest; 30.5% of the population eats fast food at least once a week.
#2. The South; 30.4%.
#3. The West Coast; 23%.
#4. The East Coast; 16.5%.

There are 525 McDonald's eateries in Japan.

THOREAU'S THOUGHTS

Thoughts from Henry Thoreau, the outspoken American iconoclast of the 19th century.

"Distrust any enterprise that requires new clothes."

"It is a characteristic of wisdom not to do desperate things."

"If Christ should appear on Earth, he would be denounced as a mistaken, misguided man, insane and crazed."

"It takes two to speak the truth—one to speak, and one to listen."

"Simplify, simplify."

"The mass of men lead lives of quiet desperation."

"What men call social virtues, good fellowship, is commonly but the virtue of pigs in a litter, which lie close together to keep each other warm."

"Blessed are they who never read a newspaper, for they shall see Nature, and through her, God."

"It is only when we forget all our learning that we begin to know."

"Do not be too moral. You may cheat yourself out of much life."

"Aim above morality. Be not simply good, be good for something."

"You cannot kill time without injuring eternity."

"The highest condition of art is artlessness."

"What man believes, God believes."

"A man is rich in proportion of the number of things he can afford to let alone."

"Business! I think there is nothing—not even crime—more opposed to poetry, to philosophy, to life itself, than this incessant business."

"There are a thousand hacking at the branches of evil to one who is striking at the root."

"Not until we are lost—in other words, not until we have lost the world—do we begin to find ourselves."

Dairy delight: The average American eats 26 lbs. of cheese every year.

THE TRUTH ABOUT SPIRO T. AGNEW

You'd think that if a Vice President of the U. S. was accused of taking bribes—and had to resign because of it—we'd all remember the incident in detail. That's not the case with Spiro Agnew; his resignation in 1973 was quickly overshadowed by Watergate. But hey—let's not forget the guy. He's part of American history.

AGNEW'S CAREER

• In 1962, he ran for Baltimore County Executive. He was elected, and served until 1966.

• In 1966, he ran for governor of Maryland as a Republican. As it happened, the Democrats nominated a reactionary who stood no chance of being elected. Agnew won.

• In 1968, ghetto riots hit Baltimore. "Agnew met with the leaders of the state's black moderates," reported *Time* magazine, "and before the TV cameras, dressed them down for not controlling the rioters. The incident established Agnew as a hard-liner on race and caught the eye of Richard Nixon."

The result: Nixon picked him as his running mate.

• In 1969, Agnew emerged, said *U.S. News & World Report*, as "one of the most controversial Vice Presidents the United States has seen in many a day." He was a strident moralist and a "law and order" man whose trademark was violent verbal attacks. His speeches were peppered with phrases like "parasites of passion," and "nattering nabobs of negativism."

• He was reelected with Nixon in 1972, and looked like the heir apparent to the Presidency. Then it all collapsed. In 1973, the *Wall Street Journal* learned that Agnew was under investigation in Maryland for having taken kickbacks from building contractors while he was both county executive and governor.

• On Oct. 10, 1973, after months of negotiating, Agnew resigned. He appeared in court and pled "No Contest" to income tax evasion—which the judge pointed out was equivalent to a guilty plea. It was part of an extensive plea-bargaining process that enabled him to avoid jail. The Government insisted, however, that they be allowed to make their case aginst him public.

In 1976, the theme song from the TV show "Happy Days" hit #5 on the *Billboard* charts.

THE GOVERNMENT'S EVIDENCE

One of several contractors who admitted paying bribes to Agnew was named Lester Matz. Here's a part of the government's report on one of the incidents he recaled. It took place in 1969, a few months after Agnew had become V.P.:

"Matz called the Vice President's office in Washington and set up an appointment to meet with Mr. Agnew. On a piece of yellow legal-sized paper, Matz calculated the sum then 'owed' to Mr. Agnew for work received by Matz's company from the State of Maryland. He met with Mr. Agnew, showed him the calculations, and briefly reviewed them for him. He then handed him an enveloped containing approximately $10,000 in cash....Mr. Agnew placed this envelope in his desk drawer.

"Matz also told the Vice President that the company might 'owe' him more money in the future....They agreed that Matz was to call Mr. Agnew's secretary when he was ready to make the next payment and to tell her that he had more 'information' for Mr. Agnew. This was to be a signal to Mr. Agnew that Mr. Matz had more money for him.

"After this meeting, Matz returned to Baltimore and told [an associate] of the payment. He also told [him] that he was shaken by his own actions, because he had just made a payoff to the Vice President of the United States."

AGNEW'S STATEMENT IN COURT

In a cleverly worded statement, Agnew made it seem as though he was denying the charges against him.

For example: The government said he took kickbacks. As Agnew explained it: "I admit that I did receive payments during the year 1967 which were not expended for political purposes, and...that contracts were awarded by State agencies in 1967 and other years to those who made such payments, and that I was aware of such awards....I stress, however, that no contracts were awarded to contractors who were not competent to perform the work, and in most instances State contracts were awarded without...payment of money by the contractor."

Careful reading of the text, however, shows that he was really saying something like: "Sure I took money, but not all the time, and only from good contractors."

According to *Billboard*: Elvis was the #1 artist of the '50s, #2 in the '60s, & #13 in the '70s.

ELEMENTARY, MY DEAR STEVE

Can you match wits with the world-famous sleuth, Leslie Boies? Here are more mysteries for you to solve. Answers are on p. 454.

It was a dark, rainy night. Leslie Boies, the celebrated solver-of-mysteries, was driving north from Thomasville on a narrow country road in her 1957 DeSoto coupe. Her faithful companion, Steve, was at the wheel. It was a critical situation—they had to reach the little town of Montez before sunrise if they were going to save Raymond Redel, the famous chair designer, from his nefarious son-in-law.

Suddenly they came to a crossroads...and they discovered that the signpost had been knocked down. Steve hopped out to take a look. One of the arrows on the sign said "Montez, 23 miles"...But there was no way to tell which road it had been pointing to.

"We're lost, Leslie," Steve exclaimed forlornly.

"I declare, Steve, sometimes you are so dense," Leslie sighed. Then she informed Steve how to tell which road was the right one.

How did Leslie know which way to go?

2. Steve was lounging around the apartment, reading the paper. "Hey, Les," he called, "There's a town I was reading about where nobody ever shaves himself—they all let the barber do it."

Leslie walked in, practicing yo-yo tricks she planned to perform in the upcoming Detective's Follies. "Well, Steve, if that's true, then who shaves the barber?"

Steve looked puzzled. "Maybe there are two barbers in town."

Leslie shook her head. "No, my uncle lives there and I know there's only one."

Steve shrugged. "I give up."

Who does shave the barber?

3. Steve came home one day and found Leslie hard at work on a new murder case.

"Sorry to bother you, Honey, but I'm a little perplexed about

The Ancient Egyptians had bowling alleys similar to ours.

NICKNAMES

What would you call celebrities if you knew them personally? According to Carl Sifakis in The Dictionary of Historic Nicknames, *you might know them by names like these:*

Johann Sebastian Bach. In his lifetime, the great composer's music was considered so boring and out of date that even his own family called him "The Old Wig."

Humphrey Bogart. If you were a Hollywood acquaintance, you night have known him as "Whiskey Straight."

Claudette Colbert. The Oscar-winning actress worried so much about the way she looked during filming that her cameramen dubbed her "The Fretting Frog."

Christopher Columbus. Historians call him a great explorer, but his own crew wasn't so kind. When his quest for riches led them to insect-infested tropical islands instead of gold and silver, they christened him "The Admiral of the Mosquitoes."

Davy Crockett. No one who knew Davy believed a word of his outrageous stories about his exploits in the wild. Acquaintances called him "The Munchausen of the West"—a name inspired by Baron von Munchausen, the popular fictional character of the late 1700s, whose trademark was absurdly exaggerated claims about his own life.

Wyatt Earp and Bat Masterson. The heroes of Western legends and prime-time TV shows were apparently as interested in other pursuits as they were in law and order. On various occasions they owned saloons, gambling establishments, and even a brothel or two. In their home, Dodge City, Kansas, they were known as "The Fighting Pimps."

Dwight David Eisenhower. In his hometown of Abilene, Kansas, the other kids knew him as "Ugly Ike."

U.S. families fight more about money than anything else. 2nd place: kids; 3rd place: chores.

Billy Graham. In his early days, the famous crusading evangelist was known as "The Preaching Windmill" because of "his exuberant arm flailing."

Sam Houston. The most celebrated hero in Texas' fight for independence from Mexico during the 1830s is known today as "The Father of Texas." But Indians who knew him called him "Big Drunk."

Robert F. Kennedy. America remembers him as RFK, or Bobby. Lyndon Johnson always called him "The Little Shit."

Spiro T. Agnew. Nixon's vice president was known by adversaries as "Spiro T. Eggplant."

Abraham Lincoln. "Honest Abe's" nickname didn't come from politics—it came from his youthful efforts as "a judge and referee at cockfights."

Richard Nixon. Nicknames haven't been kind to the ex-prez. When he was in college, he was so humorless that classmates called him "Gloomy Gus." And he spent so much time studying that he was dubbed "Iron Butt." When he ran for Congress in 1950, he earned the title "Tricky Dick."

Leo Tolstoy. The author of *War and Peace* is considered one of the greatest novelists in history. But people who knew him as a child—even his own family and close friends—called the troubled youth "Crybaby Leo."

Henri de Toulouse-Lautrec. The famous French painter suffered through childhood accidents that gave him the appearance of a dwarf—but not in every way. When he lived in a brothel, the prostitutes, amused by the contrast in size between "his large male member" and the rest of his body, dubbed him "the Teapot."

Warren G. Harding. Probably should have been called "The Rodney Dangerfield of Politics," but in 1920 when he was elected president, Rodney wasn't around yet. Instead, he was called "Everybody's Second Choice," because he was nominated as a compromise candidate in a "smoke-filled room."

Last roundup: In 1962 "Chief," the last U.S. Cavalry horse, was retired.

MT. RUSHMORE

Here's Charles Panati's version of how the four big faces got there, from Extraordinary Origins of Everyday Things.

HOW IT GOT ITS NAME.

"The full story of the origin of Mount Rushmore begins 60 million years ago, when pressures deep within the earth pushed up layers of rock. The forces created an elongated granite-and-limestone dome towering several thousand feet above the Dakota prairie lands. The first sculpting of the mountain was done by nature. The erosive forces of wind and water fashioned one particularly protuberant peak, which was unnamed until 1885.

"That year, a New York attorney, Charles E. Rushmore, was surveying the mountain range on horseback with a guide. Rushmore inquired about the impressive peak's name, and the guide, ribbing the city lawyer, answered, 'Hell, it never had a name. But from now on we'll call the damn thing Rushmore.' The label stuck. And later, with a gift of five thousand dollars, Charles Rushmore became one of the earliest contributors to the presidential memorial."

THE MEMORIAL

"The idea to transform a gigantic mountaintop into a colossus of human figures sprang from the mind of a South Dakota historian, Doane Robinson. In 1923, Robinson presented to the state his plan to simultaneously increase South Dakota's tourism, strengthen its economy, and immortalize three 'romantic western heroes.' [Ed. note: The original plan was to sculpt the heads of Kit Carson, Jim Bridger, and John Colter.] A commission then sought the skills of renowned sculptor John Gutzon de la Mothe Borglum, an authority on colossi.

"Idaho born, Borglum started as a painter, then switched to sculpture, and his fame grew in proportion to the size of his works. The year Doane Robinson conceived the idea for a Mount Rushmore memorial, Borglum accepted a commission from the United Daughters of the Confederacy to carve a head of General Robert E. Lee on Stone Mountain in Georgia.

"Mount Rushmore, though, beckoned with the greater challenge. Borglum opposed sculpting Western heroes. The notion was provincial, he argued. A colossus should capture prominent figures. In a letter dated August 14, 1925, Borglum proposed the faces of four influential American presidents."

THE SCULPTURE.

"Construction on the 6,200-foot-high wilderness peak was fraught with dangers. And the mountain itself was inaccessible except by foot or horseback, which necessitated countless climbs to lug up drills and scaffolding. But for Borglum, two features made the remote Rushmore peak ideal. The rocks faced southeast, ensuring maximum sunlight for construction, and later for viewing. And the peak's inaccessibility would protect the monument from vandals.

"Bitter winters, compounded by a chronic shortage of funds, continually threatened to terminate construction. Weathered surface rock had to be blasted away to expose suitably firm stone for sculpting. The chin of George Washington, for instance, was begun thirty feet back from the original mountain surface, and Theodore Roosevelt's forehead was undertaken only after 120 feet of surface rock were peeled away.

"Borglum worked from a scale model. Critical 'points' were measured on the model, then transferred to the mountain to indicate the depth of rock to be removed point by point.

"In 1941, fourteen years after construction began—and at a total cost of $990,000—a new world wonder was unveiled. There stood George Washington, whom Borglum selected because he was 'Father of the Nation'; Abraham Lincoln, 'Preserver of the Union'; Thomas Jefferson, 'The Expansionist'; and Theodore Roosevelt, 'Protector of the Working Man.'

"The figures measure sixty feet from chin to top of head. Each nose is twenty feet long, each mouth eighteen feet wide, and the eyes are eleven feet across. 'A monument's dimensions,' Borglum believed, 'should be determined by the importance to civilization of the events commemorated.'

"Gutzon Borglum died on March 6, 1941, aged 74. The monument was essentially completed. His son, also a sculptor, added the finishing touches."

From *Roadside America*: "The Black Hills can get foggy....Many a tourist Dad has been known to blow his top after driving umpteen miles...only to find he can't see those giant faces, goddammit."

THE BIRTH OF KLEENEX

Feel a sneeze coming on? If you're like most Americans, you reach for a kleenex without even thinking about it. But that wasn't always true. In fact, not so long ago there was no such thing. Here's how they were invented.

MILITARY SUPPLIES

The Kimberly-Clark Corporation originally designed the product that evolved into Kleenex tissues for *military* use.

• It started in 1914. World War I was being fought in Europe, and the cotton soldiers needed for bandages was starting to run out.

• So Kimberly-Clark devised a product called Cellucotton—an absorbent, soft paper that could be used to dress wounds.

• It was so effective that the army looked for other uses. And they found one: They used it as an air filter for soldiers' gas masks.

PEACETIME PROBLEM

Kimberly-Clark got too enthusiastic about their new material and overproduced it. After the war, they had warehouses full of Cellucotton left over; they *had* to find a new way to sell the stuff.

• Their clever solution: They marketed it as a modern women's tool for cleaning off makeup, and a "sanitary cold cream remover."

• Calling it Kleenex Kerchiefs, they hired movie stars to endorse it as a secret path to glamour. It was a big success.

SURPRISE SOLUTION

But Americans found another use for the product. Kimberly-Clark was inundated with letters that informed them the Kleenex Kerchiefs were great for nose-blowing.

•Men, in particular, wanted to know why Kleenex had to be a woman's product. And women griped that men were stealing their Kleenex to sneeze into.

• During the 1920s, Kimberly-Clark introduced a pop-up box that always left one tissue sticking out of the box, waiting to be grabbed.

• But the question remained—were people buying Kleenex as a cold cream remover, or a nose-blower? A survey showed that 60% of the people used it as the latter. So that's what K-C emphasized, and that's how we think of it today.

You can only smell 1/20th as well as a dog.

ROCK ME, SUE ME

It's not all peace and love in the rock 'n' roll world. It's big bucks... and as the stakes get higher, the lawsuits get bigger. Here are a few.

GHOSTBUSTERS

The "Ghostbusters" theme song, by Ray Parker, Jr. sounded a lot like Huey Lewis and the News' "I Want a New Drug." And sure enough, it turns out that the film's producers originally wanted Lewis, himself, to pen their theme song. When he refused, they hired Parker and requested something similar to Lewis's hit. Lewis sued for copyright infringement, and the case was settled out of court.

HEY, HEY, HEY

The Beatles' version of "Kansas City" was written by Jerry Leiber and Mike Stoller—or at least that's the way the song was credited when it came out in 1964. But it turned out the Beatles had recorded a medley of "Kansas City" and "Hey, Hey, Hey," a Little Richard composition that originally appeared on the B-side of his 1956 hit "Good Golly Miss Molly." It took Little Richard about 20 years to figure out what had happened, but when he did—and took it to court—it paid off in big numbers: $500,000.

MY SWEET LORD

George Harrison's "My Sweet Lord" casually borrowed the melody of the Chiffons' 1963 hit "He's So Fine," written by Ronald Mack. One strange aspect of the case: Ronald Mack was dead by the time his estate pressed charges and won. Another: Although Harrison had to pay, he was absolved of plagiarism. It was, according to the judge, "unconscious plagiarism."

STAIRWAY TO GILLIGAN'S ISLAND

Led Zeppelin, the biggest-selling band of the 1970s, were known among music experts for stealing songs from old blues artists and then crediting themselves. Their first hit, "Whole Lotta Love," was virtually a note-for-note recreation of Willie Dixon's "I Need Love." And "How Much More" was a direct lift of Howling Wolf's "Killing Floor."

But when someone messed with one of *their* tunes, it was time for legal action. A San Francisco-based band called Roger and The Goosebumps recorded a hilarious parody of the group's "Stairway to Heaven," matching Zep's melody with the lyrics of the theme song to "Gilligan's Island." Led Zepplin quickly had its lawyers block the song's release."It was a real blow," said one of the Goosebumps later. "We were getting airplay all over the country—I think we had a hit on our hands." Later, the same band did an equally funny take-off of the Beatles' "Fool on the Hill," called "Fudd on the Hill," sung in an Elmer Fudd voice. Thankfully, the Beatles didn't sue.

SURFIN' USA

The Beach Boys' big hit of 1963 sounded vaguely familiar to Chuck Berry...and it should have; he wrote the melody. Brian Wilson had appropriated it from Berry's 1958 tune, "Sweet Little Sixteen." Berry's publisher sued on his behalf, and won. The result: Berry owns 100% of the rights to both his own tune and Wilson's.

OLD MAN DOWN THE ROAD

The strangest case of an artist being sued for copyright infringement must be the one involvng John Fogerty's 1984 comeback hit, "The Old Man Down The Road."

He was sued for copying himself.

The story: "Old Man Down the Road" bore more than a little resemblence to "Run Through the Jungle," a tune Fogarty had previously written and recorded with Creedence Clearwater Revival, The problem: Fogarty no longer owned the rights to his original song, and there was bad blood between him and Saul Zaentz, the man who did.

Zaentz owned Fantasy Records, the label Creedence Clearwater Revival had recorded on. He and Fogerty had been embroiled in a long, bitter lawsuit over royalties that Creedence said were still owed to them. And when Fogerty included a tune on his solo album (the same one with "Old Man" on it) called "Zaentz Can't Dance," Saul sued him for defamation of character. Fogerty had to change it to "Vanz Can't Dance."

The highlight of the "Old Man" case was Fogerty's appearance in court, where he demonstrated to the jury how he composes tunes. They must have enjoyed it; he won.

LOST IN SPACE

This show still has a cult following; Why? Don't ask us. We've never even been able to figure out why the Robinsons didn't just push that whining SOB Dr. Smith out the airlock and forget him.

HOW IT STARTED

After producing everything from documentaries to comedies in the '50s, filmmaker Irwin Allen discovered kids' science fiction/adventure films in the '60s. He made *The Lost World* (1960), *Voyage to the Bottom of the Sea* (1961), and Jules Verne's *Five Weeks In a Balloon* (1963). All were successful. But special-effects films are hard to finance, so Allen decided to move to TV.

His first effort was a popular 1964 adaptation of *Voyage to the Bottom of the Sea.* His second was to be a live-action version of a comic book called *Space Family Robinson* (Swiss Family Robinson in space). But while Allen was still making the 2-hour pilot in 1964, Walt Disney, who owned the rights to the name, decided that Allen couldn't use it. So Allen changed it to "Lost In Space."

It was supposed to be a serious space adventure show, like "Star Trek" (no kidding), but when Allen showed it to CBS executives for the first time, he got a rude shock. One of the men who was there that day recalls: "Irwin, who has absolutely no sense of humor, thought he was making a very serious program. But in the viewing room, the network executives who were watching the pilot were absolutely hysterical, laughing . . . Irwin got furious and wanted to stop the showing...But his assistant kicked him under the table and whispered, 'Never mind. They love it.' " And they did. CBS bought the show and ran it for 3 years, from 1965 to 1968. Allen went on to make films like *The Poseidon Adventure* and *Towering Inferno*, for which he is known as "The Master of Disaster."

INSIDE FACTS

You Bet Your Life

The man who financed "Lost In Space" was "the one, the only... GROUCHO!" Marx and Irwin Allen were good friends. Groucho included a photo of himself and Allen in his book, *The Groucho-Phile*. The caption: "I taught him everything he knows about 'disaster' pictures. This picture was taken either at his wedding or mine."

Vivien Leigh made only $15,000 for playing Scarlett O'Hara in *Gone With the Wind.*

Saved By the Mail
Dr. Smith (Jonathan Harris) was originally meant to be killed off after 6 weeks. In fact, he was such a "minor" character that his contact stated that he couldn't be billed higher than 7th in the credits! But fan mail was overwhelmingly in favor of keeping him.

Adventures of Zorro
Dr. Smith's popularity was particularly frustrating to Guy Williams (John Robinson), who—guaranteed top billing—assumed he'd be the star. Instead, he rarely got *any* important dialogue. "I must be getting paid more per word than Lawrence Olivier," he groused.

Special Effects
Irwin Allen was notoriously cheap. For example, the dome on the frog alien's space ship in the episode "The Golden Man" was actually a giant champagne glass from a Marilyn Monroe film, salvaged by the director from the 20th Century Fox junk pile. Originally, the space ship in the episode was budgeted at $10,000. But when Allen was told the cost, he hit the roof. "Let the frog walk," he screamed. So the director had to scrounge and get it for free.

TV Robotics
- The Robot (no name) bore a striking resemblance to Robby, the famous robot from the film *Forbidden Planet* (1956). No coincidence. He was created by Bob Kinoshita, Robby's co-designer.
- Lights flashed on the robot in synchronization with his voice. An electronic innovation? No. A little actor was inside, pressing a telegraph key in the left claw as he spoke.
- The actor in the robot saw out via the robot's plastic collar. Viewers couldn't see him in the shell, because he was in black-face.

Phony Numbers
The Robinsons traveled on planet surfaces in a vehicle with the official-looking call numbers "277-2211 IA" painted on it. Actually, the 7 digits are 20th-Century Fox's phone number. And the IA is producer Irwin Allen's initials.

Surprise!
Every member of the cast learned the show was cancelled by reading about it in the newspapers.

The opposite sides of a dice cube always add up to 7.

NOTABLE & QUOTABLE

Memorable comments from memorable personalities.

JOHN WAYNE

• "Westerns are closer to art than anything else in the motion picture business."

• "I don't feel we did wrong in taking this great country away from [the Indians]. There were great numbers of people who needed new land and the Indians were selfishly trying to keep it for themselves."

• [About liberated women] "They have a right to work wherever they want to—as long as they have dinner ready when you get home."

• "There's been no top authority saying what marijuana does to you. I really don't know that much about it. I tried it once, but it didn't do anything to me."

J. EDGAR HOOVER

• "Justice is incidental to law and order."

• "We are a fact-gathering organization only. We don't clear anybody. We don't condemn anybody. Just the minute the F.B.I. begins making recommendations on what should be done with its information, it becomes a Gestapo."

AL CAPONE

• "Don't get the idea that I'm one of those goddamn radicals. Don't get the idea that I'm knocking the American system."

• "Vote early and vote often."

• "When I sell liquor, it's called bootlegging; when my patrons serve it on silver trays on Lake Shore Drive, it's called hospitality."

• "I'm like any other man. All I do is supply a demand."

• "[Communism] is knocking at our gates, and we can't afford to let it in.... We must keep America whole and safe and unspoiled. We must keep the worker away from Red literature and Red ruses; we must see that his mind remains healthy."

The leaves of an adult oak tree give off 7 tons of water every day.

DINER LORE

As Richard Gutman said in American Diner: *"One nice thing about a diner is that anyone who shares American values and American ways of doing things can function there."*

ORIGIN OF THE LUNCHWAGON

The year was 1872.
The city was Providence, Rhode Island.

Thousands of late-night factory workers had a problem—every restaurant in town closed promptly at 8:00 p.m., and they couldn't get anything to eat when their shifts let out.

The solution was provided by an enterprising pushcart peddler named Walter Scott. He outfitted a horsedrawn wagon with a stove and storage space and drove around the streets selling sandwiches, boiled eggs, and coffee for a nickel. The wagon only provided shelter for Scott—his customers had to stand out on the street. But it was a welcome service and an instant success. Before long, "after hours lunchwagons" were operating all over town.

INDOOR SEATING

Fifteen years later, an enterprising worker named Sam Jones introduced the first custom-made, walk-in lunchwagon—complete with a kitchen, a counter, and stools. It seated four to five people, and it, was immediately successful. Walk-in lunchwagons became popular all over the Northeast; soon they were being made in factories.

THE DINER EVOLVES

By 1910 dozens of lunchwagons—many of them rundown eyesores—were rumbling around the streets of most New England cities. Although they were only allowed to operate between dusk and dawn, many were staying on the streets until noon—which outraged many "respectable" citizens. Cities began cracking down on them, forcing the wagons off the streets by 10:00 A.M.

Lunchcart owners didn't like the idea of closing up when there was plenty of business around, so they came up with a way to skirt the rules—they just picked a good site where they could set up their lunchcarts permanently. Then they took off the wheels and hooked up to power, water, and gas lines and expanded their kitchens. Now they were officially called "street cafes," and they could operate all day and all night. They were the original 24-hour diners.

DINER FACTS

• The term *diner* originated with manufacturer Patrick J. Tierney, who called his prefab early-1900s restaurants "dining cars." Salesmen shortened them to "diners."
• Tierney was proud that, in 1911, his company built the first diner with an indoor toilet.
• Contrary to popular belief, diners were never converted from railroad dining cars. Rather, in the late '30s manufacturers were so impressed by the streamlined look of modern locomotives that they imitated the style. They called these diners "Streamliners."
• Diners reflect technological advances. When, in the late '30s, materials like stainless steel, Naugahyde, and Formica became available, diner-makers put them to use. So what we call a "classic" diner was actually "state of the art" in its time.
• At their peak in the late '40s, there were some 7,000 diners. Today there are only 2,000.

DINER DIALOGUE (from the film, *Five Easy Pieces*)

Jack Nicholson: "I'd like a plain omelette—no potatoes on the plate—a cup of coffee, and a side order of wheat toast."
Waitress: "I'm sorry, we don't have any side orders here."
Nicholson: "No side orders? You've got bread and a toaster of some kind?"
Waitress: "I don't make the rules."
Nicholson: "Okay, I'll make it as easy for you as I can. I'd like an omelette—plain—a chicken salad sandwich on wheat toast—no mayonnaise, no butter, no lettuce, and a cup of coffee."
Waitress: "A Number Two, chicken salad sandwich—no butter, no mayo, no lettuce, and a cup of coffee. Anything else?"
Nicholson: "Yeah. Now all you have to do is hold the chicken, bring me the toast, give me a check for the chicken salad sandwich, and you haven't broken any rules."
Waitress: "You want me to hold the chicken, huh?"
Nicholson: "I want you to hold it between your knees."

DINER LINGO

Diner waitresses and short order cooks have a language all their own—a sort of restaurant jazz, with clever variations on standard menu themes. Here's a little collection of some of the best.

Burn the British: Gimme an English muffin
Draw one in the Dark: A black coffee
Balloon Juice: Seltzer
An M.D.: A Dr. Pepper
Hold the hail: No ice
Wreck 'em: Scrambled eggs
Sweep the kitchen: A plate of hash
Adam and Eve on a raft: Two poached eggs on toast
A spot with a twist: A cup of tea with lemon
Bossy in a Bowl: Beef stew
A Blonde with Sand: Coffee with cream and sugar
Break It and Shake It: Add an egg to a drink
A Stack of Vermont: Pancakes with maple syrup.
Million on a Platter: A plate of baked beans
A White Cow: A vanilla milkshake
Let it Walk: It's to go
Noah's Boy on Bread: A ham sandwich
A Murphy: A potato
Nervous Pudding: Jello
Paint a Bow-wow Red: Gimme a hot dog with ketchup
Eve with a lid: A piece of apple pie
Burn one, take it through the garden, and pin a rose on it: Gimme a burger with lettuce and onion
Mike and Ike: Salt and pepper shakers
Angels on Horseback: Oysters rolled in bacon and placed on toast
Cow Paste: Butter
Lighthouse: Bottle of ketchup
Hounds on an Island: Franks and beans
Frog Sticks: French fries
Houseboat: A banana split
Wax: American cheese
Fry Two, let the sun shine: 2 fried eggs with unbroken yolks
Throw it in the Mud: Add chocolate syrup
Hug One: Squeeze a glass of orange juice
Life Preservers: Doughnuts
Put out the lights and cry: An order of liver and onions
One from the Alps: A Swiss cheese sandwich
Put a Hat on It: Add ice cream
A Splash of Red Noise: A bowl of tomato soup

Americans watch more TV in January and February than any other time of year.

WILL POWER

A will is the last chance the deceased has to drive the living nuts. Here are a few true-life examples of slightly offbeat wills.

THE DECEASED: Ms. Eleanor Ritchey, the unmarried granddaughter of the founder of Quaker State Oil (Philip John Bayer).

THE BEQUEST: Ms. Ritchey died in 1968, with an estate worth around $12 million. According to Scott Bieber in *Trusts and Estates* magazine: "Under her will, she left over 1,700 pairs of shoes and 1,200 boxes of stationery to the Salvation Army. The rest of her estate went to the dogs." Real dogs, he means—a pack of 150 strays that Ritchey had adopted as pets. The will set up a trust that permitted the mutts to live in the lap of luxury for up to 20 years. At the end of that period—or on the death of the last of the dogs, whichever came first—the remainder of the estate went to Auburn University.

WHAT HAPPENED: In 1984, Musketeer, the richest dog in America and the last of the original 150, went to that great kennel in the sky. Auburn got its money.

THE DECEASED: Patrick Henry, American patriot.

THE BEQUEST: Everything he owned was left to his wife—as long as she never married again. If she did, she forfeited the whole thing. "It would make me unhappy," he explained, "to feel I have worked all my life only to support another man's wife!"

WHAT HAPPENED: She remarried anyway.

THE DECEASED: Charles Millar, famed Canadian lawyer.

THE BEQUEST: According to Thomas Bedell in *Having the Last Word*, his will "consisted mainly of practical jokes. He willed shares in the Ontario Jockey Club to 2 crusaders against gambling. To 3 men who hated one another, he left equal shares of the same house. And part of his estate was promised to the Toronto mother giving birth to the largest number of children in the decade after his birth."

WHAT HAPPENED: The public either loved or hated it. Newspapers called it "the Stork Derby." Moralists tried to invalidate the will on the grounds that it promoted promiscuity. But in the end, a half a million dollars was split between a quartet of women who had each had 9 kids in the 10 ensuing years.

THE DECEASED: Robert Louis Stevenson, author of *Treasure Island*, etc.
THE BEQUEST: In addition to his normal earthly goods, Stevenson tried to leave his birthday. He willed it to a good friend who'd complained that since she was born on Christmas, she never got to have a real birthday celebration.

THE DECEASED: Felipe Segrandez, the sole survivor of the wreck of the Spanish ship *Santa Cecilia*. At the time he made out his will, he was a castaway on an island somewhere west of Africa.
THE BEQUEST: His will divided his estate between his relatives. It was written in his own blood, sealed in a bottle, and tossed into the ocean.
WHAT HAPPENED: The bottle was found on a South African beach by a prospector and was forwarded to Spanish authorities. Unfortunately, they couldn't execute the will; it was found in 1934, but had been written 178 years earlier, in 1756.

THE DECEASED: An attorney in France.
THE BEQUEST: $10,000 to "a local madhouse." The gentleman declared that "it was simply an act of restitution to his clients."

THE DECEASED: An Australian named Francis R. Lord.
THE BEQUEST: One shilling to his wife "for tram fare so she can go somewhere and drown herself."
WHAT HAPPENED: The inheritance was never claimed.

THE DECEASED: Sandra West, wealthy 37-year-old Beverly Hills socialite.
THE BEQUEST: Her estate was worth about $3 million, most of which she left to her brother—provided he made sure she was buried "in my lace nightgown and my Ferrari, with the seat slanted comfortably."

WHAT HAPPENED: That's how they buried her, surrounding the Ferrari with concrete so no one would be tempted to dig it up and drive it away.

THE DECEASED: A woman in Cherokee County, North Carolina.
THE BEQUEST: She left her entire estate to God.
WHAT HAPPENED: The court instructed the county sheriff to find the beneficiary. A few days later, the sheriff returned and submitted his report: "After due and diligent search, God cannot be found in this county."

THE DECEASED: Edgar Bergen, famed ventriloquist.
THE BEQUEST: $10,000 to the Actor's Fund of America—so they could take care of his dummy, Charlie McCarthy, and put him in a show once a year.
WHAT HAPPENED: They went along with it.

THE DECEASED: A rich, unmarried New Yorker. Died: 1880.
THE BEQUEST: He left everything to his nephews and nieces, with the exception of 71 pairs of pants. He wrote: "I enjoin my executors to hold a public sale at which these trousers shall be sold to the highest bidder, and the proceeds distributed to the poor. No one purchaser is to buy more than one pair."
WHAT HAPPENED: The auction took place. Each person who bought a pair of pants, upon examining their purchase, discovered "a $1,000 bill sewn into a pocket."

THE DECEASED: A merchant.
THE BEQUEST: Quoted in *To Will or Not to Will:* "My overdraft at the bank goes to my wife—she can explain it. My car goes to my son—he will have to go to work to keep up the payments....I want six of my creditors for pallbearers—they have carried me so long they might as well finish the job."

Only 55% of all Americans know that the sun is a star.

ONE GOOD YAWN DESERVES ANOTHER

Wonder why you cover your mouth when you yawn? Charles Panati did, and here's what he said about it in his book, Extraordinary Origins of Everyday Things.

THE POLITE YAWN

"Today, covering the mouth when yawning is considered an essential of good manners. But the original custom stemmed not from politeness but from fear—a fear that in one giant exhalation the soul, and life itself, might depart the body. A hand to the lips held back the life force."

THE DEADLY YAWN

"Ancient man had accurately observed (though incorrectly interpreted) that a newborn, struggling to survive, yawns shortly after birth (a reflexive response to draw additional oxygen into the lungs). With infant mortality extraordinarily high, early physicians, at a loss to account for frequent deaths, blamed the yawn. The helpless baby simply could not cover its mouth with a protective hand. Roman physicians actually recommended that a mother be particularly vigilant during the early months of life and cover any of her newborn's yawns."

THE CONTAGIOUS YAWN

"Today it is also considered good manners when yawning to turn one's head. But courtesy had nothing to do with the origin of the custom, nor with the apology that follows a yawn. Ancient man had also accurately observed that a yawn is contagious to witnesses. Thus, if a yawn was dangerous to a yawner, this danger could be 'caught' by others, like the Plague. The apology was for exposing friends to mortal danger."

WHAT GOES HERE?

Since we've got a space at the bottom of the page, we'll throw in a recommendation for a favorite bathroom book: *Rules of Thumb*, by Tom Parker. Includes 896 bite-size, bizarre rules for living, about everything from ostrich eggs to "Getting Emotionally Involved."

Genghis Khan is said to have killed over a million people in *one hour* in the year 1221.

THE SHOWER SCENE

Facts about one of the most chilling scenes in movie history.

Alfred Hitchcock has provided filmgoers with some of the cinema's most thrilling moments, but most movie historians agree that in terms of pure shock value, the shower scene in *Psycho* tops the list.

It is probably the most famous single scene in film history.

It's admired for its masterful editing (approximately 65 edits in 45 seconds), its skillful use of music (Bernard Herrman's screeching violins) and its shocking conclusion, where the movie's apparent protagonist (played by Janet Leigh) is suddenly butchered to death in a shower.

• Although there's practically no graphic violence in the scene, it has literally scared some people out of taking showers—including Janet Leigh, who says in her autobiography that *she* refuses to take them anymore.

• Amazingly, Hitchcock later claimed he had made the film as a *joke*.

• The screenplay was adapted from Robert Bloch's novel of the same name in 1959 (by Joseph Stefano, who later created TV's "The Outer Limits"), and was shot on the set of the "Alfred Hitchcock Presents" television series.

FACTS:

Since *Psycho*'s release in 1960, film students have dissected every frame of film in the shower scene. Among the interesting details:

• It took seven days to shoot the 45-second scene.

• By far, the most difficult shot was of Marion Crane's (Janet Leigh's) open-eyed stare as she lay dead outside the shower. At first Hitchcock attempted to get special contact lenses for Leigh, but time constraints prevented it. Instead, Hitchcock used an ingenious three-shot method: (1) a close-up of Leigh's eye from a still photograph, which cuts away to (2) a shower spigot and running water and then back to "live action" of (3) Leigh staring, wide-eyed, on the bathroom floor . . . trying desperately not to blink. It is one of the film's many legends that if you look closely, you can see Leigh blink (Mrs. Hitchcock said she saw it).

• Another legend has it that a stand-in model was used for Leigh—but she denies that. Leigh says the only model used was when her body is carried out in a sheet by police in a later scene.

• The blood washing down the drain was really chocolate sauce.

• Only one shot in the entire shower scene montage shows a knife entering the body and no blood is seen in the shot.

• Some shots use as little as eight frames of film (i.e., one-third of a second).

• Anthony Perkins (as Norman Bates) did not actually act in the scene. He was on Broadway at the time of the shooting, starring in a play; a stand-in filled in as "Mom."

• Mixed-up priorities: According to Hitchcock, studio executives were more concerned about having a toilet flushing onscreen than they were about the implicit violence.

• Janet Leigh refused to let her daughter (actress Jamie Lee Curtis) watch the movie as a child when it appeared on TV.

• Hitchcock got the movie past censors by first submitting a script with many more horrible scenes, knowing that by allowing them to be cut he would get more leverage on the others.

JANET LEIGH ON THE SHOWER SCENE:

"What I was to wear in the shower scene gave the wardrobe supervisor migraines. I had to appear nude, without being nude. She and I pored over striptease magazines, hoping one of their costumes would be the answer. . . . There was an impressive display of pinwheels, feathers, sequins, etc., but nothing suitable for our needs. Finally, the supervisor came up with a simple solution: flesh-colored moleskin. . . . So each morning for seven shooting days and seventy-one setups, we covered my private parts, and we were in business."

"For sundry reasons, we had to do [the scene] over and over. At long last a take was near completion without a mishap. Abruptly I felt something strange happening around my breasts. The steam from the hot water had melted the adhesive on the moleskin, and I sensed the napped cotton fabric peeling away from my skin. What to do?...I opted for immodesty...and made the correct judgment. That was the printed take."

No surprise: Casinos in Las Vegas don't have clocks in them.

A FOOD IS BORN

These foods are fairly common, but you've probably never wondered where they came from. Here are the answers anyway.

FROZEN CONCENTRATED ORANGE JUICE. During World War II, the U.S. government wanted an easy-to-carry, powdered orange juice for soldiers in the field. They commissioned the Minute Maid Company to develop it, but the effort only succeeded a few weeks before the war ended—so the powder was never produced. However, as a by-product of their research, Minute Maid discovered that o.j. could be concentrated and frozen. When the war was over, they took advantage of the discovery and marketed it.

McDONALD'S FILET-O-FISH SANDWICH. The first successful non-burger "entree" in McDonald's history was a concession to organized religion. In the early '60s, the McDonald's in Cincinnati lost sales every Friday because the large Catholic population couldn't eat meat—and McDonald's had nothing else to offer. The owner asked Mac chairman Ray Kroc for permission to expand the menu. Kroc resisted at first ("Let 'em eat burgers, like everyone else!"), but ultimately supported research into selling a fish sandwich. McDonald's researchers decided to use codfish, but didn't call it that for two reasons: One, they were legally allowed to call it the much classier "North Atlantic Whitefish," and two, Kroc's childhood memories of cod liver oil were too unpleasant. After successful test-marketing, the fish sandwich went on the McDonald's menu permanently in 1963.

LIFESAVERS. In 1912 a Cleveland candymaker named Clarence Crane decided to make a mint to sell in the summer. Until then, most mints were imported from Europe; Crane figured he could cut the price by making them in the U.S. He had the candy manufactured by a pill-maker—who discovered that his machinery would only work if it punched a hole in the middle of each candy. So Crane cleverly called the mints LifeSavers.

A-1 STEAK SAUCE. The Royal Chef for England's King George IV (1820-1830) whipped up this sauce as a treat for His Majesty, a devoted epicure. How did George like it? "Absolutely A-1," he reputedly declared. The sauce became so popular around the Court that when the chef—a gentleman named Brand—retired from his position, he started a company specifically to manufacture it. After World War I, an American company licensed it and distributed it in the States. It's still the biggest-selling sauce of its kind.

CAESAR SALAD. The name of this unique salad doesn't refer to the Roman conqueror, but to the man who created it—a Tijuana restaurateur named Caesar Cardini. Here's one account of its origin: "Cardini started several restaurants in Tijuana, Mexico in the early '20s. He devised the salad in 1924 during the Fourth of July weekend at Caesar's Place. He served it as finger food, arranging the garlic-scented lettuce leaves on platters. Later, he shredded the leaves into bite-sized pieces. The salad became a hit with the Hollywood movie stars who visited Tijuana, and soon was a specialty of such prestigious restauants as Chasen's and Romanoff's."

MAXWELL HOUSE COFFEE. In the 1880s, a young Tennesseean named Joel Cheek became obsessed with the idea of roasting the perfect blend of coffee. After years of experiments, he came up with the blend he liked. Then, in 1892, he persuaded the owners of Nashville's ritzy Maxwell House Hotel to serve it exclusively. Cheek was so encouraged by the clientele's enthusiastic response to the coffee that he named it after the hotel.

BISQUICK. The first instant biscuit mix was inspired by a train ride. In 1930, an executive of General Mills was traveling by train and ordered some biscuits in the dining car. He expected them to be cold and stale, since it was long past the usual dinner hour. But instead, they were hot and fresh—and they arrived almost instantly. He inquired how this was possible, and was told that the bread dough had been mixed in advance and stored in the refrigerator. The executive thought it was a great idea. He worked with General Mills chemists and created a similar product—but one that could be kept in a box, unrefrigerated. It was so popular when it was introduced in the '30s that it revolutionized American baking habits.

The sound of E.T. walking was made by someone squishing her hands in Jello.

PRIME-TIME PROVERBS

More words of wisdom from Prime Time Proverbs, *by Jack Mingo and John Javna.*

ON EXISTENCE
"I reek, therefore I am."
—Diane Chambers, *Cheers*

"There's more to life than sitting around in the sun in your underwear playing the clarinet."
—Lt. Larry Casey, *Baa Baa Black Sheep*

ON THE GOOD LIFE
"I'm a lucky guy—I mean, life has been good to me. I've got a good job, good health, a good wife, and a fantastic barber."
—Ted Baxter, *The Mary Tyler Moore Show*

ON THE LEGAL SYSTEM
"This is America. You can't make a horse testify against himself."
—Mr. Ed, *Mr. Ed*

Venus Flytrap: "I'm not gonna sit here and let her lie!"
Lawyer: "You have to. This is a court of law."
—WKRP in Cincinnati

ON INDIVIDUALITY
Frank Burns: "Don't you understand? The man is not normal."
Hawkeye Pierce: "What's normal, Frank?"
Frank: "Normal is everybody doing the same thing."
Trapper McIntyre: "What about individuality?"
Frank: "Well, individuality is fine. As long as we do it together."
—M*A*S*H

ON WOMEN
"It's been proven through history that wimmin's a mystery."
—Popeye, *The Popeye Cartoon Show*

ON LOVE
"Love makes you do funny things. It made me get married."
—Buddy Sorrel, *The Dick Van Dyke Show*

"Love's the only thing in life you've got to earn. Everything else you can steal."
—Pappy Maverick, *Maverick*

.According to a *Money* magazine poll, women like money more than sex.

THE MINI-SKIRT SAGA

Today, when practically anything goes in fashion, people have forgotten how revolutionary the mini-skirt was in its day. In the mid-'60s, when it caught on, it was more than a fashion—it was a philosophy, a political statement, a news event. Here are some facts to remind you.

HISTORY.
The mini-skirt was created by an English seamstress named Mary Quant. As a girl, Mary hated the straightlaced clothes grown-ups wore. So when she got older, she made unconventional clothes for herself.

In 1955, she opened the world's first boutique in London, selling "wild and kinky" handmade clothes, like the ones she wore. She used bright colors, lots of plastic, and kept hemlines shorter than normal (though they weren't minis yet). Her fashions caught on with hip Londoners. They became known as "mod" (for modern) clothes, and Mary became a local celebrity.

In 1965, young girls in London were beginning to wear their dresses shorter than ever. Taking a cue from them, Quant began manufacturing skirts that were outrageously short for the time. She called them "mini-skirts." They took off like wildfire.

Later that year, respected French designer Andre Courreges brought the mini-skirt and go-go boots (his own creation) to the world of high fashion. This made the mini a "style" instead of a "fad" and inspired influential women—movie stars, models, heiresses—to shorten their skirts. But the largest American clothing manufacturers weren't sure whether to hop on the mini bandwagon until the day in 1965 that Jackie Kennedy appeared in public with a shortened hemline. After that, it was full speed ahead.

The mini fad lasted for less than a decade. But it permanently altered the concept of what was acceptable in women's attire, and helped break down traditional barriers for women in other areas of society.

The Meaning of the Mini-Skirt, Part I
In 1965, Mary Quant, creator of the mini-skirt, was asked to reveal the meaning of the mini-skirt. Her reply: "Sex."

The Meaning of the Mini-Skirt, Part II
"Without a doubt, the pill bred the mini, just as it bred the topless bathing suit by Rudi Gernreich in 1964. They were intended to prove that women were in control of their destiny and could choose whom they wished to mate with."

—*In Fashion*, by Prudence Glynn

THE MINI-SKIRT — INTERNATIONAL CONTROVERSY
Today, the mini-skirt is a fashion, not a political issue, but in the '60s, it was a major controversy. Here's how some people reacted:

- **In the Vatican:** Women in mini-skirts were not allowed to enter Vatican City.
- **In the Malagasy Republic:** An anti-mini-skirt law went into effect in 1967. Violators were subject to ten days in jail.
- **In the Congo:** In 1967 police arrested three hundred women wearing mini-skirts, which were banned.
- **In Venezuela:** Churches in Caracas put up signs telling people to give up their minis or "be condemned to hell."
- **In Egypt:** Women in minis were subject to a charge of indecent behavior. This law was passed because two women wore mini-skirts in the center of the city and caused a two-hour traffic jam.
- **In Zambia:** Gangs of youths roamed the streets assaulting girls in mini-skirts and forcibly lowering their hemlines. After a week, the war against mini-skirts was declared officially over when women went on television and said they "realized their mistake."
- **In Greece:** Anyone wearing a mini-skirt was jailed.
- **In the Philippines:** A congressman proposed that mini-skirts be banned. But the proposal was withdrawn when a congresswoman threatened to retaliate by outlawing elevator shoes.
- **In Rio De Janeiro:** In 1966, a sixty-three-year-old man on a bus was overcome when a young woman wearing a mini-skirt crossed her legs in the seat next to him. He bit her on the thigh and was sentenced to three days in jail.
- **In the U.S.A.:** Disneyland outlawed mini-skirts—the gatekeepers measured the distance from the woman's knee to her hemline and restricted her entrance until she ripped out the hem.

In most schools during the '60s, if the hem of a dress didn't touch the floor when a girl was kneeling, it was considered a mini, and the guilty party was sent home. "And don't come back until you look respectable, young lady."

THE ORIGIN OF DRACULA

Dracula first appeared in 1897 in a book written by Irish author Bram Stoker. Extraordinary Origins of Everyday Things *says:*

The nineteenth-century Irish writer Bram Stoker came serendipitously upon the subject matter for his novel *Dracula* while engaged in research at the British Museum. He discovered a manuscript of traditional Eastern European folklore concerning Vlad the Impaler, a fifteenth-century warrior prince of Walachia. According to Romanian legend, the sadistic Prince Vlad took his meals al fresco, amidst a forest of impaled, groaning victims. And Vlad washed down each course with his victims' blood, in the belief that it imbued him with supernatural strength.

Vlad's crimes were legend. On red-hot pokers, he impaled male friends who had fallen from favor, and women unfaithful to him were impaled, then skinned alive. Imprisoned himself, he tortured mice and birds for amusement. His mountaintop retreat, known as Castle Drakula, suggested the title for Stoker's novel.

Although Stoker had found his model for Dracula, it was a friend, a professor from the University of Budapest, who suggested a locale for the fiction by relating lore of the vampires of Transylvania. The novelist traveled to the area and was...impressed with its dark, brooding mountains, morning fogs, and sinister-looking castles.

Dracula was an immense success when published in 1897, wrapped in a brown paper cover. And the novel was responsible for reviving interest in the Gothic horror romance, which has continued into the present day in books and films.

EEAGH! TWO AWFUL VAMPIRE RIDDLES

"How can you spot a Vampire jockey?"
"He always wins by a neck."

"Why aren't Vampires good gamblers?"
"Because they always make sucker bets."

The Empire State Building contains more than 10 million bricks.

...L SPEAKS

...om from the quotable ...nston Churchill.

..., for

...red for ma... that it be postpon...

"If you have an important point, don't try to be subtle or clever. Use a pile driver. Hit the point once. Then come back and hit it again. Then hit it a third time—a tremendous whack."

"It is a mistake to look too far ahead. The chain of destiny can only be grasped one link at a time."

"In war you can only be killed once, but in politics, many times."

"I have taken more out of alcohol than alcohol has taken out of me."

"A fantatic is one who can't change his mind and won't change the subject."

"Eating words has never given me indigestion."

"I like a man who grins when he fights."

"I am always ready to learn, although I do not always like being taught."

"The inherent vice of Capitalism is the unequal sharing of its blessings; the inherent vice of Socialism is the equal sharing of its miseries."

"A hopeful disposition is not the sole qualification to be a prophet."

"We are all worms, but I do believe I'm a glow worm."

"It is a fine thing to be honest, but it is also important to be right."

"Never turn your back on a threatened danger and try to run away from it. If you do that, you will double the danger. But if you meet it promptly and without flinching, you will reduce the danger by half. Never run away from anything. Never!"

The #1 TV show of 1961 was a Western called "Wagon Train."

WHO WAS THAT MAN?

Some songs leave you wondering who they're about. Here are the stories behind a few, from Behind the Hits, *by Bob Shannon and John Javna.*

I WRITE THE SONGS; BARRY MANILOW

Most people associate this tune with Barry Manilow, because his version sold millions of records. But it actually has nothing to do with him. He didn't write it—Bruce Johnston, one of the Beach Boys, did. And Johnston didn't write it about Manilow—or himself. He was inspired by someone he considers a truly great songwriter.

Who was that man?

Johnston says: "I guess it's pretty obvious that I wrote the song about Brian Wilson."

Wilson, the leader of the Beach Boys, really *has* written songs the whole world sings. For example: "Good Vibrations," "In My Room," "Fun, Fun, Fun," "I Get Around," "Surfer Girl," "Help Me Rhonda," and so on. Good choice.

KILLING ME SOFTLY WITH HIS SONG; ROBERTA FLACK

Roberta Flack didn't write this song; a poet and folksinger named Lori Lieberman did.

The Story. One evening in 1972, Lori went to L.A.'s Troubador to see a singer who had earned the nickname "The Hudson River Troubador" when he sailed from Maine to New York with Pete Seeger, trying to call attention to pollution. She was impressed by what she saw and heard. "I thought he was just incredible," she recalled. "He was singing songs that I felt pertained to my life at that time. I was going though some difficult things, and what he was singing about made me think, 'Whoa! This person knows me! I don't understand.' Never having met him, how could he know me so well? I went home and wrote a poem and showed it to the two men I was working with at the time."

Those two men, Norman Gimbel and Charles Fox, thought the poem could be adapted into a great song. They quickly reworked it and gave it back to Lieberman to record on her own album.

America's most popular names for female cats: Samantha, Fluffy, Misty, and Muffin.

In its original form it was ten minutes long—too long for radio play—so it was edited and released as a single. It got a little airplay, but never sold. It did, however, get included on a tape of music created especially for airline headsets.

How It Became a Hit: On a flight from Los Angeles to New York, Roberta Flack plugged in her personal headphones and began leafing through the in-flight magazine to see what songs were included on the 10 channels of music that were available. Her main interest was to see if any of her recordings were among the offerings. They weren't.

But Flack happened to notice the listing for a song she'd never heard. The title seemed interesting, so she tuned it in. By the time she reached New York she knew she had to record it. "When I heard it," Flack said, "I absolutely freaked. In New York, I started calling people, asking how to find the guys who wrote that song."

Flack felt she had stumbled on an "uncut diamond," a song that she could restructure and improve and make her own. It became the most important project in her life, and she spent eight months on it. "Roberta came out with the most wonderful version," says Lieberman. "Killing Me Softly" was released in January; it became the top-selling song in the nation by February, and won three Grammy awards for Flack.

Who was that man?

The gentle "killer" was folksinger Don McLean. He had just completed his second album, "American Pie," and his rendition of the title song was the performance that inspired Lieberman. McLean says: "After she announced it, somebody called me up and said, 'Hey, somebody's written a song about you.' The first question I asked was, 'Is it any good?' "

YOU'RE SO VAIN; CARLY SIMON

This is probably old news by now, but it's worth repeating. Carly Simon's first big hit created a controversy. As soon as it was released, people began speculating about its subject. Who was "so vain"? Was it Mick Jagger? Her husband, James Taylor?

Who was that man?

Simon wanted to keep an air of mystery around the song, so she was reluctant to reveal her secret. But producer Richard Perry wasn't so shy. "It's about a compilation of men," he said, "but primarily Warren Beatty."

39% of Americans think that the best way to get rich is to win a lottery.

WORDPLAY

More origins of common phrases.

KEEP THE BALL ROLLING
Meaning: To keep things going, to maintain momentum.
Background: Comes from the presidential election of 1840, which was won by Whig party candidate William Henry Harrison. The election campaign included the usual pamphlets, buttons, banners, and one unique item—a giant 6-foot paper ball with all the Whig slogans written on it (e.g., "Tippecanoe and Tyler Too!"). Harrison's supporters took it from town to town, rolling it down the streets shouting "Keep the ball rolling!"

GET UP ON THE WRONG SIDE OF BED
Meaning: To start the day feeling bad, or to wake up in a bad mood.
Background: Reflects a long-standing cultural bias against the left side of the body. The phrase was originally "get out of bed the wrong way"—which meant with your left foot first, or while you were lying on your left side—a sure sign, people believed, that things were destined to go wrong that day. The phrase evolved into "get up on the wrong side of bed."

BEAT AROUND THE BUSH
Meaning: To avoid dealing with the main issue.
Background: In the Middle Ages, people trapped birds for food by dropping a net over a bush and beating the ground around it with a club. As frightened birds perched in the bush tried to fly away, they were caught in the net. Someone who kept beating around the bush after the birds were trapped never got to the point of the activity—actually getting the birds and eating them.

BARK UP THE WRONG TREE
Meaning: To focus on the wrong object or idea.
Background: A hunting term. In Colonial days, pioneers used hounds to trap raccoons and possums. The dogs would chase the animals up trees, then sit and bay at the tree trunk. Occasionally, the hound would get fooled and the hunter would find his pet barking "up" the wrong tree.

On the average, American men carry more cash than women do.

THE FABULOUS '60S

More miscellany from the pop decade, courtesy of Gordon and John Javna's great bathroom reader, 60s!

WAR GAMES

One of the forgotten footnotes of the Vietnam war is the toys it inspired. In 1961 JFK committed our first troops to Vietnam...and in 1962, toys relating to Vietnam began to appear. "We've discovered through dealer interviews and consumer mail that our customers are demanding toys about Vietnam," explained the sales manager of a major toy company. Among the big sellers:

• **The Mattel "Guerilla Gun."** In 1963, Mattel painted its Dick Tracy Submachine guns camouflage green and packaged each one with a poncho, toy hand grenades, and a beret. They immediately sold 2 million of them, twice as many as they had when the product was just a Dick Tracy gun.

• **The Green Beret hobby kit.** Aurora Plastics marketed a plastic assemble-it-yourself model of a Green Beret holding a machine gun and tossing a hand grenade. "Inspired by the great motion picture *The Green Berets*, starring John Wayne," it said on the box. No mention of the real war, though.

• **"Viet Nam, a Game for Interested Americans."** The next best thing to being there—an educational board game for people who liked role-playing.

WHO CARES ABOUT THE CEREAL?

In 1965 kids discovered an animated TV commercial for a brand-new cereal. It actually had a cast of characters the way cartoons did: lovable old Cap'n Crunch, his crew of kids, his faithful pet, Seadog, and the villains, archenemy Magnolia Bulkhead and Jean LaFoot, the barefoot pirate. The kiddie videophiles loved the commercials and, of course, made their parents buy the cereal. It quickly became the most popular new cereal of the decade, giving its manufacturer, Quaker Oats, the sweet taste of success.

What consumers didn't know: Cap'n Crunch was carefully

The sex organ on a male spider is located at the end of one of its legs.

planned out as a TV promotion *before the cereal even existed.* Quaker hired Jay Ward, creator of Bullwinkle, to come up with a cartoon character and produce one-minute commercials—cereal serials—of Cap'n Crunch sailing the high seas, keeping the world safe for breakfast. Then, when they were satisfied with the ads, Quaker produced the actual cereal. It became the best-selling new cereal of the decade.

WHO DUNNIT?

The first James Bond film, *Dr. No*, came out in 1963. But Ian Fleming's books were already selling well in America by then. Here's how it happened: In 1961, a well-known intellectual was asked by a reporter from *Life* magazine to name his favorite books. The man, who was known to read a book a day, quickly supplied a list of 10 of them. Most were scholarly works . . . except one—*From Russia with Love*, a James Bond thriller.

This was the only book on the list that most Americans would even consider buying. And they did. The guy had so much influence that James Bond became an overnight sensation in bookstores.

Who was the man whose list started the Bond craze?

President John F. Kennedy.

MACHINE AGE MAN

They sang it on TV in 1962: "Here he comes, here he comes, greatest toy you've ever seen, and his name is Mr. Machine. . . ." Mr. Machine was a plastic wind-up robot with a top hat, who clunked and whirred, and walked mechanically. Manufactured by the Ideal Toy Company in 1962, he became one of the most popular toys of the early sixties.

But kids and their parents never realized that Mr. Machine was more than a toy—it was actually a comment on the condition of modern man.

It was created by Marvin Glass, a neurotic toy designer who considered himself something of a philosopher. One day Glass was having a typical argument with his ex-wife. Just before she hung up, she screamed at him: "You're nothing but a machine!" Glass pondered the comment. Maybe she was right, he thought. . . . Maybe the 20th century had turned all of us into machines. Inspired, Glass designed his homage to modern life, Mr. Machine.

Indestructible: Even if you cut off a cockroach's head, it can live for several weeks.

LUNACY

We've heard enough about moons and Junes to last a lifetime. But the joke is that some of the old fables about the power of the moon might actually be true.

MOON CHILD:

- The average menstrual cycle for women is 29.5 days—precisely the same as a lunar month.
- The human gestation period is 9 months. But whose months? The average birth occurs 265.5 days after conception—which happens to be the exact equivalent of 9 lunar months.

STUDIES SHOW THAT:

- More children are born after new and full moons than at any other time.
- More boys are born after a full moon, and more girls are born after a new moon.
- People who are experiencing a lot of stress have an increase in pulse rates during a full or new moon.
- Surgeons have found that around the full or new moons, their patients bleed more.
- When full and new moons occur, more people are admitted into mental hospitals and hospital emergency rooms are busier.
- There's an increase in certain crimes (rape, robbery, assault) during a full moon.

THE WORD

- "Lunacy" refers to the Roman moon goddess, Luna.
- In ancient times, people thought that exposure to the moon could "affect the mind."
- People were advised not to sleep with moonlight shining on their faces, or they would become "moonstruck" (crazy).
- The word *lunacy* is probably derived from ancient observations that during a full moon, mad people became more frenzied.
- The term *lunatic fringe* was coined by Teddy Roosevelt, who was describing some of his followers in the Bullmoose Party during the 1912 presidential election.

From the bottom of a well, you can actually see the stars during the daytime.

THE GUMBY STORY

He's the "Clayboy of the Western World," an American icon. But what does he stand for, and where did he come from? Now it can be told.

A STAR IS BORN. Gumby was created in the mid-'50s by Art Clokey, a filmmaker who had learned "stop-motion animation" (film is shot one frame at a time and the inanimate subject is moved between shots) at the University of Southern California, working with a world-famous expert.

• After graduating, Clokey experimented with his "stop-motion" techniques in an art film he called *Gumbasia*. The stars of the film were geometric clay forms ("It was cheaper than getting actors") that metamorphized to the rhythm of a jazz soundtrack.

• Clokey took *Gumbasia* to a Hollywood producer, hoping to make feature films. Instead, the producer decided Clokey ought to make a kids' TV show. He put up the money for a pilot, and Clokey created the star—a clay character named Gumby. NBC then commissioned several 6-minute films.

• Gumby made his first appearance on "The Howdy Doody Show" in 1956. Then in March, 1957 he got his own NBC program.

• Beginning in 1958, "The Adventures of Gumby" was offered as a syndicated show. By the mid-'60s, he was everywhere.

GUMBY: PERSONAL DATA

• His name came from a type of sticky clay soil found in Michigan, known as "gumbo."

• The shape of his head was inspired by a photo of Clokey's father. In it, the senior Clokey had a cowlick that looked to his son like "the bump of wisdom that Buddhists have." So Art passed it on to Gumby.

• According to Clokey: "His green color represents the chlorophyll found in plants, while his bluish tint reflects the sky. He's got his feet on the ground and his head in the sky."

• His pal, Pokey, is orange because, says Clokey, "Pokey represents the critical, doubting, more earthy side of life."

• His voice was supplied by Dick Beals. Pokey's voice was supplied by Clokey himself.

HIS FALL AND RESURRECTION

Gumby's popularity lasted through the '60s and into the early '70s. But by the late '70s, he was washed up; TV stations had dropped the show, and toymakers had stopped manufacturing Gumby toys.

• Art Clokey was nearly broke. His house was about to be foreclosed on, and the new toy product in which he had invested heavily—something called Moody Rudy—was proving to be a bomb. Worse, his daughter had recently been killed in a car accident. Life was not going Art's way.

• In 1979, he went to Hong Kong to take a look at the Moody Rudy manufacturing facilities. While he was there, he decided to visit Satya Sai Baba, an Indian holy man he'd once seen in a film.

• As journalist Sean Elder describes it: "On that day in 1979, Clokey and his wife, Gloria, were among the faithful hundreds sitting outside Baba's ashram, awaiting...a glimpse of the Master. Once or twice a day Baba would make the rounds, pouring ash from his hand onto objects that the devout held up to be blessed: books, photographs, religious statues. That afternoon, Sai Baba found Clokey in the lotus position, holding a small likeness of Gumby. Ash poured forth from his hand onto Gumby's sloping head, and the master moved on. 'Then I went home,' says Clokey, 'and things began happening.' "

THE GUMBY REVIVAL

• It started at the Pasadena Art Center, where Clokey gave a talk on animation. The Gumby-philes who attended enjoyed it so much that they set up some screenings of Gumby films (remember, it was pre-video, and they hadn't been seen on TV for years) in the auditorium of the Beverly Hills Library.

• This was sold out for two weeks in a row—which prompted the owners of a chain of movie theaters to send Clokey around the country, appearing with his Gumby films. He was a hit everywhere.

• Inspired by the Gumby revival, a couple of cadets painted a Gumby sign and flew it during the 1980 Army-Navy football game. This, in turn, was spotted by the producer of "Saturday Night Live," who decided it would be a kick to dress Eddie Murphy in a Gumby suit. Suddenly Gumby was a star again.

• Clokey is clear about who's responsible for his turn in fortunes—Satya Sai Baba. "He's the epitome of cosmic creation in human form," he explains. "He taught me that Gumby is me, and since we're all alike, Gumby is everyone."

Gumby and his friends are sometimes moved as many as 9,000 times in a Gumby film.

EARTH TRIVIA

A few fascinating facts about the planet to help you while away the time:

The earth isn't round. It's slightly flattened on the top and bottom.

❖

There are over 300,000 miles of coastline on the planet.

❖

The longest mountain range in the world is the Andes, in South America. It is 4525 miles long. Next longest: The Rockies, followed by the Himalayas, the Great Dividing Range in Australia, and the Trans-Antarctic Mountains.

On a mountain, the temperature drops about 3-1/2° for every 984 feet you climb.

❖

The atmosphere extends about 5,000 miles above the earth. It consists of five separate layers: the exosphere, thermosphere, mesosphere, stratosphere, and troposphere.

❖

The troposphere is the life-supporting layer closest to the earth. It is also the smallest—only10 miles high.

❖

There are about a million earthquakes every year. Most are so small they don't even register.

❖

The deepest lake in the world is the U.S.S.R.'s Lake Baikal. Its size: 30 miles wide by 400 miles long. Its depth: over a mile (approx. 6,360 feet). "It's so deep," says one source, "that all five of the Great Lakes could be emptied into it."

❖

The largest lake (or inland sea) in the world is the Caspian Sea, on the border of Iran and the U.S.S.R.

❖

About 20% of the Earth's surface is desert. However, most deserts are not sand (only about 15% are). Deserts are frequently bare rock or gravel.

The Sahara Desert takes up about 1/3 of Africa. It is almost as big as the continental United States.

❖

If you could take all of the salt out of the ocean and spread it on land, you'd have a five hundred-foot layer of salt covering the Earth's surface.

You can only see a rainbow in the morning or late in the afternoon.

THE STORY OF LAYLA

Several B.R.I. members wrote and asked for the inside story on this classic Eric Clapton tune—one of the most popular rock songs of all time.

Eric Clapton could play the blues as few other guitarists could—a talent which both satisfied and tortured him. Unlike some of his fellow British "bluesmen," Clapton was keenly aware that he was a white musician imitating an essentially black art form. This created a terrible conflict; playing the blues was his first love, but was he really entitled to practice his craft? In order to reconcile the feelings, Clapton became a blues purist. He believed that you had to suffer in order to be able to play the blues—so he was miserable a lot of the time. He was particularly unhappy when he wrote his most famous composition, "Layla."

THE BIRTH OF LAYLA

The real "Layla's" real name was Patti Boyd—or more accurately, Patti Boyd Harrison. She was the wife of Beatle George Harrison when Eric Clapton began pursuing her.

• Harrison first met her on the set of *A Hard Day's Night* in 1964. A stunning nineteen-year-old blonde model, she was only supposed to make a brief appearance in the film and leave; instead, she and George fell in love and eventually married.

• George and Eric were close friends. They'd known each other since the days when the Beatles and the Yardbirds (Eric's group at the time) were becoming popular. As they both became superstars, they hung out together more and more. They even contributed to each other's recordings. Eric played a magnificent solo on "While My Guitar Gently Weeps"; George co-wrote and played on Cream's "Badge." George wrote "Here Comes the Sun" while sitting in Eric's garden; he wrote "Savoy Truffle" specifically for Eric, who was having dental problems but still couldn't resist chocolates. George joined Eric when he toured with a band called Delaney and Bonnie and Friends, etc.

• George didn't realize, however, that over the years Eric had quietly fallen in love with his wife. Eric told Patti (but not George) about his feelings, but she wouldn't hear anything of it. She remained dedicated to the man who had written "Something" for her.

• Already a tortured soul, Eric was plunged into despair. In an outburst of emotion, he wrote "Layla." Later, when people asked him who he was singing for, all he would say was, " 'Layla' was about a woman I felt really deeply about and who turned me down, and I had to pour it out in some way."

• You may be wondering how "Patti" became "Layla." The answer: Clapton lifted the name "Layla" from a Persian love story called "Layla and Mashoun." The tale had little similarity to the Eric/Patti/George love triangle. Clapton just liked the title. The song was recorded and released in 1970, but it flopped. The reason: the record was attributed to Derek and the Dominoes; no one knew it was Clapton, so it didn't get airplay.

• Eric, who had poured his heart and soul into the record, threw in the towel. He gave up music and took up heroin. "I basically stayed in the house with my girlfriend for two and-a-half years," he told *Rolling Stone* magazine, "and we got very strung out. Dying from drugs didn't seem to me then to be a terrible thing."

• Ironically, during this low point in his life, "Layla" was re-released and became one of the all-time FM favorites...and then struck gold as a Top 10 single.

• In 1974, Clapton kicked the heroin habit and re-emerged on the music scene with "I Shot the Sheriff," his first #1 song.

• A happy ending for Eric: Patti eventually divorced George and, in a secret ceremony in Tucson, Arizona, in 1979, married Clapton. The ultimate irony: Patti and Eric later joined George in a recording of the Everly Brothers' old hit, "Bye, Bye Love."

UNRELATED MORBID TRIVIA

From Fred Worth's Hollywood Trivia:

• George Reeves, the star of TV's "Superman," was buried wearing the grey double-breasted suit he wore when he played Clark Kent.

• Bela Lugosi, who played the vampire Dracula in many films, was buried in his Dracula cape.

BATMAN ON TV

Holy bonanza! In the summer of 1989, Batman *became one of the biggest-grossing films of all time. But the Batman TV series in 1966 was just as much of a smash on the small screen.*

HOW IT STARTED

Back in 1939, cartoonist Bob Kane created Batman as a stablemate for the popular DC Comics character, Superman. A skilled detective who kept his identity hidden under a cape and mask, this "Batman" hunted down criminals in the night . . . and murdered them. He was an instant smash.

After his comic book success, Batman became a radio series, then made the jump to movie serials in the late '40s.

By 1965, pop art was big and a comic book revival was on, and the time was right for Batman to make a bat-leap onto TV. As it happened, ABC was hard up for anything that would bolster its sagging ratings. So when Douglas Cramer suggested the idea to network executives, they agreed to give Batman a shot. What could they lose? William Dozier, who had never even heard of Batman, was hired to produce the series, and he recruited "the most bizarre thinker I knew," Lorenzo Semple, to develop scripts. Then fate lent a hand. As production for the series was beginning in fall 1965, Columbia Pictures released four hours of old Batman movie serials under the title *An Evening With Batman and Robin*. It played to packed houses at college campuses around the country and ignited "Batmania." Dozier rushed production to take advantage of this good fortune. And Batman premiered in January of 1966. Holy ratings! It shot up to #1 immediately, becoming an instant cult classic.

INSIDE FACTS

Holy Bat-Craze

TV ignited a Batman merchandise boom. In 1966, over 60 manufacturers made more than 500 Batman products and sold more than $60 million worth of them . . . making Batman the biggest fad America had ever seen. Suddenly consumers could buy Batbath bubble soap, Batman peanut butter, Batman greeting cards, Batman pajamas, and so on. The fad was repeated 23 years later, in 1989.

Who Is That Masked Man?

The actors chosen to play the Dynamic Duo were virtual unknowns. Adam West (Batman) had co-starred for a season in a 1961 TV series called "The Detectives," but other than that, had endured 7 years of bit parts in TV shows and Italian Westerns before becoming an "overnight success." Burt Ward (Robin) had even less experience, and was flat broke when he got the part. To celebrate, he and his new bride cashed in 25¢ worth of Coke bottles and bought 8 chicken wings.

Top Priorities

When ABC broke into the middle of a "Batman" episode to announce the emergency landing of the Gemini 8 spacecraft, they were flooded with irate phone calls. Holy priorities! Apparently, Bat-fans cared more about the fictional exploits of the Caped Crusader than the real-life ones of the astronauts.

Follow that Car

The TV Batmobile was a modified Lincoln Continental, customized by George Barris for the show at a cost of $30,000. Despite the impressive fireball that burst from the rear of the car upon ignition, it ran on plain old gasoline.

Guardian Angel

Aunt Harriet, Bruce's kindly old relative, was not in the original comic book. She was added to the Wayne household by Dozier to parry charges of homosexual overtones in the show (3 men living together). "She watches everything," said a network representative.

So Bad, He's Good

In 1966, Frank Gorshin was nominated for an Emmy for his performance as the Riddler, making him the most critically acclaimed villain on TV.

Status

Viewers will spot plenty of familiar faces in "Batman" reruns. "Batman" was the show it was "in" to be "on"; and guest stars included Joan Collins, Milton Berle, Liberace, Vincent Price, Cliff Robertson, Otto Preminger, Zsa Zsa Gabor, Burgess Meredith, et al.

The world population of chickens is about equal to the number of people.

NAZI OR NOT?

These celebrities have been accused of being Nazis. But were they? Or are they just the victims of nasty rumors?

THE ACCUSED: Errol Flynn, swashbuckling screen idol of the '30s and '40s.

THE CHARGE: Flynn actively worked as a Nazi spy.

THE EVIDENCE:

• *Exhibit A*: Flynn was apparently a rabid anti-semite.

• *Exhibit B*: One of Flynn's closest friends, Dr. Hermann Erben, was unmasked as a Nazi spy after the war. He and Flynn traveled extensively together (e.g., during the Spanish Civil War, they went to Spain and posed as journalists), and when Erben was booted out of America by the U.S. Government, Flynn smuggled him back into Mexico.

• *Exhibit C*: During the war, the U.S. Government had Flynn under surveillance, calling him a potential subversive.

• *Exhibit D*: He insisted that the 1941 film *Dive Bomber* be shot on location at the San Diego naval base. His accusers say it was to give "Japanese military planners a look at American defense installations and aircraft carriers."

THE DEFENSE: Flynn died in 1959, and the charge was made 21 years later by author Charles Higham, in his book *Errol Flynn: The Untold Story*.

• Ex-spy Erben denies Flynn had ever worked with him.

• Flynn's Hollywood cohorts scoff at the charges, saying that at worst, Flynn was guilty only of standing by a pal.

• It has been pointed out that although he was watched, Flynn was never picked up by the government

• Flynn's daughters sued Higham for libel. "We're hoping... we might discourage authors like Higham from writing about people who aren't even alive to defend themselves," explained one. The California Supreme Court refused to hear the case.

NAZI OR NOT? The evidence is too thin to convict anyone, but it's an intriguing possibility.

THE ACCUSED: Charles Lindbergh, the first man to fly solo nonstop across the Atlantic. A national hero.

THE CHARGE: Lindbergh was either America's "number one Nazi sympathizer," as many politicians charged, or worse. FDR is quoted as having told Henry Morganthau, his secretary of the Treasury, in 1940: "If I should die tomorrow, I want you to know this. I am absolutely convinced Lindbergh is a Nazi."

THE EVIDENCE:

- *Exhibit A*: In 1938, Lindbergh accepted a medal from Adolf Hitler, and publicly expressed his admiration for Germany.
- *Exhibit B*: Returning to America, he began making speeches in favor of the U.S. staying out of any European conflict at all costs. This was—coincidentally?—a policy priority for the German government as well.
- *Exhibit C*: He became a central figure in the America First Committee (stay out of Europe, take care of America first), tirelessly giving speeches and radio addresses directed not only at keeping America out of World War II, but at preventing the U.S. from supporting Britain.
- *Exhibit D*: When "interventionist" politicians attacked him as a Nazi, his political allies urged him to repudiate fascism and Hitler. He refused to do so.
- *Exhibit E*: Pre-war cables from the German consulate in Washington described his efforts as a wonderful propaganda tool, and urged the Nazi government not to publicly support his position, lest he be branded a traitor.
- *Exhibit F*: In an October, 1941 speech he blamed the British and the Jews for the public pressure to get America into the war. "The leaders of the British and Jewish races...for reasons which are not American, wish to involve us in the war," he said.

THE DEFENSE: When America went to war, Lindbergh wrote in his diary: "I have always stood for what I thought would be to the best interest of this country, and now we are at war I want to take part in it, foolish and disastrous as I think the war will prove to be. Our decision has been made, and now we must fight to preserve our national honor and our national future." He got a job working with Ford Motor Company, developing bomber manufacturing capacity. And in 1944, he went to Germany to help the U.S. study their rocket-building facilities.

NAZI OR NOT? Yes and no. He considered himself a patriotic American and joined in the war effort (even though he disagreed with it). But his sympathies clearly lay with the Nazis. Even in his diaries, he never criticized Hitler or fascism. And the prospect of a Nazi-dominated Europe was a positive one to him; he admired their efficiency and orderliness. When the war was over, he still maintained we should never have become involved. Confronted with the sight of a concentration camp, he merely said it was no worse than America had treated the Japanese, and added: "Judge not, that ye not be judged."

THE ACCUSED: Gary Cooper.

THE CHARGE: Cooper was a " strong Nazi sympathizer." This allegation, too, was made by Charles Higham in his book, *Cary Grant: The Lonely Heart*.

THE EVIDENCE:

- *Exhibit A:* In 1938, Cooper visited Germany.
- *Exhibit B:* While there, he met with high government officials and may even have had a secret meeting with Hitler.
- *Exhibit C:* Hitler's favorite movie was Cooper's *Lives of the Bengal Lancers*.

THE DEFENSE:

- According to Cooper's wife at the time, the charge is "a despicable, bald-faced lie." She says Cooper never went to Germany in 1938.
- Origin of the rumor, according to the ex-wife: she and Gary accompanied her mother and stepfather to Germany in 1939. It was a special favor to FDR, with whom her stepfather was friends.
- Says the ex-wife: "It was shortly after Lindbergh said what he did about the power of the German Air Force. FDR wanted to know about Germany's finances, and my stepfather made contact with a Goering—not Hermann Goering, but his half-brother...to look at some plants."

NAZI OR NOT? The evidence is embarrassingly scanty. Unless more turns up, there's no case at all.

From age 5 to age 15, an American kid will see about 13,500 people killed on TV.

THE BIRDS

Some inside dope on one of Alfred Hitchcock's spookiest films.

Alfred Hitchcock's 1963 film *The Birds* was a milestone: no one had ever tried to work with so many animals at once; and no one has ever used live animals so effectively in a suspense film.

Much of the credit goes to Hollywood's #1 bird expert, Ray Berwick. He was familiar with the Daphne DuMaurier short story on which *The Birds* was based, but never imagined anyone would try to film it. Then, one morning at 6:30, he got a call telling him to be at Hitchcock's office in an hour. He walked in on a *Birds* production meeting, where he was told that $250,000 had already been spent on mechanical birds that didn't work. Could they use live birds? Not even Berwick was sure. But he agreed to try.

BERWICK'S APPROACH

- Although thousands of untrained birds—sparrows, finches, buntings, seagulls, and ravens—were ultimately used, Berwick only trained 100-150 ravens, blackbirds, and seagulls for the film.
- Of the trained birds, only 25 or 30 were well-trained; that's all they needed. Birds, says Berwick, have a tendency to follow leaders, so the well-trained birds lead the others wherever the director wants them to go.
- The small birds weren't trained—and they didn't have to be. In one convincing scene, for example, they were just "dumped down a chimney."
- According to Berwick: Once the wild birds were tame, they lost their fear of humans and actually became "the birds," attacking members of the cast and crew.
- Hitchcock wanted to include an owl among his feathered fiends, but had to cut the owl's scene because it looked comical.

BEHIND THE SCENES

Years after the film was released, Berwick revealed the secret of making seagulls look as though were attacking humans:

- He taught the birds to land on people's heads whenever people were standing still. And each time they performed that stunt successfully, they were fed.

• In the film, the audience saw what *looked* like people running down a street being chased by seagulls; in reality, the seagulls were flying along *with* the people, waiting for the people to stop moving so the birds could perform their trick.

• As soon as the director yelled "Cut!" the actors stopped running and the birds landed on their heads—and received their food rewards.

• **Postscript:** After the film was completed, the seagulls that had been used in the film were taken to the Pacific shore and set free. According to Berwick, trained seagulls will forget what they've been taught in about a week, if no one's working with them. But for the first week after the birds were released, there were strange reports of seagulls landing on people's heads at the beach. No one believed the reports, of course—except the people who'd worked on *The Birds*. And they weren't about to explain it to anyone.

ADVENTURES IN CINEMAGIC

In one carefully crafted scene, co-star Tippi Hedren was rowing across a lake when a seagull seemed to swipe her across the head—leaving her bloodied. Here's how Hitchcock's crew did it:

• They ran two tubes up Hedren's dress: one, which went to her forehead, spurted "blood" ; the other, which went to the top of her head, was attached to an air compressor.

• Then they released the gull, which was one of the birds trained to land on people's heads.

• The gull started to land on Hedren's head. But at the moment it touched her, the air compressor was turned on. The burst of air scared the bird into flying away.

• At the same moment, the "blood" squirted through the other tube, making it seem as though the bird had attacked. A complicated stunt, but clever and effective.

AFTERMATH

Hitchcock and Berwick made a lot of enemies in pet shops wth *The Birds*. After the film was released, sales of pet birds plummeted.

• Turnabout: Years later, Berwick was also responsible for a bird "boom" when he brought Fred the cockatoo to the screen in the TV show "Baretta."

STRANGE LAWSUITS

More examples of the American legal system gone slightly nuts.

THE PLAINTIFFS: Michael and Geraldine S., of Bridgehampton, New York.

THE DEFENDANT: The Hampton Day School.

THE LAWSUIT: The S. family was angry that their 6-year-old son Philip, a first-grader, wasn't getting any homework. So they sued the school for $1,500.

THE RESULT: The jury rejected the S.'s claim and "ordered them to hand over the $975 in tuition they had refused to pay the school."

THE PLAINTIFF: Andrew Freese, a 23-year-old silver miner.

THE DEFENDANT: The state of Idaho.

THE LAWSUIT: Freese objected to the slogan on the Idaho license plate, "Famous Potatoes," because it forced him to advertise potatoes against his will. "This imposition has been borne by the long-suffering citizens of Idaho for the last 12 years," he said in his complaint. He added that mentioning only potatoes discriminated against Idaho's other major products, like lumber...and silver.

VERDICT: Unknown.

THE PLAINTIFFS: The family of Tomontra Mangrum, a 15-year-old West Palm Beach girl.

THE DEFENDANT: Marlon Shadd, a 17-year-old West Palm Beach boy.

THE LAWSUIT: Tomontra claimed she was stood up by Marlon on prom night. "I talked to him a few days before, and he said he already had his tux and the tickets," she told reporters. "I was very upset when he didn't show up." Marlon, on the other hand, insisted he'd called off the date a week before the prom. "I told her I fractured my ankle," he said. Tomontra's mother filed suit against Shadd, seeking $49.53 for the cost of the shoes, flowers, and hairdo her daughter had gotten for the prom. Shadd's mother tried to

settle out of court: "I offered her the money. You know what she tells me? She tells me the boy has to be punished."
VERDICT: Pending.

THE PLAINTIFF: Lori C.
THE DEFENDANT: Jack Lee C.
THE LAWSUIT: When Jack met his future bride at a party, he told her his parents had been killed in an auto accident some ten years before. After they were married, Lori "became suspicious when her husband started waving guns around at home. She investigated and found that Jack had shot his parents to death, but was cleared on insanity grounds." She not only sued for divorce, she asked for an additional $20,000 for "emotional distress."
THE VERDICT: Settled out of court.

THE PLAINTIFF: Virginia N., a dental hygenist from Naperville, Illinois.
THE DEFENDANT: James L., her former employer.
THE LAWSUIT: Ms. N. charged that Mr. L. forced his employees to hug him each day before leaving work. She asserted that if she had been informed that to hug and be hugged was part of the job description, she "would not have taken the job." She also said that whenever she tried to "dash from work hugless," her employer complained bitterly. Did she quit or was she fired?
VERDICT: Pending.

THE PLAINTIFF: Randall Dale Adams.
THE DEFENDANT: Filmmaker Errol Morris.
THE LAWSUIT: Adams was convicted of murder in 1977. Ten years later, Morris made a film about the Adams case and as he did, he became convinced that Adams was innocent. The movie, *The Thin Blue Line*, presented the case for Adams's innocence so effectively that he was released from prison. Morris's reward? When Adams got out of jail, he sued the filmmaker for $60,000 for using his story.
VERDICT: Settled out of court. Adams dropped the suit, and Morris agreed that Adams should receive full rights to any further commercial uses—notably films or books—of his life.

PRIME-TIME PROVERBS

More words of wisdom from Prime-Time Proverbs.

ON CHANGING
"Some of us change, some of us mutate."

—**Joyce Davenport,**
Hill Street Blues

ON HELPING
New Yorker (Victim): "Lemme get this straight—you're saying that you saw me in trouble, so you came over for no reason, with nothing in it for you, and saved my life?"
Good Samaritan: "Yep."
Victim: "You're sick!"

—Barney Miller

ON GRATITUDE
Radar O'Reilly: "How can I ever thank you?"
Hawkeye Pierce: "Well, you can give us your firstborn."
B.J. Hunnicut: "And an order of fries."

—M*A*S*H

ON NICE GIRLS
Jack Tripper: "She's pure and wholesome and virtuous. Whatever happened to girls like that?"
Janet Wood: "They all go out with guys like you."

—Three's Company

Sue Ann Nivens: "Mary, what do you think turns on a man?"
Mary Richards (exasperated): "Sue Ann, I haven't the slightest idea."
Sue Ann: "I know that, dear. I was just trying to make your day."

—The Mary Tyler Moore Show

ON NUCLEAR WAR
Agent 99: "Oh, Max, what a terrible weapon of destruction."
Maxwell Smart: "Yes. You know, China, Russia, and France should outlaw all nuclear weapons. We should insist upon it."
99: "What if they won't?"
Smart: "Then we may have to blast them. That's the only way to keep peace in the world."

—Get Smart

ON EXERCISE
"Relaxation helps you live longer. Don't exercise, it could kill you."

—Roger Addison,
Mr. Ed

Not just people: Dogs, too, are either left-handed or right-handed.

SEE EUROPE IN THE U.S.

Tip from the B.R.I. travel director: Want to see Europe? Why bother? As fast as you can think up places to visit overseas, we'll find you a nicer, more sanitary, air-conditioned domestic version as an alternative.

THE LEANING TOWER OF PISA

May we suggest a trip to Niles, Illinois.? There, out in front of the local YMCA, is a half-scale replica, with a gift store at the bottom and an observation deck on top. And after you've taken some souvenir photos of your family holding up the Leaning Tower, why not head for a day under the Eiffel Tower? No, not the one in France. Of course, we're referring to the Eiffel Tower at the King's Island Theme Park near Cincinnati, Ohio.

THE STATUE OF DAVID

Why spend 10 billion lira for a cold-water hotel to stay to see this? It doesn't even move, and what else is there to do, once you've seen it? Wouldn't you rather see an exact replica inside Caesar's Palace in Atlantic City, N.J., at the Ringling Brothers Museum of Art in Sarasota, Fla., or in Sioux Falls, S.D., where it is dedicated to Tom Fawich, inventor of the four-door automobile? You bet you would.

THE LAST SUPPER

By all accounts the original Last Supper is peeling and dingy. No need to head to Rome—not only does America have carloads of Last Suppers to see, we've got them made out of such an ingenious variety of materials that even Leonardo himself would've been hard-pressed to match them.

• See one crafted from gourd seeds at the Gourd Museum in Angler, N.C.

• See one made of butterfly wings at the Christ Only Art Gallery, Eureka Springs, Ark.

• There are life-sized versions made of wood at Kissimmee, Florida's Woodcarving Museum, of plaster in Rhyolite, Nev., and a bas-relief in Yucca Valley, California's Desert Christ Park.

There's about a 50-50 chance you were still a virgin when you were 16.

• The best one, though, is the larger-than-life stained glass Last Supper in Glendale, California's Forest Lawn Cemetery. This window comes complete with narration...and back-lighting to show the coming of evening to the Holy Land.

STONEHENGE

America has two! There's one in North Salem, N.H., but the best (in the world) is in Mary Hill, Wash. It is full-sized and complete, not just a ruined pile of dusty rocks like the original. And the parking lot is big enough for a car to do "doughnuts" in, something the fun-loving ancient Druids would've appreciated.

THE BLARNEY STONE

With all the trouble in Ireland, you'd be much better off visiting the Blarney Stones in either Shamrock, Texas, or in Irish Hills, Michigan. The latter is heartily recommended, due to its proximity to both the Michigan International Speedway and The Prehistoric Forest dinosaur park. Let 'em match that in Erin.

AFRICA

You can visit Cleopatra's Needle in New York City, Cleopatra's Barge in Las Vegas, and the Rosicrucian Egyptian Shrine in San Jose, California.

• What about actual pyramids? Well, Bedford, Indiana, tried to construct a replica out of limestone (along with a replica of the Great Wall of China) but ran out of funds. But don't pack your bags for Giza yet. Not before you visit the aptly designed Pyramid Supper Club in Beaver Dam, Wisconsin, and sample their specialty after-dinner drink, the "Yummy Mummy."

• After drinks in Wisconsin, why not travel to the Oyotunji African Village near Sheldon, S.C.? There, King Adefunmi I, Ooni of Life, will treat you to a splendid afternoon of traditional Nigerian garb and customs. And remember this: If happy exhaustion catches up with you after your long day, it won't be from a tsetse-fly bite.

GREECE

Tourist disappointment with polluted Athens is well-chronicled. But don't whine about missing history, when a trip to Nashville, Tennessee, will place you in front of a full-scale, clean version of

Watch out for German shepherds—they bite more people than any other breed of dog.

the Parthenon. And in Greece you can't visit Loretta Lynn's Dude Ranch and motocross attractions after your day of pointless rubble-rousing.

• If that doesn't sate your Grecian yearning, spend the weekend at the Greek Spongers' Village in Tarpon Springs, Florida.

INDIA

From the quiet rolling hills of West Virginia, suddenly there bursts forth the spectacular Hari Krishna Palace of Gold in the town of New Vrindavan. This tremendous palace recreates the mystical buildings and gardens of India—sans untouchables—in a truly fabulous manner. Now you know what gets done with all that money the Krishnas raise in airports.

• The illusion of India is not yet complete, the Krishnas say, but will be by the time they finish the adjoining Krishnaland theme park, complete with live elephants to transport guests from the Temple of Understanding to the Diety Swan Boat rides. All this is forecast to cost $50 million.

DENMARK

There are a number of "little Denmarks" in the United States, but there is none better than Solvang, Calif. Danish windmills and thatched roofs appear as one drives through the warm countryside of Southern California. Is Solvang better than Denmark? Is Denmark 30 minutes from the beautiful beaches of Santa Barbara? Does Denmark have MTV? Case closed.

SWITZERLAND

Sugarcreek, Ohio, and the surrounding towns one up this land of neutral nebbishes. If Switzerland is so proud of its cheeses, how come they don't have the world's largest cheese wheel, like they do at Heine's Place (in nearby Berlin, Ohio)? And don't believe the Swiss travel brochures if they tell you that Switzerland is the home of the world champion of Steinstossen, or stone-tossing, because he lives in Sugarcreek. (Stone-tossing is a big deal in Switzerland. Isn't that exciting?) Sugarcreek has gas stations that look like ski chalets, the world's largest cuckoo clock and, if that weren't enough, John F. Kennedy's Navy footlocker is exhibited in the town museum.

Every time Beethoven sat down to write music, he poured ice water over his head.

MORE FAMOUS CHEATERS

The culprits here are a small-time trio of crooks and a big-time corporation.

CULPRITS: Clifford Irving and friends.

CIRCUMSTANCES: In 1971, billionaire Howard Hughes was the most famous recluse alive. For fifteen years he had refused to give interviews, refused to be photographed, refused even to be seen in public. So when a little-known author named Clifford Irving stepped forward as co-author of Hughes's authorized autobiography, it created a sensation. Irving had proof—letters scrawled in Hughes's own handwriting, checked and verified by the world's leading handwriting experts, attesting to the fact that the project was genuine.

Life magazine paid Irving an enormous sum for the magazine rights. "We've checked this thing out. We have proof," a Time, Inc. spokeman declared. Then McGraw-Hill gave Irving $650,000 for the right to publish the book, and the author delivered a 1050-page manuscript with Hughes's own notes in the margins.

Then the scheme fell apart. Irving had guessed that Hughes would remain aloof rather than becoming embroiled in a messy public confrontation. But he guessed wrong. In 1972 Hughes publicly disavowed the book; at the same time, Swiss authorities found out that Irving's wife, Edith, had been depositing checks made out to Hughes. Further investigation revealed that while Irving was in Mexico supposedly interviewing the rich hermit, he was actually having an affair with a German actress.

VERDICT: The Irvings and an accomplice named Dick Suskind were arrested and tried on various charges, ranging from conspiracy to breaking Swiss banking laws. They were convicted.

AFTERMATH: First of all, they had to give the money back. Then Clifford served 17 months in prison; he was paroled in 1974. Edith served 2 months in a U.S. jail and 14 in a Swiss one. Suskind served 5 months. When it was over, the Irvings got a divorce. Edith

More Hollywood films have been made about boxing than about any other sport.

remarried and moved to Spain. Suskind moved to Spain, too. Irving moved to Easthampton, Long Island and started writing again. In 1982 he published a moderately successful novel called *Tom Mix and Pancho Villa.*

CULPRIT: General Motors, America's auto manufacturing giant.

CIRCUMSTANCES: In the '30s, General Motors was looking for ways to expand its bus manufacturing business. So, along with Greyhound, Standard Oil, Firestone Tires, and several other corporations, they formed a company to buy municipal streetcar systems and dismantle them.

They started in 1932 with a few small urban public transportation systems—the streetcar lines in Kalamazoo, Michigan; Saginaw, Michigan; and Springfield, Ohio. When that worked, they moved on to bigger cities.

In 1936, they "engineered the conversion of New York City's stretcars to GM buses." Later, they moved on to Los Angeles.

As anti-trust lawyer Bernard Snell tells it: "In December 1944, [a company] financed by GM and Standard Oil...purchased the local system, scrapped its electric transit cars, tore down its power transmission lines, ripped up the tracks, and placed GM diesel buses fueled by Standard Oil on Los Angeles' crowded streets."

VERDICT: "In April of 1949," says *Environmental Action*, "a Chicago federal jury convicted GM of criminally conspiring with Standard Oil and Firestone to replace electric transportation with buses and to monopolize sale of buses. GM was fined $5,000."

AFTERMATH: While once there was a "vibrant public transportation" system of non-polluting electric trolleys and streetcars in America, we now have buses spewing tons of carbon monoxide into the air, doing their part to make urban air unbreathable. And, of course, General Motors has a lucrative bus business.

Footnote: The head of GM once said, "What's good for General Motors is good for America." Would he still think so? By the summer of 1989, Los Angeles—with its abnormally heavy dependence on cars—had the worst quality air in the U.S. It was so bad that L.A. was forced to adopt an emergency plan to cut down on pollution. Ironically, the measures suggested included: "Cleaner-running buses," and "cleaner fuel for all buses." Plus: "The use of electric cars will be encouraged."

A common housefly's life span is only two weeks.

FOOTBALL NAMES

Football fans know these names by heart. But they probably don't know how the teams got them. Here are the stories behind some famous names; info from Name That Team!

Los Angeles Rams. When they were founded in Cleveland in 1937, the team's owner resisted public pressure to call his club the Indians, after the local baseball team. Instead, he named them after a college football team—the Fordham Rams. In 1945, the Rams became the first N.F.L. franchise to switch cities when they moved to L.A.

Cleveland Browns. When the Rams left Cleveland, a new N.F.L. franchise took its place, and a contest was held to pick a new name. The winner was the "Panthers" ...but the owners found out there was already a semipro Ohio football team called the Panthers—and they stunk. So another contest was held. This time the winner was "Brown Bombers," inspired by boxing champion Joe Louis. The name was then shortened to "Browns," probably because the coach's name was Paul Brown.

Houston Oilers. The owner of the team made all his money in oil, and picked the name "for sentimental reasons."

Los Angeles Raiders. Originally located in Oakland, California, the team was first called the "Metropolitan Oakland Area Football Club." That was too unwieldy, so the Oakland Chamber of Commerce held a contest to find a new one. The winner: the "Oakland Senors." The team's reaction: "Forget it." The owners came up with "Raiders" on their own.

Green Bay Packers. The club was named for the Indian Packing Company, which sponsored the team when it was formed in 1919. Ironically, the company went out of business during the Packers' first season. But the team was a success; they joined the N.F.L. two years later.

New Orleans Saints. The team was admitted to the N.F.L. on November 1, 1966—which happens to be All Saints' Day. But the team probably got its name from the classic New Orleans jazz tune, "When the Saints Go Marching In."

Philadelphia Eagles. When they first began playing, in 1924, they were a pathetic club called the Frankford Yellowjackets (Frankford was the section of Philly they played in). The team went belly-up during the Depression, and two local businessmen bought it for $2500. F.D.R. had just been elected President; his two major economic programs—the New Deal and the National Recovery Act—used an eagle as their symbol. The team's new owners adopted the New Deal eagle as their symbol, too.

Phoenix Cardinals. Originally the Chicago Cardinals. They got their name when the team's owner bought a batch of second-hand jerseys from the University of Chicago. Someone commented they looked like the University's maroon shirts, and the owner replied defensively that they weren't maroon—they were "cardinal red." The name stuck.

Washington Redskins. They started out as the Duluth (Minnesota) Eskimos in 1928. In 1932, because they were having a tough time surviving, they moved to Boston. Their new home was the stadium owned by baseball's Boston Braves (now the Atlanta Braves), so they changed their name to the Boston Braves as well. But the arrangement didn't work out; the following season, the football team moved across to Fenway Park, home of the Boston Red Sox. To avoid offending the Red Sox (by keeping the name of the local rivals), the football team changed its name from Braves to Redskins. In 1938, the Redskins moved to Washington.

New York Giants. When the team was formed in 1925, they played in the Polo Grounds—home of the New York Giants baseball team. Owner Timothy Mara was a Giants fan already, so he named his team after them.

Chicago Bears, Detroit Lions, and **New York Jets.** All derived their names from local baseball teams—the Chicago Cubs, Detroit Tigers, and New York Mets.

Amazing garden: 50% of all species of flowers in the world are found in South America.

VONNEGUT SAYS...

A few thoughts from novelist Kurt Vonnegut, Jr.

"What passes for culture in my head is really a bunch of commercials."

"Laughing or crying is what a human being does when there's nothing else he can do."

"It strikes me as gruesome and comical that in our culture we have an expectation that a man can always solve his problems. This is so untrue that it makes me want to laugh—or cry."

"People don't come to church for preachments, of course, but to daydream about God."

"The canary bird in the coal mine theory of the arts: Artists should be treasured as alarm systems."

"People need good lies. There are too many bad ones."

"Thinking doesn't seem to help very much. The human brain is too high-powered to have many practical uses in this particular universe."

"We are healthy only to the extent that our ideas are humane."

"Beware of the man who works hard to learn something, learns it, then finds himself no wiser than before."

"Any reviewer who expresses rage and loathing for a novel is preposterous. He or she is like a person who has put on full armor and attacked a hot fudge sundae."

"I can think of no more stirring symbol of man's humanity to man than a fire engine."

"There is no reason why good cannot triumph as often as evil. The triumph of anything is a matter of organization. If there are such things as angels, I hope they are organized along the lines of the Mafia."

"Say what you will about the sweet miracle of unquestioning faith. I consider a capacity for it terrifying."

"We are what we pretend to be."

The $ Barometer: *Citizen Kane*, considered the best movie ever made, was a box office flop.

96 TEARS

"96 Tears" is as popular today as it was when it was first released in 1966. Here's the story behind the song, from Behind the Hits.

One of the all-time classic rock tunes is a simple song called "96 Tears." The band responsible for it, Question Mark and the Mysterians, were the embodiment of a number of rock phenomena: They were the ultimate "garage band"; they were living proof that anyone could be discovered and become a star; and finally, they were the classic one-hit wonder, a band that zoomed to the top and suddenly disappeared.

THE MYSTERY

Maybe you had to be there to appreciate this, but part of the excitement about "96 Tears" when it originally hit the airwaves in 1966 was trying to figure out who'd recorded it. They called themselves "Question Mark and the Mysterians." But who were they, really? Why wouldn't they reveal their true identities? It gave the deejays something to talk about when they played the record ("Friends, I have it on authority that Question Mark is actually Bob Dylan"), and it lent a little glamour to an otherwise ordinary garage-band tune. As a matter of fact, it's more interesting not to know who recorded "96 Tears." Does the name Rudy Martinez mean anything to you? That's Question Mark's real name.

BACKGROUND

The band's members were actually five young guys from Mexico whose families had all migrated to work in Michigan's Saginaw Valley. They took their group name from a Japanese alien-invasion movie, and they adopted their pattern of secrecy from their lead singer. Rudy always sported dark glasses and called himself "Question Mark." Early in the band's career, he wanted everyone else to go incognito, too; he suggested that the group be called XYZ, and that each member be referred to only by initials. Maybe he'd seen too many James Bond movies.

The band played around the Saginaw area for a few years in the mid-'60s, developing a repertoire that included an original number called "Too Many Teardrops," a poem that Rudy had written and

Left in the dark: there's no sun at the North Pole for 186 days each year.

set to very simple music. The rest of the group liked the tune, but not the title. They wanted to call it "69 Tears." But they decided they'd never get it onto the radio with a title like that. So they eventually began calling it "96 Tears" instead.

THEIR BIG BREAK

Like millions of other garage bands in the '60s, Question Mark and the Mysterians wanted to make a record. But no big label would talk to them, so they contacted a woman named Lilly Gonzales, who owned a little outfit in Texas called Pa-Go-Go Records. They told her they had some good songs, and she set them up with a recording session in a Bay City, Michigan, studio. (Actually, it wasn't a real studio—it was a converted living room).

They hauled their instruments—guitar, bass, drums, and Farfisa organ—to the studio, and played a few tunes. Then Pa-Go-Go pressed 500 records and sent them back to the band to distribute to deejays in the area.

The boys carried their discs around, asking jocks to listen...and surprisingly, several did. Particularly Bob Dell at WTAC in Flint and Tom Shannon at CKLW in Detroit, who played "96 Tears" regularly.

Then a funny thing happened. Executives at a national label that was almost bankrupt, Cameo Records, heard "96 Tears" on CKLW, and picked it up for distribution. They began selling it in other parts of the country. And suddenly, it took off. The song was recorded in February. By October, seven months later, it achieved the ultimate rock 'n' roll fantasy—#1 in America.

A PERFECT ENDING

The band broke up, according to lead guitarist Robert Balderrama, because its anonymous lead singer, Question Mark, "was on kind of an ego trip." Figure that one out.

IRRELEVANT ASIDE

In 1989, the Federal government financed a study on tuxedos to find out how to tax them. In a 54-page report, they revealed thought-provoking data like: "There are two major types of tuxedos—basic black tuxedos and fashion tuxedos." Their "principal findings" were that a rental tux lasts an average of 1.9 years, while the privately owned tux might last as long as 3.7 years.

John Wayne appeared in 153 movies. In all but 11 of them, he was the star.

THE ORIGIN OF FRANKENSTEIN

The original Frankenstein's monster wasn't Boris Karloff—it was (believe it or not) a character created by a 19-year-old author named Mary Shelley...more than 170 years ago.

BACKGROUND

In the summer of 1816, 19-year-old Mary Wollstonecraft Shelley and her 24-year-old husband, the poet Percy Bysshe Shelley, visited Switzerland. "It proved a wet, uncongenial summer," she wrote some 15 years later, "and incessant rain often confined us for days to the house."

To pass the time, the Shelleys and their neighbors—28-year-old Lord Byron, his 23-year-old personal physician, and his 18-year-old lover—read German ghost stories aloud. They enjoyed it so much that one day, Byron announced, "We will each write a ghost story." Everyone agreed, but apparently the poets, unaccustomed to prose writing, couldn't come up with anything very scary.

Mary was determined to do better. "I busied myself to think of a story," she recalled, "One which would speak to the mysterious fears of our nature and awaken thrilling horror." Yet she couldn't come up with anything. Every morning, her companions asked: "Have you thought of a story?" "And each morning," she wrote later, " I was forced to reply with a mortifying negative."

A FLASH OF INSPIRATION

One evening Mary sat by the fireplace, listening to her husband and Byron discuss the possibility of reanimating a corpse with electricity, giving it what they called "vital warmth."

The discussion finally ended well after midnight, and Shelley retired. But Mary, "transfixed in speculation," couldn't sleep.

"When I placed my head on the pillow," she recalled, " I did not sleep, nor could I be said to think. My imagination, unbidden, possessed and guided me, gifting the successive images that arose in my mind with a vividness far beyond the usual bounds of reverie. I saw—with shut eyes but acute mental vision—I saw the pale student of unhallowed arts kneeling beside the thing he had put together....I saw the hideous phantasm of a man stretched out, and then, on the working of some powerful engine, show signs of life and stir with an uneasy, half-vital motion.

"Frightful must it be; for supremely frightful would be the effect of any human endeavor to mock the stupendous mechanism of the Creator of the world. His success would terrify the artist; he would rush away from his odious handiwork, horror-stricken. He would hope that, left to itself, the slight spark of light which he had communicated would fade; that this thing would subside into dead matter; and he might sleep in the belief that the silence of the grave would quench forever the transient existence of the hideous corpse which he had looked upon as the cradle of life. He sleeps; but he is awakened; the horrid thing stands at his bedside, opening his curtains, and looking on him with yellow, watery eyes...."

THE PERFECT HORROR STORY

At this point, Mary opened her eyes in terror—so frightened that she needed reassurance it had all just been her imagination. She gazed around the room, but just couldn't shake the image of "my hideous phantom." Finally, to take her mind off the creature, she went back to the ghost story she'd been trying to compose all week. "If only I could contrive one," she thought, "that would frighten people as I myself had been frightened that night!" Then she realized that her vision was, in fact, the story she'd been reaching for.

As she recounted: "Swift as light and as cheering was the idea that broke in upon me. 'I have found it! What terrified me will terrify others; and I need only describe the spectre which had haunted my midnight pillow.' On the morrow I announced I had thought of a story. I began the day with the words, 'It was on a dreary night in November,' making only a transcript of the grim terrors of my waking dream."

THE NOVEL

The first version of Frankenstein was a short story. But Mary's husband encouraged her to develop it further, and she eventually turned it into a novel. It was published anonymously in 3 parts in 1818. "Mary," notes one critic, "did not think it important enough to sign her name to the book....And since her husband wrote the book's preface, people assumed he had written the rest of the book as well....It was not until a later edition of *Frankenstein* that the book was revealed as the work of a young girl."

The Carpenters won more Grammy awards for "Best Pop Group" than the Beatles ever did.

HOW PANTYHOSE HATCHED

Today, you can find pantyhose in every supermarket, clothes store, department store, drug store, and so on. Surprisingly, they've only been around since the mid-'60s.

In the early '60s, women were still wearing traditional stockings with garter belts, as they had since 1939, when DuPont first introduced nylons.

But as the mini-skirt caught on, stockings became impossible to wear. Whenever a woman sat down, the tops of her stockings showed. It was embarrassing. But what could she do instead?

Hosiery manufacturers looked desperately for a solution to the problem. They tried all kinds of bizarre things—stocking glue (roll it onto the top of your leg, and the stocking will stick there—no garters needed), decorating the tops of the stockings (so it looked like they were meant to be seen), even girdles with stockings already attached. But the only alternative that really made sense was a new kind of sheer tights called pantyhose. And they were much more expensive than stockings. Would women pay for them?

Enter Mary Quant, the creator of the mini-skirt. She added patterns to tights and—accompanied by a huge publicity campaign—introduced them as an integral part of the mini-skirt outfit. It was not only the solution to embarrassing stocking problems, she said, but an essential element of the "mini-look." Since it was in fashion, woman gladly paid the price.

Once the market for pantyhose was established, manufacturers developed ways to cut prices. Soon, undecorated pantyhose were cheaper than traditional stockings, and—since they were more convenient—they quickly replaced the old-fashioned kind. By the early '70s, 95% of all women's hosiery sold was pantyhose.

FASHION FLOP: In the mid-'60s, Coty tried cashing in on the colored pantyhose craze by offering "Body Paint." Why bother wearing expensive pantyhose, they asked, when you can paint your legs? The "mini, kicky, bare-as-you-dare fashion" was packaged in a paint can, and came complete with a roller and paint tray. There were four colors: Blue, green, mauve, or "flesh." It bombed.

BY GEORGE!

George Burns was always a popular performer. But by lasting longer than his compatriots, he's become an elder statesman, too.

"Too bad that all the people who know how to run the country are driving taxicabs and cutting hair."

"By the time you're eighty years old, you've learned everything. You only have to remember it."

"I must be getting absent-minded. Whenever I complain that things aren't what they used to be, I forget to include myself."

"The most important thing in acting is honesty. If you can fake that, you've got it made."

"I don't believe in dying—it's been done. I'm working on a new exit. Besides, I can't die now—I'm booked."

"I smoke cigars because at my age, if I don't have something to hold onto, I might fall down."

"Retirement at 65 is ridiculous. When I was 65, I still had pimples."

"Happiness? A good cigar, a good meal, a good cigar, and a good woman—or a bad woman; it depends on how much happiness you can handle."

"If you live to the age of a hundred, you've got it made, because very few people die past the age of a hundred."

"I don't worry about getting old. I'm old already. Only young people worry about getting old."

"I was married by a judge. I should have asked for a jury."

"Happiness is having a large, loving, caring, close-knit family in another city."

"Critics are eunuchs at a gang-bang."

"To be perfectly honest, I don't think acting is very hard. They say the most important thing to be able to do is laugh and cry. Well, if I have to cry I think of my sex life, and if I have to laugh, I think of my sex life."

80% of the people who get migraine headaches are women.

THE THREE STOOGES

There's nothing like the sound of a good "Nyuk, nyuk, nyuk" to make a Three Stooges fan smile. Even if you don't like them, you have to be impressed by their enduring popularity.

HOW THEY STARTED.

There are so many different stories about the Stooges' origin that it's hard to know which is correct. Probably none of them. Anyway, here's one that sounds good.

• There was a vaudevillian named Ted Healy, a boyhood friend of Moe and Shemp Horwitz. One night in 1922, some acrobats working for him walked out just before a show. Desperate, he asked Moe to fill in temporarily, as a favor.

• Moe, in turn, got his brother Shemp out of the audience, and the 3 of them did an impromptu routine that had the audience in stitches. Moe and Shemp loved the stage, so they changed their names from Horwitz to Howard and hit the road with their friend as Ted Healy and the Gang (or Ted Healy and his Stooges, depending on who tells the story).

• In 1925, the trio was on the lookout for another member and spotted Larry Fine (real name: Louis Feinberg) playing violin with the "Haney Sisters and Fine." Exactly why they thought he'd be a good Stooge isn't clear, since he'd never done comedy before, but he joined as the third Stooge anyway.

• They traveled the vaudeville circuit for years under a variety of names, including Ted Healy and his Racketeers, his Southern Gentlemen, his Stooges, etc. Then they wound up in a Broadway revue in 1929, which led to a movie contract.

• In 1931, Shemp quit and was replaced by his younger brother, Jerry. At the time, Jerry had a full head of hair and a handsome mustache—but Healy insisted he shave them both off...hence the nickname "Curly."

• Three years later, after a bitter dispute, the boys broke up with Healy. They quickly got a Columbia film contract on their own, and The Three Stooges were born.

• Over the next 23 years, they made 190 short films—but no features. For some reason, Harry Cohn, head of Columbia Pictures, wouldn't allow it (despite the Stooges' popularity and the fact they

J. Paul Getty—at one time, the richest man in the world—had a pay phone in his mansion.

were once nominated for an Oscar).

• Between the '30s and the '50s, the Stooges made four personnel changes: In 1946, Curly suffered a stroke and retired; Shemp then returned to the Stooges until his death in 1955; he, in turn, was replaced by Joe Besser (Joe) and Joe DeRita (Curly Joe).

INSIDE FACTS.

Two-Fingered Poker

One day backstage in the '30s, Larry, Shemp and Moe were playing cards. Shemp accused Larry of cheating. After a heated argument, Shemp reached over and stuck his fingers in Larry's eyes. Moe, watching, thought it was hilarious...and that's how his famous poke-in-the eyes routine was born.

Profitable Experience

By the mid-'50s, the average budget for a Three Stooges' episode—including the stars' salaries—was about $16,000. Depending on the time slot, Columbia Pictures can now earn more than that with one showing of the same film...in one city.

So What If He's Dead?

The last four Stooges episodes featuring Shemp were filmed after he died. The films' producer, Jules White, brought in a Shemp "double" who was only seen from behind.

The Stooges' Resurrection

By the mid-'50s the demand for short films had petered out. So in 1957, Columbia unceremoniously announced they weren't renewing the Stooges' contracts. Moe and Larry were devastated. After 23 years, what else could they do? Moe was rich from real estate investments, but Larry was broke—which made it even harder. They decided to get a third Stooge (Curly and Shemp were dead) and go back on tour. Joe DeRita, "Curly Joe," was selected. They started making appearances in 3rd-rate clubs, just to have work.

Meanwhile, Columbia, looking for a way to get a few bucks out of its old Stooge films, released them to TV at bargain prices. They had no expectations, so everyone (particularly Moe and Larry) was shocked when, in 1959, the Stooges emerged as the hottest kids' program in America. Suddenly the Stooges had offers to make big-time personal appearances and new films. And they've been modern American cult heroes ever since.

In 75% of American households, women manage the money and pay the bills.

A BIZARRE GENIUS

Great geniuses are often said to be "born ahead of their time." William James Sidis, on the other hand, seems to have been born out of his time completely; on the wrong world, in the wrong dimension. Perhaps someday the world will understand Sidis's strange genius. Probably not.

William James Sidis was born in 1898. His father, Boris Sidis, taught psychology at Harvard and was considered one of the foremost psychologists of his day. Boris argued that traditional approaches to childrearing obstructed the learning process. The elder Sidis was determined not to make that mistake with his son.

• He started by stringing words together with alphabet blocks above the child's crib.

• He eschewed the usual "googley-goo" babytalk that adults lapse into around infants, speaking instead to the child the same way he would speak to an adult. If the boy showed any interest in a subject, Boris encouraged his curiosity and study.

The effect of all this on the boy was astounding. By the time he was two, Willie was reading literature meant for adults; by age four he was typing letters in French and English; at age five he wrote a treatise on anatomy and dazzled everyone with a mathematical expertise few adults could match.

HIGHER EDUCATION

William Sidis graduated from Brookline High School when he was eight years old. When he applied to Harvard, the entrance board suggested he take a few years off to let his personality catch up to his intellect.

• Willie spent the time between high school and college reading books in French, German, Latin, Greek, Russian, Turkish, and Armenian.

• The boy entered Harvard at age eleven, becoming the youngest student ever to attend the school.

• Later that year, he gave a speech in front of the Harvard Mathematical Society on the subject of "Four-Dimensional Bodies." After the speech, Professor Daniel Comstock of MIT told reporters that the boy would someday be the greatest mathematician of the century.

DOWNHILL

From that moment on, William Sidis's world was never the same. Reporters followed his every move. He was a celebrity. His classmates treated him differently.

- The boy kept to himself, walking to his classes alone.
- At some point, Sidis realized his intellect was not admired—it was stared at. He wasn't merely intelligent—he was a freak.
- Within a year, at age 12, he suffered a nervous breakdown. He was taken to his father's Psycho-therapeutic Institute and treated.
- A few months later, Willie was back at Harvard, studying as diligently as ever. He graduated cum laude at the age of sixteen.
- In 1918, he began teaching mathematics at Rice University in Texas. But the annoyance of constant media attention finally took its toll. Quitting his teaching post, the young man moved back to Boston and, after a notorious arrest at a socialist march, disappeared from sight.
- In 1924, a reporter found him in New York City, working in a Wall Street office for menial pay. Sidis told the reporter that he was not the boy-wonder he once was. (Although this was probably not true. At one point, Sidis's knowledge of mathematics led him to completely rework his employer's statistical tables in his spare time, for amusement.) He wanted anonymity and a menial job that made no demands on him. Soon afterwards, he dropped out of sight again.

A STRANGE OBSESSION

- As an adult, Sidis had one great passion, a passion that has intrigued psychologists and writers for years. Sidis spent hours every day in search of streetcar transfers. He would chase them through windy lots, chisel them from icy sidewalks, and rescue them from rainy gutters. During his lifetime, he collected over two thousand of them, all different.
- In 1926, he published a book on the subject of his hobby. The book, *Notes on the Collection of Transfers*, is—to say the least—esoteric. Sidis filled it with page after page of detailed information on how the transfers are interpreted, how to use them to their best advantage, and techniques used by the devoted "peridromophile"

The longest that any high jumper has ever been able to stay in the air is one second.

(his term for someone who collects streetcar transfers) to find abandoned transfers.

• For those with merely a passing interest in the subject, he provided a chapter of bad streetcar jokes.

• Sidis used the pseudonym "Frank Folupa" to throw the press off the track, but it did not work. The book was quickly ascribed to him and once again, Sidis had to flee from the curious eyes of the press, losing himself in the crowded streets of New York City.

• Sidis managed to stay out of view for many years after that. In 1937, a writer working for *The New Yorker* magazine found him in a rundown rooming house in South Boston.

• Sidis told the reporter that he was no longer a mathematical genius. "The very sight of a mathematical formula," he claimed, "makes me physically ill." When the *New Yorker* article appeared, Sidis sued for invasion of privacy. Acting as his own attorney, Sidis offered to take an I.Q. test to prove just how normal he was. The suit was thrown out of court.

• Again the world forgot about him—until 1944, when, at the age of 46, William James Sidis died of a cerebral hemorrhage.

No one can explain his life. But one thing is certain: he knew more about streetcar transfers than anyone in history. And for this, we salute him.

ANOTHER "UNUSUAL" COLLECTOR

George Wahlert, of New York, has what he believes to be the world's largest collection of Apollo 11 memorabilia. He hasn't got any moon rocks or lunar modules yet, but he does have stamps, plates, mugs, cups, plaques, medals, flags, towels, curtains, T-shirts, hats, pencils, spoons, watches, clocks, models, lunchboxes...and even a bedspread—all commemorating the first flight to the moon.

How did George become hooked on the subject? Apollo 11 landed on the moon on his birthday.

Now he has enough stuff to fill a museum.

Would he like to go to the moon someday? He already has his Pan Am ticket.

He even bought two acres of moon land, and has a moon deed to prove it. "There's probably a lunar rover parked on my property right now," he says.

When they grow up: 1 in 100 American boys, and 1 in 150 girls, will become lawyers.

MACK THE KNIFE

A classic tune with a classy history. From Behind the Hits, *by Bob Shannon and John Javna.*

Bobby Darin's version of "Mack the Knife" was the #1 song of 1959. But few people who enjoyed it then—or have since—had any idea of its strange 30-year history.

THE SHARK BITES...

"Mack" debuted in Germany in 1929, in the Kurt Weill / Bertolt Brecht production of the *Threepenny Opera*, a scathing social commentary with parallels to the rise of Adolf Hitler. It was then known as "The Ballad of Mac the Knife" and was a song about MacHeath, the central character of the play. It was quite candid about Mac's bloody escapades.

The Nazis didn't particularly like Weill; he, Brecht, and Weill's wife, Lotte Lenya—who had created the role of Jenny in the original play—fled to the United States.

NEVER A TRACE OF RED

But it wasn't until the early '50s that the *Threepenny Opera* was performed here—and when it was, "The Ballad of Mac the Knife" became a very different song. In the conservative atmosphere of the times, the German lyrics were considered too violent to be translated literally. So an American named Marc Blitzstein was assigned to rewrite it.

MACKIE'S BACK

By 1956, millions of Americans had heard the melody of "Mac the Knife"...but they still hadn't heard either the German *or* American version of the lyrics—because the Dick Hyman Trio had recorded it as an instrumental. Hyman called it "Moritat," and it sold over a million copies.

Around that time, Louis Armstrong also recorded it, using Blitzstein's lyrics. But when Satchmo sang the song, he made a mistake in the list of characters near the end; he added singer/actress Lotte Lenya's name to the roll-call of ladies who'd succumbed to "Mackie." It was this version that got to Bobby Darin.

DARIN'S "MACK" ATTACK

An up-and-coming rock 'n' roll singer who had already scored with "Splish Splash," "Queen of the Hop," and "Dream Lover," Darin was hesitant about "Mack the Knife." He recorded it as part of an album called "That's All," but never envisioned it as a single. His friend Dick Clark agreed, telling Darin that it could never be a hit—it was too different. Besides, about twenty different versions of the song had already been recorded in 1956.

But Darin didn't have the last word on the subject. His record label, Atco, decided to release it as a single over his objections. To his surprise, "Mack the Knife" rocketed up the charts immediately. It was not only the most popular record of the year—selling over two million copies—but also won the Grammy for "Record of the Year." Darin was named "Best New Artist," although he'd been around the Top 10 for a while, and the song transformed him into a Frank Sinatra-type entertainer.

MACKIE'S BACK...AGAIN

In all, between 1956 and 1960 "Mack the Knife" appeared in the Top 40 seven times. The most memorable of these was the last one, by Ella Fitzgerald. Her version—a tribute to Satchmo and Darin—was recorded live at a concert in Berlin, and she forgot the words. It wasn't a problem, though. Ella is one of the all-time great improvisers, and the Germans had no idea what the English meant. She just made up the lyrics, which was all anyone had been doing since the original English translation anyway.

• **Final note:** The song keeps going and changing. In the late '80s, Frank Sinatra attempted a version of "Mack the Knife." He didn't start with Weill's, or Armstrong's or Darin's version, though—instead, he copied Ella's.

ABOUT BOBBY DARIN:

- His real name was Walden Robert Cassotto.
- He picked the named "Darin" out of a phone book.
- While he was a scuffling young singer, he and Connie Francis fell in love. Her father chased him away. She never got over it; Darin went on to marry teenage heartthrob Sandra Dee.
- Darin's first big hit, "Splish Splash," was written by the mother of a popular New York deejay, Murray the K.
- His congenitally weak heart gave out in 1973; he died at age 37.

The oldest tree in the world is the macrozamia tree of Australia. It lives for 7,000 years.

"LET'S DO THE TWIST"

Looking back 30 years, past slam-dancing and Flashdancing and Dirty Dancing, *it's hard to believe how significant—and scandalous—the tame Twist was when it first appeared. It's considered nostalgic fun today, but it was a powerful force in its time. It helped change American society in the '60s, and its impact is still being felt. Here's a quick retrospective.*

ITS ORIGIN

Everyone knows that "Mr. Twister" is Chubby Checker. "You know," he said, "I taught the world how to dance as they know it today. I'm almost like Einstein creating atomic power. Whatever dances came after the Twist, it all started here."

But "The Twist" was not originally done by Chubby Checker. The original version was written and recorded by a rhythm and blues performer named Hank Ballard.

• In the '50s, Ballard was a popular R&B singer who toured with his band, the Midnighters. The band often danced while they played, and one night . . . . "I was just watching them go through their routines, seeing them twisting their bodies," Ballard recalls, "and the lyric just came to me—'Twist.' " He wrote the rest of the lyrics to go along with their movements, taking the melody from an old R&B song, "What'cha Gonna Do."

• In 1959 he recorded the song and it was released as the flip side of "Teardrops on My Letter." He thought it should be the hit side, but couldn't convince his record company. "They thought it was just another mediocre record," he sighs.

• Ballard and his group tried to popularize the dance as they toured the country, and when they got to Baltimore it finally caught on. There, a deejay named Buddy Dean (who hosted a TV dance party) watched Baltimore teenagers Twisting up a storm. "He saw these kids doing the dance," says Ballard, "so he called up Dick Clark and told him to come over and see them."

• Clark, hosting "American Bandstand" in nearby Philadelphia, liked what he saw. He played the song on his show, and was impressed by the audience response, so he offered Ballard a chance to introduce the dance on "Bandstand." It would have been Ballard's big break, but it fell through. Instead, Clark got someone to do a new version. "He was trying to find someone to emulate my voice," Ballard says.

ENTER CHUBBY CHECKER

Clark found just the right person—Ernest Evans, an expert at mimicking other singers. Ernest changed his name to Chubby Checker at the suggestion of Clark's wife ("He looks just like a little Fats Domino—let's call him Chubby Checker"), and the new version of "The Twist" was released.

• Chubby copied Ballard's version exactly—it's almost impossible to tell the difference between them.

• With Dick Clark pushing it, Checker's record became a #1 smash in 1960, and the dance became a teenage craze. Then, like all fads, it died down.

• In 1962, however, adults discovered it. Society celebs like Zsa Zsa Gabor were photographed twisting at the Peppermint Lounge . . .and suddenly the dance was bigger than ever. Chubby's version of "The Twist" zoomed back up the charts to #1 again. It is still the only record ever to reach #1 in two different years. It was on the charts for 8 months, longer than any other #1 record in history.

• Twist records were released by the carload. Joey Dee and the Starliters hit #1 with "The Peppermint Twist"; young Rod McKuen sang "Oliver Twist"; Ray Charles put out a Twist album; Chubby did "Let's Twist Again"; Sam Cooke did "Twistin' the Night Away"; even Frank Sinatra got into the act. Everyone in America, it seemed, was doing the Twist. Except Hank Ballard.

AS A DANCE

The "Twist" made social dancing accessible to everyone; it was the first dance that anybody—young or old, athletic or uncoordinated, etc.—could do. There was nothing special to learn, no need to take lessons, and no need to practice. Instructions for the Twist could be summed up in one sentence. "It's like putting out a cigarette with both feet," explained Chubby Checker, "and coming out of a shower and wiping your bottom with a towel to the beat of the music. It's that simple."

• It was the first modern dance that people did without touching each other. Practically every popular dance since 1960 (except disco) is a direct outgrowth of the Twist.

• And finally, after howling about the immorality of rock 'n' roll in the late '50s, parents gave up their protests in 1962 and joined in . . .doing the Twist. It was the first time adults accepted rock. Until then, it was associated with juvenile delinquency.

AS A MERCHANDISING BOOM

While the Twist was *the* popular dance, Twist merchandise sold like hot cakes. You could get "twist" anything.

• Clothes became "Twist clothes" if you put fringes on them (fringes would fly out when you twisted);

• A "Twister chair" was so twisted that you couldn't sit on it;

• "Twist cigars" (bent stogies) were available;

• You could even eat a misshapen hot dog called a "Twistfurter." "The Twist has now danced its way onto the dinner table," announced its manufacturer.

AS A SCANDAL. Some examples of the international furor caused by the Twist:

1961: The Associated Press reported a scandalous scoop. "Under a secret service guard," AP claimed, "Mrs. Jacqueline Kennedy slipped out of Palm Beach last night and for an hour and a half danced the Twist in a Fort Lauderdale nightclub." AP turned out to be wrong—Jackie was home all night. AP had to publish a public apology. . .its first since it announced the end of World War II prematurely.

1962: Tampa, Florida, banned the Twist in its community centers.

1962: The United Arab Republic banned the Twist.

1962: Red Chinese newspapers castigated "ugly displays" of young people doing the Twist in Maoming Cultural Park in China.

1962: The Twist was banned by the Buffalo, New York, diocese in parish, school, and Catholic Youth Organization events.

1962: The South African foreign minister deplored the fact that South African youth were doing the Twist, calling it a "strange god from the United States."

1963: The Twist was East Germany's most popular dance, despite the fact that the Communist Party had denounced it.

1963: The South Vietnamese government said the Twist "was not compatible with the anti-Communist struggle," and banned it.

There have been 69 movies featuring the character Zorro.

MUHAMMAD ALI SPEAKS

The great boxer was also known as a talker. A few of his comments:

"Pleasure is not happiness. It has no more importance than a shadow following a man."

"Everybody's negotiable."

"I'm so fast I could hit you before God gets the news."

"When you're as great as I am, it's hard to be humble."

"A nation is only as good as its women."

"My toughest fight was with my first wife."

[Explaining his retirement] "There are more pleasant things to do than beat up people."

"I'll beat him so bad he'll need a shoehorn to put his hat on."

"There are no pleasures in a fight, but some of my fights have been a pleasure to win."

"It's just a job. Grass grows. Birds fly. Waves pound the sand. I beat people up."

"I'm not only the greatest, I'm the double greatest."

"When you can whip any man in the world, you never know peace."

"No one knows what to say in the loser's room."

"Wars on nations change maps. Wars on poverty map change."

"The man who views the world at 50 the same as he did at 20 has wasted 30 years of his life."

"I fear Allah, thunderstorms, and airplane rides."

"I'm one black man who got loose."

"Christianity is a good philosophy if you live it, but it's controlled by white people who preach it but don't practice it. They just organize it and use it any which way they want to."

"I just *said* I was the greatest—I never thought I was."

At one time, Hawaiian women were forbidden by law to eat coconuts.

AMERICA'S NOSTRADAMUS

If you read the National Enquirer *at the checkout counter of your local supermarket, you've seen that people like Jeanne Dixon are always trying to predict the future. They rarely get it right, of course. But in 1900 John Watkins did. In an article written for* The Ladies' Home Journal, *he looked a century into the future and foresaw subways, air-conditioning, Satellite TV, and lots more. No one has ever come close to this prognosticating feat—except maybe Nostradamus. Here's a small excerpt from Watkins' amazing 1900 article.*

BACKGROUND. John Elspeth Watkins was a Philadelphia newspaperman whose predictions were recently rediscovered by two Indiana professors. They call him "The Seer of the Century," and note that he was lucky enough to see many of his predictions come true before dying in the '40s.

What's amazing about these predictions? Remember what was going on in 1900: Production on primitive autos had just begun; they were still just a novelty. People lived in squalor and ill health, and died young. There was no such thing as an airplane. There was no radio; the first feature movie hadn't yet been made; the telephone had been invented a scant 25 years earlier. It was a whole different world—yet somehow, Watkins described ours in detail.

"These prophecies," he wrote in his introduction, "will seem strange, almost impossible."

It's a fascinating measure of how things have changed to realize that our way of life seemed like science fiction to the average American of 1900.

EXCERPTS FROM WATKINS' PREDICTIONS

"Man Will See Around the World. Persons and things of all kinds will be brought within focus of cameras connected electrically with screens at opposite ends of circuits, thousands of miles at a span. American audiences in their theatres will view upon huge curtains before them the coronations of kings in Europe or the progress of battles in the Orient. The instrument bringing these distant scenes to the very doors of people will be connected with a giant telephone apparatus transmitting each incidental sound into its appropriate place. Thus the guns of a distant battle will be heard to boom when seen to blaze, and thus the lips of a remote actor or singer will be heard to utter words or music when seen to move."

"The American Will Be Taller by from one to two inches. His increase in stature will result from better health, due to vast reforms in medicine, sanitation, food, and athletics. He will live fifty years instead of thirty-five as at present—for he will reside in the suburbs."

"Hot and Cold Air from Spigots. Hot or cold air will be turned on from spigots to regulate the temperature of a house as we now turn on hot or cold water from spigots to regulate the temperature of the bath....Rising early to build the furnace fire will be a task of the olden times. Homes will have no chimneys, because no smoke will be created within their walls."

"No Mosquitoes nor Flies. Boards of health will have destroyed all mosquito haunts and breeding grounds, drained all stagnant pools, filled in all swamp-lands, and chemically treated all still-water streams. The extermination of the horse and its stable will reduce the house-fly."

"Ready-Cooked Meals Will Be Bought from establishments similar to our bakeries of today. Such wholesale cookery will be done in electric laboratories...equipped with electric stoves, and all sorts of electric devices, such as coffee-grinders, egg-beaters, stirrers, shakers, parers, meat-choppers, meat-saws, potato-mashers, lemon-squeezers, dishwashers, dish-dryers and the like. All such utensils will be washed in chemicals fatal to disease microbes."

"There will Be No Street Cars in Our Large Cities. All traffic will be below or high above ground when brought within city limits. In most cities it will be confined to broad subways or tunnels, well lighted and well ventilated, or to high trestles with "moving-sidewalk" stairways leading to the top. These underground or overhead streets will teem with automobile passenger coaches and freight wagons, with cushioned wheels. Subways or trestles will be reserved for express trains. Cities, therefore, will be

The Boy Scouts were founded in 1910.

free from all noises." [Ed. note: not quite.]

"**Photographs Will Be Telegraphed from any distance.** If there be a battle in China a hundred years hence snapshots of its most striking events will be published in the newspapers an hour later. Even today photographs are being telegraphed over short distances. Photographs will reproduce all of Nature's colors."

"**Automobiles Will Be Cheaper Than Horses are today.** Farmers will own automobile hay-wagons, plows, harrows, and hay-rakes. A one-pound motor in one of these vehicles will do the work of a pair of horses or more....Automobiles will have been substituted for every horse vehicle now known....The horse in harness will be as scarce, if, indeed, not scarcer, then as the yoked ox is today."

"**Everybody Will Walk Ten Miles.** Gymnastics will begin in the nursery, where toys and games will be designed to strengthen the muscles. Exercise will be compulsory in the schools. Every school, college, and community will have a complete gymnasium....A man or woman unable to walk ten miles at a stretch will be regarded as a weakling."

"**There Will Be No Wild Animals except in menageries.** Rats and mice will have been exterminated. The horse will have become practically extinct....The automobile will have driven out the horse. Cattle and sheep will have no horns. They will be unable to run faster than the fattened hog of to-day. Food animals will be bred to expend practically all of their life energy in producing meat, milk, wool, and other by-products. Horns, bones, muscles and lungs will have been neglected."

"**Submarine boats** submerged for days will be capable of wiping a whole navy off the face of the deep."

"**To England in Two Days.** Fast electric ships, crossing the ocean at more than a mile a minute, will go from New York to Liverpool in two days. The bodies of these ships will be built above the waves. They will be supported upon runners, somewhat like those of the sleigh. These runners will be very buoyant. Upon their undersides will be apertures expelling jets of air. In this way a film of

Until 1857, foreign coins were considered U.S. money if they were made of a precious metal.

air will be kept between them and the water's surface. This film, together with the small surface of the runners, will reduce friction against the waves to the smallest possible degree." [Ed. note: Wow! He's predicting hydrofoils.]

"Telephones Around the World. Wireless telephone and telegraph circuits will span the world. A husband in the middle of the Atlantic will be able to converse with his wife sitting in her boudoir in Chicago. We will be able to telephone to China quite as readily as we now talk from New York to Brooklyn. By an automatic signal they will connect with any circuit in their locality without the intervention of a 'hello girl.' "

"Automatic instruments reproducing original airs exactly will bring the best music to the families of the untalented. In great cities there will be public opera-houses whose singers and musicians are paid from funds endowed by philanthropists and by the government. The piano will be capable of changing its tone from cheerful to sad. Many devices will add to the emotional effect of music."

"How Children Will Be Taught. A university education will be free to every man and woman. Several great national universities will have been established. Children will study a simple English grammar adapted to simplified English, and not copied after the Latin. Time will be saved by grouping like studies...Medical inspectors regularly visiting the public schools will furnish poor children free eyeglasses, free dentistry, and free medical attention of every kind. The very poor will, when necessary, get free rides to and from school and free lunches between sessions." [Ed. note: An incredible, revolutionary concept in 1900.]

"Oranges...in Philadelphia. Fast-flying refrigerators on land and sea will bring delicious fruits from the tropics and southern temperate zone within a few days. The farmer of South America, South Africa, Australia, and the South Sea Islands, whose seasons are directly opposite to ours, will thus supply us in winter with fresh summer foods which cannot be grown here. Scientists will have discovered how to raise here many fruits now confined to much hotter or colder climates."

LEAVE IT TO BEAVER

The Cleavers and their clan are classic TV creations—from June, who wore pearls while she vacuumed...to the rotten Eddie Haskell...to Beaver Cleaver, the quintessential '50s innocent.

HOW IT STARTED.

By 1957, shows like "The Danny Thomas Show" and "Father Knows Best"—sitcoms that portrayed modern American family life from an adult point of view—were hits. But Bob Mosher and Joe Connelly, who'd written together since 1942 (their major credit was over 1500 "Amos 'n' Andy" TV and radio scripts) came up with a new twist—a family sitcom that centered on the kids, not the parents. They called the program "Wally and Beaver" and modelled the characters after their own children. The stories they proposed were based on real-life occurrences in their own households.

When the pilot was filmed in 1957, it featured a slightly different cast than the one America eventually came to know: Barbara Billingsley (June) and Jerry Mathers (Beaver) were in it, but Hugh Beaumont (Ward Cleaver) and Tony Dow (Wally) were not.

CBS liked it anyway, and bought it for the 1957-58 season. Beaumont and Dow were hired to join the permanent cast, and production began.

However, the producers made one last change—they gave their show a new title. "Wally and the Beaver" didn't work, they said, because "it sounded like a show about a boy and his pet." Instead, they appropriated the title of a 1954 sitcom, "Leave It to Larry," and altered it slightly.

"Beaver" ran from 1957 to 1963. Surprsingly, though, it was never a huge hit. In its six seasons on the air, it didn't place among the Top 25 shows of a year even once.

INSIDE FACTS

Meet the Beave

At age 8, Jerry "Beaver" Mathers was already a professional actor, with TV appearances and a major film role (in Alfred Hitchcock's *The Trouble With Harry*) under his belt. But he was so fidgety when he was auditioning for the role of Beaver that the producers asked him what the trouble was. He blurted out: "I gotta go to my scout meeting." Rather than disqualifying him, that won Jerry the job. His honesty and "little boy" qualities were exactly what they were looking for in their main character.

Big Boys Don't Cry

After the pilot, "Beaver's" producers began searching for a new actor to play Ward. One day, Jerry Mathers was called in to read with Hugh Beaumont, who'd befriended him when they co-starred in a religious film. In one scene, tears had been required, but Jerry just couldn't do it. Beaumont gave the boy invaluable advice: "Cover your face with your hands and laugh—it'll sound the same." It worked. So now, here was the man who'd been so kind to him, reading for the part of his father. When Jerry got home that night, he prayed Beaumont would get the part of Ward. And he did.

Those Pearls

June Cleaver caused a nation of TV-viewing kids to wonder why their moms didn't wear pearls while doing the laundry, too. The secret: Barbara Billingsley wore them in each episode not for aesthetics or even character development, but because the ex-model had a very skinny neck.

But Don't Flush It!

The first "Beaver" episode ever filmed, "Captain Jack," wasn't the first one aired—because it was censored! It included scenes of Wally and Beaver keeping a pet alligator in their toilet tank, and showing a toilet on camera was against CBS policy. It was finally shown as the 4th episode.

Monstrous Copy

After "Beaver," Mosher and Connelly created another family sitcom—"The Munsters"! Oddly enough, several "Munsters" episodes re-worked Beaver plots, with child werewolf Eddie Munster filling in for the Beave.

Historic Coincidence

Two events make Oct. 4, 1957 a historic date to remember: on that day, both "Leave It to Beaver" and Russia's first satellite, Sputnik 1, were launched.

During the Plague many people thought they could cure themselves by sniffing human waste.

THE GREAT ROCKEFELLER

John D. Rockefeller, one of the most famous Americans who ever lived, is a hero to some, a villain to others. Here are some facts about his life that you may not have heard before, excerpted from Everybody's Business.

HIS PARENTS

"Rockefeller, born in 1839, seems to have inherited his character in equal portions from his con artist father and his stern, Calvinist mother."

The Father: "William Avery Rockefeller, was a tall, effusive, barrelchested man who amassed great sums of money first by flimflamming the Iroquois Indians near his home in upstate New York and later by selling patent medicines, including an elixir he claimed could cure cancer."

- "He gave medical consultations to the gullible country folk for $25—a good two months' wages."
- "In 1849 he was indicted for the rape of a young woman who had worked in the Rockefeller household...."
- "He moved his family to Cleveland in 1853 so that he could take advantage of the settlers streaming west in covered wagons with their life savings."
- "He often went away for long periods, and finally he disappeared altogether. Years later, a reporter working for Joseph Pulitzer discovered that the elder Rockefeller survived to the age of 96 and spent his last 40 years living under an assumed name in South Dakota in a bigamous marriage with a woman 20 years his junior."

The Mother: "The task of setting the children on the path of righteousness fell to the mother, Eliza Davison Rockefeller, described as a 'thin, hatchet-faced woman with flaming red hair and equally stark blue eyes.' "

- "A devout Baptist, she studied the Bible and filled young John with maxims he carried through life, such as 'Willful waste makes woeful want.' "

ROCKEFELLER GOES INTO BUSINESS

"Upon graduating from high school in 1855, Rockefeller chose to go into business rather than to college."

• "He got a job as a bookkeeper with a Cleveland commodity merchant for $3.50 a week—10% of which he faithfully donated to the Baptist church."

• "After three years he had saved $800 and he decided to start his own commodity business with a partner, Maurice Clark."

• "Needing another $1,000, he turned to his father, who had promised each of his children that amount when they turned 21. John was only 19-1/2, but his father agreed to lend him the money at 10% interest until he came of age. 'I cheat my boys every chance get,' the father liked to say. 'I want to make 'em sharp.' "

ROCKEFELLER DISCOVERS OIL

"Commodity prices rose sharply during the Civil War, and the new firm of Clark & Rockefeller made impressive profits. But a development even more far-reaching than the war was emerging around Titusville, Pennsylvania, where Edwin Drake had drilled the world's first successful oil well in 1859."

• "Oil was established as the cheapest, most efficient of illuminants, and...quickly started to replace candles and whale oil. The 'oil regions' sprouted derricks overnight, and dozens of refineries sprang up, first in Pittsburgh and New York and then...Cleveland."

• "In 1863 an acquaintance of Clark came to the partners with a proposition to start a refinery. Rockefeller dipped into his savings and invested $4,000 as a silent partner. At first he saw it as an unimportant sideline, but as the oil boom continued he began to devote more of his attention to it. In 1865, at the age of 26, he bought out the others and took control of the business."

• "His refinery was already the largest in Cleveland, and he was determined to expand. Around this time a startled bystander happened to see Rockefeller in his office, jumping into the air, clicking his heels, and rejoicing to himself, 'I'm bound to be rich! Bound to be rich! Bound to be rich!' "

ROCKFELLER DESTROYS HIS COMPETITION

"Rockefeller now set out to control the oil industry. He realized that the big money in oil would not be made at the well, since prices collapsed every time someone struck a new find."

• "The key to his success, Rockefeller saw, was to control the refining and transportation of oil. Borrowing heavily from Cleveland banks, he expanded his refining capacity and leased all the available tank cars from the railroads, leaving his competitors with no way to ship their oil out of Cleveland."

• "Next he negotiated an agreement with the Lake Shore Railroad to give him secret rebates on the crude oil he shipped from the oil regions to Cleveland and the refined oil he sent from Cleveland to the East Coast.... With his freight advantage secure, Rockefeller formed a new company in 1870, called Standard Oil."

• "In the same year several railroads came up with a new plan: they would secretly combine with the largest refiners in each major refining center, to the benefit of both parties. Freight rates would go up, but the refiners in the scheme would get their money back through rebates on their shipments and additional 'drawbacks' on the shipments of other refiners who were not in on the arrangement. Rockefeller saw it as a way to get rid of his bothersome competitors in Cleveland: they could either collapse their businesses into his, in exchange for stock, or they would be bankrupted by the rebate scheme."

BROTHERLY LOVE

"Rockefeller's younger brother, Frank, was a partner in a firm competing with Standard Oil. John D. told him: 'We have a combination with the railroads. We are going to buy out all the refiners in Cleveland. We will give everyone a chance to come in.... Those who refuse will be crushed. If you don't sell your property to us, it will be valueless.' Frank did not sell, and he went bankrupt. He remained bitter for the rest of his life and eventually moved his two children's bodies from the family burial plot in Cleveland so they would not have to spend eternity in the company of John D. Rockefeller."

GOOD MR. ROCKEFELLER

"Rockefeller looked back on this period with great piety. 'The Standard was an angel of mercy,' John D. told a biographer late in life. It was a situation, he explained, of 'the strongest and most prosperous concern in the business...turning to its less fortunate competitors...and saying to them, "We will stand in for the risks and hazards of the refining business....Come with us, and we will do you good." ' "

Men live longest in Japan (79.7 years). 2nd place: Norway (79.4 years).

ROCKEFELLER WANTS IT ALL

"Within three months, Rockefeller bought up all but 3 of his 25 competitors in Cleveland. Standard Oil controlled one-quarter of the nation's refining capacity, but he was not satisfied."

• "Rockefeller raised his sights and convinced more independent refiners in New York, Philadelphia, Pittsburgh, and the oil regions to come into the Standard combine. He did it with such secrecy that almost no one knew about his oil monopoly until it was a fait accompli."

• "By 1880 Rockefeller was refining 95% of the nation's oil."

• "At the time, American companies were prohibited from owning shares in other companies in other states. To get around this restriction, Rockefeller devised an 'oil trust,' which owned shares in each of the component companies—pretending all the while that the companies were independent."

• "He lavished bribes and 'deals' on state legislators."

• "He drove his competitors out of business by undercutting their prices until they gave up, and he expanded his power by buying oil-fields across the country."

CHANGING HIS IMAGE

Rockefeller was one of the most powerful men in the world when, in a 1911 anti-trust action, the Supreme Court forced Standard Oil to divide itself into into 31 different companies—but it wasn't as big a blow as it seemed to the public—because behind the scenes, Rockefeller held the bulk of the stock in all of them.

• With the aid of a publicist named Ivy Lee, the Rockefellers began a concerted effort to change his image. The Rockefeller Foundation was created; at Lee's behest, Rockefeller began giving away nickels (to children) and dimes (to adults) on the street; newspapers were encouraged by Lee to cover John D.'s golf games instead of his business practices.

• The effort was so effective that when he died in at age 97, John D. Rockefeller was known as a philanthropist by most Americans.

• His obituaries did little to contradict the image. Ivy Lee had seen to it that they were rewritten to include only data supplied by an "authorized" biographer.

About 70% of Americans who go to college do it just to make more money.

ELEMENTARY, MY DEAR STEVE

Once again, here's the famous woman sleuth, Leslie Boies, with a few simple mysteries for you to solve. Answers on page 454.

Leslie Boies, beautiful blonde detective, was reading a report on the "Penge Bungalow Case" to her faithful companion, Steve.

"Mrs. Krojanker was making biscuits in the kitchen and accidentally dropped her diamond ring into some coffee," she read. "Strangely enough, though, the diamond didn't get wet."

"Wait a minute," Steve interjected. "How is that possible?"

"It's elementary, Steve," Leslie replied.

What happened?

2. "You know, Steve," Leslie said, "Once, I was captured and almost bumped off by my arch-enemy, Fritz von Springmeyer."

Steve was surprised. "I didn't know that."

"Yes, the only thing that saved me was his gang's code of honor. They had a tradition—they always gave their captives an even chance to escape death. They took two pieces of paper, wrote "death" on one and "freedom" on the other. Then they told me to pick one. Now, I knew that that von Springmeyer couldn't afford to let me live, so he'd probably written "death" on both papers. But I thought fast, and they had to free me."

Steve was stumped. "How'd you, do it, Les?"

How *did* she do it?

3. Leslie and Steve were having coffee, discussing Leslie's latest case. The famous detective happened to glance down and saw there was a fly in her coffee.

"Yuck! Waiter!" she called, "Take this coffee away and bring me a fresh cup."

The waiter took her coffee away, and returned with more.

Leslie took a sip. Then she exploded angrily—"Waiter, this is the same cup of coffee I had before!"

How did she know?

THE NUT BEHIND GRAPE NUTS

To appreciate this story, first read "The Birth of a Flake" on page 294. Then come back and read this.

One of the guests in John Kellogg's Battle Creek sanitarium (The San) was a feeble 37-year-old named Charles W. Post, who arrived there in 1891. His story is told in the strangely fascinating book, *The New Nuts Among the Berries*:

Born in Springfield, Illinois in 1854, Post had wandered in search of success until, at age 37, he had become a well-to-do real estate salesman and blanket manufacturer in Fort Worth, Texas. He had also become a sick man, although we do not know the nature of his illness.

We do know that Dr. Kellogg promptly put Post in a wheelchair, and that after a few months Post hadn't enough cash left to remain a San resident; he had to become an outpatient. So he and his wife and daughter lived in a rented room in town, while Mrs. Post sewed suspenders to pay her husband's medical bills.

By the end of 9 months, Post was getting desperate. He still felt sick, and now he was destitute to boot. He pleaded with Dr. Kellogg to keep him on as a patient. He had spent quite a little time around the San's experimental kitchen. He knew that Kellogg had a new cereal coffee, called Minute Brew, and begged to help promote and sell the coffee in exchange for treatment and a little share of the profits. Post was coldly refused. John Harvey was not a loose man with money. And he did not believe in sharing profits with anyone.... Why take Post in?

So Post studied the powers of the mind, took up Christian Science, determinedly repeated to himself, "I am well," got out of his wheelchair and went to work. He had studied the economics of The San and liked what he saw. So with his gift of persuasion, he raised some money and by 1892 established his small La Vita Inn on a plot of 10 acres. Here diet and mental healing were combined, and at prices much lower than those of The San. Meat was allowed to lure those who wanted it. But despite these and other inducements, Mrs. Post still had to go on sewing suspenders.

Post got some of Kellogg's overflow, some of his malcontent clients, and some of his employees. He talked up his own powers to heal with faith and hypnosis. But things were still so slow that he went back to Kellogg and offered to pray for San patients for only $50 a week. The answer was the usual no.

So now Post began writing a book—*I Am Well! The Modern Practice of Natural Suggestion as Distinct from Hypnotic or Unnatural Influence*.....The book featured amazing stories of instant cures—no waiting around for months and taking all those enemas. In some cases of bad teeth, dyspepsia, or troubled bladder, one could hope for same-day service. He also knocked out a pamphlet, *The Road to Wellville*, which he gave away. In both the book and the pamphlet he criticized Kellogg, making the Doctor his certain enemy.

Later on, the San magazine, *Good Health*, would say that Post had spent a lot of time around the San kitchen. The clear implication was that Post had borrowed some of the formulas for his products. *Good Health* quoted Kellogg as saying, "Let him see everything that we are doing. I shall be delighted if he makes a cereal coffee and wish him every success. The more he sells of it the less coffee will be consumed, and this will be of great benefit to the American people."

In January of 1895, the year Dr. Kellogg discovered and launched the cereal flake, C.W. Post put out [a coffee substitute he called] Postum Cereal Food Coffee. The original marketing tool was a handcart which was pushed through the town of Battle Creek.

Soon Post took samples to Grand Rapids, Michigan. Almost without capital, he told wholesale grocers they could pay him if and when they sold their Postum. He talked newspapers into ad credit on the strength of the line, "It Makes Red Blood." By the end of the year, his sales amounted to over $250,000. In three years, they tripled.

American law: Less than 50% of the lawsuits filed actually go to court.

Steadily Post opened wider and wider markets, using ads for which he invented such ailments as "coffee neuralgia" and "coffee heart." Postum could cure them, he said. "Lost Eyesight Through Coffee Drinking" was another of his gambits. And they worked; 50 years later Postum was still being sold as the answer to "coffee nerves." He ploughed a fortune into advertising, using every cent of profit and borrowing more. He began to take ads in the New York Magazine of Mysteries, offering spot cash to get testimonials of cures.

Largely because sales of Postum fell off in summer, Post came up with a cereal to try and take up the warm-weather slack.... It was broken into rock-hard bits crumbled from sheets of baked wheat. He called it Grape Nuts, and he pulled out all the stops to announce its curative properties. According to ads which first ran in 1898, it was almost a specific for appendicitis. It tightened up loose teeth, fed the brain through what was implied to be almost a direct pipeline, and quickly disposed of tuberculosis and malaria. Of course, it worked better when consumed with a certain amount of faith; so Post put a copy of *The Road to Wellville* in each package. By 1901, C.W. Post was netting a million dollars a year.

In 1904, C.W. Post [scandalized the religious community of Battle Creek when he] divorced his suspender-sewing wife and married his typist. He was in his fifties; she was in her twenties. He also introduced a new cereal called "Elijah's Manna." Actually, it was corn flakes, which he had appropriated from Kellogg. But the cereal was unsuccessful until he changed its name to "Post Toasties." Then it became the cornerstone of Post Cereals, and later, General Foods.

In 1914, having tried to build his own city in Texas, and having failed to make it flourish by setting off explosions to bring rain, C.W. Post became depressed. In his Santa Barbara, California, home, he fired one of his own fine rifles into his head.

UNRELATED ASIDE

When Harry Truman was told there were ghosts in the White House, he replied: "I'm sure they're here and I'm not half so alarmed at meeting up with any of them as I am at having to meet the live nuts I have to see every day."

WHAT'S THE BEEF?

What's the real difference between Burger King and McDonald's? Not what you'd think. An examination by Mike Wilkins.

For years, Americans have watched as the world's two largest and most successful hamburger chains—Burger King and McDonald's—battled it out over supposed differences:

- Flame-broiling vs. frying
- *Doing It All For You* vs. *Having It Your Way*
- Whoppers vs. Big Macs.

And so on. To the uninitiated, these distinctions may seem like advertising hyperbole...But the fact is, the differences between McDonald's (10,000 restaurants, $13 billion in sales) and Burker King (4,500, $1.5 billion) are quite real.

BACKGROUND

McDonald's

The mythology of the birth of the McDonald's chain is fairly well known. In 1954, Ray Kroc, a fifty-year-old paper cup and milkshake-mixer salesman (actually owner of the company that made them), visited the McDonald Brothers' bustling restaurant in San Bernardino, California in 1954, after they placed a large order for his mixers. Impressed with their volume of business and the simplicity of their limited menu operation, he struck a deal for franchise rights, opened his first restaurant in Des Plaines, Illinois in 1955, and built McDonald's into the burger behemoth it is today.

Burger King

Surprisingly, Burger King also began with a visit to the original McDonald's. In 1952—two years before Kroc arrived—Keith Cramer, owner of a small Florida drive-in restaurant, made a pilgimage to watch the McDonald brothers in action. He was so impressed that he adapted their methods and began franchising his "Insta-Burger King" concept. A year later, the enterprise was taken over by franchisees Jim McLamore and David Edgerton. At first, Burger King was concentrated in the Southeast. But in 1967 it was acquired by Pillsbury, which began to expand the chain nationawide. With Pillsbury's economic muscle behind it, Burger King

63% of the Americans who earn minimum wage are women.

could challenge McDonald's in head-to-head competition. Their ad strategy: Burger King encouraged consumers to compare the "differences" between the two giants.

None of the ads, however, pinpointed the *real* differences.

WHAT'S THE DIFFERENCE?

The biggest difference between Burger King and McDonald's is this: McDonald's cooks their hamburgers using a batch process. Burger King cooks theirs using a machine-paced assembly process.

• Check it out: Next time you go into one of these restaurants, watch how the burgers are cooked. McDonald's fries their hamburgers on a large platen, in batches, or groups, of up to twelve. Two or more batches may be on the platen at one time, in various stages of cooking. When the guy in the back says "Quarter Pounders Up," a whole batch is ready at the same time.

• Burger King is built around its "continuous chain broiler." Raw hamburgers are placed at one end, and 80 seconds later they come out the other end, cooked. This machine-paced assembly process is common in most industrial manufacturing processes. It turns hamburger production into an assembly line, much like the type Henry Ford introduced to automobiles in the early 1900s.

IT'S BIGGER THAN IT LOOKS

As simple as this distinction (broiled vs. fried) seems, it is, in fact, at the core of each chain's operation, and is responsible for the corporate culture of each.

• For example: When hiring workers, McDonald's makes a big point about joining the McDonald's team, of the many incentives for doing good jobs, of its nonsalary benefits. Most McDonald's have a framed picture of the "Crew Member Of The Month" on a wall near the cash registers. McDonald's holds an Olympic-style competition to reward the best workers from around the country at each aspect of its food preparation. Not long ago, its advertising featured successful people who had once worked at McD's. When ordering, look at the McD uniforms. Many of the workers have pins or special nametags that signify proficiency or accomplishment at a task.

• Go to Burger King and all you see is a "Help Wanted" sign. There are no incentives to join the "Burger King Pit Crew" and the non-salary benefits are much less than those offered by McDonald's. (Total compensation was nearly $1 per hour greater at McDonald's in 1984.)

TEAMWORK VS. ASSEMBLY LINE

How does this relate to production methods? In a batch process, the speed of delivery is dependent upon the worker. At McDonald's, 12 burgers are made at one time. They are hand-seared after 20 seconds on the grill, turned at 60 seconds, and pulled at 100. When they come off the grill, workers must quickly add condiments, wrap and shelve them. If there are two batches going in different stages of cooking, it means that speed is even more essential to keep the production moving. And this means that the crew must all be motivated, or the process gums up. People must be willing and able to help in another's area in case of backup. Teamwork and a sense of team must be present. Thus the motivational and non-salary rewards.

At Burger King, on the other hand, no matter how fast the burgers are prepared once they are cooked, the rate-limiting step is the cooking itself. One burger at a time comes off the chain broiler at the rate of eight per minute, maximum. The machine paces the process. (Again, in slow times this is not entirely accurate because at these points in the day, BK keeps an inventory of already cooked patties in a steam tray at the end of the broiler. That is why BK sometimes has to microwave its burgers.) As long as you can do your part of the assembly process in 7.5 seconds per burger (adding pickles and onions in 7 seconds is easy even if you're not very motivated—try it someday), that's all that is required. If you get excited and love your work, and can do it faster, so what? You still have to wait for the machine to spit out the next patty. This means that Burger King saves money on wages and hiring expense, by not paying for all the motivation-inspired cross-talk.

HAVE IT WHOSE WAY?

Batch processing also means less room for individual differences in members of the batch. Twelve burgers come up, 12 burgers are all done exactly the same. At Burger King, since one patty comes out at a time, each can be made to individual order. Thus the *Have It Your Way* point of difference (vs. *We Do It All For You*) harped on by Burger King stems directly from the difference in production methods.

Also, batch processing means that twelve burgers will be ready (or 10 Quarter Pounders, or 6 Macs, since 12 patties = 6 Macs), whether or not customers are ready for them. During rush hour this is not a problem, but at other times it can be—especially in a business that promises fresh food. McDonald's and Burger King throw old food out—after 10 minutes in McDonald's case. That is what those cards with the numbers are doing on the McDonald's food shelves. When the minute hand gets to that number, all food in front of the card gets pitched.

WASTE NOT...

Since a product may stay in the bin nine minutes, keeping it warm is a problem. That is why McDonald's uses those Styrofoam containers, especially for its larger sandwiches. Styrofoam is much more expensive (and less ecologically sound) than the cardboard Burger King uses. Burger King doesn't need to keep finished burgers warm as long, so it doesn't spend for the fancy packaging. A McDonald's restaurant spends about 1¢ per revenue dollar more on paper costs than does a Burger King. That adds up to a yearly $15 million savings systemwide for BK.

• As one might guess, McDonald's throws away much more food than Burger King does. In fact, in the seedy Tenderloin area of San Francisco, the derelicts paint stars on the wastecans of the nearby restaurants and stores. The only four-star can in the neighborhood? McDonald's.

BATCHES MEAN BUCKS

How can McDonald's stay on top—or even competitive—with its system? The answer is that, when it is running right, the batch process allows for much greater throughput and faster speed of service. And speed is one big reason for the popularity of fast food in the first place. If an item is waiting in a bin, it obviously takes less time to serve than one made "your way."

• The batch process can deliver 300 burgers an hour vs. 200 for the continuous chain broiler.

• Speed standards given to individual restaurants by each headquarters bear this out. At side-by-side locations, the standard for a McDonald's is up to twice as fast as for a Burger King (a customer wait of, say, 90 seconds vs. three minutes).

• This difference may not be that noticeable per individual customer, but it means that McDonald's can do twice the dollar volume at peak than can a similarly sized Burger King.

Even customer flow is regulated by the speed of the broiler. Once the steam tray and bin reserves are gone, Burger King simply cannot serve more than eight burgers per minute. This accounts for at least some of the tremendous difference in the dollar volume per store between the two chains ($1.5 Billion over 4,500 stores, vs. $13 billion over 10,000). McDonald's is systemically better equipped to handle crowded areas. It is only during off-peak times when Burger King comes close in dollar volume, and is actually more efficient because of less waste, paper, and salary expenses.

So there you have it. An enormous "hidden" difference at the heart of the two chains. Next time you hear either of them make a claim about their service or products, check to see if it's based on their methods of production. Chances are, it will be.

UNRELATED INFO:

These were the #1 songs in America during the first week of each of the following years, according to *Billboard* magazine:

- 1958: "At the Hop," by Danny and the Juniors
- 1960: "El Paso," by Marty Robbins
- 1963: "Go Away Little Girl," by Steve Lawrence
- 1965: "Downtown," by Petula Clark
- 1966: "The Sounds of Silence," by Simon and Garfunkel
- 1967: "Kind of a Drag," by the Buckinghams
- 1969: "Crimson and Clover," by Tommy James & the Shondells
- 1971: "Knock Three Times," by Dawn
- 1972: "American Pie," by Don McLean
- 1973: "You're So Vain," by Carly Simon
- 1974: "The Joker," by the Steve Miller Band
- 1975: " Lucy In the Sky," by Elton John
- 1976: "Saturday Night," by the Bay City Rollers
- 1979: "Too Much Heaven," by the Bee Gees
- 1980: "Please Don't Go," by KC & the Sunshine Band
- 1982: "I Can't Go for That," by Hall & Oates
- 1983: "Down Under," by Men At Work

On the average: You can get about 6 glasses of wine from a standard-size bottle.

ELEMENTARY MY DEAR STEVE: SOLUTIONS

PAGE 247

1. A man with the hiccups was cured when the bartender scared him. The man—who happened to own a carnival—was very grateful, and when he died, he left the bartender his Funhouse.

2. If the nightwatchman had a dream that the 5:30 train crashed, that meant he was sleeping on the job. It turned out well for the night watchman; he was such a sound sleeper that he was able to get a job demonstrating mattresses for department stores.

PAGE 358–359

1. Remember, they had just come from Thomasville. All they had to do was reposition the signpost so that the "Thomasville" arrow was correct. That way, the road to Montez was obvious. They got their in time, and thwarted the evil son-in-law just as he was breaking into the wall-safe

2. No one shaves the barber—she's a woman. Good barber, too.

3. They're two of three triplets. Leslie made Steve promise never to see them again.

4. The poison was in the ice cubes. Arnie luckily saved his own life when he gulped down his drink and left before the ice melted. Mingo wasn't so lucky. The bartender, it turned out, was working for a used car dealer on the side, and wanted Mingo's '64 Mustang convertible.

PAGE 445

1. She dropped her ring into a bag of dry, ground coffee.

2. She quickly grabbed one of the pieces of paper, and ripped it up. Then she said, "I've chosen my fate. Let us see which one is left." The paper that was left said "death," which meant she'd chosen "freedom." Von Springmeyer was forced by the rest of the gang to let Leslie go.

3. Leslie had a sweet tooth, and always put sugar in her coffee. When she tasted the coffee, it was sweet.

"The Star Spangled Banner" became America's national anthem in 1931.

Uncle John's

THIRD BATHROOM READER

"Blowin' in the Wind," "The Archies," "Black & White," "The Australian Beatles," "Monkee Business," "Blue Suede Shoes," "Ain't That a Shame," and "Real People" originally appeared in *Behind the Hits*, Copyright © 1985, by Bob Shannon and John Javna. Reprinted by permission of the authors.

"Moore to Come," "The Best of Groucho," "Saturday Night Live," "Bewitched," "Say Goodnight, Gracie," and "Alfred Hitchcock Presents" originally appeared in *Cult TV*. Copyright © 1985, by John Javna. Reprinted by permission of the author.

"Landslide Lyndon" Copyright © 1990 by Michael Dorman. Reprinted by permission of the author.

Disney Stories Copyright © 1990 by Jim Morton. Reprinted by permission.

Excerpts from *UNAUTHORIZED AMERICA* ("Elvis-O-Rama," "Elvis: Still Dead?") by Vince Staten. Copyright © 1990 by Vince Staten. Reprinted by permission of Harper Collins Publishers.

"The Paper Chase" Copyright © 1989 by Ron Barlow, originally appeared in *The Vanishing American Outhouse*, published by Windmill Publishing House. Reprinted by permission of the author.

"Tissue Talk" by Harry L. Rinker, originally appeared in *Antiques and Collecting* magazine. Reprinted by permission of the publisher.

THANK YOU

The Bathroom Readers' Institute sincerely thanks the people whose advice and assistance made this book possible.

Eric Lefcowitz
Larry Kelp
John Javna
Derek Goldberg
Michael Goldberger
John Dollison
Jim Morton
Michael Brunsfeld
Richard Kizu-Blair
Gordon Van Gelder
Stuart Moore
Fifth Street Computers
Jay Nitschke
Penelope Houston
Bob Shannon
Jack Mingo
Patty Glikbarg
Robin Kipke Alkire
Lyn Speakman

The city of Domme
"Weird Brain"
Antiques and Collecting magazine
Harry L. Rinker
Ron Barlow
Michael Dorman
Vince Staten
Anita Sethi
Dan Simon
Bill Batson
David Davis
Duane Dimock
Sandra Konte
The EarthWorks Group
Reddy Kilowatt
Rocky
Bob Migdal
Lenna Lebovich
The Sharp Fax Machine

UNCLE JOHN'S MAILBAG

Our first two Bathroom Readers brought in lots of mail with interesting stories and comments...Here's a random sample:

Gentlemen:
If you recall, several weeks ago, astronomers discovered rings around Uranus. Well, after spending several hours engrossed in your book, so did I!

—*John M., Fort Mill, South Carolina*

Fellow Bathroom Readers:
Whenever I have a relative or guest at my house, they always come out of the bathroom and ask me why there is a stack of magazines on the back of the toilet. When I answer them, they just chuckle and call me "silly."

I'm glad to see there's finally an offical bathroom reader's publication that I can leave on the toilet so people can answer the question for themselves. Keep up the good work!

—*Duane J., Palm Bay, Florida*

Dear Uncle John:
I was beginning to think that Excremeditation was a dying cultural phenomenon, a lost art. Uncle John's Second Bathroom Reader is the simmering potpourri in the Great Outhouse of Life.

—*F. Lee S., Charlottesville, Virginia*

Dear B.R.I.:
We would like to sit down and be counted. We read the first book in the bathroom, but since we're traveling for a year, we read the second book out loud to each other while driving. We enjoyed driving on Route 66...which we didn't even know existed until we read your book...And, hey, whatever happened to Burger Chef, Burger Queen, and Jack-in-the-Box? Any chance you'll write about them in a future edition?...FYI: Your books make great housewarming gifts! We are waiting with our pants around our ankles for book #3!

—*Amy & Rex Y., Athens, Michigan*

Before 1859, baseball umpires didn't crouch behind the catcher—they sat in rocking chairs.

Dear Uncle John:
I was reading the Bathroom Reader when I noticed I was out of toilet paper. Unfortunately, I had to make the most out of what I had. Will you please send me a copy of pages 38-39? Thanks.

Arnie P., Seattle, Washington

Dear B.R.I.:
I'd like to admit that one day I read the Bathroom Reader in 20° weather in an outhouse. Thanks, you guys helped me keep my mind off the cold.

—Robert W., Old Tappan, New Jersey

Dear Uncle John:
Thanks a ton. Now my husband *lives* in the john.

—Renee G., Los Angeles, California

Dear Uncle John:
Info on Kelsey—

1. My nickname is Kelley.
2. I'm 14 years old.
3. I love to read (especially on the pot).

—Kelsey B., Cedar Rapids, Iowa

Dear Sirs:
After reading your book, I had to take time out from the "business at hand" to write this letter. Having been a bathroom reader for many years, I found your book to be very "moving." There's a lot of very good information to "pass" on to others.

—Jim B., Canyon Country, California

Dear Uncle John:
Who is that guy on the back cover of both your books? Is it you? And what's he doing with the clipboard? I've just got to know—I read both your books cover-to-cover, and have spent hours staring at that picture, "passing" the time.

—Glenn W., Montpelier, Vermont

Glad you asked, Glenn. He's not Uncle John; he's Larry Kelp, a music critic at an urban newspaper. Of course, he's busy recording data about America's bathroom reading habits. Keep up the great work, Lar!

THE PAPER CHASE

At the B.R.I., we get a lot of questions about toilet paper. Heck, we even get them written on toilet paper. Recently, one of our "field representatives" discovered a couple of selections that should satisfy even the most finicky T.P. afficianado. The first is this piece adapted from a self-published book called The Vanishing American Outhouse, *by Ronald Barlow It should unroll a few mysteries.*

YESTERDAY'S PAPER

"Toilet paper is a fairly modern invention. Today's thoughtfully perforated product was patented by an Englishman named Walter J. Alcock, in the early 1880s. At first there was little demand for toilet paper by the roll. British pharmacy owners stocked this item under their counters and out of sight; T. P. was an affront to Victorian sensibilities.

"But Mr. Alcock was undaunted by the public's reserve and promoted his product religiously. His singleminded missionary zeal eventually paid off. By 1888 toilet paper fixtures (roll-holders) were stocked in most hardware stores, and today Alcock's original factory exports two-ply tissue to a world-wide market."

★ ★ ★

BEFORE PAPER

"What did folks use before paper was in wide circulation? Affluent Romans used sponges, wool, and rosewater. The rest of the world grabbed whatever was at hand, including shells, sticks, stones, leaves, hay, or dry bones. Royalty in the Middle Ages was fond of silk or goose feathers (still attached to a pliable neck) for this delicate clean-up task."

★ ★ ★

NO CORNY JOKE

"Rural Americans traditionally relied on corncobs instead of T.P. James Whitcomb Riley wrote a poem commemorating the experience:

The torture of that icy seat could make a Spartan sob,
For needs must scrape the gooseflesh with a lacerating cob.

Riley's family privy must have had an outdated supply of corncobs because old timers tell me that fresh ones are not all that uncomfortable. The term: 'rough as a cob' could perhaps apply to produce left out in the sun and rain for a year or so, but not to the supply of month-old corncobs used in privy confines. Guests often had a choice of colors, even before the invention of toilet paper. According to privy folklore, red cobs outnumbered white ones by a two to one ratio. The modus operandi was to use a red cob first and then follow up with a white one to see if another of the red variety was necessary."

★ ★ ★

T.P. BY MAIL

"Mail order catalogs came into general outhouse use in the late 1880s. Prior to that time they consisted of less than a dozen pages and could not compete with newspapers, dress patterns and other *uncoated* paper stock. Concerned mothers routinely removed the 'female undergarment' and 'personal hygiene' sections of these catalogs before consigning them to the outhouse. By the early 1930s most magazines and mail-order catalogs had converted to slick clay-coated pages and fell into general disuse as a T.P. substitute.

"The following letters, adapted from Bob Sherwood's 1929 book, *Hold Everything*, illustrate how important the thick semi-annual Sears catalogs were to many country households:

The Letter

Dear Sears & Roebuck:

Please find enclosed money order for one dollar ($1.00) for which please send me ten packages of your Peerless Toilet Paper.

Yours sincerely, Abner Bewley, Sr.

The Reply

Dear Sir:

We acknowledge receipt of your order with enclosure of $1.00 in payment for ten packages of Peerless Toilet paper. We assume you have taken this price from one of our old catalogs. On account of the recent increase in the cost of manufacturing this article, the price is now listed at $1.50 for ten packages. On receipt of an additional fifty cents, we will forward at once.

Very respectfully, SEARS & CO.

The Back-Fire

Gentlemen:

I am in receipt of your reply to my letter ordering ten packages of Peerless Toilet Paper.

If I had had one of your old catalogs, I would not have needed any toilet paper.

Please send me your latest catalog, and return my money.

Yours Sincerely, Abner Bewley, Sr.

P.S. After thinking the matter over you had better send two catalogs, as we have a very large family."

★ ★ ★

FOREIGN PAPER

"There are enough different varieties of toilet paper to inspire a major collection. (Smithsonian...are you listening?)

- One can write very easily in pen and ink on modern day Czechoslovakian toilet issue, which is of the consistency of writing paper. My son's college roommate just sent him a long letter on some of this 'poor man's stationery.'
- German-made bathroom tissue is light gray in color and rather coarse textured. The brand used on railway trains is imprinted 'Deutsche Bundesbahn' on every single sheet.
- In England, museum-going tourists are quick to notice that each square of paper is plainly marked 'Official Government Property.'
- In some Scandinavian restrooms the extra heavy roll is simply too large to carry away.
- Mexico solved her paper pilfering problem in airport and bus station 'baños' by not supplying any at all. Be prepared and bring your own, or you'll be forced to borrow from an adjacent stall-holder.
- Upscale European consumers are switching to a new luxury brand of paper; the pre-moistened, perfumed squares, sealed separately in foil envelopes, are not unlike the 'wet wipes' mothers buy

in American supermarkets.

★ ★ ★

AUTOMATIC WIPE

According to a 1988 article in *The San Diego Union*, fully 11.5% of all Japanese homes are now equipped with deluxe flush toilets which have built-in hot-water cleansing and hot-air drying mechanisms; these features preclude the need for any sort of tissue at all.

What are the chances of a Japanese-owned electronic-potty-maker locating its manufacturing facilities in San Diego, or some other U.S. city? 'Almost nil,' stated a spokesman. 'Only the quality control standards in Japan are strict enough to produce these devices without fear of public-liability lawsuits.' "

★ ★ ★

RECOMMENDED READING

The Vanishing American Outhouse is an oversized paperback full of color photos of outhouses, and goes where no man has gone before in its detailed study of American outhouse history. To order a copy, send $15.95 plus $1.50 for postage and handling to: Windmill Publishing Co., 2147 Windmill View Rd., El Cajon, CA 92020.

✍ ✍ ✍

TWINKIE POWER

• It's been estimated that the cake in a Twinkie will outlast the wrapper—which is made of plastic, and probably takes about 200 years to decompose. But according to William Poundstone in *Bigger Secrets*, that's just a rumor. He says that the Continental Baking Company, makers of America's favorite cremed cake, pulls unsold boxes of Twinkies off grocery store shelves every four days. Believe it or not.

• When James A. Deware invented the Twinkie in 1930, he called it, "The best darn-tootin' idea I ever had." How good was it? A Continental Baking Company executive claims that one man lived for 7 years solely on a diet of Twinkies and Cutty Sark.

Every day, more than 20,000,000 Americans read their horoscope.

COMMON PHRASES

What do these familiar phrases really mean? Entymologists have researched them and come up with these explanations.

SIAMESE TWINS
Meaning: Identical twins who are physically attached.
Background: Eng and Chang Bunker were always close—in fact, the twin brothers from Siam were born joined at the liver. P.T. Barnum hired the Bunkers and exploited them on the carnival and sideshow circuit during the mid-1800s. Though the brothers were really three-quarters Chinese, Barnum thought "Siamese" had a more exotic ring, and coined the term we still use today. (Side note: Eng and Chang lived long lives, married twin sisters and fathered more than twenty children).

LONG IN THE TOOTH
Meaning: Old.
Background: Originally used to describe old horses. As horses age, their gums recede, giving the impression that their teeth are growing. The longer the teeth look, the older the horse.

TO GO BERSERK
Meaning: To go mad, or to act with reckless abandon.
Background: Viking warriors were incredibly wild and ferocious in battle, probably because they ate hallucinogenic mushrooms in pre-battle ceremonies. They charged their enemies recklessly, wearing nothing more than bearskin, which in Old Norse was pronounced "berserkr" or "bear-sark."

TO FACE THE MUSIC
Meaning: To deal with a troubling situation.
Background: All actors have experienced stage fright, but eventually they must stand upon the stage and face the audience and orchestra (the music).

A-OKAY
Meaning: All correct, or all systems working.
Background: NASA engineers added 'A' onto "OKAY" because the 'O' sound sometimes got lost in radio static.

Toto's real name was Terry.

EDIBLE NAMES

st food? Try this list. You still may not know what e eating, but at least know what's it's named after.

McDONALD'S. Named after two brothers who were scenery movers in Hollywood during the 1920s—Richard and Maurice ("Mac") McDonald. They started the first modern fast food joint in San Bernardino, California after World War II and sold out to Ray Kroc for $2.7 million in 1961.

• Sidelight: They gave up the rights to use their own names, so when they wanted to open another fast food restaurant, they had to call it "Mac's." Kroc was so incensed they were competing with him that he opened a McDonald's across the street from "Mac's" and drove the McDonald brothers out of business.

ARBY'S. Forest and Leroy Raffel wanted to open a fast food restaurant called Big Tex, in Akron, Ohio...but someone else already owned the name. So they settled for Arby's—R.B.'s—after the first initials of *R*affel *b*rothers.

TACO BELL. No, it has nothing to do with mission bells. The chain was founded in 1962 by Glen W. Bell.

JACK IN THE BOX. There was a huge, square metal ventilation unit on the roof of Robert Peterson's restaurant. It was really ugly, but he couldn't remove it...So he covered it up instead, disguising it as a jack-in-the-box. Then he changed the name of his restaurant, making it seem as though the whole thing had been planned.

HARDEE'S. Founded by Wilbur Hardee, who opened the first Hardee's in Greenville, North Carolina in 1960.

BOB'S BIG BOY. In 1937, local orchestra members told 19-year-old Bob Wian they wanted "something different"; so the young owner of the ten-stool Bob's Pantry served up the "Big Boy" double-decker hamburger. It became so popular that Bob changed the name of his eatery to match it.

In Italy, a whole year's salary is the proper amount to pay for an enagement ring.

PIZZA HUT. Frank Carney, a 19-year-old engineering student at the University of Wichita, opened a pizza parlor in 1958 with his older brother Dan. It was in a rented, hut-shaped building with a sign that only had room for eight letters and a single space. Pizza Hut was the perfect name because it described the restaurant *and* fit the sign.

CHURCH'S FRIED CHICKEN. George W. Church, who'd previously sold incubators and run a chicken hatchery, founded the chain after he retired.

DAIRY QUEEN. In 1938, Sherb Noble put together a 10¢ All-You-Can-Eat promotion for his Kankakee, Illinois store. He offered a brand new kind of "semi-frozen" ice cream called "Dairy Queen," and was dumbfounded by the public's response—they bought 16,000 servings of it in two hours. Two years later, Noble opened a food stand that sold nothing but Dairy Queen.

KENTUCKY FRIED CHICKEN. "Colonel" Harlan Sanders had a restaurant in Corbin, Kentucky. His speciality was fried chicken.

WHITE CASTLE. In 1921, Walter Anderson needed money to open his fourth hamburger stand. He borrowed the money—$700—from a local real-estate and insurance salesman named Billy Ingram, who suggested that the restaurant be called the "White Castle," symbolizing cleanliness and strength. Since it was Ingram's money, Anderson humored him.

WENDY'S. Dave Thomas, an executive at Kentucky Fried Chicken, decided to open his own chain of fast food restaurants in 1969. The first one was located in Columbus, Ohio. It was named for Thomas's third daughter, Wendy.

NOW THAT YOU'RE HUNGRY... SOME NUTRITION INFO

• From *Best Worst And Most Unusual*: "If one is really starving, consider licking some postage stamps. The glue is a mixture of cassava (the source of tapioca) and corn...starchy but nutritious."

OH, ZSA ZSA!

Sure, you've read about her in the National Enquirer (only while you're waiting in line at the supermarket, of course). But what do you really know about Zsa Zsa Gabor? You might surprised to learn that a century ago, while she was still a young lady, she was quite beautiful and...yes, we admit it—pretty clever. A few words from, and about, this national institution.

WHAT ABOUT ZSA ZSA?

"She not only worships the golden calf, she barbecues it for lunch."

—*Oscar Levant*

"I feel a little like Zsa Zsa Gabor's fifth husband. I know what I'm supposed to do, but I'm not sure how to make it interesting."

—*Senator Al Gore, the 24th speaker at a political dinner*

"As a graduate of the Zsa Zsa Gabor School of Creative Mathematics, I honestly do not know how old I am."

—*Erma Bombeck*

ZSA ZSA SAYS...

- "I'm a marvelous housekeeper...Every time I leave a man, I keep his house."
- "You never really know a man until you've divorced him."
- "Macho does not prove mucho."
- "A man in love is incomplete until he has married. Then he's finished."
- "I want a man who's kind and understanding. Is that too much to ask of a millionaire?"
- "I never hated a man enough to give him his diamonds back."
- "Husbands are like fires. They go out when unattended."
- "I know nothing about sex because I was always married."

...BUT THEY'RE NOT ALL BIMBOS

"I will do anything to initiate world peace."

—*Jayne Mansfield*

Confederate General Robert E. Lee didn't own slaves. He didn't believe in it.

TRAVELS WITH RAY

Perplexing adventures of the brilliant egghead Ray "Weird Brain" Redel. Answers are on page 672.

Only a few men in modern history have been known specifically for their ability to think. There's Albert Einstein, Buckminster Fuller, and of course the most famous of all, Ray "Weird Brain" Redel. As I'm sure you've heard, "Weird Brain" 's reputation for solving word problems inspired friends to spring practical jokes on him constantly. Everyone wanted to be the one to say he or she had stumped him.

A few years ago, "Weird Brain" and I went to Egypt together for the International Smart Guys Conference. After listening to boring highbrow discussions for two days, we escaped to the local marketplace. It was refreshing to wander through the crowd, listening to people bark prices at each other instead of scientific theories.

Suddenly, a man in a white suit appeared before us, clutching something in his hand. He staggered and groaned and pointed to the object in his hand. I felt as though I was in a Hitchcock movie. The man managed to gasp, "*If you feed it, it will live. If you give it water, it will die.*" Then he swooned.

Alarmed, I looked for the police. But Ray just reached into his pocket, pulled out something, and tossed it to the prostrate man. "Here, Humphrey," he said—for the "dying" man was really "Weird Brain" 's Hollywood drinking buddy, Humphrey Bogart—"Nice try, but I think this is what you want."

What did "Weird Brain" toss Bogart?

The next day, we decided to do a little sightseeing. The cab driver offered to suggest a destination. "Sure," I said, "where should we go?" The driver grinned and said in broken English, "*It has a bed, but never sleeps; and has a mouth, but never eats.*" "Weird Brain" yawned. "Casey," he told the driver, who was New York Yankees manager Casey Stengel, an old pal, in disguise—that one's so old everyone knows it. But if it'll make you happy, take us there.

Where did Casey take us?

BONEHEAD ADS

Businesses spend billions of bucks on ads every year—but some of them backfire. A few amusing examples:

SAY WHAT?

Translating U.S. ad slogans into other languages doesn't always work.

• In China, a Coca-Cola ad used Chinese symbols to sound out "Coca-Cola" phonetically. The soda company withdrew the ad after learning the symbols "Co" "Ca" "Co" " La" meant "Bite the wax tadpole."

• In Brazil, an American airline advertised that its planes had "rendezvous" lounges, not realizing that in Portuguese "rendezvous" means a place to have sex.

• "In Taiwan," according to a book called *The Want Makers*, "Pepsi's 'Come Alive with the Pepsi Generation' was reportedly translated on billboards as 'Pepsi brings your ancestors back from the dead.'"

• "In French Canada, Hunt-Wesson attempted to use its 'Big John' brand name by translating it into French as 'Gros Jos,' a colloquial French phrase that denotes a woman with huge breasts."

• When the gringos at General Motors introduced the Chevrolet *Nova* in Latin America, it was obvious they didn't know their Spanish. Ads all across Latin America heralded the arrival of the new, reliable *Nova*, which in Spanish means "Doesn't go."

SMELL IT LIKE IT IS

Two of the most ludicrous Scratch'n'Sniff ads ever:

• In June, 1977, the Rolls-Royce Motor Car Company introduced a campaign entitled "This, In Essence, Is Rolls Royce." Apparently, the company's executives hired scientists to analyze the smell inside a Rolls. They came up with a scent strip that was supposed to smell like leather upholstery.

• In 1989, BEI Defense Systems ran a Scratch'n'Sniff ad for its Hydra 70 weapons system in *The Armed Forces Journal*. It pictured two battling helicopters; when scratched, it gave off the smell of cordite, the odor left in the air after a rocket explosion.

Dirt Cheap: The United States bought Alaska from the Russia for about 2 cents an acre.

CELEBRITY HYPOCHONDRIACS

Everyone's at least a little afraid of getting sick, but some people take it to extremes. Here are some of history's most famous hypochondriacs:

THE CELEBRITY: Howard Hughes

THE SYMPTOMS: When he was a little boy, the billionaire-to-be's mother fussed over every change in Howard's physical and emotional conditions. One result: Hughes developed a low tolerance to pain.

• After crashing one of his planes in Hollywood in 1946, Hughes began to display an irrational fear of dust and germs. He used Kleenex tissues on everything, and refused to touch doorknobs or let other people use his bathroom. (He once spent 26 straight hours in the bathroom; he also suffered from severe constipation).

• His fastidiousness got out of hand when he wrote out nine-step instructions to his housekeepers on how to open a can of fruit. He became a virtual recluse.

• One of the most bizarre manifestations of his obsession with health was a urine collection, purportedly for medical testing.

• Ironically, towards the end of his life, Hughes lost all pretenses of hygiene. He stopped taking care of himself—letting his hair and fingernails grow outrageously long—and stopped eating; he weighed only 93 pounds when he died.

THE CELEBRITY: Charles Darwin

THE SYMPTOMS: The father of the theory of evolution, staunch believer in the "survival of the fittest," apparently wasn't such a hardy specimen himself. Darwin was a life-long hypochondriac who suffered from stomach aches, chronic insomnia and fatigue.

• In 1849, he began a daily diary which included a running commentary on the state of his health. He kept it up for six straight years.

• In one entry, he wrote gloomily, "It has been a bitter mortification for me to digest the conclusion that the 'race is for the strong' and that I shall probably do little more but be content to admire the strides others made in science." He lived forty-one years after making that statement.

• Some have speculated that Darwin's ailments were brought about by the stress of his "heretical" theories; others have claimed they were an easy solution to meeting social obligations.

THE CELEBRITY: Napoleon Bonaparte

THE SYMPTOMS: Napoleon had a lifelong fear and hatred of medicine. As a student, he studied anatomy but was too squeamish to continue. He reportedly claimed, "I believe in the doctor, not medicine."

• The "Little Emperor" suffered a plethora of maladies, most of them the result of stress, including: skin disorders, ulcers, dysuria (difficulty urinating) and a nervous cough.

• To combat his hypochondria, Napoleon took steaming hot baths, sometimes 1-1/2 hours long. He also developed meticulous grooming habits, including gargling with brandy and water, and showering himself with eau-du-cologne.

• One doctor's report of Napoleon from the battlefields of Russia said, "The constitution of the Emperor was highly nervous. He was very susceptible to emotional influences...divided between the stomach and the bladder."

•Some scholars even doubted the diagnosis of Napoleon's death (stomach cancer) during his exile in St. Helena, claiming he died of hysteria brought on by boredom.

THE CELEBRITY: Alfred Lord Tennyson

THE SYMPTOMS: According to one of Tennyson's friends, the poet laureate of England worried "more about his bowels and nerves than about the Laureate wreath he was born to inherit."

• Throughout his life, Tennyson was beset by seizures, fits and trances, which including seeing animals floating across his field of vision.

• An admitted hypochondriac, Tennyson was obsessed with going bald and blind. Among the treatments he sought was a radical form of water therapy called hydropathy, which included being rolled naked into wet blankets and then plunged into water.

• Three of his major poems, "In Memoriam," "The Princess" and "Maud" alluded to his preoccupation with mental illness.

Home-Sweet-Home: One-fifth of Americans spend their vacations at home.

• In reference to his hypochondria, Tennyson was once quoted as saying, "I'm black-blooded like all Tennysons." He lived past 80.

THE CELEBRITY: H.L. Mencken

THE SYMPTOMS: The irascible essayist, one of the most respected American journalists of the 20th century, rationalized his hypochondria by once stating "the human body is a complex organism in a state of dubious equilibrium. It is almost unthinkable for all parts of it be operating perfectly at any one time."

• Mencken suffered an obsessive-compulsive need to continually wash his hands.

• Among his real-or-imagined maladies was a chronic sore throat (which resulted in three operations), hives, low blood pressure, lumbago, sinus infections, ulcers and hemorrhoids. He also suffered from terrible allergies, which, Mencken wrote, "I accept philosphically as a reasonable punishment for my errors."

• For years, Mencken kept a medical diary of his hay fever, which included log entries of his temperature, the weather conditions and the medicine he was taking. He also subjected himself to many new miracle cures, which lead him to describe himself as a "sort of laboratory animal" for medical experimentation.

THE CELEBRITY: Florence Nightingale

THE SYMPTOMS: The woman who revolutioned modern nursing was also a confirmed hypochondriac; she suffered from migraine headaches, chronic coughs, breathlessness, fainting and nervous distress.

• After her heroic deeds in the Crimean War, Nightingale became convinced that her heart trouble placed her in imminent danger.

• Starting in 1859, she became a virtual recluse, confined to bed and sofa, where she continued to write letters and books about nursing.

• Though she often claimed she was on the edge of death, Nightingale lived a long life. She died in 1910, at the age of 90.

AND DON'T FORGET... Michael Jackson. The thriller of pop and dance music is often seen in public wearing a surgical mask. Once, he tried to buy a germ-free hyperbaric oxygen chamber to sleep in, but the manufacturer refused to sell it to him.

People in the Southern U.S. watch more TV than people in any other region.

BOMBS AWAY!

Sitcoms don't have to be dumb...but they usually are. Here are the premises of some of the dumbest and most obscure sitcoms flops ever. Yes, they really aired on national TV.

MY LIVING DOLL (1964-65) An Army psychiatrist who lives with his sister brings home a gorgeous woman one day, explaining that she's got severe mental problems and needs constant care. He neglects to explain that she's not really a person at all—she's a robot who's so lifelike and sexy that men lust after her. She calls the psychiatrist "Master," and she'll do anything (yes, anything) he tells her to. So what does he do? What would you do? Well, all he wants is to teach her good manners. That's more than enough to make this show unbelievable.

MONA McCLUSKEY (1965) A Hollywood star makes 40 times as much money as her husband, an Air Force sergeant (he gets $500 a month, she gets $5000 a week). But the guy won't let her spend any of her dough—they live on his salary or nothing. Well, she's so in love that she agrees: She moves into a two-bedroom apartment and then spends all her time trying to figure out ways to secretly use her own money. The show lasted longer than the marriage would have—seven months.

IT'S ABOUT TIME (1966-67) Two astronauts accidentally break through the time barrier and wind up in a prehistoric era. There they coexist with a bunch of Neanderthals until they fix their space capsule—and then they head for L.A. But whoops! A couple of cavemen hitch a lift into the present. Intelligently, the astronauts hide the Neanderthals in an apartment and try to teach them about modern life. This inanity could only come from the fertile mind that also gave us "Gilligan's Island" and "The Brady Bunch."

RUN BUDDY RUN (1966-67) A couple of goofy assassins try to catch and kill a guy who accidentally overheard their secret plans in a Turkish bath. Some fun.

THE SECOND HUNDRED YEARS (1967-68) The cryogenics sitcom. A 33-year-old prospector is frozen alive in an avalanche in 1900. Sixty-eight years later he thaws out. Surprise! He's still 33 and full of pep. He goes to live with his son, who's now older than ol' dad, and his grandson, who's the same age. In fact, he and his grandson look exactly alike. What a coincidence!

THE GIRL WITH SOMETHING EXTRA (1973-74) Sally Field gave up her nun's habit and stopped flying. Now she's got ESP. And she's married to John Davidson. She says she can read his mind, but how can she be sure there's really something in it? The premise sounds like a *National Enquirer* story.

THE WAVERLY WONDERS (1978) Among television critics, this show is already a legend. Who thought it up? Is he still allowed into Hollywood? Joe Namath was the star, playing a basketball coach/history teacher at a small Wisconsin high school. Joe didn't know anything about history, as you might imagine. And his players didn't know anything about basketball. So what's the joke? The inept teacher? The inept basketball team? The inept TV network?

APPLE PIE (1978) The ultimate absurdity in family sitcoms. It broke all sitcom records for brevity too, lasting exactly two weeks. The plot: In 1933, a hairdresser decided she wanted a family. So she advertised for one in the local paper. The result: a collection of weirdos that rivals *King of Hearts*—a con-man "husband," a "son" who thinks he's a bird, a "grandpa" who's barely still moving, and a "daughter" who likes to tap dance around the house.

TURNABOUT (1978) A husband and wife, in an idle moment, wish they could switch places. They're only kidding around, but they speak in the presence of a magic Buddha statue—and Buddha *doesn't* kid around. Overnight, their spirits switch bodies—the man becomes a cosmetics exec in a woman's body, and the woman becomes a male sports reporter.

MR. MERLIN (1981-82) Merlin the Magician shows up in the 1980's as a garage mechanic. Merlin the Mechanic. Next time you tell a repairman he's a real wizard, think twice. You might be inventing a sitcom.

The U.S. Department of Defense spends about $6,000,000 on recruiting—every day.

PRIME-TIME PROVERBS

Here are some more TV quotes from the book Primetime Proverbs, *by Jack Mingo and John Javna.*

ON LOVE

"Ah—love— the walks over soft grass, the smiles over candlelight, the arguments over just about everything else..."

Max Headroom,
Max Headroom

"I'm looking for a serious commitment—someone who'll stay the night."

—Stewardess,
Married...With Children

THE FACTS OF LIFE

"There's an old Moroccan saying—trust in God, but tie your camel tight."

—Annie McGuire
Annie McGuire

"There are three things you don't get over in hurry—losing a woman, eating bad possum, and eating good possum."

—Beau La Barre
Welcome Back, Kotter

"Reservations are the condoms in the birth of new ideas."

—Twiggy Rathbone
Heavy Metal

ON SEX

"If sex were fast food, you'd have an arch over your head."

—Carlotta Winchester,
Filthy Rich

[After his first time] "I'm so excited. It's like discovering America, or a third arm or something. This is the greatest thing that ever happened to me. I should have started this ten years ago. I mean, the hell with television."

—Billy Tate,
Soap

"I haven't had much experience saying 'No' to a woman. The closest I've ever come is, 'Not now, we're landing.' "

—Sam Malone,
Cheers

ON WOMEN

Dwayne Schneider: "A woman is like a bathtub full of water— once you get it hot, it doesn't cool off too fast."

Barbara Cooper: " And once it does, it has a ring."

—One Day at a Time

FAMILIAR NAMES

Some people achieve immortality because their names become commonly associated with an item or activity. You already know the names—now here are the people.

Giovanni Casanova. A European diplomat. At age 16, his "immoral behavior" got him expelled from a seminary. Later, he was so notorious as a lover that his name became synonymous with seduction.

Count Paul Stroganoff. A 19th-century Russian diplomat. He funded archaeological expeditions, supervised a Russian educational district, and ate huge amounts of the sauce now named after him.

Daniel Elmer Salmon. A veterinary surgeon. He first identified the rod-shaped bacteria, *salmonella*, that causes food poisoning.

Adolphe Sax. A Belgian musical-instrument maker. In the early 1840s, he turned the music world on its ear with his invention, the *saxophone*.

Ambrose Everett Burnside. A Union General in the Civil War. His full side-whiskers (to complement his moustache) were so distinctive that they were called "burnsides." Over time, the word has been transformed into *sideburns*.

James Smithson. An English chemist. It took ten years of debate before Congress accepted his bequest for a Washington, D.C. *Smithsonian Institution*, for "the increase and diffusion of knowledge among men."

Oliver Fisher Winchester. An American men's shirt manufacturer. His special talent was improving on others' inventions, notably the Winchester repeating rifle invented by Benjamin Henry.

Mr. and Mrs. Legrand Benedict. After complaining that there was nothing new being served by New York restaurants, this "high society" couple cooked up the idea of *eggs benedict*.

According to M magazine, 84 percent of bicyclists think about sex while cycling.

Rudolph Boysen. An American horticulturist. After years of experimentation breeding hybrid berries, he finally came up with a *boysenberry*.

John Montague. The 4th Earl of Sandwich. A compulsive gambler who would not leave any game to dine, he had his valet serve him a piece of cold meat placed between two slices of bread.

Captain Bo. A legendary English fighter. His exploits inspired other combatants, who used a variation of his name, *boo*, as a bloodcurdling war cry.

Julius Caesar. The Roman Emperor was allegedly the first person delivered via *caesarian section*, through his mother's abdominal wall.

James Thomas Brudenell. The 7th Earl of Cardigan. The button-up sweater is named after him.

Thomas "Stonewall" Jackson. A Confederate General in the Civil War. He is credited for "standing like a stone wall" against Union troops at the first battle of Bull Run. Today we call similar holding actions *stonewalling*.

John Macadam. An Australian chemist. He discovered the *Macadamia nut*.

Vidkun Quisling. Leader of Norway in 1940. His surname became synonymous with *traitor* after he collaborated when they occupied his country.

Joseph Pulitzer. A newspaper publisher. His will created and funded the Pulitzer Prize for journalism.

Josh Billings. A 19th century humorist. He popularized a bantering comedy style which became known as *joshing*.

Charles Moncke. A British blacksmith. He is credited with inventing the monkey wrench (which the British call a "spanner").

ASSORTED MANIACS

You've heard of pyromaniacs and kleptomaniacs, but chances are you've never heard of these loonies. Do you know a...

Coprolalomaniac: Someone who compulsively uses foul language.

Doromaniac: Someone who compulsively gives presents.

Cresomaniac: Someone suffering from delusions of wealth.

Timromaniacs: Someone obsessed with postage stamps.

Emetomaniac: A person who always feels like throwing up.

Ablutomaniac: Someone obsessed with taking baths.

Hellenomaniac: Someone who compulsively uses Greek or Latin words.

Ailuromaniac: A person obsessed with cats.

Philopatridomaniac: Someone who's always homesick.

Dromomaniac: A compulsive traveler.

Phagomaniac: Someone who constantly craves food.

Xenomaniac: Someone obsessed with foreign customs.

Oniomaniac: A person who compulsively buys things.

Klazomaniac: Someone who always feels like shouting.

Micromaniac: Someone suffering from delusions of a shrinking body.

Titillomaniac: A compulsive scratcher.

Erythromaniac: Someone who's always blushing.

Catapedamaniac: Someone who always feels like jumping from high places.

Chionomaniac: Someone obsessed with snow.

Theomaniac: Someone who's sure he or she is God.

Nudomaniac: A person obsessed with nudity.

Ichthyomaniac: Someone who's just crazy about fish.

Arithomaniac: Someone who compulsively counts objects.

Cynomaniac: Someone obsessed with dogs.

Onychotillomaniac: A person who constantly picks his or her nails.

Bruxomaniac: Someone who grinds his or her teeth all the time.

Lycomaniac: Someone suffering from delusions of being a wolf.

There are three museums in the world which only exhibit footwear.

VIEWER'S CHOICE

Hollywood producers often use sneak previews to shape the way their movies end. Here are some examples of the ways preview audiences have influenced the final versions of recent films.

COCKTAIL

Initial tests by the Disney Company revealed that audiences found this Tom Cruise vehicle a snooze. So Disney executives decided to shoot more footage—including bar scenes of Cruise mixing drinks and dancing up a storm in front of bikini-clad bathing beauties and presto!—they had a hit. *Cocktail* went on to gross $160 million.

PRETTY IN PINK

In the original ending of the film, Molly Ringwald ended up with her awkward friend Duckie (Jon Cryer) instead of the slick and wealthy Blaine (Andrew McCarthy). When preview audiences disapproved, director John Hughes re-filmed the ending to conform to their wishes, including a romantic liason between Ringwald and McCarthy.

LITTLE SHOP OF HORRORS

In both the original film and off-Broadway musical production, the "Little Shop Of Horrors" ended with Audrey, the people-eating plant, munching down the lead characters. During preview tests for the 1986 film version of the musical, however, audiences expressed their displeasure that Rick Moranis and Ellen Greene became plant food. The cast and crew flew back to England to film an entirely new—and happy—ending where the plant was killed instead.

FIRST BLOOD

Preview audiences were asked to vote on whether Rambo, played by Sylvester Stallone, should die at the end of movie. Two endings had already been filmed. One showed Rambo shot by his enemy, Richard Crenna (which was how the 1972 novel on which the movie is based, ended). The other showed an emotionally-drained Rambo being led away by Crenna alive. Audiences were split on the decision, but apparently the producers made the correct choice by letting Rambo live. The sequels, *Rambo: First Blood Part II* and *Rambo III*, were box-office bonanzas.

THE BIG CHILL

Lawrence Kasdan's cult movie about '60s college pals reuniting in the '80s originally had a different ending—a flashback to the group's hippie days at the University of Michigan. Preview audiences, however, refused to accept the actors dressed up as college-age kids and the ending was cut.

An exception to the rule:

STAR WARS

Marketing research for the 1976 mega-hit was conducted by the staff of Twentieth Century Fox. It concluded that "you can't use war in the title," and that "robots could turn off the mass majority of moviegoers." Director George Lucas ignored the advice and obviously the force was with him—*Star Wars* is one of the top-grossing films of all time.

MISCELLANEOUS MOVIE FACTS:

• **Bizarre Movie Titles:** *Betta, Betta in the Wall, Who's the Fattest Fish of All* (United States, 1969), *She Ee Clit Soak* (United States, 1971), *Recharge Grandmothers Exactly!* (Czechoslovakia, 1984), *I Go Oh No* (Taiwan, 1984), *Egg! Egg?* (Sweden, 1975), *Phfft* (United States, 1954), and *Film Without Title* (East Germany, 1947).

• **Sound Stomachs:** To create the language of the mutants in *Island of Lost Souls* (United States 1932), sound-man Loren L. Ryder recorded a mixture of animal sounds and foreign languages, then played them backwards at alternating speeds. The effect: the sound induced nausea—audiences vomited in the theaters.

• **The Amazing van der Zyl:** Sometimes beautiful movie actresses don't have beautiful voices to go with their good looks. Enter Nikki van der Zyl, the voice of the James Bond Girls. In *Doctor No* (1962) Miss van der Zyl is the voice of all but two women in the film. She also dubbed the neanderthal grunts for Racquel Welch in *One Million Years BC (1962)*. Of course, the films don't credit her.

That's the breaks: A major league baseball team can break $150,000 worth of bats in one year.

QUAYLE QUIPS

Vice President Dan Quayle may not be articulate, but he's quotable. Here are some of his more memorable remarks.

"What a waste it is to lose one's mind. Or not to have a mind. Do I mean that?"

"Republicans understand the importance of the bondage between parent and child."

"We're going to have the best-educated American people in the world."

When asked by state GOP chairman to consider running for Congress: "I'll have to check with my dad."

"Hawaii has always been a very pivotal role in the Pacific. It is in the Pacific. It is part of the United States that is an island that is right here."

On his decision to join the National Guard in 1969:
"Well, growing up in Huntington, Indiana, the first thing you think about is education."

On which vice president he might model himself after:
"I don't know if there's one that comes to mind."

"It's rural America. It's where I come from. We always refer to ourselves as real America. Rural America, real America, real, real America."

On the ethics of his admission into law school:
"I deserve respect for the things I did not do."

On the Holocaust:
"An obscene period of our nation's history."

"Verbosity leads to unclear, inarticulate things."

On the meaning of Thanksgiving:
"The first would be our family. Your family, my family—which is composed of an immediate family of a wife and three children, a larger family with grandparents and aunts and uncles. We all have our family, whichever that may be."

At the Inauguration:
"I'm not used to going in front of President Reagan, so we went out behind the Bushes."

Dan Quayle's favorite film is "Ferris Bueller's Day Off."

DISNEY STORIES: SNOW WHITE

"Snow White and the Seven Dwarfs" was Walt Disney's first full-length cartoon feature, and it was nearly his last. Hollywood, appalled at the money he was pouring into it, dubbed it "Disney's Folly." It premiered in L.A. on December 21, 1937—and received a standing ovation. It also received a special Academy Award—"a full-size Oscar and seven little ones." Of course, the Disney version and the Grimm fairy tale were substantially different. Here are some examples of how the tale was changed.

THE DISNEY VERSION

Snow White's stepmother, the Wicked Queen, is jealous of Snow White's beauty. So she sends Snow White to the forest with one of her hunters. He's supposed to kill the young Princess and bring her heart to the queen as proof the girl is dead...but he can't do it. He lets Snow White go free, kills a wild boar and brings the boar's heart to the Queen instead.

• This trick almost works. But the queen consults her magic mirror and learns that Snow White is still alive.

• Meanwhile, Snow takes up residence with the seven dwarfs.

• One day, the wicked queen shows up looking like a hag and offers Snow White a poison apple. The dwarfs catch the queen in the act, but they're too late; Snow White dies. The dwarfs chase the queen to a rocky cliff where she falls to her death.

• A handsome Prince shows up and kisses the dead princess. Snow White is revived; she and the Prince live happily ever after.

THE ORIGINAL VERSION

• To small children, Disney's version is nightmarish enough. We can only wonder what children would think of the gruesome goings-on in the original fairy tale.

• The Queen doesn't ask for Snow White's heart—she wants the princess's lungs and liver. When the hunter brings her the boar's innards, the Queen—thinking they're Snow White's—has them boiled in salt and eats them.

• In the original story, the Queen tries to kill Snow White three times. The first two attempts fail. Since the Queen uses the same disguise all three times, we have to assume Snow White, although pretty, is a little short in the brains department.

• The dwarfs—who don't have cute names like Sneezy and Grumpy—do put Snow White in a glass coffin. But the Prince doesn't wake her with a kiss. In fact, kissing her never enters his mind. He just thinks she's pretty (albeit dead), and wants to keep her around his castle.

• On the way back to the castle, servants carrying the casket trip and drop it. This dislodges the poison apple from Snow White's throat and she's revived.

• In this tale, the Queen makes it back to her castle after apparently killing Snow White. A little later, she's invited to a wedding. The wedding, it turns out, is Snow White's. When the Queen arrives, Snow and the Prince have a pair of red-hot iron shoes waiting in the fireplace. The Queen is forced to wear the shoes and dance until she drops dead.

SAMPLE PASSAGES (FROM THE ORIGINAL)

"The Queen summoned a huntsman and said, 'Take the child out into the forest. I never want to lay eyes on her again. You are to kill her and bring me back her lungs and liver as proof of your deed'...The cook was ordered to boil [the boar's organs] in salt, and the wicked woman ate them and thought that she had eaten Snow White's lungs and liver."

The Queen receives an invitation to Snow White's wedding. She's stunned, because she was sure Snow White was dead.

"The evil woman uttered a loud curse and became so terribly afraid that she did not know what to do. At first she didn't want to go to the wedding celebration. But she couldn't calm herself until she saw the young queen. When she entered the hall, she recognized Snow White...and she was so petrified with fright that she couldn't move. Iron slippers had already been heated over a fire, and they were brought over to her with tongs. Finally, she had to put on the red-hot slippers and dance until she fell down dead."

JUST YOUR TYPE

Have you ever wondered why the letters on a typewriter are arranged so strangely? Here's the answer:

BUILT FOR SPEED

In 1872, Charles Latham Sholes and two partners developed a bizarre-looking machine they called the "Type-Writer." It wasn't the original typewriting machine, but it was the first to go beyond the experimental stage.

However, shortly after Sholes and his partners started selling it, they ran into a problem: The machine couldn't keep up with quick-fingered typists; the keys would jam if they were struck too closely in succession. Sholes spent long hours in his workshop, but still couldn't find a way to quicken the machine's keystrokes.

NOT SO FAST

One day in his lab, the desperate inventor had a brainstorm—a clever idea which still affects typists today. Since he couldn't speed up the machine to accomodate typists, he decided to slow down typists to accommodate the machine. He set out to design the most inconvenient, awkward, and confusing arrangement of typewriter keys possible.

After weeks of research, Sholes settled on what is now called the QWERTY keyboard (after the first six letters of the typewriter's third row). With this new keyboard, Sholes was confident everyone would have to "hunt and peck"—and even an expert typist would be slowed enough to use his machine. He marketed a model with the altered keyboard as a "groundbreaking advancement," boasting that a typist could now type the word "typewriter" without having to leave the third row.

Today we type on high-speed machines that Sholes couldn't have imagined in his wildest dreams. But we still use the keyboard he devised to save his primitive machine.

SWEET DREAMS... Where did the term *lollipop* come from? According to *How Did They Do That*: "George Smith, who invented the candy on a stick in the early 1900s, had other money-making interests: Lolly Pop was one of the finest racehorses of the time."

Recent poll results: 1/3 of U.S. women say men aren't as good in bed as they think they are.

CARTOON CORNER

A few facts about the origins of your favorite cartoon characters.

THE FLINTSTONES. This half-hour cartoon, introduced in 1960, was TV's first animated sitcom...and the first prime-time cartoon show ever. Hanna-Barbera Studios originally planned to take a standard sitcom—"a young couple with a kid and a dog"—and transpose it to prehistoric times. But that wound up too much like "Blondie." So Joseph Hanna turned it into a prehistoric "Honeymooners" instead, complete with an Art Carney-type next-door neighbor.

The original stars were Fred and Wilma Flagstone; the program was going to be called "Rally 'Round the Flagstones." But Mort Walker, creator of the comic strip "Hi and Lois," objected. Pointing out that Hi and Lois's last name is Flagston, he insisted that "Flagstone" was too similar to his creation, and asked Hanna-Barbera to change the name.

Receiving this news, one furious Hanna-Barbera producer suddenly had a vision of a Stone Age man rubbing two stones together to make fire—two flint stones. And that became the new name. Footnote: "The Flintstones" was the first cartoon ever to rank among the Top 20 shows of a year, ranking at #18 in 1960.

MIGHTY MOUSE. In 1939, DC comics introduced Superman; by the early 1940s, Superman was so popular that the comics had been joined by a Superman radio show and a series of animated cartoons. Paul Terry, a veteran cartoon-maker (Terrytoons), decided to capitalize on the Superman craze. So in 1942, he introduced an invulnerable flying rodent (dressed in a Superman-style costume, complete with a red cape) named Super Mouse. The public loved it. A year later, anxious to avoid a lawsuit, Terry changed Our Hero's name to Mighty Mouse.

ROCKY AND BULLWINKLE. In 1948 Jay Ward and his partner, Alex Anderson, decided to create a cartoon series especially for TV—which had never been done. For their stars, they had in mind an animal duo—a smart little creature (the hero) and a big dumb one (the sidekick). They proposed two shows:

• "Crusader Rabbit," featuring a rabbit and his towering, dimwitted tiger buddy.

• "Frostbite Follies," featuring a flying squirrel and a big, dumb moose.

The first one they developed, "Crusader Rabbit," was immediately successful...so they didn't bother working out the second one. Then, in the mid-1950s, Ward sold his rights to "Crusader" and started work on a new cartoon show that adults would appreciate, too. He went back to the squirrel and moose concept.

He'd already picked the name Bullwinkle for the moose. It was inspired by a car salesman in Berkeley, California, where Ward lived. "Every day I'd drive by this sign, Bullwinkle Chevrolet or something," he recalled several decades later, "and I'd think to myself, 'If I ever do another cartoon character, I'm gonna name it Bullwinkle.'" The name Rocky for the little squirrel was a takeoff on tough-guy, macho names. Ward worked on the show for several years. It finally debuted as "Rocky and His Friends" in 1959.

GOOFY. Mickey Mouse's pal made his screen debut in the 1932 cartoon Mickey's Review, as Dippy Dawg. (At the time, "dippy" was popular slang for "someone foolish or slightly mad.") The inspiration: country folks whom Pinto Colvig, Goofy's voice, had known in Oregon. Over the next 6 years Dippy Dawg became a regular character, but his name was changed to Dippy, then Dippy the Goof, and finally Goofy (although for a while in the '40s, his name changed again, to Mr. Geef). His first-ever appearance as Goofy was in the 1939 short, *Goofy and Wilbur*.

TWEETY BIRD. Created by Bob Clampett, a Warner Brothers animator. The inspiration for Tweety's wide-eyed stare and little body was a nude baby photograph of Clampett himself. The canary's famous phrase, "I tawt I taw a puddy-tat," originated in a letter Clampett wrote to a friend on MGM stationery. He drew a surprised baby bird pointing at Leo the Lion, saying "I tink I taw a titty-tat!" Clampett's friend wrote back that he got "quite a kick" out of the "titty-tat" gag. (It was a little off-color for the times). "Titty-tat" was turned into "Puddy-tat" for the big screen.

MEL BLANC. Believe it or not, the man who provided Bugs Bunny's voice was allergic to carrots.

MYTH AMERICA

You may have believed these myths all your life; after all, they were taught to us as sacred truths. But here's another look...

REMEMBER THE ALAMO

The Myth: The defenders of the Alamo fought for justice, political freedom, and independence.

The Truth: It was as much an issue of slavery as it was independence. In the 1820s Texas was a part of Mexico, and much of its land was being settled by slave-owning farmers and ranchers from the southern U.S. But in 1830, the Mexican government passed a law outlawing slavery. Soon after, American settlers revolted, and the Alamo was defended—at least in part because American settlers wanted to keep their slaves.

BAR-B-COW

The Myth: Mrs. O'Leary's cow kicked over a lantern while being milked and started the Great Chicago Fire of October 8, 1871.

Background: The cow was merely a scapegoat . . .or scapecow. Michael Aherns, a reporter whose newspaper account first broke the legendary cow story, later admitted he made the whole thing up to boost his paper's circulation.

The Truth: The fire did start somewhere near the O'Leary house, but the Chicago Fire Department never found the real cause of the blaze.

THE FATHER OF OUR COUNTRY

The Myth: George Washington was the first president of the United States.

The Truth: Washington was the first to serve as America's president under the Constitution of 1789, but the United States was a sovereign nation 13 years before the Constitution was written. In 1777, the Congress adopted the Articles of Confederation, which were ratified by the states in 1781. Later in 1781, this new legislative body convened and elected John Hanson as "President of the U.S. in Congress assembled." Hanson had been a member of the Maryland assembly and the Continental Congress, where he played a key role in convincing Maryland, the only state against the Articles of Confederation, to ratify them. Washington himself sent Hanson a letter of congratulations on his "appointment to fill the most important seat in the United States." However, Hanson and the *seven* other presidents who served before George Washington have been forgotten.

THOREAU-LY SURPRISING

The Myth: Henry David Thoreau was a recluse who spent his Walden years in solitude, far from civilization.

The Truth: During his two years at Walden, Thoreau kept a pretty busy social schedule. He made frequent trips to the nearby town of Concord to spend time with friends and enjoy some of his mother's home cooking. In addition, he often played host to whole groups of visitors in his "secluded" cabin. Ralph Waldo Emerson was a frequent visitor, as was Bronson Alcott, who dropped by weekly. One day, April 1, 1846, Thoreau had about 30 people over for a meeting. According to Walter Harding's *The Days of Henry Thoreau*, "hardly a day went by that Thoreau did not visit the village or was not visited at the pond."

The Myth: Thoreau spent an extended period of time in prison for refusing to pay poll taxes which would support the Mexican War of 1846 and slavery.

The Truth: Thoreau did do jail time for his act of civil disobedience—one night of it. He was bailed out the following morning by an unidentified woman rumored to be his Aunt Maria, or Ralph Waldo Emerson in disguise. Legend has it Thoreau begged to stay in jail, but the jailer would have none of it.

CHARGE!

The Myth: Teddy Roosevelt commanded his hardy band of Rough Riders on their charge up Cuba's San Juan Hill in the Spanish-American War.

The Truth: Contrary to the popular image of the courageous cavalry charge on horseback, the cavalry unit was on foot; their horses had accidentally been left in Florida. And Roosevelt wasn't even on San Juan Hill. He did take part in the charge on nearby Kettle Hill, but only watched from there as Colonel C. Wood led the Rough Riders up San Juan Hill.

One out of five American families doesn't have a bank account.

REEL GANGSTERS

If you're an old movie buff, you've probably seen classic gangster films like Scarface, Little Caesar, *and* Public Enemy. *Here's some behind-the-scenes trivia about how the films were made.*

BIG AL IS WATCHING YOU

Scarface (1932) was the best known of all early gangster films. Director Howard Hughes and screenwriter Ben Hecht modeled the main character, Tony Camonte (played by Paul Muni), after Chicago mobster Al Capone. Capone heard about it. And just to make sure *Scarface* was to his liking, he sent some of his own men to monitor the filming, as "advisors."

How do you spell relief? Capone enjoyed the film so much he bought a print of it and threw a huge party for Hawks in Chicago.

THE UN-NATURAL LOOK

Edward G. Robinson's portrayal of vicious killer Caesar Enrico Bandello in *Litte Caesar* (1930) made him a star. But he actually hated firing guns; in fact, every time he shot one in the film, he shut his eyes. Director Mervin LeRoy wanted a "cold and unblinking" killer, so he taped Robinson's eyelids open.

RIGHT GUY, WRONG PART

James Cagney was brought to Hollywood by Darryl Zanuck, and was immediately miscast as a smooth character in *The Millionaire*. One day Zanuck was watching unedited cuts of the film, wondering why Cagney wasn't working out. A scene ended; Cagney turned to the camera, sneered, and said, "For God's sake, who wrote this crap?" Zanuck realized the tough-talking Cagney was perfect for the gangster roles he was having such a hard time casting. It made Cagney's career.

In the most famous 1930s gangster scene, Cagney (*Public Enemy*, 1931), smashed half a grapefruit in Mae Clark's face. It wasn't in the script. Cagney and Clark staged it as a practical joke to shock the film crew, but director William Wellman liked it and left it in. Later in life, Cagney wasn't able to finish a meal in a restaurant without being offered a free half-grapefruit.

At the wedding of Ronald Reagan's daughter Patti: 134 guests and 180 security personnel.

FIT FOR A KING

A few thoughts from Maring Luther King, Jr., winner of the Nobel Peace Prize and one of the greatest leaders of the 20th Century.

"Human salvation lies in the hands of the creatively maladjusted."

"I live each day under a threat of death. I know I can meet a violent end."

"Philanthropy is commendable, but it must not cause the philanthropists to overlook the circumstances of economic injustice which make philanthropy necessary."

"He who passively accepts evil is as much involved in it as he who helps to perpetrate it."

"Freeedom is never voluntarily given by the oppressor; it must be demanded by the oppressed."

"War is a poor chisel to carve out tomorrows."

"All progress is precarious, and the solution of one problem brings us face to face with another problem."

"Nothing pains some people more than having to think."

"We will have to repent in this generation not merely for the vitriolic words and actions of the bad people, but for the appalling silence of the good people."

"Injustice anywhere is a threat to justice everywhere."

"The means by which we live have outdistanced the ends for which we live."

"Our scientific power has outrun our spiritual power. We have guided missiles and misguided men."

"A man has no right to live until he has found something to die for."

"Shallow understanding from people of goodwill is more frustrating than absolute misunderstanding from people of ill will."

MARS ATTACKS

*On October 30, 1938, over a million-and-a-half listeners tuned in to the most famous radio broadcast of all-time—*War Of The Worlds, *a dramatization of* H.G. Wells' *classic science fiction novel about a Martian invasion. Here's what happened.*

HERE THEY COME

The radio version of *War of the Worlds* was just an elaborate Halloween joke played by actor Orson Welles and the regulars of "Mercury Theatre on the Air." But it caused a nationwide panic. Some terrified families fled from their homes; others prepared for a full-scale Martian war.

ON THE SPOT

Welles insisted on making the broadcast of *War of the Worlds* as realistic-sounding as possible. At first, the announcements that Martians had landed came in the form of news bulletins interspersed between live big-band remotes. Gradually the tone of the broadcast became more hysterical. Some of the bulletins ("We take you now to Washington for a special broadcast on the national emergency...") sounded particularly unnerving to a nation on the verge of World War II.

I CAN'T LOOK

Since the show had no sponsors, there were only a few interruptions to announce that the show was a dramatic presentation. Listeners tuning in mid-broadcast heard frightening "on the scene" descriptions of the attacking Martians. "Good heavens, something's wriggling out of the shadow like a grey snake. Now it's another one, and another. They look like tentacles to me. There, I can see the thing's body. It's large as bear and it glistens like wet leather. But that face...it's indescribable. I can hardly force myself to look at it. The eyes are black and gleam like a serpent. The mouth is V-shaped with saliva dripping from its rimless lips that seem to quiver and pulsate."

Although he was oblivious to the hysteria his program was stirring up, Welles was still clever enough to give the show a happy ending—the Martians are conquered and calm is restored. Welles concluded the broadcast by saying, "And if your doorbell rings and nobody's 'there,' that was no Martian...it's Halloween."

THE PANIC

By the time the broadcast was completed, millions of Americans were convinced that a Martian invasion had occurred. Police switchboards were flooded from coast to coast by calls from terrified listeners. Among the reactions:

- One New Jersey resident mistook a water tower for the Martians and blasted it with a shotgun.
- Twenty families from one apartment building evacuated their homes with wet towels on their faces to avoid deadly Martian rays.
- Pennsylvania's governor offered troop support to New Jersey, where the invasion was supposedly taking place.
- A woman paged her husband at a Broadway play to warn him of the attack—and many audience members fled with him.
- A husband in Pittsburgh came home to find his wife with a bottle of poison in her hand, saying "I'd rather die this way than that."

Despite the hysteria, no deaths resulting from the broadcast have ever been documented.

FALL OUT

- Police stormed CBS studios after the broadcast and held the cast and crew for questioning (Mercury employees hid the tape of the show, fearing that it would be confiscated). After a few hours of intense grilling, the police let everybody go.
- Welles became an instant nationwide celebrity. The day after the broadcast, he seemed as incredulous as anybody about all the hoopla: "I'm extremely surprised to learn that a story, which has become familiar to children through the medium of comic strips and many succeeding novels and adventure stories, should have had such an immediate and profound effect upon radio listeners."
- In 1947, the citizens of Ecuador had a similar hysterical reaction to Radio Quito's dramatization of the Mercury script. Once again, panic-stricken residents fled into the streets. Later, when a mob of terrified listeners found out the broadcast wasn't real, they burned down the radio station (Ecuador's oldest) in anger. One radio station employee died in the blaze.

DICK NIXON, FOOTBALL COACH

Judging from Watergate, you might say strategy wasn't Richard Nixon's strongest suit. But that didn't keep Nixon from trying to "coach" two football teams—the Washington Redskins and the Miami Dolphins—while he was serving as president.

BACKGROUND

• Nixon was an acknowledged football freak, an armchair quarterback who often peppered his speeches with allusions to the game.
• He once referred to Congress as "a fourth-quarter team," adding, "in the last quarter, we have to score a lot of points."
• The White House used the code name "Operation Linebacker," for a secret Pentagon strategy in Vietnam during Nixon's presidency. Nixon's personal code name was "Quarterback."

COLLEGE DAYS

• Nixon was never much of a football player. He made the freshman squad at Whittier College in California, but later in his college career was only allowed to practice with the team and sit on the bench.
• He later recalled: "I played on the C team...and I didn't even make that."
• In 1969, a few days before being inaugurated, he finally received a varsity letter from Whittier.

THE COACH AND THE PREZ

• George Allen, who coached the Redskins during Nixon's tenure at the White House, had previously been Whittier's football coach.
• The two met at a college sports banquet in 1952 and became very close. Allen, who spoke often to the president, publicly praised him, saying, "The president thinks football is a way of life. He is a competitor."
• Allen, like Nixon, wasn't known for his scruples. Once, while he was coach of the Redskins, Allen traded away a draft choice he didn't have. Football officials fined him $5,000.

PEP TALK

• In November, 1971, President Nixon visited the Redskins at their practice camp in Virginia. He gave them a pep talk: "I've always said that in life, as well as in sports, politics, and business, what really makes a team or a country is when it has lost one, it doesn't lose its spirit. I think this team has the spirit it takes. I think government has it. You're going to go on and win."

• The president was wrong. Washington lost the National Football Conference championship game that season to the San Francisco 49ers, partly due to Nixon's playmaking.

• Late in the second quarter of the game, with the Redskins on the verge of a touchdown, Coach Allen ran a play that Nixon had especially requested—a flanker reverse with Roy Jefferson. The play resulted in a 13-yard loss, throwing the Redskins from the 49ers' 8-yard line to the 21-yard line. The Skins had to settle for a field goal.

• When the 49ers won the game, 24-20, many sportwriters claimed Nixon's play had been the turning point of the game.

SWITCHING SIDES

• Following the Redskins' loss to the 49ers, Nixon quickly switched allegiances to the Miami Dolphins, claiming he had followed the team from his vacation home in Key Biscayne, Florida.

• The Dolphins defeated the Baltimore Colts, 21-0, for the American Football Conference title. That night, their coach, Don Shula, received a 1:30 am phone call from the president. "I thought it might be some nut calling," Shula later recounted. "But his aide said, 'Is this Mr. Shula?' Then he said, 'The president is calling.' I thought it might be a hoax. I was listening to make sure it was his voice."

SINKING THE DOLPHINS

• Shula would soon regret Nixon's interest.

• Somehow it became public knowledge that the President had suggested the Dolphins run a specific play for their star wide-receiver, Paul Warfield, against the Dallas Cowboys in the upcoming Super Bowl. "I think you can hit Warfield on that down-and-in pattern," Nixon told Shula.

• The Dolphins failed to complete the play three times in the 1972 Super Bowl, which the Cowboys won handily, 24- 3.

• After the game, Warfield complained that the Cowboys had keyed on him thanks to Nixon. "They had two weeks to prepare and they made sure that under any circumstances we wouldn't be able to catch that pass," he said.

NO BONES ABOUT IT

• More than a few Cowboys fans took umbrage at Nixon's support of the Dolphins. The Bonehead Club of Dallas, a group of Dallas businessmen, awarded their annual "Bonehead of the Year Award" to Nixon two days prior to the Super Bowl.

• Nixon accepted the award "in the spirit in which it is given . . . in good humor."

CSONKA'S COMPAINT

• Larry Csonka, the Dolphins' star running back, wasn't all that pleased with Nixon's playmaking either. He later complained, "President Nixon may identify with football players, but I don't identify with him, and I haven't met a player yet who does. The man upset me with his role as superjock. Here he is, the one man in the world who has, at his fingertips, all the information and influence to make a lot of people's lives better. But what's he doing calling football players on the telephone and giving pep talks to teams? It just brainwashes people more, makes people think football is a lot more important to them than it really is. He's either hung up on the violence or else he's pulling off a master con job on a lot of sports fans. He's implying that he's one of them and he's hoping to get their votes in return."

KILMER'S COMPAINT

• Despite his coaching ineptitude, Nixon kept meddling with the Redskins the following season.

• Billy Kilmer, the Redskins' quarterback, became so frustrated that he told the *Washington Post*, "He's really hurting us. He calls all the time. He told some guy from Cleveland he met in New York that Cleveland had a good team but they had quarterback problems. Then Cleveland got all psyched up and they were much harder to beat. I think I'm going to ask George Allen to tell the president not to talk about the game until after we've played it."

POSTSCRIPT

• By 1978, both Nixon and Coach Allen had lost their jobs. But unlike the ex-President, Allen had landed a new one as the head coach of the Rams.

• Surfacing to express confidence in his old pal, Nixon fearlessly predicted that Allen would coach the Rams to the Super Bowl.

• "I'm not saying they will win the Super Bowl," he told the *Los Angeles Herald Examiner* in 1978, "but I think he'll get them there at least."

• Not exactly. Allen was fired early in the season; the Rams lost in the playoffs. Nixon was later spotted in Yankee Stadium, rooting for the New York Yankees. Apparently, he'd become a baseball fan.

☛ ☛ ☛

AD-VERSARIES: WOULD YOU BUY A USED CAR FROM THESE GUYS?

• **Mr. Clean versus Mr. Bush:** In 1985, Procter & Gamble took a poll to see how many people could identify Mr. Clean, the genie character used as a trademark for one of their cleaning products. 93% of consumers could identify him. That year, *People* magazine also took a poll and found that only 56% of the same shoppers could identify then-Vice President George Bush.

• **TV Time:** The average American teenager will see some 350,000 TV commercials by the time he or she graduates from high school.

Obsolescent Ads

• **Planned:** During the 1984 Super Bowl, Apple Computer showed a commercial that depicted a procession of robot-like people marching off a cliff. The idea: Most computer buyers pick the same old thing, but choosing an Apple is daring to be different. The widely-praised ad, which cost over $500,000 to produce, was intentionally never shown again.

• **Un-Planned:** In 1989, Pepsi paid Madonna a whopping $5 million for one two-minute commercial featuring her new hit "Like A Prayer." Ironically, the ad was abruptly cancelled by Pepsi after a month when consumers confused the commercial with Madonna's video of the same song, which featured "sacreligious" images like burning crosses.

A horse has 10 more bones than a man.

SPACE JUNK

Since Sputnik I was launched in 1957, nearly four thousand satellites have been put into orbit. Many just exploded; others have been deliberately blown up. As a result, there are literally billions of pieces of man-made debris now circling the earth...a veritable junkyard in space. So here's some "space junk" trivia.

Seven U.S. Delta rockets and a French observation satellite have exploded in space.

In 1961, Cuban premier Fidel Castro charged that a chunk of a U.S. spacecraft had fallen on Cuba and killed a cow.

In 1962, a 21-lb. fragment of Soviet Sputnik IV landed at the intersection of Park and North 8th Streets in Manitowoc, Wisconsin.

In 1978, a Soviet satellite came crashing back to Earth, contaminating hundreds of square miles of Canadian territory with radiation. What caused the crash? Scientists' best guess: the satellite collided with space junk, which caused it to go off its orbit.

Lost and never found: Astronaut Ed White lost a white glove during the Gemini 4 flight in 1965; George "Pinky" Nelson lost two minature screws while attempting to repair a satellite on a space shuttle mission in 1984.

In 1981, a Soviet navigation satellite exploded into 135 pieces after colliding with space debris.

Over 7,000 objects floating in space are being tracked from earth; only five percent are satellites.

Dodging space junk is a dangerous occupation. A 0.5 millimeter metal chip could puncture a space suit and kill an astronaut walking in space. A particle as small as ten millimeters could damage and possibly even destroy an orbiting space vehicle.

Before it blew up in 1986, the space shuttle Challenger was hit by a flake of paint measuring 0.2 millimeters, which damaged a window during one of its missions.

Americans make $500 million worth of illegal long distance phone calls annually.

JUST SAY NO-HIT!

Although quite a few public figures dabbled in pyschedelics during the late '60s and early '70s, few played major league baseball. Dock Ellis did...and pitched a no-hitter on LSD.

BACKGROUND

Dock Ellis was a premier pitcher from 1968 through 1979, winning 138 games while playing for the Pittsburgh Pirates, New York Yankees, Oakland Athletics, Texas Rangers and New York Mets. Of all his achievements, which include pitching in two World Series, his biggest was the no-hitter he pitched as a Pittsburgh Pirate against the San Diego Padres on June 12, 1970.

Fourteen years later, Ellis revealed he had accomplished this feat while under the influence of LSD.

A LONG STRANGE TRIP

Apparently, Ellis took the dose at noon and then realized he had to pitch at 6:05 p.m. that night. "I was in Los Angeles and the team was playing in San Diego, but I didn't know it," Ellis told the *Pittsburgh Press* in 1984. "I had taken LSD. I thought it was an off-day."

THE ACID TEST

The game was the first in a twi-night doubleheader between the Pirates and the Padres. Despite the powerful effects of the LSD, Ellis pitched brilliantly for nine innings, allowing no hits (he walked eight and hit a batter). "I can only remember bits of pieces of the game," Ellis later recounted. "I was psyched. I had a feeling of euphoria." According to one source, Ellis believed the ball was talking to him, telling him what pitches to throw.

THE AFTERMATH

Ellis didn't dare admit what he'd done. In fact, he never pitched on psychedelics again. Years later, Ellis was treated for drug dependency and became the coordinator of an anti-drug program in Los Angeles.

FABULOUS FAKES

There are plenty of little lies and hoaxes in the newspapers every day—from President Reagan pretending to light the White House Christmas tree, to votes of confidence for baseball managers about to be fired. But some hoaxes capture the public's imagination, and fool the experts at the same time. Here are some classics.

THE PILTDOWN MAN

THE DISCOVERY: In 1912, the remains of the fabled "missing link" between man and ape were found at an English excavation site. The exciting discovery included nine pieces of a skull and a jawbone.

THE HOAX: Charles Dawson was a British lawyer and amateur archeologist when he "discovered" the remains of the half-ape/half-man in a pit at Piltdown Common near Sussex, England. Dawson claimed the fossils were proof that human life had origins in England—a notion that appealed to British sensibilities.

In 1915, Dawson made a similar discovery two miles away from the first, proving the "Piltdown Man" was part of a race of people. The problem was, no one could get close enough to the bones to either prove or disprove Dawson's theory—he kept them locked up and only provided plaster cast models of the fossils.

THE UNMASKING: Dawson died in 1916, but it wasn't until 1953 that scientists finally got a chance to test the authenticity of the bones. They quickly proved the "Piltdown Man" was a fraud and concluded that Dawson probably bought the bones in an auction and tried to pass them off as "the missing link" as a practical joke.

THE CARDIFF GIANT

THE DISCOVERY: In 1869, workers digging near a well in Cardiff, New York discovered the petrified remains of a ten-foot tall man. Newspapers dubbed him "the Cardiff Giant" and hailed the discovery as the paleontogical "find of the century." "Cardiff Giant fever" swept the country.

THE SCHEME: The Cardiff Giant was the brainchild of a cigar manufacturer named George Hull, from Binghamton, New York.

Hull bought a 5-ton block of gypsum in Iowa and had it shipped to Chicago, where two marble cutters, with him as their model, spent three months carving out a likeness of a naked man.

According to Stephen Jay Gould in *Natural History* magazine: "Hull made some crude and minimal attempts to give his statue an aged appearance. He chipped off the carved hair and beard because experts told him that such items would not petrify. He drove darning needles into a wooden block and hammered the statue, hoping to simulate skin pores. Finally, he dumped a gallon of sulfuric acid all over his creation to simulate extended erosion." Hull then had the statue buried in Cardiff (in the backyard of a friend who was in on the hoax), where it was not-so-accidentally "discovered" by two unsuspecting workmen hired to dig a well there.

THE UNMASKING: A Yale paleontologist named O.C. Marsh exposed the fraud a few weeks later. After giving the Cardiff Giant the once-over, he declared that the Giant "was of very recent origin and a decided humbug." Shortly thereafter, under intense pressure, Hull confessed to his fraud.

AFTERMATH: Hull had managed to sell the rights to the Cardiff Giant—for $30,000 to a consortium of businessmen—before revealing the hoax. Although the Cardiff Giant was no longer the acknowledged "Eighth Wonder of the World," people still paid 50¢ apiece to see it. P.T. Barnum later made a copy of the fake and also put it on exhibition in New York City. Reportedly, his model outdrew the original when both were on display at the same time. The original Cardiff Giant is still on display at the Farmer's Museum in Cooperstown, New York.

THE ORANGE MOONMEN

THE DISCOVERY: In 1835, a New York *Sun* writer named Richard Adams Locke broke the stunning news that a British astronomer had seen furry, orange creatures living on the moon. The public was fascinated.

THE HOAX: Locke claimed that British astronomer Sir John Herschel had been trying out a new telescope when he noticed bison grazing on the moon. Supposedly, Herschel also saw blue goats, tropical forests and white beaches. Locke made the moon sound like a vacation spot. And the most amazing revelation was...there were apparently orange humanoid creatures, sporting leather wings, living on the lunar surface.

THE UNMASKING: Locke's chicanery was quickly exposed. Herschel disavowed the story and Locke owned up. He made up the entire thing to satirize an astronomer from Scotland who'd been claiming that he had discovered plant life on the moon.

BATS IN THE BELLE-FRY

THE DISCOVERY: During the Civil War, Ida Mayfield, a beautiful belle from Louisiana, became the toast of New York society. She was among the most beautiful, well-bred women in the city, and married Ben Wood, a newspaper magnate and congressman. She wore the finest gowns and jewels, danced with the Prince of Wales, was presented to Empress Eugenie of Austria, and entertained President Cleveland. Then, during the financial panic of 1907, she disappeared without a trace.

THE HOAX: Ida Mayfield was really Ellen Walsh, the penniless daughter of an immigrant textile worker, using a borrowed dress, the name of respected Louisiana family, and her innate charm. Wood never knew her real identity.

THE UNMASKING: In 1931, Ida Mayfield was found blind, deaf and shrunken. She was 94 years old, and living in a dingy New York hotel room, wearing a "dress" made only of two hotel towels pinned together. Her room was a mess of yellowed newspapers, letters and boxes, all scattered in disarray. She was judged incompetent and was made a ward of the court.

However, when they opened the boxes, they found securities worth hundreds of thousands of dollars. A diamond and emerald necklace was hidden in a box of crackers. And to top it off, fifty $10,000 dollar bills were contained inside a pouch tied around her waist. When collectors took this from her, she died.

FABULOUS FAKES ADDENDUM:

In 1708, English writer Jonathan Swift was so sick and tired of an astrologer that he wrote and published a fake obituary about the man, whose career subsequently took a dive.

DEFINITIONS

How's your vocabulary? In the first two Bathroom Readers we included some obscure words and their meanings, so you could impress your friends and neighbors. Here's another batch.

Labrose: Thick-lipped
Xenoepist: Someone with a foreign accent
Nosocomephrenia: Depression resulting from prolonged stay in the hospital
Hebetate: To become stupid or boring
Palpebrate: To wink
Quakebuttock: A coward
Glock: To swallow in large gulps
Brumous: Foggy or misty
Noyade: Mass execution by drowning
Ergophile: A workaholic
Weener: A trustworthy or believable person
Phrontistery: A place to study
Crurophilous: Liking legs
Dactylgram: Fingerprint
Valgus: Knock-kneed or bow-legged
Fample: To feed a child
Thuften: Having webbed toes
Errhine: Causing sneezing
Sphragistics: The study of engraved seals
Subrahend: The amount subtracted
Cygnet: A young swan
Misocapnist: Someone who dislikes tobacco smoke
Culch: Meat scraps
Recrement: A bodily secretion that is re-absorbed
Dentiscalp: A toothpick
Sorbile: Drinkable
Glabella: The space on your forehead between your eyebrows
Vespertilonize: To turn into a bat
Misodoctakleidist: Someone who dislikes practicing the piano
Deglutible: Capable of being swallowed
Spasmatomancy: Fortune-telling based upon body twitches
Bonnyclabber: Sour, coagulated milk
Peen: The end of a hammer opposite the striking end
Opsigamy: Marriage late in life
Hesternal: Having to do with yesterday
Shoding: The part in a person's hair

The chairman of Hyundai is called "The Chairman," even by his wife and kids.

BLACK AND WHITE

In 1972, Three Dog Night hit #1 on the pop charts with a tune called "Black and White" ("The ink is black, the page is white..."). Here's the amazing true story behind it.

LEGAL HISTORY

In 1896, in a decision called *Plessy v. Ferguson*, the United States Supreme Court ruled that racial segregation was constitutional—as long as blacks were given facilities which were "separate but equal" to those provided to whites. This ruling was the basis for institutionalized segregation in America.

Fifty-eight years later, the NAACP and a group of black families, with the support of Attorney General Herbert Brownell, sued the Topeka, Kansas school system, claiming that segregation was discriminatory and violated their constitutional rights. In an historic decision known as *Brown v. the Board of Education*, the court ruled in their favor, unanimously overturning the *Plessy* verdict. "In the field of public education, the doctrine of 'separate but equal' has no place," the court ruled.

During the months following the decision, more than 150 school districts integrated. Others fought the decision, and eventually lost. But the decision's impact was not merely on schools. It was one of the turning points of the Civil Rights movement, and marked an awakening of black activism that changed the face of American culture forever.

A SONG IS BORN

To jubilant Americans like Earl Robinson, an activist-songwriter who composed "Joe Hill," the *Brown v. Board of Education* ruling was a triumph. He and David Arkin, actor Alan Arkin's father, wrote "Black and White" to commemorate the event. It was a modern folk song.

"It was done in the '50s to celebrate a Supreme Court decision on segregation in the schools," Robinson says. "It was a famous decision, and this was kind of a celebration song, written actually, with children in mind, and no ideas whatsoever about it going popular."

Robinson was a performer himself, and sang the song whenever he gave concerts ("The first place it was performed was in Elizabeth Irwin High School in the New York area, by the junior high school class there"). Thus it was passed around among New York folksingers , until it landed in...Guyana?

Robinson says: "In the late '50s, I got a call from CBS, which wanted to use my song, 'The Ink Is Black'—which isn't the title—for a documentary film they were making. It seems there was some kind of a Peace Corps that was working in French Guyana, and CBS wanted to clear the song because it was being used by them there, to teach the French Guyanese how to speak English! In the film, they showed a blackboard with a pointer, so you would hear [sings] 'The Ink Is Black...' and they'd point to the words as it went along. That became a theme song for this whole film, which was about how the American group was helping them build a recreation hall."

BACK TO AMERICA

"So then Sammy Davis Jr. got ahold of it through a publisher of mine, and he sang it and pressed 5,000 copies for the Anti-Defamation League of B'nai B'rith, which he was strongly connected with—and this was kind of like a flash in the pan. Pete Seeger also recorded it. He did it with a bunch of kids, and I wasn't too impressed, although I was happy that Pete did it.

"Anyway, it kept on being sung around, spreading slowly, by word of mouth until I got called on the phone in the early '70s. Someone told me, 'Three Dog Night is singing your song, did you know that?' I didn't even know who the Three Dogs were, to tell you the truth. I had no concept of it. You know, they told me later, when I went to attend a concert where they were singing, that they had heard the song in Holland, over a radio, where it was being sung by a Jamaican group. Now, I remembered this Jamaican group, but we paid very little attention to them because very little royalties were coming in from them. But the guys in Three Dog Night told me that they knew immediately it was going to be a hit when they heard it." And it was. Six weeks after it was released, it reached #1 in the nation. But virtually none of the millions of fans who bought it had any idea of what it was really about.

REAL ADS

Some ad characters—Charmin's Mr. Whipple, for instance—are so believable that we forget they're simply actors playing parts. Just to remind us, here's some inside info on a few of them.

THE STAR: Clara Peller in "Where's the Beef?"
BACKGROUND: Joe Sedelmaier, a producer of commercials, was filming a scene in a Chicago barbershop when he discovered that nobody had hired a manicurist. He sent an assistant to a local beauty shop to find one and she returned with Clara Peller, an octogenarian manicurist who had worked in a nearby salon for 35 years. She looked at Sedelmaier and said gruffly: "How ya doin', honey?" Sedelmaier realized he had found a "natural." "She's a counterpart to all those sweet little old ladies," he explained.
THE AD: In 1984, Sedelmaier convinced Wendy's Old Fashioned Hamburgers to design an ad campaign around Peller, who growled the catchy phrase, "Where's the beef?" Almost immediately, Wendy's sales jumped 15%. The slogan "Where's the beef?" entered the popular lexicon when Presidential candidate Walter Mondale used the phrase against his Democratic rival, Gary Hart, in the primary campaigns.

Meanwhile, the 82-year-old Peller became an instant cult star with a national fan club. She ended up making $500,000 for the Wendy's ad, plus merchandising. Before she passed away in 1987, Peller said "I made some money, which is nice for an older person, but Wendy's made millions because of me."

THE STAR: Jim Varney in "Hey, Vern!"
BACKGROUND: John R. Cherry III, a Nashville ad executive, was searching for an innovative ad campaign to publicize an amusement park that, in his words, was "so bad we couldn't show it on television." His solution: a fictional character named Ernest P. Worrell, a nosy country bumpkin with a penchant for injuring himself, who continually harasses an off-screen character named Vern.

To fill Ernest's silly shoes, Cherry picked Jim Varney, who'd appeared on the TV show "Fernwood 2-Night," as a "mobile home daredevil." Ironically, Varney was a trained Shakespearean actor.

Every year, Americans buy 5 million copies of *Cliffs Notes* for *The Scarlet Letter*.

THE AD: Although the amusement park closed after three months, Ernest was an immediate success. Sensing Ernest's potential, Cherry and Varney cleverly decided to license the character to any company that wanted him—rather than identifying Ernest with one particular product. Eventually, the duo collaborated on over 3,000 Ernest commercials (sometimes filming as many as 20 a day) plugging everything from Toyota cars to Snickers bars. In 1987, Ernest made it to the movies in "Ernest Goes To Camp," a $4 million feature that outdrew its competition, the $45 million "Ishtar." Since then, two other features, "Ernest's Christmas" and "Ernest Goes To Jail"—both huge box-office successes—have been released. No doubt more are on the way.

THE STAR: David Leisure in "You Have My Word On It."
BACKGROUND: David Leisure was an unemployed actor when an ad agency chose him to star in a series of Isuzu TV ads that were based on the character of "The Liar," popularized by Jon Luvitz on "Saturday Night Live." After auditioning several candidates, the agency hired Leisure "because he could lie like a pro." Leisure's previous biggest screen role had been as a Hare Krishna in the film "Airplane!"
THE AD: The ads featured Leisure playing Joe Isuzu, a car salesman who made outlandish claims about Isuzu cars while the words "he's lying" appeared under him. The campaign caught the public's imagination and Isuzu car sales jumped 18%. Meanwhile, the character became a household name. In the 1988 Presidential race, Michael Dukakis compared George Bush's tax promises to Joe Isuzu.

THE STAR: Dick Wilson in "Don't Squeeze The Charmin."
BACKGROUND: In 1964, Proctor and Gamble was looking for an actor to portray Mr. Whipple, an uptight supermarket manager who (for some strange reason never fully explained) begged his shoppers to stop squeezing Charmin toilet paper. Dick Wilson, an ex-vaudevillian, won the role over 80 potential Mr. Whipples. The first ads were filmed in Flushing, New York.
THE AD: Mr. Whipple caught on; Charmin became the bestselling toilet paper in the country. One 1970s survey found that more people recognized Mr. Whipple than Jimmy Carter. Unfortunately, Wilson became typecast. "When I go through the toilet paper section," he told People magazine, "I get some very strange looks."

Poetry in Ocean: According to experts, whale songs rhyme.

MOORE TO COME

In a recent poll, TV critics called "The Mary Tyler Moore Show" one of the 5 best sitcoms ever. As the first program to feature a single career woman competing on equal terms with men, it was certainly among the most influential. Here are some interesting facts about the show:

HOW IT STARTED

From 1961 to 1965, Mary Tyler Moore co-starred in the popular TV program "The Dick Van Dyke Show." But after she left the show, her career didn't fare too well. She tried movies, and wound up in films like *Change of Habit*, with Elvis Presley (she played a nun). She gave Broadway a shot (a musical version of *Breakfast At Tiffany's*), and the play closed before opening night. People began to notice that she'd never made it on her own, and suspected that she'd just been lucky on TV. She needed to do something to prove herself.

Then in 1969 she was invited to co-star with Dick Van Dyke in a TV special called "Dick Van Dyke and the Other Woman." Van Dyke's previous TV special, which co-starred singer Leslie Uggams, hadn't done well. But the Moore-Van Dyke show got high ratings, and Mary got the credit. The result: she received an offer from CBS that was too good to pass up; if she'd star in a new sitcom for them, they'd give her total creative freedom in developing it—plus part-ownership of the series. If it succeeded, she'd be rich. She accepted the offer.

Moore chose her new character carefully. She didn't want to be a housewife because she'd been "married" in "The Dick Van Dyke Show" (and wanted to avoid typecasting). She didn't want to be another sitcom "widow." So she decided to become a divorcee. Her writers created a pilot in which a recently-divorced woman (Mary) struggled with a career as an associate TV producer, and CBS loved it—except for the divorce. America wasn't quite that liberated yet. The network requested a change, saying they were afraid viewers would assume she had "divorced" Van Dyke. So the part was re-written to make Mary a refugee from a love affair. That was fine with CBS. The series debuted in Sept. 1970, and was a hit from the start. For three years in a row, it was among the Top 10 TV shows in America.

According to a Yale study, you think better in the winter than in summer.

SCOREBOARD

• The *Mary Tyler Moore Show* was the most honored show in Emmy history. It received 27 awards, including three for best comedy show, one for directing, and five for writing. Moore, Ed Asner (Lou Grant), and Valerie Harper (Rhoda Morgenstern) received three Emmys each; Ted Knight (Ted Baxter) and Betty White (Sue Ann Nivens) received two apiece; and Cloris Leachman (Phyllis, the land-lady) was presented with one.

• Even more impressive, the show spawned more successful spinoffs than any other sitcoms: *Rhoda*, *Phyllis*, and *Lou Grant*. In the 1975 season, two of the spinoffs placed in the Top Ten of the Year (*Phyllis* was #6, *Rhoda* was #8), outstripping even *Mary*, which ranked at #19.

REVENGE

Ironically, the only major cast-member who never received an Emmy for his work on the *MTM Show*—Gavin Macleod (Murray)—went on to the biggest TV success of all of them. He wound up as captain of the *Love Boat*, which ranked in the Top 5 several years in a row—higher than Mary or any of its spinoffs ever got. Amazing, but true.

HOME SWEET HOME

Remember that quaint house at 119 North Weatherly, where Mary supposedly had her apartment? It was owned by a University of Minnesota humanities professor. She was initially delighted to let MTM Productions shoot its exterior for use on the show (the interior scenes were done in the studio).

But when the program became popular, doorbell ringers began showing up regularly, asking for Mary, Rhoda, and Phyllis. The professor's life was so disrupted that she refused to let MTM film the outside of her house anymore. When MTM ignored her wishes and showed up to film the outside of her house anyway, the professor hung banners reading "Impeach Nixon" out of the windows that were supposed to be Mary's. That stopped the film crew.

Soon after, Mary "moved" to a high rise.

ANGLERS TAKE NOTE: In Tennessee and Washington, it's illegal to fish with a lasso.

JOCKS IN POLITICS

Are all jocks dumb? Not necessarily. Some wind up making laws, starting revolutions, even running countries. A few examples:

George Bush. Right after World War II, Yale had the best baseball team in the East; it won the Eastern Division NCAA championships twice. Bush was the team's starting first baseman, and was even named captain in his senior year (1948). Five members of the Yale team signed pro contracts after graduation. Bush supposedly thought about going pro, too.

Mario Cuomo (governor of New York). Tried professional baseball for a single season, then quit. In 1952, he played with a minor league team in the lowly Class D Georgia-Florida League. His record: A .244 batting average, with one homer in 254 at bats. His strength, according to a scouting report was that he would "run right over you."

Fidel Castro. A star pitcher at the University of Havana in the 1940s. Cuba once had a minor league team (the Havana Sugar Kings) and when Castro took over the country, he enthusiastically supported it. In fact, Premier Castro once pitched an inning in the minors, striking out 2 batters—on called strikes (after which he left the mound and shook the umpire's hand). In another game, his team was losing in the 9th inning—so he declared that the game would go into extra innings. They played until Castro's team won.

Jack Kemp (former New York congressman, secretary of HUD). Spent 13 years as a pro quarterback, leading the AFL's Buffalo Bills to championships in 1964 and 1965. He used his standing as a local Buffalo hero to run for Congress—and won.

Bill Bradley (U.S. senator from New Jersey). Star of the Princeton University "Cinderella" basketball team in 1965, Rhodes Scholar who returned to the U.S. and signed with the New York Knicks. He was a starting guard on their world championship 1970 and 1973 teams. In 1978, he was elected senator; and in the '80s, he was the architect of major tax reform legislation.

An ice cream sundae will warm you more than hot chocolate. The reason: more calories.

SECRET RECIPES

Here's some fascinating data we found in a wonderful book called Big Secrets *by William Poundstone.*

TWINKIES

In 1976, the *Snack Food Yearbook* reported "[Twinkies inventor James] Deware says [the Twinkies] formula is a secret...He always refers to [the filling] as a creamed filling, emphasizing the need to add the 'ed.' " So what's really in the filling? Among other things:

• Sugar and corn syrup. (40%)

• Shortening content (25%). Here's what's written on the label: "partially hydrogenated vegetable and/or animal shortening (contains one or more of the following: soybean oil, cottonseed oil, palm oil, beef fat, lard)." Hydrogenated vegetable shortening is oil turned into a wax-like solid. Beef fat is...well...the fat from beef.

• Skim milk (7%). The "nutritional" part.

• Butter flavoring (1%).

KENTUCKY FRIED CHICKEN

The Colonel's "secret recipe" is a special combination of eleven herbs and spices, right? Not even close. In a laboratory analysis, the "eleven herbs and spices" were revealed to be a sum total of zero herbs and only four spices, namely salt, pepper, flour, and Monosodium Glutamate (MSG).

OREOS

What's the creme filling in America's favorite sandwich cookie? Mostly sugar and shortening, with hydrogenated coconut oil the favored shortening. Lard is also used occasionally, but not beef fat.

COCA-COLA

Does Coca-Cola, which is made with coca leaves, have any cocaine in it? Trace amounts, almost certainly. Even if 99.99999999 percent of the cocaine from the coca leaves was removed, millions of cocaine molecules would remain floating in each can of Coke. Regardless, Coca-Cola is still 99.5% sugar water.

In a single year, over 200,000 pounds of barnacles collect on the bottom of a steamship.

INVASION! PART I

European history is full of invasions. But since it became a nation in 1776, the U.S. has rarely been the target of foreign attacks. In fact, we could only think of five of them. Here's one.

THE INVADERS: The British.

THE DATE: August 24, 1814.

BACKGROUND: During the early 1800s, relations between Britain and America were strained. One reason: the English had broken their promise to leave Canada after the Revolutionary War. Another: the British fleet had begun seizing American ships that were headed for France (which was at war with England).

Ultimately, the dispute over free trade led to open conflict—on June 18, 1812 President James Monroe declared war. (Historians call it the War of 1812). Two years of fighting ensued. In 1814, the U.S. mounted a particularly destructive attack on the British stronghold in York, Canada, burning down several government buildings. The British decided to retaliate.

THE INVASION: Under the command of British General Robert Ross, 4,000 British troops sailed through Chesapeake Bay, headed for Washington. There was virtually no resistance. British soldiers marched into America's capital and burned down government buildings—including the Capitol, the Library of Congress, and the White House.

President James Madison and his wife, Dolly, were warned of the attack and managed to escape, taking only the White House drapes, Gilbert Stuart's famous portrait of George Washington, and some fine china with them. Ravenous British soldiers raided the White House and polished off all the food they could find. Then, using rockets and gunpowder, they incinerated the place. That night, a drenching thunderstorm put out the fire, but not in time to save the young nation's symbol of power.

AFTERMATH: Later that year, the Treaty of Ghent was signed between the two nations, ending the War of 1812. Conquered territories were returned and hostilities ceased. Four years later, on January 1, 1818, the Madisons moved into the newly restored White House. No foreign power ever occupied it again.

WORD PLAY

Here are some more origins of common phrases.

SON OF A GUN

Meaning: An epithet.

Background: In the 1800s, British sailors took their wives along on extended voyages. When babies were born at sea, the mothers delivered them in a partitioned section of the gundeck. Because no one could be sure who the *true* fathers were, each of these "gunnery" babies was called a "son of a gun."

PUT UP YOUR DUKES

Meaning: Raise your fists and get ready to fight.

Background: In the early 1800s, the Duke of York, Frederick Augustus, shocked English society by taking up boxing. He gained such admiration from boxers that many started referrring to their fists as the "Dukes of York," and later, "dukes."

HAVING AN AXE TO GRIND

Meaning: Having a hidden agenda.

Background: The expression comes from a story told by Benjamin Franklin. A man once praised Franklin's father's grindstone and asked young Benjamin to demonstrate how the grindstone worked. As Franklin complied, the stranger placed his own axe upon the grindstone, praising the young boy for his cleverness and vigor. When the axe was sharpened, the man laughed at Franklin and walked away, giving the boy a valuable lesson about people with "an axe to grind."

NO BONES ABOUT IT

Meaning: Without a doubt.

Background: The *Oxford English Dictionary* traces this phrase to a 1459 reference to eating stew. Stew-eaters had to be careful not to swallow bones. If a bowl of stew had no bones in it, one could eat it without hesitation. Bone appetit.

People in the Soviet Union don't chew gum.

UPPER CRUST

Meaning: Elite.

Backround: In the Middle Ages, nobility and royalty were served the choice part of a loaf of bread, the upper crust, before it was offered to other diners.

HIS NAME IS MUD

Meaning: Fallen into ill-repute or disrespect.

Backround: John Wilkes Booth, the man who assassinated President Lincoln, broke his leg as he escaped the scene of the crime. Samuel Mudd, a country doctor who hadn't heard of the assassination yet, treated Booth's injury. When he received news of the assassination the following day, Mudd notified the authorties that his patient might have been the assassin. But the doctor had a second surprise coming—he was arrested as a conspirator and sentenced to life in prison.

President Andrew Johnson, Lincoln's successor, commuted Mudd's sentence after the doctor helped stop a yellow fever outbreak at the jail. However, Mudd's family was still trying to clear his name as recently as the 1980s.

MEET A DEADLINE

Meaning: Finish a project by an appointed time.

Backround: The phrase originated in prisoner-of-war camps during the Civil War. Because resources were scarce, the prison camps were sometimes nothing more than a plot of land surrounded by a marked line. If a prisoner tried to cross the line, he would be shot. So it became known as the "deadline."

TOE THE LINE

Meaning: To behave or act in accordance with the rules.

Backround: In the early days of the British Parliament, members of Parliament wore swords in the House of Commons. To keep the Members from fighting during heated debates, the Speaker of the House of Commons forced the Government and Opposition party to sit on opposite sides of the chamber. Lines, two sword-lengths plus one foot apart, were drawn in the carpet. Members were required to stand behind the lines when the House was in session. To this day, when a member steps over the line during a debate, the speaker yells: "Toe the Line."

AMAZING COINCIDENCES

How many bizarre coincidences have you experienced in your life? We'll bet that none of them were as weird as these.

PSYCHIC LINC

Abraham Lincoln's eldest son, Robert Todd Lincoln, was on the scene of *three* separate presidential assassinations.

• First, he was summoned to his father's side after his father was mortally wounded at Ford's Theatre in 1865.

• The second occurred in 1881, when Lincoln was Secretary of War under President Garfield. Lincoln went to Union Station in Washington to inform the president he could not travel with him due to work overload. By the time Lincoln arrived, Garfield had been shot by Charles Guiteau.

• The third assassination occurred 20 years later in 1901, when Lincoln accepted an invitation from President William McKinley to meet him at the Pan-American Exposition in Buffalo, New York. When Lincoln entered the festival he noticed a crowd had gathered—William McKinley had just been mortally wounded by Leon Czolgosz.

WHAT ABOUT HYMN?

In 1950, *Life* magazine reported that 15 people barely missed disaster by an intricate stroke of luck. The 15, members of a church choir in Beatrice, Nebraska, were supposed to meet at 7:15 pm for practice. Each one got delayed...each for a different reason! For example, one had car trouble, another was finishing house chores, another was catching a radio show, etc. Whatever the reason, they were all lucky to be late: The church was destroyed in an explosion at 7:25.

BASIC TRAINING

A distraught architect threw himself in front of a train in the London Underground in a suicide attempt. Luckily, the train stopped inches from his body; in fact, it had to be jacked off its tracks to allow his removal. When questioned, however, the driver informed officials he hadn't stopped the train. An investigation revealed that one of the passengers, unaware of the suicide attempt, had independently pulled the emergency brake. Postscript: London Transport officials considered prosecuting the passenger for illegal use of the emergency brake but ultimately decided against it.

GEORGE, BY GEORGE

George D. Bryson, a businessman from Connecticut, decided to change his travel plans and stop in Louisville, Kentucky, a place he'd never visited before. He went into a local hotel and made preparations to check into Room 307. Before he could do so, a hotel employee handed him a letter addressed to his exact name. It turned out the previous occupant of Room 307 was another George D. Bryson.

NUMBER, PLEASE

In 1983, a woman told British Rail authorities about a disturbing vision she had of a fatal train crash involving an engine with the numbers 47 216. Two years later, a train had a fatal accident, similar to one the woman had described. The engine number, however, was 47 299. Later, someone noticed that the number had previously been changed by nervous British Rail officials. The original number: 47 216.

WHAT'S THE GOOD WORD?

Several secret code words were devised by Allied military commanders during their preparations to invade Normandy in World War II. Among them: "Utah," "Neptune," "Mulberry," "Omaha," and "Overlord." Before the invasion could begin, however, all of these words appeared in a crossword puzzle in the *London Daily Telegraph.* After interrogating the puzzle's author, an English school teacher, authorities became convinced that it was sheer, inexplicable coincidence.

THE MOST AMAZING

On three separate occasions—in the years 1664, 1785, and 1860—there was a shipwreck in which only one person survived the accident. Each time that one person was named Hugh Williams.

TRAVELS WITH RAY

Perplexing adventures of the brilliant egghead Ray "Weird Brain" Redel. Answers are on page 672.

One weekend Ray "Weird Brain" Redel, the man who inspired Rodin's statue "The Thinker," decided to go backpacking at Yosemite National Park. "I've been pushing this old brain too hard," he told me as we set off for the mountains.

"I don't see how you can tell," I muttered.

At that, "Weird Brain" slapped his forehead. "Here's proof," he groaned. "I just realized I've forgotten something terribly important."

"Did you forget to turn off the stove at home?" I grumbled.

"No, no, nothing like that. I just forgot to bring something."

I was getting exasperated. "What? What did you forget to bring?"

He glared at me. "Don't use that tone of voice. You want to know what I forgot? Figure this out: *It has cities, but no houses; it has forests but no trees; it has rivers but no fish.*"

I smiled. "Well, why didn't you say so. Let's just get another one."

What did "Weird Brain" forget?

When we finally got to Yosemite, "Weird Brain" ran into an old friend—a photographer named Ansel Adams.

"Anse, m'boy, what are you doing around here?" he asked the shutterbug.

"Well, Weirdo, I think Yosemite's the best place to enjoy my favorite thing in nature."

"Which is..."

Adams smiled, and I could tell he was testing "Weird Brain"'s fabled ability to solve riddles. "*What can pass before the sun without making a shadow?*" he asked. "That's what I love best.

What was Adams saying he loved?

BATHROOM NEWS

Here are a few of the stories we flushed out during the past year.

JUST WHAT WE NEEDED

October, 1989: A North Carolina company has introduced "Talking Tissue," a novelty gadget which fits the standard toilet paper dispenser. Each time you pull the tissue, you hear one of four recordings: "Yuk-yuk," "Stinky-stinky," "Nice one-nice one," or alarm bells. Batteries not included.

DOWN IN THE DUMPS

January, 1990: A man in Lawrence, Kansas, spent a night underneath an outhouse after he fell through the seat trying to retrieve his wallet. He was rescued by Sheriff Loren Anderson, who said the man wasn't injured, "but in a pretty ugly mood."

UNCLE SAM SAT HERE

November 6, 1989: Archaeologists recently discovered Uncle Sam's toilet six feet under Ferry Street in Troy, New York. The site is where 19th century meatpacker Sam Wilson used to live (see *Uncle John's Second Bathroom Reader* for more info). During the War of 1812, Sam labelled his meat-crates "U.S.," which led American soldiers to joke that they were being fed by Uncle Sam. A developer is building a supermarket and a park on the site, but Uncle Sam's bathroom floor and house foundation will be preserved for visitors to view.

RIGHT BACK AT YA

January, 1990: Over 20 toilets and urinals in the King County, Washington, Court House erupted after being flushed. Apparently, a plumber who was making repairs mistakenly switched an air compressor with a water line.

SINGAPORE STAKE OUT

June, 1989: Undercover agents arrested six men for not flushing urinals in Singapore public restrooms.

In a separate investigation, Singapore courts fined a man $75 for urinating in an elevator. Police nabbed him in the elevator after the *urine detector* locked the elevator doors. A hidden video camera recorded the whole event and the footage was later used as evidence.

THE JOHN POLICE

December 19, 1989: Police employees in Concord, California, filed a $30 million lawsuit against the Concord Police Department after they found a hidden camera installed above a urinal in the men's room. Police Chief George Straka explained that the surveillance was necessary to catch the culprit who had clogged the urinal a few times, causing it to flood the chief's office downstairs.

HIGH-TECH TOILETS

October 29, 1989: "New high-tech toilets from Japan can do it all, including check your health. Here are a few features of some of the latest models:"

• No paper is needed. The push of a button sends a jet of cleansing water upward. A control panel allows the user to adjust the angle, pressure and temperature of the stream. Drying blasts of hot air and mists of perfume follow seconds after. As the commercial for the Toto Ltd. *Toto Queen* says, "Even your bottom wants to be washed."

• The "intelligent bowl" automatically drops a strip of litmus paper into the bowl. Optical sensors analyze urine levels of protein, sugar and other substances. Blood pressure and pulse data are measured if the user inserts his finger in the blood pressure device on the side of the toilet. All test results are revealed on a display screen beside the toilet.

POTTY-PARITY

Setpember, 1989: The American Society of Interior Designers honored Sandra Rawls, an assistant Professor at the University of Missouri, Columbia, for her research which revealed that women's restrooms need more toilets, because women need more time than men. The states of California, New York and Virginia have listened to Rawls's advice and have intoduced so-called "potty-parity" laws.

That's stretching it: An ounce of gold can be drawn into a wire 50 miles long.

THE SIMPUL SPELLING MOOVMENT

At the turn of the century, Andrew Carnegie spent over $200,000 in an attempt to simplify spelling. Here are a few of the details of that forgotten episode in American history.

E-Z DUZ IT: In 1906, millionaire industrialist Andrew Carnegie was approached by Melvin Dewey, the head of the New York libraries, and Brander Matthews, a Columbia University professor, with a revolutionary plan to simplify spelling. Carnegie was enthusiastic. He believed that easier spelling could lead to world peace. Together, the threesome formed the Simplified Spelling Board; their expressed goal was to convince authorities to begin changing the spelling of 300 words.

Among the words targeted were though (tho), confessed (confest), dropped (dropt), through (thru), kissed (kist), fixed (fixt), enough (enuf), prologue (prolog), thoroughfare (thorofare) and depressed (deprest).

ENUF ALREDDEE: Theodore Roosevelt was an instant convert to the simplified spelling plan. On August 29, 1906, he ordered the U.S. Printer to use the new spelling on all executive branch publications. For an instant, it looked as if simplified spelling would be instituted nationwide.

Roosevelt's plan met instant oppostion. It even made front-page news—both here *and* abroad. In England, the *London Times* ridiculed the American president with a headline reading "Roosevelt Spelling Makes Britons Laugh."

Congress was equally outraged by Roosevelt's decree. In late 1906, they debated the idea on the floor of the House. Sensing an embarrassing political defeat, Roosevelt quickly withdrew his support for the plan.

WEL, THATZ THAT: Carnegie was deeply disappointed. Eventually he dropped his financial support for the Simplified Spelling Board, writing, "I think I hav been patient long enuf...I have a much better use of $25,000 a year."

GREAT NEWSPAPER LEADS

The first paragraph in a newspaper story is called the "lead." Technically, it's supposed to answer five questions: Who? What? Where? When? and Why? Here are some of the greatest leads in newspaper history.

"John Dillinger, ace bad man of the world, got his last night—two slugs through his heart and one through his head. He was tough and he was shrewd, but he wasn't as tough and shrewd as the Federals, who never close a case until the end. It took 27 of them to end Dillinger's career, and their strength came out of his weakness—a woman."

—Jack Lait for the *International News Service*, July 23, 1934

"Death and destruction have been the fate of San Francisco. Shaken by a trembler at 5:13 o'clock yesterday morning, the shock lasting 48 seconds, and scourged by flames that raged diametrically in all directions, the city is a mass of smouldering ruins."

— *The San Francisco Call, Chronicle and Examiner*, April 19, 1906

"In the darkness of night and in water two miles deep the *Titanic*, newest of the White Star fleet and greatest of all ocean steamships, sank to the bottom of the sea at twenty minutes past two o'clock yesterday morning. The loss of the *Titanic*—costliest, most powerful, greatest of all the ocean fleet—while speeding westward on her maiden voyage will take rank in maritime history as the most terrible of all recorded disasters at sea."

—*New York Herald*, April 15, 1912

"Steel-nerved Alan B. Shepard Jr., rode a rocket into space today, exclaimed 'What a beautiful sight' as he looked down on the earth, and then dropped to a safe landing in the Atlantic ocean. To the wiry, 37-year-old navy commander, the historic adventure obviously was no more frightening than many earlier flights he had made

In 1936, a cabin on the Hindenburg airship cost $750 for a trans-Atlantic flight.

in experimental aircraft. 'It's a beautiful day,' he told marines on the helicopter that plucked his space capsule out of the water after a soaring flight 115 miles above the earth and 302 miles southeast from the Cape Canaveral launching pad. Then his nonchalance gave way to excitement as he declared: 'Boy, what a ride!' "

—Ralph Dighton for the *Associated Press*, May 5, 1961

"War broke with lightning suddeness in the Pacific today when waves of Japanese bombers attacked Hawaii this morning and the United States Fleet struck back with a thunder of big naval rifles. Japanese bombers, including four-engine dive bombers and torpedo-carrying planes, blasted at Pearl Harbor, the great United States naval base, the city of Honolulu and several outlying American military bases on the Island of Oahu. There were causalities of unstated numbers."

—*The New York Times*, December 8, 1941

OTHER NEWS:

Here are some items from a great "bathroom reader" called *News Of the Weird*.

• An Alaskan assemblyman authored legislation to punish "public flatulence, crepitation, gaseous emission, and miasmic effluence," with a $100 penalty.

• Firefighters in Thurston, Washington slept through a fire in their own station. A passing police officer noticed the blaze and called in the alarm.

• In 1986, firefighters used wire cutters and pliers to free a San Jose, California woman from a tight pair of designer jeans.

• In the 1988 Massachusetts Democratic primary, Herbert Connolly dashed from a late campaign appearance to the polling place to cast his ballot. He got there fifteen minutes late, and lost his seat on the Governor's council. The final tally: 14,716 to 14,715.

• The Internal Revenue Service fined George Wittmeier $159.78 for not paying all of his taxes. He was a penny short on his return.

Only one of the Seven Wonders of the Ancient World still exists—the Sphinx.

FLAKE-OUT

When financial analysts say baseball cards are a better investment than the stock market, you know collecting has become a way of life. But cereal boxes? It's strange but true. Here are some examples.

CORN FLAKES. One of the most collectible cereal boxes is the 1984 Kelloggs' Miss America commerative Corn Flakes Box. The box features Vanessa Williams, the first black Miss America, with a congratulatory endorsement on the back panel that claims the limited edition box is "a lasting reminder that America remains the land of opportunity...and we must continue to promote the American dream and encourage all Americans to freely pursue life, liberty and happiness." Ironically, the box was recalled immediately after *Penthouse* magazine published pictures of Williams in the buff.

WHEATIES. In the 1950s Wheaties stopped using athletes on their boxes and started using Walt Disney figures. Within a year, sales went down 15%. General Mills had a huddle, kicked Disney out, and recalled their sports stars. But the Disney boxes are valuable today.

SWISS MIX. The psychedelic generation of the late 1960s didn't miss out on cereal boxes—pop-artist Peter Max designed a surreal cereal box for an imported Swiss Mix cereal called LOVE. It's now collectible.

WHEAT AND RICE HONEYS. A pair of 1969 Wheat and Rice Honeys boxes featuring the Beatles in "Yellow Submarine" recently sold for $7000.

COUNT CHOCULA. In 1981, General Mills released a cereal called Count Chocula. The box featured a cartoon Count Dracula in front with a Bela Lugosi Dracula in the background. The "Bela" Dracula was wearing a six-point star pendant. A religious group objected to what they felt was a "Star of David" and the box was recalled. Today collectors pursue it religiously.

PARDON ME

The Constitution gives our president the power to grant pardons. This doesn't mean he can overturn guilty verdicts—it only gives him the authority to remove the legal penalties. You hardly ever hear about presidential pardons, but they're granted all the time. Here are a few of the more interesting ones.

RICHARD NIXON

The most famous pardon in U.S. history occurred on September 8, 1974, when Gerald Ford granted Richard Nixon "a full, free, and absolute pardon" for any crimes connected with the Watergate scandal. The decision was extremely controversial. A Gallup Poll conducted after the pardon found that 56% of the American public thought Nixon should have been brought to trial for Watergate.

An August, 1983 article in *Atlantic* magazine by journalist Seymour Hersh alleged that Ford and Nixon had cut a deal for a pardon before the latter's resignation on August 9, 1974. According to the article, Nixon made a threatening phone call to Ford on September 7—one day before the pardon—to make sure the deal was still on. Ford "really resented it," an unnamed Ford aide told Hersh.

ARMAND HAMMER

Armand Hammer, multi-millionaire head of Occidental Petroleum, was pardoned by George Bush in August, 1989, for making an illegal $54,000 contribution to Nixon's 1972 re-election campaign. Hammer was found guilty and placed on a year's probation for the offense—making a political contribution in the name of another person—in March, 1976. He was fined $3,000.

GEORGE STEINBRENNER

In January, 1989, George Steinbrenner, shipbuilder and ex-owner of the New York Yankees, was pardoned by Ronald Reagan. Steinbrenner had been convicted of making an illegal $100,000 contribution to Richard Nixon's re-election campaign in 1972.

Steinbrenner was fined $15,000 in 1974 and later suspended for two years by Baseball Commissioner Bowie Kuhn after pleading not guilty to the charges. Kuhn lifted the suspension in March 1976 after 16 months had been served.

TOKYO ROSE

In one of his last official acts as president in 1977, Ford pardoned Iva Toguri D'Aquino (aka, Tokyo Rose), who had served six years in jail for making pro-Japanese propaganda broadcasts during World War II. D'Aquino, an American citizen of Japanese descent, had gone to Japan to visit a sick aunt in July, 1941, just before war broke out between the two countries. Unable to return to the U.S., she was recruited by Japanese authorities to try to demoralize American troops. According to the *New York Times*, "For the G.I.s in the South Pacific, the broadcasts were as much a part of the routine as Spam. In between familiar selections of American music there was the voice of a woman telling American servicemen that their wives and girlfriends were being taken over by the civilians who remained behind and that there was really no point in fighting on any further because the Japanese were going to win anyway. The G.I.s began calling her Tokyo Rose. To most soldiers and sailors the broadcasts were a pleasant joke."

D'Aquino was indicted for treason and was sentenced to 10 years in prison beginning in 1949 (she was released in 1956 for good behavior). She also paid a $10,000 fine.

DRAFT RESISTERS

On January 21, 1977, in his first act as president, Jimmy Carter issued an unconditional presidential pardon to Vietnam draft resisters. Prior to Carter's proclamation, Gerald Ford had granted a limited amnesty to Vietnam draft resisters in 1974 if they swore allegiance to the U.S. and agreed to perform two years of public service. 21,700 people took advantage of Ford's program. Carter's unconditional pardon—which excluded deserters and veterans with less-than-honorable discharges—affected between 100,000 and 500,000 people.

Holy cow!: 2.2 pounds of steak costs $1.50 in Buenos Aires, and $51 in Tokyo.

...AND TWO PARDONS REFUSED

• Samuel A. Mudd, a physician who aided assassin John Wilkes Booth, (he set his broken leg after the assassination) pleaded for a pardon for his inadvertant role in the death of Abraham Lincoln. Mudd was paroled in 1869 from a life sentence, but was never pardoned. In 1988, his grandson, Dr. Richard Mudd, gave up a 61-year campaign to clear his name after the Reagan White House refused to grant one.

• In 1914, journalist George Burdick, a writer for the *New York Tribune*, broke a story about prominent officials who were going to be indicted for smuggling. A Federal grand jury demanded to know his sources, but Burdick refused to reveal them. President Wilson stepped in and offered a full pardon, but Burdick refused. This set a precedent—no one had ever refused a pardon before. Eventually, the Supreme Court upheld Burdick's right to refuse Wilson's pardon, arguing it preserved the privilege against self-incrimination. The case was widely regarded as a major victory for freedom of the press. Burdick never revealed his source.

ODDS & ENDS

• In 1795, George Washington issued the first presidential pardon to two instigators of the Whiskey Rebellion. They'd led a mob that attacked and burned a tax collector's home on July 17, 1794.

• During the War of 1812, President James Madison announced amnesty for pirates and smugglers "in the vicinity of New Orleans who helped fight the British."

• Abraham Lincoln pardoned over 10,000 Confederate soldiers for their role in the Civil War. His successor, Andrew Johnson, issued a full pardon in 1865 to all Confederates, except leaders, as long as they took an oath of allegiance to the United States. Then in 1868, Johnson granted an unconditional amnesty to "all persons engaged in the late rebellion."

• During his two terms as president, Ronald Reagan granted 380 pardons. Among the offenses for which people were pardoned were tax evasion, possession of untaxed whiskey, possession with intent to distribute cocaine, illegal transfer of machine guns, and copyright infringement.

NAME & PLACE

Would you want to live in Hell Station, Accident, or Dildo? You can. Here are the strange names of some real places.

Frozen Run, West Virginia: A man saved his own life by wrapping himself in the skin of a recently killed buffalo. His friends had to thaw it to get him out.

Preacher's Head, New Mexico: A rock resembling the face of a serious-looking man overlooks the town.

Dildo, Newfoundland: Coincidentally, it's the birthplace of Shannon Tweed, *Playboy* magazine's 1982 Playmate of the Year.

Anxiety Point, Alaska: Sir John Franklin, a British explorer, was afraid that bad weather would prevent his team from reaching a point on the Alaskan coast. They made it, and left this permanent reminder of his nervousness.

Nipple Mountain, Colorado: One formation on the mountain is named "Clara's Bird's Nipple."

Chilly Buttes, Idaho: A cold place in the winter.

Chicago, Illinois: From the Algonquin word meaning "onion-place."

Hell Station, Michigan: Locals say it freezes over every winter.

Art, Texas: As one resident explained, "Well, it's not for Arthur or Artesian, and far as I know people here weren't ever especially arty. We've heard they picked it just because they wanted a real short name."

Sacul, Texas: A reverse spelling of (John) Lucas, an early settler in the area.

Lake Italy, California: The lake is shaped like a boot.

Accident, Maryland: In 1774, surveyors marked off a parcel of land by mistake. They decided to immortalize the error.

YOU BET YOUR LIFE

To a generation of viewers who only know the Marx Brothers from their films, it may come as a surprise that Groucho was also a radio and TV star...as the host of a quiz show called "You Bet Your Life," which aired from 1950 to 1961.

HOW IT STARTED

In 1947, radio was the most popular entertainment medium in America. Groucho Marx was no longer a movie star, but he did a guest spot on *The Bob Hope Show* that turned into a hilarious ad-lib free-for-all. The act impressed a successful radio producer named John Guedel, who happened to be in the audience that night. When it was over, Guedel approached Groucho and asked him if he could ad-lib like that all the time. Groucho replied that he'd done it all his life.

Guedel was excited. He thought Groucho's talent was wasted with scripts—he ought to do a show in which he was allowed to interact with "real people," ad-libbing. Groucho, who'd hosted four different radio shows and had bombed every time, was open to anything. But when Guedel suggested a quiz show, Groucho balked. He said he had to think about it.

Groucho wondered if he could live with himself as a game-show host...and decided he could. ("What the hell, nothing else had worked.") So he made an audition tape. But no network was interested. So Guedel, convinced that America would love tuning in to the real Groucho, took the tape directly to a sponsor and got it on the air that way. Within a few years Guedel looked like a genius and Groucho's career was revived—"You Bet Your Life" was one of America's top 10 radio shows.

At that time, TV networks were snapping up popular radio programs and adapting them to television. Everything from "Burns and Allen" and "The Jack Benny Show," to "Gangbusters" and "The Lone Ranger" wound up on the tube. Naturally, Groucho was approached about bringing his show to TV. CBS and NBC both wanted it—but in the ensuing battle for Marx's talents, CBS head William Paley offended Groucho by referring to the fact that they were both Jewish and that Jews should stick together. NBC head Robert Sarnoff was also Jewish. Groucho chose NBC.

All continents have deserts—except for Europe.

INSIDE INFO

Stiff Upper Lip.

Without his mustache, Groucho was unrecognizable to the public; he could walk the streets without being stopped by fans. For radio and TV he refused to use the phony mustache he wore in his movie days ("That character is dead," he said). But he did agree to grow a real mustache.

TV or Not TV?

When Groucho's show moved to TV, NBC wanted to add all kinds of visual gimmicks "to make it more interesting." They also wanted to resurrect his movie persona. But Groucho insisted on keeping things simple, as they had been in the radio format. No funny walks, no costumes. Just Groucho in a business suit, sitting in front of a curtain with his guests. It turned out to be a good idea: From the time the show debuted in 1950 to the time it was cancelled 11 years later, "You Bet Your Life" was the most consistently popular game show on TV.

Nobody Loses.

Groucho wasn't comfortable with some aspects of being a game show host. He complained, for example, that he felt bad when people had to leave the show broke. He said, "Can't we ask them a simple question, like who's the President of the U. S., or who's buried in Grant's Tomb?" So that became part of the show. Whenever someone lost, Groucho asked the easiest question possible, and the contestant got a few bucks as a consolation.

Close Encounters.

In 1973, NBC started burning original negatives of the 250 reels of *You Bet Your Life* to make space in their warehouse. Fortunately, someone thought to call the show's producer, John Guedel, and ask if he wanted a few negatives as souvenirs; they'd already burned 15 of them. A shocked Guedel stopped the destruction and made a deal with NBC to take over syndication of *The Best of Groucho*. In 1973, a Los Angeles TV station aired reruns at 11:00 p.m. as a favor to Groucho. The ratings were so good that stations all over the country picked it up, and the show was revived.

Video Mania: On average, Americans rent over 6 million videos a day.

GROUCHO & GUESTS

No one could ad-lib like Groucho. Here are a few spontaneous remarks from "You Bet Your Life."

Groucho: "What's it like in South Carolina?"
Woman: "Oh, it's wonderful, Goucho, Southern hospitality and wonderful folks."
Groucho: "Well, we want you to feel at home here, Marie, so we'll pay you in Confederate money."

Groucho: "How did you meet your wife?"
Man: "A friend of mine."
Groucho: "Do you still regard him as a friend?"

Groucho (to husband & wife with arms around each other): "How long have you been married?"
Wife: "Two and a half years, Groucho."
Groucho: "Why are you holding on to each other? Are you afraid if you let go, you'll kill each other?"

Groucho: "What are you gonna do with your money?"
Man: "I'm gonna make my wife happy, Groucho."
Groucho: "What are you gonna do—get a divorce?"

Groucho: "You don't mind if I ask you a few questions, do you?"
Woman: "If they're not too embarrassing."
Groucho: "Don't give it a second thought. I've asked thousands of questions on this show, and I've yet to be embarrassed."

Woman (explaining herself): "I'm afraid you don't follow me."
Groucho: "Even if I did, you'd have nothing to be afraid of."

Groucho (to the father of triplets): "Do you have a job?
Man: "Yeah."
Groucho: "What is it?"
Man: "I work for the California Power Company."
Groucho: "My boy, you don't work for the California Power Company. You *are* the California Power Company."

Groucho: "What's your husband's name?"
Woman: "Milton August."
Groucho: "What's his name in September?"

In Helsinki, Finland, police rarely give parking tickets—they deflate tires.

BANNED IN THE U.S.A.

Censorship is a big issue for bathroom readers. After all, we don't want anyone telling us what we can read in here...or if we can read in here at all! So we've included a few tidbits on censorship in this edition, to remind us all to sit down and be counted.

AND STAY OUT!

Bring us your tired, your wretched...etc.? Not in the early '50s. In 1952, at the height of our Cold War hysteria, a provision was added to the Immigration and Nationality Act of 1952 to keep certain "undesirable" people from entering the U.S. The law, known as the McCarran-Walter Immigration Act, was vetoed by then-President Harry S Truman, but overriden by Congress. Usually, "undesirable" meant "suspected Commies," although the 33 provisions included categories for people who engaged in espionage, polygamy and "deviant sexual behavior."

But the bill was actually a political tool, designed to keep people with controversial views (like John Lennon) out of the country. In 1984 alone—32 years after the act was passed—8,000 people from 98 different countries were banned from the U.S.A. under the auspices of the bill, because of their political beliefs.

WHO'S WHO?

Among the people banned from the U.S.A. since 1952 were actors, singers, writers, and politicians. Two examples:

• *Gabriel García Márquez*, Colombian author and winner of the Nobel Prize. Márquez, a critic of U.S. foreign policy, was denied a visa in 1963. Eight years later, he was allowed in temporarily to accept an honorary degree from Columbia University. The terms of Márquez's restricted visa included the stipulation that an FBI agent would accompany him everywhere he went.

• *Pierre Trudeau*, future Prime Minister of Canada. He was denied entry because he had participated in an economic conference in Moscow in 1952 and was labeled a "Communist sympathizer." Trudeau was eventually allowed to travel in the U.S. after immigration officials interviewed him in Montreal and gave him "clearance."

Postscript: Congress finally repealed the law in January, 1990.

91% of Americans surveyed have bought their pets holiday gifts.

DISNEY STORIES: SLEEPING BEAUTY

In 1959, Walt Disney released Sleeping Beauty, an adaptation of the classic fairy tale. It took 6 years and $6 million (an incredible sum at the time) to finish. But it was a disappointment at the box office, taking in just $5.3 million that year. Since then, it has grossed almost 5 times that much. Of course, the Disney version and the original story were substantially different. Here are some examples of how the tale was changed.

THE DISNEY VERSION

A King and a Queen in a faraway kingdom throw a party for their newborn daughter. They invite everyone from miles around...except a Wicked Witch, who's really upset about it. She shows up anyway, and casts this spell on the baby: On her 15th birthday, the young Princess will prick her finger on a spinning wheel spindle and die.

• A Good Fairy attending the party softens the curse, changing it to 100 years of sleep instead of death.

• The King tries to avoid the curse by burning every spinning wheel in the kingdom. No luck; on her 15th birthday, the Princess discovers a tower chamber where an old woman is working a spinning wheel. The Princess tries her hand at it, pricks her finger, and falls asleep. So does everyone else in the kingdom.

• Thick, impenetrable brambles grow around the castle. 100 years later, a young Prince shows up.

• The Witch throws the Prince into her dungeon. When he escapes, the Witch turns herself into a dragon and attacks him. The Prince slays her, enters the castle, and kisses the Princess, who wakes up (along with the rest of the people in the castle). The Prince and Princess live happily ever after.

THE ORIGINAL VERSION

• Disney's version of Sleeping Beauty is based loosely on Charles Perrault's telling of this ancient fairy tale. But Disney only tells half the story.

• In the original, the Wicked Witch disappears from the story after casting her spell. No brambles grow up around the castle.

• The Prince just happens to arrive at exactly the moment Sleeping Beauty is supposed to wake up. The Prince secretly marries her, and they have two children—a daughter (Aurora) and son (Day). It isn't until his father dies and he becomes king that the Prince invites Sleeping Beauty to his castle.

• The Prince's mother, it turns out, is an Ogress. While he's away at war, the Queen Mother orders the chef to slaughter and cook the daughter, then the son, and eventually Sleeping Beauty herself. The chef can't bring himself to do it—he hides the trio and serves other animals instead.

• Eventually the Queen Mother discovers the truth. She orders Sleeping Beauty and her children to be thrown into a cauldron of carnivorous reptiles. In the nick of time, the new King arrives home and the Queen Mother leaps into the cauldron herself.

SAMPLE PASSAGE (FROM THE ORIGINAL)

"The Prince—now the King—had no sooner left than the Queen Mother sent her daughter-in-law and the children to a country house in the wood so that she might more easily gratify her horrible longing. She followed them there a few days later, and one evening she said to her head cook, 'I will eat little Aurora for dinner tomorrow.'

"'Oh no, Madam,' the cook exlaimed.

"'Yes, I will.' said the Queen Mother, and she said it in a voice of an Ogress longing to eat fresh meat. 'And I want her served with my favorite sauce.'

"The cook, seeing that an Ogress isn't someone to trifle with, took his knife and went up to Aurora's room. She was about four years old, and she came jumping and laughing toward him, threw her arms around his neck, and asked him if he had any candy for her. He burst into tears, dropping the knife; then he went into the farmyard and killed a little lamb, which he served up with such a delicious sauce that the Ogress assured him she'd never eaten anything so tasty. Meanwhile, he carried Aurora to his own home and gave her to his wife to hide, so the Queen Mother wouldn't find her."

Mr. Green Jeans's nickname in real life was "Lumpy."

THE AUSTRALIAN BEATLES

When Beatlemania and the British Invasion hit the U.S. in the mid-sixties, many musicians suddenly found themselves out of work. Here's the story of a creative solution that turned into one of the all-time great rock'n'roll hoaxes.

It was rock 'n' roll news in 1965. A new band had arrived in America. Direct from the outbacks of Australia—Armstrong, Australia, aborigine country—came the "Down Under" continent's answer to the Beatles! The Strange brothers, Miles, Niles and Giles, known professionally as the Strangeloves. They were strange, indeed. They dressed in loud striped outfits and wore native hats. And the three didn't look at all alike. But that, they explained, was because they had the same mother and different fathers.

The boys had rhythm, too. Playing jungle drums, they brought back the old Bo Diddley beat with a great song called "I Want Candy," which took off like a frightened kangaroo, hopping up the American charts into the Top 10. The Strangeloves toured three times with the Beach Boys, who thought the brothers were the most insane people they'd ever met. They appeared on Radio Caroline in England. And they had the time of their lives on NBC-TV's "Hullabaloo." An unbelievable feat for a group that didn't exist. They were real people, of course, but they weren't named Strange. And they weren't from Australia. The Strangeloves came straight from the Brill Building in New York City.

The Brill Building was rock'n'roll's Tin Pan Alley in the early '60s. It was the home of songwriters like Ellie Greenwich and Jeff Barry, Carole King and Gerry Goffin, and Neil Sedaka and Howie Greenfield, who had been the source of hundreds of hit songs in the early sixties. But in 1965, no one wanted to hear American groups. So songwriters/producers Bob Feldman, Jerry Goldstein, and Richard Gotterher got the idea to put together a fake "British Invasion" act. They donned bizarre costumes, learned their accents from a Britisher named Doug Moody, and the Strangeloves were born. After writing "I Want Candy" and recording it for their record label, Bang Records, the act went on tour. First stop, the dome at Virginia Beach, where Feldman recalls, "There were 3,000 kids with banners saying, 'Welcome to the U.S., Strangeloves.' And the mayor gave us the key to the city and there we were. We had to go through with it!"

The Beach Boys knew the truth; nobody else did, except the Strangeloves' immediate families. In fact, the group turned down a $10,000 offer to appear on "The Ed Sullivan Show" because Richard didn't want his elderly Jewish grandmother to see him on TV in a wild leopard-skin outfit. The Strangeloves' "Australian" accents, filtered through their native Brooklynese, must have sounded pretty authentic. They eventually appeared with almost every major British act and they never got caught. But the ruse did lead to some unexpected close calls. One time on a local Pittsburgh dance show, host Clark Race unexpectedly brought out a boomerang and handed it to Miles (Feldman), who was supposedly a champion thrower. As Bob was about to throw it, Clark stopped him and said, "Miles, that's not the way to hold a boomerang." Bob looked right into the camera and said, "Clark, that's why I'm the champion and you're not." "Miles" then proceeded to throw it. He hit the cameraman on the shoulder, barely missing his head, and knocked him to the floor. As the cameraman fell, his camera went with him.

At nearby Kennywood Park, the Strangeloves were hired without a backup band. They had their jungle drums with them and wowed the crowd with a 45-minute version of "Shout." Bob then went for some fun on an amusement park ride called "The Magic Carpet Ride," forgot to hug his knees as instructed, and fell over the top. He was carried to the infirmary where they tended to his injured shoulder...but he found out that he couldn't even drop his pose there! The head nurse was from Sydney, Australia, and she recognized him. As Bob tells it, "She said, 'You're one of those Strange boys, aren't you?'...Now I had to cry out in pain with an accent, too!"

Mercifully, the Strangeloves' pose only lasted until 1966.

The song sung most often in America is "Happy Birthday to You."

DUMB SCIENCE

Ever wonder what scientists do in their laboratories all day? Here are a few real-life examples.

THE EXPERIMENT: James McConnell, head of the University of Michigan's Planaria Research group, wanted to see if memory "can be eaten and reused." So he trained a batch of worms, ground them up, and fed them to a second group of untrained worms.
THE CONCLUSION: According to McConnell, it worked. The untrained worms demonstrated behavior he'd taught the ground up worms. Minor problem: He never got the same results again.

THE EXPERIMENT: A scientist named Spalding brilliantly theorized that a baby chick's instinct to follow a mother hen originates in its brain. In an 1873 experiment, he removed the brains of baby chicks and placed the chicks a few yards from a mother hen.
THE CONCLUSION: Spalding's groundbreaking paper, "Instinct," tells us: "Decerebrated chicks will not move towards a clucking or retreating object."

THE EXPERIMENT: To test the rumor that Coca-Cola is an effective spermicide, Harvard University researchers added sperm samples to test tubes, each containing a different type of Coke.
THE CONCLUSION: A minor success. Diet Coke was the most effective, followed by Classic Coke, New Caffeine-Free, and in last place, New Coke. Researchers suggest that levels of acidic pH and perhaps some secret formula components were the determining factors. In any event, a Coca-Cola official was quoted to say: "We do not promote Coca-Cola for medical purposes. It is a soft drink."

THE EXPERIMENT: Are rats psychic? In 1974, two parapsychologists named Craig and Treuriniet decided to find out. They put rats in a lab maze with only two exits—one leading to freedom, the other to death. (They would kill the rats).
THE CONCLUSION: Half chose the correct path; half didn't. Unsatisfied with the results, Craig and Treuriniet theorized a correlation between the rat's psychic powers and phases of the moon.

According to a recent study, housewives feel more stressed than working women.

HONESTLY, ABE

Abraham Lincoln, our 16th president, was surprisingly quotable. Here are a few of his better-known sayings.

"The best way to destroy your enemy is to make him your friend."

"God must love the common man, he made so many of them."

"No man is good enough to govern another man without that other's consent."

"It's been my experience that people who have no vices have very few virtues."

"No matter how much cats fight, there always seems to be plenty of kittens."

"People who like this sort of thing will find this the sort of thing they like."

"Public opinion in this country is everything."

"Human action can be modified to some extent, but human nature cannot be changed."

"A man's legs must be long enough to reach the ground."

"Those who deny freedom for others deserve it not for themselves."

"My father taught me to work, but not to love it. I never did like to work, and I don't deny it. I'd rather read, tell stories, crack jokes, talk, laugh—anything but work."

"Tact is the ability to describe others as they see themselves."

"The things I want to know are in books; my best friend is the man who'll get me a book I ain't read."

"The man who is incapable of making a mistake is incapable of anything."

"The ballot is stronger than the bullet."

"As I would not be a slave, so I would not be a master. This expresses my idea of democracy."

"The best thing about the future is that it comes only one day at a time."

YOU BE THE JUDGE

Blowin' In The Wind is one of the best-known folk songs in American history. It was written by Bob Dylan, of course . . . or was it? Here's an analysis from the book Behind the Hits, *by Bob Shannon and John Javna.*

This appeared in *Newsweek* on November 4, 1963. . ."There is a rumor circulating that Dylan did not write "Blowin' in the Wind," but that it was written by a Millburn, New Jersey high school student named Lorre Wyatt, who sold it to the singer. Dylan says he did write the song, and Wyatt denies authorship, but several Millburn students claim they heard the song from Wyatt before Dylan ever sang it." Who is really responsible for the song? Here is all the info we could find...what do you think?

CLUE #1

Dylan comes to New York in autumn of 1960, or February of 1961 (there are two stories), to visit Woody Guthrie at Greystone Hospital. He continues to visit through 1963.

- "In the autumn of 1960, Dylan quit the University of Minnesota and decided to visit Guthrie at Greystone Hospital, in New Jersey."—Nat Hentoff, in the *New Yorker*, 1964.
- "In February 1961, Dylan came East, primarily to visit Woody Guthrie at Greystone Hospital in New Jersey. The visits have continued..."—liner notes to "The Freewheelin' Bob Dylan," in 1963.

CLUE #2

Lorre Wyatt is doing volunteer work at Greystone at the same time Dylan is visiting it, from Autumn 1960, to Spring 1963.

- Among activities listed for Wyatt in his 1963 high school yearbook: "Folksinging at Hospitals, 1, 2, 3."
- "Lorre's sense of humor, musical ability, and strong desire to help people have made him a welcome sight to the ill and mentally retarded children at Kessler Institute and Greystone Hospital."—liner notes from "A Time To Sing," an album released in 1963 by a Millburn High School folksinging group called the Millburnaires.

CLUE #3

Both Dylan (according to many sources), and Lorre Wyatt (according to Millburn High graduates whom we interviewed) are hanging out in Greenwich Village in 1961 and 1962. So the two might have met in either Greystone or the Village. Or both.

CLUE #4

Although "The Freewheelin' Bob Dylan," the LP on which "Blowin' In the Wind" first appears, will not be released until May 1963, Dylan actually records the song on July 9, 1962 (according to Columbia Records). This would seem to indicate that the song is legitimately his—but there is one irregularity.

CLUE #5

The song is not published and copyrighted in Dylan's name until July 30, 1962—three weeks after Dylan records it. This is highly unusual; the normal procedure is for a songwriter to write a song, get it published, and then record it. Hypothetical situation: Dylan learns the song from Wyatt, takes it into a recording session, and gets such a favorable reaction that he takes credit for it. After learning from Wyatt that he hasn't published it, Dylan has his own publisher, M. Witmark and Sons, do it in his name. Alternative hypothesis: Dylan just never bothers with the legal details until a few weeks after recording it. Would he take his own songs that lightly?

CLUE #6

A December 1962 issue of *The Miller*, the Millburn High School newspaper, mentions that Wyatt had written the song in the summer.

- "Last summer Lorre, an amateur folk singer and guitarist, put together a melody that had come to him in snatches."
- The article then adds: "He began writing lyrics to it in early autumn, inspired by Student President Steve Oxman's welcoming speech [in September of 1962]." This, of course, is at odds with the fact that Dylan recorded the song in July. However, we contacted Oxman, and he explained that the article had things reversed—his speech was inspired by the already existing song.

CLUE #7

According to *The Miller*, Wyatt sells the song to Dylan for $1000. He donates the money to CARE in memory of his deceased mother. "Blowin' in the Wind," says the paper, "a song written by senior Lorre Wyatt, and expressing the singer's own philosophy concerning the world's problems, is now the property of a well-known folk-singer. Recently, the singer heard 'Blowin' In the Wind' while in New York and bought the song and the rights to it for one thousand dollars. Shortly after this, Lorre donated the money to CARE. When asked why, he replied, 'Just listen to the words in the song, and I think you'll understand.' "

CLUE #8

The Chad Mitchell Trio records "Blowin' in the Wind" for Kapp Records in early 1963.

• *The Miller* says this in its February 2, 1963 issue: "The Chad Mitchell Trio has added 'Blowin' In the Wind,' a song written by MHS senior Lorre Wyatt, to its latest album, 'Chad Mitchell in Action.'. . .The publicity department at Kapp Studios said, 'Lorre has created a beautiful ballad. A song of this nature takes longer to write and to become well-known, but it has a greater meaning and a richer melody than most of today's popular rock and roll tunes.'"

• However, when the record comes out, the song is credited to Dylan on the label.

CLUE #9

The Millburnaires, of which Wyatt is a member, record an album in April of 1963. It is called "A Time to Sing." "Blowin' in the Wind" is on the album, and is credited to Wyatt. The Millburnaires make a deal with Riverside Records to release the LP nationally.

CLUE #10

"The Freewheelin' Bob Dylan" is released on Columbia Records on May 27, 1963.

CLUE #11

Here is what Lorre says in the liner notes on the back of the Millburnaires' album: "Did you ever stop to ask yourself why the hate, the greed, the hunger—the fear?...No, they're not 'pretty' questions, but they're ones that must be asked. But we must do more than just ask: we must do something about them. It is our duty to God, ourselves, and to our fellow man. 'None is so blind as he who will not see.' The biggest criminals are people like you and I, who see things that are wrong, and know that they're wrong, and yet do nothing about them. How many times can a man turn his head and pretend that he just doesn't see?"

CLUE #12

From the liner notes of "Freewheelin':" "The first of Dylan's songs in this set is 'Blowin' in the Wind.' In 1962, Dylan said of the song's background: "I still say that some of the biggest criminals are those that turn their heads away when they see wrong and they know it's wrong."

CLUE #13

The Millburnaires' album is re-released nationally in the fall of 1963 as "Teenage Hootenanny" but gives no credits for authorship of "Blowin' in the Wind." It does have Wyatt's liner notes about "criminals," though.

CLUE #14

Dylan in his "Biograph" LP: "It was just another song that I wrote and got thrown into all the songs I was doing at the time. I wrote it in a cafe across the street from the Gaslight. Although I thought it was special, I didn't know to what degree. I wrote it for the moment."

CLUE #15

Interviews with Millburn students and teachers reveal that many recall the song being sung by the Millburnaires in a school performance in either the fall of 1962 or the spring of 1963. It was definitely introduced as Wyatt's song, and it was before the Dylan album was released. Sample interview (with Bill McCormick, M.H.S. history teacher): "[What people understood], was that one of the contingencies of the buyout was that, whatever monetary arrangements were made, it was to the effect that [Wyatt] had sold all rights and was not to ever claim that it was his. I shouldn't say it was common knowledge, but that was the hot rumor back 10, 12, 15 years ago, whatever." Ray Fowler, engineer on the

Millburnaires' LP: "Everyone I talked to at the time, said that Wyatt wrote the song."

CLUE #16

When columnist Mike Royko contacted Lorre in 1974 and asked him if he'd written "Blowin' in the Wind," Wyatt's answer was, "I don't want to talk about it." Royko: "[I told him that] all he had to do was deny writing "Blowin' in the Wind" and the matter would be closed for good. Did Wyatt deny writing it? He said, 'No comment.'" Royko contacted Anthony Scaduto, who wrote a Dylan biography, and asked what he thought. Scaduto said he believed the Wyatt story was phony, and that Dylan wrote "Blowin' in the Wind."

Did Dylan write Blowin' in the Wind? You be the judge.

✔ ✔ ✔

WORKING GIRL

Mary Tyler Moore, head of the MTM TV production company, is one of the world's wealthiest women. Some interesting facts about her:

• At age 18, she landed her first TV role. It didn't exactly make her a star. She played "Happy Hotpoint," a tiny elf with pointy ears. She jumped out of an icetray in a Hotpoint refrigerator ad and said, "Hi, Harriet. Aren't you glad you bought a Hotpoint?"

• She finally landed a regular part in a prime time series in 1959. It was on *Richard Diamond*, and she played Sam, the sexy switchboard operator. The only catch: all they ever showed of her was her legs.

• She kept auditioning. But all she could get were bit parts. Then she got a call from her agent. "He told me, 'Get over to Carl Reiner's office. He wants to talk to you about playing Dick Van Dyke's wife. I said 'No, I may just as well stay home. I'm not going to get it.'" He finally convinced her to go, and she got the part.

• With her husband, she created MTM Enterprises, which owned TV shows like "Newhart," "WKRP in Cincinnati," and "Rhoda."

• She said: "Three things help me get through life successfully: An understanding husband, an extremely good analyst, and millions and millions of dollars."

ELVIS-O-RAMA

Here's some info from Vince Staten's irreverent guidebook, Unauthorized America.

ALL SHOOK UP

"Elvis hated Robet Goulet.

"Detested him.

"Any time he saw Goulet on TV, he became violently angry. Unfortunately, in the days when Mike Douglas and Merv Griffin ruled the airwaves, Goulet was on TV a lot. Elvis shot up the TV with Goulet on it several times, usually in his suite at the Las Vegas Hilton Hotel. The most famous time Elvis pulled a derringer out of his boot and fired it into the set, sending sparks everywhere."

"Elvis didn't limit his gunplay to shooting up TV sets. He shot up lots of small appliances and a few large ones. In February 1974, he fired at light switch in his Vegas suite. The bullet penetrated the wall and just missed his girlfriend at the time, Linda Thompson. She came running into his room trembling, but Elvis was able to soothe her by saying, 'Hey now, hon, just don't get excited.'

"From then on he confined his shooting to the TV and the chandelier, explaining to his boys, 'We're in the penthouse. Nobody's gonna get hit as long as you shoot straight up.'"

THE FIRST SWIVEL

"The question of the ages is: what did he shake, and when did he shake it? Let's face it, his swivel hips were the one thing that set him apart from the other young singers of his day. They didn't call him Elvis the Pelvis for nothing.

"So when and where did he first shake his hips while singing?

"Country music legend Webb Pierce says it happened July 30, 1954, on a country music package tour that played Overton Park in Memphis. 'Elvis told me that it was the first time he had ever sung before a big crowd and that he was real scared. He said he thought he was gonna faint out there on stage, so he started flapping his legs, just to keep from passing out. Then he noticed the crowd was reacting to it, so he just kept doing it.'"

The pastry we call a "Danish" is called "Vienna Bread" in Denmark.

PRIME-TIME PROVERBS

Here are some more TV quotes from the book Primetime Proverbs, *by Jack Mingo and John Javna.*

ON POLITICS

"When I was in third grade, there was a kid running for office. His slogan was: 'Vote for me and I'll show you my wee-wee.' He won by a landslide."

—Dorothy, ***The Golden Girls***

ON "FREE LOVE"

"You American girls have such big breasts all the time...So please, give us the number of your apartment so we can go up there and have sex with you now!"

—Dan Aykroyd (The Wild and Crazy Guy), ***Saturday Night Live***

ON PETS

[To his dog] "You're glad to see me every minute of your life. I come home, you jump around and wag your tail. I go to the closet, I come out, you jump around and wag your tail. I turn my face away and turn it back, you wag your tail. Either you love me very much or your short-term memory is shot."

Dr. Harry Weston, —*Empty Nest*

"The only good cat is a stir-fried cat."

—Alf, ***ALF***

COP TALK

Witness [refusing to testify because he doesn't want to "get involved"]: "Mr. Friday, if you were me, would you want to get involved?"
Sgt. Joe Friday: "Can I wait a while?"
Witness: "Huh?"
Friday: "Before I'm you."

—***Dragnet***

Killer: "You made a mistake, and I'm not going to pay for it."
Sgt. Joe Friday: "You're going to use a credit card?"

—***Dragnet***

ON LINGUISTICS

"Due to the shape of the North American elk's esophagus, even if it could speak, it could not pronounce the word *lasagna*."

—Cliff Clavin, ***Cheers***

"You must always keep abreast of other tongues."

—Batman, ***Batman***

OH SAY CAN YOU SEE?

A Bathroom Reader's dilemma: What would do if you heard the National Anthem right now? Stay seated? Stand? Well, no one's watching. Hum it to yourself while you read this, and do whatever you want.

THE PRISONER

During the War of 1812, British troops marched on Washington, D.C. and burned down the White House. Then, with their sights set on Baltimore, they sailed up the Chesapeake River, taking a civilian prisoner with them—a Dr. William Beanes, who'd supposedly helped arrest 3 English soldiers in Washington.

THE RESCUE.

The next day Francis Scott Key, a prominent young lawyer from Washington, met with British military commanders on the Chesapeake Bay and persuaded them to release Beanes (who'd actually *assisted* wounded British soldiers). But the Brits wouldn't let Key go until the planned bombardment of Baltimore's Fort McHenry was over. So he was detained on the British boat overnight.

THE DEFENSE

During the night, Key got a first-hand look at the raging battle. He assumed that the British would take Baltimore, as they had Washington. But in the morning, he awoke to find that the American flag was still flying over Fort McHenry. Inspired by the American defense, he jotted down an emotional poem.

THE SONG

On his way back to shore, Key wrote the words down on an envelope. The next day, he showed the poem to his wife's sister. She found it so inspiring that she took it to a printer, made handbills, and circulated the poem around Baltimore. The next week, the *Baltimore American* newspaper became the first to publish it.

Surprise: the words were set to the melody of a *British* song called "Anacreon in Heaven." Another surprise: It didn't become the National Anthem until 1931—after being voted down in 1929 because it's a British tune, and a poor marching song.

CUSTOM-MADE

You know these customs. Now, here's where they came from.

CLINKING GLASSES AFTER A TOAST

Nobles and knights were sometimes assassinated by enemies who'd poisoned their wine. So when they got together socially, each poured a little of his own wine into everyone else's goblet, as a precaution. That way, if one man poisoned another, he poisoned everyone—including himself...Over the years, the tradition of exchanging wine has been simplied into this gesture of friendship.

SPLITTING THE WISHBONE

In ancient Rome, soothsayers used the bones and entrails of birds to predict the future. In fact, one Latin term for "soothsayer," *auspex*, means "one who looks at birds." The soothsayer would " throw the bones" (a precursor of throwing dice) or dissect the bird to receive insight. Nowadays, we just break the wishbone, hoping to get the larger—and luckier—piece.

BUTTONS ON COAT SLEEVES

Researchers credit this to Napoleon Bonaparte. Apparently, while inspecting some of his troops, he spotted a soldier wiping his nose on his jacket sleeve. Disgusted, Napoleon ordered all new shirts and jackets for his army—this time with buttons on the sleeves.

WEARING BLACK FOR MOURNING

Until King Charles VIII died in the late fifteenth century, Europeans in mourning wore white (for hope or renewal). But when Anne Brittany, Charles' widow, went into mourning, she donned black. The result: a funeral fashion that continues today.

THROWING RICE & EATING CAKE AT WEDDINGS

For the Romans, wheat was a symbol of fertility. In fact, the Latin term for wedding, *conferreatio*, means "eating wheat together." Weddings began with the bride holding wheat sheaves and ended with the married couple eating wheat cakes. Over the years, wheat sheaves and wheat loaves have been replaced by throwing rice and serving multi-tiered cakes.

RADIO STUNTS

Radio stations will do practically anything for a little publicity. Three cases in point...

In 1990, WKRL in St. Petersburg, Florida introduced an all-Led Zeppelin format by playing the song "Stairway to Heaven" for 24 hours straight. According to *Pulse* magazine: "Two hours into the marathon the police showed up...Evidently a lot of listeners had called them thinking the DJ had a heart attack or was being held up at gunpoint." After 12 days of playing nothing but Led Zeppelin songs, the station decided to add another group to their format: Pink Floyd.

In 1988, the Baltimore Orioles opened their season by losing 21 straight games—a major league record. Ten games into the losing streak, Bob Rivers, a disc jockey at WIYY in Baltimore, vowed to stay on the air until the Orioles won their first game. At first it seemed like a fun idea...but then the Orioles kept losing.

Rivers kept his word—he stayed on the air 24 hours a day, sleeping only between songs. His plight made international headlines. But 258 hours later, the ordeal was finally over: the Orioles defeated the Chicago White Sox, 9-0. After playing the Who song "I'm Free," Rivers went home for some well-deserved rest.

In 1982, WSAN in Allentown, Pennsylvania announced a contest—three randomly drawn contestants would climb on top of a WSAN billboard...and live there. The one who stayed there the longest would win a mobile home. Sleeping bags and portable toilets were provided by WSAN; the rest was up to the contestants.

On September 20, 1982 the marathon began. Three men perched on a billboard off Interstate 22 in Allentown. Even through freezing winter temperatures, none would give up. Newspapers worldwide picked up the story. In March, 1983, one of the contestants was busted for selling marijuana. The two remaining billboard-sitters stayed until May 4, 1983, seven months after the contest began. Finally, WSAN declared both men winners. Each received a mobile home, a car, clothes and a free vacation. The third guy was awarded free rent for a year, a color TV and a three month supply of Big Macs.

That's a mouthful: Over 200 different languages are spoken in the African country of Zaire.

THE HAYS OFFICE

From 1922-1945, Will H. Hays—the acknowledged "czar" of Hollywood—wielded an iron hand over the Motion Pictures Producers and Directors Association (MPAA). As the moral guardian of American moviegoers, he alone decided what did and didn't make it to the screen.

BACKGROUND

Films have been censored from the beginning. In 1894, just two weeks after Edison introduced the Kinescope in Atlantic City, New Jersey, residents complained about the primitive scenes in *Dulorita in the Passion Dance*. In 1897 a New York judge closed a film that depicted a bride preparing for her wedding night, calling it "an outrage upon public decency."

By the time America entered the "Roaring Twenties," however, religious groups had upped the ante, calling for a boycott if certain moral standards were not upheld. In 1921, when popular comic Fatty Arbuckle was accused of raping and killing an actress named Virginia Rappe, America was scandalized. Arbuckle was later acquitted of the charges (although his career was ruined), but the damage was already done.

THE CZAR

To forestall public criticism, Hollywood named Will Hays as "chief censor." He was the perfect man for the job. One contemporary commentaror called him "as indigenous as sassafras root. He is one of us. He is folks."

Hays had been a rising star in the Republican Party, serving as the party's chairman in 1918. He was even briefly nominated for president in the 1920 Republican Convention and later served as Postmaster General under President Warren G. Harding.

By 1924, Hays had issued a Code of Standards which stipulated what kind of films could and could not be made. It prevented 67 books and plays from becoming films that year.

THE FORBIDDEN

In 1927, Hays issued a pamphlet called "Don'ts and Be Carefuls," which included 11 subjects "to be avoided" and 26 to "handle with care." Among the "avoided" were:

• "Scenes of actual childbirth—in fact or in silhouette."

• "Branding of people or animals."

• "Excessive or lustful kissing, particularly when one character is a 'heavy.' "

• Also banned: revealing dresses, lingerie and shots which showed a woman's inner thigh.

Several years later, the Hays Office issued amended codes including 43 words that were banned, including "broad," "cripes," "fairy," "hot" (as applied to a woman) and the phrase "in your hat."

THE PRODUCTION CODE

Despite pressure from the Hays Office, motion pictures became increasingly racy in the early 1930's due to diminishing Depression-era receipts. One Catholic group threatened a nationwide boycott, saying, "The pesthole that infects the entire country with its obscene and lascivious moving pictures must be cleansed and disinfected."

Enter Joseph Breen, appointed by Hays to enforce a strict 1934 Production Code. Among the rules of the code were: no machine guns, no gambling, no graphic killings, no dying policeman, no exposed bosoms, no excessive drinking, no lace lingerie and no drugs.

Without the Production Code Seal, a film was virtually dead in the water. Anyone distributing or exhibiting a film without the seal could be severely fined.

CHANGES

Rather than risk not getting the Production Seal refused, most movie companies made whatever changes the "Hays Office" recommended. Among the decisions were:

• Forbidding Walt Disney to show a cow's udder in a cartoon.

• Altering a Joan Crawford film title from *Infidelity* to *Fidelity*.

• Removing all references to the city of Chicago in *Scarface* and forcing producer Howard Hughes to add "Shame of the Nation" to the title.

• Ruling that adultery could not be directly mentioned in the 1935 screen adaptation of *Anna Karenina*, starring Greta Garbo—despite the fact that adultery was the subject of the book it was based on.

BODY PARTS

A few fascinating facts about your body to entertain you while you pass the…uh…time.

Your brain weighs around three pounds. All but ten ounces is water.

☛

It takes 200,000 frowns to make a permanent wrinkle.

☛

While you're resting, the air you breathe passes through your nose at about four miles per hour. At this rate, you breathe over 400 gallons of air every hour.

☛

If you stub your toe, your brain will register pain in 1/50 of a second.

☛

It takes about 150 days for your fingernails to grow from your cuticles to your fingertips.

☛

The cartilage in your nose doesn't stop growing. Expect it to grow 1/2 inch longer and wider as you age.

☛

New freckles generally stop appearing after age 19 or 20.

Bone is about four times stronger than steel. It can endure 24,000 pounds of pressure per square inch.

☛

The average adult has about 18 square feet of skin.

☛

To say one word, you use over 70 muscles.

☛

Your brain uses less power than a 100-watt bulb.

☛

Women have a more developed sense of smell than men do.

☛

The average man shrinks a little more than one inch between the ages of 30 and 70. In the same period of time, the average woman shrinks two inches.

☛

There are over 200 taste buds on each of the small bumps on your tongue.

In 1989, Americans bought over 7,000 Harlequin romance books…every hour.

LUCY THE RED

Everyone loved Lucy. When she died in 1989, newspaper obituaries mourned the passing of the brilliant red-headed comedienne. But few mentioned her brief affiliation with the Communist party in 1936...and the way it almost destroyed her career.

BACKGROUND

In the early 1950s, during the height of Senator Joe McCarthy's "red menace" witch-hunts, an appearance before McCarthy and the House Un-American Activities Committee (HUAC) could ruin anybody—especially a Hollywood celebrity. At the time, "I Love Lucy" was the number one television show in the country. But that didn't make Lucy exempt from scrutiny. In 1953, Lucille Ball's political beliefs became a nationwide controversy.

REVELATION

In 1953, in his popular newsparer gossip column, Walter Winchell reported this shocking news: Lucille Ball, "America's sitcom sweetheart," had been a "commie!" Lucy denied it, of course; and Desi emotionally proclaimed, "The only thing red about Lucy is her hair. And that's not even real!"

THE INVESTIGATION

On September 4, 1953, Ball was asked to explain to the House Un-American Activities Committee (HUAC) why she had registered as a Communist on March 19, 1936.

William A. Wheeler, an investigator for HUAC, flew to Hollywood for Lucy's testimony. In the transcripts later released, Ball explained that she had registered as a Communist "to appease an old man," namely, her grandfather Fred C. Hunt, an ardent socialist.

"How we got to signing a few things," she told Wheeler, "or going among some people that thought differently, that has happened to to all of us out here in the last ten or twelve years, and it is unfortunate, but I certainly will do anything in the world to prove that we made a bad mistake."

But why had Ball voted for the Communist candidate in a primary election? While not really denying she had, Ball claimed she "had really racked my brain...and all I remember was something like a garage and a flag, like a voting day."

As for her political leanings, Ball was more conclusive. "I am not a Communist now," she testified. "I never have been. I never want to be. Nothing in the world could ever change my mind."

THE AFTERMATH

Both the Congress and the country forgave Lucy's "mistake." After her testimony, Representative Donald J. Jackson of California revealed that the committee had known of her Communist party registration for over a year and only divulged it to quell growing rumours that Lucy was a red.

Letters of sympathy poured in from all over the nation. But a few people, including J. Edgar Hoover, apparently had their doubts.

THE FBI

According to Jack Anderson's 12/7/89 column in the *Washington Post*, Hoover kept an open file on Lucy and her husband Desi Arnaz. Among the contents:

• Lucy went to great lengths to "make her grandfather happy." Besides registering as a Communist Party member, she signed a nominating petition of the Communist candidate for the California State Assembly in 1936. She was also named as a member of the Communist party's State Central Committee in California, although Lucy later denied any knowledge of her membership.

• In testimony before the State Legistative Committee on Un-American Activities in 1943, a Hollywood writer claimed to have attended Communist Party meetings at 1344 North Ogden Drive in Hollywood—Lucy's address at the time. According to Anderson, "The writer said Ball was not there but approved of the meeting."

• In 1951, the Communist newspaper, the *Daily Worker*, alleged that Lucy had once been more outspoken in her opposition to McCarthy but had been warned to keep quiet.

• While many movie people were pilloried for less, Lucy escaped unscathed. "My conscience has always been clean," she told a press conference after her testimony in 1953. "And I have great faith in the American people. They have been very good to me in the past and I'm sure they will be now."

Two out of three Soviet doctors are women.

PIGS IN SPACE

We honor astronauts like Neil Armstrong and John Glenn for their pioneering feats in space. But animals have been the real "guinea pigs" of flight since the first balloon took off in the 1700s.

UP, UP, AND AWAY

One month before the first manned balloon flight, a sheep, duck and a chicken were loaded onto a ballon and launched in Versailles, France on September 19, 1783. They survived the eight minute, two mile flight, achieving a peak altitude of 1,700 feet. The event was witnessed by King Louis XVI and Marie Antoinette.

FLYING PIGS

• On October 30, 1909, the first pig flew on an airplane. The stunt was inspired by the expression "pigs might fly," a phrase commonly used to express skepicism about flying. Lord Barbazon of England, wanting to put the expression to rest, kept a pig in a basket during an airplane flight.

• On February 18, 1930 the first cow flew from St. Louis. In a publicity stunt, the cow was milked during the flight. The milk was parachuted to the ground in sealed paper cartons.

A DOG'S LIFE

• The first living creature to orbit the Earth was a Russian dog named Laika, who was launched in a Russian satellite on November 3, 1957. The satellite orbited the Earth 2,370 times before burning up—with Laika aboard—during re-entry.

• The first animals to orbit Earth and survive were two dogs named Belka and Strelka on Sputnik 5, which was launched August 19, 1960.

MONKEY BUSINESS

• The U.S. also sent up animals before sending a human into space. On May 28, 1959, two monkeys named Able and Baker were launched 300 miles into space from Cape Canaveral, Florida. They were recovered alive the next day in the Caribbean.

ROCK NAMES

Where do rock groups get their outrageous names? From movies, books, and medieval torture devices. Some examples:

ABBA: An acronymn of the first letters of the band's four members, Agnetha Ulugeus, Bjorn Ulugeus, Benny Anderson and Annifred Anderson.

The Bay City Rollers: Came up with their name by sticking a pin in a map of the world. It landed on Bay City, Michigan.

The Beatles: A tribute to Buddy Holly's Crickets. The "a" was added by John Lennon, who later explained that it came to him in a dream.

Buffalo Springfield: Members of the legendary L.A.-based group were stumped for a name. A member of the band was looking out their manager's window at a construction site in Hollywood, when he spotted a steamroller with the brand name "Buffalo Springfield."

The Doors: Jim Morrison got the band's name from Aldous Huxley's book *The Doors Of Perception*, which dealt with Huxley's experimentation with psychedelic drugs.

Duran Duran: Named after a character in the film *Barbarella*, starring Jane Fonda.

The Grateful Dead: The name of an Egyptian prayer which band member Jerry Garcia spotted in a dictionary.

Iron Maiden: A medieval torture device.

Jefferson Airplane: Slang for a roach clip.

Jethro Tull: Named after the 18th century British inventor of the seed drill.

Led Zeppelin: Based on a comment by the late Who drummer Keith Moon, who jokingly remarked that an early live appearance of the band "went down like a lead balloon."

Lynard Skynard: Inspired by Leonard Skinner, a teacher who once suspended the original band members from high school for having long hair.

Manhattan Transfer: After the 1920 novel by John Dos Passos.

Pink Floyd: An amalgam of two American blues artists, Pink Anderson and Floyd Council.

The Ramones: After Phil Ramone, the name Paul McCartney adopted for himself when the Beatles were the Silver Beatles.

The Rolling Stones: Taken from Muddy Waters' song, "Rolling Stone Blues."

Sha Na Na: Supposedly the doo-wop lyrics from "Get A Job," a 1957 hit by the Silhouettes.

Steely Dan: Based on the name of a dildo in William Burrough's novel, *The Naked Lunch*.

The Thompson Twins: There are no Thompsons or twins in the band, which took its name from characters in the Belgian comic book, *Tintin*.

Three Dog Night: It is a practice of Australian aborigines to sleep with three dogs on particularly cold nights.

UB40: Named after the British unemployment benefit form.

The Velvet Underground: Lou Reed lifted the name from a title of a cheap paperback novel.

The Yardbirds: A tribute to legendary be-bop saxophonist Charlie "Yardbird" Parker.

About half of American men polled say they enjoy money more than sex.

MYTH AMERICA

Here we are again: You may have believed these stories since you were a kid—after all, they were taught as sacred truths. Well, it's time to take another look...

TEA TIME

The Myth: The Boston Tea Party was held because the British imposed a tax on tea.

The Truth: The exact opposite is actually true. The British did impose the Townsend Act, which taxed a number of goods—including tea—quite heavily. However, the tax on tea didn't really affect the colonists—they drank a smuggled, less expensive Dutch tea (John Hancock was a big Dutch tea smuggler).

To undercut the American tea-smuggling operation, the British rounded up between 15 and 20 million pounds of surplus tea, passed the Tea Act which eliminated taxes on British tea, and priced their huge supply below the price of the smuggled Dutch tea.

Colonists responded to this British interference by dumping the British tea before it was unloaded. That was the event called the Boston Tea Party.

FOR WHOM THE BELL TOLLS

The Myth: Alexander Graham Bell invented the telephone.

Background: About 15 years before Bell uttered the famous words, "Mr. Watson, come here; I want you," German scientist Phillip Reis had developed a crude working telephone. And about five years before Bell's historic race to the patent office, an Italian scientist named Antonio Meucci offered the patent office a rough description of a telephone's structure and principles. But nothing ever came of it.

The Truth: Bell wasn't the first to develop the device—but he was the first to patent it...barely. Many scientists were working on a telephone at the same time; one of them—Elisha Gray—arrived at the U.S. Patent Office with a model telephone just two hours *after* Bell. In fact, some say Gray's telephone was better than Bell's and more like the one we use today. By the time Bell received his patent, so many people claimed the telephone as their own invention that Bell had to defend the patent in court. In fact, the case went all the way to the *Supreme Court*. The verdict: the high court was divided in his favor, allowing him to the rights to the phone.

FULTON'S FOLLY

The Myth: Robert Fulton invented the steamboat.

The Truth: Twenty years before Fulton built his first steamboat, *Fulton's Folly*, in 1807, James Rumsey had a steamboat chugging up the Potomac and John Fitch had one traveling the Delaware. In some states, Fitch even secured exclusive rights to run passenger and freight steamboat trips. So why does Fulton get the credit for the invention 20 years later? Rumsey and Fitch died broke, while Fulton had a knack for promotion and fund-raising. But Fulton did fail to make one key sale—to Napoleon Bonaparte, who thought the idea of steamships impractical. Some historians say the little conqueror's bad decision might have saved the English.

FORD FACTS

The Myth: Henry Ford produced the first automobile.

The Truth: Karl Benz and Gottlieb Daimler, two German engineers who went on to form Mercedes-Benz, each developed working gasoline engine automobiles in 1885. The first American car was built by Charles and J. Frank Duryea in 1893. By then, Benz already had a model, the Velo, ready for sale to the general public.

The Myth: O.K., if Ford didn't invent the car, at least he invented the auto assembly line.

The Truth: No, chalk this one up to Ransom E. Olds, creator of the Oldsmobile. Olds introduced the moving assembly line in the early 1900s and boosted car production by 500%. The previous year, the Olds Motor Vehicle Company had turned out 425 cars. The year after they made over 2,500 of them. Ford improved Olds's system by introducing the conveyor belt, which moved both the cars *and* needed parts along the production line. The belt cut Ford's production time from a day to about two hours. A significant contribution, but not the original.

Disney animators drew nearly 6.5 million black spots for the film *101 Dalmations*.

WHO'S ON FIRST?

The Abbott and Costello baseball routine "Who's On First?" is considered a landmark in the history of comedy.

Abbot and Costello's recording of "Who's On First?" became the first gold record placed in the Baseball Hall of Fame in Cooperstown, New York.

• "The Baseball Scene," as it was known before it was given the title "Who's On First?" was a burlesque standard long before Abbot and Costello popularized it. In fact, Abbott and Costello each performed it with other vaudeville partners before teaming up in 1936.

• When the duo first performed the routine on radio's "The Kate Smith Hour," they were forced to change the ending from "I don't give a damn!" / "Oh, that's our shortstop" to "I don't care" / "Oh, that's our shortstop." President Roosevelt was listening; he enjoyed it so much that he called them personally to offer congratulations after the show.

HERE'S THE ROUTINE

BUD: You know, strange as it may seem, they give baseball players peculiar names nowadays. On the St. Louis team Who's on first, What's on second, I Don't Know is on third.

LOU: That's what I want to find out. I want you to tell me the names of the fellows on the St. Louis team.

BUD: I'm telling you. Who's on first, What's on second, I Don't Know is on third.

LOU: You know the fellows' names?

BUD: Yes.

LOU: Well, then, who's playin' first?

BUD: Yes.

LOU: I mean the fellow's name on first base.

BUD: Who.

BUD: The fellow's name on first base for St. Louis.

LOU: Who.

BUD: The guy on first base.

LOU: Well, what are you askin' me for?

BUD: I'm not asking you. I'm telling you. Who is on first.

LOU: I'm askin' you, who is on first?

BUD: That's the man's name.

LOU: That's whose name?

BUD: Yes.

LOU: Well, go ahead and tell me.

BUD: Who?

LOU: The guy on first.

BUD: Who.

LOU: The first baseman.

BUD: Who is on first.

LOU: *(Trying to stay calm)* Have you got a first baseman on first?

BUD: Certainly.

LOU: Well, all I'm trying to find out is what's the guy's name on first base.

BUD: Oh, no, no. What is on *second* base.

LOU: I'm not askin' you who's on second.

BUD: Who's on first.

LOU: That's what I'm tryin' to find out.

BUD: Well, don't change the players around.

LOU: (*starting to get angry*) I'm not changin' anybody.

BUD: Now take it easy.

LOU: What's the guy's name on first base?

BUD: What's the guy's name on *second* base.

LOU: I'm not askin' you who's on second.

BUD: Who's on first.

LOU: I don't know.

BUD: He's on third. We're not talking about him.

LOU: (*begging*) How could I get on third base?

BUD: You mentioned his name.

LOU: If I mentioned the third baseman's name, who did I say is playing third?

BUD: (*starting all over again*) No, Who's playing first.

LOU: Stay offa first, will ya?
BUD: Please, now what is it you'd like to know?
LOU: What is the fellow's name on third base?
BUD: What is the fellow's name on second base.
LOU: I'm not askin' ya who's on second.
BUD: Who's on first.
LOU: I don't know.
BUD & LOU: (*together*) Third base!
LOU: (*tries again*) You got an outfield?
BUD: Certainly.
LOU: St. Louis got a good outfield?
BUD: Oh, absolutely.
LOU: The left fielder's name.
BUD: Why.
LOU: I don't know. I just thought I'd ask.
BUD: Well, I just thought I'd tell you.
LOU: Then tell me who's playing left field.
BUD: Who's playing first.
LOU: Stay outa the infield!
BUD: Don't mention any names there.
LOU: (*firmly*) I wanta know what's the fellow's name in left field.
BUD: What is on second.
LOU: I'm not askin' you who's on second.
BUD: Who is on first.
LOU: I don't know!
BUD & LOU: (*together*) Third base! (*Lou makes funny noises*)
BUD: Now take it easy, man.
LOU: And the left fielder's name?
BUD: Why?
LOU: Because.
BUD: Oh, he's center field.
LOU: Wait a minute. You got a pitcher on the team?
BUD: Wouldn't this be a fine team without a pitcher?
LOU: I dunno. Tell me the pitcher's name.

BUD: Tomorrow.
LOU: You don't want to tell me today?
BUD: I'm telling you, man.
LOU: Then go ahead.
BUD: Tomorrow.
LOU: What time?
BUD: What time what?
LOU: What time tomorrow are you gonna tell me who's pitching?
BUD: Now listen, who is not pitching. Who is on—
LOU: (*excited*) I'll break your arm if you say who is on first.
BUD: Then why come up here and ask?
LOU: I want to know what's the pitcher's name!
BUD: What's on second.
LOU: (*sighs*) I don't know.
BUD & LOU: (*together*) Third base!
LOU: You gotta catcher?
BUD: Yes.
LOU: The catcher's name.
BUD: Today.
LOU: Today. And Tomorrow's pitching.
BUD: Now you've got it.
LOU: That's all. St. Louis got a couple of days on their team. That's all.
BUD: Well, I can't help that. What do you want me to do?
LOU: Gotta catcher?
BUD: Yes.
LOU: I'm a good catcher, too, you know.
BUD: I know that.
LOU: I would like to play for St. Louis.
BUD: Well, I might arrange that.
LOU: I would like to catch. Now Tomorrow's pitching on the team and I'm catching.
BUD: Yes.
LOU: Tomorrow throws the ball and the guy up bunts the ball.

BUD: Yes.

LOU: So when he bunts the ball, me, bein' a good catcher, I want to throw the guy out at first base. So I pick up the ball and I throw it to who?

BUD: Now that's the first thing you've said right!

LOU: *I don't even know what I'm talkin' about!*

BUD: Well, that's all you have to do.

LOU: I throw it to first base.

BUD: Yes.

LOU: Now who's got it?

BUD: Naturally.

LOU: Naturally.

BUD: Naturally.

LOU: I throw the ball to naturally.

BUD: You throw it to Who.

LOU: Naturally.

BUD: Naturally, well, say it that way.

LOU: That's what I'm saying!

BUD: Now don't get excited, don't get excited.

LOU: I throw the ball to first base.

BUD: Then Who gets it.

LOU: He'd better get it.

BUD: That's it. All right now, don't get excited. Take it easy.

LOU: (*beside himself*) Now I throw the ball to first base, whoever it is grabs the ball, so the guy runs to second.

BUD: Uh-huh.

LOU: Who picks up the ball and throws it to What. What throws it to I Don't Know. I Don't Know throws it back to Tomorrow. A triple play!

BUD: Yeah, could be.

LOU: Another guy goes up and it's a long fly ball to center. Why? I don't know. And I don't give a damn!

BUD: What was that?

LOU: I said, I don't give a damn!

BUD: Oh, that's our shortstop.

STRANGE LAWSUITS

Tired of being sprayed by department store employees? Are headless cartoon characters terrorizing your children? Don't take the law into your own hands. Take 'em to court.

THE PLAINTIFF: Deborah Martorano.
THE DEFENDANT: Bloomingdale's Department Store.
THE LAWSUIT: Martorano claimed she was wrongfully sprayed with perfume by a store employee. On April 30, 1984, she was shopping for a blouse on her lunch hour when a roving perfume-demonstrator approached her and squirted her with fragrance. Martorano's lawyer claimed his client, a lifelong asthma and allergy sufferer, spent 10 days in a New York hospital recovering from "respiratory distress" resulting from the unsolicited spritz.
VERDICT: She accepted a $75,000 settlement from the store.

THE PLAINTIFF: John Moore.
THE DEFENDANT: Regents of the University of California.
THE LAWSUIT: Moore claimed one of his organs was pirated. In 1976, University of California-Los Angeles Medical Center doctors removed Moore's spleen in a successful effort to cure his cancer. Doctors later found that the spleen possessed unique cancer-fighting cells; experiments with the cells led to a new discovery worth an estimated $3 billion. Moore, who was never told that his ex-organ had commercial value, sued for part of the profits.
VERDICT: In 1990, 14 years after the operation, Moore lost the case.

THE PLAINTIFF: The estate of an unidentified 34-year-old co-pilot.
THE DEFENDANT: Gates Lear Jet Corporation.
THE LAWSUIT: The estate claimed that a jet's windshield wasn't thick enough. In 1987, an 11.5 pound loon crashed through the windshield of a state-of-the-art jet during takeoff, killing the loon and the co-pilot. The man's estate contended that the windshield should have been "birdproofed." It was, Gates Lear said, but

only for birds weighing up to four pounds.
VERDICT: A Michigan circuit court awarded the man's estate $1.5 million in compensatory damages.

THE PLAINTIFF: McDonald's.
THE DEFENDANT: McDharma's Natural Fast Foods.
THE LAWSUIT: McDonald's hadn't a clue that McDharma's, a 15-employee vegetarian restaurant where cashiers wear T-shirts, shorts, and sandals, even existed until the three-year-old Santa Cruz, California eatery sought its own national trademark. McDonald's had nothing against the top-selling "Brahma Burger," a burger made of beans, nuts, seeds, grains, and soy, but objected to the McDharma's use of the trademarked "Mc." "It's such a joke," McDharma's co-owner Bernie Shapiro said, "and they're the only ones taking it seriously."
VERDICT: McDharma's was forced to drop the "Mc," but instead of removing the two letters from their sign, McDharma's painted a red circle with a slash over them. McDonald's sued again; McDharma's eventually removed the "Mc." However, McDharma's received a handful of offers for franchises.

THE PLAINTIFF: Mr. and Mrs. Lonnie and Karen B.
THE DEFENDANT: The Walt Disney Corporation
THE LAWSUIT: The couple claimed that they were falsely arrested for shoplifting while they and their daughters, Lindsay, 6, and Melissa, 2, were visiting Disneyland. They were detained for questioning. Apparently, while they waited, Lindsay caught sight of several actors dressed as Disney characters who had taken their costume headpieces off...and she freaked out. The couple sued for damages, claiming their daughter suffered nightmares and had to undergo therapy as a result of the experience.
THE VERDICT: Pending.

MISC. DID WE MENTION THIS?
From the book *George Washington Had No Middle Name:* "A biography of George Armstrong Custer, by James Warner Bellah, reads in its entirety: 'To put it mildly, this was an oddball.' "

In the Olympics, men and women compete together in rifle shooting.

LATE NIGHT WITH DAVID LETTERMAN

A few words from America's favorite gap-toothed talk show host.

"This warning from the New York City Department of Health Fraud: Be suspicious of any doctor who tries to take your temperature with his finger."

"Martin Levine has passed away at age 75. Mr Levine had owned a movie theater chain here in New York. The funeral will be held on Thursday at 2:15, 4:20, 6:30, 8:40, and 10:50."

"A professor at Johns Hopkins has come forth with an intriguing thought about a perennial question: He says that if an infinite number of monkeys sat typing at an infinite number of typewriters, the smell in the room would be unbearable."

"Interesting survey in the *Journal of Abnormal Psychology*. New York City has a higher percentage of people you shouldn't make any sudden moves around than any other city in the world."

"Tip to out-of-town visitors: If you buy something here in New York and want to have it shipped home, be suspicious if the clerk tells you they don't need your name and address."

"Every year when it's Chinese New Year here in New York, there are fireworks going off at all hours. New York mothers calm their children by telling them it's just gunfire."

"New Jersey announced today that they were adopting a new license plate slogan: 'Try Our Creamy Thick Shakes.'"

"Someone did a study of the three most often heard phrases in New York City. One is, 'Hey, taxi.' Two is, 'What train do I take to get to Bloomingdales?' And three is, 'Don't worry. It's just a flesh wound.' "

"High insurance rates are what really killed the dinosaurs."

American teenagers spend over $70 billion a year.

MONKEE BUSINESS

The Monkees were one of the most popular bands in the world, but weren't allowed to play on their own records—until they went on strike. Here's the inside story, from Behind the Hits, *by Bob Shannon and John Javna.*

From the outside, everything looked great for the Monkees in 1967. In one year they had leaped from semi—or total—obscurity to overnight superstardom. They had a hit TV series, two #1 singles ("Last Train to Clarksville," and "I'm A Believer"), and two #1 albums ("The Monkees," and "More of the Monkees"). The only problem was the Monkees weren't allowed to play on their own records. Why not? Because Don Kirshner, the musical supervisor of the Monkees, said so. It was...well...embarrassing. Here they were, pretending to be a real group, when in fact they had almost nothing to do with "their" music. Critics made fun of them. Even worse, teenyboppers idolized them for something they weren't doing. And to add insult to injury, Kirshner made more money from their records than they did. They each got a 1.5% royalty, but Kirshner got 15%! They had their pride, after all.

Trouble had been brewing for some time between Kirshner and the group, particularly Mike Nesmith, who wasn't even allowed to play guitar on the songs he *wrote*. That was Kirshner's studio policy; the Monkees just sang vocals while studio musicians played on the tracks. But what the hell, Kirshner reasoned, he was getting results—hits—and that was his job. So what if Nesmith had to stand by and watch Glen Campbell put the guitar licks on his own song, "Mary Mary"? This was the only way management could be sure it was right. The bottom line was what counted, after all. Nesmith, a genuinely creative individual, just stewed.

"Essentially, the big collision I had with Don Kirshner was this," said Nesmith; "he kept saying, 'You can't make the music; it would be no good, it won't be a hit.' And I was saying, 'Hey, the music isn't a hit because somebody wonderful is making it, the music is a hit because of the television show. So, at least let us put out music that is closer to our personas, closer to who we are artistically, so

Legendary lawman Wyatt Earp was kicked out of California for horse-stealing.

that we don't have to walk around and have people throwing eggs at us,' which they were."

Eventually the feud came to a showdown in early '67 at Kirshner's suite at the Beverly Hills Hotel. Kirshner had just handed the four Monkees some new demos (including "Sugar, Sugar," a bubblegum hit later for Kirshner's Archies) that they would be putting vocals on. Nesmith stepped forward and demanded that musical control be give to the Monkees. When Kirshner refused, Nesmith angrily smashed his fist through the wall, declaring, "That could have been your face!" Then the Monkees went off to record some original material *without* Kirshner's approval.

What happened next is a little unclear. While the Monkees were working out their own songs, Kirshner appears to have approached Davy Jones, one of the members of the group, and talked him into going into the studio without the rest of the Monkees. Jones put the vocals on several tunes, one of which was "A Little Bit Me, A Little Bit You." But the Monkees weren't doing the backing vocals. Who was it? Eric Lefcowitz, author of *The Monkees Tale*, speculates, "Kirshner was quoted once as saying that Neil Diamond and Carole King had sung back-up vocals on some Monkees songs, and I think that if you listen closely to 'A Little Bit Me,' you can hear them. It sounds like Neil Diamond to me." And why would Jones record without the rest of his group? "I don't know, of course," Lefcowitz says, "but Davy Jones hadn't ever had the chance to sing lead before. This was *his* session. Maybe that had something to do with it."

Whatever. The important thing is that in a power play, Kirshner recorded and released "A Little Bit Me, A Little Bit You" without even telling the Monkees he was doing it! That was the last straw. Monkees' producers Bert Schnieder and Bob Rafelson wanted hits, but they weren't going to put up with that from anyone. They fired Kirshner, and yanked the single out of American record stores. Then they re-released it with a Monkees' original—Nesmith's "The Girl I Knew Somewhere"—on the B side. Finally the Monkees could smile. They were out from under Kirshner...and a song they'd actually played on made the Top 40—"The Girl I Knew Somewhere" reached #39 on the charts.

Layne Hall of New York, age 109, has been driving 75 years—without an accident.

GIVE US A HAND

You probably can't put a finger on the origins of these common gestures, but here's some info you might find handy.

THE FINGER
It doesn't matter what you call it—"the bird," "the finger," or the "freeway salute"— the middle finger is among the most well-known symbols in America. Believe it or not, the gesture can be traced to the ancient Romans, who called it the "finger without shame" or *digitus impudicus*. Psychologists say it's a symbol of phallic aggressiveness.

THE RING FINGER
Over two-thousand years ago, Greek physicians believed that a special "vein of love" connected this finger to the heart. It logically became the finger to be "bound" by an affair of the heart.

CROSSING FINGERS
Ever cross your fingers for good luck? Historians suggest this popular gesture comes from the pre-Christian belief that a cross symbolizes perfect unity. The intersection point of the fingers was said to possess a mystical quality which would hold the wish until it was fulfilled.

THUMBS UP OR THUMBS DOWN
This symbol wasn't always used to rate new movies or hitch rides. According to popular lore, it was a matter of life or death. Roman emperors would use "thumbs up" to spare a defeated gladiator's life, and "thumbs down" to order his death.

THUMBING YOUR NOSE
You've done it before—touching your thumb to the tip of your nose and extending your fingers like a fan. It's understood as an insult all over the world, but what does it mean? Some folklorists say it's a mock military salute. Others maintain that it's a graphic suggestion that someone stinks.

THE GREAT *TITANIC*

You've probably heard of the Titantic. We had, but we didn't really know much about it. So this piece by Eric Lefcowitz was particularly interesting.

BACKGROUND

Steamships were the most viable means of trans-Atlantic travel when the White Star Company decided to build the world'd largest ship, the *Titanic* in 1912. Its proposed measurements—900 feet (3-1/2 city blocks) long and 11 stories high—were enough to make it front-page news. But size wasn't all it had to offer. The company announced a breakthrough in steamship design; with 16 watertight compartments and a double bottom, the *Titanic* would be "unsinkable." If water got through the first hull, spokesmen explained, the second one would still keep the boat afloat.

The construction of the Titanic captured the public's imagination. Newspapers billed it as a "floating Camelot." By the time it was ready to sail, the whole world was watching.

THE VOYAGE

On April 12, the *Titanic* left for its maiden voyage from Southhampton, England to New York. Accommodations varied: There were cramped, low-cost quarters in the bowels of the boat for arriving immigrants; and there were luxurious upper-deck suites for the upper class. A one-way luxury ticket cost an incredible $4,350.

Fatal mistake: The captain, intent on breaking the world's record with the fastest trans-Atlantic journey ever, ignored warnings about icebergs.

The result: On April 15, four days, 17 hours, and 35 minutes later, the "unsinkable" Titanic hit an iceberg in the North Atlantic. It was 350 miles from Newfoundland. In the darkness of night, the mighty boat plunged into water two miles deep.

It was the most dramatic ship disaster of all-time; 1,512 passengers were killed.

TITANIC FACTS

• The *Titanic*'s band played on deck as the ship was sinking. The song they played was "Autumn," a popular British waltz.

• There was lifeboat space for only 1,200 of the 2,227 passengers.

• Only 705 people, most of them women and children, survived the disaster. They were picked up by the Cunard liner *Carpathia*.

• Among the rich and famous who went down with the ship were John Jacob Astor and Benjamin Guggenheim.

• Unlike the 1898 disaster of the French ship, *La Bourgogne*—where women and children were trampled by hysterical passengers attempting to get on lifeboats—chivalry and honor prevailed on the *Titanic*; most of the women and children survived. However, a greater proportion of first-class passengers survived than lower-class travelers, including immigrants, who were on the lower decks.

• The *California*, a freighter only 10 miles away, saw eight distress flares fired from the *Titanic* but did not respond, figuring they had been set off in celebration.

• Several changes in sea travel regulations occurred after the disaster. Every ship was required to have enough lifeboats to accommodate every passenger. The International Ice Patrol was also organized.

• Only one ship has struck an iceberg since the *Titanic* sank—it happened during World War II.

• A song called "The Wreck of the *Titanic*" became popular shortly after the disaster. Sample lyrics: "Oh, they built the ship *Titanic* to sail the ocean blue. And they thought they had a ship that the water couldn't get through. But an iceberg on the wave, Sent it to its watery grave. It was sad when that great ship went down."

DISCOVERING THE WRECK

Still controversial: For years people searched for the most famous wreck of all-time. Finally, in 1985, the *Titanic* was discovered by a U.S./French exploratory team. To keep potential looters away, its location wasn't divulged. But in 1987, the French members returned to the site and—contrary to the wishes of the U.S. team, who thought the site should be preserved out of respect to the dead—salvaged 800 artifacts from the wreck. In response, the U.S. Senate, whose members agreed the site should be left alone, passed a resolution banning the display of the recovered *Titanic* items for profit in the United States.

WEIRD COINCIDENCES

A reader sent us this list of the bizarre similarities between the assassinations of Lincoln and Kennedy. It's hard to believe, but they're true. Rod Serling, where are you?

Abraham Lincoln was elected in 1860, and John Kennedy in 1960, 100 years later.

Both Lincoln and Kennedy mentioned having premonitions of death before their assassinations.

Lincoln's secretary, named Kennedy, warned him not to go to the theater that fatal night. Kennedy's secretary, named Lincoln, tried to talk him out of going to Dallas.

Both men died of bullet wounds to the head.

Both were killed as they sat beside their wives.

Both were ardent proponents of civil rights.

John Wilkes Booth, Lincoln's assassin, was born in 1839, and Lee Harvey Oswald, Kennedy's assassin, was born in 1939, exactly 100 years later.

The names John Wilkes Booth and Lee Harvey Oswald each contain 15 letters.

Booth shot Lincoln in a theater and fled to a warehouse. Oswald shot Kennedy from a warehouse and fled to a theater.

Both Presidents were succeeded by vice-presidents named Johnson. Andrew Johnson followed Lincoln, and Lyndon B. Johnson followed Kennedy.

Andrew Johnson was born in 1808, and Lyndon B. Johnson was born in 1908, 100 years later.

Both were killed on Friday.

Both Johnsons were Democrats, southern, and former senators.

The names Kennedy and Lincoln each contain seven letters.

The names Andrew Johnson and Lyndon Johnson each contain 13 letters.

Both Booth and Oswald were killed before reaching trial.

SATURDAY NIGHT LIVE

The original version of Saturday Night Live, which ran from 1975 to about 1980, was a milestone in modern TV. Some say its hip, bold, innovative humor hasn't been matched since then. Here's how it got on the air.

HOW IT STARTED

In early 1975, NBC executives were looking to improve Saturday night ratings in the 11:30-1:00 a.m. time slot. "Tonight Show" reruns were getting stale, and research showed that viewers were constantly changing channels, indicating that a restless audience was looking for something new. . . and not finding it. "The problem," Producer Lorne Michaels explained a few years later, "was that no one in TV was accurately expressing what was going on. Carol Burnett sketches were dealing with the problems of another generation—divorce, Valium, crab-grass, adultery. It used to drive me crazy to see Bob Hope doing a sketch about marijuana and acting drunk."

When Michaels and NBC vice president Dick Ebersol suggested a 90-minute variety show featuring "rock'n'roll, satire, changing hosts, and a cast of unknown regulars who'd done almost no TV," NBC brass shocked them by accepting. Michaels also proposed going "live," sensing that the young, hip, late-nite crowd would be drawn to the "anything goes" atmosphere of such a format. "I felt that American kids knew TV as well as French kids knew wine and that there was such a thing as good TV."

Michaels began casting. He recruited some of the best young talent available, including Dan Aykroyd, Chevy Chase, Gilda Radner, and John Belushi. On Oct. 11, 1975, unaware of the profound effect they were about to have on an entire generation of American youth, the Not Ready for Prime Time Players appeared for the first time on "Saturday Night Live."

INSIDE INFO

Peanuts. The Not Ready For Prime Time Players' starting weekly salaries in 1975 were $750 per week.

Employment Opportunity. Four of the original eleven writers on SNL had just graduated from college, and the show was their first post-college job.

THE ORIGINAL CAST

• On his 21st birthday Bill Murray was in a Chicago jail (busted with eight lbs. of marijuana on him). After his release, jobless and penniless, he decided to try comedy. He joined his brother (Brian Doyle-Murray) at the Second City comedy troupe. There he found his niche; soon afterwards, SNL called and offered him a spot.

• John Belushi was the last cast-member hired for SNL. Lorne Michaels had sincere reservations about unleashing such a volatile, "on-the-edge" talent in front of a live camera, but after seeing John's "Samurai Pool Hustler," how could he resist? "Everyone in the group wanted him," Dick Ebersol said, "but we heard horrendous tales of his being a discipline problem." Said writer Michael O'Donoghue: "He wanted to grab the world and snort it."

• An experienced writer with "The Smothers' Brothers Show," Chevy Chase was originally hired only to write for SNL. But he wanted to act. One night, after dinner with Lorne Michaels, Chase took off down the street, threw himself into the air, and landed in "the biggest puddle I'd ever seen. We figured," says Michaels, "that if he wanted it that badly, we might as well give him a shot." But he'd only signed a one-year contract, so after the first season he left.

• Dan Aykroyd was hired for the show at the last minute, and for a while had to commute between Canada and the U.S. on his motorcycle.

• Laraine Newman auditioned for SNL in a hospital room, where Dick Ebersol was recuperating from an illness.

• Jane Curtin was hired out of a Boston improv group. There were equally talented applicants for the spot, but says Dick Ebersol, "we thought we needed someone who was white bread."

• The best physical comedian in the troupe, Gilda Radner was the first person hired for SNL. She was also from Second City.

• The only cast member without formal comic training (though he had formal music training at Julliard), Garrett Morris was first hired as a writer. When Michaels saw him acting in *Cooley High*, Morris was added to the cast.

FROG FACTS

Kermit the Frog says, "It's not easy being green." Maybe this is what he means.

There are around 2,600 different species of frogs. They live in every continent except Antarctica.

Frogs don't drink water—they absorb water through their skin.

Every species of frog as its own special mating call, made only by the males. The call has two parts—"a whine," which the whole species uses, and a "chuck" which is the individual frog's calling card. Females listen to the chuck carefully—the larger, more desirable frogs make longer, deeper chucks. The drawback: bats, which eat frogs, also listen for long, deep chucks.

One expert reports "A frog from Ethiopa has teethlike protusions and eats snails—shells and all."

An Australian frog hatches its offspring in its stomach, then spits out fully developed frogs—sometimes more than 20 at once.

The skin of some poisonous frogs is so toxic that it will kill any creature that bites it. Only 1/100,000 of a gram of skin poison from one species is enough to kill a man.

Have you ever heard of flying frogs? They do exist, but they don't really fly—they can't gain height in the air. Instead, they glide. Top speed: 24 kilometers per hour, fastest of all amphibians.

According to an expert, "One frog in Colombia is so toxic that local Indians merely wipe their arrows across its skin to poison the tips."

Reputedly, there's a frog in Australia that excretes a hallucenogenic slime. Natives lick it to get high.

Film for frog-fans: *Frogs*, a ludicrous 1972 horror flick starring Ray Milland. "Thousands of frogs overrun a remote, inhabited island off the southern U.S. coast, devouring any human who gets in their way." An absolutely ribbeting film.

The hamburgers McDonald's serves in a week equal more than 16,000 head of cattle.

THE NAME IS FAMILIAR

Some people have achieved immortality because their names have become product brand names. You already know the names—now here are the people.

King C. Gillette. William Painter—the man who invented the bottle cap—suggested that Gillette, a traveling salesman, invent something that people could use a few times and throw away. In 1895, while cursing his dull razor, Gillette realized that disposable razors would be a perfect invention. Devising a thin enough blade was the problem; Gillette tinkered with 700 blades and 51 razors before getting it right in 1903. Within three years, he was selling over 500,000 blades annually.

Sir Joseph Lister. Even before the mouthwash that bears his name was invented, Lister fought germs; he campaigned against filthy hospitals and against doctors who performed surgery in their street clothes. When St. Louis chemist Joseph Lawrence invented the famous mouthwash, he named it 'Listerine' both to honor and to take advantage of Lister's well-known obsession with cleanliness .

Clarence Birdseye. Brooklyn-born "Bob" Birdseye was the first person to figure out how to freeze fresh food and still preserve its taste and nutrition. Birdseye's insight came from an Arctic expedition; he observed that Caribou meat, quickly frozen in the sub-zero temperatures, retained its flavor when cooked months later. He returned to America and worked for years to develop a quick-freezing process. When he succeeded in 1929, he sold his invention for the then-enormous sum of $22 million; Birdseye foods still bears his name.

Charles Fleischmann. An Austrian native who first visited the United States during the Civil War, he found our bread almost as appalling as our political situation. At the time bread was mostly home-baked, using yeast made from potato peelings, and its taste was unpredictable. The next time he came to America,

Fleischmann brought along samples of the yeast used to make Viennese bread. In 1868, he began to sell his yeast in compressed cakes of uniform size that removed the guesswork from baking. In 1937, yeast sales reached $20 million a year. After Prohibition ended, Fleischmann and his brother Maximillian found another use for their yeast—Fleischmann's distilled gin.

William and Andrew Smith. The makers of the Smith Brothers Cough Drops were the sons of Poughkeepsie, New York restauranteur and candymaker James Smith. In 1870, one of Smith's customers gave him a recipe for a "cough candy." Smith made a batch and quickly sold it all. People in the windswept Hudson Valley—plagued by constant colds during the long winters—clamored for more... And so the Smith family became America's cough drop kings. When copycat "Smith" cough drops appeared, the bearded brothers introduced the famous box that bears their pictures, as a means of guaranteeing authenticity.

John B. Stetson. While traveling out west in the 1850s, Stetson became adept at trapping animals and sewing the skins together, making them hats for sun protection. When he returned to Philadephia, he started a hat business for $100; his mainstay, "The Boss of the Plains" hat, became the classic symbol of the Wild West.

William Scholl. As apprentice to the local shoemaker, "Billy" Scholl's work led him to two conclusions: feet were abused, and nobody cared. So, in a burst of idealism, Scholl appointed himself the future foot doctor to the world. Strangely enough, it actually happened. By the time he became a M.D. at 22, Dr. Scholl had invented and patented his first arch support; in fact, he held over 300 patents for foot treatments and machines for making foot comfort aids. And his customers seemed to appreciate it—a widow once wrote him that she buried her husband with his "Foot-Eazers" so he would be as comfortable as he was in life. Until he died, in his eighties, Dr. Scholl devoted himself to saving the world's feet, adhering always to his credo: "Early to bed, early to rise, work like hell, and advertise."

FULLER IDEAS

Buckminster Fuller, an architect, inventor, scientist, mathematician, philosopher, and we don't know what else, was considered one of the most original thinkers of the 20th century.

"Faith is much better than belief. Belief is when someone *else* does the thinking."

"If nature had wanted you to be a specialist she'd have had you born with one eye with a microscope fastened to it."

"Either war is obsolete or men are."

"Don't oppose forces, use them."

"It struck me that nature's system must be a real beauty, because in chemistry we find that the associations are always in beautiful whole numbers—there are no fractions."

"Politics is an accessory after the fact."

"People should think things out fresh and not just accept conventional terms and the conventional way of doing things."

"God to me…is a verb, not a noun, proper or improper."

"I am a passenger on the spaceship Earth."

"The most important thing about Spaceship Earth—an instruction booklet didn't come with it."

"If we do more with less, our resources will be adequate to take care of everybody."

"The end move in politics is to pick up a gun."

"When I'm working on a problem, I never think about beauty. I think only how to solve the problem. But when I have finished, if the solution is not beautiful, I know it is wrong."

"You can't reorder the world by talking to it."

"We are not going to be able to operate our spaceship Earth successfully nor for much longer unless we see it as a whole spaceship and our fate as common. It has to be everybody or nobody."

CLOSE CALLS

Four presidents—Abraham Lincoln (1865), James Garfield (1881), William McKinley (1901) and John F. Kennedy (1963)— have lost their lives to assassins. Others have barely escaped assassination attempts. Here are the most famous "close calls" in American history.

THE ATTEMPT: On January 30, 1835, President Andrew Jackson was in the Capitol rotunda, attending funeral services for Congressman Warren B. Davis of South Carolina. He was approached by Richard Lawrence, a 35 year-old house painter, who drew two revolvers and pointed them at the president...but both guns misfired. Jackson was so incensed that he rushed at Lawrence and started to beat him with his cane.

THE MOTIVE: Lawrence had approached Jackson a week before on the White House grounds and begged the president for money. Jackson thought he was a "harmless lunatic" and dismissed him.

THE SENTENCE: Lawrence was tried by prosecutor Francis Scott Key, author of "The Star Spangled Banner." He pled insanity, claiming he was the King of England, but the verdict was "guilty." He later died in a mental institution.

THE ATTEMPT: On October 14, 1912, former President Theodore Roosevelt was campaigning for a third term in Milwaukee, Wisconsin, running as the Progressive Party candidate. Roosevelt was approaching an automobile on his way to a speech when a New Yorker named John Schrank pulled a revolver, pointed it between two spectators, and pulled the trigger. Roosevelt staggered but didn't fall. Although there was no blood, Roosevelt's handlers begged him to go to the hospital. Roosevelt refused. "I shall deliver this speech or die," he reportedly said. And that's what he did; he delivered a fifty-minute speech to a cheering throng at the Milwaukee Auditorium. When he pulled the 100-page speech out of his vest, however, he noticed a bullet hole in it. A bullet had penetrated four inches into his body, right under his right nipple. Finally, after the speech was completed, Roosevelt consented to go to the hospital where he was treated for shock and loss of blood.

THE MOTIVE: Schrank claimed that William McKinley, who'd been assassinated in 1901, had revealed in a dream that Teddy Roosevelt was behind his death...and that Schrank should avenge him. Schrank had stalked Roosevelt from New Orleans to Chicago and then to Milwaukee to accomplish this.

THE SENTENCE: Schrank was later found guilty of attempted murder, and was sent to an insane asylum where he spent 32 years. He died in 1943.

THE ATTEMPT: In 1933, Guiseppe Zangara wanted to kill a president—it didn't matter which one. As it happened, Franklin D. Roosevelt had just defeated Herbert Hoover in the 1932 election and was the new president-elect. So he became Zangara's target.

Roosevelt had just finished giving a speech in Chicago when Zangara approached the podium and fired his revolver five times. One shot hit Anton Cermak, Chicago's mayor; another wounded a spectator seriously. Three others were hit—but Roosevelt was untouched. Reportedly, the mortally wounded Cermak told FDR "better me than you." He died two days after FDR's inauguration.

THE MOTIVE: Zangara was a brick-layer who had emigrated from Italy. He was a self-professed anarchist and had previously considered killing Hoover and Calvin Coolidge.

THE SENTENCE: Zangara was found guilty of murder and sentenced to the electric chair. In jail, he wrote his autobiography, which ended with "I go contented because I go for my idea. I salute all the poor of the world." On the day of his execution in Florida, Zangara became enraged when he saw that no photographers were present. He reportedly said, "No pictures? All capitalists are a lousy bunch of crooks."

THE ATTEMPT: On November 1, 1950, Harry S Truman was taking a nap at the Blair House, his temporary quarters while the White House was being restored. Outside, three policeman and a Secret Service agent were on guard when two men approached the Blair House from different directions, in an attempt to kill Truman. The first, Oscar Collazo, tried to shoot an officer, but the gun didn't fire. He eventually shot the guard in the leg and ran for the steps. Meanwhile, the other conspirator, Griselio Torresola, approached and fired at an officer, Leslie Coffert, who was hit but managed to shoot Torresola in the head. Both Coffert and Torresola died later.

THE MOTIVE: Collazo, who suffered slight injuries, later stood trial. He claimed that he and Terresola—both of whom were Puerto Rican—were fighting for Puerto Rico's independence, and hoped to get attention for their cause by assassinating Truman.

THE SENTENCE: He was found guilty and sentenced to death. In a surprise move, Truman commuted Collazo's sentence to life in prison eight days before he was scheduled to die.

THE ATTEMPT: On September 5, 1975, Lynette "Squeaky" Fromme drew a Colt .45 loaded with four bullets and aimed it at President Gerald Ford during a campaign stop in Sacramento, California. Fromme managed to squeeze the trigger but the firing chamber was empty. She was wrestled to the ground by Secret Service agents.

THE MOTIVE: Fromme, a follower of Charles Manson, had once declared, "I'll die for Charlie; I'll kill for him, I'll do whatever is necessary."

THE SENTENCE: She was tried under the post-JFK-assassination law that made any attempt on a president's life a Federal offense. She was found guilty and imprisoned. On December 24, 1987, Fromme escaped from a West Virginia prison, after hearing a rumor that Manson was dying and wanted to see her. Two days later she was apprehended on a country road.

THE ATTEMPT: On September 22, 1975, a few weeks after Fromme's attempt on Ford's life, another woman in California attempted to kill the president. The woman was Sarah Jane Moore, a 45-year old police and FBI informant, who, only the day before, had been interrogated by the police for threatening the president's life (they confiscated her .44 gun). Moore's shot at Ford was deflected by a bystander in the crowd who knocked her arm as she pulled the trigger of her .38. The shot ricocheted off a concrete wall and slightly injured a nearby cab driver.

THE MOTIVE: Moore later claimed, "it was kind of an ultimate protest against the system."

Famous Myth: You use more calories eating celery than are in the celery itself.

THE SENTENCE: She was convicted and jailed. Like Fromme, Moore made a jail break in 1979 but was later apprehended.

THE ATTEMPT: On March 29, 1981, John Hinckley arrived in Washington, D.C. after a three-day cross-country bus trip from Los Angeles. The next day he checked out of his hotel, went over the Washington Hilton and waited for President Reagan to come out after a speech to union representatives. When Reagan emerged from the hotel, Hinckley drew out a .22 caliber "Saturday Night Special" and fired six Devastator bullets. One shot ricocheted off a waiting limousine and struck Reagan, who later recovered.

THE MOTIVE: Apparently, it was a "gift of love" to actress Jody Foster. Hinckley left a note to Foster which said "there is a definite possibility that I will be killed in my attempt to get Reagan...I'm asking you to please look into your heart and at least give me the chance with this historical deed to gain your respect and love."

THE SENTENCE: On June 21, 1982, Hinckley was found "not guilty" of attempting to assassinate the president for reasons of insanity and was admitted to St. Elizabeth's Hospital in Washington.

P.S. There is no precedent for letting attempted assassins out of jail. None have ever been released from custody alive.

A LITTLE MORE PRESIDENTIAL TRIVIA

From Sid Frank and Arden Davis Melick's book *Presidents: Tidbits and Trivia*: "On April 10, 1865, Washington crowds, overjoyed at the news of Robert E. Lee's surrender, surged around the White House, cheering and calling for the President to make a speech.

"Abraham Lincoln appeared, quieted the throng, and promised to make a few remarks. But first, he said, turning toward the members of a band which was at the scene, he had a request. He would like the band to play 'Dixie.'

" 'Dixie?' The Confederate song? Why 'Dixie?' The crowd stirred restlessly. Was this another of Lincoln's jokes?

" ' "Dixie," ' he said, 'is one of the best tunes I have ever heard, and now we have captured it.' A mighty cheer went up from the crowd and the band played 'Dixie.' "

Check a map: Reno, Nevada is west of Los Angeles, California.

TRAVELS WITH RAY

Perplexing adventures of the brilliant egghead Ray "Weird Brain" Redel. Answers are on page 672.

One morning, "Weird Brain" Redel, the most renowned thinker of our time, called and asked if I wanted to go to the gym with him and lift weights. I have to admit that weight-lifting isn't really my bag, but the prospect of spending a few hours with a brilliant man like "Weird Brain" was too good to pass up. I agreed.

When we got there, I discovered that our trainer for the day was Charles Atlas—the guy I used to see on the back of comic books. Wow!

But even Mr. Atlas, who taught thousands of people how to keep bullies from kicking sand in their faces, couldn't resist trying push "Weird Brain" around with a little weightlifter's riddle. "Okay Brain," he said to his old buddy, "try this one: *Light as a feather, Nothing in it, But a big guy can't hold it for more than a minute.*"

"Weird Brain" rolled his eyes and said, "Charlie, you ask me that every time I come to the gym. It's the same answer as last week."

What WAS the answer?

When my friend, "Weird Brain" Redel returned from the month-long Western Hemisphere Egghead Conference in Panama, I picked him up at the airport.

"I hope you brought your 1953 Chevy panel truck," he said.

"Of course I did," I replied; "You asked me to on the phone. But I don't understand why."

"Well," "Weird Brain" explained, "As you know, I had my new pre-sotonic-zorperator along, and the only thing I could find that was big enough and padded enough to ship it in was..." I saw that horrible gleam in his eye, and I knew he was going to answer me in a riddle. "Was *what?*' I shuddered. He replied: "*The man who made it didn't want it, the man who bought it didn't use it, the man who used it didn't know it.*"

What did "Weird Brain" use for a shipping crate?

INVASION! PART II

Most invasions of the U.S. aren't any big deal, except as footnotes in history...and as excellent bathroom reading (although we're sure that wasn't on anyone's mind at the time). Take these invasions, for example:

THE INVADERS: Pancho Villa and his guerilla army.

THE DATE: March 9, 1916.

BACKGROUND: Many folk heroes—Emiliano Zapata and Albert Obregon, for instance—emerged during the Mexican revolution in 1910. But the most notorious was a former cattle rustler named Francisco "Pancho" Villa. To the people of Chihuahua, Mexico's largest state, he and his guerilla army of 40,000 men seemed like Robin Hood, stealing from rich landlords and giving to the poor.

At first, the U.S. government supported Villa and his outlaw army. But after the war was won, Washington was forced to ally itself with a single faction of the splintered Mexican revolutionary movement...and it chose Villa's rival, Venustian Carranza. Villa was furious. He felt betrayed, and decided to retaliate against the U.S.

THE INVASION: Villa led an army of 1500 guerrillas across the border and attacked the 13th U.S. Cavalry in Columbus, New Mexico. During the raid, Villa's men killed 18 Americans, burned down several buildings, and stole a quantity of weapons. But as they retreated across the border into Mexico, 50 of Villa's troops were killed by U.S. Army personnel.

AFTERMATH: The American public was seething. U.S. president Woodrow Wilson responded to the attack by ordering John J. "Black Jack" Pershing to cross the Mexican border and capture Villa. The so-called "Punitive Expedition" was a dismal failure; the nimble Villa eluded Pershing's troops. Months later, the American army gave up and retreated emptyhanded. Pershing later claimed the campaign had given his men field experience for future battles in World War I.

Villa was assassinated in Parral, South Chihuahua in 1923.

THE INVADERS: Eight Nazi terrorists.

THE DATES: June 13 and June 17, 1942.

BACKGROUND: In early 1942, German U-boats were a menacing presence in the waters off the East Coast. Fearing a secret Nazi invasion, the U.S. ordered the approaches to harbors in New York, Boston, and Portland, Maine to be mined.

U.S. authorities had no inkling, however, that the invasion being planned by Nazi strategists involved only eight men—specially trained terrorists with instructions to bomb selected factories and bridges and shake the confidence of the American public.

THE INVASION: On the night of June 13, four Nazi agents rowed a collapsible boat from a German U-boat to a beach in Amagansett, Long Island. Fortunately for the U.S. John C. Cullen, a 21-year-old second class seaman in the Coast Guard, stumbled onto the four Germans while patrolling the beach. The nervous Nazis claimed to be shipwrecked fisherman.

Cullen was suspicious, particularly when the group's leader, Johann Dasch, tried to bribe Cullen with $300 to shut up. Cullen took the money and rushed back to Coast Guard headquarters to tell his superiors. The FBI instantly rushed in and found a cache of weapons and explosives that the Germans had buried on the beach. An extensive search was conducted but the agents had already fled.

Four days later, another Nazi foursome landed without detection on the beach of Ponte Vedra, Florida.

AFTERMATH: Dasch, leader of the Nazi mission, was unnerved by his run-in with Cullen. The Nazi spy convinced his partner E.P Burger to abandon their intricately conceived plan. The duo traveled to Washington, D.C., and turned themselves in to the FBI.

Thanks to Dasch's information, FBI officials tracked down the other six Nazis before they could carry out their mission. Dasch and Burger were sentenced to jail (Truman later commuted their sentences and sent them back to Germany, where Dasch wrote a book about the mission). The other six were executed within a month of their capture, before the public was informed.

BEN FRANKLIN SPEAKLIN': "Our Constitution is in actual operation; everything promises that it will last; but in this world nothing is certain but death and taxes."

DISNEY STORIES: CINDERELLA

In 1949, Uncle Walt released the musical cartoon version of Cinderella, which "combined realism with caricature." The people—Cinderella, her family, and the Prince, were drawn from life; the animals were just cartoon characters. Of course, the Disney version and the original story were substantially different. Here are Jim Morton's examples of how the tale was changed:

THE DISNEY VERSION

Cinderella is horribly mistreated by her mean step-mother and step-sisters. She's stuck dreaming while she scrubs floors.

• When the Prince holds a ball for the women of the Kingdom, trying to find a wife, Cinderella isn't allowed to go—she has to finish her chores. But Cinderella's Fairy Godmother appears. With her magic wand (bibbety, bobbety, boo), the Fairy turns a pumpkin into a coach and makes a beautiful gown for the girl. She warns Cinderella to be home by midnight; that's when the spell wears off.

• When the Prince sees Cinderella he immediately falls in love, and spends the entire evening with her. Cinderella loses all track of time; before she knows it, the clock strikes twelve. She flees the palace, leaving behind only a glass slipper.

• The Prince searches his Kingdom for the woman whose foot fits the glass slipper. The step-sisters try to squeeze into it, but can't. When Cinderella tries it on, the Prince realizes she's the one he's looking for. They marry and live happily ever after.

THE ORIGINAL STORY

• Most people don't realize there are two popular versions of Cinderella (it's actually a very old folktale, and there are dozens of variations all over Europe). Disney's film is a remarkably accurate retelling of Charles Perrault's version. But what about kids who don't have the Perrault fairy tales around the house and turn, instead, to the Brothers Grimm version? Boy, are they in for a surprise!

• The differences between the Perrault and the Grimm versions are startling. The Grimm tale is so gruesome it approaches Grand Guignol, and has more in common with Alfred Hitchcock's *The Birds* than it does with the Disney film.

• There is no Fairy Godmother in the Grimm story. Cinderella is helped by two pigeons, who bring her a gown and slippers, and help with her chores. The slippers in the Grimm version are gold, not glass. (In other versions, the slippers are made of fur.)

• It's not a ball, but a three-day festival, that Cinderella attends. So the Prince has three chances to find her, and narrows the search down to one household—he doesn't have to try the shoe on every woman in the kingdom. (Cinderella doesn't lose her slipper by chance, either. On the third day of the festival, the Prince, after losing Cinderella on two previous occasions, has the palace stairway coated with pitch.)

• When the Prince tries the gold slipper on Cinderella's stepsisters, the shoe is too small. The first step-sister cuts her big toe off to get her foot into the slipper. The second step-sister cuts her heel off to fit into the slipper. Each time, the blood on the slipper (pointed out by the two pigeons) betrays the women. Finally the Prince tries the slipper on Cinderella, and of course, it fits.

• Cinderella and the Prince marry, and at Cinderella's wedding, the pigeons appear once more and peck out the eyes of the two step-sisters. Gruesome.

SAMPLE PASSAGE (FROM THE GRIMM VERSION)

The Prince brings the gold slipper to Cinderella's house, and the step-sister tries it on first.

"The oldest took the shoe into a room to try it on, and her mother stood by her side. However, the shoe was too small for her, and she could not get her big toe into it. So her mother handed her a knife and said, 'Cut your toe off. Once you become Queen, you won't have to walk anymore.'

"The maiden cut her toe off, forced her foot into the shoe, and went out to the Prince. He took her on his horse as his bride, and rode off. But they had to pass the grave where the two pigeons were sitting on the hazel tree, and they cried out: '*Looky, look, look, At the shoe that she took; There's blood all over, and her foot's too small. She's not the bride you met at the ball.*' "

FILM TERMS

Every business has its slang. Here are some of the terms movie people use, some of which you've probably seen on screen.

Annie Oakley: A free ticket to a movie screening.
Apple Box: A box that actors stand on while filming a scene.
Best Boy: Assistant to the head gaffer (see gaffer).
Clapsticks: The wood sticks that are struck together to signify the beginning of filming a scene.
Click Track: Audible click used in musical scoring.
Dolly Shot: Wheeling the camera on tracks for motion in a film shot.
Dope Sheet: Storyboards (see storyboards) used in animation films.
Final Cut: The last edited version of a film ready for release.
Gaffer: Electrician on a film set.
The Grip: Head fix-it person on the set.
Juicer: Electrician in charge of the main power source.
Lap Dissolve: Editing together two shots, one fading in, the other fading out.
Matte Shot: Film editing technique where foreground and background images are placed together to form one shot.
Oater: A Western.
Outtake: Footage not used in final cut.
P-O-V: Acronym for point-of-view. Camera is positioned to simulate a character's line of sight.
Rear Projection: Cost-cutting filming technique where actors stand in front of a projection on a translucent screen.
Rushes: Daily screenings of footage from a work-in-progress.
SFX: Acronymn for sound effects.
Sky Pan: Huge floodlights used for large areas to be lit.
Slate: Board used with clapsticks (see left column) to identify scenes during editing.
Splice: Editing two pieces of film together.
Space Opera: Slang for science fiction film.
Storyboards: Sketches drawn to depict, shot-for-shot, the action to be filmed.
Swish Pan: Rapid camera movement causing a blurring sensation.
Weenie: A plot device that is considered to be a gimmick.
Walla Walla: Background noise in a scene.

Who suffers the most on-the-job back injuries? Garbage collectors & warehouse workers.

CARTOON CORNER

Miscellaneous facts about your favorite cartoon characters.

DAFFY DUCK

Daffy first appeared in the 1937 cartoon, "Porky's Duck Hunt." According to animator / director Chuck Jones in *Chuck Amuck*, he and his co-workers were looking for a voice to complete this new character—"a duck who enjoyed being nutty." While they were brainstorming, someone did an impression of their boss, producer Leon Schlesinger, who had a heavy lisp. Pressed for time, the crew impulsively decided to use that voice.

It wasn't until later that it occured to them what they'd done. Schlesinger would have to screen the cartoon and approve the new character—lisp and all. He wasn't going to think it was funny to hear his own voice coming from the duck.

Expecting to be fired, the animators wrote out their resignations and took them to the cartoon's first screening. Schlesinger arrived, the lights were dimmed, and at the producer's cry of "Roll the garbage!" Daffy Duck lit up the screen. A few minutes later, the lights went back on and all eyes focused on Schlesinger. His reaction? Jones recalls: "He said, 'Jesus Crithe, that's a funny voithe! Where'd you get that voithe?' "...He didn't have a clue!

FELIX THE CAT

You may find it hard to believe, but Felix was the first cartoon superstar—the Mickey Mouse of the silent film years. In 1919 he appeared in a short called "Feline Follies," and was so popular that Pat Sullivan's production studio could barely keep up with the demand. They turned out 26 cartoons a year—one every two weeks. Among Felix's early achievements:

- In 1922 he appeared as the New York Yankees' lucky mascot.
- In 1923, he shared the screen with Charlie Chaplin.
- In 1927, a Felix doll was Charles Lindbergh's companion on his historic trans-Atlantic flight.
- In 1928, he became the first image ever to appear on TV. When the first experimental television broadcast occurred, the subject was a Felix doll.

So what happened? Why didn't Felix remain popular? Like a lot of movie-industry people, Felix's owner, Pat Sullivan didn't believe in "talkies." So silent star Felix the Cat was eclipsed by the new talking cartoons.

YOGI BEAR

When Hanna-Barbera produced Jellystone's smarter-than-the-average-bear, New York Yankees catcher Yogi Berra threatened to sue them. The grounds: Among other things, defamation of character. Although everyone in America made the connection between Yogi and Yogi, a Hanna-Barbera executive producer swore "it was just a coincidence." He said the character was inspired by Ed Norton (Art Carney), the next-door neighbor in "The Honeymooners."

HUEY, LOUIE, & DEWEY

This is one of the greatest "naming" stories we've ever heard. It comes from a fascinating book called *Cartoon Monickers*, by Walter M. Brasch.

"One day in the late 1930s, Harry Reeves, a gagman working on the Donald Duck cartoons, burst into the work area of Jim Carmichael, a layout man, proclaiming, 'Jim, we've got three new characters. Donald's nephews. And we're gonna work them into a lot of screwy situations with the duck. But we haven't got name for 'em. Got any ideas for naming three cute li'l ducks?'"

"Carmichael recalls that he 'wasn't too interested that morning in the nomenclature of three cute li'l ducks, so I glanced at the front page of the newspaper...Thomas E. Dewey was doing something political in New York, and Huey P. Long was blabbering in New Orleans. So, off-handedly, I said, 'Why don't you call them Huey and Dewey?' A friend, Louie Schmitt, was passing in the hall and gave a big hello. Inspired, I said, 'Hell, call the little clunkers Huey, Louie, and Dewey.' Harry leaped up, yelping 'That's it!' "

POPEYE

The sailor man was a popular comic strip character before he made his screen appearance—in an early '30s Betty Boop cartoon. A few years later, in 1936, he won an Oscar for *Sinbad the Sailor*. If the dialogue between Popeye and Olive Oyle often seems informal, it's because a lot of it was ad-libbed.

Spectators drink more than 1,800 gallons of mint julips at each Kentucky Derby.

THE OLD BALL GAME

Baseball's unofficial anthem, "Take Me Out To The Ballgame," is one of the best-known songs in America. But only a few trivia buffs know the story behind it. Here it is:

THE WORDS: In the summer of 1908, a vaudevillian named Jack Norworth was riding the New York City subway when he noticed an advertisement that read "Baseball Today—Polo Grounds." He'd never been to a baseball game, but he knew the sport was getting popular...and it hit him that a baseball song might fit into his act. Inspired, he jotted down some lyrics about a woman named Katie who was crazy about baseball games.

THE MUSIC: Norworth rushed to the office of a music-publisher friend named Albert von Tilzer. Von Tilzer had never seen a baseball game either, but he quickly set the words to music.

THE FLOP: Norworth was convinced he had a hit...But when he sang "Take Me Out To The Ballgame" during his vaudeville act in Brooklyn that night, the crowd seemed bored. No one complained ...but no one paid much attention to it, either.

THE HIT: So Norworth tried a different approach; he turned the song into a "Nickelodeon slide show"—a sort of turn-of-the-century MTV. Slide shows, featuring sing-along lyrics and illustrations (in this case, photos of pretty Miss Katie Casey at a Polo Grounds game), were shown at movie theaters between films. Audiences "followed the bouncing ball," and sang along. Norworth's ploy worked. "Take Me Out To The Ballgame" became a hit. Ironically, it wasn't until *after* the song was popular that Norworth finally went to an "old ballgame."

THE MISSING LINK: Everybody knows the chorus to "Take Me Out To The Ballgame." But here are the verses: *Katie Casey was baseball mad. Had the fever and had it bad. Just to root for the hometown crew, Ev'ry sou, Katie blew. On a Saturday her young beau, Called to see if she'd like to go. To see a show but Miss Kate said "No I tell you what you can do..."*

Every minute, more than 70 million gallons of water pass over Victoria falls in Africa.

LOOSE ENDS

What would a Bathroom Reader be without flushing out some new information on toilets?

TOILET ART

Two toilets have figured prominently in the art world:

• Marcel Duchamp rocked the art world in 1917 when he made a urinal into sculpture by turning it upside down and signing it "R. Mutt." The piece, entitled "The Fountain," upset an art committee's dignified sensibilites—they refused to exhibit it. According to the *New York Times*, however, the work "is now considered a masterwork," although it exists only in a photograph taken by Alfred Stieglitz.

• Another "art toilet" surfaced in 1985 when a three-hole outhouse seat was discovered to have been "painted" by famed artist Willem de Kooning in 1954. Apparently, de Kooning splattered some paint on the seat to make it resemble a marble surface as a joke for a party he was throwing in a rented home in Bridgehampton, New York. An art dealer spotted the 22" X 99" toilet seat in an auction, and bought it for $50. Theoretically, the three-seater could be worth millions, which is how much de Kooning's regular work sells for.

LOOK OUT BELOW

Gene Gordon of Fort Worth, Texas was in his backyard in late 1987 when he heard a loud bang in his house. He checked it out, and found a large hole in his roof and chunks of blue ice melting in his attic. After an investigation, it was determined that the ice originated from an airplane toilet. Apparently, blue cleaning fluid had leaked from the airplane's toilet, frozen in mid-air, and dropped to earth.

THE BOTTOM LINE

• In 1985, Lockheed Corporation charged the U.S. government $34,560 for 54 toilet seats (or about $600 a piece) for the Navy's P-3C Orion anti-submarine planes. When government officals told

Lockheed that the same seat could be purchased by mobile-home owners for $25, the price was lowered to $100 apiece.

• The most expensive toilet ever made was the one developed for the space shuttle. The price tag for NASA's waste collector: $3,000,000.

LOO-SELY SPEAKING

The popular British slang for *toilet* is the "loo." Where did the term come from? One theory suggests its roots are in a pay toilet with an L-shaped handle followed by two O-shaped coin slots—spelling out the word "loo." A more plausible explanation: it derives from the phrase "gardyloo," which Scottish people shouted before throwing trash out of the window and onto the street. Another longshot: it's a pun on the words "water closet" and "Waterloo."

EXPENSIVE TOILET PAPER

Billy Edd Wheeler, the country songwriter who penned "Coward of the County" for Kenny Rogers, also wrote a little gem of a book called *Outhouse Humor* (published by August House).

Here's a sample joke from the volume:

"At a filling station near Bland, Virginia, before they got indoor plumbing, customers had to use the outhouse if they wanted to go to the bathroom.

Actually, they had two outhouses under one roof, with side doors, but they were separated in the middle only by a partition built about a foot off the floor, and running up to about six feet...similar to the rows of stalls in restrooms in airports.

One time two men were in this outhouse at the same time. After one man finished going he noticed there wasn't any toilet paper left on the spool, so he pecked on the wall and said, 'Hey bud, would you kindly share some of your paper with me? This one's empty over here.' The voice came back from the other side: 'Sorry, pal, but there ain't much left over here, either. I'm afraid there's just enough for me.'

A few minutes passed. There was another peck on the wall, and the first man said, 'Uh, buddy...you ain't got five ones for a five, have you? Or maybe two fives for a ten?' "

BLUE SUEDE SHOES

And now, the mystery of the most famous pair of shoes in rock 'n' roll history.

Pop culture is full of contradictions. Stories about the beginnings of fads, products, books and songs are fun to tell, but you can't be sure if they're true. To illustrate the point, here are two versions of the origin of the rock'n'roll classic, "Blue Suede Shoes," each told by believable sources. One, Carl Perkins, wrote the tune. The other, Johnny Cash, has been a friend of Perkins' since the days when "Blue Suede" was recorded. If anyone should know the story, Carl should. But Johnny Cash seems to be pretty sure about his version, too. We'll never know exactly which of these stories is true.

STORY A—*"Blue Suede Shoes," according to Carl Perkins*: On December 4, 1955, a Jackson, Tennessee musician named Carl Perkins played at a local dance tht changed his life. "[I was] playin' a club in my hometown," he remembers, "for a high school sorority dance. A beautiful girl was dancin' with a boy who had on a pair of blue suede shoes...He said, 'Uh-uh, don't step on my suedes!' "

Carl couldn't believe it—this kid was with a gorgeous girl, but all he cared about were his shoes! What a nut! When the dance ended, Perkins went home and went to sleep. And then at 3:00 A.M. he suddenly awoke with a song in his head. He jumped out of bed, grabbed the first piece of paper he could find—which happened to be a brown paper potato sack—and wrote down the lyrics to "Blue Suede Shoes."

STORY B—*"Blue Suede Shoes," according to Johnny Cash*: Carl Perkins and Johnny Cash were part of Sam Phillips' fabled Sun Records stable, which included Jerry Lee Lewis, Roy Orbison, and a certain Mr. Elvis Presley. One night, Cash, Presley and Perkins were performing in Amory, Mississippi. Cash and Perkins had already done their shows and Presley was onstage. In the wings, Cash told Perkins that he really had a "feel for the 'bop' kind of song," and asked why didn't he record one? Perkins said he'd tried, but he could never come up with the right song. So Cash gave him an idea for a tune. He told Carl a story about his Air Force days. His sergeant, Cash said, was a black man named C. V. White, who was always immaculately dressed. White would come into Cash's room and ask how he looked. After Cash replied, White would say, "Just don't step on my blue suede shoes," and leave the room. Cash would yell after him that those were Air Force regulation shoes, not blue suede, and White would say, "Tonight when I get to town they're gonna be blue suede, man!" Perkins exclaimed, "That's a great idea for a bop song!" He grabbed a pencil and before Elvis was offstage, Perkins had written it.

FOR THE RECORD

• The original intro was "One for the money, two for the show, three to get ready and go, man, go." As they were recording, Perkins said "Go, cat, go" instead. The record producer asked, "This word 'cat,' what did you mean?" Perkins: "I have no idea where it came from." "Cat" was actually a slang word for "black person."

• Released on New Year's Day, 1956, "Blue Suede" took about three months to break out of the South. By March it was headed for the top of all three music charts (Pop, Country, R&B). But as Perkins was driving to appear on "The Perry Como Show," where he was to make his first national appearance and receive his gold record for "Blue Suede," he got into a serious car accident that killed one of his brothers and put him in the hospital. His interrupted career was never the same again.

THE TOP FIVE—Week of April 21, 1956

1. **Heartbreak Hotel**
   —*Elvis Presley*
2. **Hot Diggity Dog/Jukebox Baby**
   —*Perry Como*
3. **Poor People of Paris**
   —*Les Baxter*
4. **Blue Suede Shoes**
   —*Carl Perkins*
5. **Lisbon Antiqua**
   —*Nelson Riddle & His Orchestra*

PRIMETIME PROVERBS

Here are some more TV quotes from the book Primetime Proverbs, *by Jack Mingo and John Javna.*

ON GOD

"God don't make no mistakes —that's how he got to be God."

—**Archie Bunker,**
All in the Family

"Well, I certainly don't believe God's a woman, because if He were, men would be the ones walking around wearing high heels, taking Midol, and having their upper lips waxed."

—**Julia Sugarbaker,**
Designing Women

Archie Bunker: "All the pictures I ever seen, God is white."
George Jefferson: "Maybe you were looking at the negatives."

—***All in the Family***

ON BOOZE

"Never cry over spilt milk. It could've been whiskey."

—**Pappy Maverick,**
Maverick

"Oh, I just adore beer. It's so... so...democratic."

—**Kookie's Girlfriend,**
77 Sunset Strip

ON THE ARMY

"What other job lets you die for a living?"

—**Hawkeye Pierce,**
M*A*S*H*

THE RICH

"He's got a purse the size of an elephant's scrotum, and it's just as hard to get your hands on."

—**Edmund Blackadder,**
Blackadder II

[*To Mama's rich boyfriend*]
"It's a pleasure to meet a man of your charming credit rating."

—**Kingfish,**
Amos'n'Andy

SKEWERED SAYINGS

"You've buttered your bread, now sleep in it."

—**Gracie Allen,**
The George Burns and Gracie Allen Show

"People in stucco houses should not throw quiche."

—**Sonny Crockett,**
Miami Vice

BEWITCHED

From 1964 to 1972, Elizabeth Montgomery starred in TV's "Bewitched" as Samantha Stevens, the perky blonde housewitch who could take care of household chores with a twitch of her nose.

HOW IT STARTED

In 1942, Veronica Lake starred in the title role of a movie comedy called *I Married a Witch*. The plot: an upright, middle-class American guy discovers his bride is literally an enchanting young woman.

In 1958, Kim Novak played a witch with her sights set on future husband James Stewart in the romantic comedy, *Bell, Book and Candle*.

In 1963, William Dozier and Harry Ackerman, two executives at Screen Gems TV, decided to make a suburban family sitcom with a "brand new" twist: The husband unwittingly marries a pretty, young witch. Well it was new for TV, anyway.

They wrote the pilot script and took it to Tammy Grimes, an English actress who'd been starring in Broadway's "The Unsinkable Molly Brown." Grimes had a TV contract with Screen Gems, didn't like the script, but she refused to say whether she'd do the show or not. "Why not rewrite it," she suggested, infuriating Dozier. But he obliged; commissioning a new script.

While he was waiting, Dozier got a call from an old friend he'd been dying to work with—Liz Montgomery. Liz, it seems, had fallen in love with a TV director named William Asher and the two of them wanted to spend all their time together—so they were interested in a TV show in which she could star, while he directed. Dozier immediately decided that Montgomery would make the perfect witch, but he couldn't offer her the part in "Bewitched" ("I couldn't even mention it,")—he was already committed to Tammy Grimes.

Fortunately, Grimes didn't like the new script either. She held out for a show in which she played the part of a befuddled English heiress. (It went on the air as "The Tammy Grimes Show," and lasted about two months.) Montgomery, meanwhile, took the part of Samantha, and "Bewitched" became the hottest new show of 1964. It was in the Top 10 for five straight years.

Most Oscars: Walt Disney won 20.

JUST KIDDING

When filming for the show began, Liz Montgomery was eight months pregnant. So Asher (by now her husband, as well as the director), had to shoot the first five shows without her, adding in her parts later. A few weeks after the baby was born, Montgomery was out on the set making up for lost time.

THE NOSE KNOWS

Some people can wiggle their ears. Elizabeth Montgomery can wiggle her nose. (It's not as easy as it looks—try it.) "Bewitched" 's producers put the trick to good use by making Sam's nose her magic wand. No one else on the show could do it, so they had to settle for hand gestures, or—in the case of Tabitha (the daughter), moving her nose with her finger.

MOON SHOT

Agnes Moorhead, who played Sam's mother, Endora, was invited to Cape Kennedy by NASA to witness the Apollo 12 moon flight in 1969. She was the honorary "technical advisor," since, as Endora, she had been on the moon herself. "I distinctly remember," she said, "being on the moon at least 7 times over the past 6 years."

WHICH WITCH?

Moorhead didn't particulary like being known as "the witch." That was understandable. She was 57 and had been performing for over 50 years when she first appeared as Endora. She had starred in almost 100 films, won an Emmy, and was nominated for 5 Oscars. She died of lung cancer in 1974, ten years later.

DARRIN'S LUCK

Viewers often ask why there were two different actors playing Darrin Stephens, Samantha's husband. Here's why: After 5 seasons as Darrin, actor Dick York had to withdraw from the series because of serious back pains. It turns out that in 1959, while working on a film with Gary Cooper, he sustained a back injury, tearing all the muscles loose from his spine. Over the years the pain got worse and by the time York got to "Bewitched," the injury had become so debilitating that he missed 14 episodes of the show. Then one day he had a seizure; he was rushed to the hospital and never returned to "Bewitched" again. He was replaced by Dick Sargent.

Racehorses don't run any faster than ostriches.

FAMOUS LAST WORDS

When you gotta go, you gotta go. Here are some final quotes from people who really knew how to make an exit.

"I'll be in hell before you've finished breakfast, boys...Let her rip!"

—"Black Jack" Ketchum, *murderer, before being hanged*

"The Countess Rouen sends her compliments but begs to be excused. She is engaged in dying."

—The Countess Rouen, *in a letter read by her attendant to her guests*

"Go away...I'm alright."

—H. G. Wells, *writer*

"God bless...God damn. . ."

—James Thurber, *writer*

"If this is dying, I don't think much of it."

—Lytton Strachey, *writer*

"Four o'clock. How strange. So that is the time. Strange. Enough."

—Sir Henry Stanley, *explorer*

"You sons of bitches. Give my love to mother."

—"Two Gun" Crowley, *sitting on the electric chair*

"Now comes the mystery."

—Henry Ward Beecher, *preacher*

"Oh God, here I go."

—Max Baer, *boxer*

"Friends applaud, the Comedy is over."

—Ludwig van Beethoven

"All my possessions for a moment of time."

—Elizabeth I, *Queen of England*

"And now, in keeping with Channel 40's policy of always bringing you the latest in blood and guts, in living color, you're about to see another first—an attempted suicide."

—Chris Hubbock, *newscaster who shot herself during broadcast*

"Drink to me."

—Pablo Picasso

"Why yes— a bullet-proof vest."

—James Rodgers, *murderer, before the firing squad, asked if he had final request*

Lip Service: Reuters News Service gave its founder a 17-word obituary.

ASTEROIDS

At the B.R.I. Science Department, we have a saying: A day without Bathroom Reading is like a pain in the asteroid. Ah, but what do we really know about asteroids? Read on...

BACKGROUND

• Asteroids are collections of rocks and dust half a mile or more in diameter. Scientists theorize they are leftover fragments from the Big Bang.

• Most asteroids orbit the sun in a large belt between Mars and Jupiter. Over a billion fragments reside in the belt, ranging from dust-sized particles to Ceres, an asteroid 637 miles in diameter.

• How do asteroids escape the asteroid belt? Through the Kirkwood Gap, named for Daniel Kirkwood, an American astronomer. He discovered that the belt was separated into two different regions by a mysterious gap. Asteroids that enter the gap shift into an orbit closer to Earth's. One out of five asteroids end up crossing Earth's orbit.

A MISS IS AS GOOD AS 500,000 MILES

On March 23, 1989, a huge asteroid passed within half a million miles (approximately twice the distance from the Earth to the Moon) of hitting the Earth. If the asteroid, which was traveling at 46,000 miles an hour, had actually crashed into Earth, it would have had a devastating impact, equivalent to exploding 20,000 one-megaton hydrogen bombs.

Scientists later calculated that the asteroid missed the Earth by six hours in its orbit. If it had hit Earth, the crater would have been 10 miles long and one mile deep.

ASTEROIDS IN THE PAST

• The first scientific finding that proved asteroids were not pieces of alien spacecraft occurred in 1803 in northern France.

• In 1908, an asteroid the size of a small building crashed near the Stony Tunguska River in Siberia. Its force was later measured to be equal to 12 megatons of TNT.

• In 1984, a Japan Air Lines flight saw a mushroom-like cloud 70,000 feet tall and 200 miles wide. The flight landed at a U.S. base in Anchorage, Alaska for fear it had flown through radiation, but no traces were found. Eventually, scientists concluded that the airliner may have passed through a cloud created by an exploding meteor.

• Scientists have found evidence of a huge asteroid collision around 100 miles off the coast of New Jersey from 34 million ago.

• An asteroid named Icarus came within four million miles of hitting Earth in 1968. This "near miss" prompted the notion that nuclear missiles could be deployed to deflect oncoming asteroids. In 1982, a scientific conference in Colorado concluded that a one-kilometer asteroid could be diverted by the using a nuclear device only half the power of the atomic bomb dropped on Hiroshima.

THE ODDS

• According to the *New York Times*, there are more than 80 asteroids of at least one kilometer that could threaten the Earth. Other scientists estimate there are over 1,000 asteroids with orbits that could collide with Earth's.

• Despite the danger, scientists say the chances of a giant asteroid colliding with Earth in our lifetime are relatively small—it only happens once every 100,000 years or so.

THE EFFECTS

• Scientists have argued that asteroid impacts in the past may have caused the Earth's magnetic field to reverse, triggering the ice age and ultimately continental drift, the breaking up of the continents 80 million years ago.

• The biggest recorded asteroid hit Earth 66 million years ago and spread lava over India. Some scientists have argued that its enormous impact eventually wiped out the dinosaurs by enveloping the Earth in dust and smoke, causing the Earth to cool.

• The dinosaur/asteroid theory arose after the discovery of the element iridium in the same geologic layers that existed when the dinosaurs disappeared. Iridium is abundant in asteroids.

On average, Salt Lake City citizens consume more Cracker Jacks than any other Americans.

IT'S THE LAW

Believe it or not, these laws are real.

In Logan County, Colorado, it's illegal to kiss a sleeping woman.

It's illegal to ride a camel on Nevada highways.

In North Carolina motels, it's a crime to move twin beds together or to make love on the floor.

In Miami, Florida, it's unlawful to imitate an animal.

Women in Morrisville, Pennsylvania, are required by law to purchase a permit before wearing lipstick in public.

Laws in Indianapolis, Indiana, and Eureka, Nevada, make it a crime to kiss if you wear a moustache.

New York City law entitles its horses to a 15 minute "coffee-break" after each two hours of work.

Children are prohibited from doing handstands on Denver, Colorado sidewalks—it might frighten horses.

It's a crime in Zion, Illinois to offer a cigar to a dog, cat, or any pet. No mention of cigarettes or pipes.

Laws in Boston, Massachusetts prohibit sleeping in "day clothes."

If your horse is ugly, the law prohibits you from riding it down a street in Wilbur, Washington.

In Minnesota, it's illegal for a woman to be dressed-up as Santa Claus on city streets.

Kansas law prohibits catching fish with your bare hands.

Arkansas law prohibits schoolteachers with "bob" hairdos from getting raises.

Don't even think about it—*Bull throwing* is illegal in Washington D.C.

You're breaking the law if you're wearing "form-fitting" pants in Lewes, Delaware.

A law in Hartford, Connecticut, prohibits the teaching or education of a dog.

Which beans are the most potent, flatulence-wise? Soybeans.

OPEN & CLOTHED

A few interesting tidbits about clothing.

BLUE FOR BOYS, PINK FOR GIRLS

The blue comes from an ancient superstition—the pink is sort of an afterthought.

According to *How Did They Do That?*, "The choice of blue dates back to ancient times, when evil spirits purportedly plagued young children but could be warded off with certain colors: blue, emblematic of the heavens, had an immanent power to dispel satanic forces (Many Arabs in the Mideast continue to paint their doorways blue.) Since it was of paramount importance to protect little boys, they were clothed in blue, while little girls were left to fend for themselves. Only much later did parents, somewhat guilty about the girls' lack of identity, assign them precious pink."

SUPERMAN'S CLOTHING

Every time George Reeves, TV's Superman, donned his costume for a public appearance, he risked kicks in the shins, fists in his back, and other assaults by young admirers eager to prove how strong the "Man of Steel" really was.

One afternoon in Detroit in 1953, the costume almost cost Reeves his life. He was making an appearance at a department store when a young fan pulled out his father's loaded .45 Army Colt and pointed it directly at Reeves's chest. Miraculously, Reeves talked the kid into putting it down. He assured the boy that Superman could stand the force of the shot, but "when bullets bounce off my chest, they might hurt you and others around here."

CHARLIE CHAPLIN'S TRAMP OUTFIT

In 1914, director Mack Sennet told Chaplin to "get into a comedy makeup." He scouted the dressing room and came up with baggy pants and derby belonging to the enormously overweight comedian, Fatty Arbuckle, a cutaway jacket from Roscoe Conklin, and a pair of size-14 shoes from Ford Sterling. They were so big that the only way to keep them on was to wear them on the wrong feet. The cane was the only thing Chaplin actually owned.

On July 22, 1972, a lady in Rome gave birth to quindecaplets—10 girls and 5 boys.

KUNG PHOOEY

Is it serious philosophy or TV gobbledygook? You be the judge of these quotes from TV's only "Buddhist" western, "Kung Fu."

"Grasshopper, look beyond the game, as you look beneath the surface of the pool to see its depths."

—Master Po

"The caterpillar is secure in the womb of the cocoon. And yet—to achieve its destiny—it must cast off its earthbound burden...to realize the ethereal beauty of the butterfly."

—Master Po

Master Po: "What have I told you, Grasshopper?"
Caine: "That life is a corridor and death merely a door."

"The blossom below the water knows not sunlight. And men, not knowing, will find me hard to understand."

—Caine

"Will shooting guns and making bombs make you men and not dogs?"

—Caine

"Seek always peace...We are all linked by our souls, and if one is endangered so are all."

—Caine

"To seek freedom, a man must struggle. To win it, he must choose wisely where and when he struggles, or it is like spitting in the wind."

—Caine

Caine: "Master Kan, what is it to be a man?"
Master Kan: "To be a man is to be one with the Universe."
Caine: "But what is the Universe?"
Master Kan: "Rather ask: what is *not* the Universe?"

"Remember always—a wise man walks with his head bowed, humble like the dust."

—Master Po

"The power to hope cannot be taken away with guns or fences."

—Caine

"Perceive the way of nature and no force of men can harm you. Do not meet a wave head-on, avoid it. You do not have to stop force; it is easier to redirect it."

—A *monk*

There are twice as many heart attacks in winter as in summer.

DON'T LOOK NOW

Here's a look at a few of the movies that have been banned in the U.S. over the last 75 years.

SPIRIT OF '76 (1917). A silent propaganda film made to enlist public support for America's entry into World War I. The film reenacted Revolutionary War events, like Paul Revere's ride and the signing of the Declaration of Independence.

One scene depicted British soldiers attacking women and children. Although the scene was realistic, England was America's ally in the war effort, so it was considered treasonous. Authorities seized the movie, alleging (erroneously) that the movie had been financed by Germans. The film's producer, Robert Goldstein—who later became an executive at 20th Century Fox—was convicted of violating the Espionage Act and was sentenced to jail (his sentence was later commuted by Woodrow Wilson).

THE NAKED TRUTH (1924). A silent movie about a man who gets venereal disease and marries. His brain is affected by V.D. and he kills his wife. Nudity, not subject matter, got this film banned in Newark, New Jersey due to a brief scene in which a male and female were shown partially naked.

Note: one of the main figures in the controversy, William J. Brennan (head of Newark's Public Safety Department), was the father of future Supreme Court Justice, William J. Brennan, Jr. Brennan upheld the censorship by refusing to see it and review the case. *The Naked Truth* was also banned in New York.

THE MAN WITH THE GOLDEN ARM (1955). Banned in Maryland for depicting drug use. The film, directed by Otto Preminger, was about a card shark (played by Frank Sinatra) who becomes a drug addict. The Maryland Board of Censors suggested that United Artists cut the scene of Sinatra being injected by a drug pusher. According to the *Historical Dictionary of Censorship in the United States*, the state of Maryland "was the only locality that attempted to censor this film: It was exhibited across the United States and Western Europe without problems, and even won a scientific and cultural award in the Netherlands." United Artists sued and a judge reversed the order.

TITICUT FOLLIES (1969). A documentary on the horrible conditions in a state prison for the criminally insane in Bridgewater, Massachusetts. Scenes included a forced nose-feeding of an inmate on a hunger strike.

Producer and director Frederick Wiseman received permission to make the film as long as he protected the privacy of the film's subjects. However, when the documentary was shown commercially, the state of Massachusetts filed suit, contending the film had violated their contract and the inmates' privacy. Massachusetts won, and the Supreme Court refused to hear an appeal. The result: The documentary was put under permanent court restrictions. Selected audiences were allowed to view the film as long as profits were put into a trust fund for the inmates.

Wiseman later commented, "There was no evidence introduced at the trial that the film was not an honest portrayal of the conditions...if [then State Attorney General Elliot] Richardson and the other politicians in Massachusetts were genuinely concerned about the privacy and dignity of the inmates of Bridgewater, they would not have allowed the conditions that are shown in the film to exist. They were more concerned about the film and its effect on their reputations than they were about Bridgewater."

CINDY AND DONNA (1970). The Sheriff of Pulaski Country, Kentucky went to see this X-rated film at a drive-in. After staying for the entire motion picture, the Sheriff arrested the manager of the theatre and confiscated the film. The manager was convicted of exhibiting an obscene film. He appealed to the Supreme Court, which overturned the conviction on the grounds that no warrant had been served.

CARNAL KNOWLEDGE (1971). This film starring Jack Nicholson, Art Garfunkle, Candice Bergen, and Ann-Margaret was a critically-acclaimed drama about two college friends who take different roads in life; one straight, the other a swinger. The state of Georgia ruled that the film was obscene. In 1974, the Supreme Court found that it was not obscene. William Rehnquist delivered the opinion, stating, "the subject of the picture is, in a broad sense,

Americans eat over 7 billion quarts of popcorn a year. 10% of it is eaten at movie theaters.

sex...(but) the camera does not focus on the bodies of the actors at such times."

DEEP THROAT (1972). The most-banned film in United States history (25 states brought it to trial) starred Linda Lovelace and Harry Reems. The X-rated skin flick was first ruled obscene in Georgia. Lovelace later denounced her role in the film, which made millions at the box-office.

CALIGULA (1980). *Penthouse* publisher Bob Guccione produced this screen version of Gore Vidal's novel about the bloody reign of the Roman Empire's fourth Caesar. The film, starring Malcolm McDowell, Sir John Gielgud, and Peter O'Toole (all of whom later officially "disassociated" themselves from the final product),showed explicit sex and violence, earning an X rating. It was banned in Boston and Atlanta, but a judge in Boston refused to uphold an obsenity claim, ruling the subject was related to historical facts. The Supreme Court ruled in 1984, agreeing that the film was not obscene. "Caligula" became the largest-grossing X-rated film ever produced independently, although critics hated it, and at least one of the actresses tried to sue the producer for talking her into performing in an X-rated scene.

THE WINDY CITY

Chicago is the "Big Banned" of America when it comes to motion pictures. Among the censorship battles that have taken place there:

• Chicago censors denied licenses to show newsreels criticizing Nazi Germany before WWII. They also banned Charlie Chaplin's "The Great Dictator," a parody of Hitler, for fear of upsetting the large German population of the city.

• They banned newsreels which showed scenes of Chicago policemen shooting at union protestors.

• They refused to issue a permit for the movie *Anatomy of a Murder* because the words "rape" and "contraceptive" were used.

• They deleted scenes of a buffalo giving birth in Walt Disney's "Vanishing Prairie," the 1954 Academy Award-winning documentary.

STENGEL-ESE

Legendary New York Yankees and Mets manager Casey Stengel offers a few confusing words of wisdom.

To a hitter with the bases loaded: "Let him hit 'ya; I'll get you a new neck."

"There are three things you can do in a baseball game. You can win, or you can lose, or it can rain."

"Now all you fellers line up alphabetically by height."

"You have to have a catcher, because if you don't, the pitch will roll all the way back to the screen."

"They say you can't do it, but sometimes it doesn't always work."

"Look at that guy. Can't run, can't hit, can't catch. Of course, that's why they gave him to us."

On two 20-year-old players: "In 10 years, Ed Kranepool has a chance to be a star. In 10 years, Greg Goosen has a chance to be 30."

"We're in such a slump that even the ones that are drinkin' aren't hittin'."

"Good pitching will always stop good hitting, and vice versa."

"I love signing autographs. I'll sign anything but veal cutlets. My ballpoint pen slips on veal cutlets."

"The secret of managing a club is to keep the five guys who hate you away from the five who are undecided."

"The Mets have come along slow, but fast!"

"Being with a woman all night never hurt no professional ballplayer. It's staying up all night looking for a woman that does him in."

"I'll never make the mistake again of being 70 years old."

"They say some of my stars drink whiskey, but I have found that the ones who drink milkshakes don't win many ball games."

"Most ball games are lost, not won."

The fourth most common language in the U.S. is sign language.

MYTH AMERICA

1992 is the 500th anniversary of Columbus's historic voyage. So it's a good time to clear up a few myths about him.

THE MYTH: Columbus proved the Earth was round.
THE TRUTH: The ancient Greeks knew the world wasn't flat two thousand years before Columbus was born. Pythagoras came up with the theory in the in sixth century B.C., and Ptolemy proved it in the second century A.D. Before Columbus even left on his first voyage to the New World, he studied globes and maps depicting a round planet. He had a hard time finding funding for his voyage, not because his contemporaries thought he would sail off the earth's edge, but because they thought the Orient was too far to reach by sailing west.

THE MYTH: He was the first European to discover North America.
THE TRUTH: Columbus never even set foot on the North American continent. The closest he ever came was the islands of the Caribbean and South America. The America whose "discovery" we celebrate is actually a tiny island near San Salvador, which was already inhabited anyway. Even Columbus wouldn't take credit for discovering a new continent—he died thinking he he had reached India. Actually, the Vikings were the first Europeans to reach North America, around 1000 A.D.

THE MYTH: Columbus was a friend to the Indians.
THE TRUTH: Sad to say, that's not even close. Take his Haitian exploits for example: According to historian Howard Zinn, Arawak Indians who didn't honor Columbus and his crew with regular contributions of gold "had their hands cut off and bled to death." After two years, half of Haiti's 250,000 inhabitants were dead "through murder, mutilation, or suicide." Many of the native Indians who survived were enslaved and brought back to Spain. "Let us in the name of the Holy Trinity, go on sending all the slaves that can be sold," Columbus wrote.

MILITARY DOUBLE-TALK

What is the Pentagon spending our money on this year? See if you can figure it out. Try to match these official U.S.military terms with their civilian meanings. *Answers on page 674.*

1. "Interlocking slide fastener."
2. "Portable hand-held communications transcriber."
3. "Weapons system."
4. "Hexiform rotatable surface compression unit."
5. "Special weapon."
6. "Habitability improvements."
7. "Vertically deployed anti-personnel device."
8. "Aerodynamic personnel decelerator."
9. "Wood interdental stimulator."
10. "Universal obscurant."
11. "Kinetic kill vehicle launcher."
12. "Missionized crew station."
13. "Radiation enhancement weapon."
14. "Interfibrous friction fastener."

A. Neutron bomb
B. Hammer
C. Parachute
D. Toothpick
E. Cockpit
F. Smoke from smoke bombs
G. Steel nut
H. Anti-satellite weapon
I. Bayonet
J. Pencil
K. Zipper
L. Atomic bomb
M. Furniture
N. Bomb

YOU BE THE JUDGE

On July 20, 1969, Neil Armstrong became the first human being to set foot on the moon. But his famous comment, "That's one small step for man, one giant leap for mankind" has caused some controversy. Did he write the words himself...or did someone at NASA slip him the line? No one knows for sure, but here are some clues that may help you decide for yourself.

CLUE #1

The quote doesn't make sense. Apparently, Armstrong meant to say "one small step for a man" instead of "one small step for man." What are the odds that he would have misquoted himself? (Armstrong claims he said "one small step for a man" but the "a" dropped out during transmission).

CLUE #2

In 1983, Armstrong told *Esquire* that he made the words up after—not before—landing on the Moon. With all the pressure and details to take care of, how likely is it that he could have come up with such an eloquent phrase?

CLUE #3

The quote—with the correct "a" included—appeared on a NASA press blackboard only minutes after Armstrong uttered the words. Did NASA know in advance about the quote?...And if so, doesn't that contradict Armstrong's own testimony?

CLUE #4

Armstrong is often described as the archtypical "strong and silent type." Many thought the words didn't sound like something he'd ordinarily say. Wouldn't Armstrong have asked a writer to help coin a phrase for such a momentous event?

CLUE #5

Space flight is a highly regimented process. Would NASA allow an astronaut to write the history of the space agency's finest hour with just anything that came into his mind? Don't forget—billions of people were watching and listening.

CLUE #6

One writer, Oriana Fallaci, tried to prove Armstrong would not have been allowed to improvise on the spot. She bet astronaut Pete Conrad that he wouldn't be allowed to say "It may be a small step for Neil, but it's a big step for a little fellow like me" during the Apollo 12 mission. But Conrad did say the words (he claims Fallaci never paid up the $500 bet).

YOU BE THE JUDGE

No one's ever proven whether or not Armstrong authored the phrase. Buzz Aldrin, his Apollo moonwalking partner, has defended Armstrong. So has every NASA official. What do you think?

★ ★ ★

MORE JUNK ABOUT SPACE JUNK

• After only a handful of human visits, the moon is already littered. Apollo astronauts left behind a space buggy, camera equipment (worth $5,000,000) and the two golf balls that Alan Shepard hit.

• On the average, more than three man-made objects crash into Earth each week.

• In 1969, five crewmen on a Japanese freighter in the Sea of Japan were seriously injured after debris from a Soviet spacecraft crashed into their ship.

• Thus far, the most famous object to fall to earth was the 78-ton U.S. Skylab, which caused a world scare during the days leading up to its reentry. Despite an international scare, the debris from Skylab did not kill anybody; instead it exploded over the Indian Ocean and the Australian Outback. The debris from Skylab was considered public domain; i.e., finders, keepers. A 17-year truck driver named Stan Thornton won a $10,000 prize from the *San Francisco Examiner* by being the first person to turn in a piece of Skylab.

EDISON ENLIGHTENS

Thomas Edison was a genius inventor who gave us the electric light, the phonograph, and movies. He also gave most of the credit for his accomplishments to hard work, not brilliance. Some of his ideas:

"Genius is one percent inspiration and ninety-nine percent perspiration."

"The chief function of your body is to carry your brain around."

"We don't know a millionth of one percent about anything."

"Restlessness and discontent are the first necessities of progress."

"I am glad that the eight-hour day had not been invented when I was a young man. If my life had been made up of eight-hour days I do not believe I could have accomplished a great deal. This country would not amount to as much as it does…if the young men had been afraid that they might earn more than they were paid."

"I am long on ideas, but short on time. I expect to live to be only about a hundred."

"The inventor tries to meet the demands of a crazy civilization."

"I never did anything worth doing by accident, nor did any of my inventions come by accident; they came by work."

"Everything comes to him who hustles while he waits."

"To my mind the old masters are not art; their value is in their scarcity."

"Not only will atomic power be released, but someday we will harness the rise and fall of the tides and imprison the rays of the sun."

"There is no substitute for hard work."

"When down in the mouth remember Jonah—he came out all right!"

"The English are not an inventive people; they don't eat enough pie."

RECYCLING FACTS

Here are some fascinating facts from the EarthWorks Group's handy new book, "The Recycler's Handbook."

Some 94,000 cans are recycled every minute in America.

• Americans use 100 million steel and tin cans every day. We recycle about 5% of them...which means we dump more than 30 billion into landfills every year.

• Americans use enough corrugated cardboard in a year to make a bale the size of a football field and the height of the World Trade Center. About 40% of it is recycled.

• If Americans recycled half our newsprint every year, we'd need 3,200 fewer garbage trucks to collect municipal trash.

• Americans throw away enough used motor oil every year to fill 120 supertankers. It could all be recycled.

• According to the EPA, we create enough garbage every year to fill a convoy of 10-ton garbage trucks 145,000 miles long—more than halfway from here to the moon.

• About 70 million car batteries are recycled in the U.S. each year. The other 15-20%, with 165,000 tons of lead, go to landfills.

• To make plastics, the U.S. uses about a billion barrels of petroleum by-products each year. How much is that? Enough to fill over 56,000 olympic-sized swimming pools.

• According to the Glass Packaging Institute, we now use around 41 billion glass containers a year—an average of about 165 per person. How much of that is recycled? About 30%...which means nearly 30 billion glass containers go into landfills.

• Every year, Americans dispose of 1.6 billion pens, 2 billion razors and blades, and 18 billion diapers. They're all sitting in landfills somewhere.

• In 1988, about 9 million automobile bodies—more than American automobile plants produced that year—were recycled.

New York City has been host to only 27 ticker-tape parades, total.

COLLEGE NAMES

We know the names—Cornell, Harvard, Stanford…
Here's where a few of them come from.

Brown University. Nicholas Brown, a member of a wealthy Rhode Island shipping family, gave a $5,000 endowment to Rhode Island College in 1804. By that time, Brown's family had given the school more than $160,000, and officials decided a name-change was in order.

Cornell University. Samuel Morse invented the telegraph, but it was Ezra Cornell who put it to work. He devised a practical method of stringing insulated wires along telephone poles, and provided the first telegraph service to the cities of the northeast. His initial donation of land and $500,000 put the school on its feet.

Stanford University. Amasa Leland Stanford, a robber baron who got himself elected governor of California and a U.S. senator, founded the university in memory of his son, Leland Jr., who died of typhoid fever at the age of 15.

Johns Hopkins University. Humbled by his own poor education, Johns Hopkins, a wealthy Baltimore merchant and banker, willed $7,000,000 to found the now famous university and hospital.

Duke University. Once there was a school in North Carolina called Trinity College. Then, in 1925, a wealthy tobacco, textiles and utilities magnate named James B. Duke gave them $107 million. Suddenly, the name Duke had a certain ring to it.

Harvard University. In 1638 John Harvard, a wealthy Massachusetts settler, left half his estate—$1,480—to a two-year-old local bible college. It was the largest gift to the new school at that point; the school repaid the favor by calling itself Harvard College.

Brigham Young University. Named after one of the founding fathers of the Church of Jesus Christ of Latter Day Saints (the Mormons).

There are about 800 tombstones in Tombstone, Arizona.

SPACE NAZIS

Whatever happened to the scientists who supplied Hitler's war machine with its advanced weaponry? Many of them moved to the U.S. at our government's invitation, to join our space program.

Following the defeat of Germany at the end of World War II, the United States began Project Paperclip, a secret program that employed "ex"-Nazis in U.S. scientific efforts. Many of the scientists smuggled into America by our government had committed war crimes—but U.S. officials didn't care. In fact, information about their past was deliberately covered up to circumvent laws that prohibited Nazi collaborators from entering the country.

CODE NAME: OVERCAST

According to Linda Hunt's 1985 exposé in the *Bulletin of the Atomic Scientists*, the scheme "grew from the notion that German and Austrian scientists were part of the spoils of the war which had been won against Nazi Germany." Initially, the top secret program, whose code name was Overcast, called for temporary immigration of "Nazi experts in rocketry, aircraft design, aviation, medicine, and other fields," writes Hunt. "But by early 1946, the War Department found their skills too valuable to lose and pushed for a revised program that would allow them to stay in the United States."

SEAL OF APPROVAL

In early 1946, Overcast was renamed Project Paperclip and the operation was approved by President Harry S. Truman. According to official policy, "No person found...to have been a member of the Nazi Party and more than a nominal participant in its activities or an active supporter of Naziism or militarism shall be brought to the U.S."

But government agencies ignored these regulations. Records of the German scientists' Nazi backrounds were routinely altered and sometimes deleted altogether. As a result, perpetrators of some of the most heinous war crimes in World War II soon became full-fledged American citizens. From 1945 to 1952, 765 German scientists were admitted to the U.S. All of them were committed Nazis.

CASE HISTORIES

Arthur Rudolph. Designed the Saturn 5 rocket used in the Apollo moon landings. During World War II, he was the operations director of the Mittelwerk factory at the Dora-Nordhausen concentration camp in Germany, where 20,000 workers were tortured to death. At first, Rudolph denied to U.S. officials that he had witnessed any incidents of abuse at the camp, but later admitted seeing 12 prisoners hanged from a crane ("I do know that one lifted his knees after I got there," Rudolph testified).

An earlier 1945 military file had concluded that Rudolph was "100% Nazi, dangerous type, security threat!!!" This appraisal was ignored, however, and Rudolph was allowed to become a U.S. citizen. In 1984, while under investigation for his war record, Rudolph fled to West Germany.

Wernher von Braun. Instrumental in many areas of NASA's Apollo program. In 1947, von Braun was labeled an "SS officer" and "potential security threat" to the United States. But several months later, a new security evaluation, specifically rewritten to allow von Braun to emigrate, claimed "no derogatory information is available...like the majority of members, he may have been a mere opportunist." Von Braun was subsequently allowed to come to the U.S., despite the fact that his V-2 rocket had been used to bombard London during World War II. He became an American celebrity and was even showcased as a role model for American children during the 1950s and early 1960s.

Kurt Blome. A high-ranking Nazi scientist who was put on trial at Nuremberg in 1947 for conducting human experiments. Although he was acquitted there, it was generally accepted that the charges had basis in fact: During a 1945 interrogation by the U.S. military, Blome admitted that he had been ordered in 1943 to experiment with plague vaccines on concentration camp prisoners.

Two months after his Nuremberg acquittal, Blome was being interviewed in Camp David, Maryland, for information about biological warfare. He supplied technological details and names of Nazi collaborators in his experiments.

In 1951, the U.S. Army Chemical Corps chose to ignore Blome's background when it hired him to work on chemical warfare for "Project 63," the U.S.'s secret effort to hire Germans scientists before the Russians got to them. Nowhere in Blome's files did it mention his arrest or trial at Nuremberg.

Hermann Becker-Freysing and ***Siegfried Ruff.*** Both Becker-Freysing and Ruff (and 21 others) were charged at the Nuremberg War Crimes trials for participating in cruel medical experiments on Dachau concentration camp inmates. Before the trials began, however, both were contacted by the Army Air Force Aero Center in Heidelberg, Germany. According to the *Bulletin of the Atomic Scientists*, Becker-Freysing and Ruff were paid "to write reports or conduct laboratory tests for the Army Air Force's use that were based on wartime experiments which Nuremberg prosecutors later charged had been conducted on concentration camp victims." Becker-Freysing was later found guilty and sentenced to 20 years in jail for conducting seawater experiments on prisoners at Dachau. Ruff was acquitted for conducting experiments that killed over 80 Dachau inmates who had been locked in a chamber that simulated high altitude pressure.

Konrad Schaefer. Schaefer was charged in the Nuremberg trials for his role in Becker-Freysing's sea water experiments. According to the charges, Schaefer oversaw experiments on Dachau concentration camp inmates who were starved and then force-fed sea water that had been chemically altered to make it drinkable. Like Becker-Freysing and Ruff, Schaefer was paid by the Aero Center to inform the Army and Air Force about his experiments.

In 1949, Schaefer was allowed to enter the United States in spite of the fact he had admitted to having been tried at Nuremberg (he was acquitted, despite evidence that he had attended planning meetings for the experiments.) Ironically, when Schaefer was sent back to Germany in 1951, it was not because of his war crimes—the Air Force simply could not find a job for him.

OBJECTIONS

In 1947, the *Bulletin of the Atomic Scientists* ran one of the first exposes on Project Paperclip. The two authors of the piece, Hans Bethe and H.S. Sack argued against the immigration of the

The American slogan, "In God We Trust," was not adopted until 1956.

ex-Nazi scientists: "Is it wise, from a long-range point of view, or even compatible with our moral standards, to make this bargain? Would it not have been better to restrict the stay of these scientists in this country to the absolute minimum? For it must be borne in mind that many of them, probably the majority, are diehard Nazis, or at least worked wholeheartedly with the Nazis; otherwise they would not have held their high posts so vital for the Nazi war machine."

JUSTIFICATION

Addressing the moral argument about using war criminals, Bosquet Wev, the director of the Joint intelligence Objectives Agency said in a 1947 memorandum: "The best interests of the United States have been subjugated to the efforts expended in 'beating a dead Nazi horse'...the return of these scientists to Germany would present a far greater security threat to the United States than their retention."

DENUNCIATION

In December, 1946, Albert Einstein, Norman Vincent Peale and other prominent Americans issued protests to the American government concerning Project Paperclip. But the issue quickly died down, since little information was made public.

THE END OF PAPERCLIP

Project Paperclip came to an end in 1957 after 11 years. Ironically, the government of West Germany began to complain of a "brain drain" of its best scientists. Since that time, writes Linda Hunt, many of imported ex-Nazi scientists "have received the highest honors bestowed by the military on civilians and have risen to top positions at NASA and other governmental agencies and in private industry."

And Now for Something Completely Different…

"What kind of animals were the dinosaurs? Up until the last decade, many scientists would have answered with confidence: Dinosaurs were huge, slow-moving, cold-blooded reptiles of the past… Today some paleontologists offer radically different views: Dinosaurs were active, perhaps even warm-blooded animals, comparable to modern mammals and birds." —*National Geographic*, 1978

DISNEY STORIES: PINOCCHIO

The original Pinocchio was written by an Italian educator named Carlo Lorenzini (using the name Carlo Collodi) in 1883. It was adapted by Disney at a cost of $2.5 million and released in 1940. Although it contains "some of the finest art and animation sequences every produced," it wasn't a big hit. Of course, the Disney version and the original story were substantially different. Here are Jim Morton's examples of how the tale was changed.

THE DISNEY VERSION

• Geppetto, a kindly old wood carver, makes a marionette named Pinocchio. Then he wishes (on a star) that the puppet were a real boy, so he could have a son.

• A talking bug named Jiminy Cricket is appointed Pinocchio's conscience. He follows Pinocchio on a series of adventures.

• Pinocchio is accosted by a fox and a cat—two humorous con artists—is sold to Stromboli, and sent to Pleasure Island, where dumb, selfish boys are turned into beasts. Pinocchio narrowly escapes being turned into a donkey.

• He's eventually reunited with Geppetto in the belly of a whale; Geppetto was swallowed while he was out looking for Pinocchio.

• Pinocchio helps the wood carver escape, and for his unselfishness, he's turned into a real boy. Jiminy Crickett beams and sings.

THE ORIGINAL VERSION

• Disney follows the main themes of the book, but skips over the grim moments from the original story.

• For example: When Pinocchio hides his gold coins in his mouth, the cat attempts to force Pinocchio's mouth open with a knife. Pinocchio bites the cat's paw off and spits it out. While he's running away, Pinocchio meets a zombie girl. Then the fox and cat hang him by the neck, trying to make him spit out the gold.

• The biggest difference between the Disney Version and the book is Jiminy Cricket. In the book, the cricket has no name. It appears early in the story and is promptly smashed with a hammer by Pinocchio. Later in the tale, the cricket's ghost pops up as a sort of insect Obi Wan Kenobi, offering Pinocchio guidance (rarely heeded) as he goes on his journeys.

• Also in the original, on Pleasure Island (called Playland in the book), Pinocchio does turn into a donkey and is sold at the market. He's forced to perform in a circus before going lame. Then he's sold to a man who plans to use Pinocchio's skin to make a drum. The man tries to drown Pinocchio, but fish eat the donkey skin off him, revealing the puppet inside.

• Pinocchio does rescue Geppetto, but from the belly of a shark, not a whale. This deed alone isn't enough to turn Pinocchio into a boy. The puppet works from sunrise to sundown every day for five months before his wish is finally granted.

SAMPLE PASSAGES (FROM THE ORIGINAL)

"'Why are you sorry for me?' Pinocchio asked the cricket.

"'Because you are a puppet, and—what is worse—you have a wooden head,' the cricket replied.

"At these last words, Pinocchio lost his temper and, seizing a mallet from the bench, threw it at the cricket.

"Perhaps he did not mean to hit him, but unfortunately the mallet struck the cricket right to the head. The poor insect had scarcely time to cry 'Cri-cri-cri,' and there he was, stretched out stiff, flattened against the wall."

• • •

The fox and cat are trying to rob Pinnochio.

"'Ah-ha, you rascal! So you hid your money under your tongue! Spit it out at once!'

"Pinocchio did not obey.

"'Oh, so you can't hear? Then we'll make you spit it out.'

"And one of them seized the puppet by the end of his nose, and the other by his chin, and they pulled without mercy, one up, the other down, to make him open his mouth; but it was no use.

"Then the smaller assassin drew a horrid knife and tried to force it between his lips, like a chisel, but Pinocchio, quick as lightning, bit off his hand and spat it out. Imagine his astonishment when he saw that it was a cat's paw."

The heads of a two-headed snake will fight over food—even though they share one stomach.

THE ARCHIES

When you were a kid, were Archie *comics part of your bathroom reading? Here's a new* Archie *story from* Behind the Hits, *by Bob Shannon and John Javna.*

If you grew up in post-World War II America, the chances are you've read at least one *Archie* comic book in your life. As Maurice Horn says in *The World Encyclopedia of Comics*, "Archie, like Batman, Superman, and a small handful of others, has transcended comic books into pure Americana. There will, it often seems, always be an Archie. It is inevitable as death and taxes."

THE '40s & '50s: ARCHIE'S EARLY DAYS

Archie Andrews, a red-headed, freckle-faced creation of cartoonist Bob Montana, first appeared in *Pep* comic books in 1941. He was portrayed as the "typical" American teenager of the '40s, and he was so popular that within a year he had his own comic book. His audience increased. He starred in a radio show. By the '50s, a whole cast of characters—and more comic book titles—had evolved.

Now Archie and his pals from Riverdale High were the "typical" American teenagers of the '50s. Maybe you remember that Archie had a red jalopy and a big crush on rich and snooty Veronica Lodge; Jughead Jones wore a strange-looking beanie and loved hamburgers; Betty, Veronica's best friend and rival, was hopelessly in love with Archie; Moose was a super-strong but super-dumb athlete; and so on. They all hung out at Pop's Malt Shoppe when they weren't in school under Mr. Weatherbee's watchful eye.

ARCHIE IN THE '60s

But as popular as the Archie clan was in the '40s and '50s, the '60s was their golden decade. With the help of the cartoon show that premiered on CBS in 1968, sales of everything connected to Archie characters, from lunch boxes to comic books, skyrocketed. For example, best-selling comics normally sold about 300,000 copies a month in the '60s; in 1969, at the height of the cartoon show's popularity, *Archie* comics sold over a million a month!

ARCHIE ANDREWS, ROCK STAR

Included in this fantastic marketing windfall was a scheme to

The cold season: Divorce rates rise in the winter.

merchandise the Archie characters as a Monkees-style rock 'n' roll group. The Monkees had already proven TV's effectiveness in selling records to American kids. Now the people behind the Archie TV show wanted to cash in on the same appeal. They hired the man behind the Monkees' hits, Don Kirshner, as "music supervisor," and he began putting together a session group to make records as the Archies. Since the stars of this TV series were animated, Kirshner didn't have to put up with what he must have regarded as prima donna actors again (his association with the Monkees ended on unfriendly terms). For this job, he could just hire anonymous studio singers.

DANTE'S INFERNO

Enter Ron Dante, an out-of-work jingle and demo singer whose only previous hit ("The Leader of the Laundramat") had been credited to the Detergents. Says Dante, "[Kirshner] was casting for the Archies, and he was listening to a lot of singers. I heard that a musician friend of mine was playing on the session, and I just happened to fall by and say, 'Why don't you try me?' I auditioned for it because I had just written a Broadway show that bombed, and my career in Broadway had gone down the drain. So I said, 'I think I'd better jump back into records and take anything I can get my hands on,' and that was the beginning of it. I went and auditioned; I sang for about a half-hour.

"The next day, they called me and said, 'All right, you're gonna do the season's music.' We must have done a hundred tunes that first season. Over the years, I must have done about three or four hundred songs for the Archies. I auditioned with songs like 'Bang Shang-A-Lang' and 'Truck driver,' and I said, 'Here I go again.'"

HOW SWEET IT IS

The Archies released an album in 1968, and had a moderate hit with "Bang Shang-A-Lang" that year. But their second single—"Sugar Sugar"—was a smash. It became the biggest-selling record of 1969, with total sales of over four million. It was even covered by Wilson Pickett, who turned it into a Top 25 hit as a soul song. The Archies had two more Top 40 singles in the next year. But a proposed Archies tour was not to be. "They wanted me to dye my hair and put freckles on and go out as Archie," Dante says, "and I said, 'Oh boy, is this a career move, or what?' "

In anonymous surveys, 40% of Americans confessed cheating on their taxes.

GROUCHO GOSSIP

How did the Groucho Marx and his brothers get into show business? And where did they get those funny names? Now it can be told. From Cult TV by John Javna.

Julius Henry Marx (Groucho's real name) wasn't happy when his mother pushed him into becoming a vaudevillian. His dream was to become a doctor. But soon he, two brothers and a friend were touring backwater theaters as the Four Nightingales.

WISECRACKS

They were less than successful. During a performance in Texas, the entire audience left the theater to catch an escaped mule. When they returned, the angry brothers dropped their regular act and ad-libbed a routine mocking the patrons instead. They expected boos, but they got laughter. It changed the Marx brothers' act forever: they learned they could make fun of people and get away with it.

NAME GAME

Years later, another piece fell into place. Julius and his brothers were playing poker with a friend who was making fun of a popular comic character named "Knocko the Monk." The friend made up a similar name for each of them. Leo became Chicko because he chased women constantly. Adolph became Harpo (he played the harp). Milton became Gummo (because he liked to chew gum?). And Julius, who groused constantly, became Groucho.

LUCKY BREAK

The Marx Brothers might never have become stars if it hadn't been for a lucky accident. One night in 1924, a major play-opening was cancelled in New York. Reviewers, left with nothing else to see that night, showed up at the opening of a new Marx brothers' vaudeville act instead. They expected to find a typically boring variety act—but the surprised reviewers loved the Marx Brothers. Their rave reviews made Groucho and his family instant celebrities and Broadway stars...which led to Hollywood.

BANNED BOOKS

It can't happen here? Guess again. Each year, the American Booksellers Association holds a "Banned Books Week" to call attention to the issues surrounding censorship. Here are some books that were banned, or nearly banned, during the 1980s.

The Diary of Anne Frank, by Anne Frank. In 1983 members of the Alabama State Textbook Committee wanted the book rejected because it was "a real downer."

Lord of the Flies, by William Golding. In 1981 the book was challenged by a high school in Owen, North Carolina because it was "demoralizing inasmuch as it implies that man is little more than an animal."

Biology, by Karen Arms and Pamela S. Camp. In 1985 the Garland, Texas textbook selection committee complained of "overly explicit diagrams of sexual organs."

The American Pageant: A History of the Republic, by Thomas A. Bailey and David M. Kennedy. In 1984 officials in the Racine, Wisconsin School District complained the book contained "a lot of funny pictures of Republicans and nicer pictures of Democrats."

Zen Buddhism: Selected Writings, by D.T. Suzuki. In 1987 the school system of Canton, Michigan was informed that "this book details the teaching of the religion of Buddhism in such a way that the reader could very likely embrace its teachings and choose this as his religion."

1984, by George Orwell. In 1981 the book was challenged in Jackson Country, Florida because it was "pro-communist and contained explicit sexual matter."

Slugs, by David Greenburg. In 1985 an elementary school in Escondido, California banned the book for describing "slugs being dissected with scissors."

A Light In the Attic, by Shel Silverstein. In 1986 the popular children's book was challenged at an elementary school in Mukwonago, Wisconsin because it "gloried Satan, suicide and cannibalism, and also encouraged children to be disobedient."

The Crucible, by Arthur Miller. In 1982 citizens of Harrisburg, Pennsylvania complained about staging a play with "sick words from the mouths of demon-possessed people. It should be wiped out of the schools or the school board should use them to fuel the fire of hell."

Slaughterhouse Five, by Kurt Vonnegut. In 1985 complaints were made in an Owensboro, Kentucky high school library because the book had "foul language, a section depicting a picture of an act of bestiality, a reference to 'Magic Fingers' attached to the protagonist's bed to help him sleep, and the sentence: 'The gun made a ripping sound like the opening of the fly of God Almighty.' "

Meet the Werewolf, by Georgess McHargue. In 1983 the school district of Vancouver, Oregon claimed the book was "full of comments about becoming a werewolf, use of opium, and pacts with the devil."

Album Cover Album, by Roger Dean. (A book of album covers). In 1987 the Vancouver, Washington school district objected to a photo of the "Statue of Liberty with bare breasts as exemplary of several photos that were pretty raw toward women."

The Amazing Bone, by William Steig. In 1986 a parent in Lambertville, New Jersey complained to the local school library about "the use of tobacco by the animals" in this fantasy.

The Haunting Of America, by Jean Anderson. In 1985 an elementary school in Lakeland, Florida claimed it "would lead children to believe in demons without realizing it."

SIDENOTE: Lewis Caroll's **Alice's Adventures In Wonderland** was banned in China in 1931. Authorities objected that "animals should not use human language, and that it was disastrous to put animals and human beings on the same level."

An automatic spaghetti-spinning fork was patented in 1950.

DON'T QUOTE ME ON THAT

You'd be surprised how many famous quotes were never actually said by the people they're attributed to. Here are some classic examples.

The Quote: "Play it again, Sam." —*Humphrey Bogart*
The Truth: The real line from *Casablanca* is "You played it for her, you can play it for me. If she can stand it, I can—Play it." Dooley Wilson (Sam) didn't really play it. In real life, Wilson couldn't play the piano; the accompaniment was dubbed in afterwards.

The Quote: "Elementary, my dear Watson." —*Sherlock Holmes*
The Truth: Arthur Conan Doyle wrote four novels and 56 short stories that feature his detective; Holmes doesn't say it in any of them. Basil Rathbone, an actor who portrayed the sleuth in films of the 1930s and 1940s, was the one who made the line famous.

The Quote: "I cannot tell a lie." —*George Washington*
The Truth: Washington's biographer, Mason Weems, fabricated the whole cherry tree incident six years after Washington's death.

The Quote: "Hold on, Mr. President!" —*Sam Donaldson*
The Truth: The aggressive White House television reporter claims he never said it at any of the presidential press conferences he covered, although it is the title of a recent book he wrote.

The Quote: "Win one for the Gipper." —*George Gipp*
The Truth: Knute Rockne, the Notre Dame football coach to whom dying player George Gipp allegedly spoke his final words, was known for embellishing the truth to inspire his players. Experts believe that Rockne—who first told the story a long eight years after Gipp's death—made it up.

In the United States, there are four times more astrologers than astronomers.

The Quote: "You dirty rat!" —*James Cagney*
The Truth: Cagney denied ever saying this in any of his movies.

The Quote: "Go west, young man." —*Horace Greeley*
The Truth: A man named John Babsone Soule first wrote it in an article for Indiana's *Terre Haute Express* in 1851. Greeley reprinted the article in his *New York Tribune*, but gave full credit to Soule.

The Quote: "On the whole, I'd rather be in Philadelphia."
—*W.C. Fields*

The Truth: Fields' alleged epitaph first appeared as a joke in a *Vanity Fair* magazine around 1950, after his death.

The Quote: "The government is best which governs least."
—*Thomas Jefferson*

The Truth: Historians can't find evidence that the founding father ever said it.

The Quote: "There are three kinds of lies: lies, damn lies, and statistics." — *Mark Twain*
The Truth: In his autobiography, Twain credited this saying to Benjamin Disraeli.

The Quote: "Judy, Judy, Judy." —*Cary Grant*
The Truth: The line comes from a popular impersonation of Grant by comedian Larry Storch.

The Quote: "War is hell." —*William T. Sherman*
The Truth: The Union general really said, "There is many a boy here today who looks on war as all glory, but, boys, it is all hell."

The Quote: "He who hesitates is lost." —*Joseph Addison*
The Truth: The original line from his play *Cato*, is, "The woman that deliberates is lost."

Every single day, L.A. residents drive 142 million miles—the distance from Earth to Mars.

AIN'T THAT A SHAME

Here's an interesting commentary on old-time rock, from Behind The Hits, *by Bob Shannon and John Javna.*

One of the more sordid aspects of rock'n'roll's early history was "cover artists," the white guys who imitated black artists who created the songs, the arrangements, and the harmonies. But the worst part wasn't that the cover artists were imitators—the worst part was that they copied the black artists' records while the original version was still new. So the cover versions competed with—and usually did better than—the originals. The difference between them was often minor; one rendition sounded like it was done by white singers, the other sounded like it was done by black singers. So lily-white radio stations pushed the songs done by by "acceptable" (white) artists. And these artists became stars.

MR. RIPOFF

A good example is Pat Boone. Pat, a pious fellow, got onto the charts doing cover versions of the El Dorados' "At My Front Door" (Pat: #7; the El Dorados: #17), the Charms' "Two Hearts (Pat: #16), Little Richard's "Tutti Frutti" (Pat: #12, Richard: #17), and a bunch more. Little Richard was so incensed by Boone's cover version of "Tutti Frutti" that he purposely made the follow-up, "Long Tall Sally," too fast for Boone to sing. Nonetheless, Boone figured out how to adapt "Long Tall Sally" to his style, and gave Richard a run for his money. Little Richard's version did beat Boone's, but only by one place on the charts (Richard: #7, Pat: #8).

WHITE BUCKS

There was also a huge difference in the attitudes of the artists toward their songs. To the originators, the songs were a part of life. To the rip-off artists, it was just business. Take, for example, one of Pat Boone's biggest hits, "Ain't That a Shame"—which actually belonged to Fats Domino. Fats, who was an established artist, wrote this song from a personal experience.

"I usually record my songs like things that people say everyday," Fats says. "Like 'Ain't That A Shame.' I was passin', walkin' down the street and I saw a little lady beatin' a little baby, you know, spankin' a baby. And I heard somebody say, 'Ain't that a shame.' "

In 1956, Fats released the song and it went to #10. Not bad, except that Pat Boone covered it right away, and his version went to #1, obviously taking some sales from Fats.

Pat, however, didn't really identify with the tune. In fact, he objected to it because the grammar was bad.

PROPER ENGLISH

" 'With 'Ain't That A Shame,' I balked," Boone says. "I said, 'Look, I just transferred to Columbia University, I'm an English major. I don't want to record a song called 'Ain't That A Shame.' I mean, 'ain't' wasn't an accepted word. It is now in the dictionary, but I was majoring in English and I felt that this was going to be a terrible thing if it was a hit. I tried to record it, 'Isn't That A Shame,' and it just didn't work."

Boone continues: "And I must say that I was complimented...I would go to radio studios, walk in, and the deejays were astonished to see that I was white."

Maybe they'd been listening to Fats' record.

THE STONES

The Rolling Stones have written some great original music, but they've also liberally "used" other people's music from the very beginning of their recording careers. "Stoned," the flip side of their first British hit ("I Wanna Be Your Man"), for example, was a copy of a 1964 hit called "Green Onions." An album cut called "Prodigal Son," which is credited to Jagger/Richards, is virtually a note-for-note copy of an old blues tune by Furry Lewis. Even the guitar licks are the same.

The Stones' first American Top 10 record, "Time Is On My Side," is another imitation, a note-for-note copy of the original version by New Orleans singer Irma Thomas. Even Mick Jagger's "rap" in the middle of the song is lifted from Irma's rendition. "Time On My Side" should have been the successful follow-up to her Top 20 tune, "I Wish Someone Would Care," but before Irma's record had a chance, the Stones' version was already rocketing up the charts. "I really liked the song, and I put my heart and soul into it," Irma says. "Then along comes this English group that half-sings it and gets a million-seller. And after that I stopped doing it."

America has more senior citizens than teenagers.

BODY LANGUAGE

Here are some fascinating facts about the human body.

IT'S A GAS

• An average person releases nearly a pint of intestinal gas by flatulence every day. Most is due to swallowed air. The rest is from fermentation of undigested food.

• Burping while lying on your back is a lot harder than burping while you're sitting or standing.

• The two things that make farts smell, *skatole* and *indole*, are commonly used in making perfumes.

• Your stomach produces a new lining every three days. Reason: It keeps stomach acids from digesting your stomach.

TAKE A BREATHER

• The average person breathes 70 to 80 million gallons of air in a lifetime.

• A newborn's first breath requires 50 times the suction of an ordinary breath.

• You inhale over 3,000 gallons of air every day.

• An infant breathes about three times faster than a 20-year-old.

• On the average, a person who smokes a pack of cigarettes a day will die at 67, seven years earlier than the average nonsmoker.

THE EYES HAVE IT

• Most men's pupils get 1/3 bigger when looking at pictures of sharks, but shrink in reaction to pictures of babies.

• 33% of the population has 20/20 vision.

• The muscles in the average eye move up to 100,000 times in a day.

• Every time you blink, you wash irritating contaminants out of your eyes.

• 1 out of every 500 people have one blue eye and one brown eye.

• You can't keep your eyes open when you sneeze.

DON'T SWEAT IT

• One square inch of your skin has over 600 sweat glands and 90 oil glands.

• In a hot climate, a person can perspire up to 3 gallons of sweat a day.

In a UCLA study, 87% of the people researchers smiled at smiled back.

SHARK!!!

Some fascinating factoids about the ocean's most feared predator.

Sharks lived more than 400 million years ago—200 million years before dinosaurs existed.

Shark skin is covered with small teeth-like denticles which can tear human skin on contact. It was once used as sandpaper by coastal wood-workers.

In a single year, a shark goes through more than 20,000 knife-like teeth.

Unlike other fish, sharks lack air bladders and consequently have to keep moving to avoid sinking and drowning.

To a shark, a swimmer in a black wetsuit looks a lot like a seal or sea lion.

Sand Tiger shark embryos fight to the death inside the mother's womb until only one shark is alive at birth.

In May 1945, fishermen off Cuba caught the largest Great White shark on record—measuring over 21 feet and weighing 7,302 pounds.

The Great White shark has no natural enemies and it never gets sick.

Sharks have no bones in their body—only cartilage.

Three times as many people are killed by lightning as are killed by sharks.

A plankton-eating Whale shark caught off Pakistan measured over 41 feet and weighed over 33,000 pounds.

Sharks have three eyelids on each eye to protect against the thrashing of its prey.

Don't swim or dive with cuts—some types of shark can smell one part of blood in 100 million parts of water.

An attacking shark can sometimes be confused and diverted by a hard blow to the nose, or a poke in the eye or nostrils.

Sharks live only in salt water, except for the mysterious Bull sharks, sometimes found swimming miles up rivers.

SITUATION TRAGEDY

Ever wish your family could be more like the Partridge Family or the Nelsons? It turns out, there were no families like that.

Back in the "golden age" of TV, situation comedies presented audiences with the image of an ideal Middle Class America. Parents were patient, neighbors were nice, and kids were neat (even their bedrooms were spotless). In reality, however, many of the child actors in these "perfect" TV families had less-than-perfect lives offscreen.

FATHER KNOWS BEST

From 1954-63, the "white-bread" Anderson family of Springfield, U.S.A., could do wrong. But two of the main actors ran into trouble after the show went off the air.

• Billy Gray (who played the son, Bud) spent 45 days in jail on marijuana charges and later dropped out from society. He told *TV Guide*, "I look back at the show and see it as a lie, a lie that was sold to the American people."

• Like Gray, Lauren Chapin (who played the youngest daughter, Kathy) also had drug troubles. She became addicted to heroin and speed, and did jail time for forging a check.

THE PATTY DUKE SHOW

Many people were shocked when Patty Duke revealed in her autobiography, *Call Me Anna: The Autobiography of Patty Duke*, that she had suffered from severe manic-depression during her TV sitcom days. She wrote, "I hated being less intelligent than I was, I hated pretending that I was younger than I was."

• From 1963-66, Duke starred in the popular series, but gradually the stress of playing two roles—herself and her look-alike cousin—caught up with her; she became depressed, anorexic and eventually an alcoholic and drug addict.

The screen on the first home television set was only 3 X 4 inches.

• To make matters worse, her managers, John and Ethel Ross, were not only physically and emotionally abusive (they wouldn't allow Duke to watch her own show) but, according to Duke, embezzled her savings as well.

THE PARTRIDGE FAMILY

• The happy-go-lucky Partridge Family was a favorite of pre-teens in the early 1970s.

• After the show ended, Danny Bonaduce, the cherubic bass player, developed drug problems. By age 21, he had squandered $350,000 in savings on his cocaine habit. In 1985 he was arrested for possession of cocaine, but the charges were dismissed after drug counseling. In 1989, Bonaduce resurfaced as a DJ in Philadelphia, claiming "My only reponsibility is not to promote drugs." Within a year, Bonaduce was busted again, this time for purchasing crack.

• Susan Dey, who was 16 when the show began, later claimed to have suffered from severe anxiety which resulted in anorexia and bulimia.

THE ADVENTURES OF OZZIE AND HARRIET

• For 14 years, 1952-66, Americans tuned in to "The Adventures of Ozzie and Harriet." The Nelsons were a real-life family, which certainly added to their appeal, but it didn't exclude them from real-life problems.

• Fans of Ricky Nelson were shocked when his autopsy revealed that he had been freebasing cocaine just prior to the plane crash that killed him on December 31, 1984 in DeKalb, Texas.

FAMILY AFFAIR

In 1976, Annissa Jones, who played "Buffy" on the series "Family Affair" was found dead of an overdose after a party in Oceanside, California. The coroner reported that Jones had "the largest combination of drugs in any cases I've ever encountered." Toxological tests showed massive amoungs of cocaine, Quaaludes and barbituates. Jones was 18.

The diameter of the wheel on TV's "Wheel of Fortune" is 8' 6".

NAME & PLACE

Planning to move? Why not make your home in Sodom... or Elephant's Playground? Or any of these other strangely-named places:

Sodom, Vermont: Its name was changed to Adamant, VT in 1905, by people who shuddered at the thought of having their incoming mail addressed to Sodom.

Mount Derby, Colorado: It's hat-shaped.

Coffee-Los Lake, Maine: Locals, who like to call nearby Telos Lake "tea-less lake," thought they should have a "coffee-less lake" too.

Einanuhto Hills, Alaska: From the Aleut word meaning "three breasts."

Phoenix, Arizona: Traces of an Indian or pre-Indian village were found at the site. Town founders, taking the name from the mythological bird who rises form the ashes, hoped their new town would rise from the village's ruins.

Bosom, Wyoming: A town with two peaks.

Mistake Peak, Arizona and Mistaken Creek, Kentucky: Wrong peak, wrong creek.

Elephant's Playground, California: Home of large boulders in a meadow.

"Gotham City": In England, during the reign of King John, Gotham villagers all feigned lunacy to discourage the king from establishing a hunting lodge nearby that would lead to an increase in taxes. The name now means a city overrun by madness. Washington Irving coined the phrase in a description of New York in 1807.

Bimble, Kentucky: From the names of Will and Rebecca Payne's prize oxen—Bim and Bill.

Portland, Oregon: The two men who named the city couldn't decide—Portland (like the Maine city)...or Boston? A coin flip settled the debate in favor of Portland.

The most popular American dog names are Rover, Spot, and Max—in that order.

COMMON PHRASES

In the first two Uncle John's Bathroom Readers, *we gave you the origins of some familiar phrases. Here are a few more.*

SECOND STRING
Meaning: Replacement or backup.
Background: You might have caught William Tell without an apple, but not without a second string. In medieval times, an archer always carried a second string in case the one on his bow broke.

IN THE LIMELIGHT
Meaning: The center of attention.
Background: In 1826, Thomas Drummond invented the limelight, an amazingly bright white light, by running an intense oxygen/hydrogen flame through a lime cylinder. At first, the intense light was used in lighthouses to direct ships. Later, theatres began using the limelight like a spotlight—to direct the audience's attention to a certain actor. If an actor was to be the focal point of a particular scene, he was thrust into the limelight.

MAKE THE GRADE
Meaning: To fulfill expectations, or succeed.
Background: In railroad jargon, the term "grade" refers to the slope of the hill. When a train reaches a plateau or mountaintop, it has "made the grade."

FLASH IN THE PAN
Meaning: Short-lived success.
Background: In the 1700s, the pan of a flintlock musket was the part which held the gunpowder. If all went well, sparks from the flint would ignite the charge, which would then propel the bullet out the barrel. However, sometimes the gun powder would burn without igniting a main charge. The flash would burn brightly but only briefly, with no lasting effect.

ELVIS: STILL DEAD?

Here's a piece about the Phantom of the Rock World, Elvis. It's taken from Vince Staten's irreverent guidebook, Unauthorized America.

"In 1988, for some reason, people all across America got the idea that Elvis wasn't really dead, that he had faked his death to get a little peace and quiet, and that he had actually spent the previous eleven years enjoying himself, wandering the country, seducing fat waitresses who knew who he was but decided not to tell until the *Weekly World News* called.

"He was spotted in Georgia and in Germany; in Texas and in Tennessee. But the majority of the sightings centered in the Kalamazoo, Michigan area."

INSIDE SOURCES

"The Elvis Is Alive mania began the last week in May, 1988 when the *Weekly World News* broke the story: After faking his tragic death [in 1977], exhausted idol Elvis Presley was secretly flown to Hawaii, where he began his new life under the name John Burrows.

"The newspaper quoted from a new book, *Is Elvis Alive? The Most Incredible Elvis Presley Story Ever Told*, by author Gail Brewer-Giorgio, who—just coincidentally—also wrote the novel *Orion*, about a rock star who faked his own death. The Elvis book came complete with an audiocassette tape of conversations with Elvis *after* his death."

ELVIS SPEAKS

"'Everything worked just like it was meant to be,' E said on the secret tape. 'There was an island I had learned about a long time ago. I must have spent a year there. I really needed the rest.'

"Voice analyst Len Williams of Houston verified that the voice on the tape was Elvis's, and that the tape had been edited. Brewer-Giorgio shrugged that one off, saying it was edited to take out the voice of the person talking with Elvis."

PROGRESS REPORT

"So how has Elvis been since his death? 'It's been enjoyable, but it's been a constant battle, growing a beard and this and that, to keep from being recognized...I'm hoping that a lot of people out there are not disappointed with me. I mean, I didn't mean to put anybody through any pain. It's taken a lot to have to do what I had to do. But in the long run it's going to pay off.'"

MORE ON TAPE

"The tape was supposedly made in 1981. Elvis said he hadn't had a sleeping pill in three years and didn't like the films about him. He said he plans to come out when 'the time is right.'"

HE'S BACK

"Soon America's tabloids were swamped with tales from chubby waitresses who had lived with Elvis and pimply-face teenagers who saw someone who looked like him at the local hamburger heaven.

"In the June 28, 1988, issue of the supermarket tabloid *Weekly World News*, amid such headlines as 'Space Aliens Graveyard Found!' and 'Man Keeps Wife's Body in Freezer for 23 Years!' and 'Cheeseburger Kills Space Alien!' was this shocker:

I'VE SEEN ELVIS AND HE'S ALIVE AND WELL!
Woman spots Presley at a Kalamazoo Burger King"

EYEWITNESS ACCOUNT

"The diligence of *Weekly World's* reporters had turned up an eyewitness, Louise Welling, fifty-one, a Kalamazoo, Michigan housewife, who said she saw Elvis twice; in September she had gone to Felpausch's grocery in suburban Vicksburg, Michigan, after church, and spotted him in the next checkout lane. He was buying a fuse. 'He was dressed in an all-white jumpsuit and holding a motorcycle helmet,' she said. 'He'd lost weight, and he didn't have sideburns.'

"She spotted him a second time two months later at the J. C. Penney entrance of the Crossroads Mall. And in May her children saw Elvis in a red Ferrari at a Burger King drive-through window."

TOUGH QUESTIONS

"Was Elvis Alive?

"And if so, why hadn't he had a hit lately?

"I conducted my own investigation.

"The first thing I had to answer was: why Kalamazoo?

"Why did Elvis Presley, Tupelo, Mississippi native and longtime Memphis, Tennessee resident pick Kalamazoo for his hideaway?

"I had no clue. I didn't even know where Kalamazoo was."

THE INVESTIGATION

"To help unravel the mystery, I sent for the Kalamazoo Chamber of Commerce's newcomer guide. I assume Elvis must have done this in those hectic last days before his death...What was it about Kalamazoo, I kept asking myself?...the annual Michigan Wine & Harbor Festival in September?...the Kellogg Bird sanctuary? The NASA/Michigan space center?

"Terrific stuff, sure, but nothing Elvis would have cared about.

"I couldn't find any plausible explanation until I spotted a short paragraph on the back of the Kalamazoo County 'come and see our corner of Michigan' brochure. It leaped out at me: 'Kalamazoo County...is the world headquarters of the Upjohn Company, and you can take a fascinating tour of their pharmaceutical production facility.'

"Bingo."

DRUG STORE COWBOY

In the last 7 months of his life, Elvis had 5,300 uppers, downers, and painkillers prescribed for him.

ELVIS LIVES AGAIN

"Just when you thought it was safe to read a supermarket tabloid again, the *National Examiner* was back on the Elvis Lives story. E had been spotted living on a farm near Cleveland, Alabama. He'd been glimpsed at the local pharmacy and at the Dogwood Inn in Oneonta, Alabama. He was using the name Johnny Buford during his Alabama sojourn."

The average American kid will watch 30-40,000 TV commercials this year.

GOLDWYNISMS

Samuel Goldwyn was one of Hollywood's great movie producers. He was also famous for murdering the English language—sort of the Yogi Berra of the film world. In Hollywood, his sayings were called Goldwynisms. Here are some classic examples:

"All this criticism—it's like ducks off my back."

"Too caustic? To hell with the cost—we'll make the movie anyway."

"We've all passed a lot of water since then."

Asked about the message of one of his films: "I'm not interested in messages. Messages are for Western Union."

"I'm willing to admit that I may not always be right...But I'm never wrong."

"Tell me, how did you love the picture?"

"I want a movie that starts with an earthquake and works up to a climax."

"I'll believe in color television when I see it in black and white."

"Don't let your opinions sway your judgment."

"Let's have some new clichés."

"These days, every director bites the hand that laid the golden egg."

"In two words: im possible."

"This music won't do. There's not enough sarcasm in it."

"Let's bring it up to date with some snappy 19th century dialogue."

"If you can't give me your word of honor, will you give me your promise?"

"A verbal contract isn't worth the paper it's written on."

"Anyone who goes to see a psychiatrist ought to have his head examined."

"The most important thing in acting is honesty. Once you've learned to fake that, you're in."

"If I could drop dead right now, I'd be the happiest man alive."

The island of Cyprus has one movie theater for every eight of its inhabitants.

TISSUE TALK

According to Harry L. Rinker, "all toilet paper is not created equal." Rinker should know—believe it or not, he collects the stuff. Here's "Rinker on Collectibles," a column excerpted from Antiques and Collecting *magazine.*

If you have traveled abroad or used an outhouse, you are aware of one basic truth—all toilet paper is not created equal. What a perfect excuse to collect it.

BEGINNER'S NOTE

On the surface, collecting toilet paper need not be an expensive hobby. Select pilfering from public restrooms and friends' bathrooms will provide enough examples to begin a collection. Of course, if you travel abroad to obtain examples, the costs increase considerably. However, I discovered that once my friends found out that I have a toilet paper collection...their personal contributions rolled in.

GETTING STARTED

I became aware of the collectible potential of toilet paper in the late 1970s when I learned about a woman who was appearing on the Women's Club lecture circuit talking about the wide assortment of toilet paper that she encountered during her travels. She charged a fee for her presentation and did not seem to lack bookings. She obviously was cleaning up.

After resisting the urge to follow suit for almost a decade, I simply gave up and began my own toilet paper collection. My initial beginnings were modest. I wrote to several German friends and asked them to send me some examples of German toilet paper. Udo, my friend in Hamburg, outdid himself. Among the examples he sent was toilet paper from the German railroad.

A close examination of the light gray textured paper revealed that each sheet was stamped "Deutsche Bundesbahn." This says something about a nation's character. The German railroad administration is so concerned about a roll of toilet paper that they find it necessary to stamp their name on every sheet. The ridiculousness of the German railroad administration is surpassed by the English

Mother tarantulas kill 99% of the babies they hatch.

government. When you use the public restrooms at government museums throughout England, you quickly notice that each sheet of toilet paper is marked "Official Government Property." What a subtle way to recognize that your tax dollars are at work.

GI T.P.

The U.S. military now issues its field troops camouflage toilet paper. It seems the Viet Cong used mounds of used white stuff to track our troop movements during the Vietnam War. What happened to the good old, collapsible GI shovel?

THE RULES

Since toilet paper collecting is in its infancy, now is an excellent time to create rules concerning how to validly accumulate this important new collectible. For example, how many sheets are necessary to have a valid example? Ideally, I suggest four to six; but, a minimum of two, one to keep in mint condition and the other to record the time and place of acquisition, will do in a pinch.

Do you collect single sheets or the entire roll? This is a tough one. I started out by collecting sheets. Then I began thinking about the potential value of wrappers and added them to my collection. Since I had gone that far, I figured why not save the entire roll. When I realized that same rolls were packaged in units of four to six, I was forced to save the entire package. My collection, which originally was meant to be confined to a shirt box, now occupies several large boxes.

TALKIN' TOILETS

Toilet paper collecting provides an engaging topic for cocktail parties and other social gatherings. Everyone has a toilet paper story to tell. I remember the time I had to use the facilities in the basement of the Moravian Archives in Herrnhut, East Germany. The nature of the call required my immediately locating a toilet with no regard to the toilet paper status. Later examination revealed no toilet paper, but rather an old railroad time schedule booklet with some of the pages torn out. As I tore a sheet loose, the ink on the paper came off in my fingers. You can imagine the rest. I should have saved an example, but I wasn't thinking of toilet paper collecting at the time.

BE A T.P. CONNOISSEUR

I think everyone should be required to use a farm or camp outhouse at some point in his or her life. The stories of corn cobs and Sears catalogs are true. I know. I remember the concern espressed by my rural relatives when Sears switched to glossy paper stock. I have a number of old catalogs in my collection.

As my toilet paper collection grew, I became fascinated with the composition and variety of designs and patterns of toilet paper. When I first visited Germany in the late 1960s, their extremely coarse gray toilet paper had the quality of sandpaper. It was rough, but you had confidence the job was getting done. In 1987 I found that German toilet paper tastes now matched the Americans' desire for soft, almost tissue-like paper. The significance of this shift and what is says about the development of the German character should not be overlooked.

FAVORITE THINGS

As with all my collections, I have some favorite examples, among which are a half roll of toilet paper that a friend brought me from England that has a surface texture equivalent to wax paper and a German aluminum foil package that contains toilet paper moistened and perfumed to act and smell like a wash and dry. I have a special box in which I put translucent examples, those you can see through when held up to the light. Their use gives real meaning to the phrase "doubling up."

HELLO OUT THERE

Thus far, I have been unsuccessful in locating other serious toilet paper collectors. They exist; there are collectors for everything. If I can locate them, I would be glad to discuss swapping duplicates.

Meanwhile, you can help. The next time your travels in the U.S.A. or abroad bring you into contact with the unusual during a period of daily meditation, save a few examples and send them to me (care of *Antiques and Collecting* magazine, 1006 S. Michigan Avenue, Chicago, Illinois 60605). Is there the making of a future museum collection here? Time will tell.

Americans spend over $400 million on toys every day.

SAY GOODNIGHT, GRACIE

George Burns and Gracie Allen were two of the only performers to successfully jump from vaudeville to radio to TV. Their sitcom, "The George Burns and Gracie Allen Show," aired from 1951 to 1958. It's been seen continuously in reruns for the last three decades.

HOW IT STARTED

George was a small-time vaudevillian and Gracie was jobless and broke when they met in 1924. Gracie went to a New Jersey club to watch a friend of hers perform. Also on the bill: a duo called "Burns and Lorraine." Gracie thought the dancer (Burns) would make a good partner and approached him about working together. George figured he had nothing to lose. At age 27, he had been a flop at everything he'd tried.

In their original act, Gracie was the "straight man," and George got the funny lines. But even as a "straight man," Allen got more laughs than Burns. So he rewrote the act, creating the daffy character that made Gracie famous. It was a selfless, professional gesture for which she always admired him. It was also a canny one—the new act was a hit. By the end of the '20s, the pair were vaudeville headliners. By 1932 they had their own radio show, which grew in popularity until they had a weekly audience of 45 million people.

Then, in the late '40s, George decided radio was on its way out (though not everyone realized it), and he decided to jump to television. Gracie, on the other hand, steadfastly refused to be a part of a TV show. George figured she was just afraid to see how she looked on the small screen—which he considered ridiculous. Some radio stars disappointed their fans with they way they looked, but Burns and Allen didn't have to worry. "Gracie," said George, "looked even better" than she sounded. So he offered her a deal. If she did a test shot on-camera and didn't like the way she looked, he'd forget all about television. She agreed, and he got his way.

Next question: what was the show going to be about? There were hours of meetings with CBS, and according to Burns, he finally asked why they couldn't do their radio program on TV. "Why give us a new look," he asked, "when nobody's seen the old one yet?"

Tallest man on record: Robert Wadlow— 8 feet 11 inches. He died at age 22, still growing.

It made sense. The radio series had featured Burns and Allen as themselves, and Blanche and Harry Morton as their next door neighbors. So did the TV series.

NAME & RANK

• George Burns's real name is Nat Birnbaum. He was born in New York City to a poor, Orthodox Jewish family. Trying to make it in show business before he met Gracie, he'd been "a singer, a dancer, a yodeling juggler, did a roller skating act, an act with a seal, worked with a dog...You name it, I did it."

• As a youth in San Francisco, Gracie hung around theaters, dreaming of becoming an actress. When she graduated from high school, she joined an Irish act as a "colleen," and headed for Broadway. It didn't work—the act fell apart when they got to New York. When she met George she was taking odd jobs just to keep eating, and was seriously considering giving up and going back home.

LOST TREASURE

The first 50 TV shows B&A did were live. It wasn't until their third season that the program was saved on film, so the reruns we watch today actually begin in 1953, not 1951. What did we miss? George says he appeared in an entire episode with his fly open.

HEADACHES

It's not easy being a scatterbrain. Despite her three decades in show business, Gracie suffered from severe stage fright...not to mention camera fright. And her concentration on her work was so intense that she frequently suffered from debilitating migraine headaches. She seldom had time to rest in bed, so she had their home decorated in subdued shades of green, pink, and brown to soothe herself.

SAY GOODNIGHT, GRACIE

• In 1958, Gracie retired. She died in 1964 of heart problems.

• George tried going solo, teamed up with comedienne Carol Channing, and even did a sitcom called "Wendy and Me," with Connie Stevens as a daffy blonde (a bomb). Nothing worked until 1975, when he won an Oscar for *The Sunshine Boys*. After that he became one of America's most venerated—and visible—actors.

GRACIE ALLENISMS

Gracie Allen was one of America's funniest comediennes for 40 years. Here are some of her classic TV lines.

"This recipe is certainly silly. It says to separate two eggs, but it doesn't say how far to separate them."

Harry von Zell: "You're sending your mother an empty envelope?"
Gracie: "I wanted to cheer her up. No news is good news."

"I read a book twice as fast as anybody else. First I read the beginning, and then I read the ending, and then I start in the middle and read toward whichever end I like best."

"There's so much good in the worst of us, and so many of the worst of us get the best of us, that the rest of us aren't even worth talking about."

Gracie: "Every time I bake a cake, I leave it in five minutes too long and it burns."
Harry von Zell: "So?"
Gracie: "So today I put in one cake, and I put in another five minutes later. When the first one starts to burn, I'll know the second one's finished."

Gracie: "You can't give up, Blanche. Women don't do that. Look at Betsy Ross, Martha Washington—they didn't give up. Look at Nina Jones."
Blanche Morton: "Nina Jones?"
Gracie: "I never heard of her either, because she gave up."

Harry von Zell: "Gracie, isn't that boiling water you're putting in the refrigerator?"
Gracie: "Yes, I'm freezing it."
Harry: "You're freezing it?"
Gracie: "Um-hmmm, and then whenever I want boiling water, all I have to do is defrost it."

Gracie: "Something smells good."
Peter: "It's Mr. Morton's ribs."
Gracie: "Really? George only puts cologne on his face."

George: "What's that?"
Gracie: "Electric cords. I had them shortened. This one's for the iron, this one's for the floor lamp."
George: "Why did you shorten the cords?"
Gracie: "To save electricity."

Switzerland's roads are mined in 2,000 strategic places; they can be blown up in 10 minutes.

ALL-AMERICAN SPORTS

Football and basketball are American creations, right? Well, sort of. Here's where "our" sports really come from.

FOOTBALL

Historical Origin: Football is a hybrid of soccer and rugby, two sports imported by British colonists. Rugby, which allows players to pick up the ball and run with it, was adapted by the British from a 2nd century Roman game called "harpastum." Soccer originated in Florence, Italy, in the mid-1500s.

American Origin: Harvard University is credited with establishing American football, which was introduced on the campus in 1869 as "The Boston Game." In 1875, Harvard beat Yale in the first U.S. intercollegiate game; there were 15 players on each team. The 11-man team with a quarterback was added five years later.

• Football got so violent that, in 1905, 18 men died from injuries sustained on the field. There was a public outcry to ban it, but a football enthusiast named President Theodore Roosevelt stepped in. He called an emergency meeting of college football officials and instituted safety measures that enabled football to survive.

BASKETBALL

Historical Origin: 16th century Aztecs played "ollamalitzli," a basketball-like game: Players tried to "shoot" a rubber ball through a stone ring on a stadium wall and the team that scored first won. Ollamalitzli "professionals" didn't play for huge contracts and shoe endorsements. The player who scored the goal won all of the audience's clothes. And the losing team's captain was...beheaded.

American Origin: In 1891 James Naismith, a gym teacher at the Young Men's Christian Association Training School in Springfield, Massachusetts created a game for his bored students. He hung two peach baskets on opposite ends of the gym, chose two 9-man teams, and told each team to try to score without running, or kicking the ball. Kids spread the new game to other schools.

• Two initial differences: An unlimited number of players could play at the same time (even 100), and baskets still had bottoms in them. Every time someone scored, they had to stop and get the ball out. It took two decades to come up with an open-bottom net.

PUBLIC ENEMY #1

In the '20s and '30s, gangsters like Machine Gun Kelly, Pretty-Boy Floyd, and Baby-Face Nelson literally shot their way into the headlines. All of them became legendary figures, but one captured the public's imagination more than any other—John Dillinger. Here is his story.

BACKGROUND

During the Depression, the American public developed an insatiable appetite for crime-buster stories. John Dillinger seemed to be the perfect romantic criminal—handsome, dapper, arrogant and audacious.

In reality, Dillinger's life was less romantic than his image. Born in Indianapolis in 1902, he was a chronic drifter. He enlisted in the U.S. Navy in 1923 after being dropped by his girlfriend, and five months later, deserted to take up armed robbery. His first prison sentence soon followed—ten years at the Indiana State Reformatory for a grocery store stick-up in Mooresville, Indiana. Twice Dillinger tried to escape. He failed both times.

Then, in 1933, he was released on parole. Three weeks later he robbed a factory manager in Illinois. One week after that, he pulled off his first bank robbery—$3,000 from a Daleville, Indiana bank. Seeing that crime could (at least temporarily) pay, Dillinger formed a gang. Within three weeks they robbed $10,000 from a Montpelier, Indiana bank and $28,000 in Indianapolis.

Dillinger was captured in Dayton, Ohio but his gang stormed the jail, killed the sheriff and freed their boss. Two days later they stole an arsenal of machine guns and bullet-proof vests from an Auburn, Indiana police station. Now Dillinger was officially Public Enemy Number One, according to the FBI.

THE HUNT

A nationwide manhunt ensued. By this time, Dillinger's antics were a nationwide obsession. *Time* magazine ran an article called "Dillinger Land," which included a board game listing all of his crimes.

Dillinger's gang moved onto Wisconsin, where they heisted $28,000 from a bank in Racine. In early 1934, they robbed an East

Chicago, Indiana bank, killing a bank guard in the process. Once again, Dillinger was captured—this time in Tuscon, Arizona. Dillinger was flown to Indiana to be tried for the bank guard murder.

A month later, in perhaps his most outrageous exploit, he broke out of jail again—by carving a look-alike pistol out of a washboard, which he used to threaten the sheriff, Mrs. Lillian Holley. To add insult to injury, he used the sheriff's car to escape.

Over 600 FBI agents were now assigned to capture Dillinger. But backed by a gang of bandits that included Baby Face Nelson, Dillinger eluded FBI agents. In St. Paul, Minnesota, the FBI cornered the gang but allowed Dillinger to escape through the back door. On May 15, Congress asked for the public's help—offering a $25,000 reward for his capture.

THE CAPTURE

Finally, on July 22, 1934, the FBI got their man. Thanks to a tip from Anna Sage, the so-called "Woman In Red," the FBI learned that Dillinger planned to attend a movie in Chicago that night with Sage (who ran a local brothel) and his new girlfriend, a waitress named Polly Hamilton. The trio went to see *Manhattan Melodrama* (starring Clark Gable and William Powell) at the Biograph Theater.

Sage wore a red dress for identification. When Dillinger emerged from the theater, Melvin Purvis, the head of the FBI's manhunt, lit a cigar as a signal to waiting agents. The two women disappeared. Sensing something suspicious was going on, Dillinger reached into his pocket for his pistol. Before he could fire, the FBI killed him in a volley of gunfire.

DILLINGER FACTS

• Reportedly, several people dipped their handkerchiefs in his blood outside the Biograph Theatre for a future souvenir.

• After Dillinger's death, the Chicago morgue opened its doors, so the public could view the corpse of "public enemy number one."

• FBI Chief J. Edgar Hoover kept a plaster facsimile of Dillinger's death mask at the FBI in one of his offices. Alongside it was Dillinger's straw hat and the unsmoked cigar he was carrying on the night of his death.

DISNEY STORIES: THE LITTLE MERMAID

Disney Studios' 1989 cartoon, The Little Mermaid, was adapted from a story by the Brothers Grimm. Of course, the Disney version and the original story were substantially different. Here are Jim Morton's examples of how the tale was changed.

THE DISNEY VERSION

A young mermaid, infatuated with humans, saves a Prince from drowning and immediately falls in love with him. But she realizes that there's no way he'll ever love her unless she can walk on land, so she goes to the evil Sea Witch and asks for help.

• The Witch agrees to help...but with certain conditions: The mermaid must give up her voice; and the Prince must fall in love with her within a week. The mermaid agrees without hesitation.

• When it looks like the Little Mermaid may actually win the prince's love in time, the Sea Witch uses the mermaid's voice to trick him. He falls in love with the witch instead, and—still under her spell—agrees to marry her.

• The Little Mermaid and her animal friends stop the wedding in the nick of time. Enraged by the interruption, the Witch tries to drown the Prince, but he kills her first.

• The Little Mermaid gets her wish to walk on land, and she joins the Prince she loves. They live happily ever after.

THE ORIGINAL VERSION

• The Little Mermaid does save the prince from drowning, and does go to the Sea Witch for help. But the similarities end there.

• The Sea Witch doesn't magically steal the mermaid's voice—she cuts her tongue out.

• When the Little Mermaid shows up at the prince's door, he says she reminds him of the girl who saved him from drowning. It sounds promising, but apparently the prince isn't too good with faces—while he's visiting a neighboring kingdom, he meets a princess and decides she's the one who saved him. So he decides to marry her, ruining the mermaid's chance for true love and eternal

In the United States, more than 5 million roses are cut each year for Valentine's Day.

life. (In this version mermaids don't have souls, so they can't go to heaven when they die. Only humans can).

• The Little Mermaid gets one last chance to save herself. Her sisters go to the Sea Witch and trade their hair for a magic dagger. If the mermaid kills the prince with the dagger before sunrise, she can be a mermaid again.

• She goes to kill the prince while he's sleeping, but she can't do it. Instead, she jumps into the ocean, and she dissolves into sea foam.

SAMPLE PASSAGES (FROM THE ORIGINAL)

"'You must pay me,' said the Witch; 'and it is not a trifle that I ask. You have the finest voice of all here at the bottom of the water; you think you can use it to enchant the Prince, but you have to give it to me.'

"'But if you take away my voice,' said the Little Mermaid. 'What will remain to me?'

"'Your body,' replied the Witch; 'your graceful walk, and your eyes should be enough to capture a human heart. Well, have you lost your nerve? Put out your little tongue, and I'll cut it off.'

"...And she cut off the little mermaid's tongue. Now the Princess was dumb; she could neither sing nor speak."

• • •

The Little Mermaid's sisters show up carrying a knife.

"'The witch has given us a knife; here it is...Before the sun rises you must thrust it into Prince's heart, and when the warm blood falls on your feet, they will grow together again into a fish-tail...Hurry up! Either he or you must die before the sun rises! ...Kill the Prince and come back! Hurry up!'

"And they vanished beneath the waves. The Little Mermaid drew back the curtain and saw the beautiful bride lying with her head on the Prince's breast. She bent down and kissed his brow...Then she looked at the sharp knife in her hands, and again looked at the Prince, who in his sleep murmured his bride's name ...The knife trembled in the mermaid's hand. But then she threw it far away into the waves—they turned red where it fell, and it seemed as though drops of blood spurted up out of the water. Once more she looked at the Prince; then she threw herself into the sea, and felt her frame dissolving into foam."

ALFRED HITCHCOCK PRESENTS

Alfred Hitchcock was one of the first Hollywood greats to lend his name to a TV show. His acclaimed anthology series ran from 1955 to 1965.

HOW IT STARTED

How did Alfred Hitchcock, one of the best-known film directors in the world, wind up on TV at a time when most Hollywood greats were avoiding it? Good advice, that's how. His friend and former agent, Lew Wasserman, was the head of MCA, a burgeoning "entertainment conglomerate" that was itching to get into TV. Wasserman thought Hitch was the perfect vehicle. First, he was a "name." Second, he traditionally made a cameo appearance in each of his enormously successful films, so people knew what he looked like. And third, a major magazine publisher had just contracted with Hitchcock to produce *The Alfred Hitchcock Mystery Magazine*, reinforcing his public image as master of suspense/mystery. Wasserman's immortal comment, uttered at a meeting in early 1955: "We ought to put Hitch on the air."

Wasserman then had to convince Alfred, who was unsure about getting involved. He feared it would hurt his image as a filmmaker, since the movie world looked down on the small screen. But he also trusted Wasserman, who offered him full creative control and advised that he get involved while the medium was young. Hitchcock agreed, and the show was bought by CBS. His appeal was so great that neither the network or sponsor needed a pilot—it simply went on the air. The success secured his place as the personification of "mystery and suspense" in American culture.

INSIDE FACTS

Good E-E-Evening

Hitchcock's lead-ins and closing comments often had nothing to do with the episode being aired. They were actually shot 24 at a time, 4 times a year, and spliced into completed episodes.

Crime Does Pay
The ownership of each episode of "Alfred Hitchcock Presents," after showing on TV once, reverted to Alfred Hitchcock. In 1964, he traded the rights to the series (along with ownership of *Psycho*) to MCA for 150,000 shares of the company's stock. This made him MCA's 4th largest shareholder, and an extremely wealthy man.

Unlikely Source
The Hitchcock theme song was actually a classical piece chosen by Alfred himself. It is Gounod's "Funeral March of a Marionette."

Just Kidding
Sponsors weren't happy with Alfred's constant put-downs of their commercials, until they discovered that the audience liked the companies better for having a sense of humor (which they didn't really have). Then they stopped hassling him about it.

Un-Sawn Episode
The only episode of *Hitchcock Presents* which was never shown was called "The Sorcerer's Apprentice." It was a story about a retarded boy who watched a magician saw a man in half and then killed someone trying to duplicate the trick. CBS refused to allow it on TV, saying it was too morbid.

Guest Star
In 10 years, Alfred Hitchcock actually directed only 20 out of the 362 episodes of the show.

Doodling
Hitchcock, who was once a commercial artist, drew the famous sketch of his profile that appeared on the show.

Buried Treasure
Most of the story ideas for the program came from short stories and novels. Hitchcock believed that if an author had a really good idea, he wouldn't use it in a TV script—he'd save it and use it in his own work. One year, his staff read more than 400 novels before they found 32 stories they could use.

Two cultures in the world don't use fire—Andaman islanders and Pygmies.

GOOD E-E-EVENING

Before each episode of "Alfred Hitchcock Presents," the "Master of Suspense" offered a few pearls of wisdom, like these.

"There is nothing quite so good as a burial at sea. It is simple, tidy, and not very incriminating."

"We seem to have a compulsion these days to bury time capsules in order to give those people living in the next century or so some idea of what we are like. I have prepared one of my own. I have placed some rather large samples of dynamite, gunpowder, and nitroglycerin. My time capsule is set to go off in the year 3000. It will show them what we are really like."

"The paperback is very interesting, but I find it will never replace a hardcover book—it makes a very poor doorstop."

"These are bagpipes. I understand the inventor of the bagpipes was inspired when he saw a man carrying an indignant, asthmatic pig under his arm. Unfortunately, the man-made sound never equalled the purity of the sound achieved by the pig."

"When I was a young man, I had an uncle who frequently took me out to dinner. He always accompanied these dinners with minutely detailed stories about himself. But I listened—because he was paying for the dinner. I don't know why I am reminded of this, but we are about to have one of our commercials."

"The length of a film should be directly related to the endurance of the human bladder."

"In each of our stories, we try to teach a little lesson or paint a little moral—things like Mother taught: 'Walk softly and carry a big stick'; 'Strike first, ask questions after'—that sort of thing."

"I seem to have lost some weight and I don't wish to mar my image. I cannot reveal exactly how much weight. I can only say that had I lost ten more pounds, I would have had to file a missing persons report."

INVASION! PART III

This wasn't exactly an invasion—but in 1942, the Japanese did attack California...sort of. Actually, the reaction was more memorable than the invasion itself.

THE INVADERS: A Japanese submarine.
THE DATE: February 23, 1942.
BACKGROUND: On December 7, 1941, Japan attacked Pearl Harbor. The U.S. responded by declaring war on Japan. Did Japan plan to attack the West Coast next? Californians watched the skies warily.
THE INVASION: About three months after America entered World War II, a Japanese submarine surfaced near the town of Goleta, California, eight miles north of Santa Barbara. It hurled 15 shells at refineries owned by the Bankline Oil Company, and disappeared. It escaped, despite an all-out search launched by the Navy and Air Force.

The shelling was the first attack on the U.S. mainland since 1918 when a German U-boat fired shells at Cape Cod. There was minimal damage—estimated at $500—and there were no injuries. However, reports that an airplane hangar was spotted on the submarine's rear deck caused jitters in Southern California. People began preparing for an imminent air attack.
AFTERMATH: Two days later, on February 25, shaky nerves gave way to general hysteria in Los Angeles. Early that morning, authorities believed they spotted an enemy plane. Assuming L.A. was under attack, they dispatched Army planes to defend them. The city was blacked out and air-raid alarms went off while local Army officials tried to locate equipment they'd lent to Paramount Pictures for a war movie.

According to the *San Francisco Chronicle*, authorities tried to blow the "enemy plane" out of the sky. They reported: "Anti-aircraft guns pumped thousands of rounds of ammunition toward an objective presumed fixed in the piercing beams of uncounted searchlights."

Then red-faced officials realized it was a false alarm; the object in question turned out to be the planet Venus.

THE BASEBALL MYTH

According to traditional baseball lore, our national pastime was invented by Abner Doubleday, in Cooperstown, New York. Was it? Not even close. Here's the truth.

THE MISSION

At the turn of the century, baseball was becoming a popular pastime…and a booming business. Albert G. Spalding, a wealthy sporting goods dealer, realized that the American public would be more loyal to a sport that had its origins in the U.S. than one with roots in Europe. So it became his mission to sell baseball to America as an entirely American game.

THE COMMISION

In 1905, Spalding created a commission to establish the origin of baseball "in some comprehensive and authoritative way, *for all time*." It was a tall order for any historian, but Spalding was no historian—and neither were the friends he appointed to his blue-ribbon commission.

Spalding gave six men honorary positions: Alfred J. Reach, head of another sporting goods company (known by many as the "Business Genius of Base-Ball"), A.G. Mills, the third president of the National League; Morgan G. Bulkeley, first president of the National League; George Wright, a businessman; and Arthur P. Gorman, a senator who died before the study was completed. James Sullivan, president of an amateur athletic union, functioned as secretary for the commission.

THE SUBMISSIONS

In 1907, the Special Baseball Commission issued the Official Baseball Guide of 1906-7, a report which A.G. Mills said "should forever set at rest the question as to the origin of baseball." What research had the group compiled in almost three years? Their files contained just three letters—one from Henry Chadwick, an Englishman who had helped popularize baseball; one from Spalding himself; and one from James Ward, a friend and supporter of Spalding.

In his letter, Chadwick pointed out the obvious similarities between baseball and a game called "rounders," a popular sport in England as well as Colonial America. Rounders was played on a diamond with a base on each corner. A "striker" with a bat would stand beside the fourth base and try to hit balls thrown by a "pecker." If he hit the ball fair, the striker could earn a run by "rounding" the bases. If the striker missed the ball three times, or if his hit was caught before touching the ground, he was "out." After a certain number of outs, the offensive and defensive teams switched. Ring a bell? It didn't with Spalding and his men. The commission, which selected Chadwick's letter to represent the "rounder's contingent," quickly dismissed it because Chadwick was born in England.

In deference to Spalding, James Ward supported the theory of American origin, though his letter stated that "all exact information upon the origin of Base-Ball must, in the very nature of things, be unobtainable." His testimony amounted to no more than a friendly opinion.

Spalding's letter vehemently argued "that the game of Base-Ball is entirely of American origin, and has no relation to, or connection with, any game of any other country." On what evidence did he base this argument, as well as the Doubleday/Cooperstown theory? On the letter of a mystery man named Abner Graves, a mining engineer from Denver, who claimed to recall Doubleday inventing the game of baseball *sixty-eight* years earlier (Graves was over eighty years old when he gave his account).

THE OMISSION

In his report, Spalding stated that Graves "was present when Doubleday first outlined with a stick in the dirt the present diamond-shaped field Base-Ball field, including the location of the players on the field, and afterward saw him make a diagram of the field, with a crude pencil on paper, memorandum of the rules of his new game, which he named 'Base Ball.'" However, none of this romantic imagery was actually in the Graves letter—no stick and no "crude pencil diagram of the rules"—Spalding made the whole thing up. Nor was Graves present at the first game, as Spalding claimed. Graves stated in his letter, "I do not know, nor is it possible to know, on what spot the first game was played according to Doubleday's plan." Graves' letter simply recounted the rules of the game, and how he thought Doubleday "improved" an *already existing game* called Town Ball. Spalding cleverly embellished and promoted the old miner's tale to make it the stuff of legends.

Spalding was also clever enough to know that Doubleday, a famous Civil War general, was "legend material" and would be an effective marketing tool in selling the Doubleday/Cooperstown myth. "It certainly appeals to an American's pride to have had the great national game of Base Ball created and named by a Major General in the United States Army," wrote Spalding.

DOUBLEDAY AND BASEBALL

• No record associated Doubleday and baseball before 1905.

• Doubleday entered West Point September 1, 1838, and was never in Cooperstown in 1839.

• Doubleday's obituary in the New York Times on January 28, 1893, didn't mention a thing about baseball.

• Doubleday, himself a writer, never wrote about the sport he supposedly invented. In a letter about his sporting life, Doubleday reminisced, "In my outdoor sports, I was addicted to topographical work, and even as a boy amused myself by making maps of the country." No mention of baseball.

BASEBALL IN EARLY WRITTEN RECORDS

The game of "baseball" was well documented long before its purported invention in 1839.

• In 1700, Revered Thomas Wilson, a Puritan from Maidstone, England, wrote disapprovingly about some of the events taking place on Sunday. "I have seen Morris-dancing, cudgel-playing, baseball and cricketts, and many other sports on the Lord's Day."

• In 1774, John Newberry of London published a children's book named *A Little Pretty Pocket-Book.* The 30-page book presents a number of games, each one with a rhyme and woodcut illustration. One of the games in the book is "BASE-BALL," which is described in the following rhyme:

BASE-BALL
The Ball once struck off,
Away flies the Boy
To the next destin'd Post
And then Home with Joy.

The accompanying illustrations depicts some young boys playing what is clearly a hit-the-ball-and-run kind of game. Posts mark separate bases at the corners (posts were used as bases in American baseball well into the 1860s). One boy is tossing the ball; another is waiting to strike the ball, while waiting beside a base; at a different base, another boy is poised to make a dash for "home."

Other early written references to baseball include the following:

• A 1744 book describes a rounders-like game as "base-ball."

• So does an 1829 London book called *The Boy's Own Book.*

• The acclaimed author Jane Austin refers to "baseball" in her 1798 novel, *Northanger Abbey.*

• C.A. Peverlly, in *The Book of American Pastimes*, published in 1866, clearly affirms that baseball came from the English game of rounders.

AT THE TIME

• Francis C. Richter said Spalding "...was the greatest propagandist and missionary the game ever knew and spent more time, labor, and money in spreading the gospel of Base Ball than any other man of record."

• The *New York Times* said: "The canny sports writer now refers to Abner with his tongue in cheek." *The Sun* of New York called it "a popular and harmless legend."

NUTS TO YOU

The average American eats about nine pounds of peanuts per year.

• Americans eat about 800 million pounds of peanut butter each year, enough to spread across the Grand Canyon's floor.

• The peanut wasn't popular in America until the late 1800s, when the Barnum Circus began selling them under the Big Top.

• Arachibutyophobia is the fear that peanut butter will stick to the roof of your mouth.

• One of Elvis Presley's favorite foods was a fried peanut butter and banana sandwich; Chef Julia Child loves peanut butter on corn chips.

LANDSLIDE LYNDON

In 1964, Republicans claimed that Democratic Presidential nominee Lyndon B. Johnson had a sordid past that included stealing his senate seat in 1948. It turns out they were right. This wonderful piece was contributed by B.R.I. member Michael Dorman.

THE RACE BEGINS

In 1948, while serving as a relatively obscure member of the House of Representatives, Lyndon Johnson entered the race for a vacant Texas seat in the Senate. Four other candidates were campaigning for the position in the Democratic primary. The most prominent among them was Coke Stevenson, who had served two terms as governor of Texas.

Since the Republican party fielded only token candidates in those days in Texas, victory in the Democratic primaries was equivalent to election. In the first primary for the Senate seat, Stevenson led the balloting with 477,077 votes—71,460 more than Johnson, who finished second. But because the remaining votes were divided among the other three candidates, Stevenson failed to win a majority of all ballots cast. Under Texas law, a second (or runoff) primary between Stevenson and Johnson was required to choose the winner of the Senate seat.

MR. BIG

During the period between the first and second primaries, Johnson forged a political alliance with a notoriously corrupt southern Texas political boss named George P. Parr. For almost four decades, Parr and his father before him had ruled as virtual feudal barons over a five-county area of oil-rich, sagebrush country just north of the Mexican border. Their subjects—thousands of Mexican-Americans—lived in terror of the Parr political machine.

Year after year, the frightened citizens trudged to the polls and voted the straight Parr ticket. This solid bloc of votes, guaranteed to any politician who won Parr's favor, could tip the balance in a close statewide race.

In the runoff, the initial returns from the five counties controlled by Parr gave Johnson 10,547 votes and Stevenson only 368. But Stevenson had run strongly in other parts of the state. When the statewide returns were tabulated, they showed Stevenson defeating Johnson by the razor-thin margin of 112 votes out of a total of almost 1 million cast.

HEADS I WIN, TAILS YOU LOSE

It was then that George Parr reached into his bag of political tricks and produced for Lyndon Johnson what came to be known as "the miracle of Box 13." After all the statewide returns were in and Johnson appeared to be the loser, Parr's election officials in Precinct (Box) 13 in the town of Alice suddenly claimed they had discovered some additional votes that had not previously been counted. Johnson's campaign manager, John Connally (who would later serve as Governor of Texas and U.S. Secretary of the Navy and Secretary of the Treasury), rushed to Alice to confer with the officials who would count the ballots that had supposedly been found. Former Governor Stevenson—fearing that Parr was in the process of trying to steal the election for Johnson—also hurried to the scene to protect his interests. He took with him two aides, James Gardner and Kellis Dibrell, who had formerly been FBI agents.

The ballot box from Precinct 13 was put away, purportedly for safekeeping, in a bank vault. The hitch was that the bank, along with almost everything else in the area, was controlled by George Parr.

It was not until six days after the election that Parr's officials submitted their revised tally of the votes from Box 13. They claimed they had found 203 ballots that had not previously been tabulated. Of those, they maintained, 201 had been cast for Johnson and only 2 for Stevenson. Thus, if these supposed ballots were allowed to stand, Johnson would win the primary by 87 votes.

By the time the additional votes were tabulated, a subcommittee of the Texas Democratic Executive Committee—assigned to count and certify the statewide ballots—had already issued a report declaring Stevenson the winner. But within hours after the subcommittee's declaration of what were assumed to be the final results, Johnson's aides announced that they expected the tabulation of the additional votes from Box 13 to change the outcome.

With the claim that the 201 newly discovered votes for Johnson would give him the victory, the situation in Parr's territory grew tense. Former Governor Stevenson and his aides demanded to see the list of registered voters in Precinct 13 so that they could check whether fraudulent ballots had been cast. Like the supposed ballots, the list of voters had also been locked in the bank vault. Bank officers, some of whom served as election officials for Parr, initially refused to allow Stevenson's men to see the list. Stevenson's aides had intended to examine it, note the names of the supposed voters, and then check whether such persons actually existed and had voted. Rumors swept Parr's territory that he and his henchmen were prepared to resort to gunplay, if necessary, to prevent inspection of the voting list. Standing by was his force of heavily armed *pistolero* sheriff's deputies. Stevenson appealed for help from the state capital in Austin, asking that a force of Texas Rangers be dispatched to the scene to prevent violence and ensure an honest count of the ballots. State officials responded by sending one of the most famous Texas Rangers of all time, Captain Frank Hamer, the man who had tracked down the notorious Bonnie Parker and Clyde Barrow and led the posse that killed them in a blazing Louisiana gun battle.

BULLETS AND BALLOTS

On the morning after Hamer's arrival, a showdown loomed in Wild West fashion on the street outside the bank. Five of Parr's henchmen, with loaded rifles at the ready, stood ominously across the street from the bank. A dozen others, with *pistolas* conspicuously displayed, formed a semicircle directly in front of the bank. Former Governor Stevenson, fearing Parr's men might try to shoot him and his aides and then claim self-defense, ordered his assistants to take off their coats before approaching the bank—to make clear they were carrying no concealed weapons.

Then, minutes before the bank was scheduled to open, Captain Hamer led Stevenson and his aides toward the bank. He halted a few feet from the semicircle of Parr men, stepped out in front of Stevenson's group, and stood there for a few moments to make sure everyone present recognized him.

In a scene that could have come right out of *High Noon*, Hamer crossed the street and set himself squarely in front of the five riflemen. He pointed his finger to the far end of the street and ordered, "Git!"

The men grumbled and swore for a few seconds, but then obeyed. Hamer next crossed back to the semicircle of men in front of the bank, surveyed the group silently at first, then barked, "Fall back!" The men cleared a path for Hamer, Stevenson and his aides to enter the bank.

LOOK, BUT DON'T TOUCH

Tom Donald, a Parr aide who ran the bank and also handled political chores for the local organization, opened the door. Stevenson and his assistants entered, but Hamer would not let the *pistoleros* inside. A short time later, Democratic party officials with responsibility for counting the votes and certifying the election results arrived. One of them, H. L. Adams, demanded that Donald open the bank vault and hand over the election records, since the Democratic party was entitled to serve as custodian of its own primary race documents. But Donald, acting on George Parr's orders, refused to comply.

"I will permit you to see the voting list, but not to handle it," he said. All he would agree to do was remove the voting list from the vault, hold it up, and allow the Stevenson men and party officials to view it from across a wide table. Stevenson and his aides began taking down names and immediately spotted several oddities. The persons whose ballots had been belatedly "found" had all signed their names in what seemed to be the identical handwriting.

Furthermore, their names appeared in ink that differed in color from all other names on the rolls. As if those facts were not suspicious enough, the "late" voters had somehow managed to cast their ballots in alphabetical order. Since voters usually show up at the polls in haphazard fashion, there seemed no reasonable explanation of why all these citizens would have appeared alphabetically.

After Stevenson and his men had recorded the names of only 17 voters, however, a telephone rang and was answered by Parr aide Donald. He listened for a minute, then folded the voting list and put it back in the bank vault. "That's all," he said.

Frustrated but determined to plod ahead, Stevenson's men began trying to locate the 17 persons whose names they had noted.

The smallest spider measures half the size of a printed period.

They quickly discovered that four of them could not have voted: the foursome had long been buried in a local cemetery. Another man whose name appeared on the list was found alive, in a distant Texas city. He denied even being in Parr's county on election day, much less voting there. A local housewife whose name appeared on the list said she had not voted and was not even qualified to vote. After a dogged investigation, Stevenson's aides were unable to find a single person from among the 17 who had actually voted.

AND THE WINNER IS...

Stevenson and Democratic party officials went into court, charging that Parr had tried to steal the election for Johnson. They asked the courts to take speedy action to prevent such a theft from receiving official sanction. But Johnson and his forces took court action of their own, seeking to certify Johnson as the winner of the election. They accused Texas Ranger Captain Hamer of entering into a conspiracy with Stevenson, various Democratic party officials, and others to have the belatedly "found" votes set aside as fraudulent. And they asked the court to bar any further recount of the votes. While the rival court actions were pending, the Texas Democratic Executive Committee met in Fort Worth to consider which candidate to certify as the winner. On the first ballot there was a 28-28 deadlock between Stevenson and Johnson. A second ballot produced identical results. Then Johnson, his campaign manager, John Connally, and his lawyer, John Cofer, left the room where the meeting was taking place, after being promised no additional votes would be taken until they returned. They made arrangements to have a member of the executive committee who had not been present for the prior votes flown to Fort Worth from Amarillo, almost 350 miles away. They did not return to the executive committee meeting until the previously absent member, C. C. Gibson, arrived.

On the next ballot, Gibson voted to certify Johnson as the winner—making the tally 29 to 28. The committee then adjourned its meeting.

Although winning the Democratic primary run off guaranteed election in Texas, there was still the formality of a general election. The slate certified by the Texas Democratic Executive Committee was ordinarily listed on the ballot for the general election alongside

The average duration of sexual intercourse (for humans) is 2 minutes.

token slates of candidates fielded by the Republicans and minority parties. In many races, the Republicans did not even bother to nominate candidates. But in any event, it would be necessary for the winners of the Democratic nominations to go through the motions of running in general election campaigns.

Responsibility for printing the official general election ballots rested with Paul Brown, the Texas secretary of state. At the time of the tight, controversial Democratic Executive Committee meeting, Brown was already facing the deadline for ordering the printing of the ballots. But he could not do so until he knew the outcome of the Johnson-Stevenson contest. Once the committee voted to certify Johnson, Brown ordered the ballots printed with Johnson's name as the official Democratic candidate for the Senate.

Former Governor Stevenson then went into the United States district court in Dallas and filed a new lawsuit seeking to overturn the certification of Johnson as winner by both the Democratic Executive Committee and Secretary of State Brown. Federal Judge T. Whitfield Davidson, in whose court the case was filed, had left Dallas for a weekend of relaxation at a farm he owned near Marshall, Texas. Stevenson drove all night to reach Davidson's farm and asked him to sign a court order preventing, at least temporarily, what the former governor contended was the "theft" of the election.

A BLANK SLATE

Judge Davidson, after reading the legal petition presented by Stevenson, agreed to sign the order. It instructed that all election returns and ballots from George Parr's territory be seized, pending court examination. It also barred Secretary of State Brown from printing the general election ballots until the court examination was completed. A hearing on Stevenson's suit was set for September 21.

Immediately after learning of the court order, Secretary of State Brown rushed to the print shop where the ballots were to be produced. He discovered the ballots were about to begin rolling off the presses. At the last moment, he ordered Johnson's name stricken and the ballots printed without a Democratic senatorial candidate listed.

Johnson and his forces soon counterattacked. They tried to persuade a federal appeals court to overturn Davidson's order, but the best they could do was get the appeals court to set a hearing on the matter for October 2—eleven days after Davidson's own hearing. Meanwhile, Davidson appointed a San Antonio attorney, William R. Smith, to conduct an investigation of the purported vote theft for the court. Smith was empowered to go to Parr's territory, take possession of the election records, subpoena witnesses, and gather evidence on all facts related to the run off election.

Smith lost no time in hurrying to the scene, taking with him federal marshals to help in the investigation. But when they arrived, they discovered that the election records were missing and that the Parr lieutenants whose testimony was wanted had mysteriously gone to Mexico—beyond the reach of the court—on what they claimed was urgent business. The ballot boxes were ultimately found, but all they contained were old newspapers and other trash.

JUSTICE TO THE RESCUE

Thus, when the hearing opened on September 21 in Judge Davidson's court, the most critical evidence was absent. The voting list, the ballots, and other election materials were gone. Johnson's team of attorneys, including both John Cofer and a friend of Johnson's named Leon Jaworski (later Watergate special prosecutor), seized the opportunity to claim that Stevenson had no case.

"This plaintiff [Stevenson] lost his race for United States senatorial nominee in a Democratic primary, over which only the regular Democratic officials have jurisdiction," Cofer told Judge Davidson. "This court has no jurisdiction. He [Stevenson] has no civil rights [that are being violated], as pleaded in his petition. He is merely a poor loser."

The judge, however, had little patience for such an argument. Banging his gavel to silence Cofer, Davidson denied his request to throw the case out of court. "This plaintiff, Mr. Stevenson, has alleged he has been robbed by fraud of a seat in the United States Senate," the judge said. "Not a shred of evidence has been submitted to disprove his claim. He...is entitled to a hearing in open court. And that hearing he shall have. This court will decide on the merits of his petition."

There are over 200 people on the waiting list to witness an execution in Florida.

Davidson was wrong. He would not have a chance to conclude his hearing or decide the case on its merits. Lyndon Johnson had retained a noted Washington lawyer, Abe Fortas, to file a petition with U.S. Supreme Court Justice Hugo Black asking him to order Davidson's hearing halted. (Fortas himself would later serve a controversial term on the Supreme Court, on appointment from his former client, then-President Lyndon Johnson.) Fortas's petition to Justice Black did not deal with the merits of the election fraud charges, but merely contended that the issues in the case should be resolved by the Democratic party and not by the federal courts. Justice Black signed an order forbidding Judge Davidson to proceed further with the hearing or otherwise consider Stevenson's case.

ORDER IN THE COURT

Justice Black was empowered to issue such an order on his own because the full Supreme Court was not in session at the time. Theoretically, the full court ultimately could have reversed his ruling. But the effect of the order was to halt Judge Davidson's consideration of the case indefinitely. Since the general election was quickly approaching, there would be little time for the full court to hear arguments and reverse Black's decision in time to allow Stevenson to get his name on the general election ballot.

Black's court order was flown from Washington to Texas and presented to Judge Davidson by a federal marshal. Davidson reluctantly halted his hearing. "This court has no choice but to submit to the mandate from the Supreme Court, although, in my opinion, Mr. Justice Black has acted hastily and probably illegally," Davidson said.

For all intents, Justice Black's order put an official seal on what many considered Johnson's theft of the Senate seat—with a major assist from George Parr. Time ran out on Stevenson's further efforts to win court consideration of the vote-fraud charges. Secretary of State Brown ordered Johnson's name listed on the ballot as the official Democratic Senate nominee. Johnson then easily swept to victory in the general election.

SENATOR JOHNSON

When he returned to Washington as senator, he had a new

Only 1 of 6 able-bodied men in the American colonies fought in the Revolutionary War.

nickname—"Landslide Lyndon"—derived from his 87-vote "victory" in the race against Stevenson. Within a few years, he would become the Senate majority leader and be considered the second most powerful man in Washington. Some said he was the most powerful, because President Dwight D. Eisenhower was in the White House at the time and was considered by many a weak chief executive. In 1960 Johnson would be elected vice president on John F. Kennedy's ticket; he would become president upon Kennedy's assassination in 1963 and win his own presidential election a year later.

THE COURSE OF HISTORY

Thus there is strong reason to speculate that the entire history of the United States might have been radically different if George Parr and his cohorts had not "stolen" the 1948 election for Johnson. If Stevenson had been declared the winner of the senatorial primary, Johnson would have remained in the House for at least several more years. He could not have become Senate majority leader when he did and thus probably would not have been the vice presidential candidate in 1960. As a result, he would not have become president. He himself observed many times that only a fluke could have put him or anyone else from the South or Southwest in the White House under the political conditions prevailing in the United States in the 1950s and 1960s. Actually, in his case, it took two flukes: the first was the purported "theft" of the Senate election, the second was President Kennedy's assassination.

Meanwhile, George Parr continued delivering one-sided majorities at the polls for his pet candidates. Johnson was a major beneficiary of such election manipulation. Another beneficiary was John Connally, who was elected governor of Texas with help from Parr.

NO JOY IN PARRVILLE

During the early 1970s Parr was indicted on charges of failing to list on his tax returns income of more than $287,000. In March 1974 he was found guilty and sentenced to 10 years in prison. By the time his final appeal was turned down, Parr was 74 years old. He had been convicted of other crimes in the past but had served only one prison term.

He was due to appear in court for a hearing. When he did not show up, he was listed as a fugitive. Federal marshals were sent to hunt for him, and they found him slumped over the steering wheel of his car in a pasture near his palatial home. He was dead, with a bullet wound in his head. A .45-caliber pistol and an M-14 military rifle lay on the car seat. A local justice of the peace ruled the death a suicide, apparently prompted by Parr's reluctance to serve any prison time at his advanced age.

By the time of Parr's death, Lyndon Johnson lay in his own grave. There were those who felt the story of the theft of the 1948 Senate election should be buried along with them.

✓ ✓ ✓

TV TIME: ALL IN THE FAMILY

• "All in the Family"'s twelve-and-a-half season run was second only to "Ozzie and Harriet" (which ran fourteen) among TV sitcoms.

• The original title of the show was "Those Were the Days"—hence the name of the theme song.

• The theme was performed with only a piano and two voices (Archie's and Edith's) because Norman Lear had only $800 in his budget to record it and that was the cheapest way to go.

• When Gloria gave birth to "Joey" in 1975, the event inspired another first—the "Joey" doll, billed as the first "anatomically correct male doll."

• Rob Reiner wore a toupee for his role as the long-haired Mike Stivic—he's actually as bald as his father, Carl Reiner. Even without hair, however, fans recognized him on the street wherever he went and yelled "Meathead" after him. He hated it.

• In 1974, Carroll O'Connor went on strike for more money. At first it seemed that his demands couldn't be met—so, according to *TV Guide*, the show's writers came up with an emergency plan to have Archie attend a convention, where he would be mugged and murdered. That way the show could continue with the rest of the cast. O'Connor settled for $2 million per year.

• Edith Bunker was so important to Americans that when she "died" of a stroke in 1980, *Newsweek* ran a half-page obituary, as they would have for a real world leader.

TRAVELS WITH RAY

Perplexing adventures of the brilliant egghead Ray "Weird Brain" Redel. Answers are on page 672.

On occasion, "Weird Brain" Redel, the celebrated thinker, would host a party at his plush home in the Hollywood hills. Of course, everyone who "mattered" in Tinseltown wanted an invitation. But "Weird Brain" had his own agenda... and his own friends. Some were well-known socialites, like Grace Kelly and Prince Ahmed Faroul; some were big brains like Einstein, and others were just...well, people like me.

One starry evening "Weird Brain," Al Schweitzer and Al Einstein were deeply engrossed in a discussion about biology with Jayne Mansfield. Jayne had them enthralled. "Well," she said, "you big, silly brains talk all the time about evolution and that sort of thing. That's so cute." She gave Einstein a peck on the forehead, leaving a big lipstick smear. "OOO, why, I'll bet you don't even know what a duckling becomes when it first takes to water."

"Of course we do, Miss Mansfield," Al Schweitzer interjected, "—a semi-mature aquatic web-toed aviant."

"No, honey," Jayne cooed. "That's not it." And when she explained it to them, the smartest guys in the world had to admit Jayne was right.

What DID she say?

Later that evening, "Weird Brain" and a few physicist buddies were discussing their newest discoveries. One little bearded guy with a German accent, dressed in a white smock that made him look as if he had just left Dr. Frankenstein's laboratory, volunteered some startling data. "I have stumbled upon something," he intoned, "that comes once in a minute, twice in a moment, but not once in a thousand years."

The eggheads gasped. How was this possible? "Weird Brain" reached over and gave the guy's beard a tug. It came off...revealing Peter Lorre. "Okay, Pete, enough jokes. Tell them what you mean."

What did Lorre have in mind?

The song "Satisfaction" is played over 300 times a day on American radio.

FAMOUS CHEATERS

In the last Bathroom Reader, we introduced a feature called "Famous Cheaters." Here's another installment.

BACKGROUND: In the mid-50s, quiz shows, like "Tic Tac Dough," "21," and "The $64,000 Question," were the hottest thing on TV. The public couldn't get enough of them. ("The $64,000 Question" was the only show to beat "I Love Lucy" in the annual ratings, ranking as the #1 program of 1955.) Network executives loved them, too, because they were cheap to produce, and extremely profitable. By 1958, over 24 game shows were on the air. The competition grew increasingly fierce.

QUIZ CROOKS: Unknown to the public, a number of shows, including "The $64,000 Question," had begun rigging the competition to increase their entertainment value and improve their ratings.

It turned out that answers were often provided to preferred contestants—such as Charles Van Doren, an assistant English professor at Columbia University, who'd been making $5,500 a year. In 1956, the 29-year-old Van Doren became an overnight celebrity thanks to his appearances on the show "21." After knocking off the champion Herb Stempel, Van Doren went on to win $129,000. The media dubbed him "the quiz whiz." Soon after he appeared on the cover of *Time* magazine and was hired by NBC's "Today" show for $50,000.

THE ACCUSATION: Stempel was bitter at being defeated by Van Doren. He complained to several New York newspapers that "21" was fixed. There were no immediate reactions to Stempel's revelations, but in 1958 a contestant on CBS's game show "Dotto"—where contestants connected dots to reveal celebrity faces—claimed to have found an opponent's notebook with answers in it.

THE INVESTIGATION: In response to growing speculation, the House Committee on Legislative Oversight investigated allegations that quiz shows were fixed. Among the first witnesses to come forward was actress Patty Duke, who had won $64,000 on "The

$64,000 Question." Duke claimed that the show's associate producer, Shirley Bernstein (the sister of conductor Leonard) had secretly given her the correct answers before the show.

But the most damaging revelations were made by Van Doren. In a dramatic confession on November 2, 1959, before the U.S. Senate, he admitted that all his "21" victories had been fixed. Van Doren claimed that producer Albert Freedman "told me that Herbert Stempel, the current champion, was an unbeatable contestant because he knew too much. He said that Stempel was unpopular, and was defeating opponents right and left to the detriment of the program. He asked me if, as a favor to him, I would agree to an arrangment whereby I would tie Stempel and thus increase the entertainment value of the program."

Van Doren appeared remorseful. "I would give almost anything I have to reverse the course of my life in the last three years...I was involved, deeply involved, in a deception." He immediately resigned from his teaching post at Columbia and was fired at NBC's "Today Show" as well.

THE RESULT: The nation was shocked by Van Doren's testimony: *Life* magazine wrote that it had "exposed a nation's sagging moral standards." Then-president Eisenhower was quoted as saying "it was a terrible thing to do to the American people." The *Washington Post* ran an editorial saying "it will render very little service to the public to make Charles Van Doren a scapegoat. It is an industry, not an individual, that stands in need of redemption." Almost immediately all game shows—even honest ones—were removed from the air. Congress passed legislation making quiz show fraud punishable by law.

MISCELLANEOUS

• Charles Van Doren later became an executive with *Encyclopedia Brittanica.* He refused to discuss the scandal after his congressional testimony.

• Dr. Joyce Brothers won $64,000 fielding questions on boxing; Barbara ("Get Smart") Feldon won $64,000 answering questions on Shakespeare. Consolation Prize: Anyone who made it to the big $64,000 question and blew it, still got to drive home in a new Cadillac.

REAL PEOPLE

Some rock songs are about real people, though most of us never know it. Here are three examples:

BAD, BAD LEROY BROWN, by Jim Croce
Jim Croce met the man who inspired "Leroy Brown" while he was in the Army, stationed at Fort Dix, New Jersey. He and Croce were both going to school to learn how to become telephone linemen. Croce recalls: "He stayed there about a week and one evening he turned around and said he was really fed up and tired. He went AWOL, and then came back at the end of the month to get his paycheck. They put handcuffs on him and took him away. Just to listen to him talk and see how 'bad' he was, I knew someday I was gonna write a song about him."

THE SULTANS OF SWING, by Dire Straits
The Sultans of Swing was a jazz band that Mark Knopfler, leader of Dire Straits, happened to see at a pub one night.

Knopfler: "My brother Dave was living somewhere in Greenwich and we went out to the pub—I think it was called the Swan...and we had a game of pool and a couple of pints. There was a jazz band playing and there was nobody in there except us and a couple of kids in the corner. They did a couple of requests. I asked them for 'Creole Love Call,' and it was great. There are loads of bands like that. They're postmen, accountants, milkmen, draftsmen, teachers. They just get together Sunday lunchtimes, nighttimes, and they play traditional jazz. It's funny, because they play this New Orleans music note-for-note...in Greenwich, England."

PEGGY SUE, by Buddy Holly
This was Buddy Holly's first solo record, and one of the most famous "girl-name" records in rock history. But although Buddy made Peggy Sue famous, she wasn't in love with him—she was Cricket drummer Jerry Allison's girlfriend. Later Jerry and Peggy Sue tied the knot, and Buddy celebrated with a tune called "Peggy Sue Got Married." By the time they got divorced, Buddy was dead.

MAGAZINE ORIGINS

They're American institutions now, but once they were just someone's ideas. Here's a quick look at the origins of a few U.S. mags.

Reader's Digest. A young Minnesotan named DeWitt Wallace realized that modern Americans didn't have time to get all the latest information. They needed quick, easy access to it, and he could provide it in a magazine. Why didn't people just tune in to radio or TV? It was 1920.

On October 15, 1921 DeWitt Wallace and Lila Acheson were married. They also sent out several thousand mimeographed fliers asking people to subscribe to their new digest. When they returned from their honeymoon, more than 1,000 subscriptions were waiting. *Reader's Digest* was born.

Time. In 1923, two Yale friends—Britt Hadden and Henry Luce—also created a sort of "digest." They scoured dozens of newspapers for important news and synopsized it in "approximately 100 short articles, none of which are over 400 words." The first issue (March, 1923), financed by wealthy Yale acquaintances, was a bomb. So they changed directions, hiring a news staff and developing the pointed, pun-filled, opinionated writing style that's now the standard in American magazines. That worked; *Time* flew.

Fortune. Started in February 1930 as a way to use the excess material being produced by *Time*'s business department.

Newsweek. It looks and sounds like *Time* magazine? That's because it was started by a man who'd worked at *Time*, and whose fondest wish was to drive *Time* "out of business." Thomas Martyn started it on February 17, 1933. Today it's owned by the *Washington Post*.

TV Guide. TV was becoming an American institution in 1952 when Philadelphia publisher Walter Annenberg spotted an ad for a magazine called *TV Digest*. Was there really a market for it? His staff said yes...so he decided to start a national TV magazine with regional listings. He bought up the half-dozen regional TV magazines that had already sprung up and consolidated them into a single new publication. The Apr. '53 debut issue featured Lucy's baby.

Starfish don't have brains.

SOLUTION PAGE

TRAVELS WITH RAY, PAGE 467

• Ray tossed Bogart a pack of matches. The answer to Bogart's riddle was "Fire." And since he was pointing to a cigarette, "Weird Brain" figured he wanted a light. Bogie, furious, jumped up and challenged "Weird Brain" to a drinking match. They tied three times, then both passed out.

• Casey was talking about a river, of course. I assume it was the Nile, though Casey kept calling it the "Vile."

TRAVELS WITH RAY, PAGE 515

• A map. We bought another one, but got lost anyway, and stumbled into the valley full of prehistoric creatures...but that's another story.

• The wind. Never leaves a shadow, as far as I know.

TRAVELS WITH RAY, PAGE 580

• "Your breath," Charlie guffawed.

• "Weird Brain" shipped his scientific equipment in a coffin. "I hope that doesn't mean my idea is dead, nyuk-nyuk-nyuk," he said. I told him he'd been hanging around the 3 Stooges too long.

MILITARY DOUBLE-TALK, PAGE 607

1-K, 2-J, 3-N, 4-G, 5-I, 6-M, 7-A, 8-C, 9-D, 10-F, 11-H, 12-E, 13-L, 14-B

TRAVELS WITH RAY, PAGE 667

• "You big brains are so-o-o-o goofy," Jayne giggled. "The first thing a duckling becomes when it takes to water is...wet." Not even Einstein could argue with that.

• Lorre was talking about the letter M, a letter he was quite fond of. "M" was the title of the film that made him a star.

Uncle John's FOURTH BATHROOM READER

Selections from "Prime Time Proverbs" Copyright © 1989 by Jack Mingo and John Javna. Reprinted by permission of the authors.

"The Monster Mash," "Surprise Hits," "Instant Hits," "Songwriter Stories," and "First Hits" originally appeared in *Behind the Hits*. Copyright © 1986, by Bob Shannon and John Javna. Reprinted by permission of the authors.

"Economy Class Syndrome" originally appeared in *The Airline Passenger's Guerrilla Handbook*. Copyright © 1989 by George Albert Brown. Reprinted by permission of Slawson Communications, San Marcos, California.

"Pun For The Money" originally appeared in *Get Thee To A Punnery*, published by Wyrick & Company. Copyright © 1988 by Richard Lederer. Reprinted by permission of the publisher.

"The Press and the Prez" and "In the News" originally appeared in *If No News, Send Rumors: Anecdotes of American Journalism*. Copyright © 1989 by Stephen Bates. Reprinted with permission of St. Martin's Press.

"The Compass in Your Nose" and "Zz-zz-zz" originally appeared in *The Compass In Your Nose and Other Astonishing Facts About Humans*. Copyright © by Marc McCutcheon. Reprinted by permission of Jeremy P Tarcher, Inc., Los Angeles.

"What's In a Name" originally appeared in The Best Baby Name Book in the Whole World, Copyright © 1984 by Bruce Lansky. Reprinted by permission of the publisher, Meadowbrook Press.

THANK YOU

The Bathroom Readers' Institute sincerely thanks the people whose advice and assistance made this book possible, including:

John Javna
John Dollison
Jack Mingo
Phil Catalfo
Ross Owens
Eric Lefcowitz
Mike Litchfield
Fritz Springmeyer
Lyn Speakman
Catherine Dee
Lenna Lebovich
Melanie Foster
Dayna Macy
Megan Anderson
Emma Lauriston
Denise "Hi Ho!" Silver
Nenelle Bunnin
Sharilyn Hovind
Ann Krueger Spivack
Audrey Baer Johnson
Gary the proofreader
Penelope Houston
Mike Goldberger
Gordon Van Gelder
Jay Nitschke
Mike Brunsfeld
Tia Kratter
Zoila Zegovia
Thomas Crapper
Jeff Stafford
The EarthWorks Group
...and all the bathroom readers

This page is for Emergency Use Only.

UNCLE JOHN'S BATHROOM LEADER

The Bathroom Reader offers a special "Bowl Me Over" salute to Lyndon Baines Johnson—probably the only president who actually conducted affairs of state while seated on the pot.

GETTING IT BACKWARDS

According to Doris Kearns Goodwin, in her biography, *Lyndon Johnson and the American Dream*, "Few Presidents have permitted the kind of intimacy between themselves and their staffs that Johnson encouraged. When he had to go to the bathroom in the middle of a conversation, it was not unusual for him to move the discussion there. Johnson seemed delighted as he told me of 'one of those delicate Kennedyites who came into the bathroom with me and then found it utterly impossible to look at me while I sat there on the toilet.' "

" 'You'd think he had never seen those parts of the body before. For there he was, standing as far away from me as he possibly could, keeping his back toward me the whole time, trying to carry on a conversation. I could barely hear a word he said. I kept straining my ears and then finally I asked him to come a little closer to me. Then began the most ludicrous scene I had ever witnessed. Instead of simply turning around and walking over to me, he kept his face away from me and walked backward, one rickety step at a time. For a moment I thought he was going to run right into me. It certainly made me wonder how that man had made it so far in the world.' "

THE EARLY DAYS

LBJ's habit of making the most of his "down time" actually began in the 1930s—long before he was elected president. According to biographer Robert Caro, the 24-year-old Johnson, a secretary to a Texas Congressman, bullied the other officeworkers while seated on the pot:

"The toilet in the office was set in a short corridor between its two rooms. Johnson would sit down on it, and there would come a call: "L.E.! [L.E. Jones, Johnson's assistant] L.E.!" L.E. would say,

'Oh, God,' because he hated this. At first, he attempted to stand away from the door, but Johnson insisted he come right into the doorway, so he would be standing over him, and L.E. would stand with his head and nose averted, and take dictation...The tactic was, indeed, 'a method of control'...those who observed it, knew it was being done to humiliate [Jones], and to prove who was boss."

ONE-MAN SHOW

Though a big believer in bathroom business, Johnson would not tolerate it from his staff. According to Caro, he wouldn't allow them to go to the bathroom at all while they worked: 'If he caught you reading a letter from your mother, or if you were taking a crap, he'd say, "Son, can't you *please* try a little harder to learn to do that on your own time?" '

IN THE NEWS

People in Johnson's inner circle weren't his only victims—even members of the press got a taste of his bathroom manner. Steven Bates describes CBS reporter/White House correspondent Robert Pierpont's lunch with LBJ: "After they had eaten...the President told Pierpont to stay for coffee. By about 3:00 p.m. the conversation had become an LBJ monologue. Pierpont tried again to leave. Johnson stood up and said it was time to cross the hall.

"Pierpont followed Johnson into a bedroom. The President started undressing, handing each piece of his clothing to a valet. LBJ stripped naked, continuing his monologue the whole time. He put on a pajama top and walked into a bathroom, 'speaking loudly, over the sound of passing water.' Then LBJ put on the pajama bottoms and got into bed. He talked for another fifteen minutes, then said good-bye—three hours after the conversation had begun."

CONSTITUENT SERVICE

Even *voters* occasionally saw Johnson in the altogether. Caro describes a typical scene during LBJ's 1948 campaign for the U.S. Senate: "Rooms in many small-town hotels had only hand basins, with communal toilets at the end of the hall. These bathrooms were small and hot, and it was cooler if the door was left open, so often Johnson left it open. Not a few voters therefore saw the candidate for the U.S. Senate sitting on the toilet, and described that sight to relatives and friends."

MYTH CONCEPTIONS

At the BRI, we love "facts" that aren't true. Here's some info that may surprise you.

Myth: The Great Wall of China is visible from the moon.
Truth: No manmade objects are visible from that far out in space. According to astronomers, it's about as visible as a popsicle stick from 240 miles away.

Myth: Alligator shirts have alligators on them.
Truth: They're crocodiles—René Lacoste, a French tennis star known as *le crocodile*, invented them in the 1920s.

Myth: The sardine is a species of fish.
Truth: The word "sardine" actually refers to any breed of small fish—including herring and pilchard—that's been stuffed into a sardine can.

Myth: S.O.S. stands for "Save Our Ship."
Truth: It doesn't stand for anything—it was selected as a distress signal because it's easy to transmit in morse code: 3 dots, 3 dashes, 3 dots.

Myth: I.O.U. stands for "I owe you."
Truth: Originally the borrower wrote "I Owe Unto," followed by the lender's name.

Myth: Thumb sucking causes buck teeth.
Truth: An old wive's tale. Thumb sucking may even be beneficial. Some researchers believe that it aids the development of facial muscles and bones.

Myth: Karate is a Japanese martial art.
Truth: It actually started in India and spread to China—before reaching Japan. It first became popular in Okinawa in the 1600s, when officials prohibited Okinawans from possessing weapons.

Myth: Thomas Edison invented the lightbulb in 1879.
Truth: The first incandescent bulb was invented by Sir Humphrey Davy in 1802. But the filaments he used burned out quickly. Edison pioneered the use of carbonized cotton filaments—making the bulbs practical for the first time.

Myth: Your ears are the things you see on the side of your head.
Truth: Technically, the human ear is located inside the skull, and stops at the end of the ear canal. The parts you can see are called the *pinnas*.

Myth: You can judge the nutritional content of an egg by the color of its shell.
Truth: Eggshells don't tell you anything about the egg—but they do tell you about the hen that laid it: white eggs are laid by hens with white earlobes; brown eggs are laid by chickens with red earlobes.

Myth: The Egyptians were master embalmers.
Truth: The dry climate deserves most of the credit. In fact, as Egyptian embalming methods "advanced" over time, corpses began deteriorating more quickly.

Myth: Fortune cookies were invented in China.
Truth: They were invented in the U.S. in 1918 by Charles Jung, a Chinese restaurant owner, to amuse customers while they waited for their food. Only later were they served *after* the meal.

Myth: The French poodle originated in France.
Truth: The breed was created in Germany around the 16th century. Called *puddel*, or "splash" dogs, they were bred to retrieve ducks. They didn't become popular in France until years later.

Myth: According to the Bible, Angels have wings.
Truth: Nowhere in the Bible does it say that angels have wings. The idea didn't become popular until painters and sculptors began adding them.

There are three times as many cows as people in Montana.

THE WHOLE DOUGHNUT

"Doughnuts," says Michael Lasky in his book Junk Food, *"are the ultimate junk food. Fortified with globs of sugar and then fried in oceans of hot grease, they have found a niche in our stomachs."*

Doughnuts originated in 16th-century Holland. They were cooked in oil, and were so greasy that the Dutch called them *olykoeks*, or "oily cakes."

The Pilgrims, who'd lived in Holland, brought the cakes with them when they came to America. Their version: a round doughy ball about the size of a nut—a *doughnut*.

The origin of the doughnut hole: Captain Hanson Gregory, a 19th-century Maine sea captain, was eating a doughnut while sailing through a storm. Suddenly the ship rocked violently and threw him against the ship's wheel—impaling his cake on one of its spokes. Seeing how well the spoke held his cake, Gregory began ordering all of his cakes with holes in them.

Doughnuts were popularized in the U.S. after the Salvation Army fed doughnuts—cooked in garbage pails and served on bayonets—to troops during World War I. Soldiers got so hooked on them that they were called "doughboys."

The French have a doughnut they call *pet de nonne,—"Nun's Fart."* According to legend, a nun living in the abbey of Marmoutier was preparing food for a religious feast. Suddenly she farted, and the other nuns laughed at her. She was so embarrassed that she dropped the spoonful of dough she was holding into a pot of boiling oil—accidently making a doughnut.

Doughnut-dunking was first popularized at the Roseland Ballroom in the '20s, when actress Mae Murray slipped and accidentally thrust a doughnut into a cup of coffee.

The *glazed* doughnut is almost three times as popular as any other type of doughnut.

Attention caffeine addicts: Hawaii is the only U.S. state where coffee is grown.

WEIRD BOARD GAMES

When you think of board games, you probably think of Monopoly or Risk. But there are plenty of bizarre board games you've never heard of. Here are a few examples. (No kidding—these games were really sold.)

Dr. Ruth Westheimer's Game of Good Sex. Based on her sexual advice talk shows. Couples play the game trying to accumulate Arousal Points in quest of Mutual Pleasure. Two to four couples could play but only consenting adults—over 21—were allowed to buy it.

Mafia. The purpose: to gain control of Sicilian airports, real estate, construction projects, banks, and drug trade. The rules call for each "family," assisted by henchmen, to move around a map of Sicily selling heroin and eluding the police. The Italian-made board game caused considerable controversy in its native country.

Is The Pope Catholic? In 1986, two Boston-based entrepreneurs manufactured this game. Players move around the board trying to attain the rank of pope. Among the obstacles (or temptations) along the way: nipping at holy wine and squandering the church's money on candy. Small miracles help players out. A winner is declared when a cloud of white smoke is sent by the Convocation of Cardinals, signaling the election of a pope.

Twinkies and Trolls. The proprietors of "Buddies," a well-known gay bar in Boston, invented this game, which they described as "a lighthearted reflection of gay life and the gay lifestyle." Players come out of the closet, visit their first gay bar and the "baths" in New York, San Francisco, Provincetown, and Ft. Lauderdale. The object is to amass as many "Twinkies" (gay slang for young, attractive preppies), and avoid "Trolls" (old, ugly gay men).

Class Struggle. Bertell Ollman was a Marxist professor at New York University when he invented this game. The object is to win the revolution, and each player represents a different class of society. Ollman later wrote a book about his experiences in marketing the game. It was called *Class Struggle Is The Name Of The Game: True Confessions Of A Marxist Businessman.*

Gender Bender. Makes players answer questions as if they were members of the opposite sex.

Trump: The Game. Developed by real estate tycoon Donald Trump. Like Monopoly, the object is to make the most money. But unlike Monopoly, the smallest denomination is $10 million...and each bill bears Trump's face. Trump explained: "I wanted to teach business instincts. It's great if they can learn that from a game instead of having to go out and lose your shirt." That, of course, was before Trump lost his own shirt.

NUKE: The Last Game on Earth. Developed by two architects, Chris Corday and Steve Weeks. The game gives players the chance to be world leaders, deciding the fate of the world. If they can't work out their problems, the world is destroyed.

Civil War. In 1989, Naji Tueini, a Lebanese entrepreneur, successful marketed this game based on his country's internal turmoil. It rewards strategy such as "reselling products sent as international assistance" and "taking hostages," but docks points for getting stuck in a fall-out shelter during heavy bombardment. It was translated into English and French.

It's Only Money. In 1989, more than 25 major companies (like Porsche, Seagrams, Revlon and Mastercard) paid $30,000 apiece to have their products promoted in this game. Each company got a storefront" on the board where players (or "shoppers") browsed in a bustling shopping mall, trying to avoid crowds on the escalators. The game's creator, Eric S. Medney, described the game as delivering "corporate messages to the entire family while they're having fun."

Bankruptcy. The object is to acquire as many companies as possible without going bankrupt. If you do declare bankruptcy, however, you have to play Russian roulette with a toy gun included with the set. If the gun pops, you're out. The inspiration for the game? Victor Smith, its creator, explained: "I was on the edge of bankruptcy when the idea hit me."

Women like blue bedrooms the most; men like white.

TAMMY FAYE

Remember when Tammy Faye Bakker was in the news every day? In case you're feeling nostalgic, here are some of the things she's said.

"We were raising money to be missionaries in the Amazon. Can you imagine me in the Amazon! All day long trying to keep my false eyelashes from falling off and my nails from breaking. The only way I would have fit in is that I like jewelry just as much as the natives."

"I'm a good cook. In the evening, I make mostly chicken or tuna sandwiches, or we'll go out for pizza."

"There's times I just have to quit thinking, and the only way I can quit thinking is by shopping."

"We prayed and asked God to give us the money to buy a trailer. We took this meeting in West Virginia, a tiny church up in the mountains. God began to bless and move. We started praying for the trailer in that meeting and people put $100 bills in the offering for us. We were embarrassed because we had been putting $20 and $30 in the bank. Now God was performing a miracle and giving us the most money we had ever had in our lives.... The next week, we purchased the most beautiful 30-foot Holiday Rambler trailer."

"I wear wigs all the time, and Jim never knows who I'm going to be."

"One day while eating supper, little Chi Chi, who liked lima beans, ate some and ran into another room.... When the dog didn't return, I wondered. Jim had seen the dog fall over on the carpet and not get up. Jim went and checked Chi Chi and then gently said, 'Tammy, Chi Chi is dead.'...I prayed and prayed and prayed. 'O Jesus, please raise Chi Chi from the dead.' I expected Jim to bring Chi Chi home any minute.' "

"No matter what they print, no reporter has ever seen me with black tears running down my face, 'cause I always use waterproof mascara."

"My shoppin' demons are hoppin'."

IN THE NEWS

In his book, If No News, Send Rumors, *Stephen Bates tells hundreds of fascinating stories about the news media. It's an excellent bathroom reader. Here are a few excerpts.*

In the early 1700s the price of a newspaper, twopence a copy, was steep. As later gentlemen callers would bring flowers or candy, a man of the era would sometimes bring a newspaper as a gift when calling on a woman, so that she could read of the latest Indian raids, runaway slaves, and pirate attacks.

Early Newspapers were often passed from person to person. Some papers contained one or more blank pages, which a subscriber could fill in with his own news before sending the newspaper on to friends.

A 1987 computer analysis found that these words most frequently appear in the New York Post headlines (in descending order): Cop, Kill, Judge, Wall Street, Death, No, Slay, U.S., Soviet, Court.

The choice for the lead story in *USA Today*'s September 15, 1982 inaugural edition was based on an informal survey undertaken by the newspaper's founder, Al Neuharth. Bashir Gemayel, president-elect of Lebanon had been murdered, and most *USA Today* editors assumed that story would lead the paper, as it did other papers across the country. But Monaco's Princess Grace had died in a car crash, and Neuharth suspected her death was, for most Americans, the more important story.

To find out, he visited a bar and a political gathering. In both places, nearly everyone was talking about Princess Grace. When Neuharth mentioned the Lebanon assassination, people shrugged. The next morning, *USA Today*'s lead story was headlined, "Princess Grace dies in Monaco. Gemayel ended up on an inside page.

When he learned that crucial work on the atom bomb had taken place nearby, the city editor of the *Nashville Tennessean* told a photographer to go out to the research facility and get two pictures—one of a whole atom, and one after it was split.

In the '60s *Rolling Stone* offered a free roach clip to every new subscriber. In the '80s its standard employment contract allowed the magazine to test employees for drug use.

In October, 1967, a major anti-war protest was held in Washington, D.C. Crowd estimates varied widely, in part reflecting the publications' political viewpoints:

Washington Post: 50,000
Time: 35,000
Wall St. Journal: 2,500

On several occasions, William Randolph Hearst's New York *Journal* suggested that President McKinley should be killed. One editorial, for instance, declared that "If bad institutions and bad men can be got rid of only by killing them, then the killing must be done."

For such remarks, the *Journal* was vilified when the president was assassinated in 1901. "The journalism of anarchy," the *Brooklyn Eagle* editorialized, "shares responsibility for the attack on President McKinley." Hearst's enemies spread the false story that McKinley's assassin had been arrested with a copy of the *Journal* in his pocket.

Stung by the criticism, the Journal changed the name of its morning edition to the *American.* Bad feelings remained, though, and five years later the McKinley issue helped defeat Hearst in his campaign for governor of New York.

A *Los Angeles Times* article in 1972 read "70-Car Fog Pileup." In fact, sixty-nine cars had crashed. An editor changed it, reasoning that sixty-nine was a smutty number.

Washington Post reporter Carl Bernstein nearly wasn't around to cover the Watergate scandal. Bernstein had asked executive editor Ben Bradlee to make him the full-time rock critic. Bradlee agreed, but the job had ended up going to someone else.

Resentful, Bernstein decided to leave the *Post.* He wrote to *Rolling Stone* and asked if he could replace the departing Hunter S. Thompson as political writer. Bernstein was waiting was waiting for a reply when he was assigned to cover the break-in at the Democratic National Committee's Watergate offices.

POP QUIZ

So you think you know popular culture. Here's a chance to find out. Some of the answers are in sections of this book and previous Bathroom Readers*—all of them are on page 892.*

CLASSIC TOYS

1. On the Japanese Barbie, these are even bigger, rounder and more voluptuous than the on the American Barbie. What are they?

2. What do the inventions of Silly Putty and the Slinky have in common?

3. What gives crayons their distinctive smell?

4. Where was the inventor of the Ant Farm when he came up with the idea?

STYLE

5.Who invented the Hawaiian shirt and why?

6. What animal is on the alligator shirt?

ON THE SCREEN

7. Where did Art Clokey get the idea for the bump on Gumby's little green head?

8. Who almost got the role of Dorothy in the *Wizard of Oz?* Which comic did they write the Wizard's lines for?

9. Who was first choice for the main character in *Casablanca?*

10. Which three of the Stooges were brothers?

11. How much older was Vivian Vance than Lucille Ball?

12. How did *Our Gang*'s Alfalfa die?

MUSIC

13. Before it had words, what was the working title of the Beatles' song, *Yesterday?*

14. How many record choices did you get on the first jukebox?

15. The average number of grooves on a 45 RPM record? How does that compare with the number of grooves on a 33 RPM record?

ART VS. REAL LIFE

16. Which are there more of in the world: plastic lawn flamingos or real flamingos?

17. Which lasted longer—the TV show *M*A*S*H* or the real Korean War?

18. The subject of Andy Warhol's first pop paintings was the thing he loved most. What was it?

MODERN MYTHOLOGY

A hundred years ago, Americans identified with Uncle Sam, Paul Bunyan, and Johnny Appleseed. Today, there are a new crop of cultural heroes, like these characters:

The Campbell's Soup Kids. Grace Gebbie Wiederseim grew up in Philadelphia in the mid-1800s. One morning when she was a young girl, she stood in front of her parents' mirror and drew a picture of herself. She liked it so much she saved it.

In 1904, Grace was a successful illustrator and the wife of a Campbell's Soup advertising executive. One afternoon he asked her to help create an advertising campaign for Campbell's. She pulled out her childhood self-portrait...and used it to create Dolly Drake and Bobby Blake—the Campbell's Soup Kids.

Poppin' Fresh (The Pillsbury Doughboy). In 1965 the Pillsbury Company hired ad exec Rudy Pera to design an advertising campaign for their new refrigerated dough product...But he had trouble thinking of anything that would make the brand stand out. One day he began playfully pounding on a container of the dough, hoping to drum up ideas. "I imagined what could pop out," he recalls. "A dough man? A dough baker? A *dough boy*?" Polls taken more than 20 years later show that the Pillsbury Doughboy is the most popular ad character in the U.S.—more popular than Ronald McDonald, Tony the Tiger, or Morris the Cat.

Mr. Zig Zag. During the 1850s the French army recruited Algerians to help fight in the Crimean war. One of them is still famous today—even though his name has been forgotten; his face is on the cover of Zig Zag rolling papers.

Ronald McDonald. Willard Scott, weatherman on NBC's *Today Show*, was the first McClown. Here's the story he tells:

"The folks at the NBC television station in Washington—WRC TV—had signed on a national kiddie show [called "Bozo the

During World War 1, removing straps from corsets saved enough metal to build 2 warships.

Clown"], and they tapped me to star in the thing. That's how I got to be Bozo the Clown...I did a lot of personal appearances as Bozo—at shopping malls, local fairs, that sort of thing. After a while a local McDonald's restaurant asked me to appear at an opening, and before too long my Bozo was a regular fixture at area franchises. When WRC dropped [the show], McDonald's didn't much like the idea of having to drop a successful promotion. They were hooked on clowns...And so—you guessed it—Ronald McDonald was born...Actually, he came very close to being christened Donald McDonald, but Ronald sounded just a touch more natural, so we went with that."

Rudolph the Red-Nosed Reindeer. In 1939, Montgomery Ward hired Robert May to write a Christmas poem for their department store Santas to give away during the holiday season. He came up with one he called *Rollo the Red-Nosed Reindeer*. Executives of the company loved it, but didn't like the name Rollo. So May renamed the reindeer Reginald—the only name he could think of that preserved the poem's rhythm. But Montgomery Ward execs rejected that name, too. Try as he might, May couldn't come up with another name that fit—until his four year-old daughter suggested *Rudolph*.

Teenage Mutant Ninja Turtles. Peter Laird, a 29-year-old artist, was the staff illustrator for the gardening page of a Massachusetts newspaper in 1983. His job didn't pay very well, and he was looking for ways to make extra money on the side...so a local comic magazine editor suggested he work with Kevin Eastman, a 20 year-old short-order cook and amateur cartoonist, to drum up ideas for a new comic book. Laird decided to give it a shot. One night he and Eastman were experimenting with karate themes. Eastman drew a picture of a turtle wearing a Ninja mask. They both liked the idea, and stayed up all night developing a storyline. By morning the one "Ninja Turtle" had expanded to four *Teenage Mutant* Ninja Turtles—Leonardo, Raphael, Michaelangelo, and Donatello.

Why name them after Renaissance artists? Laird explained: "The characters should have have had Japanese names, but we couldn't come up with convincing ones."

Nuns have the longest life expectancy of any demographic group in the U.S.

AT THE OSCARS

Here are a few lesser-known stories about the Academy Awards ceremonies

THAT LITTLE GOLD STATUE

• According to legend, the Oscar was named in 1931 when a secretary at the Academy saw the statuette and exclaimed, "Why, he reminds me of my Uncle Oscar!" A reporter overheard the remark and used it in a story, and the name stuck.

• In 1942, gold and bronze were being used in the war, so Oscars were made out of plaster. (Actor Barry Fitzgerald accidentally decapitated his plaster Oscar while practicing his golf swing indoors).

• When Dustin Hoffman accepted his Oscar in 1979, he described the statuette for the audience: "He has no genitalia and he's holding a sword."

HOSTS WITH THE MOST (OR LEAST)

• At the 1947 Oscar ceremony, Ronald Reagan supplied live narration for "Parade of Stars," a silent compilation of Oscar-winning films. Oblivious to the fact that the film was running upside down, backwards, and showing on the ceiling instead of on a screen, Reagan kept reading: "This picture embodies the glories of our past, the memories of our present, and the inspiration of our future."

• Comedian Jerry Lewis was the host in 1958 when the Oscar ceremony actually finished 20 minutes earlier than expected. No one realized the show was ending early until they were well into the closing number, "There's No Business Like Show Business." Lewis shouted "Twenty more times!" and tried to drag out the finale by grabbing a baton and conducting the orchestra. Actors onstage paired up and started dancing. Meanwhile, the audience started to get up and leave. Dean Martin danced by the podium and grabbed a leftover Oscar.

A few minutes later Lewis picked up a trumpet and started trying to play it. That's when NBC turned its cameras off. Eventually, NBC had to plug the hole with a short film on *pistol shooting*.

NO-SHOWS

Not everyone shows up for Oscar night:

• Robert Rich won the Best Screenplay Oscar in 1956 for *The Brave One*, but never claimed his award. That's because there *was* no Robert Rich. The winner was actually Dalton Trumbo, one of the notorious "Hollywood Ten," a group of writers who had been blacklisted for their left-wing views. Trumbo managed to sneak himself onto the nomination list by using "Robert Rich" as a pseudonym.

• In 1970 the Academy decided to give Orson Welles an honorary Oscar—presumably to make up for the fact that they'd snubbed him for *Citizen Kane* in 1941. When he didn't show up to accept it, the Academy announced he was out of the country. Actually, he was just a few miles away, watching the whole thing on television.

• That same year George C. Scott refused a Best Actor Oscar for his title role in the movie *Patton*. Instead of attending the ceremony, he says he watched a hockey game on TV, then went to bed.

• In 1979, 79-year-old Melvyn Douglas was nominated as Best Supporting Actor for *Being There*. His chief competition was child star Justin Henry, who played the contested child in the divorce drama, *Kramer vs. Kramer*. Douglas didn't show up for Oscar night, and told reporters: "The whole thing is absurd, my competing with an 8-year-old." Although Henry did show up, Douglas still won.

AND THE WINNER IS...

• In 1984, F. Murray Abraham won the Oscar for Best Actor. (He played the jealous composer Antonio Salieri in the movie *Amadeus*.) Until then, Abraham's most prominent screen role had been as a leaf in a Fruit of the Loom underwear commercial.

• In 1946, *The Razor's Edge* failed to win the Oscar for Best Picture...But it *was* named the year's best by the National Association of Barbers.

• Humphrey Bogart wasn't thrilled at winning an Oscar for *African Queen*: "Hell," he remarked, "I hope I'm never nominated again. It's meat and potatoes roles for me from now on."

In 16th century Turkey, drinking coffee was punishable by death.

• Playwrite George Bernard Shaw was livid about winning the Best Screenplay Oscar for *Pygmalion*."It's an insult," he railed. "To offer me an award of this sort is an insult, as if they have never heard of me before...and it's very likely they never have."

• The nameplate on Spencer Tracy's first Oscar was mistakenly made out to *Dick* Tracy.

WINNERS, PART II

The ultimate Oscar winner/loser story involved a little-known Polish director named Zbignew Rybcyznski, who was nominated for Best Animated Short in 1983:

• Presenter Kristy McNichol tried to pronounce his name as a nominee, but giggled and gave up halfway through. When Rybcyznski won, McNichol tried again. This time she called him "Zbigniewski Sky."

• Rybcyznski made his acceptance speech through an interpreter but they were cut off when the orchestra struck up the theme from "Loony Tunes."

• Co-presenter Matt Dillon tried to ease Rybcyznski off the stage, but the director held his ground by shaking Dillon's hand and kissing McNichol. He added some final words but the interpreter lost them in the translation. They came out, "On the occasion of the film like *Gandhi*, which will portray Lech Walesa and Solidarity."

• Later in the evening, Rybcyznski stepped out for a cigarette. He tried to return to his seat, but a guard wouldn't let him back in. The guard didn't believe that Rybcyznski, who was dressed in a tuxedo and tennis shoes, was a guest. Rybcyznski got angry, kicked the guard, and wound up in jail.

• The director asked for attorney Marvin Mitchelson, who specializes in palimony cases, because he was the only Hollywood lawyer he could think of.

• Mitchelson took the case, but on the following conditions: "First, bring me an interpreter; and then tell me how to pronounce his name." The charges were dropped.

• Rybcyznski's conclusion: "Success and defeat are quite intertwined."

PRIME TIME POLITICIANS

You see politicians on TV all the time—but not usually in shows like "The Dukes of Hazard" and "The Beverly Hillbillies." Here are a few actors who followed Ronald Reagan's footsteps into politics.

The Race: U.S. Congress (Virginia), 1984.

Candidate: Nancy Kulp (Democrat). Played Jane Hathaway, the sour-faced bank secretary on *"The Beverly Hillbillies,"* for nine seasons.

Political Background: Worked for Adlai Stevenson in the 1952 presidential race against Eisenhower; elected to the Screen Actor Guild's Board of Directors in 1982. She also worked with the Democratic State Committee of Pennsylvania.

The Race: Kulp ran unopposed in the primary and won the Democratic nomination. But Buddy Ebsen, who played Jed Clampett on "The Beverly Hillbillies," campaigned against her in the general election. He taped a radio ad for Kulp's opponent, Bud Shuster, which said: "I dropped [Nancy] a note to say, 'Hey Nancy, I love you dearly buy you're too liberal for me—I've got to go with Bud Shuster.' " Shuster beat Kulp by 117,203 to 59,449.

The Race: Mayor of Carmel-by-the-Sea, California, 1986.

The Candidate: Clint Eastwood (no party affiliation).

Political Background: Eastwood wanted to expand his Carmel restaurant, the *Hog's Breath Inn*. City Hall refused to let him. So, in true *Dirty Harry* style, he took them on and ran for mayor.

Outcome: He defeated incumbent mayor Charlotte Townshend by 2,166 votes to 799. He held the $200-a-week post for two years.

The Race: U.S. House of Representatives (Iowa), 1986.

The Candidate: Fred Grandy, Republican. Played Burl "Gopher" Smith for nine years on *The Love Boat*.

Political Background: Grandy was David Eisenhower's roommate at Exeter Academy and later was best man at Eisenhower's wedding to Julie Nixon. He also served as a speechwriter for Congressman Wiley Mayne (R-Iowa). A Harvard graduate fluent in both French and Arabic, Grandy wanted to dispel his image as the dimwitted Gopher. Even so, he told *People* magazine, "If there were no Gopher, there would be no Fred Grandy for Congress."

Outcome: Grandy's opponent, Clayton Hodgson, criticized him for not living in Iowa's Sixth district (Grandy had lived in Iowa as an orphan at 12), and aired tapes of Grandy on NBC's "Tonight Show" describing Iowa as the "only place in the world where people still use 'by golly' in a sentence." Still, Grandy won the election in 1986 by 3,000 votes.

The Race: U.S. House of Representatives (Georgia), 1988.

The Candidate: Ben Jones (Democrat). Jones played Cooter, the auto mechanic on *The Dukes of Hazard,* for seven seasons.

Political Background: Worked on Jimmy Carter's 1980 presidential campaign. Lost his first bid for Congressman Pat Swindall's House seat in 1986, but ran again in 1988. Reason for getting involved: "I awoke naked in a tattoo parlor in Talladega, Alabama. I knew it was time to change my lifestyle. So I went into politics."

Outcome: *The Washington Post* described the race as "perhaps the nastiest, most personal congressional campaign in the country." Swindall was facing a perjury indictment for lying about his involvement with an undercover cop posing as a drug money launderer. He tried to portray the four-time married Jones as a wife-beater, alluding to charges of battery against an ex-wife, for which he had been fined $50. Jones' defense: "I'm not your typical political candidate; I've seen the insides of jails." Nevertheless, he captured 60% of the vote and defeated Swindall.

The Race: Mayor of Palm Springs, California, 1988.

The Candidate: Sonny Bono (Republican). Bono and his ex-wife Cher, had a variety T.V. show in the '70s and several hit songs.

Political Background: None.

The Race: Although he faced opposition ("Clint's a big star," commented outgoing Palm Springs mayor, Frank Bogert. "Sonny's a big nothing.") Bono won the election easily. But in 1990 his opponents started a petition drive to recall him after he dropped out of an AIDS walk-a-thon. It failed.

SURPRISE HITS

Some of pop music's most popular records have become hits through totally unexpected circumstances—discovered by deejays in a 25¢ bin, featured on ads years after their first release, picked as TV themes. These flukes are the equivalent of winning the "pop lottery." Here are a few classic examples:

GET TOGETHER—THE YOUNGBLOODS

Background: The Youngbloods first album was released in 1967 on RCA records. It included the song "Get Together," which was released as a single. Unfortunately, the song only reached #62 on the national charts—a flop, as far as RCA was concerned. The record was quickly forgotten.

The Surprise: To promote Brotherhood Week in 1969, the National Conference of Christians and Jews put together a package of public service messages for TV announcers and radio deejays to read on the air. They decided to include a record for stations to use as background music, and the one they picked—without informing the Youngbloods—was "Get Together."

The Hit: After a week of national radio and TV exposure, the record started becoming popular. Radio stations began playing it...and RCA cashed in by re-releasing it. In the summer of 1969, two years after it was first released, "Get Together" hit #1, sold about 2 million copies, and made the Youngbloods stars.

"HANKY PANKY"—TOMMY JAMES & THE SHONDELLS

Background: In 1963, a Niles, Michigan high school student named Tommy Jackson made a record called "Hanky Panky" with his band, the Shondells. It became a regional hit in parts of Michigan, Illinois, and Indiana. Then it disappeared.

The Surprise: A year and a half later, a Pittsburgh, Pennsylvania, deejay named Bob Livorio found a copy of "Hanky Panky" in a pile of 25¢ records. He began playing it on the air. When it became popular with his audiences, rival deejays dug up their own copies of the record...and a "Hanky Panky" war was on. A local record company bought the rights to the record and distributed it to Pittsburgh record stores. In 3 weeks, "Hanky Panky" was the city's #1 song.

Meanwhile, Tommy Jackson—whose band had broken up when

he graduated from high school the year before—didn't know anything about this. He was at his family's house one evening when he got a phone call from a Pittsburgh deejay named "Mad Mike" Metro. As Tommy recalls it: "He said, 'Your record's #1. Can you come to Pittsburgh?' I said, 'What record? Who is this? What's your name?' I thought it was one of my friends pulling my leg. Finally, the guy started to sound official, and I started hearing radio noises in the background. I said, 'My god! He's telling the truth!' "

The Hit: When Tommy Jackson—now Tommy James—arrived in Pittsburgh, kids went wild. By this time "Hanky Panky" had gotten a lot of publicity in the record industry, and major companies were eager to distribute it nationally. The winner: Roulette Records, which bought it for $10,000. The record repeated its success on a national level, becoming the #1 song in America…and Tommy James became one of pop's biggest stars."I don't think that kind of stuff can happen anymore," Tommy muses. "We're talking an absolute Cinderella story!"

"HUMAN NATURE"—MICHAEL JACKSON

Background: Steve Porcaro was a studio musician and a member of the group Toto. One day his little daughter came home from school upset about a fight she'd had with some of her playmates. "Why do they do that?" she asked.

"It's just human nature," her father replied.

He realized that phrase might make a good title for a song….So he went into Toto's recording studio and made up a melody—which he put onto a tape cassette, singing nonsense syllables and occasionally throwing in the phrase, "It's just human nature." Then he left the cassette lying around and forgot about it.

The Surprise: About this time, Quincy Jones was looking for songs to use on Michael Jackson's new album, "Thriller." He asked David Paitch—also a member of Toto and one of the most respected songwriters in the music business—to submit material for Jackson. Paitch went into Toto's studio, picked up a used cassette, and recorded three songs. Then he sent the cassette to Quincy Jones.

Jones didn't feel any of Paitch's tunes were right for "Thriller"…but just before he turned off the tape recorder, he realized there was an extra song on the cassette—Steve Porcaro's scratch vocal of "Human Nature." It turned out that without realizing it, Paitch picked up the tape with Porcaro's song on it. Jones decided "Human Nature" was perfect for Jackson. Porcaro, who had no idea anyone had the tape, was astonished.

The Hit: All the song needed now was lyrics. Jones contacted songwriter John Bettis, who wrote the words in two days. Not only was "Human Nature" included on "Thriller," the biggest-selling album in history, it was also released as a single. It reached #7 on *Billboard's* charts, and sold over a million copies.

TIME IN A BOTTLE—JIM CROCE

Background: "Time In a Bottle" was a "throwaway" tune on a Jim Croce album. The producers didn't even bother putting the finishing touches on it because, as one of them said, "No one is ever gonna hear it."

The Surprise: Producers of a 1973 TV movie called "She Lives"—about a woman dying of cancer—heard Croce's album and liked "Time in a Bottle." They decided to make it the movie's theme.

The Hit: "The next day," Croce's record producer recalls,"we got a call from our record company telling us that they had 50,000 orders for the album, just in the Midwest. People had fallen in love with the song. It was just instantaneous. I think they sold something like 200,000 albums in the next two weeks That's why 'Time in a Bottle' was released as a single—because of that show." About three months later, the song hit #1.

"OH HAPPY DAY"—THE EDWIN HAWKINS SINGERS

Background: Edwin Hawkins assembled the 46-member Northern California State Youth Choir in mid-1967. A few months later, he needed to raise funds for the choir's trip to a convention. So he picked out 8 members of the choir and recorded an album (which included "Oh Happy Day") in the basement of his church. He was delighted when the choir sold 600 copies of it.

The Surprise: Two years later, a San Francisco rock promoter happened to find the album in a warehouse while flipping through a stack of gospel records. He gave it to a popular deejay named Abe "Voco" Kesh, who played the record on the air.

The Hit: Kesh played "Oh Happy Day" so often that it became an S.F., then a national hit. Sales jumped from 1,000 to over a million.

PUN FOR THE MONEY

"There's something irresistible about bad puns," notes BRI member Michael McDonald. "For some reason, the worse a pun is the more we like it." Well, here are some real groaners from Get Thee to a Punnery, *by Richard Lederer See if you can fill in the punch lines:*

THE STORY: An ancient jungle king tyrannized his subjects and forced them to build him one elaborate throne after another—first of mud, then bamboo, then tin, then copper, then silver, and so on. When the king became tired of each throne, he would store it in the attic of his grass hut. One day the attic collapsed, and the thrones crashed down upon the chief's head and killed him.
The moral: "*People who live in grass houses* ____________________."

THE STORY: A congregation decided to paint the walls of the church. They were doing an admirable job until they began to run out of paint, so they decided to thin the stuff in order to complete their task.

Shortly after the job was finished, the rains descended from the heavens, and the paint began to peel from the walls of the church. And a thunderous voice boomed from above:
"*Repaint, and* ___________________________"

THE STORY: In an ancient kingdom, the castle was surrounded by a treacherous swamp called the Yellow Fingers. Whenever the king would ask his lords and knights to cross the Yellow Fingers, they would reply:
"*Let your pages* ___________________________"

THE STORY: Mrs. Wong, a Chinese woman, gave birth to a blond-haired, blue-eyed Caucasian baby. When the doctor asked Mr. Wong to explain the astonishing occurrence, he replied:
"*It takes two Wongs* ________________________"

THE STORY: In days of old when knights were bold, people were a lot smaller than they are today, so much smaller, in fact, that many knights rode upon large dogs when they couldn't get horses. One dark and stormy night, as the rain blew about, a squire entered a pet store in order to purchase a large dog for his master, the Black Knight. Unfortunately, all the shopkeeper could offer the squire was one undersized, mangy mutt. Commented the squire: "*I wouldn't send a knight* ________________________"

THE STORY: In Baghdad, a worthy young man named Abdul found a beautiful urn. When he began to polish the urn, out came a magnificently bearded genie, who introduced himself as Benny. Benny granted Abdul the obligatory three wishes and bid him goodbye. Abdul knew that if he could shave Benny's beard, the genie would have to return to the urn and grant him three more wishes. Wielding a magic razor, Abdul shaved off Benny's beard, and, sure enough, Benny flew back into the enchanted vessel.
The Moral: "*A Benny shaved* ____________________"

THE STORY: A Frenchman and a Czechoslovakian went out hunting for bear. When the two had not returned after four days, their friends, fearing the worst, went out searching for them. The group came to a clearing, and, sure enough, they saw a mother and father bear each with a bloated belly. Slashing open the belly of the female, the distraught friends found therein the remains of the Frenchman. Their darkest fears confirmed, the group looked at the other bear and guessed:
"*The Czech.* ______________________."

THE STORY: A witch doctor kept the members of his tribe in subjugation by means of his powerful magic. Whenever one of the tribespeople tried to revolt against the witch doctor, the tyrant uttered a magic incantation and turned the person into an apple. One night a group of the doctor's subjects sneaked into his hut, opened his book of magic recipes, and learned the apple incantation. When the doctor awoke, the people turned him into an apple. But the magic book warned that if the apple ever dried out and changed significantly in weight, it would change back into a doctor, who would take his revenge. So every day they would place the apple on a scale to make sure that its weight remained the same.
Moral: "*A weigh a day* ______________________."

General George Patton was dyslexic.

THANKS... BUT NO THANKS

If you've written a manuscript but can't find a publisher, take heart. Even the best writers get rejection slips. For example, a newspaper editor once told Rudyard Kipling: "I'm sorry, Mr. Kipling, but you just don't know how to use the English language." Here are some other notable rejection letters from editors to authors.

Manuscript: *Madame Bovary*, by Gustave Flaubert
Editor's Comment: "You have buried your novel underneath a heap of details which are well done but utterly superfluous."

Manuscript: *Remembrance of Things Past*, by Marcel Proust
Editor's Comment: "My dear fellow, I may perhaps be dead from the neck up, but rack my brains as I may I can't see why a chap should need thirty pages to describe how he turns over in bed before going to sleep."

Manuscript: *The Diary of Anne Frank*, by Anne Frank
Editor's Comment: "The girl doesn't, it seems to me, have a special perception or feeling which would lift that book above the 'curiosity' level."

Manuscript: *Atlas Shrugged*, by Ayn Rand
Editor's Comment: "The book is *much* too long. There are too many long speeches...I regret to say that the book is unsaleable and unpublishable."

Manuscript: *Ulysses*, by James Joyce
Editor's Comment: "We have read the chapters of Mr. Joyce's novel with great interest, and we wish we could offer to print it. But the length is an insuperable difficulty to us at present. We can get no one to help us, and at our rate of progress a book of 300 pages would take at least two years to produce."

The first advertisement to discuss body odor was a 1919 ad for the deodorant Odo-Ro-No.

Manuscript: *The Postman Always Rings Twice*, by James M. Cain
Editor's Comment: "I think it is only a matter of time before you reach out into more substantial efforts that will be capable of making some real money as books."

Manuscript: *Lord of the Flies*, by William Golding
Editor's Comment: "It does not seem to us that you have been wholly successful in working out an admittedly promising idea."

Manuscript: *And to Think That I Saw It On Mulberry Street*, by Dr. Seuss
Editor's Comment: "Too different from other [books for] juveniles on the market to warrant its selling."

Manuscript: *Ironweed*, by William Kennedy
Editor's Comment: "There is much about the novel that is very good and much that I did not like. When I throw in the balance the book's unrelenting lack of commerciality, I am afraid I just have to pass."

Manuscript: *Kon-Tiki*, by Thor Heyerdahl
Editor's Comment: "The idea of men adrift on a raft does have a certain appeal, but for the most part this is a long, solemn and tedious Pacific voyage."

Manuscript: *Lady Chatterly's Lover*, by D.H. Lawrence
Editor's Comment: "For your own good, do not publish this book."

Manuscript: *Animal Farm*, by George Orwell
Editor's Comment: "It is impossible to sell animal stories in the USA."

Manuscript: *The Blessing Way*, by Tony Hillerman
Editor's Comment: "If you insist on rewriting this, get rid of all that Indian stuff."

RANDOM QUOTE: "A man can be happy with any woman as long as he does not love her." —Oscar Wilde.

The Washington Monument is sinking at a rate of 6 inches a year.

THE KING AND I

You may have already seen the famous photos of Elvis Presley and Richard Nixon in the Oval Office. Here's the inside story behind that meeting—taken directly from the memos of the White House staff.

Even Elvis was a fan. He thought J. Edgar Hoover was "the greatest living American"...and Nixon "wasn't far behind." On December 21, 1970, Elvis dropped by the White House unannounced, asking to see the President. He brought this letter with him:

DEAR MR. PRESIDENT:

First, I would like to introduce myself. I am Elvis Presley and admire you and have great respect for your office. I talked to Vice President Agnew in Palm Springs three weeks ago and expressed my concern for our country. The drug culture, the hippie elements, the SDS, Black Panthers, etc. do not consider me as their enemy or as they call it, the establishment. I call it America and I love it. Sir, I can and will be of any service that I can to help the country out. I have no concerns or motives other than helping the country out. So I wish not to be given a title or an appointed position. I can and will do more good if I were made a Federal Agent at Large and I will help out by doing it my way through my communications with people of all ages. First and foremost, I am an entertainer, but all I need is the Federal credentials. I am on this plane with Senator George Murphy and we have been discussing the problems that our country is faced with.

Sir, I am staying at the Washington Hotel, Room 505-506-507. I have two men who work with me by the name of Jerry Schilling and Sonny West. I am registered under the name of Jon Burrows. I will be here for as long as it takes to get the credentials of a Federal Agent. I have done an in-depth study of drug abuse and Communist brainwashing techniques and I am right in the middle of the whole thing where I can and will do the most good.

I am glad to help just so long as it is kept very private. You can have your staff or whomever call me anytime today, tonight, or to-

The British pound got its name because it was originally equal to the value of a pound of silver.

morrow. I was nominated this coming year one of America's Ten Most Outstanding Young Men. That will be in January 18 in my home town of Memphis, Tennessee. I am sending you the short autobiography about myself so you can better understand this approach. I would love to meet you just to say hello if you're not too busy.

Respectfully,

Elvis Presley

P.S. I believe that you, Sir, were one of the Top Ten Outstanding Men of America also. I have a personal gift for you which I would like to present to you and you can accept it or I will keep it for you until you can take it.

Dwight Chapin, the White House Appointments Secretary, met with Elvis. He wasn't sure what to do—did Nixon want to speak with the King? Was he a Presley fan? Did he even know who the singer was? Chapin passed the buck and wrote a memo to H.R. Haldeman, White House Chief of Staff:

DEAR H.R.:

Attached you will find a letter to the President from Elvis Presley. As you are aware, Presley showed up here this morning and has requested an appointment with the President. He states that he knows the President is very busy, but he would just like to say hello...I think that it would be wrong to push Presley off on the Vice President since it will take very little of the President's time and it can be extremely beneficial for the President to build some rapport with Presley.

Haldeman approached Nixon about meeting with Elvis, and Nixon agreed. Here are the official White House notes describing the meeting:

DECEMBER 21, 1970

The meeting opened with pictures taken of the President and Elvis Presley. Presley immediately began showing the President his law enforcement paraphernalia including badges from police departments in California, Colorado, and Tennessee. Presley indicated that he had been playing Las Vegas and the President indicated that he was aware of how difficult it is to perform in Las Vegas.

The President mentioned that he thought Presley could reach young people, and that it was important for Presley to retain his credibility. Presley responded that he did his thing by "just singing." He said that he could not get to the kids if he made a speech on the stage, that he had to reach them in his own way. The President nodded in agreement.

Presley indicated that he thought the Beatles had been a real force for anti-American spirit. He said that the Beatles came to this country, made their money, and then returned to England where they promoted an anti-American theme. The President nodded in agreement and expressed some surprise. The President then indicated that those who use drugs are also those in the vanguard of anti-American protest. "Violence, drug usage, dissent, protest all seem to merge in generally the same group of young people."

Presley indicated to the President in a very emotional manner that he was "on your side." Presley kept repeating that he wanted to be helpful, that he wanted to restore some respect for the flag which was being lost. He mentioned that he was just a poor boy from Tennessee who had gotten a lot from his country, which in some way he wanted to repay. He also mentioned that he is studying Communist brainwashing and the drug culture for over ten years. He mentioned that he knew a lot about this and was accepted by the hippies. He said he could go right into a group of young people or hippies and be accepted which he felt could be helpful to him in his drug drive. The President indicated again his concern that Presley retain his credibility.

At the conclusion of the meeting, Presley again told the President how much he supported him, and then, in a surprising, spontaneous gesture, put his left arm around the President and hugged him.

* * *

During a 1958 visit to Venezuela, Vice President Richard Nixon was spit upon by a protester. After Secret Service agents grabbed the man—Nixon kicked him in the shins. He admitted in his book *Six Crises* that "nothing I did all day made me feel better."

OLD NEWS IS GOOD NEWS

Are your newspapers piling up in the garage? Here's some recycling info from The Recycler's Handbook, *written by the EarthWorks Group.*

If you're one of the millions of Americans who are recycling your newspapers, here's some good news: You're making a big difference.

Not only are you saving natural resources and landfill space, you're helping to change the way the paper industry works.

Until recently, newspaper publishers believed that recycling was just a fad—that we'd "get over it." Now it's clear that Americans are committed...So they're going to give us what we want.

RECYCLING NEWS

• Every day Americans buy about 62 million newspapers…and throw out around 44 million of them. That means the equivalent of about 500,000 trees is dumped into landfills every week.

• If we recycled just half our newsprint every year, we'd need 3,200 fewer garbage trucks to collect our trash.

• If you recycled the *New York Times* every day for a year, you'd prevent 15 pounds of air pollution. That doesn't sound like much, but it adds up. If everyone who subscribes to the *New York Times* recycled, we'd keep over 6,000 *tons* of pollution out of the air.

• According to *Clean Ocean Action*, recycling a 36" tall stack of newspaper saves the equivalent of about 14% of the average household electric bill.

• Top uses for recycled newsprint: More newsprint, paperboard. Also, construction paper, insulation, egg cartons, animal bedding.

PILES OF PAPER

• One of the results of America's new enthusiasm for recycling is a "newspaper glut." More paper on the market means lower prices. This is bad for collection programs, but good for mills.

• Of the 25 newsprint mills in the U.S., only ten of them can recycle. Most of our newsprint is manufactured in Canada, and only two of the 42 newsprint mills there are set up to recycle. However, many have announced plans to recycle; some are beginning.

• It may be a while before mills catch up to the public. It takes about 18 months and $40-80 million to retool a mill to recycle.

• Does this mean we shouldn't bother recycling? No, no, no. Mill-owners and newspapers have been waiting to see if recycling is a legitimate trend before they make major investments. But because we've kept the pressure up, they're making the necessary adjustments.

SIMPLE THINGS YOU CAN DO

1. Find a Recycling Center

• It should be easy. Most recyclers accept newspaper, including curbside programs, recycling centers, charity paper drives, etc.

2. Recycle

• Ask your recycling center or curbside service if newspapers should be tied or left loose.

• If they should be tied, put them in bundles about 10" thick, so they're easy to carry. Tying tip: Lay the string in an empty box with the ends draping out over the sides. Put the paper in the box and make the knot.

• If they should be left loose, store the papers in brown grocery bags or cardboard boxes.

• Don't worry about pulling out all the glossy inserts, but don't *add* any junk mail or magazines to the pile. Try to keep the paper dry.

• If you're taking the newspaper to a recycling center, you may be asked to empty out the bags or cut the strings holding the bundles; some recyclers prefer just the newspaper.

• Don't recycle newspaper you've used for birdcages, for housebreaking your dog, or for painting or art projects.

FOR MORE INFORMATION

"Read, Then Recycle." American Newspaper Publishers Association, The Newspaper Center, 11600 Sunrise Valley Drive, Reston, VA 22091; (703) 648-1125. *A free pamphlet.*

Dog food bags can't be recycled; they have plastic linings inside.

ABOUT JAMES DEAN

What was "The Rebel Without a Cause" really like?

Dean was fascinated with death. He wrote poems about dying, and often drew pictures of himself hanging by a noose from the ceiling of his apartment. During one trip to his home town, he had a local funeral parlor photograph him lying in a casket.

★

His main body of work consisted of several TV appearances and only three motion pictures—*East of Eden*, *Rebel Without a Cause*, and *Giant*.

★

While filming *Giant*, Dean annoyed his coworkers by walking around with unfurled pastries hanging out of each nostril.

★

Once on the set he even urinated in full view of the public. His explanation: "I figured if I could piss in front of those 2,000 people, man, and I could be cool....I could get in front of the camera and do just anything, anything at all."

★

Dean didn't have any front teeth; he had to wear a special bridge to fill in the gap. He liked to startle people by smiling at them with his teeth out.

★

Dean had several gay roommates while living in Hollywood. When asked whether he was bisexual, he reportedly responded: "Well, I'm certainly not going through life with one hand tied behind my back!" He also avoided the military draft by registering as a homosexual.

★

In late 1955 Dean filmed a TV commercial on auto safety for teenagers. One of his lines: "Drive safely, the life you save may be mine..." A few weeks later, he was killed in a car wreck.

★

Dean's last words before he slammed into Donald Gene Turnupseed's 1950 Ford Tudor near Cholame, on California Highway 466: "That guy up there has to stop, he's seen us..."

★

Dean really did say, "Live fast, die young and leave a good-looking corpse."

Two animals—Rin Tin Tin and Lassie—have stars on Hollywood's walk of fame.

STRANGE LAWSUITS

Here are more of the BRI's "worst and weirdest" true-life lawsuits.

THE PLAINTIFF: The Karolinska Institute in Stockholm, Sweden
THE DEFENDENT: Olaf Olavson
THE LAWSUIT: In 1910 Olavson was desperate for cash, so he sold his body to the Karolinska Institute (to be used for medical research after he died). But in 1911 he unexpectedly inherited a fortune and decided to "buy himself back." To his surprise, the institute wouldn't cooperate.

When Olavson flatly refused to donate his body, the institute actually sued for breach of contract.
THE VERDICT: Not only did Olavson owe his body to the Institute…he actually owed them money as well. The judge decided that since he'd had two teeth removed without the Institute's permission, Olavson had illegally tampered with their property.

THE PLAINTIFF: Joyce and David W., of Berlin Heights, Ohio
THE DEFENDENT: Natalina Pizza Co. of Elyria, Ohio
THE LAWSUIT: The couple said a frozen pizza they bought on April 26, 1986 had made them "violently ill," caused "emotional distress," and led to the death of their dog, Fluffy.

Although the expiration date on the pizza was April 18, "it was labeled edible for human consumption seven days after that date"…so the pair ate a few pieces. They claimed it was "spoiled, rotten, rancid, and moldy," and made them so sick they had to seek medical help. Fluffy didn't die from eating pizza; the couple ran him over in the driveway as they headed for the hospital.

They sued the pizza company for $125,000.
THE VERDICT: Not reported.

THE PLAINTIFFS: The Cherry Sisters, an Iowa singing group
THE DEFENDENT: The Des Moines *Register*
THE LAWSUIT: At the turn of the century, the *Register* ran a scathing review of the Cherry Sisters' act. Their reporter wrote that

"Their long, skinny arms, equipped with talons at the extremeties...waved frantically at the suffering audience. The mouths of their rancid features opened like caverns, and sounds like the wailings of damned souls issued therefrom."

Outraged and humiliated, the singers sued for libel.

THE VERDICT: The judge asked the sisters to perform their act for him in court...and then ruled in favor of the newspaper. It was, as one historian says, "a landmark libel case."

THE PLAINTIFF: Sarah, a 27-year-old woman with 46 personalities

THE DEFENDENT: Mark Peterson, of Oshkosh, Wisconsin

THE LAWSUIT: Peterson, who dated Sarah, was accused of deliberately drawing out the personality of Jennifer, described as "a gullible 20-year-old who he thought would have sex with him."

He was charged with rape. During the trial, he took the stand and testified he didn't know Sarah had multiple personalities. "I thought she was talking about her brothers and sisters," he said.

THE VERDICT: After deliberating for six hours, the jury found him guilty.

THE PLAINTIFF: Edith Tyler

THE DEFENDENTS: A restaurant in Flagstaff, Arizona

THE LAWSUIT: Tyler, a patron of the restaurant, ordered stuffed cabbage. She was appalled when she dug into it and found that it "apparently contained a used rubber prophylactic." She sued for $150,000.

THE VERDICT: Settled out of court.

THE PLAINTIFF: Tom H., a 24-year-old resident of Boulder, Colorado

THE DEFENDENTS: His parents

THE LAWSUIT: The young man, who'd spent a lot of time in mental institutions, blamed his parents for screwing him up. He sued them for "psychological malparenting." It was, he explained, a healthy alternative to following through on his "desire to kill his father."

THE VERDICT: He got no money.

THE PLAINTIFFS: Eric Hubert, Jeffrey Stabile, Jr., Christopher Drake

THE DEFENDENT: Disneyland

THE LAWSUIT: In 1988, the men were slow-dancing with each other at a Disneyland concert when a security guard allegedly approached them and told them that "touch dancing is reserved for heterosexual couples only." They sued, claiming their civil rights had been violated.

THE VERDICT: They agreed to drop the suit "in exchange for a pledge from Disneyland that the park would not discriminate based on sexual orientation."

THE PLAINTIFF: Wah-Ja Kim, a 58-year-old acupuncturist from Monterey, California

THE DEFENDENTS: William Hall, her ex-husband, and Jeannie Westall, his friend

THE LAWSUIT: In December 1983 Kim dropped in at Hall's condominium and got into an argument with Westall. During the fight, Westall allegedly bit off Kim's right pinkie. Kim sued for $1 million in damages, claiming that "she could not effectively stick pins in her patients' bodies without her little finger." She also said the loss posed a spiritual problem, since "the Confucianism of her native Korea demands 'that every human being should have a perfect, whole body to join our ancestors and carry on in the next life.' "

THE VERDICT: A jury awarded her $55,000.

THE PLAINTIFF: Relatives of a recently deceased man

THE DEFENDENT: A Vallejo, California cemetary

THE LAWSUIT: At the end of a funeral, cemetary employees realized the coffin they were about to lower into the ground was too wide for the hole. They tried turning the coffin on its side, but mourners stopped them. Then the employees tried breaking off the handles; it didn't work. Finally, "they tried to force it by jumping up and down on the lid." The coffin broke, and the funeral had to be stopped. Relatives sued for $500,000.

THE VERDICT: Settled out of court.

The film *Total Recall* contained 55 paid references to 31 products.

WHAT'S THE WORD?

Here are some unusual origins of common words, provided by BRI member John Dollison.

Addict. Slaves known as *addicts* were given to Roman soldiers to reward performance in battle. Eventually, a person who was a slave to anything became known as an addict.

Appendix. In Latin it means "the part that hangs." A human appendix hangs at the end of the large intestine; appendices come at the end of books.

Bistro. In the 1812 campaign against Napoleon's armies, Russian soldiers pushed all the way into the outskirts of Paris. They became known for shouting "bistro"—"hurry up"—at slow-moving waiters in sidewalk cafes.

Quakers. During a run-in with the law, George Fox, founder of the Society of Friends, told the British judges hearing his case to "tremble at the word of God." One of them laughed back at Fox, calling him a "quaker." The nickname stuck.

Atlas. It was once a tradition for map-makers to include a scene of the Greek god Atlas carrying the Earth on his shoulders in their map books. In time the books themselves came to be known as *atlases*.

Avocado. A South American Indian word for testicle.

Escape. In Latin, *escape* means "out of cape." The ancient Romans would often avoid capture by throwing off their capes when fleeing.

Oklahoma Sooners. Before opening the Oklahoma Territory to settlers, the United States government sealed the borders temporarily to allow everyone a fair chance to claim the free land. Some settlers broke the law and entered before the deadline—getting there *sooner* than anyone else.

People removed at the last minute from the Sgt. Pepper cover: actor Leo Gorcey, Gandhi, and Hitler.

Posh. Originally stood for "Port-outbound, Starbord-home." Clever passengers traveling through the Suez canal in the 1800s ordered cabins on the left side of the ship for the trip out and cabins on the right side for the return voyage. This kept their staterooms in the shade both ways. The desirable accommodations were recorded as "P.O.S.H." in ship records.

Kangaroo. During a trip to Australia Captain Cook, the British explorer, asked a tribesman the name of the large animals he saw hopping about. The tribesman replied "kangaroo"...which means "I don't know."

Pandemonium. Coined in the 1600s by the English author John Milton in his book *Paradise Lost*. Pandemonium is the capital of Hell, where Satan and other demons plan their adventures.

Noon. Derived from the Latin word for ninth. The word "noon" originally meant the 9th hour after sunrise, or 3:00 pm.

Best Man. It was traditional in Scotland for a prospective groom to kidnap the woman he wanted for his wife. His friends would help him. The largest and strongest was called "the best man."

Sincere. *Sine Cera* means "without wax" in Latin. Legend has it that Roman stone carvers would pass off hollow columns (used for building) as solid by filling them with wax. In time *sine cera* came to refer to anything that was authentic or pure.

Coconut. Portugese explorers thought the three holes on the shell made the coconut resemble a human. They named it *coco*—"smiling face."

• • •

BAD JOKE DEPARTMENT:

Q: How many psychiatrists does it take to change a lightbulb?

A: One...But the lightbulb has to want to change.

CHEWING GUM

Does your chewing gum lose its flavor on the bedpost overnight? Not if it's in a glass of water, according to The Whole Pop Catalog. *Here are some other bits of gum trivia from the book.*

"Every year, nearly two billion dollars worth of chewing gum is sold in America alone. That's enough to give 300 pieces a year to every American over the age of three."

"Even our most primitive ancestors engaged in recreational chewing. Along with human bones and other prehistoric artifacts, archaeologists at some sites have discovered well-chewed wads of tree resin."

"The first mass-produced gum (made of spruce resin) was manufactured by John Curtis in 1848."

"Clove gum was one of America's most popular flavors during Prohibition; patrons of speakeasies used it to hide the smell of alcohol on their breath. Today the most popular flavor is mint."

"The first bubble gum was invented by Frank Fleer in 1906—but never made it to market. It was so sticky that the only way to remove it from skin was with vigorous scrubbing and turpentine."

"It took Fleer more than twenty years to fix the recipe. In 1928 the 'new improved' gum was introduced as Dubble Bubble gum. It became the largest selling penny candy within just a few years."

"Why is bubble gum pink? Pink was the only food coloring on the shelf the day the first commercial batch of Dubble Bubble was made."

"New York Central Railroad once employed a full-time gum removal man to clean discarded gum from Grand Central Station. He harvested an average of seven pounds a night. The wad grew to fourteen pounds on holiday weekends."

"On June 3, 1965, the Gemini IV astronauts chewed gum in outer space. And according to NASA, when the astronauts were finished with the gum they swallowed it."

There are an estimated 4,000 sunken ships off the coast of New England.

MYTH AMERICA

Here's a batch of historical "truths" that aren't true.

TORY, TORY, TORY

The Myth: The vast majority of American colonists supported the rebellion during the Revolutionary War.

The Truth: According to President John Adams, at the beginning of the war only about a third of the people were on the side of the revolution. Another third were on the side of the British, and the rest didn't care either way. After a while, the ratio changed as British supporters were terrorized, publicly humiliated and finally attacked. Many fled to Canada.

FOOLED AGAIN

The Myth: Abraham Lincoln said: "You can fool all the people some of the time and some of the people all of the time, but you can't fool all of the people all of the time."

Background: Claims that Lincoln said it did not surface until more than 50 years after he was supposed to have said it. The remark was not recorded in any newspapers in Lincoln's time.

The Truth: Some researchers attribute the remark to circus showman P.T. Barnum.

ASLEEP AT THE WHEEL

The Myth: John F. Kennedy was a hero in World War II; when his tiny PT-109 patrol boat was rammed and sunk by a destroyer, he singlehandedly saved three members of his own crew.

Background: In his (ghost-written) book *PT-109*, Kennedy presented this version of the events that night. Yet, while he apparently showed great endurance and courage after his boat sank, there's some question as to whether the incident might have been avoidable in the first place.

The Truth: At least one Kennedy biographer argues that Kennedy's own negligence may have doomed his boat. According to a number of the ship's crew members, Kennedy and most of the crew were sleeping when PT-109 was rammed—not attacking the destroyer as Kennedy later claimed. Naval experts point out that it is unlikely for a ship as small and quick as PT-109 to be outmaneuvered by a ship as large as a destroyer, unless the crew is caught off guard.

SWAN SONG

The Myth: General Douglas MacArthur coined the saying "Old soldiers never die; they just fade away."

The Truth: He was just quoting a British Army song from World War I.

SO HIGH, SOLO

The Myth: Charles Lindbergh was the first person to fly nonstop across the Atlantic Ocean.

The Truth: He was the *67th* person to fly nonstop across the Atlantic. The first nonstop flight was made by William Alcock and Arthur Brown in 1919, eight years before Lindbergh's flight. Lindbergh's was famous because he did it *alone*.

IN THE GROOVE

The Myth: Thomas Edison invented the phonograph to bring music to the masses.

Background: When Edison first played "Mary Had a Little Lamb" on his crude recording device, he knew he was onto something commercially significant. But he didn't have a clue what it was.

The Truth: He was actually trying to create the first telephone answering machine. The problem he saw with the phone was that, unlike the telegraph, you couldn't leave messages for people. Edison came up with an idea and—to his shock—it worked the first time he tried it. Still, it became clear that the machine wasn't suited for telephones. So Edison began marketing phonographs to businesses, believing that it was only suitable as a dictating machine. It took fifteen years and the successes of other manufacturers for him to be convinced that people would buy the machines for home music.

KISSING

This won't help you kiss any better, but it will give you something to talk about afterwards.

HOW KISSING EVOLVED

• One theory: it evolved from sniffing, a form of greeting still used by animals. In some languages "kiss me" translates literally as "smell me."

• Another theory: it's a holdover from breast feeding.

PROCEED WITH CAUTION

• Europeans of the Dark Ages took kissing very seriously. French women who kissed men other than their husbands were considered guilty of adultery, and Italian men who kissed women in public had to marry them.

• The Great Plague that struck London in 1665 killed thousands—and put kissing out of style. The "substitute" kisses Londoners developed to avoid actually kissing someone—tipping hats, waving hands, and bowing—are still used as greetings today.

• Concerned about the moral and hygienic dangers of kissing, a group of Kansas men founded the Anti-Kissing League in 1909. Members took vows never to kiss their wives again.

SCREEN KISSES

• Thomas Edison filmed the first movie featuring an onscreen kiss in 1896. The "film"—called *The Kiss*—was a 30-second clip starring May Irwin and John C. Rice. It played in nickelodeons.

• Ronald Reagan's ex-wife gets the credit for the longest kiss in Hollywood history. In the 1940 film *You're in the Army Now*, Jane Wyman's kiss with Regis Toomey lasts more than 3 minutes.

• In the mid-1980s Rock Hudson kissed Linda Evans on TV's "Dynasty." Soon afterward he died of AIDS, setting off a nationwide debate on the safety of kissing. Today the Screen Actor's Guild requires film companies to notify actors in advance if their roles require "deep kissing."

KISSING FACTS

• According to Dr. Joyce Brothers, American women kiss an average of 79 men before marrying.

• Longest kiss on record, according to the *Guiness Book of World Records:* 130 hours, 2 minutes. Bobbie Sherlock and Ray Blazina set the record at a charity "Smoochathon" held in Pittsburgh, Pennsylvania in 1979.

• The Japanese did not kiss at all before coming in contact with Westerners.

• Do you kiss your wife goodbye in the morning? Some studies have shown that you'll outlive people who don't by as much as five years.

• In the Middle Ages, where you kissed someone depended on their social status. You kissed equals on the mouth, and superiors on the hand, knee, or feet (the more "superior" they were, the lower you kissed). You didn't have to kiss inferior people at all; they kissed you.

• Studies conducted in the 1950s showed that more than 250 colonies of bacteria are transmitted from one person to another during an average kiss. The good news: most are harmless.

• • •

FROM OUR WRONG # DEPARTMENT:

In 1940 A. Douglass Thompson, a Tennessee paper boy, was delivering his papers when he was attacked and bitten by a neighborhood dog. Thompson had it taken to the pound. It was released to its owner a few days later.

But the owner of the dog, Gertrude Jamieson, was so upset at Thompson for impounding her pet that she began harassing him with obscene phone calls several times a day. She kept it up—for 43 years. Finally in 1983, at the age of 85, she stopped calling Thompson (who by now was age 59)—but not because she had forgiven him. The only reason she stopped calling was because she had suffered a minor stroke and was confined to a hospital room without a telephone.

Horses use 17 muscles to twitch their ears. Humans use only 9.

RUTH'S TRUTHS

Babe Ruth did more than hit home runs. He gave a few interviews, too.

(Responding to a comment that he made more money than President Hoover): "I had a better year than he did."

"I have only one superstition. I make sure to touch all the bases when I hit a home run."

"A man ought to get all he can earn. A man who knows he's making money for other people ought to get some of the profit he brings in. Don't make any difference if it's baseball or a bank or a vaudeville show. It's business, I tell you. There ain't no sentiment to it. Forget that stuff."

"Don't quit until every base is uphill."

"Gee, it's lonesome in the outfield. It's hard keeping awake with nothing to do."

"Hot as hell, ain't it, Prez?" (His greeting to President Calvin Coolidge, during a game at the Washington ball park.)

" I hit big or I miss big. I like to live as big as I can."

"If I'd just tried for them dinky singles, I could've batted around six hundred."

"It's hell to get older."

"I've heard people say that the trouble with the world is that we haven't enough great leaders. I think we haven't enough great followers. I have stood side by side with great thinkers—surgeons, engineers, economists; men who deserve a great following—and have heard the crowd cheer me instead...I'm proud of my profession. I like to play baseball. I like fans, too...But I think they yelled too loudly and yelled for the wrong man."

"What I am, what I have, what I am going to leave behind me—all this I owe to the game of baseball, without which I would have come out of St. Mary's Industrial School in Baltimore a tailor, and a pretty bad one, at that."

"You need a certain number of breaks in baseball...and every other calling."

In 1991 General Motors was #1 on the Fortune 500 list—but 485th in profitablilty.

THE SOUND OF MUZAK

You hear it in the elevator, in your dentist's office, at the supermarket—even in the reptile house of the Bronx Zoo. Here's the inside story on the music you love to hate:

ORIGIN

General George Squier was the head of the U.S. Signal Corps in World War I. During the war he discovered a way to transmit music over electrical lines. When the war was over, he showed his discovery to a Cleveland, Ohio utility. The company liked his invention, and in 1922 helped Squier set up the Wired Radio Company.

• Their plan: provide an alternative to radio by broadcasting music to households through their power lines (for a fee).

• Squier changed his company's name to *Muzak* in 1934. Why? He liked Kodak's name, and wanted something that sounded similar.

MUZAK AT WAR:

Squier overlooked one thing when he started his business: households receiving radio broadcasts free of charge would not see any reason to pay a monthly fee for Muzak's wire broadcasts. This made it tough to attract customers. However, events during World War II helped keep the company in business:

• To combat assembly line fatigue, the British government began broadcasting the BBC in defense factories.

• When production at these plants increased as much as 6%, the U.S. government hired Muzak to pipe sound into U.S. plants. Their productivity rose 11%.

• Studies showed that even cows and chickens increased productivity when "functional" music played in the background.

• Seeing this, the company switched its focus to increasing productivity for business customers. Today it broadcasts via satellite to

180 different Muzak "stations" around the country—and into the ears of more than 100 *million* "listeners" worldwide.

MIND CONTROL

If you thought Muzak just played songs at random, think again:

At Work

• To maximize Muzak's uplifting potential, the company gives each of its songs a "mood rating" that ranges from "Gloomy" (minus three) to "Ecstatic" (plus eight). An overall "stimulus value" is determined for each song.

• Broadcasts are divided into 15 minute "segments": 14 minutes of songs with 1 minute of silence at the end. The "stimulus value" of a segment increases with each song.

• To revive sluggish workers, Muzak plays speedier segments between 10:00 and 11:00 am.

• The songs slow down again at 1:00 pm. Why? To calm employees after lunch.

• By 3:00 pm the music picks up pace—to energize workers at the end of the day.

At the Supermarket

The broadcasts Muzak provides to supermarkets are *always* slow-paced—studies have shown that shoppers who listen to slow music spend more time shopping...and as much as 35% more money.

MUZAK FACTS

• President Dwight D. Eisenhower played Muzak in the White House—and Lyndon Johnson liked it so much he bought a local Texas franchise. He even had Muzak speakers installed in the trees of the LBJ ranch.

• Neil Armstrong listened to Muzak during the Apollo XI voyage to the moon.

• During the fall of Saigon in 1975, State Department staffers evacuated the American embassy compound with Muzak playing in the background.

• No surprise: 90% of Muzak "listeners" say they like the stuff. Andy Warhol claimed it was his favorite music.

There are enough stones in the Great Wall of China to build an 8 ft. wall around the equator.

FAMILIAR NAMES

Some people achieve immortality because their names are associated with common items or activities. You already know the names—now here are the people

Atoine de la Mothe Cadillac. A French explorer, Cadillac founded Detroit in 1701.

Ernesto Miranda. Miranda was arrested in 1963 for stealing $8 from a Phoenix, Arizona bank employee. He confessed, but the U.S. Supreme Court threw out his conviction—the police had not advised him of his rights. To avoid the same mistake, police now read the *Miranda Warning* to people they arrest.

Alexander Garden. A South Carolina botanist born in 1730. The Royal Society of Botany in London named a newly discovered tropical plant, the *gardenia*, in his honor in 1755.

Captain William Lynch. A Virginia farmer during the Revolutionary War, Lynch organized bands of townspeople to dispense justice to outlaws and British collaborators. These bands became known as "Lynch Mobs," and hanging someone without a trial became known as "Lynching."

Ludwig Doberman. A German dog breeder in the late 1800s. He is the "father" of Doberman Pinschers.

Henry Deringer. An American gunsmith of the 1840s, Deringer invented a tiny pistol that he named after himself. Imitators copied his guns—and misspelled his name. Today derringer is still spelled with two r's.

Thomas and William Bowler. The Bowlers, English hatmakers in the 1860s, made a brimmed hunting hat for one of their customers. It became known as a "bowler" hat.

Thomas Derrick. A notorious hangman in England during the 17th century, Derrick designed a hoisting apparatus for the gallows—which he used to execute more than 3,000 people. The apparatus—and the crane that resembles it—are both called derricks.

Charles Henry Dow and Edward D. Jones. Journalists at the turn of the century, Dow and Jones created the first index of U.S. stock prices—the Dow-Jones Average. It later appeared in the newspaper they founded, *The Wall St. Journal*.

Captain Fudge. Though his first name has been forgotten, Captain Fudge was a captain in the British Navy in the 1600s. His wild tales about his seafaring adventures earned him the nickname "Lying Fudge." Sailors of the day referred to his storytelling as "fudging it."

Dr. Thomas Lushington. Lushington was a heavy-drinking English chaplain in the 1600s. His reputation as a drunk was so great that the *City of Lushington*, a London drinking club, was named in his honor more than 200 years after his death. The club's inebriated clientele inspired the word *lush*.

Mr. Scheuster. Like Captain Fudge, Scheuster's first name has been forgotten. He was a crooked criminal lawyer in New York in the 1840s, whose name inspired the term *shyster*.

Admiral Edward "Old Grog" Vernon. Old Grog was famous for pacing his ship's deck in a grogram cloak—that's how he got his nickname. But he was also famously cheap. When he began watering down the rum he served to his sailors, they christened the weakened spirit "Grog."

E.A. Murphy, Jr. Murphy was not an optimist. An American engineer in the 1940s, he was the first to utter the words "Anything that can go wrong *will* go wrong"— Murphy's Law.

John Taliaferro Thompson. A general in the U.S. Army in the 1920s. He was one of the inventors of the Thompson sub-machine gun in 1921. Though the "Tommy Gun" never really caught on with the military as Thompson had hoped, by the late 1920s it was a big hit with the mob.

Antionette Perry. A popular stage actress whose career spanned from 1905 to 1949. The Tony awards are named in her honor.

Sequoya. Sequoya—who also used the name George Guess—was an Indian scholar who developed a system of writing for his native Cherokee language. Sequoia redwood trees are named after him.

IFS AND BUTTS

Warning: The Surgeon General has determined that reading about cigarettes is not harmful to your health.

Richard Joshua (R.J.) Reynolds—one of the fathers of the cigarette industry—hated cigarettes. He preferred chewing tobacco and would not allow smokes in his house.

Though Turkish tobacco is popular all over the world, 7th century Turks hated smokers. One punishment: smokers were led through town on muleback—with their pipes shoved up their noses.

In 1989, Reynolds introduced Uptown, a menthol brand designed specifically for blacks. Within days of its introduction, civil rights groups and anti-smoking organizations lit into Reynolds. Two months later, Uptown was dumped.

Who's the camel on the package of Camel cigarettes? Old Joe, a camel in Barnum and Bailey's circus. R.J. Reynolds had his personal secretary photograph him in 1913. The package is an exact copy of the photo.

Unlucky promotion: R.J. Reynolds paid Amelia Earhart to take Lucky Strikes with her on her ill-fated trip across the ~~Atlantic~~. PACIFIC

Kent cigarette filters were originally made from the same material as WW II gas masks.

In the late 1980s, R.J. Reynolds spent $300 million developing Premier, a high-tech "smokeless cigarette" that came with a 4-page set of instructions. Smokers were supposed to light the "carbon heat source" at the tip and suck flavorings out of the "flavor capsule." It flopped.

If you were a tobacco farmer in the 1930s and 40s, you wouldn't have had to fight in World War II. Pres. Roosevelt declared tobacco "an essential crop" at the outbreak of the war—exempting tobacco growers from the draft.

Mafia means "beauty, excellence, bravery" in Italian.

THE DUSTBIN OF HISTORY

They were VIPs in their time...but they're forgotten now. They've been swept into the Dustbin of History.

FORGOTTEN FIGURE: Lord Cornbury (Edward Hyde), colonial governor of New York from 1702 to 1708.

CLAIM TO FAME: Edward Hyde, a cousin of Queen Anne, was appointed governor of New York in 1702. When colonists went to welcome him, they found him rocking on his porch, knitting a doily and wearing one of his wife's dresses.

Things got weirder when he threw his first dress ball. Not only was he decked out in a formal gown; he also charged an admission fee, and insisted that his guests all feel his wife's ears...which he had described in a long poem as "conch shells."

For many years, he was the was the talk of New York—especially when it turned out he had taken the governorship to escape creditors in England. Then in 1708 he was caught embezzling public funds.

INTO THE DUSTBIN: Cornbury was confined to debtor's prison until his father died, when he inherited a title and returned to England. No monuments to his rule were built, but he did leave his family name on land along the Hudson: Hyde Park.

FORGOTTEN FIGURE: Lucy Page Gaston, 1860-1924, American anti-tobacco reformer.

CLAIM TO FAME: After legendary prohibitionist Carrie Nation, she was the most famous American female reformer of her time. In 1899 she founded the Chicago Anti-Cigarette League, which became the National Anti-Cigarette League two years later. For a while the movement she inspired was a real threat to the tobacco industry, as cigarette sales dipped by 25%.

By 1920 she was so well-known that she became a candidate in the Republican presidential race, vowing to "emancipate" the country from smoking. But she won few votes, and Warren

The golden eagle can spot a rabbit from almost 2 miles away.

Harding, a smoker, was nominated.

INTO THE DUSTBIN: In June, 1924, Gaston was hit by a trolley while crossing a street. She was taken to a hospital, but did not respond well to treatment. That's when doctors discovered she was terminally ill. She died two months later—of throat cancer.

FORGOTTEN FIGURE: Luise Rainer, a film star of the '30s.

CLAIM TO FAME: She was the first person ever to win two consecutive Academy Awards—for Best Actress in 1936 (for *The Great Ziegfield) and* in 1937 (for *The Good Earth*).

In 1936, nominations were still carefully controlled by movie studios. Rainer's first nomination was engineered by MGM to help develop her career. (It was only her second film, and it was a relatively small part.) No one thought she would actually *win* the Oscar. That's why everyone voted for her.

The following year, voting was opened up for the first time to thousands of actors, writers, etc. Rainer, who was well-liked for not acting like a "star," beat out Greta Garbo and Barbara Stanwyck.

INTO THE DUSTBIN: For some reason, MGM forced Ranier into a quick series of throwaway roles; two years and five insignificant pictures later, she was a has-been. Her downfall led gossip columnist Louella Parsons to coin the term "Oscar jinx."

FORGOTTEN FIGURE: Smedley Butler, America's most famous soldier—a U.S. Marine and two-time Medal of Honor winner, nicknamed "Old Gimlet Eye."

CLAIM TO FAME: Once called "the finest fighting man in the armed forces" by Teddy Roosevelt, Butler was renowned for personal bravery, tactical brilliance, and the ability to inspire his fellow soldiers. He joined a Marine force in China during the Boxer rebellion, and helped carry a wounded comrade 17 miles through enemy fire back to their camp. He was promoted to captain—at age 18. He later served in Cuba, Nicaragua, Panama, Honduras, and Haiti.

Butler served in France during World War I—not at the front, but as commander of a troop depot, Camp Pontanezen. Ironically, his greatest fame came from this post. The camp was practically buried in mud; and the troops were short of food and blankets. But somehow, Butler scrounged a huge supply of slats used for trench floors and created walkways and tent floors to keep the troops out

The letters "J" and "V" are the youngest letters of the alphabet. They're about 350 years old.

of the mud.

The grateful soldiers never forgot him; as one said, "I'd cross hell on a slat if Butler gave the word."

After the war, Butler was regarded as presidential material (he didn't run). He was also a popular figure on the lecture circuit.

In the early '30s, he was approached by men claiming to be associated with the American Legion. They wanted him to organize a fighting force to overthrow Franklin Roosevelt—and said there was $300 million available to fund the insurrection. Butler played along and eventually learned he was being courted by the American fascist movement. He divulged the plot before the Un-American Activities Committee in 1934, but nothing much came of it; the story was hushed up because several prominent figures were involved.

INTO THE DUSTBIN: Butler retired from the Corps in 1931, but continued to speak out on military and foreign-policy issues. He died in 1940.

FORGOTTEN FIGURE: William Walker, American journalist, physician, lawyer, and soldier of fortune.

CLAIM TO FAME: Walker is the only native-born American ever to become president of a foreign nation. From July 1856, to May 1857, he was self-appointed dictator of Nicaragua, a nation he took over with a hand-picked force of mercenaries who called themselves "The Immortals."

Walker's success made him a hero throughout the U.S., where the notion of "Manifest Destiny" was gaining wide acceptance. Crowds cheered his exploits, newspapers hailed his triumphs. But a coalition of Central American nations, financed in part by Cornelius Vanderbilt, overthrew Walker. On May 1, 1857, he and his troops fled back to the U.S.

Walker made three more attempts to win control in Central America. Finally, in the fall of 1859, he and his men attacked Honduras and were captured by British and Honduran troops.

INTO THE DUSTBIN: Walker surrendered to the British, expecting he would again be returned to the States. But he was turned over to the Hondurans instead, and was executed by a firing squad on September 12, 1860.

He was so hated by Nicaraguans that he became a symbol of "Yankee Imperialism." He is still remembered there.

U.S. Highway facts: Odd numbered highways move north and south, Even go east and west.

HOW LONG?

See if you can guess the average lifespan of the following things *(answers on page 892)*.

1. The American male in 1900: A. 32.4 years B. 46.3 years C. 66.3 years

2. American male in 1990: A. 67.3 years B. 72.1 years C. 78.6 years

3. The American female in 1900: A. 48.3 years B. 52.8 years C. 60.1 years

4. American female in 1990: A. 68.4 years B. 74.8 years C. 79.0 years

5. Beer: A. 3-5 weeks B. 12-18 months C. 3 months

6. Freeze-dried fish squares (Stored at 70° F): A. 25 years B. 12 months C. 72 months

7. Facelifts: A. 1-3 years B. 6-10 years C. 10-18 years

8. U.S. Patents: A. 17 years B. 70 years C. Unlimited

9. Lightning Bolts: A. 1-7 microseconds B. 45-55 microseconds C. 11 seconds

10. Cockroaches: A. 40 days B. 6 months C. 7 years

11. Bras: A. Up to 9 months B. Up to 2 years C. Up to 5 years

12. Ballistic missiles: A. 10-15 months B. 10 - 15 years C. 100-150 years

13. Snowflakes: A. From 7 minutes to several centuries B. From 30 seconds to 4 days C. From 1 minute to 9 months

14. Televisions: A. 7-10 years B. 10-15 years C. 15-18 years

15. Skywriting: A. 45-60 seconds B. 5-7 minutes C. 45 minutes

16. A professional football (when used in an NFL game): A. 6 minutes B. 30 minutes C. One hour

17. Moonbeams: A. 1.3 Seconds B. 12 minutes C. 1 hour

18. A dollar bill (in circulation): A. 3.8 months, or 900 folds B. 18 months, or 4,000 folds C. 2.5 years, or 10,000 folds

Three million cars are abandoned every year in the U.S.

JOIN THE CLUB

Every time you drive into a town, you see signs with info on Rotary, Kiwanis, or Elk's club chapters. How did they come up with those names? Here are some answers.

The Benevolent and Protective Order of Elks: The group started out in the 1860s as "The Jolly Corks," a drinking club for vaudevillians. Members changed the name to the Elks after they saw a stuffed elk in Barnum's Museum in New York City.

Kiwanis International: Founded as The Benevolent Order of Brothers in 1914 by Allen S. Browne, a Detroit businessman. A year later the group changed its name to Kiwanis, borrowing from the Canadian Indian expression "nun keewanis." They believed that it meant "we trade." Actual translation: "we have good time/we make noise."

The Rotarians: When a group of Chicago businessmen founded a service organization in 1905, they decided to make the meetings convenient for everyone by *rotating* the meeting place from one member's office to another. They couldn't think of a name for it—so they just named it the *Rotary* Club.

The Shriners: During a visit to France in 1867, Walter M. Fleming, a New York doctor, went to see an Arabian musical comedy. At the end of the performance, the cast initiated the audience into a "secret society." Fleming liked the idea—and in 1872 he formed the Ancient Arabic Order of the Nobles of the Mystic Shrine... commonly known as the *Shriners*.

The Freemasons: The group traces its roots back to 17th century guilds of English "freestone mason" guilds of highly skilled craftsmen who carved the ornate stonework used to build monasteries, palaces and cathedrals.

The Lion's Club: Adopted when the group was founded in 1917. It stands for what members consider "the true meaning of citizenship: Liberty, Intelligence, and Our Nation's Safety."

Vital stats: 42% of U.S. men and 31% of U.S. women say they clean their belly buttons every day.

CLASSIC MOVIES: BEHIND THE SCENES

You've seen the films—now here are the stories.

PRIDE OF THE YANKEES (1942). The film biography of New York Yankee first baseman Lou Gehrig starred Gary Cooper...who'd never played baseball in his life. He couldn't run, couldn't field, and couldn't throw.

• The studio hired an expert to teach him baseball fundamentals, but it didn't do any good. Doubles still had to be used whenever Gehrig was supposed to be out in the field.

• Cooper had a knack for batting, though; he was able to meet the ball solidly, with a fairly convincing swing. Unfortunately, he was right-handed and Gehrig had been left-handed.

• Director Sam Woods's solution: He filmed Cooper hitting right-handed and flipped the film so the actor appeared to be batting from the left side.

• That meant other details had to be reversed. For example: Special mirror-image Yankee uniforms had to be designed. And new ballpark billboards that were printed backwards were erected, so the signs would be readable.

• After all that trouble, Wood wouldn't take any chances casting an actor as Babe Ruth. He signed the Babe to play himself.

SINGIN' IN THE RAIN (1952). For years Arthur Freed, the producer of this classic musical, wanted to name a film—any film—"Singin' in the Rain" (after the popular 1920's song)...and this was his chance. It didn't matter to him that there were no rain scenes originally planned for the movie...or that its star and director, Gene Kelly, thought he was nuts.

• When Freed insisted, Kelly gave in and choreographed the film's main dance sequence around the song.

• But the splashing footsteps that audiences heard in the "Rain" dance routine weren't all Kelly's. To enhance the "puddle" effect, a young dancer sloshed through a series of water-filled buckets off-screen. (The dancer was Gwen Verdon, who later starred in *Damn Yankees*.)

• During the dance, Kelly looked joyful. Actually, he was miserable. He had a terrible cold and was afraid that prancing around in all that water would give him pneumonia.

• He was also unhappy about his 19-year-old female co-star, Debbie Reynolds. She'd never sung or danced before, and he had to tutor her for every number.

KING KONG (1933). Merian C. Cooper, the film's producer, wanted to include a scene audiences would never forget. As Paul Boller reports in his excellent book, *Hollywood Anecdotes*: "Late one afternoon in February 1930, as he was leaving his office in midtown Manhattan, Cooper heard the sound of an airplane, glanced out of the window, and saw a plane flying close to the New York Life Insurance Building, then the city's tallest building. At once it flashed into his mind: 'If I can get that gorilla logically on top of the mightiest building in the world, and then have him shot down by the most modern of weapons, the airplane, then no matter how giant he was in size, and how fierce, that gorilla was doomed by civilization.' "

• "By the time RKO came to make the picture, Cooper had had to move Kong, first to the new Chrysler Building, and then, finally, to the Empire State Building, which, when completed in 1931, was the tallest structure in the world."

• King Kong, of course, was a model. He was actually 18" tall.

HIGH NOON (1952). Gary Cooper starred as a sheriff who had to face a band of outlaws by himself. Cooper, who was 50 years old, was praised for the convincing way he made his character seem pained and worried. Actually, it wasn't all acting. Right before filming began, Cooper was hospitalized for a hernia. During the filming, he was troubled by a hip injury. After the film was finished, he went right back to the hospital—this time to have a duodenal ulcer removed.

The rest of the story: Radio personality Paul Harvey's real name is Paul Aurandt.

• He had other reasons to look worried: He thought his co-star, Grace Kelly, was too inexperienced, and that the movie was dull.

• Kelly *was* inexperienced—*High Noon* was only her second movie—but that's why the director had hired her. He wanted the character to seem innocent and naive.

• The movie *was* dull, too. It bombed in its first preview and had to be completely re-edited. Editor Elmo Williams shortened it, sped up the pace, and transformed it from a turkey to a classic. Cooper won an Oscar for Best Actor.

THE GRAPES OF WRATH (1940). The film that made Henry Fonda a star was adapted from one of the most controversial novels in America's history. The book was denounced—and even banned—in many communities as "subversive."

• Author John Steinbeck insisted that 20th Century Fox guarantee the studio would "retain the main action and social intent" of his book.

• Before agreeing, Fox hired detectives to check the accuracy of Steinbeck's portrayal of life in migrant camps. The report: conditions were even worse than Steinbeck had suggested.

• Fox was worried the film's pro-labor message might provoke a response from banks and agri-business (the novel's two villains). So they filmed it under tight security, with unusual secrecy.

• They posted armed guards at the studio door. None of the actors was given a complete script; they had to read from mimeographed sheets instead. The sheets were collected at the end of each day; no one was allowed to leave the set with a script. During shooting, the film was given a false title—*Highway 66*—so the crew could film wherever they pleased without creating a controversy.

• The cast and director John Ford went out of their way to make sure the public knew the film was "apolitical," and it won two Oscars.

AND NOW A SHORT FEATURE FROM THE BOOK,
***Hollywood Anecdotes*, by Paul Boller:**

"For the opening of Pinocchio (1940) Walt Disney's publicity department decided to hire eleven midgets, dress them in Pinocchio outfits, and have them frisk about on top of the theater marquee on opening day. At lunchtime, food and refreshments were passed up to the marquee, including a couple of quarts of liquor. By three o'clock that afternoon things had gotten out of hand and an amused crowd in Times Square was regaled by the spectacle of eleven stark-naked midgets belching noisily and enjoying a crap game atop the Broadway marquee. Police with ladders removed the gamblers in pillowcases."

CLASSIC BLOOPERS

• In *The Invisible Man*, the title character is supposed to be naked, but the footprints he leaves are of shoes instead of bare feet.

• If you look closely in the famous chariot race scene in *Ben Hur* (1959), you'll see a red sports car driving by the Coliseum in the distance.

• In *El Cid*, a 1961 movie extravaganza about an 11th century Spanish hero, a costly crowd scene was spoiled by an extra wearing sunglasses.

• *The Green Berets* features a dramatic shot of the sun...setting in the east.

• In another crowd scene, this time from the 1982 epic *Gandhi*, one of the peasants is sporting Adidas tennis shoes.

MOVIE NOTES

• A South Korean movie theater owner decided that *The Sound of Music* was too long, so he shortened the movie himself—by cutting out all of the songs.

• Why was the computer in *2001* named HAL? The director claimed the name is a hybrid of the two principal learning systems Heuristic and Algorithmic. However, a number of critics have pointed out that if you replace each initial in HAL with the letter that succeeds it, you wind up with the well-known name of a real-life computer...IBM.

• The shortest shooting schedule for a full-length, commercial film was two days...for Roger Corman's 1959 classic, *Little Shop of Horrors*.

George Reeves, TV's Superman, needed three people to help him out of his costume.

THE COMPASS IN YOUR NOSE

What do you know about your body? Here's some fascinating info from a book called, The Compass in Your Nose, *by Marc McCutcheon*

THE COMPASS IN YOUR NOSE

Magnetic Attraction

• All humans have a trace amount of iron in their noses, a rudimentary compass found in the ethmoid bone (between the eyes) to help in directional finding relative to the earth's magnetic field.

• Studies show that many people have the ability to use these magnetic deposits to orient themselves—even when blindfolded and removed from such external clues as sunlight—to within a few degrees of the North Pole, exactly as a compass does.

• Though no one knows how this "sixth" sense is processed by the brain, more than two dozen animals, including the dolphin, tuna, salmon, salamander, pigeon, and honeybee, have been found to have similar magnetic deposits in their brains to help them in navigation and migration.

The Off-Duty Nostril

• Nostrils switch on and off every three to four hours, so that one is always smelling and breathing while the other closes down and rests.

Whose Nose?

• Women have a better sense of smell than men due to higher levels of the female hormone estrogen.

• Interestingly, a woman can detect the odor of musk—a scent associated with male bodies—better than any other odor.

Scent-sational

• The sex/scent connection is a powerful one. About 25 percent of people with smell disorders—due to either head injuries, viral infections, allergies, or aging—lose interest in sex.

HAIR TODAY, GONE TOMORROW

Get Growing

• On the scalp, each hair grows continuously for 3 to 5 years, then enters a resting phase. After about 3 months of "resting," the hair falls out; a new hair starts growing 3 to 4 months later. Ninety percent of the scalp is always in the growing phase.

• Eyebrow hairs stay short because their growing phase only lasts for 10 weeks. Eyelashes are replaced every 3 months. A person will grow about 600 complete eyelashes in a lifetime.

• "Beards grow faster than any other hair on the body, and blond beards grow fastest of all. The average beard grows about 5-1/2 inches in a year—or about 30 feet in a lifetime. The longest beard on record was grown by Hans Langseth of Kensett, Iowa." When he died in 1927 his beard measured 17-1/2 feet.

Baldness

• One out of every five men begin balding rapidly in their 20s. Another one out of five will always keep their hair. The others will slowly bald over time.

• As a general rule, the more hair a man has on his chest at age 30 the less hair he'll have on his head at age 40.

• Women typically lose as much as 50 percent of their hair within 3 months of childbirth. This partial and temporary balding is caused by severe fluctuations of hormones.

Hair Growth and Loss

• The average hair grows half an inch per month, with the fastest growth generally occurring in the morning hours. Hair sprouts fastest of all when you're in love, which may also be due to fluctuations of hormones.

• A loss of about 70 hairs per day is typical, but emotional stress (including falling out of love), illness, malnourishment, and anemia can more than double this amount.

Goosebumps

• The goosebumps that break out on our skin when we're cold represent little more than the body's effort to erect the coat of fur our ancestors lost over 100,000 years ago. Raised body hair provides added insulation.

ONLY SKIN DEEP

Sags, Lines, and Wrinkles

• Collagen—the skin's network of protein fibers—breaks down and becomes less pliable with age, causing sags, lines, and wrinkles to form on the face, neck, and hands. Any expression that manipulates the skin deeply and consistently will promote wrinkling (it takes about 200,000 frowns to create one permanent brow line), but exposure to sunlight and cigarette smoke hastens the process.

Dead Skin and Where It Goes

• The body constantly sheds dead skin cells and replaces them with new ones. Thousands of these cells are lost, for example, every time we shake hands or swing a baseball bat. By the time we reach age 70, we'll have shed 40 pounds of dead skin.

• Of the dust floating around in the average house, 75 percent is made up of dead skin cells.

HEAR, HEAR

Human versus Animal Hearing

• Vampire and fruit bats can hear pitch as high as 210,000 hertz, ten times higher than humans. The dolphin's hearing is even more sensitive, with an acuity of 280,000 hertz.

• The best overall long-distance hearing, on the other hand, belongs to the fennec, a small African fox. Its oversized ears enable it to hear the movements of another animal up to one mile away.

The Future of Ear Wiggling

• The ability to wiggle the ears is a vestige of evolution, a throwback to a time when our ancestors could "cock," or adjust, the ears to aid in hearing. The musculature for ear cocking has gradually diminished over the eons through genetic reprogramming. Most of us have lost the ability to move the ears at all in such a manner.

ON ANOTHER SUBJECT...

Doo-wop Mysteries Of Life:

How can you tell if a singer is singing "Bom-Bom," or "Bomp-bomp"? And is there any way to be sure that it's "Dip-dip" rather than "Dit-dit"?

ABE LINCOLN, WARTS AND ALL

We've all heard so much about Abraham Lincoln that it's easy to assume we know everything important about him. Actually, most of us know almost nothing. For example, did you know...

THE REAL ABE

• Some photographs of Lincoln show him with a mole on the right side of his face—but other photos show it on the left. The reason: few full-length pictures of Lincoln existed when he was running for president. So when photographers needed one, they put Lincoln's head onto other people's bodies. Sometimes the head needed to be reversed to fit the body they were using—and the mole on his right cheek ended up on his left.

• Although Lincoln's voice is often portrayed in movies as being deep and booming, his actual voice was high-pitched, piercing and shrill. Though unusual, it payed off politically: It carried for hundreds of yards—a distinct advantage in open-air speeches and debates.

TRY, TRY AGAIN

Lincoln wasn't always a success:

• He lost a race for the state legislature in 1832. He also lost his job.

• His grocery business failed the following year. It took him 15 years to pay off the debt.

• He was elected to the state legislature in 1834, but he lost races for speaker of the house in 1836 and 1838.

• He was elected to Congress in 1846 but was defeated after only two years, and in 1849 lost the race for a land-office seat.

• He lost the U.S. Senate race in 1854 and again in 1858. In between, he lost the Vice Presidential nomination.

• It makes you wonder why he even bothered to run for president in 1860—but he did...and won. He was reelected in 1864.

HONEST ABE?

• Lincoln's presidential campaigns used dirty tricks to get ahead: During the 1860 Republican National Convention, his campaign managers forged convention passes in order to pack the galleries with Lincoln supporters, shutting out hundreds of his opponent's supporters in the process. Lincoln won the nomination.

• Lincoln wasn't always that honest: After one trip to Springfield, Illinois, he filed for compensation for the 3,252 miles he claimed to have traveled. The actual length of the trip was 1,800 miles.

ABE FACTS

• Lincoln hated being called "Abe"—friends called him Lincoln.

• He really did carry important documents in his stovepipe hat.

• He was the first President to support womens' suffrage. In 1832, while running for the state legislature, he provided a newspaper with a prepared statement that supported the idea.

• Though the Gettysburg Address is considered the most eloquent oration in American history, the *Chicago Times* hated it. The day after Lincoln delivered it, the *Times* wrote: "The cheek of every American must tingle with shame as he reads the silly, flat and dish-watery utterances of the man who has been pointed out to intelligent foreigners as the President of the United States."

STRANGE BUT TRUE

Lincoln took his dreams seriously, and believed that strange events foretold the future. According to some accounts, he may even have "predicted" his own assassination.

• On one occasion, he looked into an old mirror and saw two reflections of himself. His interpretation: he would serve a second term as President—but would die in office.

• About a week before his assassination, Lincoln had a dream in which he "awoke" to the sound of sobbing and went to the East Room of the White House—which had been prepared for a funeral. When he asked a guard who had died, he replied: "The President."

• The morning of the assassination, Lincoln told his aides that he had had another dream, one in which he was sailing "in an indescribable vessel and moving rapidly toward an indistinct shore."

Dr. Seuss designed the first animated color TV commercial in 1949, for Ford.

BATTLE OF THE SEXES

Looking for words of wisdom about love and life? Try TV quotes from the book Primetime Proverbs, *by Jack Mingo and John Javna.*

ALL ABOUT MEN

"Men are nothing but lazy lumps of drunken flesh. They crowd you in bed, get you all worked up, and then before you can say 'Is that all there is?' that's all there is."

—Mrs. Gravas (Latka's mom), *Taxi*

Cosmetic Clerk: "You know what the fastest way to a man's heart is?"
Rosanne: "Yeah. Through his chest."

—Roseanne

ALL ABOUT WOMEN

"It's not the frivolity of women that makes them so intolerable. It's their ghastly enthusiasm."

—Horace Rumpole, *Rumpole of the Bailey*

"There she was—dejected, desperate, and stoned. Everything I could hope for in a woman."

—Louie DePalma, *Taxi*

"It's been proven through history that wimmin's a mystery."

—Popeye

ON MARRIAGE

"In my town, we didn't have datin.' You washed your hair every Saturday night and when you were fourteen, you married your cousin."

Nurse Laverne, *Empty Nest*

"Well, well, well...So you're going to get married, ha, ha, ha. Welcome to the ranks of the living dead."

—Kingfish, *Amos & Andy*

"Men are such idiots, and I married their King."

—Peg Bundy, *Married with Children*

ABOUT SEX

"With my first husband, it was like a news bulletin: brief, unexpected, and usually a disaster."

—Mary Campbell, *Soap*

"You can point out any item in the Sears catalog and somebody wants to sleep with it."

—Det. Stanley Wojohoicz, *Barney Miller*

BREAKFAST SERIALS

You're not supposed to read this book at breakfast, of course. But you can read it after *breakfast. Here's the perfect reading fiber.*

RAISIN' DOUBTS

Everybody knows a raisin is heavier than a cereal flake. So how come all the raisins in Kellogg's Raisin Bran don't end up at the bottom of the box?

The raisins are mixed evenly with the cereal as the boxes are filled. Since the flat flakes pack so densely together, the raisins can't move around much during shipping.

GETTING FLAKY?

According to one researcher, large doses of cereal may contain enough natural LSD to induce mild euphoria. Dr. David Conning, director of the British Nutritional Foundation, suggests that eating a large bowl of shredded wheat or bran flakes in one sitting may be enough to set you off. This is because LSD is produced by ergot, a common fungal infestation of wheat that may, in some cases, survive food processing. A high-bran diet could result in a daily consumption of 100 micrograms of LSD, four times the minimum dose needed to produce an effect on an inexperienced user of the drug. Eight to ten slices of whole wheat bread, the doctor said, could have the same effect. Turn On, Tune In, Snap, Crackle Pop?

SO SWEET

Are cereals ashamed of their sugary roots? Three that have been renamed to appeal to the new nutrition-conscious consumer are: Super Sugar Crisp (has become Super Golden Crisp), Sugar Pops (now called simply Corn Pops); and Sugar Smacks (changed to the healthy-sounding but still tooth-aching sweet Honey Smacks). But that doesn't mean they're less sugary—Honey Smacks and Super Golden Crisp are right up there with Froot Loops and Apple Jacks on the list of "high sugar content" cereals, some of which contain more than half their weight in sugar.

George Washington's false teeth were made of Hippopotomus ivory.

SOMETHING USEFUL, FOR A CHANGE

A notorious "Phone Phreak" (a pre-computer hackers of the late 1960s who developed elaborate strategies for getting free phone calls through guerrilla technology), called himself Cap'n Crunch. This was in honor of a "free-inside" premium whistle from the cereal of the same name which, according to legend, was exactly the right frequency for triggering free long distance calls if blown into the phone right after dialing the number.

STATISTICS:

• Nielsen Marketing Research tells us that last year nearly 2.5 billion boxes of hot and cold cereal were sold in the US.

• The manufacturers of Post cereals use a staggering 75,000,000 pounds of corn, 1,550,000 bushels of wheat and 7,500,000 pounds of rice each year, which they sweeten with 36,000,000 pounds of liquid sugar.

• Kellogg's reports that the average American child consumes 15 pounds of cereal in a year.

• A Cheerios box with a Lone Ranger Frontier Town premium on the box sold for 18¢ in 1948. The price today for this vintage box? $165 to $350 (cereal not included). A full set of the Frontier Town (four maps and 72 models) sells for $7,200 on the collectibles market.

• Potato chips: the new breakfast of champions? A bowlful of Wheaties contains twice as much sodium as a similar size serving of potato chips, according to researchers at *Consumer Reports* Magazine.

AMERICA'S BEST-SELLING CEREALS

1. Kellogg's Corn Flakes
2. Kellogg's Frosted Flakes
3 General Mills Cheerios
4. Kellogg's Raisin Bran
5. Kellogg's Rice Krispies

CR_ _ SW_ _ D P_ZZL_S

What's an 8-letter word for the smallest library in the house? While you're pondering the answer, here's some crossword puzzle trivia.

The first crossword puzzle appeared on December 21, 1913, in the pages of the *New York World* newspaper. It was created by a reporter named Arthur Wynn.

Dick Simon, a struggling publisher, was visiting his aunt one afternoon in 1924. She wanted to give her daughter a book of crossword puzzles, but none existed. So Simon and his partner, Lincoln Schuster, published one themselves. It became a bestseller overnight—and made enough money to keep the fledgling Simon and Schuster company afloat.

Crosswords were so popular in the twenties that in 1925 the B & O Railroad put dictionaries on all its mainline trains for its many crossword-solving passengers.

During the Roaring '20s, crossword puzzles even influenced fashions: Clothes made with black and white checked fabric were the rage.

In December, 1925 Theodore Koerner, a 27-year-old employee of the New York Telephone Co., shot and wounded his wife after she refused to help him solve a crossword puzzle.

In 1926, a waiter living in Budapest, Hungary commited suicide. He left behind a note—in the form of a crossword puzzle—explaining why he killed himself. His motive: unknown. The police couldn't solve the puzzle.

Today crossword puzzles are the most popular hobby on Earth. The Bible is the most popular Crossword puzzle subject.

What's a 14-1etter word for a crossword maniac? CRUCIVERBALIST.

1ST-CLASS COACH

It seems as though Vince Lombardi is quoted more often than other football coaches. Here's an example of what he had to say.

"To play this game, you must have that fire in you, and there is nothing that stokes that fire like hate."

"Pro football...is a violent, dangerous sport. To play it other than violently would be imbecile."

"Winning isn't everything. It's the only thing."

(On his "Winning is everything" quote): "I wish to hell I'd never said the damn thing...I meant the effort...I meant having a goal...I sure as hell don't mean for people to crush human values and morality."

"I think the rights of the individual have been put above everything else...The individual has to have every respect for authority regardless of what authority is."

"The harder you work, the harder it is to surrender."

"Run to daylight."

"A real executive goes around with a worried look on his assistants."

"No one is ever hurt. Hurt is in the mind."

"If you aren't fired with enthusiasm, you'll be fired with enthusiasm."

"If you can't accept losing, you can't win."

"The greatest accomplishment is not in never falling, but in rising again after you fall."

"A school without football is in danger of deteriorating into a medieval study hall."

"There are three important things in life: family, religion, and the Green Bay Packers."

"Football isn't a contact sport. It's a collision sport. Dancing is a contact sport."

"Football is a game of clichés, and I believe in every one of them."

THE PONY EXPRESS

Remember those dramatic scenes in TV westerns where everyone's waiting for the Pony Express to arrive with the mail? It turns out that didn't happen very often…or for very long.

THE MYTH

The Pony Express was one of the most important links connecting the gold rush towns of the West and large cities in the East. For years, it was the fastest way to send a letter to California; without it the western states might never have developed.

THE TRUTH

In its short lifetime (18 months—1860-61), the Pony Express *was* the fastest way to send a letter to California. Riders could deliver a letter in 10 days—half the time to send it by sea. But it had its problems:

• Hardly anyone could afford to use it. A single letter initially cost $5.00 to mail, and never dropped below a dollar. The largest customers were newspapers that depended on late-breaking news to keep readers up to date.

• The shipping firm of Russell, Majors & Waddell—founders of the Pony Express—knew their enterprise could never make money with normal business; they counted on winning a contract with the federal government to help cover its enormous costs ($70,000 up front and $4,000 per month). They never got one. The government was more interested in Samuel Morse's telegraph.

• By 1861 the nation's first transcontinental telegraph line was completed—making the Pony Express obsolete overnight. It folded less than two years after its introduction, over $500,000 in debt.

EXPRESS FACTS

• There wasn't a single pony in the Pony Express. Ponies didn't have the stamina to carry large loads of mail over long distances.

• Few of the riders were adults. Most were teenagers, hired through newspaper advertisements that read: "Wanted: Young skinny wiry fellows, not over 18. Must be expert riders willing to risk death daily. Orphans preferred."

What state has the highest percentage of literate citizens? Iowa.

DON'T CAN IT

Here are some recycling tips from The Recycler's Handbook, *by the EarthWorks Group.*

For the recycling novice—in other words, almost all of us—aluminum cans are as close to perfect as you can get: No matter how many of them you have, they're still light enough to carry; you don't need any fancy storage containers—you can even pile them into a paper bag. And you don't have to hunt very far to find someplace to take them—cans are worth so much that there's always someone around who collects them.

The secret is that it's a lot cheaper to recycle aluminum cans than it is to make them out of new metal. So years ago, the aluminum industry set up collection services, and they've been paying top dollar to get cans back ever since.

So if you're wondering where to start recycling, put aluminum cans at the top of your list.

ALUMINATING FACTS

- Aluminum was worth more than gold when it was discovered. It was first used to make a rattle for Napoleon's son.
- In 1989, Americans used 80 billion aluminum cans. That's the equivalent of about 16 cans for every person on the planet.
- We recycled a record 60% of them that same year.
- Making cans from recycled aluminum cuts related air pollution (for example, sulfur dioxides, which create acid rain) by 95%.
- Recycling aluminum saves 95% of the energy used to make the material from scratch. That means you can make *20* cans out of recycled material with the same energy it takes to make *one* can out of new material.
- Americans throw away enough aluminum every three months to rebuild our entire commercial air fleet.

WHAT YOU CAN DO

1. Find a Place to Take Them

- Virtually all recycling programs accept aluminum cans.

Which state recycles the most? Washington.

Call recycling centers in your area for more details.

• If you're having trouble finding a recycling center, try the toll-free Reynolds Aluminum hotline: (800) 228-2525. If there's a Reynolds recycling center in your area, they'll tell you where it is.

• Check phone listings under "Scrap Metal." Many scrap dealers aren't interested in small loads, but aluminum is valuable—so they may take it.

• Contact your state recycling office.

2. Recycle

Cans

• Crushing cans makes storing and transporting them easier. But before recycling, check with your recycler to find out if crushing them is okay. In some states with deposit laws, recyclers prefer to get the cans intact; they need to see the brand and the name of the factory the can came from.

• In most places, it's not necessary to rinse cans...but a large batch of unwashed cans may attract bees and ants.

Foiled Again

• Aluminum foil, pie plates, TV dinner trays, etc. are all reusable and recyclable. Lightly rinse them off first if they're dirty (you don't have to waste water—use dishwater).

• Some places request that you keep foil and cans separate. Check with your local recycling center.

Other Items

• Containers aren't the only source of aluminum scrap. Other common items include window frames, screen doors and lawn furniture. However, check with your recycling center before including these.

• Is your scrap aluminum? Check it with a magnet; aluminum isn't magnetic. Check small pieces like screws, rivets, etc.

• Remove everything that's not aluminum.

FOR MORE INFORMATION

"Aluminum Recycling: America's Environmental Success Story." The Aluminum Association, 900 19th St., N.W., Washington, D.C. 20006. (202) 862-5100.

Americans buy two billion disposable razors and razor blades every year.

UNCLES & ANT FARMS

Ever had an ant farm? It's one of those toys people buy you when they're trying to get something "educational" instead of something you can actually play with. Even when you're a kid, you can't help but wonder: Who could have come up with an idea like this?... And where did they get the ants? Here's the answer.

THE BEGINNING

It was Independence Day, 1956, when the idea struck. "It just came to me in a flash," "Uncle" Milton Levine says. He was a 32-year-old entrepreneur looking for new products to help expand his line of mail order novelties. "I was at a Fourth of July picnic at my sister's house in the Valley [California's San Fernando Valley]. I saw a bunch of ants around the pool. I saw a bunch of kids, and they were interested in the ants. And it came to me."

• Levine's first ant farms were six inches by nine inches, and sold for $1.98. They consisted of a solid-colored plastic frame that sandwiched a layer of sand between two sheets of transparent plastic. There was a plastic farm scene—barn, silo, farmhouse, and windmill.

• To attract customers, Levine bought a 2-inch ad in the *Los Angles Times*, inviting the curious to "Watch the ants dig tunnels and build bridges" in their own Ant Farm. "I got so many orders, you wouldn't believe it," he says.

• Uncle Milton ran into an unexpected problem, though. The ants in his first farms kept dying—the result of either glue fumes (Levine's former partner's theory) or the booze the assembler used to drink (Levine's theory). Whatever the cause, the problem was eventually solved.

DOWN ON THE FARM

• The Ant Farm is an enduring product; Over 12 million farms—containing more than 360 million ants—have been sold so far. Most customers are satisfied: the company receives about 12,000 letters each year from happy Ant Farm owners. But not all the letters are positive: one child wrote in complaining that his ants weren't wearing top hats like it showed on the box.

• How do the ants survive weeks on toy store shelves? They don't—the farms are sold empty, with a certificate the owner sends to Uncle Milton Industries for a shipment of free ants.

• Every farm comes with *Uncle Milton's Ant Watchers' Manual*, which tells you how to care for your ants, and gives you information about your new livestock (Do ants talk? Yes. Do ants take baths? Yes).

• One improvement on the Ant Farms of yesteryear: Newer models have connectors for plastic tubes—so you can connect any number of ant farms together and watch the ants crawl back and forth.

THE ORIGINAL ANT FARMER

• Kenneth Gidney started digging ants in 1959 after answering an ad Uncle Milton had placed in the *Los Angeles Times*. One of his children, Robin Brenner, is still doing it today—she's one of only three diggers that supply the 15 million ants the company sends out each year.

• Not that it's an easy job, according to Brenner. You get bitten a lot. "Sometimes when I'm sitting up late at night, I think 'People don't know how hard this is. They don't know where these ants come from. They don't know how much sleep I'm missing.' "

• Every ant catcher has his or her own technique. Some take straws and blow into antholes, catching the ants as they run out. Brenner's father carefully sliced the tunnels and the kids gathered the ants into coffee cans. Brenner herself digs up the ant tunnels and then sucks up the ants using a car vacuum fixed to a Tupperware container.

• It takes about 10 hours to gather 50,000 ants, for which you can earn about $550. Afterward a half-dozen workers tediously fill little plastic vials with exactly 30 ants each, and these are mailed out to Ant Farm owners.

ANT FARM FACTS

• All the ants supplied for the Ant Farm are female. In the ant world, there aren't many males, and all they do is mate and die (an anty-climax, if you will). And since the company can't legally ship queen ants, Ant Farm colonies can't reproduce and will eventually dwindle to nothing.

• Out of thousands of varieties of ants, the harvester ant was chosen for the Ant Farm because it's big and is one of the few varieties that will dig in daylight.

• The leading cause of barnyard death is overfeeding. If you exceed the recommended ration of one birdseed or a single corn flake every two days, the food gets moldy, and your ants "buy the farm."

• The next leading dangers are too much sunlight (baked ants). Shaking the farm has been known to cause mass death by shock.

• At a funeral, the live ants always carry the dead ant to the northeastern corner of the farm. If the farm is rotated to a new direction, the pallbearers march into action again, digging up the dead ants and reburying them in the northeast. Why? Nobody knows.

• The technical name for an ant farm (or any ant habitat) is a formicarium.

• Why is Levine called "Uncle Milton"? "Everyone always said, 'You've got the ants, but where's the uncles?' So I became Uncle Milton."

• Ant farms aren't the only culturally significant product Uncle Milton Industries makes. Some others:

—the plastic shrunken heads that hang from rear-view mirrors.

—the Spud Gun, which fires potato pellets

—the once-popular insecticides Fly Cake and Roach Cake

—"100 Toy Soldiers for a Buck"

ANT FACTS

• In medieval times, it was thought that ants in the house were a sign of good luck and abundance.

• Chinese farmers use ants against pests. A large colony can capture several million insects a year.

AD NAUSEUM

Here's a horrible thought: Every day the average American is exposed to 3,000 ads. Today you get to read about them, too.

In a 1985 Procter & Gamble poll, 93% of the people questioned recognized Mr. Clean, but only 56% of the same group could identify Vice President George Bush.

More American kids age 3-5 recognize Ronald McDonald than Santa Claus or any other entity, real or mythical.

The typical 30-second prime-time TV ad costs about the same to produce as the half-hour program it interrupts.

Advertisers spend about $400 a year on each newspaper subscriber and $300 a year on each television household.

The first advertisement to discuss body odor was a 1919 ad for the deodorant Odo-Ro-No.

The infamous "this is your brain on drugs" ad had an unintentional side effect: Small kids all over the country refused to eat fried eggs, believing they were somehow laced with drugs.

In early cuts of *Die Hard II*, Bruce Willis clearly used a Black & Decker drill in a key scene. When the scene was cut, Black & Decker—which paid for the scene and had planned an expensive promotion campaign around it—sued for damages.

The first recorded singing commercial was for Moxie, the most popular soft drink of the '20s; it was released on disc (on the Moxie label) in 1921.

Michael Jackson's hair-burning Pepsi ads in the mid-1980s boosted Pepsi drinking among 12-20 year olds, the elderly and Japanese. They actually hurt sales among 25-40 year-old blacks, who saw Jackson's plastic surgery and cosmetic touches as a repudiation of his roots.

If you're an average American, you'll spend a year and a half of your life watching TV commercials.

MORE MYTH CONCEPTIONS

Here are two more pages of "facts" that everyone knows—but aren't true.

Myth: The song "Chopsticks" was named after the Chinese eating utensils with the same name.
Truth: The song was written by Euphemia Allen, a 16-year-old British girl in 1877. She advised pianists to play it with their hands turned sideways, using chopping motions.

Myth: Alan Shepard coined the phrase "A-OK" during his first spaceflight in May, 1961. Reason: "OK" by itself could not be heard over the static.
Truth: Even *we* thought he said it—we mentioned it in our *Third Bathroom Reader*. But he never did. Colonel "Shorty" Powers—NASA's public relations officer at the time—came up with the phrase himself and attributed it to Shepard, hoping it would catch on. It did—even though most astronauts hated it.

Myth: Chinese checkers were invented in China.
Truth: The game was invented in England in the 1800s. It was originally called *Halma*.

Myth: The Guinea pig originated on the island of Guinea.
Truth: It's actually from South America. And it's not a pig—it's a rodent.

Myth: Goats can eat anything—even tin cans.
Truth: Even if their jaws were strong enough to crunch metal, goats hate the taste of tin cans.

Myth: Switching from butter to margarine will help you lose weight.
Truth: Margerine may be lower in cholesterol than butter, but it has the same number of calories—so it won't help you lose weight.

Alaska is closer to the USSR than it is to the 48 contiguous United States.

Myth: The Romans used chariots in battle.
Truth: Chariots weren't effective on the battlefield—soldiers couldn't fight while holding onto the reins. The Romans used them only in sports and as transportation.

Myth: Dogs sweat through their tongues.
Truth: Dogs cool off by breathing rapidly; not by sticking their tongues out. Their tongues don't have sweat glands—and the only large sweat glands they have are in their feet.

Myth: Having so many ships in Pearl Harbor when the Japanese attacked in 1941 was one of the worst disasters of World War II.
Truth: It may actually have been *lucky:* the ships in port had better air cover, didn't sink as deep, and were much closer to repair facilities than if they had been out at sea.

Myth: If too many pores in your skin clog up, you can get sick—even die.
Truth: The pores in your skin don't breathe—and you don't need to keep them "open." It is possible to clog all the pores in your body for an extended period of time without suffering any ill effects.

Myth: You can tell the age of a rattlesnake by counting the number of rattles it has.
Truth: The number of rattles a snake has does increase with age, but not at a uniform rate. Snakes shed their skins more than once a year—and the interval varies with each individual snake.

Myth: In high winds, skyscrapers can sway as much as eight feet in any direction.
Truth: Even the most limber buildings won't move more than a few inches.

Myth: Cold-blooded animals have cold blood.
Truth: A "cold-blooded" animal's body temperature changes with the surrounding air temperature. Many cold-blooded animals have body temperatures that are higher than "warm-blooded" animals.

Given a second chance, 18% of Americans say they would not remarry their spouses.

THE GOSPEL ACCORDING TO BOB

You've heard his songs. Here are a few of his comments.

"Colleges are like old-age homes; except for the fact that more people die in colleges.

"Just because you like my stuff doesn't mean I owe you anything."

"Art is the perpetual motion of illusion."

"Rock and roll ended with Little Anthony & the Imperials."

"I'd like to see Thomas Jefferson, Benjamin Franklin and a few of those other guys come back. If they did I'd go out and vote. They knew what was happening."

"I'm just as good a singer as Caruso…I hit all those notes and I can hold my breath three times as long if I want to."

"It's always lonely where I am."

"They're just songs. Songs are transparent so you can see every bit through them."

"You can get sex anywhere. If you're looking for someone to *love* you, now that's different. I guess you have to stay in college for that."

"I sometimes dream of running the country and putting all my friends in office. That's the way it works now, anyway."

"I have no message for anyone, my songs are only me talking to myself.."

"On some of my earlier records, I sounded cross because I was poor. Lived on less than 10 cents a day in those times. Now I'm cross because I'm rich."

"Death don't come knocking at the door. It's there in the morning when you wake up. Did you ever clip your fingernails, cut your hair? Then you experience death."

"Money doesn't talk—It swears."

THE PIGMENT OF YOUR IMAGINATION

Do you remember your first box of Crayola Crayons? Here's some info you probably never knew about them:

BACKGROUND

In 1885, Joseph W. Binney founded the Peekskill Chemical Company in Peekskill, NY and began producing lampblack, charcoal and red iron oxide barn paint. In 1900 his son and nephew, Edwin Binney and C. Harold Smith, took over, renamed the company "Binney and Smith," and added schoolroom slate pencils to their line of goods.

• In selling to schools, they learned that teachers were dissatisfied with the classroom chalk and crayons available at the time. The chalk was too crumbly and dusty, the European-made crayons too expensive and their colors too anemic.

• Binney and Smith went to work, developing first a "dustless" chalk and then a better-quality crayon. Further research went into finding non-toxic pigments when they discovered that many kids then, as now, thought the colors look good enough to eat.

WHAT'S YOUR NUMBER?

In 1903 the first boxes of Crayolas rolled off the line, priced at five cents and offering eight colors: red, blue, green, yellow, orange, brown, violet and black. The number of colors available has changed several times since then: By 1949, Crayolas were up to 48 colors; by 1958, 64; and in 1972 eight fluorescent colors were added. The company has stuck with 72 colors ever since. To introduce new ones they have to retire some, most recently in 1990.

RED SCARE

Crayons, although ageless, are not exempt from the changing world. Consider these examples:

• In 1958, with Cold War xenophobia in full bloom, the company changed the name of "Prussian Blue" to "Midnight Blue."

• In 1962, heightened consciousness brought on by the civil rights movement led Binney and Smith to change the name of "Flesh" to "Peach," recognizing, as the company put it, "that not everyone's flesh is the same shade." On the other hand, the color "Indian Red" still exists.

• In 1990, with much ballyhoo, Binney and Smith discontinued eight of their less-popular colors (Blue Gray, Green Blue, Lemon Yellow, Maize, Orange Red, Orange Yellow, Raw Umber, and Violet Blue) in order to replace them with the brighter colors (Cerulean, Dandelion, Fuchsia, Jungle Green, Royal Purple, Teal Blue, Vivid Tangerine, and Wild Strawberry) that their marketing research indicated that kids wanted.

• The problem: parents. When the colors were introduced, a small knot of protesters picketed the Binney and Smith headquarters, carrying signs with slogans like "We Take Umber-age" and "Save Lemon Yellow." The company refused to back down. But it did make one concession; it promised to ensconce a five foot replica of each color in its "Crayon Hall of Fame," a new feature of its guided tours.

CRAYON FACTS

• The name *Crayola* comes from combining the French word "craie" meaning a stick of color with "ola" from the word "oleaginous," referring to the oily paraffin wax in the crayons. It was Binney's wife Alice (a schoolteacher, incidentally) who coined the term.

• Surveys have shown that the smell of crayons is one of the most recognized smells in America. Its source: stearic acid, also known as beef fat.

• Four out of five crayons sold in the U.S. are Crayolas. Each year Binney and Smith manufactures more than 2 billion of them. That's enough to produce a giant crayon 35 feet in diameter and 410 feet tall, towering 100 feet taller than the Statue of Liberty.

• 65% of all American children between the ages of 2 and 7 will pick up a crayon at least once today. American kids will spend 6.3 billion hours coloring this year—that's 27 minutes a coloring session, longer if the crayons are brand new.

James Smithson, founder of the Smithsonian Institution, never visited the U.S.

THE PHRASE IS FAMILIAR

Here are some well-known phrases and the stories behind them.

WHEN MY SHIP COMES IN

Meaning: When financial luck improves.

Background: Before steamships, cargo ships depended on wind, luck and weather. Investors who had a large financial stake in a ship's cargo often waited anxiously, hoping the ship would arrive before they ran out of money.

PULL OUT ALL THE STOPS

Meaning: To use every means at your disposal.

Background: Each pipe in an organ contains a "stop" which blocks the flow of air; pulling out specific stops allows sets of pipes to sound. An organist wanting the loudest sound possible "pulls out all the stops."

THE LION'S SHARE

Meaning: A greedily large portion.

Background: Taken from an Aesop's fable in which a lion goes hunting with a cow, a goat and a sheep. When the animals catch a deer, the lion divides it into four portions—then takes them all.

THE BOONDOCKS

Meaning: A very remote area.

Background: *Bundok* is the Philipino word for mountain. U.S. soldiers brought the term back from the Spanish-American War.

TO THE HILT

Meaning: All the way.

Background: A hilt is a handle of a sword or dagger. When you stab as far as you can, it's "to the hilt."

IN CAHOOTS WITH

Meaning: To conspire with.

Background: Thieves in medieval Germany's Black Forest often shared cabins known as *kajuetes*. They were literally "in kajuetes" with each other.

NOT WORTH HIS SALT

Meaning: Overpaid.

Background: Before the invention of money, the Romans paid their soldiers in portions of salt, then a very valuable commodity. It was believed to have magical properties. They'd throw it over their shoulder for luck or sprinkle it on food they suspected might be spoiled or poisoned, which explains another salt phrase—"Take it with a grain of salt."

A DOG EAT DOG WORLD

Meaning: A brutishly hostile world.

Background: An old English saying goes: "dog does not eat dog"—another way of saying "birds of a feather stick together." In a "dog eat dog world" life is so brutal that even natural law is overturned.

EXAMINE WITH A FINE-TOOTH COMB

Meaning: Look at thoroughly.

Background: The phrase comes from the days before chemical treatment, when the only cure for head and body lice was using a special comb with spaces small enough to trap the tiny bugs. The same device comes up in the old song *Won't You Come Home, Bill Bailey?* in which the singer says she was abandoned with "nothing but a fine-tooth comb"—in other words, a case of the crabs.

PUT A SOCK IN IT

Meaning: Shut up!

Background: In early days, handwound Victrolas didn't come with a volume control, and in a small room they could be pretty loud. People discovered that you could lower the sound level by jamming a heavy woolen stocking into the phonograph's horn.

PIRATE LEGENDS

Captain Kidd, Blackbeard...their exploits are legendary. But did you know they were real people, too?

EUSTACE THE MONK

Background: No one knows for sure who inspired the legend of Robin Hood, but Eustace is a strong candidate. He was born in the late 1100s, and really was a priest at one time. He lived in a monastery near Nottingham...until his father was murdered. Then Eustace left religious life forever.

His Exploits: At first, he lived as a hermit in Sherwood Forest. But gradually he developed new interests—killing and looting. He built a reputation as a soldier of fortune, and even delved into piracy. His attacks on ships in the English Channel were so effective that King Philip II warned English ships: "if you fall into the hands of Eustace the Monk...do not put the blame on us." Eustace's career as a pirate spanned nearly twenty years. It ended on August 24, 1217, when King Henry III defeated him in the battle of Sandwich and had him beheaded.

Note: Eustace stole from the rich, but he probably never gave to the poor. That part of the legend didn't surface until the 1300s.

CAPTAIN KIDD

Background: William Kidd was born in Greenock, Scotland in 1645. He had an unusual background for a pirate; he was a respectable ship owner in New York, and the son of a Presbyterian minister. He never even wanted to be a pirate—he seized only two ships; and only because he had no other choice.

His Exploits: The English East India Company hired him in 1695 to work as a *privateer*—a "bounty hunter" who attacks pirate ships in exchange for a share of the recovered loot. But after more than a year at sea, he hadn't caught a single pirate; he had nothing to pay his men with. So in 1697 he let his crew plunder a single ship. But they insisted on raiding another. Kidd refused; he flew into a rage and hit one of his crew members over the head with a bucket. The

The elephant tree sprays a foul smelling spray at animals that try to eat its leaves.

man died the next day. Fearing mutiny, Kidd backed down and let his crew seize a second ship.

Soon after the second adventure, Kidd and his men finally found a real pirate ship to plunder—the *Resolution,* sailing in the Indian Ocean. Kidd gave the order to attack the ship, but his men refused—and most of them jumped ship to join the pirate crew. Exasperated, Kidd gave up and sailed home.

Though he had committed acts of piracy and murder, Kidd didn't expect to be arrested when he landed in New York. He was friends with the governor, and the East India Company stood to profit enormously from his plunder. Nevertheless, he was seized as soon as he pulled into port, and extradited to England for trial. He was found guilty and was hanged on May 23, 1701.

Note: Eleven days before he was scheduled to be executed, Kidd petitioned the House of Commons with a deal: in exchange for a delay in his execution, he would lead a fleet to the spot where he claimed to have buried his treasure. His offer was denied. Searches for Kidd's "lost treasure" have been conducted all over the Northeastern United States and other parts of the world, but nothing has been found. One possibility: it's buried on Oak Island.

BLACKBEARD

Background: Edward Teach was born in Bristol, England in the late 1600s. Like Captain Kidd, he got his start on a privateering ship. But unlike Kidd, he was good at it—so good that in 1713 his captain gave him command of one of the captured ships. That was a mistake—he turned to piracy almost immediately and began plundering English ships.

His Exploits: Though his pirate career spanned only five years, Teach came about as close as anyone to living up to pirate lore—even in appearance. According to one historian: "he wore a sling over his shoulders, with three brace of pistols hanging in holsters like bandoleers; he stuck lighted matches under his hat...and his eyes looked fierce and wild...Imagination cannot form an idea of a fury from Hell to look more frightful." He tied his enormous black beard into braids, which he threw back over both ears. He had at least 14 wives—each one in a different port.

Teach operated out of several bases off the coast of South Carolina, which he set up with the help of the state's corrupt governor. But in 1717 his numerous attacks on ships off the New England coast prodded Virginia's *un*corrupt governor into action. Using his own money, he hired Lieutenant Robert Maynard, a privateer, to hunt Teach down.

On November 21, 1718 Maynard found Teach's ship anchored off the coast of the Carolinas. He pulled within shooting distance and opened fire. Teach weighed anchor and tried to flee, but his ship ran aground. He fired back with his cannon, forcing Maynard to send his crew below decks. Seeing so few people on Maynard's ship, Teach assumed that he had killed most of the crew. But when his men tried to board the ship, Maynard's men reemerged from below decks and attacked. Within minutes they had overwhelmed the pirate crew.

While this was going on, Teach and Maynard fought man-to-man—first with pistols, then with cutlasses. Teach came very close to winning. He broke Maynard's blade off at the hilt and knocked him to the ground, but as he was moving in for the kill, one of Maynard's men rushed up and slashed Teach's throat. He kept on fighting, but collapsed and died a few minutes later. Maynard cut off his head and hung it from the ship's bow. The pirates who survived the fight didn't fare any better: all but two were tried for piracy, convicted, and hanged.

ROBINSON CRUSOE

Background: Alexander Selkirk—who inspired the tale of Robinson Crusoe—was born in Largo, Scotland, in 1676.

His Exploits: In his early teens he signed up with a privateering expedition, and remained a privateer until 1704. That year he had an argument with his captain—and as punishment, was dumped on an island in the South Seas. He lived there for more than five years, off the wild goats that roamed the island.

Selkirk was rescued in 1709 after a passing ship noticed his signal fire. He returned to Scotland, but never really recovered from his isolation. He remained a recluse, spending much of his time in a cave in his father's garden. He died in 1721. By that time his story had been immortalized in *Robinson Crusoe*, a novel Daniel Defoe had written two years earlier.

SECTS SCANDALS

Sex scandals involving famous preachers? Jimmy Swaggert and Jim Bakker were only following a pulpit tradition. As the Bible says, there is nothing new under the sun.

THE SINNER: Horatio Alger. Before becoming one of the most successful American writers of the 19th century, Alger was a preacher. In 1864, at the age of 32, he became pastor of the First Unitarian Parish in Brewster, Massachusetts.

THE SCANDAL: More than a few people noticed that he "was always with the boys"—at first this seemed liked commendable interest in their spiritual development, though parishioners began wondering why the eligible bachelor didn't pay attention to any the congregation's single women. An 1866 investigation concluded that he and several of his young charges had committed acts "too revolting to relate."

JUDGMENT DAY: Alger didn't deny the charges, but admitted only that he was "imprudent." He resigned and left town. Church officials warned other parishes of his dismissal (without getting specific), and some families threatened legal action. But Alger had promised to abandon his clerical career, and the matter was allowed to die quietly. Resettling in New York, he became a literary success, writing more than 100 books about poverty-stricken boys whose hard work and diligence earned them the attention of rich older men who helped them earn fortune and honor. The shocked parish concealed its findings for more than a century, until the 1970s, when its records were finally made public.

THE SINNER: Henry Ward Beecher. The famous Congregational preacher of the 1860s and 1870s (and brother of *Uncle Tom's Cabin* author Harriet Beecher Stowe) was a skilled orator—some called him "the greatest preacher since St. Paul." Pastor of Brooklyn's prestigious Plymouth Congregational Church, where 2,500 people came to hear him weekly, Stowe's eloquent advocacy of abolition, women's rights and Darwinism brought him both fame and an enormous salary of $40,000 a year.

THE SCANDAL: In 1874, his close friend and protege, Thomas Tilton, filed suit against Beecher, charging that he had been having an affair with Tilton's wife over several years. Noted feminist writer Victoria Woodhull (with whom Tilton was also suspected of having an affair) dared Beecher to admit his adultery. Beecher would not make a forthright admission of guilt, and the suit went to trial.

The trial itself became a sensation. Ticket scalpers charged $5 for admission passes they had gotten for free; up to 3,000 people were turned away every day; vendors made a killing selling refreshments and binoculars before and after trial sessions. Up against the testimony of 95 witnesses, Beecher declared he was "unable to remember" nearly 900 times.

JUDGMENT DAY: The trial ended in a hung jury, and Beecher, free and unabashed, expelled Tilton from Plymouth Church. He continued to enjoy great popularity and influence until his death in 1887.

THE SINNER: Aimee Semple McPherson. Pentecostal evangelist, "Queen of Heaven" and founder of the International Church of the Foursquare Gospel, McPherson seemed to have it all: youth, good looks, a large following, and part ownership in the Angelus Temple, the 5,000-seat, $1.5 million Los Angeles church where she preached to the accompaniment of choirs, bell ringers, and an 80-piece xylophone band.

THE SCANDAL: On May 18, 1926, the 36-year-old McPherson vanished while swimming in the Pacific Ocean. It was feared she was drowned. Her congregation took to walking into the sea where she was last seen, looking for clues and signs, resulting in the drowning death of one. A few days later, the first of several ransom notes arrived, and police received reports of sightings in Santa Barbara, Denver, El Paso, and Tucson. On June 23, Sister Aimee staggered across the U.S.-Mexican border into Douglas, Arizona with a tale of harrowing escape from kidnapers.

But details of her story failed to check out—for one thing, her ardu-

Americans spend an average of 76 hours per week in bed; They're asleep for 45 of the hours.

ous trek across the Mexican desert somehow left her shoes unscuffed. Things got sticky for Sister Aimee. Reporters turned up accounts that McPherson and a married former employee had rented a cottage in Carmel-by-the-Sea, a few hundred miles north of Los Angeles, for ten days in May. Newspapers had a field day, calling it a "honeymoon cottage" and "love nest." A Temple worker told police the kidnaping tale was merely a cover-up for the Carmel tryst. In September, McPherson and others were arrested on charges including "conspiracy to commit acts injurious to public morals."

JUDGMENT DAY: During the trial the key prosecution witness—the Temple worker who had blown the cover story—was arrested on a bad-check charge, and it was revealed she had previously been committed to a mental hospital because of a tendency to create elaborate lies. The district attorney dropped the charges against McPherson without explanation. Sister Aimee, who fainted when she heard the news, left the next day for a "Vindication Tour" of the East Coast, but the bad publicity had its effect. She was finished as an influential evangelist. She died at the age of 53 from an accidental overdose of barbiturates.

• • •

FROM OUR "HEROES OF LITERATURE" DEPARTMENT

A few tales of Mark Twain:

• He got hundreds of photos from people who claimed they were "his exact double." After a while, he got so sick of answering them that he had a form letter printed up: "My dear Sir, I thank you very much for your letter and your photograph. In my opinion, you are more like me than any other of my numerous doubles. I may even say that you resemble me more closely than I do myself. I fact, I intend to use your picture to shave by. Yours thankfully, S. Clemens

• A ruthless businessman he knew announced that "Before I die, I'm going to make a pilgrimage to the Holy Land. I will climb Mount Sinai and read the Ten Commandments aloud at the top."

Twain's reply: "I have a better idea. Stay home in Boston and keep them."

PRODUCT NAMES

You probably have some of these products in your house…
But do you know how they got their names?

AVON PRODUCTS. Founder D.H. McConnell lived in a small New York town called Suffern on the Ramapo in the 1880s. The name reminded him of Shakespeare's Stratford-upon-Avon.

TONI HOME PERMANENTS. Richard Harris began selling "Roll-Wav" home permanent kits through the mail in 1943. For the first time, women could do at home for 25¢ what cost them $10 or more in a beauty salon. But he ran into a problem; the curling chemicals he used were too harsh. "Roll-Wav" flopped. Harris fixed the problem by using a milder curling agent, but something still wasn't right—customers weren't buying. Finally, one of his distributors gave him the advice he needed: "What you need is a *tony* name—one with class." Harris took the advice—literally.

NOXZEMA. After more than ten years of mixing up batches of skin cream in his coffeepot, Dr. Avery Bunting, a Maryland pharmacist, hit on a formula he felt was perfect in 1914. But he couldn't find the perfect name—after hundreds of tries he gave up. Then one of his customers walked into the store and said "Doc, you know your sunburn cream has sure knocked out my eczema." Bunding was inspired: The cream that "knocked eczema" became known as *Noxzema*.

SHELL OIL COMPANY. Believe it or not, the Shell Oil company got its name because it started out as a *shell shop*. Marcus Samuel owned a London novelty store in the mid-1800s; he began selling shells after getting the idea while on vacation by the sea. Over time his business grew into a large trading company and began selling things other than shells—including *kerosene*.

MURINE. Otis Hall, a banker recovering from a serious eye infection in the 1890s, was so impressed with the eye lotion his doctors made for him that he spent years trying to get them to sell it directly to the public. They finally consented—on the condition that its name be derived from its chemical formula: *mur*iate of berber*ine*.

DIXIE CUPS. Hugh Moore founded the American Water Supply Company in 1908...but decided that there was more money to be made in supplying paper cups. He changed the company's name to the Individual Drinking Cup Company, then to the Health Kup Co. But his business still wasn't successful. The company next door, The Dixie Doll Company, was doing well at the time. He thought some of their luck might rub off on him if he used their name.

PRINCE MATCHABELLI. Georges Matchabelli had it made—or so he thought. A prince with enormous land holdings in southern Russia, Matchabelli was vacationing in Europe when the Bolsheviks seized power in 1919. He lost his entire fortune overnight. But he still had his title—and when he opened an antique shop on New York's Madison Avenue, the well-to-do from all over the world flocked to his store. To maintain their interest, he began making perfumes for individual clients—perfumes he claimed matched their personalities. His customers began ignoring his antiques altogether, asking only about his perfumes. He took the hint.

PYREX GLASS. Dr. Jesse Littleton was a scientist who worked for the Corning Glass Works in New York. One morning in 1913, he brought a chocolate cake to work and shared it with the office. After his coworkers finished eating, he told them he had baked the cake in a *glass* pan he'd made out of a battery jar—something they had insisted was impossible. It wasn't. Though heat-resistant glass had been used in industry for more than 20 years, no one had thought of using it to make cooking utensils. Within three years, Corning introduced Pyrex glassware—naming it after the first product they manufactured: a glass *pie* pan.

RANDOM FACT: What do electric eels use their electricity for? To detect and kill their prey.

Renoir's last words: "What a pity I have to go now just when I was beginning to show promise!"

UNCLE JOHN'S BATHROOM NEWS

Bits and pieces of bathroom trivia we've flushed out in the past year.

TAKE A STAND

According to a 1991 survey by the Scott Paper Company:

• "You can gauge a person's education by whether they read in the bathroom. More than two-thirds of people with master's degrees and doctorates read in the stall, the survey shows. Only one in two high school grads read while in the bathroom, and 56 percent of those with college degrees do."

• "Fifty-four percent of Americans fold their toilet tissue neatly while 35 percent wad it into a ball before using it."

• "7% steal rolls of toilet paper."

• "More than 60 percent prefer that their toilet paper roll over the top, 29 percent from the bottom. The rest don't care."

LEFT OUT

• According to *Why Do Clocks Run Clockwise, and Other Imponderables*, here's why toilet flush handles are on the left side:

"Most early flush toilets were operated by a chain above the tank that had to be pulled down by hand. Almost all of the chains were located on the left side of the toilet, for the user had more leverage when pulling with the right hand while seated.

"When the smaller handles near the top of the tank were popularized in the 1940s and 1950s, many were fitted onto existing toilets then equipped with pull-chains. Therefore, it was cheaper and more convenient to place the new handles where they fitted standard plumbing and fixtures."

STRONGER THAN DIRT

According to a book called *Bigger Secrets*, by William Poundstone, here's a bit of bathroom science you should know about:

• "The combination of Sani-Flush and Comet cleansers can explode. Comet (sodium hypochlorite and grit) is a common all-purpose abrasive, and Sani-Flush (a.k.a. sodium bisulfate) is designed to keep toilet bowls clean. Many think that the combination ought to work all the better.

"The Sani-Flush label warns consumers not to mix it with a chlorine-containing cleanser lest hazardous fumes be released. But few people know which other cleansers contain chlorine, and in any case the label says nothing about explosions. In 1985 Hilton Martin of Satellite Beach, Florida, cleaned the bowl of his toilet with Comet and then hung a Sani-Flush dispenser inside the tank. He noticed the water starting to bubble when the phone rang. While he was in another room on the phone, the toilet detonated. American Home Products has denied that Sani-Flush poses an explosion hazard."

LIFE-STALLS OF THE RICH AND FAMOUS

If you're *really* famous, you can't even go to the bathroom in peace. Example: In February, 1979, Jacqueline Kennedy was on her way to her nephew's wedding in Gladwyne, Pennsylvania. She pulled into an Arco gas station to answer the call of nature. The owner of the gas station commemorated the event by mounting a plaque in the ladies room: "This room was honored by the presence of Jacqueline Bovier Kennedy Onassis on the occasion of the wedding of Joseph P. Kennedy II and Sheila B. Rauch, February 3, 1989."

ALL TOGETHER NOW

During a showing of the movie *Airport* on television, the Lafayette, Louisiana Waterworks Department recorded changes in water pressure during the show. Their findings: "At approximately 8:30, a bomb exploded in the airplane, and from then until nine p.m., when the pilot landed safely and the movie ended, almost nobody left his television to do anything—then there was a twenty-six pound drop in water pressure." The department estimates that as many as 20,000 Lafayette residents used the john at the same time. Ratings for other films: *The Good, the Bad, and the Ugly:* a 19 lb. drop in pressure; *Patton:* 22 lbs.

HERE'S LOOKING AT YOU, KID

Humphrey Bogart is one of the most popular movie stars of all time. Here are some inside facts about two of his most popular films.

THE MALTESE FALCON (1941)

The film that made Bogart a star was adapted from a 1929 novel by Dashiell Hammett (who also wrote *The Thin Man)*. Warner Brothers bought the screen rights in 1930 and milked the story for all it was worth; they made three different versions of *Falcon* in 10 years.

Bogart's film, the third version, was regarded as a minor picture by Warner Brothers...so they let a screenwriter named John Huston make his directing debut with it.

• George Raft, a popular personality who played slick gangsters, was Warners' first choice for Sam Spade. He turned it down because he didn't like the idea of working for a first-time director. "I feel strongly that *The Maltese Falcon* is not an important picture," he explained.

• It was the fifth time in five years that Bogart (a minor star who specialized in tough gangster roles) was forced to take a part Raft didn't want. Earlier in 1941 Raft even refused to appear in a film if Bogart was cast in a supporting role. He once protested to Jack Warner: "You told me I would never have to play Humphrey Bogart part." After *Falcon*, he never had the chance again.

• Sydney Greenstreet, "the Fatman," had never acted in a movie before *Falcon*. He was an English stage actor who specialized in comedy. He earned an Oscar nomination for his movie debut... and was typecast as a film heavy.

• Mary Astor prepared for her scenes as conniving, unstable Brigid Wonderly, by hyperventilating almost to the point of dizziness. "It gives me the heady feeling of thinking at cross purposes," she said.

• Real life imitates art: In 1975, one of the seven Falcons used in the movie was stolen from its exhibit in a Los Angeles art museum.

CASABLANCA (1943)

The Oscar winner for Best Film in 1943 started out as an unproduced play called *Everybody Comes to Rick's*. It was written by a New York City school teacher whose inspiration was a visit to a nightclub in southern France in 1938. The club's mix of refugees, Nazis, and French made it, he remarked to his wife, "a marvelous setting for a play."

The rights to the play were purchased by Warner Brothers the day after Pearl Harbor was attacked.

• Legend has it that George Raft was offered the leading role of Rick and, as usual, turned it down. Actually, Raft *wanted* the part...but by this time Bogart was a bigger star and got first choice.

• Ronald Reagan was one of the actors initially considered for Rick.

• *Casablanca*'s famous theme, "As Time Goes By," was included in the original play because the author had been fond of it in college. It first appeared in a 1931 Broadway show called *Everybody's Welcome*.

• Believe it or not, that classic song was nearly cut out of the movie. After *Casablanca* had been shot, the composer who'd scored it decided to write his own tune, because theme songs are worth a lot of money in royalties. But that would have meant reshooting several scenes—and Ingrid Bergman had already cut her hair for her next role (in *For Whom the Bell Tolls*). So reshooting was impossible, the song was left in.

• Dooley Wilson (Sam) didn't really know how to play the piano. He just pretended to finger the keys as he sang, while a studio musician did the playing offstage.

• *Casablanca* won the Oscar for best screenplay, yet the actors never had the luxury of a complete script. In fact, Bogart and Bergman were sometimes handed their lines just before a scene was to be shot. Other times Bogart and the screenwriters would sit around with a bottle of whiskey and argue what should happen next. Ingrid Bergman didn't even know which of the story's main characters she was supposed to love more. She found out when everyone else did—in the final scene.

• Humphrey Bogart's agents took out a $100,000 insurance policy on the actor (a huge amount in those days) during the filming. Bogart's wife was convinced that Bogie was having an affair with Ingrid Bergman and had threatened to kill him if she found them together. The agents decided they'd better not take any chances.

• Good timing may have been what turned *Casablanca* into a hit. In November 1942, Allied forces launched a successful assault on occupied cities in North Africa, including Casablanca. Less than three weeks later the movie premiered in New York. It opened throughout the rest of the country in January of '43, just as Franklin Roosevelt, Josef Stalin, and Winston Churchill were holding a secret conference—in Casablanca.

• The Germans considered *Casablanca* a propaganda film, and banned it. Even after the war, only a censored version was allowed to be shown; all references to Nazis were cut out.

• After the success of *Casablanca*, Bogart signed a contract that made him the world's highest-paid actor.

***AND NOW...*Some Miscellaneous Movie Trivia**

• Actress Jane Wyman broke up with husband Ronald Reagan because, she said, "He talked too much."

• Spencer Tracy and Humphrey Bogart never appeared in a film together because they could never agree on who'd get top billing.

• Actor Peter Lorre specialized in psychotic characters. But in his native Germany he was a student—not a patient—of Sigmund Freud and Alfred Adler.

• Garbo actually said, "I want to be *let* alone."

• Bogart got his distinctive lisp as the result of a childhood accident. A tiny piece of wood lodged in his lip, and the operation to remove it was botched. It left him with a partially paralyzed lip and a permanent speech impediment.

• *Casablanca* was turned into an ABC TV show in 1955. It flopped, and was cancelled after only a few months.

THE 7 WONDERS OF THE ANCIENT WORLD

Here's some more useless info you can use to drive your friends and family crazy, contributed by BRI member Phil Catalfo.

THE ORIGIN OF THE "7 WONDERS"

Today we think nothing of 100-story skyscrapers. But in the earliest days of civilization, huge structures were considered superhuman feats. The most impressive of these came to be known as "The Seven Wonders of the World."

• How they got that name is a pretty interesting story in itself. (After all, there were no intercontinental broadcasts to tell people about them.). It turns out that in the timewhen Greece and Rome dominated the course of history in Europe, North Africa and the Middle East, private fleets made money ferrying passengers to "exotic" lands. To tout these destinations, the world's first tourist guidebooks were created.

• Among their most popular attractions were...The Seven Wonders of the World. The earliest list of them on record was compiled by Antipater of Sidonin in the Second Century B.C.

THE EGYPTIAN PYRAMIDS AT GIZA

Built: Between 2600 and 2500 B.C.

History: Three enormous pyramids were erected as burial tombs for Egyptian pharaohs thousands of years before the golden ages of Greece and Rome. The largest, called the Great Pyramid, stands some 450 feet high at its peak; its base takes up 13 acres. The Greeks and Romans were impressed by their size, but, unaware of their religious significance, considered them extravagant.

Fate: Still standing. And they still attract millions visitors from around the globe every year.

THE HANGING GARDENS OF BABYLON

Built: Sometime in the late Seventh or early Sixth Century B.C.

History: King Nebuchadnezzar II, who ruled Babylon (near the modern city of Baghdad) between 605 and 562 B.C., built the hanging gardens for his queen, the daughter of the Median king Cyaxares. She was supposedly uncomfortable on the hot Mesopotamian flatlands, and longed for the cool, lofty heights of her mountainous homeland. So Nebuchadnezzar had the enormous garden structure designed and built with elevated terraces containing groves of trees, lush vegetation, fountains and exotic birds. According to contemporary accounts, the gardens were laid out on a brick terrace about 400 feet square and 75 feet above the ground; irrigation was provided by slaves turning screws to lift water from the nearby Euphrates River. The stone used in the construction is not found anywhere on the Mesopotamian plane; historians believe it was ferried down the Tigris River from a far-off mountain quarry.

Fate: Destroyed. Archaeologists have been unable to discover and positively identify the remains of the gardens.

THE TEMPLE OF ARTEMIS (DIANA) AT EPHESUS

Built: Circa 550 B.C.

History: One of the grandest and most architecturally advanced of ancient temples, the temple of Artemis (whom the Romans called Diana) was located in the Greek city of Ephesus, across the Aegean from modern Greece, on the west coast of what is now Turkey. According to Pliny, it took 120 years to build. It was made entirely of marble, except for its tile-covered wooden roof. It rested on a foundation measuring 377 by 180 feet, and featured 106 columns—each represented by a different king—about 40 feet high.

The Ephesians (the same ones St. Paul preached to) used an especially clever technique for lifting the giant marble stones: They built an inclined plane of sandbags up to the apex of the columns, and dragged the stones up the plane to be laid atop the columns. Then they slit the bags so the sand would empty out, leaving the marble slabs resting in place.

Fate: The original temple was destroyed by an arsonist (who said he did it to achieve immortality for his name) in 356 B.C. A replacement of similar design was erected on the same foundation. The replacement was burned by the Goths in 262 A.D. Today only the foundation and parts of the second temple remain. Sculptures from the second temple can be found in the British Museum.

THE STATUE OF ZEUS, OLYMPIA, GREECE

Built: Circa 435 B.C.

History: Built by the Greek sculptor Phidias, this depiction of the Greek king of the gods may have been the ancient world's most famous statue. It stood 40 feet high and depicted Zeus—symbol of power, thrower of thunderbolts—on his throne. His robe and ornaments were made of gold, his body of ivory. He wore a wreath on his head and held a figure of his messenger Nike in his right hand, and a scepter in his left.

Fate: Destroyed (No one is sure how or when).

THE MAUSOLEUM AT HALICARNASSUS, IN ASIA MINOR (Southwestern Turkey)

Built: About 353 B.C.

History: Originally built as a burial tomb for Mausolus, a local ruler in part of the Persian Empire, this huge, white marble edifice stood about 135 feet high, and measured 440 feet around its rectangular base. Above the base was a colonnade formed by 36 columns, and, above them, a stepped pyramid, which, historians believe, held a statue of Mausolus in a chariot.

Fate: The top part was destroyed by an earthquake. Only pieces of the building, and its decorations (called friezes) remain; the British Museum holdings include some sculptures from the site. King Mausolus has been immortalized in the word used to name any large tomb.

THE COLOSSUS OF RHODES

Built: Early Third Century B.C.

History: According to historians of the time, this huge bronze statue stood astride the harbor at Rhodes, an island in the Aegean. It took the Greek sculptor Chares twelve years to build. Created in honor of the sun god Helios, it stood 120 feet high—roughly the height of the Statue of Liberty—and was made of hollow stone blocks held together by iron bars, a construction technique still used today.

Fate: Destroyed by an earthquake in 224 B.C. The iron bars were sold for scrap some 800 years later, in 653 A.D.

THE PHAROS LIGHTHOUSE AT ALEXANDRIA

Built: Sometime during the reign of Ptolemy II (283-246 B.C.)

History: Designed by the Greek architect Sostratos, the 400-feet-high lighthouse stood on the island of Pharos in Alexandria's harbor. It achieved such renown that the word *pharos* came to mean "lighthouse." The structure's design was particularly striking: the bottom section, resting on a stone platform, was square; the middle section was eight-sided; and the top section was circular. A fire at the apex provided light.

Fate: After helping mariners enter the harbor for *1,500 years*, the lighthouse collapsed in an earthquake.

SO WHAT ELSE IS NEW?

Johnny B. Goode, by Chuck Berry

Berry says: "It sounds like it's autobiographical, but it's not. I never lived in Louisiana.... I just improvised the story, typical of what I thought a young, enthusiastic guitar-player from the South would go through. As for the log cabin, I don't think I've actually seen a real log cabin, much less lived in one."

Etch A Sketch

It was invented in France by Arthur Granjean, who called it "L'Ecran Magique" (The Magic Screen). Representatives of the Ohio Art Company saw it at the Nuremberg Toy Fair in 1959 and decided the toy had possibilities. They purchased the rights to it.

• Ohio Art management decided to introduce their version of it at the New York Toy Fair in February, 1960. They had no idea the toy would become a big success, but they got an inkling on the plane flight to the New York show when company officials started bickering about who would get to play with the prototypes next.

• The toy was officially released to the public on July 12, 1960. More than 60 million of them have been sold to date.

Einstein's brain is stored in a mason jar in a Wichita, Kansas laboratory.

CARNIVAL LINGO

Next time you wander through a carnival, listen to the hucksters chatting with each other. Here are a few things you might hear them saying, from the marvelous book, Carnival Secrets, *by Matthew Gryczan.*

Carny: Carnival employee.

Jointee: A carny who works in one of the booths.

Ride Monkey: A carny who operates a ride.

Kootch: Strippers.

Alibi agent: A game operator who uses undisclosed "rules" (player touched the rail, leaned over the foul line, etc.) to avoid giving out prizes to winners.

Fixer: The person who handles complaints about rigged games and payoffs to local police.

Marks, Tips: Players

Chumps: Naive players.

Sharpies: Practiced players who are skilled at winning games.

Lot lice: Carnival-goers who don't spend money.

Patch Money, Ice, Juice: Money that's used to pay off the police.

Hey Rube: A call for help when carnies are in trouble.

Mitt camp: Palm readers.

Circus candy: Cheap candy in an impressive box.

Floss: Cotton Candy.

Plaster, Slum: Cheap prizes.

Donniker: A toilet.

Flat stores: Games set up solely to cheat players as soon as possible.

Gaff: Rig a game so that players have absolutely no chance of winning.

Gig: Take all of a player's money in one try.

Two Way Joint: A game that quickly converts from a dishonest to an honest one in case the police come by.

Ikey Heyman, G-wheel: A wheel of fortune with brakes—so the operator can control which number it lands on.

Burn the lot: Cheat contestants outrageously because you don't expect to return to the same location again.

Build up: Excite a player into spending more money.

POP CULTURE

These pages on the history of soda are brought to you by the BRI's Snack Food Division.

POPPING OFF

In the early 1800s, the closest thing to soft drinks on the market was "impregnated water," a corked bottle of carbonated water that was sold as a "health tonic." By 1860 makers were adding sugar and flavoring—with mixed success: The corks in the bottles (metal caps hadn't been invented yet) often blew off under the extra pressure created by sugar fermenting in the bottles. This made a popping sound—and the drinks became known as "Soda Pop."

A CURE FOR WHAT ALES YOU

Selling soda pop to an unitiated public wasn't easy...so most manufacturers tried to boost sales by promoting their concoctions as cures for fever, nausea, dehydration, indigestion, and so on. If the government hadn't passed the Pure Food and Drug Act in 1906, they'd probably be making similar claims today.

Some examples:

Dr. Pepper: "Brightens the mind and clears the brain"; an "antidote" to cigarette smoking; and "alone on the bridge defending your children against an army of caffeine doped beverages." (Note: Today's version contains caffeine).

Hires Root beer: "Soothing to the nerves, vitalizing to the blood, refreshing to the brain...helps even a cynic see the brighter side of life."

Moxie "Nerve Food": "Can recover brain and nervous exhaustion; loss of manhood, imbecility and helplessness. It has recovered paralysis, softening of the brain...and insanity."

Seven Up: "Tunes tiny tummies," "For Home and Hospital Use," "Cures Seven Hangovers."

HIRES ROOT BEER: Recipes for drinks made from boiled roots date back to the colonial days. But most people didn't want to bother collecting their own roots, so in 1870 Charles F. Hires, a Pennsylvania pharmacist, began selling premixed ingredients through the mail. He originally called his drink "Root Tea," but changed its name to "Root *Beer*" after a friend suggested it would sell better with a stronger name.

Hires' mix sold well, but he realized that bottled soft drinks were the wave of the future. So in 1882 he began bottling his creation—and by 1885 was selling 3 million bottles a year.

The Sober Truth: The company ran into trouble in 1895, when the Woman's Christian Temperance Union called for a nationwide boycott of Hires. Reason: the WCTU assumed that, like regular beer, root beer contained enough alcohol to get people drunk. The boycott remained in effect (and devastated sales) until 1898, when an independent laboratory decided to finally *test* Hires' root beer and see how much alcohol it actually contained. Its finding: a bottle of Hires had as much alcohol as half a loaf of bread. The WCTU backed off, and sales returned to normal.

DR. PEPPER: In the 1880s, a Virginia pharmacist's assistant named Wade Morrison fell in love with his boss's daughter. The pharmacist "decided the assistant was too old for his daughter" and encouraged Morrison to move on. He did, moving to Waco, Texas, where he bought his own drug store. When one of his employees developed a new soft drink syrup, Morrison named it after the man who got him started in the pharmacy business—his old flame's father, Dr. Kenneth Pepper.

THE MOXIE GENERATION: You've probably heard the expression "He has plenty of moxie." But have you heard of the soft drink that inspired it? It was the most popular soda in the U.S. during the '20s—even outselling Coca-Cola.

• What went wrong? The problem wasn't that it started out as a "medicine;" so did Coke. The problem was that it *tasted* like one. It contained gentian root, which has a very bitter aftertaste. Americans wanted a sweeter drink.

ON JINGLES

• "Things go better with Coke" was the first slogan that appeared on everything Coke did. They worked on it for two and a half years, and spent millions of dollars figuring out how to present it to the public. The first "things go better" jingle was sung by the Kingston Trio. This jingle was also the first in which Coke experimented with rock music. They used the Shirelles for it.

• The "You've got a lot to live . . ." campaign of the mid-1960s was a smashing success for Pepsi.

Pepsi received over ten thousand letters congratulating them. Some people even said they were on the verge of suicide until they heard the ad. The lyrics were written by the songwriter who composed "You Light Up My Life."

SODA FACTS

• During World War II caffeine was so scarce that Coca-Cola chemists experimented with a substitute made from bat guano. Executives dumped the idea. They thought that if the public identified their drink with bat "droppings," it would doom the company.

• In 1900, Americans were drinking an average of twelve bottles and glasses of soft drink a piece. Today, it's 556 cans each.

• According to the *University of California Wellness Letter*, "If you drink only sugared soft drinks, those 566 cans (at an average of 150 calories each) would add up to about 83,400 empty calories per year."

• Only about five percent of all soft drink caffeine is taken from cola nuts. The other 95% is added during the manufacturing. Where does it come from? Usually the leftovers processed out of decaffeinated coffee.

• Which soda has the most caffeine per serving? Jolt Cola is #1, with 72 milligrams, followed by Mountain Dew (54), Coke (46), Dr. Pepper (40) and Pepsi (38). A cup of coffee contains 50-200 milligrams.

• Research suggests that as many as 950,000 Americans drink Coca-Cola for breakfast.

Listen closely: On at least one episode, George Burns was the voice of Mr. Ed (the horse).

INSTANT HITS

It usually takes work to write a hit song. But now and then a performer creates one spontaneously. Here are a few of the better-known examples.

THE SONG: "Sweet Dreams" by the Eurythmics (1983)
THE SITUATION: Annie Lenox and Dave Stewart, the Eurythmics, had never had a hit. One day they were quarreling so bitterly that it felt like the end of their partnership. Annie was lying on the floor of their studio, curled up in the fetal position. Dave was at the opposite end of the huge room, angrily playing with the recording equipment.
INSTANT HIT: As they glared at each other, Stewart fiddled around with his drum machine for a while. He came up with a catchy rhythm...then added a bass line. "It sounded so good," Annie recalls, "that I couldn't resist getting up and playing the synthesizer." Off the top of her head, Lenox began singing: "Sweet dreams are made of this." In thirty minutes the entire song was finished.

They recorded it on their eight-track as a demo tape, but when Stewart took it in to a record company, incredulous record execs told him it was "already perfect." So the "demo" was released; it sold millions of records and established them as major pop celebrities of the early '80s.

THE SONG: "What'd I Say," by Ray Charles (1959)
THE SITUATION: It was almost 1:00 AM. Ray Charles and his band were playing at a Midwestern night club; they were almost through for the night, but still had about fifteen minutes to go when they played the last song in their repertoire. So Ray just started "noodling."
INSTANT HIT: "I couldn't think of nothin' else to play," Ray says. " So I told the guys...'Look, I'm just gonna start this rhythm pattern and just follow me." He also told his back-up singers to repeat whatever he said (which is where the title "What'd I Say" came from). Charles made up the words as he went along. "People went crazy," he recalls, "and so the next night we did the same thing and got the same reaction, in a different town. Somebody came up to me and asked me, 'Listen, where can I buy this record?'

The all-aluminum can was introduced in 1964.

I said, 'Record? What record?' He said, 'But that's a great [song]!' So Charles called up his record producers and said, "Listen, I got a song and I want to record it." He went into the studio on Feb., 18, 1959 and recorded a long version ("because it was for dancing, see?") that was split into Part I and Part II. It became his first record to reach the Top 10 on the pop charts.

THE SONG: "Satisfaction," by The Rolling Stones (1965)

THE SITUATION: During their tour of North America in 1965, the Rolling Stones spent a night in a Clearwater, Florida, motel.

INSTANT HIT: In the middle of the night, Keith Richards woke up with some music running through his head. He got out of bed, recorded it on his tape recorder, and went back to sleep. "In the morning," Richards says, "I still thought it sounded pretty good. I played it to Mick and said the words that go with this are, 'I can't get no satisfaction.' That was just a working title. It could have been, 'Aunt Millie's Caught Her Left Tit in the Mangle,' I thought of it as just a little riff, an album filler. I never thought it was commercial enough to be a single." Jagger wrote lyrics as he sat by the motel swimming pool. But Richards didn't like them; he said the song "sounded too much like a folk song." The song was actually recorded over Keith Richards' objections; he thought it was too corny. It became the band's unofficial anthem, and the #1 song of 1965.

THE SONG: "When a Man Loves a Woman," by Percy Sledge (1966)

THE SITUATION: Percy Sledge worked as an orderly at Colbert County Hospital in Alabama during the day, and sang with a band called The Esquires Combo at night.

INSTANT HIT: One evening the Esquires Combo was playing at a club in Sheffield, Alabama, and Percy just couldn't keep his mind on the songs he was supposed to sing. He was upset about a woman. Overcome by emotion, he turned to bass player Cameron Lewis and organ player Andrew Wright, and begged them to play something he could sing to—anything—it didn't matter what. The musicians looked at each other, shrugged, and just started playing. Percy made up "When a Man Loves a Woman," one of the prettiest soul ballads ever written, on the spot.

The sperm whale can hold its breath for 82 minutes.

W.C. FIELDS FOREVER

Little-known facts about one of America's classic comedians.

Fields didn't get his legendary bulbous nose from drinking; he got it as a kid in street fights with neighborhood toughs.

★

His raspy voice, another trademark, was the result of a long series of colds brought on by exposure; a circus hand, he slept outdoors year-round from age 11 till age 15.

★

According to Groucho Marx, Fields had about $50,000 worth of booze stored in his attic. Groucho: "Don't you know that Prohibition is over?" Fields: "Well, it may come back!"

★

Fields' misanthropy was legendary. He liked to hide in the bushes of his San Fernando Valley home and shoot spitballs at passing tourists.

★

He left his mistress, Carlotta Monti, $25,000—to be paid out in 1,000 weekly installments of $25 each.

★

On his deathbed, Fields supposedly said: "I've been thinking about those poor little newsboys out there peddling their papers in cold and rain, working to support their mothers. I want to do something for them." But after a few minutes he sat up in bed and said "On second thought, f--- 'em."

★

Fields had a lifelong fear of returning to the crushing poverty of his youth. He opened hundreds of bank accounts as he traveled, under scores of aliases. Most of the money is still unclaimed.

★

In his 31-year acting career, Fields appeared in 42 films, many of which he wrote and directed as well. Of these, almost a third have vanished or are otherwise not available for viewing.

The title "Mr." originally applied only to ministers, schoolmasters, and property owners.

THE NUMBERS GAME

You're in the supermarket checkout line and have a few dollars to spare. Should you buy some lottery tickets, or a copy of the National Enquirer? *Here's some info to help you decide.*

THE EARLY DAYS

Lotteries in the U.S. may seem like a recent fad, but they date back at least as far as the 1700s. The original 13 colonies were financed with the help of lottery dollars, and the U.S. government used them to help pay for the Revolutionary and Civil Wars. Even the Ivy League universities—Harvard, Yale and Princeton—used them to get started.

State lotteries didn't begin until the 1960s. The first, a $100,000 sweepstakes tied to a horse race, was held in New Hampshire in 1964. Today at least 30 states have lotteries, which generate $17 billion a year in revenues.

LOTTERY FACTS

• According to *Consumer's Research* magazine, lotteries have the worst odds of any form of legalized gambling. In terms of average payouts, highest percentage is craps (98%), followed by roulette (95%), slots (75-95%), jai alai (85-87%), the race track (83-87%) and, last, the lottery (49%). Only 0.000008% of the 97 million people who play the lottery annually win a million dollars.

• Lotteries with the best odds: Delaware, Maryland, Michigan, Pennsylvania and Washington, DC. The odds of winning their jackpots are 1 in 1000. Worst odds: California and Florida. Their odds are 1 in 14 million.

WINNERS AND LOSERS

• In 1983, Joseph R. Wyatt, 29, of Union, New Jersey ripped up his lottery ticket—which read "Void if torn or altered" on the back—before realizing it was worth $1,600,000. In tears, he taped his ticket back together and presented it to New Jersey lottery officials, begging them to overlook the rule. They did—he got his money.

• In 1983, Don Temple accidentally threw away a lottery ticket worth $10,000 in a trash can outside a Seattle convenience store. When he realized his mistake, he talked the store into dumping that week's garbage onto the driveway of his father-in-law's home. Temple sifted through the trash for four days, but never found his ticket. The booby prize: he had to pay haulers $200 to take the garbage away.

• In 1985, Donna Lee Sobb won $100 in the California lottery, which qualified her for a $2,000,000 jackpot. But when her photograph appeared in a local paper, a local law officer recognized her—and arrested her on an eight-month-old shoplifting warrant.

• In 1986, California lottery winner Terry Garrett of San Diego was arrested only months after winning $1,000,000—for selling cocaine out of the sports car he had bought with his winnings.

• In 1988, Henry Rich, a computer expert from Harrisburg, Pennsylvania, used a computer at work to forge a winning ticket for a $15,200,000 lottery prize that hadn't been claimed. He had a friend come forward with the fake ticket and explain that he had been using it as a bookmark without realizing that it was the winner. The scheme almost worked: the friend was actually issued a first installment check for $469,989. But lottery officials arrested Rich and his friend when they realized the real ticket had been issued in another part of the state.

• In 1984, Hai Vo, a Vietnamese refugee, spent more than $200 of spare change he had saved up from food stamp purchases to buy California lottery tickets. One ticket won $2,000,000. A week later a couple from Mill Valley, California sued Vo to recover $616.26—the amount they paid in state income taxes that year—claiming Vo had used some of their earnings (in the form of state-subsidized food stamps) to buy the ticket. They lost; Vo kept his winnings.

THE SAD TRUTH

How much is a $1 million prize *really* worth? The IRS deducts 20% automatically—and state and local taxes are also taken out, leaving about $560,000. The state pays the first $50,000 in cash, but pays out the rest over twenty years, saving another $100,000.
Conclusion: the $1 million prize is worth about $468,000.

A *moment* used to be defined as lasting exactly 1 1/2 minutes.

DEFINITIONS

How's your vocabulary? Here's another batch of unusual words you can use to impress your friends and neighbors.

Deosculate: To kiss passionately.

Pap-hawk: A child who's breast fed.

Moirologist: A person hired to mourn at a funeral.

Philematophobe: A woman who hates to be kissed.

Hippocampine: Having to do with seahorses.

Sneckdraw: A sneaky or mean person.

Hircine: Something that smells like a goat.

Eruciform: Something that resembles a caterpillar.

Snoach: Talk through your nose.

Fripperer: A person who sells old clothes.

Clipster: A woman barber.

Girn: Bare your teeth in anger.

Snollygoster: A politician with no interest in issues or principles.

Butyric: Having to do with butter.

Cacogen: A hostile, unfriendly person.

Coprology: The study of pornographic art and writing.

Napiform: Shaped like a turnip.

Natiform: Shaped like a buttock.

Hippopotomonstrosesquipedalian: Having to do with a very long word.

Phaneromania: An obsession with picking at your skin.

Pussock: An old maid.

Smell-Feast: An uninvited guest at a feast.

Mastodont: Having teeth that look like a mastadon's.

Powsowdy: A broth made from sheep's heads.

Wallydrag: A completely useless person.

Onygophagist: A person who bites his or her nails.

Eirmonger: Someone who sells eggs.

Fagotist: A person who plays the bassoon.

There is only one diamond mine in the entire continent of North America. It's in Arkansas.

THE MYSTERY OF OAK ISLAND

The romance of searching for pirates' treasure has been celebrated in dozens of stories since Robert Louis Stevenson's Treasure Island. *But is there really any buried treasure to be found? Maybe so...on Oak Island.*

TREASURE ISLAND

In 1795, a teenager named Daniel McGuinnis discovered an unusual, saucer-shaped depression on Oak Island, a tiny island off the coast of Nova Scotia. Next to the hole was an ancient oak tree with sawed-off limbs. And according to legend, a ship's tackle hung from the tree directly over the depression—as if it had been used to lower something very heavy into the hole.

McGuinnis was certain he had found buried pirates' treasure, and with the help of two friends began digging for it. Within minutes they hit rock—which turned out to be a flagstone buried two feet below the surface. They hit another barrier made of oak logs at 10 feet deep; another at 20 feet, and a third at 30 feet. McGuinnis and his friends kept digging—but they never found any treasure and eventually gave up. Still, word of their discovery spread.

SECOND TRY

In 1803 a wealthy man named Simeon Lynds took up the search. The diggers he hired found another platform at 40 feet, and found several more deeper down. Finally, at 90 feet, the workers found a large stone with strange symbols carved into it. No one could decipher what the stone said, but the workers were convinced they were close to the treasure and kept digging. (The stone was later stolen.) At 98 feet deep, their shovels struck what felt like a wooden chest. But the sun was going down so they stopped for the night.

By the time the workers got back the next morning, the hole had flooded to the top with seawater. And it somehow kept refilling, even as the workers tried to bail it out. They never were able to drain the pit enough to finish digging.

Like McGuinnis, Lynds had hit a dead end.

AMAZING DISCOVERIES

Lynds wasn't the last person to dig for treasure on Oak Island. In fact, so many excavations have been attempted that the precise location of the original hole—known as the "Money Pit" because so much money has been spent trying to solve its mysteries—has been lost because so many other holes have been dug nearby. Even young Franklin D. Roosevelt supervised a dig in 1909; he followed Oak Island's progress even as president. And the search continues today. Some findings:

• There's at least *some* gold down there. In 1849 treasure hunters sank a drill to the 98 ft. level. Like Lynds, they hit what felt like a wooden chest. They dug through the top into what felt like "22 inches of metal in pieces (possibly gold coins)," through more wood, and into another 22 inches of metal. When they pulled the drill back up to the surface, three links of a gold chain were stuck to it. In nearly 200 years of digging, that's all the treasure that's been found.

• In 1897 another group of drillers dug down to 155 feet. They pulled up a half-inch-square piece of parchment—but that was all. They also hit what they thought was a heavy iron plate at 126 feet, but couldn't pull it up.

• In 1987, an IBM cryptologist finally deciphered an engraving of Lynds' lost stone. The message read: "Forty feet below, two million pounds are buried."

HIGH SECURITY

• Whoever dug the original pit went to a great deal of trouble to do it. In 1850 explorers resting on a nearby beach noticed that the beach "gulched forth water like a sponge being squeezed." So they dug it up—and discovered it was a *fake*. The beach was actually a manmade network of stone drains that filtered seawater and fed it into the Money Pit. The drains—designed to flood the pit whenever treasure hunters got close to the treasure—had been buried in sand to avoid detection.

• The Money Pit may even be protected by poison gas. On August 17, 1965, treasure hunter Bob Restall blacked out and fell into the pit he had dug. His son and four others tried to rescue him, but they also blacked out and fell in. Restall, his son, and two of the workers were killed. The autopsy finding: death by "marsh-gas poisoning and/or drowning."

TODAY

In 1977 the Montreal-based Triton Alliance Ltd., a consortium of 49 investors headed by David Tobias, bought the 128-acre Oak Island for $125,000. They have spent more than $3 million digging for treasure.

• During one drill, Triton's workers found bits of china, glass, wood, charcoal—even cement. But no treasure.

• Perhaps the strangest incident associated with Oak Island occurred in 1971 when Tobias' partner Dan Blankenship lowered an underwater video camera into a water-filled cavity at the bottom of a shaft. On the monitor, Blankenship suddenly saw what looked like a human hand. Horrified, he called over three crew members, who later verified his story. Asked by *Smithsonian* magazine about the legitimacy of his hand-sighting, he answered, "There's no question about it."

WHAT'S DOWN THERE?

Oak Island's "treasure," if there is one, could be worth over $100,000,000. Among the many theories of what the Money Pit could be hiding:

1) The missing crown jewels of France. The Nova Scotia area was frequented by pirates in the 16th and 17th centuries—when the jewels were stolen. The local Mahone Bay takes its name from the French word *mahonne*, a craft used by Mediterranean pirates.

2) Inca gold plundered by Spanish galleons and later pirated by Sir Francis Drake. A carbon analysis of wood samples recovered from the area dated back to 1575, around the time of Drake's explorations. However, there is no record of Drake ever having been to Nova Scotia.

3) Captain Kidd's buried treasure. Some believe Kidd buried his treasure there before being extradited and later hanged by the British. Before Kidd was executed in 1701, he offered a deal: "He would lead a fleet to the spot where he had hidden his East Indian

The *Revenge of the Creature* was Clint Eastwood's first movie.

treasure, if the authorities would put off his execution. The deal was refused—and Kidd's treasure has never been found." There is, however, no evidence that Kidd was ever near Oak Island.

• Others have their doubts. Some feel that the Money Pit is merely an elaborate decoy, and that the treasure is actually buried in a nearby swamp. Others think it is just a sinkhole. Many doubt whether pirates had the resources and engineering know-how to construct such an elaborate trap.

POST SCRIPT

Similar Money Pits are rumored to have been found in Haiti and Madagascar, although these discoveries have not been confirmed by archaeologists.

• • •

...AND NOW A LITTLE MOOD READING

Here's a brief quote from Treasure Island, *by Robert Louis Stevenson. Appropriately, it's the part where they find the spot the treasure should be...and see that it's already been dug up.*

"We were now at the margin of the thicket.

" 'Huzza, mates, altogether?' shouted Merry; and the foremost broke into a run.

"And suddenly, not ten yards further, we beheld them stop. A low cry arose. Long John Silver doubled his pace, digging away with the foot of his crutch like one possessed; and next moment he and I had come also to a dead halt.

"Before us was a great excavation, not very recent, for the sides had fallen in and grass had sprouted on the bottom. In this were the shaft of a pick broken in two and the boards of several packing-cases strewn around. On one of these boards I saw, branded with a hot iron, the name *Walrus*—the name of Flint's ship.

"All was clear to probation. The *cache* had been found and rifled: the seven hundred thousand pounds were gone!"

If you're into classic books and buried treasure, Treasure Island *could be a good bathroom reader. The chapters are all about six pages long, and a new copy shouldn't cost more than $3.*

ZZZ-Z-Z-Z-ZZZ

According to author Marc McCutcheon, your heart can stop beating for as long as 9 seconds while you're asleep. Here's some more information on sleep from his book, The Compass in Your Nose.

Sleep deprivation lasting more than 48 hours typically causes hallucinations and psychosis.

The world record for going without sleep is 11 days (264 hours and 12 minutes), a feat considered extremely dangerous by sleep researchers.

30 million Americans suffer from sleep disorders. Most men begin having problems falling asleep in their mid-twenties; women have the same difficulty during their mid-forties.

While normal sleepers change body positions about 30 times per night, insomniacs may toss and turn more than 100 times.

Dream sleep has been observed in all animals studied except the spiny anteater.

Sleep studies show that if your sleeping partner is absent in your sleep, you'll almost always move over to the side of the bed normally occupied by him or her.

An aftenoon nap is healthy. One study indicates that afternoon nappers are 30 percent less likely to suffer coronary artery disease, although the reasons behind this are not yet known.

Humans stay awake far longer than many animals. Bats, cats, porcupines, lions, gorillas, and opossums sleep 18 to 20 hours a day, and some woodchucks snooze for as long as 22 hours.

Pigeons frequently open their eyes during sleep to watch for predators. The dolphin, remarkably, only "half" sleeps: its brain shuts down only one hemisphere at a time.

Horses and rats dream 20 percent or the time during sleep. Cows kept in barns dream 40 minutes per night, while cows sleeping in meadows dream only half as much.

Idaho grows 120 billion potatoes a year—that's about 500 for every man, woman, and child in the U.S.

OFF TO SEE THE WIZARD

The Wizard of Oz is one of our most enduring modern fairy tales. In the first Bathroom Reader, we explained it as a political allegory. Here are some some other interesting facts about the book and film.

THE BIRTH OF THE BOOK

According to some accounts, the land of Oz was created when Lyman Frank Baum, the author, was weaving a tale of fantastical creatures for some neighborhood kids. When one child asked where the imaginary people lived, Baum glanced around. His eyes fell on the labels on his file cabinet; the top was labeled A-N and the bottom, O-Z.

• He didn't write the story down for some time after. But suddenly it took over and demanded to be written: "I was sitting," he wrote later, "in the hall telling the kids a [different] story and suddenly this one moved right in and took possession. I shooed the children away and grabbed a piece of paper and began to write. It really seemed to write itself. Then I couldn't find any regular paper, so I took anything at all, even a bunch of old envelopes." His pencil-written longhand manuscript went right to the typesetter.

• He called his story *The Emerald City*. But his publisher wouldn't release it under that title, citing a long-standing publishers' superstition that any book with a jewel named in its title was doomed to failure.

• So he changed it to *From Kansas to Fairyland*, then *The Fairyland of Oz*, then *The Land of Oz*. They filed for a copyright under this last name, but Baum was still looking for something more colorful and eye-catching. Right before the book was supposed to go to press, illustrator W. W. Denslow pasted a new title over the old one: *The Wonderful Wizard of Oz*.

FILM FACTS

• Panned by many critics when it was first released in 1939, the

"We're Off to See the Wizard" was used as a marching song by the Australians in World War II.

film version of the book was considered a flop. It didn't earn back its initial investment until 1959—twenty years later. Cult status only came as a result of annual TV showings, starting in 1956.

• The cast consisted of 9,200 actors and actresses, including dancing trees, flying monkeys, and 124 midgets as Munchkins. Ray Bolger and Jack Haley were paid $3000 a week; Judy Garland, only $500 a week.

• Dorothy's dog Toto was paid $125 a week, more than twice the wage of each of the 122 midgets hired to play munchkins. Although the little people of Oz were paid $100 a week, their benevolent manager, Leo Singer (Papa), pocketed half. Clearly the Lollipop Guild and Lullaby League were ineffective unions.

• Oz was nominated for five Academy Awards. But the competition was fierce and *Gone With the Wind* dominated the event, Oz did win for Original Score and Best Song—"Over the Rainbow," written in a car parked outside Schwab's drugstore.

• Ironically, "Rainbow" was the song studio execs wanted to cut out when the finished film was too long. "Why is she singing in a barnyard?" one of the producers had asked. But the director and others complained. Instead, MGM removed a scene (and song) in the Haunted Forest, where Dorothy and crew were attacked by Jitter Bugs (a kind of oversized pink and blue mosquito). The scene, which took five weeks and $80,000 to shoot, has never been found.

MEET LITTLE DOROTHY

• When the MGM movie was first planned, Shirley Temple was the unanimous choice to play Dorothy. (Likewise, Frank Morgan was the third choice for the Wizard. The lines were written with W.C. Fields in mind. Ed Wynn turned down the part, too.)

• But Shirley Temple wasn't available. While searching for another Dorothy, L.B. Mayer viewed a short called *Every Sunday* and was taken by its star, Deanna Durbin. He told his assistant: "Sign up that singer— the flat one." (He might have been referring to the pitch of Durbin's voice). What the assistant heard was, "Sign up the fat one." He thought Mayer was talking about a different girl in the short, who had a bit of baby fat...so he called Francis Gumm

The tornado in the "The Wizard of Oz" was a custom-built spinning 35 foot muslin "miniature."

(quickly renamed "Judy Garland"). But don't cry for Deanna Durbin—she went on to Universal where her movies brought in $100 million in the next 10 years.

• Judy Garland was 16, but she was playing an 11-year-old. So the studio put her on a diet to make her look younger; she was only allowed to eat four days a week. And every morning before filming, her breasts were taped flat so she'd look more like an adolescent.

• MGM's constant attempts at keeping Garland thin with pills and diets may have ultimately cost her life—Garland died in June, 1969 of a drug overdose.

INSULTS AND INJURIES

• While the Tin Man bemoaned his heartless condition, it was another vital organ that caused him the biggest problems during the filming of *Oz*. Buddy Ebsen, the original tin man, had an extreme allergic reaction when his lungs were coated by the aluminum powder dusted onto his tin makeup. Seriously ill, he spent several weeks in the hospital. He was replaced by Jack Haley.

• The Wicked Witch, Margaret Hamilton, was badly burned on face and hand while filming her dramatic exit from Munchkinland and was off the set for a month. The fire effect went off before she was safely below the trap door. Ironically, a little water thrown her way might have helped.

• She wasn't the only injury: Her double, Betty Danko, was injured when her broom exploded during a stunt shot. Two winged monkeys crashed to the stage floor when their support wires snapped. And Toto too? Yes, Toto too—out of action for a week after being stepped on by one of the witch's huge "O-EE-O"-chanting Winkie guards.

SHOE FETISH

Although 50 years have passed, at least four pairs of Dorothy's ruby slippers have survived and they bring out-of-sight auction prices (top price so far—$165,000). One pair is on exhibit at the Smithsonian, another at Walt Disney World-MGM Studios. The rest are in private hands...or feet. Over five million people visit the Smithsonian display annually.

WORLD-CLASS LOSERS

Have you ever dreamed about having a "sure thing"? It's not always that simple. Here are four stories of people who "couldn't miss"...but did.

The Losers: John Augustus Sutter & James Wilson Marshall
The Sure Thing: The largest gold strike in American history.

Background: In the 1840s, Sutter was one of Northern California's largest landowners. His headquarters was Sutter's Fort, a trading post near the Sacramento River—an important stopping-point for westward-bound immigrants. Sutter welcomed them all.

One settler, a carpenter named James Marshall, became friends with Sutter. In 1847 they started a sawmill together on the South Fork of the American River at Coloma. Sutter put up the money, Marshall ran the mill, and they split the profits.

Good Luck: In January 1848, Marshall had to deepen his mill stream to allow the wheel to turn freely. His digging turned up some bright metal that he realized, after consulting the *American Encyclopedia*, was gold.

It appeared that he and Sutter were rich beyond their wildest dreams.

Tough Luck: They kept the secret for a few months. Then word leaked out, and the Gold Rush was on.

First, all of Marshall's workers left to pan for gold. With no laborers, the mill failed.

Then thousands of gold-crazy '49ers flocked to Sutter's land. They slaughtered his livestock for food, trampled his fields and staked claims on his property. He was ruined. The land was legally his, but he couldn't afford the cost of litigation to recover it.

Marshall "became despondent and misanthropic." When he died some 35 years later, he was working as a gardener in Coloma. Sutter died broke in 1880, still petitioning Congress for compensation for his losses.

On average, Americans spend 40% of their leisure time watching TV.

The Loser: Eli Whitney

The Sure Thing: Control of the South's cotton industry.

Background: After the Revolutionary War, the outlook for agriculture in the South was pretty grim. The only thing farmers could grow easily was green-seed cotton—an unprofitable crop because it took an entire day for one person to separate a single pound of cotton from the seeds.

In 1793, a young inventor named Eli Whitney overheard several South Carolina planters discussing the possibility of a machine that could clean cotton easily. If someone could invent one, they said, it would "save the South"...and make its inventor a fortune.

Good Luck: Whitney was intrigued by the challenge. After only a few days of experimenting, he came up with a working model of a "cotton gin." He received a patent for it in 1794.

Tough Luck. Unfortunately, Whitney couldn't cash in on his own creation. The machine was so efficient and amazingly simple that "any country handy man could copy it—and they did." He sued companies that pirated his design, but the courts kept ruling against him. In fact, it took 13 years for Whitney to get even one favorable judgment...and by then the patent had nearly expired.

The cotton gin revolutionized Southern agriculture. In 1792 the U.S. exported about 140,000 lbs. of cotton; by 1800, with the help of Whitney's machine, almost 18 *million* lbs. were being exported annually. However, Whitney never benefitted from it.

The Loser: Charles Goodyear

The Sure Thing: Control of the "vulcanizing" process that makes rubber useful in manufactured products.

Background: Goodyear's hardware store went broke in 1830, and over the next decade he spent a lot of time in debtor's prison. When he wasn't in jail, he was inventing things.

In 1834, he designed a rubber inner tube. He took it to the Roxbury India Rubber company, hoping they'd manufacture it. The company's owners admired his work, but couldn't buy anything; they were broke.

Rubber products, it turned out, were essentially worthless; rubber melted in heat and cracked in cold. "The individual who could unlock the secret to India rubber," the owners assured Goodyear,

Canine toupees—which attach to the top of dogs' heads with adhesive—are sold in Tokyo.

"stood to make a fortune."

"To someone forever in debt," recounts *Yankee* magazine, "these words were like throwing a life preserver to a drowning man. The raw material was cheap, and the necessary equipment for cooking rubber could be found in his wife's kitchen: a rolling pin, a marble slab, and a few pots and pans. Vulcanizing rubber became Goodyear's mission in life."

Good Luck: After five years of dire poverty, during which he experimented constantly, Goodyear accidentally dropped a batch of rubber and sulphur mixture on a hot stove. When it didn't melt, as he expected it would, he realized he had finally discovered vulcanization.

Tough Luck: He had lived off people's charity—and dreams—for so long that none of his family or friends believed in him any more. In fact, it took him three years to find someone who was willing to invest in his discovery.

Finally, in 1854, he perfected the process enough to receive a valuable patent. But he still never made a cent from it. Other companies stole the process and challenged his rights to it. He was forced to spend all the money he could get his hands on defending himself. He died a pauper in 1860, hounded by collection agents.

The Loser: Josh J. Evans

Sure Thing: A district judgeship in Oklahoma.

Background: Frank Ogden had been a popular judge in rural northwest Oklahoma for thirteen years. He normally ran for reelection unopposed, but just before the deadline for filing to run in 1990, it was announced that he had cancer. Doctors speculated that Ogden could last another term. However, Josh Evans decided to run against him. He even tried, unsuccessfully, to get Ogden removed from the ballot.

Good Luck: On August ninth, Ogden died. Since write-ins aren't allowed in Okalhoma, Evans looked like a shoo-in.

Tough Luck: Evans couldn't even beat a dead man. The local Bar Association endorsed the deceased judge, and the electorate gave him 91% of the vote. The final tally: 9,377 for Ogden; 959 for Evans.

PRIME-TIME RELIGION

If God is everywhere, why not on Gilligan's Island*? TV quotes from the book* Primetime Proverbs, *by Jack Mingo and John Javna.*

ON RELIGION

"I'm going to take the moment to contemplate most Western religions. I'm looking for something soft on morality, generous with holidays, and with a very short initiation period."

—David Addison,
Moonlighting

"The pilgrims who drink the water of the Ganges shall trot all the way to the Mosque."

—Henry Gibson,
Laugh-In

THE RULES OF HEAVEN

"There's no plea bargaining in heaven."

—Mark McCormick,
Hardcastle & McCormack

"You don't have to be homely to get into heaven."

—Hattie Denton,
The Rifleman

Jean-Paul Sartre [arriving in heaven]: "It's not what I expected."
God: "What did you expect?"
Sartre: "Nothing."

—SCTV

ABOUT GOD

"When I was dead I saw God. She looks just like Toody from *The Facts of Life*."

—Larry,
Newhart

"God don't make no mistakes—that's how He got to be God."

—Archie Bunker,
All in the Family

Gabe Kotter: "I think God is everywhere."
Arnold Horschack: "Even in liver?"

—Welcome Back, Kotter

On FAITH

"All faith must have a little doubt thrown in. Otherwise it just becomes flabby sentimentality."

—Dr. Loveless,
The Wild, Wild West

"You have to believe in the gods to see them."

—Hopi the Indian,
Gumby

THE MONSTER MASH

This Halloween classic swept across America in 1962—and 1973—like a bat out of...Here's the inside story, from Behind the Hits, *by Bob Shannon and John Javna.*

BACKGROUND

In the late '50s, Universal Studios syndicated a package of its greatest monster movies—including *Dracula*, The *Mummy*, and *Frankenstein*, featuring Boris Karloff—to television stations around the country. That's how baby boom kids got their first look at classic horror films. It was love at first sight; by the early '60s, a monster craze was under way. There were monster models, monster trading cards, monster wallets, monster posters...and a monster song: "The Monster Mash," by Bobby "Boris" Pickett.

KARLOFF DOO-WOP

Bobby was an aspiring actor who made his living singing with a Hollywood rock 'n' roll group called the Cordials at night, while he went on casting calls during the day. He'd always done impressions, and Karloff was one of his best. So one night just for the hell of it, while the Cordials doo-wopped their way thorugh a classic tune called "Little Darlin'," Bobby did a monologue in the middle with a Karloff voice. The crowds loved it. A member of the band suggested that Bobby do more with the Karloff imitation—write an original song, perhaps.

Pickett resisted for a while, but finally he and a friend wrote a monster take-off of Dee Dee Sharp's hit, "Mashed Potato Time." They recorded it at a studio on Hollywood Boulevard, for Gary Paxton's Garpax Records.

SOUND EFFECTS

Paxton, who'd had his own hit with "Alley Oop" a few years earlier, came up with some clever low-budget techniques to produce the background noises that made the rock 'n' roll's ultimate Halloween party so effective.

For example:

• "The sound of the coffin opening was actually a rusty nail being drawn out of a two-by-four."

• The cauldron bubbling was really water being bubbled through a straw.

• The chains rattling was just the sound of chains being dropped on a tile floor.

"Boris" Pickett thought of "Monster Mash" as a cute novelty tune. But he didn't understand the power of the monster mania that was sweeping America. The song sold a million copies and became a #1 hit in October—just in time for Halloween. One of its fans, who recieved free copies from Pickett, was Boris Karloff.

RETURN FROM THE DEAD

Pickett followed "Monster Mash" with "Monster's Holiday," and with an album of monster rock 'n' roll. But he had no more monster hits until 1970, when "Monster Mash" was re-released. It was released again in 1973, and it really hit big, reaching the Top 10. Pickett, by then a cabdriver in New York City, attributed its 1973 success, in part, to Nixon's Watergate scandal. "At this point in time, with what's coming down with Watergate, people need some relief from the tension that's building up," he explained.

ROCKIN' MONSTERS

Before "Monster Mash," the most popular monster tune in rock history was "Purple People Eater," recorded in 1958 by Sheb Wooley. Here's how Wooley came up with it:

• A friend of Wooley's told him a riddle he'd heard from his kid: "What flies, has one horn, has one eye, and eats people?" The answer: "A one-eyed, one-horned flying purple people eater." Wooley thought it was amusing, and wrote a song based on it.

• A short time later,Wooley met with the president of MGM Records to decide on his next single. Wooley played every song he'd written, but still couldn't come up with one the guy liked. "You got anything else?" the president asked. "Well, yeah, one more thing, but it's nothing you'd wanna hear." "Let's hear it."

• It was "Purple People Eater." Wooley recorded it, and three weeks later it was the #1 single in the U.S.

THE REAL PURITANS

According to American folklore, the Puritans were stern martinets who wore dark clothes, burned witches and never had sex. That's only partly true.

Were the Puritans "puritanical"?
In many ways, yes. They had little tolerance for differences of opinion. They didn't think much of the concept of democracy, either—John Winthrop, first governor of the Massachusetts Bay Colony, called it "the meanest and worst of all forms of government." The religious freedom they left Europe to find was denied in their own settlements, where religious dissenters were expelled.

Colonial Christmas.
They didn't celebrate Christmas—in fact, they made it illegal to do so. A law passed in 1659 levied a 5-shilling fine against anyone "found observing, by abstinence from labor, feasting or any other way, any such days as Christmas day."

On the other hand, the Puritans' reputation for shyness about sex was a fabrication by 19th century historians who were trying to give their Colonial ancestors a moral makeover. In reality, the Puritans considered sex a public concern and regularly discussed it during meetings. They valued sexual intercourse inside marriage to such an extent that, after lengthy public discussion, they expelled a husband from the church community because he had refused to sleep with his wife for over two years. Furthermore, parents and children all slept in close proximity, so youngsters got plenty of sexual education at an early age, with visual aids.

Animal Husbandry
Still, deviations from the norm were severely dealt with. In 1647, a 16-year-old from Plymouth, Mass. was "detected of buggery with a mare, a cowe, two goats, five sheep, two calves and a turkey," as Governor Bradford put it. The boy was put to death. "A very sade spectakle it was; for first the mare, and them the cowe, and the rest of the lesser catle, were kild before his face, according to the law, Levitticus 20:15, and then he him selfe was executed."

OTHER PRESIDENTIAL FIRSTS

We all know the first president (Washington), the first to resign (Nixon), the first Catholic president (Kennedy), and so on. But who was the first to be interviewed in the nude? Here's the BRI's list of other presidential firsts.

THE PRESIDENT: Theodore Roosevelt (1901-1909)
NOTABLE FIRST: First president to coin an advertising slogan.
BACKGROUND: While he was visiting Andrew Jackson's home in Nashville, Tennessee, Roosevelt was offered a cup of the coffee sold at the nearby Maxwell House hotel. When someone asked if he'd like another cup, Roosevelt replied: "Will I have another cup? Delighted! *It's good to the last drop!*" His words were eventually used by Maxwell House in their ad campaigns.
Note: Teddy was also the first president to be blinded while in office. He liked to box, and during one White House bout was hit so hard he became permanently blind in one eye.

THE PRESIDENT: James Madison (1809-1817)
NOTABLE FIRST: First commander-in-chief to actually command a military unit while in office.
BACKGROUND: When the British attacked Washington, D.C., during the War of 1812, President Madison personally took charge of an artillery battery. But that didn't last long; when the Americans started to lose, Madison fled the city.

THE PRESIDENT: Benjamin Harrison (1889-1893)
NOTABLE FIRST: First president with a fear of electricity.
BACKGROUND: President Harrison knew two things about electricity: The White House had just been wired for it; and it could kill people (the electric chair was becoming a common form of execution). That was all he needed to know—he didn't want anything more to do with it. Throughout his entire term, he and his wife refused to turn the lights on and off themselves. They either had the servants do it or left the lights on all night.

An estimated 70% of all Americans visit shopping malls at least once a week.

THE PRESIDENT: Andrew Jackson (1829-1837)
ACCOMPLISHMENT: First president to be born in more than one place.
BACKGROUND: The following places claim themselves as Andrew Jackson's birthplace: Union County, North Carolina; Berkeley County, West Virginia; Augusta County, West Virginia; York County, Pennsylvania; as well as England, Ireland, and the Atlantic Ocean (he may have been born at sea). His "official" birthplace: Waxhaw, South Carolina.

THE PRESIDENT: John Quincy Adams (1825-1829)
ACCOMPLISHMENT: First president interviewed in the nude.
BACKGROUND: President Adams loved to skinny-dip. In hot weather he'd sneak out for a swim in the Potomac. One morning Anne Royall—a reporter who had been trying to interview him for months—sneaked up while he was swimming, sat on his clothes, and refused to leave until he granted her an interview. He did.

THE PRESIDENT: Martin Van Buren (1837-1841)
ACCOMPLISHMENT: First president to forget about his wife.
BACKGROUND: In his autobiography, Van Buren did not mention his wife Hannah even once.

THE PRESIDENT: Warren G. Harding (1921-1923)
ACCOMPLISHMENT: First president to pardon a dog.
BACKGROUND: One morning Harding read a newspaper article about Pennsylvania dog that had been ordered destroyed because it had been brought into the country illegally. Harding—who loved animals—wrote a letter to the Governor of Pennsylvania. The governor saw to it that the dog's life was spared.

THE PRESIDENT: David Rice Atchison (1849-1849)
ACCOMPLISHMENT: First president to serve for one day.
BACKGROUND: Zachary Taylor was so religious that he refused to take the oath of office on a Sunday. So Atchison, President Pro Tempore of the U.S. Senate, stood in for him until he could be sworn in the next day.

Americans buy two billion disposable razors and razor blades every year.

SMART COOKIES

Cookies keep the Girl Scouts in the green. That box of Thin Mints or Do-Si-Does you order every season is part of a tradition that's nearly 60 years old.

FOUNDING MOTHERS

After Juliette Low founded the Girl Scouts in 1912, the local troops raised money by selling knitted clothes, baked goods and chickens. Then in 1934, Philadelphia press agent Bella Spewack (who later co-wrote *Kiss Me Kate)* came up with an idea she thought would make fund-raising easier: a vanilla cookie in the shape of the Girl Scout seal. She contracted with a local bakery to make them. One day she heard that reporters were going to interview actresses at a local flower show. Figuring her Girl Scout troop would get free publicity if they showed up selling cookies, she sent a contingent of green-clad cookie-mongers. They got so much publicity and sold so many cookies that within three years, more than a hundred local councils were selling the same professionally-baked cookies. It was the beginning of an American institution.

NOW IT'S BIG BUSINESS

- In 1990 the Girl Scouts sold 130 million boxes of cookies, grossing $225 million. That's 13 cookies for every person in the U.S. Average sale per scout? About 100 boxes.
- Some troops now offer "cookie seminars" and toll-free ordering numbers to boost sales. When asked about nutritional value, scouts are coached to respond: "Our cookies contain no preservatives and no artificial colors, and are made of 100% vegetable shortening."
- The *Girl Scout Manual* offers sales tips like this: "Your words and tone of voice must generate the image of someone people trust."
- The greatest cookie seller of all time was Markita Andrews, who sold 60,000 boxes in her twelve years of Girl Scouting. She was so successful that she was hired to make motivational speeches to big companies and appear in a 12-minute sales motivational film, *The Cookie Kid*, produced by Disney.
- Most popular cookies: Thin Mint, followed by Shortbread and Peanut Butter Sandwiches. Least popular: cheese-flavored crackers.

Nice place to visit: 24% of all Iowans have some sort of ornament on their lawns.

YOU SEND ME

Here are the origins of some of the nation's largest people and package movers.

GREYHOUND BUSES

In 1914 Carl Eric Wickman opened a Hupmobile car dealership in Minnesota. When business was slow, he used one of the Hupmobiles to drive miners the 4 miles between the towns of Alice and Hibbing, charging 15¢ per trip (25¢ round trip). This enterprise turned out to be very profitable (he made $2.25 the first day), and by 1916 Wickman had expanded it to include long distance routes. He painted the Hupmobiles gray to hide the dust during long journeys...which prompted a hotel owner along one route to comment that they looked like greyhound dogs. Wickman liked the idea. He adopted the slogan "Ride the Greyhounds."

FEDERAL EXPRESS

When Fred Smith was a student at Yale University, he wrote a term paper outlining his idea for a nationwide overnight delivery service. His Professor gave him a C for the effort....but Smith (who'd inherited a fortune) invested $4 million to start the company anyway. He named it Federal Express because he thought his first major customer would be the Federal Reserve Bank. (Ironically, it wasn't).

UNITED PARCEL SERVICE

Jim Casey was 19 years old in 1907, when he started the American Messenger company in Seattle. His business consisted of only six messengers, two bicycles, and a telephone...but within a year he added 6 motorcycles and a Model T Ford. By 1918 he was handling the deliveries of 3 of Seattle's major department stores. By the end of World War I, Casey had changed the name of the business to the United Parcel Service, and focused exclusively on delivering for department stores. In 1953 UPS expanded service to 16 metropolitan areas and started expanding its service. Today UPS owns more than 300 aircraft and delivers 600,000 packages every day.

Ounce for ounce, a bumblebee is 150 times stronger than an elephant.

THE HARDER THEY FALL

The bigger they are, the harder they fall?
Sadly, that was true for these stars.

THE STAR: Veronica Lake, sultry actress known for her "peek-a-boo" hair-style (combed over one eye—in fact, practically covering one whole side of her face).
ACCOMPLISHMENTS: A leading box-office attraction of the early 1940s. Made 26 films, including *I Married a Witch* (the inspiration for the TV show, "Bewitched").
AT HER PEAK: Her hair-style was so popular that it hampered the war effort. Women working in factories kept getting their "peek-a-boo" hair caught in the machinery. U.S. government officials asked Lake to cut her hair. She did.
THE FALL: Without the hair, Lake wasn't special anymore. By the early '50s, her movie career was over. Though she found intermittent work in stage roles, she was reduced at one point to working as a barmaid in Manhattan. She died of acute hepatitis at age 53, on July 7, 1973.

THE STAR: D.W. Griffith, the genius regarded as "the father of modern cinema."
ACCOMPLISHMENTS: Griffith produced and directed nearly 500 films. The cinematic genres he created—from the epic to the psychological drama—influenced generations of directors. He launched the careers of Hollywood legends Mary Pickford, Douglas Fairbanks, Lionel Barrymore, and many others.
AT HIS PEAK: His films had such impact that Woodrow Wilson remarked, when he saw Griffith's *The Birth of a Nation* (the first film shown at the White House), that it was "like writing history with lightning."
THE FALL: Griffith's bouts with the bottle inspired him to make *The Struggle*, a 1931 exploration of alchoholism. It bombed. Griffith's own struggle with booze worsened, and his production company folded. Suddenly, he was unable to find work; in the last 17 years of his life, no one in Hollywood would give him a job.

Although his films had earned tens of millions of dollars, he left an estate of only $30,000 when he died in 1948, at the age of 73.

THE STAR: "Shoeless Joe" Jackson, one of the greatest players in baseball history. Played for the Philadelphia Athletics (1908-09), Cleveland Indians (1910-15) and Chicago White Sox (1915-20).

ACCOMPLISHMENTS: Compiled the third-highest lifetime batting average of all time: .356. Only Ty Cobb, at .367, and Rogers Hornsby, at .358, are higher. In his first full year he hit .408 (but lost the batting title to Cobb, who hit .420).

AT HIS PEAK: Between 1910 and 1915, Jackson batted no lower than .331. Cobb called Jackson the greatest natural hitter who ever lived, adding, "He never figured anything out or studied anything with the same scientific approach I gave it. He just swung."

THE FALL: After the White Sox lost the 1919 World Series to the Cincinatti Reds, officials learned that eight Chicago players—including Jackson—had agreed to "throw" the Series in exchange for bribes from gangsters. They called it the "Black Sox" scandal.

The revelation outraged the country. A sensational investigation was launched and a grand jury was convened. Jackson, who had hit .375 in the Series (leading all batters), maintained he never accepted any money. He claimed he'd agreed to the plan only because the team's owner, notoriously stingy Charles Comiskey, was paying the players next to nothing. He was found innocent of any criminal wrongdoing, but baseball executives decided to make an example of him (and his teammates). He was banned from baseball for life.

Jackson resettled in his native South Carolina, where he ran a liquor store and played sandlot and textile-league baseball. He died of a heart attack on December 5, 1951, at the age of 63.

THE STAR: Joseph McCarthy, U.S. Senator (R-Wisc.) from 1947 to 1957.

ACCOMPLISHMENTS: Senator McCarthy did not create the Cold War, but he almost single-handedly fashioned the post-World War II anti-communist hysteria that swept through American society. His 1950 claim that more than 200 Communists had infiltrated the State Department launched a national witch hunt. It ruined hundreds of careers, led to infamous blacklists (especially in the motion picture industry), and, as one magazine put it, "convinced most Americans that their government was riddled with Reds bent on its destruction."

AT HIS PEAK: He could make or break careers and reputations. Polls showed that half of all Americans approved of his efforts, while less than one-third disapproved.

THE FALL: In April, 1954, a Senate committee began investigating his charge that the U.S. Army was "coddling Communists." Two-thirds of all TV sets in the country were tuned in. TV cameras captured his cruel sneer, his bullying manner, and America saw Army counsel Joseph Welch put McCarthy in his place with the famous words, "Have you no sense of decency, sir?" Welch got a standing ovation and McCarthy's colleagues in the Senate moved to censure him. His political career was effectively over. Always known as a two-fisted drinker, he hit the bottle harder and harder, and on May 2, 1957, he died of liver disease, at the age of 48.

THE STAR: Eliot Ness, legendary G-man whose 15-year law enforcement career was highlighted by his campaign against Chicago mob boss Al Capone.

ACCOMPLISHMENTS: In 1929, during Prohibition, Ness led the special ten-man Justice Department team known as "The Untouchables," targeting Capone. In 1935, at 32, Ness became Cleveland's youngest director of public safety. He went on to rid the police department of rampant corruption, brought dozens of mobsters to trial, and reduced juvenile crime by two-thirds.

AT HIS PEAK: In two years, Ness and his men did more to curtail organized crime in Chicago than federal, state, and local officials combined had in an entire decade. In its first six months alone, the "Untouchables" unit seized nineteen Capone distilleries and six breweries. By 1931 the team had effectively shut down Capone's alcohol-production operations.

THE FALL: In the spring of 1942, Ness drove his car, with its unmistakable "EN-1" license plates, into another vehicle—then left the scene. It was reported he'd been driving drunk. Ness denied it, but resigned under pressure two months later. Over the next 15 years, he spiralled downward through a series of failed business ventures, marriages, and an abortive political career. He managed to complete his memoirs, but didn't live to see them in print. When he died of a heart attack, on May 16, 1957, he was $8,000 in debt.

BEAGLE, SHYSTER, & BEAGLE

This script from the first episode of a long-lost early radio show by the Marx Brothers was recently rediscovered. So close your ears, listen with your eyes, and travel back in time to Nov. 28. 1932, when the first episode of Five-Star Theater aired.

SCENE: *The offices of Beagle, Shyster, & Beagle, Attorneys at Law. Miss Dimple, the receptionist, is polishing her nails. Beagle (Groucho Marx) bursts in.*

MISS DIMPLE: Good morning, Mr. Beagle.

GROUCHO: Never mind that. Get President Hoover on the phone. There's a picture of me in the police station and it doesn't do me justice. It makes me look like my father. In fact, it *is* my father. Never mind calling the president. Just find out what the reward is.

MISS DIMPLE: Mr. Beagle, I've got some letters for you to sign.

GROUCHO: Not now, not now! I've had a big day in court.

MISS DIMPLE: What was the case?

GROUCHO: Disorderly conduct, but I think I'll get off. Why shouldn't I? She hit me first.

MISS DIMPLE: Mr. Beagle! You hit a woman?

GROUCHO: Well, she was my size. Even smaller. Besides, if it weren't for my own arrests, I'd never get a case. Any calls?

MISS DIMPLE: Yes, your creditors have been calling all morning. They said they're tired of phoning and that something will have to be done.

GROUCHO: All right. We'll do something. We'll have the phone taken out.

MISS DIMPLE: Okay.

GROUCHO: There's a good girl. Your salary is raised ten dollars.

MISS DIMPLE: Thank you, Mr. Beagle.

GROUCHO: It's nothing at all. Say, how about lending me that ten till payday?

MISS DIMPLE: But Mr. Beagle, I haven't been paid in weeks. Besides, you overlook the fact—

GROUCHO: I've overlooked plenty around here. A fine stenographer you are! What do you do with your time? The floors aren't washed, the windows aren't cleaned. and my pants aren't even pressed.

MISS DIMPLE: But Mr. Beagle—

GROUCHO: Enough of this small talk. Where's that ten dollars?

Groucho retires to his office. Soon after, Miss Dimple ushers in a client—a nervous, worried soul named Mr. Jones.

JONES: How do you do, Mr. Beagle. A friend of mine told me you were a good lawyer.

GROUCHO: You just *think* he's a friend of yours. Sit down. Have you got a couple of cigars?

JONES: Uh...no, I'm sorry.

GROUCHO: Well, why don't you send out for some? If you've got a quarter, I'll go myself.

JONES: Oh, no, no, Mr. Beagle.

GROUCHO: What's the matter? Don't you trust me?

JONES: Why—I'd like to talk to you. I'm having trouble with my wife.

GROUCHO: You are! Well, I'm having trouble with my wife, too, but I don't go around bragging about it. Hmm. You oughta be ashamed of yourself. Miss Dimple, show this gentleman the door. On second thought, never mind. He saw it when he came in.

JONES: But, Mr. Beagle—I came to you for advice. Let me tell you a story. My wife is in love with two men, and—

GROUCHO: Ha, ha, ha! Not a bad story. The boys are all repeating it around the club. Now let me tell you one. There were two traveling men named Pat and Mike—

JONES: No, no, Mr. Beagle. I came here with a problem. I'm looking for evidence against my wife.

GROUCHO: What you really want is someone to shadow your wife. I've got just the man for you—my new assistant, Emmanuel Ravelli. He looks like an idiot and talks like an idiot. But don't let that fool you. He really is an idiot. You and Ravelli will have a lot in common.

JONES: Mr. Beagle, my time is valuable. Let me give you the facts. I married my wife secretly.

GROUCHO: You married her secretly? You mean you haven't told her about it? No wonder she runs around with other men.

JONES: Mr. Beagle, we must get this divorce—I want your assistant, Mr. Ravelli, to follow my wife.

GROUCHO: One thing at a time. Let's get the divorce first and then we can all follow your wife.

CHICO: Here I am, boss. You callin' Ravelli?

GROUCHO: See here. I don't like your sleeping on the company's time.

CHICO: I don't like sleeping on it it, either. Why don't you buy me a bed?

JONES: Mr. Ravelli, I've just been telling Mr. Beagle that, much as I regret to say it, my wife is going around with other men.

CHICO: She's going around with other men? 'At'sa fine. Hey! You think she like me?

JONES: Well, Mr. Ravelli, as long as you're going to trail my wife, I think I ought to describe her to you. She's of medium height and…but never mind, I've got a photograph.

CHICO: Hey, 'at'sa fine. Awright. I'll take a dozen.

JONES: I'm not selling them

CHICO: You mean, I get it for nothing?

JONES: Of course.

CHICO: Awright. Then I take two dozen.

JONES: One picture ought to be enough for the present. There's one man my wife has been paying particular attention to. I'm counting on you to find out who he is. Do you think you can do it?

CHICO: Sure, you leave 'im to me. I find out who the man was with your wife. And I find out quick.

JONES: Really? How you going to do it?

CHICO: Well, first I put on a disguise ...

JONES: Yes?

CHICO: Then I get a bloodhound ...

JONES: Yes??

CHICO: Then I go to your house ...

JONES: Yes???

CHICO: Then I ask your wife.

(Applause, commercial break)

Two weeks later at the offices of Beagle, Shyster, & Beagle.

MISS DIMPLE: Law offices of Beagle, Shyster, and Beagle ...Oh, hello, Mr. Jones. I didn't recognize your voice... Yes, Mr. Ravelli is still trailing your wife ...but it hasn't been long ...just two weeks. We expect Mr. Ravelli in the office this morning. He says he has some news ...Okay, I'll tell Mr. Beagle you'll be in ...Goodbye.

(Groucho comes in).

MISS DIMPLE: Good morning, Mr. Beagle—

GROUCHO: Miss Dimple, before I forget—call Ravelli and tell him to be sure and oversleep.

MISS DIMPLE: But he phoned and said he was coming right in.

GROUCHO: In that case, I'm going right back to the poolroom *(he heads for the door)*.

MISS DIMPLE: But Mr. Jones is on his way here to talk to you about his divorce.

GROUCHO: That's all he ever talks to me about. I'm getting pretty sick of it, too.

MISS DIMPLE: But Mr. Beagle, that's your business.

Each year, Americans consume 19 billion franks—an average of 87 per person.

GROUCHO: Well, I wish he'd keep his nose out of my business. *(Door opens.)*

MISS DIMPLE: Shh! Someone's coming in. I think it's Mr. Jones. How do you do, Mr. Jones?

JONES: How do you do, Miss Dimple? Morning, Mr. Beagle. About my divorce—

GROUCHO: Divorce! You going to start that again? Listen, Jones, can I sell you a ticket to the Firemen's Ball? It's a five-dollar ticket, and it's yours for a buck and a half.

JONES: Why, this is last year's ticket.

GROUCHO: I know it is, but they had a better show last year.

JONES: Mr. Beagle, when will I find out about my divorce case?

GROUCHO: See here, Jones, don't change the subject. What about that ticket?

JONES: I don't like to appear impatient, Mr. Beagle, but your assistant was supposed to bring in some evidence against my wife. Where is Mr. Ravelli?

CHICO: Hey! Who'sa calling Ravelli? Here I am.

JONES: Ah, Mr. Ravelli, I'd like to get the results of your investigation. Have you been trailing my wife?

CHICO: Sure, I shadow her all day.

JONES: What day was that?

CHICO: That was Shadowday. I went right to your house—

JONES: What did you find out?

CHICO: I find your wife out.

JONES: Then you wasted the entire two weeks?

CHICO: No. Monday, I shadow your wife. Tuesday, I go to the ball game—she don't show up. Wednesday, she go to the ball game—I don't show up. Thursday was a doubleheader. We both no show up. Friday it rain all day—there's a no ball game, so I go fishing.

JONES: Well, what's that got to do with my wife?

CHICO: Well, I no catcha no fish, but I catch your wife.

The state with the most outhouses is Alaska.

JONES: You caught my wife—with a man? Who was he?

CHICO: I don't wanna say.

JONES: I insist that you tell me the man's name.

CHICO: I don't wanna tell.

GROUCHO: Listen, Jones, my assistant isn't the type of fellow who'd bandy a man's good name in public—

JONES: For the last time, gentlemen—who was the man?

GROUCHO: Come clean, Ravelli, who was the man with his wife?

CHICO: Awright, awright. You maka me tell, I tell you. Mr. Jones, the man with your wife was my boss, Mr. Beagle.

JONES: This is an outrage. My attorney going out with my wife!

GROUCHO: What do you mean, outrage? Don't you think I'm good enough for her?

JONES: I'm going to get a new attorney.

GROUCHO: Hmm! I suppose you think we can't get a new client?

JONES: Good day! *(He stomps out and slams the door.)*

GROUCHO: Ravelli, you did noble work. You can have the rest of the year off. And if you never come back, I'll give you a bonus.

CHICO: Well, boss, there's something I wanna tell you.

GROUCHO: Go right ahead. I'm not listening.

CHICO: You want I should never come back?

GROUCHO: In a word, yes.

CHICO: Awright, boss, I make you a proposition. If you want I should never come back, I gotta have more money.

GROUCHO: Ravelli, it's worth it. (*Applause, theme music*)

ANNOUNCER: The crowd in the studio is giving the Marx Brothers a great ovation. We hope you in the radio audience enjoyed them as much as we did. Groucho and Chico will be back again next Monday at this same time.

The first "streamlined swimsuits" of the early 1900s were made of wool and weighed as much as 20 lbs.

PICASSO ORIGINALS

Pablo Picasso was known for his skill with lines. Here are some you won't see in a museum.

"We know that art is not truth. Art is a lie that makes us realize truth."

"When I was a child my mother said to me, 'If you become a soldier you'll be a general. If you become a monk you'll become the pope.' Instead I became a painter and wound up as Picasso."

"I am only a public entertainer who has understood his time."

"There are only two kinds of women—goddesses and doormats."

"There are painters who transform the sun into a yellow spot, but there are others who, thanks to their art and intelligence, transform a yellow spot into the sun."

"One starts to get young at the age of sixty and then it is too late."

"There's nothing so similar to one poodle dog as another poodle dog and that goes for women, too."

"You never see anything very great which is not, at the same time, horrible in some respect. The genius of Einstein leads to Hiroshima."

"God is really only another artist. He invented the giraffe, the elephant, and the cat. He has no real style, he just goes on trying other things."

"Ah, good taste! What a dreadful thing! Taste is the enemy of creativeness."

"An artist must know how to convince others of the truth of his lies."

"If only we could pull out our brains and use only our eyes."

"If I like it, I say it's mine. If I don't, I say it's a fake."

"Work is a necessity for man. Man invented the alarm clock."

"You invent something, and then someone comes along and does it pretty."

Arachibutyrophobia: the fear of peanut butter sticking to the roof of your mouth.

LATIN

So you thought Latin was dead? Latin For A... *Henry Beard, brings it back to life. Here are so...*

Useful phrase: "Amicule, deliciæ, num is sum qui mentiar tibi?"
Meaning: "Baby, sweetheart, would I lie to you?"

Useful phrase: "Perscriptio in manibus tabellariorum est."
Meaning: "The check is in the mail."

Useful phrase: "Braccæ tuæ aperiuntur."
Meaning: "Your fly is open."

Useful phrase: "Da mihi sis bubulæ frustum assæ, solana tuberosa in modo Gallico fricta ac quassum lactatum coagulatum crassum."
Meaning: "I'll have a hamburger, French fries, and a thick shake."

Useful phrase: "Cur non isti mictum ex occasione?"
Meaning: "Why didn't you go when you had the chance?"

Useful phrase: "In rivo fimi sine rivo sum."
Meaning: "I'm up the creek without a paddle."

Useful phrase: "Est ... luus nummus superfluus."
Meaning: "I do not have any spare change."

Useful phrase: "Lex clavatoris designati rescindenda est."
Meaning: "The designated-hitter rule has got to go."

Useful phrase: "Observa quo vadis, cinaede!"
Meaning: "Watch where you're going, you jerk!"

Useful phrase: "Tractatorne in Germania Orinetali doctus est?"
Meaning: "Was your masseur trained in East Germany?"

Useful phrase: "Visne scire quod credam? Credo Elvem ipsum etiam vivere."
Meaning: "You know what I think? I think that Elvis is still alive."

Useful phrase: "Di! Ecce hora! Uxor mea necabit!"
Meaning: "God, look at the time! My wife will kill me!"

Hitler's favorite movie was *King Kong*.

THE TAJ MAHAL

On the banks of the Jumna River, at Agra, India is a structure considered by many to be the most beautiful edifice ever built—the Taj Mahal.

BACKGROUND

In 1628, Shah Jahan became the fifth Mogul emperor of India. Of his four wives, his favorite was one he called *Mumtaz Mahal* (which means "Ornament of the Palace").

• Shah Jahan was known as a benevolent, fatherly ruler. One ritual he—and his subjects—especially enjoyed was "Tula Dan." He would sit on a scale forty feet high, and was weighed against gold coins. When an amount equal to his weight was measured out, the coins were distributed to the poor.

• Mumtaz Mahal, on the other hand, was a bloodthirsty religious zealot and a committed foe of Christianity. She goaded her husband into destroying a Christian colony at Hooghly, on the northeast coast of India. The entire colony was razed. The survivors were marched 1,200 miles from Hooghly to Agra. There, the priests were thrown beneath elephants; the rest were sold as slaves.

THE MONUMENT

• When Mumtaz Mahal died in 1631, Shah Jahan was so grief-stricken that he disappeared into his quarters for eight days, "refusing food or wine"; all that could be heard coming from his room was a low moan.

• On the ninth day he emerged, determined to build a magnificent tomb as a monument to his beloved. Mumtaz herself, on her deathbed, supposedly whispered into Shah Jahan's ear that he should build " monument of perfect proportions" to symbolize and immortalize their perfect love.

• The project took 22 years. More than 20,000 jewelers, builders, masons and calligraphers worked on it day and night. When they finished, they had created the wondrous white mausoleum which is still regarded—nearly 340 years later—as the most remarkable

It is illegal to fly an airplane over the Taj Mahal.

piece of architecture in the world.

• The main building of the Taj Mahal is on a 186-foot square whose sides have been cut to form an octagon. This rests on a platform 2,000 feet long and 1,000 feet wide. At each of its four corners is a minaret—an Islamic prayer tower—three stories tall.

• Hundreds of tons of imported white marble were used.

• The Taj is adorned with Tibetan turquoise, Chinese jade, Arabian carnelian, and other precious metals.

• According to one account, Shah Jahan showed his appreciation for this masterpiece by ordering the hands of the master builders—and the head of the architect—to be chopped off, so the perfection of the Taj could never be duplicated.

LATER ON...

• In first centuries after it was built, the Taj Mahal wasn't a tourist attraction. Until the British Raj (occupation of India), any non-Moslem who entered it was put to death.

• Shah Jahan planned to build a second Taj Mahal, made of black marble, on the opposite bank of the Jumna. (He planned to make it his own tomb.) The two structures were to have been connected by a bridge of solid silver. Construction on this "Black Taj" supposedly was begun in the 1650s, but no traces of its foundation have ever been found. The project was halted when Shah Jahan was deposed by his sons.

• The Mogul spent his last years confined to a suite in Agra's famous Red Fort, where he was imprisoned by his son Aurangzeb, Agra's new ruler. From his window, Jahan could see his monument to Mumtaz—to whom he remained devoted (even though his entire harem was with him). Every day for eight years he sat gazing across the river.

• Jahan finally died at the age of 74, when he took an overdose of aphrodisiacs in an effort to prove his virility.

• Jahan was buried with Mumtaz in the Taj, but their actual remains are not in the main structure. The tombs upstairs are empty; the real ones are in the basement.

MODERN TIMES

• The domes and minarets of the Taj are so reflective—even in moonlight—that, during the India-Pakistan War, large sections were covered in burlap so that Pakistani aircraft could not use it as a beacon.

• Today, the Taj is threatened by pollution. The river valley where it sits tends to trap corrosive air pollutants, including coal dust and sulfur dioxide, for days at a time. Only about 1% of its surface has been affected, but formerly bright-white marble is now streaked, pitted and yellow. Some of the red sandstone of auxiliary buildings is flaking. Most of the pollution is said to come from two coal-fired power plants, a railroad switching yard and many small coal-burning foundries.

• The Indian government has installed pollution-monitoring gear and promises to relocate the power stations and foundries, but these are long-term propositions. Meanwhile, the race to save the Taj is already being run by frantic workmen who are repairing and replacing slabs of marble as fast as possible.

THE OTHER TAJ

• Taj Mahal is one of the foremost modern American bluesmen.

• His real name: Henry St. Clair Fredericks.

• Our favorite of his albums: "Natch'l Blues" and "Giant Step." Both are recommended for your bathroom CD player.

• • •

GOTTA FILL THIS SPACE

Random quotes about greatness:

• "A small man can be just as exhausted as a great man." (Arthur Miller)

• "Behind every great man is a woman with nothing to wear." (L. Grant Glickman)

• "Calvin Coolidge—the greatest man ever to come out of Plymouth Corner, Vermont." (Clarence Darrow)

• "The privilege of the great is to see catastrophes from a terrace." (Jean Giraudoux).

On average, there are more than 1,800 thunder storms on Earth at any given time.

THE PLANE TRUTH

Occasionally, we get a letter from a reader who confesses he or she has read a Bathroom Reader on an airplane. Well, that's okay with us. To prove it, here's a bit of practical airplane advice from the Airline Passenger's Guerrilla Handbook, *by George Brown.*

Believe it or not, specialists have actually discovered a medical complaint called "economy class syndrome" (ECS). According to the British medical journal, *The Lancet*, the symptoms can appear several weeks after flights as short as three hours. The syndrome can result in anything from minor body pains and shortness of breath to heart attacks and strokes.

Doctors suspect that cramped legroom in economy class combined with dehydration interrupts the blood flow which causes clots, cutting off the supply of oxygen to various parts of the body. This may account for the results of one study which showed that 18 percent of sudden deaths on airplanes are due to blood clots in the lungs.

The medical specialists reported that the syndrome most often affects smokers, heavy drinkers, those whose feet don't reach the floor (because the seat puts more pressure on the backs of their legs), the elderly and those with a predisposition to coronary heart disease. But it also can affect normally healthy people, in some recorded cases causing them to develop pneumonia-like symptons due to blood clots in the lungs.

The best ways to fight ECS: drink nonalcoholic beverages, don't smoke, take aspirin to thin your blood and exercise on the plane.

How to Exercise on the Plane

The best type of exercise on a long flight is to get out of your seat, go to the back of the plane (or, if you're shy, into a toilet cubicle) and engage in traditional calisthenics, such as touching your toes, reaching for the sky and running in place. Avoid doing jumping jacks if you're in the lavatory.

If you can't or don't want to get up, there are certain sets of exercises you can do in your seat. Before you start, be sure to inform your seatmate of what you intend to do. This will prevent him from thinking you're having some sort of seizure, which could lead to his attempting to wrestle a pencil sideways into your mouth to keep you from choking on your tongue—always an embarrassing mistake for both parties.

The exercises are as follows:

1. Tighten and release, one group at a time, the muscles in your shoulders, back, buttocks and thighs.

2. By raising your thighs, lift both feet six inches off the floor and rotate them first in one direction and then in the other.

3. Reach up repeatedly toward your overhead light with one arm and then with the other as though trying to block out the light.

4. Bend forward with all your weight, press your crossed forearms onto your knees and, keeping your toes on the floor, repeatedly lift your heels as high as possible.

5. Sitting up, arching your back, repeatedly roll both shoulders forward and then back, first together and then one at a time.

6. Pretending you are on skis, push your knees to the right and your heels and hands to the left. Lift your feet off the floor, and swing your knees to the left and heels and hands to the right. Repeat twenty times.

7. Sitting back, lower your head as far forward as you can. Then, still facing forward, lower it to the left. Then, to the right. Repeat several times.

8. Lay your head back, with your mouth hanging open, and, arching your back, look as far back on the ceiling as you can.

9. With your right hand grab the back of your left armrest and pull your upper body around until you are looking behind you. Hold for ten seconds. Repeat in the other direction.

10. Place your right hand on your left shoulder and your left hand on your right shoulder, and hug yourself. Lean forward as though giving someone a Latin lover kiss. Repeat several times.

11. Sit up slowly, turn towards the aisle and tell the crowd looking at you that you've finished your exercises, so they can all go back to their seats.

EXPERT OPINIONS

Being an expert means never having to admit you're wrong. Here are some memorable examples of "expert opinion," quoted in a great book called The Experts Speak, *by Christopher Cerf & Victor Navasky.*

ON HEALTH:

"If excessive smoking actually plays a role in the production of lung cancer, it seems to be a minor one."

—The National Cancer Institute, 1954

"How do we know? Fallout may be good for us."

—Edward Teller, 1950

"A nuclear power plant is infinitely safer than eating, because 300 people choke to death on food every day."

—Dixie Lee Ray, Washington Governor, 1977

...ON MILITARY STRATEGY:

"I tell you Wellington is a bad general, the English are bad soldiers; we will settle the matter by lunch time."

—Napoleon Bonaparte at the Battle of Waterloo, 1815

"I guess we'll get through with them in a day."

—General George Custer at Little Big Horn, 1876

...ON FILM

"The cinema is little more than a fad. It's canned drama. I'm going to get out of this business. It's too much for me. It'll never catch on."

—Charlie Chaplin, 1914

"*Gone With the Wind* is going to be the biggest flop in the history of Hollywood. I'm just glad it'll be Clark Gable who's falling flat on his face and not Gary Cooper."

—Gary Cooper, 1938

"You'd better learn secretarial work or else get married."

—Emmeline Snively (modeling agent) to Marilyn Monroe, 1944

...ON TECHNOLOGY

"Rail travel at high speed is not possible, because passengers, unable to breathe, would die of asphyxiation."

—Dr. Dionysus Lardener, 1845

"Heavier-than-air flying machines are impossible."

—William Thomson, President of the Royal Society, 1890

"Nuclear powered vacuum cleaners will probably be a reality within 10 years."

—Alex Lewyt, President, Lewyt Vacuum Cleaner Co., 1955

"My invention...can be exploited for a certain time as a scientific curiosity, but apart from that it has no commercial value whatsoever."

—Auguste Lumiere (inventor of the movie camera), 1895.

...ON COMPUTERS

"While a calculator now is equipped with 18,000 vacuum tubes and weighs 30 tons, computers in the future may have only 1,000 vacuum tubes and only weigh 1 1/2 tons."

—*Popular Mechanics*, 1949

"I think there is a world market for about five computers."

—Thomas J. Watson, Chairman of IBM, 1943

"There is no reason for any individual to have a computer in their home."

—Ken Olson, President, Digital Equipment Corporation, 1977

...ON POLITICS

"If Richard Nixon is impeached, there will be mass suicides, mass nervous breakdowns, and total demoralization of the country."

—Helen Buffington, Committee to Re-Elect the President, 1974

"Dwight D. Eisenhower is a dedicated, conscious agent of the Communist conspiracy."

—Robert Welch, President, John Birch Society, 1963

A typical "lawn" in Austria is planted with cabbages and kohlrabi.

LUCKY STRIKES

Here's proof that the BRI appreciates other kinds of "bowling," too.

BIRTH OF BOWLING

• Bowling originated in German monasteries around 300 A.D. The monks had churchgoers knock down a bottle-shaped object called a *kegel* from a distance to prove their devotion to God. The kegel represented the devil, and upsetting it meant complete absolution from sin.

• Gradually, more kegels (pins) were added and it turned into a secular game. By the 1600s, a version called "nine-pin" had become popular throughout Europe.

• Ninepins was popular in the U.S. in the early 1800s. But because many lanes were located in saloons, the game became associated with drinking. Many states banned it. Bowlers got around the laws by adding a *tenth* pin to the set. Eventually ten-pins became more popular than Ninepins.

BOWLING LINGO

Apple: a bowling ball

Barmaid: a pin that's "hiding" behind another pin.

Bedposts, Snake eyes, Mule ears, Goal posts: 7-10 split.

Body English: using body contortions to change the course of an already thrown ball.

Cherry: downing only the front pins when going for a spare.

Christmas Tree: 3-7-10 or 2-7-10 splits.

Cincinnati: an 8-10 split

Creeper, powder puff: a sluggish ball.

Dead Apple: a ball with no power when it reaches the pins.

Golden Gate: A 4-6-7-10 split.

Grasshopper: a ball that sends the pins leaping

Grandma's Teeth: a random, gap-filled group of pins left standing.

Mother-In-Law: the 7 pin

Poodle: a roll right into the gutter.

Schleifer: a suspenseful, domino-like strike.

Woolworth, Dime Store: 5-10 ("five and dime") split.

Norman Rockwell started painting Saturday Evening Post covers at the age of 21.

TEA TIME

Some things you probably never knew about one of the world's most popular beverages.

According to Chinese legend, tea was discovered in 2737 B.C. by Emperor Shen Nung, when leaves from a nearby plant fell into a pot of boiling water.

◆

Japanese legend differs—it attributes the discovery of tea to Daruma, founder of Zen Buddhism. After nine years of meditating without sleep, it says, Daruma became groggy. This made him mad, so he cut off his eyelids. Blood from his eyes spilled to the ground, and a plant grew from that spot. The drink Daruma made from the plant cured his grogginess.

◆

All teas (except herbal teas) come from the same plant—*Camellia Sinensis*. The only things that distinguish one variety of tea from another are blending, added flavors, and the length of time the leaves are allowed to dry, or "ferment."

◆

Tea grows naturally in only one part of the world: the forested region shared by China, India, Burma, and Tibet.

Before the 1700s, the English considered tea a "man's" drink—and sold it only in coffee houses, places considered too rough for women. Thomas Twining changed this in 1706 when he opened London's first tea shop for ladies.

◆

Thomas Lipton, founder of the Lipton Tea Co., owes his success to pigs. Lipton owned a general store in Glasgow, Scotland. To promote it, he dressed up pigs and led them in parades. The pigs, called "Lipton's Orphans," helped Lipton make enough money to buy a tea plantation, and get his start in the tea business.

◆

The tea bag was invented in 1908, by accident. A New York tea importer mailed his customers free samples of his tea, which he packaged in tiny silk bags. When the customers wrote back asking for more of the bags, the importer realized they were using them to steep tea...and began packaging all of his tea that way.

◆

Watch how tea leaves unfold in boiling water. Experts call this "the agony of the leaves."

The word "Kennedy" actually means "hideous head" in Irish.

DEATH OF A CLOWN

Abbie Hoffman loved to make political points by making Americans laugh. Did somebody take him too seriously? Here's information from a new book, It's a Conspiracy, *by the American Paranoid Society.*

BACKGROUND

Rabble-Rouser

Abbie Hoffman was best known for co-founding the Yippies, a band of hairy anti-war freaks who assembled outside the Democratic Convention in Chicago to nominate a pig ("Pigasus") for President of the United States in 1968.

• The riots that followed were later blamed on the police, but Hoffman and seven other activists were hauled into court on "conspiracy" charges. They were known as the Chicago 8. After one of the most publicized trials of the '60s, the case was eventually thrown out of court.

Counterculture King of Satire.

His social satire (he called it "street theater") always attracted attention:

• When he fluttered three hundred crisp dollar bills down onto the floor of the New York Stock Exchange, there was pandemonium as brokers fought for the money.

• His plan to levitate the Pentagon made the front page.

• He called his second book *Steal This Book!* When no publisher would touch it (because of the title), he published it himself, sold 200,000 copies, and gave most of the money away.

The Fugitive

After getting busted for selling cocaine to an undercover policeman, he jumped bail, had plastic surgery and emerged shortly as Barry Freed, an environmental activist in upstate New York.

• Though he was "wanted" by the law, he regularly played softball with the New York State Police, testified to a congressional committee, and was commended by New York's Governor Cuomo for his work.

• As *Newsweek* wrote, "Hoffman may have been the first fugitive

The state of Pennsylvania is not named after William Penn. It's named after his father.

surrender with a press agent and a business manager. Before giving up, he summoned ABC's Barbara Walters...for a taping session."

• After a brief sentence, he went back to protest. His next book, *Steal This Urine Test* was an attack on "Reagan's repressive policy." And in 1987 he was back on the streets, getting arrested—along with Amy Carter—in an anti-CIA protest.

GOING FOR BUSH

• Abbie next took on George Bush, then running for President. In an October, 1988, *Playboy* article he co-authored, Hoffman broke the story of the "October Surprise." He alleged that Reagan supporters had made a deal with Iran to postpone the release of the hostages and keep President Carter from getting re-elected. In his version of the story, Bush had a key role in the conspiracy.

• Presumably, Amy Carter is the person who told Hoffman of her father's suspicions. With his nose for publicity, Hoffman knew it was an explosive story.

• There were rumors Hoffman was assembling a book on the subject. If he was as effective in presenting the story as he was in championing the counterculture during the '60s—and in getting publicity for it—he could have created real headaches for the Republicans...and potentially, the CIA.

WHAT HAPPENED

On April 12, 1989, when he was unable to contact Hoffman by phone, his landlord entered his house and found him in bed, dead.

OFFICIAL EXPLANATION

Coroner Thomas J. Rosko reportedly found the residue of about 150 pills and alcohol in Abbie's system. He said, "There is no way to take that amount of phenobarbital without intent. It was intentional and self-inflicted."

SUSPICIOUS FACTS

• **Hard to swallow:** Hoffman supposedly took 150 pills. One-tenth that number would have been enough to kill anyone.

• **Bad Brakes:** According to conspiracy theorist John Judge in

Alternative Perspectives on American Democracy, "When he went to deliver the manuscript to *Playboy* Abbie had an automobile accident....He told his friend and long-time fellow activist David Dellinger, that his brakes had been tampered with."

• **That's Incredible:** The *New York Times* quoted Dellinger as saying: "I don't believe for one moment the suicide thing." The reason: He had spoken with Hoffman recently and reported that Abbie had "numerous plans for the future."

• **No Glory:** His family didn't believe it either. In fact, almost all of Abbie Hoffman's friends were puzzled by the lack of a suicide note—he had a compelling need to express himself. As one of Hoffman's sons said, "Abbie was the kind of guy who, if he was going to do it, would wrap himself in a flag and jump off the top of the ITT building."

WAS THERE A CONSPIRACY?

THEORY #1:

YES. Somebody was afraid he knew too much and he was sure to create problems for the"Establishment" in the future. A number of journalists think he was able to break the "October Surprise" story with information received from President Jimmy Carter. Moreover, he had made a lot of powerful enemies during the '60s. He was an easy target, given his history of drug use.

THEORY #2

NO. Abbie generated a lot of strong feelings, and the people who loved him had a hard time accepting a suicide verdict. Abbie Hoffman was also a long-time manic-depressive, and was taking medication for it. He was very depressed by the Eighties. One night, he may have hit bottom.

PARTING SHOTS

"It's hard to believe that Abbie committed suicide—especially so late in the day that he missed The *New York Times*'s deadline."

—Paul Krassner (Abbie's fellow prankster), in *The Nation*

SONGWRITER STORIES

Songwriters often have fascinating stories to tell about their compositions. Unfortunately, we rarely get to hear those tales. Fortunately, there's a great book called Behind the Hits, *by Bob Shannon and John Javna, full of entertaining stories like these.*

LOLA, The Kinks

As songwriter Ray Davies recounts it, he was spending the evening with record producer Robert Wace at a nightclub; Wace was having a bit of luck with a particular young lady. "I'm really onto a good thing here," Wace told Davies, indicating the sultry black woman he was dancing with. But as the night wore on, Davies got a little suspicious. He noticed stubble on the chin of Wace's new girlfriend. Davies decided "she" was a man. Presumably, Wace was so smashed he couldn't tell the difference.

Davies recalls: "I had a few dances with it...him. It became kind of obvious. It's that thrust in the pelvic region when they're on the dance floor. It's never quite the same with a woman."

Davies wrote "Lola" about that incident. But he kept the language deliberately ambiguous ("I'm glad that I'm a man / And so is Lola"), so listeners would never be able to decide whether Lola was a man, a woman...or what.

HONOLULU LULU, Jan and Dean

In the early '60s, Roger Christian was one of the top deejays in L.A. He sometimes did live shows at high schools, and his friends, Jan and Dean, often performed with him. One graduation night after a grueling schedule of personal appearances, the exhausted Christian and Jan Berry decided to go to The Copper Penny, an all-night L.A. diner, for something to eat. The two of them co-wrote many of Jan and Dean's hits and this night, as they sat at the table, they started writing another one. They based it on a title that a record company executive had suggested—"Honolulu Lulu."

Christian scribbled the lyrics down on a napkin, and then they paid and left the restaurant. Out front, they said good night. "Give me the napkin," Jan said, "and I'll take it to the studio and write out the arrangements." "I don't have it—you do," Christian replied. "No I don't—you do." "Not me." Suddenly they realized that they'd left it on the table in the restaurant.

They bolted inside to retrieve it, but it was too late. The waitress had already cleared their dishes and everything had been thrown away. Roger and Jan sat down and tried to reconstruct the song, but they just couldn't get the lyrics to work like they had the first time. There was only one thing left to do. They went out to the back of the diner and started sorting through the contents of the dumpster, looking for their napkin in the dark. At about 4:00 A.M., they finally found it. The reward for their treasure hunt? "Honolulu Lulu" hit #11 on the national charts.

THEY'RE COMING TO TAKE ME AWAY, HA-HAAA!, Napoleon XIV

In 1966, a 28-year-old New York recording engineer named Jerry Samuels went into the studio to record a song that had no melody and needed almost no instruments. It was recited, not sung, and he used only drums and a tambourine to back himself up. The total cost for studio time was $15.

But if the production of the song was a little unusual, that was nothing compared to the content. Essentially, the "singer" went insane while he was reciting the lyrics. His voice began in a normal tone, and slowly went up until it was as high-pitched as the Chipmunks. What was making him crazy? His dog had run away.

The whole thing was completely bizarre...and very funny.

The first record company Samuels played it for, Warner Brothers, snapped it up. Within a week after releasing the record, more than 500,000 copies had been sold, making it the fastest-selling record in Warner's history.

Although it went on to sell over a million copies, "They're Coming To Take Me Away" was taken off the radio almost immediately. Mental health organizations protested that the record made fun of the mentally ill...and shouldn't receive airplay. That was Napoleon XIV's Waterloo; we never heard from him again.

Note: Samuels didn't have any money—or a song—to put on the flip side, so he just reversed the tape. He called it "Aaah-Ah Yawa Em Ekat Ot Gnimoc Er-Yeht."

I PUT A SPELL ON YOU, Screamin' Jay Hawkins

In the summer of 1954, Screamin' Jay Hawkins, a blues singer with seven records—all bombs—under his belt, was performing at a joint in Atlantic City called Herman's. In the middle of his set, his live-in girlfriend walked in, marched right up to the stage and tossed his house keys at him. Then she disappeared. It looked bad...and it was. Jay went home to find "Good-bye, my love" scrawled in lipstick on the bathroom mirror.

He plopped down on the bed and let out "the most painful" scream of his life. Then he began writing a "sweet ballad" that he hoped would get her back—"I Put a Spell on You."

Hawkins recorded it for the tiny Grand Records in Philadelphia, and it, too, took a dive. He couldn't get his lover back with that record—she never heard it.

It wasn't a total loss, though. In the meantime, Jay incorporated the song into his act and the head of Columbia Records, Arnold Matson, happened to see him perform it in a typically wild manner. Matson loved it. He signed Hawkins to the Okeh label (primarily Columbia's R&B label), and they went into the studio to do a version. But something was wrong. They tried take after take, and Matson still wasn't happy with it. It just wasn't as powerful as when Jay did it live. Why? "Is there something you do when you perform that you're not doing here?" Matson asked."Well," Jay told him, "I usually drink a bit when I'm on stage."

As Hawkins tells it: "So he brought in a case of Italian Swiss Colony muscatel and we all got our heads bent...We all got blind drunk." Hawkins couldn't even remember the session when it was over. "Ten days later the record came out. I listened to it and heard all those drunken groans and screams and yells. I thought, 'Oh, my god!'" It ended in a series of sexual moans, so many radio stations refused to play it. Even after Columbia remastered it to cut out the controversial ending, they couldn't get it on the air. So it never made the charts. But it did become a cult favorite, especially in live performances when Hawkins was carried out in a coffin, wore Dracula capes, and played with snakes. It has also been recorded dozens of times by artists like Creedence Clearwater Revival, and was the theme music for the 1984 cult film, *Stranger Than Paradise*.

Note: Jay got his girlfriend back. Not, ironically, because of "Spell," but because she liked the flip side, "Little Demon."

ROYAL PAINS

Gossip about some famous kings and a queen.

KING WENCESLAS

Was the Christmas carol about "Good King Wenceslas" accurate? Apparently not. The real Wenceslas was King of Bohemia and Holy Roman Emperor in the latter part of the 14th century. According to one source, he was a tyrant who "prowled the street with his cronies at night, breaking into houses, molesting his female subjects, and generally venting his feelings in a riot of cruelty."

He did love his hunting dogs, though; he even slept with them, over the objections of his wife, Johanna. (Even after one of the dogs attacked and killed her while she slept.)

MACBETH

There really was a Scottish king named Macbeth; he ruled from 1040 to 1057. But according to David Randall in *Royal Misbehavior*, "Although little is known about him, there is no evidence that he was the henpecked social climber portrayed by Shakespeare....[In fact], he was a good and strong enough ruler to survive on the throne for 17 years—which is more than 25 other occupants of that precarious hot spot can claim." Lady Macbeth, granddaughter of King Kenneth III, was known in her time as a "patron of the church"—not as the Shakespearean "royal bitch."

RICHARD THE LIONHEARTED

Maybe it's because of the legend of Robin Hood that Richard I is remembered as a righteous hero. But according to *Royal Misbehavior*: "He was in reality an absentee monarch who spent no more than ten months of a ten-year reign in England, left the country to the vagaries of his brother John and failed to produce an heir or even, it is said, consummate his marriage. Indeed, his sexual proclivities meant that Robin Hood and his chums were not the only young men...who followed the king with expectations."

IVAN THE TERRIBLE

Monarchs aren't often as fearsome as their nicknames imply. But Ivan IV, Czar of Russia in the mid-1500s, was worse. "As a child," writes one historian, "he amused himself by throwing cats and dogs from the [200-foot-high] towers of the Kremlin. As Czar, when a group of seventy citizens complained to him of injustices in their town, he ordered hot wine poured over their heads and had them lie naked in the snow. When it was rumored that the city of Novogorod was conspiring to defect to neighboring Lithuania, Ivan exterminated the city, torturing its citizens for five weeks and killing 60,000 people."

He was so terrifying that he could actually scare people to death. In 1569 the girl he'd picked to be his third wife had a heart attack and died when she heard the news.

CATHERINE THE GREAT

From *They Went That-A-Way*, by Malcolm Forbes: "What you've probably heard about the death of Russian Empress Catherine the Great is wrong. The poor maligned woman, insatiable lover that she was, did not die *in flagrante delicto* with a horse that, according to the famous rumor, crushed her when the truss broke. No, the 67-year-old ruler was alone when she collapsed, having dismissed her lover—a 27-year-old man—earlier that morning."

Apparently Catherine had a stroke in her dressing room and was found on the floor, unconscious. She died the following night without ever coming to.

KING FAROUK

The last king of Egypt was so corrupt that he once freed a pickpocket from jail just so the prisoner could teach him how to steal. Farouk became as adept at it. "At receptions and parties," says David Randall, "he would move among the company, brushing against dignitaries and their ladies and then slipping off into an ante-room [to] empty his pockets of watches, wallets, lighters, and powder compacts. Eventually an entire warehouse was filled with these items, which even included the ceremonial sword, belt, and medals stolen from the body of the Shah of Persia as the funeral procession passed through Egypt in 1944."

A FOOD IS BORN

Those brand names on your supermarket shelf had to come from somewhere, right? Here's the inside scoop on a few famous food products.

ANIMAL COOKIES. Cookies shaped like animals were introduced in England in the 1890s, but in 1902 Nabisco added something new. Recognizing the popularity of P.T. Barnum's "Greatest Show on Earth," they designed a box that looked like a circus cage, labeling it "Barnum's Animals." And to increase sales during the holiday season, they added a string handle that would allow parents to hang the boxes on Christmas trees.

TABASCO SAUCE. When Union troops in Louisiana occupied Avery Island and seized Edmund McIhenny's salt mines in 1862, he and his wife fled to Texas. They returned after the war to find that everything they owned had been destroyed—except for a crop of capsicum hot peppers. Desperate, McIhenny decided to try to make a sauce that he could sell to raise money. He aged a concoction of salt, vinegar and peppers in wooden barrels, and poured it into tiny old cologne bottles. He called his creation "tabasco sauce," after Mexico's Tabasco river, because he liked the name.

WORCESTERSHIRE SAUCE. When Sir Marcus Sandys, a British nobleman, returned to England from Bengal in the mid-1800s, he brought with him a recipe for a spicy sauce he had tasted in the Orient. He showed it to some chemists he knew in his home county of Worcestershire—John Lea and William Perrins—and asked them to reproduce the sauce exclusively for his use. Lea and Perrins agreed, but over time the sauce became so popular that Sandys gave them permission to sell it to other customers—and eventually sold them the recipe—which the Lea & Perrins Company uses to this day.

DUNCAN HINES. Duncan Hines was a traveling restaurant critic in the 1930s. His book *Adventures in Good Eating*—a guide to restaurants along major highways—was so popular that his name be-

Can't sleep at night? Soak your feet in hot water for 10 minutes. It draws

came a household word. Hines' notoriety attracted the attention of Roy Park, a New York businessman who was looking for a way to promote his new line of baked goods. He asked Hines to become a partner in the company, and Hines agreed. Together they formed Hines-Park Foods, Inc. in 1948. Their line of cake mixes captured 48% of the American cake mix market in less than *three weeks*.

YUBAN COFFEE. John Arbuckle, a turn-of-the-century Brooklyn merchant, sold his own popular blend of coffee. He needed a brand name for it, and decided to make one up using the letters that appeared on the shipments of coffee beans he received:

A B
N Y

(Arbuckle Brothers, New York) The combination he liked best was Yban. But it still wasn't quite right—so he added the letter u.

LOG CABIN SYRUP. P.J. Towle, a St. Paul, Minnesota grocer, was the first person to blend expensive maple syrup with other, more affordable syrups without losing the maple taste. A big fan of Abraham Lincoln, Towle decided to name the syrup Log Cabin in his honor—and sold it in cabin-shaped tin containers.

ORVILLE REDENBACHER'S POPCORN. In the 1950s an agronomist named Orville Redenbacher developed a hybrid strain of popcorn with a higher moisture content than regular corn—resulting in fluffier kernels and fewer "old maids" per batch. But popcorn companies refused to buy it—they insisted the public wanted *cheap* popcorn, not *good* popcorn. Redenbacher disagreed. He began selling to the public directly. Today Orville Redenbacher's is the best selling popcorn in the U.S.

• • •

WEIGHTING FOR A TRAIN

U.S. President William Taft weighed over 300 pounds. He used it to his advantage: once while stranded at a train station in the country, he was told that the express only stopped for "large parties." He sent a wire to the conductor saying "Stop at Hicksville. Large party waiting to catch train." Once on board, he explained: "You can go ahead. I am the large party."

blood away from your brain and makes you sleepy.

TV OR NOT TV?

What's a Bathroom Reader without a little TV trivia?

THE PARTRIDGE FAMILY
Love them or hate them, *The Partridge Family* made money. Their show, records, and licensed merchandise reportedly earned $11 million a year. In addition, more than 200,000 people paid $2 each for membership in their fan club—and the *Partridge Family Magazine* sold 400,000 copies a month. They even had 7 hit singles—in spite of the fact that none of them played on the records, and only David Cassidy and Shirley Jones sang on them.

THE LOVE BOAT. This show was based on *The Love Boats:* a novel written by a former cruise hostess. She based it on her own experiences.

• The show was always filmed on a real cruise ship, with passengers acting as extras. But before the show's success, it was difficult to get passengers to cooperate; they complained that the film crew was in their way.

THE BRADY BUNCH. Executive producer Sherwood Schwartz interviewed 464 girls and boys to find the right Brady kids. He hadn't picked the adult leads yet, but he knew he wanted the kids to have the same color hair as their "parents." His solution: he picked two sets of Brady boys, and two sets of Brady girls (blonde and brunette). When Robert Reed and Florence Henderson were chosen to play the parents, he dumped the kids he didn't need.

I DREAM OF JEANNIE. Although network censors had no objection to Barbara Eden's sexy costume or the fact that Jeannie was living with a man for whom she would do anything (anything?), they *did* object to her navel showing. The solution: she had to put a cloth plug in it so it wouldn't show on film.

• Scripts were written by novelist Sidney Sheldon, who was writing scripts for "The Patty Duke Show" at the same time.

The only Hitchcock film to win the Oscar for best film of the year was *Rebecca*, in 1940.

TWO THUMBS DOWN

Are book reviews believable? When they're good reviews of Uncle John's Bathroom Reader *they are, of course. But consider these true-life comments, quoted in* Rotten Reviews *by Bill Henderson*

Subject: *Wuthering Heights*, by Emily Brönte
Reviewer's Comment: "The only consolation we have in reflecting upon it is that it will never be generally read." —James Lorimer, *North British Review*

Subject: *Gulliver's Travels*, by Jonathan Swift
Reviewer's Comment: "Evidence of a diseased mind and lacerated heart." —John Dunlop, *The History of Fiction*

Subject: *Romeo & Juliet*, by William Shakespeare:
Reviewer's Comment: "March 1 [1662]. Saw *Romeo and Juliet*, the first time it was ever acted; but it is a play of itself the worst that ever I heard in my life, and the worst acted that ever I saw these people do." —Samuel Pepys, *Diary*

Subject: *Alice in Wonderland*, by Lewis Carroll
Reviewer's Comment: "We fancy that any real child might be more puzzled than enchanted by this stiff, overwrought story." —*Children's Books*.

Subject: A *Tale of Two Cities*, by Charles Dickens
Reviewer's Comment: "It was a sheer dead pull from start to finish. It all seemed so insincere, such a transparent make-believe, a mere piece of acting."—John Burroughs, *Century* magazine

Subject: *Anna Karenina*, by Leo Tolstoy
Reviewer's Comment: " Sentimental rubbish ...Show me one page that contains an idea." —*The Odessa Courier*

Subject: A *Doll's House*, by Henrik Ibsen
Reviewer's Comment: "It is as though someone had dramatized the cooking of a sunday dinner."—Clement Scott, *Sporting & Dramatic News*

The cracks in a piece of breaking glass travel faster than 3,000 miles per hour.

Subject: *Moby Dick*, by Herman Melville
Reviewer's Comment: "A huge dose of hyperbolic slang, maudlin sentimentalism and tragic-comic bubble and squeak."—Willima Harrison Ainsworth, *New Monthly Magazine*

Subject: *The Great Gatsby*, by F. Scott Fitzgerald
Reviewer's Comment: "A little slack, a little soft, more than a little artificial, *The Great Gatsby* falls into the class of negligible novels."—*The Springfield Republican*

Subject: *The Sun Also Rises*, by Ernest Hemingway
Reviewer's Comment: "His characters are as shallow as the saucers in which they stack their daily emotions, and instead of interpreting his material—or even challenging it—he has been content merely to make a carbon copy of a not particularly significant surface life of Paris."—*The Dial*

Subject: *From Here to Eternity*, by James Jones
Reviewer's Comment: "Certainly America has something better to offer the world, along with its arms and armies, than such a confession of spiritual vacuum as this."—*Christian Science Monitor*

Subject: *Babbitt*, by Sinclair Lewis
Reviewer's Comment:"As a humorist, Mr. Lewis makes valiant attempts to be funny; he merely succeeds in being silly. In fact it is as yellow a novel as novel can be."—*Boston Evening Transcript*

AND THE MOTHER OF ALL "ROTTEN REVIEWS"

Subject: *Lady Chatterly's Lover*, by D. H. Lawrence:
Reviewer's Comments:"This pictorial account of the day-by-day life of an English gamekeeper is full of considerable interest to outdoor minded readers, as it contains many passages on pheasant-raising, the apprehending of poachers, ways to control vermin, and other chores and duties of the professional gamekeeper. Unfortunately, one is obliged to wade through many pages of extraneous material in order to discover and savor these sidelights on the management of a midland shooting estate, and in this reviewer's opinion the book cannot take the place of J. R. Miller's *Practical Gamekeeping*." —Ed Zern, *Field & Stream*

KENNEDY QUOTES

Robert Kennedy's legacy is his idealism...and his fatalism. A few of the comments he left for us:

"One-fifth of the people are against everything all the time."

"I should like to love my country and still love justice."

"Some men see things as they are and ask, 'Why?' I dream of things that could be and ask, 'Why not?' "

"My views on birth control are distorted by the fact that I was seventh of nine children."

"Who knows if any of us will still be alive in 1972? Existence is so fickle, fate is so fickle."

"We give our money and go back to our homes and...our swimming pools and wonder, 'Why don't they keep quiet, why don't they go away?' "

"A revolution is coming—a revolution which will be peaceful if we are wise enough; compassionate if we care enough; successful if we are fortunate enough—but a revolution is coming whether we will it or not. We can affect its character; we cannot alter its inevitability."

"[Freedom] proposes ends, but it does not propose means."

"Every society gets the kind of criminal it deserves."

"What is dangerous about extremists is not that they are extreme, but that they are intolerant. The evil is not what they say about their cause, but what they say about their opponents."

(On learning of his brother's assassination). "I thought they'd get one of us, but Jack, after all he's been through, never worried about it...I thought it would be me."

"Did the CIA kill my brother?"

"With all the violence and killings we've had in the United States, I think you will agree that we must keep firearms from people who have no business with guns." (5 days later, he was assassinated.)

The emperor penguin can dive to depths of 870 ft. for as long as 18 minutes.

REMEMBER THE MAINE!

In 1898, America declared war against Spain. But was it caused by Spanish atrocities or newspaper profits? Here's information from a new book, It's a Conspiracy, *by the American Paranoid Society.*

BACKGROUND

Itching for a Fight

In the late 1890s, America was bursting at the seams. Having reached the end of its frontier, the nation now looked for new lands to conquer and causes to fight for. As young Teddy Roosevelt, put it, "I should welcome almost any war, for I think this country needs one."

The Newspaper Wars

• Had Roosevelt worked for a New York City newspaper, he would have found all the fighting he wanted. The city's dailies were locked in a fierce struggle for circulation.

• With seemingly endless millions to spend, young William Randolph Hearst from California bought the *New York Journal* and took on the city's largest daily, the *World.* He started by cutting the paper's price to a penny, though he lost money doing it. Then, to further outrage the *World's* publisher, Joseph Pulitzer, Hearst lured away his most talented people with strapping raises.

• But the real war was on the front pages, and its biggest casualty was the truth. Both papers favored "crime, underwear and indignation." So when Cuban separatists tried to overthrow the rotting empire of Spain, the dailies fought to make each dispatch more lurid than the last.

Extra! Extra!

• Sample from the *World:* "No man's life, no man's property is safe. American citizens are imprisoned or slain without cause...Blood on the roadsides, blood in the fields, blood on the doorsteps, blood, blood, blood!"

• Sample headline from the *Journal*, responding to a Spanish diplomat's remark—in a private letter—that President McKinley was "a low politician":

"THE WORST INSULT TO THE UNITED STATES IN ITS HISTORY!"

DATELINE, CUBA

• Offended by press attacks against them, Spanish authorities in Cuba restricted U.S. reporters to Havana. In response, the U.S.S. *Maine* was sent to Havana harbor, "to protect American interests." A quiet three weeks passed. Then, on February 15, 1898, the *Maine* was sunk by a mysterious explosion; 260 men died.

• The *Maine*'s Captain Sigsbee, cabled Washington, "Many killed and wounded...Don't send war vessels...Public opinion should be suspended until further report."

• When Spain's captain-general in charge of Cuba heard the news, he "burst into tears...and sent officers to express regret and organize assistance." The Spanish, joined by a U.S. Navy team, began investigating the cause of the explosion immediately. Their findings were eventually released on March 17.

JUMPING THE GUN

The papers couldn't wait, though. Hearst's *Journal* led the cry for war with headlines like:

"The Warship Maine Was Split In Two By An Enemy's Secret Infernal Machine" (Feb. 17)

"The Whole Country Thrills With The War Fever" (Feb. 18)

"Havana...insults The Memory Of The Maine Victims" (Feb. 23)

"War! Sure!" (March 1)

• Although the Spanish government finally met the United States' demands about freedom for Cuba—and President McKinley urged restraint—most Americans were howling for war. For example, "Frank James, ex-bandit brother of the legendary Jesse, offered to lead a company of cowboys."

• Ultimately, though, the decision rested on the Navy's findings.

Napoleon conquered Italy at the age of twenty-six.

OFFICIAL EXPLANATION

The Naval Court of Inquiry found that "the *Maine* was destroyed by the explosion of a submarine mine"; however, it was "unable to obtain evidence fixing the responsibility...upon any person or persons." America went to war.

SUSPICIOUS FACTS

• In addition to Captain Sigsbee's plea to withhold judgment, the *Journal*'s first dispatch from Cuba was also uncertain: "The injured do not know what caused the explosion. There is some doubt as to whether the explosion took place on the *Maine*."

• According to *The Yellow Kids*, "The Navy's new coal-powered warships...like the Maine [had] coal bunkers located near the ship's [gunpowder] magazines. There had been at least a dozen reported incidents on American ships in the previous year, and during one fire...sparks actually ignited wooden ammunition crates before the blaze was brought under control."

• The Navy Secretary "publicly announced his opinion that an explosion in the *Maine*'s magazine had caused the accident," and McKinley himself thought "the catastrophe had resulted from an internal explosion."

• Two days after the explosion, the navy's leading expert on explosives told a reporter that "no torpedo [or mine] as is known to modern warfare can of itself cause an explosion as powerful as that which destroyed the *Maine*."

WAS THERE A CONSPIRACY?

Theory #1: YES. William Randolph Hearst started a war with Spain to boost circulation. His quote to artist Frederick Remington is well-known: "You supply the pictures, I'll supply the war."

• On either side of the *Journal*'s front-page masthead ran the blurb, "How Do You Like The *Journal*'s War?"—until even Hearst saw its tastelessness and removed it.

• If it was a conspiracy, it worked: For the first week after the explosion, the *Journal* averaged 8-1/2 pages on the *Maine*. And the paper's circulation "soared from 416,885 copies on January 9th to 1,036,140 on February 18th."

Theory #2: YES. But the navy was also complicit. Unless the Naval Court of Inquiry found that Spain was guilty, it would have had to admit the Navy had been negligent.

• In August, 1897, a bunker fire interrupted a dinner party Captain Sigsbee was hosting on the *Maine*. As he helped his guests down the gangplank he said, "Gentlemen, you have had a narrow escape tonight."

• During the inquiry, Sigsbee likely perjured himself. Although he was vague and "unfamiliar with the ship," he claimed that the day of the explosion he had personally inspected the bunker wall and found it cool. Nobody on the panel believed him.

• Although the navy report was supposed to be delivered to the White House under the strictest confidentiality, its findings were published in the *Journal* before President McKinley even opened the secret document.

Theory #3: NO. American industrialists needed a war to distract the public; Hearst was just a bit player, albeit a noisy one.

• A depression had begun in 1893 and showed no signs of ending soon. This was causing widespread strikes, farm revolts and a dramatic growth of the Populist movement.

• As one industrialist put it, "A little war will knock the pus out of Populism." Another noted that "it will take men's minds off domestic concerns."

• With the American frontier used up, untouched lands overseas would give businesses new lands to exploit.

• The American people were undoubtedly whipped up by Hearst and his ilk, but they overwhelmingly supported the war, at least as a fight for Cuban liberty.

RANDOM QUOTE:

"The last thing I could imagine is moving in with three other friends, no matter how much I liked them."

—Betty White, star of "Golden Girls."

The White House's first telephone was installed by Alexander Graham Bell.

GOING THROUGH A PHRASE

Here are some well-known phrases and the stories behind them.

TURN A BLIND EYE

Meaning: To ignore something.

Background: Captain Horatio Nelson of the British Navy was blind in one eye. In 1801, he was part of a force attacking French troops in Copenhagen, Denmark. As the tide of battle turned, the command ship signaled for Nelson to withdraw, but Nelson wanted to continue fighting. When he was told that his commander was signalling, Nelson held his telescope up to his sightless eye and declared that he could not see any signal. He continued his attack ...and won.

CHARLEY HORSE

Meaning: A muscle cramp.

Background: In 1640 Charles I of England expanded the London police force. The new recruits were nicknamed "Charleys." There wasn't enough money to provide the new police with horses, so they patrolled on foot. They joked that their sore feet and legs came from riding "Charley's horse."

BURY THE HATCHET

Meaning: To make peace with an enemy.

Background: Some Native American tribes declared peace by literally burying a tomahawk in the ground.

SPEAK OF THE DEVIL

Meaning: Someone appears after you mention him or her.

Background: People believed that you could actually summon the devil by saying his name (to be safe, they used nicknames and euphemisms like "the Deuce"). Over time, the expression was used to jokingly imply that your friend was "Old Nick" himself.

AT THE END OF YOUR ROPE

Meaning: Exhausted all possibilities; out of options.

Background: Horsemen tied their horses to trees with long lengths of rope so they could graze a large area of land. But when the horse ate all the grass within its reach, it was out of luck, literally "at the end of its rope." An alternate but equally plausible explanation for the phrase has to do with being strung up on the gallows.

SOW WILD OATS

Meaning: Commit youthfully foolish acts.

Background: In the 11th century, when England was in the midst of its perpetual war against invaders, many farms were left to go fallow for years, even decades. Many of the grains which had been domesticated over generations reverted to their wild strains. When things settled down on the war front, a lot of the younger men had no experience farming and—eager to get on with it—collected seeds from the wild strains of oats, which grew great leaves and trunks, but few of the "heads" which contain the edible seeds. The plants weren't even worth harvesting.

WHITE ELEPHANT

Meaning: A costly but unwanted object.

Background: When the kings of ancient Siam didn't like someone, they sometimes "honored" them with a rare, sacred White Elephant. The beasts cost a fortune to feed and keep in style befitting their high station—but because they were considered sacred, they couldn't be expected to work like normal elephants.

TO BE AT LOOSE ENDS

Meaning: Frazzled and disorganized

Background: On old sailing ships, hundreds of ropes went everywhere. If they were allowed to unravel, they quickly became a tangled, disorganized mess. A mark of a good sea captain became the condition of his neatly taped "ends"; you could tell an inefficient and disorganized ship by its number of loose ends.

Random Quote: "People don't have much of a sense of humor when they themselves are victimized." —William F. Buckley

The first electric toothbrush was developed and tested on dogs. They reportedly enjoyed it.

PASS THE KETCHUP

Can you imagine life without ketchup? One BRI member tells the story of a French visitor who automatically started to pour ketchup on pancakes. When the host stopped him, the surprised visitor asked "Don't Americans put ketchup on everything? *Here's a little ketchup history.*

ORIGIN. The Chinese invented *ke-tsiap*—a concoction of pickled fish and spices (but no tomatoes)—in the 1690s. By the early 1700s its popularity had spread to Malaysia, where British explorers first encountered it. By 1740 the sauce—renamed *ketchup*—was an English staple, and was becoming popular in the American colonies.

A BAD APPLE

Tomato ketchup wasn't invented until the 1790s, when New England colonists first mixed tomatoes into the sauce. Why did it take so long to add tomatoes? People were afraid to eat them. The tomato is a close relative of the toxic belladonna and nightshade plants; most people assumed the tomato was also poisonous. Thomas Jefferson helped dispel the myth; his highly publicized love of tomatoes helped popularize them.

KETCHUP FACTS

• Homemade tomato ketchup starts out as a watery gruel that has to be boiled down into a thick sauce—an all-day project that requires hours of stirring. Housewives of the 1870s loved the sauce, but they hated making it. So when Henry J. Heinz began selling bottled ketchup in 1875, he promoted it as a labor-saving device. He used the slogan "blessed relief for Mother and the other women of the household." Today more than half the ketchup sold in the U.S. is made by the H.J. Heinz Co.

• Note: Have you ever poured ketchup on something, wrapped it in aluminum foil, and then noticed later that there were holes in the foil? The ketchup is to blame; it's highly acidic and can actually dissolve small amounts of aluminum if it remains in contact with the metal long enough.

The average American uses two pine trees' worth of paper products each year.

GLASSIFIED INFORMATION

You don't have to throw glass bottles and containers out with the trash; they're recyclable. Here are more recycling tips from The Recycler's Handbook, *by the EarthWorks Group*

It's interesting to listen to people talk about why they like glass. The appeal is more than just being able to recycle it easily—they like the way it looks and feels, too.

It's an ancient attraction. Glass bottles and jars have been a part of human culture for more than 3,000 years. We've been recycling them just about that long, too. In fact, it's conceivable that some of the glass you'll use today was once part of a bottle used by Richard the Lion-Hearted or Catherine the Great.

Of course it's not likely, but so what? The point is that recycling glass is a time-honored tradition. It's up to us to keep it going for the next 3,000 years.

A TOUCH OF GLASS

- Before recycled glass is shipped to manufacturers, it's broken so it'll take up less space. This broken glass is called "cullet."
- When it arrives at the glass factory, the cullet is run through a device which removes metal rings from bottles. A vacuum process removes plastic coatings and paper labels.
- When it's "clean," the cullet is added to raw materials and melted down with them. Most bottles and jars contain at least 25% recycled glass.
- Glass never wears out—it can be recycled forever.

WHY RECYCLE?

- We save over a ton of resources for every ton of glass recycled. (If you want specifics, it's 1,330 pounds of sand, 433 pounds of soda ash, 433 pounds of limestone, and 151 pounds of feldspar.)
- A ton of glass produced from raw materials creates 384 pounds of

mining waste. Using 50% recycled glass cuts it by about 75%.

• We get 27.8 pounds of air pollution for every ton of new glass produced. Recycling glass reduces that pollution by 14-20%.

• Recycling glass saves 25-32% of the energy used to make glass.

• Glass makes up about 8% of America's municipal garbage.

SIMPLE THINGS YOU CAN DO

1. Precycle

• Look for refillable bottles. They're the most energy and material efficient; they can be sterilized and reused up to seven times before recycling.

• Refillables aren't easy to find any more. But if enough consumers speak up at local supermarkets, they'll reappear on shelves. Case in point: Washington's Rainier Brewery, citing its customers' environmental concerns, has recently returned to using refillables for all its single serving bottles.

• An easy way to manage refillables: Get one of the sturdy crates they come in, and store "empties" in it. When the crates are full, take them to the store and exchange the empties for full bottles.

• In some areas of the Midwest and Mountain states, glass is not accepted because there's no market for it. In these areas, consider buying aluminum cans, which are recycled virtually everywhere.

2. Store It

• It's safer to pack bottles in boxes or bins than in bags.

• Don't leave the bottles in six-pack carriers; that makes extra processing work for recyclers (they have to remove the bottles).

• If you're selling your glass at a buyback center or dropping it off, you'll probably have to separate it into brown, green and clear glass. The reason: To make recycling profitable, glass factories need to turn brown glass into brown bottles, etc. If colors are mixed, the end product is an unpredictable hue. Glass factories don't like it because their orders are for specific colors.

• If you have any blue or other colored glass containers, recycle them with the brown or green glass—but only in small amounts.

Giraffes can live longer without water than camels can.

• If the glass is even slightly tinted, sort as colored, not as clear.

• Broken bottles can be recycled, but not everyone accepts them.

• Curbside programs generally accept all colors mixed together; sorting occurs later. Keep glass unbroken if possible—it's easier for the recycling crew to handle.

3. Recycle

• Remove lids and caps. You can recycle steel caps with steel cans. (Plastic cap liners are no problem). For aluminum caps, check with the recycling center before including them with aluminum cans.

• It's okay to leave on neck rings, paper and plastic labels—they burn or blow off in the recycling process.

• Dump out food residue and lightly rinse bottles. Old food attracts animals, it's a mess for recyclers, and it stinks. Be sure to empty beer bottles. A drop of beer can turn into a slimy mold.

• Remove rocks and dirt from bottles found in parks, beaches, etc. Even a little stone can ruin a whole load of glass.

4. Absolutely Don't Include...

• Windows, drinking glasses, mirrors, Pyrex (baking dishes, coffee pots, etc.), or other glass. Any of these can ruin an entire batch of glass if they slip through at the factory. The reason: They don't melt at the same temperature as bottles.

• Ceramics (coffee mugs, mustard jars, plates, etc.). They don't melt down with the glass, so they contaminate it.

IF YOUR STATE HAS A "BOTTLE BILL..."

• Not all states accept the same bottles for redemption. Some take only beer and soft drink bottles; others include juice or liquor bottles. Check with stores or recycling centers.

• General Rules: Empty bottles; you may need to sort them by brand to get your deposit back. Broken bottles aren't redeemable.

SOURCES

"Glass Recycling: Why? How?" The Glass Packaging Institute, 1801 K St. N.W., Suite 1105-L, Washington, D.C. 20006.

ELVIS TRIVIA

It's become a Bathroom Reader tradition to include a few sections on The King in every book. Here are bits of Elvis gossip.

Elvis didn't sing well enough to make his high school glee club.

★

Although he has received many co-writing credits, Elvis never wrote a song. His manager (Col. Tom Parker) simply told songwriters that Elvis wouldn't record their songs unless he got credit—and half the royalties.

★

Over the years, Elvis bought more than 100 Cadillacs and gave away around 20 of them. The first one he bought was a pink one for his mom.

★

There are 50 dogs named Elvis registered in Los Angeles county.

★

Elvis's favorite sandwich: grilled peanut butter and banana.

★

Elvis's 1956 two-sided hit, "Hound Dog"/"Don't Be Cruel," is the most popular jukebox selection of all time.

Every day the U.S. Postal Service receives at least one letter on the advisability of issuing an Elvis stamp. Mail is currently running 6 to 1 in favor.

★

According to one author, in 1960 Elvis began secretly dating Frank Sinatra's girlfriend, Juliet Prowse. Sinatra found out and one night showed up at Elvis's dressing room with two "unpleasant companions." Frank and friends "discussed Presley's continued good health." Elvis refused to return Prowse's calls after that.

★

If it wasn't for Colonel Parker torpedoing the offers, Elvis could have starred in *Midnight Cowboy* and opposite Barbra Streisand in *A Star is Born*.

★

Elvis' autopsy revealed that he had at least 10 different drugs in his system at the time of death. Official cause of death: heart failure brought on by "straining at stool." Translation: he died on the pot.

Rule of thumb: Widowed, divorced, and separated people smoke more than other people.

UNCLE JOHN'S BATHROOM CATALOG

Looking for some "singing" toilet paper? How about "tinkle time targets"? No bathroom reader's bathroom is complete without them. Here are a few key bathroom items you can order by mail.

The Little Plastic Cup

"Everybody's had to do it. The nurse tells you to go into the bathroom at the end of the hall and 'give us a sample.' And how many times have you sat in there until they had to come looking for you and you had to confess, sheepishly, that you 'just couldn't.' Now you can practice at home, and train yourself to avoid the embarrassment (or relive the thrill, if that's your thing)."

Specimen cup,
Item No. 20120

5 oz. Jerryco Inc.
601 Linden Place
Evanston, IL 60202

Tinkle Targets

"Teaching your little boys to aim properly when they're being toilet trained (and after) can be a trying chore. This'll turn boys of any age into sharpshooters. Each pack contains 45 colorful, flushable, non-staining targets. Just float one in the bowl and fire away."

Tinkle Targets
Item # G225

The Right Start Catalog
Right Start Plaza
5334 Sterling Center Drive
Westlake Village, CA 91361

Pink Flamingo Toilet Paper

"Flamingo toilet tissue can help you with any impossible bathroom decorating task. This is an exclusive "The Cat's Pyjamas" design; order their catalog and check out some of their other great flamingo bathroom items like shower curtains, toothbrush holders and towel bars."

Flamingo Toilet Paper
Item # CP756

The Cat's Pyjamas
20 Church Street
Montclair, NJ 07042

Gag Black-Hands Soap

"Looks like regular designer soap, the manufacturers claim. But nobody would guess that when they wash their hands, the black color comes off the soap and stays on them. Easy way to tell which of your friends habitually 'forgets' to wash hands after using the bathroom."

Black Soap
Item # 2419

Johnson Smith Company
4514 19th Court East
PO Box 25500
Bradenton, FL 34206-5500

Toity Tunes

"'A musical novelty! Makes your toilet paper sing!' reads the colorful hang tag. And the battery is INCLUDED! This ingenious, maddening, little electronic device slips inside the toilet paper roll. When the tissue is pulled, what sounds like a mosquito orchestra starts loudly playing one of these old favorites: Christmas Medley, Happy Birthday, My Favorite Things, Home Sweet Home, Wedding March, Love Me Tender, Yesterday, Twinkle Twinkle Little Star, It's a Small World, Over the Rainbow, You Are My Sunshine, When the Saints Go Marching In, and our favorite: The Star Spangled Banner, since true patriots will leap to attention when this starts to play…"

Toity Tunes

Funny Side Up.
25 Stump Rd.
N. Wales, PA 19454

• • •

FROM OUR MUHAMMAD ALI FILES:

Just before takeoff on a commercial flight, a stewardess asked Ali to make sure his seat belt was fastened. "Superman don't need no seat belt," he protested. She answered: "Superman don't need no airplane, either." He fastened it.

Franklin D. Roosevelt was related by blood or marriage to 11 other presidents.

DRIVE-IN MOVIES

Although they've all but disappeared from the American landscape, drive-in movies were once the coolest thing around.

THE BIRTH OF THE DRIVE-IN

Richard M. Hollingshead Jr. had friends over one summer night in the late 1920s to see his home movies. It was a hot night, and the projector just made it hotter. Seeing his guests' discomfort, the inventor and businessman had an idea—why not show his movies outside?

He put his projector on the hood of the family's model T and projected image onto the white wall of his garage. His guests—and eventually the whole neighborhood—lounged on his car seats and lawn furniture.

Hollingshead knew he had a hit when his guests asked to see more of his home movies. While the picture flickered in front of his eyes, he started thinking about business possibilities.

COMMERCIAL POTENTIAL

His first idea was that gas stations could keep their patrons amused with short comedies or nature films while filling their tanks. That idea went nowhere. Then one night, he had a vision of an all-car outdoor movie theater where people could watch in the privacy and comfort of their own cars. He started tinkering with the idea, even watching films with his lawn sprinkler going to see if it was possible to watch a movie during a rain storm.

THE REAL THING

"The World's First Automobile Movie Theater" opened on May 6, 1933 at 2601 Admiral Wilson Boulevard in Camden, New Jersey. It was primitive, yet brilliant—room for 400 cars in seven rows of parking spots tilted at a 5% grade for better reclining and visibility. The site was provided by V. V. Smith, an early investor who happened to have made his fortune in parking lots. On opening night some 600 customers paid 25¢ per car plus 25¢ per person ($1.00 tops) to see *Wife Beware* starring Adolph Menjou.

George Washington, Thomas Jefferson, and John Adams played marbles even as adults.

Hollingshead had some trouble with sound. At first he embedded speakers in the ground under each car space, but the floorboards muffled the sounds. Next, he tried huge speakers on either side of the screen. Now everybody in cars could hear every word perfectly—but so could the unhappy neighbors and the freeloaders who watched from just outside the theatre boundary. He abandoned that, too, and next tried individual car speakers hanging on the car windows. Perfect.

Unfortunately, Hollingshead was ahead of his time. Film distributors, seeing the drive-in as a threat to indoor theatres, charged exorbitantly high rental prices and withheld their best first-runs. In 1935, a disgusted Hollingshead sold his theater.

RISE & FALL

But soon after, drive-in movies caught on. The baby boom of the late 1940s was also an automobile boom. People quickly discovered they could dress casually, bring their own food, smoke, talk, steam up the windows, and bring the kids without paying for a sitter. For teens, roomy back seats provided an arena for love's wrestling matches. The marriage of car and movie seemed perfect.

But not for long. Encroaching suburbia drove up cheap rural land prices, cars got smaller, TV became popular, the opportunities for sexual ecounters expanded, and the quality of the drive-in film fare declined from first run to B-minus. Drive-ins began disappearing from across the landscape, including Hollingshead's original one—its former site is now occupied by a fur store.

DRIVE-IN FACTS

• Some drive-in theatres even offered drive-in church services on Sunday morning. You didn't have to dress up and you said "Amen!" by honking your horn.

• In the late 1950s and early 1960s, over 4,000 drive-ins operated across the U.S.

• There are only about 1,000 operational drive-ins now. The National Association of Drive-In Operators is defunct.

Alaska does not have a state motto.

NAME THAT TOWN

The origins of the names of cities and towns are sometimes more interesting than the places themselves.

Place: Anaconda, Montana

Background: In Copperopolis, Montana during the Civil War, owners of the local copper mine were strong supporters of the Union cause. Late in the war, word reached them that General Grant's troops were circling Genreral Lee's troops "like an anaconda"—the large snake that wraps itself around its prey and squeezes it to death. To celebrate, they changed the mine's name to Anaconda, and the town eventually followed suit.

Places: Bushong and Latham, Kansas

Background: In the 1880s, workers for the Missouri Pacific railroad were building a new line through Kansas. To celebrate the success of their hometown baseball team, the St. Louis Browns (who were in the middle of a winning streak) they named 14 stations on the line for their favorite players. Twelve of the stations have been renamed, but Arlie Latham (shortstop) and Doc Bushong (pitcher) are still on the map in Kansas.

Place: Pullman, Washington

Background: The citizens of this community decided to name their town after George M. Pullman, the rich manufacturer of the Pullman Car...hoping he would shower his namesake with new libraries and other civic gifts. When they invited him to the ceremonies, he sent his regrets, a nice thank you note and a check for $50. That was the last the town heard from him.

Place: Eighty Eight, Kentucky

Background: Dabney Nunnally was the postmaster of a village 8.8 miles from Glasgow, KY. His handwriting was unreadable, but he could scrawl legible numbers. "Let's call our place 88," he proposed. "I can write that so anybody can read it." Unfortunately for Nunnally, the government insisted that the name be spelled out.

Place: Old Glory, Texas

Background: Before World War I, this town was called Brandenburg. But anti-German sentiment ran so high during the war that no one wanted to live in a place that sounded German.

Place: Naughty Girl Meadow, Arizona

Background: The US Board of Geographic Names wouldn't allow them to use the real name—Whorehouse Meadow.

Place: Lufkin, Texas

Background: Surveyor E. P. Lufkin was laying out a railroad route, and some of his workers were jailed in nearby Homer, Texas for drunkenness. In retaliation, Luflkin rerouted the tracks to miss Homer completely. The newly located station, which he named for himself, flourished; Homer disappeared.

Place: Modesto, California

Background: Named because the founders were too "modest" to name it after themselves.

Place: Truth or Consequences, New Mexico

Background: In 1950, the hit radio show *Truth or Consequences* offered free publicity and valuable prizes to any town that would change its name. Hot Springs, NM quickly volunteered and even named the park in the center of town Ralph Edwards Park, after the game show's host

Place: Titusville, Florida

Background: In 1873, Henry Titus and Charles Rice decided to play a game of dominoes to decide who to name the town after.

Place: Tarzana, California

Background: Named after Tarzan to honor his creator, Edgar Rice Burroughs, who lived there for many years.

The only known meteorite fatality was a dog hit in Egypt in 1922.

THE PRESS & THE PREZ

Presidents and the press have a peculiar love-hate relationship. Here are some anecdotes from If No News, Send Rumors, *a great bathroom reader by Stephen Bates.*

When Paul Hume of the *Washington Post* wrote a harsh critique of Margaret Truman's singing debut, her father Harry wrote back, " I have just read your lousy review buried in the back pages. You sound like a frustrated old man who never made a success, an eight-ulcer man on a four-ulcer job and all four ulcers working. I never met you, but if I do you'll need a new nose and a supporter below."

President Franklin Roosevelt inscribed a photo of himself for the White House press room: "From their victim."

During a trip to India, President Jimmy Carter was shown a pit filled with cow manure, which generated methane gas for energy. ABC's Sam Donaldson said, "If I fell in, you'd pull me out, wouldn't you, Mr. President?" Carter replied, "Certainly—after a suitable interval."

Reporters covering the Kennedys once submitted a detailed questionnaire inquiring about the family's new dog. The First Lady filled it out. When she reached the question, "What do you feed the dog," she wrote: "Reporters."

On his desk President Reagan's press secretary, Larry Speakes, posted a sign: "You don't tell us how to stage the news, and we don't tell you how to cover it."

After the Apollo 11 astronauts returned to earth, President Nixon arranged to send fragments of moon rocks to world leaders. He remarked privately that he hoped to find some "contaminated" pieces to send to reporters.

When he was angry at reporters, Pres. [Franklin] Roosevelt sometimes punished them directly. Once, for example, he ordered Robert Post of the *New York Times* to wear a dunce cap and stand in the corner.

During his 1983 visit to Japan, President Reagan gave a speech praising freedom of the press. At his request, the entire speech was off the record.

After Washington Post reporter Judith Martin described Tricia Nixon as a "24-year-old woman dressed like an ice cream cone who can give neatness and cleanliness a bad name," the White House told Martin she would not be allowed to cover Tricia's wedding.

On Richard Nixon's post-resignation flight to San Clemente, he wandered back through Air Force One. The rear section had previously held reporters; now it held the Secret Service contingent. "Well," Nixon said, "it certainly smells better back here."

When President Johnson was angry with the columnists Evans and Novak, he referred to them as "Errors and Nofacts."

NIXON ON THE PRESS

- "For sixteen years, ever since the Hiss case, you've had a lot of fun....[J]ust think of how much you're going to be missing. You won't have Nixon to kick around anymore, because , gentlemen, this is my last press conference."—*News conference, 1962*
- "Don't take it personally, but I'm not going to pay that much attention to you." —*To reporters, 1969*
- "The press is the enemy."—*To aides, 1969*
- If we treat the press with a little more contempt we'll probably get better treatment."—*To aides, 1969*
- "Kicking the press is an art."—*To aides, 1972*
- " I have never heard or seen such outrageous, vicious, distorted reporting in 27 years of public life. I am not blaming anyone for that." —*News conference, 1973*
- "Don't get the impression that you arouse my anger...You see, one can only be angry with those he respects."—*News conference, 1973*
- "I have no enemies in the press whatsoever." —*To the Society of Newspaper Editors, 1984.*

TRY, TRY AGAIN

Many products we take for granted today were flops when they were first introduced; it took a second—or even a third—effort to find a way to make them successful. Here are a few examples.

THE PRODUCT: Timex watches

Background: In 1942, the Waterbury Watch Company stopped making pocket watches and started making fuses for the U.S. military. Sales went up to $70 million, but plummeted to $300,000 after the war. To avoid bankruptcy, the company went back to manufacturing watches. They developed a line of cheap, durable timepieces anyone could afford—"Timex watches."

First Try: Salesmen took samples to jewelry stores (where watches were normally sold), expecting quick sales. But at $7.00 each, Timexes turned out to be too cheap and low-class for jewelers. They were used to a fancier product and a bigger profit margin; they refused to stock the watches.

Second Try: The company was forced to look for another place to sell its product. They sent salesmen out again, and to everyone's surprise, they found a market in drug stores. Whereas Timex products looked low-class in jewelry stores, they seemed ritzy next to aspirin and cough syrup. Within about a decade, one-third of all watches sold in the U.S. were Timexes.

THE PRODUCT: Tupperware

First Try: Earl Tupper invented Tupperware in the 1940s. Unlike glass or tin containers, Tupperware's plastic body and innovative airtight seal (based on a paint can design) made it ideal for keeping leftovers fresh. But consumers rejected it—they didn't understand how to use the plastic containers properly, and retailers rarely took the time to demonstrate them. By 1951 Tupper had given up.

Second Try: Mrs. Brownie Humphrey Wise, a "house party" saleswoman, came to Tupper's rescue. She was already selling Tupperware alongside other products at house parties, and pointed out to Tupper that the relaxed environment of a house party made it easy to demonstrate its advantages. Tupper agreed—and formed Tupperware Home Parties, Inc., in 1951. The parties worked—Tupperware was a hit. And it still is—today more than 75,000 Tupperware parties are held *every day*.

THE PRODUCT: Wisk Liquid Detergent

First Try: Unilever introduced Wisk, the first liquid laundry detergent ever, in 1956. It received a lot of publicity, but since it cost more than dry detergents, it wasn't a major success.

Second Try: A decade later, Unilever's market research revealed that housewives hated cleaning shirt collars more than any other laundry chore. So the company devised a new strategy for Wisk: They began running commercials that showed "ring around the collar" as the source of lost job promotions, husband-and-wife spats, etc. Their suggested solution: "Wisk around the collar." By 1974 sales of Wisk had tripled, and "ring around the collar" was a household phrase.

THE PRODUCT: Marlboro Cigarettes

First Try: Philip Morris introduced Marlboro in 1924 with upper-class women in mind—the cigarettes were longer and higher priced than standard brands. They also came with a "beauty tip"—an unfiltered mouthpiece that kept the smoker's lips from touching the cigarette paper. The gimmicks didn't work—Marlboro flopped. As late as 1954, it had less than 1% of the cigarette market.

Second Try: When filtered cigarettes were introduced in 1953, Philip Morris decided to dump the "beauty tip" and reintroduce Marlboro with a filter tip. (It was their worst-selling cigarette, and had the least to lose if it bombed). The company also replaced the brand's soft packaging with a new red and white "flip top" box. But women still ignored them, and the brand flopped again.

Third Try: In 1954, after 30 years of failures, Phillip Morris decided to forget about women. To attract male smokers, they gave the brand a more "manly" image, running commercials of pilots, hunters, sailors, and cowboys smoking Marlboros. Sales took off immediately; within a year, Marlboro was the fourth most popular smoke in the country. By the 1970s, it had become the most popular cigarette on Earth.

THE PRODUCT: Vaseline

Background: In 1857 a Brooklyn chemist named Robert Chesebrough visited the site of the first oil strike in U.S. history in Titusville, Pennsylvania. The oil workers he chatted with kept mentioning "rod wax" —a substance that collected on oil pumping machinery. They swore it healed their cuts and burns.

Chesebrough took a sample home to study and worked on refining it into a jelly-like product. He deliberately cut and burned himself—and rubbed the Vaseline (a combination of the German word for water—*wasser*—and the Greek word for oil—*elaion)* on his wounds. He found that it did actually speed up healing.

First Try: In 1870, Chesebrough set up a Vaseline factory and began mailing free samples to physicians and scientists. He expected to use their endorsements to convince drug stores to carry Vaseline. But they ignored him.

Second Try: He had no choice but to go directly to the public. He loaded his wagon with jars of Vaseline and rode around New York state, handing them out to everyone he met along the way. Soon these "customers" began asking local druggists to order refills, and Chesebrough's business took off. By 1912 Vaseline had been written up in medical journals all over the world.

• • •

AND NOW BACK TO THE SHOW

Worst sitcom of the '70s: *Sugar Time!* (From *The Best of TV Sitcoms* by John Javna)

"If this were a horror film, it might be called *The Attack of the Rock-and-Roll Jiggling Bombers. Sugar Time!*, starring Barbi Benton (Hugh Hefner's girlfriend), Didi Carr, and Marianne Black, was about a group of braless, spandex-clad rock-and-roll singers who dreamt of stardom, despite their precarious financial condition. The show served a dual purpose. Literally. The late '70s were the era of the jigglers, and producers were looking for any excuse to put both of the jiggling actresses' talents on display. If they could sing (or act), so much the better. Unfortunately in this case, they couldn't. The show was created by James Komack, producer of such classics as *Chico and the Man*, and *The Courtship of Eddie's Father*."

The Jesus Christ lizard actually walks on water.

WHAT'S IN A NAME?

Interesting facts about names, from The Best Baby Name Book in the Whole Wild World, *by Bruce Lansky*

UNUSUAL NAMES

• "Ann Landers wrote about a couple who has six children, all named Eugene Jerome Dupuis, Junior. The children answer to One, Two, Three, Four, Five and Six, respectively."

• "Tonsilitis Jackson has brothers and sisters named Meningitis, Appendicitis and Peritonitis."

• "A couple in Louisiana named their children after colleges: Stanford, Duke, T'Lane, Harvard, Princeton, Auburn and Cornell. The parents' names? Stanford, Sr., and Loyola."

• "In 1979, the Pennsylvania Health Department discovered these two first names among the 159,000 birth certificates issued in the state that year—Pepsi and Cola."

• "Zachary Zzzzra has been listed in the *Guinness Book of World Records* as making 'the most determined attempt to be the last personal name in a local telephone directory' in San Francisco. That happened before his place was challenged by one Vladimir Zzzzzzabakov. Zzzzra reports that he called Zzzzzzabakov and demanded to know his real name (Zzzzra's name is really his own, he says). Zzzzzzabakov told him it was none of his . . . business. At any rate... Zzzzra changed his name to regain his former position. When the new phone book appeared, he was relieved to find himself comfortably in the last place again, as Zachary Zzzzzzzzzzra. Unknown to him, the contender, Zzzzzzabakov, had disappeared."

• "One family which was not terribly successful in limiting its expansion has a series of children called, respectively, Finis, Addenda, Appendix, Supplement and (last but not least) Errata."

LETTER ALONE

• "Harry S Truman owed his middle name, the initial S with no period, to a compromise his parents worked out. By using only the initial, they were able to please both his grandfathers, whose names were Shippe and Solomon."

Tokyo dogs have a high baldness rate, because they "apparently lead very stressful lives."

• "A new recruit in the U.S. Army had only letters for his first and middle names—R B Jones. To avoid problems upon recruitment, he helpfully listed his name as ' R (only) B (only) Jones.' You guessed it—from then on he was, as far as the Army was concerned, 'Ronly Bonly Jones,' and all his records, dogtags, assignment forms and even discharge papers were issued in that name."

WHAT IN GOD'S NAME?

• "The majority of people in the Western hemisphere have names based on biblical ones. Women outnumber men, yet there are 3,037 male names in the Bible and only 181 female names, with the New Testament a more popular source than the Old."

• "Popes traditionally choose a new name upon their election. The practice began in 844 A.D. when Boca de Porco (Pig's Mouth) was elected. He changed his name to Sergious II."

• "Praise-God Barebones had a brother named If-Christ-Had-Not-Died-For-Thee-Thou-Wouldst-Have-Been-Damned Barebones, who was called 'Damned Barebones' for short."

• "Terril William Clark is listed in the phone book under his new name—God. Now he's looking for someone to publish a book he's written. 'Let's face it,' he reportedly said. 'The last book with my name on it was a blockbuster.'

LIVING UP TO THE NAME

• "Researchers have found that boys with peculiar first names have a higher incidence of mental problems than boys with common ones; no similar correlation was found for girls."

• "A recent study suggests that about two-thirds of the population of the U.S. is named to honor somebody. Of the people who are namesakes, about 60 percent are named after a relative and 40 percent for someone outside the family."

• "Many people dislike their own names. The most common reasons given for this dislike are that the names "sound too ugly," that they're old-fashioned, too hard to pronounce, too common, too uncommon, too long, sound too foreign, are too easy for people to joke about, and that they sound too effeminate (for men) or too masculine (for women)."

Cloud Nine was used by the U.S. Weather Bureau to describe the highest, least dangerous clouds.

THE LEGEND OF THE YELLOW RIBBON

When American troops came home from the Mideast in 1991, people welcomed them with yellow ribbons...as if that was a perfectly natural thing to do. Where did this "tradition" start? With a pop song—which, in turn, came from a Readers Digest *article. Here's the whole weird story, from* Behind the Hits, *by Bob Shannon and John Javna.*

INSPIRATION

Songwriter Irwin Levine leaned back and opened the January, 1972 issue of *Reader's Digest*. He skimmed through the magazine and read a few of the articles. Eventually he flipped to the story on page 64. The title said in red letters, "Going Home." And underneath: "Condensed from the New York *Post*." The piece was by newspaper columnist Pete Hamill; it had originally appeared in the New York *Post* on Oct. 14, 1971.

"I first heard this story a few years ago, from a girl I had met in New York's Greenwich Village," Hamill wrote in the introduction. "The girl told me she had been one of the participants. Since then, others...have said that they have read a version of it in some forgotten book, or been told it by an acquaintance who said that it actually happened to a friend. Probably the story is one of those mysterious bits of folklore that emerge from the national subconscious every few years, to be told anew in one form or another."

THE STORY

The two-page article was about a guy named Vingo, whom six teenagers spotted on a bus headed from New York City to Florida. The kids were going to Fort Lauderdale. Vingo, who'd been in a New York jail for the last four years, was on his way home. But he didn't know if his wife and kids would be there waiting for him. He'd told his wife when he first went in that he'd understand if she couldn't wait. Then he'd told her not to write, and she hadn't.

"Last week," said Vingo in the story, "when I was sure the parole was coming through, I wrote her again. We used to live in Brunswick, just before Jacksonville, and there's a big oak tree just as you come into town. I told her that if she'd take me back, she should put a yellow handkerchief on the tree, and I'd get off and come home. If she didn't want me, forget it—no handkerchief, and I'd go on through."

This tale was big news in the bus, so as they got to Brunswick everyone watched out the window for the tree. When they saw it, there was a massive celebration—dancing, tears, screaming. The tree was covered with ribbons. Vingo could go home.

THE SONG

Levine told his partner, Larry Brown, about the article. They both thought it could be a great song, and quickly wrote "Tie a Yellow Ribbon" based on it.

Then they gave it to a record producer, who convinced Tony Orlando to sing it. Orlando, a rhythm and blues fan, thought it was silly. But he couldn't get it out of his head. "I kept singing it around the house…against my will," he recalls.

It affected other people the same way; "Tie a Yellow Ribbon" sold three million copies in two weeks, and became the #1 record of 1973. By now, over a thousand versions have been recorded around the world.

THE FOLKLORE

A 1991 wire service report: "A yellow ribbon made by the wife of former Iranian hostage L. Bruce Laingen was donated yesterday to the Library of Congress, which accepted the bow as a genuine piece of American folklore.

"Shortly after Laingen was captured on Nov. 4, 1979 (when Muslim revolutionaries seized the U.S. Embassy in Tehran), Penne Laingen made the bow from 12 feet of yellow vinyl upholstery material and tied it around an oak tree in the front yard of the Laingen home in Bethesda, MD. When the 52 embassy hostages were freed Jan. 20, 1981, Laingen, the embassy's senior diplomat, returned home and removed the ribbon that had become a national symbol of hope for the hostages' eventual release.

"Laingen's yellow ribbon will be put on permanent display in the reading room of the library's American Folklife Center."

Nearly 13% of lawyers admit to having six or more drinks a day.

BOX OFFICE W

Who are the real movie superstars? We were surprised b
on these lists, compiled using the annual info from Quigley P

TOP 10 BOX OFFICE STARS

...OF THE 1930s

1. Clark Gable
2. Shirley Temple
3. Joan Crawford
4. Will Rogers
5. Wallace Beery
6. Fred Astaire and Ginger Rogers
7. Norma Shearer
8. Marie Dressler
9. Janet Gaynor
10. Sonja Henie

...OF THE 1950s

1. John Wayne
2. James Stewart
3. Gary Cooper
4. Bing Crosby
5. Dean Martin and Jerry Lewis
6. Bob Hope
7. Frank Sinatra
8. William Holden
9. Randolph Scott
10. Marilyn Monroe

...OF THE 1970s

1. Clint Eastwood
2. Steve McQueen
3. Paul Newman
4. Barbra Streisand
5. John Wayne
6. Robert Redford
7. Charles Bronson
8. Burt Reynolds
9. Woody Allen
10. Al Pacino

...OF THE 1940s

1. Bob Hope
2. Bing Crosby
3. Betty Grable
4. Humphrey Bogart
5. Clark Gable
6. Bud Abbott and Lou Costello
7. Gary Cooper
8. Spencer Tracy
9. Greer Garson
10. James Cagney

...OF THE 1960s

1. John Wayne
2. Elizabeth Taylor
3. Doris Day
4. Paul Newman
5. Jack Lemmon
6. Elvis Presley
7. Rock Hudson
8. Julie Andrews
9. Richard Burton
10. Sandra Dee

...OF THE 1980s

1. Clint Eastwood
2. Eddie Murphy
3. Burt Reynolds
4. Tom Cruise
5. Sylvester Stallone
6. Michael J. Fox
7. Arnold Schwarzenegger
8. Michael Douglas
9. Harrison Ford
10. Dudley Moore

Origin of the term "bigwig:" King Louis IV of France was a big fan of big wigs.

POLITICAL SYMBOLS

You know what they represent—but do you know where they come from?

The Republican Elephant: First appeared in *Harper's Weekly* in 1874, in a political cartoon drawn by Thomas Nast. Rumors were circulating that President Ulysses S. Grant, a Republican, was going to run for a third term. Fearful of what would happen if Grant were reelected, Nast drew a cartoon of the rumor, incorporating another news story: a false report that wild animals had escaped from the Central Park Zoo and were roaming the streets in search of prey. He drew the Republican Party as a stampeding elephant.

The Democratic Donkey: In the 1828 presidential elections, Andrew Jackson's opponents referred to him as a "stubborn jackass." Proud of his reputation for obstinacy, Jackson (a Democrat) began using donkeys in his campaign posters and flyers. Democrats have been doing it ever since.

The Peace Symbol: ☮ Created by Gerald Holtom, a British artist, in 1958. A member of the Campaign for Nuclear Disarmament, Holtom was looking for a symbol to promote the antinuclear group that could be easily reproduced on banners. He based it on letters in the semaphore (flag) alphabet that Navy ships use to communicate with each other. The circle stands for the word "total;" the two smaller lines represent the letter N (nuclear), and the long vertical line in the center stands for the letter D (disarmament)—"Total Nuclear Disarmament." It was first displayed at a 1958 peace march in England.

The Swastika: Originally a Hindu symbol that represented the sun's daily path across the sky—and that, ironically, was considered a "good luck" symbol before World War II. It has been found on religious artifacts all over the world, from the Middle East to Asia to North and South America. Its image was tarnished forever when Adolf Hitler adopted it as the symbol for the Nazi party.

Mickey's good news: 70% of Americans have been to Disneyland or Disney World.

UNSUNG HEROES

Everyone knows about Thomas Edison and Alexander Graham Bell. But the guy who invented the portable vacuum cleaner is anonymous. The folks at the BRI's Division of Practical Science think it's time this injustice is corrected. Here are some heroes we should all recognize.

HERO: Earl Richardson
WHAT HE DID: Designed the first practical electric iron.
THE STORY: In 1905 Richardson, a California utility worker, decided to improve the electric irons of the day. Existing models weighed as much as 15 lbs, and were warm only while they were sitting in their bases. Richardson's solution: design a lighter iron that stayed hot, even when in use. He succeeded, but still had a problem. Most power companies of the day generated power only in the evenings—their purpose was to provide power for lighting—but women liked to iron during the day. In 1906, Richardson convinced his local utility to generate electricity all day on Tuesdays... and housewives started buying his irons.

HEROINE: Josephine Cochrane
WHAT SHE DID: Invented the dishwasher.
THE STORY: Though she invented the dishwasher, Josephine never washed dishes herself. A wealthy woman of the 1890s, she invented the machine because she was tired of servants breaking her valuable china as they washed it. One afternoon, Cochrane went out into the woodshed alongside her house and began building wire compartments that would hold her dishes. She set these in a large copper boiler, and attached a motor to pump the water and rotate the dishes. Her friends convinced her to patent it; in 1893 one of her machines won top prize at the Chicago World's Fair.

HERO: James Murray Spengler
WHAT HE DID: Invented the portable vacuum cleaner
THE STORY: A failed inventor, Spengler hit rock-bottom in

Would you like to host the "Tonight Show"? A third of American men say they would.

1907 and had to take a job as a janitor in an Ohio department store. The mechanical carpet cleaner he used to clean the store's carpets kicked up dust and set off his allergies—so Spengler decided to build a better contraption. He made his first vacuum out of a pillow case, a soap box, an old fan, and some tape; he patented it in 1908. Later he sold the rights to his device to William Hoover, an Ohio businessman, and retired with the money he made.

HERO: Henry Alden Sherwin

WHAT HE DID: Developed ready-mixed paint.

THE STORY: You knew that Sherwin Williams sold ready-mixed paint, but did you know they invented it? The year was 1870, and Sherwin, co-owner of a paint company, wanted to sell pre-mixed colors, so homeowners wouldn't have to mix their own (a risky business). His partners hated the idea, and forced Sherwin out of the company. So he found a new partner, Edward Williams; together they formed Sherwin Williams in 1880.

HERO: Frederick Walton and Thomas Armstrong

WHAT THEY DID: Invented linoleum floors.

THE STORY: Frederick Walton, an Englishman, deserves the credit for inventing linoleum. But Thomas Armstrong, an American, deserves credit for making it what it is today. Walton patented his floor covering, a layer of linseed oil, resin, and cork dust with a woven backing, in 1860. When Thomas Armstrong, a cork maker, heard of Walton's invention, he developed his own cork-based floor covering. Unlike Walton, he experimented with coloring, patterns, and other ideas, giving linoleum the features that made it a fixture in American homes.

HERO: Edwin Budding

WHAT HE DID: Invented the lawn mower.

THE STORY: Edwin Budding was a foreman in an English textile plant in the late 1820s. He was obsessed with a new machine the plant used to shear excess fibers from cotton cloth. He thought a similar machine might help him keep his lawn trimmed, and he set out to make one. Today's mowers are direct descendents of the machine he invented.

A TOY IS BORN

We all grew up with them: Raggedy Ann, Legos, Lionel Trains...

RAGGEDY ANN

In the early 1900s a little girl named Marcella Gruelle was rummaging through the attic of her parents' Connecticut home when she found a hand-made doll. It was dusty and torn, but Marcella liked it so much that her father repaired it for her. He even gave it a name: Raggedy Ann, (inspired by two poems by James Whitcomb Riley: "The Raggedy Man" and "Little Orphan Annie").

In fact, Marcella spent so much time with the doll that her father (Johnny Gruelle), a cartoonist, started writing and illustrating stories about it. His books—the original *Raggedy Ann* series—made Raggedy Ann one of the most popular dolls of the 20th Century.

MATCHBOX CARS

In 1952 John Odell and Leslie Smith, owners of a British industrial die-casting factory, started casting toys at night to make extra money. Their first toy: a tiny replica of Princess Elizabeth's Royal Coach. When Elizabeth became Queen in 1953, more than a million of them were sold.

So the partners went into toymaking full time. They created a line of tiny automobiles they called *Matchbox Toys (*because the cars were tiny enough to fit in a matchbox)...then they took it a step further and decided to sell their products in packages that actually *looked* like matchboxes.

LEGOS

One afternoon in 1954, a shopkeeper complained to Godtfred Kirk-Christiansen, a Danish toymaker, that most modern toys didn't challenge children to think. That night, Christiansen came up with an idea for a new toy: building blocks that locked together, enabling children to use their imagination and build interesting structures that weren't possible with standard blocks. He called his creation *Legos*, from the Danish words *leg godt*, which means "play well." Today they're sold in more than 125 countries.

Americans spend $10 million a day on potato chips, and $2 million a day on exercise equipment.

LIONEL TRAINS

Joshua Lionel Cohen was an inventor in the late 1900s. His earliest creations included fuses for land mines, primitive versions of the electronic doorbell, and something he called a flowerpot light, (a small, battery-operated lamp which was intended to illuminate plants in hotel lobbies). He also invented a tiny electric motor, but couldn't figure out what to do with it. He finally stuffed one into a model train, named it Lionel (after himself), and sold it with 30 feet of track to a novelty store. Within a day or two the store asked for more. Cohen decided to go into train-making full time, and by 1903 his Lionel Train Company had an entire catalog of trains and accessories.

Note: Cohen's trains made him rich, but he never earned any money—or credit—for his most famous invention: the battery-operated flowerpot light. It was such a loser that he sold the design to his business partner. The partner started selling the lights *without* the flowerpots—under a new name—*The Eveready Flashlight*.

CABBAGE PATCH KIDS

Xavier Roberts, a Georgia folk artist, was selling his soft sculpture dolls at a craft fair when a customer walked up and asked him how much the dolls cost. Roberts had a splitting headache. He snapped back: "They're not for sale."—but quickly recovered and said: "They're up for adoption." The idea behind Cabbage Patch Kids was born.

Roberts carried the concept to extremes. He converted an old medical clinic into "Babyland General Hospital," where employees "delivered" his "babies" and gave them "birth certificates" with names like Bessie Sue or Billie Jo. His dolls were ugly, but they still became a national craze in 1983. Customers in one toy store rioted after waiting more than eight hours to buy the dolls. One woman broke her leg—and the store owner had to protect himself with a baseball bat.

Note: In 1980 Martha Nelson, a craft artist Roberts had worked with in the past, sued him, claiming he had stolen some of her soft sculpture techniques. The court ruled that Roberts *had* used some of Nelson's ideas, but since she never copyrighted the design, she wasn't entitled to any of the profits.

An ant can survive for 2 weeks underwater.

CHANDLER SAYS...

Raymond Chandler was a master of detective fiction. Here's a sample of his style, from his books.

"When in doubt, have two guys come in through the doors with guns."

"He didn't know the right people. That's all a police record means."

"Guns never settle anything. They're just a fast curtain to a bad second act."

"It was a blonde. A blonde to make a bishop kick a hole in a stained glass window."

"She gave me a smile I could feel in my hip pocket."

"You could tell by his eyes that he was plastered to the hairline, but otherwise he looked like any other nice young guy in a dinner jacket who had been spending too much money in a joint that exists for that purpose and no other."

On marriage: "For two people in a hundred it's wonderful. The rest just work at it. After 20 years all the guy has left is a work bench in the garage."

"She had a pair of blue-gray eyes that looked at me as if I had said a dirty word."

"She lowered her lashes until they almost cuddled her cheeks and raised them again, like a theater curtain....That was supposed to make me roll over on my back with all four paws in the air."

"The [dying] General spoke again, slowly, using his strength as carefully as an out-of-work showgirl uses her last good pair of stockings."

"I lit the cigarette and blew a lungful at him and he sniffed at it like a terrier at a rathole."

"Alcohol is like love: the first kiss is magic, the second is intimate, the third is routine. After that you just take the girl's clothes off."

"Los Angeles is a city no worse than others, a city rich and vigorous and full of pride, a city lost and beaten and full of emptiness."

$1 out of every $11 Americans spend on food goes for packaging.

CN U RD THS?

The cryptic messages on personalized license plates can be fun...or maddening—as these examples.

CAR BRAGGIN'
FSTRNU
IDSMOKU
2AHSUM
WOWZER
NUN BTR
I XLR8
UDLUUZ
WAY2BAD

CAR MODESTY
EYEZOR
HAZRDUS
JUS2LOUD
LOTECH
GASGUZ
H2OLOO
OK4NOW
SHLOMO

AUTO BIOGRAPHY
JUSAHIK
NDCENT
I 4GET 2
FMNIST
GAY1
ERLEBRD
IMON2U
IMOKUOK
NVR2OLD
WELLRED
PHAQUE
AIRHED
H82BL8
KUNFUZD
PINHEAD
REDNEK
TRCULNT
XNTRIK
2CRAY Z
BEERFAT
IMNOZEE
CURMUJN
DESPOT
EZ HUMP
FLAKEY
KARMA
I ELVIS

IT'S A LIVING
RABBI
TUPRWR
ILSTR8TR
CME4OB
I FIX BAX
MDUC2P
OPNWDE
LITIG8R
ISUEM
SHYSTERR
I ADD4U
I CALQL8
KAR2NST
PNO2R
DCOR8
EDUKTR
GESTALT
MS DONUT
SOUL DR
2THFXR
2BY CME

JUST FOR FUN
POLKA
H2O SKE
ROC4EVR
N2HRSES
W8LIFTN
XRCIZE
AV8TR
ICESK8
HAIKU
HDBANGR
ILUV10S
K9SHOW
LV2PUN
PBS YES
SGTPEPR
W8N4SUN
2DA BCHS

GOOD ADVICE
BCRE8TV
BCOOL
DOITNOW
B LOGICL
10D 2IT
UBUKLUP

"If we ever needed a brain, now is the time."—Squiggy, "Laverne and Shirley"

I'M GAME

You can't play board games in the bathroom (not yet, anyway—someone may be developing one right now)...but you can still read about them.

START HERE

• The earliest board game on record is the royal game of Ur, which was invented more than 4,000 years ago in Mesopotamia, the site of present-day Iraq. It was a "race" game; the first player to complete the course was the winner. Moves were governed by throwing dice-like objects. Archaeologists believe it is the forerunner of backgammon.

• The Egyptian game of Senet was a best-seller some 4,000 years ago. Even King Tut had one. He liked it so much he was buried with it.

• The first American board game, "The Mansion of Happiness," was produced in 1843. Its theme was Victorian: Players tried to avoid Passion, Idleness, Cruelty, Immodesty and Ingratitude. Drunkeness was punished by a trip to the stocks.

THE PLAYERS

• *Milton Bradley*: In 1860 he bought a lithographic press and began printing board games. His first game: The Checkered Game of Life. Object: Get to "happy old age" while avoiding "disgrace" and "ruin."

• *The Parker Brothers*: In 1883, about 50 years before Monopoly, George Parker went into the game business. His first product was a card game called Banking. Later, with the help of his brothers Charles and Edward, he revolutionized the toy industry by introducing mass-produced board games.

• *Mark Twain*: The great American author also invented a game. He called it "Mark Twain's Memory Builder: A Game for Acquiring and Retaining All Sorts of Facts and Dates." In the introduction to the rules he wrote: "Many public-school children seem to know only two dates—1492 and 4th of July; but as a rule they don't know what happened on either occasion. It is because they have not had a chance to play this game."

THE GAME BOARD

If you're going to go to Atlantic City to check out the properties that the Monopoly spaces are named after, be prepared for heartbreak. According to Nathan Cobb, a *Boston Globe* writer who made the pilgrimmage a few years ago:

• You can't take a ride on the Reading Railroad; it's out of business. The only railroad left is Conrail, which doesn't take passengers.

• Advance to St. Charles Place? Forget it. It's gone, replaced by a casino parking lot.

• Kentucky Avenue is a string of burger huts and seedy bars.

• Pacific Avenue is crawling with hookers.

• There's no longer a Community Chest...or the old Water Works.

• You won't find any Free Parking.

• Many of the nineteen other Monopoly streets that still exist are lined with buildings that are boarded up and run down. One wine-guzzling derelict sitting on Oriental Avenue, when told it could be had for $100 on the Monopoly board, declared, "Damn, it ain't worth that much."

TOKEN FACTS

• Parcheesi, the original male chauvinist game, was created in the 1500s in India by Akbar the Great. It was played in the palace courtyard with young women as game pawns. "Home" was originally the emperor's throne. What Akbar did with the women once he got them all "home" is not documented.

• Backgammon was once known as "Nero's Game."

• There are five legal Scrabble words using 'q' without 'u': faqir, qaid, qoph, qindar and qintar.

• In 1988, the 23rd foreign language version of Monopoly was manufactured—in the USSR. Among the changes: a Russian bear token, real estate names corresponding to Moscow locations (Broadway became the Arbat Mall) and rubles instead of dollars.

WHAT ALES YOU?

Here's a bit of information you can use to impress your friends next time you go out for a beer.

In medieval times, taverns were rough and dangerous places. Glass-bottomed beer tankards were invented so a drinker could take a hefty bottoms-up gulp while still keeping a wary eye on fellow drinkers.

Beer steins were first seen in Europe in the 1500s. Covered containers protected the beer from flies, which were thought to carry the plague.

Eberhard Anheuser, a St. Louis soap maker, bought a failing brewery in 1860 and tried to turn it around. But within 2 years he owed so much money to the local brewer's supply store—owned by Aldophus Busch—that he had to take Busch on as a partner to cancel the debt. Busch married his daughter in 1860, and assumed control of the brewery when he died.

About one out of four beers consumed in the U. S. is a Budweiser. Next most popular domestic beers are Miller Lite, Coors Light, Bud Light, Busch, Miller High Life, Milwaukee's Best, Old Milwaukee, and Coors.

In the late 1860s Adolph Coors stowed away on a ship to America to avoid serving in the German Army. He and a partner founded the Golden brewery in Golden, Colorado in 1873—which he bought outright in 1880.

The reason you spend a lot of time in the john when you drink beer: besides the bulk of liquid that passes through you, the alcohol acts as a diuretic, taking the liquids out of your body and flushing them down the tubes. This dehydration causes a lot of the hangover the next morning. Best prevention? Drink a glass of water or two every time you visit the facilities.

Frederick Miller, royal brewmaster at Germany's Hohenzollern Castle, fled to Milwaukee in 1854 to escape the political strife consuming his country. He founded the Miller Brewing Company in 1855.

Northeasterners and westerners drink more imported beer than elsewhere—more than twice the national average.

Pigeons are the only birds that can drink water without raising their heads to swallow.

NUMBER, PLEASE

Think of all the numbers you know—your phone number, your address, etc. There's no explanation for most of them. But here are a few we can give you a reason for.

NUMBER: 5280 feet (a mile).
ORIGIN: The term *mile* comes from the Latin word *mille*—meaning 1,000. To the Romans it was the distance a soldier could cover in 1,000 paces—about 5,000 feet. But British farmers measured their fields in *furlongs*, which were 660 feet long, and they didn't want to change. So when the mile was introduced in England, it was changed to 5,280 feet—exactly eight furlongs.

NUMBER: 60 feet, 6 inches (the distance between the pitcher's mound and home plate in baseball).
ORIGIN: The pitching distance was 50 feet until 1893—when some baseball executives changed it to 60 feet. But the surveyor they hired to remap their infield misread their instructions—he thought 60 feet 0 inches was 60 feet 6 inches. The extra 6 inches have been there ever since.

NUMBER: Age 65 (when Americans qualify for Social Security).
ORIGIN: German Chancellor Otto von Bismarck established the world's first Social Security program in 1881 to undercut the popularity of the socialist movement. He set the retirement age at 65 because he knew he wouldn't have to pay out many benefits—in the 1880s living to age 65 was as likely as living to 105 today. When FDR set up Social Security in the U.S., he copied the German retirement age—not realizing why it had been chosen to begin with.

NUMBER: 26 miles, 385 yards (the length of a marathon).
ORIGIN: The distance of a marathon was first standardized at 25 miles in 1896. During the 1908 London Olympics, however, Queen Alexandra wanted her grandchildren to see the start of the race. So the starting line was moved back 1 mile and 385 yards—onto the front lawn of Windsor Castle. Marathons are still that length. today.

BEN FRANKLIN'S ALMANAC

Here are more bits of wisdom from the man who thought a penny saved is a penny earned.

"A single man has not nearly the value he'd have in a state of union. He resembles the odd half of a pair of scissors."

"There are more old drunkards than old doctors."

"If a man empties a purse into his head, no man can take it away from him. An investment in knowledge always pays the best interest."

"None preaches better than the ant, and she says nothing."

"He that is good for making excuses is seldom good for anything else."

"In general, mankind, since the improvement of cookery, eats twice as much as nature requires."

"The heart of a fool is in his mouth; but the mouth of a wise man is in his heart."

"He that lives upon hope will die fasting."

"Where there's marriage without love, there will be love without marriage."

"He that falls in love with himself will have no rivals."

"God heals and the doctor takes the fee."

"He that is of the opinion that money will do everything may well be accused of doing everything for money."

"Plough deep while sluggards sleep."

"Three may keep a secret if two of them are dead."

"There was never a good war, or a bad peace."

"Nothing gives an author so much pleasure as to find his works quoted by other learned authors."

"Necessity never made a good bargain."

"At twenty years of age, the will reigns; at thirty, the wit; and at forty, the judgement."

"There are no ugly loves nor handsome prisons."

"Admiration is the daughter of ignorance."

The Roman Emperor Caligula's last words were: "I'm still alive!"

THE COLA WARS

Some competitors have friendly rivalries, but not Coke and Pepsi. These two have battled for most of this century, taking no prisoners. And the cola wars continue today.

BEFORE THE BATTLES

To understand the bitterness between Coke and Pepsi, you have to go back a hundred years to the two pharmacists (both veterans of the Confederate army) who formulated the sticky-sweet brown liquids.

COKE BEGINNINGS

John Pemberton, a pharmacist in Atlanta, created Coca-Cola as a non-alcoholic "nerve medicine" in 1886.

• He came up with the first Coke syrup by boiling a batch of herbs, coca leaves and kola nuts in his back yard.

• He mixed the syrup with tap water and sold it in his drug store.

• It wasn't until a customer with an upset stomach specifically asked him to mix the syrup with fizzy water that he realized Coke's potential as a soft drink.

• He didn't live to see Coca-Cola become a success. Shortly after he created the drink, Pemberton's health began to fail. He sold the rights to Coke to a group of druggists for about $350; he died in 1888.

THE NEW REGIME

Only one of Coca-Cola's new owners, Asa Candler, saw the drink's huge potential. By 1891, he had bought complete control of the company for $2,300, and registered *Coca-Cola* as a trademark a few years later. Candler plowed nearly all of the company's early profits back into the business, and kept costs to a minimum (one employee reported earning "$3.00 per week and lots of Coca-Cola").

He had an unmatched flair for promotion, and began the company's tradition of giving away Coca-Cola clocks, fans, calendars, urns, scales, thermometers, and other premiums to storekeepers that ordered Coke syrup.

By 1892 he was selling more than 35,000 gallons of syrup a year, and by the turn of the century, Coca-Cola had become the best known product in America.

EARLY COMPETITORS

Coca-Cola's meteoric rise had inspired scores of imitators. Coke sued dozens of them for trademark infringement, including the Koke Company, Kola Koke, Coke-Ola, Koko-Cola, Koko-Kola, Ko-Kola, and Coca & Cola. The case against the Koke Company went all the way to the Supreme Court, and Coca-Cola won.

HITTING THE BOTTLE

According to legend, a mystery man walked into Coca-Cola's offices one day in 1891. He told Candler he knew a way to double the company's sales overnight, and would share his idea for $5,000 (or, some say, $50,000). Candler paid him. The man handed Candler a slip of paper which said, "Bottle it."

Regardless of whether the story is true, Candler resisted bottling Coca-Cola for a long time, fearing that pressurized bottles might explode and expose the company to legal liability. Eventually, a Mississippi candy store owner started bottling the liquid on his own. He had enormous success (and no lawsuits), and five years later, Candler opened his first bottling plant.

At first, Coca-Cola's bottles were indistinguishable from those of other companies, but in 1915 Coke hired an Indiana glass company to design a bottle that customers would recognize "even in the dark." Loosely adapting sketches of a cola nut they found in the *Encyclopedia Britannica*, the glassworkers designed the distinctive bottle that is still in use today.

Candler ran Coca-Cola until 1916, when he turned over control of the company to his sons. His wife's death in 1919 sent him into a deep depression; he tried to shake it off by taking a trip to Europe. While he was away, his sons sold the company to Robert Woodruff, an Atlanta entrepreneur, for $25 million dollars.

In Boise, Idaho's 1985 mayoral election, Mr. Potatohead received four write-in votes.

PEPSI-COLA HITS THE SPOT

Meanwhile, back to 1893: In North Carolina, pharmacist Caleb Bradham decided he wanted to cash in on the success of Coke. At first, he called his imitation "Brad's Drink," but then decided to name it after *pepsin*, a digestive aid, hoping people would buy it as a stomach remedy. Like Pemberton, he didn't see Pepsi's potential as a soft drink until it became popular among people who *weren't* sick.

Bradham paid careful attention to advertising and sales grew to 100,000 gallons of syrup by 1898. Pepsi continued to grow until the end of World War I, when sugar prices shot up from 5 1/2¢ a pound to 22 1/2¢ a pound. To hedge against future shortages, Bradham stocked up on sugar at the higher price. But a few months later, sugar plummeted to 3 1/2¢ a pound, and the company went bankrupt. Bradham returned to his drug store, leaving the soda world.

Roy C. McGargel bought the rights to Pepsi-Cola in 1920 and tried to put the company back on its feet. But he couldn't afford a large advertising budget, and the company faltered. It went bankrupt in 1925, reorganized, and went bankrupt again in 1931.

SKIRMISH #1: LOFTY GOALS

The day after Pepsi-Cola went bankrupt in 1931, Charles Guth, the president the Loft Candy Store chain, bought it for $10,500. It didn't seem like a wise investment at the time, since Coca-Cola was already the industry giant and was getting bigger every year. But Guth wanted something more than mere money—he bought Pepsi to get *revenge*.

Guth hated the Coca-Cola Company. Even though Loft's 115 candy stores sold 4 million servings of Coke every year, the company had refused to give him a quantity discount. When Guth bought Pepsi for himself, it gave him the chance to dump Coke from Loft stores.

- Coca-Cola was furious: Guth was one of its largest customers, and losing his business hurt. It decided to fight back.

- It secretly sent its employees into Guth's stores to order "a Coke." On 620 occasions, they reported, they were served Pepsi instead. The company sued Guth, claiming he didn't have the right to serve Pepsi to customers asking for "a Coke." Coca-Cola fought the case for more than 10 years. It lost in 1942. The bitterness be-

On a typical day, your name is transmitted between computers five times.

tween the two companies was just beginning.

SKIRMISH #2: "12 FULL OUNCES, THAT'S A LOT"

Two years after buying Pepsi, Guth had had enough. He couldn't expand sales beyond his own stores, and wanted to sell out. The logical buyer was Coke. Guth offered them the company at a bargain price…and they refused.

Desperate to cut costs, Guth began bottling Pepsi in secondhand beer bottles, which held nearly twice as much soda as normal soft drink bottles. Guth saved money, and hoped the larger serving size would increase sales.

It didn't. Nearly bankrupt, Guth took one last gamble to save his company: He cut Pepsi's price from 10¢ to a nickel, offering twice as much cola as Coke for 1/2 the price. The gamble paid off. By 1938 Pepsi was making $4 million a year and growing fast.

PALACE COUP

Guth won the battle, but lost it all in an internal power play. By 1935 he had spent so much of his attention and energy building up Pepsi that Loft Candy Stores was on the verge of bankruptcy. Loft's board of directors forced him to resign and hired the Phoenix Security Company to nurse the candy company back to health.

Guth still owned Pepsi-Cola outright; he said he had bought it with his own money. But audits showed that he had bought it using Loft's funds. Upon discovering this, Phoenix Securities hatched a scheme to take control of Pepsi for itself. It bought up much of Loft's nearly worthless stock. Acting on behalf of the candy company, it then sued Guth for control of Pepsi. Phoenix won the suit in 1939. Their scheme had worked—for the bargain basement price of a nearly bankrupt chain of candy stores, Phoenix Securities had taken control of the second most successful soft drink company in the nation.

SKIRMISH #3: A SMOKING GUN

While Coca-Cola was still the undisputed leader of the cola companies, Pepsi-Cola's booming sales made it nervous. In 1934 it fired the next volley with a trademark infringement suit against Pepsi-

Cola to force it to drop the word "Cola" from its name. Coke had already won similar lawsuits against several companies, and Walter Mack, Pepsi's new president, actually expected to lose.

Everyone else thought Pepsi would lose, too. The widow of the president of Cleo-Cola, which lost a similar lawsuit, visited Mack to commiserate. "My husband thought he was right too," she said, "but they still put him out of business. And I still have a photograph of the check they gave him."

Check? What check? Purely by chance, she given Mack an important piece of evidence proving that Coca-Cola had been bribing soft drink executives to deliberately lose the lawsuits it filed against them, in order to strengthen its trademark position for future cases.

Mack asked the widow for a copy of the check, and introduced it as evidence in court. Caught red-handed, Coca-Cola asked for a two day recess. The next day Robert Woodruff, President of Coca-Cola, met with Mack in a New York hotel. He offered to withdraw the suit, and Mack agreed—but only after forcing Woodruff to sign a statement he had written out on the hotel's stationery: "I, Robert Woodruff, hereby agree that [Coca-Cola] will recognize the Pepsi-Cola trademark and never attack it in the United States."

Coke kept its word. It never again attacked Pepsi's trademark in this country. However, in other countries around the world Coke attacked Pepsi's trademark whenever and however possible.

SKIRMISH #3: BEG, BORROW & STEELE

By 1949 Pepsi was in trouble again. Coke had recaptured 84% of the U.S. soda market, and Pepsi was again near bankruptcy. The problem: Pepsi's image. Its huge bottles and low price had made it popular during the Great Depression—but they also gave the brand a reputation as a "cheap" drink for people who couldn't afford Coke. Affluent post-war America was returning to Coke.

Luckily for Pepsi, a Coca-Cola vice president named Alfred Steele jumped ship. A former circus showman, Steele's flamboyant antics had been unpopular at Coke, and his career with the company had bottomed out. He quit and become president of Pepsi-Cola, taking 15 other top executives with him. For the second time in its history, Pepsi was being run by a man bent on getting revenge on Coke.

Steele was just what Pepsi needed. He reworked Pepsi's image, updating the company's logo to the familiar circular one used for decades, and switching to fancy swirl bottles. He launched a massive advertising campaign which positioned Pepsi as a superior product, even a status symbol.

In 1955, he married actress Joan Crawford, a former Coca-Cola endorser, and she began appearing in Pepsi ads and publicity events. Her Hollywood glamour helped shake off the brand's "low class" image. Steele succeeded in breathing new life into Pepsi. By the time he died in 1959, he had cut Coke's lead in half.

SKIRMISH #5: ICE COLD WAR

During the '50s, Pepsi was active in conservative politics. It was a big supporter of Senator Joseph McCarthy and his anti-communist associate, Richard Nixon. In 1959, Vice President Nixon travelled to Moscow to attend an international trade show of American and Soviet products, including Pepsi-Cola. Soviet President Nikita Khrushchev was there, and while touring the Macy's kitchen exhibit the two men got into a heated argument over the merits of communism and capitalism.

Pepsi officials asked Nixon to bring Krushchev to their display to cool off after the debate. Nixon happily obliged, shoving a Pepsi into Krushchev's hand. Photos of the scene were a public relations bonanza for Pepsi: at the height of the cold war, the leader of the Communist world was photographed drinking a Pepsi In one stroke, Pepsi's worldwide image and prestige had finally caught up with Coca-Cola's, and Donald Kendall, Pepsi's overseas operations chief, never forgot Nixon's gesture. A few years late he got a chance to return the favor.

Nixon lost the presidential campaign in 1960, and the California gubernatorial race in 1962. Now unemployed, he was offered the presidency of several universities, considered for the chairmanship of Chrysler, and was even suggested as commissioner of baseball. But he decided to practice law so he could stay active in politics. His wife, Pat, was too embarrassed by his defeat to stay in California, so they moved to New York.

Nixon hadn't practiced law for a long time and wasn't exactly a prestigious figure any more, so he had a hard time finding a firm

In 1977 there were over 15,000 discos in the United States.

that would take him. Donald Kendall repaid the Moscow favor by presenting him with the Pepsi account, worth a considerable amount of money. And the job helped keep him in the public eye. He traveled around the world opening Pepsi bottling plants, stopping to meet world leaders. Coincidence: He was in Dallas making a Pepsi-related appearance on Nov. 22, 1963, when JFK was killed.

Even after Nixon was elected President in 1968, his relationship with the company remained close. During his years in office, Pepsi was the only soft drink served at the White House. In 1972, Pepsi won the right to begin selling soft drinks in the USSR after Nixon personally asked the Soviets to "look favorably" on Pepsi's request. Pepsi had pull even when Nixon didn't intervene directly: foreign governments knew that giving Pepsi favorable treatment would score points with the his administration.

SKIRMISH #6: COKE SHALL RISE AGAIN

In 1962, the same year Nixon became Pepsi's lawyer, a young Georgian named Jimmy Carter lost the Democratic nomination for the state senate. But he suspected election fraud, and hired King & Spalding, Atlanta's most prominent law firm, to challenge the results. They succeeded: Carter was declared the Democratic nominee, and went on to win the election.

The law firm got Carter together with officials from another of its clients: the Coca-Cola Company. Company officials saw immediately that he had potential as a national candidate. They introduced him to the inner circle of Georgia's corporate and industrial leaders, whose money and support would later prove crucial in Carter's campaigns for governor and president.

Carter remained close to Coca-Cola for the rest of his career. As governor he often used the company's jets on official trips, and when his 1976 presidential campaign started losing steam, he turned to Coke's image makers to film his campaign commercials.

As early as 1974 he admitted the company's role in developing his knowledge of foreign affairs: "We have our own built-in State Department in the Coca-Cola company. The provide me ahead of time with...penetrating analyses of what the country is, what its problems are, who its leaders are, and when I arrive there, provide me with an introduction to the leaders of that country."

Like Nixon, Carter returned the favor after being elected president. One of the first acts of his administration: removing the White House Pepsi-Cola machines and replacing them with Coke.

After Carter was elected, Portugal allowed Coke to be bottled and sold in the country—lifting a ban that was more than 50 years old. Not long afterward, U.S. government approved a $300 million emergency loan to the country. And when China opened its markets to American companies during Carter's term, Coke was the one that got the nod.

SKIRMISH #7: PEPSICO STRIKES BACK

In the mid-1960s, the Pepsi-Cola Company (renamed *Pepsico*) began diversifying into the snack-food and restaurant business eventually buying Kentucky Fried Chicken, Pizza Hut and other popular chains, in part so they could switch their soda fountains over to Pepsi-Cola. Pepsico's diversification strategy worked: by 1979 the company succeeded at the unthinkable—the company had grown larger than Coca-Cola. While undiversified Coke still sold more soft drinks and had higher profits, Pepsi was gaining even there. And now Coke's own surveys were showing that younger drinkers preferred the taste of Pepsi. Coke decided to act.

A SHOT TO THE FOOT: NEW COKE

In 1985, the Coke company announced it was replacing the old Coke formula with one a new one. Extensive marketing tests indicated that people preferred New Coke over both the old product *and* Pepsi.

But the marketing tests didn't anticipate the huge negative reaction to tinkering with a beloved old product. It was a major embarrassment for Coca-Cola. Pepsi declared victory, consumers revolted, and within two months old Coke was back—in the form of "Classic Coke." Today it outsells New Coke by a ratio of 4 to 1.

Today, the makers of the sweet liquids continue their bitter battle.

NOW AND ZEN

If all of the world can be seen in a grain of sand, as some Zen masters say, why not on TV? Cosmic quotes from the book Primetime Proverbs, *by Jack Mingo and John Javna.*

SELF KNOWLEDGE

"I am what I am and that's all that I am."

—Popeye,
The Popeye Show

"The blossom below the water knows not sunlight. And men, not knowing, will find me hard to understand."

—Caine,
Kung Fu

COSMIC THOUGHTS

"There's a time to be Daniel Boone, and there's a time to be a plumber."

—MacGyver,
MacGyver

"The butcher with the sharpest knife has the warmest heart."

—Village saying,
The Prisoner

"A day without grapes is like a day without apples."

—Kelly Robinson,
I Spy

"There's a big difference between making instant coffee and bringing a Rastafarian back from the dead."

—Ricardo Tubbs,
Miami Vice

EVERYTHING IS EVERYTHING

"I know they're blue berries, but they might not be blueberries. And while all blueberries are blue berries, not all blue berries are blueberries."

—Alex Reiger,*Taxi*"

RULES FOR LIVING

"No good deed goes unpunished."

—B.J. Hunnicut,
M*A*S*H

"Most people's lives are governed by telephone numbers."

—Narrator, *Hitchhiker's Guide to theGalaxy*

"No river is shallow to a man who cannot swim."

—Paladin,
Have Gun Will Travel

FIRST HITS

Here are the inside stories of the first hit records for three of the most successful music acts in history—the Beatles, Elvis, and Simon & Garfunkel—from Behind the Hits, *by Bob Shannon and John Javna.*

THE BEATLES

First Hit: "Love Me Do," 1962

BACKGROUND: The tune was written by Paul McCartney, who called it "our greatest philosophical song." He skipped school and wrote it when he was sixteen years old.

By the time the Beatles went to London in 1962 to try to get a recording contract, it was one of their best numbers.

They played it at their audition...but the record executive assigned to work with them, George Martin, wasn't particularly impressed. Still, he agreed to give them a contract—and even make "Love Me Do" their first single—provided they got a new drummer.

THE SESSION: The recording session took place on September 11, 1962, at Abbey Road Studios. The Beatles arrived with a new drummer, Ringo Starr...But Martin didn't trust him and brought his own session drummer, Andy White, to make the record. Ringo was despondent, so Martin took pity on him; he recorded several versions with Ringo, and several with White. (In fact, Ringo played on the English hit, and White was the drummer on the single released in America.) It took seventeen takes to get the song right. By the time they were done, John Lennon's lips were numb from playing the harmonica so much.

IT'S A HIT. On October 4, 1962, "Love Me Do" was released in England on Parlophone Records. It surged into the Top 20 and established the Beatles as a viable commercial group. But behind the scenes was manager Brian Epstein, making sure that the Beatles succeeded. He bought 10,000 copies himself, knowing that was the minimum amount their record company had to sell to make a disc a best-seller. Epstein's gimmick worked. The record company was impressed and got behind the Beatles' next single, "Please Please Me," which reached #1 in Britain and started a chain of events that revolutionized popular music.

In America, in 1962, no one wanted any part of the silly "Love Me Do." Capitol Records, which owned the rights to the song, practically gave it to Vee Jay Records, which later issued it on an album called "Introducing the Beatles."

On May 2, 1964, about a year and a half after it was first released, "Love Me Do" became the Beatles' fourth American #1 record.

ELVIS PRESLEY

First Hit: "Heartbreak Hotel," 1956

BACKGROUND: The headline on the front page of the *Miami Herald* read, "Do You Know This Man?" Below it was a photograph of a suicide victim. Who was he? The story explained that he'd left no clue about his identity behind—only a pathetic hand-written message that read, "I walk a lonely street." It asked the family—or anyone who recognized the photo—to get in touch with the police.

THE SONG: In Gainesville, Florida, a songwriter named Tommy Durden read the paper and was struck by the suicide note. Now *that* was a great line for a blues tune, he mused. The more he thought about it, the more he liked it...so he hopped in his car and drove over to Mae Axton's house to work on it. Mae was Tommy's collaborator in songwriting; she was also a local TV and radio personality. When Elvis Presley had come to town earlier in the year, she'd befriended the young singer and reportedly assured him that she'd be the one to write his first million-seller.

Mae agreed that the suicide line might make a good song, but couldn't stop thinking about how the guy's family would suffer when they found out about him. He might have walked a lonely street, but at the end of it there was surely going to be heartbreak for the people who loved him. So Mae decided there should be a "heartbreak hotel" at the end of "lonely street." From there it took fifteen minutes to write the whole song.

IT'S A HIT: A friend of Mae's named Glen Reeves dropped by her house and agreed to tape a version of the song in a pseudo-Elvis style—so Elvis would be able to imagine how he'd sound on the tune. Then Mae, demo in hand, drove up to Tennessee to play it for Elvis. "Hot dog, Mae!" Presley is said to have exclaimed, "Play it again!" Legend has it that when he recorded the song, Elvis copied Reeves's version note-for-note.

In exchange for agreeing to make it his first RCA record, Elvis got an equal share of the writer's credit. "Heartbreak Hotel" went to the top of the charts, establishing Elvis as the most popular new singer in America.

SIMON & GARFUNKEL

First Hit: "Hey Schoolgirl," 1957

BACKGROUND: Paul Simon got to know Artie Garfunkel in P.S. 164 in Queens when they both appeared in their sixth-grade graduation play, *Alice In Wonderland*. Paul was the White Rabbit, Artie was the Cheshire Cat. Because of their mutual interest in music, they became close friends, and when they were fourteen, they began writing songs together.

THE SINGERS: According to Paul Simon: "We were fifteen years old when we signed a contract with Big Records as Tom and Jerry. 'Hey Schoolgirl' was the first song we recorded. To go along with the Tom and Jerry thing, I took on the stage name of Tom Landis and Artie took Jerry Graph. I picked Landis because I was going out with a girl named Sue Landis at the time and Artie picked Graph because he used to [keep track] of all the current hit records on big sheets of graph paper.'Hey Schoolgirl' was sold in both 45 and 78 RPM; on the 45 it says by Landis-Graph, but on the 78 it's got P. Simon and A. Garfunkel."

IT'S A HIT: The song was released in 1957 and sold 120,000 copies, peaking at #54 after being on *Billboard's* "Top 100" for nine weeks. "You can't imagine," says Simon, "what it was like having a hit record behind you at the age of sixteen. One month Artie and I were watching 'American Bandstand' on television and the next month we were on the show." They had to follow Jerry Lee Lewis playing "Great Balls of Fire." It's one of the few "Bandstand" shows not preserved on tape.

"Hey Schoolgirl" was "Tom and Jerry's" only hit. Simon says he bought a red Impala convertible with the royalties.

IF THE SHOE FITS...

In ancient Inca weddings, the bride and groom weren't considered "officially" married until they had taken off their sandals and traded them with one another.

OH, MARILYN

Some little known facts about the life of the ultimate Hollywood icon.

Marilyn Monroe was born Norma Jean Mortenson, an illegitimate child, on June 1, 1926 in Los Angeles. Her mother, Gladys Pearl Baker, was a negative cutter in a Hollywood film studio. Her father, Edward Mortenson, was a baker.

★

Norma Jean's mother entered a sanitarium when she was three, and sent Norma Jean to live with her aunt. Her aunt later dumped her in a Los Angeles orphanage, where she was neglected and sexually abused.

★

Norma Jean spent much of her childhood in foster homes. She married an aircraft worker at age 16—to avoid getting sent to yet another foster home.

★

She was was discovered by an Army photographer whose boss had told him "to take some morale-building shots of pretty girls for *Yank* and *Stars and Stripes*." The photographer's boss: a soldier named Ronald Reagan.

She stuttered as a child: "It comes back sometimes," she said. "Once I had a small part with a scene in which I had to climb a staircase and I couldn't bring out my line. The director rushed over and shouted: 'You don't actually stutter?' 'Y-y-you th-think not?' I said to him."

★

Early in her career, Monroe was desperate for money. So she agreed to pose nude for a calendar, and was paid the standard modeling fee. To date more than 1 million copies of the photos have been sold, generating more than $750,000 in profits. Marilyn's share: $50.

★

Marilyn never understood why men were so attracted to her: "Why I was a siren, I hadn't the faintest idea. There were no thoughts of sex in my head...I had no thoughts of being seduced by a duke or a movie star. The truth was that with all my lipstick and mascara and precocious curves, I was as unsensual as a fossil. But I seemed to affect people otherwise."

Oops! One third of the U.S. population is reportedly the result of unwanted pregnancies.

TEARS IN THE SNOW

All's fair in love, war...and politics. But did somebody go just a little too far to win in '72? Here's information from a new book called It's a Conspiracy, *by the American Paranoid Society.*

BACKGROUND

As election year 1972 got underway, all eyes turned to New Hampshire, the nation's first primary. The Republican candidate would be President Richard Nixon, of course. But his reelection was not the foregone conclusion it seems in retrospect. Among other issues, his handling of the Vietnam war made him vulnerable.

• The Democrats' early favorite, Ted Kennedy, had been knocked out by Chappaquiddick. Of the eleven Democrats running, Senator Ed Muskie—Hubert Humphrey's 1968 running mate—looked like the strongest candidate. In the polls, a Muskie-Nixon race was dead even.

• Because Muskie was from Maine, he was expected to win the New Hampshire primary easily. But experts said a really impressive victory might clinch the nomination for him early.

WHAT HAPPENED

• William Loeb, owner and editor of New Hampshire's largest newspaper (the *Union Leader*)—and an arch-conservative—had been sniping at his liberal neighbor for years, nicknaming him "Moscow Muskie."

• Loeb also constantly repeated claims that Muskie had called French-Canadian descendants "Canucks," an unforgivable ethnic slur. This offended nearly half the state's voters.

• A little more than a week before the primary, Loeb ran a story about Mrs. Muskie headlined, "Big Daddy's Jane," slurring the candidate's wife as a heavy boozer with an itch for dirty stories.

A government study of U.S. eating habits turned up a man who drank 64 cups of coffee a day.

• It was a serious accusation in conservative New Hampshire. Muskie, terribly stung by the cheap shot at his wife, took the attack personally. He took the fight to Loeb the next day.

• Standing on a flatbed truck in a driving snowstorm outside *Union Leader* offices, the senator called Loeb ,"a gutless coward." Then Muskie, slump-shouldered and weary from campaigning, stood in the blizzard and wept.

• It was touching, but it killed him in the polls. Broadcast endlessly on the news, Muskie's emotional moment made him look like a basket case. As *Time* put it: "The moment of weakness left many voters wondering about Muskie's ability to stand up under stress."

• Muskie still won the primary, but with such a small margin that his campaign lost its momentum and soon collapsed.

THE OFFICIAL EXPLANATION

Since there were no allegations of a conspiracy at the time of the incident, there were no official explanations denying one.

SUSPICIOUS FACTS

• Loeb's source for the "Canuck" story was a letter from Paul Morrison in Deerfield Beach, Florida. However, when veteran reporter David Broder looked for Morrison, he could not be found.

• In fact, the Muskie camp was *plagued* with bizarre incidents. In March, 200 letters on *Citizens for Muskie* stationery were sent to supporters of Henry Jackson, a Muskie rival. The letters—which created tension between the Democratic camps—contended that Jackson had fathered an illegitimate child, and was later arrested on "homosexual charges."

• Some voters in largely white New Hampshire got calls at 2 or 3AM from representatives of the "Harlem for Muskie Committee" who promised "full justice for black people."

• Sometimes, the skulduggery was really intricate. "At a Muskie fund-raiser for 1300 people in Washington, D.C., several arrivals weren't planned: 200 pizzas nobody ordered, two magicians, and 16 ambassadors from African and Middle Eastern countries who, though entirely out of place, had to be treated courteously and fed."

It took 1,700 years to complete the Great Wall of China.

WAS THERE A CONSPIRACY?

Theory #1: YES. Ed Muskie was systematically harrassed and embarrassed to destroy his candidacy.

• The reporters who later broke the Watergate story said the "Canuck" letter and all the other tricks were part of a "massive campaign of political spying and sabotage conducted on behalf of the re-election effort by the White House and Nixon campaign officials."

• The "Canuck" letter was said to have been written by White House PR man Ken Clawson, but he denied it. According to Nixon's master of dirty tricks, Donald Segretti, Muskie's Washington fund raiser almost had one more guest: "We also made inquiries about renting an elephant, but were unable to make the arrangements."

• In time, all of Nixon's '72 adversaries were destroyed in one way or another. The Democrats' eventual nominee, George McGovern, was scuttled by leaks that his running mate had been in a mental hospital; George Wallace, whose strong appeal to conservatives might have drawn votes from Nixon, was shot in the stomach; and Ted Kennedy never ran because of Chappaquiddick. Coincidences?

Theory #2: NO. Loeb acted on his own.

• In light of the facts that came to light after Watergate, that's pretty hard to believe. The real question is, how far did the Nixon tricksters go in undermining the democratic process?

PARTING SHOTS

Muskie later said that though he was upset, he had not actually cried: it was melting snow running down his face. Whatever—it cost him the election. "It was," as he put it, "a bitch of a day."

SOLUTIONS

POP QUIZ, PAGE 687

1. Her eyes
2. Discovered by accident
3. Stearic acid from beef fat
4. At a picnic
5. Missionaries, because they were embarassed by all that bare skin
6. A crocodile
7. From his father's cowlick
8. Shirley Temple, W. C. Fields
9. Trick question—it *was* Bogart
10. Moe, Shemp, and Curley
11. Actually Vance was one year *younger*
12. Stabbed during a fight over a hunting dog
13. *Scrambled Eggs*
14. One
15. Two. Exactly the same. (There's one long groove on each side.)
16. Plastic
17. TV show
18. Money

HOW LONG, PAGE 727

1. B; 2. B; 3. A; 4. C; 5. C; 6. C; 7. B; 8. A; 9. B;
10. A; 11. B; 12. B; 13. A; 14. B; 15. B; 16. A; 17. A; 18. B.

PUNS:

1. "People who live in grass houses shouldn't stow thrones."
2. "Repaint, and thin no more."
3. "Let your pages do the walking through the yellow fingers."
4. "It takes two Wongs to make a white."
5. "I wouldn't send a knight out on a dog like this"
6. "A Benny shaved is a benny urned."
7. "The Czech is in the male."
8. "A weigh a day keeps the doctor an apple."

THE LAST PAGE

FELLOW BATHROOM READERS:

The fight for good bathroom reading should never be taken loosely—we must sit firmly for what we believe in, even while the rest of the world is taking pot shots at us.

Once we prove we're not simply a flush-in-the-pan, writers and publishers will find their resistance unrolling.

So we invite you to take the plunge: "Sit Down and Be Counted!" by joining The Bathroom Readers' Institute. Send a self-addressed, stamped envelope to: B.R.I., 1400 Shattuck Avenue, #25, Berkeley, CA 94709. You'll receive your attractive free membership card, a copy of the B.R.I. newsletter (if we ever get around to publishing one), and earn a permanent spot on the B.R.I. honor roll.

S0-BXW-409

FOUNDATIONS OF THE FAITH
FOR FOLLOWERS OF CHRIST

CHRISTIAN
— BASICS —
BIBLE

New Living Translation®

Tyndale House Publishers, Inc.
Carol Stream, Illinois

Visit Tyndale online at www.newlivingtranslation.com and www.tyndale.com.

Christian Basics Bible is an edition of the *Holy Bible,* New Living Translation.

For information about special discounts for bulk purchases, please contact Tyndale House Publishers at csresponse@tyndale.com or call 800-323-9400.

ISBN 978-1-4964-1355-0 Hardcover
ISBN 978-1-4964-1359-8 Hardcover Indexed
ISBN 978-1-4964-1356-7 Softcover
ISBN 978-1-4964-1357-4 LeatherLike Brown/Tan
ISBN 978-1-4964-1360-4 LeatherLike Brown/Tan Indexed

Printed in China

23 22 21 20 19 18 17
7 6 5 4 3 2 1

Tyndale House Publishers and Wycliffe Bible Translators share the vision for an understandable, accurate translation of the Bible for every person in the world. Each sale of the *Holy Bible,* New Living Translation, benefits Wycliffe Bible Translators. Wycliffe is working with partners around the world to accomplish Vision 2025—an initiative to start a Bible translation program in every language group that needs it by the year 2025.

Contents

The Old Testament

The New Testament

CONTRIBUTORS

General Editors
Mike Beaumont
Martin Manser

Editor
Timothy Belcher

Copy Editors
Ellen Richard
Jonathan Bryant
Brad Davis
Eric Huffman

Proofreading
Peachtree Editorial Services

Design
Dan Farrell

Typesetting
Audra Brady

Associate Publisher
Blaine A. Smith

Publisher
Douglas R. Knox

ACKNOWLEDGMENTS

The editors wish to thank the following for their help in compiling and checking previous material on which some parts of this work were based: Natasha Reece, Debra Reid, Martin Selman, and Stephen Travis.

In preparing this text, the editors also acknowledge their gratitude to Lion Hudson for allowing adaptation of material from *The One-Stop Bible Guide* (Lion Hudson, 2006) and *The New Lion Bible Encyclopedia* (Lion Hudson, 2012) by Mike Beaumont.

The following notes written by Mike Beaumont are adapted from *NIV Bible Handbook* (by Alister McGrath, edited by Martin Manser, Hodder & Stoughton, 2013) and are used by permission of Hodder & Stoughton: *Are the Ten Commandments still relevant today?*, page 89; *Can God still speak through "fleeces"?*, page 277; *Is there anything God won't forgive?*, page 633; *Does God mind if we are honest with him?*, page 848; *Does God really get angry?*, page 854; *Does marriage still matter to God?*, page 976; *Is God concerned about social justice?*, page 994; *Why do bad things happen in life?*, page 1025; *Does fasting have any value?*, page 1042; *Should Christians still tithe?*, page 1052; *Does it matter if I sin?*, page 1289; *Can a Christian marry a non-Christian?*, page 1329; *Can a Christian lose their salvation?*, page 1401; *How can I be sure God has forgiven me?*, page 1433.

Read This First!

The book you hold in your hands is the most exciting and life-changing book in the world! For some of you, this may be the first time you have ever picked up a Bible. Perhaps you became a Christian recently and have no Christian background whatsoever, so the thought of starting to read the Bible may seem a bit overwhelming. For others of you, you may have been part of a church for years but somehow just never got into the Bible, or whenever you did, it seemed remote and hard to grasp. Well, whichever category you fall into, this Bible is for you!

First of all, the Bible text itself is the easy-to-read New Living Translation. This means that, while it's a full Bible with nothing left out, it's translated into the language of today.

Moreover, the Bible text is accompanied by a whole range of helpful notes and features—all of them written especially for readers who know little or nothing of the Bible's story, background, or message. These supplemental materials are designed to help you engage with the Bible from scratch, to help you get hold of the basics—hence the title, the *Christian Basics Bible*.

The first additional feature that will help you is the **book introductions** at the beginning of each Bible book. Each introduction contains four sections that provide a helpful way into the book:

- *Introduction*—a short summary of the book's content
- *Overview*—an outline of the book
- *What's it all about?*—a summary of the book's content in more detail
- *What does it mean for us?*—a guide to the book's relevance for today

Second, throughout the Bible text, there are **notes** on various historical, cultural, social, biographical, practical, and theological issues—all written from the perspective of a reader who is new to all of this, and all geared toward showing the relevance of the Bible for today. Some of these notes include maps to give you an idea of where key events happened or charts that help summarize information on a wide range of topics. At the end of many notes and also throughout the Bible text you will find cross-references to related notes.

Third, at the front and back of the Bible you will find **other material** that we think you will find helpful in laying a strong foundation for your Christian faith. These include:

- three articles: "Becoming a Christian," "Now that You Are a Christian," and "What Is the Bible?"
- a timeline of the Bible to show you what happened when
- two Bible reading plans
- a section called "Basic Truths of the Christian Faith" that can be used as a starting point in finding and engaging with the answers that God's word provides on many basic questions about life and faith

- a glossary and a feature index
- "A Visual Overview of the Bible," which provides a helpful visual means of accessing the Bible's story. These maps and infographics give a survey of the biblical narrative through visually engaging historical, geographical, and thematic background material.

Our prayer is that all of this will help the Bible come alive for you! If you don't already have a relationship with God through Jesus, we pray that reading this Bible will help you come to know Jesus personally and find the difference that he makes in life. And if you are already a Christian—whether new or long-standing—our prayer is that you may find help in developing your faith, acquiring a strong foundation, and becoming a strong, mature, and fruitful Christian. The Bible has helped millions of people over countless generations to know God better and to find their place in his plans; we pray that the same may be true for you. And if, after a few years, you move on from this edition of the Bible to a different study Bible that helps you dig even deeper into its teachings, then there will be no one happier than us.

Mike Beaumont
Martin Manser

Becoming a Christian

Becoming a Christian is not about deciding to live better, trying to be more holy, going to church, or following certain religious practices or behaviors. It is about beginning a personal relationship with God. Religious rules and duties will always end up tying us up, as Jesus often reminded the highly religious Pharisees of his day. Jesus came not to tie us up but to set us free (see, e.g., John 8:31-32; Galatians 5:1). He came with good news (the meaning of the word "gospel"); and this good news is that ordinary people—even people who feel unworthy or have failed or have done bad things—can know God personally and live in harmony with him.

But before that can happen, something has to go—our old way of life, the life that always puts self first, just like Adam and Eve did (see Genesis 3). In fact, following their disobedience, something entered the human race that separates each one of us from God (see Romans 5:12). Somehow that barrier needs to be removed—though none of us, the Bible says, can do anything about it.

But what we could not do, God himself did: Such is his love for us. The way he did this was by coming into this world himself to rescue us, in the person of his Son, Jesus Christ. As the One who was God-become-man, he was uniquely capable of doing two things: As a man, he had *the right* to replace us, to be our substitute; as God, he had *the power* to deal with the sin that separated us from him. The way he did this was through his execution on the cross—a death he did not deserve, for he had lived a perfect, sinless life that deserved no condemnation, as even his judge agreed (Luke 23:4). As our substitute, he took upon himself the sins of every human being who had ever lived, and would ever live, and bore the punishment for us (see 1 Peter 2:24). He is "the Lamb of God" (John 1:29; see also 1 Peter 1:19)—the sacrifice provided by God himself. And what proved that his sacrifice had been effective was his resurrection, God's confirmation that Christ had indeed conquered sin and death for us and that the way to God was now open.

All God asks of us now is that we believe this! But this belief is not just about accepting certain facts about Jesus; it is about committing yourself to live a whole new life in light of those facts. We can do this by taking the following steps:

- First, we need to *acknowledge* that God's perspective on us is true, that "everyone has sinned; we all fall short of God's glorious standard" (Romans 3:23)—including me—and we need to repent of all wrongdoing.
- Second, we need to *believe* that Jesus is God's Son and that he died on the cross to pay the price for all our sin (Romans 10:9-10).
- Third, we need to *commit* our lives to him and promise that, from this time on, we will be his true disciples, learning from him and putting into practice all he says to us.

You could pray a prayer like this: "Dear God, I am sorry I have left you out of my life. I acknowledge that I have sinned against you in thought, word, and deed. I believe that you sent your Son, Jesus, to die on the cross to pay the price for my sins. So now please forgive all my sin. I commit my life totally into your hands, to love and serve you. Please fill me with your Holy Spirit that I may now begin to live for you alone. In Jesus' name. Amen."

If you pray this with all your heart, then from that moment on you are "born again" (John 3:3), a child of God (1 John 3:1), and part of his growing redeemed family (see Ephesians 2:19). Don't worry if you don't feel an immediate change (some people do; some don't). What matters is that you trust that Jesus has done what he promised to do (see, e.g., Revelation 3:20). His Holy Spirit *is* now at work in your life, and from this moment onward your life will begin to change, and you will never be the same again. You are now a child of the living God!

Now that You Are a Christian

Just as a baby doesn't understand what has happened to it when it is born, so we really don't understand fully what has happened to us when we are "born again" into God's family through faith in Jesus. All we know is that *something new has started* (2 Corinthians 5:17)! You are now living a new life, made possible through God's Holy Spirit bringing your human spirit to life. This new life brings several new things to you:

A NEW RELATIONSHIP

Through Jesus you have been brought into relationship with the living God. He is now your heavenly Father—a Father who is perfect and is everything you would want a father to be. He will always be there for you and promises to never leave you (Hebrews 13:5). He will provide for all your needs as you seek to put him first (Matthew 6:25-34).

Developing the relationship

Like any new relationship, your relationship with God now needs to be developed. That requires spending time together, talking and listening. The talking is done through *prayer*. Prayer (see *The Lord's Prayer*, page 1077) is simply conversation with God. Unlike in other religions, Christian prayer needs no special words, rituals, places, or times. Simply talk to God as you would to your best friend—and be honest with him (see *Does God mind if we are honest with him?*, page 848). Share everything with him—your gratitude, concerns, needs, and mistakes—and don't give up if your prayer isn't answered immediately! (See *Perseverance in prayer*, page 1184.) The listening is best achieved by *reading the Bible*, God's word to us (though you will often hear God in your heart, too, as you listen while praying). If you get into the habit of reading a portion of the Bible daily in a systematic way, you will be amazed at how just the right passage comes up at just the moment you need it.

▶ *See also* ***Studying God's word****, page 1387.*

Not being ashamed

It is important not to be ashamed of this new relationship. Be ready to tell others about it. This can be done in two ways. First, it can be done through *words*, telling others what Jesus has done for you (what Christians call a "testimony"). Be wise how you do this, but don't be embarrassed or try to hide your faith. Second, it can be done through *action*, particularly through the action of baptism (see *Baptism*, page 1238). Baptism is your badge of allegiance to Jesus, making public to everyone that you now belong to him.

A NEW FAMILY

When we come to God as our Father, we join with many others who are also his children—our new brothers and sisters in Christ. Together we form God's big family, the church. It is therefore important to express that by *joining a local church*. Churches come in many different kinds; simply find one where you feel at home. Don't just look for people like you, however—from your neighborhood, people group, or profession. The wonderful thing about the church is that it comprises people "from every nation and tribe and people and language" (Revelation 7:9), and we have the joy of experiencing and demonstrating that right now. Meet with your new spiritual family as often as you can—attending worship on Sunday and being part of its midweek or small-group structures. This is part of God's provision to help you grow strong as a Christian.

▶ *See also* ***Belonging to a church****, page 1406.*

A NEW ENEMY

Becoming a Christian isn't always easy. Not everyone will appreciate your decision; some may think you have betrayed your family or former faith and may at best mock you or at worst oppose or persecute you. Behind all this lies your new enemy, the devil, who, as Peter said, "prowls around like a roaring lion, looking for someone to devour" (1 Peter 5:8). These words are not meant to frighten us but to cause us to be alert. And that is why Paul tells us to "put on all of God's armor" (Ephesians 6:11) and lists some of the weapons God has given us to help us stand in the fight (Ephesians 6:11-17).

▶ *See also* ***Spiritual warfare****, page 1353.*

A NEW FRIEND

Thankfully, that isn't the last word! For we are not left alone. Jesus sends us his Holy Spirit, just as he promised (see John 14:15-18). The Spirit helps us both to develop our relationship with the Father and to resist the devil. That is why Paul tells us to "be filled with the Holy Spirit"—literally, to "go on being filled with the Spirit" (Ephesians 5:18). The Spirit is the One who brings God's presence and power, who guides and restrains us, who urges us on when we are timid, who helps us to witness to Jesus, and who gives us his gifts to be used in God's service. With him, our new life in Christ is an exciting adventure!

▶ *See also* ***The Christian's relationship with the Holy Spirit****, page 1350.*

What Is the Bible?

THE BIBLE'S LIBRARY

The word "Bible" comes from the Greek word *biblia*, which means "books"—yes, books, plural. That's because the Bible isn't just one book but rather a collection of sixty-six books, written by some forty authors over a period of around fifteen hundred years. That makes it a kind of "library of books." And just as in any library, those books are not gathered chronologically (in order of the time that they describe or were written in), but by category.

First, we have what we call ***The Old Testament***, with its main sections of *Law* (recording the beginnings of creation, humanity, and God's people), *history* (telling us the story of that people), the *poetry and wisdom* of that people, and the words of their *prophets*—all of which prepare for the coming of Jesus.

Then we come to ***The New Testament*** with its four *Gospels* (recording the story of the life, death, and resurrection of Jesus), *Acts* (the story of the early church and how it took the message of Jesus out to the world), *letters* written to the first churches, and a book called *Revelation*, which shows how God is ultimately in control, no matter what happens in human history, and how everything works out in the end.

Through all of these books, with all their individual stories, the Bible tells us one big, overarching story. It is the story of God's love for people and his determination to rescue them from the mess they have made of both their lives and the world and to restore them to friendship with him, putting things back to the way they were at the beginning. The Bible is therefore an amazing love story.

THE BIBLE'S WRITERS

Each part of the Bible has two writers: the person who wrote the words and God, who was actively inspiring them in what they wrote. As the apostle Paul explained, "All Scripture is inspired by God" (2 Timothy 3:16). The term "inspired" doesn't mean that the human authors were some kind of robot, mechanistically churning out words that they had no control over. Nor were they mere mail carriers, dropping off letters someone else had written. Rather, the Greek word translated "inspired" means "God-breathed." In other words, God so breathed by his Spirit upon the writers that he stirred their hearts and thoughts to write exactly what he wanted written. The apostle Peter said a similar thing, but using a different picture. He wrote that the writers of Scripture were "moved by the Holy Spirit" (2 Peter 1:21). The word "moved" in the original Greek was the word used of a ship being moved as it hoisted its sails to catch the wind. In other words, it is as if the writers of the Bible hoisted an inner sail to God's Spirit, who then moved them along in their writing.

But because these writers were human and not robots, their different styles come out in that writing. For example, Isaiah was well educated, so his prophecies are written in beautifully poetic Hebrew; but Peter, whose story probably lay behind Mark's Gospel, was a working-class man, so Mark's Gospel is written in simple, fast-moving Greek. When God comes into our lives, he doesn't override our personalities; nor did he do so with the writers of the Bible.

THE BIBLE'S LANGUAGES

The original texts of the Bible were written in three ancient languages: Hebrew, Aramaic, and Greek. The Old Testament was written entirely in Hebrew, apart from some small sections of it—Daniel 2:4–7:28; Ezra 4:8–6:18; 7:12-26; and Jeremiah 10:11. These passages were all written in Aramaic, an international language of Bible times, because they concerned nations other than Israel, and God wanted them to hear his message. The entire New Testament was written in Greek, the language used throughout the Roman Empire in the first and second centuries AD. Excellent scholarship has ensured that these languages are translated accurately for us today.

Some people worry about whether our Bible today is an accurate representation of the original manuscripts. After all, messages often get changed when passed on, even among people with the best intentions; so how can we be sure that didn't happen to the Bible? Two key things reassure us. First, we know that copyists of the ancient texts took great care in hand-copying their work (long before the invention of printing). They copied word for word, then counted how many words and letters were on each page and checked it against the original copy. So mistakes were rare—especially since they believed they were dealing with God's word. But the truth is, mistakes sometimes did happen. And that is where our second reassurance comes in—the science of the study of ancient texts. This has become a very refined skill which, through years of research and experience, has led to the development of guidelines that help us to ascertain the original text with remarkable accuracy. And if there is ever uncertainty about how a word or phrase should be translated, a footnote is made to that effect, as in this Bible.

THE BIBLE'S LAYOUT

To help us find our way around the Bible, each book is divided up into chapters and verses. The chapter and verse numbers aren't part of the original Bible text, however; they were simply added later in church history as a tool to assist us. In a reference to a specific place in the Bible (e.g., John 3:16), the **name of the book** comes first; then the first number is the **chapter**, and the second number is the **verse**. In the biblical text of this edition, chapter numbers appear in blue in a larger font, while verse numbers appear in black in a smaller font. The Table of Contents at the front will help you find each book quickly.

THE BIBLE'S MESSAGE

At the heart of the Bible's sixty-six books lies one central message: God's love for people and his determination to save them. **The Old Testament** opens with the story of creation, then tells of how things started to go wrong with the human race and of God's resolve to put this right. His plan would involve a family—a family through whom he would eventually build a nation (Israel), from which he would eventually bring a Messiah to save not just Israel but the whole world. The story unfolds slowly, and at times it even looks like it is going backward rather than forward; but God was steadily working out his plan. And then, "when the right time came, God sent his Son" (Galatians 4:4). This is where **The New Testament** comes in, telling us about the coming of God's own Son, Jesus, who was the Messiah promised in the Old Testament. It was through his life, death, resurrection, and ascension that salvation could be given, not just to Israel, but to everyone who believed in him. Through him, God's Kingdom started to break into this world—a small seed at first, but one that would grow into a worldwide harvest of people who loved God and one another. The church, God's redeemed people, has been given the responsibility and the privilege of taking this message of God's love through Jesus to others—a task that will only be completed when Jesus returns at the end of the age, destroys all evil, and makes everything new. The Bible both tells us this story and gives us insights into how to live a fulfilled life with God, serving him and others.

THE BIBLE'S IMPORTANCE

Reading the Bible is important. Why? First and foremost because it reveals God to us, showing us what he is really like. The Bible shows us that God is good and loving, always right and faithful (Exodus 34:6-7); he is the perfect Father. His character is reflected in everything he does: creating a beautiful world (Genesis 1:1-31), having a plan for when people messed up that world, steadily unfolding that plan through the story of Israel, and bringing it to a climax through sending his own Son, Jesus, to deal with sin through his death on the cross (Romans 3:23-26). How would we know all this if it were not for the Bible?

Secondly, the Bible shows us the way to have a relationship with this God. We receive this gift of relationship with him through Jesus Christ by truly turning away (the Bible's word for this is "repenting") from our own independent, anti-God (sinful) way of living and turning to God in belief (see John 1:12; Acts 20:21). Such believing includes personally accepting that Jesus died on the cross to take the punishment for our sin. As we trust Jesus, he saves us and puts us in a right relationship with God in a way no one else can (see Luke 18:9-14; John 3:16; Romans 3:21-28).

Thirdly, the Bible shows us the way to live out that relationship in daily life. Reading the Bible nurtures our faith by bringing the very life of God to us through his Spirit so we can live in relationship with God as he wants us to. Through the Bible, God helps us to grow stronger, to come to know him better, and to become more like Jesus. It answers many of the questions we face in life—questions such as, How should we behave at work, at home, with our families, and in society? (See Colossians 3:1–4:6.) Why and how should we pray? (See Luke 11:1-13.) What do we do when the going gets tough? (See Ephesians 6:10-20.) But it will also challenge our worldview, for sin has caused us to get out of step with God. So it will sometimes cut across our cultural norms or our former way of living. But as we not only read the Bible but also seek to put it into practice, we will find that it increasingly shapes us into the people God wants us to be.

READING THE BIBLE

Because some parts of the Bible are hard to understand, we sometimes need help in grasping what it means and how it applies to life today. The notes throughout this edition will help you with that. Bible devotionals and commentaries can also be very helpful (ask your pastor or a Christian friend for more information about these resources).

But here is a simple approach we can adopt when reading the Bible. First, ask yourself, what would this passage have meant *then* (to the people who first experienced or heard this)? Put yourself into the story and imagine what it must have been like and how people must have reacted or what they must have thought. Second, ask yourself, how does this apply to us *today*? What does this story reveal about what God is like? And what abiding principles does the story give us about how God wants his people to live? Always start with "then"—then move to "today." This will help you to avoid the danger of reading things back into the story that were never there.

THE OLD TESTAMENT

The Old Testament is made up of four main sections in our Christian Bibles—Law, History, Poetry and Wisdom, and Prophets—though the Jewish Bible divides it up differently and has three main sections called Law, Prophets, and Writings.

The Law

This is the name given to the first five books of the Bible. This section is also sometimes called "the Pentateuch" (from a Greek expression meaning "five books"). According to the oldest Jewish and Christian traditions, these five books were written by Moses, though they were probably shaped as we now have them by a later editor. They are partly historical, partly legal in character. ***Genesis***, meaning "beginning," tells us of the beginnings of everything—creation, humanity, the breakdown of relationship with God, and the origins of the family God would use to start his rescue program (Abraham and his descendants, the Jews). ***Exodus*** narrates God's rescue of this people from the slavery in Egypt that they ended up in. He called a man named Moses, who, backed up by miracles from God, dramatically led Israel to freedom. At Mount Sinai, God made a "covenant" or "binding agreement" with the Israelites, taking them as his own people and giving them his laws, including the Ten Commandments. ***Leviticus*** reveals what the people of Israel had to do when they disobeyed those laws and the relationship with God was broken: offer sacrifices to deal with their sin. ***Numbers*** continues the story as the Israelites left Mount Sinai and made their way toward Canaan, the land God had promised to give them. But repeated disobedience led to their spending forty years in the wilderness as that whole generation died out. In ***Deuteronomy***, Moses looked back over Israel's history and reminded them of their laws, calling them to be faithful to God as they were about to enter the Promised Land. They would enter it without Moses, however. He died within sight of the Promised Land, but he never made it there himself.

The Historical Books

This section contains twelve books covering the history of the Israelites from their entry into the Promised Land to their exile from it and eventual return. ***Joshua*** contains exciting stories of God giving them military victories—at times surprising or miraculous victories—over the Canaanites under the leadership of Moses' successor, Joshua. ***Judges*** records some sad stories as the newly established nation of Israel was repeatedly disobedient and unfaithful to God. But God stayed faithful to them. He appointed leaders or "judges" to rescue them from their various enemies; but every time, despite their initial gratitude, they soon fell back into disobedient and idolatrous ways. But the story of ***Ruth***, set in the time of the judges, shows us a glimmer of hope. It contains the story of someone who was faithful to God even in dark days and whom God used to further his rescue plan—for Ruth would be the great-grandmother of the famous King David. ***1 and 2 Samuel*** record Israel's history from the end of the period of the judges to Israel's first kings, Saul and David. The early chapters are dominated by the prophet Samuel, after whom the books are named, who helped Israel transition from a theocracy (a nation ruled directly by God) to a monarchy, which is what the people asked for. Saul started his reign well but finished badly and was rejected by God. David was God's chosen replacement through whom he promised to build a kingdom that would never end—something Christians see fulfilled through his descendant Jesus. ***1 and 2 Kings*** record the reign of David's son Solomon and the division of the kingdom into a northern kingdom (Israel) and a southern kingdom (Judah) after his death because of the foolishness of his son. Israel was conquered by Assyria in 722 BC, and Judah by Babylon in 586 BC—both because of ongoing and willful disobedience to God. Israel was scattered and dispersed; Judah was taken into exile and preserved. ***1 and 2 Chronicles*** tell the same history again, but this time from the perspective of those who returned to Judah after the seventy-year exile and who were asking the question, Is God still with us?—to which the author's answer was: Yes! ***Ezra*** records the story of the rebuilding of the Temple in Jerusalem by the returning exiles; while ***Nehemiah*** tells us of Nehemiah's bold leadership in rebuilding Jerusalem's walls and defenses, and in rebuilding Israel itself as a people who were to hold God's word as foundational. But not everyone came back from exile; ***Esther*** was a young Jewish woman who was born in exile and remained there. She rose to become queen of Persia and was able to save the Jews from a plot to exterminate them.

The Books of Poetry and Wisdom

This section of the Bible contains stories, proverbs, and poems that deal with many of "the big questions" of life: things like suffering, meaning, God, and love. ***Job*** is the story of a really good man who experienced incredible suffering—none of which was helped by the input of his friends. Job ultimately found peace, not by finding answers, but by finding God in a new way. ***Psalms*** is the hymn and prayer book of the Old Testament and contains prayers that cover the whole range of human experiences and emotions. ***Proverbs*** is a collection of short sayings that seek to bring God's wisdom to a wide range of everyday situations. They highlight what happens when people don't walk in God's ways, and the blessing that follows when they do. ***Ecclesiastes*** takes us on a journey through life from birth to death. It considers the age-old question, What is life all about?—and shows how empty it all is if lived without God. The ***Song of Songs*** (or ***Song of Solomon***) is a collection of love songs, celebrating the joy of human love and the relationship between a man and a woman.

The Books of the Prophets

This section contains the writings of four so-called Major Prophets ("major" because of the length of their works rather than the importance of their writings) and twelve Minor Prophets. The four Major Prophets are Isaiah, Jeremiah, Ezekiel, and Daniel. ***Isaiah*** repeatedly warned Judah of God's coming judgment through conquest and exile, but his great vision of God and his holiness also brought hope that when the judgment was past, God would once again restore his people. He also looked ahead to the coming of the Messiah, the one who would come to ultimately deliver God's people. ***Jeremiah*** prophesied judgment upon Judah because of their unfaithfulness, and his prophecies led to much personal suffering for him. Judgment would come in the form of exile to Babylon. Jeremiah also wrote ***Lamentations***, a lament over the destruction of Jerusalem by the Babylonians. ***Ezekiel*** was a priest taken into exile in Babylon. With his priestly work now over, God called him to be a prophet, though his language remained that of a priest. He saw both the reason for Judah's exile—their uncleanness before God—and God's restoration of them in the future. ***Daniel***, taken into captivity in Babylon, served a number of pagan kings there, but he used his position to bring God's word to them by interpreting their dreams. His own dreams gave him a glimpse of God's plan for the future and his establishing of a kingdom that, unlike human empires, would never end.

The first of the twelve Minor Prophets is ***Hosea***, who prophesied to the northern kingdom of Israel in its closing years, assuring them of God's faithfulness despite their own unfaithfulness. ***Joel*** described a devastating plague of locusts, which he interpreted as a sign of the coming "day of the LORD," and he called people back to God in light of it. ***Amos*** was passionate about social justice and called upon the rich and materialistic in Israel to change. ***Obadiah***, whose work is the shortest book in the Old Testament, prophesied against Judah's neighbor Edom, calling them to account for their behavior. ***Jonah*** is the story of a reluctant prophet whom God called to preach in Nineveh, the capital of Assyria. Jonah really didn't want to, being unwilling to accept that God loved other nations, too, and not just Israel. ***Micah*** spoke against the injustices in society and promised judgment on both Israel and Judah for their sins; yet he also promised hope, forgiveness, and restoration. ***Nahum*** prophesied that God would comfort his people through the coming destruction of Nineveh. ***Habakkuk*** questioned God about his justice, wanting to know why he would use wicked Babylon to punish his holy people. ***Zephaniah*** condemned the spiritual state of Judah and prophesied that the coming "day of the LORD" would bring judgment not just against others but also against God's own people. ***Haggai*** urged the returning exiles to renew their commitment to God and to prioritize rebuilding the Temple. ***Zechariah*** also encouraged God's people to throw off their discouragement and rebuild the Temple, assuring them that great things still lay ahead. ***Malachi*** challenged God's people to be wholehearted in their serving of God and to get ready for the coming of his messenger, who would prepare the way for the Messiah.

▸ *See also **A timeline of the Bible**, pages A22-A24.*

THE NEW TESTAMENT

The Gospels

The word *gospel* means "good news," and the news about Jesus is so good that we get not just one account of it but four—each one written from a slightly different perspective and highlighting slightly different things in order to fill out the picture we get of Jesus. These four accounts make up nearly half of the New Testament.

Matthew wrote his Gospel primarily for Jews who had become Christians. He uses many quotations from the Old Testament to prove that Jesus was the promised Messiah, and his collection of Jesus' teaching into five main blocks is a way of saying, "Here is the new Moses (the writer of the first five books of the Bible), who leads his people into freedom." ***Mark***, although second in order, was probably the first Gospel to be written. His account, written for Gentiles (non-Jews), is succinct and fast-moving. He has little time for details, so he launches straight into the start of Jesus' ministry, showing us through Jesus' teaching and miracles that he is both Messiah and Son of God. ***Luke***, the only non-Jewish Gospel writer, emphasizes that Jesus is for everybody, especially those society has rejected. His account stretches from Jesus' conception to his return to heaven (the Ascension), and it includes many details that the other Gospels do not have, such as information about Jesus' childhood. ***John*** is quite different from the other three Gospels, approaching the story of Jesus in a distinctive way. Although John knew many stories, he carefully chose just some—seven signs (miracles) and seven sayings (known as the "I am" sayings)—stating that his purpose was "that you may continue to believe that Jesus is the Messiah, the Son of God, and that by believing in him you will have life by the power of his name" (John 20:31).

Matthew, Mark, and Luke are called the "synoptic" Gospels, from a Greek word meaning "seen from the same viewpoint."

▶ *For charts showing where the parables and miracles of Jesus are recorded in the Gospels, see **Jesus' parables**, page 1089, and **Jesus' miracles**, page 1128.*

Acts

Acts of the Apostles is the second part of Luke's two-volume work (compare Luke 1:3 and Acts 1:1). In it he continues the story of Jesus that he began in his Gospel, starting with Jesus' return to heaven (the Ascension) and his sending the Holy Spirit on the Day of Pentecost. Now the story of Jesus could continue—not through Jesus in person, but through his empowered followers, the church. Acts shows how the church kept at its very core the mission to spread the Good News "in Jerusalem, throughout Judea, in Samaria, and to the ends of the earth" (Acts 1:8). Luke follows that geographic pattern in his account, highlighting the work not just of key apostles like Peter and Paul but also of ordinary church members. The book ends in an open-ended way as Paul, even though under house arrest in Rome, just kept preaching the gospel to everyone who came to him.

The Letters

The newly established church needed a lot of help, and that help was provided by the visits and letters of the apostles. These letters dealt with a wide range of matters: from right beliefs about God and Jesus to right living for those who followed Jesus. This section begins with thirteen letters written by the apostle Paul, some to churches and some to individuals.

Romans, written to prepare the way for Paul to visit a church he did not know and had not founded, outlined his gospel so that they would know they believed the same thing. In this letter, he shows that the gospel of Jesus is God's plan of salvation and righteousness for everyone who believes, Jew and Gentile alike; and he shows how the gospel, lived in the power of God's Spirit, should transform our lives. In ***1 and 2 Corinthians*** Paul deals with many of the problems the church in Corinth faced as a result of selfishness, immorality, worldliness, and super-spirituality. ***Galatians*** is one of his most strongly worded letters, challenging those who were saying that, to be a real Christian, you had to become a Jew as well (by being circumcised and keeping the Law). He makes it very clear that salvation is through faith in Jesus alone. In ***Ephesians*** Paul explains that God's great and mysterious plan is being worked out through the church, which lies at the very center of this letter. ***Philippians*** is a letter full of joy as Paul thanks his Christian friends in Philippi for their support of his ministry and as he encourages them to keep pressing on. ***Colossians*** tackles some cultural and religious ideas that had trickled into the church from the surrounding culture and which urgently needed to be addressed because they were undermining the deity and supremacy of Christ. ***1 and 2 Thessalonians***, among Paul's earliest letters, deal with people's wrong understandings about Christ's second coming. ***1 and 2 Timothy*** and ***Titus*** are letters to church leaders, containing practical advice on church leadership. ***Philemon*** is a personal letter, appealing to a man named Philemon on behalf of a runaway slave, Onesimus, who had now become a Christian.

What follows is a collection of letters by other leaders in the early church, the first of which—***Hebrews***—is completely anonymous. It was almost certainly written to Jews who had become Christians but who were being pressured to give up their Christian faith and return to Judaism. The author shows them that this would be a big mistake since everything about Jesus is better and since he fulfilled everything that the Old Testament pointed to. ***James***, one of the earliest New Testament writings, is a letter to Jewish Christians experiencing various troubles that had spilled over into church life. It is therefore full of practical teaching on how to live out the Christian life together. ***1 Peter***, written by the apostle Peter, encouraged Christians who were being persecuted for their faith, while ***2 Peter*** contains warnings against false teachers and urges believers to stand firm. ***1, 2, and 3 John*** were all written by the apostle John to help Christians be sure of their faith and to show them how to work that out in their everyday lives—lives that should be full of love. ***Jude*** encouraged believers to stand firm against false teachers and the havoc they were causing.

When reading these letters, we should always remember that they are exactly that—letters. As such, they were written to specific people at specific times for specific reasons, so it is important to understand as much as we can about the background or context to help us interpret them correctly. Nevertheless, while they are letters from people to people, they are also letters from God. His inspiration lies behind them all, as the early church leaders themselves began to see. Peter, for example, put Paul's letters on a par with "other parts of Scripture" (2 Peter 3:15-16). Therefore, even though they address issues at a certain point in history, they also contain God's eternal principles for us today.

Revelation

In many ways, the final book of the Bible, ***Revelation***, could be included in the previous section, since the book itself tells us it is a letter (Revelation 1:4), and its opening follows the standard form of a letter in those days. Yet it is more than a letter. It also describes itself as a "revelation" (Revelation 1:1) and a prophecy (Revelation 1:3; 22:18). Using spectacular and mysterious images—often puzzling to us but well-understood by the original recipients—Revelation assured believers who were being persecuted for their faith that, despite everything that was happening, Jesus was still Lord, was still seated on his throne, and would triumph at the End. And his triumph over all evil would be followed by a new heaven and a new earth, and God's redeemed people would be safe with him forever. The Paradise lost in Genesis 3 through human sin is here regained through God's own intervention!

A Timeline of the Bible

Dates in this chart are those that have been traditionally accepted. In the early period (before Israel's monarchy) all dates are approximate. A question mark (?) indicates scholarly uncertainty about the dating. Dates of kings, queens, and prophets are the dates of their reign or ministry. Where dates of kings overlap, it is where there was a "co-regency" (the next king being crowned before the death of the previous one to ensure a peaceful succession).

EARLY BIBLICAL HISTORY

Period	Key Events	Key Figures	Key Bible Passages
Beginnings	**Creation** **The Fall** **The Flood** **Babel**	**Adam** **Noah**	**Genesis 1–11**
The Patriarchs	**God's promise to Abraham**	**Abraham** *2166–1991 BC* **Isaac** *2066–1886 BC* **Jacob** *2006–1859 BC* **Joseph** *1915–1805 BC*	**Genesis 12–50**
Israel in Egypt, the Exodus, and Sinai	**Slavery in Egypt** **The Exodus** *1446 BC* **Sinai and wilderness wanderings** *1446–1406 BC*	**Moses** *1526–1406 BC*	**Exodus**
Conquest of Canaan	**Crossing the Jordan** *1406 BC* **Conquest of Canaan** *1406–1375 BC* **The judges** *1375–1050 BC*	**Joshua** *1486–1376 BC*	**Exodus—Deuteronomy** **Joshua** **Judges**
The United Monarchy		**Saul** *1050–1010 BC*	**1 Samuel**
		David *1010–970 BC*	**2 Samuel; 1 Chronicles**
		Solomon *970–930 BC*	**1 Kings; 2 Chronicles**
The kingdom splits in two *930 BC*			

THE DIVIDED MONARCHY

Prophets of Judah	Kings of Judah (the southern kingdom)	Kings of Israel (the northern kingdom)	Prophets of Israel
	Rehoboam *930–913* BC	**Jeroboam I** *930–909* BC	
	Abijah *913–910* BC **Asa** *910–869* BC	**Nadab** *909–908* BC **Baasha** *908–886* BC	
		Elah *886–885* BC **Zimri** *885* BC **Tibni** *885–880* BC **Omri** *885–874* BC	
	Jehoshaphat *872–848* BC	**Ahab** *874–853* BC **Ahaziah** *853–852* BC **Joram** *852–841* BC	**Elijah** *875–848* BC
Joel *835–825* BC *(?)*	**Jehoram** *848–841* BC **Ahaziah** *841* BC **Athaliah** *841–835* BC **Joash** *835–796* BC	**Jehu** *841–814* BC	**Elisha** *848–797* BC
		Jehoahaz *814–798* BC	
	Amaziah *796–767* BC **Uzziah (Azariah)** *792–740* BC	**Jehoash** *798–782* BC **Jeroboam II** *793–753* BC	
		Zechariah *753* BC **Shallum** *752* BC **Menahem** *752–742* BC **Pekahiah** *742–740* BC **Pekah** *752–732* BC	**Amos** *760–750* BC **Jonah** *c. 755* BC
Isaiah *740–685* BC **Micah** *735–686* BC	**Jotham** *750–735* BC **Ahaz** *735–715* BC	**Hoshea** *732–722* BC	**Hosea** *760–722* BC
	Hezekiah *715–686* BC	***Fall of Samaria and exile of the ten northern tribes*** *722* BC	
Habakkuk *640–605* BC **Zephaniah** *635–622* BC **Jeremiah** *626–580* BC	**Manasseh** *697–642* BC		
	Amon *642–640* BC **Josiah** *640–609* BC		
	Jehoahaz *609* BC **Jehoiakim** *609–598* BC	***Assyria conquered by Babylon*** *605* BC ***First Jews exiled to Babylon*** *605* BC	
Obadiah *c. 586* BC *(?)* **Joel** *(?)*	**Jehoiachin** *598–597* BC **Zedekiah** *597–586* BC		
	Fall of Jerusalem *586* BC		

EXILE AND RETURN

Prophets	Events in Judah	Events in Babylon & Persia	Key Bible Passages
Daniel *605–535 BC* Ezekiel *593–571 BC*	Temple destroyed and Judah exiled to Babylon *586 BC*		2 Kings 25; 2 Chronicles 36
Joel *(?)* Haggai *520 BC* Zechariah *520–480 BC*	Judea becomes part of Persia *539 BC* The Jewish exiles return to Jerusalem *538 BC* Temple rebuilt *536–515 BC*	Persia conquers Babylon *539 BC* Daniel continues to serve the Persian kings	Ezra, Daniel, Haggai, Zechariah
Malachi *440–430 BC* Joel *(?)*	Ezra returns to teach God's word *458 BC* Nehemiah rebuilds Jerusalem's walls *445–443 BC*	Esther *484–464 BC* Haman's attempt to exterminate the Jews	Esther Ezra Nehemiah
	Alexander the Great conquers Judea *333 BC* Growing Greek influence in Judea Maccabean revolt *167 BC* Rome conquers Judea *63 BC* Herod the Great *37–4 BC*		

THE NEW TESTAMENT PERIOD

Events in Judea and Galilee	Events elsewhere in the Roman Empire	Writing of New Testament Books
Jesus born *c. 5–4 BC*		
Jesus begins his ministry *c. AD 26* Jesus' crucifixion, resurrection, and ascension *c. AD 30* Pentecost *c. AD 30* Council of Jerusalem *AD 49*	Paul's conversion *c. AD 33–34* Paul's first missionary journey *AD 46–48*	Galatians *c. AD 48 (or AD 53)* James *c. AD 48* 1 & 2 Thessalonians *c. AD 50–51*
Jerusalem destroyed by Rome *AD 70*	Paul's second missionary journey *AD 50–52* Paul's third missionary journey *AD 53–57* Emperor Nero *AD 54–68* Paul imprisoned in Rome *AD 59–62* Peter dies *c. AD 65–67* Paul dies *c. AD 67*	1 & 2 Corinthians *c. AD 54–55* Romans *AD 57* Mark *late AD 50s/early 60s* Matthew *early AD 60s* Luke *early AD 60s* Ephesians, Philippians, Colossians, Philemon *AD 62* Acts *c. AD 62–63* 1 Peter *c. AD 62–63* 1 & 2 Timothy, Titus *AD 63–67* 2 Peter *c. AD 64–67* Jude *c. AD 65* Hebrews *c. AD 66–70*
		John's Gospel, his letters, and Revelation *c. AD 85–95*

Old Testament

Genesis *In the beginning*

The word "Genesis" means "origins." This book shows us about the origins of the world, especially the human race, and the origins of God's people, Israel.

Genesis tells us of God's creation of all things. Human beings were the high point of his creation, but their disobedience led to their expulsion not only from the Garden of Eden but also from intimate friendship with God. This sin of disobedience spread rapidly as the human race developed, but from the beginning we see that God had a plan to put things right again.

What's it all about?

Chapters 1 to 11 describe the earliest history of the world and its beginnings. They show us that the world as originally made by God was good, that the human race has a special place in that world (with both male and female being made in God's image to be like him and to be called into a relationship with him), and that humanity has a responsibility to look after God's world.

But because the first human beings disobeyed God, refusing to trust and obey him, the world in which we live is now "fallen." Brokenness in relationships, illness, suffering, trouble, and even death itself are the results of human sin. God responds to sin with judgment, but he also brings salvation, as we see in the story of the flood.

The remainder of Genesis shows us how God began his plan to mend a broken world. Even though human beings don't deserve it, God in his kindness loves the world, and so he made a covenant—a binding agreement involving a special relationship—with a man named Abraham. In this covenant he promised to bless not just Abraham and his descendants but ultimately the whole world. In return, God called for faithful obedience. So chapters 12 to 50 tell the stories of the ancestors of the people of Israel: Abraham, his son Isaac, Isaac's son Jacob, and Jacob's sons, who became the fathers of the twelve tribes of Israel. Through their descendants, God would work out his plan of salvation.

OVERVIEW

THE BEGINNING OF THE HUMAN RACE

The creation of the world
1:1–2:25

The first human beings disobey God
3:1-24

Adam's descendants and the spread of sin · *4:1–5:32*

The story of Noah and the flood
6:1–10:32

The tower of Babel
11:1-32

THE BEGINNINGS OF GOD'S PEOPLE, ISRAEL

The story of Abraham
12:1–25:34

The story of Isaac and Jacob
26:1–36:43

The story of Joseph
37:1–50:26

What does it mean for us?

Genesis gives us answers to the big questions of life: Who brought everything into being? What is God like? Why do things go wrong in the world? What is the purpose of life? Genesis shows us about God—that he is eternal, powerful, perfect; the creator and the giver of life. He is also personal and has made human beings in his image, to have a close relationship with him. He made men and women as equals, to be different, but to complement each other.

God gave the first human beings the principles of work and rest (2:2-3) and the basic social unit of marriage: the union of one man and one woman in a lifelong relationship (2:24). The rebellion of Adam and Eve led to God's judgment, which included death and suffering. Yet even in the midst of judgment, we see God's kindness and his patience with people.

Through God's special relationship with Abraham and his descendants, we see the beginning of God's plan to bring hope and salvation to the whole world, despite the reality of human sin.

The Account of Creation

1 In the beginning God created the heavens
and the earth.* 2The earth was formless
and empty, and darkness covered the deep
waters. And the Spirit of God was hovering
over the surface of the waters.

3Then God said, "Let there be light," and
there was light. 4And God saw that the
light was good. Then he separated the light
from the darkness. 5God called the light
"day" and the darkness "night."

And evening passed and morning
came, marking the first day.

6Then God said, "Let there be a space
between the waters, to separate the waters
of the heavens from the waters of the
earth." 7And that is what happened. God
made this space to separate the waters of
the earth from the waters of the heavens.
8God called the space "sky."

And evening passed and morning
came, marking the second day.

9Then God said, "Let the waters beneath
the sky flow together into one place,
so dry ground may appear." And that
is what happened. 10God called the dry
ground "land" and the waters "seas."
And God saw that it was good. 11Then
God said, "Let the land sprout with
vegetation—every sort of seed-bearing
plant, and trees that grow seed-bearing
fruit. These seeds will then produce the
kinds of plants and trees from which
they came." And that is what happened.
12The land produced vegetation—all sorts
of seed-bearing plants, and trees with
seed-bearing fruit. Their seeds produced
plants and trees of the same kind. And
God saw that it was good.

13And evening passed and morning
came, marking the third day.

14Then God said, "Let lights appear in the
sky to separate the day from the night.
Let them be signs to mark the seasons,
days, and years. 15Let these lights in
the sky shine down on the earth." And
that is what happened. 16God made two
great lights—the larger one to govern
the day, and the smaller one to govern
the night. He also made the stars. 17God
set these lights in the sky to light the
earth, 18to govern the day and night, and
to separate the light from the darkness.
And God saw that it was good.

19And evening passed and morning
came, marking the fourth day.

20Then God said, "Let the waters swarm
with fish and other life. Let the skies be
filled with birds of every kind." 21So God
created great sea creatures and every
living thing that scurries and swarms in
the water, and every sort of bird—each
producing offspring of the same kind.
And God saw that it was good. 22Then
God blessed them, saying, "Be fruitful
and multiply. Let the fish fill the seas,
and let the birds multiply on the earth."

23And evening passed and morning
came, marking the fifth day.

24Then God said, "Let the earth produce every
sort of animal, each producing offspring
of the same kind—livestock, small animals
that scurry along the ground, and wild
animals." And that is what happened.
25God made all sorts of wild animals,
livestock, and small animals, each able
to produce offspring of the same kind.
And God saw that it was good.

26 Then God said, "Let us make human
beings* in our image, to be like us. They
will reign over the fish in the sea, the
birds in the sky, the livestock, all the wild
animals on the earth,* and the small
animals that scurry along the ground."

27 So God created human beings* in his
own image.
In the image of God he created
them;
male and female he created them.

28 Then God blessed them and said,
"Be fruitful and multiply. Fill the earth
and govern it. Reign over the fish in
the sea, the birds in the sky, and all the
animals that scurry along the ground."
29 Then God said, "Look! I have given
you every seed-bearing plant throughout
the earth and all the fruit trees for your
food. 30 And I have given every green
plant as food for all the wild animals,
the birds in the sky, and the small
animals that scurry along the ground—
everything that has life." And that is
what happened.
31 Then God looked over all he had
made, and he saw that it was very good!

And evening passed and morning
came, marking the sixth day.

2 So the creation of the heavens and
the earth and everything in them was
completed. 2 On the seventh day God
had finished his work of creation, so
he rested* from all his work. 3 And God
blessed the seventh day and declared
it holy, because it was the day when he
rested from all his work of creation.

4 This is the account of the creation of the
heavens and the earth.

The Man and Woman in Eden

When the LORD God made the earth and
the heavens, 5 neither wild plants nor grains
were growing on the earth. For the LORD God
had not yet sent rain to water the earth, and
there were no people to cultivate the soil.
6 Instead, springs* came up from the ground
and watered all the land. 7 Then the LORD God
formed the man from the dust of the ground.
He breathed the breath of life into the man's
nostrils, and the man became a living person.
8 Then the LORD God planted a garden in
Eden in the east, and there he placed the
man he had made. 9 The LORD God made all
sorts of trees grow up from the ground—trees
that were beautiful and that produced delicious fruit. In the middle of the garden he
placed the tree of life and the tree of the
knowledge of good and evil.
10 A river flowed from the land of Eden,
watering the garden and then dividing into
four branches. 11 The first branch, called
the Pishon, flowed around the entire land
of Havilah, where gold is found. 12 The gold
of that land is exceptionally pure; aromatic
resin and onyx stone are also found there.
13 The second branch, called the Gihon,
flowed around the entire land of Cush. 14 The
third branch, called the Tigris, flowed east
of the land of Asshur. The fourth branch is
called the Euphrates.
15 The LORD God placed the man in the
Garden of Eden to tend and watch over
it. 16 But the LORD God warned him, "You
may freely eat the fruit of every tree in the
garden—17 except the tree of the knowledge
of good and evil. If you eat its fruit, you are
sure to die."

1:1 Or *In the beginning when God created the heavens and the earth, . . .* Or *When God began to create the heavens and the earth, . . .* **1:26a** Or *man;* Hebrew reads *adam.* **1:26b** As in Syriac version; Hebrew reads *all the earth.* **1:27** Or *the man;* Hebrew reads *ha-adam.* **2:2** Or *ceased;* also in 2:3. **2:6** Or *mist.*

Was the world really made in six days?

Some Christians believe that the world was made in six literal twenty-four-hour periods. Others consider that the periods described as days refer to extended periods of time.

The real issue is not so much the length of the periods of time that God took to create everything but the fact that he did create everything: There is a God who made everything in an orderly manner. It isn't chance or luck that controls human life; it is God. A living, personal God, not blind, impersonal fate, has guided all life from the beginning.

[18]Then the LORD God said, "It is not good for the man to be alone. I will make a helper who is just right for him." [19]So the LORD God formed from the ground all the wild animals and all the birds of the sky. He brought them to the man* to see what he would call them, and the man chose a name for each one. [20]He gave names to all the livestock, all the birds of the sky, and all the wild animals. But still there was no helper just right for him.

[21]So the LORD God caused the man to fall into a deep sleep. While the man slept, the LORD God took out one of the man's ribs* and closed up the opening. [22]Then the LORD God made a woman from the rib, and he brought her to the man.

[23]"At last!" the man exclaimed.

"This one is bone from my bone,
  and flesh from my flesh!
She will be called 'woman,'
  because she was taken from 'man.'"

[24]This explains why a man leaves his father and mother and is joined to his wife, and the two are united into one.

[25]Now the man and his wife were both naked, but they felt no shame.

The Man and Woman Sin

3 The serpent was the shrewdest of all the wild animals the LORD God had made. One day he asked the woman, "Did God really say you must not eat the fruit from any of the trees in the garden?"

[2]"Of course we may eat fruit from the trees in the garden," the woman replied. [3]"It's only the fruit from the tree in the middle of the garden that we are not allowed to eat. God said, 'You must not eat it or even touch it; if you do, you will die.'"

[4]"You won't die!" the serpent replied to the woman. [5]"God knows that your eyes will be opened as soon as you eat it, and you will be like God, knowing both good and evil."

[6]The woman was convinced. She saw that the tree was beautiful and its fruit looked delicious, and she wanted the wisdom it would give her. So she took some of the fruit and ate it. Then she gave some to her husband, who was with her, and he ate it, too. [7]At that moment their eyes were opened, and they suddenly felt shame at their nakedness. So they sewed fig leaves together to cover themselves.

[8]When the cool evening breezes were blowing, the man* and his wife heard the LORD God walking about in the garden. So they hid from the LORD God among the trees. [9]Then the LORD God called to the man, "Where are you?"

[10]He replied, "I heard you walking in the garden, so I hid. I was afraid because I was naked."

[11]"Who told you that you were naked?" the LORD God asked. "Have you eaten from the tree whose fruit I commanded you not to eat?"

[12]The man replied, "It was the woman you gave me who gave me the fruit, and I ate it."

▸ **2:24** *See **Does marriage still matter to God?**, page 976;* **3:6** *See **Sin**, page 387.*

Adam and Eve

Chapter 2 zooms in on the climax of creation portrayed in chapter 1—the creation of human beings. The Hebrew word *adam* is used in this chapter of both humanity in general and "the man" (i.e., Adam). It's as if it is telling us that the story of Adam is not just the story of an individual but also of the whole human race.

Adam alone couldn't fully reflect what God was like; for that, he needed "a helper" (Genesis 2:18). Together "Man" and "Woman"—only later called Eve (3:20)—were created to reflect God, know God, and care for his world. Sadly, disobedience would rob both them and all humanity of experiencing all this in its fullness, until Christ—"the last Adam"—came to restore it (Romans 5:12-21; see also 1 Corinthians 15:45-49).

▸ *See also **The fall of humanity**, page 7.*

13 Then the LORD God asked the woman, "What have you done?"

"The serpent deceived me," she replied. "That's why I ate it."

14 Then the LORD God said to the serpent,

"Because you have done this, you are cursed
more than all animals, domestic and wild.
You will crawl on your belly,
groveling in the dust as long as you live.
15 And I will cause hostility between you and the woman,
and between your offspring and her offspring.
He will strike* your head,
and you will strike his heel."

16 Then he said to the woman,

"I will sharpen the pain of your pregnancy,
and in pain you will give birth.
And you will desire to control your husband,
but he will rule over you.*"

17 And to the man he said,

"Since you listened to your wife and ate from the tree
whose fruit I commanded you not to eat,
the ground is cursed because of you.
All your life you will struggle to
scratch a living from it.
18 It will grow thorns and thistles for you,
though you will eat of its grains.
19 By the sweat of your brow
will you have food to eat
until you return to the ground
from which you were made.
For you were made from dust,
and to dust you will return."

Paradise Lost: God's Judgment

20 Then the man—Adam—named his wife Eve, because she would be the mother of all who live.* 21 And the LORD God made clothing from animal skins for Adam and his wife.

22 Then the LORD God said, "Look, the human beings* have become like us, knowing both good and evil. What if they reach out, take fruit from the tree of life, and eat it? Then they will live forever!" 23 So the LORD God banished them from the Garden of Eden, and he sent Adam out to cultivate the ground from which he had been made. 24 After sending them out, the LORD God stationed mighty cherubim to the east of the Garden of Eden. And he placed a flaming sword that flashed back and forth to guard the way to the tree of life.

2:19 Or *Adam,* and so throughout the chapter. **2:21** Or *took a part of the man's side.* **3:8** Or *Adam,* and so throughout the chapter. **3:15** Or *bruise;* also in 3:15b. **3:16** Or *And though you will have desire for your husband, / he will rule over you.* **3:20** *Eve* sounds like a Hebrew term that means "to give life." **3:22** Or *the man;* Hebrew reads *ha-adam.*

The fall of humanity

Adam and Eve's disobedience and their subsequent expulsion from the Garden of Eden is known as "the Fall"—so called because they fell from their place of security and intimate friendship with God. They fell into a life of uncertainty, hard labor, disharmony, and threat in the world into which they were sent. But this didn't just affect them; it affected every human descended from them (Romans 5:12). Even by Genesis 4 we see what a mixed bag humanity has now become—on the one hand, still wonderfully creative (4:21-22), yet on the other hand capable of great wickedness (4:1-16). This condition has been passed on through the human race (Romans 1:18-32), affecting even creation itself (Romans 8:20-21).

But God has not abandoned us. He even provided a note of hope to Adam and Eve by promising that one day a descendant of theirs would come and crush the head of the serpent (the devil), even at cost to himself (Genesis 3:15). This has often been seen as the first proclamation of what Jesus would do one day (see Revelation 12:9).

▶ *See also* ***Adam and Eve****, page 6.*

Cain and Abel

4 Now Adam* had sexual relations with
his wife, Eve, and she became pregnant. When she gave birth to Cain, she said,
"With the LORD's help, I have produced* a
man!" 2Later she gave birth to his brother
and named him Abel.

When they grew up, Abel became a shepherd, while Cain cultivated the ground.
3When it was time for the harvest, Cain presented some of his crops as a gift to the LORD.
4Abel also brought a gift—the best portions
of the firstborn lambs from his flock. The
LORD accepted Abel and his gift, 5but he did
not accept Cain and his gift. This made Cain
very angry, and he looked dejected.

6"Why are you so angry?" the LORD asked
Cain. "Why do you look so dejected? 7You will
be accepted if you do what is right. But if you
refuse to do what is right, then watch out! Sin
is crouching at the door, eager to control you.
But you must subdue it and be its master."

8One day Cain suggested to his brother,
"Let's go out into the fields."* And while
they were in the field, Cain attacked his
brother, Abel, and killed him.

9Afterward the LORD asked Cain, "Where
is your brother? Where is Abel?"

"I don't know," Cain responded. "Am I my
brother's guardian?"

10But the LORD said, "What have you
done? Listen! Your brother's blood cries out
to me from the ground! 11Now you are cursed
and banished from the ground, which has
swallowed your brother's blood. 12No longer
will the ground yield good crops for you, no
matter how hard you work! From now on you
will be a homeless wanderer on the earth."

13Cain replied to the LORD, "My punishment* is too great for me to bear! 14You
have banished me from the land and from
your presence; you have made me a homeless wanderer. Anyone who finds me will
kill me!"

15The LORD replied, "No, for I will give a
sevenfold punishment to anyone who kills
you." Then the LORD put a mark on Cain to
warn anyone who might try to kill him. 16So
Cain left the LORD's presence and settled in
the land of Nod,* east of Eden.

The Descendants of Cain

17Cain had sexual relations with his wife,
and she became pregnant and gave birth to
Enoch. Then Cain founded a city, which he
named Enoch, after his son. 18Enoch had a
son named Irad. Irad became the father of*
Mehujael. Mehujael became the father of
Methushael. Methushael became the father
of Lamech.

19Lamech married two women. The first
was named Adah, and the second was
Zillah. 20Adah gave birth to Jabal, who was
the first of those who raise livestock and
live in tents. 21His brother's name was Jubal,
the first of all who play the harp and flute.
22Lamech's other wife, Zillah, gave birth
to a son named Tubal-cain. He became an
expert in forging tools of bronze and iron.
Tubal-cain had a sister named Naamah.
23One day Lamech said to his wives,

"Adah and Zillah, hear my voice;
  listen to me, you wives of
    Lamech.
I have killed a man who attacked me,
  a young man who wounded me.
24 If someone who kills Cain is punished
    seven times,
  then the one who kills me will be
    punished seventy-seven times!"

Cain and Abel

Chapter 4 reveals how quickly sin spread, affecting even close family relationships. Cain, a farmer and Eve's firstborn, allowed his anger and bitterness with his brother, Abel, a shepherd, to boil over, and Cain killed Abel when God accepted Abel's offering but not Cain's. This may have been because of what was offered—Abel offered his best ("the best portions of the firstborn lambs"), while Cain simply offered ordinary farm produce (Genesis 4:3-4)—or it may have been because of Cain's heart attitude and unawareness of sin (4:7). But not only did Cain kill Abel, he coldheartedly denied any knowledge of it (4:9), leading to him being cursed and banished, driven even further away from God's presence.

The Birth of Seth

25Adam had sexual relations with his wife
again, and she gave birth to another son.
She named him Seth,* for she said, "God
has granted me another son in place of
Abel, whom Cain killed." 26When Seth grew
up, he had a son and named him Enosh. At
that time people first began to worship the
LORD by name.

The Descendants of Adam

5 This is the written account of the descendants of Adam. When God created human
beings,* he made them to be like himself.
2He created them male and female, and he
blessed them and called them "human."

3When Adam was 130 years old, he became
the father of a son who was just like
him—in his very image. He named his
son Seth. 4After the birth of Seth, Adam
lived another 800 years, and he had
other sons and daughters. 5Adam lived
930 years, and then he died.
6When Seth was 105 years old, he became
the father of* Enosh. 7After the birth of*
Enosh, Seth lived another 807 years, and
he had other sons and daughters. 8Seth
lived 912 years, and then he died.
9When Enosh was 90 years old, he became
the father of Kenan. 10After the birth of
Kenan, Enosh lived another 815 years,
and he had other sons and daughters.
11Enosh lived 905 years, and then he died.
12When Kenan was 70 years old, he became
the father of Mahalalel. 13After the
birth of Mahalalel, Kenan lived another
840 years, and he had other sons and
daughters. 14Kenan lived 910 years, and
then he died.
15When Mahalalel was 65 years old, he
became the father of Jared. 16After the
birth of Jared, Mahalalel lived another
830 years, and he had other sons and
daughters. 17Mahalalel lived 895 years,
and then he died.
18When Jared was 162 years old, he became
the father of Enoch. 19After the birth of
Enoch, Jared lived another 800 years,
and he had other sons and daughters.
20Jared lived 962 years, and then he died.
21When Enoch was 65 years old, he became
the father of Methuselah. 22After the
birth of Methuselah, Enoch lived in
close fellowship with God for another
300 years, and he had other sons and
daughters. 23Enoch lived 365 years,
24walking in close fellowship with God.
Then one day he disappeared, because
God took him.
25When Methuselah was 187 years old, he
became the father of Lamech. 26After
the birth of Lamech, Methuselah lived
another 782 years, and he had other
sons and daughters. 27Methuselah lived
969 years, and then he died.
28When Lamech was 182 years old, he
became the father of a son. 29Lamech
named his son Noah, for he said, "May
he bring us relief* from our work and
the painful labor of farming this ground
that the LORD has cursed." 30After the
birth of Noah, Lamech lived another
595 years, and he had other sons and
daughters. 31Lamech lived 777 years,
and then he died.
32After Noah was 500 years old, he became
the father of Shem, Ham, and Japheth.

A World Gone Wrong

6 Then the people began to multiply on
the earth, and daughters were born to
them. 2The sons of God saw the beautiful
women* and took any they wanted as their
wives. 3Then the LORD said, "My Spirit will
not put up with* humans for such a long
time, for they are only mortal flesh. In the
future, their normal lifespan will be no
more than 120 years."
4In those days, and for some time after,
giant Nephilites lived on the earth, for
whenever the sons of God had intercourse
with women, they gave birth to children
who became the heroes and famous warriors of ancient times.
5The LORD observed the extent of human
wickedness on the earth, and he saw that
everything they thought or imagined was
consistently and totally evil. 6So the LORD
was sorry he had ever made them and put
them on the earth. It broke his heart. 7And
the LORD said, "I will wipe this human race

4:1a Or *the man;* also in 4:25. **4:1b** Or *I have acquired. Cain* sounds like a Hebrew term that can mean "produce" or "acquire." **4:8** As in Samaritan Pentateuch, Greek and Syriac versions, and Latin Vulgate; Masoretic Text lacks *"Let's go out into the fields."* **4:13** Or *My sin.* **4:16** *Nod* means "wandering." **4:18** Or *the ancestor of,* and so throughout the verse. **4:25** *Seth* probably means "granted"; the name may also mean "appointed." **5:1** Or *man;* Hebrew reads *adam;* similarly in 5:2. **5:6** Or *the ancestor of;* also in 5:9, 12, 15, 18, 21, 25. **5:7** Or *the birth of this ancestor of;* also in 5:10, 13, 16, 19, 22, 26. **5:29** *Noah* sounds like a Hebrew term that can mean "relief" or "comfort." **6:2** Hebrew *daughters of men;* also in 6:4. **6:3** Greek version reads *will not remain in.*

I have created from the face of the earth.
Yes, and I will destroy every living thing—
all the people, the large animals, the small
animals that scurry along the ground, and
even the birds of the sky. I am sorry I ever
made them." [8]But Noah found favor with
the LORD.

The Story of Noah

[9]This is the account of Noah and his family.
Noah was a righteous man, the only blameless person living on earth at the time, and
he walked in close fellowship with God.
[10]Noah was the father of three sons: Shem,
Ham, and Japheth.

[11]Now God saw that the earth had become
corrupt and was filled with violence. [12]God
observed all this corruption in the world,
for everyone on earth was corrupt. [13]So God
said to Noah, "I have decided to destroy
all living creatures, for they have filled the
earth with violence. Yes, I will wipe them all
out along with the earth!

[14]"Build a large boat* from cypress wood*
and waterproof it with tar, inside and out.
Then construct decks and stalls throughout
its interior. [15]Make the boat 450 feet long,
75 feet wide, and 45 feet high.* [16]Leave an
18-inch opening* below the roof all the way
around the boat. Put the door on the side,
and build three decks inside the boat—
lower, middle, and upper.

[17]"Look! I am about to cover the earth
with a flood that will destroy every living
thing that breathes. Everything on earth
will die. [18]But I will confirm my covenant
with you. So enter the boat—you and your
wife and your sons and their wives. [19]Bring
a pair of every kind of animal—a male and a
female—into the boat with you to keep them
alive during the flood. [20]Pairs of every kind
of bird, and every kind of animal, and every
kind of small animal that scurries along the
ground, will come to you to be kept alive.
[21]And be sure to take on board enough food
for your family and for all the animals."

[22]So Noah did everything exactly as God
had commanded him.

The Flood Covers the Earth

7 When everything was ready, the LORD
said to Noah, "Go into the boat with all
your family, for among all the people of the
earth, I can see that you alone are righteous.
[2]Take with you seven pairs—male and
female—of each animal I have approved for
eating and for sacrifice,* and take one pair
of each of the others. [3]Also take seven pairs
of every kind of bird. There must be a male
and a female in each pair to ensure that all
life will survive on the earth after the flood.
[4]Seven days from now I will make the rains
pour down on the earth. And it will rain
for forty days and forty nights, until I have
wiped from the earth all the living things
I have created."

[5]So Noah did everything as the LORD commanded him.

[6]Noah was 600 years old when the flood
covered the earth. [7]He went on board the
boat to escape the flood—he and his wife
and his sons and their wives. [8]With them
were all the various kinds of animals—those
approved for eating and for sacrifice and
those that were not—along with all the birds
and the small animals that scurry along the
ground. [9]They entered the boat in pairs, male
and female, just as God had commanded
Noah. [10]After seven days, the waters of the
flood came and covered the earth.

[11]When Noah was 600 years old, on the
seventeenth day of the second month, all
the underground waters erupted from the
earth, and the rain fell in mighty torrents
from the sky. [12]The rain continued to fall for
forty days and forty nights.

[13]That very day Noah had gone into the
boat with his wife and his sons—Shem,
Ham, and Japheth—and their wives. [14]With
them in the boat were pairs of every kind
of animal—domestic and wild, large and
small—along with birds of every kind. [15]Two
by two they came into the boat, representing every living thing that breathes. [16]A
male and female of each kind entered, just
as God had commanded Noah. Then the
LORD closed the door behind them.

[17]For forty days the floodwaters grew
deeper, covering the ground and lifting the
boat high above the earth. [18]As the waters
rose higher and higher above the ground,
the boat floated safely on the surface.
[19]Finally, the water covered even the highest
mountains on the earth, [20]rising more than
twenty-two feet* above the highest peaks.
[21]All the living things on earth died—birds,
domestic animals, wild animals, small
animals that scurry along the ground, and
all the people. [22]Everything that breathed
and lived on dry land died. [23]God wiped

out every living thing on the earth—people, livestock, small animals that scurry along the ground, and the birds of the sky. All were destroyed. The only people who survived were Noah and those with him in the boat. [24]And the floodwaters covered the earth for 150 days.

The Flood Recedes

8 But God remembered Noah and all the wild animals and livestock with him in the boat. He sent a wind to blow across the earth, and the floodwaters began to recede. [2]The underground waters stopped flowing, and the torrential rains from the sky were stopped. [3]So the floodwaters gradually receded from the earth. After 150 days, [4]exactly five months from the time the flood began,* the boat came to rest on the mountains of Ararat. [5]Two and a half months later,* as the waters continued to go down, other mountain peaks became visible.

[6]After another forty days, Noah opened the window he had made in the boat [7]and released a raven. The bird flew back and forth until the floodwaters on the earth had dried up. [8]He also released a dove to see if the water had receded and it could find dry ground. [9]But the dove could find no place to land because the water still covered the ground. So it returned to the boat, and Noah held out his hand and drew the dove back inside. [10]After waiting another seven days, Noah released the dove again. [11]This time the dove returned to him in the evening with a fresh olive leaf in its beak. Then Noah knew that the floodwaters were almost gone. [12]He waited another seven days and then released the dove again. This time it did not come back.

[13]Noah was now 601 years old. On the first day of the new year, ten and a half months after the flood began,* the floodwaters had almost dried up from the earth. Noah lifted back the covering of the boat and saw that the surface of the ground was drying. [14]Two more months went by,* and at last the earth was dry!

[15]Then God said to Noah, [16]"Leave the boat, all of you—you and your wife, and your sons and their wives. [17]Release all the animals—the birds, the livestock, and the small animals that scurry along the ground—so they can be fruitful and multiply throughout the earth."

6:14a Traditionally rendered *an ark.* **6:14b** Or *gopher wood.* **6:15** Hebrew *300 cubits* [138 meters] *long, 50 cubits* [23 meters] *wide, and 30 cubits* [13.8 meters] *high.* **6:16** Hebrew *an opening of 1 cubit* [46 centimeters]. **7:2** Hebrew *of each clean animal;* similarly in 7:8. **7:20** Hebrew *15 cubits* [6.9 meters]. **8:4** Hebrew *on the seventeenth day of the seventh month;* see 7:11. **8:5** Hebrew *On the first day of the tenth month;* see 7:11 and note on 8:4. **8:13** Hebrew *On the first day of the first month;* see 7:11. **8:14** Hebrew *The twenty-seventh day of the second month arrived;* see note on 8:13.

The flood and the ark

Human sin became so deep and widespread that God decided to start all over again, sending a flood to destroy everyone and everything (Genesis 6:1-7). He told Noah to build an "ark"—not so much a boat as a huge, three-decked floating box—and to gather his family and pairs of animals there (6:11-22). For forty days, torrential rains fell and underground waters erupted, flooding the earth (perhaps the result of an ice age ending). Noah and his family stayed in the ark for over a year before the waters dried up completely. With wickedness removed, it was time for a new beginning, marked by a covenant between God and Noah, the sign of which was the rainbow—God's promise that he would never flood the earth again (9:1-17).

Some people struggle with this story because a flooding of the whole earth seems impossible. But the Genesis story does not require belief in a global flood; in fact, Genesis 11:9 says that it was only after the tower of Babel that God scattered people across the whole earth. Therefore, it is perhaps more likely that this was a vast regional flood that destroyed the emerging human population—though from the perspective of Middle Eastern writers, that would have been "the whole earth," as they understood the term at that time.

▶ *See also* ***Noah****, page 12.*

18 So Noah, his wife, and his sons and
their wives left the boat. 19 And all of the
large and small animals and birds came out
of the boat, pair by pair.

20 Then Noah built an altar to the LORD,
and there he sacrificed as burnt offerings
the animals and birds that had been approved for that purpose.* 21 And the LORD
was pleased with the aroma of the sacrifice and said to himself, "I will never again
curse the ground because of the human
race, even though everything they think or
imagine is bent toward evil from childhood.
I will never again destroy all living things.
22 As long as the earth remains, there will
be planting and harvest, cold and heat,
summer and winter, day and night."

God Confirms His Covenant

9 Then God blessed Noah and his sons
and told them, "Be fruitful and multiply. Fill the earth. 2 All the animals of the
earth, all the birds of the sky, all the small
animals that scurry along the ground, and
all the fish in the sea will look on you with
fear and terror. I have placed them in your
power. 3 I have given them to you for food,
just as I have given you grain and vegetables. 4 But you must never eat any meat
that still has the lifeblood in it.

5 "And I will require the blood of anyone
who takes another person's life. If a wild
animal kills a person, it must die. And
anyone who murders a fellow human must
die. 6 If anyone takes a human life, that
person's life will also be taken by human
hands. For God made human beings* in his
own image. 7 Now be fruitful and multiply,
and repopulate the earth."

8 Then God told Noah and his sons,
9 "I hereby confirm my covenant with you and
your descendants, 10 and with all the animals
that were on the boat with you—the birds,
the livestock, and all the wild animals—every
living creature on earth. 11 Yes, I am confirming my covenant with you. Never again will
floodwaters kill all living creatures; never
again will a flood destroy the earth."

12 Then God said, "I am giving you a sign
of my covenant with you and with all living
creatures, for all generations to come. 13 I
have placed my rainbow in the clouds. It
is the sign of my covenant with you and
with all the earth. 14 When I send clouds
over the earth, the rainbow will appear in
the clouds, 15 and I will remember my covenant with you and with all living creatures. Never again will the floodwaters
destroy all life. 16 When I see the rainbow
in the clouds, I will remember the eternal
covenant between God and every living
creature on earth." 17 Then God said to
Noah, "Yes, this rainbow is the sign of the
covenant I am confirming with all the creatures on earth."

Noah's Sons

18 The sons of Noah who came out of the
boat with their father were Shem, Ham,
and Japheth. (Ham is the father of Canaan.)
19 From these three sons of Noah came all the
people who now populate the earth.

20 After the flood, Noah began to cultivate
the ground, and he planted a vineyard. 21 One
day he drank some wine he had made, and
he became drunk and lay naked inside his
tent. 22 Ham, the father of Canaan, saw that
his father was naked and went outside and

Noah

In contrast to the sin depicted in these early chapters, Noah was "righteous" and "blameless" (Genesis 6:9). His faith—no doubt mocked by others as he built his enormous boat—was rewarded when God, heartbroken (6:6), resolved to destroy sinful humanity and start again. Noah obeyed God, gathering his family and the animals into the ark he had made and staying there until it was safe to come out—around a year after the rains had begun. Noah's first response on leaving the ark was to build an altar to God (8:20), and God responded by making a covenant, not just with Noah, but with all humanity, marked by the sign of the rainbow (9:1-17). Noah's faith became noteworthy for generations to come (see Hebrews 11:7).

▸ *See also* ***The flood and the ark****, page 11.*

told his brothers. [23]Then Shem and Japheth
took a robe, held it over their shoulders, and
backed into the tent to cover their father. As
they did this, they looked the other way so
they would not see him naked.
[24]When Noah woke up from his stupor, he
learned what Ham, his youngest son, had
done. [25]Then he cursed Canaan, the son of
Ham:

"May Canaan be cursed!
May he be the lowest of servants to his
relatives."

[26]Then Noah said,

"May the LORD, the God of Shem, be
blessed,
and may Canaan be his servant!
[27] May God expand the territory of Japheth!
May Japheth share the prosperity of
Shem,*
and may Canaan be his servant."

[28]Noah lived another 350 years after the
great flood. [29]He lived 950 years, and then
he died.

10 This is the account of the families of
Shem, Ham, and Japheth, the three
sons of Noah. Many children were born to
them after the great flood.

Descendants of Japheth

[2]The descendants of Japheth were Gomer,
Magog, Madai, Javan, Tubal, Meshech,
and Tiras.
[3]The descendants of Gomer were
Ashkenaz, Riphath, and Togarmah.
[4]The descendants of Javan were Elishah,
Tarshish, Kittim, and Rodanim.* [5]Their
descendants became the seafaring
peoples that spread out to various lands,
each identified by its own language,
clan, and national identity.

Descendants of Ham

[6]The descendants of Ham were Cush,
Mizraim, Put, and Canaan.
[7]The descendants of Cush were Seba,
Havilah, Sabtah, Raamah, and Sabteca.
The descendants of Raamah were Sheba
and Dedan.
[8]Cush was also the ancestor of
Nimrod, who was the first heroic warrior
on earth. [9]Since he was the greatest
hunter in the world,* his name became
proverbial. People would say, "This
man is like Nimrod, the greatest hunter
in the world." [10]He built his kingdom in
the land of Babylonia,* with the cities
of Babylon, Erech, Akkad, and Calneh.
[11]From there he expanded his territory to
Assyria,* building the cities of Nineveh,
Rehoboth-ir, Calah, [12]and Resen (the
great city located between Nineveh and
Calah).
[13]Mizraim was the ancestor of the Ludites,
Anamites, Lehabites, Naphtuhites,
[14]Pathrusites, Casluhites, and the
Caphtorites, from whom the Philistines
came.*
[15]Canaan's oldest son was Sidon, the
ancestor of the Sidonians. Canaan
was also the ancestor of the Hittites,*
[16]Jebusites, Amorites, Girgashites,
[17]Hivites, Arkites, Sinites, [18]Arvadites,
Zemarites, and Hamathites. The
Canaanite clans eventually spread out,
[19]and the territory of Canaan extended
from Sidon in the north to Gerar and
Gaza in the south, and east as far
as Sodom, Gomorrah, Admah, and
Zeboiim, near Lasha.
[20]These were the descendants of Ham,
identified by clan, language, territory, and
national identity.

Descendants of Shem

[21]Sons were also born to Shem, the older
brother of Japheth.* Shem was the
ancestor of all the descendants of Eber.
[22]The descendants of Shem were Elam,
Asshur, Arphaxad, Lud, and Aram.
[23]The descendants of Aram were Uz, Hul,
Gether, and Mash.
[24]Arphaxad was the father of Shelah,* and
Shelah was the father of Eber.
[25]Eber had two sons. The first was named
Peleg (which means "division"), for
during his lifetime the people of the
world were divided into different
language groups. His brother's name
was Joktan.

8:20 Hebrew *every clean animal and every clean bird.* **9:6** Or *man;* Hebrew reads *ha-adam.* **9:27** Hebrew *May he live in the tents of Shem.* **10:4** As in some Hebrew manuscripts and Greek version (see also 1 Chr 1:7); most Hebrew manuscripts read *Dodanim.* **10:9** Hebrew *a great hunter before the LORD;* also in 10:9b. **10:10** Hebrew *Shinar.* **10:11** Or *From that land Assyria went out.* **10:14** Hebrew *Casluhites, from whom the Philistines came, and Caphtorites.* Compare Jer 47:4; Amos 9:7. **10:15** Hebrew *ancestor of Heth.* **10:21** Or *Shem, whose older brother was Japheth.* **10:24** Greek version reads *Arphaxad was the father of Cainan, Cainan was the father of Shelah.* Compare Luke 3:36.

26 Joktan was the ancestor of Almodad,
Sheleph, Hazarmaveth, Jerah,
27 Hadoram, Uzal, Diklah, 28 Obal,
Abimael, Sheba, 29 Ophir, Havilah, and
Jobab. All these were descendants of
Joktan. 30 The territory they occupied
extended from Mesha all the way to
Sephar in the eastern mountains.

31 These were the descendants of Shem,
identified by clan, language, territory, and
national identity.

Conclusion

32 These are the clans that descended from
Noah's sons, arranged by nation according
to their lines of descent. All the nations of
the earth descended from these clans after
the great flood.

The Tower of Babel

11 At one time all the people of the world
spoke the same language and used
the same words. 2 As the people migrated to
the east, they found a plain in the land of
Babylonia* and settled there.

3 They began saying to each other, "Let's
make bricks and harden them with fire."
(In this region bricks were used instead
of stone, and tar was used for mortar.)
4 Then they said, "Come, let's build a great
city for ourselves with a tower that reaches
into the sky. This will make us famous and
keep us from being scattered all over the
world."

5 But the LORD came down to look at the
city and the tower the people were building.
6 "Look!" he said. "The people are united,
and they all speak the same language. After
this, nothing they set out to do will be impossible for them! 7 Come, let's go down and
confuse the people with different languages.
Then they won't be able to understand each
other."

8 In that way, the LORD scattered them
all over the world, and they stopped building the city. 9 That is why the city was called
Babel,* because that is where the LORD confused the people with different languages. In
this way he scattered them all over the world.

The Line of Descent from Shem to Abram

10 This is the account of Shem's family.

Two years after the great flood, when
Shem was 100 years old, he became the
father of* Arphaxad. 11 After the birth of*
Arphaxad, Shem lived another 500 years
and had other sons and daughters.

12 When Arphaxad was 35 years old, he
became the father of Shelah. 13 After the
birth of Shelah, Arphaxad lived another
403 years and had other sons and
daughters.*

14 When Shelah was 30 years old, he became
the father of Eber. 15 After the birth of
Eber, Shelah lived another 403 years and
had other sons and daughters.

16 When Eber was 34 years old, he became
the father of Peleg. 17 After the birth of
Peleg, Eber lived another 430 years and
had other sons and daughters.

18 When Peleg was 30 years old, he became
the father of Reu. 19 After the birth of
Reu, Peleg lived another 209 years and
had other sons and daughters.

20 When Reu was 32 years old, he became
the father of Serug. 21 After the birth of
Serug, Reu lived another 207 years and
had other sons and daughters.

22 When Serug was 30 years old, he became
the father of Nahor. 23 After the birth of

The tower of Babel

The tower of Babel was a *ziggurat*, a multistoried temple tower with a square base, increasingly smaller levels, and a religious shrine on the top.

People originally all spoke one language. In their pride, conceit, and insecurity, the people thought that they could become famous and boast of their great human reputation as a result of their building project. God had to come down to solve the problem—to impose some discipline on the unruly mob. The result was a confusion of languages, which was miraculously overcome centuries later at Pentecost, when the Holy Spirit enabled the apostles to speak in a variety of languages to tell the crowds what God had done in Jesus (Acts 2).

Nahor, Serug lived another 200 years
and had other sons and daughters.
24 When Nahor was 29 years old, he became
the father of Terah. 25 After the birth of
Terah, Nahor lived another 119 years and
had other sons and daughters.
26 After Terah was 70 years old, he became
the father of Abram, Nahor, and Haran.

The Family of Terah

27 This is the account of Terah's family. Terah
was the father of Abram, Nahor, and Haran;
and Haran was the father of Lot. 28 But
Haran died in Ur of the Chaldeans, the land
of his birth, while his father, Terah, was still
living. 29 Meanwhile, Abram and Nahor both
married. The name of Abram's wife was
Sarai, and the name of Nahor's wife was
Milcah. (Milcah and her sister Iscah were
daughters of Nahor's brother Haran.) 30 But
Sarai was unable to become pregnant and
had no children.
31 One day Terah took his son Abram, his
daughter-in-law Sarai (his son Abram's
wife), and his grandson Lot (his son
Haran's child) and moved away from Ur of
the Chaldeans. He was headed for the land
of Canaan, but they stopped at Haran and
settled there. 32 Terah lived for 205 years*
and died while still in Haran.

The Call of Abram

12 The LORD had said to Abram, "Leave
your native country, your relatives,
and your father's family, and go to the land
that I will show you. 2 I will make you into
a great nation. I will bless you and make
you famous, and you will be a blessing to
others. 3 I will bless those who bless you and
curse those who treat you with contempt.
All the families on earth will be blessed
through you."
4 So Abram departed as the LORD had
instructed, and Lot went with him. Abram
was seventy-five years old when he left
Haran. 5 He took his wife, Sarai, his nephew
Lot, and all his wealth—his livestock and
all the people he had taken into his household at Haran—and headed for the land
of Canaan. When they arrived in Canaan,
6 Abram traveled through the land as far as
Shechem. There he set up camp beside the
oak of Moreh. At that time, the area was inhabited by Canaanites.
7 Then the LORD appeared to Abram and
said, "I will give this land to your descendants.*" And Abram built an altar there
and dedicated it to the LORD, who had appeared to him. 8 After that, Abram traveled
south and set up camp in the hill country,
with Bethel to the west and Ai to the east.
There he built another altar and dedicated
it to the LORD, and he worshiped the LORD.
9 Then Abram continued traveling south by
stages toward the Negev.

Abram and Sarai in Egypt

10 At that time a severe famine struck the
land of Canaan, forcing Abram to go down
to Egypt, where he lived as a foreigner. 11 As
he was approaching the border of Egypt,
Abram said to his wife, Sarai, "Look, you are
a very beautiful woman. 12 When the Egyptians see you, they will say, 'This is his wife.
Let's kill him; then we can have her!' 13 So
please tell them you are my sister. Then they

11:2 Hebrew *Shinar.* **11:9** Or *Babylon. Babel* sounds like a Hebrew term that means "confusion." **11:10** Or *the ancestor of;* also in 11:12, 14, 16, 18, 20, 22, 24. **11:11** Or *the birth of this ancestor of;* also in 11:13, 15, 17, 19, 21, 23, 25. **11:12-13** Greek version reads *12 When Arphaxad was 135 years old, he became the father of Cainan. 13 After the birth of Cainan, Arphaxad lived another 430 years and had other sons and daughters, and then he died. When Cainan was 130 years old, he became the father of Shelah. After the birth of Shelah, Cainan lived another 330 years and had other sons and daughters, and then he died.* Compare Luke 3:35-36. **11:32** Some ancient versions read *145 years;* compare 11:26 and 12:4. **12:7** Hebrew *seed.*

Ur

Ur was a prosperous city in southern Mesopotamia and the original home of Abraham's family (Genesis 11:28; 15:7). It was a famous center for the worship of the moon god, known as Sin or Nanna, whose symbol was the crescent moon. So it is almost certain that Abraham too would have been a moon worshiper when God revealed himself to him. For by no means the last time, the Bible shows us that no one is ever beyond God's reach.

▶ *See also* ***Abraham***, *page 16.*

will spare my life and treat me well because
of their interest in you."
[14]And sure enough, when Abram arrived
in Egypt, everyone noticed Sarai's beauty.
[15]When the palace officials saw her, they
sang her praises to Pharaoh, their king,
and Sarai was taken into his palace. [16]Then
Pharaoh gave Abram many gifts because of
her—sheep, goats, cattle, male and female
donkeys, male and female servants, and
camels.
[17]But the LORD sent terrible plagues upon
Pharaoh and his household because of Sarai,
Abram's wife. [18]So Pharaoh summoned
Abram and accused him sharply. "What have
you done to me?" he demanded. "Why didn't
you tell me she was your wife? [19]Why did you
say, 'She is my sister,' and allow me to take
her as my wife? Now then, here is your wife.
Take her and get out of here!" [20]Pharaoh
ordered some of his men to escort them, and
he sent Abram out of the country, along with
his wife and all his possessions.

Abram and Lot Separate

13 So Abram left Egypt and traveled north
into the Negev, along with his wife
and Lot and all that they owned. [2](Abram
was very rich in livestock, silver, and gold.)
[3]From the Negev, they continued traveling by
stages toward Bethel, and they pitched their
tents between Bethel and Ai, where they had
camped before. [4]This was the same place
where Abram had built the altar, and there
he worshiped the LORD again.
[5]Lot, who was traveling with Abram, had
also become very wealthy with flocks of
sheep and goats, herds of cattle, and many
tents. [6]But the land could not support both
Abram and Lot with all their flocks and
herds living so close together. [7]So disputes
broke out between the herdsmen of Abram
and Lot. (At that time Canaanites and Perizzites were also living in the land.)
[8]Finally Abram said to Lot, "Let's not
allow this conflict to come between us or
our herdsmen. After all, we are close relatives! [9]The whole countryside is open to
you. Take your choice of any section of the
land you want, and we will separate. If you
want the land to the left, then I'll take the
land on the right. If you prefer the land on
the right, then I'll go to the left."
[10]Lot took a long look at the fertile plains
of the Jordan Valley in the direction of Zoar.
The whole area was well watered everywhere, like the garden of the LORD or the
beautiful land of Egypt. (This was before the
LORD destroyed Sodom and Gomorrah.) [11]Lot
chose for himself the whole Jordan Valley
to the east of them. He went there with his
flocks and servants and parted company
with his uncle Abram. [12]So Abram settled in
the land of Canaan, and Lot moved his tents

Abraham

Abraham (first called "Abram") was the man whom God called to be the father of the people of Israel. Even though Abraham did not know God, God revealed himself to him and called him to leave his home in Ur, promising him a new land, many descendants, a great name, and that he would become a blessing to many people. His faith and obedience in responding to God's call is often commended in the Bible, and he is held up as an example to be followed (e.g., Romans 4:1-25; Galatians 3:6-9; Hebrews 11:8-19). But when it seemed that his wife, Sarah, would never have children to inherit God's blessings, they tried to help God out. Sarah gave her servant girl Hagar to Abraham as a second wife, and so Ishmael was born (from whom the Arab nations are descended). But an angel told Sarah that a son would be born to Abraham and herself, even in their old age. God kept his promise and Isaac was born to them (Genesis 21:1-5), causing both joy (21:6-7) and tension (21:8-21). Later, Abraham's faith would be severely tested when God asked him to sacrifice Isaac—an incident that showed both Abraham's resolute faith and God's ability to surprise us (22:1-19).

▶ *See also **Ur**, page 15; **Lot**, page 17; **Ishmael**, page 20; **Sarah**, page 27; **Isaac and Rebekah**, page 28; **Faith**, page 1286; **World of the Patriarchs** map, Visual Overview Z2.*

to a place near Sodom and settled among
the cities of the plain. [13]But the people of this
area were extremely wicked and constantly
sinned against the LORD.
[14]After Lot had gone, the LORD said to
Abram, "Look as far as you can see in every
direction—north and south, east and west.
[15]I am giving all this land, as far as you can
see, to you and your descendants* as a permanent possession. [16]And I will give you
so many descendants that, like the dust of
the earth, they cannot be counted! [17]Go and
walk through the land in every direction, for
I am giving it to you."
[18]So Abram moved his camp to Hebron
and settled near the oak grove belonging to
Mamre. There he built another altar to the
LORD.

Abram Rescues Lot

14 About this time war broke out in the
region. King Amraphel of Babylonia,*
King Arioch of Ellasar, King Kedorlaomer
of Elam, and King Tidal of Goiim [2]fought
against King Bera of Sodom, King Birsha
of Gomorrah, King Shinab of Admah, King
Shemeber of Zeboiim, and the king of Bela
(also called Zoar).
[3]This second group of kings joined forces
in Siddim Valley (that is, the valley of the
Dead Sea*). [4]For twelve years they had been
subject to King Kedorlaomer, but in the thirteenth year they rebelled against him.
[5]One year later Kedorlaomer and his
allies arrived and defeated the Rephaites
at Ashteroth-karnaim, the Zuzites at Ham,
the Emites at Shaveh-kiriathaim, [6]and the
Horites at Mount Seir, as far as El-paran
at the edge of the wilderness. [7]Then they
turned back and came to En-mishpat (now
called Kadesh) and conquered all the territory of the Amalekites, and also the
Amorites living in Hazazon-tamar.
[8]Then the rebel kings of Sodom, Gomorrah,
Admah, Zeboiim, and Bela (also called Zoar)
prepared for battle in the valley of the Dead
Sea.* [9]They fought against King Kedorlaomer
of Elam, King Tidal of Goiim, King Amraphel
of Babylonia, and King Arioch of Ellasar—
four kings against five. [10]As it happened, the
valley of the Dead Sea was filled with tar pits.
And as the army of the kings of Sodom and
Gomorrah fled, some fell into the tar pits,
while the rest escaped into the mountains.
[11]The victorious invaders then plundered
Sodom and Gomorrah and headed for home,
taking with them all the spoils of war and
the food supplies. [12]They also captured Lot—
Abram's nephew who lived in Sodom—and
carried off everything he owned.
[13]But one of Lot's men escaped and reported everything to Abram the Hebrew,
who was living near the oak grove belonging
to Mamre the Amorite. Mamre and his relatives, Eshcol and Aner, were Abram's allies.
[14]When Abram heard that his nephew
Lot had been captured, he mobilized the
318 trained men who had been born into
his household. Then he pursued Kedorlaomer's army until he caught up with them
at Dan. [15]There he divided his men and attacked during the night. Kedorlaomer's
army fled, but Abram chased them as far as

13:15 Hebrew *seed;* also in 13:16. **14:1** Hebrew *Shinar;* also in 14:9. **14:3** Hebrew *Salt Sea.* **14:8** Hebrew *Siddim Valley* (see 14:3); also in 14:10.

Lot

When Abraham moved to Canaan in obedience to God, Lot, his nephew, went with him (Genesis 12:5). But these chapters give the impression that he simply seemed to "tag along," rather than going in faith. When increasing livestock numbers led them to separate (chapter 13), Lot chose with his eyes rather than his heart. He selected land near Sodom, south of the Dead Sea, which was fertile but immoral, unstable, and heading for disaster. God rescued him from his foolishness—first through Abraham from Kedorlaomer's attack (chapter 14) and then through angels from God's judgment (19:1-29). His daughters were just as faithless, getting Lot drunk and becoming pregnant by him. Their sons became the ancestors of the Moabites and Ammonites (19:30-38).

▶ *See also* ***Abraham****, page 16;* ***Sodom and Gomorrah****, page 23.*

Hobah, north of Damascus. 16 Abram recovered all the goods that had been taken, and he brought back his nephew Lot with his possessions and all the women and other captives.

Melchizedek Blesses Abram

17 After Abram returned from his victory over Kedorlaomer and all his allies, the king of Sodom went out to meet him in the valley of Shaveh (that is, the King's Valley).

18 And Melchizedek, the king of Salem and a priest of God Most High,* brought Abram some bread and wine. 19 Melchizedek blessed Abram with this blessing:

"Blessed be Abram by God Most High,
Creator of heaven and earth.
20 And blessed be God Most High,
who has defeated your enemies for you."

Then Abram gave Melchizedek a tenth of all the goods he had recovered.

21 The king of Sodom said to Abram, "Give back my people who were captured. But you may keep for yourself all the goods you have recovered."

22 Abram replied to the king of Sodom, "I solemnly swear to the LORD, God Most High, Creator of heaven and earth, 23 that I will not take so much as a single thread or sandal thong from what belongs to you. Otherwise you might say, 'I am the one who made Abram rich.' 24 I will accept only what my young warriors have already eaten, and I request that you give a fair share of the goods to my allies—Aner, Eshcol, and Mamre."

The LORD's Covenant Promise to Abram

15 Some time later, the LORD spoke to Abram in a vision and said to him, "Do not be afraid, Abram, for I will protect you, and your reward will be great."

2 But Abram replied, "O Sovereign LORD, what good are all your blessings when I don't even have a son? Since you've given me no children, Eliezer of Damascus, a servant in my household, will inherit all my wealth. 3 You have given me no descendants of my own, so one of my servants will be my heir."

4 Then the LORD said to him, "No, your servant will not be your heir, for you will have a son of your own who will be your heir." 5 Then the LORD took Abram outside and said to him, "Look up into the sky and count the stars if you can. That's how many descendants you will have!"

6 And Abram believed the LORD, and the LORD counted him as righteous because of his faith.

7 Then the LORD told him, "I am the LORD who brought you out of Ur of the Chaldeans to give you this land as your possession."

8 But Abram replied, "O Sovereign LORD, how can I be sure that I will actually possess it?"

9 The LORD told him, "Bring me a three-year-old heifer, a three-year-old female goat, a three-year-old ram, a turtledove, and a young pigeon." 10 So Abram presented all these to him and killed them. Then he cut each animal down the middle and laid the halves side by side; he did not, however, cut the birds in half. 11 Some vultures swooped down to eat the carcasses, but Abram chased them away.

12 As the sun was going down, Abram fell into a deep sleep, and a terrifying darkness came down over him. 13 Then the LORD said to Abram, "You can be sure that your descendants will be strangers in a foreign land, where they will be oppressed as slaves for 400 years. 14 But I will punish the nation that enslaves them, and in the end they will come away with great wealth. 15 (As for you, you will die in peace and be buried at a ripe old age.) 16 After four generations your descendants will return here to this land, for the sins of the Amorites do not yet warrant their destruction."

17 After the sun went down and darkness fell, Abram saw a smoking firepot and a flaming torch pass between the halves of the carcasses. 18 So the LORD made a covenant with Abram that day and said, "I have given this land to your descendants, all the way from the border of Egypt* to the great Euphrates River— 19 the land now occupied by the Kenites, Kenizzites, Kadmonites, 20 Hittites, Perizzites, Rephaites, 21 Amorites, Canaanites, Girgashites, and Jebusites."

▸ **14:17** *See* ***Melchizedek****, page 1402.*

The Birth of Ishmael

16 Now Sarai, Abram's wife, had not
been able to bear children for him.
But she had an Egyptian servant named
Hagar. 2So Sarai said to Abram, "The LORD
has prevented me from having children. Go
and sleep with my servant. Perhaps I can
have children through her." And Abram
agreed with Sarai's proposal. 3So Sarai,
Abram's wife, took Hagar the Egyptian
servant and gave her to Abram as a wife.
(This happened ten years after Abram had
settled in the land of Canaan.)
4So Abram had sexual relations with
Hagar, and she became pregnant. But when
Hagar knew she was pregnant, she began
to treat her mistress, Sarai, with contempt.
5Then Sarai said to Abram, "This is all your
fault! I put my servant into your arms, but
now that she's pregnant she treats me
with contempt. The LORD will show who's
wrong—you or me!"
6Abram replied, "Look, she is your servant,
so deal with her as you see fit." Then Sarai
treated Hagar so harshly that she finally ran
away.
7The angel of the LORD found Hagar
beside a spring of water in the wilderness,
along the road to Shur. 8The angel said to
her, "Hagar, Sarai's servant, where have you
come from, and where are you going?"
"I'm running away from my mistress,
Sarai," she replied.
9The angel of the LORD said to her,
"Return to your mistress, and submit to her
authority." 10Then he added, "I will give you
more descendants than you can count."
11And the angel also said, "You are now
pregnant and will give birth to a son. You
are to name him Ishmael (which means
'God hears'), for the LORD has heard your
cry of distress. 12This son of yours will be
a wild man, as untamed as a wild donkey!
He will raise his fist against everyone,
and everyone will be against him. Yes, he

14:18 Hebrew *El-Elyon;* also in 14:19, 20, 22. **15:18** Hebrew *the river of Egypt,* referring either to an eastern branch of the Nile River or to the Brook of Egypt in the Sinai (see Num 34:5).

Covenant

Covenants—binding commitments made between two or more parties—were very common in the ancient Near East. Covenants were ratified in several different ways: sharing a meal (e.g., Genesis 26:28-31), offering a sacrifice (e.g., Exodus 24:4-8), taking an oath (e.g., 2 Kings 11:4), or performing the ritual described in Genesis 15. In this type of ritual, animals were cut in half, and the halves were laid out opposite one another. Both participants then walked between the divided animals, through the flowing blood, a declaration that death for them too was the only outcome of breaking the covenant.

In Genesis 15, however, only God (symbolized by fire) passed between the animals, while Abraham could only watch in his dream. This underlined the fact that he could bring nothing to the covenant that God was making with him.

Covenant is a constant theme in Scripture. Some key covenants include those God made with Moses and Israel (Exodus 19:1-8) and with King David (2 Samuel 7:1-16). The prophets often challenged God's people that they were breaking God's covenant with them through their disobedience and that judgment would surely come unless they repented. Eventually the covenant became so disregarded that it could no longer be restored, but only replaced. Jeremiah prophesied God would make "a new covenant" with his people (Jeremiah 31:31-34), written in their hearts, and Ezekiel saw that this new covenant would be a work of God's Spirit (Ezekiel 36:25-27).

The theme of covenant is picked up in the New Testament, where it is seen as new, yet nevertheless a continuation of this covenant made with Abraham (Acts 3:24-25; Galatians 3:15-20).

▶ *See also* ***The Davidic covenant****, page 468;* ***The new covenant****, page 861.*

will live in open hostility against all his
relatives."
13 Thereafter, Hagar used another name to
refer to the LORD, who had spoken to her.
She said, "You are the God who sees me."*
She also said, "Have I truly seen the One
who sees me?" 14 So that well was named
Beer-lahai-roi (which means "well of the
Living One who sees me"). It can still be
found between Kadesh and Bered.
15 So Hagar gave Abram a son, and Abram
named him Ishmael. 16 Abram was eighty-six
years old when Ishmael was born.

Abram Is Named Abraham

17 When Abram was ninety-nine years
old, the LORD appeared to him and
said, "I am El-Shaddai—'God Almighty.'
Serve me faithfully and live a blameless
life. 2 I will make a covenant with you, by
which I will guarantee to give you countless
descendants."
3 At this, Abram fell face down on the
ground. Then God said to him, 4 "This is
my covenant with you: I will make you the
father of a multitude of nations! 5 What's
more, I am changing your name. It will no
longer be Abram. Instead, you will be called
Abraham,* for you will be the father of many
nations. 6 I will make you extremely fruitful. Your descendants will become many
nations, and kings will be among them!
7 "I will confirm my covenant with you
and your descendants* after you, from generation to generation. This is the everlasting
covenant: I will always be your God and the
God of your descendants after you. 8 And I
will give the entire land of Canaan, where
you now live as a foreigner, to you and your
descendants. It will be their possession
forever, and I will be their God."

The Mark of the Covenant

9 Then God said to Abraham, "Your responsibility is to obey the terms of the covenant.
You and all your descendants have this continual responsibility. 10 This is the covenant
that you and your descendants must keep:
Each male among you must be circumcised.
11 You must cut off the flesh of your foreskin
as a sign of the covenant between me and
you. 12 From generation to generation, every
male child must be circumcised on the
eighth day after his birth. This applies not
only to members of your family but also to
the servants born in your household and
the foreign-born servants whom you have
purchased. 13 All must be circumcised. Your
bodies will bear the mark of my everlasting
covenant. 14 Any male who fails to be circumcised will be cut off from the covenant
family for breaking the covenant."

Sarai Is Named Sarah

15 Then God said to Abraham, "Regarding
Sarai, your wife—her name will no longer be
Sarai. From now on her name will be Sarah.*
16 And I will bless her and give you a son from
her! Yes, I will bless her richly, and she will
become the mother of many nations. Kings
of nations will be among her descendants."
17 Then Abraham bowed down to the
ground, but he laughed to himself in disbelief. "How could I become a father at
the age of 100?" he thought. "And how
can Sarah have a baby when she is ninety
years old?" 18 So Abraham said to God, "May
Ishmael live under your special blessing!"

Ishmael

When God's promise of a son didn't happen quickly, Abraham and Sarah tried to help God out. Sarah suggested he father a child through her servant, Hagar, a common practice in those days. But when Hagar became pregnant, it led to huge family tensions and to Hagar fleeing. In the desert an angel reassured her that her son would be blessed and that she should call him Ishmael ("God hears"). When Sarah eventually bore a son of her own—Isaac—rivalry again led to Hagar and Ishmael being sent away (Genesis 21:8-21). But God promised he would make Ishmael into a great nation, and he became the ancestor of the Arab peoples.

▶ *See also* ***Childlessness****, page 25.*

19 But God replied, "No—Sarah, your wife,
will give birth to a son for you. You will name
him Isaac,* and I will confirm my covenant
with him and his descendants as an everlasting covenant. 20 As for Ishmael, I will bless
him also, just as you have asked. I will make
him extremely fruitful and multiply his descendants. He will become the father of
twelve princes, and I will make him a great
nation. 21 But my covenant will be confirmed
with Isaac, who will be born to you and Sarah
about this time next year." 22 When God had
finished speaking, he left Abraham.
23 On that very day Abraham took his son,
Ishmael, and every male in his household,
including those born there and those he had
bought. Then he circumcised them, cutting
off their foreskins, just as God had told
him. 24 Abraham was ninety-nine years old
when he was circumcised, 25 and Ishmael,
his son, was thirteen. 26 Both Abraham and
his son, Ishmael, were circumcised on that
same day, 27 along with all the other men
and boys of the household, whether they
were born there or bought as servants. All
were circumcised with him.

A Son Is Promised to Sarah

18 The LORD appeared again to Abraham near the oak grove belonging to
Mamre. One day Abraham was sitting at the
entrance to his tent during the hottest part
of the day. 2 He looked up and noticed three
men standing nearby. When he saw them,
he ran to meet them and welcomed them,
bowing low to the ground.
3 "My lord," he said, "if it pleases you, stop
here for a while. 4 Rest in the shade of this
tree while water is brought to wash your feet.
5 And since you've honored your servant with
this visit, let me prepare some food to refresh
you before you continue on your journey."
"All right," they said. "Do as you have
said."
6 So Abraham ran back to the tent and said
to Sarah, "Hurry! Get three large measures*
of your best flour, knead it into dough, and
bake some bread." 7 Then Abraham ran out to
the herd and chose a tender calf and gave it to
his servant, who quickly prepared it. 8 When
the food was ready, Abraham took some
yogurt and milk and the roasted meat, and
he served it to the men. As they ate, Abraham
waited on them in the shade of the trees.
9 "Where is Sarah, your wife?" the visitors
asked.
"She's inside the tent," Abraham replied.
10 Then one of them said, "I will return
to you about this time next year, and your
wife, Sarah, will have a son!"
Sarah was listening to this conversation
from the tent. 11 Abraham and Sarah were
both very old by this time, and Sarah was
long past the age of having children. 12 So
she laughed silently to herself and said,
"How could a worn-out woman like me
enjoy such pleasure, especially when my
master—my husband—is also so old?"
13 Then the LORD said to Abraham, "Why
did Sarah laugh? Why did she say, 'Can an old
woman like me have a baby?' 14 Is anything
too hard for the LORD? I will return about this
time next year, and Sarah will have a son."

16:13 Hebrew *El-roi.* **17:5** *Abram* means "exalted father"; *Abraham* sounds like a Hebrew term that means "father of many." **17:7** Hebrew *seed;* also in 17:7b, 8, 9, 10, 19. **17:15** *Sarai* and *Sarah* both mean "princess"; the change in spelling may reflect the difference in dialect between Ur and Canaan. **17:19** *Isaac* means "he laughs." **18:6** Hebrew *3 seahs,* about half a bushel or 22 liters.

Canaan

Canaan is the name given to the region between the Mediterranean Sea and the Jordan River, originally occupied by descendants of Canaan, Noah's grandson and Ham's son, whose line was cursed because of Ham's disrespect to his father (Genesis 9:18-27). God chose Canaan as Israel's Promised Land (15:12-16; 17:8), probably because of its location at the crossroads of the ancient world's great empires. Israel was meant to influence them all but sadly would be influenced by them instead.

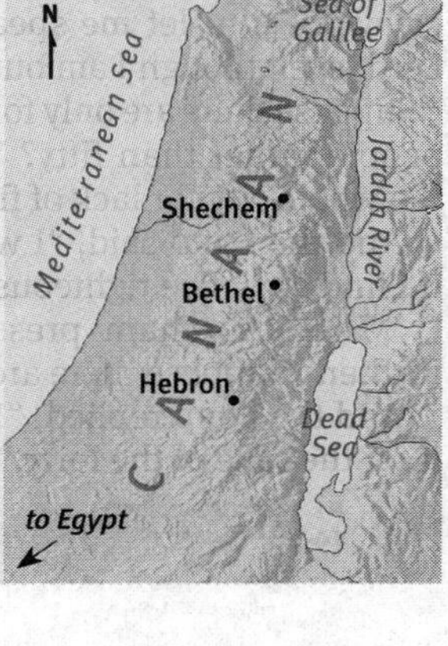

15 Sarah was afraid, so she denied it,
saying, "I didn't laugh."
But the LORD said, "No, you did laugh."

Abraham Intercedes for Sodom

16 Then the men got up from their meal and
looked out toward Sodom. As they left,
Abraham went with them to send them on
their way.
17 "Should I hide my plan from Abraham?"
the LORD asked. 18 "For Abraham will certainly become a great and mighty nation,
and all the nations of the earth will be
blessed through him. 19 I have singled him
out so that he will direct his sons and their
families to keep the way of the LORD by
doing what is right and just. Then I will do
for Abraham all that I have promised."
20 So the LORD told Abraham, "I have heard
a great outcry from Sodom and Gomorrah,
because their sin is so flagrant. 21 I am going
down to see if their actions are as wicked as
I have heard. If not, I want to know."
22 The other men turned and headed
toward Sodom, but the LORD remained with
Abraham. 23 Abraham approached him
and said, "Will you sweep away both the
righteous and the wicked? 24 Suppose you
find fifty righteous people living there in
the city—will you still sweep it away and
not spare it for their sakes? 25 Surely you
wouldn't do such a thing, destroying the
righteous along with the wicked. Why,
you would be treating the righteous and
the wicked exactly the same! Surely you
wouldn't do that! Should not the Judge of
all the earth do what is right?"
26 And the LORD replied, "If I find fifty
righteous people in Sodom, I will spare the
entire city for their sake."
27 Then Abraham spoke again. "Since
I have begun, let me speak further to my
Lord, even though I am but dust and ashes.
28 Suppose there are only forty-five righteous
people rather than fifty? Will you destroy
the whole city for lack of five?"
And the LORD said, "I will not destroy it
if I find forty-five righteous people there."
29 Then Abraham pressed his request
further. "Suppose there are only forty?"
And the LORD replied, "I will not destroy
it for the sake of the forty."
30 "Please don't be angry, my Lord,"
Abraham pleaded. "Let me speak—suppose
only thirty righteous people are found?"
And the LORD replied, "I will not destroy
it if I find thirty."
31 Then Abraham said, "Since I have dared
to speak to the Lord, let me continue—
suppose there are only twenty?"
And the LORD replied, "Then I will not
destroy it for the sake of the twenty."
32 Finally, Abraham said, "Lord, please
don't be angry with me if I speak one more
time. Suppose only ten are found there?"
And the LORD replied, "Then I will not
destroy it for the sake of the ten."
33 When the LORD had finished his conversation with Abraham, he went on his way,
and Abraham returned to his tent.

Sodom and Gomorrah Destroyed

19 That evening the two angels came to
the entrance of the city of Sodom. Lot
was sitting there, and when he saw them,
he stood up to meet them. Then he welcomed them and bowed with his face to the
ground. 2 "My lords," he said, "come to my
home to wash your feet, and be my guests
for the night. You may then get up early in
the morning and be on your way again."
"Oh no," they replied. "We'll just spend
the night out here in the city square."
3 But Lot insisted, so at last they went
home with him. Lot prepared a feast for
them, complete with fresh bread made
without yeast, and they ate. 4 But before they
retired for the night, all the men of Sodom,
young and old, came from all over the city
and surrounded the house. 5 They shouted
to Lot, "Where are the men who came to
spend the night with you? Bring them out
to us so we can have sex with them!"
6 So Lot stepped outside to talk to them,
shutting the door behind him. 7 "Please,
my brothers," he begged, "don't do such
a wicked thing. 8 Look, I have two virgin
daughters. Let me bring them out to you,
and you can do with them as you wish. But
please, leave these men alone, for they are
my guests and are under my protection."
9 "Stand back!" they shouted. "This fellow
came to town as an outsider, and now he's
acting like our judge! We'll treat you far

▸ **19:1** *See **Angels**, page 1397.*

worse than those other men!" And they
lunged toward Lot to break down the door.
10 But the two angels* reached out, pulled
Lot into the house, and bolted the door.
11 Then they blinded all the men, young and
old, who were at the door of the house, so
they gave up trying to get inside.
12 Meanwhile, the angels questioned Lot.
"Do you have any other relatives here in
the city?" they asked. "Get them out of this
place—your sons-in-law, sons, daughters,
or anyone else. 13 For we are about to destroy
this city completely. The outcry against this
place is so great it has reached the LORD,
and he has sent us to destroy it."
14 So Lot rushed out to tell his daughters'
fiancés, "Quick, get out of the city! The LORD
is about to destroy it." But the young men
thought he was only joking.
15 At dawn the next morning the angels
became insistent. "Hurry," they said to
Lot. "Take your wife and your two daughters who are here. Get out right now, or you
will be swept away in the destruction of the
city!"
16 When Lot still hesitated, the angels
seized his hand and the hands of his wife
and two daughters and rushed them to
safety outside the city, for the LORD was
merciful. 17 When they were safely out of
the city, one of the angels ordered, "Run
for your lives! And don't look back or stop
anywhere in the valley! Escape to the mountains, or you will be swept away!"
18 "Oh no, my lord!" Lot begged. 19 "You
have been so gracious to me and saved my
life, and you have shown such great kindness. But I cannot go to the mountains.
Disaster would catch up to me there, and
I would soon die. 20 See, there is a small
village nearby. Please let me go there
instead; don't you see how small it is? Then
my life will be saved."
21 "All right," the angel said, "I will grant
your request. I will not destroy the little
village. 22 But hurry! Escape to it, for I can
do nothing until you arrive there." (This explains why that village was known as Zoar,
which means "little place.")
23 Lot reached the village just as the sun
was rising over the horizon. 24 Then the
LORD rained down fire and burning sulfur
from the sky on Sodom and Gomorrah. 25 He
utterly destroyed them, along with the other
cities and villages of the plain, wiping out
all the people and every bit of vegetation.
26 But Lot's wife looked back as she was following behind him, and she turned into a
pillar of salt.
27 Abraham got up early that morning and
hurried out to the place where he had stood
in the LORD's presence. 28 He looked out
across the plain toward Sodom and Gomorrah and watched as columns of smoke rose
from the cities like smoke from a furnace.
29 But God had listened to Abraham's
request and kept Lot safe, removing him
from the disaster that engulfed the cities on
the plain.

Lot and His Daughters

30 Afterward Lot left Zoar because he was
afraid of the people there, and he went to
live in a cave in the mountains with his two
daughters. 31 One day the older daughter said
to her sister, "There are no men left anywhere
in this entire area, so we can't get married
like everyone else. And our father will soon
be too old to have children. 32 Come, let's get

19:10 Hebrew *men;* also in 19:12, 16.

Sodom and Gomorrah

Sodom and Gomorrah, located south of the Dead Sea, were prosperous yet immoral cities. Sodom's immorality led to its citizens demanding homosexual sex with Lot's guests, a violation of both social and ethical codes. The angels urged Lot and his family to flee to escape God's coming judgment. Burning sulfur rained down on them—probably the result of seismic disturbance of the region's tar pits—and they were utterly destroyed. The cities became examples of human depravity and God's consequent judgment (e.g., Matthew 10:15; 2 Peter 2:6). However, had there been as few as ten righteous people in them, the cities would have been spared (Genesis 18:32).

him drunk with wine, and then we will have sex with him. That way we will preserve our family line through our father."

33 So that night they got him drunk with wine, and the older daughter went in and had intercourse with her father. He was unaware of her lying down or getting up again.

34 The next morning the older daughter said to her younger sister, "I had sex with our father last night. Let's get him drunk with wine again tonight, and you go in and have sex with him. That way we will preserve our family line through our father." 35 So that night they got him drunk with wine again, and the younger daughter went in and had intercourse with him. As before, he was unaware of her lying down or getting up again.

36 As a result, both of Lot's daughters became pregnant by their own father. 37 When the older daughter gave birth to a son, she named him Moab.* He became the ancestor of the nation now known as the Moabites. 38 When the younger daughter gave birth to a son, she named him Ben-ammi.* He became the ancestor of the nation now known as the Ammonites.

Abraham Deceives Abimelech

20 Abraham moved south to the Negev and lived for a while between Kadesh and Shur, and then he moved on to Gerar. While living there as a foreigner, 2 Abraham introduced his wife, Sarah, by saying, "She is my sister." So King Abimelech of Gerar sent for Sarah and had her brought to him at his palace.

3 But that night God came to Abimelech in a dream and told him, "You are a dead man, for that woman you have taken is already married!"

4 But Abimelech had not slept with her yet, so he said, "Lord, will you destroy an innocent nation? 5 Didn't Abraham tell me, 'She is my sister'? And she herself said, 'Yes, he is my brother.' I acted in complete innocence! My hands are clean."

6 In the dream God responded, "Yes, I know you are innocent. That's why I kept you from sinning against me, and why I did not let you touch her. 7 Now return the woman to her husband, and he will pray for you, for he is a prophet. Then you will live. But if you don't return her to him, you can be sure that you and all your people will die."

8 Abimelech got up early the next morning and quickly called all his servants together. When he told them what had happened, his men were terrified. 9 Then Abimelech called for Abraham. "What have you done to us?" he demanded. "What crime have I committed that deserves treatment like this, making me and my kingdom guilty of this great sin? No one should ever do what you have done! 10 Whatever possessed you to do such a thing?"

11 Abraham replied, "I thought, 'This is a godless place. They will want my wife and will kill me to get her.' 12 And she really is my sister, for we both have the same father, but different mothers. And I married her. 13 When God called me to leave my father's home and to travel from place to place, I told her, 'Do me a favor. Wherever we go, tell the people that I am your brother.'"

14 Then Abimelech took some of his sheep and goats, cattle, and male and female servants, and he presented them to Abraham. He also returned his wife, Sarah, to him. 15 Then Abimelech said, "Look over my land and choose any place where you would like to live." 16 And he said to Sarah, "Look, I am giving your 'brother' 1,000 pieces of silver* in the presence of all these witnesses. This is to compensate you for any wrong I may have done to you. This will settle any claim against me, and your reputation is cleared."

17 Then Abraham prayed to God, and God healed Abimelech, his wife, and his female servants, so they could have children. 18 For the LORD had caused all the women to be infertile because of what happened with Abraham's wife, Sarah.

The Birth of Isaac

21 The LORD kept his word and did for Sarah exactly what he had promised. 2 She became pregnant, and she gave birth to a son for Abraham in his old age. This happened at just the time God had said it would. 3 And Abraham named their son Isaac. 4 Eight days after Isaac was born, Abraham circumcised him as God had commanded. 5 Abraham was 100 years old when Isaac was born.

6 And Sarah declared, "God has brought me laughter.* All who hear about this will laugh with me. 7 Who would have said to Abraham that Sarah would nurse a baby? Yet I have given Abraham a son in his old age!"

Hagar and Ishmael Are Sent Away

8When Isaac grew up and was about to
be weaned, Abraham prepared a huge
feast to celebrate the occasion. 9But
Sarah saw Ishmael—the son of Abraham
and her Egyptian servant Hagar—making
fun of her son, Isaac.* 10So she turned to
Abraham and demanded, "Get rid of that
slave woman and her son. He is not going
to share the inheritance with my son,
Isaac. I won't have it!"

11This upset Abraham very much because
Ishmael was his son. 12But God told
Abraham, "Do not be upset over the boy
and your servant. Do whatever Sarah tells
you, for Isaac is the son through whom
your descendants will be counted. 13But I
will also make a nation of the descendants
of Hagar's son because he is your son, too."

14So Abraham got up early the next
morning, prepared food and a container of
water, and strapped them on Hagar's shoulders. Then he sent her away with their son,
and she wandered aimlessly in the wilderness of Beersheba.

15When the water was gone, she put the
boy in the shade of a bush. 16Then she went
and sat down by herself about a hundred
yards* away. "I don't want to watch the boy
die," she said, as she burst into tears.

17But God heard the boy crying, and
the angel of God called to Hagar from
heaven, "Hagar, what's wrong? Do not
be afraid! God has heard the boy crying
as he lies there. 18Go to him and comfort
him, for I will make a great nation from his
descendants."

19Then God opened Hagar's eyes, and she
saw a well full of water. She quickly filled
her water container and gave the boy a
drink.

20And God was with the boy as he grew
up in the wilderness. He became a skillful
archer, 21and he settled in the wilderness
of Paran. His mother arranged for him to
marry a woman from the land of Egypt.

19:37 *Moab* sounds like a Hebrew term that means "from father." **19:38** *Ben-ammi* means "son of my kinsman." **20:16** Hebrew *1,000 [shekels] of silver,* about 25 pounds or 11.4 kilograms in weight. **21:6** The name *Isaac* means "he laughs." **21:9** As in Greek version and Latin Vulgate; Hebrew lacks *of her son, Isaac.* **21:16** Hebrew *a bowshot.*

Childlessness

Twenty-five years had passed since God had called Abraham to go to Canaan, promising him many descendants (Genesis 12:1-6). But there was a problem: His wife, Sarah, was unable to have children. So when God promised that she would conceive, Abraham had laughed in disbelief (17:1-22). But God is always faithful to his promises, and now Sarah laughed with delight as she nursed her son (21:6-7).

Up to this point, Sarah's life must have been painful, for in those days infertility was often seen as a sign of God's judgment. Abraham had tried to solve the problem—first through considering adopting his servant (15:2-3), and then through fathering a child through Sarah's servant (16:1-4), showing how desperate they were for a child. But while the Bible sees children as God's blessing (e.g., Deuteronomy 7:12-14; Psalm 127:3-5), it doesn't condemn those who cannot have children. Rather, it commends those who trust God in such circumstances—people like Hannah, Samuel's mother (1 Samuel 1:1-28), and Zechariah and Elizabeth, the parents of John the Baptist (Luke 1:5-25, 57-66). Often such faith was rewarded with children who were especially significant in God's purposes, but an inability to have children does not prove ungodliness. We should therefore be careful never to look down on those who cannot have children, but rather to love and encourage them as God himself does. And if we ourselves are facing infertility issues, we should simply keep trusting God. He may well provide a miracle in due course; but even if he doesn't, we should always remember that we are no less blessed and loved by him and that we can be significant in his purposes whether we have many children (like Jacob) or no children (like Jesus).

▶ *See also* ***Hannah****, page 306.*

Abraham's Covenant with Abimelech

22 About this time, Abimelech came with
Phicol, his army commander, to visit
Abraham. "God is obviously with you,
helping you in everything you do," Abimelech said. 23 "Swear to me in God's name
that you will never deceive me, my children,
or any of my descendants. I have been loyal
to you, so now swear that you will be
loyal to me and to this country where you
are living as a foreigner."

24 Abraham replied, "Yes, I swear to it!"
25 Then Abraham complained to Abimelech
about a well that Abimelech's servants had
taken by force from Abraham's servants.

26 "This is the first I've heard of it," Abimelech answered. "I have no idea who is
responsible. You have never complained
about this before."

27 Abraham then gave some of his sheep,
goats, and cattle to Abimelech, and they
made a treaty. 28 But Abraham also took
seven additional female lambs and set
them off by themselves. 29 Abimelech asked,
"Why have you set these seven apart from
the others?"

30 Abraham replied, "Please accept these
seven lambs to show your agreement that
I dug this well." 31 Then he named the place
Beersheba (which means "well of the
oath"), because that was where they had
sworn the oath.

32 After making their covenant at Beersheba, Abimelech left with Phicol, the
commander of his army, and they returned
home to the land of the Philistines. 33 Then
Abraham planted a tamarisk tree at Beersheba, and there he worshiped the LORD, the
Eternal God.* 34 And Abraham lived as a foreigner in Philistine country for a long time.

Abraham's Faith Tested

22 Some time later, God tested Abraham's faith. "Abraham!" God called.
"Yes," he replied. "Here I am."

2 "Take your son, your only son—yes,
Isaac, whom you love so much—and go to
the land of Moriah. Go and sacrifice him as
a burnt offering on one of the mountains,
which I will show you."

3 The next morning Abraham got up early.
He saddled his donkey and took two of his
servants with him, along with his son, Isaac.
Then he chopped wood for a fire for a burnt
offering and set out for the place God had told
him about. 4 On the third day of their journey,
Abraham looked up and saw the place in
the distance. 5 "Stay here with the donkey,"
Abraham told the servants. "The boy and I
will travel a little farther. We will worship
there, and then we will come right back."

6 So Abraham placed the wood for the
burnt offering on Isaac's shoulders, while
he himself carried the fire and the knife. As
the two of them walked on together, 7 Isaac
turned to Abraham and said, "Father?"

"Yes, my son?" Abraham replied.

"We have the fire and the wood," the boy
said, "but where is the sheep for the burnt
offering?"

8 "God will provide a sheep for the burnt
offering, my son," Abraham answered. And
they both walked on together.

9 When they arrived at the place where
God had told him to go, Abraham built an
altar and arranged the wood on it. Then he
tied his son, Isaac, and laid him on the altar
on top of the wood. 10 And Abraham picked
up the knife to kill his son as a sacrifice. 11 At
that moment the angel of the LORD called
to him from heaven, "Abraham! Abraham!"

"Yes," Abraham replied. "Here I am!"

12 "Don't lay a hand on the boy!" the angel
said. "Do not hurt him in any way, for now
I know that you truly fear God. You have
not withheld from me even your son, your
only son."

13 Then Abraham looked up and saw a ram
caught by its horns in a thicket. So he took
the ram and sacrificed it as a burnt offering in place of his son. 14 Abraham named
the place Yahweh-Yireh (which means "the
LORD will provide"). To this day, people still
use that name as a proverb: "On the mountain of the LORD it will be provided."

15 Then the angel of the LORD called again
to Abraham from heaven. 16 "This is what the
LORD says: Because you have obeyed me
and have not withheld even your son, your
only son, I swear by my own name that 17 I
will certainly bless you. I will multiply your
descendants* beyond number, like the stars
in the sky and the sand on the seashore.
Your descendants will conquer the cities of
their enemies. 18 And through your descendants all the nations of the earth will be
blessed—all because you have obeyed me."

19 Then they returned to the servants and
traveled back to Beersheba, where Abraham
continued to live.

[20]Soon after this, Abraham heard that
Milcah, his brother Nahor's wife, had
borne Nahor eight sons. [21]The oldest was
named Uz, the next oldest was Buz, followed by Kemuel (the ancestor of the Arameans), [22]Kesed, Hazo, Pildash, Jidlaph,
and Bethuel. [23](Bethuel became the father
of Rebekah.) In addition to these eight sons
from Milcah, [24]Nahor had four other children
from his concubine Reumah. Their names
were Tebah, Gaham, Tahash, and Maacah.

The Burial of Sarah

23 When Sarah was 127 years old, [2]she
died at Kiriath-arba (now called
Hebron) in the land of Canaan. There
Abraham mourned and wept for her.
[3]Then, leaving her body, he said to the
Hittite elders, [4]"Here I am, a stranger and
a foreigner among you. Please sell me a
piece of land so I can give my wife a proper
burial."
[5]The Hittites replied to Abraham, [6]"Listen,
my lord, you are an honored prince among
us. Choose the finest of our tombs and bury
her there. No one here will refuse to help
you in this way."
[7]Then Abraham bowed low before the
Hittites [8]and said, "Since you are willing to
help me in this way, be so kind as to ask
Ephron son of Zohar [9]to let me buy his cave
at Machpelah, down at the end of his field.
I will pay the full price in the presence of
witnesses, so I will have a permanent burial
place for my family."
[10]Ephron was sitting there among the
others, and he answered Abraham as the
others listened, speaking publicly before
all the Hittite elders of the town. [11]"No, my
lord," he said to Abraham, "please listen to
me. I will give you the field and the cave.
Here in the presence of my people, I give it
to you. Go and bury your dead."
[12]Abraham again bowed low before the citizens of the land, [13]and he replied to Ephron
as everyone listened. "No, listen to me. I will
buy it from you. Let me pay the full price for
the field so I can bury my dead there."
[14]Ephron answered Abraham, [15]"My
lord, please listen to me. The land is worth
400 pieces* of silver, but what is that between
friends? Go ahead and bury your dead."
[16]So Abraham agreed to Ephron's
price and paid the amount he had suggested—400 pieces of silver, weighed according to the market standard. The Hittite
elders witnessed the transaction.
[17]So Abraham bought the plot of land
belonging to Ephron at Machpelah, near
Mamre. This included the field itself, the
cave that was in it, and all the surrounding
trees. [18]It was transferred to Abraham as his
permanent possession in the presence of the
Hittite elders at the city gate. [19]Then Abraham
buried his wife, Sarah, there in Canaan, in
the cave of Machpelah, near Mamre (also
called Hebron). [20]So the field and the cave
were transferred from the Hittites to Abraham
for use as a permanent burial place.

A Wife for Isaac

24 Abraham was now a very old man,
and the LORD had blessed him in
every way. [2]One day Abraham said to his
oldest servant, the man in charge of his

21:33 Hebrew *El-Olam*. **22:17** Hebrew *seed;* also in 22:17b, 18.
23:15 Hebrew *400 shekels*, about 10 pounds or 4.6 kilograms in weight; also in 23:16.

Sarah

Abraham's wife Sarah is honored in the New Testament as a great example of a wife respecting her husband (1 Peter 3:6) and of trusting God despite the challenges (Hebrews 11:11). Her encouragement to Abraham to father a child through her servant Hagar came from a good (if misguided) heart (Genesis 16). When it seemed that Sarah's hopes of a child were in vain, God changed her name from Sarai to Sarah (though both mean "princess," the very fact of God changing her name was hugely significant) and allowed her to conceive at the age of ninety (17:17). She gave birth to Isaac (21:1-7), from whom the nation of Israel would descend.

▶ *See also* ***Abraham****, page 16;* ***Ishmael****, page 20;* ***Childlessness****, page 25;* ***Isaac and Rebekah****, page 28.*

household, "Take an oath by putting your hand under my thigh. 3Swear by the LORD, the God of heaven and earth, that you will not allow my son to marry one of these local Canaanite women. 4Go instead to my homeland, to my relatives, and find a wife there for my son Isaac."

5The servant asked, "But what if I can't find a young woman who is willing to travel so far from home? Should I then take Isaac there to live among your relatives in the land you came from?"

6"No!" Abraham responded. "Be careful never to take my son there. 7For the LORD, the God of heaven, who took me from my father's house and my native land, solemnly promised to give this land to my descendants.* He will send his angel ahead of you, and he will see to it that you find a wife there for my son. 8If she is unwilling to come back with you, then you are free from this oath of mine. But under no circumstances are you to take my son there."

9So the servant took an oath by putting his hand under the thigh of his master, Abraham. He swore to follow Abraham's instructions. 10Then he loaded ten of Abraham's camels with all kinds of expensive gifts from his master, and he traveled to distant Aram-naharaim. There he went to the town where Abraham's brother Nahor had settled. 11He made the camels kneel beside a well just outside the town. It was evening, and the women were coming out to draw water.

12"O LORD, God of my master, Abraham," he prayed. "Please give me success today, and show unfailing love to my master, Abraham. 13See, I am standing here beside this spring, and the young women of the town are coming out to draw water. 14This is my request. I will ask one of them, 'Please give me a drink from your jug.' If she says, 'Yes, have a drink, and I will water your camels, too!'—let her be the one you have selected as Isaac's wife. This is how I will know that you have shown unfailing love to my master."

15Before he had finished praying, he saw a young woman named Rebekah coming out with her water jug on her shoulder. She was the daughter of Bethuel, who was the son of Abraham's brother Nahor and his wife, Milcah. 16Rebekah was very beautiful and old enough to be married, but she was still a virgin. She went down to the spring, filled her jug, and came up again. 17Running over to her, the servant said, "Please give me a little drink of water from your jug."

18"Yes, my lord," she answered, "have a drink." And she quickly lowered her jug from her shoulder and gave him a drink. 19When she had given him a drink, she said, "I'll draw water for your camels, too, until they have had enough to drink." 20So she quickly emptied her jug into the watering trough and ran back to the well to draw water for all his camels.

21The servant watched her in silence, wondering whether or not the LORD had given him success in his mission. 22Then at last, when the camels had finished drinking, he took out a gold ring for her nose and two large gold bracelets* for her wrists.

23"Whose daughter are you?" he asked. "And please tell me, would your father have any room to put us up for the night?"

24"I am the daughter of Bethuel," she replied. "My grandparents are Nahor and Milcah. 25Yes, we have plenty of straw and feed for the camels, and we have room for guests."

Isaac and Rebekah

Born to Abraham and Sarah when, humanly speaking, they were too old to have children, Isaac was the promised son through whom God's promises to Abraham would be fulfilled (Genesis 17:19-21; 21:12; 26:1-5)—though that would be tested when God wanted to know if Abraham was ready to sacrifice him (chapter 22). Genesis 24 recounts how Abraham's servant went back to Abraham's family in Haran to find a wife for Isaac. Although initially unable to have children, Rebekah bore Isaac twin sons, Esau and Jacob (25:19-26). In his old age, when he was blind, Isaac was tricked into giving Jacob, the second-born, his inheritance-blessing (27:1-40).

▶ *See also* ***World of the Patriarchs*** *map, Visual Overview Z2.*

[26]The man bowed low and worshiped the
LORD. [27]"Praise the LORD, the God of my
master, Abraham," he said. "The LORD has
shown unfailing love and faithfulness to
my master, for he has led me straight to my
master's relatives."
[28]The young woman ran home to tell her
family everything that had happened. [29]Now
Rebekah had a brother named Laban, who
ran out to meet the man at the spring. [30]He
had seen the nose-ring and the bracelets on
his sister's wrists, and had heard Rebekah
tell what the man had said. So he rushed
out to the spring, where the man was still
standing beside his camels. [31]Laban said to
him, "Come and stay with us, you who are
blessed by the LORD! Why are you standing
here outside the town when I have a room
all ready for you and a place prepared for
the camels?"
[32]So the man went home with Laban, and
Laban unloaded the camels, gave him straw
for their bedding, fed them, and provided
water for the man and the camel drivers to
wash their feet. [33]Then food was served. But
Abraham's servant said, "I don't want to eat
until I have told you why I have come."
"All right," Laban said, "tell us."
[34]"I am Abraham's servant," he explained. [35]"And the LORD has greatly blessed
my master; he has become a wealthy man.
The LORD has given him flocks of sheep and
goats, herds of cattle, a fortune in silver and
gold, and many male and female servants
and camels and donkeys.
[36]"When Sarah, my master's wife, was
very old, she gave birth to my master's son,
and my master has given him everything
he owns. [37]And my master made me take
an oath. He said, 'Do not allow my son to
marry one of these local Canaanite women.
[38]Go instead to my father's house, to my
relatives, and find a wife there for my son.'
[39]"But I said to my master, 'What if I can't
find a young woman who is willing to go
back with me?' [40]He responded, 'The LORD,
in whose presence I have lived, will send his
angel with you and will make your mission
successful. Yes, you must find a wife for
my son from among my relatives, from my
father's family. [41]Then you will have fulfilled your obligation. But if you go to my
relatives and they refuse to let her go with
you, you will be free from my oath.'
[42]"So today when I came to the spring,
I prayed this prayer: 'O LORD, God of my
master, Abraham, please give me success
on this mission. [43]See, I am standing here
beside this spring. This is my request. When
a young woman comes to draw water, I will
say to her, "Please give me a little drink of
water from your jug." [44]If she says, "Yes,
have a drink, and I will draw water for your
camels, too," let her be the one you have
selected to be the wife of my master's son.'
[45]"Before I had finished praying in my
heart, I saw Rebekah coming out with her
water jug on her shoulder. She went down
to the spring and drew water. So I said to
her, 'Please give me a drink.' [46]She quickly
lowered her jug from her shoulder and
said, 'Yes, have a drink, and I will water
your camels, too!' So I drank, and then she
watered the camels.
[47]"Then I asked, 'Whose daughter are
you?' She replied, 'I am the daughter of
Bethuel, and my grandparents are Nahor
and Milcah.' So I put the ring on her nose,
and the bracelets on her wrists.
[48]"Then I bowed low and worshiped the
LORD. I praised the LORD, the God of my
master, Abraham, because he had led me
straight to my master's niece to be his son's
wife. [49]So tell me—will you or won't you
show unfailing love and faithfulness to my
master? Please tell me yes or no, and then
I'll know what to do next."
[50]Then Laban and Bethuel replied, "The
LORD has obviously brought you here,
so there is nothing we can say. [51]Here is
Rebekah; take her and go. Yes, let her be
the wife of your master's son, as the LORD
has directed."
[52]When Abraham's servant heard their
answer, he bowed down to the ground and
worshiped the LORD. [53]Then he brought
out silver and gold jewelry and clothing
and presented them to Rebekah. He also
gave expensive presents to her brother and
mother. [54]Then they ate their meal, and the
servant and the men with him stayed there
overnight.
But early the next morning, Abraham's
servant said, "Send me back to my master."
[55]"But we want Rebekah to stay with us
at least ten days," her brother and mother
said. "Then she can go."

24:7 Hebrew *seed;* also in 24:60. **24:22** Hebrew *a gold nose-ring weighing a beka* [0.2 ounces or 6 grams] *and two gold bracelets weighing 10 [shekels]* [4 ounces or 114 grams].

56But he said, "Don't delay me. The LORD
has made my mission successful; now send
me back so I can return to my master."
57"Well," they said, "we'll call Rebekah
and ask her what she thinks." 58So they
called Rebekah. "Are you willing to go with
this man?" they asked her.
And she replied, "Yes, I will go."
59So they said good-bye to Rebekah and
sent her away with Abraham's servant
and his men. The woman who had been
Rebekah's childhood nurse went along
with her. 60They gave her this blessing as
she parted:

"Our sister, may you become
the mother of many millions!
May your descendants be strong
and conquer the cities of their
enemies."

61Then Rebekah and her servant girls
mounted the camels and followed the man.
So Abraham's servant took Rebekah and
went on his way.
62Meanwhile, Isaac, whose home was in
the Negev, had returned from Beer-lahai-roi.
63One evening as he was walking and meditating in the fields, he looked up and saw
the camels coming. 64When Rebekah looked
up and saw Isaac, she quickly dismounted
from her camel. 65"Who is that man walking
through the fields to meet us?" she asked
the servant.
And he replied, "It is my master." So
Rebekah covered her face with her veil.
66Then the servant told Isaac everything he
had done.
67And Isaac brought Rebekah into his
mother Sarah's tent, and she became his
wife. He loved her deeply, and she was a
special comfort to him after the death of his
mother.

The Death of Abraham

25 Abraham married another wife,
whose name was Keturah. 2She gave
birth to Zimran, Jokshan, Medan, Midian,
Ishbak, and Shuah. 3Jokshan was the father
of Sheba and Dedan. Dedan's descendants
were the Asshurites, Letushites, and Leum-
mites. 4Midian's sons were Ephah, Epher,
Hanoch, Abida, and Eldaah. These were all
descendants of Abraham through Keturah.
5Abraham gave everything he owned to his
son Isaac. 6But before he died, he gave gifts
to the sons of his concubines and sent them
off to a land in the east, away from Isaac.
7Abraham lived for 175 years, 8and he died
at a ripe old age, having lived a long and satisfying life. He breathed his last and joined
his ancestors in death. 9His sons Isaac and
Ishmael buried him in the cave of Machpelah, near Mamre, in the field of Ephron
son of Zohar the Hittite. 10This was the field
Abraham had purchased from the Hittites
and where he had buried his wife Sarah.
11After Abraham's death, God blessed his
son Isaac, who settled near Beer-lahai-roi
in the Negev.

Ishmael's Descendants

12This is the account of the family of
Ishmael, the son of Abraham through
Hagar, Sarah's Egyptian servant. 13Here is a
list, by their names and clans, of Ishmael's
descendants: The oldest was Nebaioth,
followed by Kedar, Adbeel, Mibsam,
14Mishma, Dumah, Massa, 15Hadad, Tema,
Jetur, Naphish, and Kedemah. 16These
twelve sons of Ishmael became the founders of twelve tribes named after them, listed
according to the places they settled and
camped. 17Ishmael lived for 137 years. Then
he breathed his last and joined his ancestors in death. 18Ishmael's descendants occupied the region from Havilah to Shur,
which is east of Egypt in the direction of
Asshur. There they lived in open hostility
toward all their relatives.*

The Births of Esau and Jacob

19This is the account of the family of Isaac,
the son of Abraham. 20When Isaac was forty
years old, he married Rebekah, the daughter of Bethuel the Aramean from Paddan-
aram and the sister of Laban the Aramean.
21Isaac pleaded with the LORD on behalf
of his wife, because she was unable to
have children. The LORD answered Isaac's
prayer, and Rebekah became pregnant with
twins. 22But the two children struggled with
each other in her womb. So she went to ask
the LORD about it. "Why is this happening
to me?" she asked.
23And the LORD told her, "The sons in
your womb will become two nations. From
the very beginning, the two nations will be
rivals. One nation will be stronger than the
other; and your older son will serve your
younger son."

24 And when the time came to give birth, Rebekah discovered that she did indeed have twins! 25 The first one was very red at birth and covered with thick hair like a fur coat. So they named him Esau.* 26 Then the other twin was born with his hand grasping Esau's heel. So they named him Jacob.* Isaac was sixty years old when the twins were born.

Esau Sells His Birthright

27 As the boys grew up, Esau became a skillful hunter. He was an outdoorsman, but Jacob had a quiet temperament, preferring to stay at home. 28 Isaac loved Esau because he enjoyed eating the wild game Esau brought home, but Rebekah loved Jacob.

29 One day when Jacob was cooking some stew, Esau arrived home from the wilderness exhausted and hungry. 30 Esau said to Jacob, "I'm starved! Give me some of that red stew!" (This is how Esau got his other name, Edom, which means "red.")

31 "All right," Jacob replied, "but trade me your rights as the firstborn son."

32 "Look, I'm dying of starvation!" said Esau. "What good is my birthright to me now?"

33 But Jacob said, "First you must swear that your birthright is mine." So Esau swore an oath, thereby selling all his rights as the firstborn to his brother, Jacob.

34 Then Jacob gave Esau some bread and lentil stew. Esau ate the meal, then got up and left. He showed contempt for his rights as the firstborn.

Isaac Deceives Abimelech

26 A severe famine now struck the land, as had happened before in Abraham's time. So Isaac moved to Gerar, where Abimelech, king of the Philistines, lived.

2 The LORD appeared to Isaac and said, "Do not go down to Egypt, but do as I tell you. 3 Live here as a foreigner in this land, and I will be with you and bless you. I hereby confirm that I will give all these lands to you and your descendants,* just as I solemnly promised Abraham, your father. 4 I will cause your descendants to become as numerous as the stars of the sky, and I will give them all these lands. And through your descendants all the nations of the earth will be blessed. 5 I will do this because Abraham listened to me and obeyed all my requirements, commands, decrees, and instructions." 6 So Isaac stayed in Gerar.

7 When the men who lived there asked Isaac about his wife, Rebekah, he said, "She is my sister." He was afraid to say, "She is my wife." He thought, "They will kill me to get her, because she is so beautiful." 8 But some time later, Abimelech, king of the Philistines, looked out his window and saw Isaac caressing Rebekah.

9 Immediately, Abimelech called for Isaac and exclaimed, "She is obviously your wife! Why did you say, 'She is my sister'?"

"Because I was afraid someone would kill me to get her from me," Isaac replied.

10 "How could you do this to us?" Abimelech exclaimed. "One of my people might easily have taken your wife and slept with her, and you would have made us guilty of great sin."

11 Then Abimelech issued a public proclamation: "Anyone who touches this man or his wife will be put to death!"

Conflict over Water Rights

12 When Isaac planted his crops that year, he harvested a hundred times more grain than he planted, for the LORD blessed him. 13 He became a very rich man, and his wealth continued to grow. 14 He acquired so many flocks of sheep and goats, herds of cattle, and servants that the Philistines became jealous of him. 15 So the Philistines filled up all of Isaac's wells with dirt. These were the wells that had been dug by the servants of his father, Abraham.

16 Finally, Abimelech ordered Isaac to leave the country. "Go somewhere else," he said, "for you have become too powerful for us."

17 So Isaac moved away to the Gerar Valley, where he set up their tents and settled down. 18 He reopened the wells his father had dug, which the Philistines had filled in after Abraham's death. Isaac also restored the names Abraham had given them.

19 Isaac's servants also dug in the Gerar Valley and discovered a well of fresh water. 20 But then the shepherds from Gerar came and claimed the spring. "This is our water," they said, and they argued over it with Isaac's herdsmen. So Isaac named the well

25:18 The meaning of the Hebrew is uncertain. **25:25** *Esau* sounds like a Hebrew term that means "hair." **25:26** *Jacob* sounds like the Hebrew words for "heel" and "deceiver." **26:3** Hebrew *seed;* also in 26:4, 24.

Esek (which means "argument"). [21]Isaac's men then dug another well, but again there was a dispute over it. So Isaac named it Sitnah (which means "hostility"). [22]Abandoning that one, Isaac moved on and dug another well. This time there was no dispute over it, so Isaac named the place Rehoboth (which means "open space"), for he said, "At last the LORD has created enough space for us to prosper in this land."

[23]From there Isaac moved to Beersheba, [24]where the LORD appeared to him on the night of his arrival. "I am the God of your father, Abraham," he said. "Do not be afraid, for I am with you and will bless you. I will multiply your descendants, and they will become a great nation. I will do this because of my promise to Abraham, my servant." [25]Then Isaac built an altar there and worshiped the LORD. He set up his camp at that place, and his servants dug another well.

Isaac's Covenant with Abimelech

[26]One day King Abimelech came from Gerar with his adviser, Ahuzzath, and also Phicol, his army commander. [27]"Why have you come here?" Isaac asked. "You obviously hate me, since you kicked me off your land."

[28]They replied, "We can plainly see that the LORD is with you. So we want to enter into a sworn treaty with you. Let's make a covenant. [29]Swear that you will not harm us, just as we have never troubled you. We have always treated you well, and we sent you away from us in peace. And now look how the LORD has blessed you!"

[30]So Isaac prepared a covenant feast to celebrate the treaty, and they ate and drank together. [31]Early the next morning, they each took a solemn oath not to interfere with each other. Then Isaac sent them home again, and they left him in peace.

[32]That very day Isaac's servants came and told him about a new well they had dug. "We've found water!" they exclaimed. [33]So Isaac named the well Shibah (which means "oath"). And to this day the town that grew up there is called Beersheba (which means "well of the oath").

[34]At the age of forty, Esau married two Hittite wives: Judith, the daughter of Beeri, and Basemath, the daughter of Elon. [35]But Esau's wives made life miserable for Isaac and Rebekah.

Jacob Steals Esau's Blessing

27 One day when Isaac was old and turning blind, he called for Esau, his older son, and said, "My son."

"Yes, Father?" Esau replied.

[2]"I am an old man now," Isaac said, "and I don't know when I may die. [3]Take your bow and a quiver full of arrows, and go out into the open country to hunt some wild game for me. [4]Prepare my favorite dish, and bring it here for me to eat. Then I will pronounce the blessing that belongs to you, my firstborn son, before I die."

[5]But Rebekah overheard what Isaac had said to his son Esau. So when Esau left to hunt for the wild game, [6]she said to her son Jacob, "Listen. I overheard your father say to Esau, [7]'Bring me some wild game and prepare me a delicious meal. Then I will bless you in the LORD's presence before I die.' [8]Now, my son, listen to me. Do exactly as I tell you. [9]Go out to the flocks, and bring me two fine young goats. I'll use them to prepare your father's favorite dish. [10]Then take the food to your father so he can eat it and bless you before he dies."

[11]"But look," Jacob replied to Rebekah, "my brother, Esau, is a hairy man, and my skin is smooth. [12]What if my father touches me? He'll see that I'm trying to trick him, and then he'll curse me instead of blessing me."

[13]But his mother replied, "Then let the curse fall on me, my son! Just do what I tell you. Go out and get the goats for me!"

[14]So Jacob went out and got the young goats for his mother. Rebekah took them and prepared a delicious meal, just the way Isaac liked it. [15]Then she took Esau's favorite clothes, which were there in the house, and gave them to her younger son, Jacob. [16]She covered his arms and the smooth part of his neck with the skin of the young goats. [17]Then she gave Jacob the delicious meal, including freshly baked bread.

[18]So Jacob took the food to his father. "My father?" he said.

"Yes, my son," Isaac answered. "Who are you—Esau or Jacob?"

[19]Jacob replied, "It's Esau, your firstborn son. I've done as you told me. Here is the wild game. Now sit up and eat it so you can give me your blessing."

[20]Isaac asked, "How did you find it so quickly, my son?"

"The LORD your God put it in my path!"
Jacob replied.
21 Then Isaac said to Jacob, "Come closer
so I can touch you and make sure that you
really are Esau." 22 So Jacob went closer to his
father, and Isaac touched him. "The voice is
Jacob's, but the hands are Esau's," Isaac said.
23 But he did not recognize Jacob, because
Jacob's hands felt hairy just like Esau's. So
Isaac prepared to bless Jacob. 24 "But are you
really my son Esau?" he asked.

"Yes, I am," Jacob replied.

25 Then Isaac said, "Now, my son, bring
me the wild game. Let me eat it, and then
I will give you my blessing." So Jacob took
the food to his father, and Isaac ate it. He
also drank the wine that Jacob served him.
26 Then Isaac said to Jacob, "Please come a
little closer and kiss me, my son."

27 So Jacob went over and kissed him. And
when Isaac caught the smell of his clothes,
he was finally convinced, and he blessed
his son. He said, "Ah! The smell of my son
is like the smell of the outdoors, which the
LORD has blessed!

28 "From the dew of heaven
and the richness of the earth,
may God always give you abundant
harvests of grain
and bountiful new wine.
29 May many nations become your servants,
and may they bow down to you.
May you be the master over your
brothers,
and may your mother's sons bow
down to you.
All who curse you will be cursed,
and all who bless you will be
blessed."

30 As soon as Isaac had finished blessing
Jacob, and almost before Jacob had left his
father, Esau returned from his hunt. 31 Esau
prepared a delicious meal and brought it to
his father. Then he said, "Sit up, my father,
and eat my wild game so you can give me
your blessing."

32 But Isaac asked him, "Who are you?"

Esau replied, "It's your son, your first-born son, Esau."

33 Isaac began to tremble uncontrollably
and said, "Then who just served me wild
game? I have already eaten it, and I blessed
him just before you came. And yes, that
blessing must stand!"

34 When Esau heard his father's words, he
let out a loud and bitter cry. "Oh my father,
what about me? Bless me, too!" he begged.

35 But Isaac said, "Your brother was here,
and he tricked me. He has taken away your
blessing."

36 Esau exclaimed, "No wonder his name
is Jacob, for now he has cheated me twice.*

27:36 *Jacob* sounds like the Hebrew words for "heel" and "deceiver."

Cheating

The story in Genesis 27 looks, at first sight, as though God approves of cheating. After all, Jacob tricked his father to obtain the family inheritance, but God still accepted him and reaffirmed to him the promises he had made to Abraham (28:10-22). Does God approve of deception and cheating? Does he ignore it if it serves his purpose? The unfolding story shows that the clear answer is no, for Jacob's trickery caught up with him. Having cheated others, he too was cheated. His uncle Laban tricked him into marrying Leah before Rachel (29:14-30) and tried to trick him out of his growing flocks (30:25-36). He had to learn that you reap what you sow (see Galatians 6:7). Ultimately Jacob changed, but only after powerfully encountering God (32:22-32).

This story highlights the importance of reading the Bible's stories both in context (since what seems like a blessing here is seen not to be so later) and in the light of Scripture's teaching elsewhere. In fact, the Bible consistently forbids stealing and cheating (e.g., Exodus 20:15; Deuteronomy 25:13-16; 1 Corinthians 6:7-8; 1 Thessalonians 4:6).

▶ *See also **Honesty**, page 707.*

First he took my rights as the firstborn, and
now he has stolen my blessing. Oh, haven't
you saved even one blessing for me?"
37 Isaac said to Esau, "I have made Jacob
your master and have declared that all his
brothers will be his servants. I have guaranteed him an abundance of grain and wine—
what is left for me to give you, my son?"
38 Esau pleaded, "But do you have only
one blessing? Oh my father, bless me, too!"
Then Esau broke down and wept.
39 Finally, his father, Isaac, said to him,

"You will live away from the richness of
the earth,
and away from the dew of the heaven
above.
40 You will live by your sword,
and you will serve your brother.
But when you decide to break free,
you will shake his yoke from your
neck."

Jacob Flees to Paddan-Aram

41 From that time on, Esau hated Jacob
because their father had given Jacob the
blessing. And Esau began to scheme: "I will
soon be mourning my father's death. Then
I will kill my brother, Jacob."
42 But Rebekah heard about Esau's plans.
So she sent for Jacob and told him, "Listen,
Esau is consoling himself by plotting to kill
you. 43 So listen carefully, my son. Get ready
and flee to my brother, Laban, in Haran.
44 Stay there with him until your brother
cools off. 45 When he calms down and forgets
what you have done to him, I will send for
you to come back. Why should I lose both of
you in one day?"
46 Then Rebekah said to Isaac, "I'm sick
and tired of these local Hittite women!
I would rather die than see Jacob marry one
of them."

28 So Isaac called for Jacob, blessed
him, and said, "You must not marry
any of these Canaanite women. 2 Instead,
go at once to Paddan-aram, to the house of
your grandfather Bethuel, and marry one
of your uncle Laban's daughters. 3 May God
Almighty* bless you and give you many children. And may your descendants multiply
and become many nations! 4 May God pass
on to you and your descendants* the blessings he promised to Abraham. May you own
this land where you are now living as a foreigner, for God gave this land to Abraham."
5 So Isaac sent Jacob away, and he went to
Paddan-aram to stay with his uncle Laban,
his mother's brother, the son of Bethuel the
Aramean.
6 Esau knew that his father, Isaac, had
blessed Jacob and sent him to Paddan-aram
to find a wife, and that he had warned Jacob,
"You must not marry a Canaanite woman."
7 He also knew that Jacob had obeyed his
parents and gone to Paddan-aram. 8 It was
now very clear to Esau that his father did
not like the local Canaanite women. 9 So
Esau visited his uncle Ishmael's family
and married one of Ishmael's daughters,
in addition to the wives he already had. His
new wife's name was Mahalath. She was
the sister of Nebaioth and the daughter of
Ishmael, Abraham's son.

Jacob's Dream at Bethel

10 Meanwhile, Jacob left Beersheba and traveled toward Haran. 11 At sundown he arrived
at a good place to set up camp and stopped
there for the night. Jacob found a stone to
rest his head against and lay down to sleep.
12 As he slept, he dreamed of a stairway that
reached from the earth up to heaven. And
he saw the angels of God going up and
down the stairway.
13 At the top of the stairway stood the
LORD, and he said, "I am the LORD, the God
of your grandfather Abraham, and the God
of your father, Isaac. The ground you are
lying on belongs to you. I am giving it to
you and your descendants. 14 Your descendants will be as numerous as the dust of
the earth! They will spread out in all directions—to the west and the east, to the north
and the south. And all the families of the
earth will be blessed through you and your
descendants. 15 What's more, I am with you,
and I will protect you wherever you go. One
day I will bring you back to this land. I will
not leave you until I have finished giving
you everything I have promised you."
16 Then Jacob awoke from his sleep and
said, "Surely the LORD is in this place, and
I wasn't even aware of it!" 17 But he was also
afraid and said, "What an awesome place
this is! It is none other than the house of
God, the very gateway to heaven!"
18 The next morning Jacob got up very
early. He took the stone he had rested his

head against, and he set it upright as a memorial pillar. Then he poured olive oil over
it. 19He named that place Bethel (which
means "house of God"), although it was
previously called Luz.
20Then Jacob made this vow: "If God will
indeed be with me and protect me on this
journey, and if he will provide me with food
and clothing, 21and if I return safely to my
father's home, then the LORD will certainly
be my God. 22And this memorial pillar I have
set up will become a place for worshiping
God, and I will present to God a tenth of
everything he gives me."

Jacob Arrives at Paddan-Aram

29 Then Jacob hurried on, finally arriving in the land of the east. 2He
saw a well in the distance. Three flocks of
sheep and goats lay in an open field beside
it, waiting to be watered. But a heavy stone
covered the mouth of the well.
3It was the custom there to wait for all the
flocks to arrive before removing the stone
and watering the animals. Afterward the
stone would be placed back over the mouth
of the well. 4Jacob went over to the shepherds and asked, "Where are you from, my
friends?"
"We are from Haran," they answered.
5"Do you know a man there named
Laban, the grandson of Nahor?" he asked.
"Yes, we do," they replied.
6"Is he doing well?" Jacob asked.
"Yes, he's well," they answered. "Look,
here comes his daughter Rachel with the
flock now."
7Jacob said, "Look, it's still broad daylight—too early to round up the animals.
Why don't you water the sheep and goats
so they can get back out to pasture?"
8"We can't water the animals until all the
flocks have arrived," they replied. "Then the
shepherds move the stone from the mouth
of the well, and we water all the sheep and
goats."
9Jacob was still talking with them when
Rachel arrived with her father's flock, for
she was a shepherd. 10And because Rachel
was his cousin—the daughter of Laban, his
mother's brother—and because the sheep
and goats belonged to his uncle Laban,
Jacob went over to the well and moved
the stone from its mouth and watered his
uncle's flock. 11Then Jacob kissed Rachel,
and he wept aloud. 12He explained to
Rachel that he was her cousin on her
father's side—the son of her aunt Rebekah.
So Rachel quickly ran and told her father,
Laban.
13As soon as Laban heard that his nephew
Jacob had arrived, he ran out to meet him.
He embraced and kissed him and brought
him home. When Jacob had told him his
story, 14Laban exclaimed, "You really are
my own flesh and blood!"

28:3 Hebrew *El-Shaddai.* **28:4** Hebrew *seed;* also in 28:13, 14.

Jacob's family tree, showing the tribes of Israel

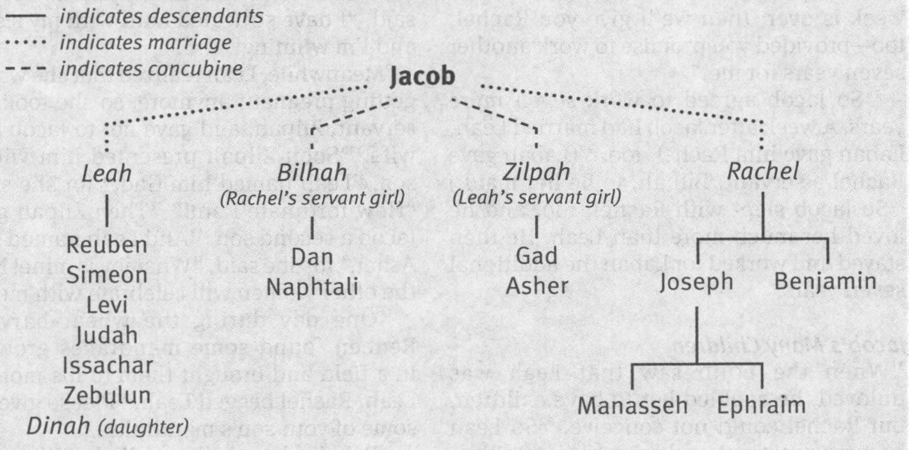

Jacob Marries Leah and Rachel

After Jacob had stayed with Laban for about a month, [15]Laban said to him, "You shouldn't work for me without pay just because we are relatives. Tell me how much your wages should be."

[16]Now Laban had two daughters. The older daughter was named Leah, and the younger one was Rachel. [17]There was no sparkle in Leah's eyes,* but Rachel had a beautiful figure and a lovely face. [18]Since Jacob was in love with Rachel, he told her father, "I'll work for you for seven years if you'll give me Rachel, your younger daughter, as my wife."

[19]"Agreed!" Laban replied. "I'd rather give her to you than to anyone else. Stay and work with me." [20]So Jacob worked seven years to pay for Rachel. But his love for her was so strong that it seemed to him but a few days.

[21]Finally, the time came for him to marry her. "I have fulfilled my agreement," Jacob said to Laban. "Now give me my wife so I can sleep with her."

[22]So Laban invited everyone in the neighborhood and prepared a wedding feast. [23]But that night, when it was dark, Laban took Leah to Jacob, and he slept with her. [24](Laban had given Leah a servant, Zilpah, to be her maid.)

[25]But when Jacob woke up in the morning—it was Leah! "What have you done to me?" Jacob raged at Laban. "I worked seven years for Rachel! Why have you tricked me?"

[26]"It's not our custom here to marry off a younger daughter ahead of the firstborn," Laban replied. [27]"But wait until the bridal week is over; then we'll give you Rachel, too—provided you promise to work another seven years for me."

[28]So Jacob agreed to work seven more years. A week after Jacob had married Leah, Laban gave him Rachel, too. [29](Laban gave Rachel a servant, Bilhah, to be her maid.) [30]So Jacob slept with Rachel, too, and he loved her much more than Leah. He then stayed and worked for Laban the additional seven years.

Jacob's Many Children

[31]When the LORD saw that Leah was unloved, he enabled her to have children, but Rachel could not conceive. [32]So Leah became pregnant and gave birth to a son. She named him Reuben,* for she said, "The LORD has noticed my misery, and now my husband will love me."

[33]She soon became pregnant again and gave birth to another son. She named him Simeon,* for she said, "The LORD heard that I was unloved and has given me another son."

[34]Then she became pregnant a third time and gave birth to another son. He was named Levi,* for she said, "Surely this time my husband will feel affection for me, since I have given him three sons!"

[35]Once again Leah became pregnant and gave birth to another son. She named him Judah,* for she said, "Now I will praise the LORD!" And then she stopped having children.

30 When Rachel saw that she wasn't having any children for Jacob, she became jealous of her sister. She pleaded with Jacob, "Give me children, or I'll die!"

[2]Then Jacob became furious with Rachel. "Am I God?" he asked. "He's the one who has kept you from having children!"

[3]Then Rachel told him, "Take my maid, Bilhah, and sleep with her. She will bear children for me,* and through her I can have a family, too." [4]So Rachel gave her servant, Bilhah, to Jacob as a wife, and he slept with her. [5]Bilhah became pregnant and presented him with a son. [6]Rachel named him Dan,* for she said, "God has vindicated me! He has heard my request and given me a son." [7]Then Bilhah became pregnant again and gave Jacob a second son. [8]Rachel named him Naphtali,* for she said, "I have struggled hard with my sister, and I'm winning!"

[9]Meanwhile, Leah realized that she wasn't getting pregnant anymore, so she took her servant, Zilpah, and gave her to Jacob as a wife. [10]Soon Zilpah presented him with a son. [11]Leah named him Gad,* for she said, "How fortunate I am!" [12]Then Zilpah gave Jacob a second son. [13]And Leah named him Asher,* for she said, "What joy is mine! Now the other women will celebrate with me."

[14]One day during the wheat harvest, Reuben found some mandrakes growing in a field and brought them to his mother, Leah. Rachel begged Leah, "Please give me some of your son's mandrakes."

[15]But Leah angrily replied, "Wasn't it

enough that you stole my husband? Now will you steal my son's mandrakes, too?"

Rachel answered, "I will let Jacob sleep with you tonight if you give me some of the mandrakes."

16So that evening, as Jacob was coming home from the fields, Leah went out to meet him. "You must come and sleep with me tonight!" she said. "I have paid for you with some mandrakes that my son found." So that night he slept with Leah. 17And God answered Leah's prayers. She became pregnant again and gave birth to a fifth son for Jacob. 18She named him Issachar,* for she said, "God has rewarded me for giving my servant to my husband as a wife." 19Then Leah became pregnant again and gave birth to a sixth son for Jacob. 20She named him Zebulun,* for she said, "God has given me a good reward. Now my husband will treat me with respect, for I have given him six sons." 21Later she gave birth to a daughter and named her Dinah.

22Then God remembered Rachel's plight and answered her prayers by enabling her to have children. 23She became pregnant and gave birth to a son. "God has removed my disgrace," she said. 24And she named him Joseph,* for she said, "May the LORD add yet another son to my family."

Jacob's Wealth Increases

25Soon after Rachel had given birth to Joseph, Jacob said to Laban, "Please release me so I can go home to my own country. 26Let me take my wives and children, for I have earned them by serving you, and let me be on my way. You certainly know how hard I have worked for you."

27"Please listen to me," Laban replied. "I have become wealthy, for* the LORD has blessed me because of you. 28Tell me how much I owe you. Whatever it is, I'll pay it."

29Jacob replied, "You know how hard I've worked for you, and how your flocks and herds have grown under my care. 30You had little indeed before I came, but your wealth has increased enormously. The LORD has blessed you through everything I've done. But now, what about me? When can I start providing for my own family?"

31"What wages do you want?" Laban asked again.

Jacob replied, "Don't give me anything. Just do this one thing, and I'll continue to tend and watch over your flocks. 32Let me inspect your flocks today and remove all the sheep and goats that are speckled or spotted, along with all the black sheep. Give these to me as my wages. 33In the future, when you check on the animals you have given me as my wages, you'll see that I have been honest. If you find in my flock any goats without speckles or spots, or any sheep that are not black, you will know that I have stolen them from you."

34"All right," Laban replied. "It will be as you say." 35But that very day Laban went out and removed the male goats that were

29:17 Or *Leah had dull eyes*, or *Leah had soft eyes*. The meaning of the Hebrew is uncertain. **29:32** *Reuben* means "Look, a son!" It also sounds like the Hebrew for "He has seen my misery." **29:33** *Simeon* probably means "one who hears." **29:34** *Levi* sounds like a Hebrew term that means "being attached" or "feeling affection for." **29:35** *Judah* is related to the Hebrew term for "praise." **30:3** Hebrew *bear children on my knees*. **30:6** *Dan* means "he judged" or "he vindicated." **30:8** *Naphtali* means "my struggle." **30:11** *Gad* means "good fortune." **30:13** *Asher* means "happy." **30:18** *Issachar* sounds like a Hebrew term that means "reward." **30:20** *Zebulun* probably means "honor." **30:24** *Joseph* means "may he add." **30:27** Or *I have learned by divination that.*

Rachel

Rachel was Jacob's beautiful cousin, the younger daughter of Laban, who lived in Haran. As soon as Jacob met her, he fell in love and asked to marry her, offering to work for Laban for seven years as the bride price. But Laban tricked Jacob and got fourteen years of service from him instead of seven, and Jacob got two wives, not one—Leah, Rachel's sister, before Rachel herself (Genesis 29:14-30). Rachel was strong-willed and came into conflict with Leah when the latter bore Jacob four sons while she herself remained unable to have children. Six more sons would follow to Leah and two servants before Rachel finally bore Joseph (30:22-24), then Benjamin (35:16-18), during whose delivery she died.

▶ *See also **Jacob's family tree, showing the tribes of Israel**, page 35; **Jacob and Esau**, page 40.*

streaked and spotted, all the female goats that were speckled and spotted or had white patches, and all the black sheep. He placed them in the care of his own sons, 36who took them a three-days' journey from where Jacob was. Meanwhile, Jacob stayed and cared for the rest of Laban's flock.

37Then Jacob took some fresh branches from poplar, almond, and plane trees and peeled off strips of bark, making white streaks on them. 38Then he placed these peeled branches in the watering troughs where the flocks came to drink, for that was where they mated. 39And when they mated in front of the white-streaked branches, they gave birth to young that were streaked, speckled, and spotted. 40Jacob separated those lambs from Laban's flock. And at mating time he turned the flock to face Laban's animals that were streaked or black. This is how he built his own flock instead of increasing Laban's.

41Whenever the stronger females were ready to mate, Jacob would place the peeled branches in the watering troughs in front of them. Then they would mate in front of the branches. 42But he didn't do this with the weaker ones, so the weaker lambs belonged to Laban, and the stronger ones were Jacob's. 43As a result, Jacob became very wealthy, with large flocks of sheep and goats, female and male servants, and many camels and donkeys.

Jacob Flees from Laban

31 But Jacob soon learned that Laban's sons were grumbling about him. "Jacob has robbed our father of everything!" they said. "He has gained all his wealth at our father's expense." 2And Jacob began to notice a change in Laban's attitude toward him.

3Then the LORD said to Jacob, "Return to the land of your father and grandfather and to your relatives there, and I will be with you."

4So Jacob called Rachel and Leah out to the field where he was watching his flock. 5He said to them, "I have noticed that your father's attitude toward me has changed. But the God of my father has been with me. 6You know how hard I have worked for your father, 7but he has cheated me, changing my wages ten times. But God has not allowed him to do me any harm. 8For if he said, 'The speckled animals will be your wages,' the whole flock began to produce speckled young. And when he changed his mind and said, 'The striped animals will be your wages,' then the whole flock produced striped young. 9In this way, God has taken your father's animals and given them to me.

10"One time during the mating season, I had a dream and saw that the male goats mating with the females were streaked, speckled, and spotted. 11Then in my dream, the angel of God said to me, 'Jacob!' And I replied, 'Yes, here I am.'

12"The angel said, 'Look up, and you will see that only the streaked, speckled, and spotted males are mating with the females of your flock. For I have seen how Laban has treated you. 13I am the God who appeared to you at Bethel,* the place where you anointed the pillar of stone and made your vow to me. Now get ready and leave this country and return to the land of your birth.'"

14Rachel and Leah responded, "That's fine with us! We won't inherit any of our father's wealth anyway. 15He has reduced our rights to those of foreign women. And after he sold us, he wasted the money you paid him for us. 16All the wealth God has given you from our father legally belongs to us and our children. So go ahead and do whatever God has told you."

17So Jacob put his wives and children on camels, 18and he drove all his livestock in front of him. He packed all the belongings he had acquired in Paddan-aram and set out for the land of Canaan, where his father, Isaac, lived. 19At the time they left, Laban was some distance away, shearing his sheep. Rachel stole her father's household idols and took them with her. 20Jacob outwitted Laban the Aramean, for they set out secretly and never told Laban they were leaving. 21So Jacob took all his possessions with him and crossed the Euphrates River,* heading for the hill country of Gilead.

Laban Pursues Jacob

22Three days later, Laban was told that Jacob had fled. 23So he gathered a group of his relatives and set out in hot pursuit. He caught up with Jacob seven days later in the hill country of Gilead. 24But the previous night God had appeared to Laban the Aramean in a dream and told him, "I'm warning you—leave Jacob alone!"

[25]Laban caught up with Jacob as he was
camped in the hill country of Gilead, and
he set up his camp not far from Jacob's.
[26]"What do you mean by deceiving me like
this?" Laban demanded. "How dare you
drag my daughters away like prisoners
of war? [27]Why did you slip away secretly?
Why did you deceive me? And why didn't
you say you wanted to leave? I would have
given you a farewell feast, with singing
and music, accompanied by tambourines
and harps. [28]Why didn't you let me kiss
my daughters and grandchildren and tell
them good-bye? You have acted very foolishly! [29]I could destroy you, but the God of
your father appeared to me last night and
warned me, 'Leave Jacob alone!' [30]I can
understand your feeling that you must go,
and your intense longing for your father's
home. But why have you stolen my gods?"

[31]"I rushed away because I was afraid,"
Jacob answered. "I thought you would take
your daughters from me by force. [32]But as
for your gods, see if you can find them, and
let the person who has taken them die! And
if you find anything else that belongs to
you, identify it before all these relatives of
ours, and I will give it back!" But Jacob did
not know that Rachel had stolen the household idols.

[33]Laban went first into Jacob's tent to
search there, then into Leah's, and then the
tents of the two servant wives—but he found
nothing. Finally, he went into Rachel's tent.
[34]But Rachel had taken the household idols
and hidden them in her camel saddle, and
now she was sitting on them. When Laban
had thoroughly searched her tent without
finding them, [35]she said to her father,
"Please, sir, forgive me if I don't get up for
you. I'm having my monthly period." So
Laban continued his search, but he could
not find the household idols.

[36]Then Jacob became very angry, and he
challenged Laban. "What's my crime?" he
demanded. "What have I done wrong to
make you chase after me as though I were
a criminal? [37]You have rummaged through
everything I own. Now show me what you
found that belongs to you! Set it out here
in front of us, before our relatives, for all to
see. Let them judge between us!

[38]"For twenty years I have been with
you, caring for your flocks. In all that time
your sheep and goats never miscarried. In
all those years I never used a single ram of
yours for food. [39]If any were attacked and
killed by wild animals, I never showed
you the carcass and asked you to reduce
the count of your flock. No, I took the loss
myself! You made me pay for every stolen
animal, whether it was taken in broad daylight or in the dark of night.

[40]"I worked for you through the scorching heat of the day and through cold and
sleepless nights. [41]Yes, for twenty years
I slaved in your house! I worked for fourteen years earning your two daughters, and
then six more years for your flock. And you
changed my wages ten times! [42]In fact, if
the God of my father had not been on my
side—the God of Abraham and the fearsome God of Isaac*—you would have sent
me away empty-handed. But God has seen
your abuse and my hard work. That is why
he appeared to you last night and rebuked
you!"

Jacob's Treaty with Laban

[43]Then Laban replied to Jacob, "These
women are my daughters, these children
are my grandchildren, and these flocks
are my flocks—in fact, everything you see
is mine. But what can I do now about my
daughters and their children? [44]So come,
let's make a covenant, you and I, and it will
be a witness to our commitment."

[45]So Jacob took a stone and set it up as
a monument. [46]Then he told his family
members, "Gather some stones." So they
gathered stones and piled them in a heap.
Then Jacob and Laban sat down beside
the pile of stones to eat a covenant meal.
[47]To commemorate the event, Laban called
the place Jegar-sahadutha (which means
"witness pile" in Aramaic), and Jacob
called it Galeed (which means "witness
pile" in Hebrew).

[48]Then Laban declared, "This pile
of stones will stand as a witness to
remind us of the covenant we have made
today." This explains why it was called
Galeed—"Witness Pile." [49]But it was also
called Mizpah (which means "watchtower"), for Laban said, "May the LORD
keep watch between us to make sure that
we keep this covenant when we are out

31:13 As in Greek version and an Aramaic Targum; Hebrew reads *the God of Bethel.* **31:21** Hebrew *the river.* **31:42** Or *and the Fear of Isaac.*

of each other's sight. 50 If you mistreat my daughters or if you marry other wives, God will see it even if no one else does. He is a witness to this covenant between us.

51 "See this pile of stones," Laban continued, "and see this monument I have set between us. 52 They stand between us as witnesses of our vows. I will never pass this pile of stones to harm you, and you must never pass these stones or this monument to harm me. 53 I call on the God of our ancestors—the God of your grandfather Abraham and the God of my grandfather Nahor—to serve as a judge between us."

So Jacob took an oath before the fearsome God of his father, Isaac,* to respect the boundary line. 54 Then Jacob offered a sacrifice to God there on the mountain and invited everyone to a covenant feast. After they had eaten, they spent the night on the mountain.

55 *Laban got up early the next morning, and he kissed his grandchildren and his daughters and blessed them. Then he left and returned home.

32 1 *As Jacob started on his way again, angels of God came to meet him. 2 When Jacob saw them, he exclaimed, "This is God's camp!" So he named the place Mahanaim.*

Jacob Sends Gifts to Esau

3 Then Jacob sent messengers ahead to his brother, Esau, who was living in the region of Seir in the land of Edom. 4 He told them, "Give this message to my master Esau: 'Humble greetings from your servant Jacob. Until now I have been living with Uncle Laban, 5 and now I own cattle, donkeys, flocks of sheep and goats, and many servants, both men and women. I have sent these messengers to inform my lord of my coming, hoping that you will be friendly to me.'"

6 After delivering the message, the messengers returned to Jacob and reported, "We met your brother, Esau, and he is already on his way to meet you—with an army of 400 men!" 7 Jacob was terrified at the news. He divided his household, along with the flocks and herds and camels, into two groups. 8 He thought, "If Esau meets one group and attacks it, perhaps the other group can escape."

9 Then Jacob prayed, "O God of my grandfather Abraham, and God of my father, Isaac—O LORD, you told me, 'Return to your own land and to your relatives.' And you promised me, 'I will treat you kindly.' 10 I am not worthy of all the unfailing love and faithfulness you have shown to me, your servant. When I left home and crossed the Jordan River, I owned nothing except a walking stick. Now my household fills two large camps! 11 O LORD, please rescue me from the hand of my brother, Esau. I am afraid that he is coming to attack me, along with my wives and children. 12 But you promised me, 'I will surely treat you kindly, and I will multiply your descendants until they become as numerous as the sands along the seashore—too many to count.'"

13 Jacob stayed where he was for the night. Then he selected these gifts from his possessions to present to his brother, Esau: 14 200 female goats, 20 male goats, 200 ewes, 20 rams, 15 30 female camels with their young, 40 cows, 10 bulls, 20 female

Jacob and Esau

Although they were twins, Esau was born before Jacob (Genesis 25:24-26). But not only did Jacob manipulate him into selling his firstborn birthright to him (25:27-34), he also tricked his father Isaac into giving him the blessing that would ensure he headed up the family after Isaac's death (27:1-40). This led to much resentment and bitterness, and to Jacob fleeing to Haran. He eventually fathered twelve sons—the founders of the twelve tribes of "Israel," the new name Jacob was given after a divine wrestling match (32:22-32; 35:10). The brothers were eventually reconciled (chapter 33), and Esau (also called Edom) moved to Seir, south of the Dead Sea, where he became the ancestor of the Edomites (36:6-43).

▶ *See also **Rachel**, page 37; **Edomites**, page 45; **World of the Patriarchs** map, Visual Overview Z2.*

donkeys, and 10 male donkeys. [16]He divided
these animals into herds and assigned each
to different servants. Then he told his servants, "Go ahead of me with the animals,
but keep some distance between the herds."
[17]He gave these instructions to the men
leading the first group: "When my brother,
Esau, meets you, he will ask, 'Whose servants are you? Where are you going? Who
owns these animals?' [18]You must reply,
'They belong to your servant Jacob, but they
are a gift for his master Esau. Look, he is
coming right behind us.'"
[19]Jacob gave the same instructions to the
second and third herdsmen and to all who
followed behind the herds: "You must say
the same thing to Esau when you meet him.
[20]And be sure to say, 'Look, your servant
Jacob is right behind us.'"
Jacob thought, "I will try to appease him
by sending gifts ahead of me. When I see
him in person, perhaps he will be friendly
to me." [21]So the gifts were sent on ahead,
while Jacob himself spent that night in the
camp.

Jacob Wrestles with God

[22]During the night Jacob got up and took his
two wives, his two servant wives, and his
eleven sons and crossed the Jabbok River
with them. [23]After taking them to the other
side, he sent over all his possessions.
[24]This left Jacob all alone in the camp,
and a man came and wrestled with him
until the dawn began to break. [25]When the
man saw that he would not win the match,
he touched Jacob's hip and wrenched it out
of its socket. [26]Then the man said, "Let me
go, for the dawn is breaking!"
But Jacob said, "I will not let you go
unless you bless me."
[27]"What is your name?" the man asked.
He replied, "Jacob."
[28]"Your name will no longer be Jacob,"
the man told him. "From now on you will
be called Israel,* because you have fought
with God and with men and have won."
[29]"Please tell me your name," Jacob said.
"Why do you want to know my name?"
the man replied. Then he blessed Jacob
there.
[30]Jacob named the place Peniel (which
means "face of God"), for he said, "I have
seen God face to face, yet my life has been
spared." [31]The sun was rising as Jacob left
Peniel,* and he was limping because of the
injury to his hip. [32](Even today the people
of Israel don't eat the tendon near the hip
socket because of what happened that
night when the man strained the tendon of
Jacob's hip.)

Jacob and Esau Make Peace

33 Then Jacob looked up and saw Esau
coming with his 400 men. So he
divided the children among Leah, Rachel,
and his two servant wives. [2]He put the
servant wives and their children at the front,
Leah and her children next, and Rachel and
Joseph last. [3]Then Jacob went on ahead. As
he approached his brother, he bowed to the
ground seven times before him. [4]Then Esau
ran to meet him and embraced him, threw
his arms around his neck, and kissed him.
And they both wept.
[5]Then Esau looked at the women and
children and asked, "Who are these people
with you?"
"These are the children God has graciously
given to me, your servant," Jacob replied.
[6]Then the servant wives came forward
with their children and bowed before him.
[7]Next came Leah with her children, and
they bowed before him. Finally, Joseph and
Rachel came forward and bowed before him.
[8]"And what were all the flocks and herds
I met as I came?" Esau asked.
Jacob replied, "They are a gift, my lord, to
ensure your friendship."
[9]"My brother, I have plenty," Esau answered. "Keep what you have for yourself."
[10]But Jacob insisted, "No, if I have found
favor with you, please accept this gift from
me. And what a relief to see your friendly
smile. It is like seeing the face of God!
[11]Please take this gift I have brought you, for
God has been very gracious to me. I have
more than enough." And because Jacob insisted, Esau finally accepted the gift.
[12]"Well," Esau said, "let's be going. I will
lead the way."
[13]But Jacob replied, "You can see, my lord,
that some of the children are very young,
and the flocks and herds have their young,
too. If they are driven too hard, even for

31:53 Or *the Fear of his father, Isaac.* **31:55** Verse 31:55 is numbered 32:1 in Hebrew text. **32:1** Verses 32:1-32 are numbered 32:2-33 in Hebrew text. **32:2** *Mahanaim* means "two camps." **32:28** *Jacob* sounds like the Hebrew words for "heel" and "deceiver." *Israel* means "God fights." **32:31** Hebrew *Penuel,* a variant spelling of Peniel.

one day, all the animals could die. [14]Please, my lord, go ahead of your servant. We will follow slowly, at a pace that is comfortable for the livestock and the children. I will meet you at Seir."

[15]"All right," Esau said, "but at least let me assign some of my men to guide and protect you."

Jacob responded, "That's not necessary. It's enough that you've received me warmly, my lord!"

[16]So Esau turned around and started back to Seir that same day. [17]Jacob, on the other hand, traveled on to Succoth. There he built himself a house and made shelters for his livestock. That is why the place was named Succoth (which means "shelters").

[18]Later, having traveled all the way from Paddan-aram, Jacob arrived safely at the town of Shechem, in the land of Canaan. There he set up camp outside the town. [19]Jacob bought the plot of land where he camped from the family of Hamor, the father of Shechem, for 100 pieces of silver.* [20]And there he built an altar and named it El-Elohe-Israel.*

Revenge against Shechem

34 One day Dinah, the daughter of Jacob and Leah, went to visit some of the young women who lived in the area. [2]But when the local prince, Shechem son of Hamor the Hivite, saw Dinah, he seized her and raped her. [3]But then he fell in love with her, and he tried to win her affection with tender words. [4]He said to his father, Hamor, "Get me this young girl. I want to marry her."

[5]Soon Jacob heard that Shechem had defiled his daughter, Dinah. But since his sons were out in the fields herding his livestock, he said nothing until they returned. [6]Hamor, Shechem's father, came to discuss the matter with Jacob. [7]Meanwhile, Jacob's sons had come in from the field as soon as they heard what had happened. They were shocked and furious that their sister had been raped. Shechem had done a disgraceful thing against Jacob's family,* something that should never be done.

[8]Hamor tried to speak with Jacob and his sons. "My son Shechem is truly in love with your daughter," he said. "Please let him marry her. [9]In fact, let's arrange other marriages, too. You give us your daughters for our sons, and we will give you our daughters for your sons. [10]And you may live among us; the land is open to you! Settle here and trade with us. And feel free to buy property in the area."

[11]Then Shechem himself spoke to Dinah's father and brothers. "Please be kind to me, and let me marry her," he begged. "I will give you whatever you ask. [12]No matter what dowry or gift you demand, I will gladly pay it—just give me the girl as my wife."

[13]But since Shechem had defiled their sister, Dinah, Jacob's sons responded deceitfully to Shechem and his father, Hamor. [14]They said to them, "We couldn't possibly allow this, because you're not circumcised. It would be a disgrace for our sister to marry a man like you! [15]But here is a solution. If every man among you will be circumcised like we are, [16]then we will give you our daughters, and we'll take your daughters for ourselves. We will live among you and become one people. [17]But if you don't agree to be circumcised, we will take her and be on our way."

Shechem

Shechem had been the first place Abraham settled in when he entered Canaan. He had built an altar there in response to God's affirmation of his promise to give Canaan to Abraham and his descendants (Genesis 12:7). Because of this, Shechem became an important religious center in Israel's history. It was here that Jacob built an altar (33:18-20), that Joshua renewed the covenant (Joshua 24:1-28), that Rehoboam, Solomon's son, was crowned, as well as the rebellious Jeroboam, who then made Shechem his capital (1 Kings 12). Shechem declined in importance, though it continued to exist after Israel's brutal conquest by Assyria. It was eventually rebuilt by refugees who fled there after Alexander the Great's conquest of Samaria, and it became the chief city of the Samaritans.

[18]Hamor and his son Shechem agreed to their proposal. [19]Shechem wasted no time in acting on this request, for he wanted Jacob's daughter desperately. Shechem was a highly respected member of his family, [20]and he went with his father, Hamor, to present this proposal to the leaders at the town gate.

[21]"These men are our friends," they said. "Let's invite them to live here among us and trade freely. Look, the land is large enough to hold them. We can take their daughters as wives and let them marry ours. [22]But they will consider staying here and becoming one people with us only if all of our men are circumcised, just as they are. [23]But if we do this, all their livestock and possessions will eventually be ours. Come, let's agree to their terms and let them settle here among us."

[24]So all the men in the town council agreed with Hamor and Shechem, and every male in the town was circumcised. [25]But three days later, when their wounds were still sore, two of Jacob's sons, Simeon and Levi, who were Dinah's full brothers, took their swords and entered the town without opposition. Then they slaughtered every male there, [26]including Hamor and his son Shechem. They killed them with their swords, then took Dinah from Shechem's house and returned to their camp.

[27]Meanwhile, the rest of Jacob's sons arrived. Finding the men slaughtered, they plundered the town because their sister had been defiled there. [28]They seized all the flocks and herds and donkeys—everything they could lay their hands on, both inside the town and outside in the fields. [29]They looted all their wealth and plundered their houses. They also took all their little children and wives and led them away as captives.

[30]Afterward Jacob said to Simeon and Levi, "You have ruined me! You've made me stink among all the people of this land—among all the Canaanites and Perizzites. We are so few that they will join forces and crush us. I will be ruined, and my entire household will be wiped out!"

[31]"But why should we let him treat our sister like a prostitute?" they retorted angrily.

Jacob's Return to Bethel

35 Then God said to Jacob, "Get ready and move to Bethel and settle there. Build an altar there to the God who appeared to you when you fled from your brother, Esau."

[2]So Jacob told everyone in his household, "Get rid of all your pagan idols, purify yourselves, and put on clean clothing. [3]We are now going to Bethel, where I will build an altar to the God who answered my prayers when I was in distress. He has been with me wherever I have gone."

33:19 Hebrew *100 kesitahs;* the value or weight of the kesitah is no longer known. **33:20** *El-Elohe-Israel* means "God, the God of Israel." **34:7** Hebrew *a disgraceful thing in Israel.*

Rape

It is a sad fact of sinful human history that some men have always seen it as their right to be able to rape women, particularly those who are vulnerable (whether through war, poverty, or other circumstances). But the Bible forbids rape and consistently condemns its perpetrators. It was forbidden in the Jewish Law and was seen as so serious as to be punishable by death in certain circumstances (Deuteronomy 22:25-27).

Rape—the enforcing of a sexual act on an unwilling partner—not only causes physical harm (e.g., Judges 19:25-28) but also leads to deep psychological damage (e.g., 2 Samuel 13:14-20). Stories of rape and other sexual violence in the Bible always show how it has devastating outcomes (e.g., Judges 19:1-20:48; 2 Samuel 13:1-39).

Rather than seeing other people—whether male or female—as mere objects of sexual attraction, we are to honor and protect them, recognizing that they too are made in the image of God. To abuse another person sexually not only violates the person against whom the act is committed but also defiles the one who commits it (see Matthew 15:16-20).

4So they gave Jacob all their pagan idols
and earrings, and he buried them under the
great tree near Shechem. 5As they set out, a
terror from God spread over the people in all
the towns of that area, so no one attacked
Jacob's family.
6Eventually, Jacob and his household
arrived at Luz (also called Bethel) in
Canaan. 7Jacob built an altar there and
named the place El-bethel (which means
"God of Bethel"), because God had appeared to him there when he was fleeing
from his brother, Esau.
8Soon after this, Rebekah's old nurse,
Deborah, died. She was buried beneath the
oak tree in the valley below Bethel. Ever
since, the tree has been called Allon-bacuth
(which means "oak of weeping").
9Now that Jacob had returned from
Paddan-aram, God appeared to him again
at Bethel. God blessed him, 10saying, "Your
name is Jacob, but you will not be called
Jacob any longer. From now on your name
will be Israel."* So God renamed him Israel.
11Then God said, "I am El-Shaddai—'God
Almighty.' Be fruitful and multiply. You will
become a great nation, even many nations.
Kings will be among your descendants!
12And I will give you the land I once gave to
Abraham and Isaac. Yes, I will give it to you
and your descendants after you." 13Then
God went up from the place where he had
spoken to Jacob.
14Jacob set up a stone pillar to mark the
place where God had spoken to him. Then
he poured wine over it as an offering to
God and anointed the pillar with olive oil.
15And Jacob named the place Bethel (which
means "house of God"), because God had
spoken to him there.

The Deaths of Rachel and Isaac

16Leaving Bethel, Jacob and his clan moved
on toward Ephrath. But Rachel went into
labor while they were still some distance
away. Her labor pains were intense. 17After
a very hard delivery, the midwife finally exclaimed, "Don't be afraid—you have another
son!" 18Rachel was about to die, but with
her last breath she named the baby Ben-oni
(which means "son of my sorrow"). The
baby's father, however, called him Benjamin
(which means "son of my right hand"). 19So
Rachel died and was buried on the way to
Ephrath (that is, Bethlehem). 20Jacob set up
a stone monument over Rachel's grave, and
it can be seen there to this day.
21Then Jacob* traveled on and camped
beyond Migdal-eder. 22While he was living
there, Reuben had intercourse with Bilhah,
his father's concubine, and Jacob soon
heard about it.

These are the names of the twelve sons
of Jacob:

23The sons of Leah were Reuben (Jacob's
oldest son), Simeon, Levi, Judah,
Issachar, and Zebulun.
24The sons of Rachel were Joseph and
Benjamin.
25The sons of Bilhah, Rachel's servant,
were Dan and Naphtali.
26The sons of Zilpah, Leah's servant, were
Gad and Asher.

These are the names of the sons who were
born to Jacob at Paddan-aram.
27So Jacob returned to his father, Isaac,
in Mamre, which is near Kiriath-arba (now
called Hebron), where Abraham and Isaac
had both lived as foreigners. 28Isaac lived
for 180 years. 29Then he breathed his last
and died at a ripe old age, joining his ancestors in death. And his sons, Esau and Jacob,
buried him.

Descendants of Esau

36 This is the account of the descendants of Esau (also known as
Edom). 2Esau married two young women
from Canaan: Adah, the daughter of Elon
the Hittite; and Oholibamah, the daughter
of Anah and granddaughter of Zibeon the
Hivite. 3He also married his cousin Basemath, who was the daughter of Ishmael and
the sister of Nebaioth. 4Adah gave birth to a
son named Eliphaz for Esau. Basemath gave
birth to a son named Reuel. 5Oholibamah
gave birth to sons named Jeush, Jalam, and
Korah. All these sons were born to Esau in
the land of Canaan.
6Esau took his wives, his children, and
his entire household, along with his livestock and cattle—all the wealth he had acquired in the land of Canaan—and moved
away from his brother, Jacob. 7There was
not enough land to support them both
because of all the livestock and possessions they had acquired. 8So Esau (also
known as Edom) settled in the hill country
of Seir.

9This is the account of Esau's descendants, the Edomites, who lived in the hill country of Seir.

10These are the names of Esau's sons:
Eliphaz, the son of Esau's wife Adah; and Reuel, the son of Esau's wife Basemath.
11The descendants of Eliphaz were Teman, Omar, Zepho, Gatam, and Kenaz.
12Timna, the concubine of Esau's son Eliphaz, gave birth to a son named Amalek. These are the descendants of Esau's wife Adah.
13The descendants of Reuel were Nahath, Zerah, Shammah, and Mizzah. These are the descendants of Esau's wife Basemath.
14Esau also had sons through Oholibamah, the daughter of Anah and granddaughter of Zibeon. Their names were Jeush, Jalam, and Korah.

15These are the descendants of Esau who became the leaders of various clans:

The descendants of Esau's oldest son, Eliphaz, became the leaders of the clans of Teman, Omar, Zepho, Kenaz,
16Korah, Gatam, and Amalek. These are the clan leaders in the land of Edom who descended from Eliphaz. All these were descendants of Esau's wife Adah.
17The descendants of Esau's son Reuel became the leaders of the clans of Nahath, Zerah, Shammah, and Mizzah. These are the clan leaders in the land of Edom who descended from Reuel. All these were descendants of Esau's wife Basemath.
18The descendants of Esau and his wife Oholibamah became the leaders of the clans of Jeush, Jalam, and Korah. These are the clan leaders who descended from Esau's wife Oholibamah, the daughter of Anah.
19These are the clans descended from Esau (also known as Edom), identified by their clan leaders.

Original Peoples of Edom

20These are the names of the tribes that descended from Seir the Horite. They lived in the land of Edom: Lotan, Shobal, Zibeon,
Anah, 21Dishon, Ezer, and Dishan. These were the Horite clan leaders, the descendants of Seir, who lived in the land of Edom.

22The descendants of Lotan were Hori and Hemam. Lotan's sister was named Timna.
23The descendants of Shobal were Alvan, Manahath, Ebal, Shepho, and Onam.
24The descendants of Zibeon were Aiah and Anah. (This is the Anah who discovered the hot springs in the wilderness while he was grazing his father's donkeys.)
25The descendants of Anah were his son, Dishon, and his daughter, Oholibamah.

35:10 *Jacob* sounds like the Hebrew words for "heel" and "deceiver." *Israel* means "God fights." **35:21** Hebrew *Israel;* also in 35:22a. The names "Jacob" and "Israel" are often interchanged throughout the Old Testament, referring sometimes to the individual patriarch and sometimes to the nation.

Edomites

The descendants of Esau, Jacob's brother, were known as Edomites—from Esau's other name, Edom, meaning "red," the name given him after the incident of the red stew (Genesis 25:27-30). They lived in the mountain region south of the Dead Sea through which the important trade route, the King's Highway, passed. Despite their family links with Israel, they refused to let them pass through their territory on their way from Mount Sinai to the Promised Land (Numbers 20:14-21), a cause of tension for years to come. After Babylon's conquest of Jerusalem in 586 BC, many Edomites migrated to southern Judah, and even more followed when Edom was conquered by the Nabateans in the third century BC. This occupied area became known as Idumea, and it was from here that Herod the Great came, which partly explains why his Jewish subjects hated him so much.

▶ *See also **Jacob and Esau**, page 40; **Exodus from Egypt** map, Visual Overview Z3.*

26 The descendants of Dishon* were
Hemdan, Eshban, Ithran, and Keran.
27 The descendants of Ezer were Bilhan,
Zaavan, and Akan.
28 The descendants of Dishan were Uz and
Aran.
29 So these were the leaders of the Horite
clans: Lotan, Shobal, Zibeon, Anah,
30 Dishon, Ezer, and Dishan. The Horite
clans are named after their clan leaders,
who lived in the land of Seir.

Rulers of Edom

31 These are the kings who ruled in the land
of Edom before any king ruled over the
Israelites*:

32 Bela son of Beor, who ruled in Edom
from his city of Dinhabah.
33 When Bela died, Jobab son of Zerah from
Bozrah became king in his place.
34 When Jobab died, Husham from the land
of the Temanites became king in his
place.
35 When Husham died, Hadad son of Bedad
became king in his place and ruled from
the city of Avith. He was the one who
defeated the Midianites in the land of
Moab.
36 When Hadad died, Samlah from the city
of Masrekah became king in his place.
37 When Samlah died, Shaul from the city
of Rehoboth-on-the-River became king
in his place.
38 When Shaul died, Baal-hanan son of
Acbor became king in his place.
39 When Baal-hanan son of Acbor died,
Hadad* became king in his place and
ruled from the city of Pau. His wife was
Mehetabel, the daughter of Matred and
granddaughter of Me-zahab.

40 These are the names of the leaders of
the clans descended from Esau, who lived
in the places named for them: Timna, Alvah,
Jetheth, 41 Oholibamah, Elah, Pinon, 42 Kenaz,
Teman, Mibzar, 43 Magdiel, and Iram. These
are the leaders of the clans of Edom, listed
according to their settlements in the land
they occupied. They all descended from
Esau, the ancestor of the Edomites.

Joseph's Dreams

37 So Jacob settled again in the land of
Canaan, where his father had lived
as a foreigner.

2 This is the account of Jacob and his
family. When Joseph was seventeen years
old, he often tended his father's flocks. He
worked for his half brothers, the sons of
his father's wives Bilhah and Zilpah. But
Joseph reported to his father some of the
bad things his brothers were doing.

3 Jacob* loved Joseph more than any of
his other children because Joseph had been
born to him in his old age. So one day Jacob
had a special gift made for Joseph—a beautiful robe.* 4 But his brothers hated Joseph
because their father loved him more than
the rest of them. They couldn't say a kind
word to him.

5 One night Joseph had a dream, and when
he told his brothers about it, they hated him
more than ever. 6 "Listen to this dream,"
he said. 7 "We were out in the field, tying
up bundles of grain. Suddenly my bundle
stood up, and your bundles all gathered
around and bowed low before mine!"

8 His brothers responded, "So you think
you will be our king, do you? Do you actually think you will reign over us?" And
they hated him all the more because of his
dreams and the way he talked about them.

9 Soon Joseph had another dream, and
again he told his brothers about it. "Listen,
I have had another dream," he said. "The
sun, moon, and eleven stars bowed low
before me!"

10 This time he told the dream to his father
as well as to his brothers, but his father
scolded him. "What kind of dream is that?"
he asked. "Will your mother and I and your
brothers actually come and bow to the
ground before you?" 11 But while his brothers were jealous of Joseph, his father wondered what the dreams meant.

12 Soon after this, Joseph's brothers went
to pasture their father's flocks at Shechem.
13 When they had been gone for some time,
Jacob said to Joseph, "Your brothers are
pasturing the sheep at Shechem. Get ready,
and I will send you to them."

"I'm ready to go," Joseph replied.

14 "Go and see how your brothers and the
flocks are getting along," Jacob said. "Then
come back and bring me a report." So Jacob
sent him on his way, and Joseph traveled to
Shechem from their home in the valley of
Hebron.

15 When he arrived there, a man from the
area noticed him wandering around the

countryside. “What are you looking for?”
he asked.
16“I’m looking for my brothers,” Joseph
replied. “Do you know where they are pasturing their sheep?”
17“Yes,” the man told him. “They have
moved on from here, but I heard them say,
‘Let’s go on to Dothan.’” So Joseph followed
his brothers to Dothan and found them
there.

Joseph Sold into Slavery

18When Joseph’s brothers saw him coming,
they recognized him in the distance. As he
approached, they made plans to kill him.
19“Here comes the dreamer!” they said.
20“Come on, let’s kill him and throw him
into one of these cisterns. We can tell our
father, ‘A wild animal has eaten him.’ Then
we’ll see what becomes of his dreams!”
21But when Reuben heard of their scheme,
he came to Joseph’s rescue. “Let’s not kill
him,” he said. 22“Why should we shed any
blood? Let’s just throw him into this empty
cistern here in the wilderness. Then he’ll die
without our laying a hand on him.” Reuben
was secretly planning to rescue Joseph and
return him to his father.
23So when Joseph arrived, his brothers ripped off the beautiful robe he was
wearing. 24Then they grabbed him and
threw him into the cistern. Now the cistern
was empty; there was no water in it. 25Then,
just as they were sitting down to eat, they
looked up and saw a caravan of camels in
the distance coming toward them. It was a
group of Ishmaelite traders taking a load of
gum, balm, and aromatic resin from Gilead
down to Egypt.
26Judah said to his brothers, “What will
we gain by killing our brother? We’d have
to cover up the crime.* 27Instead of hurting
him, let’s sell him to those Ishmaelite
traders. After all, he is our brother—our own
flesh and blood!” And his brothers agreed.
28So when the Ishmaelites, who were Midianite traders, came by, Joseph’s brothers
pulled him out of the cistern and sold him
to them for twenty pieces* of silver. And the
traders took him to Egypt.
29Some time later, Reuben returned to get
Joseph out of the cistern. When he discovered that Joseph was missing, he tore his
clothes in grief. 30Then he went back to his
brothers and lamented, “The boy is gone!
What will I do now?”
31Then the brothers killed a young goat
and dipped Joseph’s robe in its blood.
32They sent the beautiful robe to their father
with this message: “Look at what we found.
Doesn’t this robe belong to your son?”
33Their father recognized it immediately.
“Yes,” he said, “it is my son’s robe. A wild
animal must have eaten him. Joseph has
clearly been torn to pieces!” 34Then Jacob
tore his clothes and dressed himself in

36:26 Hebrew *Dishan,* a variant spelling of Dishon; compare 36:21, 28. **36:31** Or *before an Israelite king ruled over them.* **36:39** As in some Hebrew manuscripts, Samaritan Pentateuch, and Syriac version (see also 1 Chr 1:50); most Hebrew manuscripts read *Hadar.* **37:3a** Hebrew *Israel;* also in 37:13. See note on 35:21. **37:3b** Traditionally rendered *a coat of many colors.* The exact meaning of the Hebrew is uncertain. **37:26** Hebrew *cover his blood.* **37:28** Hebrew *20 [shekels],* about 8 ounces or 228 grams in weight.

Joseph

The longest story in Genesis, chapters 37–50, is devoted to the life of Joseph, Jacob’s eleventh son, whose name means “may he add.” It shows how, despite all obstacles, God adds to his people, causing them to grow, just as he promised. The story has unpromising beginnings, however. Jacob’s favoritism of Joseph and Joseph’s unwise use of his ability to interpret dreams provoked his brothers’ anger, and they sold him into slavery (chapter 37). He was taken to Egypt, where he experienced many setbacks but finally rose to become Pharaoh’s right-hand man (chapters 39–41). This enabled him to bring his family to Egypt to avoid a famine in Canaan (chapters 42–47), and here they grew and prospered. His brothers understandably feared for their lives after Jacob’s death, but Joseph understood that God’s providence had been at work through everything (50:20).

▶ *See also* ***Dreams****, page 50;* ***Trusting God when we cannot see the way ahead****, page 57;* ***God intended it all for good****, page 62.*

burlap. He mourned deeply for his son for a long time. 35His family all tried to comfort him, but he refused to be comforted. "I will go to my grave* mourning for my son," he would say, and then he would weep.

36Meanwhile, the Midianite traders* arrived in Egypt, where they sold Joseph to Potiphar, an officer of Pharaoh, the king of Egypt. Potiphar was captain of the palace guard.

Judah and Tamar

38 About this time, Judah left home and moved to Adullam, where he stayed with a man named Hirah. 2There he saw a Canaanite woman, the daughter of Shua, and he married her. When he slept with her, 3she became pregnant and gave birth to a son, and he named the boy Er. 4Then she became pregnant again and gave birth to another son, and she named him Onan. 5And when she gave birth to a third son, she named him Shelah. At the time of Shelah's birth, they were living at Kezib.

6In the course of time, Judah arranged for his firstborn son, Er, to marry a young woman named Tamar. 7But Er was a wicked man in the LORD's sight, so the LORD took his life. 8Then Judah said to Er's brother Onan, "Go and marry Tamar, as our law requires of the brother of a man who has died. You must produce an heir for your brother."

9But Onan was not willing to have a child who would not be his own heir. So whenever he had intercourse with his brother's wife, he spilled the semen on the ground. This prevented her from having a child who would belong to his brother. 10But the LORD considered it evil for Onan to deny a child to his dead brother. So the LORD took Onan's life, too.

11Then Judah said to Tamar, his daughter-in-law, "Go back to your parents' home and remain a widow until my son Shelah is old enough to marry you." (But Judah didn't really intend to do this because he was afraid Shelah would also die, like his two brothers.) So Tamar went back to live in her father's home.

12Some years later Judah's wife died. After the time of mourning was over, Judah and his friend Hirah the Adullamite went up to Timnah to supervise the shearing of his sheep. 13Someone told Tamar, "Look, your father-in-law is going up to Timnah to shear his sheep."

14Tamar was aware that Shelah had grown up, but no arrangements had been made for her to come and marry him. So she changed out of her widow's clothing and covered herself with a veil to disguise herself. Then she sat beside the road at the entrance to the village of Enaim, which is on the road to Timnah. 15Judah noticed her and thought she was a prostitute, since she had covered her face. 16So he stopped and propositioned her. "Let me have sex with you," he said, not realizing that she was his own daughter-in-law.

"How much will you pay to have sex with me?" Tamar asked.

17"I'll send you a young goat from my flock," Judah promised.

"But what will you give me to guarantee that you will send the goat?" she asked.

18"What kind of guarantee do you want?" he replied.

She answered, "Leave me your identification seal and its cord and the walking stick you are carrying." So Judah gave them to her. Then he had intercourse with her, and she became pregnant. 19Afterward she went back home, took off her veil, and put on her widow's clothing as usual.

20Later Judah asked his friend Hirah the Adullamite to take the young goat to the woman and to pick up the things he had given her as his guarantee. But Hirah couldn't find her. 21So he asked the men who lived there, "Where can I find the shrine prostitute who was sitting beside the road at the entrance to Enaim?"

"We've never had a shrine prostitute here," they replied.

22So Hirah returned to Judah and told him, "I couldn't find her anywhere, and the men of the village claim they've never had a shrine prostitute there."

23"Then let her keep the things I gave her," Judah said. "I sent the young goat as we agreed, but you couldn't find her. We'd be the laughingstock of the village if we went back again to look for her."

24About three months later, Judah was told, "Tamar, your daughter-in-law, has acted like a prostitute. And now, because of this, she's pregnant."

"Bring her out, and let her be burned!" Judah demanded.

25But as they were taking her out to kill

her, she sent this message to her father-in-law: "The man who owns these things made me pregnant. Look closely. Whose seal and cord and walking stick are these?"

[26]Judah recognized them immediately and said, "She is more righteous than I am, because I didn't arrange for her to marry my son Shelah." And Judah never slept with Tamar again.

[27]When the time came for Tamar to give birth, it was discovered that she was carrying twins. [28]While she was in labor, one of the babies reached out his hand. The midwife grabbed it and tied a scarlet string around the child's wrist, announcing, "This one came out first." [29]But then he pulled back his hand, and out came his brother! "What!" the midwife exclaimed. "How did you break out first?" So he was named Perez.* [30]Then the baby with the scarlet string on his wrist was born, and he was named Zerah.*

Joseph in Potiphar's House

39 When Joseph was taken to Egypt by the Ishmaelite traders, he was purchased by Potiphar, an Egyptian officer. Potiphar was captain of the guard for Pharaoh, the king of Egypt.

[2]The LORD was with Joseph, so he succeeded in everything he did as he served in the home of his Egyptian master. [3]Potiphar noticed this and realized that the LORD was with Joseph, giving him success in everything he did. [4]This pleased Potiphar, so he soon made Joseph his personal attendant. He put him in charge of his entire household and everything he owned. [5]From the day Joseph was put in charge of his master's household and property, the LORD began to bless Potiphar's household for Joseph's sake. All his household affairs ran smoothly, and his crops and livestock flourished. [6]So Potiphar gave Joseph complete administrative responsibility over everything he owned. With Joseph there, he didn't worry about a thing—except what kind of food to eat!

Joseph was a very handsome and well-built young man, [7]and Potiphar's wife soon began to look at him lustfully. "Come and sleep with me," she demanded.

[8]But Joseph refused. "Look," he told her, "my master trusts me with everything in his entire household. [9]No one here has more authority than I do. He has held back nothing from me except you, because you are his wife. How could I do such a wicked thing? It would be a great sin against God."

[10]She kept putting pressure on Joseph day after day, but he refused to sleep with her, and he kept out of her way as much as possible. [11]One day, however, no one else was around when he went in to do his work. [12]She came and grabbed him by his cloak, demanding, "Come on, sleep with me!" Joseph tore himself away, but he left his cloak in her hand as he ran from the house.

[13]When she saw that she was holding his cloak and he had fled, [14]she called out to her servants. Soon all the men came running. "Look!" she said. "My husband has brought this Hebrew slave here to make fools of us! He came into my room to rape me, but I screamed. [15]When he heard me scream, he ran outside and got away, but he left his cloak behind with me."

[16]She kept the cloak with her until her husband came home. [17]Then she told him her story. "That Hebrew slave you've brought into our house tried to come in and fool around with me," she said. [18]"But when I screamed, he ran outside, leaving his cloak with me!"

Joseph Put in Prison

[19]Potiphar was furious when he heard his wife's story about how Joseph had treated her. [20]So he took Joseph and threw him into the prison where the king's prisoners were held, and there he remained. [21]But the LORD was with Joseph in the prison and showed him his faithful love. And the LORD made Joseph a favorite with the prison warden. [22]Before long, the warden put Joseph in charge of all the other prisoners and over everything that happened in the prison. [23]The warden had no more worries, because Joseph took care of everything. The LORD was with him and caused everything he did to succeed.

Joseph Interprets Two Dreams

40 Some time later, Pharaoh's chief cup-bearer and chief baker offended their royal master. [2]Pharaoh became angry with these two officials, [3]and he put them in the prison where Joseph was, in the palace of the captain of the guard. [4]They

37:35 Hebrew *go down to Sheol.* **37:36** Hebrew *the Medanites.* The relationship between the Midianites and Medanites is unclear; compare 37:28. See also 25:2. **38:29** *Perez* means "breaking out." **38:30** *Zerah* means "scarlet" or "brightness."

remained in prison for quite some time, and the captain of the guard assigned them to Joseph, who looked after them.

5While they were in prison, Pharaoh's cup-bearer and baker each had a dream one night, and each dream had its own meaning. 6When Joseph saw them the next morning, he noticed that they both looked upset. 7"Why do you look so worried today?" he asked them.

8And they replied, "We both had dreams last night, but no one can tell us what they mean."

"Interpreting dreams is God's business," Joseph replied. "Go ahead and tell me your dreams."

9So the chief cup-bearer told Joseph his dream first. "In my dream," he said, "I saw a grapevine in front of me. 10The vine had three branches that began to bud and blossom, and soon it produced clusters of ripe grapes. 11I was holding Pharaoh's wine cup in my hand, so I took a cluster of grapes and squeezed the juice into the cup. Then I placed the cup in Pharaoh's hand."

12"This is what the dream means," Joseph said. "The three branches represent three days. 13Within three days Pharaoh will lift you up and restore you to your position as his chief cup-bearer. 14And please remember me and do me a favor when things go well for you. Mention me to Pharaoh, so he might let me out of this place. 15For I was kidnapped from my homeland, the land of the Hebrews, and now I'm here in prison, but I did nothing to deserve it."

16When the chief baker saw that Joseph had given the first dream such a positive interpretation, he said to Joseph, "I had a dream, too. In my dream there were three baskets of white pastries stacked on my head. 17The top basket contained all kinds of pastries for Pharaoh, but the birds came and ate them from the basket on my head."

18"This is what the dream means," Joseph told him. "The three baskets also represent three days. 19Three days from now Pharaoh will lift you up and impale your body on a pole. Then birds will come and peck away at your flesh."

20Pharaoh's birthday came three days later, and he prepared a banquet for all his officials and staff. He summoned* his chief cup-bearer and chief baker to join the other officials. 21He then restored the chief cup-bearer to his former position, so he could again hand Pharaoh his cup. 22But Pharaoh impaled the chief baker, just as Joseph had predicted when he interpreted his dream. 23Pharaoh's chief cup-bearer, however, forgot all about Joseph, never giving him another thought.

Dreams

In Bible times, it was widely accepted in all cultures that God could speak to people through dreams. We find many examples in the Old Testament of him revealing his truth, underlining his promises, or bringing guidance through dreams (e.g., Genesis 28:12-22; 31:10-13; 37:5-11; 41:1-40; 1 Kings 3:5-15; Daniel 2). Sometimes God even gave such dreams to those who didn't believe in him, like the cup-bearer and baker in this story, and even Pharaoh himself (Genesis 41). Visions are very similar to dreams, except that they occur while the recipient is awake (e.g., Genesis 15:1-11; 1 Samuel 3:1-18; Isaiah 1:1; Acts 9:10-16; 10:9-16). Joseph not only had dreams but also the God-given gift of interpreting their meaning—a gift that just as often got him into trouble (Genesis 37) as out of it (Genesis 41).

Of course, not every dream is God-given; some just may be the result of worry or thinking about our hopes and plans. But God can, and still does, speak through dreams today, just as Joel prophesied (Joel 2:28-29) and as Peter affirmed on the day of Pentecost (Acts 2:16-18). However, anything we feel we have received from God through a dream should always align with Scripture, lest we be led astray by our own desires (see Jude 1:7-8).

Pharaoh's Dreams

41 Two full years later, Pharaoh dreamed that he was standing on the bank of the Nile River. 2In his dream he saw seven fat, healthy cows come up out of the river and begin grazing in the marsh grass. 3Then he saw seven more cows come up behind them from the Nile, but these were scrawny and thin. These cows stood beside the fat cows on the riverbank. 4Then the scrawny, thin cows ate the seven healthy, fat cows! At this point in the dream, Pharaoh woke up.

5But he fell asleep again and had a second dream. This time he saw seven heads of grain, plump and beautiful, growing on a single stalk. 6Then seven more heads of grain appeared, but these were shriveled and withered by the east wind. 7And these thin heads swallowed up the seven plump, well-formed heads! Then Pharaoh woke up again and realized it was a dream.

8The next morning Pharaoh was very disturbed by the dreams. So he called for all the magicians and wise men of Egypt. When Pharaoh told them his dreams, not one of them could tell him what they meant.

9Finally, the king's chief cup-bearer spoke up. "Today I have been reminded of my failure," he told Pharaoh. 10"Some time ago, you were angry with the chief baker and me, and you imprisoned us in the palace of the captain of the guard. 11One night the chief baker and I each had a dream, and each dream had its own meaning. 12There was a young Hebrew man with us in the prison who was a slave of the captain of the guard. We told him our dreams, and he told us what each of our dreams meant. 13And everything happened just as he had predicted. I was restored to my position as cup-bearer, and the chief baker was executed and impaled on a pole."

14Pharaoh sent for Joseph at once, and he was quickly brought from the prison. After he shaved and changed his clothes, he went in and stood before Pharaoh. 15Then Pharaoh said to Joseph, "I had a dream last night, and no one here can tell me what it means. But I have heard that when you hear about a dream you can interpret it."

16"It is beyond my power to do this," Joseph replied. "But God can tell you what it means and set you at ease."

17So Pharaoh told Joseph his dream. "In my dream," he said, "I was standing on the bank of the Nile River, 18and I saw seven fat, healthy cows come up out of the river and begin grazing in the marsh grass. 19But then I saw seven sick-looking cows, scrawny and thin, come up after them. I've never seen such sorry-looking animals in all the land of Egypt. 20These thin, scrawny cows ate the seven fat cows. 21But afterward you wouldn't have known it, for they were still as thin and scrawny as before! Then I woke up.

22"In my dream I also saw seven heads of grain, full and beautiful, growing on a single stalk. 23Then seven more heads of grain appeared, but these were blighted, shriveled, and withered by the east wind. 24And the shriveled heads swallowed the seven healthy heads. I told these dreams to the magicians, but no one could tell me what they mean."

25Joseph responded, "Both of Pharaoh's dreams mean the same thing. God is telling Pharaoh in advance what he is about to do. 26The seven healthy cows and the seven healthy heads of grain both represent seven years of prosperity. 27The seven thin, scrawny cows that came up later and the seven thin heads of grain, withered by the east wind, represent seven years of famine.

28"This will happen just as I have described it, for God has revealed to Pharaoh in advance what he is about to do. 29The next seven years will be a period of great prosperity throughout the land of Egypt. 30But afterward there will be seven years of famine so great that all the prosperity will be forgotten in Egypt. Famine will destroy the land. 31This famine will be so severe that even the memory of the good years will be erased. 32As for having two similar dreams, it means that these events have been decreed by God, and he will soon make them happen.

33"Therefore, Pharaoh should find an intelligent and wise man and put him in charge of the entire land of Egypt. 34Then Pharaoh should appoint supervisors over the land and let them collect one-fifth of all the crops during the seven good years. 35Have them gather all the food produced in the good years that are just ahead and bring it to Pharaoh's storehouses. Store it away, and guard it so there will be food in the cities. 36That way there will be enough

40:20 Hebrew *He lifted up the head of.*

to eat when the seven years of famine come to the land of Egypt. Otherwise this famine will destroy the land."

Joseph Made Ruler of Egypt

37 Joseph's suggestions were well received by Pharaoh and his officials. 38 So Pharaoh asked his officials, "Can we find anyone else like this man so obviously filled with the spirit of God?" 39 Then Pharaoh said to Joseph, "Since God has revealed the meaning of the dreams to you, clearly no one else is as intelligent or wise as you are. 40 You will be in charge of my court, and all my people will take orders from you. Only I, sitting on my throne, will have a rank higher than yours."

41 Pharaoh said to Joseph, "I hereby put you in charge of the entire land of Egypt." 42 Then Pharaoh removed his signet ring from his hand and placed it on Joseph's finger. He dressed him in fine linen clothing and hung a gold chain around his neck. 43 Then he had Joseph ride in the chariot reserved for his second-in-command. And wherever Joseph went, the command was shouted, "Kneel down!" So Pharaoh put Joseph in charge of all Egypt. 44 And Pharaoh said to him, "I am Pharaoh, but no one will lift a hand or foot in the entire land of Egypt without your approval."

45 Then Pharaoh gave Joseph a new Egyptian name, Zaphenath-paneah.* He also gave him a wife, whose name was Asenath. She was the daughter of Potiphera, the priest of On.* So Joseph took charge of the entire land of Egypt. 46 He was thirty years old when he began serving in the court of Pharaoh, the king of Egypt. And when Joseph left Pharaoh's presence, he inspected the entire land of Egypt.

47 As predicted, for seven years the land produced bumper crops. 48 During those years, Joseph gathered all the crops grown in Egypt and stored the grain from the surrounding fields in the cities. 49 He piled up huge amounts of grain like sand on the seashore. Finally, he stopped keeping records because there was too much to measure.

50 During this time, before the first of the famine years, two sons were born to Joseph and his wife, Asenath, the daughter of Potiphera, the priest of On. 51 Joseph named his older son Manasseh,* for he said, "God has made me forget all my troubles and everyone in my father's family." 52 Joseph named his second son Ephraim,* for he said, "God has made me fruitful in this land of my grief."

53 At last the seven years of bumper crops throughout the land of Egypt came to an end. 54 Then the seven years of famine began, just as Joseph had predicted. The famine also struck all the surrounding countries, but throughout Egypt there was plenty of food. 55 Eventually, however, the famine spread throughout the land of Egypt as well. And when the people cried out to Pharaoh for food, he told them, "Go to Joseph, and do whatever he tells you." 56 So with severe famine everywhere, Joseph opened up the storehouses and distributed grain to the Egyptians, for the famine was severe throughout the land of Egypt. 57 And people from all around came to Egypt to buy grain from Joseph because the famine was severe throughout the world.

Joseph's Brothers Go to Egypt

42 When Jacob heard that grain was available in Egypt, he said to his sons, "Why are you standing around looking at one another? 2 I have heard there is grain in Egypt. Go down there, and buy enough grain to keep us alive. Otherwise we'll die."

3 So Joseph's ten older brothers went down to Egypt to buy grain. 4 But Jacob wouldn't let Joseph's younger brother, Benjamin, go with them, for fear some harm might come to him. 5 So Jacob's* sons arrived in Egypt along with others to buy food, for the famine was in Canaan as well.

6 Since Joseph was governor of all Egypt and in charge of selling grain to all the people, it was to him that his brothers came. When they arrived, they bowed before him with their faces to the ground. 7 Joseph recognized his brothers instantly, but he pretended to be a stranger and spoke harshly to them. "Where are you from?" he demanded.

"From the land of Canaan," they replied. "We have come to buy food."

8 Although Joseph recognized his brothers, they didn't recognize him. 9 And he remembered the dreams he'd had about them many years before. He said to them, "You are spies! You have come to see how vulnerable our land has become."

10 "No, my lord!" they exclaimed. "Your servants have simply come to buy food.

11We are all brothers—members of the same
family. We are honest men, sir! We are not
spies!"
12"Yes, you are!" Joseph insisted. "You
have come to see how vulnerable our land
has become."
13"Sir," they said, "there are actually
twelve of us. We, your servants, are all
brothers, sons of a man living in the land of
Canaan. Our youngest brother is back there
with our father right now, and one of our
brothers is no longer with us."
14But Joseph insisted, "As I said, you are
spies! 15This is how I will test your story.
I swear by the life of Pharaoh that you
will never leave Egypt unless your youngest brother comes here! 16One of you must
go and get your brother. I'll keep the rest
of you here in prison. Then we'll find out
whether or not your story is true. By the life
of Pharaoh, if it turns out that you don't
have a younger brother, then I'll know you
are spies."
17So Joseph put them all in prison for
three days. 18On the third day Joseph said to
them, "I am a God-fearing man. If you do as
I say, you will live. 19If you really are honest
men, choose one of your brothers to remain
in prison. The rest of you may go home with
grain for your starving families. 20But you
must bring your youngest brother back to
me. This will prove that you are telling the
truth, and you will not die." To this they
agreed.
21Speaking among themselves, they said,
"Clearly we are being punished because of
what we did to Joseph long ago. We saw his
anguish when he pleaded for his life, but
we wouldn't listen. That's why we're in this
trouble."
22"Didn't I tell you not to sin against the
boy?" Reuben asked. "But you wouldn't
listen. And now we have to answer for his
blood!"
23Of course, they didn't know that Joseph
understood them, for he had been speaking to them through an interpreter. 24Now
he turned away from them and began to
weep. When he regained his composure, he
spoke to them again. Then he chose Simeon
from among them and had him tied up right
before their eyes.
25Joseph then ordered his servants to fill
the men's sacks with grain, but he also gave
secret instructions to return each brother's
payment at the top of his sack. He also gave
them supplies for their journey home. 26So
the brothers loaded their donkeys with the
grain and headed for home.
27But when they stopped for the night and
one of them opened his sack to get grain for
his donkey, he found his money in the top
of his sack. 28"Look!" he exclaimed to his
brothers. "My money has been returned; it's
here in my sack!" Then their hearts sank.
Trembling, they said to each other, "What
has God done to us?"
29When the brothers came to their father,
Jacob, in the land of Canaan, they told him
everything that had happened to them.
30"The man who is governor of the land
spoke very harshly to us," they told him.
"He accused us of being spies scouting the
land. 31But we said, 'We are honest men, not
spies. 32We are twelve brothers, sons of one
father. One brother is no longer with us, and
the youngest is at home with our father in
the land of Canaan.'
33"Then the man who is governor of the
land told us, 'This is how I will find out if you
are honest men. Leave one of your brothers

41:45a *Zaphenath-paneah* probably means "God speaks and lives." **41:45b** Greek version reads of *Heliopolis;* also in 41:50. **41:51** *Manasseh* sounds like a Hebrew term that means "causing to forget." **41:52** *Ephraim* sounds like a Hebrew term that means "fruitful." **42:5** Hebrew *Israel's*. See note on 35:21.

Egypt

Egypt was one of the ancient world's great empires, rivaling those of Mesopotamia. In fact, when Abraham visited it to avoid a famine (Genesis 12:10-20), it was already over one thousand years old. Egypt comes into the Bible's story on many occasions—sometimes as a refuge (e.g., Genesis 12:10-20; Matthew 2:13-15), sometimes as an enemy (e.g., Exodus 1–11). Israel always looked back on God's miraculous deliverance of them from slavery in Egypt through the Exodus as the greatest point in their history.

here with me, and take grain for your starving families and go on home. 34But you must
bring your youngest brother back to me.
Then I will know you are honest men and not
spies. Then I will give you back your brother,
and you may trade freely in the land.'"
35As they emptied out their sacks, there
in each man's sack was the bag of money
he had paid for the grain! The brothers and
their father were terrified when they saw
the bags of money. 36Jacob exclaimed, "You
are robbing me of my children! Joseph is
gone! Simeon is gone! And now you want
to take Benjamin, too. Everything is going
against me!"
37Then Reuben said to his father, "You
may kill my two sons if I don't bring Benjamin back to you. I'll be responsible for him,
and I promise to bring him back."
38But Jacob replied, "My son will not go
down with you. His brother Joseph is dead,
and he is all I have left. If anything should
happen to him on your journey, you would
send this grieving, white-haired man to his
grave.*"

The Brothers Return to Egypt

43 But the famine continued to ravage
the land of Canaan. 2When the grain
they had brought from Egypt was almost
gone, Jacob said to his sons, "Go back and
buy us a little more food."
3But Judah said, "The man was serious
when he warned us, 'You won't see my
face again unless your brother is with you.'
4If you send Benjamin with us, we will go
down and buy more food. 5But if you don't
let Benjamin go, we won't go either. Remember, the man said, 'You won't see my
face again unless your brother is with you.'"
6"Why were you so cruel to me?" Jacob*
moaned. "Why did you tell him you had
another brother?"
7"The man kept asking us questions about
our family," they replied. "He asked, 'Is
your father still alive? Do you have another
brother?' So we answered his questions.
How could we know he would say, 'Bring
your brother down here'?"
8Judah said to his father, "Send the boy
with me, and we will be on our way. Otherwise we will all die of starvation—and not
only we, but you and our little ones. 9I personally guarantee his safety. You may hold
me responsible if I don't bring him back to
you. Then let me bear the blame forever. 10If
we hadn't wasted all this time, we could
have gone and returned twice by now."
11So their father, Jacob, finally said to
them, "If it can't be avoided, then at least do
this. Pack your bags with the best products
of this land. Take them down to the man as
gifts—balm, honey, gum, aromatic resin,
pistachio nuts, and almonds. 12Also take
double the money that was put back in your
sacks, as it was probably someone's mistake.
13Then take your brother, and go back to the
man. 14May God Almighty* give you mercy
as you go before the man, so that he will
release Simeon and let Benjamin return. But
if I must lose my children, so be it."
15So the men packed Jacob's gifts and
double the money and headed off with Benjamin. They finally arrived in Egypt and presented themselves to Joseph. 16When Joseph
saw Benjamin with them, he said to the
manager of his household, "These men will
eat with me this noon. Take them inside the
palace. Then go slaughter an animal, and
prepare a big feast." 17So the man did as
Joseph told him and took them into Joseph's
palace.
18The brothers were terrified when
they saw that they were being taken into
Joseph's house. "It's because of the money
someone put in our sacks last time we were
here," they said. "He plans to pretend that
we stole it. Then he will seize us, make us
slaves, and take our donkeys."

A Feast at Joseph's Palace

19The brothers approached the manager
of Joseph's household and spoke to him
at the entrance to the palace. 20"Sir," they
said, "we came to Egypt once before to buy
food. 21But as we were returning home,
we stopped for the night and opened our
sacks. Then we discovered that each man's
money—the exact amount paid—was in the
top of his sack! Here it is; we have brought
it back with us. 22We also have additional
money to buy more food. We have no idea
who put our money in our sacks."
23"Relax. Don't be afraid," the household
manager told them. "Your God, the God of
your father, must have put this treasure
into your sacks. I know I received your
payment." Then he released Simeon and
brought him out to them.
24The manager then led the men into

Joseph's palace. He gave them water to wash their feet and provided food for their donkeys. 25 They were told they would be eating there, so they prepared their gifts for Joseph's arrival at noon.

26 When Joseph came home, they gave him the gifts they had brought him, then bowed low to the ground before him. 27 After greeting them, he asked, "How is your father, the old man you spoke about? Is he still alive?"

28 "Yes," they replied. "Our father, your servant, is alive and well." And they bowed low again.

29 Then Joseph looked at his brother Benjamin, the son of his own mother. "Is this your youngest brother, the one you told me about?" Joseph asked. "May God be gracious to you, my son." 30 Then Joseph hurried from the room because he was overcome with emotion for his brother. He went into his private room, where he broke down and wept. 31 After washing his face, he came back out, keeping himself under control. Then he ordered, "Bring out the food!"

32 The waiters served Joseph at his own table, and his brothers were served at a separate table. The Egyptians who ate with Joseph sat at their own table, because Egyptians despise Hebrews and refuse to eat with them. 33 Joseph told each of his brothers where to sit, and to their amazement, he seated them according to age, from oldest to youngest. 34 And Joseph filled their plates with food from his own table, giving Benjamin five times as much as he gave the others. So they feasted and drank freely with him.

Joseph's Silver Cup

44 When his brothers were ready to leave, Joseph gave these instructions to his palace manager: "Fill each of their sacks with as much grain as they can carry, and put each man's money back into his sack. 2 Then put my personal silver cup at the top of the youngest brother's sack, along with the money for his grain." So the manager did as Joseph instructed him.

3 The brothers were up at dawn and were sent on their journey with their loaded donkeys. 4 But when they had gone only a short distance and were barely out of the city, Joseph said to his palace manager, "Chase after them and stop them. When you catch up with them, ask them, 'Why have you repaid my kindness with such evil? 5 Why have you stolen my master's silver cup,* which he uses to predict the future? What a wicked thing you have done!'"

6 When the palace manager caught up with the men, he spoke to them as he had been instructed.

7 "What are you talking about?" the brothers responded. "We are your servants and would never do such a thing! 8 Didn't we return the money we found in our sacks? We brought it back all the way from the land of Canaan. Why would we steal silver or gold from your master's house? 9 If you find his cup with any one of us, let that man die. And all the rest of us, my lord, will be your slaves."

10 "That's fair," the man replied. "But only the one who stole the cup will be my slave. The rest of you may go free."

11 They all quickly took their sacks from the backs of their donkeys and opened them. 12 The palace manager searched the brothers' sacks, from the oldest to the youngest. And the cup was found in Benjamin's sack! 13 When the brothers saw this, they tore their clothing in despair. Then they loaded their donkeys again and returned to the city.

14 Joseph was still in his palace when Judah and his brothers arrived, and they fell to the ground before him. 15 "What have you done?" Joseph demanded. "Don't you know that a man like me can predict the future?"

16 Judah answered, "Oh, my lord, what can we say to you? How can we explain this? How can we prove our innocence? God is punishing us for our sins. My lord, we have all returned to be your slaves—all of us, not just our brother who had your cup in his sack."

17 "No," Joseph said. "I would never do such a thing! Only the man who stole the cup will be my slave. The rest of you may go back to your father in peace."

Judah Speaks for His Brothers

18 Then Judah stepped forward and said, "Please, my lord, let your servant say just one word to you. Please, do not be angry with me, even though you are as powerful as Pharaoh himself.

19 "My lord, previously you asked us, your servants, 'Do you have a father or a brother?' 20 And we responded, 'Yes, my lord, we have

42:38 Hebrew *to Sheol.* **43:6** Hebrew *Israel;* also in 43:11. See note on 35:21. **43:14** Hebrew *El-Shaddai.* **44:5** As in Greek version; Hebrew lacks this phrase.

a father who is an old man, and his youngest son is a child of his old age. His full brother is dead, and he alone is left of his mother's children, and his father loves him very much.'

21"And you said to us, 'Bring him here so I can see him with my own eyes.' 22But we said to you, 'My lord, the boy cannot leave his father, for his father would die.' 23But you told us, 'Unless your youngest brother comes with you, you will never see my face again.'

24"So we returned to your servant, our father, and told him what you had said. 25Later, when he said, 'Go back again and buy us more food,' 26we replied, 'We can't go unless you let our youngest brother go with us. We'll never get to see the man's face unless our youngest brother is with us.'

27"Then my father said to us, 'As you know, my wife had two sons, 28and one of them went away and never returned. Doubtless he was torn to pieces by some wild animal. I have never seen him since. 29Now if you take his brother away from me, and any harm comes to him, you will send this grieving, white-haired man to his grave.*'

30"And now, my lord, I cannot go back to my father without the boy. Our father's life is bound up in the boy's life. 31If he sees that the boy is not with us, our father will die. We, your servants, will indeed be responsible for sending that grieving, white-haired man to his grave. 32My lord, I guaranteed to my father that I would take care of the boy. I told him, 'If I don't bring him back to you, I will bear the blame forever.'

33"So please, my lord, let me stay here as a slave instead of the boy, and let the boy return with his brothers. 34For how can I return to my father if the boy is not with me? I couldn't bear to see the anguish this would cause my father!"

Joseph Reveals His Identity

45 Joseph could stand it no longer. There were many people in the room, and he said to his attendants, "Out, all of you!" So he was alone with his brothers when he told them who he was. 2Then he broke down and wept. He wept so loudly the Egyptians could hear him, and word of it quickly carried to Pharaoh's palace.

3"I am Joseph!" he said to his brothers. "Is my father still alive?" But his brothers were speechless! They were stunned to realize that Joseph was standing there in front of them. 4"Please, come closer," he said to them. So they came closer. And he said again, "I am Joseph, your brother, whom you sold into slavery in Egypt. 5But don't be upset, and don't be angry with yourselves for selling me to this place. It was God who sent me here ahead of you to preserve your lives. 6This famine that has ravaged the land for two years will last five more years, and there will be neither plowing nor harvesting. 7God has sent me ahead of you to keep you and your families alive and to preserve many survivors.* 8So it was God who sent me here, not you! And he is the one who made me an adviser* to Pharaoh—the manager of his entire palace and the governor of all Egypt.

9"Now hurry back to my father and tell him, 'This is what your son Joseph says: God has made me master over all the land of Egypt. So come down to me immediately! 10You can live in the region of Goshen, where you can be near me with all your children and grandchildren, your flocks and herds, and everything you own. 11I will take care of you there, for there are still five years of famine ahead of us. Otherwise you, your household, and all your animals will starve.'"

12Then Joseph added, "Look! You can see for yourselves, and so can my brother Benjamin, that I really am Joseph! 13Go tell my father of my honored position here in Egypt. Describe for him everything you have seen, and then bring my father here quickly." 14Weeping with joy, he embraced Benjamin, and Benjamin did the same. 15Then Joseph kissed each of his brothers and wept over them, and after that they began talking freely with him.

Pharaoh Invites Jacob to Egypt

16The news soon reached Pharaoh's palace: "Joseph's brothers have arrived!" Pharaoh and his officials were all delighted to hear this.

17Pharaoh said to Joseph, "Tell your brothers, 'This is what you must do: Load your pack animals, and hurry back to the land of Canaan. 18Then get your father and all of your families, and return here to me. I will give you the very best land in Egypt, and you will eat from the best that the land produces.'"

19Then Pharaoh said to Joseph, "Tell your brothers, 'Take wagons from the land of Egypt to carry your little children and your wives, and bring your father here. 20 Don't worry about your personal belongings, for the best of all the land of Egypt is yours.'"

21 So the sons of Jacob* did as they were told. Joseph provided them with wagons, as Pharaoh had commanded, and he gave them supplies for the journey. 22 And he gave each of them new clothes—but to Benjamin he gave five changes of clothes and 300 pieces* of silver. 23 He also sent his father ten male donkeys loaded with the finest products of Egypt, and ten female donkeys loaded with grain and bread and other supplies he would need on his journey.

24 So Joseph sent his brothers off, and as they left, he called after them, "Don't quarrel about all this along the way!" 25 And they left Egypt and returned to their father, Jacob, in the land of Canaan.

26 "Joseph is still alive!" they told him. "And he is governor of all the land of Egypt!" Jacob was stunned at the news—he couldn't believe it. 27 But when they repeated to Jacob everything Joseph had told them, and when he saw the wagons Joseph had sent to carry him, their father's spirits revived.

28 Then Jacob exclaimed, "It must be true! My son Joseph is alive! I must go and see him before I die."

Jacob's Journey to Egypt

46 So Jacob* set out for Egypt with all his possessions. And when he came to Beersheba, he offered sacrifices to the God of his father, Isaac. 2 During the night God spoke to him in a vision. "Jacob! Jacob!" he called.

"Here I am," Jacob replied.

3 "I am God,* the God of your father," the voice said. "Do not be afraid to go down to Egypt, for there I will make your family into a great nation. 4 I will go with you down to Egypt, and I will bring you back again. You will die in Egypt, but Joseph will be with you to close your eyes."

44:29 Hebrew *to Sheol;* also in 44:31. **45:7** Or *and to save you with an extraordinary rescue.* The meaning of the Hebrew is uncertain. **45:8** Hebrew *a father.* **45:21** Hebrew *Israel;* also in 45:28. See note on 35:21. **45:22** Hebrew *300 [shekels],* about 7.5 pounds or 3.4 kilograms in weight. **46:1** Hebrew *Israel;* also in 46:29, 30. See note on 35:21. **46:3** Hebrew *I am El.*

Trusting God when we cannot see the way ahead

There are very few Christians who won't, at some point, have to patiently wait and trust God when everything seems to be going wrong or contrary to what they felt God said. That's what happened with Joseph. He had had dreams of becoming great, but thirteen years passed between those dreams and becoming Pharaoh's right-hand man (Genesis 37:2; 41:46). Those years were marked by constant ups and downs: from being his father's favorite, to slavery, to being in charge of Potiphar's house, to being wrongly imprisoned on false charges of attempted rape, to being in charge of prisoners, to being abandoned in the prison for a further two years by the cup-bearer whom he helped, to becoming Pharaoh's leading official. Through all of that, Joseph had to be patient and hold on to God and the dreams he had given him, believing God would bring them to pass at the right time. But those years weren't wasted, as Joseph came to realize. He saw that God had sent him to Egypt ahead of his family to save their lives (45:5), and it was a very different character who met his brothers in chapter 45 than the arrogant young man who left them in chapter 37.

Countless other Bible characters also had to learn how to hold on to God in difficult times: Abraham, who waited twenty-five years before Isaac was born; David, who waited some ten years before becoming king; Paul, who experienced imprisonment, shipwrecks, beatings, and countless dangers even though God had sent him as the apostle to the Gentiles. Through all of this, it was holding on to God that led them to see God's promises come to pass in the end.

▸ *See also* ***The character of God****, page 104;* ***God's sovereignty****, page 584;* ***Faith****, page 1286.*

5 So Jacob left Beersheba, and his sons
took him to Egypt. They carried him and
their little ones and their wives in the
wagons Pharaoh had provided for them.
6 They also took all their livestock and all the
personal belongings they had acquired in
the land of Canaan. So Jacob and his entire
family went to Egypt—7 sons and grandsons, daughters and granddaughters—all
his descendants.

8 These are the names of the descendants
of Israel—the sons of Jacob—who went to
Egypt:

Reuben was Jacob's oldest son. 9 The sons
of Reuben were Hanoch, Pallu, Hezron,
and Carmi.
10 The sons of Simeon were Jemuel, Jamin,
Ohad, Jakin, Zohar, and Shaul. (Shaul's
mother was a Canaanite woman.)
11 The sons of Levi were Gershon, Kohath,
and Merari.
12 The sons of Judah were Er, Onan, Shelah,
Perez, and Zerah (though Er and Onan
had died in the land of Canaan). The
sons of Perez were Hezron and Hamul.
13 The sons of Issachar were Tola, Puah,*
Jashub,* and Shimron.
14 The sons of Zebulun were Sered, Elon,
and Jahleel.
15 These were the sons of Leah and Jacob
who were born in Paddan-aram, in addition to their daughter, Dinah. The number
of Jacob's descendants (male and female)
through Leah was thirty-three.

16 The sons of Gad were Zephon,* Haggi,
Shuni, Ezbon, Eri, Arodi, and Areli.
17 The sons of Asher were Imnah, Ishvah,
Ishvi, and Beriah. Their sister was
Serah. Beriah's sons were Heber and
Malkiel.
18 These were the sons of Zilpah, the servant
given to Leah by her father, Laban. The
number of Jacob's descendants through
Zilpah was sixteen.

19 The sons of Jacob's wife Rachel were
Joseph and Benjamin.
20 Joseph's sons, born in the land of Egypt,
were Manasseh and Ephraim. Their
mother was Asenath, daughter of
Potiphera, the priest of On.*
21 Benjamin's sons were Bela, Beker,
Ashbel, Gera, Naaman, Ehi, Rosh,
Muppim, Huppim, and Ard.
22 These were the sons of Rachel and Jacob.
The number of Jacob's descendants through
Rachel was fourteen.

23 The son of Dan was Hushim.
24 The sons of Naphtali were Jahzeel, Guni,
Jezer, and Shillem.
25 These were the sons of Bilhah, the servant
given to Rachel by her father, Laban. The
number of Jacob's descendants through
Bilhah was seven.

26 The total number of Jacob's direct descendants who went with him to Egypt, not
counting his sons' wives, was sixty-six. 27 In
addition, Joseph had two sons* who were
born in Egypt. So altogether, there were
seventy* members of Jacob's family in the
land of Egypt.

Jacob's Family Arrives in Goshen

28 As they neared their destination, Jacob
sent Judah ahead to meet Joseph and get directions to the region of Goshen. And when
they finally arrived there, 29 Joseph prepared
his chariot and traveled to Goshen to meet
his father, Jacob. When Joseph arrived, he
embraced his father and wept, holding
him for a long time. 30 Finally, Jacob said to
Joseph, "Now I am ready to die, since I have
seen your face again and know you are still
alive."

31 And Joseph said to his brothers and
to his father's entire family, "I will go to
Pharaoh and tell him, 'My brothers and my
father's entire family have come to me from
the land of Canaan. 32 These men are shepherds, and they raise livestock. They have
brought with them their flocks and herds
and everything they own.'"

33 Then he said, "When Pharaoh calls for
you and asks you about your occupation,
34 you must tell him, 'We, your servants,
have raised livestock all our lives, as our
ancestors have always done.' When you
tell him this, he will let you live here in the
region of Goshen, for the Egyptians despise
shepherds."

Jacob Blesses Pharaoh

47 Then Joseph went to see Pharaoh and
told him, "My father and my brothers have arrived from the land of Canaan.
They have come with all their flocks and
herds and possessions, and they are now in
the region of Goshen."

[2]Joseph took five of his brothers with him and presented them to Pharaoh. [3]And Pharaoh asked the brothers, "What is your occupation?"

They replied, "We, your servants, are shepherds, just like our ancestors. [4]We have come to live here in Egypt for a while, for there is no pasture for our flocks in Canaan. The famine is very severe there. So please, we request permission to live in the region of Goshen."

[5]Then Pharaoh said to Joseph, "Now that your father and brothers have joined you here, [6]choose any place in the entire land of Egypt for them to live. Give them the best land of Egypt. Let them live in the region of Goshen. And if any of them have special skills, put them in charge of my livestock, too."

[7]Then Joseph brought in his father, Jacob, and presented him to Pharaoh. And Jacob blessed Pharaoh.

[8]"How old are you?" Pharaoh asked him.

[9]Jacob replied, "I have traveled this earth for 130 hard years. But my life has been short compared to the lives of my ancestors." [10]Then Jacob blessed Pharaoh again before leaving his court.

[11]So Joseph assigned the best land of Egypt—the region of Rameses—to his father and his brothers, and he settled them there, just as Pharaoh had commanded. [12]And Joseph provided food for his father and his brothers in amounts appropriate to the number of their dependents, including the smallest children.

Joseph's Leadership in the Famine

[13]Meanwhile, the famine became so severe that all the food was used up, and people were starving throughout the lands of Egypt and Canaan. [14]By selling grain to the people, Joseph eventually collected all the money in Egypt and Canaan, and he put the money in Pharaoh's treasury. [15]When the people of Egypt and Canaan ran out of money, all the Egyptians came to Joseph. "Our money is gone!" they cried. "But please give us food, or we will die before your very eyes!"

[16]Joseph replied, "Since your money is gone, bring me your livestock. I will give you food in exchange for your livestock." [17]So they brought their livestock to Joseph in exchange for food. In exchange for their horses, flocks of sheep and goats, herds of cattle, and donkeys, Joseph provided them with food for another year.

[18]But that year ended, and the next year they came again and said, "We cannot hide the truth from you, my lord. Our money is gone, and all our livestock and cattle are yours. We have nothing left to give but our bodies and our land. [19]Why should we die before your very eyes? Buy us and our land in exchange for food; we offer our land and ourselves as slaves for Pharaoh. Just give us grain so we may live and not die, and so the land does not become empty and desolate."

[20]So Joseph bought all the land of Egypt for Pharaoh. All the Egyptians sold him their fields because the famine was so severe, and soon all the land belonged to Pharaoh. [21]As for the people, he made them all slaves,* from one end of Egypt to the other. [22]The only land he did not buy was the land belonging to the priests. They received an allotment of food directly from Pharaoh, so they didn't need to sell their land.

[23]Then Joseph said to the people, "Look, today I have bought you and your land for Pharaoh. I will provide you with seed so you can plant the fields. [24]Then when you harvest it, one-fifth of your crop will belong to Pharaoh. You may keep the remaining four-fifths as seed for your fields and as food for you, your households, and your little ones."

[25]"You have saved our lives!" they exclaimed. "May it please you, my lord, to let us be Pharaoh's servants." [26]Joseph then issued a decree still in effect in the land of Egypt, that Pharaoh should receive one-fifth of all the crops grown on his land. Only the land belonging to the priests was not given to Pharaoh.

[27]Meanwhile, the people of Israel settled in the region of Goshen in Egypt. There they acquired property, and they were fruitful, and their population grew rapidly. [28]Jacob lived for seventeen years after his arrival in Egypt, so he lived 147 years in all.

46:13a As in Syriac version and Samaritan Pentateuch (see also 1 Chr 7:1); Hebrew reads *Puvah*. **46:13b** As in some Greek manuscripts and Samaritan Pentateuch (see also Num 26:24; 1 Chr 7:1); Hebrew reads *Iob*. **46:16** As in Greek version and Samaritan Pentateuch (see also Num 26:15); Hebrew reads *Ziphion*. **46:20** Greek version reads *of Heliopolis*. **46:27a** Greek version reads *nine sons*, probably including Joseph's grandsons through Ephraim and Manasseh (see 1 Chr 7:14-20). **46:27b** Greek version reads *seventy-five;* see note on Exod 1:5. **47:21** As in Greek version and Samaritan Pentateuch; Hebrew reads *he moved them all into the towns*.

29 As the time of his death drew near,
Jacob* called for his son Joseph and said to
him, "Please do me this favor. Put your hand
under my thigh and swear that you will treat
me with unfailing love by honoring this last
request: Do not bury me in Egypt. 30 When
I die, please take my body out of Egypt and
bury me with my ancestors."

So Joseph promised, "I will do as you ask."
31 "Swear that you will do it," Jacob insisted. So Joseph gave his oath, and Jacob
bowed humbly at the head of his bed.*

Jacob Blesses Manasseh and Ephraim

48 One day not long after this, word
came to Joseph, "Your father is
failing rapidly." So Joseph went to visit his
father, and he took with him his two sons,
Manasseh and Ephraim.

2 When Joseph arrived, Jacob was told,
"Your son Joseph has come to see you." So
Jacob* gathered his strength and sat up in
his bed.

3 Jacob said to Joseph, "God Almighty* appeared to me at Luz in the land of Canaan
and blessed me. 4 He said to me, 'I will make
you fruitful, and I will multiply your descendants. I will make you a multitude of
nations. And I will give this land of Canaan
to your descendants* after you as an everlasting possession.'

5 "Now I am claiming as my own sons
these two boys of yours, Ephraim and Manasseh, who were born here in the land of
Egypt before I arrived. They will be my sons,
just as Reuben and Simeon are. 6 But any
children born to you in the future will be
your own, and they will inherit land within
the territories of their brothers Ephraim and
Manasseh.

7 "Long ago, as I was returning from
Paddan-aram,* Rachel died in the land of
Canaan. We were still on the way, some distance from Ephrath (that is, Bethlehem). So
with great sorrow I buried her there beside
the road to Ephrath."

8 Then Jacob looked over at the two boys.
"Are these your sons?" he asked.

9 "Yes," Joseph told him, "these are the
sons God has given me here in Egypt."

And Jacob said, "Bring them closer to me,
so I can bless them."

10 Jacob was half blind because of his age
and could hardly see. So Joseph brought
the boys close to him, and Jacob kissed
and embraced them. 11 Then Jacob said to
Joseph, "I never thought I would see your
face again, but now God has let me see your
children, too!"

12 Joseph moved the boys, who were at
their grandfather's knees, and he bowed
with his face to the ground. 13 Then he positioned the boys in front of Jacob. With
his right hand he directed Ephraim toward
Jacob's left hand, and with his left hand he
put Manasseh at Jacob's right hand. 14 But
Jacob crossed his arms as he reached out to
lay his hands on the boys' heads. He put his
right hand on the head of Ephraim, though
he was the younger boy, and his left hand
on the head of Manasseh, though he was
the firstborn. 15 Then he blessed Joseph and
said,

"May the God before whom my
grandfather Abraham
and my father, Isaac, walked—
the God who has been my shepherd
all my life, to this very day,
16 the Angel who has redeemed me from
all harm—
may he bless these boys.
May they preserve my name
and the names of Abraham and Isaac.
And may their descendants multiply
greatly
throughout the earth."

17 But Joseph was upset when he saw
that his father placed his right hand on
Ephraim's head. So Joseph lifted it to move
it from Ephraim's head to Manasseh's head.
18 "No, my father," he said. "This one is the
firstborn. Put your right hand on his head."

19 But his father refused. "I know, my son;
I know," he replied. "Manasseh will also
become a great people, but his younger
brother will become even greater. And his
descendants will become a multitude of
nations."

20 So Jacob blessed the boys that day with
this blessing: "The people of Israel will
use your names when they give a blessing. They will say, 'May God make you as
prosperous as Ephraim and Manasseh.'"
In this way, Jacob put Ephraim ahead of
Manasseh.

21 Then Jacob said to Joseph, "Look, I am
about to die, but God will be with you and
will take you back to Canaan, the land of
your ancestors. 22 And beyond what I have

given your brothers, I am giving you an extra portion of the land* that I took from the Amorites with my sword and bow."

Jacob's Last Words to His Sons

49 Then Jacob called together all his sons and said, "Gather around me, and I will tell you what will happen to each of you in the days to come.

2 "Come and listen, you sons of Jacob;
listen to Israel, your father.
3 "Reuben, you are my firstborn,
my strength,
the child of my vigorous youth.
You are first in rank and first in
power.
4 But you are as unruly as a flood,
and you will be first no longer.
For you went to bed with my wife;
you defiled my marriage couch.
5 "Simeon and Levi are two of a kind;
their weapons are instruments of
violence.
6 May I never join in their meetings;
may I never be a party to their plans.
For in their anger they murdered men,
and they crippled oxen just for sport.
7 A curse on their anger, for it is fierce;
a curse on their wrath, for it is cruel.
I will scatter them among the
descendants of Jacob;
I will disperse them throughout Israel.
8 "Judah, your brothers will praise you.
You will grasp your enemies by the
neck.
All your relatives will bow before you.
9 Judah, my son, is a young lion
that has finished eating its prey.
Like a lion he crouches and lies down;
like a lioness—who dares to rouse him?
10 The scepter will not depart from Judah,
nor the ruler's staff from his
descendants,*
until the coming of the one to whom it
belongs,*
the one whom all nations will honor.
11 He ties his foal to a grapevine,
the colt of his donkey to a choice
vine.
He washes his clothes in wine,
his robes in the blood of grapes.
12 His eyes are darker than wine,
and his teeth are whiter than milk.
13 "Zebulun will settle by the seashore
and will be a harbor for ships;
his borders will extend to Sidon.
14 "Issachar is a sturdy donkey,
resting between two saddlepacks.*
15 When he sees how good the
countryside is
and how pleasant the land,
he will bend his shoulder to the load
and submit himself to hard labor.
16 "Dan will govern his people,
like any other tribe in Israel.
17 Dan will be a snake beside the road,
a poisonous viper along the path
that bites the horse's hooves
so its rider is thrown off.
18 I trust in you for salvation, O LORD!
19 "Gad will be attacked by marauding
bands,
but he will attack them when they
retreat.
20 "Asher will dine on rich foods
and produce food fit for kings.
21 "Naphtali is a doe set free
that bears beautiful fawns.
22 "Joseph is the foal of a wild donkey,
the foal of a wild donkey at a spring—
one of the wild donkeys on the ridge.*
23 Archers attacked him savagely;
they shot at him and harassed him.
24 But his bow remained taut,
and his arms were strengthened
by the hands of the Mighty One of Jacob,
by the Shepherd, the Rock of Israel.
25 May the God of your father help you;
may the Almighty bless you
with the blessings of the heavens above,
and blessings of the watery depths
below,
and blessings of the breasts and womb.
26 May my fatherly blessings on you
surpass the blessings of my
ancestors,*

47:29 Hebrew *Israel;* also in 47:31b. See note on 35:21. **47:31** Greek version reads *and Israel bowed in worship as he leaned on his staff.* Compare Heb 11:21. **48:2** Hebrew *Israel;* also in 48:8, 10, 11, 13, 14, 21. See note on 35:21. **48:3** Hebrew *El-Shaddai.* **48:4** Hebrew *seed;* also in 48:19. **48:7** Hebrew *Paddan,* referring to Paddan-aram; compare Gen 35:9. **48:22** Or *an extra ridge of land.* The meaning of the Hebrew is uncertain. **49:10a** Hebrew *from between his feet.* **49:10b** Or *until tribute is brought to him and the peoples obey;* traditionally rendered *until Shiloh comes.* **49:14** Or *sheepfolds,* or *hearths.* **49:22** Or *Joseph is a fruitful tree, / a fruitful tree beside a spring. / His branches reach over the wall.* The meaning of the Hebrew is uncertain. **49:26** Or *of the ancient mountains.*

reaching to the heights of the eternal
hills.
May these blessings rest on the head of
Joseph,
who is a prince among his brothers.

27 "Benjamin is a ravenous wolf,
devouring his enemies in the morning
and dividing his plunder in the
evening."

28These are the twelve tribes of Israel, and
this is what their father said as he told his
sons good-bye. He blessed each one with an
appropriate message.

Jacob's Death and Burial

29Then Jacob instructed them, "Soon I will
die and join my ancestors. Bury me with my
father and grandfather in the cave in the
field of Ephron the Hittite. 30This is the cave
in the field of Machpelah, near Mamre in
Canaan, that Abraham bought from Ephron
the Hittite as a permanent burial site.
31There Abraham and his wife Sarah are
buried. There Isaac and his wife, Rebekah,
are buried. And there I buried Leah. 32It is
the plot of land and the cave that my grandfather Abraham bought from the Hittites."
33When Jacob had finished this charge
to his sons, he drew his feet into the bed,
breathed his last, and joined his ancestors
in death.

50 Joseph threw himself on his father
and wept over him and kissed him.
2Then Joseph told the physicians who served
him to embalm his father's body; so Jacob*
was embalmed. 3The embalming process
took the usual forty days. And the Egyptians
mourned his death for seventy days.
4When the period of mourning was over,
Joseph approached Pharaoh's advisers and
said, "Please do me this favor and speak
to Pharaoh on my behalf. 5Tell him that
my father made me swear an oath. He said
to me, 'Listen, I am about to die. Take my
body back to the land of Canaan, and bury
me in the tomb I prepared for myself.' So
please allow me to go and bury my father.
After his burial, I will return without
delay."
6Pharaoh agreed to Joseph's request.
"Go and bury your father, as he made you
promise," he said. 7So Joseph went up to
bury his father. He was accompanied by
all of Pharaoh's officials, all the senior
members of Pharaoh's household, and all
the senior officers of Egypt. 8Joseph also
took his entire household and his brothers
and their households. But they left their
little children and flocks and herds in the
land of Goshen. 9A great number of chariots
and charioteers accompanied Joseph.
10When they arrived at the threshing floor
of Atad, near the Jordan River, they held a
very great and solemn memorial service,
with a seven-day period of mourning for
Joseph's father. 11The local residents, the
Canaanites, watched them mourning at the
threshing floor of Atad. Then they renamed
that place (which is near the Jordan) Abel-
mizraim,* for they said, "This is a place of
deep mourning for these Egyptians."
12So Jacob's sons did as he had commanded them. 13They carried his body to the
land of Canaan and buried him in the cave in

God intended it all for good

"You intended to harm me," Joseph told his brothers, "but God intended it all for good" (Genesis 50:20). His brothers had sold him into slavery, but God had used even their harmful intentions to save lives. Joseph had risen to become prime minister of Egypt and had wisely set aside food from the years of plenty for the years of famine, saving many lives as a result. And Joseph had forgiven his brothers. If we are God's children, then he not only rules over everything in our lives but also, amazingly, uses everything that happens in our lives—even our difficult family background, problems, and adversities—for good. We don't know how he does it, and sometimes we question his dealings with us, but we can trust him to do this.

▶ *See also* ***Why do bad things happen in life?****, page 1025.*

the field of Machpelah, near Mamre. This is the cave that Abraham had bought as a permanent burial site from Ephron the Hittite.

Joseph Reassures His Brothers

14 After burying Jacob, Joseph returned to Egypt with his brothers and all who had accompanied him to his father's burial. 15 But now that their father was dead, Joseph's brothers became fearful. "Now Joseph will show his anger and pay us back for all the wrong we did to him," they said.

16 So they sent this message to Joseph: "Before your father died, he instructed us 17 to say to you: 'Please forgive your brothers for the great wrong they did to you—for their sin in treating you so cruelly.' So we, the servants of the God of your father, beg you to forgive our sin." When Joseph received the message, he broke down and wept. 18 Then his brothers came and threw themselves down before Joseph. "Look, we are your slaves!" they said.

19 But Joseph replied, "Don't be afraid of me. Am I God, that I can punish you? 20 You intended to harm me, but God intended it all for good. He brought me to this position so I could save the lives of many people. 21 No, don't be afraid. I will continue to take care of you and your children." So he reassured them by speaking kindly to them.

The Death of Joseph

22 So Joseph and his brothers and their families continued to live in Egypt. Joseph lived to the age of 110. 23 He lived to see three generations of descendants of his son Ephraim, and he lived to see the birth of the children of Manasseh's son Makir, whom he claimed as his own.*

24 "Soon I will die," Joseph told his brothers, "but God will surely come to help you and lead you out of this land of Egypt. He will bring you back to the land he solemnly promised to give to Abraham, to Isaac, and to Jacob."

25 Then Joseph made the sons of Israel swear an oath, and he said, "When God comes to help you and lead you back, you must take my bones with you." 26 So Joseph died at the age of 110. The Egyptians embalmed him, and his body was placed in a coffin in Egypt.

50:2 Hebrew *Israel.* See note on 35:21. **50:11** *Abel-mizraim* means "mourning of the Egyptians." **50:23** Hebrew *who were born on Joseph's knees.*

Exodus *Let my people go*

Exodus is the gripping tale of a people's liberation from slavery and their journey into the wilderness to meet with God. Jacob's descendants, whom Joseph had brought to Egypt to avoid famine, were initially favored by Pharaoh, and they prospered. But after Joseph's death, a new king from a new dynasty, who knew nothing of how Joseph had served Egypt and who feared the fast-growing number of immigrants (1:8-10), made them slaves and put them to work on major building projects. Their increasingly cruel treatment led them to cry out to God, who resolved to deliver them. Israel came to see the miraculous rescue that followed as the decisive event that transformed them from a diverse group of slaves into a nation with God as their defender and leader. Passover—the celebration of their deliverance—became the Israelites' most important annual religious feast, and redemption one of the most important concepts in the Bible. After rescuing the Israelites from Egypt, God provided for their every need in the wilderness, despite their constant grumbling, and at Mount Sinai he established his covenant with them and gave them the Law.

What's it all about?

Chapters 1 to 15 tell the story of the Hebrews (the Israelites) in Egypt. We meet them engaged in hard labor, making bricks for Pharaoh's great building projects and suffering greatly. But God heard their groaning and remembered his promise to Abraham about giving Canaan to his descendants as "their possession forever" (Genesis 17:8), so he resolved to free them. Through a bush that seemed to burn yet was not burnt up, God spoke to Moses while he was tending a flock near Mount Sinai, commissioning him to go to Pharaoh and demand the Hebrews' release. He revealed his personal name to him: Yahweh ("I AM WHO I AM"). A reluctant Moses went to Pharaoh with God's demand, "Let my people go!" Pharaoh, unwilling to lose his workforce, stubbornly resisted, but finally relented after God sent increasingly harsh plagues that eventually cost him the life of his own son.

Deliverance, when it came, came swiftly. On the night the Hebrews left Egypt, they celebrated the first Passover, as God had commanded, while the angel of God "passed over" their homes but killed all firstborn Egyptian males, just as Pharaoh had been destroying all newborn Hebrew males. That very night Pharaoh and the Egyptians urged them to leave, giving them silver, gold, and clothing. The Hebrews headed east, with Pharaoh close behind. When they found themselves trapped between the Red Sea and the pursuing Egyptians, God made a way through the water, and they crossed over on dry land. But when Pharaoh and his army attempted to do the same, they met a watery grave.

Chapters 16 to 40 tell the story of the Hebrews' journey toward the Promised Land of Canaan. Avoiding the busy coastal road, they headed south, toward Sinai, led by God in the form of a cloud by day and a pillar of fire by night. The story is dominated by their complaining and disobedience. They even complained that life in Egypt wasn't so bad after all! But God still blessed them, miraculously providing manna and quail for them to eat and making water gush from a rock. When they reached Mount Sinai, God made a covenant with them: Henceforth they would be "my own special treasure from among all the peoples on earth . . . my kingdom of priests, my holy nation" (Exodus 19:5-6). God then gave his Law to guide his people in this new relationship and gave them sacrifices as a means of maintaining the relationship. These sacrifices would be offered at a mobile sanctuary, called the Tabernacle, which contained the Ark of the Covenant, the symbol of his intimate presence among them.

What does it mean for us?

Exodus introduces one of the Bible's most important themes: redemption. The Hebrews belonged to Pharaoh, who had enslaved them, but God claimed them for himself and shattered Pharaoh's hold over them. In doing so, God set himself against oppression in all its forms and took the side of the weak and oppressed. But God's action goes beyond the mere social or political sphere. God did not free the Israelites simply because they were oppressed, but so that they could serve him, the living God. His command to Pharaoh was "Let my people go, so they can worship me."

Exodus serves as a testimony to the great works of God, but it also gives a candid portrayal of human failure. In spite of the miracles the people experienced, each new difficulty drove them into a crisis, rather than to God. This shows us that the things that enslave us are often within us, and their grip is not easily loosened. Sin, rather than Pharaoh, was the people's most stubborn adversary. It took one night to get them out of Egypt, but many years to get Egypt out of them.

Through this portrayal of God's dealings with the people of Israel, we see his patience toward our shortsightedness. He respects our free will and allows us to bear the consequences of our actions, but he doesn't leave it there. He is still always there for us, making provision for our material and spiritual needs—most importantly our need for forgiveness. And he promises never to withdraw his presence, however long it takes us to get the message that being his people is not simply about being forgiven and freed; rather, we are called to become part of a people whose encounter with God now changes everything—our lifestyle, our service, and our sense of destiny.

OVERVIEW

The story of Moses' early years and his call · *1:1–4:31*

Pharaoh's rejection of God's demand and the plagues that follow · *5:1–11:10*

The institution of the Passover and the Hebrews' flight from Egypt · *12:1–13:16*

The parting of the Red Sea *13:17–15:27*

God provides manna, quail, and water in the wilderness · *16:1–18:27*

God makes a covenant with Israel, giving them laws to live by, including the Ten Commandments · *19:1–24:18*

God directs the people to make a tent (the Tabernacle) in which he will dwell in a special way · *25:1–31:18*

The people worship a gold calf and Moses intercedes for them · *32:1–33:11*

The covenant renewed *33:12–34:35*

The construction of the Tabernacle *35:1–40:38*

The Israelites in Egypt

1 These are the names of the sons of Israel
(that is, Jacob) who moved to Egypt with
their father, each with his family: 2Reuben,
Simeon, Levi, Judah, 3Issachar, Zebulun,
Benjamin, 4Dan, Naphtali, Gad, and Asher.
5In all, Jacob had seventy* descendants in
Egypt, including Joseph, who was already
there.

6In time, Joseph and all of his brothers
died, ending that entire generation. 7But
their descendants, the Israelites, had many
children and grandchildren. In fact, they
multiplied so greatly that they became extremely powerful and filled the land.

8Eventually, a new king came to power in
Egypt who knew nothing about Joseph or
what he had done. 9He said to his people,
"Look, the people of Israel now outnumber
us and are stronger than we are. 10We must
make a plan to keep them from growing even
more. If we don't, and if war breaks out, they
will join our enemies and fight against us.
Then they will escape from the country.*"

11So the Egyptians made the Israelites
their slaves. They appointed brutal slave
drivers over them, hoping to wear them
down with crushing labor. They forced them
to build the cities of Pithom and Rameses as
supply centers for the king. 12But the more
the Egyptians oppressed them, the more the
Israelites multiplied and spread, and the
more alarmed the Egyptians became. 13So
the Egyptians worked the people of Israel
without mercy. 14They made their lives
bitter, forcing them to mix mortar and make
bricks and do all the work in the fields. They
were ruthless in all their demands.

15Then Pharaoh, the king of Egypt, gave
this order to the Hebrew midwives, Shiphrah
and Puah: 16"When you help the Hebrew
women as they give birth, watch as they
deliver.* If the baby is a boy, kill him; if it is a
girl, let her live." 17But because the midwives
feared God, they refused to obey the king's
orders. They allowed the boys to live, too.

18So the king of Egypt called for the midwives. "Why have you done this?" he demanded. "Why have you allowed the boys
to live?"

19"The Hebrew women are not like the
Egyptian women," the midwives replied.
"They are more vigorous and have their
babies so quickly that we cannot get there
in time."

20So God was good to the midwives,
and the Israelites continued to multiply,
growing more and more powerful. 21And
because the midwives feared God, he gave
them families of their own.

22Then Pharaoh gave this order to all his
people: "Throw every newborn Hebrew boy
into the Nile River. But you may let the girls
live."

The Birth of Moses

2 About this time, a man and woman
from the tribe of Levi got married. 2The
woman became pregnant and gave birth to
a son. She saw that he was a special baby
and kept him hidden for three months. 3But
when she could no longer hide him, she
got a basket made of papyrus reeds and
waterproofed it with tar and pitch. She put
the baby in the basket and laid it among
the reeds along the bank of the Nile River.
4The baby's sister then stood at a distance,
watching to see what would happen to him.
5Soon Pharaoh's daughter came down to
bathe in the river, and her attendants walked

▸ **1:11** *See **Oppression**, page 710.*

The Nile

The Nile, into which Pharaoh commanded that all the newborn Israelite boys should be thrown, was full of crocodiles. Its origins lay in Lake Victoria in modern Uganda, from which it flowed for over 4,100 miles, breaking into a swampy delta before finally reaching the Mediterranean. It flooded every year between June and October, swollen by Africa's heavy rains and melting snows—a season called *akhet* ("the inundation"), which brought great fertility to the land along its borders. This was why Egypt often avoided famines when other regions did not.

along the riverbank. When the princess saw the basket among the reeds, she sent her maid to get it for her. 6 When the princess opened it, she saw the baby. The little boy was crying, and she felt sorry for him. "This must be one of the Hebrew children," she said.

7 Then the baby's sister approached the princess. "Should I go and find one of the Hebrew women to nurse the baby for you?" she asked.

8 "Yes, do!" the princess replied. So the girl went and called the baby's mother.

9 "Take this baby and nurse him for me," the princess told the baby's mother. "I will pay you for your help." So the woman took her baby home and nursed him.

10 Later, when the boy was older, his mother brought him back to Pharaoh's daughter, who adopted him as her own son. The princess named him Moses,* for she explained, "I lifted him out of the water."

Moses Escapes to Midian

11 Many years later, when Moses had grown up, he went out to visit his own people, the Hebrews, and he saw how hard they were forced to work. During his visit, he saw an Egyptian beating one of his fellow Hebrews. 12 After looking in all directions to make sure no one was watching, Moses killed the Egyptian and hid the body in the sand.

13 The next day, when Moses went out to visit his people again, he saw two Hebrew men fighting. "Why are you beating up your friend?" Moses said to the one who had started the fight.

14 The man replied, "Who appointed you to be our prince and judge? Are you going to kill me as you killed that Egyptian yesterday?"

Then Moses was afraid, thinking, "Everyone knows what I did." 15 And sure enough, Pharaoh heard what had happened, and he tried to kill Moses. But Moses fled from Pharaoh and went to live in the land of Midian.

When Moses arrived in Midian, he sat down beside a well. 16 Now the priest of Midian had seven daughters who came as usual to draw water and fill the water troughs for their father's flocks. 17 But some other shepherds came and chased them away. So Moses jumped up and rescued the girls from the shepherds. Then he drew water for their flocks.

18 When the girls returned to Reuel, their father, he asked, "Why are you back so soon today?"

19 "An Egyptian rescued us from the shepherds," they answered. "And then he drew water for us and watered our flocks."

20 "Then where is he?" their father asked. "Why did you leave him there? Invite him to come and eat with us."

21 Moses accepted the invitation, and he settled there with him. In time, Reuel gave Moses his daughter Zipporah to be his wife. 22 Later she gave birth to a son, and Moses named him Gershom,* for he explained, "I have been a foreigner in a foreign land."

23 Years passed, and the king of Egypt died. But the Israelites continued to groan under their burden of slavery. They cried out for help, and their cry rose up to God. 24 God heard their groaning, and he remembered his covenant promise to Abraham, Isaac, and Jacob. 25 He looked down on the people of Israel and knew it was time to act.*

1:5 Dead Sea Scrolls and Greek version read *seventy-five;* see notes on Gen 46:27. **1:10** Or *will take the country.* **1:16** Hebrew *look upon the two stones;* perhaps the reference is to a birthstool. **2:10** *Moses* sounds like a Hebrew term that means "to lift out." **2:22** *Gershom* sounds like a Hebrew term that means "a foreigner there." **2:25** Or *and acknowledged his obligation to help them.*

The Hebrews

Several times in Exodus 1–10 the Israelites are called "Hebrews." The term seems to have been used of them by foreigners in a disparaging way (e.g., Genesis 39:14; 1 Samuel 4:5-9). They may have seen it as a variant of *Habiru*, a propertyless immigrant social class mentioned in many ancient texts. But its origins are in fact rooted in Israel's own history. In Genesis 14:13 we read of "Abram the Hebrew"—probably a way of defining his ethnic background and linking him to Eber, a descendant of Shem, Noah's firstborn (Genesis 10:21). The term was gradually replaced by "Israelites."

Moses and the Burning Bush

3 One day Moses was tending the flock of his father-in-law, Jethro,* the priest of Midian. He led the flock far into the wilderness and came to Sinai,* the mountain of God. 2There the angel of the LORD appeared to him in a blazing fire from the middle of a bush. Moses stared in amazement. Though the bush was engulfed in flames, it didn't burn up. 3"This is amazing," Moses said to himself. "Why isn't that bush burning up? I must go see it."

4When the LORD saw Moses coming to take a closer look, God called to him from the middle of the bush, "Moses! Moses!"

"Here I am!" Moses replied.

5"Do not come any closer," the LORD warned. "Take off your sandals, for you are standing on holy ground. 6I am the God of your father*—the God of Abraham, the God of Isaac, and the God of Jacob." When Moses heard this, he covered his face because he was afraid to look at God.

7Then the LORD told him, "I have certainly seen the oppression of my people in Egypt. I have heard their cries of distress because of their harsh slave drivers. Yes, I am aware of their suffering. 8So I have come down to rescue them from the power of the Egyptians and lead them out of Egypt into their own fertile and spacious land. It is a land flowing with milk and honey—the land where the Canaanites, Hittites, Amorites, Perizzites, Hivites, and Jebusites now live. 9Look! The cry of the people of Israel has reached me, and I have seen how harshly the Egyptians abuse them. 10Now go, for I am sending you to Pharaoh. You must lead my people Israel out of Egypt."

11But Moses protested to God, "Who am I to appear before Pharaoh? Who am I to lead the people of Israel out of Egypt?"

12God answered, "I will be with you. And this is your sign that I am the one who has sent you: When you have brought the people out of Egypt, you will worship God at this very mountain."

13But Moses protested, "If I go to the people of Israel and tell them, 'The God of your ancestors has sent me to you,' they will ask me, 'What is his name?' Then what should I tell them?"

14God replied to Moses, "I AM WHO I AM.* Say this to the people of Israel: I AM has sent me to you." 15God also said to Moses, "Say this to the people of Israel: Yahweh,* the God of your ancestors—the God of Abraham, the God of Isaac, and the God of Jacob—has sent me to you.

This is my eternal name,
  my name to remember for all
    generations.

16"Now go and call together all the elders of Israel. Tell them, 'Yahweh, the God of your ancestors—the God of Abraham, Isaac, and Jacob—has appeared to me. He told me, "I have been watching closely, and I see how the Egyptians are treating you. 17I have promised to rescue you from your oppression in Egypt. I will lead you to a land flowing with milk and honey—the land where the Canaanites, Hittites, Amorites, Perizzites, Hivites, and Jebusites now live."'

18"The elders of Israel will accept your message. Then you and the elders must go to the king of Egypt and tell him, 'The LORD, the God of the Hebrews, has met with us. So please let us take a three-day journey into the wilderness to offer sacrifices to the LORD, our God.'

19"But I know that the king of Egypt will not let you go unless a mighty hand forces him.* 20So I will raise my hand and strike the Egyptians, performing all kinds of miracles among them. Then at last he will let you go. 21And I will cause the Egyptians to look favorably on you. They will give you gifts when you go so you will not leave empty-handed. 22Every Israelite woman will ask for articles of silver and gold and fine clothing from her Egyptian neighbors and from the foreign women in their houses. You will dress your sons and daughters with these, stripping the Egyptians of their wealth."

Signs of the LORD's Power

4 But Moses protested again, "What if they won't believe me or listen to me? What if they say, 'The LORD never appeared to you'?"

2Then the LORD asked him, "What is that in your hand?"

"A shepherd's staff," Moses replied.

▸ **3:1** *See **The wilderness**, page 784.* **4:1** *See **Doubt**, page 1414.*

3“Throw it down on the ground,” the
LORD told him. So Moses threw down the
staff, and it turned into a snake! Moses
jumped back.
4Then the LORD told him, “Reach out and
grab its tail.” So Moses reached out and
grabbed it, and it turned back into a shepherd’s staff in his hand.
5“Perform this sign,” the LORD told him.
“Then they will believe that the LORD,
the God of their ancestors—the God of
Abraham, the God of Isaac, and the God of
Jacob—really has appeared to you.”
6Then the LORD said to Moses, “Now put
your hand inside your cloak.” So Moses put
his hand inside his cloak, and when he took
it out again, his hand was white as snow
with a severe skin disease.* 7“Now put your
hand back into your cloak,” the LORD said.
So Moses put his hand back in, and when
he took it out again, it was as healthy as the
rest of his body.
8The LORD said to Moses, “If they do not
believe you and are not convinced by the first
miraculous sign, they will be convinced by
the second sign. 9And if they don’t believe
you or listen to you even after these two signs,
then take some water from the Nile River and
pour it out on the dry ground. When you do,
the water from the Nile will turn to blood on
the ground.”
10But Moses pleaded with the LORD, “O
Lord, I’m not very good with words. I never

3:1a Moses’ father-in-law went by two names, Jethro and Reuel. **3:1b** Hebrew *Horeb,* another name for Sinai. **3:6** Greek version reads *your fathers.* **3:14** Or *I WILL BE WHAT I WILL BE.* **3:15** *Yahweh* (also in 3:16) is a transliteration of the proper name *YHWH* that is sometimes rendered “Jehovah”; in this translation it is usually rendered “the LORD” (note the use of small capitals). **3:19** As in Greek and Latin versions; Hebrew reads *will not let you go, not by a mighty hand.* **4:6** Or *with leprosy.* The Hebrew word used here can describe various skin diseases.

Moses, the man who loved God’s presence

Although born a Hebrew, Moses was brought up as an Egyptian, having been rescued by Pharaoh’s daughter (Exodus 2:1-10). He felt deeply for his suffering fellow Hebrews and tried to win their acceptance, even killing an Egyptian slave driver, but he was rejected and fled for his life to Midian (2:11-22). There, an encounter with the living God changed his life forever as God revealed himself and commissioned him to free the Hebrews (chapters 3–4).

From the uncertainty and fear of this first encounter, Moses’ story becomes one of increasing intimacy with God. He boldly went where no man had gone before: not only across the Red Sea but into the very presence of God. Three times we read that his face was “radiant” “because he had spoken to the LORD” (34:29, 30, 35). He even got God to change his mind (32:14). In fact, Moses seemed far more comfortable in *God’s* presence than in the people’s presence, for God listened to him, while the people rarely did, and spoke to him “face to face, as one speaks to a friend” (33:11).

While the people feared God’s presence at Mount Sinai (19:16), Moses delighted in it. But after receiving God’s Law, he returned to find the people worshiping a gold calf (chapter 32). He was so angry that he smashed the tablets of the Ten Commandments. And yet he went back into God’s presence to intercede for the people, begging God not to abandon them (32:30–33:17). Through his intercession God not only relented from destroying them but also revealed himself to Moses in a powerful way (33:18–34:8). Later God filled the Tabernacle with his glory—so powerfully that Moses could not enter it (40:34-35)—the assurance that he had heard Moses’ prayer and would continue with Israel on their journey to the Promised Land.

The intimacy Moses experienced with God is even expressed at his death, when God himself buried him in an unknown grave in Moab on the edge of the Promised Land (Deuteronomy 34:5-6).

▶ *See also* ***Moses, the faithful servant,*** *page 239;* ***The presence of God,*** *page 1031.*

Names and titles of God

Name or title	Example verse	Significance
Ancient One	Daniel 7:9	God without beginning
Creator	Isaiah 40:28	God who brought everything into being
Eternal God	Genesis 21:33	God without beginning or ending
Father	Matthew 6:9	Relational God
First and the Last	Isaiah 44:6	Eternal God of history
God Almighty	Genesis 17:1	God of invincible power
God Most High	Genesis 14:18	God who is supreme above other so-called gods
God of Abraham, Isaac, and Jacob	Exodus 3:15	Personal God and God of those who have gone before us
God of all the peoples of the world	Jeremiah 32:27	God even of those who do not acknowledge him
God of heaven	Nehemiah 2:4	God who is above all creation
God of Israel	Joshua 24:2	God who is committed to caring for his people
God of peace	Hebrews 13:20	God who brings peace (wholeness) to us
God who sees	Genesis 16:13	God who watches over his people, especially when they are in need
Holy One	Job 6:10	God who is utterly different from all his creation
Judge of all the earth	Genesis 18:25	God of justice
King	Jeremiah 51:57	Ruler over everything
Lord	Joshua 3:11	Master of everything
Lord of lords	Deuteronomy 10:17	No ruler greater than him
LORD (Yahweh)	Exodus 3:14-15	God who is always there
LORD God	Genesis 2:4	Redeemer and creator God
LORD is my banner	Exodus 17:15	God our rallying point
LORD of Heaven's Armies	1 Samuel 1:3	God who commands all heavenly beings
LORD is peace	Judges 6:24	God who brings us peace
LORD will provide	Genesis 22:14	God who provides for all our needs
Mighty One	Luke 1:49	God with no limits to his power
Redeemer	Isaiah 41:14	God who rescues us
Rock	Deuteronomy 32:4	God of unfailing strength and our refuge
Savior	Luke 1:47	God who saves us from our circumstances
Shepherd	Genesis 49:24	God of intimate care who leads us
Shield	Deuteronomy 33:29	King and protector
Sovereign LORD	2 Samuel 7:28	God who brings all things under his rule
True God	Jeremiah 10:10	There is no other God besides him

have been, and I'm not now, even though you
have spoken to me. I get tongue-tied, and my
words get tangled."
11Then the LORD asked Moses, "Who makes
a person's mouth? Who decides whether
people speak or do not speak, hear or do not
hear, see or do not see? Is it not I, the LORD?
12Now go! I will be with you as you speak,
and I will instruct you in what to say."
13But Moses again pleaded, "Lord, please!
Send anyone else."
14Then the LORD became angry with
Moses. "All right," he said. "What about your
brother, Aaron the Levite? I know he speaks
well. And look! He is on his way to meet you
now. He will be delighted to see you. 15Talk to
him, and put the words in his mouth. I will be
with both of you as you speak, and I will instruct you both in what to do. 16Aaron will
be your spokesman to the people. He will be
your mouthpiece, and you will stand in the
place of God for him, telling him what to say.
17And take your shepherd's staff with you,
and use it to perform the miraculous signs
I have shown you."

Moses Returns to Egypt

18So Moses went back home to Jethro, his
father-in-law. "Please let me return to my
relatives in Egypt," Moses said. "I don't
even know if they are still alive."
"Go in peace," Jethro replied.
19Before Moses left Midian, the LORD said
to him, "Return to Egypt, for all those who
wanted to kill you have died."
20So Moses took his wife and sons, put
them on a donkey, and headed back to the
land of Egypt. In his hand he carried the
staff of God.
21And the LORD told Moses, "When you
arrive back in Egypt, go to Pharaoh and
perform all the miracles I have empowered
you to do. But I will harden his heart so he
will refuse to let the people go. 22Then you
will tell him, 'This is what the LORD says:
Israel is my firstborn son. 23I commanded
you, "Let my son go, so he can worship me."
But since you have refused, I will now kill
your firstborn son!'"
24On the way to Egypt, at a place where
Moses and his family had stopped for the
night, the LORD confronted him and was
about to kill him. 25But Moses' wife, Zipporah, took a flint knife and circumcised
her son. She touched his feet* with the
foreskin and said, "Now you are a bridegroom of blood to me." 26(When she said "a
bridegroom of blood," she was referring to
the circumcision.) After that, the LORD left
him alone.
27Now the LORD had said to Aaron, "Go
out into the wilderness to meet Moses." So
Aaron went and met Moses at the mountain
of God, and he embraced him. 28Moses then
told Aaron everything the LORD had commanded him to say. And he told him about
the miraculous signs the LORD had commanded him to perform.
29Then Moses and Aaron returned to Egypt
and called all the elders of Israel together.
30Aaron told them everything the LORD had
told Moses, and Moses performed the miraculous signs as they watched. 31Then the
people of Israel were convinced that the
LORD had sent Moses and Aaron. When they
heard that the LORD was concerned about
them and had seen their misery, they bowed
down and worshiped.

Moses and Aaron Speak to Pharaoh

5 After this presentation to Israel's
leaders, Moses and Aaron went and
spoke to Pharaoh. They told him, "This is
what the LORD, the God of Israel, says: Let
my people go so they may hold a festival in
my honor in the wilderness."
2"Is that so?" retorted Pharaoh. "And who
is the LORD? Why should I listen to him and
let Israel go? I don't know the LORD, and
I will not let Israel go."
3But Aaron and Moses persisted. "The
God of the Hebrews has met with us,"
they declared. "So let us take a three-day
journey into the wilderness so we can offer
sacrifices to the LORD our God. If we don't,
he will kill us with a plague or with the
sword."
4Pharaoh replied, "Moses and Aaron, why
are you distracting the people from their
tasks? Get back to work! 5Look, there are
many of your people in the land, and you
are stopping them from their work."

Making Bricks without Straw

6That same day Pharaoh sent this order to
the Egyptian slave drivers and the Israelite
foremen: 7"Do not supply any more straw
for making bricks. Make the people get it

4:25 The Hebrew word for "feet" may refer here to the male sex organ.

themselves! 8 But still require them to make the same number of bricks as before. Don't reduce the quota. They are lazy. That's why they are crying out, 'Let us go and offer sacrifices to our God.' 9 Load them down with more work. Make them sweat! That will teach them to listen to lies!"

10 So the slave drivers and foremen went out and told the people: "This is what Pharaoh says: I will not provide any more straw for you. 11 Go and get it yourselves. Find it wherever you can. But you must produce just as many bricks as before!" 12 So the people scattered throughout the land of Egypt in search of stubble to use as straw.

13 Meanwhile, the Egyptian slave drivers continued to push hard. "Meet your daily quota of bricks, just as you did when we provided you with straw!" they demanded. 14 Then they whipped the Israelite foremen they had put in charge of the work crews. "Why haven't you met your quotas either yesterday or today?" they demanded.

15 So the Israelite foremen went to Pharaoh and pleaded with him. "Please don't treat your servants like this," they begged. 16 "We are given no straw, but the slave drivers still demand, 'Make bricks!' We are being beaten, but it isn't our fault! Your own people are to blame!"

17 But Pharaoh shouted, "You're just lazy! Lazy! That's why you're saying, 'Let us go and offer sacrifices to the LORD.' 18 Now get back to work! No straw will be given to you, but you must still produce the full quota of bricks."

19 The Israelite foremen could see that they were in serious trouble when they were told, "You must not reduce the number of bricks you make each day." 20 As they left Pharaoh's court, they confronted Moses and Aaron, who were waiting outside for them. 21 The foremen said to them, "May the LORD judge and punish you for making us stink before Pharaoh and his officials. You have put a sword into their hands, an excuse to kill us!"

22 Then Moses went back to the LORD and protested, "Why have you brought all this trouble on your own people, Lord? Why did you send me? 23 Ever since I came to Pharaoh as your spokesman, he has been even more brutal to your people. And you have done nothing to rescue them!"

Promises of Deliverance

6 Then the LORD told Moses, "Now you will see what I will do to Pharaoh. When he feels the force of my strong hand, he will let the people go. In fact, he will force them to leave his land!"

2 And God said to Moses, "I am Yahweh—'the LORD.'* 3 I appeared to Abraham, to Isaac, and to Jacob as El-Shaddai—'God Almighty'*—but I did not reveal my name, Yahweh, to them. 4 And I reaffirmed my covenant with them. Under its terms, I promised to give them the land of Canaan, where they were living as foreigners. 5 You can be sure that I have heard the groans of the people of Israel, who are now slaves to the Egyptians. And I am well aware of my covenant with them.

6 "Therefore, say to the people of Israel: 'I am the LORD. I will free you from your oppression and will rescue you from your slavery in Egypt. I will redeem you with a powerful arm and great acts of judgment. 7 I will claim you as my own people, and I will be your God. Then you will know that I am the LORD your God who has freed you from your oppression in Egypt. 8 I will bring you into the land I swore to give to Abraham, Isaac, and Jacob. I will give it to you as your very own possession. I am the LORD!'"

9 So Moses told the people of Israel what the LORD had said, but they refused to listen anymore. They had become too discouraged by the brutality of their slavery.

10 Then the LORD said to Moses, 11 "Go back to Pharaoh, the king of Egypt, and tell him to let the people of Israel leave his country."

12 "But LORD!" Moses objected. "My own people won't listen to me anymore. How can I expect Pharaoh to listen? I'm such a clumsy speaker!*"

13 But the LORD spoke to Moses and Aaron and gave them orders for the Israelites and for Pharaoh, the king of Egypt. The LORD commanded Moses and Aaron to lead the people of Israel out of Egypt.

The Ancestors of Moses and Aaron

14 These are the ancestors of some of the clans of Israel:

▸ **6:6** *See **Redemption**, page 1136.*

The sons of Reuben, Israel's oldest son, were Hanoch, Pallu, Hezron, and Carmi. Their descendants became the clans of Reuben.

15The sons of Simeon were Jemuel, Jamin, Ohad, Jakin, Zohar, and Shaul. (Shaul's mother was a Canaanite woman.) Their descendants became the clans of Simeon.

16These are the descendants of Levi, as listed in their family records: The sons of Levi were Gershon, Kohath, and Merari. (Levi lived to be 137 years old.)

17The descendants of Gershon included Libni and Shimei, each of whom became the ancestor of a clan.

18The descendants of Kohath included Amram, Izhar, Hebron, and Uzziel. (Kohath lived to be 133 years old.)

19The descendants of Merari included Mahli and Mushi.

These are the clans of the Levites, as listed in their family records.

20Amram married his father's sister Jochebed, and she gave birth to his sons, Aaron and Moses. (Amram lived to be 137 years old.)

21The sons of Izhar were Korah, Nepheg, and Zicri.

22The sons of Uzziel were Mishael, Elzaphan, and Sithri.

23Aaron married Elisheba, the daughter of Amminadab and sister of Nahshon, and she gave birth to his sons, Nadab, Abihu, Eleazar, and Ithamar.

24The sons of Korah were Assir, Elkanah, and Abiasaph. Their descendants became the clans of Korah.

25Eleazar son of Aaron married one of the daughters of Putiel, and she gave birth to his son, Phinehas.

These are the ancestors of the Levite families, listed according to their clans.

26The Aaron and Moses named in this list are the same ones to whom the LORD said, "Lead the people of Israel out of the land of Egypt like an army." 27It was Moses and Aaron who spoke to Pharaoh, the king of Egypt, about leading the people of Israel out of Egypt.

28When the LORD spoke to Moses in the land of Egypt, 29he said to him, "I am the LORD! Tell Pharaoh, the king of Egypt, everything I am telling you." 30But Moses argued with the LORD, saying, "I can't do it! I'm such a clumsy speaker! Why should Pharaoh listen to me?"

Aaron's Staff Becomes a Serpent

7 Then the LORD said to Moses, "Pay close attention to this. I will make you seem like God to Pharaoh, and your brother, Aaron, will be your prophet. 2Tell Aaron everything I command you, and Aaron must command Pharaoh to let the people of Israel leave his country. 3But I will make Pharaoh's heart stubborn so I can multiply my miraculous signs and wonders in the land of Egypt. 4Even then Pharaoh will refuse to listen to you. So I will bring down my fist on Egypt. Then I will rescue my forces—my people, the Israelites—from the land of Egypt with great acts of judgment. 5When I raise my powerful hand and bring out the Israelites, the Egyptians will know that I am the LORD."

6So Moses and Aaron did just as the LORD had commanded them. 7Moses was eighty years old, and Aaron was eighty-three when they made their demands to Pharaoh.

8Then the LORD said to Moses and Aaron, 9"Pharaoh will demand, 'Show me a miracle.' When he does this, say to Aaron, 'Take your staff and throw it down in front of Pharaoh, and it will become a serpent.*'"

10So Moses and Aaron went to Pharaoh and did what the LORD had commanded them. Aaron threw down his staff before Pharaoh and his officials, and it became a serpent! 11Then Pharaoh called in his own wise men and sorcerers, and these Egyptian magicians did the same thing with their magic. 12They threw down their staffs, which also became serpents! But then Aaron's staff swallowed up their staffs. 13Pharaoh's heart, however, remained hard. He still refused to listen, just as the LORD had predicted.

A Plague of Blood

14Then the LORD said to Moses, "Pharaoh's heart is stubborn,* and he still refuses to let the people go. 15So go to Pharaoh in the morning as he goes down to the river. Stand on the bank of the Nile and meet him there.

6:2 *Yahweh* is a transliteration of the proper name *YHWH* that is sometimes rendered "Jehovah"; in this translation it is usually rendered "the LORD" (note the use of small capitals). **6:3** *El-Shaddai,* which means "God Almighty," is the name for God used in Gen 17:1; 28:3; 35:11; 43:14; 48:3. **6:12** Hebrew *I have uncircumcised lips;* also in 6:30. **7:9** Hebrew *tannin,* which elsewhere refers to a sea monster. Greek version translates it "dragon." **7:14** Hebrew *heavy.*

Be sure to take along the staff that turned
into a snake. 16Then announce to him, 'The
LORD, the God of the Hebrews, has sent me
to tell you, "Let my people go, so they can
worship me in the wilderness." Until now,
you have refused to listen to him. 17So this
is what the LORD says: "I will show you that
I am the LORD." Look! I will strike the water
of the Nile with this staff in my hand, and
the river will turn to blood. 18The fish in it
will die, and the river will stink. The Egyptians will not be able to drink any water
from the Nile.'"
19Then the LORD said to Moses: "Tell
Aaron, 'Take your staff and raise your hand
over the waters of Egypt—all its rivers,
canals, ponds, and all the reservoirs. Turn
all the water to blood. Everywhere in Egypt
the water will turn to blood, even the water
stored in wooden bowls and stone pots.'"
20So Moses and Aaron did just as the
LORD commanded them. As Pharaoh and
all of his officials watched, Aaron raised his
staff and struck the water of the Nile. Suddenly, the whole river turned to blood! 21The
fish in the river died, and the water became
so foul that the Egyptians couldn't drink it.
There was blood everywhere throughout
the land of Egypt. 22But again the magicians of Egypt used their magic, and they,
too, turned water into blood. So Pharaoh's
heart remained hard. He refused to listen to
Moses and Aaron, just as the LORD had predicted. 23Pharaoh returned to his palace and
put the whole thing out of his mind. 24Then
all the Egyptians dug along the riverbank to
find drinking water, for they couldn't drink
the water from the Nile.
25Seven days passed from the time the
LORD struck the Nile.

A Plague of Frogs

8 1*Then the LORD said to Moses, "Go
back to Pharaoh and announce to him,
'This is what the LORD says: Let my people
go, so they can worship me. 2If you refuse
to let them go, I will send a plague of frogs
across your entire land. 3The Nile River will
swarm with frogs. They will come up out
of the river and into your palace, even into
your bedroom and onto your bed! They will
enter the houses of your officials and your
people. They will even jump into your ovens
and your kneading bowls. 4Frogs will jump
on you, your people, and all your officials.'"
5*Then the LORD said to Moses, "Tell
Aaron, 'Raise the staff in your hand over all
the rivers, canals, and ponds of Egypt, and
bring up frogs over all the land.'" 6So Aaron
raised his hand over the waters of Egypt, and
frogs came up and covered the whole land!
7But the magicians were able to do the same
thing with their magic. They, too, caused
frogs to come up on the land of Egypt.
8Then Pharaoh summoned Moses and
Aaron and begged, "Plead with the LORD to
take the frogs away from me and my people.
I will let your people go, so they can offer
sacrifices to the LORD."
9"You set the time!" Moses replied. "Tell
me when you want me to pray for you, your
officials, and your people. Then you and
your houses will be rid of the frogs. They
will remain only in the Nile River."
10"Do it tomorrow," Pharaoh said.
"All right," Moses replied, "it will be as

The ten plagues

When Pharaoh would not obey God's command to release the Hebrew slaves, God applied increasing pressure on him over the coming weeks through ten plagues (Exodus 7:14–12:30): water turned to blood, frogs, gnats, flies, death of livestock, boils, hail, locusts, darkness, and death of the firstborn. Each of these plagues was a direct challenge to Egypt's gods. Each one demonstrated God's control over something that either represented an Egyptian god (such as the fly and the bull) or was thought to be a god (like the Nile and the sun). Even death itself could not be controlled, as Egyptians sought to do through their careful preparations of the deceased's body; it came without warning, taking their firstborn. The Lord God truly showed himself to be the most powerful God of all. Pharaoh had little choice but to yield.

▸ *See also* ***The Plagues of Egypt****, Visual Overview Z3.*

you have said. Then you will know that
there is no one like the LORD our God. 11The
frogs will leave you and your houses, your
officials, and your people. They will remain
only in the Nile River."
12So Moses and Aaron left Pharaoh's
palace, and Moses cried out to the LORD
about the frogs he had inflicted on Pharaoh.
13And the LORD did just what Moses had predicted. The frogs in the houses, the courtyards, and the fields all died. 14The Egyptians
piled them into great heaps, and a terrible
stench filled the land. 15But when Pharaoh
saw that relief had come, he became stubborn.* He refused to listen to Moses and
Aaron, just as the LORD had predicted.

A Plague of Gnats

16So the LORD said to Moses, "Tell Aaron,
'Raise your staff and strike the ground. The
dust will turn into swarms of gnats throughout the land of Egypt.'" 17So Moses and Aaron
did just as the LORD had commanded them.
When Aaron raised his hand and struck the
ground with his staff, gnats infested the
entire land, covering the Egyptians and their
animals. All the dust in the land of Egypt
turned into gnats. 18Pharaoh's magicians
tried to do the same thing with their secret
arts, but this time they failed. And the gnats
covered everyone, people and animals alike.
19"This is the finger of God!" the magicians exclaimed to Pharaoh. But Pharaoh's
heart remained hard. He wouldn't listen to
them, just as the LORD had predicted.

A Plague of Flies

20Then the LORD told Moses, "Get up early in
the morning and stand in Pharaoh's way as
he goes down to the river. Say to him, 'This
is what the LORD says: Let my people go, so
they can worship me. 21If you refuse, then
I will send swarms of flies on you, your officials, your people, and all the houses. The
Egyptian homes will be filled with flies, and
the ground will be covered with them. 22But
this time I will spare the region of Goshen,
where my people live. No flies will be found
there. Then you will know that I am the
LORD and that I am present even in the heart
of your land. 23I will make a clear distinction
between* my people and your people. This
miraculous sign will happen tomorrow.'"
24And the LORD did just as he had said.
A thick swarm of flies filled Pharaoh's
palace and the houses of his officials. The
whole land of Egypt was thrown into chaos
by the flies.
25Pharaoh called for Moses and Aaron.
"All right! Go ahead and offer sacrifices to
your God," he said. "But do it here in this
land."
26But Moses replied, "That wouldn't be
right. The Egyptians detest the sacrifices
that we offer to the LORD our God. Look, if
we offer our sacrifices here where the Egyptians can see us, they will stone us. 27We
must take a three-day trip into the wilderness to offer sacrifices to the LORD our God,
just as he has commanded us."
28"All right, go ahead," Pharaoh replied.
"I will let you go into the wilderness to
offer sacrifices to the LORD your God. But
don't go too far away. Now hurry and pray
for me."
29Moses answered, "As soon as I leave
you, I will pray to the LORD, and tomorrow
the swarms of flies will disappear from you
and your officials and all your people. But
I am warning you, Pharaoh, don't lie to us
again and refuse to let the people go to sacrifice to the LORD."
30So Moses left Pharaoh's palace and
pleaded with the LORD to remove all the
flies. 31And the LORD did as Moses asked
and caused the swarms of flies to disappear
from Pharaoh, his officials, and his people.
Not a single fly remained. 32But Pharaoh
again became stubborn and refused to let
the people go.

A Plague against Livestock

9 "Go back to Pharaoh," the LORD commanded Moses. "Tell him, 'This is what
the LORD, the God of the Hebrews, says: Let
my people go, so they can worship me. 2If
you continue to hold them and refuse to let
them go, 3the hand of the LORD will strike
all your livestock—your horses, donkeys,
camels, cattle, sheep, and goats—with a
deadly plague. 4But the LORD will again
make a distinction between the livestock of
the Israelites and that of the Egyptians. Not
a single one of Israel's animals will die! 5The
LORD has already set the time for the plague
to begin. He has declared that he will strike
the land tomorrow.'"

8:1 Verses 8:1-4 are numbered 7:26-29 in Hebrew text. **8:5** Verses 8:5-32 are numbered 8:1-28 in Hebrew text. **8:15** Hebrew *made his heart heavy;* also in 8:32. **8:23** As in Greek and Latin versions; Hebrew reads *I will set redemption between.*

6 And the LORD did just as he had said. The next morning all the livestock of the Egyptians died, but the Israelites didn't lose a single animal. 7 Pharaoh sent his officials to investigate, and they discovered that the Israelites had not lost a single animal! But even so, Pharaoh's heart remained stubborn,* and he still refused to let the people go.

A Plague of Festering Boils

8 Then the LORD said to Moses and Aaron, "Take handfuls of soot from a brick kiln, and have Moses toss it into the air while Pharaoh watches. 9 The ashes will spread like fine dust over the whole land of Egypt, causing festering boils to break out on people and animals throughout the land."

10 So they took soot from a brick kiln and went and stood before Pharaoh. As Pharaoh watched, Moses threw the soot into the air, and boils broke out on people and animals alike. 11 Even the magicians were unable to stand before Moses, because the boils had broken out on them and all the Egyptians. 12 But the LORD hardened Pharaoh's heart, and just as the LORD had predicted to Moses, Pharaoh refused to listen.

A Plague of Hail

13 Then the LORD said to Moses, "Get up early in the morning and stand before Pharaoh. Tell him, 'This is what the LORD, the God of the Hebrews, says: Let my people go, so they can worship me. 14 If you don't, I will send more plagues on you* and your officials and your people. Then you will know that there is no one like me in all the earth. 15 By now I could have lifted my hand and struck you and your people with a plague to wipe you off the face of the earth. 16 But I have spared you for a purpose—to show you my power* and to spread my fame throughout the earth. 17 But you still lord it over my people and refuse to let them go. 18 So tomorrow at this time I will send a hailstorm more devastating than any in all the history of Egypt. 19 Quick! Order your livestock and servants to come in from the fields to find shelter. Any person or animal left outside will die when the hail falls.'"

20 Some of Pharaoh's officials were afraid because of what the LORD had said. They quickly brought their servants and livestock in from the fields. 21 But those who paid no attention to the word of the LORD left theirs out in the open.

22 Then the LORD said to Moses, "Lift your hand toward the sky so hail may fall on the people, the livestock, and all the plants throughout the land of Egypt."

23 So Moses lifted his staff toward the sky, and the LORD sent thunder and hail, and lightning flashed toward the earth. The LORD sent a tremendous hailstorm against all the land of Egypt. 24 Never in all the history of Egypt had there been a storm like that, with such devastating hail and continuous lightning. 25 It left all of Egypt in ruins. The hail struck down everything in the open field—people, animals, and plants alike. Even the trees were destroyed. 26 The only place without hail was the region of Goshen, where the people of Israel lived.

27 Then Pharaoh quickly summoned Moses and Aaron. "This time I have sinned," he confessed. "The LORD is the righteous one, and my people and I are wrong. 28 Please beg the LORD to end this terrifying thunder and hail. We've had enough. I will let you go; you don't need to stay any longer."

29 "All right," Moses replied. "As soon as I leave the city, I will lift my hands and pray to the LORD. Then the thunder and hail will stop, and you will know that the earth

Pharaoh

The term *pharaoh* was the title of Egypt's kings. The Egyptian word, or hieroglyph (symbol), means "great house" and originally applied to the royal palace, then to the royal dynasty in that palace, and finally to the king of the dynasty himself. The rise of a new dynasty that neither knew nor cared about what Joseph had done for Egypt centuries earlier transformed Israel's peaceful existence in Egypt into a time of oppression and slavery as the new pharaoh reacted to their growing numbers (Exodus 1:8-14).

belongs to the LORD. [30]But I know that you and your officials still do not fear the LORD God."

[31](All the flax and barley were ruined by the hail, because the barley had formed heads and the flax was budding. [32]But the wheat and the emmer wheat were spared, because they had not yet sprouted from the ground.)

[33]So Moses left Pharaoh's court and went out of the city. When he lifted his hands to the LORD, the thunder and hail stopped, and the downpour ceased. [34]But when Pharaoh saw that the rain, hail, and thunder had stopped, he and his officials sinned again, and Pharaoh again became stubborn.* [35]Because his heart was hard, Pharaoh refused to let the people leave, just as the LORD had predicted through Moses.

A Plague of Locusts

10 Then the LORD said to Moses, "Return to Pharaoh and make your demands again. I have made him and his officials stubborn* so I can display my miraculous signs among them. [2]I've also done it so you can tell your children and grandchildren about how I made a mockery of the Egyptians and about the signs I displayed among them—and so you will know that I am the LORD."

[3]So Moses and Aaron went to Pharaoh and said, "This is what the LORD, the God of the Hebrews, says: How long will you refuse to submit to me? Let my people go, so they can worship me. [4]If you refuse, watch out! For tomorrow I will bring a swarm of locusts on your country. [5]They will cover the land so that you won't be able to see the ground. They will devour what little is left of your crops after the hailstorm, including all the trees growing in the fields. [6]They will overrun your palaces and the homes of your officials and all the houses in Egypt. Never in the history of Egypt have your ancestors seen a plague like this one!" And with that, Moses turned and left Pharaoh.

[7]Pharaoh's officials now came to Pharaoh and appealed to him. "How long will you let this man hold us hostage? Let the men go to worship the LORD their God! Don't you realize that Egypt lies in ruins?"

[8]So Moses and Aaron were brought back to Pharaoh. "All right," he told them, "go and worship the LORD your God. But who exactly will be going with you?"

[9]Moses replied, "We will all go—young and old, our sons and daughters, and our flocks and herds. We must all join together in celebrating a festival to the LORD."

[10]Pharaoh retorted, "The LORD will certainly need to be with you if I let you take your little ones! I can see through your evil plan. [11]Never! Only the men may go and worship the LORD, since that is what you requested." And Pharaoh threw them out of the palace.

[12]Then the LORD said to Moses, "Raise your hand over the land of Egypt to bring on the locusts. Let them cover the land and devour every plant that survived the hailstorm."

[13]So Moses raised his staff over Egypt, and the LORD caused an east wind to blow over the land all that day and through the night. When morning arrived, the east wind had brought the locusts. [14]And the locusts swarmed over the whole land of Egypt, settling in dense swarms from one end of the country to the other. It was the worst locust plague in Egyptian history, and there has never been another one like it. [15]For the locusts covered the whole country and darkened the land. They devoured every plant in the fields and all the fruit on the trees that had survived the hailstorm. Not a single leaf was left on the trees and plants throughout the land of Egypt.

[16]Pharaoh quickly summoned Moses and Aaron. "I have sinned against the LORD your God and against you," he confessed. [17]"Forgive my sin, just this once, and plead with the LORD your God to take away this death from me."

[18]So Moses left Pharaoh's court and pleaded with the LORD. [19]The LORD responded by shifting the wind, and the strong west wind blew the locusts into the Red Sea.* Not a single locust remained in all the land of Egypt. [20]But the LORD hardened Pharaoh's heart again, so he refused to let the people go.

A Plague of Darkness

[21]Then the LORD said to Moses, "Lift your hand toward heaven, and the land of Egypt will be covered with a darkness so thick you can feel it." [22]So Moses lifted his hand to the sky, and a deep darkness covered the

9:7 Hebrew *heavy.* **9:14** Hebrew *on your heart.* **9:16** Greek version reads *to display my power in you;* compare Rom 9:17. **9:34** Hebrew *made his heart heavy.* **10:1** Hebrew *have made his heart and his officials' hearts heavy.* **10:19** Hebrew *sea of reeds.*

entire land of Egypt for three days. 23During
all that time the people could not see each
other, and no one moved. But there was
light as usual where the people of Israel
lived.
24Finally, Pharaoh called for Moses. "Go
and worship the LORD," he said. "But leave
your flocks and herds here. You may even
take your little ones with you."
25"No," Moses said, "you must provide
us with animals for sacrifices and burnt offerings to the LORD our God. 26All our livestock must go with us, too; not a hoof can be
left behind. We must choose our sacrifices
for the LORD our God from among these
animals. And we won't know how we are to
worship the LORD until we get there."
27But the LORD hardened Pharaoh's heart
once more, and he would not let them go.
28"Get out of here!" Pharaoh shouted at
Moses. "I'm warning you. Never come back
to see me again! The day you see my face,
you will die!"
29"Very well," Moses replied. "I will never
see your face again."

Death for Egypt's Firstborn

11 Then the LORD said to Moses, "I will
strike Pharaoh and the land of Egypt
with one more blow. After that, Pharaoh
will let you leave this country. In fact, he
will be so eager to get rid of you that he will
force you all to leave. 2Tell all the Israelite men and women to ask their Egyptian
neighbors for articles of silver and gold."
3(Now the LORD had caused the Egyptians
to look favorably on the people of Israel.
And Moses was considered a very great man
in the land of Egypt, respected by Pharaoh's
officials and the Egyptian people alike.)
4Moses had announced to Pharaoh, "This
is what the LORD says: At midnight tonight
I will pass through the heart of Egypt. 5All
the firstborn sons will die in every family in
Egypt, from the oldest son of Pharaoh, who
sits on his throne, to the oldest son of his
lowliest servant girl who grinds the flour.
Even the firstborn of all the livestock will
die. 6Then a loud wail will rise throughout
the land of Egypt, a wail like no one has
heard before or will ever hear again. 7But
among the Israelites it will be so peaceful
that not even a dog will bark. Then you will
know that the LORD makes a distinction
between the Egyptians and the Israelites.
8All the officials of Egypt will run to me
and fall to the ground before me. 'Please
leave!' they will beg. 'Hurry! And take all
your followers with you.' Only then will
I go!" Then, burning with anger, Moses left
Pharaoh.
9Now the LORD had told Moses earlier,
"Pharaoh will not listen to you, but then
I will do even more mighty miracles in the
land of Egypt." 10Moses and Aaron performed these miracles in Pharaoh's presence, but the LORD hardened Pharaoh's
heart, and he wouldn't let the Israelites
leave the country.

The First Passover

12 While the Israelites were still in the
land of Egypt, the LORD gave the following instructions to Moses and Aaron:
2"From now on, this month will be the first
month of the year for you. 3Announce to the
whole community of Israel that on the tenth
day of this month each family must choose
a lamb or a young goat for a sacrifice, one
animal for each household. 4If a family is
too small to eat a whole animal, let them
share with another family in the neighborhood. Divide the animal according to the
size of each family and how much they can
eat. 5The animal you select must be a one-
year-old male, either a sheep or a goat, with
no defects.
6"Take special care of this chosen animal
until the evening of the fourteenth day of
this first month. Then the whole assembly
of the community of Israel must slaughter
their lamb or young goat at twilight. 7They
are to take some of the blood and smear it
on the sides and top of the doorframes of
the houses where they eat the animal. 8That
same night they must roast the meat over a
fire and eat it along with bitter salad greens
and bread made without yeast. 9Do not eat
any of the meat raw or boiled in water. The
whole animal—including the head, legs, and
internal organs—must be roasted over a fire.
10Do not leave any of it until the next morning.
Burn whatever is not eaten before morning.
11"These are your instructions for eating
this meal: Be fully dressed,* wear your
sandals, and carry your walking stick in your
hand. Eat the meal with urgency, for this is
the LORD's Passover. 12On that night I will
pass through the land of Egypt and strike
down every firstborn son and firstborn male

animal in the land of Egypt. I will execute judgment against all the gods of Egypt, for I am the LORD! [13]But the blood on your doorposts will serve as a sign, marking the houses where you are staying. When I see the blood, I will pass over you. This plague of death will not touch you when I strike the land of Egypt.

[14]"This is a day to remember. Each year, from generation to generation, you must celebrate it as a special festival to the LORD. This is a law for all time. [15]For seven days the bread you eat must be made without yeast. On the first day of the festival, remove every trace of yeast from your homes. Anyone who eats bread made with yeast during the seven days of the festival will be cut off from the community of Israel. [16]On the first day of the festival and again on the seventh day, all the people must observe an official day for holy assembly. No work of any kind may be done on these days except in the preparation of food.

[17]"Celebrate this Festival of Unleavened Bread, for it will remind you that I brought your forces out of the land of Egypt on this very day. This festival will be a permanent law for you; celebrate this day from generation to generation. [18]The bread you eat must be made without yeast from the evening of the fourteenth day of the first month until the evening of the twenty-first day of that month. [19]During those seven days, there must be no trace of yeast in your homes. Anyone who eats anything made with yeast during this week will be cut off from the community of Israel. These regulations apply both to the foreigners living among you and to the native-born Israelites. [20]During those days you must not eat anything made with yeast. Wherever you live, eat only bread made without yeast."

[21]Then Moses called all the elders of Israel together and said to them, "Go, pick out a lamb or young goat for each of your families, and slaughter the Passover animal. [22]Drain the blood into a basin. Then take a bundle of hyssop branches and dip it into the blood. Brush the hyssop across the top and sides of the doorframes of your houses. And no one may go out through the door until morning. [23]For the LORD will pass through the land to strike down the Egyptians. But when he sees the blood on the top and sides of the doorframe, the LORD will pass over your home. He will not permit his death angel to enter your house and strike you down.

[24]"Remember, these instructions are a permanent law that you and your descendants must observe forever. [25]When you enter the land the LORD has promised to give you, you will continue to observe this ceremony. [26]Then your children will ask, 'What does this ceremony mean?' [27]And you will reply, 'It is the Passover sacrifice to the LORD, for he passed over the houses of the Israelites in Egypt. And though he struck the Egyptians, he spared our families.'" When Moses had finished speaking, all the people bowed down to the ground and worshiped.

[28]So the people of Israel did just as the LORD had commanded through Moses and Aaron. [29]And that night at midnight, the LORD struck down all the firstborn sons in the land of Egypt, from the firstborn son of Pharaoh, who sat on his throne, to the firstborn son of the prisoner in the dungeon. Even the firstborn of their livestock were killed. [30]Pharaoh and all his officials and all the people of Egypt woke up during the night, and loud wailing was heard throughout the land of Egypt. There was not a single house where someone had not died.

Israel's Exodus from Egypt

[31]Pharaoh sent for Moses and Aaron during the night. "Get out!" he ordered. "Leave my people—and take the rest of the Israelites with you! Go and worship the LORD as you have requested. [32]Take your flocks and herds, as you said, and be gone. Go, but bless me as you leave." [33]All the Egyptians urged the people of Israel to get out of the land as quickly as possible, for they thought, "We will all die!"

[34]The Israelites took their bread dough before yeast was added. They wrapped their kneading boards in their cloaks and carried them on their shoulders. [35]And the people of Israel did as Moses had instructed;

12:11 Hebrew *Bind up your loins.*

▸ **12:1-39** *See **Redemption**, page 1136.*

they asked the Egyptians for clothing and
articles of silver and gold. [36]The LORD
caused the Egyptians to look favorably on
the Israelites, and they gave the Israelites
whatever they asked for. So they stripped
the Egyptians of their wealth!

[37]That night the people of Israel left
Rameses and started for Succoth. There were
about 600,000 men,* plus all the women
and children. [38]A rabble of non-Israelites
went with them, along with great flocks and
herds of livestock. [39]For bread they baked flat
cakes from the dough without yeast they had
brought from Egypt. It was made without
yeast because the people were driven out of
Egypt in such a hurry that they had no time
to prepare the bread or other food.

[40]The people of Israel had lived in Egypt*
for 430 years. [41]In fact, it was on the last day
of the 430th year that all the LORD's forces
left the land. [42]On this night the LORD kept
his promise to bring his people out of the
land of Egypt. So this night belongs to him,
and it must be commemorated every year
by all the Israelites, from generation to
generation.

Instructions for the Passover

[43]Then the LORD said to Moses and Aaron,
"These are the instructions for the festival
of Passover. No outsiders are allowed to eat
the Passover meal. [44]But any slave who has
been purchased may eat it if he has been
circumcised. [45]Temporary residents and hired
servants may not eat it. [46]Each Passover lamb
must be eaten in one house. Do not carry any
of its meat outside, and do not break any of
its bones. [47]The whole community of Israel
must celebrate this Passover festival.

[48]"If there are foreigners living among
you who want to celebrate the LORD's Passover, let all their males be circumcised.
Only then may they celebrate the Passover
with you like any native-born Israelite. But
no uncircumcised male may ever eat the
Passover meal. [49]This instruction applies to
everyone, whether a native-born Israelite or
a foreigner living among you."

[50]So all the people of Israel followed all
the LORD's commands to Moses and Aaron.
[51]On that very day the LORD brought the
people of Israel out of the land of Egypt like
an army.

Dedication of the Firstborn

13 Then the LORD said to Moses, [2]"Dedicate to me every firstborn among the
Israelites. The first offspring to be born, of
both humans and animals, belongs to me."

[3]So Moses said to the people, "This is a
day to remember forever—the day you left
Egypt, the place of your slavery. Today the
LORD has brought you out by the power of
his mighty hand. (Remember, eat no food
containing yeast.) [4]On this day in early
spring, in the month of Abib,* you have

The Passover

The Passover is one of the major festivals in the Old Testament. God gave the people of Israel this festival to commemorate their liberation from slavery in Egypt (Exodus 12; Leviticus 23:5-8; Deuteronomy 16:1-8). The Passover consisted of a ceremonial meal with lamb and unleavened bread as the main course. Its Hebrew name, *Pesach*, is related to the verb translated "to pass over," recalling how the angel of death passed over the houses of the Israelites because they had put the blood of a lamb on their doorposts, just as God had promised (Exodus 12:12-13).

The New Testament emphasizes the fact that the death of Jesus on the cross coincided with the celebration of Passover. To Jesus and his followers, that meant that he was the true Passover lamb, whose blood saves his people from sin and death (see 1 Corinthians 5:7). Hence Christians do not celebrate Passover, as the Jews still do. The Christian ceremonial meal is the Lord's Supper, which focuses on Jesus' suffering as the Lamb of God and how he brought us freedom from slavery to sin (see Matthew 26:26-28).

▶ *See also* ***Israel's Annual Calendar****, Visual Overview Z4.*

been set free. 5 You must celebrate this event in this month each year after the LORD brings you into the land of the Canaanites, Hittites, Amorites, Hivites, and Jebusites. (He swore to your ancestors that he would give you this land—a land flowing with milk and honey.) 6 For seven days the bread you eat must be made without yeast. Then on the seventh day, celebrate a feast to the LORD. 7 Eat bread without yeast during those seven days. In fact, there must be no yeast bread or any yeast at all found within the borders of your land during this time.

8 "On the seventh day you must explain to your children, 'I am celebrating what the LORD did for me when I left Egypt.' 9 This annual festival will be a visible sign to you, like a mark branded on your hand or your forehead. Let it remind you always to recite this teaching of the LORD: 'With a strong hand, the LORD rescued you from Egypt.'* 10 So observe the decree of this festival at the appointed time each year.

11 "This is what you must do when the LORD fulfills the promise he swore to you and to your ancestors. When he gives you the land where the Canaanites now live, 12 you must present all firstborn sons and firstborn male animals to the LORD, for they belong to him. 13 A firstborn donkey may be bought back from the LORD by presenting a lamb or young goat in its place. But if you do not buy it back, you must break its neck. However, you must buy back every firstborn son.

14 "And in the future, your children will ask you, 'What does all this mean?' Then you will tell them, 'With the power of his mighty hand, the LORD brought us out of Egypt, the place of our slavery. 15 Pharaoh stubbornly refused to let us go, so the LORD killed all the firstborn males throughout the land of Egypt, both people and animals. That is why I now sacrifice all the firstborn males to the LORD—except that the firstborn sons are always bought back.' 16 This ceremony will be like a mark branded on your hand or your forehead. It is a reminder that the power of the LORD's mighty hand brought us out of Egypt."

Israel's Wilderness Detour

17 When Pharaoh finally let the people go, God did not lead them along the main road that runs through Philistine territory, even though that was the shortest route to the Promised Land. God said, "If the people are faced with a battle, they might change their minds and return to Egypt." 18 So God led them in a roundabout way through the wilderness toward the Red Sea.* Thus the Israelites left Egypt like an army ready for battle.*

19 Moses took the bones of Joseph with him, for Joseph had made the sons of Israel swear to do this. He said, "God will certainly come to help you. When he does, you must take my bones with you from this place."

20 The Israelites left Succoth and camped at Etham on the edge of the wilderness. 21 The LORD went ahead of them. He guided them during the day with a pillar of cloud, and he provided light at night with a pillar of fire. This allowed them to travel by day or by night. 22 And the LORD did not remove the pillar of cloud or pillar of fire from its place in front of the people.

14 Then the LORD gave these instructions to Moses: 2 "Order the Israelites to turn back and camp by Pi-hahiroth between Migdol and the sea. Camp there along the shore, across from Baal-zephon. 3 Then Pharaoh will think, 'The Israelites are confused. They are trapped in the wilderness!' 4 And once again I will harden Pharaoh's heart, and he will chase after you.* I have planned this in order to display my glory through Pharaoh and his whole army. After this the Egyptians will know that I am the LORD!" So the Israelites camped there as they were told.

The Egyptians Pursue Israel

5 When word reached the king of Egypt that the Israelites had fled, Pharaoh and his officials changed their minds. "What have we done, letting all those Israelite slaves get away?" they asked. 6 So Pharaoh harnessed his chariot and called up his troops. 7 He took with him 600 of Egypt's best chariots, along with the rest of the chariots of Egypt, each with its commander. 8 The LORD hardened the heart of Pharaoh, the king of Egypt, so he chased after the people of Israel, who

12:37 Or *fighting men;* Hebrew reads *men on foot.*
12:40 Samaritan Pentateuch reads *in Canaan and Egypt;* Greek version reads *in Egypt and Canaan.* **13:4** Hebrew *On this day in the month of Abib.* This first month of the ancient Hebrew lunar calendar usually occurs within the months of March and April. **13:9** Or *Let it remind you always to keep the instructions of the LORD on the tip of your tongue, because with a strong hand, the LORD rescued you from Egypt.* **13:18a** Hebrew *sea of reeds.*
13:18b Greek version reads *left Egypt in the fifth generation.*
14:4 Hebrew *after them.*

had left with fists raised in defiance. [9]The Egyptians chased after them with all the forces in Pharaoh's army—all his horses and chariots, his charioteers, and his troops. The Egyptians caught up with the people of Israel as they were camped beside the shore near Pi-hahiroth, across from Baal-zephon.

[10]As Pharaoh approached, the people of Israel looked up and panicked when they saw the Egyptians overtaking them. They cried out to the LORD, [11]and they said to Moses, "Why did you bring us out here to die in the wilderness? Weren't there enough graves for us in Egypt? What have you done to us? Why did you make us leave Egypt? [12]Didn't we tell you this would happen while we were still in Egypt? We said, 'Leave us alone! Let us be slaves to the Egyptians. It's better to be a slave in Egypt than a corpse in the wilderness!'"

[13]But Moses told the people, "Don't be afraid. Just stand still and watch the LORD rescue you today. The Egyptians you see today will never be seen again. [14]The LORD himself will fight for you. Just stay calm."

Escape through the Red Sea

[15]Then the LORD said to Moses, "Why are you crying out to me? Tell the people to get moving! [16]Pick up your staff and raise your hand over the sea. Divide the water so the Israelites can walk through the middle of the sea on dry ground. [17]And I will harden the hearts of the Egyptians, and they will charge in after the Israelites. My great glory will be displayed through Pharaoh and his troops, his chariots, and his charioteers. [18]When my glory is displayed through them, all Egypt will see my glory and know that I am the LORD!"

[19]Then the angel of God, who had been leading the people of Israel, moved to the rear of the camp. The pillar of cloud also moved from the front and stood behind them. [20]The cloud settled between the Egyptian and Israelite camps. As darkness fell, the cloud turned to fire, lighting up the night. But the Egyptians and Israelites did not approach each other all night.

[21]Then Moses raised his hand over the sea, and the LORD opened up a path through the water with a strong east wind. The wind blew all that night, turning the seabed into dry land. [22]So the people of Israel walked through the middle of the sea on dry ground, with walls of water on each side!

[23]Then the Egyptians—all of Pharaoh's horses, chariots, and charioteers—chased them into the middle of the sea. [24]But just before dawn the LORD looked down on the Egyptian army from the pillar of fire and cloud, and he threw their forces into total confusion. [25]He twisted* their chariot wheels, making their chariots difficult to drive. "Let's get out of here—away from these Israelites!" the Egyptians shouted. "The LORD is fighting for them against Egypt!"

[26]When all the Israelites had reached the other side, the LORD said to Moses, "Raise your hand over the sea again. Then the waters will rush back and cover the Egyptians and

The Red Sea

An inlet of the Indian Ocean, the Red Sea separates Egypt and the Arabian Peninsula. However, it is possible that these were not the waters the Israelites actually crossed—despite tradition and Hollywood. The Hebrew text says they crossed not the Red Sea but "the Reed Sea" (Yam Suph)—see the footnotes on Exodus 13:18a and 15:4—possibly referring to one of several ancient marshy lakes within the rift that extends north from the Red Sea's western arm. In such a location "a strong east wind" (14:21) could have driven back the waters, and the Egyptians' chariot wheels could easily have gotten into difficulties (14:25). In the ancient Greek translation of the Hebrew Bible, "Reed Sea" was translated "Red Sea" (the best-known body of water in the area), and this translation has been perpetuated by tradition ever since. Considering alternative locations for the crossing doesn't take away the miraculous nature of the event, however. Wherever it occurred, God still overruled nature to ensure that his people escaped from the pursuing Egyptians, who were judged for their wickedness.

their chariots and charioteers." [27]So as the
sun began to rise, Moses raised his hand
over the sea, and the water rushed back
into its usual place. The Egyptians tried to
escape, but the LORD swept them into the
sea. [28]Then the waters returned and covered
all the chariots and charioteers—the entire
army of Pharaoh. Of all the Egyptians who
had chased the Israelites into the sea, not a
single one survived.
[29]But the people of Israel had walked
through the middle of the sea on dry
ground, as the water stood up like a wall on
both sides. [30]That is how the LORD rescued
Israel from the hand of the Egyptians that
day. And the Israelites saw the bodies of
the Egyptians washed up on the seashore.
[31]When the people of Israel saw the mighty
power that the LORD had unleashed against
the Egyptians, they were filled with awe
before him. They put their faith in the LORD
and in his servant Moses.

A Song of Deliverance

15 Then Moses and the people of Israel sang this song to the LORD:

"I will sing to the LORD,
for he has triumphed gloriously;
he has hurled both horse and rider
into the sea.
2 The LORD is my strength and my song;
he has given me victory.
This is my God, and I will praise him—
my father's God, and I will exalt him!
3 The LORD is a warrior;
Yahweh* is his name!
4 Pharaoh's chariots and army
he has hurled into the sea.
The finest of Pharaoh's officers
are drowned in the Red Sea.*
5 The deep waters gushed over them;
they sank to the bottom like a stone.

6 "Your right hand, O LORD,
is glorious in power.
Your right hand, O LORD,
smashes the enemy.
7 In the greatness of your majesty,
you overthrow those who rise against you.
You unleash your blazing fury;
it consumes them like straw.
8 At the blast of your breath,
the waters piled up!
The surging waters stood straight like a wall;
in the heart of the sea the deep waters became hard.

9 "The enemy boasted, 'I will chase them
and catch up with them.
I will plunder them
and consume them.
I will flash my sword;
my powerful hand will destroy them.'
10 But you blew with your breath,
and the sea covered them.
They sank like lead
in the mighty waters.

11 "Who is like you among the gods,
O LORD—
glorious in holiness,
awesome in splendor,
performing great wonders?
12 You raised your right hand,
and the earth swallowed our enemies.

13 "With your unfailing love you lead
the people you have redeemed.
In your might, you guide them
to your sacred home.
14 The peoples hear and tremble;
anguish grips those who live in Philistia.
15 The leaders of Edom are terrified;
the nobles of Moab tremble.
All who live in Canaan melt away;
16 terror and dread fall upon them.
The power of your arm
makes them lifeless as stone
until your people pass by, O LORD,
until the people you purchased pass by.
17 You will bring them in and plant them
on your own mountain—
the place, O LORD, reserved for your own dwelling,
the sanctuary, O Lord, that your hands have established.
18 The LORD will reign forever and ever!"

14:25 As in Greek version, Samaritan Pentateuch, and Syriac version; Hebrew reads *He removed.* **15:3** *Yahweh* is a transliteration of the proper name *YHWH* that is sometimes rendered "Jehovah"; in this translation it is usually rendered "the LORD" (note the use of small capitals). **15:4** Hebrew *sea of reeds;* also in 15:22.

▸ **15:1** *See* ***God's power,*** *page 596.*

19When Pharaoh's horses, chariots, and
charioteers rushed into the sea, the LORD
brought the water crashing down on them.
But the people of Israel had walked through
the middle of the sea on dry ground!
20Then Miriam the prophet, Aaron's sister,
took a tambourine and led all the women as
they played their tambourines and danced.
21And Miriam sang this song:

"Sing to the LORD,
for he has triumphed gloriously;
he has hurled both horse and rider
into the sea."

Bitter Water at Marah

22Then Moses led the people of Israel away
from the Red Sea, and they moved out into
the desert of Shur. They traveled in this desert
for three days without finding any water.
23When they came to the oasis of Marah, the
water was too bitter to drink. So they called
the place Marah (which means "bitter").
24Then the people complained and
turned against Moses. "What are we going
to drink?" they demanded. 25So Moses cried
out to the LORD for help, and the LORD
showed him a piece of wood. Moses threw
it into the water, and this made the water
good to drink.

It was there at Marah that the LORD set
before them the following decree as a standard
to test their faithfulness to him. 26He
said, "If you will listen carefully to the
voice of the LORD your God and do what is
right in his sight, obeying his commands
and keeping all his decrees, then I will not
make you suffer any of the diseases I sent
on the Egyptians; for I am the LORD who
heals you."
27After leaving Marah, the Israelites traveled
on to the oasis of Elim, where they
found twelve springs and seventy palm
trees. They camped there beside the water.

Manna and Quail from Heaven

16 Then the whole community of Israel
set out from Elim and journeyed into
the wilderness of Sin,* between Elim and
Mount Sinai. They arrived there on the fifteenth
day of the second month, one month
after leaving the land of Egypt.* 2There, too,
the whole community of Israel complained
about Moses and Aaron.
3"If only the LORD had killed us back in
Egypt," they moaned. "There we sat around
pots filled with meat and ate all the bread we
wanted. But now you have brought us into
this wilderness to starve us all to death."
4Then the LORD said to Moses, "Look, I'm
going to rain down food from heaven for you.
Each day the people can go out and pick up
as much food as they need for that day. I will
test them in this to see whether or not they
will follow my instructions. 5On the sixth day
they will gather food, and when they prepare
it, there will be twice as much as usual."
6So Moses and Aaron said to all the people
of Israel, "By evening you will realize it was
the LORD who brought you out of the land
of Egypt. 7In the morning you will see the
glory of the LORD, because he has heard
your complaints, which are against him,
not against us. What have we done that you
should complain about us?" 8Then Moses
added, "The LORD will give you meat to eat

Miriam

Miriam, elder sister of Moses and Aaron, played a significant role in the story of Exodus. It was she who watched from a distance when Pharaoh's daughter found Moses hidden among the reeds—a desperate attempt by his mother to save his life—and it was she who quickly offered to find a nurse for the baby, bringing Moses' own mother to do it (Exodus 2:1-10). Had it not been for Miriam, the story might have worked out completely differently, showing how even the smallest steps of faith can be used by God in ways we cannot imagine. Now, with the Israelites freed from slavery, she led the women in praise and dance (15:19-21). Sadly, she experienced God's judgment later when she criticized Moses (Numbers 12).

▶ *See also* ***Moses, the man who loved God's presence****, page 69;* ***Aaron****, page 99.*

in the evening and bread to satisfy you in the morning, for he has heard all your complaints against him. What have we done? Yes, your complaints are against the LORD, not against us."

[9]Then Moses said to Aaron, "Announce this to the entire community of Israel: 'Present yourselves before the LORD, for he has heard your complaining.'" [10]And as Aaron spoke to the whole community of Israel, they looked out toward the wilderness. There they could see the awesome glory of the LORD in the cloud.

[11]Then the LORD said to Moses, [12]"I have heard the Israelites' complaints. Now tell them, 'In the evening you will have meat to eat, and in the morning you will have all the bread you want. Then you will know that I am the LORD your God.'"

[13]That evening vast numbers of quail flew in and covered the camp. And the next morning the area around the camp was wet with dew. [14]When the dew evaporated, a flaky substance as fine as frost blanketed the ground. [15]The Israelites were puzzled when they saw it. "What is it?" they asked each other. They had no idea what it was.

And Moses told them, "It is the food the LORD has given you to eat. [16]These are the LORD's instructions: Each household should gather as much as it needs. Pick up two quarts* for each person in your tent."

[17]So the people of Israel did as they were told. Some gathered a lot, some only a little. [18]But when they measured it out,* everyone had just enough. Those who gathered a lot had nothing left over, and those who gathered only a little had enough. Each family had just what it needed.

[19]Then Moses told them, "Do not keep any of it until morning." [20]But some of them didn't listen and kept some of it until morning. But by then it was full of maggots and had a terrible smell. Moses was very angry with them.

[21]After this the people gathered the food morning by morning, each family according to its need. And as the sun became hot, the flakes they had not picked up melted and disappeared. [22]On the sixth day, they gathered twice as much as usual—four quarts* for each person instead of two. Then all the leaders of the community came and asked Moses for an explanation. [23]He told them, "This is what the LORD commanded: Tomorrow will be a day of complete rest, a holy Sabbath day set apart for the LORD. So bake or boil as much as you want today, and set aside what is left for tomorrow."

[24]So they put some aside until morning, just as Moses had commanded. And in the morning the leftover food was wholesome and good, without maggots or odor. [25]Moses said, "Eat this food today, for today is a Sabbath day dedicated to the LORD. There will be no food on the ground today. [26]You may gather the food for six days, but the seventh day is the Sabbath. There will be no food on the ground that day."

[27]Some of the people went out anyway on the seventh day, but they found no food. [28]The LORD asked Moses, "How long will these people refuse to obey my commands and instructions? [29]They must realize that the Sabbath is the LORD's gift to you. That is why he gives you a two-day supply on the sixth day, so there will be enough for two days. On the Sabbath day you must each stay in your place. Do not go out to pick up food on the seventh day." [30]So the people did not gather any food on the seventh day.

[31]The Israelites called the food manna.* It was white like coriander seed, and it tasted like honey wafers.

16:1a The geographical name *Sin* is related to *Sinai* and should not be confused with the English word *sin*. **16:1b** The Exodus had occurred on the fifteenth day of the first month (see Num 33:3). **16:16** Hebrew *1 omer* [2.2 liters]; also in 16:32, 33. **16:18** Hebrew *measured it with an omer.* **16:22** Hebrew *2 omers* [4.4 liters]. **16:31** *Manna* means "What is it?" See 16:15.

Manna: What was it?

Manna was a substance that looked like small white seeds, left on the surface of the ground when the dew lifted. It tasted like honey and looked like coriander seed. It had to be collected fresh every morning (Exodus 16:13-36; see also Numbers 11:7-9). *Manna* is a Hebrew word meaning "What is it?" This is the question that the people asked, since they had never seen anything like it before.

[32]Then Moses said, "This is what the LORD
has commanded: Fill a two-quart container
with manna to preserve it for your descendants. Then later generations will be able
to see the food I gave you in the wilderness
when I set you free from Egypt."
[33]Moses said to Aaron, "Get a jar and fill
it with two quarts of manna. Then put it in
a sacred place before the LORD to preserve
it for all future generations." [34]Aaron did
just as the LORD had commanded Moses.
He eventually placed it in the Ark of the
Covenant—in front of the stone tablets inscribed with the terms of the covenant.*
[35]So the people of Israel ate manna for
forty years until they arrived at the land
where they would settle. They ate manna
until they came to the border of the land of
Canaan.
[36]The container used to measure the
manna was an omer, which was one-tenth
of an ephah; it held about two quarts.*

Water from the Rock

17 At the LORD's command, the whole
community of Israel left the wilderness of Sin* and moved from place to place.
Eventually they camped at Rephidim, but
there was no water there for the people
to drink. [2]So once more the people complained against Moses. "Give us water to
drink!" they demanded.
"Quiet!" Moses replied. "Why are you
complaining against me? And why are you
testing the LORD?"
[3]But tormented by thirst, they continued
to argue with Moses. "Why did you bring us
out of Egypt? Are you trying to kill us, our
children, and our livestock with thirst?"
[4]Then Moses cried out to the LORD, "What
should I do with these people? They are
ready to stone me!"
[5]The LORD said to Moses, "Walk out in
front of the people. Take your staff, the one
you used when you struck the water of the
Nile, and call some of the elders of Israel to
join you. [6]I will stand before you on the rock
at Mount Sinai.* Strike the rock, and water
will come gushing out. Then the people will
be able to drink." So Moses struck the rock
as he was told, and water gushed out as the
elders looked on.
[7]Moses named the place Massah (which
means "test") and Meribah (which means
"arguing") because the people of Israel
argued with Moses and tested the LORD by
saying, "Is the LORD here with us or not?"

Israel Defeats the Amalekites

[8]While the people of Israel were still at
Rephidim, the warriors of Amalek attacked
them. [9]Moses commanded Joshua, "Choose
some men to go out and fight the army of
Amalek for us. Tomorrow, I will stand at the
top of the hill, holding the staff of God in
my hand."
[10]So Joshua did what Moses had commanded and fought the army of Amalek.
Meanwhile, Moses, Aaron, and Hur climbed
to the top of a nearby hill. [11]As long as Moses
held up the staff in his hand, the Israelites had the advantage. But whenever he
dropped his hand, the Amalekites gained
the advantage. [12]Moses' arms soon became
so tired he could no longer hold them up. So
Aaron and Hur found a stone for him to sit
on. Then they stood on each side of Moses,
holding up his hands. So his hands held
steady until sunset. [13]As a result, Joshua
overwhelmed the army of Amalek in battle.
[14]After the victory, the LORD instructed
Moses, "Write this down on a scroll as a
permanent reminder, and read it aloud to
Joshua: I will erase the memory of Amalek
from under heaven." [15]Moses built an altar
there and named it Yahweh-Nissi (which
means "the LORD is my banner"). [16]He said,
"They have raised their fist against the LORD's
throne, so now* the LORD will be at war with
Amalek generation after generation."

Jethro's Visit to Moses

18 Moses' father-in-law, Jethro, the
priest of Midian, heard about everything God had done for Moses and his
people, the Israelites. He heard especially
about how the LORD had rescued them from
Egypt.
[2]Earlier, Moses had sent his wife, Zipporah,
and his two sons back to Jethro, who had
taken them in. [3](Moses' first son was named
Gershom,* for Moses had said when the
boy was born, "I have been a foreigner in a
foreign land." [4]His second son was named
Eliezer,* for Moses had said, "The God of
my ancestors was my helper; he rescued me
from the sword of Pharaoh.") [5]Jethro, Moses'
father-in-law, now came to visit Moses in
the wilderness. He brought Moses' wife and
two sons with him, and they arrived while

Moses and the people were camped near the mountain of God. 6 Jethro had sent a message to Moses, saying, "I, Jethro, your father-in-law, am coming to see you with your wife and your two sons."

7 So Moses went out to meet his father-in-law. He bowed low and kissed him. They asked about each other's welfare and then went into Moses' tent. 8 Moses told his father-in-law everything the LORD had done to Pharaoh and Egypt on behalf of Israel. He also told about all the hardships they had experienced along the way and how the LORD had rescued his people from all their troubles. 9 Jethro was delighted when he heard about all the good things the LORD had done for Israel as he rescued them from the hand of the Egyptians.

10 "Praise the LORD," Jethro said, "for he has rescued you from the Egyptians and from Pharaoh. Yes, he has rescued Israel from the powerful hand of Egypt! 11 I know now that the LORD is greater than all other gods, because he rescued his people from the oppression of the proud Egyptians."

12 Then Jethro, Moses' father-in-law, brought a burnt offering and sacrifices to God. Aaron and all the elders of Israel came out and joined him in a sacrificial meal in God's presence.

Jethro's Wise Advice

13 The next day, Moses took his seat to hear the people's disputes against each other. They waited before him from morning till evening.

14 When Moses' father-in-law saw all that Moses was doing for the people, he asked, "What are you really accomplishing here? Why are you trying to do all this alone while everyone stands around you from morning till evening?"

15 Moses replied, "Because the people come to me to get a ruling from God. 16 When a dispute arises, they come to me, and I am the one who settles the case between the quarreling parties. I inform the people of God's decrees and give them his instructions."

17 "This is not good!" Moses' father-in-law exclaimed. 18 "You're going to wear yourself out—and the people, too. This job is too heavy a burden for you to handle all by yourself. 19 Now listen to me, and let me give you a word of advice, and may God be with you. You should continue to be the people's representative before God, bringing their disputes to him. 20 Teach them God's decrees, and give them his instructions. Show them how to conduct their lives. 21 But select from all the people some capable, honest men who fear God and hate bribes. Appoint them as leaders over groups of one thousand, one hundred, fifty, and ten. 22 They should always be available to solve the people's common disputes, but have them bring the major cases to you. Let the leaders decide the smaller matters themselves. They will help you carry the load, making the task easier for you. 23 If you follow this advice, and if God commands you to do so, then you will be able to endure the pressures, and all these people will go home in peace."

24 Moses listened to his father-in-law's advice and followed his suggestions. 25 He chose capable men from all over Israel and

16:34 Hebrew *He placed it in front of the Testimony;* see note on 25:16. **16:36** Hebrew *An omer is one-tenth of an ephah.* **17:1** The geographical name *Sin* is related to *Sinai* and should not be confused with the English word *sin.* **17:6** Hebrew *Horeb,* another name for Sinai. **17:16** Or *Hands have been lifted up to the LORD's throne, and now.* **18:3** *Gershom* sounds like a Hebrew term that means "a foreigner there." **18:4** *Eliezer* means "God is my helper."

The Amalekites

If the Israelites thought their problems were over, they were wrong. Their possession of a new water source caused the Amalekites to quickly come and attack them (chapter 17). The Amalekites were descendants of Amalek, Esau's grandson, and lived as nomads in the Sinai Peninsula and the Negev, so water was vital to them, too. Through Moses' intercession, the Israelites defeated them, and they were placed under a permanent vow of destruction. Both Saul and David would fight them in the years to come.

▶ *See also* ***Prayer as intercession****, page 922.*

appointed them as leaders over the people.
He put them in charge of groups of one thousand, one hundred, fifty, and ten. 26 These
men were always available to solve the
people's common disputes. They brought
the major cases to Moses, but they took care
of the smaller matters themselves.
27 Soon after this, Moses said good-bye to
his father-in-law, who returned to his own
land.

The LORD Reveals Himself at Sinai

19 Exactly two months after the Israelites
left Egypt,* they arrived in the wilderness of Sinai. 2 After breaking camp at Rephidim, they came to the wilderness of Sinai and
set up camp there at the base of Mount Sinai.
3 Then Moses climbed the mountain to
appear before God. The LORD called to him
from the mountain and said, "Give these instructions to the family of Jacob; announce
it to the descendants of Israel: 4 'You have
seen what I did to the Egyptians. You know
how I carried you on eagles' wings and
brought you to myself. 5 Now if you will obey
me and keep my covenant, you will be my
own special treasure from among all the
peoples on earth; for all the earth belongs to
me. 6 And you will be my kingdom of priests,
my holy nation.' This is the message you
must give to the people of Israel."
7 So Moses returned from the mountain
and called together the elders of the people
and told them everything the LORD had commanded him. 8 And all the people responded
together, "We will do everything the LORD
has commanded." So Moses brought the
people's answer back to the LORD.
9 Then the LORD said to Moses, "I will come
to you in a thick cloud, Moses, so the people
themselves can hear me when I speak with
you. Then they will always trust you."
Moses told the LORD what the people had
said. 10 Then the LORD told Moses, "Go down
and prepare the people for my arrival. Consecrate them today and tomorrow, and have
them wash their clothing. 11 Be sure they are
ready on the third day, for on that day the
LORD will come down on Mount Sinai as
all the people watch. 12 Mark off a boundary
all around the mountain. Warn the people,
'Be careful! Do not go up on the mountain
or even touch its boundaries. Anyone who
touches the mountain will certainly be put
to death. 13 No hand may touch the person or
animal that crosses the boundary; instead,
stone them or shoot them with arrows. They
must be put to death.' However, when the
ram's horn sounds a long blast, then the
people may go up on the mountain.*"
14 So Moses went down to the people. He
consecrated them for worship, and they
washed their clothes. 15 He told them, "Get
ready for the third day, and until then
abstain from having sexual intercourse."
16 On the morning of the third day,
thunder roared and lightning flashed, and
a dense cloud came down on the mountain.
There was a long, loud blast from a ram's
horn, and all the people trembled. 17 Moses
led them out from the camp to meet with
God, and they stood at the foot of the mountain. 18 All of Mount Sinai was covered with
smoke because the LORD had descended on
it in the form of fire. The smoke billowed
into the sky like smoke from a brick kiln,
and the whole mountain shook violently.
19 As the blast of the ram's horn grew louder

Mount Sinai

While scholars still debate the exact location of Mount Sinai (also called Mount Horeb and "the mountain of God"), the traditional site is Jebel Musa in the southern Sinai Peninsula. At its base is a broad plain where the Israelites could have gathered while Moses ascended the mountain—something he did not once but seven times. Sinai was an appropriate place for Moses to receive the Ten Commandments and the Law, for it was here that he had first encountered God (Exodus 3:1). The dramatic appearing of God on the mountain, accompanied by smoke, thunder, earthquakes, and fire, would be remembered for generations to come (e.g., Judges 5:5; Psalm 68:7-8; Hebrews 12:18-21).

▶ *See also **Exodus from Egypt** map, Visual Overview Z3.*

and louder, Moses spoke, and God thundered his reply. 20 The LORD came down on
the top of Mount Sinai and called Moses
to the top of the mountain. So Moses
climbed the mountain.
21 Then the LORD told Moses, "Go back
down and warn the people not to break
through the boundaries to see the LORD, or
they will die. 22 Even the priests who regularly come near to the LORD must purify
themselves so that the LORD does not break
out and destroy them."
23 "But LORD," Moses protested, "the
people cannot come up to Mount Sinai. You
already warned us. You told me, 'Mark off a
boundary all around the mountain to set it
apart as holy.'"
24 But the LORD said, "Go down and bring
Aaron back up with you. In the meantime,
do not let the priests or the people break
through to approach the LORD, or he will
break out and destroy them."
25 So Moses went down to the people and
told them what the LORD had said.

Ten Commandments for the Covenant Community

20 Then God gave the people all these
instructions*:

2 "I am the LORD your God, who rescued
you from the land of Egypt, the place of
your slavery.
3 "You must not have any other god but me.
4 "You must not make for yourself an idol of
any kind or an image of anything in the
heavens or on the earth or in the sea. 5 You
must not bow down to them or worship
them, for I, the LORD your God, am a
jealous God who will not tolerate your
affection for any other gods. I lay the sins
of the parents upon their children; the

19:1 Hebrew *In the third month after the Israelites left Egypt, on the very day*, i.e., two lunar months to the day after leaving Egypt. Compare Num 33:3. **19:13** Or *up to the mountain.* **20:1** Hebrew *all these words.*

Are the Ten Commandments still relevant today?

Spoken aloud by God to all Israel, then committed to stone tablets written by God himself, the Ten Commandments lay at the heart of God's covenant with Israel. But are they relevant to us today? If they are, why don't we keep all the other Jewish laws too?

While the New Testament teaches that Law-keeping isn't a requirement for Gentile Christians (e.g., Galatians 5:1-6), there seems to be something different about the Ten Commandments, not least their reaffirmation in some way or other by Jesus. In fact, Exodus itself distinguishes between the Ten Commandments and the rest of the Law. We read that "Moses went down to the people and repeated all the *instructions* and *regulations* the LORD had given him" (Exodus 24:3)—"instructions" referring to the Ten Commandments and "regulations" referring to "the Book of the Covenant" (Exodus 24:7), which applied those commandments to various aspects of life. This Book of the Covenant is summarized in Exodus 20:22–23:19 and further unpacked in the rest of Exodus, Leviticus, and Deuteronomy.

The same distinction is found in Deuteronomy, where Moses, recalling the Ten Commandments, said, "The LORD spoke these words to all of you. . . . *This was all he said at that time*" (Deuteronomy 5:22). Although a further unpacking then follows, it begins with, "These are the commands, decrees, and regulations that the LORD your God commanded me to teach you. You must obey them *in the land you are about to enter and occupy*" (Deuteronomy 6:1), suggesting that while the Ten Commandments are God's "words" for everyone, the further laws were specific to Israel for life in the Promised Land.

The Ten Commandments are therefore God's "words" not just for Israel, but for everyone—his wise boundaries for fulfilled living, exposing that which dehumanizes and destroys, and freeing people to enjoy life as he created it to be.

entire family is affected—even children in
the third and fourth generations of those
who reject me. 6But I lavish unfailing love
for a thousand generations on those* who
love me and obey my commands.
7"You must not misuse the name of the
LORD your God. The LORD will not let you
go unpunished if you misuse his name.
8"Remember to observe the Sabbath day
by keeping it holy. 9You have six days
each week for your ordinary work, 10but
the seventh day is a Sabbath day of rest
dedicated to the LORD your God. On
that day no one in your household may
do any work. This includes you, your
sons and daughters, your male and
female servants, your livestock, and any
foreigners living among you. 11For in six
days the LORD made the heavens, the
earth, the sea, and everything in them;
but on the seventh day he rested. That is
why the LORD blessed the Sabbath day
and set it apart as holy.
12"Honor your father and mother. Then you
will live a long, full life in the land the
LORD your God is giving you.
13"You must not murder.
14"You must not commit adultery.
15"You must not steal.
16"You must not testify falsely against your
neighbor.
17"You must not covet your neighbor's
house. You must not covet your
neighbor's wife, male or female servant,
ox or donkey, or anything else that
belongs to your neighbor."

18When the people heard the thunder and
the loud blast of the ram's horn, and when
they saw the flashes of lightning and the
smoke billowing from the mountain, they
stood at a distance, trembling with fear.
19And they said to Moses, "You speak to
us, and we will listen. But don't let God
speak directly to us, or we will die!"
20"Don't be afraid," Moses answered
them, "for God has come in this way to test
you, and so that your fear of him will keep
you from sinning!"
21As the people stood in the distance, Moses
approached the dark cloud where God was.

Proper Use of Altars

22And the LORD said to Moses, "Say this to
the people of Israel: You saw for yourselves
that I spoke to you from heaven. 23Remem-
ber, you must not make any idols of silver or
gold to rival me.
24"Build for me an altar made of earth,
and offer your sacrifices to me—your burnt
offerings and peace offerings, your sheep
and goats, and your cattle. Build my altar
wherever I cause my name to be remembered, and I will come to you and bless you.
25If you use stones to build my altar, use
only natural, uncut stones. Do not shape
the stones with a tool, for that would make
the altar unfit for holy use. 26And do not approach my altar by going up steps. If you do,
someone might look up under your clothing
and see your nakedness.

Fair Treatment of Slaves

21 "These are the regulations you must
present to Israel.
2"If you buy a Hebrew slave, he may
serve for no more than six years. Set him
free in the seventh year, and he will owe
you nothing for his freedom. 3If he was
single when he became your slave, he shall
leave single. But if he was married before
he became a slave, then his wife must be
freed with him.
4"If his master gave him a wife while he
was a slave and they had sons or daughters, then only the man will be free in the
seventh year, but his wife and children will
still belong to his master. 5But the slave may
declare, 'I love my master, my wife, and my
children. I don't want to go free.' 6If he does
this, his master must present him before
God.* Then his master must take him to the
door or doorpost and publicly pierce his ear
with an awl. After that, the slave will serve
his master for life.
7"When a man sells his daughter as a
slave, she will not be freed at the end of six
years as the men are. 8If she does not satisfy
her owner, he must allow her to be bought
back again. But he is not allowed to sell her
to foreigners, since he is the one who broke
the contract with her. 9But if the slave's
owner arranges for her to marry his son, he
may no longer treat her as a slave but as a
daughter.
10"If a man who has married a slave wife
takes another wife for himself, he must not
neglect the rights of the first wife to food,
clothing, and sexual intimacy. 11If he fails
in any of these three obligations, she may

leave as a free woman without making any payment.

Cases of Personal Injury

12"Anyone who assaults and kills another person must be put to death. 13But if it was simply an accident permitted by God, I will appoint a place of refuge where the slayer can run for safety. 14However, if someone deliberately kills another person, then the slayer must be dragged even from my altar and be put to death.

15"Anyone who strikes father or mother must be put to death.

16"Kidnappers must be put to death, whether they are caught in possession of their victims or have already sold them as slaves.

17"Anyone who dishonors* father or mother must be put to death.

18"Now suppose two men quarrel, and one hits the other with a stone or fist, and the injured person does not die but is confined to bed. 19If he is later able to walk outside again, even with a crutch, the assailant will not be punished but must compensate his victim for lost wages and provide for his full recovery.

20"If a man beats his male or female slave with a club and the slave dies as a result, the owner must be punished. 21But if the slave recovers within a day or two, then the owner shall not be punished, since the slave is his property.

22"Now suppose two men are fighting, and in the process they accidentally strike a pregnant woman so she gives birth prematurely.* If no further injury results, the man who struck the woman must pay the amount of compensation the woman's husband demands and the judges approve. 23But if there is further injury, the punishment must match the injury: a life for a life, 24an eye for an eye, a tooth for a tooth, a hand for a hand, a foot for a foot, 25a burn for a burn, a wound for a wound, a bruise for a bruise.

26"If a man hits his male or female slave in the eye and the eye is blinded, he must let the slave go free to compensate for the eye. 27And if a man knocks out the tooth of his male or female slave, he must let the slave go free to compensate for the tooth.

28"If an ox* gores a man or woman to death, the ox must be stoned, and its flesh may not be eaten. In such a case, however, the owner

20:6 Hebrew *for thousands of those.* **21:6** Or *before the judges.* **21:17** Greek version reads *Anyone who speaks disrespectfully of.* Compare Matt 15:4; Mark 7:10. **21:22** Or *so she has a miscarriage;* Hebrew reads *so her children come out.* **21:28** Or *bull, or cow;* also in 21:29-36.

Crime and punishment

Crime is the committing of an offense against society. For Israel, however, since all their laws were God-given, crime was primarily seen as an offense against God. To dishonor our fellow citizens in any way—for example, through theft, adultery, deception, or murder—is to dishonor the God in whose image they are made. God's laws were therefore given to restrain people's sinful actions that would harm their fellow citizens and dishonor God.

Crime is always a matter for the dispensing of justice—though a key Hebrew word for punishment has more to do with "correction" than "punishment." This correction takes several forms—though today's most familiar form, imprisonment, is completely disregarded in the Bible. The primary biblical means of dealing with crime is *compensation*—making good the loss caused, often together with an added penalty (e.g., Exodus 21:18-19; 22:1). The death penalty was imposed for willful (though not accidental) murder (Exodus 21:12-14) and willful negligence (e.g., Exodus 21:28-32). Punishment could not exceed the crime, however; the Law restrained it to "a life for a life, an eye for an eye, a tooth for a tooth" (Exodus 21:23-24).

The prescribed method of execution was stoning. In cases of public offense (e.g., blasphemy and adultery), the whole community had to participate in it. While stoning may seem barbaric today, it was merciful compared to many methods of execution in surrounding nations.

will not be held liable. [29]But suppose the ox had a reputation for goring, and the owner had been informed but failed to keep it under control. If the ox then kills someone, it must be stoned, and the owner must also be put to death. [30]However, the dead person's relatives may accept payment to compensate for the loss of life. The owner of the ox may redeem his life by paying whatever is demanded.

[31]"The same regulation applies if the ox gores a boy or a girl. [32]But if the ox gores a slave, either male or female, the animal's owner must pay the slave's owner thirty silver coins,* and the ox must be stoned.

[33]"Suppose someone digs or uncovers a pit and fails to cover it, and then an ox or a donkey falls into it. [34]The owner of the pit must pay full compensation to the owner of the animal, but then he gets to keep the dead animal.

[35]"If someone's ox injures a neighbor's ox and the injured ox dies, then the two owners must sell the live ox and divide the price equally between them. They must also divide the dead animal. [36]But if the ox had a reputation for goring, yet its owner failed to keep it under control, he must pay full compensation—a live ox for the dead one—but he may keep the dead ox.

Protection of Property

22 [1]*"If someone steals an ox* or sheep and then kills or sells it, the thief must pay back five oxen for each ox stolen, and four sheep for each sheep stolen.

[2]*"If a thief is caught in the act of breaking into a house and is struck and killed in the process, the person who killed the thief is not guilty of murder. [3]But if it happens in daylight, the one who killed the thief is guilty of murder.

"A thief who is caught must pay in full for everything he stole. If he cannot pay, he must be sold as a slave to pay for his theft. [4]If someone steals an ox or a donkey or a sheep and it is found in the thief's possession, then the thief must pay double the value of the stolen animal.

[5]"If an animal is grazing in a field or vineyard and the owner lets it stray into someone else's field to graze, then the animal's owner must pay compensation from the best of his own grain or grapes.

[6]"If you are burning thornbushes and the fire gets out of control and spreads into another person's field, destroying the sheaves or the uncut grain or the whole crop, the one who started the fire must pay for the lost crop.

[7]"Suppose someone leaves money or goods with a neighbor for safekeeping, and they are stolen from the neighbor's house. If the thief is caught, the compensation is double the value of what was stolen. [8]But if the thief is not caught, the neighbor must appear before God,* who will determine if he stole the property.

[9]"Suppose there is a dispute between two people who both claim to own a particular ox, donkey, sheep, article of clothing, or any lost property. Both parties must come before God, and the person whom God declares* guilty must pay double compensation to the other.

[10]"Now suppose someone leaves a donkey, ox, sheep, or any other animal with a neighbor for safekeeping, but it dies or is injured or is taken away, and no one sees what happened. [11]The neighbor must then take an oath in the presence of the LORD. If the LORD confirms that the neighbor did not steal the property, the owner must accept the verdict, and no payment will be required. [12]But if the animal was indeed stolen, the guilty person must pay compensation to the owner. [13]If it was torn to pieces by a wild animal, the remains of the carcass must be shown as evidence, and no compensation will be required.

[14]"If someone borrows an animal from a neighbor and it is injured or dies when the owner is absent, the person who borrowed it must pay full compensation. [15]But if the owner was present, no compensation is required. And no compensation is required if the animal was rented, for this loss is covered by the rental fee.

Social Responsibility

[16]"If a man seduces a virgin who is not engaged to anyone and has sex with her, he must pay the customary bride price and marry her. [17]But if her father refuses to let him marry her, the man must still pay him an amount equal to the bride price of a virgin.

[18]"You must not allow a sorceress to live.

[19]"Anyone who has sexual relations with an animal must certainly be put to death.

[20]"Anyone who sacrifices to any god other than the LORD must be destroyed.*

21 “You must not mistreat or oppress foreigners in any way. Remember, you yourselves were once foreigners in the land of
Egypt.
22 “You must not exploit a widow or an
orphan. 23 If you exploit them in any way
and they cry out to me, then I will certainly
hear their cry. 24 My anger will blaze against
you, and I will kill you with the sword. Then
your wives will be widows and your children fatherless.
25 “If you lend money to any of my people
who are in need, do not charge interest as
a money lender would. 26 If you take your
neighbor’s cloak as security for a loan, you
must return it before sunset. 27 This coat may
be the only blanket your neighbor has. How
can a person sleep without it? If you do not
return it and your neighbor cries out to me
for help, then I will hear, for I am merciful.
28 “You must not dishonor God or curse
any of your rulers.
29 “You must not hold anything back when
you give me offerings from your crops and
your wine.
“You must give me your firstborn sons.
30 “You must also give me the firstborn
of your cattle, sheep, and goats. But leave
the newborn animal with its mother for
seven days; then give it to me on the eighth
day.
31 “You must be my holy people. Therefore, do not eat any animal that has been
torn up and killed by wild animals. Throw
it to the dogs.

A Call for Justice

23 “You must not pass along false
rumors. You must not cooperate with
evil people by lying on the witness stand.
2 “You must not follow the crowd in doing
wrong. When you are called to testify in a
dispute, do not be swayed by the crowd to
twist justice. 3 And do not slant your testimony in favor of a person just because that
person is poor.
4 “If you come upon your enemy’s ox or
donkey that has strayed away, take it back
to its owner. 5 If you see that the donkey of
someone who hates you has collapsed under
its load, do not walk by. Instead, stop and
help.
6 “In a lawsuit, you must not deny justice
to the poor.
7 “Be sure never to charge anyone falsely
with evil. Never sentence an innocent or
blameless person to death, for I never
declare a guilty person to be innocent.
8 “Take no bribes, for a bribe makes you
ignore something that you clearly see.
A bribe makes even a righteous person twist
the truth.
9 “You must not oppress foreigners. You
know what it’s like to be a foreigner, for you
yourselves were once foreigners in the land
of Egypt.
10 “Plant and harvest your crops for six
years, 11 but let the land be renewed and lie
uncultivated during the seventh year. Then
let the poor among you harvest whatever
grows on its own. Leave the rest for wild
animals to eat. The same applies to your
vineyards and olive groves.
12 “You have six days each week for your
ordinary work, but on the seventh day you
must stop working. This gives your ox and
your donkey a chance to rest. It also allows
your slaves and the foreigners living among
you to be refreshed.
13 “Pay close attention to all my instructions.
You must not call on the name of any other
gods. Do not even speak their names.

Three Annual Festivals

14 “Each year you must celebrate three festivals in my honor. 15 First, celebrate the Festival of Unleavened Bread. For seven days the
bread you eat must be made without yeast,
just as I commanded you. Celebrate this festival annually at the appointed time in early
spring, in the month of Abib,* for that is the
anniversary of your departure from Egypt.
No one may appear before me without an
offering.
16 “Second, celebrate the Festival of
Harvest,* when you bring me the first crops
of your harvest.
“Finally, celebrate the Festival of the
Final Harvest* at the end of the harvest

21:32 Hebrew *30 shekels of silver,* about 12 ounces or 342 grams in weight. **22:1a** Verse 22:1 is numbered 21:37 in Hebrew text. **22:1b** Or *bull,* or *cow;* also in 22:4, 9, 10. **22:2** Verses 22:2-31 are numbered 22:1-30 in Hebrew text. **22:8** Or *before the judges.* **22:9** Or *before the judges, and the person whom the judges declare.* **22:20** The Hebrew term used here refers to the complete consecration of things or people to the LORD, either by destroying them or by giving them as an offering. **23:15** Hebrew *appointed time in the month of Abib.* This first month of the ancient Hebrew lunar calendar usually occurs within the months of March and April. **23:16a** Or *Festival of Weeks.* This was later called the Festival of Pentecost (see Acts 2:1). It is celebrated today as Shavuot (or Shabuoth). **23:16b** Or *Festival of Ingathering.* This was later called the Festival of Shelters or Festival of Tabernacles (see Lev 23:33-36). It is celebrated today as Sukkot (or Succoth).

season, when you have harvested all the
crops from your fields. 17 At these three times
each year, every man in Israel must appear
before the Sovereign, the LORD.

18 "You must not offer the blood of my sacrificial offerings together with any baked
goods containing yeast. And do not leave
the fat from the festival offerings until the
next morning.

19 "As you harvest your crops, bring the
very best of the first harvest to the house of
the LORD your God.

"You must not cook a young goat in its
mother's milk.

A Promise of the LORD's Presence

20 "See, I am sending an angel before you to
protect you on your journey and lead you
safely to the place I have prepared for you.
21 Pay close attention to him, and obey his instructions. Do not rebel against him, for he
is my representative, and he will not forgive
your rebellion. 22 But if you are careful to obey
him, following all my instructions, then I
will be an enemy to your enemies, and I will
oppose those who oppose you. 23 For my angel
will go before you and bring you into the land
of the Amorites, Hittites, Perizzites, Canaanites, Hivites, and Jebusites, so you may live
there. And I will destroy them completely.
24 You must not worship the gods of these
nations or serve them in any way or imitate
their evil practices. Instead, you must utterly
destroy them and smash their sacred pillars.

25 "You must serve only the LORD your
God. If you do, I* will bless you with food
and water, and I will protect you from
illness. 26 There will be no miscarriages or
infertility in your land, and I will give you
long, full lives.

27 "I will send my terror ahead of you and
create panic among all the people whose
lands you invade. I will make all your enemies
turn and run. 28 I will send terror* ahead of
you to drive out the Hivites, Canaanites, and
Hittites. 29 But I will not drive them out in a
single year, because the land would become
desolate and the wild animals would multiply and threaten you. 30 I will drive them out
a little at a time until your population has
increased enough to take possession of the
land. 31 And I will fix your boundaries from
the Red Sea to the Mediterranean Sea,* and
from the eastern wilderness to the Euphrates River.* I will hand over to you the people
now living in the land, and you will drive
them out ahead of you.

32 "Make no treaties with them or their
gods. 33 They must not live in your land, or
they will cause you to sin against me. If you
serve their gods, you will be caught in the
trap of idolatry."

Israel Accepts the LORD's Covenant

24 Then the LORD instructed Moses:
"Come up here to me, and bring
along Aaron, Nadab, Abihu, and seventy
of Israel's elders. All of you must worship
from a distance. 2 Only Moses is allowed to
come near to the LORD. The others must not
come near, and none of the other people
are allowed to climb up the mountain with
him."

3 Then Moses went down to the people
and repeated all the instructions and regulations the LORD had given him. All the
people answered with one voice, "We will
do everything the LORD has commanded."

4 Then Moses carefully wrote down all the
LORD's instructions. Early the next morning
Moses got up and built an altar at the foot of
the mountain. He also set up twelve pillars,
one for each of the twelve tribes of Israel.
5 Then he sent some of the young Israelite

The Book of the Covenant

The Book of the Covenant that Moses read to the Israelites (Exodus 24:7) would have included all the commandments that God had given him (20:22–23:19) and that he had written down—in contrast to the Ten Commandments, which were first spoken aloud by God and then later written down on stone tablets, the Bible says, by God himself (31:18). This Book of the Covenant is an unpacking and explaining of the Ten Commandments, and together they formed the framework of the covenant between God and Israel.

men to present burnt offerings and to sacrifice bulls as peace offerings to the LORD. 6Moses drained half the blood from these animals into basins. The other half he splattered against the altar.

7Then he took the Book of the Covenant and read it aloud to the people. Again they all responded, "We will do everything the LORD has commanded. We will obey."

8Then Moses took the blood from the basins and splattered it over the people, declaring, "Look, this blood confirms the covenant the LORD has made with you in giving you these instructions."

9Then Moses, Aaron, Nadab, Abihu, and the seventy elders of Israel climbed up the mountain. 10There they saw the God of Israel. Under his feet there seemed to be a surface of brilliant blue lapis lazuli, as clear as the sky itself. 11And though these nobles of Israel gazed upon God, he did not destroy them. In fact, they ate a covenant meal, eating and drinking in his presence!

12Then the LORD said to Moses, "Come up to me on the mountain. Stay there, and I will give you the tablets of stone on which I have inscribed the instructions and commands so you can teach the people." 13So Moses and his assistant Joshua set out, and Moses climbed up the mountain of God.

14Moses told the elders, "Stay here and wait for us until we come back. Aaron and Hur are here with you. If anyone has a dispute while I am gone, consult with them."

15Then Moses climbed up the mountain, and the cloud covered it. 16And the glory of the LORD settled down on Mount Sinai, and the cloud covered it for six days. On the seventh day the LORD called to Moses from inside the cloud. 17To the Israelites at the foot of the mountain, the glory of the LORD appeared at the summit like a consuming fire. 18Then Moses disappeared into the cloud as he climbed higher up the mountain. He remained on the mountain forty days and forty nights.

Offerings for the Tabernacle

25 The LORD said to Moses, 2"Tell the people of Israel to bring me their sacred offerings. Accept the contributions from all whose hearts are moved to offer them. 3Here is a list of sacred offerings you may accept from them:

gold, silver, and bronze;
4 blue, purple, and scarlet thread;
fine linen and goat hair for cloth;
5 tanned ram skins and fine goatskin leather;
acacia wood;
6 olive oil for the lamps;
spices for the anointing oil and the fragrant incense;
7 onyx stones, and other gemstones to be set in the ephod and the priest's chestpiece.

8"Have the people of Israel build me a holy sanctuary so I can live among them. 9You must build this Tabernacle and its furnishings exactly according to the pattern I will show you.

Plans for the Ark of the Covenant

10"Have the people make an Ark of acacia wood—a sacred chest 45 inches long, 27 inches wide, and 27 inches high.* 11Overlay it inside and outside with pure gold, and run a molding of gold all around it. 12Cast four gold rings and attach them to its four feet, two rings on each side. 13Make poles from acacia wood, and overlay them with gold. 14Insert the poles into the rings at the sides of the Ark to carry it. 15These carrying poles must stay inside the rings; never remove them. 16When the Ark is finished, place inside it the stone tablets inscribed with the terms of the covenant,* which I will give to you.

17"Then make the Ark's cover—the place of atonement—from pure gold. It must be 45 inches long and 27 inches wide.* 18Then make two cherubim from hammered gold, and place them on the two ends of the atonement cover. 19Mold the cherubim on each end of the atonement cover, making it all of one piece of gold. 20The cherubim

23:25 As in Greek and Latin versions; Hebrew reads *he.*
23:28 Often rendered *the hornet.* The meaning of the Hebrew is uncertain. **23:31a** Hebrew *from the sea of reeds to the sea of the Philistines.* **23:31b** Hebrew *from the wilderness to the river.* **25:10** Hebrew *2.5 cubits* [115 centimeters] *long, 1.5 cubits* [69 centimeters] *wide, and 1.5 cubits high.* **25:16** Hebrew *Place inside the Ark the Testimony;* similarly in 25:21. The Hebrew word for "testimony" refers to the terms of the LORD's covenant with Israel as written on stone tablets, and also to the covenant itself.
25:17 Hebrew *2.5 cubits* [115 centimeters] *long and 1.5 cubits* [69 centimeters] *wide.*

▸ **25:10** *See The Ark of the Covenant, page 311.*

will face each other and look down on the
atonement cover. With their wings spread
above it, they will protect it. 21Place inside
the Ark the stone tablets inscribed with the
terms of the covenant, which I will give to
you. Then put the atonement cover on top
of the Ark. 22I will meet with you there and
talk to you from above the atonement cover
between the gold cherubim that hover over
the Ark of the Covenant.* From there I will
give you my commands for the people of
Israel.

Plans for the Table

23"Then make a table of acacia wood,
36 inches long, 18 inches wide, and 27 inches
high.* 24Overlay it with pure gold and run a
gold molding around the edge. 25Decorate it
with a 3-inch border* all around, and run a
gold molding along the border. 26Make four
gold rings for the table and attach them
at the four corners next to the four legs.
27Attach the rings near the border to hold the
poles that are used to carry the table. 28Make
these poles from acacia wood, and overlay
them with gold. 29Make special containers
of pure gold for the table—bowls, ladles,
pitchers, and jars—to be used in pouring
out liquid offerings. 30Place the Bread of the
Presence on the table to remain before me
at all times.

Plans for the Lampstand

31"Make a lampstand of pure, hammered
gold. Make the entire lampstand and its
decorations of one piece—the base, center
stem, lamp cups, buds, and petals. 32Make it
with six branches going out from the center
stem, three on each side. 33Each of the six
branches will have three lamp cups shaped
like almond blossoms, complete with buds
and petals. 34Craft the center stem of the
lampstand with four lamp cups shaped like
almond blossoms, complete with buds and
petals. 35There will also be an almond bud
beneath each pair of branches where the
six branches extend from the center stem.
36The almond buds and branches must all
be of one piece with the center stem, and
they must be hammered from pure gold.
37Then make the seven lamps for the lampstand, and set them so they reflect their
light forward. 38The lamp snuffers and trays
must also be made of pure gold. 39You will
need 75 pounds* of pure gold for the lampstand and its accessories.

The Tabernacle

God instructed the people of Israel to make a special tent that would serve as the focal point of Israel's worship. The idea was that the people would carry the tent with them on the journey to the Promised Land. When they set up camp, they would put the Tabernacle right in the center, signifying that God was in the midst of his people.

The Tabernacle was surrounded by a courtyard where the people gathered, and the tent itself was divided into two parts by a curtain. The main section was called the Holy Place, and the innermost area the Most Holy Place (the Holy of Holies). Only the high priest was allowed to enter the latter, and only on the Day of Atonement (see Leviticus 16).

The Tabernacle furniture included the washbasin and the bronze altar of burnt offering in the courtyard; the gold incense altar, the gold lampstand, and the table for the bread of God's presence in the Holy Place; and the Ark of the Covenant with its cherubim cover in the Most Holy Place. Each of these represented different aspects of God's presence and of the covenant he had made with Israel. The Tabernacle was also equipped with various items for offering the sacrifices and sprinkling the blood of the sacrificial animals, such as sprinkling bowls, ladles, forks, and shovels. Censers were also used for offering incense or carrying burning coals.

▶ *See also* ***The tribes and the Tabernacle****, page 154.*

40“Be sure that you make everything according to the pattern I have shown you
here on the mountain.

Plans for the Tabernacle

26 “Make the Tabernacle from ten curtains of finely woven linen. Decorate
the curtains with blue, purple, and scarlet
thread and with skillfully embroidered
cherubim. 2These ten curtains must all be
exactly the same size—42 feet long and
6 feet wide.* 3Join five of these curtains together to make one long curtain, then join
the other five into a second long curtain.
4Put loops of blue yarn along the edge of
the last curtain in each set. 5The fifty loops
along the edge of one curtain are to match
the fifty loops along the edge of the other
curtain. 6Then make fifty gold clasps and
fasten the long curtains together with the
clasps. In this way, the Tabernacle will be
made of one continuous piece.

7“Make eleven curtains of goat-hair cloth
to serve as a tent covering for the Tabernacle. 8These eleven curtains must all be
exactly the same size—45 feet long and
6 feet wide.* 9Join five of these curtains together to make one long curtain, and join
the other six into a second long curtain.
Allow 3 feet of material from the second
set of curtains to hang over the front* of
the sacred tent. 10Make fifty loops for one
edge of each large curtain. 11Then make fifty
bronze clasps, and fasten the loops of the
long curtains with the clasps. In this way,
the tent covering will be made of one continuous piece. 12The remaining 3 feet* of this
tent covering will be left to hang over the
back of the Tabernacle. 13Allow 18 inches*
of remaining material to hang down over
each side, so the Tabernacle is completely
covered. 14Complete the tent covering with
a protective layer of tanned ram skins and a
layer of fine goatskin leather.

15“For the framework of the Tabernacle,
construct frames of acacia wood. 16Each
frame must be 15 feet high and 27 inches
wide,* 17with two pegs under each frame.
Make all the frames identical. 18Make
twenty of these frames to support the curtains on the south side of the Tabernacle.
19Also make forty silver bases—two bases
under each frame, with the pegs fitting securely into the bases. 20For the north side
of the Tabernacle, make another twenty
frames, 21with their forty silver bases,
two bases under each frame. 22Make six
frames for the rear—the west side of the
Tabernacle—23along with two additional
frames to reinforce the rear corners of the
Tabernacle. 24These corner frames will be
matched at the bottom and firmly attached
at the top with a single ring, forming a
single corner unit. Make both of these
corner units the same way. 25So there will
be eight frames at the rear of the Tabernacle, set in sixteen silver bases—two bases
under each frame.

26“Make crossbars of acacia wood to link
the frames, five crossbars for the north side
of the Tabernacle 27and five for the south
side. Also make five crossbars for the rear
of the Tabernacle, which will face west.
28The middle crossbar, attached halfway up
the frames, will run all the way from one
end of the Tabernacle to the other. 29Overlay
the frames with gold, and make gold rings
to hold the crossbars. Overlay the crossbars
with gold as well.

30“Set up this Tabernacle according to the
pattern you were shown on the mountain.

31“For the inside of the Tabernacle, make
a special curtain of finely woven linen.
Decorate it with blue, purple, and scarlet
thread and with skillfully embroidered
cherubim. 32Hang this curtain on gold
hooks attached to four posts of acacia
wood. Overlay the posts with gold, and set
them in four silver bases. 33Hang the inner
curtain from clasps, and put the Ark of
the Covenant* in the room behind it. This
curtain will separate the Holy Place from
the Most Holy Place.

34“Then put the Ark's cover—the place of
atonement—on top of the Ark of the Covenant inside the Most Holy Place. 35Place
the table outside the inner curtain on the
north side of the Tabernacle, and place the
lampstand across the room on the south
side.

36“Make another curtain for the entrance
to the sacred tent. Make it of finely woven

25:22 Or *Ark of the Testimony.* **25:23** Hebrew *2 cubits* [92 centimeters] *long, 1 cubit* [46 centimeters] *wide, and 1.5 cubits* [69 centimeters] *high.* **25:25** Hebrew *a border of a handbreadth* [8 centimeters]. **25:39** Hebrew *1 talent* [34 kilograms]. **26:2** Hebrew *28 cubits* [12.9 meters] *long and 4 cubits* [1.8 meters] *wide.* **26:8** Hebrew *30 cubits* [13.8 meters] *long and 4 cubits* [1.8 meters] *wide.* **26:9** Hebrew *Double over the sixth sheet at the front.* **26:12** Hebrew *The half sheet that is left over.* **26:13** Hebrew *1 cubit* [46 centimeters]. **26:16** Hebrew *10 cubits* [4.6 meters] *high and 1.5 cubits* [69 centimeters] *wide.* **26:33** Or *Ark of the Testimony;* also in 26:34.

linen and embroider it with exquisite designs, using blue, purple, and scarlet thread. 37 Craft five posts from acacia wood. Overlay them with gold, and hang the curtain from them with gold hooks. Cast five bronze bases for the posts.

Plans for the Altar of Burnt Offering

27 "Using acacia wood, construct a square altar 7½ feet wide, 7½ feet long, and 4½ feet high.* 2 Make horns for each of its four corners so that the horns and altar are all one piece. Overlay the altar with bronze. 3 Make ash buckets, shovels, basins, meat forks, and firepans, all of bronze. 4 Make a bronze grating for it, and attach four bronze rings at its four corners. 5 Install the grating halfway down the side of the altar, under the ledge. 6 For carrying the altar, make poles from acacia wood, and overlay them with bronze. 7 Insert the poles through the rings on the two sides of the altar. 8 The altar must be hollow, made from planks. Build it just as you were shown on the mountain.

Plans for the Courtyard

9 "Then make the courtyard for the Tabernacle, enclosed with curtains made of finely woven linen. On the south side, make the curtains 150 feet long.* 10 They will be held up by twenty posts set securely in twenty bronze bases. Hang the curtains with silver hooks and rings. 11 Make the curtains the same on the north side—150 feet of curtains held up by twenty posts set securely in bronze bases. Hang the curtains with silver hooks and rings. 12 The curtains on the west end of the courtyard will be 75 feet long,* supported by ten posts set into ten bases. 13 The east end of the courtyard, the front, will also be 75 feet long. 14 The courtyard entrance will be on the east end, flanked by two curtains. The curtain on the right side will be 22½ feet long,* supported by three posts set into three bases. 15 The curtain on the left side will also be 22½ feet long, supported by three posts set into three bases.

16 "For the entrance to the courtyard, make a curtain that is 30 feet long.* Make it from finely woven linen, and decorate it with beautiful embroidery in blue, purple, and scarlet thread. Support it with four posts, each securely set in its own base. 17 All the posts around the courtyard must have silver rings and hooks and bronze bases. 18 So the entire courtyard will be 150 feet long and 75 feet wide, with curtain walls 7½ feet high,* made from finely woven linen. The bases for the posts will be made of bronze.

19 "All the articles used in the rituals of the Tabernacle, including all the tent pegs used to support the Tabernacle and the courtyard curtains, must be made of bronze.

Light for the Tabernacle

20 "Command the people of Israel to bring you pure oil of pressed olives for the light, to keep the lamps burning continually. 21 The lampstand will stand in the Tabernacle, in front of the inner curtain that shields the Ark of the Covenant.* Aaron and his sons must keep the lamps burning in the LORD's presence all night. This is a permanent law for the people of Israel, and it must be observed from generation to generation.

Clothing for the Priests

28 "Call for your brother, Aaron, and his sons, Nadab, Abihu, Eleazar, and Ithamar. Set them apart from the rest of the people of Israel so they may minister to me and be my priests. 2 Make sacred garments for Aaron that are glorious and beautiful. 3 Instruct all the skilled craftsmen whom I have filled with the spirit of wisdom. Have them make garments for Aaron that will distinguish him as a priest set apart for my service. 4 These are the garments they are to make: a chestpiece, an ephod, a robe, a patterned tunic, a turban, and a sash. They are to make these sacred garments for your brother, Aaron, and his sons to wear when they serve me as priests. 5 So give them fine linen cloth, gold thread, and blue, purple, and scarlet thread.

Design of the Ephod

6 "The craftsmen must make the ephod of finely woven linen and skillfully embroider it with gold and with blue, purple, and scarlet thread. 7 It will consist of two pieces, front and back, joined at the shoulders with two shoulder-pieces. 8 The decorative sash will be made of the same materials: finely woven linen embroidered with gold and with blue, purple, and scarlet thread.

9 "Take two onyx stones, and engrave on

them the names of the tribes of Israel. [10]Six
names will be on each stone, arranged in
the order of the births of the original sons
of Israel. [11]Engrave these names on the two
stones in the same way a jeweler engraves
a seal. Then mount the stones in settings of
gold filigree. [12]Fasten the two stones on the
shoulder-pieces of the ephod as a reminder
that Aaron represents the people of Israel.
Aaron will carry these names on his shoulders as a constant reminder whenever he
goes before the LORD. [13]Make the settings of
gold filigree, [14]then braid two cords of pure
gold and attach them to the filigree settings
on the shoulders of the ephod.

Design of the Chestpiece

[15]"Then, with great skill and care, make a
chestpiece to be worn for seeking a decision from God.* Make it to match the ephod,
using finely woven linen embroidered with
gold and with blue, purple, and scarlet
thread. [16]Make the chestpiece of a single
piece of cloth folded to form a pouch nine
inches* square. [17]Mount four rows of gemstones* on it. The first row will contain a
red carnelian, a pale-green peridot, and an
emerald. [18]The second row will contain a
turquoise, a blue lapis lazuli, and a white
moonstone. [19]The third row will contain
an orange jacinth, an agate, and a purple
amethyst. [20]The fourth row will contain
a blue-green beryl, an onyx, and a green
jasper. All these stones will be set in gold
filigree. [21]Each stone will represent one of
the twelve sons of Israel, and the name of
that tribe will be engraved on it like a seal.
[22]"To attach the chestpiece to the ephod,
make braided cords of pure gold thread.
[23]Then make two gold rings and attach
them to the top corners of the chestpiece.
[24]Tie the two gold cords to the two rings on
the chestpiece. [25]Tie the other ends of the
cords to the gold settings on the shoulder-
pieces of the ephod. [26]Then make two more
gold rings and attach them to the inside
edges of the chestpiece next to the ephod.
[27]And make two more gold rings and attach
them to the front of the ephod, below the
shoulder-pieces, just above the knot where
the decorative sash is fastened to the ephod.
[28]Then attach the bottom rings of the chestpiece to the rings on the ephod with blue
cords. This will hold the chestpiece securely
to the ephod above the decorative sash.
[29]"In this way, Aaron will carry the names
of the tribes of Israel on the sacred chestpiece* over his heart when he goes into
the Holy Place. This will be a continual reminder that he represents the people when
he comes before the LORD. [30]Insert the Urim
and Thummim into the sacred chestpiece so
they will be carried over Aaron's heart when
he goes into the LORD's presence. In this way,
Aaron will always carry over his heart the
objects used to determine the LORD's will for
his people whenever he goes in before the
LORD.

27:1 Hebrew *5 cubits* [2.3 meters] *wide, 5 cubits long, a square, and 3 cubits* [1.4 meters] *high.* **27:9** Hebrew *100 cubits* [46 meters]; also in 27:11. **27:12** Hebrew *50 cubits* [23 meters]; also in 27:13. **27:14** Hebrew *15 cubits* [6.9 meters]; also in 27:15. **27:16** Hebrew *20 cubits* [9.2 meters]. **27:18** Hebrew *100 cubits* [46 meters] *long and 50 by 50* [23 meters] *wide and 5 cubits* [2.3 meters] *high.* **27:21** Hebrew *in the Tent of Meeting, outside the inner curtain that is in front of the Testimony.* See note on 25:16. **28:15** Hebrew *a chestpiece for decision.* **28:16** Hebrew *1 span* [23 centimeters]. **28:17** The identification of some of these gemstones is uncertain. **28:29** Hebrew *the chestpiece for decision;* also in 28:30. See 28:15.

Aaron

Having served as Moses' spokesman in Egypt (Exodus 4:16; 6:28–7:7), Aaron was now honored by being appointed Israel's first high priest, with his four sons appointed as priests alongside him (Exodus 28:1; Leviticus 8). Their descendants would serve forever as Israel's priests.

Sadly, Aaron was easily swayed by others, with disastrous consequences. On one occasion he made a gold calf-idol when the Israelites felt Moses wasn't returning from Sinai (Exodus 32), on another he joined in a family revolt against Moses out of jealousy (Numbers 12), and at the end of his life he was not permitted to enter Canaan because he had joined in Moses' anger (Numbers 20:1-12, 22-29).

▶ *See also* ***Moses, the man who loved God's presence****, page 69.*

Additional Clothing for the Priests

31“Make the robe that is worn with the ephod from a single piece of blue cloth, 32with an opening for Aaron’s head in the middle of it. Reinforce the opening with a woven collar* so it will not tear. 33Make pomegranates out of blue, purple, and scarlet yarn, and attach them to the hem of the robe, with gold bells between them. 34The gold bells and pomegranates are to alternate all around the hem. 35Aaron will wear this robe whenever he ministers before the LORD, and the bells will tinkle as he goes in and out of the LORD’s presence in the Holy Place. If he wears it, he will not die.

36“Next make a medallion of pure gold, and engrave it like a seal with these words: HOLY TO THE LORD. 37Attach the medallion with a blue cord to the front of Aaron’s turban, where it must remain. 38Aaron must wear it on his forehead so he may take on himself any guilt of the people of Israel when they consecrate their sacred offerings. He must always wear it on his forehead so the LORD will accept the people.

39“Weave Aaron’s patterned tunic from fine linen cloth. Fashion the turban from this linen as well. Also make a sash, and decorate it with colorful embroidery.

40“For Aaron’s sons, make tunics, sashes, and special head coverings that are glorious and beautiful. 41Clothe your brother, Aaron, and his sons with these garments, and then anoint and ordain them. Consecrate them so they can serve as my priests. 42Also make linen undergarments for them, to be worn next to their bodies, reaching from their hips to their thighs. 43These must be worn whenever Aaron and his sons enter the Tabernacle* or approach the altar in the Holy Place to perform their priestly duties. Then they will not incur guilt and die. This is a permanent law for Aaron and all his descendants after him.

Dedication of the Priests

29 “This is the ceremony you must follow when you consecrate Aaron and his sons to serve me as priests: Take a young bull and two rams with no defects. 2Then, using choice wheat flour and no yeast, make loaves of bread, thin cakes mixed with olive oil, and wafers spread with oil. 3Place them all in a single basket, and present them at the entrance of the Tabernacle, along with the young bull and the two rams.

4“Present Aaron and his sons at the entrance of the Tabernacle,* and wash them with water. 5Dress Aaron in his priestly garments—the tunic, the robe worn with the ephod, the ephod itself, and the chestpiece. Then wrap the decorative sash of the ephod around him. 6Place the turban on his head, and fasten the sacred medallion to the turban. 7Then anoint him by pouring the anointing oil over his head. 8Next present his sons, and dress them in their tunics. 9Wrap the sashes around the waists of Aaron and his sons, and put their special head coverings on them. Then the right to the priesthood will be theirs by law forever. In this way, you will ordain Aaron and his sons.

10“Bring the young bull to the entrance of the Tabernacle, where Aaron and his sons will lay their hands on its head. 11Then slaughter the bull in the LORD’s presence at the entrance of the Tabernacle. 12Put some of its blood on the horns of the altar with your finger, and pour out the rest at the base of the altar. 13Take all the fat around the internal organs, the long lobe of the liver, and the two kidneys and the fat around them, and burn it all on the altar. 14Then take the rest of the bull, including its hide, meat, and dung, and burn it outside the camp as a sin offering.

15“Next Aaron and his sons must lay their hands on the head of one of the rams. 16Then slaughter the ram, and splatter its blood against all sides of the altar. 17Cut the ram into pieces, and wash off the internal organs and the legs. Set them alongside the head and the other pieces of the body, 18then burn the entire animal on the altar. This is a burnt offering to the LORD; it is a pleasing aroma, a special gift presented to the LORD.

19“Now take the other ram, and have Aaron and his sons lay their hands on its head. 20Then slaughter it, and apply some of its blood to the right earlobes of Aaron and his sons. Also put it on the thumbs of their right hands and the big toes of their right feet. Splatter the rest of the blood against all sides of the altar. 21Then take some of the blood from the altar and some of the anointing oil, and sprinkle it on Aaron and his sons and on their garments. In this way, they and their garments will be set apart as holy.

22“Since this is the ram for the ordination

of Aaron and his sons, take the fat of the
ram, including the fat of the broad tail, the
fat around the internal organs, the long
lobe of the liver, and the two kidneys and
the fat around them, along with the right
thigh. [23]Then take one round loaf of bread,
one thin cake mixed with olive oil, and one
wafer from the basket of bread without
yeast that was placed in the LORD's presence. [24]Put all these in the hands of Aaron
and his sons to be lifted up as a special
offering to the LORD. [25]Afterward take the
various breads from their hands, and burn
them on the altar along with the burnt offering. It is a pleasing aroma to the LORD, a
special gift for him. [26]Then take the breast
of Aaron's ordination ram, and lift it up in
the LORD's presence as a special offering to
him. Then keep it as your own portion.

[27]"Set aside the portions of the ordination
ram that belong to Aaron and his sons. This
includes the breast and the thigh that were
lifted up before the LORD as a special offering. [28]In the future, whenever the people of
Israel lift up a peace offering, a portion of it
must be set aside for Aaron and his descendants. This is their permanent right, and it
is a sacred offering from the Israelites to the
LORD.

[29]"Aaron's sacred garments must be preserved for his descendants who succeed
him, and they will wear them when they are
anointed and ordained. [30]The descendant
who succeeds him as high priest will wear
these clothes for seven days as he ministers
in the Tabernacle and the Holy Place.

[31]"Take the ram used in the ordination ceremony, and boil its meat in a sacred place.
[32]Then Aaron and his sons will eat this meat,
along with the bread in the basket, at the
Tabernacle entrance. [33]They alone may eat
the meat and bread used for their purification* in the ordination ceremony. No one else
may eat them, for these things are set apart
and holy. [34]If any of the ordination meat or
bread remains until the morning, it must be
burned. It may not be eaten, for it is holy.

[35]"This is how you will ordain Aaron
and his sons to their offices, just as I have
commanded you. The ordination ceremony
will go on for seven days. [36]Each day you
must sacrifice a young bull as a sin offering to purify them, making them right with
the LORD.* Afterward, cleanse the altar by
purifying it*; make it holy by anointing it
with oil. [37]Purify the altar, and consecrate
it every day for seven days. After that, the
altar will be absolutely holy, and whatever
touches it will become holy.

[38]"These are the sacrifices you are to
offer regularly on the altar. Each day, offer
two lambs that are a year old, [39]one in the
morning and the other in the evening. [40]With
one of them, offer two quarts of choice flour
mixed with one quart of pure oil of pressed
olives; also, offer one quart of wine* as a
liquid offering. [41]Offer the other lamb in the
evening, along with the same offerings of
flour and wine as in the morning. It will be
a pleasing aroma, a special gift presented
to the LORD.

[42]"These burnt offerings are to be made
each day from generation to generation.
Offer them in the LORD's presence at the
Tabernacle entrance; there I will meet with
you and speak with you. [43]I will meet the
people of Israel there, in the place made
holy by my glorious presence. [44]Yes, I will
consecrate the Tabernacle and the altar,
and I will consecrate Aaron and his sons to
serve me as priests. [45]Then I will live among
the people of Israel and be their God, [46]and
they will know that I am the LORD their God.
I am the one who brought them out of the
land of Egypt so that I could live among
them. I am the LORD their God.

Plans for the Incense Altar

30 "Then make another altar of acacia
wood for burning incense. [2]Make it
18 inches square and 36 inches high,* with
horns at the corners carved from the same
piece of wood as the altar itself. [3]Overlay the
top, sides, and horns of the altar with pure
gold, and run a gold molding around the
entire altar. [4]Make two gold rings, and attach
them on opposite sides of the altar below
the gold molding to hold the carrying poles.
[5]Make the poles of acacia wood and overlay
them with gold. [6]Place the incense altar just
outside the inner curtain that shields the
Ark of the Covenant,* in front of the Ark's
cover—the place of atonement—that covers

28:32 The meaning of the Hebrew is uncertain. **28:43** Hebrew *Tent of Meeting.* **29:4** Hebrew *Tent of Meeting;* also in 29:10, 11, 30, 32, 42, 44. **29:33** Or *their atonement.* **29:36a** Or *to make atonement.* **29:36b** Or *by making atonement for it;* similarly in 29:37. **29:40** Hebrew 1/10 *[of an ephah]* [2.2 liters] *of choice flour . . .* 1/4 *of a hin* [1 liter] *of pure oil . . .* 1/4 *of a hin of wine.* **30:2** Hebrew *1 cubit* [46 centimeters] *long and 1 cubit wide, a square, and 2 cubits* [92 centimeters] *high.* **30:6a** Or *Ark of the Testimony;* also in 30:26.

the tablets inscribed with the terms of the covenant.* I will meet with you there.

7“Every morning when Aaron maintains the lamps, he must burn fragrant incense on the altar. 8And each evening when he lights the lamps, he must again burn incense in the LORD’s presence. This must be done from generation to generation. 9Do not offer any unholy incense on this altar, or any burnt offerings, grain offerings, or liquid offerings.

10“Once a year Aaron must purify* the altar by smearing its horns with blood from the offering made to purify the people from their sin. This will be a regular, annual event from generation to generation, for this is the LORD’s most holy altar.”

Money for the Tabernacle

11Then the LORD said to Moses, 12“Whenever you take a census of the people of Israel, each man who is counted must pay a ransom for himself to the LORD. Then no plague will strike the people as you count them. 13Each person who is counted must give a small piece of silver as a sacred offering to the LORD. (This payment is half a shekel,* based on the sanctuary shekel, which equals twenty gerahs.) 14All who have reached their twentieth birthday must give this sacred offering to the LORD. 15When this offering is given to the LORD to purify your lives, making you right with him,* the rich must not give more than the specified amount, and the poor must not give less. 16Receive this ransom money from the Israelites, and use it for the care of the Tabernacle.* It will bring the Israelites to the LORD’s attention, and it will purify your lives.”

Plans for the Washbasin

17Then the LORD said to Moses, 18“Make a bronze washbasin with a bronze stand. Place it between the Tabernacle and the altar, and fill it with water. 19Aaron and his sons will wash their hands and feet there. 20They must wash with water whenever they go into the Tabernacle to appear before the LORD and when they approach the altar to burn up their special gifts to the LORD—or they will die! 21They must always wash their hands and feet, or they will die. This is a permanent law for Aaron and his descendants, to be observed from generation to generation.”

The Anointing Oil

22Then the LORD said to Moses, 23“Collect choice spices—12½ pounds of pure myrrh, 6¼ pounds of fragrant cinnamon, 6¼ pounds of fragrant calamus,* 24and 12½ pounds of cassia*—as measured by the weight of the sanctuary shekel. Also get one gallon of olive oil.* 25Like a skilled incense maker, blend these ingredients to make a holy anointing oil. 26Use this sacred oil to anoint the Tabernacle, the Ark of the Covenant, 27the table and all its utensils, the lampstand and all its accessories, the incense altar, 28the altar of burnt offering and all its utensils, and the washbasin with its stand. 29Consecrate them to make them absolutely holy. After this, whatever touches them will also become holy.

30“Anoint Aaron and his sons also, consecrating them to serve me as priests. 31And say to the people of Israel, ‘This holy anointing oil is reserved for me from generation to generation. 32It must never be used to anoint anyone else, and you must never make any blend like it for yourselves. It is holy, and you must treat it as holy. 33Anyone who makes a blend like it or anoints someone other than a priest will be cut off from the community.’”

The Incense

34Then the LORD said to Moses, “Gather fragrant spices—resin droplets, mollusk shell, and galbanum—and mix these fragrant spices with pure frankincense, weighed out in equal amounts. 35Using the usual techniques of the incense maker, blend the spices together and sprinkle them with salt to produce a pure and holy incense. 36Grind some of the mixture into a very fine powder and put it in front of the Ark of the Covenant,* where I will meet with you in the Tabernacle. You must treat this incense as most holy. 37Never use this formula to make this incense for yourselves. It is reserved for the LORD, and you must treat it as holy. 38Anyone who makes incense like this for personal use will be cut off from the community.”

Craftsmen: Bezalel and Oholiab

31 Then the LORD said to Moses, 2“Look, I have specifically chosen Bezalel son of Uri, grandson of Hur, of the tribe of Judah. 3I have filled him with the Spirit

of God, giving him great wisdom, ability,
and expertise in all kinds of crafts. [4]He is a
master craftsman, expert in working with
gold, silver, and bronze. [5]He is skilled in
engraving and mounting gemstones and in
carving wood. He is a master at every craft!
[6]"And I have personally appointed
Oholiab son of Ahisamach, of the tribe of
Dan, to be his assistant. Moreover, I have
given special skill to all the gifted craftsmen
so they can make all the things I have commanded you to make:

7 the Tabernacle;*
the Ark of the Covenant;*
the Ark's cover—the place of atonement;
all the furnishings of the Tabernacle;
8 the table and its utensils;
the pure gold lampstand with all its accessories;
the incense altar;
9 the altar of burnt offering with all its utensils;
the washbasin with its stand;
10 the beautifully stitched garments—the sacred garments for Aaron the priest, and the garments for his sons to wear as they minister as priests;
11 the anointing oil;
the fragrant incense for the Holy Place.

The craftsmen must make everything as I have commanded you."

Instructions for the Sabbath

[12]The LORD then gave these instructions
to Moses: [13]"Tell the people of Israel: 'Be
careful to keep my Sabbath day, for the
Sabbath is a sign of the covenant between
me and you from generation to generation.
It is given so you may know that I am the
LORD, who makes you holy. [14]You must
keep the Sabbath day, for it is a holy day
for you. Anyone who desecrates it must be
put to death; anyone who works on that
day will be cut off from the community.
[15]You have six days each week for your ordinary work, but the seventh day must be
a Sabbath day of complete rest, a holy day
dedicated to the LORD. Anyone who works
on the Sabbath must be put to death. [16]The
people of Israel must keep the Sabbath day
by observing it from generation to generation. This is a covenant obligation for all
time. [17]It is a permanent sign of my covenant with the people of Israel. For in six
days the LORD made heaven and earth, but
on the seventh day he stopped working and
was refreshed.'"
[18]When the LORD finished speaking with
Moses on Mount Sinai, he gave him the
two stone tablets inscribed with the terms
of the covenant,* written by the finger of
God.

The Gold Calf

32 When the people saw how long it
was taking Moses to come back
down the mountain, they gathered around
Aaron. "Come on," they said, "make us
some gods who can lead us. We don't know
what happened to this fellow Moses, who
brought us here from the land of Egypt."
[2]So Aaron said, "Take the gold rings from
the ears of your wives and sons and daughters, and bring them to me."
[3]All the people took the gold rings from
their ears and brought them to Aaron. [4]Then
Aaron took the gold, melted it down, and
molded it into the shape of a calf. When the
people saw it, they exclaimed, "O Israel,
these are the gods who brought you out of
the land of Egypt!"
[5]Aaron saw how excited the people were,
so he built an altar in front of the calf. Then
he announced, "Tomorrow will be a festival
to the LORD!"
[6]The people got up early the next morning
to sacrifice burnt offerings and peace offerings. After this, they celebrated with feasting and drinking, and they indulged in
pagan revelry.
[7]The LORD told Moses, "Quick! Go down
the mountain! Your people whom you
brought from the land of Egypt have corrupted themselves. [8]How quickly they have
turned away from the way I commanded
them to live! They have melted down gold
and made a calf, and they have bowed
down and sacrificed to it. They are saying,
'These are your gods, O Israel, who brought
you out of the land of Egypt.'"
[9]Then the LORD said, "I have seen how

30:6b Hebrew *that covers the Testimony;* see note on 25:16. **30:10** Or *make atonement for;* also in 30:10b. **30:13** Or *0.2 ounces* [6 grams]. **30:15** Or *to make atonement for your lives;* similarly in 30:16. **30:16** Hebrew *Tent of Meeting;* also in 30:18, 20, 26, 36. **30:23** Hebrew *500 [shekels]* [5.7 kilograms] *of pure myrrh, 250 [shekels]* [2.9 kilograms] *of fragrant cinnamon, 250 [shekels] of fragrant calamus.* **30:24a** Hebrew *500 [shekels]* [5.7 kilograms] *of cassia.* **30:24b** Hebrew *1 hin* [3.8 liters] *of olive oil.* **30:36** Hebrew *in front of the Testimony;* see note on 25:16. **31:7a** Hebrew *the Tent of Meeting.* **31:7b** Hebrew *the Ark of the Testimony.* **31:18** Hebrew *the two tablets of the Testimony;* see note on 25:16.

stubborn and rebellious these people are.
10 Now leave me alone so my fierce anger can
blaze against them, and I will destroy them.
Then I will make you, Moses, into a great
nation."
11 But Moses tried to pacify the LORD his
God. "O LORD!" he said. "Why are you so
angry with your own people whom you
brought from the land of Egypt with such
great power and such a strong hand? 12 Why
let the Egyptians say, 'Their God rescued
them with the evil intention of slaughtering them in the mountains and wiping them
from the face of the earth'? Turn away from
your fierce anger. Change your mind about
this terrible disaster you have threatened
against your people! 13 Remember your servants Abraham, Isaac, and Jacob.* You
bound yourself with an oath to them, saying,
'I will make your descendants as numerous
as the stars of heaven. And I will give them all
of this land that I have promised to your descendants, and they will possess it forever.'"
14 So the LORD changed his mind about the
terrible disaster he had threatened to bring
on his people.

15 Then Moses turned and went down the
mountain. He held in his hands the two
stone tablets inscribed with the terms of
the covenant.* They were inscribed on both
sides, front and back. 16 These tablets were
God's work; the words on them were written
by God himself.
17 When Joshua heard the boisterous noise
of the people shouting below them, he exclaimed to Moses, "It sounds like war in the
camp!"
18 But Moses replied, "No, it's not a shout
of victory nor the wailing of defeat. I hear
the sound of a celebration."
19 When they came near the camp, Moses
saw the calf and the dancing, and he burned
with anger. He threw the stone tablets to
the ground, smashing them at the foot of
the mountain. 20 He took the calf they had
made and burned it. Then he ground it into
powder, threw it into the water, and forced
the people to drink it.
21 Finally, he turned to Aaron and demanded, "What did these people do to you
to make you bring such terrible sin upon
them?"

The character of God

While people often say that the God of the Old Testament seems so different from the God of the New Testament, nothing could be further from the truth. We probably already associate Jesus with compassion, but here in Exodus 32–34 is a story that clearly declares how God revealed himself as the God of compassion in Old Testament times too.

While Moses was up on Mount Sinai, Aaron had made a gold calf, which Israel worshiped in a wild party (Exodus 32:1-8). God was rightly angry with them (though his anger is not like our anger; it is the right and just response of a holy God to wickedness). They had broken a fundamental aspect of the covenant—to have no gods other than him—and so deserved his judgment. Yet even here we see God's compassion, mercy, and patience. In swift response to Moses' prayer, God forgave them (32:14), and when he called Moses up Sinai once again, he showed him what he was really like: "Yahweh! The LORD! The God of compassion and mercy! I am slow to anger and filled with unfailing love and faithfulness. I lavish unfailing love to a thousand generations. I forgive iniquity, rebellion, and sin" (34:6-7)—a revelation that utterly transformed Moses (34:29-35).

This absolute conviction that God was compassionate and merciful, always patient with his people, became an underlying theme of the Old Testament (e.g., 2 Chronicles 30:9; Nehemiah 9:17; Psalm 86:15; 103:8-18; Joel 2:13; Jonah 4:2).

▸ *See also **The compassionate God**, page 666; **The holiness of God**, page 754; **Goodness**, page 1251; **Faithfulness**, page 1307; **The love of God**, page 1437.*

22“Don’t get so upset, my lord,” Aaron
replied. “You yourself know how evil these
people are. 23They said to me, ‘Make us gods
who will lead us. We don’t know what happened to this fellow Moses, who brought
us here from the land of Egypt.’ 24So I told
them, ‘Whoever has gold jewelry, take it off.’
When they brought it to me, I simply threw it
into the fire—and out came this calf!”

25Moses saw that Aaron had let the people
get completely out of control, much to the
amusement of their enemies.* 26So he stood
at the entrance to the camp and shouted,
“All of you who are on the LORD’s side, come
here and join me.” And all the Levites gathered around him.

27Moses told them, “This is what the LORD,
the God of Israel, says: Each of you, take
your swords and go back and forth from one
end of the camp to the other. Kill everyone—
even your brothers, friends, and neighbors.”
28The Levites obeyed Moses’ command, and
about 3,000 people died that day.

29Then Moses told the Levites, “Today you
have ordained yourselves* for the service of
the LORD, for you obeyed him even though it
meant killing your own sons and brothers.
Today you have earned a blessing.”

Moses Intercedes for Israel

30The next day Moses said to the people,
“You have committed a terrible sin, but
I will go back up to the LORD on the mountain. Perhaps I will be able to obtain forgiveness* for your sin.”

31So Moses returned to the LORD and said,
“Oh, what a terrible sin these people have
committed. They have made gods of gold
for themselves. 32But now, if you will only
forgive their sin—but if not, erase my name
from the record you have written!”

33But the LORD replied to Moses, “No, I will
erase the name of everyone who has sinned
against me. 34Now go, lead the people to the
place I told you about. Look! My angel will
lead the way before you. And when I come
to call the people to account, I will certainly
hold them responsible for their sins.”

35Then the LORD sent a great plague upon
the people because they had worshiped the
calf Aaron had made.

33 The LORD said to Moses, “Get going,
you and the people you brought up
from the land of Egypt. Go up to the land
I swore to give to Abraham, Isaac, and Jacob.
I told them, ‘I will give this land to your descendants.’ 2And I will send an angel before
you to drive out the Canaanites, Amorites,
Hittites, Perizzites, Hivites, and Jebusites.
3Go up to this land that flows with milk and
honey. But I will not travel among you, for
you are a stubborn and rebellious people. If
I did, I would surely destroy you along the
way.”

4When the people heard these stern
words, they went into mourning and
stopped wearing their jewelry and fine
clothes. 5For the LORD had told Moses to tell
them, “You are a stubborn and rebellious
people. If I were to travel with you for even a
moment, I would destroy you. Remove your
jewelry and fine clothes while I decide what
to do with you.” 6So from the time they left
Mount Sinai,* the Israelites wore no more
jewelry or fine clothes.

7It was Moses’ practice to take the Tent of
Meeting* and set it up some distance from
the camp. Everyone who wanted to make a
request of the LORD would go to the Tent of
Meeting outside the camp.

8Whenever Moses went out to the Tent of
Meeting, all the people would get up and
stand in the entrances of their own tents.
They would all watch Moses until he disappeared inside. 9As he went into the tent,
the pillar of cloud would come down and
hover at its entrance while the LORD spoke
with Moses. 10When the people saw the
cloud standing at the entrance of the tent,
they would stand and bow down in front of
their own tents. 11Inside the Tent of Meeting,
the LORD would speak to Moses face to face,
as one speaks to a friend. Afterward Moses
would return to the camp, but the young
man who assisted him, Joshua son of Nun,
would remain behind in the Tent of Meeting.

Moses Sees the LORD’s Glory

12One day Moses said to the LORD, “You
have been telling me, ‘Take these people
up to the Promised Land.’ But you haven’t
told me whom you will send with me. You

32:13 Hebrew *Israel.* The names “Jacob” and “Israel” are often interchanged throughout the Old Testament, referring sometimes to the individual patriarch and sometimes to the nation. **32:15** Hebrew *the two tablets of the Testimony;* see note on 25:16. **32:25** Or *out of control, and they mocked anyone who opposed them.* The meaning of the Hebrew is uncertain. **32:29** As in Greek and Latin versions; Hebrew reads *Today ordain yourselves.* **32:30** Or *to make atonement.* **33:6** Hebrew *Horeb,* another name for Sinai. **33:7** This “Tent of Meeting” is different from the Tabernacle described in chapters 26 and 36.

have told me, 'I know you by name, and I look favorably on you.' 13If it is true that you look favorably on me, let me know your ways so I may understand you more fully and continue to enjoy your favor. And remember that this nation is your very own people."

14The LORD replied, "I will personally go with you, Moses, and I will give you rest—everything will be fine for you."

15Then Moses said, "If you don't personally go with us, don't make us leave this place. 16How will anyone know that you look favorably on me—on me and on your people—if you don't go with us? For your presence among us sets your people and me apart from all other people on the earth."

17The LORD replied to Moses, "I will indeed do what you have asked, for I look favorably on you, and I know you by name."

18Moses responded, "Then show me your glorious presence."

19The LORD replied, "I will make all my goodness pass before you, and I will call out my name, Yahweh,* before you. For I will show mercy to anyone I choose, and I will show compassion to anyone I choose. 20But you may not look directly at my face, for no one may see me and live." 21The LORD continued, "Look, stand near me on this rock. 22As my glorious presence passes by, I will hide you in the crevice of the rock and cover you with my hand until I have passed by. 23Then I will remove my hand and let you see me from behind. But my face will not be seen."

A New Copy of the Covenant

34 Then the LORD told Moses, "Chisel out two stone tablets like the first ones. I will write on them the same words that were on the tablets you smashed. 2Be ready in the morning to climb up Mount Sinai and present yourself to me on the top of the mountain. 3No one else may come with you. In fact, no one is to appear anywhere on the mountain. Do not even let the flocks or herds graze near the mountain."

4So Moses chiseled out two tablets of stone like the first ones. Early in the morning he climbed Mount Sinai as the LORD had commanded him, and he carried the two stone tablets in his hands.

5Then the LORD came down in a cloud and stood there with him; and he called out his own name, Yahweh.* 6The LORD passed in front of Moses, calling out,

"Yahweh!* The LORD!
  The God of compassion and mercy!
I am slow to anger
  and filled with unfailing love and
    faithfulness.
7 I lavish unfailing love to a thousand
    generations.*
  I forgive iniquity, rebellion, and sin.
But I do not excuse the guilty.
  I lay the sins of the parents upon their
    children and grandchildren;
the entire family is affected—
  even children in the third and fourth
    generations."

8Moses immediately threw himself to the ground and worshiped. 9And he said, "O Lord, if it is true that I have found favor with you, then please travel with us. Yes, this is a stubborn and rebellious people, but please forgive our iniquity and our sins. Claim us as your own special possession."

10The LORD replied, "Listen, I am making a covenant with you in the presence of all your people. I will perform miracles that have never been performed anywhere in all the earth or in any nation. And all the people around you will see the power of the LORD—the awesome power I will display for you. 11But listen carefully to everything I command you today. Then I will go ahead of you and drive out the Amorites, Canaanites, Hittites, Perizzites, Hivites, and Jebusites.

12"Be very careful never to make a treaty with the people who live in the land where you are going. If you do, you will follow their evil ways and be trapped. 13Instead, you must break down their pagan altars, smash their sacred pillars, and cut down their Asherah poles. 14You must worship no other gods, for the LORD, whose very name is Jealous, is a God who is jealous about his relationship with you.

15"You must not make a treaty of any kind with the people living in the land. They lust after their gods, offering sacrifices to them. They will invite you to join them in their

▸ **34:6** *See **Faithfulness**, page 1307.*

sacrificial meals, and you will go with them.
16 Then you will accept their daughters, who
sacrifice to other gods, as wives for your
sons. And they will seduce your sons to
commit adultery against me by worshiping
other gods. 17 You must not make any gods of
molten metal for yourselves.

18 "You must celebrate the Festival of Unleavened Bread. For seven days the bread
you eat must be made without yeast, just
as I commanded you. Celebrate this festival annually at the appointed time in early
spring, in the month of Abib,* for that is
the anniversary of your departure from
Egypt.

19 "The firstborn of every animal belongs to
me, including the firstborn males* from your
herds of cattle and your flocks of sheep and
goats. 20 A firstborn donkey may be bought
back from the LORD by presenting a lamb or
young goat in its place. But if you do not buy
it back, you must break its neck. However,
you must buy back every firstborn son.

"No one may appear before me without
an offering.

21 "You have six days each week for your
ordinary work, but on the seventh day you
must stop working, even during the seasons
of plowing and harvest.

22 "You must celebrate the Festival of
Harvest* with the first crop of the wheat
harvest, and celebrate the Festival of the
Final Harvest* at the end of the harvest
season. 23 Three times each year every man
in Israel must appear before the Sovereign,
the LORD, the God of Israel. 24 I will drive out
the other nations ahead of you and expand
your territory, so no one will covet and
conquer your land while you appear before
the LORD your God three times each year.

25 "You must not offer the blood of my sacrificial offerings together with any baked
goods containing yeast. And none of the
meat of the Passover sacrifice may be kept
over until the next morning.

26 "As you harvest your crops, bring the
very best of the first harvest to the house of
the LORD your God.

"You must not cook a young goat in its
mother's milk."

27 Then the LORD said to Moses, "Write
down all these instructions, for they represent the terms of the covenant I am making
with you and with Israel."

28 Moses remained there on the mountain
with the LORD forty days and forty nights.
In all that time he ate no bread and drank
no water. And the LORD* wrote the terms of
the covenant—the Ten Commandments*—
on the stone tablets.

29 When Moses came down Mount Sinai
carrying the two stone tablets inscribed
with the terms of the covenant,* he wasn't
aware that his face had become radiant
because he had spoken to the LORD. 30 So
when Aaron and the people of Israel saw
the radiance of Moses' face, they were
afraid to come near him.

31 But Moses called out to them and asked
Aaron and all the leaders of the community to come over, and he talked with them.
32 Then all the people of Israel approached
him, and Moses gave them all the instructions the LORD had given him on Mount
Sinai. 33 When Moses finished speaking with
them, he covered his face with a veil. 34 But
whenever he went into the Tent of Meeting
to speak with the LORD, he would remove
the veil until he came out again. Then he
would give the people whatever instructions the LORD had given him, 35 and the
people of Israel would see the radiant glow
of his face. So he would put the veil over
his face until he returned to speak with the
LORD.

Instructions for the Sabbath

35 Then Moses called together the
whole community of Israel and told
them, "These are the instructions the LORD
has commanded you to follow. 2 You have
six days each week for your ordinary work,
but the seventh day must be a Sabbath day
of complete rest, a holy day dedicated to
the LORD. Anyone who works on that day
must be put to death. 3 You must not even
light a fire in any of your homes on the
Sabbath."

33:19 *Yahweh* is a transliteration of the proper name *YHWH* that is sometimes rendered "Jehovah"; in this translation it is usually rendered "the LORD" (note the use of small capitals). **34:5** *Yahweh* is a transliteration of the proper name *YHWH* that is sometimes rendered "Jehovah"; in this translation it is usually rendered "the LORD" (note the use of small capitals). **34:6** See note on 34:5. **34:7** Hebrew *for thousands.* **34:18** Hebrew *appointed time in the month of Abib.* This first month of the ancient Hebrew lunar calendar usually occurs within the months of March and April. **34:19** As in Greek version; the meaning of the Hebrew word is uncertain. **34:22a** Hebrew *Festival of Weeks;* compare 23:16. This was later called the Festival of Pentecost. It is celebrated today as Shavuot (or Shabuoth). **34:22b** Or *Festival of Ingathering.* This was later called the Festival of Shelters or Festival of Tabernacles (see Lev 23:33-36). It is celebrated today as Sukkot (or Succoth). **34:28a** Hebrew *he.* **34:28b** Hebrew *the ten words.* **34:29** Hebrew *the two tablets of the Testimony;* see note on 25:16.

Offerings for the Tabernacle

4 Then Moses said to the whole community of Israel, "This is what the LORD has
commanded: 5 Take a sacred offering for
the LORD. Let those with generous hearts
present the following gifts to the LORD:

gold, silver, and bronze;
6 blue, purple, and scarlet thread;
fine linen and goat hair for cloth;
7 tanned ram skins and fine goatskin
leather;
acacia wood;
8 olive oil for the lamps;
spices for the anointing oil and the
fragrant incense;
9 onyx stones, and other gemstones to
be set in the ephod and the priest's
chestpiece.

10 "Come, all of you who are gifted craftsmen. Construct everything that the LORD
has commanded:

11 the Tabernacle and its sacred tent, its
covering, clasps, frames, crossbars,
posts, and bases;
12 the Ark and its carrying poles;
the Ark's cover—the place of atonement;
the inner curtain to shield the Ark;
13 the table, its carrying poles, and all its
utensils;
the Bread of the Presence;
14 for light, the lampstand, its accessories,
the lamp cups, and the olive oil for
lighting;
15 the incense altar and its carrying poles;
the anointing oil and fragrant incense;
the curtain for the entrance of the
Tabernacle;
16 the altar of burnt offering;
the bronze grating of the altar and its
carrying poles and utensils;
the washbasin with its stand;
17 the curtains for the walls of the courtyard;
the posts and their bases;
the curtain for the entrance to the
courtyard;
18 the tent pegs of the Tabernacle and
courtyard and their ropes;
19 the beautifully stitched garments for the
priests to wear while ministering in
the Holy Place—the sacred garments
for Aaron the priest, and the garments
for his sons to wear as they minister
as priests."

20 So the whole community of Israel left
Moses and returned to their tents. 21 All
whose hearts were stirred and whose spirits
were moved came and brought their sacred
offerings to the LORD. They brought all the
materials needed for the Tabernacle,* for
the performance of its rituals, and for the
sacred garments. 22 Both men and women
came, all whose hearts were willing. They
brought to the LORD their offerings of
gold—brooches, earrings, rings from their
fingers, and necklaces. They presented
gold objects of every kind as a special offering to the LORD. 23 All those who owned
the following items willingly brought them:
blue, purple, and scarlet thread; fine linen
and goat hair for cloth; and tanned ram
skins and fine goatskin leather. 24 And all
who had silver and bronze objects gave
them as a sacred offering to the LORD. And
those who had acacia wood brought it for
use in the project.

25 All the women who were skilled in
sewing and spinning prepared blue,
purple, and scarlet thread, and fine linen
cloth. 26 All the women who were willing
used their skills to spin the goat hair into
yarn. 27 The leaders brought onyx stones
and the special gemstones to be set in the
ephod and the priest's chestpiece. 28 They
also brought spices and olive oil for the
light, the anointing oil, and the fragrant
incense. 29 So the people of Israel—every
man and woman who was eager to help in
the work the LORD had given them through
Moses—brought their gifts and gave them
freely to the LORD.

30 Then Moses told the people of Israel,
"The LORD has specifically chosen Bezalel
son of Uri, grandson of Hur, of the tribe of
Judah. 31 The LORD has filled Bezalel with
the Spirit of God, giving him great wisdom,
ability, and expertise in all kinds of crafts.
32 He is a master craftsman, expert in
working with gold, silver, and bronze. 33 He
is skilled in engraving and mounting gemstones and in carving wood. He is a master
at every craft. 34 And the LORD has given both
him and Oholiab son of Ahisamach, of the
tribe of Dan, the ability to teach their skills
to others. 35 The LORD has given them special
skills as engravers, designers, embroider-
ers in blue, purple, and scarlet thread on
fine linen cloth, and weavers. They excel as
craftsmen and as designers.

36 "The LORD has gifted Bezalel,
Oholiab, and the other skilled craftsmen with wisdom and ability to perform
any task involved in building the sanctuary.
Let them construct and furnish the Tabernacle, just as the LORD has commanded."
2 So Moses summoned Bezalel and
Oholiab and all the others who were specially gifted by the LORD and were eager
to get to work. 3 Moses gave them the materials donated by the people of Israel
as sacred offerings for the completion of
the sanctuary. But the people continued
to bring additional gifts each morning.
4 Finally the craftsmen who were working
on the sanctuary left their work. 5 They
went to Moses and reported, "The people
have given more than enough materials to
complete the job the LORD has commanded
us to do!"

6 So Moses gave the command, and this
message was sent throughout the camp:
"Men and women, don't prepare any more
gifts for the sanctuary. We have enough!"
So the people stopped bringing their
sacred offerings. 7 Their contributions were
more than enough to complete the whole
project.

Building the Tabernacle

8 The skilled craftsmen made ten curtains
of finely woven linen for the Tabernacle.
Then Bezalel* decorated the curtains with
blue, purple, and scarlet thread and with
skillfully embroidered cherubim. 9 All ten
curtains were exactly the same size—42 feet
long and 6 feet wide.* 10 Five of these curtains were joined together to make one
long curtain, and the other five were joined
to make a second long curtain. 11 He made
fifty loops of blue yarn and put them along
the edge of the last curtain in each set. 12 The
fifty loops along the edge of one curtain
matched the fifty loops along the edge of
the other curtain. 13 Then he made fifty gold
clasps and fastened the long curtains together with the clasps. In this way, the Tabernacle was made of one continuous piece.
14 He made eleven curtains of goat-hair
cloth to serve as a tent covering for the Tabernacle. 15 These eleven curtains were all exactly
the same size—45 feet long and 6 feet wide.*
16 Bezalel joined five of these curtains together
to make one long curtain, and the other six
were joined to make a second long curtain.
17 He made fifty loops for the edge of each large
curtain. 18 He also made fifty bronze clasps to
fasten the long curtains together. In this way,
the tent covering was made of one continuous piece. 19 He completed the tent covering
with a layer of tanned ram skins and a layer
of fine goatskin leather.
20 For the framework of the Tabernacle,

35:21 Hebrew *Tent of Meeting.* **36:8** Hebrew *he;* also in 36:16, 20, 35. See 37:1. **36:9** Hebrew *28 cubits* [12.9 meters] *long and 4 cubits* [1.8 meters] *wide.* **36:15** Hebrew *30 cubits* [13.8 meters] *long and 4 cubits* [1.8 meters] *wide.*

Creative skills

It is sometimes easy to think that only church leaders are gifted by God and can be used by him. The story of Bezalel shows us how wrong such thinking is!

Bezalel was as gifted as any leader, but in a different way. God filled him with his Holy Spirit, not to preach or lead, but to be creative: "He is a master craftsman, expert in working with gold, silver, and bronze. He is skilled in engraving and mounting gemstones and in carving wood. He is a master at every craft"—including engraving, design, and embroidery (Exodus 35:32-35). Moreover, he and his colleague Oholiab were skilled not only to do such creative work but to teach others how to do it too (35:34). Without their contribution, the people would not have had a beautiful place to which to bring their offerings, and the priests would have had no place to offer sacrifices.

Therefore, what we often call our "natural" abilities are as much God-given as any of the "spiritual gifts" Paul refers to (e.g., 1 Corinthians 12:7-11). As Paul writes, "There are different kinds of spiritual gifts, but the same Spirit is the source of them all" (1 Corinthians 12:4). Never despise the gifts and abilities God has given you, but rather believe he wants to use them in his service.

Bezalel constructed frames of acacia wood.
21 Each frame was 15 feet high and 27 inches
wide,* 22 with two pegs under each frame.
All the frames were identical. 23 He made
twenty of these frames to support the curtains on the south side of the Tabernacle.
24 He also made forty silver bases—two bases
under each frame, with the pegs fitting securely into the bases. 25 For the north side
of the Tabernacle, he made another twenty
frames, 26 with their forty silver bases, two
bases under each frame. 27 He made six
frames for the rear—the west side of the Tabernacle—28 along with two additional frames
to reinforce the rear corners of the Tabernacle. 29 These corner frames were matched
at the bottom and firmly attached at the top
with a single ring, forming a single corner
unit. Both of these corner units were made
the same way. 30 So there were eight frames
at the rear of the Tabernacle, set in sixteen
silver bases—two bases under each frame.

31 Then he made crossbars of acacia wood
to link the frames, five crossbars for the
north side of the Tabernacle 32 and five for
the south side. He also made five crossbars
for the rear of the Tabernacle, which faced
west. 33 He made the middle crossbar to
attach halfway up the frames; it ran all the
way from one end of the Tabernacle to the
other. 34 He overlaid the frames with gold and
made gold rings to hold the crossbars. Then
he overlaid the crossbars with gold as well.

35 For the inside of the Tabernacle, Bezalel
made a special curtain of finely woven
linen. He decorated it with blue, purple,
and scarlet thread and with skillfully embroidered cherubim. 36 For the curtain, he
made four posts of acacia wood and four
gold hooks. He overlaid the posts with gold
and set them in four silver bases.

37 Then he made another curtain for the
entrance to the sacred tent. He made it of
finely woven linen and embroidered it with
exquisite designs using blue, purple, and
scarlet thread. 38 This curtain was hung on
gold hooks attached to five posts. The posts
with their decorated tops and hooks were
overlaid with gold, and the five bases were
cast from bronze.

Building the Ark of the Covenant

37 Next Bezalel made the Ark of acacia
wood—a sacred chest 45 inches
long, 27 inches wide, and 27 inches high.*
2 He overlaid it inside and outside with
pure gold, and he ran a molding of gold
all around it. 3 He cast four gold rings and
attached them to its four feet, two rings on
each side. 4 Then he made poles from acacia
wood and overlaid them with gold. 5 He inserted the poles into the rings at the sides of
the Ark to carry it.

6 Then he made the Ark's cover—the
place of atonement—from pure gold. It was
45 inches long and 27 inches wide.* 7 He
made two cherubim from hammered gold
and placed them on the two ends of the
atonement cover. 8 He molded the cherubim
on each end of the atonement cover, making
it all of one piece of gold. 9 The cherubim
faced each other and looked down on the
atonement cover. With their wings spread
above it, they protected it.

Building the Table

10 Then Bezalel* made the table of acacia
wood, 36 inches long, 18 inches wide, and
27 inches high.* 11 He overlaid it with pure
gold and ran a gold molding around the
edge. 12 He decorated it with a 3-inch border*
all around, and he ran a gold molding along
the border. 13 Then he cast four gold rings
for the table and attached them at the four
corners next to the four legs. 14 The rings
were attached near the border to hold the
poles that were used to carry the table. 15 He
made these poles from acacia wood and
overlaid them with gold. 16 Then he made
special containers of pure gold for the
table—bowls, ladles, jars, and pitchers—to
be used in pouring out liquid offerings.

Building the Lampstand

17 Then Bezalel made the lampstand of pure,
hammered gold. He made the entire lampstand and its decorations of one piece—the
base, center stem, lamp cups, buds, and
petals. 18 The lampstand had six branches
going out from the center stem, three on each
side. 19 Each of the six branches had three
lamp cups shaped like almond blossoms,
complete with buds and petals. 20 The center
stem of the lampstand was crafted with four
lamp cups shaped like almond blossoms,
complete with buds and petals. 21 There
was an almond bud beneath each pair of
branches where the six branches extended
from the center stem, all made of one piece.
22 The almond buds and branches were all

of one piece with the center stem, and they were hammered from pure gold.

[23]He also made seven lamps for the lampstand, lamp snuffers, and trays, all of pure gold. [24]The entire lampstand, along with its accessories, was made from 75 pounds* of pure gold.

Building the Incense Altar

[25]Then Bezalel made the incense altar of acacia wood. It was 18 inches square and 36 inches high,* with horns at the corners carved from the same piece of wood as the altar itself. [26]He overlaid the top, sides, and horns of the altar with pure gold, and he ran a gold molding around the entire altar. [27]He made two gold rings and attached them on opposite sides of the altar below the gold molding to hold the carrying poles. [28]He made the poles of acacia wood and overlaid them with gold.

[29]Then he made the sacred anointing oil and the fragrant incense, using the techniques of a skilled incense maker.

Building the Altar of Burnt Offering

38 Next Bezalel* used acacia wood to construct the square altar of burnt offering. It was 7½ feet wide, 7½ feet long, and 4½ feet high.* [2]He made horns for each of its four corners so that the horns and altar were all one piece. He overlaid the altar with bronze. [3]Then he made all the altar utensils of bronze—the ash buckets, shovels, basins, meat forks, and firepans. [4]Next he made a bronze grating and installed it halfway down the side of the altar, under the ledge. [5]He cast four rings and attached them to the corners of the bronze grating to hold the carrying poles. [6]He made the poles from acacia wood and overlaid them with bronze. [7]He inserted the poles through the rings on the sides of the altar. The altar was hollow and was made from planks.

Building the Washbasin

[8]Bezalel made the bronze washbasin and its bronze stand from bronze mirrors donated by the women who served at the entrance of the Tabernacle.*

Building the Courtyard

[9]Then Bezalel made the courtyard, which was enclosed with curtains made of finely woven linen. On the south side the curtains were 150 feet long.* [10]They were held up by twenty posts set securely in twenty bronze bases. He hung the curtains with silver hooks and rings. [11]He made a similar set of curtains for the north side—150 feet of curtains held up by twenty posts set securely in bronze bases. He hung the curtains with silver hooks and rings. [12]The curtains on the west end of the courtyard were 75 feet long,* hung with silver hooks and rings and supported by ten posts set into ten bases. [13]The east end, the front, was also 75 feet long.

[14]The courtyard entrance was on the east end, flanked by two curtains. The curtain on the right side was 22½ feet long* and was supported by three posts set into three bases. [15]The curtain on the left side was also 22½ feet long and was supported by three posts set into three bases. [16]All the curtains used in the courtyard were made of finely woven linen. [17]Each post had a bronze base, and all the hooks and rings were silver. The tops of the posts of the courtyard were overlaid with silver, and the rings to hold up the curtains were made of silver.

[18]He made the curtain for the entrance to the courtyard of finely woven linen, and he decorated it with beautiful embroidery in blue, purple, and scarlet thread. It was 30 feet long, and its height was 7½ feet,* just like the curtains of the courtyard walls. [19]It was supported by four posts, each set securely in its own bronze base. The tops of the posts were overlaid with silver, and the hooks and rings were also made of silver.

[20]All the tent pegs used in the Tabernacle and courtyard were made of bronze.

Inventory of Materials

[21]This is an inventory of the materials used in building the Tabernacle of the Covenant.* The Levites compiled the figures, as Moses directed, and Ithamar son of Aaron the priest

36:21 Hebrew *10 cubits* [4.6 meters] *high and 1.5 cubits* [69 centimeters] *wide.* **37:1** Hebrew *2.5 cubits* [115 centimeters] *long, 1.5 cubits* [69 centimeters] *wide, and 1.5 cubits high.* **37:6** Hebrew *2.5 cubits* [115 centimeters] *long and 1.5 cubits* [69 centimeters] *wide.* **37:10a** Hebrew *he;* also in 37:17, 25. **37:10b** Hebrew *2 cubits* [92 centimeters] *long, 1 cubit* [46 centimeters] *wide, and 1.5 cubits* [69 centimeters] *high.* **37:12** Hebrew *a border of a handbreadth* [8 centimeters]. **37:24** Hebrew *1 talent* [34 kilograms]. **37:25** Hebrew *1 cubit* [46 centimeters] *long and 1 cubit wide, a square, and 2 cubits* [92 centimeters] *high.* **38:1a** Hebrew *he;* also in 38:8, 9. **38:1b** Hebrew *5 cubits* [2.3 meters] *wide, 5 cubits long, a square, and 3 cubits* [1.4 meters] *high.* **38:8** Hebrew *Tent of Meeting;* also in 38:30. **38:9** Hebrew *100 cubits* [46 meters]; also in 38:11. **38:12** Hebrew *50 cubits* [23 meters]; also in 38:13. **38:14** Hebrew *15 cubits* [6.9 meters]; also in 38:15. **38:18** Hebrew *20 cubits* [9.2 meters] *long and 5 cubits* [2.3 meters] *high.* **38:21** Hebrew *the Tabernacle, the Tabernacle of the Testimony.*

served as recorder. [22]Bezalel son of Uri, grandson of Hur, of the tribe of Judah, made everything just as the LORD had commanded Moses. [23]He was assisted by Oholiab son of Ahisamach, of the tribe of Dan, a craftsman expert at engraving, designing, and embroidering with blue, purple, and scarlet thread on fine linen cloth.

[24]The people brought special offerings of gold totaling 2,193 pounds,* as measured by the weight of the sanctuary shekel. This gold was used throughout the Tabernacle.

[25]The whole community of Israel gave 7,545 pounds* of silver, as measured by the weight of the sanctuary shekel. [26]This silver came from the tax collected from each man registered in the census. (The tax is one beka, which is half a shekel,* based on the sanctuary shekel.) The tax was collected from 603,550 men who had reached their twentieth birthday. [27]The hundred bases for the frames of the sanctuary walls and for the posts supporting the inner curtain required 7,500 pounds of silver, about 75 pounds for each base.* [28]The remaining 45 pounds* of silver was used to make the hooks and rings and to overlay the tops of the posts.

[29]The people also brought as special offerings 5,310 pounds* of bronze, [30]which was used for casting the bases for the posts at the entrance to the Tabernacle, and for the bronze altar with its bronze grating and all the altar utensils. [31]Bronze was also used to make the bases for the posts that supported the curtains around the courtyard, the bases for the curtain at the entrance of the courtyard, and all the tent pegs for the Tabernacle and the courtyard.

Clothing for the Priests

39 The craftsmen made beautiful sacred garments of blue, purple, and scarlet cloth—clothing for Aaron to wear while ministering in the Holy Place, just as the LORD had commanded Moses.

Making the Ephod

[2]Bezalel* made the ephod of finely woven linen and embroidered it with gold and with blue, purple, and scarlet thread. [3]He made gold thread by hammering out thin sheets of gold and cutting it into fine strands. With great skill and care, he worked it into the fine linen with the blue, purple, and scarlet thread.

[4]The ephod consisted of two pieces, front and back, joined at the shoulders with two shoulder-pieces. [5]The decorative sash was made of the same materials: finely woven linen embroidered with gold and with blue, purple, and scarlet thread, just as the LORD had commanded Moses. [6]They mounted the two onyx stones in settings of gold filigree. The stones were engraved with the names of the tribes of Israel, just as a seal is engraved. [7]He fastened these stones on the shoulder-pieces of the ephod as a reminder that the priest represents the people of Israel. All this was done just as the LORD had commanded Moses.

Making the Chestpiece

[8]Bezalel made the chestpiece with great skill and care. He made it to match the ephod, using finely woven linen embroidered with gold and with blue, purple, and scarlet thread. [9]He made the chestpiece of a single piece of cloth folded to form a pouch nine inches* square. [10]They mounted four rows of gemstones* on it. The first row contained a red carnelian, a pale-green peridot, and an emerald. [11]The second row contained a turquoise, a blue lapis lazuli, and a white moonstone. [12]The third row contained an orange jacinth, an agate, and a purple amethyst. [13]The fourth row contained a blue-green beryl, an onyx, and a green jasper. All these stones were set in gold filigree. [14]Each stone represented one of the twelve sons of Israel, and the name of that tribe was engraved on it like a seal.

[15]To attach the chestpiece to the ephod, they made braided cords of pure gold thread. [16]They also made two settings of gold filigree and two gold rings and attached them to the top corners of the chestpiece. [17]They tied the two gold cords to the rings on the chestpiece. [18]They tied the other ends of the cords to the gold settings on the shoulder-pieces of the ephod. [19]Then they made two more gold rings and attached them to the inside edges of the chestpiece next to the ephod. [20]Then they made two more gold rings and attached them to the front of the ephod, below the shoulder-pieces, just above the knot where the decorative sash was fastened to the ephod. [21]They attached the bottom rings of the chestpiece to the rings on the ephod with blue cords. In this way, the chestpiece

was held securely to the ephod above the
decorative sash. All this was done just as
the LORD had commanded Moses.

Additional Clothing for the Priests

22Bezalel made the robe that is worn with the
ephod from a single piece of blue woven cloth,
23with an opening for Aaron's head in the
middle of it. The opening was reinforced with
a woven collar* so it would not tear. 24They
made pomegranates of blue, purple, and
scarlet yarn, and attached them to the hem of
the robe. 25They also made bells of pure gold
and placed them between the pomegranates
along the hem of the robe, 26with bells and
pomegranates alternating all around the hem.
This robe was to be worn whenever the priest
ministered before the LORD, just as the LORD
had commanded Moses.

27They made tunics for Aaron and his
sons from fine linen cloth. 28The turban
and the special head coverings were made
of fine linen, and the undergarments were
also made of finely woven linen. 29The
sashes were made of finely woven linen and
embroidered with blue, purple, and scarlet
thread, just as the LORD had commanded
Moses.

30Finally, they made the sacred medallion—the badge of holiness—of pure gold.
They engraved it like a seal with these
words: HOLY TO THE LORD. 31They attached
the medallion with a blue cord to Aaron's
turban, just as the LORD had commanded
Moses.

Moses Inspects the Work

32And so at last the Tabernacle* was finished. The Israelites had done everything
just as the LORD had commanded Moses.
33And they brought the entire Tabernacle to
Moses:

the sacred tent with all its furnishings,
clasps, frames, crossbars, posts, and
bases;
34 the tent coverings of tanned ram skins
and fine goatskin leather;
the inner curtain to shield the Ark;
35 the Ark of the Covenant* and its
carrying poles;
the Ark's cover—the place of atonement;
36 the table and all its utensils;
the Bread of the Presence;
37 the pure gold lampstand with its
symmetrical lamp cups, all its
accessories, and the olive oil for
lighting;
38 the gold altar;
the anointing oil and fragrant incense;
the curtain for the entrance of the sacred
tent;
39 the bronze altar;
the bronze grating and its carrying poles
and utensils;
the washbasin with its stand;
40 the curtains for the walls of the courtyard;
the posts and their bases;
the curtain for the entrance to the
courtyard;

38:24 Hebrew *29 talents and 730 shekels* [994 kilograms]. Each shekel weighed about 0.4 ounces or 11 grams. **38:25** Hebrew *100 talents and 1,775 shekels* [3,420 kilograms]. **38:26** Or *0.2 ounces* [6 grams]. **38:27** Hebrew *100 talents* [3,400 kilograms] *of silver, 1 talent* [34 kilograms] *for each base.* **38:28** Hebrew *1,775 [shekels]* [20.2 kilograms]. **38:29** Hebrew *70 talents and 2,400 shekels* [2,407 kilograms]. **39:2** Hebrew *He;* also in 39:8, 22. **39:9** Hebrew *1 span* [23 centimeters]. **39:10** The identification of some of these gemstones is uncertain. **39:23** The meaning of the Hebrew is uncertain. **39:32** Hebrew *the Tabernacle, the Tent of Meeting;* also in 39:40. **39:35** Or *Ark of the Testimony.*

The high priest's garments

The high priest was given special robes for his work in the Tabernacle. These comprised: a blue robe hemmed with pomegranates made of yarn and gold bells; an "ephod" (sleeveless overgarment) made of linen and gold, blue, purple, and scarlet yarns, with two onyx stones engraved with the names of the twelve tribes fastened to its straps so he could bring them symbolically before God; a chestpiece set with twelve stones to represent the twelve tribes and a pouch for the Urim and Thummim stones, which were used to determine God's will (see Exodus 28:30); and a turban with a gold medallion with the words "HOLY TO THE LORD." Ordinary priests wore simple linen tunics, sashes, and headbands.

▶ *See also **Every Christian is a priest**, page 1422.*

the ropes and tent pegs;
all the furnishings to be used in worship
at the Tabernacle;
41 the beautifully stitched garments for the
priests to wear while ministering in
the Holy Place—the sacred garments
for Aaron the priest, and the garments
for his sons to wear as they minister
as priests.

42 So the people of Israel followed all of the LORD's instructions to Moses. 43 Then Moses inspected all their work. When he found it had been done just as the LORD had commanded him, he blessed them.

The Tabernacle Completed

40 Then the LORD said to Moses, 2 "Set up the Tabernacle* on the first day of the new year.* 3 Place the Ark of the Covenant* inside, and install the inner curtain to enclose the Ark within the Most Holy Place. 4 Then bring in the table, and arrange the utensils on it. And bring in the lampstand, and set up the lamps.

5 "Place the gold incense altar in front of the Ark of the Covenant. Then hang the curtain at the entrance of the Tabernacle. 6 Place the altar of burnt offering in front of the Tabernacle entrance. 7 Set the washbasin between the Tabernacle* and the altar, and fill it with water. 8 Then set up the courtyard around the outside of the tent, and hang the curtain for the courtyard entrance.

9 "Take the anointing oil and anoint the Tabernacle and all its furnishings to consecrate them and make them holy. 10 Anoint the altar of burnt offering and its utensils to consecrate them. Then the altar will become absolutely holy. 11 Next anoint the washbasin and its stand to consecrate them.

12 "Present Aaron and his sons at the entrance of the Tabernacle, and wash them with water. 13 Dress Aaron with the sacred garments and anoint him, consecrating him to serve me as a priest. 14 Then present his sons and dress them in their tunics. 15 Anoint them as you did their father, so they may also serve me as priests. With their anointing, Aaron's descendants are set apart for the priesthood forever, from generation to generation."

16 Moses proceeded to do everything just as the LORD had commanded him. 17 So the Tabernacle was set up on the first day of the first month of the second year. 18 Moses erected the Tabernacle by setting down its bases, inserting the frames, attaching the crossbars, and setting up the posts. 19 Then he spread the coverings over the Tabernacle framework and put on the protective layers, just as the LORD had commanded him.

20 He took the stone tablets inscribed with the terms of the covenant and placed them* inside the Ark. Then he attached the carrying poles to the Ark, and he set the Ark's cover—the place of atonement—on top of it. 21 Then he brought the Ark of the Covenant into the Tabernacle and hung the inner curtain to shield it from view, just as the LORD had commanded him.

22 Next Moses placed the table in the Tabernacle, along the north side of the Holy Place, just outside the inner curtain. 23 And he arranged the Bread of the Presence on the table before the LORD, just as the LORD had commanded him.

24 He set the lampstand in the Tabernacle across from the table on the south side of the Holy Place. 25 Then he lit the lamps in the LORD's presence, just as the LORD had commanded him. 26 He also placed the gold incense altar in the Tabernacle, in the Holy Place in front of the inner curtain. 27 On it he burned the fragrant incense, just as the LORD had commanded him.

28 He hung the curtain at the entrance of the Tabernacle, 29 and he placed the altar of burnt offering near the Tabernacle entrance. On it he offered a burnt offering and a grain offering, just as the LORD had commanded him.

30 Next Moses placed the washbasin between the Tabernacle and the altar. He filled it with water so the priests could wash themselves. 31 Moses and Aaron and Aaron's sons used water from it to wash their hands and feet. 32 Whenever they approached the altar and entered the Tabernacle, they washed themselves, just as the LORD had commanded Moses.

33 Then he hung the curtains forming the courtyard around the Tabernacle and the altar. And he set up the curtain at the entrance of the courtyard. So at last Moses finished the work.

The LORD's Glory Fills the Tabernacle

34 Then the cloud covered the Tabernacle, and the glory of the LORD filled the

Tabernacle. [35]Moses could no longer enter the Tabernacle because the cloud had settled down over it, and the glory of the LORD filled the Tabernacle.

[36]Now whenever the cloud lifted from the Tabernacle, the people of Israel would set out on their journey, following it. [37]But if the cloud did not rise, they remained where they were until it lifted. [38]The cloud of the LORD hovered over the Tabernacle during the day, and at night fire glowed inside the cloud so the whole family of Israel could see it. This continued throughout all their journeys.

40:2a Hebrew *the Tabernacle, the Tent of Meeting;* also in 40:6, 29. **40:2b** Hebrew *the first day of the first month.* This day of the ancient Hebrew lunar calendar occurred in March or April. **40:3** Or *Ark of the Testimony;* also in 40:5, 21. **40:7** Hebrew *Tent of Meeting;* also in 40:12, 22, 24, 26, 30, 32, 34, 35. **40:20** Hebrew *He placed the Testimony;* see note on 25:16.

▸ **40:34** *See* ***Glory****, page 946.*

The glory of God

Exodus ends with the glory of God coming and filling the Tabernacle (or Tent of Meeting), the tent that symbolized how God now "tabernacled" (or lived) among his people Israel. The word translated "glory" comes from a Hebrew root meaning "heaviness" or "weight." The idea behind the word, therefore, is that when God is present there is such a weight of splendor, worthiness, and honor that all we can do is bow down before him in worship (e.g., 2 Chronicles 7:3), and sometimes we are not even able to stand before him (e.g., Exodus 40:35; 2 Chronicles 7:2). Glory is the distinctive feature of his presence.

The Bible says that God reveals his glory both in creation (e.g., Psalm 19:1) and through his people (e.g., Isaiah 44:23; 2 Corinthians 3:18), but it is seen supremely in Jesus Christ, his Son (e.g., John 1:14; Hebrews 1:3). When Christ returns, we will experience God's glory in all its fullness (e.g., Romans 8:18; Colossians 3:4), but he wants us to begin to experience that glory in ever-increasing measure right now as we yield our lives to him, just as Moses did.

▸ *See also* ***Glory****, page 946.*

Leviticus *Laws for life and worship*

Set in the period when the Israelites were slowly traveling toward their Promised Land of Canaan, Leviticus records Moses' instructions, received from God on Mount Sinai, about how they should approach and relate to God, both individually and as a nation. If Exodus is about the establishing of the covenant, Leviticus is about the maintaining of that covenant.

Leviticus emphasizes the holiness of God. This characteristic made the provision of sacrifice essential, for human sinfulness is a bar to relationship with a completely holy God. The repeated instruction is "be holy because I am holy" (11:44-45), but people cannot achieve this by themselves. However, other aspects of God's character make relationship with him possible: his grace, favor, faithfulness, provision, and presence, as 26:3-13 beautifully illustrates.

The name of the book comes from the Levites, the descendants of Levi, who were responsible for worship and maintaining holiness among the people of Israel.

What's it all about?

Leviticus provides detailed instructions about how Israel was to worship while they were in the desert.

Chapters 1 to 7 provide the means by which a sinful people could safely approach a holy God. The answer is found in a system of sacrifices and offerings, which are described in great detail. The point is that sin can only be atoned for with blood (though unlike in some surrounding nations, it always had to be the blood of an animal, never a human being). Forgiveness is not cheap: If a sin is committed, someone or something has to pay for it if the guilty person is to go free. In addition to the sacrifices to atone for sin, we are given details about offerings that the people would bring to the priest as a means of honoring God. They always involved the gift of something precious (like fine flour mixed with oil and frankincense, or the firstfruits of harvest)—a reminder that an offering or sacrifice always *costs*.

In chapter 8, Aaron and his sons are ordained as priests. From then on, when the people approached God, they did so primarily

OVERVIEW

Detailed instructions on sacrifices and offerings · *1:1–7:38*

The ordination and consecration of Aaron and his sons · *8:1–9:24*

Nadab and Abihu's presumption and punishment · *10:1-20*

Various laws about ritual purity
11:1–15:33

The Day of Atonement
16:1-34

Laws about holy and just living
17:1–22:33

Laws about holy days, religious festivals, and the Year of Jubilee
23:1–25:55

Promised blessings for obedience and punishments for disobedience
26:1-46

Rules about vows and gifts
27:1-34

through Aaron, rather than through Moses. But Aaron was not a free agent. His entry into God's presence was restricted and carefully regulated, with the recurring warning that disobedience would lead to death (see 16:2, 13).

Chapter 10 tells the tragic story of two of Aaron's sons, Nadab and Abihu. They tried to invent their own kind of sacrifice, but God rejected the fire of their sacrifice and burned them up in his own fire instead—a salutary reminder not to play with God's holiness.

Chapters 11 to 15 describe various laws on ritual cleanliness and purification, highlighting the difference that existed between the people of Israel and their pagan neighbors. This is an outworking of the key conviction of Leviticus, namely that there is a distinction between the holy and the ordinary. Chapter 16 introduces the great Day of Atonement, an annual ceremony with very elaborate rituals that dealt with any sin the nation may have neglected to confess.

The remaining chapters cover laws governing the Israelites' behavior and national life, with an overriding emphasis on caring for the weak and needy, for they themselves were once weak and needy in Egypt. The book ends with a list of blessings and punishments, which put the people's future firmly in their own hands.

What does it mean for us?

Leviticus contains God's principles for living as a holy people. God is holy, and so his people must be holy too. From their behavior in Exodus it is clear that they could never achieve this on their own. So God took the initiative: The sacrificial system to maintain their covenant relationship with him was his idea, not theirs. All they had to do was obey him, and such obedience *was* within their reach.

Since they had shown how forgetful they were, God made sure his people couldn't forget him. The many rules and regulations brought him into every aspect of their daily lives. The message of Leviticus is that God's demands do not restrain our freedom; on the contrary, they guarantee our welfare. But will we go down this route, or will we follow Nadab and Abihu in not wanting to be told what to do?

Procedures for the Burnt Offering

1 The LORD called to Moses from the Tabernacle* and said to him, 2"Give the
following instructions to the people of
Israel. When you present an animal as an
offering to the LORD, you may take it from
your herd of cattle or your flock of sheep
and goats.
3"If the animal you present as a burnt offering is from the herd, it must be a male
with no defects. Bring it to the entrance of
the Tabernacle so you* may be accepted by
the LORD. 4Lay your hand on the animal's
head, and the LORD will accept its death in
your place to purify you, making you right
with him.* 5Then slaughter the young bull
in the LORD's presence, and Aaron's sons,
the priests, will present the animal's blood
by splattering it against all sides of the altar
that stands at the entrance to the Tabernacle.
6Then skin the animal and cut it into pieces.
7The sons of Aaron the priest will build a
wood fire on the altar. 8They will arrange the
pieces of the offering, including the head
and fat, on the wood burning on the altar.
9But the internal organs and the legs must
first be washed with water. Then the priest
will burn the entire sacrifice on the altar as a
burnt offering. It is a special gift, a pleasing
aroma to the LORD.
10"If the animal you present as a burnt offering is from the flock, it may be either a
sheep or a goat, but it must be a male with no
defects. 11Slaughter the animal on the north
side of the altar in the LORD's presence, and
Aaron's sons, the priests, will splatter its
blood against all sides of the altar. 12Then
cut the animal in pieces, and the priests will

1:1 Hebrew *Tent of Meeting;* also in 1:3, 5. **1:3** Or *it.* **1:4** Or *to make atonement for you.*

Old Testament sacrifices and offerings

Type of offering	Key verses	Elements used	Action involved	Purpose
Burnt offering	Leviticus 1:1-17; 6:8-13; 8:18-21	Perfect male animal from the herd or flock; dove or pigeon for the poor	Blood sprinkled on the sides of the altar; whole carcass burned on the altar	Atonement for unintentional sin; expression of dedication to God
Grain offering	Leviticus 2:1-16; 6:14-23	Grain (raw, baked, cooked, or fried, but with no yeast) with oil, incense, and salt	Partly burned on the altar; partly given to the priests to eat	To remind the worshiper of God (especially his provision) and to remind God of the worshiper as he smelled its aroma
Peace or fellowship offering	Leviticus 3:1-17; 7:11-36	Perfect male or female from the herd or flock	Blood sprinkled on the sides of the altar; kidneys and fat around the internal organs burned on the altar; meat eaten by worshipers	To celebrate fellowship with God, but also to express gratitude, fulfill a vow, or be a freewill offering
Sin offering	Leviticus 4:1–5:13; 6:24-30; 16:1-22	Bull (for priests or the whole community), male goat (for leaders), female goat or lamb (for the common people), two doves or pigeons (for the poor), fine flour (for the very poor)	Blood sprinkled on the sanctuary curtain and daubed on the horns of the altar; kidneys and fat around the internal organs burned on the altar; rest of the animal burned outside the sanctuary and dumped	Compulsory offering to atone for unintentional sin; also to be cleansed from impurity
Guilt offering	Leviticus 5:14–6:7; 7:1-10	Perfect ram from the flock, or its value in silver	Blood sprinkled on the sides of the altar; kidneys and fat around the internal organs burned on the altar; restitution paid for anything stolen plus twenty percent	Atonement for desecration of sacred things or violation of others' property

Notes:

1. All animal sacrifices involved shedding blood to atone for sin. For the Israelites, blood wasn't seen as something mystical or magical, but rather as symbolizing life offered up in death as the price of sin.
2. If more than one offering was required, this order was followed: first, the sin or guilt offering; second, the burnt offering; third; the fellowship and grain offering. This order underlined the fact that sin had to be dealt with and recommitment to God made before fellowship with him and others could be reestablished.

▶ *See also* ***The importance of blood****, page 136.*

arrange the pieces of the offering, including the head and fat, on the wood burning on the altar. [13]But the internal organs and the legs must first be washed with water. Then the priest will burn the entire sacrifice on the altar as a burnt offering. It is a special gift, a pleasing aroma to the LORD.

[14]"If you present a bird as a burnt offering to the LORD, choose either a turtledove or a young pigeon. [15]The priest will take the bird to the altar, wring off its head, and burn it on the altar. But first he must drain its blood against the side of the altar. [16]The priest must also remove the crop and the feathers* and throw them in the ashes on the east side of the altar. [17]Then, grasping the bird by its wings, the priest will tear the bird open, but without tearing it apart. Then he will burn it as a burnt offering on the wood burning on the altar. It is a special gift, a pleasing aroma to the LORD.

Procedures for the Grain Offering

2 "When you present grain as an offering to the LORD, the offering must consist of choice flour. You are to pour olive oil on it, sprinkle it with frankincense, [2]and bring it to Aaron's sons, the priests. The priest will scoop out a handful of the flour moistened with oil, together with all the frankincense, and burn this representative portion on the altar. It is a special gift, a pleasing aroma to the LORD. [3]The rest of the grain offering will then be given to Aaron and his sons. This offering will be considered a most holy part of the special gifts presented to the LORD.

[4]"If your offering is a grain offering baked in an oven, it must be made of choice flour, but without any yeast. It may be presented in the form of thin cakes mixed with olive oil or wafers spread with olive oil. [5]If your grain offering is cooked on a griddle, it must be made of choice flour mixed with olive oil but without any yeast. [6]Break it in pieces and pour olive oil on it; it is a grain offering. [7]If your grain offering is prepared in a pan, it must be made of choice flour and olive oil.

[8]"No matter how a grain offering for the LORD has been prepared, bring it to the priest, who will present it at the altar. [9]The priest will take a representative portion of the grain offering and burn it on the altar. It is a special gift, a pleasing aroma to the LORD. [10]The rest of the grain offering will then be given to Aaron and his sons as their food. This offering will be considered a most holy part of the special gifts presented to the LORD.

[11]"Do not use yeast in preparing any of the grain offerings you present to the LORD, because no yeast or honey may be burned as a special gift presented to the LORD. [12]You may add yeast and honey to an offering of the first crops of your harvest, but these must never be offered on the altar as a pleasing aroma to the LORD. [13]Season all your grain offerings with salt to remind you of God's eternal covenant. Never forget to add salt to your grain offerings.

[14]"If you present a grain offering to the LORD from the first portion of your harvest, bring fresh grain that is coarsely ground and roasted on a fire. [15]Put olive oil on this grain offering, and sprinkle it with frankincense. [16]The priest will take a representative portion of the grain moistened with oil, together with all the frankincense, and burn it as a special gift presented to the LORD.

Procedures for the Peace Offering

3 "If you present an animal from the herd as a peace offering to the LORD, it may be a male or a female, but it must have no defects. [2]Lay your hand on the animal's head, and slaughter it at the entrance of the Tabernacle.* Then Aaron's sons, the priests, will splatter its blood against all sides of the altar. [3]The priest must present part of this peace offering as a special gift to the LORD. This includes all the fat around the internal organs, [4]the two kidneys and the fat around them near the loins, and the long lobe of the liver. These must be removed with the kidneys, [5]and Aaron's sons will burn them on top of the burnt offering on the wood burning on the altar. It is a special gift, a pleasing aroma to the LORD.

[6]"If you present an animal from the flock as a peace offering to the LORD, it may be a male or a female, but it must have no defects. [7]If you present a sheep as your offering, bring it to the LORD, [8]lay your hand on its head, and slaughter it in front of the Tabernacle. Aaron's sons will then splatter the sheep's blood against all sides of the altar. [9]The priest must present the fat of this peace offering as a special gift to the LORD.

1:16 Or *the crop and its contents*. The meaning of the Hebrew is uncertain. **3:2** Hebrew *Tent of Meeting;* also in 3:8, 13.

This includes the fat of the broad tail cut off near the backbone, all the fat around the internal organs, 10the two kidneys and the fat around them near the loins, and the long lobe of the liver. These must be removed with the kidneys, 11and the priest will burn them on the altar. It is a special gift of food presented to the LORD.

12"If you present a goat as your offering, bring it to the LORD, 13lay your hand on its head, and slaughter it in front of the Tabernacle. Aaron's sons will then splatter the goat's blood against all sides of the altar. 14The priest must present part of this offering as a special gift to the LORD. This includes all the fat around the internal organs, 15the two kidneys and the fat around them near the loins, and the long lobe of the liver. These must be removed with the kidneys, 16and the priest will burn them on the altar. It is a special gift of food, a pleasing aroma to the LORD. All the fat belongs to the LORD.

17"You must never eat any fat or blood. This is a permanent law for you, and it must be observed from generation to generation, wherever you live."

Procedures for the Sin Offering

4 Then the LORD said to Moses, 2"Give the following instructions to the people of Israel. This is how you are to deal with those who sin unintentionally by doing anything that violates one of the LORD's commands.

3"If the high priest* sins, bringing guilt upon the entire community, he must give a sin offering for the sin he has committed. He must present to the LORD a young bull with no defects. 4He must bring the bull to the LORD at the entrance of the Tabernacle,* lay his hand on the bull's head, and slaughter it before the LORD. 5The high priest will then take some of the bull's blood into the Tabernacle, 6dip his finger in the blood, and sprinkle it seven times before the LORD in front of the inner curtain of the sanctuary. 7The priest will then put some of the blood on the horns of the altar for fragrant incense that stands in the LORD's presence inside the Tabernacle. He will pour out the rest of the bull's blood at the base of the altar for burnt offerings at the entrance of the Tabernacle. 8Then the priest must remove all the fat of the bull to be offered as a sin offering. This includes all the fat around the internal organs, 9the two kidneys and the fat around them near the loins, and the long lobe of the liver. He must remove these along with the kidneys, 10just as he does with cattle offered as a peace offering, and burn them on the altar of burnt offerings. 11But he must take whatever is left of the bull—its hide, meat, head, legs, internal organs, and dung—12and carry it away to a place outside the camp that is ceremonially clean, the place where the ashes are dumped. There, on the ash heap, he will burn it on a wood fire.

13"If the entire Israelite community sins by violating one of the LORD's commands, but the people don't realize it, they are still guilty. 14When they become aware of their sin, the people must bring a young bull as an offering for their sin and present it before the Tabernacle. 15The elders of the community must then lay their hands on the bull's head and slaughter it before the LORD. 16The high priest will then take some of the bull's blood into the Tabernacle, 17dip his finger in the blood, and sprinkle it seven times before the LORD in front of the inner curtain. 18He will then put some of the blood on the horns of the altar for fragrant incense that stands in the LORD's presence inside the Tabernacle. He will pour out the rest of the blood at the base of the altar for burnt offerings at the entrance of the Tabernacle. 19Then the priest must remove all the animal's fat and burn it on the altar, 20just as he does with the bull offered as a sin offering for the high priest. Through this process, the priest will purify the people, making them right with the LORD,* and they will be forgiven. 21Then the priest must take what is left of the bull and carry it outside the camp and burn it there, just as is done with the sin offering for the high priest. This offering is for the sin of the entire congregation of Israel.

22"If one of Israel's leaders sins by violating one of the commands of the LORD his God but doesn't realize it, he is still guilty. 23When he becomes aware of his sin, he must bring as his offering a male goat with no defects. 24He must lay his hand on the goat's head and slaughter it at the place where burnt offerings are slaughtered before the LORD. This is an offering for his sin. 25Then the priest will dip his finger in the blood of the sin offering and put it on the horns of the altar for burnt offerings.

He will pour out the rest of the blood at the
base of the altar. 26 Then he must burn all the
goat's fat on the altar, just as he does with
the peace offering. Through this process,
the priest will purify the leader from his sin,
making him right with the LORD, and he will
be forgiven.

27 "If any of the common people sin by
violating one of the LORD's commands, but
they don't realize it, they are still guilty.
28 When they become aware of their sin,
they must bring as an offering for their sin
a female goat with no defects. 29 They must
lay a hand on the head of the sin offering
and slaughter it at the place where burnt
offerings are slaughtered. 30 Then the priest
will dip his finger in the blood and put it
on the horns of the altar for burnt offerings.
He will pour out the rest of the blood at the
base of the altar. 31 Then he must remove all
the goat's fat, just as he does with the fat
of the peace offering. He will burn the fat on
the altar, and it will be a pleasing aroma
to the LORD. Through this process, the priest
will purify the people, making them right
with the LORD, and they will be forgiven.

32 "If the people bring a sheep as their sin
offering, it must be a female with no defects.
33 They must lay a hand on the head of the
sin offering and slaughter it at the place
where burnt offerings are slaughtered.
34 Then the priest will dip his finger in the
blood of the sin offering and put it on the
horns of the altar for burnt offerings. He will
pour out the rest of the blood at the base
of the altar. 35 Then he must remove all the
sheep's fat, just as he does with the fat of a
sheep presented as a peace offering. He will
burn the fat on the altar on top of the special
gifts presented to the LORD. Through this
process, the priest will purify the people
from their sin, making them right with the
LORD, and they will be forgiven.

Sins Requiring a Sin Offering

5 "If you are called to testify about something you have seen or that you know
about, it is sinful to refuse to testify, and
you will be punished for your sin.

2 "Or suppose you unknowingly touch
something that is ceremonially unclean,
such as the carcass of an unclean animal.
When you realize what you have done, you
must admit your defilement and your guilt.
This is true whether it is a wild animal, a
domestic animal, or an animal that scurries
along the ground.

3 "Or suppose you unknowingly touch
something that makes a person unclean.
When you realize what you have done, you
must admit your guilt.

4 "Or suppose you make a foolish vow of
any kind, whether its purpose is for good or
for bad. When you realize its foolishness,
you must admit your guilt.

5 "When you become aware of your guilt
in any of these ways, you must confess your
sin. 6 Then you must bring to the LORD as
the penalty for your sin a female from the
flock, either a sheep or a goat. This is a sin
offering with which the priest will purify
you from your sin, making you right with
the LORD.*

7 "But if you cannot afford to bring a
sheep, you may bring to the LORD two turtledoves or two young pigeons as the penalty
for your sin. One of the birds will be for a sin
offering, and the other for a burnt offering.
8 You must bring them to the priest, who will

4:3 Hebrew *the anointed priest;* also in 4:5, 16. **4:4** Hebrew *Tent of Meeting;* also in 4:5, 7, 14, 16, 18. **4:20** Or *will make atonement for the people;* similarly in 4:26, 31, 35. **5:6** Or *will make atonement for you for your sin;* similarly in 5:10, 13, 16, 18.

The role of the priests

These chapters cover in great detail two key aspects of the work of Israel's priests: to offer the sacrifices that people brought to God so that their sin might be atoned for, and to present their offerings that honored God. At this stage in Israel's history it is clear that the priests did not slaughter the animal to be sacrificed; the sinner did. The role of the priest was to serve as an intermediary, catching the blood in a bowl and presenting it at the altar as a way of atoning for sin (e.g., Leviticus 1:3-5). But priests had many other responsibilities too, including teaching God's law, acting as judges, and serving as public health inspectors.

present the first bird as the sin offering. He will wring its neck but without severing its head from the body. [9]Then he will sprinkle some of the blood of the sin offering against the sides of the altar, and the rest of the blood will be drained out at the base of the altar. This is an offering for sin. [10]The priest will then prepare the second bird as a burnt offering, following all the procedures that have been prescribed. Through this process the priest will purify you from your sin, making you right with the LORD, and you will be forgiven.

[11]"If you cannot afford to bring two turtledoves or two young pigeons, you may bring two quarts* of choice flour for your sin offering. Since it is an offering for sin, you must not moisten it with olive oil or put any frankincense on it. [12]Take the flour to the priest, who will scoop out a handful as a representative portion. He will burn it on the altar on top of the special gifts presented to the LORD. It is an offering for sin. [13]Through this process, the priest will purify those who are guilty of any of these sins, making them right with the LORD, and they will be forgiven. The rest of the flour will belong to the priest, just as with the grain offering."

Procedures for the Guilt Offering

[14]Then the LORD said to Moses, [15]"If one of you commits a sin by unintentionally defiling the LORD's sacred property, you must bring a guilt offering to the LORD. The offering must be your own ram with no defects, or you may buy one of equal value with silver, as measured by the weight of the sanctuary shekel.* [16]You must make restitution for the sacred property you have harmed by paying for the loss, plus an additional 20 percent. When you give the payment to the priest, he will purify you with the ram sacrificed as a guilt offering, making you right with the LORD, and you will be forgiven.

[17]"Suppose you sin by violating one of the LORD's commands. Even if you are unaware of what you have done, you are guilty and will be punished for your sin. [18]For a guilt offering, you must bring to the priest your own ram with no defects, or you may buy one of equal value. Through this process the priest will purify you from your unintentional sin, making you right with the LORD, and you will be forgiven. [19]This is a guilt offering, for you have been guilty of an offense against the LORD."

Sins Requiring a Guilt Offering

6 [1]*Then the LORD said to Moses, [2]"Suppose one of you sins against your associate and is unfaithful to the LORD. Suppose you cheat in a deal involving a security deposit, or you steal or commit fraud, [3]or you find lost property and lie about it, or you lie while swearing to tell the truth, or you commit any other such sin. [4]If you have sinned in any of these ways, you are guilty. You must give back whatever you stole, or the money you took by extortion, or the security deposit, or the lost property you found, [5]or anything obtained by swearing falsely. You must make restitution by paying the full price plus an additional 20 percent to the person you have harmed. On the same day you must present a guilt offering. [6]As a guilt offering to the LORD, you must bring to the priest your own ram with no defects, or you may buy one of equal value. [7]Through this process, the priest will purify you before the LORD, making you right with him,* and you will be forgiven for any of these sins you have committed."

Further Instructions for the Burnt Offering

[8]*Then the LORD said to Moses, [9]"Give Aaron and his sons the following instructions regarding the burnt offering. The burnt offering must be left on top of the altar until the next morning, and the fire on the altar must be kept burning all night. [10]In the morning, after the priest on duty has put on his official linen clothing and linen undergarments, he must clean out the ashes of the burnt offering and put them beside the altar. [11]Then he must take off these garments, change back into his regular clothes, and carry the ashes outside the camp to a place that is ceremonially clean. [12]Meanwhile, the fire on the altar must be kept burning; it must never go out. Each morning the priest will add fresh wood to the fire and arrange the burnt offering on it. He will then burn the fat of the peace offerings on it. [13]Remember, the fire must be kept burning on the altar at all times. It must never go out.

Further Instructions for the Grain Offering

[14]"These are the instructions regarding the grain offering. Aaron's sons must present

this offering to the LORD in front of the altar.
[15]The priest on duty will take from the grain
offering a handful of the choice flour moistened with olive oil, together with all the
frankincense. He will burn this representative portion on the altar as a pleasing aroma
to the LORD. [16]Aaron and his sons may eat
the rest of the flour, but it must be baked
without yeast and eaten in a sacred place
within the courtyard of the Tabernacle.*
[17]Remember, it must never be prepared
with yeast. I have given it to the priests as
their share of the special gifts presented to
me. Like the sin offering and the guilt offering, it is most holy. [18]Any of Aaron's male
descendants may eat from the special gifts
presented to the LORD. This is their permanent right from generation to generation.
Anyone or anything that touches these offerings will become holy."

Procedures for the Ordination Offering

[19]Then the LORD said to Moses, [20]"On the
day Aaron and his sons are anointed, they
must present to the LORD the standard grain
offering of two quarts* of choice flour, half
to be offered in the morning and half to be
offered in the evening. [21]It must be carefully mixed with olive oil and cooked on a
griddle. Then slice* this grain offering and
present it as a pleasing aroma to the LORD.
[22]In each generation, the high priest* who
succeeds Aaron must prepare this same offering. It belongs to the LORD and must be
burned up completely. This is a permanent
law. [23]All such grain offerings of a priest
must be burned up entirely. None of it may
be eaten."

Further Instructions for the Sin Offering

[24]Then the LORD said to Moses, [25]"Give
Aaron and his sons the following instructions regarding the sin offering. The animal
given as an offering for sin is a most holy
offering, and it must be slaughtered in the
LORD's presence at the place where the
burnt offerings are slaughtered. [26]The priest
who offers the sacrifice as a sin offering
must eat his portion in a sacred place within
the courtyard of the Tabernacle. [27]Anyone
or anything that touches the sacrificial
meat will become holy. If any of the sacrificial blood spatters on a person's clothing,
the soiled garment must be washed in a
sacred place. [28]If a clay pot is used to boil
the sacrificial meat, it must then be broken.
If a bronze pot is used, it must be scoured
and thoroughly rinsed with water. [29]Any
male from a priest's family may eat from
this offering; it is most holy. [30]But the offering for sin may not be eaten if its blood was
brought into the Tabernacle as an offering
for purification* in the Holy Place. It must
be completely burned with fire.

Further Instructions for the Guilt Offering

7 "These are the instructions for the guilt
offering. It is most holy. [2]The animal
sacrificed as a guilt offering must be slaughtered at the place where the burnt offerings are slaughtered, and its blood must
be splattered against all sides of the altar.
[3]The priest will then offer all its fat on the
altar, including the fat of the broad tail, the
fat around the internal organs, [4]the two
kidneys and the fat around them near the
loins, and the long lobe of the liver. These
are to be removed with the kidneys, [5]and
the priests will burn them on the altar as
a special gift presented to the LORD. This is
the guilt offering. [6]Any male from a priest's
family may eat the meat. It must be eaten in
a sacred place, for it is most holy.

[7]"The same instructions apply to both
the guilt offering and the sin offering. Both
belong to the priest who uses them to purify
someone, making that person right with the
LORD.* [8]In the case of the burnt offering,
the priest may keep the hide of the sacrificed animal. [9]Any grain offering that has
been baked in an oven, prepared in a pan,
or cooked on a griddle belongs to the priest
who presents it. [10]All other grain offerings,
whether made of dry flour or flour moistened
with olive oil, are to be shared equally among
all the priests, the descendants of Aaron.

Further Instructions for the Peace Offering

[11]"These are the instructions regarding the
different kinds of peace offerings that may
be presented to the LORD. [12]If you present
your peace offering as an expression of
thanksgiving, the usual animal sacrifice

5:11 Hebrew *1/10 of an ephah* [2.2 liters]. **5:15** Each shekel was about 0.4 ounces or 11 grams in weight. **6:1** Verses 6:1-7 are numbered 5:20-26 in Hebrew text. **6:7** Or *will make atonement for you before the LORD.* **6:8** Verses 6:8-30 are numbered 6:1-23 in Hebrew text. **6:16** Hebrew *Tent of Meeting;* also in 6:26, 30. **6:20** Hebrew *1/10 of an ephah* [2.2 liters]. **6:21** The meaning of this Hebrew term is uncertain. **6:22** Hebrew *the anointed priest.* **6:30** Or *an offering to make atonement.* **7:7** Or *to make atonement.*

must be accompanied by various kinds of bread made without yeast—thin cakes mixed with olive oil, wafers spread with oil, and cakes made of choice flour mixed with olive oil. [13]This peace offering of thanksgiving must also be accompanied by loaves of bread made with yeast. [14]One of each kind of bread must be presented as a gift to the LORD. It will then belong to the priest who splatters the blood of the peace offering against the altar. [15]The meat of the peace offering of thanksgiving must be eaten on the same day it is offered. None of it may be saved for the next morning.

[16]"If you bring an offering to fulfill a vow or as a voluntary offering, the meat must be eaten on the same day the sacrifice is offered, but whatever is left over may be eaten on the second day. [17]Any meat left over until the third day must be completely burned up. [18]If any of the meat from the peace offering is eaten on the third day, the person who presented it will not be accepted by the LORD. You will receive no credit for offering it. By then the meat will be contaminated; if you eat it, you will be punished for your sin.

[19]"Meat that touches anything ceremonially unclean may not be eaten; it must be completely burned up. The rest of the meat may be eaten, but only by people who are ceremonially clean. [20]If you are ceremonially unclean and you eat meat from a peace offering that was presented to the LORD, you will be cut off from the community. [21]If you touch anything that is unclean (whether it is human defilement or an unclean animal or any other unclean, detestable thing) and then eat meat from a peace offering presented to the LORD, you will be cut off from the community."

The Forbidden Blood and Fat

[22]Then the LORD said to Moses, [23]"Give the following instructions to the people of Israel. You must never eat fat, whether from cattle, sheep, or goats. [24]The fat of an animal found dead or torn to pieces by wild animals must never be eaten, though it may be used for any other purpose. [25]Anyone who eats fat from an animal presented as a special gift to the LORD will be cut off from the community. [26]No matter where you live, you must never consume the blood of any bird or animal. [27]Anyone who consumes blood will be cut off from the community."

A Portion for the Priests

[28]Then the LORD said to Moses, [29]"Give the following instructions to the people of Israel. When you present a peace offering to the LORD, bring part of it as a gift to the LORD. [30]Present it to the LORD with your own hands as a special gift to the LORD. Bring the fat of the animal, together with the breast, and lift up the breast as a special offering to the LORD. [31]Then the priest will burn the fat on the altar, but the breast will belong to Aaron and his descendants. [32]Give the right thigh of your peace offering to the priest as a gift. [33]The right thigh must always be given to the priest who offers the blood and the fat of the peace offering. [34]For I have reserved the breast of the special offering and the right thigh of the sacred offering for the priests. It is the permanent right of Aaron and his descendants to share in the peace offerings brought by the people of Israel. [35]This is their rightful share. The special gifts presented to the LORD have been reserved for Aaron and his descendants from the time they were set apart to serve the LORD as priests. [36]On the day they were anointed, the LORD commanded the Israelites to give these portions to the priests as their permanent share from generation to generation."

[37]These are the instructions for the burnt offering, the grain offering, the sin offering, and the guilt offering, as well as the ordination offering and the peace offering. [38]The LORD gave these instructions to Moses on Mount Sinai when he commanded the Israelites to present their offerings to the LORD in the wilderness of Sinai.

Ordination of the Priests

8 Then the LORD said to Moses, [2]"Bring Aaron and his sons, along with their sacred garments, the anointing oil, the bull for the sin offering, the two rams, and the basket of bread made without yeast, [3]and call the entire community of Israel together at the entrance of the Tabernacle.*"

[4]So Moses followed the LORD's instructions, and the whole community assembled at the Tabernacle entrance. [5]Moses announced to them, "This is what the LORD has commanded us to do!" [6]Then he presented Aaron and his sons and washed them with water. [7]He put the official tunic on Aaron and tied the sash around his

waist. He dressed him in the robe, placed the ephod on him, and attached the ephod securely with its decorative sash. [8]Then Moses placed the chestpiece on Aaron and put the Urim and the Thummim inside it. [9]He placed the turban on Aaron's head and attached the gold medallion—the badge of holiness—to the front of the turban, just as the LORD had commanded him.

[10]Then Moses took the anointing oil and anointed the Tabernacle and everything in it, making them holy. [11]He sprinkled the oil on the altar seven times, anointing it and all its utensils, as well as the washbasin and its stand, making them holy. [12]Then he poured some of the anointing oil on Aaron's head, anointing him and making him holy for his work. [13]Next Moses presented Aaron's sons. He clothed them in their tunics, tied their sashes around them, and put their special head coverings on them, just as the LORD had commanded him.

[14]Then Moses presented the bull for the sin offering. Aaron and his sons laid their hands on the bull's head, [15]and Moses slaughtered it. Moses took some of the blood, and with his finger he put it on the four horns of the altar to purify it. He poured out the rest of the blood at the base of the altar. Through this process, he made the altar holy by purifying it.* [16]Then Moses took all the fat around the internal organs, the long lobe of the liver, and the two kidneys and the fat around them, and he burned it all on the altar. [17]He took the rest of the bull, including its hide, meat, and dung, and burned it on a fire outside the camp, just as the LORD had commanded him.

[18]Then Moses presented the ram for the burnt offering. Aaron and his sons laid their hands on the ram's head, [19]and Moses slaughtered it. Then Moses took the ram's blood and splattered it against all sides of the altar. [20]Then he cut the ram into pieces, and he burned the head, some of its pieces, and the fat on the altar. [21]After washing the internal organs and the legs with water, Moses burned the entire ram on the altar as a burnt offering. It was a pleasing aroma, a special gift presented to the LORD, just as the LORD had commanded him.

[22]Then Moses presented the other ram, which was the ram of ordination. Aaron and his sons laid their hands on the ram's head, [23]and Moses slaughtered it. Then Moses took some of its blood and applied it to the lobe of Aaron's right ear, the thumb of his right hand, and the big toe of his right foot. [24]Next Moses presented Aaron's sons and applied some of the blood to the lobes of their right ears, the thumbs of their right hands, and the big toes of their right feet. He then splattered the rest of the blood against all sides of the altar.

[25]Next Moses took the fat, including the fat of the broad tail, the fat around the internal organs, the long lobe of the liver, and the two kidneys and the fat around them, along with the right thigh. [26]On top of these he placed a thin cake of bread made without yeast, a cake of bread mixed with olive oil, and a wafer spread with olive oil. All these were taken from the basket of bread made without yeast that was placed in the LORD's presence. [27]He put all these in the hands of Aaron and his sons, and he lifted these gifts as a special offering to the LORD. [28]Moses then took all the offerings back from them and burned them on the altar on top of the burnt offering. This was the ordination offering. It was a pleasing aroma, a special gift presented to the LORD. [29]Then Moses took the breast and lifted it up as a special offering to the LORD. This was Moses' portion of the ram of ordination, just as the LORD had commanded him.

[30]Next Moses took some of the anointing oil and some of the blood that was on the altar, and he sprinkled them on Aaron and his garments and on his sons and their garments. In this way, he made Aaron and his sons and their garments holy.

[31]Then Moses said to Aaron and his sons, "Boil the remaining meat of the offerings at the Tabernacle entrance, and eat it there, along with the bread that is in the basket of offerings for the ordination, just as I commanded when I said, 'Aaron and his sons will eat it.' [32]Any meat or bread that is left over must then be burned up. [33]You must not leave the Tabernacle entrance for seven days, for that is when the ordination ceremony will be completed. [34]Everything we have done today was commanded by the LORD in order to purify you, making you right with him.* [35]Now stay at the entrance of the Tabernacle day and night for seven

8:3 Hebrew *Tent of Meeting;* also in 8:4, 31, 33, 35. **8:15** Or *by making atonement for it;* or *that offerings for purification might be made on it.* **8:34** Or *to make atonement for you.*

days, and do everything the LORD requires. If you fail to do this, you will die, for this is what the LORD has commanded." 36So Aaron and his sons did everything the LORD had commanded through Moses.

The Priests Begin Their Work

9 After the ordination ceremony, on the eighth day, Moses called together Aaron and his sons and the elders of Israel. 2He said to Aaron, "Take a young bull for a sin offering and a ram for a burnt offering, both without defects, and present them to the LORD. 3Then tell the Israelites, 'Take a male goat for a sin offering, and take a calf and a lamb, both a year old and without defects, for a burnt offering. 4Also take a bull* and a ram for a peace offering and flour moistened with olive oil for a grain offering. Present all these offerings to the LORD because the LORD will appear to you today.'"

5So the people presented all these things at the entrance of the Tabernacle,* just as Moses had commanded. Then the whole community came forward and stood before the LORD. 6And Moses said, "This is what the LORD has commanded you to do so that the glory of the LORD may appear to you."

7Then Moses said to Aaron, "Come to the altar and sacrifice your sin offering and your burnt offering to purify yourself and the people. Then present the offerings of the people to purify them, making them right with the LORD,* just as he has commanded."

8So Aaron went to the altar and slaughtered the calf as a sin offering for himself. 9His sons brought him the blood, and he dipped his finger in it and put it on the horns of the altar. He poured out the rest of the blood at the base of the altar. 10Then he burned on the altar the fat, the kidneys, and the long lobe of the liver from the sin offering, just as the LORD had commanded Moses. 11The meat and the hide, however, he burned outside the camp.

12Next Aaron slaughtered the animal for the burnt offering. His sons brought him the blood, and he splattered it against all sides of the altar. 13Then they handed him each piece of the burnt offering, including the head, and he burned them on the altar. 14Then he washed the internal organs and the legs and burned them on the altar along with the rest of the burnt offering.

15Next Aaron presented the offerings of the people. He slaughtered the people's goat and presented it as an offering for their sin, just as he had first done with the offering for his own sin. 16Then he presented the burnt offering and sacrificed it in the prescribed way. 17He also presented the grain offering, burning a handful of the flour mixture on the altar, in addition to the regular burnt offering for the morning.

18Then Aaron slaughtered the bull and the ram for the people's peace offering. His sons brought him the blood, and he splattered it against all sides of the altar. 19Then he took the fat of the bull and the ram—the fat of the broad tail and from around the internal organs—along with the kidneys and the long lobes of the livers. 20He placed these fat portions on top of the breasts of these animals and burned them on the altar. 21Aaron then lifted up the breasts and right thighs as a special offering to the LORD, just as Moses had commanded.

22After that, Aaron raised his hands toward the people and blessed them. Then, after presenting the sin offering, the burnt offering, and the peace offering, he stepped down from the altar. 23Then Moses and Aaron went into the Tabernacle, and when they came back out, they blessed the people again, and the glory of the LORD appeared to the whole community. 24Fire blazed forth from the LORD's presence and consumed the burnt offering and the fat on the altar. When the people saw this, they shouted with joy and fell face down on the ground.

The Sin of Nadab and Abihu

10 Aaron's sons Nadab and Abihu put coals of fire in their incense burners and sprinkled incense over them. In this way, they disobeyed the LORD by burning before him the wrong kind of fire, different than he had commanded. 2So fire blazed forth from the LORD's presence and burned them up, and they died there before the LORD.

3Then Moses said to Aaron, "This is what the LORD meant when he said,

'I will display my holiness
  through those who come near me.
I will display my glory
  before all the people.'"

And Aaron was silent.

[4]Then Moses called for Mishael and Elzaphan, Aaron's cousins, the sons of Aaron's
uncle Uzziel. He said to them, "Come
forward and carry away the bodies of your
relatives from in front of the sanctuary to
a place outside the camp." [5]So they came
forward and picked them up by their garments and carried them out of the camp,
just as Moses had commanded.

[6]Then Moses said to Aaron and his sons
Eleazar and Ithamar, "Do not show grief by
leaving your hair uncombed* or by tearing
your clothes. If you do, you will die, and
the LORD's anger will strike the whole
community of Israel. However, the rest of
the Israelites, your relatives, may mourn
because of the LORD's fiery destruction of
Nadab and Abihu. [7]But you must not leave
the entrance of the Tabernacle* or you will
die, for you have been anointed with the
LORD's anointing oil." So they did as Moses
commanded.

Instructions for Priestly Conduct

[8]Then the LORD said to Aaron, [9]"You and
your descendants must never drink wine
or any other alcoholic drink before going
into the Tabernacle. If you do, you will die.
This is a permanent law for you, and it must
be observed from generation to generation. [10]You must distinguish between what
is sacred and what is common, between
what is ceremonially unclean and what is
clean. [11]And you must teach the Israelites
all the decrees that the LORD has given them
through Moses."

[12]Then Moses said to Aaron and his remaining sons, Eleazar and Ithamar, "Take
what is left of the grain offering after a
portion has been presented as a special gift
to the LORD, and eat it beside the altar. Make
sure it contains no yeast, for it is most holy.
[13]You must eat it in a sacred place, for it has
been given to you and your descendants as
your portion of the special gifts presented
to the LORD. These are the commands I have
been given. [14]But the breast and thigh that
were lifted up as a special offering may
be eaten in any place that is ceremonially
clean. These parts have been given to you
and your descendants as your portion of the
peace offerings presented by the people of
Israel. [15]You must lift up the thigh and breast
as a special offering to the LORD, along with
the fat of the special gifts. These parts will
belong to you and your descendants as
your permanent right, just as the LORD has
commanded."

[16]Moses then asked them what had happened to the goat of the sin offering. When
he discovered it had been burned up, he
became very angry with Eleazar and Ithamar,
Aaron's remaining sons. [17]"Why didn't you
eat the sin offering in the sacred area?" he
demanded. "It is a holy offering! The LORD
has given it to you to remove the guilt of
the community and to purify the people,
making them right with the LORD.* [18]Since
the animal's blood was not brought into the
Holy Place, you should have eaten the meat
in the sacred area as I ordered you."

[19]Then Aaron answered Moses, "Today
my sons presented both their sin offering
and their burnt offering to the LORD. And
yet this tragedy has happened to me. If I
had eaten the people's sin offering on such
a tragic day as this, would the LORD have
been pleased?" [20]And when Moses heard
this, he was satisfied.

9:4 Or *cow;* also in 9:18, 19. **9:5** Hebrew *Tent of Meeting;* also in 9:23. **9:7** Or *to make atonement for them.* **10:6** Or *by uncovering your heads.* **10:7** Hebrew *Tent of Meeting;* also in 10:9. **10:17** Or *to make atonement for the people before the LORD.*

Nadab and Abihu

Not satisfied with their role as priests, or perhaps with the way it was to be carried out, Nadab and Abihu wanted to do things differently. They "disobeyed the LORD by burning before him the wrong kind of fire, different than he had commanded" (Leviticus 10:1). What exactly this involved we aren't sure—though since God goes on to warn Aaron that priests shouldn't enter the sanctuary after drinking alcohol (10:8-9), it may have been that they were drunk. But whatever it was, their godless action and attitude displeased God greatly. Judgment came in the form of fire from God's presence that consumed them where they stood.

Ceremonially Clean and Unclean Animals

11 Then the LORD said to Moses and Aaron, 2“Give the following instructions to the people of Israel.

“Of all the land animals, these are the ones you may use for food. 3You may eat any animal that has completely split hooves and chews the cud. 4You may not, however, eat the following animals* that have split hooves or that chew the cud, but not both. The camel chews the cud but does not have split hooves, so it is ceremonially unclean for you. 5The hyrax* chews the cud but does not have split hooves, so it is unclean. 6The hare chews the cud but does not have split hooves, so it is unclean. 7The pig has evenly split hooves but does not chew the cud, so it is unclean. 8You may not eat the meat of these animals or even touch their carcasses. They are ceremonially unclean for you.

9“Of all the marine animals, these are ones you may use for food. You may eat anything from the water if it has both fins and scales, whether taken from salt water or from streams. 10But you must never eat animals from the sea or from rivers that do not have both fins and scales. They are detestable to you. This applies both to little creatures that live in shallow water and to all creatures that live in deep water. 11They will always be detestable to you. You must never eat their meat or even touch their dead bodies. 12Any marine animal that does not have both fins and scales is detestable to you.

13“These are the birds that are detestable to you. You must never eat them: the griffon vulture, the bearded vulture, the black vulture, 14the kite, falcons of all kinds, 15ravens of all kinds, 16the eagle owl, the short-eared owl, the seagull, hawks of all kinds, 17the little owl, the cormorant, the great owl, 18the barn owl, the desert owl, the Egyptian vulture, 19the stork, herons of all kinds, the hoopoe, and the bat.

20“You must not eat winged insects that walk along the ground; they are detestable to you. 21You may, however, eat winged insects that walk along the ground and have jointed legs so they can jump. 22The insects you are permitted to eat include all kinds of locusts, bald locusts, crickets, and grasshoppers. 23All other winged insects that walk along the ground are detestable to you.

Holiness

God’s people are called to be holy, different from everything around them, in order to reflect what he himself is like. Sometimes a false division is drawn between holiness in the Old Testament and in the New Testament. But in both testaments, God’s command is identical: “Be holy, because I am holy” (Leviticus 11:44; 1 Peter 1:16)—a holiness that is to affect not just faith but every aspect of life.

What is different between the Old Testament and the New Testament, however, is *how* this holiness was to be expressed. In the Old Testament, holiness was carefully prescribed through detailed commands, covering how God’s people worshiped, lived, ate, dressed, kept hygienic, cared for the poor, etc. It was following these commands that demonstrated you were truly part of God’s covenant people.

In the New Testament, Christians are still called to holiness—though now, not through external laws, but by an internal enabler, the Holy Spirit. Throughout the Bible, holiness is the *consequence*, not the *cause*, of a relationship with God.

Christians are not called to live by following rules, even less by following rules they expect others to live by (e.g., Colossians 2:16-23). Rather they are told to live by following the Holy Spirit and his leadings. “Let the Holy Spirit guide your lives. Then you won’t be doing what your sinful nature craves” (Galatians 5:16) is God’s promise to us.

▶ *See also* ***The holiness of God****, page 754;* ***Becoming like Christ****, page 1435.*

24 “The following creatures will make you ceremonially unclean. If any of you touch their carcasses, you will be defiled until evening. 25 If you pick up their carcasses, you must wash your clothes, and you will remain defiled until evening.

26 “Any animal that has split hooves that are not evenly divided or that does not chew the cud is unclean for you. If you touch the carcass of such an animal, you will be defiled. 27 Of the animals that walk on all fours, those that have paws are unclean. If you touch the carcass of such an animal, you will be defiled until evening. 28 If you pick up its carcass, you must wash your clothes, and you will remain defiled until evening. These animals are unclean for you.

29 “Of the small animals that scurry along the ground, these are unclean for you: the mole rat, the rat, large lizards of all kinds, 30 the gecko, the monitor lizard, the common lizard, the sand lizard, and the chameleon. 31 All these small animals are unclean for you. If any of you touch the dead body of such an animal, you will be defiled until evening. 32 If such an animal dies and falls on something, that object will be unclean. This is true whether the object is made of wood, cloth, leather, or burlap. Whatever its use, you must dip it in water, and it will remain defiled until evening. After that, it will be ceremonially clean and may be used again.

33 “If such an animal falls into a clay pot, everything in the pot will be defiled, and the pot must be smashed. 34 If the water from such a container spills on any food, the food will be defiled. And any beverage in such a container will be defiled. 35 Any object on which the carcass of such an animal falls will be defiled. If it is an oven or hearth, it must be destroyed, for it is defiled, and you must treat it accordingly.

36 “However, if the carcass of such an animal falls into a spring or a cistern, the water will still be clean. But anyone who touches the carcass will be defiled. 37 If the carcass falls on seed grain to be planted in the field, the seed will still be considered clean. 38 But if the seed is wet when the carcass falls on it, the seed will be defiled.

39 “If an animal you are permitted to eat dies and you touch its carcass, you will be defiled until evening. 40 If you eat any of its meat or carry away its carcass, you must wash your clothes, and you will remain defiled until evening.

41 “All small animals that scurry along the ground are detestable, and you must never eat them. 42 This includes all animals that slither along on their bellies, as well as those with four legs and those with many feet. All such animals that scurry along the ground are detestable, and you must never eat them. 43 Do not defile yourselves by touching them. You must not make yourselves ceremonially unclean because of them. 44 For I am the LORD your God. You must consecrate yourselves and be holy, because I am holy. So do not defile yourselves with any of these small animals that scurry along the ground. 45 For I, the LORD, am the one who brought you up from the land of Egypt, that I might be your God. Therefore, you must be holy because I am holy.

46 “These are the instructions regarding land animals, birds, marine creatures, and animals that scurry along the ground. 47 By these instructions you will know what is unclean and clean, and which animals may be eaten and which may not be eaten.”

Purification after Childbirth

12 The LORD said to Moses, 2 “Give the following instructions to the people of Israel. If a woman becomes pregnant and gives birth to a son, she will be ceremonially unclean for seven days, just as she is unclean during her menstrual period. 3 On the eighth day the boy’s foreskin must be circumcised. 4 After waiting thirty-three days, she will be purified from the bleeding of childbirth. During this time of purification, she must not touch anything that is set apart as holy. And she must not enter the sanctuary until her time of purification is over. 5 If a woman gives birth to a daughter, she will be ceremonially unclean for two weeks, just as she is unclean during her menstrual period. After waiting sixty-six days, she will be purified from the bleeding of childbirth.

6 “When the time of purification is completed for either a son or a daughter, the woman must bring a one-year-old lamb for a burnt offering and a young pigeon or turtledove for a purification offering. She

11:4 The identification of some of the animals, birds, and insects in this chapter is uncertain. **11:5** Or *coney,* or *rock badger.*

must bring her offerings to the priest at the entrance of the Tabernacle.* 7The priest will then present them to the LORD to purify her.* Then she will be ceremonially clean again after her bleeding at childbirth. These are the instructions for a woman after the birth of a son or a daughter.

8"If a woman cannot afford to bring a lamb, she must bring two turtledoves or two young pigeons. One will be for the burnt offering and the other for the purification offering. The priest will sacrifice them to purify her, and she will be ceremonially clean."

Serious Skin Diseases

13 The LORD said to Moses and Aaron, 2"If anyone has a swelling or a rash or discolored skin that might develop into a serious skin disease,* that person must be brought to Aaron the priest or to one of his sons.* 3The priest will examine the affected area of the skin. If the hair in the affected area has turned white and the problem appears to be more than skin-deep, it is a serious skin disease, and the priest who examines it must pronounce the person ceremonially unclean.

4"But if the affected area of the skin is only a white discoloration and does not appear to be more than skin-deep, and if the hair on the spot has not turned white, the priest will quarantine the person for seven days. 5On the seventh day the priest will make another examination. If he finds the affected area has not changed and the problem has not spread on the skin, the priest will quarantine the person for seven more days. 6On the seventh day the priest will make another examination. If he finds the affected area has faded and has not spread, the priest will pronounce the person ceremonially clean. It was only a rash. The person's clothing must be washed, and the person will be ceremonially clean. 7But if the rash continues to spread after the person has been examined by the priest and has been pronounced clean, the infected person must return to be examined again. 8If the priest finds that the rash has spread, he must pronounce the person ceremonially unclean, for it is indeed a skin disease.

9"Anyone who develops a serious skin disease must go to the priest for an examination. 10If the priest finds a white swelling on the skin, and some hair on the spot has turned white, and there is an open sore in the affected area, 11it is a chronic skin disease, and the priest must pronounce the person ceremonially unclean. In such cases the person need not be quarantined, for it is obvious that the skin is defiled by the disease.

12"Now suppose the disease has spread all over the person's skin, covering the body from head to foot. 13When the priest examines the infected person and finds that the disease covers the entire body, he will pronounce the person ceremonially clean. Since the skin has turned completely white, the person is clean. 14But if any open sores appear, the infected person will be pronounced ceremonially unclean. 15The priest must make this pronouncement as soon as he sees an open sore, since open sores indicate the presence of a skin disease. 16However, if the open sores heal and turn white like the rest of the skin, the person must return to the priest 17for another examination. If the affected areas have indeed turned white, the priest will then pronounce the person ceremonially clean by declaring, 'You are clean!'

18"If anyone has a boil on the skin that has started to heal, 19but a white swelling or a reddish white spot develops in its place, that person must go to the priest to be examined. 20If the priest examines it and finds it to be more than skin-deep, and if the hair in the affected area has turned white, the priest must pronounce the person ceremonially unclean. The boil has become a serious skin disease. 21But if the priest finds no white hair on the affected area and the problem appears to be no more than skin-deep and has faded, the priest must quarantine the person for seven days. 22If during that time the affected area spreads on the skin, the priest must pronounce the person ceremonially unclean, because it is a serious disease. 23But if the area grows no larger and does not spread, it is merely the scar from the boil, and the priest will pronounce the person ceremonially clean.

24"If anyone has suffered a burn on the skin and the burned area changes color, becoming either reddish white or shiny white, 25the priest must examine it. If he finds that the hair in the affected area has turned white and the problem appears to be more than skin-deep, a skin disease has broken out in the burn. The priest must then pronounce the person ceremonially unclean, for it is clearly a serious skin disease. [26]But if the priest finds no white hair on the affected area and the problem appears to be no more than skin-deep and has faded, the priest must quarantine the infected person for seven days. [27]On the seventh day the priest must examine the person again. If the affected area has spread on the skin, the priest must pronounce that person ceremonially unclean, for it is clearly a serious skin disease. [28]But if the affected area has not changed or spread on the skin and has faded, it is simply a swelling from the burn. The priest will then pronounce the person ceremonially clean, for it is only the scar from the burn.

[29]"If anyone, either a man or woman, has a sore on the head or chin, [30]the priest must examine it. If he finds it is more than skin-deep and has fine yellow hair on it, the priest must pronounce the person ceremonially unclean. It is a scabby sore of the head or chin. [31]If the priest examines the scabby sore and finds that it is only skin-deep but there is no black hair on it, he must quarantine the person for seven days. [32]On the seventh day the priest must examine the sore again. If he finds that the scabby sore has not spread, and there is no yellow hair on it, and it appears to be only skin-deep, [33]the person must shave off all hair except the hair on the affected area. Then the priest must quarantine the person for another seven days. [34]On the seventh day he will examine the sore again. If it has not spread and appears to be no more than skin-deep, the priest will pronounce the person ceremonially clean. The person's clothing must be washed, and the person will be ceremonially clean. [35]But if the scabby sore begins to spread after the person is pronounced clean, [36]the priest must do another examination. If he finds that the sore has spread, the priest does not need to look for yellow hair. The infected person is ceremonially unclean. [37]But if the color of the scabby sore does not change and black hair has grown on it, it has healed. The priest will then pronounce the person ceremonially clean.

[38]"If anyone, either a man or woman, has shiny white patches on the skin, [39]the priest must examine the affected area. If he finds that the shiny patches are only pale white, this is a harmless skin rash, and the person is ceremonially clean.

[40]"If a man loses his hair and his head becomes bald, he is still ceremonially clean. [41]And if he loses hair on his forehead, he simply has a bald forehead; he is still clean. [42]However, if a reddish white sore appears on the bald area on top of his head or on his forehead, this is a skin disease. [43]The priest must examine him, and if he finds swelling around the reddish white sore anywhere on the man's head and it looks like a skin disease, [44]the man is indeed infected with a skin disease and is unclean. The priest must pronounce him ceremonially unclean because of the sore on his head.

[45]"Those who suffer from a serious skin disease must tear their clothing and leave their hair uncombed.* They must cover their mouth and call out, 'Unclean! Unclean!' [46]As long as the serious disease lasts, they will be ceremonially unclean. They must live in isolation in their place outside the camp.

Treatment of Contaminated Clothing

[47]"Now suppose mildew* contaminates some woolen or linen clothing, [48]woolen or linen fabric, the hide of an animal, or anything made of leather. [49]If the contaminated area in the clothing, the animal hide, the fabric, or the leather article has turned greenish or reddish, it is contaminated with mildew and must be shown to the priest. [50]After examining the affected spot, the priest will put the article in quarantine for seven days. [51]On the seventh day the priest must inspect it again. If the contaminated area has spread, the clothing or fabric or leather is clearly contaminated by a serious mildew and is ceremonially unclean. [52]The priest must burn the item—the clothing, the woolen or linen fabric, or piece of leather—for it has been contaminated by a serious mildew. It must be completely destroyed by fire.

[53]"But if the priest examines it and finds that the contaminated area has not spread in the clothing, the fabric, or the leather,

12:6 Hebrew *Tent of Meeting.* **12:7** Or *to make atonement for her;* also in 12:8. **13:2a** Traditionally rendered *leprosy.* The Hebrew word used throughout this passage is used to describe various skin diseases. **13:2b** Or *one of his descendants.* **13:45** Or *and uncover their heads.* **13:47** Traditionally rendered *leprosy.* The Hebrew term used throughout this passage is the same term used for the various skin diseases described in 13:1-46.

54the priest will order the object to be washed and then quarantined for seven more days. 55Then the priest must examine the object again. If he finds that the contaminated area has not changed color after being washed, even if it did not spread, the object is defiled. It must be completely burned up, whether the contaminated spot* is on the inside or outside. 56But if the priest examines it and finds that the contaminated area has faded after being washed, he must cut the spot from the clothing, the fabric, or the leather. 57If the spot later reappears on the clothing, the fabric, or the leather article, the mildew is clearly spreading, and the contaminated object must be burned up. 58But if the spot disappears from the clothing, the fabric, or the leather article after it has been washed, it must be washed again; then it will be ceremonially clean.

59"These are the instructions for dealing with mildew that contaminates woolen or linen clothing or fabric or anything made of leather. This is how the priest will determine whether these items are ceremonially clean or unclean."

Cleansing from Skin Diseases

14 And the LORD said to Moses, 2"The following instructions are for those seeking ceremonial purification from a skin disease.* Those who have been healed must be brought to the priest, 3who will examine them at a place outside the camp. If the priest finds that someone has been healed of a serious skin disease, 4he will perform a purification ceremony, using two live birds that are ceremonially clean, a stick of cedar,* some scarlet yarn, and a hyssop branch. 5The priest will order that one bird be slaughtered over a clay pot filled with fresh water. 6He will take the live bird, the cedar stick, the scarlet yarn, and the hyssop branch, and dip them into the blood of the bird that was slaughtered over the fresh water. 7The priest will then sprinkle the blood of the dead bird seven times on the person being purified of the skin disease. When the priest has purified the person, he will release the live bird in the open field to fly away.

8"The persons being purified must then wash their clothes, shave off all their hair, and bathe themselves in water. Then they will be ceremonially clean and may return to the camp. However, they must remain outside their tents for seven days. 9On the seventh day they must again shave all the hair from their heads, including the hair of the beard and eyebrows. They must also wash their clothes and bathe themselves in water. Then they will be ceremonially clean.

10"On the eighth day each person being purified must bring two male lambs and a one-year-old female lamb, all with no defects, along with a grain offering of six quarts* of choice flour moistened with olive oil, and a cup* of olive oil. 11Then the officiating priest will present that person for purification, along with the offerings, before the LORD at the entrance of the Tabernacle.* 12The priest will take one of the male lambs and the olive oil and present them as a guilt offering, lifting them up as a special offering before the LORD. 13He will then slaughter the male lamb in the sacred area where sin offerings and burnt offerings are slaughtered. As with the sin offering, the guilt offering belongs to the priest. It is a most holy offering. 14The priest will then take some of the blood of the guilt offering and apply it to the lobe of the right ear, the thumb of the right hand, and the big toe of the right foot of the person being purified.

15"Then the priest will pour some of the olive oil into the palm of his own left hand. 16He will dip his right finger into the oil in his palm and sprinkle some of it with his finger seven times before the LORD. 17The priest will then apply some of the oil in his palm over the blood from the guilt offering that is on the lobe of the right ear, the thumb of the right hand, and the big toe of the right foot of the person being purified. 18The priest will apply the oil remaining in his hand to the head of the person being purified. Through this process, the priest will purify* the person before the LORD.

19"Then the priest must present the sin offering to purify the person who was cured of the skin disease. After that, the priest will slaughter the burnt offering 20and offer it on the altar along with the grain offering. Through this process, the priest will purify the person who was healed, and the person will be ceremonially clean.

21"But anyone who is too poor and cannot afford these offerings may bring one male lamb for a guilt offering, to be lifted up as a special offering for purification. The person must also bring two quarts* of choice flour moistened with olive oil for the grain offering and a cup of olive oil. [22]The offering must also include two turtledoves or two young pigeons, whichever the person can afford. One of the pair must be used for the sin offering and the other for a burnt offering. [23]On the eighth day of the purification ceremony, the person being purified must bring the offerings to the priest in the LORD's presence at the entrance of the Tabernacle. [24]The priest will take the lamb for the guilt offering, along with the olive oil, and lift them up as a special offering to the LORD. [25]Then the priest will slaughter the lamb for the guilt offering. He will take some of its blood and apply it to the lobe of the right ear, the thumb of the right hand, and the big toe of the right foot of the person being purified.

[26]"The priest will also pour some of the olive oil into the palm of his own left hand. [27]He will dip his right finger into the oil in his palm and sprinkle some of it seven times before the LORD. [28]The priest will then apply some of the oil in his palm over the blood from the guilt offering that is on the lobe of the right ear, the thumb of the right hand, and the big toe of the right foot of the person being purified. [29]The priest will apply the oil remaining in his hand to the head of the person being purified. Through this process, the priest will purify the person before the LORD.

[30]"Then the priest will offer the two turtledoves or the two young pigeons, whichever the person can afford. [31]One of them is for a sin offering and the other for a burnt offering, to be presented along with the grain offering. Through this process, the priest will purify the person before the LORD. [32]These are the instructions for purification for those who have recovered from a serious skin disease but who cannot afford to bring the offerings normally required for the ceremony of purification."

Treatment of Contaminated Houses

[33]Then the LORD said to Moses and Aaron, [34]"When you arrive in Canaan, the land I am giving you as your own possession, I may contaminate some of the houses in your land with mildew.* [35]The owner of such a house must then go to the priest and say, 'It appears that my house has some kind of mildew.' [36]Before the priest goes in to inspect the house, he must have the house emptied so nothing inside will be pronounced ceremonially unclean. [37]Then the priest will go in and examine the mildew on the walls. If he finds greenish or reddish streaks and the contamination appears to go deeper than the wall's surface, [38]the priest will step outside the door and put the house in quarantine for seven days. [39]On the seventh day the priest must return for another inspection. If he finds that the mildew on the walls of the house has spread, [40]the priest must order that the stones from those areas be removed. The contaminated material will then be taken outside the town to an area designated as ceremonially unclean. [41]Next the inside walls of the entire house must be scraped thoroughly and the scrapings dumped in the unclean place outside the town. [42]Other stones will be brought in to replace the ones that were removed, and the walls will be replastered.

[43]"But if the mildew reappears after all the stones have been replaced and the house has been scraped and replastered, [44]the priest must return and inspect the house again. If he finds that the mildew has spread, the walls are clearly contaminated with a serious mildew, and the house is defiled. [45]It must be torn down, and all its stones, timbers, and plaster must be carried out of town to the place designated as ceremonially unclean. [46]Those who enter the house during the period of quarantine will be ceremonially unclean until evening, [47]and all who sleep or eat in the house must wash their clothing.

[48]"But if the priest returns for his inspection and finds that the mildew has not reappeared in the house after the fresh plastering, he will pronounce it clean because the mildew is clearly gone. [49]To purify the house the priest must take two birds, a stick of cedar, some scarlet yarn, and a hyssop branch. [50]He will slaughter one of the birds over a clay pot filled with fresh water. [51]He will take the cedar stick, the hyssop branch, the scarlet yarn, and the live bird,

13:55 The meaning of the Hebrew is uncertain. **14:2** Traditionally rendered *leprosy;* see note on 13:2a. **14:4** Or *juniper;* also in 14:6, 49, 51. **14:10a** Hebrew *3/10 of an ephah* [6.6 liters]. **14:10b** Hebrew *1 log* [0.3 liters]; also in 14:21. **14:11** Hebrew *Tent of Meeting;* also in 14:23. **14:18** Or *will make atonement for;* similarly in 14:19, 20, 21, 29, 31, 53. **14:21** Hebrew *1/10 of an ephah* [2.2 liters]. **14:34** Traditionally rendered *leprosy;* see note on 13:47.

and dip them into the blood of the slaughtered bird and into the fresh water. Then he will sprinkle the house seven times. [52]When the priest has purified the house in exactly this way, [53]he will release the live bird in the open fields outside the town. Through this process, the priest will purify the house, and it will be ceremonially clean.

[54]"These are the instructions for dealing with serious skin diseases,* including scabby sores; [55]and mildew,* whether on clothing or in a house; [56]and a swelling on the skin, a rash, or discolored skin. [57]This procedure will determine whether a person or object is ceremonially clean or unclean.

"These are the instructions regarding skin diseases and mildew."

Bodily Discharges

15 The LORD said to Moses and Aaron, [2]"Give the following instructions to the people of Israel.

"Any man who has a bodily discharge is ceremonially unclean. [3]This defilement is caused by his discharge, whether the discharge continues or stops. In either case the man is unclean. [4]Any bed on which the man with the discharge lies and anything on which he sits will be ceremonially unclean. [5]So if you touch the man's bed, you must wash your clothes and bathe yourself in water, and you will remain unclean until evening. [6]If you sit where the man with the discharge has sat, you must wash your clothes and bathe yourself in water, and you will remain unclean until evening. [7]If you touch the man with the discharge, you must wash your clothes and bathe yourself in water, and you will remain unclean until evening. [8]If the man spits on you, you must wash your clothes and bathe yourself in water, and you will remain unclean until evening. [9]Any saddle blanket on which the man rides will be ceremonially unclean. [10]If you touch anything that was under the man, you will be unclean until evening. You must wash your clothes and bathe yourself in water, and you will remain unclean until evening. [11]If the man touches you without first rinsing his hands, you must wash your clothes and bathe yourself in water, and you will remain unclean until evening. [12]Any clay pot the man touches must be broken, and any wooden utensil he touches must be rinsed with water.

[13]"When the man with the discharge is healed, he must count off seven days for the period of purification. Then he must wash his clothes and bathe himself in fresh water, and he will be ceremonially clean. [14]On the eighth day he must get two turtledoves or two young pigeons and come before the LORD at the entrance of the Tabernacle* and give his offerings to the priest. [15]The priest will offer one bird for a sin offering and the other for a burnt offering. Through this process, the priest will purify* the man before the LORD for his discharge.

[16]"Whenever a man has an emission of semen, he must bathe his entire body in water, and he will remain ceremonially unclean until the next evening.* [17]Any clothing or leather with semen on it must be washed in water, and it will remain unclean until evening. [18]After a man and a woman have sexual intercourse, they must each bathe in water, and they will remain unclean until the next evening.

[19]"Whenever a woman has her menstrual period, she will be ceremonially unclean for seven days. Anyone who touches her during that time will be unclean until evening. [20]Anything on which the woman lies or sits during the time of her period will be unclean. [21]If any of you touch her bed, you must wash your clothes and bathe yourself in water, and you will remain unclean until evening. [22]If you touch any object she has sat on, you must wash your clothes and bathe yourself in water, and you will remain unclean until evening. [23]This includes her bed or any other object she has sat on; you will be unclean until evening if you touch it. [24]If a man has sexual intercourse with her and her blood touches him, her menstrual impurity will be transmitted to him. He will remain unclean for seven days, and any bed on which he lies will be unclean.

[25]"If a woman has a flow of blood for many days that is unrelated to her menstrual period, or if the blood continues beyond the normal period, she is ceremonially unclean. As during her menstrual period, the woman will be unclean as long as the discharge continues. [26]Any bed she lies on and any object she sits on during that time will be unclean, just as during her normal menstrual period. [27]If any of you touch these things, you will be ceremonially unclean. You must wash your clothes and

bathe yourself in water, and you will remain unclean until evening.

28“When the woman’s bleeding stops, she must count off seven days. Then she will be ceremonially clean. 29On the eighth day she must bring two turtledoves or two young pigeons and present them to the priest at the entrance of the Tabernacle. 30The priest will offer one for a sin offering and the other for a burnt offering. Through this process, the priest will purify her before the LORD for the ceremonial impurity caused by her bleeding.

31“This is how you will guard the people of Israel from ceremonial uncleanness. Otherwise they would die, for their impurity would defile my Tabernacle that stands among them. 32These are the instructions for dealing with anyone who has a bodily discharge—a man who is unclean because of an emission of semen 33or a woman during her menstrual period. It applies to any man or woman who has a bodily discharge, and to a man who has sexual intercourse with a woman who is ceremonially unclean.”

The Day of Atonement

16 The LORD spoke to Moses after the death of Aaron’s two sons, who died after they entered the LORD’s presence and burned the wrong kind of fire before him. 2The LORD said to Moses, “Warn your brother, Aaron, not to enter the Most Holy Place behind the inner curtain whenever he chooses; if he does, he will die. For the Ark’s cover—the place of atonement—is there, and I myself am present in the cloud above the atonement cover.

3“When Aaron enters the sanctuary area, he must follow these instructions fully. He must bring a young bull for a sin offering and a ram for a burnt offering. 4He must put on his linen tunic and the linen undergarments worn next to his body. He must tie the linen sash around his waist and put the linen turban on his head. These are sacred garments, so he must bathe himself in water before he puts them on. 5Aaron must take from the community of Israel two male goats for a sin offering and a ram for a burnt offering.

6“Aaron will present his own bull as a sin offering to purify himself and his family, making them right with the LORD.* 7Then he must take the two male goats and present them to the LORD at the entrance of the Tabernacle.* 8He is to cast sacred lots to determine which goat will be reserved as an offering to the LORD and which will carry the sins of the people to the wilderness of

14:54 Traditionally rendered *leprosy;* see note on 13:2a.
14:55 Traditionally rendered *leprosy;* see note on 13:47.
15:14 Hebrew *Tent of Meeting;* also in 15:29. **15:15** Or *will make atonement for;* also in 15:30. **15:16** Hebrew *until evening;* also in 15:18. **16:6** Or *to make atonement for himself and his family;* similarly in 16:11, 17b, 24, 34. **16:7** Hebrew *Tent of Meeting;* also in 16:16, 17, 20, 23, 33.

The Day of Atonement

The Day of Atonement was a solemn annual festival when all work was prohibited and a fast commanded to reflect its seriousness.

God commanded Aaron to select a bull, a ram, and two goats, and then to wash and to wear special garments. First, he had to offer a sacrifice to atone for his own sin and that of his fellow priests. This involved slaughtering the bull, offering incense so that its smoke would prevent him from seeing God’s presence in the Most Holy Place—the only occasion he could enter there—and sprinkling the bull’s blood on and before the atonement cover. Only then could he deal with Israel’s sin. One goat, chosen by casting lots, was to be sacrificed and its blood sprinkled in the same way. Then he had to lay his hands on the second goat’s head, confessing Israel’s sin over it, and send it off into the wilderness—a symbol of sin being carried away. After more ritual washing and putting on his ordinary garments, Aaron would offer the ram as a burnt offering.

The New Testament sees this ritual as a picture of Christ’s work on the cross (Hebrews 9:6-14), both atoning for our sin and carrying it away so we might enter God’s holy presence.

Azazel. [9]Aaron will then present as a sin offering the goat chosen by lot for the LORD.
[10]The other goat, the scapegoat chosen by
lot to be sent away, will be kept alive, standing before the LORD. When it is sent away
to Azazel in the wilderness, the people will
be purified and made right with the LORD.*

[11]"Aaron will present his own bull as a sin
offering to purify himself and his family,
making them right with the LORD. After he
has slaughtered the bull as a sin offering,
[12]he will fill an incense burner with burning
coals from the altar that stands before the
LORD. Then he will take two handfuls of fragrant powdered incense and will carry the
burner and the incense behind the inner
curtain. [13]There in the LORD's presence he
will put the incense on the burning coals
so that a cloud of incense will rise over the
Ark's cover—the place of atonement—that
rests on the Ark of the Covenant.* If he
follows these instructions, he will not die.
[14]Then he must take some of the blood of
the bull, dip his finger in it, and sprinkle
it on the east side of the atonement cover.
He must sprinkle blood seven times with his
finger in front of the atonement cover.

[15]"Then Aaron must slaughter the first
goat as a sin offering for the people and
carry its blood behind the inner curtain.
There he will sprinkle the goat's blood over
the atonement cover and in front of it, just
as he did with the bull's blood. [16]Through
this process, he will purify* the Most Holy
Place, and he will do the same for the entire
Tabernacle, because of the defiling sin and
rebellion of the Israelites. [17]No one else is
allowed inside the Tabernacle when Aaron
enters it for the purification ceremony in the
Most Holy Place. No one may enter until he
comes out again after purifying himself, his
family, and all the congregation of Israel,
making them right with the LORD.

[18]"Then Aaron will come out to purify
the altar that stands before the LORD. He
will do this by taking some of the blood
from the bull and the goat and putting it
on each of the horns of the altar. [19]Then
he must sprinkle the blood with his finger
seven times over the altar. In this way, he
will cleanse it from Israel's defilement and
make it holy.

[20]"When Aaron has finished purifying the
Most Holy Place and the Tabernacle and the
altar, he must present the live goat. [21]He will
lay both of his hands on the goat's head and
confess over it all the wickedness, rebellion,
and sins of the people of Israel. In this way,
he will transfer the people's sins to the head
of the goat. Then a man specially chosen for
the task will drive the goat into the wilderness. [22]As the goat goes into the wilderness,
it will carry all the people's sins upon itself
into a desolate land.

[23]"When Aaron goes back into the Tabernacle, he must take off the linen garments
he was wearing when he entered the Most
Holy Place, and he must leave the garments
there. [24]Then he must bathe himself with
water in a sacred place, put on his regular
garments, and go out to sacrifice a burnt offering for himself and a burnt offering for
the people. Through this process, he will
purify himself and the people, making them
right with the LORD. [25]He must then burn all
the fat of the sin offering on the altar.

The importance of blood

For Israel, blood represented life—"the life of the body is in its blood," God said, before adding, "I have given you the blood on the altar to purify you, making you right with the LORD. It is the blood, given in exchange for a life, that makes purification possible" (Leviticus 17:11). And yet, all the blood of all those Old Testament sacrifices could never really deal with sin, for "it is not possible for the blood of bulls and goats to take away sins" (Hebrews 10:4). Rather, these sacrifices were serving as a pointer to Christ, the perfect sacrifice who would come and shed his blood as the price for all sin. In the meantime, Israel was to treat blood as holy, ensuring that it was drained from animals before eating them (Leviticus 17:10-12).

▸ *See also **Old Testament sacrifices and offerings**, page 118.*

26“The man chosen to drive the scapegoat into the wilderness of Azazel must wash his clothes and bathe himself in water. Then he may return to the camp.

27“The bull and the goat presented as sin offerings, whose blood Aaron takes into the Most Holy Place for the purification ceremony, will be carried outside the camp. The animals’ hides, internal organs, and dung are all to be burned. 28The man who burns them must wash his clothes and bathe himself in water before returning to the camp.

29“On the tenth day of the appointed month in early autumn,* you must deny yourselves.* Neither native-born Israelites nor foreigners living among you may do any kind of work. This is a permanent law for you. 30On that day offerings of purification will be made for you,* and you will be purified in the LORD’s presence from all your sins. 31It will be a Sabbath day of complete rest for you, and you must deny yourselves. This is a permanent law for you. 32In future generations, the purification* ceremony will be performed by the priest who has been anointed and ordained to serve as high priest in place of his ancestor Aaron. He will put on the holy linen garments 33and purify the Most Holy Place, the Tabernacle, the altar, the priests, and the entire congregation. 34This is a permanent law for you, to purify the people of Israel from their sins, making them right with the LORD once each year.”

Moses followed all these instructions exactly as the LORD had commanded him.

Prohibitions against Eating Blood

17 Then the LORD said to Moses, 2“Give the following instructions to Aaron and his sons and all the people of Israel. This is what the LORD has commanded.

3“If any native Israelite sacrifices a bull* or a lamb or a goat anywhere inside or outside the camp 4instead of bringing it to the entrance of the Tabernacle* to present it as an offering to the LORD, that person will be as guilty as a murderer.* Such a person has shed blood and will be cut off from the community. 5The purpose of this rule is to stop the Israelites from sacrificing animals in the open fields. It will ensure that they bring their sacrifices to the priest at the entrance of the Tabernacle, so he can present them to the LORD as peace offerings. 6Then the priest will be able to splatter the blood against the LORD’s altar at the entrance of the Tabernacle, and he will burn the fat as a pleasing aroma to the LORD. 7The people must no longer be unfaithful to the LORD by offering sacrifices to the goat idols.* This is a permanent law for them, to be observed from generation to generation.

8“Give them this command as well. If any native Israelite or foreigner living among you offers a burnt offering or a sacrifice 9but does not bring it to the entrance of the Tabernacle to offer it to the LORD, that person will be cut off from the community.

10“And if any native Israelite or foreigner living among you eats or drinks blood in any form, I will turn against that person and cut him off from the community of your people, 11for the life of the body is in its blood. I have given you the blood on the altar to purify you, making you right with the LORD.* It is the blood, given in exchange for a life, that makes purification possible. 12That is why I have said to the people of Israel, ‘You must never eat or drink blood—neither you nor the foreigners living among you.’

13“And if any native Israelite or foreigner living among you goes hunting and kills an animal or bird that is approved for eating, he must drain its blood and cover it with earth. 14The life of every creature is in its blood. That is why I have said to the people of Israel, ‘You must never eat or drink blood, for the life of any creature is in its blood.’ So whoever consumes blood will be cut off from the community.

15“And if any native-born Israelites or foreigners eat the meat of an animal that died naturally or was torn up by wild animals, they must wash their clothes and bathe themselves in water. They will remain ceremonially unclean until evening, but then they will be clean. 16But if they do not wash their clothes and bathe themselves, they will be punished for their sin.”

16:10 Or *wilderness, it will make atonement for the people.* **16:13** Hebrew *that is above the Testimony.* The Hebrew word for “testimony” refers to the terms of the LORD’s covenant with Israel as written on stone tablets, which were kept in the Ark, and also to the covenant itself. **16:16** Or *make atonement for;* similarly in 16:17a, 18, 20, 27, 33. **16:29a** Hebrew *On the tenth day of the seventh month.* This day in the ancient Hebrew lunar calendar occurred in September or October. **16:29b** Or *must fast;* also in 16:31. **16:30** Or *atonement will be made for you, to purify you.* **16:32** Or *atonement.* **17:3** Or *cow.* **17:4a** Hebrew *Tent of Meeting;* also in 17:5, 6, 9. **17:4b** Hebrew *will be guilty of blood.* **17:7** Or *goat demons.* **17:11** Or *to make atonement for you.*

Forbidden Sexual Practices

18 Then the LORD said to Moses, 2“Give the following instructions to the people of Israel. I am the LORD your God. 3So do not act like the people in Egypt, where you used to live, or like the people of Canaan, where I am taking you. You must not imitate their way of life. 4You must obey all my regulations and be careful to obey my decrees, for I am the LORD your God. 5If you obey my decrees and my regulations, you will find life through them. I am the LORD.

6“You must never have sexual relations with a close relative, for I am the LORD.

7“Do not violate your father by having sexual relations with your mother. She is your mother; you must not have sexual relations with her.

8“Do not have sexual relations with any of your father’s wives, for this would violate your father.

9“Do not have sexual relations with your sister or half sister, whether she is your father’s daughter or your mother’s daughter, whether she was born into your household or someone else’s.

10“Do not have sexual relations with your granddaughter, whether she is your son’s daughter or your daughter’s daughter, for this would violate yourself.

11“Do not have sexual relations with your stepsister, the daughter of any of your father’s wives, for she is your sister.

12“Do not have sexual relations with your father’s sister, for she is your father’s close relative.

13“Do not have sexual relations with your mother’s sister, for she is your mother’s close relative.

14“Do not violate your uncle, your father’s brother, by having sexual relations with his wife, for she is your aunt.

15“Do not have sexual relations with your daughter-in-law; she is your son’s wife, so you must not have sexual relations with her.

16“Do not have sexual relations with your brother’s wife, for this would violate your brother.

17“Do not have sexual relations with both a woman and her daughter. And do not take* her granddaughter, whether her son’s daughter or her daughter’s daughter, and have sexual relations with her. They are close relatives, and this would be a wicked act.

18“While your wife is living, do not marry her sister and have sexual relations with her, for they would be rivals.

19“Do not have sexual relations with a woman during her period of menstrual impurity.

20“Do not defile yourself by having sexual intercourse with your neighbor’s wife.

21“Do not permit any of your children to be offered as a sacrifice to Molech, for you must not bring shame on the name of your God. I am the LORD.

22“Do not practice homosexuality, having sex with another man as with a woman. It is a detestable sin.

23“A man must not defile himself by having sex with an animal. And a woman must not offer herself to a male animal to have intercourse with it. This is a perverse act.

24“Do not defile yourselves in any of these ways, for the people I am driving out before you have defiled themselves in all these ways. 25Because the entire land has become defiled, I am punishing the people who live there. I will cause the land to vomit them out. 26You must obey all my decrees and regulations. You must not commit any of these detestable sins. This applies both to native-born Israelites and to the foreigners living among you.

27“All these detestable activities are practiced by the people of the land where I am taking you, and this is how the land has become defiled. 28So do not defile the land and give it a reason to vomit you out, as it will vomit out the people who live there now. 29Whoever commits any of these detestable sins will be cut off from the community of Israel. 30So obey my instructions, and do not defile yourselves by committing any of these detestable practices that were committed by the people who lived in the land before you. I am the LORD your God.”

Holiness in Personal Conduct

19 The LORD also said to Moses, 2“Give the following instructions to the entire community of Israel. You must be holy because I, the LORD your God, am holy.

3“Each of you must show great respect for your mother and father, and you must always observe my Sabbath days of rest. I am the LORD your God.

4“Do not put your trust in idols or make metal images of gods for yourselves. I am the LORD your God.

5 "When you sacrifice a peace offering to the LORD, offer it properly so you*
will be accepted by God. 6 The sacrifice
must be eaten on the same day you offer
it or on the next day. Whatever is left over
until the third day must be completely
burned up. 7 If any of the sacrifice is eaten
on the third day, it will be contaminated,
and I will not accept it. 8 Anyone who eats it
on the third day will be punished for defiling what is holy to the LORD and will be cut
off from the community.
9 "When you harvest the crops of your
land, do not harvest the grain along the
edges of your fields, and do not pick up
what the harvesters drop. 10 It is the same
with your grape crop—do not strip every
last bunch of grapes from the vines, and
do not pick up the grapes that fall to the
ground. Leave them for the poor and the
foreigners living among you. I am the LORD
your God.
11 "Do not steal.
"Do not deceive or cheat one another.
12 "Do not bring shame on the name of
your God by using it to swear falsely. I am
the LORD.
13 "Do not defraud or rob your neighbor.
"Do not make your hired workers wait
until the next day to receive their pay.
14 "Do not insult the deaf or cause the
blind to stumble. You must fear your God;
I am the LORD.
15 "Do not twist justice in legal matters by
favoring the poor or being partial to the rich
and powerful. Always judge people fairly.
16 "Do not spread slanderous gossip
among your people.*
"Do not stand idly by when your neighbor's life is threatened. I am the LORD.
17 "Do not nurse hatred in your heart for any
of your relatives.* Confront people directly so
you will not be held guilty for their sin.
18 "Do not seek revenge or bear a grudge
against a fellow Israelite, but love your
neighbor as yourself. I am the LORD.
19 "You must obey all my decrees.
"Do not mate two different kinds of
animals. Do not plant your field with two
different kinds of seed. Do not wear clothing
woven from two different kinds of thread.
20 "If a man has sex with a slave girl whose
freedom has never been purchased but
who is committed to become another man's
wife, he must pay full compensation to her
master. But since she is not a free woman,
neither the man nor the woman will be put
to death. 21 The man, however, must bring
a ram as a guilt offering and present it to
the LORD at the entrance of the Tabernacle.*
22 The priest will then purify him* before the
LORD with the ram of the guilt offering, and
the man's sin will be forgiven.
23 "When you enter the land and plant

18:17 Or *do not marry.* **19:5** Or *it.* **19:16** Hebrew *Do not act as a merchant toward your own people.* **19:17** Hebrew *for your brother.* **19:21** Hebrew *Tent of Meeting.* **19:22** Or *make atonement for him.*

Love your neighbor as yourself

If ever there was a Bible book that gathers dust, it must surely be Leviticus. We start out with our New Year's resolution to read through our Bible in a year . . . and then all too often get stuck in all the sacrifices of Leviticus. And yet, buried deep in its pages is this amazing command (Leviticus 19:18), quoted by Jesus as the second greatest commandment (Matthew 22:39) and also quoted in the Sermon on the Mount (Matthew 5:43). Paul refers to it twice (Romans 13:9; Galatians 5:14) and James once, calling it "the royal law" (James 2:8). In New Testament times, the Pharisees added what they thought must be the natural consequence of this verse: Hate your enemy. But Jesus brought people back to God's true intention: We are to love even our enemies (Matthew 5:43-48). Why? Because God loved us when we were still his enemies because of our sin. Loving even our enemies is an essential part of being in covenant with God. If we are followers of Jesus, then there can be no social or ethnic group outside the circle of our love.

▶ *See also* ***Loving others****, page 1220.*

fruit trees, leave the fruit unharvested for the first three years and consider it forbidden.* Do not eat it. 24 In the fourth year the entire crop must be consecrated to the LORD as a celebration of praise. 25 Finally, in the fifth year you may eat the fruit. If you follow this pattern, your harvest will increase. I am the LORD your God.

26 "Do not eat meat that has not been drained of its blood.

"Do not practice fortune-telling or witchcraft.

27 "Do not trim off the hair on your temples or trim your beards.

28 "Do not cut your bodies for the dead, and do not mark your skin with tattoos. I am the LORD.

29 "Do not defile your daughter by making her a prostitute, or the land will be filled with prostitution and wickedness.

30 "Keep my Sabbath days of rest, and show reverence toward my sanctuary. I am the LORD.

31 "Do not defile yourselves by turning to mediums or to those who consult the spirits of the dead. I am the LORD your God.

32 "Stand up in the presence of the elderly, and show respect for the aged. Fear your God. I am the LORD.

33 "Do not take advantage of foreigners who live among you in your land. 34 Treat them like native-born Israelites, and love them as you love yourself. Remember that you were once foreigners living in the land of Egypt. I am the LORD your God.

35 "Do not use dishonest standards when measuring length, weight, or volume. 36 Your scales and weights must be accurate. Your containers for measuring dry materials or liquids must be accurate.* I am the LORD your God who brought you out of the land of Egypt.

37 "You must be careful to keep all of my decrees and regulations by putting them into practice. I am the LORD."

Punishments for Disobedience

20 The LORD said to Moses, 2 "Give the people of Israel these instructions, which apply both to native Israelites and to the foreigners living in Israel.

"If any of them offer their children as a sacrifice to Molech, they must be put to death. The people of the community must stone them to death. 3 I myself will turn against them and cut them off from the community, because they have defiled my sanctuary and brought shame on my holy name by offering their children to Molech. 4 And if the people of the community ignore those who offer their children to Molech and refuse to execute them, 5 I myself will turn against them and their families and will cut them off from the community. This will happen to all who commit spiritual prostitution by worshiping Molech.

6 "I will also turn against those who commit spiritual prostitution by putting their trust in mediums or in those who consult the spirits of the dead. I will cut them off from the community. 7 So set yourselves apart to be holy, for I am the LORD your God. 8 Keep all my decrees by putting them into practice, for I am the LORD who makes you holy.

9 "Anyone who dishonors* father or mother must be put to death. Such a person is guilty of a capital offense.

10 "If a man commits adultery with his neighbor's wife, both the man and the woman who have committed adultery must be put to death.

11 "If a man violates his father by having sex with one of his father's wives, both the man and the woman must be put to death, for they are guilty of a capital offense.

12 "If a man has sex with his daughter-in-law, both must be put to death. They have committed a perverse act and are guilty of a capital offense.

13 "If a man practices homosexuality, having sex with another man as with a woman, both men have committed a detestable act. They must both be put to death, for they are guilty of a capital offense.

14 "If a man marries both a woman and her mother, he has committed a wicked act. The man and both women must be burned to death to wipe out such wickedness from among you.

15 "If a man has sex with an animal, he must be put to death, and the animal must be killed.

16 "If a woman presents herself to a male

▸ **19:26** *See **The occult**, page 337.* **19:32** *See **Respect for those who are older**, page 415.*

animal to have intercourse with it, she
and the animal must both be put to death.
You must kill both, for they are guilty of a
capital offense.

17“If a man marries his sister, the daughter
of either his father or his mother, and they
have sexual relations, it is a shameful disgrace. They must be publicly cut off from
the community. Since the man has violated
his sister, he will be punished for his sin.

18“If a man has sexual relations with a
woman during her menstrual period, both
of them must be cut off from the community, for together they have exposed the
source of her blood flow.

19“Do not have sexual relations with your
aunt, whether your mother’s sister or your
father’s sister. This would dishonor a close
relative. Both parties are guilty and will be
punished for their sin.

20“If a man has sex with his uncle’s wife,
he has violated his uncle. Both the man and
woman will be punished for their sin, and
they will die childless.

21“If a man marries his brother’s wife, it
is an act of impurity. He has violated his
brother, and the guilty couple will remain
childless.

22“You must keep all my decrees and
regulations by putting them into practice;
otherwise the land to which I am bringing
you as your new home will vomit you out.
23Do not live according to the customs of
the people I am driving out before you. It
is because they do these shameful things
that I detest them. 24But I have promised
you, ‘You will possess their land because
I will give it to you as your possession—a
land flowing with milk and honey.’ I am the
LORD your God, who has set you apart from
all other people.

25“You must therefore make a distinction
between ceremonially clean and unclean
animals, and between clean and unclean
birds. You must not defile yourselves by
eating any unclean animal or bird or creature that scurries along the ground. I have
identified them as being unclean for you.
26You must be holy because I, the LORD,
am holy. I have set you apart from all other
people to be my very own.

27“Men and women among you who act
as mediums or who consult the spirits of the
dead must be put to death by stoning. They
are guilty of a capital offense.”

Instructions for the Priests

21 The LORD said to Moses, “Give the following instructions to the priests, the
descendants of Aaron.

“A priest must not make himself ceremonially unclean by touching the dead body of a
relative. 2The only exceptions are his closest
relatives—his mother or father, son or daughter, brother, 3or his virgin sister who depends
on him because she has no husband. 4But
a priest must not defile himself and make
himself unclean for someone who is related
to him only by marriage.

5“The priests must not shave their heads
or trim their beards or cut their bodies.
6They must be set apart as holy to their God
and must never bring shame on the name
of God. They must be holy, for they are the
ones who present the special gifts to the
LORD, gifts of food for their God.

7“Priests may not marry a woman defiled
by prostitution, and they may not marry a
woman who is divorced from her husband,
for the priests are set apart as holy to their
God. 8You must treat them as holy because
they offer up food to your God. You must
consider them holy because I, the LORD, am
holy, and I make you holy.

9“If a priest’s daughter defiles herself by
becoming a prostitute, she also defiles her
father’s holiness, and she must be burned
to death.

10“The high priest has the highest rank of
all the priests. The anointing oil has been
poured on his head, and he has been ordained to wear the priestly garments. He
must never leave his hair uncombed* or tear
his clothing. 11He must not defile himself by
going near a dead body. He may not make
himself ceremonially unclean even for his
father or mother. 12He must not defile the
sanctuary of his God by leaving it to attend to
a dead person, for he has been made holy by
the anointing oil of his God. I am the LORD.

13“The high priest may marry only a virgin.
14He may not marry a widow, a woman who
is divorced, or a woman who has defiled
herself by prostitution. She must be a virgin
from his own clan, 15so that he will not dishonor his descendants among his clan, for
I am the LORD who makes him holy.”

19:23 Hebrew *consider it uncircumcised.* **19:36** Hebrew *Use an honest ephah* [a dry measure] *and an honest hin* [a liquid measure]. **20:9** Greek version reads *Anyone who speaks disrespectfully of.* Compare Matt 15:4; Mark 7:10. **21:10** Or *never uncover his head.*

[16]Then the LORD said to Moses, [17]“Give
the following instructions to Aaron: In all
future generations, none of your descendants who has any defect will qualify to
offer food to his God. [18]No one who has a
defect qualifies, whether he is blind, lame,
disfigured, deformed, [19]or has a broken foot
or arm, [20]or is hunchbacked or dwarfed, or
has a defective eye, or skin sores or scabs,
or damaged testicles. [21]No descendant of
Aaron who has a defect may approach the
altar to present special gifts to the LORD.
Since he has a defect, he may not approach
the altar to offer food to his God. [22]However,
he may eat from the food offered to God,
including the holy offerings and the most
holy offerings. [23]Yet because of his physical
defect, he may not enter the room behind
the inner curtain or approach the altar, for
this would defile my holy places. I am the
LORD who makes them holy.”

[24]So Moses gave these instructions to
Aaron and his sons and to all the Israelites.

22 The LORD said to Moses, [2]“Tell Aaron
and his sons to be very careful with
the sacred gifts that the Israelites set apart
for me, so they do not bring shame on my
holy name. I am the LORD. [3]Give them the
following instructions.

“In all future generations, if any of your
descendants is ceremonially unclean when
he approaches the sacred offerings that the
people of Israel consecrate to the LORD,
he must be cut off from my presence. I am
the LORD.

[4]“If any of Aaron’s descendants has a skin
disease* or any kind of discharge that makes
him ceremonially unclean, he may not eat
from the sacred offerings until he has been
pronounced clean. He also becomes unclean
by touching a corpse, or by having an emission of semen, [5]or by touching a small animal
that is unclean, or by touching someone who
is ceremonially unclean for any reason. [6]The
man who is defiled in any of these ways will
remain unclean until evening. He may not
eat from the sacred offerings until he has
bathed himself in water. [7]When the sun goes
down, he will be ceremonially clean again
and may eat from the sacred offerings, for
this is his food. [8]He may not eat an animal
that has died a natural death or has been
torn apart by wild animals, for this would
defile him. I am the LORD.

[9]“The priests must follow my instructions
carefully. Otherwise they will be punished
for their sin and will die for violating my instructions. I am the LORD who makes them
holy.

[10]“No one outside a priest’s family may eat
the sacred offerings. Even guests and hired
workers in a priest’s home are not allowed
to eat them. [11]However, if the priest buys a
slave for himself, the slave may eat from
the sacred offerings. And if his slaves have
children, they also may share his food. [12]If a
priest’s daughter marries someone outside
the priestly family, she may no longer eat
the sacred offerings. [13]But if she becomes a
widow or is divorced and has no children to
support her, and she returns to live in her
father’s home as in her youth, she may eat
her father’s food again. Otherwise, no one
outside a priest’s family may eat the sacred
offerings.

[14]“Any such person who eats the sacred
offerings without realizing it must pay the
priest for the amount eaten, plus an additional 20 percent. [15]The priests must not
let the Israelites defile the sacred offerings brought to the LORD [16]by allowing unauthorized people to eat them. This would
bring guilt upon them and require them
to pay compensation. I am the LORD who
makes them holy.”

Worthy and Unworthy Offerings

[17]And the LORD said to Moses, [18]“Give Aaron
and his sons and all the Israelites these instructions, which apply both to native Israelites and to the foreigners living among
you.

“If you present a gift as a burnt offering to
the LORD, whether it is to fulfill a vow or is
a voluntary offering, [19]you* will be accepted
only if your offering is a male animal with
no defects. It may be a bull, a ram, or a
male goat. [20]Do not present an animal with
defects, because the LORD will not accept it
on your behalf.

[21]“If you present a peace offering to the
LORD from the herd or the flock, whether
it is to fulfill a vow or is a voluntary offering, you must offer a perfect animal. It may
have no defect of any kind. [22]You must not
offer an animal that is blind, crippled, or
injured, or that has a wart, a skin sore, or
scabs. Such animals must never be offered
on the altar as special gifts to the LORD. [23]If

a bull* or lamb has a leg that is too long or too short, it may be offered as a voluntary offering, but it may not be offered to fulfill a vow. [24]If an animal has damaged testicles or is castrated, you may not offer it to the LORD. You must never do this in your own land, [25]and you must not accept such an animal from foreigners and then offer it as a sacrifice to your God. Such animals will not be accepted on your behalf, for they are mutilated or defective."

[26]And the LORD said to Moses, [27]"When a calf or lamb or goat is born, it must be left with its mother for seven days. From the eighth day on, it will be acceptable as a special gift to the LORD. [28]But you must not slaughter a mother animal and her offspring on the same day, whether from the herd or the flock. [29]When you bring a thanksgiving offering to the LORD, sacrifice it properly so you will be accepted. [30]Eat the entire sacrificial animal on the day it is presented. Do not leave any of it until the next morning. I am the LORD.

[31]"You must faithfully keep all my commands by putting them into practice, for I am the LORD. [32]Do not bring shame on my holy name, for I will display my holiness among the people of Israel. I am the LORD who makes you holy. [33]It was I who rescued you from the land of Egypt, that I might be your God. I am the LORD."

The Appointed Festivals

23 The LORD said to Moses, [2]"Give the following instructions to the people of Israel. These are the LORD's appointed festivals, which you are to proclaim as official days for holy assembly.

[3]"You have six days each week for your ordinary work, but the seventh day is a Sabbath day of complete rest, an official day for holy assembly. It is the LORD's Sabbath day, and it must be observed wherever you live.

[4]"In addition to the Sabbath, these are the LORD's appointed festivals, the official days for holy assembly that are to be celebrated at their proper times each year.

Passover and the Festival of Unleavened Bread

[5]"The LORD's Passover begins at sundown on the fourteenth day of the first month.* [6]On the next day, the fifteenth day of the month, you must begin celebrating the Festival of Unleavened Bread. This festival to the LORD continues for seven days, and during that time the bread you eat must be made without yeast. [7]On the first day of the festival, all the people must stop their ordinary work and observe an official day for holy assembly. [8]For seven days you must present special gifts to the LORD. On the seventh day the people must again stop all their ordinary work to observe an official day for holy assembly."

Celebration of First Harvest

[9]Then the LORD said to Moses, [10]"Give the following instructions to the people of Israel. When you enter the land I am giving you and you harvest its first crops, bring the priest a bundle of grain from the first cutting of your grain harvest. [11]On the day after the Sabbath, the priest will lift it up before the LORD so it may be accepted on your behalf. [12]On that same day you must sacrifice a one-year-old male lamb with no defects as a burnt offering to the LORD. [13]With it you must present a grain offering consisting of four quarts* of choice flour moistened with olive oil. It will be a special gift, a pleasing aroma to the LORD. You must also offer one quart* of wine as a liquid offering. [14]Do not eat any bread or roasted grain or fresh kernels on that day until you bring this offering to your God. This is a permanent law for you, and it must be observed from generation to generation wherever you live.

The Festival of Harvest

[15]"From the day after the Sabbath—the day you bring the bundle of grain to be lifted up as a special offering—count off seven full weeks. [16]Keep counting until the day after the seventh Sabbath, fifty days later. Then present an offering of new grain to the LORD. [17]From wherever you live, bring two loaves of bread to be lifted up before the LORD as a special offering. Make these loaves from four quarts of choice flour, and bake them with yeast. They will be an offering to the LORD from the first of your crops. [18]Along with the bread, present seven one-year-old male lambs with no defects, one young bull, and two rams as burnt offerings

22:4 Traditionally rendered *leprosy;* see note on 13:2a. **22:19** Or *it.* **22:23** Or *cow.* **23:5** This day in the ancient Hebrew lunar calendar occurred in late March, April, or early May. **23:13a** Hebrew *2/10 of an ephah* [4.4 liters]; also in 23:17. **23:13b** Hebrew *1/4 of a hin* [1 liter].

Key Jewish religious festivals

God said that Israel's year was to be marked by key festivals. These were located at important points in the agricultural year and were often linked with key points in Israel's history. Three of the festivals—Passover, the Festival of Harvest, and the Festival of Shelters—required all Jewish men to be present at the central sanctuary (Deuteronomy 16:16-17). The chart below shows some of these key Old Testament festivals. Bible references in italics show particular festivals either being commemorated in New Testament times or being reinterpreted in light of the coming of Jesus.

Festival	Key references	Requirements	Significance
Sabbath	Exodus 20:8-11; 31:12-17; Leviticus 23:3; *Matthew 12:1-14; Hebrews 4:1-11*	A weekly day of rest for both people and animals	Remembering God's rest after the work of creation and his covenant with Israel
Passover and the Festival of Unleavened Bread	Exodus 12:11-20; Leviticus 23:5-8; Numbers 28:16-25; *Matthew 26:17-30; 1 Corinthians 5:6-8*	Passover: a day of rest, with a family meal of roast lamb and unleavened bread; all men were to attend the sanctuary; Unleavened Bread: a joyful week-long festival during which bread could not contain yeast, beginning and ending with a "day for holy assembly"	Recalling Israel's dramatic rescue by God from slavery in Egypt
First Harvest (Firstfruits)	Leviticus 23:9-14; *1 Corinthians 15:20-23*	Dedication of the first bundle of grain of the harvest to God; offering a burnt offering and a grain offering	Thanksgiving for the harvest and dedication to God for the future
Festival of Harvest (Feast of Weeks/ Pentecost)	Leviticus 23:15-22; Numbers 28:26-31; Deuteronomy 16:9-12; *Acts 2:1-4*	A day of rest and "holy assembly"; offering a burnt offering and a grain offering	Celebration of the harvest and God's faithfulness; by New Testament times it also included commemoration of the giving of the Law
Festival of Trumpets	Leviticus 23:23-25; Numbers 29:1-6	A day of rest, "holy assembly," and presenting special offerings to God	Commemorating the start of a new year (today known as Jewish New Year or Rosh Hashanah)
Day of Atonement (Yom Kippur)	Leviticus 16:1-34; 23:26-32; Numbers 29:7-11; *Romans 3:23-26; Hebrews 9:6–10:22*	A solemn day of rest, fasting (the only occasion this is commanded in Scripture), and special sacrifices	Atonement for Israel's sin and purification of the Most Holy Place
Festival of Shelters (Feast of Tabernacles/Feast of Booths)	Leviticus 23:33-43; Numbers 29:12-40; Deuteronomy 16:13-15; *John 7:1-52*	Seven-day festival during which people lived in rough shelters and made special offerings; began and ended with days of "holy assembly" and rest from work	Celebration of the grape harvest; remembrance of Israel's forty years in the wilderness and God's provision in Canaan
Purim	Esther 9:1-32	A day of celebration, feasting, and giving gifts	Remembrance of God's deliverance of the Jews at the time of Esther

to the LORD. These burnt offerings, together
with the grain offerings and liquid offerings, will be a special gift, a pleasing aroma
to the LORD. [19]Then you must offer one male
goat as a sin offering and two one-year-old
male lambs as a peace offering.
[20]"The priest will lift up the two lambs
as a special offering to the LORD, together
with the loaves representing the first of your
crops. These offerings, which are holy to the
LORD, belong to the priests. [21]That same day
will be proclaimed an official day for holy
assembly, a day on which you do no ordinary work. This is a permanent law for you,
and it must be observed from generation to
generation wherever you live.*
[22]"When you harvest the crops of your
land, do not harvest the grain along the
edges of your fields, and do not pick up
what the harvesters drop. Leave it for the
poor and the foreigners living among you.
I am the LORD your God."

The Festival of Trumpets

[23]The LORD said to Moses, [24]"Give the following instructions to the people of Israel.
On the first day of the appointed month in
early autumn,* you are to observe a day of
complete rest. It will be an official day for
holy assembly, a day commemorated with
loud blasts of a trumpet. [25]You must do no
ordinary work on that day. Instead, you are
to present special gifts to the LORD."

The Day of Atonement

[26]Then the LORD said to Moses, [27]"Be
careful to celebrate the Day of Atonement
on the tenth day of that same month—nine
days after the Festival of Trumpets.* You
must observe it as an official day for holy
assembly, a day to deny yourselves* and
present special gifts to the LORD. [28]Do no
work during that entire day because it is
the Day of Atonement, when offerings of
purification are made for you, making you
right with* the LORD your God. [29]All who
do not deny themselves that day will be cut
off from God's people. [30]And I will destroy
anyone among you who does any work on
that day. [31]You must not do any work at all!
This is a permanent law for you, and it must
be observed from generation to generation
wherever you live. [32]This will be a Sabbath
day of complete rest for you, and on that day
you must deny yourselves. This day of rest
will begin at sundown on the ninth day of
the month and extend until sundown on the
tenth day."

The Festival of Shelters

[33]And the LORD said to Moses, [34]"Give the
following instructions to the people of
Israel. Begin celebrating the Festival of
Shelters* on the fifteenth day of the appointed month—five days after the Day of
Atonement.* This festival to the LORD will
last for seven days. [35]On the first day of the
festival you must proclaim an official day
for holy assembly, when you do no ordinary
work. [36]For seven days you must present
special gifts to the LORD. The eighth day
is another holy day on which you present
your special gifts to the LORD. This will be
a solemn occasion, and no ordinary work
may be done that day.
[37]("These are the LORD's appointed festivals. Celebrate them each year as official days for holy assembly by presenting
special gifts to the LORD—burnt offerings,
grain offerings, sacrifices, and liquid offerings—each on its proper day. [38]These festivals must be observed in addition to the
LORD's regular Sabbath days, and the offerings are in addition to your personal gifts,
the offerings you give to fulfill your vows,
and the voluntary offerings you present to
the LORD.)
[39]"Remember that this seven-day festival to the LORD—the Festival of Shelters—begins on the fifteenth day of the
appointed month,* after you have harvested all the produce of the land. The first
day and the eighth day of the festival will
be days of complete rest. [40]On the first day
gather branches from magnificent trees*—
palm fronds, boughs from leafy trees, and
willows that grow by the streams. Then celebrate with joy before the LORD your God

23:21 This celebration, called the Festival of Harvest or the Festival of Weeks, was later called the Festival of Pentecost (see Acts 2:1). It is celebrated today as Shavuot (or Shabuoth). **23:24** Hebrew *On the first day of the seventh month.* This day in the ancient Hebrew lunar calendar occurred in September or October. This festival is celebrated today as Rosh Hashanah, the Jewish new year. **23:27a** Hebrew *on the tenth day of the seventh month;* see 23:24 and the note there. This day in the ancient Hebrew lunar calendar occurred in September or October. It is celebrated today as Yom Kippur. **23:27b** Or *to fast;* similarly in 23:29, 32. **23:28** Or *when atonement is made for you before.* **23:34a** Or *Festival of Booths,* or *Festival of Tabernacles.* This was earlier called the Festival of the Final Harvest or Festival of Ingathering (see Exod 23:16b). It is celebrated today as Sukkot (or Succoth). **23:34b** Hebrew *on the fifteenth day of the seventh month;* see 23:27a and the note there. **23:39** Hebrew *on the fifteenth day of the seventh month.* **23:40** Or *gather fruit from majestic trees.*

for seven days. 41You must observe this festival to the LORD for seven days every year.
This is a permanent law for you, and it must
be observed in the appointed month* from
generation to generation. 42For seven days
you must live outside in little shelters. All
native-born Israelites must live in shelters.
43This will remind each new generation of
Israelites that I made their ancestors live in
shelters when I rescued them from the land
of Egypt. I am the LORD your God."
44So Moses gave the Israelites these instructions regarding the annual festivals of
the LORD.

Pure Oil and Holy Bread

24 The LORD said to Moses, 2"Command
the people of Israel to bring you pure
oil of pressed olives for the light, to keep
the lamps burning continually. 3This is the
lampstand that stands in the Tabernacle,
in front of the inner curtain that shields
the Ark of the Covenant.* Aaron must keep
the lamps burning in the LORD's presence
all night. This is a permanent law for you,
and it must be observed from generation
to generation. 4Aaron and the priests must
tend the lamps on the pure gold lampstand
continually in the LORD's presence.
5"You must bake twelve flat loaves of
bread from choice flour, using four quarts*
of flour for each loaf. 6Place the bread
before the LORD on the pure gold table, and
arrange the loaves in two stacks, with six
loaves in each stack. 7Put some pure frankincense near each stack to serve as a representative offering, a special gift presented
to the LORD. 8Every Sabbath day this bread
must be laid out before the LORD as a gift
from the Israelites; it is an ongoing expression of the eternal covenant. 9The loaves of
bread will belong to Aaron and his descendants, who must eat them in a sacred place,
for they are most holy. It is the permanent
right of the priests to claim this portion of
the special gifts presented to the LORD."

An Example of Just Punishment

10One day a man who had an Israelite
mother and an Egyptian father came out of
his tent and got into a fight with one of the
Israelite men. 11During the fight, this son of
an Israelite woman blasphemed the Name
of the LORD* with a curse. So the man was
brought to Moses for judgment. His mother
was Shelomith, the daughter of Dibri of the
tribe of Dan. 12They kept the man in custody
until the LORD's will in the matter should
become clear to them.
13Then the LORD said to Moses, 14"Take
the blasphemer outside the camp, and tell
all those who heard the curse to lay their
hands on his head. Then let the entire community stone him to death. 15Say to the
people of Israel: Those who curse their God
will be punished for their sin. 16Anyone who
blasphemes the Name of the LORD must be
stoned to death by the whole community of
Israel. Any native-born Israelite or foreigner
among you who blasphemes the Name of
the LORD must be put to death.
17"Anyone who takes another person's life
must be put to death.
18"Anyone who kills another person's
animal must pay for it in full—a live animal
for the animal that was killed.
19"Anyone who injures another person
must be dealt with according to the injury
inflicted—20a fracture for a fracture, an eye
for an eye, a tooth for a tooth. Whatever
anyone does to injure another person must
be paid back in kind.
21"Whoever kills an animal must pay for
it in full, but whoever kills another person
must be put to death.
22"This same standard applies both to
native-born Israelites and to the foreigners
living among you. I am the LORD your God."
23After Moses gave all these instructions
to the Israelites, they took the blasphemer
outside the camp and stoned him to death.
The Israelites did just as the LORD had commanded Moses.

The Sabbath Year

25 While Moses was on Mount Sinai,
the LORD said to him, 2"Give the following instructions to the people of Israel.
When you have entered the land I am giving
you, the land itself must observe a Sabbath
rest before the LORD every seventh year.
3For six years you may plant your fields
and prune your vineyards and harvest your
crops, 4but during the seventh year the land
must have a Sabbath year of complete rest.
It is the LORD's Sabbath. Do not plant your
fields or prune your vineyards during that
year. 5And don't store away the crops that
grow on their own or gather the grapes
from your unpruned vines. The land must

have a year of complete rest. 6But you may eat whatever the land produces on its own during its Sabbath. This applies to you, your male and female servants, your hired workers, and the temporary residents who live with you. 7Your livestock and the wild animals in your land will also be allowed to eat what the land produces.

The Year of Jubilee

8"In addition, you must count off seven Sabbath years, seven sets of seven years, adding up to forty-nine years in all. 9Then on the Day of Atonement in the fiftieth year,* blow the ram's horn loud and long throughout the land. 10Set this year apart as holy, a time to proclaim freedom throughout the land for all who live there. It will be a jubilee year for you, when each of you may return to the land that belonged to your ancestors and return to your own clan. 11This fiftieth year will be a jubilee for you. During that year you must not plant your fields or store away any of the crops that grow on their own, and don't gather the grapes from your unpruned vines. 12It will be a jubilee year for you, and you must keep it holy. But you may eat whatever the land produces on its own. 13In the Year of Jubilee each of you may return to the land that belonged to your ancestors.

14"When you make an agreement with your neighbor to buy or sell property, you must not take advantage of each other. 15When you buy land from your neighbor, the price you pay must be based on the number of years since the last jubilee. The seller must set the price by taking into account the number of years remaining until the next Year of Jubilee. 16The more years until the next jubilee, the higher the price; the fewer years, the lower the price. After all, the person selling the land is actually selling you a certain number of harvests. 17Show your fear of God by not taking advantage of each other. I am the LORD your God.

18"If you want to live securely in the land, follow my decrees and obey my regulations. 19Then the land will yield large crops, and you will eat your fill and live securely in it. 20But you might ask, 'What will we eat during the seventh year, since we are not allowed to plant or harvest crops that year?' 21Be assured that I will send my blessing for you in the sixth year, so the land will produce a crop large enough for three years. 22When you plant your fields in the eighth year, you will still be eating from the large crop of the sixth year. In fact, you will still be eating from that large crop when the new crop is harvested in the ninth year.

Redemption of Property

23"The land must never be sold on a permanent basis, for the land belongs to me. You are only foreigners and tenant farmers working for me.

24"With every purchase of land you must grant the seller the right to buy it back. 25If one of your fellow Israelites falls into poverty and is forced to sell some family land, then a

23:41 Hebrew *the seventh month.* **24:3** Hebrew *in the Tent of Meeting, outside the inner curtain of the Testimony;* see note on 16:13. **24:5** Hebrew *2/10 of an ephah* [4.4 liters]. **24:11** Hebrew *the Name;* also in 24:16b. **25:9** Hebrew *on the tenth day of the seventh month, on the Day of Atonement;* see 23:27a and the note there.

The Year of Jubilee

Nowhere is God's concern for the poor, needy, and downtrodden seen more than in the Year of Jubilee (Leviticus 25). Every fiftieth year all debts were to be canceled, all slaves freed, and all land returned to its original owners. The purpose was to prevent the endemic poverty that so easily arises in society, as it does even today. This law deeply challenges human selfishness and our sense of what is "fair," but God is never fair—he is always more than fair. This idea of Jubilee was picked up by the prophet Isaiah, who saw Israel's release from Babylonian captivity as a kind of Jubilee (Isaiah 58 and 61), and by Jesus himself, who proclaimed himself as the herald of God's long-awaited Jubilee Year (Luke 4:18-21).

▶ *See also* ***Debt****, page 219.*

close relative should buy it back for him. [26]If
there is no close relative to buy the land, but
the person who sold it gets enough money to
buy it back, [27]he then has the right to redeem
it from the one who bought it. The price of
the land will be discounted according to
the number of years until the next Year of
Jubilee. In this way the original owner can
then return to the land. [28]But if the original
owner cannot afford to buy back the land,
it will remain with the new owner until the
next Year of Jubilee. In the jubilee year, the
land must be returned to the original owners
so they can return to their family land.

[29]"Anyone who sells a house inside a
walled town has the right to buy it back for
a full year after its sale. During that year, the
seller retains the right to buy it back. [30]But if
it is not bought back within a year, the sale
of the house within the walled town cannot
be reversed. It will become the permanent
property of the buyer. It will not be returned
to the original owner in the Year of Jubilee.
[31]But a house in a village—a settlement
without fortified walls—will be treated like
property in the countryside. Such a house
may be bought back at any time, and it must
be returned to the original owner in the Year
of Jubilee.

[32]"The Levites always have the right to
buy back a house they have sold within
the towns allotted to them. [33]And any property that is sold by the Levites—all houses
within the Levitical towns—must be returned in the Year of Jubilee. After all, the
houses in the towns reserved for the Levites
are the only property they own in all Israel.
[34]The open pastureland around the Levitical towns may never be sold. It is their permanent possession.

Redemption of the Poor and Enslaved

[35]"If one of your fellow Israelites falls
into poverty and cannot support himself,
support him as you would a foreigner or a
temporary resident and allow him to live
with you. [36]Do not charge interest or make
a profit at his expense. Instead, show your
fear of God by letting him live with you as
your relative. [37]Remember, do not charge
interest on money you lend him or make a
profit on food you sell him. [38]I am the LORD
your God, who brought you out of the land
of Egypt to give you the land of Canaan and
to be your God.

[39]"If one of your fellow Israelites falls
into poverty and is forced to sell himself to
you, do not treat him as a slave. [40]Treat him
instead as a hired worker or as a temporary
resident who lives with you, and he will
serve you only until the Year of Jubilee. [41]At
that time he and his children will no longer
be obligated to you, and they will return to
their clans and go back to the land originally
allotted to their ancestors. [42]The people of
Israel are my servants, whom I brought out
of the land of Egypt, so they must never be
sold as slaves. [43]Show your fear of God by
not treating them harshly.

[44]"However, you may purchase male
and female slaves from among the nations
around you. [45]You may also purchase the
children of temporary residents who live
among you, including those who have been
born in your land. You may treat them as
your property, [46]passing them on to your
children as a permanent inheritance. You
may treat them as slaves, but you must
never treat your fellow Israelites this way.

[47]"Suppose a foreigner or temporary
resident becomes rich while living among
you. If any of your fellow Israelites fall
into poverty and are forced to sell themselves to such a foreigner or to a member
of his family, [48]they still retain the right to
be bought back, even after they have been
purchased. They may be bought back by
a brother, [49]an uncle, or a cousin. In fact,
anyone from the extended family may buy
them back. They may also redeem themselves if they have prospered. [50]They will
negotiate the price of their freedom with
the person who bought them. The price
will be based on the number of years from
the time they were sold until the next Year
of Jubilee—whatever it would cost to hire
a worker for that period of time. [51]If many
years still remain until the jubilee, they will
repay the proper proportion of what they received when they sold themselves. [52]If only
a few years remain until the Year of Jubilee,
they will repay a small amount for their redemption. [53]The foreigner must treat them
as workers hired on a yearly basis. You must

▸ **25:35** *See **Poverty**, page 1142.*

not allow a foreigner to treat any of your
fellow Israelites harshly. 54 If any Israelites
have not been bought back by the time the
Year of Jubilee arrives, they and their children must be set free at that time. 55 For the
people of Israel belong to me. They are my
servants, whom I brought out of the land of
Egypt. I am the LORD your God.

Blessings for Obedience

26 "Do not make idols or set up carved
images, or sacred pillars, or sculp-
tured stones in your land so you may
worship them. I am the LORD your God.
2 You must keep my Sabbath days of rest
and show reverence for my sanctuary. I am
the LORD.
3 "If you follow my decrees and are careful
to obey my commands, 4 I will send you the
seasonal rains. The land will then yield its
crops, and the trees of the field will produce
their fruit. 5 Your threshing season will
overlap with the grape harvest, and your
grape harvest will overlap with the season
of planting grain. You will eat your fill and
live securely in your own land.
6 "I will give you peace in the land, and
you will be able to sleep with no cause for
fear. I will rid the land of wild animals and
keep your enemies out of your land. 7 In
fact, you will chase down your enemies and
slaughter them with your swords. 8 Five of
you will chase a hundred, and a hundred
of you will chase ten thousand! All your
enemies will fall beneath your sword.
9 "I will look favorably upon you, making
you fertile and multiplying your people.
And I will fulfill my covenant with you.
10 You will have such a surplus of crops that
you will need to clear out the old grain to
make room for the new harvest! 11 I will live
among you, and I will not despise you.
12 I will walk among you; I will be your God,
and you will be my people. 13 I am the LORD
your God, who brought you out of the land
of Egypt so you would no longer be their
slaves. I broke the yoke of slavery from your
neck so you can walk with your heads held
high.

Punishments for Disobedience

14 "However, if you do not listen to me or obey
all these commands, 15 and if you break my
covenant by rejecting my decrees, treating
my regulations with contempt, and refusing
to obey my commands, 16 I will punish you.
I will bring sudden terrors upon you—
wasting diseases and burning fevers that
will cause your eyes to fail and your life to
ebb away. You will plant your crops in vain
because your enemies will eat them. 17 I will
turn against you, and you will be defeated
by your enemies. Those who hate you will
rule over you, and you will run even when
no one is chasing you!
18 "And if, in spite of all this, you still
disobey me, I will punish you seven times
over for your sins. 19 I will break your proud
spirit by making the skies as unyielding as
iron and the earth as hard as bronze. 20 All
your work will be for nothing, for your land
will yield no crops, and your trees will bear
no fruit.
21 "If even then you remain hostile toward
me and refuse to obey me, I will inflict disaster on you seven times over for your sins.
22 I will send wild animals that will rob you
of your children and destroy your livestock.
Your numbers will dwindle, and your roads
will be deserted.
23 "And if you fail to learn the lesson and
continue your hostility toward me, 24 then
I myself will be hostile toward you. I will
personally strike you with calamity seven
times over for your sins. 25 I will send armies
against you to carry out the curse of the covenant you have broken. When you run to
your towns for safety, I will send a plague to
destroy you there, and you will be handed
over to your enemies. 26 I will destroy your
food supply, so that ten women will need
only one oven to bake bread for their families. They will ration your food by weight,
and though you have food to eat, you will
not be satisfied.
27 "If in spite of all this you still refuse to
listen and still remain hostile toward me,
28 then I will give full vent to my hostility.
I myself will punish you seven times over
for your sins. 29 Then you will eat the flesh
of your own sons and daughters. 30 I will
destroy your pagan shrines and knock down
your places of worship. I will leave your
lifeless corpses piled on top of your lifeless
idols,* and I will despise you. 31 I will make
your cities desolate and destroy your places
of pagan worship. I will take no pleasure in
your offerings that should be a pleasing

26:30 The Hebrew term (literally *round things*) probably alludes to dung.

aroma to me. 32Yes, I myself will devastate your land, and your enemies who come to occupy it will be appalled at what they see. 33I will scatter you among the nations and bring out my sword against you. Your land will become desolate, and your cities will lie in ruins. 34Then at last the land will enjoy its neglected Sabbath years as it lies desolate while you are in exile in the land of your enemies. Then the land will finally rest and enjoy the Sabbaths it missed. 35As long as the land lies in ruins, it will enjoy the rest you never allowed it to take every seventh year while you lived in it.

36"And for those of you who survive, I will demoralize you in the land of your enemies. You will live in such fear that the sound of a leaf driven by the wind will send you fleeing. You will run as though fleeing from a sword, and you will fall even when no one pursues you. 37Though no one is chasing you, you will stumble over each other as though fleeing from a sword. You will have no power to stand up against your enemies. 38You will die among the foreign nations and be devoured in the land of your enemies. 39Those of you who survive will waste away in your enemies' lands because of their sins and the sins of their ancestors.

40"But at last my people will confess their sins and the sins of their ancestors for betraying me and being hostile toward me. 41When I have turned their hostility back on them and brought them to the land of their enemies, then at last their stubborn hearts will be humbled, and they will pay for their sins. 42Then I will remember my covenant with Jacob and my covenant with Isaac and my covenant with Abraham, and I will remember the land. 43For the land must be abandoned to enjoy its years of Sabbath rest as it lies deserted. At last the people will pay for their sins, for they have continually rejected my regulations and despised my decrees.

44"But despite all this, I will not utterly reject or despise them while they are in exile in the land of their enemies. I will not cancel my covenant with them by wiping them out, for I am the LORD their God. 45For their sakes I will remember my ancient covenant with their ancestors, whom I brought out of the land of Egypt in the sight of all the nations, that I might be their God. I am the LORD."

46These are the decrees, regulations, and instructions that the LORD gave through Moses on Mount Sinai as evidence of the relationship between himself and the Israelites.

Redemption of Gifts Offered to the LORD

27 The LORD said to Moses, 2"Give the following instructions to the people of Israel. If anyone makes a special vow to dedicate someone to the LORD by paying the value of that person, 3here is the scale of values to be used. A man between the ages of twenty and sixty is valued at fifty shekels* of silver, as measured by the sanctuary shekel. 4A woman of that age is valued at thirty shekels* of silver. 5A boy between the ages of five and twenty is valued at twenty shekels of silver; a girl of that age is valued at ten shekels* of silver. 6A boy between the ages of one month and five years is valued at five shekels of silver; a girl of that age is valued at three shekels* of silver. 7A man older than sixty is valued at fifteen shekels of silver; a woman of that age is valued at ten shekels* of silver. 8If you desire to make such a vow but cannot afford to pay the required amount, take the person to the priest. He will determine the amount for you to pay based on what you can afford.

9"If your vow involves giving an animal that is acceptable as an offering to the LORD, any gift to the LORD will be considered holy. 10You may not exchange or substitute it for another animal—neither a good animal for a bad one nor a bad animal for a good one. But if you do exchange one animal for another, then both the original animal and its substitute will be considered holy. 11If your vow involves an unclean animal—one that is not acceptable as an offering to the LORD—then you must bring the animal to the priest. 12He will assess its value, and his assessment will be final, whether high or low. 13If you want to buy back the animal, you must pay the value set by the priest, plus 20 percent.

14"If someone dedicates a house to the LORD, the priest will come to assess its value. The priest's assessment will be final, whether high or low. 15If the person who dedicated the house wants to buy it back, he must pay the value set by the priest, plus 20 percent. Then the house will again be his.

16"If someone dedicates to the LORD a piece of his family property, its value will be

assessed according to the amount of seed required to plant it—fifty shekels of silver for
a field planted with five bushels of barley
seed.* 17If the field is dedicated to the LORD
in the Year of Jubilee, then the entire assessment will apply. 18But if the field is dedicated after the Year of Jubilee, the priest will
assess the land's value in proportion to the
number of years left until the next Year of
Jubilee. Its assessed value is reduced each
year. 19If the person who dedicated the field
wants to buy it back, he must pay the value
set by the priest, plus 20 percent. Then the
field will again be legally his. 20But if he
does not want to buy it back, and it is sold
to someone else, the field can no longer be
bought back. 21When the field is released in
the Year of Jubilee, it will be holy, a field specially set apart* for the LORD. It will become
the property of the priests.

22"If someone dedicates to the LORD a
field he has purchased but which is not part
of his family property, 23the priest will assess
its value based on the number of years left
until the next Year of Jubilee. On that day
he must give the assessed value of the land
as a sacred donation to the LORD. 24In the
Year of Jubilee the field must be returned
to the person from whom he purchased it,
the one who inherited it as family property.
25(All the payments must be measured by
the weight of the sanctuary shekel,* which
equals twenty gerahs.)

26"You may not dedicate a firstborn animal
to the LORD, for the firstborn of your cattle,
sheep, and goats already belong to him.
27However, you may buy back the firstborn
of a ceremonially unclean animal by paying
the priest's assessment of its worth, plus
20 percent. If you do not buy it back, the
priest will sell it at its assessed value.

28"However, anything specially set apart
for the LORD—whether a person, an animal,
or family property—must never be sold or
bought back. Anything devoted in this way
has been set apart as holy, and it belongs
to the LORD. 29No person specially set apart
for destruction may be bought back. Such a
person must be put to death.

30"One-tenth of the produce of the land,
whether grain from the fields or fruit from
the trees, belongs to the LORD and must be
set apart to him as holy. 31If you want to buy
back the LORD's tenth of the grain or fruit,
you must pay its value, plus 20 percent.
32Count off every tenth animal from your
herds and flocks and set them apart for the
LORD as holy. 33You may not pick and choose
between good and bad animals, and you may
not substitute one for another. But if you do
exchange one animal for another, then both
the original animal and its substitute will be
considered holy and cannot be bought back."

34These are the commands that the LORD
gave through Moses on Mount Sinai for the
Israelites.

27:3 Or *20 ounces* [570 grams]. **27:4** Or *12 ounces* [342 grams]. **27:5** Or *A boy . . . 8 ounces* [228 grams] *of silver; a girl . . . 4 ounces* [114 grams]. **27:6** Or *A boy . . . 2 ounces* [57 grams] *of silver; a girl . . . 1.2 ounces* [34 grams]. **27:7** Or *A man . . . 6 ounces* [171 grams] *of silver; a woman . . . 4 ounces* [114 grams]. **27:16** Hebrew *50 shekels* [20 ounces or 570 grams] *of silver for a homer* [220 liters] *of barley seed.* **27:21** The Hebrew term used here refers to the complete consecration of things or people to the LORD, either by destroying them or by giving them as an offering; also in 27:28, 29. **27:25** Each shekel was about 0.4 ounces [11 grams] in weight.

Numbers *Wandering through the desert*

The book of Numbers continues the story of the Israelites' journey toward the Promised Land of Canaan. It opens with a census (from which the book's name "Numbers" comes), and there are plenty of what seem to be dry statistics—with more of the laws and regulations we met in Exodus. But there is far more to the book than this.

Numbers chronicles some of the saddest and most critical events in Israel's history. The people's failures to obey God, which seem to build up as the story unfolds, resulted in death for the entire adult population who left Egypt. They spent thirty-eight years wandering through a desert that even in those days traders could cross in a week or so. It was left to their children, the new generation, to inherit the land that God had intended to give to them.

What's it all about?

Numbers is dominated by the vivid stories of Israel's journey to Canaan and their failure to enter the Promised Land. When they set out, they were led by God's presence in the form of a cloud; but even this visible presence wasn't enough to convince them of God's good intentions toward them. When life became hard, they grumbled and questioned God's motives.

When Moses couldn't accept the responsibility for the people on his own any longer, God provided him with seventy elders to share the burden with (chapter 11). But the distinction between them and Moses is brought into clear relief: While they prophesied once, to show they were chosen by God, Moses spent time in God's presence constantly and repeatedly brought God's word to the people. When Miriam and Aaron joined in criticizing Moses, God made clear whose side he was on.

Chapter 13 marks the beginning of a new phase. On the threshold of the Promised Land, Moses commissioned twelve scouts to go and bring back a report. They returned, confirming that it was indeed a land "flowing with milk and honey." But then they soured their report with fears about the size and strength of the existing inhabitants (13:33). This negative report was seized on by the people, who were

OVERVIEW

The census and arrangement of the tribes · *1:1–4:49*

Various purity laws and regulations for worship · *5:1–10:10*

The Israelites leave Sinai for Canaan *10:11–12:16*

Twelve leaders spy out the Promised Land but bring back a discouraging report that leads to rebellion and judgment · *13:1–14:45*

A collection of laws on offerings, Sabbath, and clothing · *15:1-41*

Another rebellion and the budding of Aaron's staff · *16:1–17:13*

Further priestly regulations *18:1–19:22*

The sin of Moses and the journey to Moab · *20:1–21:35*

The prophecies of Balaam *22:1–24:25*

Disobedience and a new census *25:1–27:11*

The commissioning of Joshua *27:12-23*

Instructions for the new generation who will enter Canaan · *28:1–36:13*

thrown into despair. When Caleb and Joshua tried to calm them and build their spirits, they even tried to stone them.

God threatened to kill all the people there and then, and to start all over again with Moses. But Moses interceded for them, and God's anger was again placated. However, their behavior was unacceptable, and God told them that they would stay in the wilderness until every adult had died there (chapter 14). The remaining chapters record the key events of this wilderness period. In chapter 27, Moses commissioned Joshua, at God's instruction, to succeed him, for Moses himself could not enter the Promised Land because of his earlier anger (20:1-13). Joshua's faithfulness had been rewarded. He would lead the new generation of Israelites to conquer Canaan.

What does it mean for us?

Numbers reminds us of the part we can play in seeing God's promises come to pass. It is our responsibility whether we experience his blessings or not. God promises a bright future, but his blessings don't come to us like fruit falling off a tree; they have to be taken hold of and fought for. The Israelites were completely unprepared to play their part in securing the Promised Land. They were expecting everything to be easy and failed to cope with any setbacks.

Numbers reminds us that how we respond to setbacks can determine our outcomes in life. And what we *say* under pressure can affect our whole future. The Israelites said, "We wish we had died in this desert," and they did. Joshua and Caleb said, "We can conquer this land," and they did. Our words—and especially our spontaneous reactions—reveal what we really believe. Numbers invites us to get our words and lives in line with what *God* says.

Registration of Israel's Troops

1 A year after Israel's departure from Egypt,
the LORD spoke to Moses in the Tabernacle* in the wilderness of Sinai. On the first
day of the second month* of that year he said,
2 "From the whole community of Israel, record
the names of all the warriors by their clans and
families. List all the men 3 twenty years old or
older who are able to go to war. You and Aaron
must register the troops, 4 and you will be assisted by one family leader from each tribe.
5 "These are the tribes and the names of the
leaders who will assist you:

Tribe	*Leader*
Reuben	Elizur son of Shedeur
6 Simeon	Shelumiel son of Zurishaddai
7 Judah	Nahshon son of Amminadab
8 Issachar	Nethanel son of Zuar
9 Zebulun	Eliab son of Helon
10 Ephraim son of Joseph	Elishama son of Ammihud
Manasseh son of Joseph	Gamaliel son of Pedahzur
11 Benjamin	Abidan son of Gideoni
12 Dan	Ahiezer son of Ammishaddai
13 Asher	Pagiel son of Ocran
14 Gad	Eliasaph son of Deuel
15 Naphtali	Ahira son of Enan

16 These are the chosen leaders of the community, the leaders of their ancestral tribes,
the heads of the clans of Israel."
17 So Moses and Aaron called together
these chosen leaders, 18 and they assembled
the whole community of Israel on that very
day.* All the people were registered according to their ancestry by their clans and families. The men of Israel who were twenty years
old or older were listed one by one, 19 just as
the LORD had commanded Moses. So Moses
recorded their names in the wilderness of
Sinai.
20-21 This is the number of men twenty years
old or older who were able to go to war, as
their names were listed in the records of their
clans and families*:

Tribe	*Number*
Reuben (Jacob's* oldest son)	46,500
22-23 Simeon	59,300
24-25 Gad	45,650
26-27 Judah	74,600

1:1a Hebrew *the Tent of Meeting.* **1:1b** This day in the ancient Hebrew lunar calendar occurred in April or May. **1:18** Hebrew *on the first day of the second month;* see 1:1. **1:20-21a** In the Hebrew text, this sentence (*This is the number of men twenty years old or older who were able to go to war, as their names were listed in the records of their clans and families*) is repeated in 1:22, 24, 26, 28, 30, 32, 34, 36, 38, 40, 42. **1:20-21b** Hebrew *Israel's.* The names "Jacob" and "Israel" are often interchanged throughout the Old Testament, referring sometimes to the individual patriarch and sometimes to the nation.

28-29 Issachar 54,400
30-31 Zebulun 57,400
32-33 Ephraim son of Joseph 40,500
34-35 Manasseh son of Joseph 32,200
36-37 Benjamin 35,400
38-39 Dan 62,700
40-41 Asher.........................41,500
42-43 Naphtali 53,400

44These were the men registered by Moses
and Aaron and the twelve leaders of Israel,
all listed according to their ancestral
descent. 45They were registered by families—
all the men of Israel who were twenty years
old or older and able to go to war. 46The total
number was 603,550.
47But this total did not include the Levites.
48For the LORD had said to Moses, 49"Do not
include the tribe of Levi in the registration;
do not count them with the rest of the Israelites. 50Put the Levites in charge of the
Tabernacle of the Covenant,* along with
all its furnishings and equipment. They
must carry the Tabernacle and all its furnishings as you travel, and they must take
care of it and camp around it. 51Whenever
it is time for the Tabernacle to move, the
Levites will take it down. And when it is
time to stop, they will set it up again. But
any unauthorized person who goes too near
the Tabernacle must be put to death. 52Each
tribe of Israel will camp in a designated
area with its own family banner. 53But the
Levites will camp around the Tabernacle of
the Covenant to protect the community of
Israel from the LORD's anger. The Levites
are responsible to stand guard around the
Tabernacle."
54So the Israelites did everything just as
the LORD had commanded Moses.

Organization for Israel's Camp

2 Then the LORD gave these instructions
to Moses and Aaron: 2"When the Israelites set up camp, each tribe will be assigned
its own area. The tribal divisions will camp
beneath their family banners on all four
sides of the Tabernacle,* but at some distance from it.
3-4"The divisions of Judah, Issachar, and
Zebulun are to camp toward the sunrise on
the east side of the Tabernacle, beneath
their family banners. These are the names
of the tribes, their leaders, and the numbers
of their registered troops:

	Tribe	*Leader*	*Number*
	Judah	Nahshon son of Amminadab	74,600
5-6	Issachar	Nethanel son of Zuar	54,400
7-8	Zebulun	Eliab son of Helon	57,400

9So the total of all the troops on Judah's side
of the camp is 186,400. These three tribes
are to lead the way whenever the Israelites
travel to a new campsite.
10-11"The divisions of Reuben, Simeon, and
Gad are to camp on the south side of the Tabernacle, beneath their family banners. These
are the names of the tribes, their leaders, and
the numbers of their registered troops:

	Tribe	*Leader*	*Number*
	Reuben	Elizur son of Shedeur	46,500
12-13	Simeon	Shelumiel son of Zurishaddai	59,300
14-15	Gad	Eliasaph son of Deuel*	45,650

16So the total of all the troops on Reuben's
side of the camp is 151,450. These three

The tribes and the Tabernacle

God told the Israelites to ensure that the Tabernacle, which represented his presence, was always at the heart of the tribes. When they camped, the Tabernacle was to be at the center, surrounded by the Levites, who were there to protect it. Three of the twelve tribes would then camp on each side of it. When they were on the move, a similar pattern was maintained, with two groups of three tribes each leading the march, the Tabernacle and the Levites in the middle, and two groups of three tribes each at the rear. This is a vivid reminder of the importance of keeping God at the center of all we do.

▸ *See also* ***The Tabernacle****, page 96.*

tribes will be second in line whenever the
Israelites travel.
17“Then the Tabernacle, carried by the
Levites, will set out from the middle of
the camp. All the tribes are to travel in the
same order that they camp, each in position
under the appropriate family banner.
18-19“The divisions of Ephraim, Manasseh, and Benjamin are to camp on the west
side of the Tabernacle, beneath their family
banners. These are the names of the tribes,
their leaders, and the numbers of their registered troops:

Tribe	*Leader*	*Number*
Ephraim	Elishama son of Ammihud	40,500
20-21 Manasseh	Gamaliel son of Pedahzur	32,200
22-23 Benjamin	Abidan son of Gideoni	35,400

24So the total of all the troops on Ephraim's
side of the camp is 108,100. These three
tribes will be third in line whenever the Israelites travel.
25-26“The divisions of Dan, Asher, and Naphtali are to camp on the north side of the Tabernacle, beneath their family banners. These
are the names of the tribes, their leaders, and
the numbers of their registered troops:

Tribe	*Leader*	*Number*
Dan	Ahiezer son of Ammishaddai	62,700
27-28 Asher	Pagiel son of Ocran	41,500
29-30 Naphtali	Ahira son of Enan	53,400

31So the total of all the troops on Dan's side
of the camp is 157,600. These three tribes
will be last, marching under their banners
whenever the Israelites travel.”
32In summary, the troops of Israel listed
by their families totaled 603,550. 33But as
the LORD had commanded, the Levites
were not included in this registration. 34So
the people of Israel did everything as the
LORD had commanded Moses. Each clan
and family set up camp and marched under
their banners exactly as the LORD had instructed them.

Levites Appointed for Service

3 This is the family line of Aaron and
Moses as it was recorded when the
LORD spoke to Moses on Mount Sinai:
2The names of Aaron's sons were Nadab
(the oldest), Abihu, Eleazar, and Ithamar.
3These sons of Aaron were anointed and
ordained to minister as priests. 4But Nadab
and Abihu died in the LORD's presence in
the wilderness of Sinai when they burned
before the LORD the wrong kind of fire,
different than he had commanded. Since
they had no sons, this left only Eleazar and
Ithamar to serve as priests with their father,
Aaron.
5Then the LORD said to Moses, 6“Call
forward the tribe of Levi, and present them
to Aaron the priest to serve as his assistants.
7They will serve Aaron and the whole community, performing their sacred duties in
and around the Tabernacle.* 8They will also
maintain all the furnishings of the sacred
tent,* serving in the Tabernacle on behalf
of all the Israelites. 9Assign the Levites to
Aaron and his sons. They have been given
from among all the people of Israel to serve
as their assistants. 10Appoint Aaron and his
sons to carry out the duties of the priesthood. But any unauthorized person who
goes too near the sanctuary must be put to
death.”
11And the LORD said to Moses, 12“Look,
I have chosen the Levites from among the
Israelites to serve as substitutes for all
the firstborn sons of the people of Israel.
The Levites belong to me, 13for all the firstborn males are mine. On the day I struck
down all the firstborn sons of the Egyptians, I set apart for myself all the firstborn
in Israel, both of people and of animals.
They are mine; I am the LORD.”

Registration of the Levites

14The LORD spoke again to Moses in the
wilderness of Sinai. He said, 15“Record
the names of the members of the tribe of
Levi by their families and clans. List every
male who is one month old or older.” 16So
Moses listed them, just as the LORD had
commanded.

17Levi had three sons, whose names were
Gershon, Kohath, and Merari.
18The clans descended from Gershon were
named after two of his descendants,
Libni and Shimei.

1:50 Or *Tabernacle of the Testimony;* also in 1:53. **2:2** Hebrew *the Tent of Meeting;* also in 2:17. **2:14-15** As in many Hebrew manuscripts, Samaritan Pentateuch, and Latin Vulgate (see also 1:14); most Hebrew manuscripts read *son of Reuel.* **3:7** Hebrew *around the Tent of Meeting, doing service at the Tabernacle.* **3:8** Hebrew *the Tent of Meeting;* also in 3:25.

[19]The clans descended from Kohath were named after four of his descendants, Amram, Izhar, Hebron, and Uzziel.
[20]The clans descended from Merari were named after two of his descendants, Mahli and Mushi.

These were the Levite clans, listed according to their family groups.

[21]The descendants of Gershon were composed of the clans descended from Libni and Shimei. [22]There were 7,500 males one month old or older among these Gershonite clans. [23]They were assigned the area to the west of the Tabernacle for their camp. [24]The leader of the Gershonite clans was Eliasaph son of Lael. [25]These two clans were responsible to care for the Tabernacle, including the sacred tent with its layers of coverings, the curtain at its entrance, [26]the curtains of the courtyard that surrounded the Tabernacle and altar, the curtain at the courtyard entrance, the ropes, and all the equipment related to their use.

[27]The descendants of Kohath were composed of the clans descended from Amram, Izhar, Hebron, and Uzziel. [28]There were 8,600* males one month old or older among these Kohathite clans. They were responsible for the care of the sanctuary, [29]and they were assigned the area south of the Tabernacle for their camp. [30]The leader of the Kohathite clans was Elizaphan son of Uzziel. [31]These four clans were responsible for the care of the Ark, the table, the lampstand, the altars, the various articles used in the sanctuary, the inner curtain, and all the equipment related to their use. [32]Eleazar, son of Aaron the priest, was the chief administrator over all the Levites, with special responsibility for the oversight of the sanctuary.

[33]The descendants of Merari were composed of the clans descended from Mahli and Mushi. [34]There were 6,200 males one month old or older among these Merarite clans. [35]They were assigned the area north of the Tabernacle for their camp. The leader of the Merarite clans was Zuriel son of Abihail. [36]These two clans were responsible for the care of the frames supporting the Tabernacle, the crossbars, the pillars, the bases, and all the equipment related to their use. [37]They were also responsible for the posts of the courtyard and all their bases, pegs, and ropes.

[38]The area in front of the Tabernacle, in the east toward the sunrise,* was reserved for the tents of Moses and of Aaron and his sons, who had the final responsibility for the sanctuary on behalf of the people of Israel. Anyone other than a priest or Levite who went too near the sanctuary was to be put to death.

[39]When Moses and Aaron counted the Levite clans at the LORD's command, the total number was 22,000 males one month old or older.

Redeeming the Firstborn Sons

[40]Then the LORD said to Moses, "Now count all the firstborn sons in Israel who are one month old or older, and make a list of their names. [41]The Levites must be reserved for me as substitutes for the firstborn sons of Israel; I am the LORD. And the Levites' livestock must be reserved for me as substitutes for the firstborn livestock of the whole nation of Israel."

[42]So Moses counted the firstborn sons of the people of Israel, just as the LORD had commanded. [43]The number of firstborn sons who were one month old or older was 22,273.

Levites

The Levites were descendants of Levi, Jacob's third son with Leah (Genesis 29:34). As a reward for their zeal for God at the gold calf incident (Exodus 32:25-29), they were set apart to God. When all the Egyptian firstborn sons had died (Exodus 12:29-30), God spared all Israel's firstborn sons, though he could have taken them too. Now he said, "I have chosen the Levites from among the Israelites to serve as substitutes for all the firstborn sons of the people of Israel. The Levites belong to me" (Numbers 3:12). Set apart in this special way, they were given the privilege of caring for the Tabernacle and all its equipment (1:50-53).

44Then the LORD said to Moses, 45"Take
the Levites as substitutes for the firstborn
sons of the people of Israel. And take the
livestock of the Levites as substitutes for the
firstborn livestock of the people of Israel.
The Levites belong to me; I am the LORD.
46There are 273 more firstborn sons of Israel
than there are Levites. To redeem these
extra firstborn sons, 47collect five pieces of
silver* for each of them (each piece weighing the same as the sanctuary shekel, which
equals twenty gerahs). 48Give the silver to
Aaron and his sons as the redemption price
for the extra firstborn sons."
49So Moses collected the silver for redeeming the firstborn sons of Israel who
exceeded the number of Levites. 50He collected 1,365 pieces of silver* on behalf of
these firstborn sons of Israel (each piece
weighing the same as the sanctuary shekel).
51And Moses gave the silver for the redemption to Aaron and his sons, just as the LORD
had commanded.

Duties of the Kohathite Clan

4 Then the LORD said to Moses and Aaron,
2"Record the names of the members of
the clans and families of the Kohathite division of the tribe of Levi. 3List all the men
between the ages of thirty and fifty who are
eligible to serve in the Tabernacle.*
4"The duties of the Kohathites at the
Tabernacle will relate to the most sacred
objects. 5When the camp moves, Aaron and
his sons must enter the Tabernacle first to
take down the inner curtain and cover the
Ark of the Covenant* with it. 6Then they
must cover the inner curtain with fine goatskin leather and spread over that a single
piece of blue cloth. Finally, they must put
the carrying poles of the Ark in place.
7"Next they must spread a blue cloth over
the table where the Bread of the Presence is
displayed, and on the cloth they will place
the bowls, ladles, jars, pitchers, and the
special bread. 8They must spread a scarlet
cloth over all of this, and finally a covering
of fine goatskin leather on top of the scarlet
cloth. Then they must insert the carrying
poles into the table.
9"Next they must cover the lampstand
with a blue cloth, along with its lamps,
lamp snuffers, trays, and special jars of
olive oil. 10Then they must cover the lampstand and its accessories with fine goatskin
leather and place the bundle on a carrying
frame.
11"Next they must spread a blue cloth
over the gold incense altar and cover this
cloth with fine goatskin leather. Then they
must attach the carrying poles to the altar.
12They must take all the remaining furnishings of the sanctuary and wrap them in a
blue cloth, cover them with fine goatskin
leather, and place them on the carrying
frame.
13"They must remove the ashes from the
altar for sacrifices and cover the altar with
a purple cloth. 14All the altar utensils—the
firepans, meat forks, shovels, basins, and
all the containers—must be placed on
the cloth, and a covering of fine goatskin
leather must be spread over them. Finally,
they must put the carrying poles in place.
15The camp will be ready to move when
Aaron and his sons have finished covering
the sanctuary and all the sacred articles.
The Kohathites will come and carry these
things to the next destination. But they
must not touch the sacred objects, or they

3:28 Some Greek manuscripts read *8,300;* see total in 3:39. **3:38** Hebrew *toward the sunrise, in front of the Tent of Meeting.* **3:47** Hebrew *5 shekels* [2 ounces or 57 grams]. **3:50** Hebrew *1,365 [shekels] of silver* [34 pounds or 15.5 kilograms]. **4:3** Hebrew *the Tent of Meeting;* also in 4:4, 15, 23, 25, 28, 30, 31, 33, 35, 37, 39, 41, 43, 47. **4:5** Or *Ark of the Testimony.*

Kohathites, Gershonites, and Merarites

The Kohathites, Gershonites, and Merarites were all clans within the tribe of Levi, the tribe responsible for caring for the Tabernacle. Each clan was given very specific responsibilities for different aspects of the care and transportation of the Tabernacle. The Kohathites had responsibility for all the articles within the Tabernacle; the Gershonites, for its curtains, hangings, and screens; the Merarites, for its structural components. This meant that everyone knew their role and was empowered to get on with it—still a crucial principle for church life today.

will die. So these are the things from the Tabernacle that the Kohathites must carry.

16 “Eleazar son of Aaron the priest will be responsible for the oil of the lampstand, the fragrant incense, the daily grain offering, and the anointing oil. In fact, Eleazar will be responsible for the entire Tabernacle and everything in it, including the sanctuary and its furnishings.”

17 Then the LORD said to Moses and Aaron, 18 “Do not let the Kohathite clans be destroyed from among the Levites! 19 This is what you must do so they will live and not die when they approach the most sacred objects. Aaron and his sons must always go in with them and assign a specific duty or load to each person. 20 The Kohathites must never enter the sanctuary to look at the sacred objects for even a moment, or they will die.”

Duties of the Gershonite Clan

21 And the LORD said to Moses, 22 “Record the names of the members of the clans and families of the Gershonite division of the tribe of Levi. 23 List all the men between the ages of thirty and fifty who are eligible to serve in the Tabernacle.

24 “These Gershonite clans will be responsible for general service and carrying loads. 25 They must carry the curtains of the Tabernacle, the Tabernacle itself with its coverings, the outer covering of fine goatskin leather, and the curtain for the Tabernacle entrance. 26 They are also to carry the curtains for the courtyard walls that surround the Tabernacle and altar, the curtain across the courtyard entrance, the ropes, and all the equipment related to their use. The Gershonites are responsible for all these items. 27 Aaron and his sons will direct the Gershonites regarding all their duties, whether it involves moving the equipment or doing other work. They must assign the Gershonites responsibility for the loads they are to carry. 28 So these are the duties assigned to the Gershonite clans at the Tabernacle. They will be directly responsible to Ithamar son of Aaron the priest.

Duties of the Merarite Clan

29 “Now record the names of the members of the clans and families of the Merarite division of the tribe of Levi. 30 List all the men between the ages of thirty and fifty who are eligible to serve in the Tabernacle.

31 “Their only duty at the Tabernacle will be to carry loads. They will carry the frames of the Tabernacle, the crossbars, the posts, and the bases; 32 also the posts for the courtyard walls with their bases, pegs, and ropes; and all the accessories and everything else related to their use. Assign the various loads to each man by name. 33 So these are the duties of the Merarite clans at the Tabernacle. They are directly responsible to Ithamar son of Aaron the priest.”

Summary of the Registration

34 So Moses, Aaron, and the other leaders of the community listed the members of the Kohathite division by their clans and families. 35 The list included all the men between thirty and fifty years of age who were eligible for service in the Tabernacle, 36 and the total number came to 2,750. 37 So this was the total of all those from the Kohathite clans who were eligible to serve at the Tabernacle. Moses and Aaron listed them, just as the LORD had commanded through Moses.

38 The Gershonite division was also listed by its clans and families. 39 The list included all the men between thirty and fifty years of age who were eligible for service in the Tabernacle, 40 and the total number came to 2,630. 41 So this was the total of all those from the Gershonite clans who were eligible to serve at the Tabernacle. Moses and Aaron listed them, just as the LORD had commanded.

42 The Merarite division was also listed by its clans and families. 43 The list included all the men between thirty and fifty years of age who were eligible for service in the Tabernacle, 44 and the total number came to 3,200. 45 So this was the total of all those from the Merarite clans who were eligible for service. Moses and Aaron listed them, just as the LORD had commanded through Moses.

46 So Moses, Aaron, and the leaders of Israel listed all the Levites by their clans and families. 47 All the men between thirty and fifty years of age who were eligible for service in the Tabernacle and for its transportation 48 numbered 8,580. 49 When their names were recorded, as the LORD had commanded through Moses, each man was assigned his task and told what to carry.

And so the registration was completed, just as the LORD had commanded Moses.

Purity in Israel's Camp

5 The LORD gave these instructions to Moses: 2“Command the people of Israel to remove from the camp anyone who has a skin disease* or a discharge, or who has become ceremonially unclean by touching a dead person. 3This command applies to men and women alike. Remove them so they will not defile the camp in which I live among them.” 4So the Israelites did as the LORD had commanded Moses and removed such people from the camp.

5Then the LORD said to Moses, 6“Give the following instructions to the people of Israel: If any of the people—men or women—betray the LORD by doing wrong to another person, they are guilty. 7They must confess their sin and make full restitution for what they have done, adding an additional 20 percent and returning it to the person who was wronged. 8But if the person who was wronged is dead, and there are no near relatives to whom restitution can be made, the payment belongs to the LORD and must be given to the priest. Those who are guilty must also bring a ram as a sacrifice, and they will be purified and made right with the LORD.* 9All the sacred offerings that the Israelites bring to a priest will belong to him. 10Each priest may keep all the sacred donations that he receives.”

Protecting Marital Faithfulness

11And the LORD said to Moses, 12“Give the following instructions to the people of Israel.

“Suppose a man's wife goes astray, and she is unfaithful to her husband 13and has sex with another man, but neither her husband nor anyone else knows about it. She has defiled herself, even though there was no witness and she was not caught in the act. 14If her husband becomes jealous and is suspicious of his wife and needs to know whether or not she has defiled herself, 15the husband must bring his wife to the priest. He must also bring an offering of two quarts* of barley flour to be presented on her behalf. Do not mix it with olive oil or frankincense, for it is a jealousy offering—an offering to prove whether or not she is guilty.

16“The priest will then present her to stand trial before the LORD. 17He must take some holy water in a clay jar and pour into it dust he has taken from the Tabernacle floor. 18When the priest has presented the woman before the LORD, he must unbind her hair and place in her hands the offering of proof—the jealousy offering to determine whether her husband's suspicions are justified. The priest will stand before her, holding the jar of bitter water that brings a curse to those who are guilty. 19The priest will then put the woman under oath and say to her, ‘If no other man has had sex with you, and you have not gone astray and defiled yourself while under your husband's authority, may you be immune from the effects of this bitter water that brings on the curse. 20But if you have gone astray by being unfaithful to your husband, and have defiled yourself by having sex with another man—’

21“At this point the priest must put the woman under oath by saying, ‘May the people know that the LORD's curse is upon you when he makes you infertile, causing your womb to shrivel* and your abdomen to swell. 22Now may this water that brings the curse enter your body and cause your abdomen to swell and your womb to shrivel.*’ And the woman will be required to say, ‘Yes, let it be so.’ 23And the priest will write these curses on a piece of leather and wash them off into the bitter water. 24He will make the woman drink the bitter water that brings on the curse. When the water enters her body, it will cause bitter suffering if she is guilty.

25“The priest will take the jealousy offering from the woman's hand, lift it up before the LORD, and carry it to the altar. 26He will take a handful of the flour as a token portion and burn it on the altar, and he will require the woman to drink the water. 27If she has defiled herself by being unfaithful to her husband, the water that brings on the curse will cause bitter suffering. Her abdomen will swell and her womb will shrink,* and her name will become a curse among her people. 28But if she has not defiled herself and is pure, then she will be unharmed and will still be able to have children.

29“This is the ritual law for dealing with suspicion. If a woman goes astray and defiles herself while under her husband's authority, 30or if a man becomes jealous

5:2 Traditionally rendered *leprosy.* The Hebrew word used here describes various skin diseases. **5:8** Or *bring a ram for atonement, which will make atonement for them.* **5:15** Hebrew *1/10 of an ephah* [2.2 liters]. **5:21** Hebrew *when he causes your thigh to waste away.* **5:22** Hebrew *and your thigh to waste away.* **5:27** Hebrew *and her thigh will waste away.*

and is suspicious that his wife has been
unfaithful, the husband must present his
wife before the LORD, and the priest will
apply this entire ritual law to her. 31The
husband will be innocent of any guilt in
this matter, but his wife will be held accountable for her sin."

Nazirite Laws

6 Then the LORD said to Moses, 2"Give the
following instructions to the people of
Israel.

"If any of the people, either men or
women, take the special vow of a Nazirite,
setting themselves apart to the LORD in a
special way, 3they must give up wine and
other alcoholic drinks. They must not use
vinegar made from wine or from other alcoholic drinks, they must not drink fresh
grape juice, and they must not eat grapes or
raisins. 4As long as they are bound by their
Nazirite vow, they are not allowed to eat or
drink anything that comes from a grapevine—not even the grape seeds or skins.

5"They must never cut their hair throughout the time of their vow, for they are holy
and set apart to the LORD. Until the time of
their vow has been fulfilled, they must let
their hair grow long. 6And they must not go
near a dead body during the entire period
of their vow to the LORD. 7Even if the dead
person is their own father, mother, brother,
or sister, they must not defile themselves,
for the hair on their head is the symbol of
their separation to God. 8This requirement
applies as long as they are set apart to the
LORD.

9"If someone falls dead beside them, the
hair they have dedicated will be defiled.
They must wait for seven days and then
shave their heads. Then they will be
cleansed from their defilement. 10On the
eighth day they must bring two turtledoves
or two young pigeons to the priest at the entrance of the Tabernacle.* 11The priest will
offer one of the birds for a sin offering and
the other for a burnt offering. In this way,
he will purify them* from the guilt they in-
curred through contact with the dead body.
Then they must reaffirm their commitment
and let their hair begin to grow again. 12The
days of their vow that were completed
before their defilement no longer count.
They must rededicate themselves to the
LORD as a Nazirite for the full term of their
vow, and each must bring a one-year-old
male lamb for a guilt offering.

13"This is the ritual law for Nazirites. At the
conclusion of their time of separation as Nazirites, they must each go to the entrance of
the Tabernacle 14and offer their sacrifices to
the LORD: a one-year-old male lamb without
defect for a burnt offering, a one-year-old
female lamb without defect for a sin offering,
a ram without defect for a peace offering, 15a
basket of bread made without yeast—cakes
of choice flour mixed with olive oil and
wafers spread with olive oil—along with

The power of blessing

Blessings—and their opposite, curses—were taken seriously in Bible times, not simply as thoughtful words but as declarations that had power to bring about what was spoken. Once given, a blessing could not be taken back, as Esau discovered when his brother, Jacob, robbed him of their father's blessing (Genesis 27:1-40). While it was recognized that God was the source of all blessing, people believed they could pray that blessing onto others, conferring God's presence, favor, and help.

But if human words given in blessing were seen as powerful, how much more so were words spoken by God himself. Having just spoken of the blessing that was on those who chose to take a Nazirite vow (Numbers 6:1-21), God now gave Moses words that the priests were to use in blessing *all* God's people (6:24-26)—words that have been used throughout the history of Israel and the church. The threefold repetition of the divine name—the LORD—underlines who it is that is giving the blessing.

The New Testament sees Jesus Christ as God's ultimate blessing.

their prescribed grain offerings and liquid offerings. [16]The priest will present these offerings before the LORD: first the sin offering and the burnt offering; [17]then the ram for a peace offering, along with the basket of bread made without yeast. The priest must also present the prescribed grain offering and liquid offering to the LORD.

[18]"Then the Nazirites will shave their heads at the entrance of the Tabernacle. They will take the hair that had been dedicated and place it on the fire beneath the peace-offering sacrifice. [19]After the Nazirite's head has been shaved, the priest will take for each of them the boiled shoulder of the ram, and he will take from the basket a cake and a wafer made without yeast. He will put them all into the Nazirite's hands. [20]Then the priest will lift them up as a special offering before the LORD. These are holy portions for the priest, along with the breast of the special offering and the thigh of the sacred offering that are lifted up before the LORD. After this ceremony the Nazirites may again drink wine.

[21]"This is the ritual law of the Nazirites, who vow to bring these offerings to the LORD. They may also bring additional offerings if they can afford it. And they must be careful to do whatever they vowed when they set themselves apart as Nazirites."

The Priestly Blessing

[22]Then the LORD said to Moses, [23]"Tell Aaron and his sons to bless the people of Israel with this special blessing:

[24] 'May the LORD bless you
    and protect you.
[25] May the LORD smile on you
    and be gracious to you.
[26] May the LORD show you his favor
    and give you his peace.'

[27]Whenever Aaron and his sons bless the people of Israel in my name, I myself will bless them."

Offerings of Dedication

7 On the day Moses set up the Tabernacle, he anointed it and set it apart as holy. He also anointed and set apart all its furnishings and the altar with its utensils. [2]Then the leaders of Israel—the tribal leaders who had registered the troops—came and brought their offerings. [3]Together they brought six large wagons and twelve oxen. There was a wagon for every two leaders and an ox for each leader. They presented these to the LORD in front of the Tabernacle.

[4]Then the LORD said to Moses, [5]"Receive their gifts, and use these oxen and wagons for transporting the Tabernacle.* Distribute them among the Levites according to the work they have to do." [6]So Moses took the wagons and oxen and presented them to the Levites. [7]He gave two wagons and four oxen to the Gershonite division for their work, [8]and he gave four wagons and eight oxen to the Merarite division for their work. All their work was done under the leadership of Ithamar son of Aaron the priest. [9]But he gave none of the wagons or oxen to the Kohathite division, since they were required to carry the sacred objects of the Tabernacle on their shoulders.

[10]The leaders also presented dedication gifts for the altar at the time it was anointed. They each placed their gifts before the altar. [11]The LORD said to Moses, "Let one leader bring his gift each day for the dedication of the altar."

[12]On the first day Nahshon son of Amminadab, leader of the tribe of Judah, presented his offering.

[13]His offering consisted of a silver platter weighing 3¼ pounds and a silver basin weighing 1¾ pounds* (as measured by the weight of the sanctuary shekel). These were both filled with grain offerings of choice flour moistened with olive oil. [14]He also brought a gold container weighing four ounces,* which was filled with incense. [15]He brought a young bull, a ram, and a one-year-old male lamb for a burnt offering, [16]and a male goat for a sin offering. [17]For a peace offering he brought two bulls, five rams, five male goats, and five one-year-old male lambs. This was the offering brought by Nahshon son of Amminadab.

[18]On the second day Nethanel son of Zuar, leader of the tribe of Issachar, presented his offering.

6:10 Hebrew *the Tent of Meeting;* also in 6:13, 18. **6:11** Or *make atonement for them.* **7:5** Hebrew *the Tent of Meeting;* also in 7:89. **7:13** Hebrew *silver platter weighing 130 [shekels]* [1.5 kilograms] *and a silver basin weighing 70 shekels* [800 grams]; also in 7:19, 25, 31, 37, 43, 49, 55, 61, 67, 73, 79, 85. **7:14** Hebrew *10 [shekels]* [114 grams]; also in 7:20, 26, 32, 38, 44, 50, 56, 62, 68, 74, 80, 86.

19 His offering consisted of a silver platter
weighing 3¼ pounds and a silver basin
weighing 1¾ pounds (as measured by
the weight of the sanctuary shekel).
These were both filled with grain
offerings of choice flour moistened
with olive oil. 20 He also brought a gold
container weighing four ounces, which
was filled with incense. 21 He brought a
young bull, a ram, and a one-year-old
male lamb for a burnt offering, 22 and a
male goat for a sin offering. 23 For a peace
offering he brought two bulls, five rams,
five male goats, and five one-year-old
male lambs. This was the offering
brought by Nethanel son of Zuar.

24 On the third day Eliab son of Helon,
leader of the tribe of Zebulun, presented
his offering.
25 His offering consisted of a silver platter
weighing 3¼ pounds and a silver basin
weighing 1¾ pounds (as measured by
the weight of the sanctuary shekel).
These were both filled with grain
offerings of choice flour moistened
with olive oil. 26 He also brought a gold
container weighing four ounces, which
was filled with incense. 27 He brought a
young bull, a ram, and a one-year-old
male lamb for a burnt offering, 28 and
a male goat for a sin offering. 29 For a
peace offering he brought two bulls,
five rams, five male goats, and five
one-year-old male lambs. This was the
offering brought by Eliab son of Helon.

30 On the fourth day Elizur son of Shedeur,
leader of the tribe of Reuben, presented his
offering.
31 His offering consisted of a silver platter
weighing 3¼ pounds and a silver basin
weighing 1¾ pounds (as measured by
the weight of the sanctuary shekel).
These were both filled with grain
offerings of choice flour moistened
with olive oil. 32 He also brought a gold
container weighing four ounces, which
was filled with incense. 33 He brought a
young bull, a ram, and a one-year-old
male lamb for a burnt offering, 34 and a
male goat for a sin offering. 35 For a peace
offering he brought two bulls, five rams,
five male goats, and five one-year-old
male lambs. This was the offering
brought by Elizur son of Shedeur.

36 On the fifth day Shelumiel son of Zurishaddai, leader of the tribe of Simeon, presented his offering.
37 His offering consisted of a silver platter
weighing 3¼ pounds and a silver basin
weighing 1¾ pounds (as measured by
the weight of the sanctuary shekel).
These were both filled with grain
offerings of choice flour moistened
with olive oil. 38 He also brought a gold
container weighing four ounces, which
was filled with incense. 39 He brought a
young bull, a ram, and a one-year-old
male lamb for a burnt offering, 40 and
a male goat for a sin offering. 41 For a
peace offering he brought two bulls,
five rams, five male goats, and five
one-year-old male lambs. This was the
offering brought by Shelumiel son of
Zurishaddai.

42 On the sixth day Eliasaph son of Deuel,
leader of the tribe of Gad, presented his
offering.
43 His offering consisted of a silver platter
weighing 3¼ pounds and a silver basin
weighing 1¾ pounds (as measured by
the weight of the sanctuary shekel).
These were both filled with grain
offerings of choice flour moistened
with olive oil. 44 He also brought a gold
container weighing four ounces, which
was filled with incense. 45 He brought a
young bull, a ram, and a one-year-old
male lamb for a burnt offering, 46 and a
male goat for a sin offering. 47 For a peace
offering he brought two bulls, five rams,
five male goats, and five one-year-old
male lambs. This was the offering
brought by Eliasaph son of Deuel.

48 On the seventh day Elishama son of
Ammihud, leader of the tribe of Ephraim,
presented his offering.
49 His offering consisted of a silver platter
weighing 3¼ pounds and a silver basin
weighing 1¾ pounds (as measured by
the weight of the sanctuary shekel).
These were both filled with grain
offerings of choice flour moistened
with olive oil. 50 He also brought a gold
container weighing four ounces, which
was filled with incense. 51 He brought a
young bull, a ram, and a one-year-old
male lamb for a burnt offering, 52 and a
male goat for a sin offering. 53 For a peace

offering he brought two bulls, five rams,
five male goats, and five one-year-old
male lambs. This was the offering
brought by Elishama son of Ammihud.

54 On the eighth day Gamaliel son of Pedahzur, leader of the tribe of Manasseh, presented his offering.
55 His offering consisted of a silver platter
weighing 3¼ pounds and a silver basin
weighing 1¾ pounds (as measured by
the weight of the sanctuary shekel).
These were both filled with grain
offerings of choice flour moistened
with olive oil. 56 He also brought a gold
container weighing four ounces, which
was filled with incense. 57 He brought a
young bull, a ram, and a one-year-old
male lamb for a burnt offering, 58 and a
male goat for a sin offering. 59 For a peace
offering he brought two bulls, five rams,
five male goats, and five one-year-old
male lambs. This was the offering
brought by Gamaliel son of Pedahzur.

60 On the ninth day Abidan son of Gideoni,
leader of the tribe of Benjamin, presented
his offering.
61 His offering consisted of a silver platter
weighing 3¼ pounds and a silver basin
weighing 1¾ pounds (as measured by
the weight of the sanctuary shekel).
These were both filled with grain
offerings of choice flour moistened
with olive oil. 62 He also brought a gold
container weighing four ounces, which
was filled with incense. 63 He brought a
young bull, a ram, and a one-year-old
male lamb for a burnt offering, 64 and a
male goat for a sin offering. 65 For a peace
offering he brought two bulls, five rams,
five male goats, and five one-year-old
male lambs. This was the offering
brought by Abidan son of Gideoni.

66 On the tenth day Ahiezer son of Ammishaddai, leader of the tribe of Dan, presented his offering.
67 His offering consisted of a silver platter
weighing 3¼ pounds and a silver basin
weighing 1¾ pounds (as measured by
the weight of the sanctuary shekel).
These were both filled with grain
offerings of choice flour moistened
with olive oil. 68 He also brought a gold
container weighing four ounces, which
was filled with incense. 69 He brought a
young bull, a ram, and a one-year-old
male lamb for a burnt offering, 70 and a
male goat for a sin offering. 71 For a peace
offering he brought two bulls, five rams,
five male goats, and five one-year-old
male lambs. This was the offering
brought by Ahiezer son of Ammishaddai.

72 On the eleventh day Pagiel son of Ocran,
leader of the tribe of Asher, presented his
offering.
73 His offering consisted of a silver platter
weighing 3¼ pounds and a silver basin
weighing 1¾ pounds (as measured by
the weight of the sanctuary shekel).
These were both filled with grain
offerings of choice flour moistened
with olive oil. 74 He also brought a gold
container weighing four ounces, which
was filled with incense. 75 He brought a
young bull, a ram, and a one-year-old
male lamb for a burnt offering, 76 and a
male goat for a sin offering. 77 For a peace
offering he brought two bulls, five rams,
five male goats, and five one-year-old
male lambs. This was the offering
brought by Pagiel son of Ocran.

78 On the twelfth day Ahira son of Enan,
leader of the tribe of Naphtali, presented
his offering.
79 His offering consisted of a silver platter
weighing 3¼ pounds and a silver basin
weighing 1¾ pounds (as measured by
the weight of the sanctuary shekel).
These were both filled with grain
offerings of choice flour moistened
with olive oil. 80 He also brought a gold
container weighing four ounces, which
was filled with incense. 81 He brought a
young bull, a ram, and a one-year-old
male lamb for a burnt offering, 82 and
a male goat for a sin offering. 83 For a
peace offering he brought two bulls,
five rams, five male goats, and five
one-year-old male lambs. This was the
offering brought by Ahira son of Enan.

84 So this was the dedication offering
brought by the leaders of Israel at the time
the altar was anointed: twelve silver platters, twelve silver basins, and twelve gold
incense containers. 85 Each silver platter
weighed 3¼ pounds, and each silver basin
weighed 1¾ pounds. The total weight of

the silver was 60 pounds* (as measured by the weight of the sanctuary shekel). [86]Each of the twelve gold containers that was filled with incense weighed four ounces (as measured by the weight of the sanctuary shekel). The total weight of the gold was three pounds.* [87]Twelve young bulls, twelve rams, and twelve one-year-old male lambs were donated for the burnt offerings, along with their prescribed grain offerings. Twelve male goats were brought for the sin offerings. [88]Twenty-four bulls, sixty rams, sixty male goats, and sixty one-year-old male lambs were donated for the peace offerings. This was the dedication offering for the altar after it was anointed.

[89]Whenever Moses went into the Tabernacle to speak with the LORD, he heard the voice speaking to him from between the two cherubim above the Ark's cover—the place of atonement—that rests on the Ark of the Covenant.* The LORD spoke to him from there.

Preparing the Lamps

8 The LORD said to Moses, [2]"Give Aaron the following instructions: When you set up the seven lamps in the lampstand, place them so their light shines forward in front of the lampstand." [3]So Aaron did this. He set up the seven lamps so they reflected their light forward, just as the LORD had commanded Moses. [4]The entire lampstand, from its base to its decorative blossoms, was made of beaten gold. It was built according to the exact design the LORD had shown Moses.

The Levites Dedicated

[5]Then the LORD said to Moses, [6]"Now set the Levites apart from the rest of the people of Israel and make them ceremonially clean. [7]Do this by sprinkling them with the water of purification, and have them shave their entire body and wash their clothing. Then they will be ceremonially clean. [8]Have them bring a young bull and a grain offering of choice flour moistened with olive oil, along with a second young bull for a sin offering. [9]Then assemble the whole community of Israel, and present the Levites at the entrance of the Tabernacle.* [10]When you present the Levites before the LORD, the people of Israel must lay their hands on them. [11]Raising his hands, Aaron must then present the Levites to the LORD as a special offering from the people of Israel, thus dedicating them to the LORD's service.

[12]"Next the Levites will lay their hands on the heads of the young bulls. Present one as a sin offering and the other as a burnt offering to the LORD, to purify the Levites and make them right with the LORD.* [13]Then have the Levites stand in front of Aaron and his sons, and raise your hands and present them as a special offering to the LORD. [14]In this way, you will set the Levites apart from the rest of the people of Israel, and the Levites will belong to me. [15]After this, they may go into the Tabernacle to do their work, because you have purified them and presented them as a special offering.

[16]"Of all the people of Israel, the Levites are reserved for me. I have claimed them for myself in place of all the firstborn sons of the Israelites; I have taken the Levites as their substitutes. [17]For all the firstborn males among the people of Israel are mine, both of people and of animals. I set them apart for myself on the day I struck down all the firstborn sons of the Egyptians. [18]Yes, I have claimed the Levites in place of all the firstborn sons of Israel. [19]And of all the Israelites, I have assigned the Levites to Aaron and his sons. They will serve in the Tabernacle on behalf of the Israelites and make sacrifices to purify* the people so no plague will strike them when they approach the sanctuary."

[20]So Moses, Aaron, and the whole community of Israel dedicated the Levites, carefully following all the LORD's instructions to Moses. [21]The Levites purified themselves from sin and washed their clothes, and Aaron lifted them up and presented them to the LORD as a special offering. He then offered a sacrifice to purify them and make them right with the LORD.* [22]After that the Levites went into the Tabernacle to perform their duties, assisting Aaron and his sons. So they carried out all the commands that the LORD gave Moses concerning the Levites.

[23]The LORD also instructed Moses, [24]"This is the rule the Levites must follow: They must begin serving in the Tabernacle at the age of twenty-five, [25]and they must retire at the age of fifty. [26]After retirement they may assist their fellow Levites by serving as guards at the Tabernacle, but they may not

officiate in the service. This is how you must assign duties to the Levites."

The Second Passover

9 A year after Israel's departure from Egypt, the LORD spoke to Moses in the wilderness of Sinai. In the first month* of that year he said, 2"Tell the Israelites to celebrate the Passover at the prescribed time, 3at twilight on the fourteenth day of the first month.* Be sure to follow all my decrees and regulations concerning this celebration."

4So Moses told the people to celebrate the Passover 5in the wilderness of Sinai as twilight fell on the fourteenth day of the month. And they celebrated the festival there, just as the LORD had commanded Moses. 6But some of the men had been ceremonially defiled by touching a dead body, so they could not celebrate the Passover that day. They came to Moses and Aaron that day 7and said, "We have become ceremonially unclean by touching a dead body. But why should we be prevented from presenting the LORD's offering at the proper time with the rest of the Israelites?"

8Moses answered, "Wait here until I have received instructions for you from the LORD."

9This was the LORD's reply to Moses. 10"Give the following instructions to the people of Israel: If any of the people now or in future generations are ceremonially unclean at Passover time because of touching a dead body, or if they are on a journey and cannot be present at the ceremony, they may still celebrate the LORD's Passover. 11They must offer the Passover sacrifice one month later, at twilight on the fourteenth day of the second month.* They must eat the Passover lamb at that time with bitter salad greens and bread made without yeast. 12They must not leave any of the lamb until the next morning, and they must not break any of its bones. They must follow all the normal regulations concerning the Passover.

13"But those who neglect to celebrate the Passover at the regular time, even though they are ceremonially clean and not away on a trip, will be cut off from the community of Israel. If they fail to present the LORD's offering at the proper time, they will suffer the consequences of their guilt. 14And if foreigners living among you want to celebrate the Passover to the LORD, they must follow these same decrees and regulations. The same laws apply both to native-born Israelites and to the foreigners living among you."

The Fiery Cloud

15On the day the Tabernacle was set up, the cloud covered it.* But from evening until morning the cloud over the Tabernacle looked like a pillar of fire. 16This was the regular pattern—at night the cloud that covered the Tabernacle had the appearance of fire. 17Whenever the cloud lifted from over the sacred tent, the people of Israel would break camp and follow it. And wherever the cloud settled, the people of Israel would set up camp. 18In this way, they traveled and camped at the LORD's command wherever he told them to go. Then they remained in their camp as long as the cloud stayed over the Tabernacle. 19If the cloud remained over the Tabernacle for a long time, the

7:85 Hebrew *2,400 [shekels]* [27.6 kilograms]. **7:86** Hebrew *120 [shekels]* [1.4 kilograms]. **7:89** Or *Ark of the Testimony.* **8:9** Hebrew *the Tent of Meeting;* also in 8:15, 19, 22, 24, 26. **8:12** Or *to make atonement for the Levites.* **8:19** Or *make atonement for.* **8:21** Or *then made atonement for them to purify them.* **9:1** The first month of the ancient Hebrew lunar calendar usually occurs within the months of March and April. **9:3** This day in the ancient Hebrew lunar calendar occurred in late March, April, or early May. **9:11** This day in the ancient Hebrew lunar calendar occurred in late April, May, or early June. **9:15** Hebrew *covered the Tabernacle, the Tent of the Testimony.*

The cloud of God's presence—Israel's GPS

Since God is the God of all creation, it shouldn't surprise us that he sometimes uses creation for his purposes, whether it be the star that led the wise men to Jesus (Matthew 2:2) or the cloud that served as a GPS in guiding the Israelites (Exodus 13:21; Numbers 9:17). Not only did that cloud lead the way, it indicated when they were to stop and when they were to move (Numbers 9:15-23). Christians today do not have a cloud, but we do have the Holy Spirit within us who is there to lead and guide, if only we will listen to him.

Israelites stayed and performed their duty
to the LORD. 20Sometimes the cloud would
stay over the Tabernacle for only a few days,
so the people would stay for only a few
days, as the LORD commanded. Then at the
LORD's command they would break camp
and move on. 21Sometimes the cloud stayed
only overnight and lifted the next morning.
But day or night, when the cloud lifted,
the people broke camp and moved on.
22Whether the cloud stayed above the Tabernacle for two days, a month, or a year, the
people of Israel stayed in camp and did not
move on. But as soon as it lifted, they broke
camp and moved on. 23So they camped or
traveled at the LORD's command, and they
did whatever the LORD told them through
Moses.

The Silver Trumpets

10 Now the LORD said to Moses, 2"Make
two trumpets of hammered silver for
calling the community to assemble and for
signaling the breaking of camp. 3When both
trumpets are blown, everyone must gather
before you at the entrance of the Tabernacle.* 4But if only one trumpet is blown,
then only the leaders—the heads of the
clans of Israel—must present themselves to
you.

5"When you sound the signal to move
on, the tribes camped on the east side of
the Tabernacle must break camp and move
forward. 6When you sound the signal a
second time, the tribes camped on the south
will follow. You must sound short blasts as
the signal for moving on. 7But when you
call the people to an assembly, blow the
trumpets with a different signal. 8Only the
priests, Aaron's descendants, are allowed to
blow the trumpets. This is a permanent law
for you, to be observed from generation to
generation.

9"When you arrive in your own land and
go to war against your enemies who attack
you, sound the alarm with the trumpets.
Then the LORD your God will remember you
and rescue you from your enemies. 10Blow
the trumpets in times of gladness, too,
sounding them at your annual festivals and
at the beginning of each month. And blow
the trumpets over your burnt offerings and
peace offerings. The trumpets will remind
your God of his covenant with you. I am the
LORD your God."

The Israelites Leave Sinai

11In the second year after Israel's departure
from Egypt—on the twentieth day of the
second month*—the cloud lifted from the
Tabernacle of the Covenant.* 12So the Israelites set out from the wilderness of Sinai
and traveled on from place to place until the
cloud stopped in the wilderness of Paran.

13When the people set out for the first
time, following the instructions the LORD
had given through Moses, 14Judah's troops
led the way. They marched behind their
banner, and their leader was Nahshon son
of Amminadab. 15They were joined by the
troops of the tribe of Issachar, led by Nethanel son of Zuar, 16and the troops of the
tribe of Zebulun, led by Eliab son of Helon.

17Then the Tabernacle was taken down,
and the Gershonite and Merarite divisions of the Levites were next in the line of
march, carrying the Tabernacle with them.
18Reuben's troops went next, marching
behind their banner. Their leader was Elizur
son of Shedeur. 19They were joined by the
troops of the tribe of Simeon, led by Shelumiel son of Zurishaddai, 20and the troops of
the tribe of Gad, led by Eliasaph son of Deuel.

21Next came the Kohathite division of the
Levites, carrying the sacred objects from the
Tabernacle. Before they arrived at the next
camp, the Tabernacle would already be set
up at its new location. 22Ephraim's troops
went next, marching behind their banner.
Their leader was Elishama son of Ammihud.
23They were joined by the troops of the tribe
of Manasseh, led by Gamaliel son of Pedahzur, 24and the troops of the tribe of Benjamin, led by Abidan son of Gideoni.

25Dan's troops went last, marching
behind their banner and serving as the rear
guard for all the tribal camps. Their leader
was Ahiezer son of Ammishaddai. 26They
were joined by the troops of the tribe of
Asher, led by Pagiel son of Ocran, 27and the
troops of the tribe of Naphtali, led by Ahira
son of Enan.

28This was the order in which the Israelites marched, division by division.

29One day Moses said to his brother-in-
law, Hobab son of Reuel the Midianite, "We
are on our way to the place the LORD promised us, for he said, 'I will give it to you.'
Come with us and we will treat you well, for
the LORD has promised wonderful blessings
for Israel!"

30But Hobab replied, "No, I will not go. I must return to my own land and family."

31"Please don't leave us," Moses pleaded. "You know the places in the wilderness where we should camp. Come, be our guide. 32If you do, we'll share with you all the blessings the LORD gives us."

33They marched for three days after leaving the mountain of the LORD, with the Ark of the LORD's Covenant moving ahead of them to show them where to stop and rest. 34As they moved on each day, the cloud of the LORD hovered over them. 35And whenever the Ark set out, Moses would shout, "Arise, O LORD, and let your enemies be scattered! Let them flee before you!" 36And when the Ark was set down, he would say, "Return, O LORD, to the countless thousands of Israel!"

The People Complain to Moses

11 Soon the people began to complain about their hardship, and the LORD heard everything they said. Then the LORD's anger blazed against them, and he sent a fire to rage among them, and he destroyed some of the people in the outskirts of the camp. 2Then the people screamed to Moses for help, and when he prayed to the LORD, the fire stopped. 3After that, the area was known as Taberah (which means "the place of burning"), because fire from the LORD had burned among them there.

4Then the foreign rabble who were traveling with the Israelites began to crave the good things of Egypt. And the people of Israel also began to complain. "Oh, for some meat!" they exclaimed. 5"We remember the fish we used to eat for free in Egypt. And we had all the cucumbers, melons, leeks, onions, and garlic we wanted. 6But now our appetites are gone. All we ever see is this manna!"

7The manna looked like small coriander seeds, and it was pale yellow like gum resin. 8The people would go out and gather it from the ground. They made flour by grinding it with hand mills or pounding it in mortars. Then they boiled it in a pot and made it into flat cakes. These cakes tasted like pastries baked with olive oil. 9The manna came down on the camp with the dew during the night.

10Moses heard all the families standing in the doorways of their tents whining, and the LORD became extremely angry. Moses was also very aggravated. 11And Moses said to the LORD, "Why are you treating me, your servant, so harshly? Have mercy on me! What did I do to deserve the burden of all these people? 12Did I give birth to them? Did I bring them into the world? Why did you tell me to carry them in my arms like a mother carries a nursing baby? How can I carry them to the land you swore to give their ancestors? 13Where am I supposed to get meat for all these people? They keep whining to me, saying, 'Give us meat to eat!' 14I can't carry all these people by myself! The load is far too heavy! 15If this is how you intend to treat me, just go ahead and kill me. Do me a favor and spare me this misery!"

Moses Chooses Seventy Leaders

16Then the LORD said to Moses, "Gather before me seventy men who are recognized as elders and leaders of Israel. Bring them to the Tabernacle* to stand there with you. 17I will come down and talk to you there. I will take some of the Spirit that is upon you, and I will put the Spirit upon them also. They will bear the burden of the people along with you, so you will not have to carry it alone.

18"And say to the people, 'Purify yourselves, for tomorrow you will have meat to eat. You were whining, and the LORD heard you when you cried, "Oh, for some meat! We were better off in Egypt!" Now the LORD will give you meat, and you will have to eat it. 19And it won't be for just a day or two, or for five or ten or even twenty. 20You will eat it for a whole month until you gag and are sick of it. For you have rejected the LORD, who is here among you, and you have whined to him, saying, "Why did we ever leave Egypt?"'"

21But Moses responded to the LORD, "There are 600,000 foot soldiers here with me, and yet you say, 'I will give them meat for a whole month!' 22Even if we butchered all our flocks and herds, would that satisfy them? Even if we caught all the fish in the sea, would that be enough?"

23Then the LORD said to Moses, "Has my arm lost its power? Now you will see whether or not my word comes true!"

10:3 Hebrew *Tent of Meeting.* **10:11a** This day in the ancient Hebrew lunar calendar occurred in late April, May, or early June. **10:11b** Or *Tabernacle of the Testimony.* **11:16** Hebrew *the Tent of Meeting.*

24 So Moses went out and reported the LORD's words to the people. He gathered the seventy elders and stationed them around the Tabernacle.* 25 And the LORD came down in the cloud and spoke to Moses. Then he gave the seventy elders the same Spirit that was upon Moses. And when the Spirit rested upon them, they prophesied. But this never happened again.

26 Two men, Eldad and Medad, had stayed behind in the camp. They were listed among the elders, but they had not gone out to the Tabernacle. Yet the Spirit rested upon them as well, so they prophesied there in the camp. 27 A young man ran and reported to Moses, "Eldad and Medad are prophesying in the camp!"

28 Joshua son of Nun, who had been Moses' assistant since his youth, protested, "Moses, my master, make them stop!"

29 But Moses replied, "Are you jealous for my sake? I wish that all the LORD's people were prophets and that the LORD would put his Spirit upon them all!" 30 Then Moses returned to the camp with the elders of Israel.

The LORD Sends Quail

31 Now the LORD sent a wind that brought quail from the sea and let them fall all around the camp. For miles in every direction there were quail flying about three feet above the ground.* 32 So the people went out and caught quail all that day and throughout the night and all the next day, too. No one gathered less than fifty bushels*! They spread the quail all around the camp to dry. 33 But while they were gorging themselves on the meat—while it was still in their mouths—the anger of the LORD blazed against the people, and he struck them with a severe plague. 34 So that place was called Kibroth-hattaavah (which means "graves of gluttony") because there they buried the people who had craved meat from Egypt. 35 From Kibroth-hattaavah the Israelites traveled to Hazeroth, where they stayed for some time.

The Complaints of Miriam and Aaron

12 While they were at Hazeroth, Miriam and Aaron criticized Moses because he had married a Cushite woman. 2 They said, "Has the LORD spoken only through Moses? Hasn't he spoken through us, too?" But the LORD heard them. 3 (Now Moses was very humble—more humble than any other person on earth.)

4 So immediately the LORD called to Moses, Aaron, and Miriam and said, "Go out to the Tabernacle,* all three of you!" So the three of them went to the Tabernacle. 5 Then the LORD descended in the pillar of cloud and stood at the entrance of the Tabernacle.* "Aaron and Miriam!" he called, and they stepped forward. 6 And the LORD said to them, "Now listen to what I say:

"If there were prophets among you,
I, the LORD, would reveal myself in visions.
I would speak to them in dreams.
7 But not with my servant Moses.
Of all my house, he is the one I trust.
8 I speak to him face to face,
clearly, and not in riddles!
He sees the LORD as he is.
So why were you not afraid
to criticize my servant Moses?"

9 The LORD was very angry with them, and he departed. 10 As the cloud moved from above the Tabernacle, there stood Miriam, her skin as white as snow from leprosy.* When Aaron saw what had happened to her, 11 he cried out to Moses, "Oh, my master! Please don't punish us for this sin we have so foolishly committed. 12 Don't let her be like a stillborn baby, already decayed at birth."

13 So Moses cried out to the LORD, "O God, I beg you, please heal her!"

14 But the LORD said to Moses, "If her father had done nothing more than spit in her face, wouldn't she be defiled for seven days? So keep her outside the camp for seven days, and after that she may be accepted back."

15 So Miriam was kept outside the camp for seven days, and the people waited until she was brought back before they traveled again. 16 Then they left Hazeroth and camped in the wilderness of Paran.

Twelve Scouts Explore Canaan

13 The LORD now said to Moses, 2 "Send out men to explore the land of Canaan, the land I am giving to the Israelites. Send

▸ **12:10** *See **Leprosy**, page 508.*

one leader from each of the twelve ancestral tribes." 3 So Moses did as the LORD commanded him. He sent out twelve men, all
tribal leaders of Israel, from their camp in
the wilderness of Paran. 4 These were the
tribes and the names of their leaders:

Tribe	*Leader*
Reuben	Shammua son of Zaccur
5 Simeon	Shaphat son of Hori
6 Judah	Caleb son of Jephunneh
7 Issachar	Igal son of Joseph
8 Ephraim	Hoshea son of Nun
9 Benjamin	Palti son of Raphu
10 Zebulun	Gaddiel son of Sodi
11 Manasseh son of Joseph	Gaddi son of Susi
12 Dan	Ammiel son of Gemalli
13 Asher	Sethur son of Michael
14 Naphtali	Nahbi son of Vophsi
15 Gad	Geuel son of Maki

16 These are the names of the men Moses
sent out to explore the land. (Moses
called Hoshea son of Nun by the name
Joshua.)

17 Moses gave the men these instructions
as he sent them out to explore the land:
"Go north through the Negev into the hill
country. 18 See what the land is like, and
find out whether the people living there
are strong or weak, few or many. 19 See what
kind of land they live in. Is it good or bad?
Do their towns have walls, or are they unprotected like open camps? 20 Is the soil
fertile or poor? Are there many trees? Do
your best to bring back samples of the crops
you see." (It happened to be the season for
harvesting the first ripe grapes.)

21 So they went up and explored the land
from the wilderness of Zin as far as Rehob,
near Lebo-hamath. 22 Going north, they
passed through the Negev and arrived
at Hebron, where Ahiman, Sheshai, and
Talmai—all descendants of Anak—lived.
(The ancient town of Hebron was founded
seven years before the Egyptian city of
Zoan.) 23 When they came to the valley
of Eshcol, they cut down a branch with a
single cluster of grapes so large that it took
two of them to carry it on a pole between
them! They also brought back samples of
the pomegranates and figs. 24 That place was
called the valley of Eshcol (which means
"cluster"), because of the cluster of grapes
the Israelite men cut there.

The Scouting Report

25 After exploring the land for forty days, the
men returned 26 to Moses, Aaron, and the
whole community of Israel at Kadesh
in the wilderness of Paran. They reported
to the whole community what they had
seen and showed them the fruit they had
taken from the land. 27 This was their report
to Moses: "We entered the land you sent
us to explore, and it is indeed a bountiful country—a land flowing with milk and
honey. Here is the kind of fruit it produces.
28 But the people living there are powerful,
and their towns are large and fortified. We
even saw giants there, the descendants of
Anak! 29 The Amalekites live in the Negev,
and the Hittites, Jebusites, and Amorites
live in the hill country. The Canaanites live
along the coast of the Mediterranean Sea*
and along the Jordan Valley."

30 But Caleb tried to quiet the people as
they stood before Moses. "Let's go at once
to take the land," he said. "We can certainly
conquer it!"

31 But the other men who had explored
the land with him disagreed. "We can't go
up against them! They are stronger than
we are!" 32 So they spread this bad report
about the land among the Israelites: "The
land we traveled through and explored will
devour anyone who goes to live there. All
the people we saw were huge. 33 We even
saw giants* there, the descendants of Anak.
Next to them we felt like grasshoppers, and
that's what they thought, too!"

The People Rebel

14 Then the whole community began
weeping aloud, and they cried all
night. 2 Their voices rose in a great chorus
of protest against Moses and Aaron. "If
only we had died in Egypt, or even here in
the wilderness!" they complained. 3 "Why
is the LORD taking us to this country only
to have us die in battle? Our wives and our
little ones will be carried off as plunder!
Wouldn't it be better for us to return to
Egypt?" 4 Then they plotted among themselves, "Let's choose a new leader and go
back to Egypt!"

11:24 Hebrew *the tent;* also in 11:26. **11:31** Or *there were quail about 3 feet* [2 cubits or 92 centimeters] *deep on the ground.* **11:32** Hebrew *10 homers* [2.2 kiloliters]. **12:4** Hebrew *the Tent of Meeting.* **12:5** Hebrew *the tent;* also in 12:10. **12:10** Or *with a skin disease.* The Hebrew word used here can describe various skin diseases. **13:29** Hebrew *the sea.* **13:33** Hebrew *nephilim.*

5 Then Moses and Aaron fell face down on
the ground before the whole community of
Israel. 6 Two of the men who had explored
the land, Joshua son of Nun and Caleb son
of Jephunneh, tore their clothing. 7 They said
to all the people of Israel, “The land we traveled through and explored is a wonderful
land! 8 And if the LORD is pleased with us, he
will bring us safely into that land and give
it to us. It is a rich land flowing with milk
and honey. 9 Do not rebel against the LORD,
and don’t be afraid of the people of the land.
They are only helpless prey to us! They have
no protection, but the LORD is with us! Don’t
be afraid of them!”

10 But the whole community began to talk
about stoning Joshua and Caleb. Then the
glorious presence of the LORD appeared to
all the Israelites at the Tabernacle.* 11 And
the LORD said to Moses, “How long will
these people treat me with contempt? Will
they never believe me, even after all the miraculous signs I have done among them? 12 I
will disown them and destroy them with a
plague. Then I will make you into a nation
greater and mightier than they are!”

Moses Intercedes for the People

13 But Moses objected. “What will the Egyptians think when they hear about it?” he
asked the LORD. “They know full well
the power you displayed in rescuing your
people from Egypt. 14 Now if you destroy
them, the Egyptians will send a report to the
inhabitants of this land, who have already
heard that you live among your people. They
know, LORD, that you have appeared to your
people face to face and that your pillar of
cloud hovers over them. They know that
you go before them in the pillar of cloud by
day and the pillar of fire by night. 15 Now if
you slaughter all these people with a single
blow, the nations that have heard of your
fame will say, 16 ‘The LORD was not able to
bring them into the land he swore to give
them, so he killed them in the wilderness.’

17 “Please, Lord, prove that your power
is as great as you have claimed. For you
said, 18 ‘The LORD is slow to anger and filled
with unfailing love, forgiving every kind of
sin and rebellion. But he does not excuse
the guilty. He lays the sins of the parents
upon their children; the entire family is

The kind of leaders God wants

Moses had had the unenviable task of leading God’s people since they had left Egypt, and worse was to come. But despite the people’s grumbling and their proposal that they should appoint a new leader and return to Egypt, Moses and Aaron fell into neither self-pity nor anger. They simply fell on their faces before God and laid the matter before him (Numbers 14:5). Such *humility* and *willingness to trust God*, rather than attempting to manipulate people and outcomes, is a true mark of the godly leader. If we are fulfilling God’s mandate, then God will defend us, as he defended Moses and Aaron in this incident.

Another two godly leaders in this story are Joshua and Caleb, two of the twelve scouts who had been sent to explore Canaan. Here they demonstrate another quality necessary for the godly leader: the *ability to speak in faith* when things look hopeless (14:7-9). They were not burying their heads in the sand when faced with the facts—Canaan’s inhabitants were indeed strong, and their cities were indeed fortified, as the other spies had reported (13:28); but Joshua and Caleb did not focus on that but on God’s presence and promise (14:8-9). Canaan was the Promised Land. Who had promised it to them? God had. So the matter was settled for them. Armed with this conviction, they urged God’s people to move ahead in confidence. Joshua and Caleb’s faith would be rewarded (they would be the only ones over the age of twenty to survive the wilderness and enter the Promised Land), while the grumblers would experience the negative outcome they had spoken of: death in the desert (14:2).

▶ *See also* ***Leaders in the church,*** *page 1390.*

affected—even children in the third and
fourth generations.’ [19]In keeping with your
magnificent, unfailing love, please pardon
the sins of this people, just as you have forgiven them ever since they left Egypt.”
[20]Then the LORD said, “I will pardon them
as you have requested. [21]But as surely as I
live, and as surely as the earth is filled with
the LORD’s glory, [22]not one of these people
will ever enter that land. They have all seen
my glorious presence and the miraculous
signs I performed both in Egypt and in the
wilderness, but again and again they have
tested me by refusing to listen to my voice.
[23]They will never even see the land I swore
to give their ancestors. None of those who
have treated me with contempt will ever
see it. [24]But my servant Caleb has a different attitude than the others have. He has
remained loyal to me, so I will bring him
into the land he explored. His descendants
will possess their full share of that land.
[25]Now turn around, and don’t go on toward
the land where the Amalekites and Canaanites live. Tomorrow you must set out for the
wilderness in the direction of the Red Sea.*”

The LORD Punishes the Israelites

[26]Then the LORD said to Moses and Aaron,
[27]“How long must I put up with this wicked
community and its complaints about me?
Yes, I have heard the complaints the Israelites are making against me. [28]Now tell them
this: ‘As surely as I live, declares the LORD,
I will do to you the very things I heard you
say. [29]You will all drop dead in this wilderness! Because you complained against me,
every one of you who is twenty years old or
older and was included in the registration
will die. [30]You will not enter and occupy the
land I swore to give you. The only exceptions will be Caleb son of Jephunneh and
Joshua son of Nun.
[31]“‘You said your children would be
carried off as plunder. Well, I will bring
them safely into the land, and they will
enjoy what you have despised. [32]But as for
you, you will drop dead in this wilderness.
[33]And your children will be like shepherds,
wandering in the wilderness for forty years.
In this way, they will pay for your faithlessness, until the last of you lies dead in the
wilderness.
[34]“‘Because your men explored the land
for forty days, you must wander in the
wilderness for forty years—a year for each
day, suffering the consequences of your
sins. Then you will discover what it is like
to have me for an enemy.’ [35]I, the LORD, have
spoken! I will certainly do these things to
every member of the community who has
conspired against me. They will be destroyed here in this wilderness, and here
they will die!”
[36]The ten men Moses had sent to explore
the land—the ones who incited rebellion
against the LORD with their bad report—
[37]were struck dead with a plague before the
LORD. [38]Of the twelve who had explored the
land, only Joshua and Caleb remained alive.
[39]When Moses reported the LORD’s
words to all the Israelites, the people were
filled with grief. [40]Then they got up early
the next morning and went to the top of
the range of hills. “Let’s go,” they said.
“We realize that we have sinned, but now
we are ready to enter the land the LORD has
promised us.”
[41]But Moses said, “Why are you now disobeying the LORD’s orders to return to the
wilderness? It won’t work. [42]Do not go up
into the land now. You will only be crushed
by your enemies because the LORD is not
with you. [43]When you face the Amalekites and Canaanites in battle, you will be
slaughtered. The LORD will abandon you
because you have abandoned the LORD.”
[44]But the people defiantly pushed ahead
toward the hill country, even though neither
Moses nor the Ark of the LORD’s Covenant
left the camp. [45]Then the Amalekites and
the Canaanites who lived in those hills
came down and attacked them and chased
them back as far as Hormah.

Laws concerning Offerings

15 Then the LORD told Moses, [2]“Give the
following instructions to the people
of Israel.
“When you finally settle in the land I am
giving you, [3]you will offer special gifts as
a pleasing aroma to the LORD. These gifts
may take the form of a burnt offering, a sacrifice to fulfill a vow, a voluntary offering, or
an offering at any of your annual festivals,
and they may be taken from your herds of
cattle or your flocks of sheep and goats.
[4]When you present these offerings, you
must also give the LORD a grain offering of

14:10 Hebrew *the Tent of Meeting.* **14:25** Hebrew *sea of reeds.*

two quarts* of choice flour mixed with one quart* of olive oil. [5]For each lamb offered as a burnt offering or a special sacrifice, you must also present one quart of wine as a liquid offering.

[6]"If the sacrifice is a ram, give a grain offering of four quarts* of choice flour mixed with a third of a gallon* of olive oil, [7]and give a third of a gallon of wine as a liquid offering. This will be a pleasing aroma to the LORD.

[8]"When you present a young bull as a burnt offering or as a sacrifice to fulfill a vow or as a peace offering to the LORD, [9]you must also give a grain offering of six quarts* of choice flour mixed with two quarts* of olive oil, [10]and give two quarts of wine as a liquid offering. This will be a special gift, a pleasing aroma to the LORD.

[11]"Each sacrifice of a bull, ram, lamb, or young goat should be prepared in this way. [12]Follow these instructions with each offering you present. [13]All of you native-born Israelites must follow these instructions when you offer a special gift as a pleasing aroma to the LORD. [14]And if any foreigners visit you or live among you and want to present a special gift as a pleasing aroma to the LORD, they must follow these same procedures. [15]Native-born Israelites and foreigners are equal before the LORD and are subject to the same decrees. This is a permanent law for you, to be observed from generation to generation. [16]The same instructions and regulations will apply both to you and to the foreigners living among you."

[17]Then the LORD said to Moses, [18]"Give the following instructions to the people of Israel.

"When you arrive in the land where I am taking you, [19]and you eat the crops that grow there, you must set some aside as a sacred offering to the LORD. [20]Present a cake from the first of the flour you grind, and set it aside as a sacred offering, as you do with the first grain from the threshing floor. [21]Throughout the generations to come, you are to present a sacred offering to the LORD each year from the first of your ground flour.

[22]"But suppose you unintentionally fail to carry out all these commands that the LORD has given you through Moses. [23]And suppose your descendants in the future fail to do everything the LORD has commanded through Moses. [24]If the mistake was made unintentionally, and the community was unaware of it, the whole community must present a young bull for a burnt offering as a pleasing aroma to the LORD. It must be offered along with its prescribed grain offering and liquid offering and with one male goat for a sin offering. [25]With it the priest will purify the whole community of Israel, making them right with the LORD,* and they will be forgiven. For it was an unintentional sin, and they have corrected it with their offerings to the LORD—the special gift and the sin offering. [26]The whole community of Israel will be forgiven, including the foreigners living among you, for all the people were involved in the sin.

[27]"If one individual commits an unintentional sin, the guilty person must bring a one-year-old female goat for a sin offering. [28]The priest will sacrifice it to purify* the guilty person before the LORD, and that person will be forgiven. [29]These same instructions apply both to native-born Israelites and to the foreigners living among you.

[30]"But those who brazenly violate the LORD's will, whether native-born Israelites or foreigners, have blasphemed the LORD, and they must be cut off from the community. [31]Since they have treated the LORD's word with contempt and deliberately disobeyed his command, they must be completely cut off and suffer the punishment for their guilt."

Penalty for Breaking the Sabbath

[32]One day while the people of Israel were in the wilderness, they discovered a man gathering wood on the Sabbath day. [33]The people who found him doing this took him before Moses, Aaron, and the rest of the community. [34]They held him in custody because they did not know what to do with him. [35]Then the LORD said to Moses, "The man must be put to death! The whole community must stone him outside the camp." [36]So the whole community took the man outside the camp and stoned him to death, just as the LORD had commanded Moses.

Tassels on Clothing

[37]Then the LORD said to Moses, [38]"Give the following instructions to the people of Israel: Throughout the generations to come you must make tassels for the hems of your

clothing and attach them with a blue cord.
39When you see the tassels, you will remember and obey all the commands of the LORD
instead of following your own desires and
defiling yourselves, as you are prone to do.
40The tassels will help you remember that
you must obey all my commands and be holy
to your God. 41I am the LORD your God who
brought you out of the land of Egypt that I
might be your God. I am the LORD your God!"

Korah's Rebellion

16 One day Korah son of Izhar, a descendant of Kohath son of Levi, conspired with Dathan and Abiram, the sons of
Eliab, and On son of Peleth, from the tribe
of Reuben. 2They incited a rebellion against
Moses, along with 250 other leaders of the
community, all prominent members of the
assembly. 3They united against Moses and
Aaron and said, "You have gone too far!
The whole community of Israel has been
set apart by the LORD, and he is with all of
us. What right do you have to act as though
you are greater than the rest of the LORD's
people?"
4When Moses heard what they were
saying, he fell face down on the ground.
5Then he said to Korah and his followers,
"Tomorrow morning the LORD will show us
who belongs to him* and who is holy. The
LORD will allow only those whom he selects
to enter his own presence. 6Korah, you
and all your followers must prepare your
incense burners. 7Light fires in them tomorrow, and burn incense before the LORD.
Then we will see whom the LORD chooses as
his holy one. You Levites are the ones who
have gone too far!"
8Then Moses spoke again to Korah: "Now
listen, you Levites! 9Does it seem insignificant to you that the God of Israel has
chosen you from among all the community
of Israel to be near him so you can serve in
the LORD's Tabernacle and stand before the
people to minister to them? 10Korah, he has
already given this special ministry to you
and your fellow Levites. Are you now demanding the priesthood as well? 11The LORD
is the one you and your followers are really
revolting against! For who is Aaron that you
are complaining about him?"
12Then Moses summoned Dathan and
Abiram, the sons of Eliab, but they replied,
"We refuse to come before you! 13Isn't it
enough that you brought us out of Egypt, a
land flowing with milk and honey, to kill us
here in this wilderness, and that you now
treat us like your subjects? 14What's more,
you haven't brought us into another land
flowing with milk and honey. You haven't
given us a new homeland with fields and
vineyards. Are you trying to fool these
men?* We will not come."
15Then Moses became very angry and said
to the LORD, "Do not accept their grain offerings! I have not taken so much as a donkey
from them, and I have never hurt a single
one of them." 16And Moses said to Korah,
"You and all your followers must come here
tomorrow and present yourselves before the
LORD. Aaron will also be here. 17You and

15:4a Hebrew *1/10 of an ephah* [2.2 liters]. **15:4b** Hebrew *1/4 of a hin* [1 liter]; also in 15:5. **15:6a** Hebrew *2/10 of an ephah* [4.4 liters]. **15:6b** Hebrew *1/3 of a hin* [1.3 liters]; also in 15:7. **15:9a** Hebrew *3/10 of an ephah* [6.6 liters]. **15:9b** Hebrew *1/2 of a hin* [2 liters]; also in 15:10. **15:25** Or *will make atonement for the whole community of Israel.* **15:28** Or *to make atonement for.* **16:5** Greek version reads *God has visited and knows those who are his.* Compare 2 Tim 2:19. **16:14** Hebrew *Are you trying to put out the eyes of these men?*

Korah

Not content with being merely a Levite, even with his tribe's special privileges (Numbers 16:9), Korah complained against Moses and Aaron, feeling they were setting themselves up over others (16:3). He no doubt felt that he too should be a priest. Complaints usually gather more complaints, and before long others had joined the protest, complaining about life's hardships (16:12-14). The campaign of 250 leaders (16:2) quickly developed into a full-blown protest by "the entire community" (16:19). But God defended Moses and Aaron in a miraculous way (16:31-35), and only Aaron's priestly intervention prevented the whole community from experiencing judgment. The whole story is a sad lesson in the dangers of grumbling and rebellion.

each of your 250 followers must prepare an
incense burner and put incense on it, so you
can all present them before the LORD. Aaron
will also bring his incense burner."
18 So each of these men prepared an
incense burner, lit the fire, and placed
incense on it. Then they all stood at the entrance of the Tabernacle* with Moses and
Aaron. 19 Meanwhile, Korah had stirred up
the entire community against Moses and
Aaron, and they all gathered at the Tabernacle entrance. Then the glorious presence
of the LORD appeared to the whole community, 20 and the LORD said to Moses and
Aaron, 21 "Get away from all these people so
that I may instantly destroy them!"
22 But Moses and Aaron fell face down on
the ground. "O God," they pleaded, "you
are the God who gives breath to all creatures. Must you be angry with all the people
when only one man sins?"
23 And the LORD said to Moses, 24 "Then tell
all the people to get away from the tents of
Korah, Dathan, and Abiram."
25 So Moses got up and rushed over to the
tents of Dathan and Abiram, followed by
the elders of Israel. 26 "Quick!" he told the
people. "Get away from the tents of these
wicked men, and don't touch anything that
belongs to them. If you do, you will be destroyed for their sins." 27 So all the people
stood back from the tents of Korah, Dathan,
and Abiram. Then Dathan and Abiram came
out and stood at the entrances of their tents,
together with their wives and children and
little ones.
28 And Moses said, "This is how you will
know that the LORD has sent me to do all
these things that I have done—for I have
not done them on my own. 29 If these men
die a natural death, or if nothing unusual
happens, then the LORD has not sent me.
30 But if the LORD does something entirely
new and the ground opens its mouth and
swallows them and all their belongings,
and they go down alive into the grave,* then
you will know that these men have shown
contempt for the LORD."
31 He had hardly finished speaking the
words when the ground suddenly split
open beneath them. 32 The earth opened
its mouth and swallowed the men, along
with their households and all their followers who were standing with them, and
everything they owned. 33 So they went
down alive into the grave, along with all
their belongings. The earth closed over
them, and they all vanished from among
the people of Israel. 34 All the people
around them fled when they heard their
screams. "The earth will swallow us, too!"
they cried. 35 Then fire blazed forth from the
LORD and burned up the 250 men who were
offering incense.
36* And the LORD said to Moses, 37 "Tell
Eleazar son of Aaron the priest to pull
all the incense burners from the fire, for
they are holy. Also tell him to scatter the
burning coals. 38 Take the incense burners
of these men who have sinned at the cost
of their lives, and hammer the metal into a
thin sheet to overlay the altar. Since these
burners were used in the LORD's presence,
they have become holy. Let them serve as a
warning to the people of Israel."
39 So Eleazar the priest collected the
250 bronze incense burners that had been
used by the men who died in the fire, and
the bronze was hammered into a thin sheet
to overlay the altar. 40 This would warn the
Israelites that no unauthorized person—no
one who was not a descendant of Aaron—
should ever enter the LORD's presence to
burn incense. If anyone did, the same thing
would happen to him as happened to Korah
and his followers. So the LORD's instructions to Moses were carried out.
41 But the very next morning the whole
community of Israel began muttering
again against Moses and Aaron, saying,
"You have killed the LORD's people!" 42 As
the community gathered to protest against
Moses and Aaron, they turned toward the
Tabernacle and saw that the cloud had
covered it, and the glorious presence of the
LORD appeared.
43 Moses and Aaron came and stood in
front of the Tabernacle, 44 and the LORD said
to Moses, 45 "Get away from all these people
so that I can instantly destroy them!" But
Moses and Aaron fell face down on the
ground.
46 And Moses said to Aaron, "Quick, take
an incense burner and place burning coals
on it from the altar. Lay incense on it, and
carry it out among the people to purify them
and make them right with the LORD.* The
LORD's anger is blazing against them—the
plague has already begun."
47 Aaron did as Moses told him and ran out

among the people. The plague had already begun to strike down the people, but Aaron burned the incense and purified* the people. [48]He stood between the dead and the living, and the plague stopped. [49]But 14,700 people died in that plague, in addition to those who had died in the affair involving Korah. [50]Then because the plague had stopped, Aaron returned to Moses at the entrance of the Tabernacle.

The Budding of Aaron's Staff

17 [1]*Then the LORD said to Moses, [2]"Tell the people of Israel to bring you twelve wooden staffs, one from each leader of Israel's ancestral tribes, and inscribe each leader's name on his staff. [3]Inscribe Aaron's name on the staff of the tribe of Levi, for there must be one staff for the leader of each ancestral tribe. [4]Place these staffs in the Tabernacle in front of the Ark containing the tablets of the Covenant,* where I meet with you. [5]Buds will sprout on the staff belonging to the man I choose. Then I will finally put an end to the people's murmuring and complaining against you."

[6]So Moses gave the instructions to the people of Israel, and each of the twelve tribal leaders, including Aaron, brought Moses a staff. [7]Moses placed the staffs in the LORD's presence in the Tabernacle of the Covenant.* [8]When he went into the Tabernacle of the Covenant the next day, he found that Aaron's staff, representing the tribe of Levi, had sprouted, budded, blossomed, and produced ripe almonds!

[9]When Moses brought all the staffs out from the LORD's presence, he showed them to the people. Each man claimed his own staff. [10]And the LORD said to Moses: "Place Aaron's staff permanently before the Ark of the Covenant* to serve as a warning to rebels. This should put an end to their complaints against me and prevent any further deaths." [11]So Moses did as the LORD commanded him.

[12]Then the people of Israel said to Moses, "Look, we are doomed! We are dead! We are ruined! [13]Everyone who even comes close to the Tabernacle of the LORD dies. Are we all doomed to die?"

Duties of Priests and Levites

18 Then the LORD said to Aaron: "You, your sons, and your relatives from the tribe of Levi will be held responsible for any offenses related to the sanctuary. But you and your sons alone will be held responsible for violations connected with the priesthood.

[2]"Bring your relatives of the tribe of Levi—your ancestral tribe—to assist you and your sons as you perform the sacred duties in front of the Tabernacle of the Covenant.* [3]But as the Levites go about all their assigned duties at the Tabernacle, they must be careful not to go near any of the sacred objects or the altar. If they do, both you and they will die. [4]The Levites must join you in fulfilling their responsibilities for the care and maintenance of the Tabernacle,* but no unauthorized person may assist you.

[5]"You yourselves must perform the sacred duties inside the sanctuary and at the altar. If you follow these instructions, the LORD's anger will never again blaze against the people of Israel. [6]I myself have chosen your fellow Levites from among the Israelites to be your special assistants. They are a gift to you, dedicated to the LORD for service in the Tabernacle. [7]But you and your sons, the priests, must personally handle all the priestly rituals associated with the altar and with everything behind the inner curtain. I am giving you the priesthood as your special privilege of service. Any unauthorized person who comes too near the sanctuary will be put to death."

Support for the Priests and Levites

[8]The LORD gave these further instructions to Aaron: "I myself have put you in charge of all the holy offerings that are brought to me by the people of Israel. I have given all these consecrated offerings to you and your sons as your permanent share. [9]You are allotted the portion of the most holy offerings that is not burned on the fire. This portion of all the most holy offerings—including the grain offerings, sin offerings, and guilt offerings—will be most holy, and it belongs to you and your sons. [10]You must eat it as a

16:18 Hebrew *the Tent of Meeting;* also in 16:19, 42, 43, 50. **16:30** Hebrew *into Sheol;* also in 16:33. **16:36** Verses 16:36-50 are numbered 17:1-15 in Hebrew text. **16:46** Or *to make atonement for them.* **16:47** Or *and made atonement for.* **17:1** Verses 17:1-13 are numbered 17:16-28 in Hebrew text. **17:4** Hebrew *in the Tent of Meeting before the Testimony.* The Hebrew word for "testimony" refers to the terms of the LORD's covenant with Israel as written on stone tablets, which were kept in the Ark, and also to the covenant itself. **17:7** Or *Tabernacle of the Testimony;* also in 17:8. **17:10** Hebrew *before the Testimony;* see note on 17:4. **18:2** Or *Tabernacle of the Testimony.* **18:4** Hebrew *the Tent of Meeting;* also in 18:6, 21, 22, 23, 31.

most holy offering. All the males may eat of
it, and you must treat it as most holy.
11 “All the sacred offerings and special offerings presented to me when the Israelites
lift them up before the altar also belong to
you. I have given them to you and to your
sons and daughters as your permanent
share. Any member of your family who
is ceremonially clean may eat of these
offerings.
12 “I also give you the harvest gifts brought
by the people as offerings to the LORD—the
best of the olive oil, new wine, and grain.
13 All the first crops of their land that the
people present to the LORD belong to you.
Any member of your family who is ceremonially clean may eat this food.
14 “Everything in Israel that is specially set
apart for the LORD* also belongs to you.
15 “The firstborn of every mother, whether
human or animal, that is offered to the LORD
will be yours. But you must always redeem
your firstborn sons and the firstborn of ceremonially unclean animals. 16 Redeem them
when they are one month old. The redemption price is five pieces of silver* (as measured by the weight of the sanctuary shekel,
which equals twenty gerahs).
17 “However, you may not redeem the
firstborn of cattle, sheep, or goats. They are
holy and have been set apart for the LORD.
Sprinkle their blood on the altar, and burn
their fat as a special gift, a pleasing aroma
to the LORD. 18 The meat of these animals
will be yours, just like the breast and right
thigh that are presented by lifting them up
as a special offering before the altar. 19 Yes,
I am giving you all these holy offerings that
the people of Israel bring to the LORD. They
are for you and your sons and daughters,
to be eaten as your permanent share. This
is an eternal and unbreakable covenant*
between the LORD and you, and it also
applies to your descendants.”
20 And the LORD said to Aaron, “You
priests will receive no allotment of land
or share of property among the people of
Israel. I am your share and your allotment.
21 As for the tribe of Levi, your relatives, I will
compensate them for their service in the
Tabernacle. Instead of an allotment of land,
I will give them the tithes from the entire
land of Israel.
22 “From now on, no Israelites except
priests or Levites may approach the
Tabernacle. If they come too near, they will
be judged guilty and will die. 23 Only the
Levites may serve at the Tabernacle, and
they will be held responsible for any offenses
against it. This is a permanent law for you,
to be observed from generation to generation. The Levites will receive no allotment of
land among the Israelites, 24 because I have
given them the Israelites’ tithes, which have
been presented as sacred offerings to the
LORD. This will be the Levites’ share. That is
why I said they would receive no allotment
of land among the Israelites.”
25 The LORD also told Moses, 26 “Give
these instructions to the Levites: When you
receive from the people of Israel the tithes
I have assigned as your allotment, give a
tenth of the tithes you receive—a tithe of
the tithe—to the LORD as a sacred offering.
27 The LORD will consider this offering to be
your harvest offering, as though it were the
first grain from your own threshing floor or
wine from your own winepress. 28 You must
present one-tenth of the tithe received from
the Israelites as a sacred offering to the
LORD. This is the LORD’s sacred portion, and
you must present it to Aaron the priest. 29 Be
sure to give to the LORD the best portions of
the gifts given to you.
30 “Also, give these instructions to the
Levites: When you present the best part
as your offering, it will be considered as
though it came from your own threshing
floor or winepress. 31 You Levites and your
families may eat this food anywhere you
wish, for it is your compensation for serving
in the Tabernacle. 32 You will not be considered guilty for accepting the LORD’s tithes
if you give the best portion to the priests.
But be careful not to treat the holy gifts of
the people of Israel as though they were
common. If you do, you will die.”

The Water of Purification

19 The LORD said to Moses and Aaron,
2 “Here is another legal requirement
commanded by the LORD: Tell the people
of Israel to bring you a red heifer, a perfect
animal that has no defects and has never
been yoked to a plow. 3 Give it to Eleazar the
priest, and it will be taken outside the camp
and slaughtered in his presence. 4 Eleazar
will take some of its blood on his finger and
sprinkle it seven times toward the front of
the Tabernacle.* 5 As Eleazar watches, the

heifer must be burned—its hide, meat, blood, and dung. [6]Eleazar the priest must then take a stick of cedar,* a hyssop branch, and some scarlet yarn and throw them into the fire where the heifer is burning.

[7]"Then the priest must wash his clothes and bathe himself in water. Afterward he may return to the camp, though he will remain ceremonially unclean until evening. [8]The man who burns the animal must also wash his clothes and bathe himself in water, and he, too, will remain unclean until evening. [9]Then someone who is ceremonially clean will gather up the ashes of the heifer and deposit them in a purified place outside the camp. They will be kept there for the community of Israel to use in the water for the purification ceremony. This ceremony is performed for the removal of sin. [10]The man who gathers up the ashes of the heifer must also wash his clothes, and he will remain ceremonially unclean until evening. This is a permanent law for the people of Israel and any foreigners who live among them.

[11]"All those who touch a dead human body will be ceremonially unclean for seven days. [12]They must purify themselves on the third and seventh days with the water of purification; then they will be purified. But if they do not do this on the third and seventh days, they will continue to be unclean even after the seventh day. [13]All those who touch a dead body and do not purify themselves in the proper way defile the LORD's Tabernacle, and they will be cut off from the community of Israel. Since the water of purification was not sprinkled on them, their defilement continues.

[14]"This is the ritual law that applies when someone dies inside a tent: All those who enter that tent and those who were inside when the death occurred will be ceremonially unclean for seven days. [15]Any open container in the tent that was not covered with a lid is also defiled. [16]And if someone in an open field touches the corpse of someone who was killed with a sword or who died a natural death, or if someone touches a human bone or a grave, that person will be defiled for seven days.

[17]"To remove the defilement, put some of the ashes from the burnt purification offering in a jar, and pour fresh water over them. [18]Then someone who is ceremonially clean must take a hyssop branch and dip it into the water. That person must sprinkle the water on the tent, on all the furnishings in the tent, and on the people who were in the tent; also on the person who touched a human bone, or touched someone who was killed or who died naturally, or touched a grave. [19]On the third and seventh days the person who is ceremonially clean must sprinkle the water on those who are defiled. Then on the seventh day the people being cleansed must wash their clothes and bathe themselves, and that evening they will be cleansed of their defilement.

[20]"But those who become defiled and do not purify themselves will be cut off from the community, for they have defiled the sanctuary of the LORD. Since the water of purification has not been sprinkled on them, they remain defiled. [21]This is a permanent law for the people. Those who sprinkle the water of purification must afterward wash their clothes, and anyone who then touches the water used for purification will remain defiled until evening. [22]Anything and anyone that a defiled person touches will be ceremonially unclean until evening."

Moses Strikes the Rock

20 In the first month of the year,* the whole community of Israel arrived in the wilderness of Zin and camped at Kadesh. While they were there, Miriam died and was buried.

[2]There was no water for the people to drink at that place, so they rebelled against Moses and Aaron. [3]The people blamed Moses and said, "If only we had died in the LORD's presence with our brothers! [4]Why have you brought the congregation of the LORD's people into this wilderness to die, along with all our livestock? [5]Why did you make us leave Egypt and bring us here to this terrible place? This land has no grain, no figs, no grapes, no pomegranates, and no water to drink!"

[6]Moses and Aaron turned away from the people and went to the entrance of the Tabernacle,* where they fell face down on the

18:14 The Hebrew term used here refers to the complete consecration of things or people to the LORD, either by destroying them or by giving them as an offering. **18:16** Hebrew *5 shekels* [2 ounces or 57 grams] *of silver.* **18:19** Hebrew *a covenant of salt.* **19:4** Hebrew *the Tent of Meeting.* **19:6** Or *juniper.* **20:1** The first month of the ancient Hebrew lunar calendar usually occurs within the months of March and April. The number of years since leaving Egypt is not specified. **20:6** Hebrew *the Tent of Meeting.*

ground. Then the glorious presence of the
LORD appeared to them, 7and the LORD said
to Moses, 8"You and Aaron must take the
staff and assemble the entire community.
As the people watch, speak to the rock over
there, and it will pour out its water. You
will provide enough water from the rock
to satisfy the whole community and their
livestock."

9So Moses did as he was told. He took the
staff from the place where it was kept before
the LORD. 10Then he and Aaron summoned
the people to come and gather at the rock.
"Listen, you rebels!" he shouted. "Must
we bring you water from this rock?" 11Then
Moses raised his hand and struck the rock
twice with the staff, and water gushed out.
So the entire community and their livestock
drank their fill.

12But the LORD said to Moses and Aaron,
"Because you did not trust me enough to
demonstrate my holiness to the people of
Israel, you will not lead them into the land
I am giving them!" 13This place was known
as the waters of Meribah (which means
"arguing") because there the people of
Israel argued with the LORD, and there he
demonstrated his holiness among them.

Edom Refuses Israel Passage

14While Moses was at Kadesh, he sent ambassadors to the king of Edom with this
message:

> "This is what your relatives, the
> people of Israel, say: You know all the
> hardships we have been through. 15Our
> ancestors went down to Egypt, and we
> lived there a long time, and we and
> our ancestors were brutally mistreated
> by the Egyptians. 16But when we cried
> out to the LORD, he heard us and sent
> an angel who brought us out of Egypt.
> Now we are camped at Kadesh, a town
> on the border of your land. 17Please let
> us travel through your land. We will be
> careful not to go through your fields and
> vineyards. We won't even drink water
> from your wells. We will stay on the
> king's road and never leave it until we
> have passed through your territory."

Water

In the desert, water is crucial. Several times the Israelites had complained about a lack of it, but each time God had provided (Exodus 15:22-27; 17:1-7). Now, in frustration, Moses struck the rock, as he had been told to do previously (Exodus 17:6). But this time God had told him simply to speak to the rock (Numbers 20:8), and this disobedience led to God forbidding him to enter the Promised Land.

In Canaan, the Israelites would need to depend continually on God to provide water. Unlike Mesopotamia and Egypt, it had no great rivers, and even the Jordan was of little use since it was below sea level and thus useless for irrigation, so the land was wholly dependent on God sending the rains. When the Israelites became tempted by Canaanite nature gods, Elijah prophesied that there would be no more rain until he commanded it (1 Kings 17:1; 18:36-46) to show the supremacy of the LORD (Yahweh).

But water is also used symbolically in the Bible—sometimes as a picture of distress (e.g., Psalm 42:7) or judgment (e.g., Exodus 15:8-10), but more often as a symbol of cleansing (e.g., Ephesians 5:26) or new beginnings (e.g., Acts 22:16). Isaiah used it as a symbol of the Holy Spirit (Isaiah 44:3), and Jesus used this idea at the Festival of Shelters (or Feast of Tabernacles), where, against the background of daily water rituals, he declared, "Anyone who is thirsty may come to me! Anyone who believes in me may come and drink! For the Scriptures declare, 'Rivers of living water will flow from his heart'" (John 7:37-38), which John goes on to explain was a picture of the Holy Spirit. God's provision for us isn't temporary, as it was for the Israelites in the desert, but rather a daily experience as we are filled with his Spirit.

18 But the king of Edom said, "Stay out of my land, or I will meet you with an army!"

19 The Israelites answered, "We will stay on the main road. If our livestock drink your water, we will pay for it. Just let us pass through your country. That's all we ask."

20 But the king of Edom replied, "Stay out! You may not pass through our land." With that he mobilized his army and marched out against them with an imposing force. 21 Because Edom refused to allow Israel to pass through their country, Israel was forced to turn around.

The Death of Aaron

22 The whole community of Israel left Kadesh and arrived at Mount Hor. 23 There, on the border of the land of Edom, the LORD said to Moses and Aaron, 24 "The time has come for Aaron to join his ancestors in death. He will not enter the land I am giving the people of Israel, because the two of you rebelled against my instructions concerning the water at Meribah. 25 Now take Aaron and his son Eleazar up Mount Hor. 26 There you will remove Aaron's priestly garments and put them on Eleazar, his son. Aaron will die there and join his ancestors."

27 So Moses did as the LORD commanded. The three of them went up Mount Hor together as the whole community watched. 28 At the summit, Moses removed the priestly garments from Aaron and put them on Eleazar, Aaron's son. Then Aaron died there on top of the mountain, and Moses and Eleazar went back down. 29 When the people realized that Aaron had died, all Israel mourned for him thirty days.

Victory over the Canaanites

21 The Canaanite king of Arad, who lived in the Negev, heard that the Israelites were approaching on the road through Atharim. So he attacked the Israelites and took some of them as prisoners. 2 Then the people of Israel made this vow to the LORD: "If you will hand these people over to us, we will completely destroy* all their towns." 3 The LORD heard the Israelites' request and gave them victory over the Canaanites. The Israelites completely destroyed them and their towns, and the place has been called Hormah* ever since.

The Bronze Snake

4 Then the people of Israel set out from Mount Hor, taking the road to the Red Sea* to go around the land of Edom. But the people grew impatient with the long journey, 5 and they began to speak against God and Moses. "Why have you brought us out of Egypt to die here in the wilderness?" they complained. "There is nothing to eat here and nothing to drink. And we hate this horrible manna!"

6 So the LORD sent poisonous snakes among the people, and many were bitten and died. 7 Then the people came to Moses and cried out, "We have sinned by speaking against the LORD and against you. Pray that the LORD will take away the snakes." So Moses prayed for the people.

8 Then the LORD told him, "Make a replica of a poisonous snake and attach it to a pole. All who are bitten will live if they simply look at it!" 9 So Moses made a snake out of bronze and attached it to a pole. Then anyone who was bitten by a snake could look at the bronze snake and be healed!

Israel's Journey to Moab

10 The Israelites traveled next to Oboth and camped there. 11 Then they went on to Iye-abarim, in the wilderness on the eastern border of Moab. 12 From there they traveled to the valley of Zered Brook and set up camp. 13 Then they moved out and camped on the far side of the Arnon River, in the wilderness adjacent to the territory of the Amorites. The Arnon is the boundary line between the Moabites and the Amorites. 14 For this reason *The Book of the Wars of the LORD* speaks of "the town of Waheb in the area of Suphah, and the ravines of the Arnon River, 15 and the ravines that extend as far as the settlement of Ar on the border of Moab."

16 From there the Israelites traveled to Beer,* which is the well where the LORD said to Moses, "Assemble the people, and I will give them water." 17 There the Israelites sang this song:

"Spring up, O well!
  Yes, sing its praises!
18 Sing of this well,
  which princes dug,

21:2 The Hebrew term used here refers to the complete consecration of things or people to the LORD, either by destroying them or by giving them as an offering; also in 21:3. **21:3** *Hormah* means "destruction." **21:4** Hebrew *sea of reeds.* **21:16** *Beer* means "well."

which great leaders hollowed out
with their scepters and staffs."

Then the Israelites left the wilderness
and proceeded on through Mattanah, 19Na-
haliel, and Bamoth. 20After that they went
to the valley in Moab where Pisgah Peak
overlooks the wasteland.*

Victory over Sihon and Og

21The Israelites sent ambassadors to King
Sihon of the Amorites with this message:

22"Let us travel through your land. We
will be careful not to go through your
fields and vineyards. We won't even
drink water from your wells. We will stay
on the king's road until we have passed
through your territory."

23But King Sihon refused to let them
cross his territory. Instead, he mobilized
his entire army and attacked Israel in the
wilderness, engaging them in battle at
Jahaz. 24But the Israelites slaughtered them
with their swords and occupied their land
from the Arnon River to the Jabbok River.
They went only as far as the Ammonite
border because the boundary of the Ammonites was fortified.*

25So Israel captured all the towns of the
Amorites and settled in them, including
the city of Heshbon and its surrounding
villages. 26Heshbon had been the capital of
King Sihon of the Amorites. He had defeated
a former Moabite king and seized all his
land as far as the Arnon River. 27Therefore,
the ancient poets wrote this about him:

"Come to Heshbon and let it be rebuilt!
Let the city of Sihon be restored.
28 A fire flamed forth from Heshbon,
a blaze from the city of Sihon.
It burned the city of Ar in Moab;
it destroyed the rulers of the Arnon
heights.
29 What sorrow awaits you, O people of
Moab!
You are finished, O worshipers of
Chemosh!
Chemosh has left his sons as refugees,
his daughters as captives of Sihon, the
Amorite king.
30 We have utterly destroyed them,
from Heshbon to Dibon.
We have completely wiped them out
as far away as Nophah and Medeba.*"

31So the people of Israel occupied the territory of the Amorites. 32After Moses sent men
to explore the Jazer area, they captured all the
towns in the region and drove out the Amorites who lived there. 33Then they turned and
marched up the road to Bashan, but King Og
of Bashan and all his people attacked them at
Edrei. 34The LORD said to Moses, "Do not be
afraid of him, for I have handed him over to
you, along with all his people and his land.
Do the same to him as you did to King Sihon
of the Amorites, who ruled in Heshbon."
35And Israel killed King Og, his sons, and all
his subjects; not a single survivor remained.
Then Israel occupied their land.

Balak Sends for Balaam

22 Then the people of Israel traveled
to the plains of Moab and camped
east of the Jordan River, across from Jericho.
2Balak son of Zippor, the Moabite king, had
seen everything the Israelites did to the
Amorites. 3And when the people of Moab
saw how many Israelites there were, they
were terrified. 4The king of Moab said to
the elders of Midian, "This mob will devour
everything in sight, like an ox devours grass
in the field!"

So Balak, king of Moab, 5sent messengers
to call Balaam son of Beor, who was living
in his native land of Pethor* near the Euphrates River.* His message said:

"Look, a vast horde of people has
arrived from Egypt. They cover the face
of the earth and are threatening me.
6Please come and curse these people
for me because they are too powerful
for me. Then perhaps I will be able to
conquer them and drive them from the
land. I know that blessings fall on any
people you bless, and curses fall on
people you curse."

7Balak's messengers, who were elders of
Moab and Midian, set out with money to
pay Balaam to place a curse upon Israel.*
They went to Balaam and delivered Balak's
message to him. 8"Stay here overnight,"
Balaam said. "In the morning I will tell you
whatever the LORD directs me to say." So
the officials from Moab stayed there with
Balaam.

9That night God came to Balaam and
asked him, "Who are these men visiting
you?"

10Balaam said to God, "Balak son of
Zippor, king of Moab, has sent me this
message: 11'Look, a vast horde of people has
arrived from Egypt, and they cover the face
of the earth. Come and curse these people
for me. Then perhaps I will be able to stand
up to them and drive them from the land.'"
12But God told Balaam, "Do not go with
them. You are not to curse these people, for
they have been blessed!"
13The next morning Balaam got up and
told Balak's officials, "Go on home! The
LORD will not let me go with you."
14So the Moabite officials returned to
King Balak and reported, "Balaam refused
to come with us." 15Then Balak tried again.
This time he sent a larger number of even
more distinguished officials than those
he had sent the first time. 16They went to
Balaam and delivered this message to him:

"This is what Balak son of Zippor says:
Please don't let anything stop you from
coming to help me. 17I will pay you very
well and do whatever you tell me. Just
come and curse these people for me!"

18But Balaam responded to Balak's messengers, "Even if Balak were to give me his
palace filled with silver and gold, I would be
powerless to do anything against the will of
the LORD my God. 19But stay here one more
night, and I will see if the LORD has anything else to say to me."
20That night God came to Balaam and told
him, "Since these men have come for you,
get up and go with them. But do only what
I tell you to do."

Balaam and His Donkey

21So the next morning Balaam got up,
saddled his donkey, and started off with
the Moabite officials. 22But God was angry
that Balaam was going, so he sent the
angel of the LORD to stand in the road
to block his way. As Balaam and two servants were riding along, 23Balaam's donkey
saw the angel of the LORD standing in the
road with a drawn sword in his hand. The
donkey bolted off the road into a field, but
Balaam beat it and turned it back onto the
road. 24Then the angel of the LORD stood at
a place where the road narrowed between
two vineyard walls. 25When the donkey saw
the angel of the LORD, it tried to squeeze by
and crushed Balaam's foot against the wall.
So Balaam beat the donkey again. 26Then
the angel of the LORD moved farther down
the road and stood in a place too narrow
for the donkey to get by at all. 27This time
when the donkey saw the angel, it lay down
under Balaam. In a fit of rage Balaam beat
the animal again with his staff.
28Then the LORD gave the donkey the
ability to speak. "What have I done to you
that deserves your beating me three times?"
it asked Balaam.
29"You have made me look like a fool!"
Balaam shouted. "If I had a sword with me,
I would kill you!"
30"But I am the same donkey you have
ridden all your life," the donkey answered.
"Have I ever done anything like this before?"
"No," Balaam admitted.
31Then the LORD opened Balaam's eyes,
and he saw the angel of the LORD standing
in the roadway with a drawn sword in his
hand. Balaam bowed his head and fell face
down on the ground before him.
32"Why did you beat your donkey those

21:20 Or *overlooks Jeshimon.* **21:24** Or *because the terrain of the Ammonite frontier was rugged;* Hebrew reads *because the boundary of the Ammonites was strong.* **21:30** Or *until fire spread to Medeba.* The meaning of the Hebrew is uncertain. **22:5a** Or *who was at Pethor in the land of the Amavites.* **22:5b** Hebrew *the river.* **22:7** Hebrew *set out with the money of divination in their hand.*

The Moabites

Balak was king of Moab, a country to the east of the Dead Sea, with Ammon to its north and Edom to its south. Balak tried to stop the Israelites from passing through Moab on their way to Canaan (Numbers 22–24). Although the Moabites and Israelites were related—Moab was the grandson of Lot (Genesis 19:36-37)—through most of the Old Testament story they were in conflict with one another, particularly over the very fertile land that lay to Moab's north, and that region often changed hands.

three times?" the angel of the LORD demanded. "Look, I have come to block your
way because you are stubbornly resisting
me. 33Three times the donkey saw me and
shied away; otherwise, I would certainly
have killed you by now and spared the
donkey."
34Then Balaam confessed to the angel of
the LORD, "I have sinned. I didn't realize
you were standing in the road to block my
way. I will return home if you are against
my going."
35But the angel of the LORD told Balaam,
"Go with these men, but say only what I
tell you to say." So Balaam went on with
Balak's officials. 36When King Balak heard
that Balaam was on the way, he went out to
meet him at a Moabite town on the Arnon
River at the farthest border of his land.
37"Didn't I send you an urgent invitation?
Why didn't you come right away?" Balak
asked Balaam. "Didn't you believe me when
I said I would reward you richly?"
38Balaam replied, "Look, now I have
come, but I have no power to say whatever
I want. I will speak only the message that
God puts in my mouth." 39Then Balaam
accompanied Balak to Kiriath-huzoth,
40where the king sacrificed cattle and sheep.
He sent portions of the meat to Balaam and
the officials who were with him. 41The next
morning Balak took Balaam up to Bamoth-
baal. From there he could see some of the
people of Israel spread out below him.

Balaam Blesses Israel

23 Then Balaam said to King Balak,
"Build me seven altars here, and
prepare seven young bulls and seven rams
for me to sacrifice." 2Balak followed his
instructions, and the two of them sacrificed
a young bull and a ram on each altar.
3Then Balaam said to Balak, "Stand here
by your burnt offerings, and I will go to see if
the LORD will respond to me. Then I will tell
you whatever he reveals to me." So Balaam
went alone to the top of a bare hill, 4and God
met him there. Balaam said to him, "I have
prepared seven altars and have sacrificed a
young bull and a ram on each altar."
5The LORD gave Balaam a message for
King Balak. Then he said, "Go back to Balak
and give him my message."
6So Balaam returned and found the king
standing beside his burnt offerings with all
the officials of Moab. 7This was the message
Balaam delivered:

"Balak summoned me to come from
    Aram;
  the king of Moab brought me from the
    eastern hills.
'Come,' he said, 'curse Jacob for me!
  Come and announce Israel's doom.'
8 But how can I curse those
  whom God has not cursed?
How can I condemn those
  whom the LORD has not condemned?
9 I see them from the cliff tops;
  I watch them from the hills.
I see a people who live by themselves,
  set apart from other nations.
10 Who can count Jacob's descendants,
    as numerous as dust?
  Who can count even a fourth of
    Israel's people?
Let me die like the righteous;
  let my life end like theirs."

11Then King Balak demanded of Balaam,
"What have you done to me? I brought you

Balaam

Balaam son of Beor, a pagan prophet from Mesopotamia, was hired by King Balak of Moab to curse Israel when they wanted to pass through his territory. Suitably rewarded for his trouble, Balaam set off for Moab—though he encountered more than he had bargained for when God broke into his life and spoke to him in such an unusual way that even he could recognize God was at work (Numbers 22:21-35). He quickly agreed to speak only what God told him to, which meant that rather than curse Israel he could only bless them (chapters 23–24). An ancient inscription referring to "Balaam son of Beor . . . divine seer" was discovered north of the plains of Moab in 1967.

to curse my enemies. Instead, you have
blessed them!"
12 But Balaam replied, "I will speak only
the message that the LORD puts in my
mouth."

Balaam's Second Message

13 Then King Balak told him, "Come with
me to another place. There you will see
another part of the nation of Israel, but not
all of them. Curse at least that many!" 14 So
Balak took Balaam to the plateau of Zophim
on Pisgah Peak. He built seven altars there
and offered a young bull and a ram on each
altar.
15 Then Balaam said to the king, "Stand
here by your burnt offerings while I go over
there to meet the LORD."
16 And the LORD met Balaam and gave him
a message. Then he said, "Go back to Balak
and give him my message."
17 So Balaam returned and found the king
standing beside his burnt offerings with all
the officials of Moab. "What did the LORD
say?" Balak asked eagerly.
18 This was the message Balaam delivered:

"Rise up, Balak, and listen!
Hear me, son of Zippor.
19 God is not a man, so he does not lie.
He is not human, so he does not
change his mind.
Has he ever spoken and failed to act?
Has he ever promised and not carried
it through?
20 Listen, I received a command to bless;
God has blessed, and I cannot
reverse it!
21 No misfortune is in his plan for Jacob;
no trouble is in store for Israel.
For the LORD their God is with them;
he has been proclaimed their king.
22 God brought them out of Egypt;
for them he is as strong as a wild ox.
23 No curse can touch Jacob;
no magic has any power against
Israel.
For now it will be said of Jacob,
'What wonders God has done for
Israel!'
24 These people rise up like a lioness,
like a majestic lion rousing itself.
They refuse to rest
until they have feasted on prey,
drinking the blood of the slaughtered!"

25 Then Balak said to Balaam, "Fine, but
if you won't curse them, at least don't bless
them!"
26 But Balaam replied to Balak, "Didn't
I tell you that I can do only what the LORD
tells me?"

Balaam's Third Message

27 Then King Balak said to Balaam, "Come,
I will take you to one more place. Perhaps it
will please God to let you curse them from
there."
28 So Balak took Balaam to the top of
Mount Peor, overlooking the wasteland.*
29 Balaam again told Balak, "Build me seven
altars, and prepare seven young bulls and
seven rams for me to sacrifice." 30 So Balak
did as Balaam ordered and offered a young
bull and a ram on each altar.

24

By now Balaam realized that the
LORD was determined to bless Israel,
so he did not resort to divination as before.
Instead, he turned and looked out toward
the wilderness, 2 where he saw the people
of Israel camped, tribe by tribe. Then the
Spirit of God came upon him, 3 and this is
the message he delivered:

"This is the message of Balaam son of
Beor,
the message of the man whose eyes
see clearly,
4 the message of one who hears the words
of God,
who sees a vision from the Almighty,
who bows down with eyes wide open:
5 How beautiful are your tents, O Jacob;
how lovely are your homes, O Israel!
6 They spread before me like palm groves,*
like gardens by the riverside.
They are like tall trees planted by the
LORD,
like cedars beside the waters.
7 Water will flow from their buckets;
their offspring have all they need.
Their king will be greater than Agag;
their kingdom will be exalted.
8 God brought them out of Egypt;
for them he is as strong as a wild ox.
He devours all the nations that oppose
him,
breaking their bones in pieces,
shooting them with arrows.

23:28 Or *overlooking Jeshimon.* **24:6** Or *like a majestic valley.*

[9] Like a lion, Israel crouches and lies
down;
like a lioness, who dares to arouse
her?
Blessed is everyone who blesses you,
O Israel,
and cursed is everyone who curses
you."

[10]King Balak flew into a rage against
Balaam. He angrily clapped his hands and
shouted, "I called you to curse my enemies!
Instead, you have blessed them three times.
[11]Now get out of here! Go back home! I promised to reward you richly, but the LORD has
kept you from your reward."

[12]Balaam told Balak, "Don't you remember
what I told your messengers? I said, [13]'Even if
Balak were to give me his palace filled with
silver and gold, I would be powerless to do
anything against the will of the LORD.' I told
you that I could say only what the LORD says!
[14]Now I am returning to my own people. But
first let me tell you what the Israelites will do
to your people in the future."

Balaam's Final Messages

[15]This is the message Balaam delivered:

"This is the message of Balaam son of
Beor,
the message of the man whose eyes
see clearly,
[16] the message of one who hears the words
of God,
who has knowledge from the Most
High,
who sees a vision from the Almighty,
who bows down with eyes wide open:
[17] I see him, but not here and now.
I perceive him, but far in the distant
future.
A star will rise from Jacob;
a scepter will emerge from Israel.
It will crush the heads of Moab's people,
cracking the skulls* of the people of
Sheth.
[18] Edom will be taken over,
and Seir, its enemy, will be conquered,
while Israel marches on in triumph.
[19] A ruler will rise in Jacob
who will destroy the survivors of Ir."

[20]Then Balaam looked over toward the people
of Amalek and delivered this message:

"Amalek was the greatest of nations,
but its destiny is destruction!"

[21]Then he looked over toward the Kenites
and delivered this message:

"Your home is secure;
your nest is set in the rocks.
[22] But the Kenites will be destroyed
when Assyria* takes you
captive."

[23]Balaam concluded his messages by saying:

"Alas, who can survive
unless God has willed it?
[24] Ships will come from the coasts of
Cyprus*;
they will oppress Assyria and afflict
Eber,
but they, too, will be utterly destroyed."

[25]Then Balaam left and returned home,
and Balak also went on his way.

Moab Seduces Israel

25 While the Israelites were camped
at Acacia Grove,* some of the men
defiled themselves by having* sexual relations with local Moabite women. [2]These
women invited them to attend sacrifices

The Midianites

Flouting the ban on intermarriage between God's people and others, and right on the heels of an example of what it can lead to (Numbers 25:1-5), an Israelite man "brought a Midianite woman into his tent, right before the eyes of Moses and all the people" (25:6). The Midianites were descendants of Midian, son of Abraham's second wife, Keturah (Genesis 25:1-4), and they lived as a nomadic group on the edges of Canaan, raiding and trading. They not only resisted the Israelites on their way to Canaan but also were involved in seducing them to worship Baal at Peor (Numbers 25:16-18).

to their gods, so the Israelites feasted with them and worshiped the gods of Moab. 3In this way, Israel joined in the worship of Baal of Peor, causing the LORD's anger to blaze against his people.

4The LORD issued the following command to Moses: "Seize all the ringleaders and execute them before the LORD in broad daylight, so his fierce anger will turn away from the people of Israel."

5So Moses ordered Israel's judges, "Each of you must put to death the men under your authority who have joined in worshiping Baal of Peor."

6Just then one of the Israelite men brought a Midianite woman into his tent, right before the eyes of Moses and all the people, as everyone was weeping at the entrance of the Tabernacle.* 7When Phinehas son of Eleazar and grandson of Aaron the priest saw this, he jumped up and left the assembly. He took a spear 8and rushed after the man into his tent. Phinehas thrust the spear all the way through the man's body and into the woman's stomach. So the plague against the Israelites was stopped, 9but not before 24,000 people had died.

10Then the LORD said to Moses, 11"Phinehas son of Eleazar and grandson of Aaron the priest has turned my anger away from the Israelites by being as zealous among them as I was. So I stopped destroying all Israel as I had intended to do in my zealous anger. 12Now tell him that I am making my special covenant of peace with him. 13In this covenant, I give him and his descendants a permanent right to the priesthood, for in his zeal for me, his God, he purified the people of Israel, making them right with me.*"

14The Israelite man killed with the Midianite woman was named Zimri son of Salu, the leader of a family from the tribe of Simeon. 15The woman's name was Cozbi; she was the daughter of Zur, the leader of a Midianite clan.

16Then the LORD said to Moses, 17"Attack the Midianites and destroy them, 18because they assaulted you with deceit and tricked you into worshiping Baal of Peor, and because of Cozbi, the daughter of a Midianite leader, who was killed at the time of the plague because of what happened at Peor."

The Second Registration of Israel's Troops

26 After the plague had ended,* the LORD said to Moses and to Eleazar son of Aaron the priest, 2"From the whole community of Israel, record the names of all the warriors by their families. List all the men twenty years old or older who are able to go to war."

3So there on the plains of Moab beside the Jordan River, across from Jericho, Moses and Eleazar the priest issued these instructions to the leaders of Israel: 4"List all the men of Israel twenty years old and older, just as the LORD commanded Moses."

This is the record of all the descendants of Israel who came out of Egypt.

The Tribe of Reuben

5These were the clans descended from the sons of Reuben, Jacob's* oldest son:

The Hanochite clan, named after their ancestor Hanoch.
The Palluite clan, named after their ancestor Pallu.
6 The Hezronite clan, named after their ancestor Hezron.
The Carmite clan, named after their ancestor Carmi.

7These were the clans of Reuben. Their registered troops numbered 43,730.

8Pallu was the ancestor of Eliab, 9and Eliab was the father of Nemuel, Dathan, and Abiram. This Dathan and Abiram are the same community leaders who conspired with Korah against Moses and Aaron, rebelling against the LORD. 10But the earth opened up its mouth and swallowed them with Korah, and fire devoured 250 of their followers. This served as a warning to the entire nation of Israel. 11However, the sons of Korah did not die that day.

The Tribe of Simeon

12These were the clans descended from the sons of Simeon:

The Jemuelite clan, named after their ancestor Jemuel.*

24:17 As in Samaritan Pentateuch; the meaning of the Hebrew word is uncertain. **24:22** Hebrew *Asshur;* also in 24:24. **24:24** Hebrew *Kittim.* **25:1a** Hebrew *Shittim.* **25:1b** As in Greek version; Hebrew reads *some of the men began having.* **25:6** Hebrew *the Tent of Meeting.* **25:13** Or *he made atonement for the people of Israel.* **26:1** The initial phrase in verse 26:1 is numbered 25:19 in Hebrew text. **26:5** Hebrew *Israel's;* see note on 1:20-21b. **26:12** As in Syriac version (see also Gen 46:10; Exod 6:15); Hebrew reads *Nemuelite . . . Nemuel.*

The Jaminite clan, named after their ancestor Jamin.
The Jakinite clan, named after their ancestor Jakin.
13 The Zoharite clan, named after their ancestor Zohar.*
The Shaulite clan, named after their ancestor Shaul.

14 These were the clans of Simeon. Their registered troops numbered 22,200.

The Tribe of Gad

15 These were the clans descended from the sons of Gad:
The Zephonite clan, named after their ancestor Zephon.
The Haggite clan, named after their ancestor Haggi.
The Shunite clan, named after their ancestor Shuni.
16 The Oznite clan, named after their ancestor Ozni.
The Erite clan, named after their ancestor Eri.
17 The Arodite clan, named after their ancestor Arodi.*
The Arelite clan, named after their ancestor Areli.

18 These were the clans of Gad. Their registered troops numbered 40,500.

The Tribe of Judah

19 Judah had two sons, Er and Onan, who had died in the land of Canaan.
20 These were the clans descended from Judah's surviving sons:
The Shelanite clan, named after their ancestor Shelah.
The Perezite clan, named after their ancestor Perez.
The Zerahite clan, named after their ancestor Zerah.

21 These were the subclans descended from the Perezites:
The Hezronites, named after their ancestor Hezron.
The Hamulites, named after their ancestor Hamul.

22 These were the clans of Judah. Their registered troops numbered 76,500.

The Tribe of Issachar

23 These were the clans descended from the sons of Issachar:
The Tolaite clan, named after their ancestor Tola.
The Puite clan, named after their ancestor Puah.*
24 The Jashubite clan, named after their ancestor Jashub.
The Shimronite clan, named after their ancestor Shimron.

25 These were the clans of Issachar. Their registered troops numbered 64,300.

The Tribe of Zebulun

26 These were the clans descended from the sons of Zebulun:
The Seredite clan, named after their ancestor Sered.
The Elonite clan, named after their ancestor Elon.
The Jahleelite clan, named after their ancestor Jahleel.

27 These were the clans of Zebulun. Their registered troops numbered 60,500.

The Tribe of Manasseh

28 Two clans were descended from Joseph through Manasseh and Ephraim.

29 These were the clans descended from Manasseh:
The Makirite clan, named after their ancestor Makir.
The Gileadite clan, named after their ancestor Gilead, Makir's son.

30 These were the subclans descended from the Gileadites:
The Iezerites, named after their ancestor Iezer.
The Helekites, named after their ancestor Helek.
31 The Asrielites, named after their ancestor Asriel.
The Shechemites, named after their ancestor Shechem.
32 The Shemidaites, named after their ancestor Shemida.
The Hepherites, named after their ancestor Hepher.
33 (One of Hepher's descendants, Zelophehad, had no sons, but his daughters' names were Mahlah, Noah, Hoglah, Milcah, and Tirzah.)

34 These were the clans of Manasseh. Their registered troops numbered 52,700.

The Tribe of Ephraim

35These were the clans descended from the sons of Ephraim:

The Shuthelahite clan, named after their ancestor Shuthelah.
The Bekerite clan, named after their ancestor Beker.
The Tahanite clan, named after their ancestor Tahan.

36This was the subclan descended from the Shuthelahites:

The Eranites, named after their ancestor Eran.

37These were the clans of Ephraim. Their registered troops numbered 32,500.

These clans of Manasseh and Ephraim were all descendants of Joseph.

The Tribe of Benjamin

38These were the clans descended from the sons of Benjamin:

The Belaite clan, named after their ancestor Bela.
The Ashbelite clan, named after their ancestor Ashbel.
The Ahiramite clan, named after their ancestor Ahiram.
39 The Shuphamite clan, named after their ancestor Shupham.*
The Huphamite clan, named after their ancestor Hupham.

40These were the subclans descended from the Belaites:

The Ardites, named after their ancestor Ard.*
The Naamites, named after their ancestor Naaman.

41These were the clans of Benjamin. Their registered troops numbered 45,600.

The Tribe of Dan

42These were the clans descended from the sons of Dan:

The Shuhamite clan, named after their ancestor Shuham.

43These were the Shuhamite clans of Dan. Their registered troops numbered 64,400.

The Tribe of Asher

44These were the clans descended from the sons of Asher:

The Imnite clan, named after their ancestor Imnah.
The Ishvite clan, named after their ancestor Ishvi.
The Beriite clan, named after their ancestor Beriah.

45These were the subclans descended from the Beriites:

The Heberites, named after their ancestor Heber.
The Malkielites, named after their ancestor Malkiel.

46Asher also had a daughter named Serah.

47These were the clans of Asher. Their registered troops numbered 53,400.

The Tribe of Naphtali

48These were the clans descended from the sons of Naphtali:

The Jahzeelite clan, named after their ancestor Jahzeel.
The Gunite clan, named after their ancestor Guni.
49 The Jezerite clan, named after their ancestor Jezer.
The Shillemite clan, named after their ancestor Shillem.

50These were the clans of Naphtali. Their registered troops numbered 45,400.

Results of the Registration

51In summary, the registered troops of all Israel numbered 601,730.

52Then the LORD said to Moses, 53"Divide the land among the tribes, and distribute the grants of land in proportion to the tribes' populations, as indicated by the number of names on the list. 54Give the larger tribes more land and the smaller tribes less land, each group receiving a grant in proportion to the size of its population. 55But you must assign the land by lot, and give land to each ancestral tribe according to the number of names on the list. 56Each grant of land must be assigned

26:13 As in parallel texts at Gen 46:10 and Exod 6:15; Hebrew reads *Zerahite . . . Zerah.* **26:17** As in Samaritan Pentateuch and Greek and Syriac versions (see also Gen 46:16); Hebrew reads *Arod.* **26:23** As in Samaritan Pentateuch, Greek and Syriac versions, and Latin Vulgate (see also 1 Chr 7:1); Hebrew reads *The Punite clan, named after its ancestor Puvah.* **26:39** As in some Hebrew manuscripts, Samaritan Pentateuch, Greek and Syriac versions, and Latin Vulgate; most Hebrew manuscripts read *Shephupham.* **26:40** As in Samaritan Pentateuch, some Greek manuscripts, and Latin Vulgate; Hebrew lacks *named after their ancestor Ard.*

by lot among the larger and smaller tribal groups."

The Tribe of Levi

57 This is the record of the Levites who were counted according to their clans:

> The Gershonite clan, named after their ancestor Gershon.
> The Kohathite clan, named after their ancestor Kohath.
> The Merarite clan, named after their ancestor Merari.

58 The Libnites, the Hebronites, the Mahlites, the Mushites, and the Korahites were all subclans of the Levites.

Now Kohath was the ancestor of Amram, 59 and Amram's wife was named Jochebed. She also was a descendant of Levi, born among the Levites in the land of Egypt. Amram and Jochebed became the parents of Aaron, Moses, and their sister, Miriam. 60 To Aaron were born Nadab, Abihu, Eleazar, and Ithamar. 61 But Nadab and Abihu died when they burned before the LORD the wrong kind of fire, different than he had commanded.

62 The men from the Levite clans who were one month old or older numbered 23,000. But the Levites were not included in the registration of the rest of the people of Israel because they were not given an allotment of land when it was divided among the Israelites.

63 So these are the results of the registration of the people of Israel as conducted by Moses and Eleazar the priest on the plains of Moab beside the Jordan River, across from Jericho. 64 Not one person on this list had been among those listed in the previous registration taken by Moses and Aaron in the wilderness of Sinai. 65 For the LORD had said of them, "They will all die in the wilderness." Not one of them survived except Caleb son of Jephunneh and Joshua son of Nun.

The Daughters of Zelophehad

27 One day a petition was presented by the daughters of Zelophehad—Mahlah, Noah, Hoglah, Milcah, and Tirzah. Their father, Zelophehad, was a descendant of Hepher son of Gilead, son of Makir, son of Manasseh, son of Joseph. 2 These women stood before Moses, Eleazar the priest, the tribal leaders, and the entire community at the entrance of the Tabernacle.* 3 "Our father died in the wilderness," they said. "He was not among Korah's followers, who rebelled against the LORD; he died because of his own sin. But he had no sons. 4 Why should the name of our father disappear from his clan just because he had no sons? Give us property along with the rest of our relatives."

5 So Moses brought their case before the LORD. 6 And the LORD replied to Moses, 7 "The claim of the daughters of Zelophehad is legitimate. You must give them a grant of land along with their father's relatives. Assign them the property that would have been given to their father.

8 "And give the following instructions to the people of Israel: If a man dies and has no son, then give his inheritance to his daughters. 9 And if he has no daughter either, transfer his inheritance to his brothers. 10 If he has no brothers, give his inheritance to his father's brothers. 11 But if his father has no brothers, give his inheritance to the nearest relative in his clan. This is a legal requirement for the people of Israel, just as the LORD commanded Moses."

Joshua Chosen to Lead Israel

12 One day the LORD said to Moses, "Climb one of the mountains east of the river,* and look out over the land I have given the people of Israel. 13 After you have seen it, you will die like your brother, Aaron, 14 for you both rebelled against my instructions in the wilderness of Zin. When the people of Israel rebelled, you failed to demonstrate my holiness to them at the waters." (These are the waters of Meribah at Kadesh* in the wilderness of Zin.)

15 Then Moses said to the LORD, 16 "O LORD, you are the God who gives breath to all creatures. Please appoint a new man as leader for the community. 17 Give them someone who will guide them wherever they go and will lead them into battle, so the community of the LORD will not be like sheep without a shepherd."

18 The LORD replied, "Take Joshua son of Nun, who has the Spirit in him, and lay your hands on him. 19 Present him to Eleazar the priest before the whole community, and publicly commission him to lead the people. 20 Transfer some of your authority to

him so the whole community of Israel will
obey him. [21]When direction from the LORD
is needed, Joshua will stand before Eleazar
the priest, who will use the Urim—one of
the sacred lots cast before the LORD—to determine his will. This is how Joshua and the
rest of the community of Israel will determine everything they should do."

[22]So Moses did as the LORD commanded.
He presented Joshua to Eleazar the priest
and the whole community. [23]Moses laid his
hands on him and commissioned him to
lead the people, just as the LORD had commanded through Moses.

The Daily Offerings

28 The LORD said to Moses, [2]"Give
these instructions to the people of
Israel: The offerings you present as special
gifts are a pleasing aroma to me; they are
my food. See to it that they are brought at
the appointed times and offered according
to my instructions.

[3]"Say to the people: This is the special gift
you must present to the LORD as your daily
burnt offering. You must offer two one-year-
old male lambs with no defects. [4]Sacrifice
one lamb in the morning and the other in
the evening. [5]With each lamb you must offer
a grain offering of two quarts* of choice
flour mixed with one quart* of pure oil of
pressed olives. [6]This is the regular burnt offering instituted at Mount Sinai as a special
gift, a pleasing aroma to the LORD. [7]Along
with it you must present the proper liquid
offering of one quart of alcoholic drink with
each lamb, poured out in the Holy Place as
an offering to the LORD. [8]Offer the second
lamb in the evening with the same grain
offering and liquid offering. It, too, is a
special gift, a pleasing aroma to the LORD.

The Sabbath Offerings

[9]"On the Sabbath day, sacrifice two one-
year-old male lambs with no defects. They

27:2 Hebrew *the Tent of Meeting.* **27:12** Or *the mountains of Abarim.* **27:14** Hebrew *waters of Meribath-kadesh.*
28:5a Hebrew *1/10 of an ephah* [2.2 liters]; also in 28:13, 21, 29.
28:5b Hebrew *1/4 of a hin* [1 liter]; also in 28:7.

Success and successors

Most people today measure success by how high they have climbed in their workplace, or how much money they earn, or what kind of home they live in or car they drive. But the Bible doesn't measure success in this way; rather, it sees success as being able to produce successors.

In Numbers 27, we see Moses—a man who, humanly speaking, was very successful—recognizing that without a successor, his lifetime's work would be a failure. He therefore asked God to appoint someone as his successor (Numbers 27:15-17). Imagine Moses' delight when God designated Joshua, the man he had spent all these years training and who had been constantly at his side. True success—whether in church or workplace—is about producing successors, for without a successor the vision and work will fail to flourish and may even die. Sadly, Joshua did not produce his own successors, which led to the godless period of the judges.

In Christian ministry today, an outgoing leader's successor may turn out to be a family member, if that is what God says, as he did to Aaron concerning the priesthood and David concerning kingship. But family membership itself is not the major biblical criterion for a successor, or a guarantee of success. In fact, both Aaron's and David's descendants would lose their roles through unfaithfulness. What matters ultimately in succession is the call of God. Indeed, the most successful successions in the Bible never involved family membership, as we see with Moses and Joshua, or Elijah and Elisha, or Paul and Timothy. True successors are those who are anointed and appointed by God, not by us; so we should always look for that anointing when we are seeking our successors in ministry, for that alone will guarantee success.

must be accompanied by a grain offering of
four quarts* of choice flour moistened with
olive oil, and a liquid offering. 10This is the
burnt offering to be presented each Sabbath
day, in addition to the regular burnt offering
and its accompanying liquid offering.

The Monthly Offerings

11"On the first day of each month, present
an extra burnt offering to the LORD of two
young bulls, one ram, and seven one-year-
old male lambs, all with no defects. 12These
must be accompanied by grain offerings of
choice flour moistened with olive oil—six
quarts* with each bull, four quarts with
the ram, 13and two quarts with each lamb.
This burnt offering will be a special gift, a
pleasing aroma to the LORD. 14You must also
present a liquid offering with each sacrifice:
two quarts* of wine for each bull, a third of a
gallon* for the ram, and one quart* for each
lamb. Present this monthly burnt offering
on the first day of each month throughout
the year.

15"On the first day of each month, you
must also offer one male goat for a sin offering to the LORD. This is in addition to the
regular burnt offering and its accompanying liquid offering.

Offerings for the Passover

16"On the fourteenth day of the first month,*
you must celebrate the LORD's Passover.
17On the following day—the fifteenth day of
the month—a joyous, seven-day festival will
begin, but no bread made with yeast may
be eaten. 18The first day of the festival will
be an official day for holy assembly, and no
ordinary work may be done on that day. 19As
a special gift you must present a burnt offering to the LORD—two young bulls, one ram,
and seven one-year-old male lambs, all with
no defects. 20These will be accompanied by
grain offerings of choice flour moistened
with olive oil—six quarts with each bull,
four quarts with the ram, 21and two quarts
with each of the seven lambs. 22You must
also offer a male goat as a sin offering to
purify yourselves and make yourselves right
with the LORD.* 23Present these offerings in
addition to your regular morning burnt offering. 24On each of the seven days of the
festival, this is how you must prepare the
food offering that is presented as a special
gift, a pleasing aroma to the LORD. These
will be offered in addition to the regular
burnt offerings and liquid offerings. 25The
seventh day of the festival will be another
official day for holy assembly, and no ordinary work may be done on that day.

Offerings for the Festival of Harvest

26"At the Festival of Harvest,* when you
present the first of your new grain to the
LORD, you must call an official day for holy
assembly, and you may do no ordinary work
on that day. 27Present a special burnt offering on that day as a pleasing aroma to the
LORD. It will consist of two young bulls, one
ram, and seven one-year-old male lambs.
28These will be accompanied by grain offerings of choice flour moistened with olive
oil—six quarts with each bull, four quarts
with the ram, 29and two quarts with each of
the seven lambs. 30Also, offer one male goat
to purify yourselves and make yourselves
right with the LORD. 31Prepare these special
burnt offerings, along with their liquid offerings, in addition to the regular burnt offering and its accompanying grain offering.
Be sure that all the animals you sacrifice
have no defects.

Offerings for the Festival of Trumpets

29 "Celebrate the Festival of Trumpets
each year on the first day of the appointed month in early autumn.* You must
call an official day for holy assembly, and
you may do no ordinary work. 2On that day
you must present a burnt offering as a pleasing aroma to the LORD. It will consist of one
young bull, one ram, and seven one-year-
old male lambs, all with no defects. 3These
must be accompanied by grain offerings of
choice flour moistened with olive oil—six
quarts* with the bull, four quarts* with the
ram, 4and two quarts* with each of the seven
lambs. 5In addition, you must sacrifice a
male goat as a sin offering to purify yourselves and make yourselves right with the
LORD.* 6These special sacrifices are in addition to your regular monthly and daily burnt
offerings, and they must be given with their
prescribed grain offerings and liquid offerings. These offerings are given as a special
gift to the LORD, a pleasing aroma to him.

Offerings for the Day of Atonement

7"Ten days later, on the tenth day of the
same month,* you must call another holy

assembly. On that day, the Day of Atonement, the people must go without food and must do no ordinary work. [8]You must present a burnt offering as a pleasing aroma to the LORD. It will consist of one young bull, one ram, and seven one-year-old male lambs, all with no defects. [9]These offerings must be accompanied by the prescribed grain offerings of choice flour moistened with olive oil—six quarts of choice flour with the bull, four quarts of choice flour with the ram, [10]and two quarts of choice flour with each of the seven lambs. [11]You must also sacrifice one male goat for a sin offering. This is in addition to the sin offering of atonement and the regular daily burnt offering with its grain offering, and their accompanying liquid offerings.

Offerings for the Festival of Shelters

[12]"Five days later, on the fifteenth day of the same month,* you must call another holy assembly of all the people, and you may do no ordinary work on that day. It is the beginning of the Festival of Shelters,* a seven-day festival to the LORD. [13]On the first day of the festival, you must present a burnt offering as a special gift, a pleasing aroma to the LORD. It will consist of thirteen young bulls, two rams, and fourteen one-year-old male lambs, all with no defects. [14]Each of these offerings must be accompanied by a grain offering of choice flour moistened with olive oil—six quarts for each of the thirteen bulls, four quarts for each of the two rams, [15]and two quarts for each of the fourteen lambs. [16]You must also sacrifice a male goat as a sin offering, in addition to the regular burnt offering with its accompanying grain offering and liquid offering.

[17]"On the second day of this seven-day festival, sacrifice twelve young bulls, two rams, and fourteen one-year-old male lambs, all with no defects. [18]Each of these offerings of bulls, rams, and lambs must be accompanied by its prescribed grain offering and liquid offering. [19]You must also sacrifice a male goat as a sin offering, in addition to the regular burnt offering with its accompanying grain offering and liquid offering.

[20]"On the third day of the festival, sacrifice eleven young bulls, two rams, and fourteen one-year-old male lambs, all with no defects. [21]Each of these offerings of bulls, rams, and lambs must be accompanied by its prescribed grain offering and liquid offering. [22]You must also sacrifice a male goat as a sin offering, in addition to the regular burnt offering with its accompanying grain offering and liquid offering.

[23]"On the fourth day of the festival, sacrifice ten young bulls, two rams, and fourteen one-year-old male lambs, all with no defects. [24]Each of these offerings of bulls, rams, and lambs must be accompanied by its prescribed grain offering and liquid offering. [25]You must also sacrifice a male goat as a sin offering, in addition to the regular burnt offering with its accompanying grain offering and liquid offering.

[26]"On the fifth day of the festival, sacrifice nine young bulls, two rams, and fourteen one-year-old male lambs, all with no defects. [27]Each of these offerings of bulls, rams, and lambs must be accompanied by its prescribed grain offering and liquid offering. [28]You must also sacrifice a male goat as a sin offering, in addition to the regular burnt offering with its accompanying grain offering and liquid offering.

[29]"On the sixth day of the festival, sacrifice eight young bulls, two rams, and fourteen one-year-old male lambs, all with no defects. [30]Each of these offerings of bulls, rams, and lambs must be accompanied by its prescribed grain offering and liquid offering. [31]You must also sacrifice a male goat as a sin offering, in addition to the regular burnt offering with its accompanying grain offering and liquid offering.

[32]"On the seventh day of the festival, sacrifice seven young bulls, two rams, and fourteen one-year-old male lambs, all with

28:9 Hebrew *2/10 of an ephah* [4.4 liters]; also in 28:12, 20, 28. **28:12** Hebrew *3/10 of an ephah* [6.6 liters]; also in 28:20, 28. **28:14a** Hebrew *1/2 of a hin* [2 liters]. **28:14b** Hebrew *1/3 of a hin* [1.3 liters]. **28:14c** Hebrew *1/4 of a hin* [1 liter]. **28:16** This day in the ancient Hebrew lunar calendar occurred in late March, April, or early May. **28:22** Or *to make atonement for yourselves;* also in 28:30. **28:26** Hebrew *Festival of Weeks.* This was later called the Festival of Pentecost (see Acts 2:1). It is celebrated today as Shavuot (or Shabuoth). **29:1** Hebrew *the first day of the seventh month.* This day in the ancient Hebrew lunar calendar occurred in September or October. This festival is celebrated today as Rosh Hashanah, the Jewish new year. **29:3a** Hebrew *3/10 of an ephah* [6.6 liters]; also in 29:9, 14. **29:3b** Hebrew *2/10 of an ephah* [4.4 liters]; also in 29:9, 14. **29:4** Hebrew *1/10 of an ephah* [2.2 liters]; also in 29:10, 15. **29:5** Or *to make atonement for yourselves.* **29:7** Hebrew *On the tenth day of the seventh month;* see 29:1 and the note there. This day in the ancient Hebrew lunar calendar occurred in September or October. It is celebrated today as Yom Kippur. **29:12a** Hebrew *On the fifteenth day of the seventh month;* see 29:1, 7 and the notes there. This day in the ancient Hebrew lunar calendar occurred in late September, October, or early November. **29:12b** Or *Festival of Booths,* or *Festival of Tabernacles.* This was earlier called the Festival of the Final Harvest or Festival of Ingathering (see Exod 23:16b). It is celebrated today as Sukkot (or Succoth).

no defects. [33]Each of these offerings of bulls, rams, and lambs must be accompanied by its prescribed grain offering and liquid offering. [34]You must also sacrifice one male goat as a sin offering, in addition to the regular burnt offering with its accompanying grain offering and liquid offering.

[35]"On the eighth day of the festival, proclaim another holy day. You must do no ordinary work on that day. [36]You must present a burnt offering as a special gift, a pleasing aroma to the LORD. It will consist of one young bull, one ram, and seven one-year-old male lambs, all with no defects. [37]Each of these offerings must be accompanied by its prescribed grain offering and liquid offering. [38]You must also sacrifice one male goat as a sin offering, in addition to the regular burnt offering with its accompanying grain offering and liquid offering.

[39]"You must present these offerings to the LORD at your annual festivals. These are in addition to the sacrifices and offerings you present in connection with vows, or as voluntary offerings, burnt offerings, grain offerings, liquid offerings, or peace offerings."

[40]*So Moses gave all of these instructions to the people of Israel as the LORD had commanded him.

Laws concerning Vows

30 [1]*Then Moses summoned the leaders of the tribes of Israel and told them, "This is what the LORD has commanded: [2]A man who makes a vow to the LORD or makes a pledge under oath must never break it. He must do exactly what he said he would do.

[3]"If a young woman makes a vow to the LORD or a pledge under oath while she is still living at her father's home, [4]and her father hears of the vow or pledge and does not object to it, then all her vows and pledges will stand. [5]But if her father refuses to let her fulfill the vow or pledge on the day he hears of it, then all her vows and pledges will become invalid. The LORD will forgive her because her father would not let her fulfill them.

[6]"Now suppose a young woman makes a vow or binds herself with an impulsive pledge and later marries. [7]If her husband learns of her vow or pledge and does not object on the day he hears of it, her vows and pledges will stand. [8]But if her husband refuses to accept her vow or impulsive pledge on the day he hears of it, he nullifies her commitments, and the LORD will forgive her. [9]If, however, a woman is a widow or is divorced, she must fulfill all her vows and pledges.

[10]"But suppose a woman is married and living in her husband's home when she makes a vow or binds herself with a pledge. [11]If her husband hears of it and does not object to it, her vow or pledge will stand. [12]But if her husband refuses to accept it on the day he hears of it, her vow or pledge will be nullified, and the LORD will forgive her. [13]So her husband may either confirm or nullify any vows or pledges she makes to deny herself. [14]But if he does not object on the day he hears of it, then he is agreeing to all her vows and pledges. [15]If he waits more than a day and then tries to nullify a vow or pledge, he will be punished for her guilt."

[16]These are the regulations the LORD gave Moses concerning relationships between a man and his wife, and between a father and a young daughter who still lives at home.

Conquest of the Midianites

31 Then the LORD said to Moses, [2]"On behalf of the people of Israel, take revenge on the Midianites for leading them into idolatry. After that, you will die and join your ancestors."

[3]So Moses said to the people, "Choose some men, and arm them to fight the LORD's war of revenge against Midian. [4]From each tribe of Israel, send 1,000 men into battle." [5]So they chose 1,000 men from each tribe of Israel, a total of 12,000 men armed for battle. [6]Then Moses sent them out, 1,000 men from each tribe, and Phinehas son of Eleazar the priest led them into battle. They carried along the holy objects of the sanctuary and the trumpets for sounding the charge. [7]They attacked Midian as the LORD had commanded Moses, and they killed all the men. [8]All five of the Midianite kings—Evi, Rekem, Zur, Hur, and Reba—died in the battle. They also killed Balaam son of Beor with the sword.

[9]Then the Israelite army captured the Midianite women and children and seized their cattle and flocks and all their wealth as plunder. [10]They burned all the towns and villages where the Midianites had lived. [11]After they had gathered the plunder and

captives, both people and animals, 12they
brought them all to Moses and Eleazar
the priest, and to the whole community of
Israel, which was camped on the plains of
Moab beside the Jordan River, across from
Jericho. 13Moses, Eleazar the priest, and all
the leaders of the community went to meet
them outside the camp. 14But Moses was
furious with all the generals and captains*
who had returned from the battle.

15"Why have you let all the women live?"
he demanded. 16"These are the very ones
who followed Balaam's advice and caused
the people of Israel to rebel against the LORD
at Mount Peor. They are the ones who caused
the plague to strike the LORD's people. 17So
kill all the boys and all the women who
have had intercourse with a man. 18Only the
young girls who are virgins may live; you
may keep them for yourselves. 19And all of
you who have killed anyone or touched a
dead body must stay outside the camp for
seven days. You must purify yourselves and
your captives on the third and seventh days.
20Purify all your clothing, too, and everything made of leather, goat hair, or wood."

21Then Eleazar the priest said to the men
who were in the battle, "The LORD has
given Moses this legal requirement: 22Any-
thing made of gold, silver, bronze, iron,
tin, or lead—23that is, all metals that do not
burn—must be passed through fire in order
to be made ceremonially pure. These metal
objects must then be further purified with
the water of purification. But everything
that burns must be purified by the water
alone. 24On the seventh day you must wash
your clothes and be purified. Then you may
return to the camp."

Division of the Plunder

25And the LORD said to Moses, 26"You and
Eleazar the priest and the family leaders of
each tribe are to make a list of all the plunder
taken in the battle, including the people
and animals. 27Then divide the plunder
into two parts, and give half to the men who
fought the battle and half to the rest of the
people. 28From the army's portion, first give
the LORD his share of the plunder—one of
every 500 of the prisoners and of the cattle,
donkeys, sheep, and goats. 29Give this share

29:40 Verse 29:40 is numbered 30:1 in Hebrew text. **30:1** Verses 30:1-16 are numbered 30:2-17 in Hebrew text. **31:14** Hebrew *the commanders of thousands, and the commanders of hundreds;* also in 31:48, 52, 54.

What does the Bible teach about revenge?

In Numbers 31:2, God tells Moses to "take revenge" on Israel's enemies, but in Romans 12:19, God tells us not to take revenge. How do we reconcile this apparent contradiction?

The Bible tells us that God alone has all the knowledge necessary for just judgment (e.g., Romans 2:1-16; Hebrews 4:13)—and that his judgment is very different from human revenge, which is based on emotion. That is why we are told not to take justice into our own hands but to leave it to God. But because God does have all the knowledge necessary for just judgment, there are times when he tells us to enforce that judgment on his behalf, as here where he commands the destruction of the Midianites for enticing Israel into sexual immorality and Baal worship (Numbers 25:1-3, 16-18)—an attempt to destroy God's holy people.

Such passages are indeed challenging, but remember the following: First, such judgments were extremely rare and occurred only at crucial moments when Israel's very survival and future were at stake. Second, it was always possible to escape such destruction, as Rahab discovered (Joshua 2:8-21; 6:22-25). Third, the cultures that were destroyed had a wicked side, practicing fertility religion with its ritual prostitution and sometimes child sacrifice. Fourth, God had given them plenty of time to change: When he promised Canaan to Abraham (Genesis 15:12-20), he said he couldn't do so immediately "for the sins of the Amorites do not yet warrant their destruction" (Genesis 15:16). Generations later, when they still had not changed, God's judgment came, as it always does.

of the army's half to Eleazar the priest as
an offering to the LORD. 30From the half that
belongs to the people of Israel, take one of
every fifty of the prisoners and of the cattle,
donkeys, sheep, goats, and other animals.
Give this share to the Levites, who are in
charge of maintaining the LORD's Tabernacle." 31So Moses and Eleazar the priest
did as the LORD commanded Moses.

32The plunder remaining from everything
the fighting men had taken totaled 675,000
sheep and goats, 3372,000 cattle, 3461,000
donkeys, 35and 32,000 virgin girls.

36Half of the plunder was given to the
fighting men. It totaled 337,500 sheep and
goats, 37of which 675 were the LORD's share;
3836,000 cattle, of which 72 were the LORD's
share; 3930,500 donkeys, of which 61 were
the LORD's share; 40and 16,000 virgin girls,
of whom 32 were the LORD's share. 41Moses
gave all the LORD's share to Eleazar the
priest, just as the LORD had directed him.

42Half of the plunder belonged to the
people of Israel, and Moses separated it
from the half belonging to the fighting
men. 43It totaled 337,500 sheep and goats,
4436,000 cattle, 4530,500 donkeys, 46and
16,000 virgin girls. 47From the half-share
given to the people, Moses took one of every
fifty prisoners and animals and gave them
to the Levites, who maintained the LORD's
Tabernacle. All this was done as the LORD
had commanded Moses.

48Then all the generals and captains
came to Moses 49and said, "We, your servants, have accounted for all the men who
went out to battle under our command;
not one of us is missing! 50So we are presenting the items of gold we captured as an
offering to the LORD from our share of the
plunder—armbands, bracelets, rings, earrings, and necklaces. This will purify our
lives before the LORD and make us right
with him.*"

51So Moses and Eleazar the priest received
the gold from all the military commanders—
all kinds of jewelry and crafted objects. 52In
all, the gold that the generals and captains
presented as a gift to the LORD weighed
about 420 pounds.* 53All the fighting men
had taken some of the plunder for themselves. 54So Moses and Eleazar the priest
accepted the gifts from the generals and
captains and brought the gold to the Tabernacle* as a reminder to the LORD that the
people of Israel belong to him.

The Tribes East of the Jordan

32 The tribes of Reuben and Gad owned
vast numbers of livestock. So when
they saw that the lands of Jazer and Gilead
were ideally suited for their flocks and herds,
2they came to Moses, Eleazar the priest, and
the other leaders of the community. They
said, 3"Notice the towns of Ataroth, Dibon,
Jazer, Nimrah, Heshbon, Elealeh, Sibmah,*
Nebo, and Beon. 4The LORD has conquered
this whole area for the community of Israel,
and it is ideally suited for all our livestock.
5If we have found favor with you, please let
us have this land as our property instead of
giving us land across the Jordan River."

6"Do you intend to stay here while your
brothers go across and do all the fighting?"
Moses asked the men of Gad and Reuben.
7"Why do you want to discourage the rest of
the people of Israel from going across to the
land the LORD has given them? 8Your ancestors did the same thing when I sent them
from Kadesh-barnea to explore the land.

The Transjordan tribes

Arriving at land on the east of the Jordan, opposite Canaan, two of Israel's tribes—Reuben and Gad—decided that this would be excellent land in which to settle since it was so suitable for their livestock. Moses was shocked, fearing they were making the same mistakes as the scouts had many years previously, but the two tribes promised that they would help the remaining tribes take their inheritance in the Promised Land first and only return to the land across the Jordan when the task was completed. Moses accepted their proposal, which half of the tribe of Manasseh also asked to be part of. Two and a half tribes from the twelve therefore eventually settled in this Transjordan region (Joshua 13:15-32).

9 After they went up to the valley of Eshcol and explored the land, they discouraged the people of Israel from entering the land the LORD was giving them. 10 Then the LORD was very angry with them, and he vowed, 11 'Of all those I rescued from Egypt, no one who is twenty years old or older will ever see the land I swore to give to Abraham, Isaac, and Jacob, for they have not obeyed me wholeheartedly. 12 The only exceptions are Caleb son of Jephunneh the Kenizzite and Joshua son of Nun, for they have wholeheartedly followed the LORD.'

13 "The LORD was angry with Israel and made them wander in the wilderness for forty years until the entire generation that sinned in the LORD's sight had died. 14 But here you are, a brood of sinners, doing exactly the same thing! You are making the LORD even angrier with Israel. 15 If you turn away from him like this and he abandons them again in the wilderness, you will be responsible for destroying this entire nation!"

16 But they approached Moses and said, "We simply want to build pens for our livestock and fortified towns for our wives and children. 17 Then we will arm ourselves and lead our fellow Israelites into battle until we have brought them safely to their land. Meanwhile, our families will stay in the fortified towns we build here, so they will be safe from any attacks by the local people. 18 We will not return to our homes until all the people of Israel have received their portions of land. 19 But we do not claim any of the land on the other side of the Jordan. We would rather live here on the east side and accept this as our grant of land."

20 Then Moses said, "If you keep your word and arm yourselves for the LORD's battles, 21 and if your troops cross the Jordan and keep fighting until the LORD has driven out his enemies, 22 then you may return when the LORD has conquered the land. You will have fulfilled your duty to the LORD and to the rest of the people of Israel. And the land on the east side of the Jordan will be your property from the LORD. 23 But if you fail to keep your word, then you will have sinned against the LORD, and you may be sure that your sin will find you out. 24 Go ahead and build towns for your families and pens for your flocks, but do everything you have promised."

25 Then the men of Gad and Reuben replied, "We, your servants, will follow your instructions exactly. 26 Our children, wives, flocks, and cattle will stay here in the towns of Gilead. 27 But all who are able to bear arms will cross over to fight for the LORD, just as you have said."

28 So Moses gave orders to Eleazar the priest, Joshua son of Nun, and the leaders of the clans of Israel. 29 He said, "The men of Gad and Reuben who are armed for battle must cross the Jordan with you to fight for the LORD. If they do, give them the land of Gilead as their property when the land is conquered. 30 But if they refuse to arm themselves and cross over with you, then they must accept land with the rest of you in the land of Canaan."

31 The tribes of Gad and Reuben said again, "We are your servants, and we will do as the LORD has commanded! 32 We will cross the Jordan into Canaan fully armed to fight for the LORD, but our property will be here on this side of the Jordan."

33 So Moses assigned land to the tribes of Gad, Reuben, and half the tribe of Manasseh son of Joseph. He gave them the territory of King Sihon of the Amorites and the land of King Og of Bashan—the whole land with its cities and surrounding lands.

34 The descendants of Gad built the towns of Dibon, Ataroth, Aroer, 35 Atroth-shophan, Jazer, Jogbehah, 36 Beth-nimrah, and Beth-haran. These were all fortified towns with pens for their flocks.

37 The descendants of Reuben built the towns of Heshbon, Elealeh, Kiriathaim, 38 Nebo, Baal-meon, and Sibmah. They changed the names of some of the towns they conquered and rebuilt.

39 Then the descendants of Makir of the tribe of Manasseh went to Gilead and conquered it, and they drove out the Amorites living there. 40 So Moses gave Gilead to the Makirites, descendants of Manasseh, and they settled there. 41 The people of Jair, another clan of the tribe of Manasseh, captured many of the towns in Gilead and changed the name of that region to the Towns of Jair.* 42 Meanwhile, a man named Nobah captured the town of Kenath and its surrounding villages, and he renamed that area Nobah after himself.

31:50 Or *will make atonement for our lives before the LORD.* **31:52** Hebrew *16,750 shekels* [191 kilograms]. **31:54** Hebrew *the Tent of Meeting.* **32:3** As in Samaritan Pentateuch and Greek version (see also 32:38); Hebrew reads *Sebam.* **32:41** Hebrew *Havvoth-jair.*

Remembering Israel's Journey

33 This is the route the Israelites followed as they marched out of Egypt
under the leadership of Moses and Aaron.
2 At the LORD's direction, Moses kept a written
record of their progress. These are the stages
of their march, identified by the different
places where they stopped along the way.
3 They set out from the city of Rameses
in early spring—on the fifteenth day of the
first month*—on the morning after the first
Passover celebration. The people of Israel
left defiantly, in full view of all the Egyptians. 4 Meanwhile, the Egyptians were
burying all their firstborn sons, whom the
LORD had killed the night before. The LORD
had defeated the gods of Egypt that night
with great acts of judgment!

5 After leaving Rameses, the Israelites set up camp at Succoth.
6 Then they left Succoth and camped at Etham on the edge of the wilderness.
7 They left Etham and turned back toward Pi-hahiroth, opposite Baal-zephon, and camped near Migdol.
8 They left Pi-hahiroth* and crossed the Red Sea* into the wilderness beyond. Then they traveled for three days into the Etham wilderness and camped at Marah.
9 They left Marah and camped at Elim, where there were twelve springs of water and seventy palm trees.
10 They left Elim and camped beside the Red Sea.*
11 They left the Red Sea and camped in the wilderness of Sin.*
12 They left the wilderness of Sin and camped at Dophkah.
13 They left Dophkah and camped at Alush.
14 They left Alush and camped at Rephidim, where there was no water for the people to drink.
15 They left Rephidim and camped in the wilderness of Sinai.
16 They left the wilderness of Sinai and camped at Kibroth-hattaavah.
17 They left Kibroth-hattaavah and camped at Hazeroth.
18 They left Hazeroth and camped at Rithmah.
19 They left Rithmah and camped at Rimmon-perez.
20 They left Rimmon-perez and camped at Libnah.
21 They left Libnah and camped at Rissah.
22 They left Rissah and camped at Kehelathah.
23 They left Kehelathah and camped at Mount Shepher.
24 They left Mount Shepher and camped at Haradah.
25 They left Haradah and camped at Makheloth.
26 They left Makheloth and camped at Tahath.
27 They left Tahath and camped at Terah.
28 They left Terah and camped at Mithcah.
29 They left Mithcah and camped at Hashmonah.
30 They left Hashmonah and camped at Moseroth.
31 They left Moseroth and camped at Bene-jaakan.
32 They left Bene-jaakan and camped at Hor-haggidgad.
33 They left Hor-haggidgad and camped at Jotbathah.
34 They left Jotbathah and camped at Abronah.
35 They left Abronah and camped at Ezion-geber.
36 They left Ezion-geber and camped at Kadesh in the wilderness of Zin.
37 They left Kadesh and camped at Mount
Hor, at the border of Edom. 38 While they
were at the foot of Mount Hor, Aaron the
priest was directed by the LORD to go up
the mountain, and there he died. This
happened in midsummer, on the first
day of the fifth month* of the fortieth
year after Israel's departure from Egypt.
39 Aaron was 123 years old when he died
there on Mount Hor.
40 At that time the Canaanite king of Arad, who lived in the Negev in the land of Canaan, heard that the people of Israel were approaching his land.
41 Meanwhile, the Israelites left Mount Hor and camped at Zalmonah.
42 Then they left Zalmonah and camped at Punon.
43 They left Punon and camped at Oboth.
44 They left Oboth and camped at Iye-abarim on the border of Moab.
45 They left Iye-abarim* and camped at Dibon-gad.
46 They left Dibon-gad and camped at Almon-diblathaim.
47 They left Almon-diblathaim and camped

in the mountains east of the river,* near
Mount Nebo.
48 They left the mountains east of the river
and camped on the plains of Moab
beside the Jordan River, across from
Jericho. 49 Along the Jordan River they
camped from Beth-jeshimoth as far as
the meadows of Acacia* on the plains
of Moab.

50 While they were camped near the
Jordan River on the plains of Moab opposite Jericho, the LORD said to Moses, 51 "Give
the following instructions to the people of
Israel: When you cross the Jordan River
into the land of Canaan, 52 you must drive
out all the people living there. You must
destroy all their carved and molten images
and demolish all their pagan shrines.
53 Take possession of the land and settle in
it, because I have given it to you to occupy.
54 You must distribute the land among the
clans by sacred lot and in proportion to
their size. A larger portion of land will be
allotted to each of the larger clans, and a
smaller portion will be allotted to each of
the smaller clans. The decision of the sacred
lot is final. In this way, the portions of land
will be divided among your ancestral tribes.
55 But if you fail to drive out the people who
live in the land, those who remain will be
like splinters in your eyes and thorns in
your sides. They will harass you in the land
where you live. 56 And I will do to you what
I had planned to do to them."

Boundaries of the Land

34 Then the LORD said to Moses, 2 "Give
these instructions to the Israelites:
When you come into the land of Canaan,
which I am giving you as your special possession, these will be the boundaries. 3 The
southern portion of your country will extend
from the wilderness of Zin, along the edge of
Edom. The southern boundary will begin on
the east at the Dead Sea.* 4 It will then run
south past Scorpion Pass* in the direction of
Zin. Its southernmost point will be Kadesh-
barnea, from which it will go to Hazar-addar,
and on to Azmon. 5 From Azmon the boundary will turn toward the Brook of Egypt and
end at the Mediterranean Sea.*

6 "Your western boundary will be the
coastline of the Mediterranean Sea.

7 "Your northern boundary will begin
at the Mediterranean Sea and run east to
Mount Hor, 8 then to Lebo-hamath, and on
through Zedad 9 and Ziphron to Hazar-enan.
This will be your northern boundary.

10 "The eastern boundary will start at
Hazar-enan and run south to Shepham,
11 then down to Riblah on the east side of
Ain. From there the boundary will run down
along the eastern edge of the Sea of Galilee,*
12 and then along the Jordan River to the Dead
Sea. These are the boundaries of your land."

13 Then Moses told the Israelites, "This
territory is the homeland you are to divide
among yourselves by sacred lot. The LORD
has commanded that the land be divided
among the nine and a half remaining tribes.
14 The families of the tribes of Reuben, Gad,
and half the tribe of Manasseh have already
received their grants of land 15 on the east
side of the Jordan River, across from Jericho
toward the sunrise."

Leaders to Divide the Land

16 And the LORD said to Moses, 17 "Eleazar
the priest and Joshua son of Nun are the
men designated to divide the grants of land
among the people. 18 Enlist one leader from
each tribe to help them with the task. 19 These
are the tribes and the names of the leaders:

Tribe	*Leader*
Judah	Caleb son of Jephunneh
20 Simeon	Shemuel son of Ammihud
21 Benjamin	Elidad son of Kislon
22 Dan	Bukki son of Jogli
23 Manasseh son of Joseph	Hanniel son of Ephod
24 Ephraim son of Joseph	Kemuel son of Shiphtan
25 Zebulun	Elizaphan son of Parnach
26 Issachar	Paltiel son of Azzan
27 Asher	Ahihud son of Shelomi
28 Naphtali	Pedahel son of Ammihud

29 These are the men the LORD has appointed
to divide the grants of land in Canaan
among the Israelites."

33:3 This day in the ancient Hebrew lunar calendar occurred in late March, April, or early May. **33:8a** As in many Hebrew manuscripts, Samaritan Pentateuch, and Latin Vulgate (see also 33:7); most Hebrew manuscripts read *left from in front of Hahiroth.* **33:8b** Hebrew *the sea.* **33:10** Hebrew *sea of reeds;* also in 33:11. **33:11** The geographical name *Sin* is related to *Sinai* and should not be confused with the English word *sin.* **33:38** This day in the ancient Hebrew lunar calendar occurred in July or August. **33:45** As in 33:44; Hebrew reads *Iyim,* another name for Iye-abarim. **33:47** Or *the mountains of Abarim;* also in 33:48. **33:49** Hebrew *as far as Abel-shittim.* **34:3** Hebrew *Salt Sea;* also in 34:12. **34:4** Or *the ascent of Akrabbim.* **34:5** Hebrew *the sea;* also in 34:6, 7. **34:11** Hebrew *Sea of Kinnereth.*

Towns for the Levites

35 While Israel was camped beside the Jordan on the plains of Moab across from Jericho, the LORD said to Moses, 2“Command the people of Israel to give to the Levites from their property certain towns to live in, along with the surrounding pasturelands. 3These towns will be for the Levites to live in, and the surrounding lands will provide pasture for their cattle, flocks, and other livestock. 4The pastureland assigned to the Levites around these towns will extend 1,500 feet* from the town walls in every direction. 5Measure off 3,000 feet* outside the town walls in every direction—east, south, west, north—with the town at the center. This area will serve as the larger pastureland for the towns.

6“Six of the towns you give the Levites will be cities of refuge, where a person who has accidentally killed someone can flee for safety. In addition, give them forty-two other towns. 7In all, forty-eight towns with the surrounding pastureland will be given to the Levites. 8These towns will come from the property of the people of Israel. The larger tribes will give more towns to the Levites, while the smaller tribes will give fewer. Each tribe will give property in proportion to the size of its land.”

Cities of Refuge

9The LORD said to Moses, 10“Give the following instructions to the people of Israel.

“When you cross the Jordan into the land of Canaan, 11designate cities of refuge to which people can flee if they have killed someone accidentally. 12These cities will be places of protection from a dead person’s relatives who want to avenge the death. The slayer must not be put to death before being tried by the community. 13Designate six cities of refuge for yourselves, 14three on the east side of the Jordan River and three on the west in the land of Canaan. 15These cities are for the protection of Israelites, foreigners living among you, and traveling merchants. Anyone who accidentally kills someone may flee there for safety.

16“But if someone strikes and kills another person with a piece of iron, it is murder, and the murderer must be executed. 17Or if someone with a stone in his hand strikes and kills another person, it is murder, and the murderer must be put to death. 18Or if someone strikes and kills another person with a wooden object, it is murder, and the murderer must be put to death. 19The victim’s nearest relative is responsible for putting the murderer to death. When they meet, the avenger must put the murderer to death. 20So if someone hates another person and waits in ambush, then pushes him or throws something at him and he dies, it is murder. 21Or if someone hates another person and hits him with a fist and he dies, it is murder. In such cases, the avenger must put the murderer to death when they meet.

22“But suppose someone pushes another person without having shown previous hostility, or throws something that unintentionally hits another person, 23or accidentally drops a huge stone on someone, though they were not enemies, and the person dies. 24If this should happen, the community must follow these regulations in making a judgment between the slayer and the avenger, the victim’s nearest relative: 25The community must protect the slayer from the avenger and must escort the slayer back to live in the city of refuge to which he fled. There he must remain until the death of the high priest, who was anointed with the sacred oil.

26“But if the slayer ever leaves the limits of the city of refuge, 27and the avenger finds him outside the city and kills him, it will not be considered murder. 28The slayer should have stayed inside the city of refuge until the death of the high priest. But after the death of the high priest, the slayer may return to his own property. 29These are legal requirements for you to observe from generation to generation, wherever you may live.

30“All murderers must be put to death, but only if evidence is presented by more than one witness. No one may be put to death on the testimony of only one witness. 31Also, you must never accept a ransom payment for the life of someone judged guilty of murder and subject to execution; murderers must always be put to death. 32And never accept a ransom payment from someone who has fled to a city of refuge, allowing a slayer to return to his property before the death of the high priest. 33This will ensure that the land where you live will not be polluted, for murder pollutes the land. And no sacrifice except the execution of the murderer can purify the land from murder.*

34 You must not defile the land where you live, for I live there myself. I am the LORD, who lives among the people of Israel."

Women Who Inherit Property

36 Then the heads of the clans of Gilead—descendants of Makir, son of Manasseh, son of Joseph—came to Moses and the family leaders of Israel with a petition. 2 They said, "Sir, the LORD instructed you to divide the land by sacred lot among the people of Israel. You were told by the LORD to give the grant of land owned by our brother Zelophehad to his daughters. 3 But if they marry men from another tribe, their grants of land will go with them to the tribe into which they marry. In this way, the total area of our tribal land will be reduced. 4 Then when the Year of Jubilee comes, their portion of land will be added to that of the new tribe, causing it to be lost forever to our ancestral tribe."

5 So Moses gave the Israelites this command from the LORD: "The claim of the men of the tribe of Joseph is legitimate. 6 This is what the LORD commands concerning the daughters of Zelophehad: Let them marry anyone they like, as long as it is within their own ancestral tribe. 7 None of the territorial land may pass from tribe to tribe, for all the land given to each tribe must remain within the tribe to which it was first allotted. 8 The daughters throughout the tribes of Israel who are in line to inherit property must marry within their tribe, so that all the Israelites will keep their ancestral property. 9 No grant of land may pass from one tribe to another; each tribe of Israel must keep its allotted portion of land."

10 The daughters of Zelophehad did as the LORD commanded Moses. 11 Mahlah, Tirzah, Hoglah, Milcah, and Noah all married cousins on their father's side. 12 They married into the clans of Manasseh son of Joseph. Thus, their inheritance of land remained within their ancestral tribe.

13 These are the commands and regulations that the LORD gave to the people of Israel through Moses while they were camped on the plains of Moab beside the Jordan River, across from Jericho.

35:4 Hebrew *1,000 cubits* [460 meters]. **35:5** Hebrew *2,000 cubits* [920 meters]. **35:33** Or *can make atonement for murder.*

Deuteronomy *The challenge to obey God*

Deuteronomy is a collection of speeches given by Moses just before the Israelites entered the Promised Land of Canaan. He reviewed their history up to that point and prepared them for what lay ahead. He also reviewed the covenant that God had made with them and both the blessings that they could expect to experience in return for their obedience and the curses in return for their disobedience. Moses repeatedly called them to be faithful and to choose God. They could do this by remembering his faithfulness and his words, whatever the new circumstances of settled life in Canaan.

What's it all about?

Deuteronomy opens with Moses reviewing Israel's thirty-eight-year history since leaving Mount Sinai (also called Mount Horeb). He reminded them of God's faithfulness, and of the heavy price they paid for disobedience. Now, on the threshold of the Promised Land, he urged a new generation to be faithful to God's covenant, a covenant that proved his love for them, and called them to respond by loving God with all their heart, soul, and strength (6:5). He reminded them that God had not chosen them because they were special, but because of his love and purposes (7:7-9); therefore they should be careful how they lived. In contrast to the hardships of Egypt, life in Canaan would be much easier, but therefore they must guard against complacency and the temptation to follow Canaanite customs and religion. If they remained faithful, they could expect a healthy, peaceful, and productive life; if not, they would forfeit everything. In light of this, Moses summarized his message with these words: "What does the LORD your God require of you? He requires only that you fear the LORD your God, and live in a way that pleases him, and love him and serve him with all your heart and soul. And you must always obey the LORD's commands and decrees that I am giving you today for your own good" (10:12-13).

OVERVIEW

In chapters 12 to 26, Moses set out the laws that would govern life in the Israelites' new environment. It was their "constitution." Underpinning everything was the fact that the Israelites were different; their God was not like other gods, so they must act accordingly. Moses commanded them to set up some large stones, coated with plaster, on which these laws would be written to serve as a permanent reminder (chapter 27). He then outlined the blessings and curses that would follow, depending on their obedience or disobedience to God's laws.

God then made a covenant with this new generation, reaffirming the one made with their parents at Sinai (chapter 29), and told them that keeping it was well within their reach (30:11). Finally, Joshua was commissioned to take Moses' place, and Moses blessed the tribes one by one. He died at the age of 120.

What does it mean for us?

According to Deuteronomy, every area of life hinges on our relationship with God. Sometimes we would rather that this wasn't so: We rarely warm to the idea that our successes and failures really depend on someone else. But instead of going it alone, why not enjoy the benefits of partnership, a partnership based on a personal relationship with God, and the blessings that brings as we obey him?

Deuteronomy revels in the material blessings of health, wealth, and peace—and makes no apology for doing so. It is not God's will that his people experience lack in any form (though the New Testament shows that following Christ will sometimes lead to suffering and lack for his sake—something we sometimes prefer to forget!). The people's prosperity would be both a blessing and a sign to the surrounding nations that God was among them. But the people were also reminded that God, not material things, was their true life and goal. It was only through keeping his word that "you will enjoy a long life in the land you will occupy when you cross the Jordan River" (32:47). Their happiness was directly linked to the attention they gave to his words.

Deuteronomy repeats many of the laws given in Exodus, Leviticus, and Numbers as Moses looks back and recalls them, but it has a slightly different emphasis. It focuses on people's motives, on *why* they should obey God's laws: because of his love and faithfulness. At least fifteen times Moses tells the Israelites to love God and cling to him in return. Obedience should spring from love, not a sense of duty.

Introduction to Moses' First Address

1 These are the words that Moses spoke to
all the people of Israel while they were
in the wilderness east of the Jordan River.
They were camped in the Jordan Valley*
near Suph, between Paran on one side and
Tophel, Laban, Hazeroth, and Di-zahab on
the other.
[2]Normally it takes only eleven days
to travel from Mount Sinai* to Kadesh-
barnea, going by way of Mount Seir. [3]But
forty years after the Israelites left Egypt,
on the first day of the eleventh month,*
Moses addressed the people of Israel,
telling them everything the LORD had
commanded him to say. [4]This took place
after he had defeated King Sihon of the
Amorites, who ruled in Heshbon, and at
Edrei had defeated King Og of Bashan, who
ruled in Ashtaroth.
[5]While the Israelites were in the land of
Moab east of the Jordan River, Moses carefully explained the LORD's instructions as
follows.

The Command to Leave Sinai

[6]"When we were at Mount Sinai, the LORD
our God said to us, 'You have stayed at this
mountain long enough. [7]It is time to break
camp and move on. Go to the hill country
of the Amorites and to all the neighboring
regions—the Jordan Valley, the hill country,
the western foothills,* the Negev, and the
coastal plain. Go to the land of the Canaanites and to Lebanon, and all the way to the
great Euphrates River. [8]Look, I am giving all
this land to you! Go in and occupy it, for it
is the land the LORD swore to give to your
ancestors Abraham, Isaac, and Jacob, and
to all their descendants.'"

Moses Appoints Leaders from Each Tribe

[9]Moses continued, "At that time I told you,
'You are too great a burden for me to carry
all by myself. [10]The LORD your God has

1:1 Hebrew *the Arabah;* also in 1:7. **1:2** Hebrew *Horeb,* another name for Sinai; also in 1:6, 19. **1:3** Hebrew *In the fortieth year, on the first day of the eleventh month.* This day in the ancient Hebrew lunar calendar occurred in January or February. **1:7** Hebrew *the Shephelah.*

increased your population, making you
as numerous as the stars! [11]And may the
LORD, the God of your ancestors, multiply
you a thousand times more and bless you
as he promised! [12]But you are such a heavy
load to carry! How can I deal with all your
problems and bickering? [13]Choose some
well-respected men from each tribe who are
known for their wisdom and understanding,
and I will appoint them as your leaders.'
[14]"Then you responded, 'Your plan is a
good one.' [15]So I took the wise and respected
men you had selected from your tribes and
appointed them to serve as judges and officials over you. Some were responsible for a
thousand people, some for a hundred, some
for fifty, and some for ten.
[16]"At that time I instructed the judges,
'You must hear the cases of your fellow
Israelites and the foreigners living among
you. Be perfectly fair in your decisions [17]and
impartial in your judgments. Hear the cases
of those who are poor as well as those who
are rich. Don't be afraid of anyone's anger,
for the decision you make is God's decision.
Bring me any cases that are too difficult for
you, and I will handle them.'
[18]"At that time I gave you instructions
about everything you were to do.

Scouts Explore the Land

[19]"Then, just as the LORD our God commanded us, we left Mount Sinai and traveled
through the great and terrifying wilderness,
as you yourselves remember, and headed
toward the hill country of the Amorites. When
we arrived at Kadesh-barnea, [20]I said to you,
'You have now reached the hill country of
the Amorites that the LORD our God is giving
us. [21]Look! He has placed the land in front of
you. Go and occupy it as the LORD, the God
of your ancestors, has promised you. Don't
be afraid! Don't be discouraged!'
[22]"But you all came to me and said, 'First,
let's send out scouts to explore the land for
us. They will advise us on the best route to
take and which towns we should enter.'
[23]"This seemed like a good idea to me,
so I chose twelve scouts, one from each
of your tribes. [24]They headed for the hill
country and came to the valley of Eshcol
and explored it. [25]They picked some of its
fruit and brought it back to us. And they
reported, 'The land the LORD our God has
given us is indeed a good land.'

Israel's Rebellion against the LORD

[26]"But you rebelled against the command
of the LORD your God and refused to go in.
[27]You complained in your tents and said,
'The LORD must hate us. That's why he
has brought us here from Egypt—to hand
us over to the Amorites to be slaughtered.
[28]Where can we go? Our brothers have de-
moralized us with their report. They tell us,
"The people of the land are taller and more
powerful than we are, and their towns are
large, with walls rising high into the sky! We
even saw giants there—the descendants of
Anak!"'
[29]"But I said to you, 'Don't be shocked
or afraid of them! [30]The LORD your God is
going ahead of you. He will fight for you,
just as you saw him do in Egypt. [31]And
you saw how the LORD your God cared
for you all along the way as you traveled
through the wilderness, just as a father
cares for his child. Now he has brought you
to this place.'
[32]"But even after all he did, you refused to
trust the LORD your God, [33]who goes before
you looking for the best places to camp,
guiding you with a pillar of fire by night and
a pillar of cloud by day.
[34]"When the LORD heard your complaining, he became very angry. So he solemnly
swore, [35]'Not one of you from this wicked
generation will live to see the good land I
swore to give your ancestors, [36]except Caleb
son of Jephunneh. He will see this land
because he has followed the LORD completely. I will give to him and his descendants some of the very land he explored
during his scouting mission.'
[37]"And the LORD was also angry with me
because of you. He said to me, 'Moses, not
even you will enter the Promised Land!
[38]Instead, your assistant, Joshua son of
Nun, will lead the people into the land. Encourage him, for he will lead Israel as they
take possession of it. [39]I will give the land
to your little ones—your innocent children.
You were afraid they would be captured,
but they will be the ones who occupy it.
[40]As for you, turn around now and go on
back through the wilderness toward the
Red Sea.*'
[41]"Then you confessed, 'We have sinned
against the LORD! We will go into the land
and fight for it, as the LORD our God has
commanded us.' So your men strapped on

their weapons, thinking it would be easy to
attack the hill country.
42 “But the LORD told me to tell you, ‘Do
not attack, for I am not with you. If you go
ahead on your own, you will be crushed by
your enemies.’
43 “This is what I told you, but you would
not listen. Instead, you again rebelled
against the LORD’s command and arrogantly went into the hill country to fight.
44 But the Amorites who lived there came
out against you like a swarm of bees. They
chased and battered you all the way from
Seir to Hormah. 45 Then you returned and
wept before the LORD, but he refused to
listen. 46 So you stayed there at Kadesh for
a long time.

Remembering Israel’s Wanderings

2 “Then we turned around and headed
back across the wilderness toward the
Red Sea,* just as the LORD had instructed
me, and we wandered around in the region
of Mount Seir for a long time.
2 “Then at last the LORD said to me, 3 ‘You
have been wandering around in this hill
country long enough; turn to the north.
4 Give these orders to the people: “You will
pass through the country belonging to
your relatives the Edomites, the descendants of Esau, who live in Seir. The Edomites will feel threatened, so be careful. 5 Do
not bother them, for I have given them all
the hill country around Mount Seir as their
property, and I will not give you even one
square foot of their land. 6 If you need food
to eat or water to drink, pay them for it.
7 For the LORD your God has blessed you in
everything you have done. He has watched
your every step through this great wilderness. During these forty years, the LORD
your God has been with you, and you have
lacked nothing.”’
8 “So we bypassed the territory of our
relatives, the descendants of Esau, who live
in Seir. We avoided the road through the
Arabah Valley that comes up from Elath and
Ezion-geber.
“Then as we turned north along the desert
route through Moab, 9 the LORD warned us,
‘Do not bother the Moabites, the descendants of Lot, or start a war with them. I have
given them Ar as their property, and I will
not give you any of their land.’”
10 (A race of giants called the Emites had
once lived in the area of Ar. They were
as strong and numerous and tall as the
Anakites, another race of giants. 11 Both the
Emites and the Anakites are also known
as the Rephaites, though the Moabites call
them Emites. 12 In earlier times the Horites
had lived in Seir, but they were driven out
and displaced by the descendants of Esau,
just as Israel drove out the people of Canaan
when the LORD gave Israel their land.)
13 Moses continued, “Then the LORD said
to us, ‘Get moving. Cross the Zered Brook.’
So we crossed the brook.
14 “Thirty-eight years passed from the time
we first left Kadesh-barnea until we finally
crossed the Zered Brook! By then, all the
men old enough to fight in battle had died
in the wilderness, as the LORD had vowed
would happen. 15 The LORD struck them
down until they had all been eliminated
from the community.
16 “When all the men of fighting age had
died, 17 the LORD said to me, 18 ‘Today you
will cross the border of Moab at Ar 19 and
enter the land of the Ammonites, the descendants of Lot. But do not bother them
or start a war with them. I have given the
land of Ammon to them as their property,
and I will not give you any of their land.’”
20 (That area was once considered the

1:40 Hebrew *sea of reeds.* **2:1** Hebrew *sea of reeds.*

The Ammonites

Descended from one of Lot’s daughters (Genesis 19:36-38), the Ammonites lived in Transjordan, to the east of the Jordan River. Because of this ancient family relationship God forbade the Israelites to fight against them on their journey to the Promised Land (Deuteronomy 2:18-19). The Ammonites still attacked Israel, however, on many occasions (Judges 3:12-13; 10:6-18; 1 Samuel 11:1-15; 2 Samuel 10:1-19) until King David finally defeated them (2 Samuel 11:1; 12:26-31).

land of the Rephaites, who had lived there,
though the Ammonites call them Zam-
zummites. 21They were also as strong and
numerous and tall as the Anakites. But the
LORD destroyed them so the Ammonites
could occupy their land. 22He had done
the same for the descendants of Esau who
lived in Seir, for he destroyed the Horites so
they could settle there in their place. The
descendants of Esau live there to this day.
23A similar thing happened when the Caphtorites from Crete* invaded and destroyed
the Avvites, who had lived in villages in the
area of Gaza.)

24Moses continued, "Then the LORD said,
'Now get moving! Cross the Arnon Gorge.
Look, I will hand over to you Sihon the
Amorite, king of Heshbon, and I will give you
his land. Attack him and begin to occupy the
land. 25Beginning today I will make people
throughout the earth terrified because of
you. When they hear reports about you, they
will tremble with dread and fear.'"

Victory over Sihon of Heshbon

26Moses continued, "From the wilderness of
Kedemoth I sent ambassadors to King Sihon
of Heshbon with this proposal of peace:

> 27'Let us travel through your land. We
> will stay on the main road and won't
> turn off into the fields on either side.
> 28Sell us food to eat and water to drink,
> and we will pay for it. All we want is
> permission to pass through your land.
> 29The descendants of Esau who live
> in Seir allowed us to go through their
> country, and so did the Moabites, who
> live in Ar. Let us pass through until we
> cross the Jordan into the land the LORD
> our God is giving us.'

30"But King Sihon of Heshbon refused to
allow us to pass through, because the LORD
your God made Sihon stubborn and defiant
so he could help you defeat him, as he has
now done.

31"Then the LORD said to me, 'Look, I have
begun to hand King Sihon and his land over
to you. Begin now to conquer and occupy
his land.'

32"Then King Sihon declared war on us
and mobilized his forces at Jahaz. 33But
the LORD our God handed him over to us,
and we crushed him, his sons, and all his
people. 34We conquered all his towns and
completely destroyed* everyone—men,
women, and children. Not a single person
was spared. 35We took all the livestock as
plunder for ourselves, along with anything
of value from the towns we ransacked.

36"The LORD our God also helped us
conquer Aroer on the edge of the Arnon
Gorge, and the town in the gorge, and
the whole area as far as Gilead. No town
had walls too strong for us. 37However,
we avoided the land of the Ammonites all
along the Jabbok River and the towns in the
hill country—all the places the LORD our
God had commanded us to leave alone.

Victory over Og of Bashan

3 "Next we turned and headed for the
land of Bashan, where King Og and his
entire army attacked us at Edrei. 2But the
LORD told me, 'Do not be afraid of him, for
I have given you victory over Og and his
entire army, and I will give you all his land.
Treat him just as you treated King Sihon of
the Amorites, who ruled in Heshbon.'

3"So the LORD our God handed King Og
and all his people over to us, and we killed
them all. Not a single person survived. 4We
conquered all sixty of his towns—the entire
Argob region in his kingdom of Bashan. Not
a single town escaped our conquest. 5These
towns were all fortified with high walls and

The Amorites

As Moses recalled Israel's history on the edge of the Promised Land, he reminded them of God's many interventions on their behalf, and in particular their first victories over the Amorites (2:26–3:11). The Amorites were a large and diverse group of seminomadic peoples from Mesopotamia who had spread to Syria and Canaan. Often the Bible uses the term "Amorites" simply to refer generally, as in Deuteronomy 1:27, to all the inhabitants of Canaan.

barred gates. We also took many unwalled villages at the same time. [6]We completely destroyed* the kingdom of Bashan, just as we had destroyed King Sihon of Heshbon. We destroyed all the people in every town we conquered—men, women, and children alike. [7]But we kept all the livestock for ourselves and took plunder from all the towns.

[8]"So we took the land of the two Amorite kings east of the Jordan River—all the way from the Arnon Gorge to Mount Hermon. [9](Mount Hermon is called Sirion by the Sidonians, and the Amorites call it Senir.) [10]We had now conquered all the cities on the plateau and all Gilead and Bashan, as far as the towns of Salecah and Edrei, which were part of Og's kingdom in Bashan. [11](King Og of Bashan was the last survivor of the giant Rephaites. His bed was made of iron and was more than thirteen feet long and six feet wide.* It can still be seen in the Ammonite city of Rabbah.)

Land Division East of the Jordan

[12]"When we took possession of this land, I gave to the tribes of Reuben and Gad the territory beyond Aroer along the Arnon Gorge, plus half of the hill country of Gilead with its towns. [13]Then I gave the rest of Gilead and all of Bashan—Og's former kingdom—to the half-tribe of Manasseh. (This entire Argob region of Bashan used to be known as the land of the Rephaites. [14]Jair, a leader from the tribe of Manasseh, conquered the whole Argob region in Bashan, all the way to the border of the Geshurites and Maacathites. Jair renamed this region after himself, calling it the Towns of Jair,* as it is still known today.) [15]I gave Gilead to the clan of Makir. [16]But I also gave part of Gilead to the tribes of Reuben and Gad. The area I gave them extended from the middle of the Arnon Gorge in the south to the Jabbok River on the Ammonite frontier. [17]They also received the Jordan Valley, all the way from the Sea of Galilee down to the Dead Sea,* with the Jordan River serving as the western boundary. To the east were the slopes of Pisgah.

[18]"At that time I gave this command to the tribes that would live east of the Jordan: 'Although the LORD your God has given you this land as your property, all your fighting men must cross the Jordan ahead of your Israelite relatives, armed and ready to assist them. [19]Your wives, children, and numerous livestock, however, may stay behind in the towns I have given you. [20]When the LORD has given security to the rest of the Israelites, as he has to you, and when they occupy the land the LORD your God is giving them across the Jordan River, then you may all return here to the land I have given you.'

Moses Forbidden to Enter the Land

[21]"At that time I gave Joshua this charge: 'You have seen for yourself everything the LORD your God has done to these two kings. He will do the same to all the kingdoms on the west side of the Jordan. [22]Do not be afraid of the nations there, for the LORD your God will fight for you.'

[23]"At that time I pleaded with the LORD and said, [24]'O Sovereign LORD, you have only begun to show your greatness and the strength of your hand to me, your servant. Is there any god in heaven or on earth who can perform such great and mighty deeds as you do? [25]Please let me cross the Jordan to see the wonderful land on the other side, the beautiful hill country and the Lebanon mountains.'

[26]"But the LORD was angry with me because of you, and he would not listen to me. 'That's enough!' he declared. 'Speak of it no more. [27]But go up to Pisgah Peak, and look over the land in every direction. Take a good look, but you may not cross the Jordan River. [28]Instead, commission Joshua and encourage and strengthen him, for he will lead the people across the Jordan. He will give them all the land you now see before you as their possession.' [29]So we stayed in the valley near Beth-peor.

Moses Urges Israel to Obey

4 "And now, Israel, listen carefully to these decrees and regulations that I am about to teach you. Obey them so that you may live, so you may enter and occupy the land that the LORD, the God of your ancestors, is giving you. [2]Do not add to or subtract from these commands I am giving you. Just obey the commands of the LORD your God that I am giving you.

2:23 Hebrew *from Caphtor.* **2:34** The Hebrew term used here refers to the complete consecration of things or people to the LORD, either by destroying them or by giving them as an offering. **3:6** The Hebrew term used here refers to the complete consecration of things or people to the LORD, either by destroying them or by giving them as an offering; also in 3:6b. **3:11** Hebrew *9 cubits* [4.1 meters] *long and 4 cubits* [1.8 meters] *wide.* **3:14** Hebrew *Havvoth-jair.* **3:17** Hebrew *from Kinnereth to the Sea of the Arabah, the Salt Sea.*

3“You saw for yourself what the LORD
did to you at Baal-peor. There the LORD
your God destroyed everyone who had worshiped Baal, the god of Peor. 4But all of you
who were faithful to the LORD your God are
still alive today—every one of you.

5“Look, I now teach you these decrees
and regulations just as the LORD my God
commanded me, so that you may obey
them in the land you are about to enter and
occupy. 6Obey them completely, and you
will display your wisdom and intelligence
among the surrounding nations. When they
hear all these decrees, they will exclaim,
‘How wise and prudent are the people of
this great nation!’ 7For what great nation
has a god as near to them as the LORD our
God is near to us whenever we call on him?
8And what great nation has decrees and regulations as righteous and fair as this body
of instructions that I am giving you today?

9“But watch out! Be careful never to
forget what you yourself have seen. Do
not let these memories escape from your
mind as long as you live! And be sure to
pass them on to your children and grandchildren. 10Never forget the day when you
stood before the LORD your God at Mount
Sinai,* where he told me, ‘Summon the
people before me, and I will personally instruct them. Then they will learn to fear me
as long as they live, and they will teach their
children to fear me also.’

11“You came near and stood at the foot of
the mountain, while flames from the mountain shot into the sky. The mountain was
shrouded in black clouds and deep darkness.
12And the LORD spoke to you from the heart of
the fire. You heard the sound of his words but
didn’t see his form; there was only a voice.
13He proclaimed his covenant—the Ten Commandments*—which he commanded you
to keep, and which he wrote on two stone
tablets. 14It was at that time that the LORD
commanded me to teach you his decrees and
regulations so you would obey them in the
land you are about to enter and occupy.

A Warning against Idolatry

15“But be very careful! You did not see the
LORD’s form on the day he spoke to you
from the heart of the fire at Mount Sinai.
16So do not corrupt yourselves by making
an idol in any form—whether of a man or a
woman, 17an animal on the ground, a bird in
the sky, 18a small animal that scurries along
the ground, or a fish in the deepest sea.
19And when you look up into the sky and
see the sun, moon, and stars—all the forces
of heaven—don’t be seduced into worshiping them. The LORD your God gave them to
all the peoples of the earth. 20Remember
that the LORD rescued you from the iron-
smelting furnace of Egypt in order to make
you his very own people and his special
possession, which is what you are today.

21“But the LORD was angry with me
because of you. He vowed that I would not
cross the Jordan River into the good land the
LORD your God is giving you as your special
possession. 22You will cross the Jordan to
occupy the land, but I will not. Instead,
I will die here on the east side of the river.
23So be careful not to break the covenant
the LORD your God has made with you. Do
not make idols of any shape or form, for the
LORD your God has forbidden this. 24The
LORD your God is a devouring fire; he is a
jealous God.

25“In the future, when you have children
and grandchildren and have lived in the
land a long time, do not corrupt yourselves
by making idols of any kind. This is evil
in the sight of the LORD your God and will
arouse his anger.

26“Today I call on heaven and earth as
witnesses against you. If you break my covenant, you will quickly disappear from the
land you are crossing the Jordan to occupy.
You will live there only a short time; then
you will be utterly destroyed. 27For the LORD
will scatter you among the nations, where
only a few of you will survive. 28There, in a
foreign land, you will worship idols made
from wood and stone—gods that neither see
nor hear nor eat nor smell. 29But from there
you will search again for the LORD your
God. And if you search for him with all your
heart and soul, you will find him.

30“In the distant future, when you are
suffering all these things, you will finally
return to the LORD your God and listen to
what he tells you. 31For the LORD your God is
a merciful God; he will not abandon you or
destroy you or forget the solemn covenant
he made with your ancestors.

There Is Only One God

32“Now search all of history, from the time
God created people on the earth until now,

and search from one end of the heavens to
the other. Has anything as great as this ever
been seen or heard before? 33 Has any nation
ever heard the voice of God* speaking from
fire—as you did—and survived? 34 Has any
other god dared to take a nation for himself
out of another nation by means of trials,
miraculous signs, wonders, war, a strong
hand, a powerful arm, and terrifying acts?
Yet that is what the LORD your God did for
you in Egypt, right before your eyes.

35 "He showed you these things so you
would know that the LORD is God and there
is no other. 36 He let you hear his voice from
heaven so he could instruct you. He let you
see his great fire here on earth so he could
speak to you from it. 37 Because he loved your
ancestors, he chose to bless their descendants, and he personally brought you out
of Egypt with a great display of power. 38 He
drove out nations far greater than you, so he
could bring you in and give you their land as
your special possession, as it is today.

39 "So remember this and keep it firmly in
mind: The LORD is God both in heaven and
on earth, and there is no other. 40 If you obey
all the decrees and commands I am giving
you today, all will be well with you and your
children. I am giving you these instructions
so you will enjoy a long life in the land the
LORD your God is giving you for all time."

Eastern Cities of Refuge

41 Then Moses set apart three cities of refuge
east of the Jordan River. 42 Anyone who killed
another person unintentionally, without
previous hostility, could flee there to live in
safety. 43 These were the cities: Bezer on the
wilderness plateau for the tribe of Reuben;
Ramoth in Gilead for the tribe of Gad; Golan
in Bashan for the tribe of Manasseh.

Introduction to Moses' Second Address

44 This is the body of instruction that Moses
presented to the Israelites. 45 These are the
laws, decrees, and regulations that Moses
gave to the people of Israel when they left
Egypt, 46 and as they camped in the valley
near Beth-peor east of the Jordan River. (This
land was formerly occupied by the Amorites
under King Sihon, who ruled from Heshbon.
But Moses and the Israelites destroyed him
and his people when they came up from
Egypt. 47 Israel took possession of his land
and that of King Og of Bashan—the two
Amorite kings east of the Jordan. 48 So Israel
conquered the entire area from Aroer at
the edge of the Arnon Gorge all the way to
Mount Sirion,* also called Mount Hermon.
49 And they conquered the eastern bank of
the Jordan River as far south as the Dead
Sea,* below the slopes of Pisgah.)

Ten Commandments for the Covenant Community

5 Moses called all the people of Israel together and said, "Listen carefully, Israel.
Hear the decrees and regulations I am
giving you today, so you may learn them
and obey them!

2 "The LORD our God made a covenant
with us at Mount Sinai.* 3 The LORD did not
make this covenant with our ancestors, but
with all of us who are alive today. 4 At the
mountain the LORD spoke to you face to
face from the heart of the fire. 5 I stood as an
intermediary between you and the LORD, for
you were afraid of the fire and did not want
to approach the mountain. He spoke to me,
and I passed his words on to you. This is
what he said:

6 "I am the LORD your God, who rescued
you from the land of Egypt, the place of
your slavery.
7 "You must not have any other god but me.
8 "You must not make for yourself an idol
of any kind, or an image of anything
in the heavens or on the earth or in the
sea. 9 You must not bow down to them or
worship them, for I, the LORD your God,
am a jealous God who will not tolerate
your affection for any other gods. I
lay the sins of the parents upon their
children; the entire family is affected—
even children in the third and fourth
generations of those who reject me. 10 But
I lavish unfailing love for a thousand
generations on those* who love me and
obey my commands.

4:10 Hebrew *Horeb*, another name for Sinai; also in 4:15.
4:13 Hebrew *the ten words*. **4:33** Or *voice of a god*.
4:48 As in Syriac version (see also 3:9); Hebrew reads *Mount Sion*. **4:49** Hebrew *took the Arabah on the east side of the Jordan as far as the sea of the Arabah*. **5:2** Hebrew *Horeb*, another name for Sinai. **5:10** Hebrew *for thousands of those*.

▸ **5:1** *See* ***Are the Ten Commandments still relevant today?***, *page 89.*

11“You must not misuse the name of the
LORD your God. The LORD will not let
you go unpunished if you misuse his
name.
12“Observe the Sabbath day by keeping
it holy, as the LORD your God has
commanded you. 13You have six days
each week for your ordinary work,
14but the seventh day is a Sabbath day
of rest dedicated to the LORD your God.
On that day no one in your household
may do any work. This includes you,
your sons and daughters, your male
and female servants, your oxen and
donkeys and other livestock, and any
foreigners living among you. All your
male and female servants must rest as
you do. 15Remember that you were once
slaves in Egypt, but the LORD your God
brought you out with his strong hand
and powerful arm. That is why the LORD
your God has commanded you to rest on
the Sabbath day.
16“Honor your father and mother, as the
LORD your God commanded you. Then
you will live a long, full life in the land
the LORD your God is giving you.
17“You must not murder.
18“You must not commit adultery.
19“You must not steal.
20“You must not testify falsely against your
neighbor.
21“You must not covet your neighbor’s
wife. You must not covet your neighbor’s
house or land, male or female servant,
ox or donkey, or anything else that
belongs to your neighbor.

22“The LORD spoke these words to all
of you assembled there at the foot of the
mountain. He spoke with a loud voice from
the heart of the fire, surrounded by clouds
and deep darkness. This was all he said at
that time, and he wrote his words on two
stone tablets and gave them to me.

23“But when you heard the voice from the
heart of the darkness, while the mountain
was blazing with fire, all your tribal leaders
and elders came to me. 24They said, ‘Look,
the LORD our God has shown us his glory
and greatness, and we have heard his voice
from the heart of the fire. Today we have
seen that God can speak to us humans, and
yet we live! 25But now, why should we risk
death again? If the LORD our God speaks
to us again, we will certainly die and be
consumed by this awesome fire. 26Can any
living thing hear the voice of the living God
from the heart of the fire as we did and yet
survive? 27Go yourself and listen to what the
LORD our God says. Then come and tell us
everything he tells you, and we will listen
and obey.’

28“The LORD heard the request you made
to me. And he said, ‘I have heard what the
people said to you, and they are right. 29Oh,
that they would always have hearts like
this, that they might fear me and obey all
my commands! If they did, they and their
descendants would prosper forever. 30Go
and tell them, “Return to your tents.” 31But
you stand here with me so I can give you
all my commands, decrees, and regulations.
You must teach them to the people so they
can obey them in the land I am giving them
as their possession.’”

32So Moses told the people, “You must
be careful to obey all the commands of the
LORD your God, following his instructions
in every detail. 33Stay on the path that the
LORD your God has commanded you to
follow. Then you will live long and prosperous lives in the land you are about to enter
and occupy.

A Call for Wholehearted Commitment

6 “These are the commands, decrees,
and regulations that the LORD your God
commanded me to teach you. You must
obey them in the land you are about to
enter and occupy, 2and you and your children and grandchildren must fear the LORD
your God as long as you live. If you obey all
his decrees and commands, you will enjoy
a long life. 3Listen closely, Israel, and be
careful to obey. Then all will go well with
you, and you will have many children in the
land flowing with milk and honey, just as
the LORD, the God of your ancestors, promised you.

4“Listen, O Israel! The LORD is our God,
the LORD alone.* 5And you must love the
LORD your God with all your heart, all your
soul, and all your strength. 6And you must
commit yourselves wholeheartedly to these
commands that I am giving you today.
7Repeat them again and again to your children. Talk about them when you are at home
and when you are on the road, when you are
going to bed and when you are getting up.

8 Tie them to your hands and wear them on
your forehead as reminders. 9 Write them on
the doorposts of your house and on your
gates.
10 "The LORD your God will soon bring you
into the land he swore to give you when he
made a vow to your ancestors Abraham,
Isaac, and Jacob. It is a land with large,
prosperous cities that you did not build.
11 The houses will be richly stocked with
goods you did not produce. You will draw
water from cisterns you did not dig, and you
will eat from vineyards and olive trees you
did not plant. When you have eaten your
fill in this land, 12 be careful not to forget the
LORD, who rescued you from slavery in the
land of Egypt. 13 You must fear the LORD your
God and serve him. When you take an oath,
you must use only his name.
14 "You must not worship any of the gods
of neighboring nations, 15 for the LORD your
God, who lives among you, is a jealous God.
His anger will flare up against you, and he
will wipe you from the face of the earth.
16 You must not test the LORD your God as
you did when you complained at Massah.
17 You must diligently obey the commands
of the LORD your God—all the laws and
decrees he has given you. 18 Do what is right
and good in the LORD's sight, so all will
go well with you. Then you will enter and
occupy the good land that the LORD swore
to give your ancestors. 19 You will drive out
all the enemies living in the land, just as the
LORD said you would.
20 "In the future your children will ask
you, 'What is the meaning of these laws,
decrees, and regulations that the LORD our
God has commanded us to obey?'
21 "Then you must tell them, 'We were
Pharaoh's slaves in Egypt, but the LORD
brought us out of Egypt with his strong
hand. 22 The LORD did miraculous signs and
wonders before our eyes, dealing terrifying
blows against Egypt and Pharaoh and all
his people. 23 He brought us out of Egypt so
he could give us this land he had sworn to
give our ancestors. 24 And the LORD our God
commanded us to obey all these decrees
and to fear him so he can continue to bless
us and preserve our lives, as he has done to
this day. 25 For we will be counted as righteous when we obey all the commands the
LORD our God has given us.'

The Privilege of Holiness

7 "When the LORD your God brings you
into the land you are about to enter and
occupy, he will clear away many nations
ahead of you: the Hittites, Girgashites,

6:4 Or *The LORD our God is one LORD;* or *The LORD our God, the LORD is one;* or *The LORD is our God, the LORD is one.*

The one true God

With Israel about to enter Canaan, with its many religions and various gods and idols, Moses needed to underline that there was only one true God: "Listen, O Israel! The LORD is our God, the LORD alone" (Deuteronomy 6:4). In declaring the uniqueness of Israel's God, Moses was affirming what the Bible says from the beginning. "In the beginning *God* . . ."—not *a* god, or *the* gods, but *God*. This belief in one God lay at the heart of Israelite faith—though sometimes they would forget that and so would be challenged by the prophets (e.g., 1 Kings 18:16-18; 2 Kings 17:7-20).

In light of this affirmation of the uniqueness of God, Israel was called, first, to have no other gods (Deuteronomy 5:6-7) and not to make any idols that might lead them astray (4:15-19; 5:8-10), and second, to "love the LORD your God with all your heart, all your soul, and all your strength" (6:5). Why? Because if there were no other gods, they need not keep anything in reserve to offer to them. Why? They simply do not exist.

Jesus himself said that this commandment, to love the one God with all our heart, soul, mind, and strength, was the greatest of all the commandments, and that it, along with the commandment to love our neighbor as ourselves, was the basis of God's entire law (Matthew 22:37-40).

Amorites, Canaanites, Perizzites, Hivites,
and Jebusites. These seven nations are
greater and more numerous than you.
[2]When the LORD your God hands these
nations over to you and you conquer them,
you must completely destroy* them. Make
no treaties with them and show them no
mercy. [3]You must not intermarry with them.
Do not let your daughters and sons marry
their sons and daughters, [4]for they will lead
your children away from me to worship
other gods. Then the anger of the LORD
will burn against you, and he will quickly
destroy you. [5]This is what you must do. You
must break down their pagan altars and
shatter their sacred pillars. Cut down their
Asherah poles and burn their idols. [6]For
you are a holy people, who belong to the
LORD your God. Of all the people on earth,
the LORD your God has chosen you to be his
own special treasure.

[7]"The LORD did not set his heart on you
and choose you because you were more
numerous than other nations, for you were
the smallest of all nations! [8]Rather, it was
simply that the LORD loves you, and he was
keeping the oath he had sworn to your ancestors. That is why the LORD rescued you
with such a strong hand from your slavery
and from the oppressive hand of Pharaoh,
king of Egypt. [9]Understand, therefore, that
the LORD your God is indeed God. He is the
faithful God who keeps his covenant for
a thousand generations and lavishes his
unfailing love on those who love him and
obey his commands. [10]But he does not hesitate to punish and destroy those who reject
him. [11]Therefore, you must obey all these
commands, decrees, and regulations I am
giving you today.

[12]"If you listen to these regulations and
faithfully obey them, the LORD your God
will keep his covenant of unfailing love with
you, as he promised with an oath to your
ancestors. [13]He will love you and bless you,
and he will give you many children. He will
give fertility to your land and your animals.
When you arrive in the land he swore to
give your ancestors, you will have large
harvests of grain, new wine, and olive oil,
and great herds of cattle, sheep, and goats.
[14]You will be blessed above all the nations of
the earth. None of your men or women will
be childless, and all your livestock will bear
young. [15]And the LORD will protect you from
all sickness. He will not let you suffer from
the terrible diseases you knew in Egypt, but
he will inflict them on all your enemies!

[16]"You must destroy all the nations the
LORD your God hands over to you. Show
them no mercy, and do not worship their
gods, or they will trap you. [17]Perhaps you
will think to yourselves, 'How can we ever
conquer these nations that are so much
more powerful than we are?' [18]But don't
be afraid of them! Just remember what the
LORD your God did to Pharaoh and to all the
land of Egypt. [19]Remember the great terrors
the LORD your God sent against them. You
saw it all with your own eyes! And remember the miraculous signs and wonders, and
the strong hand and powerful arm with
which he brought you out of Egypt. The
LORD your God will use this same power
against all the people you fear. [20]And then
the LORD your God will send terror* to drive
out the few survivors still hiding from you!

[21]"No, do not be afraid of those nations,
for the LORD your God is among you, and
he is a great and awesome God. [22]The LORD
your God will drive those nations out ahead
of you little by little. You will not clear them
away all at once, otherwise the wild animals
would multiply too quickly for you. [23]But
the LORD your God will hand them over
to you. He will throw them into complete
confusion until they are destroyed. [24]He
will put their kings in your power, and you

All those "-ites"

In these accounts of Israel's early history we often find reference to various nations and people groups with strange-sounding names that all end in "-ites" (e.g., Genesis 15:19-20; Exodus 3:17; 34:11; Deuteronomy 7:1). The listing of these nations in this way was meant to underline how complete God's gift of Canaan to Israel as the Promised Land was.

will erase their names from the face of the earth. No one will be able to stand against you, and you will destroy them all.

[25]"You must burn their idols in fire, and you must not covet the silver or gold that covers them. You must not take it or it will become a trap to you, for it is detestable to the LORD your God. [26]Do not bring any detestable objects into your home, for then you will be destroyed, just like them. You must utterly detest such things, for they are set apart for destruction.

A Call to Remember and Obey

8 "Be careful to obey all the commands I am giving you today. Then you will live and multiply, and you will enter and occupy the land the LORD swore to give your ancestors. [2]Remember how the LORD your God led you through the wilderness for these forty years, humbling you and testing you to prove your character, and to find out whether or not you would obey his commands. [3]Yes, he humbled you by letting you go hungry and then feeding you with manna, a food previously unknown to you and your ancestors. He did it to teach you that people do not live by bread alone; rather, we live by every word that comes from the mouth of the LORD. [4]For all these forty years your clothes didn't wear out, and your feet didn't blister or swell. [5]Think about it: Just as a parent disciplines a child, the LORD your God disciplines you for your own good.

[6]"So obey the commands of the LORD your God by walking in his ways and fearing him. [7]For the LORD your God is bringing you into a good land of flowing streams and pools of water, with fountains and springs that gush out in the valleys and hills. [8]It is a land of wheat and barley; of grapevines, fig trees, and pomegranates; of olive oil and honey. [9]It is a land where food is plentiful and nothing is lacking. It is a land where iron is as common as stone, and copper is abundant in the hills. [10]When you have eaten your fill, be sure to praise the LORD your God for the good land he has given you.

[11]"But that is the time to be careful! Beware that in your plenty you do not forget the LORD your God and disobey his commands, regulations, and decrees that I am giving you today. [12]For when you have become full and prosperous and have built fine homes to live in, [13]and when your flocks and herds have become very large and your silver and gold have multiplied along with everything else, be careful! [14]Do not become proud at that time and forget the LORD your God, who rescued you from slavery in the land of Egypt. [15]Do not forget that he led you through the great and terrifying wilderness with its poisonous snakes and scorpions, where it was so hot and dry. He gave you water from the rock! [16]He fed you with manna in the wilderness, a food unknown to your ancestors. He did this to humble you and test you for your own good. [17]He did all this so you would never say to yourself, 'I have achieved this wealth with my own strength and energy.' [18]Remember the LORD your God. He is the one who gives you power to be successful, in order to fulfill the covenant he confirmed to your ancestors with an oath.

[19]"But I assure you of this: If you ever forget the LORD your God and follow other gods, worshiping and bowing down to them, you will certainly be destroyed. [20]Just as the LORD has destroyed other nations in your path, you also will be destroyed if you refuse to obey the LORD your God.

Victory by God's Grace

9 "Listen, O Israel! Today you are about to cross the Jordan River to take over the land belonging to nations much greater and more powerful than you. They live in cities with walls that reach to the sky! [2]The people are strong and tall—descendants of the famous Anakite giants. You've heard the saying, 'Who can stand up to the Anakites?' [3]But recognize today that the LORD your God is the one who will cross over ahead of you like a devouring fire to destroy them. He will subdue them so that you will quickly conquer them and drive them out, just as the LORD has promised.

[4]"After the LORD your God has done this for you, don't say in your hearts, 'The

7:2 The Hebrew term used here refers to the complete consecration of things or people to the LORD, either by destroying them or by giving them as an offering; also in 7:26. **7:20** Often rendered *the hornet*. The meaning of the Hebrew is uncertain.

▸ **8:10** *See **Money**, page 1417.*

LORD has given us this land because we are such good people!' No, it is because of the wickedness of the other nations that he is pushing them out of your way. [5]It is not because you are so good or have such integrity that you are about to occupy their land. The LORD your God will drive these nations out ahead of you only because of their wickedness, and to fulfill the oath he swore to your ancestors Abraham, Isaac, and Jacob. [6]You must recognize that the LORD your God is not giving you this good land because you are good, for you are not—you are a stubborn people.

Remembering the Gold Calf

[7]"Remember and never forget how angry you made the LORD your God out in the wilderness. From the day you left Egypt until now, you have been constantly rebelling against him. [8]Even at Mount Sinai* you made the LORD so angry he was ready to destroy you. [9]This happened when I was on the mountain receiving the tablets of stone inscribed with the words of the covenant that the LORD had made with you. I was there for forty days and forty nights, and all that time I ate no food and drank no water. [10]The LORD gave me the two tablets on which God had written with his own finger all the words he had spoken to you from the heart of the fire when you were assembled at the mountain.

[11]"At the end of the forty days and nights, the LORD handed me the two stone tablets inscribed with the words of the covenant. [12]Then the LORD said to me, 'Get up! Go down immediately, for the people you brought out of Egypt have corrupted themselves. How quickly they have turned away from the way I commanded them to live! They have melted gold and made an idol for themselves!'

[13]"The LORD also said to me, 'I have seen how stubborn and rebellious these people are. [14]Leave me alone so I may destroy them and erase their name from under heaven. Then I will make a mighty nation of your descendants, a nation larger and more powerful than they are.'

[15]"So while the mountain was blazing with fire I turned and came down, holding in my hands the two stone tablets inscribed with the terms of the covenant. [16]There below me I could see that you had sinned against the LORD your God. You had melted gold and made a calf idol for yourselves. How quickly you had turned away from the path the LORD had commanded you to follow! [17]So I took the stone tablets and threw them to the ground, smashing them before your eyes.

[18]"Then, as before, I threw myself down before the LORD for forty days and nights. I ate no bread and drank no water because of the great sin you had committed by doing what the LORD hated, provoking him to anger. [19]I feared that the furious anger of the LORD, which turned him against you, would drive him to destroy you. But again he listened to me. [20]The LORD was so angry with Aaron that he wanted to destroy him, too. But I prayed for Aaron, and the LORD spared him. [21]I took your sin—the calf you had made—and I melted it down in the fire and ground it into fine dust. Then I threw the dust into the stream that flows down the mountain.

[22]"You also made the LORD angry at Taberah,* Massah,* and Kibroth-hattaavah.* [23]And at Kadesh-barnea the LORD sent you out with this command: 'Go up and take over the land I have given you.' But you rebelled against the command of the LORD your God and refused to put your trust in him or obey him. [24]Yes, you have been rebelling against the LORD as long as I have known you.

[25]"That is why I threw myself down before the LORD for forty days and nights—for the LORD said he would destroy you. [26]I prayed to the LORD and said, 'O Sovereign LORD, do not destroy them. They are your own people. They are your special possession, whom you redeemed from Egypt by your mighty power and your strong hand. [27]Please overlook the stubbornness and the awful sin of these people, and remember instead your servants Abraham, Isaac, and Jacob. [28]If you destroy these people, the Egyptians will say, "The Israelites died because the LORD wasn't able to bring them to the land he had promised to give them." Or they might say, "He destroyed them because he hated them; he deliberately took them into the wilderness to slaughter them." [29]But they are your people and your special possession, whom you brought out of Egypt by your great strength and powerful arm.'

A New Copy of the Covenant

10 "At that time the LORD said to me,
'Chisel out two stone tablets like
the first ones. Also make a wooden Ark—a
sacred chest to store them in. Come up to
me on the mountain, 2 and I will write on
the tablets the same words that were on the
ones you smashed. Then place the tablets
in the Ark.'

3 "So I made an Ark of acacia wood and
cut two stone tablets like the first two. Then
I went up the mountain with the tablets in
my hand. 4 Once again the LORD wrote the
Ten Commandments* on the tablets and
gave them to me. They were the same words
the LORD had spoken to you from the heart
of the fire on the day you were assembled
at the foot of the mountain. 5 Then I turned
and came down the mountain and placed
the tablets in the Ark of the Covenant,
which I had made, just as the LORD commanded me. And the tablets are still there
in the Ark."

6 (The people of Israel set out from the
wells of the people of Jaakan* and traveled to Moserah, where Aaron died and was
buried. His son Eleazar ministered as high
priest in his place. 7 Then they journeyed to
Gudgodah, and from there to Jotbathah, a
land with many brooks and streams. 8 At that
time the LORD set apart the tribe of Levi to
carry the Ark of the LORD's Covenant, and
to stand before the LORD as his ministers,
and to pronounce blessings in his name.
These are their duties to this day. 9 That is
why the Levites have no share of property or
possession of land among the other Israelite
tribes. The LORD himself is their special possession, as the LORD your God told them.)

10 "As for me, I stayed on the mountain
in the LORD's presence for forty days and
nights, as I had done the first time. And
once again the LORD listened to my pleas
and agreed not to destroy you. 11 Then the
LORD said to me, 'Get up and resume the
journey, and lead the people to the land
I swore to give to their ancestors, so they
may take possession of it.'

A Call to Love and Obedience

12 "And now, Israel, what does the LORD
your God require of you? He requires only
that you fear the LORD your God, and live
in a way that pleases him, and love him
and serve him with all your heart and soul.
13 And you must always obey the LORD's
commands and decrees that I am giving you
today for your own good.

14 "Look, the highest heavens and the earth
and everything in it all belong to the LORD
your God. 15 Yet the LORD chose your ancestors
as the objects of his love. And he chose you,
their descendants, above all other nations,
as is evident today. 16 Therefore, change your
hearts* and stop being stubborn.

17 "For the LORD your God is the God of
gods and Lord of lords. He is the great God,
the mighty and awesome God, who shows
no partiality and cannot be bribed. 18 He
ensures that orphans and widows receive
justice. He shows love to the foreigners
living among you and gives them food and
clothing. 19 So you, too, must show love to
foreigners, for you yourselves were once
foreigners in the land of Egypt. 20 You must
fear the LORD your God and worship him
and cling to him. Your oaths must be in his
name alone. 21 He alone is your God, the only
one who is worthy of your praise, the one
who has done these mighty miracles that
you have seen with your own eyes. 22 When
your ancestors went down into Egypt, there
were only seventy of them. But now the
LORD your God has made you as numerous
as the stars in the sky!

11 "You must love the LORD your God
and always obey his requirements,
decrees, regulations, and commands. 2 Keep
in mind that I am not talking now to your
children, who have never experienced the
discipline of the LORD your God or seen his
greatness and his strong hand and powerful
arm. 3 They didn't see the miraculous signs
and wonders he performed in Egypt against
Pharaoh and all his land. 4 They didn't see
what the LORD did to the armies of Egypt
and to their horses and chariots—how he
drowned them in the Red Sea* as they were

9:8 Hebrew *Horeb,* another name for Sinai. **9:22a** *Taberah* means "place of burning." See Num 11:1-3. **9:22b** *Massah* means "place of testing." See Exod 17:1-7. **9:22c** *Kibroth-hattaavah* means "graves of gluttony." See Num 11:31-34. **10:4** Hebrew *the ten words.* **10:6** Or *set out from Beeroth of Bene-jaakan.* **10:16** Hebrew *circumcise the foreskin of your hearts.* **11:4** Hebrew *sea of reeds.*

▸ **10:17** *See **Bribery**, page 736.*

chasing you. He destroyed them, and they have not recovered to this very day!

5 "Your children didn't see how the LORD cared for you in the wilderness until you arrived here. 6 They didn't see what he did to Dathan and Abiram (the sons of Eliab, a descendant of Reuben) when the earth opened its mouth in the Israelite camp and swallowed them, along with their households and tents and every living thing that belonged to them. 7 But you have seen the LORD perform all these mighty deeds with your own eyes!

The Blessings of Obedience

8 "Therefore, be careful to obey every command I am giving you today, so you may have strength to go in and take over the land you are about to enter. 9 If you obey, you will enjoy a long life in the land the LORD swore to give to your ancestors and to you, their descendants—a land flowing with milk and honey! 10 For the land you are about to enter and take over is not like the land of Egypt from which you came, where you planted your seed and made irrigation ditches with your foot as in a vegetable garden. 11 Rather, the land you will soon take over is a land of hills and valleys with plenty of rain—12 a land that the LORD your God cares for. He watches over it through each season of the year!

13 "If you carefully obey the commands I am giving you today, and if you love the LORD your God and serve him with all your heart and soul, 14 then he will send the rains in their proper seasons—the early and late rains—so you can bring in your harvests of grain, new wine, and olive oil. 15 He will give you lush pastureland for your livestock, and you yourselves will have all you want to eat.

16 "But be careful. Don't let your heart be deceived so that you turn away from the LORD and serve and worship other gods. 17 If you do, the LORD's anger will burn against you. He will shut up the sky and hold back the rain, and the ground will fail to produce its harvests. Then you will quickly die in that good land the LORD is giving you.

18 "So commit yourselves wholeheartedly to these words of mine. Tie them to your hands and wear them on your forehead as reminders. 19 Teach them to your children. Talk about them when you are at home and when you are on the road, when you are going to bed and when you are getting up. 20 Write them on the doorposts of your house and on your gates, 21 so that as long as the sky remains above the earth, you and your children may flourish in the land the LORD swore to give your ancestors.

22 "Be careful to obey all these commands I am giving you. Show love to the LORD your God by walking in his ways and holding tightly to him. 23 Then the LORD will drive out all the nations ahead of you, though they are much greater and stronger than you, and you will take over their land. 24 Wherever you set foot, that land will be yours. Your frontiers will stretch from the wilderness in the south to Lebanon in the north, and from the Euphrates River in the east to the Mediterranean Sea in the west.* 25 No one will be able to stand against you, for the LORD your God will cause the people to fear and dread you, as he promised, wherever you go in the whole land.

26 "Look, today I am giving you the choice between a blessing and a curse! 27 You will be blessed if you obey the commands of the LORD your God that I am giving you today. 28 But you will be cursed if you reject the commands of the LORD your God and turn away from him and worship gods you have not known before.

29 "When the LORD your God brings you into the land and helps you take possession of it, you must pronounce the blessing at Mount Gerizim and the curse at Mount Ebal. 30 (These two mountains are west of the Jordan River in the land of the Canaanites who live in the Jordan Valley,* near the town of Gilgal, not far from the oaks of Moreh.) 31 For you are about to cross the Jordan River to take over the land the LORD your God is giving you. When you take that land and are living in it, 32 you must be careful to obey all the decrees and regulations I am giving you today.

The LORD's Chosen Place for Worship

12 "These are the decrees and regulations you must be careful to obey when you live in the land that the LORD, the God of your ancestors, is giving you. You must obey them as long as you live.

2 "When you drive out the nations that live there, you must destroy all the places where they worship their gods—high on the mountains, up on the hills, and under every green tree. 3 Break down their altars and smash

their sacred pillars. Burn their Asherah
poles and cut down their carved idols. Completely erase the names of their gods!
4 "Do not worship the LORD your God in
the way these pagan peoples worship their
gods. 5 Rather, you must seek the LORD your
God at the place of worship he himself will
choose from among all the tribes—the place
where his name will be honored. 6 There you
will bring your burnt offerings, your sacrifices, your tithes, your sacred offerings,
your offerings to fulfill a vow, your voluntary offerings, and your offerings of the
firstborn animals of your herds and flocks.
7 There you and your families will feast in
the presence of the LORD your God, and you
will rejoice in all you have accomplished
because the LORD your God has blessed
you.
8 "Your pattern of worship will change.
Today all of you are doing as you please,
9 because you have not yet arrived at the
place of rest, the land the LORD your God is
giving you as your special possession. 10 But
you will soon cross the Jordan River and
live in the land the LORD your God is giving
you. When he gives you rest from all your
enemies and you're living safely in the land,
11 you must bring everything I command
you—your burnt offerings, your sacrifices,
your tithes, your sacred offerings, and your
offerings to fulfill a vow—to the designated
place of worship, the place the LORD your
God chooses for his name to be honored.
12 "You must celebrate there in the presence of the LORD your God with your sons
and daughters and all your servants. And
remember to include the Levites who live
in your towns, for they will receive no allotment of land among you. 13 Be careful
not to sacrifice your burnt offerings just
anywhere you like. 14 You may do so only at
the place the LORD will choose within one
of your tribal territories. There you must
offer your burnt offerings and do everything
I command you.
15 "But you may butcher your animals
and eat their meat in any town whenever
you want. You may freely eat the animals
with which the LORD your God blesses you.
All of you, whether ceremonially clean or
unclean, may eat that meat, just as you
now eat gazelle and deer. 16 But you must
not consume the blood. You must pour it
out on the ground like water.
17 "But you may not eat your offerings in
your hometown—neither the tithe of your
grain and new wine and olive oil, nor the

11:24 Hebrew *to the western sea.* **11:30** Hebrew *the Arabah.*

Where can we worship?

Initially the Israelites had no special places of worship. The patriarchs worshiped and prayed anywhere, and even places that came to be seen as "holy" were only seen like that because they served as reminders of what God had done.

In the wilderness God provided the Israelites with a Tabernacle for their sacrifices—a tent that could be dismantled and moved to new locations, showing that God had no fixed abode. But now, on the edge of the Promised Land, Moses told them to "seek the LORD your God at the place of worship he himself will choose from among all the tribes—the place where his name will be honored" (Deuteronomy 12:5). Moses may simply have meant that they were not to worship at the many Canaanite shrines, but only in a place of *God's* choice, or he may have been saying that there really would only be one place where they could worship and offer sacrifices. His words were later interpreted as justification for seeing the Jerusalem Temple as the chief place of worship. Sadly, the people would come to put their trust in the Temple of God rather than the God of the Temple, so God allowed it to be destroyed, not once but twice—in Old Testament times by the Babylonians and in New Testament times by the Romans.

In his discussion with the woman at the well, Jesus stressed that God is not interested in *where* we worship but *how* we worship (John 4:21-24), saying his only requirement is that it be "in spirit and in truth."

firstborn of your flocks and herds, nor any offering to fulfill a vow, nor your voluntary offerings, nor your sacred offerings. 18You must eat these in the presence of the LORD your God at the place he will choose. Eat them there with your children, your servants, and the Levites who live in your towns, celebrating in the presence of the LORD your God in all you do. 19And be very careful never to neglect the Levites as long as you live in your land.

20"When the LORD your God expands your territory as he has promised, and you have the urge to eat meat, you may freely eat meat whenever you want. 21It might happen that the designated place of worship—the place the LORD your God chooses for his name to be honored—is a long way from your home. If so, you may butcher any of the cattle, sheep, or goats the LORD has given you, and you may freely eat the meat in your hometown, as I have commanded you. 22Anyone, whether ceremonially clean or unclean, may eat that meat, just as you do now with gazelle and deer. 23But never consume the blood, for the blood is the life, and you must not consume the lifeblood with the meat. 24Instead, pour out the blood on the ground like water. 25Do not consume the blood, so that all may go well with you and your children after you, because you will be doing what pleases the LORD.

26"Take your sacred gifts and your offerings given to fulfill a vow to the place the LORD chooses. 27You must offer the meat and blood of your burnt offerings on the altar of the LORD your God. The blood of your other sacrifices must be poured out on the altar of the LORD your God, but you may eat the meat. 28Be careful to obey all my commands, so that all will go well with you and your children after you, because you will be doing what is good and pleasing to the LORD your God.

29"When the LORD your God goes ahead of you and destroys the nations and you drive them out and live in their land, 30do not fall into the trap of following their customs and worshiping their gods. Do not inquire about their gods, saying, 'How do these nations worship their gods? I want to follow their example.' 31You must not worship the LORD your God the way the other nations worship their gods, for they perform for their gods every detestable act that the LORD hates. They even burn their sons and daughters as sacrifices to their gods.

32*"So be careful to obey all the commands I give you. You must not add anything to them or subtract anything from them.

A Warning against Idolatry

13 1*"Suppose there are prophets among you or those who dream dreams about the future, and they promise you signs or miracles, 2and the predicted signs or miracles occur. If they then say, 'Come, let us worship other gods'—gods you have not known before—3do not listen to them. The LORD your God is testing you to see if you truly love him with all your heart and soul. 4Serve only the LORD your God and fear him alone. Obey his commands, listen to his voice, and cling to him. 5The false prophets or visionaries who try to lead you astray must be put to death, for they encourage rebellion against the LORD your God, who redeemed you from slavery and brought you out of the land of Egypt. Since they try to lead you astray from the way the LORD your God commanded you to live, you must put them to death. In this way you will purge the evil from among you.

6"Suppose someone secretly entices you—even your brother, your son or daughter, your beloved wife, or your closest friend—and says, 'Let us go worship other gods'—gods that neither you nor your ancestors have known. 7They might suggest that you worship the gods of peoples who live nearby or who come from the ends of the earth. 8But do not give in or listen. Have no pity, and do not spare or protect them. 9You must put them to death! Strike the first blow yourself, and then all the people must join in. 10Stone the guilty ones to death because they have tried to draw you away from the LORD your God, who rescued you from the land of Egypt, the place of slavery. 11Then all Israel will hear about it and be afraid, and no one will act so wickedly again.

12"When you begin living in the towns the LORD your God is giving you, you may hear 13that scoundrels among you are leading their fellow citizens astray by saying, 'Let us go worship other gods'—gods you have not known before. 14In such cases, you must examine the facts carefully. If you find that the report is true and such a detestable act has been committed among you, 15 you must attack that town and completely destroy* all its inhabitants, as well as all the livestock. 16 Then you must pile all the plunder in the middle of the open square and burn it. Burn the entire town as a burnt offering to the LORD your God. That town must remain a ruin forever; it may never be rebuilt. 17 Keep none of the plunder that has been set apart for destruction. Then the LORD will turn from his fierce anger and be merciful to you. He will have compassion on you and make you a large nation, just as he swore to your ancestors.

18 "The LORD your God will be merciful only if you listen to his voice and keep all his commands that I am giving you today, doing what pleases him.

Ceremonially Clean and Unclean Animals

14 "Since you are the people of the LORD your God, never cut yourselves or shave the hair above your foreheads in mourning for the dead. 2 You have been set apart as holy to the LORD your God, and he has chosen you from all the nations of the earth to be his own special treasure.

3 "You must not eat any detestable animals that are ceremonially unclean. 4 These are the animals* you may eat: the ox, the sheep, the goat, 5 the deer, the gazelle, the roe deer, the wild goat, the addax, the antelope, and the mountain sheep.

6 "You may eat any animal that has completely split hooves and chews the cud, 7 but if the animal doesn't have both, it may not be eaten. So you may not eat the camel, the hare, or the hyrax.* They chew the cud but do not have split hooves, so they are ceremonially unclean for you. 8 And you may not eat the pig. It has split hooves but does not chew the cud, so it is ceremonially unclean for you. You may not eat the meat of these animals or even touch their carcasses.

9 "Of all the marine animals, you may eat whatever has both fins and scales. 10 You may not, however, eat marine animals that do not have both fins and scales. They are ceremonially unclean for you.

11 "You may eat any bird that is ceremonially clean. 12 These are the birds you may not eat: the griffon vulture, the bearded vulture, the black vulture, 13 the kite, the falcon, buzzards of all kinds, 14 ravens of all kinds, 15 the eagle owl, the short-eared owl, the seagull, hawks of all kinds, 16 the little owl, the great owl, the barn owl, 17 the desert owl, the Egyptian vulture, the cormorant, 18 the stork, herons of all kinds, the hoopoe, and the bat.

19 "All winged insects that walk along the ground are ceremonially unclean for you and may not be eaten. 20 But you may eat any winged bird or insect that is ceremonially clean.

21 "You must not eat anything that has died a natural death. You may give it to a foreigner living in your town, or you may sell it to a stranger. But do not eat it yourselves, for you are set apart as holy to the LORD your God.

"You must not cook a young goat in its mother's milk.

The Giving of Tithes

22 "You must set aside a tithe of your crops—one-tenth of all the crops you harvest each year. 23 Bring this tithe to the designated place of worship—the place the LORD your God chooses for his name to be honored—and eat it there in his presence. This applies to your tithes of grain, new wine, olive oil, and the firstborn males of your flocks and herds. Doing this will teach you always to fear the LORD your God.

24 "Now when the LORD your God blesses you with a good harvest, the place of worship he chooses for his name to be honored might be too far for you to bring the tithe. 25 If so, you may sell the tithe portion of your crops and herds, put the money in a pouch, and go to the place the LORD your God has chosen. 26 When you arrive, you may use the money to buy any kind of food you want—cattle, sheep, goats, wine, or other alcoholic drink. Then feast there in the presence of the LORD your God and celebrate with your household. 27 And do not neglect the Levites in your town, for they will receive no allotment of land among you.

28 "At the end of every third year, bring the entire tithe of that year's harvest and store it in the nearest town. 29 Give it to the Levites, who will receive no allotment of

12:32 Verse 12:32 is numbered 13:1 in Hebrew text. **13:1** Verses 13:1-18 are numbered 13:2-19 in Hebrew text. **13:15** The Hebrew term used here refers to the complete consecration of things or people to the LORD, either by destroying them or by giving them as an offering; similarly in 13:17. **14:4** The identification of some of the animals and birds listed in this chapter is uncertain. **14:7** Or *coney*, or *rock badger*.

land among you, as well as to the foreigners living among you, the orphans, and the
widows in your towns, so they can eat and
be satisfied. Then the LORD your God will
bless you in all your work.

Release for Debtors

15 "At the end of every seventh year you
must cancel the debts of everyone
who owes you money. 2This is how it must
be done. Everyone must cancel the loans
they have made to their fellow Israelites.
They must not demand payment from their
neighbors or relatives, for the LORD's time of
release has arrived. 3This release from debt,
however, applies only to your fellow Israelites—not to the foreigners living among you.
4"There should be no poor among you,
for the LORD your God will greatly bless
you in the land he is giving you as a special
possession. 5You will receive this blessing
if you are careful to obey all the commands
of the LORD your God that I am giving you
today. 6The LORD your God will bless you
as he has promised. You will lend money to
many nations but will never need to borrow.
You will rule many nations, but they will
not rule over you.
7"But if there are any poor Israelites in
your towns when you arrive in the land
the LORD your God is giving you, do not be
hard-hearted or tightfisted toward them.
8Instead, be generous and lend them whatever they need. 9Do not be mean-spirited
and refuse someone a loan because the
year for canceling debts is close at hand. If
you refuse to make the loan and the needy
person cries out to the LORD, you will be
considered guilty of sin. 10Give generously
to the poor, not grudgingly, for the LORD
your God will bless you in everything you
do. 11There will always be some in the land
who are poor. That is why I am commanding
you to share freely with the poor and with
other Israelites in need.

Release for Hebrew Slaves

12"If a fellow Hebrew sells himself or herself
to be your servant* and serves you for six
years, in the seventh year you must set that
servant free.
13"When you release a male servant, do
not send him away empty-handed. 14Give
him a generous farewell gift from your
flock, your threshing floor, and your winepress. Share with him some of the bounty
with which the LORD your God has blessed
you. 15Remember that you were once slaves
in the land of Egypt and the LORD your God
redeemed you! That is why I am giving you
this command.
16"But suppose your servant says, 'I will
not leave you,' because he loves you and
your family, and he has done well with
you. 17In that case, take an awl and push
it through his earlobe into the door. After
that, he will be your servant for life. And do
the same for your female servants.
18"You must not consider it a hardship
when you release your servants. Remember that for six years they have given you
services worth double the wages of hired
workers, and the LORD your God will bless
you in all you do.

Sacrificing Firstborn Male Animals

19"You must set aside for the LORD your God
all the firstborn males from your flocks
and herds. Do not use the firstborn of your
herds to work your fields, and do not shear
the firstborn of your flocks. 20Instead, you
and your family must eat these animals in
the presence of the LORD your God each
year at the place he chooses. 21But if this
firstborn animal has any defect, such as
lameness or blindness, or if anything else
is wrong with it, you must not sacrifice it
to the LORD your God. 22Instead, use it for
food for your family in your hometown.
Anyone, whether ceremonially clean or
unclean, may eat it, just as anyone may
eat a gazelle or deer. 23But you must not
consume the blood. You must pour it out
on the ground like water.

Passover and the Festival of Unleavened Bread

16 "In honor of the LORD your God, celebrate the Passover each year in the
early spring, in the month of Abib,* for that
was the month in which the LORD your God
brought you out of Egypt by night. 2Your
Passover sacrifice may be from either the
flock or the herd, and it must be sacrificed

▸ **15:1-11** *See **Poverty**, page 1142.*

to the LORD your God at the designated
place of worship—the place he chooses
for his name to be honored. 3Eat it with
bread made without yeast. For seven days
the bread you eat must be made without
yeast, as when you escaped from Egypt
in such a hurry. Eat this bread—the bread
of suffering—so that as long as you live
you will remember the day you departed
from Egypt. 4Let no yeast be found in any
house throughout your land for those seven
days. And when you sacrifice the Passover
lamb on the evening of the first day, do not
let any of the meat remain until the next
morning.
5"You may not sacrifice the Passover in
just any of the towns that the LORD your
God is giving you. 6You must offer it only
at the designated place of worship—the
place the LORD your God chooses for his
name to be honored. Sacrifice it there in
the evening as the sun goes down on the
anniversary of your exodus from Egypt.
7Roast the lamb and eat it in the place the
LORD your God chooses. Then you may
go back to your tents the next morning.
8For the next six days you may not eat any
bread made with yeast. On the seventh day
proclaim another holy day in honor of the
LORD your God, and no work may be done
on that day.

The Festival of Harvest

9"Count off seven weeks from when you
first begin to cut the grain at the time of
harvest. 10Then celebrate the Festival of
Harvest* to honor the LORD your God.
Bring him a voluntary offering in proportion to the blessings you have received
from him. 11This is a time to celebrate
before the LORD your God at the designated
place of worship he will choose for his
name to be honored. Celebrate with your
sons and daughters, your male and female
servants, the Levites from your towns, and
the foreigners, orphans, and widows who
live among you. 12Remember that you were

15:12 Or *If a Hebrew man or woman is sold to you.* **16:1** Hebrew *Observe the month of Abib, and keep the Passover unto the LORD your God.* Abib, the first month of the ancient Hebrew lunar calendar, usually occurs within the months of March and April. **16:10** Hebrew *Festival of Weeks;* also in 16:16. This was later called the Festival of Pentecost (see Acts 2:1). It is celebrated today as Shavuot (or Shabuoth).

Debt

Deuteronomy 15:1-18 is utterly radical in its approach to loans and debt, unparalleled in any economy. To ensure the Israelites did not fall into an endless cycle of poverty and debt, God told his people that every seventh year all outstanding debts must be canceled (15:1). This would guarantee that "there should be no poor among you" (15:4). And to guard against hard-heartedness, they were not allowed to refuse a loan simply because the seventh year was near (15:9). Such laws seem shocking by the standards of most modern economies, but they were designed to prevent severe poverty, like the poverty that so many people endure in the world today.

And yet, this was not an excuse to take debt lightly. Indeed, if an Israelite could not repay his debt, he had to become the slave of the one to whom he was indebted (e.g., 2 Kings 4:1; Matthew 18:25) and pay off the debt through his work. Such slavery was not permanent, however, but was also limited to seven years, after which the debt was considered paid (Deuteronomy 15:12-18).

Paying off a debt was seen as a priority, as Elisha reminded the widow for whom God provided (2 Kings 4:1-7), and Paul urges Christians to "owe nothing to anyone—except for your obligation to love one another" (Romans 13:8).

If you do find yourself in debt, seek advice quickly, either from your pastor or from a Christian friend who is good at handling their finances. Whatever you do, don't ignore it, hoping it will go away. God is as concerned about seeing you get out of your debt as he is about anything else in life that holds you back.

▶ *See also* ***The Year of Jubilee****, page 147.*

once slaves in Egypt, so be careful to obey
all these decrees.

The Festival of Shelters

13“You must observe the Festival of Shelters* for seven days at the end of the harvest
season, after the grain has been threshed
and the grapes have been pressed. 14This
festival will be a happy time of celebrating
with your sons and daughters, your male
and female servants, and the Levites, foreigners, orphans, and widows from your
towns. 15For seven days you must celebrate
this festival to honor the LORD your God at
the place he chooses, for it is he who blesses
you with bountiful harvests and gives you
success in all your work. This festival will
be a time of great joy for all.

16“Each year every man in Israel must celebrate these three festivals: the Festival of
Unleavened Bread, the Festival of Harvest,
and the Festival of Shelters. On each of these
occasions, all men must appear before the
LORD your God at the place he chooses,
but they must not appear before the LORD
without a gift for him. 17All must give as they
are able, according to the blessings given to
them by the LORD your God.

Justice for the People

18“Appoint judges and officials for yourselves from each of your tribes in all the
towns the LORD your God is giving you.
They must judge the people fairly. 19You
must never twist justice or show partiality.
Never accept a bribe, for bribes blind the
eyes of the wise and corrupt the decisions
of the godly. 20Let true justice prevail, so you
may live and occupy the land that the LORD
your God is giving you.

21“You must never set up a wooden
Asherah pole beside the altar you build
for the LORD your God. 22And never set up
sacred pillars for worship, for the LORD your
God hates them.

17 “Never sacrifice sick or defective
cattle, sheep, or goats to the LORD
your God, for he detests such gifts.

2“When you begin living in the towns
the LORD your God is giving you, a man
or woman among you might do evil in the
sight of the LORD your God and violate the
covenant. 3For instance, they might serve
other gods or worship the sun, the moon,
or any of the stars—the forces of heaven—
which I have strictly forbidden. 4When
you hear about it, investigate the matter
thoroughly. If it is true that this detestable
thing has been done in Israel, 5then the
man or woman who has committed such
an evil act must be taken to the gates of the
town and stoned to death. 6But never put
a person to death on the testimony of only
one witness. There must always be two or
three witnesses. 7The witnesses must throw
the first stones, and then all the people may
join in. In this way, you will purge the evil
from among you.

8“Suppose a case arises in a local court
that is too hard for you to decide—for
instance, whether someone is guilty of
murder or only of manslaughter, or a difficult lawsuit, or a case involving different
kinds of assault. Take such legal cases to the
place the LORD your God will choose, 9and
present them to the Levitical priests or the
judge on duty at that time. They will hear
the case and declare the verdict. 10You must
carry out the verdict they announce and
the sentence they prescribe at the place the
LORD chooses. You must do exactly what
they say. 11After they have interpreted the
law and declared their verdict, the sentence
they impose must be fully executed; do not
modify it in any way. 12Anyone arrogant
enough to reject the verdict of the judge or of
the priest who represents the LORD your God
must die. In this way you will purge the evil
from Israel. 13Then everyone else will hear
about it and be afraid to act so arrogantly.

Guidelines for a King

14“You are about to enter the land the LORD
your God is giving you. When you take it
over and settle there, you may think, ‘We
should select a king to rule over us like the
other nations around us.’ 15If this happens,
be sure to select as king the man the LORD
your God chooses. You must appoint a
fellow Israelite; he may not be a foreigner.

16“The king must not build up a large
stable of horses for himself or send his
people to Egypt to buy horses, for the LORD
has told you, ‘You must never return to
Egypt.’ 17The king must not take many wives
for himself, because they will turn his heart
away from the LORD. And he must not accumulate large amounts of wealth in silver
and gold for himself.

18 “When he sits on the throne as king, he must copy for himself this body of instruction on a scroll in the presence of the Levitical priests. 19 He must always keep that copy with him and read it daily as long as he lives. That way he will learn to fear the LORD his God by obeying all the terms of these instructions and decrees. 20 This regular reading will prevent him from becoming proud and acting as if he is above his fellow citizens. It will also prevent him from turning away from these commands in the smallest way. And it will ensure that he and his descendants will reign for many generations in Israel.

Gifts for the Priests and Levites

18 “Remember that the Levitical priests—that is, the whole of the tribe of Levi—will receive no allotment of land among the other tribes in Israel. Instead, the priests and Levites will eat from the special gifts given to the LORD, for that is their share. 2 They will have no land of their own among the Israelites. The LORD himself is their special possession, just as he promised them.

3 “These are the parts the priests may claim as their share from the cattle, sheep, and goats that the people bring as offerings: the shoulder, the cheeks, and the stomach. 4 You must also give to the priests the first share of the grain, the new wine, the olive oil, and the wool at shearing time. 5 For the LORD your God chose the tribe of Levi out of all your tribes to minister in the LORD’s name forever.

6 “Suppose a Levite chooses to move from his town in Israel, wherever he is living, to the place the LORD chooses for worship. 7 He may minister there in the name of the LORD his God, just like all his fellow Levites who are serving the LORD there. 8 He may eat his share of the sacrifices and offerings, even if he also receives support from his family.

A Call to Holy Living

9 “When you enter the land the LORD your God is giving you, be very careful not to imitate the detestable customs of the nations living there. 10 For example, never sacrifice your son or daughter as a burnt offering.* And do not let your people practice fortune-telling, or use sorcery, or interpret omens, or engage in witchcraft, 11 or cast spells, or function as mediums or psychics, or call forth the spirits of the dead. 12 Anyone who does these things is detestable to the LORD. It is because the other nations have done these detestable things that the LORD your God will drive them out ahead of you. 13 But you must be blameless before the LORD your God. 14 The nations you are about to displace consult sorcerers and fortune-tellers, but the LORD your God forbids you to do such things.”

True and False Prophets

15 Moses continued, “The LORD your God will raise up for you a prophet like me from among your fellow Israelites. You must listen to him. 16 For this is what you yourselves requested of the LORD your God when you were assembled at Mount Sinai.* You said, ‘Don’t let us hear the voice of the LORD our God anymore or see this blazing fire, for we will die.’

17 “Then the LORD said to me, ‘What they have said is right. 18 I will raise up a prophet like you from among their fellow Israelites. I will put my words in his mouth, and he will tell the people everything I command him. 19 I will personally deal with anyone who will not listen to the messages the prophet proclaims on my behalf. 20 But any prophet who falsely claims to speak in my name or who speaks in the name of another god must die.’

21 “But you may wonder, ‘How will we know whether or not a prophecy is from the LORD?’ 22 If the prophet speaks in the LORD’s name but his prediction does not happen or come true, you will know that the LORD did not give that message. That prophet has spoken without my authority and need not be feared.

Cities of Refuge

19 “When the LORD your God destroys the nations whose land he is giving you, you will take over their land and settle

16:13 Or *Festival of Booths,* or *Festival of Tabernacles;* also in 16:16. This was earlier called the Festival of the Final Harvest or Festival of Ingathering (see Exod 23:16b). It is celebrated today as Sukkot (or Succoth). **18:10** Or *never make your son or daughter pass through the fire.* **18:16** Hebrew *Horeb,* another name for Sinai.

▸ **18:9-14** *See* ***The occult,*** *page 337.* **18:17-22** *See* ***False prophecy,*** *page 911.*

in their towns and homes. 2 Then you must set apart three cities of refuge in the land the LORD your God is giving you. 3 Survey the territory,* and divide the land the LORD your God is giving you into three districts, with one of these cities in each district. Then anyone who has killed someone can flee to one of the cities of refuge for safety.

4 "If someone kills another person unintentionally, without previous hostility, the slayer may flee to any of these cities to live in safety. 5 For example, suppose someone goes into the forest with a neighbor to cut wood. And suppose one of them swings an ax to chop down a tree, and the ax head flies off the handle, killing the other person. In such cases, the slayer may flee to one of the cities of refuge to live in safety.

6 "If the distance to the nearest city of refuge is too far, an enraged avenger might be able to chase down and kill the person who caused the death. Then the slayer would die unfairly, since he had never shown hostility toward the person who died. 7 That is why I am commanding you to set aside three cities of refuge.

8 "And if the LORD your God enlarges your territory, as he swore to your ancestors, and gives you all the land he promised them, 9 you must designate three additional cities of refuge. (He will give you this land if you are careful to obey all the commands I have given you—if you always love the LORD your God and walk in his ways.) 10 That way you will prevent the death of innocent people in the land the LORD your God is giving you as your special possession. You will not be held responsible for the death of innocent people.

11 "But suppose someone is hostile toward a neighbor and deliberately ambushes and murders him and then flees to one of the cities of refuge. 12 In that case, the elders of the murderer's hometown must send agents to the city of refuge to bring him back and hand him over to the dead person's avenger to be put to death. 13 Do not feel sorry for that murderer! Purge from Israel the guilt of murdering innocent people; then all will go well with you.

Concern for Justice

14 "When you arrive in the land the LORD your God is giving you as your special possession, you must never steal anyone's land by moving the boundary markers your ancestors set up to mark their property.

15 "You must not convict anyone of a crime on the testimony of only one witness. The facts of the case must be established by the testimony of two or three witnesses.

16 "If a malicious witness comes forward and accuses someone of a crime, 17 then both the accuser and accused must appear before the LORD by coming to the priests and judges in office at that time. 18 The judges must investigate the case thoroughly. If the accuser has brought false charges against his fellow Israelite, 19 you must impose on the accuser the sentence he intended for the other person. In this way, you will purge such evil from among you. 20 Then the rest of the people will hear about it and be afraid to do such an evil thing. 21 You must show no pity for the guilty! Your rule should be life for life, eye for eye, tooth for tooth, hand for hand, foot for foot.

Regulations concerning War

20 "When you go out to fight your enemies and you face horses and chariots and an army greater than your own, do not be afraid. The LORD your God, who brought you out of the land of Egypt, is with you! 2 When you prepare for battle, the priest must come forward to speak to the

Cities of refuge

In order to prevent vigilantes from taking the law into their own hands, Moses provided cities of refuge to which anyone who had killed someone accidentally could flee (Deuteronomy 19:1-13). These cities were to be established in easily accessible locations, with provision for more if ever Israel's territory expanded. In these cities those taking refuge could stay safely until they had the opportunity for a fair trial. Joshua 20 tells of the six cities that were eventually chosen.

troops. 3He will say to them, 'Listen to me,
all you men of Israel! Do not be afraid as you
go out to fight your enemies today! Do not
lose heart or panic or tremble before them.
4For the LORD your God is going with you!
He will fight for you against your enemies,
and he will give you victory!'

5"Then the officers of the army must
address the troops and say, 'Has anyone
here just built a new house but not yet dedicated it? If so, you may go home! You might
be killed in the battle, and someone else
would dedicate your house. 6Has anyone
here just planted a vineyard but not yet
eaten any of its fruit? If so, you may go
home! You might die in battle, and someone
else would eat the first fruit. 7Has anyone
here just become engaged to a woman but
not yet married her? Well, you may go home
and get married! You might die in the battle,
and someone else would marry her.'

8"Then the officers will also say, 'Is
anyone here afraid or worried? If you are,
you may go home before you frighten
anyone else.' 9When the officers have finished speaking to their troops, they will
appoint the unit commanders.

10"As you approach a town to attack it, you
must first offer its people terms for peace. 11If
they accept your terms and open the gates to
you, then all the people inside will serve you
in forced labor. 12But if they refuse to make
peace and prepare to fight, you must attack
the town. 13When the LORD your God hands
the town over to you, use your swords to kill
every man in the town. 14But you may keep
for yourselves all the women, children, livestock, and other plunder. You may enjoy the
plunder from your enemies that the LORD
your God has given you.

15"But these instructions apply only
to distant towns, not to the towns of the
nations in the land you will enter. 16In those
towns that the LORD your God is giving you
as a special possession, destroy every living
thing. 17You must completely destroy* the
Hittites, Amorites, Canaanites, Perizzites,
Hivites, and Jebusites, just as the LORD
your God has commanded you. 18This will
prevent the people of the land from teaching you to imitate their detestable customs
in the worship of their gods, which would
cause you to sin deeply against the LORD
your God.

19"When you are attacking a town and
the war drags on, you must not cut down
the trees with your axes. You may eat the
fruit, but do not cut down the trees. Are the
trees your enemies, that you should attack
them? 20You may only cut down trees that
you know are not valuable for food. Use
them to make the equipment you need to
attack the enemy town until it falls.

Cleansing for Unsolved Murder

21 "When you are in the land the LORD
your God is giving you, someone may
be found murdered in a field, and you don't
know who committed the murder. 2In such a
case, your elders and judges must measure
the distance from the site of the crime to the
nearby towns. 3When the nearest town has
been determined, that town's elders must
select from the herd a heifer that has never
been trained or yoked to a plow. 4They must
lead it down to a valley that has not been
plowed or planted and that has a stream
running through it. There in the valley they
must break the heifer's neck. 5Then the Levitical priests must step forward, for the
LORD your God has chosen them to minister before him and to pronounce blessings
in the LORD's name. They are to decide all
legal and criminal cases.

6"The elders of the town must wash their
hands over the heifer whose neck was
broken. 7Then they must say, 'Our hands did
not shed this person's blood, nor did we see it
happen. 8O LORD, forgive your people Israel
whom you have redeemed. Do not charge
your people with the guilt of murdering an
innocent person.' Then they will be absolved
of the guilt of this person's blood. 9By following these instructions, you will do what is
right in the LORD's sight and will cleanse the
guilt of murder from your community.

Marriage to a Captive Woman

10"Suppose you go out to war against your
enemies and the LORD your God hands
them over to you, and you take some of
them as captives. 11And suppose you see
among the captives a beautiful woman, and
you are attracted to her and want to marry
her. 12If this happens, you may take her to
your home, where she must shave her head,
cut her nails, 13and change the clothes she

19:3 Or *Keep the roads in good repair.* **20:17** The Hebrew term used here refers to the complete consecration of things or people to the LORD, either by destroying them or by giving them as an offering.

was wearing when she was captured. She
will stay in your home, but let her mourn
for her father and mother for a full month.
Then you may marry her, and you will be
her husband and she will be your wife. 14But
if you marry her and she does not please
you, you must let her go free. You may not
sell her or treat her as a slave, for you have
humiliated her.

Rights of the Firstborn

15"Suppose a man has two wives, but he
loves one and not the other, and both have
given him sons. And suppose the firstborn
son is the son of the wife he does not love.
16When the man divides his inheritance, he
may not give the larger inheritance to his
younger son, the son of the wife he loves, as
if he were the firstborn son. 17He must recognize the rights of his oldest son, the son
of the wife he does not love, by giving him
a double portion. He is the first son of his
father's virility, and the rights of the firstborn belong to him.

Dealing with a Rebellious Son

18"Suppose a man has a stubborn and rebellious son who will not obey his father
or mother, even though they discipline
him. 19In such a case, the father and mother
must take the son to the elders as they hold
court at the town gate. 20The parents must
say to the elders, 'This son of ours is stubborn and rebellious and refuses to obey. He
is a glutton and a drunkard.' 21Then all the
men of his town must stone him to death.
In this way, you will purge this evil from
among you, and all Israel will hear about
it and be afraid.

Various Regulations

22"If someone has committed a crime
worthy of death and is executed and hung
on a tree,* 23the body must not remain
hanging from the tree overnight. You must
bury the body that same day, for anyone
who is hung* is cursed in the sight of God.
In this way, you will prevent the defilement
of the land the LORD your God is giving you
as your special possession.

22

"If you see your neighbor's ox or
sheep or goat wandering away,
don't ignore your responsibility.* Take it
back to its owner. 2If its owner does not live
nearby or you don't know who the owner
is, take it to your place and keep it until
the owner comes looking for it. Then you
must return it. 3Do the same if you find your
neighbor's donkey, clothing, or anything
else your neighbor loses. Don't ignore your
responsibility.

4"If you see that your neighbor's donkey
or ox has collapsed on the road, do not look
the other way. Go and help your neighbor
get it back on its feet!

5"A woman must not put on men's clothing, and a man must not wear women's
clothing. Anyone who does this is detestable in the sight of the LORD your God.

6"If you happen to find a bird's nest in a
tree or on the ground, and there are young
ones or eggs in it with the mother sitting in
the nest, do not take the mother with the
young. 7You may take the young, but let the
mother go, so that you may prosper and
enjoy a long life.

8"When you build a new house, you must
build a railing around the edge of its flat
roof. That way you will not be considered
guilty of murder if someone falls from the
roof.

9"You must not plant any other crop
between the rows of your vineyard. If you
do, you are forbidden to use either the
grapes from the vineyard or the other crop.

10"You must not plow with an ox and a
donkey harnessed together.

11"You must not wear clothing made of
wool and linen woven together.

12"You must put four tassels on the hem of
the cloak with which you cover yourself—on
the front, back, and sides.

Regulations for Sexual Purity

13"Suppose a man marries a woman, but
after sleeping with her, he turns against
her 14and publicly accuses her of shameful conduct, saying, 'When I married this
woman, I discovered she was not a virgin.'
15Then the woman's father and mother must
bring the proof of her virginity to the elders
as they hold court at the town gate. 16Her
father must say to them, 'I gave my daughter to this man to be his wife, and now he
has turned against her. 17He has accused her
of shameful conduct, saying, "I discovered
that your daughter was not a virgin." But
here is the proof of my daughter's virginity.'
Then they must spread her bed sheet before

the elders. 18 The elders must then take the
man and punish him. 19 They must also fine
him 100 pieces of silver,* which he must
pay to the woman's father because he publicly accused a virgin of Israel of shameful
conduct. The woman will then remain the
man's wife, and he may never divorce her.
20 "But suppose the man's accusations are
true, and he can show that she was not a
virgin. 21 The woman must be taken to the
door of her father's home, and there the
men of the town must stone her to death,
for she has committed a disgraceful crime
in Israel by being promiscuous while living
in her parents' home. In this way, you will
purge this evil from among you.
22 "If a man is discovered committing
adultery, both he and the woman must die.
In this way, you will purge Israel of such
evil.
23 "Suppose a man meets a young woman,
a virgin who is engaged to be married, and
he has sexual intercourse with her. If this
happens within a town, 24 you must take
both of them to the gates of that town and
stone them to death. The woman is guilty
because she did not scream for help. The
man must die because he violated another
man's wife. In this way, you will purge this
evil from among you.
25 "But if the man meets the engaged
woman out in the country, and he rapes her,
then only the man must die. 26 Do nothing to
the young woman; she has committed no
crime worthy of death. She is as innocent
as a murder victim. 27 Since the man raped
her out in the country, it must be assumed
that she screamed, but there was no one to
rescue her.
28 "Suppose a man has intercourse with
a young woman who is a virgin but is not
engaged to be married. If they are discovered, 29 he must pay her father fifty pieces
of silver.* Then he must marry the young
woman because he violated her, and he
may never divorce her as long as he lives.
30* "A man must not marry his father's
former wife, for this would violate his
father.

Regulations concerning Worship

23 1* "If a man's testicles are crushed or
his penis is cut off, he may not be
admitted to the assembly of the LORD.
2 "If a person is illegitimate by birth,
neither he nor his descendants for ten generations may be admitted to the assembly
of the LORD.
3 "No Ammonite or Moabite or any of their
descendants for ten generations may be admitted to the assembly of the LORD. 4 These
nations did not welcome you with food and
water when you came out of Egypt. Instead,
they hired Balaam son of Beor from Pethor
in distant Aram-naharaim to curse you.
5 But the LORD your God refused to listen to
Balaam. He turned the intended curse into
a blessing because the LORD your God loves
you. 6 As long as you live, you must never
promote the welfare and prosperity of the
Ammonites or Moabites.
7 "Do not detest the Edomites or the Egyptians, because the Edomites are your relatives and you lived as foreigners among the
Egyptians. 8 The third generation of Edomites and Egyptians may enter the assembly
of the LORD.

Miscellaneous Regulations

9 "When you go to war against your enemies,
be sure to stay away from anything that is
impure.
10 "Any man who becomes ceremonially
defiled because of a nocturnal emission
must leave the camp and stay away all day.
11 Toward evening he must bathe himself,
and at sunset he may return to the camp.
12 "You must have a designated area outside
the camp where you can go to relieve yourself.
13 Each of you must have a spade as part of
your equipment. Whenever you relieve yourself, dig a hole with the spade and cover the
excrement. 14 The camp must be holy, for the
LORD your God moves around in your camp
to protect you and to defeat your enemies. He
must not see any shameful thing among you,
or he will turn away from you.
15 "If slaves should escape from their
masters and take refuge with you, you
must not hand them over to their masters.
16 Let them live among you in any town they
choose, and do not oppress them.
17 "No Israelite, whether man or woman,
may become a temple prostitute. 18 When you

21:22 Or *impaled on a pole;* similarly in 21:23. **21:23** Greek version reads *for everyone who is hung on a tree.* Compare Gal 3:13. **22:1** Hebrew *don't hide yourself;* similarly in 22:3. **22:19** Hebrew *100 [shekels] of silver,* about 2.5 pounds or 1.1 kilograms in weight. **22:29** Hebrew *50 [shekels] of silver,* about 1.25 pounds or 570 grams in weight. **22:30** Verse 22:30 is numbered 23:1 in Hebrew text. **23:1** Verses 23:1-25 are numbered 23:2-26 in Hebrew text.

are bringing an offering to fulfill a vow, you must not bring to the house of the LORD your God any offering from the earnings of a prostitute, whether a man* or a woman, for both are detestable to the LORD your God.

19“Do not charge interest on the loans you make to a fellow Israelite, whether you loan money, or food, or anything else. 20You may charge interest to foreigners, but you may not charge interest to Israelites, so that the LORD your God may bless you in everything you do in the land you are about to enter and occupy.

21“When you make a vow to the LORD your God, be prompt in fulfilling whatever you promised him. For the LORD your God demands that you promptly fulfill all your vows, or you will be guilty of sin. 22However, it is not a sin to refrain from making a vow. 23But once you have voluntarily made a vow, be careful to fulfill your promise to the LORD your God.

24“When you enter your neighbor’s vineyard, you may eat your fill of grapes, but you must not carry any away in a basket. 25And when you enter your neighbor’s field of grain, you may pluck the heads of grain with your hand, but you must not harvest it with a sickle.

24 “Suppose a man marries a woman but she does not please him. Having discovered something wrong with her, he writes a document of divorce, hands it to her, and sends her away from his house. 2When she leaves his house, she is free to marry another man. 3But if the second husband also turns against her, writes a document of divorce, hands it to her, and sends her away, or if he dies, 4the first husband may not marry her again, for she has been defiled. That would be detestable to the LORD. You must not bring guilt upon the land the LORD your God is giving you as a special possession.

5“A newly married man must not be drafted into the army or be given any other official responsibilities. He must be free to spend one year at home, bringing happiness to the wife he has married.

6“It is wrong to take a set of millstones, or even just the upper millstone, as security for a loan, for the owner uses it to make a living.

7“If anyone kidnaps a fellow Israelite and treats him as a slave or sells him, the kidnapper must die. In this way, you will purge the evil from among you.

8“In all cases involving serious skin diseases,* be careful to follow the instructions of the Levitical priests; obey all the commands I have given them. 9Remember what the LORD your God did to Miriam as you were coming from Egypt.

10“If you lend anything to your neighbor, do not enter his house to pick up the item he is giving as security. 11You must wait outside while he goes in and brings it out to you. 12If your neighbor is poor and gives you his cloak as security for a loan, do not keep the cloak overnight. 13Return the cloak to its owner by sunset so he can stay warm through the night and bless you, and the LORD your God will count you as righteous.

14“Never take advantage of poor and destitute laborers, whether they are fellow Israelites or foreigners living in your towns. 15You must pay them their wages each day before sunset because they are poor and are

Provision for the poor

Many Old Testament laws command God’s people to show practical concern for the poor and needy and not to be “hard-hearted or tightfisted toward them” (Deuteronomy 15:7). Here (24:19-22), they are told not to return to collect sheaves of grain left in the fields or to go back a second time to pick olives or grapes, but to leave them all for the poor. Elsewhere they are told not to harvest to the edges of their fields, but to leave something for the poor (Leviticus 19:9), a practice that Ruth benefited from (Ruth 2:2). The reason for this was to remind the Israelites that they themselves were once in great need when they were slaves in Egypt (Deuteronomy 24:22).

▶ *See also **Poverty**, page 1142.*

counting on it. If you don't, they might cry out to the LORD against you, and it would be counted against you as sin.

16“Parents must not be put to death for the sins of their children, nor children for the sins of their parents. Those deserving to die must be put to death for their own crimes.

17“True justice must be given to foreigners living among you and to orphans, and you must never accept a widow's garment as security for her debt. 18Always remember that you were slaves in Egypt and that the LORD your God redeemed you from your slavery. That is why I have given you this command.

19“When you are harvesting your crops and forget to bring in a bundle of grain from your field, don't go back to get it. Leave it for the foreigners, orphans, and widows. Then the LORD your God will bless you in all you do. 20When you beat the olives from your olive trees, don't go over the boughs twice. Leave the remaining olives for the foreigners, orphans, and widows. 21When you gather the grapes in your vineyard, don't glean the vines after they are picked. Leave the remaining grapes for the foreigners, orphans, and widows. 22Remember that you were slaves in the land of Egypt. That is why I am giving you this command.

25 “Suppose two people take a dispute to court, and the judges declare that one is right and the other is wrong. 2If the person in the wrong is sentenced to be flogged, the judge must command him to lie down and be beaten in his presence with the number of lashes appropriate to the crime. 3But never give more than forty lashes; more than forty lashes would publicly humiliate your neighbor.

4“You must not muzzle an ox to keep it from eating as it treads out the grain.

5“If two brothers are living together on the same property and one of them dies without a son, his widow may not be married to anyone from outside the family. Instead, her husband's brother should marry her and have intercourse with her to fulfill the duties of a brother-in-law. 6The first son she bears to him will be considered the son of the dead brother, so that his name will not be forgotten in Israel.

7“But if the man refuses to marry his brother's widow, she must go to the town gate and say to the elders assembled there, ‘My husband's brother refuses to preserve his brother's name in Israel—he refuses to fulfill the duties of a brother-in-law by marrying me.’ 8The elders of the town will then summon him and talk with him. If he still refuses and says, ‘I don't want to marry her,’ 9the widow must walk over to him in the presence of the elders, pull his sandal from his foot, and spit in his face. Then she must declare, ‘This is what happens to a man who refuses to provide his brother with children.’ 10Ever afterward in Israel his family will be referred to as ‘the family of the man whose sandal was pulled off’!

11“If two Israelite men get into a fight and the wife of one tries to rescue her husband by grabbing the testicles of the other man, 12you must cut off her hand. Show her no pity.

13“You must use accurate scales when you weigh out merchandise, 14and you must use full and honest measures. 15Yes, always use honest weights and measures, so that you may enjoy a long life in the land the LORD your God is giving you. 16All who cheat with dishonest weights and measures are detestable to the LORD your God.

17“Never forget what the Amalekites did to you as you came from Egypt. 18They attacked you when you were exhausted and weary, and they struck down those who were straggling behind. They had no fear of God. 19Therefore, when the LORD your God has given you rest from all your enemies in the land he is giving you as a special possession, you must destroy the Amalekites and erase their memory from under heaven. Never forget this!

Harvest Offerings and Tithes

26 “When you enter the land the LORD your God is giving you as a special possession and you have conquered it and settled there, 2put some of the first produce from each crop you harvest into a basket and bring it to the designated place

23:18 Hebrew *a dog.* **24:8** Traditionally rendered *leprosy.* The Hebrew word used here can describe various skin diseases.

▸ **24:17** *See **Widows**, page 400.* **25:13** *See **Honesty**, page 707.*

of worship—the place the LORD your God
chooses for his name to be honored. 3Go
to the priest in charge at that time and say
to him, 'With this gift I acknowledge to the
LORD your God that I have entered the land
he swore to our ancestors he would give us.'
4The priest will then take the basket from
your hand and set it before the altar of the
LORD your God.
5"You must then say in the presence of
the LORD your God, 'My ancestor Jacob was
a wandering Aramean who went to live as a
foreigner in Egypt. His family arrived few in
number, but in Egypt they became a large
and mighty nation. 6When the Egyptians
oppressed and humiliated us by making
us their slaves, 7we cried out to the LORD,
the God of our ancestors. He heard our cries
and saw our hardship, toil, and oppression.
8So the LORD brought us out of Egypt with
a strong hand and powerful arm, with overwhelming terror, and with miraculous signs
and wonders. 9He brought us to this place
and gave us this land flowing with milk and
honey! 10And now, O LORD, I have brought
you the first portion of the harvest you have
given me from the ground.' Then place the
produce before the LORD your God, and bow
to the ground in worship before him. 11After-
ward you may go and celebrate because of
all the good things the LORD your God has
given to you and your household. Remember to include the Levites and the foreigners
living among you in the celebration.
12"Every third year you must offer a special
tithe of your crops. In this year of the special
tithe you must give your tithes to the Levites,
foreigners, orphans, and widows, so that
they will have enough to eat in your towns.
13Then you must declare in the presence of
the LORD your God, 'I have taken the sacred
gift from my house and have given it to the
Levites, foreigners, orphans, and widows,
just as you commanded me. I have not violated or forgotten any of your commands.
14I have not eaten any of it while in mourning;
I have not handled it while I was ceremonially unclean; and I have not offered any of it
to the dead. I have obeyed the LORD my God
and have done everything you commanded
me. 15Now look down from your holy dwelling
place in heaven and bless your people Israel
and the land you swore to our ancestors to
give us—a land flowing with milk and honey.'

A Call to Obey the LORD's Commands

16"Today the LORD your God has commanded you to obey all these decrees and
regulations. So be careful to obey them
wholeheartedly. 17You have declared today
that the LORD is your God. And you have
promised to walk in his ways, and to obey
his decrees, commands, and regulations,
and to do everything he tells you. 18The
LORD has declared today that you are his
people, his own special treasure, just as
he promised, and that you must obey all
his commands. 19And if you do, he will set
you high above all the other nations he has
made. Then you will receive praise, honor,
and renown. You will be a nation that is holy
to the LORD your God, just as he promised."

The Altar on Mount Ebal

27 Then Moses and the leaders of Israel
gave this charge to the people: "Obey
all these commands that I am giving you
today. 2When you cross the Jordan River and
enter the land the LORD your God is giving
you, set up some large stones and coat

The Arameans

As Moses outlined a prayer for the Israelites that looked back on their history, he began with the words, "My ancestor Jacob was a wandering Aramean" (Deuteronomy 26:5). The Arameans were a seminomadic group scattered across Syria and Mesopotamia, and it was from this people group that the Israelite patriarchs came. Their nomadic nature was reflected in the life of Jacob, who wandered to Haran and back (Genesis 27–35), having married two Aramean women, and finally to Egypt (Genesis 46:3-7). Later, in the period of Israel's kings, Arameans (or Syrians) had formed powerful city-states with which Israel had mixed relationships.

them with plaster. [3]Write this whole body
of instruction on them when you cross the
river to enter the land the LORD your God is
giving you—a land flowing with milk and
honey, just as the LORD, the God of your ancestors, promised you. [4]When you cross the
Jordan, set up these stones at Mount Ebal
and coat them with plaster, as I am commanding you today.
[5]"Then build an altar there to the LORD
your God, using natural, uncut stones. You
must not shape the stones with an iron tool.
[6]Build the altar of uncut stones, and use it to
offer burnt offerings to the LORD your God.
[7]Also sacrifice peace offerings on it, and celebrate by feasting there before the LORD your
God. [8]You must clearly write all these instructions on the stones coated with plaster."
[9]Then Moses and the Levitical priests addressed all Israel as follows: "O Israel, be
quiet and listen! Today you have become
the people of the LORD your God. [10]So you
must obey the LORD your God by keeping
all these commands and decrees that I am
giving you today."

Curses from Mount Ebal

[11]That same day Moses also gave this charge
to the people: [12]"When you cross the Jordan
River, the tribes of Simeon, Levi, Judah, Issachar, Joseph, and Benjamin must stand
on Mount Gerizim to proclaim a blessing
over the people. [13]And the tribes of Reuben,
Gad, Asher, Zebulun, Dan, and Naphtali
must stand on Mount Ebal to proclaim a
curse.
[14]"Then the Levites will shout to all the
people of Israel:

[15]'Cursed is anyone who carves or casts an idol and secretly sets it up. These idols, the work of craftsmen, are detestable to the LORD.'
And all the people will reply, 'Amen.'

[16]'Cursed is anyone who dishonors father or mother.'
And all the people will reply, 'Amen.'

[17]'Cursed is anyone who steals property from a neighbor by moving a boundary marker.'
And all the people will reply, 'Amen.'

[18]'Cursed is anyone who leads a blind person astray on the road.'
And all the people will reply, 'Amen.'

[19]'Cursed is anyone who denies justice to foreigners, orphans, or widows.'
And all the people will reply, 'Amen.'

[20]'Cursed is anyone who has sexual intercourse with one of his father's wives, for he has violated his father.'
And all the people will reply, 'Amen.'

[21]'Cursed is anyone who has sexual intercourse with an animal.'
And all the people will reply, 'Amen.'

[22]'Cursed is anyone who has sexual intercourse with his sister, whether she is the daughter of his father or his mother.'
And all the people will reply, 'Amen.'

[23]'Cursed is anyone who has sexual intercourse with his mother-in-law.'
And all the people will reply, 'Amen.'

[24]'Cursed is anyone who attacks a neighbor in secret.'
And all the people will reply, 'Amen.'

[25]'Cursed is anyone who accepts payment to kill an innocent person.'
And all the people will reply, 'Amen.'

[26]'Cursed is anyone who does not affirm and obey the terms of these instructions.'
And all the people will reply, 'Amen.'

Blessings for Obedience

28 "If you fully obey the LORD your God
and carefully keep all his commands
that I am giving you today, the LORD your
God will set you high above all the nations
of the world. [2]You will experience all these
blessings if you obey the LORD your God:

[3] Your towns and your fields
will be blessed.
[4] Your children and your crops
will be blessed.
The offspring of your herds and flocks
will be blessed.
[5] Your fruit baskets and breadboards
will be blessed.
[6] Wherever you go and whatever you do,
you will be blessed.

[7]"The LORD will conquer your enemies
when they attack you. They will attack you
from one direction, but they will scatter
from you in seven!

8"The LORD will guarantee a blessing on everything you do and will fill your storehouses with grain. The LORD your God will bless you in the land he is giving you.

9"If you obey the commands of the LORD your God and walk in his ways, the LORD will establish you as his holy people as he swore he would do. 10Then all the nations of the world will see that you are a people claimed by the LORD, and they will stand in awe of you.

11"The LORD will give you prosperity in the land he swore to your ancestors to give you, blessing you with many children, numerous livestock, and abundant crops. 12The LORD will send rain at the proper time from his rich treasury in the heavens and will bless all the work you do. You will lend to many nations, but you will never need to borrow from them. 13If you listen to these commands of the LORD your God that I am giving you today, and if you carefully obey them, the LORD will make you the head and not the tail, and you will always be on top and never at the bottom. 14You must not turn away from any of the commands I am giving you today, nor follow after other gods and worship them.

Curses for Disobedience

15"But if you refuse to listen to the LORD your God and do not obey all the commands and decrees I am giving you today, all these curses will come and overwhelm you:

16 Your towns and your fields
will be cursed.
17 Your fruit baskets and breadboards
will be cursed.
18 Your children and your crops
will be cursed.
The offspring of your herds and flocks
will be cursed.
19 Wherever you go and whatever you do,
you will be cursed.

20"The LORD himself will send on you curses, confusion, and frustration in everything you do, until at last you are completely destroyed for doing evil and abandoning me. 21The LORD will afflict you with diseases until none of you are left in the land you are about to enter and occupy. 22The LORD will strike you with wasting diseases, fever, and inflammation, with scorching heat and drought, and with blight and mildew. These disasters will pursue you until you die. 23The skies above will be as unyielding as bronze, and the earth beneath will be as hard as iron. 24The LORD will change the rain that falls on your land into powder, and dust will pour down from the sky until you are destroyed.

25"The LORD will cause you to be defeated by your enemies. You will attack your enemies from one direction, but you will scatter from them in seven! You will be an object of horror to all the kingdoms of the earth. 26Your corpses will be food for all

Disobedience

Disobedience is the refusal to submit to God. It first raises its head at the beginning of the human story when Adam and Eve, putting selfish desire first, chose to disobey God's command about not eating from the tree of the knowledge of good and evil, which led to their banishment from Eden and God's intimate presence.

While disobedience has many expressions, its origin is always the same: the sinfulness of the human heart, which wants to assert its independence and do as it pleases rather than as God directs us.

Disobedience always has dire consequences, as Moses outlined in Deuteronomy 28:15-68. The consequences may not always be seen immediately. For example, David thought he had gotten away with his disobedience in committing adultery with Bathsheba, but while God forgave him when he repented (2 Samuel 12:13), David lived with the consequences in his family for years to come.

While the Bible warns us of the dangers of disobedience, it also stresses the other side: the huge blessing that comes when we choose obedience to our heavenly Father, who always knows what is best for us.

the scavenging birds and wild animals, and no one will be there to chase them away.

[27]"The LORD will afflict you with the boils of Egypt and with tumors, scurvy, and the itch, from which you cannot be cured. [28]The LORD will strike you with madness, blindness, and panic. [29]You will grope around in broad daylight like a blind person groping in the darkness, but you will not find your way. You will be oppressed and robbed continually, and no one will come to save you.

[30]"You will be engaged to a woman, but another man will sleep with her. You will build a house, but someone else will live in it. You will plant a vineyard, but you will never enjoy its fruit. [31]Your ox will be butchered before your eyes, but you will not eat a single bite of the meat. Your donkey will be taken from you, never to be returned. Your sheep and goats will be given to your enemies, and no one will be there to help you. [32]You will watch as your sons and daughters are taken away as slaves. Your heart will break for them, but you won't be able to help them. [33]A foreign nation you have never heard about will eat the crops you worked so hard to grow. You will suffer under constant oppression and harsh treatment. [34]You will go mad because of all the tragedy you see around you. [35]The LORD will cover your knees and legs with incurable boils. In fact, you will be covered from head to foot.

[36]"The LORD will exile you and your king to a nation unknown to you and your ancestors. There in exile you will worship gods of wood and stone! [37]You will become an object of horror, ridicule, and mockery among all the nations to which the LORD sends you.

[38]"You will plant much but harvest little, for locusts will eat your crops. [39]You will plant vineyards and care for them, but you will not drink the wine or eat the grapes, for worms will destroy the vines. [40]You will grow olive trees throughout your land, but you will never use the olive oil, for the fruit will drop before it ripens. [41]You will have sons and daughters, but you will lose them, for they will be led away into captivity. [42]Swarms of insects will destroy your trees and crops.

[43]"The foreigners living among you will become stronger and stronger, while you become weaker and weaker. [44]They will lend money to you, but you will not lend to them. They will be the head, and you will be the tail!

[45]"If you refuse to listen to the LORD your God and to obey the commands and decrees he has given you, all these curses will pursue and overtake you until you are destroyed. [46]These horrors will serve as a sign and warning among you and your descendants forever. [47]If you do not serve the LORD your God with joy and enthusiasm for the abundant benefits you have received, [48]you will serve your enemies whom the LORD will send against you. You will be left hungry, thirsty, naked, and lacking in everything. The LORD will put an iron yoke on your neck, oppressing you harshly until he has destroyed you.

[49]"The LORD will bring a distant nation against you from the end of the earth, and it will swoop down on you like a vulture. It is a nation whose language you do not understand, [50]a fierce and heartless nation that shows no respect for the old and no pity for the young. [51]Its armies will devour your livestock and crops, and you will be destroyed. They will leave you no grain, new wine, olive oil, calves, or lambs, and you will starve to death. [52]They will attack your cities until all the fortified walls in your land—the walls you trusted to protect you—are knocked down. They will attack all the towns in the land the LORD your God has given you.

[53]"The siege and terrible distress of the enemy's attack will be so severe that you will eat the flesh of your own sons and daughters, whom the LORD your God has given you. [54]The most tenderhearted man among you will have no compassion for his own brother, his beloved wife, and his surviving children. [55]He will refuse to share with them the flesh he is devouring—the flesh of one of his own children—because he has nothing else to eat during the siege and terrible distress that your enemy will inflict on all your towns. [56]The most tender and delicate woman among you—so delicate she would not so much as touch the ground with her foot—will be selfish toward the husband she loves and toward her own son or daughter. [57]She will hide from them the afterbirth and the new baby she has borne, so that she herself can secretly eat them. She will have nothing else to eat during the siege and terrible distress that your enemy will inflict on all your towns.

[58]"If you refuse to obey all the words of

instruction that are written in this book, and
if you do not fear the glorious and awesome
name of the LORD your God, 59 then the LORD
will overwhelm you and your children with
indescribable plagues. These plagues will
be intense and without relief, making you
miserable and unbearably sick. 60 He will
afflict you with all the diseases of Egypt that
you feared so much, and you will have no
relief. 61 The LORD will afflict you with every
sickness and plague there is, even those not
mentioned in this Book of Instruction, until
you are destroyed. 62 Though you become as
numerous as the stars in the sky, few of you
will be left because you would not listen to
the LORD your God.

63 "Just as the LORD has found great pleasure in causing you to prosper and multiply,
the LORD will find pleasure in destroying
you. You will be torn from the land you are
about to enter and occupy. 64 For the LORD
will scatter you among all the nations from
one end of the earth to the other. There you
will worship foreign gods that neither you
nor your ancestors have known, gods made
of wood and stone! 65 There among those
nations you will find no peace or place to
rest. And the LORD will cause your heart
to tremble, your eyesight to fail, and your
soul to despair. 66 Your life will constantly
hang in the balance. You will live night and
day in fear, unsure if you will survive. 67 In
the morning you will say, 'If only it were
night!' And in the evening you will say, 'If
only it were morning!' For you will be terrified by the awful horrors you see around
you. 68 Then the LORD will send you back to
Egypt in ships, to a destination I promised
you would never see again. There you will
offer to sell yourselves to your enemies as
slaves, but no one will buy you."

29 1* These are the terms of the covenant the LORD commanded Moses
to make with the Israelites while they were
in the land of Moab, in addition to the covenant he had made with them at Mount
Sinai.*

Moses Reviews the Covenant

2* Moses summoned all the Israelites and
said to them, "You have seen with your own
eyes everything the LORD did in the land of
Egypt to Pharaoh and to all his servants and
to his whole country— 3 all the great tests of
strength, the miraculous signs, and the
amazing wonders. 4 But to this day the LORD
has not given you minds that understand,
nor eyes that see, nor ears that hear! 5 For
forty years I led you through the wilderness,
yet your clothes and sandals did not wear
out. 6 You ate no bread and drank no wine
or other alcoholic drink, but he provided for
you so you would know that he is the LORD
your God.

7 "When we came here, King Sihon of
Heshbon and King Og of Bashan came out
to fight against us, but we defeated them.
8 We took their land and gave it to the tribes
of Reuben and Gad and to the half-tribe of
Manasseh as their grant of land.

9 "Therefore, obey the terms of this covenant so that you will prosper in everything
you do. 10 All of you—tribal leaders, elders,
officers, all the men of Israel—are standing today in the presence of the LORD your
God. 11 Your little ones and your wives are
with you, as well as the foreigners living
among you who chop your wood and carry
your water. 12 You are standing here today
to enter into the covenant of the LORD your
God. The LORD is making this covenant,
including the curses. 13 By entering into the
covenant today, he will establish you as his
people and confirm that he is your God, just
as he promised you and as he swore to your
ancestors Abraham, Isaac, and Jacob.

14 "But you are not the only ones with
whom I am making this covenant with its
curses. 15 I am making this covenant both
with you who stand here today in the presence of the LORD our God, and also with
the future generations who are not standing here today.

16 "You remember how we lived in the land
of Egypt and how we traveled through the
lands of enemy nations as we left. 17 You
have seen their detestable practices and
their idols* made of wood, stone, silver,
and gold. 18 I am making this covenant with
you so that no one among you—no man,
woman, clan, or tribe—will turn away from
the LORD our God to worship these gods of
other nations, and so that no root among
you bears bitter and poisonous fruit.

19 "Those who hear the warnings of
this curse should not congratulate themselves, thinking, 'I am safe, even though
I am following the desires of my own stubborn heart.' This would lead to utter ruin!

20The LORD will never pardon such people.
Instead his anger and jealousy will burn
against them. All the curses written in this
book will come down on them, and the
LORD will erase their names from under
heaven. 21The LORD will separate them from
all the tribes of Israel, to pour out on them
all the curses of the covenant recorded in
this Book of Instruction.

22"Then the generations to come, both
your own descendants and the foreigners
who come from distant lands, will see the
devastation of the land and the diseases
the LORD inflicts on it. 23They will exclaim,
'The whole land is devastated by sulfur and
salt. It is a wasteland with nothing planted
and nothing growing, not even a blade of
grass. It is like the cities of Sodom and Gomorrah, Admah and Zeboiim, which the
LORD destroyed in his intense anger.'

24"And all the surrounding nations will
ask, 'Why has the LORD done this to this
land? Why was he so angry?'

25"And the answer will be, 'This happened because the people of the land abandoned the covenant that the LORD, the God
of their ancestors, made with them when
he brought them out of the land of Egypt.
26Instead, they turned away to serve and
worship gods they had not known before,
gods that were not from the LORD. 27That is
why the LORD's anger has burned against
this land, bringing down on it every curse
recorded in this book. 28In great anger and
fury the LORD uprooted his people from
their land and banished them to another
land, where they still live today!'

29"The LORD our God has secrets known
to no one. We are not accountable for them,
but we and our children are accountable
forever for all that he has revealed to us,
so that we may obey all the terms of these
instructions.

A Call to Return to the LORD

30 "In the future, when you experience all these blessings and curses I
have listed for you, and when you are living
among the nations to which the LORD your
God has exiled you, take to heart all these
instructions. 2If at that time you and your
children return to the LORD your God, and
if you obey with all your heart and all your
soul all the commands I have given you
today, 3then the LORD your God will restore
your fortunes. He will have mercy on you
and gather you back from all the nations
where he has scattered you. 4Even though
you are banished to the ends of the earth,*
the LORD your God will gather you from
there and bring you back again. 5The LORD
your God will return you to the land that
belonged to your ancestors, and you will
possess that land again. Then he will make
you even more prosperous and numerous
than your ancestors!

6"The LORD your God will change your
heart* and the hearts of all your descendants, so that you will love him with all
your heart and soul and so you may live!
7The LORD your God will inflict all these
curses on your enemies and on those who
hate and persecute you. 8Then you will
again obey the LORD and keep all his commands that I am giving you today.

9"The LORD your God will then make
you successful in everything you do. He
will give you many children and numerous
livestock, and he will cause your fields to
produce abundant harvests, for the LORD
will again delight in being good to you as
he was to your ancestors. 10The LORD your
God will delight in you if you obey his
voice and keep the commands and decrees
written in this Book of Instruction, and if
you turn to the LORD your God with all your
heart and soul.

The Choice of Life or Death

11"This command I am giving you today is
not too difficult for you, and it is not beyond
your reach. 12It is not kept in heaven, so
distant that you must ask, 'Who will go up
to heaven and bring it down so we can hear
it and obey?' 13It is not kept beyond the sea,
so far away that you must ask, 'Who will
cross the sea to bring it to us so we can hear
it and obey?' 14No, the message is very close
at hand; it is on your lips and in your heart
so that you can obey it.

15"Now listen! Today I am giving you a
choice between life and death, between
prosperity and disaster. 16For I command
you this day to love the LORD your God and
to keep his commands, decrees, and regulations by walking in his ways. If you do this,

29:1a Verse 29:1 is numbered 28:69 in Hebrew text. **29:1b** Hebrew *Horeb*, another name for Sinai. **29:2** Verses 29:2-29 are numbered 29:1-28 in Hebrew text. **29:17** The Hebrew term (literally *round things*) probably alludes to dung. **30:4** Hebrew *of the heavens*. **30:6** Hebrew *circumcise your heart*.

you will live and multiply, and the LORD
your God will bless you and the land you
are about to enter and occupy.
17“But if your heart turns away and you
refuse to listen, and if you are drawn away to
serve and worship other gods, 18then I warn
you now that you will certainly be destroyed.
You will not live a long, good life in the land
you are crossing the Jordan to occupy.
19“Today I have given you the choice
between life and death, between blessings and curses. Now I call on heaven and
earth to witness the choice you make. Oh,
that you would choose life, so that you and
your descendants might live! 20You can
make this choice by loving the LORD your
God, obeying him, and committing yourself
firmly to him. This* is the key to your life.
And if you love and obey the LORD, you will
live long in the land the LORD swore to give
your ancestors Abraham, Isaac, and Jacob.”

Joshua Becomes Israel’s Leader

31 When Moses had finished giving
these instructions* to all the people
of Israel, 2he said, “I am now 120 years
old, and I am no longer able to lead you.
The LORD has told me, ‘You will not cross
the Jordan River.’ 3But the LORD your God
himself will cross over ahead of you. He will
destroy the nations living there, and you
will take possession of their land. Joshua
will lead you across the river, just as the
LORD promised.
4“The LORD will destroy the nations living
in the land, just as he destroyed Sihon and
Og, the kings of the Amorites. 5The LORD
will hand over to you the people who live
there, and you must deal with them as I
have commanded you. 6So be strong and
courageous! Do not be afraid and do not
panic before them. For the LORD your God
will personally go ahead of you. He will
neither fail you nor abandon you.”
7Then Moses called for Joshua, and as
all Israel watched, he said to him, “Be
strong and courageous! For you will lead
these people into the land that the LORD
swore to their ancestors he would give
them. You are the one who will divide it
among them as their grants of land. 8Do
not be afraid or discouraged, for the LORD
will personally go ahead of you. He will
be with you; he will neither fail you nor
abandon you.”

Public Reading of the Book of Instruction

9So Moses wrote this entire body of instruction in a book and gave it to the priests,
who carried the Ark of the LORD’s Covenant, and to the elders of Israel. 10Then
Moses gave them this command: “At the
end of every seventh year, the Year of
Release, during the Festival of Shelters,
11you must read this Book of Instruction to
all the people of Israel when they assemble
before the LORD your God at the place he
chooses. 12Call them all together—men,
women, children, and the foreigners living
in your towns—so they may hear this Book
of Instruction and learn to fear the LORD
your God and carefully obey all the terms
of these instructions. 13Do this so that your
children who have not known these instructions will hear them and will learn to
fear the LORD your God. Do this as long as
you live in the land you are crossing the
Jordan to occupy.”

Israel’s Disobedience Predicted

14Then the LORD said to Moses, “The time
has come for you to die. Call Joshua and
present yourselves at the Tabernacle,* so
that I may commission him there.” So Moses
and Joshua went and presented themselves
at the Tabernacle. 15And the LORD appeared
to them in a pillar of cloud that stood at the
entrance to the sacred tent.
16The LORD said to Moses, “You are about
to die and join your ancestors. After you are
gone, these people will begin to worship
foreign gods, the gods of the land where
they are going. They will abandon me and
break my covenant that I have made with
them. 17Then my anger will blaze forth
against them. I will abandon them, hiding
my face from them, and they will be devoured. Terrible trouble will come down on
them, and on that day they will say, ‘These
disasters have come down on us because
God is no longer among us!’ 18At that time
I will hide my face from them on account
of all the evil they commit by worshiping
other gods.
19“So write down the words of this song,
and teach it to the people of Israel. Help
them learn it, so it may serve as a witness for
me against them. 20For I will bring them into
the land I swore to give their ancestors—a
land flowing with milk and honey. There
they will become prosperous, eat all the

food they want, and become fat. But they
will begin to worship other gods; they will
despise me and break my covenant.
21 And
when great disasters come down on them,
this song will stand as evidence against
them, for it will never be forgotten by their
descendants. I know the intentions of these
people, even now before they have entered
the land I swore to give them."

22 So that very day Moses wrote down
the words of the song and taught it to the
Israelites.

23 Then the LORD commissioned Joshua
son of Nun with these words: "Be strong
and courageous, for you must bring the
people of Israel into the land I swore to give
them. I will be with you."

24 When Moses had finished writing this
entire body of instruction in a book,
25 he
gave this command to the Levites who
carried the Ark of the LORD's Covenant:
26 "Take this Book of Instruction and place
it beside the Ark of the Covenant of the
LORD your God, so it may remain there as
a witness against the people of Israel.
27 For
I know how rebellious and stubborn you
are. Even now, while I am still alive and am
here with you, you have rebelled against the
LORD. How much more rebellious will you
be after my death!

28 "Now summon all the elders and officials of your tribes, so that I can speak to
them directly and call heaven and earth to
witness against them.
29 I know that after my
death you will become utterly corrupt and
will turn from the way I have commanded
you to follow. In the days to come, disaster
will come down on you, for you will do what
is evil in the LORD's sight, making him very
angry with your actions."

The Song of Moses

30 So Moses recited this entire song publicly
to the assembly of Israel:

32

1 "Listen, O heavens, and I will speak!
Hear, O earth, the words that I say!
2 Let my teaching fall on you like rain;
let my speech settle like dew.
Let my words fall like rain on tender grass,
like gentle showers on young plants.
3 I will proclaim the name of the LORD;
how glorious is our God!
4 He is the Rock; his deeds are perfect.
Everything he does is just and fair.
He is a faithful God who does no wrong;
how just and upright he is!

5 "But they have acted corruptly toward him;
when they act so perversely,
are they really his children?*
They are a deceitful and twisted generation.
6 Is this the way you repay the LORD,
you foolish and senseless people?
Isn't he your Father who created you?
Has he not made you and established you?
7 Remember the days of long ago;
think about the generations past.
Ask your father, and he will inform you.
Inquire of your elders, and they will tell you.
8 When the Most High assigned lands to the nations,
when he divided up the human race,
he established the boundaries of the peoples
according to the number in his heavenly court.*

9 "For the people of Israel belong to the LORD;
Jacob is his special possession.
10 He found them in a desert land,
in an empty, howling wasteland.
He surrounded them and watched over them;
he guarded them as he would guard his own eyes.*
11 Like an eagle that rouses her chicks
and hovers over her young,
so he spread his wings to take them up
and carried them safely on his pinions.
12 The LORD alone guided them;
they followed no foreign gods.
13 He let them ride over the highlands
and feast on the crops of the fields.
He nourished them with honey from the rock
and olive oil from the stony ground.

30:20 Or *He.* **31:1** As in Dead Sea Scrolls and Greek version; Masoretic Text reads *Moses went and spoke.* **31:14** Hebrew *Tent of Meeting;* also in 31:14b. **32:5** The meaning of the Hebrew is uncertain. **32:8** As in Dead Sea Scrolls, which read *the number of the sons of God,* and Greek version, which reads *the number of the angels of God;* Masoretic Text reads *the number of the sons of Israel.* **32:10** Hebrew *as the pupil of his eye.*

14 He fed them yogurt from the herd
and milk from the flock,
together with the fat of lambs.
He gave them choice rams from Bashan,
and goats,
together with the choicest wheat.
You drank the finest wine,
made from the juice of grapes.

15 "But Israel* soon became fat and unruly;
the people grew heavy, plump, and
stuffed!
Then they abandoned the God who had
made them;
they made light of the Rock of their
salvation.
16 They stirred up his jealousy by
worshiping foreign gods;
they provoked his fury with detestable
deeds.
17 They offered sacrifices to demons, which
are not God,
to gods they had not known before,
to new gods only recently arrived,
to gods their ancestors had never
feared.
18 You neglected the Rock who had
fathered you;
you forgot the God who had given you
birth.
19 "The LORD saw this and drew back,
provoked to anger by his own sons
and daughters.
20 He said, 'I will abandon them;
then see what becomes of them.
For they are a twisted generation,
children without integrity.
21 They have roused my jealousy by
worshiping things that are not God;
they have provoked my anger with
their useless idols.
Now I will rouse their jealousy through
people who are not even a people;
I will provoke their anger through the
foolish Gentiles.
22 For my anger blazes forth like fire
and burns to the depths of the grave.*
It devours the earth and all its crops
and ignites the foundations of the
mountains.
23 I will heap disasters upon them
and shoot them down with my arrows.
24 I will weaken them with famine,
burning fever, and deadly disease.
I will send the fangs of wild beasts
and poisonous snakes that glide in
the dust.
25 Outside, the sword will bring death,
and inside, terror will strike
both young men and young women,
both infants and the aged.
26 I would have annihilated them,
wiping out even the memory of them.
27 But I feared the taunt of Israel's enemy,
who might misunderstand and say,
"Our own power has triumphed!
The LORD had nothing to do with this!"'
28 "But Israel is a senseless nation;
the people are foolish, without
understanding.
29 Oh, that they were wise and could
understand this!
Oh, that they might know their fate!

Singing

Deuteronomy ends with Moses singing praise to God for his faithfulness and then blessing the twelve tribes. Singing played an important part in Israel's faith, sometimes spontaneously, as here (see also, e.g., Exodus 15:1-21; Numbers 21:17-18; Judges 5:1-31; 1 Samuel 21:11; 2 Chronicles 20:21), sometimes using the Psalms ("psalms" means "songs of praise," showing they were originally sung, not spoken). Many psalms encourage us to sing to God (e.g., Psalm 5:11; 9:11; 33:1-3; 66:1-4; 95:1-7), and modern research shows that singing is good for us at every level. Whether we feel we have a good voice or not, we should all respond to Paul's encouragement to be "filled with the Holy Spirit, singing psalms and hymns and spiritual songs among yourselves, and making music to the Lord in your hearts" (Ephesians 5:18-19).

▸ *See also **The ministry of music and singing**, page 475; **The power of praise**, page 501.*

30 How could one person chase a thousand
of them,
and two people put ten thousand to
flight,
unless their Rock had sold them,
unless the LORD had given them up?
31 But the rock of our enemies is not like
our Rock,
as even they recognize.*
32 Their vine grows from the vine of Sodom,
from the vineyards of Gomorrah.
Their grapes are poison,
and their clusters are bitter.
33 Their wine is the venom of serpents,
the deadly poison of cobras.

34 "The LORD says, 'Am I not storing up
these things,
sealing them away in my treasury?
35 I will take revenge; I will pay them back.
In due time their feet will slip.
Their day of disaster will arrive,
and their destiny will overtake them.'

36 "Indeed, the LORD will give justice to his
people,
and he will change his mind about*
his servants,
when he sees their strength is gone
and no one is left, slave or free.
37 Then he will ask, 'Where are their gods,
the rocks they fled to for refuge?
38 Where now are those gods,
who ate the fat of their sacrifices
and drank the wine of their offerings?
Let those gods arise and help you!
Let them provide you with shelter!
39 Look now; I myself am he!
There is no other god but me!
I am the one who kills and gives life;
I am the one who wounds and
heals;
no one can be rescued from my
powerful hand!
40 Now I raise my hand to heaven
and declare, "As surely as I live,
41 when I sharpen my flashing sword
and begin to carry out justice,
I will take revenge on my enemies
and repay those who reject me.
42 I will make my arrows drunk with
blood,
and my sword will devour flesh—
the blood of the slaughtered and the
captives,
and the heads of the enemy leaders."'

43 "Rejoice with him, you heavens,
and let all of God's angels worship
him.*
Rejoice with his people, you
Gentiles,
and let all the angels be strengthened
in him.*
For he will avenge the blood of his
children*;
he will take revenge against his
enemies.
He will repay those who hate him*
and cleanse his people's
land."

44 So Moses came with Joshua* son of Nun
and recited all the words of this song to the
people.
45 When Moses had finished reciting all
these words to the people of Israel, 46 he
added: "Take to heart all the words of
warning I have given you today. Pass them
on as a command to your children so they
will obey every word of these instructions.
47 These instructions are not empty words—
they are your life! By obeying them you will
enjoy a long life in the land you will occupy
when you cross the Jordan River."

Moses' Death Foretold

48 That same day the LORD said to Moses,
49 "Go to Moab, to the mountains east of
the river,* and climb Mount Nebo, which
is across from Jericho. Look out across the
land of Canaan, the land I am giving to the
people of Israel as their own special possession. 50 Then you will die there on the
mountain. You will join your ancestors, just
as Aaron, your brother, died on Mount Hor
and joined his ancestors. 51 For both of you
betrayed me with the Israelites at the waters
of Meribah at Kadesh* in the wilderness of
Zin. You failed to demonstrate my holiness
to the people of Israel there. 52 So you will
see the land from a distance, but you may
not enter the land I am giving to the people
of Israel."

32:15 Hebrew *Jeshurun,* a term of endearment for Israel. **32:22** Hebrew *of Sheol.* **32:31** The meaning of the Hebrew is uncertain. Greek version reads *our enemies are fools.* **32:36** Or *will take revenge for.* **32:43a** As in Dead Sea Scrolls and Greek version; Masoretic Text lacks the first two lines. Compare Heb 1:6. **32:43b** As in Greek version; Hebrew text lacks this sentence. Compare Rom 15:10. **32:43c** As in Dead Sea Scrolls and Greek version; Masoretic Text reads *his servants.* **32:43d** As in Dead Sea Scrolls and Greek version; Masoretic Text lacks this line. **32:44** Hebrew *Hoshea,* a variant name for Joshua. **32:49** Hebrew *the mountains of Abarim.* **32:51** Hebrew *waters of Meribath-kadesh.*

Moses Blesses the People

33 This is the blessing that Moses, the man of God, gave to the people of Israel before his death:

2 "The LORD came from Mount Sinai
and dawned upon us* from Mount Seir;
he shone forth from Mount Paran
and came from Meribah-kadesh
with flaming fire at his right hand.*
3 Indeed, he loves his people;*
all his holy ones are in his hands.
They follow in his steps
and accept his teaching.
4 Moses gave us the LORD's instruction,
the special possession of the people
of Israel.*
5 The LORD became king in Israel*—
when the leaders of the people
assembled,
when the tribes of Israel gathered as
one."

6 Moses said this about the tribe of Reuben:*

"Let the tribe of Reuben live and not die
out,
though they are few in number."

7 Moses said this about the tribe of Judah:

"O LORD, hear the cry of Judah
and bring them together as a people.
Give them strength to defend their cause;
help them against their enemies!"

8 Moses said this about the tribe of Levi:

"O LORD, you have given your Thummim
and Urim—the sacred lots—
to your faithful servants the Levites.*
You put them to the test at Massah
and struggled with them at the waters
of Meribah.
9 The Levites obeyed your word
and guarded your covenant.
They were more loyal to you
than to their own parents.
They ignored their relatives
and did not acknowledge their own
children.
10 They teach your regulations to Jacob;
they give your instructions to Israel.
They present incense before you
and offer whole burnt offerings on the
altar.
11 Bless the ministry of the Levites, O LORD,
and accept all the work of their hands.
Hit their enemies where it hurts the most;
strike down their foes so they never
rise again."

12 Moses said this about the tribe of Benjamin:

"The people of Benjamin are loved by
the LORD
and live in safety beside him.
He surrounds them continuously
and preserves them from every harm."

13 Moses said this about the tribes of Joseph:

"May their land be blessed by the LORD
with the precious gift of dew from the
heavens
and water from beneath the earth;
14 with the rich fruit that grows in the sun,
and the rich harvest produced each
month;
15 with the finest crops of the ancient
mountains,
and the abundance from the
everlasting hills;
16 with the best gifts of the earth and its
bounty,
and the favor of the one who appeared
in the burning bush.
May these blessings rest on Joseph's head,
crowning the brow of the prince
among his brothers.
17 Joseph has the majesty of a young bull;
he has the horns of a wild ox.
He will gore distant nations,
even to the ends of the earth.
This is my blessing for the multitudes of
Ephraim
and the thousands of Manasseh."

18 Moses said this about the tribes of Zebulun and Issachar*:

"May the people of Zebulun prosper in
their travels.
May the people of Issachar prosper at
home in their tents.
19 They summon the people to the
mountain
to offer proper sacrifices there.
They benefit from the riches of the sea
and the hidden treasures in the sand."

20 Moses said this about the tribe of Gad:

"Blessed is the one who enlarges Gad's
territory!
Gad is poised there like a lion
to tear off an arm or a head.

21 The people of Gad took the best land for
themselves;
a leader's share was assigned to
them.
When the leaders of the people were
assembled,
they carried out the LORD's justice
and obeyed his regulations for Israel."

22 Moses said this about the tribe of Dan:

"Dan is a lion's cub,
leaping out from Bashan."

23 Moses said this about the tribe of Naphtali:

"O Naphtali, you are rich in favor
and full of the LORD's blessings;
may you possess the west and the
south."

24 Moses said this about the tribe of Asher:

"May Asher be blessed above other sons;
may he be esteemed by his brothers;
may he bathe his feet in olive oil.
25 May the bolts of your gates be of iron
and bronze;
may you be secure all your days."

26 "There is no one like the God of Israel.*
He rides across the heavens to help
you,
across the skies in majestic splendor.
27 The eternal God is your refuge,
and his everlasting arms are under
you.
He drives out the enemy before you;
he cries out, 'Destroy them!'
28 So Israel will live in safety,
prosperous Jacob in security,
in a land of grain and new wine,
while the heavens drop down
dew.
29 How blessed you are, O Israel!
Who else is like you, a people saved
by the LORD?
He is your protecting shield
and your triumphant sword!
Your enemies will cringe before you,
and you will stomp on their backs!"

The Death of Moses

34 Then Moses went up to Mount Nebo from the plains of Moab and climbed Pisgah Peak, which is across from Jericho.

33:2a As in Greek and Syriac versions; Hebrew reads *upon them.* **33:2b** Or *came from myriads of holy ones, from the south, from his mountain slopes.* The meaning of the Hebrew is uncertain. **33:3** As in Greek version; Hebrew reads *Indeed, lover of the peoples.* **33:4** Hebrew *of Jacob.* The names "Jacob" and "Israel" are often interchanged throughout the Old Testament, referring sometimes to the individual patriarch and sometimes to the nation. **33:5** Hebrew *in Jeshurun,* a term of endearment for Israel. **33:6** Hebrew lacks *Moses said this about the tribe of Reuben.* **33:8** As in Greek version; Hebrew lacks *the Levites.* **33:18** Hebrew lacks *and Issachar.* **33:26** Hebrew *of Jeshurun,* a term of endearment for Israel.

Moses, the faithful servant

Moses had spent the last forty years bringing Israel safely through the wilderness. Now, within sight of the Promised Land and without ever entering it, he died. Moses had not been perfect: He had killed an Egyptian overseer, had been fearful about obeying God and going to Pharaoh, had become angry at times with God's people, and had been self-pitying. But through it all, this man whom the Bible calls "very humble—more humble than any other person on earth" (Numbers 12:3) had continued to be a faithful servant of God, despite many trials and much opposition—often even from his own people. He had resolved that he would do only what God had spoken to him and would seek to faithfully carry that out, come what may. This is why the writer of Hebrews says of him that "Moses was certainly faithful in God's house as a servant" (Hebrews 3:5). His faithfulness was honored when he was buried by the very hand of God (Deuteronomy 34:6).

Faithfulness to what God calls us to do is still the hallmark of a true servant. The key thing we will be judged on is not whether we did what others felt were great things, but whether we did the things God has asked us to do and used our gifts in his service. If we did, then we, like the servants in Jesus' parable, will one day hear the words, "Well done, my good and faithful servant" (Matthew 25:21).

▶ *See also* ***Moses, the man who loved God's presence****, page 69.*

And the LORD showed him the whole land, from Gilead as far as Dan; 2all the land of Naphtali; the land of Ephraim and Manasseh; all the land of Judah, extending to the Mediterranean Sea*; 3the Negev; the Jordan Valley with Jericho—the city of palms—as far as Zoar. 4Then the LORD said to Moses, "This is the land I promised on oath to Abraham, Isaac, and Jacob when I said, 'I will give it to your descendants.' I have now allowed you to see it with your own eyes, but you will not enter the land."

5So Moses, the servant of the LORD, died there in the land of Moab, just as the LORD had said. 6The LORD buried him* in a valley near Beth-peor in Moab, but to this day no one knows the exact place. 7Moses was 120 years old when he died, yet his eyesight was clear, and he was as strong as ever. 8The people of Israel mourned for Moses on the plains of Moab for thirty days, until the customary period of mourning was over.

9Now Joshua son of Nun was full of the spirit of wisdom, for Moses had laid his hands on him. So the people of Israel obeyed him, doing just as the LORD had commanded Moses.

10There has never been another prophet in Israel like Moses, whom the LORD knew face to face. 11The LORD sent him to perform all the miraculous signs and wonders in the land of Egypt against Pharaoh, and all his servants, and his entire land. 12With mighty power, Moses performed terrifying acts in the sight of all Israel.

34:2 Hebrew *the western sea.* **34:6** Hebrew *He buried him;* Samaritan Pentateuch and some Greek manuscripts read *They buried him.*

Joshua *Taking possession of the land*

Joshua is a book of exciting history. Moses had just died, so what would happen to God's people now? After all, Moses had been the only leader they had ever known. They had been in the desert for forty years and were now on the brink of entering the Promised Land of Canaan. How would Joshua fare as their new leader? And would they fall apart under his leadership? No; Joshua would lead them successfully and would prove noteworthy for his obedience to God.

What's it all about?

Having been encouraged by God to be strong after Moses' death, Joshua sent out spies to see what lay ahead of the Israelites. At God's command, the people crossed the Jordan River, the Ark of the Covenant leading the way into the Promised Land. At that time Canaan consisted of many small independent city-states, each with its own ruler and fortified settlement. But God had promised the land to the Israelites hundreds of years before. In giving Joshua victory, God was at last judging the evil of the Canaanites, just as he had said he would (Genesis 15:16). Joshua's first aim was to capture the ancient walled town of Jericho (Joshua 5:13–6:27), which the Israelites did in a miraculous way. After a surprising setback at Ai—due to the disobedience of one individual (Achan, chapter 7)—Joshua marched on to Shechem, where the people renewed the covenant at Mount Gerizim and Mount Ebal, in obedience to Moses' instructions (Joshua 8:30-35; see Deuteronomy 27). Joshua had now divided the country in two. There followed military campaigns in the south and north that resulted in significant victories (chapters 10 and 11).

The Israelites were made up of twelve tribes, descended from the twelve sons of Jacob. The conquered land was allocated to these different tribes by casting lots to ensure fairness (chapters 13–21), though two and a half tribes were allowed to return to land they had requested east of the Jordan. Chapter 20 records laws about six cities of refuge, three on either side of the Jordan, where those who were guilty of accidental killing could live in safety (see *Cities of refuge*, page 222). The final chapters of the book relate a story about the danger of disunity between the tribes who lived east and west of the Jordan (chapter 22), Joshua's farewell to the leaders (chapter 23), the renewal of the covenant with God (chapter 24), and the burial of Joshua and Joseph's bones (24:29-33).

OVERVIEW

God calls the people to get ready to enter Canaan; spies are sent to explore · *1:1–2:24*

Israel crosses the Jordan River *3:1–5:1*

The covenant sign of circumcision is reestablished · *5:2-12*

The conquest of Canaan *5:13–12:24*

The allocation of land to the tribes of Israel · *13:1–22:34*

Joshua's farewell and the renewal of the covenant · *23:1–24:33*

What does it mean for us?

The book of Joshua shows that God always keeps his promises. God had promised Canaan to Abraham (Genesis 12:1-3; 15:7, 12-20; 17:7-8), and now it was time for the Israelites to take it. Through it all God looked after his people, constantly giving them victory as they took possession of the Promised Land. But there is also a tension in the book: a tension between God's ideal way of living and the people's limited obedience to him. Despite Joshua's good leadership—expressed in both his military skill and his commitment to God—and despite God's faithful provision, the people of Israel failed to fully occupy the land, leaving behind small areas of resistance that would come to trouble them greatly in future years. The fact that the people did not serve God and obey him completely was a serious threat not only to their future occupation of the land but also to their very relationship with him.

▸ *See also* ***Twelve Tribes of Israel*** *map, Visual Overview Z5.*

The LORD's Charge to Joshua

1 After the death of Moses the LORD's
servant, the LORD spoke to Joshua son
of Nun, Moses' assistant. He said, 2"Moses
my servant is dead. Therefore, the time
has come for you to lead these people, the
Israelites, across the Jordan River into the
land I am giving them. 3I promise you what
I promised Moses: 'Wherever you set foot,
you will be on land I have given you—4from
the Negev wilderness in the south to the
Lebanon mountains in the north, from the
Euphrates River in the east to the Mediterranean Sea* in the west, including all the
land of the Hittites.' 5No one will be able to
stand against you as long as you live. For
I will be with you as I was with Moses. I will
not fail you or abandon you.
6"Be strong and courageous, for you are
the one who will lead these people to possess
all the land I swore to their ancestors I would
give them. 7Be strong and very courageous.
Be careful to obey all the instructions Moses
gave you. Do not deviate from them, turning
either to the right or to the left. Then you will
be successful in everything you do. 8Study
this Book of Instruction continually. Meditate
on it day and night so you will be sure to obey
everything written in it. Only then will you
prosper and succeed in all you do. 9This is
my command—be strong and courageous!
Do not be afraid or discouraged. For the LORD
your God is with you wherever you go."

Joshua's Charge to the Israelites

10Joshua then commanded the officers of
Israel, 11"Go through the camp and tell the
people to get their provisions ready. In three
days you will cross the Jordan River and
take possession of the land the LORD your
God is giving you."
12Then Joshua called together the tribes of
Reuben, Gad, and the half-tribe of Manasseh.
He told them, 13"Remember what Moses, the
servant of the LORD, commanded you: 'The
LORD your God is giving you a place of rest.
He has given you this land.' 14Your wives,
children, and livestock may remain here in
the land Moses assigned to you on the east
side of the Jordan River. But your strong warriors, fully armed, must lead the other tribes
across the Jordan to help them conquer their
territory. Stay with them 15until the LORD
gives them rest, as he has given you rest, and
until they, too, possess the land the LORD
your God is giving them. Only then may you
return and settle here on the east side of
the Jordan River in the land that Moses, the
servant of the LORD, assigned to you."
16They answered Joshua, "We will do
whatever you command us, and we will go
wherever you send us. 17We will obey you
just as we obeyed Moses. And may the LORD
your God be with you as he was with Moses.
18Anyone who rebels against your orders
and does not obey your words and everything you command will be put to death. So
be strong and courageous!"

Rahab Protects the Spies

2 Then Joshua secretly sent out two
spies from the Israelite camp at Acacia
Grove.* He instructed them, "Scout out the
land on the other side of the Jordan River,
especially around Jericho." So the two men
set out and came to the house of a prostitute
named Rahab and stayed there that night.
2But someone told the king of Jericho,
"Some Israelites have come here tonight to
spy out the land." 3So the king of Jericho
sent orders to Rahab: "Bring out the men
who have come into your house, for they
have come here to spy out the whole land."
4Rahab had hidden the two men, but she

replied, "Yes, the men were here earlier, but
I didn't know where they were from. [5]They
left the town at dusk, as the gates were about
to close. I don't know where they went. If
you hurry, you can probably catch up with
them." [6](Actually, she had taken them up to
the roof and hidden them beneath bundles
of flax she had laid out.) [7]So the king's men
went looking for the spies along the road
leading to the shallow crossings of the
Jordan River. And as soon as the king's men
had left, the gate of Jericho was shut.

[8]Before the spies went to sleep that night,
Rahab went up on the roof to talk with
them. [9]"I know the LORD has given you this
land," she told them. "We are all afraid of
you. Everyone in the land is living in terror.
[10]For we have heard how the LORD made
a dry path for you through the Red Sea*
when you left Egypt. And we know what
you did to Sihon and Og, the two Amorite
kings east of the Jordan River, whose people
you completely destroyed.* [11]No wonder our
hearts have melted in fear! No one has the
courage to fight after hearing such things.
For the LORD your God is the supreme God
of the heavens above and the earth below.

[12]"Now swear to me by the LORD that you
will be kind to me and my family since I have
helped you. Give me some guarantee that
[13]when Jericho is conquered, you will let me
live, along with my father and mother, my
brothers and sisters, and all their families."

[14]"We offer our own lives as a guarantee for
your safety," the men agreed. "If you don't
betray us, we will keep our promise and
be kind to you when the LORD gives us the
land."

[15]Then, since Rahab's house was built
into the town wall, she let them down by a
rope through the window. [16]"Escape to the
hill country," she told them. "Hide there for
three days from the men searching for you.
Then, when they have returned, you can go
on your way."

[17]Before they left, the men told her, "We
will be bound by the oath we have taken
only if you follow these instructions.
[18]When we come into the land, you must
leave this scarlet rope hanging from the
window through which you let us down.
And all your family members—your father,
mother, brothers, and all your relatives—
must be here inside the house. [19]If they go
out into the street and are killed, it will not
be our fault. But if anyone lays a hand on
people inside this house, we will accept the

1:4 Hebrew *the Great Sea*. **2:1** Hebrew *Shittim*. **2:10a** Hebrew *sea of reeds*. **2:10b** The Hebrew term used here refers to the complete consecration of things or people to the LORD, either by destroying them or by giving them as an offering.

Courage

The book of Joshua opens with God telling Joshua that it was time to cross the Jordan and take the Promised Land. God promised to be with him and called him—four times—to "be strong and courageous" (Joshua 1:6, 7, 9, 18). Why? Presumably because Joshua felt anything but strong and courageous! For the past forty years, Israel had been led by Moses, that great man of God, alongside whom Joshua must have felt so small. But Moses had trained him and God had called him; now it was time to step up to the task.

That is what true courage is all about: not acting foolishly or rashly, but simply stepping up to the task to which God has called us. Courage doesn't somehow drop out of heaven to remove our fear *before* we act; rather, it comes as we say yes to what God is asking us to do, just as Jesus promised (e.g., Luke 21:12-19).

It is natural (for most of us at least) to feel daunted when asked to take on larger responsibilities, whether at work or in the church. We perhaps look at others who went before us and feel inadequate in light of their experience or knowledge. But Joshua felt the same—and still God did not let him off the hook. Courage is about knowing what God has called us to do and responding in obedience, believing he will meet us as we do so.

▶ *See also **Confidence**, page 1399.*

responsibility for their death. [20]If you betray
us, however, we are not bound by this oath
in any way."
[21]"I accept your terms," she replied. And
she sent them on their way, leaving the
scarlet rope hanging from the window.
[22]The spies went up into the hill country
and stayed there three days. The men who
were chasing them searched everywhere
along the road, but they finally returned
without success.
[23]Then the two spies came down from the
hill country, crossed the Jordan River, and
reported to Joshua all that had happened to
them. [24]"The LORD has given us the whole
land," they said, "for all the people in the
land are terrified of us."

The Israelites Cross the Jordan

3 Early the next morning Joshua and all
the Israelites left Acacia Grove* and
arrived at the banks of the Jordan River,
where they camped before crossing. [2]Three
days later the Israelite officers went through
the camp, [3]giving these instructions to the
people: "When you see the Levitical priests
carrying the Ark of the Covenant of the LORD
your God, move out from your positions and
follow them. [4]Since you have never traveled
this way before, they will guide you. Stay
about half a mile* behind them, keeping
a clear distance between you and the Ark.
Make sure you don't come any closer."
[5]Then Joshua told the people, "Purify
yourselves, for tomorrow the LORD will do
great wonders among you."
[6]In the morning Joshua said to the priests,
"Lift up the Ark of the Covenant and lead
the people across the river." And so they
started out and went ahead of the people.
[7]The LORD told Joshua, "Today I will
begin to make you a great leader in the eyes
of all the Israelites. They will know that I am
with you, just as I was with Moses. [8]Give
this command to the priests who carry the
Ark of the Covenant: 'When you reach the
banks of the Jordan River, take a few steps
into the river and stop there.'"
[9]So Joshua told the Israelites, "Come
and listen to what the LORD your God says.
[10]Today you will know that the living God
is among you. He will surely drive out the
Canaanites, Hittites, Hivites, Perizzites,
Girgashites, Amorites, and Jebusites ahead
of you. [11]Look, the Ark of the Covenant,
which belongs to the Lord of the whole
earth, will lead you across the Jordan River!
[12]Now choose twelve men from the tribes of
Israel, one from each tribe. [13]The priests will
carry the Ark of the LORD, the Lord of all the
earth. As soon as their feet touch the water,
the flow of water will be cut off upstream,
and the river will stand up like a wall."

The Jordan River

The Jordan is Israel's main river, flowing from Mount Hermon in the north, through the Sea of Galilee, and on to the Dead Sea (also called the Salt Sea or the Sea of the Arabah) in the south. Its name, meaning "Descender," comes from the fact that it drops 2,380 feet as it winds its narrow and meandering way. Because it was mainly below sea level, it was useless for irrigation purposes, unlike the mighty Nile and Euphrates Rivers.

While the Jordan is often used symbolically in Christian hymns of passing through death into eternal life in heaven, its significance in the Bible has much more to do with new beginnings in this life, as here where Joshua led Israel into its Promised Land at last (Joshua 3:1-17).

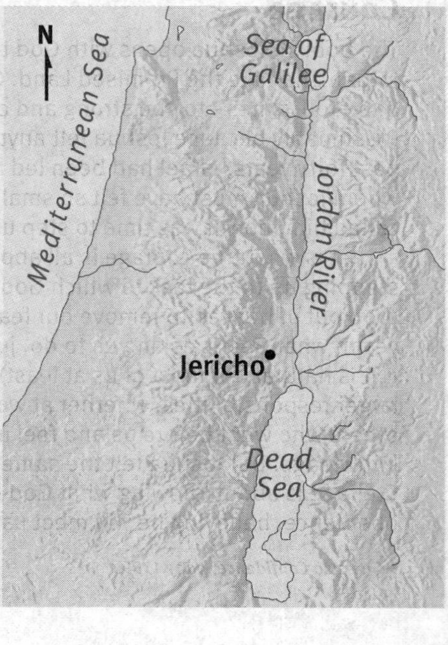

14So the people left their camp to cross the
Jordan, and the priests who were carrying
the Ark of the Covenant went ahead of them.
15It was the harvest season, and the Jordan
was overflowing its banks. But as soon as the
feet of the priests who were carrying the Ark
touched the water at the river's edge, 16the
water above that point began backing up a
great distance away at a town called Adam,
which is near Zarethan. And the water below
that point flowed on to the Dead Sea* until
the riverbed was dry. Then all the people
crossed over near the town of Jericho.

17Meanwhile, the priests who were
carrying the Ark of the LORD's Covenant
stood on dry ground in the middle of the
riverbed as the people passed by. They
waited there until the whole nation of Israel
had crossed the Jordan on dry ground.

Memorials to the Jordan Crossing

4 When all the people had crossed the
Jordan, the LORD said to Joshua, 2"Now
choose twelve men, one from each tribe. 3Tell
them, 'Take twelve stones from the very place
where the priests are standing in the middle
of the Jordan. Carry them out and pile them
up at the place where you will camp tonight.'"

4So Joshua called together the twelve men
he had chosen—one from each of the tribes
of Israel. 5He told them, "Go into the middle
of the Jordan, in front of the Ark of the LORD
your God. Each of you must pick up one stone
and carry it out on your shoulder—twelve
stones in all, one for each of the twelve tribes
of Israel. 6We will use these stones to build
a memorial. In the future your children will
ask you, 'What do these stones mean?' 7Then
you can tell them, 'They remind us that the
Jordan River stopped flowing when the Ark
of the LORD's Covenant went across.' These
stones will stand as a memorial among the
people of Israel forever."

8So the men did as Joshua had commanded them. They took twelve stones
from the middle of the Jordan River, one for
each tribe, just as the LORD had told Joshua.
They carried them to the place where they
camped for the night and constructed the
memorial there.

9Joshua also set up another pile of twelve
stones in the middle of the Jordan, at the
place where the priests who carried the Ark
of the Covenant were standing. And they
are there to this day.

10The priests who were carrying the Ark
stood in the middle of the river until all of
the LORD's commands that Moses had given
to Joshua were carried out. Meanwhile, the
people hurried across the riverbed. 11And
when everyone was safely on the other side,
the priests crossed over with the Ark of the
LORD as the people watched.

12The armed warriors from the tribes of
Reuben, Gad, and the half-tribe of Manasseh led the Israelites across the Jordan, just
as Moses had directed. 13These armed men—
about 40,000 strong—were ready for battle,
and the LORD was with them as they crossed
over to the plains of Jericho.

14That day the LORD made Joshua a great
leader in the eyes of all the Israelites, and
for the rest of his life they revered him as
much as they had revered Moses.

15The LORD had said to Joshua,
16"Command the priests carrying the Ark of
the Covenant* to come up out of the riverbed." 17So Joshua gave the command. 18As
soon as the priests carrying the Ark of the
LORD's Covenant came up out of the riverbed and their feet were on high ground,
the water of the Jordan returned and overflowed its banks as before.

19The people crossed the Jordan on the
tenth day of the first month.* Then they
camped at Gilgal, just east of Jericho. 20It
was there at Gilgal that Joshua piled up the
twelve stones taken from the Jordan River.

21Then Joshua said to the Israelites, "In
the future your children will ask, 'What do
these stones mean?' 22Then you can tell
them, 'This is where the Israelites crossed
the Jordan on dry ground.' 23For the LORD
your God dried up the river right before your
eyes, and he kept it dry until you were all
across, just as he did at the Red Sea* when
he dried it up until we had all crossed
over. 24He did this so all the nations of the
earth might know that the LORD's hand is
powerful, and so you might fear the LORD
your God forever."

5 When all the Amorite kings west of the
Jordan and all the Canaanite kings who
lived along the Mediterranean coast* heard
how the LORD had dried up the Jordan River

3:1 Hebrew *Shittim.* **3:4** Hebrew *about 2,000 cubits* [920 meters].
3:16 Hebrew *the sea of the Arabah, the Salt Sea.* **4:16** Hebrew
Ark of the Testimony. **4:19** This day in the ancient Hebrew
lunar calendar occurred in late March, April, or early May.
4:23 Hebrew *sea of reeds.* **5:1** Hebrew *along the sea.*

so the people of Israel could cross, they lost
heart and were paralyzed with fear because
of them.

Israel Reestablishes Covenant Ceremonies

2At that time the LORD told Joshua, "Make
flint knives and circumcise this second
generation of Israelites.*" 3So Joshua made
flint knives and circumcised the entire male
population of Israel at Gibeath-haaraloth.*
4Joshua had to circumcise them because
all the men who were old enough to fight
in battle when they left Egypt had died in
the wilderness. 5Those who left Egypt had
all been circumcised, but none of those
born after the Exodus, during the years in
the wilderness, had been circumcised. 6The
Israelites had traveled in the wilderness for
forty years until all the men who were old
enough to fight in battle when they left
Egypt had died. For they had disobeyed the
LORD, and the LORD vowed he would not let
them enter the land he had sworn to give
us—a land flowing with milk and honey. 7So
Joshua circumcised their sons—those who
had grown up to take their fathers' places—
for they had not been circumcised on the
way to the Promised Land. 8After all the
males had been circumcised, they rested in
the camp until they were healed.
9Then the LORD said to Joshua, "Today
I have rolled away the shame of your slavery
in Egypt." So that place has been called
Gilgal* to this day.
10While the Israelites were camped
at Gilgal on the plains of Jericho, they
celebrated Passover on the evening of the
fourteenth day of the first month.* 11The
very next day they began to eat unleavened
bread and roasted grain harvested from the
land. 12No manna appeared on the day they
first ate from the crops of the land, and it
was never seen again. So from that time on
the Israelites ate from the crops of Canaan.

The LORD's Commander Confronts Joshua

13When Joshua was near the town of Jericho,
he looked up and saw a man standing in front
of him with sword in hand. Joshua went up to
him and demanded, "Are you friend or foe?"
14"Neither one," he replied. "I am the commander of the LORD's army."
At this, Joshua fell with his face to
the ground in reverence. "I am at your
command," Joshua said. "What do you want
your servant to do?"
15The commander of the LORD's army
replied, "Take off your sandals, for the
place where you are standing is holy." And
Joshua did as he was told.

The Fall of Jericho

6 Now the gates of Jericho were tightly
shut because the people were afraid
of the Israelites. No one was allowed to go
out or in. 2But the LORD said to Joshua, "I
have given you Jericho, its king, and all its
strong warriors. 3You and your fighting men
should march around the town once a day
for six days. 4Seven priests will walk ahead
of the Ark, each carrying a ram's horn. On
the seventh day you are to march around the
town seven times, with the priests blowing
the horns. 5When you hear the priests give
one long blast on the rams' horns, have all
the people shout as loud as they can. Then
the walls of the town will collapse, and the
people can charge straight into the town."
6So Joshua called together the priests
and said, "Take up the Ark of the LORD's

Gilgal

Having crossed the Jordan, it would have been easy to rush ahead. But Joshua knew that, first, it was important to remind God's people of who they were. He did this through reinstituting the covenant sign of circumcision (to remind them of their relationship with God) and the ceremony of Passover (to remind them of how God had redeemed them). This he did at Gilgal, which would later become an Israelite sanctuary. It was here that Saul was both confirmed as king (1 Samuel 11:15) and later rejected as king (1 Samuel 13). Sadly, by the eighth century BC Gilgal had become a center of idolatry and was denounced by Hosea (Hosea 9:15) and Amos (Amos 4:4).

Covenant, and assign seven priests to walk in front of it, each carrying a ram's horn." [7]Then he gave orders to the people: "March around the town, and the armed men will lead the way in front of the Ark of the LORD."

[8]After Joshua spoke to the people, the seven priests with the rams' horns started marching in the presence of the LORD, blowing the horns as they marched. And the Ark of the LORD's Covenant followed behind them. [9]Some of the armed men marched in front of the priests with the horns and some behind the Ark, with the priests continually blowing the horns. [10]"Do not shout; do not even talk," Joshua commanded. "Not a single word from any of you until I tell you to shout. Then shout!" [11]So the Ark of the LORD was carried around the town once that day, and then everyone returned to spend the night in the camp.

[12]Joshua got up early the next morning, and the priests again carried the Ark of the LORD. [13]The seven priests with the rams' horns marched in front of the Ark of the LORD, blowing their horns. Again the armed men marched both in front of the priests with the horns and behind the Ark of the LORD. All this time the priests were blowing their horns. [14]On the second day they again marched around the town once and returned to the camp. They followed this pattern for six days.

[15]On the seventh day the Israelites got up at dawn and marched around the town as they had done before. But this time they went around the town seven times. [16]The seventh time around, as the priests sounded the long blast on their horns, Joshua commanded the people, "Shout! For the LORD has given you the town! [17]Jericho and everything in it must be completely destroyed* as an offering to the LORD. Only Rahab the prostitute and the others in her house will be spared, for she protected our spies.

[18]"Do not take any of the things set apart for destruction, or you yourselves will be completely destroyed, and you will bring trouble on the camp of Israel. [19]Everything made from silver, gold, bronze, or iron is sacred to the LORD and must be brought into his treasury."

[20]When the people heard the sound of the rams' horns, they shouted as loud as they could. Suddenly, the walls of Jericho collapsed, and the Israelites charged straight into the town and captured it. [21]They completely destroyed everything in it with their swords—men and women, young and old, cattle, sheep, goats, and donkeys.

[22]Meanwhile, Joshua said to the two spies, "Keep your promise. Go to the prostitute's house and bring her out, along with all her family."

[23]The men who had been spies went in and brought out Rahab, her father, mother, brothers, and all the other relatives who were with her. They moved her whole family to a safe place near the camp of Israel.

[24]Then the Israelites burned the town and everything in it. Only the things made from silver, gold, bronze, or iron were kept for the

5:2 Or *circumcise the Israelites a second time.* **5:3** *Gibeath-haaraloth* means "hill of foreskins." **5:9** *Gilgal* sounds like the Hebrew word *galal,* meaning "to roll." **5:10** This day in the ancient Hebrew lunar calendar occurred in late March, April, or early May. **6:17** The Hebrew term used here refers to the complete consecration of things or people to the LORD, either by destroying them or by giving them as an offering; similarly in 6:18, 21.

Jericho

Jericho, one of the oldest fortified cities in the world, must have seemed impregnable to the Israelites. Archaeologists have unearthed its walls, which were four and a half feet thick, and one of its huge round stone towers. As an oasis, it had a good water supply, leading it to become known as "the city of palms" (2 Chronicles 28:15), and water meant a city could hold out against attack. And yet conquering this city was crucial for two reasons. First, it guarded the key road-link between the King's Highway to the east of the Jordan and the Great Trunk Road (or "Way of the Sea") by the Mediterranean. Second, it was probably a center of moon worship, for its name sounds like the Hebrew word for "moon"; so overcoming this seemingly impregnable fortress would be a demonstration of who was truly God.

treasury of the LORD's house. 25 So Joshua
spared Rahab the prostitute and her relatives
who were with her in the house, because she
had hidden the spies Joshua sent to Jericho.
And she lives among the Israelites to this day.
26 At that time Joshua invoked this curse:

"May the curse of the LORD fall on
anyone
who tries to rebuild the town of
Jericho.
At the cost of his firstborn son,
he will lay its foundation.
At the cost of his youngest son,
he will set up its gates."

27 So the LORD was with Joshua, and his
reputation spread throughout the land.

Ai Defeats the Israelites

7 But Israel violated the instructions
about the things set apart for the LORD.*
A man named Achan had stolen some of
these dedicated things, so the LORD was
very angry with the Israelites. Achan was
the son of Carmi, a descendant of Zimri*
son of Zerah, of the tribe of Judah.
2 Joshua sent some of his men from Jericho
to spy out the town of Ai, east of Bethel,
near Beth-aven. 3 When they returned, they
told Joshua, "There's no need for all of us
to go up there; it won't take more than two
or three thousand men to attack Ai. Since
there are so few of them, don't make all our
people struggle to go up there."
4 So approximately 3,000 warriors were
sent, but they were soundly defeated. The
men of Ai 5 chased the Israelites from the
town gate as far as the quarries,* and they
killed about thirty-six who were retreating
down the slope. The Israelites were paralyzed with fear at this turn of events, and
their courage melted away.
6 Joshua and the elders of Israel tore their
clothing in dismay, threw dust on their
heads, and bowed face down to the ground
before the Ark of the LORD until evening.
7 Then Joshua cried out, "Oh, Sovereign
LORD, why did you bring us across the Jordan
River if you are going to let the Amorites kill
us? If only we had been content to stay on
the other side! 8 Lord, what can I say now
that Israel has fled from its enemies? 9 For
when the Canaanites and all the other
people living in the land hear about it, they
will surround us and wipe our name off the
face of the earth. And then what will happen
to the honor of your great name?"
10 But the LORD said to Joshua, "Get up!
Why are you lying on your face like this?
11 Israel has sinned and broken my covenant!
They have stolen some of the things that
I commanded must be set apart for me. And
they have not only stolen them but have lied
about it and hidden the things among their
own belongings. 12 That is why the Israelites
are running from their enemies in defeat.
For now Israel itself has been set apart for
destruction. I will not remain with you any
longer unless you destroy the things among
you that were set apart for destruction.
13 "Get up! Command the people to purify
themselves in preparation for tomorrow.
For this is what the LORD, the God of Israel,
says: Hidden among you, O Israel, are
things set apart for the LORD. You will never
defeat your enemies until you remove these
things from among you.
14 "In the morning you must present yourselves by tribes, and the LORD will point out
the tribe to which the guilty man belongs.
That tribe must come forward with its clans,
and the LORD will point out the guilty clan.
That clan will then come forward, and
the LORD will point out the guilty family.
Finally, each member of the guilty family
must come forward one by one. 15 The one
who has stolen what was set apart for
destruction will himself be burned with
fire, along with everything he has, for he
has broken the covenant of the LORD and
has done a horrible thing in Israel."

Achan's Sin

16 Early the next morning Joshua brought
the tribes of Israel before the LORD, and the
tribe of Judah was singled out. 17 Then the
clans of Judah came forward, and the clan
of Zerah was singled out. Then the families
of Zerah came forward, and the family of
Zimri was singled out. 18 Every member of
Zimri's family was brought forward person
by person, and Achan was singled out.

▸ **6:25** *See **Prostitution**, page 285.*

19 Then Joshua said to Achan, "My son, give
glory to the LORD, the God of Israel, by telling
the truth. Make your confession and tell me
what you have done. Don't hide it from me."
20 Achan replied, "It is true! I have sinned
against the LORD, the God of Israel. 21 Among
the plunder I saw a beautiful robe from
Babylon,* 200 silver coins,* and a bar
of gold weighing more than a pound.* I
wanted them so much that I took them. They
are hidden in the ground beneath my tent,
with the silver buried deeper than the rest."
22 So Joshua sent some men to make a
search. They ran to the tent and found the
stolen goods hidden there, just as Achan
had said, with the silver buried beneath
the rest. 23 They took the things from the
tent and brought them to Joshua and all
the Israelites. Then they laid them on the
ground in the presence of the LORD.
24 Then Joshua and all the Israelites took
Achan, the silver, the robe, the bar of gold,
his sons, daughters, cattle, donkeys, sheep,
goats, tent, and everything he had, and
they brought them to the valley of Achor.
25 Then Joshua said to Achan, "Why have
you brought trouble on us? The LORD will
now bring trouble on you." And all the
Israelites stoned Achan and his family and
burned their bodies. 26 They piled a great
heap of stones over Achan, which remains
to this day. That is why the place has been
called the Valley of Trouble* ever since. So
the LORD was no longer angry.

The Israelites Defeat Ai

8 Then the LORD said to Joshua, "Do not
be afraid or discouraged. Take all your
fighting men and attack Ai, for I have given
you the king of Ai, his people, his town, and
his land. 2 You will destroy them as you destroyed Jericho and its king. But this time
you may keep the plunder and the livestock
for yourselves. Set an ambush behind the
town."
3 So Joshua and all the fighting men set
out to attack Ai. Joshua chose 30,000 of his
best warriors and sent them out at night
4 with these orders: "Hide in ambush close
behind the town and be ready for action.
5 When our main army attacks, the men of
Ai will come out to fight as they did before,
and we will run away from them. 6 We will
let them chase us until we have drawn

7:1a The Hebrew term used here refers to the complete consecration of things or people to the LORD, either by destroying them or by giving them as an offering; similarly in 7:11, 12, 13, 15. **7:1b** As in parallel text at 1 Chr 2:6; Hebrew reads *Zabdi*. Also in 7:17, 18. **7:5** Or *as far as Shebarim*. **7:21a** Hebrew *Shinar*. **7:21b** Hebrew *200 shekels of silver*, about 5 pounds or 2.3 kilograms in weight. **7:21c** Hebrew *50 shekels*, about 20 ounces or 570 grams in weight. **7:26** Hebrew *valley of Achor*.

The deceitfulness of Achan

This story, with its execution not just of Achan but of his whole family simply for stealing, seems so unjust to modern thinking. But what lay at the heart of this incident was an important question: What sort of people would Israel be? Those who loved and obeyed God? Or those who deceived and used religion for their own ends?

Joshua had commanded that Jericho and everything in it be devoted to God, either by destruction or by being given to the sanctuary (Joshua 6:17-19). But Achan thought he knew better, so when he saw a beautiful robe, some silver, and a gold bar, he took them and hid them under his tent (7:21). But his greed and deceitfulness brought disaster on the whole nation, for as a result they were defeated at Ai, and thirty-six Israelites were killed—blood on Achan's hands. What Achan failed to realize was that he had broken the covenant with God by identifying himself with something under God's curse. Even worse, he then tried to cover it up, implicating his whole family.

God didn't stop him—he never does. But he always ultimately exposes our sin. And sadly, our sin often affects others, and they suffer too, as we see here as Joshua enforces the judgment necessary to bring Israel out from the curse that Achan had brought upon it. As Paul writes, "Don't be misled—you cannot mock the justice of God. You will always harvest what you plant" (Galatians 6:7).

them away from the town. For they will say, 'The Israelites are running away from us as they did before.' Then, while we are running from them, [7]you will jump up from your ambush and take possession of the town, for the LORD your God will give it to you. [8]Set the town on fire, as the LORD has commanded. You have your orders."

[9]So they left and went to the place of ambush between Bethel and the west side of Ai. But Joshua remained among the people in the camp that night. [10]Early the next morning Joshua roused his men and started toward Ai, accompanied by the elders of Israel. [11]All the fighting men who were with Joshua marched in front of the town and camped on the north side of Ai, with a valley between them and the town. [12]That night Joshua sent about 5,000 men to lie in ambush between Bethel and Ai, on the west side of the town. [13]So they stationed the main army north of the town and the ambush west of the town. Joshua himself spent that night in the valley.

[14]When the king of Ai saw the Israelites across the valley, he and all his army hurried out early in the morning and attacked the Israelites at a place overlooking the Jordan Valley.* But he didn't realize there was an ambush behind the town. [15]Joshua and the Israelite army fled toward the wilderness as though they were badly beaten. [16]Then all the men in the town were called out to chase after them. In this way, they were lured away from the town. [17]There was not a man left in Ai or Bethel* who did not chase after the Israelites, and the town was left wide open.

[18]Then the LORD said to Joshua, "Point the spear in your hand toward Ai, for I will hand the town over to you." Joshua did as he was commanded. [19]As soon as Joshua gave this signal, all the men in ambush jumped up from their position and poured into the town. They quickly captured it and set it on fire.

[20]When the men of Ai looked behind them, smoke from the town was filling the sky, and they had nowhere to go. For the Israelites who had fled in the direction of the wilderness now turned on their pursuers. [21]When Joshua and all the other Israelites saw that the ambush had succeeded and that smoke was rising from the town, they turned and attacked the men of Ai. [22]Meanwhile, the Israelites who were inside the town came out and attacked the enemy from the rear. So the men of Ai were caught in the middle, with Israelite fighters on both sides. Israel attacked them, and not a single person survived or escaped. [23]Only the king of Ai was taken alive and brought to Joshua.

[24]When the Israelite army finished chasing and killing all the men of Ai in the open fields, they went back and finished off everyone inside. [25]So the entire population of Ai, including men and women, was wiped out that day—12,000 in all. [26]For Joshua kept holding out his spear until everyone who had lived in Ai was completely destroyed.* [27]Only the livestock and the treasures of the town were not destroyed, for the Israelites kept these as plunder for themselves, as the LORD had commanded Joshua. [28]So Joshua burned the town of Ai,* and it became a permanent mound of ruins, desolate to this very day.

[29]Joshua impaled the king of Ai on a sharpened pole and left him there until evening. At sunset the Israelites took down the body, as Joshua commanded, and threw it in front of the town gate. They piled a great heap of stones over him that can still be seen today.

The LORD's Covenant Renewed

[30]Then Joshua built an altar to the LORD, the God of Israel, on Mount Ebal. [31]He followed the commands that Moses the LORD's servant had written in the Book of Instruction: "Make me an altar from stones that are uncut and have not been shaped with iron tools."* Then on the altar they presented burnt offerings and peace offerings to the LORD. [32]And as the Israelites watched, Joshua copied onto the stones of the altar* the instructions Moses had given them.

[33]Then all the Israelites—foreigners and native-born alike—along with the elders, officers, and judges, were divided into two groups. One group stood in front of Mount Gerizim, the other in front of Mount Ebal. Each group faced the other, and between them stood the Levitical priests carrying the Ark of the LORD's Covenant. This was all done according to the commands that Moses, the servant of the LORD, had previously given for blessing the people of Israel.

[34]Joshua then read to them all the blessings and curses Moses had written in the Book of Instruction. [35]Every word of every

command that Moses had ever given was
read to the entire assembly of Israel, including the women and children and the
foreigners who lived among them.

The Gibeonites Deceive Israel

9 Now all the kings west of the Jordan
River heard about what had happened.
These were the kings of the Hittites, Amorites, Canaanites, Perizzites, Hivites, and
Jebusites, who lived in the hill country, in
the western foothills,* and along the coast
of the Mediterranean Sea* as far north as
the Lebanon mountains. 2 These kings combined their armies to fight as one against
Joshua and the Israelites.
3 But when the people of Gibeon heard
what Joshua had done to Jericho and Ai,
4 they resorted to deception to save themselves. They sent ambassadors to Joshua,
loading their donkeys with weathered
saddlebags and old, patched wineskins.
5 They put on worn-out, patched sandals
and ragged clothes. And the bread they took
with them was dry and moldy. 6 When they
arrived at the camp of Israel at Gilgal, they
told Joshua and the men of Israel, "We have
come from a distant land to ask you to make
a peace treaty with us."
7 The Israelites replied to these Hivites,
"How do we know you don't live nearby?
For if you do, we cannot make a treaty with
you."
8 They replied, "We are your servants."
"But who are you?" Joshua demanded.
"Where do you come from?"
9 They answered, "Your servants have
come from a very distant country. We
have heard of the might of the LORD your
God and of all he did in Egypt. 10 We have
also heard what he did to the two Amorite
kings east of the Jordan River—King Sihon
of Heshbon and King Og of Bashan (who
lived in Ashtaroth). 11 So our elders and all
our people instructed us, 'Take supplies for
a long journey. Go meet with the people of
Israel and tell them, "We are your servants;
please make a treaty with us."'
12 "This bread was hot from the ovens
when we left our homes. But now, as you
can see, it is dry and moldy. 13 These wineskins were new when we filled them, but
now they are old and split open. And our
clothing and sandals are worn out from our
very long journey."
14 So the Israelites examined their food,
but they did not consult the LORD. 15 Then
Joshua made a peace treaty with them and
guaranteed their safety, and the leaders
of the community ratified their agreement
with a binding oath.
16 Three days after making the treaty, they
learned that these people actually lived
nearby! 17 The Israelites set out at once to
investigate and reached their towns in
three days. The names of these towns were
Gibeon, Kephirah, Beeroth, and Kiriath-
jearim. 18 But the Israelites did not attack the
towns, for the Israelite leaders had made a

8:14 Hebrew *the Arabah*. **8:17** Some manuscripts lack *or Bethel*. **8:26** The Hebrew term used here refers to the complete consecration of things or people to the LORD, either by destroying them or by giving them as an offering. **8:28** *Ai* means "ruin." **8:31** Exod 20:25; Deut 27:5-6. **8:32** Hebrew *onto the stones*. **9:1a** Hebrew *the Shephelah*. **9:1b** Hebrew *the Great Sea*.

The Gibeonites

Joshua 9 warns of the dangers of making decisions based purely on common sense but without involving God. When the residents of Gibeon, six miles northwest of Jerusalem, tried to trick the Israelites into thinking they lived a long way off so that they would make a peace treaty with them, "the Israelites examined their food, but they did not consult the LORD" (9:14). Only when it was too late, when they had already made a treaty with them, did the Israelites discover the truth. As a result the Gibeonites were made "woodcutters and water carriers" (9:21), their presence reminding Israel of the importance of seeking God's guidance in everything.

Gibeon became the home of the Tabernacle, and it was here that God appeared to Solomon (1 Kings 3:4-15).

▸ *See also* ***Guidance****, page 1261.*

vow to them in the name of the LORD, the
God of Israel.
The people of Israel grumbled against
their leaders because of the treaty. 19But the
leaders replied, "Since we have sworn an
oath in the presence of the LORD, the God of
Israel, we cannot touch them. 20This is what
we must do. We must let them live, for divine
anger would come upon us if we broke our
oath. 21Let them live." So they made them
woodcutters and water carriers for the entire
community, as the Israelite leaders directed.
22Joshua called together the Gibeonites
and said, "Why did you lie to us? Why did
you say that you live in a distant land when
you live right here among us? 23May you be
cursed! From now on you will always be servants who cut wood and carry water for the
house of my God."
24They replied, "We did it because we—
your servants—were clearly told that the
LORD your God commanded his servant
Moses to give you this entire land and to
destroy all the people living in it. So we
feared greatly for our lives because of you.
That is why we have done this. 25Now we are
at your mercy—do to us whatever you think
is right."
26So Joshua did not allow the people of
Israel to kill them. 27But that day he made
the Gibeonites the woodcutters and water
carriers for the community of Israel and for
the altar of the LORD—wherever the LORD
would choose to build it. And that is what
they do to this day.

Israel Defeats the Southern Armies

10 Adoni-zedek, king of Jerusalem,
heard that Joshua had captured and
completely destroyed* Ai and killed its
king, just as he had destroyed the town of
Jericho and killed its king. He also learned
that the Gibeonites had made peace with
Israel and were now their allies. 2He and
his people became very afraid when they
heard all this because Gibeon was a large
town—as large as the royal cities and larger
than Ai. And the Gibeonite men were strong
warriors.
3So King Adoni-zedek of Jerusalem sent
messengers to several other kings: Hoham
of Hebron, Piram of Jarmuth, Japhia of
Lachish, and Debir of Eglon. 4"Come and
help me destroy Gibeon," he urged them,
"for they have made peace with Joshua and
the people of Israel." 5So these five Amorite
kings combined their armies for a united
attack. They moved all their troops into
place and attacked Gibeon.
6The men of Gibeon quickly sent messengers to Joshua at his camp in Gilgal. "Don't
abandon your servants now!" they pleaded.
"Come at once! Save us! Help us! For all the
Amorite kings who live in the hill country
have joined forces to attack us."
7So Joshua and his entire army, including his best warriors, left Gilgal and set out
for Gibeon. 8"Do not be afraid of them," the
LORD said to Joshua, "for I have given you
victory over them. Not a single one of them
will be able to stand up to you."
9Joshua traveled all night from Gilgal and
took the Amorite armies by surprise. 10The
LORD threw them into a panic, and the Israelites slaughtered great numbers of them
at Gibeon. Then the Israelites chased the
enemy along the road to Beth-horon, killing
them all along the way to Azekah and Makkedah. 11As the Amorites retreated down the
road from Beth-horon, the LORD destroyed
them with a terrible hailstorm from heaven
that continued until they reached Azekah.
The hail killed more of the enemy than the
Israelites killed with the sword.
12On the day the LORD gave the Israelites
victory over the Amorites, Joshua prayed to
the LORD in front of all the people of Israel.
He said,

"Let the sun stand still over Gibeon,
and the moon over the valley of
Aijalon."

13So the sun stood still and the moon stayed
in place until the nation of Israel had defeated its enemies.
Is this event not recorded in *The Book of
Jashar**? The sun stayed in the middle of the
sky, and it did not set as on a normal day.*
14There has never been a day like this one
before or since, when the LORD answered
such a prayer. Surely the LORD fought for
Israel that day!
15Then Joshua and the Israelite army
returned to their camp at Gilgal.

Joshua Kills the Five Southern Kings

16During the battle the five kings escaped
and hid in a cave at Makkedah. 17When
Joshua heard that they had been found, 18he
issued this command: "Cover the opening

of the cave with large rocks, and place
guards at the entrance to keep the kings
inside. 19 The rest of you continue chasing
the enemy and cut them down from the rear.
Don't give them a chance to get back to their
towns, for the LORD your God has given you
victory over them."
20 So Joshua and the Israelite army continued the slaughter and completely crushed
the enemy. They totally wiped out the
five armies except for a tiny remnant that
managed to reach their fortified towns.
21 Then the Israelites returned safely to
Joshua in the camp at Makkedah. After that,
no one dared to speak even a word against
Israel.
22 Then Joshua said, "Remove the rocks
covering the opening of the cave, and bring
the five kings to me." 23 So they brought the
five kings out of the cave—the kings of Jerusalem, Hebron, Jarmuth, Lachish, and
Eglon. 24 When they brought them out,
Joshua told the commanders of his army,
"Come and put your feet on the kings'
necks." And they did as they were told.
25 "Don't ever be afraid or discouraged,"
Joshua told his men. "Be strong and courageous, for the LORD is going to do this to
all of your enemies." 26 Then Joshua killed
each of the five kings and impaled them on
five sharpened poles, where they hung until
evening.
27 As the sun was going down, Joshua gave
instructions for the bodies of the kings to
be taken down from the poles and thrown
into the cave where they had been hiding.
Then they covered the opening of the cave
with a pile of large rocks, which remains to
this very day.

Israel Destroys the Southern Towns

28 That same day Joshua captured and destroyed the town of Makkedah. He killed
everyone in it, including the king, leaving
no survivors. He destroyed them all, and
he killed the king of Makkedah as he had
killed the king of Jericho. 29 Then Joshua
and the Israelites went to Libnah and attacked it. 30 There, too, the LORD gave them
the town and its king. He killed everyone in
it, leaving no survivors. Then Joshua killed
the king of Libnah as he had killed the king
of Jericho.
31 From Libnah, Joshua and the Israelites
went to Lachish and attacked it. 32 Here
again, the LORD gave them Lachish. Joshua
took it on the second day and killed everyone in it, just as he had done at Libnah.
33 During the attack on Lachish, King Horam
of Gezer arrived with his army to help
defend the town. But Joshua's men killed
him and his army, leaving no survivors.
34 Then Joshua and the Israelite army
went on to Eglon and attacked it. 35 They
captured it that day and killed everyone in
it. He completely destroyed everyone, just
as he had done at Lachish. 36 From Eglon,
Joshua and the Israelite army went up to
Hebron and attacked it. 37 They captured
the town and killed everyone in it, including its king, leaving no survivors. They did
the same thing to all of its surrounding villages. And just as he had done at Eglon, he
completely destroyed the entire population.
38 Then Joshua and the Israelites turned
back and attacked Debir. 39 He captured the
town, its king, and all of its surrounding villages. He completely destroyed everyone in
it, leaving no survivors. He did to Debir and
its king just what he had done to Hebron
and to Libnah and its king.
40 So Joshua conquered the whole region—
the kings and people of the hill country,
the Negev, the western foothills,* and the
mountain slopes. He completely destroyed
everyone in the land, leaving no survivors,
just as the LORD, the God of Israel, had commanded. 41 Joshua slaughtered them from
Kadesh-barnea to Gaza and from the region
around the town of Goshen up to Gibeon.
42 Joshua conquered all these kings and their
land in a single campaign, for the LORD, the
God of Israel, was fighting for his people.
43 Then Joshua and the Israelite army
returned to their camp at Gilgal.

Israel Defeats the Northern Armies

11 When King Jabin of Hazor heard what
had happened, he sent messages to the
following kings: King Jobab of Madon; the
king of Shimron; the king of Acshaph; 2 all
the kings of the northern hill country; the
kings in the Jordan Valley south of Galilee*;
the kings in the Galilean foothills*; the
kings of Naphoth-dor on the west; 3 the kings

10:1 The Hebrew term used here refers to the complete consecration of things or people to the LORD, either by destroying them or by giving them as an offering; also in 10:28, 35, 37, 39, 40. **10:13a** Or *The Book of the Upright.* **10:13b** Or *did not set for about a whole day.* **10:40** Hebrew *the Shephelah.* **11:2a** Hebrew *in the Arabah south of Kinnereth.* **11:2b** Hebrew *the Shephelah;* also in 11:16.

of Canaan, both east and west; the kings of the Amorites, the Hittites, the Perizzites, the Jebusites in the hill country, and the Hivites in the towns on the slopes of Mount Hermon in the land of Mizpah.

4 All these kings came out to fight. Their combined armies formed a vast horde. And with all their horses and chariots, they covered the landscape like the sand on the seashore. 5 The kings joined forces and established their camp around the water near Merom to fight against Israel.

6 Then the LORD said to Joshua, "Do not be afraid of them. By this time tomorrow I will hand all of them over to Israel as dead men. Then you must cripple their horses and burn their chariots."

7 So Joshua and all his fighting men traveled to the water near Merom and attacked suddenly. 8 And the LORD gave them victory over their enemies. The Israelites chased them as far as Greater Sidon and Misrephoth-maim, and eastward into the valley of Mizpah, until not one enemy warrior was left alive. 9 Then Joshua crippled the horses and burned all the chariots, as the LORD had instructed.

10 Joshua then turned back and captured Hazor and killed its king. (Hazor had at one time been the capital of all these kingdoms.) 11 The Israelites completely destroyed* every living thing in the city, leaving no survivors. Not a single person was spared. And then Joshua burned the city.

12 Joshua slaughtered all the other kings and their people, completely destroying them, just as Moses, the servant of the LORD, had commanded. 13 But the Israelites did not burn any of the towns built on mounds except Hazor, which Joshua burned. 14 And the Israelites took all the plunder and livestock of the ravaged towns for themselves. But they killed all the people, leaving no survivors. 15 As the LORD had commanded his servant Moses, so Moses commanded Joshua. And Joshua did as he was told, carefully obeying all the commands that the LORD had given to Moses.

16 So Joshua conquered the entire region—the hill country, the entire Negev, the whole area around the town of Goshen, the western foothills, the Jordan Valley,* the mountains of Israel, and the Galilean foothills. 17 The Israelite territory now extended all the way from Mount Halak, which leads up to Seir in the south, as far north as Baal-gad at the foot of Mount Hermon in the valley of Lebanon. Joshua killed all the kings of those territories, 18 waging war for a long time to accomplish this. 19 No one in this region made peace with the Israelites except the Hivites of Gibeon. All the others were defeated. 20 For the LORD hardened their hearts and caused them to fight the Israelites. So they were completely destroyed without mercy, as the LORD had commanded Moses.

21 During this period Joshua destroyed all the descendants of Anak, who lived in the hill country of Hebron, Debir, Anab, and the entire hill country of Judah and Israel. He killed them all and completely destroyed their towns. 22 None of the descendants of Anak were left in all the land of Israel, though some still remained in Gaza, Gath, and Ashdod.

23 So Joshua took control of the entire land, just as the LORD had instructed Moses. He gave it to the people of Israel as their special possession, dividing the land among the tribes. So the land finally had rest from war.

Kings Defeated East of the Jordan

12 These are the kings east of the Jordan River who had been killed by the Israelites and whose land was taken. Their territory extended from the Arnon Gorge to Mount Hermon and included all the land east of the Jordan Valley.*

2 King Sihon of the Amorites, who lived in Heshbon, was defeated. His kingdom included Aroer, on the edge of the Arnon Gorge, and extended from the middle of the Arnon Gorge to the Jabbok River, which serves as a border for the Ammonites. This territory included the southern half of the territory of Gilead. 3 Sihon also controlled the Jordan Valley and regions to the east—from as far north as the Sea of Galilee to as far south as the Dead Sea,* including the road to Beth-jeshimoth and southward to the slopes of Pisgah.

4 King Og of Bashan, the last of the Rephaites, lived at Ashtaroth and Edrei. 5 He ruled a territory stretching from Mount Hermon to Salecah in the north and to all of Bashan in the east, and westward to the borders of the kingdoms of Geshur and Maacah. This territory included the northern half of Gilead, as far as the boundary of King Sihon of Heshbon.

6 Moses, the servant of the LORD, and the
Israelites had destroyed the people of King
Sihon and King Og. And Moses gave their
land as a possession to the tribes of Reuben,
Gad, and the half-tribe of Manasseh.

Kings Defeated West of the Jordan

7 The following is a list of the kings that
Joshua and the Israelite armies defeated on
the west side of the Jordan, from Baal-gad
in the valley of Lebanon to Mount Halak,
which leads up to Seir. (Joshua gave this
land to the tribes of Israel as their possession, 8 including the hill country, the
western foothills,* the Jordan Valley, the
mountain slopes, the Judean wilderness,
and the Negev. The people who lived in this
region were the Hittites, the Amorites, the
Canaanites, the Perizzites, the Hivites, and
the Jebusites.) These are the kings Israel
defeated:

9 The king of Jericho
The king of Ai, near Bethel
10 The king of Jerusalem
The king of Hebron
11 The king of Jarmuth
The king of Lachish
12 The king of Eglon
The king of Gezer
13 The king of Debir
The king of Geder
14 The king of Hormah
The king of Arad
15 The king of Libnah
The king of Adullam
16 The king of Makkedah
The king of Bethel
17 The king of Tappuah
The king of Hepher
18 The king of Aphek
The king of Lasharon
19 The king of Madon
The king of Hazor
20 The king of Shimron-meron
The king of Acshaph
21 The king of Taanach
The king of Megiddo
22 The king of Kedesh
The king of Jokneam in Carmel
23 The king of Dor in the town of
Naphoth-dor*
The king of Goyim in Gilgal*
24 The king of Tirzah.

In all, thirty-one kings were defeated.

The Land Yet to Be Conquered

13 When Joshua was an old man, the
LORD said to him, "You are growing
old, and much land remains to be conquered. 2 This is the territory that remains:
all the regions of the Philistines and the
Geshurites, 3 and the larger territory of the
Canaanites, extending from the stream of
Shihor on the border of Egypt, northward to
the boundary of Ekron. It includes the territory of the five Philistine rulers of Gaza,
Ashdod, Ashkelon, Gath, and Ekron. The
land of the Avvites 4 in the south also remains
to be conquered. In the north, the following area has not yet been conquered: all the
land of the Canaanites, including Mearah
(which belongs to the Sidonians), stretching northward to Aphek on the border of the
Amorites; 5 the land of the Gebalites and all
of the Lebanon mountain area to the east,
from Baal-gad below Mount Hermon to
Lebo-hamath; 6 and all the hill country from
Lebanon to Misrephoth-maim, including all
the land of the Sidonians.

"I myself will drive these people out of
the land ahead of the Israelites. So be sure
to give this land to Israel as a special possession, just as I have commanded you.
7 Include all this territory as Israel's possession when you divide this land among the
nine tribes and the half-tribe of Manasseh."

The Land Divided East of the Jordan

8 Half the tribe of Manasseh and the tribes of
Reuben and Gad had already received their
grants of land on the east side of the Jordan,
for Moses, the servant of the LORD, had previously assigned this land to them.

9 Their territory extended from Aroer on
the edge of the Arnon Gorge (including
the town in the middle of the gorge)
to the plain beyond Medeba, as far as
Dibon. 10 It also included all the towns
of King Sihon of the Amorites, who had
reigned in Heshbon, and extended as far
as the borders of Ammon. 11 It included
Gilead, the territory of the kingdoms
of Geshur and Maacah, all of Mount
Hermon, all of Bashan as far as Salecah,

11:11 The Hebrew term used here refers to the complete consecration of things or people to the LORD, either by destroying them or by giving them as an offering; also in 11:12, 20, 21. **11:16** Hebrew *the Shephelah, the Arabah.* **12:1** Hebrew *the Arabah;* also in 12:3, 8. **12:3** Hebrew *from the Sea of Kinnereth to the Sea of the Arabah, which is the Salt Sea.* **12:8** Hebrew *the Shephelah.* **12:23a** Hebrew *Naphath-dor,* a variant spelling of Naphoth-dor. **12:23b** Greek version reads *Goyim in Galilee.*

[12]and all the territory of King Og of
Bashan, who had reigned in Ashtaroth
and Edrei. King Og was the last of the
Rephaites, for Moses had attacked them
and driven them out. [13]But the Israelites
failed to drive out the people of Geshur
and Maacah, so they continue to live
among the Israelites to this day.

An Allotment for the Tribe of Levi

[14]Moses did not assign any allotment of land
to the tribe of Levi. Instead, as the LORD had
promised them, their allotment came from
the offerings burned on the altar to the
LORD, the God of Israel.

The Land Given to the Tribe of Reuben

[15]Moses had assigned the following area to
the clans of the tribe of Reuben.

[16]Their territory extended from Aroer on
the edge of the Arnon Gorge (including
the town in the middle of the gorge)
to the plain beyond Medeba. [17]It
included Heshbon and the other towns
on the plain—Dibon, Bamoth-baal,
Beth-baal-meon, [18]Jahaz, Kedemoth,
Mephaath, [19]Kiriathaim, Sibmah,
Zereth-shahar on the hill above the
valley, [20]Beth-peor, the slopes of Pisgah,
and Beth-jeshimoth.

[21]The land of Reuben also included
all the towns of the plain and the
entire kingdom of Sihon. Sihon was
the Amorite king who had reigned in
Heshbon and was killed by Moses along
with the leaders of Midian—Evi, Rekem,
Zur, Hur, and Reba—princes living in the
region who were allied with Sihon. [22]The
Israelites had also killed Balaam son of
Beor, who used magic to tell the future.
[23]The Jordan River marked the western
boundary for the tribe of Reuben. The
towns and their surrounding villages in
this area were given as a homeland to
the clans of the tribe of Reuben.

The Land Given to the Tribe of Gad

[24]Moses had assigned the following area to
the clans of the tribe of Gad.

[25]Their territory included Jazer, all the
towns of Gilead, and half of the land
of Ammon, as far as the town of Aroer
just west of* Rabbah. [26]It extended
from Heshbon to Ramath-mizpeh
and Betonim, and from Mahanaim
to the territory of Lo-debar.* [27]In the
valley were Beth-haram, Beth-nimrah,
Succoth, Zaphon, and the rest of the
kingdom of King Sihon of Heshbon.
The western boundary ran along the
Jordan River, extended as far north as
the tip of the Sea of Galilee,* and then
turned eastward. [28]The towns and their
surrounding villages in this area were
given as a homeland to the clans of the
tribe of Gad.

The Land Given to the Half-Tribe of Manasseh

[29]Moses had assigned the following area to
the clans of the half-tribe of Manasseh.

[30]Their territory extended from
Mahanaim, including all of Bashan,
all the former kingdom of King Og,
and the sixty towns of Jair in Bashan.
[31]It also included half of Gilead and
King Og's royal cities of Ashtaroth and
Edrei. All this was given to the clans
of the descendants of Makir, who was
Manasseh's son.

[32]These are the allotments Moses had
made while he was on the plains of Moab,
across the Jordan River, east of Jericho. [33]But
Moses gave no allotment of land to the tribe
of Levi, for the LORD, the God of Israel, had
promised that he himself would be their
allotment.

The Land Divided West of the Jordan

14 The remaining tribes of Israel received land in Canaan as allotted
by Eleazar the priest, Joshua son of Nun,
and the tribal leaders. [2]These nine and a
half tribes received their grants of land
by means of sacred lots, in accordance
with the LORD's command through Moses.
[3]Moses had already given a grant of land
to the two and a half tribes on the east side
of the Jordan River, but he had given the
Levites no such allotment. [4]The descendants of Joseph had become two separate
tribes—Manasseh and Ephraim. And the
Levites were given no land at all, only
towns to live in with surrounding pasturelands for their livestock and all their possessions. [5]So the land was distributed in
strict accordance with the LORD's commands to Moses.

Caleb Requests His Land

6A delegation from the tribe of Judah, led by
Caleb son of Jephunneh the Kenizzite, came
to Joshua at Gilgal. Caleb said to Joshua,
"Remember what the LORD said to Moses,
the man of God, about you and me when we
were at Kadesh-barnea. 7I was forty years
old when Moses, the servant of the LORD,
sent me from Kadesh-barnea to explore
the land of Canaan. I returned and gave
an honest report, 8but my brothers who
went with me frightened the people from
entering the Promised Land. For my part, I
wholeheartedly followed the LORD my God.
9So that day Moses solemnly promised me,
'The land of Canaan on which you were just
walking will be your grant of land and that
of your descendants forever, because you
wholeheartedly followed the LORD my God.'
10"Now, as you can see, the LORD has
kept me alive and well as he promised for
all these forty-five years since Moses made
this promise—even while Israel wandered
in the wilderness. Today I am eighty-five
years old. 11I am as strong now as I was
when Moses sent me on that journey, and
I can still travel and fight as well as I could
then. 12So give me the hill country that the
LORD promised me. You will remember that
as scouts we found the descendants of Anak
living there in great, walled towns. But if
the LORD is with me, I will drive them out of
the land, just as the LORD said."
13So Joshua blessed Caleb son of Jephunneh and gave Hebron to him as his portion
of land. 14Hebron still belongs to the descendants of Caleb son of Jephunneh the Kenizzite because he wholeheartedly followed
the LORD, the God of Israel. 15(Previously
Hebron had been called Kiriath-arba. It had
been named after Arba, a great hero of the
descendants of Anak.)
And the land had rest from war.

The Land Given to the Tribe of Judah

15 The allotment for the clans of the tribe
of Judah reached southward to the
border of Edom, as far south as the wilderness of Zin.

2The southern boundary began at
the south bay of the Dead Sea,* 3ran
south of Scorpion Pass* into the
wilderness of Zin, and then went south
of Kadesh-barnea to Hezron. Then
it went up to Addar, where it turned
toward Karka. 4From there it passed
to Azmon until it finally reached the
Brook of Egypt, which it followed to the
Mediterranean Sea.* This was their*
southern boundary.
5The eastern boundary extended
along the Dead Sea to the mouth of the
Jordan River.
The northern boundary began at the
bay where the Jordan River empties
into the Dead Sea, 6went up from
there to Beth-hoglah, then proceeded
north of Beth-arabah to the Stone of
Bohan. (Bohan was Reuben's son.)
7From that point it went through the
valley of Achor to Debir, turning north
toward Gilgal, which is across from the

13:25 Hebrew *in front of.* **13:26** Hebrew *Li-debir,* apparently a variant spelling of Lo-debar (compare 2 Sam 9:4; 17:27; Amos 6:13). **13:27** Hebrew *Sea of Kinnereth.* **15:2** Hebrew *the Salt Sea;* also in 15:5. **15:3** Hebrew *Akrabbim.* **15:4a** Hebrew *the sea;* also in 15:11. **15:4b** Hebrew *your.*

Caleb

Caleb had been one of the twelve scouts sent by Moses to explore Canaan. Only he and Joshua had returned with a report that was full of faith (Numbers 13:25–14:9), a report that led God to say of him, "My servant Caleb has a different attitude than the others have. He has remained loyal to me" (Numbers 14:24). Now here in Joshua 14, we see him still as full of faith as ever at the age of eighty-five, wanting to take the inheritance that God had given him. This was in the hill country with its fortified cities, but this did not deter Caleb. He knew that God had made a promise, so he boldly declared, "If the LORD is with me, I will drive them out of the land, just as the LORD said" (Joshua 14:12). Caleb is a wonderful example of an obedient, faithful, and daring servant of God. He also shows us that we are never too old to serve God!

slopes of Adummim on the south side
of the valley. From there the boundary
extended to the springs at En-shemesh
and on to En-rogel. 8 The boundary
then passed through the valley of
Ben-Hinnom, along the southern
slopes of the Jebusites, where the city
of Jerusalem is located. Then it went
west to the top of the mountain above
the valley of Hinnom, and on up to the
northern end of the valley of Rephaim.
9 From there the boundary extended
from the top of the mountain to the
spring at the waters of Nephtoah,*
and from there to the towns on Mount
Ephron. Then it turned toward Baalah
(that is, Kiriath-jearim). 10 The boundary
circled west of Baalah to Mount Seir,
passed along to the town of Kesalon on
the northern slope of Mount Jearim, and
went down to Beth-shemesh and on to
Timnah. 11 The boundary then proceeded
to the slope of the hill north of Ekron,
where it turned toward Shikkeron and
Mount Baalah. It passed Jabneel and
ended at the Mediterranean Sea.
12 The western boundary was the
shoreline of the Mediterranean Sea.*

These are the boundaries for the clans of
the tribe of Judah.

The Land Given to Caleb

13 The LORD commanded Joshua to assign
some of Judah's territory to Caleb son of Jephunneh. So Caleb was given the town of
Kiriath-arba (that is, Hebron), which had
been named after Anak's ancestor. 14 Caleb
drove out the three groups of Anakites—
the descendants of Sheshai, Ahiman, and
Talmai, the sons of Anak.
15 From there he went to fight against
the people living in the town of Debir (formerly called Kiriath-sepher). 16 Caleb said,
"I will give my daughter Acsah in marriage to the one who attacks and captures
Kiriath-sepher." 17 Othniel, the son of Caleb's
brother Kenaz, was the one who conquered
it, so Acsah became Othniel's wife.
18 When Acsah married Othniel, she urged
him* to ask her father for a field. As she
got down off her donkey, Caleb asked her,
"What's the matter?"
19 She said, "Give me another gift. You
have already given me land in the Negev;
now please give me springs of water, too."
So Caleb gave her the upper and lower
springs.

The Towns Allotted to Judah

20 This was the homeland allocated to the
clans of the tribe of Judah.

21 The towns of Judah situated along
the borders of Edom in the extreme
south were Kabzeel, Eder, Jagur,
22 Kinah, Dimonah, Adadah, 23 Kedesh,
Hazor, Ithnan, 24 Ziph, Telem, Bealoth,
25 Hazor-hadattah, Kerioth-hezron (that
is, Hazor), 26 Amam, Shema, Moladah,
27 Hazar-gaddah, Heshmon, Beth-pelet,
28 Hazar-shual, Beersheba, Biziothiah,
29 Baalah, Iim, Ezem, 30 Eltolad, Kesil,
Hormah, 31 Ziklag, Madmannah,
Sansannah, 32 Lebaoth, Shilhim, Ain,
and Rimmon—twenty-nine towns with
their surrounding villages.
33 The following towns situated in
the western foothills* were also given
to Judah: Eshtaol, Zorah, Ashnah,
34 Zanoah, En-gannim, Tappuah, Enam,
35 Jarmuth, Adullam, Socoh, Azekah,
36 Shaaraim, Adithaim, Gederah, and
Gederothaim—fourteen towns with their
surrounding villages.
37 Also included were Zenan,
Hadashah, Migdal-gad, 38 Dilean,
Mizpeh, Joktheel, 39 Lachish, Bozkath,
Eglon, 40 Cabbon, Lahmam, Kitlish,
41 Gederoth, Beth-dagon, Naamah, and
Makkedah—sixteen towns with their
surrounding villages.
42 Besides these, there were Libnah,
Ether, Ashan, 43 Iphtah, Ashnah, Nezib,
44 Keilah, Aczib, and Mareshah—nine
towns with their surrounding villages.
45 The territory of the tribe of Judah
also included Ekron and its surrounding
settlements and villages. 46 From Ekron
the boundary extended west and
included the towns near Ashdod with
their surrounding villages. 47 It also
included Ashdod with its surrounding
settlements and villages and Gaza with
its settlements and villages, as far as the
Brook of Egypt and along the coast of
the Mediterranean Sea.
48 Judah also received the following
towns in the hill country: Shamir, Jattir,
Socoh, 49 Dannah, Kiriath-sannah (that

is, Debir), [50]Anab, Eshtemoh, Anim, [51]Goshen, Holon, and Giloh—eleven towns with their surrounding villages.

[52]Also included were the towns of Arab, Dumah, Eshan, [53]Janim, Beth-tappuah, Aphekah, [54]Humtah, Kiriath-arba (that is, Hebron), and Zior—nine towns with their surrounding villages.

[55]Besides these, there were Maon, Carmel, Ziph, Juttah, [56]Jezreel, Jokdeam, Zanoah, [57]Kain, Gibeah, and Timnah—ten towns with their surrounding villages.

[58]In addition, there were Halhul, Beth-zur, Gedor, [59]Maarath, Beth-anoth, and Eltekon—six towns with their surrounding villages.

[60]There were also Kiriath-baal (that is, Kiriath-jearim) and Rabbah—two towns with their surrounding villages.

[61]In the wilderness there were the towns of Beth-arabah, Middin, Secacah, [62]Nibshan, the City of Salt, and En-gedi—six towns with their surrounding villages.

[63]But the tribe of Judah could not drive out the Jebusites, who lived in the city of Jerusalem, so the Jebusites live there among the people of Judah to this day.

The Land Given to Ephraim and West Manasseh

16 The allotment for the descendants of Joseph extended from the Jordan River near Jericho, east of the springs of Jericho, through the wilderness and into the hill country of Bethel. [2]From Bethel (that is, Luz)* it ran over to Ataroth in the territory of the Arkites. [3]Then it descended westward to the territory of the Japhletites as far as Lower Beth-horon, then to Gezer and over to the Mediterranean Sea.*

[4]This was the homeland allocated to the families of Joseph's sons, Manasseh and Ephraim.

The Land Given to Ephraim

[5]The following territory was given to the clans of the tribe of Ephraim.

The boundary of their homeland began at Ataroth-addar in the east. From there it ran to Upper Beth-horon, [6]then on to the Mediterranean Sea. From Micmethath on the north, the boundary curved eastward past Taanath-shiloh to the east of Janoah. [7]From Janoah it turned southward to Ataroth and Naarah, touched Jericho, and ended at the Jordan River. [8]From Tappuah the boundary extended westward, following the Kanah Ravine to the Mediterranean Sea. This is the homeland allocated to the clans of the tribe of Ephraim.

[9]In addition, some towns with their surrounding villages in the territory allocated to the half-tribe of Manasseh were set aside for the tribe of Ephraim. [10]They did not drive the Canaanites out of Gezer, however, so the people of Gezer live as slaves among the people of Ephraim to this day.

The Land Given to West Manasseh

17 The next allotment of land was given to the half-tribe of Manasseh, the descendants of Joseph's older son. Makir, the firstborn son of Manasseh, was the father of Gilead. Because his descendants were experienced soldiers, the regions of Gilead and Bashan on the east side of the Jordan had already been given to them. [2]So the allotment on the west side of the Jordan was for the remaining families within the clans of the tribe of Manasseh: Abiezer, Helek, Asriel, Shechem, Hepher, and Shemida. These clans represent the male descendants of Manasseh son of Joseph.

[3]However, Zelophehad, a descendant of Hepher son of Gilead, son of Makir, son of Manasseh, had no sons. He had only daughters, whose names were Mahlah, Noah, Hoglah, Milcah, and Tirzah. [4]These women came to Eleazar the priest, Joshua son of Nun, and the Israelite leaders and said, "The LORD commanded Moses to give us a grant of land along with the men of our tribe."

So Joshua gave them a grant of land along with their uncles, as the LORD had commanded. [5]As a result, Manasseh's total allocation came to ten parcels of land, in addition to the land of Gilead and Bashan

15:9 Or *the spring at Me-nephtoah.* **15:12** Hebrew *the Great Sea;* also in 15:47. **15:18** Some Greek manuscripts read *he urged her.* **15:33** Hebrew *the Shephelah.* **16:2** As in Greek version (also see 18:13); Hebrew reads *From Bethel to Luz.* **16:3** Hebrew *the sea;* also in 16:6, 8.

across the Jordan River, 6because the female descendants of Manasseh received a grant of land along with the male descendants. (The land of Gilead was given to the rest of the male descendants of Manasseh.)

7The boundary of the tribe of Manasseh extended from the border of Asher to Micmethath, near Shechem. Then the boundary went south from Micmethath to the settlement near the spring of Tappuah. 8The land surrounding Tappuah belonged to Manasseh, but the town of Tappuah itself, on the border of Manasseh's territory, belonged to the tribe of Ephraim. 9From the spring of Tappuah, the boundary of Manasseh followed the Kanah Ravine to the Mediterranean Sea.* Several towns south of the ravine were inside Manasseh's territory, but they actually belonged to the tribe of Ephraim. 10In general, however, the land south of the ravine belonged to Ephraim, and the land north of the ravine belonged to Manasseh. Manasseh's boundary ran along the northern side of the ravine and ended at the Mediterranean Sea. North of Manasseh was the territory of Asher, and to the east was the territory of Issachar.

11The following towns within the territory of Issachar and Asher, however, were given to Manasseh: Beth-shan,* Ibleam, Dor (that is, Naphoth-dor),* Endor, Taanach, and Megiddo, each with their surrounding settlements.

12But the descendants of Manasseh were unable to occupy these towns because the Canaanites were determined to stay in that region. 13Later, however, when the Israelites became strong enough, they forced the Canaanites to work as slaves. But they did not drive them out of the land.

14The descendants of Joseph came to Joshua and asked, "Why have you given us only one portion of land as our homeland when the LORD has blessed us with so many people?"

15Joshua replied, "If there are so many of you, and if the hill country of Ephraim is not large enough for you, clear out land for yourselves in the forest where the Perizzites and Rephaites live."

16The descendants of Joseph responded, "It's true that the hill country is not large enough for us. But all the Canaanites in the lowlands have iron chariots, both those in Beth-shan and its surrounding settlements and those in the valley of Jezreel. They are too strong for us."

17Then Joshua said to the tribes of Ephraim and Manasseh, the descendants of Joseph, "Since you are so large and strong, you will be given more than one portion. 18The forests of the hill country will be yours as well. Clear as much of the land as you wish, and take possession of its farthest corners. And you will drive out the Canaanites from the valleys, too, even though they are strong and have iron chariots."

The Allotments of the Remaining Land

18 Now that the land was under Israelite control, the entire community of Israel gathered at Shiloh and set up the Tabernacle.* 2But there remained seven tribes who had not yet been allotted their grants of land.

3Then Joshua asked them, "How long are you going to wait before taking possession of the remaining land the LORD, the God of your ancestors, has given to you? 4Select three men from each tribe, and I will send them out to explore the land and map it out. They will then return to me with a written report of their proposed divisions of their new homeland. 5Let them divide the land into seven sections, excluding Judah's territory in the south and Joseph's territory in the north. 6And when you record the seven divisions of the land and bring them to me, I will cast sacred lots in the presence of the LORD our God to assign land to each tribe.

7"The Levites, however, will not receive any allotment of land. Their role as priests of the LORD is their allotment. And the tribes of Gad, Reuben, and the half-tribe of Manasseh won't receive any more land, for they have already received their grant of land, which Moses, the servant of the LORD, gave them on the east side of the Jordan River."

8As the men started on their way to map out the land, Joshua commanded them, "Go and explore the land and write a description of it. Then return to me, and I will assign the land to the tribes by casting sacred lots here in the presence of the LORD at Shiloh." 9The men did as they were told and mapped the entire territory into seven sections, listing the towns in each section. They made a written record and then returned to Joshua in the camp at Shiloh. [10]And there at Shiloh, Joshua cast sacred lots in the presence of the LORD to determine which tribe should have each section.

The Land Given to Benjamin

[11]The first allotment of land went to the clans of the tribe of Benjamin. It lay between the territory assigned to the tribes of Judah and Joseph.

[12]The northern boundary of Benjamin's land began at the Jordan River, went north of the slope of Jericho, then west through the hill country and the wilderness of Beth-aven. [13]From there the boundary went south to Luz (that is, Bethel) and proceeded down to Ataroth-addar on the hill that lies south of Lower Beth-horon.

[14]The boundary then made a turn and swung south along the western edge of the hill facing Beth-horon, ending at the village of Kiriath-baal (that is, Kiriath-jearim), a town belonging to the tribe of Judah. This was the western boundary.

[15]The southern boundary began at the outskirts of Kiriath-jearim. From that western point it ran* to the spring at the waters of Nephtoah,* [16]and down to the base of the mountain beside the valley of Ben-Hinnom, at the northern end of the valley of Rephaim. From there it went down the valley of Hinnom, crossing south of the slope where the Jebusites lived, and continued down to En-rogel. [17]From En-rogel the boundary proceeded in a northerly direction and came to En-shemesh and on to Geliloth (which is across from the slopes of Adummim). Then it went down to the Stone of Bohan. (Bohan was Reuben's son.) [18]From there it passed along the north side of the slope overlooking the Jordan Valley.* The border then went down into the valley, [19]ran past the north slope of Beth-hoglah, and ended at the north bay of the Dead Sea,* which is the southern end of the Jordan River. This was the southern boundary.

[20]The eastern boundary was the Jordan River.

These were the boundaries of the homeland allocated to the clans of the tribe of Benjamin.

The Towns Given to Benjamin

[21]These were the towns given to the clans of the tribe of Benjamin.

Jericho, Beth-hoglah, Emek-keziz,
[22]Beth-arabah, Zemaraim,
Bethel, [23]Avvim, Parah, Ophrah,
[24]Kephar-ammoni, Ophni, and Geba—
twelve towns with their surrounding
villages. [25]Also Gibeon, Ramah, Beeroth,
[26]Mizpah, Kephirah, Mozah, [27]Rekem,
Irpeel, Taralah, [28]Zela, Haeleph, the
Jebusite town (that is, Jerusalem),
Gibeah, and Kiriath-jearim*—fourteen
towns with their surrounding villages.

This was the homeland allocated to the clans of the tribe of Benjamin.

17:9 Hebrew *the sea;* also in 17:10. **17:11a** Hebrew *Beth-shean,* a variant spelling of Beth-shan; also in 17:16. **17:11b** The meaning of the Hebrew here is uncertain. **18:1** Hebrew *Tent of Meeting.* **18:15a** Or *From there it went to Mozah.* The meaning of the Hebrew is uncertain. **18:15b** Or *the spring at Me-nephtoah.* **18:18** Hebrew *overlooking the Arabah,* or *overlooking Beth-arabah.* **18:19** Hebrew *Salt Sea.* **18:28** As in Greek version; Hebrew reads *Kiriath.*

Shiloh

Moses had told the Israelites that God would choose a central location for the Tabernacle once they were settled in the Promised Land (Deuteronomy 12:8-14). That place proved to be Shiloh, a city in the hills in the middle of the country, where Joshua set up the Tabernacle (Joshua 18:1). It was here that Eli would serve as a priest and Samuel begin his ministry (1 Samuel 3). Shiloh was eventually destroyed by the Philistines around 1050 BC, an event recalled by Jeremiah many years later as a solemn warning to Jerusalem that religious shrines, in themselves, are of no value to God (Jeremiah 7:12-15).

The Land Given to Simeon

19 The second allotment of land went to the clans of the tribe of Simeon. Their homeland was surrounded by Judah's territory.

2Simeon's homeland included
Beersheba, Sheba, Moladah,
3Hazar-shual, Balah, Ezem,
4Eltolad, Bethul, Hormah, 5Ziklag,
Beth-marcaboth, Hazar-susah,
6Beth-lebaoth, and Sharuhen—thirteen
towns with their surrounding villages.
7It also included Ain, Rimmon, Ether,
and Ashan—four towns with their
villages, 8including all the surrounding
villages as far south as Baalath-beer
(also known as Ramah of the Negev).

This was the homeland allocated to the clans of the tribe of Simeon. 9Their allocation of land came from part of what had been given to Judah because Judah's territory was too large for them. So the tribe of Simeon received an allocation within the territory of Judah.

The Land Given to Zebulun

10The third allotment of land went to the clans of the tribe of Zebulun.

The boundary of Zebulun's homeland
started at Sarid. 11From there it went
west, going past Maralah, touching
Dabbesheth, and proceeding to the
brook east of Jokneam. 12In the other
direction, the boundary went east from
Sarid to the border of Kisloth-tabor, and
from there to Daberath and up to Japhia.
13Then it continued east to Gath-hepher,
Eth-kazin, and Rimmon and turned
toward Neah. 14The northern boundary of
Zebulun passed Hannathon and ended
at the valley of Iphtah-el. 15The towns in
these areas included Kattath, Nahalal,
Shimron, Idalah, and Bethlehem—twelve
towns with their surrounding villages.

16The homeland allocated to the clans of the tribe of Zebulun included these towns and their surrounding villages.

The Land Given to Issachar

17The fourth allotment of land went to the clans of the tribe of Issachar.

18Its boundaries included the following
towns: Jezreel, Kesulloth, Shunem,
19Hapharaim, Shion, Anaharath,
20Rabbith, Kishion, Ebez, 21Remeth,
En-gannim, En-haddah, and
Beth-pazzez. 22The boundary also
touched Tabor, Shahazumah, and
Beth-shemesh, ending at the Jordan
River—sixteen towns with their
surrounding villages.

Why does the Bible have passages like these?

Let's face it, some parts of the Bible can (if we are really honest) seem quite boring: passages like these detailed accounts of which tribe was allotted which parts of the Promised Land (Joshua 15–19); or lists of Temple equipment returned to Jerusalem (Ezra 1:7-11) along with the names of the returning exiles (Ezra 2:1-70); or long genealogies (e.g., 1 Chronicles 1–9). These are the parts that most Christians usually skim over when reading their Bibles. So why are they there?

What we need to remember is that, long before the Old Testament was part of our Christian Bible, it was Israel's "Bible"—the account of their faith-walk with God. And that faith-walk did not just affect spiritual matters, but rather every area of life, including who should live where, and whether precious artifacts were faithfully delivered to their destination, and whether someone was truly descended from Abraham and so a true Jew.

These chapters of Joshua serve as a "map in words," for maps as we understand them didn't exist. The only way to "map" a region was by noting where its boundaries ran, what rivers, hills, towns, and villages were there, and so on. While such particulars are of little direct relevance to us, what they do demonstrate is God's concern for every detail of our lives.

23 The homeland allocated to the clans of the
tribe of Issachar included these towns and
their surrounding villages.

The Land Given to Asher

24 The fifth allotment of land went to the
clans of the tribe of Asher.

25 Its boundaries included these
towns: Helkath, Hali, Beten, Acshaph,
26 Allammelech, Amad, and Mishal.
The boundary on the west touched
Carmel and Shihor-libnath, 27 then it
turned east toward Beth-dagon, and
ran as far as Zebulun in the valley of
Iphtah-el, going north to Beth-emek
and Neiel. It then continued north to
Cabul, 28 Abdon,* Rehob, Hammon,
Kanah, and as far as Greater Sidon.
29 Then the boundary turned toward
Ramah and the fortress of Tyre,
where it turned toward Hosah
and came to the Mediterranean
Sea.* The territory alsoincluded
Mehebel, Aczib, 30 Ummah, Aphek,
and Rehob—twenty-two towns with
their surrounding villages.

31 The homeland allocated to the clans of
the tribe of Asher included these towns and
their surrounding villages.

The Land Given to Naphtali

32 The sixth allotment of land went to the
clans of the tribe of Naphtali.

33 Its boundary ran from Heleph, from
the oak at Zaanannim, and extended
across to Adami-nekeb, Jabneel, and
as far as Lakkum, ending at the Jordan
River. 34 The western boundary ran
past Aznoth-tabor, then to Hukkok,
and touched the border of Zebulun
in the south, the border of Asher
on the west, and the Jordan River*
on the east. 35 The fortified towns
included in this territory were Ziddim,
Zer, Hammath, Rakkath, Kinnereth,
36 Adamah, Ramah, Hazor,
37 Kedesh, Edrei, En-hazor, 38 Yiron,
Migdal-el, Horem, Beth-anath, and
Beth-shemesh—nineteen towns with
their surrounding villages.

39 The homeland allocated to the clans of the
tribe of Naphtali included these towns and
their surrounding villages.

The Land Given to Dan

40 The seventh allotment of land went to the
clans of the tribe of Dan.

41 The land allocated as their homeland
included the following towns: Zorah,
Eshtaol, Ir-shemesh, 42 Shaalabbin,
Aijalon, Ithlah, 43 Elon, Timnah, Ekron,
44 Eltekeh, Gibbethon, Baalath, 45 Jehud,
Bene-berak, Gath-rimmon, 46 Me-jarkon,
Rakkon, and the territory across from
Joppa.

47 But the tribe of Dan had trouble
taking possession of their land,* so
they attacked the town of Laish.* They
captured it, slaughtered its people, and
settled there. They renamed the town
Dan after their ancestor.

48 The homeland allocated to the clans of the
tribe of Dan included these towns and their
surrounding villages.

The Land Given to Joshua

49 After all the land was divided among the
tribes, the Israelites gave a piece of land to
Joshua as his allocation. 50 For the LORD had
said he could have any town he wanted. He
chose Timnath-serah in the hill country
of Ephraim. He rebuilt the town and lived
there.

51 These are the territories that Eleazar the
priest, Joshua son of Nun, and the tribal
leaders allocated as grants of land to the
tribes of Israel by casting sacred lots in
the presence of the LORD at the entrance of
the Tabernacle* at Shiloh. So the division
of the land was completed.

The Cities of Refuge

20 The LORD said to Joshua, 2 "Now tell
the Israelites to designate the cities
of refuge, as I instructed Moses. 3 Anyone
who kills another person accidentally and
unintentionally can run to one of these
cities; they will be places of refuge from relatives seeking revenge for the person who
was killed.

4 "Upon reaching one of these cities, the
one who caused the death will appear before
the elders at the city gate and present his
case. They must allow him to enter the city

19:28 As in some Hebrew manuscripts (see also 21:30); most Hebrew manuscripts read *Ebron.* **19:29** Hebrew *the sea.* **19:34** Hebrew *and Judah at the Jordan River.* **19:47a** Or *had trouble holding on to their land.* **19:47b** Hebrew *Leshem,* a variant spelling of Laish. **19:51** Hebrew *Tent of Meeting.*

and give him a place to live among them. [5]If
the relatives of the victim come to avenge
the killing, the leaders must not release the
slayer to them, for he killed the other person
unintentionally and without previous hostility. [6]But the slayer must stay in that city and
be tried by the local assembly, which will
render a judgment. And he must continue to
live in that city until the death of the high
priest who was in office at the time of the accident. After that, he is free to return to his
own home in the town from which he fled."

[7]The following cities were designated as
cities of refuge: Kedesh of Galilee, in the hill
country of Naphtali; Shechem, in the hill
country of Ephraim; and Kiriath-arba (that
is, Hebron), in the hill country of Judah.
[8]On the east side of the Jordan River, across
from Jericho, the following cities were designated: Bezer, in the wilderness plain of
the tribe of Reuben; Ramoth in Gilead, in
the territory of the tribe of Gad; and Golan
in Bashan, in the land of the tribe of Manasseh. [9]These cities were set apart for all
the Israelites as well as the foreigners living
among them. Anyone who accidentally
killed another person could take refuge in
one of these cities. In this way, they could
escape being killed in revenge prior to
standing trial before the local assembly.

The Towns Given to the Levites

21 Then the leaders of the tribe of Levi
came to consult with Eleazar the
priest, Joshua son of Nun, and the leaders
of the other tribes of Israel. [2]They came to
them at Shiloh in the land of Canaan and
said, "The LORD commanded Moses to give
us towns to live in and pasturelands for our
livestock." [3]So by the command of the LORD
the people of Israel gave the Levites the following towns and pasturelands out of their
own grants of land.

[4]The descendants of Aaron, who were
members of the Kohathite clan within the
tribe of Levi, were allotted thirteen towns
that were originally assigned to the tribes
of Judah, Simeon, and Benjamin. [5]The other
families of the Kohathite clan were allotted
ten towns from the tribes of Ephraim, Dan,
and the half-tribe of Manasseh.

[6]The clan of Gershon was allotted thirteen
towns from the tribes of Issachar, Asher,
Naphtali, and the half-tribe of Manasseh in
Bashan.

[7]The clan of Merari was allotted twelve
towns from the tribes of Reuben, Gad, and
Zebulun.

[8]So the Israelites obeyed the LORD's
command to Moses and assigned these
towns and pasturelands to the Levites by
casting sacred lots.

[9]The Israelites gave the following towns
from the tribes of Judah and Simeon [10]to the
descendants of Aaron, who were members
of the Kohathite clan within the tribe of
Levi, since the sacred lot fell to them first:
[11]Kiriath-arba (that is, Hebron), in the hill
country of Judah, along with its surrounding pasturelands. (Arba was an ancestor of
Anak.) [12]But the open fields beyond the town
and the surrounding villages were given to
Caleb son of Jephunneh as his possession.

[13]The following towns with their pasturelands were given to the descendants of
Aaron the priest: Hebron (a city of refuge
for those who accidentally killed someone),
Libnah, [14]Jattir, Eshtemoa, [15]Holon, Debir,
[16]Ain, Juttah, and Beth-shemesh—nine
towns from these two tribes.

[17]From the tribe of Benjamin the priests
were given the following towns with their
pasturelands: Gibeon, Geba, [18]Anathoth,
and Almon—four towns. [19]So in all, thirteen
towns with their pasturelands were given to
the priests, the descendants of Aaron.

[20]The rest of the Kohathite clan from
the tribe of Levi was allotted the following
towns and pasturelands from the tribe of
Ephraim: [21]Shechem in the hill country of
Ephraim (a city of refuge for those who accidentally killed someone), Gezer, [22]Kibzaim,
and Beth-horon—four towns.

[23]The following towns and pasturelands
were allotted to the priests from the tribe
of Dan: Eltekeh, Gibbethon, [24]Aijalon, and
Gath-rimmon—four towns.

[25]The half-tribe of Manasseh allotted the
following towns with their pasturelands to
the priests: Taanach and Gath-rimmon—
two towns. [26]So in all, ten towns with their
pasturelands were given to the rest of the
Kohathite clan.

[27]The descendants of Gershon, another
clan within the tribe of Levi, received the
following towns with their pasturelands
from the half-tribe of Manasseh: Golan in
Bashan (a city of refuge for those who accidentally killed someone) and Be-eshterah—
two towns.

[28]From the tribe of Issachar they received
the following towns with their pasturelands: Kishion, Daberath, [29]Jarmuth, and
En-gannim—four towns.
[30]From the tribe of Asher they received the
following towns with their pasturelands:
Mishal, Abdon, [31]Helkath, and Rehob—four
towns.
[32]From the tribe of Naphtali they received
the following towns with their pasturelands: Kedesh in Galilee (a city of refuge for
those who accidentally killed someone),
Hammoth-dor, and Kartan—three towns.
[33]So in all, thirteen towns with their pasturelands were allotted to the clan of Gershon.
[34]The rest of the Levites—the Merari
clan—were given the following towns
with their pasturelands from the tribe of
Zebulun: Jokneam, Kartah, [35]Dimnah, and
Nahalal—four towns.
[36]From the tribe of Reuben they received
the following towns with their pasturelands: Bezer, Jahaz,* [37]Kedemoth, and
Mephaath—four towns.
[38]From the tribe of Gad they received the
following towns with their pasturelands:
Ramoth in Gilead (a city of refuge for those
who accidentally killed someone), Mahanaim, [39]Heshbon, and Jazer—four towns.
[40]So in all, twelve towns were allotted to the
clan of Merari.
[41]The total number of towns and pasturelands within Israelite territory given to
the Levites came to forty-eight. [42]Every
one of these towns had pasturelands
surrounding it.
[43]So the LORD gave to Israel all the land
he had sworn to give their ancestors, and
they took possession of it and settled there.
[44]And the LORD gave them rest on every side,
just as he had solemnly promised their ancestors. None of their enemies could stand
against them, for the LORD helped them
conquer all their enemies. [45]Not a single one
of all the good promises the LORD had given
to the family of Israel was left unfulfilled;
everything he had spoken came true.

The Eastern Tribes Return Home

22 Then Joshua called together the
tribes of Reuben, Gad, and the half-
tribe of Manasseh. [2]He told them, "You have
done as Moses, the servant of the LORD, commanded you, and you have obeyed every
order I have given you. [3]During all this time
you have not deserted the other tribes. You
have been careful to obey the commands of
the LORD your God right up to the present
day. [4]And now the LORD your God has given
the other tribes rest, as he promised them.
So go back home to the land that Moses, the
servant of the LORD, gave you as your possession on the east side of the Jordan River.
[5]But be very careful to obey all the commands and the instructions that Moses gave
to you. Love the LORD your God, walk in all
his ways, obey his commands, hold firmly to
him, and serve him with all your heart and
all your soul." [6]So Joshua blessed them and
sent them away, and they went home.
[7]Moses had given the land of Bashan, east
of the Jordan River, to the half-tribe of Manasseh. (The other half of the tribe was given
land west of the Jordan.) As Joshua sent them
away and blessed them, [8]he said to them,
"Go back to your homes with the great wealth
you have taken from your enemies—the vast
herds of livestock, the silver, gold, bronze,
and iron, and the large supply of clothing.
Share the plunder with your relatives."
[9]So the men of Reuben, Gad, and the half-
tribe of Manasseh left the rest of Israel at
Shiloh in the land of Canaan. They started
the journey back to their own land of Gilead,
the territory that belonged to them according to the LORD's command through Moses.

The Eastern Tribes Build an Altar

[10]But while they were still in Canaan, and
when they came to a place called Geliloth*
near the Jordan River, the men of Reuben,
Gad, and the half-tribe of Manasseh stopped
to build a large and imposing altar.
[11]The rest of Israel heard that the people
of Reuben, Gad, and the half-tribe of Manasseh had built an altar at Geliloth at the edge
of the land of Canaan, on the west side of
the Jordan River. [12]So the whole community
of Israel gathered at Shiloh and prepared
to go to war against them. [13]First, however,
they sent a delegation led by Phinehas son
of Eleazar, the priest, to talk with the tribes
of Reuben, Gad, and the half-tribe of Manasseh. [14]In this delegation were ten leaders
of Israel, one from each of the ten tribes,
and each the head of his family within the
clans of Israel.
[15]When they arrived in the land of Gilead,

21:36 Hebrew *Jahzah,* a variant spelling of Jahaz. **22:10** Or *to the circle of stones;* similarly in 22:11.

they said to the tribes of Reuben, Gad, and
the half-tribe of Manasseh, 16“The whole
community of the LORD demands to know
why you are betraying the God of Israel. How
could you turn away from the LORD and build
an altar for yourselves in rebellion against
him? 17Was our sin at Peor not enough? To
this day we are not fully cleansed of it, even
after the plague that struck the entire community of the LORD. 18And yet today you are
turning away from following the LORD. If
you rebel against the LORD today, he will be
angry with all of us tomorrow.

19“If you need the altar because the land
you possess is defiled, then join us in the
LORD’s land, where the Tabernacle of the
LORD is situated, and share our land with
us. But do not rebel against the LORD or
against us by building an altar other than
the one true altar of the LORD our God.
20Didn’t divine anger fall on the entire community of Israel when Achan, a member of
the clan of Zerah, sinned by stealing the
things set apart for the LORD*? He was not
the only one who died because of his sin.”

21Then the people of Reuben, Gad, and the
half-tribe of Manasseh answered the heads of
the clans of Israel: 22“The LORD, the Mighty
One, is God! The LORD, the Mighty One, is
God! He knows the truth, and may Israel
know it, too! We have not built the altar in
treacherous rebellion against the LORD. If
we have done so, do not spare our lives this
day. 23If we have built an altar for ourselves to
turn away from the LORD or to offer burnt offerings or grain offerings or peace offerings,
may the LORD himself punish us.

24“The truth is, we have built this altar
because we fear that in the future your descendants will say to ours, ‘What right do you
have to worship the LORD, the God of Israel?
25The LORD has placed the Jordan River as a
barrier between our people and you people
of Reuben and Gad. You have no claim to the
LORD.’ So your descendants may prevent our
descendants from worshiping the LORD.

26“So we decided to build the altar, not
for burnt offerings or sacrifices, 27but as a
memorial. It will remind our descendants
and your descendants that we, too, have
the right to worship the LORD at his sanctuary with our burnt offerings, sacrifices, and
peace offerings. Then your descendants
will not be able to say to ours, ‘You have no
claim to the LORD.’

28“If they say this, our descendants can
reply, ‘Look at this copy of the LORD’s altar
that our ancestors made. It is not for burnt
offerings or sacrifices; it is a reminder of the
relationship both of us have with the LORD.’
29Far be it from us to rebel against the LORD
or turn away from him by building our own
altar for burnt offerings, grain offerings, or
sacrifices. Only the altar of the LORD our
God that stands in front of the Tabernacle
may be used for that purpose.”

30When Phinehas the priest and the
leaders of the community—the heads of the
clans of Israel—heard this from the tribes of
Reuben, Gad, and the half-tribe of Manasseh, they were satisfied. 31Phinehas son of
Eleazar, the priest, replied to them, “Today
we know the LORD is among us because you
have not committed this treachery against
the LORD as we thought. Instead, you have
rescued Israel from being destroyed by the
hand of the LORD.”

32Then Phinehas son of Eleazar, the
priest, and the other leaders left the tribes
of Reuben and Gad in Gilead and returned
to the land of Canaan to tell the Israelites
what had happened. 33And all the Israelites
were satisfied and praised God and spoke
no more of war against Reuben and Gad.

34The people of Reuben and Gad named
the altar “Witness,”* for they said, “It is a
witness between us and them that the LORD
is our God, too.”

Joshua’s Final Words to Israel

23 The years passed, and the LORD had
given the people of Israel rest from
all their enemies. Joshua, who was now
very old, 2called together all the elders,
leaders, judges, and officers of Israel. He
said to them, “I am now a very old man.
3You have seen everything the LORD your
God has done for you during my lifetime.
The LORD your God has fought for you
against your enemies. 4I have allotted to
you as your homeland all the land of the
nations yet unconquered, as well as the
land of those we have already conquered—
from the Jordan River to the Mediterranean
Sea* in the west. 5This land will be yours,
for the LORD your God will himself drive out
all the people living there now. You will take
possession of their land, just as the LORD
your God promised you.

6“So be very careful to follow everything

Moses wrote in the Book of Instruction. Do
not deviate from it, turning either to the right
or to the left. 7 Make sure you do not associate
with the other people still remaining in the
land. Do not even mention the names of their
gods, much less swear by them or serve them
or worship them. 8 Rather, cling tightly to the
LORD your God as you have done until now.
9 "For the LORD has driven out great and
powerful nations for you, and no one has
yet been able to defeat you. 10 Each one of
you will put to flight a thousand of the
enemy, for the LORD your God fights for you,
just as he has promised. 11 So be very careful
to love the LORD your God.
12 "But if you turn away from him and
cling to the customs of the survivors of
these nations remaining among you, and
if you intermarry with them, 13 then know
for certain that the LORD your God will no
longer drive them out of your land. Instead,
they will be a snare and a trap to you, a
whip for your backs and thorny brambles
in your eyes, and you will vanish from this
good land the LORD your God has given you.
14 "Soon I will die, going the way of everything on earth. Deep in your hearts you know
that every promise of the LORD your God has
come true. Not a single one has failed! 15 But
as surely as the LORD your God has given you
the good things he promised, he will also
bring disaster on you if you disobey him. He
will completely destroy you from this good
land he has given you. 16 If you break the covenant of the LORD your God by worshiping
and serving other gods, his anger will burn
against you, and you will quickly vanish
from the good land he has given you."

The LORD's Covenant Renewed

24 Then Joshua summoned all the
tribes of Israel to Shechem, including their elders, leaders, judges, and
officers. So they came and presented themselves to God.
2 Joshua said to the people, "This is what
the LORD, the God of Israel, says: Long ago
your ancestors, including Terah, the father
of Abraham and Nahor, lived beyond the
Euphrates River,* and they worshiped other
gods. 3 But I took your ancestor Abraham
from the land beyond the Euphrates and
led him into the land of Canaan. I gave him
many descendants through his son Isaac.
4 To Isaac I gave Jacob and Esau. To Esau I
gave the mountains of Seir, while Jacob and
his children went down into Egypt.
5 "Then I sent Moses and Aaron, and
I brought terrible plagues on Egypt; and
afterward I brought you out as a free people.
6 But when your ancestors arrived at the Red
Sea,* the Egyptians chased after you with
chariots and charioteers. 7 When your ancestors cried out to the LORD, I put darkness
between you and the Egyptians. I brought
the sea crashing down on the Egyptians,

22:20 The Hebrew term used here refers to the complete consecration of things or people to the LORD, either by destroying them or by giving them as an offering. **22:34** Some manuscripts lack this word. **23:4** Hebrew *the Great Sea*. **24:2** Hebrew *the river;* also in 24:3, 14, 15. **24:6** Hebrew *sea of reeds*.

Consecration

With the conquest completed, Joshua was about to renew the covenant between God and his people. But first, he recalled their history, going back to its beginnings with Abraham, and reminding them of God's faithfulness to them over the years. In light of all this, it was now decision time, time to "choose today whom you will serve" (Joshua 24:15). His own choice was clear: "As for me and my family, we will serve the LORD" (24:15). Although the people were quick to agree, Joshua saw that their response was shallow and challenged them again. At last they made a wholehearted decision (24:21).

There comes a time in all our lives when we too have to decide, once and for all. Yes, we have been following God, but there remain elements of the old life in us, just like these Israelites who had kept pagan idols while still worshiping God (24:23). Consecration is about putting everything that is not of God to one side and yielding our lives completely to be his and only his. Only then can we truly know the joy of what it means to be his people.

drowning them. With your very own eyes
you saw what I did. Then you lived in the
wilderness for many years.
8“Finally, I brought you into the land of
the Amorites on the east side of the Jordan.
They fought against you, but I destroyed
them before you. I gave you victory over
them, and you took possession of their
land. 9Then Balak son of Zippor, king of
Moab, started a war against Israel. He summoned Balaam son of Beor to curse you,
10but I would not listen to him. Instead,
I made Balaam bless you, and so I rescued
you from Balak.
11“When you crossed the Jordan River and
came to Jericho, the men of Jericho fought
against you, as did the Amorites, the Perizzites, the Canaanites, the Hittites, the
Girgashites, the Hivites, and the Jebusites.
But I gave you victory over them. 12And I
sent terror* ahead of you to drive out the
two kings of the Amorites. It was not your
swords or bows that brought you victory.
13I gave you land you had not worked on,
and I gave you towns you did not build—the
towns where you are now living. I gave you
vineyards and olive groves for food, though
you did not plant them.
14“So fear the LORD and serve him wholeheartedly. Put away forever the idols your
ancestors worshiped when they lived
beyond the Euphrates River and in Egypt.
Serve the LORD alone. 15But if you refuse to
serve the LORD, then choose today whom
you will serve. Would you prefer the gods
your ancestors served beyond the Euphrates? Or will it be the gods of the Amorites in
whose land you now live? But as for me and
my family, we will serve the LORD.”
16The people replied, “We would never
abandon the LORD and serve other gods.
17For the LORD our God is the one who
rescued us and our ancestors from slavery
in the land of Egypt. He performed mighty
miracles before our very eyes. As we traveled through the wilderness among our
enemies, he preserved us. 18It was the LORD
who drove out the Amorites and the other
nations living here in the land. So we, too,
will serve the LORD, for he alone is our God.”
19Then Joshua warned the people, “You
are not able to serve the LORD, for he is a
holy and jealous God. He will not forgive
your rebellion and your sins. 20If you
abandon the LORD and serve other gods, he
will turn against you and destroy you, even
though he has been so good to you.”
21But the people answered Joshua, “No,
we will serve the LORD!”
22“You are a witness to your own decision,” Joshua said. “You have chosen to
serve the LORD.”
“Yes,” they replied, “we are witnesses to
what we have said.”
23“All right then,” Joshua said, “destroy
the idols among you, and turn your hearts
to the LORD, the God of Israel.”
24The people said to Joshua, “We will
serve the LORD our God. We will obey him
alone.”
25So Joshua made a covenant with the
people that day at Shechem, committing
them to follow the decrees and regulations
of the LORD. 26Joshua recorded these things
in the Book of God’s Instructions. As a
reminder of their agreement, he took a huge
stone and rolled it beneath the terebinth
tree beside the Tabernacle of the LORD.
27Joshua said to all the people, “This
stone has heard everything the LORD said
to us. It will be a witness to testify against
you if you go back on your word to God.”
28Then Joshua sent all the people away to
their own homelands.

Leaders Buried in the Promised Land

29After this, Joshua son of Nun, the servant
of the LORD, died at the age of 110. 30They
buried him in the land he had been allocated, at Timnath-serah in the hill country
of Ephraim, north of Mount Gaash.
31The people of Israel served the LORD
throughout the lifetime of Joshua and of the
elders who outlived him—those who had
personally experienced all that the LORD
had done for Israel.
32The bones of Joseph, which the Israelites had brought along with them when
they left Egypt, were buried at Shechem, in
the plot of land Jacob had bought from the
sons of Hamor for 100 pieces of silver.* This
land was located in the territory allotted to
the descendants of Joseph.
33Eleazar son of Aaron also died. He was
buried in the hill country of Ephraim, in the
town of Gibeah, which had been given to his
son Phinehas.

24:12 Often rendered *the hornet*. The meaning of the Hebrew is uncertain. **24:32** Hebrew *100 kesitahs;* the value or weight of the kesitah is no longer known.

Judges *An endless cycle of Israelite sin*

The book of Judges covers the years between the Israelites' conquest of Canaan and their first king. It was a bleak period marked by repeated complacency and disobedience that led to domination by their enemies. Yet despite the people's unfaithfulness, God raised up leaders ("judges") to deliver them from their oppressors and to lead the different tribes (though probably never the whole nation). Again and again, we see a cycle of the Israelites' sin and worship of other gods, which led to their defeat and oppression by the Canaanites and other invading nations. The Israelites then cried out to God in repentance, and God sent a judge to rescue them from their oppressors. There was peace for a while until the cycle was repeated all over again.

The judges were leaders who were spontaneously empowered by God to rescue and lead the tribes. Some of the judges had very questionable sides to their character (like Samson) or were ambitious (like Jephthah), and Gideon's son Abimelech wanted to be not just a judge but a king. Nevertheless God used them since they were often the best he could find—a reflection of how dark these days were.

What's it all about?

The story begins ominously, noting the decline that followed Joshua's death. The Israelites had not eliminated their enemies from the land, they had intermarried with the Canaanites and were worshiping their gods, and foreign enemies were invading various tribal territories.

In chapter 3 the endless cycle begins: The Israelites sinned, suffered at the hands of their enemies, cried out to God, and were delivered. The first judges were Othniel, Ehud, and Shamgar (chapter 3). In chapters 4 and 5, Deborah, the only woman leader at this time, and her general, Barak, defeated the Canaanites, and Deborah celebrated their victory in song. Gideon defeated the Midianites, a nomadic people who lived on the edges of Canaan, with just three hundred men (chapters 6–8). As a result, Israel invited him to become their king, but he refused, reminding them that God alone was king (8:22-23). Abimelech, Gideon's son, was much more ambitious, however (chapter 9). Later, Jephthah defeated the Ammonites, a people who lived to the east of the Jordan. Other minor judges are also briefly mentioned. Chapters 13 to 16 relate the story of Samson, who was raised as a Nazirite—which involved not drinking alcohol, going near a dead body, or cutting his hair. Samson had extraordinary strength and used it to gain personal revenge on the Philistines. But he broke his Nazirite vows and failed to deliver Israel from oppression. His love affair with the Philistine Delilah led to disaster: She conspired against him and organized his capture (16:4-22). But he called out to God one last time, and

OVERVIEW

The failure of Israel to take the whole land of Canaan · *1:1–3:6*

The rescue of Israel by the judges *3:7–16:31*

The moral and spiritual decline of Israel · *17:1–21:25*

even in his death he brought destruction to many Philistines (16:23-30). Samson was not a godly man; but he was the best that God could find, showing how bad things had become in Israel by this time—as the remaining chapters of Judges reveal. Micah and the Danites became involved in idol worship (chapters 17–18); wicked men threatened a Levite with homosexual rape, and he surrendered his concubine to them instead (chapter 19); and the tribe of Benjamin, who defended the rapists, were attacked by the other tribes (chapter 20). Israel was falling apart.

What does it mean for us?

Judges shows us how destructive complacency can be. The Israelites let their commitment to a close relationship with God wane. They drifted along with the lifestyle of those around them, making their own choices rather than listening to God. They preferred the Canaanites' religion with its less demanding standards and highly sexualized worship, and they mixed some of it with their own faith. But mixing faith in this way is ultimately always destructive, weakening our commitment to God.

Judges is also a testimony to the effectiveness of prayer, even when it is offered in desperation. Whenever the Israelites called out to God for help, he always answered their prayers because he loved his people. Though the Judges period was a dark age in Israel's history, God did not—and does not—let his people go.

Judah and Simeon Conquer the Land

1 After the death of Joshua, the Israelites
asked the LORD, "Which tribe should go
first to attack the Canaanites?"
[2]The LORD answered, "Judah, for I have
given them victory over the land."
[3]The men of Judah said to their relatives
from the tribe of Simeon, "Join with us to
fight against the Canaanites living in the
territory allotted to us. Then we will help
you conquer your territory." So the men of
Simeon went with Judah.
[4]When the men of Judah attacked, the
LORD gave them victory over the Canaanites
and Perizzites, and they killed 10,000 enemy
warriors at the town of Bezek. [5]While at
Bezek they encountered King Adoni-bezek
and fought against him, and the Canaanites
and Perizzites were defeated. [6]Adoni-bezek
escaped, but the Israelites soon captured
him and cut off his thumbs and big toes.
[7]Adoni-bezek said, "I once had seventy
kings with their thumbs and big toes cut off,
eating scraps from under my table. Now God
has paid me back for what I did to them."
They took him to Jerusalem, and he died
there.
[8]The men of Judah attacked Jerusalem and
captured it, killing all its people and setting
the city on fire. [9]Then they went down to fight
the Canaanites living in the hill country, the
Negev, and the western foothills.* [10]Judah
marched against the Canaanites in Hebron
(formerly called Kiriath-arba), defeating the
forces of Sheshai, Ahiman, and Talmai.
[11]From there they went to fight against
the people living in the town of Debir (formerly called Kiriath-sepher). [12]Caleb said, "I
will give my daughter Acsah in marriage to
the one who attacks and captures Kiriath-
sepher." [13]Othniel, the son of Caleb's younger
brother, Kenaz, was the one who conquered
it, so Acsah became Othniel's wife.
[14]When Acsah married Othniel, she urged
him* to ask her father for a field. As she
got down off her donkey, Caleb asked her,
"What's the matter?"
[15]She said, "Let me have another gift. You
have already given me land in the Negev;
now please give me springs of water, too." So
Caleb gave her the upper and lower springs.
[16]When the tribe of Judah left Jericho—the
city of palms—the Kenites, who were descendants of Moses' father-in-law, traveled with
them into the wilderness of Judah. They
settled among the people there, near the
town of Arad in the Negev.
[17]Then Judah joined with Simeon to fight
against the Canaanites living in Zephath,
and they completely destroyed* the town.
So the town was named Hormah.* [18]In addition, Judah captured the towns of Gaza,
Ashkelon, and Ekron, along with their surrounding territories.

Israel Fails to Conquer the Land

19 The LORD was with the people of Judah, and they took possession of the hill country. But they failed to drive out the people living in the plains, who had iron chariots. 20 The town of Hebron was given to Caleb as Moses had promised. And Caleb drove out the people living there, who were descendants of the three sons of Anak.

21 The tribe of Benjamin, however, failed to drive out the Jebusites, who were living in Jerusalem. So to this day the Jebusites live in Jerusalem among the people of Benjamin.

22 The descendants of Joseph attacked the town of Bethel, and the LORD was with them. 23 They sent men to scout out Bethel (formerly known as Luz). 24 They confronted a man coming out of the town and said to him, "Show us a way into the town, and we will have mercy on you." 25 So he showed them a way in, and they killed everyone in the town except that man and his family. 26 Later the man moved to the land of the Hittites, where he built a town. He named it Luz, which is its name to this day.

27 The tribe of Manasseh failed to drive out the people living in Beth-shan,* Taanach, Dor, Ibleam, Megiddo, and all their surrounding settlements, because the Canaanites were determined to stay in that region. 28 When the Israelites grew stronger, they forced the Canaanites to work as slaves, but they never did drive them completely out of the land.

29 The tribe of Ephraim failed to drive out the Canaanites living in Gezer, so the Canaanites continued to live there among them.

30 The tribe of Zebulun failed to drive out the residents of Kitron and Nahalol, so the Canaanites continued to live among them. But the Canaanites were forced to work as slaves for the people of Zebulun.

31 The tribe of Asher failed to drive out the residents of Acco, Sidon, Ahlab, Aczib, Helbah, Aphik, and Rehob. 32 Instead, the people of Asher moved in among the Canaanites, who controlled the land, for they failed to drive them out.

33 Likewise, the tribe of Naphtali failed to drive out the residents of Beth-shemesh and Beth-anath. Instead, they moved in among the Canaanites, who controlled the land. Nevertheless, the people of Beth-shemesh and Beth-anath were forced to work as slaves for the people of Naphtali.

34 As for the tribe of Dan, the Amorites forced them back into the hill country and would not let them come down into the plains. 35 The Amorites were determined to stay in Mount Heres, Aijalon, and Shaalbim, but when the descendants of Joseph became stronger, they forced the Amorites to work as slaves. 36 The boundary of the Amorites ran from Scorpion Pass* to Sela and continued upward from there.

The LORD's Messenger Comes to Bokim

2 The angel of the LORD went up from Gilgal to Bokim and said to the Israelites, "I brought you out of Egypt into this land that I swore to give your ancestors, and I said I would never break my covenant with you. 2 For your part, you were not to make any covenants with the people living in this land;

1:9 Hebrew *the Shephelah.* **1:14** Greek version and Latin Vulgate read *he urged her.* **1:17a** The Hebrew term used here refers to the complete consecration of things or people to the LORD, either by destroying them or by giving them as an offering. **1:17b** *Hormah* means "destruction." **1:27** Hebrew *Beth-shean,* a variant spelling of Beth-shan. **1:36** Hebrew *Akrabbim.*

The angel of the LORD

"The angel of the LORD" is a figure who frequently appears in the Old Testament—for example, to Hagar (Genesis 16:7-14), Abraham (Genesis 22:9-19), Moses (Exodus 3:1–4:17), Balaam (Numbers 22:21-35), Elijah (1 Kings 19:3-9), David (1 Chronicles 21:13-16), and Zechariah (Zechariah 3). He also makes frequent appearances throughout the book of Judges (2:1-5; 6:11-24; 13:1-25). At times he simply seems to be God's special messenger, but at other times he seems to be equated with God himself. While some Christians have seen these as pre-incarnation manifestations of Christ, it is far more likely that, as the personal messenger of the LORD (Yahweh), he had authority to speak not just on God's behalf but also in his name.

instead, you were to destroy their altars. But you disobeyed my command. Why did you do this? 3So now I declare that I will no longer drive out the people living in your land. They will be thorns in your sides,* and their gods will be a constant temptation to you."

4When the angel of the LORD finished speaking to all the Israelites, the people wept loudly. 5So they called the place Bokim (which means "weeping"), and they offered sacrifices there to the LORD.

The Death of Joshua

6After Joshua sent the people away, each of the tribes left to take possession of the land allotted to them. 7And the Israelites served the LORD throughout the lifetime of Joshua and the leaders who outlived him—those who had seen all the great things the LORD had done for Israel.

8Joshua son of Nun, the servant of the LORD, died at the age of 110. 9They buried him in the land he had been allocated, at Timnath-serah* in the hill country of Ephraim, north of Mount Gaash.

Israel Disobeys the LORD

10After that generation died, another generation grew up who did not acknowledge the LORD or remember the mighty things he had done for Israel.

11The Israelites did evil in the LORD's sight and served the images of Baal. 12They abandoned the LORD, the God of their ancestors, who had brought them out of Egypt. They went after other gods, worshiping the gods of the people around them. And they angered the LORD. 13They abandoned the LORD to serve Baal and the images of Ashtoreth. 14This made the LORD burn with anger against Israel, so he handed them over to raiders who stole their possessions. He turned them over to their enemies all around, and they were no longer able to resist them. 15Every time Israel went out to battle, the LORD fought against them, causing them to be defeated, just as he had warned. And the people were in great distress.

The LORD Rescues His People

16Then the LORD raised up judges to rescue the Israelites from their attackers. 17Yet Israel did not listen to the judges but prostituted themselves by worshiping other gods. How quickly they turned away from the path of their ancestors, who had walked in obedience to the LORD's commands.

18Whenever the LORD raised up a judge over Israel, he was with that judge and rescued the people from their enemies throughout the judge's lifetime. For the LORD took pity on his people, who were burdened by oppression and suffering. 19But when the judge died, the people returned to their corrupt ways, behaving worse than those who had lived before them. They went after other gods, serving and worshiping them. And they refused to give up their evil practices and stubborn ways.

20So the LORD burned with anger against Israel. He said, "Because these people have violated my covenant, which I made with their ancestors, and have ignored my commands, 21I will no longer drive out the nations that Joshua left unconquered when he died. 22I did this to test Israel—to see whether or not they would follow the ways of the LORD as their ancestors did." 23That is why the LORD left those nations in place. He did not quickly drive them out or allow Joshua to conquer them all.

The Nations Left in Canaan

3 These are the nations that the LORD left in the land to test those Israelites who had not experienced the wars of Canaan. 2He did this to teach warfare to generations of Israelites who had no experience in battle. 3These are the nations: the Philistines (those living under the five Philistine rulers), all the Canaanites, the Sidonians, and the Hivites living in the mountains of Lebanon from Mount Baal-hermon to Lebo-hamath. 4These people were left to test the Israelites—to see whether they would obey the commands the LORD had given to their ancestors through Moses.

5So the people of Israel lived among the Canaanites, Hittites, Amorites, Perizzites, Hivites, and Jebusites, 6and they intermarried with them. Israelite sons married their daughters, and Israelite daughters were given in marriage to their sons. And the Israelites served their gods.

▸ **3:3** *See* ***The Philistines****, page 310.*

Othniel Becomes Israel's Judge

7The Israelites did evil in the LORD's sight. They forgot about the LORD their God, and they served the images of Baal and the Asherah poles. 8Then the LORD burned with anger against Israel, and he turned them over to King Cushan-rishathaim of Aram-naharaim.* And the Israelites served Cushan-rishathaim for eight years.

9But when the people of Israel cried out to the LORD for help, the LORD raised up a rescuer to save them. His name was Othniel, the son of Caleb's younger brother, Kenaz. 10The Spirit of the LORD came upon him, and he became Israel's judge. He went to war against King Cushan-rishathaim of Aram, and the LORD gave Othniel victory over him. 11So there was peace in the land for forty years. Then Othniel son of Kenaz died.

Ehud Becomes Israel's Judge

12Once again the Israelites did evil in the LORD's sight, and the LORD gave King Eglon of Moab control over Israel because of their evil. 13Eglon enlisted the Ammonites and Amalekites as allies, and then he went out and defeated Israel, taking possession of Jericho, the city of palms. 14And the Israelites served Eglon of Moab for eighteen years.

15But when the people of Israel cried out to the LORD for help, the LORD again raised up a rescuer to save them. His name was Ehud son of Gera, a left-handed man of the tribe of Benjamin. The Israelites sent Ehud to deliver their tribute money to King Eglon of Moab. 16So Ehud made a double-edged dagger that was about a foot* long, and he strapped it to his right thigh, keeping it hidden under his clothing. 17He brought the tribute money to Eglon, who was very fat.

18After delivering the payment, Ehud started home with those who had helped carry the tribute. 19But when Ehud reached the stone idols near Gilgal, he turned back. He came to Eglon and said, "I have a secret message for you."

So the king commanded his servants, "Be quiet!" and he sent them all out of the room.

20Ehud walked over to Eglon, who was sitting alone in a cool upstairs room. And Ehud said, "I have a message from God for you!" As King Eglon rose from his seat, 21Ehud reached with his left hand, pulled out the dagger strapped to his right thigh, and plunged it into the king's belly. 22The dagger went so deep that the handle disappeared beneath the king's fat. So Ehud did not pull out the dagger, and the king's bowels emptied.* 23Then Ehud closed and locked the doors of the room and escaped down the latrine.*

24After Ehud was gone, the king's servants returned and found the doors to the upstairs room locked. They thought he might be using the latrine in the room, 25so they waited. But when the king didn't come out after a long delay, they became concerned and got a key. And when they opened the doors, they found their master dead on the floor.

26While the servants were waiting, Ehud escaped, passing the stone idols on his

2:3 Hebrew *They will be in your sides;* compare Num 33:55. **2:9** As in parallel text at Josh 24:30; Hebrew reads *Timnath-heres,* a variant spelling of Timnath-serah. **3:8** *Aram-naharaim* means "Aram of the two rivers," thought to have been located between the Euphrates and Balih Rivers in northwestern Mesopotamia. **3:16** Hebrew *gomed,* the length of which is uncertain. **3:22** Or *and it came out behind.* **3:23** Or *and went out through the porch;* the meaning of the Hebrew is uncertain.

Baal and Asherah

One of the greatest challenges the Israelites faced over these years was from Canaanite religion, a highly sexualized fertility religion. Two of its most popular gods were Baal (meaning "Lord"), who was the son of El, the chief god, and El's consort Asherah (see Judges 3:7). Baal was often depicted standing on a bull, holding a spear of lightning, representing his control over nature. Asherah was depicted holding enlarged breasts, symbolizing her fertility. Canaanite worship involved sacred prostitution in the belief that the sexual act provoked the gods to reproduce and release fertility onto the land. At times it even involved child sacrifice. It was this abuse of religion, sexuality, and life itself that caused such vehement protests from Israel's prophets.

way to Seirah. 27
When he arrived in the hill country of Ephraim, Ehud sounded a call to arms. Then he led a band of Israelites down from the hills.

28
"Follow me," he said, "for the LORD has given you victory over Moab your enemy." So they followed him. And the Israelites took control of the shallow crossings of the Jordan River across from Moab, preventing anyone from crossing.

29
They attacked the Moabites and killed about 10,000 of their strongest and most able-bodied warriors. Not one of them escaped. 30
So Moab was conquered by Israel that day, and there was peace in the land for eighty years.

Shamgar Becomes Israel's Judge

31
After Ehud, Shamgar son of Anath rescued Israel. He once killed 600 Philistines with an ox goad.

Deborah Becomes Israel's Judge

4 After Ehud's death, the Israelites again did evil in the LORD's sight. 2
So the LORD turned them over to King Jabin of Hazor, a Canaanite king. The commander of his army was Sisera, who lived in Harosheth-haggoyim. 3
Sisera, who had 900 iron chariots, ruthlessly oppressed the Israelites for twenty years. Then the people of Israel cried out to the LORD for help.

4
Deborah, the wife of Lappidoth, was a prophet who was judging Israel at that time. 5
She would sit under the Palm of Deborah, between Ramah and Bethel in the hill country of Ephraim, and the Israelites would go to her for judgment. 6
One day she sent for Barak son of Abinoam, who lived in Kedesh in the land of Naphtali. She said to him, "This is what the LORD, the God of Israel, commands you: Call out 10,000 warriors from the tribes of Naphtali and Zebulun at Mount Tabor. 7
And I will call out Sisera, commander of Jabin's army, along with his chariots and warriors, to the Kishon River. There I will give you victory over him."

8
Barak told her, "I will go, but only if you go with me."

9
"Very well," she replied, "I will go with you. But you will receive no honor in this venture, for the LORD's victory over Sisera will be at the hands of a woman." So Deborah went with Barak to Kedesh. 10
At Kedesh, Barak called together the tribes of Zebulun and Naphtali, and 10,000 warriors went up with him. Deborah also went with him.

11
Now Heber the Kenite, a descendant of Moses' brother-in-law* Hobab, had moved away from the other members of his tribe and pitched his tent by the oak of Zaanannim near Kedesh.

12
When Sisera was told that Barak son of Abinoam had gone up to Mount Tabor, 13
he called for all 900 of his iron chariots and all of his warriors, and they marched from Harosheth-haggoyim to the Kishon River.

14
Then Deborah said to Barak, "Get ready! This is the day the LORD will give you victory over Sisera, for the LORD is marching ahead of you." So Barak led his 10,000 warriors down the slopes of Mount Tabor into battle. 15
When Barak attacked, the LORD threw Sisera and all his chariots and warriors into a panic. Sisera leaped down from his chariot and escaped on foot. 16
Then Barak chased the chariots and the enemy army all the way to Harosheth-haggoyim, killing all of Sisera's warriors. Not a single one was left alive.

17
Meanwhile, Sisera ran to the tent of Jael, the wife of Heber the Kenite, because Heber's

Deborah

Of all the judges that God raised up in this period, only one of them was a woman—Deborah. Deborah was a prophet, living in the hill country of Ephraim in the center of the country, and "the Israelites would go to her for judgment" (Judges 4:5). It was as a prophet that she called upon Barak to raise an army against the ongoing oppression of Jabin, the nearby Canaanite king of Hazor, promising God's intervention. Deborah's faith, in stark contrast to Barak's timidity, led to a great victory for Israel, which she celebrated in a prophetic song (chapter 5).

family was on friendly terms with King Jabin of Hazor. [18]Jael went out to meet Sisera and said to him, "Come into my tent, sir. Come in. Don't be afraid." So he went into her tent, and she covered him with a blanket.

[19]"Please give me some water," he said. "I'm thirsty." So she gave him some milk from a leather bag and covered him again.

[20]"Stand at the door of the tent," he told her. "If anybody comes and asks you if there is anyone here, say no."

[21]But when Sisera fell asleep from exhaustion, Jael quietly crept up to him with a hammer and tent peg in her hand. Then she drove the tent peg through his temple and into the ground, and so he died.

[22]When Barak came looking for Sisera, Jael went out to meet him. She said, "Come, and I will show you the man you are looking for." So he followed her into the tent and found Sisera lying there dead, with the tent peg through his temple.

[23]So on that day Israel saw God defeat Jabin, the Canaanite king. [24]And from that time on Israel became stronger and stronger against King Jabin until they finally destroyed him.

The Song of Deborah

5 On that day Deborah and Barak son of Abinoam sang this song:

2 "Israel's leaders took charge,
and the people gladly followed.
Praise the LORD!

3 "Listen, you kings!
Pay attention, you mighty rulers!
For I will sing to the LORD.
I will make music to the LORD, the God of Israel.

4 "LORD, when you set out from Seir
and marched across the fields of Edom,
the earth trembled,
and the cloudy skies poured down rain.
5 The mountains quaked in the presence of the LORD,
the God of Mount Sinai—
in the presence of the LORD,
the God of Israel.

6 "In the days of Shamgar son of Anath,
and in the days of Jael,
people avoided the main roads,
and travelers stayed on winding pathways.
7 There were few people left in the villages of Israel*—
until Deborah arose as a mother for Israel.
8 When Israel chose new gods,
war erupted at the city gates.
Yet not a shield or spear could be seen
among forty thousand warriors in Israel!
9 My heart is with the commanders of Israel,
with those who volunteered for war.
Praise the LORD!

10 "Consider this, you who ride on fine donkeys,
you who sit on fancy saddle blankets,
and you who walk along the road.
11 Listen to the village musicians*
gathered at the watering holes.
They recount the righteous victories of the LORD
and the victories of his villagers in Israel.
Then the people of the LORD
marched down to the city gates.

12 "Wake up, Deborah, wake up!
Wake up, wake up, and sing a song!
Arise, Barak!
Lead your captives away, son of Abinoam!

13 "Down from Tabor marched the few
against the nobles.
The people of the LORD marched
down against mighty warriors.
14 They came down from Ephraim—
a land that once belonged to the Amalekites;
they followed you, Benjamin, with your troops.
From Makir the commanders marched down;
from Zebulun came those who carry a commander's staff.
15 The princes of Issachar were with
Deborah and Barak.
They followed Barak, rushing into the valley.
But in the tribe of Reuben
there was great indecision.*

4:11 Or *father-in-law.* **5:7** The meaning of the Hebrew is uncertain. **5:11** The meaning of the Hebrew is uncertain. **5:15** As in some Hebrew manuscripts and Syriac version, which read *searchings of heart;* Masoretic Text reads *resolve of heart.*

16 Why did you sit at home among the sheepfolds—
to hear the shepherds whistle for their flocks?
Yes, in the tribe of Reuben
there was great indecision.
17 Gilead remained east of the Jordan.
And why did Dan stay home?
Asher sat unmoved at the seashore,
remaining in his harbors.
18 But Zebulun risked his life,
as did Naphtali, on the heights of the battlefield.

19 "The kings of Canaan came and fought,
at Taanach near Megiddo's springs,
but they carried off no silver treasures.
20 The stars fought from heaven.
The stars in their orbits fought against Sisera.
21 The Kishon River swept them away—
that ancient torrent, the Kishon.
March on with courage, my soul!
22 Then the horses' hooves hammered the ground,
the galloping, galloping of Sisera's mighty steeds.
23 'Let the people of Meroz be cursed,' said the angel of the LORD.
'Let them be utterly cursed,
because they did not come to help the LORD—
to help the LORD against the mighty warriors.'

24 "Most blessed among women is Jael,
the wife of Heber the Kenite.
May she be blessed above all women who live in tents.
25 Sisera asked for water,
and she gave him milk.
In a bowl fit for nobles,
she brought him yogurt.
26 Then with her left hand she reached for a tent peg,
and with her right hand for the workman's hammer.
She struck Sisera with the hammer,
crushing his head.
With a shattering blow, she pierced his temples.
27 He sank, he fell,
he lay still at her feet.
And where he sank,
there he died.

28 "From the window Sisera's mother looked out.
Through the window she watched for his return, saying,
'Why is his chariot so long in coming?
Why don't we hear the sound of chariot wheels?'

29 "Her wise women answer,
and she repeats these words to herself:
30 'They must be dividing the captured plunder—
with a woman or two for every man.
There will be colorful robes for Sisera,
and colorful, embroidered robes for me.
Yes, the plunder will include
colorful robes embroidered on both sides.'

31 "LORD, may all your enemies die like Sisera!
But may those who love you rise like the sun in all its power!"
Then there was peace in the land for forty years.

Gideon Becomes Israel's Judge

6 The Israelites did evil in the LORD's sight. So the LORD handed them over to the Midianites for seven years. 2The Midianites were so cruel that the Israelites made hiding places for themselves in the mountains, caves, and strongholds. 3Whenever the Israelites planted their crops, marauders from Midian, Amalek, and the people of the east would attack Israel, 4camping in the land and destroying crops as far away as Gaza. They left the Israelites with nothing to eat, taking all the sheep, goats, cattle, and donkeys. 5These enemy hordes, coming with their livestock and tents, were as thick as locusts; they arrived on droves of camels too numerous to count. And they stayed until the land was stripped bare. 6So Israel was reduced to starvation by the Midianites. Then the Israelites cried out to the LORD for help.

7When they cried out to the LORD because of Midian, 8the LORD sent a prophet to the Israelites. He said, "This is what the LORD, the God of Israel, says: I brought you up out of slavery in Egypt. 9I rescued you from the Egyptians and from all who oppressed you.

I drove out your enemies and gave you their
land. [10]I told you, 'I am the LORD your God.
You must not worship the gods of the Amorites, in whose land you now live.' But you
have not listened to me."
[11]Then the angel of the LORD came and
sat beneath the great tree at Ophrah, which
belonged to Joash of the clan of Abiezer.
Gideon son of Joash was threshing wheat at
the bottom of a winepress to hide the grain
from the Midianites. [12]The angel of the LORD
appeared to him and said, "Mighty hero, the
LORD is with you!"
[13]"Sir," Gideon replied, "if the LORD is
with us, why has all this happened to us?
And where are all the miracles our ancestors told us about? Didn't they say, 'The
LORD brought us up out of Egypt'? But now
the LORD has abandoned us and handed us
over to the Midianites."
[14]Then the LORD turned to him and said,
"Go with the strength you have, and rescue
Israel from the Midianites. I am sending
you!"
[15]"But Lord," Gideon replied, "how can
I rescue Israel? My clan is the weakest in the
whole tribe of Manasseh, and I am the least
in my entire family!"
[16]The LORD said to him, "I will be with
you. And you will destroy the Midianites as
if you were fighting against one man."
[17]Gideon replied, "If you are truly going
to help me, show me a sign to prove that it
is really the LORD speaking to me. [18]Don't
go away until I come back and bring my offering to you."

He answered, "I will stay here until you
return."
[19]Gideon hurried home. He cooked a
young goat, and with a basket* of flour he
baked some bread without yeast. Then,
carrying the meat in a basket and the broth
in a pot, he brought them out and presented
them to the angel, who was under the great
tree.
[20]The angel of God said to him, "Place
the meat and the unleavened bread on

6:19 Hebrew *an ephah* [20 quarts or 22 liters].

Can God still speak through "fleeces"?

Some Christians sometimes suggest "putting out a fleece" as a way of seeking God's will. The expression refers to the incident in Judges 6:36-40 where Gideon, wanting reassurance of his call to lead Israel into battle, took a wool fleece, laid it on a threshing floor, and then prayed, asking that if God truly wanted to save Israel through him then the next morning dew would cover the fleece but not the ground. When that happened, he asked God to do the same thing, but the other way around, and again it happened. Now convinced God was speaking, he led Israel to great victory. But is such an approach an authentic way of discovering God's will today? In seeking an answer, we must note the context of Gideon's experience, for actually, this was an expression of his unbelief rather than his faith. After all, an angel had already visited him, answering his doubts, commissioning him, and assuring him that God would be with him (6:11-16). When his lack of faith had still led him to request a sign, the angel had graciously granted it (6:17-24). God had then protected him the next day when the town was angry with him for cutting down their idols (6:25-32). Yet despite all this, Gideon *still* wanted another sign. This was unbelief, not faith! So should we do this sort of thing? God is undoubtedly gracious and no doubt answers such requests at times, but we should remember that it shows the absence of faith rather than its presence. With the Holy Spirit, the Bible, and Christian counsel, God has provided ample resources for us today to seek and confirm his will without needing to resort to such "fleeces," which can often be excuses for not facing up to responsibility rather than genuine expressions of courageous faith.

▶ *See also* ***Guidance****, page 1261.*

this rock, and pour the broth over it." And Gideon did as he was told. 21 Then the angel of the LORD touched the meat and bread with the tip of the staff in his hand, and fire flamed up from the rock and consumed all he had brought. And the angel of the LORD disappeared.

22 When Gideon realized that it was the angel of the LORD, he cried out, "Oh, Sovereign LORD, I'm doomed! I have seen the angel of the LORD face to face!"

23 "It is all right," the LORD replied. "Do not be afraid. You will not die." 24 And Gideon built an altar to the LORD there and named it Yahweh-Shalom (which means "the LORD is peace"). The altar remains in Ophrah in the land of the clan of Abiezer to this day.

25 That night the LORD said to Gideon, "Take the second bull from your father's herd, the one that is seven years old. Pull down your father's altar to Baal, and cut down the Asherah pole standing beside it. 26 Then build an altar to the LORD your God here on this hilltop sanctuary, laying the stones carefully. Sacrifice the bull as a burnt offering on the altar, using as fuel the wood of the Asherah pole you cut down."

27 So Gideon took ten of his servants and did as the LORD had commanded. But he did it at night because he was afraid of the other members of his father's household and the people of the town.

28 Early the next morning, as the people of the town began to stir, someone discovered that the altar of Baal had been broken down and that the Asherah pole beside it had been cut down. In their place a new altar had been built, and on it were the remains of the bull that had been sacrificed. 29 The people said to each other, "Who did this?" And after asking around and making a careful search, they learned that it was Gideon, the son of Joash.

30 "Bring out your son," the men of the town demanded of Joash. "He must die for destroying the altar of Baal and for cutting down the Asherah pole."

31 But Joash shouted to the mob that confronted him, "Why are you defending Baal? Will you argue his case? Whoever pleads his case will be put to death by morning! If Baal truly is a god, let him defend himself and destroy the one who broke down his altar!" 32 From then on Gideon was called Jerub-baal, which means "Let Baal defend himself," because he broke down Baal's altar.

Gideon Asks for a Sign

33 Soon afterward the armies of Midian, Amalek, and the people of the east formed an alliance against Israel and crossed the Jordan, camping in the valley of Jezreel. 34 Then the Spirit of the LORD clothed Gideon with power. He blew a ram's horn as a call to arms, and the men of the clan of Abiezer came to him. 35 He also sent messengers throughout Manasseh, Asher, Zebulun, and Naphtali, summoning their warriors, and all of them responded.

36 Then Gideon said to God, "If you are truly going to use me to rescue Israel as you promised, 37 prove it to me in this way. I will put a wool fleece on the threshing floor tonight. If the fleece is wet with dew in the morning but the ground is dry, then I will know that you are going to help me rescue Israel as you promised." 38 And that is just what happened. When Gideon got up early the next morning, he squeezed the fleece and wrung out a whole bowlful of water.

39 Then Gideon said to God, "Please don't be angry with me, but let me make one more request. Let me use the fleece for one more test. This time let the fleece remain dry while the ground around it is wet with dew." 40 So that night God did as Gideon asked. The fleece was dry in the morning, but the ground was covered with dew.

Gideon Defeats the Midianites

7 So Jerub-baal (that is, Gideon) and his army got up early and went as far as the spring of Harod. The armies of Midian were camped north of them in the valley near the hill of Moreh. 2 The LORD said to Gideon, "You have too many warriors with you. If I let all of you fight the Midianites, the Israelites will boast to me that they saved themselves by their own strength. 3 Therefore, tell the people, 'Whoever is timid or afraid may leave this mountain* and go home.'" So 22,000 of them went home, leaving only 10,000 who were willing to fight.

4 But the LORD told Gideon, "There are still too many! Bring them down to the spring, and I will test them to determine who will go with you and who will not." 5 When Gideon took his warriors down to the water,

the LORD told him, "Divide the men into two
groups. In one group put all those who cup
water in their hands and lap it up with their
tongues like dogs. In the other group put
all those who kneel down and drink with
their mouths in the stream." 6Only 300 of
the men drank from their hands. All the
others got down on their knees and drank
with their mouths in the stream.
7The LORD told Gideon, "With these
300 men I will rescue you and give you
victory over the Midianites. Send all the
others home." 8So Gideon collected the provisions and rams' horns of the other warriors and sent them home. But he kept the
300 men with him.

The Midianite camp was in the valley just
below Gideon. 9That night the LORD said,
"Get up! Go down into the Midianite camp,
for I have given you victory over them! 10But
if you are afraid to attack, go down to the
camp with your servant Purah. 11Listen to
what the Midianites are saying, and you
will be greatly encouraged. Then you will
be eager to attack."

So Gideon took Purah and went down to
the edge of the enemy camp. 12The armies
of Midian, Amalek, and the people of the
east had settled in the valley like a swarm
of locusts. Their camels were like grains of
sand on the seashore—too many to count!
13Gideon crept up just as a man was telling
his companion about a dream. The man
said, "I had this dream, and in my dream
a loaf of barley bread came tumbling down
into the Midianite camp. It hit a tent, turned
it over, and knocked it flat!"
14His companion answered, "Your dream
can mean only one thing—God has given
Gideon son of Joash, the Israelite, victory
over Midian and all its allies!"
15When Gideon heard the dream and its
interpretation, he bowed in worship before
the LORD.* Then he returned to the Israelite
camp and shouted, "Get up! For the LORD
has given you victory over the Midianite
hordes!" 16He divided the 300 men into
three groups and gave each man a ram's
horn and a clay jar with a torch in it.
17Then he said to them, "Keep your eyes
on me. When I come to the edge of the camp,
do just as I do. 18As soon as I and those with
me blow the rams' horns, blow your horns,
too, all around the entire camp, and shout,
'For the LORD and for Gideon!'"
19It was just after midnight,* after the
changing of the guard, when Gideon and
the 100 men with him reached the edge
of the Midianite camp. Suddenly, they blew
the rams' horns and broke their clay jars.
20Then all three groups blew their horns

7:3 Hebrew *may leave Mount Gilead.* The identity of Mount Gilead is uncertain in this context. It is perhaps used here as another name for Mount Gilboa. **7:15** As in Greek version; Hebrew reads *he bowed.* **7:19** Hebrew *at the beginning of the second watch.*

Gideon

Gideon was a real mixture—called "mighty hero" by an angel (Judges 6:12), yet hiding from the Midianites in a winepress as he threshed his wheat; obeying God by destroying the village idols, yet doing it by night because he was afraid (6:25-27); having God's Spirit come upon him to fight against the Midianites (6:33-35), yet needing further reassurance (6:36-40). God reduced his army of thirty-two thousand men to just three hundred, for he knew they would become proud when they won (7:1-8), but he encouraged Gideon with a further sign (7:9-15). Gideon used cunning to panic the Midianites, who killed one another and fled (7:15-25). But then he seemed to forget God, so while the pursuit was a complete rout (8:10-12), it came at significant cost to relationships within Israel (8:1-17). The Israelites then wanted to make him king, but Gideon refused (8:22-23). But from their gifts he made an ephod, causing Israel to engage in idolatry once again (8:24-27), which only got worse after his death (8:33-35). Gideon shows that God can and does use us despite the mixture that is in us, but wholehearted devotion and trust make things so much more straightforward.

▸ *See also* ***Can God still speak through "fleeces"?****, page 277.*

and broke their jars. They held the blazing
torches in their left hands and the horns in
their right hands, and they all shouted, "A
sword for the LORD and for Gideon!"
[21]Each man stood at his position around
the camp and watched as all the Midianites
rushed around in a panic, shouting as they
ran to escape. [22]When the 300 Israelites
blew their rams' horns, the LORD caused
the warriors in the camp to fight against
each other with their swords. Those who
were not killed fled to places as far away as
Beth-shittah near Zererah and to the border
of Abel-meholah near Tabbath.
[23]Then Gideon sent for the warriors of
Naphtali, Asher, and Manasseh, who joined
in chasing the army of Midian. [24]Gideon also
sent messengers throughout the hill country
of Ephraim, saying, "Come down to attack
the Midianites. Cut them off at the shallow
crossings of the Jordan River at Beth-barah."
So all the men of Ephraim did as they
were told. [25]They captured Oreb and Zeeb,
the two Midianite commanders, killing
Oreb at the rock of Oreb, and Zeeb at the
winepress of Zeeb. And they continued to
chase the Midianites. Afterward the Israelites brought the heads of Oreb and Zeeb
to Gideon, who was by the Jordan River.

Gideon Kills Zebah and Zalmunna

8 Then the people of Ephraim asked
Gideon, "Why have you treated us this
way? Why didn't you send for us when you
first went out to fight the Midianites?" And
they argued heatedly with Gideon.
[2]But Gideon replied, "What have I accomplished compared to you? Aren't even
the leftover grapes of Ephraim's harvest
better than the entire crop of my little clan
of Abiezer? [3]God gave you victory over Oreb
and Zeeb, the commanders of the Midianite
army. What have I accomplished compared
to that?" When the men of Ephraim heard
Gideon's answer, their anger subsided.
[4]Gideon then crossed the Jordan River with
his 300 men, and though exhausted, they
continued to chase the enemy. [5]When they
reached Succoth, Gideon asked the leaders
of the town, "Please give my warriors some
food. They are very tired. I am chasing Zebah
and Zalmunna, the kings of Midian."
[6]But the officials of Succoth replied,
"Catch Zebah and Zalmunna first, and then
we will feed your army."
[7]So Gideon said, "After the LORD gives
me victory over Zebah and Zalmunna, I will
return and tear your flesh with the thorns
and briers from the wilderness."
[8]From there Gideon went up to Peniel*
and again asked for food, but he got the
same answer. [9]So he said to the people of
Peniel, "After I return in victory, I will tear
down this tower."
[10]By this time Zebah and Zalmunna were
in Karkor with about 15,000 warriors—all
that remained of the allied armies of the
east, for 120,000 had already been killed.
[11]Gideon circled around by the caravan
route east of Nobah and Jogbehah, taking
the Midianite army by surprise. [12]Zebah and
Zalmunna, the two Midianite kings, fled,
but Gideon chased them down and captured all their warriors.
[13]After this, Gideon returned from the
battle by way of Heres Pass. [14]There he captured a young man from Succoth and demanded that he write down the names of
all the seventy-seven officials and elders in
the town. [15]Gideon then returned to Succoth
and said to the leaders, "Here are Zebah
and Zalmunna. When we were here before,
you taunted me, saying, 'Catch Zebah and
Zalmunna first, and then we will feed your
exhausted army.'" [16]Then Gideon took the
elders of the town and taught them a lesson,
punishing them with thorns and briers from
the wilderness. [17]He also tore down the tower
of Peniel and killed all the men in the town.
[18]Then Gideon asked Zebah and Zalmunna, "The men you killed at Tabor—
what were they like?"
"Like you," they replied. "They all had
the look of a king's son."
[19]"They were my brothers, the sons of my
own mother!" Gideon exclaimed. "As surely
as the LORD lives, I wouldn't kill you if you
hadn't killed them."
[20]Turning to Jether, his oldest son, he
said, "Kill them!" But Jether did not draw
his sword, for he was only a boy and was
afraid.
[21]Then Zebah and Zalmunna said to
Gideon, "Be a man! Kill us yourself!" So
Gideon killed them both and took the royal
ornaments from the necks of their camels.

Gideon's Sacred Ephod

[22]Then the Israelites said to Gideon, "Be our
ruler! You and your son and your grandson

will be our rulers, for you have rescued us
from Midian."
23 But Gideon replied, "I will not rule over
you, nor will my son. The LORD will rule
over you! 24 However, I do have one request—
that each of you give me an earring from
the plunder you collected from your fallen
enemies." (The enemies, being Ishmaelites,
all wore gold earrings.)
25 "Gladly!" they replied. They spread
out a cloak, and each one threw in a gold
earring he had gathered from the plunder.
26 The weight of the gold earrings was forty-
three pounds,* not including the royal ornaments and pendants, the purple clothing
worn by the kings of Midian, or the chains
around the necks of their camels.
27 Gideon made a sacred ephod from the
gold and put it in Ophrah, his hometown.
But soon all the Israelites prostituted themselves by worshiping it, and it became a
trap for Gideon and his family.
28 That is the story of how the people
of Israel defeated Midian, which never
recovered. Throughout the rest of Gideon's
lifetime—about forty years—there was peace
in the land.
29 Then Gideon* son of Joash returned
home. 30 He had seventy sons born to him,
for he had many wives. 31 He also had a concubine in Shechem, who gave birth to a son,
whom he named Abimelech. 32 Gideon died
when he was very old, and he was buried in
the grave of his father, Joash, at Ophrah in
the land of the clan of Abiezer.
33 As soon as Gideon died, the Israelites
prostituted themselves by worshiping the
images of Baal, making Baal-berith their
god. 34 They forgot the LORD their God, who
had rescued them from all their enemies
surrounding them. 35 Nor did they show any
loyalty to the family of Jerub-baal (that is,
Gideon), despite all the good he had done
for Israel.

Abimelech Rules over Shechem

9 One day Gideon's* son Abimelech went
to Shechem to visit his uncles—his
mother's brothers. He said to them and to
the rest of his mother's family, 2 "Ask the
leading citizens of Shechem whether they
want to be ruled by all seventy of Gideon's
sons or by one man. And remember that
I am your own flesh and blood!"
3 So Abimelech's uncles gave his message
to all the citizens of Shechem on his behalf.
And after listening to this proposal, the
people of Shechem decided in favor of
Abimelech because he was their relative.
4 They gave him seventy silver coins from the
temple of Baal-berith, which he used to hire
some reckless troublemakers who agreed to
follow him. 5 He went to his father's home
at Ophrah, and there, on one stone, they
killed all seventy of his half brothers, the
sons of Gideon.* But the youngest brother,
Jotham, escaped and hid.
6 Then all the leading citizens of Shechem
and Beth-millo called a meeting under the
oak beside the pillar* at Shechem and made
Abimelech their king.

Jotham's Parable

7 When Jotham heard about this, he climbed
to the top of Mount Gerizim and shouted,

"Listen to me, citizens of Shechem!
Listen to me if you want God to listen
to you!
8 Once upon a time the trees decided to
choose a king.
First they said to the olive tree,
'Be our king!'
9 But the olive tree refused, saying,
'Should I quit producing the olive oil
that blesses both God and people,
just to wave back and forth over the
trees?'

10 "Then they said to the fig tree,
'You be our king!'
11 But the fig tree also refused, saying,
'Should I quit producing my sweet fruit
just to wave back and forth over the
trees?'

12 "Then they said to the grapevine,
'You be our king!'
13 But the grapevine also refused, saying,
'Should I quit producing the wine
that cheers both God and people,
just to wave back and forth over the
trees?'

14 "Then all the trees finally turned to the
thornbush and said,
'Come, you be our king!'
15 And the thornbush replied to the trees,

8:8 Hebrew *Penuel*, a variant spelling of Peniel; also in 8:9, 17. **8:26** Hebrew *1,700 [shekels]* [19.4 kilograms]. **8:29** Hebrew *Jerub-baal;* see 6:32. **9:1** Hebrew *Jerub-baal's* (see 6:32); also in 9:2, 24. **9:5** Hebrew *Jerub-baal* (see 6:32); also in 9:16, 19, 28, 57. **9:6** The meaning of the Hebrew is uncertain.

'If you truly want to make me your king,
come and take shelter in my shade.
If not, let fire come out from me
and devour the cedars of Lebanon.'"

16 Jotham continued, "Now make sure you
have acted honorably and in good faith by
making Abimelech your king, and that you
have done right by Gideon and all of his descendants. Have you treated him with the
honor he deserves for all he accomplished?
17 For he fought for you and risked his life
when he rescued you from the Midianites.
18 But today you have revolted against my
father and his descendants, killing his
seventy sons on one stone. And you have
chosen his slave woman's son, Abimelech,
to be your king just because he is your
relative.
19 "If you have acted honorably and in
good faith toward Gideon and his descendants today, then may you find joy in Abimelech, and may he find joy in you. 20 But if
you have not acted in good faith, then may
fire come out from Abimelech and devour
the leading citizens of Shechem and Beth-
millo; and may fire come out from the citizens of Shechem and Beth-millo and devour
Abimelech!"
21 Then Jotham escaped and lived in
Beer because he was afraid of his brother
Abimelech.

Shechem Rebels against Abimelech

22 After Abimelech had ruled over Israel for
three years, 23 God sent a spirit that stirred
up trouble between Abimelech and the
leading citizens of Shechem, and they revolted. 24 God was punishing Abimelech for
murdering Gideon's seventy sons, and the
citizens of Shechem for supporting him in
this treachery of murdering his brothers.
25 The citizens of Shechem set an ambush
for Abimelech on the hilltops and robbed
everyone who passed that way. But someone
warned Abimelech about their plot.
26 One day Gaal son of Ebed moved to
Shechem with his brothers and gained
the confidence of the leading citizens of
Shechem. 27 During the annual harvest festival at Shechem, held in the temple of the
local god, the wine flowed freely, and everyone began cursing Abimelech. 28 "Who is
Abimelech?" Gaal shouted. "He's not a true
son of Shechem,* so why should we be his
servants? He's merely the son of Gideon,
and this Zebul is merely his deputy. Serve
the true sons of Hamor, the founder of
Shechem. Why should we serve Abimelech?
29 If I were in charge here, I would get rid of
Abimelech. I would say* to him, 'Get some
soldiers, and come out and fight!'"
30 But when Zebul, the leader of the
city, heard what Gaal was saying, he was
furious. 31 He sent messengers to Abimelech in Arumah,* telling him, "Gaal son of
Ebed and his brothers have come to live in
Shechem, and now they are inciting the city
to rebel against you. 32 Come by night with
an army and hide out in the fields. 33 In the
morning, as soon as it is daylight, attack the
city. When Gaal and those who are with him
come out against you, you can do with them
as you wish."
34 So Abimelech and all his men went by
night and split into four groups, stationing
themselves around Shechem. 35 Gaal was

Abimelech

Although his father, Gideon, had refused to become Israel's king, reminding them that God alone was king (Judges 8:22-23), Abimelech had no such qualms. He made a violent grab for power by gathering mercenaries in Shechem and murdering his own seventy half brothers (9:5). But the Bible says that "you will always harvest what you plant" (Galatians 6:7), and three years later, Abimelech reaped the harvest of the dissension he had sown. Shechem rebelled against him (Judges 9:22-25)—a rebellion he put down violently (9:26-49). But once again, God's justice caught up with him. During Abimelech's attack on another town, a woman dropped a millstone on his head from a tower, seriously wounding him and leaving him begging to be killed (9:53-54). Israel's first experiment with kingship had ended disastrously.

standing at the city gates when Abimelech and his army came out of hiding. 36When Gaal saw them, he said to Zebul, "Look, there are people coming down from the hilltops!"

Zebul replied, "It's just the shadows on the hills that look like men."

37But again Gaal said, "No, people are coming down from the hills.* And another group is coming down the road past the Diviners' Oak.*"

38Then Zebul turned on him and asked, "Now where is that big mouth of yours? Wasn't it you that said, 'Who is Abimelech, and why should we be his servants?' The men you mocked are right outside the city! Go out and fight them!"

39So Gaal led the leading citizens of Shechem into battle against Abimelech. 40But Abimelech chased him, and many of Shechem's men were wounded and fell along the road as they retreated to the city gate. 41Abimelech returned to Arumah, and Zebul drove Gaal and his brothers out of Shechem.

42The next day the people of Shechem went out into the fields to battle. When Abimelech heard about it, 43he divided his men into three groups and set an ambush in the fields. When Abimelech saw the people coming out of the city, he and his men jumped up from their hiding places and attacked them. 44Abimelech and his group stormed the city gate to keep the men of Shechem from getting back in, while Abimelech's other two groups cut them down in the fields. 45The battle went on all day before Abimelech finally captured the city. He killed the people, leveled the city, and scattered salt all over the ground.

46When the leading citizens who lived in the tower of Shechem heard what had happened, they ran and hid in the temple of Baal-berith.* 47Someone reported to Abimelech that the citizens had gathered in the temple, 48so he led his forces to Mount Zalmon. He took an ax and chopped some branches from a tree, then put them on his shoulder. "Quick, do as I have done!" he told his men. 49So each of them cut down some branches, following Abimelech's example. They piled the branches against the walls of the temple and set them on fire. So all the people who had lived in the tower of Shechem died—about 1,000 men and women.

50Then Abimelech attacked the town of Thebez and captured it. 51But there was a strong tower inside the town, and all the men and women—the entire population—fled to it. They barricaded themselves in and climbed up to the roof of the tower. 52Abimelech followed them to attack the tower. But as he prepared to set fire to the entrance, 53a woman on the roof dropped a millstone that landed on Abimelech's head and crushed his skull.

54He quickly said to his young armor bearer, "Draw your sword and kill me! Don't let it be said that a woman killed Abimelech!" So the young man ran him through with his sword, and he died. 55When Abimelech's men saw that he was dead, they disbanded and returned to their homes.

56In this way, God punished Abimelech for the evil he had done against his father by murdering his seventy brothers. 57God also punished the men of Shechem for all their evil. So the curse of Jotham son of Gideon was fulfilled.

Tola Becomes Israel's Judge

10 After Abimelech died, Tola son of Puah, son of Dodo, was the next person to rescue Israel. He was from the tribe of Issachar but lived in the town of Shamir in the hill country of Ephraim. 2He judged Israel for twenty-three years. When he died, he was buried in Shamir.

Jair Becomes Israel's Judge

3After Tola died, Jair from Gilead judged Israel for twenty-two years. 4His thirty sons rode around on thirty donkeys, and they owned thirty towns in the land of Gilead, which are still called the Towns of Jair.* 5When Jair died, he was buried in Kamon.

The Ammonites Oppress Israel

6Again the Israelites did evil in the LORD's sight. They served the images of Baal and Ashtoreth, and the gods of Aram, Sidon, Moab, Ammon, and Philistia. They abandoned the LORD and no longer served him at all. 7So the LORD burned with anger against Israel, and he turned them over to the Philistines and the Ammonites, 8who began to

9:28 Hebrew *Who is Shechem?* **9:29** As in Greek version; Hebrew reads *And he said.* **9:31** Or *in secret;* Hebrew reads *in Tormah;* compare 9:41. **9:37a** Or *the center of the land.* **9:37b** Hebrew *Elon-meonenim.* **9:46** Hebrew *El-berith,* another name for Baal-berith; compare 9:4. **10:4** Hebrew *Havvoth-jair.*

oppress them that year. For eighteen years they oppressed all the Israelites east of the Jordan River in the land of the Amorites (that is, in Gilead). 9 The Ammonites also crossed to the west side of the Jordan and attacked Judah, Benjamin, and Ephraim.

The Israelites were in great distress. 10 Finally, they cried out to the LORD for help, saying, "We have sinned against you because we have abandoned you as our God and have served the images of Baal."

11 The LORD replied, "Did I not rescue you from the Egyptians, the Amorites, the Ammonites, the Philistines, 12 the Sidonians, the Amalekites, and the Maonites? When they oppressed you, you cried out to me for help, and I rescued you. 13 Yet you have abandoned me and served other gods. So I will not rescue you anymore. 14 Go and cry out to the gods you have chosen! Let them rescue you in your hour of distress!"

15 But the Israelites pleaded with the LORD and said, "We have sinned. Punish us as you see fit, only rescue us today from our enemies." 16 Then the Israelites put aside their foreign gods and served the LORD. And he was grieved by their misery.

17 At that time the armies of Ammon had gathered for war and were camped in Gilead, and the people of Israel assembled and camped at Mizpah. 18 The leaders of Gilead said to each other, "Whoever attacks the Ammonites first will become ruler over all the people of Gilead."

Jephthah Becomes Israel's Judge

11 Now Jephthah of Gilead was a great warrior. He was the son of Gilead, but his mother was a prostitute. 2 Gilead's wife also had several sons, and when these half brothers grew up, they chased Jephthah off the land. "You will not get any of our father's inheritance," they said, "for you are the son of a prostitute." 3 So Jephthah fled from his brothers and lived in the land of Tob. Soon he had a band of worthless rebels following him.

4 At about this time, the Ammonites began their war against Israel. 5 When the Ammonites attacked, the elders of Gilead sent for Jephthah in the land of Tob. 6 The elders said, "Come and be our commander! Help us fight the Ammonites!"

7 But Jephthah said to them, "Aren't you the ones who hated me and drove me from my father's house? Why do you come to me now when you're in trouble?"

8 "Because we need you," the elders replied. "If you lead us in battle against the Ammonites, we will make you ruler over all the people of Gilead."

9 Jephthah said to the elders, "Let me get this straight. If I come with you and if the LORD gives me victory over the Ammonites, will you really make me ruler over all the people?"

10 "The LORD is our witness," the elders replied. "We promise to do whatever you say."

11 So Jephthah went with the elders of Gilead, and the people made him their ruler and commander of the army. At Mizpah, in the presence of the LORD, Jephthah repeated what he had said to the elders.

12 Then Jephthah sent messengers to the king of Ammon, asking, "Why have you come out to fight against my land?"

13 The king of Ammon answered Jephthah's messengers, "When the Israelites came out of Egypt, they stole my land from the Arnon River to the Jabbok River and all the way to the Jordan. Now then, give back the land peaceably."

14 Jephthah sent this message back to the Ammonite king:

> 15 "This is what Jephthah says: Israel did not steal any land from Moab or Ammon. 16 When the people of Israel arrived at Kadesh on their journey from Egypt after crossing the Red Sea,* 17 they sent messengers to the king of Edom asking for permission to pass through his land. But their request was denied. Then they asked the king of Moab for similar permission, but he wouldn't let them pass through either. So the people of Israel stayed in Kadesh.
>
> 18 "Finally, they went around Edom and Moab through the wilderness. They traveled along Moab's eastern border and camped on the other side of the Arnon River. But they never once crossed the Arnon River into Moab, for the Arnon was the border of Moab.
>
> 19 "Then Israel sent messengers to King Sihon of the Amorites, who ruled from Heshbon, asking for permission to cross through his land to get to their destination. 20 But King Sihon didn't

trust Israel to pass through his land.
Instead, he mobilized his army at Jahaz
and attacked them. 21But the LORD, the
God of Israel, gave his people victory
over King Sihon. So Israel took control
of all the land of the Amorites, who lived
in that region, 22from the Arnon River to
the Jabbok River, and from the eastern
wilderness to the Jordan.
23"So you see, it was the LORD, the
God of Israel, who took away the land
from the Amorites and gave it to Israel.
Why, then, should we give it back to
you? 24You keep whatever your god
Chemosh gives you, and we will keep
whatever the LORD our God gives us.
25Are you any better than Balak son of
Zippor, king of Moab? Did he try to make
a case against Israel for disputed land?
Did he go to war against them?
26"Israel has been living here for
300 years, inhabiting Heshbon and its
surrounding settlements, all the way to
Aroer and its settlements, and in all the
towns along the Arnon River. Why have
you made no effort to recover it before
now? 27Therefore, I have not sinned
against you. Rather, you have wronged
me by attacking me. Let the LORD, who
is judge, decide today which of us is
right—Israel or Ammon."

28But the king of Ammon paid no attention
to Jephthah's message.

Jephthah's Vow

29At that time the Spirit of the LORD came
upon Jephthah, and he went throughout
the land of Gilead and Manasseh, including Mizpah in Gilead, and from there he
led an army against the Ammonites. 30And
Jephthah made a vow to the LORD. He said,
"If you give me victory over the Ammonites,
31I will give to the LORD whatever comes
out of my house to meet me when I return

11:16 Hebrew *sea of reeds.*

Prostitution

The mention of Jephthah's mother as a prostitute (Judges 11:1) is not meant to commend prostitution, but rather to highlight that Jephthah would have been seen as an outcast—and yet God still used him. Prostitutes—or "commercial sex workers"—were used in Bible times not just for sexual pleasure, but also in some expressions of worship (in Canaanite fertility religions, for example). But the Bible shows that God hates prostitution, for it undermines his purpose for marriage as a lifelong, faithful relationship between one man and one woman (Genesis 2:24; Matthew 19:4-6). This is why it is forbidden to God's people (e.g., Leviticus 19:29; 1 Corinthians 6:12-20), why Proverbs warns of its dangers (Proverbs 6:20-29; 7:6-27), and why the prophets often described Israel as a prostitute for abandoning her faithful relationship with God alone (e.g., Jeremiah 2:20-25; Ezekiel 16:1-34; Hosea 2:2-7).

Yet while the Bible constantly opposes prostitution, it is important to remember that not all prostitutes become so by choice. Today some end up in prostitution through poverty, abuse, human trafficking, or slavery; in Bible times it could be through poverty, abandonment, or conquest. Christians should therefore not simply oppose prostitution, but do all they can to work against the unjust causes of it.

And if you have been involved in prostitution, or any kind of casual sex, in the past, don't despair. There is as much hope for you as anyone else. Rahab the prostitute was saved because of her faith (Joshua 6:24-25; Hebrews 11:31; James 2:25), and many prostitutes found forgiveness from Jesus (e.g., Matthew 21:31) and became part of the church (1 Corinthians 6:11). With Jesus, there is no sin that cannot be forgiven.

▸ *See also **Sexuality**, page 742; **Casual sex**, page 1309.*

in triumph. I will sacrifice it as a burnt offering."

32 So Jephthah led his army against the Ammonites, and the LORD gave him victory. 33 He crushed the Ammonites, devastating about twenty towns from Aroer to an area near Minnith and as far away as Abel-keramim. In this way Israel defeated the Ammonites.

34 When Jephthah returned home to Mizpah, his daughter came out to meet him, playing on a tambourine and dancing for joy. She was his one and only child; he had no other sons or daughters. 35 When he saw her, he tore his clothes in anguish. "Oh, my daughter!" he cried out. "You have completely destroyed me! You've brought disaster on me! For I have made a vow to the LORD, and I cannot take it back."

36 And she said, "Father, if you have made a vow to the LORD, you must do to me what you have vowed, for the LORD has given you a great victory over your enemies, the Ammonites. 37 But first let me do this one thing: Let me go up and roam in the hills and weep with my friends for two months, because I will die a virgin."

38 "You may go," Jephthah said. And he sent her away for two months. She and her friends went into the hills and wept because she would never have children. 39 When she returned home, her father kept the vow he had made, and she died a virgin.

So it has become a custom in Israel 40 for young Israelite women to go away for four days each year to lament the fate of Jephthah's daughter.

Ephraim Fights with Jephthah

12 Then the people of Ephraim mobilized an army and crossed over the Jordan River to Zaphon. They sent this message to Jephthah: "Why didn't you call for us to help you fight against the Ammonites? We are going to burn down your house with you in it!"

2 Jephthah replied, "I summoned you at the beginning of the dispute, but you refused to come! You failed to help us in our struggle against Ammon. 3 So when I realized you weren't coming, I risked my life and went to battle without you, and the LORD gave me victory over the Ammonites. So why have you now come to fight me?"

4 The people of Ephraim responded, "You men of Gilead are nothing more than fugitives from Ephraim and Manasseh." So Jephthah gathered all the men of Gilead and attacked the men of Ephraim and defeated them.

5 Jephthah captured the shallow crossings of the Jordan River, and whenever a fugitive from Ephraim tried to go back across, the men of Gilead would challenge him. "Are you a member of the tribe of Ephraim?" they would ask. If the man said, "No, I'm not," 6 they would tell him to say "Shibboleth." If he was from Ephraim, he would say "Sibboleth," because people from Ephraim cannot pronounce the word correctly. Then they would take him and kill him at the shallow crossings of the Jordan. In all, 42,000 Ephraimites were killed at that time.

7 Jephthah judged Israel for six years. When he died, he was buried in one of the towns of Gilead.

Ibzan Becomes Israel's Judge

8 After Jephthah died, Ibzan from Bethlehem judged Israel. 9 He had thirty sons and thirty daughters. He sent his daughters to marry men outside his clan, and he brought in thirty young women from outside his clan to marry his sons. Ibzan judged Israel for seven years. 10 When he died, he was buried at Bethlehem.

Elon Becomes Israel's Judge

11 After Ibzan died, Elon from the tribe of Zebulun judged Israel for ten years. 12 When he died, he was buried at Aijalon in Zebulun.

Abdon Becomes Israel's Judge

13 After Elon died, Abdon son of Hillel, from Pirathon, judged Israel. 14 He had forty sons and thirty grandsons, who rode on seventy donkeys. He judged Israel for eight years. 15 When he died, he was buried at Pirathon in Ephraim, in the hill country of the Amalekites.

The Birth of Samson

13 Again the Israelites did evil in the LORD's sight, so the LORD handed them over to the Philistines, who oppressed them for forty years.

2 In those days a man named Manoah from the tribe of Dan lived in the town of Zorah. His wife was unable to become pregnant, and they had no children. 3 The angel of the LORD appeared to Manoah's wife and said,

"Even though you have been unable to have
children, you will soon become pregnant
and give birth to a son. 4So be careful; you
must not drink wine or any other alcoholic
drink nor eat any forbidden food.* 5You will
become pregnant and give birth to a son, and
his hair must never be cut. For he will be dedicated to God as a Nazirite from birth. He will
begin to rescue Israel from the Philistines."
6The woman ran and told her husband,
"A man of God appeared to me! He looked
like one of God's angels, terrifying to see. I
didn't ask where he was from, and he didn't
tell me his name. 7But he told me, 'You will
become pregnant and give birth to a son.
You must not drink wine or any other alcoholic drink nor eat any forbidden food. For
your son will be dedicated to God as a Nazirite from the moment of his birth until the
day of his death.'"
8Then Manoah prayed to the LORD,
saying, "Lord, please let the man of God
come back to us again and give us more instructions about this son who is to be born."
9God answered Manoah's prayer, and the
angel of God appeared once again to his
wife as she was sitting in the field. But her
husband, Manoah, was not with her. 10So
she quickly ran and told her husband, "The
man who appeared to me the other day is
here again!"
11Manoah ran back with his wife and
asked, "Are you the man who spoke to my
wife the other day?"
"Yes," he replied, "I am."
12So Manoah asked him, "When your
words come true, what kind of rules should
govern the boy's life and work?"
13The angel of the LORD replied, "Be sure
your wife follows the instructions I gave
her. 14She must not eat grapes or raisins,
drink wine or any other alcoholic drink, or
eat any forbidden food."
15Then Manoah said to the angel of
the LORD, "Please stay here until we can
prepare a young goat for you to eat."
16"I will stay," the angel of the LORD
replied, "but I will not eat anything.
However, you may prepare a burnt offering
as a sacrifice to the LORD." (Manoah didn't
realize it was the angel of the LORD.)
17Then Manoah asked the angel of the
LORD, "What is your name? For when all
this comes true, we want to honor you."
18"Why do you ask my name?" the angel
of the LORD replied. "It is too wonderful for
you to understand."
19Then Manoah took a young goat and a
grain offering and offered it on a rock as a
sacrifice to the LORD. And as Manoah and
his wife watched, the LORD did an amazing
thing. 20As the flames from the altar shot up
toward the sky, the angel of the LORD ascended in the fire. When Manoah and his
wife saw this, they fell with their faces to
the ground.
21The angel did not appear again to
Manoah and his wife. Manoah finally realized it was the angel of the LORD, 22and he
said to his wife, "We will certainly die, for
we have seen God!"
23But his wife said, "If the LORD were
going to kill us, he wouldn't have accepted
our burnt offering and grain offering. He
wouldn't have appeared to us and told us this
wonderful thing and done these miracles."
24When her son was born, she named him

13:4 Hebrew *any unclean thing;* also in 13:7, 14.

Nazirites

Samson's childless parents were delighted when an angel told his mother she would become pregnant and was to dedicate their son to be a Nazirite (Judges 13:5). A Nazirite vow (Numbers 6:1-21) was normally both voluntary and limited in time—though in Samson's case it was imposed upon him and lasted until his death (Judges 13:7). It indicated special dedication to God for a period, involving abstinence from wine and other alcohol, not cutting one's hair, and avoiding defilement through touching dead bodies. Samson seemed to resent having the vow imposed upon him, which is perhaps why he broke all three of these aspects during his life. The Nazirite vow was still practiced in New Testament times (Acts 18:18; 21:23-26).

Samson. And the LORD blessed him as he
grew up. 25 And the Spirit of the LORD began
to stir him while he lived in Mahaneh-dan,
which is located between the towns of
Zorah and Eshtaol.

Samson's Riddle

14 One day when Samson was in
Timnah, one of the Philistine women
caught his eye. 2 When he returned home,
he told his father and mother, "A young Philistine woman in Timnah caught my eye.
I want to marry her. Get her for me."

3 His father and mother objected. "Isn't
there even one woman in our tribe or among
all the Israelites you could marry?" they
asked. "Why must you go to the pagan Philistines to find a wife?"

But Samson told his father, "Get her for
me! She looks good to me." 4 His father and
mother didn't realize the LORD was at work
in this, creating an opportunity to work
against the Philistines, who ruled over
Israel at that time.

5 As Samson and his parents were going
down to Timnah, a young lion suddenly
attacked Samson near the vineyards of
Timnah. 6 At that moment the Spirit of the
LORD came powerfully upon him, and he
ripped the lion's jaws apart with his bare
hands. He did it as easily as if it were a
young goat. But he didn't tell his father or
mother about it. 7 When Samson arrived in
Timnah, he talked with the woman and was
very pleased with her.

8 Later, when he returned to Timnah for
the wedding, he turned off the path to look
at the carcass of the lion. And he found that
a swarm of bees had made some honey in
the carcass. 9 He scooped some of the honey
into his hands and ate it along the way. He
also gave some to his father and mother, and
they ate it. But he didn't tell them he had
taken the honey from the carcass of the lion.

10 As his father was making final arrangements for the marriage, Samson threw a
party at Timnah, as was the custom for elite
young men. 11 When the bride's parents* saw
him, they selected thirty young men from
the town to be his companions.

12 Samson said to them, "Let me tell you a
riddle. If you solve my riddle during these
seven days of the celebration, I will give
you thirty fine linen robes and thirty sets
of festive clothing. 13 But if you can't solve
it, then you must give me thirty fine linen
robes and thirty sets of festive clothing."

"All right," they agreed, "let's hear your
riddle."

14 So he said:

"Out of the one who eats came
something to eat;
out of the strong came something
sweet."

Three days later they were still trying to
figure it out. 15 On the fourth* day they said
to Samson's wife, "Entice your husband to
explain the riddle for us, or we will burn
down your father's house with you in it.
Did you invite us to this party just to make
us poor?"

16 So Samson's wife came to him in tears
and said, "You don't love me; you hate me!
You have given my people a riddle, but you
haven't told me the answer."

"I haven't even given the answer to my
father or mother," he replied. "Why should
I tell you?" 17 So she cried whenever she was
with him and kept it up for the rest of the
celebration. At last, on the seventh day he
told her the answer because she was tormenting him with her nagging. Then she
explained the riddle to the young men.

18 So before sunset of the seventh day, the
men of the town came to Samson with their
answer:

"What is sweeter than honey?
What is stronger than a lion?"

Samson replied, "If you hadn't plowed
with my heifer, you wouldn't have solved
my riddle!"

19 Then the Spirit of the LORD came powerfully upon him. He went down to the town
of Ashkelon, killed thirty men, took their
belongings, and gave their clothing to the
men who had solved his riddle. But Samson
was furious about what had happened, and
he went back home to live with his father
and mother. 20 So his wife was given in marriage to the man who had been Samson's
best man at the wedding.

Samson's Vengeance on the Philistines

15 Later on, during the wheat harvest,
Samson took a young goat as a
present to his wife. He said, "I'm going into
my wife's room to sleep with her," but her
father wouldn't let him in.

2“I truly thought you must hate her,” her
father explained, “so I gave her in marriage
to your best man. But look, her younger
sister is even more beautiful than she is.
Marry her instead.”
3Samson said, “This time I cannot be
blamed for everything I am going to do to
you Philistines.” 4Then he went out and
caught 300 foxes. He tied their tails together
in pairs, and he fastened a torch to each
pair of tails. 5Then he lit the torches and
let the foxes run through the grain fields of
the Philistines. He burned all their grain to
the ground, including the sheaves and the
uncut grain. He also destroyed their vineyards and olive groves.
6“Who did this?” the Philistines demanded.
“Samson,” was the reply, “because his
father-in-law from Timnah gave Samson’s
wife to be married to his best man.” So the
Philistines went and got the woman and her
father and burned them to death.
7“Because you did this,” Samson vowed,
“I won’t rest until I take my revenge on
you!” 8So he attacked the Philistines with
great fury and killed many of them. Then
he went to live in a cave in the rock of Etam.
9The Philistines retaliated by setting up
camp in Judah and spreading out near the
town of Lehi. 10The men of Judah asked the
Philistines, “Why are you attacking us?”
The Philistines replied, “We’ve come to
capture Samson. We’ve come to pay him
back for what he did to us.”
11So 3,000 men of Judah went down to
get Samson at the cave in the rock of Etam.
They said to Samson, “Don’t you realize the
Philistines rule over us? What are you doing
to us?”
But Samson replied, “I only did to them
what they did to me.”
12But the men of Judah told him, “We have
come to tie you up and hand you over to the
Philistines.”
“All right,” Samson said. “But promise
that you won’t kill me yourselves.”
13“We will only tie you up and hand you
over to the Philistines,” they replied. “We
won’t kill you.” So they tied him up with
two new ropes and brought him up from
the rock.
14As Samson arrived at Lehi, the Philistines
came shouting in triumph. But the Spirit of
the LORD came powerfully upon Samson,
and he snapped the ropes on his arms as if
they were burnt strands of flax, and they fell
from his wrists. 15Then he found the jawbone
of a recently killed donkey. He picked it up
and killed 1,000 Philistines with it. 16Then
Samson said,

14:11 Hebrew *they*. **14:15** As in Greek version; Hebrew reads *seventh*.

Why does God use bad people?

It is sobering to recall that the Bible shows us that just because God uses us does not mean that everything we do has his approval. Actually, God used many bad people to further his purposes, even though they didn’t realize they were doing so: people like Egypt’s pharaoh, whose cruelty drove Israel to cry out to God and so find freedom; or Babylon’s King Nebuchadnezzar, whose conquest of Judah and the subsequent exile led God’s people to seek him in a new way.

But Samson falls into a different category. Although one of God’s people and dedicated to God in a special way at his birth (Judges 13), he didn’t live in a godly way. He didn’t rule his sexual appetite (14:1-3), married a non-Israelite in disobedience to God’s Law (chapter 14), could easily be manipulated (14:15-17), and was extremely cruel (15:3-5). Yet despite all this, God used him. Why? Simply put, this was the best man that God could find for the task of defeating the Philistines, which reflects what dark days these were in Israel.

God uses bad people sometimes—not for their sake, but for his; not to further their purposes, but his. Such examples remind us that God is sovereign over all things and all people—even those who don’t acknowledge him or obey him—and that he is constantly working in every situation to bring about his good purposes (Romans 8:28).

“With the jawbone of a donkey,
I’ve piled them in heaps!
With the jawbone of a donkey,
I’ve killed a thousand men!”

17 When he finished his boasting, he threw
away the jawbone; and the place was
named Jawbone Hill.*
18 Samson was now very thirsty, and he
cried out to the LORD, “You have accomplished this great victory by the strength of
your servant. Must I now die of thirst and
fall into the hands of these pagans?” 19 So
God caused water to gush out of a hollow in
the ground at Lehi, and Samson was revived
as he drank. Then he named that place “The
Spring of the One Who Cried Out,”* and it is
still in Lehi to this day.
20 Samson judged Israel for twenty years
during the period when the Philistines
dominated the land.

Samson Carries Away Gaza’s Gates

16 One day Samson went to the Philistine town of Gaza and spent the
night with a prostitute. 2 Word soon spread*
that Samson was there, so the men of Gaza
gathered together and waited all night at
the town gates. They kept quiet during the
night, saying to themselves, “When the
light of morning comes, we will kill him.”
3 But Samson stayed in bed only until
midnight. Then he got up, took hold of the
doors of the town gate, including the two
posts, and lifted them up, bar and all. He
put them on his shoulders and carried them
all the way to the top of the hill across from
Hebron.

Samson and Delilah

4 Some time later Samson fell in love with
a woman named Delilah, who lived in the
valley of Sorek. 5 The rulers of the Philistines
went to her and said, “Entice Samson to tell
you what makes him so strong and how he
can be overpowered and tied up securely.
Then each of us will give you 1,100 pieces*
of silver.”
6 So Delilah said to Samson, “Please tell
me what makes you so strong and what it
would take to tie you up securely.”
7 Samson replied, “If I were tied up with
seven new bowstrings that have not yet
been dried, I would become as weak as
anyone else.”
8 So the Philistine rulers brought Delilah
seven new bowstrings, and she tied Samson
up with them. 9 She had hidden some men
in one of the inner rooms of her house, and
she cried out, “Samson! The Philistines
have come to capture you!” But Samson
snapped the bowstrings as a piece of string
snaps when it is burned by a fire. So the
secret of his strength was not discovered.
10 Afterward Delilah said to him, “You’ve
been making fun of me and telling me lies!
Now please tell me how you can be tied up
securely.”
11 Samson replied, “If I were tied up with
brand-new ropes that had never been used,
I would become as weak as anyone else.”
12 So Delilah took new ropes and tied him
up with them. The men were hiding in the
inner room as before, and again Delilah
cried out, “Samson! The Philistines have
come to capture you!” But again Samson
snapped the ropes from his arms as if they
were thread.
13 Then Delilah said, “You’ve been making
fun of me and telling me lies! Now tell me
how you can be tied up securely.”
Samson replied, “If you were to weave
the seven braids of my hair into the fabric
on your loom and tighten it with the loom
shuttle, I would become as weak as anyone
else.”
So while he slept, Delilah wove the seven
braids of his hair into the fabric. 14 Then she
tightened it with the loom shuttle.* Again
she cried out, “Samson! The Philistines
have come to capture you!” But Samson
woke up, pulled back the loom shuttle, and
yanked his hair away from the loom and the
fabric.
15 Then Delilah pouted, “How can you
tell me, ‘I love you,’ when you don’t share
your secrets with me? You’ve made fun of
me three times now, and you still haven’t
told me what makes you so strong!” 16 She
tormented him with her nagging day after
day until he was sick to death of it.
17 Finally, Samson shared his secret with
her. “My hair has never been cut,” he confessed, “for I was dedicated to God as a Nazirite from birth. If my head were shaved,
my strength would leave me, and I would
become as weak as anyone else.”
18 Delilah realized he had finally told
her the truth, so she sent for the Philistine
rulers. “Come back one more time,” she

said, "for he has finally told me his secret."
So the Philistine rulers returned with the
money in their hands. [19]Delilah lulled
Samson to sleep with his head in her lap,
and then she called in a man to shave off
the seven locks of his hair. In this way she
began to bring him down,* and his strength
left him.
[20]Then she cried out, "Samson! The Philistines have come to capture you!"
When he woke up, he thought, "I will do
as before and shake myself free." But he
didn't realize the LORD had left him.
[21]So the Philistines captured him and
gouged out his eyes. They took him to Gaza,
where he was bound with bronze chains
and forced to grind grain in the prison.
[22]But before long, his hair began to grow
back.

Samson's Final Victory

[23]The Philistine rulers held a great festival,
offering sacrifices and praising their god,
Dagon. They said, "Our god has given us
victory over our enemy Samson!"
[24]When the people saw him, they praised
their god, saying, "Our god has delivered
our enemy to us! The one who killed so
many of us is now in our power!"
[25]Half drunk by now, the people demanded, "Bring out Samson so he can
amuse us!" So he was brought from the
prison to amuse them, and they had him
stand between the pillars supporting the
roof.
[26]Samson said to the young servant
who was leading him by the hand, "Place
my hands against the pillars that hold up
the temple. I want to rest against them."
[27]Now the temple was completely filled
with people. All the Philistine rulers were
there, and there were about 3,000 men and
women on the roof who were watching as
Samson amused them.
[28]Then Samson prayed to the LORD, "Sovereign LORD, remember me again. O God,
please strengthen me just one more time.
With one blow let me pay back the Philistines for the loss of my two eyes." [29]Then
Samson put his hands on the two center
pillars that held up the temple. Pushing
against them with both hands, [30]he prayed,
"Let me die with the Philistines." And the
temple crashed down on the Philistine
rulers and all the people. So he killed more
people when he died than he had during his
entire lifetime.
[31]Later his brothers and other relatives
went down to get his body. They took him
back home and buried him between Zorah
and Eshtaol, where his father, Manoah,
was buried. Samson had judged Israel for
twenty years.

Micah's Idols

17 There was a man named Micah, who
lived in the hill country of Ephraim.
[2]One day he said to his mother, "I heard you
place a curse on the person who stole 1,100
pieces* of silver from you. Well, I have the
money. I was the one who took it."
"The LORD bless you for admitting it,"
his mother replied. [3]He returned the money
to her, and she said, "I now dedicate these
silver coins to the LORD. In honor of my
son, I will have an image carved and an
idol cast."
[4]So when he returned the money to his
mother, she took 200 silver coins and gave
them to a silversmith, who made them into
an image and an idol. And these were placed
in Micah's house. [5]Micah set up a shrine for
the idol, and he made a sacred ephod and
some household idols. Then he installed
one of his sons as his personal priest.
[6]In those days Israel had no king; all the
people did whatever seemed right in their
own eyes.
[7]One day a young Levite, who had been
living in Bethlehem in Judah, arrived in that
area. [8]He had left Bethlehem in search of
another place to live, and as he traveled,
he came to the hill country of Ephraim.
He happened to stop at Micah's house as
he was traveling through. [9]"Where are you
from?" Micah asked him.
He replied, "I am a Levite from Bethlehem in Judah, and I am looking for a place
to live."
[10]"Stay here with me," Micah said, "and
you can be a father and priest to me. I will
give you ten pieces of silver* a year, plus a

15:17 Hebrew *Ramath-lehi.* **15:19** Hebrew *En-hakkore.* **16:2** As in Greek and Syriac versions and Latin Vulgate; Hebrew lacks *Word soon spread.* **16:5** Hebrew *1,100 [shekels],* about 28 pounds or 12.5 kilograms in weight. **16:13-14** As in Greek version and Latin Vulgate; Hebrew lacks *I would become as weak as anyone else. / So while he slept, Delilah wove the seven braids of his hair into the fabric. [14]Then she tightened it with the loom shuttle.* **16:19** Or *she began to torment him.* Greek version reads *He began to grow weak.* **17:2** Hebrew *1,100 [shekels],* about 28 pounds or 12.5 kilograms in weight. **17:10** Hebrew *10 [shekels] of silver,* about 4 ounces or 114 grams in weight.

change of clothes and your food." 11The Levite
agreed to this, and the young man became
like one of Micah's sons.
12So Micah installed the Levite as his personal priest, and he lived in Micah's house.
13"I know the LORD will bless me now,"
Micah said, "because I have a Levite serving
as my priest."

Idolatry in the Tribe of Dan

18 Now in those days Israel had no king.
And the tribe of Dan was trying to
find a place where they could settle, for they
had not yet moved into the land assigned to
them when the land was divided among the
tribes of Israel. 2So the men of Dan chose
from their clans five capable warriors from
the towns of Zorah and Eshtaol to scout out
a land for them to settle in.
When these warriors arrived in the hill
country of Ephraim, they came to Micah's
house and spent the night there. 3While at
Micah's house, they recognized the young
Levite's accent, so they went over and asked
him, "Who brought you here, and what
are you doing in this place? Why are you
here?" 4He told them about his agreement
with Micah and that he had been hired as
Micah's personal priest.
5Then they said, "Ask God whether or not
our journey will be successful."
6"Go in peace," the priest replied. "For
the LORD is watching over your journey."
7So the five men went on to the town of
Laish, where they noticed the people living
carefree lives, like the Sidonians; they were
peaceful and secure.* The people were also
wealthy because their land was very fertile.
And they lived a great distance from Sidon
and had no allies nearby.
8When the men returned to Zorah and
Eshtaol, their relatives asked them, "What
did you find?"
9The men replied, "Come on, let's attack
them! We have seen the land, and it is very
good. What are you waiting for? Don't hesitate to go and take possession of it. 10When
you get there, you will find the people living
carefree lives. God has given us a spacious
and fertile land, lacking in nothing!"
11So 600 men from the tribe of Dan, armed
with weapons of war, set out from Zorah
and Eshtaol. 12They camped at a place west
of Kiriath-jearim in Judah, which is called
Mahaneh-dan* to this day. 13Then they
went on from there into the hill country of
Ephraim and came to the house of Micah.
14The five men who had scouted out the
land around Laish explained to the others,
"These buildings contain a sacred ephod,
as well as some household idols, a carved
image, and a cast idol. What do you think
you should do?" 15Then the five men turned
off the road and went over to Micah's house,
where the young Levite lived, and greeted
him kindly. 16As the 600 armed warriors
from the tribe of Dan stood at the entrance of
the gate, 17the five scouts entered the shrine
and removed the carved image, the sacred
ephod, the household idols, and the cast
idol. Meanwhile, the priest was standing at
the gate with the 600 armed warriors.
18When the priest saw the men carrying
all the sacred objects out of Micah's shrine,
he said, "What are you doing?"
19"Be quiet and come with us," they said.
"Be a father and priest to all of us. Isn't it
better to be a priest for an entire tribe and
clan of Israel than for the household of just
one man?"
20The young priest was quite happy to
go with them, so he took along the sacred
ephod, the household idols, and the carved
image. 21They turned and started on their
way again, placing their children, livestock,
and possessions in front of them.
22When the people from the tribe of Dan
were quite a distance from Micah's house,
the people who lived near Micah came
chasing after them. 23They were shouting as
they caught up with them. The men of Dan
turned around and said to Micah, "What's
the matter? Why have you called these men
together and chased after us like this?"
24"What do you mean, 'What's the
matter?'" Micah replied. "You've taken
away all the gods I have made, and my
priest, and I have nothing left!"
25The men of Dan said, "Watch what you
say! There are some short-tempered men
around here who might get angry and kill
you and your family." 26So the men of Dan
continued on their way. When Micah saw
that there were too many of them for him to
attack, he turned around and went home.
27Then, with Micah's idols and his priest,
the men of Dan came to the town of Laish,
whose people were peaceful and secure.
They attacked with swords and burned
the town to the ground. 28There was no

one to rescue the people, for they lived a
great distance from Sidon and had no allies
nearby. This happened in the valley near
Beth-rehob.

Then the people of the tribe of Dan rebuilt
the town and lived there. 29They renamed
the town Dan after their ancestor, Israel's
son, but it had originally been called Laish.

30Then they set up the carved image, and
they appointed Jonathan son of Gershom,
son of Moses,* as their priest. This family
continued as priests for the tribe of Dan
until the Exile. 31So Micah's carved image
was worshiped by the tribe of Dan as long as
the Tabernacle of God remained at Shiloh.

The Levite and His Concubine

19 Now in those days Israel had no king.
There was a man from the tribe of Levi
living in a remote area of the hill country of
Ephraim. One day he brought home a woman
from Bethlehem in Judah to be his concubine. 2But she became angry with him* and
returned to her father's home in Bethlehem.

After about four months, 3her husband
set out for Bethlehem to speak personally
to her and persuade her to come back.
He took with him a servant and a pair of
donkeys. When he arrived at* her father's
house, her father saw him and welcomed
him. 4Her father urged him to stay awhile,
so he stayed three days, eating, drinking,
and sleeping there.

5On the fourth day the man was up early,
ready to leave, but the woman's father
said to his son-in-law, "Have something
to eat before you go." 6So the two men sat
down together and had something to eat
and drink. Then the woman's father said,
"Please stay another night and enjoy yourself." 7The man got up to leave, but his
father-in-law kept urging him to stay, so he
finally gave in and stayed the night.

8On the morning of the fifth day he was
up early again, ready to leave, and again
the woman's father said, "Have something
to eat; then you can leave later this afternoon." So they had another day of feasting.
9Later, as the man and his concubine and
servant were preparing to leave, his father-
in-law said, "Look, it's almost evening. Stay
the night and enjoy yourself. Tomorrow you
can get up early and be on your way."

10But this time the man was determined to
leave. So he took his two saddled donkeys
and his concubine and headed in the direction of Jebus (that is, Jerusalem). 11It was late
in the day when they neared Jebus, and the
man's servant said to him, "Let's stop at this
Jebusite town and spend the night there."

12"No," his master said, "we can't stay
in this foreign town where there are no Israelites. Instead, we will go on to Gibeah.
13Come on, let's try to get as far as Gibeah
or Ramah, and we'll spend the night in one
of those towns." 14So they went on. The sun
was setting as they came to Gibeah, a town in
the land of Benjamin, 15so they stopped there
to spend the night. They rested in the town
square, but no one took them in for the night.

18:7 The meaning of the Hebrew is uncertain. **18:12** *Mahaneh-dan* means "the camp of Dan." **18:30** As in an ancient Hebrew tradition, some Greek manuscripts, and Latin Vulgate; Masoretic Text reads *son of Manasseh.* **19:2** Or *she was unfaithful to him.* **19:3** As in Greek version; Hebrew reads *When she brought him to.*

Concubines

This horrific story of the concubine's fate (Judges 19) shows the depths into which Israel had sunk—gang rape, murder, and callousness, leading to civil war (chapter 20). A concubine was a servant or slave whose role was to enlarge the family—a common practice in an age when child mortality was high and having many children ensured that at least some would survive, thus maintaining the family line (e.g., Genesis 16:1-4; 30:1-13). While some concubines were treated well and considered as part of the family, others were treated as mere possessions, as here, where the concubine is seen as expendable. Both polygamy and having concubines were a significant drift from God's original design of one man living with one woman faithfully for life (Genesis 2:24; Matthew 19:4-6).

▸ *See also* ***Ishmael****, page 20.*

16That evening an old man came home
from his work in the fields. He was from the
hill country of Ephraim, but he was living
in Gibeah, where the people were from the
tribe of Benjamin. 17When he saw the travelers sitting in the town square, he asked
them where they were from and where they
were going.

18"We have been in Bethlehem in Judah,"
the man replied. "We are on our way to a
remote area in the hill country of Ephraim,
which is my home. I traveled to Bethlehem,
and now I'm returning home.* But no one
has taken us in for the night, 19even though
we have everything we need. We have straw
and feed for our donkeys and plenty of
bread and wine for ourselves."

20"You are welcome to stay with me," the
old man said. "I will give you anything you
might need. But whatever you do, don't
spend the night in the square." 21So he took
them home with him and fed the donkeys.
After they washed their feet, they ate and
drank together.

22While they were enjoying themselves,
a crowd of troublemakers from the town
surrounded the house. They began beating
at the door and shouting to the old man,
"Bring out the man who is staying with you
so we can have sex with him."

23The old man stepped outside to talk to
them. "No, my brothers, don't do such an
evil thing. For this man is a guest in my
house, and such a thing would be shameful. 24Here, take my virgin daughter and this
man's concubine. I will bring them out to
you, and you can abuse them and do whatever you like. But don't do such a shameful
thing to this man."

25But they wouldn't listen to him. So
the Levite took hold of his concubine and
pushed her out the door. The men of the
town abused her all night, taking turns
raping her until morning. Finally, at dawn
they let her go. 26At daybreak the woman
returned to the house where her husband
was staying. She collapsed at the door of the
house and lay there until it was light.

27When her husband opened the door to
leave, there lay his concubine with her hands
on the threshold. 28He said, "Get up! Let's
go!" But there was no answer.* So he put her
body on his donkey and took her home.

29When he got home, he took a knife
and cut his concubine's body into twelve
pieces. Then he sent one piece to each tribe
throughout all the territory of Israel.

30Everyone who saw it said, "Such a horrible crime has not been committed in all
the time since Israel left Egypt. Think about
it! What are we going to do? Who's going to
speak up?"

Israel's War with Benjamin

20 Then all the Israelites were united
as one man, from Dan in the north
to Beersheba in the south, including those
from across the Jordan in the land of
Gilead. The entire community assembled
in the presence of the LORD at Mizpah.
2The leaders of all the people and all the
tribes of Israel—400,000 warriors armed
with swords—took their positions in the
assembly of the people of God. 3(Word
soon reached the land of Benjamin that the
other tribes had gone up to Mizpah.) The Israelites then asked how this terrible crime
had happened.

4The Levite, the husband of the woman
who had been murdered, said, "My concubine and I came to spend the night in Gibeah,
a town that belongs to the people of Benjamin. 5That night some of the leading citizens
of Gibeah surrounded the house, planning
to kill me, and they raped my concubine
until she was dead. 6So I cut her body into
twelve pieces and sent the pieces throughout the territory assigned to Israel, for these
men have committed a terrible and shameful
crime. 7Now then, all of you—the entire community of Israel—must decide here and now
what should be done about this!"

8And all the people rose to their feet in
unison and declared, "None of us will return
home! No, not even one of us! 9Instead, this
is what we will do to Gibeah; we will draw
lots to decide who will attack it. 10One-tenth
of the men* from each tribe will be chosen
to supply the warriors with food, and the
rest of us will take revenge on Gibeah* of
Benjamin for this shameful thing they have
done in Israel." 11So all the Israelites were
completely united, and they gathered together to attack the town.

12The Israelites sent messengers to the
tribe of Benjamin, saying, "What a terrible
thing has been done among you! 13Give up
those evil men, those troublemakers from
Gibeah, so we can execute them and purge
Israel of this evil."

But the people of Benjamin would not listen. [14]Instead, they came from their towns and gathered at Gibeah to fight the Israelites. [15]In all, 26,000 of their warriors armed with swords arrived in Gibeah to join the 700 elite troops who lived there. [16]Among Benjamin's elite troops, 700 were left-handed, and each of them could sling a rock and hit a target within a hairsbreadth without missing. [17]Israel had 400,000 experienced soldiers armed with swords, not counting Benjamin's warriors.

[18]Before the battle the Israelites went to Bethel and asked God, "Which tribe should go first to attack the people of Benjamin?"

The LORD answered, "Judah is to go first."

[19]So the Israelites left early the next morning and camped near Gibeah. [20]Then they advanced toward Gibeah to attack the men of Benjamin. [21]But Benjamin's warriors, who were defending the town, came out and killed 22,000 Israelites on the battlefield that day.

[22]But the Israelites encouraged each other and took their positions again at the same place they had fought the previous day. [23]For they had gone up to Bethel and wept in the presence of the LORD until evening. They had asked the LORD, "Should we fight against our relatives from Benjamin again?"

And the LORD had said, "Go out and fight against them."

[24]So the next day they went out again to fight against the men of Benjamin, [25]but the men of Benjamin killed another 18,000 Israelites, all of whom were experienced with the sword.

[26]Then all the Israelites went up to Bethel and wept in the presence of the LORD and fasted until evening. They also brought burnt offerings and peace offerings to the LORD. [27]The Israelites went up seeking direction from the LORD. (In those days the Ark of the Covenant of God was in Bethel, [28]and Phinehas son of Eleazar and grandson of Aaron was the priest.) The Israelites asked the LORD, "Should we fight against our relatives from Benjamin again, or should we stop?"

The LORD said, "Go! Tomorrow I will hand them over to you."

[29]So the Israelites set an ambush all around Gibeah. [30]They went out on the third day and took their positions at the same place as before. [31]When the men of Benjamin came out to attack, they were drawn away from the town. And as they had done before, they began to kill the Israelites. About thirty Israelites died in the open fields and along the roads, one leading to Bethel and the other leading back to Gibeah.

[32]Then the warriors of Benjamin shouted, "We're defeating them as we did before!" But the Israelites had planned in advance to run away so that the men of Benjamin would chase them along the roads and be drawn away from the town.

[33]When the main group of Israelite warriors reached Baal-tamar, they turned and took up their positions. Meanwhile, the Israelites hiding in ambush to the west* of Gibeah jumped up to fight. [34]There were 10,000 elite Israelite troops who advanced against Gibeah. The fighting was so heavy that Benjamin didn't realize the impending

19:18 As in Greek version (see also 19:29); Hebrew reads *now I'm going to the Tabernacle of the LORD.* **19:28** Greek version adds *for she was dead.* **20:10a** Hebrew *10 men from every hundred, 100 men from every thousand, and 1,000 men from every 10,000.* **20:10b** Hebrew *Geba,* in this case a variant spelling of Gibeah; also in 20:33. **20:33** As in Greek and Syriac versions and Latin Vulgate; Hebrew reads *hiding in the open space.*

Bethel

The outrageous assault and murder of the concubine in Judges 19 led the Israelites to come together to deal with the citizens of Gibeah. But first they assembled at Bethel (Judges 20:18), whose name means "house of God," the name given to it by Jacob after his dream of the stairway to heaven (Genesis 28:10-22). Abraham had camped near Bethel (Genesis 12:8); eventually, it became the home of the Ark of the Covenant (Judges 20:26-27) and was known as a place of seeking God (Judges 21:2-3). After the kingdom split following Solomon's death, Jeroboam established a shrine for idol worship here (1 Kings 12:26-33).

disaster. 35So the LORD helped Israel defeat Benjamin, and that day the Israelites killed 25,100 of Benjamin's warriors, all of whom were experienced swordsmen. 36Then the men of Benjamin saw that they were beaten.

The Israelites had retreated from Benjamin's warriors in order to give those hiding in ambush more room to maneuver against Gibeah. 37Then those who were hiding rushed in from all sides and killed everyone in the town. 38They had arranged to send up a large cloud of smoke from the town as a signal. 39When the Israelites saw the smoke, they turned and attacked Benjamin's warriors.

By that time Benjamin's warriors had killed about thirty Israelites, and they shouted, "We're defeating them as we did in the first battle!" 40But when the warriors of Benjamin looked behind them and saw the smoke rising into the sky from every part of the town, 41the men of Israel turned and attacked. At this point the men of Benjamin became terrified, because they realized disaster was close at hand. 42So they turned around and fled before the Israelites toward the wilderness. But they couldn't escape the battle, and the people who came out of the nearby towns were also killed.* 43The Israelites surrounded the men of Benjamin and chased them relentlessly, finally overtaking them east of Gibeah.* 44That day 18,000 of Benjamin's strongest warriors died in battle. 45The survivors fled into the wilderness toward the rock of Rimmon, but Israel killed 5,000 of them along the road. They continued the chase until they had killed another 2,000 near Gidom.

46So that day the tribe of Benjamin lost 25,000 strong warriors armed with swords, 47leaving only 600 men who escaped to the rock of Rimmon, where they lived for four months. 48And the Israelites returned and slaughtered every living thing in all the towns—the people, the livestock, and everything they found. They also burned down all the towns they came to.

Israel Provides Wives for Benjamin

21 The Israelites had vowed at Mizpah, "We will never give our daughters in marriage to a man from the tribe of Benjamin." 2Now the people went to Bethel and sat in the presence of God until evening, weeping loudly and bitterly. 3"O LORD, God of Israel," they cried out, "why has this happened in Israel? Now one of our tribes is missing from Israel!"

4Early the next morning the people built an altar and presented their burnt offerings and peace offerings on it. 5Then they said, "Who among the tribes of Israel did not join us at Mizpah when we held our assembly in the presence of the LORD?" At that time they had taken a solemn oath in the LORD's presence, vowing that anyone who refused to come would be put to death.

6The Israelites felt sorry for their brother Benjamin and said, "Today one of the tribes of Israel has been cut off. 7How can we find wives for the few who remain, since we have sworn by the LORD not to give them our daughters in marriage?"

8So they asked, "Who among the tribes of Israel did not join us at Mizpah when we assembled in the presence of the LORD?" And they discovered that no one from Jabesh-gilead had attended the assembly. 9For after they counted all the people, no one from Jabesh-gilead was present.

10So the assembly sent 12,000 of their best warriors to Jabesh-gilead with orders to kill everyone there, including women and children. 11"This is what you are to do," they said. "Completely destroy* all the males and every woman who is not a virgin." 12Among the residents of Jabesh-gilead they found 400 young virgins who had never slept with a man, and they brought them to the camp at Shiloh in the land of Canaan.

13The Israelite assembly sent a peace delegation to the remaining people of Benjamin who were living at the rock of Rimmon. 14Then the men of Benjamin returned to their homes, and the 400 women of Jabesh-gilead who had been spared were given to them as wives. But there were not enough women for all of them.

15The people felt sorry for Benjamin because the LORD had made this gap among the tribes of Israel. 16So the elders of the assembly asked, "How can we find wives for the few who remain, since the women of the tribe of Benjamin are dead? 17There must be heirs for the survivors so that an entire tribe of Israel is not wiped out. 18But we cannot give them our own daughters in marriage because we have sworn with a solemn oath

that anyone who does this will fall under
God's curse."
[19]Then they thought of the annual festival of the LORD held in Shiloh, south of
Lebonah and north of Bethel, along the east
side of the road that goes from Bethel to
Shechem. [20]They told the men of Benjamin
who still needed wives, "Go and hide in the
vineyards. [21]When you see the young women
of Shiloh come out for their dances, rush out
from the vineyards, and each of you can take
one of them home to the land of Benjamin to
be your wife! [22]And when their fathers and
brothers come to us in protest, we will tell
them, 'Please be sympathetic. Let them have
your daughters, for we didn't find wives
for all of them when we destroyed Jabesh-
gilead. And you are not guilty of breaking
the vow since you did not actually give your
daughters to them in marriage.'"
[23]So the men of Benjamin did as they were
told. Each man caught one of the women as
she danced in the celebration and carried
her off to be his wife. They returned to their
own land, and they rebuilt their towns and
lived in them.
[24]Then the people of Israel departed by
tribes and families, and they returned to
their own homes.
[25]In those days Israel had no king; all the
people did whatever seemed right in their
own eyes.

20:42 Or *battle, for the people from the nearby towns also came out and killed them.* **20:43** The meaning of the Hebrew is uncertain. **21:11** The Hebrew term used here refers to the complete consecration of things or people to the LORD, either by destroying them or by giving them as an offering.

Ruth *Love and loyalty*

This delightful short book contains a love story . . . and a little slice of history. Ruth was a non-Israelite woman from neighboring Moab who chose to follow Israel's God. For her love for, and loyalty to, her mother-in-law, Ruth was not only rewarded by finding a husband and a home, but she became the ancestor of a king (David) and the Messiah (Jesus). The story is a wonderful ray of light and hope in the very dark times of the judges (1:1).

What's it all about?

During a time of famine, Elimelech, his wife, Naomi, and their two sons left their native town of Bethlehem in Israel and settled in Moab. However, while they were there, Elimelech died. His sons married Moabite women, but they also died, leaving their wives and widowed mother behind, now with no one to provide for them. But then, hearing that the famine back home was over, Naomi decided to return to Judah. Although her name means "pleasant," she wanted to change her name to *Mara*, meaning "bitter," because of the bitter tragedies that she had suffered. One of her daughters-in-law, Ruth, insisted on accompanying her and, in beautiful words, promised that she would never leave her (1:16-17). They resettled in Bethlehem, where Ruth went searching in the fields for any grain left behind by the harvesters (a practice known as gleaning).

OVERVIEW

Naomi, accompanied by Ruth, returns to her home town of Bethlehem · *1:1-22*

Ruth meets Boaz, her and Naomi's family redeemer · *2:1-23*

Naomi's plan for Ruth *3:1-18*

Ruth marries Boaz and becomes the ancestor of King David · *4:1-22*

One day she happened to come to a field belonging to a wealthy family relative named Boaz, though she did not know he was a family member. Boaz heard about Ruth and her decision to remain with her mother-in-law, and he was kind to her. Soon Naomi noticed Boaz's interest in Ruth and devised a plan to bring the two together in marriage. She sent Ruth to Boaz with a request for him to take care of her. Boaz and Ruth married and had a son, whom they named Obed ("servant"). He was to become the grandfather of David, Israel's greatest king. He was also an ancestor of Jesus Christ (see the genealogy in Matthew 1).

What does it mean for us?

The book of Ruth is all about the covenant faithfulness of God. Even though Naomi had given up hope of a solution and had become embittered, God still had a plan for her, and through her for his people, Israel. He drew in a complete outsider—a woman from Moab, a traditional enemy of Israel—and through her turned Naomi's situation around completely. The story powerfully demonstrates God's determination to save his people.

Love and loyalty are key themes of this little book. While both Orpah and Ruth loved Naomi, Orpah only kissed her mother-in-law and then left her, whereas Ruth clung to her and would not abandon her. Ruth remained loyal and gave practical expression to her love by staying with Naomi constantly, even in difficult times. Her example shows love in action. While Ruth's pledge to Naomi (1:16-17) is sometimes used in wedding services, its true setting is Ruth's relationship with her mother-in-law. Naomi and Ruth are a beautiful example of loyalty, friendship, and commitment. The love and respect shared by Ruth, Boaz, and Naomi is an example for both family and church life today.

Elimelech Moves His Family to Moab

1 In the days when the judges ruled in
Israel, a severe famine came upon the
land. So a man from Bethlehem in Judah left
his home and went to live in the country of
Moab, taking his wife and two sons with him.
[2]The man's name was Elimelech, and his wife
was Naomi. Their two sons were Mahlon and
Kilion. They were Ephrathites from Bethlehem in the land of Judah. And when they
reached Moab, they settled there.
[3]Then Elimelech died, and Naomi was left
with her two sons. [4]The two sons married
Moabite women. One married a woman
named Orpah, and the other a woman named
Ruth. But about ten years later, [5]both Mahlon
and Kilion died. This left Naomi alone,
without her two sons or her husband.

Naomi and Ruth Return

[6]Then Naomi heard in Moab that the LORD
had blessed his people in Judah by giving
them good crops again. So Naomi and her
daughters-in-law got ready to leave Moab
to return to her homeland. [7]With her two
daughters-in-law she set out from the place
where she had been living, and they took the
road that would lead them back to Judah.
[8]But on the way, Naomi said to her two
daughters-in-law, "Go back to your mothers'
homes. And may the LORD reward you for
your kindness to your husbands and to me.
[9]May the LORD bless you with the security
of another marriage." Then she kissed them
good-bye, and they all broke down and wept.
[10]"No," they said. "We want to go with you
to your people."
[11]But Naomi replied, "Why should you go
on with me? Can I still give birth to other
sons who could grow up to be your husbands? [12]No, my daughters, return to your
parents' homes, for I am too old to marry
again. And even if it were possible, and
I were to get married tonight and bear sons,
then what? [13]Would you wait for them to
grow up and refuse to marry someone else?
No, of course not, my daughters! Things
are far more bitter for me than for you,
because the LORD himself has raised his fist
against me."
[14]And again they wept together, and Orpah
kissed her mother-in-law good-bye. But Ruth
clung tightly to Naomi. [15]"Look," Naomi said
to her, "your sister-in-law has gone back to
her people and to her gods. You should do
the same."
[16]But Ruth replied, "Don't ask me to leave
you and turn back. Wherever you go, I will
go; wherever you live, I will live. Your people
will be my people, and your God will be my
God. [17]Wherever you die, I will die, and there
I will be buried. May the LORD punish me severely if I allow anything but death to separate us!" [18]When Naomi saw that Ruth was
determined to go with her, she said nothing
more.
[19]So the two of them continued on their
journey. When they came to Bethlehem, the
entire town was excited by their arrival. "Is it
really Naomi?" the women asked.
[20]"Don't call me Naomi," she responded.
"Instead, call me Mara,* for the Almighty
has made life very bitter for me. [21]I went away
full, but the LORD has brought me home
empty. Why call me Naomi when the LORD
has caused me to suffer* and the Almighty
has sent such tragedy upon me?"
[22]So Naomi returned from Moab, accompanied by her daughter-in-law Ruth, the young
Moabite woman. They arrived in Bethlehem
in late spring, at the beginning of the barley
harvest.

1:20 *Naomi* means "pleasant"; *Mara* means "bitter." **1:21** Or *has testified against me.*

▸ **1:16** *See* ***Faithfulness****, page 1307.*

Ruth Works in Boaz's Field

2 Now there was a wealthy and influential man in Bethlehem named Boaz, who was a relative of Naomi's husband, Elimelech.

2 One day Ruth the Moabite said to Naomi, "Let me go out into the harvest fields to pick up the stalks of grain left behind by anyone who is kind enough to let me do it."

Naomi replied, "All right, my daughter, go
ahead." 3 So Ruth went out to gather grain behind the harvesters. And as it happened, she found herself working in a field that belonged to Boaz, the relative of her father-in-law, Elimelech.

4 While she was there, Boaz arrived from Bethlehem and greeted the harvesters. "The LORD be with you!" he said.

"The LORD bless you!" the harvesters replied.

5 Then Boaz asked his foreman, "Who is that young woman over there? Who does she belong to?"

6 And the foreman replied, "She is the young woman from Moab who came back
with Naomi. 7 She asked me this morning if she could gather grain behind the harvesters. She has been hard at work ever since, except for a few minutes' rest in the shelter."

8 Boaz went over and said to Ruth, "Listen, my daughter. Stay right here with us when you gather grain; don't go to any other fields. Stay right behind the young women
working in my field. 9 See which part of the field they are harvesting, and then follow them. I have warned the young men not to treat you roughly. And when you are thirsty, help yourself to the water they have drawn from the well."

10 Ruth fell at his feet and thanked him warmly. "What have I done to deserve such kindness?" she asked. "I am only a foreigner."

11 "Yes, I know," Boaz replied. "But I also know about everything you have done for your mother-in-law since the death of your husband. I have heard how you left your father and mother and your own land to live
here among complete strangers. 12 May the LORD, the God of Israel, under whose wings you have come to take refuge, reward you fully for what you have done."

13 "I hope I continue to please you, sir," she replied. "You have comforted me by speaking so kindly to me, even though I am not one of your workers."

14 At mealtime Boaz called to her, "Come over here, and help yourself to some food. You can dip your bread in the sour wine."

Immigrants

Ruth 1 is all about the plight of immigrants. Elimelech and his family were immigrants in Moab, one of Israel's traditional enemies; yet they had to resist their pride and go there to avoid famine. Naomi experienced how abandoned an immigrant can feel when her family died and she was left alone. Then it was Ruth's turn to be an immigrant as she accompanied Naomi to Israel. Naomi and Ruth must both have felt very vulnerable.

Immigrants still feel vulnerable today. They don't know the language, culture, or practices of the people they now live among. They are also frequently despised, which can make finding accommodation or employment difficult. But God has a big heart for immigrants, and for all who are vulnerable to ill-treatment by society. That is why he legislated for their protection in the Law (e.g., Leviticus 19:33-34; Deuteronomy 24:17-18), reminding Israel that they too had once been immigrants in Egypt and had experienced mistreatment firsthand. The New Testament too urges Christians to show hospitality to strangers, reminding them that "some who have done this have entertained angels without realizing it!" (Hebrews 13:2).

Of course, it is not just people from other nations who can feel as though they are strangers, but even people from other parts of our own nation or from different ethnic groups. But disrespecting such people is utterly ungodly and can find no place in the church, where God sees all his people as equal.

So she sat with his harvesters, and Boaz
gave her some roasted grain to eat. She ate
all she wanted and still had some left over.
[15]When Ruth went back to work again,
Boaz ordered his young men, "Let her
gather grain right among the sheaves
without stopping her. [16]And pull out some
heads of barley from the bundles and drop
them on purpose for her. Let her pick them
up, and don't give her a hard time!"
[17]So Ruth gathered barley there all day, and
when she beat out the grain that evening, it
filled an entire basket.* [18]She carried it back
into town and showed it to her mother-in-
law. Ruth also gave her the roasted grain that
was left over from her meal.
[19]"Where did you gather all this grain
today?" Naomi asked. "Where did you
work? May the LORD bless the one who
helped you!"

So Ruth told her mother-in-law about
the man in whose field she had worked.
She said, "The man I worked with today is
named Boaz."
[20]"May the LORD bless him!" Naomi
told her daughter-in-law. "He is showing
his kindness to us as well as to your dead
husband.* That man is one of our closest
relatives, one of our family redeemers."
[21]Then Ruth* said, "What's more, Boaz
even told me to come back and stay with
his harvesters until the entire harvest is
completed."
[22]"Good!" Naomi exclaimed. "Do as he
said, my daughter. Stay with his young
women right through the whole harvest.
You might be harassed in other fields, but
you'll be safe with him."
[23]So Ruth worked alongside the women in
Boaz's fields and gathered grain with them
until the end of the barley harvest. Then she
continued working with them through the
wheat harvest in early summer. And all
the while she lived with her mother-in-law.

Ruth at the Threshing Floor

3 One day Naomi said to Ruth, "My
daughter, it's time that I found a permanent home for you, so that you will be provided for. [2]Boaz is a close relative of ours,
and he's been very kind by letting you gather
grain with his young women. Tonight he will
be winnowing barley at the threshing floor.
[3]Now do as I tell you—take a bath and put
on perfume and dress in your nicest clothes.
Then go to the threshing floor, but don't let
Boaz see you until he has finished eating
and drinking. [4]Be sure to notice where he
lies down; then go and uncover his feet and
lie down there. He will tell you what to do."
[5]"I will do everything you say," Ruth
replied. [6]So she went down to the threshing
floor that night and followed the instructions of her mother-in-law.
[7]After Boaz had finished eating and drinking and was in good spirits, he lay down at
the far end of the pile of grain and went to
sleep. Then Ruth came quietly, uncovered
his feet, and lay down. [8]Around midnight
Boaz suddenly woke up and turned over. He
was surprised to find a woman lying at his
feet! [9]"Who are you?" he asked.

"I am your servant Ruth," she replied.
"Spread the corner of your covering over
me, for you are my family redeemer."
[10]"The LORD bless you, my daughter!"

2:17 Hebrew *it was about an ephah* [20 quarts or 22 liters]. **2:20** Hebrew *to the living and to the dead.* **2:21** Hebrew *Ruth the Moabite.*

The family redeemer

In Bible times, the family redeemer (Ruth 2:20) was the closest surviving relative, who had an obligation to care for a widow and her family. This involved providing an heir where there was none, redeeming land that had been sold outside the family, and even avenging the killing of a relative.

Boaz knew that there was a family member closer in line to fulfill these responsibilities for Ruth. This man was eager to buy the field, but as soon as he heard the field came with obligations to father a child to continue the family line, he quickly lost interest, opening up the way for Boaz (4:1-8).

Many Christians see in Boaz's redemption of Ruth a picture of Jesus Christ redeeming us.

Boaz exclaimed. "You are showing even more family loyalty now than you did before, for you have not gone after a younger man, whether rich or poor. 11Now don't worry about a thing, my daughter. I will do what is necessary, for everyone in town knows you are a virtuous woman. 12But while it's true that I am one of your family redeemers, there is another man who is more closely related to you than I am. 13Stay here tonight, and in the morning I will talk to him. If he is willing to redeem you, very well. Let him marry you. But if he is not willing, then as surely as the LORD lives, I will redeem you myself! Now lie down here until morning."

14So Ruth lay at Boaz's feet until the morning, but she got up before it was light enough for people to recognize each other. For Boaz had said, "No one must know that a woman was here at the threshing floor." 15Then Boaz said to her, "Bring your cloak and spread it out." He measured six scoops* of barley into the cloak and placed it on her back. Then he* returned to the town.

16When Ruth went back to her mother-in-law, Naomi asked, "What happened, my daughter?"

Ruth told Naomi everything Boaz had done for her, 17and she added, "He gave me these six scoops of barley and said, 'Don't go back to your mother-in-law empty-handed.'"

18Then Naomi said to her, "Just be patient, my daughter, until we hear what happens. The man won't rest until he has settled things today."

Boaz Marries Ruth

4 Boaz went to the town gate and took a seat there. Just then the family redeemer he had mentioned came by, so Boaz called out to him, "Come over here and sit down, friend. I want to talk to you." So they sat down together. 2Then Boaz called ten leaders from the town and asked them to sit as witnesses. 3And Boaz said to the family redeemer, "You know Naomi, who came back from Moab. She is selling the land that belonged to our relative Elimelech. 4I thought I should speak to you about it so that you can redeem it if you wish. If you want the land, then buy it here in the presence of these witnesses. But if you don't want it, let me know right away, because I am next in line to redeem it after you."

The man replied, "All right, I'll redeem it."

5Then Boaz told him, "Of course, your purchase of the land from Naomi also requires that you marry Ruth, the Moabite widow. That way she can have children who will carry on her husband's name and keep the land in the family."

6"Then I can't redeem it," the family redeemer replied, "because this might endanger my own estate. You redeem the land; I cannot do it."

7Now in those days it was the custom in Israel for anyone transferring a right of purchase to remove his sandal and hand it to the other party. This publicly validated the transaction. 8So the other family redeemer drew off his sandal as he said to Boaz, "You buy the land."

9Then Boaz said to the elders and to the crowd standing around, "You are witnesses that today I have bought from Naomi all the property of Elimelech, Kilion, and Mahlon. 10And with the land I have acquired Ruth, the Moabite widow of Mahlon, to be my wife. This way she can have a son to carry on the family name of her dead husband and to inherit the family

Threshing floors

The threshing floor, the scene of events in Ruth 3, would have been a flat rocky outcrop or a clay-covered patch of land. The harvested grain was taken there on carts, then the sheaves were scattered across its floor and either beaten with sticks or broken up by animals dragging a threshing sledge. The stalks were then tossed into the air with a wooden fork, allowing the lighter straw to be blown aside by the breeze and the heavier grain to fall back onto the ground to be gathered. There was often just one threshing floor for a whole town or village, so the whole harvesting process was a real communal event, as is evident in this chapter.

property here in his hometown. You are all
witnesses today."
11 Then the elders and all the people standing in the gate replied, "We are witnesses!
May the LORD make this woman who is
coming into your home like Rachel and
Leah, from whom all the nation of Israel
descended! May you prosper in Ephrathah
and be famous in Bethlehem. 12 And may the
LORD give you descendants by this young
woman who will be like those of our ancestor Perez, the son of Tamar and Judah."

The Descendants of Boaz

13 So Boaz took Ruth into his home, and she
became his wife. When he slept with her, the
LORD enabled her to become pregnant, and
she gave birth to a son. 14 Then the women of
the town said to Naomi, "Praise the LORD,
who has now provided a redeemer for your
family! May this child be famous in Israel.
15 May he restore your youth and care for you
in your old age. For he is the son of your
daughter-in-law who loves you and has
been better to you than seven sons!"
16 Naomi took the baby and cuddled him
to her breast. And she cared for him as if
he were her own. 17 The neighbor women
said, "Now at last Naomi has a son again!"
And they named him Obed. He became the
father of Jesse and the grandfather of David.
18 This is the genealogical record of their
ancestor Perez:

Perez was the father of Hezron.
19 Hezron was the father of Ram.
Ram was the father of Amminadab.
20 Amminadab was the father of Nahshon.
Nahshon was the father of Salmon.*
21 Salmon was the father of Boaz.
Boaz was the father of Obed.
22 Obed was the father of Jesse.
Jesse was the father of David.

3:15a Hebrew *six measures,* an unknown quantity. **3:15b** Most Hebrew manuscripts read *he;* many Hebrew manuscripts, Syriac version, and Latin Vulgate read *she.* **4:20** As in some Greek manuscripts (see also 4:21); Hebrew reads *Salma.*

▶ **4:18** *See **Genealogies**, page 454.*

Naomi

Although this book is named after Ruth, it is actually Naomi's problem that lies at the heart of the story. After the death of her husband and sons, Naomi had no one to provide for her and her daughters-in-law. She hit rock bottom, even wanting to change her name from Naomi ("pleasant") to Mara ("bitter"). She eventually returned to her hometown of Bethlehem, where the family had once owned land that poverty, it seems, had forced them to sell. It is her realization that she has a forgotten family redeemer that turns the story around and provides hope for her and Ruth. Although at times deeply depressed on account of her circumstances, Naomi always wanted the best for her daughters-in-law, and her dogged determination eventually brought her through.

▶ *See also **The family redeemer**, page 301.*

1 Samuel *Samuel, Saul, and David*

Both 1 and 2 Samuel are named after the prophet God used to establish kingship in Israel—though he himself was very much against it. At God's leading, Samuel anointed Saul, Israel's first king—a man full of promise but who ruined it by wanting to do things his way. When God rejected Saul, Samuel anointed David, whom God described as "a man after my own heart," to replace him. Yet Saul was still on the throne and unwilling to give way, so the second half of the book records his struggles to remain as king, but also David's quiet rise to prominence.

What's it all about?

First Samuel picks up Israel's story at the end of the period of the judges. Eli, a priest, led the people from Shiloh; but the influence of the priesthood was waning, largely due to the sinful behavior of Eli's sons. The era of prophets and kings was about to begin. First and Second Samuel are concerned with the establishment of a united monarchy in Israel, in response to frequent incursions on their territory, mainly by the Philistines. Spiritually, the nation was barely alive. "Now in those days messages from the LORD were very rare, and visions were quite uncommon" (1 Samuel 3:1).

The book opens with the touching story of Elkanah's wife Hannah. She was unable to have children, but when she prayed for a son, God enabled her to bear Samuel. She offered him for God's service, and he became Eli's assistant. While still young, Samuel heard God speaking to him for the first time (chapter 3). He grew up to become one of Israel's greatest prophets and the last of its judges. But his own sons, whom he appointed as judges, were no better than Eli's sons.

Worried by the ongoing threat of the Philistines, Israel's leaders demanded a king "like all the other nations have" (8:5). Although God made it clear that "they are rejecting me, not you. They don't want me to be their king any longer" (8:7), he told Samuel to go ahead, and he led him to Saul (chapters 9–10). Saul started out well: He was a striking but humble figure, and very brave. But he quickly began to disobey God (chapter 13). However, God gave him a second chance (chapter 15), but he failed again, and so God rejected him as king.

OVERVIEW

The boy Samuel is entrusted to Eli the priest · *1:1–2:36*

Samuel's call as a prophet *3:1-21*

The Philistines capture the Ark of the Covenant, but disaster leads to its return · *4:1–7:2*

Samuel leads the nation *7:3-17*

Israel asks for a king *8:1-22*

Samuel anoints Saul as king *9:1–10:27*

Saul's early successes and Samuel's farewell speech · *11:1–12:25*

Saul's disobedience and rejection as king · *13:1–15:35*

David anointed as the new king *16:1-23*

David kills Goliath, the Philistine champion · *17:1-58*

Declining relationships with Saul lead David to flee · *18:1–30:31*

Saul's death in battle *31:1-13*

At God's direction, Samuel secretly anointed a new king, David, a young shepherd boy from Bethlehem. His courage and complete trust in God are seen in his killing of the dreaded Philistine warrior, Goliath (chapter 17), and David was invited to join Saul's court. Saul quickly became jealous of David's ongoing successes and consequent fame, however, and turned against him. Saul's son Jonathan helped David and remained his closest friend (chapters 18–20). The remaining chapters cover David's success in battle and the ten years or so that he spent evading Saul's murderous plans. In the final chapter, Saul and his son Jonathan died in battle, Saul taking his own life. The story of Israel's first king ended disastrously.

What does it mean for us?

At the heart of 1 and 2 Samuel lies the message of the importance of doing things God's way. Under constant oppression from their Philistine overlords, Israel's leaders decided that having a king to lead them would solve all their problems—whereas the reality was, they needed to get back to obeying God so that all the blessings of the covenant would follow. So God let them try it their way. He gave them the sort of king they were looking for, the best he could find by the standards they had chosen. When it inevitably failed, he gave them the sort of king that he had in mind, "a man after his own heart" (1 Samuel 13:14), who loved God and sought to put him first. But even this king wasn't perfect; and he discovered that when he did things his own way, they went disastrously wrong, as his adultery with Bathsheba showed. But the difference between Saul and David was this: David was quick to repent, whereas Saul always wanted to blame others. God can do anything with the one whose heart is tender.

▶ *See also* ***A timeline of the Bible****, pages A22–A24.*

Elkanah and His Family

1 There was a man named Elkanah who
lived in Ramah in the region of Zuph* in
the hill country of Ephraim. He was the son
of Jeroham, son of Elihu, son of Tohu, son of
Zuph, of Ephraim. 2Elkanah had two wives,
Hannah and Peninnah. Peninnah had children, but Hannah did not.
3Each year Elkanah would travel to Shiloh
to worship and sacrifice to the LORD of
Heaven's Armies at the Tabernacle. The
priests of the LORD at that time were the
two sons of Eli—Hophni and Phinehas. 4On
the days Elkanah presented his sacrifice, he
would give portions of the meat to Peninnah and each of her children. 5And though
he loved Hannah, he would give her only
one choice portion* because the LORD had
given her no children. 6So Peninnah would
taunt Hannah and make fun of her because
the LORD had kept her from having children.
7Year after year it was the same—Peninnah
would taunt Hannah as they went to the
Tabernacle.* Each time, Hannah would be
reduced to tears and would not even eat.
8"Why are you crying, Hannah?" Elkanah
would ask. "Why aren't you eating? Why
be downhearted just because you have no
children? You have me—isn't that better than
having ten sons?"

Hannah's Prayer for a Son

9Once after a sacrificial meal at Shiloh,
Hannah got up and went to pray. Eli the priest
was sitting at his customary place beside
the entrance of the Tabernacle.* 10Hannah
was in deep anguish, crying bitterly as she
prayed to the LORD. 11And she made this vow:
"O LORD of Heaven's Armies, if you will look
upon my sorrow and answer my prayer and
give me a son, then I will give him back to
you. He will be yours for his entire lifetime,
and as a sign that he has been dedicated to
the LORD, his hair will never be cut.*"
12As she was praying to the LORD, Eli
watched her. 13Seeing her lips moving but
hearing no sound, he thought she had been
drinking. 14"Must you come here drunk?" he
demanded. "Throw away your wine!"
15"Oh no, sir!" she replied. "I haven't been
drinking wine or anything stronger. But I
am very discouraged, and I was pouring out

1:1 As in Greek version; Hebrew reads *in Ramathaim-zophim;* compare 1:19. **1:5** Or *And because he loved Hannah, he would give her a choice portion.* The meaning of the Hebrew is uncertain. **1:7** Hebrew *the house of the LORD;* also in 1:24. **1:9** Hebrew *the Temple of the LORD.* **1:11** Some manuscripts add *He will drink neither wine nor intoxicants.*

my heart to the LORD. [16]Don't think I am a
wicked woman! For I have been praying out
of great anguish and sorrow."
[17]"In that case," Eli said, "go in peace!
May the God of Israel grant the request you
have asked of him."
[18]"Oh, thank you, sir!" she exclaimed.
Then she went back and began to eat again,
and she was no longer sad.

Samuel's Birth and Dedication

[19]The entire family got up early the next
morning and went to worship the LORD
once more. Then they returned home to
Ramah. When Elkanah slept with Hannah,
the LORD remembered her plea, [20]and in
due time she gave birth to a son. She named
him Samuel,* for she said, "I asked the
LORD for him."
[21]The next year Elkanah and his family
went on their annual trip to offer a sacrifice to the LORD and to keep his vow. [22]But
Hannah did not go. She told her husband,
"Wait until the boy is weaned. Then I will
take him to the Tabernacle and leave him
there with the LORD permanently.*"
[23]"Whatever you think is best," Elkanah
agreed. "Stay here for now, and may the
LORD help you keep your promise.*" So
she stayed home and nursed the boy until
he was weaned.
[24]When the child was weaned, Hannah
took him to the Tabernacle in Shiloh. They
brought along a three-year-old bull* for
the sacrifice and a basket* of flour and
some wine. [25]After sacrificing the bull,
they brought the boy to Eli. [26]"Sir, do you
remember me?" Hannah asked. "I am the
very woman who stood here several years
ago praying to the LORD. [27]I asked the LORD
to give me this boy, and he has granted
my request. [28]Now I am giving him to the
LORD, and he will belong to the LORD his
whole life." And they* worshiped the LORD
there.

Hannah's Prayer of Praise

2 Then Hannah prayed:
"My heart rejoices in the LORD!
The LORD has made me strong.*
Now I have an answer for my enemies;
I rejoice because you rescued me.
2 No one is holy like the LORD!
There is no one besides you;
there is no Rock like our God.

3 "Stop acting so proud and haughty!
Don't speak with such arrogance!
For the LORD is a God who knows what
you have done;
he will judge your actions.
4 The bow of the mighty is now broken,
and those who stumbled are now
strong.
5 Those who were well fed are now
starving,
and those who were starving are now
full.

Hannah

Hannah was Elkanah's wife and was childless for a long time. She had to endure constant taunting from Elkanah's other wife and, in desperation, she prayed to God for a son. She promised to dedicate him to God's service, and God answered her prayer: Samuel was born. When Samuel was old enough, she took him to Shiloh and presented him to Eli, the high priest.

Hannah celebrated God's goodness to her with a beautiful song (1 Samuel 2:1-10), praising him who acts on behalf of those who have nothing yet keep trusting him. Her story shows the importance of not giving up when prayer isn't answered quickly. God always hears our cry, though in his wisdom and perfect planning he does not always answer immediately or in the way we might like. It is important not to become discouraged or angry at such times but, like Hannah, to keep praying to God, trusting that our prayers are being heard and that God is working out his plan.

▸ *See also* ***Childlessness***, *page 25.*

The childless woman now has seven
children,
and the woman with many children
wastes away.
6 The LORD gives both death and life;
he brings some down to the grave*
but raises others up.
7 The LORD makes some poor and others
rich;
he brings some down and lifts others
up.
8 He lifts the poor from the dust
and the needy from the garbage
dump.
He sets them among princes,
placing them in seats of honor.
For all the earth is the LORD's,
and he has set the world in order.

9 "He will protect his faithful ones,
but the wicked will disappear in
darkness.
No one will succeed by strength alone.
10 Those who fight against the LORD will
be shattered.
He thunders against them from heaven;
the LORD judges throughout the earth.
He gives power to his king;
he increases the strength* of his
anointed one."

11 Then Elkanah returned home to Ramah
without Samuel. And the boy served the
LORD by assisting Eli the priest.

Eli's Wicked Sons

12 Now the sons of Eli were scoundrels who
had no respect for the LORD 13 or for their
duties as priests. Whenever anyone offered
a sacrifice, Eli's sons would send over a
servant with a three-pronged fork. While
the meat of the sacrificed animal was still
boiling, 14 the servant would stick the fork
into the pot and demand that whatever it
brought up be given to Eli's sons. All the Israelites who came to worship at Shiloh were
treated this way. 15 Sometimes the servant
would come even before the animal's fat
had been burned on the altar. He would
demand raw meat before it had been boiled
so that it could be used for roasting.
16 The man offering the sacrifice might
reply, "Take as much as you want, but the
fat must be burned first." Then the servant
would demand, "No, give it to me now, or
I'll take it by force." 17 So the sin of these
young men was very serious in the LORD's
sight, for they treated the LORD's offerings
with contempt.
18 But Samuel, though he was only a boy,
served the LORD. He wore a linen garment
like that of a priest.* 19 Each year his mother
made a small coat for him and brought it to
him when she came with her husband for
the sacrifice. 20 Before they returned home,
Eli would bless Elkanah and his wife and
say, "May the LORD give you other children
to take the place of this one she gave to the
LORD.*" 21 And the LORD blessed Hannah,
and she conceived and gave birth to three

1:20 *Samuel* sounds like the Hebrew term for "asked of God" or "heard by God." **1:22** Some manuscripts add *I will offer him as a Nazirite for all time.* **1:23** As in Dead Sea Scrolls and Greek version; Masoretic Text reads *may the LORD keep his promise.* **1:24a** As in Dead Sea Scrolls, Greek and Syriac versions; Masoretic Text reads *three bulls.* **1:24b** Hebrew *and an ephah* [20 quarts or 22 liters]. **1:28** Hebrew *he.* **2:1** Hebrew *has exalted my horn.* **2:6** Hebrew *to Sheol.* **2:10** Hebrew *he exalts the horn.* **2:18** Hebrew *He wore a linen ephod.* **2:20** As in Dead Sea Scrolls and Greek version; Masoretic Text reads *this one he requested of the LORD.*

Eli

Based at the Tabernacle at Shiloh, Eli was both a priest (1 Samuel 1:9) and a judge (4:18). He prayed a blessing on the childless Hannah, and when the child she bore (Samuel) was weaned, he was brought to the sanctuary and left in Eli's care. Eli trained him to serve the Lord, and it was he who first recognized that Samuel was starting to hear God speak to him and told him what to do (chapter 3). Although a godly man, Eli failed to raise his sons to follow God and live in a godly way. They began to abuse their position as priests and wouldn't respond to Eli's appeals (1:12-25), and it was not long before Eli himself fell into bad ways (2:29) and experienced God's judgment (2:27-36; 4:12-18)—a warning of how easy it is to start well and finish badly.

▶ *See also* ***Hannah****, page 306;* ***Samuel****, page 309.*

sons and two daughters. Meanwhile, Samuel grew up in the presence of the LORD.

22Now Eli was very old, but he was aware of what his sons were doing to the people of Israel. He knew, for instance, that his sons were seducing the young women who assisted at the entrance of the Tabernacle.* 23Eli said to them, "I have been hearing reports from all the people about the wicked things you are doing. Why do you keep sinning? 24You must stop, my sons! The reports I hear among the LORD's people are not good. 25If someone sins against another person, God* can mediate for the guilty party. But if someone sins against the LORD, who can intercede?" But Eli's sons wouldn't listen to their father, for the LORD was already planning to put them to death.

26Meanwhile, the boy Samuel grew taller and grew in favor with the LORD and with the people.

A Warning for Eli's Family

27One day a man of God came to Eli and gave him this message from the LORD: "I revealed myself* to your ancestors when they were Pharaoh's slaves in Egypt. 28I chose your ancestor Aaron* from among all the tribes of Israel to be my priest, to offer sacrifices on my altar, to burn incense, and to wear the priestly vest* as he served me. And I assigned the sacrificial offerings to you priests. 29So why do you scorn my sacrifices and offerings? Why do you give your sons more honor than you give me—for you and they have become fat from the best offerings of my people Israel!

30"Therefore, the LORD, the God of Israel, says: I promised that your branch of the tribe of Levi* would always be my priests. But I will honor those who honor me, and I will despise those who think lightly of me. 31The time is coming when I will put an end to your family, so it will no longer serve as my priests. All the members of your family will die before their time. None will reach old age. 32You will watch with envy as I pour out prosperity on the people of Israel. But no members of your family will ever live out their days. 33The few not cut off from serving at my altar will survive, but only so their eyes can go blind and their hearts break, and their children will die a violent death.* 34And to prove that what I have said will come true, I will cause your two sons, Hophni and Phinehas, to die on the same day!

35"Then I will raise up a faithful priest who will serve me and do what I desire. I will establish his family, and they will be priests to my anointed kings forever. 36Then all of your surviving family will bow before him, begging for money and food. 'Please,' they will say, 'give us jobs among the priests so we will have enough to eat.'"

The LORD Speaks to Samuel

3 Meanwhile, the boy Samuel served the LORD by assisting Eli. Now in those days messages from the LORD were very rare, and visions were quite uncommon.

2One night Eli, who was almost blind by now, had gone to bed. 3The lamp of God had not yet gone out, and Samuel was sleeping in the Tabernacle* near the Ark of God. 4Suddenly the LORD called out, "Samuel!"

"Yes?" Samuel replied. "What is it?" 5He got up and ran to Eli. "Here I am. Did you call me?"

"I didn't call you," Eli replied. "Go back to bed." So he did.

6Then the LORD called out again, "Samuel!"

Again Samuel got up and went to Eli. "Here I am. Did you call me?"

"I didn't call you, my son," Eli said. "Go back to bed."

7Samuel did not yet know the LORD because he had never had a message from the LORD before. 8So the LORD called a third time, and once more Samuel got up and went to Eli. "Here I am. Did you call me?"

Then Eli realized it was the LORD who was calling the boy. 9So he said to Samuel, "Go and lie down again, and if someone calls again, say, 'Speak, LORD, your servant is listening.'" So Samuel went back to bed.

10And the LORD came and called as before, "Samuel! Samuel!"

And Samuel replied, "Speak, your servant is listening."

11Then the LORD said to Samuel, "I am about to do a shocking thing in Israel. 12I am going to carry out all my threats against Eli and his family, from beginning to end. 13I have warned him that judgment is coming upon his family forever, because his sons are blaspheming God* and he hasn't disciplined them. 14So I have vowed that the sins of Eli and his sons will never be forgiven by sacrifices or offerings."

Samuel Speaks for the LORD

15Samuel stayed in bed until morning, then
got up and opened the doors of the Tabernacle* as usual. He was afraid to tell Eli
what the LORD had said to him. 16But Eli
called out to him, "Samuel, my son."

"Here I am," Samuel replied.

17"What did the LORD say to you? Tell me
everything. And may God strike you and
even kill you if you hide anything from me!"
18So Samuel told Eli everything; he didn't
hold anything back. "It is the LORD's will,"
Eli replied. "Let him do what he thinks best."

19As Samuel grew up, the LORD was with
him, and everything Samuel said proved to
be reliable. 20And all Israel, from Dan in the
north to Beersheba in the south, knew that
Samuel was confirmed as a prophet of the
LORD. 21The LORD continued to appear at
Shiloh and gave messages to Samuel there
at the Tabernacle. 4:1And Samuel's words
went out to all the people of Israel.

The Philistines Capture the Ark

4 At that time Israel was at war with
the Philistines. The Israelite army was
camped near Ebenezer, and the Philistines
were at Aphek. 2The Philistines attacked
and defeated the army of Israel, killing
4,000 men. 3After the battle was over, the
troops retreated to their camp, and the
elders of Israel asked, "Why did the LORD
allow us to be defeated by the Philistines?"
Then they said, "Let's bring the Ark of the
Covenant of the LORD from Shiloh. If we
carry it into battle with us, it* will save us
from our enemies."

4So they sent men to Shiloh to bring the
Ark of the Covenant of the LORD of Heaven's
Armies, who is enthroned between the cherubim. Hophni and Phinehas, the sons of Eli,
were also there with the Ark of the Covenant
of God. 5When all the Israelites saw the Ark
of the Covenant of the LORD coming into the
camp, their shout of joy was so loud it made
the ground shake!

6"What's going on?" the Philistines asked.
"What's all the shouting about in the
Hebrew camp?" When they were told it was
because the Ark of the LORD had arrived,
7they panicked. "The gods have* come into
their camp!" they cried. "This is a disaster!
We have never had to face anything like this
before! 8Help! Who can save us from these
mighty gods of Israel? They are the same gods
who destroyed the Egyptians with plagues
when Israel was in the wilderness. 9Fight as
never before, Philistines! If you don't, we will
become the Hebrews' slaves just as they have
been ours! Stand up like men and fight!"

10So the Philistines fought desperately,
and Israel was defeated again. The slaughter was great; 30,000 Israelite soldiers died
that day. The survivors turned and fled to
their tents. 11The Ark of God was captured,
and Hophni and Phinehas, the two sons of
Eli, were killed.

The Death of Eli

12A man from the tribe of Benjamin ran
from the battlefield and arrived at Shiloh

2:22 Hebrew *Tent of Meeting.* Some manuscripts lack this entire sentence. **2:25** Or *the judges.* **2:27** As in Greek and Syriac versions; Hebrew reads *Did I reveal myself.* **2:28a** Hebrew *your father.* **2:28b** Hebrew *an ephod.* **2:30** Hebrew *that your house and your father's house.* **2:33** As in Dead Sea Scrolls and Greek version, which read *die by the sword;* Masoretic Text reads *die like mortals.* **3:3** Hebrew *the Temple of the LORD.* **3:13** As in Greek version; Hebrew reads *his sons have made themselves contemptible.* **3:15** Hebrew *the house of the LORD.* **4:3** Or *he.* **4:7** Or *A god has.*

Samuel

Dedicated to God from childhood (1 Samuel 1:27-28), Samuel grew up to become both a prophet (3:19–4:1) and a judge (7:15). As such, he was able to lead Israel in overcoming the Philistines (7:3-14) and to help them transition to having a king—though this was something he deeply resented, believing they were rejecting God as their true king (chapter 8). He both anointed Saul as God's chosen king (chapters 9–10) and rejected him when he disobeyed (chapters 13 and 15). He was then led to anoint David in Saul's place (chapter 16), after which he withdrew from public life, his work done. The New Testament lists him among the heroes of faith (Hebrews 11:32).

▶ *See also* ***Anointing****, page 315;* ***Prophecy in the Old Testament****, page 903.*

later that same day. He had torn his clothes
and put dust on his head to show his grief.
13Eli was waiting beside the road to hear the
news of the battle, for his heart trembled
for the safety of the Ark of God. When the
messenger arrived and told what had happened, an outcry resounded throughout the
town.
14"What is all the noise about?" Eli asked.
The messenger rushed over to Eli, 15who
was ninety-eight years old and blind. 16He
said to Eli, "I have just come from the battlefield—I was there this very day."
"What happened, my son?" Eli demanded.
17"Israel has been defeated by the Philistines," the messenger replied. "The people
have been slaughtered, and your two sons,
Hophni and Phinehas, were also killed. And
the Ark of God has been captured."
18When the messenger mentioned what
had happened to the Ark of God, Eli fell
backward from his seat beside the gate. He
broke his neck and died, for he was old and
overweight. He had been Israel's judge for
forty years.
19Eli's daughter-in-law, the wife of Phinehas, was pregnant and near her time of
delivery. When she heard that the Ark of
God had been captured and that her father-
in-law and husband were dead, she went
into labor and gave birth. 20She died in
childbirth, but before she passed away the
midwives tried to encourage her. "Don't be
afraid," they said. "You have a baby boy!"
But she did not answer or pay attention to
them.
21She named the child Ichabod (which
means "Where is the glory?"), for she said,
"Israel's glory is gone." She named him this
because the Ark of God had been captured
and because her father-in-law and husband
were dead. 22Then she said, "The glory has
departed from Israel, for the Ark of God has
been captured."

The Ark in Philistia

5 After the Philistines captured the Ark of
God, they took it from the battleground
at Ebenezer to the town of Ashdod. 2They
carried the Ark of God into the temple of
Dagon and placed it beside an idol of Dagon.
3But when the citizens of Ashdod went to see
it the next morning, Dagon had fallen with
his face to the ground in front of the Ark of
the LORD! So they took Dagon and put him
in his place again. 4But the next morning the
same thing happened—Dagon had fallen
face down before the Ark of the LORD again.
This time his head and hands had broken
off and were lying in the doorway. Only the
trunk of his body was left intact. 5That is
why to this day neither the priests of Dagon
nor anyone who enters the temple of Dagon
in Ashdod will step on its threshold.
6Then the LORD's heavy hand struck the
people of Ashdod and the nearby villages

The Philistines

The Philistines originally came from Greece and Crete. They had tried to invade Egypt but were driven back, so they retreated and settled in five cities on Canaan's coastal strip—Gaza, Ashkelon, Ashdod, Gath, and Ekron—thus controlling the international coastal highway. As they outgrew these cities, they sought new territory inland, leading to constant clashes with the Israelites. During the Judges period they were a constant threat, and it was their attacks, in part, that led Israel to demand a king (1 Samuel 8). What gave them their superiority was their iron weapons. They had learned how to smelt iron, probably from the Hittites, whom they had defeated, and jealously guarded the secret, especially from Israel (13:19-22). Israel was terrified of them (13:5-7), and Saul, who never managed to defeat them, was finally killed in battle against them (chapter 31). It was left to David to finally subdue them.

The Philistines continued to live in Canaan until the eighth century BC, when they were defeated by Assyria before being finally swallowed up into the Babylonian Empire in the sixth century BC. Their legacy was to leave a name for the region—Palestine.

with a plague of tumors.* [7]When the people realized what was happening, they cried out, "We can't keep the Ark of the God of Israel here any longer! He is against us! We will all be destroyed along with Dagon, our god." [8]So they called together the rulers of the Philistine towns and asked, "What should we do with the Ark of the God of Israel?"

The rulers discussed it and replied, "Move it to the town of Gath." So they moved the Ark of the God of Israel to Gath. [9]But when the Ark arrived at Gath, the LORD's heavy hand fell on its men, young and old; he struck them with a plague of tumors, and there was a great panic.

[10]So they sent the Ark of God to the town of Ekron, but when the people of Ekron saw it coming they cried out, "They are bringing the Ark of the God of Israel here to kill us, too!" [11]The people summoned the Philistine rulers again and begged them, "Please send the Ark of the God of Israel back to its own country, or it* will kill us all." For the deadly plague from God had already begun, and great fear was sweeping across the town. [12]Those who didn't die were afflicted with tumors; and the cry from the town rose to heaven.

The Philistines Return the Ark

6 The Ark of the LORD remained in Philistine territory seven months in all. [2]Then the Philistines called in their priests and diviners and asked them, "What should we do about the Ark of the LORD? Tell us how to return it to its own country."

[3]"Send the Ark of the God of Israel back with a gift," they were told. "Send a guilt offering so the plague will stop. Then, if you are healed, you will know it was his hand that caused the plague."

[4]"What sort of guilt offering should we send?" they asked.

And they were told, "Since the plague has struck both you and your five rulers, make five gold tumors and five gold rats, just like those that have ravaged your land. [5]Make these things to show honor to the God of Israel. Perhaps then he will stop afflicting you, your gods, and your land. [6]Don't be stubborn and rebellious as Pharaoh and the Egyptians were. By the time God was finished with them, they were eager to let Israel go.

[7]"Now build a new cart, and find two cows that have just given birth to calves. Make sure the cows have never been yoked to a cart. Hitch the cows to the cart, but shut their calves away from them in a pen. [8]Put the Ark of the LORD on the cart, and beside it place a chest containing the gold rats and gold tumors you are sending as a guilt offering. Then let the cows go wherever they want. [9]If they cross the border of our land and go to Beth-shemesh, we will know it was the LORD who brought this great disaster upon us. If they don't, we will know it was not his hand that caused the plague. It came simply by chance."

[10]So these instructions were carried out. Two cows were hitched to the cart, and their newborn calves were shut up in a pen. [11]Then the Ark of the LORD and the chest containing the gold rats and gold tumors were placed on the cart. [12]And sure enough,

5:6 Greek version and Latin Vulgate read *tumors; and rats appeared in their land, and death and destruction were throughout the city.* **5:11** Or *he.*

The Ark of the Covenant

The Ark of the Covenant was a wooden box covered with pure gold, with a lid on which were two large gold cherubim with outstretched wings, which symbolized the throne of God (Exodus 25:17-22). It was kept in the Most Holy Place in the Tabernacle and, later, the Temple. It contained the stone tablets with the Ten Commandments, a jar of manna, and Aaron's rod that had budded. Sadly, the Ark was sometimes regarded as no more than a lucky charm whose presence would ensure victory in battle (e.g., 1 Samuel 4:3) and which could be dangerous for the unwary (1 Samuel 5:1-12; 2 Samuel 6:6-11). However, it primarily symbolized God's presence among his people and his commitment to his covenant promises to them.

without veering off in other directions, the
cows went straight along the road toward
Beth-shemesh, lowing as they went. The
Philistine rulers followed them as far as the
border of Beth-shemesh.
13The people of Beth-shemesh were harvesting wheat in the valley, and when they
saw the Ark, they were overjoyed! 14The
cart came into the field of a man named
Joshua and stopped beside a large rock. So
the people broke up the wood of the cart
for a fire and killed the cows and sacrificed them to the LORD as a burnt offering.
15Several men of the tribe of Levi lifted the
Ark of the LORD and the chest containing
the gold rats and gold tumors from the
cart and placed them on the large rock.
Many sacrifices and burnt offerings were
offered to the LORD that day by the people
of Beth-shemesh. 16The five Philistine
rulers watched all this and then returned
to Ekron that same day.
17The five gold tumors sent by the Philistines as a guilt offering to the LORD were
gifts from the rulers of Ashdod, Gaza, Ashkelon, Gath, and Ekron. 18The five gold rats
represented the five Philistine towns and
their surrounding villages, which were controlled by the five rulers. The large rock* at
Beth-shemesh, where they set the Ark of the
LORD, still stands in the field of Joshua as a
witness to what happened there.

The Ark Moved to Kiriath-Jearim

19But the LORD killed seventy men* from
Beth-shemesh because they looked into
the Ark of the LORD. And the people
mourned greatly because of what the LORD
had done. 20"Who is able to stand in the
presence of the LORD, this holy God?" they
cried out. "Where can we send the Ark
from here?"
21So they sent messengers to the people
at Kiriath-jearim and told them, "The Philistines have returned the Ark of the LORD.
Come here and get it!"

7 So the men of Kiriath-jearim came to get
the Ark of the LORD. They took it to the
hillside home of Abinadab and ordained
Eleazar, his son, to be in charge of it. 2The
Ark remained in Kiriath-jearim for a long
time—twenty years in all. During that time
all Israel mourned because it seemed the
LORD had abandoned them.

Samuel Leads Israel to Victory

3Then Samuel said to all the people of Israel,
"If you want to return to the LORD with all
your hearts, get rid of your foreign gods and
your images of Ashtoreth. Turn your hearts
to the LORD and obey him alone; then he
will rescue you from the Philistines." 4So the
Israelites got rid of their images of Baal and
Ashtoreth and worshiped only the LORD.
5Then Samuel told them, "Gather all
of Israel to Mizpah, and I will pray to the
LORD for you." 6So they gathered at Mizpah
and, in a great ceremony, drew water from
a well and poured it out before the LORD.
They also went without food all day and
confessed that they had sinned against
the LORD. (It was at Mizpah that Samuel
became Israel's judge.)
7When the Philistine rulers heard that
Israel had gathered at Mizpah, they mobilized their army and advanced. The Israelites were badly frightened when they
learned that the Philistines were approaching. 8"Don't stop pleading with the LORD our
God to save us from the Philistines!" they
begged Samuel. 9So Samuel took a young
lamb and offered it to the LORD as a whole
burnt offering. He pleaded with the LORD
to help Israel, and the LORD answered him.
10Just as Samuel was sacrificing the burnt
offering, the Philistines arrived to attack
Israel. But the LORD spoke with a mighty
voice of thunder from heaven that day, and
the Philistines were thrown into such confusion that the Israelites defeated them. 11The
men of Israel chased them from Mizpah to
a place below Beth-car, slaughtering them
all along the way.
12Samuel then took a large stone and
placed it between the towns of Mizpah and
Jeshanah.* He named it Ebenezer (which
means "the stone of help"), for he said, "Up
to this point the LORD has helped us!"
13So the Philistines were subdued and
didn't invade Israel again for some time.
And throughout Samuel's lifetime, the
LORD's powerful hand was raised against
the Philistines. 14The Israelite villages near
Ekron and Gath that the Philistines had
captured were restored to Israel, along with
the rest of the territory that the Philistines
had taken. And there was peace between
Israel and the Amorites in those days.
15Samuel continued as Israel's judge for
the rest of his life. 16Each year he traveled

around, setting up his court first at Bethel,
then at Gilgal, and then at Mizpah. He
judged the people of Israel at each of these
places. 17Then he would return to his home
at Ramah, and he would hear cases there,
too. And Samuel built an altar to the LORD
at Ramah.

Israel Requests a King

8 As Samuel grew old, he appointed his
sons to be judges over Israel. 2Joel and
Abijah, his oldest sons, held court in Beersheba. 3But they were not like their father,
for they were greedy for money. They accepted bribes and perverted justice.
4Finally, all the elders of Israel met at
Ramah to discuss the matter with Samuel.
5"Look," they told him, "you are now old,
and your sons are not like you. Give us a
king to judge us like all the other nations
have."
6Samuel was displeased with their
request and went to the LORD for guidance.
7"Do everything they say to you," the LORD
replied, "for they are rejecting me, not you.
They don't want me to be their king any
longer. 8Ever since I brought them from
Egypt they have continually abandoned me
and followed other gods. And now they are
giving you the same treatment. 9Do as they
ask, but solemnly warn them about the way
a king will reign over them."

Samuel Warns against a Kingdom

10So Samuel passed on the LORD's warning
to the people who were asking him for a
king. 11"This is how a king will reign over
you," Samuel said. "The king will draft your
sons and assign them to his chariots and
his charioteers, making them run before
his chariots. 12Some will be generals and
captains in his army,* some will be forced
to plow in his fields and harvest his crops,
and some will make his weapons and
chariot equipment. 13The king will take your
daughters from you and force them to cook
and bake and make perfumes for him. 14He
will take away the best of your fields and
vineyards and olive groves and give them
to his own officials. 15He will take a tenth of
your grain and your grape harvest and distribute it among his officers and attendants.
16He will take your male and female slaves
and demand the finest of your cattle* and
donkeys for his own use. 17He will demand
a tenth of your flocks, and you will be his
slaves. 18When that day comes, you will beg
for relief from this king you are demanding,
but then the LORD will not help you."
19But the people refused to listen to
Samuel's warning. "Even so, we still want
a king," they said. 20"We want to be like the
nations around us. Our king will judge us
and lead us into battle."
21So Samuel repeated to the LORD what
the people had said, 22and the LORD replied,
"Do as they say, and give them a king." Then
Samuel agreed and sent the people home.

Saul Meets Samuel

9 There was a wealthy, influential man
named Kish from the tribe of Benjamin.
He was the son of Abiel, son of Zeror, son

6:18 As in some Hebrew manuscripts and Greek version; most Hebrew manuscripts read *great meadow* or *Abel-haggedolah.* **6:19** As in a few Hebrew manuscripts; most Hebrew manuscripts read *70 men, 50,000 men.* Perhaps the text should be understood to read *the LORD killed 70 men and 50 oxen.* **7:12** As in Greek and Syriac versions; Hebrew reads *Shen.* **8:12** Hebrew *commanders of thousands and commanders of fifties.* **8:16** As in Greek version; Hebrew reads *young men.*

Why did Israel ask for a king?

Sometimes people ask for things to get them out of a problem without thinking of the long-term consequences, and that's what Israel did here in 1 Samuel 8. With Samuel getting older and his sons not walking in his godly ways, Israel started to think about the need for a new leader (1 Samuel 8:1-5). Looking at surrounding successful nations, they realized the one thing those nations had that Israel didn't was a king (8:5, 19-20). Jumping to the conclusion that this must be the key, they demanded that Samuel give them one. Samuel was angry and warned them what a king would do (8:10-18), but God told him to go ahead, saying, "They are rejecting me, not you" (8:7). Israel's first experience of a king would prove disastrous, but thankfully God still had further plans for them.

of Becorath, son of Aphiah, of the tribe of Benjamin. 2His son Saul was the most handsome man in Israel—head and shoulders taller than anyone else in the land.

3One day Kish's donkeys strayed away, and he told Saul, "Take a servant with you, and go look for the donkeys." 4So Saul took one of the servants and traveled through the hill country of Ephraim, the land of Shalishah, the Shaalim area, and the entire land of Benjamin, but they couldn't find the donkeys anywhere.

5Finally, they entered the region of Zuph, and Saul said to his servant, "Let's go home. By now my father will be more worried about us than about the donkeys!"

6But the servant said, "I've just thought of something! There is a man of God who lives here in this town. He is held in high honor by all the people because everything he says comes true. Let's go find him. Perhaps he can tell us which way to go."

7"But we don't have anything to offer him," Saul replied. "Even our food is gone, and we don't have a thing to give him."

8"Well," the servant said, "I have one small silver piece.* We can at least offer it to the man of God and see what happens!" 9(In those days if people wanted a message from God, they would say, "Let's go and ask the seer," for prophets used to be called seers.)

10"All right," Saul agreed, "let's try it!" So they started into the town where the man of God lived.

11As they were climbing the hill to the town, they met some young women coming out to draw water. So Saul and his servant asked, "Is the seer here today?"

12"Yes," they replied. "Stay right on this road. He is at the town gates. He has just arrived to take part in a public sacrifice up at the place of worship. 13Hurry and catch him before he goes up there to eat. The guests won't begin eating until he arrives to bless the food."

14So they entered the town, and as they passed through the gates, Samuel was coming out toward them to go up to the place of worship.

15Now the LORD had told Samuel the previous day, 16"About this time tomorrow I will send you a man from the land of Benjamin. Anoint him to be the leader of my people, Israel. He will rescue them from the Philistines, for I have looked down on my people in mercy and have heard their cry."

17When Samuel saw Saul, the LORD said, "That's the man I told you about! He will rule my people."

18Just then Saul approached Samuel at the gateway and asked, "Can you please tell me where the seer's house is?"

19"I am the seer!" Samuel replied. "Go up to the place of worship ahead of me. We will eat there together, and in the morning I'll tell you what you want to know and send you on your way. 20And don't worry about those donkeys that were lost three days ago, for they have been found. And I am here to tell you that you and your family are the focus of all Israel's hopes."

21Saul replied, "But I'm only from the tribe of Benjamin, the smallest tribe in Israel, and my family is the least important of all the families of that tribe! Why are you talking like this to me?"

22Then Samuel brought Saul and his servant into the hall and placed them at the head of the table, honoring them above the thirty special guests. 23Samuel then instructed the cook to bring Saul the finest cut of meat, the piece that had been set aside for the guest of honor. 24So the cook brought in the meat and placed it before Saul. "Go ahead and eat it," Samuel said. "I was saving it for you even before I invited these others!" So Saul ate with Samuel that day.

25When they came down from the place of worship and returned to town, Samuel took Saul up to the roof of the house and prepared a bed for him there.* 26At daybreak the next morning, Samuel called to Saul, "Get up! It's time you were on your way." So Saul got ready, and he and Samuel left the house together. 27When they reached the edge of town, Samuel told Saul to send his servant on ahead. After the servant was gone, Samuel said, "Stay here, for I have received a special message for you from God."

Samuel Anoints Saul as King

10 Then Samuel took a flask of olive oil and poured it over Saul's head. He kissed Saul and said, "I am doing this because the LORD has appointed you to be the ruler over Israel, his special possession.* 2When you leave me today, you will see two men beside Rachel's tomb at Zelzah, on the border of Benjamin. They will tell you that the donkeys have been found and that your father has stopped worrying about them and is now worried about you. He is asking, 'Have you seen my son?'

3 "When you get to the oak of Tabor, you will see three men coming toward you who are on their way to worship God at Bethel. One will be bringing three young goats, another will have three loaves of bread, and the third will be carrying a wineskin full of wine. 4 They will greet you and offer you two of the loaves, which you are to accept.

5 "When you arrive at Gibeah of God,* where the garrison of the Philistines is located, you will meet a band of prophets coming down from the place of worship. They will be playing a harp, a tambourine, a flute, and a lyre, and they will be prophesying. 6 At that time the Spirit of the LORD will come powerfully upon you, and you will prophesy with them. You will be changed into a different person. 7 After these signs take place, do what must be done, for God is with you. 8 Then go down to Gilgal ahead of me. I will join you there to sacrifice burnt offerings and peace offerings. You must wait for seven days until I arrive and give you further instructions."

Samuel's Signs Are Fulfilled

9 As Saul turned and started to leave, God gave him a new heart, and all Samuel's signs were fulfilled that day. 10 When Saul and his servant arrived at Gibeah, they saw a group of prophets coming toward them. Then the Spirit of God came powerfully upon Saul, and he, too, began to prophesy. 11 When those who knew Saul heard about it, they exclaimed, "What? Is even Saul a prophet? How did the son of Kish become a prophet?"

12 And one of those standing there said, "Can anyone become a prophet, no matter who his father is?"* So that is the origin of the saying "Is even Saul a prophet?"

13 When Saul had finished prophesying, he went up to the place of worship. 14 "Where have you been?" Saul's uncle asked him and his servant.

"We were looking for the donkeys," Saul replied, "but we couldn't find them. So we went to Samuel to ask him where they were."

15 "Oh? And what did he say?" his uncle asked.

9:8 Hebrew 1/4 *shekel of silver,* about 0.1 ounces or 3 grams in weight. **9:25** As in Greek version; Hebrew reads *and talked with him there.* **10:1** Greek version reads *over Israel. And you will rule over the LORD's people and save them from their enemies around them. This will be the sign to you that the LORD has appointed you to be leader over his special possession.* **10:5** Hebrew *Gibeath-haelohim.* **10:12** Hebrew *said, "Who is their father?"*

Anointing

The practice of pouring oil over someone's head to set them apart for a task that God had called them to was known as anointing. It was used especially for priests (e.g., Exodus 30:22-33), kings (e.g., 1 Samuel 10:1), and prophets (e.g., 1 Kings 19:16) and symbolized God's gift of his Holy Spirit to both consecrate them to their work and empower them to do it (1 Samuel 10:6, 9-10). It was a way of saying, "As this oil is poured over your head, so may God's Spirit be poured into your life to enable you to do what God has called you to do." And it was not just a little bit of oil as is sometimes used in some Christian ceremonies today. Samuel took a whole flask of oil and poured it over Saul (see also 1 Kings 1:39; Psalm 133:1-2). The holiness of someone anointed in this way is reflected in David's unwillingness to lay a hand on Saul (1 Samuel 26:5-25; see also 1 Chronicles 16:22).

The New Testament continues to use anointing as an image of being filled with the Holy Spirit. Having been filled with the Spirit (Luke 3:21-22; 4:14), Jesus saw himself as now anointed for his ministry (Luke 4:18-19; see also Acts 10:38). But the image is also used of all Christians to reassure them of the presence and power of the Holy Spirit within (1 John 2:20, 27; see footnotes).

▶ *See also* ***The Holy Spirit in Acts****, page 1236;* ***Life in the Spirit****, page 1291.*

16“He told us that the donkeys had already been found,” Saul replied. But Saul didn’t tell his uncle what Samuel said about the kingdom.

Saul Is Acclaimed King

17Later Samuel called all the people of Israel to meet before the LORD at Mizpah. 18And he said, “This is what the LORD, the God of Israel, has declared: I brought you from Egypt and rescued you from the Egyptians and from all of the nations that were oppressing you. 19But though I have rescued you from your misery and distress, you have rejected your God today and have said, ‘No, we want a king instead!’ Now, therefore, present yourselves before the LORD by tribes and clans.”

20So Samuel brought all the tribes of Israel before the LORD, and the tribe of Benjamin was chosen by lot. 21Then he brought each family of the tribe of Benjamin before the LORD, and the family of the Matrites was chosen. And finally Saul son of Kish was chosen from among them. But when they looked for him, he had disappeared! 22So they asked the LORD, “Where is he?”

And the LORD replied, “He is hiding among the baggage.” 23So they found him and brought him out, and he stood head and shoulders above anyone else.

24Then Samuel said to all the people, “This is the man the LORD has chosen as your king. No one in all Israel is like him!”

And all the people shouted, “Long live the king!”

25Then Samuel told the people what the rights and duties of a king were. He wrote them down on a scroll and placed it before the LORD. Then Samuel sent the people home again.

26When Saul returned to his home at Gibeah, a group of men whose hearts God had touched went with him. 27But there were some scoundrels who complained, “How can this man save us?” And they scorned him and refused to bring him gifts. But Saul ignored them.

[Nahash, king of the Ammonites, had been grievously oppressing the people of Gad and Reuben who lived east of the Jordan River. He gouged out the right eye of each of the Israelites living there, and he didn’t allow anyone to come and rescue them. In fact, of all the Israelites east of the Jordan, there wasn’t a single one whose right eye Nahash had not gouged out. But there were 7,000 men who had escaped from the Ammonites, and they had settled in Jabesh-gilead.]*

Saul Defeats the Ammonites

11 About a month later,* King Nahash of Ammon led his army against the Israelite town of Jabesh-gilead. But all the citizens of Jabesh asked for peace. “Make a treaty with us, and we will be your servants,” they pleaded.

2“All right,” Nahash said, “but only on one condition. I will gouge out the right eye of every one of you as a disgrace to all Israel!”

3“Give us seven days to send messengers throughout Israel!” replied the elders of Jabesh. “If no one comes to save us, we will agree to your terms.”

4When the messengers came to Gibeah of Saul and told the people about their plight, everyone broke into tears. 5Saul had been plowing a field with his oxen, and when he returned to town, he asked, “What’s the matter? Why is everyone crying?” So they told him about the message from Jabesh.

6Then the Spirit of God came powerfully upon Saul, and he became very angry. 7He took two oxen and cut them into pieces and sent the messengers to carry them throughout Israel with this message: “This is what will happen to the oxen of anyone who refuses to follow Saul and Samuel into battle!” And the LORD made the people afraid of Saul’s anger, and all of them came out together as one. 8When Saul mobilized them at Bezek, he found that there were 300,000 men from Israel and 30,000* men from Judah.

9So Saul sent the messengers back to Jabesh-gilead to say, “We will rescue you by noontime tomorrow!” There was great joy throughout the town when that message arrived!

10The men of Jabesh then told their enemies, “Tomorrow we will come out to you, and you can do to us whatever you wish.” 11But before dawn the next morning, Saul arrived, having divided his army into three detachments. He launched a surprise attack against the Ammonites and slaughtered them the whole morning. The remnant of their army was so badly scattered that no two of them were left together.

12 Then the people exclaimed to Samuel,
"Now where are those men who said, 'Why
should Saul rule over us?' Bring them here,
and we will kill them!"
13 But Saul replied, "No one will be executed today, for today the LORD has rescued
Israel!"
14 Then Samuel said to the people, "Come,
let us all go to Gilgal to renew the kingdom."
15 So they all went to Gilgal, and in a solemn
ceremony before the LORD they made Saul
king. Then they offered peace offerings to
the LORD, and Saul and all the Israelites
were filled with joy.

Samuel's Farewell Address

12 Then Samuel addressed all Israel:
"I have done as you asked and given
you a king. 2 Your king is now your leader. I
stand here before you—an old, gray-haired
man—and my sons serve you. I have served
as your leader from the time I was a boy to
this very day. 3 Now testify against me in
the presence of the LORD and before his
anointed one. Whose ox or donkey have
I stolen? Have I ever cheated any of you?
Have I ever oppressed you? Have I ever
taken a bribe and perverted justice? Tell me
and I will make right whatever I have done
wrong."
4 "No," they replied, "you have never
cheated or oppressed us, and you have
never taken even a single bribe."
5 "The LORD and his anointed one are my
witnesses today," Samuel declared, "that
my hands are clean."
"Yes, he is a witness," they replied.
6 "It was the LORD who appointed Moses
and Aaron," Samuel continued. "He
brought your ancestors out of the land
of Egypt. 7 Now stand here quietly before
the LORD as I remind you of all the great
things the LORD has done for you and your
ancestors.
8 "When the Israelites were* in Egypt and
cried out to the LORD, he sent Moses and
Aaron to rescue them from Egypt and to
bring them into this land. 9 But the people
soon forgot about the LORD their God, so
he handed them over to Sisera, the commander of Hazor's army, and also to the
Philistines and to the king of Moab, who
fought against them.
10 "Then they cried to the LORD again and
confessed, 'We have sinned by turning away
from the LORD and worshiping the images
of Baal and Ashtoreth. But we will worship
you and you alone if you will rescue us from
our enemies.' 11 Then the LORD sent Gideon,*
Bedan,* Jephthah, and Samuel* to save
you, and you lived in safety.
12 "But when you were afraid of Nahash,
the king of Ammon, you came to me and
said that you wanted a king to reign over
you, even though the LORD your God was
already your king. 13 All right, here is the
king you have chosen. You asked for him,
and the LORD has granted your request.
14 "Now if you fear and worship the LORD
and listen to his voice, and if you do not rebel
against the LORD's commands, then both
you and your king will show that you recognize the LORD as your God. 15 But if you rebel
against the LORD's commands and refuse to
listen to him, then his hand will be as heavy
upon you as it was upon your ancestors.
16 "Now stand here and see the great thing
the LORD is about to do. 17 You know that it
does not rain at this time of the year during
the wheat harvest. I will ask the LORD to
send thunder and rain today. Then you will
realize how wicked you have been in asking
the LORD for a king!"
18 So Samuel called to the LORD, and the
LORD sent thunder and rain that day. And
all the people were terrified of the LORD and
of Samuel. 19 "Pray to the LORD your God for
us, or we will die!" they all said to Samuel.
"For now we have added to our sins by
asking for a king."
20 "Don't be afraid," Samuel reassured
them. "You have certainly done wrong, but
make sure now that you worship the LORD
with all your heart, and don't turn your back
on him. 21 Don't go back to worshiping worthless idols that cannot help or rescue you—
they are totally useless! 22 The LORD will not
abandon his people, because that would
dishonor his great name. For it has pleased
the LORD to make you his very own people.
23 "As for me, I will certainly not sin
against the LORD by ending my prayers for
you. And I will continue to teach you what

10:27 This paragraph, which is not included in the Masoretic Text, is found in Dead Sea Scroll 4QSam[a]. **11:1** As in Dead Sea Scroll 4QSam[a] and Greek version; Masoretic Text lacks *About a month later.* **11:8** Dead Sea Scrolls and Greek version read *70,000.* **12:8** Hebrew *When Jacob was.* The names "Jacob" and "Israel" are often interchanged throughout the Old Testament, referring sometimes to the individual patriarch and sometimes to the nation. **12:11a** Hebrew *Jerub-baal,* another name for Gideon; see Judg 6:32. **12:11b** Greek and Syriac versions read *Barak.* **12:11c** Greek and Syriac versions read *Samson.*

is good and right. 24But be sure to fear the
LORD and faithfully serve him. Think of all
the wonderful things he has done for you.
25But if you continue to sin, you and your
king will be swept away."

Continued War with Philistia

13 Saul was thirty* years old when he
became king, and he reigned for
forty-two years.*
2Saul selected 3,000 special troops from
the army of Israel and sent the rest of the
men home. He took 2,000 of the chosen men
with him to Micmash and the hill country of
Bethel. The other 1,000 went with Saul's son
Jonathan to Gibeah in the land of Benjamin.
3Soon after this, Jonathan attacked and
defeated the garrison of Philistines at Geba.
The news spread quickly among the Philistines. So Saul blew the ram's horn throughout the land, saying, "Hebrews, hear this!
Rise up in revolt!" 4All Israel heard the news
that Saul had destroyed the Philistine garrison at Geba and that the Philistines now
hated the Israelites more than ever. So the
entire Israelite army was summoned to join
Saul at Gilgal.
5The Philistines mustered a mighty army
of 3,000* chariots, 6,000 charioteers, and as
many warriors as the grains of sand on the
seashore! They camped at Micmash east of
Beth-aven. 6The men of Israel saw what a
tight spot they were in; and because they
were hard pressed by the enemy, they tried to
hide in caves, thickets, rocks, holes, and cisterns. 7Some of them crossed the Jordan River
and escaped into the land of Gad and Gilead.

Saul's Disobedience and Samuel's Rebuke

Meanwhile, Saul stayed at Gilgal, and his
men were trembling with fear. 8Saul waited
there seven days for Samuel, as Samuel
had instructed him earlier, but Samuel still
didn't come. Saul realized that his troops
were rapidly slipping away. 9So he demanded, "Bring me the burnt offering and
the peace offerings!" And Saul sacrificed
the burnt offering himself.
10Just as Saul was finishing with the burnt
offering, Samuel arrived. Saul went out to
meet and welcome him, 11but Samuel said,
"What is this you have done?"
Saul replied, "I saw my men scattering
from me, and you didn't arrive when you
said you would, and the Philistines are at
Micmash ready for battle. 12So I said, 'The
Philistines are ready to march against us
at Gilgal, and I haven't even asked for the
LORD's help!' So I felt compelled to offer the
burnt offering myself before you came."
13"How foolish!" Samuel exclaimed. "You
have not kept the command the LORD your
God gave you. Had you kept it, the LORD
would have established your kingdom over
Israel forever. 14But now your kingdom
must end, for the LORD has sought out a
man after his own heart. The LORD has
already appointed him to be the leader of
his people, because you have not kept the
LORD's command."

Israel's Military Disadvantage

15Samuel then left Gilgal and went on his
way, but the rest of the troops went with
Saul to meet the army. They went up from

King Saul

When God gave Israel their first king, he gave them the best he could find according to the standards they were looking for—a successful military leader (1 Samuel 8:20). Saul was both physically impressive (9:2) and very humble (9:21; 10:20-22), and he soon showed his military prowess (11:1-11). But power went to his head, and he disobeyed God's command through Samuel the prophet (13:7-14), thereby putting his own authority above God's. Although God then rejected him as king (13:13-14), he gave him another chance; but Saul disobeyed once again, and his rejection was now complete (chapter 15). The remaining chapters of 1 Samuel record his sad decline as he fought not just the Philistines but also his own fear of David replacing him. He finally took his own life after being seriously wounded in a fierce battle against the Philistines on Mount Gilboa (chapter 31).

▶ *See also **Kingdoms of Israel** maps, Visual Overview Z6.*

Gilgal to Gibeah in the land of Benjamin.* When Saul counted the men who were still with him, he found only 600 were left! [16]Saul and Jonathan and the troops with them were staying at Geba in the land of Benjamin. The Philistines set up their camp at Micmash. [17]Three raiding parties soon left the camp of the Philistines. One went north toward Ophrah in the land of Shual, [18]another went west to Beth-horon, and the third moved toward the border above the valley of Zeboim near the wilderness.

[19]There were no blacksmiths in the land of Israel in those days. The Philistines wouldn't allow them for fear they would make swords and spears for the Hebrews. [20]So whenever the Israelites needed to sharpen their plowshares, picks, axes, or sickles,* they had to take them to a Philistine blacksmith. [21]The charges were as follows: a quarter of an ounce* of silver for sharpening a plowshare or a pick, and an eighth of an ounce* for sharpening an ax or making the point of an ox goad. [22]So on the day of the battle none of the people of Israel had a sword or spear, except for Saul and Jonathan.

[23]The pass at Micmash had meanwhile been secured by a contingent of the Philistine army.

Jonathan's Daring Plan

14 One day Jonathan said to his armor bearer, "Come on, let's go over to where the Philistines have their outpost." But Jonathan did not tell his father what he was doing.

[2]Meanwhile, Saul and his 600 men were camped on the outskirts of Gibeah, around the pomegranate tree* at Migron. [3]Among Saul's men was Ahijah the priest, who was wearing the ephod, the priestly vest. Ahijah was the son of Ichabod's brother Ahitub, son of Phinehas, son of Eli, the priest of the LORD who had served at Shiloh.

No one realized that Jonathan had left the Israelite camp. [4]To reach the Philistine outpost, Jonathan had to go down between two rocky cliffs that were called Bozez and Seneh. [5]The cliff on the north was in front of Micmash, and the one on the south was in front of Geba. [6]"Let's go across to the outpost of those pagans," Jonathan said to his armor bearer. "Perhaps the LORD will help us, for nothing can hinder the LORD. He can win a battle whether he has many warriors or only a few!"

[7]"Do what you think is best," the armor bearer replied. "I'm with you completely, whatever you decide."

[8]"All right, then," Jonathan told him. "We will cross over and let them see us. [9]If they say to us, 'Stay where you are or we'll kill you,' then we will stop and not go up to them. [10]But if they say, 'Come on up and fight,' then we will go up. That will be the LORD's sign that he will help us defeat them."

[11]When the Philistines saw them coming, they shouted, "Look! The Hebrews are crawling out of their holes!" [12]Then the men from the outpost shouted to Jonathan, "Come on up here, and we'll teach you a lesson!"

"Come on, climb right behind me," Jonathan said to his armor bearer, "for the LORD will help us defeat them!"

[13]So they climbed up using both hands and feet, and the Philistines fell before Jonathan, and his armor bearer killed those who came behind them. [14]They killed some twenty men in all, and their bodies were scattered over about half an acre.*

[15]Suddenly, panic broke out in the Philistine army, both in the camp and in the field, including even the outposts and raiding parties. And just then an earthquake struck, and everyone was terrified.

Israel Defeats the Philistines

[16]Saul's lookouts in Gibeah of Benjamin saw a strange sight—the vast army of Philistines began to melt away in every direction.* [17]"Call the roll and find out who's missing," Saul ordered. And when they checked, they found that Jonathan and his armor bearer were gone.

[18]Then Saul shouted to Ahijah, "Bring the ephod here!" For at that time Ahijah was wearing the ephod in front of the Israelites.* [19]But while Saul was talking to the

13:1a As in a few Greek manuscripts; the number is missing in the Hebrew. **13:1b** Hebrew *reigned . . . and two;* the number is incomplete in the Hebrew. Compare Acts 13:21. **13:5** As in Greek and Syriac versions; Hebrew reads *30,000.* **13:15** As in Greek version; Hebrew reads *Samuel then left Gilgal and went to Gibeah in the land of Benjamin.* **13:20** As in Greek version; Hebrew reads *or plowshares.* **13:21a** Hebrew *1 pim* [8 grams]. **13:21b** Hebrew *⅓ [of a shekel]* [4 grams]. **14:2** Or *around the rock of Rimmon;* compare Judg 20:45, 47; 21:13. **14:14** Hebrew *half a yoke;* a "yoke" was the amount of land plowed by a pair of yoked oxen in one day. **14:16** As in Greek version; Hebrew reads *they went and there.* **14:18** As in some Greek manuscripts; Hebrew reads *"Bring the Ark of God." For at that time the Ark of God was with the Israelites.*

priest, the confusion in the Philistine camp grew louder and louder. So Saul said to the priest, "Never mind; let's get going!"*

20Then Saul and all his men rushed out to the battle and found the Philistines killing each other. There was terrible confusion everywhere. 21Even the Hebrews who had previously gone over to the Philistine army revolted and joined in with Saul, Jonathan, and the rest of the Israelites. 22Likewise, the men of Israel who were hiding in the hill country of Ephraim joined the chase when they saw the Philistines running away. 23So the LORD saved Israel that day, and the battle continued to rage even beyond Beth-aven.

Saul's Foolish Oath

24Now the men of Israel were pressed to exhaustion that day, because Saul had placed them under an oath, saying, "Let a curse fall on anyone who eats before evening—before I have full revenge on my enemies." So no one ate anything all day, 25even though they had all found honeycomb on the ground in the forest. 26They didn't dare touch the honey because they all feared the oath they had taken.

27But Jonathan had not heard his father's command, and he dipped the end of his stick into a piece of honeycomb and ate the honey. After he had eaten it, he felt refreshed.* 28But one of the men saw him and said, "Your father made the army take a strict oath that anyone who eats food today will be cursed. That is why everyone is weary and faint."

29"My father has made trouble for us all!" Jonathan exclaimed. "A command like that only hurts us. See how refreshed I am now that I have eaten this little bit of honey. 30If the men had been allowed to eat freely from the food they found among our enemies, think how many more Philistines we could have killed!"

31They chased and killed the Philistines all day from Micmash to Aijalon, growing more and more faint. 32That evening they rushed for the battle plunder and butchered the sheep, goats, cattle, and calves, but they ate them without draining the blood. 33Someone reported to Saul, "Look, the men are sinning against the LORD by eating meat that still has blood in it."

"That is very wrong," Saul said. "Find a large stone and roll it over here. 34Then go out among the troops and tell them, 'Bring the cattle, sheep, and goats here to me. Kill them here, and drain the blood before you eat them. Do not sin against the LORD by eating meat with the blood still in it.'"

So that night all the troops brought their animals and slaughtered them there. 35Then Saul built an altar to the LORD; it was the first of the altars he built to the LORD.

36Then Saul said, "Let's chase the Philistines all night and plunder them until sunrise. Let's destroy every last one of them."

His men replied, "We'll do whatever you think is best."

But the priest said, "Let's ask God first."

37So Saul asked God, "Should we go after the Philistines? Will you help us defeat them?" But God made no reply that day.

38Then Saul said to the leaders, "Something's wrong! I want all my army commanders to come here. We must find out what sin was committed today. 39I vow by the name of the LORD who rescued Israel that the sinner will surely die, even if it is my own son Jonathan!" But no one would tell him what the trouble was.

40Then Saul said, "Jonathan and I will stand over here, and all of you stand over there."

And the people responded to Saul, "Whatever you think is best."

41Then Saul prayed, "O LORD, God of Israel, please show us who is guilty and who is innocent.*" Then they cast sacred lots, and Jonathan and Saul were chosen as the guilty ones, and the people were declared innocent.

42Then Saul said, "Now cast lots again and choose between me and Jonathan." And Jonathan was shown to be the guilty one.

43"Tell me what you have done," Saul demanded of Jonathan.

"I tasted a little honey," Jonathan admitted. "It was only a little bit on the end of my stick. Does that deserve death?"

44"Yes, Jonathan," Saul said, "you must die! May God strike me and even kill me if you do not die for this."

45But the people broke in and said to Saul, "Jonathan has won this great victory for Israel. Should he die? Far from it! As surely as the LORD lives, not one hair on his head will be touched, for God helped him do a great deed today." So the people rescued Jonathan, and he was not put to death.

46Then Saul called back the army from chasing the Philistines, and the Philistines returned home.

Saul's Military Successes

47Now when Saul had secured his grasp on Israel's throne, he fought against his enemies in every direction—against Moab, Ammon, Edom, the kings of Zobah, and the Philistines. And wherever he turned, he was victorious.* 48He performed great deeds and conquered the Amalekites, saving Israel from all those who had plundered them.

49Saul's sons included Jonathan, Ishbosheth,* and Malkishua. He also had two daughters: Merab, who was older, and Michal. 50Saul's wife was Ahinoam, the daughter of Ahimaaz. The commander of Saul's army was Abner, the son of Saul's uncle Ner. 51Saul's father, Kish, and Abner's father, Ner, were both sons of Abiel.

52The Israelites fought constantly with the Philistines throughout Saul's lifetime. So whenever Saul observed a young man who was brave and strong, he drafted him into his army.

Saul Defeats the Amalekites

15 One day Samuel said to Saul, "It was the LORD who told me to anoint you as king of his people, Israel. Now listen to this message from the LORD! 2This is what the LORD of Heaven's Armies has declared: I have decided to settle accounts with the nation of Amalek for opposing Israel when they came from Egypt. 3Now go and completely destroy* the entire Amalekite nation—men, women, children, babies, cattle, sheep, goats, camels, and donkeys."

4So Saul mobilized his army at Telaim. There were 200,000 soldiers from Israel and 10,000 men from Judah. 5Then Saul and his army went to a town of the Amalekites and lay in wait in the valley. 6Saul sent this warning to the Kenites: "Move away from where the Amalekites live, or you will die with them. For you showed kindness to all the people of Israel when they came up from Egypt." So the Kenites packed up and left.

7Then Saul slaughtered the Amalekites from Havilah all the way to Shur, east of Egypt. 8He captured Agag, the Amalekite king, but completely destroyed everyone else. 9Saul and his men spared Agag's life and kept the best of the sheep and goats, the cattle, the fat calves, and the lambs—everything, in fact, that appealed to them. They destroyed only what was worthless or of poor quality.

The LORD Rejects Saul

10Then the LORD said to Samuel, 11"I am sorry that I ever made Saul king, for he has not been loyal to me and has refused to obey my command." Samuel was so deeply moved when he heard this that he cried out to the LORD all night.

12Early the next morning Samuel went to find Saul. Someone told him, "Saul went to the town of Carmel to set up a monument to himself; then he went on to Gilgal."

13When Samuel finally found him, Saul greeted him cheerfully. "May the LORD bless you," he said. "I have carried out the LORD's command!"

14"Then what is all the bleating of sheep and goats and the lowing of cattle I hear?" Samuel demanded.

15"It's true that the army spared the best of the sheep, goats, and cattle," Saul admitted. "But they are going to sacrifice them to the LORD your God. We have destroyed everything else."

16Then Samuel said to Saul, "Stop! Listen to what the LORD told me last night!"

"What did he tell you?" Saul asked.

17And Samuel told him, "Although you may think little of yourself, are you not the leader of the tribes of Israel? The LORD has anointed you king of Israel. 18And the LORD sent you on a mission and told you, 'Go and completely destroy the sinners, the Amalekites, until they are all dead.' 19Why haven't you obeyed the LORD? Why did you rush for the plunder and do what was evil in the LORD's sight?"

20"But I did obey the LORD," Saul insisted. "I carried out the mission he gave me. I brought back King Agag, but I destroyed everyone else. 21Then my troops brought

14:19 Hebrew *Withdraw your hand.* **14:27** Or *his eyes brightened;* similarly in 14:29. **14:41** Greek version adds *If the fault is with me or my son Jonathan, respond with Urim; but if the men of Israel are at fault, respond with Thummim.* **14:47** As in Greek version; Hebrew reads *he acted wickedly.* **14:49** Hebrew *Ishvi*, a variant name for Ishbosheth; also known as Esh-baal. **15:3** The Hebrew term used here refers to the complete consecration of things or people to the LORD, either by destroying them or by giving them as an offering; also in 15:8, 9, 15, 18, 20, 21.

in the best of the sheep, goats, cattle, and plunder to sacrifice to the LORD your God in Gilgal."

22 But Samuel replied,

"What is more pleasing to the LORD:
your burnt offerings and sacrifices
or your obedience to his voice?
Listen! Obedience is better than
sacrifice,
and submission is better than offering
the fat of rams.
23 Rebellion is as sinful as witchcraft,
and stubbornness as bad as
worshiping idols.
So because you have rejected the
command of the LORD,
he has rejected you as king."

Saul Pleads for Forgiveness

24 Then Saul admitted to Samuel, "Yes, I have sinned. I have disobeyed your instructions and the LORD's command, for I was afraid of the people and did what they demanded. 25 But now, please forgive my sin and come back with me so that I may worship the LORD."

26 But Samuel replied, "I will not go back with you! Since you have rejected the LORD's command, he has rejected you as king of Israel."

27 As Samuel turned to go, Saul tried to hold him back and tore the hem of his robe. 28 And Samuel said to him, "The LORD has torn the kingdom of Israel from you today and has given it to someone else—one who is better than you. 29 And he who is the Glory of Israel will not lie, nor will he change his mind, for he is not human that he should change his mind!"

30 Then Saul pleaded again, "I know I have sinned. But please, at least honor me before the elders of my people and before Israel by coming back with me so that I may worship the LORD your God." 31 So Samuel finally agreed and went back with him, and Saul worshiped the LORD.

Samuel Executes King Agag

32 Then Samuel said, "Bring King Agag to me." Agag arrived full of hope, for he thought, "Surely the worst is over, and I have been spared!"* 33 But Samuel said, "As your sword has killed the sons of many mothers, now your mother will be childless." And Samuel cut Agag to pieces before the LORD at Gilgal.

34 Then Samuel went home to Ramah, and Saul returned to his house at Gibeah of Saul. 35 Samuel never went to meet with Saul again, but he mourned constantly for him.

Rebellion

Rebellion is a very strong word, but that's what Samuel accused Saul of when he disobeyed—for the second time—God's clear instructions.

God had been very clear that a fundamental condition on which he would give Israel a king was that both king and people would not rebel against God but would always obey him (1 Samuel 12:13-15). Here now was Saul disobeying. Just like the first man, Adam, he tried to blame others for his actions—at first the impending Philistine attack and Samuel's apparent delay (13:11-12), and then his soldiers (15:15); but Samuel (and God!) saw through it all. This was sheer disobedience (13:13), pride (15:12), and greed (15:19). The whole matter amounted to outright rebellion against God—saying no to him and yes to self. Its horrific nature is summed up when Samuel says, "Rebellion is as sinful as witchcraft" (15:23).

It is sobering to recall that whenever *we* disobey God's clear word to us—for example, by ignoring some clear teaching in the Bible—that we are being *rebellious*. Of course, the devil will try to convince us that it isn't really rebellion; it's simply a weakness, or something quite understandable. But this is not how God sees it. What delights God more than anything is not our extravagant worship or giving ("burnt offerings and sacrifices") but simply obeying him (15:22).

▶ *See also **Satan**, page 566.*

And the LORD was sorry he had ever made
Saul king of Israel.

Samuel Anoints David as King

16 Now the LORD said to Samuel, “You
have mourned long enough for Saul.
I have rejected him as king of Israel, so fill
your flask with olive oil and go to Bethlehem. Find a man named Jesse who lives
there, for I have selected one of his sons to
be my king.”
2 But Samuel asked, “How can I do that? If
Saul hears about it, he will kill me.”
“Take a heifer with you,” the LORD
replied, “and say that you have come to
make a sacrifice to the LORD. 3 Invite Jesse
to the sacrifice, and I will show you which
of his sons to anoint for me.”
4 So Samuel did as the LORD instructed.
When he arrived at Bethlehem, the elders
of the town came trembling to meet him.
“What’s wrong?” they asked. “Do you come
in peace?”
5 “Yes,” Samuel replied. “I have come
to sacrifice to the LORD. Purify yourselves
and come with me to the sacrifice.” Then
Samuel performed the purification rite for
Jesse and his sons and invited them to the
sacrifice, too.
6 When they arrived, Samuel took one
look at Eliab and thought, “Surely this is
the LORD’s anointed!”
7 But the LORD said to Samuel, “Don’t
judge by his appearance or height, for I
have rejected him. The LORD doesn’t see
things the way you see them. People judge
by outward appearance, but the LORD looks
at the heart.”
8 Then Jesse told his son Abinadab to
step forward and walk in front of Samuel.
But Samuel said, “This is not the one the
LORD has chosen.” 9 Next Jesse summoned
Shimea,* but Samuel said, “Neither is this

15:32 Dead Sea Scrolls and Greek version read *Agag arrived hesitantly, for he thought, “Surely this is the bitterness of death.”*
16:9 Hebrew *Shammah*, a variant spelling of Shimea; compare 1 Chr 2:13; 20:7.

King David

The “man after his own heart” (1 Samuel 13:14) that God had chosen to replace Saul was David. At the time, he was a young teenager, dismissed as a possible contender by his father (16:11). Samuel anointed him in his family’s presence (16:1-13), though it would be some ten years before David came to the throne. He first came to Saul’s attention as a musician (16:14-23), fighter (chapter 17), and the best friend of Saul’s son Jonathan (18:1-4). But as a result of David's military successes, Saul became jealous of him and began to see him as a threat (18:5-9), and he tried to kill him. David fled, and he spent the following years hiding in caves, hills, and forests, but also gathering supporters. Only after Saul’s death was the way clear for him to become king as Samuel had promised.

David’s story continues in 2 Samuel where we see him becoming king, at first of Judah (2 Samuel 2:1-7) and then, seven years later, of all Israel (2 Samuel 5:1-16). During his reign Israel’s enemies were defeated and its borders strengthened. David wanted to build a temple for God, but God said he would build a “house” for David instead, making him the founder of an everlasting kingdom (2 Samuel 7:1-29)—a promise Christians see fulfilled in Jesus (e.g., Luke 1:30-33). Although David loved God, he wasn’t perfect. His adultery with Bathsheba (2 Samuel 11:1-27), his failure to properly discipline his son Amnon (2 Samuel 13:1-39), and his blindness to what his son Absalom was doing (2 Samuel 15:1-12) were all disastrous, both for himself and for Israel. But David’s quick repentance always enabled God to forgive and bless him and turn the circumstances around (e.g., 2 Samuel 12:1-25). And it was ultimately his heart, not his failures or successes, that God loved. It remains the same for us today.

▶ *See **The Davidic covenant**, page 468; **Kingdoms of Israel** map, Visual Overview Z6.*

the one the LORD has chosen." 10In the same
way all seven of Jesse's sons were presented
to Samuel. But Samuel said to Jesse, "The
LORD has not chosen any of these." 11Then
Samuel asked, "Are these all the sons you
have?"
"There is still the youngest," Jesse
replied. "But he's out in the fields watching
the sheep and goats."
"Send for him at once," Samuel said. "We
will not sit down to eat until he arrives."
12So Jesse sent for him. He was dark and
handsome, with beautiful eyes.
And the LORD said, "This is the one;
anoint him."
13So as David stood there among his
brothers, Samuel took the flask of olive oil
he had brought and anointed David with
the oil. And the Spirit of the LORD came
powerfully upon David from that day on.
Then Samuel returned to Ramah.

David Serves in Saul's Court

14Now the Spirit of the LORD had left Saul,
and the LORD sent a tormenting spirit* that
filled him with depression and fear.
15Some of Saul's servants said to him,
"A tormenting spirit from God is troubling
you. 16Let us find a good musician to play
the harp whenever the tormenting spirit
troubles you. He will play soothing music,
and you will soon be well again."
17"All right," Saul said. "Find me someone
who plays well, and bring him here."
18One of the servants said to Saul, "One
of Jesse's sons from Bethlehem is a talented
harp player. Not only that—he is a brave
warrior, a man of war, and has good judgment. He is also a fine-looking young man,
and the LORD is with him."
19So Saul sent messengers to Jesse to say,
"Send me your son David, the shepherd."
20Jesse responded by sending David to Saul,
along with a young goat, a donkey loaded
with bread, and a wineskin full of wine.
21So David went to Saul and began
serving him. Saul loved David very much,
and David became his armor bearer.
22Then Saul sent word to Jesse asking,
"Please let David remain in my service, for
I am very pleased with him."
23And whenever the tormenting spirit
from God troubled Saul, David would play
the harp. Then Saul would feel better, and
the tormenting spirit would go away.

Goliath Challenges the Israelites

17 The Philistines now mustered
their army for battle and camped
between Socoh in Judah and Azekah at
Ephes-dammim. 2Saul countered by gathering his Israelite troops near the valley of
Elah. 3So the Philistines and Israelites faced
each other on opposite hills, with the valley
between them.
4Then Goliath, a Philistine champion
from Gath, came out of the Philistine ranks
to face the forces of Israel. He was over nine
feet* tall! 5He wore a bronze helmet, and his
bronze coat of mail weighed 125 pounds.*
6He also wore bronze leg armor, and he
carried a bronze javelin on his shoulder.
7The shaft of his spear was as heavy and
thick as a weaver's beam, tipped with an
iron spearhead that weighed 15 pounds.*
His armor bearer walked ahead of him carrying a shield.
8Goliath stood and shouted a taunt across
to the Israelites. "Why are you all coming
out to fight?" he called. "I am the Philistine
champion, but you are only the servants of
Saul. Choose one man to come down here
and fight me! 9If he kills me, then we will be
your slaves. But if I kill him, you will be our
slaves! 10I defy the armies of Israel today!
Send me a man who will fight me!" 11When
Saul and the Israelites heard this, they were
terrified and deeply shaken.

Jesse Sends David to Saul's Camp

12Now David was the son of a man named
Jesse, an Ephrathite from Bethlehem in
the land of Judah. Jesse was an old man at
that time, and he had eight sons. 13Jesse's
three oldest sons—Eliab, Abinadab, and
Shimea*—had already joined Saul's army
to fight the Philistines. 14David was the
youngest son. David's three oldest brothers
stayed with Saul's army, 15but David went
back and forth so he could help his father
with the sheep in Bethlehem.
16For forty days, every morning and
evening, the Philistine champion strutted
in front of the Israelite army.
17One day Jesse said to David, "Take this
basket* of roasted grain and these ten
loaves of bread, and carry them quickly
to your brothers. 18And give these ten cuts
of cheese to their captain. See how your
brothers are getting along, and bring back
a report on how they are doing.*" 19David's

brothers were with Saul and the Israelite
army at the valley of Elah, fighting against
the Philistines.
20 So David left the sheep with another
shepherd and set out early the next morning
with the gifts, as Jesse had directed him. He
arrived at the camp just as the Israelite army
was leaving for the battlefield with shouts
and battle cries. 21 Soon the Israelite and
Philistine forces stood facing each other,
army against army. 22 David left his things
with the keeper of supplies and hurried out
to the ranks to greet his brothers. 23 As he
was talking with them, Goliath, the Philistine champion from Gath, came out from
the Philistine ranks. Then David heard him
shout his usual taunt to the army of Israel.
24 As soon as the Israelite army saw him,
they began to run away in fright. 25 "Have
you seen the giant?" the men asked. "He
comes out each day to defy Israel. The king
has offered a huge reward to anyone who
kills him. He will give that man one of his
daughters for a wife, and the man's entire
family will be exempted from paying taxes!"
26 David asked the soldiers standing
nearby, "What will a man get for killing this
Philistine and ending his defiance of Israel?
Who is this pagan Philistine anyway, that
he is allowed to defy the armies of the living
God?"
27 And these men gave David the same
reply. They said, "Yes, that is the reward for
killing him."
28 But when David's oldest brother, Eliab,
heard David talking to the men, he was
angry. "What are you doing around here
anyway?" he demanded. "What about those
few sheep you're supposed to be taking care
of? I know about your pride and deceit. You
just want to see the battle!"
29 "What have I done now?" David replied.
"I was only asking a question!" 30 He walked
over to some others and asked them the
same thing and received the same answer.
31 Then David's question was reported to
King Saul, and the king sent for him.

David Kills Goliath

32 "Don't worry about this Philistine," David
told Saul. "I'll go fight him!"
33 "Don't be ridiculous!" Saul replied.
"There's no way you can fight this Philistine
and possibly win! You're only a boy, and
he's been a man of war since his youth."
34 But David persisted. "I have been taking
care of my father's sheep and goats," he
said. "When a lion or a bear comes to steal a
lamb from the flock, 35 I go after it with a club
and rescue the lamb from its mouth. If the
animal turns on me, I catch it by the jaw and
club it to death. 36 I have done this to both
lions and bears, and I'll do it to this pagan
Philistine, too, for he has defied the armies
of the living God! 37 The LORD who rescued
me from the claws of the lion and the bear
will rescue me from this Philistine!"
Saul finally consented. "All right, go
ahead," he said. "And may the LORD be
with you!"

16:14 Or *an evil spirit;* also in 16:15, 16, 23. **17:4** Hebrew *6 cubits and 1 span* [which totals about 9.75 feet or 3 meters]; Dead Sea Scrolls and Greek version read *4 cubits and 1 span* [which totals about 6.75 feet or 2 meters]. **17:5** Hebrew *5,000 shekels* [57 kilograms]. **17:7** Hebrew *600 shekels* [6.8 kilograms]. **17:13** Hebrew *Shammah,* a variant spelling of Shimea; compare 1 Chr 2:13; 20:7. **17:17** Hebrew *ephah* [20 quarts or 22 liters]. **17:18** Hebrew *and take their pledge.*

Goliath

First Samuel 17 is an example of what the ancient world called "battle by champion." Rather than two armies fighting each other, with the losses that entailed, each side appointed a champion, and whoever won claimed victory for their side (17:8-9). But the problem here was that the Philistine champion was over nine feet tall and equipped with incredible armor and weapons (17:4-7). But Goliath's arrogance proved to be his downfall; he despised David without understanding his skill with a sling (which used stones the size of a baseball), let alone his confidence in the LORD (Yahweh; 17:34-37). David's shot found the gap in Goliath's helmet, the giant crashed down, and David rushed in to finish him off with Goliath's own sword.

▶ *See **The Philistines**, page 310.*

38 Then Saul gave David his own armor—a
bronze helmet and a coat of mail. 39 David
put it on, strapped the sword over it, and
took a step or two to see what it was like,
for he had never worn such things before.

"I can't go in these," he protested to Saul.
"I'm not used to them." So David took them
off again. 40 He picked up five smooth stones
from a stream and put them into his shepherd's bag. Then, armed only with his shepherd's staff and sling, he started across the
valley to fight the Philistine.

41 Goliath walked out toward David with
his shield bearer ahead of him, 42 sneering
in contempt at this ruddy-faced boy. 43 "Am
I a dog," he roared at David, "that you come
at me with a stick?" And he cursed David by
the names of his gods. 44 "Come over here,
and I'll give your flesh to the birds and wild
animals!" Goliath yelled.

45 David replied to the Philistine, "You
come to me with sword, spear, and javelin,
but I come to you in the name of the LORD of
Heaven's Armies—the God of the armies of
Israel, whom you have defied. 46 Today the
LORD will conquer you, and I will kill you
and cut off your head. And then I will give
the dead bodies of your men to the birds
and wild animals, and the whole world will
know that there is a God in Israel! 47 And
everyone assembled here will know that
the LORD rescues his people, but not with
sword and spear. This is the LORD's battle,
and he will give you to us!"

48 As Goliath moved closer to attack,
David quickly ran out to meet him. 49 Reaching into his shepherd's bag and taking out a
stone, he hurled it with his sling and hit the
Philistine in the forehead. The stone sank
in, and Goliath stumbled and fell face down
on the ground.

50 So David triumphed over the Philistine
with only a sling and a stone, for he had no
sword. 51 Then David ran over and pulled
Goliath's sword from its sheath. David used
it to kill him and cut off his head.

Israel Routs the Philistines

When the Philistines saw that their champion was dead, they turned and ran. 52 Then
the men of Israel and Judah gave a great
shout of triumph and rushed after the
Philistines, chasing them as far as Gath*
and the gates of Ekron. The bodies of the
dead and wounded Philistines were strewn
all along the road from Shaaraim, as far as
Gath and Ekron. 53 Then the Israelite army
returned and plundered the deserted Philistine camp. 54 (David took the Philistine's
head to Jerusalem, but he stored the man's
armor in his own tent.)

55 As Saul watched David go out to fight
the Philistine, he asked Abner, the commander of his army, "Abner, whose son is
this young man?"

"I really don't know," Abner declared.

56 "Well, find out who he is!" the king told
him.

57 As soon as David returned from killing
Goliath, Abner brought him to Saul with the
Philistine's head still in his hand. 58 "Tell me
about your father, young man," Saul said.

And David replied, "His name is Jesse,
and we live in Bethlehem."

Saul Becomes Jealous of David

18 After David had finished talking
with Saul, he met Jonathan, the
king's son. There was an immediate bond
between them, for Jonathan loved David.
2 From that day on Saul kept David with him
and wouldn't let him return home. 3 And
Jonathan made a solemn pact with David,
because he loved him as he loved himself.
4 Jonathan sealed the pact by taking off his
robe and giving it to David, together with
his tunic, sword, bow, and belt.

5 Whatever Saul asked David to do, David
did it successfully. So Saul made him a commander over the men of war, an appointment that was welcomed by the people and
Saul's officers alike.

6 When the victorious Israelite army was
returning home after David had killed the
Philistine, women from all the towns of
Israel came out to meet King Saul. They
sang and danced for joy with tambourines
and cymbals.* 7 This was their song:

"Saul has killed his thousands,
    and David his ten thousands!"

8 This made Saul very angry. "What's this?"
he said. "They credit David with ten thousands and me with only thousands. Next
they'll be making him their king!" 9 So from
that time on Saul kept a jealous eye on David.

10 The very next day a tormenting spirit*
from God overwhelmed Saul, and he began
to rave in his house like a madman. David
was playing the harp, as he did each day.

But Saul had a spear in his hand, 11and he
suddenly hurled it at David, intending to
pin him to the wall. But David escaped him
twice.
12Saul was then afraid of David, for the
LORD was with David and had turned away
from Saul. 13Finally, Saul sent him away
and appointed him commander over 1,000
men, and David faithfully led his troops into
battle.
14David continued to succeed in everything he did, for the LORD was with him.
15When Saul recognized this, he became
even more afraid of him. 16But all Israel and
Judah loved David because he was so successful at leading his troops into battle.

David Marries Saul's Daughter

17One day Saul said to David, "I am ready
to give you my older daughter, Merab, as
your wife. But first you must prove yourself
to be a real warrior by fighting the LORD's
battles." For Saul thought, "I'll send him
out against the Philistines and let them kill
him rather than doing it myself."
18"Who am I, and what is my family in
Israel that I should be the king's son-in-
law?" David exclaimed. "My father's family
is nothing!" 19So* when the time came for
Saul to give his daughter Merab in marriage
to David, he gave her instead to Adriel, a
man from Meholah.
20In the meantime, Saul's daughter
Michal had fallen in love with David, and
Saul was delighted when he heard about it.
21"Here's another chance to see him killed
by the Philistines!" Saul said to himself. But
to David he said, "Today you have a second
chance to become my son-in-law!"
22Then Saul told his men to say to David,
"The king really likes you, and so do we.
Why don't you accept the king's offer and
become his son-in-law?"
23When Saul's men said these things to
David, he replied, "How can a poor man
from a humble family afford the bride price
for the daughter of a king?"
24When Saul's men reported this back to
the king, 25he told them, "Tell David that
all I want for the bride price is 100 Philistine foreskins! Vengeance on my enemies
is all I really want." But what Saul had in
mind was that David would be killed in the
fight.
26David was delighted to accept the offer.
Before the time limit expired, 27he and his
men went out and killed 200 Philistines.
Then David fulfilled the king's requirement
by presenting all their foreskins to him. So
Saul gave his daughter Michal to David to
be his wife.
28When Saul realized that the LORD was
with David and how much his daughter
Michal loved him, 29Saul became even more
afraid of him, and he remained David's
enemy for the rest of his life.
30Every time the commanders of the
Philistines attacked, David was more
successful against them than all the rest
of Saul's officers. So David's name became
very famous.

17:52 As in some Greek manuscripts; Hebrew reads *a valley.*
18:6 The type of instrument represented by the word *cymbals* is uncertain. **18:10** Or *an evil spirit.* **18:19** Or *But.*

Jonathan

Jonathan is a wonderful example of someone not clinging to their own "rights." As Saul's eldest son, he would have been seen as the natural heir to the throne. Yet he seemed to recognize early on that David was God's chosen future king, which he demonstrated by giving him his prince's robe (1 Samuel 18:4), and they became the closest of friends (18:1-4). He always portrayed David in a good light (19:4-6), made a pact with him (20:16-17), and helped him escape Saul's efforts to kill him (chapters 19–20). It was during David's time on the run that Jonathan "went to find David and encouraged him to stay strong in his faith in God" (23:16)—one of the best acts a true friend can do. Yet he remained loyal to his father to the end, eventually dying alongside him in a fierce battle against the Philistines on Mount Gilboa (chapter 31).

▶ *See also **Friendship**, page 725.*

Saul Tries to Kill David

19 Saul now urged his servants and his son Jonathan to assassinate David. But Jonathan, because of his strong affection for David, 2told him what his father was planning. "Tomorrow morning," he warned him, "you must find a hiding place out in the fields. 3I'll ask my father to go out there with me, and I'll talk to him about you. Then I'll tell you everything I can find out."

4The next morning Jonathan spoke with his father about David, saying many good things about him. "The king must not sin against his servant David," Jonathan said. "He's never done anything to harm you. He has always helped you in any way he could. 5Have you forgotten about the time he risked his life to kill the Philistine giant and how the LORD brought a great victory to all Israel as a result? You were certainly happy about it then. Why should you murder an innocent man like David? There is no reason for it at all!"

6So Saul listened to Jonathan and vowed, "As surely as the LORD lives, David will not be killed."

7Afterward Jonathan called David and told him what had happened. Then he brought David to Saul, and David served in the court as before.

8War broke out again after that, and David led his troops against the Philistines. He attacked them with such fury that they all ran away.

9But one day when Saul was sitting at home, with spear in hand, the tormenting spirit* from the LORD suddenly came upon him again. As David played his harp, 10Saul hurled his spear at David. But David dodged out of the way, and leaving the spear stuck in the wall, he fled and escaped into the night.

Michal Saves David's Life

11Then Saul sent troops to watch David's house. They were told to kill David when he came out the next morning. But Michal, David's wife, warned him, "If you don't escape tonight, you will be dead by morning." 12So she helped him climb out through a window, and he fled and escaped. 13Then she took an idol* and put it in his bed, covered it with blankets, and put a cushion of goat's hair at its head.

14When the troops came to arrest David, she told them he was sick and couldn't get out of bed.

15But Saul sent the troops back to get David. He ordered, "Bring him to me in his bed so I can kill him!" 16But when they came to carry David out, they discovered that it was only an idol in the bed with a cushion of goat's hair at its head.

17"Why have you betrayed me like this and let my enemy escape?" Saul demanded of Michal.

"I had to," Michal replied. "He threatened to kill me if I didn't help him."

18So David escaped and went to Ramah to see Samuel, and he told him all that Saul had done to him. Then Samuel took David with him to live at Naioth. 19When the report reached Saul that David was at Naioth in Ramah, 20he sent troops to capture him. But when they arrived and saw Samuel leading a group of prophets who were prophesying, the Spirit of God came upon Saul's men, and they also began to prophesy. 21When Saul heard what had happened, he sent other troops, but they, too, prophesied! The same thing happened a third time. 22Finally, Saul himself went to Ramah and arrived at the great well in Secu. "Where are Samuel and David?" he demanded.

"They are at Naioth in Ramah," someone told him.

23But on the way to Naioth in Ramah the Spirit of God came even upon Saul, and he, too, began to prophesy all the way to Naioth! 24He tore off his clothes and lay naked on the ground all day and all night, prophesying in the presence of Samuel. The people who were watching exclaimed, "What? Is even Saul a prophet?"

Jonathan Helps David

20 David now fled from Naioth in Ramah and found Jonathan. "What have I done?" he exclaimed. "What is my crime? How have I offended your father that he is so determined to kill me?"

2"That's not true!" Jonathan protested. "You're not going to die. He always tells me everything he's going to do, even the little things. I know my father wouldn't hide something like this from me. It just isn't so!"

3Then David took an oath before Jonathan and said, "Your father knows perfectly well about our friendship, so he has said to himself, 'I won't tell Jonathan—why should

I hurt him?' But I swear to you that I am only a step away from death! I swear it by the LORD and by your own soul!"

[4]"Tell me what I can do to help you," Jonathan exclaimed.

[5]David replied, "Tomorrow we celebrate the new moon festival. I've always eaten with the king on this occasion, but tomorrow I'll hide in the field and stay there until the evening of the third day. [6]If your father asks where I am, tell him I asked permission to go home to Bethlehem for an annual family sacrifice. [7]If he says, 'Fine!' you will know all is well. But if he is angry and loses his temper, you will know he is determined to kill me. [8]Show me this loyalty as my sworn friend—for we made a solemn pact before the LORD—or kill me yourself if I have sinned against your father. But please don't betray me to him!"

[9]"Never!" Jonathan exclaimed. "You know that if I had the slightest notion my father was planning to kill you, I would tell you at once."

[10]Then David asked, "How will I know whether or not your father is angry?"

[11]"Come out to the field with me," Jonathan replied. And they went out there together. [12]Then Jonathan told David, "I promise by the LORD, the God of Israel, that by this time tomorrow, or the next day at the latest, I will talk to my father and let you know at once how he feels about you. If he speaks favorably about you, I will let you know. [13]But if he is angry and wants you killed, may the LORD strike me and even kill me if I don't warn you so you can escape and live. May the LORD be with you as he used to be with my father. [14]And may you treat me with the faithful love of the LORD as long as I live. But if I die, [15]treat my family with this faithful love, even when the LORD destroys all your enemies from the face of the earth."

[16]So Jonathan made a solemn pact with David,* saying, "May the LORD destroy all your enemies!" [17]And Jonathan made David reaffirm his vow of friendship again, for Jonathan loved David as he loved himself.

[18]Then Jonathan said, "Tomorrow we celebrate the new moon festival. You will be missed when your place at the table is empty. [19]The day after tomorrow, toward evening, go to the place where you hid before, and wait there by the stone pile.* [20]I will come out and

19:9 Or *evil spirit.* **19:13** Hebrew *teraphim;* also in 19:16. **20:16** Hebrew *with the house of David.* **20:19** Hebrew *the stone Ezel.* The meaning of the Hebrew is uncertain.

Waiting for God's timing

David's confusion and frustration can clearly be felt in his question to Jonathan, Saul's son (1 Samuel 20:1). Despite David's complete loyalty to Saul and his faithful service, Saul was out to kill him. Saul was becoming increasingly jealous of David's success and fame, feeling he was a threat to his position as king (18:6-9). But even though Samuel had anointed David as Saul's replacement (16:1-13), David always refused to take matters into his own hands by killing Saul, even though he twice had the opportunity to do so (chapters 24, 26).

Saul himself increasingly came to recognize that David would be the next king (24:20), but he was not about to give up power easily. In fact, David would spend the next ten years on the run, fleeing for his life as Saul pursued him. He would hide in forests, caves, deserts—even in Philistine cities pretending to be their mercenary (chapters 20–28). But through all this God was training David, both in the skills of battle and in leadership, as people began to gather to him (e.g., 1 Samuel 22:1-2; 1 Chronicles 12:1-22).

It had only taken a moment for David to be anointed as king, but it took at least ten years for that to be worked out in his life and for him to be installed as king over Judah, and then a further seven years before he became king of the whole nation. God is rarely in a hurry—though we generally are. We always want him to act quickly, and according to our schedules. But those who truly want to be used by God must learn to wait for his timing.

shoot three arrows to the side of the stone
pile as though I were shooting at a target.
21 Then I will send a boy to bring the arrows
back. If you hear me tell him, 'They're on
this side,' then you will know, as surely as
the LORD lives, that all is well, and there is
no trouble. 22 But if I tell him, 'Go farther—
the arrows are still ahead of you,' then it will
mean that you must leave immediately, for
the LORD is sending you away. 23 And may
the LORD make us keep our promises to each
other, for he has witnessed them."

24 So David hid himself in the field, and
when the new moon festival began, the
king sat down to eat. 25 He sat at his usual
place against the wall, with Jonathan sitting
opposite him* and Abner beside him. But
David's place was empty. 26 Saul didn't say
anything about it that day, for he said to
himself, "Something must have made David
ceremonially unclean." 27 But when David's
place was empty again the next day, Saul
asked Jonathan, "Why hasn't the son of
Jesse been here for the meal either yesterday or today?"

28 Jonathan replied, "David earnestly
asked me if he could go to Bethlehem. 29 He
said, 'Please let me go, for we are having a
family sacrifice. My brother demanded that
I be there. So please let me get away to see
my brothers.' That's why he isn't here at the
king's table."

30 Saul boiled with rage at Jonathan. "You
stupid son of a whore!"* he swore at him.
"Do you think I don't know that you want
him to be king in your place, shaming yourself and your mother? 31 As long as that son
of Jesse is alive, you'll never be king. Now go
and get him so I can kill him!"

32 "But why should he be put to death?"
Jonathan asked his father. "What has he
done?" 33 Then Saul hurled his spear at
Jonathan, intending to kill him. So at last
Jonathan realized that his father was really
determined to kill David.

34 Jonathan left the table in fierce anger
and refused to eat on that second day of the
festival, for he was crushed by his father's
shameful behavior toward David.

35 The next morning, as agreed, Jonathan
went out into the field and took a young
boy with him to gather his arrows. 36 "Start
running," he told the boy, "so you can find
the arrows as I shoot them." So the boy
ran, and Jonathan shot an arrow beyond
him. 37 When the boy had almost reached
the arrow, Jonathan shouted, "The arrow
is still ahead of you. 38 Hurry, hurry, don't
wait." So the boy quickly gathered up the
arrows and ran back to his master. 39 He,
of course, suspected nothing; only Jonathan and David understood the signal.
40 Then Jonathan gave his bow and arrows
to the boy and told him to take them back
to town.

41 As soon as the boy was gone, David
came out from where he had been hiding
near the stone pile.* Then David bowed
three times to Jonathan with his face to the
ground. Both of them were in tears as they
embraced each other and said good-bye,
especially David.

42 At last Jonathan said to David, "Go in
peace, for we have sworn loyalty to each
other in the LORD's name. The LORD is the
witness of a bond between us and our children forever." Then David left, and Jonathan returned to the town.*

David Runs from Saul

21 1* David went to the town of Nob to
see Ahimelech the priest. Ahimelech trembled when he saw him. "Why are
you alone?" he asked. "Why is no one with
you?"

2 "The king has sent me on a private
matter," David said. "He told me not to tell
anyone why I am here. I have told my men
where to meet me later. 3 Now, what is there
to eat? Give me five loaves of bread or anything else you have."

4 "We don't have any regular bread," the
priest replied. "But there is the holy bread,
which you can have if your young men have
not slept with any women recently."

5 "Don't worry," David replied. "I never
allow my men to be with women when we
are on a campaign. And since they stay
clean even on ordinary trips, how much
more on this one!"

6 Since there was no other food available,
the priest gave him the holy bread—the
Bread of the Presence that was placed before
the LORD in the Tabernacle. It had just been
replaced that day with fresh bread.

7 Now Doeg the Edomite, Saul's chief
herdsman, was there that day, having been
detained before the LORD.*

8 David asked Ahimelech, "Do you have a
spear or sword? The king's business was so

urgent that I didn't even have time to grab
a weapon!"
9"I only have the sword of Goliath the
Philistine, whom you killed in the valley of
Elah," the priest replied. "It is wrapped in
a cloth behind the ephod. Take that if you
want it, for there is nothing else here."
"There is nothing like it!" David replied.
"Give it to me!"
10So David escaped from Saul and went
to King Achish of Gath. 11But the officers of
Achish were unhappy about his being there.
"Isn't this David, the king of the land?" they
asked. "Isn't he the one the people honor
with dances, singing,

'Saul has killed his thousands,
and David his ten thousands'?"

12David heard these comments and was
very afraid of what King Achish of Gath
might do to him. 13So he pretended to be
insane, scratching on doors and drooling
down his beard.
14Finally, King Achish said to his men,
"Must you bring me a madman? 15We
already have enough of them around here!
Why should I let someone like this be my
guest?"

David at the Cave of Adullam

22 So David left Gath and escaped to the
cave of Adullam. Soon his brothers
and all his other relatives joined him there.
2Then others began coming—men who were
in trouble or in debt or who were just discontented—until David was the captain of
about 400 men.
3Later David went to Mizpeh in Moab,
where he asked the king, "Please allow my
father and mother to live here with you until
I know what God is going to do for me." 4So
David's parents stayed in Moab with the
king during the entire time David was living
in his stronghold.
5One day the prophet Gad told David,
"Leave the stronghold and return to the
land of Judah." So David went to the forest
of Hereth.
6The news of his arrival in Judah soon
reached Saul. At the time, the king was
sitting beneath the tamarisk tree on the
hill at Gibeah, holding his spear and surrounded by his officers.
7"Listen here, you men of Benjamin!"
Saul shouted to his officers when he heard
the news. "Has that son of Jesse promised
every one of you fields and vineyards? Has
he promised to make you all generals and
captains in his army?* 8Is that why you have
conspired against me? For not one of you
told me when my own son made a solemn
pact with the son of Jesse. You're not even
sorry for me. Think of it! My own son—
encouraging him to kill me, as he is trying
to do this very day!"
9Then Doeg the Edomite, who was standing there with Saul's men, spoke up. "When
I was at Nob," he said, "I saw the son of
Jesse talking to the priest, Ahimelech son of
Ahitub. 10Ahimelech consulted the LORD for
him. Then he gave him food and the sword
of Goliath the Philistine."

The Slaughter of the Priests

11King Saul immediately sent for Ahimelech
and all his family, who served as priests
at Nob. 12When they arrived, Saul shouted
at him, "Listen to me, you son of Ahitub!"
"What is it, my king?" Ahimelech asked.
13"Why have you and the son of Jesse
conspired against me?" Saul demanded.
"Why did you give him food and a sword?
Why have you consulted God for him? Why
have you encouraged him to kill me, as he
is trying to do this very day?"
14"But sir," Ahimelech replied, "is anyone
among all your servants as faithful as David,
your son-in-law? Why, he is the captain
of your bodyguard and a highly honored
member of your household! 15This was certainly not the first time I had consulted God
for him! May the king not accuse me and my
family in this matter, for I knew nothing at
all of any plot against you."
16"You will surely die, Ahimelech, along
with your entire family!" the king shouted.
17And he ordered his bodyguards, "Kill
these priests of the LORD, for they are allies
and conspirators with David! They knew he
was running away from me, but they didn't
tell me!" But Saul's men refused to kill the
LORD's priests.
18Then the king said to Doeg, "You do it."
So Doeg the Edomite turned on them and
killed them that day, eighty-five priests in

20:25 As in Greek version; Hebrew reads *with Jonathan standing.* **20:30** Hebrew *You son of a perverse and rebellious woman.* **20:41** As in Greek version; Hebrew reads *near the south edge.* **20:42** This sentence is numbered 21:1 in Hebrew text. **21:1** Verses 21:1-15 are numbered 21:2-16 in Hebrew text. **21:7** The meaning of the Hebrew is uncertain. **22:7** Hebrew *commanders of thousands and commanders of hundreds?*

all, still wearing their priestly garments. 19 Then he went to Nob, the town of the priests, and killed the priests' families—men and women, children and babies—and all the cattle, donkeys, sheep, and goats.

20 Only Abiathar, one of the sons of Ahimelech, escaped and fled to David. 21 When he told David that Saul had killed the priests of the LORD, 22 David exclaimed, "I knew it! When I saw Doeg the Edomite there that day, I knew he was sure to tell Saul. Now I have caused the death of all your father's family. 23 Stay here with me, and don't be afraid. I will protect you with my own life, for the same person wants to kill us both."

David Protects the Town of Keilah

23 One day news came to David that the Philistines were at Keilah stealing grain from the threshing floors. 2 David asked the LORD, "Should I go and attack them?"

"Yes, go and save Keilah," the LORD told him.

3 But David's men said, "We're afraid even here in Judah. We certainly don't want to go to Keilah to fight the whole Philistine army!"

4 So David asked the LORD again, and again the LORD replied, "Go down to Keilah, for I will help you conquer the Philistines."

5 So David and his men went to Keilah. They slaughtered the Philistines and took all their livestock and rescued the people of Keilah. 6 Now when Abiathar son of Ahimelech fled to David at Keilah, he brought the ephod with him.

7 Saul soon learned that David was at Keilah. "Good!" he exclaimed. "We've got him now! God has handed him over to me, for he has trapped himself in a walled town!" 8 So Saul mobilized his entire army to march to Keilah and besiege David and his men.

9 But David learned of Saul's plan and told Abiathar the priest to bring the ephod and ask the LORD what he should do. 10 Then David prayed, "O LORD, God of Israel, I have heard that Saul is planning to come and destroy Keilah because I am here. 11 Will the leaders of Keilah betray me to him?* And will Saul actually come as I have heard? O LORD, God of Israel, please tell me."

And the LORD said, "He will come."

12 Again David asked, "Will the leaders of Keilah betray me and my men to Saul?"

And the LORD replied, "Yes, they will betray you."

David Hides in the Wilderness

13 So David and his men—about 600 of them now—left Keilah and began roaming the countryside. Word soon reached Saul that David had escaped, so he didn't go to Keilah after all. 14 David now stayed in the strongholds of the wilderness and in the hill country of Ziph. Saul hunted him day after day, but God didn't let Saul find him.

15 One day near Horesh, David received the news that Saul was on the way to Ziph to search for him and kill him. 16 Jonathan went to find David and encouraged him to stay strong in his faith in God. 17 "Don't be afraid," Jonathan reassured him. "My father will never find you! You are going to be the king of Israel, and I will be next to you, as my father, Saul, is well aware." 18 So the two of them renewed their solemn pact before the LORD. Then Jonathan returned home, while David stayed at Horesh.

19 But now the men of Ziph went to Saul in Gibeah and betrayed David to him. "We know where David is hiding," they said. "He is in the strongholds of Horesh on the hill of Hakilah, which is in the southern part of Jeshimon. 20 Come down whenever you're ready, O king, and we will catch him and hand him over to you!"

21 "The LORD bless you," Saul said. "At last someone is concerned about me! 22 Go and check again to be sure of where he is staying and who has seen him there, for I know that he is very crafty. 23 Discover his hiding places, and come back when you are sure. Then I'll go with you. And if he is in the area at all, I'll track him down, even if I have to search every hiding place in Judah!" 24 So the men of Ziph returned home ahead of Saul.

Meanwhile, David and his men had moved into the wilderness of Maon in the Arabah Valley south of Jeshimon. 25 When David heard that Saul and his men were searching for him, he went even farther into the wilderness to the great rock, and he remained there in the wilderness of Maon. But Saul kept after him in the wilderness.

26 Saul and David were now on opposite sides of a mountain. Just as Saul and his men began to close in on David and his men, 27 an urgent message reached Saul that

the Philistines were raiding Israel again.
[28]So Saul quit chasing David and returned
to fight the Philistines. Ever since that time,
the place where David was camped has
been called the Rock of Escape.* [29]*David
then went to live in the strongholds of
En-gedi.

David Spares Saul's Life

24 [1]*After Saul returned from fighting the Philistines, he was told
that David had gone into the wilderness of
En-gedi. [2]So Saul chose 3,000 elite troops
from all Israel and went to search for David
and his men near the rocks of the wild goats.
[3]At the place where the road passes some
sheepfolds, Saul went into a cave to relieve
himself. But as it happened, David and his
men were hiding farther back in that very
cave!
[4]"Now's your opportunity!" David's
men whispered to him. "Today the LORD is
telling you, 'I will certainly put your enemy
into your power, to do with as you wish.'"
So David crept forward and cut off a piece
of the hem of Saul's robe.
[5]But then David's conscience began
bothering him because he had cut Saul's
robe. [6]He said to his men, "The LORD forbid
that I should do this to my lord the king. I
shouldn't attack the LORD's anointed one,
for the LORD himself has chosen him." [7]So
David restrained his men and did not let
them kill Saul.
After Saul had left the cave and gone on
his way, [8]David came out and shouted after
him, "My lord the king!" And when Saul
looked around, David bowed low before him.
[9]Then he shouted to Saul, "Why do you
listen to the people who say I am trying to
harm you? [10]This very day you can see with
your own eyes it isn't true. For the LORD
placed you at my mercy back there in the
cave. Some of my men told me to kill you,
but I spared you. For I said, 'I will never
harm the king—he is the LORD's anointed
one.' [11]Look, my father, at what I have in my
hand. It is a piece of the hem of your robe!
I cut it off, but I didn't kill you. This proves
that I am not trying to harm you and that I
have not sinned against you, even though
you have been hunting for me to kill me.
[12]"May the LORD judge between us.
Perhaps the LORD will punish you for what
you are trying to do to me, but I will never
harm you. [13]As that old proverb says, 'From
evil people come evil deeds.' So you can be
sure I will never harm you. [14]Who is the king
of Israel trying to catch anyway? Should
he spend his time chasing one who is as
worthless as a dead dog or a single flea?

23:11 Some manuscripts lack the first sentence of 23:11. **23:28** Hebrew *Sela-hammahlekoth.* **23:29** Verse 23:29 is numbered 24:1 in Hebrew text. **24:1** Verses 24:1-22 are numbered 24:2-23 in Hebrew text.

Conscience

Conscience is the innate ability to discern right from wrong. It is God's law written in our heart (Romans 2:15), that little inner voice that whispers, "That was wrong, and you know it!"—no matter how much we might try to explain it away.

That's what happened with David. When Saul unknowingly entered the cave where David and his men were hiding, logic said it was a God-given opportunity to take Saul's life (1 Samuel 24:1-4). But David was unwilling to kill Saul, as his soldiers urged; he simply cut off a piece of his robe, perhaps to show Saul that he had nothing to fear from him. But as soon as he had done it, his conscience pricked him; after all, this was God's anointed king.

It is so important to listen to our conscience when it tells us that we have done or said or are planning something wrong. If we don't, our conscience can become "corrupted" (Titus 1:15), and even "seared" (1 Timothy 4:2; see footnote)—burnt to the point where it can feel nothing. That is why Paul said, "I always try to maintain a clear conscience before God and all people" (Acts 24:16). Thankfully, if we have done wrong and our conscience does prick us, we can confess it and be assured that "our guilty consciences have been sprinkled with Christ's blood to make us clean" (Hebrews 10:22).

[15]May the LORD therefore judge which of us is right and punish the guilty one. He is my advocate, and he will rescue me from your power!"

[16]When David had finished speaking, Saul called back, "Is that really you, my son David?" Then he began to cry. [17]And he said to David, "You are a better man than I am, for you have repaid me good for evil. [18]Yes, you have been amazingly kind to me today, for when the LORD put me in a place where you could have killed me, you didn't do it. [19]Who else would let his enemy get away when he had him in his power? May the LORD reward you well for the kindness you have shown me today. [20]And now I realize that you are surely going to be king, and that the kingdom of Israel will flourish under your rule. [21]Now swear to me by the LORD that when that happens you will not kill my family and destroy my line of descendants!"

[22]So David promised this to Saul with an oath. Then Saul went home, but David and his men went back to their stronghold.

The Death of Samuel

25 Now Samuel died, and all Israel gathered for his funeral. They buried him at his house in Ramah.

Nabal Angers David

Then David moved down to the wilderness of Maon.* [2]There was a wealthy man from Maon who owned property near the town of Carmel. He had 3,000 sheep and 1,000 goats, and it was sheep-shearing time. [3]This man's name was Nabal, and his wife, Abigail, was a sensible and beautiful woman. But Nabal, a descendant of Caleb, was crude and mean in all his dealings.

[4]When David heard that Nabal was shearing his sheep, [5]he sent ten of his young men to Carmel with this message for Nabal: [6]"Peace and prosperity to you, your family, and everything you own! [7]I am told that it is sheep-shearing time. While your shepherds stayed among us near Carmel, we never harmed them, and nothing was ever stolen from them. [8]Ask your own men, and they will tell you this is true. So would you be kind to us, since we have come at a time of celebration? Please share any provisions you might have on hand with us and with your friend David." [9]David's young men gave this message to Nabal in David's name, and they waited for a reply.

[10]"Who is this fellow David?" Nabal sneered to the young men. "Who does this son of Jesse think he is? There are lots of servants these days who run away from their masters. [11]Should I take my bread and my water and my meat that I've slaughtered for my shearers and give it to a band of outlaws who come from who knows where?"

[12]So David's young men returned and told him what Nabal had said. [13]"Get your swords!" was David's reply as he strapped on his own. Then 400 men started off with David, and 200 remained behind to guard their equipment.

[14]Meanwhile, one of Nabal's servants went to Abigail and told her, "David sent messengers from the wilderness to greet our master, but he screamed insults at them. [15]These men have been very good to us, and we never suffered any harm from them. Nothing was stolen from us the whole time they were with us. [16]In fact, day and night they were like a wall of protection to us and the sheep. [17]You need to know this and figure out what to do, for there is going to be trouble for our master and his whole family. He's so ill-tempered that no one can even talk to him!"

[18]Abigail wasted no time. She quickly gathered 200 loaves of bread, two wineskins full of wine, five sheep that had been slaughtered, nearly a bushel* of roasted grain, 100 clusters of raisins, and 200 fig cakes. She packed them on donkeys [19]and said to her servants, "Go on ahead. I will follow you shortly." But she didn't tell her husband Nabal what she was doing.

[20]As she was riding her donkey into a mountain ravine, she saw David and his men coming toward her. [21]David had just been saying, "A lot of good it did to help this fellow. We protected his flocks in the wilderness, and nothing he owned was lost or stolen. But he has repaid me evil for good. [22]May God strike me and kill me* if even one man of his household is still alive tomorrow morning!"

Abigail Intercedes for Nabal

[23]When Abigail saw David, she quickly got off her donkey and bowed low before him. [24]She fell at his feet and said, "I accept all blame in this matter, my lord. Please listen to what I have to say. [25]I know Nabal is a

wicked and ill-tempered man; please don't pay any attention to him. He is a fool, just as his name suggests.* But I never even saw the young men you sent.

[26]"Now, my lord, as surely as the LORD lives and you yourself live, since the LORD has kept you from murdering and taking vengeance into your own hands, let all your enemies and those who try to harm you be as cursed as Nabal is. [27]And here is a present that I, your servant, have brought to you and your young men. [28]Please forgive me if I have offended you in any way. The LORD will surely reward you with a lasting dynasty, for you are fighting the LORD's battles. And you have not done wrong throughout your entire life.

[29]"Even when you are chased by those who seek to kill you, your life is safe in the care of the LORD your God, secure in his treasure pouch! But the lives of your enemies will disappear like stones shot from a sling! [30]When the LORD has done all he promised and has made you leader of Israel, [31]don't let this be a blemish on your record. Then your conscience won't have to bear the staggering burden of needless bloodshed and vengeance. And when the LORD has done these great things for you, please remember me, your servant!"

[32]David replied to Abigail, "Praise the LORD, the God of Israel, who has sent you to meet me today! [33]Thank God for your good sense! Bless you for keeping me from murder and from carrying out vengeance with my own hands. [34]For I swear by the LORD, the God of Israel, who has kept me from hurting you, that if you had not hurried out to meet me, not one of Nabal's men would still be alive tomorrow morning." [35]Then David accepted her present and told her, "Return home in peace. I have heard what you said. We will not kill your husband."

[36]When Abigail arrived home, she found that Nabal was throwing a big party and was celebrating like a king. He was very drunk, so she didn't tell him anything about her meeting with David until dawn the next day. [37]In the morning when Nabal was sober, his wife told him what had happened. As a result he had a stroke,* and he lay paralyzed on his bed like a stone. [38]About ten days later, the LORD struck him, and he died.

David Marries Abigail

[39]When David heard that Nabal was dead, he said, "Praise the LORD, who has avenged the insult I received from Nabal and has kept me from doing it myself. Nabal has received the punishment for his sin." Then David sent messengers to Abigail to ask her to become his wife.

[40]When the messengers arrived at Carmel, they told Abigail, "David has sent us to take you back to marry him."

[41]She bowed low to the ground and responded, "I, your servant, would be happy to marry David. I would even be willing to become a slave, washing the feet of his servants!" [42]Quickly getting ready, she took along five of her servant girls as attendants, mounted her donkey, and went with David's messengers. And so she became his wife. [43]David also married Ahinoam from Jezreel, making both of them his wives. [44]Saul, meanwhile, had given his daughter Michal, David's wife, to a man from Gallim named Palti son of Laish.

David Spares Saul Again

26 Now some men from Ziph came to Saul at Gibeah to tell him, "David is hiding on the hill of Hakilah, which overlooks Jeshimon."

[2]So Saul took 3,000 of Israel's elite troops and went to hunt him down in the wilderness of Ziph. [3]Saul camped along the road beside the hill of Hakilah, near Jeshimon, where David was hiding. When David learned that Saul had come after him into the wilderness, [4]he sent out spies to verify the report of Saul's arrival.

[5]David slipped over to Saul's camp one night to look around. Saul and Abner son of Ner, the commander of his army, were sleeping inside a ring formed by the slumbering warriors. [6]"Who will volunteer to go in there with me?" David asked Ahimelech the Hittite and Abishai son of Zeruiah, Joab's brother.

"I'll go with you," Abishai replied. [7]So David and Abishai went right into Saul's camp and found him asleep, with his spear stuck in the ground beside his head. Abner and the soldiers were lying asleep around him.

25:1 As in Greek version (see also 25:2); Hebrew reads *Paran.*
25:18 Hebrew *5 seahs* [36.5 liters]. **25:22** As in Greek version; Hebrew reads *May God strike and kill the enemies of David.*
25:25 The name *Nabal* means "fool." **25:37** Hebrew *his heart failed him.*

8“God has surely handed your enemy over to you this time!” Abishai whispered to David. “Let me pin him to the ground with one thrust of the spear; I won’t need to strike twice!”

9“No!” David said. “Don’t kill him. For who can remain innocent after attacking the LORD’s anointed one? 10Surely the LORD will strike Saul down someday, or he will die of old age or in battle. 11The LORD forbid that I should kill the one he has anointed! But take his spear and that jug of water beside his head, and then let’s get out of here!”

12So David took the spear and jug of water that were near Saul’s head. Then he and Abishai got away without anyone seeing them or even waking up, because the LORD had put Saul’s men into a deep sleep.

13David climbed the hill opposite the camp until he was at a safe distance. 14Then he shouted down to the soldiers and to Abner son of Ner, “Wake up, Abner!”

“Who is it?” Abner demanded.

15“Well, Abner, you’re a great man, aren’t you?” David taunted. “Where in all Israel is there anyone as mighty? So why haven’t you guarded your master the king when someone came to kill him? 16This isn’t good at all! I swear by the LORD that you and your men deserve to die, because you failed to protect your master, the LORD’s anointed! Look around! Where are the king’s spear and the jug of water that were beside his head?”

17Saul recognized David’s voice and called out, “Is that you, my son David?”

And David replied, “Yes, my lord the king. 18Why are you chasing me? What have I done? What is my crime? 19But now let my lord the king listen to his servant. If the LORD has stirred you up against me, then let him accept my offering. But if this is simply a human scheme, then may those involved be cursed by the LORD. For they have driven me from my home, so I can no longer live among the LORD’s people, and they have said, ‘Go, worship pagan gods.’ 20Must I die on foreign soil, far from the presence of the LORD? Why has the king of Israel come out to search for a single flea? Why does he hunt me down like a partridge on the mountains?”

21Then Saul confessed, “I have sinned. Come back home, my son, and I will no longer try to harm you, for you valued my life today. I have been a fool and very, very wrong.”

22“Here is your spear, O king,” David replied. “Let one of your young men come over and get it. 23The LORD gives his own reward for doing good and for being loyal, and I refused to kill you even when the LORD placed you in my power, for you are the LORD’s anointed one. 24Now may the LORD value my life, even as I have valued yours today. May he rescue me from all my troubles.”

25And Saul said to David, “Blessings on you, my son David. You will do many heroic deeds, and you will surely succeed.” Then David went away, and Saul returned home.

David among the Philistines

27 But David kept thinking to himself, “Someday Saul is going to get me. The best thing I can do is escape to the Philistines. Then Saul will stop hunting for me in Israelite territory, and I will finally be safe.”

2So David took his 600 men and went over and joined Achish son of Maoch, the king of Gath. 3David and his men and their families settled there with Achish at Gath. David brought his two wives along with him—Ahinoam from Jezreel and Abigail, Nabal’s widow from Carmel. 4Word soon reached Saul that David had fled to Gath, so he stopped hunting for him.

5One day David said to Achish, “If it is all right with you, we would rather live in one of the country towns instead of here in the royal city.”

6So Achish gave him the town of Ziklag (which still belongs to the kings of Judah to this day), 7and they lived there among the Philistines for a year and four months.

8David and his men spent their time raiding the Geshurites, the Girzites, and the Amalekites—people who had lived near Shur, toward the land of Egypt, since ancient times. 9David did not leave one person alive in the villages he attacked. He took the sheep, goats, cattle, donkeys, camels, and clothing before returning home to see King Achish.

10“Where did you make your raid today?” Achish would ask.

And David would reply, “Against the south of Judah, the Jerahmeelites, and the Kenites.”

11No one was left alive to come to Gath and

tell where he had really been. This happened again and again while he was living among the Philistines. 12 Achish believed David and thought to himself, "By now the people of Israel must hate him bitterly. Now he will have to stay here and serve me forever!"

Saul Consults a Medium

28 About that time the Philistines mustered their armies for another war with Israel. King Achish told David, "You and your men will be expected to join me in battle."

2 "Very well!" David agreed. "Now you will see for yourself what we can do."

Then Achish told David, "I will make you my personal bodyguard for life."

3 Meanwhile, Samuel had died, and all Israel had mourned for him. He was buried in Ramah, his hometown. And Saul had banned from the land of Israel all mediums and those who consult the spirits of the dead.

4 The Philistines set up their camp at Shunem, and Saul gathered all the army of Israel and camped at Gilboa. 5 When Saul saw the vast Philistine army, he became frantic with fear. 6 He asked the LORD what he should do, but the LORD refused to answer him, either by dreams or by sacred lots* or by the prophets. 7 Saul then said to his advisers, "Find a woman who is a medium, so I can go and ask her what to do."

His advisers replied, "There is a medium at Endor."

8 So Saul disguised himself by wearing ordinary clothing instead of his royal robes. Then he went to the woman's home at night, accompanied by two of his men.

"I have to talk to a man who has died," he said. "Will you call up his spirit for me?"

9 "Are you trying to get me killed?" the woman demanded. "You know that Saul has outlawed all the mediums and all who consult the spirits of the dead. Why are you setting a trap for me?"

10 But Saul took an oath in the name of the LORD and promised, "As surely as the LORD lives, nothing bad will happen to you for doing this."

11 Finally, the woman said, "Well, whose spirit do you want me to call up?"

"Call up Samuel," Saul replied.

12 When the woman saw Samuel, she screamed, "You've deceived me! You are Saul!"

13 "Don't be afraid!" the king told her. "What do you see?"

"I see a god* coming up out of the earth," she said.

28:6 Hebrew *by Urim.* **28:13** Or *gods.*

The occult

Saul's increasing desperation is reflected in his visit to a medium. With Samuel now dead and God not answering his requests for guidance (1 Samuel 28:3-6), Saul turned to the occult—stupidly, for the Law clearly forbade this (Leviticus 19:26, 31; Deuteronomy 18:9-13), and God had said he would turn against people who did such things (Leviticus 20:6). Whether it was a deceiving spirit that Saul saw, or truly Samuel's spirit—unusual, but not beyond God's ability—the experience terrified the witch and resulted in a message of judgment on Saul (1 Samuel 28:12, 16-20). Dark powers only ever bring despair, not hope.

Because Satan is a deceiver, he loves to make people think they are hearing something good through such things. But this is not the case, for Satan is the father of lies (John 8:44). Paul exposed fortune-telling as demonic (Acts 16:16-18), which is why the Bible consistently forbids and denounces things like divination, sorcery, magic, witchcraft, casting spells, astrology, consulting mediums, and spiritism (e.g., Isaiah 8:19-22; Acts 8:9-24; 13:6-12). God does reveal things, through genuine gifts of the Spirit like prophecy or dreams; but some things he chooses to keep silent about. "The LORD our God has secrets known to no one" (Deuteronomy 29:29).

▶ *See also* ***Satan****, page 566;* ***Mediums****, page 768.*

14“What does he look like?” Saul asked.
“He is an old man wrapped in a robe,”
she replied. Saul realized it was Samuel,
and he fell to the ground before him.
15“Why have you disturbed me by calling
me back?” Samuel asked Saul.
“Because I am in deep trouble,” Saul
replied. “The Philistines are at war with
me, and God has left me and won’t reply by
prophets or dreams. So I have called for you
to tell me what to do.”
16But Samuel replied, “Why ask me, since
the LORD has left you and has become your
enemy? 17The LORD has done just as he said
he would. He has torn the kingdom from
you and given it to your rival, David. 18The
LORD has done this to you today because
you refused to carry out his fierce anger
against the Amalekites. 19What’s more, the
LORD will hand you and the army of Israel
over to the Philistines tomorrow, and you
and your sons will be here with me. The
LORD will bring down the entire army of
Israel in defeat.”
20Saul fell full length on the ground,
paralyzed with fright because of Samuel’s
words. He was also faint with hunger, for
he had eaten nothing all day and all night.
21When the woman saw how distraught he
was, she said, “Sir, I obeyed your command
at the risk of my life. 22Now do what I say,
and let me give you a little something to eat
so you can regain your strength for the trip
back.”
23But Saul refused to eat anything. Then
his advisers joined the woman in urging
him to eat, so he finally yielded and got up
from the ground and sat on the couch.
24The woman had been fattening a calf, so
she hurried out and killed it. She took some
flour, kneaded it into dough and baked unleavened bread. 25She brought the meal to
Saul and his advisers, and they ate it. Then
they went out into the night.

The Philistines Reject David

29 The entire Philistine army now mobilized at Aphek, and the Israelites
camped at the spring in Jezreel. 2As the
Philistine rulers were leading out their troops
in groups of hundreds and thousands, David
and his men marched at the rear with King
Achish. 3But the Philistine commanders demanded, “What are these Hebrews doing
here?”
And Achish told them, “This is David,
the servant of King Saul of Israel. He’s been
with me for years, and I’ve never found a
single fault in him from the day he arrived
until today.”
4But the Philistine commanders were
angry. “Send him back to the town you’ve
given him!” they demanded. “He can’t go
into the battle with us. What if he turns
against us in battle and becomes our adversary? Is there any better way for him to
reconcile himself with his master than by
handing our heads over to him? 5Isn’t this
the same David about whom the women of
Israel sing in their dances,

‘Saul has killed his thousands,
and David his ten thousands’?”

6So Achish finally summoned David and
said to him, “I swear by the LORD that you
have been a trustworthy ally. I think you
should go with me into battle, for I’ve never
found a single flaw in you from the day you
arrived until today. But the other Philistine
rulers won’t hear of it. 7Please don’t upset
them, but go back quietly.”
8“What have I done to deserve this treatment?” David demanded. “What have you
ever found in your servant, that I can’t go
and fight the enemies of my lord the king?”
9But Achish insisted, “As far as I’m concerned, you’re as perfect as an angel of God.
But the Philistine commanders are afraid
to have you with them in the battle. 10Now
get up early in the morning, and leave with
your men as soon as it gets light.”
11So David and his men headed back into
the land of the Philistines, while the Philistine army went on to Jezreel.

David Destroys the Amalekites

30 Three days later, when David and his
men arrived home at their town of
Ziklag, they found that the Amalekites had
made a raid into the Negev and Ziklag; they
had crushed Ziklag and burned it to the
ground. 2They had carried off the women
and children and everyone else but without
killing anyone.
3When David and his men saw the ruins
and realized what had happened to their
families, 4they wept until they could weep
no more. 5David’s two wives, Ahinoam from
Jezreel and Abigail, the widow of Nabal
from Carmel, were among those captured.

[6]David was now in great danger because all
his men were very bitter about losing their
sons and daughters, and they began to talk
of stoning him. But David found strength in
the LORD his God.
[7]Then he said to Abiathar the priest, "Bring
me the ephod!" So Abiathar brought it. [8]Then
David asked the LORD, "Should I chase after
this band of raiders? Will I catch them?"
And the LORD told him, "Yes, go after
them. You will surely recover everything
that was taken from you!"
[9]So David and his 600 men set out, and
they came to the brook Besor. [10]But 200 of
the men were too exhausted to cross the
brook, so David continued the pursuit with
400 men.
[11]Along the way they found an Egyptian
man in a field and brought him to David.
They gave him some bread to eat and water
to drink. [12]They also gave him part of a
fig cake and two clusters of raisins, for he
hadn't had anything to eat or drink for three
days and nights. Before long his strength
returned.
[13]"To whom do you belong, and where do
you come from?" David asked him.
"I am an Egyptian—the slave of an Amalekite," he replied. "My master abandoned
me three days ago because I was sick. [14]We
were on our way back from raiding the Kerethites in the Negev, the territory of Judah,
and the land of Caleb, and we had just
burned Ziklag."
[15]"Will you lead me to this band of
raiders?" David asked.
The young man replied, "If you take an
oath in God's name that you will not kill me
or give me back to my master, then I will
guide you to them."
[16]So he led David to them, and they found
the Amalekites spread out across the fields,
eating and drinking and dancing with joy
because of the vast amount of plunder they
had taken from the Philistines and the land
of Judah. [17]David and his men rushed in
among them and slaughtered them throughout that night and the entire next day until
evening. None of the Amalekites escaped
except 400 young men who fled on camels.
[18]David got back everything the Amalekites
had taken, and he rescued his two wives.
[19]Nothing was missing: small or great, son
or daughter, nor anything else that had
been taken. David brought everything back.
[20]He also recovered all the flocks and herds,
and his men drove them ahead of the other
livestock. "This plunder belongs to David!"
they said.
[21]Then David returned to the brook Besor
and met up with the 200 men who had been
left behind because they were too exhausted
to go with him. They went out to meet David
and his men, and David greeted them joyfully. [22]But some evil troublemakers among
David's men said, "They didn't go with us,
so they can't have any of the plunder we
recovered. Give them their wives and children, and tell them to be gone."
[23]But David said, "No, my brothers! Don't
be selfish with what the LORD has given us.
He has kept us safe and helped us defeat
the band of raiders that attacked us. [24]Who
will listen when you talk like this? We share
and share alike—those who go to battle and
those who guard the equipment." [25]From
then on David made this a decree and
regulation for Israel, and it is still followed
today.
[26]When he arrived at Ziklag, David sent
part of the plunder to the elders of Judah,
who were his friends. "Here is a present for
you, taken from the LORD's enemies," he
said.

Ziklag

Toward the end of his years on the run from Saul, David ended up playing a dangerous double game. He pretended to be a mercenary for the Philistines, hired to fight against Israel, yet actually fighting mutual enemies of both the Philistines and the Israelites (1 Samuel 27:8-12). The Philistine king Achish gave David the town of Ziklag as his base (27:6), a town in the Negev scrubland in southern Judah. It was here that many who had deserted Saul came to join David and where his loyal inner core of supporters developed (1 Chronicles 12).

27The gifts were sent to the people of the following towns David had visited: Bethel, Ramoth-negev, Jattir, 28Aroer, Siphmoth, Eshtemoa, 29Racal,* the towns of the Jerahmeelites, the towns of the Kenites, 30Hormah, Bor-ashan, Athach, 31Hebron, and all the other places David and his men had visited.

The Death of Saul

31 Now the Philistines attacked Israel, and the men of Israel fled before them. Many were slaughtered on the slopes of Mount Gilboa. 2The Philistines closed in on Saul and his sons, and they killed three of his sons—Jonathan, Abinadab, and Malkishua. 3The fighting grew very fierce around Saul, and the Philistine archers caught up with him and wounded him severely.

4Saul groaned to his armor bearer, "Take your sword and kill me before these pagan Philistines come to run me through and taunt and torture me."

But his armor bearer was afraid and would not do it. So Saul took his own sword and fell on it. 5When his armor bearer realized that Saul was dead, he fell on his own sword and died beside the king. 6So Saul, his three sons, his armor bearer, and his troops all died together that same day.

7When the Israelites on the other side of the Jezreel Valley and beyond the Jordan saw that the Israelite army had fled and that Saul and his sons were dead, they abandoned their towns and fled. So the Philistines moved in and occupied their towns.

8The next day, when the Philistines went out to strip the dead, they found the bodies of Saul and his three sons on Mount Gilboa. 9So they cut off Saul's head and stripped off his armor. Then they proclaimed the good news of Saul's death in their pagan temple and to the people throughout the land of Philistia. 10They placed his armor in the temple of the Ashtoreths, and they fastened his body to the wall of the city of Beth-shan.

11But when the people of Jabesh-gilead heard what the Philistines had done to Saul, 12all their mighty warriors traveled through the night to Beth-shan and took the bodies of Saul and his sons down from the wall. They brought them to Jabesh, where they burned the bodies. 13Then they took their bones and buried them beneath the tamarisk tree at Jabesh, and they fasted for seven days.

30:29 Greek version reads *Carmel.*

Mount Gilboa

When the Philistines left their base at Aphek, Saul and his army withdrew, taking up defensive positions on the slopes of Mount Gilboa. The mountain overlooked the Jezreel Valley, so Saul hoped that taking the higher ground would give them the advantage. But the better-equipped Philistine army overwhelmed the Israelites (1 Samuel 31:1). Three of Saul's sons were killed in the battle, and Saul himself was so seriously wounded that he took his own life. David so mourned the loss of Saul and Jonathan that he composed a lament in which he not only praised them but cursed Mount Gilboa as the place of their downfall (2 Samuel 1).

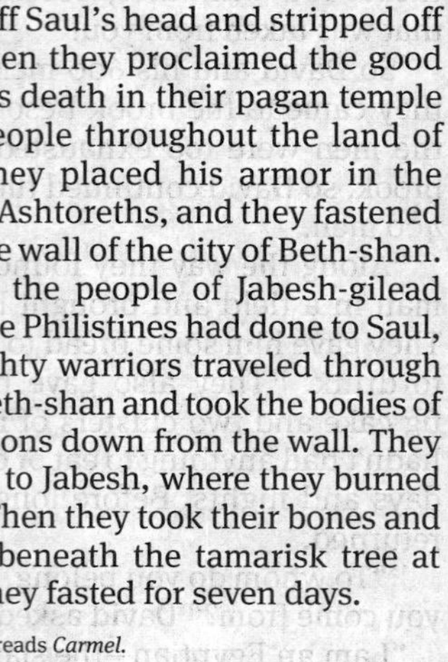

2 Samuel *Kingship and covenant*

The book of 2 Samuel continues where 1 Samuel ended and shows how Saul's death opened up the way for David to be acknowledged as God's chosen king, at first over Judah and seven years later over all Israel. The book is very honest in portraying not only David's great successes but also his abysmal failures. But through it all we continue to see that he was a man after God's own heart.

What's it all about?

David mourned the deaths of Saul and Jonathan and was officially made king of Judah (the southern part of the nation), while Saul's son Ishbosheth succeeded Saul in Israel (the northern part of the nation). A seven-year struggle between Israel and Judah followed, but eventually David was also made king of Israel, uniting the two parts under him. He arranged for the Ark of the Covenant to be brought up to Jerusalem, his newly established capital (chapter 6), and then decided to build a permanent home for it. But God prevented him. David was told that this task would come to his son, though seeing his heart, God promised to build a "house" for David (chapter 7).

Second Samuel 11–12 tells the dark story of David's adulterous affair with Bathsheba and his murder of her husband, Uriah, in the hope of covering it up. David's wrongdoing blighted what had been a good story so far. But when Nathan the prophet confronted him with his sin (chapter 12), David was quick to repent, unlike Saul (see also Psalm 51). When David and Bathsheba's baby died, God blessed them with another—the future King Solomon.

OVERVIEW

The remainder of 2 Samuel records David's endless family problems (chapters 13–19), largely a result of his failure as a father to discipline his children. These problems include rape, murder, conspiracy, and civil war. The final chapter tells the story of another of David's misjudgments—the decision to take a census (chapter 24), probably as a result of pride.

David's story does not end in tragedy, however. Although he had to live with the consequences of his sin, he enjoyed God's favor. Second Samuel records his final words (chapter 23)—but we have to wait until the book of 1 Kings to learn how his life ended.

What does it mean for us?

The book of 2 Samuel continues the message of 1 Samuel of the importance of doing things God's way—and shows us the mess we can get into when we

page 342

don't. Although David was a man after God's own heart (1 Samuel 13:14), who genuinely loved God and tried to put him first, he wasn't perfect. His adultery with Bathsheba and his weakness as a father both had disastrous results, not just for David personally but also for others. Doing things our own way, rather than God's way, never works in the long run. But whereas Saul always tried to blame circumstances or others for his failures and disobedience, David was always quick to repent; and God can do anything with people whose hearts are tender.

▶ *See also* ***A timeline of the Bible****, pages A22-A24.*

David Learns of Saul's Death

1 After the death of Saul, David returned
from his victory over the Amalekites and
spent two days in Ziklag. 2 On the third day a
man arrived from Saul's army camp. He had
torn his clothes and put dirt on his head to
show that he was in mourning. He fell to the
ground before David in deep respect.
3 "Where have you come from?" David
asked.
"I escaped from the Israelite camp," the
man replied.
4 "What happened?" David demanded.
"Tell me how the battle went."
The man replied, "Our entire army fled
from the battle. Many of the men are dead,
and Saul and his son Jonathan are also
dead."
5 "How do you know Saul and Jonathan
are dead?" David demanded of the young
man.
6 The man answered, "I happened to be on
Mount Gilboa, and there was Saul leaning
on his spear with the enemy chariots and
charioteers closing in on him. 7 When he
turned and saw me, he cried out for me to
come to him. 'How can I help?' I asked him.
8 "He responded, 'Who are you?'
"'I am an Amalekite,' I told him.
9 "Then he begged me, 'Come over here
and put me out of my misery, for I am in
terrible pain and want to die.'
10 "So I killed him," the Amalekite told
David, "for I knew he couldn't live. Then I
took his crown and his armband, and I have
brought them here to you, my lord."
11 David and his men tore their clothes in
sorrow when they heard the news. 12 They
mourned and wept and fasted all day for Saul
and his son Jonathan, and for the LORD's
army and the nation of Israel, because they
had died by the sword that day.
13 Then David said to the young man who
had brought the news, "Where are you
from?"
And he replied, "I am a foreigner, an Amalekite, who lives in your land."
14 "Why were you not afraid to kill the
LORD's anointed one?" David asked.
15 Then David said to one of his men, "Kill
him!" So the man thrust his sword into
the Amalekite and killed him. 16 "You have
condemned yourself," David said, "for
you yourself confessed that you killed the
LORD's anointed one."

David's Song for Saul and Jonathan

17 Then David composed a funeral song for
Saul and Jonathan, 18 and he commanded
that it be taught to the people of Judah. It
is known as the Song of the Bow, and it is
recorded in *The Book of Jashar*.*

19 Your pride and joy, O Israel, lies dead on
the hills!
Oh, how the mighty heroes have fallen!
20 Don't announce the news in Gath,
don't proclaim it in the streets of
Ashkelon,
or the daughters of the Philistines will
rejoice
and the pagans will laugh in triumph.

21 O mountains of Gilboa,
let there be no dew or rain upon you,
nor fruitful fields producing offerings
of grain.*
For there the shield of the mighty heroes
was defiled;
the shield of Saul will no longer be
anointed with oil.
22 The bow of Jonathan was powerful,
and the sword of Saul did its mighty
work.
They shed the blood of their enemies
and pierced the bodies of mighty
heroes.

23 How beloved and gracious were Saul
 and Jonathan!
They were together in life and in
 death.
They were swifter than eagles,
 stronger than lions.
24 O women of Israel, weep for Saul,
 for he dressed you in luxurious scarlet
 clothing,
 in garments decorated with gold.

25 Oh, how the mighty heroes have fallen
 in battle!
Jonathan lies dead on the hills.
26 How I weep for you, my brother
 Jonathan!
Oh, how much I loved you!
And your love for me was deep,
 deeper than the love of women!

27 Oh, how the mighty heroes have fallen!
 Stripped of their weapons, they lie
 dead.

David Anointed King of Judah

2 After this, David asked the LORD, "Should I move back to one of the towns of Judah?"

"Yes," the LORD replied.

Then David asked, "Which town should I go to?"

"To Hebron," the LORD answered.

2 David's two wives were Ahinoam from Jezreel and Abigail, the widow of Nabal from Carmel. So David and his wives 3 and his men and their families all moved to Judah, and they settled in the villages near Hebron. 4 Then the men of Judah came to David and anointed him king over the people of Judah.

When David heard that the men of Jabesh-gilead had buried Saul, 5 he sent them this message: "May the LORD bless you for being so loyal to your master Saul and giving him a decent burial. 6 May the LORD be loyal to you in return and reward you with his unfailing love! And I, too, will reward you for what you have done. 7 Now that Saul is dead, I ask you to be my strong and loyal subjects like the people of Judah, who have anointed me as their new king."

Ishbosheth Proclaimed King of Israel

8 But Abner son of Ner, the commander of Saul's army, had already gone to Mahanaim with Saul's son Ishbosheth.* 9 There he proclaimed Ishbosheth king over Gilead, Jezreel, Ephraim, Benjamin, the land of the Ashurites, and all the rest of Israel.

10 Ishbosheth, Saul's son, was forty years old when he became king, and he ruled from Mahanaim for two years. Meanwhile, the people of Judah remained loyal to David. 11 David made Hebron his capital, and he ruled as king of Judah for seven and a half years.

War between Israel and Judah

12 One day Abner led Ishbosheth's troops from Mahanaim to Gibeon. 13 About the same time, Joab son of Zeruiah led David's troops out and met them at the pool of Gibeon. The two groups sat down there, facing each other from opposite sides of the pool.

14 Then Abner suggested to Joab, "Let's have a few of our warriors fight hand to hand here in front of us."

"All right," Joab agreed. 15 So twelve men were chosen to fight from each side—twelve men of Benjamin representing Ishbosheth son of Saul, and twelve representing David. 16 Each one grabbed his opponent by the hair and thrust his sword into the other's side so that all of them died. So this place at Gibeon has been known ever since as the Field of Swords.*

17 A fierce battle followed that day, and Abner and the men of Israel were defeated by the forces of David.

The Death of Asahel

18 Joab, Abishai, and Asahel—the three sons of Zeruiah—were among David's forces that day. Asahel could run like a gazelle, 19 and he began chasing Abner. He pursued him relentlessly, not stopping for anything. 20 When Abner looked back and saw him coming, he called out, "Is that you, Asahel?"

"Yes, it is," he replied.

21 "Go fight someone else!" Abner warned. "Take on one of the younger men, and strip him of his weapons." But Asahel kept right on chasing Abner.

22 Again Abner shouted to him, "Get away from here! I don't want to kill you. How could I ever face your brother Joab again?"

23 But Asahel refused to turn back, so

1:18 Or *The Book of the Upright.* **1:21** The meaning of the Hebrew is uncertain. **2:8** *Ishbosheth* is another name for Esh-baal. **2:16** Hebrew *Helkath-hazzurim.*

Abner thrust the butt end of his spear through Asahel's stomach, and the spear came out through his back. He stumbled to the ground and died there. And everyone who came by that spot stopped and stood still when they saw Asahel lying there.

24When Joab and Abishai found out what had happened, they set out after Abner. The sun was just going down as they arrived at the hill of Ammah near Giah, along the road to the wilderness of Gibeon. 25Abner's troops from the tribe of Benjamin regrouped there at the top of the hill to take a stand.

26Abner shouted down to Joab, "Must we always be killing each other? Don't you realize that bitterness is the only result? When will you call off your men from chasing their Israelite brothers?"

27Then Joab said, "God only knows what would have happened if you hadn't spoken, for we would have chased you all night if necessary." 28So Joab blew the ram's horn, and his men stopped chasing the troops of Israel.

29All that night Abner and his men retreated through the Jordan Valley.* They crossed the Jordan River, traveling all through the morning,* and didn't stop until they arrived at Mahanaim.

30Meanwhile, Joab and his men also returned home. When Joab counted his casualties, he discovered that only 19 men were missing in addition to Asahel. 31But 360 of Abner's men had been killed, all from the tribe of Benjamin. 32Joab and his men took Asahel's body to Bethlehem and buried him there in his father's tomb. Then they traveled all night and reached Hebron at daybreak.

3 That was the beginning of a long war between those who were loyal to Saul and those loyal to David. As time passed David became stronger and stronger, while Saul's dynasty became weaker and weaker.

David's Sons Born in Hebron

2These are the sons who were born to David in Hebron:

The oldest was Amnon, whose mother was Ahinoam from Jezreel.
3 The second was Daniel,* whose mother was Abigail, the widow of Nabal from Carmel.
The third was Absalom, whose mother was Maacah, the daughter of Talmai, king of Geshur.
4 The fourth was Adonijah, whose mother was Haggith.
The fifth was Shephatiah, whose mother was Abital.
5 The sixth was Ithream, whose mother was Eglah, David's wife.

These sons were all born to David in Hebron.

Abner Joins Forces with David

6As the war between the house of Saul and the house of David went on, Abner became a powerful leader among those loyal to Saul. 7One day Ishbosheth,* Saul's son, accused Abner of sleeping with one of his father's concubines, a woman named Rizpah, daughter of Aiah.

8Abner was furious. "Am I some Judean dog to be kicked around like this?" he shouted. "After all I have done for your father, Saul, and his family and friends by not handing you over to David, is this my reward—that you

Hebron

Hebron, where David was proclaimed king—initially just of Judah—was a city in the Judean hills. It had been a base for the patriarchs (Genesis 13:18; 35:27) and was where Abraham bought a field to bury Sarah (Genesis 23:1-20). Later Abraham, Isaac, Rebekah, Jacob, and Leah would all be buried here. It is not surprising, therefore, in light of such a rich history, that "David made Hebron his capital" (2 Samuel 2:11). Seven and a half years later, the northern tribes also came to him at Hebron, asking him to be their king too (5:1-5). David then wisely moved his capital to Jerusalem (5:6-10), which lay on the border between north and south, thus avoiding any claims of favoritism.

▶ *See also **Jerusalem**, page 347.*

find fault with me about this woman? [9]May
God strike me and even kill me if I don't do
everything I can to help David get what the
LORD has promised him! [10]I'm going to take
Saul's kingdom and give it to David. I will establish the throne of David over Israel as well
as Judah, all the way from Dan in the north to
Beersheba in the south." [11]Ishbosheth didn't
dare say another word because he was afraid
of what Abner might do.

[12]Then Abner sent messengers to David,
saying, "Doesn't the entire land belong to
you? Make a solemn pact with me, and I will
help turn over all of Israel to you."

[13]"All right," David replied, "but I will not
negotiate with you unless you bring back
my wife Michal, Saul's daughter, when you
come."

[14]David then sent this message to Ishbosheth, Saul's son: "Give me back my wife
Michal, for I bought her with the lives* of
100 Philistines."

[15]So Ishbosheth took Michal away from
her husband, Palti* son of Laish. [16]Palti followed along behind her as far as Bahurim,
weeping as he went. Then Abner told him,
"Go back home!" So Palti returned.

[17]Meanwhile, Abner had consulted with
the elders of Israel. "For some time now," he
told them, "you have wanted to make David
your king. [18]Now is the time! For the LORD
has said, 'I have chosen David to save my
people Israel from the hands of the Philistines and from all their other enemies.'"
[19]Abner also spoke with the men of Benjamin. Then he went to Hebron to tell David
that all the people of Israel and Benjamin
had agreed to support him.

[20]When Abner and twenty of his men
came to Hebron, David entertained them
with a great feast. [21]Then Abner said to
David, "Let me go and call an assembly of
all Israel to support my lord the king. They
will make a covenant with you to make you
their king, and you will rule over everything
your heart desires." So David sent Abner
safely on his way.

Joab Murders Abner

[22]But just after David had sent Abner away in
safety, Joab and some of David's troops returned from a raid, bringing much plunder
with them. [23]When Joab arrived, he was told
that Abner had just been there visiting the
king and had been sent away in safety.

[24]Joab rushed to the king and demanded,
"What have you done? What do you mean
by letting Abner get away? [25]You know perfectly well that he came to spy on you and
find out everything you're doing!"

[26]Joab then left David and sent messengers to catch up with Abner, asking him to
return. They found him at the well of Sirah
and brought him back, though David knew
nothing about it. [27]When Abner arrived
back at Hebron, Joab took him aside at the
gateway as if to speak with him privately.
But then he stabbed Abner in the stomach
and killed him in revenge for killing his
brother Asahel.

[28]When David heard about it, he declared,

2:29a Hebrew *the Arabah*. **2:29b** Or *continued on through the Bithron*. The meaning of the Hebrew is uncertain. **3:3** As in parallel text at 1 Chr 3:1 (see also Greek version, which reads *Daluia*, and possible support by Dead Sea Scrolls); Hebrew reads *Kileab*. **3:7** *Ishbosheth* is another name for Esh-baal. **3:14** Hebrew *the foreskins*. **3:15** As in 1 Sam 25:44; Hebrew reads *Paltiel*, a variant spelling of Palti.

"From Dan to Beersheba"

"From Dan in the north to Beersheba in the south" (2 Samuel 3:10; literally, "from Dan to Beersheba") was a common expression in Bible times. Dan was Israel's most northern city and Beersheba lay in the far south, so the expression became a way of saying "the whole land of Israel." Dan was situated by the largest of the four sources of the Jordan River at the base of Mount Hermon. In later history it became a false sanctuary under King Jeroboam I, one of two centers of calf-worship, along with Bethel (1 Kings 12:29-30). Beersheba, in the Negev, had associations with all three patriarchs—Abraham (Genesis 21:8-34; 22:19), Isaac (Genesis 26:32-33), and Jacob (Genesis 28:10; 46:1). Like Dan, it too became an idolatrous shrine in later history and was condemned by Amos (Amos 5:4-5).

▶ *See also* ***Beersheba****, page 997.*

"I vow by the LORD that I and my kingdom are
forever innocent of this crime against Abner
son of Ner. [29]Joab and his family are the guilty
ones. May the family of Joab be cursed in
every generation with a man who has open
sores or leprosy* or who walks on crutches*
or dies by the sword or begs for food!"
[30]So Joab and his brother Abishai killed
Abner because Abner had killed their
brother Asahel at the battle of Gibeon.

David Mourns Abner's Death

[31]Then David said to Joab and all those who
were with him, "Tear your clothes and put
on burlap. Mourn for Abner." And King
David himself walked behind the procession to the grave. [32]They buried Abner in
Hebron, and the king and all the people
wept at his graveside. [33]Then the king sang
this funeral song for Abner:

"Should Abner have died as fools die?
[34] Your hands were not bound;
your feet were not chained.
No, you were murdered—
the victim of a wicked plot."

All the people wept again for Abner.
[35]David had refused to eat anything on
the day of the funeral, and now everyone
begged him to eat. But David had made a
vow, saying, "May God strike me and even
kill me if I eat anything before sundown."
[36]This pleased the people very much. In
fact, everything the king did pleased them!
[37]So everyone in Judah and all Israel understood that David was not responsible for
Abner's murder.
[38]Then King David said to his officials,
"Don't you realize that a great commander
has fallen today in Israel? [39]And even
though I am the anointed king, these two
sons of Zeruiah—Joab and Abishai—are too
strong for me to control. So may the LORD
repay these evil men for their evil deeds."

The Murder of Ishbosheth

4 When Ishbosheth,* Saul's son, heard
about Abner's death at Hebron, he lost
all courage, and all Israel became paralyzed with fear. [2]Now there were two brothers, Baanah and Recab, who were captains
of Ishbosheth's raiding parties. They were
sons of Rimmon, a member of the tribe of
Benjamin who lived in Beeroth. The town of
Beeroth is now part of Benjamin's territory
[3]because the original people of Beeroth fled
to Gittaim, where they still live as foreigners.
[4](Saul's son Jonathan had a son named
Mephibosheth,* who was crippled as a
child. He was five years old when the report
came from Jezreel that Saul and Jonathan
had been killed in battle. When the child's
nurse heard the news, she picked him up
and fled. But as she hurried away, she
dropped him, and he became crippled.)
[5]One day Recab and Baanah, the sons
of Rimmon from Beeroth, went to Ishbosheth's house around noon as he was taking
his midday rest. [6]The doorkeeper, who had
been sifting wheat, became drowsy and fell
asleep. So Recab and Baanah slipped past
her.* [7]They went into the house and found
Ishbosheth sleeping on his bed. They struck
and killed him and cut off his head. Then,
taking his head with them, they fled across
the Jordan Valley* through the night. [8]When
they arrived at Hebron, they presented Ishbosheth's head to David. "Look!" they exclaimed to the king. "Here is the head of
Ishbosheth, the son of your enemy Saul
who tried to kill you. Today the LORD has
given my lord the king revenge on Saul and
his entire family!"
[9]But David said to Recab and Baanah,
"The LORD, who saves me from all my
enemies, is my witness. [10]Someone once
told me, 'Saul is dead,' thinking he was
bringing me good news. But I seized him
and killed him at Ziklag. That's the reward
I gave him for his news! [11]How much more
should I reward evil men who have killed an
innocent man in his own house and on his
own bed? Shouldn't I hold you responsible
for his blood and rid the earth of you?"
[12]So David ordered his young men to kill
them, and they did. They cut off their hands
and feet and hung their bodies beside the
pool in Hebron. Then they took Ishbosheth's head and buried it in Abner's tomb
in Hebron.

David Becomes King of All Israel

5 Then all the tribes of Israel went to
David at Hebron and told him, "We are
your own flesh and blood. [2]In the past,*
when Saul was our king, you were the one
who really led the forces of Israel. And the
LORD told you, 'You will be the shepherd
of my people Israel. You will be Israel's
leader.'"

3So there at Hebron, King David made a covenant before the LORD with all the elders of Israel. And they anointed him king of Israel.

4David was thirty years old when he began to reign, and he reigned forty years in all. 5He had reigned over Judah from Hebron for seven years and six months, and from Jerusalem he reigned over all Israel and Judah for thirty-three years.

David Captures Jerusalem

6David then led his men to Jerusalem to fight against the Jebusites, the original inhabitants of the land who were living there. The Jebusites taunted David, saying, "You'll never get in here! Even the blind and lame could keep you out!" For the Jebusites thought they were safe. 7But David captured the fortress of Zion, which is now called the City of David.

8On the day of the attack, David said to his troops, "I hate those 'lame' and 'blind' Jebusites.* Whoever attacks them should strike by going into the city through the water tunnel.*" That is the origin of the saying, "The blind and the lame may not enter the house."*

9So David made the fortress his home, and he called it the City of David. He extended the city, starting at the supporting terraces* and working inward. 10And David became more and more powerful, because the LORD God of Heaven's Armies was with him.

11Then King Hiram of Tyre sent messengers to David, along with cedar timber and carpenters and stonemasons, and they built David a palace. 12And David realized that the LORD had confirmed him as king over Israel and had blessed his kingdom for the sake of his people Israel.

13After moving from Hebron to Jerusalem, David married more concubines and wives, and they had more sons and daughters. 14These are the names of David's sons who were born in Jerusalem: Shammua, Shobab, Nathan, Solomon, 15Ibhar, Elishua, Nepheg, Japhia, 16Elishama, Eliada, and Eliphelet.

3:29a Or *or a contagious skin disease*. The Hebrew word used here can describe various skin diseases. **3:29b** Or *who is effeminate;* Hebrew reads *who handles a spindle*. **4:1** *Ishbosheth* is another name for Esh-baal. **4:4** *Mephibosheth* is another name for Merib-baal. **4:6** As in Greek version; Hebrew reads *So they went into the house pretending to fetch wheat, but they stabbed him in the stomach. Then Recab and Baanah escaped.* **4:7** Hebrew *the Arabah*. **5:2** Or *For some time*. **5:8a** Or *Those 'lame' and 'blind' Jebusites hate me*. **5:8b** Or *with scaling hooks*. The meaning of the Hebrew is uncertain. **5:8c** The meaning of this saying is uncertain. **5:9** Hebrew *the millo*. The meaning of the Hebrew is uncertain.

Jerusalem

For seven years David had ruled Judah in the south, but now the northern tribes (known as Israel) had asked him to be their king too. David realized he needed a new capital for this newly united kingdom. To avoid any accusations of favoritism, he decided to establish his capital at Jerusalem, located right on the border between north and south—a shrewd decision. It had been a Jebusite stronghold that the Israelites had been unable to capture, but David's men gained entry by climbing up the water tunnel into the city and conquering it from within. It became known as the City of David, or Zion, after the hill on which it was built. When it later became home to the Temple and the Ark of the Covenant, it also became known as "the city of the great King" (that is, God himself; see Psalm 48:2; Matthew 5:35).

Yet while Jerusalem symbolized devotion to God, it also came to symbolize unfaithfulness as its kings and people turned away from God. The prophets therefore warned that God would destroy it. He did this through the Babylonians in the sixth century BC and again through the Romans in the first century AD.

The New Testament shows less interest in Jerusalem, its purpose now completed. It focuses rather on God's *people* instead of a particular place and looks forward to the coming of the new Jerusalem from heaven when Christ returns (Revelation 21:2).

▸ *See also **Zion**, page 649.*

David Conquers the Philistines
17When the Philistines heard that David had
been anointed king of Israel, they mobilized
all their forces to capture him. But David
was told they were coming, so he went into
the stronghold. 18The Philistines arrived and
spread out across the valley of Rephaim.
19So David asked the LORD, "Should I go out
to fight the Philistines? Will you hand them
over to me?"
The LORD replied to David, "Yes, go
ahead. I will certainly hand them over to
you."
20So David went to Baal-perazim and defeated the Philistines there. "The LORD did
it!" David exclaimed. "He burst through my
enemies like a raging flood!" So he named
that place Baal-perazim (which means "the
Lord who bursts through"). 21The Philistines
had abandoned their idols there, so David
and his men confiscated them.
22But after a while the Philistines returned and again spread out across the
valley of Rephaim. 23And again David asked
the LORD what to do. "Do not attack them
straight on," the LORD replied. "Instead,
circle around behind and attack them
near the poplar* trees. 24When you hear a
sound like marching feet in the tops of the
poplar trees, be on the alert! That will be
the signal that the LORD is moving ahead of
you to strike down the Philistine army." 25So
David did what the LORD commanded, and
he struck down the Philistines all the way
from Gibeon* to Gezer.

Moving the Ark to Jerusalem
6 Then David again gathered all the elite
troops in Israel, 30,000 in all. 2He led
them to Baalah of Judah* to bring back
the Ark of God, which bears the name of
the LORD of Heaven's Armies,* who is enthroned between the cherubim. 3They placed
the Ark of God on a new cart and brought
it from Abinadab's house, which was on
a hill. Uzzah and Ahio, Abinadab's sons,
were guiding the cart 4that carried the Ark of
God.* Ahio walked in front of the Ark. 5David
and all the people of Israel were celebrating
before the LORD, singing songs* and playing
all kinds of musical instruments—lyres,
harps, tambourines, castanets, and cymbals.
6But when they arrived at the threshing
floor of Nacon, the oxen stumbled, and
Uzzah reached out his hand and steadied
the Ark of God. 7Then the LORD's anger was
aroused against Uzzah, and God struck him
dead because of this.* So Uzzah died right
there beside the Ark of God.
8David was angry because the LORD's
anger had burst out against Uzzah. He
named that place Perez-uzzah (which
means "to burst out against Uzzah"), as it
is still called today.
9David was now afraid of the LORD, and
he asked, "How can I ever bring the Ark of
the LORD back into my care?" 10So David
decided not to move the Ark of the LORD
into the City of David. Instead, he took it
to the house of Obed-edom of Gath. 11The
Ark of the LORD remained there in Obed-
edom's house for three months, and the
LORD blessed Obed-edom and his entire
household.
12Then King David was told, "The LORD
has blessed Obed-edom's household and
everything he has because of the Ark of
God." So David went there and brought the
Ark of God from the house of Obed-edom to
the City of David with a great celebration.
13After the men who were carrying the Ark
of the LORD had gone six steps, David sacrificed a bull and a fattened calf. 14And David
danced before the LORD with all his might,
wearing a priestly garment.* 15So David and
all the people of Israel brought up the Ark of
the LORD with shouts of joy and the blowing
of rams' horns.

Michal's Contempt for David
16But as the Ark of the LORD entered the
City of David, Michal, the daughter of Saul,
looked down from her window. When she
saw King David leaping and dancing before
the LORD, she was filled with contempt for
him.
17They brought the Ark of the LORD and
set it in its place inside the special tent
David had prepared for it. And David sacrificed burnt offerings and peace offerings to
the LORD. 18When he had finished his sacrifices, David blessed the people in the name
of the LORD of Heaven's Armies. 19Then he
gave to every Israelite man and woman in

▸ **6:5** *See **The ministry of music and singing**, page 475.* **6:6-11** *See **The Ark of the Covenant**, page 311.*

the crowd a loaf of bread, a cake of dates,*
and a cake of raisins. Then all the people
returned to their homes.

[20]When David returned home to bless his
own family, Michal, the daughter of Saul,
came out to meet him. She said in disgust,
"How distinguished the king of Israel
looked today, shamelessly exposing himself
to the servant girls like any vulgar person
might do!"

[21]David retorted to Michal, "I was dancing
before the LORD, who chose me above your
father and all his family! He appointed me
as the leader of Israel, the people of the
LORD, so I celebrate before the LORD. [22]Yes,
and I am willing to look even more foolish
than this, even to be humiliated in my own
eyes! But those servant girls you mentioned
will indeed think I am distinguished!" [23]So
Michal, the daughter of Saul, remained
childless throughout her entire life.

The LORD's Covenant Promise to David

7 When King David was settled in his
palace and the LORD had given him rest
from all the surrounding enemies, [2]the king
summoned Nathan the prophet. "Look,"
David said, "I am living in a beautiful cedar
palace,* but the Ark of God is out there in
a tent!"

[3]Nathan replied to the king, "Go ahead
and do whatever you have in mind, for the
LORD is with you."

[4]But that same night the LORD said to
Nathan,

[5]"Go and tell my servant David, 'This
is what the LORD has declared: Are
you the one to build a house for me to
live in? [6]I have never lived in a house,
from the day I brought the Israelites
out of Egypt until this very day. I
have always moved from one place to
another with a tent and a Tabernacle
as my dwelling. [7]Yet no matter where
I have gone with the Israelites, I have
never once complained to Israel's tribal
leaders, the shepherds of my people
Israel. I have never asked them, "Why
haven't you built me a beautiful cedar
house?"'

[8]"Now go and say to my servant
David, 'This is what the LORD of
Heaven's Armies has declared: I took
you from tending sheep in the pasture
and selected you to be the leader of my
people Israel. [9]I have been with you
wherever you have gone, and I have
destroyed all your enemies before your
eyes. Now I will make your name as
famous as anyone who has ever lived
on the earth! [10]And I will provide a
homeland for my people Israel, planting
them in a secure place where they
will never be disturbed. Evil nations
won't oppress them as they've done
in the past, [11]starting from the time I
appointed judges to rule my people
Israel. And I will give you rest from all
your enemies.

"'Furthermore, the LORD declares that
he will make a house for you—a dynasty
of kings! [12]For when you die and are
buried with your ancestors, I will raise
up one of your descendants, your own
offspring, and I will make his kingdom
strong. [13]He is the one who will build a
house—a temple—for my name. And I
will secure his royal throne forever. [14]I
will be his father, and he will be my son.
If he sins, I will correct and discipline
him with the rod, like any father would
do. [15]But my favor will not be taken
from him as I took it from Saul, whom I
removed from your sight. [16]Your house
and your kingdom will continue before
me* for all time, and your throne will be
secure forever.'"

[17]So Nathan went back to David and told
him everything the LORD had said in this
vision.

David's Prayer of Thanks

[18]Then King David went in and sat before
the LORD and prayed,

"Who am I, O Sovereign LORD, and what
is my family, that you have brought me
this far? [19]And now, Sovereign LORD, in
addition to everything else, you speak

5:23 Or *aspen*, or *balsam;* also in 5:24. The exact identification of this tree is uncertain. **5:25** As in Greek version (see also 1 Chr 14:16); Hebrew reads *Geba.* **6:2a** Hebrew *Baale of Judah,* another name for Kiriath-jearim; compare 1 Chr 13:6. **6:2b** Or *the Ark of God where the Name is proclaimed—the name of the LORD of Heaven's Armies.* **6:4** As in Dead Sea Scrolls and some Greek manuscripts; Masoretic Text reads [4]*and they brought it from Abinadab's house, which was on a hill, with the Ark of God.* **6:5** As in Dead Sea Scrolls and Greek version (see also 1 Chr 13:8); Masoretic Text reads *before the LORD with all manner of cypress wood.* **6:7** As in Dead Sea Scrolls; Masoretic Text reads *because of his irreverence.* **6:14** Hebrew *a linen ephod.* **6:19** Or *a portion of meat.* The meaning of the Hebrew is uncertain. **7:2** Hebrew *a house of cedar.* **7:16** As in Greek version and some Hebrew manuscripts; Masoretic Text reads *before you.*

of giving your servant a lasting dynasty!
Do you deal with everyone this way,
O Sovereign LORD?*
20“What more can I say to you? You
know what your servant is really like,
Sovereign LORD. 21Because of your
promise and according to your will,
you have done all these great things
and have made them known to your
servant.
22“How great you are, O Sovereign
LORD! There is no one like you. We have
never even heard of another God like
you! 23What other nation on earth is like
your people Israel? What other nation,
O God, have you redeemed from slavery
to be your own people? You made
a great name for yourself when you
redeemed your people from Egypt. You
performed awesome miracles and drove
out the nations and gods that stood in
their way.* 24You made Israel your very
own people forever, and you, O LORD,
became their God.
25“And now, O LORD God, I am your
servant; do as you have promised
concerning me and my family. Confirm it
as a promise that will last forever. 26And
may your name be honored forever so
that everyone will say, ‘The LORD of
Heaven’s Armies is God over Israel!’ And
may the house of your servant David
continue before you forever.
27“O LORD of Heaven’s Armies, God of
Israel, I have been bold enough to pray
this prayer to you because you have
revealed all this to your servant, saying,
‘I will build a house for you—a dynasty
of kings!’ 28For you are God, O Sovereign
LORD. Your words are truth, and you
have promised these good things to your
servant. 29And now, may it please you to
bless the house of your servant, so that
it may continue forever before you. For
you have spoken, and when you grant
a blessing to your servant, O Sovereign
LORD, it is an eternal blessing!”

David’s Military Victories

8 After this, David defeated and subdued
the Philistines by conquering Gath,
their largest town.* 2David also conquered
the land of Moab. He made the people lie
down on the ground in a row, and he measured them off in groups with a length of
rope. He measured off two groups to be executed for every one group to be spared.
The Moabites who were spared became
David’s subjects and paid him tribute
money.
3David also destroyed the forces of Hadadezer son of Rehob, king of Zobah, when
Hadadezer marched out to strengthen his
control along the Euphrates River. 4David
captured 1,000 chariots, 7,000 charioteers,*
and 20,000 foot soldiers. He crippled

An everlasting kingdom

Out of his love for God, David wanted to build a more permanent home for the Ark of the Covenant, which symbolized God’s presence. Now that David had a palace of his own, it didn’t seem right to him that the Ark was still in a tent, so he planned to build a temple for it. At first Nathan the prophet encouraged him to go ahead, but that night God spoke to Nathan, who immediately told David what God had said. God said he had never needed a house thus far and didn’t need one now (2 Samuel 7:5-7). He saw David’s good intentions but turned things around on him: Rather than David building a house for God, God was going to build a “house” for David—a house of descendants in a kingdom that would last forever (7:16). This promise, often called “the Davidic covenant,” wouldn’t find fulfillment in Israel’s monarchy, for the rule of David’s dynasty eventually did come to an end; rather, the New Testament sees it fulfilled in Christ, who was descended from David and who rules over an everlasting kingdom (e.g., Luke 1:26-33; Acts 2:29-37).

▸ *See also **The Davidic covenant**, page 468.*

all the chariot horses except enough for 100 chariots.

5 When Arameans from Damascus arrived to help King Hadadezer, David killed 22,000 of them. 6 Then he placed several army garrisons in Damascus, the Aramean capital, and the Arameans became David's subjects and paid him tribute money. So the LORD made David victorious wherever he went.

7 David brought the gold shields of Hadadezer's officers to Jerusalem, 8 along with a large amount of bronze from Hadadezer's towns of Tebah* and Berothai.

9 When King Toi of Hamath heard that David had destroyed the entire army of Hadadezer, 10 he sent his son Joram to congratulate King David for his successful campaign. Hadadezer and Toi had been enemies and were often at war. Joram presented David with many gifts of silver, gold, and bronze.

11 King David dedicated all these gifts to the LORD, as he did with the silver and gold from the other nations he had defeated—12 from Edom,* Moab, Ammon, Philistia, and Amalek—and from Hadadezer son of Rehob, king of Zobah.

13 So David became even more famous when he returned from destroying 18,000 Edomites* in the Valley of Salt. 14 He placed army garrisons throughout Edom, and all the Edomites became David's subjects. In fact, the LORD made David victorious wherever he went.

15 So David reigned over all Israel and did what was just and right for all his people. 16 Joab son of Zeruiah was commander of the army. Jehoshaphat son of Ahilud was the royal historian. 17 Zadok son of Ahitub and Ahimelech son of Abiathar were the priests. Seraiah was the court secretary. 18 Benaiah son of Jehoiada was captain of the king's bodyguard.* And David's sons served as priestly leaders.*

David's Kindness to Mephibosheth

9 One day David asked, "Is anyone in Saul's family still alive—anyone to whom I can show kindness for Jonathan's sake?" 2 He summoned a man named Ziba, who had been one of Saul's servants. "Are you Ziba?" the king asked.

"Yes sir, I am," Ziba replied.

3 The king then asked him, "Is anyone still alive from Saul's family? If so, I want to show God's kindness to them."

Ziba replied, "Yes, one of Jonathan's sons is still alive. He is crippled in both feet."

4 "Where is he?" the king asked.

"In Lo-debar," Ziba told him, "at the home of Makir son of Ammiel."

5 So David sent for him and brought him from Makir's home. 6 His name was Mephibosheth*; he was Jonathan's son and Saul's grandson. When he came to David, he bowed low to the ground in deep respect. David said, "Greetings, Mephibosheth."

Mephibosheth replied, "I am your servant."

7 "Don't be afraid!" David said. "I intend to show kindness to you because of my promise to your father, Jonathan. I will give you all the property that once belonged to your grandfather Saul, and you will eat here with me at the king's table!"

8 Mephibosheth bowed respectfully and exclaimed, "Who is your servant, that you should show such kindness to a dead dog like me?"

9 Then the king summoned Saul's servant Ziba and said, "I have given your master's grandson everything that belonged to Saul and his family. 10 You and your sons and servants are to farm the land for him to produce food for your master's household.* But Mephibosheth, your master's grandson, will eat here at my table." (Ziba had fifteen sons and twenty servants.)

11 Ziba replied, "Yes, my lord the king; I am your servant, and I will do all that you have commanded." And from that time on, Mephibosheth ate regularly at David's table,* like one of the king's own sons.

12 Mephibosheth had a young son named Mica. From then on, all the members of Ziba's household were Mephibosheth's

7:19 Or *This is your instruction for all humanity, O Sovereign LORD.* **7:23** As in Greek version (see also 1 Chr 17:21); Hebrew reads *You made a name for yourself and awesome miracles for your land in the sight of your people, whom you redeemed from Egypt, the nations and their gods.* **8:1** Hebrew *by conquering Metheg-ammah,* a name that means "the bridle," possibly referring to the size of the town or the tribute money taken from it. Compare 1 Chr 18:1. **8:4** As in Dead Sea Scrolls and Greek version (see also 1 Chr 18:4); Masoretic Text reads *captured 1,700 charioteers.* **8:8** As in some Greek manuscripts (see also 1 Chr 18:8); Hebrew reads *Betah.* **8:12** As in a few Hebrew manuscripts and Greek and Syriac versions (see also 8:14; 1 Chr 18:11); most Hebrew manuscripts read *Aram.* **8:13** As in a few Hebrew manuscripts and Greek and Syriac versions (see also 8:14; 1 Chr 18:12); most Hebrew manuscripts read *Arameans.* **8:18a** Hebrew *of the Kerethites and Pelethites.* **8:18b** Hebrew *David's sons were priests;* compare parallel text at 1 Chr 18:17. **9:6** *Mephibosheth* is another name for Merib-baal. **9:10** As in Greek version; Hebrew reads *your master's grandson.* **9:11** As in Greek version; Hebrew reads *my table.*

servants. [13]And Mephibosheth, who was crippled in both feet, lived in Jerusalem and ate regularly at the king's table.

David Defeats the Ammonites

10 Some time after this, King Nahash* of the Ammonites died, and his son Hanun became king. [2]David said, "I am going to show loyalty to Hanun just as his father, Nahash, was always loyal to me." So David sent ambassadors to express sympathy to Hanun about his father's death.

But when David's ambassadors arrived in the land of Ammon, [3]the Ammonite commanders said to Hanun, their master, "Do you really think these men are coming here to honor your father? No! David has sent them to spy out the city so they can come in and conquer it!" [4]So Hanun seized David's ambassadors and shaved off half of each man's beard, cut off their robes at the buttocks, and sent them back to David in shame.

[5]When David heard what had happened, he sent messengers to tell the men, "Stay at Jericho until your beards grow out, and then come back." For they felt deep shame because of their appearance.

[6]When the people of Ammon realized how seriously they had angered David, they sent and hired 20,000 Aramean foot soldiers from the lands of Beth-rehob and Zobah, 1,000 from the king of Maacah, and 12,000 from the land of Tob. [7]When David heard about this, he sent Joab and all his warriors to fight them. [8]The Ammonite troops came out and drew up their battle lines at the entrance of the city gate, while the Arameans from Zobah and Rehob and the men from Tob and Maacah positioned themselves to fight in the open fields.

[9]When Joab saw that he would have to fight on both the front and the rear, he chose some of Israel's elite troops and placed them under his personal command to fight the Arameans in the fields. [10]He left the rest of the army under the command of his brother Abishai, who was to attack the Ammonites. [11]"If the Arameans are too strong for me, then come over and help me," Joab told his brother. "And if the Ammonites are too strong for you, I will come and help you. [12]Be courageous! Let us fight bravely for our people and the cities of our God. May the LORD's will be done."

[13]When Joab and his troops attacked, the Arameans began to run away. [14]And when the Ammonites saw the Arameans running, they ran from Abishai and retreated into the city. After the battle was over, Joab returned to Jerusalem.

[15]The Arameans now realized that they were no match for Israel. So when they regrouped, [16]they were joined by additional Aramean troops summoned by Hadadezer from the other side of the Euphrates River.* These troops arrived at Helam under the command of Shobach, the commander of Hadadezer's forces.

[17]When David heard what was happening, he mobilized all Israel, crossed the Jordan River, and led the army to Helam. The Arameans positioned themselves in battle formation and fought against David. [18]But again the Arameans fled from the Israelites. This time David's forces killed 700 charioteers and 40,000 foot soldiers,* including Shobach, the commander of their army. [19]When all the kings allied with Hadadezer saw that they had been defeated by Israel, they surrendered to Israel and became their subjects. After that, the Arameans were afraid to help the Ammonites.

David and Bathsheba

11 In the spring of the year,* when kings normally go out to war, David sent Joab and the Israelite army to fight the Ammonites. They destroyed the Ammonite army and laid siege to the city of Rabbah. However, David stayed behind in Jerusalem.

[2]Late one afternoon, after his midday rest, David got out of bed and was walking on the roof of the palace. As he looked out over the city, he noticed a woman of unusual beauty taking a bath. [3]He sent someone to find out who she was, and he was told, "She is Bathsheba, the daughter of Eliam and the wife of Uriah the Hittite." [4]Then David sent messengers to get her; and when she came to the palace, he slept with her. She had just completed the purification rites after having her menstrual period. Then she returned home. [5]Later, when Bathsheba discovered that she was pregnant, she sent David a message, saying, "I'm pregnant."

[6]Then David sent word to Joab: "Send me Uriah the Hittite." So Joab sent him to David. [7]When Uriah arrived, David asked him how Joab and the army were getting along and

how the war was progressing. 8 Then he
told Uriah, "Go on home and relax.*" David
even sent a gift to Uriah after he had left the
palace. 9 But Uriah didn't go home. He slept
that night at the palace entrance with the
king's palace guard.
10 When David heard that Uriah had not
gone home, he summoned him and asked,
"What's the matter? Why didn't you go
home last night after being away for so
long?"
11 Uriah replied, "The Ark and the armies
of Israel and Judah are living in tents,* and
Joab and my master's men are camping in
the open fields. How could I go home to
wine and dine and sleep with my wife? I
swear that I would never do such a thing."
12 "Well, stay here today," David told
him, "and tomorrow you may return to the
army." So Uriah stayed in Jerusalem that
day and the next. 13 Then David invited him
to dinner and got him drunk. But even then
he couldn't get Uriah to go home to his wife.
Again he slept at the palace entrance with
the king's palace guard.

David Arranges for Uriah's Death

14 So the next morning David wrote a letter
to Joab and gave it to Uriah to deliver. 15 The
letter instructed Joab, "Station Uriah on the
front lines where the battle is fiercest. Then
pull back so that he will be killed." 16 So Joab
assigned Uriah to a spot close to the city
wall where he knew the enemy's strongest
men were fighting. 17 And when the enemy
soldiers came out of the city to fight, Uriah
the Hittite was killed along with several
other Israelite soldiers.
18 Then Joab sent a battle report to David.
19 He told his messenger, "Report all the
news of the battle to the king. 20 But he might
get angry and ask, 'Why did the troops go
so close to the city? Didn't they know there
would be shooting from the walls? 21 Wasn't
Abimelech son of Gideon* killed at Thebez
by a woman who threw a millstone down
on him from the wall? Why would you get
so close to the wall?' Then tell him, 'Uriah
the Hittite was killed, too.'"
22 So the messenger went to Jerusalem and gave a complete report to David.
23 "The enemy came out against us in the
open fields," he said. "And as we chased
them back to the city gate, 24 the archers
on the wall shot arrows at us. Some of the
king's men were killed, including Uriah the
Hittite."
25 "Well, tell Joab not to be discouraged,"

10:1 As in parallel text at 1 Chr 19:1; Hebrew reads *the king.* **10:16** Hebrew *the river.* **10:18** As in some Greek manuscripts (see also 1 Chr 19:18); Hebrew reads *charioteers.* **11:1** Hebrew *At the turn of the year.* The first day of the year in the ancient Hebrew lunar calendar occurred in March or April. **11:8** Hebrew *and wash your feet,* an expression that may also have a connotation of ritualistic washing. **11:11** Or *at Succoth.* **11:21** Hebrew *son of Jerub-besheth.* Jerub-besheth is a variation on the name Jerub-baal, which is another name for Gideon; see Judg 6:32.

Adultery

Adultery—sexual intercourse by a married person with someone other than their partner—is plainly forbidden in God's Word. Its seriousness is seen in the fact that its prohibition is included in the Ten Commandments (Exodus 20:14), the very heart of God's ways for his people. Proverbs has much to say about it, warning that "the man who commits adultery is an utter fool, for he destroys himself" (Proverbs 6:32).

David's adultery with Bathsheba shows just how far that destruction can reach: It affected David's godliness and integrity, Bathsheba's purity, Uriah's life, the child's life—all destroyed by a moment's selfish desire. Of course, David thought he had covered it all up, especially after Uriah was killed and David married Bathsheba to make it look like the child was his. But he could not hide it from God (2 Samuel 11:27). Yes, he was forgiven when he repented, but the effects of this one act stretched ahead for many years, just as Nathan the prophet declared (12:10-12). A moment of pleasure had a lifetime of consequences.

▸ *See also* ***Does marriage still matter to God?****, page 976.*

David said. "The sword devours this one today and that one tomorrow! Fight harder next time, and conquer the city!"

[26]When Uriah's wife heard that her husband was dead, she mourned for him. [27]When the period of mourning was over, David sent for her and brought her to the palace, and she became one of his wives. Then she gave birth to a son. But the LORD was displeased with what David had done.

Nathan Rebukes David

12 So the LORD sent Nathan the prophet to tell David this story: "There were two men in a certain town. One was rich, and one was poor. [2]The rich man owned a great many sheep and cattle. [3]The poor man owned nothing but one little lamb he had bought. He raised that little lamb, and it grew up with his children. It ate from the man's own plate and drank from his cup. He cuddled it in his arms like a baby daughter. [4]One day a guest arrived at the home of the rich man. But instead of killing an animal from his own flock or herd, he took the poor man's lamb and killed it and prepared it for his guest."

[5]David was furious. "As surely as the LORD lives," he vowed, "any man who would do such a thing deserves to die! [6]He must repay four lambs to the poor man for the one he stole and for having no pity."

[7]Then Nathan said to David, "You are that man! The LORD, the God of Israel, says: I anointed you king of Israel and saved you from the power of Saul. [8]I gave you your master's house and his wives and the kingdoms of Israel and Judah. And if that had not been enough, I would have given you much, much more. [9]Why, then, have you despised the word of the LORD and done this horrible deed? For you have murdered Uriah the Hittite with the sword of the Ammonites and stolen his wife. [10]From this time on, your family will live by the sword because you have despised me by taking Uriah's wife to be your own.

[11]"This is what the LORD says: Because of what you have done, I will cause your own household to rebel against you. I will give your wives to another man before your very eyes, and he will go to bed with them in public view. [12]You did it secretly, but I will make this happen to you openly in the sight of all Israel."

David Confesses His Guilt

[13]Then David confessed to Nathan, "I have sinned against the LORD."

Nathan replied, "Yes, but the LORD has forgiven you, and you won't die for this sin. [14]Nevertheless, because you have shown utter contempt for the word of the LORD* by doing this, your child will die."

[15]After Nathan returned to his home, the LORD sent a deadly illness to the child of David and Uriah's wife. [16]David begged God to spare the child. He went without food and lay all night on the bare ground. [17]The elders of his household pleaded with him to get up and eat with them, but he refused.

[18]Then on the seventh day the child died. David's advisers were afraid to tell him. "He wouldn't listen to reason while the child was ill," they said. "What drastic thing will he do when we tell him the child is dead?"

Nathan

Although utterly loyal to David, expressed in his prompt action when Adonijah made a bid for the throne (1 Kings 1), the prophet Nathan wasn't afraid to confront him with God's truth, knowing it was for his good. When God gave Nathan his promise of an eternal kingdom to share with David (2 Samuel 7:4-17), he also made it clear that kings weren't allowed to do whatever they liked, and if they did, there would be consequences (7:14). This was demonstrated when David foolishly committed adultery with Bathsheba. It could not have been easy for Nathan when God revealed to him what had happened. But he confronted David by sharing a parable, causing David to condemn himself by his own words (chapter 12). It must have been hard for Nathan to say, "You are that man!" (12:7). Yet when David quickly confessed, Nathan assured him of God's forgiveness (12:13). Real friendship will always speak the truth.

[19]When David saw them whispering, he realized what had happened. "Is the child dead?" he asked.

"Yes," they replied, "he is dead."

[20]Then David got up from the ground, washed himself, put on lotions,* and changed his clothes. He went to the Tabernacle and worshiped the LORD. After that, he returned to the palace and was served food and ate.

[21]His advisers were amazed. "We don't understand you," they told him. "While the child was still living, you wept and refused to eat. But now that the child is dead, you have stopped your mourning and are eating again."

[22]David replied, "I fasted and wept while the child was alive, for I said, 'Perhaps the LORD will be gracious to me and let the child live.' [23]But why should I fast when he is dead? Can I bring him back again? I will go to him one day, but he cannot return to me."

[24]Then David comforted Bathsheba, his wife, and slept with her. She became pregnant and gave birth to a son, and David* named him Solomon. The LORD loved the child [25]and sent word through Nathan the prophet that they should name him Jedidiah (which means "beloved of the LORD"), as the LORD had commanded.*

David Captures Rabbah

[26]Meanwhile, Joab was fighting against Rabbah, the capital of Ammon, and he captured the royal fortifications.* [27]Joab sent messengers to tell David, "I have fought against Rabbah and captured its water supply.* [28]Now bring the rest of the army and capture the city. Otherwise, I will capture it and get credit for the victory."

[29]So David gathered the rest of the army and went to Rabbah, and he fought against it and captured it. [30]David removed the crown from the king's head,* and it was placed on his own head. The crown was made of gold and set with gems, and it weighed seventy-five pounds.* David took a vast amount of plunder from the city. [31]He also made slaves of the people of Rabbah and forced them to labor with* saws, iron picks, and iron axes, and to work in the brick kilns.* That is how he dealt with the people of all the Ammonite towns. Then David and all the army returned to Jerusalem.

The Rape of Tamar

13 Now David's son Absalom had a beautiful sister named Tamar. And Amnon, her half brother, fell desperately in love with her. [2]Amnon became so obsessed with Tamar that he became ill. She was a virgin, and Amnon thought he could never have her.

[3]But Amnon had a very crafty friend—his cousin Jonadab. He was the son of David's brother Shimea.* [4]One day Jonadab said to Amnon, "What's the trouble? Why should the son of a king look so dejected morning after morning?"

So Amnon told him, "I am in love with Tamar, my brother Absalom's sister."

[5]"Well," Jonadab said, "I'll tell you what to do. Go back to bed and pretend you are ill. When your father comes to see you, ask him to let Tamar come and prepare some food for you. Tell him you'll feel better if she prepares it as you watch and feeds you with her own hands."

[6]So Amnon lay down and pretended to be sick. And when the king came to see him, Amnon asked him, "Please let my sister Tamar come and cook my favorite dish* as I watch. Then I can eat it from her own hands." [7]So David agreed and sent Tamar to Amnon's house to prepare some food for him.

[8]When Tamar arrived at Amnon's house, she went to the place where he was lying down so he could watch her mix some dough. Then she baked his favorite dish for him. [9]But when she set the serving tray before him, he refused to eat. "Everyone get out of here," Amnon told his servants. So they all left.

[10]Then he said to Tamar, "Now bring the food into my bedroom and feed it to me here." So Tamar took his favorite dish

12:14 As in Dead Sea Scrolls; Masoretic Text reads *the enemies of the LORD.* **12:20** Hebrew *anointed himself.* **12:24** Hebrew *he;* an alternate Hebrew reading and some Hebrew manuscripts read *she.* **12:25** As in Greek version; Hebrew reads *because of the LORD.* **12:26** Or *the royal city.* **12:27** Or *captured the city of water.* **12:30a** Or *from the head of Milcom* (as in Greek version). Milcom, also called Molech, was the god of the Ammonites. **12:30b** Hebrew *1 talent* [34 kilograms]. **12:31a** Hebrew *He also brought out the people [of Rabbah] and put them under.* **12:31b** Hebrew *and he made them pass through the brick kilns.* **13:3** Hebrew *Shimeah* (also in 13:32), a variant spelling of Shimea; compare 1 Chr 2:13. **13:6** Or *a couple of cakes;* also in 13:8, 10.

▸ **12:19-25** *See* ***Mourning****, page 892.*

to him. [11]But as she was feeding him, he grabbed her and demanded, "Come to bed with me, my darling sister."

[12]"No, my brother!" she cried. "Don't be foolish! Don't do this to me! Such wicked things aren't done in Israel. [13]Where could I go in my shame? And you would be called one of the greatest fools in Israel. Please, just speak to the king about it, and he will let you marry me."

[14]But Amnon wouldn't listen to her, and since he was stronger than she was, he raped her. [15]Then suddenly Amnon's love turned to hate, and he hated her even more than he had loved her. "Get out of here!" he snarled at her.

[16]"No, no!" Tamar cried. "Sending me away now is worse than what you've already done to me."

But Amnon wouldn't listen to her. [17]He shouted for his servant and demanded, "Throw this woman out, and lock the door behind her!"

[18]So the servant put her out and locked the door behind her. She was wearing a long, beautiful robe,* as was the custom in those days for the king's virgin daughters. [19]But now Tamar tore her robe and put ashes on her head. And then, with her face in her hands, she went away crying.

[20]Her brother Absalom saw her and asked, "Is it true that Amnon has been with you? Well, my sister, keep quiet for now, since he's your brother. Don't you worry about it." So Tamar lived as a desolate woman in her brother Absalom's house.

[21]When King David heard what had happened, he was very angry.* [22]And though Absalom never spoke to Amnon about this, he hated Amnon deeply because of what he had done to his sister.

Absalom's Revenge on Amnon

[23]Two years later, when Absalom's sheep were being sheared at Baal-hazor near Ephraim, Absalom invited all the king's sons to come to a feast. [24]He went to the king and said, "My sheep-shearers are now at work. Would the king and his servants please come to celebrate the occasion with me?"

[25]The king replied, "No, my son. If we all came, we would be too much of a burden on you." Absalom pressed him, but the king would not come, though he gave Absalom his blessing.

[26]"Well, then," Absalom said, "if you can't come, how about sending my brother Amnon with us?"

"Why Amnon?" the king asked. [27]But Absalom kept on pressing the king until he finally agreed to let all his sons attend, including Amnon. So Absalom prepared a feast fit for a king.*

[28]Absalom told his men, "Wait until Amnon gets drunk; then at my signal, kill him! Don't be afraid. I'm the one who has given the command. Take courage and do it!" [29]So at Absalom's signal they murdered Amnon. Then the other sons of the king jumped on their mules and fled.

[30]As they were on the way back to Jerusalem, this report reached David: "Absalom has killed all the king's sons; not one is left alive!" [31]The king got up, tore his robe, and threw himself on the ground. His advisers also tore their clothes in horror and sorrow.

[32]But just then Jonadab, the son of David's

Amnon

Amnon was David's firstborn son (2 Samuel 3:2) and as such expected to be the future king, no doubt thinking therefore that he could do what he liked. He fell in love with Tamar, his half-sister, but she didn't respond, leaving him more and more obsessed with her. He finally raped her, but he quickly turned against her once his desires were satisfied. Sadly, David took no action—perhaps he felt he had lost one son already (chapter 12) and didn't want to lose another. So Tamar's brother, Absalom, decided to take matters into his own hands. He waited two years but then took revenge on Amnon by killing him while he was drunk at a party. It seems everyone had seen this coming except David (13:32).

▸ *See also **Rape**, page 43.*

brother Shimea, arrived and said, "No, don't believe that all the king's sons have been killed! It was only Amnon! Absalom has been plotting this ever since Amnon raped his sister Tamar. 33No, my lord the king, your sons aren't all dead! It was only Amnon." 34Meanwhile Absalom escaped.

Then the watchman on the Jerusalem wall saw a great crowd coming down the hill on the road from the west. He ran to tell the king, "I see a crowd of people coming from the Horonaim road along the side of the hill."*

35"Look!" Jonadab told the king. "There they are now! The king's sons are coming, just as I said."

36They soon arrived, weeping and sobbing, and the king and all his servants wept bitterly with them. 37And David mourned many days for his son Amnon.

Absalom fled to his grandfather, Talmai son of Ammihud, the king of Geshur. 38He stayed there in Geshur for three years. 39And King David,* now reconciled to Amnon's death, longed to be reunited with his son Absalom.*

Joab Arranges for Absalom's Return

14 Joab realized how much the king longed to see Absalom. 2So he sent for a woman from Tekoa who had a reputation for great wisdom. He said to her, "Pretend you are in mourning; wear mourning clothes and don't put on lotions.* Act like a woman who has been mourning for the dead for a long time. 3Then go to the king and tell him the story I am about to tell you." Then Joab told her what to say.

4When the woman from Tekoa approached* the king, she bowed with her face to the ground in deep respect and cried out, "O king! Help me!"

5"What's the trouble?" the king asked.

"Alas, I am a widow!" she replied. "My husband is dead. 6My two sons had a fight out in the field. And since no one was there to stop it, one of them was killed. 7Now the rest of the family is demanding, 'Let us have your son. We will execute him for murdering his brother. He doesn't deserve to inherit his family's property.' They want to extinguish the only coal I have left, and my husband's name and family will disappear from the face of the earth."

8"Leave it to me," the king told her. "Go home, and I'll see to it that no one touches him."

9"Oh, thank you, my lord the king," the woman from Tekoa replied. "If you are criticized for helping me, let the blame fall on me and on my father's house, and let the king and his throne be innocent."

10"If anyone objects," the king said, "bring him to me. I can assure you he will never harm you again!"

11Then she said, "Please swear to me by the LORD your God that you won't let anyone take vengeance against my son. I want no more bloodshed."

"As surely as the LORD lives," he replied, "not a hair on your son's head will be disturbed!"

12"Please allow me to ask one more thing of my lord the king," she said.

"Go ahead and speak," he responded.

13She replied, "Why don't you do as much for the people of God as you have promised to do for me? You have convicted yourself in making this decision, because you have refused to bring home your own banished son. 14All of us must die eventually. Our lives are like water spilled out on the ground, which cannot be gathered up again. But God does not just sweep life away; instead, he devises ways to bring us back when we have been separated from him.

15"I have come to plead with my lord the king because people have threatened me. I said to myself, 'Perhaps the king will listen to me 16and rescue us from those who would cut us off from the inheritance* God has given us. 17Yes, my lord the king will give us peace of mind again.' I know that you are like an angel of God in discerning good from evil. May the LORD your God be with you."

18"I must know one thing," the king replied, "and tell me the truth."

"Yes, my lord the king," she responded.

19"Did Joab put you up to this?"

And the woman replied, "My lord the king, how can I deny it? Nobody can hide anything from you. Yes, Joab sent me and

13:18 Or *a robe with sleeves,* or *an ornamented robe.* The meaning of the Hebrew is uncertain. **13:21** Dead Sea Scrolls and Greek version add *But he did not punish his son Amnon, because he loved him, for he was his firstborn.* **13:27** As in Greek and Latin versions (compare also Dead Sea Scrolls); the Hebrew text lacks this sentence. **13:34** As in Greek version; Hebrew lacks this sentence. **13:39a** Dead Sea Scrolls and Greek version read *And the spirit of the king.* **13:39b** Or *no longer felt a need to go out after Absalom.* **14:2** Hebrew *don't anoint yourself with oil.* **14:4** As in many Hebrew manuscripts and Greek and Syriac versions; Masoretic Text reads *spoke to.* **14:16** Or *the property;* or *the people.*

told me what to say. 20He did it to place the
matter before you in a different light. But
you are as wise as an angel of God, and
you understand everything that happens
among us!"
21So the king sent for Joab and told him,
"All right, go and bring back the young man
Absalom."
22Joab bowed with his face to the ground
in deep respect and said, "At last I know that
I have gained your approval, my lord the
king, for you have granted me this request!"
23Then Joab went to Geshur and brought
Absalom back to Jerusalem. 24But the king
gave this order: "Absalom may go to his own
house, but he must never come into my
presence." So Absalom did not see the king.

Absalom Reconciled to David

25Now Absalom was praised as the most
handsome man in all Israel. He was flawless from head to foot. 26He cut his hair only
once a year, and then only because it was so
heavy. When he weighed it out, it came to
five pounds!* 27He had three sons and one
daughter. His daughter's name was Tamar,
and she was very beautiful.
28Absalom lived in Jerusalem for two
years, but he never got to see the king.
29Then Absalom sent for Joab to ask him to
intercede for him, but Joab refused to come.
Absalom sent for him a second time, but
again Joab refused to come. 30So Absalom
said to his servants, "Go and set fire to
Joab's barley field, the field next to mine."
So they set his field on fire, as Absalom had
commanded.
31Then Joab came to Absalom at his house
and demanded, "Why did your servants set
my field on fire?"
32And Absalom replied, "Because I
wanted you to ask the king why he brought
me back from Geshur if he didn't intend to
see me. I might as well have stayed there.
Let me see the king; if he finds me guilty of
anything, then let him kill me."
33So Joab told the king what Absalom
had said. Then at last David summoned
Absalom, who came and bowed low before
the king, and the king kissed him.

Absalom's Rebellion

15 After this, Absalom bought a chariot
and horses, and he hired fifty bodyguards to run ahead of him. 2He got up early
every morning and went out to the gate of
the city. When people brought a case to
the king for judgment, Absalom would ask
where in Israel they were from, and they
would tell him their tribe. 3Then Absalom

The Absalom spirit

Absalom, David's third son, murdered his brother Amnon for his rape of Absalom's sister Tamar (2 Samuel 13:23-39), and when David didn't punish him, Absalom interpreted this as weakness. In his ambition for status and power, he slowly started undermining David's rule, commiserating with those who came to bring their causes to David, who was too busy to see them. He started saying things like, "If only I were in a position to do something about it . . ."

Over a period of four years behaving like this, Absalom gradually "stole the hearts of all the people of Israel" (15:6). At last, he made his bid for power and had his followers proclaim him king. But rather than dealing with his son, David fled. Things went from bad to worse, climaxing in a civil war. It was only through the action of ruthless Joab that Absalom was hunted down and killed and the rightful king restored.

The Absalom spirit is still at work whenever people start grumbling about leaders behind their backs, or start exacerbating others' discontent, or start positioning themselves to take over, forgetting that the Bible warns us that "wherever there is jealousy and selfish ambition, there you will find disorder and evil of every kind" (James 3:16). If ever we see such tendencies in ourselves, this story shows the importance of dealing with them ruthlessly. Otherwise we are doing Satan's work for him.

would say, "You've really got a strong case here! It's too bad the king doesn't have anyone to hear it. 4I wish I were the judge. Then everyone could bring their cases to me for judgment, and I would give them justice!"

5When people tried to bow before him, Absalom wouldn't let them. Instead, he took them by the hand and kissed them. 6Absalom did this with everyone who came to the king for judgment, and so he stole the hearts of all the people of Israel.

7After four years,* Absalom said to the king, "Let me go to Hebron to offer a sacrifice to the LORD and fulfill a vow I made to him. 8For while your servant was at Geshur in Aram, I promised to sacrifice to the LORD in Hebron* if he would bring me back to Jerusalem."

9"All right," the king told him. "Go and fulfill your vow."

So Absalom went to Hebron. 10But while he was there, he sent secret messengers to all the tribes of Israel to stir up a rebellion against the king. "As soon as you hear the ram's horn," his message read, "you are to say, 'Absalom has been crowned king in Hebron.'" 11He took 200 men from Jerusalem with him as guests, but they knew nothing of his intentions. 12While Absalom was offering the sacrifices, he sent for Ahithophel, one of David's counselors who lived in Giloh. Soon many others also joined Absalom, and the conspiracy gained momentum.

David Escapes from Jerusalem

13A messenger soon arrived in Jerusalem to tell David, "All Israel has joined Absalom in a conspiracy against you!"

14"Then we must flee at once, or it will be too late!" David urged his men. "Hurry! If we get out of the city before Absalom arrives, both we and the city of Jerusalem will be spared from disaster."

15"We are with you," his advisers replied. "Do what you think is best."

16So the king and all his household set out at once. He left no one behind except ten of his concubines to look after the palace. 17The king and all his people set out on foot, pausing at the last house 18to let all the king's men move past to lead the way. There were 600 men from Gath who had come with David, along with the king's bodyguard.*

19Then the king turned and said to Ittai, a leader of the men from Gath, "Why are you coming with us? Go on back to King Absalom, for you are a guest in Israel, a foreigner in exile. 20You arrived only recently, and should I force you today to wander with us? I don't even know where we will go. Go on back and take your kinsmen with you, and may the LORD show you his unfailing love and faithfulness.*"

21But Ittai said to the king, "I vow by the LORD and by your own life that I will go wherever my lord the king goes, no matter what happens—whether it means life or death."

22David replied, "All right, come with us." So Ittai and all his men and their families went along.

23Everyone cried loudly as the king and his followers passed by. They crossed the Kidron Valley and then went out toward the wilderness.

24Zadok and all the Levites also came along, carrying the Ark of the Covenant of God. They set down the Ark of God, and Abiathar offered sacrifices* until everyone had passed out of the city.

25Then the king instructed Zadok to take the Ark of God back into the city. "If the LORD sees fit," David said, "he will bring me back to see the Ark and the Tabernacle* again. 26But if he is through with me, then let him do what seems best to him."

27The king also told Zadok the priest, "Look,* here is my plan. You and Abiathar* should return quietly to the city with your son Ahimaaz and Abiathar's son Jonathan. 28I will stop at the shallows of the Jordan River* and wait there for a report from you." 29So Zadok and Abiathar took the Ark of God back to the city and stayed there.

30David walked up the road to the Mount of Olives, weeping as he went. His head was covered and his feet were bare as a sign of mourning. And the people who were with him covered their heads and wept as they climbed the hill. 31When someone told David that his adviser Ahithophel was now

14:26 Hebrew *200 shekels* [2.3 kilograms] *by the royal standard.* **15:7** As in Greek and Syriac versions; Hebrew reads *forty years.* **15:8** As in some Greek manuscripts; Hebrew lacks *in Hebron.* **15:18** Hebrew *the Kerethites and Pelethites.* **15:20** As in Greek version; Hebrew reads *and may unfailing love and faithfulness go with you.* **15:24** Or *Abiathar went up.* **15:25** Hebrew *and his dwelling place.* **15:27a** As in Greek version; Hebrew reads *Are you a seer?* or *Do you see?* **15:27b** Hebrew lacks *and Abiathar;* compare 15:29. **15:28** Hebrew *at the crossing points of the wilderness.*

backing Absalom, David prayed, "O LORD,
let Ahithophel give Absalom foolish
advice!"
[32]When David reached the summit of the
Mount of Olives where people worshiped
God, Hushai the Arkite was waiting there
for him. Hushai had torn his clothing and
put dirt on his head as a sign of mourning.
[33]But David told him, "If you go with me,
you will only be a burden. [34]Return to Jerusalem and tell Absalom, 'I will now be your
adviser, O king, just as I was your father's
adviser in the past.' Then you can frustrate
and counter Ahithophel's advice. [35]Zadok
and Abiathar, the priests, will be there. Tell
them about the plans being made in the
king's palace, [36]and they will send their
sons Ahimaaz and Jonathan to tell me what
is going on."
[37]So David's friend Hushai returned to
Jerusalem, getting there just as Absalom
arrived.

David and Ziba

16 When David had gone a little beyond
the summit of the Mount of Olives,
Ziba, the servant of Mephibosheth,* was
waiting there for him. He had two donkeys
loaded with 200 loaves of bread, 100 clusters of raisins, 100 bunches of summer fruit,
and a wineskin full of wine.
[2]"What are these for?" the king asked
Ziba.
Ziba replied, "The donkeys are for the
king's people to ride on, and the bread
and summer fruit are for the young men to
eat. The wine is for those who become exhausted in the wilderness."
[3]"And where is Mephibosheth, Saul's
grandson?" the king asked him.
"He stayed in Jerusalem," Ziba replied.
"He said, 'Today I will get back the kingdom
of my grandfather Saul.'"
[4]"In that case," the king told Ziba, "I give
you everything Mephibosheth owns."
"I bow before you," Ziba replied. "May
I always be pleasing to you, my lord the
king."

Shimei Curses David

[5]As King David came to Bahurim, a man
came out of the village cursing them. It was
Shimei son of Gera, from the same clan as
Saul's family. [6]He threw stones at the king
and the king's officers and all the mighty
warriors who surrounded him. [7]"Get out
of here, you murderer, you scoundrel!" he
shouted at David. [8]"The LORD is paying you
back for all the bloodshed in Saul's clan.
You stole his throne, and now the LORD has
given it to your son Absalom. At last you will
taste some of your own medicine, for you
are a murderer!"
[9]"Why should this dead dog curse my
lord the king?" Abishai son of Zeruiah demanded. "Let me go over and cut off his
head!"
[10]"No!" the king said. "Who asked your
opinion, you sons of Zeruiah! If the LORD
has told him to curse me, who are you to
stop him?"
[11]Then David said to Abishai and to all
his servants, "My own son is trying to kill
me. Doesn't this relative of Saul* have even
more reason to do so? Leave him alone and
let him curse, for the LORD has told him to
do it. [12]And perhaps the LORD will see that
I am being wronged* and will bless me
because of these curses today." [13]So David
and his men continued down the road, and
Shimei kept pace with them on a nearby
hillside, cursing and throwing stones and
dirt at David.
[14]The king and all who were with him
grew weary along the way, so they rested
when they reached the Jordan River.*

Ahithophel Advises Absalom

[15]Meanwhile, Absalom and all the army of
Israel arrived at Jerusalem, accompanied by
Ahithophel. [16]When David's friend Hushai
the Arkite arrived, he went immediately to
see Absalom. "Long live the king!" he exclaimed. "Long live the king!"
[17]"Is this the way you treat your friend
David?" Absalom asked him. "Why aren't
you with him?"
[18]"I'm here because I belong to the man
who is chosen by the LORD and by all the
men of Israel," Hushai replied. [19]"And
anyway, why shouldn't I serve you? Just as I
was your father's adviser, now I will be your
adviser!"
[20]Then Absalom turned to Ahithophel
and asked him, "What should I do next?"
[21]Ahithophel told him, "Go and sleep with
your father's concubines, for he has left
them here to look after the palace. Then all
Israel will know that you have insulted your
father beyond hope of reconciliation, and

they will throw their support to you." 22 So they set up a tent on the palace roof where everyone could see it, and Absalom went in and had sex with his father's concubines.

23 Absalom followed Ahithophel's advice, just as David had done. For every word Ahithophel spoke seemed as wise as though it had come directly from the mouth of God.

17 Now Ahithophel urged Absalom, "Let me choose 12,000 men to start out after David tonight. 2 I will catch up with him while he is weary and discouraged. He and his troops will panic, and everyone will run away. Then I will kill only the king, 3 and I will bring all the people back to you as a bride returns to her husband. After all, it is only one man's life that you seek.* Then you will be at peace with all the people." 4 This plan seemed good to Absalom and to all the elders of Israel.

Hushai Counters Ahithophel's Advice

5 But then Absalom said, "Bring in Hushai the Arkite. Let's see what he thinks about this." 6 When Hushai arrived, Absalom told him what Ahithophel had said. Then he asked, "What is your opinion? Should we follow Ahithophel's advice? If not, what do you suggest?"

7 "Well," Hushai replied to Absalom, "this time Ahithophel has made a mistake. 8 You know your father and his men; they are mighty warriors. Right now they are as enraged as a mother bear who has been robbed of her cubs. And remember that your father is an experienced man of war. He won't be spending the night among the troops. 9 He has probably already hidden in some pit or cave. And when he comes out and attacks and a few of your men fall, there will be panic among your troops, and the word will spread that Absalom's men are being slaughtered. 10 Then even the bravest soldiers, though they have the heart of a lion, will be paralyzed with fear. For all Israel knows what a mighty warrior your father is and how courageous his men are.

11 "I recommend that you mobilize the entire army of Israel, bringing them from as far away as Dan in the north and Beersheba in the south. That way you will have an army as numerous as the sand on the seashore. And I advise that you personally lead the troops. 12 When we find David, we'll fall on him like dew that falls on the ground. Then neither he nor any of his men will be left alive. 13 And if David were to escape into some town, you will have all Israel there at your command. Then we can take ropes and drag the walls of the town into the nearest valley until every stone is torn down."

14 Then Absalom and all the men of Israel said, "Hushai's advice is better than Ahithophel's." For the LORD had determined to defeat the counsel of Ahithophel, which really was the better plan, so that he could bring disaster on Absalom!

Hushai Warns David to Escape

15 Hushai told Zadok and Abiathar, the priests, what Ahithophel had said to Absalom and the elders of Israel and what he himself had advised instead. 16 "Quick!" he told them. "Find David and urge him not to stay at the shallows of the Jordan River* tonight. He must go across at once into the wilderness beyond. Otherwise he will die and his entire army with him."

17 Jonathan and Ahimaaz had been staying at En-rogel so as not to be seen entering and leaving the city. Arrangements had been made for a servant girl to bring them the message they were to take to King David. 18 But a boy spotted them at En-rogel, and he told Absalom about it. So they quickly escaped to Bahurim, where a man hid them down inside a well in his courtyard. 19 The man's wife put a cloth over the top of the well and scattered grain on it to dry in the sun; so no one suspected they were there.

20 When Absalom's men arrived, they asked her, "Have you seen Ahimaaz and Jonathan?"

The woman replied, "They were here, but they crossed over the brook." Absalom's men looked for them without success and returned to Jerusalem.

21 Then the two men crawled out of the well and hurried on to King David. "Quick!" they told him, "cross the Jordan tonight!" And they told him how Ahithophel had advised that he be captured and killed. 22 So

16:1 *Mephibosheth* is another name for Merib-baal. **16:11** Hebrew *this Benjaminite.* **16:12** As in Greek and Syriac versions; Hebrew reads *see my iniquity.* **16:14** As in Greek version (see also 17:16); Hebrew reads *when they reached their destination.* **17:3** As in Greek version; Hebrew reads *like the return of all is the man whom you seek.* **17:16** Hebrew *at the crossing points of the wilderness.*

David and all the people with him went across the Jordan River during the night, and they were all on the other bank before dawn.

[23]When Ahithophel realized that his advice had not been followed, he saddled his donkey, went to his hometown, set his affairs in order, and hanged himself. He died there and was buried in the family tomb.

[24]David soon arrived at Mahanaim. By now, Absalom had mobilized the entire army of Israel and was leading his troops across the Jordan River. [25]Absalom had appointed Amasa as commander of his army, replacing Joab, who had been commander under David. (Amasa was Joab's cousin. His father was Jether,* an Ishmaelite.* His mother, Abigail daughter of Nahash, was the sister of Joab's mother, Zeruiah.) [26]Absalom and the Israelite army set up camp in the land of Gilead.

[27]When David arrived at Mahanaim, he was warmly greeted by Shobi son of Nahash, who came from Rabbah of the Ammonites, and by Makir son of Ammiel from Lo-debar, and by Barzillai of Gilead from Rogelim. [28]They brought sleeping mats, cooking pots, serving bowls, wheat and barley, flour and roasted grain, beans, lentils, [29]honey, butter, sheep, goats, and cheese for David and those who were with him. For they said, "You must all be very hungry and tired and thirsty after your long march through the wilderness."

Absalom's Defeat and Death

18 David now mustered the men who were with him and appointed generals and captains* to lead them. [2]He sent the troops out in three groups, placing one group under Joab, one under Joab's brother Abishai son of Zeruiah, and one under Ittai, the man from Gath. The king told his troops, "I am going out with you."

[3]But his men objected strongly. "You must not go," they urged. "If we have to turn and run—and even if half of us die—it will make no difference to Absalom's troops; they will be looking only for you. You are worth 10,000 of us,* and it is better that you stay here in the town and send help if we need it."

[4]"If you think that's the best plan, I'll do it," the king answered. So he stood alongside the gate of the town as all the troops marched out in groups of hundreds and of thousands.

[5]And the king gave this command to Joab, Abishai, and Ittai: "For my sake, deal gently with young Absalom." And all the troops heard the king give this order to his commanders.

[6]So the battle began in the forest of Ephraim, [7]and the Israelite troops were beaten back by David's men. There was a great slaughter that day, and 20,000 men laid down their lives. [8]The battle raged all across the countryside, and more men died because of the forest than were killed by the sword.

[9]During the battle, Absalom happened to come upon some of David's men. He tried to

Joab

Joab, David's nephew, became commander of David's army as a reward for leading the successful attack on Jerusalem (1 Chronicles 11:4-7). While utterly loyal to David, he was also utterly ruthless to gain his end results. So we find him murdering Abner, commander of the northern armies, when he thought David had been too gracious to him (2 Samuel 3:22-30). When Absalom stirred up a rebellion against David, David told Joab not to harm his son (18:5), but Joab, believing he understood the situation better than David, disobeyed and personally killed him (18:14-15). And when David grieved for Absalom, Joab told him to pull himself together and act like a king (19:1-7). Perhaps weary of David's constant weakness, he sided in later life with David's eldest surviving son, Adonijah, when he made a bid to become king rather than Solomon. But Joab died as he lived, by the sword—killed by one of Solomon's men as he clung to the horns of the altar in an attempt to seek clemency (1 Kings 2:28-34; see also Exodus 21:12-14). He had given no mercy in life, and now he found none.

escape on his mule, but as he rode beneath the thick branches of a great tree, his hair* got caught in the tree. His mule kept going and left him dangling in the air. 10One of David's men saw what had happened and told Joab, "I saw Absalom dangling from a great tree."

11"What?" Joab demanded. "You saw him there and didn't kill him? I would have rewarded you with ten pieces of silver* and a hero's belt!"

12"I would not kill the king's son for even a thousand pieces of silver,*" the man replied to Joab. "We all heard the king say to you and Abishai and Ittai, 'For my sake, please spare young Absalom.' 13And if I had betrayed the king by killing his son—and the king would certainly find out who did it—you yourself would be the first to abandon me."

14"Enough of this nonsense," Joab said. Then he took three daggers and plunged them into Absalom's heart as he dangled, still alive, in the great tree. 15Ten of Joab's young armor bearers then surrounded Absalom and killed him.

16Then Joab blew the ram's horn, and his men returned from chasing the army of Israel. 17They threw Absalom's body into a deep pit in the forest and piled a great heap of stones over it. And all Israel fled to their homes.

18During his lifetime, Absalom had built a monument to himself in the King's Valley, for he said, "I have no son to carry on my name." He named the monument after himself, and it is known as Absalom's Monument to this day.

David Mourns Absalom's Death

19Then Zadok's son Ahimaaz said, "Let me run to the king with the good news that the LORD has rescued him from his enemies."

20"No," Joab told him, "it wouldn't be good news to the king that his son is dead. You can be my messenger another time, but not today."

21Then Joab said to a man from Ethiopia,* "Go tell the king what you have seen." The man bowed and ran off.

22But Ahimaaz continued to plead with Joab, "Whatever happens, please let me go, too."

"Why should you go, my son?" Joab replied. "There will be no reward for your news."

23"Yes, but let me go anyway," he begged.

Joab finally said, "All right, go ahead." So Ahimaaz took the less demanding route by way of the plain and ran to Mahanaim ahead of the Ethiopian.

24While David was sitting between the inner and outer gates of the town, the watchman climbed to the roof of the gateway by the wall. As he looked, he saw a lone man running toward them. 25He shouted the news down to David, and the king replied, "If he is alone, he has news."

As the messenger came closer, 26the watchman saw another man running toward them. He shouted down, "Here comes another one!"

The king replied, "He also will have news."

27"The first man runs like Ahimaaz son of Zadok," the watchman said.

"He is a good man and comes with good news," the king replied.

28Then Ahimaaz cried out to the king, "Everything is all right!" He bowed before the king with his face to the ground and said, "Praise to the LORD your God, who has handed over the rebels who dared to stand against my lord the king."

29"What about young Absalom?" the king demanded. "Is he all right?"

Ahimaaz replied, "When Joab told me to come, there was a lot of commotion. But I didn't know what was happening."

30"Wait here," the king told him. So Ahimaaz stepped aside.

31Then the man from Ethiopia arrived and said, "I have good news for my lord the king. Today the LORD has rescued you from all those who rebelled against you."

32"What about young Absalom?" the king demanded. "Is he all right?"

And the Ethiopian replied, "May all of your enemies, my lord the king, both now and in the future, share the fate of that young man!"

33*The king was overcome with emotion. He went up to the room over the gateway and burst into tears. And as he went, he

17:25a Hebrew *Ithra,* a variant spelling of Jether. **17:25b** As in some Greek manuscripts (see also 1 Chr 2:17); Hebrew reads *an Israelite.* **18:1** Hebrew *appointed commanders of thousands and commanders of hundreds.* **18:3** As in two Hebrew manuscripts and some Greek and Latin manuscripts; most Hebrew manuscripts read *Now there are 10,000 like us.* **18:9** Hebrew *his head.* **18:11** Hebrew *10 [shekels] of silver,* about 4 ounces or 114 grams in weight. **18:12** Hebrew *1,000 [shekels] of silver,* about 25 pounds or 11.4 kilograms in weight. **18:21** Hebrew *from Cush;* similarly in 18:23, 31, 32. **18:33** Verse 18:33 is numbered 19:1 in Hebrew text.

cried, "O my son Absalom! My son, my son
Absalom! If only I had died instead of you!
O Absalom, my son, my son."

Joab Rebukes the King

19 1*Word soon reached Joab that the
king was weeping and mourning for
Absalom. 2As all the people heard of the
king's deep grief for his son, the joy of that
day's victory was turned into deep sadness.
3They crept back into the town that day as
though they were ashamed and had deserted in battle. 4The king covered his face
with his hands and kept on crying, "O my
son Absalom! O Absalom, my son, my son!"
5Then Joab went to the king's room and
said to him, "We saved your life today
and the lives of your sons, your daughters,
and your wives and concubines. Yet you act
like this, making us feel ashamed of ourselves. 6You seem to love those who hate you
and hate those who love you. You have made
it clear today that your commanders and
troops mean nothing to you. It seems that
if Absalom had lived and all of us had died,
you would be pleased. 7Now go out there and
congratulate your troops, for I swear by the
LORD that if you don't go out, not a single one
of them will remain here tonight. Then you
will be worse off than ever before."
8So the king went out and took his seat
at the town gate, and as the news spread
throughout the town that he was there,
everyone went to him.

Meanwhile, the Israelites who had supported Absalom fled to their homes. 9And
throughout all the tribes of Israel there was
much discussion and argument going on.
The people were saying, "The king rescued
us from our enemies and saved us from the
Philistines, but Absalom chased him out
of the country. 10Now Absalom, whom we
anointed to rule over us, is dead. Why not
ask David to come back and be our king
again?"
11Then King David sent Zadok and Abiathar, the priests, to say to the elders
of Judah, "Why are you the last ones to
welcome back the king into his palace? For
I have heard that all Israel is ready. 12You are
my relatives, my own tribe, my own flesh
and blood! So why are you the last ones to
welcome back the king?" 13And David told
them to tell Amasa, "Since you are my own
flesh and blood, like Joab, may God strike
me and even kill me if I do not appoint you
as commander of my army in his place."
14Then Amasa* convinced all the men of
Judah, and they responded unanimously.
They sent word to the king, "Return to us,
and bring back all who are with you."

David's Return to Jerusalem

15So the king started back to Jerusalem. And
when he arrived at the Jordan River, the
people of Judah came to Gilgal to meet him
and escort him across the river. 16Shimei
son of Gera, the man from Bahurim in Benjamin, hurried across with the men of Judah
to welcome King David. 17A thousand other
men from the tribe of Benjamin were with
him, including Ziba, the chief servant of the
house of Saul, and Ziba's fifteen sons and
twenty servants. They rushed down to the
Jordan to meet the king. 18They crossed the
shallows of the Jordan to bring the king's
household across the river, helping him in
every way they could.

David's Mercy to Shimei

As the king was about to cross the river,
Shimei fell down before him. 19"My lord
the king, please forgive me," he pleaded.
"Forget the terrible thing your servant did
when you left Jerusalem. May the king put
it out of his mind. 20I know how much I
sinned. That is why I have come here today,
the very first person in all Israel* to greet my
lord the king."
21Then Abishai son of Zeruiah said,
"Shimei should die, for he cursed the
LORD's anointed king!"
22"Who asked your opinion, you sons of
Zeruiah!" David exclaimed. "Why have you
become my adversary* today? This is not a
day for execution, for today I am once again
the king of Israel!" 23Then, turning to Shimei,
David vowed, "Your life will be spared."

David's Kindness to Mephibosheth

24Now Mephibosheth,* Saul's grandson,
came down from Jerusalem to meet the
king. He had not cared for his feet, trimmed
his beard, or washed his clothes since the
day the king left Jerusalem. 25"Why didn't
you come with me, Mephibosheth?" the
king asked him.
26Mephibosheth replied, "My lord the
king, my servant Ziba deceived me. I told
him, 'Saddle my donkey* so I can go with the

king.' For as you know I am crippled. [27]Ziba has slandered me by saying that I refused to come. But I know that my lord the king is like an angel of God, so do what you think is best. [28]All my relatives and I could expect only death from you, my lord, but instead you have honored me by allowing me to eat at your own table! What more can I ask?"

[29]"You've said enough," David replied. "I've decided that you and Ziba will divide your land equally between you."

[30]"Give him all of it," Mephibosheth said. "I am content just to have you safely back again, my lord the king!"

David's Kindness to Barzillai

[31]Barzillai of Gilead had come down from Rogelim to escort the king across the Jordan. [32]He was very old—eighty years of age—and very wealthy. He was the one who had provided food for the king during his stay in Mahanaim. [33]"Come across with me and live in Jerusalem," the king said to Barzillai. "I will take care of you there."

[34]"No," he replied, "I am far too old to go with the king to Jerusalem. [35]I am eighty years old today, and I can no longer enjoy anything. Food and wine are no longer tasty, and I cannot hear the singers as they sing. I would only be a burden to my lord the king. [36]Just to go across the Jordan River with the king is all the honor I need! [37]Then let me return again to die in my own town, where my father and mother are buried. But here is your servant, my son Kimham. Let him go with my lord the king and receive whatever you want to give him."

[38]"Good," the king agreed. "Kimham will go with me, and I will help him in any way you would like. And I will do for you anything you want." [39]So all the people crossed the Jordan with the king. After David had blessed Barzillai and kissed him, Barzillai returned to his own home.

[40]The king then crossed over to Gilgal, taking Kimham with him. All the troops of Judah and half the troops of Israel escorted the king on his way.

An Argument over the King

[41]But all the men of Israel complained to the king, "The men of Judah stole the king and didn't give us the honor of helping take you, your household, and all your men across the Jordan."

[42]The men of Judah replied, "The king is one of our own kinsmen. Why should this make you angry? We haven't eaten any of the king's food or received any special favors!"

[43]"But there are ten tribes in Israel," the others replied. "So we have ten times as much right to the king as you do. What right do you have to treat us with such contempt? Weren't we the first to speak of bringing him back to be our king again?" The argument continued back and forth, and the men of Judah spoke even more harshly than the men of Israel.

The Revolt of Sheba

20 There happened to be a troublemaker there named Sheba son of Bicri, a man from the tribe of Benjamin. Sheba blew a ram's horn and began to chant:

"Down with the dynasty of David!
  We have no interest in the son of Jesse.
Come on, you men of Israel,
  back to your homes!"

[2]So all the men of Israel deserted David and followed Sheba son of Bicri. But the men of Judah stayed with their king and escorted him from the Jordan River to Jerusalem.

[3]When David came to his palace in Jerusalem, he took the ten concubines he had left to look after the palace and placed them in seclusion. Their needs were provided for, but he no longer slept with them. So each of them lived like a widow until she died.

[4]Then the king told Amasa, "Mobilize the army of Judah within three days, and report back at that time." [5]So Amasa went out to notify Judah, but it took him longer than the time he had been given.

[6]Then David said to Abishai, "Sheba son of Bicri is going to hurt us more than Absalom did. Quick, take my troops and chase after him before he gets into a fortified town where we can't reach him."

[7]So Abishai and Joab,* together with the king's bodyguard* and all the mighty

19:1 Verses 19:1-43 are numbered 19:2-44 in Hebrew text. **19:14** Or *David;* Hebrew reads *he.* **19:20** Hebrew *in the house of Joseph.* **19:22** Or *my prosecutor.* **19:24** *Mephibosheth* is another name for Merib-baal. **19:26** As in Greek, Syriac, and Latin versions; Hebrew reads *I will saddle a donkey for myself.* **20:7a** Hebrew *So Joab's men.* **20:7b** Hebrew *the Kerethites and Pelethites;* also in 20:23.

warriors, set out from Jerusalem to go after Sheba. 8 As they arrived at the great stone in Gibeon, Amasa met them. Joab was wearing his military tunic with a dagger strapped to his belt. As he stepped forward to greet Amasa, he slipped the dagger from its sheath.*

9 "How are you, my cousin?" Joab said and took him by the beard with his right hand as though to kiss him. 10 Amasa didn't notice the dagger in his left hand, and Joab stabbed him in the stomach with it so that his insides gushed out onto the ground. Joab did not need to strike again, and Amasa soon died. Joab and his brother Abishai left him lying there and continued after Sheba.

11 One of Joab's young men shouted to Amasa's troops, "If you are for Joab and David, come and follow Joab." 12 But Amasa lay in his blood in the middle of the road, and Joab's man saw that everyone was stopping to stare at him. So he pulled him off the road into a field and threw a cloak over him. 13 With Amasa's body out of the way, everyone went on with Joab to capture Sheba son of Bicri.

14 Meanwhile, Sheba traveled through all the tribes of Israel and eventually came to the town of Abel-beth-maacah. All the members of his own clan, the Bicrites,* assembled for battle and followed him into the town. 15 When Joab's forces arrived, they attacked Abel-beth-maacah. They built a siege ramp against the town's fortifications and began battering down the wall. 16 But a wise woman in the town called out to Joab, "Listen to me, Joab. Come over here so I can talk to you." 17 As he approached, the woman asked, "Are you Joab?"

"I am," he replied.

So she said, "Listen carefully to your servant."

"I'm listening," he said.

18 Then she continued, "There used to be a saying, 'If you want to settle an argument, ask advice at the town of Abel.' 19 I am one who is peace loving and faithful in Israel. But you are destroying an important town in Israel.* Why do you want to devour what belongs to the LORD?"

20 And Joab replied, "Believe me, I don't want to devour or destroy your town! 21 That's not my purpose. All I want is a man named Sheba son of Bicri from the hill country of Ephraim, who has revolted against King David. If you hand over this one man to me, I will leave the town in peace."

"All right," the woman replied, "we will throw his head over the wall to you." 22 Then the woman went to all the people with her wise advice, and they cut off Sheba's head and threw it out to Joab. So he blew the ram's horn and called his troops back from the attack. They all returned to their homes, and Joab returned to the king at Jerusalem.

23 Now Joab was the commander of the army of Israel. Benaiah son of Jehoiada was captain of the king's bodyguard. 24 Adoniram* was in charge of forced labor. Jehoshaphat son of Ahilud was the royal historian. 25 Sheva was the court secretary. Zadok and Abiathar were the priests. 26 And Ira, a descendant of Jair, was David's personal priest.

David Avenges the Gibeonites

21 There was a famine during David's reign that lasted for three years, so David asked the LORD about it. And the LORD said, "The famine has come because Saul and his family are guilty of murdering the Gibeonites."

2 So the king summoned the Gibeonites. They were not part of Israel but were all that was left of the nation of the Amorites. The people of Israel had sworn not to kill them, but Saul, in his zeal for Israel and Judah, had tried to wipe them out. 3 David asked them, "What can I do for you? How can I make amends so that you will bless the LORD's people again?"

4 "Well, money can't settle this matter between us and the family of Saul," the Gibeonites replied. "Neither can we demand the life of anyone in Israel."

"What can I do then?" David asked. "Just tell me and I will do it for you."

5 Then they replied, "It was Saul who planned to destroy us, to keep us from having any place at all in the territory of Israel. 6 So let seven of Saul's sons be handed over to us, and we will execute them before the LORD at Gibeon, on the mountain of the LORD.*"

"All right," the king said, "I will do it." 7 The king spared Jonathan's son Mephibosheth,* who was Saul's grandson, because of the oath David and Jonathan had sworn before the LORD. 8 But he gave them Saul's two sons Armoni and Mephibosheth, whose mother was Rizpah daughter of Aiah. He also gave them the five sons of Saul's daughter Merab,* the wife of Adriel son of Barzillai from Meholah. 9The men of Gibeon executed them on the mountain before the LORD. So all seven of them died together at the beginning of the barley harvest.

10Then Rizpah daughter of Aiah, the mother of two of the men, spread burlap on a rock and stayed there the entire harvest season. She prevented the scavenger birds from tearing at their bodies during the day and stopped wild animals from eating them at night. 11When David learned what Rizpah, Saul's concubine, had done, 12he went to the people of Jabesh-gilead and retrieved the bones of Saul and his son Jonathan. (When the Philistines had killed Saul and Jonathan on Mount Gilboa, the people of Jabesh-gilead stole their bodies from the public square of Beth-shan, where the Philistines had hung them.) 13So David obtained the bones of Saul and Jonathan, as well as the bones of the men the Gibeonites had executed.

14Then the king ordered that they bury the bones in the tomb of Kish, Saul's father, at the town of Zela in the land of Benjamin. After that, God ended the famine in the land.

Battles against Philistine Giants

15Once again the Philistines were at war with Israel. And when David and his men were in the thick of battle, David became weak and exhausted. 16Ishbi-benob was a descendant of the giants*; his bronze spearhead weighed more than seven pounds,* and he was armed with a new sword. He had cornered David and was about to kill him. 17But Abishai son of Zeruiah came to David's rescue and killed the Philistine. Then David's men declared, "You are not going out to battle with us again! Why risk snuffing out the light of Israel?"

18After this, there was another battle against the Philistines at Gob. As they fought, Sibbecai from Hushah killed Saph, another descendant of the giants.

19During another battle at Gob, Elhanan son of Jair* from Bethlehem killed the brother of Goliath of Gath.* The handle of his spear was as thick as a weaver's beam!

20In another battle with the Philistines at Gath, they encountered a huge man* with six fingers on each hand and six toes on each foot, twenty-four in all, who was also a descendant of the giants. 21But when he defied and taunted Israel, he was killed by Jonathan, the son of David's brother Shimea.*

22These four Philistines were descendants of the giants of Gath, but David and his warriors killed them.

David's Song of Praise

22 David sang this song to the LORD on the day the LORD rescued him from all his enemies and from Saul. 2He sang:

"The LORD is my rock, my fortress, and
my savior;
3 my God is my rock, in whom I find
protection.
He is my shield, the power that
saves me,
and my place of safety.
He is my refuge, my savior,
the one who saves me from violence.
4 I called on the LORD, who is worthy of
praise,
and he saved me from my enemies.

5 "The waves of death overwhelmed me;
floods of destruction swept over me.
6 The grave* wrapped its ropes
around me;
death laid a trap in my path.
7 But in my distress I cried out to the
LORD;
yes, I cried to my God for help.
He heard me from his sanctuary;
my cry reached his ears.

8 "Then the earth quaked and trembled.
The foundations of the heavens
shook;
they quaked because of his anger.
9 Smoke poured from his nostrils;
fierce flames leaped from his mouth.
Glowing coals blazed forth from him.

20:8 Hebrew *As he stepped forward, it fell out.* **20:14** As in Greek and Latin versions; Hebrew reads *All the Berites.* **20:19** Hebrew *a town that is a mother in Israel.* **20:24** As in Greek version (see also 1 Kgs 4:6; 5:14); Hebrew reads *Adoram.* **21:6** As in Greek version (see also 21:9); Hebrew reads *at Gibeah of Saul, the chosen of the LORD.* **21:7** *Mephibosheth* is another name for Merib-baal. **21:8** As in a few Hebrew and Greek manuscripts and Syriac version (see also 1 Sam 18:19); most Hebrew manuscripts read *Michal.* **21:16a** Or *a descendant of the Rapha;* also in 21:18, 20, 22. **21:16b** Hebrew *300 [shekels]* [3.4 kilograms]. **21:19a** As in parallel text at 1 Chr 20:5; Hebrew reads *son of Jaare-oregim.* **21:19b** As in parallel text at 1 Chr 20:5; Hebrew reads *killed Goliath of Gath.* **21:20** As in parallel text at 1 Chr 20:6; Hebrew reads *a Midianite.* **21:21** As in parallel text at 1 Chr 20:7; Hebrew reads *Shimei,* a variant spelling of Shimea. **22:6** Hebrew *Sheol.*

10 He opened the heavens and came down;
dark storm clouds were beneath his feet.
11 Mounted on a mighty angelic being,* he flew,
soaring* on the wings of the wind.
12 He shrouded himself in darkness,
veiling his approach with dense rain clouds.
13 A great brightness shone around him,
and burning coals* blazed forth.
14 The LORD thundered from heaven;
the voice of the Most High resounded.
15 He shot arrows and scattered his enemies;
his lightning flashed, and they were confused.
16 Then at the command of the LORD,
at the blast of his breath,
the bottom of the sea could be seen,
and the foundations of the earth were laid bare.

17 "He reached down from heaven and rescued me;
he drew me out of deep waters.
18 He rescued me from my powerful enemies,
from those who hated me and were too strong for me.
19 They attacked me at a moment when I was in distress,
but the LORD supported me.
20 He led me to a place of safety;
he rescued me because he delights in me.
21 The LORD rewarded me for doing right;
he restored me because of my innocence.
22 For I have kept the ways of the LORD;
I have not turned from my God to follow evil.
23 I have followed all his regulations;
I have never abandoned his decrees.
24 I am blameless before God;
I have kept myself from sin.
25 The LORD rewarded me for doing right.
He has seen my innocence.

26 "To the faithful you show yourself faithful;
to those with integrity you show integrity.
27 To the pure you show yourself pure,
but to the crooked you show yourself shrewd.
28 You rescue the humble,
but your eyes watch the proud and humiliate them.
29 O LORD, you are my lamp.
The LORD lights up my darkness.
30 In your strength I can crush an army;
with my God I can scale any wall.

31 "God's way is perfect.
All the LORD's promises prove true.
He is a shield for all who look to him for protection.
32 For who is God except the LORD?
Who but our God is a solid rock?
33 God is my strong fortress,
and he makes my way perfect.
34 He makes me as surefooted as a deer,
enabling me to stand on mountain heights.
35 He trains my hands for battle;
he strengthens my arm to draw a bronze bow.
36 You have given me your shield of victory;
your help* has made me great.
37 You have made a wide path for my feet
to keep them from slipping.

38 "I chased my enemies and destroyed them;
I did not stop until they were conquered.
39 I consumed them;
I struck them down so they did not get up;
they fell beneath my feet.
40 You have armed me with strength for the battle;
you have subdued my enemies under my feet.
41 You placed my foot on their necks.
I have destroyed all who hated me.
42 They looked for help, but no one came to their rescue.
They even cried to the LORD, but he refused to answer.
43 I ground them as fine as the dust of the earth;
I trampled them* in the gutter like dirt.

44 "You gave me victory over my accusers.
You preserved me as the ruler over nations;
people I don't even know now serve me.

45 Foreign nations cringe before me;
as soon as they hear of me, they submit.
46 They all lose their courage
and come trembling* from their strongholds.
47 "The LORD lives! Praise to my Rock!
May God, the Rock of my salvation, be exalted!
48 He is the God who pays back those who harm me;
he brings down the nations under me
49 and delivers me from my enemies.
You hold me safe beyond the reach of my enemies;
you save me from violent opponents.
50 For this, O LORD, I will praise you among the nations;
I will sing praises to your name.
51 You give great victories to your king;
you show unfailing love to your anointed,
to David and all his descendants forever."

David's Last Words

23 These are the last words of David:
"David, the son of Jesse, speaks—
David, the man who was raised up so high,
David, the man anointed by the God of Jacob,
David, the sweet psalmist of Israel.*
2 "The Spirit of the LORD speaks through me;
his words are upon my tongue.
3 The God of Israel spoke.
The Rock of Israel said to me:
'The one who rules righteously,
who rules in the fear of God,
4 is like the light of morning at sunrise,
like a morning without clouds,
like the gleaming of the sun
on new grass after rain.'

5 "Is it not my family God has chosen?
Yes, he has made an everlasting covenant with me.
His agreement is arranged and guaranteed in every detail.
He will ensure my safety and success.
6 But the godless are like thorns to be thrown away,
for they tear the hand that touches them.
7 One must use iron tools to chop them down;
they will be totally consumed by fire."

David's Mightiest Warriors

8These are the names of David's mightiest warriors. The first was Jashobeam
the Hacmonite,* who was leader of the
Three*—the three mightiest warriors among
David's men. He once used his spear to kill
800 enemy warriors in a single battle.*
9Next in rank among the Three was Eleazar
son of Dodai, a descendant of Ahoah. Once
Eleazar and David stood together against
the Philistines when the entire Israelite
army had fled. 10He killed Philistines until
his hand was too tired to lift his sword, and
the LORD gave him a great victory that day.
The rest of the army did not return until it
was time to collect the plunder!
11Next in rank was Shammah son of Agee
from Harar. One time the Philistines gathered
at Lehi and attacked the Israelites in a field
full of lentils. The Israelite army fled, 12but
Shammah* held his ground in the middle of
the field and beat back the Philistines. So the
LORD brought about a great victory.
13Once during the harvest, when David
was at the cave of Adullam, the Philistine
army was camped in the valley of Rephaim.
The Three (who were among the Thirty—an
elite group among David's fighting men)
went down to meet him there. 14David was
staying in the stronghold at the time, and
a Philistine detachment had occupied the
town of Bethlehem.
15David remarked longingly to his men,

22:11a Hebrew *a cherub.* **22:11b** As in some Hebrew manuscripts (see also Ps 18:10); other Hebrew manuscripts read *appearing.* **22:13** Or *and lightning bolts.* **22:36** As in Dead Sea Scrolls; Masoretic Text reads *your answering.* **22:43** As in Dead Sea Scrolls (see also Ps 18:42); Masoretic Text reads *I crushed and trampled them.* **22:46** As in parallel text at Ps 18:45; Hebrew reads *come girding themselves.* **23:1** Or *the favorite subject of the songs of Israel;* or *the favorite of the Strong One of Israel.* **23:8a** As in parallel text at 1 Chr 11:11; Hebrew reads *Josheb-basshebeth the Tahkemonite.* **23:8b** As in Greek and Latin versions (see also 1 Chr 11:11); the meaning of the Hebrew is uncertain. **23:8c** As in some Greek manuscripts (see also 1 Chr 11:11); the meaning of the Hebrew is uncertain, though it might be rendered *the Three. It was Adino the Eznite who killed 800 men at one time.* **23:12** Hebrew *he.*

▸ **23:8** *See **Serving one another**, page 461.*

“Oh, how I would love some of that good
water from the well by the gate in Bethlehem.” 16So the Three broke through the
Philistine lines, drew some water from the
well by the gate in Bethlehem, and brought
it back to David. But he refused to drink it.
Instead, he poured it out as an offering to
the LORD. 17“The LORD forbid that I should
drink this!” he exclaimed. “This water is as
precious as the blood of these men* who
risked their lives to bring it to me.” So David
did not drink it. These are examples of the
exploits of the Three.

David’s Thirty Mighty Men

18Abishai son of Zeruiah, the brother of
Joab, was the leader of the Thirty.* He once
used his spear to kill 300 enemy warriors in
a single battle. It was by such feats that he
became as famous as the Three. 19Abishai
was the most famous of the Thirty* and was
their commander, though he was not one of
the Three.

20There was also Benaiah son of Jehoiada, a valiant warrior* from Kabzeel. He did
many heroic deeds, which included killing
two champions* of Moab. Another time, on
a snowy day, he chased a lion down into a pit
and killed it. 21Once, armed only with a club,
he killed an imposing Egyptian warrior who
was armed with a spear. Benaiah wrenched
the spear from the Egyptian’s hand and
killed him with it. 22Deeds like these made
Benaiah as famous as the Three mightiest
warriors. 23He was more honored than the
other members of the Thirty, though he was
not one of the Three. And David made him
captain of his bodyguard.

24Other members of the Thirty included:

Asahel, Joab’s brother;
Elhanan son of Dodo from Bethlehem;
25 Shammah from Harod;
Elika from Harod;
26 Helez from Pelon*;
Ira son of Ikkesh from Tekoa;
27 Abiezer from Anathoth;
Sibbecai* from Hushah;
28 Zalmon from Ahoah;
Maharai from Netophah;
29 Heled* son of Baanah from Netophah;
Ithai* son of Ribai from Gibeah (in the land of Benjamin);
30 Benaiah from Pirathon;
Hurai* from Nahale-gaash*;
31 Abi-albon from Arabah;
Azmaveth from Bahurim;
32 Eliahba from Shaalbon;
the sons of Jashen;
Jonathan 33son of Shagee* from Harar;
Ahiam son of Sharar from Harar;
34 Eliphelet son of Ahasbai from Maacah;
Eliam son of Ahithophel from Giloh;
35 Hezro from Carmel;
Paarai from Arba;
36 Igal son of Nathan from Zobah;
Bani from Gad;
37 Zelek from Ammon;
Naharai from Beeroth, the armor bearer of Joab son of Zeruiah;
38 Ira from Jattir;
Gareb from Jattir;
39 Uriah the Hittite.

There were thirty-seven in all.

David Takes a Census

24 Once again the anger of the LORD
burned against Israel, and he caused
David to harm them by taking a census. “Go
and count the people of Israel and Judah,”
the LORD told him.

2So the king said to Joab and the commanders* of the army, “Take a census of all
the tribes of Israel—from Dan in the north to
Beersheba in the south—so I may know how
many people there are.”

3But Joab replied to the king, “May the
LORD your God let you live to see a hundred
times as many people as there are now! But
why, my lord the king, do you want to do
this?”

4But the king insisted that they take the
census, so Joab and the commanders of the
army went out to count the people of Israel.
5First they crossed the Jordan and camped
at Aroer, south of the town in the valley, in
the direction of Gad. Then they went on to
Jazer, 6then to Gilead in the land of Tahtim-
hodshi* and to Dan-jaan and around to
Sidon. 7Then they came to the fortress of
Tyre, and all the towns of the Hivites and
Canaanites. Finally, they went south to
Judah* as far as Beersheba.

8Having gone through the entire land for
nine months and twenty days, they returned
to Jerusalem. 9Joab reported the number
of people to the king. There were 800,000
capable warriors in Israel who could handle
a sword, and 500,000 in Judah.

Judgment for David's Sin

[10]But after he had taken the census, David's
conscience began to bother him. And he
said to the LORD, "I have sinned greatly by
taking this census. Please forgive my guilt,
LORD, for doing this foolish thing."
[11]The next morning the word of the LORD
came to the prophet Gad, who was David's
seer. This was the message: [12]"Go and say
to David, 'This is what the LORD says: I
will give you three choices. Choose one of
these punishments, and I will inflict it on
you.'"
[13]So Gad came to David and asked him,
"Will you choose three* years of famine
throughout your land, three months of
fleeing from your enemies, or three days of
severe plague throughout your land? Think
this over and decide what answer I should
give the LORD who sent me."
[14]"I'm in a desperate situation!" David
replied to Gad. "But let us fall into the
hands of the LORD, for his mercy is great.
Do not let me fall into human hands."
[15]So the LORD sent a plague upon Israel
that morning, and it lasted for three days.*
A total of 70,000 people died throughout
the nation, from Dan in the north to Beersheba in the south. [16]But as the angel was
preparing to destroy Jerusalem, the LORD
relented and said to the death angel, "Stop!
That is enough!" At that moment the angel
of the LORD was by the threshing floor of
Araunah the Jebusite.
[17]When David saw the angel, he said to
the LORD, "I am the one who has sinned and
done wrong! But these people are as innocent as sheep—what have they done? Let
your anger fall against me and my family."

David Builds an Altar

[18]That day Gad came to David and said
to him, "Go up and build an altar to the
LORD on the threshing floor of Araunah the
Jebusite."

23:17 Hebrew *Shall I drink the blood of these men?* **23:18** As in a few Hebrew manuscripts and Syriac version; most Hebrew manuscripts read *the Three.* **23:19** As in Syriac version; Hebrew reads *the Three.* **23:20a** Or *son of Jehoiada, son of Ish-hai.* **23:20b** Hebrew *two of Ariel.* **23:26** As in parallel text at 1 Chr 11:27 (see also 1 Chr 27:10); Hebrew reads *from Palti.* **23:27** As in some Greek manuscripts (see also 1 Chr 11:29); Hebrew reads *Mebunnai.* **23:29a** As in some Hebrew manuscripts (see also 1 Chr 11:30); most Hebrew manuscripts read *Heleb.* **23:29b** As in parallel text at 1 Chr 11:31; Hebrew reads *Ittai.* **23:30a** As in some Greek manuscripts (see also 1 Chr 11:32); Hebrew reads *Hiddai.* **23:30b** Or *from the ravines of Gaash.* **23:33** As in parallel text at 1 Chr 11:34; Hebrew reads *Jonathan, Shammah;* some Greek manuscripts read *Jonathan son of Shammah.* **24:2** As in Greek version (see also 24:4 and 1 Chr 21:2); Hebrew reads *Joab the commander.* **24:6** Greek version reads *to Gilead and to Kadesh in the land of the Hittites.* **24:7** Or *they went to the Negev of Judah.* **24:13** As in Greek version (see also 1 Chr 21:12); Hebrew reads *seven.* **24:15** Hebrew *for the designated time.*

Why was David wrong to take a census?

This strange story in 2 Samuel 24 reminds us of the dangers of becoming comfortable and complacent, feeling that because we have God's blessing we can now sit back, take life easy, and not worry too much about every little detail of obedience to him. That was the trap that David fell into. At some point in later life when his battles were over and the nation was secure and prospering, David decided to take a census. While we aren't told the reason for his doing this, Joab's surprised reaction (24:3) shows he knew that David's motives were questionable. The account in 2 Samuel sees the provocation to do this as coming from God (24:1), perhaps to test what was truly in David's heart; while the account in 1 Chronicles, written much later, sees it as Satan's provocation (1 Chronicles 21:1), for even Satan must ultimately obey God. Either way, it suggests there was something in David's heart that could be provoked, for God himself does not cause us to sin (e.g., James 1:12-15). Perhaps it was pride, wanting to know how big and strong his nation now was; perhaps it was a lack of faith, needing to put his trust in the strength of his army instead of in God. Moreover, David may well have neglected to pay the census tax as the Law required—perhaps showing a casualness to God's Word for plague was promised for failure to do so (Exodus 30:11-16)—But whatever the cause, the outcome was disastrous for the nation. Only the mercy of God ultimately spared them and brought good out of bad: a site for the new Temple.

19So David went up to do what the LORD
had commanded him. 20When Araunah saw
the king and his men coming toward him,
he came and bowed before the king with his
face to the ground. 21"Why have you come,
my lord the king?" Araunah asked.

David replied, "I have come to buy your
threshing floor and to build an altar to
the LORD there, so that he will stop the
plague."

22"Take it, my lord the king, and use it as
you wish," Araunah said to David. "Here
are oxen for the burnt offering, and you
can use the threshing boards and ox yokes
for wood to build a fire on the altar. 23I will
give it all to you, Your Majesty, and may the
LORD your God accept your sacrifice."

24But the king replied to Araunah, "No,
I insist on buying it, for I will not present
burnt offerings to the LORD my God that
have cost me nothing." So David paid him
fifty pieces of silver* for the threshing floor
and the oxen.

25David built an altar there to the LORD
and sacrificed burnt offerings and peace offerings. And the LORD answered his prayer
for the land, and the plague on Israel was
stopped.

24:24 Hebrew *50 shekels of silver,* about 20 ounces or 570 grams in weight.

1 Kings *A divided kingdom*

First and Second Kings were originally one book but were divided into two when the Hebrew text was translated into Greek and Latin, and most modern translations followed this tradition. Their contents follow on from where the books of Samuel left off. We learn about David's death, the reign of his son Solomon, the division of Solomon's kingdom into two kingdoms, Judah and Israel (and the reason for it), and the generally bad reigns of their kings, which led to God's judgment. We also meet two passionate prophets—Elijah and Elisha—who brought God's word to his people and performed spectacular miracles to authenticate their message. Their ministry demonstrated that the nations of Israel and Judah were not like the other nations. They prospered only when they, and their kings, chose to obey God.

What's it all about?

First Kings opens with Solomon being appointed king by his father, David—though not before his brother Adonijah had made a bid for the throne. Solomon took the advice of David and trusted in God to give him success. In a dream, God appeared to Solomon, who asked him for wisdom to govern the people, and God gave it to him in extraordinary measure (chapter 3). Peace and prosperity flowed as a result throughout Solomon's forty-year reign. Solomon undertook many successful construction projects, including a splendid Temple in Jerusalem. But sadly, out of political expediency, Solomon formed marriage alliances with surrounding nations. His foreign wives and their pagan beliefs had a bad influence on Solomon's relationship with God, and we are told that in later life "they turned his heart to worship other gods instead of being completely faithful to the LORD his God, as his father, David, had been" (11:4).

On Solomon's death, his son Rehoboam succeeded him as king. When the northern tribes asked him to lighten the oppressive tax burden on their people, brought about by Solomon's building projects and lavish lifestyle, he increased it instead. The ten northern tribes immediately rebelled, and the kingdom split into two, never to come together again. They established Israel (the northern kingdom) as a separate nation with Jeroboam (merely a former official of Solomon and not a descendant of David) as their king (12:1–14:20). The southern kingdom became known as Judah. The book tells the story of each kingdom in parallel,

OVERVIEW

David dies and Solomon becomes king · *1:1–2:46*

Solomon's wisdom and wealth *3:1–4:34*

Solomon builds and dedicates the Temple · *5:1–8:66*

Solomon's experience of God *9:1-9*

Solomon's great achievements—and mistakes · *9:10–11:13*

Opposition to Solomon, and his death · *11:14-43*

The foolishness of Rehoboam and the division of the kingdom · *12:1-24*

The early kings of Israel and Judah *12:25–16:28*

Ahab and the prophet Elijah *16:29–22:53*

always beginning with Judah and then going back to look at what had been happening in Israel over the same period. From now on, the story of both kingdoms is dominated by the reigns of wicked and idolatrous kings, of whom Ahab was the most notorious.

First Kings ends with the prophet Elijah's conflict with Ahab and his Phoenician wife, Jezebel (chapters 16–22). In a confrontation on Mount Carmel, Elijah called down fire from heaven and defeated the prophets of the pagan god Baal.

What does it mean for us?

The books of Kings are about God's faithfulness to his people even when they were unfaithful to him for generation after generation. God's faithfulness shone like a light in the darkness, as the spiritual life of God's people gradually declined. At the start, God provided so much for them: a permanent dynasty to rule Israel on God's behalf, a Temple as a house of prayer for all nations, Jerusalem as the city of God, and a succession of prophets to proclaim God's word. The lives of Elijah and Elisha show the importance of prophecy in this period of Israel's history as a vehicle for bringing people back to living in line with God's word. But again and again, kings and people alike turned their backs on God, despite some outstanding exceptions in kings like Hezekiah and Josiah. Their faith could not prevent the punishment of God—Israel's ultimate destruction and Judah's exile—but even that was not the end. The book of 2 Kings ends with a flickering flame of hope in the deepest darkness that God still had a future for his wayward people.

▶ *See also* ***A timeline of the Bible,*** *pages A22-A24.*

David in His Old Age

1 King David was now very old, and no
matter how many blankets covered him,
he could not keep warm. 2 So his advisers told
him, "Let us find a young virgin to wait on
you and look after you, my lord. She will lie
in your arms and keep you warm."
3 So they searched throughout the land of
Israel for a beautiful girl, and they found
Abishag from Shunem and brought her to
the king. 4 The girl was very beautiful, and she
looked after the king and took care of him.
But the king had no sexual relations with her.

Adonijah Claims the Throne

5 About that time David's son Adonijah,
whose mother was Haggith, began boasting,
"I will make myself king." So he provided
himself with chariots and charioteers and
recruited fifty men to run in front of him.
6 Now his father, King David, had never disciplined him at any time, even by asking,
"Why are you doing that?" Adonijah had
been born next after Absalom, and he was
very handsome.
7 Adonijah took Joab son of Zeruiah and
Abiathar the priest into his confidence, and
they agreed to help him become king. 8 But
Zadok the priest, Benaiah son of Jehoiada,
Nathan the prophet, Shimei, Rei, and David's
personal bodyguard refused to support
Adonijah.
9 Adonijah went to the Stone of Zoheleth*
near the spring of En-rogel, where he sacrificed sheep, cattle, and fattened calves.
He invited all his brothers—the other sons
of King David—and all the royal officials of
Judah. 10 But he did not invite Nathan the
prophet or Benaiah or the king's bodyguard
or his brother Solomon.
11 Then Nathan went to Bathsheba, Solomon's mother, and asked her, "Haven't
you heard that Haggith's son, Adonijah,
has made himself king, and our lord David
doesn't even know about it? 12 If you want to
save your own life and the life of your son
Solomon, follow my advice. 13 Go at once
to King David and say to him, 'My lord the
king, didn't you make a vow and say to me,
"Your son Solomon will surely be the next
king and will sit on my throne"? Why then
has Adonijah become king?' 14 And while you
are still talking with him, I will come and
confirm everything you have said."
15 So Bathsheba went into the king's
bedroom. (He was very old now, and Abishag
was taking care of him.) 16 Bathsheba bowed
down before the king.

"What can I do for you?" he asked her.
[17]She replied, "My lord, you made a vow before the LORD your God when you said to me, 'Your son Solomon will surely be the next king and will sit on my throne.' [18]But instead, Adonijah has made himself king, and my lord the king does not even know about it. [19]He has sacrificed many cattle, fattened calves, and sheep, and he has invited all the king's sons to attend the celebration. He also invited Abiathar the priest and Joab, the commander of the army. But he did not invite your servant Solomon. [20]And now, my lord the king, all Israel is waiting for you to announce who will become king after you. [21]If you do not act, my son Solomon and I will be treated as criminals as soon as my lord the king has died."

[22]While she was still speaking with the king, Nathan the prophet arrived. [23]The king's officials told him, "Nathan the prophet is here to see you."

Nathan went in and bowed before the king with his face to the ground. [24]Nathan asked, "My lord the king, have you decided that Adonijah will be the next king and that he will sit on your throne? [25]Today he has sacrificed many cattle, fattened calves, and sheep, and he has invited all the king's sons to attend the celebration. He also invited the commanders of the army and Abiathar the priest. They are feasting and drinking with him and shouting, 'Long live King Adonijah!' [26]But he did not invite me or Zadok the priest or Benaiah or your servant Solomon. [27]Has my lord the king really done this without letting any of his officials know who should be the next king?"

David Makes Solomon King

[28]King David responded, "Call Bathsheba!" So she came back in and stood before the king. [29]And the king repeated his vow: "As surely as the LORD lives, who has rescued me from every danger, [30]your son Solomon will be the next king and will sit on my throne this very day, just as I vowed to you before the LORD, the God of Israel."

[31]Then Bathsheba bowed down with her face to the ground before the king and exclaimed, "May my lord King David live forever!"

[32]Then King David ordered, "Call Zadok the priest, Nathan the prophet, and Benaiah son of Jehoiada." When they came into the king's presence, [33]the king said to them, "Take Solomon and my officials down to Gihon Spring. Solomon is to ride on my own mule. [34]There Zadok the priest and Nathan the prophet are to anoint him king over Israel. Blow the ram's horn and shout, 'Long live King Solomon!' [35]Then escort him back here, and he will sit on my throne. He will succeed me as king, for I have appointed him to be ruler over Israel and Judah."

[36]"Amen!" Benaiah son of Jehoiada replied. "May the LORD, the God of my lord the king, decree that it happen. [37]And may the LORD be with Solomon as he has been with you, my lord the king, and may he

1:9 Or *to the Serpent's Stone;* Greek version supports reading *Zoheleth* as a proper name.

Zadok

Zadok is a great example of faithfulness. A priest descended from Aaron (1 Chronicles 6:50-53), he was with David from his earliest days as king (2 Samuel 8:17). He was given responsibility for bringing the Ark of the Covenant to Jerusalem (1 Chronicles 15:11-15) and helped David allocate responsibilities for the future Temple (1 Chronicles 24:3-5). He remained utterly loyal to David throughout his reign and was entrusted with the Ark when David fled Jerusalem during Absalom's revolt (2 Samuel 15:23-29), and he helped arrange David's return to Jerusalem (2 Samuel 19:11-15). When David's days were coming to an end, Zadok ensured that David's chosen successor, Solomon, was anointed as king (1 Kings 1:32-40). His descendants served as high priests until 171 BC when Antiochus IV Epiphanes, a godless Greek ruler, transferred the role to Menelaus, though the Qumran community stayed loyal to the Zadokite priesthood.

▸ *See also* ***Faithfulness,*** *page 1307.*

make Solomon's reign even greater than
yours!"
38So Zadok the priest, Nathan the
prophet, Benaiah son of Jehoiada, and the
king's bodyguard* took Solomon down to
Gihon Spring, with Solomon riding on King
David's own mule. 39There Zadok the priest
took the flask of olive oil from the sacred
tent and anointed Solomon with the oil.
Then they sounded the ram's horn and
all the people shouted, "Long live King
Solomon!" 40And all the people followed
Solomon into Jerusalem, playing flutes and
shouting for joy. The celebration was so
joyous and noisy that the earth shook with
the sound.
41Adonijah and his guests heard the
celebrating and shouting just as they were
finishing their banquet. When Joab heard
the sound of the ram's horn, he asked,
"What's going on? Why is the city in such
an uproar?"
42And while he was still speaking, Jonathan son of Abiathar the priest arrived.
"Come in," Adonijah said to him, "for you
are a good man. You must have good news."
43"Not at all!" Jonathan replied. "Our lord
King David has just declared Solomon king!
44The king sent him down to Gihon Spring
with Zadok the priest, Nathan the prophet,
and Benaiah son of Jehoiada, protected by
the king's bodyguard. They had him ride
on the king's own mule, 45and Zadok and
Nathan have anointed him at Gihon Spring
as the new king. They have just returned, and
the whole city is celebrating and rejoicing.
That's what all the noise is about. 46What's
more, Solomon is now sitting on the royal
throne as king. 47And all the royal officials
have gone to King David and congratulated
him, saying, 'May your God make Solomon's
fame even greater than your own, and may
Solomon's reign be even greater than yours!'
Then the king bowed his head in worship
as he lay in his bed, 48and he said, 'Praise
the LORD, the God of Israel, who today has
chosen a successor to sit on my throne while
I am still alive to see it.'"
49Then all of Adonijah's guests jumped up
in panic from the banquet table and quickly
scattered. 50Adonijah was afraid of Solomon,
so he rushed to the sacred tent and grabbed
on to the horns of the altar. 51Word soon
reached Solomon that Adonijah had seized
the horns of the altar in fear, and that he was
pleading, "Let King Solomon swear today
that he will not kill me!"
52Solomon replied, "If he proves himself
to be loyal, not a hair on his head will
be touched. But if he makes trouble, he
will die." 53So King Solomon summoned
Adonijah, and they brought him down from
the altar. He came and bowed respectfully
before King Solomon, who dismissed him,
saying, "Go on home."

David's Final Instructions to Solomon

2 As the time of King David's death approached, he gave this charge to his son
Solomon:
2"I am going where everyone on earth
must someday go. Take courage and be a
man. 3Observe the requirements of the LORD
your God, and follow all his ways. Keep the
decrees, commands, regulations, and laws
written in the Law of Moses so that you will
be successful in all you do and wherever
you go. 4If you do this, then the LORD will
keep the promise he made to me. He told
me, 'If your descendants live as they should
and follow me faithfully with all their heart
and soul, one of them will always sit on the
throne of Israel.'
5"And there is something else. You know
what Joab son of Zeruiah did to me when
he murdered my two army commanders,
Abner son of Ner and Amasa son of Jether.
He pretended that it was an act of war, but
it was done in a time of peace,* staining his
belt and sandals with innocent blood.* 6Do
with him what you think best, but don't let
him grow old and go to his grave in peace.*
7"Be kind to the sons of Barzillai of Gilead.
Make them permanent guests at your table,
for they took care of me when I fled from
your brother Absalom.
8"And remember Shimei son of Gera, the
man from Bahurim in Benjamin. He cursed
me with a terrible curse as I was fleeing to
Mahanaim. When he came down to meet
me at the Jordan River, I swore by the LORD
that I would not kill him. 9But that oath
does not make him innocent. You are a wise
man, and you will know how to arrange a
bloody death for him.*"
10Then David died and was buried with
his ancestors in the City of David. 11David
had reigned over Israel for forty years,
seven of them in Hebron and thirty-three in
Jerusalem. 12Solomon became king and sat

on the throne of David his father, and his
kingdom was firmly established.

Solomon Establishes His Rule

13 One day Adonijah, whose mother was
Haggith, came to see Bathsheba, Solomon's
mother. "Have you come with peaceful intentions?" she asked him.
"Yes," he said, "I come in peace. 14 In fact,
I have a favor to ask of you."
"What is it?" she asked.
15 He replied, "As you know, the kingdom
was rightfully mine; all Israel wanted me to
be the next king. But the tables were turned,
and the kingdom went to my brother
instead; for that is the way the LORD wanted
it. 16 So now I have just one favor to ask of
you. Please don't turn me down."
"What is it?" she asked.
17 He replied, "Speak to King Solomon
on my behalf, for I know he will do anything you request. Ask him to let me marry
Abishag, the girl from Shunem."
18 "All right," Bathsheba replied. "I will
speak to the king for you."
19 So Bathsheba went to King Solomon to
speak on Adonijah's behalf. The king rose
from his throne to meet her, and he bowed
down before her. When he sat down on his
throne again, the king ordered that a throne
be brought for his mother, and she sat at his
right hand.
20 "I have one small request to make of
you," she said. "I hope you won't turn me
down."
"What is it, my mother?" he asked. "You
know I won't refuse you."
21 "Then let your brother Adonijah marry
Abishag, the girl from Shunem," she replied.
22 "How can you possibly ask me to give
Abishag to Adonijah?" King Solomon
demanded. "You might as well ask me to give
him the kingdom! You know that he is my
older brother, and that he has Abiathar the
priest and Joab son of Zeruiah on his side."
23 Then King Solomon made a vow before
the LORD: "May God strike me and even kill
me if Adonijah has not sealed his fate with
this request. 24 The LORD has confirmed me
and placed me on the throne of my father,
David; he has established my dynasty as he
promised. So as surely as the LORD lives,
Adonijah will die this very day!" 25 So King
Solomon ordered Benaiah son of Jehoiada to
execute him, and Adonijah was put to death.
26 Then the king said to Abiathar the
priest, "Go back to your home in Anathoth.
You deserve to die, but I will not kill you
now, because you carried the Ark of the
Sovereign LORD for David my father and
you shared all his hardships." 27 So Solomon
deposed Abiathar from his position as priest
of the LORD, thereby fulfilling the prophecy
the LORD had given at Shiloh concerning
the descendants of Eli.
28 Joab had not joined Absalom's earlier rebellion, but he had joined Adonijah's rebellion. So when Joab heard about Adonijah's
death, he ran to the sacred tent of the LORD

1:38 Hebrew *the Kerethites and Pelethites;* also in 1:44. **2:5a** Or *He murdered them during a time of peace as revenge for deaths they had caused in time of war.* **2:5b** As in some Greek and Old Latin manuscripts; Hebrew reads *with the blood of war.* **2:6** Hebrew *don't let his white head go down to Sheol in peace.* **2:9** Hebrew *how to bring his white head down to Sheol in blood.*

King Solomon

Solomon, Israel's third king, was a strange mixture. On the one hand, he was a great ruler, renowned for his wisdom (1 Kings 3:5-28; 4:29-34; Matthew 12:42), who expanded and strengthened the nation (1 Kings 4:20-25; 9:15-19), built the Temple (chapters 6–8), and developed international trade (9:26-28). Yet there was another, much darker, side to Solomon. His ambition led to him imposing taxation and conscripted labor (5:13-14). And he was driven by both a huge sexual appetite and political expediency—which came together in his marrying hundreds of foreign wives (11:1-3). And these foreign wives brought with them their foreign gods, and "they turned his heart to worship other gods instead of being completely faithful to the LORD" (11:4). Solomon shows us the danger of trying to develop a relationship with God while leaving underlying issues undealt with.

▶ *See also **Kingdoms of Israel** maps, Visual Overview Z6.*

and grabbed on to the horns of the altar.
29When this was reported to King Solomon,
he sent Benaiah son of Jehoiada to execute
him.

30Benaiah went to the sacred tent of the
LORD and said to Joab, "The king orders you
to come out!"

But Joab answered, "No, I will die here."

So Benaiah returned to the king and told
him what Joab had said.

31"Do as he said," the king replied. "Kill
him there beside the altar and bury him.
This will remove the guilt of Joab's senseless murders from me and from my father's
family. 32The LORD will repay him* for the
murders of two men who were more righteous and better than he. For my father
knew nothing about the deaths of Abner
son of Ner, commander of the army of Israel,
and of Amasa son of Jether, commander of
the army of Judah. 33May their blood be on
Joab and his descendants forever, and may
the LORD grant peace forever to David, his
descendants, his dynasty, and his throne."

34So Benaiah son of Jehoiada returned
to the sacred tent and killed Joab, and he
was buried at his home in the wilderness.
35Then the king appointed Benaiah to
command the army in place of Joab, and he
installed Zadok the priest to take the place
of Abiathar.

36The king then sent for Shimei and told
him, "Build a house here in Jerusalem and
live there. But don't step outside the city to go
anywhere else. 37On the day you so much as
cross the Kidron Valley, you will surely die;
and your blood will be on your own head."

38Shimei replied, "Your sentence is fair;
I will do whatever my lord the king commands." So Shimei lived in Jerusalem for a
long time.

39But three years later two of Shimei's
slaves ran away to King Achish son of
Maacah of Gath. When Shimei learned
where they were, 40he saddled his donkey
and went to Gath to search for them. When
he found them, he brought them back to
Jerusalem.

41Solomon heard that Shimei had left
Jerusalem and had gone to Gath and returned. 42So the king sent for Shimei and
demanded, "Didn't I make you swear by the
LORD and warn you not to go anywhere else
or you would surely die? And you replied,
'The sentence is fair; I will do as you say.'
43Then why haven't you kept your oath to
the LORD and obeyed my command?"

44The king also said to Shimei, "You
certainly remember all the wicked things
you did to my father, David. May the LORD
now bring that evil on your own head. 45But
may I, King Solomon, receive the LORD's
blessings, and may one of David's descendants always sit on this throne in the presence of the LORD." 46Then, at the king's
command, Benaiah son of Jehoiada took
Shimei outside and killed him.

So the kingdom was now firmly in Solomon's grip.

Solomon Asks for Wisdom

3 Solomon made an alliance with Pharaoh,
the king of Egypt, and married one of his
daughters. He brought her to live in the City
of David until he could finish building his
palace and the Temple of the LORD and the
wall around the city. 2At that time the people
of Israel sacrificed their offerings at local
places of worship, for a temple honoring
the name of the LORD had not yet been built.

3Solomon loved the LORD and followed all
the decrees of his father, David, except that
Solomon, too, offered sacrifices and burned
incense at the local places of worship. 4The
most important of these places of worship
was at Gibeon, so the king went there and
sacrificed 1,000 burnt offerings. 5That night
the LORD appeared to Solomon in a dream,
and God said, "What do you want? Ask, and
I will give it to you!"

6Solomon replied, "You showed great and
faithful love to your servant my father, David,
because he was honest and true and faithful
to you. And you have continued to show this
great and faithful love to him today by giving
him a son to sit on his throne.

7"Now, O LORD my God, you have made
me king instead of my father, David, but I
am like a little child who doesn't know his
way around. 8And here I am in the midst of
your own chosen people, a nation so great
and numerous they cannot be counted!
9Give me an understanding heart so that I
can govern your people well and know the
difference between right and wrong. For
who by himself is able to govern this great
people of yours?"

10The Lord was pleased that Solomon had
asked for wisdom. 11So God replied, "Because
you have asked for wisdom in governing my

people with justice and have not asked for
a long life or wealth or the death of your
enemies—12 I will give you what you asked
for! I will give you a wise and understanding
heart such as no one else has had or ever will
have! 13 And I will also give you what you did
not ask for—riches and fame! No other king in
all the world will be compared to you for the
rest of your life! 14 And if you follow me and
obey my decrees and my commands as your
father, David, did, I will give you a long life."

15 Then Solomon woke up and realized it
had been a dream. He returned to Jerusalem
and stood before the Ark of the Lord's Covenant, where he sacrificed burnt offerings
and peace offerings. Then he invited all his
officials to a great banquet.

Solomon Judges Wisely

16 Some time later two prostitutes came to the
king to have an argument settled. 17 "Please,
my lord," one of them began, "this woman
and I live in the same house. I gave birth to
a baby while she was with me in the house.
18 Three days later this woman also had a
baby. We were alone; there were only two
of us in the house.

19 "But her baby died during the night
when she rolled over on it. 20 Then she got
up in the night and took my son from beside
me while I was asleep. She laid her dead
child in my arms and took mine to sleep
beside her. 21 And in the morning when
I tried to nurse my son, he was dead! But
when I looked more closely in the morning
light, I saw that it wasn't my son at all."

22 Then the other woman interrupted, "It
certainly was your son, and the living child
is mine."

"No," the first woman said, "the living
child is mine, and the dead one is yours."
And so they argued back and forth before
the king.

23 Then the king said, "Let's get the facts
straight. Both of you claim the living child
is yours, and each says that the dead one
belongs to the other. 24 All right, bring me a
sword." So a sword was brought to the king.

25 Then he said, "Cut the living child in
two, and give half to one woman and half
to the other!"

26 Then the woman who was the real
mother of the living child, and who loved
him very much, cried out, "Oh no, my lord!
Give her the child—please do not kill him!"

But the other woman said, "All right, he
will be neither yours nor mine; divide him
between us!"

27 Then the king said, "Do not kill the
child, but give him to the woman who wants
him to live, for she is his mother!"

28 When all Israel heard the king's decision, the people were in awe of the king, for
they saw the wisdom God had given him for
rendering justice.

Solomon's Officials and Governors

4 King Solomon now ruled over all Israel,
2 and these were his high officials:

Azariah son of Zadok was the priest.
3 Elihoreph and Ahijah, the sons of
Shisha, were court secretaries.
Jehoshaphat son of Ahilud was the royal
historian.
4 Benaiah son of Jehoiada was
commander of the army.
Zadok and Abiathar were priests.
5 Azariah son of Nathan was in charge
of the district governors.
Zabud son of Nathan, a priest, was a
trusted adviser to the king.
6 Ahishar was manager of the palace
property.
Adoniram son of Abda was in charge
of forced labor.

7 Solomon also had twelve district governors who were over all Israel. They were responsible for providing food for the king's
household. Each of them arranged provisions for one month of the year. 8 These are
the names of the twelve governors:

Ben-hur, in the hill country of Ephraim.
9 Ben-deker, in Makaz, Shaalbim,
Beth-shemesh, and Elon-bethhanan.
10 Ben-hesed, in Arubboth, including
Socoh and all the land of Hepher.
11 Ben-abinadab, in all of Naphoth-dor.*
(He was married to Taphath, one of
Solomon's daughters.)
12 Baana son of Ahilud, in Taanach
and Megiddo, all of Beth-shan*
near Zarethan below Jezreel, and
all the territory from Beth-shan to
Abel-meholah and over to Jokmeam.
13 Ben-geber, in Ramoth-gilead, including
the Towns of Jair (named for Jair of the

2:32 Hebrew *will return his blood on his own head.* **4:11** Hebrew *Naphath-dor,* a variant spelling of Naphoth-dor. **4:12** Hebrew *Beth-shean,* a variant spelling of Beth-shan; also in 4:12b.

tribe of Manasseh*) in Gilead, and in the Argob region of Bashan, including sixty large fortified towns with bronze bars on their gates.
14 Ahinadab son of Iddo, in Mahanaim.
15 Ahimaaz, in Naphtali. (He was married to Basemath, another of Solomon's daughters.)
16 Baana son of Hushai, in Asher and in Aloth.
17 Jehoshaphat son of Paruah, in Issachar.
18 Shimei son of Ela, in Benjamin.
19 Geber son of Uri, in the land of Gilead,* including the territories of King Sihon of the Amorites and King Og of Bashan.
There was also one governor over the land of Judah.*

Solomon's Prosperity and Wisdom

20The people of Judah and Israel were as numerous as the sand on the seashore. They
were very contented, with plenty to eat and
drink. 21*Solomon ruled over all the kingdoms from the Euphrates River* in the
north to the land of the Philistines and the
border of Egypt in the south. The conquered
peoples of those lands sent tribute money
to Solomon and continued to serve him
throughout his lifetime.
22The daily food requirements for Solomon's palace were 150 bushels of choice
flour and 300 bushels of meal*; 23also
10 oxen from the fattening pens, 20 pasture-
fed cattle, 100 sheep or goats, as well as deer,
gazelles, roe deer, and choice poultry.*
24Solomon's dominion extended over all
the kingdoms west of the Euphrates River,
from Tiphsah to Gaza. And there was peace
on all his borders. 25During the lifetime of
Solomon, all of Judah and Israel lived in
peace and safety. And from Dan in the north
to Beersheba in the south, each family had
its own home and garden.*
26Solomon had 4,000* stalls for his chariot
horses, and he had 12,000 horses.*
27The district governors faithfully
provided food for King Solomon and his
court; each made sure nothing was lacking
during the month assigned to him. 28They
also brought the necessary barley and straw
for the royal horses in the stables.
29God gave Solomon very great wisdom
and understanding, and knowledge as vast
as the sands of the seashore. 30In fact, his
wisdom exceeded that of all the wise men
of the East and the wise men of Egypt. 31He
was wiser than anyone else, including Ethan
the Ezrahite and the sons of Mahol—Heman,
Calcol, and Darda. His fame spread throughout all the surrounding nations. 32He composed some 3,000 proverbs and wrote 1,005
songs. 33He could speak with authority about
all kinds of plants, from the great cedar of
Lebanon to the tiny hyssop that grows from
cracks in a wall. He could also speak about
animals, birds, small creatures, and fish.
34And kings from every nation sent their ambassadors to listen to the wisdom of Solomon.

Preparations for Building the Temple

5 1*King Hiram of Tyre had always been
a loyal friend of David. When Hiram
learned that David's son Solomon was the

Adoniram and forced labor

Hidden in the list of Solomon's officials (1 Kings 4:1-6) is a comment whose significance it is easy to miss. We read that Adoniram was "in charge of forced labor" (4:6; see also 5:14). Solomon's building projects—his palace and the Temple—were so great that he "conscripted a labor force of 30,000 men from all Israel. He sent them to Lebanon in shifts, 10,000 every month, so that each man would be one month in Lebanon and two months at home" (5:13-14). He also had 70,000 laborers, 80,000 quarry workers, and 3,600 supervisors (5:15-16). All this generated huge resentment, for another term for "conscripted labor" is "slavery," and slavery was what God had freed his people from in Egypt. Little wonder, therefore, that at Solomon's death the people had had enough. The ten northern tribes stoned Adoniram to death and rebelled against Rehoboam, Solomon's son (12:18-19).

new king of Israel, he sent ambassadors to
congratulate him.
[2]Then Solomon sent this message back to
Hiram:

> [3]"You know that my father, David, was
> not able to build a Temple to honor the
> name of the LORD his God because of
> the many wars waged against him by
> surrounding nations. He could not build
> until the LORD gave him victory over all
> his enemies. [4]But now the LORD my God
> has given me peace on every side; I have
> no enemies, and all is well. [5]So I am
> planning to build a Temple to honor
> the name of the LORD my God, just as
> he had instructed my father, David. For
> the LORD told him, 'Your son, whom I
> will place on your throne, will build the
> Temple to honor my name.'
> [6]"Therefore, please command that
> cedars from Lebanon be cut for me. Let
> my men work alongside yours, and I will
> pay your men whatever wages you ask.
> As you know, there is no one among us
> who can cut timber like you Sidonians!"

[7]When Hiram received Solomon's
message, he was very pleased and said,
"Praise the LORD today for giving David a
wise son to be king of the great nation of
Israel." [8]Then he sent this reply to Solomon:

> "I have received your message, and I
> will supply all the cedar and cypress
> timber you need. [9]My servants will bring
> the logs from the Lebanon mountains
> to the Mediterranean Sea* and make
> them into rafts and float them along
> the coast to whatever place you choose.
> Then we will break the rafts apart so you
> can carry the logs away. You can pay
> me by supplying me with food for my
> household."

[10]So Hiram supplied as much cedar
and cypress timber as Solomon desired.
[11]In return, Solomon sent him an annual
payment of 100,000 bushels* of wheat
for his household and 110,000 gallons* of
pure olive oil. [12]So the LORD gave wisdom
to Solomon, just as he had promised. And
Hiram and Solomon made a formal alliance
of peace.
[13]Then King Solomon conscripted a labor
force of 30,000 men from all Israel. [14]He
sent them to Lebanon in shifts, 10,000
every month, so that each man would be
one month in Lebanon and two months at
home. Adoniram was in charge of this labor
force. [15]Solomon also had 70,000 common
laborers, 80,000 quarry workers in the hill
country, [16]and 3,600* foremen to supervise the work. [17]At the king's command,
they quarried large blocks of high-quality
stone and shaped them to make the foundation of the Temple. [18]Men from the city
of Gebal helped Solomon's and Hiram's
builders prepare the timber and stone for
the Temple.

Solomon Builds the Temple

6 It was in midspring, in the month of
Ziv,* during the fourth year of Solomon's
reign, that he began to construct the Temple
of the LORD. This was 480 years after the
people of Israel were rescued from their
slavery in the land of Egypt.
[2]The Temple that King Solomon built for
the LORD was 90 feet long, 30 feet wide, and
45 feet high.* [3]The entry room at the front
of the Temple was 30 feet* wide, running
across the entire width of the Temple. It
projected outward 15 feet* from the front
of the Temple. [4]Solomon also made narrow
recessed windows throughout the Temple.
[5]He built a complex of rooms against
the outer walls of the Temple, all the way
around the sides and rear of the building.
[6]The complex was three stories high, the
bottom floor being 7½ feet wide, the second
floor 9 feet wide, and the top floor 10½ feet
wide.* The rooms were connected to the
walls of the Temple by beams resting on
ledges built out from the wall. So the beams
were not inserted into the walls themselves.

4:13 Hebrew *Jair son of Manasseh;* compare 1 Chr 2:22. **4:19a** Greek version reads *of Gad;* compare 4:13. **4:19b** As in some Greek manuscripts; Hebrew lacks *of Judah.* The meaning of the Hebrew is uncertain. **4:21a** Verses 4:21-34 are numbered 5:1-14 in Hebrew text. **4:21b** Hebrew *the river;* also in 4:24. **4:22** Hebrew *30 cors* [6.6 kiloliters] *of choice flour and 60 cors* [13.2 kiloliters] *of meal.* **4:23** Or *and fattened geese.* **4:25** Hebrew *each family lived under its own grapevine and under its own fig tree.* **4:26a** As in some Greek manuscripts (see also 2 Chr 9:25); Hebrew reads *40,000.* **4:26b** Or *12,000 charioteers.* **5:1** Verses 5:1-18 are numbered 5:15-32 in Hebrew text. **5:9** Hebrew *the sea.* **5:11a** Hebrew *20,000 cors* [4,400 kiloliters]. **5:11b** As in Greek version, which reads *20,000 baths* [420 kiloliters] (see also 2 Chr 2:10); Hebrew reads *20 cors,* about 1,000 gallons or 4.4 kiloliters in volume. **5:16** As in some Greek manuscripts (see also 2 Chr 2:2, 18); Hebrew reads *3,300.* **6:1** Hebrew *It was in the month of Ziv, which is the second month.* This month of the ancient Hebrew lunar calendar usually occurs within the months of April and May. **6:2** Hebrew *60 cubits* [27.6 meters] *long, 20 cubits* [9.2 meters] *wide, and 30 cubits* [13.8 meters] *high.* **6:3a** Hebrew *20 cubits* [9.2 meters]; also in 6:16, 20. **6:3b** Hebrew *10 cubits* [4.6 meters]. **6:6** Hebrew *the bottom floor being 5 cubits* [2.3 meters] *wide, the second floor 6 cubits* [2.8 meters] *wide, and the top floor 7 cubits* [3.2 meters] *wide.*

7 The stones used in the construction of
the Temple were finished at the quarry, so
there was no sound of hammer, ax, or any
other iron tool at the building site.
8 The entrance to the bottom floor* was
on the south side of the Temple. There
were winding stairs going up to the second
floor, and another flight of stairs between
the second and third floors. 9 After completing the Temple structure, Solomon put in a
ceiling made of cedar beams and planks.
10 As already stated, he built a complex
of rooms along the sides of the building,
attached to the Temple walls by cedar
timbers. Each story of the complex was
7½ feet* high.
11 Then the LORD gave this message to
Solomon: 12 "Concerning this Temple you
are building, if you keep all my decrees and
regulations and obey all my commands, I
will fulfill through you the promise I made
to your father, David. 13 I will live among
the Israelites and will never abandon my
people Israel."

The Temple's Interior

14 So Solomon finished building the Temple.
15 The entire inside, from floor to ceiling, was
paneled with wood. He paneled the walls
and ceilings with cedar, and he used planks
of cypress for the floors. 16 He partitioned off
an inner sanctuary—the Most Holy Place—
at the far end of the Temple. It was 30 feet
deep and was paneled with cedar from floor
to ceiling. 17 The main room of the Temple,
outside the Most Holy Place, was 60 feet*
long. 18 Cedar paneling completely covered
the stone walls throughout the Temple, and
the paneling was decorated with carvings of
gourds and open flowers.
19 He prepared the inner sanctuary at
the far end of the Temple, where the Ark
of the LORD's Covenant would be placed.
20 This inner sanctuary was 30 feet long,
30 feet wide, and 30 feet high. He overlaid
the inside with solid gold. He also overlaid
the altar made of cedar.* 21 Then Solomon
overlaid the rest of the Temple's interior
with solid gold, and he made gold chains

The Temple

Solomon's Temple was Israel's first permanent sanctuary. Twice the size of the Tabernacle that it replaced, it took seven years to build. Solomon used Phoenician craftsmen, so it followed the pattern of other Canaanite temples, divided into three main parts: an entrance portico; a large hall called "the Holy Place," which contained an altar, a table, and ten lampstands—all made of gold; and the much smaller "Most Holy Place," which contained the Ark of the Covenant and which only the high priest could enter, and then only once a year. While the Holy Place was lit by candles and light from high windows, the Most Holy Place was completely dark.

After the Temple's dedication, God told Solomon that he had "set this Temple apart to be holy" and that his name would be honored forever there (1 Kings 9:3). With the promise of an everlasting royal dynasty (2 Samuel 7:16) and a Temple where God promised to dwell and be honored forever, God's people now felt extremely secure. But they forgot that God had put conditions to his blessing the Temple and remaining there (1 Kings 9:6-9), and when they broke these conditions, God brought the judgment that he had promised. Dismissive of the prophets' challenges about their lifestyle, they started trusting in the Temple of God rather than the God of the Temple (e.g., Jeremiah 1:1-15). In 586 BC God therefore allowed the Babylonians to besiege Jerusalem, destroy its Temple, and exile its people. The Temple was rebuilt on a much smaller scale after the Exile, grieving those who remembered the magnificent original (Ezra 3:8-13). By New Testament times Herod the Great had built another Temple that far surpassed Solomon's in splendor, but it too would end up in ruins.

▸ *See also **David's preparations for building the Temple**, page 472.*

to protect the entrance* to the Most Holy
Place. 22So he finished overlaying the entire
Temple with gold, including the altar that
belonged to the Most Holy Place.

23He made two cherubim of wild olive*
wood, each 15 feet* tall, and placed them
in the inner sanctuary. 24The wingspan of
each of the cherubim was 15 feet, each wing
being 7½ feet* long. 25The two cherubim
were identical in shape and size; 26each
was 15 feet tall. 27He placed them side by
side in the inner sanctuary of the Temple.
Their outspread wings reached from wall
to wall, while their inner wings touched at
the center of the room. 28He overlaid the two
cherubim with gold.

29He decorated all the walls of the inner
sanctuary and the main room with carvings
of cherubim, palm trees, and open flowers.
30He overlaid the floor in both rooms with
gold.

31For the entrance to the inner sanctuary,
he made double doors of wild olive wood
with five-sided doorposts.* 32These double
doors were decorated with carvings of cherubim, palm trees, and open flowers. The
doors, including the decorations of cherubim and palm trees, were overlaid with gold.

33Then he made four-sided doorposts
of wild olive wood for the entrance to the
Temple. 34There were two folding doors of
cypress wood, and each door was hinged
to fold back upon itself. 35These doors were
decorated with carvings of cherubim, palm
trees, and open flowers—all overlaid evenly
with gold.

36The walls of the inner courtyard were
built so that there was one layer of cedar
beams between every three layers of finished stone.

37The foundation of the LORD's Temple
was laid in midspring, in the month of Ziv,*
during the fourth year of Solomon's reign.
38The entire building was completed in
every detail by midautumn, in the month of
Bul,* during the eleventh year of his reign.
So it took seven years to build the Temple.

Solomon Builds His Palace

7 Solomon also built a palace for himself,
and it took him thirteen years to complete the construction.

2One of Solomon's buildings was called
the Palace of the Forest of Lebanon. It was
150 feet long, 75 feet wide, and 45 feet high.*
There were four rows of cedar pillars, and
great cedar beams rested on the pillars.
3The hall had a cedar roof. Above the beams
on the pillars were forty-five side rooms,*
arranged in three tiers of fifteen each. 4On
each end of the long hall were three rows
of windows facing each other. 5All the
doorways and doorposts* had rectangular
frames and were arranged in sets of three,
facing each other.

6Solomon also built the Hall of Pillars,
which was 75 feet long and 45 feet wide.*
There was a porch in front, along with a
canopy supported by pillars.

7Solomon also built the throne room,
known as the Hall of Justice, where he sat to
hear legal matters. It was paneled with cedar
from floor to ceiling.* 8Solomon's living
quarters surrounded a courtyard behind this
hall, and they were constructed the same
way. He also built similar living quarters for
Pharaoh's daughter, whom he had married.

9From foundation to eaves, all these
buildings were built from huge blocks
of high-quality stone, cut with saws and
trimmed to exact measure on all sides.
10Some of the huge foundation stones were
15 feet long, and some were 12 feet* long.
11The blocks of high-quality stone used in
the walls were also cut to measure, and
cedar beams were also used. 12The walls of
the great courtyard were built so that there
was one layer of cedar beams between every
three layers of finished stone, just like the
walls of the inner courtyard of the LORD's
Temple with its entry room.

Furnishings for the Temple

13King Solomon then asked for a man
named Huram* to come from Tyre. 14He was

6:8 As in Greek version; Hebrew reads *middle floor.* **6:10** Hebrew *5 cubits* [2.3 meters]. **6:17** Hebrew *40 cubits* [18.4 meters]. **6:20** Or *overlaid the altar with cedar.* The meaning of the Hebrew is uncertain. **6:21** Or *to draw curtains across.* The meaning of the Hebrew is uncertain. **6:23a** Or *pine;* Hebrew reads *oil tree;* also in 6:31, 33. **6:23b** Hebrew *10 cubits* [4.6 meters]; also in 6:24, 26. **6:24** Hebrew *5 cubits* [2.3 meters]. **6:31** The meaning of the Hebrew is uncertain. **6:37** Hebrew *was laid in the month of Ziv.* This month of the ancient Hebrew lunar calendar usually occurs within the months of April and May. **6:38** Hebrew *by the month of Bul, which is the eighth month.* This month of the ancient Hebrew lunar calendar usually occurs within the months of October and November. **7:2** Hebrew *100 cubits* [46 meters] *long, 50 cubits* [23 meters] *wide, and 30 cubits* [13.8 meters] *high.* **7:3** Or *45 rafters,* or *45 beams,* or *45 pillars.* The architectural details in 7:2-6 can be interpreted in many different ways. **7:5** Greek version reads *windows.* **7:6** Hebrew *50 cubits* [23 meters] *long and 30 cubits* [13.8 meters] *wide.* **7:7** As in Syriac version and Latin Vulgate; Hebrew reads *from floor to floor.* **7:10** Hebrew *10 cubits* [4.6 meters] . . . *8 cubits* [3.7 meters]. **7:13** Hebrew *Hiram* (also in 7:40, 45); compare 2 Chr 2:13. This is not the same person mentioned in 5:1.

half Israelite, since his mother was a widow from the tribe of Naphtali, and his father had been a craftsman in bronze from Tyre. Huram was extremely skillful and talented in any work in bronze, and he came to do all the metal work for King Solomon.

[15]Huram cast two bronze pillars, each 27 feet tall and 18 feet in circumference.* [16]For the tops of the pillars he cast bronze capitals, each 7½ feet* tall. [17]Each capital was decorated with seven sets of latticework and interwoven chains. [18]He also encircled the latticework with two rows of pomegranates to decorate the capitals over the pillars. [19]The capitals on the columns inside the entry room were shaped like water lilies, and they were six feet* tall. [20]The capitals on the two pillars had 200 pomegranates in two rows around them, beside the rounded surface next to the latticework. [21]Huram set the pillars at the entrance of the Temple, one toward the south and one toward the north. He named the one on the south Jakin, and the one on the north Boaz.* [22]The capitals on the pillars were shaped like water lilies. And so the work on the pillars was finished.

[23]Then Huram cast a great round basin, 15 feet across from rim to rim, called the Sea. It was 7½ feet deep and about 45 feet in circumference.* [24]It was encircled just below its rim by two rows of decorative gourds. There were about six gourds per foot* all the way around, and they were cast as part of the basin.

[25]The Sea was placed on a base of twelve bronze oxen,* all facing outward. Three faced north, three faced west, three faced south, and three faced east, and the Sea rested on them. [26]The walls of the Sea were about three inches* thick, and its rim flared out like a cup and resembled a water lily blossom. It could hold about 11,000 gallons* of water.

[27]Huram also made ten bronze water carts, each 6 feet long, 6 feet wide, and 4½ feet tall.* [28]They were constructed with side panels braced with crossbars. [29]Both the panels and the crossbars were decorated with carved lions, oxen, and cherubim. Above and below the lions and oxen were wreath decorations. [30]Each of these carts had four bronze wheels and bronze axles. There were supporting posts for the bronze basins at the corners of the carts; these supports were decorated on each side with carvings of wreaths. [31]The top of each cart had a rounded frame for the basin. It projected 1½ feet* above the cart's top like a round pedestal, and its opening was 2¼ feet* across; it was decorated on the outside with carvings of wreaths. The panels of the carts were square, not round. [32]Under the panels were four wheels that were connected to axles that had been cast as one unit with the cart. The wheels were 2¼ feet in diameter [33]and were similar to chariot wheels. The axles, spokes, rims, and hubs were all cast from molten bronze. [34]There were handles at each of the four corners of the carts, and these, too, were cast as one unit with the cart. [35]Around the top of each cart was a rim nine inches wide.* The corner supports and side panels were cast as one unit with the cart. [36]Carvings of cherubim, lions, and palm trees decorated the panels and corner supports wherever there was room, and there were wreaths all around. [37]All ten water carts were the same size and were made alike, for each was cast from the same mold.

[38]Huram also made ten smaller bronze basins, one for each cart. Each basin was six feet across and could hold 220 gallons* of water. [39]He set five water carts on the south side of the Temple and five on the north side. The great bronze basin called the Sea was placed near the southeast corner of the Temple. [40]He also made the necessary washbasins, shovels, and bowls.

So at last Huram completed everything King Solomon had assigned him to make for the Temple of the LORD:

41 the two pillars;
the two bowl-shaped capitals on top of the pillars;
the two networks of interwoven chains that decorated the capitals;
42 the 400 pomegranates that hung from the chains on the capitals (two rows of pomegranates for each of the chain networks that decorated the capitals on top of the pillars);
43 the ten water carts holding the ten basins;
44 the Sea and the twelve oxen under it;
45 the ash buckets, the shovels, and the bowls.

Huram made all these things of burnished bronze for the Temple of the LORD, just as

King Solomon had directed. 46 The king had
them cast in clay molds in the Jordan Valley
between Succoth and Zarethan. 47 Solomon
did not weigh all these things because there
were so many; the weight of the bronze
could not be measured.

48 Solomon also made all the furnishings
of the Temple of the LORD:

the gold altar;
the gold table for the Bread of the
Presence;
49 the lampstands of solid gold, five on the
south and five on the north, in front of
the Most Holy Place;
the flower decorations, lamps, and
tongs—all of gold;
50 the small bowls, lamp snuffers, bowls,
ladles, and incense burners—all of
solid gold;
the doors for the entrances to the Most
Holy Place and the main room of the
Temple, with their fronts overlaid
with gold.

51 So King Solomon finished all his work
on the Temple of the LORD. Then he brought
all the gifts his father, David, had dedicated—the silver, the gold, and the various
articles—and he stored them in the treasuries of the LORD's Temple.

The Ark Brought to the Temple

8 Solomon then summoned to Jerusalem
the elders of Israel and all the heads of
the tribes—the leaders of the ancestral families of the Israelites. They were to bring the
Ark of the LORD's Covenant to the Temple
from its location in the City of David, also
known as Zion. 2 So all the men of Israel assembled before King Solomon at the annual
Festival of Shelters, which is held in early
autumn in the month of Ethanim.*

3 When all the elders of Israel arrived,
the priests picked up the Ark. 4 The priests
and Levites brought up the Ark of the LORD
along with the special tent* and all the
sacred items that had been in it. 5 There,
before the Ark, King Solomon and the entire
community of Israel sacrificed so many
sheep, goats, and cattle that no one could
keep count!

6 Then the priests carried the Ark of the
LORD's Covenant into the inner sanctuary
of the Temple—the Most Holy Place—and
placed it beneath the wings of the cherubim.
7 The cherubim spread their wings over the
Ark, forming a canopy over the Ark and its
carrying poles. 8 These poles were so long
that their ends could be seen from the Holy
Place, which is in front of the Most Holy
Place, but not from the outside. They are
still there to this day. 9 Nothing was in the
Ark except the two stone tablets that Moses
had placed in it at Mount Sinai,* where the
LORD made a covenant with the people of
Israel when they left the land of Egypt.

10 When the priests came out of the Holy
Place, a thick cloud filled the Temple of the
LORD. 11 The priests could not continue their
service because of the cloud, for the glorious presence of the LORD filled the Temple
of the LORD.

Solomon Praises the LORD

12 Then Solomon prayed, "O LORD, you have
said that you would live in a thick cloud
of darkness. 13 Now I have built a glorious
Temple for you, a place where you can live
forever!*"

14 Then the king turned around to the
entire community of Israel standing before
him and gave this blessing: 15 "Praise the
LORD, the God of Israel, who has kept the
promise he made to my father, David. For
he told my father, 16 'From the day I brought
my people Israel out of Egypt, I have never
chosen a city among any of the tribes of
Israel as the place where a Temple should
be built to honor my name. But I have
chosen David to be king over my people
Israel.'"

17 Then Solomon said, "My father, David,
wanted to build this Temple to honor the
name of the LORD, the God of Israel. 18 But
the LORD told him, 'You wanted to build the
Temple to honor my name. Your intention is

7:15 Hebrew *18 cubits* [8.3 meters] *tall and 12 cubits* [5.5 meters] *in circumference.* **7:16** Hebrew *5 cubits* [2.3 meters]. **7:19** Hebrew *4 cubits* [1.8 meters]; also in 7:38. **7:21** *Jakin* probably means "he establishes"; *Boaz* probably means "in him is strength." **7:23** Hebrew *10 cubits* [4.6 meters] *across. . . . 5 cubits* [2.3 meters] *deep and 30 cubits* [13.8 meters] *in circumference.* **7:24** Or *20 gourds per meter;* Hebrew reads *10 per cubit.* **7:25** Hebrew *12 oxen;* compare 2 Kgs 16:17, which specifies *bronze oxen.* **7:26a** Hebrew *a handbreadth* [8 centimeters]. **7:26b** Hebrew *2,000 baths* [42 kiloliters]. **7:27** Hebrew *4 cubits* [1.8 meters] *long, 4 cubits wide, and 3 cubits* [1.4 meters] *high.* **7:31a** Hebrew *a cubit* [46 centimeters]. **7:31b** Hebrew *1½ cubits* [69 centimeters]; also in 7:32. **7:35** Hebrew *half a cubit wide* [23 centimeters]. **7:38** Hebrew *40 baths* [840 liters]. **8:2** Hebrew *at the festival in the month Ethanim, which is the seventh month.* The Festival of Shelters began on the fifteenth day of the seventh month of the ancient Hebrew lunar calendar. This day occurred in late September, October, or early November. **8:4** Hebrew *the Tent of Meeting;* i.e., the tent mentioned in 2 Sam 6:17 and 1 Chr 16:1. **8:9** Hebrew *at Horeb*, another name for Sinai. **8:13** Some Greek texts add the line *Is this not written in the Book of Jashar?*

good, 19but you are not the one to do it. One
of your own sons will build the Temple to
honor me.'
20"And now the LORD has fulfilled the
promise he made, for I have become king
in my father's place, and now I sit on the
throne of Israel, just as the LORD promised.
I have built this Temple to honor the name
of the LORD, the God of Israel. 21And I have
prepared a place there for the Ark, which
contains the covenant that the LORD made
with our ancestors when he brought them
out of Egypt."

Solomon's Prayer of Dedication

22Then Solomon stood before the altar of
the LORD in front of the entire community
of Israel. He lifted his hands toward heaven,
23and he prayed,

"O LORD, God of Israel, there is no God
like you in all of heaven above or on the
earth below. You keep your covenant
and show unfailing love to all who walk
before you in wholehearted devotion.
24You have kept your promise to your
servant David, my father. You made that
promise with your own mouth, and with
your own hands you have fulfilled it
today.
25"And now, O LORD, God of Israel,
carry out the additional promise you
made to your servant David, my father.
For you said to him, 'If your descendants
guard their behavior and faithfully
follow me as you have done, one of
them will always sit on the throne of
Israel.' 26Now, O God of Israel, fulfill this
promise to your servant David, my father.
27"But will God really live on earth?
Why, even the highest heavens cannot
contain you. How much less this Temple
I have built! 28Nevertheless, listen to
my prayer and my plea, O LORD my
God. Hear the cry and the prayer that
your servant is making to you today.
29May you watch over this Temple night
and day, this place where you have
said, 'My name will be there.' May you
always hear the prayers I make toward
this place. 30May you hear the humble
and earnest requests from me and your
people Israel when we pray toward this
place. Yes, hear us from heaven where
you live, and when you hear, forgive.
31"If someone wrongs another
person and is required to take an oath
of innocence in front of your altar in
this Temple, 32then hear from heaven
and judge between your servants—
the accuser and the accused. Punish
the guilty as they deserve. Acquit the
innocent because of their innocence.
33"If your people Israel are defeated by
their enemies because they have sinned
against you, and if they turn to you
and acknowledge your name and pray
to you here in this Temple, 34then hear
from heaven and forgive the sin of your
people Israel and return them to this
land you gave their ancestors.
35"If the skies are shut up and there
is no rain because your people have
sinned against you, and if they pray
toward this Temple and acknowledge
your name and turn from their sins
because you have punished them, 36then
hear from heaven and forgive the sins of
your servants, your people Israel. Teach
them to follow the right path, and send
rain on your land that you have given to
your people as their special possession.
37"If there is a famine in the land or
a plague or crop disease or attacks of
locusts or caterpillars, or if your people's
enemies are in the land besieging their
towns—whatever disaster or disease
there is—38and if your people Israel pray
about their troubles, raising their hands
toward this Temple, 39then hear from
heaven where you live, and forgive. Give
your people what their actions deserve,
for you alone know each human heart.
40Then they will fear you as long as
they live in the land you gave to our
ancestors.
41"In the future, foreigners who do not
belong to your people Israel will hear of
you. They will come from distant lands
because of your name, 42for they will
hear of your great name and your strong
hand and your powerful arm. And when
they pray toward this Temple, 43then hear
from heaven where you live, and grant
what they ask of you. In this way, all the
people of the earth will come to know
and fear you, just as your own people
Israel do. They, too, will know that this
Temple I have built honors your name.
44"If your people go out where you

send them to fight their enemies, and if
they pray to the LORD by turning toward
this city you have chosen and toward
this Temple I have built to honor your
name, 45 then hear their prayers from
heaven and uphold their cause.
46 "If they sin against you—and who
has never sinned?—you might become
angry with them and let their enemies
conquer them and take them captive to
their land far away or near. 47 But in that
land of exile, they might turn to you in
repentance and pray, 'We have sinned,
done evil, and acted wickedly.' 48 If they
turn to you with their whole heart and
soul in the land of their enemies and
pray toward the land you gave to their
ancestors—toward this city you have
chosen, and toward this Temple I have
built to honor your name—49 then hear
their prayers and their petition from
heaven where you live, and uphold
their cause. 50 Forgive your people who
have sinned against you. Forgive all the
offenses they have committed against
you. Make their captors merciful to them,
51 for they are your people—your special
possession—whom you brought out of
the iron-smelting furnace of Egypt.
52 "May your eyes be open to my
requests and to the requests of your
people Israel. May you hear and answer
them whenever they cry out to you. 53 For
when you brought our ancestors out of
Egypt, O Sovereign LORD, you told your
servant Moses that you had set Israel
apart from all the nations of the earth
to be your own special possession."

The Dedication of the Temple

54 When Solomon finished making these
prayers and petitions to the LORD, he stood
up in front of the altar of the LORD, where
he had been kneeling with his hands raised
toward heaven. 55 He stood and in a loud
voice blessed the entire congregation of
Israel:
56 "Praise the LORD who has given rest to
his people Israel, just as he promised. Not
one word has failed of all the wonderful
promises he gave through his servant
Moses. 57 May the LORD our God be with us
as he was with our ancestors; may he never
leave us or abandon us. 58 May he give us
the desire to do his will in everything and
to obey all the commands, decrees, and regulations that he gave our ancestors. 59 And
may these words that I have prayed in the

Sin

Sin is primarily disobedience to God. That is the first picture of sin we see in the Bible: Adam and Eve disobeyed God and bore the consequences—expulsion from the Garden of Eden and God's intimate presence (Genesis 3). From that point on, sin infected the whole human race (see *The fall of humanity*, page 7)—the point of Solomon's rhetorical question, "Who has never sinned?" (1 Kings 8:46). As Paul puts it, "everyone has sinned; we all fall short of God's glorious standard" (Romans 3:23)—no matter how great, important, or holy we might think ourselves to be. In fact the Bible says that "if we claim we have no sin, we are only fooling ourselves and not living in the truth" (1 John 1:8).

Our word "sin" translates several different words in the Bible describing disobedience to God. In the Old Testament, key words for sin mean missing the mark, rebellion, twisting things, and straying from the right path. In the New Testament, key words mean missing a target or taking a wrong road, making a mistake, transgression, ungodliness, evil, and wickedness. Sin is very wide-ranging; it is not just bad things we do, but also good things we fail to do.

But here is the good news: The Bible says that "if we confess our sins to him, he is faithful and just to forgive us our sins and to cleanse us from all wickedness" (1 John 1:9).

▸ *See also* ***How can I be sure God has forgiven me?****, page 1433.*

presence of the LORD be before him constantly, day and night, so that the LORD our
God may give justice to me and to his people
Israel, according to each day's needs.
[60]Then people all over the earth will know
that the LORD alone is God and there is no
other. [61]And may you be completely faithful
to the LORD our God. May you always obey
his decrees and commands, just as you are
doing today."

[62]Then the king and all Israel with him
offered sacrifices to the LORD. [63]Solomon
offered to the LORD a peace offering of
22,000 cattle and 120,000 sheep and goats.
And so the king and all the people of Israel
dedicated the Temple of the LORD.

[64]That same day the king consecrated the
central area of the courtyard in front of the
LORD's Temple. He offered burnt offerings,
grain offerings, and the fat of peace offerings there, because the bronze altar in the
LORD's presence was too small to hold all
the burnt offerings, grain offerings, and the
fat of the peace offerings.

[65]Then Solomon and all Israel celebrated
the Festival of Shelters* in the presence of
the LORD our God. A large congregation had
gathered from as far away as Lebo-hamath in
the north and the Brook of Egypt in the south.
The celebration went on for fourteen days in
all—seven days for the dedication of the altar
and seven days for the Festival of Shelters.*
[66]After the festival was over,* Solomon sent
the people home. They blessed the king and
went to their homes joyful and glad because
the LORD had been good to his servant David
and to his people Israel.

The LORD's Response to Solomon

9 So Solomon finished building the
Temple of the LORD, as well as the royal
palace. He completed everything he had
planned to do. [2]Then the LORD appeared
to Solomon a second time, as he had done
before at Gibeon. [3]The LORD said to him,

"I have heard your prayer and your
petition. I have set this Temple apart to
be holy—this place you have built where
my name will be honored forever. I will
always watch over it, for it is dear to my
heart.

[4]"As for you, if you will follow me with
integrity and godliness, as David your
father did, obeying all my commands,
decrees, and regulations, [5]then I will
establish the throne of your dynasty
over Israel forever. For I made this
promise to your father, David: 'One of
your descendants will always sit on the
throne of Israel.'

[6]"But if you or your descendants
abandon me and disobey the commands
and decrees I have given you, and if
you serve and worship other gods,
[7]then I will uproot Israel from this land
that I have given them. I will reject this
Temple that I have made holy to honor
my name. I will make Israel an object of
mockery and ridicule among the nations.
[8]And though this Temple is impressive
now, all who pass by will be appalled
and will gasp in horror. They will ask,
'Why did the LORD do such terrible
things to this land and to this Temple?'

Hazor, Megiddo, and Gezer

As part of his strengthening of Israel's defenses, Solomon fortified three strategic cities: Hazor, north of the Sea of Kinnereth (later called the Sea of Galilee); Megiddo, which controlled the pass through the Mount Carmel range from the Valley of Jezreel to the coastal Plain of Sharon; and Gezer, which lay northwest of Jerusalem. Together these three fortified cities gave Solomon control of the main north–south highway.

Megiddo's strategic position and the huge size of its plain meant it was the site of many battles. The book of Revelation picks up this fact and uses Megiddo (almost certainly symbolically) as the setting for the final battle of Armageddon ("the Hill of Megiddo"), when God's enemies make their final stand against him (Revelation 16:16).

▶ *See also* ***Armageddon****, page 1461;* ***Kingdoms of Israel*** *maps, Visual Overview Z6.*

9 “And the answer will be, ‘Because
his people abandoned the LORD their
God, who brought their ancestors out of
Egypt, and they worshiped other gods
instead and bowed down to them. That
is why the LORD has brought all these
disasters on them.’”

Solomon's Agreement with Hiram

10 It took Solomon twenty years to build the
LORD's Temple and his own royal palace.
At the end of that time, 11 he gave twenty
towns in the land of Galilee to King Hiram
of Tyre. (Hiram had previously provided all
the cedar and cypress timber and gold that
Solomon had requested.) 12 But when Hiram
came from Tyre to see the towns Solomon
had given him, he was not at all pleased
with them. 13 “What kind of towns are these,
my brother?” he asked. So Hiram called that
area Cabul (which means “worthless”), as it
is still known today. 14 Nevertheless, Hiram
paid* Solomon 9,000 pounds* of gold.

Solomon's Many Achievements

15 This is the account of the forced labor
that King Solomon conscripted to build the
LORD's Temple, the royal palace, the supporting terraces,* the wall of Jerusalem,
and the cities of Hazor, Megiddo, and Gezer.
16 (Pharaoh, the king of Egypt, had attacked
and captured Gezer, killing the Canaanite
population and burning it down. He gave
the city to his daughter as a wedding gift
when she married Solomon. 17 So Solomon
rebuilt the city of Gezer.) He also built up
the towns of Lower Beth-horon, 18 Baalath,
and Tamar* in the wilderness within his
land. 19 He built towns as supply centers and
constructed towns where his chariots and
horses* could be stationed. He built everything he desired in Jerusalem and Lebanon
and throughout his entire realm.

20 There were still some people living in
the land who were not Israelites, including
Amorites, Hittites, Perizzites, Hivites, and
Jebusites. 21 These were descendants of the
nations whom the people of Israel had not
completely destroyed.* So Solomon conscripted them as slaves, and they serve as
forced laborers to this day. 22 But Solomon did
not conscript any of the Israelites for forced
labor. Instead, he assigned them to serve as
fighting men, government officials, officers
and captains in his army, commanders of
his chariots, and charioteers. 23 Solomon appointed 550 of them to supervise the people
working on his various projects.

24 Solomon moved his wife, Pharaoh's
daughter, from the City of David to the new
palace he had built for her. Then he constructed the supporting terraces.

25 Three times each year Solomon presented burnt offerings and peace offerings
on the altar he had built for the LORD. He
also burned incense to the LORD. And so he
finished the work of building the Temple.

26 King Solomon also built a fleet of ships
at Ezion-geber, a port near Elath* in the
land of Edom, along the shore of the Red
Sea.* 27 Hiram sent experienced crews of
sailors to sail the ships with Solomon's men.
28 They sailed to Ophir and brought back to
Solomon some sixteen tons* of gold.

Visit of the Queen of Sheba

10 When the queen of Sheba heard of
Solomon's fame, which brought honor
to the name of the LORD,* she came to test
him with hard questions. 2 She arrived in Jerusalem with a large group of attendants and
a great caravan of camels loaded with spices,
large quantities of gold, and precious jewels.
When she met with Solomon, she talked with
him about everything she had on her mind.
3 Solomon had answers for all her questions;
nothing was too hard for the king to explain
to her. 4 When the queen of Sheba realized
how very wise Solomon was, and when she
saw the palace he had built, 5 she was overwhelmed. She was also amazed at the food
on his tables, the organization of his officials
and their splendid clothing, the cup-bearers,
and the burnt offerings Solomon made at the
Temple of the LORD.

6 She exclaimed to the king, “Everything
I heard in my country about your achievements* and wisdom is true! 7 I didn't believe
what was said until I arrived here and saw it

8:65a Hebrew *the festival;* see note on 8:2. **8:65b** Hebrew *seven days and seven days, fourteen days;* compare parallel text at 2 Chr 7:8-10. **8:66** Hebrew *On the eighth day,* probably referring to the day following the seven-day Festival of Shelters; compare parallel text at 2 Chr 7:9-10. **9:14a** Or *For Hiram had paid.* **9:14b** Hebrew *120 talents* [4,000 kilograms]. **9:15** Hebrew *the millo;* also in 9:24. The meaning of the Hebrew is uncertain. **9:18** An alternate reading in the Masoretic Text reads *Tadmor.* **9:19** Or *and charioteers.* **9:21** The Hebrew term used here refers to the complete consecration of things or people to the LORD, either by destroying them or by giving them as an offering. **9:26a** As in Greek version (see also 2 Kgs 14:22; 16:6); Hebrew reads *Eloth,* a variant spelling of Elath. **9:26b** Hebrew *sea of reeds.* **9:28** Hebrew *420 talents* [14 metric tons]. **10:1** Or *which was due to the name of the LORD.* The meaning of the Hebrew is uncertain. **10:6** Hebrew *your words.*

with my own eyes. In fact, I had not heard the half of it! Your wisdom and prosperity are far beyond what I was told. [8]How happy your people* must be! What a privilege for your officials to stand here day after day, listening to your wisdom! [9]Praise the LORD your God, who delights in you and has placed you on the throne of Israel. Because of the LORD's eternal love for Israel, he has made you king so you can rule with justice and righteousness."

[10]Then she gave the king a gift of 9,000 pounds* of gold, great quantities of spices, and precious jewels. Never again were so many spices brought in as those the queen of Sheba gave to King Solomon.

[11](In addition, Hiram's ships brought gold from Ophir, and they also brought rich cargoes of red sandalwood* and precious jewels. [12]The king used the sandalwood to make railings for the Temple of the LORD and the royal palace, and to construct lyres and harps for the musicians. Never before or since has there been such a supply of sandalwood.)

[13]King Solomon gave the queen of Sheba whatever she asked for, besides all the customary gifts he had so generously given. Then she and all her attendants returned to their own land.

Solomon's Wealth and Splendor

[14]Each year Solomon received about 25 tons* of gold. [15]This did not include the additional revenue he received from merchants and traders, all the kings of Arabia, and the governors of the land.

[16]King Solomon made 200 large shields of hammered gold, each weighing more than fifteen pounds.* [17]He also made 300 smaller shields of hammered gold, each weighing nearly four pounds.* The king placed these shields in the Palace of the Forest of Lebanon.

[18]Then the king made a huge throne, decorated with ivory and overlaid with fine gold. [19]The throne had six steps and a rounded back. There were armrests on both sides of the seat, and the figure of a lion stood on each side of the throne. [20]There were also twelve other lions, one standing on each end of the six steps. No other throne in all the world could be compared with it!

[21]All of King Solomon's drinking cups were solid gold, as were all the utensils in the Palace of the Forest of Lebanon. They were not made of silver, for silver was considered worthless in Solomon's day!

[22]The king had a fleet of trading ships of Tarshish that sailed with Hiram's fleet. Once every three years the ships returned, loaded with gold, silver, ivory, apes, and peacocks.*

[23]So King Solomon became richer and wiser than any other king on earth. [24]People from every nation came to consult him and to hear the wisdom God had given him. [25]Year after year everyone who visited brought him gifts of silver and gold, clothing, weapons, spices, horses, and mules.

[26]Solomon built up a huge force of chariots and horses.* He had 1,400 chariots and 12,000 horses. He stationed some of them in the chariot cities and some near him in Jerusalem. [27]The king made silver as plentiful in Jerusalem as stone. And valuable cedar timber was as common as the sycamore-fig trees that grow in the foothills of Judah.* [28]Solomon's horses were imported from Egypt* and from Cilicia*; the king's traders acquired them from Cilicia at the standard price. [29]At that time chariots from Egypt could be purchased for 600 pieces of silver,* and horses for 150 pieces of silver.* They were then exported to the kings of the Hittites and the kings of Aram.

Solomon's Many Wives

11 Now King Solomon loved many foreign women. Besides Pharaoh's daughter, he married women from Moab, Ammon, Edom, Sidon, and from among the Hittites. [2]The LORD had clearly instructed the people of Israel, "You must not marry them, because they will turn your hearts to their gods." Yet Solomon insisted on loving them anyway. [3]He had 700 wives of royal birth and 300 concubines. And in fact, they did turn his heart away from the LORD.

[4]In Solomon's old age, they turned his heart to worship other gods instead of being completely faithful to the LORD his God, as his father, David, had been. [5]Solomon worshiped Ashtoreth, the goddess of the Sidonians, and Molech,* the detestable god of the Ammonites. [6]In this way, Solomon did what was evil in the LORD's sight; he refused to follow the LORD completely, as his father, David, had done.

[7]On the Mount of Olives, east of Jerusalem,* he even built a pagan shrine for

Chemosh, the detestable god of Moab, and
another for Molech, the detestable god of
the Ammonites. 8Solomon built such shrines
for all his foreign wives to use for burning
incense and sacrificing to their gods.
9The LORD was very angry with Solomon,
for his heart had turned away from the LORD,
the God of Israel, who had appeared to him
twice. 10He had warned Solomon specifically
about worshiping other gods, but Solomon
did not listen to the LORD's command. 11So
now the LORD said to him, "Since you have
not kept my covenant and have disobeyed
my decrees, I will surely tear the kingdom
away from you and give it to one of your
servants. 12But for the sake of your father,
David, I will not do this while you are still
alive. I will take the kingdom away from your
son. 13And even so, I will not take away the
entire kingdom; I will let him be king of one
tribe, for the sake of my servant David and
for the sake of Jerusalem, my chosen city."

Solomon's Adversaries

14Then the LORD raised up Hadad the
Edomite, a member of Edom's royal family,
to be Solomon's adversary. 15Years before,
David had defeated Edom. Joab, his army
commander, had stayed to bury some of the
Israelite soldiers who had died in battle.
While there, they killed every male in Edom.
16Joab and the army of Israel had stayed
there for six months, killing them.
17But Hadad and a few of his father's royal
officials escaped and headed for Egypt.
(Hadad was just a boy at the time.) 18They set
out from Midian and went to Paran, where
others joined them. Then they traveled to
Egypt and went to Pharaoh, who gave them a
home, food, and some land. 19Pharaoh grew
very fond of Hadad, and he gave him his
wife's sister in marriage—the sister of Queen
Tahpenes. 20She bore him a son named Ge-
nubath. Tahpenes raised him* in Pharaoh's
palace among Pharaoh's own sons.
21When the news reached Hadad in Egypt
that David and his commander Joab were
both dead, he said to Pharaoh, "Let me
return to my own country."
22"Why?" Pharaoh asked him. "What do
you lack here that makes you want to go
home?"
"Nothing," he replied. "But even so,
please let me return home."
23God also raised up Rezon son of Eliada
as Solomon's adversary. Rezon had fled
from his master, King Hadadezer of Zobah,
24and had become the leader of a gang of
rebels. After David conquered Hadadezer,
Rezon and his men fled to Damascus, where
he became king. 25Rezon was Israel's bitter
adversary for the rest of Solomon's reign,
and he made trouble, just as Hadad did.

10:8 Greek and Syriac versions and Latin Vulgate read *your wives.* **10:10** Hebrew *120 talents* [4,000 kilograms]. **10:11** Hebrew *almug wood;* also in 10:12. **10:14** Hebrew *666 talents* [23 metric tons]. **10:16** Hebrew *600 [shekels] of gold* [6.8 kilograms]. **10:17** Hebrew *3 minas* [1.8 kilograms]. **10:22** Or *and baboons.* **10:26** Or *charioteers;* also in 10:26b. **10:27** Hebrew *the Shephelah.* **10:28a** Possibly *Muzur,* a district near Cilicia; also in 10:29. **10:28b** Hebrew *Kue,* probably another name for Cilicia. **10:29a** Hebrew *600 [shekels] of silver,* about 15 pounds or 6.8 kilograms in weight. **10:29b** Hebrew *150 [shekels],* about 3.8 pounds or 1.7 kilograms in weight. **11:5** Hebrew *Milcom,* a variant spelling of Molech; also in 11:33. **11:7** Hebrew *On the mountain east of Jerusalem.* **11:20** As in Greek version; Hebrew reads *weaned him.*

Chemosh and Molech

When Solomon allowed his foreign wives to bring their gods with them, he perhaps thought he was simply being kind or accommodating. But he didn't think of the consequences, and he certainly didn't pay attention to what God said. For God said these gods were "detestable" (1 Kings 11:7) and had told his people before they entered Canaan that they were to have nothing to do with them (e.g., Exodus 23:23-26; 34:15-16; Deuteronomy 7:1-6). Neither Chemosh nor Molech reflected anything of what the true God was like: Chemosh, a Moabite god, was associated with death, plague, drought, and famine; Molech, an Ammonite god, was associated with child sacrifice. Perhaps Solomon thought no harm would come from letting his wives worship these gods privately, but they would soon take hold in Israel, and future kings would themselves worship them and practice child sacrifice (e.g., 2 Kings 16:1-4; 21:1-6). Failing to think of long-term consequences is always disastrous.

Rezon hated Israel intensely and continued
to reign in Aram.

Jeroboam Rebels against Solomon

26 Another rebel leader was Jeroboam son of
Nebat, one of Solomon's own officials. He
came from the town of Zeredah in Ephraim,
and his mother was Zeruah, a widow.

27 This is the story behind his rebellion.
Solomon was rebuilding the supporting
terraces* and repairing the walls of the city
of his father, David. 28 Jeroboam was a very
capable young man, and when Solomon saw
how industrious he was, he put him in charge
of the labor force from the tribes of Ephraim
and Manasseh, the descendants of Joseph.

29 One day as Jeroboam was leaving Jerusalem, the prophet Ahijah from Shiloh met
him along the way. Ahijah was wearing a new
cloak. The two of them were alone in a field,
30 and Ahijah took hold of the new cloak he
was wearing and tore it into twelve pieces.
31 Then he said to Jeroboam, "Take ten of these
pieces, for this is what the LORD, the God of
Israel, says: 'I am about to tear the kingdom
from the hand of Solomon, and I will give ten
of the tribes to you! 32 But I will leave him one
tribe for the sake of my servant David and for
the sake of Jerusalem, which I have chosen
out of all the tribes of Israel. 33 For Solomon
has* abandoned me and worshiped Ashtoreth, the goddess of the Sidonians; Chemosh,
the god of Moab; and Molech, the god of the
Ammonites. He has not followed my ways
and done what is pleasing in my sight. He
has not obeyed my decrees and regulations
as David his father did.

34 "'But I will not take the entire kingdom
from Solomon at this time. For the sake of
my servant David, the one whom I chose
and who obeyed my commands and
decrees, I will keep Solomon as leader
for the rest of his life. 35 But I will take the
kingdom away from his son and give ten
of the tribes to you. 36 His son will have one
tribe so that the descendants of David my
servant will continue to reign, shining like
a lamp in Jerusalem, the city I have chosen
to be the place for my name. 37 And I will
place you on the throne of Israel, and you
will rule over all that your heart desires. 38 If
you listen to what I tell you and follow my
ways and do whatever I consider to be right,
and if you obey my decrees and commands,
as my servant David did, then I will always
be with you. I will establish an enduring
dynasty for you as I did for David, and I will
give Israel to you. 39 Because of Solomon's
sin I will punish the descendants of David—
though not forever.'"

40 Solomon tried to kill Jeroboam, but he
fled to King Shishak of Egypt and stayed
there until Solomon died.

Summary of Solomon's Reign

41 The rest of the events in Solomon's reign,
including all his deeds and his wisdom, are
recorded in *The Book of the Acts of Solomon.*
42 Solomon ruled in Jerusalem over all Israel
for forty years. 43 When he died, he was
buried in the City of David, named for his
father. Then his son Rehoboam became the
next king.

The Northern Tribes Revolt

12 Rehoboam went to Shechem, where
all Israel had gathered to make him
king. 2 When Jeroboam son of Nebat heard
of this, he returned from Egypt,* for he had
fled to Egypt to escape from King Solomon.
3 The leaders of Israel summoned him, and
Jeroboam and the whole assembly of Israel
went to speak with Rehoboam. 4 "Your father
was a hard master," they said. "Lighten the
harsh labor demands and heavy taxes that
your father imposed on us. Then we will be
your loyal subjects."

5 Rehoboam replied, "Give me three days
to think this over. Then come back for my
answer." So the people went away.

6 Then King Rehoboam discussed the
matter with the older men who had counseled his father, Solomon. "What is your
advice?" he asked. "How should I answer
these people?"

7 The older counselors replied, "If you are
willing to be a servant to these people today
and give them a favorable answer, they will
always be your loyal subjects."

8 But Rehoboam rejected the advice of the
older men and instead asked the opinion
of the young men who had grown up with
him and were now his advisers. 9 "What is
your advice?" he asked them. "How should
I answer these people who want me to
lighten the burdens imposed by my father?"

10 The young men replied, "This is what

11:27 Hebrew *the millo.* The meaning of the Hebrew is uncertain.
11:33 As in Greek, Syriac, and Latin Vulgate; Hebrew reads *For they have.* **12:2** As in Greek version and Latin Vulgate (see also 2 Chr 10:2); Hebrew reads *he lived in Egypt.*

Rulers of Israel and Judah

RULERS OF UNITED ISRAEL

Saul | 1 Samuel 8–31; 1 Chronicles 10 | ***see page 318***
David | 1 Samuel 16:1—1 Kings 2:12; 1 Chronicles 11–29 | ***see page 323***
Solomon | 1 Kings 1–11; 2 Chronicles 1–9 | ***see page 377***

RULERS OF JUDAH
Southern Kingdom

Rehoboam | 1 Kings 12:1-24; 14:21-31; 2 Chronicles 10–12 | ***see page 394***
Abijah | 1 Kings 15:1-8; 2 Chronicles 13:1–14:1
Asa | 1 Kings 15:9-24; 2 Chronicles 14:2–16:14 | ***see page 496***
Jehoshaphat | 1 Kings 22:41-50; 2 Chronicles 17:1–21:1 | ***see page 498***
Jehoram | 2 Kings 8:16-24; 2 Chronicles 21:2-20
Ahaziah | 2 Kings 8:25-29; 2 Chronicles 22:1-9
Queen Athaliah | 2 Kings 11:1-16; 2 Chronicles 22:10–23:15
Joash | 2 Kings 12; 2 Chronicles 24 ***see page 504***
Amaziah | 2 Kings 14:1-22; 2 Chronicles 25
Uzziah/Azariah | 2 Kings 15:1-7; 2 Chronicles 26
Jotham | 2 Kings 15:32-38; 2 Chronicles 27
Ahaz | 2 Kings 16; 2 Chronicles 28
Hezekiah | 2 Kings 18:1–20:21; 2 Chronicles 29–32 | ***see page 786***
Manasseh | 2 Kings 21:1-18; 2 Chronicles 33:1-20 | ***see page 439***
Amon | 2 Kings 21:19-26; 2 Chronicles 33:21-25
Josiah | 2 Kings 22:1–23:30; 2 Chronicles 34:1–36:1
Jehoahaz | 2 Kings 23:31-34; 2 Chronicles 36:2-4
Jehoiakim | 2 Kings 23:34–24:7; 2 Chronicles 36:5-8 | ***see page 867***
Jehoiachin | 2 Kings 24:8-17; 25:27-30; 2 Chronicles 36:9-10
Zedekiah | 2 Kings 24:18–25:26; 2 Chronicles 36:11-20 | ***see page 444***

RULERS OF ISRAEL
Northern Kingdom

Jeroboam I | 1 Kings 12:25–14:20 ***see page 396***
Nadab | 1 Kings 15:25-31
Baasha | 1 Kings 15:32–16:7
Elah | 1 Kings 16:8-14
Zimri | 1 Kings 16:15-20
Omri | 1 Kings 16:21-28
Ahab | 1 Kings 16:29–22:40 ***see page 407***
Ahaziah | 1 Kings 22:51—2 Kings 1:18
Joram | 2 Kings 3:1–8:15
Jehu | 2 Kings 9:1–10:36
Jehoahaz | 2 Kings 13:1-9
Jehoash | 2 Kings 13:10-25
Jeroboam II | 2 Kings 14:23-29
Zechariah | 2 Kings 15:8-12
Shallum | 2 Kings 15:13-15
Menahem | 2 Kings 15:16-22
Pekahiah | 2 Kings 15:23-26
Pekah | 2 Kings 15:27-31
Hoshea | 2 Kings 17:1-6

▶ *See also* ***A timeline of the Bible****, pages A22-A24;* ***Kingdoms of Israel*** *maps, Visual Overview Z6.*

you should tell those complainers who want
a lighter burden: 'My little finger is thicker
than my father's waist! 11Yes, my father laid
heavy burdens on you, but I'm going to make
them even heavier! My father beat you with
whips, but I will beat you with scorpions!'"
12Three days later Jeroboam and all the
people returned to hear Rehoboam's decision, just as the king had ordered. 13But Rehoboam spoke harshly to the people, for he
rejected the advice of the older counselors
14and followed the counsel of his younger
advisers. He told the people, "My father laid
heavy burdens on you, but I'm going to make
them even heavier! My father beat you with
whips, but I will beat you with scorpions!"
15So the king paid no attention to the
people. This turn of events was the will of
the LORD, for it fulfilled the LORD's message
to Jeroboam son of Nebat through the
prophet Ahijah from Shiloh.
16When all Israel realized that the
king had refused to listen to them, they
responded,

"Down with the dynasty of David!
We have no interest in the son of
Jesse.
Back to your homes, O Israel!
Look out for your own house,
O David!"

So the people of Israel returned home.
17But Rehoboam continued to rule over the
Israelites who lived in the towns of Judah.
18King Rehoboam sent Adoniram,* who
was in charge of forced labor, to restore
order, but the people of Israel stoned him
to death. When this news reached King Rehoboam, he quickly jumped into his chariot
and fled to Jerusalem. 19And to this day the
northern tribes of Israel have refused to be
ruled by a descendant of David.
20When the people of Israel learned of Jeroboam's return from Egypt, they called an
assembly and made him king over all Israel.
So only the tribe of Judah remained loyal to
the family of David.

Shemaiah's Prophecy

21When Rehoboam arrived at Jerusalem, he
mobilized the men of Judah and the tribe of
Benjamin—180,000 select troops—to fight
against the men of Israel and to restore the
kingdom to himself.
22But God said to Shemaiah, the man of
God, 23"Say to Rehoboam son of Solomon,
king of Judah, and to all the people of Judah
and Benjamin, and to the rest of the people,
24'This is what the LORD says: Do not fight
against your relatives, the Israelites. Go back
home, for what has happened is my doing!'"
So they obeyed the message of the LORD and
went home, as the LORD had commanded.

Jeroboam Makes Gold Calves

25Jeroboam then built up the city of
Shechem in the hill country of Ephraim,
and it became his capital. Later he went and
built up the town of Peniel.*
26Jeroboam thought to himself, "Unless I
am careful, the kingdom will return to the
dynasty of David. 27When these people go to
Jerusalem to offer sacrifices at the Temple of
the LORD, they will again give their allegiance

King Rehoboam

If Solomon had been renowned for his wisdom, then his son Rehoboam would become known for his stupidity. When Israel's leaders asked him for relief from the burdens Solomon had put upon them, Rehoboam completely rejected the elders' wisdom and took his young friends' advice instead, threatening to be even tougher than his father. As a result the ten northern tribes broke away, setting up a new kingdom (called Israel) under the leadership of Jeroboam, one of Solomon's officials. Rehoboam was left with a much smaller nation, now called Judah. He reigned for seventeen years (930–913 BC), but his heart was never devoted to God. He permitted idolatry, religious prostitution, and shrines to pagan gods (1 Kings 14:21-24). So God allowed Egypt to attack Judah, and they confiscated some of the Temple's treasures (14:25-27).

▸ *see also **Kingdoms of Israel** maps, Visual Overview Z6.*

to King Rehoboam of Judah. They will kill me
and make him their king instead."
28 So on the advice of his counselors, the
king made two gold calves. He said to the
people,* "It is too much trouble for you to
worship in Jerusalem. Look, Israel, these
are the gods who brought you out of Egypt!"
29 He placed these calf idols in Bethel and
in Dan—at either end of his kingdom. 30 But
this became a great sin, for the people worshiped the idols, traveling as far north as
Dan to worship the one there.
31 Jeroboam also erected buildings at the
pagan shrines and ordained priests from the
common people—those who were not from
the priestly tribe of Levi. 32 And Jeroboam instituted a religious festival in Bethel, held
on the fifteenth day of the eighth month,* in
imitation of the annual Festival of Shelters
in Judah. There at Bethel he himself offered
sacrifices to the calves he had made, and
he appointed priests for the pagan shrines
he had made. 33 So on the fifteenth day of
the eighth month, a day that he himself had
designated, Jeroboam offered sacrifices on
the altar at Bethel. He instituted a religious
festival for Israel, and he went up to the
altar to burn incense.

A Prophet Denounces Jeroboam

13 At the LORD's command, a man of
God from Judah went to Bethel, arriving there just as Jeroboam was approaching the altar to burn incense. 2 Then at the
LORD's command, he shouted, "O altar,
altar! This is what the LORD says: A child
named Josiah will be born into the dynasty
of David. On you he will sacrifice the priests
from the pagan shrines who come here to
burn incense, and human bones will be
burned on you." 3 That same day the man
of God gave a sign to prove his message. He
said, "The LORD has promised to give this
sign: This altar will split apart, and its ashes
will be poured out on the ground."
4 When King Jeroboam heard the man of
God speaking against the altar at Bethel,
he pointed at him and shouted, "Seize that
man!" But instantly the king's hand became
paralyzed in that position, and he couldn't
pull it back. 5 At the same time a wide crack
appeared in the altar, and the ashes poured
out, just as the man of God had predicted in
his message from the LORD.
6 The king cried out to the man of God,
"Please ask the LORD your God to restore my
hand again!" So the man of God prayed to
the LORD, and the king's hand was restored
and he could move it again.
7 Then the king said to the man of God,
"Come to the palace with me and have
something to eat, and I will give you a gift."
8 But the man of God said to the king,
"Even if you gave me half of everything you
own, I would not go with you. I would not
eat or drink anything in this place. 9 For the
LORD gave me this command: 'You must not
eat or drink anything while you are there,
and do not return to Judah by the same way
you came.'" 10 So he left Bethel and went
home another way.
11 As it happened, there was an old prophet
living in Bethel, and his sons* came home
and told him what the man of God had
done in Bethel that day. They also told their
father what the man had said to the king.
12 The old prophet asked them, "Which way
did he go?" So they showed their father*
which road the man of God had taken.
13 "Quick, saddle the donkey," the old man
said. So they saddled the donkey for him,
and he mounted it.
14 Then he rode after the man of God and
found him sitting under a great tree. The
old prophet asked him, "Are you the man of
God who came from Judah?"
"Yes, I am," he replied.
15 Then he said to the man of God, "Come
home with me and eat some food."
16 "No, I cannot," he replied. "I am not
allowed to eat or drink anything here in
this place. 17 For the LORD gave me this
command: 'You must not eat or drink anything while you are there, and do not return
to Judah by the same way you came.'"
18 But the old prophet answered, "I am a
prophet, too, just as you are. And an angel
gave me this command from the LORD:
'Bring him home with you so he can have

12:18 As in some Greek manuscripts and Syriac version (see also 4:6; 5:14); Hebrew reads *Adoram*. **12:25** Hebrew *Penuel*, a variant spelling of Peniel. **12:28** Hebrew *to them*. **12:32** This day of the ancient Hebrew lunar calendar occurred in late October or early November, exactly one month after the annual Festival of Shelters in Judah (see Lev 23:34). **13:11** As in Greek version; Hebrew reads *son*. **13:12** As in Greek version; Hebrew reads *They had seen*.

▸ **12:31** *See **Pagan shrines**, page 427.*

something to eat and drink.'" But the old man was lying to him. [19]So they went back together, and the man of God ate and drank at the prophet's home.

[20]Then while they were sitting at the table, a command from the LORD came to the old prophet. [21]He cried out to the man of God from Judah, "This is what the LORD says: You have defied the word of the LORD and have disobeyed the command the LORD your God gave you. [22]You came back to this place and ate and drank where he told you not to eat or drink. Because of this, your body will not be buried in the grave of your ancestors."

[23]After the man of God had finished eating and drinking, the old prophet saddled his own donkey for him, [24]and the man of God started off again. But as he was traveling along, a lion came out and killed him. His body lay there on the road, with the donkey and the lion standing beside it. [25]People who passed by saw the body lying in the road and the lion standing beside it, and they went and reported it in Bethel, where the old prophet lived.

[26]When the prophet heard the report, he said, "It is the man of God who disobeyed the LORD's command. The LORD has fulfilled his word by causing the lion to attack and kill him."

[27]Then the prophet said to his sons, "Saddle a donkey for me." So they saddled a donkey, [28]and he went out and found the body lying in the road. The donkey and lion were still standing there beside it, for the lion had not eaten the body nor attacked the donkey. [29]So the prophet laid the body of the man of God on the donkey and took it back to the town to mourn over him and bury him. [30]He laid the body in his own grave, crying out in grief, "Oh, my brother!"

[31]Afterward the prophet said to his sons, "When I die, bury me in the grave where the man of God is buried. Lay my bones beside his bones. [32]For the message the LORD told him to proclaim against the altar in Bethel and against the pagan shrines in the towns of Samaria will certainly come true."

[33]But even after this, Jeroboam did not turn from his evil ways. He continued to choose priests from the common people. He appointed anyone who wanted to become a priest for the pagan shrines. [34]This became a great sin and resulted in the utter destruction of Jeroboam's dynasty from the face of the earth.

Ahijah's Prophecy against Jeroboam

14 At that time Jeroboam's son Abijah became very sick. [2]So Jeroboam told his wife, "Disguise yourself so that no one will recognize you as my wife. Then go to the prophet Ahijah at Shiloh—the man who told me I would become king. [3]Take him a gift of ten loaves of bread, some cakes, and a jar of honey, and ask him what will happen to the boy."

[4]So Jeroboam's wife went to Ahijah's home at Shiloh. He was an old man now and could no longer see. [5]But the LORD had told Ahijah, "Jeroboam's wife will come here, pretending to be someone else. She will ask you about her son, for he is very sick. Give her the answer I give you."

King Jeroboam I

Jeroboam, one of Solomon's aides (1 Kings 11:26-28), had received a prophecy from Ahijah that part of the kingdom would be given to him as judgment for Solomon's sin (11:29-33). This happened when Rehoboam, Solomon's son, wouldn't listen to appeals from the ten northern tribes for relief from the burdens Solomon had imposed. They therefore broke away and set up their own nation, making Jeroboam their king (12:1-24). To stop people from going to Jerusalem to worship, he established two shrines—one in Dan and one in Bethel, each with a gold calf—and appointed non-Levitical priests (12:25-33). This was the beginning of the idolatry that would eventually lead to Israel's exile. When Jeroboam continued in his ways, God used the same prophet, Ahijah, to prophesy that judgment would come upon him, his descendants, and the whole nation (14:7-16).

▶ *See also* ***Kingdoms of Israel*** *maps, Visual Overview Z6.*

6So when Ahijah heard her footsteps at
the door, he called out, "Come in, wife of
Jeroboam! Why are you pretending to be
someone else?" Then he told her, "I have
bad news for you. 7Give your husband, Jeroboam, this message from the LORD, the God
of Israel: 'I promoted you from the ranks
of the common people and made you ruler
over my people Israel. 8I ripped the kingdom
away from the family of David and gave it to
you. But you have not been like my servant
David, who obeyed my commands and followed me with all his heart and always did
whatever I wanted. 9You have done more
evil than all who lived before you. You
have made other gods for yourself and have
made me furious with your gold calves.
And since you have turned your back on
me, 10I will bring disaster on your dynasty
and will destroy every one of your male descendants, slave and free alike, anywhere
in Israel. I will burn up your royal dynasty
as one burns up trash until it is all gone.
11The members of Jeroboam's family who
die in the city will be eaten by dogs, and
those who die in the field will be eaten by
vultures. I, the LORD, have spoken.'"
12Then Ahijah said to Jeroboam's wife,
"Go on home, and when you enter the city,
the child will die. 13All Israel will mourn for
him and bury him. He is the only member of
your family who will have a proper burial,
for this child is the only good thing that the
LORD, the God of Israel, sees in the entire
family of Jeroboam.
14"In addition, the LORD will raise up a
king over Israel who will destroy the family
of Jeroboam. This will happen today, even
now! 15Then the LORD will shake Israel like
a reed whipped about in a stream. He will
uproot the people of Israel from this good
land that he gave their ancestors and will
scatter them beyond the Euphrates River,*
for they have angered the LORD with the
Asherah poles they have set up for worship.
16He will abandon Israel because Jeroboam
sinned and made Israel sin along with him."
17So Jeroboam's wife returned to Tirzah,
and the child died just as she walked through
the door of her home. 18And all Israel buried
him and mourned for him, as the LORD had
promised through the prophet Ahijah.
19The rest of the events in Jeroboam's
reign, including all his wars and how he
ruled, are recorded in *The Book of the
History of the Kings of Israel.* 20Jeroboam
reigned in Israel twenty-two years. When
Jeroboam died, his son Nadab became the
next king.

Rehoboam Rules in Judah

21Meanwhile, Rehoboam son of Solomon was
king in Judah. He was forty-one years old
when he became king, and he reigned seventeen years in Jerusalem, the city the LORD had
chosen from among all the tribes of Israel as
the place to honor his name. Rehoboam's
mother was Naamah, an Ammonite woman.
22During Rehoboam's reign, the people
of Judah did what was evil in the LORD's
sight, provoking his anger with their sin,
for it was even worse than that of their ancestors. 23For they also built for themselves
pagan shrines and set up sacred pillars and
Asherah poles on every high hill and under
every green tree. 24There were even male
and female shrine prostitutes throughout
the land. The people imitated the detestable
practices of the pagan nations the LORD had
driven from the land ahead of the Israelites.
25In the fifth year of King Rehoboam's
reign, King Shishak of Egypt came up and
attacked Jerusalem. 26He ransacked the
treasuries of the LORD's Temple and the
royal palace; he stole everything, including all the gold shields Solomon had made.
27King Rehoboam later replaced them with
bronze shields as substitutes, and he entrusted them to the care of the commanders
of the guard who protected the entrance to
the royal palace. 28Whenever the king went
to the Temple of the LORD, the guards would
also take the shields and then return them
to the guardroom.
29The rest of the events in Rehoboam's
reign and everything he did are recorded in
The Book of the History of the Kings of Judah.
30There was constant war between Rehoboam and Jeroboam. 31When Rehoboam
died, he was buried among his ancestors in
the City of David. His mother was Naamah,
an Ammonite woman. Then his son Abijam*
became the next king.

14:15 Hebrew *the river.* **14:31** Also known as *Abijah.*

14:27 *See **Keeping up appearances**, page 494.*

Abijam Rules in Judah

15 Abijam* began to rule over Judah in the eighteenth year of Jeroboam's reign in Israel. 2He reigned in Jerusalem three years. His mother was Maacah, the granddaughter of Absalom.*

3He committed the same sins as his father before him, and he was not faithful to the LORD his God, as his ancestor David had been. 4But for David's sake, the LORD his God allowed his descendants to continue ruling, shining like a lamp, and he gave Abijam a son to rule after him in Jerusalem. 5For David had done what was pleasing in the LORD's sight and had obeyed the LORD's commands throughout his life, except in the affair concerning Uriah the Hittite.

6There was war between Abijam and Jeroboam* throughout Abijam's reign. 7The rest of the events in Abijam's reign and everything he did are recorded in *The Book of the History of the Kings of Judah*. There was constant war between Abijam and Jeroboam. 8When Abijam died, he was buried in the City of David. Then his son Asa became the next king.

Asa Rules in Judah

9Asa began to rule over Judah in the twentieth year of Jeroboam's reign in Israel. 10He reigned in Jerusalem forty-one years. His grandmother* was Maacah, the granddaughter of Absalom.

11Asa did what was pleasing in the LORD's sight, as his ancestor David had done. 12He banished the male and female shrine prostitutes from the land and got rid of all the idols* his ancestors had made. 13He even deposed his grandmother Maacah from her position as queen mother because she had made an obscene Asherah pole. He cut down her obscene pole and burned it in the Kidron Valley. 14Although the pagan shrines were not removed, Asa's heart remained completely faithful to the LORD throughout his life. 15He brought into the Temple of the LORD the silver and gold and the various items that he and his father had dedicated.

16There was constant war between King Asa of Judah and King Baasha of Israel. 17King Baasha of Israel invaded Judah and fortified Ramah in order to prevent anyone from entering or leaving King Asa's territory in Judah.

18Asa responded by removing all the silver and gold that was left in the treasuries of the Temple of the LORD and the royal palace. He sent it with some of his officials to Ben-hadad son of Tabrimmon, son of Hezion, the king of Aram, who was ruling in Damascus, along with this message:

> 19"Let there be a treaty* between you and me like the one between your father and my father. See, I am sending you a gift of silver and gold. Break your treaty with King Baasha of Israel so that he will leave me alone."

20Ben-hadad agreed to King Asa's request and sent the commanders of his army to attack the towns of Israel. They conquered the towns of Ijon, Dan, Abel-beth-maacah, and all Kinnereth, and all the land of Naphtali. 21As soon as Baasha of Israel heard what was happening, he abandoned his project of fortifying Ramah and withdrew to Tirzah. 22Then King Asa sent an order throughout Judah, requiring that everyone, without exception, help to carry away the building stones and timbers that Baasha had been using to fortify Ramah. Asa used these materials to fortify the town of Geba in Benjamin and the town of Mizpah.

23The rest of the events in Asa's reign—the extent of his power, everything he did, and the names of the cities he built—are recorded in *The Book of the History of the Kings of Judah*. In his old age his feet became diseased. 24When Asa died, he was buried with his ancestors in the City of David.

Then Jehoshaphat, Asa's son, became the next king.

Nadab Rules in Israel

25Nadab son of Jeroboam began to rule over Israel in the second year of King Asa's reign in Judah. He reigned in Israel two years. 26But he did what was evil in the LORD's sight and followed the example of his father, continuing the sins that Jeroboam had led Israel to commit.

▸ **15:9** *See* ***King Asa****, page 496.*

[27]Then Baasha son of Ahijah, from the
tribe of Issachar, plotted against Nadab and
assassinated him while he and the Israelite
army were laying siege to the Philistine town
of Gibbethon. [28]Baasha killed Nadab in the
third year of King Asa's reign in Judah, and
he became the next king of Israel.
[29]He immediately slaughtered all the descendants of King Jeroboam, so that not
one of the royal family was left, just as the
LORD had promised concerning Jeroboam
by the prophet Ahijah from Shiloh. [30]This
was done because Jeroboam had provoked
the anger of the LORD, the God of Israel, by
the sins he had committed and the sins he
had led Israel to commit.
[31]The rest of the events in Nadab's reign
and everything he did are recorded in *The
Book of the History of the Kings of Israel.*

Baasha Rules in Israel

[32]There was constant war between King
Asa of Judah and King Baasha of Israel.
[33]Baasha son of Ahijah began to rule over
all Israel in the third year of King Asa's reign
in Judah. Baasha reigned in Tirzah twenty-
four years. [34]But he did what was evil in the
LORD's sight and followed the example of
Jeroboam, continuing the sins that Jeroboam had led Israel to commit.

16 This message from the LORD was delivered to King Baasha by the prophet
Jehu son of Hanani: [2]"I lifted you out of the
dust to make you ruler of my people Israel,
but you have followed the evil example of
Jeroboam. You have provoked my anger by
causing my people Israel to sin. [3]So now I
will destroy you and your family, just as I
destroyed the descendants of Jeroboam son
of Nebat. [4]The members of Baasha's family
who die in the city will be eaten by dogs, and
those who die in the field will be eaten by
vultures."
[5]The rest of the events in Baasha's reign
and the extent of his power are recorded
in *The Book of the History of the Kings of
Israel.* [6]When Baasha died, he was buried
in Tirzah. Then his son Elah became the
next king.
[7]The message from the LORD against
Baasha and his family came through the
prophet Jehu son of Hanani. It was delivered because Baasha had done what was
evil in the LORD's sight (just as the family
of Jeroboam had done), and also because
Baasha had destroyed the family of Jeroboam. The LORD's anger was provoked by
Baasha's sins.

Elah Rules in Israel

[8]Elah son of Baasha began to rule over Israel
in the twenty-sixth year of King Asa's reign
in Judah. He reigned in the city of Tirzah for
two years.
[9]Then Zimri, who commanded half of
the royal chariots, made plans to kill him.
One day in Tirzah, Elah was getting drunk
at the home of Arza, the supervisor of
the palace. [10]Zimri walked in and struck
him down and killed him. This happened

15:1 Also known as *Abijah.* **15:2** Hebrew *Abishalom* (also in 15:10), a variant spelling of Absalom; compare 2 Chr 11:20. **15:6** As in a few Hebrew and Greek manuscripts; most Hebrew manuscripts read *between Rehoboam and Jeroboam.* **15:10** Or *The queen mother;* Hebrew reads *His mother* (also in 15:13); compare 15:2. **15:12** The Hebrew term (literally *round things*) probably alludes to dung. **15:19** As in Greek version; Hebrew reads *There is a treaty.*

Samaria

When the northern tribes split away from the south, Jeroboam first chose Shechem (1 Kings 12:25), then Tirzah (14:17), as the capital of the new nation. Four other kings of Israel followed before Omri established a much grander capital at what became known as Samaria, seven miles northwest of Shechem (16:23-24). He built it from nothing on a hill rising three hundred feet above the surrounding valleys and dominating the crossroads below. His son Ahab built a splendid palace here (22:39) and, sadly, a temple to Baal (16:32). Samaria's location made the city almost impregnable, and it would take Assyria three years of besieging it before it finally fell in 722 BC (2 Kings 17:5-6). After this time Samaria became the name of the surrounding region (2 Kings 17:24).

▸ *See also* ***The Samaritans****, page 1204.*

in the twenty-seventh year of King Asa's
reign in Judah. Then Zimri became the
next king.
11 Zimri immediately killed the entire
royal family of Baasha, leaving him not
even a single male child. He even destroyed
distant relatives and friends. 12 So Zimri destroyed the dynasty of Baasha as the LORD
had promised through the prophet Jehu.
13 This happened because of all the sins
Baasha and his son Elah had committed,
and because of the sins they led Israel to
commit. They provoked the anger of the
LORD, the God of Israel, with their worthless idols.
14 The rest of the events in Elah's reign and
everything he did are recorded in *The Book
of the History of the Kings of Israel*.

Zimri Rules in Israel

15 Zimri began to rule over Israel in the
twenty-seventh year of King Asa's reign in
Judah, but his reign in Tirzah lasted only
seven days. The army of Israel was then attacking the Philistine town of Gibbethon.
16 When they heard that Zimri had committed treason and had assassinated the king,
that very day they chose Omri, commander
of the army, as the new king of Israel. 17 So
Omri led the entire army of Israel up from
Gibbethon to attack Tirzah, Israel's capital.
18 When Zimri saw that the city had been
taken, he went into the citadel of the palace
and burned it down over himself and died
in the flames. 19 For he, too, had done what
was evil in the LORD's sight. He followed the
example of Jeroboam in all the sins he had
committed and led Israel to commit.
20 The rest of the events in Zimri's reign
and his conspiracy are recorded in *The Book
of the History of the Kings of Israel*.

Omri Rules in Israel

21 But now the people of Israel were split into
two factions. Half the people tried to make
Tibni son of Ginath their king, while the other
half supported Omri. 22 But Omri's supporters defeated the supporters of Tibni. So Tibni
was killed, and Omri became the next king.
23 Omri began to rule over Israel in the
thirty-first year of King Asa's reign in Judah.
He reigned twelve years in all, six of them
in Tirzah. 24 Then Omri bought the hill now
known as Samaria from its owner, Shemer,
for 150 pounds of silver.* He built a city on
it and called the city Samaria in honor of
Shemer.
25 But Omri did what was evil in the LORD's
sight, even more than any of the kings
before him. 26 He followed the example of
Jeroboam son of Nebat in all the sins he
had committed and led Israel to commit.
The people provoked the anger of the LORD,
the God of Israel, with their worthless idols.
27 The rest of the events in Omri's reign,
the extent of his power, and everything he
did are recorded in *The Book of the History
of the Kings of Israel*. 28 When Omri died, he
was buried in Samaria. Then his son Ahab
became the next king.

Ahab Rules in Israel

29 Ahab son of Omri began to rule over Israel
in the thirty-eighth year of King Asa's reign
in Judah. He reigned in Samaria twenty-two
years. 30 But Ahab son of Omri did what was
evil in the LORD's sight, even more than any
of the kings before him. 31 And as though it

Widows

To be a widow in Bible times was to be completely without hope. It meant that not only had your husband died but also there were no surviving members of your extended family who could take care of you, as the Jewish Law required. Little wonder, then, that the Bible says that God has a special place in his heart for widows (Psalm 68:5). In both Old and New Testaments he said that they were to be the object of special care (e.g., Deuteronomy 24:17-21; Isaiah 1:17; 1 Timothy 5:3-16; James 1:27), and those who oppressed them are considered as bad as sorcerers and adulterers (Malachi 3:5). The early church laid great stress on the importance of caring for widows (e.g., Acts 6:1-7; James 1:27), and it should still be a hallmark of any true church today.

were not enough to follow the sinful example
of Jeroboam, he married Jezebel, the daughter of King Ethbaal of the Sidonians, and
he began to bow down in worship of Baal.
32First Ahab built a temple and an altar for
Baal in Samaria. 33Then he set up an Asherah
pole. He did more to provoke the anger of the
LORD, the God of Israel, than any of the other
kings of Israel before him.
34It was during his reign that Hiel, a man
from Bethel, rebuilt Jericho. When he laid
its foundations, it cost him the life of his
oldest son, Abiram. And when he completed it and set up its gates, it cost him the
life of his youngest son, Segub.* This all
happened according to the message from
the LORD concerning Jericho spoken by
Joshua son of Nun.

Elijah Fed by Ravens

17 Now Elijah, who was from Tishbe in
Gilead, told King Ahab, "As surely as
the LORD, the God of Israel, lives—the God
I serve—there will be no dew or rain during
the next few years until I give the word!"
2Then the LORD said to Elijah, 3"Go to the
east and hide by Kerith Brook, near where
it enters the Jordan River. 4Drink from the
brook and eat what the ravens bring you, for
I have commanded them to bring you food."
5So Elijah did as the LORD told him and
camped beside Kerith Brook, east of the
Jordan. 6The ravens brought him bread
and meat each morning and evening, and
he drank from the brook. 7But after a while
the brook dried up, for there was no rainfall
anywhere in the land.

The Widow at Zarephath

8Then the LORD said to Elijah, 9"Go and live
in the village of Zarephath, near the city of
Sidon. I have instructed a widow there to
feed you."
10So he went to Zarephath. As he arrived
at the gates of the village, he saw a widow
gathering sticks, and he asked her, "Would
you please bring me a little water in a cup?"
11As she was going to get it, he called to her,
"Bring me a bite of bread, too."
12But she said, "I swear by the LORD your
God that I don't have a single piece of bread
in the house. And I have only a handful of
flour left in the jar and a little cooking oil in
the bottom of the jug. I was just gathering a
few sticks to cook this last meal, and then
my son and I will die."
13But Elijah said to her, "Don't be afraid!
Go ahead and do just what you've said, but
make a little bread for me first. Then use
what's left to prepare a meal for yourself
and your son. 14For this is what the LORD,
the God of Israel, says: There will always
be flour and olive oil left in your containers until the time when the LORD sends rain
and the crops grow again!"
15So she did as Elijah said, and she and
Elijah and her family continued to eat for
many days. 16There was always enough flour
and olive oil left in the containers, just as
the LORD had promised through Elijah.
17Some time later the woman's son
became sick. He grew worse and worse, and
finally he died. 18Then she said to Elijah,
"O man of God, what have you done to me?
Have you come here to point out my sins
and kill my son?"
19But Elijah replied, "Give me your son."
And he took the child's body from her arms,
carried him up the stairs to the room where
he was staying, and laid the body on his
bed. 20Then Elijah cried out to the LORD,
"O LORD my God, why have you brought
tragedy to this widow who has opened her
home to me, causing her son to die?"
21And he stretched himself out over the
child three times and cried out to the LORD,
"O LORD my God, please let this child's life
return to him." 22The LORD heard Elijah's
prayer, and the life of the child returned,
and he revived! 23Then Elijah brought him
down from the upper room and gave him
to his mother. "Look!" he said. "Your son
is alive!"
24Then the woman told Elijah, "Now I
know for sure that you are a man of God, and
that the LORD truly speaks through you."

The Contest on Mount Carmel

18 Later on, in the third year of the
drought, the LORD said to Elijah, "Go
and present yourself to King Ahab. Tell him

16:24 Hebrew *for 2 talents* [68 kilograms] *of silver.* **16:34** An ancient Hebrew scribal tradition reads *He killed his oldest son when he laid its foundations, and he killed his youngest son when he set up its gates.*

▸ **17:8-16** *See* ***Hospitality****, page 1410.*

that I will soon send rain!" [2]So Elijah went
to appear before Ahab.
Meanwhile, the famine had become very
severe in Samaria. [3]So Ahab summoned
Obadiah, who was in charge of the palace.
(Obadiah was a devoted follower of the LORD.
[4]Once when Jezebel had tried to kill all the
LORD's prophets, Obadiah had hidden 100 of
them in two caves. He put fifty prophets in
each cave and supplied them with food and
water.) [5]Ahab said to Obadiah, "We must
check every spring and valley in the land
to see if we can find enough grass to save
at least some of my horses and mules." [6]So
they divided the land between them. Ahab
went one way by himself, and Obadiah went
another way by himself.
[7]As Obadiah was walking along, he
suddenly saw Elijah coming toward him.
Obadiah recognized him at once and bowed
low to the ground before him. "Is it really
you, my lord Elijah?" he asked.
[8]"Yes, it is," Elijah replied. "Now go and
tell your master, 'Elijah is here.'"
[9]"Oh, sir," Obadiah protested, "what harm
have I done to you that you are sending me
to my death at the hands of Ahab? [10]For I
swear by the LORD your God that the king
has searched every nation and kingdom on
earth from end to end to find you. And each
time he was told, 'Elijah isn't here,' King
Ahab forced the king of that nation to swear
to the truth of his claim. [11]And now you say,
'Go and tell your master, "Elijah is here."'
[12]But as soon as I leave you, the Spirit of
the LORD will carry you away to who knows
where. When Ahab comes and cannot
find you, he will kill me. Yet I have been a
true servant of the LORD all my life. [13]Has
no one told you, my lord, about the time
when Jezebel was trying to kill the LORD's
prophets? I hid 100 of them in two caves
and supplied them with food and water.
[14]And now you say, 'Go and tell your master,
"Elijah is here."' Sir, if I do that, Ahab will
certainly kill me."
[15]But Elijah said, "I swear by the LORD
Almighty, in whose presence I stand, that
I will present myself to Ahab this very day."
[16]So Obadiah went to tell Ahab that
Elijah had come, and Ahab went out to
meet Elijah. [17]When Ahab saw him, he exclaimed, "So, is it really you, you troublemaker of Israel?"
[18]"I have made no trouble for Israel,"
Elijah replied. "You and your family are the
troublemakers, for you have refused to obey
the commands of the LORD and have worshiped the images of Baal instead. [19]Now
summon all Israel to join me at Mount
Carmel, along with the 450 prophets of Baal
and the 400 prophets of Asherah who are
supported by Jezebel.*"
[20]So Ahab summoned all the people of
Israel and the prophets to Mount Carmel.
[21]Then Elijah stood in front of them and

Elijah

Elijah (whose name means "the LORD is my God") was a prophet who confronted the northern kingdom of Israel with their increasing idolatry and worship of Baal, a Canaanite nature god. His first prophecy was a direct challenge to Baal's supposed control over the weather and fertility, declaring that it wouldn't rain for three years (1 Kings 17:1)—and it didn't (18:41-46). In a dramatic confrontation with Baal's prophets (chapter 18), he called upon the people to decide once and for all between Baal and the LORD (Yahweh; 18:21). He demonstrated the LORD's superiority as fire fell from heaven, and then he had Baal's prophets killed. This enraged Jezebel, King Ahab's wife, who was a promoter of Baal worship, and Elijah fled for his life (chapter 19). A further confrontation with Ahab and Jezebel occurred over their unrighteous taking of Naboth's vineyard (chapter 21). Elijah's ministry was authenticated by significant miracles, and his life ended, not in death, but by his being taken up to heaven in a chariot of fire (2 Kings 2). He would next appear at Jesus' transfiguration (Matthew 17:1-13).

▶ *See also* ***Baal and Asherah****, page 273;* ***Prophecy in the Old Testament****, page 903;* ***King Ahab and Queen Jezebel****, page 407;* ***The Transfiguration****, page 1169.*

said, "How much longer will you waver, hobbling between two opinions? If the LORD is God, follow him! But if Baal is God, then follow him!" But the people were completely silent.

[22]Then Elijah said to them, "I am the only prophet of the LORD who is left, but Baal has 450 prophets. [23]Now bring two bulls. The prophets of Baal may choose whichever one they wish and cut it into pieces and lay it on the wood of their altar, but without setting fire to it. I will prepare the other bull and lay it on the wood on the altar, but not set fire to it. [24]Then call on the name of your god, and I will call on the name of the LORD. The god who answers by setting fire to the wood is the true God!" And all the people agreed.

[25]Then Elijah said to the prophets of Baal, "You go first, for there are many of you. Choose one of the bulls, and prepare it and call on the name of your god. But do not set fire to the wood."

[26]So they prepared one of the bulls and placed it on the altar. Then they called on the name of Baal from morning until noontime, shouting, "O Baal, answer us!" But there was no reply of any kind. Then they danced, hobbling around the altar they had made.

[27]About noontime Elijah began mocking them. "You'll have to shout louder," he scoffed, "for surely he is a god! Perhaps he is daydreaming, or is relieving himself.* Or maybe he is away on a trip, or is asleep and needs to be wakened!"

[28]So they shouted louder, and following their normal custom, they cut themselves with knives and swords until the blood gushed out. [29]They raved all afternoon until the time of the evening sacrifice, but still there was no sound, no reply, no response.

[30]Then Elijah called to the people, "Come over here!" They all crowded around him as he repaired the altar of the LORD that had been torn down. [31]He took twelve stones, one to represent each of the tribes of Israel,* [32]and he used the stones to rebuild the altar in the name of the LORD. Then he dug a trench around the altar large enough to hold about three gallons.* [33]He piled wood on the altar, cut the bull into pieces, and laid the pieces on the wood.*

Then he said, "Fill four large jars with water, and pour the water over the offering and the wood."

[34]After they had done this, he said, "Do the same thing again!" And when they were finished, he said, "Now do it a third time!" So they did as he said, [35]and the water ran around the altar and even filled the trench.

[36]At the usual time for offering the evening sacrifice, Elijah the prophet walked up to the altar and prayed, "O LORD, God of Abraham, Isaac, and Jacob,* prove today that you are God in Israel and that I am your servant. Prove that I have done all this at your command. [37]O LORD, answer me! Answer me so these people will know that you, O LORD, are God and that you have brought them back to yourself."

[38]Immediately the fire of the LORD flashed down from heaven and burned up the young bull, the wood, the stones, and the dust. It even licked up all the water in the trench! [39]And when all the people saw it, they fell face down on the ground and cried out, "The LORD—he is God! Yes, the LORD is God!"

[40]Then Elijah commanded, "Seize all the prophets of Baal. Don't let a single one escape!" So the people seized them all, and Elijah took them down to the Kishon Valley and killed them there.

Elijah Prays for Rain

[41]Then Elijah said to Ahab, "Go get something to eat and drink, for I hear a mighty rainstorm coming!"

[42]So Ahab went to eat and drink. But Elijah climbed to the top of Mount Carmel and bowed low to the ground and prayed with his face between his knees.

[43]Then he said to his servant, "Go and look out toward the sea."

The servant went and looked, then returned to Elijah and said, "I didn't see anything."

Seven times Elijah told him to go and look. [44]Finally the seventh time, his servant told him, "I saw a little cloud about the size of a man's hand rising from the sea."

Then Elijah shouted, "Hurry to Ahab and tell him, 'Climb into your chariot and go back home. If you don't hurry, the rain will stop you!'"

18:19 Hebrew *who eat at Jezebel's table.* **18:27** Or *is busy somewhere else,* or *is engaged in business.* **18:31** Hebrew *each of the tribes of the sons of Jacob to whom the LORD had said, "Your name will be Israel."* **18:32** Hebrew *2 seahs* [14.6 liters] *of seed.* **18:33** Verse 18:34 in the Hebrew text begins here. **18:36** Hebrew *and Israel.* The names "Jacob" and "Israel" are often interchanged throughout the Old Testament, referring sometimes to the individual patriarch and sometimes to the nation.

45 And soon the sky was black with clouds.
A heavy wind brought a terrific rainstorm,
and Ahab left quickly for Jezreel. 46 Then
the LORD gave special strength to Elijah.
He tucked his cloak into his belt* and ran
ahead of Ahab's chariot all the way to the
entrance of Jezreel.

Elijah Flees to Sinai

19 When Ahab got home, he told Jezebel
everything Elijah had done, including the way he had killed all the prophets of
Baal. 2 So Jezebel sent this message to Elijah:
"May the gods strike me and even kill me if
by this time tomorrow I have not killed you
just as you killed them."
3 Elijah was afraid and fled for his life. He
went to Beersheba, a town in Judah, and he
left his servant there. 4 Then he went on alone
into the wilderness, traveling all day. He sat
down under a solitary broom tree and prayed
that he might die. "I have had enough, LORD,"
he said. "Take my life, for I am no better than
my ancestors who have already died."
5 Then he lay down and slept under the
broom tree. But as he was sleeping, an
angel touched him and told him, "Get up
and eat!" 6 He looked around and there
beside his head was some bread baked on
hot stones and a jar of water! So he ate and
drank and lay down again.
7 Then the angel of the LORD came again
and touched him and said, "Get up and eat
some more, or the journey ahead will be too
much for you."
8 So he got up and ate and drank, and the
food gave him enough strength to travel
forty days and forty nights to Mount Sinai,*
the mountain of God. 9 There he came to a
cave, where he spent the night.

The LORD Speaks to Elijah

But the LORD said to him, "What are you
doing here, Elijah?"
10 Elijah replied, "I have zealously served
the LORD God Almighty. But the people of
Israel have broken their covenant with you,
torn down your altars, and killed every one
of your prophets. I am the only one left, and
now they are trying to kill me, too."
11 "Go out and stand before me on the
mountain," the LORD told him. And as
Elijah stood there, the LORD passed by, and
a mighty windstorm hit the mountain. It was
such a terrible blast that the rocks were torn
loose, but the LORD was not in the wind.
After the wind there was an earthquake, but
the LORD was not in the earthquake. 12 And
after the earthquake there was a fire, but
the LORD was not in the fire. And after the
fire there was the sound of a gentle whisper.
13 When Elijah heard it, he wrapped his face

Depression

Elijah's opposition to the worship of Baal had brought him into confrontation with Ahab and Jezebel. Its climax—the contest with Baal's prophets on Mount Carmel (1 Kings 18)—led Jezebel to threaten his life (19:2). Suddenly, it was all too much; emotionally and spiritually exhausted, and feeling the relentless stress of his work as a prophet, Elijah fell into deep depression.

Depression is more than sadness; it is profound discouragement and despondency, and feeling unable to do anything about it. It can have many causes: for Elijah, fear; for Job, circumstances (Job 6:1-13); for Hagar, hopelessness (Genesis 21:15-16); for Moses, weariness (Numbers 11:11-15); for Judas, sin (Matthew 27:3-5). It also has many expressions: despair, loneliness, escapism, loathing life, feeling abandoned by God.

However, whatever its causes and expressions, the solution is the same: beginning to see once again who God is and that he has a purpose for us. Elijah's encounter with God through a quiet voice (1 Kings 19:12-13) started to turn things around for him. God would not share in Elijah's self-pity, but he did deal with him tenderly, providing food and rest, giving him a task to do, reassuring him he was not alone, and providing a companion, Elisha, to share his work (19:15-18). Practical solutions can often be the first step out of depression.

in his cloak and went out and stood at the entrance of the cave.

And a voice said, "What are you doing here, Elijah?"

14 He replied again, "I have zealously served the LORD God Almighty. But the people of Israel have broken their covenant with you, torn down your altars, and killed every one of your prophets. I am the only one left, and now they are trying to kill me, too."

15 Then the LORD told him, "Go back the same way you came, and travel to the wilderness of Damascus. When you arrive there, anoint Hazael to be king of Aram. 16 Then anoint Jehu grandson of Nimshi* to be king of Israel, and anoint Elisha son of Shaphat from the town of Abel-meholah to replace you as my prophet. 17 Anyone who escapes from Hazael will be killed by Jehu, and those who escape Jehu will be killed by Elisha! 18 Yet I will preserve 7,000 others in Israel who have never bowed down to Baal or kissed him!"

The Call of Elisha

19 So Elijah went and found Elisha son of Shaphat plowing a field. There were twelve teams of oxen in the field, and Elisha was plowing with the twelfth team. Elijah went over to him and threw his cloak across his shoulders and then walked away. 20 Elisha left the oxen standing there, ran after Elijah, and said to him, "First let me go and kiss my father and mother good-bye, and then I will go with you!"

Elijah replied, "Go on back, but think about what I have done to you."

21 So Elisha returned to his oxen and slaughtered them. He used the wood from the plow to build a fire to roast their flesh. He passed around the meat to the townspeople, and they all ate. Then he went with Elijah as his assistant.

Ben-Hadad Attacks Samaria

20 About that time King Ben-hadad of Aram mobilized his army, supported by the chariots and horses of thirty-two allied kings. They went to besiege Samaria, the capital of Israel, and launched attacks against it. 2 Ben-hadad sent messengers into the city to relay this message to King Ahab of Israel: "This is what Ben-hadad says: 3 'Your silver and gold are mine, and so are your wives and the best of your children!'"

4 "All right, my lord the king," Israel's king replied. "All that I have is yours!"

5 Soon Ben-hadad's messengers returned again and said, "This is what Ben-hadad says: 'I have already demanded that you give me your silver, gold, wives, and children. 6 But about this time tomorrow I will send my officials to search your palace and the homes of your officials. They will take away everything you consider valuable!'"

7 Then Ahab summoned all the elders of the land and said to them, "Look how this man is stirring up trouble! I already agreed with his demand that I give him my wives and children and silver and gold."

8 "Don't give in to any more demands," all the elders and the people advised.

9 So Ahab told the messengers from Ben-hadad, "Say this to my lord the king: 'I will give you everything you asked for the first time, but I cannot accept this last demand of yours.'" So the messengers returned to Ben-hadad with that response.

10 Then Ben-hadad sent this message to Ahab: "May the gods strike me and even kill me if there remains enough dust from Samaria to provide even a handful for each of my soldiers."

11 The king of Israel sent back this answer: "A warrior putting on his sword for battle should not boast like a warrior who has already won."

12 Ahab's reply reached Ben-hadad and the other kings as they were drinking in their tents.* "Prepare to attack!" Ben-hadad commanded his officers. So they prepared to attack the city.

Ahab's Victory over Ben-Hadad

13 Then a certain prophet came to see King Ahab of Israel and told him, "This is what the LORD says: Do you see all these enemy forces? Today I will hand them all over to you. Then you will know that I am the LORD."

14 Ahab asked, "How will he do it?"

And the prophet replied, "This is what the LORD says: The troops of the provincial commanders will do it."

18:46 Hebrew *He bound up his loins.* **19:8** Hebrew *to Horeb,* another name for Sinai. **19:16** Hebrew *descendant of Nimshi;* compare 2 Kgs 9:2, 14. **20:12** Or *in Succoth;* also in 20:16.

▸ **19:1-21** *See* ***Doubt****, page 1414.*

"Should we attack first?" Ahab asked.
"Yes," the prophet answered.
15 So Ahab mustered the troops of the
232 provincial commanders. Then he called
out the rest of the army of Israel, some 7,000
men. 16 About noontime, as Ben-hadad and
the thirty-two allied kings were still in their
tents drinking themselves into a stupor,
17 the troops of the provincial commanders
marched out of the city as the first contingent.
As they approached, Ben-hadad's scouts
reported to him, "Some troops are coming
from Samaria."
18 "Take them alive," Ben-hadad commanded, "whether they have come for
peace or for war."
19 But Ahab's provincial commanders
and the entire army had now come out
to fight. 20 Each Israelite soldier killed his
Aramean opponent, and suddenly the
entire Aramean army panicked and fled.
The Israelites chased them, but King Ben-
hadad and a few of his charioteers escaped
on horses. 21 However, the king of Israel destroyed the other horses and chariots and
slaughtered the Arameans.
22 Afterward the prophet said to King
Ahab, "Get ready for another attack. Begin
making plans now, for the king of Aram will
come back next spring.*"

Ben-Hadad's Second Attack

23 After their defeat, Ben-hadad's officers
said to him, "The Israelite gods are gods of
the hills; that is why they won. But we can
beat them easily on the plains. 24 Only this
time replace the kings with field commanders! 25 Recruit another army like the one you
lost. Give us the same number of horses,
chariots, and men, and we will fight against
them on the plains. There's no doubt that
we will beat them." So King Ben-hadad did
as they suggested.
26 The following spring he called up the
Aramean army and marched out against
Israel, this time at Aphek. 27 Israel then
mustered its army, set up supply lines, and
marched out for battle. But the Israelite
army looked like two little flocks of goats in
comparison to the vast Aramean forces that
filled the countryside!
28 Then the man of God went to the king of
Israel and said, "This is what the LORD says:
The Arameans have said, 'The LORD is a god
of the hills and not of the plains.' So I will
defeat this vast army for you. Then you will
know that I am the LORD."
29 The two armies camped opposite each
other for seven days, and on the seventh
day the battle began. The Israelites killed
100,000 Aramean foot soldiers in one day.
30 The rest fled into the town of Aphek, but
the wall fell on them and killed another
27,000. Ben-hadad fled into the town and
hid in a secret room.
31 Ben-hadad's officers said to him, "Sir,
we have heard that the kings of Israel are
merciful. So let's humble ourselves by
wearing burlap around our waists and
putting ropes on our heads, and surrender
to the king of Israel. Then perhaps he will
let you live."
32 So they put on burlap and ropes, and
they went to the king of Israel and begged,
"Your servant Ben-hadad says, 'Please let
me live!'"
The king of Israel responded, "Is he still
alive? He is my brother!"
33 The men took this as a good sign and
quickly picked up on his words. "Yes," they
said, "your brother Ben-hadad!"
"Go and get him," the king of Israel told
them. And when Ben-hadad arrived, Ahab
invited him up into his chariot.
34 Ben-hadad told him, "I will give back
the towns my father took from your father,
and you may establish places of trade in
Damascus, as my father did in Samaria."
Then Ahab said, "I will release you under
these conditions." So they made a new
treaty, and Ben-hadad was set free.

A Prophet Condemns Ahab

35 Meanwhile, the LORD instructed one of
the group of prophets to say to another
man, "Hit me!" But the man refused to hit
the prophet. 36 Then the prophet told him,
"Because you have not obeyed the voice of
the LORD, a lion will kill you as soon as you
leave me." And when he had gone, a lion
did attack and kill him.
37 Then the prophet turned to another
man and said, "Hit me!" So he struck the
prophet and wounded him.
38 The prophet placed a bandage over his
eyes to disguise himself and then waited
beside the road for the king. 39 As the king
passed by, the prophet called out to him,
"Sir, I was in the thick of battle, and suddenly a man brought me a prisoner. He said,

'Guard this man; if for any reason he gets
away, you will either die or pay a fine of
seventy-five pounds* of silver!' [40]But while
I was busy doing something else, the prisoner disappeared!"
"Well, it's your own fault," the king
replied. "You have brought the judgment
on yourself."
[41]Then the prophet quickly pulled the
bandage from his eyes, and the king
of Israel recognized him as one of the
prophets. [42]The prophet said to him, "This
is what the LORD says: Because you have
spared the man I said must be destroyed,*
now you must die in his place, and your
people will die instead of his people." [43]So
the king of Israel went home to Samaria
angry and sullen.

Naboth's Vineyard

21 Now there was a man named Naboth,
from Jezreel, who owned a vineyard
in Jezreel beside the palace of King Ahab
of Samaria. [2]One day Ahab said to Naboth,
"Since your vineyard is so convenient to
my palace, I would like to buy it to use as
a vegetable garden. I will give you a better
vineyard in exchange, or if you prefer, I will
pay you for it."
[3]But Naboth replied, "The LORD forbid
that I should give you the inheritance that
was passed down by my ancestors."
[4]So Ahab went home angry and sullen
because of Naboth's answer. The king went
to bed with his face to the wall and refused
to eat!
[5]"What's the matter?" his wife Jezebel
asked him. "What's made you so upset that
you're not eating?"
[6]"I asked Naboth to sell me his vineyard
or trade it, but he refused!" Ahab told her.
[7]"Are you the king of Israel or not?"
Jezebel demanded. "Get up and eat something, and don't worry about it. I'll get you
Naboth's vineyard!"
[8]So she wrote letters in Ahab's name,
sealed them with his seal, and sent them
to the elders and other leaders of the town
where Naboth lived. [9]In her letters she
commanded: "Call the citizens together for
a time of fasting, and give Naboth a place
of honor. [10]And then seat two scoundrels
across from him who will accuse him of
cursing God and the king. Then take him
out and stone him to death."
[11]So the elders and other town leaders followed the instructions Jezebel had written
in the letters. [12]They called for a fast and
put Naboth at a prominent place before the
people. [13]Then the two scoundrels came
and sat down across from him. And they
accused Naboth before all the people,
saying, "He cursed God and the king."
So he was dragged outside the town and
stoned to death. [14]The town leaders then
sent word to Jezebel, "Naboth has been
stoned to death."

20:22 Hebrew *at the turn of the year;* similarly in 20:26. The first day of the year in the ancient Hebrew lunar calendar occurred in March or April. **20:39** Hebrew *1 talent* [34 kilograms]. **20:42** The Hebrew term used here refers to the complete consecration of things or people to the LORD, either by destroying them or by giving them as an offering.

King Ahab and Queen Jezebel

Ahab's twenty-two-year reign (874–853 BC) was marked by significant growth in Baal worship. Ahab married Jezebel from Sidon, a Baal worshiper, contrary to God's commands (e.g., Deuteronomy 7:3-4). She brought many prophets of Baal, encouraging Ahab to worship her Canaanite god (1 Kings 16:31-33). As a result, the people increasingly worshiped Baal as well as the LORD (Yahweh), something Elijah described as "hobbling between two opinions" (18:21). Ahab and Jezebel came into conflict with Elijah, who fearlessly confronted them, as we see in the contest with Baal's prophets (chapter 18) and his exposing of their ruthlessness concerning Naboth's vineyard (chapter 21). Although Ahab was politically quite successful, the book of Kings only condemns him, such was the depth of his sin. He was killed in a battle against Aram (Syria; 22:29-38), his blood licked up by dogs as judgment for his murder of Naboth, just as Elijah had prophesied (21:17-19).

▶ *See also* ***Elijah****, page 402;* ***Can a Christian marry a non-Christian?****, page 1329.*

15 When Jezebel heard the news, she said to Ahab, "You know the vineyard Naboth wouldn't sell you? Well, you can have it now! He's dead!" 16 So Ahab immediately went down to the vineyard of Naboth to claim it.

17 But the LORD said to Elijah,* 18 "Go down to meet King Ahab of Israel, who rules in Samaria. He will be at Naboth's vineyard in Jezreel, claiming it for himself. 19 Give him this message: 'This is what the LORD says: Wasn't it enough that you killed Naboth? Must you rob him, too? Because you have done this, dogs will lick your blood at the very place where they licked the blood of Naboth!'"

20 "So, my enemy, you have found me!" Ahab exclaimed to Elijah.

"Yes," Elijah answered, "I have come because you have sold yourself to what is evil in the LORD's sight. 21 So now the LORD says,* 'I will bring disaster on you and consume you. I will destroy every one of your male descendants, slave and free alike, anywhere in Israel! 22 I am going to destroy your family as I did the family of Jeroboam son of Nebat and the family of Baasha son of Ahijah, for you have made me very angry and have led Israel into sin.'

23 "And regarding Jezebel, the LORD says, 'Dogs will eat Jezebel's body at the plot of land in Jezreel.*'

24 "The members of Ahab's family who die in the city will be eaten by dogs, and those who die in the field will be eaten by vultures."

25 (No one else so completely sold himself to what was evil in the LORD's sight as Ahab did under the influence of his wife Jezebel. 26 His worst outrage was worshiping idols* just as the Amorites had done—the people whom the LORD had driven out from the land ahead of the Israelites.)

27 But when Ahab heard this message, he tore his clothing, dressed in burlap, and fasted. He even slept in burlap and went about in deep mourning.

28 Then another message from the LORD came to Elijah: 29 "Do you see how Ahab has humbled himself before me? Because he has done this, I will not do what I promised during his lifetime. It will happen to his sons; I will destroy his dynasty."

Jehoshaphat and Ahab

22 For three years there was no war between Aram and Israel. 2 Then during the third year, King Jehoshaphat of Judah went to visit King Ahab of Israel. 3 During the visit, the king of Israel said to his officials, "Do you realize that the town of Ramoth-gilead belongs to us? And yet we've done nothing to recapture it from the king of Aram!"

4 Then he turned to Jehoshaphat and asked, "Will you join me in battle to recover Ramoth-gilead?"

Jehoshaphat replied to the king of Israel, "Why, of course! You and I are as one. My troops are your troops, and my horses are your horses." 5 Then Jehoshaphat added, "But first let's find out what the LORD says."

6 So the king of Israel summoned the prophets, about 400 of them, and asked them, "Should I go to war against Ramoth-gilead, or should I hold back?"

They all replied, "Yes, go right ahead! The Lord will give the king victory."

7 But Jehoshaphat asked, "Is there not also a prophet of the LORD here? We should ask him the same question."

8 The king of Israel replied to Jehoshaphat, "There is one more man who could consult the LORD for us, but I hate him. He never prophesies anything but trouble for me! His name is Micaiah son of Imlah."

Jehoshaphat replied, "That's not the way a king should talk! Let's hear what he has to say."

9 So the king of Israel called one of his officials and said, "Quick! Bring Micaiah son of Imlah."

Micaiah Prophesies against Ahab

10 King Ahab of Israel and King Jehoshaphat of Judah, dressed in their royal robes, were sitting on thrones at the threshing floor near the gate of Samaria. All of Ahab's prophets were prophesying there in front of them. 11 One of them, Zedekiah son of Kenaanah, made some iron horns and proclaimed, "This is what the LORD says: With these horns you will gore the Arameans to death!"

12 All the other prophets agreed. "Yes," they said, "go up to Ramoth-gilead and be victorious, for the LORD will give the king victory!"

▸ **21:1-16** *See* ***Oppression****, page 710.*

13 Meanwhile, the messenger who went
to get Micaiah said to him, "Look, all the
prophets are promising victory for the
king. Be sure that you agree with them and
promise success."
14 But Micaiah replied, "As surely as the
LORD lives, I will say only what the LORD
tells me to say."
15 When Micaiah arrived before the king,
Ahab asked him, "Micaiah, should we go to
war against Ramoth-gilead, or should we
hold back?"
Micaiah replied sarcastically, "Yes, go up
and be victorious, for the LORD will give the
king victory!"
16 But the king replied sharply, "How
many times must I demand that you speak
only the truth to me when you speak for the
LORD?"
17 Then Micaiah told him, "In a vision
I saw all Israel scattered on the mountains,
like sheep without a shepherd. And the
LORD said, 'Their master has been killed.*
Send them home in peace.'"
18 "Didn't I tell you?" the king of Israel exclaimed to Jehoshaphat. "He never prophesies anything but trouble for me."
19 Then Micaiah continued, "Listen to
what the LORD says! I saw the LORD sitting
on his throne with all the armies of heaven
around him, on his right and on his left.
20 And the LORD said, 'Who can entice Ahab
to go into battle against Ramoth-gilead so
he can be killed?'
"There were many suggestions, 21 and
finally a spirit approached the LORD and
said, 'I can do it!'
22 "'How will you do this?' the LORD asked.
"And the spirit replied, 'I will go out and
inspire all of Ahab's prophets to speak lies.'
"'You will succeed,' said the LORD. 'Go
ahead and do it.'
23 "So you see, the LORD has put a lying
spirit in the mouths of all your prophets. For
the LORD has pronounced your doom."
24 Then Zedekiah son of Kenaanah walked
up to Micaiah and slapped him across the
face. "Since when did the Spirit of the LORD
leave me to speak to you?" he demanded.
25 And Micaiah replied, "You will find out
soon enough when you are trying to hide in
some secret room!"
26 "Arrest him!" the king of Israel ordered.
"Take him back to Amon, the governor of
the city, and to my son Joash. 27 Give them
this order from the king: 'Put this man in
prison, and feed him nothing but bread and
water until I return safely from the battle!'"
28 But Micaiah replied, "If you return
safely, it will mean that the LORD has not
spoken through me!" Then he added to
those standing around, "Everyone mark
my words!"

The Death of Ahab

29 So King Ahab of Israel and King Jehoshaphat of Judah led their armies against
Ramoth-gilead. 30 The king of Israel said to
Jehoshaphat, "As we go into battle, I will
disguise myself so no one will recognize me,
but you wear your royal robes." So the king
of Israel disguised himself, and they went
into battle.
31 Meanwhile, the king of Aram had issued
these orders to his thirty-two chariot commanders: "Attack only the king of Israel.
Don't bother with anyone else!" 32 So when
the Aramean chariot commanders saw Jehoshaphat in his royal robes, they went
after him. "There is the king of Israel!" they
shouted. But when Jehoshaphat called out,
33 the chariot commanders realized he was
not the king of Israel, and they stopped
chasing him.
34 An Aramean soldier, however, randomly shot an arrow at the Israelite troops
and hit the king of Israel between the joints
of his armor. "Turn the horses* and get me
out of here!" Ahab groaned to the driver of
his chariot. "I'm badly wounded!"
35 The battle raged all that day, and the
king remained propped up in his chariot
facing the Arameans. The blood from his
wound ran down to the floor of his chariot,
and as evening arrived he died. 36 Just as the
sun was setting, the cry ran through his
troops: "We're done for! Run for your lives!"
37 So the king died, and his body was
taken to Samaria and buried there. 38 Then
his chariot was washed beside the pool
of Samaria, and dogs came and licked his
blood at the place where the prostitutes
bathed,* just as the LORD had promised.
39 The rest of the events in Ahab's reign

21:17 Hebrew *Elijah the Tishbite;* also in 21:28. **21:21** As in Greek version; Hebrew lacks *So now the LORD says.* **21:23** As in several Hebrew manuscripts, Syriac, and Latin Vulgate (see also 2 Kgs 9:26, 36); most Hebrew manuscripts read *at the city wall.* **21:26** The Hebrew term (literally *round things*) probably alludes to dung. **22:17** Hebrew *These people have no master.* **22:34** Hebrew *Turn your hand.* **22:38** Or *his blood, and the prostitutes bathed [in it];* or *his blood, and they washed his armor.*

and everything he did, including the story of the ivory palace and the towns he built, are recorded in *The Book of the History of the Kings of Israel.* [40]So Ahab died, and his son Ahaziah became the next king.

Jehoshaphat Rules in Judah

[41]Jehoshaphat son of Asa began to rule over Judah in the fourth year of King Ahab's reign in Israel. [42]Jehoshaphat was thirty-five years old when he became king, and he reigned in Jerusalem twenty-five years. His mother was Azubah, the daughter of Shilhi.

[43]Jehoshaphat was a good king, following the example of his father, Asa. He did what was pleasing in the LORD's sight. *During his reign, however, he failed to remove all the pagan shrines, and the people still offered sacrifices and burned incense there. [44]Jehoshaphat also made peace with the king of Israel.

[45]The rest of the events in Jehoshaphat's reign, the extent of his power, and the wars he waged are recorded in *The Book of the History of the Kings of Judah.* [46]He banished from the land the rest of the male and female shrine prostitutes, who still continued their practices from the days of his father, Asa.

[47](There was no king in Edom at that time, only a deputy.)

[48]Jehoshaphat also built a fleet of trading ships* to sail to Ophir for gold. But the ships never set sail, for they met with disaster in their home port of Ezion-geber. [49]At one time Ahaziah son of Ahab had proposed to Jehoshaphat, "Let my men sail with your men in the ships." But Jehoshaphat refused the request.

[50]When Jehoshaphat died, he was buried with his ancestors in the City of David. Then his son Jehoram became the next king.

Ahaziah Rules in Israel

[51]Ahaziah son of Ahab began to rule over Israel in the seventeenth year of King Jehoshaphat's reign in Judah. He reigned in Samaria two years. [52]But he did what was evil in the LORD's sight, following the example of his father and mother and the example of Jeroboam son of Nebat, who had led Israel to sin. [53]He served Baal and worshiped him, provoking the anger of the LORD, the God of Israel, just as his father had done.

22:43 Verses 22:43b-53 are numbered 22:44-54 in Hebrew text.
22:48 Hebrew *fleet of ships of Tarshish.*

▸ **22:41** *See **King Jehoshaphat**, page 498.*

2 Kings *Decline and disaster*

Second Kings continues the story begun in 1 Kings, showing the ongoing spiritual decline of both the northern kingdom of Israel and the southern kingdom of Judah. When neither would hear the prophets' calls to repent, God's judgment finally fell on them both. Within 150 years of each other, both Israel and Judah were invaded, plundered, and taken into exile. The ten northern tribes that made up Israel were scattered across the Assyrian Empire, never to come back together again; but those from the south would be allowed to stay together during their exile in Babylon, giving the possibility of hope for the future.

What's it all about?

In 2 Kings, the prophet Elisha succeeded Elijah. Elisha performed many mighty miracles, many of them miracles of compassion for individuals (2 Kings 1–8). At Elisha's instruction, Jehu was anointed the next king of Israel, and he went on to overthrow the house of Ahab (chapters 9–10).

Chapters 11 to 16 record the reigns of other kings of Israel and Judah. Again and again the writer of 2 Kings tells us that the king "did what was evil in the LORD's sight." The northern kingdom (Israel) was finally conquered by Assyria, a mighty empire from the east, in 722 BC (2 Kings 17). This judgment of God brought the northern tribes to an end as they were scattered across Assyria's empire.

Chapters 18 to 21 relate the reigns of good King Hezekiah and his wicked son Manasseh in Judah. Hezekiah was loyal to God, so God rescued Jerusalem from Assyria's attack (2 Kings 18–19) and healed him of a life-threatening illness (2 Kings 20). Another good king, Josiah, who was only eight years old when he became king, led the nation back to God. When the Book of the Law was rediscovered during building work in the Temple, Josiah reformed Judah (2 Kings 22–23) and led the people to rededicate themselves to God. But the nation began to fall away from God again, so eventually it too was conquered and destroyed, this time by Babylon, the new rising empire in the east, in 586 BC. Many residents were deported to Babylon, just as Jeremiah had prophesied. But the book ends with a possible glimmer of hope—the release of the exiled King Jehoiachin from prison.

OVERVIEW

Elijah's death and his succession by Elisha · *1:1–2:18*

Elisha's ministry and miracles *2:19–8:15*

The reigns of kings in Israel and Judah · *8:16–16:20*

The fall and exile of the northern kingdom (Israel) · *17:1-41*

Hezekiah's reforms and God's rescue of Jerusalem · *18:1–20:21*

The wicked kings Manasseh and Amon · *21:1-26*

Josiah's reforms *22:1–23:30*

Judah's final kings, destruction, and exile · *23:31–25:30*

What does it mean for us?

Second Kings continues the message of 1 Kings, that God remained loving and faithful to Israel and Judah even when they were unfaithful to him. But it also reminds us that his love does not mean he lets us get away with doing whatever we like. As a loving and faithful Father he disciplined his people when they stubbornly maintained their disobedience, allowing the judgment to come upon them that he had said would come if they were not faithful. God does the same today. But when hardship or discipline come our way, we should always remember that it is not because God doesn't love us, but because he does. He is treating us like his own children (see Hebrews 12:5-13). And no matter how bad things get, the way this story ends shows that there is always hope.

▶ *See also* ***A timeline of the Bible,*** *pages A22-A24.*

Elijah Confronts King Ahaziah

1 After King Ahab's death, the land of Moab
rebelled against Israel.
2 One day Israel's new king, Ahaziah, fell
through the latticework of an upper room
at his palace in Samaria and was seriously
injured. So he sent messengers to the temple
of Baal-zebub, the god of Ekron, to ask
whether he would recover.
3 But the angel of the LORD told Elijah, who
was from Tishbe, "Go and confront the messengers of the king of Samaria and ask them,
'Is there no God in Israel? Why are you going to
Baal-zebub, the god of Ekron, to ask whether
the king will recover? 4 Now, therefore, this is
what the LORD says: You will never leave the
bed you are lying on; you will surely die.'" So
Elijah went to deliver the message.
5 When the messengers returned to the
king, he asked them, "Why have you returned so soon?"
6 They replied, "A man came up to us and
told us to go back to the king and give him
this message. 'This is what the LORD says: Is
there no God in Israel? Why are you sending
men to Baal-zebub, the god of Ekron, to ask
whether you will recover? Therefore, because
you have done this, you will never leave the
bed you are lying on; you will surely die.'"
7 "What sort of man was he?" the king demanded. "What did he look like?"
8 They replied, "He was a hairy man,* and
he wore a leather belt around his waist."
"Elijah from Tishbe!" the king exclaimed.
9 Then he sent an army captain with fifty
soldiers to arrest him. They found him sitting
on top of a hill. The captain said to him,
"Man of God, the king has commanded you
to come down with us."
10 But Elijah replied to the captain, "If I am a
man of God, let fire come down from heaven
and destroy you and your fifty men!" Then
fire fell from heaven and killed them all.
11 So the king sent another captain with
fifty men. The captain said to him, "Man of
God, the king demands that you come down
at once."
12 Elijah replied, "If I am a man of God, let
fire come down from heaven and destroy
you and your fifty men!" And again the fire
of God fell from heaven and killed them all.
13 Once more the king sent a third captain
with fifty men. But this time the captain
went up the hill and fell to his knees before
Elijah. He pleaded with him, "O man of God,
please spare my life and the lives of these,
your fifty servants. 14 See how the fire from
heaven came down and destroyed the first
two groups. But now please spare my life!"
15 Then the angel of the LORD said to Elijah,
"Go down with him, and don't be afraid of
him." So Elijah got up and went with him to
the king.
16 And Elijah said to the king, "This is what
the LORD says: Why did you send messengers to Baal-zebub, the god of Ekron, to ask
whether you will recover? Is there no God in
Israel to answer your question? Therefore,
because you have done this, you will never
leave the bed you are lying on; you will
surely die."
17 So Ahaziah died, just as the LORD had
promised through Elijah. Since Ahaziah did
not have a son to succeed him, his brother
Joram* became the next king. This took place
in the second year of the reign of Jehoram
son of Jehoshaphat, king of Judah.
18 The rest of the events in Ahaziah's reign
and everything he did are recorded in *The
Book of the History of the Kings of Israel.*

Elijah Taken into Heaven

2 When the LORD was about to take Elijah
up to heaven in a whirlwind, Elijah and
Elisha were traveling from Gilgal. 2 And Elijah
said to Elisha, "Stay here, for the LORD has
told me to go to Bethel."
But Elisha replied, "As surely as the LORD

lives and you yourself live, I will never leave
you!" So they went down together to Bethel.
3The group of prophets from Bethel came
to Elisha and asked him, "Did you know
that the LORD is going to take your master
away from you today?"
"Of course I know," Elisha answered.
"But be quiet about it."
4Then Elijah said to Elisha, "Stay here, for
the LORD has told me to go to Jericho."
But Elisha replied again, "As surely as
the LORD lives and you yourself live, I will
never leave you." So they went on together
to Jericho.
5Then the group of prophets from Jericho
came to Elisha and asked him, "Did you
know that the LORD is going to take your
master away from you today?"
"Of course I know," Elisha answered.
"But be quiet about it."
6Then Elijah said to Elisha, "Stay here,
for the LORD has told me to go to the Jordan
River."
But again Elisha replied, "As surely as the
LORD lives and you yourself live, I will never
leave you." So they went on together.
7Fifty men from the group of prophets
also went and watched from a distance as
Elijah and Elisha stopped beside the Jordan
River. 8Then Elijah folded his cloak together
and struck the water with it. The river
divided, and the two of them went across
on dry ground!
9When they came to the other side, Elijah
said to Elisha, "Tell me what I can do for
you before I am taken away."
And Elisha replied, "Please let me inherit
a double share of your spirit and become
your successor."
10"You have asked a difficult thing," Elijah
replied. "If you see me when I am taken
from you, then you will get your request.
But if not, then you won't."
11As they were walking along and talking,
suddenly a chariot of fire appeared, drawn
by horses of fire. It drove between the two
men, separating them, and Elijah was
carried by a whirlwind into heaven. 12Elisha
saw it and cried out, "My father! My father!
I see the chariots and charioteers of Israel!"
And as they disappeared from sight, Elisha
tore his clothes in distress.
13Elisha picked up Elijah's cloak, which
had fallen when he was taken up. Then
Elisha returned to the bank of the Jordan
River. 14He struck the water with Elijah's
cloak and cried out, "Where is the LORD,
the God of Elijah?" Then the river divided,
and Elisha went across.
15When the group of prophets from
Jericho saw from a distance what happened,
they exclaimed, "Elijah's spirit rests upon
Elisha!" And they went to meet him and
bowed to the ground before him. 16"Sir,"
they said, "just say the word and fifty of our
strongest men will search the wilderness for
your master. Perhaps the Spirit of the LORD
has left him on some mountain or in some
valley."
"No," Elisha said, "don't send them." 17But

1:8 Or *He was wearing clothing made of hair.* **1:17** Hebrew *Jehoram*, a variant spelling of Joram.

Elisha

Elisha, whose name means "my God saves," had been anointed as Elijah's successor at God's command (1 Kings 19:16), though Elijah seemed reluctant to mentor him (19:19-21). But Elisha continued to work alongside him and refused to leave him when Elijah's ministry was nearing its end (2 Kings 2:6). When Elijah was taken up to heaven, Elisha received the "double share of your spirit" (2:9) he had asked Elijah for—not a request to be twice the man, but to be seen as his successor, which he became. Elisha's ministry was characterized by many miracles—some of them at a personal, compassionate level, as in chapter 4, and some with a more national or international significance (3:4-27; 5:1-27; 6:8-23). A small, yet very significant, act was his command to anoint Jehu as king to replace the wicked dynasty of Ahab (9:1-13). Elisha stayed a prophet to the end, even with his final breaths (13:14-20).

▶ *See also* ***Elijah****, page 402;* ***Prophecy in the Old Testament****, page 903.*

they kept urging him until they shamed him into agreeing, and he finally said, "All right, send them." So fifty men searched for three days but did not find Elijah. 18 Elisha was still at Jericho when they returned. "Didn't I tell you not to go?" he asked.

Elisha's First Miracles

19 One day the leaders of the town of Jericho visited Elisha. "We have a problem, my lord," they told him. "This town is located in pleasant surroundings, as you can see. But the water is bad, and the land is unproductive."

20 Elisha said, "Bring me a new bowl with salt in it." So they brought it to him. 21 Then he went out to the spring that supplied the town with water and threw the salt into it. And he said, "This is what the LORD says: I have purified this water. It will no longer cause death or infertility.*" 22 And the water has remained pure ever since, just as Elisha said.

23 Elisha left Jericho and went up to Bethel. As he was walking along the road, a group of boys from the town began mocking and making fun of him. "Go away, baldy!" they chanted. "Go away, baldy!" 24 Elisha turned around and looked at them, and he cursed them in the name of the LORD. Then two bears came out of the woods and mauled forty-two of them. 25 From there Elisha went to Mount Carmel and finally returned to Samaria.

War between Israel and Moab

3 Ahab's son Joram* began to rule over Israel in the eighteenth year of King Jehoshaphat's reign in Judah. He reigned in Samaria twelve years. 2 He did what was evil in the LORD's sight, but not to the same extent as his father and mother. He at least tore down the sacred pillar of Baal that his father had set up. 3 Nevertheless, he continued in the sins that Jeroboam son of Nebat had committed and led the people of Israel to commit.

4 King Mesha of Moab was a sheep breeder. He used to pay the king of Israel an annual tribute of 100,000 lambs and the wool of 100,000 rams. 5 But after Ahab's death, the king of Moab rebelled against the king of Israel. 6 So King Joram promptly mustered the army of Israel and marched from Samaria. 7 On the way, he sent this message to King Jehoshaphat of Judah: "The king of Moab has rebelled against me. Will you join me in battle against him?"

And Jehoshaphat replied, "Why, of course! You and I are as one. My troops are your troops, and my horses are your horses." 8 Then Jehoshaphat asked, "What route will we take?"

"We will attack from the wilderness of Edom," Joram replied.

9 The king of Edom and his troops joined them, and all three armies traveled along a roundabout route through the wilderness for seven days. But there was no water for the men or their animals.

10 "What should we do?" the king of Israel cried out. "The LORD has brought the three of us here to let the king of Moab defeat us."

11 But King Jehoshaphat of Judah asked, "Is there no prophet of the LORD with us? If there is, we can ask the LORD what to do through him."

One of King Joram's officers replied, "Elisha son of Shaphat is here. He used to be Elijah's personal assistant.*"

12 Jehoshaphat said, "Yes, the LORD speaks through him." So the king of Israel, King Jehoshaphat of Judah, and the king of Edom went to consult with Elisha.

13 "Why are you coming to me?"* Elisha asked the king of Israel. "Go to the pagan prophets of your father and mother!"

But King Joram of Israel said, "No! For it was the LORD who called us three kings here—only to be defeated by the king of Moab!"

14 Elisha replied, "As surely as the LORD Almighty lives, whom I serve, I wouldn't even bother with you except for my respect for King Jehoshaphat of Judah. 15 Now bring me someone who can play the harp."

While the harp was being played, the power* of the LORD came upon Elisha, 16 and he said, "This is what the LORD says: This dry valley will be filled with pools of water! 17 You will see neither wind nor rain, says the LORD, but this valley will be filled with water. You will have plenty for yourselves and your cattle and other animals. 18 But this is only a simple thing for the LORD, for he will make you victorious over the army of Moab! 19 You will conquer the best of their towns, even the fortified ones. You will cut down all their good trees, stop up all their springs, and ruin all their good land with stones."

20 The next day at about the time when
the morning sacrifice was offered, water
suddenly appeared! It was flowing from
the direction of Edom, and soon there was
water everywhere.
21 Meanwhile, when the people of Moab
heard about the three armies marching
against them, they mobilized every man
who was old enough to strap on a sword,
and they stationed themselves along
their border. 22 But when they got up the
next morning, the sun was shining across
the water, making it appear red to the
Moabites—like blood. 23 "It's blood!" the
Moabites exclaimed. "The three armies must
have attacked and killed each other! Let's
go, men of Moab, and collect the plunder!"
24 But when the Moabites arrived at the
Israelite camp, the army of Israel rushed
out and attacked them until they turned
and ran. The army of Israel chased them
into the land of Moab, destroying everything as they went.* 25 They destroyed the
towns, covered their good land with stones,
stopped up all the springs, and cut down
all the good trees. Finally, only Kir-hareseth
and its stone walls were left, but men with
slings surrounded and attacked it.
26 When the king of Moab saw that he
was losing the battle, he led 700 of his
swordsmen in a desperate attempt to break
through the enemy lines near the king of
Edom, but they failed. 27 Then the king of
Moab took his oldest son, who would have
been the next king, and sacrificed him as
a burnt offering on the wall. So there was
great anger against Israel,* and the Israelites withdrew and returned to their own
land.

Elisha Helps a Poor Widow

4 One day the widow of a member of the
group of prophets came to Elisha and
cried out, "My husband who served you
is dead, and you know how he feared the
LORD. But now a creditor has come, threatening to take my two sons as slaves."
2 "What can I do to help you?" Elisha asked.
"Tell me, what do you have in the house?"
"Nothing at all, except a flask of olive
oil," she replied.
3 And Elisha said, "Borrow as many empty
jars as you can from your friends and neighbors. 4 Then go into your house with your
sons and shut the door behind you. Pour
olive oil from your flask into the jars, setting
each one aside when it is filled."
5 So she did as she was told. Her sons kept
bringing jars to her, and she filled one after
another. 6 Soon every container was full to
the brim!
"Bring me another jar," she said to one
of her sons.

2:21 Or *or make the land unproductive;* Hebrew reads *or barrenness.* **3:1** Hebrew *Jehoram,* a variant spelling of Joram; also in 3:6. **3:11** Hebrew *He used to pour water on the hands of Elijah.* **3:13** Hebrew *What is there in common between you and me?* **3:15** Hebrew *the hand.* **3:24** The meaning of the Hebrew is uncertain. **3:27** Or *So Israel's anger was great.* The meaning of the Hebrew is uncertain.

Respect for those who are older

The story of the gang of boys attacked by bears as a result of mocking Elisha (2 Kings 2:23-24) sounds shocking to our modern ears, but it shows the importance the Bible attaches to showing respect for those who are older than us. Leviticus 19:32 says, "Stand up in the presence of the elderly, and show respect for the aged. Fear your God. I am the LORD." The inclusion of this command within God's Law shows how important respect for the elderly is to God. After all, none of us would be here without the previous generation, and much of what we enjoy is owing to them.

Of course, respect should not just be demanded; it must also be earned, which is why Paul told Titus to "teach the older men . . . to be worthy of respect" (Titus 2:2).

In an increasingly globalized culture, where youth is frequently honored and age despised, the church must ensure that it promotes godly attitudes from both young to old and old to young.

▶ *See also* ***Old age****, page 660.*

"There aren't any more!" he told her. And then the olive oil stopped flowing.

7When she told the man of God what had happened, he said to her, "Now sell the olive oil and pay your debts, and you and your sons can live on what is left over."

Elisha and the Woman from Shunem

8One day Elisha went to the town of Shunem. A wealthy woman lived there, and she urged him to come to her home for a meal. After that, whenever he passed that way, he would stop there for something to eat.

9She said to her husband, "I am sure this man who stops in from time to time is a holy man of God. 10Let's build a small room for him on the roof and furnish it with a bed, a table, a chair, and a lamp. Then he will have a place to stay whenever he comes by."

11One day Elisha returned to Shunem, and he went up to this upper room to rest. 12He said to his servant Gehazi, "Tell the woman from Shunem I want to speak to her." When she appeared, 13Elisha said to Gehazi, "Tell her, 'We appreciate the kind concern you have shown us. What can we do for you? Can we put in a good word for you to the king or to the commander of the army?'"

"No," she replied, "my family takes good care of me."

14Later Elisha asked Gehazi, "What can we do for her?"

Gehazi replied, "She doesn't have a son, and her husband is an old man."

15"Call her back again," Elisha told him. When the woman returned, Elisha said to her as she stood in the doorway, 16"Next year at this time you will be holding a son in your arms!"

"No, my lord!" she cried. "O man of God, don't deceive me and get my hopes up like that."

17But sure enough, the woman soon became pregnant. And at that time the following year she had a son, just as Elisha had said.

18One day when her child was older, he went out to help his father, who was working with the harvesters. 19Suddenly he cried out, "My head hurts! My head hurts!"

His father said to one of the servants, "Carry him home to his mother."

20So the servant took him home, and his mother held him on her lap. But around noontime he died. 21She carried him up and laid him on the bed of the man of God, then shut the door and left him there. 22She sent a message to her husband: "Send one of the servants and a donkey so that I can hurry to the man of God and come right back."

23"Why go today?" he asked. "It is neither a new moon festival nor a Sabbath."

But she said, "It will be all right."

24So she saddled the donkey and said to the servant, "Hurry! Don't slow down unless I tell you to."

25As she approached the man of God at Mount Carmel, Elisha saw her in the distance. He said to Gehazi, "Look, the woman from Shunem is coming. 26Run out to meet her and ask her, 'Is everything all right with you, your husband, and your child?'"

"Yes," the woman told Gehazi, "everything is fine."

27But when she came to the man of God at the mountain, she fell to the ground before him and caught hold of his feet. Gehazi began to push her away, but the man of God said, "Leave her alone. She is deeply troubled, but the LORD has not told me what it is."

28Then she said, "Did I ask you for a son, my lord? And didn't I say, 'Don't deceive me and get my hopes up'?"

29Then Elisha said to Gehazi, "Get ready to travel*; take my staff and go! Don't talk to anyone along the way. Go quickly and lay the staff on the child's face."

30But the boy's mother said, "As surely as the LORD lives and you yourself live, I won't go home unless you go with me." So Elisha returned with her.

31Gehazi hurried on ahead and laid the staff on the child's face, but nothing happened. There was no sign of life. He returned to meet Elisha and told him, "The child is still dead."

32When Elisha arrived, the child was indeed dead, lying there on the prophet's bed. 33He went in alone and shut the door behind him and prayed to the LORD. 34Then he lay down on the child's body, placing his mouth on the child's mouth, his eyes on the child's eyes, and his hands on the child's hands. And as he stretched out on him, the child's body began to grow warm again! 35Elisha got up, walked back and forth across the room once, and then stretched himself out again on the child. This time the boy sneezed seven times and opened his eyes!

36 Then Elisha summoned Gehazi. "Call
the child's mother!" he said. And when
she came in, Elisha said, "Here, take your
son!" 37 She fell at his feet and bowed before
him, overwhelmed with gratitude. Then she
took her son in her arms and carried him
downstairs.

Miracles during a Famine

38 Elisha now returned to Gilgal, and there
was a famine in the land. One day as the
group of prophets was seated before him,
he said to his servant, "Put a large pot on
the fire, and make some stew for the rest of
the group."
39 One of the young men went out into the
field to gather herbs and came back with a
pocketful of wild gourds. He shredded them
and put them into the pot without realizing
they were poisonous. 40 Some of the stew
was served to the men. But after they had
eaten a bite or two they cried out, "Man of
God, there's poison in this stew!" So they
would not eat it.
41 Elisha said, "Bring me some flour."
Then he threw it into the pot and said, "Now
it's all right; go ahead and eat." And then it
did not harm them.
42 One day a man from Baal-shalishah
brought the man of God a sack of fresh grain
and twenty loaves of barley bread made
from the first grain of his harvest. Elisha
said, "Give it to the people so they can eat."
43 "What?" his servant exclaimed. "Feed a
hundred people with only this?"
But Elisha repeated, "Give it to the people
so they can eat, for this is what the LORD
says: Everyone will eat, and there will even
be some left over!" 44 And when they gave
it to the people, there was plenty for all
and some left over, just as the LORD had
promised.

The Healing of Naaman

5 The king of Aram had great admiration for Naaman, the commander of
his army, because through him the LORD
had given Aram great victories. But though
Naaman was a mighty warrior, he suffered
from leprosy.*
2 At this time Aramean raiders had
invaded the land of Israel, and among their
captives was a young girl who had been
given to Naaman's wife as a maid. 3 One
day the girl said to her mistress, "I wish
my master would go to see the prophet in
Samaria. He would heal him of his leprosy."
4 So Naaman told the king what the young
girl from Israel had said. 5 "Go and visit the
prophet," the king of Aram told him. "I will
send a letter of introduction for you to take
to the king of Israel." So Naaman started
out, carrying as gifts 750 pounds of silver,
150 pounds of gold,* and ten sets of clothing.
6 The letter to the king of Israel said: "With
this letter I present my servant Naaman.
I want you to heal him of his leprosy."
7 When the king of Israel read the letter,
he tore his clothes in dismay and said, "Am
I God, that I can give life and take it away?
Why is this man asking me to heal someone
with leprosy? I can see that he's just trying
to pick a fight with me."
8 But when Elisha, the man of God, heard
that the king of Israel had torn his clothes in
dismay, he sent this message to him: "Why
are you so upset? Send Naaman to me, and
he will learn that there is a true prophet
here in Israel."
9 So Naaman went with his horses and
chariots and waited at the door of Elisha's
house. 10 But Elisha sent a messenger out to
him with this message: "Go and wash yourself seven times in the Jordan River. Then
your skin will be restored, and you will be
healed of your leprosy."
11 But Naaman became angry and stalked
away. "I thought he would certainly come
out to meet me!" he said. "I expected him
to wave his hand over the leprosy and call
on the name of the LORD his God and heal
me! 12 Aren't the rivers of Damascus, the
Abana and the Pharpar, better than any of
the rivers of Israel? Why shouldn't I wash in
them and be healed?" So Naaman turned
and went away in a rage.
13 But his officers tried to reason with him
and said, "Sir,* if the prophet had told you
to do something very difficult, wouldn't you
have done it? So you should certainly obey
him when he says simply, 'Go and wash
and be cured!'" 14 So Naaman went down to
the Jordan River and dipped himself seven
times, as the man of God had instructed
him. And his skin became as healthy as the
skin of a young child, and he was healed!

4:29 Hebrew *Bind up your loins.* **5:1** Or *from a contagious skin disease.* The Hebrew word used here and throughout this passage can describe various skin diseases. **5:5** Hebrew *10 talents* [340 kilograms] *of silver, 6,000 [shekels]* [68 kilograms] *of gold.* **5:13** Hebrew *My father.*

15Then Naaman and his entire party went
back to find the man of God. They stood
before him, and Naaman said, "Now I know
that there is no God in all the world except
in Israel. So please accept a gift from your
servant."
16But Elisha replied, "As surely as the
LORD lives, whom I serve, I will not accept
any gifts." And though Naaman urged him
to take the gift, Elisha refused.
17Then Naaman said, "All right, but please
allow me to load two of my mules with
earth from this place, and I will take it back
home with me. From now on I will never
again offer burnt offerings or sacrifices to
any other god except the LORD. 18However,
may the LORD pardon me in this one thing:
When my master the king goes into the
temple of the god Rimmon to worship there
and leans on my arm, may the LORD pardon
me when I bow, too."
19"Go in peace," Elisha said. So Naaman
started home again.

The Greed of Gehazi

20But Gehazi, the servant of Elisha, the man
of God, said to himself, "My master should
not have let this Aramean get away without
accepting any of his gifts. As surely as the
LORD lives, I will chase after him and get
something from him." 21So Gehazi set off
after Naaman.

When Naaman saw Gehazi running after
him, he climbed down from his chariot and
went to meet him. "Is everything all right?"
Naaman asked.
22"Yes," Gehazi said, "but my master has
sent me to tell you that two young prophets
from the hill country of Ephraim have just
arrived. He would like 75 pounds* of silver
and two sets of clothing to give to them."
23"By all means, take twice as much*
silver," Naaman insisted. He gave him two
sets of clothing, tied up the money in two
bags, and sent two of his servants to carry
the gifts for Gehazi. 24But when they arrived
at the citadel,* Gehazi took the gifts from
the servants and sent the men back. Then
he went and hid the gifts inside the house.
25When he went in to his master, Elisha
asked him, "Where have you been, Gehazi?"

"I haven't been anywhere," he replied.
26But Elisha asked him, "Don't you realize
that I was there in spirit when Naaman
stepped down from his chariot to meet
you? Is this the time to receive money and
clothing, olive groves and vineyards, sheep
and cattle, and male and female servants?
27Because you have done this, you and your
descendants will suffer from Naaman's
leprosy forever." When Gehazi left the
room, he was covered with leprosy; his skin
was white as snow.

The Floating Ax Head

6 One day the group of prophets came to
Elisha and told him, "As you can see,
this place where we meet with you is too
small. 2Let's go down to the Jordan River,
where there are plenty of logs. There we can
build a new place for us to meet."

"All right," he told them, "go ahead."
3"Please come with us," someone
suggested.

"I will," he said. 4So he went with them.

When they arrived at the Jordan, they
began cutting down trees. 5But as one of
them was cutting a tree, his ax head fell
into the river. "Oh, sir!" he cried. "It was a
borrowed ax!"
6"Where did it fall?" the man of God
asked. When he showed him the place,
Elisha cut a stick and threw it into the water
at that spot. Then the ax head floated to the
surface. 7"Grab it," Elisha said. And the
man reached out and grabbed it.

Elisha Traps the Arameans

8When the king of Aram was at war with
Israel, he would confer with his officers and
say, "We will mobilize our forces at such
and such a place."
9But immediately Elisha, the man of God,
would warn the king of Israel, "Do not go
near that place, for the Arameans are planning to mobilize their troops there." 10So
the king of Israel would send word to the
place indicated by the man of God. Time
and again Elisha warned the king, so that
he would be on the alert there.
11The king of Aram became very upset
over this. He called his officers together and
demanded, "Which of you is the traitor?
Who has been informing the king of Israel
of my plans?"
12"It's not us, my lord the king," one of
the officers replied. "Elisha, the prophet
in Israel, tells the king of Israel even the
words you speak in the privacy of your
bedroom!"

13 “Go and find out where he is,” the king
commanded, “so I can send troops to seize
him.”
And the report came back: “Elisha is at
Dothan.” 14 So one night the king of Aram
sent a great army with many chariots and
horses to surround the city.
15 When the servant of the man of
God got up early the next morning and
went outside, there were troops, horses,
and chariots everywhere. “Oh, sir, what
will we do now?” the young man cried to
Elisha.
16 “Don’t be afraid!” Elisha told him. “For
there are more on our side than on theirs!”
17 Then Elisha prayed, “O LORD, open his
eyes and let him see!” The LORD opened
the young man’s eyes, and when he
looked up, he saw that the hillside around
Elisha was filled with horses and chariots
of fire.
18 As the Aramean army advanced toward
him, Elisha prayed, “O LORD, please make
them blind.” So the LORD struck them with
blindness as Elisha had asked.
19 Then Elisha went out and told them,
“You have come the wrong way! This isn’t
the right city! Follow me, and I will take you
to the man you are looking for.” And he led
them to the city of Samaria.
20 As soon as they had entered Samaria,
Elisha prayed, “O LORD, now open their
eyes and let them see.” So the LORD opened
their eyes, and they discovered that they
were in the middle of Samaria.
21 When the king of Israel saw them, he
shouted to Elisha, “My father, should I kill
them? Should I kill them?”
22 “Of course not!” Elisha replied. “Do we
kill prisoners of war? Give them food and
drink and send them home again to their
master.”
23 So the king made a great feast for them
and then sent them home to their master.
After that, the Aramean raiders stayed away
from the land of Israel.

Ben-Hadad Besieges Samaria

24 Some time later, however, King Ben-hadad
of Aram mustered his entire army and besieged Samaria. 25 As a result, there was a
great famine in the city. The siege lasted so
long that a donkey’s head sold for eighty
pieces of silver, and a cup of dove’s dung
sold for five pieces* of silver.
26 One day as the king of Israel was
walking along the wall of the city, a woman
called to him, “Please help me, my lord the
king!”
27 He answered, “If the LORD doesn’t help
you, what can I do? I have neither food from
the threshing floor nor wine from the press
to give you.” 28 But then the king asked,
“What is the matter?”
She replied, “This woman said to me:
‘Come on, let’s eat your son today, then we
will eat my son tomorrow.’ 29 So we cooked
my son and ate him. Then the next day
I said to her, ‘Kill your son so we can eat
him,’ but she has hidden her son.”
30 When the king heard this, he tore his
clothes in despair. And as the king walked
along the wall, the people could see that he
was wearing burlap under his robe next to
his skin. 31 “May God strike me and even kill
me if I don’t separate Elisha’s head from his
shoulders this very day,” the king vowed.
32 Elisha was sitting in his house with the
elders of Israel when the king sent a messenger to summon him. But before the messenger arrived, Elisha said to the elders, “A
murderer has sent a man to cut off my head.
When he arrives, shut the door and keep
him out. We will soon hear his master’s
steps following him.”
33 While Elisha was still saying this, the
messenger arrived. And the king* said, “All
this misery is from the LORD! Why should
I wait for the LORD any longer?”

7 Elisha replied, “Listen to this message
from the LORD! This is what the LORD
says: By this time tomorrow in the markets
of Samaria, six quarts of choice flour will
cost only one piece of silver,* and twelve
quarts of barley grain will cost only one
piece of silver.*”
2 The officer assisting the king said to the
man of God, “That couldn’t happen even if
the LORD opened the windows of heaven!”
But Elisha replied, “You will see it happen
with your own eyes, but you won’t be able
to eat any of it!”

5:22 Hebrew *1 talent* [34 kilograms]. **5:23** Hebrew *take 2 talents* [150 pounds or 68 kilograms]. **5:24** Hebrew *the Ophel.* **6:25** Hebrew *sold for 80 [shekels]* [2 pounds or 0.9 kilograms] *of silver, and 1/4 of a cab* [0.3 liters] *of dove’s dung sold for 5 [shekels]* [2 ounces or 57 grams]. *Dove’s dung* may be a variety of wild vegetable. **6:33** Hebrew *he.* **7:1a** Hebrew *1 seah* [7.3 liters] *of choice flour will cost 1 shekel* [0.4 ounces or 11 grams]; also in 7:16, 18. **7:1b** Hebrew *2 seahs* [14.6 liters] *of barley grain will cost 1 shekel* [0.4 ounces or 11 grams]; also in 7:16, 18.

Outcasts Visit the Enemy Camp

3Now there were four men with leprosy*
sitting at the entrance of the city gates. "Why
should we sit here waiting to die?" they asked
each other. 4"We will starve if we stay here,
but with the famine in the city, we will starve
if we go back there. So we might as well go
out and surrender to the Aramean army. If
they let us live, so much the better. But if they
kill us, we would have died anyway."
5So at twilight they set out for the camp of
the Arameans. But when they came to the
edge of the camp, no one was there! 6For the
Lord had caused the Aramean army to hear
the clatter of speeding chariots and the galloping of horses and the sounds of a great
army approaching. "The king of Israel has
hired the Hittites and Egyptians* to attack
us!" they cried to one another. 7So they panicked and ran into the night, abandoning
their tents, horses, donkeys, and everything
else, as they fled for their lives.
8When the men with leprosy arrived at
the edge of the camp, they went into one
tent after another, eating and drinking
wine; and they carried off silver and gold
and clothing and hid it. 9Finally, they said
to each other, "This is not right. This is a
day of good news, and we aren't sharing it
with anyone! If we wait until morning, some
calamity will certainly fall upon us. Come
on, let's go back and tell the people at the
palace."
10So they went back to the city and told
the gatekeepers what had happened. "We
went out to the Aramean camp," they said,
"and no one was there! The horses and
donkeys were tethered and the tents were
all in order, but there wasn't a single person
around!" 11Then the gatekeepers shouted
the news to the people in the palace.

Israel Plunders the Camp

12The king got out of bed in the middle of
the night and told his officers, "I know what
has happened. The Arameans know we are
starving, so they have left their camp and
have hidden in the fields. They are expecting us to leave the city, and then they will
take us alive and capture the city."
13One of his officers replied, "We had
better send out scouts to check into this.
Let them take five of the remaining horses.
If something happens to them, it will be no
worse than if they stay here and die with
the rest of us."
14So two chariots with horses were prepared, and the king sent scouts to see what
had happened to the Aramean army. 15They
went all the way to the Jordan River, following a trail of clothing and equipment that
the Arameans had thrown away in their
mad rush to escape. The scouts returned
and told the king about it. 16Then the people
of Samaria rushed out and plundered the
Aramean camp. So it was true that six quarts
of choice flour were sold that day for one
piece of silver, and twelve quarts of barley

Good news is for sharing!

"This is not right. This is a day of good news, and we aren't sharing it with anyone!" (2 Kings 7:9). It is understandable that these men with leprosy, having found a rich supply of food and resources, should be eager to enjoy it. After all, they would have been constantly shunned because of their leprosy. But as they returned for more, their conscience pricked them, and they realized they must share this good news with their fellow Israelites, trapped inside Samaria by this army that had now fled. They were none the poorer for sharing, but their fellow citizens would be far the richer for their having shared.

The same is true with our sharing of the Good News. If we have discovered that the one who has been attacking us and trying to destroy our lives (the devil) has been conquered, that there is no longer any need to live trapped within our prisons, and that God has made such rich provision for us all, why would we not want to tell as many others as possible about this? We lose nothing and they gain everything! Keeping good news to ourselves is, as these men discovered, simply not right!

grain were sold for one piece of silver, just as the LORD had promised. [17]The king appointed his officer to control the traffic at the gate, but he was knocked down and trampled to death as the people rushed out.

So everything happened exactly as the man of God had predicted when the king came to his house. [18]The man of God had said to the king, "By this time tomorrow in the markets of Samaria, six quarts of choice flour will cost one piece of silver, and twelve quarts of barley grain will cost one piece of silver."

[19]The king's officer had replied, "That couldn't happen even if the LORD opened the windows of heaven!" And the man of God had said, "You will see it happen with your own eyes, but you won't be able to eat any of it!" [20]And so it was, for the people trampled him to death at the gate!

The Woman from Shunem Returns Home

8 Elisha had told the woman whose son he had brought back to life, "Take your family and move to some other place, for the LORD has called for a famine on Israel that will last for seven years." [2]So the woman did as the man of God instructed. She took her family and settled in the land of the Philistines for seven years.

[3]After the famine ended she returned from the land of the Philistines, and she went to see the king about getting back her house and land. [4]As she came in, the king was talking with Gehazi, the servant of the man of God. The king had just said, "Tell me some stories about the great things Elisha has done." [5]And Gehazi was telling the king about the time Elisha had brought a boy back to life. At that very moment, the mother of the boy walked in to make her appeal to the king about her house and land.

"Look, my lord the king!" Gehazi exclaimed. "Here is the woman now, and this is her son—the very one Elisha brought back to life!"

[6]"Is this true?" the king asked her. And she told him the story. So he directed one of his officials to see that everything she had lost was restored to her, including the value of any crops that had been harvested during her absence.

Hazael Murders Ben-Hadad

[7]Elisha went to Damascus, the capital of Aram, where King Ben-hadad lay sick. When someone told the king that the man of God had come, [8]the king said to Hazael, "Take a gift to the man of God. Then tell him to ask the LORD, 'Will I recover from this illness?'"

[9]So Hazael loaded down forty camels with the finest products of Damascus as a gift for Elisha. He went to him and said, "Your servant Ben-hadad, the king of Aram, has sent me to ask, 'Will I recover from this illness?'"

[10]And Elisha replied, "Go and tell him, 'You will surely recover.' But actually the LORD has shown me that he will surely die!" [11]Elisha stared at Hazael* with a fixed gaze until Hazael became uneasy.* Then the man of God started weeping.

[12]"What's the matter, my lord?" Hazael asked him.

Elisha replied, "I know the terrible things you will do to the people of Israel. You will burn their fortified cities, kill their young men with the sword, dash their little children to the ground, and rip open their pregnant women!"

[13]Hazael responded, "How could a nobody like me* ever accomplish such great things?"

Elisha answered, "The LORD has shown me that you are going to be the king of Aram."

[14]When Hazael left Elisha and went back, the king asked him, "What did Elisha tell you?"

And Hazael replied, "He told me that you will surely recover."

[15]But the next day Hazael took a blanket, soaked it in water, and held it over the king's face until he died. Then Hazael became the next king of Aram.

Jehoram Rules in Judah

[16]Jehoram son of King Jehoshaphat of Judah began to rule over Judah in the fifth year of the reign of Joram son of Ahab, king of

7:3 Or *with a contagious skin disease*. The Hebrew word used here and throughout this passage can describe various skin diseases. **7:6** Possibly *and the people of Muzur*, a district near Cilicia. **8:11a** Hebrew *He stared at him*. **8:11b** The meaning of the Hebrew is uncertain. **8:13** Hebrew *a dog*.

▸ **8:16** *See **Rulers of Israel and Judah**, page 393.*

Israel. 17 Jehoram was thirty-two years old
when he became king, and he reigned in Jerusalem eight years. 18 But Jehoram followed
the example of the kings of Israel and was
as wicked as King Ahab, for he had married
one of Ahab's daughters. So Jehoram did
what was evil in the LORD's sight. 19 But the
LORD did not want to destroy Judah, for he
had promised his servant David that his descendants would continue to rule, shining
like a lamp forever.

20 During Jehoram's reign, the Edomites
revolted against Judah and crowned their
own king. 21 So Jehoram* went with all his
chariots to attack the town of Zair.* The
Edomites surrounded him and his chariot
commanders, but he went out at night and
attacked them* under cover of darkness.
But Jehoram's army deserted him and fled
to their homes. 22 So Edom has been independent from Judah to this day. The town of
Libnah also revolted about that same time.

23 The rest of the events in Jehoram's reign
and everything he did are recorded in *The
Book of the History of the Kings of Judah*.
24 When Jehoram died, he was buried with
his ancestors in the City of David. Then his
son Ahaziah became the next king.

Ahaziah Rules in Judah

25 Ahaziah son of Jehoram began to rule
over Judah in the twelfth year of the reign
of Joram son of Ahab, king of Israel.

26 Ahaziah was twenty-two years old when
he became king, and he reigned in Jerusalem one year. His mother was Athaliah,
a granddaughter of King Omri of Israel.
27 Ahaziah followed the evil example of
King Ahab's family. He did what was evil in
the LORD's sight, just as Ahab's family had
done, for he was related by marriage to the
family of Ahab.

28 Ahaziah joined Joram son of Ahab in his
war against King Hazael of Aram at Ramoth-
gilead. When the Arameans wounded King
Joram in the battle, 29 he returned to Jezreel to
recover from the wounds he had received at
Ramoth.* Because Joram was wounded, King
Ahaziah of Judah went to Jezreel to visit him.

Jehu Anointed King of Israel

9 Meanwhile, Elisha the prophet had
summoned a member of the group of
prophets. "Get ready to travel,"* he told
him, "and take this flask of olive oil with
you. Go to Ramoth-gilead, 2 and find Jehu
son of Jehoshaphat, son of Nimshi. Call him
into a private room away from his friends,
3 and pour the oil over his head. Say to him,
'This is what the LORD says: I anoint you to
be the king over Israel.' Then open the door
and run for your life!"

4 So the young prophet did as he was
told and went to Ramoth-gilead. 5 When he
arrived there, he found Jehu sitting around
with the other army officers. "I have a
message for you, Commander," he said.

"For which one of us?" Jehu asked.

"For you, Commander," he replied.

6 So Jehu left the others and went into the
house. Then the young prophet poured the
oil over Jehu's head and said, "This is what
the LORD, the God of Israel, says: I anoint you
king over the LORD's people, Israel. 7 You are
to destroy the family of Ahab, your master.
In this way, I will avenge the murder of my
prophets and all the LORD's servants who
were killed by Jezebel. 8 The entire family of
Ahab must be wiped out. I will destroy every
one of his male descendants, slave and free
alike, anywhere in Israel. 9 I will destroy the
family of Ahab as I destroyed the families of
Jeroboam son of Nebat and of Baasha son of
Ahijah. 10 Dogs will eat Ahab's wife Jezebel
at the plot of land in Jezreel, and no one will
bury her." Then the young prophet opened
the door and ran.

11 Jehu went back to his fellow officers,
and one of them asked him, "What did that
madman want? Is everything all right?"

"You know how a man like that babbles
on," Jehu replied.

12 "You're hiding something," they said.
"Tell us."

So Jehu told them, "He said to me, 'This
is what the LORD says: I have anointed you
to be king over Israel.'"

13 Then they quickly spread out their
cloaks on the bare steps and blew the ram's
horn, shouting, "Jehu is king!"

Jehu Kills Joram and Ahaziah

14 So Jehu son of Jehoshaphat, son of Nimshi,
led a conspiracy against King Joram. (Now
Joram had been with the army at Ramoth-
gilead, defending Israel against the forces
of King Hazael of Aram. 15 But King Joram*
was wounded in the fighting and returned
to Jezreel to recover from his wounds.) So
Jehu told the men with him, "If you want me

to be king, don't let anyone leave town and go to Jezreel to report what we have done."

16 Then Jehu got into a chariot and rode to Jezreel to find King Joram, who was lying there wounded. King Ahaziah of Judah was there, too, for he had gone to visit him. 17 The watchman on the tower of Jezreel saw Jehu and his company approaching, so he shouted to Joram, "I see a company of troops coming!"

"Send out a rider to ask if they are coming in peace," King Joram ordered.

18 So a horseman went out to meet Jehu and said, "The king wants to know if you are coming in peace."

Jehu replied, "What do you know about peace? Fall in behind me!"

The watchman called out to the king, "The messenger has met them, but he's not returning."

19 So the king sent out a second horseman. He rode up to them and said, "The king wants to know if you come in peace."

Again Jehu answered, "What do you know about peace? Fall in behind me!"

20 The watchman exclaimed, "The messenger has met them, but he isn't returning either! It must be Jehu son of Nimshi, for he's driving like a madman."

21 "Quick! Get my chariot ready!" King Joram commanded.

Then King Joram of Israel and King Ahaziah of Judah rode out in their chariots to meet Jehu. They met him at the plot of land that had belonged to Naboth of Jezreel. 22 King Joram demanded, "Do you come in peace, Jehu?"

Jehu replied, "How can there be peace as long as the idolatry and witchcraft of your mother, Jezebel, are all around us?"

23 Then King Joram turned the horses around* and fled, shouting to King Ahaziah, "Treason, Ahaziah!" 24 But Jehu drew his bow and shot Joram between the shoulders. The arrow pierced his heart, and he sank down dead in his chariot.

25 Jehu said to Bidkar, his officer, "Throw him into the plot of land that belonged to Naboth of Jezreel. Do you remember when you and I were riding along behind his father, Ahab? The LORD pronounced this message against him: 26 'I solemnly swear that I will repay him here on this plot of land, says the LORD, for the murder of Naboth and his sons that I saw yesterday.' So throw him out on Naboth's property, just as the LORD said."

27 When King Ahaziah of Judah saw what was happening, he fled along the road to Beth-haggan. Jehu rode after him, shouting, "Shoot him, too!" So they shot Ahaziah* in his chariot at the Ascent of Gur, near Ibleam. He was able to go on as far as Megiddo, but he died there. 28 His servants took him by chariot to Jerusalem, where they buried him with his ancestors in the City of David. 29 Ahaziah had become king over Judah in the eleventh year of the reign of Joram son of Ahab.

The Death of Jezebel

30 When Jezebel, the queen mother, heard that Jehu had come to Jezreel, she painted her eyelids and fixed her hair and sat at a window. 31 When Jehu entered the gate of the palace, she shouted at him, "Have you come in peace, you murderer? You're just like Zimri, who murdered his master!"*

32 Jehu looked up and saw her at the window and shouted, "Who is on my side?" And two or three eunuchs looked out at him. 33 "Throw her down!" Jehu yelled. So they threw her out the window, and her blood spattered against the wall and on the horses. And Jehu trampled her body under his horses' hooves.

34 Then Jehu went into the palace and ate and drank. Afterward he said, "Someone go and bury this cursed woman, for she is the daughter of a king." 35 But when they went out to bury her, they found only her skull, her feet, and her hands.

36 When they returned and told Jehu, he stated, "This fulfills the message from the LORD, which he spoke through his servant Elijah from Tishbe: 'At the plot of land in Jezreel, dogs will eat Jezebel's body. 37 Her remains will be scattered like dung on the plot of land in Jezreel, so that no one will be able to recognize her.'"

Jehu Kills Ahab's Family

10 Ahab had seventy sons living in the city of Samaria. So Jehu wrote letters and sent them to Samaria, to the elders and officials of the city,* and to the guardians

8:21a Hebrew *Joram*, a variant spelling of Jehoram; also in 8:23, 24. **8:21b** Greek version reads *Seir*. **8:21c** Or *he went out and escaped*. The meaning of the Hebrew is uncertain. **8:29** Hebrew *Ramah*, a variant spelling of Ramoth. **9:1** Hebrew *Bind up your loins*. **9:15** Hebrew *Jehoram*, a variant spelling of Joram; also in 9:17, 21, 22, 23, 24. **9:23** Hebrew *turned his hands*. **9:27** As in Greek and Syriac versions; Hebrew lacks *So they shot Ahaziah*. **9:31** See 1 Kgs 16:9-10, where Zimri killed his master, King Elah. **10:1** As in some Greek manuscripts and Latin Vulgate (see also 10:6); Hebrew reads *of Jezreel*.

of King Ahab's sons. He said, 2"The king's sons are with you, and you have at your disposal chariots, horses, a fortified city, and weapons. As soon as you receive this letter, 3select the best qualified of your master's sons to be your king, and prepare to fight for Ahab's dynasty."

4But they were paralyzed with fear and said, "We've seen that two kings couldn't stand against this man! What can we do?"

5So the palace and city administrators, together with the elders and the guardians of the king's sons, sent this message to Jehu: "We are your servants and will do anything you tell us. We will not make anyone king; do whatever you think is best."

6Jehu responded with a second letter: "If you are on my side and are going to obey me, bring the heads of your master's sons to me at Jezreel by this time tomorrow." Now the seventy sons of the king were being cared for by the leaders of Samaria, where they had been raised since childhood. 7When the letter arrived, the leaders killed all seventy of the king's sons. They placed their heads in baskets and presented them to Jehu at Jezreel.

8A messenger went to Jehu and said, "They have brought the heads of the king's sons."

So Jehu ordered, "Pile them in two heaps at the entrance of the city gate, and leave them there until morning."

9In the morning he went out and spoke to the crowd that had gathered around them. "You are not to blame," he told them. "I am the one who conspired against my master and killed him. But who killed all these? 10You can be sure that the message of the LORD that was spoken concerning Ahab's family will not fail. The LORD declared through his servant Elijah that this would happen." 11Then Jehu killed all who were left of Ahab's relatives living in Jezreel and all his important officials, his personal friends, and his priests. So Ahab was left without a single survivor.

12Then Jehu set out for Samaria. Along the way, while he was at Beth-eked of the Shepherds, 13he met some relatives of King Ahaziah of Judah. "Who are you?" he asked them.

And they replied, "We are relatives of King Ahaziah. We are going to visit the sons of King Ahab and the sons of the queen mother."

14"Take them alive!" Jehu shouted to his men. And they captured all forty-two of them and killed them at the well of Beth-eked. None of them escaped.

15When Jehu left there, he met Jehonadab son of Recab, who was coming to meet him. After they had greeted each other, Jehu said to him, "Are you as loyal to me as I am to you?"

"Yes, I am," Jehonadab replied.

"If you are," Jehu said, "then give me your hand." So Jehonadab put out his hand, and Jehu helped him into the chariot. 16Then Jehu said, "Now come with me, and see how devoted I am to the LORD." So Jehonadab rode along with him.

17When Jehu arrived in Samaria, he killed everyone who was left there from Ahab's family, just as the LORD had promised through Elijah.

Jehu Kills the Priests of Baal

18Then Jehu called a meeting of all the people of the city and said to them, "Ahab's worship of Baal was nothing compared to the way I will worship him! 19Therefore, summon all the prophets and worshipers of Baal, and call together all his priests. See to it that every one of them comes, for I am going to offer a great sacrifice to Baal. Anyone who fails to come will be put to death." But Jehu's cunning plan was to destroy all the worshipers of Baal.

20Then Jehu ordered, "Prepare a solemn assembly to worship Baal!" So they did. 21He sent messengers throughout all Israel summoning those who worshiped Baal. They all came—not a single one remained behind—and they filled the temple of Baal from one end to the other. 22And Jehu instructed the keeper of the wardrobe, "Be sure that every worshiper of Baal wears one of these robes." So robes were given to them.

23Then Jehu went into the temple of Baal with Jehonadab son of Recab. Jehu said to the worshipers of Baal, "Make sure no one who worships the LORD is here—only those who worship Baal." 24So they were all inside the temple to offer sacrifices and burnt offerings. Now Jehu had stationed eighty of his men outside the building and had warned them, "If you let anyone escape, you will pay for it with your own life."

25As soon as Jehu had finished sacrificing

the burnt offering, he commanded his
guards and officers, "Go in and kill all of
them. Don't let a single one escape!" So
they killed them all with their swords, and
the guards and officers dragged their bodies
outside.* Then Jehu's men went into the
innermost fortress* of the temple of Baal.
26 They dragged out the sacred pillar* used
in the worship of Baal and burned it. 27 They
smashed the sacred pillar and wrecked the
temple of Baal, converting it into a public
toilet, as it remains to this day.
28 In this way, Jehu destroyed every trace
of Baal worship from Israel. 29 He did not,
however, destroy the gold calves at Bethel
and Dan, with which Jeroboam son of Nebat
had caused Israel to sin.
30 Nonetheless the LORD said to Jehu, "You
have done well in following my instructions
to destroy the family of Ahab. Therefore,
your descendants will be kings of Israel
down to the fourth generation." 31 But Jehu
did not obey the Law of the LORD, the God of
Israel, with all his heart. He refused to turn
from the sins that Jeroboam had led Israel
to commit.

The Death of Jehu

32 At about that time the LORD began to cut
down the size of Israel's territory. King
Hazael conquered several sections of the
country 33 east of the Jordan River, including
all of Gilead, Gad, Reuben, and Manasseh.
He conquered the area from the town of
Aroer by the Arnon Gorge to as far north as
Gilead and Bashan.
34 The rest of the events in Jehu's reign—
everything he did and all his achievements—are recorded in *The Book of the
History of the Kings of Israel*.
35 When Jehu died, he was buried in
Samaria. Then his son Jehoahaz became the
next king. 36 In all, Jehu reigned over Israel
from Samaria for twenty-eight years.

Queen Athaliah Rules in Judah

11 When Athaliah, the mother of King
Ahaziah of Judah, learned that her
son was dead, she began to destroy the rest
of the royal family. 2 But Ahaziah's sister Jehosheba, the daughter of King Jehoram,*
took Ahaziah's infant son, Joash, and stole
him away from among the rest of the king's
children, who were about to be killed. She
put Joash and his nurse in a bedroom, and
they hid him from Athaliah, so the child
was not murdered. 3 Joash remained hidden
in the Temple of the LORD for six years while
Athaliah ruled over the land.

Revolt against Athaliah

4 In the seventh year of Athaliah's reign, Jehoiada the priest summoned the commanders, the Carite mercenaries, and the palace
guards to come to the Temple of the LORD.
He made a solemn pact with them and
made them swear an oath of loyalty there
in the LORD's Temple; then he showed them
the king's son.
5 Jehoiada told them, "This is what you
must do. A third of you who are on duty on
the Sabbath are to guard the royal palace
itself. 6 Another third of you are to stand
guard at the Sur Gate. And the final third
must stand guard behind the palace guard.
These three groups will all guard the palace.
7 The other two units who are off duty on the
Sabbath must stand guard for the king at the
LORD's Temple. 8 Form a bodyguard around
the king and keep your weapons in hand.
Kill anyone who tries to break through. Stay
with the king wherever he goes."
9 So the commanders did everything as
Jehoiada the priest ordered. The commanders took charge of the men reporting for
duty that Sabbath, as well as those who
were going off duty. They brought them all
to Jehoiada the priest, 10 and he supplied
them with the spears and small shields
that had once belonged to King David and
were stored in the Temple of the LORD.
11 The palace guards stationed themselves
around the king, with their weapons ready.
They formed a line from the south side of
the Temple around to the north side and all
around the altar.
12 Then Jehoiada brought out Joash, the
king's son, placed the crown on his head,
and presented him with a copy of God's
laws.* They anointed him and proclaimed
him king, and everyone clapped their hands
and shouted, "Long live the king!"

The Death of Athaliah

13 When Athaliah heard the noise made
by the palace guards and the people, she

10:25a Or *and they left their bodies lying there;* or *and they threw them out into the outermost court.* **10:25b** Hebrew *city.* **10:26** As in Greek and Syriac versions and Latin Vulgate; Hebrew reads *sacred pillars.* **11:2** Hebrew *Joram,* a variant spelling of Jehoram. **11:12** Or *a copy of the covenant.*

hurried to the LORD's Temple to see what was happening. [14]When she arrived, she saw the newly crowned king standing in his place of authority by the pillar, as was the custom at times of coronation. The commanders and trumpeters were surrounding him, and people from all over the land were rejoicing and blowing trumpets. When Athaliah saw all this, she tore her clothes in despair and shouted, "Treason! Treason!"

[15]Then Jehoiada the priest ordered the commanders who were in charge of the troops, "Take her to the soldiers in front of the Temple,* and kill anyone who tries to rescue her." For the priest had said, "She must not be killed in the Temple of the LORD." [16]So they seized her and led her out to the gate where horses enter the palace grounds, and she was killed there.

Jehoiada's Religious Reforms

[17]Then Jehoiada made a covenant between the LORD and the king and the people that they would be the LORD's people. He also made a covenant between the king and the people. [18]And all the people of the land went over to the temple of Baal and tore it down. They demolished the altars and smashed the idols to pieces, and they killed Mattan the priest of Baal in front of the altars.

Jehoiada the priest stationed guards at the Temple of the LORD. [19]Then the commanders, the Carite mercenaries, the palace guards, and all the people of the land escorted the king from the Temple of the LORD. They went through the gate of the guards and into the palace, and the king took his seat on the royal throne. [20]So all the people of the land rejoiced, and the city was peaceful because Athaliah had been killed at the king's palace.

[21]*Joash* was seven years old when he became king.

Joash Repairs the Temple

12 [1]*Joash* began to rule over Judah in the seventh year of King Jehu's reign in Israel. He reigned in Jerusalem forty years. His mother was Zibiah from Beersheba. [2]All his life Joash did what was pleasing in the LORD's sight because Jehoiada the priest instructed him. [3]Yet even so, he did not destroy the pagan shrines, and the people still offered sacrifices and burned incense there.

[4]One day King Joash said to the priests, "Collect all the money brought as a sacred offering to the LORD's Temple, whether it is a regular assessment, a payment of vows, or a voluntary gift. [5]Let the priests take some of that money to pay for whatever repairs are needed at the Temple."

[6]But by the twenty-third year of Joash's reign, the priests still had not repaired the Temple. [7]So King Joash called for Jehoiada and the other priests and asked them, "Why haven't you repaired the Temple? Don't use any more money for your own needs. From now on, it must all be spent on Temple repairs." [8]So the priests agreed not to accept any more money from the people, and they also agreed to let others take responsibility for repairing the Temple.

[9]Then Jehoiada the priest bored a hole in the lid of a large chest and set it on the right-hand side of the altar at the entrance of the Temple of the LORD. The priests guarding the entrance put all of the people's contributions into the chest. [10]Whenever the chest became full, the court secretary and the high priest counted the money that had been brought to the LORD's Temple and put it into bags. [11]Then they gave the money to the construction supervisors, who used it to pay the people working on the LORD's Temple—the carpenters, the builders, [12]the masons, and the stonecutters. They also used the money to buy the timber and the finished stone needed for repairing the LORD's Temple, and they paid any other expenses related to the Temple's restoration.

[13]The money brought to the Temple was not used for making silver bowls, lamp snuffers, basins, trumpets, or other articles of gold or silver for the Temple of the LORD. [14]It was paid to the workmen, who used it for the Temple repairs. [15]No accounting of this money was required from the construction supervisors, because they were honest and trustworthy men. [16]However, the money that was contributed for guilt offerings and sin offerings was not brought into the LORD's Temple. It was given to the priests for their own use.

▸ **12:1** *See **King Joash**, page 504.*

The End of Joash's Reign

17 About this time King Hazael of Aram went to war against Gath and captured it. Then he turned to attack Jerusalem. 18 King Joash collected all the sacred objects that Jehoshaphat, Jehoram, and Ahaziah, the previous kings of Judah, had dedicated, along with what he himself had dedicated. He sent them all to Hazael, along with all the gold in the treasuries of the LORD's Temple and the royal palace. So Hazael called off his attack on Jerusalem.

19 The rest of the events in Joash's reign and everything he did are recorded in *The Book of the History of the Kings of Judah.*

20 Joash's officers plotted against him and assassinated him at Beth-millo on the road to Silla. 21 The assassins were Jozacar* son of Shimeath and Jehozabad son of Shomer—both trusted advisers. Joash was buried with his ancestors in the City of David. Then his son Amaziah became the next king.

Jehoahaz Rules in Israel

13 Jehoahaz son of Jehu began to rule over Israel in the twenty-third year of King Joash's reign in Judah. He reigned in Samaria seventeen years. 2 But he did what was evil in the LORD's sight. He followed the example of Jeroboam son of Nebat, continuing the sins that Jeroboam had led Israel to commit. 3 So the LORD was very angry with Israel, and he allowed King Hazael of Aram and his son Ben-hadad to defeat them repeatedly.

4 Then Jehoahaz prayed for the LORD's help, and the LORD heard his prayer, for he could see how severely the king of Aram was oppressing Israel. 5 So the LORD provided someone to rescue the Israelites from the tyranny of the Arameans. Then Israel lived in safety again as they had in former days.

6 But they continued to sin, following the evil example of Jeroboam. They also allowed the Asherah pole in Samaria to remain standing. 7 Finally, Jehoahaz's army was reduced to 50 charioteers, 10 chariots, and 10,000 foot soldiers. The king of Aram had killed the others, trampling them like dust under his feet.

8 The rest of the events in Jehoahaz's reign—everything he did and the extent of his power—are recorded in *The Book of the*

11:15 Or *Bring her out from between the ranks;* or *Take her out of the Temple precincts.* The meaning of the Hebrew is uncertain. **11:21a** Verse 11:21 is numbered 12:1 in Hebrew text. **11:21b** Hebrew *Jehoash,* a variant spelling of Joash. **12:1a** Verses 12:1-21 are numbered 12:2-22 in Hebrew text. **12:1b** Hebrew *Jehoash,* a variant spelling of Joash; also in 12:2, 4, 6, 7, 18. **12:21** As in Greek and Syriac versions; Hebrew reads *Jozabad.*

Pagan shrines

In the Hebrew text of the Old Testament pagan shrines are called "high places." All military leaders know that holding the high ground gives you an advantage and control. This probably lay behind the choice of high places for religious shrines; people believed it gave the god lordship over that particular region. Despite the Lord's command that Canaanite high places were to be destroyed (Deuteronomy 12:1-3), Israel adopted them, sometimes for worshiping him, but increasingly to follow Canaanite religious practices. When Israel, the northern kingdom, split away, Jeroboam built shrines on many high places (1 Kings 12:31) in the hope of stopping people from going to Jerusalem to worship. This became a major cause of Israel's idolatry.

But even in Judah some kings built high places, including Solomon, despite his having built the Temple. Whenever reforming kings—Asa, Jehoshaphat, Hezekiah, and Josiah—destroyed them, their successors simply rebuilt them. Joash, despite repairing the Temple, failed to see the importance of removing them (2 Kings 12:3). This ongoing use of high places was a chief cause of the Exile (17:7-23).

High places are still favored spots for temples and shrines in many religions today. Their presence can seem dominating, especially if the Christian community is small. But we should not fear them. For even if demonic strongholds have taken hold there, Christ is seated in the highest place of all (Ephesians 1:20-22), and nothing is higher than him.

History of the Kings of Israel. 9When Jehoahaz died, he was buried in Samaria. Then
his son Jehoash* became the next king.

Jehoash Rules in Israel

10Jehoash son of Jehoahaz began to rule
over Israel in the thirty-seventh year of
King Joash's reign in Judah. He reigned in
Samaria sixteen years. 11But he did what
was evil in the LORD's sight. He refused
to turn from the sins that Jeroboam son of
Nebat had led Israel to commit.

12The rest of the events in Jehoash's
reign and everything he did, including the
extent of his power and his war with King
Amaziah of Judah, are recorded in *The Book
of the History of the Kings of Israel.* 13When
Jehoash died, he was buried in Samaria
with the kings of Israel. Then his son Jeroboam II became the next king.

Elisha's Final Prophecy

14When Elisha was in his last illness, King
Jehoash of Israel visited him and wept
over him. "My father! My father! I see the
chariots and charioteers of Israel!" he cried.

15Elisha told him, "Get a bow and some
arrows." And the king did as he was told.
16Elisha told him, "Put your hand on the
bow," and Elisha laid his own hands on the
king's hands.

17Then he commanded, "Open that eastern
window," and he opened it. Then he said,
"Shoot!" So he shot an arrow. Elisha proclaimed, "This is the LORD's arrow, an arrow
of victory over Aram, for you will completely
conquer the Arameans at Aphek."

18Then he said, "Now pick up the other
arrows and strike them against the ground."
So the king picked them up and struck the
ground three times. 19But the man of God was
angry with him. "You should have struck
the ground five or six times!" he exclaimed.
"Then you would have beaten Aram until it
was entirely destroyed. Now you will be victorious only three times."

20Then Elisha died and was buried.

Groups of Moabite raiders used to invade
the land each spring. 21Once when some Israelites were burying a man, they spied a band
of these raiders. So they hastily threw the
corpse into the tomb of Elisha and fled. But
as soon as the body touched Elisha's bones,
the dead man revived and jumped to his feet!

22King Hazael of Aram had oppressed
Israel during the entire reign of King Jehoahaz. 23But the LORD was gracious and merciful to the people of Israel, and they were not
totally destroyed. He pitied them because
of his covenant with Abraham, Isaac, and
Jacob. And to this day he still has not completely destroyed them or banished them
from his presence.

24King Hazael of Aram died, and his son
Ben-hadad became the next king. 25Then
Jehoash son of Jehoahaz recaptured from
Ben-hadad son of Hazael the towns that had
been taken from Jehoash's father, Jehoahaz.
Jehoash defeated Ben-hadad on three occa-
sions, and he recovered the Israelite towns.

Amaziah Rules in Judah

14 Amaziah son of Joash began to rule
over Judah in the second year of the
reign of King Jehoash* of Israel. 2Amaziah
was twenty-five years old when he became
king, and he reigned in Jerusalem twenty-
nine years. His mother was Jehoaddin from
Jerusalem. 3Amaziah did what was pleasing
in the LORD's sight, but not like his ancestor
David. Instead, he followed the example of
his father, Joash. 4Amaziah did not destroy
the pagan shrines, and the people still
offered sacrifices and burned incense there.

5When Amaziah was well established as
king, he executed the officials who had assassinated his father. 6However, he did not
kill the children of the assassins, for he
obeyed the command of the LORD as written
by Moses in the Book of the Law: "Parents
must not be put to death for the sins of their
children, nor children for the sins of their
parents. Those deserving to die must be put
to death for their own crimes."*

7Amaziah also killed 10,000 Edomites in
the Valley of Salt. He also conquered Sela
and changed its name to Joktheel, as it is
called to this day.

8One day Amaziah sent messengers with
this challenge to Israel's king Jehoash, the
son of Jehoahaz and grandson of Jehu:
"Come and meet me in battle!"*

9But King Jehoash of Israel replied to King
Amaziah of Judah with this story: "Out in
the Lebanon mountains, a thistle sent a
message to a mighty cedar tree: 'Give your
daughter in marriage to my son.' But just
then a wild animal of Lebanon came by and
stepped on the thistle, crushing it!

10"You have indeed defeated Edom, and

you are proud of it. But be content with
your victory and stay at home! Why stir up
trouble that will only bring disaster on you
and the people of Judah?"
11 But Amaziah refused to listen, so King
Jehoash of Israel mobilized his army against
King Amaziah of Judah. The two armies
drew up their battle lines at Beth-shemesh
in Judah. 12 Judah was routed by the army
of Israel, and its army scattered and fled
for home. 13 King Jehoash of Israel captured
Judah's king, Amaziah son of Joash and
grandson of Ahaziah, at Beth-shemesh. Then
he marched to Jerusalem, where he demolished 600 feet* of Jerusalem's wall, from the
Ephraim Gate to the Corner Gate. 14 He carried
off all the gold and silver and all the articles
from the Temple of the LORD. He also seized
the treasures from the royal palace, along
with hostages, and then returned to Samaria.
15 The rest of the events in Jehoash's
reign and everything he did, including the
extent of his power and his war with King
Amaziah of Judah, are recorded in *The Book
of the History of the Kings of Israel.* 16 When
Jehoash died, he was buried in Samaria
with the kings of Israel. And his son Jeroboam II became the next king.
17 King Amaziah of Judah lived for fifteen
years after the death of King Jehoash of
Israel. 18 The rest of the events in Amaziah's
reign are recorded in *The Book of the History
of the Kings of Judah.*
19 There was a conspiracy against
Amaziah's life in Jerusalem, and he fled
to Lachish. But his enemies sent assassins
after him, and they killed him there. 20 They
brought his body back to Jerusalem on a
horse, and he was buried with his ancestors
in the City of David.
21 All the people of Judah had crowned
Amaziah's sixteen-year-old son, Uzziah,* as
king in place of his father, Amaziah. 22 After
his father's death, Uzziah rebuilt the town
of Elath and restored it to Judah.

Jeroboam II Rules in Israel

23 Jeroboam II, the son of Jehoash, began to
rule over Israel in the fifteenth year of King
Amaziah's reign in Judah. He reigned in
Samaria forty-one years. 24 He did what was
evil in the LORD's sight. He refused to turn
from the sins that Jeroboam son of Nebat had
led Israel to commit. 25 Jeroboam II recovered
the territories of Israel between Lebo-hamath
and the Dead Sea,* just as the LORD, the God
of Israel, had promised through Jonah son of
Amittai, the prophet from Gath-hepher.
26 For the LORD saw the bitter suffering of
everyone in Israel, and that there was no
one in Israel, slave or free, to help them.
27 And because the LORD had not said he
would blot out the name of Israel completely, he used Jeroboam II, the son of
Jehoash, to save them.
28 The rest of the events in the reign of Jeroboam II and everything he did—including
the extent of his power, his wars, and how
he recovered for Israel both Damascus and
Hamath, which had belonged to Judah*—
are recorded in *The Book of the History of
the Kings of Israel.* 29 When Jeroboam II died,
he was buried in Samaria* with the kings of
Israel. Then his son Zechariah became the
next king.

Uzziah Rules in Judah

15 Uzziah* son of Amaziah began to rule
over Judah in the twenty-seventh year
of the reign of King Jeroboam II of Israel. 2 He
was sixteen years old when he became king,
and he reigned in Jerusalem fifty-two years.
His mother was Jecoliah from Jerusalem.
3 He did what was pleasing in the LORD's
sight, just as his father, Amaziah, had done.
4 But he did not destroy the pagan shrines,
and the people still offered sacrifices and
burned incense there. 5 The LORD struck the
king with leprosy,* which lasted until the
day he died. He lived in isolation in a separate house. The king's son Jotham was put
in charge of the royal palace, and he governed the people of the land.
6 The rest of the events in Uzziah's reign
and everything he did are recorded in *The
Book of the History of the Kings of Judah.*
7 When Uzziah died, he was buried with his

13:9 Hebrew *Joash*, a variant spelling of Jehoash; also in 13:10, 12, 13, 14, 25. **14:1** Hebrew *Joash*, a variant spelling of Jehoash; also in 14:13, 23, 27. **14:6** Deut 24:16. **14:8** Hebrew *Come, let us look one another in the face.* **14:13** Hebrew *400 cubits* [180 meters]. **14:21** Hebrew *Azariah*, a variant spelling of Uzziah. **14:25** Hebrew *the sea of the Arabah.* **14:28** Or *to Yaudi.* The meaning of the Hebrew is uncertain. **14:29** As in some Greek manuscripts; Hebrew lacks *he was buried in Samaria.* **15:1** Hebrew *Azariah*, a variant spelling of Uzziah; also in 15:6, 7, 8, 17, 23, 27. **15:5** Or *with a contagious skin disease.* The Hebrew word used here and throughout this passage can describe various skin diseases.

▸ **15:5** *See **Leprosy**, page 508.*

ancestors in the City of David. And his son
Jotham became the next king.

Zechariah Rules in Israel

8 Zechariah son of Jeroboam II began to
rule over Israel in the thirty-eighth year of
King Uzziah's reign in Judah. He reigned in
Samaria six months. 9 Zechariah did what
was evil in the LORD's sight, as his ancestors
had done. He refused to turn from the sins
that Jeroboam son of Nebat had led Israel
to commit. 10 Then Shallum son of Jabesh
conspired against Zechariah, assassinated
him in public,* and became the next king.

11 The rest of the events in Zechariah's reign are recorded in *The Book of the
History of the Kings of Israel.* 12 So the LORD's
message to Jehu came true: "Your descendants will be kings of Israel down to the
fourth generation."

Shallum Rules in Israel

13 Shallum son of Jabesh began to rule over
Israel in the thirty-ninth year of King Uzziah's
reign in Judah. Shallum reigned in Samaria
only one month. 14 Then Menahem son of
Gadi went to Samaria from Tirzah and assassinated him, and he became the next king.

15 The rest of the events in Shallum's reign,
including his conspiracy, are recorded in
The Book of the History of the Kings of Israel.

Menahem Rules in Israel

16 At that time Menahem destroyed the
town of Tappuah* and all the surrounding countryside as far as Tirzah, because
its citizens refused to surrender the town.
He killed the entire population and ripped
open the pregnant women.

17 Menahem son of Gadi began to rule over
Israel in the thirty-ninth year of King Uzziah's
reign in Judah. He reigned in Samaria ten
years. 18 But Menahem did what was evil in
the LORD's sight. During his entire reign, he
refused to turn from the sins that Jeroboam
son of Nebat had led Israel to commit.

19 Then King Tiglath-pileser* of Assyria
invaded the land. But Menahem paid him
thirty-seven tons* of silver to gain his
support in tightening his grip on royal
power. 20 Menahem extorted the money from
the rich of Israel, demanding that each of
them pay fifty pieces* of silver to the king of
Assyria. So the king of Assyria turned from
attacking Israel and did not stay in the land.

21 The rest of the events in Menahem's
reign and everything he did are recorded in
The Book of the History of the Kings of Israel.
22 When Menahem died, his son Pekahiah
became the next king.

Pekahiah Rules in Israel

23 Pekahiah son of Menahem began to
rule over Israel in the fiftieth year of King
Uzziah's reign in Judah. He reigned in
Samaria two years. 24 But Pekahiah did what
was evil in the LORD's sight. He refused to
turn from the sins that Jeroboam son of
Nebat had led Israel to commit.

25 Then Pekah son of Remaliah, the commander of Pekahiah's army, conspired
against him. With fifty men from Gilead,
Pekah assassinated the king, along with
Argob and Arieh, in the citadel of the palace
at Samaria. And Pekah reigned in his place.

26 The rest of the events in Pekahiah's
reign and everything he did are recorded in
The Book of the History of the Kings of Israel.

Pekah Rules in Israel

27 Pekah son of Remaliah began to rule
over Israel in the fifty-second year of King
Uzziah's reign in Judah. He reigned in
Samaria twenty years. 28 But Pekah did what
was evil in the LORD's sight. He refused to
turn from the sins that Jeroboam son of
Nebat had led Israel to commit.

29 During Pekah's reign, King Tiglath-
pileser of Assyria attacked Israel again, and
he captured the towns of Ijon, Abel-beth-
maacah, Janoah, Kedesh, and Hazor. He also
conquered the regions of Gilead, Galilee,
and all of Naphtali, and he took the people
to Assyria as captives. 30 Then Hoshea son of
Elah conspired against Pekah and assassinated him. He began to rule over Israel in
the twentieth year of Jotham son of Uzziah.

31 The rest of the events in Pekah's reign
and everything he did are recorded in *The
Book of the History of the Kings of Israel.*

Jotham Rules in Judah

32 Jotham son of Uzziah began to rule over
Judah in the second year of King Pekah's
reign in Israel. 33 He was twenty-five years
old when he became king, and he reigned
in Jerusalem sixteen years. His mother was
Jerusha, the daughter of Zadok.

34 Jotham did what was pleasing in the
LORD's sight. He did everything his father,

Uzziah, had done. [35]But he did not destroy the pagan shrines, and the people still offered sacrifices and burned incense there. He rebuilt the upper gate of the Temple of the LORD.

[36]The rest of the events in Jotham's reign and everything he did are recorded in *The Book of the History of the Kings of Judah.* [37]In those days the LORD began to send King Rezin of Aram and King Pekah of Israel to attack Judah. [38]When Jotham died, he was buried with his ancestors in the City of David. And his son Ahaz became the next king.

Ahaz Rules in Judah

16 Ahaz son of Jotham began to rule over Judah in the seventeenth year of King Pekah's reign in Israel. [2]Ahaz was twenty years old when he became king, and he reigned in Jerusalem sixteen years. He did not do what was pleasing in the sight of the LORD his God, as his ancestor David had done. [3]Instead, he followed the example of the kings of Israel, even sacrificing his own son in the fire.* In this way, he followed the detestable practices of the pagan nations the LORD had driven from the land ahead of the Israelites. [4]He offered sacrifices and burned incense at the pagan shrines and on the hills and under every green tree.

[5]Then King Rezin of Aram and King Pekah of Israel came up to attack Jerusalem. They besieged Ahaz but could not conquer him. [6]At that time the king of Edom* recovered the town of Elath for Edom.* He drove out the people of Judah and sent Edomites* to live there, as they do to this day.

[7]King Ahaz sent messengers to King Tiglath-pileser of Assyria with this message: "I am your servant and your vassal.* Come up and rescue me from the attacking armies of Aram and Israel." [8]Then Ahaz took the silver and gold from the Temple of the LORD and the palace treasury and sent it as a payment to the Assyrian king. [9]So the king of Assyria attacked the Aramean capital of Damascus and led its population away as captives, resettling them in Kir. He also killed King Rezin.

[10]King Ahaz then went to Damascus to meet with King Tiglath-pileser of Assyria. While he was there, he took special note of the altar. Then he sent a model of the altar to Uriah the priest, along with its design in full detail. [11]Uriah followed the king's instructions and built an altar just like it, and it was ready before the king returned from Damascus. [12]When the king returned, he inspected the altar and made offerings on it. [13]He presented a burnt offering and a grain offering, he poured out a liquid offering, and he sprinkled the blood of peace offerings on the altar.

15:10 Or *at Ibleam.* **15:16** As in some Greek manuscripts; Hebrew reads *Tiphsah.* **15:19a** Hebrew *Pul,* another name for Tiglath-pileser. **15:19b** Hebrew *1,000 talents* [34 metric tons]. **15:20** Hebrew *50 shekels* [20 ounces or 570 grams]. **16:3** Or *even making his son pass through the fire.* **16:6a** As in Latin Vulgate; Hebrew reads *Rezin king of Aram.* **16:6b** As in Latin Vulgate; Hebrew reads *Aram.* **16:6c** As in Greek version, Latin Vulgate, and an alternate reading of the Masoretic Text; the other alternate reads *Arameans.* **16:7** Hebrew *your son.*

Assyria

When Aram (Syria) and Israel joined forces to attack Judah, King Ahaz appealed to Assyria for help (2 Kings 16:7). Eager to expand its empire, Assyria obliged, conquering Syria and, soon afterwards, Israel too. The Assyrians came from northern Mesopotamia, where they had settled in city-states around 2300 BC. Over the centuries they had become a leading regional power, and by the ninth century BC they had become fearsome warriors and hungry expansionists. Although highly cultured, they were also brutal in warfare, inflicting maximum suffering to intimidate opponents. Those who survived their onslaughts were forced to pay heavy tributes or were deported. (It is estimated they deported four million people.) Yet even such great empires are not beyond God's control; he used them as "the rod of my anger" (Isaiah 10:5) to bring his judgment on wicked Israel. Assyria conquered Israel in 722 BC and exiled and scattered its people (2 Kings 17).

▸ *See also* ***The Exile****, page 433;* ***The Exile*** *map, Visual Overview Z9.*

14Then King Ahaz removed the old bronze
altar from its place in front of the LORD's
Temple, between the entrance and the new
altar, and placed it on the north side of the
new altar. 15He told Uriah the priest, "Use
the new altar* for the morning sacrifices of
burnt offering, the evening grain offering,
the king's burnt offering and grain offering,
and the burnt offerings of all the people, as
well as their grain offerings and liquid offerings. Sprinkle the blood from all the burnt
offerings and sacrifices on the new altar.
The bronze altar will be for my personal
use only." 16Uriah the priest did just as King
Ahaz commanded him.

17Then the king removed the side panels
and basins from the portable water carts.
He also removed the great bronze basin
called the Sea from the backs of the bronze
oxen and placed it on the stone pavement.
18In deference to the king of Assyria, he
also removed the canopy that had been
constructed inside the palace for use on the
Sabbath day,* as well as the king's outer entrance to the Temple of the LORD.

19The rest of the events in Ahaz's reign
and everything he did are recorded in *The
Book of the History of the Kings of Judah.*
20When Ahaz died, he was buried with his
ancestors in the City of David. Then his son
Hezekiah became the next king.

Hoshea Rules in Israel

17 Hoshea son of Elah began to rule
over Israel in the twelfth year of
King Ahaz's reign in Judah. He reigned in
Samaria nine years. 2He did what was evil
in the LORD's sight, but not to the same
extent as the kings of Israel who ruled
before him.

3King Shalmaneser of Assyria attacked
King Hoshea, so Hoshea was forced to
pay heavy tribute to Assyria. 4But Hoshea
stopped paying the annual tribute and conspired against the king of Assyria by asking
King So of Egypt* to help him shake free of
Assyria's power. When the king of Assyria
discovered this treachery, he seized Hoshea
and put him in prison.

Samaria Falls to Assyria

5Then the king of Assyria invaded the entire
land, and for three years he besieged the
city of Samaria. 6Finally, in the ninth year of
King Hoshea's reign, Samaria fell, and the
people of Israel were exiled to Assyria. They
were settled in colonies in Halah, along the
banks of the Habor River in Gozan, and in
the cities of the Medes.

7This disaster came upon the people of
Israel because they worshiped other gods.
They sinned against the LORD their God,
who had brought them safely out of Egypt
and had rescued them from the power of
Pharaoh, the king of Egypt. 8They had followed the practices of the pagan nations
the LORD had driven from the land ahead
of them, as well as the practices the kings
of Israel had introduced. 9The people of
Israel had also secretly done many things
that were not pleasing to the LORD their
God. They built pagan shrines for themselves in all their towns, from the smallest
outpost to the largest walled city. 10They set
up sacred pillars and Asherah poles at the
top of every hill and under every green tree.
11They offered sacrifices on all the hilltops,
just like the nations the LORD had driven
from the land ahead of them. So the people
of Israel had done many evil things, arousing the LORD's anger. 12Yes, they worshiped
idols,* despite the LORD's specific and repeated warnings.

13Again and again the LORD had sent his
prophets and seers to warn both Israel and
Judah: "Turn from all your evil ways. Obey
my commands and decrees—the entire law
that I commanded your ancestors to obey,
and that I gave you through my servants the
prophets."

14But the Israelites would not listen. They
were as stubborn as their ancestors who had
refused to believe in the LORD their God.
15They rejected his decrees and the covenant
he had made with their ancestors, and they
despised all his warnings. They worshiped
worthless idols, so they became worthless
themselves. They followed the example of
the nations around them, disobeying the
LORD's command not to imitate them.

16They rejected all the commands of the
LORD their God and made two calves from
metal. They set up an Asherah pole and
worshiped Baal and all the forces of heaven.
17They even sacrificed their own sons and
daughters in the fire.* They consulted
fortune-tellers and practiced sorcery and sold
themselves to evil, arousing the LORD's anger.

18Because the LORD was very angry
with Israel, he swept them away from his

presence. Only the tribe of Judah remained
in the land. 19 But even the people of Judah
refused to obey the commands of the LORD
their God, for they followed the evil practices that Israel had introduced. 20 The LORD
rejected all the descendants of Israel. He
punished them by handing them over to
their attackers until he had banished Israel
from his presence.
21 For when the LORD* tore Israel away
from the kingdom of David, they chose Jeroboam son of Nebat as their king. But Jeroboam drew Israel away from following
the LORD and made them commit a great
sin. 22 And the people of Israel persisted in
all the evil ways of Jeroboam. They did not
turn from these sins 23 until the LORD finally
swept them away from his presence, just as
all his prophets had warned. So Israel was
exiled from their land to Assyria, where
they remain to this day.

Foreigners Settle in Israel

24 The king of Assyria transported groups of
people from Babylon, Cuthah, Avva, Hamath,
and Sepharvaim and resettled them in the
towns of Samaria, replacing the people of

16:15 Hebrew *the great altar.* **16:18** The meaning of the Hebrew is uncertain. **17:4** Or *by asking the king of Egypt at Sais.* **17:12** The Hebrew term (literally *round things*) probably alludes to dung. **17:17** Or *They even made their sons and daughters pass through the fire.* **17:21** Hebrew *he;* compare 1 Kgs 11:31-32.

The Exile

As the Israelites prepared to enter the Promised Land, God had warned them not to stray from his commands. In Deuteronomy he predicted the drought, plagues, and military defeats that would result from disobedience. Worst of all he had warned them that "you will be torn from the land you are about to enter and occupy. For the LORD will scatter you among all the nations from one end of the earth to the other" (Deuteronomy 28:63-64).

In spite of repeated warnings by the prophets, the unthinkable did happen. First Israel, then later Judah, fell to the superpowers of the day—Israel to Assyria and Judah to Babylon. The Israelites, who had once been slaves in Egypt, were captives once again. This surely cannot have been God's purpose for them.

Israel was invaded by the Assyrians several times, the last time in 722 BC. The armies surrounded and conquered Samaria, its capital. Then they deported many of the Israelites and repopulated the land with foreigners from other parts of the empire. (This mixture of peoples the Assyrians resettled in Israel came to be known as Samaritans, and by New Testament times they would be hated because they were seen as "impure" and not God's true people.) The Israelites from the ten northern tribes never returned. We have no idea what happened to them; as Assyria itself was conquered by the Babylonians and Medes in 605 BC, they were scattered to the four winds.

Judah (the southern kingdom) was invaded by the Babylonians three times between 605 and 586 BC. The armies finally marched into Jerusalem, burned down the Temple, took all its treasures, tore down the city's massive walls, and carried off the people into captivity. Unlike the Assyrians, the Babylonians took captives only among the strong and skilled, leaving the poor and weak behind. Judah's leaders were allowed to settle in Babylon and build homes and find jobs, just as Jeremiah had encouraged them to (Jeremiah 29:4-7). Some (like Daniel) became an important part of Babylonian society.

Eventually, as the prophets had predicted, the Exile came to an end. In 539 BC the Babylonian Empire was itself conquered by the Persians, who had a policy of allowing exiled peoples to go home, which God's people began to do the following year.

▶ *See also* ***Assyria****, page 431;* ***The Exile*** *map, Visual Overview Z9.*

Israel. They took possession of Samaria and lived in its towns. 25 But since these foreign settlers did not worship the LORD when they first arrived, the LORD sent lions among them, which killed some of them.

26 So a message was sent to the king of Assyria: "The people you have sent to live in the towns of Samaria do not know the religious customs of the God of the land. He has sent lions among them to destroy them because they have not worshiped him correctly."

27 The king of Assyria then commanded, "Send one of the exiled priests back to Samaria. Let him live there and teach the new residents the religious customs of the God of the land." 28 So one of the priests who had been exiled from Samaria returned to Bethel and taught the new residents how to worship the LORD.

29 But these various groups of foreigners also continued to worship their own gods. In town after town where they lived, they placed their idols at the pagan shrines that the people of Samaria had built. 30 Those from Babylon worshiped idols of their god Succoth-benoth. Those from Cuthah worshiped their god Nergal. And those from Hamath worshiped Ashima. 31 The Avvites worshiped their gods Nibhaz and Tartak. And the people from Sepharvaim even burned their own children as sacrifices to their gods Adrammelech and Anammelech.

32 These new residents worshiped the LORD, but they also appointed from among themselves all sorts of people as priests to offer sacrifices at their places of worship. 33 And though they worshiped the LORD, they continued to follow their own gods according to the religious customs of the nations from which they came. 34 And this is still going on today. They continue to follow their former practices instead of truly worshiping the LORD and obeying the decrees, regulations, instructions, and commands he gave the descendants of Jacob, whose name he changed to Israel.

35 For the LORD had made a covenant with the descendants of Jacob and commanded them: "Do not worship any other gods or bow before them or serve them or offer sacrifices to them. 36 But worship only the LORD, who brought you out of Egypt with great strength and a powerful arm. Bow down to him alone, and offer sacrifices only to him. 37 Be careful at all times to obey the decrees, regulations, instructions, and commands that he wrote for you. You must not worship other gods. 38 Do not forget the covenant I made with you, and do not worship other gods. 39 You must worship only the LORD your God. He is the one who will rescue you from all your enemies."

40 But the people would not listen and continued to follow their former practices. 41 So while these new residents worshiped the LORD, they also worshiped their idols. And to this day their descendants do the same.

Hezekiah Rules in Judah

18 Hezekiah son of Ahaz began to rule over Judah in the third year of King Hoshea's reign in Israel. 2 He was twenty-five years old when he became king, and he reigned in Jerusalem twenty-nine years. His mother was Abijah,* the daughter of Zechariah. 3 He did what was pleasing in the LORD's sight, just as his ancestor David had done. 4 He removed the pagan shrines, smashed the sacred pillars, and cut down the Asherah poles. He broke up the bronze serpent that Moses had made, because the people of Israel had been offering sacrifices to it. The bronze serpent was called Nehushtan.*

5 Hezekiah trusted in the LORD, the God of Israel. There was no one like him among all the kings of Judah, either before or after his time. 6 He remained faithful to the LORD in everything, and he carefully obeyed all the commands the LORD had given Moses. 7 So the LORD was with him, and Hezekiah was successful in everything he did. He revolted against the king of Assyria and refused to pay him tribute. 8 He also conquered the Philistines as far distant as Gaza and its territory, from their smallest outpost to their largest walled city.

9 During the fourth year of Hezekiah's reign, which was the seventh year of King Hoshea's reign in Israel, King Shalmaneser of Assyria attacked the city of Samaria and began a siege against it. 10 Three years later, during the sixth year of King Hezekiah's reign and the ninth year of King Hoshea's reign in Israel, Samaria fell. 11 At that time the

▸ **18:1** *See* ***King Hezekiah****, page 786.*

king of Assyria exiled the Israelites to Assyria and placed them in colonies in Halah, along the banks of the Habor River in Gozan, and in the cities of the Medes. 12 For they refused to listen to the LORD their God and obey him. Instead, they violated his covenant—all the laws that Moses the LORD's servant had commanded them to obey.

Assyria Invades Judah

13 In the fourteenth year of King Hezekiah's reign,* King Sennacherib of Assyria came to attack the fortified towns of Judah and conquered them. 14 King Hezekiah sent this message to the king of Assyria at Lachish: "I have done wrong. I will pay whatever tribute money you demand if you will only withdraw." The king of Assyria then demanded a settlement of more than eleven tons of silver and one ton of gold.* 15 To gather this amount, King Hezekiah used all the silver stored in the Temple of the LORD and in the palace treasury. 16 Hezekiah even stripped the gold from the doors of the LORD's Temple and from the doorposts he had overlaid with gold, and he gave it all to the Assyrian king.

17 Nevertheless, the king of Assyria sent his commander in chief, his field commander, and his chief of staff* from Lachish with a huge army to confront King Hezekiah in Jerusalem. The Assyrians took up a position beside the aqueduct that feeds water into the upper pool, near the road leading to the field where cloth is washed.* 18 They summoned King Hezekiah, but the king sent these officials to meet with them: Eliakim son of Hilkiah, the palace administrator; Shebna the court secretary; and Joah son of Asaph, the royal historian.

Sennacherib Threatens Jerusalem

19 Then the Assyrian king's chief of staff told them to give this message to Hezekiah:

"This is what the great king of Assyria says: What are you trusting in that makes you so confident? 20 Do you think that mere words can substitute for military skill and strength? Who are you counting on, that you have rebelled against me? 21 On Egypt? If you lean on Egypt, it will be like a reed that splinters beneath your weight and pierces your hand. Pharaoh, the king of Egypt, is completely unreliable!

22 "But perhaps you will say to me, 'We are trusting in the LORD our God!' But isn't he the one who was insulted by Hezekiah? Didn't Hezekiah tear down his shrines and altars and make everyone in Judah and Jerusalem

18:2 As in parallel text at 2 Chr 29:1; Hebrew reads *Abi,* a variant spelling of Abijah. **18:4** *Nehushtan* sounds like the Hebrew terms that mean "snake," "bronze," and "unclean thing." **18:13** The fourteenth year of Hezekiah's reign was 701 B.C. **18:14** Hebrew *300 talents* [10 metric tons] *of silver and 30 talents* [1 metric ton] *of gold.* **18:17a** Or *the rabshakeh;* also in 18:19, 26, 27, 28, 37. **18:17b** Or *bleached.*

▸ **18:17** *See **Sennacherib's siege of Jerusalem**, page 514.*

Lachish

Having conquered Israel in the north, it wasn't long before Assyria decided to attack Judah too. In 701 BC King Sennacherib invaded Judah with an army of at least 185,000 men. One of the cities he captured was Lachish (2 Kings 18:14), twenty-five miles southwest of Jerusalem, and Judah's second most important city at that time. Its siege was depicted in low-relief sculpture in Sennacherib's palace at Nineveh, showing siege engines and towers set up against the walls and bowmen, slingers, and spearmen marching up ramps to take the city. Although strongly fortified, the city was defeated, sacked, and razed to the ground. Hoping Sennacherib would spare Jerusalem, King Hezekiah paid a huge financial tribute. But unsatisfied with what Hezekiah paid, Sennacherib threatened to destroy Jerusalem (18:19-25), which was spared only by Hezekiah trusting God's promise to him through Isaiah (chapter 19). The Bible consistently encourages us to look to God, not our natural resources, if we want to have success.

worship only at the altar here in
Jerusalem?
23“I’ll tell you what! Strike a bargain
with my master, the king of Assyria.
I will give you 2,000 horses if you can
find that many men to ride on them!
24With your tiny army, how can you
think of challenging even the weakest
contingent of my master’s troops,
even with the help of Egypt’s chariots
and charioteers? 25What’s more, do
you think we have invaded your land
without the LORD’s direction? The LORD
himself told us, ‘Attack this land and
destroy it!’”

26Then Eliakim son of Hilkiah, Shebna,
and Joah said to the Assyrian chief of staff,
“Please speak to us in Aramaic, for we
understand it well. Don’t speak in Hebrew,*
for the people on the wall will hear.”
27But Sennacherib’s chief of staff replied,
“Do you think my master sent this message
only to you and your master? He wants all
the people to hear it, for when we put this
city under siege, they will suffer along with
you. They will be so hungry and thirsty that
they will eat their own dung and drink their
own urine.”
28Then the chief of staff stood and shouted
in Hebrew to the people on the wall, “Listen
to this message from the great king of
Assyria! 29This is what the king says: Don’t
let Hezekiah deceive you. He will never be
able to rescue you from my power. 30Don’t
let him fool you into trusting in the LORD
by saying, ‘The LORD will surely rescue us.
This city will never fall into the hands of the
Assyrian king!’
31“Don’t listen to Hezekiah! These are the
terms the king of Assyria is offering: Make
peace with me—open the gates and come
out. Then each of you can continue eating
from your own grapevine and fig tree and
drinking from your own well. 32Then I will
arrange to take you to another land like this
one—a land of grain and new wine, bread
and vineyards, olive groves and honey.
Choose life instead of death!
“Don’t listen to Hezekiah when he tries
to mislead you by saying, ‘The LORD will
rescue us!’ 33Have the gods of any other
nations ever saved their people from the
king of Assyria? 34What happened to the
gods of Hamath and Arpad? And what
about the gods of Sepharvaim, Hena, and
Ivvah? Did any god rescue Samaria from my
power? 35What god of any nation has ever
been able to save its people from my power?
So what makes you think that the LORD can
rescue Jerusalem from me?”
36But the people were silent and did not
utter a word because Hezekiah had commanded them, “Do not answer him.”
37Then Eliakim son of Hilkiah, the palace
administrator; Shebna the court secretary;
and Joah son of Asaph, the royal historian,
went back to Hezekiah. They tore their
clothes in despair, and they went in to see
the king and told him what the Assyrian
chief of staff had said.

Hezekiah Seeks the LORD’s Help

19 When King Hezekiah heard their
report, he tore his clothes and put
on burlap and went into the Temple of the
LORD. 2And he sent Eliakim the palace administrator, Shebna the court secretary, and
the leading priests, all dressed in burlap,
to the prophet Isaiah son of Amoz. 3They
told him, “This is what King Hezekiah
says: Today is a day of trouble, insults, and
disgrace. It is like when a child is ready to
be born, but the mother has no strength
to deliver the baby. 4But perhaps the LORD
your God has heard the Assyrian chief of
staff,* sent by the king to defy the living
God, and will punish him for his words. Oh,
pray for those of us who are left!”
5After King Hezekiah’s officials delivered
the king’s message to Isaiah, 6the prophet
replied, “Say to your master, ‘This is what
the LORD says: Do not be disturbed by
this blasphemous speech against me from
the Assyrian king’s messengers. 7Listen!
I myself will move against him,* and the
king will receive a message that he is
needed at home. So he will return to his
land, where I will have him killed with a
sword.’”
8Meanwhile, the Assyrian chief of staff
left Jerusalem and went to consult the king
of Assyria, who had left Lachish and was
attacking Libnah.
9Soon afterward King Sennacherib received word that King Tirhakah of Ethiopia*
was leading an army to fight against him.
Before leaving to meet the attack, he sent
messengers back to Hezekiah in Jerusalem
with this message:

10 “This message is for King Hezekiah of Judah. Don’t let your God, in whom you trust, deceive you with promises that Jerusalem will not be captured by the king of Assyria. 11 You know perfectly well what the kings of Assyria have done wherever they have gone. They have completely destroyed everyone who stood in their way! Why should you be any different? 12 Have the gods of other nations rescued them—such nations as Gozan, Haran, Rezeph, and the people of Eden who were in Tel-assar? My predecessors destroyed them all! 13 What happened to the king of Hamath and the king of Arpad? What happened to the kings of Sepharvaim, Hena, and Ivvah?”

14 After Hezekiah received the letter from the messengers and read it, he went up to the LORD’s Temple and spread it out before the LORD. 15 And Hezekiah prayed this prayer before the LORD: “O LORD, God of Israel, you are enthroned between the mighty cherubim! You alone are God of all the kingdoms of the earth. You alone created the heavens and the earth. 16 Bend down, O LORD, and listen! Open your eyes, O LORD, and see! Listen to Sennacherib’s words of defiance against the living God.

17 “It is true, LORD, that the kings of Assyria have destroyed all these nations. 18 And they have thrown the gods of these nations into the fire and burned them. But of course the Assyrians could destroy them! They were not gods at all—only idols of wood and stone shaped by human hands. 19 Now, O LORD our God, rescue us from his power; then all the kingdoms of the earth will know that you alone, O LORD, are God.”

Isaiah Predicts Judah’s Deliverance

20 Then Isaiah son of Amoz sent this message to Hezekiah: “This is what the LORD, the God of Israel, says: I have heard your prayer about King Sennacherib of Assyria. 21 And the LORD has spoken this word against him:

“The virgin daughter of Zion
despises you and laughs at you.
The daughter of Jerusalem
shakes her head in derision as you flee.
22 “Whom have you been defying and ridiculing?
Against whom did you raise your voice?
At whom did you look with such haughty eyes?
It was the Holy One of Israel!
23 By your messengers you have defied the Lord.
You have said, ‘With my many chariots
I have conquered the highest mountains—
yes, the remotest peaks of Lebanon.
I have cut down its tallest cedars
and its finest cypress trees.
I have reached its farthest corners
and explored its deepest forests.
24 I have dug wells in many foreign lands
and refreshed myself with their water.
With the sole of my foot
I stopped up all the rivers of Egypt!’
25 “But have you not heard?
I decided this long ago.
Long ago I planned it,
and now I am making it happen.
I planned for you to crush fortified cities
into heaps of rubble.
26 That is why their people have so little power
and are so frightened and confused.
They are as weak as grass,
as easily trampled as tender green shoots.
They are like grass sprouting on a housetop,
scorched before it can grow lush and tall.
27 “But I know you well—
where you stay
and when you come and go.
I know the way you have raged against me.
28 And because of your raging against me
and your arrogance, which I have heard for myself,
I will put my hook in your nose
and my bit in your mouth.
I will make you return
by the same road on which you came.”

29 Then Isaiah said to Hezekiah, “Here is the proof that what I say is true:

18:26 Hebrew *in the dialect of Judah;* also in 18:28. **19:4** Or *the rabshakeh;* also in 19:8. **19:7** Hebrew *I will put a spirit in him.* **19:9** Hebrew *of Cush.*

“This year you will eat only what grows
up by itself,
and next year you will eat what
springs up from that.
But in the third year you will plant crops
and harvest them;
you will tend vineyards and eat their
fruit.
30 And you who are left in Judah,
who have escaped the ravages of the
siege,
will put roots down in your own soil
and will grow up and flourish.
31 For a remnant of my people will spread
out from Jerusalem,
a group of survivors from Mount Zion.
The passionate commitment of the LORD
of Heaven’s Armies*
will make this happen!

[32]“And this is what the LORD says about the
king of Assyria:

“His armies will not enter Jerusalem.
They will not even shoot an arrow at it.
They will not march outside its gates
with their shields
nor build banks of earth against its
walls.
33 The king will return to his own country
by the same road on which he came.
He will not enter this city,
says the LORD.
34 For my own honor and for the sake of
my servant David,
I will defend this city and protect it.”

[35]That night the angel of the LORD went
out to the Assyrian camp and killed 185,000
Assyrian soldiers. When the surviving Assyrians* woke up the next morning, they
found corpses everywhere. [36]Then King
Sennacherib of Assyria broke camp and returned to his own land. He went home to his
capital of Nineveh and stayed there.
[37]One day while he was worshiping in the
temple of his god Nisroch, his sons* Adrammelech and Sharezer killed him with their
swords. They then escaped to the land of
Ararat, and another son, Esarhaddon,
became the next king of Assyria.

Hezekiah’s Sickness and Recovery

20 About that time Hezekiah became
deathly ill, and the prophet Isaiah
son of Amoz went to visit him. He gave the
king this message: “This is what the LORD
says: Set your affairs in order, for you are
going to die. You will not recover from this
illness.”
[2]When Hezekiah heard this, he turned
his face to the wall and prayed to the LORD,
[3]“Remember, O LORD, how I have always
been faithful to you and have served you
single-mindedly, always doing what pleases
you.” Then he broke down and wept bitterly.
[4]But before Isaiah had left the middle
courtyard,* this message came to him from
the LORD: [5]“Go back to Hezekiah, the leader
of my people. Tell him, ‘This is what the
LORD, the God of your ancestor David, says:
I have heard your prayer and seen your
tears. I will heal you, and three days from
now you will get out of bed and go to the
Temple of the LORD. [6]I will add fifteen years
to your life, and I will rescue you and this
city from the king of Assyria. I will defend
this city for my own honor and for the sake
of my servant David.’”
[7]Then Isaiah said, “Make an ointment
from figs.” So Hezekiah’s servants spread
the ointment over the boil, and Hezekiah
recovered!
[8]Meanwhile, Hezekiah had said to Isaiah,
“What sign will the LORD give to prove that
he will heal me and that I will go to the
Temple of the LORD three days from now?”
[9]Isaiah replied, “This is the sign from the
LORD to prove that he will do as he promised.
Would you like the shadow on the sundial to
go forward ten steps or backward ten steps?*”
[10]“The shadow always moves forward,”
Hezekiah replied, “so that would be easy.
Make it go ten steps backward instead.”
[11]So Isaiah the prophet asked the LORD to
do this, and he caused the shadow to move
ten steps backward on the sundial* of Ahaz!

Envoys from Babylon

[12]Soon after this, Merodach-baladan* son
of Baladan, king of Babylon, sent Hezekiah
his best wishes and a gift, for he had heard
that Hezekiah had been very sick. [13]Heze-
kiah received the Babylonian envoys and
showed them everything in his treasure-
houses—the silver, the gold, the spices, and
the aromatic oils. He also took them to see
his armory and showed them everything
in his royal treasuries! There was nothing
in his palace or kingdom that Hezekiah did
not show them.

[14]Then Isaiah the prophet went to King
Hezekiah and asked him, "What did those
men want? Where were they from?"
Hezekiah replied, "They came from the
distant land of Babylon."
[15]"What did they see in your palace?"
Isaiah asked.
"They saw everything," Hezekiah replied.
"I showed them everything I own—all my
royal treasuries."
[16]Then Isaiah said to Hezekiah, "Listen to
this message from the LORD: [17]The time is
coming when everything in your palace—all
the treasures stored up by your ancestors
until now—will be carried off to Babylon.
Nothing will be left, says the LORD. [18]Some
of your very own sons will be taken away
into exile. They will become eunuchs who
will serve in the palace of Babylon's king."
[19]Then Hezekiah said to Isaiah, "This
message you have given me from the LORD
is good." For the king was thinking, "At
least there will be peace and security during
my lifetime."
[20]The rest of the events in Hezekiah's
reign, including the extent of his power
and how he built a pool and dug a tunnel*
to bring water into the city, are recorded in
The Book of the History of the Kings of Judah.
[21]Hezekiah died, and his son Manasseh
became the next king.

Manasseh Rules in Judah

21 Manasseh was twelve years old when
he became king, and he reigned
in Jerusalem fifty-five years. His mother
was Hephzibah. [2]He did what was evil in
the LORD's sight, following the detestable
practices of the pagan nations that the
LORD had driven from the land ahead of
the Israelites. [3]He rebuilt the pagan shrines
his father, Hezekiah, had destroyed. He
constructed altars for Baal and set up an
Asherah pole, just as King Ahab of Israel
had done. He also bowed before all the
powers of the heavens and worshiped them.
[4]He built pagan altars in the Temple of the
LORD, the place where the LORD had said,
"My name will remain in Jerusalem forever."
[5]He built these altars for all the powers of
the heavens in both courtyards of the LORD's
Temple. [6]Manasseh also sacrificed his own
son in the fire.* He practiced sorcery and
divination, and he consulted with mediums
and psychics. He did much that was evil in
the LORD's sight, arousing his anger.
[7]Manasseh even made a carved image of
Asherah and set it up in the Temple, the
very place where the LORD had told David
and his son Solomon: "My name will be
honored forever in this Temple and in Jerusalem—the city I have chosen from among
all the tribes of Israel. [8]If the Israelites will
be careful to obey my commands—all the
laws my servant Moses gave them—I will
not send them into exile from this land
that I gave their ancestors." [9]But the people

19:31 As in Greek and Syriac versions, Latin Vulgate, and an alternate reading of the Masoretic Text (see also Isa 37:32); the other alternate reads *the LORD*. **19:35** Hebrew *When they.* **19:37** As in Greek version and an alternate reading of the Masoretic Text (see also Isa 37:38); the other alternate reading lacks *his sons.* **20:4** As in Greek version and an alternate reading in the Masoretic Text; the other alternate reads *the middle of the city.* **20:9** Or *The shadow on the sundial has gone forward ten steps; do you want it to go backward ten steps?* **20:11** Hebrew *the steps.* **20:12** As in some Hebrew manuscripts and Greek and Syriac versions (see also Isa 39:1); Masoretic Text reads *Berodach-baladan.* **20:20** Hebrew *watercourse.* **21:6** Or *also made his son pass through the fire.*

King Manasseh

Manasseh was one of Judah's most wicked kings. He came to the throne at the age of twelve and reigned for fifty-five years (697–642 BC)—the longest reign of any king of Israel or Judah. Sadly he did not walk in his father Hezekiah's godly ways but led Israel into idolatry. He rebuilt shrines to Baal, worshiped the stars, encouraged sorcery, divination, and spiritism, and violated the Temple; he even sacrificed his own son in the fire to pagan gods (2 Kings 21:1-6). His sin would be seen as largely responsible for Judah's exile (2 Kings 21:10-15; Jeremiah 15:3-4). Most of his reign was spent under Assyrian domination, and as judgment for his sin God allowed Assyria to take him into exile. It was only here that he repented (2 Chronicles 33:13), leading to his return to Jerusalem. His reign ended on a more godly note (2 Chronicles 33:15-17), showing that it is never too late to change.

refused to listen, and Manasseh led them to do even more evil than the pagan nations that the LORD had destroyed when the people of Israel entered the land.

10 Then the LORD said through his servants the prophets: 11 "King Manasseh of Judah has done many detestable things. He is even more wicked than the Amorites, who lived in this land before Israel. He has caused the people of Judah to sin with his idols.* 12 So this is what the LORD, the God of Israel, says: I will bring such disaster on Jerusalem and Judah that the ears of those who hear about it will tingle with horror. 13 I will judge Jerusalem by the same standard I used for Samaria and the same measure* I used for the family of Ahab. I will wipe away the people of Jerusalem as one wipes a dish and turns it upside down. 14 Then I will reject even the remnant of my own people who are left, and I will hand them over as plunder for their enemies. 15 For they have done great evil in my sight and have angered me ever since their ancestors came out of Egypt."

16 Manasseh also murdered many innocent people until Jerusalem was filled from one end to the other with innocent blood. This was in addition to the sin that he caused the people of Judah to commit, leading them to do evil in the LORD's sight.

17 The rest of the events in Manasseh's reign and everything he did, including the sins he committed, are recorded in *The Book of the History of the Kings of Judah.* 18 When Manasseh died, he was buried in the palace garden, the garden of Uzza. Then his son Amon became the next king.

Amon Rules in Judah

19 Amon was twenty-two years old when he became king, and he reigned in Jerusalem two years. His mother was Meshullemeth, the daughter of Haruz from Jotbah. 20 He did what was evil in the LORD's sight, just as his father, Manasseh, had done. 21 He followed the example of his father, worshiping the same idols his father had worshiped. 22 He abandoned the LORD, the God of his ancestors, and he refused to follow the LORD's ways.

23 Then Amon's own officials conspired against him and assassinated him in his palace. 24 But the people of the land killed all those who had conspired against King Amon, and they made his son Josiah the next king.

25 The rest of the events in Amon's reign and what he did are recorded in *The Book of the History of the Kings of Judah.* 26 He was buried in his tomb in the garden of Uzza. Then his son Josiah became the next king.

Josiah Rules in Judah

22 Josiah was eight years old when he became king, and he reigned in Jerusalem thirty-one years. His mother was Jedidah, the daughter of Adaiah from Bozkath. 2 He did what was pleasing in the LORD's sight and followed the example of his ancestor David. He did not turn away from doing what was right.

3 In the eighteenth year of his reign, King Josiah sent Shaphan son of Azaliah and grandson of Meshullam, the court secretary, to the Temple of the LORD. He told him, 4 "Go to Hilkiah the high priest and have him count the money the gatekeepers have collected from the people at the LORD's Temple. 5 Entrust this money to the men assigned to supervise the restoration of the LORD's Temple. Then they can use it to pay workers to repair the Temple. 6 They will need to hire carpenters, builders, and masons. Also have them buy the timber and the finished stone needed to repair the Temple. 7 But don't require the construction supervisors to keep account of the money they receive, for they are honest and trustworthy men."

Hilkiah Discovers God's Law

8 Hilkiah the high priest said to Shaphan the court secretary, "I have found the Book of the Law in the LORD's Temple!" Then Hilkiah gave the scroll to Shaphan, and he read it.

9 Shaphan went to the king and reported, "Your officials have turned over the money collected at the Temple of the LORD to the workers and supervisors at the Temple." 10 Shaphan also told the king, "Hilkiah the priest has given me a scroll." So Shaphan read it to the king.

11 When the king heard what was written in the Book of the Law, he tore his clothes in despair. 12 Then he gave these orders to Hilkiah the priest, Ahikam son of Shaphan, Acbor son of Micaiah, Shaphan the court secretary, and Asaiah the king's personal adviser: 13 "Go to the Temple and speak to the LORD for me and for the people and for all Judah. Inquire about the words written in this scroll that has been found. For the

LORD's great anger is burning against us
because our ancestors have not obeyed the
words in this scroll. We have not been doing
everything it says we must do."
[14]So Hilkiah the priest, Ahikam, Acbor,
Shaphan, and Asaiah went to the New
Quarter* of Jerusalem to consult with
the prophet Huldah. She was the wife of
Shallum son of Tikvah, son of Harhas, the
keeper of the Temple wardrobe.
[15]She said to them, "The LORD, the God of
Israel, has spoken! Go back and tell the man
who sent you, [16]'This is what the LORD says:
I am going to bring disaster on this city* and
its people. All the words written in the scroll
that the king of Judah has read will come
true. [17]For my people have abandoned me
and offered sacrifices to pagan gods, and
I am very angry with them for everything
they have done. My anger will burn against
this place, and it will not be quenched.'
[18]"But go to the king of Judah who sent you
to seek the LORD and tell him: 'This is what
the LORD, the God of Israel, says concerning
the message you have just heard: [19]You were
sorry and humbled yourself before the LORD
when you heard what I said against this city
and its people—that this land would be
cursed and become desolate. You tore your
clothing in despair and wept before me in repentance. And I have indeed heard you, says
the LORD. [20]So I will not send the promised
disaster until after you have died and been
buried in peace. You will not see the disaster
I am going to bring on this city.'"
So they took her message back to the king.

Josiah's Religious Reforms

23 Then the king summoned all the
elders of Judah and Jerusalem. [2]And
the king went up to the Temple of the LORD
with all the people of Judah and Jerusalem,
along with the priests and the prophets—
all the people from the least to the greatest.
There the king read to them the entire Book
of the Covenant that had been found in the
LORD's Temple. [3]The king took his place
of authority beside the pillar and renewed
the covenant in the LORD's presence. He
pledged to obey the LORD by keeping all his
commands, laws, and decrees with all his
heart and soul. In this way, he confirmed all
the terms of the covenant that were written
in the scroll, and all the people pledged
themselves to the covenant.
[4]Then the king instructed Hilkiah the
high priest and the priests of the second
rank and the Temple gatekeepers to remove
from the LORD's Temple all the articles that
were used to worship Baal, Asherah, and
all the powers of the heavens. The king had
all these things burned outside Jerusalem
on the terraces of the Kidron Valley, and he
carried the ashes away to Bethel. [5]He did
away with the idolatrous priests, who had
been appointed by the previous kings of
Judah, for they had offered sacrifices at the
pagan shrines throughout Judah and even
in the vicinity of Jerusalem. They had also

21:11 The Hebrew term (literally *round things*) probably alludes to dung; also in 21:21. **21:13** Hebrew *the same plumb line I used for Samaria and the same plumb bob.* **22:14** Or *the Second Quarter,* a newer section of Jerusalem. Hebrew reads *the Mishneh.* **22:16** Hebrew *this place;* also in 22:19, 20.

King Josiah

Only eight years old when he came to the throne, Josiah became one of Judah's most godly kings. At the age of sixteen he "began to seek the God of his ancestor David" (2 Chronicles 34:3). By twenty, he was purging the land of idolatry and destroying shrines to Baal and all idols (2 Chronicles 34:3-7). But it was when Josiah was twenty-six (2 Kings 22:3) that the biggest transformation took place. During renovations in the Temple, "the Book of the Law" (22:8) was discovered—probably the book of Deuteronomy. As it was read to him, Josiah was appalled at how far God's people had fallen from his ways; he immediately led the nation in a covenant renewal ceremony (chapter 23) and completed his spiritual reforms in the land. He died in battle, trying to stop Egypt from marching to Assyria's aid (2 Kings 23:29). Josiah shows us that we don't understand everything about God at the beginning, but if we keep our hearts open, we can keep growing, changing, and having a powerful impact.

offered sacrifices to Baal, and to the sun,
the moon, the constellations, and to all the
powers of the heavens. [6]The king removed
the Asherah pole from the LORD's Temple
and took it outside Jerusalem to the Kidron
Valley, where he burned it. Then he ground
the ashes of the pole to dust and threw the
dust over the graves of the people. [7]He also
tore down the living quarters of the male and
female shrine prostitutes that were inside
the Temple of the LORD, where the women
wove coverings for the Asherah pole.

[8]Josiah brought to Jerusalem all the
priests who were living in other towns of
Judah. He also defiled the pagan shrines,
where they had offered sacrifices—all the
way from Geba to Beersheba. He destroyed
the shrines at the entrance to the gate of
Joshua, the governor of Jerusalem. This gate
was located to the left of the city gate as one
enters the city. [9]The priests who had served
at the pagan shrines were not allowed to
serve at* the LORD's altar in Jerusalem, but
they were allowed to eat unleavened bread
with the other priests.

[10]Then the king defiled the altar of
Topheth in the valley of Ben-Hinnom, so
no one could ever again use it to sacrifice
a son or daughter in the fire* as an offering
to Molech. [11]He removed from the entrance
of the LORD's Temple the horse statues that
the former kings of Judah had dedicated
to the sun. They were near the quarters
of Nathan-melech the eunuch, an officer
of the court.* The king also burned the
chariots dedicated to the sun.

[12]Josiah tore down the altars that the kings
of Judah had built on the palace roof above
the upper room of Ahaz. The king destroyed
the altars that Manasseh had built in the two
courtyards of the LORD's Temple. He smashed
them to bits* and scattered the pieces in the
Kidron Valley. [13]The king also desecrated
the pagan shrines east of Jerusalem, to the
south of the Mount of Corruption, where
King Solomon of Israel had built shrines for
Ashtoreth, the detestable goddess of the Sidonians; and for Chemosh, the detestable
god of the Moabites; and for Molech,* the
vile god of the Ammonites. [14]He smashed
the sacred pillars and cut down the Asherah
poles. Then he desecrated these places by
scattering human bones over them.

[15]The king also tore down the altar at
Bethel—the pagan shrine that Jeroboam
son of Nebat had made when he caused
Israel to sin. He burned down the shrine
and ground it to dust, and he burned the
Asherah pole. [16]Then Josiah turned around
and noticed several tombs in the side of the
hill. He ordered that the bones be brought
out, and he burned them on the altar at
Bethel to desecrate it. (This happened just
as the LORD had promised through the man
of God when Jeroboam stood beside the
altar at the festival.)

Then Josiah turned and looked up at the
tomb of the man of God* who had predicted
these things. [17]"What is that monument
over there?" Josiah asked.

And the people of the town told him, "It is
the tomb of the man of God who came from
Judah and predicted the very things that
you have just done to the altar at Bethel!"

[18]Josiah replied, "Leave it alone. Don't
disturb his bones." So they did not burn
his bones or those of the old prophet from
Samaria.

[19]Then Josiah demolished all the buildings at the pagan shrines in the towns of
Samaria, just as he had done at Bethel.
They had been built by the various kings of
Israel and had made the LORD* very angry.
[20]He executed the priests of the pagan
shrines on their own altars, and he burned
human bones on the altars to desecrate
them. Finally, he returned to Jerusalem.

Josiah Celebrates Passover

[21]King Josiah then issued this order to all
the people: "You must celebrate the Passover to the LORD your God, as required
in this Book of the Covenant." [22]There
had not been a Passover celebration like
that since the time when the judges ruled
in Israel, nor throughout all the years of
the kings of Israel and Judah. [23]But in the
eighteenth year of King Josiah's reign, this
Passover was celebrated to the LORD in
Jerusalem.

[24]Josiah also got rid of the mediums and
psychics, the household gods, the idols,*
and every other kind of detestable practice, both in Jerusalem and throughout the
land of Judah. He did this in obedience to
the laws written in the scroll that Hilkiah
the priest had found in the LORD's Temple.
[25]Never before had there been a king like
Josiah, who turned to the LORD with all his
heart and soul and strength, obeying all the

laws of Moses. And there has never been a king like him since.

[26]Even so, the LORD was very angry with Judah because of all the wicked things Manasseh had done to provoke him. [27]For the LORD said, "I will also banish Judah from my presence just as I have banished Israel. And I will reject my chosen city of Jerusalem and the Temple where my name was to be honored."

[28]The rest of the events in Josiah's reign and all his deeds are recorded in *The Book of the History of the Kings of Judah*.

[29]While Josiah was king, Pharaoh Neco, king of Egypt, went to the Euphrates River to help the king of Assyria. King Josiah and his army marched out to fight him,* but King Neco* killed him when they met at Megiddo. [30]Josiah's officers took his body back in a chariot from Megiddo to Jerusalem and buried him in his own tomb. Then the people of the land anointed Josiah's son Jehoahaz and made him the next king.

Jehoahaz Rules in Judah

[31]Jehoahaz was twenty-three years old when he became king, and he reigned in Jerusalem three months. His mother was Hamutal, the daughter of Jeremiah from Libnah. [32]He did what was evil in the LORD's sight, just as his ancestors had done.

[33]Pharaoh Neco put Jehoahaz in prison at Riblah in the land of Hamath to prevent him from ruling* in Jerusalem. He also demanded that Judah pay 7,500 pounds of silver and 75 pounds of gold* as tribute.

Jehoiakim Rules in Judah

[34]Pharaoh Neco then installed Eliakim, another of Josiah's sons, to reign in place of his father, and he changed Eliakim's name to Jehoiakim. Jehoahaz was taken to Egypt as a prisoner, where he died.

[35]In order to get the silver and gold demanded as tribute by Pharaoh Neco, Jehoiakim collected a tax from the people of Judah, requiring them to pay in proportion to their wealth.

[36]Jehoiakim was twenty-five years old when he became king, and he reigned in Jerusalem eleven years. His mother was Zebidah, the daughter of Pedaiah from Rumah. [37]He did what was evil in the LORD's sight, just as his ancestors had done.

24 During Jehoiakim's reign, King Nebuchadnezzar of Babylon invaded the land of Judah. Jehoiakim surrendered and paid him tribute for three years but then rebelled. [2]Then the LORD sent bands of Babylonian,* Aramean, Moabite, and Ammonite raiders against Judah to destroy it, just as the LORD had promised through his prophets. [3]These disasters happened to Judah because of the LORD's command. He had decided to banish Judah from his presence because of the many sins of Manasseh, [4]who had filled Jerusalem with innocent blood. The LORD would not forgive this.

[5]The rest of the events in Jehoiakim's reign and all his deeds are recorded in *The Book of the History of the Kings of Judah*. [6]When Jehoiakim died, his son Jehoiachin became the next king.

[7]The king of Egypt did not venture out of his country after that, for the king of Babylon captured the entire area formerly claimed by Egypt—from the Brook of Egypt to the Euphrates River.

Jehoiachin Rules in Judah

[8]Jehoiachin was eighteen years old when he became king, and he reigned in Jerusalem three months. His mother was Nehushta, the daughter of Elnathan from Jerusalem. [9]Jehoiachin did what was evil in the LORD's sight, just as his father had done.

[10]During Jehoiachin's reign, the officers of King Nebuchadnezzar of Babylon came up against Jerusalem and besieged it. [11]Nebuchadnezzar himself arrived at the city during the siege. [12]Then King Jehoiachin, along with the queen mother, his advisers, his commanders, and his officials, surrendered to the Babylonians.

In the eighth year of Nebuchadnezzar's

23:9 Hebrew *did not come up to.* **23:10** Or *to make a son or daughter pass through the fire.* **23:11** The meaning of the Hebrew is uncertain. **23:12** Or *He quickly removed them.* **23:13** Hebrew *Milcom,* a variant spelling of Molech. **23:16** As in Greek version; Hebrew lacks *when Jeroboam stood beside the altar at the festival. Then Josiah turned and looked up at the tomb of the man of God.* **23:19** As in Greek and Syriac versions and Latin Vulgate; Hebrew lacks *the LORD.* **23:24** The Hebrew term (literally *round things*) probably alludes to dung. **23:29a** Or *Josiah went out to meet him.* **23:29b** Hebrew *he.* **23:33a** The meaning of the Hebrew is uncertain. **23:33b** Hebrew *100 talents* [3,400 kilograms] *of silver and 1 talent* [34 kilograms] *of gold.* **24:2** Or *Chaldean.*

▸ **23:34** See ***King Jehoiakim***, page 867.

reign, he took Jehoiachin prisoner. 13As the
Lord had said beforehand, Nebuchadnezzar carried away all the treasures from the
Lord's Temple and the royal palace. He
stripped away* all the gold objects that King
Solomon of Israel had placed in the Temple.
14King Nebuchadnezzar took all of Jerusalem captive, including all the commanders
and the best of the soldiers, craftsmen, and
artisans—10,000 in all. Only the poorest
people were left in the land.
15Nebuchadnezzar led King Jehoiachin
away as a captive to Babylon, along with the
queen mother, his wives and officials, and
all Jerusalem's elite. 16He also exiled 7,000
of the best troops and 1,000 craftsmen and
artisans, all of whom were strong and fit for
war. 17Then the king of Babylon installed
Mattaniah, Jehoiachin's* uncle, as the next
king, and he changed Mattaniah's name to
Zedekiah.

Zedekiah Rules in Judah

18Zedekiah was twenty-one years old when
he became king, and he reigned in Jerusalem eleven years. His mother was Hamutal,
the daughter of Jeremiah from Libnah. 19But
Zedekiah did what was evil in the Lord's
sight, just as Jehoiakim had done. 20These
things happened because of the Lord's
anger against the people of Jerusalem and
Judah, until he finally banished them from
his presence and sent them into exile.

The Fall of Jerusalem

Zedekiah rebelled against the king of
Babylon.

25 So on January 15,* during the ninth
year of Zedekiah's reign, King Nebuchadnezzar of Babylon led his entire army
against Jerusalem. They surrounded the
city and built siege ramps against its walls.
2Jerusalem was kept under siege until the
eleventh year of King Zedekiah's reign.
3By July 18 in the eleventh year of Zedekiah's reign,* the famine in the city had
become very severe, and the last of the food
was entirely gone. 4Then a section of the
city wall was broken down. Since the city
was surrounded by the Babylonians,* the
soldiers waited for nightfall and escaped*
through the gate between the two walls
behind the king's garden. Then they headed
toward the Jordan Valley.*
5But the Babylonian* troops chased the
king and overtook him on the plains of
Jericho, for his men had all deserted him
and scattered. 6They captured the king and
took him to the king of Babylon at Riblah,
where they pronounced judgment upon
Zedekiah. 7They made Zedekiah watch
as they slaughtered his sons. Then they
gouged out Zedekiah's eyes, bound him
in bronze chains, and led him away to
Babylon.

The Temple Destroyed

8On August 14 of that year,* which was the
nineteenth year of King Nebuchadnezzar's
reign, Nebuzaradan, the captain of the
guard and an official of the Babylonian
king, arrived in Jerusalem. 9He burned
down the Temple of the Lord, the royal
palace, and all the houses of Jerusalem.

▸ **25:1** *See* ***The fall of Jerusalem,*** *page 871.*

King Zedekiah

Zedekiah was Judah's last king. Previously known as Mattaniah, he was uncle to King Jehoiachin, whom Babylon forcibly removed and replaced with Mattaniah, whose name they changed (2 Kings 24:15-17). Although Babylon's vassal, Zedekiah eventually rebelled against King Nebuchadnezzar; so Babylon marched against Jerusalem (2 Kings 24:20–25:2). After a two-year siege the city finally fell in 586 BC. Zedekiah fled but was captured, and his sons were killed in front of him before his eyes were put out and he was taken in chains to Babylon. Jerusalem's great buildings, including the Temple, were looted and destroyed, and the people taken into exile (2 Kings 25). Unless God did something special, Judah's history was now over.

He destroyed all the important buildings*
in the city. 10 Then he supervised the entire
Babylonian army as they tore down the
walls of Jerusalem on every side. 11 Then
Nebuzaradan, the captain of the guard,
took as exiles the rest of the people who
remained in the city, the defectors who
had declared their allegiance to the king
of Babylon, and the rest of the population.
12 But the captain of the guard allowed some
of the poorest people to stay behind to care
for the vineyards and fields.

13 The Babylonians broke up the bronze
pillars in front of the LORD's Temple, the
bronze water carts, and the great bronze
basin called the Sea, and they carried all
the bronze away to Babylon. 14 They also
took all the ash buckets, shovels, lamp
snuffers, ladles, and all the other bronze
articles used for making sacrifices at the
Temple. 15 The captain of the guard also
took the incense burners and basins, and
all the other articles made of pure gold or
silver.

16 The weight of the bronze from the two
pillars, the Sea, and the water carts was too
great to be measured. These things had been
made for the LORD's Temple in the days of
Solomon. 17 Each of the pillars was 27 feet*
tall. The bronze capital on top of each pillar
was 7½ feet* high and was decorated with
a network of bronze pomegranates all the
way around.

18 Nebuzaradan, the captain of the guard,
took with him as prisoners Seraiah the high
priest, Zephaniah the priest of the second
rank, and the three chief gatekeepers. 19 And
from among the people still hiding in the
city, he took an officer who had been in
charge of the Judean army; five of the king's
personal advisers; the army commander's
chief secretary, who was in charge of recruitment; and sixty other citizens. 20 Nebuzaradan, the captain of the guard, took them all
to the king of Babylon at Riblah. 21 And there
at Riblah, in the land of Hamath, the king
of Babylon had them all put to death. So the
people of Judah were sent into exile from
their land.

Gedaliah Governs in Judah

22 Then King Nebuchadnezzar appointed
Gedaliah son of Ahikam and grandson of
Shaphan as governor over the people he
had left in Judah. 23 When all the army commanders and their men learned that the
king of Babylon had appointed Gedaliah as
governor, they went to see him at Mizpah.
These included Ishmael son of Nethaniah, Johanan son of Kareah, Seraiah son

24:13 Or *He cut apart.* **24:17** Hebrew *his.* **25:1** Hebrew *on the tenth day of the tenth month,* of the ancient Hebrew lunar calendar. A number of events in 2 Kings can be cross-checked with dates in surviving Babylonian records and related accurately to our modern calendar. This day was January 15, 588 B.C. **25:3** Hebrew *By the ninth day of the [fourth] month* [in the eleventh year of Zedekiah's reign] (compare Jer 39:2; 52:6 and the notes there). This day was July 18, 586 B.C.; also see note on 25:1. **25:4a** Or *the Chaldeans;* also in 25:13, 25, 26. **25:4b** As in Greek version (see also Jer 39:4; 52:7); Hebrew lacks *escaped.* **25:4c** Hebrew *the Arabah.* **25:5** Or *Chaldean*; also in 25:10, 24. **25:8** Hebrew *On the seventh day of the fifth month,* of the ancient Hebrew lunar calendar. This day was August 14, 586 B.C.; also see note on 25:1. **25:9** Or *destroyed the houses of all the important people.* **25:17a** Hebrew *18 cubits* [8.3 meters]. **25:17b** As in parallel texts at 1 Kgs 7:16, 2 Chr 3:15, and Jer 52:22, all of which read *5 cubits* [2.3 meters]; Hebrew reads *3 cubits,* which is 4.5 feet or 1.4 meters.

Babylon

In 612 BC Babylon had conquered Nineveh, the Assyrian capital, and over the next few years thoroughly defeated Assyria, swallowing up its empire and wealth. The mighty King Nebuchadnezzar (mentioned in the Bible more than any other foreign ruler) embarked on a program of expansion, of which Judah became a part. Using the riches from his conquests, Nebuchadnezzar set about making Babylon the greatest city in the world. It had two great walls, the outer one ten miles long and twelve feet thick, the inner one five and a half miles long and twenty-one feet thick. The city had eight beautiful gateways, towers every fifty-five feet along its walls, and fabulous palaces and buildings. It was to this very different kind of city, and others like it, that the people of Judah were exiled, including Daniel, who would serve several different Babylonian kings.

▶ *See also* ***Assyria****, page 431;* ***King Nebuchadnezzar****, page 957;* ***Babylon in Revelation****, page 1459;* ***The Exile*** *map, Visual Overview Z9.*

of Tanhumeth the Netophathite, Jezaniah* son of the Maacathite, and all their men.

[24]Gedaliah vowed to them that the Babylonian officials meant them no harm. "Don't be afraid of them. Live in the land and serve the king of Babylon, and all will go well for you," he promised.

[25]But in midautumn of that year,* Ishmael son of Nethaniah and grandson of Elishama, who was a member of the royal family, went to Mizpah with ten men and killed Gedaliah. He also killed all the Judeans and Babylonians who were with him at Mizpah.

[26]Then all the people of Judah, from the least to the greatest, as well as the army commanders, fled in panic to Egypt, for they were afraid of what the Babylonians would do to them.

Hope for Israel's Royal Line

[27]In the thirty-seventh year of the exile of King Jehoiachin of Judah, Evil-merodach ascended to the Babylonian throne. He was kind to* Jehoiachin and released him* from prison on April 2 of that year.* [28]He spoke kindly to Jehoiachin and gave him a higher place than all the other exiled kings in Babylon. [29]He supplied Jehoiachin with new clothes to replace his prison garb and allowed him to dine in the king's presence for the rest of his life. [30]So the king gave him a regular food allowance as long as he lived.

25:23 As in parallel text at Jer 40:8; Hebrew reads *Jaazaniah,* a variant spelling of Jezaniah. **25:25** Hebrew *in the seventh month,* of the ancient Hebrew lunar calendar. This month occurred within the months of October and November 586 B.C.; also see note on 25:1. **25:27a** Hebrew *He raised the head of.* **25:27b** As in some Hebrew manuscripts and Greek and Syriac versions (see also Jer 52:31); Masoretic Text lacks *released him.* **25:27c** Hebrew *on the twenty-seventh day of the twelfth month,* of the ancient Hebrew lunar calendar. This day was April 2, 561 B.C.; also see note on 25:1.

1 Chronicles *God is still with us!*

The books of Chronicles give an alternative version of the history recorded in Samuel and Kings. They cover much of the same period of history but answer a different question. Kings had been written during the Exile to answer the exiles' question, "How did we end up here?"—and the answer the author gave was: "Disobedience! Just look at our history and see." But Chronicles, written after the return from exile—according to ancient Jewish tradition, by Ezra, and certainly by a Levite—is now concerned with a different question: "Is God still with us?" And the answer this author gave was: "Yes! And we can be sure of that because of God's promises to David."

This explains the books' great interest in King David's line and why, in telling us David's story, it focuses on his triumphs rather than his mistakes. First Chronicles encourages the returning exiles that they are still part of God's people of old and are still the inheritors of all the promises made to King David—hence the book's focus on David and Solomon.

What's it all about?

The first nine chapters of 1 Chronicles contain genealogies, stretching right back to Adam to show that the Israel that returned from exile was still at the heart of God's purposes from the beginning. Chapters 11 to 16 record the story of how David became king and conquered Jerusalem, making it his new capital and bringing the Ark of the Covenant there. The book goes on to record his great deeds and presents him as the great man of God who served God wholeheartedly, reorganized how worship was carried out, and laid out the plans for the construction of the Temple. It is because of God's promise to David that the Jews could still have hope after the Exile.

OVERVIEW

Genealogies from Adam to Saul
1:1–9:44

Saul's sad end; David established as king in Jerusalem · *10:1–16:43*

God promises David an eternal dynasty · *17:1-27*

David's military exploits · *18:1–20:8*

David's census
21:1–22:1

Preparations for building the Temple
22:2–29:20

Solomon succeeds David as king and David's death · *29:21-30*

What does it mean for us?

The books of Chronicles are full of choices. Each of the kings we meet had to make a choice, either to obey God or to reject him. Some had good role models to follow, others didn't; but they each had to make a choice of their own, for good or bad. In Chronicles, the thought that they had to behave like their fathers is not valid; each was responsible for making his own choice before God.

Chronicles shows how the promises and warnings contained in Israel's covenant worked out in reality. The kings who chose to follow God wholeheartedly (like King David in 1 Chronicles) prospered; those who turned to worshiping idols didn't, and they brought disaster to the land. It was all as God had spoken through Moses long ago (Deuteronomy 28). But even when they were disobedient, God was ready to forgive. Manasseh provides the living proof that, no matter how bad anyone might become, if they will turn back to God, then God will receive them.

▶ See also **A timeline of the Bible**, pages A22-A24.

From Adam to Noah's Sons

1 The descendants of Adam were Seth,
Enosh, [2]Kenan, Mahalalel, Jared,
[3]Enoch, Methuselah, Lamech, [4]and Noah.
The sons of Noah were* Shem, Ham, and Japheth.

Descendants of Japheth

[5]The descendants of Japheth were Gomer, Magog, Madai, Javan, Tubal, Meshech, and Tiras.
[6]The descendants of Gomer were Ashkenaz, Riphath,* and Togarmah.
[7]The descendants of Javan were Elishah, Tarshish, Kittim, and Rodanim.

Descendants of Ham

[8]The descendants of Ham were Cush, Mizraim,* Put, and Canaan.
[9]The descendants of Cush were Seba, Havilah, Sabtah, Raamah, and Sabteca.
The descendants of Raamah were Sheba
and Dedan. [10]Cush was also the ancestor of Nimrod, who was the first heroic warrior on earth.
[11]Mizraim was the ancestor of the Ludites, Anamites, Lehabites, Naphtuhites,
[12]Pathrusites, Casluhites, and the Caphtorites, from whom the Philistines came.*
[13]Canaan's oldest son was Sidon, the ancestor of the Sidonians. Canaan was also the ancestor of the Hittites,*
[14]Jebusites, Amorites, Girgashites,
[15]Hivites, Arkites, Sinites, [16]Arvadites,
Zemarites, and Hamathites.

Descendants of Shem

[17]The descendants of Shem were Elam, Asshur, Arphaxad, Lud, and Aram.
The descendants of Aram were* Uz, Hul, Gether, and Mash.*
[18]Arphaxad was the father of Shelah.
Shelah was the father of Eber.
[19]Eber had two sons. The first was named Peleg (which means "division"), for during his lifetime the people of the world were divided into different language groups. His brother's name was Joktan.
[20]Joktan was the ancestor of Almodad,
Sheleph, Hazarmaveth, Jerah, [21]Hadoram,
Uzal, Diklah, [22]Obal,* Abimael, Sheba,
[23]Ophir, Havilah, and Jobab. All these were descendants of Joktan.
[24]So this is the family line descended from
Shem: Arphaxad, Shelah,* [25]Eber, Peleg,
Reu, [26]Serug, Nahor, Terah, [27]and Abram,
later known as Abraham.

Descendants of Abraham

[28]The sons of Abraham were Isaac and
Ishmael. [29]These are their genealogical records:
The sons of Ishmael were Nebaioth (the oldest), Kedar, Adbeel, Mibsam,
[30]Mishma, Dumah, Massa, Hadad, Tema,
[31]Jetur, Naphish, and Kedemah. These were the sons of Ishmael.
[32]The sons of Keturah, Abraham's concubine, were Zimran, Jokshan, Medan, Midian, Ishbak, and Shuah.
The sons of Jokshan were Sheba and Dedan.
[33]The sons of Midian were Ephah, Epher, Hanoch, Abida, and Eldaah.
All these were descendants of Abraham through his concubine Keturah.

Descendants of Isaac

[34]Abraham was the father of Isaac. The sons of Isaac were Esau and Israel.*

Descendants of Esau

[35]The sons of Esau were Eliphaz, Reuel, Jeush, Jalam, and Korah.
[36]The descendants of Eliphaz
were Teman, Omar, Zepho,*
Gatam, Kenaz, and Amalek, who was born to Timna.*
[37]The descendants of Reuel were Nahath, Zerah, Shammah, and Mizzah.

Original Peoples of Edom

[38]The descendants of Seir were Lotan, Shobal, Zibeon, Anah, Dishon, Ezer, and Dishan.

39 The descendants of Lotan were Hori and Hemam.* Lotan's sister was named Timna.
40 The descendants of Shobal were Alvan,* Manahath, Ebal, Shepho,* and Onam.
The descendants of Zibeon were Aiah and Anah.
41 The son of Anah was Dishon.
The descendants of Dishon were Hemdan,* Eshban, Ithran, and Keran.
42 The descendants of Ezer were Bilhan, Zaavan, and Akan.*
The descendants of Dishan* were Uz and Aran.

Rulers of Edom

43 These are the kings who ruled in the land of Edom before any king ruled over the Israelites*:

Bela son of Beor, who ruled from his city of Dinhabah.
44 When Bela died, Jobab son of Zerah from Bozrah became king in his place.
45 When Jobab died, Husham from the land of the Temanites became king in his place.
46 When Husham died, Hadad son of Bedad became king in his place and ruled from the city of Avith. He was the one who destroyed the Midianite army in the land of Moab.
47 When Hadad died, Samlah from the city of Masrekah became king in his place.
48 When Samlah died, Shaul from the city of Rehoboth-on-the-River became king in his place.
49 When Shaul died, Baal-hanan son of Acbor became king in his place.
50 When Baal-hanan died, Hadad became king in his place and ruled from the city of Pau.* His wife was Mehetabel, the daughter of Matred and granddaughter
of Me-zahab.
51 Then Hadad died.

The clan leaders of Edom were Timna, Alvah,* Jetheth,
52 Oholibamah, Elah, Pinon,
53 Kenaz, Teman, Mibzar,
54 Magdiel, and Iram. These are the clan leaders of Edom.

Descendants of Israel

2 The sons of Israel* were Reuben, Simeon, Levi, Judah, Issachar, Zebulun,
2 Dan, Joseph, Benjamin, Naphtali, Gad, and Asher.

Descendants of Judah

3 Judah had three sons from Bathshua, a Canaanite woman. Their names were Er, Onan, and Shelah. But the LORD saw that the oldest son, Er, was a wicked man, so he killed him.
4 Later Judah had twin sons from Tamar, his widowed daughter-in-law. Their names were Perez and Zerah. So Judah had five sons in all.
5 The sons of Perez were Hezron and Hamul.
6 The sons of Zerah were Zimri, Ethan, Heman, Calcol, and Darda*—five in all.
7 The son of Carmi (a descendant of Zimri) was Achan,* who brought disaster on Israel by taking plunder that had been set apart for the LORD.*
8 The son of Ethan was Azariah.

From Judah's Grandson Hezron to David

9 The sons of Hezron were Jerahmeel, Ram, and Caleb.*
10 Ram was the father of Amminadab.
Amminadab was the father of Nahshon, a leader of Judah.
11 Nahshon was the father of Salmon.*
Salmon was the father of Boaz.
12 Boaz was the father of Obed.
Obed was the father of Jesse.
13 Jesse's first son was Eliab, his second

1:4 As in Greek version (see also Gen 5:3-32); Hebrew lacks *The sons of Noah were.* **1:6** As in some Hebrew manuscripts and Greek version (see also Gen 10:3); most Hebrew manuscripts read *Diphath.* **1:8** Or *Egypt;* also in 1:11. **1:12** Hebrew *Casluhites, from whom the Philistines came, Caphtorites.* See Jer 47:4; Amos 9:7. **1:13** Hebrew *ancestor of Heth.* **1:17a** As in one Hebrew manuscript and some Greek manuscripts (see also Gen 10:23); most Hebrew manuscripts lack *The descendants of Aram were.* **1:17b** As in parallel text at Gen 10:23; Hebrew reads *and Meshech.* **1:22** As in some Hebrew manuscripts and Syriac version (see also Gen 10:28); most Hebrew manuscripts read *Ebal.* **1:24** Some Greek manuscripts read *Arphaxad, Cainan, Shelah.* See notes on Gen 10:24; 11:12-13. **1:34** *Israel* is the name that God gave to Jacob. **1:36a** As in many Hebrew manuscripts and a few Greek manuscripts (see also Gen 36:11); most Hebrew manuscripts read *Zephi.* **1:36b** As in some Greek manuscripts (see also Gen 36:12); Hebrew reads *Kenaz, Timna, and Amalek.* **1:39** As in parallel text at Gen 36:22; Hebrew reads *and Homam.* **1:40a** As in many Hebrew manuscripts and a few Greek manuscripts (see also Gen 36:23); most Hebrew manuscripts read *Alian.* **1:40b** As in some Hebrew manuscripts (see also Gen 36:23); most Hebrew manuscripts read *Shephi.* **1:41** As in many Hebrew manuscripts and some Greek manuscripts (see also Gen 36:26); most Hebrew manuscripts read *Hamran.* **1:42a** As in many Hebrew and Greek manuscripts (see also Gen 36:27); most Hebrew manuscripts read *Jaakan.* **1:42b** Hebrew *Dishon;* compare 1:38 and parallel text at Gen 36:28. **1:43** Or *before an Israelite king ruled over them.* **1:50** As in many Hebrew manuscripts, some Greek manuscripts, Syriac version, and Latin Vulgate (see also Gen 36:39); most Hebrew manuscripts read *Pai.* **1:51** As in an alternate reading of the Masoretic Text (see also Gen 36:40); the other alternate reads *Aliah.* **2:1** *Israel* is the name that God gave to Jacob. **2:6** As in many Hebrew manuscripts, some Greek manuscripts, and Syriac version (see also 1 Kgs 4:31); Hebrew reads *Dara.* **2:7a** Hebrew *Achar;* compare Josh 7:1. *Achar* means "disaster." **2:7b** The Hebrew term used here refers to the complete consecration of things or people to the LORD, either by destroying them or by giving them as an offering. **2:9** Hebrew *Kelubai,* a variant spelling of Caleb; compare 2:18. **2:11** As in Greek version (see also Ruth 4:20); Hebrew reads *Salma.*

was Abinadab, his third was Shimea,
14 his fourth was Nethanel, his fifth was
Raddai, 15 his sixth was Ozem, and his
seventh was David.
16 Their sisters were named Zeruiah
and Abigail. Zeruiah had three sons
named Abishai, Joab, and Asahel.
17 Abigail married a man named Jether,
an Ishmaelite, and they had a son
named Amasa.

Other Descendants of Hezron

18 Hezron's son Caleb had sons from his
wife Azubah and from Jerioth.* Her sons
were named Jesher, Shobab, and Ardon.
19 After Azubah died, Caleb married
Ephrathah,* and they had a son named
Hur. 20 Hur was the father of Uri. Uri was
the father of Bezalel.
21 When Hezron was sixty years old, he
married Gilead's sister, the daughter of
Makir. They had a son named Segub.
22 Segub was the father of Jair, who ruled
twenty-three towns in the land of Gilead.
23 (But Geshur and Aram captured the
Towns of Jair* and also took Kenath and
its sixty surrounding villages.) All these
were descendants of Makir, the father of
Gilead.
24 Soon after Hezron died in the town of
Caleb-ephrathah, his wife Abijah gave
birth to a son named Ashhur (the father
of* Tekoa).

Descendants of Hezron's Son Jerahmeel

25 The sons of Jerahmeel, the oldest son
of Hezron, were Ram (the firstborn),
Bunah, Oren, Ozem, and Ahijah.
26 Jerahmeel had a second wife named
Atarah. She was the mother of Onam.
27 The sons of Ram, the oldest son of
Jerahmeel, were Maaz, Jamin, and Eker.
28 The sons of Onam were Shammai and
Jada.
The sons of Shammai were Nadab and
Abishur.
29 The sons of Abishur and his wife Abihail
were Ahban and Molid.
30 The sons of Nadab were Seled and
Appaim. Seled died without children,
31 but Appaim had a son named Ishi. The
son of Ishi was Sheshan. Sheshan had a
descendant named Ahlai.
32 The sons of Jada, Shammai's brother,
were Jether and Jonathan. Jether died
without children, 33 but Jonathan had
two sons named Peleth and Zaza.
These were all descendants of Jerahmeel.
34 Sheshan had no sons, though he did
have daughters. He also had an Egyptian
servant named Jarha. 35 Sheshan gave
one of his daughters to be the wife of
Jarha, and they had a son named Attai.
36 Attai was the father of Nathan.
Nathan was the father of Zabad.
37 Zabad was the father of Ephlal.
Ephlal was the father of Obed.
38 Obed was the father of Jehu.
Jehu was the father of Azariah.
39 Azariah was the father of Helez.
Helez was the father of Eleasah.
40 Eleasah was the father of Sismai.
Sismai was the father of Shallum.
41 Shallum was the father of Jekamiah.
Jekamiah was the father of Elishama.

Descendants of Hezron's Son Caleb

42 The descendants of Caleb, the brother
of Jerahmeel, included Mesha (the
firstborn), who became the father of
Ziph. Caleb's descendants also included
the sons of Mareshah, the father of
Hebron.*
43 The sons of Hebron were Korah,
Tappuah, Rekem, and Shema. 44 Shema
was the father of Raham. Raham was the
father of Jorkeam. Rekem was the father
of Shammai. 45 The son of Shammai was
Maon. Maon was the father of Beth-zur.
46 Caleb's concubine Ephah gave birth to
Haran, Moza, and Gazez. Haran was the
father of Gazez.
47 The sons of Jahdai were Regem, Jotham,
Geshan, Pelet, Ephah, and Shaaph.
48 Another of Caleb's concubines, Maacah,
gave birth to Sheber and Tirhanah. 49 She
also gave birth to Shaaph (the father of
Madmannah) and Sheva (the father of
Macbenah and Gibea). Caleb also had
a daughter named Acsah.
50 These were all descendants of Caleb.

Descendants of Caleb's Son Hur

The sons of Hur, the oldest son of
Caleb's wife Ephrathah, were
Shobal (the founder of Kiriath-jearim),
51 Salma (the founder of Bethlehem), and
Hareph (the founder of Beth-gader).
52 The descendants of Shobal (the founder
of Kiriath-jearim) were Haroeh, half

the Manahathites, 53 and the families of
Kiriath-jearim—the Ithrites, Puthites,
Shumathites, and Mishraites, from whom
came the people of Zorah and Eshtaol.
54 The descendants of Salma were the
people of Bethlehem, the Netophathites,
Atroth-beth-joab, the other half of the
Manahathites, the Zorites, 55 and
the families of scribes living at Jabez—
the Tirathites, Shimeathites, and
Sucathites. All these were Kenites who
descended from Hammath, the father of
the family of Recab.*

Descendants of David

3 These are the sons of David who were
born in Hebron:

The oldest was Amnon, whose mother
was Ahinoam from Jezreel.
The second was Daniel, whose mother
was Abigail from Carmel.
2 The third was Absalom, whose mother
was Maacah, the daughter of Talmai,
king of Geshur.
The fourth was Adonijah, whose mother
was Haggith.
3 The fifth was Shephatiah, whose mother
was Abital.
The sixth was Ithream, whose mother
was Eglah, David's wife.

4 These six sons were born to David in
Hebron, where he reigned seven and a half
years.

Then David reigned another thirty-three
years in Jerusalem. 5 The sons born to David
in Jerusalem included Shammua,* Shobab,
Nathan, and Solomon. Their mother was
Bathsheba,* the daughter of Ammiel.
6 David also had nine other sons: Ibhar,
Elishua,* Elpelet,* 7 Nogah, Nepheg, Japhia,
8 Elishama, Eliada, and Eliphelet.
9 These were the sons of David, not including his sons born to his concubines.
Their sister was named Tamar.

Descendants of Solomon

10 The descendants of Solomon were
Rehoboam, Abijah, Asa, Jehoshaphat,
11 Jehoram,* Ahaziah, Joash, 12 Amaziah,
Uzziah,* Jotham, 13 Ahaz, Hezekiah,
Manasseh, 14 Amon, and Josiah.
15 The sons of Josiah were Johanan (the
oldest), Jehoiakim (the second), Zedekiah
(the third), and Jehoahaz* (the fourth).
16 The successors of Jehoiakim were his son
Jehoiachin and his brother Zedekiah.*

Descendants of Jehoiachin

17 The sons of Jehoiachin,* who was
taken prisoner by the Babylonians,
were Shealtiel, 18 Malkiram, Pedaiah,
Shenazzar, Jekamiah, Hoshama, and
Nedabiah.
19 The sons of Pedaiah were Zerubbabel and
Shimei.
The sons of Zerubbabel were Meshullam
and Hananiah. (Their sister was
Shelomith.) 20 His five other sons were
Hashubah, Ohel, Berekiah, Hasadiah,
and Jushab-hesed.
21 The sons of Hananiah were Pelatiah and
Jeshaiah. Jeshaiah's son was Rephaiah.
Rephaiah's son was Arnan. Arnan's
son was Obadiah. Obadiah's son was
Shecaniah.
22 The descendants of Shecaniah were
Shemaiah and his sons, Hattush, Igal,
Bariah, Neariah, and Shaphat—six in
all.
23 The sons of Neariah were Elioenai,
Hizkiah, and Azrikam—three in all.
24 The sons of Elioenai were Hodaviah,
Eliashib, Pelaiah, Akkub, Johanan,
Delaiah, and Anani—seven in all.

Other Descendants of Judah

4 The descendants of Judah were Perez,
Hezron, Carmi, Hur, and Shobal.
2 Shobal's son Reaiah was the father of
Jahath. Jahath was the father of Ahumai
and Lahad. These were the families of
the Zorathites.
3 The descendants of* Etam were Jezreel,
Ishma, Idbash, their sister Hazzelelponi,
4 Penuel (the father of* Gedor), and Ezer
(the father of Hushah). These were the

2:18 Or *Caleb had a daughter named Jerioth from his wife, Azubah.* The meaning of the Hebrew is uncertain. **2:19** Hebrew *Ephrath,* a variant spelling of Ephrathah; compare 2:50 and 4:4. **2:23** Or *captured Havvoth-jair.* **2:24** Or *the founder of;* also in 2:42, 45, 49. **2:42** Or *who founded Hebron.* The meaning of the Hebrew is uncertain. **2:55** Or *the founder of Beth-recab.* **3:5a** As in Syriac version (see also 14:4; 2 Sam 5:14); Hebrew reads *Shimea.* **3:5b** Hebrew *Bathshua,* a variant spelling of Bathsheba. **3:6a** As in some Hebrew and Greek manuscripts (see also 14:5-7 and 2 Sam 5:15); most Hebrew manuscripts read *Elishama.* **3:6b** Hebrew *Eliphelet;* compare parallel text at 14:5-7. **3:11** Hebrew *Joram,* a variant spelling of Jehoram. **3:12** Hebrew *Azariah,* a variant spelling of Uzziah. **3:15** Hebrew *Shallum,* another name for Jehoahaz. **3:16** Hebrew *The sons of Jehoiakim were his son Jeconiah* [a variant spelling of Jehoiachin] *and his son Zedekiah.* **3:17** Hebrew *Jeconiah,* a variant spelling of Jehoiachin. **4:3** As in Greek version; Hebrew reads *father of.* The meaning of the Hebrew is uncertain. **4:4** Or *the founder of;* also in 4:5, 12, 14, 17, 18, and perhaps other instances where the text reads *the father of.*

descendants of Hur (the firstborn of Ephrathah), the ancestor of Bethlehem.
5Ashhur (the father of Tekoa) had two wives, named Helah and Naarah.
6Naarah gave birth to Ahuzzam, Hepher, Temeni, and Haahashtari. 7Helah gave birth to Zereth, Izhar,* Ethnan, 8and Koz, who became the ancestor of Anub, Zobebah, and all the families of Aharhel son of Harum.
9There was a man named Jabez who was more honorable than any of his brothers. His mother named him Jabez* because his birth had been so painful. 10He was the one who prayed to the God of Israel, "Oh, that you would bless me and expand my territory! Please be with me in all that I do, and keep me from all trouble and pain!" And God granted him his request.
11Kelub (the brother of Shuhah) was the father of Mehir. Mehir was the father of Eshton. 12Eshton was the father of Beth-rapha, Paseah, and Tehinnah. Tehinnah was the father of Ir-nahash. These were the descendants of Recah.
13The sons of Kenaz were Othniel and Seraiah. Othniel's sons were Hathath and Meonothai.* 14Meonothai was the father of Ophrah. Seraiah was the father of Joab, the founder of the Valley of Craftsmen,* so called because they were craftsmen.
15The sons of Caleb son of Jephunneh were Iru, Elah, and Naam. The son of Elah was Kenaz.
16The sons of Jehallelel were Ziph, Ziphah, Tiria, and Asarel.
17The sons of Ezrah were Jether, Mered, Epher, and Jalon. One of Mered's wives became* the mother of Miriam, Shammai, and Ishbah (the father of Eshtemoa).
18He married a woman from Judah, who became the mother of Jered (the father of Gedor), Heber (the father of Soco), and Jekuthiel (the father of Zanoah). Mered also married Bithia, a daughter of Pharaoh, and she bore him children.
19Hodiah's wife was the sister of Naham. One of her sons was the father of Keilah the Garmite, and another was the father of Eshtemoa the Maacathite.
20The sons of Shimon were Amnon, Rinnah, Ben-hanan, and Tilon.
The descendants of Ishi were Zoheth and Ben-zoheth.

Descendants of Judah's Son Shelah

21Shelah was one of Judah's sons. The descendants of Shelah were Er (the father of Lecah); Laadah (the father of Mareshah); the families of linen workers at Beth-ashbea; 22Jokim; the men of Cozeba; and Joash and Saraph, who ruled over Moab and Jashubi-lehem. These names all come from ancient records. 23They were the pottery makers who lived in Netaim and Gederah. They lived there and worked for the king.

Descendants of Simeon

24The sons of Simeon were Jemuel,* Jamin, Jarib, Zohar,* and Shaul.
25The descendants of Shaul were Shallum, Mibsam, and Mishma.
26The descendants of Mishma were Hammuel, Zaccur, and Shimei.
27Shimei had sixteen sons and six daughters, but none of his brothers had

Jabez

Jabez shows us how important it is not to skim our Bibles when we get to challenging passages or lists, like these in Chronicles. For tucked away in the list of Judah's descendants are two verses about Jabez that should challenge us all. Jabez, whose name sounds like the Hebrew word for "pain," was so called because his mother bore him in pain. But he refused to live life under what he saw as a curse and cried out to God: "'Oh, that you would bless me and expand my territory! Please be with me in all that I do, and keep me from all trouble and pain!' And God granted him his request" (1 Chronicles 4:10). Jabez shows us that none of us have to live life limited by how others have seen us or what we have been in the past.

large families. So Simeon's tribe never
grew as large as the tribe of Judah.
28 They lived in Beersheba, Moladah,
Hazar-shual, 29 Bilhah, Ezem,
Tolad, 30 Bethuel, Hormah, Ziklag,
31 Beth-marcaboth, Hazar-susim, Beth-biri,
and Shaaraim. These towns were under
their control until the time of King David.
32 Their descendants also lived in Etam,
Ain, Rimmon, Token, and Ashan—five
towns 33 and their surrounding villages
as far away as Baalath.* This was their
territory, and these names are listed in
their genealogical records.
34 Other descendants of Simeon included
Meshobab, Jamlech, Joshah son of
Amaziah, 35 Joel, Jehu son of Joshibiah,
son of Seraiah, son of Asiel, 36 Elioenai,
Jaakobah, Jeshohaiah, Asaiah, Adiel,
Jesimiel, Benaiah, 37 and Ziza son of
Shiphi, son of Allon, son of Jedaiah, son
of Shimri, son of Shemaiah.

38 These were the names of some of the
leaders of Simeon's wealthy clans. Their
families grew, 39 and they traveled to the
region of Gerar,* in the east part of the
valley, seeking pastureland for their flocks.
40 They found lush pastures there, and the
land was spacious, quiet, and peaceful.

Some of Ham's descendants had been
living in that region. 41 But during the reign
of King Hezekiah of Judah, these leaders of
Simeon invaded the region and completely
destroyed* the homes of the descendants of
Ham and of the Meunites. No trace of them
remains today. They killed everyone who
lived there and took the land for themselves,
because they wanted its good pastureland
for their flocks. 42 Five hundred of these
invaders from the tribe of Simeon went to
Mount Seir, led by Pelatiah, Neariah, Rephaiah, and Uzziel—all sons of Ishi. 43 They
destroyed the few Amalekites who had survived, and they have lived there ever since.

Descendants of Reuben

5 The oldest son of Israel* was Reuben.
But since he dishonored his father by
sleeping with one of his father's concubines, his birthright was given to the sons of
his brother Joseph. For this reason, Reuben
is not listed in the genealogical records
as the firstborn son. 2 The descendants of
Judah became the most powerful tribe and
provided a ruler for the nation,* but the
birthright belonged to Joseph.

3 The sons of Reuben, the oldest son of
Israel, were Hanoch, Pallu, Hezron, and
Carmi.
4 The descendants of Joel were Shemaiah,
Gog, Shimei, 5 Micah, Reaiah, Baal, 6 and
Beerah. Beerah was the leader of the
Reubenites when they were taken into
captivity by King Tiglath-pileser* of
Assyria.
7 Beerah's* relatives are listed in their
genealogical records by their clans: Jeiel
(the leader), Zechariah, 8 and Bela son of
Azaz, son of Shema, son of Joel.
The Reubenites lived in the area that
stretches from Aroer to Nebo and
Baal-meon. 9 And since they had so many
livestock in the land of Gilead, they
spread east toward the edge of the desert
that stretches to the Euphrates River.
10 During the reign of Saul, the Reubenites
defeated the Hagrites in battle. Then
they moved into the Hagrite settlements
all along the eastern edge of Gilead.

Descendants of Gad

11 Next to the Reubenites, the descendants
of Gad lived in the land of Bashan as far
east as Salecah. 12 Joel was the leader in
the land of Bashan, and Shapham was
second-in-command, followed by Janai
and Shaphat.
13 Their relatives, the leaders of seven other
clans, were Michael, Meshullam, Sheba,
Jorai, Jacan, Zia, and Eber. 14 These were
all descendants of Abihail son of Huri,
son of Jaroah, son of Gilead, son of
Michael, son of Jeshishai, son of Jahdo,
son of Buz. 15 Ahi son of Abdiel, son of
Guni, was the leader of their clans.

16 The Gadites lived in the land of Gilead,
in Bashan and its villages, and throughout

4:7 As in an alternate reading in the Masoretic Text (see also Latin Vulgate); the other alternate and the Greek version read *Zohar.* **4:9** *Jabez* sounds like a Hebrew word meaning "distress" or "pain." **4:13** As in some Greek manuscripts and Latin Vulgate; Hebrew lacks *and Meonothai.* **4:14** Or *Joab, the father of Ge-harashim.* **4:17** Or *Jether's wife became;* Hebrew reads *She became.* **4:24a** As in Syriac version (see also Gen 46:10; Exod 6:15); Hebrew reads *Nemuel.* **4:24b** As in parallel texts at Gen 46:10 and Exod 6:15; Hebrew reads *Zerah.* **4:33** As in some Greek manuscripts (see also Josh 19:8); Hebrew reads *Baal.* **4:39** As in Greek version; Hebrew reads *Gedor.* **4:41** The Hebrew term used here refers to the complete consecration of things or people to the LORD, either by destroying them or by giving them as an offering. **5:1** *Israel* is the name that God gave to Jacob. **5:2** Or *and from Judah came a prince.* **5:6** Hebrew *Tilgath-pilneser,* a variant spelling of Tiglath-pileser; also in 5:26. **5:7** Hebrew *His.*

all the pasturelands of Sharon. 17 All of these
were listed in the genealogical records
during the days of King Jotham of Judah and
King Jeroboam of Israel.

The Tribes East of the Jordan

18 There were 44,760 capable warriors in
the armies of Reuben, Gad, and the half-
tribe of Manasseh. They were all skilled in
combat and armed with shields, swords,
and bows. 19 They waged war against the
Hagrites, the Jeturites, the Naphishites,
and the Nodabites. 20 They cried out to God
during the battle, and he answered their
prayer because they trusted in him. So the
Hagrites and all their allies were defeated.
21 The plunder taken from the Hagrites included 50,000 camels, 250,000 sheep and
goats, 2,000 donkeys, and 100,000 captives. 22 Many of the Hagrites were killed in
the battle because God was fighting against
them. The people of Reuben, Gad, and Manasseh lived in their land until they were
taken into exile.
23 The half-tribe of Manasseh was very
large and spread through the land from
Bashan to Baal-hermon, Senir, and Mount
Hermon. 24 These were the leaders of their
clans: Epher,* Ishi, Eliel, Azriel, Jeremiah,
Hodaviah, and Jahdiel. These men had a
great reputation as mighty warriors and
leaders of their clans.
25 But these tribes were unfaithful to the
God of their ancestors. They worshiped the
gods of the nations that God had destroyed.
26 So the God of Israel caused King Pul of
Assyria (also known as Tiglath-pileser) to
invade the land and take away the people of
Reuben, Gad, and the half-tribe of Manasseh as captives. The Assyrians exiled them
to Halah, Habor, Hara, and the Gozan River,
where they remain to this day.

The Priestly Line

6 1*The sons of Levi were Gershon,
Kohath, and Merari.
2 The descendants of Kohath included
Amram, Izhar, Hebron, and Uzziel.
3 The children of Amram were Aaron,
Moses, and Miriam.
The sons of Aaron were Nadab, Abihu,
Eleazar, and Ithamar.
4 Eleazar was the father of Phinehas.
Phinehas was the father of Abishua.
5 Abishua was the father of Bukki.
Bukki was the father of Uzzi.
6 Uzzi was the father of Zerahiah.
Zerahiah was the father of Meraioth.
7 Meraioth was the father of Amariah.
Amariah was the father of Ahitub.
8 Ahitub was the father of Zadok.
Zadok was the father of Ahimaaz.
9 Ahimaaz was the father of Azariah.
Azariah was the father of Johanan.

Genealogies

Let's be honest, these long genealogies (family records) don't strike us as the most exciting bits of the Bible! But for people in Bible times they were absolutely crucial. Sometimes long (as here in 1 Chronicles) and sometimes short (e.g., Ruth 4:18-22), they helped people establish a clear link with their ancestors and God's promises to them. Once you had grasped that link, you could start to understand who you were in the present and what God's purposes were for you in the future.

The long genealogy of 1 Chronicles 1–9 is meant to show that God's people who had returned from exile still stood at the center of his purposes, both for them as descendants of Abraham and also for the whole of humanity as descendants of Adam. God had not given up on them!

Genealogies were especially important for hereditary offices like priests and kings and also for establishing land rights. The early church was at pains to show that Jesus was a true descendant of Abraham and David (Matthew 1; Luke 3) and therefore qualified to receive God's promises to them and to fulfill his messianic calling.

▸ *See also* ***Why does the Bible have passages like these?****, page 262.*

10 Johanan was the father of Azariah, the
high priest at the Temple* built by
Solomon in Jerusalem.
11 Azariah was the father of Amariah.
Amariah was the father of Ahitub.
12 Ahitub was the father of Zadok.
Zadok was the father of Shallum.
13 Shallum was the father of Hilkiah.
Hilkiah was the father of Azariah.
14 Azariah was the father of Seraiah.
Seraiah was the father of Jehozadak,
15 who went into exile when the
LORD sent the people of Judah and
Jerusalem into captivity under
Nebuchadnezzar.

The Levite Clans

16* The sons of Levi were Gershon,* Kohath,
and Merari.
17 The descendants of Gershon included
Libni and Shimei.
18 The descendants of Kohath included
Amram, Izhar, Hebron, and Uzziel.
19 The descendants of Merari included
Mahli and Mushi.

The following were the Levite clans, listed according to their ancestral descent:

20 The descendants of Gershon included
Libni, Jahath, Zimmah, 21 Joah, Iddo,
Zerah, and Jeatherai.
22 The descendants of Kohath included
Amminadab, Korah, Assir, 23 Elkanah,
Abiasaph,* Assir, 24 Tahath, Uriel,
Uzziah, and Shaul.
25 The descendants of Elkanah included
Amasai, Ahimoth, 26 Elkanah, Zophai,
Nahath, 27 Eliab, Jeroham, Elkanah, and
Samuel.*
28 The sons of Samuel were Joel* (the older)
and Abijah (the second).
29 The descendants of Merari included
Mahli, Libni, Shimei, Uzzah, 30 Shimea,
Haggiah, and Asaiah.

The Temple Musicians

31 David assigned the following men to lead
the music at the house of the LORD after
the Ark was placed there. 32 They ministered with music at the Tabernacle* until
Solomon built the Temple of the LORD in
Jerusalem. They carried out their work, following all the regulations handed down
to them. 33 These are the men who served,
along with their sons:

Heman the musician was from the clan
of Kohath. His genealogy was traced
back through Joel, Samuel, 34 Elkanah,
Jeroham, Eliel, Toah, 35 Zuph, Elkanah,
Mahath, Amasai, 36 Elkanah, Joel,
Azariah, Zephaniah, 37 Tahath, Assir,
Abiasaph, Korah, 38 Izhar, Kohath, Levi,
and Israel.*
39 Heman's first assistant was Asaph from
the clan of Gershon.* Asaph's genealogy
was traced back through Berekiah,
Shimea, 40 Michael, Baaseiah, Malkijah,
41 Ethni, Zerah, Adaiah, 42 Ethan, Zimmah,
Shimei, 43 Jahath, Gershon, and Levi.
44 Heman's second assistant was Ethan
from the clan of Merari. Ethan's
genealogy was traced back through
Kishi, Abdi, Malluch, 45 Hashabiah,
Amaziah, Hilkiah, 46 Amzi, Bani, Shemer,
47 Mahli, Mushi, Merari, and Levi.

48 Their fellow Levites were appointed to
various other tasks in the Tabernacle, the
house of God.

Aaron's Descendants

49 Only Aaron and his descendants served
as priests. They presented the offerings on
the altar of burnt offering and the altar of
incense, and they performed all the other
duties related to the Most Holy Place. They
made atonement for Israel by doing everything that Moses, the servant of God, had
commanded them.

50 The descendants of Aaron were Eleazar,
Phinehas, Abishua, 51 Bukki, Uzzi,
Zerahiah, 52 Meraioth, Amariah, Ahitub,
53 Zadok, and Ahimaaz.

Territory for the Levites

54 This is a record of the towns and territory
assigned by means of sacred lots to the descendants of Aaron, who were from the clan
of Kohath. 55 This territory included Hebron
and its surrounding pasturelands in Judah,
56 but the fields and outlying areas belonging to the city were given to Caleb son of

5:24 As in Greek version and Latin Vulgate; Hebrew reads *and Epher.* **6:1** Verses 6:1-15 are numbered 5:27-41 in Hebrew text. **6:10** Hebrew *the house.* **6:16a** Verses 6:16-81 are numbered 6:1-66 in Hebrew text. **6:16b** Hebrew *Gershom,* a variant spelling of Gershon (see 6:1); also in 6:17, 20, 43, 62, 71. **6:23** Hebrew *Ebiasaph,* a variant spelling of Abiasaph (also in 6:37); compare parallel text at Exod 6:24. **6:27** As in some Greek manuscripts (see also 6:33-34); Hebrew lacks *and Samuel.* **6:28** As in some Greek manuscripts and the Syriac version (see also 6:33 and 1 Sam 8:2); Hebrew lacks *Joel.* **6:32** Hebrew *the Tabernacle, the Tent of Meeting.* **6:38** *Israel* is the name that God gave to Jacob. **6:39** Hebrew lacks *from the clan of Gershon;* see 6:43.

Jephunneh. 57 So the descendants of Aaron
were given the following towns, each with
its pasturelands: Hebron (a city of refuge),*
Libnah, Jattir, Eshtemoa, 58 Holon,* Debir,
59 Ain,* Juttah,* and Beth-shemesh. 60 And
from the territory of Benjamin they were
given Gibeon,* Geba, Alemeth, and Anathoth, each with its pasturelands. So thirteen towns were given to the descendants
of Aaron. 61 The remaining descendants of
Kohath received ten towns from the territory of the half-tribe of Manasseh by means
of sacred lots.

62 The descendants of Gershon received
by sacred lots thirteen towns from the territories of Issachar, Asher, Naphtali, and
from the Bashan area of Manasseh, east of
the Jordan.

63 The descendants of Merari received by
sacred lots twelve towns from the territories
of Reuben, Gad, and Zebulun.

64 So the people of Israel assigned all these
towns and pasturelands to the Levites. 65 The
towns in the territories of Judah, Simeon,
and Benjamin, mentioned above, were assigned to them by means of sacred lots.

66 The descendants of Kohath were given
the following towns from the territory
of Ephraim, each with its pasturelands:
67 Shechem (a city of refuge in the hill
country of Ephraim),* Gezer, 68 Jokmeam,
Beth-horon, 69 Aijalon, and Gath-rimmon.
70 The remaining descendants of Kohath
were assigned the towns of Aner and Bileam
from the territory of the half-tribe of Manasseh, each with its pasturelands.

71 The descendants of Gershon received
the towns of Golan (in Bashan) and Ashtaroth from the territory of the half-tribe
of Manasseh, each with its pasturelands.
72 From the territory of Issachar, they were
given Kedesh, Daberath, 73 Ramoth, and
Anem, each with its pasturelands. 74 From
the territory of Asher, they received Mashal,
Abdon, 75 Hukok, and Rehob, each with its
pasturelands. 76 From the territory of Naphtali, they were given Kedesh in Galilee,
Hammon, and Kiriathaim, each with its
pasturelands.

77 The remaining descendants of Merari
received the towns of Jokneam, Kartah,*
Rimmon,* and Tabor from the territory
of Zebulun, each with its pasturelands.
78 From the territory of Reuben, east of the
Jordan River opposite Jericho, they received
Bezer (a desert town), Jahaz,* 79 Kedemoth,
and Mephaath, each with its pasturelands.
80 And from the territory of Gad, they received
Ramoth in Gilead, Mahanaim, 81 Heshbon,
and Jazer, each with its pasturelands.

Descendants of Issachar

7 The four sons of Issachar were Tola,
Puah, Jashub, and Shimron.
2 The sons of Tola were Uzzi, Rephaiah,
Jeriel, Jahmai, Ibsam, and Shemuel.
Each of them was the leader of an
ancestral clan. At the time of King
David, the total number of mighty
warriors listed in the records of these
clans was 22,600.
3 The son of Uzzi was Izrahiah. The sons
of Izrahiah were Michael, Obadiah,
Joel, and Isshiah. These five became
the leaders of clans. 4 All of them had
many wives and many sons, so the total
number of men available for military
service among their descendants was
36,000.
5 The total number of mighty warriors from
all the clans of the tribe of Issachar was
87,000. All of them were listed in their genealogical records.

Descendants of Benjamin

6 Three of Benjamin's sons were Bela,
Beker, and Jediael.
7 The five sons of Bela were Ezbon, Uzzi,
Uzziel, Jerimoth, and Iri. Each of them
was the leader of an ancestral clan. The
total number of mighty warriors from
these clans was 22,034, as listed in their
genealogical records.
8 The sons of Beker were Zemirah, Joash,
Eliezer, Elioenai, Omri, Jeremoth,
Abijah, Anathoth, and Alemeth.
9 Each of them was the leader of an
ancestral clan. The total number of
mighty warriors and leaders from these
clans was 20,200, as listed in their
genealogical records.
10 The son of Jediael was Bilhan. The sons
of Bilhan were Jeush, Benjamin, Ehud,
Kenaanah, Zethan, Tarshish, and
Ahishahar. 11 Each of them was the leader
of an ancestral clan. From these clans
the total number of mighty warriors
ready for war was 17,200.
12 The sons of Ir were Shuppim and
Huppim. Hushim was the son of Aher.

Descendants of Naphtali

13 The sons of Naphtali were Jahzeel,*
Guni, Jezer, and Shillem.* They were
all descendants of Jacob's concubine
Bilhah.

Descendants of Manasseh

14 The descendants of Manasseh through
his Aramean concubine included Asriel.
She also bore Makir, the father of Gilead.
15 Makir found wives for* Huppim and
Shuppim. Makir had a sister named
Maacah. One of his descendants was
Zelophehad, who had only daughters.
16 Makir's wife, Maacah, gave birth to
a son whom she named Peresh. His
brother's name was Sheresh. The sons
of Peresh were Ulam and Rakem. 17 The
son of Ulam was Bedan. All these were
considered Gileadites, descendants of
Makir son of Manasseh.
18 Makir's sister Hammoleketh gave birth
to Ishhod, Abiezer, and Mahlah.
19 The sons of Shemida were Ahian,
Shechem, Likhi, and Aniam.

Descendants of Ephraim

20 The descendants of Ephraim were
Shuthelah, Bered, Tahath, Eleadah,
Tahath, 21 Zabad, Shuthelah, Ezer, and
Elead. These two were killed trying to
steal livestock from the local farmers
near Gath. 22 Their father, Ephraim,
mourned for them a long time, and
his relatives came to comfort him.
23 Afterward Ephraim slept with his
wife, and she became pregnant and
gave birth to a son. Ephraim named
him Beriah* because of the tragedy his
family had suffered. 24 He had a daughter
named Sheerah. She built the towns
of Lower and Upper Beth-horon and
Uzzen-sheerah.
25 The descendants of Ephraim included
Rephah, Resheph, Telah, Tahan,
26 Ladan, Ammihud, Elishama, 27 Nun,
and Joshua.

28 The descendants of Ephraim lived in
the territory that included Bethel and its
surrounding towns to the south, Naaran to
the east, Gezer and its villages to the west,
and Shechem and its surrounding villages
to the north as far as Ayyah and its towns.
29 Along the border of Manasseh were the
towns of Beth-shan,* Taanach, Megiddo,
Dor, and their surrounding villages. The
descendants of Joseph son of Israel* lived
in these towns.

Descendants of Asher

30 The sons of Asher were Imnah, Ishvah,
Ishvi, and Beriah. They had a sister
named Serah.
31 The sons of Beriah were Heber and
Malkiel (the father of Birzaith).
32 The sons of Heber were Japhlet, Shomer,
and Hotham. They had a sister named
Shua.
33 The sons of Japhlet were Pasach, Bimhal,
and Ashvath.
34 The sons of Shomer were Ahi,* Rohgah,
Hubbah, and Aram.
35 The sons of his brother Helem* were
Zophah, Imna, Shelesh, and Amal.
36 The sons of Zophah were Suah,
Harnepher, Shual, Beri, Imrah, 37 Bezer,
Hod, Shamma, Shilshah, Ithran,* and
Beera.
38 The sons of Jether were Jephunneh,
Pispah, and Ara.
39 The sons of Ulla were Arah, Hanniel, and
Rizia.
40 Each of these descendants of Asher was
the head of an ancestral clan. They were
all select men—mighty warriors and outstanding leaders. The total number of men
available for military service was 26,000, as
listed in their genealogical records.

Descendants of Benjamin

8 Benjamin's first son was Bela, the
second was Ashbel, the third was
Aharah, 2 the fourth was Nohah, and the
fifth was Rapha.

6:57 As in parallel text at Josh 21:13; Hebrew reads *were given the cities of refuge: Hebron, and the following towns, each with its pasturelands.* **6:58** As in parallel text at Josh 21:15; Masoretic Text reads *Hilez;* other manuscripts read *Hilen.* **6:59a** As in parallel text at Josh 21:16; Hebrew reads *Ashan.* **6:59b** As in Syriac version (see also Josh 21:16); Hebrew lacks *Juttah.* **6:60** As in parallel text at Josh 21:17; Hebrew lacks *Gibeon.* **6:66-67** As in parallel text at Josh 21:21; Hebrew text reads *were given the cities of refuge: Shechem in the hill country of Ephraim, and the following towns, each with its pasturelands.* **6:77a** As in Greek version (see also Josh 21:34); Hebrew lacks *Jokneam, Kartah.* **6:77b** As in Greek version (see also Josh 19:13); Hebrew reads *Rimmono.* **6:78** Hebrew *Jahzah,* a variant spelling of Jahaz. **7:13a** As in parallel text at Gen 46:24; Hebrew reads *Jahziel,* a variant spelling of Jahzeel. **7:13b** As in some Hebrew and Greek manuscripts (see also Gen 46:24; Num 26:49); most Hebrew manuscripts read *Shallum.* **7:15** Or *Makir took a wife from.* The meaning of the Hebrew is uncertain. **7:23** *Beriah* sounds like a Hebrew term meaning "tragedy" or "misfortune." **7:29a** Hebrew *Beth-shean,* a variant spelling of Beth-shan. **7:29b** *Israel* is the name that God gave to Jacob. **7:34** Or *The sons of Shomer, his brother, were.* **7:35** Possibly another name for *Hotham;* compare 7:32. **7:37** Possibly another name for *Jether;* compare 7:38.

3The sons of Bela were Addar, Gera,
Abihud,* 4Abishua, Naaman, Ahoah,
5Gera, Shephuphan, and Huram.
6The sons of Ehud, leaders of the clans
living at Geba, were exiled to Manahath.
7Ehud's sons were Naaman, Ahijah, and
Gera. Gera, who led them into exile, was
the father of Uzza and Ahihud.*
8After Shaharaim divorced his wives
Hushim and Baara, he had children in
the land of Moab. 9His wife Hodesh gave
birth to Jobab, Zibia, Mesha, Malcam,
10Jeuz, Sakia, and Mirmah. These sons
all became the leaders of clans.
11Shaharaim's wife Hushim had already
given birth to Abitub and Elpaal. 12The
sons of Elpaal were Eber, Misham,
Shemed (who built the towns of Ono and
Lod and their nearby villages), 13Beriah,
and Shema. They were the leaders of the
clans living in Aijalon, and they drove
out the inhabitants of Gath.
14Ahio, Shashak, Jeremoth, 15Zebadiah,
Arad, Eder, 16Michael, Ishpah, and Joha
were the sons of Beriah.
17Zebadiah, Meshullam, Hizki, Heber,
18Ishmerai, Izliah, and Jobab were the
sons of Elpaal.
19Jakim, Zicri, Zabdi, 20Elienai, Zillethai,
Eliel, 21Adaiah, Beraiah, and Shimrath
were the sons of Shimei.
22Ishpan, Eber, Eliel, 23Abdon, Zicri,
Hanan, 24Hananiah, Elam, Anthothijah,
25Iphdeiah, and Penuel were the sons of
Shashak.
26Shamsherai, Shehariah, Athaliah,
27Jaareshiah, Elijah, and Zicri were the
sons of Jeroham.
28These were the leaders of the ancestral
clans; they were listed in their genealogical
records, and they all lived in Jerusalem.

The Family of Saul

29Jeiel* (the father of* Gibeon) lived in the
town of Gibeon. His wife's name was
Maacah, 30and his oldest son was named
Abdon. Jeiel's other sons were Zur,
Kish, Baal, Ner,* Nadab, 31Gedor, Ahio,
Zechariah,* 32and Mikloth, who was the
father of Shimeam.* All these families
lived near each other in Jerusalem.
33 Ner was the father of Kish.
Kish was the father of Saul.
Saul was the father of Jonathan,
Malkishua, Abinadab, and Esh-baal.
34 Jonathan was the father of Merib-baal.
Merib-baal was the father of Micah.
35 Micah was the father of Pithon, Melech,
Tahrea,* and Ahaz.
36 Ahaz was the father of Jadah.*
Jadah was the father of Alemeth,
Azmaveth, and Zimri.
Zimri was the father of Moza.
37 Moza was the father of Binea.
Binea was the father of Rephaiah.*
Rephaiah was the father of Eleasah.
Eleasah was the father of Azel.
38Azel had six sons: Azrikam, Bokeru,
Ishmael, Sheariah, Obadiah, and
Hanan. These were the sons of Azel.
39Azel's brother Eshek had three sons: the
first was Ulam, the second was Jeush,
and the third was Eliphelet. 40Ulam's
sons were all mighty warriors and
expert archers. They had many sons and
grandsons—150 in all.

All these were descendants of Benjamin.

9 So all Israel was listed in the genealogical records in *The Book of the Kings of
Israel.*

The Returning Exiles

The people of Judah were exiled to Babylon
because they were unfaithful to the LORD.
2The first of the exiles to return to their
property in their former towns were priests,
Levites, Temple servants, and other Israelites. 3Some of the people from the tribes
of Judah, Benjamin, Ephraim, and Manasseh came and settled in Jerusalem.

4One family that returned was that of Uthai
son of Ammihud, son of Omri, son of
Imri, son of Bani, a descendant of Perez
son of Judah.
5Others returned from the Shilonite clan,
including Asaiah (the oldest) and his
sons.
6From the Zerahite clan, Jeuel returned
with his relatives.

In all, 690 families from the tribe of Judah
returned.

7From the tribe of Benjamin came Sallu
son of Meshullam, son of Hodaviah, son
of Hassenuah; 8Ibneiah son of Jeroham;
Elah son of Uzzi, son of Micri; and
Meshullam son of Shephatiah, son of
Reuel, son of Ibnijah.

9 These men were all leaders of clans,
and they were listed in their genealogical
records. In all, 956 families from the tribe
of Benjamin returned.

The Returning Priests

10 Among the priests who returned were
Jedaiah, Jehoiarib, Jakin, 11 Azariah son
of Hilkiah, son of Meshullam, son of
Zadok, son of Meraioth, son of Ahitub.
Azariah was the chief officer of the
house of God.
12 Other returning priests were Adaiah
son of Jeroham, son of Pashhur, son of
Malkijah, and Maasai son of Adiel, son
of Jahzerah, son of Meshullam, son of
Meshillemith, son of Immer.
13 In all, 1,760 priests returned. They were
heads of clans and very able men. They
were responsible for ministering at the
house of God.

The Returning Levites

14 The Levites who returned were Shemaiah
son of Hasshub, son of Azrikam, son
of Hashabiah, a descendant of Merari;
15 Bakbakkar; Heresh; Galal; Mattaniah
son of Mica, son of Zicri, son of Asaph;
16 Obadiah son of Shemaiah, son of
Galal, son of Jeduthun; and Berekiah
son of Asa, son of Elkanah, who lived in
the area of Netophah.
17 The gatekeepers who returned were
Shallum, Akkub, Talmon, Ahiman, and
their relatives. Shallum was the chief
gatekeeper. 18 Prior to this time, they
were responsible for the King's Gate
on the east side. These men served
as gatekeepers for the camps of the
Levites. 19 Shallum was the son of Kore,
a descendant of Abiasaph,* from the
clan of Korah. He and his relatives,
the Korahites, were responsible for
guarding the entrance to the sanctuary,
just as their ancestors had guarded the
Tabernacle in the camp of the LORD.
20 Phinehas son of Eleazar had been in
charge of the gatekeepers in earlier times,
and the LORD had been with him. 21 And
later Zechariah son of Meshelemiah was
responsible for guarding the entrance to
the Tabernacle.*

22 In all, there were 212 gatekeepers in
those days, and they were listed according
to the genealogies in their villages. David
and Samuel the seer had appointed their
ancestors because they were reliable men.
23 These gatekeepers and their descendants, by their divisions, were responsible
for guarding the entrance to the house of
the LORD when that house was a tent. 24 The
gatekeepers were stationed on all four
sides—east, west, north, and south. 25 Their
relatives in the villages came regularly to
share their duties for seven-day periods.

26 The four chief gatekeepers, all Levites,
were trusted officials, for they were responsible for the rooms and treasuries at the
house of God. 27 They would spend the night
around the house of God, since it was their
duty to guard it and to open the gates every
morning.

28 Some of the gatekeepers were assigned
to care for the various articles used in
worship. They checked them in and out to
avoid any loss. 29 Others were responsible
for the furnishings, the items in the sanctuary, and the supplies, such as choice flour,
wine, olive oil, frankincense, and spices.
30 But it was the priests who blended the
spices. 31 Mattithiah, a Levite and the oldest
son of Shallum the Korahite, was entrusted
with baking the bread used in the offerings.
32 And some members of the clan of Kohath
were in charge of preparing the bread to be
set on the table each Sabbath day.

33 The musicians, all prominent Levites,
lived at the Temple. They were exempt from
other responsibilities since they were on
duty at all hours. 34 All these men lived in Jerusalem. They were the heads of Levite families and were listed as prominent leaders in
their genealogical records.

King Saul's Family Tree

35 Jeiel (the father of* Gibeon) lived in the
town of Gibeon. His wife's name was
Maacah, 36 and his oldest son was named
Abdon. Jeiel's other sons were Zur,

8:3 Possibly *Gera the father of Ehud;* compare 8:6. **8:7** Or *Gera, that is Heglam, was the father of Uzza and Ahihud.* **8:29a** As in some Greek manuscripts (see also 9:35); Hebrew lacks *Jeiel.* **8:29b** Or *the founder of.* **8:30** As in some Greek manuscripts (see also 9:36); Hebrew lacks *Ner.* **8:31** As in parallel text at 9:37; Hebrew reads *Zeker,* a variant spelling of Zechariah. **8:32** As in parallel text at 9:38; Hebrew reads *Shimeah,* a variant spelling of Shimeam. **8:35** As in parallel text at 9:41; Hebrew reads *Tarea,* a variant spelling of Tahrea. **8:36** As in parallel text at 9:42; Hebrew reads *Jehoaddah,* a variant spelling of Jadah. **8:37** As in parallel text at 9:43; Hebrew reads *Raphah,* a variant spelling of Rephaiah. **9:19** Hebrew *Ebiasaph,* a variant spelling of Abiasaph; compare Exod 6:24. **9:21** Hebrew *Tent of Meeting.* **9:35** Or *the founder of.*

Kish, Baal, Ner, Nadab, [37]Gedor, Ahio,
Zechariah, and Mikloth. [38]Mikloth was
the father of Shimeam. All these families
lived near each other in Jerusalem.

39 Ner was the father of Kish.
Kish was the father of Saul.
Saul was the father of Jonathan,
Malkishua, Abinadab, and Esh-baal.
40 Jonathan was the father of Merib-baal.
Merib-baal was the father of Micah.
41 The sons of Micah were Pithon, Melech,
Tahrea, and Ahaz.*
42 Ahaz was the father of Jadah.*
Jadah was the father of Alemeth,
Azmaveth, and Zimri.
Zimri was the father of Moza.
43 Moza was the father of Binea.
Binea's son was Rephaiah.
Rephaiah's son was Eleasah.
Eleasah's son was Azel.
[44]Azel had six sons, whose names were
Azrikam, Bokeru, Ishmael, Sheariah,
Obadiah, and Hanan. These were the
sons of Azel.

The Death of King Saul

10 Now the Philistines attacked Israel,
and the men of Israel fled before
them. Many were slaughtered on the slopes
of Mount Gilboa. [2]The Philistines closed
in on Saul and his sons, and they killed
three of his sons—Jonathan, Abinadab, and
Malkishua. [3]The fighting grew very fierce
around Saul, and the Philistine archers
caught up with him and wounded him.

[4]Saul groaned to his armor bearer, "Take
your sword and kill me before these pagan
Philistines come to taunt and torture me."

But his armor bearer was afraid and would
not do it. So Saul took his own sword and fell
on it. [5]When his armor bearer realized that
Saul was dead, he fell on his own sword and
died. [6]So Saul and his three sons died there
together, bringing his dynasty to an end.

[7]When all the Israelites in the Jezreel
Valley saw that their army had fled and that
Saul and his sons were dead, they abandoned their towns and fled. So the Philistines moved in and occupied their towns.

[8]The next day, when the Philistines went
out to strip the dead, they found the bodies
of Saul and his sons on Mount Gilboa. [9]So
they stripped off Saul's armor and cut off
his head. Then they proclaimed the good
news of Saul's death before their idols and
to the people throughout the land of Philistia. [10]They placed his armor in the temple
of their gods, and they fastened his head to
the temple of Dagon.

[11]But when everyone in Jabesh-gilead
heard about everything the Philistines
had done to Saul, [12]all their mighty warriors brought the bodies of Saul and his
sons back to Jabesh. Then they buried their
bones beneath the great tree at Jabesh, and
they fasted for seven days.

[13]So Saul died because he was unfaithful
to the LORD. He failed to obey the LORD's
command, and he even consulted a medium
[14]instead of asking the LORD for guidance.
So the LORD killed him and turned the
kingdom over to David son of Jesse.

David Becomes King of All Israel

11 Then all Israel gathered before David
at Hebron and told him, "We are your
own flesh and blood. [2]In the past,* even
when Saul was king, you were the one who
really led the forces of Israel. And the LORD
your God told you, 'You will be the shepherd of my people Israel. You will be the
leader of my people Israel.'"

[3]So there at Hebron, David made a covenant before the LORD with all the elders of
Israel. And they anointed him king of Israel,
just as the LORD had promised through
Samuel.

David Captures Jerusalem

[4]Then David and all Israel went to Jerusalem (or Jebus, as it used to be called), where
the Jebusites, the original inhabitants of
the land, were living. [5]The people of Jebus
taunted David, saying, "You'll never get in
here!" But David captured the fortress of
Zion, which is now called the City of David.

[6]David had said to his troops, "Whoever
is first to attack the Jebusites will become
the commander of my armies!" And Joab,
the son of David's sister Zeruiah, was first
to attack, so he became the commander of
David's armies.

[7]David made the fortress his home, and
that is why it is called the City of David. [8]He

▸ **10:1-14** *See* ***King Saul****, page 318.* **11:1** *See* ***King David****, page 323.* **11:4** *See* ***Jerusalem****, page 347.*

extended the city from the supporting terraces* to the surrounding area, while Joab
rebuilt the rest of Jerusalem. 9And David
became more and more powerful, because
the LORD of Heaven's Armies was with him.

David's Mightiest Warriors

10These are the leaders of David's mighty
warriors. Together with all Israel, they
decided to make David their king, just as
the LORD had promised concerning Israel.
11Here is the record of David's mightiest
warriors: The first was Jashobeam the Hacmonite, who was leader of the Three—the
mightiest warriors among David's men.* He
once used his spear to kill 300 enemy warriors in a single battle.
12Next in rank among the Three was
Eleazar son of Dodai,* a descendant of
Ahoah. 13He was with David when the Philistines gathered for battle at Pas-dammim
and attacked the Israelites in a field full of
barley. The Israelite army fled, 14but Eleazar
and David* held their ground in the middle
of the field and beat back the Philistines.
So the LORD saved them by giving them a
great victory.
15Once when David was at the rock near
the cave of Adullam, the Philistine army
was camped in the valley of Rephaim. The
Three (who were among the Thirty—an
elite group among David's fighting men)
went down to meet him there. 16David was
staying in the stronghold at the time, and
a Philistine detachment had occupied the
town of Bethlehem.
17David remarked longingly to his men,
"Oh, how I would love some of that good
water from the well by the gate in Bethlehem." 18So the Three broke through the
Philistine lines, drew some water from the
well by the gate in Bethlehem, and brought
it back to David. But David refused to drink
it. Instead, he poured it out as an offering to
the LORD. 19"God forbid that I should drink
this!" he exclaimed. "This water is as precious as the blood of these men* who risked
their lives to bring it to me." So David did
not drink it. These are examples of the
exploits of the Three.

David's Thirty Mighty Men

20Abishai, the brother of Joab, was the leader
of the Thirty.* He once used his spear to kill
300 enemy warriors in a single battle. It was
by such feats that he became as famous as
the Three. 21Abishai was the most famous
of the Thirty and was their commander,
though he was not one of the Three.
22There was also Benaiah son of Jehoiada, a valiant warrior from Kabzeel. He did

9:41 As in Syriac version and Latin Vulgate (see also 8:35); Hebrew lacks *and Ahaz.* **9:42** As in some Hebrew manuscripts and Greek version (see also 8:36); Hebrew reads *Jarah.* **11:2** Or *For some time.* **11:8** Hebrew *the millo.* The meaning of the Hebrew is uncertain. **11:11** As in some Greek manuscripts (see also 2 Sam 23:8); Hebrew reads *leader of the Thirty,* or *leader of the captains.* **11:12** As in parallel text at 2 Sam 23:9 (see also 1 Chr 27:4); Hebrew reads *Dodo,* a variant spelling of Dodai. **11:14** Hebrew *they.* **11:19** Hebrew *Shall I drink the lifeblood of these men?* **11:20** As in Syriac version; Hebrew reads *the Three;* also in 11:21.

Serving one another

First Chronicles 11 and 12 give us an insight into the character of some of David's fellow leaders—in particular, the thirty mighty warriors who had served him during those waiting years between his being anointed by Samuel and his finally becoming king (covered in 1 Samuel but not in 1 Chronicles). While they were all gifted and courageous individuals—"brave and experienced warriors . . . expert with both shield and spear" (1 Chronicles 12:8)—their sole desire was not to push themselves forward but to serve David and the call they recognized that God had put on his life. Hence they "decided to make David their king" (11:10). Their character comes out in a Spirit-anointed song sung by Amasai, leader of the Thirty: "We are yours, David! We are on your side, son of Jesse. Peace and prosperity be with you, and success to all who help you, for your God is the one who helps you" (12:18). This should be the mark of all who are called to work alongside God's appointed leader: a total commitment to the leader they are called to work with and a desire for that leader's success rather than their own. Without this we are in danger of becoming another Absalom (see *The Absalom spirit*, page 358).

many heroic deeds, which included killing
two champions* of Moab. Another time, on
a snowy day, he chased a lion down into a
pit and killed it. 23 Once, armed only with
a club, he killed an Egyptian warrior who
was 7½ feet* tall and who was armed with a
spear as thick as a weaver's beam. Benaiah
wrenched the spear from the Egyptian's
hand and killed him with it. 24 Deeds like
these made Benaiah as famous as the three
mightiest warriors. 25 He was more honored
than the other members of the Thirty,
though he was not one of the Three. And
David made him captain of his bodyguard.
26 David's mighty warriors also included:

Asahel, Joab's brother;
Elhanan son of Dodo from Bethlehem;
27 Shammah from Harod;*
Helez from Pelon;
28 Ira son of Ikkesh from Tekoa;
Abiezer from Anathoth;
29 Sibbecai from Hushah;
Zalmon* from Ahoah;
30 Maharai from Netophah;
Heled son of Baanah from Netophah;
31 Ithai son of Ribai from Gibeah (in the land of Benjamin);
Benaiah from Pirathon;
32 Hurai from near Nahale-gaash*;
Abi-albon* from Arabah;
33 Azmaveth from Bahurim*;
Eliahba from Shaalbon;
34 the sons of Jashen* from Gizon;
Jonathan son of Shagee from Harar;
35 Ahiam son of Sharar* from Harar;
Eliphal son of Ur;
36 Hepher from Mekerah;
Ahijah from Pelon;
37 Hezro from Carmel;
Paarai* son of Ezbai;
38 Joel, the brother of Nathan;
Mibhar son of Hagri;
39 Zelek from Ammon;
Naharai from Beeroth, the armor bearer of Joab son of Zeruiah;
40 Ira from Jattir;
Gareb from Jattir;
41 Uriah the Hittite;
Zabad son of Ahlai;
42 Adina son of Shiza, the Reubenite leader who had thirty men with him;
43 Hanan son of Maacah;
Joshaphat from Mithna;
44 Uzzia from Ashtaroth;
Shama and Jeiel, the sons of Hotham, from Aroer;
45 Jediael son of Shimri;
Joha, his brother, from Tiz;
46 Eliel from Mahavah;
Jeribai and Joshaviah, the sons of Elnaam;
Ithmah from Moab;
47 Eliel and Obed;
Jaasiel from Zobah.*

Warriors Join David's Army

12 The following men joined David at
Ziklag while he was hiding from Saul
son of Kish. They were among the warriors
who fought beside David in battle. 2 All of
them were expert archers, and they could
shoot arrows or sling stones with their left
hand as well as their right. They were all
relatives of Saul from the tribe of Benjamin.
3 Their leader was Ahiezer son of Shemaah
from Gibeah; his brother Joash was second-
in-command. These were the other warriors:

Jeziel and Pelet, sons of Azmaveth;
Beracah;
Jehu from Anathoth;
4 Ishmaiah from Gibeon, a famous warrior and leader among the Thirty;
*Jeremiah, Jahaziel, Johanan, and Jozabad from Gederah;
5 Eluzai, Jerimoth, Bealiah, Shemariah, and Shephatiah from Haruph;
6 Elkanah, Isshiah, Azarel, Joezer, and Jashobeam, who were Korahites;
7 Joelah and Zebadiah, sons of Jeroham from Gedor.

8 Some brave and experienced warriors
from the tribe of Gad also defected to David
while he was at the stronghold in the wilderness. They were expert with both shield and
spear, as fierce as lions and as swift as deer
on the mountains.

9 Ezer was their leader.
Obadiah was second.
Eliab was third.
10 Mishmannah was fourth.
Jeremiah was fifth.
11 Attai was sixth.
Eliel was seventh.
12 Johanan was eighth.
Elzabad was ninth.
13 Jeremiah was tenth.
Macbannai was eleventh.

14These warriors from Gad were army commanders. The weakest among them could take on a hundred regular troops, and the strongest could take on a thousand! 15These were the men who crossed the Jordan River during its seasonal flooding at the beginning of the year and drove out all the people living in the lowlands on both the east and west banks.

16Others from Benjamin and Judah came to David at the stronghold. 17David went out to meet them and said, "If you have come in peace to help me, we are friends. But if you have come to betray me to my enemies when I am innocent, then may the God of our ancestors see it and punish you."

18Then the Spirit came upon Amasai, the leader of the Thirty, and he said,

"We are yours, David!
 We are on your side, son of Jesse.
Peace and prosperity be with you,
 and success to all who help you,
 for your God is the one who helps you."

So David let them join him, and he made them officers over his troops.

19Some men from Manasseh defected from the Israelite army and joined David when he set out with the Philistines to fight against Saul. But as it turned out, the Philistine rulers refused to let David and his men go with them. After much discussion, they sent them back, for they said, "It will cost us our heads if David switches loyalties to Saul and turns against us."

20Here is a list of the men from Manasseh who defected to David as he was returning to Ziklag: Adnah, Jozabad, Jediael, Michael, Jozabad, Elihu, and Zillethai. Each commanded 1,000 troops from the tribe of Manasseh. 21They helped David chase down bands of raiders, for they were all brave and able warriors who became commanders in his army. 22Day after day more men joined David until he had a great army, like the army of God.

23These are the numbers of armed warriors who joined David at Hebron. They were all eager to see David become king instead of Saul, just as the LORD had promised.

24From the tribe of Judah, there were 6,800 warriors armed with shields and spears.
25From the tribe of Simeon, there were 7,100 brave warriors.
26From the tribe of Levi, there were 4,600 warriors. 27This included Jehoiada, leader of the family of Aaron, who had 3,700 under his command. 28This also included Zadok, a brave young warrior, with 22 members of his family who were all officers.
29From the tribe of Benjamin, Saul's relatives, there were 3,000 warriors. Most of the men from Benjamin had remained loyal to Saul until this time.
30From the tribe of Ephraim, there were 20,800 brave warriors, each highly respected in his own clan.
31From the half-tribe of Manasseh west of the Jordan, 18,000 men were designated by name to help David become king.
32From the tribe of Issachar, there were 200 leaders of the tribe with their relatives. All these men understood the signs of the times and knew the best course for Israel to take.
33From the tribe of Zebulun, there were 50,000 skilled warriors. They were fully armed and prepared for battle and completely loyal to David.
34From the tribe of Naphtali, there were 1,000 officers and 37,000 warriors armed with shields and spears.
35From the tribe of Dan, there were 28,600 warriors, all prepared for battle.
36From the tribe of Asher, there were 40,000 trained warriors, all prepared for battle.
37From the east side of the Jordan River—where the tribes of Reuben and Gad and the half-tribe of Manasseh lived—there were 120,000 troops armed with every kind of weapon.

38All these men came in battle array to Hebron with the single purpose of making David the king over all Israel. In fact, everyone in Israel agreed that David should be their king. 39They feasted and drank with David for three days, for preparations had been made by their relatives for their arrival. 40And people from as far away as

11:22 Or *two sons of Ariel.* **11:23** Hebrew *5 cubits* [2.3 meters]. **11:27** As in parallel text at 2 Sam 23:25; Hebrew reads *Shammoth from Haror.* **11:29** As in parallel text at 2 Sam 23:28; Hebrew reads *Ilai.* **11:32a** Or *from the ravines of Gaash.* **11:32b** As in parallel text at 2 Sam 23:31; Hebrew reads *Abiel.* **11:33** As in parallel text at 2 Sam 23:31; Hebrew reads *Baharum.* **11:34** As in parallel text at 2 Sam 23:32; Hebrew reads *sons of Hashem.* **11:35** As in parallel text at 2 Sam 23:33; Hebrew reads *son of Sacar.* **11:37** As in parallel text at 2 Sam 23:35; Hebrew reads *Naarai.* **11:47** Or *the Mezobaite.* **12:4** Verses 12:4b-40 are numbered 12:5-41 in Hebrew text.

Issachar, Zebulun, and Naphtali brought
food on donkeys, camels, mules, and oxen.
Vast supplies of flour, fig cakes, clusters of
raisins, wine, olive oil, cattle, sheep, and
goats were brought to the celebration. There
was great joy throughout the land of Israel.

David Attempts to Move the Ark

13 David consulted with all his officials, including the generals and
captains of his army.* [2]Then he addressed
the entire assembly of Israel as follows: "If
you approve and if it is the will of the LORD
our God, let us send messages to all the
Israelites throughout the land, including
the priests and Levites in their towns and
pasturelands. Let us invite them to come
and join us. [3]It is time to bring back the Ark
of our God, for we neglected it during the
reign of Saul."
[4]The whole assembly agreed to this, for
the people could see it was the right thing
to do. [5]So David summoned all Israel, from
the Shihor Brook of Egypt in the south all
the way to the town of Lebo-hamath in the
north, to join in bringing the Ark of God
from Kiriath-jearim. [6]Then David and all
Israel went to Baalah of Judah (also called
Kiriath-jearim) to bring back the Ark of God,
which bears the name* of the LORD who is
enthroned between the cherubim. [7]They
placed the Ark of God on a new cart and
brought it from Abinadab's house. Uzzah
and Ahio were guiding the cart. [8]David and
all Israel were celebrating before God with
all their might, singing songs and playing all
kinds of musical instruments—lyres, harps,
tambourines, cymbals, and trumpets.
[9]But when they arrived at the threshing
floor of Nacon,* the oxen stumbled, and
Uzzah reached out his hand to steady the
Ark. [10]Then the LORD's anger was aroused
against Uzzah, and he struck him dead
because he had laid his hand on the Ark.
So Uzzah died there in the presence of God.
[11]David was angry because the LORD's
anger had burst out against Uzzah. He
named that place Perez-uzzah (which
means "to burst out against Uzzah"), as it
is still called today.
[12]David was now afraid of God, and he
asked, "How can I ever bring the Ark of God
back into my care?" [13]So David did not move
the Ark into the City of David. Instead, he
took it to the house of Obed-edom of Gath.
[14]The Ark of God remained there in Obed-
edom's house for three months, and the
LORD blessed the household of Obed-edom
and everything he owned.

David's Palace and Family

14 Then King Hiram of Tyre sent messengers to David, along with cedar
timber, and stonemasons and carpenters to
build him a palace. [2]And David realized that
the LORD had confirmed him as king over

Uzzah

Uzzah was one of Abinadab's two sons who guided the cart on which the Ark of the Covenant was placed when it was brought to Jerusalem. When the cart jolted, Uzzah instinctively reached out to steady the Ark and was instantly struck dead for touching it (1 Chronicles 13:9-10). To us this seems so unfair. After all, Uzzah no doubt had good intentions. But good intentions are no substitute for obedience. God had made it clear in the Law that the Ark was to be carried on poles, and only by the Levites (Exodus 25:12-14; Numbers 4:5-6, 15). Since the Ark had spent twenty years in Abinadab's house after its return from the Philistines (1 Samuel 7:1-2), perhaps Uzzah had become overfamiliar with it and so forgot what God had said. Still today it is all too easy to become overfamiliar with spiritual things and take them for granted rather than appreciate them—privileges like being able to pray or read God's word, which we can easily neglect in our busyness; or being able to worship with others each week, which we can skip if something else comes along. When this overfamiliarity sets in, we might find ourselves becoming somewhat cynical about spiritual things. At such times we need to remember the lesson of Uzzah.

Israel and had greatly blessed his kingdom for the sake of his people Israel.

[3]Then David married more wives in Jerusalem, and they had more sons and daughters. [4]These are the names of David's sons who were born in Jerusalem: Shammua, Shobab, Nathan, Solomon, [5]Ibhar, Elishua, Elpelet, [6]Nogah, Nepheg, Japhia, [7]Elishama, Eliada,* and Eliphelet.

David Conquers the Philistines

[8]When the Philistines heard that David had been anointed king over all Israel, they mobilized all their forces to capture him. But David was told they were coming, so he marched out to meet them. [9]The Philistines arrived and made a raid in the valley of Rephaim. [10]So David asked God, "Should I go out to fight the Philistines? Will you hand them over to me?"

The LORD replied, "Yes, go ahead. I will hand them over to you."

[11]So David and his troops went up to Baal-perazim and defeated the Philistines there. "God did it!" David exclaimed. "He used me to burst through my enemies like a raging flood!" So they named that place Baal-perazim (which means "the Lord who bursts through"). [12]The Philistines had abandoned their gods there, so David gave orders to burn them.

[13]But after a while the Philistines returned and raided the valley again. [14]And once again David asked God what to do. "Do not attack them straight on," God replied. "Instead, circle around behind and attack them near the poplar* trees. [15]When you hear a sound like marching feet in the tops of the poplar trees, go out and attack! That will be the signal that God is moving ahead of you to strike down the Philistine army." [16]So David did what God commanded, and they struck down the Philistine army all the way from Gibeon to Gezer.

[17]So David's fame spread everywhere, and the LORD caused all the nations to fear David.

Preparing to Move the Ark

15 David now built several buildings for himself in the City of David. He also prepared a place for the Ark of God and set up a special tent for it. [2]Then he commanded, "No one except the Levites may carry the Ark of God. The LORD has chosen them to carry the Ark of the LORD and to serve him forever."

[3]Then David summoned all Israel to Jerusalem to bring the Ark of the LORD to the place he had prepared for it. [4]This is the number of the descendants of Aaron (the priests) and the Levites who were called together:

[5]From the clan of Kohath, 120, with Uriel as their leader.
[6]From the clan of Merari, 220, with Asaiah as their leader.
[7]From the clan of Gershon,* 130, with Joel as their leader.
[8]From the descendants of Elizaphan, 200, with Shemaiah as their leader.
[9]From the descendants of Hebron, 80, with Eliel as their leader.
[10]From the descendants of Uzziel, 112, with Amminadab as their leader.

[11]Then David summoned the priests, Zadok and Abiathar, and these Levite leaders: Uriel, Asaiah, Joel, Shemaiah, Eliel, and Amminadab. [12]He said to them, "You are the leaders of the Levite families. You must purify yourselves and all your fellow Levites, so you can bring the Ark of the LORD, the God of Israel, to the place I have prepared for it. [13]Because you Levites did not carry the Ark the first time, the anger of the LORD our God burst out against us. We failed to ask God how to move it properly." [14]So the priests and the Levites purified themselves in order to bring the Ark of the LORD, the God of Israel, to Jerusalem. [15]Then the Levites carried the Ark of God on their shoulders with its carrying poles, just as the LORD had instructed Moses.

[16]David also ordered the Levite leaders to appoint a choir of Levites who were singers and musicians to sing joyful songs to the accompaniment of harps, lyres, and cymbals. [17]So the Levites appointed Heman son of Joel along with his fellow Levites: Asaph son of Berekiah, and Ethan son of Kushaiah from the clan of Merari. [18]The following men were chosen as their assistants: Zechariah, Jaaziel,* Shemiramoth, Jehiel, Unni, Eliab,

13:1 Hebrew *the commanders of thousands and of hundreds.* **13:6** Or *the Ark of God, where the Name is proclaimed—the name.* **13:9** As in parallel text at 2 Sam 6:6; Hebrew reads *Kidon.* **14:7** Hebrew *Beeliada,* a variant spelling of Eliada; compare 3:8 and parallel text at 2 Sam 5:16. **14:14** Or *aspen,* or *balsam;* also in 14:15. The exact identification of this tree is uncertain. **15:7** Hebrew *Gershom,* a variant spelling of Gershon. **15:18** As in several Hebrew manuscripts and Greek version (see also parallel lists in 15:20; 16:5); Masoretic Text reads *Zechariah ben Jaaziel.*

Benaiah, Maaseiah, Mattithiah, Eliphelehu,
Mikneiah, and the gatekeepers—Obed-
edom and Jeiel.
19 The musicians Heman, Asaph, and
Ethan were chosen to sound the bronze
cymbals. 20 Zechariah, Aziel, Shemiramoth,
Jehiel, Unni, Eliab, Maaseiah, and Benaiah
were chosen to play the harps.* 21 Mattithiah,
Eliphelehu, Mikneiah, Obed-edom, Jeiel,
and Azaziah were chosen to play the lyres.*
22 Kenaniah, the head Levite, was chosen as
the choir leader because of his skill.
23 Berekiah and Elkanah were chosen to
guard* the Ark. 24 Shebaniah, Joshaphat,
Nethanel, Amasai, Zechariah, Benaiah, and
Eliezer—all of whom were priests—were
chosen to blow the trumpets as they marched
in front of the Ark of God. Obed-edom and
Jehiah were chosen to guard the Ark.

Moving the Ark to Jerusalem

25 Then David and the elders of Israel and
the generals of the army* went to the house
of Obed-edom to bring the Ark of the LORD's
Covenant up to Jerusalem with a great celebration. 26 And because God was clearly
helping the Levites as they carried the Ark
of the LORD's Covenant, they sacrificed
seven bulls and seven rams.
27 David was dressed in a robe of fine
linen, as were all the Levites who carried
the Ark, and also the singers, and Kenaniah
the choir leader. David was also wearing a
priestly garment.* 28 So all Israel brought up
the Ark of the LORD's Covenant with shouts
of joy, the blowing of rams' horns and trumpets, the crashing of cymbals, and loud
playing on harps and lyres.
29 But as the Ark of the LORD's Covenant
entered the City of David, Michal, the
daughter of Saul, looked down from her
window. When she saw King David skip-
ping about and laughing with joy, she was
filled with contempt for him.

16 They brought the Ark of God and
placed it inside the special tent David
had prepared for it. And they presented
burnt offerings and peace offerings to God.
2 When he had finished his sacrifices, David
blessed the people in the name of the LORD.
3 Then he gave to every man and woman in
all Israel a loaf of bread, a cake of dates,*
and a cake of raisins.
4 David appointed the following Levites to
lead the people in worship before the Ark of
the LORD—to invoke his blessings, to give
thanks, and to praise the LORD, the God
of Israel. 5 Asaph, the leader of this group,
sounded the cymbals. Second to him was
Zechariah, followed by Jeiel, Shemiramoth,
Jehiel, Mattithiah, Eliab, Benaiah, Obed-
edom, and Jeiel. They played the harps and
lyres. 6 The priests, Benaiah and Jahaziel,
played the trumpets regularly before the
Ark of God's Covenant.

David's Song of Praise

7 On that day David gave to Asaph and his
fellow Levites this song of thanksgiving to
the LORD:

8 Give thanks to the LORD and proclaim
his greatness.
Let the whole world know what he
has done.
9 Sing to him; yes, sing his praises.
Tell everyone about his wonderful
deeds.
10 Exult in his holy name;
rejoice, you who worship the LORD.
11 Search for the LORD and for his strength;
continually seek him.
12 Remember the wonders he has
performed,
his miracles, and the rulings he has
given,
13 you children of his servant Israel,
you descendants of Jacob, his chosen
ones.
14 He is the LORD our God.
His justice is seen throughout the
land.
15 Remember his covenant forever—
the commitment he made to a
thousand generations.
16 This is the covenant he made with
Abraham
and the oath he swore to Isaac.
17 He confirmed it to Jacob as a decree,
and to the people of Israel as a
never-ending covenant:
18 "I will give you the land of Canaan
as your special possession."
19 He said this when you were few in
number,
a tiny group of strangers in Canaan.
20 They wandered from nation to nation,
from one kingdom to another.

21 Yet he did not let anyone oppress them.
He warned kings on their behalf:
22 "Do not touch my chosen people,
and do not hurt my prophets."

23 Let the whole earth sing to the LORD!
Each day proclaim the good news that he saves.
24 Publish his glorious deeds among the nations.
Tell everyone about the amazing things he does.
25 Great is the LORD! He is most worthy of praise!
He is to be feared above all gods.
26 The gods of other nations are mere idols,
but the LORD made the heavens!
27 Honor and majesty surround him;
strength and joy fill his dwelling.

28 O nations of the world, recognize the LORD,
recognize that the LORD is glorious and strong.
29 Give to the LORD the glory he deserves!
Bring your offering and come into his presence.
Worship the LORD in all his holy splendor.
30 Let all the earth tremble before him.
The world stands firm and cannot be shaken.

31 Let the heavens be glad, and the earth rejoice!
Tell all the nations, "The LORD reigns!"
32 Let the sea and everything in it shout his praise!
Let the fields and their crops burst out with joy!
33 Let the trees of the forest sing for joy before the LORD,
for he is coming to judge the earth.

34 Give thanks to the LORD, for he is good!
His faithful love endures forever.
35 Cry out, "Save us, O God of our salvation!
Gather and rescue us from among the nations,
so we can thank your holy name
and rejoice and praise you."

36 Praise the LORD, the God of Israel,
who lives from everlasting to everlasting!

And all the people shouted "Amen!" and praised the LORD.

Worship at Jerusalem and Gibeon

37 David arranged for Asaph and his fellow
Levites to serve regularly before the Ark
of the LORD's Covenant, doing whatever
needed to be done each day. 38 This group
included Obed-edom (son of Jeduthun),
Hosah, and sixty-eight other Levites as
gatekeepers.
39 Meanwhile, David stationed Zadok the
priest and his fellow priests at the Tabernacle of the LORD at the place of worship
in Gibeon, where they continued to minister before the LORD. 40 They sacrificed
the regular burnt offerings to the LORD
each morning and evening on the altar set
aside for that purpose, obeying everything
written in the Law of the LORD, as he had
commanded Israel. 41 David also appointed
Heman, Jeduthun, and the others chosen by
name to give thanks to the LORD, for "his
faithful love endures forever." 42 They used
their trumpets, cymbals, and other instruments to accompany their songs of praise
to God.* And the sons of Jeduthun were appointed as gatekeepers.
43 Then all the people returned to their
homes, and David turned and went home
to bless his own family.

The LORD's Covenant Promise to David

17 When David was settled in his palace,
he summoned Nathan the prophet.
"Look," David said, "I am living in a beautiful cedar palace,* but the Ark of the LORD's
Covenant is out there under a tent!"
2 Nathan replied to David, "Do whatever
you have in mind, for God is with you."
3 But that same night God said to Nathan,

4 "Go and tell my servant David, 'This is
what the LORD has declared: You are not
the one to build a house for me to live in.
5 I have never lived in a house, from the
day I brought the Israelites out of Egypt
until this very day. My home has always
been a tent, moving from one place to
another in a Tabernacle. 6 Yet no matter
where I have gone with the Israelites,

15:20 Hebrew adds *according to Alamoth,* which is probably a musical term. The meaning of the Hebrew is uncertain. **15:21** Hebrew adds *according to the Sheminith,* which is probably a musical term. The meaning of the Hebrew is uncertain. **15:23** Hebrew *chosen as gatekeepers for;* also in 15:24. **15:25** Hebrew *the commanders of thousands.* **15:27** Hebrew *a linen ephod.* **16:3** Or *a portion of meat.* The meaning of the Hebrew is uncertain. **16:42** Or *to accompany the sacred music;* or *to accompany singing to God.* **17:1** Hebrew *a house of cedar.*

I have never once complained to Israel's
leaders, the shepherds of my people.
I have never asked them, "Why haven't
you built me a beautiful cedar house?"'
7"Now go and say to my servant
David, 'This is what the LORD of
Heaven's Armies has declared: I took
you from tending sheep in the pasture
and selected you to be the leader of my
people Israel. 8I have been with you
wherever you have gone, and I have
destroyed all your enemies before your
eyes. Now I will make your name as
famous as anyone who has ever lived
on the earth! 9And I will provide a
homeland for my people Israel, planting
them in a secure place where they will
never be disturbed. Evil nations won't
oppress them as they've done in the
past, 10starting from the time I appointed
judges to rule my people Israel. And
I will defeat all your enemies.
"'Furthermore, I declare that the LORD
will build a house for you—a dynasty of
kings! 11For when you die and join your
ancestors, I will raise up one of your
descendants, one of your sons, and I will
make his kingdom strong. 12He is the one
who will build a house—a temple—for
me. And I will secure his throne forever.
13I will be his father, and he will be my
son. I will never take my favor from him
as I took it from the one who ruled before
you. 14I will confirm him as king over my
house and my kingdom for all time, and
his throne will be secure forever.'"

15So Nathan went back to David and told
him everything the LORD had said in this
vision.

David's Prayer of Thanks

16Then King David went in and sat before
the LORD and prayed,

"Who am I, O LORD God, and what is
my family, that you have brought me
this far? 17And now, O God, in addition
to everything else, you speak of giving
your servant a lasting dynasty! You
speak as though I were someone very
great,* O LORD God!
18"What more can I say to you about
the way you have honored me? You
know what your servant is really like.
19For the sake of your servant, O LORD,
and according to your will, you have
done all these great things and have
made them known.
20"O LORD, there is no one like you.
We have never even heard of another
God like you! 21What other nation on
earth is like your people Israel? What
other nation, O God, have you redeemed
from slavery to be your own people? You

The Davidic covenant

David loved God deeply and longed to build a temple worthy of him. But God did not allow him to do so because he had shed too much blood (1 Chronicles 22:7-8). Rather, he told him that it would be his son Solomon who would build the Temple. But God saw the good intention of David's heart, so he turned events around: David would not build a "house" for God—God would build a "house" for David, a house not of stones but of descendants, and a house that would last forever (17:12-14; see also 2 Samuel 7).

Humanly speaking, however, this did not happen. Israel lost its Davidic rulers when it was exiled to Babylon, and although the Israelites returned to the Promised Land, they never became an independent nation again under a king who was a descendant of David. It seemed as if God's promise had failed—until we consider Jesus Christ, whom the New Testament shows was both a member of the tribe of Judah and a direct descendant of King David. At his ascension, Jesus took up his rightful kingly throne, and he now reigns over the one people of God, Jew and Gentile, never to be replaced or removed, just as God promised.

▶ *See also **Covenant**, page 19; **The new covenant**, page 861.*

made a great name for yourself when
you redeemed your people from Egypt.
You performed awesome miracles and
drove out the nations that stood in their
way. 22 You chose Israel to be your very
own people forever, and you, O LORD,
became their God.

23 "And now, O LORD, I am your
servant; do as you have promised
concerning me and my family. May
it be a promise that will last forever.
24 And may your name be established
and honored forever so that everyone
will say, 'The LORD of Heaven's Armies,
the God of Israel, is Israel's God!' And
may the house of your servant David
continue before you forever.

25 "O my God, I have been bold
enough to pray to you because you have
revealed to your servant that you will
build a house for him—a dynasty of
kings! 26 For you are God, O LORD. And
you have promised these good things to
your servant. 27 And now, it has pleased
you to bless the house of your servant,
so that it will continue forever before
you. For when you grant a blessing,
O LORD, it is an eternal blessing!"

David's Military Victories

18 After this, David defeated and
subdued the Philistines by conquering Gath and its surrounding towns. 2 David
also conquered the land of Moab, and the
Moabites who were spared became David's
subjects and paid him tribute money.

3 David also destroyed the forces of Hadadezer, king of Zobah, as far as Hamath,*
when Hadadezer marched out to strengthen
his control along the Euphrates River.
4 David captured 1,000 chariots, 7,000 charioteers, and 20,000 foot soldiers. He crippled
all the chariot horses except enough for
100 chariots.

5 When Arameans from Damascus arrived
to help King Hadadezer, David killed 22,000
of them. 6 Then he placed several army garrisons* in Damascus, the Aramean capital,
and the Arameans became David's subjects
and paid him tribute money. So the LORD
made David victorious wherever he went.

7 David brought the gold shields of Hadadezer's officers to Jerusalem, 8 along with
a large amount of bronze from Hadadezer's
towns of Tebah* and Cun. Later Solomon
melted the bronze and molded it into the
great bronze basin called the Sea, the
pillars, and the various bronze articles used
at the Temple.

9 When King Toi* of Hamath heard that
David had destroyed the entire army of
King Hadadezer of Zobah, 10 he sent his son
Joram* to congratulate King David for his
successful campaign. Hadadezer and Toi
had been enemies and were often at war.
Joram presented David with many gifts of
gold, silver, and bronze.

11 King David dedicated all these gifts to
the LORD, along with the silver and gold
he had taken from the other nations—
from Edom, Moab, Ammon, Philistia, and
Amalek.

12 Abishai son of Zeruiah destroyed 18,000
Edomites in the Valley of Salt. 13 He placed
army garrisons in Edom, and all the Edomites became David's subjects. In fact, the
LORD made David victorious wherever he
went.

14 So David reigned over all Israel and did
what was just and right for all his people.
15 Joab son of Zeruiah was commander of
the army. Jehoshaphat son of Ahilud was
the royal historian. 16 Zadok son of Ahitub
and Ahimelech* son of Abiathar were the
priests. Seraiah* was the court secretary.
17 Benaiah son of Jehoiada was captain of
the king's bodyguard.* And David's sons
served as the king's chief assistants.

David Defeats the Ammonites

19 Some time after this, King Nahash
of the Ammonites died, and his son
Hanun* became king. 2 David said, "I am
going to show loyalty to Hanun because his
father, Nahash, was always loyal to me." So
David sent messengers to express sympathy
to Hanun about his father's death.

But when David's ambassadors arrived
in the land of Ammon, 3 the Ammonite
commanders said to Hanun, "Do you really
think these men are coming here to honor

17:17 The meaning of the Hebrew is uncertain. **18:3** The meaning of the Hebrew is uncertain. **18:6** As in Greek version and Latin Vulgate (see also 2 Sam 8:6); Hebrew lacks *several army garrisons.* **18:8** Hebrew reads *Tibhath,* a variant spelling of Tebah; compare parallel text at 2 Sam 8:8. **18:9** As in parallel text at 2 Sam 8:9; Hebrew reads *Tou;* also in 18:10. **18:10** As in parallel text at 2 Sam 8:10; Hebrew reads *Hadoram,* a variant spelling of Joram. **18:16a** As in some Hebrew manuscripts, Syriac version, and Latin Vulgate (see also 2 Sam 8:17); most Hebrew manuscripts read *Abimelech.* **18:16b** As in parallel text at 2 Sam 8:17; Hebrew reads *Shavsha.* **18:17** Hebrew *of the Kerethites and Pelethites.* **19:1** As in parallel text at 2 Sam 10:1; Hebrew lacks *Hanun.*

your father? No! David has sent them to
spy out the land so they can come in and
conquer it!" 4So Hanun seized David's ambassadors and shaved them, cut off their
robes at the buttocks, and sent them back
to David in shame.
5When David heard what had happened
to the men, he sent messengers to tell them,
"Stay at Jericho until your beards grow out,
and then come back." For they felt deep
shame because of their appearance.
6When the people of Ammon realized how
seriously they had angered David, Hanun
and the Ammonites sent 75,000 pounds* of
silver to hire chariots and charioteers from
Aram-naharaim, Aram-maacah, and Zobah.
7They also hired 32,000 chariots and secured
the support of the king of Maacah and his
army. These forces camped at Medeba,
where they were joined by the Ammonite
troops that Hanun had recruited from his
own towns. 8When David heard about this,
he sent Joab and all his warriors to fight
them. 9The Ammonite troops came out and
drew up their battle lines at the entrance of
the city, while the other kings positioned
themselves to fight in the open fields.
10When Joab saw that he would have to
fight on both the front and the rear, he chose
some of Israel's elite troops and placed
them under his personal command to fight
the Arameans in the fields. 11He left the
rest of the army under the command of his
brother Abishai, who was to attack the Ammonites. 12"If the Arameans are too strong
for me, then come over and help me," Joab
told his brother. "And if the Ammonites are
too strong for you, I will help you. 13Be courageous! Let us fight bravely for our people
and the cities of our God. May the LORD's
will be done."
14When Joab and his troops attacked,
the Arameans began to run away. 15And
when the Ammonites saw the Arameans
running, they also ran from Abishai and
retreated into the city. Then Joab returned
to Jerusalem.
16The Arameans now realized that they
were no match for Israel, so they sent
messengers and summoned additional
Aramean troops from the other side of the
Euphrates River.* These troops were under
the command of Shobach,* the commander
of Hadadezer's forces.
17When David heard what was happening, he mobilized all Israel, crossed the
Jordan River, and positioned his troops in
battle formation. Then David engaged the
Arameans in battle, and they fought against
him. 18But again the Arameans fled from the
Israelites. This time David's forces killed
7,000 charioteers and 40,000 foot soldiers,
including Shobach, the commander of their
army. 19When Hadadezer's allies saw that
they had been defeated by Israel, they surrendered to David and became his subjects.
After that, the Arameans were no longer
willing to help the Ammonites.

David Captures Rabbah

20 In the spring of the year,* when
kings normally go out to war, Joab
led the Israelite army in successful attacks
against the land of the Ammonites. In the
process he laid siege to the city of Rabbah,
attacking and destroying it. However, David
stayed behind in Jerusalem.
2Then David went to Rabbah and removed
the crown from the king's head,* and it was
placed on his own head. The crown was
made of gold and set with gems, and he
found that it weighed seventy-five pounds.*
David took a vast amount of plunder from
the city. 3He also made slaves of the people
of Rabbah and forced them to labor with
saws, iron picks, and iron axes.* That is
how David dealt with the people of all the
Ammonite towns. Then David and all the
army returned to Jerusalem.

Battles against Philistine Giants

4After this, war broke out with the Philistines at Gezer. As they fought, Sibbecai
from Hushah killed Saph,* a descendant
of the giants,* and so the Philistines were
subdued.
5During another battle with the Philistines,
Elhanan son of Jair killed Lahmi, the brother
of Goliath of Gath. The handle of Lahmi's
spear was as thick as a weaver's beam!
6In another battle with the Philistines at
Gath, they encountered a huge man with
six fingers on each hand and six toes on
each foot, twenty-four in all, who was also

▸ **20:4** *See* ***The Philistines****, page 310.*

a descendant of the giants. [7]But when he
defied and taunted Israel, he was killed by
Jonathan, the son of David's brother Shimea.
[8]These Philistines were descendants of
the giants of Gath, but David and his warriors killed them.

David Takes a Census

21 Satan rose up against Israel and
caused David to take a census of the
people of Israel. [2]So David said to Joab and
the commanders of the army, "Take a census
of all the people of Israel—from Beersheba
in the south to Dan in the north—and bring
me a report so I may know how many there
are."
[3]But Joab replied, "May the LORD increase
the number of his people a hundred times
over! But why, my lord the king, do you
want to do this? Are they not all your servants? Why must you cause Israel to sin?"
[4]But the king insisted that they take the
census, so Joab traveled throughout all
Israel to count the people. Then he returned
to Jerusalem [5]and reported the number of
people to David. There were 1,100,000
warriors in all Israel who could handle a
sword, and 470,000 in Judah. [6]But Joab did
not include the tribes of Levi and Benjamin
in the census because he was so distressed
at what the king had made him do.

Judgment for David's Sin

[7]God was very displeased with the census,
and he punished Israel for it. [8]Then David
said to God, "I have sinned greatly by taking
this census. Please forgive my guilt for
doing this foolish thing."
[9]Then the LORD spoke to Gad, David's
seer. This was the message: [10]"Go and say
to David, 'This is what the LORD says: I will
give you three choices. Choose one of these
punishments, and I will inflict it on you.'"
[11]So Gad came to David and said, "These
are the choices the LORD has given you.
[12]You may choose three years of famine,
three months of destruction by the sword of
your enemies, or three days of severe plague
as the angel of the LORD brings devastation
throughout the land of Israel. Decide what
answer I should give the LORD who sent me."
[13]"I'm in a desperate situation!" David
replied to Gad. "But let me fall into the
hands of the LORD, for his mercy is very
great. Do not let me fall into human hands."
[14]So the LORD sent a plague upon Israel,
and 70,000 people died as a result. [15]And God
sent an angel to destroy Jerusalem. But just
as the angel was preparing to destroy it, the
LORD relented and said to the death angel,
"Stop! That is enough!" At that moment
the angel of the LORD was standing by the
threshing floor of Araunah* the Jebusite.
[16]David looked up and saw the angel of the
LORD standing between heaven and earth
with his sword drawn, reaching out over Jerusalem. So David and the leaders of Israel
put on burlap to show their deep distress
and fell face down on the ground. [17]And
David said to God, "I am the one who called
for the census! I am the one who has sinned
and done wrong! But these people are as
innocent as sheep—what have they done?
O LORD my God, let your anger fall against
me and my family, but do not destroy your
people."

David Builds an Altar

[18]Then the angel of the LORD told Gad
to instruct David to go up and build an
altar to the LORD on the threshing floor of
Araunah the Jebusite. [19]So David went up
to do what the LORD had commanded him
through Gad. [20]Araunah, who was busy
threshing wheat at the time, turned and
saw the angel there. His four sons, who
were with him, ran away and hid. [21]When
Araunah saw David approaching, he left
his threshing floor and bowed before David
with his face to the ground.
[22]David said to Araunah, "Let me buy this
threshing floor from you at its full price.
Then I will build an altar to the LORD there,
so that he will stop the plague."
[23]"Take it, my lord the king, and use it as

19:6 Hebrew *1,000 talents* [34,000 kilograms]. **19:16a** Hebrew *the river.* **19:16b** As in parallel text at 2 Sam 10:16; Hebrew reads *Shophach;* also in 19:18. **20:1** Hebrew *At the turn of the year.* The first day of the year in the ancient Hebrew lunar calendar occurred in March or April. **20:2a** Or *from the head of Milcom* (as in Greek version and Latin Vulgate). Milcom, also called Molech, was the god of the Ammonites. **20:2b** Hebrew *1 talent* [34 kilograms]. **20:3** As in parallel text at 2 Sam 12:31; Hebrew reads *and cut them with saws, iron picks, and saws.* **20:4a** As in parallel text at 2 Sam 21:18; Hebrew reads *Sippai.* **20:4b** Hebrew *descendant of the Rephaites;* also in 20:6, 8. **21:15** As in parallel text at 2 Sam 24:16; Hebrew reads *Ornan,* another name for Araunah; also in 21:18-28.

▸ **21:1** *See **Why was David wrong to take a census?**, page 371.*

you wish," Araunah said to David. "I will
give the oxen for the burnt offerings, and
the threshing boards for wood to build a fire
on the altar, and the wheat for the grain offering. I will give it all to you."
24But King David replied to Araunah,
"No, I insist on buying it for the full price.
I will not take what is yours and give it to
the LORD. I will not present burnt offerings
that have cost me nothing!" 25So David gave
Araunah 600 pieces of gold* in payment for
the threshing floor.
26David built an altar there to the LORD
and sacrificed burnt offerings and peace offerings. And when David prayed, the LORD
answered him by sending fire from heaven
to burn up the offering on the altar. 27Then
the LORD spoke to the angel, who put the
sword back into its sheath.
28When David saw that the LORD had
answered his prayer, he offered sacrifices
there at Araunah's threshing floor. 29At that
time the Tabernacle of the LORD and the
altar of burnt offering that Moses had made
in the wilderness were located at the place
of worship in Gibeon. 30But David was not
able to go there to inquire of God, because
he was terrified by the drawn sword of the
angel of the LORD.

22 Then David said, "This will be the
location for the Temple of the LORD
God and the place of the altar for Israel's
burnt offerings!"

Preparations for the Temple

2So David gave orders to call together the
foreigners living in Israel, and he assigned
them the task of preparing finished stone
for building the Temple of God. 3David provided large amounts of iron for the nails
that would be needed for the doors in the
gates and for the clamps, and he gave more
bronze than could be weighed. 4He also
provided innumerable cedar logs, for the
men of Tyre and Sidon had brought vast
amounts of cedar to David.
5David said, "My son Solomon is still young
and inexperienced. And since the Temple to
be built for the LORD must be a magnificent
structure, famous and glorious throughout
the world, I will begin making preparations
for it now." So David collected vast amounts
of building materials before his death.
6Then David sent for his son Solomon
and instructed him to build a Temple for the
LORD, the God of Israel. 7"My son, I wanted
to build a Temple to honor the name of the
LORD my God," David told him. 8"But the
LORD said to me, 'You have killed many men
in the battles you have fought. And since
you have shed so much blood in my sight,
you will not be the one to build a Temple
to honor my name. 9But you will have a son
who will be a man of peace. I will give him
peace with his enemies in all the surrounding lands. His name will be Solomon,* and I
will give peace and quiet to Israel during his
reign. 10He is the one who will build a Temple
to honor my name. He will be my son, and
I will be his father. And I will secure the
throne of his kingdom over Israel forever.'
11"Now, my son, may the LORD be with
you and give you success as you follow his
directions in building the Temple of the
LORD your God. 12And may the LORD give

David's preparations for building the Temple

God had prevented David from building the Temple (2 Samuel 7; 1 Chronicles 17), and here, in 1 Chronicles 22, we discover why. It was because he had shed too much blood in battle (22:8). So God said that David's son Solomon, "a man of peace" (22:9), would build it instead. But David played his part by making preparations for the Temple's construction. He bought the land on which it would be built (21:18–22:1) and provided the material for its construction (22:14-16), as well as making plans for worship there (chapters 23–26).

Sometimes our role is simply to prepare the ground for others rather than seeing things through ourselves. When that happens, it is a good test of where our hearts really lie.

▶ *See also **An everlasting kingdom**, page 350; **The Temple**, page 382.*

you wisdom and understanding, that you may obey the Law of the LORD your God as you rule over Israel. 13 For you will be successful if you carefully obey the decrees and regulations that the LORD gave to Israel through Moses. Be strong and courageous; do not be afraid or lose heart!

14 "I have worked hard to provide materials for building the Temple of the LORD—nearly 4,000 tons of gold, 40,000 tons of silver,* and so much iron and bronze that it cannot be weighed. I have also gathered timber and stone for the walls, though you may need to add more. 15 You have a large number of skilled stonemasons and carpenters and craftsmen of every kind. 16 You have expert goldsmiths and silversmiths and workers of bronze and iron. Now begin the work, and may the LORD be with you!"

17 Then David ordered all the leaders of Israel to assist Solomon in this project. 18 "The LORD your God is with you," he declared. "He has given you peace with the surrounding nations. He has handed them over to me, and they are now subject to the LORD and his people. 19 Now seek the LORD your God with all your heart and soul. Build the sanctuary of the LORD God so that you can bring the Ark of the LORD's Covenant and the holy vessels of God into the Temple built to honor the LORD's name."

Duties of the Levites

23 When David was an old man, he appointed his son Solomon to be king over Israel. 2 David summoned all the leaders of Israel, together with the priests and Levites. 3 All the Levites who were thirty years old or older were counted, and the total came to 38,000. 4 Then David said, "From all the Levites, 24,000 will supervise the work at the Temple of the LORD. Another 6,000 will serve as officials and judges. 5 Another 4,000 will work as gatekeepers, and 4,000 will praise the LORD with the musical instruments I have made." 6 Then David divided the Levites into divisions named after the clans descended from the three sons of Levi—Gershon, Kohath, and Merari.

The Gershonites

7 The Gershonite family units were defined
by their lines of descent from Libni* and
Shimei, the sons of Gershon. 8 Three of
the descendants of Libni were Jehiel (the
family leader), Zetham, and Joel. 9 These
were the leaders of the family of Libni.
Three of the descendants of Shimei
were Shelomoth, Haziel, and Haran.
10 Four other descendants of Shimei
were Jahath, Ziza,* Jeush, and Beriah.
11 Jahath was the family leader, and
Ziza was next. Jeush and Beriah were
counted as a single family because
neither had many sons.

The Kohathites

12 Four of the descendants of Kohath were
Amram, Izhar, Hebron, and Uzziel.
13 The sons of Amram were Aaron and
Moses. Aaron and his descendants
were set apart to dedicate the most holy
things, to offer sacrifices in the LORD's
presence, to serve the LORD, and to
pronounce blessings in his name forever.
14 As for Moses, the man of God, his
sons were included with the tribe of
Levi. 15 The sons of Moses were Gershom
and Eliezer. 16 The descendants of
Gershom included Shebuel, the family
leader. 17 Eliezer had only one son,
Rehabiah, the family leader. Rehabiah
had numerous descendants.
18 The descendants of Izhar included
Shelomith, the family leader.
19 The descendants of Hebron included
Jeriah (the family leader), Amariah
(the second), Jahaziel (the third), and
Jekameam (the fourth).
20 The descendants of Uzziel included
Micah (the family leader) and Isshiah
(the second).

The Merarites

21 The descendants of Merari included
Mahli and Mushi.
The sons of Mahli were Eleazar and
Kish. 22 Eleazar died with no sons, only
daughters. His daughters married their
cousins, the sons of Kish.
23 Three of the descendants of Mushi were
Mahli, Eder, and Jerimoth.

24 These were the descendants of Levi by clans, the leaders of their family groups,

21:25 Hebrew *600 shekels of gold,* about 15 pounds or 6.8 kilograms in weight. **22:9** *Solomon* sounds like and is probably derived from the Hebrew word for "peace." **22:14** Hebrew *100,000 talents* [3,400 metric tons] *of gold, 1,000,000 talents* [34,000 metric tons] *of silver.* **23:7** Hebrew *Ladan* (also in 23:8, 9), a variant spelling of Libni; compare 6:17. **23:10** As in Greek version and Latin Vulgate (see also 23:11); Hebrew reads *Zina.*

registered carefully by name. Each had to
be twenty years old or older to qualify for
service in the house of the LORD. 25 For David
said, "The LORD, the God of Israel, has given
us peace, and he will always live in Jerusalem. 26 Now the Levites will no longer need to
carry the Tabernacle and its furnishings from
place to place." 27 In accordance with David's
final instructions, all the Levites twenty
years old or older were registered for service.
28 The work of the Levites was to assist the
priests, the descendants of Aaron, as they
served at the house of the LORD. They also
took care of the courtyards and side rooms,
helped perform the ceremonies of purification, and served in many other ways in the
house of God. 29 They were in charge of the
sacred bread that was set out on the table,
the choice flour for the grain offerings,
the wafers made without yeast, the cakes
cooked in olive oil, and the other mixed
breads. They were also responsible to check
all the weights and measures. 30 And each
morning and evening they stood before the
LORD to sing songs of thanks and praise to
him. 31 They assisted with the burnt offerings that were presented to the LORD on
Sabbath days, at new moon celebrations,
and at all the appointed festivals. The required number of Levites served in the
LORD's presence at all times, following all
the procedures they had been given.
32 And so, under the supervision of the
priests, the Levites watched over the Tabernacle and the Temple* and faithfully
carried out their duties of service at the
house of the LORD.

Duties of the Priests

24 This is how Aaron's descendants,
the priests, were divided into groups
for service. The sons of Aaron were Nadab,
Abihu, Eleazar, and Ithamar. 2 But Nadab
and Abihu died before their father, and they
had no sons. So only Eleazar and Ithamar
were left to carry on as priests.
3 With the help of Zadok, who was a descendant of Eleazar, and of Ahimelech, who
was a descendant of Ithamar, David divided
Aaron's descendants into groups according to
their various duties. 4 Eleazar's descendants
were divided into sixteen groups and Ithamar's into eight, for there were more family
leaders among the descendants of Eleazar.
5 All tasks were assigned to the various
groups by means of sacred lots so that no
preference would be shown, for there were
many qualified officials serving God in the
sanctuary from among the descendants of
both Eleazar and Ithamar. 6 Shemaiah son
of Nethanel, a Levite, acted as secretary and
wrote down the names and assignments
in the presence of the king, the officials,
Zadok the priest, Ahimelech son of Abiathar, and the family leaders of the priests
and Levites. The descendants of Eleazar
and Ithamar took turns casting lots.

7 The first lot fell to Jehoiarib.
The second lot fell to Jedaiah.
8 The third lot fell to Harim.
The fourth lot fell to Seorim.
9 The fifth lot fell to Malkijah.
The sixth lot fell to Mijamin.
10 The seventh lot fell to Hakkoz.
The eighth lot fell to Abijah.
11 The ninth lot fell to Jeshua.
The tenth lot fell to Shecaniah.
12 The eleventh lot fell to Eliashib.
The twelfth lot fell to Jakim.
13 The thirteenth lot fell to Huppah.
The fourteenth lot fell to Jeshebeab.
14 The fifteenth lot fell to Bilgah.
The sixteenth lot fell to Immer.
15 The seventeenth lot fell to Hezir.
The eighteenth lot fell to Happizzez.
16 The nineteenth lot fell to Pethahiah.
The twentieth lot fell to Jehezkel.
17 The twenty-first lot fell to Jakin.
The twenty-second lot fell to Gamul.
18 The twenty-third lot fell to Delaiah.
The twenty-fourth lot fell to Maaziah.

19 Each group carried out its appointed
duties in the house of the LORD according
to the procedures established by their ancestor Aaron in obedience to the commands
of the LORD, the God of Israel.

Family Leaders among the Levites

20 These were the other family leaders descended from Levi:

From the descendants of Amram, the
leader was Shebuel.*
From the descendants of Shebuel, the
leader was Jehdeiah.
21 From the descendants of Rehabiah, the
leader was Isshiah.
22 From the descendants of Izhar, the
leader was Shelomith.*

From the descendants of Shelomith, the leader was Jahath.
23 From the descendants of Hebron, Jeriah was the leader,* Amariah was second, Jahaziel was third, and Jekameam was fourth.
24 From the descendants of Uzziel, the leader was Micah.
From the descendants of Micah, the leader was Shamir, 25along with Isshiah, the brother of Micah.
From the descendants of Isshiah, the leader was Zechariah.
26 From the descendants of Merari, the leaders were Mahli and Mushi.
From the descendants of Jaaziah, the leader was Beno.
27 From the descendants of Merari through Jaaziah, the leaders were Beno, Shoham, Zaccur, and Ibri.
28 From the descendants of Mahli, the leader was Eleazar, though he had no sons.
29 From the descendants of Kish, the leader was Jerahmeel.
30 From the descendants of Mushi, the leaders were Mahli, Eder, and Jerimoth.

These were the descendants of Levi in
their various families. 31Like the descendants
of Aaron, they were assigned to their duties
by means of sacred lots, without regard to
age or rank. Lots were drawn in the presence
of King David, Zadok, Ahimelech, and the
family leaders of the priests and the Levites.

Duties of the Musicians

25 David and the army commanders then appointed men from the families of Asaph, Heman, and Jeduthun to proclaim God's messages to the accompaniment of lyres, harps, and cymbals. Here is a list of their names and their work:

2From the sons of Asaph, there were Zaccur, Joseph, Nethaniah, and Asarelah. They worked under the direction of their father, Asaph, who proclaimed God's messages by the king's orders.
3From the sons of Jeduthun, there were Gedaliah, Zeri, Jeshaiah, Shimei,* Hashabiah, and Mattithiah, six in all. They worked under the direction of their father, Jeduthun, who proclaimed God's messages to the accompaniment of the lyre, offering thanks and praise to the LORD.
4From the sons of Heman, there were Bukkiah, Mattaniah, Uzziel, Shubael,* Jerimoth, Hananiah, Hanani, Eliathah, Giddalti, Romamti-ezer, Joshbekashah,
Mallothi, Hothir, and Mahazioth. 5All
these were the sons of Heman, the king's seer, for God had honored him with fourteen sons and three daughters.

23:32 Hebrew *the Tent of Meeting and the sanctuary.* **24:20** Hebrew *Shubael* (also in 24:20b), a variant spelling of Shebuel; compare 23:16 and 26:24. **24:22** Hebrew *Shelomoth* (also in 24:22b), a variant spelling of Shelomith; compare 23:18. **24:23** Hebrew *From the descendants of Jeriah;* compare 23:19. **25:3** As in one Hebrew manuscript and some Greek manuscripts (see also 25:17); most Hebrew manuscripts lack *Shimei.* **25:4** Hebrew *Shebuel,* a variant spelling of Shubael; compare 25:20.

The ministry of music and singing

Music and singing played an important part in worship among God's people. Their significance is seen here in how David set apart musicians and singers "to proclaim God's messages to the accompaniment of lyres, harps, and cymbals" (1 Chronicles 25:1). In other words, he recognized that music and song can bring God's word to us as much as a spoken prophecy or sermon, and they can often reach deep into our hearts where words alone cannot reach.

Temple worship was a noisy and lively affair, with all kinds of instruments—stringed, wind, and percussion—being used and lots of singing, clapping, and dancing. We see this reflected in many of the psalms (e.g., Psalm 33:1-3; 47:1-6; 95:1-2; 98:4-6). David himself was an exuberant worshiper (e.g., 2 Samuel 6:5).

Those who minister in music and song today play an important role, and those involved should treat it seriously—not seeing it as an opportunity to perform or simply play their instrument, but as a ministry to God and a help to God's people as they worship.

[6]All these men were under the direction
of their fathers as they made music at the
house of the LORD. Their responsibilities included the playing of cymbals, harps, and
lyres at the house of God. Asaph, Jeduthun,
and Heman reported directly to the king.
[7]They and their families were all trained in
making music before the LORD, and each
of them—288 in all—was an accomplished
musician. [8]The musicians were appointed
to their term of service by means of sacred
lots, without regard to whether they were
young or old, teacher or student.

9 The first lot fell to Joseph of the Asaph clan and twelve of his sons and relatives.*
The second lot fell to Gedaliah and twelve of his sons and relatives.
10 The third lot fell to Zaccur and twelve of his sons and relatives.
11 The fourth lot fell to Zeri* and twelve of his sons and relatives.
12 The fifth lot fell to Nethaniah and twelve of his sons and relatives.
13 The sixth lot fell to Bukkiah and twelve of his sons and relatives.
14 The seventh lot fell to Asarelah* and twelve of his sons and relatives.
15 The eighth lot fell to Jeshaiah and twelve of his sons and relatives.
16 The ninth lot fell to Mattaniah and twelve of his sons and relatives.
17 The tenth lot fell to Shimei and twelve of his sons and relatives.
18 The eleventh lot fell to Uzziel* and twelve of his sons and relatives.
19 The twelfth lot fell to Hashabiah and twelve of his sons and relatives.
20 The thirteenth lot fell to Shubael and twelve of his sons and relatives.
21 The fourteenth lot fell to Mattithiah and twelve of his sons and relatives.
22 The fifteenth lot fell to Jerimoth* and twelve of his sons and relatives.
23 The sixteenth lot fell to Hananiah and twelve of his sons and relatives.
24 The seventeenth lot fell to Joshbekashah* and twelve of his sons and relatives.
25 The eighteenth lot fell to Hanani and twelve of his sons and relatives.
26 The nineteenth lot fell to Mallothi and twelve of his sons and relatives.
27 The twentieth lot fell to Eliathah and twelve of his sons and relatives.
28 The twenty-first lot fell to Hothir and twelve of his sons and relatives.
29 The twenty-second lot fell to Giddalti and twelve of his sons and relatives.
30 The twenty-third lot fell to Mahazioth and twelve of his sons and relatives.
31 The twenty-fourth lot fell to Romamti-ezer and twelve of his sons and relatives.

Duties of the Gatekeepers

26 These are the divisions of the gatekeepers:

From the Korahites, there was
Meshelemiah son of Kore, of the family
of Abiasaph.* [2]The sons of Meshelemiah
were Zechariah (the oldest), Jediael
(the second), Zebadiah (the third),
Jathniel (the fourth), [3]Elam (the fifth),
Jehohanan (the sixth), and Eliehoenai
(the seventh).
[4]The sons of Obed-edom, also gatekeepers,
were Shemaiah (the oldest), Jehozabad
(the second), Joah (the third), Sacar (the
fourth), Nethanel (the fifth), [5]Ammiel
(the sixth), Issachar (the seventh), and
Peullethai (the eighth). God had richly
blessed Obed-edom.
[6]Obed-edom's son Shemaiah had sons
with great ability who earned positions
of great authority in the clan. [7]Their
names were Othni, Rephael, Obed,
and Elzabad. Their relatives, Elihu and
Semakiah, were also very capable men.
[8]All of these descendants of
Obed-edom, including their sons and
grandsons—sixty-two of them in all—
were very capable men, well qualified
for their work.
[9]Meshelemiah's eighteen sons and
relatives were also very capable men.
[10]Hosah, of the Merari clan, appointed
Shimri as the leader among his sons,
though he was not the oldest. [11]His other
sons included Hilkiah (the second),
Tebaliah (the third), and Zechariah (the
fourth). Hosah's sons and relatives,
who served as gatekeepers, numbered
thirteen in all.

[12]These divisions of the gatekeepers were
named for their family leaders, and like the
other Levites, they served at the house of
the LORD. [13]They were assigned by families

for guard duty at the various gates, without
regard to age or training, for it was all
decided by means of sacred lots.
[14]The responsibility for the east gate went
to Meshelemiah* and his group. The north
gate was assigned to his son Zechariah, a
man of unusual wisdom. [15]The south gate
went to Obed-edom, and his sons were put
in charge of the storehouse. [16]Shuppim and
Hosah were assigned the west gate and the
gateway leading up to the Temple.* Guard
duties were divided evenly. [17]Six Levites
were assigned each day to the east gate,
four to the north gate, four to the south gate,
and two pairs at the storehouse. [18]Six were
assigned each day to the west gate, four to
the gateway leading up to the Temple, and
two to the courtyard.*
[19]These were the divisions of the gatekeepers from the clans of Korah and Merari.

Treasurers and Other Officials

[20]Other Levites, led by Ahijah, were in
charge of the treasuries of the house of God
and the treasuries of the gifts dedicated
to the LORD. [21]From the family of Libni* in
the clan of Gershon, Jehiel* was the leader.
[22]The sons of Jehiel, Zetham and his brother
Joel, were in charge of the treasuries of the
house of the LORD.
[23]These are the leaders that descended
from Amram, Izhar, Hebron, and Uzziel:

[24]From the clan of Amram, Shebuel was a
descendant of Gershom son of Moses.
He was the chief officer of the treasuries.
[25]His relatives through Eliezer were
Rehabiah, Jeshaiah, Joram, Zicri, and
Shelomoth.
[26]Shelomoth and his relatives were in
charge of the treasuries containing the
gifts that King David, the family leaders,
and the generals and captains* and
other officers of the army had dedicated
to the LORD. [27]These men dedicated
some of the plunder they had gained
in battle to maintain the house of the
LORD. [28]Shelomoth* and his relatives
also cared for the gifts dedicated to the
LORD by Samuel the seer, Saul son of
Kish, Abner son of Ner, and Joab son of
Zeruiah. All the other dedicated gifts
were in their care, too.
[29]From the clan of Izhar came
Kenaniah. He and his sons were given
administrative responsibilities* over
Israel as officials and judges.
[30]From the clan of Hebron came
Hashabiah. He and his relatives—1,700
capable men—were put in charge of the
Israelite lands west of the Jordan River.
They were responsible for all matters
related to the things of the LORD and the
service of the king in that area.
[31]Also from the clan of Hebron
came Jeriah,* who was the leader
of the Hebronites according to the
genealogical records. (In the fortieth
year of David's reign, a search was made
in the records, and capable men from
the clan of Hebron were found at Jazer
in the land of Gilead.) [32]There were 2,700
capable men among the relatives of
Jeriah. King David sent them to the east
side of the Jordan River and put them in
charge of the tribes of Reuben and Gad
and the half-tribe of Manasseh. They
were responsible for all matters related
to God and to the king.

Military Commanders and Divisions

27 This is the list of Israelite generals and captains,* and their officers, who served the king by supervising
the army divisions that were on duty each
month of the year. Each division served for
one month and had 24,000 troops.

[2]Jashobeam son of Zabdiel was
commander of the first division of
24,000 troops, which was on duty
during the first month. [3]He was a
descendant of Perez and was in charge
of all the army officers for the first
month.
[4]Dodai, a descendant of Ahoah, was
commander of the second division

25:9 As in Greek version; Hebrew lacks *and twelve of his sons and relatives.* **25:11** Hebrew *Izri,* a variant spelling of Zeri; compare 25:3. **25:14** Hebrew *Jesarelah,* a variant spelling of Asarelah; compare 25:2. **25:18** Hebrew *Azarel,* a variant spelling of Uzziel; compare 25:4. **25:22** Hebrew *Jeremoth,* a variant spelling of Jerimoth; compare 25:4. **25:24** Hebrew *Joshbekasha,* a variant spelling of Joshbekashah; compare 25:4. **26:1** As in Greek version (see also Exod 6:24); Hebrew reads *Asaph.* **26:14** Hebrew *Shelemiah,* a variant spelling of Meshelemiah; compare 26:2. **26:16** Or *the gate of Shalleketh on the upper road* (also in 26:18). The meaning of the Hebrew is uncertain. **26:18** Or *the colonnade.* The meaning of the Hebrew is uncertain. **26:21a** Hebrew *Ladan,* a variant spelling of Libni; compare 6:17. **26:21b** Hebrew *Jehieli* (also in 26:22), a variant spelling of Jehiel; compare 23:8. **26:26** Hebrew *the commanders of thousands and of hundreds.* **26:28** Hebrew *Shelomith,* a variant spelling of Shelomoth. **26:29** Or *were given outside work;* or *were given work away from the Temple area.* **26:31** Hebrew *Jerijah,* a variant spelling of Jeriah; compare 23:19. **27:1** Hebrew *commanders of thousands and of hundreds.*

of 24,000 troops, which was on duty
during the second month. Mikloth was
his chief officer.
5 Benaiah son of Jehoiada the priest was
commander of the third division of
24,000 troops, which was on duty
during the third month. 6 This was the
Benaiah who commanded David's elite
military group known as the Thirty. His
son Ammizabad was his chief officer.
7 Asahel, the brother of Joab, was
commander of the fourth division of
24,000 troops, which was on duty
during the fourth month. Asahel was
succeeded by his son Zebadiah.
8 Shammah* the Izrahite was commander
of the fifth division of 24,000 troops,
which was on duty during the fifth
month.
9 Ira son of Ikkesh from Tekoa was
commander of the sixth division of
24,000 troops, which was on duty
during the sixth month.
10 Helez, a descendant of Ephraim from
Pelon, was commander of the seventh
division of 24,000 troops, which was on
duty during the seventh month.
11 Sibbecai, a descendant of Zerah from
Hushah, was commander of the eighth
division of 24,000 troops, which was on
duty during the eighth month.
12 Abiezer from Anathoth in the territory of
Benjamin was commander of the ninth
division of 24,000 troops, which was on
duty during the ninth month.
13 Maharai, a descendant of Zerah from
Netophah, was commander of the tenth
division of 24,000 troops, which was on
duty during the tenth month.
14 Benaiah from Pirathon in Ephraim was
commander of the eleventh division
of 24,000 troops, which was on duty
during the eleventh month.
15 Heled,* a descendant of Othniel from
Netophah, was commander of the
twelfth division of 24,000 troops, which
was on duty during the twelfth month.

Leaders of the Tribes

16 The following were the tribes of Israel and
their leaders:

Tribe	*Leader*
Reuben	Eliezer son of Zicri
Simeon	Shephatiah son of Maacah
17 Levi	Hashabiah son of Kemuel
Aaron (the priests)	Zadok
18 Judah	Elihu (a brother of David)
Issachar	Omri son of Michael
19 Zebulun	Ishmaiah son of Obadiah
Naphtali	Jeremoth son of Azriel
20 Ephraim	Hoshea son of Azaziah
Manasseh (west)	Joel son of Pedaiah
21 Manasseh in Gilead (east)	Iddo son of Zechariah
Benjamin	Jaasiel son of Abner
22 Dan	Azarel son of Jeroham

These were the leaders of the tribes of Israel.
23 When David took his census, he did not
count those who were younger than twenty
years of age, because the LORD had promised to make the Israelites as numerous as
the stars in heaven. 24 Joab son of Zeruiah
began the census but never finished it
because* the anger of God fell on Israel.
The total number was never recorded in
King David's official records.

Officials of David's Kingdom

25 Azmaveth son of Adiel was in charge of
the palace treasuries.
Jonathan son of Uzziah was in charge of
the regional treasuries throughout the
towns, villages, and fortresses of Israel.
26 Ezri son of Kelub was in charge of the field
workers who farmed the king's lands.
27 Shimei from Ramah was in charge of the
king's vineyards.
Zabdi from Shepham was responsible for
the grapes and the supplies of wine.
28 Baal-hanan from Geder was in charge of
the king's olive groves and sycamore-fig
trees in the foothills of Judah.*
Joash was responsible for the supplies of
olive oil.
29 Shitrai from Sharon was in charge of the
cattle on the Sharon Plain.
Shaphat son of Adlai was responsible for
the cattle in the valleys.
30 Obil the Ishmaelite was in charge of the
camels.
Jehdeiah from Meronoth was in charge of
the donkeys.
31 Jaziz the Hagrite was in charge of the
king's flocks of sheep and goats.
All these officials were overseers of King
David's property.

32 Jonathan, David's uncle, was a wise
counselor to the king, a man of great

insight, and a scribe. Jehiel the Hacmonite
was responsible for teaching the king's
sons. [33]Ahithophel was the royal adviser.
Hushai the Arkite was the king's friend.
[34]Ahithophel was succeeded by Jehoiada
son of Benaiah and by Abiathar. Joab was
commander of the king's army.

David's Instructions to Solomon

28 David summoned all the officials
of Israel to Jerusalem—the leaders
of the tribes, the commanders of the army
divisions, the other generals and captains,*
the overseers of the royal property and
livestock, the palace officials, the mighty
men, and all the other brave warriors in
the kingdom. [2]David rose to his feet and
said: "My brothers and my people! It was
my desire to build a Temple where the Ark
of the LORD's Covenant, God's footstool,
could rest permanently. I made the necessary preparations for building it, [3]but God
said to me, 'You must not build a Temple to
honor my name, for you are a warrior and
have shed much blood.'

[4]"Yet the LORD, the God of Israel, has
chosen me from among all my father's
family to be king over Israel forever. For he
has chosen the tribe of Judah to rule, and
from among the families of Judah he chose
my father's family. And from among my
father's sons the LORD was pleased to make
me king over all Israel. [5]And from among
my sons—for the LORD has given me many—
he chose Solomon to succeed me on the
throne of Israel and to rule over the LORD's
kingdom. [6]He said to me, 'Your son Solomon
will build my Temple and its courtyards, for
I have chosen him as my son, and I will be
his father. [7]And if he continues to obey my
commands and regulations as he does now,
I will make his kingdom last forever.'

[8]"So now, with God as our witness, and
in the sight of all Israel—the LORD's assembly—I give you this charge. Be careful to
obey all the commands of the LORD your
God, so that you may continue to possess
this good land and leave it to your children
as a permanent inheritance.

[9]"And Solomon, my son, learn to know the
God of your ancestors intimately. Worship
and serve him with your whole heart and
a willing mind. For the LORD sees every
heart and knows every plan and thought. If
you seek him, you will find him. But if you
forsake him, he will reject you forever. [10]So
take this seriously. The LORD has chosen
you to build a Temple as his sanctuary. Be
strong, and do the work."

[11]Then David gave Solomon the plans for
the Temple and its surroundings, including
the entry room, the storerooms, the upstairs
rooms, the inner rooms, and the inner sanctuary—which was the place of atonement.
[12]David also gave Solomon all the plans
he had in mind* for the courtyards of the
LORD's Temple, the outside rooms, the treasuries, and the rooms for the gifts dedicated
to the LORD. [13]The king also gave Solomon
the instructions concerning the work of the
various divisions of priests and Levites in
the Temple of the LORD. And he gave specifications for the items in the Temple that
were to be used for worship.

[14]David gave instructions regarding how
much gold and silver should be used to
make the items needed for service. [15]He told
Solomon the amount of gold needed for
the gold lampstands and lamps, and the
amount of silver for the silver lampstands
and lamps, depending on how each would
be used. [16]He designated the amount of gold
for the table on which the Bread of the Presence would be placed and the amount of
silver for other tables.

[17]David also designated the amount of
gold for the solid gold meat hooks used
to handle the sacrificial meat and for the
basins, pitchers, and dishes, as well as the
amount of silver for every dish. [18]He designated the amount of refined gold for the
altar of incense. Finally, he gave him a plan
for the LORD's "chariot"—the gold cherubim* whose wings were stretched out over
the Ark of the LORD's Covenant. [19]"Every
part of this plan," David told Solomon,
"was given to me in writing from the hand
of the LORD.*"

[20]Then David continued, "Be strong and
courageous, and do the work. Don't be
afraid or discouraged, for the LORD God,
my God, is with you. He will not fail you
or forsake you. He will see to it that all the
work related to the Temple of the LORD is

27:8 Hebrew *Shamhuth,* a variant spelling of Shammah; compare 11:27 and 2 Sam 23:25. **27:15** Hebrew *Heldai,* a variant spelling of Heled; compare 11:30 and 2 Sam 23:29. **27:24** Or *never finished it, and yet.* **27:28** Hebrew *the Shephelah.* **28:1** Hebrew *the commanders of thousands and commanders of hundreds.* **28:12** Or *the plans of the spirit that was with him.* **28:18** Hebrew *for the gold cherub chariot.* **28:19** Or *was written under the direction of the LORD.*

finished correctly. 21The various divisions of priests and Levites will serve in the Temple of God. Others with skills of every kind will volunteer, and the officials and the entire nation are at your command."

Gifts for Building the Temple

29 Then King David turned to the entire assembly and said, "My son Solomon, whom God has clearly chosen as the next king of Israel, is still young and inexperienced. The work ahead of him is enormous, for the Temple he will build is not for mere mortals—it is for the LORD God himself! 2Using every resource at my command, I have gathered as much as I could for building the Temple of my God. Now there is enough gold, silver, bronze, iron, and wood, as well as great quantities of onyx, other precious stones, costly jewels, and all kinds of fine stone and marble.

3"And now, because of my devotion to the Temple of my God, I am giving all of my own private treasures of gold and silver to help in the construction. This is in addition to the building materials I have already collected for his holy Temple. 4I am donating more than 112 tons of gold* from Ophir and 262 tons of refined silver* to be used for overlaying the walls of the buildings 5and for the other gold and silver work to be done by the craftsmen. Now then, who will follow my example and give offerings to the LORD today?"

6Then the family leaders, the leaders of the tribes of Israel, the generals and captains of the army,* and the king's administrative officers all gave willingly. 7For the construction of the Temple of God, they gave about 188 tons of gold,* 10,000 gold coins,* 375 tons of silver,* 675 tons of bronze,* and 3,750 tons of iron.* 8They also contributed numerous precious stones, which were deposited in the treasury of the house of the LORD under the care of Jehiel, a descendant of Gershon. 9The people rejoiced over the offerings, for they had given freely and wholeheartedly to the LORD, and King David was filled with joy.

David's Prayer of Praise

10Then David praised the LORD in the presence of the whole assembly:

"O LORD, the God of our ancestor
Israel,* may you be praised forever and
ever! 11Yours, O LORD, is the greatness,
the power, the glory, the victory, and
the majesty. Everything in the heavens
and on earth is yours, O LORD, and this
is your kingdom. We adore you as the
one who is over all things. 12Wealth and
honor come from you alone, for you rule
over everything. Power and might are in
your hand, and at your discretion people
are made great and given strength.

13"O our God, we thank you and praise
your glorious name! 14But who am I, and
who are my people, that we could give
anything to you? Everything we have has
come from you, and we give you only
what you first gave us! 15We are here for
only a moment, visitors and strangers
in the land as our ancestors were before
us. Our days on earth are like a passing
shadow, gone so soon without a trace.

16"O LORD our God, even this material
we have gathered to build a Temple to
honor your holy name comes from you!
It all belongs to you! 17I know, my God,
that you examine our hearts and rejoice
when you find integrity there. You know
I have done all this with good motives,
and I have watched your people offer
their gifts willingly and joyously.

18"O LORD, the God of our ancestors
Abraham, Isaac, and Israel, make
your people always want to obey you.
See to it that their love for you never
changes. 19Give my son Solomon the
wholehearted desire to obey all your
commands, laws, and decrees, and to
do everything necessary to build this
Temple, for which I have made these
preparations."

20Then David said to the whole assembly, "Give praise to the LORD your God!" And the entire assembly praised the LORD, the God of their ancestors, and they bowed low and knelt before the LORD and the king.

Solomon Named as King

21The next day they brought 1,000 bulls, 1,000 rams, and 1,000 male lambs as burnt offerings to the LORD. They also brought liquid offerings and many other sacrifices on behalf of all Israel. 22They feasted and drank in the LORD's presence with great joy that day.

And again they crowned David's son Solomon as their new king. They anointed

him before the LORD as their leader,
and they anointed Zadok as priest. [23]So
Solomon took the throne of the LORD in
place of his father, David, and he succeeded in everything, and all Israel obeyed
him. [24]All the officials, the warriors, and the
sons of King David pledged their loyalty to
King Solomon. [25]And the LORD exalted
Solomon in the sight of all Israel, and he
gave Solomon greater royal splendor than
any king in Israel before him.

Summary of David's Reign

[26]So David son of Jesse reigned over all Israel.
[27]He reigned over Israel for forty years, seven
of them in Hebron and thirty-three in Jerusalem. [28]He died at a ripe old age, having
enjoyed long life, wealth, and honor. Then
his son Solomon ruled in his place.

[29]All the events of King David's reign,
from beginning to end, are written in *The
Record of Samuel the Seer, The Record of
Nathan the Prophet,* and *The Record of
Gad the Seer.* [30]These accounts include the
mighty deeds of his reign and everything
that happened to him and to Israel and to
all the surrounding kingdoms.

29:4a Hebrew *3,000 talents* [102 metric tons] *of gold.*
29:4b Hebrew *7,000 talents* [238 metric tons] *of silver.*
29:6 Hebrew *the commanders of thousands and commanders of hundreds.* **29:7a** Hebrew *5,000 talents* [170 metric tons] *of gold.* **29:7b** Hebrew *10,000 darics* [a Persian coin] *of gold,* about 185 pounds or 84 kilograms in weight. **29:7c** Hebrew *10,000 talents* [340 metric tons] *of silver.* **29:7d** Hebrew *18,000 talents* [612 metric tons] *of bronze.* **29:7e** Hebrew *100,000 talents* [3,400 metric tons] *of iron.* **29:10** *Israel* is the name that God gave to Jacob.

2 Chronicles *God does what he promised*

The book of 2 Chronicles parallels 1 and 2 Kings—though with one big difference: It focuses entirely on the history of the southern kingdom, Judah, ignoring the history of Israel, the northern kingdom, since it had not returned from exile but rather had been dispersed. The book covers Judah's history from its third king, Solomon, to its last king, Zedekiah. But although the story climaxes in God's judgment because of their unfaithfulness, it ends on a note of hope for the future. Whether through judgment or hope, God will be faithful to what he promised.

What's it all about?

Second Chronicles begins with the story of Solomon. The first nine chapters repeat the stories of his reign narrated in 1 Kings, but concentrate on the construction of the magnificent Temple at Jerusalem. The author sees Solomon's great work as a parallel to the construction of the Tabernacle. There, Bezalel and Oholiab worked together as a team (Exodus 35:30–36:1); now it was Solomon and Huram-abi (2 Chronicles 2:13-14). And in both cases it was God who gave the plans (Exodus 25:1–30:38; 1 Chronicles 28:11-19). The parallel could not be clearer.

OVERVIEW

The reign of Solomon
1:1–9:31

The nation splits in two
10:1–11:4

The history of the kings of Judah
11:5–36:16

The fall of Jerusalem and Judah's exile · *36:17-23*

Under Solomon the nation enjoyed great peace and prosperity, but the foolishness of his son Rehoboam led to the kingdom splitting after Solomon's death (chapter 10). The rest of the book focuses on his successors in Judah, showing that proper kingly rule is always exercised by kings descended from David who followed God's word. Some of them, such as Jehoshaphat and Hezekiah, took a stand against idolatry and sought God in times of national crisis. God remembered his promises to David and intervened to give them victory in the face of overwhelming difficulties. Josiah, just eight years old when he became king, "began to seek the God of his ancestor David" (34:3) when he was sixteen, and four years later systematically removed idolatry from the land. During renovations on the Temple, a priest discovered "the Book of the Law of the LORD" (34:14-15), which many scholars think was the book of Deuteronomy—imagine, a whole book of the Law lost and no one had noticed! This led to a renewal of the covenant and a recommitment to walk in God's ways. But despite these godly interludes, ongoing disobedience on the part of the nation ultimately led to its conquest by Babylon and to exile (36:15-21). But God's promise to David meant that this is not where the story would end (36:22-23)—though we need to wait until the books of Ezra and Nehemiah to see what happens next.

What does it mean for us?

Second Chronicles continues the message of 1 Chronicles, that all of us have choices to make about how we live—not just at the moment when we first encounter God, but in an ongoing way throughout life. Good choices lead to good consequences—though that doesn't necessarily mean that we won't face hardships or challenges at times, as some of the godly kings discovered; but good and godly choices ensure that God will always be with us. Equally, bad choices lead to bad outcomes—not just for us but for others, too. But the book ends on a note of hope: For while Judah's sin led to judgment through exile, God in his faithfulness did not abandon his people. He ensured that they were eventually sent back home again. But how much easier it would have been for them if they had obeyed God in the first place!

▶ *See also* ***A timeline of the Bible****, pages A22-A24.*

Solomon Asks for Wisdom

1 Solomon son of David took firm control
of his kingdom, for the LORD his God was
with him and made him very powerful.
2 Solomon called together all the leaders
of Israel—the generals and captains of the
army,* the judges, and all the political and
clan leaders. 3 Then he led the entire assembly to the place of worship in Gibeon, for
God's Tabernacle* was located there. (This
was the Tabernacle that Moses, the LORD's
servant, had made in the wilderness.)
4 David had already moved the Ark of God
from Kiriath-jearim to the tent he had prepared for it in Jerusalem. 5 But the bronze altar
made by Bezalel son of Uri and grandson of
Hur was there* at Gibeon in front of the Tabernacle of the LORD. So Solomon and the people
gathered in front of it to consult the LORD.*
6 There in front of the Tabernacle, Solomon
went up to the bronze altar in the LORD's presence and sacrificed 1,000 burnt offerings on it.
7 That night God appeared to Solomon and
said, "What do you want? Ask, and I will give
it to you!"
8 Solomon replied to God, "You showed great
and faithful love to David, my father, and now
you have made me king in his place. 9 O LORD
God, please continue to keep your promise to
David my father, for you have made me king
over a people as numerous as the dust of the
earth! 10 Give me the wisdom and knowledge
to lead them properly,* for who could possibly
govern this great people of yours?"
11 God said to Solomon, "Because your greatest desire is to help your people, and you
did not ask for wealth, riches, fame, or even
the death of your enemies or a long life, but
rather you asked for wisdom and knowledge
to properly govern my people— 12 I will certainly give you the wisdom and knowledge
you requested. But I will also give you wealth,
riches, and fame such as no other king has
had before you or will ever have in the future!"
13 Then Solomon returned to Jerusalem
from the Tabernacle at the place of worship
in Gibeon, and he reigned over Israel.
14 Solomon built up a huge force of chariots
and horses.* He had 1,400 chariots and
12,000 horses. He stationed some of them
in the chariot cities and some near him in
Jerusalem. 15 The king made silver and gold
as plentiful in Jerusalem as stone. And valuable cedar timber was as common as the
sycamore-fig trees that grow in the foothills
of Judah.* 16 Solomon's horses were imported
from Egypt* and from Cilicia*; the king's
traders acquired them from Cilicia at the
standard price. 17 At that time chariots from
Egypt could be purchased for 600 pieces of
silver,* and horses for 150 pieces of silver.*
They were then exported to the kings of the
Hittites and the kings of Aram.

Preparations for Building the Temple

2 1 *Solomon decided to build a Temple to
honor the name of the LORD, and also a
royal palace for himself. 2 *He enlisted a force
of 70,000 laborers, 80,000 men to quarry
stone in the hill country, and 3,600 foremen.

1:2 Hebrew *the commanders of thousands and of hundreds.* **1:3** Hebrew *Tent of Meeting;* also in 1:6, 13. **1:5a** As in Greek version and Latin Vulgate, and some Hebrew manuscripts; Masoretic Text reads *he placed.* **1:5b** Hebrew *to consult him.* **1:10** Hebrew *to go out and come in before this people.* **1:14** Or *charioteers;* also in 1:14b. **1:15** Hebrew *the Shephelah.* **1:16a** Possibly *Muzur,* a district near Cilicia; also in 1:17. **1:16b** Hebrew *Kue,* probably another name for Cilicia. **1:17a** Hebrew *600 [shekels] of silver,* about 15 pounds or 6.8 kilograms in weight. **1:17b** Hebrew *150 [shekels],* about 3.8 pounds or 1.7 kilograms in weight. **2:1** Verse 2:1 is numbered 1:18 in Hebrew text. **2:2** Verses 2:2-18 are numbered 2:1-17 in Hebrew text.

▶ **1:1** *See* ***King Solomon****, page 377.*

[3]Solomon also sent this message to King Hiram* at Tyre:

"Send me cedar logs as you did for my father, David, when he was building his palace. [4]I am about to build a Temple to honor the name of the LORD my God. It will be a place set apart to burn fragrant incense before him, to display the special sacrificial bread, and to sacrifice burnt offerings each morning and evening, on the Sabbaths, at new moon celebrations, and at the other appointed festivals of the LORD our God. He has commanded Israel to do these things forever.

[5]"This must be a magnificent Temple because our God is greater than all other gods. [6]But who can really build him a worthy home? Not even the highest heavens can contain him! So who am I to consider building a Temple for him, except as a place to burn sacrifices to him?

[7]"So send me a master craftsman who can work with gold, silver, bronze, and iron, as well as with purple, scarlet, and blue cloth. He must be a skilled engraver who can work with the craftsmen of Judah and Jerusalem who were selected by my father, David.

[8]"Also send me cedar, cypress, and red sandalwood* logs from Lebanon, for I know that your men are without equal at cutting timber in Lebanon. I will send my men to help them. [9]An immense amount of timber will be needed, for the Temple I am going to build will be very large and magnificent. [10]In payment for your woodcutters, I will send 100,000 bushels of crushed wheat, 100,000 bushels of barley,* 110,000 gallons of wine, and 110,000 gallons of olive oil.*"

[11]King Hiram sent this letter of reply to Solomon:

"It is because the LORD loves his people that he has made you their king! [12]Praise the LORD, the God of Israel, who made the heavens and the earth! He has given King David a wise son, gifted with skill and understanding, who will build a Temple for the LORD and a royal palace for himself.

[13]"I am sending you a master craftsman named Huram-abi, who is extremely talented. [14]His mother is from the tribe of Dan in Israel, and his father is from Tyre. He is skillful at making things from gold, silver, bronze, and iron, and he also works with stone and wood. He can work with purple, blue, and scarlet cloth and fine linen. He is also an engraver and can follow any design given to him. He will work with your craftsmen and those appointed by my lord David, your father.

[15]"Send along the wheat, barley, olive oil, and wine that my lord has mentioned. [16]We will cut whatever timber you need from the Lebanon mountains and will float the logs in rafts down the coast of the Mediterranean Sea* to Joppa. From there you can transport the logs up to Jerusalem."

[17]Solomon took a census of all foreigners in the land of Israel, like the census his father had taken, and he counted 153,600. [18]He assigned 70,000 of them as common laborers, 80,000 as quarry workers in the hill country, and 3,600 as foremen.

Solomon Builds the Temple

3 So Solomon began to build the Temple of the LORD in Jerusalem on Mount Moriah, where the LORD had appeared to David, his father. The Temple was built on the threshing floor of Araunah* the Jebusite, the site that David had selected. [2]The construction began in midspring,* during the fourth year of Solomon's reign.

[3]These are the dimensions Solomon used for the foundation of the Temple of God (using the old standard of measurement).* It was 90 feet long and 30 feet wide.* [4]The entry room at the front of the Temple was 30 feet* wide, running across the entire width of the Temple, and 30 feet* high. He overlaid the inside with pure gold.

[5]He paneled the main room of the Temple with cypress wood, overlaid it with fine gold, and decorated it with carvings of palm trees and chains. [6]He decorated the walls of the Temple with beautiful jewels and with gold from the land of Parvaim. [7]He overlaid the beams, thresholds, walls, and doors

▸ **3:1** *See* ***The Temple****, page 382.*

throughout the Temple with gold, and he
carved figures of cherubim on the walls.
8He made the Most Holy Place 30 feet
wide, corresponding to the width of the
Temple, and 30 feet deep. He overlaid its
interior with 23 tons* of fine gold. 9The gold
nails that were used weighed 20 ounces*
each. He also overlaid the walls of the upper
rooms with gold.
10He made two figures shaped like cherubim, overlaid them with gold, and placed
them in the Most Holy Place. 11The total
wingspan of the two cherubim standing side by side was 30 feet. One wing of
the first figure was 7½ feet* long, and it
touched the Temple wall. The other wing,
also 7½ feet long, touched one of the wings
of the second figure. 12In the same way, the
second figure had one wing 7½ feet long
that touched the opposite wall. The other
wing, also 7½ feet long, touched the wing
of the first figure. 13So the wingspan of the
two cherubim side by side was 30 feet. They
stood on their feet and faced out toward the
main room of the Temple.
14Across the entrance of the Most Holy
Place he hung a curtain made of fine linen,
decorated with blue, purple, and scarlet
thread and embroidered with figures of
cherubim.
15For the front of the Temple, he made two
pillars that were 27 feet* tall, each topped
by a capital extending upward another
7½ feet. 16He made a network of interwoven
chains* and used them to decorate the tops
of the pillars. He also made 100 decorative
pomegranates and attached them to the
chains. 17Then he set up the two pillars at
the entrance of the Temple, one to the south
of the entrance and the other to the north.
He named the one on the south Jakin, and
the one on the north Boaz.*

Furnishings for the Temple

4 Solomon* also made a bronze altar
30 feet long, 30 feet wide, and 15 feet
high.* 2Then he cast a great round basin,
15 feet across from rim to rim, called the
Sea. It was 7½ feet deep and about 45 feet in
circumference.* 3It was encircled just below
its rim by two rows of figures that resembled
oxen. There were about six oxen per foot*
all the way around, and they were cast as
part of the basin.
4The Sea was placed on a base of twelve
bronze oxen, all facing outward. Three faced
north, three faced west, three faced south,
and three faced east, and the Sea rested on
them. 5The walls of the Sea were about three
inches* thick, and its rim flared out like a

2:3 Hebrew *Huram*, a variant spelling of Hiram; also in 2:11. **2:8** Or *juniper;* Hebrew reads *algum*, perhaps a variant spelling of *almug;* compare 9:10-11 and parallel text at 1 Kgs 10:11-12. **2:10a** Hebrew *20,000 cors* [4,400 kiloliters] *of crushed wheat, 20,000 cors of barley.* **2:10b** Hebrew *20,000 baths* [420 kiloliters] *of wine, and 20,000 baths of olive oil.* **2:16** Hebrew *the sea.* **3:1** Hebrew reads *Ornan*, a variant spelling of Araunah; compare 2 Sam 24:16. **3:2** Hebrew *on the second [day] of the second month.* This day of the ancient Hebrew lunar calendar occurred in April or May. **3:3a** The "old standard of measurement" was a cubit equal to 18 inches [46 centimeters]. The new standard was a cubit of approximately 21 inches [53 centimeters]. **3:3b** Hebrew *60 cubits* [27.6 meters] *long and 20 cubits* [9.2 meters] *wide.* **3:4a** Hebrew *20 cubits* [9.2 meters]; also in 3:8, 11, 13. **3:4b** As in some Greek and Syriac manuscripts, which read *20 cubits* [9.2 meters]; Hebrew reads *120 [cubits]*, which is 180 feet or 55 meters. **3:8** Hebrew *600 talents* [20.4 metric tons]. **3:9** Hebrew *50 shekels* [570 grams]. **3:11** Hebrew *5 cubits* [2.3 meters]; also in 3:11b, 12, 15. **3:15** As in Syriac version (see also 1 Kgs 7:15; 2 Kgs 25:17; Jer 52:21), which reads *18 cubits* [8.3 meters]; Hebrew reads *35 cubits*, which is 52.5 feet or 16.5 meters. **3:16** Hebrew *He made chains in the inner sanctuary.* The meaning of the Hebrew is uncertain. **3:17** *Jakin* probably means "he establishes"; *Boaz* probably means "in him is strength." **4:1a** Or *Huram-abi;* Hebrew reads *He.* **4:1b** Hebrew *20 cubits* [9.2 meters] *long, 20 cubits wide, and 10 cubits* [4.6 meters] *high.* **4:2** Hebrew *10 cubits* [4.6 meters] *across . . . 5 cubits* [2.3 meters] *deep and 30 cubits* [13.8 meters] *in circumference.* **4:3** Or *20 oxen per meter;* Hebrew reads *10 per cubit.* **4:5a** Hebrew *a handbreadth* [8 centimeters].

Mount Moriah

The Temple was built on a threshing floor David bought from Araunah that was located on Mount Moriah (2 Chronicles 3:1). This was where an angel appeared to David after the plague that came upon Israel was stopped (2 Samuel 24; 1 Chronicles 21), so it spoke of God's faithfulness to his covenant people. But it also reminded them of their history. For Mount Moriah was where Abraham, the founder of the Israelite people, had been prepared to offer his son Isaac to God but where God had intervened and himself provided a sacrifice instead (Genesis 22). It was as if God were saying that all the sacrifices offered here at this Temple would not be able to deal with human sin, but only the sacrifice that he himself would one day offer—that of his Son.

cup and resembled a water lily blossom. It
could hold about 16,500 gallons* of water.
6 He also made ten smaller basins for
washing the utensils for the burnt offerings.
He set five on the south side and five on the
north. But the priests washed themselves in
the Sea.
7 He then cast ten gold lampstands according to the specifications that had been
given, and he put them in the Temple. Five
were placed against the south wall, and five
were placed against the north wall.
8 He also built ten tables and placed them
in the Temple, five along the south wall and
five along the north wall. Then he molded
100 gold basins.
9 He then built a courtyard for the priests,
and also the large outer courtyard. He made
doors for the courtyard entrances and overlaid them with bronze. 10 The great bronze
basin called the Sea was placed near the
southeast corner of the Temple.
11 Huram-abi also made the necessary
washbasins, shovels, and bowls.

So at last Huram-abi completed everything King Solomon had assigned him to make for the Temple of God:

12 the two pillars;
the two bowl-shaped capitals on top of the pillars;
the two networks of interwoven chains that decorated the capitals;
13 the 400 pomegranates that hung from the chains on the capitals (two rows of pomegranates for each of the chain networks that decorated the capitals on top of the pillars);
14 the water carts holding the basins;
15 the Sea and the twelve oxen under it;
16 the ash buckets, the shovels, the meat hooks, and all the related articles.

Huram-abi made all these things of burnished bronze for the Temple of the LORD,
just as King Solomon had directed. 17 The
king had them cast in clay molds in the
Jordan Valley between Succoth and Zarethan.* 18 Solomon used such great quantities of bronze that its weight could not be
determined.
19 Solomon also made all the furnishings
for the Temple of God:

the gold altar;
the tables for the Bread of the Presence;
20 the lampstands and their lamps of solid gold, to burn in front of the Most Holy Place as prescribed;
21 the flower decorations, lamps, and tongs—all of the purest gold;
22 the lamp snuffers, bowls, ladles, and incense burners—all of solid gold;
the doors for the entrances to the Most Holy Place and the main room of the Temple, overlaid with gold.

5 So Solomon finished all his work on the
Temple of the LORD. Then he brought
all the gifts his father, David, had dedicated—the silver, the gold, and the various
articles—and he stored them in the treasuries of the Temple of God.

The Ark Brought to the Temple

2 Solomon then summoned to Jerusalem
the elders of Israel and all the heads of
tribes—the leaders of the ancestral families
of Israel. They were to bring the Ark of the
LORD's Covenant to the Temple from its location in the City of David, also known as
Zion. 3 So all the men of Israel assembled
before the king at the annual Festival of
Shelters, which is held in early autumn.*
4 When all the elders of Israel arrived, the
Levites picked up the Ark. 5 The priests and
Levites brought up the Ark along with the
special tent* and all the sacred items that
had been in it. 6 There, before the Ark, King
Solomon and the entire community of Israel
sacrificed so many sheep, goats, and cattle
that no one could keep count!
7 Then the priests carried the Ark of the
LORD's Covenant into the inner sanctuary
of the Temple—the Most Holy Place—and
placed it beneath the wings of the cherubim. 8 The cherubim spread their wings over
the Ark, forming a canopy over the Ark and
its carrying poles. 9 These poles were so long
that their ends could be seen from the Holy
Place,* which is in front of the Most Holy
Place, but not from the outside. They are
still there to this day. 10 Nothing was in the
Ark except the two stone tablets that Moses
had placed in it at Mount Sinai,* where the
LORD made a covenant with the people of
Israel when they left Egypt.
11 Then the priests left the Holy Place. All
the priests who were present had purified
themselves, whether or not they were on
duty that day. 12 And the Levites who were

musicians—Asaph, Heman, Jeduthun, and all their sons and brothers—were dressed in fine linen robes and stood at the east side of the altar playing cymbals, lyres, and harps. They were joined by 120 priests who were playing trumpets. [13]The trumpeters and singers performed together in unison to praise and give thanks to the LORD. Accompanied by trumpets, cymbals, and other instruments, they raised their voices and praised the LORD with these words:

"He is good!
His faithful love endures forever!"

At that moment a thick cloud filled the Temple of the LORD. [14]The priests could not continue their service because of the cloud, for the glorious presence of the LORD filled the Temple of God.

Solomon Praises the LORD

6 Then Solomon prayed, "O LORD, you have said that you would live in a thick cloud of darkness. [2]Now I have built a glorious Temple for you, a place where you can live forever!"

[3]Then the king turned around to the entire community of Israel standing before him and gave this blessing: [4]"Praise the LORD, the God of Israel, who has kept the promise he made to my father, David. For he told my father, [5]'From the day I brought my people out of the land of Egypt, I have never chosen a city among any of the tribes of Israel as the place where a Temple should be built to honor my name. Nor have I chosen a king to lead my people Israel. [6]But now I have chosen Jerusalem as the place for my name to be honored, and I have chosen David to be king over my people Israel.'"

[7]Then Solomon said, "My father, David, wanted to build this Temple to honor the name of the LORD, the God of Israel. [8]But the LORD told him, 'You wanted to build the Temple to honor my name. Your intention is good, [9]but you are not the one to do it. One of your own sons will build the Temple to honor me.'

[10]"And now the LORD has fulfilled the promise he made, for I have become king in my father's place, and now I sit on the throne of Israel, just as the LORD promised. I have built this Temple to honor the name of the LORD, the God of Israel. [11]There I have placed the Ark, which contains the covenant that the LORD made with the people of Israel."

Solomon's Prayer of Dedication

[12]Then Solomon stood before the altar of the LORD in front of the entire community of Israel, and he lifted his hands in prayer. [13]Now Solomon had made a bronze platform 7½ feet long, 7½ feet wide, and 4½ feet high* and had placed it at the center of the Temple's outer courtyard. He stood on the platform, and then he knelt in front of the entire community of Israel and lifted his hands toward heaven. [14]He prayed,

"O LORD, God of Israel, there is no God
like you in all of heaven and earth. You
keep your covenant and show unfailing
love to all who walk before you in
wholehearted devotion. [15]You have kept
your promise to your servant David, my
father. You made that promise with your
own mouth, and with your own hands
you have fulfilled it today.

[16]"And now, O LORD, God of Israel,
carry out the additional promise you
made to your servant David, my father.
For you said to him, 'If your descendants
guard their behavior and faithfully
follow my Law as you have done, one
of them will always sit on the throne
of Israel.' [17]Now, O LORD, God of Israel,
fulfill this promise to your servant David.

[18]"But will God really live on earth
among people? Why, even the highest
heavens cannot contain you. How
much less this Temple I have built!
[19]Nevertheless, listen to my prayer and
my plea, O LORD my God. Hear the cry
and the prayer that your servant is
making to you. [20]May you watch over
this Temple day and night, this place
where you have said you would put your
name. May you always hear the prayers
I make toward this place. [21]May you hear
the humble and earnest requests from
me and your people Israel when we pray
toward this place. Yes, hear us from

4:5b Hebrew *3,000 baths* [63 kiloliters]. **4:17** As in parallel text at 1 Kgs 7:46; Hebrew reads *Zeredah.* **5:3** Hebrew *at the festival that is in the seventh month.* The Festival of Shelters began on the fifteenth day of the seventh month of the ancient Hebrew lunar calendar. This day occurred in late September, October, or early November. **5:5** Hebrew *the Tent of Meeting;* i.e., the tent mentioned in 2 Sam 6:17 and 1 Chr 16:1. **5:9** As in some Hebrew manuscripts and Greek version (see also 1 Kgs 8:8); Masoretic Text reads *from the Ark.* **5:10** Hebrew *Horeb,* another name for Sinai. **6:13** Hebrew *5 cubits* [2.3 meters] *long, 5 cubits wide, and 3 cubits* [1.4 meters] *high.*

heaven where you live, and when you
hear, forgive.
22"If someone wrongs another
person and is required to take an oath
of innocence in front of your altar at
this Temple, 23then hear from heaven
and judge between your servants—the
accuser and the accused. Pay back
the guilty as they deserve. Acquit the
innocent because of their innocence.
24"If your people Israel are defeated by
their enemies because they have sinned
against you, and if they turn back and
acknowledge your name and pray to you
here in this Temple, 25then hear from
heaven and forgive the sin of your people
Israel and return them to this land you
gave to them and to their ancestors.
26"If the skies are shut up and there
is no rain because your people have
sinned against you, and if they pray
toward this Temple and acknowledge
your name and turn from their sins
because you have punished them, 27then
hear from heaven and forgive the sins of
your servants, your people Israel. Teach
them to follow the right path, and send
rain on your land that you have given to
your people as their special possession.
28"If there is a famine in the land or
a plague or crop disease or attacks of
locusts or caterpillars, or if your people's
enemies are in the land besieging their
towns—whatever disaster or disease there
is—29and if your people Israel pray about
their troubles or sorrow, raising their
hands toward this Temple, 30then hear
from heaven where you live, and forgive.
Give your people what their actions
deserve, for you alone know each human
heart. 31Then they will fear you and walk
in your ways as long as they live in the
land you gave to our ancestors.
32"In the future, foreigners who do not
belong to your people Israel will hear of
you. They will come from distant lands
when they hear of your great name and
your strong hand and your powerful
arm. And when they pray toward this
Temple, 33then hear from heaven where
you live, and grant what they ask of you.
In this way, all the people of the earth
will come to know and fear you, just as
your own people Israel do. They, too,
will know that this Temple I have built
honors your name.
34"If your people go out where you
send them to fight their enemies, and if
they pray to you by turning toward this
city you have chosen and toward this
Temple I have built to honor your name,
35then hear their prayers from heaven
and uphold their cause.
36"If they sin against you—and who
has never sinned?—you might become
angry with them and let their enemies
conquer them and take them captive to
a foreign land far away or near. 37But in
that land of exile, they might turn to you
in repentance and pray, 'We have sinned,
done evil, and acted wickedly.' 38If they
turn to you with their whole heart and
soul in the land of their captivity and
pray toward the land you gave to their
ancestors—toward this city you have
chosen, and toward this Temple I have
built to honor your name—39then hear
their prayers and their petitions from
heaven where you live, and uphold their
cause. Forgive your people who have
sinned against you.
40"O my God, may your eyes be open
and your ears attentive to all the prayers
made to you in this place.

41 "And now arise, O LORD God, and
enter your resting place,
along with the Ark, the symbol of
your power.
May your priests, O LORD God, be
clothed with salvation;
may your loyal servants rejoice in
your goodness.
42 O LORD God, do not reject the king
you have anointed.
Remember your unfailing love for
your servant David."

The Dediction of the Temple

7 When Solomon finished praying, fire
flashed down from heaven and burned
up the burnt offerings and sacrifices, and
the glorious presence of the LORD filled the
Temple. 2The priests could not enter the
Temple of the LORD because the glorious

▸ **6:36** *See **Sin**, page 387.*

presence of the LORD filled it. 3When all the
people of Israel saw the fire coming down and
the glorious presence of the LORD filling the
Temple, they fell face down on the ground
and worshiped and praised the LORD, saying,

"He is good!
His faithful love endures forever!"

4Then the king and all the people offered
sacrifices to the LORD. 5King Solomon offered
a sacrifice of 22,000 cattle and 120,000 sheep
and goats. And so the king and all the people
dedicated the Temple of God. 6The priests
took their assigned positions, and so did
the Levites who were singing, "His faithful
love endures forever!" They accompanied
the singing with music from the instruments
King David had made for praising the LORD.
Across from the Levites, the priests blew the
trumpets, while all Israel stood.

7Solomon then consecrated the central
area of the courtyard in front of the LORD's
Temple. He offered burnt offerings and the
fat of peace offerings there, because the
bronze altar he had built could not hold
all the burnt offerings, grain offerings, and
sacrificial fat.

8For the next seven days Solomon and all
Israel celebrated the Festival of Shelters.* A
large congregation had gathered from as far
away as Lebo-hamath in the north and the
Brook of Egypt in the south. 9On the eighth
day they had a closing ceremony, for they
had celebrated the dedication of the altar
for seven days and the Festival of Shelters
for seven days. 10Then at the end of the celebration,* Solomon sent the people home.
They were all joyful and glad because the
LORD had been so good to David and to
Solomon and to his people Israel.

The LORD's Response to Solomon

11So Solomon finished the Temple of the
LORD, as well as the royal palace. He completed everything he had planned to do
in the construction of the Temple and the
palace. 12Then one night the LORD appeared
to Solomon and said,

"I have heard your prayer and have
chosen this Temple as the place for
making sacrifices. 13At times I might
shut up the heavens so that no rain falls,
or command grasshoppers to devour
your crops, or send plagues among
you. 14Then if my people who are called
by my name will humble themselves
and pray and seek my face and turn
from their wicked ways, I will hear
from heaven and will forgive their sins
and restore their land. 15My eyes will

7:8 Hebrew *the festival* (also in 7:9); see note on 5:3. **7:10** Hebrew *Then on the twenty-third day of the seventh month.* This day of the ancient Hebrew lunar calendar occurred in October or early November.

▸ **7:14** *See* ***Revival****, page 817;* ***Repentance****, page 1253.*

Seeking God for the nation

"If my people who are called by my name will humble themselves and pray and seek my face and turn from their wicked ways, I will hear from heaven and will forgive their sins and restore their land" (2 Chronicles 7:14). These were the words God promised to Solomon at the Temple's dedication; and there were many times when they would be fulfilled as God's people cried out to him in time of need, despair, or realization of their wickedness.

But does this promise still apply to us today? After all, we live in a secular nation, where not everyone believes in the living God, rather than a theocratic (God-ruled) nation like Israel. But while our situation is not *identical* to Israel's, it is certainly *parallel*. God always delights to hear any prayer, especially for the unsaved and for ungodliness to be changed. And Paul encourages us to pray "for kings and all who are in authority" adding that "this is good and pleases God our Savior, who wants everyone to be saved and to understand the truth" (1 Timothy 2:1-4). If God's heart is for all to be saved, then this surely gives us boldness to pray for many, many people to be saved in our nation—so many that the nation itself is transformed.

be open and my ears attentive to every prayer made in this place. 16 For I have chosen this Temple and set it apart to be holy—a place where my name will be honored forever. I will always watch over it, for it is dear to my heart.

17 "As for you, if you faithfully follow me as David your father did, obeying all my commands, decrees, and regulations, 18 then I will establish the throne of your dynasty. For I made this covenant with your father, David, when I said, 'One of your descendants will always rule over Israel.'

19 "But if you or your descendants abandon me and disobey the decrees and commands I have given you, and if you serve and worship other gods, 20 then I will uproot the people from this land that I have given them. I will reject this Temple that I have made holy to honor my name. I will make it an object of mockery and ridicule among the nations. 21 And though this Temple is impressive now, all who pass by will be appalled. They will ask, 'Why did the LORD do such terrible things to this land and to this Temple?'

22 "And the answer will be, 'Because his people abandoned the LORD, the God of their ancestors, who brought them out of Egypt, and they worshiped other gods instead and bowed down to them. That is why he has brought all these disasters on them.'"

Solomon's Many Achievements

8 It took Solomon twenty years to build the LORD's Temple and his own royal palace. At the end of that time, 2 Solomon turned his attention to rebuilding the towns that King Hiram* had given him, and he settled Israelites in them.

3 Solomon also fought against the town of Hamath-zobah and conquered it. 4 He rebuilt Tadmor in the wilderness and built towns in the region of Hamath as supply centers. 5 He fortified the towns of Upper Beth-horon and Lower Beth-horon, rebuilding their walls and installing barred gates. 6 He also rebuilt Baalath and other supply centers and constructed towns where his chariots and horses* could be stationed. He built everything he desired in Jerusalem and Lebanon and throughout his entire realm.

7 There were still some people living in the land who were not Israelites, including the Hittites, Amorites, Perizzites, Hivites, and Jebusites. 8 These were descendants of the nations whom the people of Israel had not destroyed. So Solomon conscripted them for his labor force, and they serve as forced laborers to this day. 9 But Solomon did not conscript any of the Israelites for his labor force. Instead, he assigned them to serve as fighting men, officers in his army, commanders of his chariots, and charioteers. 10 King Solomon appointed 250 of them to supervise the people.

11 Solomon moved his wife, Pharaoh's daughter, from the City of David to the new palace he had built for her. He said, "My wife must not live in King David's palace, for the Ark of the LORD has been there, and it is holy ground."

12 Then Solomon presented burnt offerings to the LORD on the altar he had built for him in front of the entry room of the Temple. 13 He offered the sacrifices for the Sabbaths, the new moon festivals, and the three annual festivals—the Passover celebration, the Festival of Harvest,* and the Festival of Shelters—as Moses had commanded.

14 In assigning the priests to their duties, Solomon followed the regulations of his father, David. He also assigned the Levites to lead the people in praise and to assist the priests in their daily duties. And he assigned the gatekeepers to their gates by their divisions, following the commands of David, the man of God. 15 Solomon did not deviate in any way from David's commands concerning the priests and Levites and the treasuries.

16 So Solomon made sure that all the work related to building the Temple of the LORD was carried out, from the day its foundation was laid to the day of its completion.

17 Later Solomon went to Ezion-geber and Elath,* ports along the shore of the Red Sea* in the land of Edom. 18 Hiram sent him ships commanded by his own officers and manned by experienced crews of sailors. These ships sailed to Ophir with Solomon's men and brought back to Solomon almost seventeen tons* of gold.

Visit of the Queen of Sheba

9 When the queen of Sheba heard of Solomon's fame, she came to Jerusalem to test him with hard questions. She arrived

with a large group of attendants and a great
caravan of camels loaded with spices, large
quantities of gold, and precious jewels.
When she met with Solomon, she talked
with him about everything she had on her
mind. 2 Solomon had answers for all her
questions; nothing was too hard for him to
explain to her. 3 When the queen of Sheba realized how wise Solomon was, and when she
saw the palace he had built, 4 she was overwhelmed. She was also amazed at the food
on his tables, the organization of his officials
and their splendid clothing, the cup-bearers
and their robes, and the burnt offerings*
Solomon made at the Temple of the LORD.
5 She exclaimed to the king, "Everything
I heard in my country about your achievements* and wisdom is true! 6 I didn't believe
what was said until I arrived here and saw it
with my own eyes. In fact, I had not heard
the half of your great wisdom! It is far
beyond what I was told. 7 How happy your
people must be! What a privilege for your
officials to stand here day after day, listening to your wisdom! 8 Praise the LORD your
God, who delights in you and has placed
you on the throne as king to rule for him.
Because God loves Israel and desires this
kingdom to last forever, he has made you
king over them so you can rule with justice
and righteousness."
9 Then she gave the king a gift of 9,000
pounds* of gold, great quantities of spices,
and precious jewels. Never before had there
been spices as fine as those the queen of
Sheba gave to King Solomon.
10 (In addition, the crews of Hiram and
Solomon brought gold from Ophir, and they
also brought red sandalwood* and precious
jewels. 11 The king used the sandalwood to
make steps* for the Temple of the LORD and
the royal palace, and to construct lyres and
harps for the musicians. Never before had
such beautiful things been seen in Judah.)
12 King Solomon gave the queen of Sheba
whatever she asked for—gifts of greater
value than the gifts she had given him.
Then she and all her attendants returned to
their own land.

Solomon's Wealth and Splendor

13 Each year Solomon received about 25 tons*
of gold. 14 This did not include the additional
revenue he received from merchants and
traders. All the kings of Arabia and the governors of the provinces also brought gold
and silver to Solomon.
15 King Solomon made 200 large shields of
hammered gold, each weighing more than
15 pounds.* 16 He also made 300 smaller
shields of hammered gold, each weighing
more than 7½ pounds.* The king placed
these shields in the Palace of the Forest of
Lebanon.
17 Then the king made a huge throne, decorated with ivory and overlaid with pure gold.
18 The throne had six steps, with a footstool
of gold. There were armrests on both sides
of the seat, and the figure of a lion stood on
each side of the throne. 19 There were also
twelve other lions, one standing on each end
of the six steps. No other throne in all the
world could be compared with it!
20 All of King Solomon's drinking cups

8:2 Hebrew *Huram,* a variant spelling of Hiram; also in 8:18. **8:6** Or *and charioteers.* **8:13** Or *Festival of Weeks.* **8:17a** As in Greek version (see also 2 Kgs 14:22; 16:6); Hebrew reads *Eloth,* a variant spelling of Elath. **8:17b** As in parallel text at 1 Kgs 9:26; Hebrew reads *the sea.* **8:18** Hebrew *450 talents* [15.3 metric tons]. **9:4** As in Greek and Syriac versions (see also 1 Kgs 10:5); Hebrew reads *and the ascent.* **9:5** Hebrew *your words.* **9:9** Hebrew *120 talents* [4,000 kilograms]. **9:10** Hebrew *algum wood* (also in 9:11); perhaps a variant spelling of *almug.* Compare parallel text at 1 Kgs 10:11-12. **9:11** Or *gateways.* The meaning of the Hebrew is uncertain. **9:13** Hebrew *666 talents* [23 metric tons]. **9:15** Hebrew *600 [shekels] of hammered gold* [6.8 kilograms]. **9:16** Hebrew *300 [shekels] of gold* [3.4 kilograms].

The Queen of Sheba

Sheba was a trading nation in southwest Arabia that imported exotic goods from India and Africa and sent them north to Damascus on the caravan routes. While 2 Chronicles 9:1-12 tells us that Sheba's queen came to visit Solomon because she had heard of his wisdom and wealth, the context suggests there may have been another motive. For chapter 8 ends by telling us that Solomon was developing a trading fleet based at Ezion-geber on the Red Sea—something that would certainly have alarmed her. The story demonstrates that behind people's flattery of us there often lie other motives.

were solid gold, as were all the utensils in the Palace of the Forest of Lebanon. They were not made of silver, for silver was considered worthless in Solomon's day!

21 The king had a fleet of trading ships of Tarshish manned by the sailors sent by Hiram.* Once every three years the ships returned, loaded with gold, silver, ivory, apes, and peacocks.*

22 So King Solomon became richer and wiser than any other king on earth. 23 Kings from every nation came to consult him and to hear the wisdom God had given him. 24 Year after year everyone who visited brought him gifts of silver and gold, clothing, weapons, spices, horses, and mules.

25 Solomon had 4,000 stalls for his horses and chariots, and he had 12,000 horses.* He stationed some of them in the chariot cities, and some near him in Jerusalem. 26 He ruled over all the kings from the Euphrates River* in the north to the land of the Philistines and the border of Egypt in the south. 27 The king made silver as plentiful in Jerusalem as stone. And valuable cedar timber was as common as the sycamore-fig trees that grow in the foothills of Judah.* 28 Solomon's horses were imported from Egypt* and many other countries.

Summary of Solomon's Reign

29 The rest of the events of Solomon's reign, from beginning to end, are recorded in *The Record of Nathan the Prophet*, and *The Prophecy of Ahijah from Shiloh*, and also in *The Visions of Iddo the Seer*, concerning Jeroboam son of Nebat. 30 Solomon ruled in Jerusalem over all Israel for forty years. 31 When he died, he was buried in the City of David, named for his father. Then his son Rehoboam became the next king.

The Northern Tribes Revolt

10 Rehoboam went to Shechem, where all Israel had gathered to make him king. 2 When Jeroboam son of Nebat heard of this, he returned from Egypt, for he had fled to Egypt to escape from King Solomon. 3 The leaders of Israel summoned him, and Jeroboam and all Israel went to speak with Rehoboam. 4 "Your father was a hard master," they said. "Lighten the harsh labor demands and heavy taxes that your father imposed on us. Then we will be your loyal subjects."

5 Rehoboam replied, "Come back in three days for my answer." So the people went away.

6 Then King Rehoboam discussed the matter with the older men who had counseled his father, Solomon. "What is your advice?" he asked. "How should I answer these people?"

7 The older counselors replied, "If you are good to these people and do your best to please them and give them a favorable answer, they will always be your loyal subjects."

8 But Rehoboam rejected the advice of the older men and instead asked the opinion of the young men who had grown up with him and were now his advisers. 9 "What is your advice?" he asked them. "How should I answer these people who want me to lighten the burdens imposed by my father?"

10 The young men replied, "This is what you should tell those complainers who want a lighter burden: 'My little finger is thicker than my father's waist! 11 Yes, my father laid heavy burdens on you, but I'm going to make them even heavier! My father beat you with whips, but I will beat you with scorpions!'"

12 Three days later Jeroboam and all the people returned to hear Rehoboam's decision, just as the king had ordered. 13 But Rehoboam spoke harshly to them, for he rejected the advice of the older counselors 14 and followed the counsel of his younger advisers. He told the people, "My father laid* heavy burdens on you, but I'm going to make them even heavier! My father beat you with whips, but I will beat you with scorpions!"

15 So the king paid no attention to the people. This turn of events was the will of God, for it fulfilled the LORD's message to Jeroboam son of Nebat through the prophet Ahijah from Shiloh.

16 When all Israel realized* that the king had refused to listen to them, they responded,

"Down with the dynasty of David!
We have no interest in the son of
Jesse.

▸ **10:1** *See* ***Rulers of Israel and Judah****, page 393;* ***King Rehoboam****, page 394.*

Back to your homes, O Israel!
  Look out for your own house,
    O David!"

So all the people of Israel returned home. 17But Rehoboam continued to rule over the Israelites who lived in the towns of Judah.

18King Rehoboam sent Adoniram,* who was in charge of forced labor, to restore order, but the people of Israel stoned him to death. When this news reached King Rehoboam, he quickly jumped into his chariot and fled to Jerusalem. 19And to this day the northern tribes of Israel have refused to be ruled by a descendant of David.

Shemaiah's Prophecy

11 When Rehoboam arrived at Jerusalem, he mobilized the men of Judah and Benjamin—180,000 select troops—to fight against Israel and to restore the kingdom to himself.

2But the LORD said to Shemaiah, the man of God, 3"Say to Rehoboam son of Solomon, king of Judah, and to all the Israelites in Judah and Benjamin: 4'This is what the LORD says: Do not fight against your relatives. Go back home, for what has happened is my doing!'" So they obeyed the message of the LORD and did not fight against Jeroboam.

Rehoboam Fortifies Judah

5Rehoboam remained in Jerusalem and fortified various towns for the defense of Judah. 6He built up Bethlehem, Etam, Tekoa, 7Beth-zur, Soco, Adullam, 8Gath, Mareshah, Ziph, 9Adoraim, Lachish, Azekah, 10Zorah, Aijalon, and Hebron. These became the fortified towns of Judah and Benjamin. 11Rehoboam strengthened their defenses and stationed commanders in them, and he stored supplies of food, olive oil, and wine. 12He also put shields and spears in these towns as a further safety measure. So only Judah and Benjamin remained under his control.

13But all the priests and Levites living among the northern tribes of Israel sided with Rehoboam. 14The Levites even abandoned their pasturelands and property and moved to Judah and Jerusalem, because Jeroboam and his sons would not allow them to serve the LORD as priests. 15Jeroboam appointed his own priests to serve at the pagan shrines, where they worshiped the goat and calf idols he had made. 16From all the tribes of Israel, those who sincerely wanted to worship the LORD, the God of Israel, followed the Levites to Jerusalem, where they could offer sacrifices to the LORD, the God of their ancestors. 17This strengthened the kingdom of Judah, and for three years they supported Rehoboam son of Solomon, for during those years they faithfully followed in the footsteps of David and Solomon.

Rehoboam's Family

18Rehoboam married his cousin Mahalath, the daughter of David's son Jerimoth and of Abihail, the daughter of Eliab son of Jesse. 19Mahalath had three sons—Jeush, Shemariah, and Zaham.

20Later Rehoboam married another cousin, Maacah, the granddaughter of Absalom. Maacah gave birth to Abijah, Attai, Ziza, and Shelomith. 21Rehoboam loved Maacah more than any of his other wives and concubines. In all, he had eighteen wives and sixty concubines, and they gave birth to twenty-eight sons and sixty daughters.

22Rehoboam appointed Maacah's son Abijah as leader among the princes, making it clear that he would be the next king. 23Rehoboam also wisely gave responsibilities to his other sons and stationed some of them in the fortified towns throughout the land of Judah and Benjamin. He provided them with generous provisions, and he found many wives for them.

Egypt Invades Judah

12 But when Rehoboam was firmly established and strong, he abandoned the Law of the LORD, and all Israel followed him in this sin. 2Because they were unfaithful to the LORD, King Shishak of Egypt came up and attacked Jerusalem in the fifth year of King Rehoboam's reign. 3He came with 1,200 chariots, 60,000 horses,* and a countless army of foot soldiers, including Libyans, Sukkites, and Ethiopians.* 4Shishak conquered Judah's fortified towns and then advanced to attack Jerusalem.

9:21a Hebrew *Huram,* a variant spelling of Hiram. **9:21b** Or *and baboons.* **9:25** Or *12,000 charioteers.* **9:26** Hebrew *the river.* **9:27** Hebrew *the Shephelah.* **9:28** Possibly *Muzur,* a district near Cilicia. **10:14** As in Greek version and many Hebrew manuscripts (see also 1 Kgs 12:14); Masoretic Text reads *I will lay.* **10:16** As in Syriac version, Latin Vulgate, and many Hebrew manuscripts (see also 1 Kgs 12:16); Masoretic Text lacks *realized.* **10:18** Hebrew *Hadoram,* a variant spelling of Adoniram; compare 1 Kgs 4:6; 5:14; 12:18. **12:3a** Or *charioteers,* or *horsemen.* **12:3b** Hebrew *and Cushites.*

[5]The prophet Shemaiah then met with Rehoboam and Judah's leaders, who had all fled to Jerusalem because of Shishak. Shemaiah told them, "This is what the LORD says: You have abandoned me, so I am abandoning you to Shishak."

[6]Then the leaders of Israel and the king humbled themselves and said, "The LORD is right in doing this to us!"

[7]When the LORD saw their change of heart, he gave this message to Shemaiah: "Since the people have humbled themselves, I will not completely destroy them and will soon give them some relief. I will not use Shishak to pour out my anger on Jerusalem. [8]But they will become his subjects, so they will know the difference between serving me and serving earthly rulers."

[9]So King Shishak of Egypt came up and attacked Jerusalem. He ransacked the treasuries of the LORD's Temple and the royal palace; he stole everything, including all the gold shields Solomon had made. [10]King Rehoboam later replaced them with bronze shields as substitutes, and he entrusted them to the care of the commanders of the guard who protected the entrance to the royal palace. [11]Whenever the king went to the Temple of the LORD, the guards would also take the shields and then return them to the guardroom. [12]Because Rehoboam humbled himself, the LORD's anger was turned away, and he did not destroy him completely. There were still some good things in the land of Judah.

Summary of Rehoboam's Reign

[13]King Rehoboam firmly established himself in Jerusalem and continued to rule. He was forty-one years old when he became king, and he reigned seventeen years in Jerusalem, the city the LORD had chosen from among all the tribes of Israel as the place to honor his name. Rehoboam's mother was Naamah, a woman from Ammon. [14]But he was an evil king, for he did not seek the LORD with all his heart.

[15]The rest of the events of Rehoboam's reign, from beginning to end, are recorded in *The Record of Shemaiah the Prophet* and *The Record of Iddo the Seer,* which are part of the genealogical record. Rehoboam and Jeroboam were continually at war with each other. [16]When Rehoboam died, he was buried in the City of David. Then his son Abijah became the next king.

Abijah's War with Jeroboam

13 Abijah began to rule over Judah in the eighteenth year of Jeroboam's reign in Israel. [2]He reigned in Jerusalem three years. His mother was Maacah,* the daughter of Uriel from Gibeah.

Then war broke out between Abijah and Jeroboam. [3]Judah, led by King Abijah, fielded 400,000 select warriors, while

Keeping up appearances

In 925 BC Egypt's armies swept through Judah and Israel, attacking Jerusalem as they went. King Rehoboam of Judah had started out so well, walking in God's ways for the first three years of his reign and so enjoying God's blessing (2 Chronicles 11:17). But in his fourth year he turned from God (12:1), so God brought Egypt's attack as his judgment. The Egyptians seized the treasures from the palace and Temple, including Solomon's special gold shields. Rehoboam could not face up to the shame of this, so he tried to make it look as if nothing had changed. He had new bronze shields made to replace them. Bronze was far less valuable, but from a distance they would look like gold as they glinted in the sun. Rehoboam was trying to keep up appearances rather than owning up to the truth of the situation.

People still try to do the same. They cover up the truth of the situation (perhaps the fact that their marriage is in difficulty, or they have lost their job, or they have fallen into sin) and try to carry on as though nothing has happened. But God cannot bless us when we walk this way; it is only when we come clean and confess our sin that God's hand is released to bless us again.

Jeroboam mustered 800,000 select troops
from Israel.
4When the army of Judah arrived in the
hill country of Ephraim, Abijah stood on
Mount Zemaraim and shouted to Jeroboam
and all Israel: "Listen to me! 5Don't you
realize that the LORD, the God of Israel,
made a lasting covenant* with David, giving
him and his descendants the throne of Israel
forever? 6Yet Jeroboam son of Nebat, a mere
servant of David's son Solomon, rebelled
against his master. 7Then a whole gang of
scoundrels joined him, defying Solomon's
son Rehoboam when he was young and inexperienced and could not stand up to them.
8"Do you really think you can stand
against the kingdom of the LORD that is led
by the descendants of David? You may have
a vast army, and you have those gold calves
that Jeroboam made as your gods. 9But you
have chased away the priests of the LORD
(the descendants of Aaron) and the Levites,
and you have appointed your own priests,
just like the pagan nations. You let anyone
become a priest these days! Whoever comes
to be dedicated with a young bull and seven
rams can become a priest of these so-called
gods of yours!
10"But as for us, the LORD is our God,
and we have not abandoned him. Only the
descendants of Aaron serve the LORD as
priests, and the Levites alone may help them
in their work. 11They present burnt offerings and fragrant incense to the LORD every
morning and evening. They place the Bread
of the Presence on the holy table, and they
light the gold lampstand every evening. We
are following the instructions of the LORD
our God, but you have abandoned him. 12So
you see, God is with us. He is our leader.
His priests blow their trumpets and lead us
into battle against you. O people of Israel,
do not fight against the LORD, the God of
your ancestors, for you will not succeed!"
13Meanwhile, Jeroboam had secretly sent
part of his army around behind the men of
Judah to ambush them. 14When Judah realized that they were being attacked from
the front and the rear, they cried out to the
LORD for help. Then the priests blew the
trumpets, 15and the men of Judah began to
shout. At the sound of their battle cry, God
defeated Jeroboam and all Israel and routed
them before Abijah and the army of Judah.
16The Israelite army fled from Judah, and
God handed them over to Judah in defeat.
17Abijah and his army inflicted heavy losses
on them; 500,000 of Israel's select troops
were killed that day. 18So Judah defeated
Israel on that occasion because they trusted
in the LORD, the God of their ancestors.
19Abijah and his army pursued Jeroboam's
troops and captured some of his towns,
including Bethel, Jeshanah, and Ephron,
along with their surrounding villages.
20So Jeroboam of Israel never regained his
power during Abijah's lifetime, and finally
the LORD struck him down and he died.
21Meanwhile, Abijah of Judah grew more
and more powerful. He married fourteen
wives and had twenty-two sons and sixteen
daughters.
22The rest of the events of Abijah's reign,
including his words and deeds, are recorded
in *The Commentary of Iddo the Prophet*.

Early Years of Asa's Reign

14 1*When Abijah died, he was buried in
the City of David. Then his son Asa
became the next king. There was peace in
the land for ten years. 2*Asa did what was
pleasing and good in the sight of the LORD
his God. 3He removed the foreign altars and
the pagan shrines. He smashed the sacred
pillars and cut down the Asherah poles. 4He
commanded the people of Judah to seek
the LORD, the God of their ancestors, and
to obey his law and his commands. 5Asa
also removed the pagan shrines, as well as
the incense altars from every one of Judah's
towns. So Asa's kingdom enjoyed a period
of peace. 6During those peaceful years, he
was able to build up the fortified towns
throughout Judah. No one tried to make war
against him at this time, for the LORD was
giving him rest from his enemies.
7Asa told the people of Judah, "Let us
build towns and fortify them with walls,
towers, gates, and bars. The land is still
ours because we sought the LORD our God,
and he has given us peace on every side."
So they went ahead with these projects and
brought them to completion.
8King Asa had an army of 300,000 warriors from the tribe of Judah, armed with
large shields and spears. He also had an

13:2 As in most Greek manuscripts and Syriac version (see also 2 Chr 11:20-21; 1 Kgs 15:2); Hebrew reads *Micaiah*, a variant spelling of Maacah. **13:5** Hebrew *a covenant of salt*. **14:1** Verse 14:1 is numbered 13:23 in Hebrew text. **14:2** Verses 14:2-15 are numbered 14:1-14 in Hebrew text.

army of 280,000 warriors from the tribe of
Benjamin, armed with small shields and
bows. Both armies were composed of well-
trained fighting men.
9 Once an Ethiopian* named Zerah attacked Judah with an army of 1,000,000
men* and 300 chariots. They advanced to
the town of Mareshah, 10 so Asa deployed his
armies for battle in the valley north of Mareshah.* 11 Then Asa cried out to the LORD
his God, "O LORD, no one but you can help
the powerless against the mighty! Help us,
O LORD our God, for we trust in you alone.
It is in your name that we have come against
this vast horde. O LORD, you are our God; do
not let mere men prevail against you!"
12 So the LORD defeated the Ethiopians* in
the presence of Asa and the army of Judah,
and the enemy fled. 13 Asa and his army
pursued them as far as Gerar, and so many
Ethiopians fell that they were unable to
rally. They were destroyed by the LORD and
his army, and the army of Judah carried off
a vast amount of plunder.
14 While they were at Gerar, they attacked
all the towns in that area, and terror from
the LORD came upon the people there. As a
result, a vast amount of plunder was taken
from these towns, too. 15 They also attacked
the camps of herdsmen and captured many
sheep, goats, and camels before finally returning to Jerusalem.

Asa's Religious Reforms

15 Then the Spirit of God came upon
Azariah son of Oded, 2 and he went out
to meet King Asa as he was returning from
the battle. "Listen to me, Asa!" he shouted.
"Listen, all you people of Judah and Benjamin! The LORD will stay with you as long
as you stay with him! Whenever you seek
him, you will find him. But if you abandon
him, he will abandon you. 3 For a long time
Israel was without the true God, without a
priest to teach them, and without the Law to
instruct them. 4 But whenever they were in
trouble and turned to the LORD, the God of
Israel, and sought him out, they found him.
5 "During those dark times, it was not safe
to travel. Problems troubled the people of
every land. 6 Nation fought against nation,
and city against city, for God was troubling
them with every kind of problem. 7 But as
for you, be strong and courageous, for your
work will be rewarded."
8 When Asa heard this message from
Azariah the prophet,* he took courage
and removed all the detestable idols from
the land of Judah and Benjamin and in the
towns he had captured in the hill country
of Ephraim. And he repaired the altar of
the LORD, which stood in front of the entry
room of the LORD's Temple.
9 Then Asa called together all the people
of Judah and Benjamin, along with the
people of Ephraim, Manasseh, and Simeon
who had settled among them. For many
from Israel had moved to Judah during
Asa's reign when they saw that the LORD
his God was with him. 10 The people gathered at Jerusalem in late spring,* during the
fifteenth year of Asa's reign.
11 On that day they sacrificed to the LORD
700 cattle and 7,000 sheep and goats from

King Asa

Asa's reign started out really well: He removed pagan shrines and idols and strengthened the nation at every level (2 Chronicles 14:1-8); when the Ethiopians attacked, he both led his army and depended upon God (14:9-11); and he responded quickly to prophecy and led Judah in renewing the covenant with God (15:1-15). As a result, Judah prospered—so much so that Israelites came south to join them (15:9; 16:1). But in his final years he drifted from his early faith. Rather than trusting God, he made an alliance with Aram (Syria) when Israel attacked, for which he was rebuked by a prophet (16:7-9). But rather than repent, Asa simply imprisoned the prophet and began to oppress his own people. He developed a serious foot disease, but "he did not seek the LORD's help but turned only to his physicians" (16:12). Asa shows us that starting well is not enough; we need to finish well too.

the plunder they had taken in the battle.
12 Then they entered into a covenant to
seek the LORD, the God of their ancestors,
with all their heart and soul. 13 They agreed
that anyone who refused to seek the LORD,
the God of Israel, would be put to death—
whether young or old, man or woman.
14 They shouted out their oath of loyalty to
the LORD with trumpets blaring and rams'
horns sounding. 15 All in Judah were happy
about this covenant, for they had entered
into it with all their heart. They earnestly
sought after God, and they found him. And
the LORD gave them rest from their enemies
on every side.

16 King Asa even deposed his grandmother* Maacah from her position as queen
mother because she had made an obscene
Asherah pole. He cut down her obscene
pole, broke it up, and burned it in the
Kidron Valley. 17 Although the pagan shrines
were not removed from Israel, Asa's heart
remained completely faithful throughout
his life. 18 He brought into the Temple of God
the silver and gold and the various items
that he and his father had dedicated.

19 So there was no more war until the
thirty-fifth year of Asa's reign.

Final Years of Asa's Reign

16 In the thirty-sixth year of Asa's reign,
King Baasha of Israel invaded Judah
and fortified Ramah in order to prevent
anyone from entering or leaving King Asa's
territory in Judah.

2 Asa responded by removing the silver
and gold from the treasuries of the Temple
of the LORD and the royal palace. He sent it
to King Ben-hadad of Aram, who was ruling
in Damascus, along with this message:

> 3 "Let there be a treaty* between you and
> me like the one between your father and
> my father. See, I am sending you silver
> and gold. Break your treaty with King
> Baasha of Israel so that he will leave
> me alone."

4 Ben-hadad agreed to King Asa's request
and sent the commanders of his army to
attack the towns of Israel. They conquered
the towns of Ijon, Dan, Abel-beth-maacah,*
and all the store cities in Naphtali. 5 As soon
as Baasha of Israel heard what was happening, he abandoned his project of fortifying
Ramah and stopped all work on it. 6 Then
King Asa called out all the men of Judah to
carry away the building stones and timbers
that Baasha had been using to fortify
Ramah. Asa used these materials to fortify
the towns of Geba and Mizpah.

7 At that time Hanani the seer came to
King Asa and told him, "Because you have
put your trust in the king of Aram instead
of in the LORD your God, you missed your
chance to destroy the army of the king of
Aram. 8 Don't you remember what happened to the Ethiopians* and Libyans and
their vast army, with all of their chariots and
charioteers?* At that time you relied on the
LORD, and he handed them over to you. 9 The
eyes of the LORD search the whole earth in
order to strengthen those whose hearts are
fully committed to him. What a fool you
have been! From now on you will be at war."

10 Asa became so angry with Hanani for
saying this that he threw him into prison
and put him in stocks. At that time Asa also
began to oppress some of his people.

Summary of Asa's Reign

11 The rest of the events of Asa's reign, from
beginning to end, are recorded in *The Book
of the Kings of Judah and Israel.* 12 In the
thirty-ninth year of his reign, Asa developed a serious foot disease. Yet even with
the severity of his disease, he did not seek
the LORD's help but turned only to his physicians. 13 So he died in the forty-first year of
his reign. 14 He was buried in the tomb he had
carved out for himself in the City of David.
He was laid on a bed perfumed with sweet
spices and fragrant ointments, and the
people built a huge funeral fire in his honor.

Jehoshaphat Rules in Judah

17 Then Jehoshaphat, Asa's son, became
the next king. He strengthened Judah
to stand against any attack from Israel. 2 He
stationed troops in all the fortified towns
of Judah, and he assigned additional garrisons to the land of Judah and to the towns of
Ephraim that his father, Asa, had captured.

14:9a Hebrew *a Cushite.* **14:9b** Or *an army of thousands and thousands;* Hebrew reads *an army of a thousand thousands.* **14:10** As in Greek version; Hebrew reads *valley of Zephathah near Mareshah.* **14:12** Hebrew *Cushites;* also in 14:13. **15:8** As in Syriac version and Latin Vulgate (see also 15:1); Hebrew reads *from Oded the prophet.* **15:10** Hebrew *in the third month.* This month of the ancient Hebrew lunar calendar usually occurs within the months of May and June. **15:16** Hebrew *his mother.* **16:3** As in Greek version; Hebrew reads *There is a treaty.* **16:4** As in parallel text at 1 Kgs 15:20; Hebrew reads *Abel-maim,* another name for Abel-beth-maacah. **16:8a** Hebrew *Cushites.* **16:8b** Or *and horsemen?*

3The LORD was with Jehoshaphat because
he followed the example of his father's early
years* and did not worship the images of
Baal. 4He sought his father's God and obeyed
his commands instead of following the evil
practices of the kingdom of Israel. 5So the
LORD established Jehoshaphat's control
over the kingdom of Judah. All the people
of Judah brought gifts to Jehoshaphat, so he
became very wealthy and highly esteemed.
6He was deeply committed to* the ways of
the LORD. He removed the pagan shrines
and Asherah poles from Judah.

7In the third year of his reign Jehoshaphat
sent his officials to teach in all the towns of
Judah. These officials included Ben-hail,
Obadiah, Zechariah, Nethanel, and Micaiah.
8He sent Levites along with them, including
Shemaiah, Nethaniah, Zebadiah, Asahel,
Shemiramoth, Jehonathan, Adonijah,
Tobijah, and Tob-adonijah. He also sent out
the priests Elishama and Jehoram. 9They
took copies of the Book of the Law of the
LORD and traveled around through all the
towns of Judah, teaching the people.

10Then the fear of the LORD fell over all the
surrounding kingdoms so that none of them
wanted to declare war on Jehoshaphat.
11Some of the Philistines brought him gifts
and silver as tribute, and the Arabs brought
7,700 rams and 7,700 male goats.

12So Jehoshaphat became more and more
powerful and built fortresses and storage
cities throughout Judah. 13He stored numerous supplies in Judah's towns and stationed
an army of seasoned troops at Jerusalem.
14His army was enrolled according to ancestral clans.

From Judah there were 300,000 troops
organized in units of 1,000, under the
command of Adnah. 15Next in command
was Jehohanan, who commanded
280,000 troops. 16Next was Amasiah son
of Zicri, who volunteered for the LORD's
service, with 200,000 troops under his
command.

17From Benjamin there were 200,000
troops equipped with bows and
shields. They were under the command
of Eliada, a veteran soldier. 18Next
in command was Jehozabad, who
commanded 180,000 armed men.

19These were the troops stationed in Jerusalem to serve the king, besides those Jehoshaphat stationed in the fortified towns
throughout Judah.

Jehoshaphat and Ahab

18 Jehoshaphat enjoyed great riches
and high esteem, and he made an
alliance with Ahab of Israel by having his
son marry Ahab's daughter. 2A few years
later he went to Samaria to visit Ahab, who

King Jehoshaphat

Jehoshaphat was one of Judah's good kings. Politically, he strengthened Judah's defenses (2 Chronicles 17:2, 12-19) and reorganized its legal system (19:4-11); spiritually, "he was deeply committed to the ways of the LORD" (17:6), removing pagan shrines, obeying God, and sending Levites across the nation to teach God's Law (17:7-9). As a consequence, Judah was blessed (17:5, 10-11). When Judah was invaded by Moabites and Ammonites (chapter 20), Jehoshaphat kept his eyes fixed on God, telling his people, "Don't be discouraged by this mighty army, for the battle is not yours, but God's" (20:15). Judah didn't have to even fight; for as they began to worship God, their enemies turned against one another (20:22-26). But Jehoshaphat also made a big mistake: He allied himself with Israel's wicked King Ahab by marriage, which, despite his best efforts, led to his compromising his faith (chapter 18) and being rebuked (19:1-3). He did exactly the same later with another king of Israel (20:35-37). Jehoshaphat reminds us that, no matter how close we think our relationship with God might be, we always need to be on our guard against compromise.

▸ *See also* ***The power of praise****, page 501.*

prepared a great banquet for him and his
officials. They butchered great numbers of
sheep, goats, and cattle for the feast. Then
Ahab enticed Jehoshaphat to join forces
with him to recover Ramoth-gilead.
3"Will you go with me to Ramoth-gilead?"
King Ahab of Israel asked King Jehoshaphat
of Judah.

Jehoshaphat replied, "Why, of course!
You and I are as one, and my troops are your
troops. We will certainly join you in battle."
4Then Jehoshaphat added, "But first let's
find out what the LORD says."
5So the king of Israel summoned the
prophets, 400 of them, and asked them,
"Should we go to war against Ramoth-gilead, or should I hold back?"

They all replied, "Yes, go right ahead!
God will give the king victory."
6But Jehoshaphat asked, "Is there not
also a prophet of the LORD here? We should
ask him the same question."
7The king of Israel replied to Jehoshaphat, "There is one more man who could
consult the LORD for us, but I hate him. He
never prophesies anything but trouble for
me! His name is Micaiah son of Imlah."

Jehoshaphat replied, "That's not the way
a king should talk! Let's hear what he has
to say."
8So the king of Israel called one of his officials and said, "Quick! Bring Micaiah son
of Imlah."

Micaiah Prophesies against Ahab

9King Ahab of Israel and King Jehoshaphat
of Judah, dressed in their royal robes, were
sitting on thrones at the threshing floor near
the gate of Samaria. All of Ahab's prophets
were prophesying there in front of them.
10One of them, Zedekiah son of Kenaanah,
made some iron horns and proclaimed,
"This is what the LORD says: With these
horns you will gore the Arameans to death!"
11All the other prophets agreed. "Yes,"
they said, "go up to Ramoth-gilead and be
victorious, for the LORD will give the king
victory!"
12Meanwhile, the messenger who went
to get Micaiah said to him, "Look, all the
prophets are promising victory for the
king. Be sure that you agree with them and
promise success."
13But Micaiah replied, "As surely as the
LORD lives, I will say only what my God says."
14When Micaiah arrived before the king,
Ahab asked him, "Micaiah, should we go
to war against Ramoth-gilead, or should
I hold back?"

Micaiah replied sarcastically, "Yes, go up
and be victorious, for you will have victory
over them!"
15But the king replied sharply, "How
many times must I demand that you speak
only the truth to me when you speak for the
LORD?"
16Then Micaiah told him, "In a vision
I saw all Israel scattered on the mountains,
like sheep without a shepherd. And the
LORD said, 'Their master has been killed.*
Send them home in peace.'"
17"Didn't I tell you?" the king of Israel exclaimed to Jehoshaphat. "He never prophesies anything but trouble for me."
18Then Micaiah continued, "Listen to
what the LORD says! I saw the LORD sitting
on his throne with all the armies of heaven
around him, on his right and on his left.
19And the LORD said, 'Who can entice King
Ahab of Israel to go into battle against
Ramoth-gilead so he can be killed?'

"There were many suggestions, 20and
finally a spirit approached the LORD and
said, 'I can do it!'

"'How will you do this?' the LORD asked.
21"And the spirit replied, 'I will go out and
inspire all of Ahab's prophets to speak lies.'

"'You will succeed,' said the LORD. 'Go
ahead and do it.'
22"So you see, the LORD has put a lying
spirit in the mouths of your prophets. For
the LORD has pronounced your doom."
23Then Zedekiah son of Kenaanah walked
up to Micaiah and slapped him across the
face. "Since when did the Spirit of the LORD
leave me to speak to you?" he demanded.
24And Micaiah replied, "You will find out
soon enough when you are trying to hide in
some secret room!"
25"Arrest him!" the king of Israel ordered.
"Take him back to Amon, the governor of
the city, and to my son Joash. 26Give them
this order from the king: 'Put this man in
prison, and feed him nothing but bread and
water until I return safely from the battle!'"
27But Micaiah replied, "If you return
safely, it will mean that the LORD has not

17:3 Some Hebrew manuscripts read *the example of his father, David.* **17:6** Hebrew *His heart was courageous in.* **18:16** Hebrew *These people have no master.*

spoken through me!" Then he added to
those standing around, "Everyone mark
my words!"

The Death of Ahab

[28]So King Ahab of Israel and King Jehoshaphat of Judah led their armies against
Ramoth-gilead. [29]The king of Israel said to
Jehoshaphat, "As we go into battle, I will
disguise myself so no one will recognize me,
but you wear your royal robes." So the king
of Israel disguised himself, and they went
into battle.
[30]Meanwhile, the king of Aram had issued
these orders to his chariot commanders:
"Attack only the king of Israel! Don't bother
with anyone else." [31]So when the Aramean
chariot commanders saw Jehoshaphat in
his royal robes, they went after him. "There
is the king of Israel!" they shouted. But Jehoshaphat called out, and the LORD saved
him. God helped him by turning the attackers away from him. [32]As soon as the chariot
commanders realized he was not the king of
Israel, they stopped chasing him.
[33]An Aramean soldier, however, randomly shot an arrow at the Israelite troops
and hit the king of Israel between the joints
of his armor. "Turn the horses* and get me
out of here!" Ahab groaned to the driver of
the chariot. "I'm badly wounded!"
[34]The battle raged all that day, and the
king of Israel propped himself up in his
chariot facing the Arameans. In the evening,
just as the sun was setting, he died.

Jehoshaphat Appoints Judges

19 When King Jehoshaphat of Judah
arrived safely home in Jerusalem,
[2]Jehu son of Hanani the seer went out
to meet him. "Why should you help the
wicked and love those who hate the LORD?"
he asked the king. "Because of what you
have done, the LORD is very angry with
you. [3]Even so, there is some good in you,
for you have removed the Asherah poles
throughout the land, and you have committed yourself to seeking God."
[4]Jehoshaphat lived in Jerusalem, but he
went out among the people, traveling from
Beersheba to the hill country of Ephraim,
encouraging the people to return to the
LORD, the God of their ancestors. [5]He appointed judges throughout the nation in all
the fortified towns, [6]and he said to them,
"Always think carefully before pronounc-
ing judgment. Remember that you do not
judge to please people but to please the
LORD. He will be with you when you render
the verdict in each case. [7]Fear the LORD and
judge with integrity, for the LORD our God
does not tolerate perverted justice, partiality, or the taking of bribes."
[8]In Jerusalem, Jehoshaphat appointed
some of the Levites and priests and clan
leaders in Israel to serve as judges* for
cases involving the LORD's regulations and
for civil disputes. [9]These were his instructions to them: "You must always act in the
fear of the LORD, with faithfulness and an
undivided heart. [10]Whenever a case comes
to you from fellow citizens in an outlying
town, whether a murder case or some
other violation of God's laws, commands,
decrees, or regulations, you must warn
them not to sin against the LORD, so that he
will not be angry with you and them. Do this
and you will not be guilty.
[11]"Amariah the high priest will have final
say in all cases involving the LORD. Zebadiah son of Ishmael, a leader from the
tribe of Judah, will have final say in all civil
cases. The Levites will assist you in making
sure that justice is served. Take courage as
you fulfill your duties, and may the LORD be
with those who do what is right."

War with Surrounding Nations

20 After this, the armies of the Moabites, Ammonites, and some of the
Meunites* declared war on Jehoshaphat.
[2]Messengers came and told Jehoshaphat, "A
vast army from Edom* is marching against
you from beyond the Dead Sea.* They are
already at Hazazon-tamar." (This was
another name for En-gedi.)
[3]Jehoshaphat was terrified by this news
and begged the LORD for guidance. He also
ordered everyone in Judah to begin fasting.
[4]So people from all the towns of Judah came
to Jerusalem to seek the LORD's help.
[5]Jehoshaphat stood before the community of Judah and Jerusalem in front of the
new courtyard at the Temple of the LORD.
[6]He prayed, "O LORD, God of our ancestors,
you alone are the God who is in heaven. You
are ruler of all the kingdoms of the earth.
You are powerful and mighty; no one can
stand against you! [7]O our God, did you not
drive out those who lived in this land when

your people Israel arrived? And did you not
give this land forever to the descendants of
your friend Abraham? 8 Your people settled
here and built this Temple to honor your
name. 9 They said, 'Whenever we are faced
with any calamity such as war,* plague, or
famine, we can come to stand in your presence before this Temple where your name is
honored. We can cry out to you to save us,
and you will hear us and rescue us.'

10 "And now see what the armies of Ammon,
Moab, and Mount Seir are doing. You would
not let our ancestors invade those nations
when Israel left Egypt, so they went around
them and did not destroy them. 11 Now see
how they reward us! For they have come to
throw us out of your land, which you gave
us as an inheritance. 12 O our God, won't you
stop them? We are powerless against this
mighty army that is about to attack us. We
do not know what to do, but we are looking
to you for help."

13 As all the men of Judah stood before the
LORD with their little ones, wives, and children, 14 the Spirit of the LORD came upon one
of the men standing there. His name was Jahaziel son of Zechariah, son of Benaiah, son
of Jeiel, son of Mattaniah, a Levite who was
a descendant of Asaph.

15 He said, "Listen, all you people of Judah
and Jerusalem! Listen, King Jehoshaphat!
This is what the LORD says: Do not be afraid!
Don't be discouraged by this mighty army, for
the battle is not yours, but God's. 16 Tomorrow,
march out against them. You will find them
coming up through the ascent of Ziz at the
end of the valley that opens into the wilderness of Jeruel. 17 But you will not even need
to fight. Take your positions; then stand still
and watch the LORD's victory. He is with you,
O people of Judah and Jerusalem. Do not be
afraid or discouraged. Go out against them
tomorrow, for the LORD is with you!"

18 Then King Jehoshaphat bowed low with
his face to the ground. And all the people
of Judah and Jerusalem did the same, worshiping the LORD. 19 Then the Levites from
the clans of Kohath and Korah stood to
praise the LORD, the God of Israel, with a
very loud shout.

20 Early the next morning the army of
Judah went out into the wilderness of Tekoa.
On the way Jehoshaphat stopped and said,
"Listen to me, all you people of Judah and
Jerusalem! Believe in the LORD your God,
and you will be able to stand firm. Believe
in his prophets, and you will succeed."

21 After consulting the people, the king appointed singers to walk ahead of the army,
singing to the LORD and praising him for his
holy splendor. This is what they sang:

"Give thanks to the LORD;
his faithful love endures forever!"

22 At the very moment they began to sing
and give praise, the LORD caused the armies

18:33 Hebrew *Turn your hand.* **19:8** As in Greek version; the meaning of the Hebrew is uncertain. **20:1** As in some Greek manuscripts (see also 26:7); Hebrew repeats *Ammonites.* **20:2a** As in one Hebrew manuscript; most Hebrew manuscripts and ancient versions read *Aram.* **20:2b** Hebrew *the sea.* **20:9** Or *sword of judgment;* or *sword, judgment.*

The power of praise

When the Moabites and Ammonites attacked Judah, everything seemed to be going wrong for Jehoshaphat. But he "begged the LORD for guidance" (2 Chronicles 20:3). His prayer was utterly God-focused, recalling who God was, what God had done in the past, and what God had promised (20:5-9). He acknowledged that "we do not know what to do, but we are looking to you for help" (20:12). God replied through one of the prophets, reminding him that "the battle is not yours, but God's" (20:15) and encouraging him to stand firm.

The next morning Jehoshaphat did something unusual—he appointed a choir to lead his army into battle (20:21). As the singers began to praise, God turned Judah's enemies on one another, and they were completely slaughtered. God's people had not had to raise a finger, such was the power of praise.

Praise is powerful—but it isn't magic! Praise helps us set our eyes on *God*, who is the answer to our need or situation. It was God who defeated Judah's enemies, not praise.

of Ammon, Moab, and Mount Seir to start
fighting among themselves. 23The armies
of Moab and Ammon turned against their
allies from Mount Seir and killed every one
of them. After they had destroyed the army
of Seir, they began attacking each other.
24So when the army of Judah arrived at the
lookout point in the wilderness, all they
saw were dead bodies lying on the ground
as far as they could see. Not a single one of
the enemy had escaped.

25King Jehoshaphat and his men went
out to gather the plunder. They found vast
amounts of equipment, clothing,* and
other valuables—more than they could
carry. There was so much plunder that it
took them three days just to collect it all!
26On the fourth day they gathered in the
Valley of Blessing,* which got its name
that day because the people praised and
thanked the LORD there. It is still called the
Valley of Blessing today.

27Then all the men returned to Jerusalem,
with Jehoshaphat leading them, overjoyed
that the LORD had given them victory over
their enemies. 28They marched into Jerusalem to the music of harps, lyres, and trumpets, and they proceeded to the Temple of
the LORD.

29When all the surrounding kingdoms
heard that the LORD himself had fought
against the enemies of Israel, the fear of
God came over them. 30So Jehoshaphat's
kingdom was at peace, for his God had
given him rest on every side.

Summary of Jehoshaphat's Reign

31So Jehoshaphat ruled over the land of
Judah. He was thirty-five years old when he
became king, and he reigned in Jerusalem
twenty-five years. His mother was Azubah,
the daughter of Shilhi.

32Jehoshaphat was a good king, following
the ways of his father, Asa. He did what was
pleasing in the LORD's sight. 33During his
reign, however, he failed to remove all the
pagan shrines, and the people never fully
committed themselves to follow the God of
their ancestors.

34The rest of the events of Jehoshaphat's
reign, from beginning to end, are recorded
in *The Record of Jehu Son of Hanani,* which
is included in *The Book of the Kings of Israel.*

35Some time later King Jehoshaphat of
Judah made an alliance with King Ahaziah
of Israel, who was very wicked.* 36Together
they built a fleet of trading ships* at the
port of Ezion-geber. 37Then Eliezer son
of Dodavahu from Mareshah prophesied
against Jehoshaphat. He said, "Because you
have allied yourself with King Ahaziah, the
LORD will destroy your work." So the ships
met with disaster and never put out to sea.*

Jehoram Rules in Judah

21 When Jehoshaphat died, he was
buried with his ancestors in the City
of David. Then his son Jehoram became the
next king.

2Jehoram's brothers—the other sons of
Jehoshaphat—were Azariah, Jehiel, Zechariah, Azariahu, Michael, and Shephatiah;
all these were the sons of Jehoshaphat king
of Judah.* 3Their father had given each of
them valuable gifts of silver, gold, and costly
items, and also some of Judah's fortified
towns. However, he designated Jehoram
as the next king because he was the oldest.
4But when Jehoram had become solidly established as king, he killed all his brothers
and some of the other leaders of Judah.

5Jehoram was thirty-two years old when
he became king, and he reigned in Jerusalem eight years. 6But Jehoram followed the
example of the kings of Israel and was as
wicked as King Ahab, for he had married one
of Ahab's daughters. So Jehoram did what
was evil in the LORD's sight. 7But the LORD
did not want to destroy David's dynasty, for
he had made a covenant with David and
promised that his descendants would continue to rule, shining like a lamp forever.

8During Jehoram's reign, the Edomites
revolted against Judah and crowned their
own king. 9So Jehoram went out with his
full army and all his chariots. The Edomites
surrounded him and his chariot commanders, but he went out at night and attacked
them* under cover of darkness. 10Even so,
Edom has been independent from Judah to
this day. The town of Libnah also revolted
about that same time. All this happened
because Jehoram had abandoned the LORD,
the God of his ancestors. 11He had built
pagan shrines in the hill country of Judah
and had led the people of Jerusalem and
Judah to give themselves to pagan gods and
to go astray.

12Then Elijah the prophet wrote Jehoram
this letter:

"This is what the LORD, the God of your ancestor David, says: You have not followed the good example of your father, Jehoshaphat, or your grandfather King Asa of Judah. [13]Instead, you have been as evil as the kings of Israel. You have led the people of Jerusalem and Judah to worship idols, just as King Ahab did in Israel. And you have even killed your own brothers, men who were better than you. [14]So now the LORD is about to strike you, your people, your children, your wives, and all that is yours with a heavy blow. [15]You yourself will suffer with a severe intestinal disease that will get worse each day until your bowels come out."

[16]Then the LORD stirred up the Philistines and the Arabs, who lived near the Ethiopians,* to attack Jehoram. [17]They marched against Judah, broke down its defenses, and carried away everything of value in the royal palace, including the king's sons and his wives. Only his youngest son, Ahaziah,* was spared.

[18]After all this, the LORD struck Jehoram with an incurable intestinal disease. [19]The disease grew worse and worse, and at the end of two years it caused his bowels to come out, and he died in agony. His people did not build a great funeral fire to honor him as they had done for his ancestors.

[20]Jehoram was thirty-two years old when he became king, and he reigned in Jerusalem eight years. No one was sorry when he died. They buried him in the City of David, but not in the royal cemetery.

Ahaziah Rules in Judah

22 Then the people of Jerusalem made Ahaziah, Jehoram's youngest son, their next king, since the marauding bands who came with the Arabs* had killed all the older sons. So Ahaziah son of Jehoram reigned as king of Judah.

[2]Ahaziah was twenty-two* years old when he became king, and he reigned in Jerusalem one year. His mother was Athaliah, a granddaughter of King Omri. [3]Ahaziah also followed the evil example of King Ahab's family, for his mother encouraged him in doing wrong. [4]He did what was evil in the LORD's sight, just as Ahab's family had done. They even became his advisers after the death of his father, and they led him to ruin.

[5]Following their evil advice, Ahaziah joined Joram,* the son of King Ahab of Israel, in his war against King Hazael of Aram at Ramoth-gilead. When the Arameans* wounded Joram in the battle, [6]he returned to Jezreel to recover from the wounds he had received at Ramoth.* Because Joram was wounded, King Ahaziah* of Judah went to Jezreel to visit him.

[7]But God had decided that this visit would be Ahaziah's downfall. While he was there, Ahaziah went out with Joram to meet Jehu grandson of Nimshi,* whom the LORD had appointed to destroy the dynasty of Ahab.

[8]While Jehu was executing judgment against the family of Ahab, he happened to meet some of Judah's officials and Ahaziah's relatives* who were traveling with Ahaziah. So Jehu killed them all. [9]Then Jehu's men searched for Ahaziah, and they found him hiding in the city of Samaria. They brought him to Jehu, who killed him. Ahaziah was given a decent burial because the people said, "He was the grandson of Jehoshaphat—a man who sought the LORD with all his heart." But none of the surviving members of Ahaziah's family was capable of ruling the kingdom.

Queen Athaliah Rules in Judah

[10]When Athaliah, the mother of King Ahaziah of Judah, learned that her son was dead, she began to destroy the rest of Judah's royal family. [11]But Ahaziah's sister Jehosheba,* the daughter of King Jehoram, took Ahaziah's infant son, Joash, and stole him away from among the rest of the king's

20:25 As in some Hebrew manuscripts and Latin Vulgate; most Hebrew manuscripts read *corpses.* **20:26** Hebrew *valley of Beracah.* **20:35** Or *who made him do what was wicked.* **20:36** Hebrew *fleet of ships that could go to Tarshish.* **20:37** Hebrew *never set sail for Tarshish.* **21:2** Masoretic Text reads *of Israel;* also in 21:4. The author of Chronicles sees Judah as representative of the true Israel. (Some Hebrew manuscripts, Greek and Syriac versions, and Latin Vulgate read *of Judah.*) **21:9** Or *he went out and escaped.* The meaning of the Hebrew is uncertain. **21:16** Hebrew *the Cushites.* **21:17** Hebrew *Jehoahaz,* a variant spelling of Ahaziah; compare 22:1. **22:1** Or *marauding bands of Arabs.* **22:2** As in some Greek manuscripts and Syriac version (see also 2 Kgs 8:26); Hebrew reads *forty-two.* **22:5a** Hebrew *Jehoram,* a variant spelling of Joram; also in 22:6, 7. **22:5b** As in two Hebrew manuscripts and Latin Vulgate (see also 2 Kgs 8:28); Masoretic Text reads *the archers.* **22:6a** Hebrew *Ramah,* a variant spelling of Ramoth. **22:6b** As in some Hebrew manuscripts, Greek and Syriac versions, and Latin Vulgate (see also 2 Kgs 8:29); most Hebrew manuscripts read *Azariah.* **22:7** Hebrew *descendant of Nimshi;* compare 2 Kgs 9:2, 14. **22:8** As in Greek version (see also 2 Kgs 10:13); Hebrew reads *and sons of the brothers of Ahaziah.* **22:11** As in parallel text at 2 Kgs 11:2; Hebrew lacks *Ahaziah's sister* and reads *Jehoshabeath* [a variant spelling of Jehosheba].

children, who were about to be killed. She
put Joash and his nurse in a bedroom. In
this way, Jehosheba, wife of Jehoiada the
priest and sister of Ahaziah, hid the child so
that Athaliah could not murder him. 12 Joash
remained hidden in the Temple of God for
six years while Athaliah ruled over the land.

Revolt against Athaliah

23 In the seventh year of Athaliah's reign,
Jehoiada the priest decided to act. He
summoned his courage and made a pact
with five army commanders: Azariah son of
Jeroham, Ishmael son of Jehohanan, Azariah
son of Obed, Maaseiah son of Adaiah, and
Elishaphat son of Zicri. 2 These men traveled
secretly throughout Judah and summoned
the Levites and clan leaders in all the towns
to come to Jerusalem. 3 They all gathered at
the Temple of God, where they made a solemn
pact with Joash, the young king.

Jehoiada said to them, "Here is the king's
son! The time has come for him to reign!
The LORD has promised that a descendant
of David will be our king. 4 This is what you
must do. When you priests and Levites
come on duty on the Sabbath, a third of you
will serve as gatekeepers. 5 Another third
will go over to the royal palace, and the
final third will be at the Foundation Gate.
Everyone else should stay in the courtyards
of the LORD's Temple. 6 Remember, only the
priests and Levites on duty may enter the
Temple of the LORD, for they are set apart
as holy. The rest of the people must obey
the LORD's instructions and stay outside.
7 You Levites, form a bodyguard around the
king and keep your weapons in hand. Kill
anyone who tries to enter the Temple. Stay
with the king wherever he goes."

8 So the Levites and all the people of
Judah did everything as Jehoiada the priest
ordered. The commanders took charge of
the men reporting for duty that Sabbath,
as well as those who were going off duty.
Jehoiada the priest did not let anyone go
home after their shift ended. 9 Then Jehoiada supplied the commanders with the
spears and the large and small shields that
had once belonged to King David and were
stored in the Temple of God. 10 He stationed
all the people around the king, with their
weapons ready. They formed a line from
the south side of the Temple around to the
north side and all around the altar.

11 Then Jehoiada and his sons brought out
Joash, the king's son, placed the crown on
his head, and presented him with a copy of
God's laws.* They anointed him and pro-
claimed him king, and everyone shouted,
"Long live the king!"

The Death of Athaliah

12 When Athaliah heard the noise of the
people running and the shouts of praise to
the king, she hurried to the LORD's Temple
to see what was happening. 13 When she
arrived, she saw the newly crowned king
standing in his place of authority by the
pillar at the Temple entrance. The commanders and trumpeters were surrounding
him, and people from all over the land were

King Joash

When Ahaziah was killed (2 Chronicles 22:7-9), his mother Athaliah—granddaughter of Israel's King Omri, so not a descendant of David—"began to destroy the rest of Judah's royal family" (22:10), seizing the throne for herself. But the infant Joash was rescued and hidden in the Temple for the next six years by Jehoiada, the high priest (22:1-12). Jehoiada then instigated a coup in order to put Joash, a true descendant of David, on the throne and had Athaliah killed (chapter 23). Joash was therefore just seven years old when he became king (24:1). He "did what was pleasing in the LORD's sight throughout the lifetime of Jehoiada the priest" (24:2) and undertook major repairs of the Temple (24:4-16). But after Jehoiada's death he came under the influence of others who led him into idolatry (24:17-22). As judgment, Judah was invaded by Aram (Syria). Joash was wounded in battle and returned only to be killed by his own officials (24:23-25). Joash serves as an example of the importance of choosing our friends well.

rejoicing and blowing trumpets. Singers with musical instruments were leading the people in a great celebration. When Athaliah saw all this, she tore her clothes in despair and shouted, "Treason! Treason!"

[14]Then Jehoiada the priest ordered the commanders who were in charge of the troops, "Take her to the soldiers in front of the Temple,* and kill anyone who tries to rescue her." For the priest had said, "She must not be killed in the Temple of the LORD." [15]So they seized her and led her out to the entrance of the Horse Gate on the palace grounds, and they killed her there.

Jehoiada's Religious Reforms

[16]Then Jehoiada made a covenant between himself and the king and the people that they would be the LORD's people. [17]And all the people went over to the temple of Baal and tore it down. They demolished the altars and smashed the idols, and they killed Mattan the priest of Baal in front of the altars.

[18]Jehoiada now put the priests and Levites in charge of the Temple of the LORD, following all the directions given by David. He also commanded them to present burnt offerings to the LORD, as prescribed by the Law of Moses, and to sing and rejoice as David had instructed. [19]He also stationed gatekeepers at the gates of the LORD's Temple to keep out those who for any reason were ceremonially unclean.

[20]Then the commanders, nobles, rulers, and all the people of the land escorted the king from the Temple of the LORD. They went through the upper gate and into the palace, and they seated the king on the royal throne. [21]So all the people of the land rejoiced, and the city was peaceful because Athaliah had been killed.

Joash Repairs the Temple

24 Joash was seven years old when he became king, and he reigned in Jerusalem forty years. His mother was Zibiah from Beersheba. [2]Joash did what was pleasing in the LORD's sight throughout the lifetime of Jehoiada the priest. [3]Jehoiada chose two wives for Joash, and he had sons and daughters.

[4]At one point Joash decided to repair and restore the Temple of the LORD. [5]He summoned the priests and Levites and gave them these instructions: "Go to all the towns of Judah and collect the required annual offerings, so that we can repair the Temple of your God. Do not delay!" But the Levites did not act immediately.

[6]So the king called for Jehoiada the high priest and asked him, "Why haven't you demanded that the Levites go out and collect the Temple taxes from the towns of Judah and from Jerusalem? Moses, the servant of the LORD, levied this tax on the community of Israel in order to maintain the Tabernacle of the Covenant.*"

[7]Over the years the followers of wicked Athaliah had broken into the Temple of God, and they had used all the dedicated things from the Temple of the LORD to worship the images of Baal.

[8]So now the king ordered a chest to be made and set outside the gate leading to the Temple of the LORD. [9]Then a proclamation was sent throughout Judah and Jerusalem, telling the people to bring to the LORD the tax that Moses, the servant of God, had required of the Israelites in the wilderness. [10]This pleased all the leaders and the people, and they gladly brought their money and filled the chest with it.

[11]Whenever the chest became full, the Levites would carry it to the king's officials. Then the court secretary and an officer of the high priest would come and empty the chest and take it back to the Temple again. This went on day after day, and a large amount of money was collected. [12]The king and Jehoiada gave the money to the construction supervisors, who hired masons and carpenters to restore the Temple of the LORD. They also hired metalworkers, who made articles of iron and bronze for the LORD's Temple.

[13]The men in charge of the renovation worked hard and made steady progress. They restored the Temple of God according to its original design and strengthened it. [14]When all the repairs were finished, they brought the remaining money to the king and Jehoiada. It was used to make various articles for the Temple of the LORD—articles for worship services and for burnt offerings, including ladles and other articles made of gold and silver. And the burnt offerings

23:11 Or *a copy of the covenant.* **23:14** Or *Bring her out from between the ranks;* or *Take her out of the Temple precincts.* The meaning of the Hebrew is uncertain. **24:6** Hebrew *Tent of the Testimony.*

were sacrificed continually in the Temple
of the LORD during the lifetime of Jehoiada
the priest.
[15]Jehoiada lived to a very old age, finally
dying at 130. [16]He was buried among the
kings in the City of David, because he had
done so much good in Israel for God and
his Temple.

Jehoiada's Reforms Reversed

[17]But after Jehoiada's death, the leaders of
Judah came and bowed before King Joash
and persuaded him to listen to their advice.
[18]They decided to abandon the Temple of
the LORD, the God of their ancestors, and
they worshiped Asherah poles and idols
instead! Because of this sin, divine anger
fell on Judah and Jerusalem. [19]Yet the LORD
sent prophets to bring them back to him.
The prophets warned them, but still the
people would not listen.
[20]Then the Spirit of God came upon Zechariah son of Jehoiada the priest. He stood
before the people and said, "This is what
God says: Why do you disobey the LORD's
commands and keep yourselves from prospering? You have abandoned the LORD, and
now he has abandoned you!"
[21]Then the leaders plotted to kill Zechariah, and King Joash ordered that they stone
him to death in the courtyard of the LORD's
Temple. [22]That was how King Joash repaid
Jehoiada for his loyalty—by killing his son.
Zechariah's last words as he died were,
"May the LORD see what they are doing and
avenge my death!"

The End of Joash's Reign

[23]In the spring of the year* the Aramean
army marched against Joash. They invaded
Judah and Jerusalem and killed all the
leaders of the nation. Then they sent all the
plunder back to their king in Damascus.
[24]Although the Arameans attacked with
only a small army, the LORD helped them
conquer the much larger army of Judah. The
people of Judah had abandoned the LORD,
the God of their ancestors, so judgment was
carried out against Joash.
[25]The Arameans withdrew, leaving Joash
severely wounded. But his own officials
plotted to kill him for murdering the son* of
Jehoiada the priest. They assassinated him
as he lay in bed. Then he was buried in the
City of David, but not in the royal cemetery.
[26]The assassins were Jozacar,* the son of an
Ammonite woman named Shimeath, and
Jehozabad, the son of a Moabite woman
named Shomer.*
[27]The account of the sons of Joash, the
prophecies about him, and the record of his
restoration of the Temple of God are written
in *The Commentary on the Book of the Kings.*
His son Amaziah became the next king.

Amaziah Rules in Judah

25 Amaziah was twenty-five years
old when he became king, and he
reigned in Jerusalem twenty-nine years.
His mother was Jehoaddin* from Jerusalem. [2]Amaziah did what was pleasing in the
LORD's sight, but not wholeheartedly.
[3]When Amaziah was well established as
king, he executed the officials who had assassinated his father. [4]However, he did not
kill the children of the assassins, for he
obeyed the command of the LORD as written
by Moses in the Book of the Law: "Parents
must not be put to death for the sins of their
children, nor children for the sins of their
parents. Those deserving to die must be put
to death for their own crimes."*
[5]Then Amaziah organized the army,
assigning generals and captains* for all
Judah and Benjamin. He took a census
and found that he had an army of 300,000
select troops, twenty years old and older, all
trained in the use of spear and shield. [6]He
also paid about 7,500 pounds* of silver to
hire 100,000 experienced fighting men from
Israel.
[7]But a man of God came to him and said,
"Your Majesty, do not hire troops from Israel,
for the LORD is not with Israel. He will not
help those people of Ephraim! [8]If you let
them go with your troops into battle, you will
be defeated by the enemy no matter how well
you fight. God will overthrow you, for he has
the power to help you or to trip you up."
[9]Amaziah asked the man of God, "But
what about all that silver I paid to hire the
army of Israel?"

The man of God replied, "The LORD is
able to give you much more than this!" [10]So
Amaziah discharged the hired troops and
sent them back to Ephraim. This made them
very angry with Judah, and they returned
home in a great rage.
[11]Then Amaziah summoned his courage
and led his army to the Valley of Salt, where

they killed 10,000 Edomite troops from Seir. 12 They captured another 10,000 and took them to the top of a cliff and threw them off, dashing them to pieces on the rocks below.

13 Meanwhile, the hired troops that Amaziah had sent home raided several of the towns of Judah between Samaria and Beth-horon. They killed 3,000 people and carried off great quantities of plunder.

14 When King Amaziah returned from slaughtering the Edomites, he brought with him idols taken from the people of Seir. He set them up as his own gods, bowed down in front of them, and offered sacrifices to them! 15 This made the LORD very angry, and he sent a prophet to ask, "Why do you turn to gods who could not even save their own people from you?"

16 But the king interrupted him and said, "Since when have I made you the king's counselor? Be quiet now before I have you killed!"

So the prophet stopped with this warning: "I know that God has determined to destroy you because you have done this and have refused to accept my counsel."

17 After consulting with his advisers, King Amaziah of Judah sent this challenge to Israel's king Jehoash,* the son of Jehoahaz and grandson of Jehu: "Come and meet me in battle!"*

18 But King Jehoash of Israel replied to King Amaziah of Judah with this story: "Out in the Lebanon mountains, a thistle sent a message to a mighty cedar tree: 'Give your daughter in marriage to my son.' But just then a wild animal of Lebanon came by and stepped on the thistle, crushing it!

19 "You are saying, 'I have defeated Edom,' and you are very proud of it. But my advice is to stay at home. Why stir up trouble that will only bring disaster on you and the people of Judah?"

20 But Amaziah refused to listen, for God was determined to destroy him for turning to the gods of Edom. 21 So King Jehoash of Israel mobilized his army against King Amaziah of Judah. The two armies drew up their battle lines at Beth-shemesh in Judah. 22 Judah was routed by the army of Israel, and its army scattered and fled for home. 23 King Jehoash of Israel captured Judah's king, Amaziah son of Joash and grandson of Ahaziah, at Beth-shemesh. Then he brought him to Jerusalem, where he demolished 600 feet* of Jerusalem's wall, from the Ephraim Gate to the Corner Gate. 24 He carried off all the gold and silver and all the articles from the Temple of God that had been in the care of Obed-edom. He also seized the treasures of the royal palace, along with hostages, and then returned to Samaria.

25 King Amaziah of Judah lived for fifteen years after the death of King Jehoash of Israel. 26 The rest of the events in Amaziah's reign, from beginning to end, are recorded in *The Book of the Kings of Judah and Israel.*

27 After Amaziah turned away from the LORD, there was a conspiracy against his life in Jerusalem, and he fled to Lachish. But his enemies sent assassins after him, and they killed him there. 28 They brought his body back on a horse, and he was buried with his ancestors in the City of David.*

Uzziah Rules in Judah

26 All the people of Judah had crowned Amaziah's sixteen-year-old son, Uzziah, as king in place of his father. 2 After his father's death, Uzziah rebuilt the town of Elath* and restored it to Judah.

3 Uzziah was sixteen years old when he became king, and he reigned in Jerusalem fifty-two years. His mother was Jecoliah from Jerusalem. 4 He did what was pleasing in the LORD's sight, just as his father, Amaziah, had done. 5 Uzziah sought God during the days of Zechariah, who taught him to fear God.* And as long as the king sought guidance from the LORD, God gave him success.

6 Uzziah declared war on the Philistines and broke down the walls of Gath, Jabneh, and Ashdod. Then he built new towns in the Ashdod area and in other parts of Philistia. 7 God helped him in his wars against

24:23 Hebrew *At the turn of the year.* The first day of the year in the ancient Hebrew lunar calendar occurred in March or April. **24:25** As in Greek version and Latin Vulgate; Hebrew reads *sons.* **24:26a** As in parallel text at 2 Kgs 12:21; Hebrew reads *Zabad.* **24:26b** As in parallel text at 2 Kgs 12:21; Hebrew reads *Shimrith,* a variant spelling of Shomer. **25:1** As in parallel text at 2 Kgs 14:2; Hebrew reads *Jehoaddan,* a variant spelling of Jehoaddin. **25:4** Deut 24:16. **25:5** Hebrew *commanders of thousands and commanders of hundreds.* **25:6** Hebrew *100 talents* [3,400 kilograms]. **25:17a** Hebrew *Joash,* a variant spelling of Jehoash; also in 25:18, 21, 23, 25. **25:17b** Hebrew *Come, let us look one another in the face.* **25:23** Hebrew *400 cubits* [180 meters]. **25:28** As in some Hebrew manuscripts and other ancient versions (see also 2 Kgs 14:20); most Hebrew manuscripts read *the city of Judah.* **26:2** As in Greek version (see also 2 Kgs 14:22; 16:6); Hebrew reads *Eloth,* a variant spelling of Elath. **26:5** As in Syriac and Greek versions; Hebrew reads *who instructed him in divine visions.*

the Philistines, his battles with the Arabs of
Gur,* and his wars with the Meunites. 8 The
Meunites* paid annual tribute to him, and
his fame spread even to Egypt, for he had
become very powerful.
9 Uzziah built fortified towers in Jerusalem
at the Corner Gate, at the Valley Gate, and at
the angle in the wall. 10 He also constructed
forts in the wilderness and dug many water
cisterns, because he kept great herds of livestock in the foothills of Judah* and on the
plains. He was also a man who loved the
soil. He had many workers who cared for his
farms and vineyards, both on the hillsides
and in the fertile valleys.
11 Uzziah had an army of well-trained
warriors, ready to march into battle, unit
by unit. This army had been mustered and
organized by Jeiel, the secretary of the army,
and his assistant, Maaseiah. They were
under the direction of Hananiah, one of the
king's officials. 12 These regiments of mighty
warriors were commanded by 2,600 clan
leaders. 13 The army consisted of 307,500
men, all elite troops. They were prepared to
assist the king against any enemy.
14 Uzziah provided the entire army with
shields, spears, helmets, coats of mail,
bows, and sling stones. 15 And he built
structures on the walls of Jerusalem, designed by experts to protect those who
shot arrows and hurled large stones* from
the towers and the corners of the wall. His
fame spread far and wide, for the LORD gave
him marvelous help, and he became very
powerful.

Uzziah's Sin and Punishment

16 But when he had become powerful, he
also became proud, which led to his downfall. He sinned against the LORD his God by
entering the sanctuary of the LORD's Temple
and personally burning incense on the
incense altar. 17 Azariah the high priest went
in after him with eighty other priests of the
LORD, all brave men. 18 They confronted King
Uzziah and said, "It is not for you, Uzziah,
to burn incense to the LORD. That is the
work of the priests alone, the descendants
of Aaron who are set apart for this work. Get
out of the sanctuary, for you have sinned.
The LORD God will not honor you for this!"
19 Uzziah, who was holding an incense
burner, became furious. But as he was
standing there raging at the priests before
the incense altar in the LORD's Temple,
leprosy* suddenly broke out on his forehead. 20 When Azariah the high priest and
all the other priests saw the leprosy, they
rushed him out. And the king himself was
eager to get out because the LORD had
struck him. 21 So King Uzziah had leprosy
until the day he died. He lived in isolation in
a separate house, for he was excluded from
the Temple of the LORD. His son Jotham was
put in charge of the royal palace, and he
governed the people of the land.
22 The rest of the events of Uzziah's reign,

Leprosy

Uzziah's story is one of the occasions in the Bible where illness was a clear mark of God's judgment. While there are a number of examples of this (e.g., Exodus 12:29-30; Numbers 12:1-15; 1 Samuel 5:9; 2 Kings 19:35; Acts 12:23; 1 Corinthians 11:27-32), we should not assume this means that *all* sickness is the result of sin. Indeed when this kind of link was put to Jesus, he specifically corrected it (John 9:1-3).

The illness that came upon Uzziah as punishment for his anger toward God's priests who challenged his right to burn incense in the Temple (2 Chronicles 26:16-21) was known as leprosy. In Bible times the term referred to a wide variety of skin diseases, not necessarily the condition known today as Hansen's disease. But whatever its exact nature, Uzziah's ailment was clearly contagious, reflected in how the priests rushed out of the Temple. The Law gave detailed instructions for establishing whether a skin condition was a serious disease or not (Leviticus 13); if it was, it required isolation, as Uzziah himself would experience (2 Chronicles 26:21).

from beginning to end, are recorded by the prophet Isaiah son of Amoz. [23]When Uzziah died, he was buried with his ancestors; his grave was in a nearby burial field belonging to the kings, for the people said, "He had leprosy." And his son Jotham became the next king.

Jotham Rules in Judah

27 Jotham was twenty-five years old when he became king, and he reigned in Jerusalem sixteen years. His mother was Jerusha, the daughter of Zadok.

[2]Jotham did what was pleasing in the LORD's sight. He did everything his father, Uzziah, had done, except that Jotham did not sin by entering the Temple of the LORD. But the people continued in their corrupt ways.

[3]Jotham rebuilt the upper gate of the Temple of the LORD. He also did extensive rebuilding on the wall at the hill of Ophel. [4]He built towns in the hill country of Judah and constructed fortresses and towers in the wooded areas. [5]Jotham went to war against the Ammonites and conquered them. Over the next three years he received from them an annual tribute of 7,500 pounds* of silver, 50,000 bushels of wheat, and 50,000 bushels of barley.*

[6]King Jotham became powerful because he was careful to live in obedience to the LORD his God.

[7]The rest of the events of Jotham's reign, including all his wars and other activities, are recorded in *The Book of the Kings of Israel and Judah*. [8]He was twenty-five years old when he became king, and he reigned in Jerusalem sixteen years. [9]When Jotham died, he was buried in the City of David. And his son Ahaz became the next king.

Ahaz Rules in Judah

28 Ahaz was twenty years old when he became king, and he reigned in Jerusalem sixteen years. He did not do what was pleasing in the sight of the LORD, as his ancestor David had done. [2]Instead, he followed the example of the kings of Israel. He cast metal images for the worship of Baal. [3]He offered sacrifices in the valley of Ben-Hinnom, even sacrificing his own sons in the fire.* In this way, he followed the detestable practices of the pagan nations the LORD had driven from the land ahead of the Israelites. [4]He offered sacrifices and burned incense at the pagan shrines and on the hills and under every green tree.

[5]Because of all this, the LORD his God allowed the king of Aram to defeat Ahaz and to exile large numbers of his people to Damascus. The armies of the king of Israel also defeated Ahaz and inflicted many casualties on his army. [6]In a single day Pekah son of Remaliah, Israel's king, killed 120,000 of Judah's troops, all of them experienced warriors, because they had abandoned the LORD, the God of their ancestors. [7]Then Zicri, a warrior from Ephraim, killed Maaseiah, the king's son; Azrikam, the king's palace commander; and Elkanah, the king's second-in-command. [8]The armies of Israel captured 200,000 women and children from Judah and seized tremendous amounts of plunder, which they took back to Samaria.

[9]But a prophet of the LORD named Oded was there in Samaria when the army of Israel returned home. He went out to meet them and said, "The LORD, the God of your ancestors, was angry with Judah and let you defeat them. But you have gone too far, killing them without mercy, and all heaven is disturbed. [10]And now you are planning to make slaves of these people from Judah and Jerusalem. What about your own sins against the LORD your God? [11]Listen to me and return these prisoners you have taken, for they are your own relatives. Watch out, because now the LORD's fierce anger has been turned against you!"

[12]Then some of the leaders of Israel*—Azariah son of Jehohanan, Berekiah son of Meshillemoth, Jehizkiah son of Shallum, and Amasa son of Hadlai—agreed with this and confronted the men returning from battle. [13]"You must not bring the prisoners here!" they declared. "We cannot afford to add to our sins and guilt. Our guilt is already great, and the LORD's fierce anger is already turned against Israel."

[14]So the warriors released the prisoners and handed over the plunder in the sight of the leaders and all the people. [15]Then the

26:7 As in Greek version; Hebrew reads *Gur-baal.* **26:8** As in Greek version; Hebrew reads *Ammonites.* Compare 26:7. **26:10** Hebrew *the Shephelah.* **26:15** Or *to shoot arrows and hurl large stones.* **26:19** Or *a contagious skin disease.* The Hebrew word used here and throughout this passage can describe various skin diseases. **27:5a** Hebrew *100 talents* [3,400 kilograms]. **27:5b** Hebrew *10,000 cors* [2,200 kiloliters] *of wheat, and 10,000 cors of barley.* **28:3** Or *even making his sons pass through the fire.* **28:12** Hebrew *Ephraim,* referring to the northern kingdom of Israel.

four men just mentioned by name came
forward and distributed clothes from the
plunder to the prisoners who were naked.
They provided clothing and sandals to
wear, gave them enough food and drink,
and dressed their wounds with olive oil.
They put those who were weak on donkeys
and took all the prisoners back to their own
people in Jericho, the city of palms. Then
they returned to Samaria.

Ahaz Closes the Temple

16 At that time King Ahaz of Judah asked
the king of Assyria for help. 17 The armies of
Edom had again invaded Judah and taken
captives. 18 And the Philistines had raided
towns located in the foothills of Judah* and
in the Negev of Judah. They had already
captured and occupied Beth-shemesh,
Aijalon, Gederoth, Soco with its villages,
Timnah with its villages, and Gimzo with
its villages. 19 The LORD was humbling Judah
because of King Ahaz of Judah,* for he had
encouraged his people to sin and had been
utterly unfaithful to the LORD.

20 So when King Tiglath-pileser* of Assyria
arrived, he attacked Ahaz instead of helping
him. 21 Ahaz took valuable items from the
LORD's Temple, the royal palace, and from
the homes of his officials and gave them to
the king of Assyria as tribute. But this did
not help him.

22 Even during this time of trouble, King
Ahaz continued to reject the LORD. 23 He
offered sacrifices to the gods of Damascus
who had defeated him, for he said, "Since
these gods helped the kings of Aram, they
will help me, too, if I sacrifice to them." But
instead, they led to his ruin and the ruin of
all Judah.

24 The king took the various articles from the
Temple of God and broke them into pieces.
He shut the doors of the LORD's Temple so
that no one could worship there, and he set
up altars to pagan gods in every corner of Jerusalem. 25 He made pagan shrines in all the
towns of Judah for offering sacrifices to other
gods. In this way, he aroused the anger of the
LORD, the God of his ancestors.

26 The rest of the events of Ahaz's reign
and everything he did, from beginning to
end, are recorded in *The Book of the Kings*
of Judah and Israel. 27 When Ahaz died, he
was buried in Jerusalem but not in the royal
cemetery of the kings of Judah. Then his son
Hezekiah became the next king.

Hezekiah Rules in Judah

29 Hezekiah was twenty-five years old
when he became the king of Judah,
and he reigned in Jerusalem twenty-nine
years. His mother was Abijah, the daughter
of Zechariah. 2 He did what was pleasing in
the LORD's sight, just as his ancestor David
had done.

Hezekiah Reopens the Temple

3 In the very first month of the first year of
his reign, Hezekiah reopened the doors of
the Temple of the LORD and repaired them.
4 He summoned the priests and Levites
to meet him at the courtyard east of the
Temple. 5 He said to them, "Listen to me,
you Levites! Purify yourselves, and purify
the Temple of the LORD, the God of your ancestors. Remove all the defiled things from
the sanctuary. 6 Our ancestors were unfaithful and did what was evil in the sight of the
LORD our God. They abandoned the LORD
and his dwelling place; they turned their
backs on him. 7 They also shut the doors to
the Temple's entry room, and they snuffed
out the lamps. They stopped burning
incense and presenting burnt offerings at
the sanctuary of the God of Israel.

8 "That is why the LORD's anger has fallen
upon Judah and Jerusalem. He has made
them an object of dread, horror, and ridicule, as you can see with your own eyes.
9 Because of this, our fathers have been
killed in battle, and our sons and daughters and wives have been captured. 10 But
now I will make a covenant with the LORD,
the God of Israel, so that his fierce anger
will turn away from us. 11 My sons, do not
neglect your duties any longer! The LORD
has chosen you to stand in his presence, to
minister to him, and to lead the people in
worship and present offerings to him."

12 Then these Levites got right to work:

From the clan of Kohath: Mahath son of
Amasai and Joel son of Azariah.
From the clan of Merari: Kish son of
Abdi and Azariah son of Jehallelel.

▸ **29:1** *See* ***King Hezekiah****, page 786.*

From the clan of Gershon: Joah son of Zimmah and Eden son of Joah.
13 From the family of Elizaphan: Shimri and Jeiel.
From the family of Asaph: Zechariah and Mattaniah.
14 From the family of Heman: Jehiel and Shimei.
From the family of Jeduthun: Shemaiah and Uzziel.

15These men called together their fellow Levites, and they all purified themselves. Then they began to cleanse the Temple of the LORD, just as the king had commanded. They were careful to follow all the LORD's
instructions in their work. 16The priests went into the sanctuary of the Temple of the LORD to cleanse it, and they took out to the Temple courtyard all the defiled things they found. From there the Levites carted it all out to the Kidron Valley.

17They began the work in early spring, on the first day of the new year,* and in eight days they had reached the entry room of the LORD's Temple. Then they purified the Temple of the LORD itself, which took another eight days. So the entire task was completed in sixteen days.

The Temple Rededication

18Then the Levites went to King Hezekiah and gave him this report: "We have cleansed the entire Temple of the LORD, the altar of burnt offering with all its utensils, and the table of the Bread of the Presence with all
its utensils. 19We have also recovered all the items discarded by King Ahaz when he was unfaithful and closed the Temple. They are now in front of the altar of the LORD, purified and ready for use."

20Early the next morning King Hezekiah gathered the city officials and went to the
Temple of the LORD. 21They brought seven bulls, seven rams, and seven male lambs as a burnt offering, together with seven male goats as a sin offering for the kingdom, for the Temple, and for Judah. The king commanded the priests, who were descendants of Aaron, to sacrifice the animals on the altar of the LORD.

22So they killed the bulls, and the priests took the blood and sprinkled it on the altar. Next they killed the rams and sprinkled their blood on the altar. And finally, they
did the same with the male lambs. 23The male goats for the sin offering were then brought before the king and the assembly of
people, who laid their hands on them. 24The priests then killed the goats as a sin offering and sprinkled their blood on the altar to make atonement for the sins of all Israel. The king had specifically commanded that this burnt offering and sin offering should be made for all Israel.

25King Hezekiah then stationed the Levites at the Temple of the LORD with cymbals, lyres, and harps. He obeyed all the commands that the LORD had given to King David through Gad, the king's seer, and the
prophet Nathan. 26The Levites then took their positions around the Temple with the instruments of David, and the priests took their positions with the trumpets.

27Then Hezekiah ordered that the burnt offering be placed on the altar. As the burnt offering was presented, songs of praise to the LORD were begun, accompanied by the trumpets and other instruments of David,
the former king of Israel. 28The entire assembly worshiped the LORD as the singers sang and the trumpets blew, until all the
burnt offerings were finished. 29Then the king and everyone with him bowed down in
worship. 30King Hezekiah and the officials ordered the Levites to praise the LORD with the psalms written by David and by Asaph the seer. So they offered joyous praise and bowed down in worship.

31Then Hezekiah declared, "Now that you have consecrated yourselves to the LORD, bring your sacrifices and thanksgiving offerings to the Temple of the LORD." So the people brought their sacrifices and thanksgiving offerings, and all whose hearts were willing brought burnt offerings, too.
32The people brought to the LORD 70 bulls, 100 rams, and 200 male lambs for burnt of-
ferings. 33They also brought 600 cattle and 3,000 sheep and goats as sacred offerings.

34But there were too few priests to prepare all the burnt offerings. So their relatives the Levites helped them until the work was finished and more priests had been purified, for the Levites had been more conscientious

28:18 Hebrew *the Shephelah.* **28:19** Masoretic Text reads *of Israel;* also in 28:23, 27. The author of Chronicles sees Judah as representative of the true Israel. (Some Hebrew manuscripts and Greek version read *of Judah.*) **28:20** Hebrew *Tilgath-pilneser,* a variant spelling of Tiglath-pileser. **29:17** Hebrew *on the first day of the first month.* This day in the ancient Hebrew lunar calendar occurred in March or early April, 715 B.C.

about purifying themselves than the priests
had been. 35 There was an abundance of
burnt offerings, along with the usual liquid
offerings, and a great deal of fat from the
many peace offerings.

So the Temple of the LORD was restored to
service. 36 And Hezekiah and all the people
rejoiced because of what God had done for
the people, for everything had been accomplished so quickly.

Preparations for Passover

30 King Hezekiah now sent word to
all Israel and Judah, and he wrote
letters of invitation to the people of Ephraim
and Manasseh. He asked everyone to come
to the Temple of the LORD at Jerusalem to
celebrate the Passover of the LORD, the God
of Israel. 2 The king, his officials, and all the
community of Jerusalem decided to celebrate Passover a month later than usual.*
3 They were unable to celebrate it at the prescribed time because not enough priests
could be purified by then, and the people
had not yet assembled at Jerusalem.

4 This plan for keeping the Passover seemed
right to the king and all the people. 5 So they
sent a proclamation throughout all Israel,
from Beersheba in the south to Dan in the
north, inviting everyone to come to Jerusalem
to celebrate the Passover of the LORD, the God
of Israel. The people had not been celebrating it in great numbers as required in the Law.

6 At the king's command, runners were
sent throughout Israel and Judah. They
carried letters that said:

> "O people of Israel, return to the LORD,
> the God of Abraham, Isaac, and Israel,*
> so that he will return to the few of us
> who have survived the conquest of the
> Assyrian kings. 7 Do not be like your
> ancestors and relatives who abandoned
> the LORD, the God of their ancestors,
> and became an object of derision, as you
> yourselves can see. 8 Do not be stubborn,
> as they were, but submit yourselves to
> the LORD. Come to his Temple, which he
> has set apart as holy forever. Worship
> the LORD your God so that his fierce
> anger will turn away from you.
>
> 9 "For if you return to the LORD, your
> relatives and your children will be treated
> mercifully by their captors, and they will
> be able to return to this land. For the
> LORD your God is gracious and merciful.
> If you return to him, he will not continue
> to turn his face from you."

Celebration of Passover

10 The runners went from town to town
throughout Ephraim and Manasseh and
as far as the territory of Zebulun. But most
of the people just laughed at the runners
and made fun of them. 11 However, some
people from Asher, Manasseh, and Zebulun
humbled themselves and went to Jerusalem.

12 At the same time, God's hand was on the
people in the land of Judah, giving them all
one heart to obey the orders of the king and
his officials, who were following the word of
the LORD. 13 So a huge crowd assembled at Jerusalem in midspring* to celebrate the Festival of Unleavened Bread. 14 They set to work
and removed the pagan altars from Jerusalem. They took away all the incense altars
and threw them into the Kidron Valley.

15 On the fourteenth day of the second
month, one month later than usual,* the
people slaughtered the Passover lamb. This
shamed the priests and Levites, so they
purified themselves and brought burnt offerings to the Temple of the LORD. 16 Then
they took their places at the Temple as
prescribed in the Law of Moses, the man
of God. The Levites brought the sacrificial
blood to the priests, who then sprinkled it
on the altar.

17 Since many of the people had not purified themselves, the Levites had to slaughter their Passover lamb for them, to set them
apart for the LORD. 18 Most of those who
came from Ephraim, Manasseh, Issachar,
and Zebulun had not purified themselves.
But King Hezekiah prayed for them, and
they were allowed to eat the Passover meal
anyway, even though this was contrary to
the requirements of the Law. For Hezekiah
said, "May the LORD, who is good, pardon
those 19 who decide to follow the LORD, the
God of their ancestors, even though they are
not properly cleansed for the ceremony."
20 And the LORD listened to Hezekiah's
prayer and healed the people.

21 So the people of Israel who were present
in Jerusalem joyously celebrated the Festival of Unleavened Bread for seven days.
Each day the Levites and priests sang to the
LORD, accompanied by loud instruments.*
22 Hezekiah encouraged all the Levites

regarding the skill they displayed as they served the LORD. The celebration continued for seven days. Peace offerings were sacrificed, and the people gave thanks to the LORD, the God of their ancestors.

[23]The entire assembly then decided to continue the festival another seven days, so they celebrated joyfully for another week. [24]King Hezekiah gave the people 1,000 bulls and 7,000 sheep and goats for offerings, and the officials donated 1,000 bulls and 10,000 sheep and goats. Meanwhile, many more priests purified themselves.

[25]The entire assembly of Judah rejoiced, including the priests, the Levites, all who came from the land of Israel, the foreigners who came to the festival, and all those who lived in Judah. [26]There was great joy in the city, for Jerusalem had not seen a celebration like this one since the days of Solomon, King David's son. [27]Then the priests and Levites stood and blessed the people, and God heard their prayer from his holy dwelling in heaven.

Hezekiah's Religious Reforms

31 When the festival ended, the Israelites who attended went to all the towns of Judah, Benjamin, Ephraim, and Manasseh, and they smashed all the sacred pillars, cut down the Asherah poles, and removed the pagan shrines and altars. After this, the Israelites returned to their own towns and homes.

[2]Hezekiah then organized the priests and Levites into divisions to offer the burnt offerings and peace offerings, and to worship and give thanks and praise to the LORD at the gates of the Temple. [3]The king also made a personal contribution of animals for the daily morning and evening burnt offerings, the weekly Sabbath festivals, the monthly new moon festivals, and the annual festivals as prescribed in the Law of the LORD. [4]In addition, he required the people in Jerusalem to bring a portion of their goods to the priests and Levites, so they could devote themselves fully to the Law of the LORD.

[5]When the people of Israel heard these requirements, they responded generously by bringing the first share of their grain, new wine, olive oil, honey, and all the produce of their fields. They brought a large quantity—a tithe of all they produced. [6]The people who had moved to Judah from Israel, and the people of Judah themselves, brought in the tithes of their cattle, sheep, and goats and a tithe of the things that had been dedicated to the LORD their God, and they piled them up in great heaps. [7]They began piling them up in late spring, and the heaps continued to grow until early autumn.* [8]When Hezekiah and his officials came and saw these huge piles, they thanked the LORD and his people Israel!

[9]"Where did all this come from?" Hezekiah asked the priests and Levites.

[10]And Azariah the high priest, from the family of Zadok, replied, "Since the people began bringing their gifts to the LORD's Temple, we have had enough to eat and plenty to spare. The LORD has blessed his people, and all this is left over."

[11]Hezekiah ordered that storerooms be prepared in the Temple of the LORD. When this was done, [12]the people faithfully brought all the gifts, tithes, and other items dedicated for use in the Temple. Conaniah the Levite was put in charge, assisted by his brother Shimei. [13]The supervisors under them were Jehiel, Azaziah, Nahath, Asahel, Jerimoth, Jozabad, Eliel, Ismakiah, Mahath, and Benaiah. These appointments were made by King Hezekiah and Azariah, the chief official in the Temple of God.

[14]Kore son of Imnah the Levite, who was the gatekeeper at the East Gate, was put in charge of distributing the voluntary offerings given to God, the gifts, and the things that had been dedicated to the LORD. [15]His faithful assistants were Eden, Miniamin, Jeshua, Shemaiah, Amariah, and Shecaniah. They distributed the gifts among the families of priests in their towns by their divisions, dividing the gifts fairly among old and young alike. [16]They distributed the gifts to all males three years old or older, regardless of their place in the genealogical records. The distribution went to all who would come to the LORD's Temple to perform their daily duties according to their divisions. [17]They distributed gifts to the

30:2 Hebrew *in the second month.* Passover was normally observed in the first month (of the ancient Hebrew lunar calendar). **30:6** *Israel* is the name that God gave to Jacob. **30:13** Hebrew *in the second month.* The second month of the ancient Hebrew lunar calendar usually occurs within the months of April and May. **30:15** Hebrew *On the fourteenth day of the second month.* Passover normally began on the fourteenth day of the first month (see Lev 23:5). **30:21** Or *sang to the LORD with all their strength.* **31:7** Hebrew *in the third month . . . until the seventh month.* The third month of the ancient Hebrew lunar calendar usually occurs within the months of May and June; the seventh month usually occurs within September and October.

priests who were listed by their families in
the genealogical records, and to the Levites
twenty years old or older who were listed
according to their jobs and their divisions.
18 Food allotments were also given to the
families of all those listed in the genealogical records, including their little babies,
wives, sons, and daughters. For they had all
been faithful in purifying themselves.

19 As for the priests, the descendants of
Aaron, who were living in the open villages
around the towns, men were appointed by
name to distribute portions to every male
among the priests and to all the Levites
listed in the genealogical records.

20 In this way, King Hezekiah handled the
distribution throughout all Judah, doing
what was pleasing and good in the sight
of the LORD his God. 21 In all that he did in
the service of the Temple of God and in his
efforts to follow God's laws and commands,
Hezekiah sought his God wholeheartedly.
As a result, he was very successful.

Assyria Invades Judah

32 After Hezekiah had faithfully carried
out this work, King Sennacherib of
Assyria invaded Judah. He laid siege to the
fortified towns, giving orders for his army to
break through their walls. 2 When Hezekiah
realized that Sennacherib also intended to
attack Jerusalem, 3 he consulted with his officials and military advisers, and they decided
to stop the flow of the springs outside the
city. 4 They organized a huge work crew to
stop the flow of the springs, cutting off the
brook that ran through the fields. For they
said, "Why should the kings of Assyria come
here and find plenty of water?"

5 Then Hezekiah worked hard at repairing
all the broken sections of the wall, erecting towers, and constructing a second wall
outside the first. He also reinforced the supporting terraces* in the City of David and
manufactured large numbers of weapons
and shields. 6 He appointed military officers
over the people and assembled them before
him in the square at the city gate. Then
Hezekiah encouraged them by saying: 7 "Be
strong and courageous! Don't be afraid or
discouraged because of the king of Assyria
or his mighty army, for there is a power far
greater on our side! 8 He may have a great
army, but they are merely men. We have the
LORD our God to help us and to fight our
battles for us!" Hezekiah's words greatly
encouraged the people.

Sennacherib Threatens Jerusalem

9 While King Sennacherib of Assyria was
still besieging the town of Lachish, he sent
his officers to Jerusalem with this message
for Hezekiah and all the people in the city:

10 "This is what King Sennacherib of
Assyria says: What are you trusting in
that makes you think you can survive my
siege of Jerusalem? 11 Hezekiah has said,
'The LORD our God will rescue us from
the king of Assyria.' Surely Hezekiah
is misleading you, sentencing you to
death by famine and thirst! 12 Don't you
realize that Hezekiah is the very person
who destroyed all the LORD's shrines
and altars? He commanded Judah and
Jerusalem to worship only at the altar at
the Temple and to offer sacrifices on it
alone.

13 "Surely you must realize what I and
the other kings of Assyria before me have
done to all the people of the earth! Were

Sennacherib's siege of Jerusalem

Sennacherib laid siege to Jerusalem in 701 BC and sent messengers to threaten and taunt the people (2 Chronicles 32:9-15). When Hezekiah, the king of Judah, heard them, he immediately humbled himself before God and prayed (32:20). The account in Kings tells us that when he received a threatening letter from Sennacherib, he spread it out before God in the Temple and prayed over it (2 Kings 19:14-19). That very night Sennacherib's army was annihilated when God sent an angel to strike their camp, and Sennacherib returned to Nineveh, one of the capital cities of Assyria. The judgment on him was completed when he was murdered by his own sons while worshiping in his temple.

any of the gods of those nations able
to rescue their people from my power?
[14]Which of their gods was able to rescue
its people from the destructive power of
my predecessors? What makes you think
your God can rescue you from me? [15]Don't
let Hezekiah deceive you! Don't let him
fool you like this! I say it again—no god of
any nation or kingdom has ever yet been
able to rescue his people from me or my
ancestors. How much less will your God
rescue you from my power!"

[16]And Sennacherib's officers further
mocked the LORD God and his servant Hezekiah, heaping insult upon insult. [17]The
king also sent letters scorning the LORD,
the God of Israel. He wrote, "Just as the
gods of all the other nations failed to rescue
their people from my power, so the God of
Hezekiah will also fail." [18]The Assyrian officials who brought the letters shouted this
in Hebrew* to the people gathered on the
walls of the city, trying to terrify them so it
would be easier to capture the city. [19]These
officers talked about the God of Jerusalem
as though he were one of the pagan gods,
made by human hands.

[20]Then King Hezekiah and the prophet
Isaiah son of Amoz cried out in prayer to
God in heaven. [21]And the LORD sent an angel
who destroyed the Assyrian army with all
its commanders and officers. So Sennacherib was forced to return home in disgrace
to his own land. And when he entered the
temple of his god, some of his own sons
killed him there with a sword.

[22]That is how the LORD rescued Hezekiah
and the people of Jerusalem from King Sennacherib of Assyria and from all the others
who threatened them. So there was peace
throughout the land. [23]From then on King
Hezekiah became highly respected among
all the surrounding nations, and many gifts
for the LORD arrived at Jerusalem, with
valuable presents for King Hezekiah, too.

Hezekiah's Sickness and Recovery

[24]About that time Hezekiah became deathly
ill. He prayed to the LORD, who healed him
and gave him a miraculous sign. [25]But Hezekiah did not respond appropriately to the
kindness shown him, and he became proud.
So the LORD's anger came against him and
against Judah and Jerusalem. [26]Then Hezekiah humbled himself and repented of his
pride, as did the people of Jerusalem. So the
LORD's anger did not fall on them during
Hezekiah's lifetime.

[27]Hezekiah was very wealthy and highly
honored. He built special treasury buildings for his silver, gold, precious stones, and
spices, and for his shields and other valuable
items. [28]He also constructed many storehouses for his grain, new wine, and olive oil;
and he made many stalls for his cattle and
pens for his flocks of sheep and goats. [29]He
built many towns and acquired vast flocks
and herds, for God had given him great
wealth. [30]He blocked up the upper spring of
Gihon and brought the water down through
a tunnel to the west side of the City of David.
And so he succeeded in everything he did.

[31]However, when ambassadors arrived
from Babylon to ask about the remarkable
events that had taken place in the land, God
withdrew from Hezekiah in order to test him
and to see what was really in his heart.

Summary of Hezekiah's Reign

[32]The rest of the events in Hezekiah's reign
and his acts of devotion are recorded in *The
Vision of the Prophet Isaiah Son of Amoz,*
which is included in *The Book of the Kings
of Judah and Israel.* [33]When Hezekiah died,
he was buried in the upper area of the royal
cemetery, and all Judah and Jerusalem
honored him at his death. And his son Manasseh became the next king.

Manasseh Rules in Judah

33 Manasseh was twelve years old when
he became king, and he reigned in
Jerusalem fifty-five years. [2]He did what was
evil in the LORD's sight, following the detestable practices of the pagan nations that
the LORD had driven from the land ahead of
the Israelites. [3]He rebuilt the pagan shrines
his father, Hezekiah, had broken down. He
constructed altars for the images of Baal
and set up Asherah poles. He also bowed
before all the powers of the heavens and
worshiped them.

32:5 Hebrew *the millo.* The meaning of the Hebrew is uncertain.
32:18 Hebrew *in the dialect of Judah.*

▸ **33:1** See ***King Manasseh***, *page 439.*

4He built pagan altars in the Temple of the LORD, the place where the LORD had said, "My name will remain in Jerusalem forever." 5He built these altars for all the powers of the heavens in both courtyards of the LORD's Temple. 6Manasseh also sacrificed his own sons in the fire* in the valley of Ben-Hinnom. He practiced sorcery, divination, and witchcraft, and he consulted with mediums and psychics. He did much that was evil in the LORD's sight, arousing his anger.

7Manasseh even took a carved idol he had made and set it up in God's Temple, the very place where God had told David and his son Solomon: "My name will be honored forever in this Temple and in Jerusalem—the city I have chosen from among all the tribes of Israel. 8If the Israelites will be careful to obey my commands—all the laws, decrees, and regulations given through Moses—I will not send them into exile from this land that I set aside for your ancestors." 9But Manasseh led the people of Judah and Jerusalem to do even more evil than the pagan nations that the LORD had destroyed when the people of Israel entered the land.

10The LORD spoke to Manasseh and his people, but they ignored all his warnings. 11So the LORD sent the commanders of the Assyrian armies, and they took Manasseh prisoner. They put a ring through his nose, bound him in bronze chains, and led him away to Babylon. 12But while in deep distress, Manasseh sought the LORD his God and sincerely humbled himself before the God of his ancestors. 13And when he prayed, the LORD listened to him and was moved by his request. So the LORD brought Manasseh back to Jerusalem and to his kingdom. Then Manasseh finally realized that the LORD alone is God!

14After this Manasseh rebuilt the outer wall of the City of David, from west of the Gihon Spring in the Kidron Valley to the Fish Gate, and continuing around the hill of Ophel. He built the wall very high. And he stationed his military officers in all of the fortified towns of Judah. 15Manasseh also removed the foreign gods and the idol from the LORD's Temple. He tore down all the altars he had built on the hill where the Temple stood and all the altars that were in Jerusalem, and he dumped them outside the city. 16Then he restored the altar of the LORD and sacrificed peace offerings and thanksgiving offerings on it. He also encouraged the people of Judah to worship the LORD, the God of Israel. 17However, the people still sacrificed at the pagan shrines, though only to the LORD their God.

18The rest of the events of Manasseh's reign, his prayer to God, and the words the seers spoke to him in the name of the LORD, the God of Israel, are recorded in *The Book of the Kings of Israel.* 19Manasseh's prayer, the account of the way God answered him, and an account of all his sins and unfaithfulness are recorded in *The Record of the Seers.** It includes a list of the locations where he built pagan shrines and set up Asherah poles and idols before he humbled himself and repented. 20When Manasseh died, he was buried in his palace. Then his son Amon became the next king.

Amon Rules in Judah

21Amon was twenty-two years old when he became king, and he reigned in Jerusalem two years. 22He did what was evil in the LORD's sight, just as his father, Manasseh, had done. He worshiped and sacrificed to all the idols his father had made. 23But unlike his father, he did not humble himself before the LORD. Instead, Amon sinned even more.

24Then Amon's own officials conspired against him and assassinated him in his palace. 25But the people of the land killed all those who had conspired against King Amon, and they made his son Josiah the next king.

Josiah Rules in Judah

34 Josiah was eight years old when he became king, and he reigned in Jerusalem thirty-one years. 2He did what was pleasing in the LORD's sight and followed the example of his ancestor David. He did not turn away from doing what was right.

3During the eighth year of his reign, while he was still young, Josiah began to seek the God of his ancestor David. Then in the twelfth year he began to purify Judah and Jerusalem, destroying all the pagan shrines, the Asherah poles, and the carved idols and cast images. 4He ordered that the altars of Baal be demolished and that the incense altars which stood

▸ **34:1** *See **King Josiah**, page 441.*

above them be broken down. He also made sure that the Asherah poles, the carved idols, and the cast images were smashed and scattered over the graves of those who had sacrificed to them. [5]He burned the bones of the pagan priests on their own altars, and so he purified Judah and Jerusalem.

[6]He did the same thing in the towns of Manasseh, Ephraim, and Simeon, even as far as Naphtali, and in the regions* all around them. [7]He destroyed the pagan altars and the Asherah poles, and he crushed the idols into dust. He cut down all the incense altars throughout the land of Israel. Finally, he returned to Jerusalem.

[8]In the eighteenth year of his reign, after he had purified the land and the Temple, Josiah appointed Shaphan son of Azaliah, Maaseiah the governor of Jerusalem, and Joah son of Joahaz, the royal historian, to repair the Temple of the LORD his God. [9]They gave Hilkiah the high priest the money that had been collected by the Levites who served as gatekeepers at the Temple of God. The gifts were brought by people from Manasseh, Ephraim, and from all the remnant of Israel, as well as from all Judah, Benjamin, and the people of Jerusalem.

[10]He entrusted the money to the men assigned to supervise the restoration of the LORD's Temple. Then they paid the workers who did the repairs and renovation of the Temple. [11]They hired carpenters and builders, who purchased finished stone for the walls and timber for the rafters and beams. They restored what earlier kings of Judah had allowed to fall into ruin.

[12]The workers served faithfully under the leadership of Jahath and Obadiah, Levites of the Merarite clan, and Zechariah and Meshullam, Levites of the Kohathite clan. Other Levites, all of whom were skilled musicians, [13]were put in charge of the laborers of the various trades. Still others assisted as secretaries, officials, and gatekeepers.

Hilkiah Discovers God's Law

[14]While they were bringing out the money collected at the LORD's Temple, Hilkiah the priest found the Book of the Law of the LORD that was written by Moses. [15]Hilkiah said to Shaphan the court secretary, "I have found the Book of the Law in the LORD's Temple!" Then Hilkiah gave the scroll to Shaphan.

[16]Shaphan took the scroll to the king and reported, "Your officials are doing everything they were assigned to do. [17]The money that was collected at the Temple of the LORD has been turned over to the supervisors and workmen." [18]Shaphan also told the king, "Hilkiah the priest has given me a scroll." So Shaphan read it to the king.

[19]When the king heard what was written in the Law, he tore his clothes in despair. [20]Then he gave these orders to Hilkiah, Ahikam son of Shaphan, Acbor son of Micaiah,* Shaphan the court secretary, and Asaiah the king's personal adviser: [21]"Go to the Temple and speak to the LORD for me and for all the remnant of Israel and Judah. Inquire about the words written in the scroll that has been found. For the LORD's great anger has been poured out on us because our ancestors have not obeyed the word of the LORD. We have not been doing everything this scroll says we must do."

[22]So Hilkiah and the other men went to the New Quarter* of Jerusalem to consult with the prophet Huldah. She was the wife of Shallum son of Tikvah, son of Harhas,* the keeper of the Temple wardrobe.

[23]She said to them, "The LORD, the God of Israel, has spoken! Go back and tell the man who sent you, [24]'This is what the LORD says: I am going to bring disaster on this city* and its people. All the curses written in the scroll that was read to the king of Judah will come true. [25]For my people have abandoned me and offered sacrifices to pagan gods, and I am very angry with them for everything they have done. My anger will be poured out on this place, and it will not be quenched.'

[26]"But go to the king of Judah who sent you to seek the LORD and tell him: 'This is what the LORD, the God of Israel, says concerning the message you have just heard: [27]You were sorry and humbled yourself before God when you heard his words against this city and its people. You humbled yourself and tore your clothing in despair and wept before me in repentance. And I have indeed heard you, says the LORD. [28]So I will not send the promised disaster until after you have died and been buried in peace. You

33:6 Or *also made his sons pass through the fire*. **33:19** Or *The Record of Hozai*. **34:6** As in Syriac version; Hebrew reads *in their temples*, or *in their ruins*. The meaning of the Hebrew is uncertain. **34:20** As in parallel text at 2 Kgs 22:12; Hebrew reads *Abdon son of Micah*. **34:22a** Or *the Second Quarter*, a newer section of Jerusalem. Hebrew reads *the Mishneh*. **34:22b** As in parallel text at 2 Kgs 22:14; Hebrew reads *son of Tokhath, son of Hasrah*. **34:24** Hebrew *this place;* also in 34:27, 28.

yourself will not see the disaster I am going to bring on this city and its people.'"

So they took her message back to the king.

Josiah's Religious Reforms

29 Then the king summoned all the elders of Judah and Jerusalem. 30 And the king went up to the Temple of the LORD with all the people of Judah and Jerusalem, along with the priests and the Levites—all the people from the greatest to the least. There the king read to them the entire Book of the Covenant that had been found in the LORD's Temple. 31 The king took his place of authority beside the pillar and renewed the covenant in the LORD's presence. He pledged to obey the LORD by keeping all his commands, laws, and decrees with all his heart and soul. He promised to obey all the terms of the covenant that were written in the scroll. 32 And he required everyone in Jerusalem and the people of Benjamin to make a similar pledge. The people of Jerusalem did so, renewing their covenant with God, the God of their ancestors.

33 So Josiah removed all detestable idols from the entire land of Israel and required everyone to worship the LORD their God. And throughout the rest of his lifetime, they did not turn away from the LORD, the God of their ancestors.

Josiah Celebrates Passover

35 Then Josiah announced that the Passover of the LORD would be celebrated in Jerusalem, and so the Passover lamb was slaughtered on the fourteenth day of the first month.* 2 Josiah also assigned the priests to their duties and encouraged them in their work at the Temple of the LORD. 3 He issued this order to the Levites, who were to teach all Israel and who had been set apart to serve the LORD: "Put the holy Ark in the Temple that was built by Solomon son of David, the king of Israel. You no longer need to carry it back and forth on your shoulders. Now spend your time serving the LORD your God and his people Israel. 4 Report for duty according to the family divisions of your ancestors, following the directions of King David of Israel and the directions of his son Solomon.

5 "Then stand in the sanctuary at the place appointed for your family division and help the families assigned to you as they bring their offerings to the Temple. 6 Slaughter the Passover lambs, purify yourselves, and prepare to help those who come. Follow all the directions that the LORD gave through Moses."

7 Then Josiah provided 30,000 lambs and young goats for the people's Passover offerings, along with 3,000 cattle, all from the king's own flocks and herds. 8 The king's officials also made willing contributions to the people, priests, and Levites. Hilkiah, Zechariah, and Jehiel, the administrators of God's Temple, gave the priests 2,600 lambs and young goats and 300 cattle as Passover offerings. 9 The Levite leaders—Conaniah and his brothers Shemaiah and Nethanel, as well as Hashabiah, Jeiel, and Jozabad—gave 5,000 lambs and young goats and 500 cattle to the Levites for their Passover offerings.

10 When everything was ready for the Passover celebration, the priests and the Levites took their places, organized by their divisions, as the king had commanded. 11 The Levites then slaughtered the Passover lambs and presented the blood to the priests, who sprinkled the blood on the altar while the Levites prepared the animals. 12 They divided the burnt offerings among the people by their family groups, so they could offer them to the LORD as prescribed in the Book of Moses. They did the same with the cattle. 13 Then they roasted the Passover lambs as prescribed; and they boiled the holy offerings in pots, kettles, and pans, and brought them out quickly so the people could eat them.

14 Afterward the Levites prepared Passover offerings for themselves and for the priests—the descendants of Aaron—because the priests had been busy from morning till night offering the burnt offerings and the fat portions. The Levites took responsibility for all these preparations.

15 The musicians, descendants of Asaph, were in their assigned places, following the commands that had been given by David, Asaph, Heman, and Jeduthun, the king's seer. The gatekeepers guarded the gates and did not need to leave their posts of duty, for their Passover offerings were prepared for them by their fellow Levites.

▸ **34:33** *See **Idols**, page 836.*

16 The entire ceremony for the LORD's
Passover was completed that day. All the
burnt offerings were sacrificed on the
altar of the LORD, as King Josiah had commanded. 17 All the Israelites present in Jerusalem celebrated Passover and the Festival
of Unleavened Bread for seven days. 18 Never
since the time of the prophet Samuel had
there been such a Passover. None of the
kings of Israel had ever kept a Passover
as Josiah did, involving all the priests and
Levites, all the people of Jerusalem, and
people from all over Judah and Israel. 19 This
Passover was celebrated in the eighteenth
year of Josiah's reign.

Josiah Dies in Battle

20 After Josiah had finished restoring the
Temple, King Neco of Egypt led his army up
from Egypt to do battle at Carchemish on the
Euphrates River, and Josiah and his army
marched out to fight him.* 21 But King Neco
sent messengers to Josiah with this message:

> "What do you want with me, king of
> Judah? I have no quarrel with you today!
> I am on my way to fight another nation,
> and God has told me to hurry! Do not
> interfere with God, who is with me, or
> he will destroy you."

22 But Josiah refused to listen to Neco, to
whom God had indeed spoken, and he would
not turn back. Instead, he disguised himself
and led his army into battle on the plain of
Megiddo. 23 But the enemy archers hit King
Josiah with their arrows and wounded him.
He cried out to his men, "Take me from the
battle, for I am badly wounded!"
24 So they lifted Josiah out of his chariot
and placed him in another chariot. Then
they brought him back to Jerusalem, where
he died. He was buried there in the royal
cemetery. And all Judah and Jerusalem
mourned for him. 25 The prophet Jeremiah
composed funeral songs for Josiah, and to
this day choirs still sing these sad songs
about his death. These songs of sorrow have
become a tradition and are recorded in *The
Book of Laments*.
26 The rest of the events of Josiah's reign and
his acts of devotion (carried out according to
what was written in the Law of the LORD),
27 from beginning to end—all are recorded in
The Book of the Kings of Israel and Judah.

Jehoahaz Rules in Judah

36 Then the people of the land took Josiah's son Jehoahaz and made him
the next king in Jerusalem.
2 Jehoahaz* was twenty-three years old
when he became king, and he reigned in Jerusalem three months.
3 Then he was deposed by the king of Egypt,
who demanded that Judah pay 7,500 pounds
of silver and 75 pounds of gold* as tribute.

Jehoiakim Rules in Judah

4 The king of Egypt then installed Eliakim,
the brother of Jehoahaz, as the next king
of Judah and Jerusalem, and he changed
Eliakim's name to Jehoiakim. Then Neco
took Jehoahaz to Egypt as a prisoner.

35:1 This day in the ancient Hebrew lunar calendar was April 5, 622 B.C. **35:20** Or *Josiah went out to meet him.* **36:2** Hebrew *Joahaz*, a variant spelling of Jehoahaz; also in 36:4. **36:3** Hebrew *100 talents* [3,400 kilograms] *of silver and 1 talent* [34 kilograms] *of gold.*

▸ **36:4** *See **King Jehoiakim**, page 867.*

Persia

While Chronicles narrates the events that led to the fall and destruction of Jerusalem, it ends on a positive note by looking ahead to Babylon's conquest by Persia, which would enable the Jews to return home (2 Chronicles 36:22-23). Persia was originally a nation to the east of Mesopotamia. It had steadily grown in power and eventually conquered mighty Babylon, becoming an even greater empire with enormous wealth. It stretched from as far as India in the east to the Aegean Sea in the west and to Egypt in the south. Daniel prophesied its defeat of Babylon, and its ultimate own defeat by Greece.

▸ *See also **Kings of Persia**, page 523; **King Cyrus**, page 798.*

5 Jehoiakim was twenty-five years old
when he became king, and he reigned in Jerusalem eleven years. He did what was evil
in the sight of the LORD his God.
6 Then King Nebuchadnezzar of Babylon
came to Jerusalem and captured it, and he
bound Jehoiakim in bronze chains and led
him away to Babylon. 7 Nebuchadnezzar
also took some of the treasures from the
Temple of the LORD, and he placed them in
his palace* in Babylon.
8 The rest of the events in Jehoiakim's reign,
including all the evil things he did and everything found against him, are recorded in *The
Book of the Kings of Israel and Judah.* Then
his son Jehoiachin became the next king.

Jehoiachin Rules in Judah

9 Jehoiachin was eighteen* years old when
he became king, and he reigned in Jerusalem three months and ten days. Jehoiachin
did what was evil in the LORD's sight.
10 In the spring of the year* King Nebuchadnezzar took Jehoiachin to Babylon.
Many treasures from the Temple of the LORD
were also taken to Babylon at that time. And
Nebuchadnezzar installed Jehoiachin's
uncle,* Zedekiah, as the next king in Judah
and Jerusalem.

Zedekiah Rules in Judah

11 Zedekiah was twenty-one years old when
he became king, and he reigned in Jerusalem eleven years. 12 But Zedekiah did what
was evil in the sight of the LORD his God,
and he refused to humble himself when the
prophet Jeremiah spoke to him directly from
the LORD. 13 He also rebelled against King
Nebuchadnezzar, even though he had taken
an oath of loyalty in God's name. Zedekiah
was a hard and stubborn man, refusing to
turn to the LORD, the God of Israel.
14 Likewise, all the leaders of the priests
and the people became more and more
unfaithful. They followed all the pagan
practices of the surrounding nations, des-
ecrating the Temple of the LORD that had
been consecrated in Jerusalem.
15 The LORD, the God of their ancestors,
repeatedly sent his prophets to warn them,
for he had compassion on his people and
his Temple. 16 But the people mocked these
messengers of God and despised their
words. They scoffed at the prophets until
the LORD's anger could no longer be restrained and nothing could be done.

The Fall of Jerusalem

17 So the LORD brought the king of Babylon
against them. The Babylonians* killed
Judah's young men, even chasing after
them into the Temple. They had no pity
on the people, killing both young men and
young women, the old and the infirm. God
handed all of them over to Nebuchadnezzar. 18 The king took home to Babylon all
the articles, large and small, used in the
Temple of God, and the treasures from both
the LORD's Temple and from the palace of
the king and his officials. 19 Then his army
burned the Temple of God, tore down the
walls of Jerusalem, burned all the palaces,
and completely destroyed everything of
value.* 20 The few who survived were taken
as exiles to Babylon, and they became
servants to the king and his sons until the
kingdom of Persia came to power.
21 So the message of the LORD spoken
through Jeremiah was fulfilled. The land
finally enjoyed its Sabbath rest, lying desolate until the seventy years were fulfilled,
just as the prophet had said.

Cyrus Allows the Exiles to Return

22 In the first year of King Cyrus of Persia,*
the LORD fulfilled the prophecy he had given
through Jeremiah.* He stirred the heart of
Cyrus to put this proclamation in writing
and to send it throughout his kingdom:

23 "This is what King Cyrus of Persia says:
"The LORD, the God of heaven, has
given me all the kingdoms of the earth.
He has appointed me to build him a
Temple at Jerusalem, which is in Judah.
Any of you who are his people may go
there for this task. And may the LORD
your God be with you!"

36:7 Or *temple.* **36:9** As in one Hebrew manuscript, some Greek manuscripts, and Syriac version (see also 2 Kgs 24:8); most Hebrew manuscripts read *eight.* **36:10a** Hebrew *At the turn of the year.* The first day of this year in the ancient Hebrew lunar calendar was April 13, 597 B.C. **36:10b** As in parallel text at 2 Kgs 24:17; Hebrew reads *brother,* or *relative.* **36:17** Or *Chaldeans.* **36:19** Or *destroyed all the valuable articles from the Temple.* **36:22a** The first year of Cyrus's reign over Babylon was 538 B.C. **36:22b** See Jer 25:11-12; 29:10.

▸ **36:11** *See* ***King Zedekiah****, page 444.* **36:17** *See* ***The fall of Jerusalem****, page 871.*

Ezra *Returning to Jerusalem*

The book of Ezra covers the period from the start of the return from exile in 538 BC to the ministry of Ezra around the mid-fifth century BC. It tells how the Jews—as the exiles were now called, referring to their origins in Judah—returned to Jerusalem after their exile in Babylon and how, despite opposition, they rebuilt the Temple. Ezra was a priest who returned with a later group of returning exiles and who challenged the people's disobedience to God's Law, especially concerning marriage to unbelievers. He reappears in the book of Nehemiah, where he is found teaching God's Law (Nehemiah 8).

Most scholars think, because of the great similarity of language, that the author of Ezra and Nehemiah was also the author of 1 and 2 Chronicles.

What's it all about?

When Persia conquered Babylon, Judah was swallowed up into its empire, becoming part of the province called "Beyond the River" (Trans-Euphrates). Cyrus, king of Persia, had a policy of allowing conquered exiles to return home, believing they would then be less likely to rebel. He encouraged the Jews to return to Jerusalem to build a house for God and provided them with the resources to do it. Over forty-two thousand returned—by no means the whole Jewish population.

On their arrival, the first thing they did was to build an altar, and then they began to rebuild the Temple itself (chapter 3). But local inhabitants opposed the work, and the project was put on hold (chapter 4). The prophets Zechariah and Haggai continued to encourage the people until King Darius issued a decree ordering the work to continue unhindered (chapter 6). The Temple was finally dedicated in March 515 BC, seventy years after its destruction, just as Jeremiah had prophesied (Jeremiah 29:10).

Almost sixty years later, Ezra led a second group of exiles back to Judah. On his arrival, he discovered that many Jews had married local unbelievers, contrary to God's Law (e.g., Deuteronomy 7:3-4). This was not prohibited because of their ethnic origins, but because they were not believers in the LORD (Yahweh). In fact, foreigners had always been welcomed into Israelite society. Ezra's primary concern was to reestablish Israelite society on the fundamental principle of belief in the one true God, which is why he and Nehemiah were so against marriages to people who worshiped idols. Idol worship had led to God's people being exiled in the first place; so now, after they had returned from that exile, was not a time to start worshiping idols again!

Convicted by Ezra's challenge, the people returned to God and determined to put aside their foreign wives, thus preserving their religious purity. A national revival followed. The Temple had now been rebuilt, but the city walls remained

OVERVIEW

The first group of exiles returns to Jerusalem with Sheshbazzar · *1:1–2:70*

The Temple is restored despite opposition · *3:1–6:22*

Ezra returns and teaches the exiles God's Law · *7:1–10:44*

page 522

in ruins. The task of rebuilding those would fall to Nehemiah (see the book of Nehemiah, page 535).

What does it mean for us?

By returning to their land, both Ezra and the people showed that they believed that God's promises remained true in spite of the people's past failures. Their faith enabled them to continue with their building work despite much opposition and suspicion. They were strengthened by the preaching of God's word by prophets like Haggai and Zechariah and (about eighty years later) Malachi.

Ezra shows that, when we choose to obey God, God will come to us. He will send people to encourage us and will even change circumstances to our advantage. Cyrus and Darius were both pagan rulers, but God used them to help his people, Israel.

▶ *See also* ***A timeline of the Bible***, *pages A22-A24.*

Cyrus Allows the Exiles to Return

1 In the first year of King Cyrus of Persia,*
the LORD fulfilled the prophecy he had
given through Jeremiah.* He stirred the heart
of Cyrus to put this proclamation in writing
and to send it throughout his kingdom:

2 "This is what King Cyrus of Persia says:
"The LORD, the God of heaven, has
given me all the kingdoms of the earth.
He has appointed me to build him a
Temple at Jerusalem, which is in Judah.
3 Any of you who are his people may go
to Jerusalem in Judah to rebuild this
Temple of the LORD, the God of Israel,
who lives in Jerusalem. And may your
God be with you! 4 Wherever this Jewish
remnant is found, let their neighbors
contribute toward their expenses by
giving them silver and gold, supplies for
the journey, and livestock, as well as a
voluntary offering for the Temple of God
in Jerusalem."

5 Then God stirred the hearts of the priests
and Levites and the leaders of the tribes of
Judah and Benjamin to go to Jerusalem to
rebuild the Temple of the LORD. 6 And all
their neighbors assisted by giving them
articles of silver and gold, supplies for the
journey, and livestock. They gave them many
valuable gifts in addition to all the voluntary
offerings.
7 King Cyrus himself brought out the
articles that King Nebuchadnezzar had taken
from the LORD's Temple in Jerusalem and
had placed in the temple of his own gods.
8 Cyrus directed Mithredath, the treasurer
of Persia, to count these items and present
them to Sheshbazzar, the leader of the exiles
returning to Judah.* 9 This is a list of the items
that were returned:

gold basins 30
silver basins 1,000
silver incense burners* 29
10 gold bowls 30
silver bowls 410
other items 1,000

11 In all, there were 5,400 articles of gold
and silver. Sheshbazzar brought all of these
along when the exiles went from Babylon to
Jerusalem.

Exiles Who Returned with Zerubbabel

2 Here is the list of the Jewish exiles of the
provinces who returned from their captivity. King Nebuchadnezzar had deported
them to Babylon, but now they returned to Jerusalem and the other towns in Judah where
they originally lived. 2 Their leaders were
Zerubbabel, Jeshua, Nehemiah, Seraiah,
Reelaiah, Mordecai, Bilshan, Mispar, Bigvai,
Rehum, and Baanah.

This is the number of the men of Israel who
returned from exile:

3 The family of Parosh 2,172
4 The family of Shephatiah 372
5 The family of Arah 775
6 The family of Pahath-moab (descendants
of Jeshua and Joab) 2,812
7 The family of Elam 1,254
8 The family of Zattu 945
9 The family of Zaccai 760
10 The family of Bani 642
11 The family of Bebai 623

[12] The family of Azgad 1,222
[13] The family of Adonikam. 666
[14] The family of Bigvai 2,056
[15] The family of Adin. 454
[16] The family of Ater (descendants of Hezekiah). 98
[17] The family of Bezai 323
[18] The family of Jorah 112
[19] The family of Hashum 223
[20] The family of Gibbar 95
[21] The people of Bethlehem 123
[22] The people of Netophah 56
[23] The people of Anathoth 128
[24] The people of Beth-azmaveth* 42
[25] The people of Kiriath-jearim,* Kephirah, and Beeroth 743
[26] The people of Ramah and Geba. 621
[27] The people of Micmash 122
[28] The people of Bethel and Ai. 223
[29] The citizens of Nebo 52
[30] The citizens of Magbish 156
[31] The citizens of West Elam*. 1,254
[32] The citizens of Harim 320
[33] The citizens of Lod, Hadid, and Ono 725
[34] The citizens of Jericho. 345
[35] The citizens of Senaah 3,630

[36] These are the priests who returned from exile:
The family of Jedaiah (through the line of Jeshua) 973
[37] The family of Immer 1,052
[38] The family of Pashhur 1,247
[39] The family of Harim 1,017

[40] These are the Levites who returned from exile:
The families of Jeshua and Kadmiel (descendants of Hodaviah) 74
[41] The singers of the family of Asaph . . 128
[42] The gatekeepers of the families of Shallum, Ater, Talmon, Akkub, Hatita, and Shobai 139

[43] The descendants of the following Temple servants returned from exile:
Ziha, Hasupha, Tabbaoth,
[44] Keros, Siaha, Padon,
[45] Lebanah, Hagabah, Akkub,
[46] Hagab, Shalmai,* Hanan,
[47] Giddel, Gahar, Reaiah,
[48] Rezin, Nekoda, Gazzam,
[49] Uzza, Paseah, Besai,
[50] Asnah, Meunim, Nephusim,
[51] Bakbuk, Hakupha, Harhur,
[52] Bazluth, Mehida, Harsha,
[53] Barkos, Sisera, Temah,
[54] Neziah, and Hatipha.

[55] The descendants of these servants of King Solomon returned from exile:
Sotai, Hassophereth, Peruda,
[56] Jaalah, Darkon, Giddel,
[57] Shephatiah, Hattil, Pokereth-hazzebaim, and Ami.

[58] In all, the Temple servants and the descendants of Solomon's servants numbered 392.

[59] Another group returned at this time from the towns of Tel-melah, Tel-harsha, Kerub, Addan, and Immer. However, they could not prove that they or their families were descendants of Israel. [60] This group included the families of Delaiah, Tobiah, and Nekoda—a total of 652 people.

[61] Three families of priests—Hobaiah, Hakkoz, and Barzillai—also returned. (This Barzillai had married a woman who was a descendant of Barzillai of Gilead, and he had taken her family name.) [62] They searched for their names in the genealogical records, but they were not found, so they were

1:1a The first year of Cyrus's reign over Babylon was 538 B.C.
1:1b See Jer 25:11-12; 29:10. **1:8** Hebrew *Sheshbazzar, the prince of Judah.* **1:9** The meaning of this Hebrew word is uncertain.
2:24 As in parallel text at Neh 7:28; Hebrew reads *Azmaveth.*
2:25 As in some Hebrew manuscripts and Greek version (see also Neh 7:29); Hebrew reads *Kiriath-arim.* **2:31** Or *of the other Elam.*
2:46 As in an alternate reading of the Masoretic Text (see also Neh 7:48); the other alternate reads *Shamlai.*

Kings of Persia

- **Cyrus** (ruled 550–530 BC) established a policy of allowing exiles to return to their homelands. See *King Cyrus*, page 798.
- **Darius** (ruled 521–486 BC) permitted construction of the Temple to continue after opposition had brought it to a halt. See *King Darius*, page 527.
- **Artaxerxes I** (ruled 465–424 BC) temporarily stopped construction of the city of Jerusalem. He allowed Ezra and Nehemiah to return to Jerusalem.

disqualified from serving as priests. [63]The governor told them not to eat the priests' share of food from the sacrifices until a priest could consult the LORD about the matter by using the Urim and Thummim—the sacred lots.

[64]So a total of 42,360 people returned to Judah, [65]in addition to 7,337 servants and 200 singers, both men and women. [66]They took with them 736 horses, 245 mules, [67]435 camels, and 6,720 donkeys.

[68]When they arrived at the Temple of the LORD in Jerusalem, some of the family leaders made voluntary offerings toward the rebuilding of God's Temple on its original site, [69]and each leader gave as much as he could. The total of their gifts came to 61,000 gold coins,* 6,250 pounds* of silver, and 100 robes for the priests.

[70]So the priests, the Levites, the singers, the gatekeepers, the Temple servants, and some of the common people settled in villages near Jerusalem. The rest of the people returned to their own towns throughout Israel.

The Altar Is Rebuilt

3 In early autumn,* when the Israelites had settled in their towns, all the people assembled in Jerusalem with a unified purpose. [2]Then Jeshua son of Jehozadak* joined his fellow priests and Zerubbabel son of Shealtiel with his family in rebuilding the altar of the God of Israel. They wanted to sacrifice burnt offerings on it, as instructed in the Law of Moses, the man of God. [3]Even though the people were afraid of the local residents, they rebuilt the altar at its old site. Then they began to sacrifice burnt offerings on the altar to the LORD each morning and evening.

[4]They celebrated the Festival of Shelters as prescribed in the Law, sacrificing the number of burnt offerings specified for each day of the festival. [5]They also offered the regular burnt offerings and the offerings required for the new moon celebrations and the annual festivals as prescribed by the LORD. The people also gave voluntary offerings to the LORD. [6]Fifteen days before the Festival of Shelters began,* the priests had begun to sacrifice burnt offerings to the LORD. This was even before they had started to lay the foundation of the LORD's Temple.

The People Begin to Rebuild the Temple

[7]Then the people hired masons and carpenters and bought cedar logs from the people of Tyre and Sidon, paying them with food, wine, and olive oil. The logs were brought down from the Lebanon mountains and floated along the coast of the Mediterranean Sea* to Joppa, for King Cyrus had given permission for this.

[8]The construction of the Temple of God began in midspring,* during the second

Lists in the Bible

When we come to passages that contain lists of things (as in Ezra 1:9-10) or lists of people (as here in chapter 2) our hearts can often sink. How can we get any blessing from reading this? Why did God even include this in the Bible?

But such passages show two things. First, they show *God's faithfulness*. He had preserved not only a remnant of his people to return to Judah but even the Temple utensils that they would need to recommence worship once they got there (1:7-11). And the listing of family names and numbers in chapter 2 shows his faithfulness in preserving a remnant who were true descendants of his covenant people and who were therefore inheritors of his promises with a legal right to the land to which they were returning.

Second, they show *God's concern*. God is concerned for even the smallest details of our lives. Not one Temple utensil and not one family member is insignificant to him. He is not just a God of the big issues, but also a God of the smallest detail. In fact, Jesus said that not even a sparrow falls to the ground without him knowing (Matthew 10:29)—such is his knowledge and love.

▶ *See also* ***Why does the Bible have passages like these?***, *page 262.*

year after they arrived in Jerusalem. The work force was made up of everyone who had returned from exile, including Zerubbabel son of Shealtiel, Jeshua son of Jehozadak and his fellow priests, and all the Levites. The Levites who were twenty years old or older were put in charge of rebuilding the LORD's Temple. 9 The workers at the Temple of God were supervised by Jeshua with his sons and relatives, and Kadmiel and his sons, all descendants of Hodaviah.* They were helped in this task by the Levites of the family of Henadad.

10 When the builders completed the foundation of the LORD's Temple, the priests put on their robes and took their places to blow their trumpets. And the Levites, descendants of Asaph, clashed their cymbals to praise the LORD, just as King David had prescribed. 11 With praise and thanks, they sang this song to the LORD:

"He is so good!
His faithful love for Israel endures
forever!"

Then all the people gave a great shout, praising the LORD because the foundation of the LORD's Temple had been laid.

12 But many of the older priests, Levites, and other leaders who had seen the first Temple wept aloud when they saw the new Temple's foundation. The others, however, were shouting for joy. 13 The joyful shouting and weeping mingled together in a loud noise that could be heard far in the distance.

Enemies Oppose the Rebuilding

4 The enemies of Judah and Benjamin heard that the exiles were rebuilding a Temple to the LORD, the God of Israel. 2 So they approached Zerubbabel and the other leaders and said, "Let us build with you, for we worship your God just as you do. We have sacrificed to him ever since King Esarhaddon of Assyria brought us here."

3 But Zerubbabel, Jeshua, and the other leaders of Israel replied, "You may have no part in this work. We alone will build the Temple for the LORD, the God of Israel, just as King Cyrus of Persia commanded us."

4 Then the local residents tried to discourage and frighten the people of Judah to keep them from their work. 5 They bribed agents to work against them and to frustrate their plans. This went on during the entire reign of King Cyrus of Persia and lasted until King Darius of Persia took the throne.*

Later Opposition under Xerxes and Artaxerxes

6 Years later when Xerxes* began his reign, the enemies of Judah wrote a letter of accusation against the people of Judah and Jerusalem.

7 Even later, during the reign of King Artaxerxes of Persia,* the enemies of Judah, led by Bishlam, Mithredath, and Tabeel, sent a letter to Artaxerxes in the Aramaic

2:69a Hebrew *61,000 darics of gold,* about 1,100 pounds or 500 kilograms in weight. **2:69b** Hebrew *5,000 minas* [3,000 kilograms]. **3:1** Hebrew *In the seventh month.* The year is not specified, so it may have been during Cyrus's first year (538 B.C.) or second year (537 B.C.). The seventh month of the ancient Hebrew lunar calendar occurred within the months of September/October 538 B.C. and October/November 537 B.C. **3:2** Hebrew *Jozadak,* a variant spelling of Jehozadak; also in 3:8. **3:6** Hebrew *On the first day of the seventh month.* This day in the ancient Hebrew lunar calendar occurred in September or October. The Festival of Shelters began on the fifteenth day of the seventh month. **3:7** Hebrew *the sea.* **3:8** Hebrew *in the second month.* This month in the ancient Hebrew lunar calendar occurred within the months of April and May 536 B.C. **3:9** Hebrew *sons of Judah* (i.e., *bene Yehudah*). *Bene* might also be read here as the proper name Binnui; *Yehudah* is probably another name for Hodaviah. Compare 2:40; Neh 7:43; 1 Esdras 5:58. **4:5** Darius reigned 521–486 B.C. **4:6** Hebrew *Ahasuerus,* another name for Xerxes. He reigned 486–465 B.C. **4:7** Artaxerxes reigned 465–424 B.C.

Zerubbabel

Coming back home was in some ways the easiest part of the exiles' task; the hardest was facing up to what needed to be done when they got there. Clearly there was a lot of fear around (Ezra 3:3); but inspired by Zerubbabel—King Jehoiachin's grandson, and therefore a descendant of King David—the people set to work, first rebuilding the altar, and then the Temple itself. When opposition arose and the work was hindered, it was once again Zerubbabel who took the lead (Ezra 5–6; Haggai 1–2). His name means "Seed of Babylon" and suggests he had been born in exile. Yet despite never having seen Jerusalem, he embraced his heritage and played a significant role in Judah's reestablishment.

language, and it was translated for the
king.
8*Rehum the governor and Shimshai
the court secretary wrote the letter, telling
King Artaxerxes about the situation in Jerusalem. 9They greeted the king for all their
colleagues—the judges and local leaders,
the people of Tarpel, the Persians, the Babylonians, and the people of Erech and Susa
(that is, Elam). 10They also sent greetings
from the rest of the people whom the great
and noble Ashurbanipal* had deported
and relocated in Samaria and throughout
the neighboring lands of the province west
of the Euphrates River.* 11This is a copy of
their letter:

"To King Artaxerxes, from your loyal
subjects in the province west of the
Euphrates River.
12"The king should know that the
Jews who came here to Jerusalem from
Babylon are rebuilding this rebellious
and evil city. They have already laid the
foundation and will soon finish its walls.
13And the king should know that if this
city is rebuilt and its walls are completed,
it will be much to your disadvantage,
for the Jews will then refuse to pay their
tribute, customs, and tolls to you.
14"Since we are your loyal subjects*
and do not want to see the king
dishonored in this way, we have sent
the king this information. 15We suggest
that a search be made in your ancestors'
records, where you will discover what a
rebellious city this has been in the past.
In fact, it was destroyed because of its
long and troublesome history of revolt
against the kings and countries who
controlled it. 16We declare to the king
that if this city is rebuilt and its walls
are completed, the province west of the
Euphrates River will be lost to you."

17Then King Artaxerxes sent this reply:

"To Rehum the governor, Shimshai the
court secretary, and their colleagues
living in Samaria and throughout the
province west of the Euphrates River.
Greetings.
18"The letter you sent has been
translated and read to me. 19I ordered
a search of the records and have found
that Jerusalem has indeed been a hotbed
of insurrection against many kings. In
fact, rebellion and revolt are normal
there! 20Powerful kings have ruled
over Jerusalem and the entire province
west of the Euphrates River, receiving
tribute, customs, and tolls. 21Therefore,
issue orders to have these men stop
their work. That city must not be rebuilt
except at my express command. 22Be
diligent, and don't neglect this matter,
for we must not permit the situation to
harm the king's interests."

23When this letter from King Artaxerxes
was read to Rehum, Shimshai, and their
colleagues, they hurried to Jerusalem.
Then, with a show of strength, they forced
the Jews to stop building.

The Rebuilding Resumes

24So the work on the Temple of God in Jerusalem had stopped, and it remained at a
standstill until the second year of the reign
of King Darius of Persia.*

5 At that time the prophets Haggai and
Zechariah son of Iddo prophesied to the
Jews in Judah and Jerusalem. They prophesied in the name of the God of Israel who
was over them. 2Zerubbabel son of Shealtiel
and Jeshua son of Jehozadak* responded by
starting again to rebuild the Temple of God
in Jerusalem. And the prophets of God were
with them and helped them.
3But Tattenai, governor of the province
west of the Euphrates River,* and Shethar-
bozenai and their colleagues soon arrived in
Jerusalem and asked, "Who gave you permission to rebuild this Temple and restore
this structure?" 4They also asked for* the
names of all the men working on the Temple.
5But because their God was watching over
them, the leaders of the Jews were not prevented from building until a report was sent
to Darius and he returned his decision.

Tattenai's Letter to King Darius

6This is a copy of the letter that Tattenai the
governor, Shethar-bozenai, and the other
officials of the province west of the Euphrates River sent to King Darius:

7"To King Darius. Greetings.
8"The king should know that we went
to the construction site of the Temple of
the great God in the province of Judah. It

is being rebuilt with specially prepared
stones, and timber is being laid in its
walls. The work is going forward with
great energy and success.
9“We asked the leaders, ‘Who gave
you permission to rebuild this Temple
and restore this structure?’ 10And we
demanded their names so that we could
tell you who the leaders were.
11“This was their answer: ‘We are
the servants of the God of heaven
and earth, and we are rebuilding the
Temple that was built here many years
ago by a great king of Israel. 12But
because our ancestors angered the
God of heaven, he abandoned them
to King Nebuchadnezzar of Babylon,*
who destroyed this Temple and exiled
the people to Babylonia. 13However,
King Cyrus of Babylon,* during the
first year of his reign, issued a decree
that the Temple of God should be
rebuilt. 14King Cyrus returned the gold
and silver cups that Nebuchadnezzar
had taken from the Temple of God in
Jerusalem and had placed in the temple
of Babylon. These cups were taken from
that temple and presented to a man
named Sheshbazzar, whom King Cyrus
appointed as governor of Judah. 15The
king instructed him to return the cups to
their place in Jerusalem and to rebuild
the Temple of God there on its original
site. 16So this Sheshbazzar came and
laid the foundations of the Temple of
God in Jerusalem. The people have been
working on it ever since, though it is not
yet completed.’
17“Therefore, if it pleases the king,
we request that a search be made in the
royal archives of Babylon to discover
whether King Cyrus ever issued a decree
to rebuild God’s Temple in Jerusalem.
And then let the king send us his
decision in this matter.”

Darius Approves the Rebuilding

6 So King Darius issued orders that a
search be made in the Babylonian
archives, which were stored in the treasury.
2But it was at the fortress at Ecbatana in the
province of Media that a scroll was found.
This is what it said:

“Memorandum:
3“In the first year of King Cyrus’s
reign, a decree was sent out concerning
the Temple of God at Jerusalem.
“Let the Temple be rebuilt on the site
where Jews used to offer their sacrifices,
using the original foundations. Its height
will be ninety feet, and its width will
be ninety feet.* 4Every three layers of
specially prepared stones will be topped
by a layer of timber. All expenses will be
paid by the royal treasury. 5Furthermore,
the gold and silver cups, which were

4:8 The original text of 4:8–6:18 is in Aramaic. **4:10a** Aramaic *Osnappar,* another name for Ashurbanipal. **4:10b** Aramaic *the province beyond the river;* also in 4:11, 16, 17, 20. **4:14** Aramaic *Since we eat the salt of the palace.* **4:24** The second year of Darius’s reign was 520 B.C. The narrative started in 4:1-5 is resumed at verse 24. **5:2** Aramaic *Jozadak,* a variant spelling of Jehozadak. **5:3** Aramaic *the province beyond the river;* also in 5:6. **5:4** As in one Hebrew manuscript and Greek and Syriac versions; Masoretic Text reads *Then we told them.* **5:12** Aramaic *Nebuchadnezzar the Chaldean.* **5:13** King Cyrus of Persia is here identified as the king of Babylon because Persia had conquered the Babylonian Empire. **6:3** Aramaic *Its height will be 60 cubits* [27.6 meters], *and its width will be 60 cubits.* It is commonly held that this verse should be emended to read: “Its height will be 30 cubits [45 feet or 13.8 meters], its length will be 60 cubits [90 feet or 27.6 meters], and its width will be 20 cubits [30 feet or 9.2 meters]”; compare 1 Kgs 6:2. The emendation regarding the width is supported by the Syriac version.

King Darius

The Jews’ opponents tried everything to stop them from rebuilding the Temple, including a letter sent by Tattenai, the local Persian governor, direct to King Darius (Ezra 5:6-17). Darius I, known as Darius the Great, ruled Persia from 521 to 486 BC and was a successful soldier, builder, and administrator. Persian documents confirm that he took enormous interest in every detail of his empire, so letters like this one to him were quite common. Tattenai’s objections rebounded, however, for Darius had the royal archives searched and discovered that King Cyrus had given the Jews permission to rebuild the Temple. Darius therefore replied that not only were the Jews not to be hindered, but that the expenses for the rebuilding should come out of Tattenai’s budget.

taken to Babylon by Nebuchadnezzar
from the Temple of God in Jerusalem,
must be returned to Jerusalem and put
back where they belong. Let them be
taken back to the Temple of God."

6 So King Darius sent this message:

"Now therefore, Tattenai, governor
of the province west of the Euphrates
River,* and Shethar-bozenai, and your
colleagues and other officials west of
the Euphrates River—stay away from
there! 7 Do not disturb the construction
of the Temple of God. Let it be rebuilt on
its original site, and do not hinder the
governor of Judah and the elders of the
Jews in their work.
8 "Moreover, I hereby decree that you
are to help these elders of the Jews as
they rebuild this Temple of God. You
must pay the full construction costs,
without delay, from my taxes collected in
the province west of the Euphrates River
so that the work will not be interrupted.
9 "Give the priests in Jerusalem
whatever is needed in the way of young
bulls, rams, and male lambs for the
burnt offerings presented to the God of
heaven. And without fail, provide them
with as much wheat, salt, wine, and
olive oil as they need each day. 10 Then
they will be able to offer acceptable
sacrifices to the God of heaven and pray
for the welfare of the king and his sons.
11 "Those who violate this decree in
any way will have a beam pulled from
their house. Then they will be lifted up
and impaled on it, and their house will
be reduced to a pile of rubble.* 12 May
the God who has chosen the city of
Jerusalem as the place to honor his name
destroy any king or nation that violates
this command and destroys this Temple.
"I, Darius, have issued this decree. Let
it be obeyed with all diligence."

The Temple's Dedication

13 Tattenai, governor of the province west of
the Euphrates River, and Shethar-bozenai
and their colleagues complied at once with
the command of King Darius. 14 So the Jewish
elders continued their work, and they were
greatly encouraged by the preaching of the
prophets Haggai and Zechariah son of Iddo.
The Temple was finally finished, as had
been commanded by the God of Israel and
decreed by Cyrus, Darius, and Artaxerxes,
the kings of Persia. 15 The Temple was completed on March 12,* during the sixth year
of King Darius's reign.
16 The Temple of God was then dedicated
with great joy by the people of Israel, the
priests, the Levites, and the rest of the people
who had returned from exile. 17 During the
dedication ceremony for the Temple of God,
100 young bulls, 200 rams, and 400 male
lambs were sacrificed. And 12 male goats
were presented as a sin offering for the
twelve tribes of Israel. 18 Then the priests and
Levites were divided into their various divisions to serve at the Temple of God in Jerusalem, as prescribed in the Book of Moses.

Celebration of Passover

19 On April 21* the returned exiles celebrated
Passover. 20 The priests and Levites had
purified themselves and were ceremonially
clean. So they slaughtered the Passover
lamb for all the returned exiles, for their
fellow priests, and for themselves. 21 The
Passover meal was eaten by the people of
Israel who had returned from exile and by
the others in the land who had turned from
their corrupt practices to worship the LORD,
the God of Israel. 22 Then they celebrated
the Festival of Unleavened Bread for seven
days. There was great joy throughout the
land because the LORD had caused the king
of Assyria* to be favorable to them, so that
he helped them to rebuild the Temple of
God, the God of Israel.

Ezra Arrives in Jerusalem

7 Many years later, during the reign of King
Artaxerxes of Persia,* there was a man
named Ezra. He was the son* of Seraiah, son
of Azariah, son of Hilkiah, 2 son of Shallum,
son of Zadok, son of Ahitub, 3 son of Amariah,
son of Azariah, son* of Meraioth, 4 son of
Zerahiah, son of Uzzi, son of Bukki, 5 son of
Abishua, son of Phinehas, son of Eleazar,
son of Aaron the high priest.* 6 This Ezra was
a scribe who was well versed in the Law of
Moses, which the LORD, the God of Israel,
had given to the people of Israel. He came
up to Jerusalem from Babylon, and the king
gave him everything he asked for, because
the gracious hand of the LORD his God was
on him. 7 Some of the people of Israel, as
well as some of the priests, Levites, singers,

gatekeepers, and Temple servants, traveled
up to Jerusalem with him in the seventh year
of King Artaxerxes' reign.
8Ezra arrived in Jerusalem in August* of
that year. 9He had arranged to leave Babylon
on April 8, the first day of the new year,* and
he arrived at Jerusalem on August 4,* for the
gracious hand of his God was on him. 10This
was because Ezra had determined to study
and obey the Law of the LORD and to teach
those decrees and regulations to the people
of Israel.

Artaxerxes' Letter to Ezra

11King Artaxerxes had given a copy of the
following letter to Ezra, the priest and scribe
who studied and taught the commands and
decrees of the LORD to Israel:

12*"From Artaxerxes, the king of kings,
to Ezra the priest, the teacher of the law
of the God of heaven. Greetings.
13"I decree that any of the people of
Israel in my kingdom, including the
priests and Levites, may volunteer to
return to Jerusalem with you. 14I and my
council of seven hereby instruct you to
conduct an inquiry into the situation
in Judah and Jerusalem, based on your
God's law, which is in your hand. 15We
also commission you to take with you
silver and gold, which we are freely
presenting as an offering to the God of
Israel who lives in Jerusalem.
16"Furthermore, you are to take any
silver and gold that you may obtain from
the province of Babylon, as well as the
voluntary offerings of the people and the
priests that are presented for the Temple
of their God in Jerusalem. 17These

6:6 Aramaic *the province beyond the river;* also in 6:6b, 8, 13. **6:11** Aramaic *a dunghill.* **6:15** Aramaic *on the third day of the month Adar,* of the ancient Hebrew lunar calendar. A number of events in Ezra can be cross-checked with dates in surviving Persian records and related accurately to our modern calendar. This day was March 12, 515 B.C. **6:19** Hebrew *On the fourteenth day of the first month,* of the ancient Hebrew lunar calendar. This day was April 21, 515 B.C.; also see note on 6:15. **6:22** King Darius of Persia is here identified as the king of Assyria because Persia had conquered the Babylonian Empire, which included the earlier Assyrian Empire. **7:1a** Artaxerxes reigned 465–424 B.C. **7:1b** Or *descendant;* see 1 Chr 6:14. **7:3** Or *descendant;* see 1 Chr 6:6-10. **7:5** Or *the first priest.* **7:8** Hebrew *in the fifth month.* This month in the ancient Hebrew lunar calendar occurred within the months of August and September 458 B.C. **7:9a** Hebrew *on the first day of the first month,* of the ancient Hebrew lunar calendar. This day was April 8, 458 B.C.; also see note on 6:15. **7:9b** Hebrew *on the first day of the fifth month,* of the ancient Hebrew lunar calendar. This day was August 4, 458 B.C.; also see note on 6:15. **7:12** The original text of 7:12-26 is in Aramaic.

Bible teaching

Ezra stands out as one of the leading teachers of God's word in the Old Testament. His teaching laid foundations for God's people at a crucial time, calling them back to godly living and to building their lives upon God's word. His teaching contributed to a time of revival, and he serves as an excellent model for today.

In Ezra 7:10 we see three essential keys to becoming a good Bible teacher or preacher. First, Ezra determined to *study God's word*. God's people are not fed by human opinions, ideas, or stories, but by God's word. That means preachers and teachers must study the text to understand it before daring to open their mouths to teach others. Ezra "determined" in advance to do this—for him, no hurried or last-minute preparation!

Second, he determined to *live God's word*. He observed God's Law himself before daring to teach others to do so. Without this preachers lack credibility—and people know if they are teaching things that are not their experience.

Third, he determined to *teach God's word*. Only now—after studying it and seeking to live it out—did he dare to start teaching others. But his concern wasn't just for his *teaching* but for the people's *learning*. Just because preachers speak (even passionately!) doesn't mean that the people they are talking to understand. So later we find Ezra putting Levites among his congregation to ensure that people were understanding what he was saying (Nehemiah 8:7-8).

Here is truly a great model for teachers and preachers today.

▸ *See also **The Scriptures in public worship**, page 544; **Teaching God's word**, page 1268; **Studying God's word**, page 1387.*

donations are to be used specifically for
the purchase of bulls, rams, male lambs,
and the appropriate grain offerings
and liquid offerings, all of which will
be offered on the altar of the Temple
of your God in Jerusalem. 18 Any silver
and gold that is left over may be used in
whatever way you and your colleagues
feel is the will of your God.
19 "But as for the cups we are
entrusting to you for the service of the
Temple of your God, deliver them all
to the God of Jerusalem. 20 If you need
anything else for your God's Temple or
for any similar needs, you may take it
from the royal treasury.
21 "I, Artaxerxes the king, hereby send
this decree to all the treasurers in the
province west of the Euphrates River*:
'You are to give Ezra, the priest and
teacher of the law of the God of heaven,
whatever he requests of you. 22 You are to
give him up to 7,500 pounds* of silver,
500 bushels* of wheat, 550 gallons of
wine, 550 gallons of olive oil,* and an
unlimited supply of salt. 23 Be careful
to provide whatever the God of heaven
demands for his Temple, for why should
we risk bringing God's anger against
the realm of the king and his sons? 24 I
also decree that no priest, Levite, singer,
gatekeeper, Temple servant, or other
worker in this Temple of God will be
required to pay tribute, customs, or tolls
of any kind.'
25 "And you, Ezra, are to use the
wisdom your God has given you to
appoint magistrates and judges who
know your God's laws to govern all
the people in the province west of
the Euphrates River. Teach the law to
anyone who does not know it. 26 Anyone
who refuses to obey the law of your
God and the law of the king will be
punished immediately, either by death,
banishment, confiscation of goods, or
imprisonment."

Ezra Praises the LORD

27 Praise the LORD, the God of our ancestors, who made the king want to beautify
the Temple of the LORD in Jerusalem! 28 And
praise him for demonstrating such unfailing love to me by honoring me before the
king, his council, and all his mighty nobles!
I felt encouraged because the gracious hand
of the LORD my God was on me. And I gathered some of the leaders of Israel to return
with me to Jerusalem.

Exiles Who Returned with Ezra

8 Here is a list of the family leaders and
the genealogies of those who came with
me from Babylon during the reign of King
Artaxerxes:

2 From the family of Phinehas: Gershom.
From the family of Ithamar: Daniel.
From the family of David: Hattush,
3 a descendant of Shecaniah.
From the family of Parosh: Zechariah
and 150 other men were registered.
4 From the family of Pahath-moab:
Eliehoenai son of Zerahiah and
200 other men.
5 From the family of Zattu*: Shecaniah
son of Jahaziel and 300 other men.
6 From the family of Adin: Ebed son of
Jonathan and 50 other men.
7 From the family of Elam: Jeshaiah son
of Athaliah and 70 other men.
8 From the family of Shephatiah: Zebadiah
son of Michael and 80 other men.
9 From the family of Joab: Obadiah son of
Jehiel and 218 other men.
10 From the family of Bani*: Shelomith son
of Josiphiah and 160 other men.
11 From the family of Bebai: Zechariah son
of Bebai and 28 other men.
12 From the family of Azgad: Johanan son
of Hakkatan and 110 other men.
13 From the family of Adonikam, who came
later*: Eliphelet, Jeuel, Shemaiah,
and 60 other men.
14 From the family of Bigvai: Uthai,
Zaccur,* and 70 other men.

Ezra's Journey to Jerusalem

15 I assembled the exiles at the Ahava Canal,
and we camped there for three days while
I went over the lists of the people and the
priests who had arrived. I found that not
one Levite had volunteered to come along.
16 So I sent for Eliezer, Ariel, Shemaiah, Elnathan, Jarib, Elnathan, Nathan, Zechariah, and Meshullam, who were leaders of
the people. I also sent for Joiarib and Elnathan, who were men of discernment. 17 I sent
them to Iddo, the leader of the Levites at Ca-
siphia, to ask him and his relatives and the

Temple servants to send us ministers for the
Temple of God at Jerusalem.
18 Since the gracious hand of our God was
on us, they sent us a man named Sherebiah, along with eighteen of his sons and
brothers. He was a very astute man and a
descendant of Mahli, who was a descendant of Levi son of Israel.* 19 They also sent
Hashabiah, together with Jeshaiah from the
descendants of Merari, and twenty of his
sons and brothers, 20 and 220 Temple servants. The Temple servants were assistants
to the Levites—a group of Temple workers
first instituted by King David and his officials. They were all listed by name.
21 And there by the Ahava Canal, I gave
orders for all of us to fast and humble ourselves before our God. We prayed that he
would give us a safe journey and protect
us, our children, and our goods as we traveled. 22 For I was ashamed to ask the king for
soldiers and horsemen* to accompany us
and protect us from enemies along the way.
After all, we had told the king, "Our God's
hand of protection is on all who worship
him, but his fierce anger rages against those
who abandon him." 23 So we fasted and earnestly prayed that our God would take care
of us, and he heard our prayer.
24 I appointed twelve leaders of the
priests—Sherebiah, Hashabiah, and ten
other priests—25 to be in charge of transporting the silver, the gold, the gold bowls, and
the other items that the king, his council,
his officials, and all the people of Israel had
presented for the Temple of God. 26 I weighed
the treasure as I gave it to them and found
the totals to be as follows:

24 tons* of silver,
7,500 pounds* of silver articles,
7,500 pounds of gold,
27 20 gold bowls, equal in value to 1,000
gold coins,*
2 fine articles of polished bronze,
as precious as gold.

28 And I said to these priests, "You and
these treasures have been set apart as holy
to the LORD. This silver and gold is a voluntary offering to the LORD, the God of our
ancestors. 29 Guard these treasures well until
you present them to the leading priests, the
Levites, and the leaders of Israel, who will
weigh them at the storerooms of the LORD's
Temple in Jerusalem." 30 So the priests and
the Levites accepted the task of transporting these treasures of silver and gold to the
Temple of our God in Jerusalem.
31 We broke camp at the Ahava Canal on
April 19* and started off to Jerusalem. And
the gracious hand of our God protected us
and saved us from enemies and bandits
along the way. 32 So we arrived safely in Jerusalem, where we rested for three days.
33 On the fourth day after our arrival,
the silver, gold, and other valuables were
weighed at the Temple of our God and entrusted to Meremoth son of Uriah the priest
and to Eleazar son of Phinehas, along with
Jozabad son of Jeshua and Noadiah son
of Binnui—both of whom were Levites.
34 Everything was accounted for by number
and weight, and the total weight was officially recorded.
35 Then the exiles who had come out of
captivity sacrificed burnt offerings to the
God of Israel. They presented twelve bulls
for all the people of Israel, as well as ninety-
six rams and seventy-seven male lambs.
They also offered twelve male goats as a sin
offering. All this was given as a burnt offering to the LORD. 36 The king's decrees were
delivered to his highest officers and the governors of the province west of the Euphrates
River,* who then cooperated by supporting
the people and the Temple of God.

Ezra's Prayer concerning Intermarriage

9 When these things had been done, the
Jewish leaders came to me and said,
"Many of the people of Israel, and even some
of the priests and Levites, have not kept
themselves separate from the other peoples
living in the land. They have taken up the
detestable practices of the Canaanites,
Hittites, Perizzites, Jebusites, Ammonites,
Moabites, Egyptians, and Amorites. 2 For
the men of Israel have married women from
these people and have taken them as wives

7:21 Aramaic *the province beyond the river;* also in 7:25. **7:22a** Aramaic *100 talents* [3,400 kilograms]. **7:22b** Aramaic *100 cors* [22 kiloliters]. **7:22c** Aramaic *100 baths* [2.1 kiloliters] *of wine, 100 baths of olive oil.* **8:5** As in some Greek manuscripts (see also 1 Esdras 8:32); Hebrew lacks *Zattu.* **8:10** As in some Greek manuscripts (see also 1 Esdras 8:36); Hebrew lacks *Bani.* **8:13** Or *who were the last of his family.* **8:14** As in Greek and Syriac versions and an alternate reading of the Masoretic Text; the other alternate reads *Zabbud.* **8:18** *Israel* is the name that God gave to Jacob. **8:22** Or *charioteers.* **8:26a** Hebrew *650 talents* [22 metric tons]. **8:26b** Hebrew *100 talents* [3,400 kilograms]; also in 8:26c. **8:27** Hebrew *1,000 darics,* about 19 pounds or 8.6 kilograms in weight. **8:31** Hebrew *on the twelfth day of the first month,* of the ancient Hebrew lunar calendar. This day was April 19, 458 B.C.; also see note on 6:15. **8:36** Hebrew *the province beyond the river.*

for their sons. So the holy race has become
polluted by these mixed marriages. Worse
yet, the leaders and officials have led the
way in this outrage."
[3]When I heard this, I tore my cloak and
my shirt, pulled hair from my head and
beard, and sat down utterly shocked. [4]Then
all who trembled at the words of the God of
Israel came and sat with me because of this
outrage committed by the returned exiles.
And I sat there utterly appalled until the
time of the evening sacrifice.
[5]At the time of the sacrifice, I stood up
from where I had sat in mourning with my
clothes torn. I fell to my knees and lifted my
hands to the LORD my God. [6]I prayed,

"O my God, I am utterly ashamed;
I blush to lift up my face to you. For
our sins are piled higher than our
heads, and our guilt has reached to the
heavens. [7]From the days of our ancestors
until now, we have been steeped in sin.
That is why we and our kings and our
priests have been at the mercy of the
pagan kings of the land. We have been
killed, captured, robbed, and disgraced,
just as we are today.
[8]"But now we have been given a brief
moment of grace, for the LORD our God
has allowed a few of us to survive as a
remnant. He has given us security in this
holy place. Our God has brightened our
eyes and granted us some relief from our
slavery. [9]For we were slaves, but in his
unfailing love our God did not abandon
us in our slavery. Instead, he caused
the kings of Persia to treat us favorably.
He revived us so we could rebuild the
Temple of our God and repair its ruins.
He has given us a protective wall in
Judah and Jerusalem.
[10]"And now, O our God, what can we
say after all of this? For once again we
have abandoned your commands! [11]Your
servants the prophets warned us when
they said, 'The land you are entering
to possess is totally defiled by the
detestable practices of the people living
there. From one end to the other, the
land is filled with corruption. [12]Don't let
your daughters marry their sons! Don't
take their daughters as wives for your
sons. Don't ever promote the peace and
prosperity of those nations. If you follow
these instructions, you will be strong
and will enjoy the good things the

Mixed marriages

The shortage of returning Jewish women led some of the Jewish men to choose wives from the local non-Jewish population. No doubt they tried to rationalize their decision: There were simply not enough Jewish women to go around; surely God would not want them to remain single all their lives; they could surely hope to win them over to the one true God. But when the leaders made Ezra aware of what they described as an outrage and a pollution of the holy race (Ezra 9:2), he was "utterly appalled" and showed his deep distress (9:3-4). He had good grounds for reacting in this way. After all, the Scriptures are clear and consistent in teaching that God's people should not marry unbelievers (e.g., Deuteronomy 7:3-4; 2 Corinthians 6:14-18). Every example of this command being disobeyed in Scripture always ended in disaster (e.g., Samson, Solomon, Ahab). However, the Bible says that if both spouses were unbelievers when they married and then one is converted to Christ, the marriage should not be ended (for marriage is a covenant); rather the believing partner should pray that their spouse might be saved (1 Corinthians 7:12-16).

The situation in Ezra's day is often paralleled in the church today, especially when people feel there is no suitable Christian match for them and so look elsewhere for a spouse. While this may be understandable, we need to be clear that it is unfaithfulness and that we cannot claim God's blessing on it.

▸ *See also* ***Can a Christian marry a non-Christian?****, page 1329.*

land produces, and you will leave this
prosperity to your children forever.’
13“Now we are being punished
because of our wickedness and our
great guilt. But we have actually been
punished far less than we deserve, for
you, our God, have allowed some of us
to survive as a remnant. 14But even so,
we are again breaking your commands
and intermarrying with people who
do these detestable things. Won’t your
anger be enough to destroy us, so
that even this little remnant no longer
survives? 15O LORD, God of Israel, you
are just. We come before you in our guilt
as nothing but an escaped remnant,
though in such a condition none of us
can stand in your presence.”

The People Confess Their Sin

10 While Ezra prayed and made this confession, weeping and lying face down
on the ground in front of the Temple of God,
a very large crowd of people from Israel—
men, women, and children—gathered and
wept bitterly with him. 2Then Shecaniah
son of Jehiel, a descendant of Elam, said to
Ezra, “We have been unfaithful to our God,
for we have married these pagan women of
the land. But in spite of this there is hope
for Israel. 3Let us now make a covenant with
our God to divorce our pagan wives and to
send them away with their children. We will
follow the advice given by you and by the
others who respect the commands of our
God. Let it be done according to the Law of
God. 4Get up, for it is your duty to tell us
how to proceed in setting things straight.
We are behind you, so be strong and take
action.”
5So Ezra stood up and demanded that
the leaders of the priests and the Levites
and all the people of Israel swear that they
would do as Shecaniah had said. And they
all swore a solemn oath. 6Then Ezra left the
front of the Temple of God and went to the
room of Jehohanan son of Eliashib. He spent
the night* there without eating or drinking
anything. He was still in mourning because
of the unfaithfulness of the returned exiles.
7Then a proclamation was made throughout Judah and Jerusalem that all the exiles
should come to Jerusalem. 8Those who
failed to come within three days would, if
the leaders and elders so decided, forfeit
all their property and be expelled from the
assembly of the exiles.
9Within three days, all the people of
Judah and Benjamin had gathered in Jerusalem. This took place on December 19,*
and all the people were sitting in the square
before the Temple of God. They were trembling both because of the seriousness of the
matter and because it was raining. 10Then
Ezra the priest stood and said to them: “You
have committed a terrible sin. By marrying
pagan women, you have increased Israel’s
guilt. 11So now confess your sin to the LORD,
the God of your ancestors, and do what he
demands. Separate yourselves from the
people of the land and from these pagan
women.”
12Then the whole assembly raised their
voices and answered, “Yes, you are right;
we must do as you say!” 13Then they added,
“This isn’t something that can be done in a
day or two, for many of us are involved in
this extremely sinful affair. And this is the
rainy season, so we cannot stay out here
much longer. 14Let our leaders act on behalf
of us all. Let everyone who has a pagan wife
come at a scheduled time, accompanied by
the leaders and judges of his city, so that
the fierce anger of our God concerning this
affair may be turned away from us.”
15Only Jonathan son of Asahel and Jah-
zeiah son of Tikvah opposed this course of
action, and they were supported by Meshullam and Shabbethai the Levite.
16So this was the plan they followed. Ezra
selected leaders to represent their families,
designating each of the representatives
by name. On December 29,* the leaders
sat down to investigate the matter. 17By
March 27, the first day of the new year,* they
had finished dealing with all the men who
had married pagan wives.

Those Guilty of Intermarriage

18These are the priests who had married
pagan wives:
From the family of Jeshua son of
Jehozadak* and his brothers: Maaseiah,

10:6 As in parallel text at 1 Esdras 9:2; Hebrew reads *He went.*
10:9 Hebrew *on the twentieth day of the ninth month,* of the ancient Hebrew lunar calendar. This day was December 19, 458 B.C.; also see note on 6:15. **10:16** Hebrew *On the first day of the tenth month,* of the ancient Hebrew lunar calendar. This day was December 29, 458 B.C.; also see note on 6:15. **10:17** Hebrew *By the first day of the first month,* of the ancient Hebrew lunar calendar. This day was March 27, 457 B.C.; also see note on 6:15.
10:18 Hebrew *Jozadak,* a variant spelling of Jehozadak.

Eliezer, Jarib, and Gedaliah. [19]They vowed to divorce their wives, and they each acknowledged their guilt by offering a ram as a guilt offering.

[20]From the family of Immer: Hanani and Zebadiah.

[21]From the family of Harim: Maaseiah, Elijah, Shemaiah, Jehiel, and Uzziah.

[22]From the family of Pashhur: Elioenai, Maaseiah, Ishmael, Nethanel, Jozabad, and Elasah.

[23]These are the Levites who were guilty: Jozabad, Shimei, Kelaiah (also called Kelita), Pethahiah, Judah, and Eliezer.

[24]This is the singer who was guilty: Eliashib.

These are the gatekeepers who were guilty: Shallum, Telem, and Uri.

[25]These are the other people of Israel who were guilty:

From the family of Parosh: Ramiah, Izziah, Malkijah, Mijamin, Eleazar, Hashabiah,* and Benaiah.

[26]From the family of Elam: Mattaniah, Zechariah, Jehiel, Abdi, Jeremoth, and Elijah.

[27]From the family of Zattu: Elioenai, Eliashib, Mattaniah, Jeremoth, Zabad, and Aziza.

[28]From the family of Bebai: Jehohanan, Hananiah, Zabbai, and Athlai.

[29]From the family of Bani: Meshullam, Malluch, Adaiah, Jashub, Sheal, and Jeremoth.

[30]From the family of Pahath-moab: Adna, Kelal, Benaiah, Maaseiah, Mattaniah, Bezalel, Binnui, and Manasseh.

[31]From the family of Harim: Eliezer, Ishijah, Malkijah, Shemaiah, Shimeon,
[32]Benjamin, Malluch, and Shemariah.

[33]From the family of Hashum: Mattenai, Mattattah, Zabad, Eliphelet, Jeremai, Manasseh, and Shimei.

[34]From the family of Bani: Maadai,
Amram, Uel, [35]Benaiah, Bedeiah,
Keluhi, [36]Vaniah, Meremoth, Eliashib,
[37]Mattaniah, Mattenai, and Jaasu.

[38]From the family of Binnui*: Shimei,
[39]Shelemiah, Nathan, Adaiah,
[40]Macnadebai, Shashai, Sharai, [41]Azarel,
Shelemiah, Shemariah, [42]Shallum,
Amariah, and Joseph.

[43]From the family of Nebo: Jeiel, Mattithiah, Zabad, Zebina, Jaddai, Joel, and Benaiah.

[44]Each of these men had a pagan wife, and some even had children by these wives.*

10:25 As in parallel text at 1 Esdras 9:26; Hebrew reads *Malkijah.* **10:37-38** As in Greek version; Hebrew reads *Jaasu, [38]Bani, Binnui.* **10:44** Or *and they sent them away with their children.* The meaning of the Hebrew is uncertain.

Nehemiah *Rebuilding the walls*

Nehemiah was a Jewish servant in Persia who led a small group of exiles back to Jerusalem, where the city walls still lay in ruins many years after the return of the first exiles. Nehemiah set to work rebuilding the walls. Despite much opposition, just fifty-two days later, the project was complete. Nehemiah also enabled Ezra (see the book of Ezra, page 521) to lay again the foundation of God's Law in the nation (chapter 8). Together, these two leaders restored not just buildings, but also the spiritual life of God's people. The reading of the Law became the basis of a renewal of the covenant.

What's it all about?

Nehemiah, a Jewish servant at the Persian royal court, heard that Jerusalem's walls still lay in ruins. He prayed for his people and sought God's direction. When God gave him favor with his master, King Artaxerxes, he asked for permission to return home and was sent to Jerusalem as Judah's new governor. He secretly inspected the wall, made a plan, and got everyone involved in the rebuilding (chapters 1–3).

Local Samaritan officials opposed the work with threats and taunts (chapters 4 and 6); but Nehemiah remained determined, refusing to be sidetracked, and regularly prayed for God's blessing and direction. The people rallied, and the work was completed in just fifty-two days (6:15). Nehemiah organized a guard to protect the wall and registered the people (chapter 7).

Chapters 8 to 13 tell how Nehemiah reformed the life of God's people. He gathered them together to hear Ezra read God's Law, and the people wept when they realized their wrongdoing. The people promised to keep God's commandments and not intermarry with the people of the surrounding nations. They occupied the restored city, and the city wall was dedicated. Arrangements were made for the priests and Levites to be supported. Nehemiah then had to return to Persia, for the king had only given him a temporary leave of absence.

When he next visited Jerusalem, Nehemiah found that one of his main opponents, Tobiah, had been given a room in the Temple precincts, the Levites had been neglected, the Sabbath was being broken by traders, and some Jews had taken foreign wives. He rebuked the people severely and did all he could to purge sin from the land.

OVERVIEW

Nehemiah's anguish on receiving news that Jerusalem's walls were in ruins · *1:1-11*

Nehemiah is commissioned by the king to return to Jerusalem to rebuild its walls · *2:1-20*

Work on the wall begins
3:1–4:23

Nehemiah's social reforms
5:1-19

The rebuilding of the wall is completed despite opposition, and the people are numbered · *6:1–7:73*

Ezra and Nehemiah renew the covenant · *8:1–10:39*

Various reforms
11:1–13:31

What does it mean for us?

The book of Nehemiah shows how much can be accomplished through prayer and hard work. Nehemiah was a gifted leader, but he didn't try to get the job done with his own resources. He constantly prayed to God, asking God to help him, and he drew others in to work alongside him. Nehemiah remained steady, refusing to give in to intimidation and threats. Knowing that God was with him, he put all his energy into the project of rebuilding the walls. Nehemiah was ruthless in expelling pagan influences and in confronting the laxity of God's people. Their history proved that the Jews couldn't afford either. Nehemiah learned from his people's past mistakes and believed the future could be different. His experience shows how faith in God can bring success in spite of great difficulties.

▸ *See also **A timeline of the Bible**, pages A22-A24.*

1 These are the memoirs of Nehemiah son
of Hacaliah.

Nehemiah's Concern for Jerusalem

In late autumn, in the month of Kislev, in the
twentieth year of King Artaxerxes' reign,*
I was at the fortress of Susa. 2 Hanani, one
of my brothers, came to visit me with some
other men who had just arrived from Judah.
I asked them about the Jews who had returned there from captivity and about how
things were going in Jerusalem.

3 They said to me, "Things are not going
well for those who returned to the province of
Judah. They are in great trouble and disgrace.
The wall of Jerusalem has been torn down,
and the gates have been destroyed by fire."

4 When I heard this, I sat down and wept.
In fact, for days I mourned, fasted, and
prayed to the God of heaven. 5 Then I said,

"O LORD, God of heaven, the great and
awesome God who keeps his covenant
of unfailing love with those who love him
and obey his commands, 6 listen to my
prayer! Look down and see me praying
night and day for your people Israel.
I confess that we have sinned against
you. Yes, even my own family and I have
sinned! 7 We have sinned terribly by not
obeying the commands, decrees, and
regulations that you gave us through
your servant Moses.

8 "Please remember what you told your
servant Moses: 'If you are unfaithful
to me, I will scatter you among the
nations. 9 But if you return to me and
obey my commands and live by them,
then even if you are exiled to the ends
of the earth,* I will bring you back to the
place I have chosen for my name to be
honored.'

10 "The people you rescued by your
great power and strong hand are your
servants. 11 O Lord, please hear my prayer!
Listen to the prayers of those of us who
delight in honoring you. Please grant
me success today by making the king
favorable to me.* Put it into his heart
to be kind to me."

In those days I was the king's cup-bearer.

Nehemiah Goes to Jerusalem

2 Early the following spring, in the month
of Nisan,* during the twentieth year of
King Artaxerxes' reign, I was serving the
king his wine. I had never before appeared
sad in his presence. 2 So the king asked me,
"Why are you looking so sad? You don't look
sick to me. You must be deeply troubled."

Then I was terrified, 3 but I replied, "Long
live the king! How can I not be sad? For the
city where my ancestors are buried is in ruins,
and the gates have been destroyed by fire."

4 The king asked, "Well, how can I help
you?"

With a prayer to the God of heaven,
5 I replied, "If it please the king, and if you
are pleased with me, your servant, send me
to Judah to rebuild the city where my ancestors are buried."

6 The king, with the queen sitting beside
him, asked, "How long will you be gone?
When will you return?" After I told him how
long I would be gone, the king agreed to my
request.

7 I also said to the king, "If it please the
king, let me have letters addressed to the governors of the province west of the Euphrates

▸ **1:5-11** *See **Prayer as intercession**, page 922.*

River,* instructing them to let me travel safely through their territories on my way to Judah. 8And please give me a letter addressed to Asaph, the manager of the king's forest, instructing him to give me timber. I will need it to make beams for the gates of the Temple fortress, for the city walls, and for a house for myself." And the king granted these requests, because the gracious hand of God was on me.

9When I came to the governors of the province west of the Euphrates River, I delivered the king's letters to them. The king, I should add, had sent along army officers and horsemen* to protect me. 10But when Sanballat the Horonite and Tobiah the Ammonite official heard of my arrival, they were very displeased that someone had come to help the people of Israel.

Nehemiah Inspects Jerusalem's Wall

11So I arrived in Jerusalem. Three days later, 12I slipped out during the night, taking only a few others with me. I had not told anyone about the plans God had put in my heart for Jerusalem. We took no pack animals with us except the donkey I was riding. 13After dark I went out through the Valley Gate, past the Jackal's Well,* and over to the Dung Gate to inspect the broken walls and burned gates. 14Then I went to the Fountain Gate and to the King's Pool, but my donkey couldn't get through the rubble. 15So, though it was still dark, I went up the Kidron Valley* instead, inspecting the wall before I turned back and entered again at the Valley Gate.

16The city officials did not know I had been out there or what I was doing, for I had not yet said anything to anyone about my plans. I had not yet spoken to the Jewish leaders—the priests, the nobles, the officials, or anyone else in the administration. 17But now I said to them, "You know very well what trouble we are in. Jerusalem lies in ruins, and its gates have been destroyed by fire. Let us rebuild the wall of Jerusalem and end this disgrace!" 18Then I told them about how the gracious hand of God had been on me, and about my conversation with the king.

1:1 Hebrew *In the month of Kislev of the twentieth year.* A number of dates in the book of Nehemiah can be cross-checked with dates in surviving Persian records and related accurately to our modern calendar. This month of the ancient Hebrew lunar calendar occurred within the months of November and December 446 B.C. The *twentieth year* probably refers to the reign of King Artaxerxes I; compare 2:1; 5:14. **1:9** Hebrew *of the heavens.* **1:11** Hebrew *today in the sight of this man.* **2:1** Hebrew *In the month of Nisan.* This month of the ancient Hebrew lunar calendar occurred within the months of April and May 445 B.C. **2:7** Hebrew *the province beyond the river;* also in 2:9. **2:9** Or *charioteers.* **2:13** Or *Serpent's Well.* **2:15** Hebrew *the valley.*

Praying in the moment

Nehemiah was one of the king's most trusted servants; as cup-bearer he ensured that the wine wasn't poisoned. But he was still a servant, and being sad in the king's presence could have been interpreted as a sign of disloyalty, which was a serious offense. Little wonder he was afraid (Nehemiah 2:2).

Nevertheless he told the king the cause of his sadness: His home city, Jerusalem, lay in ruins. Rather than rebuke him, the king asked what he wanted. Nehemiah shot a quick prayer heavenward. "With a prayer to the God of heaven, I replied . . ." (2:4-5). Note that prayer came before action. So often we speak first then pray later. But Nehemiah knew he needed God's favor, so he fired a prayer toward heaven, like an archer firing a speedy arrow, and then spoke.

Of course, this wasn't the sum total of Nehemiah's prayer life. When he first heard about Jerusalem's condition, we read that "for days I mourned, fasted, and prayed . . ." (1:4). He had been laying a foundation of daily prayer for four months, which gave him confidence to step out now with his request. His "arrow prayer" worked because it was rooted in a lifestyle of prayer.

Many of us want to live a life of only arrow prayers, then wonder why those prayers aren't answered. But investing in our relationship with God through regular prayer is crucial. It is not that these other prayers have bought us the right to be heard; it is simply that time with God increases our confidence before him and shapes our desires to increasingly reflect God's own desires.

They replied at once, "Yes, let's rebuild the wall!" So they began the good work.

[19]But when Sanballat, Tobiah, and Geshem the Arab heard of our plan, they scoffed contemptuously. "What are you doing? Are you rebelling against the king?" they asked.

[20]I replied, "The God of heaven will help us succeed. We, his servants, will start rebuilding this wall. But you have no share, legal right, or historic claim in Jerusalem."

Rebuilding the Wall of Jerusalem

3 Then Eliashib the high priest and the other priests started to rebuild at the Sheep Gate. They dedicated it and set up its doors, building the wall as far as the Tower of the Hundred, which they dedicated, and the Tower of Hananel. [2]People from the town of Jericho worked next to them, and beyond them was Zaccur son of Imri.

[3]The Fish Gate was built by the sons of Hassenaah. They laid the beams, set up its doors, and installed its bolts and bars. [4]Meremoth son of Uriah and grandson of Hakkoz repaired the next section of wall. Beside him were Meshullam son of Berekiah and grandson of Meshezabel, and then Zadok son of Baana. [5]Next were the people from Tekoa, though their leaders refused to work with the construction supervisors.

[6]The Old City Gate* was repaired by Joiada son of Paseah and Meshullam son of Besodeiah. They laid the beams, set up its doors, and installed its bolts and bars. [7]Next to them were Melatiah from Gibeon, Jadon from Meronoth, people from Gibeon, and people from Mizpah, the headquarters of the governor of the province west of the Euphrates River.* [8]Next was Uzziel son of Harhaiah, a goldsmith by trade, who also worked on the wall. Beyond him was Hananiah, a manufacturer of perfumes. They left out a section of Jerusalem as they built the Broad Wall.*

[9]Rephaiah son of Hur, the leader of half the district of Jerusalem, was next to them on the wall. [10]Next Jedaiah son of Harumaph repaired the wall across from his own house, and next to him was Hattush son of Hashabneiah. [11]Then came Malkijah son of Harim and Hasshub son of Pahath-moab, who repaired another section of the wall and the Tower of the Ovens. [12]Shallum son of Hallohesh and his daughters repaired the next section. He was the leader of the other half of the district of Jerusalem.

[13]The Valley Gate was repaired by the people from Zanoah, led by Hanun. They set up its doors and installed its bolts and bars. They also repaired the 1,500 feet* of wall to the Dung Gate.

Vision and planning

Some Christians seem to despise vision and planning, as though it were "less spiritual," suggesting that "responding to the Spirit" is all we need. But these are not opposites, requiring us to choose one and reject the other. In fact the Bible opens with the account of creation, for which God had a clear vision and which was planned in an orderly way, while all the time the Holy Spirit was "hovering" over everything (Genesis 1:2).

Nehemiah had a God-given vision of what he wanted to achieve: Jerusalem's restoration, as he made clear to the king (Nehemiah 2:5). This vision was birthed out of four months' praying and fasting—the months of Kislev (1:1) and Nisan (2:1) are four months apart. But while vision comes through prayer, its outworking comes through action. Nehemiah's next step was to establish how that vision could be implemented. So he planned. First he undertook a secret nighttime inspection of the walls (2:11-16), then he shared his plan with his fellow leaders (2:17-20). Then, rather than just letting people get on with it, he assigned different families to different sections of the wall, making them responsible for the section opposite their own homes to ensure the work was done well.

Through this combination of vision birthed through prayer and planning realized through action, the walls were rebuilt in an astonishing fifty-two days (6:15).

14The Dung Gate was repaired by Malkijah son of Recab, the leader of the Beth-hakkerem district. He rebuilt it, set up its doors, and installed its bolts and bars.

15The Fountain Gate was repaired by Shallum* son of Col-hozeh, the leader of the Mizpah district. He rebuilt it, roofed it, set up its doors, and installed its bolts and bars. Then he repaired the wall of the pool of Siloam* near the king's garden, and he rebuilt the wall as far as the stairs that descend from the City of David. 16Next to him was Nehemiah son of Azbuk, the leader of half the district of Beth-zur. He rebuilt the wall from a place across from the tombs of David's family as far as the water reservoir and the House of the Warriors.

17Next to him, repairs were made by a group of Levites working under the supervision of Rehum son of Bani. Then came Hashabiah, the leader of half the district of Keilah, who supervised the building of the wall on behalf of his own district. 18Next down the line were his countrymen led by Binnui* son of Henadad, the leader of the other half of the district of Keilah.

19Next to them, Ezer son of Jeshua, the leader of Mizpah, repaired another section of wall across from the ascent to the armory near the angle in the wall. 20Next to him was Baruch son of Zabbai, who zealously repaired an additional section from the angle to the door of the house of Eliashib the high priest. 21Meremoth son of Uriah and grandson of Hakkoz rebuilt another section of the wall extending from the door of Eliashib's house to the end of the house.

22The next repairs were made by the priests from the surrounding region. 23After them, Benjamin and Hasshub repaired the section across from their house, and Azariah son of Maaseiah and grandson of Ananiah repaired the section across from his house. 24Next was Binnui son of Henadad, who rebuilt another section of the wall from Azariah's house to the angle and the corner. 25Palal son of Uzai carried on the work from a point opposite the angle and the tower that projects up from the king's upper house beside the court of the guard. Next to him were Pedaiah son of Parosh, 26with the Temple servants living on the hill of Ophel, who repaired the wall as far as a point across from the Water Gate to the east and the projecting tower. 27Then came the people of Tekoa, who repaired another section across from the great projecting tower and over to the wall of Ophel.

28Above the Horse Gate, the priests repaired the wall. Each one repaired the section immediately across from his own house. 29Next Zadok son of Immer also rebuilt the wall across from his own house, and beyond him was Shemaiah son of Shecaniah, the gatekeeper of the East Gate. 30Next Hananiah son of Shelemiah and Hanun, the sixth son of Zalaph, repaired another section, while Meshullam son of Berekiah rebuilt the wall across from where he lived. 31Malkijah, one of the goldsmiths, repaired the wall as far as the housing for the Temple servants and merchants, across from the Inspection Gate. Then he continued as far as the upper room at the corner. 32The other goldsmiths and merchants repaired the wall from that corner to the Sheep Gate.

Enemies Oppose the Rebuilding

4 1*Sanballat was very angry when he learned that we were rebuilding the wall. He flew into a rage and mocked the Jews, 2saying in front of his friends and the Samarian army officers, "What does this bunch of poor, feeble Jews think they're doing? Do they think they can build the wall in a single day by just offering a few sacrifices?* Do they actually think they can make something of stones from a rubbish heap—and charred ones at that?"

3Tobiah the Ammonite, who was standing beside him, remarked, "That stone wall would collapse if even a fox walked along the top of it!"

4Then I prayed, "Hear us, our God, for we are being mocked. May their scoffing fall back on their own heads, and may they themselves become captives in a foreign land! 5Do not ignore their guilt. Do not blot out their sins, for they have provoked you to anger here in front of* the builders."

6At last the wall was completed to half its

3:6 Or *The Mishneh Gate*, or *The Jeshanah Gate*. **3:7** Hebrew *the province beyond the river*. **3:8** Or *They fortified Jerusalem up to the Broad Wall*. **3:13** Hebrew *1,000 cubits* [460 meters]. **3:15a** As in Syriac version; Hebrew reads *Shallun*. **3:15b** Hebrew *pool of Shelah*, another name for the pool of Siloam. **3:18** As in a few Hebrew manuscripts, some Greek manuscripts, and Syriac version (see also 3:24; 10:9); most Hebrew manuscripts read *Bavvai*. **4:1** Verses 4:1-6 are numbered 3:33-38 in Hebrew text. **4:2** The meaning of the Hebrew is uncertain. **4:5** Or *for they have thrown insults in the face of*.

height around the entire city, for the people
had worked with enthusiasm.
7*But when Sanballat and Tobiah and
the Arabs, Ammonites, and Ashdodites
heard that the work was going ahead and
that the gaps in the wall of Jerusalem were
being repaired, they were furious. 8They all
made plans to come and fight against Jerusalem and throw us into confusion. 9But we
prayed to our God and guarded the city day
and night to protect ourselves.
10Then the people of Judah began to
complain, "The workers are getting tired,
and there is so much rubble to be moved.
We will never be able to build the wall by
ourselves."
11Meanwhile, our enemies were saying,
"Before they know what's happening, we
will swoop down on them and kill them and
end their work."
12The Jews who lived near the enemy
came and told us again and again, "They
will come from all directions and attack
us!"* 13So I placed armed guards behind
the lowest parts of the wall in the exposed
areas. I stationed the people to stand guard
by families, armed with swords, spears, and
bows.
14Then as I looked over the situation,
I called together the nobles and the rest
of the people and said to them, "Don't be
afraid of the enemy! Remember the Lord,
who is great and glorious, and fight for your
brothers, your sons, your daughters, your
wives, and your homes!"
15When our enemies heard that we knew
of their plans and that God had frustrated
them, we all returned to our work on the
wall. 16But from then on, only half my men
worked while the other half stood guard with
spears, shields, bows, and coats of mail. The
leaders stationed themselves behind the
people of Judah 17who were building the wall.
The laborers carried on their work with one
hand supporting their load and one hand
holding a weapon. 18All the builders had a
sword belted to their side. The trumpeter
stayed with me to sound the alarm.
19Then I explained to the nobles and officials and all the people, "The work is very
spread out, and we are widely separated
from each other along the wall. 20When you
hear the blast of the trumpet, rush to wherever it is sounding. Then our God will fight
for us!"
21We worked early and late, from sunrise
to sunset. And half the men were always on
guard. 22I also told everyone living outside
the walls to stay in Jerusalem. That way
they and their servants could help with
guard duty at night and work during the
day. 23During this time, none of us—not
I, nor my relatives, nor my servants, nor
the guards who were with me—ever took
off our clothes. We carried our weapons
with us at all times, even when we went
for water.*

Nehemiah Defends the Oppressed

5 About this time some of the men and
their wives raised a cry of protest against
their fellow Jews. 2They were saying, "We
have such large families. We need more
food to survive."
3Others said, "We have mortgaged our
fields, vineyards, and homes to get food
during the famine."
4And others said, "We have had to borrow
money on our fields and vineyards to pay
our taxes. 5We belong to the same family
as those who are wealthy, and our children
are just like theirs. Yet we must sell our children into slavery just to get enough money
to live. We have already sold some of our
daughters, and we are helpless to do anything about it, for our fields and vineyards
are already mortgaged to others."
6When I heard their complaints, I was
very angry. 7After thinking it over, I spoke
out against these nobles and officials. I told
them, "You are hurting your own relatives
by charging interest when they borrow
money!" Then I called a public meeting to
deal with the problem.
8At the meeting I said to them, "We are
doing all we can to redeem our Jewish relatives who have had to sell themselves to
pagan foreigners, but you are selling them
back into slavery again. How often must we
redeem them?" And they had nothing to say
in their defense.
9Then I pressed further, "What you are
doing is not right! Should you not walk in
the fear of our God in order to avoid being
mocked by enemy nations? 10I myself, as
well as my brothers and my workers, have
been lending the people money and grain,
but now let us stop this business of charging interest. 11You must restore their fields,
vineyards, olive groves, and homes to them

this very day. And repay the interest you charged when you lent them money, grain, new wine, and olive oil."

12They replied, "We will give back everything and demand nothing more from the people. We will do as you say." Then I called the priests and made the nobles and officials swear to do what they had promised.

13I shook out the folds of my robe and said, "If you fail to keep your promise, may God shake you like this from your homes and from your property!"

The whole assembly responded, "Amen," and they praised the LORD. And the people did as they had promised.

14For the entire twelve years that I was governor of Judah—from the twentieth year to the thirty-second year of the reign of King Artaxerxes*—neither I nor my officials drew on our official food allowance. 15The former governors, in contrast, had laid heavy burdens on the people, demanding a daily ration of food and wine, besides forty pieces* of silver. Even their assistants took advantage of the people. But because I feared God, I did not act that way.

16I also devoted myself to working on the wall and refused to acquire any land. And I required all my servants to spend time working on the wall. 17I asked for nothing, even though I regularly fed 150 Jewish officials at my table, besides all the visitors from other lands! 18The provisions I paid for each day included one ox, six choice sheep or goats, and a large number of poultry. And every ten days we needed a large supply of all kinds of wine. Yet I refused to claim the governor's food allowance because the people already carried a heavy burden.

19Remember, O my God, all that I have
done for these people, and bless me for it.

Continued Opposition to Rebuilding

6 Sanballat, Tobiah, Geshem the Arab, and the rest of our enemies found out that I had finished rebuilding the wall and that no gaps remained—though we had not yet set up the doors in the gates. 2So Sanballat and Geshem sent a message asking me to meet them at one of the villages* in the plain of Ono.

But I realized they were plotting to harm me, 3so I replied by sending this message to them: "I am engaged in a great work, so I can't come. Why should I stop working to come and meet with you?"

4Four times they sent the same message, and each time I gave the same reply. 5The fifth time, Sanballat's servant came with an open letter in his hand, 6and this is what it said:

"There is a rumor among the surrounding
nations, and Geshem* tells me it is true,
that you and the Jews are planning to
rebel and that is why you are building the
wall. According to his reports, you plan
to be their king. 7He also reports that you
have appointed prophets in Jerusalem
to proclaim about you, 'Look! There is
a king in Judah!'

4:7 Verses 4:7-23 are numbered 4:1-17 in Hebrew text. **4:12** The meaning of the Hebrew is uncertain. **4:23** Or *Each carried his weapon in his right hand.* Hebrew reads *Each his weapon the water.* The meaning of the Hebrew is uncertain. **5:14** That is, 445-433 B.C. **5:15** Hebrew *40 shekels* [1 pound or 456 grams]. **6:2** As in Greek version; Hebrew reads *at Kephirim.* **6:6** Hebrew *Gashmu,* a variant spelling of Geshem.

Interest on loans

In times of economic hardship it is common for the rich to get richer and the poor to get poorer. To help prevent that, God established certain commands in the Law to protect the poor—things like the canceling of all debts in the Year of Jubilee and leaving crops at the edge of fields when harvesting for the poor to take. Another restraint was the forbidding of interest on loans to fellow Israelites (Exodus 22:25-27; Leviticus 25:36; Deuteronomy 23:19-20)—a prohibition that was clearly being ignored here and that Nehemiah demanded be upheld (Nehemiah 5:1-13). God wants his people to be kind and generous, especially to those who are less fortunate than themselves.

▶ *See also* ***The Year of Jubilee****, page 147;* ***Provision for the poor****, page 226.*

"You can be very sure that this report
will get back to the king, so I suggest
that you come and talk it over with me."

8I replied, "There is no truth in any part
of your story. You are making up the whole
thing."

9They were just trying to intimidate us,
imagining that they could discourage us
and stop the work. So I continued the work
with even greater determination.*

10Later I went to visit Shemaiah son of
Delaiah and grandson of Mehetabel, who
was confined to his home. He said, "Let
us meet together inside the Temple of God
and bolt the doors shut. Your enemies are
coming to kill you tonight."

11But I replied, "Should someone in my
position run from danger? Should someone
in my position enter the Temple to save his
life? No, I won't do it!" 12I realized that God
had not spoken to him, but that he had
uttered this prophecy against me because
Tobiah and Sanballat had hired him. 13They
were hoping to intimidate me and make me
sin. Then they would be able to accuse and
discredit me.

14Remember, O my God, all the evil
things that Tobiah and Sanballat have
done. And remember Noadiah the
prophet and all the prophets like her
who have tried to intimidate me.

The Builders Complete the Wall

15So on October 2* the wall was finished—
just fifty-two days after we had begun.
16When our enemies and the surrounding
nations heard about it, they were frightened
and humiliated. They realized this work
had been done with the help of our God.

17During those fifty-two days, many letters
went back and forth between Tobiah and
the nobles of Judah. 18For many in Judah
had sworn allegiance to him because his
father-in-law was Shecaniah son of Arah,
and his son Jehohanan was married to the
daughter of Meshullam son of Berekiah.
19They kept telling me about Tobiah's good
deeds, and then they told him everything I
said. And Tobiah kept sending threatening
letters to intimidate me.

7 After the wall was finished and I had set
up the doors in the gates, the gatekeepers,
singers, and Levites were appointed. 2I gave
the responsibility of governing Jerusalem to
my brother Hanani, along with Hananiah,
the commander of the fortress, for he was
a faithful man who feared God more than
most. 3I said to them, "Do not leave the gates
open during the hottest part of the day.*
And even while the gatekeepers are on duty,
have them shut and bar the doors. Appoint
the residents of Jerusalem to act as guards,
everyone on a regular watch. Some will serve
at sentry posts and some in front of their own
homes."

Nehemiah Registers the People

4At that time the city was large and spacious, but the population was small, and
none of the houses had been rebuilt. 5So my
God gave me the idea to call together all the
nobles and leaders of the city, along with
the ordinary citizens, for registration. I had
found the genealogical record of those who
had first returned to Judah. This is what was
written there:

6Here is the list of the Jewish exiles
of the provinces who returned from
their captivity. King Nebuchadnezzar
had deported them to Babylon, but
now they returned to Jerusalem and
the other towns in Judah where they
originally lived. 7Their leaders were
Zerubbabel, Jeshua, Nehemiah,
Seraiah,* Reelaiah,* Nahamani,
Mordecai, Bilshan, Mispar,* Bigvai,
Rehum,* and Baanah.

This is the number of the men of Israel
who returned from exile:

8 The family of Parosh 2,172
9 The family of Shephatiah 372
10 The family of Arah. 652
11 The family of Pahath-moab
(descendants of Jeshua
and Joab) 2,818
12 The family of Elam 1,254
13 The family of Zattu 845
14 The family of Zaccai 760
15 The family of Bani* 648
16 The family of Bebai 628
17 The family of Azgad 2,322
18 The family of Adonikam 667
19 The family of Bigvai 2,067
20 The family of Adin. 655
21 The family of Ater (descendants
of Hezekiah). 98
22 The family of Hashum 328

23 The family of Bezai 324
24 The family of Jorah* 112
25 The family of Gibbar* 95
26 The people of Bethlehem and
Netophah 188
27 The people of Anathoth 128
28 The people of Beth-azmaveth 42
29 The people of Kiriath-jearim,
Kephirah, and Beeroth 743
30 The people of Ramah and Geba. . . 621
31 The people of Micmash. 122
32 The people of Bethel and Ai. 123
33 The people of West Nebo* 52
34 The citizens of West Elam*. 1,254
35 The citizens of Harim 320
36 The citizens of Jericho. 345
37 The citizens of Lod, Hadid,
and Ono 721
38 The citizens of Senaah 3,930

39 These are the priests who returned
from exile:
The family of Jedaiah (through
the line of Jeshua) 973
40 The family of Immer 1,052
41 The family of Pashhur. 1,247
42 The family of Harim 1,017

43 These are the Levites who returned
from exile:
The families of Jeshua and Kadmiel
(descendants of Hodaviah*) 74
44 The singers of the family of Asaph. .148
45 The gatekeepers of the families
of Shallum, Ater, Talmon,
Akkub, Hatita, and Shobai. 138

46 The descendants of the following
Temple servants returned from exile:
Ziha, Hasupha, Tabbaoth,
47 Keros, Siaha,* Padon,
48 Lebanah, Hagabah, Shalmai,
49 Hanan, Giddel, Gahar,
50 Reaiah, Rezin, Nekoda,
51 Gazzam, Uzza, Paseah,
52 Besai, Meunim, Nephusim,*
53 Bakbuk, Hakupha, Harhur,
54 Bazluth,* Mehida, Harsha,
55 Barkos, Sisera, Temah,
56 Neziah, and Hatipha.

57 The descendants of these servants of
King Solomon returned from exile:
Sotai, Hassophereth, Peruda,*
58 Jaalah,* Darkon, Giddel,
59 Shephatiah, Hattil,
Pokereth-hazzebaim, and Ami.*

60 In all, the Temple servants and the
descendants of Solomon's servants
numbered 392.

61 Another group returned at this time
from the towns of Tel-melah, Tel-harsha,
Kerub, Addan,* and Immer. However,
they could not prove that they or their
families were descendants of Israel.
62 This group included the families of
Delaiah, Tobiah, and Nekoda—a total of
642 people.

63 Three families of priests—Hobaiah,
Hakkoz, and Barzillai—also returned.
(This Barzillai had married a woman
who was a descendant of Barzillai of
Gilead, and he had taken her family
name.) 64 They searched for their
names in the genealogical records,
but they were not found, so they were
disqualified from serving as priests.
65 The governor told them not to eat the
priests' share of food from the sacrifices
until a priest could consult the LORD
about the matter by using the Urim and
Thummim—the sacred lots.

66 So a total of 42,360 people returned to
Judah, 67 in addition to 7,337 servants and
245 singers, both men and women. 68 They
took with them 736 horses, 245 mules,*
69 435 camels, and 6,720 donkeys.

70 Some of the family leaders gave
gifts for the work. The governor gave to
the treasury 1,000 gold coins,* 50 gold
basins, and 530 robes for the priests.
71 The other leaders gave to the treasury
a total of 20,000 gold coins* and some
2,750 pounds* of silver for the work.

6:9 As in Greek version; Hebrew reads *But now to strengthen my hands.* **6:15** Hebrew *on the twenty-fifth day of the month Elul,* of the ancient Hebrew lunar calendar. This day was October 2, 445 B.C.; also see note on 1:1. **7:3** Or *Keep the gates of Jerusalem closed until the sun is hot.* **7:7a** As in parallel text at Ezra 2:2; Hebrew reads *Azariah.* **7:7b** As in parallel text at Ezra 2:2; Hebrew reads *Raamiah.* **7:7c** As in parallel text at Ezra 2:2; Hebrew reads *Mispereth.* **7:7d** As in parallel text at Ezra 2:2; Hebrew reads *Nehum.* **7:15** As in parallel text at Ezra 2:10; Hebrew reads *Binnui.* **7:24** As in parallel text at Ezra 2:18; Hebrew reads *Hariph.* **7:25** As in parallel text at Ezra 2:20; Hebrew reads *Gibeon.* **7:33** Or *of the other Nebo.* **7:34** Or *of the other Elam.* **7:43** As in parallel text at Ezra 2:40; Hebrew reads *Hodevah.* **7:47** As in parallel text at Ezra 2:44; Hebrew reads *Sia.* **7:52** As in parallel text at Ezra 2:50; Hebrew reads *Nephushesim.* **7:54** As in parallel text at Ezra 2:52; Hebrew reads *Bazlith.* **7:57** As in parallel text at Ezra 2:55; Hebrew reads *Sotai, Sophereth, Perida.* **7:58** As in parallel text at Ezra 2:56; Hebrew reads *Jaala.* **7:59** As in parallel text at Ezra 2:57; Hebrew reads *Amon.* **7:61** As in parallel text at Ezra 2:59; Hebrew reads *Addon.* **7:68** As in some Hebrew manuscripts (see also Ezra 2:66); most Hebrew manuscripts lack this verse. Verses 7:69-73 are numbered 7:68-72 in Hebrew text. **7:70** Hebrew *1,000 darics of gold,* about 19 pounds or 8.6 kilograms in weight. **7:71a** Hebrew *20,000 darics of gold,* about 375 pounds or 170 kilograms in weight; also in 7:72. **7:71b** Hebrew *2,200 minas* [1,300 kilograms].

[72]The rest of the people gave 20,000 gold coins, about 2,500 pounds* of silver, and 67 robes for the priests.

[73]So the priests, the Levites, the gatekeepers, the singers, the Temple servants, and some of the common people settled near Jerusalem. The rest of the people returned to their own towns throughout Israel.

Ezra Reads the Law

8 In October,* when the Israelites had settled in their towns, [8:1]all the people assembled with a unified purpose at the square just inside the Water Gate. They asked Ezra the scribe to bring out the Book of the Law of Moses, which the LORD had given for Israel to obey.

[2]So on October 8* Ezra the priest brought the Book of the Law before the assembly, which included the men and women and all the children old enough to understand. [3]He faced the square just inside the Water Gate from early morning until noon and read aloud to everyone who could understand. All the people listened closely to the Book of the Law.

[4]Ezra the scribe stood on a high wooden platform that had been made for the occasion. To his right stood Mattithiah, Shema, Anaiah, Uriah, Hilkiah, and Maaseiah. To his left stood Pedaiah, Mishael, Malkijah, Hashum, Hashbaddanah, Zechariah, and Meshullam. [5]Ezra stood on the platform in full view of all the people. When they saw him open the book, they all rose to their feet.

[6]Then Ezra praised the LORD, the great God, and all the people chanted, "Amen! Amen!" as they lifted their hands. Then they bowed down and worshiped the LORD with their faces to the ground.

[7]The Levites—Jeshua, Bani, Sherebiah, Jamin, Akkub, Shabbethai, Hodiah, Maaseiah, Kelita, Azariah, Jozabad, Hanan, and Pelaiah—then instructed the people in the Law while everyone remained in their places. [8]They read from the Book of the Law of God and clearly explained the meaning of what was being read, helping the people understand each passage.

[9]Then Nehemiah the governor, Ezra the priest and scribe, and the Levites who were interpreting for the people said to them, "Don't mourn or weep on such a day as this! For today is a sacred day before the LORD your God." For the people had all been weeping as they listened to the words of the Law.

The Scriptures in public worship

Ezra had returned to Judah thirteen years earlier than Nehemiah and had already sought to implement reforms. But now, backed by Nehemiah the governor, Ezra was able to make further progress in teaching God's people. On the first day of the New Year, Ezra gathered them in a large square and, standing on a high platform, read to them from "the Book of the Law of Moses" (Nehemiah 8:1). And it wasn't a short reading! In fact, he read aloud "from early morning until noon" and "all the people listened closely" (8:3). To ensure they understood what they were hearing, he scattered Levites among them to explain what the Scriptures were saying (8:7-8). Ezra probably read a section of Scripture and then paused while the Levites did their work. For Ezra, ensuring that everyone had not only heard the word but had also understood it was crucial, for he was about to call them to make a covenant to keep it (chapter 10).

Scripture reading should still play a central role in Christian meetings today. Churches with a liturgical tradition follow a set reading for each Sunday; other churches allow preachers more freedom to choose their own Bible passage for their theme. But whatever our tradition, this story shows that the reading of Scripture—and the reading of lengthy sections of Scripture, together with ensuring people have understood—should be a key part of our corporate life.

▶ *See also* ***Bible teaching****, page 529;* ***Teaching God's word****, page 1268;* ***Studying God's word****, page 1387.*

10 And Nehemiah* continued, "Go and
celebrate with a feast of rich foods and
sweet drinks, and share gifts of food with
people who have nothing prepared. This
is a sacred day before our Lord. Don't be
dejected and sad, for the joy of the LORD is
your strength!"

11 And the Levites, too, quieted the people,
telling them, "Hush! Don't weep! For this is
a sacred day." 12 So the people went away
to eat and drink at a festive meal, to share
gifts of food, and to celebrate with great joy
because they had heard God's words and
understood them.

The Festival of Shelters

13 On October 9* the family leaders of all
the people, together with the priests and
Levites, met with Ezra the scribe to go over
the Law in greater detail. 14 As they studied
the Law, they discovered that the LORD had
commanded through Moses that the Israelites should live in shelters during the
festival to be held that month.* 15 He had
said that a proclamation should be made
throughout their towns and in Jerusalem,
telling the people to go to the hills to get
branches from olive, wild olive,* myrtle,
palm, and other leafy trees. They were
to use these branches to make shelters in
which they would live during the festival,
as prescribed in the Law.

16 So the people went out and cut branches
and used them to build shelters on the
roofs of their houses, in their courtyards,
in the courtyards of God's Temple, or in the
squares just inside the Water Gate and the
Ephraim Gate. 17 So everyone who had returned from captivity lived in these shelters
during the festival, and they were all filled
with great joy! The Israelites had not celebrated like this since the days of Joshua*
son of Nun.

18 Ezra read from the Book of the Law of
God on each of the seven days of the festival. Then on the eighth day they held a
solemn assembly, as was required by law.

The People Confess Their Sins

9 On October 31* the people assembled
again, and this time they fasted and
dressed in burlap and sprinkled dust on
their heads. 2 Those of Israelite descent
separated themselves from all foreigners as
they confessed their own sins and the sins
of their ancestors. 3 They remained standing in place for three hours* while the Book
of the Law of the LORD their God was read
aloud to them. Then for three more hours
they confessed their sins and worshiped the
LORD their God. 4 The Levites—Jeshua, Bani,
Kadmiel, Shebaniah, Bunni, Sherebiah,
Bani, and Kenani—stood on the stairway of
the Levites and cried out to the LORD their
God with loud voices.

5 Then the leaders of the Levites—Jeshua,
Kadmiel, Bani, Hashabneiah, Sherebiah,
Hodiah, Shebaniah, and Pethahiah—called
out to the people: "Stand up and praise the
LORD your God, for he lives from everlasting
to everlasting!" Then they prayed:

"May your glorious name be praised!
May it be exalted above all blessing and
praise!

6 "You alone are the LORD. You made
the skies and the heavens and all the
stars. You made the earth and the seas
and everything in them. You preserve
them all, and the angels of heaven
worship you.

7 "You are the LORD God, who chose
Abram and brought him from Ur of the
Chaldeans and renamed him Abraham.
8 When he had proved himself faithful,
you made a covenant with him to give
him and his descendants the land of
the Canaanites, Hittites, Amorites,
Perizzites, Jebusites, and Girgashites.
And you have done what you promised,
for you are always true to your word.

9 "You saw the misery of our ancestors
in Egypt, and you heard their cries from
beside the Red Sea.* 10 You displayed

7:72 Hebrew *2,000 minas* [1,200 kilograms]. **7:73** Hebrew *In the seventh month.* This month of the ancient Hebrew lunar calendar occurred within the months of October and November 445 B.C. **8:2** Hebrew *on the first day of the seventh month,* of the ancient Hebrew lunar calendar. This day was October 8, 445 B.C.; also see note on 1:1. **8:10** Hebrew *he.* **8:13** Hebrew *On the second day,* of the seventh month of the ancient Hebrew lunar calendar. This day was October 9, 445 B.C.; also see notes on 1:1 and 8:2. **8:14** Hebrew *in the seventh month.* This month of the ancient Hebrew lunar calendar usually occurs within the months of September and October. See Lev 23:39-43. **8:15** Or *pine;* Hebrew reads *oil tree.* **8:17** Hebrew *Jeshua,* a variant spelling of Joshua. **9:1** Hebrew *On the twenty-fourth day of that same month,* the seventh month of the ancient Hebrew lunar calendar. This day was October 31, 445 B.C.; also see notes on 1:1 and 8:2. **9:3** Hebrew *for a quarter of a day.* **9:9** Hebrew *sea of reeds.*

▸ **8:10** *See **Joy**, page 1360.*

miraculous signs and wonders against Pharaoh, his officials, and all his people, for you knew how arrogantly they were treating our ancestors. You have a glorious reputation that has never been forgotten. 11You divided the sea for your people so they could walk through on dry land! And then you hurled their enemies into the depths of the sea. They sank like stones beneath the mighty waters. 12You led our ancestors by a pillar of cloud during the day and a pillar of fire at night so that they could find their way.

13"You came down at Mount Sinai and spoke to them from heaven. You gave them regulations and instructions that were just, and decrees and commands that were good. 14You instructed them concerning your holy Sabbath. And you commanded them, through Moses your servant, to obey all your commands, decrees, and instructions.

15"You gave them bread from heaven when they were hungry and water from the rock when they were thirsty. You commanded them to go and take possession of the land you had sworn to give them.

16"But our ancestors were proud and stubborn, and they paid no attention to your commands. 17They refused to obey and did not remember the miracles you had done for them. Instead, they became stubborn and appointed a leader to take them back to their slavery in Egypt.* But you are a God of forgiveness, gracious and merciful, slow to become angry, and rich in unfailing love. You did not abandon them, 18even when they made an idol shaped like a calf and said, 'This is your god who brought you out of Egypt!' They committed terrible blasphemies.

19"But in your great mercy you did not abandon them to die in the wilderness. The pillar of cloud still led them forward by day, and the pillar of fire showed them the way through the night. 20You sent your good Spirit to instruct them, and you did not stop giving them manna from heaven or water for their thirst. 21For forty years you sustained them in the wilderness, and they lacked nothing. Their clothes did not wear out, and their feet did not swell!

22"Then you helped our ancestors conquer kingdoms and nations, and you placed your people in every corner of the land.* They took over the land of King Sihon of Heshbon and the land of King Og of Bashan. 23You made their descendants as numerous as the stars in the sky and brought them into the land you had promised to their ancestors.

24"They went in and took possession of the land. You subdued whole nations before them. Even the Canaanites, who inhabited the land, were powerless! Your people could deal with these nations and their kings as they pleased. 25Our ancestors captured fortified cities and fertile land. They took over houses full of good things, with cisterns already dug and vineyards and olive groves and fruit trees in abundance. So they ate until they were full and grew fat and enjoyed themselves in all your blessings.

26"But despite all this, they were disobedient and rebelled against you. They turned their backs on your Law, they killed your prophets who warned them to return to you, and they committed terrible blasphemies. 27So you handed them over to their enemies, who made them suffer. But in their time of trouble they cried to you, and you heard them from heaven. In your great mercy, you sent them liberators who rescued them from their enemies.

28"But as soon as they were at peace, your people again committed evil in your sight, and once more you let their enemies conquer them. Yet whenever your people turned and cried to you again for help, you listened once more from heaven. In your wonderful mercy, you rescued them many times!

29"You warned them to return to your Law, but they became proud and obstinate and disobeyed your commands. They did not follow your regulations, by which people will find life if only they obey. They stubbornly turned their backs on you and refused to listen. 30In your love, you were patient with them for many years. You sent your Spirit, who warned them through the prophets. But still they wouldn't listen! So once again

you allowed the peoples of the land to
conquer them. 31But in your great mercy,
you did not destroy them completely or
abandon them forever. What a gracious
and merciful God you are!

32"And now, our God, the great and
mighty and awesome God, who keeps
his covenant of unfailing love, do not
let all the hardships we have suffered
seem insignificant to you. Great trouble
has come upon us and upon our kings
and leaders and priests and prophets
and ancestors—all of your people—from
the days when the kings of Assyria first
triumphed over us until now. 33Every time
you punished us you were being just.
We have sinned greatly, and you gave
us only what we deserved. 34Our kings,
leaders, priests, and ancestors did not
obey your Law or listen to the warnings
in your commands and laws. 35Even
while they had their own kingdom, they
did not serve you, though you showered
your goodness on them. You gave them
a large, fertile land, but they refused to
turn from their wickedness.

36"So now today we are slaves in
the land of plenty that you gave our
ancestors for their enjoyment! We are
slaves here in this good land. 37The lush
produce of this land piles up in the
hands of the kings whom you have set
over us because of our sins. They have
power over us and our livestock. We
serve them at their pleasure, and we are
in great misery."

The People Agree to Obey

38*The people responded, "In view of all this,* we are making a solemn promise and putting it in writing. On this sealed document are the names of our leaders and Levites and priests."

10 1*The document was ratified and sealed with the following names:

The governor:
Nehemiah son of Hacaliah, and also
Zedekiah.

2The following priests:
Seraiah, Azariah, Jeremiah, 3Pashhur,
Amariah, Malkijah, 4Hattush, Shebaniah,
Malluch, 5Harim, Meremoth, Obadiah,
6Daniel, Ginnethon, Baruch, 7Meshullam,
Abijah, Mijamin, 8Maaziah, Bilgai, and
Shemaiah. These were the priests.

9The following Levites:
Jeshua son of Azaniah, Binnui from
the family of Henadad, Kadmiel,
10and their fellow Levites: Shebaniah,
Hodiah, Kelita, Pelaiah, Hanan, 11Mica,
Rehob, Hashabiah, 12Zaccur, Sherebiah,
Shebaniah, 13Hodiah, Bani, and Beninu.

14The following leaders:
Parosh, Pahath-moab, Elam, Zattu,
Bani, 15Bunni, Azgad, Bebai, 16Adonijah,
Bigvai, Adin, 17Ater, Hezekiah, Azzur,
18Hodiah, Hashum, Bezai, 19Hariph,
Anathoth, Nebai, 20Magpiash,
Meshullam, Hezir, 21Meshezabel,
Zadok, Jaddua, 22Pelatiah, Hanan,
Anaiah, 23Hoshea, Hananiah, Hasshub,
24Hallohesh, Pilha, Shobek, 25Rehum,
Hashabnah, Maaseiah, 26Ahiah, Hanan,
Anan, 27Malluch, Harim, and Baanah.

The Vow of the People

28Then the rest of the people—the priests, Levites, gatekeepers, singers, Temple servants, and all who had separated themselves from the pagan people of the land in order to obey the Law of God, together with their wives, sons, daughters, and all who were
old enough to understand—29joined their
leaders and bound themselves with an oath. They swore a curse on themselves if they failed to obey the Law of God as issued by his servant Moses. They solemnly promised to carefully follow all the commands, regulations, and decrees of the LORD our Lord:

30"We promise not to let our daughters
marry the pagan people of the land,
and not to let our sons marry their
daughters.

31"We also promise that if the
people of the land should bring any
merchandise or grain to be sold on the
Sabbath or on any other holy day, we
will refuse to buy it. Every seventh year
we will let our land rest, and we will
cancel all debts owed to us.

32"In addition, we promise to obey
the command to pay the annual Temple
tax of one-eighth of an ounce of silver*

9:17 As in Greek version; Hebrew reads *in their rebellion.*
9:22 The meaning of the Hebrew is uncertain. **9:38a** Verse 9:38 is numbered 10:1 in Hebrew text. **9:38b** Or *In spite of all this.* **10:1** Verses 10:1-39 are numbered 10:2-40 in Hebrew text.
10:32 Hebrew *tax of 1/3 of a shekel* [4 grams].

for the care of the Temple of our God.
[33]This will provide for the Bread of the
Presence; for the regular grain offerings
and burnt offerings; for the offerings
on the Sabbaths, the new moon
celebrations, and the annual festivals;
for the holy offerings; and for the sin
offerings to make atonement for Israel. It
will provide for everything necessary for
the work of the Temple of our God.

[34]"We have cast sacred lots to
determine when—at regular times each
year—the families of the priests, Levites,
and the common people should bring
wood to God's Temple to be burned
on the altar of the LORD our God, as is
written in the Law.

[35]"We promise to bring the first part
of every harvest to the LORD's Temple
year after year—whether it be a crop
from the soil or from our fruit trees. [36]We
agree to give God our oldest sons and the
firstborn of all our herds and flocks, as
prescribed in the Law. We will present
them to the priests who minister in the
Temple of our God. [37]We will store the
produce in the storerooms of the Temple
of our God. We will bring the best of our
flour and other grain offerings, the best
of our fruit, and the best of our new wine
and olive oil. And we promise to bring to
the Levites a tenth of everything our land
produces, for it is the Levites who collect
the tithes in all our rural towns.

[38]"A priest—a descendant of Aaron—
will be with the Levites as they receive
these tithes. And a tenth of all that is
collected as tithes will be delivered by
the Levites to the Temple of our God
and placed in the storerooms. [39]The
people and the Levites must bring
these offerings of grain, new wine, and
olive oil to the storerooms and place
them in the sacred containers near the
ministering priests, the gatekeepers, and
the singers.

"We promise together not to neglect
the Temple of our God."

The People Occupy Jerusalem

11 The leaders of the people were living
in Jerusalem, the holy city. A tenth of
the people from the other towns of Judah
and Benjamin were chosen by sacred lots to
live there, too, while the rest stayed where
they were. [2]And the people commended
everyone who volunteered to resettle in
Jerusalem.

[3]Here is a list of the names of the provincial officials who came to live in Jerusalem.
(Most of the people, priests, Levites, Temple
servants, and descendants of Solomon's
servants continued to live in their own
homes in the various towns of Judah, [4]but
some of the people from Judah and Benjamin resettled in Jerusalem.)

From the tribe of Judah:
Athaiah son of Uzziah, son of Zechariah,
son of Amariah, son of Shephatiah,
son of Mahalalel, of the family of Perez.
[5]Also Maaseiah son of Baruch, son
of Col-hozeh, son of Hazaiah, son of
Adaiah, son of Joiarib, son of Zechariah,
of the family of Shelah.* [6]There were
468 descendants of Perez who lived in
Jerusalem—all outstanding men.

[7]From the tribe of Benjamin:
Sallu son of Meshullam, son of Joed,
son of Pedaiah, son of Kolaiah, son of
Maaseiah, son of Ithiel, son of Jeshaiah.
[8]After him were Gabbai and Sallai and
a total of 928 relatives. [9]Their chief
officer was Joel son of Zicri, who was
assisted by Judah son of Hassenuah,
second-in-command over the city.

[10]From the priests:
Jedaiah son of Joiarib; Jakin; [11]and
Seraiah son of Hilkiah, son of
Meshullam, son of Zadok, son of
Meraioth, son of Ahitub, the supervisor
of the Temple of God. [12]Also 822 of their
associates, who worked at the Temple.
Also Adaiah son of Jeroham, son of
Pelaliah, son of Amzi, son of Zechariah,
son of Pashhur, son of Malkijah, [13]along
with 242 of his associates, who were
heads of their families. Also Amashsai
son of Azarel, son of Ahzai, son of
Meshillemoth, son of Immer, [14]and 128 of
his* outstanding associates. Their chief
officer was Zabdiel son of Haggedolim.

[15]From the Levites:
Shemaiah son of Hasshub, son of
Azrikam, son of Hashabiah, son of
Bunni. [16]Also Shabbethai and Jozabad,
who were in charge of the work outside
the Temple of God. [17]Also Mattaniah
son of Mica, son of Zabdi, a descendant
of Asaph, who led in thanksgiving

and prayer. Also Bakbukiah, who
was Mattaniah's assistant, and Abda
son of Shammua, son of Galal, son of
Jeduthun. 18 In all, there were 284 Levites
in the holy city.
19 From the gatekeepers:
Akkub, Talmon, and 172 of their
associates, who guarded the gates.

20 The other priests, Levites, and the rest
of the Israelites lived wherever their family
inheritance was located in any of the towns
of Judah. 21 The Temple servants, however,
whose leaders were Ziha and Gishpa, all
lived on the hill of Ophel.

22 The chief officer of the Levites in Jerusalem was Uzzi son of Bani, son of Hashabiah,
son of Mattaniah, son of Mica, a descendant
of Asaph, whose family served as singers at
God's Temple. 23 Their daily responsibilities
were carried out according to the terms of a
royal command.

24 Pethahiah son of Meshezabel, a descendant of Zerah son of Judah, was
the royal adviser in all matters of public
administration.

25 As for the surrounding villages with
their open fields, some of the people of
Judah lived in Kiriath-arba with its settlements, Dibon with its settlements, and Je-
kabzeel with its villages. 26 They also lived
in Jeshua, Moladah, Beth-pelet, 27 Hazar-
shual, Beersheba with its settlements,
28 Ziklag, and Meconah with its settlements.
29 They also lived in En-rimmon, Zorah,
Jarmuth, 30 Zanoah, and Adullam with their
surrounding villages. They also lived in
Lachish with its nearby fields and Azekah
with its surrounding villages. So the people
of Judah were living all the way from Beersheba in the south to the valley of Hinnom.

31 Some of the people of Benjamin lived
at Geba, Micmash, Aija, and Bethel with its
settlements. 32 They also lived in Anathoth,
Nob, Ananiah, 33 Hazor, Ramah, Gittaim,
34 Hadid, Zeboim, Neballat, 35 Lod, Ono, and
the Valley of Craftsmen.* 36 Some of the
Levites who lived in Judah were sent to live
with the tribe of Benjamin.

A History of the Priests and Levites

12 Here is the list of the priests and
Levites who returned with Zerubbabel son of Shealtiel and Jeshua the high
priest:

Seraiah, Jeremiah, Ezra,
2 Amariah, Malluch, Hattush,
3 Shecaniah, Harim,* Meremoth,
4 Iddo, Ginnethon,* Abijah,
5 Miniamin, Moadiah,* Bilgah,
6 Shemaiah, Joiarib, Jedaiah,
7 Sallu, Amok, Hilkiah, and Jedaiah.

These were the leaders of the priests and
their associates in the days of Jeshua.

8 The Levites who returned with them were
Jeshua, Binnui, Kadmiel, Sherebiah, Judah,
and Mattaniah, who with his associates
was in charge of the songs of thanksgiving.
9 Their associates, Bakbukiah and Unni,
stood opposite them during the service.

10 Jeshua the high priest was the father of
Joiakim.
Joiakim was the father of Eliashib.
Eliashib was the father of Joiada.
11 Joiada was the father of Johanan.*
Johanan was the father of Jaddua.

12 Now when Joiakim was high priest, the
family leaders of the priests were as follows:

Meraiah was leader of the family of
Seraiah.
Hananiah was leader of the family of
Jeremiah.
13 Meshullam was leader of the family of
Ezra.
Jehohanan was leader of the family of
Amariah.
14 Jonathan was leader of the family of
Malluch.*
Joseph was leader of the family of
Shecaniah.*
15 Adna was leader of the family of Harim.
Helkai was leader of the family of
Meremoth.*
16 Zechariah was leader of the family of
Iddo.
Meshullam was leader of the family of
Ginnethon.
17 Zicri was leader of the family of Abijah.
There was also a* leader of the family of
Miniamin.

11:5 Hebrew *son of the Shilonite.* **11:14** As in Greek version; Hebrew reads *their.* **11:35** Or *and Ge-harashim.* **12:3** Hebrew *Rehum;* compare 7:42; 12:15; Ezra 2:39. **12:4** As in some Hebrew manuscripts and Latin Vulgate (see also 12:16); most Hebrew manuscripts read *Ginnethoi.* **12:5** Hebrew *Mijamin, Maadiah;* compare 12:17. **12:11** Hebrew *Jonathan;* compare 12:22. **12:14a** As in Greek version (see also 10:4; 12:2); Hebrew reads *Malluchi.* **12:14b** As in many Hebrew manuscripts, some Greek manuscripts, and Syriac version (see also 12:3); most Hebrew manuscripts read *Shebaniah.* **12:15** As in some Greek manuscripts (see also 12:3); Hebrew reads *Meraioth.* **12:17** Hebrew lacks the name of this family leader.

Piltai was leader of the family of Moadiah.
18 Shammua was leader of the family of Bilgah.
Jehonathan was leader of the family of Shemaiah.
19 Mattenai was leader of the family of Joiarib.
Uzzi was leader of the family of Jedaiah.
20 Kallai was leader of the family of Sallu.*
Eber was leader of the family of Amok.
21 Hashabiah was leader of the family of Hilkiah.
Nethanel was leader of the family of Jedaiah.

22 A record of the Levite families was kept during the years when Eliashib, Joiada, Johanan, and Jaddua served as high priest. Another record of the priests was kept during the reign of Darius the Persian.*
23 A record of the heads of the Levite families was kept in *The Book of History* down to the days of Johanan, the grandson* of Eliashib.

24 These were the family leaders of the Levites: Hashabiah, Sherebiah, Jeshua, Binnui,* Kadmiel, and other associates, who stood opposite them during the ceremonies of praise and thanksgiving, one section responding to the other, as commanded by David, the man of God.
25 This included Mattaniah, Bakbukiah, and Obadiah.

Meshullam, Talmon, and Akkub were the gatekeepers in charge of the storerooms at the gates.
26 These all served in the days of Joiakim son of Jeshua, son of Jehozadak,* and in the days of Nehemiah the governor and of Ezra the priest and scribe.

Dedication of Jerusalem's Wall

27 For the dedication of the new wall of Jerusalem, the Levites throughout the land were asked to come to Jerusalem to assist in the ceremonies. They were to take part in the joyous occasion with their songs of thanksgiving and with the music of cymbals, harps, and lyres.
28 The singers were brought together from the region around Jerusalem and from the villages of the Netophathites.
29 They also came from Beth-gilgal and the rural areas near Geba and Azmaveth, for the singers had built their own settlements around Jerusalem.
30 The priests and Levites first purified themselves; then they purified the people, the gates, and the wall.

31 I led the leaders of Judah to the top of the wall and organized two large choirs to give thanks. One of the choirs proceeded southward* along the top of the wall to the Dung Gate.
32 Hoshaiah and half the leaders of Judah followed them,
33 along with Azariah, Ezra, Meshullam,
34 Judah, Benjamin, Shemaiah, and Jeremiah.
35 Then came some priests who played trumpets, including Zechariah son of Jonathan, son of Shemaiah, son of Mattaniah, son of Micaiah, son of Zaccur, a descendant of Asaph.
36 And Zechariah's colleagues were Shemaiah, Azarel, Milalai, Gilalai, Maai, Nethanel, Judah, and Hanani. They used the musical instruments prescribed by David, the man of God. Ezra the scribe led this procession.
37 At the Fountain Gate they went straight up the steps on the ascent of the city wall toward the City of David. They passed the house of David and then proceeded to the Water Gate on the east.

38 The second choir giving thanks went

Scribes

One of the choirs that led the great procession around the walls was led by "Ezra the scribe" (Nehemiah 12:36). This word "scribe" (often translated in NLT as "secretary") was originally used of those who copied God's Law. In the days before printing, everything was copied by hand, and scribes took great care and followed strict rules (like counting the number of words and letters on each page) to ensure no mistakes were made. But during the Exile, scribes like Ezra took on another role—that of interpreting and applying the Law for the new situation that Jews found themselves in. By New Testament times the scribes' interpretations were considered as important as the Law itself, and this often brought them into conflict with Jesus.

northward* around the other way to meet
them. I followed them, together with the
other half of the people, along the top of
the wall past the Tower of the Ovens to the
Broad Wall, 39then past the Ephraim Gate to
the Old City Gate,* past the Fish Gate and
the Tower of Hananel, and on to the Tower
of the Hundred. Then we continued on to the
Sheep Gate and stopped at the Guard Gate.

40The two choirs that were giving thanks
then proceeded to the Temple of God, where
they took their places. So did I, together
with the group of leaders who were with
me. 41We went together with the trumpet-
playing priests—Eliakim, Maaseiah, Miniamin, Micaiah, Elioenai, Zechariah, and
Hananiah—42and the singers—Maaseiah,
Shemaiah, Eleazar, Uzzi, Jehohanan, Malkijah, Elam, and Ezer. They played and sang
loudly under the direction of Jezrahiah the
choir director.

43Many sacrifices were offered on that
joyous day, for God had given the people
cause for great joy. The women and children
also participated in the celebration, and
the joy of the people of Jerusalem could be
heard far away.

Provisions for Temple Worship

44On that day men were appointed to be in
charge of the storerooms for the offerings,
the first part of the harvest, and the tithes.
They were responsible to collect from the
fields outside the towns the portions required by the Law for the priests and Levites.
For all the people of Judah took joy in the
priests and Levites and their work. 45They
performed the service of their God and the
service of purification, as commanded by
David and his son Solomon, and so did the
singers and the gatekeepers. 46The custom
of having choir directors to lead the choirs
in hymns of praise and thanksgiving to
God began long ago in the days of David
and Asaph. 47So now, in the days of Zerubbabel and of Nehemiah, all Israel brought
a daily supply of food for the singers, the
gatekeepers, and the Levites. The Levites, in
turn, gave a portion of what they received to
the priests, the descendants of Aaron.

Nehemiah's Various Reforms

13 On that same day, as the Book of
Moses was being read to the people,
the passage was found that said no
Ammonite or Moabite should ever be permitted to enter the assembly of God.* 2For
they had not provided the Israelites with
food and water in the wilderness. Instead,
they hired Balaam to curse them, though
our God turned the curse into a blessing.
3When this passage of the Law was read, all
those of foreign descent were immediately
excluded from the assembly.

4Before this had happened, Eliashib the
priest, who had been appointed as supervisor of the storerooms of the Temple of our
God and who was also a relative of Tobiah,
5had converted a large storage room and
placed it at Tobiah's disposal. The room
had previously been used for storing the
grain offerings, the frankincense, various
articles for the Temple, and the tithes of
grain, new wine, and olive oil (which were
prescribed for the Levites, the singers, and
the gatekeepers), as well as the offerings for
the priests.

6I was not in Jerusalem at that time, for I
had returned to King Artaxerxes of Babylon
in the thirty-second year of his reign,*
though I later asked his permission to
return. 7When I arrived back in Jerusalem,
I learned about Eliashib's evil deed in providing Tobiah with a room in the courtyards
of the Temple of God. 8I became very upset
and threw all of Tobiah's belongings out of
the room. 9Then I demanded that the rooms
be purified, and I brought back the articles
for God's Temple, the grain offerings, and
the frankincense.

10I also discovered that the Levites had not
been given their prescribed portions of food,
so they and the singers who were to conduct
the worship services had all returned to
work their fields. 11I immediately confronted
the leaders and demanded, "Why has the
Temple of God been neglected?" Then I
called all the Levites back again and restored
them to their proper duties. 12And once more
all the people of Judah began bringing their
tithes of grain, new wine, and olive oil to the
Temple storerooms.

12:20 Hebrew *Sallai;* compare 12:7. **12:22** *Darius the Persian* is probably Darius II, who reigned 423–404 B.C., or possibly Darius III, who reigned 336–331 B.C. **12:23** Hebrew *descendant;* compare 12:10-11. **12:24** Hebrew *son of* (i.e., *ben*), which should probably be read here as the proper name Binnui; compare Ezra 3:9 and the note there. **12:26** Hebrew *Jozadak,* a variant spelling of Jehozadak. **12:31** Hebrew *to the right.* **12:38** Hebrew *to the left.* **12:39** Or *the Mishneh Gate,* or *the Jeshanah Gate.* **13:1** See Deut 23:3-6. **13:6** King Artaxerxes of Persia is here identified as the king of Babylon because Persia had conquered the Babylonian Empire. The thirty-second year of Artaxerxes was 433 B.C.

13 I assigned supervisors for the storerooms: Shelemiah the priest, Zadok the scribe, and Pedaiah, one of the Levites. And I appointed Hanan son of Zaccur and grandson of Mattaniah as their assistant. These men had an excellent reputation, and it was their job to make honest distributions to their fellow Levites.

> 14 Remember this good deed, O my God, and do not forget all that I have faithfully done for the Temple of my God and its services.

15 In those days I saw men of Judah treading out their winepresses on the Sabbath. They were also bringing in grain, loading it on donkeys, and bringing their wine, grapes, figs, and all sorts of produce to Jerusalem to sell on the Sabbath. So I rebuked them for selling their produce on that day. 16 Some men from Tyre, who lived in Jerusalem, were bringing in fish and all kinds of merchandise. They were selling it on the Sabbath to the people of Judah—and in Jerusalem at that!

17 So I confronted the nobles of Judah. "Why are you profaning the Sabbath in this evil way?" I asked. 18 "Wasn't it just this sort of thing that your ancestors did that caused our God to bring all this trouble upon us and our city? Now you are bringing even more wrath upon Israel by permitting the Sabbath to be desecrated in this way!"

19 Then I commanded that the gates of Jerusalem should be shut as darkness fell every Friday evening,* not to be opened until the Sabbath ended. I sent some of my own servants to guard the gates so that no merchandise could be brought in on the Sabbath day. 20 The merchants and tradesmen with a variety of wares camped outside Jerusalem once or twice. 21 But I spoke sharply to them and said, "What are you doing out here, camping around the wall? If you do this again, I will arrest you!" And that was the last time they came on the Sabbath. 22 Then I commanded the Levites to purify themselves and to guard the gates in order to preserve the holiness of the Sabbath.

> Remember this good deed also, O my God! Have compassion on me according to your great and unfailing love.

23 About the same time I realized that some of the men of Judah had married women from Ashdod, Ammon, and Moab. 24 Furthermore, half their children spoke the language of Ashdod or of some other people and could not speak the language of Judah at all. 25 So I confronted them and called down curses on them. I beat some of them and pulled out their hair. I made them swear in the name of God that they would not let their children intermarry with the pagan people of the land.

26 "Wasn't this exactly what led King Solomon of Israel into sin?" I demanded. "There was no king from any nation who could compare to him, and God loved him and made him king over all Israel. But even he was led into sin by his foreign wives. 27 How could you even think of committing this sinful deed and acting unfaithfully toward God by marrying foreign women?"

28 One of the sons of Joiada son of Eliashib the high priest had married a daughter of Sanballat the Horonite, so I banished him from my presence.

> 29 Remember them, O my God, for they have defiled the priesthood and the solemn vows of the priests and Levites.

30 So I purged out everything foreign and assigned tasks to the priests and Levites, making certain that each knew his work. 31 I also made sure that the supply of wood for the altar and the first portions of the harvest were brought at the proper times.

> Remember this in my favor, O my God.

13:19 Hebrew *on the day before the Sabbath.*

Esther *God rules behind the scenes*

The book of Esther is the story of a young Jewish woman who became the queen of Persia and so was well placed to help rescue her people from threatened annihilation. It is a story of drama, romance, power, and intrigue—but with no direct mention of God! But behind the scenes, God's plans were being carefully worked out. The story unfolds in Susa in Persia during the reign of Xerxes I (king of Persia from 486 to 465 BC), about thirty years before the events recorded in the book of Nehemiah. It tells of life for those Jews who chose not to return from exile.

What's it all about?

Esther's story begins in 484 BC, about one hundred years after Nebuchadnezzar had taken the Jews into captivity and twenty-five years before Ezra led his group of exiles back to Jerusalem. King Xerxes I (Ahasuerus) called his queen, Vashti, to appear before him. When she declined the command, he was furious and deposed her. His officials advised him to have the land searched for a beautiful woman, and Esther, a Jew, was one of those who was presented to the king. He immediately fell in love with her, and she became his queen.

Meanwhile, an ambitious court official named Haman was steadily being promoted. Full of self-importance, he insisted that all the palace officials bow down to him; but when Mordecai, a Jew, refused to do so, he plotted revenge against the entire Jewish people, not realizing that Queen Esther was a Jew and that Mordecai was her cousin. Blinded by his pride and self-importance, Haman was convinced that he would achieve his aim. On his wife's advice, he even had a sharpened pole set up on which he planned to impale Mordecai.

At great risk to herself, Esther responded to her cousin's promptings and, by gaining the king's favor, was able to expose Haman's plot. Haman was impaled on the very pole that he intended for Mordecai, and Mordecai assumed Haman's vacated role. The Jews were given permission to destroy their enemies, and they celebrated their victory with the Festival of Purim (from a Hebrew word meaning "lot," since the festival's date in the twelfth month was originally chosen by lot).

OVERVIEW

Esther becomes queen
1:1–2:23

Haman's conspiracy against the Jews
3:1-15

Mordecai persuades Esther to seek the king's help · *4:1–5:14*

Mordecai is honored and Haman is hanged · *6:1–7:10*

The king permits the Jews to destroy their enemies · *8:1–9:19*

The Festival of Purim is established
9:20-32

The greatness of Mordecai
10:1-3

What does it mean for us?

The book of Esther is a remarkable story of God's providence and human courage. Queen Esther and her cousin Mordecai kept faith in God, sometimes at great risk to their own personal safety. We see that God is always at work behind the scenes, even though he is never mentioned by name in the book. When the ultimate threat came to annihilate all the Jews in the Persian Empire,

page 554

Esther was willing to risk her life and reputation for the sake of her people. Just at that moment, events began to unfold in a most unexpected way, and both she and the rest of the Jews were saved. The book shows that God's plans are never frustrated by evil human plans, and that God can be trusted even when our very lives are under threat. The book of Esther is a call to God's people to stand up and be counted (like Esther) and to celebrate God's victories (as they did in the Festival of Purim).

▶ *See also* ***A timeline of the Bible****, pages A22-A24.*

The King's Banquet

1 These events happened in the days of
King Xerxes,* who reigned over 127 provinces stretching from India to Ethiopia.* 2At
that time Xerxes ruled his empire from his
royal throne at the fortress of Susa. 3In the
third year of his reign, he gave a banquet for
all his nobles and officials. He invited all the
military officers of Persia and Media as well
as the princes and nobles of the provinces.
4The celebration lasted 180 days—a tremendous display of the opulent wealth of his
empire and the pomp and splendor of his
majesty.

5When it was all over, the king gave a
banquet for all the people, from the greatest
to the least, who were in the fortress of Susa.
It lasted for seven days and was held in the
courtyard of the palace garden. 6The courtyard was beautifully decorated with white
cotton curtains and blue hangings, which
were fastened with white linen cords and
purple ribbons to silver rings embedded in
marble pillars. Gold and silver couches stood
on a mosaic pavement of porphyry, marble,
mother-of-pearl, and other costly stones.

7Drinks were served in gold goblets of
many designs, and there was an abundance
of royal wine, reflecting the king's generosity. 8By edict of the king, no limits were
placed on the drinking, for the king had instructed all his palace officials to serve each
man as much as he wanted.

9At the same time, Queen Vashti gave a
banquet for the women in the royal palace
of King Xerxes.

Queen Vashti Deposed

10On the seventh day of the feast, when King
Xerxes was in high spirits because of the wine,
he told the seven eunuchs who attended
him—Mehuman, Biztha, Harbona, Bigtha,
Abagtha, Zethar, and Carcas—11to bring
Queen Vashti to him with the royal crown on
her head. He wanted the nobles and all the
other men to gaze on her beauty, for she was
a very beautiful woman. 12But when they conveyed the king's order to Queen Vashti, she
refused to come. This made the king furious,
and he burned with anger.

13He immediately consulted with his wise
advisers, who knew all the Persian laws and
customs, for he always asked their advice.
14The names of these men were Carshena,
Shethar, Admatha, Tarshish, Meres, Marsena,
and Memucan—seven nobles of Persia and
Media. They met with the king regularly and
held the highest positions in the empire.

15"What must be done to Queen Vashti?"
the king demanded. "What penalty does the
law provide for a queen who refuses to obey
the king's orders, properly sent through his
eunuchs?"

16Memucan answered the king and his
nobles, "Queen Vashti has wronged not only
the king but also every noble and citizen
throughout your empire. 17Women everywhere will begin to despise their husbands
when they learn that Queen Vashti has
refused to appear before the king. 18Before
this day is out, the wives of all the king's
nobles throughout Persia and Media will
hear what the queen did and will start treating their husbands the same way. There will
be no end to their contempt and anger.

19"So if it please the king, we suggest that
you issue a written decree, a law of the Persians and Medes that cannot be revoked. It
should order that Queen Vashti be forever banished from the presence of King Xerxes, and
that the king should choose another queen
more worthy than she. 20When this decree is
published throughout the king's vast empire,
husbands everywhere, whatever their rank,
will receive proper respect from their wives!"

21The king and his nobles thought this
made good sense, so he followed Memucan's
counsel. 22He sent letters to all parts of the

empire, to each province in its own script and language, proclaiming that every man should be the ruler of his own home and should say whatever he pleases.*

Esther Becomes Queen

2 But after Xerxes' anger had subsided, he began thinking about Vashti and what she had done and the decree he had made. 2So his personal attendants suggested, "Let us search the empire to find beautiful young virgins for the king. 3Let the king appoint agents in each province to bring these beautiful young women into the royal harem at the fortress of Susa. Hegai, the king's eunuch in charge of the harem, will see that they are all given beauty treatments. 4After that, the young woman who most pleases the king will be made queen instead of Vashti." This advice was very appealing to the king, so he put the plan into effect.

5At that time there was a Jewish man in the fortress of Susa whose name was Mordecai son of Jair. He was from the tribe of Benjamin and was a descendant of Kish and Shimei. 6His family* had been among those who, with King Jehoiachin* of Judah, had been exiled from Jerusalem to Babylon by King Nebuchadnezzar. 7This man had a very beautiful and lovely young cousin, Hadassah, who was also called Esther. When her father and mother died, Mordecai adopted her into his family and raised her as his own daughter.

8As a result of the king's decree, Esther, along with many other young women, was brought to the king's harem at the fortress of Susa and placed in Hegai's care. 9Hegai was very impressed with Esther and treated her kindly. He quickly ordered a special menu for her and provided her with beauty treatments. He also assigned her seven maids specially chosen from the king's palace, and he moved her and her maids into the best place in the harem.

10Esther had not told anyone of her nationality and family background, because Mordecai had directed her not to do so. 11Every day Mordecai would take a walk near the courtyard of the harem to find out about Esther and what was happening to her.

12Before each young woman was taken to the king's bed, she was given the prescribed twelve months of beauty treatments—six months with oil of myrrh, followed by six months with special perfumes and ointments. 13When it was time for her to go to the king's palace, she was given her choice of whatever clothing or jewelry she wanted to take from the harem. 14That evening she was taken to the king's private rooms, and the next morning she was brought to the second harem,* where the king's wives lived. There she would be under the care of Shaashgaz, the king's eunuch in charge of the concubines. She would never go to the king again unless he had especially enjoyed her and requested her by name.

15Esther was the daughter of Abihail, who was Mordecai's uncle. (Mordecai had adopted his younger cousin Esther.) When it was Esther's turn to go to the king, she accepted the advice of Hegai, the eunuch in charge of the harem. She asked for nothing except what he suggested, and she was admired by everyone who saw her.

16Esther was taken to King Xerxes at the royal palace in early winter* of the seventh

1:1a Hebrew *Ahasuerus,* another name for Xerxes; also throughout the book of Esther. Xerxes reigned 486–465 B.C. **1:1b** Hebrew *to Cush.* **1:22** Or *and should speak in the language of his own people.* **2:6a** Hebrew *He.* **2:6b** Hebrew *Jeconiah,* a variant spelling of Jehoiachin. **2:14** Or *to another part of the harem.* **2:16** Hebrew *in the tenth month, the month of Tebeth.* A number of dates in the book of Esther can be cross-checked with dates in surviving Persian records and related accurately to our modern calendar. This month of the ancient Hebrew lunar calendar occurred within the months of December 479 B.C. and January 478 B.C.

Fascinating facts about the book of Esther

- The book does not explicitly refer to God, but his activity is seen throughout the book.
- It is one of only two books in the Bible named after a woman; the other is Ruth.
- The activities of the Persian court are prominent, including beauty treatments (2:12) and especially feasting (e.g., 1:3-4, 5-8).
- It tells of the last attempt in the Old Testament to wipe out God's people.

year of his reign. 17And the king loved Esther more than any of the other young women. He was so delighted with her that he set the royal crown on her head and declared her queen instead of Vashti. 18To celebrate the occasion, he gave a great banquet in Esther's honor for all his nobles and officials, declaring a public holiday for the provinces and giving generous gifts to everyone.

19Even after all the young women had been transferred to the second harem* and Mordecai had become a palace official,* 20Esther continued to keep her family background and nationality a secret. She was still following Mordecai's directions, just as she did when she lived in his home.

Mordecai's Loyalty to the King

21One day as Mordecai was on duty at the king's gate, two of the king's eunuchs, Bigthana* and Teresh—who were guards at the door of the king's private quarters—became angry at King Xerxes and plotted to assassinate him. 22But Mordecai heard about the plot and gave the information to Queen Esther. She then told the king about it and gave Mordecai credit for the report. 23When an investigation was made and Mordecai's story was found to be true, the two men were impaled on a sharpened pole. This was all recorded in *The Book of the History of King Xerxes' Reign*.

Haman's Plot against the Jews

3 Some time later King Xerxes promoted Haman son of Hammedatha the Agagite over all the other nobles, making him the most powerful official in the empire. 2All the king's officials would bow down before Haman to show him respect whenever he passed by, for so the king had commanded. But Mordecai refused to bow down or show him respect.

3Then the palace officials at the king's gate asked Mordecai, "Why are you disobeying the king's command?" 4They spoke to him day after day, but still he refused to comply with the order. So they spoke to Haman about this to see if he would tolerate Mordecai's conduct, since Mordecai had told them he was a Jew.

5When Haman saw that Mordecai would not bow down or show him respect, he was filled with rage. 6He had learned of Mordecai's nationality, so he decided it was not enough to lay hands on Mordecai alone. Instead, he looked for a way to destroy all the Jews throughout the entire empire of Xerxes.

7So in the month of April,* during the twelfth year of King Xerxes' reign, lots were cast in Haman's presence (the lots were called *purim*) to determine the best day and month to take action. And the day selected was March 7, nearly a year later.*

8Then Haman approached King Xerxes and said, "There is a certain race of people scattered through all the provinces of your empire who keep themselves separate from everyone else. Their laws are different from those of any other people, and they refuse to obey the laws of the king. So it is not in the king's interest to let them live. 9If it please the king, issue a decree that they be destroyed, and I will give 10,000 large sacks* of silver to the government administrators to be deposited in the royal treasury."

10The king agreed, confirming his decision by removing his signet ring from his finger and giving it to Haman son of Hammedatha the Agagite, the enemy of the Jews. 11The king said, "The money and the people are both yours to do with as you see fit."

12So on April 17* the king's secretaries were summoned, and a decree was written exactly as Haman dictated. It was sent to the king's highest officers, the governors of the respective provinces, and the nobles of each province in their own scripts and languages.

Susa

The events of Esther took place in the royal palace in Susa in southwest Persia (Esther 2:3). This beautiful palace-fortress had been built by Darius I and served as the winter residence of the Persian kings. Susa was also where Nehemiah worked as cup-bearer to the king (Nehemiah 1:1) and was where one of Daniel's visions was set (Daniel 8:2).

The decree was written in the name of King Xerxes and sealed with the king's signet ring. [13]Dispatches were sent by swift messengers into all the provinces of the empire, giving the order that all Jews—young and old, including women and children—must be killed, slaughtered, and annihilated on a single day. This was scheduled to happen on March 7 of the next year.* The property of the Jews would be given to those who killed them.

[14]A copy of this decree was to be issued as law in every province and proclaimed to all peoples, so that they would be ready to do their duty on the appointed day. [15]At the king's command, the decree went out by swift messengers, and it was also proclaimed in the fortress of Susa. Then the king and Haman sat down to drink, but the city of Susa fell into confusion.

Mordecai Requests Esther's Help

4 When Mordecai learned about all that had been done, he tore his clothes, put on burlap and ashes, and went out into the city, crying with a loud and bitter wail. [2]He went as far as the gate of the palace, for no one was allowed to enter the palace gate while wearing clothes of mourning. [3]And as news of the king's decree reached all the provinces, there was great mourning among the Jews. They fasted, wept, and wailed, and many people lay in burlap and ashes.

[4]When Queen Esther's maids and eunuchs came and told her about Mordecai, she was deeply distressed. She sent clothing to him to replace the burlap, but he refused it. [5]Then Esther sent for Hathach, one of the king's eunuchs who had been appointed as her attendant. She ordered him to go to Mordecai and find out what was troubling him and why he was in mourning. [6]So Hathach went out to Mordecai in the square in front of the palace gate.

[7]Mordecai told him the whole story, including the exact amount of money Haman had promised to pay into the royal treasury for the destruction of the Jews. [8]Mordecai gave Hathach a copy of the decree issued in Susa that called for the death of all Jews. He asked Hathach to show it to Esther and explain the situation to her. He also asked Hathach to direct her to go to the king to beg for mercy and plead for her people. [9]So Hathach returned to Esther with Mordecai's message.

[10]Then Esther told Hathach to go back and relay this message to Mordecai: [11]"All the king's officials and even the people in the provinces know that anyone who appears before the king in his inner court without being invited is doomed to die unless the king holds out his gold scepter. And the king has not called for me to come to him for thirty days." [12]So Hathach* gave Esther's message to Mordecai.

2:19a The meaning of the Hebrew is uncertain. **2:19b** Hebrew *and Mordecai was sitting in the gate of the king.* **2:21** Hebrew *Bigthan*; compare 6:2. **3:7a** Hebrew *in the first month, the month of Nisan.* This month of the ancient Hebrew lunar calendar occurred within the months of April and May 474 B.C.; also see note on 2:16. **3:7b** As in 3:13, which reads *the thirteenth day of the twelfth month, the month of Adar;* Hebrew reads *in the twelfth month,* of the ancient Hebrew lunar calendar. The date selected was March 7, 473 B.C.; also see note on 2:16. **3:9** Hebrew *10,000 talents,* about 375 tons or 340 metric tons in weight. **3:12** Hebrew *On the thirteenth day of the first month,* of the ancient Hebrew lunar calendar. This day was April 17, 474 B.C.; also see note on 2:16. **3:13** Hebrew *on the thirteenth day of the twelfth month, the month of Adar,* of the ancient Hebrew lunar calendar. The date selected was March 7, 473 B.C.; also see note on 2:16. **4:12** As in Greek version; Hebrew reads *they.*

Haman

Haman was a descendant of King Agag, king of the Amalekites, who had been Israel's enemies ever since they attacked the Israelites on their way to the Promised Land. Like Daniel and Nehemiah, Haman had served his foreign masters well, working his way up to become chief minister of King Xerxes of Persia—a position he tried to use to exterminate the Jews. When he discovered that Mordecai, a Jew, wouldn't bow down to him like everyone else, he was furious and resolved to take revenge not just on Mordecai but on the entire Jewish race. But he didn't know that Queen Esther was a Jew and that Mordecai was her cousin. Esther exposed his plans to the king, who promptly had Haman impaled on the very pole he had prepared for Mordecai. The attempt to exterminate God's people had failed, and God's justice against those who seek to abuse their power for their own ends had been demonstrated.

13 Mordecai sent this reply to Esther:
"Don't think for a moment that because
you're in the palace you will escape when
all other Jews are killed. 14 If you keep quiet
at a time like this, deliverance and relief for
the Jews will arise from some other place,
but you and your relatives will die. Who
knows if perhaps you were made queen for
just such a time as this?"
15 Then Esther sent this reply to Mordecai:
16 "Go and gather together all the Jews of Susa
and fast for me. Do not eat or drink for three
days, night or day. My maids and I will do
the same. And then, though it is against the
law, I will go in to see the king. If I must die,
I must die." 17 So Mordecai went away and did
everything as Esther had ordered him.

Esther's Request to the King

5 On the third day of the fast, Esther put
on her royal robes and entered the inner
court of the palace, just across from the
king's hall. The king was sitting on his royal
throne, facing the entrance. 2 When he saw
Queen Esther standing there in the inner
court, he welcomed her and held out the
gold scepter to her. So Esther approached
and touched the end of the scepter.
3 Then the king asked her, "What do you
want, Queen Esther? What is your request?
I will give it to you, even if it is half the
kingdom!"
4 And Esther replied, "If it please the king,
let the king and Haman come today to a
banquet I have prepared for the king."
5 The king turned to his attendants and
said, "Tell Haman to come quickly to a
banquet, as Esther has requested." So the
king and Haman went to Esther's banquet.
6 And while they were drinking wine, the
king said to Esther, "Now tell me what you
really want. What is your request? I will give
it to you, even if it is half the kingdom!"
7 Esther replied, "This is my request and
deepest wish. 8 If I have found favor with
the king, and if it pleases the king to grant
my request and do what I ask, please come
with Haman tomorrow to the banquet I will
prepare for you. Then I will explain what
this is all about."

Haman's Plan to Kill Mordecai

9 Haman was a happy man as he left the
banquet! But when he saw Mordecai sitting
at the palace gate, not standing up or trembling nervously before him, Haman became

Waiting

Most of us hate waiting. We want things *now*. But the Bible teaches the importance of waiting—especially waiting for God to act. Isaiah said, "For since the world began, no ear has heard and no eye has seen a God like you, who works for those who wait for him!" (Isaiah 64:4). In other words, God acts while we wait—though most of us, if we are honest, prefer to turn that on its head and keep God waiting while we act! Esther had learned how to wait for God's moment. She didn't tell the king immediately she was Jewish (Esther 2:10); she didn't rush to tell him about Haman's plan to exterminate the Jews, but rather called people to prayer (4:15-16); she didn't even answer the king immediately when he asked her what she wanted (5:3-4). She was waiting for God's moment and for God to act so that he alone would receive the credit.

But there is also a flip side to waiting. Sometimes we can wait so long—perhaps out of timidity or fear—that God needs to push us to get on with things. In the story of Esther, it took an appeal from Mordecai to make Esther realize that now was the time for her to act and that all God had done for her had been leading up to this very moment (4:14). And because she now stepped out, the Jews were saved.

Working out when we need to wait and when we have waited too long isn't always easy! But the more we grow as Christians, the more we learn to trust the nudges of the Holy Spirit to lead us.

▶ *See also* ***The use of time****, page 732.*

furious. [10]However, he restrained himself and went on home.

Then Haman gathered together his friends and Zeresh, his wife, [11]and boasted to them about his great wealth and his many children. He bragged about the honors the king had given him and how he had been promoted over all the other nobles and officials.

[12]Then Haman added, "And that's not all! Queen Esther invited only me and the king himself to the banquet she prepared for us. And she has invited me to dine with her and the king again tomorrow!" [13]Then he added, "But this is all worth nothing as long as I see Mordecai the Jew just sitting there at the palace gate."

[14]So Haman's wife, Zeresh, and all his friends suggested, "Set up a sharpened pole that stands seventy-five feet* tall, and in the morning ask the king to impale Mordecai on it. When this is done, you can go on your merry way to the banquet with the king." This pleased Haman, and he ordered the pole set up.

The King Honors Mordecai

6 That night the king had trouble sleeping, so he ordered an attendant to bring the book of the history of his reign so it could be read to him. [2]In those records he discovered an account of how Mordecai had exposed the plot of Bigthana and Teresh, two of the eunuchs who guarded the door to the king's private quarters. They had plotted to assassinate King Xerxes.

[3]"What reward or recognition did we ever give Mordecai for this?" the king asked.

His attendants replied, "Nothing has been done for him."

[4]"Who is that in the outer court?" the king inquired. As it happened, Haman had just arrived in the outer court of the palace to ask the king to impale Mordecai on the pole he had prepared.

[5]So the attendants replied to the king, "Haman is out in the court."

"Bring him in," the king ordered. [6]So Haman came in, and the king said, "What should I do to honor a man who truly pleases me?"

Haman thought to himself, "Whom would the king wish to honor more than me?" [7]So he replied, "If the king wishes to honor someone, [8]he should bring out one of the king's own royal robes, as well as a horse that the king himself has ridden—one with a royal emblem on its head. [9]Let the

5:14 Hebrew *50 cubits* [23 meters].

Pride

When Haman was promoted to become chief official in the palace, his pride quickly got the better of him. The king had ordered that other officials should bow down to Haman, and Haman was furious when Mordecai would not do so (Esther 3:1-5). He felt he was better than Mordecai and became increasingly angry at what he felt was a lack of respect for someone as important as him (5:9). But his pride overtook him, as pride always does. When the king asked, "What should I do to honor a man who truly pleases me?" (6:6), Haman's pride blinded him to the fact that the king could be referring to someone other than him. So he was outraged when he discovered the man to be honored was Mordecai. His pride quickly turned to despondency (6:12), and even his wife saw that disaster lay ahead. The very same day Haman was impaled on the pole he had set up for Mordecai.

Pride always leads to ultimate disaster (even if it brings some immediate success) for it blinds us to what is really going on. In the Bible we see pride leading to self-deception, hardness of heart, contempt, and quarreling, to name but a few results. But since pride has its origins in Satan himself (e.g., as Ezekiel sees in the prophetic imagery of Ezekiel 28:2, 17), it is not surprising that its outcome is always devilish and disastrous. That is why Jesus taught us to humble, rather than exalt, ourselves (Matthew 23:12).

▶ *See also* ***Humility****, page 1134.*

robes and the horse be handed over to one of the king's most noble officials. And let him see that the man whom the king wishes to honor is dressed in the king's robes and led through the city square on the king's horse. Have the official shout as they go, 'This is what the king does for someone he wishes to honor!'"

10 "Excellent!" the king said to Haman. "Quick! Take the robes and my horse, and do just as you have said for Mordecai the Jew, who sits at the gate of the palace. Leave out nothing you have suggested!"

11 So Haman took the robes and put them on Mordecai, placed him on the king's own horse, and led him through the city square, shouting, "This is what the king does for someone he wishes to honor!" 12 Afterward Mordecai returned to the palace gate, but Haman hurried home dejected and completely humiliated.

13 When Haman told his wife, Zeresh, and all his friends what had happened, his wise advisers and his wife said, "Since Mordecai—this man who has humiliated you—is of Jewish birth, you will never succeed in your plans against him. It will be fatal to continue opposing him."

14 While they were still talking, the king's eunuchs arrived and quickly took Haman to the banquet Esther had prepared.

The King Executes Haman

7 So the king and Haman went to Queen Esther's banquet. 2 On this second occasion, while they were drinking wine, the king again said to Esther, "Tell me what you want, Queen Esther. What is your request? I will give it to you, even if it is half the kingdom!"

3 Queen Esther replied, "If I have found favor with the king, and if it pleases the king to grant my request, I ask that my life and the lives of my people will be spared. 4 For my people and I have been sold to those who would kill, slaughter, and annihilate us. If we had merely been sold as slaves, I could remain quiet, for that would be too trivial a matter to warrant disturbing the king."

5 "Who would do such a thing?" King Xerxes demanded. "Who would be so presumptuous as to touch you?"

6 Esther replied, "This wicked Haman is our adversary and our enemy." Haman grew pale with fright before the king and queen. 7 Then the king jumped to his feet in a rage and went out into the palace garden.

Haman, however, stayed behind to plead for his life with Queen Esther, for he knew that the king intended to kill him. 8 In despair he fell on the couch where Queen Esther was reclining, just as the king was returning from the palace garden.

The king exclaimed, "Will he even assault the queen right here in the palace, before my very eyes?" And as soon as the king spoke, his attendants covered Haman's face, signaling his doom.

9 Then Harbona, one of the king's eunuchs, said, "Haman has set up a sharpened pole that stands seventy-five feet* tall in his own courtyard. He intended to use it to impale Mordecai, the man who saved the king from assassination."

"Then impale Haman on it!" the king ordered. 10 So they impaled Haman on the pole he had set up for Mordecai, and the king's anger subsided.

A Decree to Help the Jews

8 On that same day King Xerxes gave the property of Haman, the enemy of the Jews, to Queen Esther. Then Mordecai was brought before the king, for Esther had told the king how they were related. 2 The king took off his signet ring—which he had taken back from Haman—and gave it to Mordecai. And Esther appointed Mordecai to be in charge of Haman's property.

3 Then Esther went again before the king, falling down at his feet and begging him with tears to stop the evil plot devised by Haman the Agagite against the Jews. 4 Again the king held out the gold scepter to Esther. So she rose and stood before him.

5 Esther said, "If it please the king, and if I have found favor with him, and if he thinks it is right, and if I am pleasing to him, let there be a decree that reverses the orders of Haman son of Hammedatha the Agagite, who ordered that Jews throughout all the king's provinces should be destroyed. 6 For how can I endure to see my people and my family slaughtered and destroyed?"

7 Then King Xerxes said to Queen Esther and Mordecai the Jew, "I have given Esther the property of Haman, and he has been impaled on a pole because he tried to destroy the Jews. 8 Now go ahead and send

a message to the Jews in the king's name,
telling them whatever you want, and seal
it with the king's signet ring. But remember
that whatever has already been written in
the king's name and sealed with his signet
ring can never be revoked."
9 So on June 25* the king's secretaries
were summoned, and a decree was written
exactly as Mordecai dictated. It was sent to
the Jews and to the highest officers, the governors, and the nobles of all the 127 provinces stretching from India to Ethiopia.*
The decree was written in the scripts and
languages of all the peoples of the empire,
including that of the Jews. 10 The decree was
written in the name of King Xerxes and
sealed with the king's signet ring. Mordecai sent the dispatches by swift messengers,
who rode fast horses especially bred for the
king's service.
11 The king's decree gave the Jews in
every city authority to unite to defend their
lives. They were allowed to kill, slaughter,
and annihilate anyone of any nationality or province who might attack them or
their children and wives, and to take the
property of their enemies. 12 The day chosen
for this event throughout all the provinces
of King Xerxes was March 7 of the next
year.*
13 A copy of this decree was to be issued
as law in every province and proclaimed to
all peoples, so that the Jews would be ready
to take revenge on their enemies on the
appointed day. 14 So urged on by the king's
command, the messengers rode out swiftly
on fast horses bred for the king's service.
The same decree was also proclaimed in the
fortress of Susa.
15 Then Mordecai left the king's presence,
wearing the royal robe of blue and white,
the great crown of gold, and an outer cloak
of fine linen and purple. And the people
of Susa celebrated the new decree. 16 The
Jews were filled with joy and gladness and
were honored everywhere. 17 In every province and city, wherever the king's decree
arrived, the Jews rejoiced and had a great
celebration and declared a public festival
and holiday. And many of the people of
the land became Jews themselves, for they
feared what the Jews might do to them.

The Victory of the Jews

9 So on March 7* the two decrees of the
king were put into effect. On that day,
the enemies of the Jews had hoped to overpower them, but quite the opposite happened. It was the Jews who overpowered
their enemies. 2 The Jews gathered in their
cities throughout all the king's provinces to
attack anyone who tried to harm them. But
no one could make a stand against them,
for everyone was afraid of them. 3 And all
the nobles of the provinces, the highest officers, the governors, and the royal officials
helped the Jews for fear of Mordecai. 4 For
Mordecai had been promoted in the king's
palace, and his fame spread throughout all
the provinces as he became more and more
powerful.
5 So the Jews went ahead on the appointed

7:9 Hebrew *50 cubits* [23 meters]. **8:9a** Hebrew *on the twenty-third day of the third month, the month of Sivan,* of the ancient Hebrew lunar calendar. This day was June 25, 474 B.C.; also see note on 2:16. **8:9b** Hebrew *to Cush.* **8:12** Hebrew *the thirteenth day of the twelfth month, the month of Adar,* of the ancient Hebrew lunar calendar. The date selected was March 7, 473 B.C.; also see note on 2:16. **9:1** Hebrew *on the thirteenth day of the twelfth month, the month of Adar,* of the ancient Hebrew lunar calendar. This day was March 7, 473 B.C.; also see note on 2:16.

The Festival of Purim

The Jewish Festival of Purim recalls the thwarting of Haman's attempt to exterminate the Jewish people, and God's special protection of them. Unlike other Jewish festivals, which had been commanded in the Law, this one arose as a spontaneous response to God's protection and faithfulness. The word Purim means "lots" and comes from the lots that Haman cast to determine the date on which the Jews should be killed (Esther 9:26). This joyful festival is still celebrated by Jews to this day; they read the book of Esther, dress up as characters from the story, and give gifts to one another. It stands as a reminder that no one can thwart God's plan of building a family descended from Abraham that will one day fill the whole earth (Genesis 12:1-3; 15:1-5; 17:3-7).

day and struck down their enemies with the sword. They killed and annihilated their enemies and did as they pleased with those who hated them. [6]In the fortress of Susa itself, the Jews killed 500 men. [7]They also killed Parshandatha, Dalphon, Aspatha, [8]Poratha, Adalia, Aridatha, [9]Parmashta, Arisai, Aridai, and Vaizatha—[10]the ten sons of Haman son of Hammedatha, the enemy of the Jews. But they did not take any plunder.

[11]That very day, when the king was informed of the number of people killed in the fortress of Susa, [12]he called for Queen Esther. He said, "The Jews have killed 500 men in the fortress of Susa alone, as well as Haman's ten sons. If they have done that here, what has happened in the rest of the provinces? But now, what more do you want? It will be granted to you; tell me and I will do it."

[13]Esther responded, "If it please the king, give the Jews in Susa permission to do again tomorrow as they have done today, and let the bodies of Haman's ten sons be impaled on a pole."

[14]So the king agreed, and the decree was announced in Susa. And they impaled the bodies of Haman's ten sons. [15]Then the Jews at Susa gathered together on March 8* and killed 300 more men, and again they took no plunder.

[16]Meanwhile, the other Jews throughout the king's provinces had gathered together to defend their lives. They gained relief from all their enemies, killing 75,000 of those who hated them. But they did not take any plunder. [17]This was done throughout the provinces on March 7, and on March 8 they rested,* celebrating their victory with a day of feasting and gladness. [18](The Jews at Susa killed their enemies on March 7 and again on March 8, then rested on March 9,* making that their day of feasting and gladness.) [19]So to this day, rural Jews living in remote villages celebrate an annual festival and holiday on the appointed day in late winter,* when they rejoice and send gifts of food to each other.

The Festival of Purim

[20]Mordecai recorded these events and sent letters to the Jews near and far, throughout all the provinces of King Xerxes, [21]calling on them to celebrate an annual festival on these two days.* [22]He told them to celebrate these days with feasting and gladness and by giving gifts of food to each other and presents to the poor. This would commemorate a time when the Jews gained relief from their enemies, when their sorrow was turned into gladness and their mourning into joy.

[23]So the Jews accepted Mordecai's proposal and adopted this annual custom. [24]Haman son of Hammedatha the Agagite, the enemy of the Jews, had plotted to crush and destroy them on the date determined by casting lots (the lots were called *purim*). [25]But when Esther came before the king, he issued a decree causing Haman's evil plot to backfire, and Haman and his sons were impaled on a sharpened pole. [26]That is why this celebration is called Purim, because it is the ancient word for casting lots.

So because of Mordecai's letter and because of what they had experienced, [27]the Jews throughout the realm agreed to inaugurate this tradition and to pass it on to their descendants and to all who became Jews. They declared they would never fail to celebrate these two prescribed days at the appointed time each year. [28]These days would be remembered and kept from generation to generation and celebrated by every family throughout the provinces and cities of the empire. This Festival of Purim would never cease to be celebrated among the Jews, nor would the memory of what happened ever die out among their descendants.

[29]Then Queen Esther, the daughter of Abihail, along with Mordecai the Jew, wrote another letter putting the queen's full authority behind Mordecai's letter to establish the Festival of Purim. [30]Letters wishing peace and security were sent to the Jews throughout the 127 provinces of the empire of Xerxes. [31]These letters established the Festival of Purim—an annual celebration of these days at the appointed time, decreed by both Mordecai the Jew and Queen Esther. (The people decided to observe this festival, just as they had decided for themselves and their descendants to establish the times of fasting and mourning.) [32]So the command of Esther confirmed the practices of Purim, and it was all written down in the records.

The Greatness of Xerxes and Mordecai

10 King Xerxes imposed a tribute throughout his empire, even to the distant coastlands. [2]His great achievements and the full account of the greatness of Mordecai, whom the king had promoted, are recorded in *The Book of the History of the Kings of Media and Persia.* [3]Mordecai the Jew became the prime minister, with authority next to that of King Xerxes himself. He was very great among the Jews, who held him in high esteem, because he continued to work for the good of his people and to speak up for the welfare of all their descendants.

9:15 Hebrew *the fourteenth day of the month of Adar,* of the ancient Hebrew lunar calendar. This day was March 8, 473 B.C.; also see note on 2:16. **9:17** Hebrew *on the thirteenth day of the month of Adar, and on the fourteenth day they rested.* These days were March 7 and 8, 473 B.C.; also see note on 2:16. **9:18** Hebrew *killed their enemies on the thirteenth day and the fourteenth day, and then rested on the fifteenth day,* of the Hebrew month of Adar. **9:19** Hebrew *on the fourteenth day of the month of Adar.* This day of the ancient Hebrew lunar calendar occurs in February or March. **9:21** Hebrew *on the fourteenth and fifteenth days of Adar,* of the ancient Hebrew lunar calendar.

Job *Faith under trial*

Job is the first of the books of the Bible known as "Wisdom Literature"—a collection of varied styles of writing (proverbs, stories, and poems) that are united by their interest in how life in this world works out in reality with God actively involved in the hopes, joys, and fears of our everyday lives. The polished and poetic language of Job tells a gripping and disturbing story. Job was a good and godly man who, through no fault of his own, lost everything: house, family, and health. But even in the midst of this great suffering, Job refused to abandon his faith in God—though he had lots of questions.

Almost all of the book is set as a poetic dialogue between Job and his friends, as his friends seek to help him understand what is happening, at least from their viewpoint. But Job found their answers unsatisfactory, and only an encounter with the living God settled matters for him.

What's it all about?

The story opens by introducing Job, a devout, prosperous farmer living in the land of Uz, which probably lay east of the Jordan. He was "blameless—a man of complete integrity" (1:1), but Satan came before God and argued that Job worshiped God only because he was so blessed. Satan challenged God to see what would happen if Job experienced misfortune instead. So God gave Satan permission to test Job. Why? Perhaps it was because Job had so much faith in God. Or perhaps it was intended to bring Job closer to God, so he could be blessed even more after his suffering. Satan was allowed to destroy Job's children, livestock, and servants, but Job still continued to trust God. Job was then afflicted with painful boils, and even his wife turned against him. She invited him to curse God and die. But Job remained silent.

Three of Job's friends heard about his misfortunes and came to visit him, hoping to be of help. They were appalled by what they saw, and at first they said nothing. But they soon began to offer their own perspective on events. They blamed Job for his misfortune. After all, bad things only happen to people who do wrong, they said. So there must have been some sin in Job's life that had brought all these disasters on him. Yet Job maintained his innocence throughout his dialogue with them.

Eventually, the three friends ran out of arguments and stopped talking. It was then that a young man called Elihu, who seemed to have been standing on the sidelines listening, spoke up. But he simply repeated what the others had already said, blaming Job for his problems.

OVERVIEW

Job's suffering
1:1–2:13

Job's dialogue with his three friends
3:1–27:23

True wisdom
28:1-28

Job sums up his plight
29:1–31:40

Elihu's speeches
32:1–37:24

God reveals himself to Job
38:1–42:6

Job is restored
42:7-17

Finally, God spoke to them all out of a storm. He rebuked Job's three friends for their empty words and confronted Job with his majesty—which reduces any human being to silence. Job at last realized that what he needed was not answers, but a revelation of God's presence and nature. Finally, God more than restored all Job's good fortunes, including giving him ten children, leaving his friends to rethink their bad advice.

What does it mean for us?

We do not have to look too hard in the world today to see that the harsh realities of human life often include undeserved suffering. At such times, it is inevitable that people ask "Why?" But in such circumstances we should trust God, who holds the intricacies of creation's wonders in his hands and who works things out in ways we do not always understand. The book of Job is therefore good news: The God who loves to bless his people is there to redeem and restore. And it is often in adversity that God's greatness and love are discovered by us afresh.

Job kept his faith in God in the midst of all his suffering. He endured difficulties, misfortunes, and great pressure with steady perseverance (see James 5:11). He serves as an example to us to do the same when things don't go well in our own lives.

Prologue

1 There once was a man named Job who lived in the land of Uz. He was blameless—a man of complete integrity. He feared God and stayed away from evil. 2He had seven sons and three daughters. 3He owned 7,000 sheep, 3,000 camels, 500 teams of oxen, and 500 female donkeys. He also had many servants. He was, in fact, the richest person in that entire area.

4Job's sons would take turns preparing feasts in their homes, and they would also invite their three sisters to celebrate with them. 5When these celebrations ended—sometimes after several days—Job would purify his children. He would get up early in the morning and offer a burnt offering for each of them. For Job said to himself, "Perhaps my children have sinned and have cursed God in their hearts." This was Job's regular practice.

Job's First Test

6One day the members of the heavenly court* came to present themselves before the LORD, and the Accuser, Satan,* came with them. 7"Where have you come from?" the LORD asked Satan.

Satan answered the LORD, "I have been patrolling the earth, watching everything that's going on."

8Then the LORD asked Satan, "Have you noticed my servant Job? He is the finest man in all the earth. He is blameless—a man of complete integrity. He fears God and stays away from evil."

9Satan replied to the LORD, "Yes, but Job has good reason to fear God. 10You have always put a wall of protection around him and his home and his property. You have made him prosper in everything he does. Look how rich he is! 11But reach out and take away everything he has, and he will surely curse you to your face!"

12"All right, you may test him," the LORD said to Satan. "Do whatever you want with everything he possesses, but don't harm him physically." So Satan left the LORD's presence.

13One day when Job's sons and daughters were feasting at the oldest brother's house, 14a messenger arrived at Job's home with this news: "Your oxen were plowing, with the donkeys feeding beside them, 15when the Sabeans raided us. They stole all the animals and killed all the farmhands. I am the only one who escaped to tell you."

16While he was still speaking, another messenger arrived with this news: "The fire of God has fallen from heaven and burned up your sheep and all the shepherds. I am the only one who escaped to tell you."

17While he was still speaking, a third messenger arrived with this news: "Three bands of Chaldean raiders have stolen your camels and killed your servants. I am the only one who escaped to tell you."

18While he was still speaking, another messenger arrived with this news: "Your sons

1:6a Hebrew *the sons of God.* **1:6b** Hebrew *and the satan;* similarly throughout this chapter.

and daughters were feasting in their oldest
brother's home. 19Suddenly, a powerful
wind swept in from the wilderness and hit
the house on all sides. The house collapsed,
and all your children are dead. I am the only
one who escaped to tell you."
20Job stood up and tore his robe in grief.
Then he shaved his head and fell to the
ground to worship. 21He said,

"I came naked from my mother's womb,
and I will be naked when I leave.
The LORD gave me what I had,
and the LORD has taken it away.
Praise the name of the LORD!"

22In all of this, Job did not sin by blaming
God.

Job's Second Test

2 One day the members of the heavenly
court* came again to present themselves before the LORD, and the Accuser,
Satan,* came with them. 2"Where have you
come from?" the LORD asked Satan.
Satan answered the LORD, "I have been
patrolling the earth, watching everything
that's going on."
3Then the LORD asked Satan, "Have you
noticed my servant Job? He is the finest man
in all the earth. He is blameless—a man of
complete integrity. He fears God and stays
away from evil. And he has maintained
his integrity, even though you urged me to
harm him without cause."
4Satan replied to the LORD, "Skin for skin!
A man will give up everything he has to save
his life. 5But reach out and take away his
health, and he will surely curse you to your
face!"
6"All right, do with him as you please,"
the LORD said to Satan. "But spare his life."
7So Satan left the LORD's presence, and he
struck Job with terrible boils from head to
foot.
8Job scraped his skin with a piece of
broken pottery as he sat among the ashes.
9His wife said to him, "Are you still trying
to maintain your integrity? Curse God and
die."
10But Job replied, "You talk like a foolish
woman. Should we accept only good things
from the hand of God and never anything
bad?" So in all this, Job said nothing wrong.

Job's Three Friends Share His Anguish

11When three of Job's friends heard of the
tragedy he had suffered, they got together
and traveled from their homes to comfort
and console him. Their names were Eliphaz
the Temanite, Bildad the Shuhite, and

Satan

Christians often fall into one of two extremes concerning Satan: ascribing too much power to him, or ignoring him completely, forgetting they have a spiritual enemy. The story of Job reminds us that Satan is indeed real and is constantly seeking to oppose God's people, but that his power is limited and that he can do no more than God permits.

His name (Satan) means "the accuser," reflected here in his accusations against Job (Job 1:9-11). He is still found accusing God's people at the end of human history—though his accusations can be easily overcome (Revelation 12:10-11). Traditionally understood to be a fallen angel, based on the prophetic imagery of Isaiah 14:12-15 and Ezekiel 28:12-19, he is also called "the tempter" (Matthew 4:3; see footnote), "the devil" (Matthew 4:5), "the evil one" (John 17:15), and the "serpent" (Revelation 20:2). Satan leads those spiritual forces that are opposed to God. His major tactics against God's people are deceit and temptation.

It is important to remember that Satan is never seen as an "opposite equal" of God. He is merely a created being who became rebellious but who has been completely overcome by Christ at the cross (Colossians 2:15) and who is destined for eternal torment (Revelation 20:7-10).

▶ *See also* ***The origins of Satan****, page 928;* ***Spiritual warfare****, page 1353.*

Zophar the Naamathite. 12 When they saw Job from a distance, they scarcely recognized him. Wailing loudly, they tore their robes and threw dust into the air over their heads to show their grief. 13 Then they sat on the ground with him for seven days and nights. No one said a word to Job, for they saw that his suffering was too great for words.

Job's First Speech

3 At last Job spoke, and he cursed the day of his birth. 2 He said:

3 "Let the day of my birth be erased,
and the night I was conceived.
4 Let that day be turned to darkness.
Let it be lost even to God on high,
and let no light shine on it.
5 Let the darkness and utter gloom claim that day for its own.
Let a black cloud overshadow it,
and let the darkness terrify it.
6 Let that night be blotted off the calendar,
never again to be counted among the days of the year,
never again to appear among the months.
7 Let that night be childless.
Let it have no joy.
8 Let those who are experts at cursing—
whose cursing could rouse Leviathan*—
curse that day.
9 Let its morning stars remain dark.
Let it hope for light, but in vain;
may it never see the morning light.
10 Curse that day for failing to shut my mother's womb,
for letting me be born to see all this trouble.

11 "Why wasn't I born dead?
Why didn't I die as I came from the womb?
12 Why was I laid on my mother's lap?
Why did she nurse me at her breasts?
13 Had I died at birth, I would now be at peace.
I would be asleep and at rest.
14 I would rest with the world's kings and prime ministers,
whose great buildings now lie in ruins.

2:1a Hebrew *the sons of God.* **2:1b** Hebrew *and the satan;* similarly throughout this chapter. **3:8** The identification of Leviathan is disputed, ranging from an earthly creature to a mythical sea monster in ancient literature.

Suffering: Why do bad things happen to good people?

Job's intense suffering led him to ask that abiding question: Why? After all, if he had been wicked, he could have understood. But he was "blameless—a man of complete integrity. He feared God and stayed away from evil" (Job 1:1)—yet everything was going wrong. So several times in Job 3, and repeatedly throughout the book, we find him asking "Why?"

Of course, some suffering can be the result of our own stupidity or sin; but most is simply the result of life in a fallen world, as Jesus explained (Luke 13:1-5; John 9:1-3). Such things happen because sin has gotten into the very fabric of human life (Romans 8:19-22) and will not cease until God's new creation (Revelation 21:4). We should therefore refrain from telling those who suffer that this is the result of their personal sin.

Rather than seeing suffering as an enemy, the Bible encourages us to see it as a friend. After all, Christ embraced suffering, confident that God's glory would be revealed through it (Luke 24:26), and called his followers to do the same (Matthew 16:24-25). Put into God's hands, bad things can turn out for our good—refining our character, changing our attitudes, deepening our dependence on him, revealing our need of others, and preparing us to help others when they suffer—which is why we should rejoice when suffering comes (James 1:2-4). It is merely God's discipline in our lives for our good (Hebrews 12:5-13).

▸ *See also* ***Why do bad things happen in life?***, *page 1025.*

15 I would rest with princes, rich in gold,
whose palaces were filled with silver.
16 Why wasn't I buried like a stillborn child,
like a baby who never lives to see the light?
17 For in death the wicked cause no trouble,
and the weary are at rest.
18 Even captives are at ease in death,
with no guards to curse them.
19 Rich and poor are both there,
and the slave is free from his master.

20 "Oh, why give light to those in misery,
and life to those who are bitter?
21 They long for death, and it won't come.
They search for death more eagerly than for hidden treasure.
22 They're filled with joy when they finally die,
and rejoice when they find the grave.
23 Why is life given to those with no future,
those God has surrounded with difficulties?
24 I cannot eat for sighing;
my groans pour out like water.
25 What I always feared has happened to me.
What I dreaded has come true.
26 I have no peace, no quietness.
I have no rest; only trouble comes."

Eliphaz's First Response to Job

4 Then Eliphaz the Temanite replied to Job:

2 "Will you be patient and let me say a word?
For who could keep from speaking out?
3 "In the past you have encouraged many people;
you have strengthened those who were weak.
4 Your words have supported those who were falling;
you encouraged those with shaky knees.
5 But now when trouble strikes, you lose heart.
You are terrified when it touches you.
6 Doesn't your reverence for God give you confidence?
Doesn't your life of integrity give you hope?

7 "Stop and think! Do the innocent die?
When have the upright been destroyed?
8 My experience shows that those who plant trouble
and cultivate evil will harvest the same.
9 A breath from God destroys them.
They vanish in a blast of his anger.
10 The lion roars and the wildcat snarls,
but the teeth of strong lions will be broken.
11 The fierce lion will starve for lack of prey,
and the cubs of the lioness will be scattered.

12 "This truth was given to me in secret,
as though whispered in my ear.
13 It came to me in a disturbing vision at night,
when people are in a deep sleep.
14 Fear gripped me,
and my bones trembled.
15 A spirit* swept past my face,
and my hair stood on end.*
16 The spirit stopped, but I couldn't see its shape.
There was a form before my eyes.
In the silence I heard a voice say,
17 'Can a mortal be innocent before God?
Can anyone be pure before the Creator?'

18 "If God does not trust his own angels
and has charged his messengers with foolishness,
19 how much less will he trust people made of clay!
They are made of dust, crushed as easily as a moth.
20 They are alive in the morning but dead by evening,
gone forever without a trace.
21 Their tent-cords are pulled and the tent collapses,
and they die in ignorance.

Eliphaz's Response Continues

5 1 "Cry for help, but will anyone answer you?
Which of the angels* will help you?
2 Surely resentment destroys the fool,
and jealousy kills the simple.
3 I have seen that fools may be successful for the moment,
but then comes sudden disaster.

4 Their children are abandoned far from help;
they are crushed in court with no one to defend them.
5 The hungry devour their harvest,
even when it is guarded by brambles.*
The thirsty pant after their wealth.*
6 But evil does not spring from the soil,
and trouble does not sprout from the earth.
7 People are born for trouble
as readily as sparks fly up from a fire.

8 "If I were you, I would go to God
and present my case to him.
9 He does great things too marvelous to understand.
He performs countless miracles.
10 He gives rain for the earth
and water for the fields.
11 He gives prosperity to the poor
and protects those who suffer.
12 He frustrates the plans of schemers
so the work of their hands will not succeed.
13 He traps the wise in their own cleverness
so their cunning schemes are thwarted.
14 They find it is dark in the daytime,
and they grope at noon as if it were night.
15 He rescues the poor from the cutting words of the strong,
and rescues them from the clutches of the powerful.
16 And so at last the poor have hope,
and the snapping jaws of the wicked are shut.

17 "But consider the joy of those corrected by God!
Do not despise the discipline of the Almighty when you sin.
18 For though he wounds, he also bandages.
He strikes, but his hands also heal.
19 From six disasters he will rescue you;
even in the seventh, he will keep you from evil.
20 He will save you from death in time of famine,
from the power of the sword in time of war.
21 You will be safe from slander
and have no fear when destruction comes.
22 You will laugh at destruction and famine;
wild animals will not terrify you.
23 You will be at peace with the stones of the field,
and its wild animals will be at peace with you.
24 You will know that your home is safe.
When you survey your possessions, nothing will be missing.
25 You will have many children;
your descendants will be as plentiful as grass!
26 You will go to the grave at a ripe old age,
like a sheaf of grain harvested at the proper time!

27 "We have studied life and found all this to be true.
Listen to my counsel, and apply it to yourself."

Job's Second Speech: A Response to Eliphaz

6 Then Job spoke again:
2 "If my misery could be weighed
and my troubles be put on the scales,
3 they would outweigh all the sands of the sea.
That is why I spoke impulsively.
4 For the Almighty has struck me down with his arrows.
Their poison infects my spirit.
God's terrors are lined up against me.
5 Don't I have a right to complain?
Don't wild donkeys bray when they find no grass,
and oxen bellow when they have no food?
6 Don't people complain about unsalted food?
Does anyone want the tasteless white of an egg?*
7 My appetite disappears when I look at it;
I gag at the thought of eating it!

8 "Oh, that I might have my request,
that God would grant my desire.
9 I wish he would crush me.
I wish he would reach out his hand and kill me.

4:15a Or *wind;* also in 4:16. **4:15b** Or *its wind sent shivers up my spine.* **5:1** Hebrew *the holy ones.* **5:5a** The meaning of the Hebrew for this phrase is uncertain. **5:5b** As in Greek and Syriac versions; Hebrew reads *A snare snatches their wealth.* **6:6** Or *the tasteless juice of the mallow plant?*

10 At least I can take comfort in this:
Despite the pain,
I have not denied the words of the
Holy One.
11 But I don't have the strength to endure.
I have nothing to live for.
12 Do I have the strength of a stone?
Is my body made of bronze?
13 No, I am utterly helpless,
without any chance of success.

14 "One should be kind to a fainting friend,
but you accuse me without any fear of
the Almighty.*
15 My brothers, you have proved as
unreliable as a seasonal brook
that overflows its banks in the spring
16 when it is swollen with ice and
melting snow.
17 But when the hot weather arrives, the
water disappears.
The brook vanishes in the heat.
18 The caravans turn aside to be refreshed,
but there is nothing to drink, so they
die.
19 The caravans from Tema search for this
water;
the travelers from Sheba hope to
find it.
20 They count on it but are disappointed.
When they arrive, their hopes are
dashed.
21 You, too, have given no help.
You have seen my calamity, and you
are afraid.
22 But why? Have I ever asked you for a
gift?
Have I begged for anything of yours
for myself?
23 Have I asked you to rescue me from my
enemies,
or to save me from ruthless people?
24 Teach me, and I will keep quiet.
Show me what I have done wrong.
25 Honest words can be painful,
but what do your criticisms
amount to?
26 Do you think your words are convincing
when you disregard my cry of
desperation?
27 You would even send an orphan into
slavery*
or sell a friend.
28 Look at me!
Would I lie to your face?
29 Stop assuming my guilt,
for I have done no wrong.
30 Do you think I am lying?
Don't know the difference between
right and wrong?

7

1 "Is not all human life a struggle?
Our lives are like that of a hired
hand,
2 like a worker who longs for the shade,
like a servant waiting to be paid.
3 I, too, have been assigned months of
futility,
long and weary nights of misery.
4 Lying in bed, I think, 'When will it be
morning?'
But the night drags on, and I toss till
dawn.
5 My body is covered with maggots and
scabs.
My skin breaks open, oozing with pus.

Job Cries Out to God

6 "My days fly faster than a weaver's
shuttle.
They end without hope.
7 O God, remember that my life is but a
breath,
and I will never again feel happiness.
8 You see me now, but not for long.
You will look for me, but I will be
gone.
9 Just as a cloud dissipates and vanishes,
those who die* will not come back.
10 They are gone forever from their home—
never to be seen again.

11 "I cannot keep from speaking.
I must express my anguish.
My bitter soul must complain.
12 Am I a sea monster or a dragon
that you must place me under guard?
13 I think, 'My bed will comfort me,
and sleep will ease my misery,'
14 but then you shatter me with dreams
and terrify me with visions.
15 I would rather be strangled—
rather die than suffer like this.
16 I hate my life and don't want to go on
living.
Oh, leave me alone for my few
remaining days.

17 "What are people, that you should make
so much of us,
that you should think of us so often?

18 For you examine us every morning
and test us every moment.
19 Why won't you leave me alone,
at least long enough for me to swallow!
20 If I have sinned, what have I done to
you,
O watcher of all humanity?
Why make me your target?
Am I a burden to you?*
21 Why not just forgive my sin
and take away my guilt?
For soon I will lie down in the dust and
die.
When you look for me, I will be gone."

Bildad's First Response to Job

8 Then Bildad the Shuhite replied to Job:
2 "How long will you go on like this?
You sound like a blustering wind.
3 Does God twist justice?
Does the Almighty twist what is right?
4 Your children must have sinned against
him,
so their punishment was well
deserved.
5 But if you pray to God
and seek the favor of the Almighty,
6 and if you are pure and live with
integrity,
he will surely rise up and restore your
happy home.
7 And though you started with little,
you will end with much.

8 "Just ask the previous generation.
Pay attention to the experience of our
ancestors.
9 For we were born but yesterday and
know nothing.
Our days on earth are as fleeting as a
shadow.
10 But those who came before us will teach
you.
They will teach you the wisdom of old.

11 "Can papyrus reeds grow tall without a
marsh?
Can marsh grass flourish without
water?
12 While they are still flowering, not ready
to be cut,
they begin to wither more quickly
than grass.
13 The same happens to all who forget God.
The hopes of the godless evaporate.
14 Their confidence hangs by a thread.
They are leaning on a spider's web.
15 They cling to their home for security, but
it won't last.
They try to hold it tight, but it will not
endure.
16 The godless seem like a lush plant
growing in the sunshine,
its branches spreading across the
garden.
17 Its roots grow down through a pile of
stones;
it takes hold on a bed of rocks.
18 But when it is uprooted,
it's as though it never existed!
19 That's the end of its life,
and others spring up from the earth to
replace it.

20 "But look, God will not reject a person of
integrity,
nor will he lend a hand to the wicked.
21 He will once again fill your mouth with
laughter
and your lips with shouts of joy.
22 Those who hate you will be clothed with
shame,
and the home of the wicked will be
destroyed."

Job's Third Speech: A Response to Bildad

9 Then Job spoke again:
2 "Yes, I know all this is true in
principle.
But how can a person be declared
innocent in God's sight?
3 If someone wanted to take God to court,*
would it be possible to answer him
even once in a thousand times?
4 For God is so wise and so mighty.
Who has ever challenged him
successfully?

5 "Without warning, he moves the
mountains,
overturning them in his anger.
6 He shakes the earth from its place,
and its foundations tremble.
7 If he commands it, the sun won't rise
and the stars won't shine.
8 He alone has spread out the heavens
and marches on the waves of the sea.

6:14 Or *friend, / or he might lose his fear of the Almighty.* **6:27** Hebrew *even gamble over an orphan.* **7:9** Hebrew *who go down to Sheol.* **7:20** As in Greek version; Hebrew reads *target, so that I am a burden to myself?* **9:3** Or *If God wanted to take someone to court.*

9 He made all the stars—the Bear and Orion,
the Pleiades and the constellations of the southern sky.
10 He does great things too marvelous to understand.
He performs countless miracles.

11 "Yet when he comes near, I cannot see him.
When he moves by, I do not see him go.
12 If he snatches someone in death, who can stop him?
Who dares to ask, 'What are you doing?'
13 And God does not restrain his anger.
Even the monsters of the sea* are crushed beneath his feet.

14 "So who am I, that I should try to answer God
or even reason with him?
15 Even if I were right, I would have no defense.
I could only plead for mercy.
16 And even if I summoned him and he responded,
I'm not sure he would listen to me.
17 For he attacks me with a storm
and repeatedly wounds me without cause.
18 He will not let me catch my breath,
but fills me instead with bitter sorrows.
19 If it's a question of strength, he's the strong one.
If it's a matter of justice, who dares to summon him* to court?
20 Though I am innocent, my own mouth would pronounce me guilty.
Though I am blameless, it* would prove me wicked.

21 "I am innocent,
but it makes no difference to me—
I despise my life.
22 Innocent or wicked, it is all the same to God.
That's why I say, 'He destroys both the blameless and the wicked.'
23 When a plague* sweeps through,
he laughs at the death of the innocent.
24 The whole earth is in the hands of the wicked,
and God blinds the eyes of the judges.
If he's not the one who does it, who is?

25 "My life passes more swiftly than a runner.
It flees away without a glimpse of happiness.
26 It disappears like a swift papyrus boat,
like an eagle swooping down on its prey.
27 If I decided to forget my complaints,
to put away my sad face and be cheerful,
28 I would still dread all the pain,
for I know you will not find me innocent, O God.
29 Whatever happens, I will be found guilty.
So what's the use of trying?
30 Even if I were to wash myself with soap
and clean my hands with lye,
31 you would plunge me into a muddy ditch,
and my own filthy clothing would hate me.

32 "God is not a mortal like me,
so I cannot argue with him or take him to trial.
33 If only there were a mediator between us,
someone who could bring us together.
34 The mediator could make God stop beating me,
and I would no longer live in terror of his punishment.
35 Then I could speak to him without fear,
but I cannot do that in my own strength.

Job Frames His Plea to God

10 1 "I am disgusted with my life.
Let me complain freely.
My bitter soul must complain.
2 I will say to God, 'Don't simply condemn me—
tell me the charge you are bringing against me.
3 What do you gain by oppressing me?
Why do you reject me, the work of your own hands,
while smiling on the schemes of the wicked?
4 Are your eyes like those of a human?
Do you see things only as people see them?
5 Is your lifetime only as long as ours?
Is your life so short
6 that you must quickly probe for my guilt
and search for my sin?

▸ **10:1** *See **Does God mind if we are honest with him?**, page 848.*

7 Although you know I am not guilty,
no one can rescue me from your hands.
8 "'You formed me with your hands; you made me,
yet now you completely destroy me.
9 Remember that you made me from dust—
will you turn me back to dust so soon?
10 You guided my conception
and formed me in the womb.*
11 You clothed me with skin and flesh,
and you knit my bones and sinews together.
12 You gave me life and showed me your unfailing love.
My life was preserved by your care.

13 "'Yet your real motive—
your true intent—
14 was to watch me, and if I sinned,
you would not forgive my guilt.
15 If I am guilty, too bad for me;
and even if I'm innocent, I can't hold my head high,
because I am filled with shame and misery.
16 And if I hold my head high, you hunt me like a lion
and display your awesome power against me.
17 Again and again you witness against me.
You pour out your growing anger on me
and bring fresh armies against me.

18 "'Why, then, did you deliver me from my mother's womb?
Why didn't you let me die at birth?
19 It would be as though I had never existed,
going directly from the womb to the grave.
20 I have only a few days left, so leave me alone,
that I may have a moment of comfort
21 before I leave—never to return—
for the land of darkness and utter gloom.
22 It is a land as dark as midnight,
a land of gloom and confusion,
where even the light is dark as midnight.'"

Zophar's First Response to Job

11 Then Zophar the Naamathite replied to Job:

2 "Shouldn't someone answer this torrent of words?
Is a person proved innocent just by a lot of talking?
3 Should I remain silent while you babble on?
When you mock God, shouldn't someone make you ashamed?
4 You claim, 'My beliefs are pure,'
and 'I am clean in the sight of God.'
5 If only God would speak;
if only he would tell you what he thinks!
6 If only he would tell you the secrets of wisdom,
for true wisdom is not a simple matter.
Listen! God is doubtless punishing you
far less than you deserve!

7 "Can you solve the mysteries of God?
Can you discover everything about the Almighty?
8 Such knowledge is higher than the heavens—
and who are you?
It is deeper than the underworld*—
what do you know?
9 It is broader than the earth
and wider than the sea.
10 If God comes and puts a person in prison
or calls the court to order, who can stop him?
11 For he knows those who are false,
and he takes note of all their sins.
12 An empty-headed person won't become wise
any more than a wild donkey can bear a human child.*

13 "If only you would prepare your heart
and lift up your hands to him in prayer!
14 Get rid of your sins,
and leave all iniquity behind you.
15 Then your face will brighten with innocence.
You will be strong and free of fear.

9:13 Hebrew *the helpers of Rahab,* the name of a mythical sea monster that represents chaos in ancient literature. **9:19** As in Greek version; Hebrew reads *me.* **9:20** Or *he.* **9:23** Or *disaster.* **10:10** Hebrew *You poured me out like milk / and curdled me like cheese.* **11:8** Hebrew *than Sheol.* **11:12** Or *than a wild male donkey can bear a tame colt.*

16 You will forget your misery;
it will be like water flowing away.
17 Your life will be brighter than the noonday.
Even darkness will be as bright as morning.
18 Having hope will give you courage.
You will be protected and will rest in safety.
19 You will lie down unafraid,
and many will look to you for help.
20 But the wicked will be blinded.
They will have no escape.
Their only hope is death."

Job's Fourth Speech: A Response to Zophar

12 Then Job spoke again:
2 "You people really know everything, don't you?
And when you die, wisdom will die with you!
3 Well, I know a few things myself—
and you're no better than I am.
Who doesn't know these things you've been saying?
4 Yet my friends laugh at me,
for I call on God and expect an answer.
I am a just and blameless man,
yet they laugh at me.
5 People who are at ease mock those in trouble.
They give a push to people who are stumbling.
6 But robbers are left in peace,
and those who provoke God live in safety—
though God keeps them in his power.*

7 "Just ask the animals, and they will teach you.
Ask the birds of the sky, and they will tell you.
8 Speak to the earth, and it will instruct you.
Let the fish in the sea speak to you.
9 For they all know
that my disaster* has come from the hand of the LORD.
10 For the life of every living thing is in his hand,
and the breath of every human being.
11 The ear tests the words it hears
just as the mouth distinguishes between foods.
12 Wisdom belongs to the aged,
and understanding to the old.

13 "But true wisdom and power are found in God;
counsel and understanding are his.
14 What he destroys cannot be rebuilt.
When he puts someone in prison,
there is no escape.
15 If he holds back the rain, the earth becomes a desert.
If he releases the waters, they flood the earth.
16 Yes, strength and wisdom are his;
deceivers and deceived are both in his power.
17 He leads counselors away, stripped of good judgment;
wise judges become fools.
18 He removes the royal robe of kings.
They are led away with ropes around their waist.
19 He leads priests away, stripped of status;
he overthrows those with long years in power.
20 He silences the trusted adviser
and removes the insight of the elders.
21 He pours disgrace upon princes
and disarms the strong.

22 "He uncovers mysteries hidden in darkness;
he brings light to the deepest gloom.
23 He builds up nations, and he destroys them.
He expands nations, and he abandons them.
24 He strips kings of understanding
and leaves them wandering in a pathless wasteland.
25 They grope in the darkness without a light.
He makes them stagger like drunkards.

Job Wants to Argue His Case with God

13 1 "Look, I have seen all this with my own eyes
and heard it with my own ears, and now I understand.
2 I know as much as you do.
You are no better than I am.
3 As for me, I would speak directly to the Almighty.
I want to argue my case with God himself.

4 As for you, you smear me with lies.
As physicians, you are worthless quacks.
5 If only you could be silent!
That's the wisest thing you could do.
6 Listen to my charge;
pay attention to my arguments.

7 "Are you defending God with lies?
Do you make your dishonest arguments for his sake?
8 Will you slant your testimony in his favor?
Will you argue God's case for him?
9 What will happen when he finds out what you are doing?
Can you fool him as easily as you fool people?
10 No, you will be in trouble with him
if you secretly slant your testimony in his favor.
11 Doesn't his majesty terrify you?
Doesn't your fear of him overwhelm you?
12 Your platitudes are as valuable as ashes.
Your defense is as fragile as a clay pot.

13 "Be silent now and leave me alone.
Let me speak, and I will face the consequences.
14 Why should I put myself in mortal danger*
and take my life in my own hands?
15 God might kill me, but I have no other hope.*
I am going to argue my case with him.
16 But this is what will save me—I am not godless.
If I were, I could not stand before him.

17 "Listen closely to what I am about to say.
Hear me out.
18 I have prepared my case;
I will be proved innocent.
19 Who can argue with me over this?
And if you prove me wrong, I will remain silent and die.

Job Asks How He Has Sinned

20 "O God, grant me these two things,
and then I will be able to face you.
21 Remove your heavy hand from me,
and don't terrify me with your awesome presence.
22 Now summon me, and I will answer!
Or let me speak to you, and you reply.

12:6 Or *safety—those who try to manipulate God.* The meaning of the Hebrew is uncertain. **12:9** Hebrew *that this.* **13:14** Hebrew *Why should I take my flesh in my teeth.* **13:15** An alternate reading in the Masoretic Text reads *God might kill me, but I hope in him.*

Being there

Job had become weary of his three friends' words. He had heard it all before, knew their answers better than they did (Job 13:1-2), and just longed for them to be quiet (13:5). What his friends failed to understand was that there are times when people do not need our words; they just need us. They need us to simply be there with them and, by our simple presence, be a support in their time of need.

That's what Jesus wanted in Gethsemane (Matthew 26:36-46) when he took Peter, James, and John with him. He didn't need answers from them (he knew far better than them what was happening!); he just wanted them there so he could be encouraged and draw support from their presence. It's what Paul wanted when, alone and chained up in prison, he lamented his friends not being with him (2 Timothy 4:9-11).

Having friends who will simply be there in difficult times brings immense support. When a friend is going through hard times, we should not feel we have to come up with answers. Just sitting with someone who has been bereaved or received bad news can bring tremendous emotional and spiritual support. It is a tangible expression of the God who is always there.

▸ *See also* ***The power of encouragement****, page 578;* ***Friendship****, page 725.*

23 Tell me, what have I done wrong?
Show me my rebellion and my sin.
24 Why do you turn away from me?
Why do you treat me as your enemy?
25 Would you terrify a leaf blown by the wind?
Would you chase dry straw?

26 "You write bitter accusations against me
and bring up all the sins of my youth.
27 You put my feet in stocks.
You examine all my paths.
You trace all my footprints.
28 I waste away like rotting wood,
like a moth-eaten coat.

14

1 "How frail is humanity!
How short is life, how full of trouble!
2 We blossom like a flower and then wither.
Like a passing shadow, we quickly disappear.
3 Must you keep an eye on such a frail creature
and demand an accounting from me?
4 Who can bring purity out of an impure person?
No one!
5 You have decided the length of our lives.
You know how many months we will live,
and we are not given a minute longer.
6 So leave us alone and let us rest!
We are like hired hands, so let us finish our work in peace.

7 "Even a tree has more hope!
If it is cut down, it will sprout again
and grow new branches.
8 Though its roots have grown old in the earth
and its stump decays,
9 at the scent of water it will bud
and sprout again like a new seedling.

10 "But when people die, their strength is gone.
They breathe their last, and then where are they?
11 As water evaporates from a lake
and a river disappears in drought,
12 people are laid to rest and do not rise again.
Until the heavens are no more, they will not wake up
nor be roused from their sleep.

13 "I wish you would hide me in the grave*
and forget me there until your anger has passed.
But mark your calendar to think of me again!
14 Can the dead live again?
If so, this would give me hope through all my years of struggle,
and I would eagerly await the release of death.
15 You would call and I would answer,
and you would yearn for me, your handiwork.
16 For then you would guard my steps,
instead of watching for my sins.
17 My sins would be sealed in a pouch,
and you would cover my guilt.

18 "But instead, as mountains fall and crumble
and as rocks fall from a cliff,
19 as water wears away the stones
and floods wash away the soil,
so you destroy people's hope.
20 You always overpower them, and they pass from the scene.
You disfigure them in death and send them away.
21 They never know if their children grow up in honor
or sink to insignificance.
22 They suffer painfully;
their life is full of trouble."

Eliphaz's Second Response to Job

15

Then Eliphaz the Temanite replied:
2 "A wise man wouldn't answer with such empty talk!
You are nothing but a windbag.
3 The wise don't engage in empty chatter.
What good are such words?
4 Have you no fear of God,
no reverence for him?
5 Your sins are telling your mouth what to say.
Your words are based on clever deception.
6 Your own mouth condemns you, not I.
Your own lips testify against you.

7 "Were you the first person ever born?
Were you born before the hills were made?
8 Were you listening at God's secret council?
Do you have a monopoly on wisdom?

[9] What do you know that we don't?
What do you understand that we do not?
[10] On our side are aged, gray-haired men
much older than your father!

[11] "Is God's comfort too little for you?
Is his gentle word not enough?
[12] What has taken away your reason?
What has weakened your vision,*
[13] that you turn against God
and say all these evil things?
[14] Can any mortal be pure?
Can anyone born of a woman be just?
[15] Look, God does not even trust the angels.*
Even the heavens are not absolutely pure in his sight.
[16] How much less pure is a corrupt and sinful person
with a thirst for wickedness!

[17] "If you will listen, I will show you.
I will answer you from my own experience.
[18] And it is confirmed by the reports of wise men
who have heard the same thing from their fathers—
[19] from those to whom the land was given
long before any foreigners arrived.

[20] "The wicked writhe in pain throughout their lives.
Years of trouble are stored up for the ruthless.
[21] The sound of terror rings in their ears,
and even on good days they fear the attack of the destroyer.
[22] They dare not go out into the darkness
for fear they will be murdered.
[23] They wander around, saying, 'Where can I find bread?'*
They know their day of destruction is near.
[24] That dark day terrifies them.
They live in distress and anguish,
like a king preparing for battle.
[25] For they shake their fists at God,
defying the Almighty.
[26] Holding their strong shields,
they defiantly charge against him.

[27] "These wicked people are heavy and prosperous;
their waists bulge with fat.
[28] But their cities will be ruined.
They will live in abandoned houses
that are ready to tumble down.
[29] Their riches will not last,
and their wealth will not endure.
Their possessions will no longer
spread across the horizon.

[30] "They will not escape the darkness.
The burning sun will wither their shoots,
and the breath of God will destroy them.
[31] Let them no longer fool themselves by trusting in empty riches,
for emptiness will be their only reward.
[32] They will be cut down in the prime of life;
their branches will never again be green.
[33] They will be like a vine whose grapes are harvested too early,
like an olive tree that loses its blossoms before the fruit can form.
[34] For the godless are barren.
Their homes, enriched through bribery, will burn.
[35] They conceive trouble and give birth to evil.
Their womb produces deceit."

Job's Fifth Speech: A Response to Eliphaz

16 Then Job spoke again:
[2] "I have heard all this before.
What miserable comforters you are!
[3] Won't you ever stop blowing hot air?
What makes you keep on talking?
[4] I could say the same things if you were in my place.
I could spout off criticism and shake my head at you.
[5] But if it were me, I would encourage you.
I would try to take away your grief.
[6] Instead, I suffer if I defend myself,
and I suffer no less if I refuse to speak.

[7] "O God, you have ground me down
and devastated my family.
[8] As if to prove I have sinned, you've
reduced me to skin and bones.
My gaunt flesh testifies against me.

14:13 Hebrew *in Sheol.* **15:12** Or *Why do your eyes flash with anger;* Hebrew reads *Why do your eyes blink.* **15:15** Hebrew *the holy ones.* **15:23** Greek version reads *He is appointed to be food for a vulture.*

9 God hates me and angrily tears me
apart.
He snaps his teeth at me
and pierces me with his eyes.
10 People jeer and laugh at me.
They slap my cheek in contempt.
A mob gathers against me.
11 God has handed me over to sinners.
He has tossed me into the hands of
the wicked.

12 "I was living quietly until he
shattered me.
He took me by the neck and broke me
in pieces.
Then he set me up as his target,
13 and now his archers surround me.
His arrows pierce me without mercy.
The ground is wet with my blood.*
14 Again and again he smashes against me,
charging at me like a warrior.
15 I wear burlap to show my grief.
My pride lies in the dust.
16 My eyes are red with weeping;
dark shadows circle my eyes.
17 Yet I have done no wrong,
and my prayer is pure.

18 "O earth, do not conceal my blood.
Let it cry out on my behalf.
19 Even now my witness is in heaven.
My advocate is there on high.
20 My friends scorn me,
but I pour out my tears to God.
21 I need someone to mediate between God
and me,
as a person mediates between friends.
22 For soon I must go down that road
from which I will never return.

Job Continues to Defend His Innocence

17 1 "My spirit is crushed,
and my life is nearly snuffed
out.
The grave is ready to receive me.
2 I am surrounded by mockers.
I watch how bitterly they taunt me.

3 "You must defend my innocence, O God,
since no one else will stand up for me.
4 You have closed their minds to
understanding,
but do not let them triumph.
5 They betray their friends for their own
advantage,
so let their children faint with hunger.

6 "God has made a mockery of me among
the people;
they spit in my face.
7 My eyes are swollen with weeping,
and I am but a shadow of my former
self.
8 The virtuous are horrified when they
see me.
The innocent rise up against the
ungodly.
9 The righteous keep moving forward,
and those with clean hands become
stronger and stronger.

10 "As for all of you, come back with a
better argument,
though I still won't find a wise man
among you.
11 My days are over.
My hopes have disappeared.
My heart's desires are
broken.

The power of encouragement

What Job really needed was encouragement, not lectures from these "miserable comforters" (Job 16:2). There is nothing weak about needing encouragement—God encouraged Joshua (Joshua 1:1-9); Jonathan encouraged David (1 Samuel 23:16); Jesus needed encouragement in Gethsemane (Matthew 26:36-38); Paul rejoiced that "God, who encourages those who are discouraged, encouraged us by the arrival of Titus" (2 Corinthians 7:6). But if we want to receive encouragement, then we need to be ready to give it too. A man called Joseph was a great encourager—so much so that the apostles nicknamed him "Barnabas," meaning "Son of Encouragement" (Acts 4:36). Encouragement had a big place in the early church (e.g., Acts 11:23; 14:22; 15:32; 16:40; 20:1-2; 28:15).

▸ *See also* ***Being there****, page 575;* ***Barnabas****, page 1242.*

12 These men say that night is day;
they claim that the darkness is light.
13 What if I go to the grave*
and make my bed in darkness?
14 What if I call the grave my father,
and the maggot my mother or my sister?
15 Where then is my hope?
Can anyone find it?
16 No, my hope will go down with me to the grave.
We will rest together in the dust!"

Bildad's Second Response to Job

18 Then Bildad the Shuhite replied:
2 "How long before you stop talking?
Speak sense if you want us to answer!
3 Do you think we are mere animals?
Do you think we are stupid?
4 You may tear out your hair in anger,
but will that destroy the earth?
Will it make the rocks tremble?

5 "Surely the light of the wicked will be snuffed out.
The sparks of their fire will not glow.
6 The light in their tent will grow dark.
The lamp hanging above them will be quenched.
7 The confident stride of the wicked will be shortened.
Their own schemes will be their downfall.
8 The wicked walk into a net.
They fall into a pit.
9 A trap grabs them by the heel.
A snare holds them tight.
10 A noose lies hidden on the ground.
A rope is stretched across their path.
11 "Terrors surround the wicked
and trouble them at every step.
12 Hunger depletes their strength,
and calamity waits for them to stumble.
13 Disease eats their skin;
death devours their limbs.
14 They are torn from the security of their homes
and are brought down to the king of terrors.
15 The homes of the wicked will burn down;
burning sulfur rains on their houses.
16 Their roots will dry up,
and their branches will wither.
17 All memory of their existence will fade from the earth;
no one will remember their names.
18 They will be thrust from light into darkness,
driven from the world.
19 They will have neither children nor grandchildren,
nor any survivor in the place where they lived.
20 People in the west are appalled at their fate;
people in the east are horrified.
21 They will say, 'This was the home of a wicked person,
the place of one who rejected God.'"

Job's Sixth Speech: A Response to Bildad

19 Then Job spoke again:
2 "How long will you torture me?
How long will you try to crush me with your words?
3 You have already insulted me ten times.
You should be ashamed of treating me so badly.
4 Even if I have sinned,
that is my concern, not yours.
5 You think you're better than I am,
using my humiliation as evidence of my sin.
6 But it is God who has wronged me,
capturing me in his net.*

7 "I cry out, 'Help!' but no one answers me.
I protest, but there is no justice.
8 God has blocked my way so I cannot move.
He has plunged my path into darkness.
9 He has stripped me of my honor
and removed the crown from my head.
10 He has demolished me on every side,
and I am finished.
He has uprooted my hope like a fallen tree.
11 His fury burns against me;
he counts me as an enemy.
12 His troops advance.
They build up roads to attack me.
They camp all around my tent.

16:13 Hebrew *my gall.* **17:13** Hebrew *to Sheol;* also in 17:16.
19:6 Or *for I am like a city under siege.*

[13] "My relatives stay far away,
and my friends have turned against me.
[14] My family is gone,
and my close friends have forgotten me.
[15] My servants and maids consider me a stranger.
I am like a foreigner to them.
[16] When I call my servant, he doesn't come;
I have to plead with him!
[17] My breath is repulsive to my wife.
I am rejected by my own family.
[18] Even young children despise me.
When I stand to speak, they turn their backs on me.
[19] My close friends detest me.
Those I loved have turned against me.
[20] I have been reduced to skin and bones
and have escaped death by the skin of my teeth.

[21] "Have mercy on me, my friends, have mercy,
for the hand of God has struck me.
[22] Must you also persecute me, like God does?
Haven't you chewed me up enough?

[23] "Oh, that my words could be recorded.
Oh, that they could be inscribed on a monument,
[24] carved with an iron chisel and filled with lead,
engraved forever in the rock.

[25] "But as for me, I know that my Redeemer lives,
and he will stand upon the earth at last.
[26] And after my body has decayed,
yet in my body I will see God!*
[27] I will see him for myself.
Yes, I will see him with my own eyes.
I am overwhelmed at the thought!

[28] "How dare you go on persecuting me,
saying, 'It's his own fault'?
[29] You should fear punishment yourselves,
for your attitude deserves punishment.
Then you will know that there is indeed a judgment."

Zophar's Second Response to Job

20 Then Zophar the Naamathite replied:
[2] "I must reply
because I am greatly disturbed.
[3] I've had to endure your insults,
but now my spirit prompts me to reply.

[4] "Don't you realize that from the beginning of time,
ever since people were first placed on the earth,

Loneliness

"It is not good for the man to be alone" (Genesis 2:18). From the very beginning, God's intention for human beings was for them to live in community with others. Yet one expression of sin's wickedness is that it seeks to break that sense of community and to leave people feeling isolated, unloved, and unwanted.

Loneliness can have a variety of causes. Sometimes it is the result of our own sin: Cain was banished because he murdered his brother Abel (Genesis 4:10-16), Zacchaeus was friendless because of his corrupt tax collecting (Luke 19:1-10), and the woman at the well was an outcast because of her sexual immorality (John 4:1-42). But often loneliness comes simply from living in a fallen world, through things like abandonment (2 Timothy 4:16), bereavement (Luke 7:12), depression (1 Kings 19:3-4), or old age (2 Samuel 19:34-35). It can even arise from God's call on our lives (1 Kings 19:10; Jeremiah 15:16-17). Job felt alone not only because some had abandoned him but also because his three friends failed to understand his situation (Job 19:13-14).

Whatever the cause of our loneliness, we should remember that even Jesus experienced loneliness (Matthew 27:46) and can therefore understand our feelings of loneliness and comfort us. Above all, we should remember that "Even if my father and mother abandon me, the LORD will hold me close" (Psalm 27:10).

5 the triumph of the wicked has been short lived
and the joy of the godless has been only temporary?
6 Though the pride of the godless reaches to the heavens
and their heads touch the clouds,
7 yet they will vanish forever,
thrown away like their own dung.
Those who knew them will ask,
'Where are they?'
8 They will fade like a dream and not be found.
They will vanish like a vision in the night.
9 Those who once saw them will see them no more.
Their families will never see them again.
10 Their children will beg from the poor,
for they must give back their stolen riches.
11 Though they are young,
their bones will lie in the dust.

12 "They enjoyed the sweet taste of wickedness,
letting it melt under their tongue.
13 They savored it,
holding it long in their mouths.
14 But suddenly the food in their bellies turns sour,
a poisonous venom in their stomach.
15 They will vomit the wealth they swallowed.
God won't let them keep it down.
16 They will suck the poison of cobras.
The viper will kill them.
17 They will never again enjoy streams of olive oil
or rivers of milk and honey.
18 They will give back everything they worked for.
Their wealth will bring them no joy.
19 For they oppressed the poor and left them destitute.
They foreclosed on their homes.
20 They were always greedy and never satisfied.
Nothing remains of all the things they dreamed about.
21 Nothing is left after they finish gorging themselves.
Therefore, their prosperity will not endure.

22 "In the midst of plenty, they will run into trouble
and be overcome by misery.
23 May God give them a bellyful of trouble.
May God rain down his anger upon them.
24 When they try to escape an iron weapon,
a bronze-tipped arrow will pierce them.
25 The arrow is pulled from their back,
and the arrowhead glistens with blood.*
The terrors of death are upon them.
26 Their treasures will be thrown into deepest darkness.
A wildfire will devour their goods,
consuming all they have left.
27 The heavens will reveal their guilt,
and the earth will testify against them.
28 A flood will sweep away their house.
God's anger will descend on them in torrents.
29 This is the reward that God gives the wicked.
It is the inheritance decreed by God."

Job's Seventh Speech: A Response to Zophar

21 Then Job spoke again:
2 "Listen closely to what I am saying.
That's one consolation you can give me.
3 Bear with me, and let me speak.
After I have spoken, you may resume mocking me.

4 "My complaint is with God, not with people.
I have good reason to be so impatient.
5 Look at me and be stunned.
Put your hand over your mouth in shock.
6 When I think about what I am saying,
I shudder.
My body trembles.

7 "Why do the wicked prosper,
growing old and powerful?
8 They live to see their children grow up and settle down,
and they enjoy their grandchildren.

19:26 Or *without my body I will see God.* The meaning of the Hebrew is uncertain. **20:25** Hebrew *with gall.*

9 Their homes are safe from every fear,
and God does not punish them.
10 Their bulls never fail to breed.
Their cows bear calves and never miscarry.
11 They let their children frisk about like lambs.
Their little ones skip and dance.
12 They sing with tambourine and harp.
They celebrate to the sound of the flute.
13 They spend their days in prosperity,
then go down to the grave* in peace.
14 And yet they say to God, 'Go away.
We want no part of you and your ways.
15 Who is the Almighty, and why should we obey him?
What good will it do us to pray?'
16 (They think their prosperity is of their own doing,
but I will have nothing to do with that kind of thinking.)

17 "Yet the light of the wicked never seems to be extinguished.
Do they ever have trouble?
Does God distribute sorrows to them in anger?
18 Are they driven before the wind like straw?
Are they carried away by the storm like chaff?
Not at all!

19 "'Well,' you say, 'at least God will punish their children!'
But I say he should punish the ones who sin,
so that they understand his judgment.
20 Let them see their destruction with their own eyes.
Let them drink deeply of the anger of the Almighty.
21 For they will not care what happens to their family
after they are dead.

22 "But who can teach a lesson to God,
since he judges even the most powerful?
23 One person dies in prosperity,
completely comfortable and secure,
24 the picture of good health,
vigorous and fit.
25 Another person dies in bitter poverty,
never having tasted the good life.
26 But both are buried in the same dust,
both eaten by the same maggots.

27 "Look, I know what you're thinking.
I know the schemes you plot against me.
28 You will tell me of rich and wicked people
whose houses have vanished because of their sins.
29 But ask those who have been around,
and they will tell you the truth.
30 Evil people are spared in times of calamity
and are allowed to escape disaster.
31 No one criticizes them openly
or pays them back for what they have done.
32 When they are carried to the grave,
an honor guard keeps watch at their tomb.
33 A great funeral procession goes to the cemetery.
Many pay their respects as the body is laid to rest,
and the earth gives sweet repose.

34 "How can your empty clichés comfort me?
All your explanations are lies!"

Eliphaz's Third Response to Job

22 Then Eliphaz the Temanite replied:
2 "Can a person do anything to help God?
Can even a wise person be helpful to him?
3 Is it any advantage to the Almighty if you are righteous?
Would it be any gain to him if you were perfect?
4 Is it because you're so pious that he accuses you
and brings judgment against you?
5 No, it's because of your wickedness!
There's no limit to your sins.

6 "For example, you must have lent money to your friend
and demanded clothing as security.
Yes, you stripped him to the bone.
7 You must have refused water for the thirsty
and food for the hungry.
8 You probably think the land belongs to the powerful

and only the privileged have a right
to it!
9 You must have sent widows away
empty-handed
and crushed the hopes of orphans.
10 That is why you are surrounded by
traps
and tremble from sudden fears.
11 That is why you cannot see in the
darkness,
and waves of water cover you.

12 "God is so great—higher than the
heavens,
higher than the farthest stars.
13 But you reply, 'That's why God can't see
what I am doing!
How can he judge through the thick
darkness?
14 For thick clouds swirl about him, and he
cannot see us.
He is way up there, walking on the
vault of heaven.'

15 "Will you continue on the old paths
where evil people have walked?
16 They were snatched away in the prime
of life,
the foundations of their lives washed
away.
17 For they said to God, 'Leave us alone!
What can the Almighty do to us?'
18 Yet he was the one who filled their
homes with good things,
so I will have nothing to do with that
kind of thinking.

19 "The righteous will be happy to see the
wicked destroyed,
and the innocent will laugh in
contempt.
20 They will say, 'See how our enemies
have been destroyed.
The last of them have been consumed
in the fire.'

21 "Submit to God, and you will have
peace;
then things will go well for you.
22 Listen to his instructions,
and store them in your heart.
23 If you return to the Almighty, you will
be restored—
so clean up your life.
24 If you give up your lust for money
and throw your precious gold into the
river,
25 the Almighty himself will be your
treasure.
He will be your precious silver!

26 "Then you will take delight in the
Almighty
and look up to God.
27 You will pray to him, and he will hear
you,
and you will fulfill your vows to him.
28 You will succeed in whatever you choose
to do,
and light will shine on the road ahead
of you.
29 If people are in trouble and you say,
'Help them,'
God will save them.
30 Even sinners will be rescued;
they will be rescued because your
hands are pure."

Job's Eighth Speech: A Response to Eliphaz

23 Then Job spoke again:
2 "My complaint today is still a
bitter one,
and I try hard not to groan aloud.
3 If only I knew where to find God,
I would go to his court.
4 I would lay out my case
and present my arguments.
5 Then I would listen to his reply
and understand what he says to me.
6 Would he use his great power to argue
with me?
No, he would give me a fair hearing.
7 Honest people can reason with him,
so I would be forever acquitted by my
judge.
8 I go east, but he is not there.
I go west, but I cannot find him.
9 I do not see him in the north, for he is
hidden.
I look to the south, but he is
concealed.

10 "But he knows where I am going.
And when he tests me, I will come out
as pure as gold.
11 For I have stayed on God's paths;
I have followed his ways and not
turned aside.
12 I have not departed from his commands,
but have treasured his words more
than daily food.

21:13 Hebrew *to Sheol.*

[13] But once he has made his decision, who
can change his mind?
Whatever he wants to do, he does.
[14] So he will do to me whatever he has
planned.
He controls my destiny.
[15] No wonder I am so terrified in his
presence.
When I think of it, terror grips me.
[16] God has made me sick at heart;
the Almighty has terrified me.
[17] Darkness is all around me;
thick, impenetrable darkness is
everywhere.

Job Asks Why the Wicked Are Not Punished

24 [1] "Why doesn't the Almighty bring
the wicked to judgment?
Why must the godly wait for him in
vain?
[2] Evil people steal land by moving the
boundary markers.
They steal livestock and put them in
their own pastures.
[3] They take the orphan's donkey
and demand the widow's ox as
security for a loan.
[4] The poor are pushed off the path;
the needy must hide together for safety.
[5] Like wild donkeys in the wilderness,
the poor must spend all their time
looking for food,
searching even in the desert for food
for their children.
[6] They harvest a field they do not own,
and they glean in the vineyards of the
wicked.
[7] All night they lie naked in the cold,
without clothing or covering.
[8] They are soaked by mountain showers,
and they huddle against the rocks for
want of a home.

[9] "The wicked snatch a widow's child
from her breast,
taking the baby as security for a loan.
[10] The poor must go about naked, without
any clothing.
They harvest food for others while
they themselves are starving.
[11] They press out olive oil without being
allowed to taste it,
and they tread in the winepress as
they suffer from thirst.
[12] The groans of the dying rise from the
city,
and the wounded cry for help,
yet God ignores their moaning.

[13] "Wicked people rebel against the light.
They refuse to acknowledge its ways
or stay in its paths.
[14] The murderer rises in the early dawn
to kill the poor and needy;
at night he is a thief.

God's sovereignty

One of the things that Job needed to learn about God was that he does "whatever he wants to do" (Job 23:13), not what we want him to do, no matter how badly we might want it or plead for it. God is absolutely free in his decisions (Psalm 135:6) and absolutely able to fulfill those decisions (Luke 1:37), whatever might come against him (2 Chronicles 20:6). And because he is God, no one else has the right to question or pass judgment on his decisions (see Job 38:2-3; 40:1-5). If this were a description of any human being, we might have just cause to be fearful. But this is God, the God who is good! That is why Paul could confidently write, "We know that God causes everything to work together for the good of those who love God" (Romans 8:28). God is able to bring everything together, even things that resist him, to bring about an outcome that is perfectly in line with what he wanted. And this sovereignty is at work from the smallest detail of life (Matthew 10:29) to the great events of history (Jeremiah 18:6-10).

Grasping this truth helps us to hold on to God even when we do not understand what he is doing or what is going on.

▸ *See also* ***The God who is everywhere and knows everything****, page 689.*

[15] The adulterer waits for the twilight,
saying, 'No one will see me then.'
He hides his face so no one will know him.
[16] Thieves break into houses at night
and sleep in the daytime.
They are not acquainted with the light.
[17] The black night is their morning.
They ally themselves with the terrors of the darkness.

[18] "But they disappear like foam down a river.
Everything they own is cursed,
and they are afraid to enter their own vineyards.
[19] The grave* consumes sinners
just as drought and heat consume snow.
[20] Their own mothers will forget them.
Maggots will find them sweet to eat.
No one will remember them.
Wicked people are broken like a tree in the storm.
[21] They cheat the woman who has no son to help her.
They refuse to help the needy widow.

[22] "God, in his power, drags away the rich.
They may rise high, but they have no assurance of life.
[23] They may be allowed to live in security,
but God is always watching them.
[24] And though they are great now,
in a moment they will be gone like all others,
cut off like heads of grain.
[25] Can anyone claim otherwise?
Who can prove me wrong?"

Bildad's Third Response to Job

25 Then Bildad the Shuhite replied:

[2] "God is powerful and dreadful.
He enforces peace in the heavens.
[3] Who is able to count his heavenly army?
Doesn't his light shine on all the earth?
[4] How can a mortal be innocent before God?
Can anyone born of a woman be pure?
[5] God is more glorious than the moon;
he shines brighter than the stars.
[6] In comparison, people are maggots;
we mortals are mere worms."

Job's Ninth Speech: A Response to Bildad

26 Then Job spoke again:

[2] "How you have helped the powerless!
How you have saved the weak!
[3] How you have enlightened my stupidity!
What wise advice you have offered!
[4] Where have you gotten all these wise sayings?
Whose spirit speaks through you?

[5] "The dead tremble—
those who live beneath the waters.
[6] The underworld* is naked in God's presence.
The place of destruction* is uncovered.
[7] God stretches the northern sky over empty space
and hangs the earth on nothing.
[8] He wraps the rain in his thick clouds,
and the clouds don't burst with the weight.
[9] He covers the face of the moon,*
shrouding it with his clouds.
[10] He created the horizon when he separated the waters;
he set the boundary between day and night.
[11] The foundations of heaven tremble;
they shudder at his rebuke.
[12] By his power the sea grew calm.
By his skill he crushed the great sea monster.*
[13] His Spirit made the heavens beautiful,
and his power pierced the gliding serpent.
[14] These are just the beginning of all that he does,
merely a whisper of his power.
Who, then, can comprehend the thunder of his power?"

Job's Final Speech

27 Job continued speaking:

[2] "I vow by the living God, who has taken away my rights,
by the Almighty who has embittered my soul—
[3] As long as I live,
while I have breath from God,

24:19 Hebrew *Sheol.* **26:6a** Hebrew *Sheol.* **26:6b** Hebrew *Abaddon.* **26:9** Or *covers his throne.* **26:12** Hebrew *Rahab,* the name of a mythical sea monster that represents chaos in ancient literature.

4 my lips will speak no evil,
and my tongue will speak no lies.
5 I will never concede that you are right;
I will defend my integrity until I die.
6 I will maintain my innocence without wavering.
My conscience is clear for as long as I live.

7 "May my enemy be punished like the wicked,
my adversary like those who do evil.
8 For what hope do the godless have when God cuts them off
and takes away their life?
9 Will God listen to their cry
when trouble comes upon them?
10 Can they take delight in the Almighty?
Can they call to God at any time?
11 I will teach you about God's power.
I will not conceal anything concerning the Almighty.
12 But you have seen all this,
yet you say all these useless things to me.

13 "This is what the wicked will receive from God;
this is their inheritance from the Almighty.
14 They may have many children,
but the children will die in war or starve to death.
15 Those who survive will die of a plague,
and not even their widows will mourn them.

16 "Evil people may have piles of money
and may store away mounds of clothing.
17 But the righteous will wear that clothing,
and the innocent will divide that money.
18 The wicked build houses as fragile as a spider's web,*
as flimsy as a shelter made of branches.
19 The wicked go to bed rich
but wake to find that all their wealth is gone.
20 Terror overwhelms them like a flood,
and they are blown away in the storms of the night.
21 The east wind carries them away, and they are gone.
It sweeps them away.
22 It whirls down on them without mercy.
They struggle to flee from its power.
23 But everyone jeers at them
and mocks them.

Mining for treasure

Anything worth having in life takes effort to get. This was certainly true of mining for minerals or precious metals in ancient times, a task that was both difficult and dangerous.

Mining lies at the heart of the imagery of Job 28, a poem on wisdom. We see the miners cutting a shaft deep into the earth, dangling precariously at the end of ropes as they do so (28:4). They chip away at the rock and tunnel through it (28:9-10), seeking a treasure of silver, gold, iron, or copper (28:1-2). It is hard work, but ultimately worthwhile as they find what they are looking for and "bring to light the hidden treasures" (28:11).

Yet despite human ability to find this kind of treasure, "do people know where to find wisdom?" (28:12, 20). Wisdom—the answers to life's challenges and questions—always seems beyond us, hidden from us. Yet such wisdom can be found, Job says. It comes as we grow in "the fear of the Lord" (28:28)—that is, honoring him in everything we are, think, and do. Wisdom can be found by those who truly value it, desire it, and search for it—though it will demand effort, persistence, and hard work, just like that of the miners. It will call for time spent digging into God's word, where God reveals his wisdom, unseen by others. And yet, like the treasure found by the miners, wisdom is always ultimately so worthwhile when it is discovered.

Job Speaks of Wisdom and Understanding

28 1 "People know where to mine
silver
and how to refine gold.
2 They know where to dig iron from the
earth
and how to smelt copper from rock.
3 They know how to shine light in the
darkness
and explore the farthest regions of the
earth
as they search in the dark for ore.
4 They sink a mine shaft into the earth
far from where anyone lives.
They descend on ropes, swinging
back and forth.
5 Food is grown on the earth above,
but down below, the earth is melted
as by fire.
6 Here the rocks contain precious lapis
lazuli,
and the dust contains gold.
7 These are treasures no bird of prey can
see,
no falcon's eye observe.
8 No wild animal has walked upon these
treasures;
no lion has ever set his paw there.
9 People know how to tear apart flinty rocks
and overturn the roots of mountains.
10 They cut tunnels in the rocks
and uncover precious stones.
11 They dam up the trickling streams
and bring to light the hidden
treasures.

12 "But do people know where to find
wisdom?
Where can they find understanding?
13 No one knows where to find it,*
for it is not found among the living.
14 'It is not here,' says the ocean.
'Nor is it here,' says the sea.
15 It cannot be bought with gold.
It cannot be purchased with silver.
16 It's worth more than all the gold of Ophir,
greater than precious onyx or lapis
lazuli.
17 Wisdom is more valuable than gold and
crystal.
It cannot be purchased with jewels
mounted in fine gold.
18 Coral and jasper are worthless in trying
to get it.
The price of wisdom is far above rubies.
19 Precious peridot from Ethiopia* cannot
be exchanged for it.
It's worth more than the purest gold.

20 "But do people know where to find
wisdom?
Where can they find understanding?
21 It is hidden from the eyes of all humanity.
Even the sharp-eyed birds in the sky
cannot discover it.
22 Destruction* and Death say,
'We've heard only rumors of where
wisdom can be found.'

23 "God alone understands the way to
wisdom;
he knows where it can be found,
24 for he looks throughout the whole earth
and sees everything under the heavens.
25 He decided how hard the winds should
blow
and how much rain should fall.
26 He made the laws for the rain
and laid out a path for the lightning.
27 Then he saw wisdom and evaluated it.
He set it in place and examined it
thoroughly.
28 And this is what he says to all humanity:
'The fear of the Lord is true wisdom;
to forsake evil is real understanding.'"

Job Speaks of His Former Blessings

29 Job continued speaking:
2 "I long for the years gone by
when God took care of me,
3 when he lit up the way before me
and I walked safely through the
darkness.
4 When I was in my prime,
God's friendship was felt in my home.
5 The Almighty was still with me,
and my children were around me.
6 My steps were awash in cream,
and the rocks gushed olive oil for me.

7 "Those were the days when I went to the
city gate
and took my place among the honored
leaders.
8 The young stepped aside when they
saw me,
and even the aged rose in respect at
my coming.

27:18 As in Greek and Syriac versions (see also 8:14); Hebrew reads *a moth.* **28:13** As in Greek version; Hebrew reads *knows its value.* **28:19** Hebrew *from Cush.* **28:22** Hebrew *Abaddon.*

[9] The princes stood in silence
and put their hands over their mouths.
[10] The highest officials of the city stood
quietly,
holding their tongues in respect.

[11] "All who heard me praised me.
All who saw me spoke well of me.
[12] For I assisted the poor in their need
and the orphans who required help.
[13] I helped those without hope, and they
blessed me.
And I caused the widows' hearts to
sing for joy.
[14] Everything I did was honest.
Righteousness covered me like a robe,
and I wore justice like a turban.
[15] I served as eyes for the blind
and feet for the lame.
[16] I was a father to the poor
and assisted strangers who needed
help.
[17] I broke the jaws of godless oppressors
and plucked their victims from their
teeth.

[18] "I thought, 'Surely I will die surrounded
by my family
after a long, good life.*
[19] For I am like a tree whose roots reach
the water,
whose branches are refreshed with
the dew.
[20] New honors are constantly bestowed
on me,
and my strength is continually
renewed.'

[21] "Everyone listened to my advice.
They were silent as they waited for me
to speak.
[22] And after I spoke, they had nothing to
add,
for my counsel satisfied them.
[23] They longed for me to speak as people
long for rain.
They drank my words like a refreshing
spring rain.
[24] When they were discouraged, I smiled at
them.
My look of approval was precious to
them.
[25] Like a chief, I told them what to do.
I lived like a king among his troops
and comforted those who
mourned.

Job Speaks of His Anguish

30 [1] "But now I am mocked by people
younger than I,
by young men whose fathers are not
worthy to run with my sheepdogs.
[2] A lot of good they are to me—
those worn-out wretches!
[3] They are gaunt from poverty and hunger.
They claw the dry ground in desolate
wastelands.
[4] They pluck wild greens from among the
bushes
and eat from the roots of broom trees.
[5] They are driven from human society,
and people shout at them as if they
were thieves.
[6] So now they live in frightening ravines,
in caves and among the rocks.
[7] They sound like animals howling among
the bushes,
huddled together beneath the nettles.
[8] They are nameless fools,
outcasts from society.

[9] "And now they mock me with vulgar
songs!
They taunt me!
[10] They despise me and won't come
near me,
except to spit in my face.
[11] For God has cut my bowstring.
He has humbled me,
so they have thrown off all restraint.
[12] These outcasts oppose me to my face.
They send me sprawling
and lay traps in my path.
[13] They block my road
and do everything they can to
destroy me.
They know I have no one to help me.
[14] They come at me from all directions.
They jump on me when I am down.
[15] I live in terror now.
My honor has blown away in the wind,
and my prosperity has vanished like
a cloud.

[16] "And now my life seeps away.
Depression haunts my days.
[17] At night my bones are filled with pain,
which gnaws at me relentlessly.
[18] With a strong hand, God grabs my
shirt.*
He grips me by the collar of my coat.
[19] He has thrown me into the mud.
I'm nothing more than dust and ashes.

20 "I cry to you, O God, but you don't
answer.
I stand before you, but you don't even
look.
21 You have become cruel toward me.
You use your power to persecute me.
22 You throw me into the whirlwind
and destroy me in the storm.
23 And I know you are sending me to my
death—
the destination of all who live.

24 "Surely no one would turn against the
needy
when they cry for help in their
trouble.
25 Did I not weep for those in trouble?
Was I not deeply grieved for the needy?
26 So I looked for good, but evil came
instead.
I waited for the light, but darkness fell.
27 My heart is troubled and restless.
Days of suffering torment me.
28 I walk in gloom, without sunlight.
I stand in the public square and cry
for help.
29 Instead, I am considered a brother to
jackals
and a companion to owls.
30 My skin has turned dark,
and my bones burn with fever.
31 My harp plays sad music,
and my flute accompanies those who
weep.

Job's Final Protest of Innocence

31 1 "I made a covenant with my eyes
not to look with lust at a young
woman.
2 For what has God above chosen for us?
What is our inheritance from the
Almighty on high?
3 Isn't it calamity for the wicked
and misfortune for those who do evil?
4 Doesn't he see everything I do
and every step I take?

5 "Have I lied to anyone
or deceived anyone?
6 Let God weigh me on the scales of
justice,
for he knows my integrity.
7 If I have strayed from his pathway,
or if my heart has lusted for what my
eyes have seen,
or if I am guilty of any other sin,

29:18 Hebrew *after I have counted my days like sand.* **30:18** As in Greek version; Hebrew reads *hand, my garment is disfigured.*

Lust

Lust is an overpowering desire for sexual fulfillment, affecting both married people and single people. The Bible frequently warns against lust, shows how it develops if not handled properly, and demonstrates the dangers of failing to control it, for ourselves and others.

In Ephesians 4:17-19 Paul describes how sin works. It begins as we harden our hearts toward God, which in turn leads to our minds being dark and our thinking wrong thoughts, which then finds expression in all kinds of shameful things, including "lustful pleasure" and "every kind of impurity" (Ephesians 4:19). In other words, lust starts in our hearts and minds; and if it is not dealt with at an early stage, it grows, as King David discovered with Bathsheba (2 Samuel 11:1-5).

It is because lust is so powerful and deceptive that the Bible calls us to be ruthless in dealing with it (e.g., Matthew 5:27-30; Colossians 3:5-6) and to develop self-control, lest we wrong both God and others (1 Thessalonians 4:3-8). That is why Job said that he had made a covenant with his eyes in order to avoid it (Job 31:1).

In days when sexual imagery and opportunity are freely available and accepted as normal, this is not something Christians can treat lightly. Lust is powerful, and even the greatest servants of God have succumbed to its attack, destroying lives and ministries. Openness and accountability to a fellow Christian is one practical way of guarding ourselves in this area.

▶ *See also **Sexuality**, page 742.*

8 then let someone else eat the crops
I have planted.
Let all that I have planted be
uprooted.

9 "If my heart has been seduced by a
woman,
or if I have lusted for my neighbor's
wife,
10 then let my wife serve* another man;
let other men sleep with her.
11 For lust is a shameful sin,
a crime that should be punished.
12 It is a fire that burns all the way to hell.*
It would wipe out everything I own.

13 "If I have been unfair to my male or
female servants
when they brought their complaints
to me,
14 how could I face God?
What could I say when he
questioned me?
15 For God created both me and my
servants.
He created us both in the womb.

16 "Have I refused to help the poor,
or crushed the hopes of widows?
17 Have I been stingy with my food
and refused to share it with orphans?
18 No, from childhood I have cared for
orphans like a father,
and all my life I have cared for
widows.
19 Whenever I saw the homeless without
clothes
and the needy with nothing to wear,
20 did they not praise me
for providing wool clothing to keep
them warm?

21 "If I raised my hand against an orphan,
knowing the judges would take my
side,
22 then let my shoulder be wrenched out of
place!
Let my arm be torn from its socket!
23 That would be better than facing God's
judgment.
For if the majesty of God opposes me,
what hope is there?

24 "Have I put my trust in money
or felt secure because of my gold?
25 Have I gloated about my wealth
and all that I own?
26 "Have I looked at the sun shining in the
skies,
or the moon walking down its silver
pathway,
27 and been secretly enticed in my heart
to throw kisses at them in worship?
28 If so, I should be punished by the
judges,
for it would mean I had denied the
God of heaven.

29 "Have I ever rejoiced when disaster
struck my enemies,
or become excited when harm came
their way?
30 No, I have never sinned by cursing
anyone
or by asking for revenge.

31 "My servants have never said,
'He let others go hungry.'
32 I have never turned away a stranger
but have opened my doors to everyone.

33 "Have I tried to hide my sins like other
people do,
concealing my guilt in my heart?
34 Have I feared the crowd
or the contempt of the masses,
so that I kept quiet and stayed
indoors?

35 "If only someone would listen to me!
Look, I will sign my name to my
defense.
Let the Almighty answer me.
Let my accuser write out the charges
against me.
36 I would face the accusation proudly.
I would wear it like a crown.
37 For I would tell him exactly what I have
done.
I would come before him like a prince.

38 "If my land accuses me
and all its furrows cry out together,
39 or if I have stolen its crops
or murdered its owners,
40 then let thistles grow on that land
instead of wheat,
and weeds instead of barley."

Job's words are ended.

Elihu Responds to Job's Friends

32 Job's three friends refused to reply
further to him because he kept insisting on his innocence.

[2]Then Elihu son of Barakel the Buzite,
of the clan of Ram, became angry. He was
angry because Job refused to admit that he
had sinned and that God was right in punishing him. [3]He was also angry with Job's
three friends, for they made God* appear to
be wrong by their inability to answer Job's
arguments. [4]Elihu had waited for the others
to speak to Job because they were older
than he. [5]But when he saw that they had no
further reply, he spoke out angrily. [6]Elihu
son of Barakel the Buzite said,

"I am young and you are old,
so I held back from telling you what I think.
7 I thought, 'Those who are older should speak,
for wisdom comes with age.'
8 But there is a spirit* within people,
the breath of the Almighty within them,
that makes them intelligent.
9 Sometimes the elders are not wise.
Sometimes the aged do not understand justice.
10 So listen to me,
and let me tell you what I think.

11 "I have waited all this time,
listening very carefully to your arguments,
listening to you grope for words.
12 I have listened,
but not one of you has refuted Job
or answered his arguments.
13 And don't tell me, 'He is too wise for us.
Only God can convince him.'
14 If Job had been arguing with me,
I would not answer with your kind of logic!
15 You sit there baffled,
with nothing more to say.
16 Should I continue to wait, now that you are silent?
Must I also remain silent?
17 No, I will say my piece.
I will speak my mind.
18 For I am full of pent-up words,
and the spirit within me urges me on.
19 I am like a cask of wine without a vent,
like a new wineskin ready to burst!
20 I must speak to find relief,
so let me give my answers.
21 I won't play favorites
or try to flatter anyone.
22 For if I tried flattery,
my Creator would soon destroy me.

Elihu Presents His Case against Job

33 1 "Listen to my words, Job;
pay attention to what I have to say.
2 Now that I have begun to speak,
let me continue.
3 I speak with all sincerity;
I speak the truth.
4 For the Spirit of God has made me,
and the breath of the Almighty gives me life.
5 Answer me, if you can;
make your case and take your stand.
6 Look, you and I both belong to God.
I, too, was formed from clay.
7 So you don't need to be afraid of me.
I won't come down hard on you.

8 "You have spoken in my hearing,
and I have heard your very words.
9 You said, 'I am pure; I am without sin;
I am innocent; I have no guilt.
10 God is picking a quarrel with me,
and he considers me his enemy.
11 He puts my feet in the stocks
and watches my every move.'

12 "But you are wrong, and I will show you why.
For God is greater than any human being.
13 So why are you bringing a charge against him?
Why say he does not respond to people's complaints?
14 For God speaks again and again,
though people do not recognize it.
15 He speaks in dreams, in visions of the night,
when deep sleep falls on people
as they lie in their beds.
16 He whispers in their ears
and terrifies them with warnings.
17 He makes them turn from doing wrong;
he keeps them from pride.
18 He protects them from the grave,
from crossing over the river of death.

19 "Or God disciplines people with pain on their sickbeds,
with ceaseless aching in their bones.

31:10 Hebrew *grind for.* **31:12** Hebrew *to Abaddon.* **32:3** As in ancient Hebrew scribal tradition; the Masoretic Text reads *Job.* **32:8** Or *Spirit;* also in 32:18.

20 They lose their appetite
for even the most delicious food.
21 Their flesh wastes away,
and their bones stick out.
22 They are at death's door;
the angels of death wait for them.

23 "But if an angel from heaven appears—
a special messenger to intercede for a person
and declare that he is upright—
24 he will be gracious and say,
'Rescue him from the grave,
for I have found a ransom for his life.'
25 Then his body will become as healthy as a child's,
firm and youthful again.
26 When he prays to God,
he will be accepted.
And God will receive him with joy
and restore him to good standing.
27 He will declare to his friends,
'I sinned and twisted the truth,
but it was not worth it.*
28 God rescued me from the grave,
and now my life is filled with light.'

29 "Yes, God does these things
again and again for people.
30 He rescues them from the grave
so they may enjoy the light of life.
31 Mark this well, Job. Listen to me,
for I have more to say.
32 But if you have anything to say, go ahead.
Speak, for I am anxious to see you justified.
33 But if not, then listen to me.
Keep silent and I will teach you wisdom!"

Elihu Accuses Job of Arrogance

34 Then Elihu said:
2 "Listen to me, you wise men.
Pay attention, you who have knowledge.
3 Job said, 'The ear tests the words it hears
just as the mouth distinguishes between foods.'
4 So let us discern for ourselves what is right;
let us learn together what is good.
5 For Job also said, 'I am innocent,
but God has taken away my rights.
6 I am innocent, but they call me a liar.
My suffering is incurable, though I have not sinned.'

7 "Tell me, has there ever been a man like Job,
with his thirst for irreverent talk?
8 He chooses evil people as companions.
He spends his time with wicked men.
9 He has even said, 'Why waste time
trying to please God?'

10 "Listen to me, you who have understanding.
Everyone knows that God doesn't sin!
The Almighty can do no wrong.
11 He repays people according to their deeds.
He treats people as they deserve.
12 Truly, God will not do wrong.
The Almighty will not twist justice.
13 Did someone else put the world in his care?
Who set the whole world in place?
14 If God were to take back his spirit
and withdraw his breath,
15 all life would cease,
and humanity would turn again to dust.

16 "Now listen to me if you are wise.
Pay attention to what I say.
17 Could God govern if he hated justice?
Are you going to condemn the almighty judge?
18 For he says to kings, 'You are wicked,'
and to nobles, 'You are unjust.'
19 He doesn't care how great a person may be,
and he pays no more attention to the rich than to the poor.
He made them all.
20 In a moment they die.
In the middle of the night they pass away;
the mighty are removed without human hand.

21 "For God watches how people live;
he sees everything they do.
22 No darkness is thick enough
to hide the wicked from his eyes.
23 We don't set the time
when we will come before God in judgment.

24 He brings the mighty to ruin without
asking anyone,
and he sets up others in their place.
25 He knows what they do,
and in the night he overturns and
destroys them.
26 He strikes them down because they are
wicked,
doing it openly for all to see.
27 For they turned away from following
him.
They have no respect for any of his
ways.
28 They cause the poor to cry out, catching
God's attention.
He hears the cries of the needy.
29 But if he chooses to remain quiet,
who can criticize him?
When he hides his face, no one can find
him,
whether an individual or a nation.
30 He prevents the godless from ruling
so they cannot be a snare to the
people.

31 "Why don't people say to God, 'I have
sinned,
but I will sin no more'?
32 Or 'I don't know what evil I have done—
tell me.
If I have done wrong, I will stop at
once'?
33 "Must God tailor his justice to your
demands?
But you have rejected him!
The choice is yours, not mine.
Go ahead, share your wisdom with us.
34 After all, bright people will tell me,
and wise people will hear me say,
35 'Job speaks out of ignorance;
his words lack insight.'
36 Job, you deserve the maximum penalty
for the wicked way you have talked.
37 For you have added rebellion to your
sin;
you show no respect,
and you speak many angry words
against God."

Elihu Reminds Job of God's Justice

35 Then Elihu said:
2 "Do you think it is right for you
to claim,
'I am righteous before God'?
3 For you also ask, 'What's in it for me?
What's the use of living a righteous
life?'
4 "I will answer you
and all your friends, too.
5 Look up into the sky,
and see the clouds high above you.
6 If you sin, how does that affect God?
Even if you sin again and again,
what effect will it have on him?
7 If you are good, is this some great gift
to him?
What could you possibly give him?
8 No, your sins affect only people like
yourself,
and your good deeds also affect only
humans.

9 "People cry out when they are
oppressed.
They groan beneath the power of the
mighty.
10 Yet they don't ask, 'Where is God my
Creator,
the one who gives songs in the night?
11 Where is the one who makes us smarter
than the animals
and wiser than the birds of the sky?'
12 And when they cry out, God does not
answer
because of their pride.
13 But it is wrong to say God doesn't listen,
to say the Almighty isn't concerned.
14 You say you can't see him,
but he will bring justice if you will
only wait.*
15 You say he does not respond to sinners
with anger
and is not greatly concerned about
wickedness.*
16 But you are talking nonsense, Job.
You have spoken like a fool."

36 Elihu continued speaking:
2 "Let me go on, and I will show
you the truth.
For I have not finished defending God!
3 I will present profound arguments
for the righteousness of my Creator.

33:27 Greek version reads *but he* [God] *did not punish me as my sin deserved.* **35:13-14** These verses can also be translated as follows: [13]*Indeed, God doesn't listen to their empty plea; / the Almighty is not concerned. /* [14]*How much less will he listen when you say you don't see him, / and that your case is before him and you're waiting for justice.* **35:15** As in Greek and Latin versions; the meaning of this Hebrew word is uncertain.

4 I am telling you nothing but the truth,
for I am a man of great knowledge.

5 "God is mighty, but he does not despise
anyone!
He is mighty in both power and
understanding.
6 He does not let the wicked live
but gives justice to the afflicted.
7 He never takes his eyes off the innocent,
but he sets them on thrones with kings
and exalts them forever.
8 If they are bound in chains
and caught up in a web of trouble,
9 he shows them the reason.
He shows them their sins of pride.
10 He gets their attention
and commands that they turn from
evil.

11 "If they listen and obey God,
they will be blessed with prosperity
throughout their lives.
All their years will be pleasant.
12 But if they refuse to listen to him,
they will cross over the river of death,
dying from lack of understanding.
13 For the godless are full of resentment.
Even when he punishes them,
they refuse to cry out to him for help.
14 They die when they are young,
after wasting their lives in immoral
living.
15 But by means of their suffering, he
rescues those who suffer.
For he gets their attention through
adversity.

16 "God is leading you away from danger,
Job,
to a place free from distress.
He is setting your table with the best
food.
17 But you are obsessed with whether the
godless will be judged.
Don't worry, judgment and justice will
be upheld.
18 But watch out, or you may be seduced
by wealth.*
Don't let yourself be bribed into sin.
19 Could all your wealth*
or all your mighty efforts
keep you from distress?
20 Do not long for the cover of night,
for that is when people will be
destroyed.*
21 Be on guard! Turn back from evil,
for God sent this suffering
to keep you from a life of evil.

Elihu Reminds Job of God's Power

22 "Look, God is all-powerful.
Who is a teacher like him?
23 No one can tell him what to do,
or say to him, 'You have done wrong.'
24 Instead, glorify his mighty works,
singing songs of praise.
25 Everyone has seen these things,
though only from a distance.

26 "Look, God is greater than we can
understand.
His years cannot be counted.
27 He draws up the water vapor
and then distills it into rain.
28 The rain pours down from the clouds,
and everyone benefits.
29 Who can understand the spreading of
the clouds
and the thunder that rolls forth from
heaven?
30 See how he spreads the lightning
around him
and how it lights up the depths of the
sea.
31 By these mighty acts he nourishes* the
people,
giving them food in abundance.
32 He fills his hands with lightning bolts
and hurls each at its target.
33 The thunder announces his presence;
the storm announces his indignant
anger.*

37 1 "My heart pounds as I think of
this.
It trembles within me.
2 Listen carefully to the thunder of God's
voice
as it rolls from his mouth.
3 It rolls across the heavens,
and his lightning flashes in every
direction.
4 Then comes the roaring of the thunder—
the tremendous voice of his majesty.
He does not restrain it when he speaks.
5 God's voice is glorious in the thunder.
We can't even imagine the greatness
of his power.

6 "He directs the snow to fall on the earth
and tells the rain to pour down.

7 Then everyone stops working
so they can watch his power.
8 The wild animals take cover
and stay inside their dens.
9 The stormy wind comes from its chamber,
and the driving winds bring the cold.
10 God's breath sends the ice,
freezing wide expanses of water.
11 He loads the clouds with moisture,
and they flash with his lightning.
12 The clouds churn about at his direction.
They do whatever he commands
throughout the earth.
13 He makes these things happen either to
punish people
or to show his unfailing love.

14 "Pay attention to this, Job.
Stop and consider the wonderful
miracles of God!
15 Do you know how God controls the storm
and causes the lightning to flash from
his clouds?
16 Do you understand how he moves the
clouds
with wonderful perfection and skill?
17 When you are sweltering in your clothes
and the south wind dies down and
everything is still,
18 he makes the skies reflect the heat like
a bronze mirror.
Can you do that?

19 "So teach the rest of us what to say to
God.
We are too ignorant to make our own
arguments.
20 Should God be notified that I want to
speak?
Can people even speak when they are
confused?*
21 We cannot look at the sun,
for it shines brightly in the sky
when the wind clears away the
clouds.
22 So also, golden splendor comes from the
mountain of God.*
He is clothed in dazzling splendor.
23 We cannot imagine the power of the
Almighty;
but even though he is just and
righteous,
he does not destroy us.
24 No wonder people everywhere fear him.
All who are wise show him
reverence.*"

The LORD Challenges Job

38 Then the LORD answered Job from
the whirlwind:

2 "Who is this that questions my wisdom
with such ignorant words?
3 Brace yourself like a man,
because I have some questions for you,
and you must answer them.

4 "Where were you when I laid the
foundations of the earth?
Tell me, if you know so much.
5 Who determined its dimensions
and stretched out the surveying line?
6 What supports its foundations,
and who laid its cornerstone
7 as the morning stars sang together
and all the angels* shouted for joy?

8 "Who kept the sea inside its boundaries
as it burst from the womb,
9 and as I clothed it with clouds
and wrapped it in thick darkness?
10 For I locked it behind barred gates,
limiting its shores.
11 I said, 'This far and no farther will you
come.
Here your proud waves must stop!'

12 "Have you ever commanded the
morning to appear
and caused the dawn to rise in the
east?
13 Have you made daylight spread to the
ends of the earth,
to bring an end to the night's
wickedness?
14 As the light approaches,
the earth takes shape like clay pressed
beneath a seal;
it is robed in brilliant colors.*
15 The light disturbs the wicked
and stops the arm that is raised in
violence.

16 "Have you explored the springs from
which the seas come?
Have you explored their depths?
17 Do you know where the gates of death
are located?

36:18 Or *But don't let your anger lead you to mockery.* **36:19** Or *Could all your cries for help.* **36:16-20** The meaning of the Hebrew in this passage is uncertain. **36:31** Or *he governs.* **36:33** Or *even the cattle know when a storm is coming.* The meaning of the Hebrew is uncertain. **37:20** Or *speak without being swallowed up?* **37:22** Or *from the north;* or *from the abode.* **37:24** As in Greek version; Hebrew reads *He is not impressed by the wise.* **38:7** Hebrew *the sons of God.* **38:14** Or *its features stand out like folds in a robe.*

Have you seen the gates of utter gloom?
18 Do you realize the extent of the earth?
Tell me about it if you know!
19 "Where does light come from,
and where does darkness go?
20 Can you take each to its home?
Do you know how to get there?
21 But of course you know all this!
For you were born before it was all created,
and you are so very experienced!
22 "Have you visited the storehouses of the snow
or seen the storehouses of hail?
23 (I have reserved them as weapons for the time of trouble,
for the day of battle and war.)
24 Where is the path to the source of light?
Where is the home of the east wind?
25 "Who created a channel for the torrents of rain?
Who laid out the path for the lightning?
26 Who makes the rain fall on barren land,
in a desert where no one lives?
27 Who sends rain to satisfy the parched ground
and make the tender grass spring up?
28 "Does the rain have a father?
Who gives birth to the dew?
29 Who is the mother of the ice?
Who gives birth to the frost from the heavens?
30 For the water turns to ice as hard as rock,
and the surface of the water freezes.
31 "Can you direct the movement of the stars—
binding the cluster of the Pleiades
or loosening the cords of Orion?
32 Can you direct the constellations through the seasons
or guide the Bear with her cubs across the heavens?
33 Do you know the laws of the universe?
Can you use them to regulate the earth?
34 "Can you shout to the clouds
and make it rain?
35 Can you make lightning appear
and cause it to strike as you direct?
36 Who gives intuition to the heart
and instinct to the mind?
37 Who is wise enough to count all the clouds?
Who can tilt the water jars of heaven
38 when the parched ground is dry
and the soil has hardened into clods?

God's power

In Job 31:35 Job had exclaimed, "Let the Almighty answer me"! And now God did just that—though in a way that neither Job nor his friends expected. In fact, God answered none of Job's questions; he simply appeared to him in a storm and demanded that Job answer him. In two speeches, broken only by Job's admission of unworthiness and ignorance (Job 40:3-5), God revealed his great power. In the first (38:1–40:2), he asked Job if he knew how creation came into being or was sustained; in the second (40:6–41:34), if he understood how this creation related to its powerful Creator. In the face of such a revelation of power from the one the Bible calls "God Almighty" (El-Shaddai), all Job could do was to humbly submit and admit he had spoken about things he did not understand (42:1-6).

But it is not just in creation that we see God's power, the Bible says. We see it in redemption too—supremely in the Exodus in the Old Testament (e.g., Exodus 15:1-21) and in Christ's resurrection in the New Testament (e.g., Ephesians 1:19-21).

Although God's power is without limits, it is constantly guided by his loving and righteous character. He will never use his power for evil or for selfish purposes, but only to further his saving purposes. It is this power that believers are constantly urged to rely on through the Holy Spirit (e.g., Acts 1:8).

▸ *See also* ***Redemption****, page 1136;* ***Christ's resurrection and ours****, page 1320.*

39 "Can you stalk prey for a lioness
and satisfy the young lions' appetites
40 as they lie in their dens
or crouch in the thicket?
41 Who provides food for the ravens
when their young cry out to God
and wander about in hunger?

The LORD's Challenge Continues

39 1 "Do you know when the wild goats give birth?
Have you watched as deer are born in the wild?
2 Do you know how many months they carry their young?
Are you aware of the time of their delivery?
3 They crouch down to give birth to their young
and deliver their offspring.
4 Their young grow up in the open fields,
then leave home and never return.

5 "Who gives the wild donkey its freedom?
Who untied its ropes?
6 I have placed it in the wilderness;
its home is the wasteland.
7 It hates the noise of the city
and has no driver to shout at it.
8 The mountains are its pastureland,
where it searches for every blade of grass.

9 "Will the wild ox consent to being tamed?
Will it spend the night in your stall?
10 Can you hitch a wild ox to a plow?
Will it plow a field for you?
11 Given its strength, can you trust it?
Can you leave and trust the ox to do your work?
12 Can you rely on it to bring home your grain
and deliver it to your threshing floor?

13 "The ostrich flaps her wings grandly,
but they are no match for the feathers of the stork.
14 She lays her eggs on top of the earth,
letting them be warmed in the dust.
15 She doesn't worry that a foot might crush them
or a wild animal might destroy them.
16 She is harsh toward her young,
as if they were not her own.
She doesn't care if they die.
17 For God has deprived her of wisdom.
He has given her no understanding.
18 But whenever she jumps up to run,
she passes the swiftest horse with its rider.

19 "Have you given the horse its strength
or clothed its neck with a flowing mane?
20 Did you give it the ability to leap like a locust?
Its majestic snorting is terrifying!
21 It paws the earth and rejoices in its strength
when it charges out to battle.
22 It laughs at fear and is unafraid.
It does not run from the sword.
23 The arrows rattle against it,
and the spear and javelin flash.
24 It paws the ground fiercely
and rushes forward into battle when the ram's horn blows.
25 It snorts at the sound of the horn.
It senses the battle in the distance.
It quivers at the captain's commands
and the noise of battle.

26 "Is it your wisdom that makes the hawk soar
and spread its wings toward the south?
27 Is it at your command that the eagle rises
to the heights to make its nest?
28 It lives on the cliffs,
making its home on a distant, rocky crag.
29 From there it hunts its prey,
keeping watch with piercing eyes.
30 Its young gulp down blood.
Where there's a carcass, there you'll find it."

40 Then the LORD said to Job,
2 "Do you still want to argue with the Almighty?
You are God's critic, but do you have the answers?"

Job Responds to the LORD

3 Then Job replied to the LORD,

4 "I am nothing—how could I ever find the answers?
I will cover my mouth with my hand.
5 I have said too much already.
I have nothing more to say."

The LORD Challenges Job Again

6Then the LORD answered Job from the whirlwind:

7 "Brace yourself like a man,
because I have some questions for you,
and you must answer them.

8 "Will you discredit my justice
and condemn me just to prove you are right?
9 Are you as strong as God?
Can you thunder with a voice like his?
10 All right, put on your glory and splendor,
your honor and majesty.
11 Give vent to your anger.
Let it overflow against the proud.
12 Humiliate the proud with a glance;
walk on the wicked where they stand.
13 Bury them in the dust.
Imprison them in the world of the dead.
14 Then even I would praise you,
for your own strength would save you.

15 "Take a look at Behemoth,*
which I made, just as I made you.
It eats grass like an ox.
16 See its powerful loins
and the muscles of its belly.
17 Its tail is as strong as a cedar.
The sinews of its thighs are knit tightly together.
18 Its bones are tubes of bronze.
Its limbs are bars of iron.
19 It is a prime example of God's handiwork,
and only its Creator can threaten it.
20 The mountains offer it their best food,
where all the wild animals play.
21 It lies under the lotus plants,*
hidden by the reeds in the marsh.
22 The lotus plants give it shade
among the willows beside the stream.
23 It is not disturbed by the raging river,
not concerned when the swelling Jordan rushes around it.
24 No one can catch it off guard
or put a ring in its nose and lead it away.

The LORD's Challenge Continues

41 1*"Can you catch Leviathan* with a hook
or put a noose around its jaw?
2 Can you tie it with a rope through the nose
or pierce its jaw with a spike?
3 Will it beg you for mercy
or implore you for pity?
4 Will it agree to work for you,
to be your slave for life?
5 Can you make it a pet like a bird,
or give it to your little girls to play with?
6 Will merchants try to buy it
to sell it in their shops?
7 Will its hide be hurt by spears
or its head by a harpoon?
8 If you lay a hand on it,
you will certainly remember the battle that follows.
You won't try that again!
9*No, it is useless to try to capture it.
The hunter who attempts it will be knocked down.
10 And since no one dares to disturb it,
who then can stand up to me?
11 Who has given me anything that I need to pay back?
Everything under heaven is mine.

12 "I want to emphasize Leviathan's limbs
and its enormous strength and graceful form.
13 Who can strip off its hide,
and who can penetrate its double layer of armor?*
14 Who could pry open its jaws?
For its teeth are terrible!
15 The scales on its back are like* rows of shields
tightly sealed together.
16 They are so close together
that no air can get between them.
17 Each scale sticks tight to the next.
They interlock and cannot be penetrated.

18 "When it sneezes, it flashes light!
Its eyes are like the red of dawn.
19 Lightning leaps from its mouth;
flames of fire flash out.
20 Smoke streams from its nostrils
like steam from a pot heated over burning rushes.
21 Its breath would kindle coals,
for flames shoot from its mouth.

22 "The tremendous strength in Leviathan's neck
strikes terror wherever it goes.

[23] Its flesh is hard and firm
and cannot be penetrated.
[24] Its heart is hard as rock,
hard as a millstone.
[25] When it rises, the mighty are afraid,
gripped by terror.
[26] No sword can stop it,
no spear, dart, or javelin.
[27] Iron is nothing but straw to that
creature,
and bronze is like rotten wood.
[28] Arrows cannot make it flee.
Stones shot from a sling are like bits
of grass.
[29] Clubs are like a blade of grass,
and it laughs at the swish of javelins.
[30] Its belly is covered with scales as sharp
as glass.
It plows up the ground as it drags
through the mud.
[31] "Leviathan makes the water boil with its
commotion.
It stirs the depths like a pot of ointment.
[32] The water glistens in its wake,
making the sea look white.
[33] Nothing on earth is its equal,
no other creature so fearless.
[34] Of all the creatures, it is the
proudest.
It is the king of beasts."

Job Responds to the LORD

42 Then Job replied to the LORD:
[2] "I know that you can do anything,
and no one can stop you.
[3] You asked, 'Who is this that questions
my wisdom with such ignorance?'
It is I—and I was talking about things
I knew nothing about,
things far too wonderful for me.
[4] You said, 'Listen and I will speak!
I have some questions for you,
and you must answer them.'
[5] I had only heard about you before,

40:15 The identification of Behemoth is disputed, ranging from an earthly creature to a mythical sea monster in ancient literature. **40:21** Or *bramble bushes;* also in 40:22. **41:1a** Verses 41:1-8 are numbered 40:25-32 in Hebrew text. **41:1b** The identification of Leviathan is disputed, ranging from an earthly creature to a mythical sea monster in ancient literature. **41:9** Verses 41:9-34 are numbered 41:1-26 in Hebrew text. **41:13** As in Greek version; Hebrew reads *its bridle?* **41:15** As in some Greek manuscripts and Latin Vulgate; Hebrew reads *Its pride is in its.*

Knowledge and revelation

For thirty-seven chapters Job had struggled with his suffering. He had asked "Why?" many times. He had listened to the counsel of his friends. He had put his arguments to God. He had justified himself often. But only now, when Job ran out of words, did God step in, revealing himself through a whirlwind—not to answer Job's questions, nor to explain Satan's original challenge. No; God simply *revealed himself.*

Through four chapters (Job 38–41) God challenged Job about whether he could understand or bring about the wonders and intricacies of creation. At last Job understood the message, recognizing that "I was talking about things I knew nothing about" (Job 42:3) and confessing, "I had only heard about you before, but now I have seen you with my own eyes" (42:5).

Job had at last understood the difference between knowledge and revelation, between *knowing about* God and *knowing* God. He had known a lot about God, had sought to live a godly life and to trust him (1:8), but he had never really *known* God in an intimate way. But when that moment came, everything changed. Job didn't need answers anymore; he could simply trust.

The challenge Job faced remains a challenge for us today: Are we living at the level of knowledge or the level of revelation—knowing about God, or knowing God himself; knowing the facts of a theological truth, or living out that truth in daily life? It is only when we stop airing our own opinions that God can break in, reveal himself, and speak to us.

▶ *See also* ***Revelation****, page 612.*

but now I have seen you with my own
eyes.
6 I take back everything I said,
and I sit in dust and ashes to show my
repentance."

Conclusion: The LORD Blesses Job

7 After the LORD had finished speaking to
Job, he said to Eliphaz the Temanite: "I am
angry with you and your two friends, for
you have not spoken accurately about me,
as my servant Job has. 8 So take seven bulls
and seven rams and go to my servant Job
and offer a burnt offering for yourselves.
My servant Job will pray for you, and I will
accept his prayer on your behalf. I will not
treat you as you deserve, for you have not
spoken accurately about me, as my servant
Job has." 9 So Eliphaz the Temanite, Bildad
the Shuhite, and Zophar the Naamathite
did as the LORD commanded them, and the
LORD accepted Job's prayer.
10 When Job prayed for his friends, the LORD
restored his fortunes. In fact, the LORD gave
him twice as much as before! 11 Then all his
brothers, sisters, and former friends came
and feasted with him in his home. And they
consoled him and comforted him because of
all the trials the LORD had brought against
him. And each of them brought him a gift of
money* and a gold ring.
12 So the LORD blessed Job in the second
half of his life even more than in the beginning. For now he had 14,000 sheep,
6,000 camels, 1,000 teams of oxen, and
1,000 female donkeys. 13 He also gave Job
seven more sons and three more daughters.
14 He named his first daughter Jemimah,
the second Keziah, and the third Keren-
happuch. 15 In all the land no women were
as lovely as the daughters of Job. And their
father put them into his will along with
their brothers.
16 Job lived 140 years after that, living to
see four generations of his children and
grandchildren. 17 Then he died, an old man
who had lived a long, full life.

42:11 Hebrew *a kesitah;* the value or weight of the kesitah is no longer known.

Psalms *Songs of worship*

The book of Psalms was and is the songbook of the Jewish people. Written over several centuries, its 150 prayers, poems, and hymns were gathered together and used by God's people in worship. They continued to be used in worship in the early church (e.g., Ephesians 5:19) and are still used in many churches today.

The psalmists held nothing back, pouring out their feelings to God, whatever they were. They asked for his help, thanked him for meeting their needs, confessed their sins, cried out in their need, and made their complaints. They expressed almost every kind of emotion, and their song-prayers are as memorable today as they were then. We find intense joy and a secure sense of intimacy with God, yet also on occasion feelings of extreme abandonment and perplexity. These are truly songs for those "who have set their minds on a pilgrimage" (Psalm 84:5).

What's it all about?

The Psalms are primarily songs of praise to God for his creation, redemption, help, forgiveness, and kingship. They were all designed to be sung, not spoken, reflected in the Hebrew title of the book—*Tehillim*, meaning "Songs of Praise." While many Christians think that King David wrote all the psalms, he in fact wrote only seventy-three of them; the rest were written over a period of one thousand years between the time of Moses (Psalm 90) and the return from exile (Psalm 126).

In the Psalms we find:

- psalms of lament (for times of trouble)
- psalms thanking God for things he has done
- hymns of praise
- psalms that celebrate God's kingship
- royal psalms about the nation's kings
- wisdom psalms (wise teachings)
- psalms that Jesus and the church saw as looking ahead to him

OVERVIEW

Book 1: Psalms 1–41 · psalms mainly by King David reflecting his experiences of God in life

Book 2: Psalms 42–72 · psalms by "the descendants of Korah," Asaph, and David, calling on God's people to trust in the face of distress

Book 3: Psalms 73–89 · psalms mainly by Asaph and the sons of Korah, written in hard times

Book 4: Psalms 90–106 · mainly anonymous psalms, reminding Israel of God's sovereignty and his dealings with them

Book 5: Psalms 107–150 · psalms of praise and calls to trust in God

The final psalm in each book concludes with a doxology, a song of praise giving glory to God.

Some of the psalms are corporate; some are personal; but all are united in their focus on God. The most dominant theme in Psalms is the sovereignty of God, the great King over all the earth, who rules everything and can therefore answer every request and deal with every situation, who is righteous and good, and whose kingdom will surely be established. Praise, worship, thanksgiving, and petition find a large place, therefore, as worshipers are encouraged to bring everything in life before this sovereign God.

page 602

Another key theme is God's choice of David as king. David is God's "son" (Psalm 2:7) and the people's "shepherd" (78:70-72), his representative on earth, ruling from Zion. Both Jesus and the early church would see anticipations of his ministry in many of these royal psalms.

What does it mean for us?

The Psalms are a rich source for our worship and prayers. When we run out of words or can't seem to find the right ones for a particular situation, the Psalms often come to our rescue! However, when we read the Psalms, we should always remember that they are both *poetry* and *prayers*. As *poetry* they are full of imagery, hyperbole, and emotion, so they cannot always be read literally. As *prayers* they are words addressed *to* God rather than words *from* God; the psalmist's appeal to God to smash his enemy's teeth, for example (3:7; 58:6), may reflect how he felt at that moment, but we should not assume that this is how God felt. Such prayers simply show us that we can bring all our feelings into God's presence. The content of Psalms shows us that it is not only our worship that we can bring to him, but also all our thoughts, emotions, concerns, expectations, hopes, and fears. God knows about them already, so we do not need to fear telling him what we are thinking!

▶ *See also* ***Musical directions in the Psalms****, page 608;* ***Acrostic psalms****, page 624;* ***Asaph****, page 647;* ***The Book of Psalms****, Visual Overview Z7.*

BOOK ONE (Psalms 1–41)

1
1 Oh, the joys of those who do not
follow the advice of the
wicked,
or stand around with sinners,
or join in with mockers.
2 But they delight in the law of the LORD,
meditating on it day and night.
3 They are like trees planted along the
riverbank,
bearing fruit each season.
Their leaves never wither,
and they prosper in all they do.

4 But not the wicked!
They are like worthless chaff, scattered
by the wind.
5 They will be condemned at the time of
judgment.
Sinners will have no place among the
godly.
6 For the LORD watches over the path of the
godly,
but the path of the wicked leads to
destruction.

2
1 Why are the nations so angry?
Why do they waste their time with
futile plans?
2 The kings of the earth prepare for battle;
the rulers plot together
against the LORD
and against his anointed one.
3 "Let us break their chains," they cry,
"and free ourselves from slavery to God."

4 But the one who rules in heaven laughs.
The Lord scoffs at them.
5 Then in anger he rebukes them,
terrifying them with his fierce fury.
6 For the Lord declares, "I have placed my
chosen king on the throne
in Jerusalem,* on my holy mountain."

7 The king proclaims the LORD's decree:
"The LORD said to me, 'You are my son.*
Today I have become your Father.*
8 Only ask, and I will give you the nations
as your inheritance,
the whole earth as your possession.
9 You will break* them with an iron rod
and smash them like clay pots.'"

10 Now then, you kings, act wisely!
Be warned, you rulers of the earth!
11 Serve the LORD with reverent fear,
and rejoice with trembling.
12 Submit to God's royal son,* or he will
become angry,
and you will be destroyed in the midst
of all your activities—
for his anger flares up in an instant.
But what joy for all who take refuge
in him!

▶ **1:2** *See* ***Delight in God's Law****, page 678.*

3

A psalm of David, regarding the time David fled from his son Absalom.

1 O LORD, I have so many enemies;
so many are against me.
2 So many are saying,
"God will never rescue him!"
*Interlude**
3 But you, O LORD, are a shield around me;
you are my glory, the one who holds
my head high.
4 I cried out to the LORD,
and he answered me from his holy
mountain. *Interlude*
5 I lay down and slept,
yet I woke up in safety,
for the LORD was watching over me.
6 I am not afraid of ten thousand
enemies
who surround me on every side.

7 Arise, O LORD!
Rescue me, my God!
Slap all my enemies in the face!
Shatter the teeth of the wicked!
8 Victory comes from you, O LORD.
May you bless your people. *Interlude*

4

For the choir director: A psalm of David, to be accompanied by stringed instruments.

1 Answer me when I call to you,
O God who declares me innocent.
Free me from my troubles.
Have mercy on me and hear my
prayer.

2 How long will you people ruin my
reputation?
How long will you make groundless
accusations?
How long will you continue your lies?
Interlude
3 You can be sure of this:
The LORD set apart the godly for
himself.
The LORD will answer when I call to
him.
4 Don't sin by letting anger control you.
Think about it overnight and remain
silent. *Interlude*
5 Offer sacrifices in the right spirit,
and trust the LORD.

6 Many people say, "Who will show us
better times?"
Let your face smile on us, LORD.
7 You have given me greater joy
than those who have abundant
harvests of grain and new wine.
8 In peace I will lie down and sleep,
for you alone, O LORD, will keep me
safe.

5

For the choir director: A psalm of David, to be accompanied by the flute.

1 O LORD, hear me as I pray;
pay attention to my groaning.

2:6 Hebrew *on Zion.* **2:7a** Or *Son;* also in 2:12. **2:7b** Or *Today I reveal you as my son.* **2:9** Greek version reads *rule.* Compare Rev 2:27. **2:12** The meaning of the Hebrew is uncertain. **3:2** Hebrew *Selah.* The meaning of this word is uncertain, though it is probably a musical or literary term. It is rendered *Interlude* throughout the Psalms.

Meditation

For the first of many times in the Psalms, God's people are reminded of the blessing of meditation (Psalm 1:2). Meditation involves reflecting on something deeply, quietly, and at length, shutting the door to everything else and focusing on just one thing—perhaps a verse of Scripture, or an aspect of God's nature, or an object (like a cross or something in creation). Through meditation we are seeking to be drawn deeper into God's love and God's ways.

The fact that meditation is practiced in other religions does not make it wrong; it is what they focus on that is wrong, not the meditation itself. The Psalms encourage us to meditate on God's word (e.g., Psalm 1:1-3), God's love (e.g., 48:9), and God's works (e.g., 77:10-12).

In today's busy world, where many of us find it hard to stop in the midst of all our activity, meditation can be a challenge. It was, however, a key feature of life for many of God's people in the Bible and throughout church history. Christian meditation can only enrich our lives.

2 Listen to my cry for help, my King and
my God,
for I pray to no one but you.
3 Listen to my voice in the morning, LORD.
Each morning I bring my requests to
you and wait expectantly.

4 O God, you take no pleasure in
wickedness;
you cannot tolerate the sins of the
wicked.
5 Therefore, the proud may not stand in
your presence,
for you hate all who do evil.
6 You will destroy those who tell lies.
The LORD detests murderers and
deceivers.

7 Because of your unfailing love, I can
enter your house;
I will worship at your Temple with
deepest awe.
8 Lead me in the right path, O LORD,
or my enemies will conquer me.
Make your way plain for me to follow.

9 My enemies cannot speak a truthful
word.
Their deepest desire is to destroy
others.
Their talk is foul, like the stench from an
open grave.
Their tongues are filled with flattery.*
10 O God, declare them guilty.
Let them be caught in their own traps.
Drive them away because of their many
sins,
for they have rebelled against you.

11 But let all who take refuge in you rejoice;
let them sing joyful praises forever.
Spread your protection over them,
that all who love your name may be
filled with joy.
12 For you bless the godly, O LORD;
you surround them with your shield
of love.

6

*For the choir director: A psalm of David, to be accompanied by an eight-stringed instrument.**

1 O LORD, don't rebuke me in your anger
or discipline me in your rage.
2 Have compassion on me, LORD, for I am
weak.
Heal me, LORD, for my bones are in
agony.
3 I am sick at heart.
How long, O LORD, until you
restore me?

4 Return, O LORD, and rescue me.
Save me because of your unfailing love.
5 For the dead do not remember you.
Who can praise you from the grave?*
6 I am worn out from sobbing.
All night I flood my bed with weeping,
drenching it with my tears.
7 My vision is blurred by grief;
my eyes are worn out because of all
my enemies.

8 Go away, all you who do evil,
for the LORD has heard my weeping.
9 The LORD has heard my plea;
the LORD will answer my prayer.

The Psalms can help you when you are feeling . . .

Abandoned: 13, 22, 31, 42
Afraid: 27, 34, 46, 55, 56
Angry: 4, 37, 73, 109
Bereaved: 23, 27, 71, 116
Betrayed: 41, 52, 55
Confused: 12, 73, 107
Depressed: 6, 25, 42, 143
Despairing: 13, 42, 130, 142
Discouraged: 31, 40, 61, 93, 121
Doubting: 10, 27, 53, 77
Far from God: 13, 22, 42, 139
Guilty: 25, 32, 51, 103, 130
Helpless: 27, 42, 46, 71, 121
Ill or weak: 6, 31, 41, 42, 103
Insecure: 27, 46, 71, 93, 125
Joyful: 33, 47, 66, 92, 103
Lonely: 3, 13, 25, 40, 139
Overwhelmed: 9, 24, 61, 142
Proud: 36, 49, 75
Stressed: 25, 31, 62, 142
Tempted: 51, 125, 141
Thankful: 100, 116, 136, 138
Threatened: 3, 7, 31, 35, 57
Trapped: 25, 27, 31, 88, 118
Troubled: 4, 20, 34, 37, 46
Undecided: 23, 25, 37, 125

10 May all my enemies be disgraced and
terrified.
May they suddenly turn back in shame.

7

A psalm of David, which he sang to the LORD concerning Cush of the tribe of Benjamin.*

1 I come to you for protection, O LORD
my God.
Save me from my persecutors—
rescue me!
2 If you don't, they will maul me like a lion,
tearing me to pieces with no one to
rescue me.
3 O LORD my God, if I have done wrong
or am guilty of injustice,
4 if I have betrayed a friend
or plundered my enemy without
cause,
5 then let my enemies capture me.
Let them trample me into the ground
and drag my honor in the dust.
Interlude
6 Arise, O LORD, in anger!
Stand up against the fury of my
enemies!
Wake up, my God, and bring
justice!
7 Gather the nations before you.
Rule over them from on high.
8 The LORD judges the nations.
Declare me righteous, O LORD,
for I am innocent, O Most High!
9 End the evil of those who are
wicked,
and defend the righteous.
For you look deep within the mind and
heart,
O righteous God.
10 God is my shield,
saving those whose hearts are true
and right.
11 God is an honest judge.
He is angry with the wicked every day.
12 If a person does not repent,
God* will sharpen his sword;
he will bend and string his bow.
13 He will prepare his deadly weapons
and shoot his flaming arrows.
14 The wicked conceive evil;
they are pregnant with trouble
and give birth to lies.
15 They dig a deep pit to trap others,
then fall into it themselves.
16 The trouble they make for others
backfires on them.
The violence they plan falls on their
own heads.
17 I will thank the LORD because he is
just;
I will sing praise to the name of the
LORD Most High.

8

*For the choir director: A psalm of David, to be accompanied by a stringed instrument.**

1 O LORD, our Lord, your majestic name
fills the earth!
Your glory is higher than the
heavens.
2 You have taught children and infants
to tell of your strength,*
silencing your enemies
and all who oppose you.
3 When I look at the night sky and see the
work of your fingers—
the moon and the stars you set in
place—
4 what are mere mortals that you should
think about them,

5:9 Greek version reads *with lies.* Compare Rom 3:13.
6:TITLE Hebrew *with stringed instruments; according to the sheminith.* **6:5** Hebrew *from Sheol?* **7:TITLE** Hebrew *A shiggaion,* probably indicating a musical setting for the psalm. **7:12** Hebrew *he.* **8:TITLE** Hebrew *according to the gittith.* **8:2** Greek version reads *to give you praise.* Compare Matt 21:16.

"Interlude"

At several points in the Psalms we find the word "Interlude"—in Hebrew, *Selah*. It is used seventy-one times in thirty-nine of the Psalms. Scholars are actually uncertain of its exact meaning, but it is probably some kind of musical indication, perhaps calling for a response from the worshipers or serving as an instruction to the musicians. It seems to serve the function of our saying today, "Let's pause and think about that!"

human beings that you should care
for them?*
5 Yet you made them only a little lower
than God*
and crowned them* with glory and
honor.
6 You gave them charge of everything you
made,
putting all things under their
authority—
7 the flocks and the herds
and all the wild animals,
8 the birds in the sky, the fish in the sea,
and everything that swims the ocean
currents.

9 O LORD, our Lord, your majestic name
fills the earth!

9 *For the choir director: A psalm of David, to be sung to the tune "Death of the Son."*

1 I will praise you, LORD, with all my
heart;
I will tell of all the marvelous things
you have done.
2 I will be filled with joy because of you.
I will sing praises to your name,
O Most High.

3 My enemies retreated;
they staggered and died when you
appeared.
4 For you have judged in my favor;
from your throne you have judged
with fairness.
5 You have rebuked the nations and
destroyed the wicked;
you have erased their names forever.
6 The enemy is finished, in endless ruins;
the cities you uprooted are now
forgotten.

7 But the LORD reigns forever,
executing judgment from his throne.
8 He will judge the world with justice
and rule the nations with fairness.
9 The LORD is a shelter for the oppressed,
a refuge in times of trouble.
10 Those who know your name trust in you,
for you, O LORD, do not abandon
those who search for you.

11 Sing praises to the LORD who reigns in
Jerusalem.*
Tell the world about his unforgettable
deeds.
12 For he who avenges murder cares for the
helpless.
He does not ignore the cries of those
who suffer.

13 LORD, have mercy on me.
See how my enemies torment me.
Snatch me back from the jaws of death.

The environment

Psalm 8 is a wonderful hymn of praise to the Creator for his creation. Creation belongs not to the devil, but to God—"the earth is the LORD's, and everything in it" (Psalm 24:1). It is not bad but good—indeed, "very good" (Genesis 1:31). It has not been abandoned by God but is rather sustained by "the mighty power of his command" (Hebrews 1:3), and even its smallest detail is watched over by him (e.g., Matthew 10:29). Creation should therefore be greatly respected (though never worshiped).

At the beginning, God delegated to humanity the responsibility to rule and care for creation on his behalf (Genesis 1:26-28), later giving specific commands governing the care of creation (e.g., Exodus 23:10-11; Deuteronomy 20:19). At the end, we see God renewing his creation, not destroying it (e.g., Revelation 21:1-5; 22:1-5).

We should therefore care for the world like God himself does. We all have a part to play in caring for the environment, especially when there is increasing evidence that careless human behavior is rapidly destroying our planet. Even resolving to do small things, like not throwing trash onto the street and not spoiling beautiful places, but rather seeking to recycle whenever we can, is to start to play our part.

14 Save me so I can praise you publicly at
Jerusalem's gates,
so I can rejoice that you have
rescued me.
15 The nations have fallen into the pit they
dug for others.
Their own feet have been caught in
the trap they set.
16 The LORD is known for his justice.
The wicked are trapped by their own
deeds. *Quiet Interlude**
17 The wicked will go down to the grave.*
This is the fate of all the nations who
ignore God.
18 But the needy will not be ignored
forever;
the hopes of the poor will not always
be crushed.
19 Arise, O LORD!
Do not let mere mortals defy you!
Judge the nations!
20 Make them tremble in fear, O LORD.
Let the nations know they are merely
human. *Interlude*

10

1 O LORD, why do you stand so far
away?
Why do you hide when I am in trouble?
2 The wicked arrogantly hunt down the
poor.
Let them be caught in the evil they
plan for others.
3 For they brag about their evil desires;
they praise the greedy and curse the
LORD.
4 The wicked are too proud to seek God.
They seem to think that God is dead.
5 Yet they succeed in everything they do.
They do not see your punishment
awaiting them.
They sneer at all their enemies.
6 They think, "Nothing bad will ever
happen to us!
We will be free of trouble forever!"
7 Their mouths are full of cursing, lies,
and threats.*
Trouble and evil are on the tips of
their tongues.
8 They lurk in ambush in the villages,
waiting to murder innocent people.
They are always searching for helpless
victims.
9 Like lions crouched in hiding,
they wait to pounce on the helpless.
Like hunters they capture the helpless
and drag them away in nets.
10 Their helpless victims are crushed;
they fall beneath the strength of the
wicked.
11 The wicked think, "God isn't watching us!
He has closed his eyes and won't even
see what we do!"
12 Arise, O LORD!
Punish the wicked, O God!
Do not ignore the helpless!
13 Why do the wicked get away with
despising God?
They think, "God will never call us
to account."
14 But you see the trouble and grief they
cause.
You take note of it and punish
them.
The helpless put their trust in you.
You defend the orphans.
15 Break the arms of these wicked, evil
people!
Go after them until the last one is
destroyed.
16 The LORD is king forever and ever!
The godless nations will vanish from
the land.
17 LORD, you know the hopes of the
helpless.
Surely you will hear their cries and
comfort them.
18 You will bring justice to the orphans and
the oppressed,
so mere people can no longer terrify
them.

11

For the choir director: A psalm of David.

1 I trust in the LORD for protection.
So why do you say to me,
"Fly like a bird to the mountains for
safety!
2 The wicked are stringing their bows
and fitting their arrows on the
bowstrings.

8:4 Hebrew *what is man that you should think of him, / the son of man that you should care for him?* **8:5a** Or *Yet you made them only a little lower than the angels;* Hebrew reads *Yet you made him* [i.e., man] *a little lower than Elohim.* **8:5b** Hebrew *him* [i.e., man]; similarly in 8:6. **9:11** Hebrew *Zion;* also in 9:14. **9:16** Hebrew *Higgaion Selah.* The meaning of this phrase is uncertain. **9:17** Hebrew *to Sheol.* **10:7** Greek version reads *cursing and bitterness.* Compare Rom 3:14.

They shoot from the shadows
at those whose hearts are right.
3 The foundations of law and order have collapsed.
What can the righteous do?"
4 But the LORD is in his holy Temple;
the LORD still rules from heaven.
He watches everyone closely,
examining every person on earth.
5 The LORD examines both the righteous and the wicked.
He hates those who love violence.
6 He will rain down blazing coals and burning sulfur on the wicked,
punishing them with scorching winds.
7 For the righteous LORD loves justice.
The virtuous will see his face.

12

*For the choir director: A psalm of David, to be accompanied by an eight-stringed instrument.**

1 Help, O LORD, for the godly are fast disappearing!
The faithful have vanished from the earth!
2 Neighbors lie to each other,
speaking with flattering lips and deceitful hearts.
3 May the LORD cut off their flattering lips
and silence their boastful tongues.
4 They say, "We will lie to our hearts' content.
Our lips are our own—who can stop us?"
5 The LORD replies, "I have seen violence done to the helpless,
and I have heard the groans of the poor.
Now I will rise up to rescue them,
as they have longed for me to do."
6 The LORD's promises are pure,
like silver refined in a furnace,
purified seven times over.
7 Therefore, LORD, we know you will protect the oppressed,
preserving them forever from this lying generation,
8 even though the wicked strut about,
and evil is praised throughout the land.

13

For the choir director: A psalm of David.

1 O LORD, how long will you forget me? Forever?
How long will you look the other way?
2 How long must I struggle with anguish in my soul,
with sorrow in my heart every day?
How long will my enemy have the upper hand?
3 Turn and answer me, O LORD my God!
Restore the sparkle to my eyes, or I will die.
4 Don't let my enemies gloat, saying, "We have defeated him!"
Don't let them rejoice at my downfall.
5 But I trust in your unfailing love.
I will rejoice because you have rescued me.
6 I will sing to the LORD
because he is good to me.

14

For the choir director: A psalm of David.

1 Only fools say in their hearts,
"There is no God."
They are corrupt, and their actions are evil;
not one of them does good!

Musical directions in the Psalms

Many of the Psalms have the heading, "For the choir director," often with instructions on how the psalm was to be performed. Sometimes the heading notes what musical instruments should accompany the psalm; sometimes it has a note about the psalm's original setting, probably to help with the mood in which it was to be sung (e.g., Psalm 18); and sometimes it includes instructions on what tune was to be used (e.g., Psalm 22). All of these serve to remind us that the psalms were originally written to be sung, not spoken. We don't need to be musicians to try that out; we can make up our own tunes as we go along and just sing with joy to God.

2 The LORD looks down from heaven
on the entire human race;
he looks to see if anyone is truly wise,
if anyone seeks God.
3 But no, all have turned away;
all have become corrupt.*
No one does good,
not a single one!

4 Will those who do evil never learn?
They eat up my people like bread
and wouldn't think of praying to the
LORD.
5 Terror will grip them,
for God is with those who obey him.
6 The wicked frustrate the plans of the
oppressed,
but the LORD will protect his people.

7 Who will come from Mount Zion to
rescue Israel?
When the LORD restores his people,
Jacob will shout with joy, and Israel
will rejoice.

15
A psalm of David.

1 Who may worship in your sanctuary,
LORD?
Who may enter your presence on your
holy hill?
2 Those who lead blameless lives and do
what is right,
speaking the truth from sincere hearts.
3 Those who refuse to gossip
or harm their neighbors
or speak evil of their friends.
4 Those who despise flagrant sinners,
and honor the faithful followers of the
LORD,
and keep their promises even when it
hurts.
5 Those who lend money without
charging interest,
and who cannot be bribed to lie about
the innocent.
Such people will stand firm forever.

16
A psalm of David.*

1 Keep me safe, O God,
for I have come to you for refuge.

2 I said to the LORD, "You are my Master!
Every good thing I have comes from
you."
3 The godly people in the land
are my true heroes!
I take pleasure in them!

12:TITLE Hebrew *according to the sheminith.* **14:3** Greek version reads *have become useless.* Compare Rom 3:12. **16:TITLE** Hebrew *miktam.* This may be a literary or musical term.

Foolishness

Today, we often think of a fool as someone who has not succeeded academically, or who has made bad decisions in business. But in the Bible, fools are those who say, "There is no God" (Psalm 14:1). Of course, fools may not speak those words aloud, which is why this verse speaks of them saying this "in their hearts." But the heart is revealed in actions—daily life lived without reference to God. This is true foolishness.

It is easy to think that such foolishness concerns only others, not people like us. But when we look at the wide-ranging actions that the Bible considers foolish, we may need to think again. Here are some examples: not trusting God (2 Chronicles 16:7-9); engaging in ungodly speech or actions (Isaiah 32:5-7); dishonest business practices (Jeremiah 17:11); disobeying God's word (1 Samuel 13:13); not expressing our faith through good works (James 2:20); spreading slander about others (Proverbs 10:18); enjoying arguments (Proverbs 20:3); not putting Christ's words into practice (Matthew 7:24-27); being greedy to get more money (Luke 12:16-21); not being ready for Christ's return (Matthew 25:1-13).

In light of these examples, there are more fools in the church than we would like to admit. The question each of us must ask ourselves is, am I one of them?

▶ *See also **Wisdom**, page 701.*

4 Troubles multiply for those who chase
after other gods.
I will not take part in their sacrifices
of blood
or even speak the names of their gods.

5 LORD, you alone are my inheritance, my
cup of blessing.
You guard all that is mine.
6 The land you have given me is a
pleasant land.
What a wonderful inheritance!
7 I will bless the LORD who guides me;
even at night my heart instructs me.
8 I know the LORD is always with me.
I will not be shaken, for he is right
beside me.

9 No wonder my heart is glad, and
I rejoice.*
My body rests in safety.
10 For you will not leave my soul among
the dead*
or allow your holy one* to rot in the
grave.
11 You will show me the way of life,
granting me the joy of your presence
and the pleasures of living with you
forever.*

17

A prayer of David.

1 O LORD, hear my plea for justice.
Listen to my cry for help.
Pay attention to my prayer,
for it comes from honest lips.
2 Declare me innocent,
for you see those who do right.

3 You have tested my thoughts and
examined my heart in the night.
You have scrutinized me and found
nothing wrong.
I am determined not to sin in what
I say.
4 I have followed your commands,
which keep me from following cruel
and evil people.
5 My steps have stayed on your path;
I have not wavered from following you.

6 I am praying to you because I know you
will answer, O God.
Bend down and listen as I pray.
7 Show me your unfailing love in
wonderful ways.
By your mighty power you rescue
those who seek refuge from their
enemies.
8 Guard me as you would guard your own
eyes.*
Hide me in the shadow of your wings.
9 Protect me from wicked people who
attack me,
from murderous enemies who
surround me.
10 They are without pity.
Listen to their boasting!
11 They track me down and surround me,
watching for the chance to throw me
to the ground.
12 They are like hungry lions, eager to tear
me apart—
like young lions hiding in ambush.

13 Arise, O LORD!
Stand against them, and bring them
to their knees!
Rescue me from the wicked with your
sword!
14 By the power of your hand, O LORD,
destroy those who look to this world
for their reward.
But satisfy the hunger of your treasured
ones.
May their children have plenty,
leaving an inheritance for their
descendants.
15 Because I am righteous, I will see you.
When I awake, I will see you face to
face and be satisfied.

18

For the choir director: A psalm of David, the servant of the LORD. He sang this song to the LORD on the day the LORD rescued him from all his enemies and from Saul. He sang:

1 I love you, LORD;
you are my strength.
2 The LORD is my rock, my fortress, and
my savior;
my God is my rock, in whom I find
protection.
He is my shield, the power that saves me,
and my place of safety.
3 I called on the LORD, who is worthy of
praise,
and he saved me from my enemies.

4 The ropes of death entangled me;
floods of destruction swept over me.
5 The grave* wrapped its ropes around me;
death laid a trap in my path.

6 But in my distress I cried out to the LORD;
yes, I prayed to my God for help.
He heard me from his sanctuary;
my cry to him reached his ears.

7 Then the earth quaked and trembled.
The foundations of the mountains shook;
they quaked because of his anger.
8 Smoke poured from his nostrils;
fierce flames leaped from his mouth.
Glowing coals blazed forth from him.
9 He opened the heavens and came down;
dark storm clouds were beneath his feet.
10 Mounted on a mighty angelic being,*
he flew,
soaring on the wings of the wind.
11 He shrouded himself in darkness,
veiling his approach with dark rain clouds.
12 Thick clouds shielded the brightness around him
and rained down hail and burning coals.*
13 The LORD thundered from heaven;
the voice of the Most High resounded
amid the hail and burning coals.
14 He shot his arrows and scattered his enemies;
great bolts of lightning flashed, and they were confused.
15 Then at your command, O LORD,
at the blast of your breath,
the bottom of the sea could be seen,
and the foundations of the earth were laid bare.

16 He reached down from heaven and rescued me;
he drew me out of deep waters.
17 He rescued me from my powerful enemies,
from those who hated me and were too strong for me.
18 They attacked me at a moment when I was in distress,
but the LORD supported me.
19 He led me to a place of safety;
he rescued me because he delights in me.
20 The LORD rewarded me for doing right;
he restored me because of my innocence.
21 For I have kept the ways of the LORD;
I have not turned from my God to follow evil.
22 I have followed all his regulations;
I have never abandoned his decrees.
23 I am blameless before God;
I have kept myself from sin.
24 The LORD rewarded me for doing right.
He has seen my innocence.

25 To the faithful you show yourself faithful;
to those with integrity you show integrity.
26 To the pure you show yourself pure,
but to the crooked you show yourself shrewd.
27 You rescue the humble,
but you humiliate the proud.
28 You light a lamp for me.
The LORD, my God, lights up my darkness.
29 In your strength I can crush an army;
with my God I can scale any wall.

30 God's way is perfect.
All the LORD's promises prove true.
He is a shield for all who look to him for protection.
31 For who is God except the LORD?
Who but our God is a solid rock?
32 God arms me with strength,
and he makes my way perfect.
33 He makes me as surefooted as a deer,
enabling me to stand on mountain heights.
34 He trains my hands for battle;
he strengthens my arm to draw a bronze bow.
35 You have given me your shield of victory.
Your right hand supports me;
your help* has made me great.
36 You have made a wide path for my feet
to keep them from slipping.

37 I chased my enemies and caught them;
I did not stop until they were conquered.
38 I struck them down so they could not get up;
they fell beneath my feet.

16:9 Greek version reads *and my tongue shouts his praises.* Compare Acts 2:26. **16:10a** Hebrew *in Sheol.* **16:10b** Or *your Holy One.* **16:11** Greek version reads *You have shown me the way of life, / and you will fill me with the joy of your presence.* Compare Acts 2:28. **17:8** Hebrew *as the pupil of your eye.* **18:5** Hebrew *Sheol.* **18:10** Hebrew *a cherub.* **18:12** Or *and lightning bolts;* also in 18:13. **18:35** Hebrew *your humility;* compare 2 Sam 22:36.

[39] You have armed me with strength for the battle;
you have subdued my enemies under my feet.
[40] You placed my foot on their necks.
I have destroyed all who hated me.
[41] They called for help, but no one came to their rescue.
They even cried to the LORD, but he refused to answer.
[42] I ground them as fine as dust in the wind.
I swept them into the gutter like dirt.
[43] You gave me victory over my accusers.
You appointed me ruler over nations;
people I don't even know now serve me.
[44] As soon as they hear of me, they submit;
foreign nations cringe before me.
[45] They all lose their courage
and come trembling from their strongholds.

[46] The LORD lives! Praise to my Rock!
May the God of my salvation be exalted!
[47] He is the God who pays back those who harm me;
he subdues the nations under me
[48] and rescues me from my enemies.
You hold me safe beyond the reach of my enemies;
you save me from violent opponents.
[49] For this, O LORD, I will praise you among the nations;
I will sing praises to your name.
[50] You give great victories to your king;
you show unfailing love to your anointed,
to David and all his descendants forever.

19

For the choir director: A psalm of David.

[1] The heavens proclaim the glory of God.
The skies display his craftsmanship.
[2] Day after day they continue to speak;
night after night they make him known.
[3] They speak without a sound or word;
their voice is never heard.*
[4] Yet their message has gone throughout the earth,
and their words to all the world.

God has made a home in the heavens for the sun.
[5] It bursts forth like a radiant bridegroom after his wedding.

Revelation

The opening words of Psalm 19 are an example of what theologians call "general" or "natural" revelation. That is, by merely looking at the world around us, we should be able to realize that—no matter what mechanism brought it all into being—creation's very existence means someone must have designed it and made it, such is its beauty, intricacy, and interdependence. Indeed, not to recognize such a Creator is to willfully close our eyes to God. As Paul put it, "For ever since the world was created, people have seen the earth and sky. Through everything God made, they can clearly see his invisible qualities—his eternal power and divine nature. So they have no excuse for not knowing God" (Romans 1:20). Jesus too reasoned from creation that there is a God, and a God who cares: "Look at the lilies of the field and how they grow. . . . If God cares so wonderfully for wildflowers . . . he will certainly care for you. Why do you have so little faith?" (Matthew 6:28, 30).

Yet the Bible also recognizes that natural revelation in itself cannot do everything. It may awaken our sensitivity to God, but it cannot lead us to salvation. That is why the psalmist moves on from his delight in creation (Psalm 19:1-6) to his delight in God's word (19:7-14). It is God's word, God's truth alone, that can revive our souls (19:7).

▸ *See also* ***Knowledge and revelation****, page 599;* ***Delight in God's Law****, page 678.*

It rejoices like a great athlete eager to
run the race.
6 The sun rises at one end of the heavens
and follows its course to the other end.
Nothing can hide from its heat.

7 The instructions of the LORD are perfect,
reviving the soul.
The decrees of the LORD are trustworthy,
making wise the simple.
8 The commandments of the LORD are
right,
bringing joy to the heart.
The commands of the LORD are clear,
giving insight for living.
9 Reverence for the LORD is pure,
lasting forever.
The laws of the LORD are true;
each one is fair.
10 They are more desirable than gold,
even the finest gold.
They are sweeter than honey,
even honey dripping from the comb.
11 They are a warning to your servant,
a great reward for those who obey
them.

12 How can I know all the sins lurking in
my heart?
Cleanse me from these hidden faults.
13 Keep your servant from deliberate sins!
Don't let them control me.
Then I will be free of guilt
and innocent of great sin.

14 May the words of my mouth
and the meditation of my heart
be pleasing to you,
O LORD, my rock and my redeemer.

20 *For the choir director: A psalm of David.*

1 In times of trouble, may the LORD
answer your cry.
May the name of the God of Jacob
keep you safe from all harm.
2 May he send you help from his
sanctuary
and strengthen you from Jerusalem.*
3 May he remember all your gifts
and look favorably on your burnt
offerings. *Interlude*

4 May he grant your heart's desires
and make all your plans succeed.
5 May we shout for joy when we hear of
your victory
and raise a victory banner in the name
of our God.
May the LORD answer all your prayers.

6 Now I know that the LORD rescues his
anointed king.
He will answer him from his holy
heaven
and rescue him by his great power.
7 Some nations boast of their chariots and
horses,
but we boast in the name of the LORD
our God.
8 Those nations will fall down and
collapse,
but we will rise up and stand firm.

9 Give victory to our king, O LORD!
Answer our cry for help.

21 *For the choir director: A psalm of David.*

1 How the king rejoices in your strength,
O LORD!
He shouts with joy because you give
him victory.
2 For you have given him his heart's
desire;
you have withheld nothing he
requested. *Interlude*

3 You welcomed him back with success
and prosperity.
You placed a crown of finest gold on
his head.
4 He asked you to preserve his life,
and you granted his request.
The days of his life stretch on forever.
5 Your victory brings him great honor,
and you have clothed him with
splendor and majesty.
6 You have endowed him with eternal
blessings
and given him the joy of your presence.
7 For the king trusts in the LORD.
The unfailing love of the Most High
will keep him from stumbling.

8 You will capture all your enemies.
Your strong right hand will seize all
who hate you.
9 You will throw them in a flaming furnace
when you appear.
The LORD will consume them in his anger;
fire will devour them.

19:3 Or *There is no speech or language where their voice is not heard.* **20:2** Hebrew *Zion.*

10 You will wipe their children from the
face of the earth;
they will never have descendants.
11 Although they plot against you,
their evil schemes will never
succeed.
12 For they will turn and run
when they see your arrows aimed at
them.
13 Rise up, O LORD, in all your power.
With music and singing we celebrate
your mighty acts.

22 *For the choir director: A psalm of David, to be sung to the tune "Doe of the Dawn."*

1 My God, my God, why have you
abandoned me?
Why are you so far away when I groan
for help?
2 Every day I call to you, my God, but you
do not answer.
Every night I lift my voice, but I find
no relief.
3 Yet you are holy,
enthroned on the praises of Israel.
4 Our ancestors trusted in you,
and you rescued them.
5 They cried out to you and were saved.
They trusted in you and were never
disgraced.
6 But I am a worm and not a man.
I am scorned and despised by all!
7 Everyone who sees me mocks me.
They sneer and shake their heads,
saying,
8 "Is this the one who relies on the LORD?
Then let the LORD save him!
If the LORD loves him so much,
let the LORD rescue him!"
9 Yet you brought me safely from my
mother's womb
and led me to trust you at my mother's
breast.
10 I was thrust into your arms at my birth.
You have been my God from the
moment I was born.
11 Do not stay so far from me,
for trouble is near,
and no one else can help me.
12 My enemies surround me like a herd of
bulls;
fierce bulls of Bashan have hemmed
me in!
13 Like lions they open their jaws
against me,
roaring and tearing into their prey.
14 My life is poured out like water,
and all my bones are out of joint.
My heart is like wax,
melting within me.

Jesus Christ in the Psalms

The early Christians believed that many psalms foreshadowed aspects of the life and work of Jesus Christ. Jesus was the "son of David" and, while not all the psalms were written by David, Jesus frequently quoted from psalms attributed to David, especially toward the end of his life. Many of David's psalms parallel Jesus' experiences:

- betrayed by a close friend (Psalm 41:9; Matthew 26:23-24)
- hated without cause (Psalm 35:19; John 15:25)
- abandoned by God (Psalm 22:1; Matthew 27:46)
- offered wine and gall on the cross (Psalm 69:21; Matthew 27:34)
- mocked by enemies (Psalm 22:7-8; Luke 23:35)
- dice thrown for his clothing (Psalm 22:18; Matthew 27:35)
- his bones were not broken (Psalm 34:20; John 19:36-37)
- his resurrection from the dead (Psalm 16:10; Acts 13:35)
- David's son and David's Lord (Psalm 110:1; Matthew 22:44)

▶ *See also* ***The Messianic King****, page 674;* ***Prophecies about Christ****, page 806;* ***Prophecies of the Messiah****, page 1044;* ***Jesus and the Old Testament****, page 1079;* ***The Old Testament in the New Testament****, page 1403;* ***Prophecies of the Messiah****, Visual Overview Z12.*

15 My strength has dried up like sunbaked
clay.
My tongue sticks to the roof of my
mouth.
You have laid me in the dust and left
me for dead.
16 My enemies surround me like a pack of
dogs;
an evil gang closes in on me.
They have pierced* my hands and feet.
17 I can count all my bones.
My enemies stare at me and gloat.
18 They divide my garments among
themselves
and throw dice* for my clothing.

19 O LORD, do not stay far away!
You are my strength; come quickly to
my aid!
20 Save me from the sword;
spare my precious life from these dogs.
21 Snatch me from the lion's jaws
and from the horns of these wild oxen.

22 I will proclaim your name to my brothers
and sisters.*
I will praise you among your
assembled people.
23 Praise the LORD, all you who fear him!
Honor him, all you descendants of
Jacob!
Show him reverence, all you
descendants of Israel!
24 For he has not ignored or belittled the
suffering of the needy.
He has not turned his back on them,
but has listened to their cries for help.

25 I will praise you in the great assembly.
I will fulfill my vows in the presence
of those who worship you.
26 The poor will eat and be satisfied.
All who seek the LORD will praise him.
Their hearts will rejoice with
everlasting joy.
27 The whole earth will acknowledge the
LORD and return to him.
All the families of the nations will
bow down before him.
28 For royal power belongs to the LORD.
He rules all the nations.

29 Let the rich of the earth feast and
worship.
Bow before him, all who are mortal,
all whose lives will end as dust.
30 Our children will also serve him.
Future generations will hear about the
wonders of the Lord.
31 His righteous acts will be told to those
not yet born.
They will hear about everything he
has done.

23 *A psalm of David.*

1 The LORD is my shepherd;
I have all that I need.
2 He lets me rest in green meadows;
he leads me beside peaceful streams.
3 He renews my strength.
He guides me along right paths,
bringing honor to his name.
4 Even when I walk
through the darkest valley,*
I will not be afraid,
for you are close beside me.
Your rod and your staff
protect and comfort me.
5 You prepare a feast for me
in the presence of my enemies.
You honor me by anointing my head
with oil.
My cup overflows with blessings.
6 Surely your goodness and unfailing love
will pursue me
all the days of my life,
and I will live in the house of the LORD
forever.

24 *A psalm of David.*

1 The earth is the LORD's, and everything
in it.
The world and all its people belong
to him.
2 For he laid the earth's foundation on the
seas
and built it on the ocean depths.
3 Who may climb the mountain of the
LORD?
Who may stand in his holy place?

22:16 As in some Hebrew manuscripts and Greek and Syriac versions; most Hebrew manuscripts read *They are like a lion at.* **22:18** Hebrew *cast lots.* **22:22** Hebrew *my brothers.* **23:4** Or *the dark valley of death.*

▸ **23:1-6** *See **Shepherds**, page 936.* **24:1** *See **The environment**, page 606.*

[4] Only those whose hands and hearts are pure,
who do not worship idols
and never tell lies.
[5] They will receive the LORD's blessing
and have a right relationship with God their savior.
[6] Such people may seek you
and worship in your presence, O God of Jacob.* *Interlude*

[7] Open up, ancient gates!
Open up, ancient doors,
and let the King of glory enter.
[8] Who is the King of glory?
The LORD, strong and mighty;
the LORD, invincible in battle.
[9] Open up, ancient gates!
Open up, ancient doors,
and let the King of glory enter.
[10] Who is the King of glory?
The LORD of Heaven's Armies—
he is the King of glory. *Interlude*

25*

A psalm of David.

[1] O LORD, I give my life to you.
[2] I trust in you, my God!
Do not let me be disgraced,
or let my enemies rejoice in my defeat.
[3] No one who trusts in you will ever be disgraced,
but disgrace comes to those who try to deceive others.

[4] Show me the right path, O LORD;
point out the road for me to follow.
[5] Lead me by your truth and teach me,
for you are the God who saves me.
All day long I put my hope in you.
[6] Remember, O LORD, your compassion and unfailing love,
which you have shown from long ages past.
[7] Do not remember the rebellious sins of my youth.
Remember me in the light of your unfailing love,
for you are merciful, O LORD.

[8] The LORD is good and does what is right;
he shows the proper path to those who go astray.
[9] He leads the humble in doing right,
teaching them his way.
[10] The LORD leads with unfailing love and faithfulness
all who keep his covenant and obey his demands.

[11] For the honor of your name, O LORD,
forgive my many, many sins.
[12] Who are those who fear the LORD?
He will show them the path they should choose.
[13] They will live in prosperity,
and their children will inherit the land.
[14] The LORD is a friend to those who fear him.
He teaches them his covenant.
[15] My eyes are always on the LORD,
for he rescues me from the traps of my enemies.

[16] Turn to me and have mercy,
for I am alone and in deep distress.
[17] My problems go from bad to worse.
Oh, save me from them all!
[18] Feel my pain and see my trouble.
Forgive all my sins.
[19] See how many enemies I have
and how viciously they hate me!
[20] Protect me! Rescue my life from them!
Do not let me be disgraced, for in you I take refuge.
[21] May integrity and honesty protect me,
for I put my hope in you.

[22] O God, ransom Israel
from all its troubles.

26

A psalm of David.

[1] Declare me innocent, O LORD,
for I have acted with integrity;
I have trusted in the LORD without wavering.
[2] Put me on trial, LORD, and cross-examine me.
Test my motives and my heart.
[3] For I am always aware of your unfailing love,
and I have lived according to your truth.
[4] I do not spend time with liars
or go along with hypocrites.
[5] I hate the gatherings of those who do evil,
and I refuse to join in with the wicked.
[6] I wash my hands to declare my innocence.
I come to your altar, O LORD,

7 singing a song of thanksgiving
and telling of all your wonders.
8 I love your sanctuary, LORD,
the place where your glorious
presence dwells.
9 Don't let me suffer the fate of sinners.
Don't condemn me along with
murderers.
10 Their hands are dirty with evil
schemes,
and they constantly take bribes.
11 But I am not like that; I live with
integrity.
So redeem me and show me mercy.
12 Now I stand on solid ground,
and I will publicly praise the
LORD.

27

A psalm of David.

1 The LORD is my light and my
salvation—
so why should I be afraid?
The LORD is my fortress, protecting me
from danger,
so why should I tremble?
2 When evil people come to devour me,
when my enemies and foes attack me,
they will stumble and fall.
3 Though a mighty army surrounds me,
my heart will not be afraid.
Even if I am attacked,
I will remain confident.
4 The one thing I ask of the LORD—
the thing I seek most—
is to live in the house of the LORD all the
days of my life,
delighting in the LORD's perfections
and meditating in his Temple.
5 For he will conceal me there when
troubles come;
he will hide me in his sanctuary.
He will place me out of reach on
a high rock.
6 Then I will hold my head high
above my enemies who surround me.
At his sanctuary I will offer sacrifices
with shouts of joy,
singing and praising the LORD with
music.
7 Hear me as I pray, O LORD.
Be merciful and answer me!
8 My heart has heard you say, "Come and
talk with me."

24:6 As in two Hebrew manuscripts and Greek and Syriac versions; most Hebrew manuscripts read *O Jacob.* **25** This psalm is a Hebrew acrostic poem; each verse begins with a successive letter of the Hebrew alphabet.

▸ **27:1-14** See ***Thanksgiving***, page 665.

Rejection

Feeling rejected—believing that no one likes us or wants us—can be a profound and crippling human emotion. Sometimes the rejection may be real, as when the Jewish leaders rejected Christ; but often, the rejection is in our own thinking. This was the case here for David, who was fearful that God had rejected him (Psalm 27:9)—something the Bible says he will never do.

If our rejection is real, we need to ask, "Is there anything I can do about it?" It may be something in our own attitudes or behavior that makes people reject us, and if we pray, God will reveal it. But if the rejection is real yet undeserved, then we need to remember that Christ himself was rejected (e.g., Isaiah 53:3). He therefore understands how we feel and can strengthen us. But how do we know if our rejection is more imagined than real? That is when we need a loving friend whom we will allow to tell us the truth and call us to see things as they really are.

Above all, we should remember that the Bible says God will never reject us, even if people do. Jesus promised that "those the Father has given me will come to me, and I will never reject them" (John 6:37); and having come to him, we can be absolutely sure of the next promise: "I will never fail you. I will never abandon you" (Hebrews 13:5; see also Deuteronomy 31:6).

And my heart responds, "LORD, I am coming."
9 Do not turn your back on me.
Do not reject your servant in anger.
You have always been my helper.
Don't leave me now; don't abandon me,
O God of my salvation!
10 Even if my father and mother abandon me,
the LORD will hold me close.
11 Teach me how to live, O LORD.
Lead me along the right path,
for my enemies are waiting for me.
12 Do not let me fall into their hands.
For they accuse me of things I've never done;
with every breath they threaten me with violence.
13 Yet I am confident I will see the LORD's goodness
while I am here in the land of the living.

14 Wait patiently for the LORD.
Be brave and courageous.
Yes, wait patiently for the LORD.

28 *A psalm of David.*

1 I pray to you, O LORD, my rock.
Do not turn a deaf ear to me.
For if you are silent,
I might as well give up and die.
2 Listen to my prayer for mercy
as I cry out to you for help,
as I lift my hands toward your holy sanctuary.

3 Do not drag me away with the wicked—
with those who do evil—
those who speak friendly words to their neighbors
while planning evil in their hearts.
4 Give them the punishment they so richly deserve!
Measure it out in proportion to their wickedness.
Pay them back for all their evil deeds!
Give them a taste of what they have done to others.
5 They care nothing for what the LORD has done
or for what his hands have made.
So he will tear them down,
and they will never be rebuilt!

6 Praise the LORD!
For he has heard my cry for mercy.
7 The LORD is my strength and shield.
I trust him with all my heart.
He helps me, and my heart is filled with joy.
I burst out in songs of thanksgiving.

8 The LORD gives his people strength.
He is a safe fortress for his anointed king.
9 Save your people!
Bless Israel, your special possession.*
Lead them like a shepherd,
and carry them in your arms forever.

29 *A psalm of David.*

1 Honor the LORD, you heavenly beings*;
honor the LORD for his glory and strength.
2 Honor the LORD for the glory of his name.
Worship the LORD in the splendor of his holiness.

3 The voice of the LORD echoes above the sea.
The God of glory thunders.
The LORD thunders over the mighty sea.
4 The voice of the LORD is powerful;
the voice of the LORD is majestic.
5 The voice of the LORD splits the mighty cedars;
the LORD shatters the cedars of Lebanon.
6 He makes Lebanon's mountains skip like a calf;
he makes Mount Hermon* leap like a young wild ox.
7 The voice of the LORD strikes
with bolts of lightning.
8 The voice of the LORD makes the barren wilderness quake;
the LORD shakes the wilderness of Kadesh.
9 The voice of the LORD twists mighty oaks*
and strips the forests bare.
In his Temple everyone shouts,
"Glory!"

10 The LORD rules over the floodwaters.
The LORD reigns as king forever.
11 The LORD gives his people strength.
The LORD blesses them with peace.

30 *A psalm of David. A song for the dedication of the Temple.*

[1] I will exalt you, LORD, for you rescued me.
You refused to let my enemies triumph over me.
[2] O LORD my God, I cried to you for help,
and you restored my health.
[3] You brought me up from the grave,* O LORD.
You kept me from falling into the pit of death.

[4] Sing to the LORD, all you godly ones!
Praise his holy name.
[5] For his anger lasts only a moment,
but his favor lasts a lifetime!
Weeping may last through the night,
but joy comes with the morning.

[6] When I was prosperous, I said,
"Nothing can stop me now!"
[7] Your favor, O LORD, made me as secure as a mountain.
Then you turned away from me, and I was shattered.

[8] I cried out to you, O LORD.
I begged the Lord for mercy, saying,
[9] "What will you gain if I die,
if I sink into the grave?
Can my dust praise you?
Can it tell of your faithfulness?
[10] Hear me, LORD, and have mercy on me.
Help me, O LORD."

[11] You have turned my mourning into joyful dancing.
You have taken away my clothes of mourning and clothed me with joy,
[12] that I might sing praises to you and not be silent.
O LORD my God, I will give you thanks forever!

31 *For the choir director: A psalm of David.*

[1] O LORD, I have come to you for protection;
don't let me be disgraced.
Save me, for you do what is right.
[2] Turn your ear to listen to me;
rescue me quickly.
Be my rock of protection,
a fortress where I will be safe.
[3] You are my rock and my fortress.
For the honor of your name, lead me out of this danger.
[4] Pull me from the trap my enemies set for me,
for I find protection in you alone.
[5] I entrust my spirit into your hand.
Rescue me, LORD, for you are a faithful God.

[6] I hate those who worship worthless idols.
I trust in the LORD.
[7] I will be glad and rejoice in your unfailing love,
for you have seen my troubles,
and you care about the anguish of my soul.
[8] You have not handed me over to my enemies
but have set me in a safe place.

[9] Have mercy on me, LORD, for I am in distress.
Tears blur my eyes.
My body and soul are withering away.
[10] I am dying from grief;
my years are shortened by sadness.
Sin has drained my strength;
I am wasting away from within.
[11] I am scorned by all my enemies
and despised by my neighbors—
even my friends are afraid to come near me.
When they see me on the street,
they run the other way.
[12] I am ignored as if I were dead,
as if I were a broken pot.
[13] I have heard the many rumors about me,
and I am surrounded by terror.
My enemies conspire against me,
plotting to take my life.

[14] But I am trusting you, O LORD,
saying, "You are my God!"
[15] My future is in your hands.
Rescue me from those who hunt me down relentlessly.
[16] Let your favor shine on your servant.
In your unfailing love, rescue me.
[17] Don't let me be disgraced, O LORD,
for I call out to you for help.
Let the wicked be disgraced;
let them lie silent in the grave.*

28:9 Hebrew *Bless your inheritance.* **29:1** Hebrew *you sons of God.* **29:6** Hebrew *Sirion,* another name for Mount Hermon. **29:9** Or *causes the deer to writhe in labor.* **30:3** Hebrew *from Sheol.* **31:17** Hebrew *in Sheol.*

[18] Silence their lying lips—
those proud and arrogant lips that
accuse the godly.
[19] How great is the goodness
you have stored up for those who fear
you.
You lavish it on those who come to you
for protection,
blessing them before the watching
world.
[20] You hide them in the shelter of your
presence,
safe from those who conspire against
them.
You shelter them in your presence,
far from accusing tongues.
[21] Praise the LORD,
for he has shown me the wonders of
his unfailing love.
He kept me safe when my city was
under attack.
[22] In panic I cried out,
"I am cut off from the LORD!"
But you heard my cry for mercy
and answered my call for help.
[23] Love the LORD, all you godly ones!
For the LORD protects those who are
loyal to him,
but he harshly punishes the arrogant.
[24] So be strong and courageous,
all you who put your hope in the
LORD!

32

A psalm of David.*

[1] Oh, what joy for those
whose disobedience is forgiven,
whose sin is put out of sight!
[2] Yes, what joy for those
whose record the LORD has cleared
of guilt,*
whose lives are lived in complete
honesty!
[3] When I refused to confess my sin,
my body wasted away,
and I groaned all day long.
[4] Day and night your hand of discipline
was heavy on me.
My strength evaporated like water in
the summer heat. *Interlude*
[5] Finally, I confessed all my sins to you
and stopped trying to hide my guilt.
I said to myself, "I will confess my
rebellion to the LORD."
And you forgave me! All my guilt is
gone. *Interlude*
[6] Therefore, let all the godly pray to you
while there is still time,

Guilt

Guilt is the feeling that our conscience produces when we have done wrong, causing us to feel shame, disgrace, despair, unworthiness, or uncleanness. As such, guilt is a good thing—providing it drives us back to God. But unresolved guilt eats away at us, accusing and nagging us, even affecting our mental and physical health, just as David discovered (Psalm 32:3-4). But the minute he confessed his sin to God, the guilt instantly lifted (Psalm 32:5).

Satan tries to get us to hide our sin or explain it away, just as he did with Adam and Eve, for he does not want us to discover God's grace. It is therefore God's kindness that he does not let us get away with things but, through his Holy Spirit, keeps nagging at our conscience, stirring up guilt—not so he can condemn us but so he can forgive us and free us as we confess our sin to him.

When we do not respond to our conscience but try to bury the guilt, deep spiritual, mental, or physical harm begins to develop. There are few things more dangerous than a hardened conscience. But guilt provokes us to keep our conscience clear before God by quickly confessing our sin to him and instantly, like the psalmist, finding freedom and forgiveness as we do so (1 John 1:9).

▶ *See also* ***Is there anything God won't forgive?****, page 633;* ***How can I be sure God has forgiven me?****, page 1433.*

that they may not drown in the
floodwaters of judgment.
7 For you are my hiding place;
you protect me from trouble.
You surround me with songs of
victory. *Interlude*

8 The LORD says, "I will guide you along
the best pathway for your life.
I will advise you and watch over you.
9 Do not be like a senseless horse or mule
that needs a bit and bridle to keep it
under control."

10 Many sorrows come to the wicked,
but unfailing love surrounds those
who trust the LORD.
11 So rejoice in the LORD and be glad, all
you who obey him!
Shout for joy, all you whose hearts are
pure!

33

1 Let the godly sing for joy to the
LORD;
it is fitting for the pure to praise him.
2 Praise the LORD with melodies on the
lyre;
make music for him on the
ten-stringed harp.
3 Sing a new song of praise to him;
play skillfully on the harp, and sing
with joy.
4 For the word of the LORD holds true,
and we can trust everything he does.
5 He loves whatever is just and good;
the unfailing love of the LORD fills the
earth.

6 The LORD merely spoke,
and the heavens were created.
He breathed the word,
and all the stars were born.
7 He assigned the sea its boundaries
and locked the oceans in vast reservoirs.
8 Let the whole world fear the LORD,
and let everyone stand in awe of him.
9 For when he spoke, the world began!
It appeared at his command.

10 The LORD frustrates the plans of the
nations
and thwarts all their schemes.
11 But the LORD's plans stand firm forever;
his intentions can never be shaken.
12 What joy for the nation whose God is the
LORD,
whose people he has chosen as his
inheritance.

13 The LORD looks down from heaven
and sees the whole human race.
14 From his throne he observes
all who live on the earth.
15 He made their hearts,
so he understands everything they do.
16 The best-equipped army cannot save a
king,
nor is great strength enough to save
a warrior.
17 Don't count on your warhorse to give
you victory—
for all its strength, it cannot save you.

18 But the LORD watches over those who
fear him,
those who rely on his unfailing love.
19 He rescues them from death
and keeps them alive in times of
famine.

20 We put our hope in the LORD.
He is our help and our shield.
21 In him our hearts rejoice,
for we trust in his holy name.
22 Let your unfailing love surround us,
LORD,
for our hope is in you alone.

34

** A psalm of David, regarding the time he pretended to be insane in front of Abimelech, who sent him away.*

1 I will praise the LORD at all times.
I will constantly speak his praises.
2 I will boast only in the LORD;
let all who are helpless take heart.
3 Come, let us tell of the LORD's greatness;
let us exalt his name together.

4 I prayed to the LORD, and he
answered me.
He freed me from all my fears.
5 Those who look to him for help will be
radiant with joy;
no shadow of shame will darken their
faces.

32:TITLE Hebrew *maskil.* This may be a literary or musical term. **32:2** Greek version reads *of sin.* Compare Rom 4:8. **34** This psalm is a Hebrew acrostic poem; each verse begins with a successive letter of the Hebrew alphabet.

▸ **33:1** *See **The ministry of music and singing,** page 475.*

[6] In my desperation I prayed, and the
LORD listened;
he saved me from all my troubles.
[7] For the angel of the LORD is a guard;
he surrounds and defends all who
fear him.
[8] Taste and see that the LORD is good.
Oh, the joys of those who take refuge
in him!
[9] Fear the LORD, you his godly people,
for those who fear him will have all
they need.
[10] Even strong young lions sometimes go
hungry,
but those who trust in the LORD will
lack no good thing.

[11] Come, my children, and listen to me,
and I will teach you to fear the LORD.
[12] Does anyone want to live a life
that is long and prosperous?
[13] Then keep your tongue from speaking
evil
and your lips from telling lies!
[14] Turn away from evil and do good.
Search for peace, and work to
maintain it.

[15] The eyes of the LORD watch over those
who do right;
his ears are open to their cries for help.
[16] But the LORD turns his face against
those who do evil;
he will erase their memory from the
earth.
[17] The LORD hears his people when they
call to him for help.
He rescues them from all their
troubles.
[18] The LORD is close to the brokenhearted;
he rescues those whose spirits are
crushed.

[19] The righteous person faces many
troubles,
but the LORD comes to the rescue each
time.
[20] For the LORD protects the bones of the
righteous;
not one of them is broken!

[21] Calamity will surely destroy the wicked,
and those who hate the righteous will
be punished.
[22] But the LORD will redeem those who
serve him.
No one who takes refuge in him will
be condemned.

35 *A psalm of David.*

[1] O LORD, oppose those who oppose me.
Fight those who fight against me.
[2] Put on your armor, and take up your
shield.
Prepare for battle, and come to my aid.
[3] Lift up your spear and javelin
against those who pursue me.
Let me hear you say,
"I will give you victory!"
[4] Bring shame and disgrace on those
trying to kill me;
turn them back and humiliate those
who want to harm me.
[5] Blow them away like chaff in the wind—
a wind sent by the angel of the LORD.
[6] Make their path dark and slippery,
with the angel of the LORD pursuing
them.
[7] I did them no wrong, but they laid a trap
for me.
I did them no wrong, but they dug a
pit to catch me.
[8] So let sudden ruin come upon them!
Let them be caught in the trap they set
for me!
Let them be destroyed in the pit they
dug for me.
[9] Then I will rejoice in the LORD.
I will be glad because he rescues me.
[10] With every bone in my body I will praise
him:
"LORD, who can compare with you?
Who else rescues the helpless from the
strong?
Who else protects the helpless and
poor from those who rob them?"

[11] Malicious witnesses testify against me.
They accuse me of crimes I know
nothing about.
[12] They repay me evil for good.
I am sick with despair.
[13] Yet when they were ill, I grieved for
them.
I denied myself by fasting for them,
but my prayers returned unanswered.
[14] I was sad, as though they were my
friends or family,
as if I were grieving for my own
mother.

15 But they are glad now that I am in trouble;
they gleefully join together against me.
I am attacked by people I don't even know;
they slander me constantly.
16 They mock me and call me names;
they snarl at me.

17 How long, O Lord, will you look on and do nothing?
Rescue me from their fierce attacks.
Protect my life from these lions!
18 Then I will thank you in front of the great assembly.
I will praise you before all the people.
19 Don't let my treacherous enemies rejoice over my defeat.
Don't let those who hate me without cause gloat over my sorrow.
20 They don't talk of peace;
they plot against innocent people who mind their own business.
21 They shout, "Aha! Aha!
With our own eyes we saw him do it!"
22 O LORD, you know all about this.
Do not stay silent.
Do not abandon me now, O Lord.
23 Wake up! Rise to my defense!
Take up my case, my God and my Lord.
24 Declare me not guilty, O LORD my God, for you give justice.
Don't let my enemies laugh about me in my troubles.
25 Don't let them say, "Look, we got what we wanted!
Now we will eat him alive!"

26 May those who rejoice at my troubles
be humiliated and disgraced.
May those who triumph over me
be covered with shame and dishonor.
27 But give great joy to those who came to my defense.
Let them continually say, "Great is the LORD,
who delights in blessing his servant with peace!"
28 Then I will proclaim your justice,
and I will praise you all day long.

36

For the choir director: A psalm of David, the servant of the LORD.

1 Sin whispers to the wicked, deep within their hearts.*
They have no fear of God at all.
2 In their blind conceit,
they cannot see how wicked they really are.
3 Everything they say is crooked and deceitful.
They refuse to act wisely or do good.
4 They lie awake at night, hatching sinful plots.
Their actions are never good.
They make no attempt to turn from evil.

5 Your unfailing love, O LORD, is as vast as the heavens;
your faithfulness reaches beyond the clouds.
6 Your righteousness is like the mighty mountains,
your justice like the ocean depths.
You care for people and animals alike, O LORD.
7 How precious is your unfailing love, O God!
All humanity finds shelter
in the shadow of your wings.
8 You feed them from the abundance of your own house,
letting them drink from your river of delights.
9 For you are the fountain of life,
the light by which we see.

10 Pour out your unfailing love on those who love you;
give justice to those with honest hearts.
11 Don't let the proud trample me
or the wicked push me around.
12 Look! Those who do evil have fallen!
They are thrown down, never to rise again.

37*

A psalm of David.

1 Don't worry about the wicked
or envy those who do wrong.
2 For like grass, they soon fade away.
Like spring flowers, they soon wither.

3 Trust in the LORD and do good.
Then you will live safely in the land and prosper.

36:1 As in some Hebrew manuscripts and Syriac version, which read *in his heart*. Masoretic Text reads *in my heart*. **37** This psalm is a Hebrew acrostic poem; each stanza begins with a successive letter of the Hebrew alphabet.

PSALM 37 • page 624

4 Take delight in the LORD,
and he will give you your heart's desires.

5 Commit everything you do to the LORD.
Trust him, and he will help you.
6 He will make your innocence radiate like the dawn,
and the justice of your cause will shine like the noonday sun.

7 Be still in the presence of the LORD,
and wait patiently for him to act.
Don't worry about evil people who prosper
or fret about their wicked schemes.

8 Stop being angry!
Turn from your rage!
Do not lose your temper—
it only leads to harm.
9 For the wicked will be destroyed,
but those who trust in the LORD will possess the land.

10 Soon the wicked will disappear.
Though you look for them, they will be gone.
11 The lowly will possess the land
and will live in peace and prosperity.

12 The wicked plot against the godly;
they snarl at them in defiance.
13 But the Lord just laughs,
for he sees their day of judgment coming.

14 The wicked draw their swords
and string their bows
to kill the poor and the oppressed,
to slaughter those who do right.
15 But their swords will stab their own hearts,
and their bows will be broken.

16 It is better to be godly and have little
than to be evil and rich.
17 For the strength of the wicked will be shattered,
but the LORD takes care of the godly.

18 Day by day the LORD takes care of the innocent,
and they will receive an inheritance that lasts forever.
19 They will not be disgraced in hard times;
even in famine they will have more than enough.

20 But the wicked will die.
The LORD's enemies are like flowers in a field—
they will disappear like smoke.

21 The wicked borrow and never repay,
but the godly are generous givers.
22 Those the LORD blesses will possess the land,
but those he curses will die.

23 The LORD directs the steps of the godly.
He delights in every detail of their lives.
24 Though they stumble, they will never fall,
for the LORD holds them by the hand.

25 Once I was young, and now I am old.
Yet I have never seen the godly abandoned
or their children begging for bread.
26 The godly always give generous loans to others,
and their children are a blessing.

Acrostic psalms

Poetry is always really difficult to translate into another language. Individual words can have a particular nuance, imagery can be hard to express succinctly, and rhyme can be almost impossible to reproduce. Hebrew poetry has neither rhyme nor regular meter like Western poetry; instead it uses things like parallel ideas, word plays, grouping, and symmetry. One common, and extremely clever, device was the *acrostic*. An acrostic involved beginning each line of the psalm or poem with the next letter in the Hebrew alphabet (as in Psalms 25, 34, and 145). Sometimes, as in Psalm 37, the next letter started the next two lines; and Psalm 119 has blocks of eight lines, with the next letter of the alphabet beginning every line of the next block. All of this shows us the careful reflection that went into writing the psalms.

27 Turn from evil and do good,
and you will live in the land forever.
28 For the LORD loves justice,
and he will never abandon the godly.

He will keep them safe forever,
but the children of the wicked will die.
29 The godly will possess the land
and will live there forever.

30 The godly offer good counsel;
they teach right from wrong.
31 They have made God's law their own,
so they will never slip from his path.

32 The wicked wait in ambush for the godly,
looking for an excuse to kill them.
33 But the LORD will not let the wicked succeed
or let the godly be condemned when they are put on trial.

34 Put your hope in the LORD.
Travel steadily along his path.
He will honor you by giving you the land.
You will see the wicked destroyed.

35 I have seen wicked and ruthless people
flourishing like a tree in its native soil.
36 But when I looked again, they were gone!
Though I searched for them, I could not find them!

37 Look at those who are honest and good,
for a wonderful future awaits those who love peace.
38 But the rebellious will be destroyed;
they have no future.

39 The LORD rescues the godly;
he is their fortress in times of trouble.
40 The LORD helps them,
rescuing them from the wicked.
He saves them,
and they find shelter in him.

38

A psalm of David, asking God to remember him.

1 O LORD, don't rebuke me in your anger
or discipline me in your rage!
2 Your arrows have struck deep,
and your blows are crushing me.
3 Because of your anger, my whole body is sick;
my health is broken because of my sins.
4 My guilt overwhelms me—
it is a burden too heavy to bear.
5 My wounds fester and stink
because of my foolish sins.
6 I am bent over and racked with pain.
All day long I walk around filled with grief.
7 A raging fever burns within me,
and my health is broken.
8 I am exhausted and completely crushed.
My groans come from an anguished heart.

9 You know what I long for, Lord;
you hear my every sigh.
10 My heart beats wildly, my strength fails,
and I am going blind.
11 My loved ones and friends stay away,
fearing my disease.
Even my own family stands at a distance.
12 Meanwhile, my enemies lay traps to kill me.
Those who wish me harm make plans to ruin me.
All day long they plan their treachery.

13 But I am deaf to all their threats.
I am silent before them as one who cannot speak.
14 I choose to hear nothing,
and I make no reply.
15 For I am waiting for you, O LORD.
You must answer for me, O Lord my God.
16 I prayed, "Don't let my enemies gloat over me
or rejoice at my downfall."

17 I am on the verge of collapse,
facing constant pain.
18 But I confess my sins;
I am deeply sorry for what I have done.
19 I have many aggressive enemies;
they hate me without reason.
20 They repay me evil for good
and oppose me for pursuing good.
21 Do not abandon me, O LORD.
Do not stand at a distance, my God.
22 Come quickly to help me,
O Lord my savior.

39

For Jeduthun, the choir director: A psalm of David.

1 I said to myself, "I will watch what I do
and not sin in what I say.
I will hold my tongue
when the ungodly are around me."

[2] But as I stood there in silence—
not even speaking of good things—
the turmoil within me grew worse.
[3] The more I thought about it,
the hotter I got,
igniting a fire of words:
[4] "LORD, remind me how brief my time on earth will be.
Remind me that my days are numbered—
how fleeting my life is.
[5] You have made my life no longer than the width of my hand.
My entire lifetime is just a moment to you;
at best, each of us is but a breath."
Interlude

[6] We are merely moving shadows,
and all our busy rushing ends in nothing.
We heap up wealth,
not knowing who will spend it.
[7] And so, Lord, where do I put my hope?
My only hope is in you.
[8] Rescue me from my rebellion.
Do not let fools mock me.
[9] I am silent before you; I won't say a word,
for my punishment is from you.
[10] But please stop striking me!
I am exhausted by the blows from your hand.
[11] When you discipline us for our sins,
you consume like a moth what is precious to us.
Each of us is but a breath. *Interlude*

[12] Hear my prayer, O LORD!
Listen to my cries for help!
Don't ignore my tears.
For I am your guest—
a traveler passing through,
as my ancestors were before me.
[13] Leave me alone so I can smile again
before I am gone and exist no more.

40

For the choir director: A psalm of David.

[1] I waited patiently for the LORD to help me,
and he turned to me and heard my cry.
[2] He lifted me out of the pit of despair,
out of the mud and the mire.
He set my feet on solid ground
and steadied me as I walked along.
[3] He has given me a new song to sing,
a hymn of praise to our God.
Many will see what he has done and be amazed.
They will put their trust in the LORD.

[4] Oh, the joys of those who trust the LORD,
who have no confidence in the proud
or in those who worship idols.
[5] O LORD my God, you have performed many wonders for us.
Your plans for us are too numerous to list.
You have no equal.
If I tried to recite all your wonderful deeds,
I would never come to the end of them.

[6] You take no delight in sacrifices or offerings.
Now that you have made me listen,
I finally understand*—
you don't require burnt offerings or sin offerings.
[7] Then I said, "Look, I have come.
As is written about me in the Scriptures:
[8] I take joy in doing your will, my God,
for your instructions are written on my heart."

[9] I have told all your people about your justice.
I have not been afraid to speak out,
as you, O LORD, well know.
[10] I have not kept the good news of your justice hidden in my heart;
I have talked about your faithfulness and saving power.
I have told everyone in the great assembly
of your unfailing love and faithfulness.

[11] LORD, don't hold back your tender mercies from me.
Let your unfailing love and faithfulness always protect me.
[12] For troubles surround me—
too many to count!
My sins pile up so high
I can't see my way out.
They outnumber the hairs on my head.
I have lost all courage.

[13] Please, LORD, rescue me!
Come quickly, LORD, and help me.
[14] May those who try to destroy me
be humiliated and put to shame.

May those who take delight in my trouble
be turned back in disgrace.
15 Let them be horrified by their shame,
for they said, "Aha! We've got him
now!"
16 But may all who search for you
be filled with joy and gladness in you.
May those who love your salvation
repeatedly shout, "The LORD is great!"
17 As for me, since I am poor and needy,
let the Lord keep me in his thoughts.
You are my helper and my savior.
O my God, do not delay.

41

For the choir director: A psalm of David.

1 Oh, the joys of those who are kind to the
poor!
The LORD rescues them when they are
in trouble.
2 The LORD protects them
and keeps them alive.
He gives them prosperity in the land
and rescues them from their enemies.
3 The LORD nurses them when they are sick
and restores them to health.
4 "O LORD," I prayed, "have mercy on me.
Heal me, for I have sinned against
you."
5 But my enemies say nothing but evil
about me.
"How soon will he die and be
forgotten?" they ask.
6 They visit me as if they were my friends,
but all the while they gather gossip,
and when they leave, they spread it
everywhere.
7 All who hate me whisper about me,
imagining the worst.
8 "He has some fatal disease," they say.
"He will never get out of that bed!"
9 Even my best friend, the one I trusted
completely,
the one who shared my food, has
turned against me.
10 LORD, have mercy on me.
Make me well again, so I can pay them
back!
11 I know you are pleased with me,
for you have not let my enemies
triumph over me.
12 You have preserved my life because I am
innocent;
you have brought me into your
presence forever.
13 Praise the LORD, the God of Israel,
who lives from everlasting to
everlasting.
Amen and amen!

BOOK TWO (Psalms 42–72)

42

For the choir director: A psalm of the descendants of Korah.*

1 As the deer longs for streams of water,
so I long for you, O God.
2 I thirst for God, the living God.
When can I go and stand before him?
3 Day and night I have only tears for food,
while my enemies continually taunt
me, saying,
"Where is this God of yours?"
4 My heart is breaking
as I remember how it used to be:
I walked among the crowds of
worshipers,
leading a great procession to the
house of God,
singing for joy and giving thanks
amid the sound of a great
celebration!
5 Why am I discouraged?
Why is my heart so sad?
I will put my hope in God!
I will praise him again—
my Savior and 6 my God!

Now I am deeply discouraged,
but I will remember you—
even from distant Mount Hermon,
the source of the Jordan,
from the land of Mount Mizar.
7 I hear the tumult of the raging seas
as your waves and surging tides
sweep over me.
8 But each day the LORD pours his
unfailing love upon me,
and through each night I sing his
songs,
praying to God who gives me life.
9 "O God my rock," I cry,
"Why have you forgotten me?
Why must I wander around in grief,
oppressed by my enemies?"

40:6 Greek version reads *You have given me a body.* Compare Heb 10:5. **42:TITLE** Hebrew *maskil.* This may be a literary or musical term.

10 Their taunts break my bones.
They scoff, "Where is this God of yours?"
11 Why am I discouraged?
Why is my heart so sad?
I will put my hope in God!
I will praise him again—
my Savior and my God!

43

1 Declare me innocent, O God!
Defend me against these ungodly people.
Rescue me from these unjust liars.
2 For you are God, my only safe haven.
Why have you tossed me aside?
Why must I wander around in grief,
oppressed by my enemies?
3 Send out your light and your truth;
let them guide me.
Let them lead me to your holy mountain,
to the place where you live.
4 There I will go to the altar of God,
to God—the source of all my joy.
I will praise you with my harp,
O God, my God!

5 Why am I discouraged?
Why is my heart so sad?
I will put my hope in God!
I will praise him again—
my Savior and my God!

44

For the choir director: A psalm of the descendants of Korah.*

1 O God, we have heard it with our own ears—
our ancestors have told us
of all you did in their day,
in days long ago:
2 You drove out the pagan nations by your power
and gave all the land to our ancestors.
You crushed their enemies
and set our ancestors free.
3 They did not conquer the land with their swords;
it was not their own strong arm that gave them victory.
It was your right hand and strong arm
and the blinding light from your face that helped them,
for you loved them.

4 You are my King and my God.
You command victories for Israel.*
5 Only by your power can we push back our enemies;
only in your name can we trample our foes.
6 I do not trust in my bow;
I do not count on my sword to save me.
7 You are the one who gives us victory over our enemies;
you disgrace those who hate us.

Longing for God

Many Christians say that they long to know God better and to have a closer sense of his presence. Yet their lives do not reflect their claims. For what they really long for is often so very different.

We each need to ask ourselves, what do I get hungry for? Well, food, obviously. Our favorite food, certainly. But do we not also get hungry to meet our friends, or watch our favorite TV program, or check our favorite website, or play our favorite computer game, or have a few minutes' sleep? Is it not these things that so often take up our time, especially our free time? If so, these are the things that we really long for.

But we will never really get to know God as we say we want to unless we start to long for it—and then do something about it. That's what characterized the psalmist. He was as desperate to find God as a deer is desperate to find water, knowing that its very life depends on it (Psalm 42:1). How desperate are we?

True longing for God is satisfied not by religious rituals, pilgrimages, or offerings; it is satisfied only by beginning and developing a personal relationship with Jesus Christ, as Jesus said to the woman at the well (John 4:13-14).

[8] O God, we give glory to you all day long
and constantly praise your name.
Interlude

[9] But now you have tossed us aside in dishonor.
You no longer lead our armies to battle.
[10] You make us retreat from our enemies
and allow those who hate us to plunder our land.
[11] You have butchered us like sheep
and scattered us among the nations.
[12] You sold your precious people for a pittance,
making nothing on the sale.
[13] You let our neighbors mock us.
We are an object of scorn and derision
to those around us.
[14] You have made us the butt of their jokes;
they shake their heads at us in scorn.
[15] We can't escape the constant humiliation;
shame is written across our faces.
[16] All we hear are the taunts of our mockers.
All we see are our vengeful enemies.

[17] All this has happened though we have not forgotten you.
We have not violated your covenant.
[18] Our hearts have not deserted you.
We have not strayed from your path.
[19] Yet you have crushed us in the jackal's desert home.
You have covered us with darkness and death.
[20] If we had forgotten the name of our God
or spread our hands in prayer to foreign gods,
[21] God would surely have known it,
for he knows the secrets of every heart.
[22] But for your sake we are killed every day;
we are being slaughtered like sheep.

[23] Wake up, O Lord! Why do you sleep?
Get up! Do not reject us forever.
[24] Why do you look the other way?
Why do you ignore our suffering and oppression?
[25] We collapse in the dust,
lying face down in the dirt.
[26] Rise up! Help us!
Ransom us because of your unfailing love.

45 *For the choir director: A love song to be sung to the tune "Lilies." A psalm* of the descendants of Korah.*

[1] Beautiful words stir my heart.
I will recite a lovely poem about the king,
for my tongue is like the pen of a skillful poet.

[2] You are the most handsome of all.
Gracious words stream from your lips.
God himself has blessed you forever.
[3] Put on your sword, O mighty warrior!
You are so glorious, so majestic!
[4] In your majesty, ride out to victory,
defending truth, humility, and justice.
Go forth to perform awe-inspiring deeds!
[5] Your arrows are sharp, piercing your enemies' hearts.
The nations fall beneath your feet.

[6] Your throne, O God,* endures forever and ever.
You rule with a scepter of justice.
[7] You love justice and hate evil.
Therefore God, your God, has anointed you,
pouring out the oil of joy on you more than on anyone else.
[8] Myrrh, aloes, and cassia perfume your robes.
In ivory palaces the music of strings entertains you.
[9] Kings' daughters are among your noble women.
At your right side stands the queen,
wearing jewelry of finest gold from Ophir!

[10] Listen to me, O royal daughter; take to heart what I say.
Forget your people and your family far away.
[11] For your royal husband delights in your beauty;
honor him, for he is your lord.
[12] The princess of Tyre* will shower you with gifts.
The wealthy will beg your favor.
[13] The bride, a princess, looks glorious
in her golden gown.

44:TITLE Hebrew *maskil.* This may be a literary or musical term. **44:4** Hebrew *for Jacob.* The names "Jacob" and "Israel" are often interchanged throughout the Old Testament, referring sometimes to the individual patriarch and sometimes to the nation. **45:TITLE** Hebrew *maskil.* This may be a literary or musical term. **45:6** Or *Your divine throne.* **45:12** Hebrew *The daughter of Tyre.*

[14] In her beautiful robes, she is led to the king,
accompanied by her bridesmaids.
[15] What a joyful and enthusiastic procession
as they enter the king's palace!
[16] Your sons will become kings like their father.
You will make them rulers over many lands.
[17] I will bring honor to your name in every generation.
Therefore, the nations will praise you forever and ever.

46 *For the choir director: A song of the descendants of Korah, to be sung by soprano voices.**

[1] God is our refuge and strength,
always ready to help in times of trouble.
[2] So we will not fear when earthquakes come
and the mountains crumble into the sea.
[3] Let the oceans roar and foam.
Let the mountains tremble as the waters surge! *Interlude*

[4] A river brings joy to the city of our God,
the sacred home of the Most High.
[5] God dwells in that city; it cannot be destroyed.
From the very break of day, God will protect it.
[6] The nations are in chaos,
and their kingdoms crumble!
God's voice thunders,
and the earth melts!
[7] The LORD of Heaven's Armies is here among us;
the God of Israel* is our fortress. *Interlude*

Fear

While some fears are natural (like the fear of danger that makes you run), much fear is paralyzing and destructive. The over 450 biblical references to fear show that this is not an uncommon problem. Whenever fear overcomes us, behind it simply lies a lack of trust in God, his promises, and his sovereignty. If not dealt with, the fear will destroy us, just as Saul experienced (1 Samuel 13:2-13; 18:5-15).

Here are five steps to dealing with fear:

1. Acknowledge your fear—and if it is the kind of fear that implies lack of trust in God, then acknowledge it for what it is—sin. Don't excuse it.
2. Confront your situation with the truth that God is always with us, knows everything about our lives, and is completely for us.
3. Declare the greatness of God and his promises into your situation, just as the psalmist does in Psalm 46. Remind yourself that his presence changes things. The more we focus on our big God, the smaller other difficulties appear.
4. Ask God to help you change your thinking patterns. "Let God transform you into a new person by changing the way you think" (Romans 12:2). Don't let your imagination run wild; instead, bring your thoughts to God and ask his Spirit to renew them. Ask God to deliver you from any stronghold of fear (2 Corinthians 10:4-5) or indeed any other stronghold that controls how your mind thinks.
5. Step out despite the fear, trusting that God will be with you as you do so.

▶ *See also* ***Courage****, page 243;* ***The fear of the LORD****, page 705;* ***Peace****, page 774;* ***Thought****, page 808.*

8 Come, see the glorious works of the LORD:
See how he brings destruction upon the world.
9 He causes wars to end throughout the earth.
He breaks the bow and snaps the spear;
he burns the shields with fire.

10 "Be still, and know that I am God!
I will be honored by every nation.
I will be honored throughout the world."

11 The LORD of Heaven's Armies is here among us;
the God of Israel is our fortress.
Interlude

47 *For the choir director: A psalm of the descendants of Korah.*

1 Come, everyone! Clap your hands!
Shout to God with joyful praise!
2 For the LORD Most High is awesome.
He is the great King of all the earth.
3 He subdues the nations before us,
putting our enemies beneath our feet.
4 He chose the Promised Land as our inheritance,
the proud possession of Jacob's descendants, whom he loves.
Interlude

5 God has ascended with a mighty shout.
The LORD has ascended with trumpets blaring.
6 Sing praises to God, sing praises;
sing praises to our King, sing praises!
7 For God is the King over all the earth.
Praise him with a psalm.*
8 God reigns above the nations,
sitting on his holy throne.
9 The rulers of the world have gathered together
with the people of the God of Abraham.
For all the kings of the earth belong to God.
He is highly honored everywhere.

48 *A song. A psalm of the descendants of Korah.*

1 How great is the LORD,
how deserving of praise,
in the city of our God,
which sits on his holy mountain!
2 It is high and magnificent;
the whole earth rejoices to see it!
Mount Zion, the holy mountain,*
is the city of the great King!
3 God himself is in Jerusalem's towers,
revealing himself as its defender.

4 The kings of the earth joined forces
and advanced against the city.
5 But when they saw it, they were stunned;
they were terrified and ran away.
6 They were gripped with terror
and writhed in pain like a woman in labor.
7 You destroyed them like the mighty ships of Tarshish
shattered by a powerful east wind.

8 We had heard of the city's glory,
but now we have seen it ourselves—
the city of the LORD of Heaven's Armies.
It is the city of our God;
he will make it safe forever. *Interlude*

9 O God, we meditate on your unfailing love
as we worship in your Temple.
10 As your name deserves, O God,
you will be praised to the ends of the earth.
Your strong right hand is filled with victory.
11 Let the people on Mount Zion rejoice.
Let all the towns of Judah be glad
because of your justice.

12 Go, inspect the city of Jerusalem.*
Walk around and count the many towers.
13 Take note of the fortified walls,
and tour all the citadels,
that you may describe them
to future generations.
14 For that is what God is like.
He is our God forever and ever,
and he will guide us until we die.

49 *For the choir director: A psalm of the descendants of Korah.*

1 Listen to this, all you people!
Pay attention, everyone in the world!
2 High and low,
rich and poor—listen!
3 For my words are wise,
and my thoughts are filled with insight.

46:TITLE Hebrew *according to alamoth.* **46:7** Hebrew *of Jacob;* also in 46:11. See note on 44:4. **47:7** Hebrew *maskil.* This may be a literary or musical term. **48:2** Or *Mount Zion, in the far north;* Hebrew reads *Mount Zion, the heights of Zaphon.* **48:12** Hebrew *Zion.*

4 I listen carefully to many proverbs
and solve riddles with inspiration
from a harp.
5 Why should I fear when trouble
comes,
when enemies surround me?
6 They trust in their wealth
and boast of great riches.
7 Yet they cannot redeem themselves from
death*
by paying a ransom to God.
8 Redemption does not come so easily,
for no one can ever pay enough
9 to live forever
and never see the grave.

10 Those who are wise must finally die,
just like the foolish and senseless,
leaving all their wealth behind.
11 The grave* is their eternal home,
where they will stay forever.
They may name their estates after
themselves,
12 but their fame will not last.
They will die, just like animals.
13 This is the fate of fools,
though they are remembered as being
wise.* *Interlude*

14 Like sheep, they are led to the grave,*
where death will be their shepherd.
In the morning the godly will rule over
them.
Their bodies will rot in the grave,
far from their grand estates.
15 But as for me, God will redeem my life.
He will snatch me from the power of
the grave. *Interlude*

16 So don't be dismayed when the wicked
grow rich
and their homes become ever more
splendid.
17 For when they die, they take nothing
with them.
Their wealth will not follow them into
the grave.
18 In this life they consider themselves
fortunate
and are applauded for their success.
19 But they will die like all before
them
and never again see the light of day.
20 People who boast of their wealth don't
understand;
they will die, just like animals.

50

A psalm of Asaph.

1 The LORD, the Mighty One, is God,
and he has spoken;
he has summoned all humanity
from where the sun rises to where it
sets.
2 From Mount Zion, the perfection of
beauty,
God shines in glorious radiance.
3 Our God approaches,
and he is not silent.
Fire devours everything in his way,
and a great storm rages around him.
4 He calls on the heavens above and earth
below
to witness the judgment of his people.
5 "Bring my faithful people to me—
those who made a covenant with me
by giving sacrifices."
6 Then let the heavens proclaim his justice,
for God himself will be the judge.
Interlude

7 "O my people, listen as I speak.
Here are my charges against you,
O Israel:
I am God, your God!
8 I have no complaint about your sacrifices
or the burnt offerings you constantly
offer.
9 But I do not need the bulls from your
barns
or the goats from your pens.
10 For all the animals of the forest are mine,
and I own the cattle on a thousand
hills.
11 I know every bird on the mountains,
and all the animals of the field are
mine.
12 If I were hungry, I would not tell you,
for all the world is mine and
everything in it.
13 Do I eat the meat of bulls?
Do I drink the blood of goats?
14 Make thankfulness your sacrifice to God,
and keep the vows you made to the
Most High.
15 Then call on me when you are in trouble,
and I will rescue you,
and you will give me glory."

16 But God says to the wicked:
"Why bother reciting my decrees
and pretending to obey my covenant?

17 For you refuse my discipline
and treat my words like trash.
18 When you see thieves, you approve of them,
and you spend your time with adulterers.
19 Your mouth is filled with wickedness,
and your tongue is full of lies.
20 You sit around and slander your brother—
your own mother's son.
21 While you did all this, I remained silent,
and you thought I didn't care.
But now I will rebuke you,
listing all my charges against you.
22 Repent, all of you who forget me,
or I will tear you apart,
and no one will help you.
23 But giving thanks is a sacrifice that truly honors me.
If you keep to my path,
I will reveal to you the salvation of God."

51 *For the choir director: A psalm of David, regarding the time Nathan the prophet came to him after David had committed adultery with Bathsheba.*

1 Have mercy on me, O God,
because of your unfailing love.
Because of your great compassion,
blot out the stain of my sins.
2 Wash me clean from my guilt.
Purify me from my sin.
3 For I recognize my rebellion;
it haunts me day and night.
4 Against you, and you alone, have I sinned;
I have done what is evil in your sight.
You will be proved right in what you say,
and your judgment against me is just.*
5 For I was born a sinner—
yes, from the moment my mother conceived me.
6 But you desire honesty from the womb,*
teaching me wisdom even there.
7 Purify me from my sins,* and I will be clean;
wash me, and I will be whiter than snow.
8 Oh, give me back my joy again;
you have broken me—
now let me rejoice.

49:7 Some Hebrew manuscripts read *no one can redeem the life of another.* **49:11** As in Greek and Syriac versions; Hebrew reads *Their inward [thought].* **49:13** The meaning of the Hebrew is uncertain. **49:14** Hebrew *Sheol;* also in 49:14b, 15. **51:4** Greek version reads *and you will win your case in court.* Compare Rom 3:4. **51:6** Or *from the heart;* Hebrew reads *in the inward parts.* **51:7** Hebrew *Purify me with the hyssop branch.*

Is there anything God won't forgive?

Most church leaders have had someone come and tell them they have committed the unforgivable sin. The sin might range from the apparently trivial to something serious, like David's adultery confessed in Psalm 51. But Jesus made clear there is only one sin that cannot be forgiven—and being worried you have committed it is a sure sign that you haven't.

It is important to read Jesus' teaching about the unforgivable sin in context (see Matthew 12:22-32; Mark 3:20-30). Yes, he speaks of sinners who "will never be forgiven, either in this world or in the world to come" (Matthew 12:32); but the context explains what he means. The Pharisees had just attributed his miracles, not to God, but to the devil. But rejecting Jesus' victory over Satan is to reject God's long-awaited Kingdom that was now breaking into this world. Not to align with Jesus, therefore, is to align with Satan.

It is this willful, stubborn, persistent rejection of the Spirit's witness to Jesus ("blasphemy against the Holy Spirit"; Matthew 12:31) that alone is unforgivable; for if we reject Jesus, and the Spirit who points us to him, how can we hope to be forgiven and saved? All other sins—no matter how bad they are—are forgivable, as David discovered and as Jesus made clear: "I tell you the truth, all sin and blasphemy can be forgiven" (Mark 3:28).

▶ *See also* ***Repentance****, page 1253;* ***How can I be sure God has forgiven me?****, page 1433.*

9 Don't keep looking at my sins.
Remove the stain of my guilt.
10 Create in me a clean heart, O God.
Renew a loyal spirit within me.
11 Do not banish me from your presence,
and don't take your Holy Spirit*
from me.

12 Restore to me the joy of your salvation,
and make me willing to obey you.
13 Then I will teach your ways to rebels,
and they will return to you.
14 Forgive me for shedding blood, O God
who saves;
then I will joyfully sing of your
forgiveness.
15 Unseal my lips, O Lord,
that my mouth may praise you.

16 You do not desire a sacrifice, or I would
offer one.
You do not want a burnt offering.
17 The sacrifice you desire is a broken spirit.
You will not reject a broken and
repentant heart, O God.
18 Look with favor on Zion and help her;
rebuild the walls of Jerusalem.
19 Then you will be pleased with sacrifices
offered in the right spirit—
with burnt offerings and whole burnt
offerings.
Then bulls will again be sacrificed on
your altar.

52

For the choir director: A psalm of David, regarding the time Doeg the Edomite said to Saul, "David has gone to see Ahimelech."*

1 Why do you boast about your crimes,
great warrior?
Don't you realize God's justice
continues forever?
2 All day long you plot destruction.
Your tongue cuts like a sharp razor;
you're an expert at telling lies.
3 You love evil more than good
and lies more than truth. *Interlude*

4 You love to destroy others with your words,
you liar!
5 But God will strike you down once and
for all.
He will pull you from your home
and uproot you from the land of the
living. *Interlude*

6 The righteous will see it and be amazed.
They will laugh and say,
7 "Look what happens to mighty warriors
who do not trust in God.
They trust their wealth instead
and grow more and more bold in their
wickedness."

8 But I am like an olive tree, thriving in
the house of God.
I will always trust in God's unfailing
love.
9 I will praise you forever, O God,
for what you have done.
I will trust in your good name
in the presence of your faithful people.

53

For the choir director: A meditation; a psalm of David.*

1 Only fools say in their hearts,
"There is no God."
They are corrupt, and their actions are
evil;
not one of them does good!

2 God looks down from heaven
on the entire human race;
he looks to see if anyone is truly wise,
if anyone seeks God.
3 But no, all have turned away;
all have become corrupt.*
No one does good,
not a single one!

4 Will those who do evil never learn?
They eat up my people like bread
and wouldn't think of praying to God.
5 Terror will grip them,
terror like they have never known
before.
God will scatter the bones of your enemies.
You will put them to shame, for God
has rejected them.

6 Who will come from Mount Zion to
rescue Israel?
When God restores his people,
Jacob will shout with joy, and Israel
will rejoice.

54

For the choir director: A psalm of David, regarding the time the Ziphites came and said to Saul, "We know where David is hiding." To be accompanied by stringed instruments.*

1 Come with great power, O God, and
rescue me!
Defend me with your might.
2 Listen to my prayer, O God.
Pay attention to my plea.

3 For strangers are attacking me;
violent people are trying to kill me.
They care nothing for God. *Interlude*

4 But God is my helper.
The Lord keeps me alive!
5 May the evil plans of my enemies be
turned against them.
Do as you promised and put an end to
them.

6 I will sacrifice a voluntary offering to you;
I will praise your name, O LORD,
for it is good.
7 For you have rescued me from my troubles
and helped me to triumph over my
enemies.

55

For the choir director: A psalm of David, to be accompanied by stringed instruments.*

1 Listen to my prayer, O God.
Do not ignore my cry for help!
2 Please listen and answer me,
for I am overwhelmed by my troubles.
3 My enemies shout at me,
making loud and wicked threats.
They bring trouble on me
and angrily hunt me down.

4 My heart pounds in my chest.
The terror of death assaults me.
5 Fear and trembling overwhelm me,
and I can't stop shaking.
6 Oh, that I had wings like a dove;
then I would fly away and rest!
7 I would fly far away
to the quiet of the wilderness. *Interlude*
8 How quickly I would escape—
far from this wild storm of hatred.

9 Confuse them, Lord, and frustrate their
plans,
for I see violence and conflict in the
city.
10 Its walls are patrolled day and night
against invaders,
but the real danger is wickedness
within the city.
11 Everything is falling apart;
threats and cheating are rampant in
the streets.

12 It is not an enemy who taunts me—
I could bear that.
It is not my foes who so arrogantly
insult me—
I could have hidden from them.
13 Instead, it is you—my equal,
my companion and close friend.
14 What good fellowship we once enjoyed
as we walked together to the house of
God.

15 Let death stalk my enemies;
let the grave* swallow them alive,
for evil makes its home within
them.

16 But I will call on God,
and the LORD will rescue me.
17 Morning, noon, and night
I cry out in my distress,
and the LORD hears my voice.
18 He ransoms me and keeps me safe
from the battle waged against me,
though many still oppose me.
19 God, who has ruled forever,
will hear me and humble them.
Interlude
For my enemies refuse to change their
ways;
they do not fear God.

20 As for my companion, he betrayed his
friends;
he broke his promises.
21 His words are as smooth as butter,
but in his heart is war.
His words are as soothing as
lotion,
but underneath are daggers!

22 Give your burdens to the LORD,
and he will take care of you.
He will not permit the godly to slip
and fall.

23 But you, O God, will send the wicked
down to the pit of destruction.
Murderers and liars will die young,
but I am trusting you to save me.

56

For the choir director: A psalm of David, regarding the time the Philistines seized him in Gath. To be sung to the tune "Dove on Distant Oaks."*

1 O God, have mercy on me,
for people are hounding me.
My foes attack me all day long.

51:11 Or *your spirit of holiness.* **52:TITLE** Hebrew *maskil.* This may be a literary or musical term. **53:TITLE** Hebrew *According to mahalath; a maskil.* These may be literary or musical terms. **53:3** Greek version reads *have become useless.* Compare Rom 3:12. **54:TITLE** Hebrew *maskil.* This may be a literary or musical term. **55:TITLE** Hebrew *maskil.* This may be a literary or musical term. **55:15** Hebrew *let Sheol.* **56:TITLE** Hebrew *miktam.* This may be a literary or musical term.

2 I am constantly hounded by those who
slander me,
and many are boldly attacking me.
3 But when I am afraid,
I will put my trust in you.
4 I praise God for what he has promised.
I trust in God, so why should I be
afraid?
What can mere mortals do to me?

5 They are always twisting what I say;
they spend their days plotting to
harm me.
6 They come together to spy on me—
watching my every step, eager to
kill me.
7 Don't let them get away with their
wickedness;
in your anger, O God, bring them
down.

8 You keep track of all my sorrows.*
You have collected all my tears in your
bottle.
You have recorded each one in your
book.

9 My enemies will retreat when I call to
you for help.
This I know: God is on my side!
10 I praise God for what he has promised;
yes, I praise the LORD for what he has
promised.
11 I trust in God, so why should I be afraid?
What can mere mortals do to me?

12 I will fulfill my vows to you, O God,
and will offer a sacrifice of thanks for
your help.
13 For you have rescued me from death;
you have kept my feet from slipping.
So now I can walk in your presence,
O God,
in your life-giving light.

57

For the choir director: A psalm of David, regarding the time he fled from Saul and went into the cave. To be sung to the tune "Do Not Destroy!"*

1 Have mercy on me, O God, have mercy!
I look to you for protection.
I will hide beneath the shadow of your
wings
until the danger passes by.
2 I cry out to God Most High,*
to God who will fulfill his purpose
for me.
3 He will send help from heaven to
rescue me,
disgracing those who hound me.
Interlude
My God will send forth his unfailing love
and faithfulness.

4 I am surrounded by fierce lions
who greedily devour human prey—
whose teeth pierce like spears and
arrows,
and whose tongues cut like swords.

5 Be exalted, O God, above the highest
heavens!
May your glory shine over all the earth.

6 My enemies have set a trap for me.
I am weary from distress.
They have dug a deep pit in my path,
but they themselves have fallen
into it. *Interlude*

7 My heart is confident in you, O God;
my heart is confident.
No wonder I can sing your praises!
8 Wake up, my heart!
Wake up, O lyre and harp!
I will wake the dawn with my song.
9 I will thank you, Lord, among all the
people.
I will sing your praises among the
nations.
10 For your unfailing love is as high as the
heavens.
Your faithfulness reaches to the clouds.

11 Be exalted, O God, above the highest
heavens.
May your glory shine over all the earth.

58

For the choir director: A psalm of David, to be sung to the tune "Do Not Destroy!"*

1 Justice—do you rulers* know the
meaning of the word?
Do you judge the people fairly?
2 No! You plot injustice in your hearts.
You spread violence throughout the
land.
3 These wicked people are born sinners;
even from birth they have lied and
gone their own way.
4 They spit venom like deadly snakes;
they are like cobras that refuse to
listen,
5 ignoring the tunes of the snake charmers,
no matter how skillfully they play.

[6] Break off their fangs, O God!
Smash the jaws of these lions, O LORD!
[7] May they disappear like water into thirsty ground.
Make their weapons useless in their hands.*
[8] May they be like snails that dissolve into slime,
like a stillborn child who will never see the sun.
[9] God will sweep them away, both young and old,
faster than a pot heats over burning thorns.
[10] The godly will rejoice when they see injustice avenged.
They will wash their feet in the blood of the wicked.
[11] Then at last everyone will say,
"There truly is a reward for those who live for God;
surely there is a God who judges justly here on earth."

59 *For the choir director: A psalm* of David, regarding the time Saul sent soldiers to watch David's house in order to kill him. To be sung to the tune "Do Not Destroy!"*

[1] Rescue me from my enemies, O God.
Protect me from those who have come to destroy me.
[2] Rescue me from these criminals;
save me from these murderers.
[3] They have set an ambush for me.
Fierce enemies are out there waiting, LORD,
though I have not sinned or offended them.
[4] I have done nothing wrong,
yet they prepare to attack me.
Wake up! See what is happening and help me!

56:8 Or *my wanderings.* **57:TITLE** Hebrew *miktam.* This may be a literary or musical term. **57:2** Hebrew *Elohim-Elyon.* **58:TITLE** Hebrew *miktam.* This may be a literary or musical term. **58:1** Or *you gods.* **58:7** Or *Let them be trodden down and wither like grass.* The meaning of the Hebrew is uncertain. **59:TITLE** Hebrew *miktam.* This may be a literary or musical term.

Vengeance in the Psalms

The psalmists often cried out to God to vindicate them—and sometimes their pleas were couched in strong expressive language! They firmly believed that God would reward the good and punish wrongdoers *in this life* . . . and they knew what such punishment would look like:

O God, declare them guilty.
Let them be caught in their own traps. (Psalm 5:10)

Blow them away like chaff in the wind—
a wind sent by the angel of the LORD.
Make their path dark and slippery,
with the angel of the LORD pursuing them. (35:5-6)

Break off their fangs, O God!
Smash the jaws of these lions, O LORD! (58:6)

May they be like snails that dissolve into slime,
like a stillborn child who will never see the sun. (58:8)

This is very strong language indeed! But the desire for vengeance in the Psalms is never about being spiteful or getting even. It springs from a burning concern for God's honor. It is rooted in the belief that God is just—and that eventually people will reap what they have sown. Wrongdoers may prosper for a while, but eventually they will have to reckon with the God they have ignored. Confident of this, the psalmists never took matters into their own hands; rather, they trusted God and waited for him to act on their behalf.

▶ *See also* ***What does the Bible teach about revenge?**, page 193.*

5 O LORD God of Heaven's Armies, the God
of Israel,
wake up and punish those hostile
nations.
Show no mercy to wicked traitors.
Interlude

6 They come out at night,
snarling like vicious dogs
as they prowl the streets.
7 Listen to the filth that comes from their
mouths;
their words cut like swords.
"After all, who can hear us?" they
sneer.
8 But LORD, you laugh at them.
You scoff at all the hostile nations.
9 You are my strength; I wait for you to
rescue me,
for you, O God, are my fortress.
10 In his unfailing love, my God will stand
with me.
He will let me look down in triumph
on all my enemies.

11 Don't kill them, for my people soon
forget such lessons;
stagger them with your power, and
bring them to their knees,
O Lord our shield.
12 Because of the sinful things they say,
because of the evil that is on their
lips,
let them be captured by their pride,
their curses, and their lies.
13 Destroy them in your anger!
Wipe them out completely!
Then the whole world will know
that God reigns in Israel.* *Interlude*
14 My enemies come out at night,
snarling like vicious dogs
as they prowl the streets.
15 They scavenge for food
but go to sleep unsatisfied.*

16 But as for me, I will sing about your
power.
Each morning I will sing with joy
about your unfailing love.
For you have been my refuge,
a place of safety when I am in
distress.
17 O my Strength, to you I sing praises,
for you, O God, are my refuge,
the God who shows me unfailing
love.

60

For the choir director: A psalm of David useful for teaching, regarding the time David fought Aram-naharaim and Aram-zobah, and Joab returned and killed 12,000 Edomites in the Valley of Salt. To be sung to the tune "Lily of the Testimony."*

1 You have rejected us, O God, and broken
our defenses.
You have been angry with us; now
restore us to your favor.
2 You have shaken our land and split it
open.
Seal the cracks, for the land trembles.
3 You have been very hard on us,
making us drink wine that sent us
reeling.
4 But you have raised a banner for those
who fear you—
a rallying point in the face of attack.
Interlude
5 Now rescue your beloved people.
Answer and save us by your power.
6 God has promised this by his holiness*:
"I will divide up Shechem with joy.
I will measure out the valley of
Succoth.
7 Gilead is mine,
and Manasseh, too.
Ephraim, my helmet, will produce my
warriors,
and Judah, my scepter, will produce
my kings.
8 But Moab, my washbasin, will become
my servant,
and I will wipe my feet on Edom
and shout in triumph over Philistia."
9 Who will bring me into the fortified city?
Who will bring me victory over Edom?
10 Have you rejected us, O God?
Will you no longer march with our
armies?
11 Oh, please help us against our enemies,
for all human help is useless.
12 With God's help we will do mighty
things,
for he will trample down our foes.

61

For the choir director: A psalm of David, to be accompanied by stringed instruments.

1 O God, listen to my cry!
Hear my prayer!
2 From the ends of the earth,
I cry to you for help
when my heart is overwhelmed.

Lead me to the towering rock of safety,
3 for you are my safe refuge,
a fortress where my enemies cannot reach me.
4 Let me live forever in your sanctuary,
safe beneath the shelter of your wings! *Interlude*
5 For you have heard my vows, O God.
You have given me an inheritance reserved for those who fear your name.
6 Add many years to the life of the king!
May his years span the generations!
7 May he reign under God's protection forever.
May your unfailing love and faithfulness watch over him.
8 Then I will sing praises to your name forever
as I fulfill my vows each day.

62

For Jeduthun, the choir director: A psalm of David.

1 I wait quietly before God,
for my victory comes from him.
2 He alone is my rock and my salvation,
my fortress where I will never be shaken.
3 So many enemies against one man—
all of them trying to kill me.
To them I'm just a broken-down wall
or a tottering fence.
4 They plan to topple me from my high position.
They delight in telling lies about me.
They praise me to my face
but curse me in their hearts. *Interlude*
5 Let all that I am wait quietly before God,
for my hope is in him.
6 He alone is my rock and my salvation,
my fortress where I will not be shaken.
7 My victory and honor come from God alone.
He is my refuge, a rock where no enemy can reach me.
8 O my people, trust in him at all times.
Pour out your heart to him,
for God is our refuge. *Interlude*
9 Common people are as worthless as a puff of wind,
and the powerful are not what they appear to be.
If you weigh them on the scales,
together they are lighter than a breath of air.
10 Don't make your living by extortion
or put your hope in stealing.
And if your wealth increases,
don't make it the center of your life.
11 God has spoken plainly,
and I have heard it many times:
Power, O God, belongs to you;
12 unfailing love, O Lord, is yours.
Surely you repay all people
according to what they have done.

63

A psalm of David, regarding a time when David was in the wilderness of Judah.

1 O God, you are my God;
I earnestly search for you.
My soul thirsts for you;
my whole body longs for you
in this parched and weary land
where there is no water.
2 I have seen you in your sanctuary
and gazed upon your power and glory.
3 Your unfailing love is better than life itself;
how I praise you!
4 I will praise you as long as I live,
lifting up my hands to you in prayer.
5 You satisfy me more than the richest feast.
I will praise you with songs of joy.
6 I lie awake thinking of you,
meditating on you through the night.
7 Because you are my helper,
I sing for joy in the shadow of your wings.
8 I cling to you;
your strong right hand holds me securely.
9 But those plotting to destroy me will come to ruin.
They will go down into the depths of the earth.
10 They will die by the sword
and become the food of jackals.
11 But the king will rejoice in God.
All who swear to tell the truth will praise him,
while liars will be silenced.

59:13 Hebrew *in Jacob.* See note on 44:4. **59:15** Or *and growl if they don't get enough.* **60:TITLE** Hebrew *miktam.* This may be a literary or musical term. **60:6** Or *in his sanctuary.*

64

For the choir director: A psalm of David.

1 O God, listen to my complaint.
Protect my life from my enemies' threats.
2 Hide me from the plots of this evil mob,
from this gang of wrongdoers.
3 They sharpen their tongues like swords
and aim their bitter words like arrows.
4 They shoot from ambush at the innocent,
attacking suddenly and fearlessly.
5 They encourage each other to do evil
and plan how to set their traps in secret.
"Who will ever notice?" they ask.
6 As they plot their crimes, they say,
"We have devised the perfect plan!"
Yes, the human heart and mind are cunning.
7 But God himself will shoot them with his arrows,
suddenly striking them down.
8 Their own tongues will ruin them,
and all who see them will shake their heads in scorn.
9 Then everyone will be afraid;
they will proclaim the mighty acts of God
and realize all the amazing things he does.
10 The godly will rejoice in the LORD
and find shelter in him.
And those who do what is right
will praise him.

65

For the choir director: A song. A psalm of David.

1 What mighty praise, O God,
belongs to you in Zion.
We will fulfill our vows to you,
2 for you answer our prayers.
All of us must come to you.
3 Though we are overwhelmed by our sins,
you forgive them all.
4 What joy for those you choose to bring near,
those who live in your holy courts.
What festivities await us
inside your holy Temple.
5 You faithfully answer our prayers with awesome deeds,
O God our savior.
You are the hope of everyone on earth,
even those who sail on distant seas.
6 You formed the mountains by your power
and armed yourself with mighty strength.
7 You quieted the raging oceans
with their pounding waves
and silenced the shouting of the nations.
8 Those who live at the ends of the earth
stand in awe of your wonders.
From where the sun rises to where it sets,
you inspire shouts of joy.
9 You take care of the earth and water it,
making it rich and fertile.
The river of God has plenty of water;
it provides a bountiful harvest of grain,
for you have ordered it so.
10 You drench the plowed ground with rain,
melting the clods and leveling the ridges.
You soften the earth with showers
and bless its abundant crops.
11 You crown the year with a bountiful harvest;
even the hard pathways overflow with abundance.
12 The grasslands of the wilderness
become a lush pasture,
and the hillsides blossom with joy.
13 The meadows are clothed with flocks of sheep,
and the valleys are carpeted with grain.
They all shout and sing for joy!

66

For the choir director: A song. A psalm.

1 Shout joyful praises to God, all the earth!
2 Sing about the glory of his name!
Tell the world how glorious he is.
3 Say to God, "How awesome are your deeds!
Your enemies cringe before your mighty power.
4 Everything on earth will worship you;
they will sing your praises,
shouting your name in glorious songs." *Interlude*
5 Come and see what our God has done,
what awesome miracles he performs for people!

[6] He made a dry path through the Red
Sea,*
and his people went across on foot.
There we rejoiced in him.
[7] For by his great power he rules forever.
He watches every movement of the
nations;
let no rebel rise in defiance. *Interlude*

[8] Let the whole world bless our God
and loudly sing his praises.
[9] Our lives are in his hands,
and he keeps our feet from stumbling.
[10] You have tested us, O God;
you have purified us like silver.
[11] You captured us in your net
and laid the burden of slavery on our
backs.
[12] Then you put a leader over us.*
We went through fire and flood,
but you brought us to a place of great
abundance.

[13] Now I come to your Temple with burnt
offerings
to fulfill the vows I made to you—
[14] yes, the sacred vows that I made
when I was in deep trouble.
[15] That is why I am sacrificing burnt
offerings to you—
the best of my rams as a pleasing
aroma,
and a sacrifice of bulls and male
goats. *Interlude*

[16] Come and listen, all you who fear God,
and I will tell you what he did for me.
[17] For I cried out to him for help,
praising him as I spoke.
[18] If I had not confessed the sin in my
heart,
the Lord would not have listened.
[19] But God did listen!
He paid attention to my prayer.
[20] Praise God, who did not ignore my
prayer
or withdraw his unfailing love
from me.

67

For the choir director: A song. A psalm, to be accompanied by stringed instruments.

[1] May God be merciful and bless us.
May his face smile with favor on us.
Interlude

66:6 Hebrew *the sea.* **66:12** Or *You made people ride over our heads.*

Why doesn't God always answer prayer?

There is nothing more discouraging than being told that if your prayers are not answered it must be because of sin. At first sight, it looks like that is what Psalm 66:18 is implying: "If I had not confessed the sin in my heart, the Lord would not have listened." But while unconfessed sin can lead to unanswered prayer, that does not automatically imply the reverse, that unanswered prayer is always the result of sin. Moreover, if sin blocked prayer entirely, then no one would ever have their prayers answered, for none of us is ever completely free of sin.

Yes, sin can block prayer sometimes. But the Bible speaks of far more "ordinary" reasons for unanswered prayer—things that are in fact still sin but which we have learned to live with or excuse: things like selfish requests (James 4:3); conflicts with others, which need resolving first (Matthew 5:23-24); thinking we can tell God what to do (Isaiah 45:11); giving up asking (Luke 18:1); and not believing God can do what we ask (James 1:5-7). And sometimes there are reasons from God's side: He may want to do something in us that we cannot see (2 Corinthians 12:7-10) or that is far greater than we had imagined (Genesis 50:20)—things we don't understand until later.

But when we ask, "Why hasn't God answered my prayer?" we are forgetting what prayer is about—that it is not primarily bringing our request list to God, but developing a relationship with him. And the more that relationship grows, the more we will see why our prayers are sometimes not answered.

▶ *See also* ***The Lord's Prayer****, page 1077;* ***Perseverance in prayer****, page 1184.*

[2] May your ways be known throughout the earth,
your saving power among people everywhere.
[3] May the nations praise you, O God.
Yes, may all the nations praise you.
[4] Let the whole world sing for joy,
because you govern the nations with justice
and guide the people of the whole world. *Interlude*
[5] May the nations praise you, O God.
Yes, may all the nations praise you.
[6] Then the earth will yield its harvests,
and God, our God, will richly bless us.
[7] Yes, God will bless us,
and people all over the world will fear him.

68

For the choir director: A song. A psalm of David.

[1] Rise up, O God, and scatter your enemies.
Let those who hate God run for their lives.
[2] Blow them away like smoke.
Melt them like wax in a fire.
Let the wicked perish in the presence of God.
[3] But let the godly rejoice.
Let them be glad in God's presence.
Let them be filled with joy.
[4] Sing praises to God and to his name!
Sing loud praises to him who rides the clouds.*
His name is the LORD—
rejoice in his presence!

[5] Father to the fatherless, defender of widows—
this is God, whose dwelling is holy.
[6] God places the lonely in families;
he sets the prisoners free and gives them joy.
But he makes the rebellious live in a sun-scorched land.

[7] O God, when you led your people out from Egypt,
when you marched through the dry wasteland, *Interlude*
[8] the earth trembled, and the heavens poured down rain
before you, the God of Sinai,
before God, the God of Israel.

Singleness

People can find themselves single for many reasons—they may be widowed, or divorced, or may not have found a spouse, or may have chosen not to marry, or may even be refugees who have had to leave all family behind. Whatever the cause of the singleness, God calls his people to have a big heart for such people, for he himself shows special care for them (e.g., Deuteronomy 10:17-19). His people are called to ensure there is a proper place and, where necessary, proper provision for them, for "God places the lonely in families" (Psalm 68:6). To ensure this bigheartedness actually happened, God gave specific laws about it (e.g., Leviticus 19:33-34; Deuteronomy 14:28-29; 25:5-10). And in the New Testament this call to care for single people is reaffirmed (e.g., 1 Timothy 5:3-8; James 1:27). This concept of God placing the lonely in families brings a big challenge to Westerners today with our idea of the nuclear family and invites us to reconsider how we do things.

Because the church emphasizes (rightly) the importance of godly marriage, singles can sometimes feel excluded or like second-class citizens. But we should remember that some choose singleness because of the call of God on their lives (e.g., 1 Corinthians 7:7), and those who do not choose their singleness need encouragement to see the opportunities that singleness can bring (e.g., 1 Corinthians 7:32-35). Meanwhile those who are married need to remember that marriage will not exist in heaven (Matthew 22:30)—presumably because whatever God has for us there will be even better!

9 You sent abundant rain, O God,
to refresh the weary land.
10 There your people finally settled,
and with a bountiful harvest, O God,
you provided for your needy people.

11 The Lord gives the word,
and a great army* brings the good news.
12 Enemy kings and their armies flee,
while the women of Israel divide the plunder.
13 Even those who lived among the sheepfolds found treasures—
doves with wings of silver
and feathers of gold.
14 The Almighty scattered the enemy kings
like a blowing snowstorm on Mount Zalmon.
15 The mountains of Bashan are majestic,
with many peaks stretching high into the sky.
16 Why do you look with envy, O rugged mountains,
at Mount Zion, where God has chosen to live,
where the LORD himself will live forever?

17 Surrounded by unnumbered thousands of chariots,
the Lord came from Mount Sinai into his sanctuary.
18 When you ascended to the heights,
you led a crowd of captives.
You received gifts from the people,
even from those who rebelled against you.
Now the LORD God will live among us there.

19 Praise the Lord; praise God our savior!
For each day he carries us in his arms.
Interlude

20 Our God is a God who saves!
The Sovereign LORD rescues us from death.

21 But God will smash the heads of his enemies,
crushing the skulls of those who love their guilty ways.
22 The Lord says, "I will bring my enemies down from Bashan;
I will bring them up from the depths of the sea.
23 You, my people, will wash* your feet in their blood,
and even your dogs will get their share!"

24 Your procession has come into view, O God—
the procession of my God and King as he goes into the sanctuary.
25 Singers are in front, musicians behind;
between them are young women playing tambourines.
26 Praise God, all you people of Israel;
praise the LORD, the source of Israel's life.
27 Look, the little tribe of Benjamin leads the way.
Then comes a great throng of rulers from Judah
and all the rulers of Zebulun and Naphtali.

28 Summon your might, O God.*
Display your power, O God, as you have in the past.
29 The kings of the earth are bringing tribute
to your Temple in Jerusalem.
30 Rebuke these enemy nations—
these wild animals lurking in the reeds,
this herd of bulls among the weaker calves.
Make them bring bars of silver in humble tribute.
Scatter the nations that delight in war.
31 Let Egypt come with gifts of precious metals*;
let Ethiopia* bring tribute to God.
32 Sing to God, you kingdoms of the earth.
Sing praises to the Lord. *Interlude*
33 Sing to the one who rides across the ancient heavens,
his mighty voice thundering from the sky.
34 Tell everyone about God's power.
His majesty shines down on Israel;
his strength is mighty in the heavens.
35 God is awesome in his sanctuary.
The God of Israel gives power and strength to his people.

Praise be to God!

68:4 Or *rides through the deserts.* **68:11** Or *a host of women.* **68:23** As in Greek and Syriac versions; Hebrew reads *shatter.* **68:28** As in some Hebrew manuscripts and Greek and Syriac versions; most Hebrew manuscripts read *Your God has commanded your strength.* **68:31a** Or *of rich cloth.* **68:31b** Hebrew *Cush.*

69

For the choir director: A psalm of David, to be sung to the tune "Lilies."

1 Save me, O God,
for the floodwaters are up to my neck.
2 Deeper and deeper I sink into the mire;
I can't find a foothold.
I am in deep water,
and the floods overwhelm me.
3 I am exhausted from crying for help;
my throat is parched.
My eyes are swollen with weeping,
waiting for my God to help me.
4 Those who hate me without cause
outnumber the hairs on my head.
Many enemies try to destroy me with lies,
demanding that I give back what I didn't steal.

5 O God, you know how foolish I am;
my sins cannot be hidden from you.
6 Don't let those who trust in you be ashamed because of me,
O Sovereign LORD of Heaven's Armies.
Don't let me cause them to be humiliated,
O God of Israel.
7 For I endure insults for your sake;
humiliation is written all over my face.
8 Even my own brothers pretend they don't know me;
they treat me like a stranger.

9 Passion for your house has consumed me,
and the insults of those who insult you have fallen on me.
10 When I weep and fast,
they scoff at me.
11 When I dress in burlap to show sorrow,
they make fun of me.
12 I am the favorite topic of town gossip,
and all the drunks sing about me.

13 But I keep praying to you, LORD,
hoping this time you will show me favor.
In your unfailing love, O God,
answer my prayer with your sure salvation.
14 Rescue me from the mud;
don't let me sink any deeper!
Save me from those who hate me,
and pull me from these deep waters.
15 Don't let the floods overwhelm me,
or the deep waters swallow me,
or the pit of death devour me.

16 Answer my prayers, O LORD,
for your unfailing love is wonderful.
Take care of me,
for your mercy is so plentiful.
17 Don't hide from your servant;
answer me quickly, for I am in deep trouble!
18 Come and redeem me;
free me from my enemies.
19 You know of my shame, scorn, and disgrace.
You see all that my enemies are doing.
20 Their insults have broken my heart,
and I am in despair.
If only one person would show some pity;
if only one would turn and comfort me.
21 But instead, they give me poison* for food;
they offer me sour wine for my thirst.

22 Let the bountiful table set before them become a snare
and their prosperity become a trap.*
23 Let their eyes go blind so they cannot see,
and make their bodies shake continually.*
24 Pour out your fury on them;
consume them with your burning anger.
25 Let their homes become desolate
and their tents be deserted.
26 To the one you have punished, they add insult to injury;
they add to the pain of those you have hurt.
27 Pile their sins up high,
and don't let them go free.
28 Erase their names from the Book of Life;
don't let them be counted among the righteous.

29 I am suffering and in pain.
Rescue me, O God, by your saving power.

30 Then I will praise God's name with singing,
and I will honor him with thanksgiving.
31 For this will please the LORD more than sacrificing cattle,
more than presenting a bull with its horns and hooves.

[32] The humble will see their God at work
and be glad.
Let all who seek God's help be
encouraged.
[33] For the LORD hears the cries of the
needy;
he does not despise his imprisoned
people.
[34] Praise him, O heaven and earth,
the seas and all that move in them.
[35] For God will save Jerusalem*
and rebuild the towns of Judah.
His people will live there
and settle in their own land.
[36] The descendants of those who obey him
will inherit the land,
and those who love him will live there
in safety.

70

For the choir director: A psalm of David, asking God to remember him.

[1] Please, God, rescue me!
Come quickly, LORD, and help me.
[2] May those who try to kill me
be humiliated and put to shame.
May those who take delight in my
trouble
be turned back in disgrace.
[3] Let them be horrified by their shame,
for they said, "Aha! We've got him
now!"
[4] But may all who search for you
be filled with joy and gladness in you.
May those who love your salvation
repeatedly shout, "God is great!"
[5] But as for me, I am poor and needy;
please hurry to my aid, O God.
You are my helper and my savior;
O LORD, do not delay.

71

[1] O LORD, I have come to you for
protection;
don't let me be disgraced.
[2] Save me and rescue me,
for you do what is right.
Turn your ear to listen to me,
and set me free.
[3] Be my rock of safety
where I can always hide.
Give the order to save me,
for you are my rock and my fortress.
[4] My God, rescue me from the power of
the wicked,
from the clutches of cruel oppressors.
[5] O Lord, you alone are my hope.
I've trusted you, O LORD, from
childhood.
[6] Yes, you have been with me from birth;
from my mother's womb you have
cared for me.
No wonder I am always praising you!
[7] My life is an example to many,
because you have been my strength
and protection.
[8] That is why I can never stop praising you;
I declare your glory all day long.
[9] And now, in my old age, don't set me
aside.
Don't abandon me when my strength
is failing.
[10] For my enemies are whispering
against me.
They are plotting together to kill me.
[11] They say, "God has abandoned him.
Let's go and get him,
for no one will help him now."
[12] O God, don't stay away.
My God, please hurry to help me.
[13] Bring disgrace and destruction on my
accusers.
Humiliate and shame those who want
to harm me.
[14] But I will keep on hoping for your help;
I will praise you more and more.
[15] I will tell everyone about your
righteousness.
All day long I will proclaim your
saving power,
though I am not skilled with words.*
[16] I will praise your mighty deeds,
O Sovereign LORD.
I will tell everyone that you alone are
just.
[17] O God, you have taught me from my
earliest childhood,
and I constantly tell others about the
wonderful things you do.
[18] Now that I am old and gray,
do not abandon me, O God.
Let me proclaim your power to this new
generation,
your mighty miracles to all who come
after me.

69:21 Or *gall.* **69:22** Greek version reads *Let their bountiful table set before them become a snare, / a trap that makes them think all is well. / Let their blessings cause them to stumble, / and let them get what they deserve.* Compare Rom 11:9. **69:23** Greek version reads *and let their backs be bent forever.* Compare Rom 11:10. **69:35** Hebrew *Zion.* **71:15** Or *though I cannot count it.*

19 Your righteousness, O God, reaches to
the highest heavens.
You have done such wonderful things.
Who can compare with you, O God?
20 You have allowed me to suffer much
hardship,
but you will restore me to life again
and lift me up from the depths of the
earth.
21 You will restore me to even greater
honor
and comfort me once again.
22 Then I will praise you with music on the
harp,
because you are faithful to your
promises, O my God.
I will sing praises to you with a lyre,
O Holy One of Israel.
23 I will shout for joy and sing your praises,
for you have ransomed me.
24 I will tell about your righteous deeds
all day long,
for everyone who tried to hurt me
has been shamed and humiliated.

72 *A psalm of Solomon.*

1 Give your love of justice to the king,
O God,
and righteousness to the king's son.
2 Help him judge your people in the right
way;
let the poor always be treated fairly.
3 May the mountains yield prosperity for
all,
and may the hills be fruitful.
4 Help him to defend the poor,
to rescue the children of the needy,
and to crush their oppressors.
5 May they fear you* as long as the sun
shines,
as long as the moon remains in the
sky.
Yes, forever!
6 May the king's rule be refreshing like
spring rain on freshly cut grass,
like the showers that water the earth.
7 May all the godly flourish during his
reign.
May there be abundant prosperity
until the moon is no more.
8 May he reign from sea to sea,
and from the Euphrates River* to the
ends of the earth.
9 Desert nomads will bow before him;
his enemies will fall before him in the
dust.
10 The western kings of Tarshish and other
distant lands
will bring him tribute.
The eastern kings of Sheba and Seba
will bring him gifts.
11 All kings will bow before him,
and all nations will serve him.
12 He will rescue the poor when they cry to
him;
he will help the oppressed, who have
no one to defend them.
13 He feels pity for the weak and the needy,
and he will rescue them.
14 He will redeem them from oppression
and violence,
for their lives are precious to him.
15 Long live the king!
May the gold of Sheba be given to him.
May the people always pray for him
and bless him all day long.
16 May there be abundant grain throughout
the land,
flourishing even on the hilltops.
May the fruit trees flourish like the trees
of Lebanon,
and may the people thrive like grass
in a field.
17 May the king's name endure forever;
may it continue as long as the sun
shines.
May all nations be blessed through him
and bring him praise.
18 Praise the LORD God, the God of Israel,
who alone does such wonderful things.
19 Praise his glorious name forever!
Let the whole earth be filled with his
glory.
Amen and amen!
20 (This ends the prayers of David son of
Jesse.)

BOOK THREE (Psalms 73–89)

73 *A psalm of Asaph.*

1 Truly God is good to Israel,
to those whose hearts are pure.
2 But as for me, I almost lost my footing.
My feet were slipping, and I was
almost gone.

3 For I envied the proud
when I saw them prosper despite their wickedness.
4 They seem to live such painless lives;
their bodies are so healthy and strong.
5 They don't have troubles like other people;
they're not plagued with problems like everyone else.
6 They wear pride like a jeweled necklace
and clothe themselves with cruelty.
7 These fat cats have everything
their hearts could ever wish for!
8 They scoff and speak only evil;
in their pride they seek to crush others.
9 They boast against the very heavens,
and their words strut throughout the earth.
10 And so the people are dismayed and confused,
drinking in all their words.
11 "What does God know?" they ask.
"Does the Most High even know what's happening?"
12 Look at these wicked people—
enjoying a life of ease while their riches multiply.

13 Did I keep my heart pure for nothing?
Did I keep myself innocent for no reason?
14 I get nothing but trouble all day long;
every morning brings me pain.

15 If I had really spoken this way to others,
I would have been a traitor to your people.
16 So I tried to understand why the wicked prosper.
But what a difficult task it is!
17 Then I went into your sanctuary, O God,
and I finally understood the destiny of the wicked.
18 Truly, you put them on a slippery path
and send them sliding over the cliff to destruction.
19 In an instant they are destroyed,
completely swept away by terrors.
20 When you arise, O Lord,
you will laugh at their silly ideas
as a person laughs at dreams in the morning.

21 Then I realized that my heart was bitter,
and I was all torn up inside.
22 I was so foolish and ignorant—
I must have seemed like a senseless animal to you.
23 Yet I still belong to you;
you hold my right hand.
24 You guide me with your counsel,
leading me to a glorious destiny.
25 Whom have I in heaven but you?
I desire you more than anything on earth.
26 My health may fail, and my spirit may grow weak,
but God remains the strength of my heart;
he is mine forever.

27 Those who desert him will perish,
for you destroy those who abandon you.
28 But as for me, how good it is to be near God!
I have made the Sovereign LORD my shelter,
and I will tell everyone about the wonderful things you do.

72:5 Greek version reads *May they endure.* **72:8** Hebrew *the river.*

Asaph

Not all of the psalms were written by King David. Other authors include "the descendants of Korah" (eleven psalms), Solomon (two psalms), and Moses (one psalm)—while quite a number are anonymous. Psalm 73 was written by Asaph, who was one of three Levitical choir directors appointed by King David (1 Chronicles 6:31-48). He was in the choir that accompanied the return of the Ark of the Covenant to Jerusalem (1 Chronicles 15:16-19) and that sang at the dedication of the Temple (2 Chronicles 5:12-13). He also played the cymbals. His descendants were still singing in the choir when the Jews returned from exile (Ezra 2:41).

74

A psalm of Asaph.*

1 O God, why have you rejected us so long?
Why is your anger so intense against
the sheep of your own pasture?
2 Remember that we are the people you
chose long ago,
the tribe you redeemed as your own
special possession!
And remember Jerusalem,* your home
here on earth.
3 Walk through the awful ruins of the city;
see how the enemy has destroyed your
sanctuary.
4 There your enemies shouted their
victorious battle cries;
there they set up their battle
standards.
5 They swung their axes
like woodcutters in a forest.
6 With axes and picks,
they smashed the carved paneling.
7 They burned your sanctuary to the
ground.
They defiled the place that bears your
name.
8 Then they thought, "Let's destroy
everything!"
So they burned down all the places
where God was worshiped.

9 We no longer see your miraculous signs.
All the prophets are gone,
and no one can tell us when it will
end.
10 How long, O God, will you allow our
enemies to insult you?
Will you let them dishonor your name
forever?
11 Why do you hold back your strong right
hand?
Unleash your powerful fist and
destroy them.

12 You, O God, are my king from ages past,
bringing salvation to the earth.
13 You split the sea by your strength
and smashed the heads of the sea
monsters.
14 You crushed the heads of Leviathan*
and let the desert animals eat him.
15 You caused the springs and streams to
gush forth,
and you dried up rivers that never run
dry.
16 Both day and night belong to you;
you made the starlight* and the sun.
17 You set the boundaries of the earth,
and you made both summer and
winter.

18 See how these enemies insult you, LORD.
A foolish nation has dishonored your
name.
19 Don't let these wild beasts destroy your
turtledoves.
Don't forget your suffering people
forever.

20 Remember your covenant promises,
for the land is full of darkness and
violence!
21 Don't let the downtrodden be humiliated
again.
Instead, let the poor and needy praise
your name.

22 Arise, O God, and defend your cause.
Remember how these fools insult you
all day long.
23 Don't overlook what your enemies have
said
or their growing uproar.

75

For the choir director: A psalm of Asaph. A song to be sung to the tune "Do Not Destroy!"

1 We thank you, O God!
We give thanks because you are near.
People everywhere tell of your
wonderful deeds.

2 God says, "At the time I have planned,
I will bring justice against the wicked.
3 When the earth quakes and its people
live in turmoil,
I am the one who keeps its
foundations firm. *Interlude*

4 "I warned the proud, 'Stop your
boasting!'
I told the wicked, 'Don't raise your
fists!
5 Don't raise your fists in defiance at the
heavens
or speak with such arrogance.'"
6 For no one on earth—from east or west,
or even from the wilderness—
should raise a defiant fist.*
7 It is God alone who judges;
he decides who will rise and who will
fall.

8 For the LORD holds a cup in his hand
that is full of foaming wine mixed
with spices.
He pours out the wine in judgment,
and all the wicked must drink it,
draining it to the dregs.
9 But as for me, I will always proclaim
what God has done;
I will sing praises to the God of Jacob.
10 For God says, "I will break the strength
of the wicked,
but I will increase the power of the
godly."

76

For the choir director: A psalm of Asaph. A song to be accompanied by stringed instruments.

1 God is honored in Judah;
his name is great in Israel.
2 Jerusalem* is where he lives;
Mount Zion is his home.
3 There he has broken the fiery arrows
of the enemy,
the shields and swords and weapons
of war. *Interlude*
4 You are glorious and more majestic
than the everlasting mountains.*
5 Our boldest enemies have been
plundered.
They lie before us in the sleep of
death.
No warrior could lift a hand
against us.
6 At the blast of your breath, O God
of Jacob,
their horses and chariots lay still.
7 No wonder you are greatly feared!
Who can stand before you when your
anger explodes?
8 From heaven you sentenced your
enemies;
the earth trembled and stood silent
before you.
9 You stand up to judge those who do evil,
O God,
and to rescue the oppressed of the
earth. *Interlude*
10 Human defiance only enhances your
glory,
for you use it as a weapon.*
11 Make vows to the LORD your God, and
keep them.
Let everyone bring tribute to the
Awesome One.
12 For he breaks the pride of princes,
and the kings of the earth fear him.

77

For Jeduthun, the choir director: A psalm of Asaph.

1 I cry out to God; yes, I shout.
Oh, that God would listen to me!
2 When I was in deep trouble,
I searched for the Lord.
All night long I prayed, with hands lifted
toward heaven,
but my soul was not comforted.

74:TITLE Hebrew *maskil*. This may be a literary or musical term. **74:2** Hebrew *Mount Zion*. **74:14** The identification of Leviathan is disputed, ranging from an earthly creature to a mythical sea monster in ancient literature. **74:16** Or *moon;* Hebrew reads *light*. **75:6** Hebrew *should lift*. **76:2** Hebrew *Salem*, another name for Jerusalem. **76:4** As in Greek version; Hebrew reads *than mountains filled with beasts of prey*. **76:10** The meaning of the Hebrew is uncertain.

Zion

Quite often in the Psalms and prophetic books we find the name "Zion" or "Mount Zion" used of Jerusalem (e.g., Psalm 76:2). Zion was originally the name of a hill on which a Jebusite city stood—one that hadn't been conquered originally by the Israelites. Because it lay on the border of Judah and Israel, King David decided it would make an excellent neutral capital for his newly united kingdom and so captured it (2 Samuel 5:6-10). As the city expanded, "Zion" came to be used of the whole city, underlining its links with David and God's promises to him; and because the Temple stood there, it was seen as God's dwelling place on earth and a place he especially loved. In the New Testament, Zion is used as a symbol of the people of God—not confined to a hill in Israel anymore, but now filling both heaven and earth (Hebrews 12:22-23).

▶ *See also* ***Jerusalem****, page 347;* ***The New Jerusalem****, page 1466.*

3 I think of God, and I moan,
overwhelmed with longing for his help. *Interlude*
4 You don't let me sleep.
I am too distressed even to pray!
5 I think of the good old days,
long since ended,
6 when my nights were filled with joyful songs.
I search my soul and ponder the difference now.
7 Has the Lord rejected me forever?
Will he never again be kind to me?
8 Is his unfailing love gone forever?
Have his promises permanently failed?
9 Has God forgotten to be gracious?
Has he slammed the door on his compassion? *Interlude*
10 And I said, "This is my fate;
the Most High has turned his hand against me."
11 But then I recall all you have done, O LORD;
I remember your wonderful deeds of long ago.
12 They are constantly in my thoughts.
I cannot stop thinking about your mighty works.
13 O God, your ways are holy.
Is there any god as mighty as you?
14 You are the God of great wonders!
You demonstrate your awesome power among the nations.
15 By your strong arm, you redeemed your people,
the descendants of Jacob and Joseph. *Interlude*
16 When the Red Sea* saw you, O God,
its waters looked and trembled!
The sea quaked to its very depths.
17 The clouds poured down rain;
the thunder rumbled in the sky.
Your arrows of lightning flashed.
18 Your thunder roared from the whirlwind;
the lightning lit up the world!
The earth trembled and shook.
19 Your road led through the sea,
your pathway through the mighty waters—
a pathway no one knew was there!
20 You led your people along that road like a flock of sheep,
with Moses and Aaron as their shepherds.

78

A psalm of Asaph.*

1 O my people, listen to my instructions.
Open your ears to what I am saying,
2 for I will speak to you in a parable.
I will teach you hidden lessons from our past—
3 stories we have heard and known,
stories our ancestors handed down to us.
4 We will not hide these truths from our children;
we will tell the next generation
about the glorious deeds of the LORD,
about his power and his mighty wonders.
5 For he issued his laws to Jacob;
he gave his instructions to Israel.
He commanded our ancestors
to teach them to their children,
6 so the next generation might know them—
even the children not yet born—
and they in turn will teach their own children.
7 So each generation should set its hope anew on God,
not forgetting his glorious miracles
and obeying his commands.
8 Then they will not be like their ancestors—
stubborn, rebellious, and unfaithful,
refusing to give their hearts to God.
9 The warriors of Ephraim, though armed with bows,
turned their backs and fled on the day of battle.
10 They did not keep God's covenant
and refused to live by his instructions.
11 They forgot what he had done—
the great wonders he had shown them,
12 the miracles he did for their ancestors
on the plain of Zoan in the land of Egypt.
13 For he divided the sea and led them through,
making the water stand up like walls!
14 In the daytime he led them by a cloud,
and all night by a pillar of fire.

15 He split open the rocks in the wilderness
to give them water, as from a gushing
spring.
16 He made streams pour from the rock,
making the waters flow down like a
river!
17 Yet they kept on sinning against him,
rebelling against the Most High in the
desert.
18 They stubbornly tested God in their
hearts,
demanding the foods they craved.
19 They even spoke against God himself,
saying,
"God can't give us food in the
wilderness.
20 Yes, he can strike a rock so water gushes
out,
but he can't give his people bread and
meat."
21 When the LORD heard them, he was
furious.
The fire of his wrath burned against
Jacob.
Yes, his anger rose against Israel,
22 for they did not believe God
or trust him to care for them.
23 But he commanded the skies to
open;
he opened the doors of heaven.
24 He rained down manna for them to eat;
he gave them bread from heaven.
25 They ate the food of angels!
God gave them all they could hold.
26 He released the east wind in the heavens
and guided the south wind by his
mighty power.
27 He rained down meat as thick as dust—
birds as plentiful as the sand on the
seashore!
28 He caused the birds to fall within their
camp
and all around their tents.
29 The people ate their fill.
He gave them what they craved.
30 But before they satisfied their craving,
while the meat was yet in their
mouths,
31 the anger of God rose against them,
and he killed their strongest men.
He struck down the finest of Israel's
young men.
32 But in spite of this, the people kept
sinning.
Despite his wonders, they refused to
trust him.
33 So he ended their lives in failure,
their years in terror.

77:16 Hebrew *the waters.* **78:TITLE** Hebrew *maskil.* This may be a literary or musical term.

From one generation to another

A constant theme of Scripture is the importance of passing on God's truth and God's actions on behalf of his people from one generation to another. In Psalm 78:3-4 the psalmist pledges that what his own generation has known of God, and what they received from the previous generation, will be passed on to the next generation. And in 78:5-6 he sees this happening through five generations: "our ancestors . . . their children . . . the next generation . . . children not yet born . . . their own children." Paul also understood the importance of faithful transmission of God's truth across the generations (2 Timothy 2:2).

Whenever God's truth and actions are not passed on, disaster follows. The book of Judges states, "After that generation died, another generation grew up who did not acknowledge the LORD or remember the mighty things he had done for Israel" (Judges 2:10). And the book goes on to record the disastrous history of the next three centuries. Even some of the greatest saints failed in the area of faithful transmission: Samuel did not raise his sons to follow godly ways (1 Samuel 8:1-3); and the godly Hezekiah failed to mentor his son Manasseh, who became one of Judah's most wicked kings.

The faithful transmission of God's truth and God's story to the next generation should always be a priority for Christian families and church leaders.

34 When God began killing them,
they finally sought him.
They repented and took God seriously.
35 Then they remembered that God was their rock,
that God Most High* was their redeemer.
36 But all they gave him was lip service;
they lied to him with their tongues.
37 Their hearts were not loyal to him.
They did not keep his covenant.
38 Yet he was merciful and forgave their sins
and did not destroy them all.
Many times he held back his anger
and did not unleash his fury!
39 For he remembered that they were merely mortal,
gone like a breath of wind that never returns.
40 Oh, how often they rebelled against him in the wilderness
and grieved his heart in that dry wasteland.
41 Again and again they tested God's patience
and provoked the Holy One of Israel.
42 They did not remember his power
and how he rescued them from their enemies.
43 They did not remember his miraculous signs in Egypt,
his wonders on the plain of Zoan.
44 For he turned their rivers into blood,
so no one could drink from the streams.
45 He sent vast swarms of flies to consume them
and hordes of frogs to ruin them.
46 He gave their crops to caterpillars;
their harvest was consumed by locusts.
47 He destroyed their grapevines with hail
and shattered their sycamore-figs with sleet.
48 He abandoned their cattle to the hail,
their livestock to bolts of lightning.
49 He loosed on them his fierce anger—
all his fury, rage, and hostility.
He dispatched against them
a band of destroying angels.
50 He turned his anger against them;
he did not spare the Egyptians' lives
but ravaged them with the plague.
51 He killed the oldest son in each Egyptian family,
the flower of youth throughout the land of Egypt.*
52 But he led his own people like a flock of sheep,
guiding them safely through the wilderness.
53 He kept them safe so they were not afraid;
but the sea covered their enemies.
54 He brought them to the border of his holy land,
to this land of hills he had won for them.
55 He drove out the nations before them;
he gave them their inheritance by lot.
He settled the tribes of Israel into their homes.
56 But they kept testing and rebelling against God Most High.
They did not obey his laws.
57 They turned back and were as faithless as their parents.
They were as undependable as a crooked bow.
58 They angered God by building shrines to other gods;
they made him jealous with their idols.
59 When God heard them, he was very angry,
and he completely rejected Israel.
60 Then he abandoned his dwelling at Shiloh,
the Tabernacle where he had lived among the people.
61 He allowed the Ark of his might to be captured;
he surrendered his glory into enemy hands.
62 He gave his people over to be butchered by the sword,
because he was so angry with his own people—his special possession.
63 Their young men were killed by fire;
their young women died before singing their wedding songs.
64 Their priests were slaughtered,
and their widows could not mourn their deaths.
65 Then the Lord rose up as though waking from sleep,
like a warrior aroused from a drunken stupor.

[66] He routed his enemies
and sent them to eternal shame.
[67] But he rejected Joseph's descendants;
he did not choose the tribe of Ephraim.
[68] He chose instead the tribe of Judah,
and Mount Zion, which he loved.
[69] There he built his sanctuary as high as the heavens,
as solid and enduring as the earth.
[70] He chose his servant David,
calling him from the sheep pens.
[71] He took David from tending the ewes and lambs
and made him the shepherd of Jacob's descendants—
God's own people, Israel.
[72] He cared for them with a true heart
and led them with skillful hands.

79

A psalm of Asaph.

[1] O God, pagan nations have conquered your land,
your special possession.
They have defiled your holy Temple
and made Jerusalem a heap of ruins.
[2] They have left the bodies of your servants
as food for the birds of heaven.
The flesh of your godly ones
has become food for the wild animals.
[3] Blood has flowed like water all around Jerusalem;
no one is left to bury the dead.
[4] We are mocked by our neighbors,
an object of scorn and derision to those around us.
[5] O LORD, how long will you be angry with us? Forever?
How long will your jealousy burn like fire?
[6] Pour out your wrath on the nations that refuse to acknowledge you—
on kingdoms that do not call upon your name.
[7] For they have devoured your people Israel,*
making the land a desolate wilderness.
[8] Do not hold us guilty for the sins of our ancestors!
Let your compassion quickly meet our needs,
for we are on the brink of despair.
[9] Help us, O God of our salvation!
Help us for the glory of your name.
Save us and forgive our sins
for the honor of your name.
[10] Why should pagan nations be allowed to scoff,
asking, "Where is their God?"
Show us your vengeance against the nations,
for they have spilled the blood of your servants.
[11] Listen to the moaning of the prisoners.
Demonstrate your great power by saving those condemned to die.
[12] O Lord, pay back our neighbors seven times
for the scorn they have hurled at you.
[13] Then we your people, the sheep of your pasture,
will thank you forever and ever,
praising your greatness from generation to generation.

80

For the choir director: A psalm of Asaph, to be sung to the tune "Lilies of the Covenant."

[1] Please listen, O Shepherd of Israel,
you who lead Joseph's descendants like a flock.
O God, enthroned above the cherubim,
display your radiant glory
[2] to Ephraim, Benjamin, and Manasseh.
Show us your mighty power.
Come to rescue us!
[3] Turn us again to yourself, O God.
Make your face shine down upon us.
Only then will we be saved.
[4] O LORD God of Heaven's Armies,
how long will you be angry with our prayers?
[5] You have fed us with sorrow
and made us drink tears by the bucketful.
[6] You have made us the scorn* of neighboring nations.
Our enemies treat us as a joke.
[7] Turn us again to yourself, O God of Heaven's Armies.
Make your face shine down upon us.
Only then will we be saved.

78:35 Hebrew *El-Elyon*. **78:51** Hebrew *in the tents of Ham*. **79:7** Hebrew *devoured Jacob*. See note on 44:4. **80:6** As in Syriac version; Hebrew reads *the strife*.

8 You brought us from Egypt like a
grapevine;
you drove away the pagan nations and
transplanted us into your land.
9 You cleared the ground for us,
and we took root and filled the
land.
10 Our shade covered the mountains;
our branches covered the mighty
cedars.
11 We spread our branches west to the
Mediterranean Sea;
our shoots spread east to the
Euphrates River.*
12 But now, why have you broken down our
walls
so that all who pass by may steal our
fruit?
13 The wild boar from the forest devours it,
and the wild animals feed on it.

14 Come back, we beg you, O God of
Heaven's Armies.
Look down from heaven and see our
plight.
Take care of this grapevine
15 that you yourself have planted,
this son you have raised for yourself.
16 For we are chopped up and burned by
our enemies.
May they perish at the sight of your
frown.
17 Strengthen the man you love,
the son of your choice.
18 Then we will never abandon you again.
Revive us so we can call on your name
once more.

19 Turn us again to yourself, O LORD God of
Heaven's Armies.
Make your face shine down upon us.
Only then will we be saved.

81

*For the choir director: A psalm of Asaph, to be accompanied by a stringed instrument.**

1 Sing praises to God, our strength.
Sing to the God of Jacob.
2 Sing! Beat the tambourine.
Play the sweet lyre and the harp.
3 Blow the ram's horn at new moon,
and again at full moon to call a
festival!
4 For this is required by the decrees of
Israel;
it is a regulation of the God of Jacob.
5 He made it a law for Israel*
when he attacked Egypt to set us
free.

I heard an unknown voice say,
6 "Now I will take the load from your
shoulders;
I will free your hands from their heavy
tasks.
7 You cried to me in trouble, and I saved
you;
I answered out of the thundercloud
and tested your faith when there was
no water at Meribah. *Interlude*

8 "Listen to me, O my people, while I give
you stern warnings.
O Israel, if you would only listen
to me!
9 You must never have a foreign god;
you must not bow down before a false
god.
10 For it was I, the LORD your God,
who rescued you from the land of
Egypt.
Open your mouth wide, and I will fill
it with good things.

11 "But no, my people wouldn't listen.
Israel did not want me around.
12 So I let them follow their own stubborn
desires,
living according to their own ideas.
13 Oh, that my people would listen to me!
Oh, that Israel would follow me,
walking in my paths!
14 How quickly I would then subdue their
enemies!
How soon my hands would be upon
their foes!
15 Those who hate the LORD would cringe
before him;
they would be doomed forever.
16 But I would feed you with the finest
wheat.
I would satisfy you with wild honey
from the rock."

82

A psalm of Asaph.

1 God presides over heaven's court;
he pronounces judgment on the
heavenly beings:
2 "How long will you hand down unjust
decisions
by favoring the wicked? *Interlude*

[3] "Give justice to the poor and the orphan;
uphold the rights of the oppressed and the destitute.
[4] Rescue the poor and helpless;
deliver them from the grasp of evil people.
[5] But these oppressors know nothing;
they are so ignorant!
They wander about in darkness,
while the whole world is shaken to the core.
[6] I say, 'You are gods;
you are all children of the Most High.
[7] But you will die like mere mortals
and fall like every other ruler.'"

[8] Rise up, O God, and judge the earth,
for all the nations belong to you.

83

A song. A psalm of Asaph.

[1] O God, do not be silent!
Do not be deaf.
Do not be quiet, O God.
[2] Don't you hear the uproar of your enemies?
Don't you see that your arrogant enemies are rising up?
[3] They devise crafty schemes against your people;
they conspire against your precious ones.
[4] "Come," they say, "let us wipe out Israel as a nation.
We will destroy the very memory of its existence."
[5] Yes, this was their unanimous decision.
They signed a treaty as allies against you—
[6] these Edomites and Ishmaelites;
Moabites and Hagrites;
[7] Gebalites, Ammonites, and Amalekites;
and people from Philistia and Tyre.
[8] Assyria has joined them, too,
and is allied with the descendants of Lot. *Interlude*

[9] Do to them as you did to the Midianites
and as you did to Sisera and Jabin at the Kishon River.
[10] They were destroyed at Endor,
and their decaying corpses fertilized the soil.
[11] Let their mighty nobles die as Oreb and Zeeb did.
Let all their princes die like Zebah and Zalmunna,
[12] for they said, "Let us seize for our own use
these pasturelands of God!"
[13] O my God, scatter them like tumbleweed,
like chaff before the wind!
[14] As a fire burns a forest
and as a flame sets mountains ablaze,
[15] chase them with your fierce storm;
terrify them with your tempest.
[16] Utterly disgrace them
until they submit to your name, O LORD.
[17] Let them be ashamed and terrified forever.
Let them die in disgrace.
[18] Then they will learn that you alone are called the LORD,
that you alone are the Most High,
supreme over all the earth.

84

*For the choir director: A psalm of the descendants of Korah, to be accompanied by a stringed instrument.**

[1] How lovely is your dwelling place,
O LORD of Heaven's Armies.
[2] I long, yes, I faint with longing
to enter the courts of the LORD.
With my whole being, body and soul,
I will shout joyfully to the living God.
[3] Even the sparrow finds a home,
and the swallow builds her nest and raises her young
at a place near your altar,
O LORD of Heaven's Armies, my King and my God!
[4] What joy for those who can live in your house,
always singing your praises. *Interlude*

[5] What joy for those whose strength comes from the LORD,
who have set their minds on a pilgrimage to Jerusalem.
[6] When they walk through the Valley of Weeping,*
it will become a place of refreshing springs.
The autumn rains will clothe it with blessings.

80:11 Hebrew *west to the sea, . . . east to the river.*
81:TITLE Hebrew *according to the gittith.* **81:5** Hebrew *for Joseph.*
84:TITLE Hebrew *according to the gittith.* **84:6** Or *Valley of Poplars;* Hebrew reads *valley of Baca.*

7 They will continue to grow stronger,
and each of them will appear before
God in Jerusalem.*

8 O LORD God of Heaven's Armies, hear
my prayer.
Listen, O God of Jacob. *Interlude*

9 O God, look with favor upon the king,
our shield!
Show favor to the one you have
anointed.

10 A single day in your courts
is better than a thousand anywhere
else!
I would rather be a gatekeeper in the
house of my God
than live the good life in the homes
of the wicked.

11 For the LORD God is our sun and our
shield.
He gives us grace and glory.
The LORD will withhold no good thing
from those who do what is right.

12 O LORD of Heaven's Armies,
what joy for those who trust in you.

85

For the choir director: A psalm of the descendants of Korah.

1 LORD, you poured out blessings on your
land!
You restored the fortunes of Israel.*

2 You forgave the guilt of your people—
yes, you covered all their sins.
Interlude

3 You held back your fury.
You kept back your blazing
anger.

4 Now restore us again, O God of our
salvation.
Put aside your anger against us once
more.

5 Will you be angry with us always?
Will you prolong your wrath to all
generations?

6 Won't you revive us again,
so your people can rejoice in you?

7 Show us your unfailing love, O LORD,
and grant us your salvation.

8 I listen carefully to what God the LORD
is saying,
for he speaks peace to his faithful
people.
But let them not return to their foolish
ways.

9 Surely his salvation is near to those who
fear him,
so our land will be filled with his glory.

10 Unfailing love and truth have met
together.
Righteousness and peace have kissed!

11 Truth springs up from the earth,
and righteousness smiles down from
heaven.

12 Yes, the LORD pours down his blessings.
Our land will yield its bountiful
harvest.

13 Righteousness goes as a herald before
him,
preparing the way for his steps.

86

A prayer of David.

1 Bend down, O LORD, and hear my prayer;
answer me, for I need your help.

Pilgrimage

Pilgrimage—a journey to a holy place as an act of devotion—played an important part in Old Testament faith (e.g., Psalm 84:5). Jews were expected to make pilgrimages to Jerusalem three times a year (Exodus 34:23) for the great festivals of Passover, Harvest (Pentecost), and Shelters (Tabernacles); and some of the psalms were written for pilgrims to sing on their way, as the introductions to Psalms 120–134 show. But, like all other religious activities, pilgrimage has no value in itself. If it is not accompanied by true heart devotion, it is meaningless to God (e.g., Amos 5:21-24).

Life itself was sometimes seen as a pilgrimage (Genesis 47:9), and the New Testament sees this world as a temporary place that we are just passing through (Hebrews 11:13; 1 Peter 2:11).

[2] Protect me, for I am devoted to you.
Save me, for I serve you and trust you.
You are my God.
[3] Be merciful to me, O Lord,
for I am calling on you constantly.
[4] Give me happiness, O Lord,
for I give myself to you.
[5] O Lord, you are so good, so ready to
forgive,
so full of unfailing love for all who ask
for your help.
[6] Listen closely to my prayer, O LORD;
hear my urgent cry.
[7] I will call to you whenever I'm in trouble,
and you will answer me.

[8] No pagan god is like you, O Lord.
None can do what you do!
[9] All the nations you made
will come and bow before you, Lord;
they will praise your holy name.
[10] For you are great and perform wonderful
deeds.
You alone are God.

[11] Teach me your ways, O LORD,
that I may live according to your truth!
Grant me purity of heart,
so that I may honor you.
[12] With all my heart I will praise you,
O Lord my God.
I will give glory to your name forever,
[13] for your love for me is very great.
You have rescued me from the depths
of death.*

[14] O God, insolent people rise up against me;
a violent gang is trying to kill me.
You mean nothing to them.
[15] But you, O Lord,
are a God of compassion and mercy,
slow to get angry
and filled with unfailing love and
faithfulness.
[16] Look down and have mercy on me.
Give your strength to your servant;
save me, the son of your servant.
[17] Send me a sign of your favor.
Then those who hate me will be put
to shame,
for you, O LORD, help and comfort me.

87

A song. A psalm of the descendants of Korah.

[1] On the holy mountain
stands the city founded by the LORD.
[2] He loves the city of Jerusalem
more than any other city in Israel.*
[3] O city of God,
what glorious things are said of you!
Interlude

[4] I will count Egypt* and Babylon among
those who know me—
also Philistia and Tyre, and even
distant Ethiopia.*
They have all become citizens of
Jerusalem!
[5] Regarding Jerusalem* it will be said,
"Everyone enjoys the rights of
citizenship there."
And the Most High will personally
bless this city.
[6] When the LORD registers the nations,
he will say,
"They have all become citizens of
Jerusalem." *Interlude*

[7] The people will play flutes* and sing,
"The source of my life springs from
Jerusalem!"

88

For the choir director: A psalm of the descendants of Korah. A song to be sung to the tune "The Suffering of Affliction." A psalm of Heman the Ezrahite.*

[1] O LORD, God of my salvation,
I cry out to you by day.
I come to you at night.
[2] Now hear my prayer;
listen to my cry.
[3] For my life is full of troubles,
and death* draws near.
[4] I am as good as dead,
like a strong man with no strength left.
[5] They have left me among the dead,
and I lie like a corpse in a grave.
I am forgotten,
cut off from your care.
[6] You have thrown me into the lowest pit,
into the darkest depths.
[7] Your anger weighs me down;
with wave after wave you have
engulfed me. *Interlude*

[8] You have driven my friends away
by making me repulsive to them.

84:7 Hebrew *Zion*. **85:1** Hebrew *of Jacob*. See note on 44:4. **86:13** Hebrew *of Sheol*. **87:2** Hebrew *He loves the gates of Zion more than all the dwellings of Jacob*. See note on 44:4. **87:4a** Hebrew *Rahab*, the name of a mythical sea monster that represents chaos in ancient literature. The name is used here as a poetic name for Egypt. **87:4b** Hebrew *Cush*. **87:5** Hebrew *Zion*. **87:7** Or *will dance*. **88:TITLE** Hebrew *maskil*. This may be a literary or musical term. **88:3** Hebrew *Sheol*.

I am in a trap with no way of escape.
9 My eyes are blinded by my tears.
Each day I beg for your help,
O LORD;
I lift my hands to you for mercy.
10 Are your wonderful deeds of any use to
the dead?
Do the dead rise up and praise you?
Interlude
11 Can those in the grave declare your
unfailing love?
Can they proclaim your faithfulness
in the place of destruction?*
12 Can the darkness speak of your
wonderful deeds?
Can anyone in the land of
forgetfulness talk about your
righteousness?
13 O LORD, I cry out to you.
I will keep on pleading day by day.
14 O LORD, why do you reject me?
Why do you turn your face from me?
15 I have been sick and close to death since
my youth.
I stand helpless and desperate before
your terrors.
16 Your fierce anger has overwhelmed me.
Your terrors have paralyzed me.
17 They swirl around me like floodwaters
all day long.
They have engulfed me completely.
18 You have taken away my companions
and loved ones.
Darkness is my closest friend.

89

A psalm of Ethan the Ezrahite.*

1 I will sing of the LORD's unfailing love
forever!
Young and old will hear of your
faithfulness.
2 Your unfailing love will last forever.
Your faithfulness is as enduring as the
heavens.
3 The LORD said, "I have made a covenant
with David, my chosen servant.
I have sworn this oath to him:
4 'I will establish your descendants as
kings forever;
they will sit on your throne from now
until eternity.'" *Interlude*
5 All heaven will praise your great
wonders, LORD;
myriads of angels will praise you for
your faithfulness.
6 For who in all of heaven can compare
with the LORD?
What mightiest angel is anything like
the LORD?
7 The highest angelic powers stand in awe
of God.
He is far more awesome than all who
surround his throne.
8 O LORD God of Heaven's Armies!
Where is there anyone as mighty as
you, O LORD?
You are entirely faithful.
9 You rule the oceans.
You subdue their storm-tossed waves.
10 You crushed the great sea monster.*
You scattered your enemies with your
mighty arm.
11 The heavens are yours, and the earth is
yours;
everything in the world is yours—you
created it all.
12 You created north and south.
Mount Tabor and Mount Hermon
praise your name.
13 Powerful is your arm!
Strong is your hand!
Your right hand is lifted high in
glorious strength.
14 Righteousness and justice are the
foundation of your throne.
Unfailing love and truth walk before
you as attendants.
15 Happy are those who hear the joyful call
to worship,
for they will walk in the light of your
presence, LORD.
16 They rejoice all day long in your
wonderful reputation.
They exult in your righteousness.
17 You are their glorious strength.
It pleases you to make us strong.
18 Yes, our protection comes from the
LORD,
and he, the Holy One of Israel, has
given us our king.
19 Long ago you spoke in a vision to your
faithful people.
You said, "I have raised up a warrior.
I have selected him from the common
people to be king.
20 I have found my servant David.
I have anointed him with my holy oil.

21 I will steady him with my hand;
with my powerful arm I will make him strong.
22 His enemies will not defeat him,
nor will the wicked overpower him.
23 I will beat down his adversaries before him
and destroy those who hate him.
24 My faithfulness and unfailing love will be with him,
and by my authority he will grow in power.
25 I will extend his rule over the sea,
his dominion over the rivers.
26 And he will call out to me, 'You are my Father,
my God, and the Rock of my salvation.'
27 I will make him my firstborn son,
the mightiest king on earth.
28 I will love him and be kind to him forever;
my covenant with him will never end.
29 I will preserve an heir for him;
his throne will be as endless as the days of heaven.
30 But if his descendants forsake my instructions
and fail to obey my regulations,
31 if they do not obey my decrees
and fail to keep my commands,
32 then I will punish their sin with the rod,
and their disobedience with beating.
33 But I will never stop loving him
nor fail to keep my promise to him.
34 No, I will not break my covenant;
I will not take back a single word I said.
35 I have sworn an oath to David,
and in my holiness I cannot lie:
36 His dynasty will go on forever;
his kingdom will endure as the sun.
37 It will be as eternal as the moon,
my faithful witness in the sky!" *Interlude*

38 But now you have rejected him and cast him off.
You are angry with your anointed king.
39 You have renounced your covenant with him;
you have thrown his crown in the dust.
40 You have broken down the walls protecting him
and ruined every fort defending him.
41 Everyone who comes along has robbed him,
and he has become a joke to his neighbors.
42 You have strengthened his enemies
and made them all rejoice.
43 You have made his sword useless
and refused to help him in battle.
44 You have ended his splendor
and overturned his throne.
45 You have made him old before his time
and publicly disgraced him. *Interlude*

46 O LORD, how long will this go on?
Will you hide yourself forever?
How long will your anger burn like fire?
47 Remember how short my life is,
how empty and futile this human existence!
48 No one can live forever; all will die.
No one can escape the power of the grave.* *Interlude*

49 Lord, where is your unfailing love?
You promised it to David with a faithful pledge.
50 Consider, Lord, how your servants are disgraced!
I carry in my heart the insults of so many people.
51 Your enemies have mocked me, O LORD;
they mock your anointed king
wherever he goes.

52 Praise the LORD forever!
Amen and amen!

BOOK FOUR (Psalms 90–106)

90

A prayer of Moses, the man of God.

1 Lord, through all the generations
you have been our home!
2 Before the mountains were born,
before you gave birth to the earth and the world,
from beginning to end, you are God.

3 You turn people back to dust, saying,
"Return to dust, you mortals!"
4 For you, a thousand years are as a passing day,
as brief as a few night hours.
5 You sweep people away like dreams that disappear.

88:11 Hebrew *in Abaddon?* **89:TITLE** Hebrew *maskil.* This may be a literary or musical term. **89:10** Hebrew *Rahab,* the name of a mythical sea monster that represents chaos in ancient literature. **89:48** Hebrew *of Sheol.*

They are like grass that springs up in
the morning.
6 In the morning it blooms and flourishes,
but by evening it is dry and
withered.
7 We wither beneath your anger;
we are overwhelmed by your fury.
8 You spread out our sins before you—
our secret sins—and you see them all.
9 We live our lives beneath your wrath,
ending our years with a groan.
10 Seventy years are given to us!
Some even live to eighty.
But even the best years are filled with
pain and trouble;
soon they disappear, and we fly away.
11 Who can comprehend the power of your
anger?
Your wrath is as awesome as the fear
you deserve.
12 Teach us to realize the brevity of life,
so that we may grow in wisdom.
13 O LORD, come back to us!
How long will you delay?
Take pity on your servants!
14 Satisfy us each morning with your
unfailing love,
so we may sing for joy to the end
of our lives.
15 Give us gladness in proportion to our
former misery!
Replace the evil years with good.
16 Let us, your servants, see you work
again;
let our children see your glory.
17 And may the Lord our God show us his
approval
and make our efforts successful.
Yes, make our efforts successful!

91

1 Those who live in the shelter
of the Most High
will find rest in the shadow of the
Almighty.
2 This I declare about the LORD:
He alone is my refuge, my place of
safety;
he is my God, and I trust him.
3 For he will rescue you from every trap
and protect you from deadly disease.
4 He will cover you with his feathers.
He will shelter you with his wings.
His faithful promises are your armor
and protection.
5 Do not be afraid of the terrors of the night,
nor the arrow that flies in the day.
6 Do not dread the disease that stalks in
darkness,
nor the disaster that strikes at midday.

Old age

In contrast to God, who alone is eternal (Psalm 90:2), the one thing common to all humanity is that we get older and die—even if we reach the seventy or eighty years the psalmist speaks of (90:10). Getting older is simply a part of life in this world, and old age can therefore be embraced as much as any other stage in life. Those who are older should remember both the challenges and opportunities of increasing age. The opportunities include growth in wisdom and experience that can be passed on. The challenge is to remain youthful at heart and strong in spirit, just like Caleb (Joshua 14:10-12).

To the young, the Bible's call is to respect the elderly (e.g., Leviticus 19:32; 1 Peter 5:5), and disrespect of them is seen as a sign of evil days (e.g., Isaiah 3:5). Eastern cultures have generally respected the elderly better than those in the West—though increasing Western influence is becoming a challenge to Eastern traditions in this area. Christians, however, should always be at the forefront of respecting and caring for the elderly.

Many key people God used were older, so we should never dismiss older people as unimportant or useless. But equally, older people should train up and prepare younger people to accept responsibility, as Paul did with Timothy.

▸ *See also* ***Respect for those who are older****, page 415;* ***Mentoring****, page 1385.*

7 Though a thousand fall at your side,
though ten thousand are dying around you,
these evils will not touch you.
8 Just open your eyes,
and see how the wicked are punished.

9 If you make the LORD your refuge,
if you make the Most High your shelter,
10 no evil will conquer you;
no plague will come near your home.
11 For he will order his angels
to protect you wherever you go.
12 They will hold you up with their hands
so you won't even hurt your foot on a stone.
13 You will trample upon lions and cobras;
you will crush fierce lions and serpents under your feet!

14 The LORD says, "I will rescue those who love me.
I will protect those who trust in my name.
15 When they call on me, I will answer;
I will be with them in trouble.
I will rescue and honor them.
16 I will reward them with a long life
and give them my salvation."

92

A psalm. A song to be sung on the Sabbath Day.

1 It is good to give thanks to the LORD,
to sing praises to the Most High.
2 It is good to proclaim your unfailing love in the morning,
your faithfulness in the evening,
3 accompanied by a ten-stringed instrument, a harp,
and the melody of a lyre.

4 You thrill me, LORD, with all you have done for me!
I sing for joy because of what you have done.
5 O LORD, what great works you do!
And how deep are your thoughts.
6 Only a simpleton would not know,
and only a fool would not understand this:
7 Though the wicked sprout like weeds
and evildoers flourish,
they will be destroyed forever.

8 But you, O LORD, will be exalted forever.
9 Your enemies, LORD, will surely perish;
all evildoers will be scattered.
10 But you have made me as strong as a wild ox.
You have anointed me with the finest oil.
11 My eyes have seen the downfall of my enemies;
my ears have heard the defeat of my wicked opponents.
12 But the godly will flourish like palm trees
and grow strong like the cedars of Lebanon.
13 For they are transplanted to the LORD's own house.
They flourish in the courts of our God.
14 Even in old age they will still produce fruit;
they will remain vital and green.
15 They will declare, "The LORD is just!
He is my rock!
There is no evil in him!"

93

1 The LORD is king! He is robed in majesty.
Indeed, the LORD is robed in majesty
and armed with strength.
The world stands firm
and cannot be shaken.

2 Your throne, O LORD, has stood from time immemorial.
You yourself are from the everlasting past.
3 The floods have risen up, O LORD.
The floods have roared like thunder;
the floods have lifted their pounding waves.
4 But mightier than the violent raging of the seas,
mightier than the breakers on the shore—
the LORD above is mightier than these!
5 Your royal laws cannot be changed.
Your reign, O LORD, is holy forever and ever.

94

1 O LORD, the God of vengeance,
O God of vengeance, let your glorious justice shine forth!
2 Arise, O Judge of the earth.
Give the proud what they deserve.
3 How long, O LORD?
How long will the wicked be allowed to gloat?

[4] How long will they speak with
arrogance?
How long will these evil people boast?
[5] They crush your people, LORD,
hurting those you claim as your own.
[6] They kill widows and foreigners
and murder orphans.
[7] "The LORD isn't looking," they say,
"and besides, the God of Israel*
doesn't care."

[8] Think again, you fools!
When will you finally catch on?
[9] Is he deaf—the one who made your ears?
Is he blind—the one who formed your
eyes?
[10] He punishes the nations—won't he also
punish you?
He knows everything—doesn't he also
know what you are doing?
[11] The LORD knows people's thoughts;
he knows they are worthless!

[12] Joyful are those you discipline, LORD,
those you teach with your
instructions.
[13] You give them relief from troubled
times
until a pit is dug to capture the
wicked.
[14] The LORD will not reject his people;
he will not abandon his special
possession.
[15] Judgment will again be founded on
justice,
and those with virtuous hearts will
pursue it.

[16] Who will protect me from the wicked?
Who will stand up for me against
evildoers?
[17] Unless the LORD had helped me,
I would soon have settled in the
silence of the grave.
[18] I cried out, "I am slipping!"
but your unfailing love, O LORD,
supported me.
[19] When doubts filled my mind,
your comfort gave me renewed hope
and cheer.

[20] Can unjust leaders claim that God is
on their side—
leaders whose decrees permit
injustice?
[21] They gang up against the righteous
and condemn the innocent to death.
[22] But the LORD is my fortress;
my God is the mighty rock where
I hide.

Worship

We do not worship God because he needs it; we worship him because he is worthy. When an artist has painted a great picture, we stand in awe; when musicians have performed a great piece, we applaud; when our football team wins, we shout; when the beauty of nature astounds us, we sigh in wonder. How much more, then, is the Creator and Sustainer of the whole universe—yet the One who also cares for our individual lives—worthy of such a response!

The Bible is full of invitations to worship, as in Psalm 95. But why do we need reminding to worship? If God is so great, shouldn't worship be instinctive? Indeed it should, but in the busyness of life we often get distracted and forgetful—just like Israel did, with disastrous results (95:8-11). This is why we need to encourage one another to worship—to declare the greatness of our Creator and Savior.

However, God is not like some divine battery that decreases in power if he isn't recharged through worship, or some megalomaniac who will sulk if we don't praise him. Worship adds nothing to God. He remains God whether we worship him or not. But worship adds something to us! It reminds us of both who we are and who God is, and of our dependence on him and his ability. In light of that, we can face anything that comes our way.

▶ *See also **Preparing for worship**, page 683; **Hallelujah!**, page 693.*

23 God will turn the sins of evil people back
on them.
He will destroy them for their sins.
The LORD our God will destroy them.

95

1 Come, let us sing to the LORD!
Let us shout joyfully to the
Rock of our salvation.
2 Let us come to him with thanksgiving.
Let us sing psalms of praise to him.
3 For the LORD is a great God,
a great King above all gods.
4 He holds in his hands the depths of the
earth
and the mightiest mountains.
5 The sea belongs to him, for he made it.
His hands formed the dry land, too.

6 Come, let us worship and bow down.
Let us kneel before the LORD our maker,
7 for he is our God.
We are the people he watches over,
the flock under his care.

If only you would listen to his voice today!
8 The LORD says, "Don't harden your
hearts as Israel did at Meribah,
as they did at Massah in the
wilderness.
9 For there your ancestors tested and tried
my patience,
even though they saw everything I did.
10 For forty years I was angry with them,
and I said,
'They are a people whose hearts turn
away from me.
They refuse to do what I tell them.'
11 So in my anger I took an oath:
'They will never enter my place of
rest.'"

96

1 Sing a new song to the LORD!
Let the whole earth sing to the
LORD!
2 Sing to the LORD; praise his name.
Each day proclaim the good news that
he saves.
3 Publish his glorious deeds among the
nations.
Tell everyone about the amazing
things he does.
4 Great is the LORD! He is most worthy of
praise!
He is to be feared above all gods.
5 The gods of other nations are mere idols,
but the LORD made the heavens!
6 Honor and majesty surround him;
strength and beauty fill his sanctuary.

7 O nations of the world, recognize the
LORD;
recognize that the LORD is glorious
and strong.
8 Give to the LORD the glory he deserves!
Bring your offering and come into his
courts.
9 Worship the LORD in all his holy
splendor.
Let all the earth tremble before him.
10 Tell all the nations, "The LORD reigns!"
The world stands firm and cannot be
shaken.
He will judge all peoples fairly.

11 Let the heavens be glad, and the earth
rejoice!
Let the sea and everything in it shout
his praise!
12 Let the fields and their crops burst out
with joy!
Let the trees of the forest sing for joy
13 before the LORD, for he is coming!
He is coming to judge the earth.
He will judge the world with justice,
and the nations with his truth.

97

1 The LORD is king!
Let the earth rejoice!
Let the farthest coastlands be glad.
2 Dark clouds surround him.
Righteousness and justice are the
foundation of his throne.
3 Fire spreads ahead of him
and burns up all his foes.
4 His lightning flashes out across the
world.
The earth sees and trembles.
5 The mountains melt like wax before
the LORD,
before the Lord of all the earth.
6 The heavens proclaim his
righteousness;
every nation sees his glory.
7 Those who worship idols are disgraced—
all who brag about their worthless
gods—
for every god must bow to him.
8 Jerusalem* has heard and rejoiced,
and all the towns of Judah are glad
because of your justice, O LORD!

94:7 Hebrew *of Jacob.* See note on 44:4. **97:8** Hebrew *Zion.*

9 For you, O LORD, are supreme over all
the earth;
you are exalted far above all gods.
10 You who love the LORD, hate evil!
He protects the lives of his godly people
and rescues them from the power of
the wicked.
11 Light shines on the godly,
and joy on those whose hearts are right.
12 May all who are godly rejoice in the LORD
and praise his holy name!

98 *A psalm.*

1 Sing a new song to the LORD,
for he has done wonderful deeds.
His right hand has won a mighty victory;
his holy arm has shown his saving
power!
2 The LORD has announced his victory
and has revealed his righteousness to
every nation!
3 He has remembered his promise to love
and be faithful to Israel.
The ends of the earth have seen the
victory of our God.
4 Shout to the LORD, all the earth;
break out in praise and sing for joy!
5 Sing your praise to the LORD with the
harp,
with the harp and melodious song,
6 with trumpets and the sound of the
ram's horn.
Make a joyful symphony before the
LORD, the King!
7 Let the sea and everything in it shout his
praise!
Let the earth and all living things
join in.
8 Let the rivers clap their hands in glee!
Let the hills sing out their songs of joy
9 before the LORD,
for he is coming to judge the earth.
He will judge the world with justice,
and the nations with fairness.

99

1 The LORD is king!
Let the nations tremble!
He sits on his throne between the
cherubim.
Let the whole earth quake!
2 The LORD sits in majesty in Jerusalem,*
exalted above all the nations.
3 Let them praise your great and awesome
name.
Your name is holy!
4 Mighty King, lover of justice,
you have established fairness.
You have acted with justice
and righteousness throughout Israel.*
5 Exalt the LORD our God!
Bow low before his feet, for he is holy!
6 Moses and Aaron were among his
priests;
Samuel also called on his name.
They cried to the LORD for help,
and he answered them.
7 He spoke to Israel from the pillar of cloud,
and they followed the laws and
decrees he gave them.
8 O LORD our God, you answered them.
You were a forgiving God to them,
but you punished them when they
went wrong.
9 Exalt the LORD our God,
and worship at his holy mountain in
Jerusalem,
for the LORD our God is holy!

100 *A psalm of thanksgiving.*

1 Shout with joy to the LORD, all the earth!
2 Worship the LORD with gladness.
Come before him, singing with joy.
3 Acknowledge that the LORD is God!
He made us, and we are his.*
We are his people, the sheep of his
pasture.
4 Enter his gates with thanksgiving;
go into his courts with praise.
Give thanks to him and praise his
name.
5 For the LORD is good.
His unfailing love continues forever,
and his faithfulness continues to each
generation.

101 *A psalm of David.*

1 I will sing of your love and justice, LORD.
I will praise you with songs.
2 I will be careful to live a blameless life—
when will you come to help me?
I will lead a life of integrity
in my own home.
3 I will refuse to look at
anything vile and vulgar.

I hate all who deal crookedly;
I will have nothing to do with them.
4 I will reject perverse ideas
and stay away from every evil.
5 I will not tolerate people who slander
their neighbors.
I will not endure conceit and pride.

6 I will search for faithful people
to be my companions.
Only those who are above reproach
will be allowed to serve me.
7 I will not allow deceivers to serve in my
house,
and liars will not stay in my presence.
8 My daily task will be to ferret out the
wicked
and free the city of the LORD from
their grip.

102

A prayer of one overwhelmed with trouble, pouring out problems before the LORD.

1 LORD, hear my prayer!
Listen to my plea!
2 Don't turn away from me
in my time of distress.
Bend down to listen,
and answer me quickly when I call
to you.
3 For my days disappear like smoke,
and my bones burn like red-hot coals.
4 My heart is sick, withered like grass,
and I have lost my appetite.
5 Because of my groaning,
I am reduced to skin and bones.
6 I am like an owl in the desert,
like a little owl in a far-off
wilderness.
7 I lie awake,
lonely as a solitary bird on the roof.
8 My enemies taunt me day after day.
They mock and curse me.
9 I eat ashes for food.
My tears run down into my drink
10 because of your anger and wrath.
For you have picked me up and
thrown me out.
11 My life passes as swiftly as the evening
shadows.
I am withering away like grass.

99:2 Hebrew *Zion*. **99:4** Hebrew *Jacob*. See note on 44:4.
100:3 As in an alternate reading in the Masoretic Text; the other alternate and some ancient versions read *and not we ourselves*.

Thanksgiving

Through three simple steps, Psalm 100 gives us a model for how to be more thankful. First, "come" (100:2). This is our invitation, the assurance that we are welcome, which needs a response. We have to choose not to stay in our present feelings but to fix our thoughts on God. Second, "acknowledge" (100:3). This is a provocation to forget about ourselves and focus on God as we remember all that he has done for us. Third, "give thanks" (100:4). As we recall what he has done for us, it becomes easy to be thankful.

Here are some of the things the psalmists encourage us to thank God for:

- His creation (Psalm 104:1-30)
- His care of us (Psalm 95:6-7)
- His knowledge of us (Psalm 139:13-16)
- His salvation (Psalm 27:1-14)
- His answering of our prayers (Psalm 118:21)
- His provision (Psalm 147:7-9)
- His healing (Psalm 30:1-2)
- His rescue (Psalm 31:21-22)
- His victory (Psalm 118:10-16)

Thanksgiving needs to become a way of life for us. As Paul wrote, "Always be joyful. Never stop praying. Be thankful in all circumstances" (1 Thessalonians 5:16-18).

▶ *See also **Thankfulness**, page 1366.*

12 But you, O LORD, will sit on your throne
forever.
Your fame will endure to every
generation.
13 You will arise and have mercy on
Jerusalem*—
and now is the time to pity her,
now is the time you promised to help.
14 For your people love every stone in her
walls
and cherish even the dust in her streets.
15 Then the nations will tremble before the
LORD.
The kings of the earth will tremble
before his glory.
16 For the LORD will rebuild Jerusalem.
He will appear in his glory.
17 He will listen to the prayers of the
destitute.
He will not reject their pleas.

18 Let this be recorded for future
generations,
so that a people not yet born will
praise the LORD.
19 Tell them the LORD looked down
from his heavenly sanctuary.
He looked down to earth from heaven
20 to hear the groans of the prisoners,
to release those condemned to die.
21 And so the LORD's fame will be
celebrated in Zion,
his praises in Jerusalem,
22 when multitudes gather together
and kingdoms come to worship the
LORD.

23 He broke my strength in midlife,
cutting short my days.
24 But I cried to him, "O my God, who lives
forever,
don't take my life while I am so young!
25 Long ago you laid the foundation of the
earth
and made the heavens with your
hands.
26 They will perish, but you remain forever;
they will wear out like old clothing.
You will change them like a
garment
and discard them.
27 But you are always the same;
you will live forever.
28 The children of your people
will live in security.
Their children's children
will thrive in your presence."

103

A psalm of David.

1 Let all that I am praise the LORD;
with my whole heart, I will praise his
holy name.
2 Let all that I am praise the LORD;
may I never forget the good things he
does for me.
3 He forgives all my sins
and heals all my diseases.
4 He redeems me from death
and crowns me with love and tender
mercies.
5 He fills my life with good things.
My youth is renewed like the eagle's!
6 The LORD gives righteousness
and justice to all who are treated
unfairly.

The compassionate God

To many people's surprise, the picture of God in the Old Testament is not one of an angry deity, but rather of a God who is full of compassion. Compassion is a kind understanding of another's weakness and acting to help them in their need. Psalm 103 recalls that God never deals with us "as we deserve" (103:10), for he knows what we are like; rather, he goes to the opposite extreme, showing his kindness and compassion in ways far beyond what we could expect. God's compassion is a constant Old Testament theme (e.g., Exodus 34:6; 2 Chronicles 36:15; Psalm 86:15; 103:8-18; 145:8-9; Joel 2:13; Jonah 4:2); so it shouldn't surprise us to find that when Jesus came, his ministry was always characterized by compassion (e.g., Matthew 14:14; Mark 1:41; Philippians 1:8).

▸ *See also **The character of God**, page 104; **Compassion**, page 983.*

7 He revealed his character to Moses
and his deeds to the people of Israel.
8 The LORD is compassionate and merciful,
slow to get angry and filled with
unfailing love.
9 He will not constantly accuse us,
nor remain angry forever.
10 He does not punish us for all our sins;
he does not deal harshly with us, as
we deserve.
11 For his unfailing love toward those who
fear him
is as great as the height of the heavens
above the earth.
12 He has removed our sins as far from us
as the east is from the west.
13 The LORD is like a father to his children,
tender and compassionate to those
who fear him.
14 For he knows how weak we are;
he remembers we are only dust.
15 Our days on earth are like grass;
like wildflowers, we bloom and die.
16 The wind blows, and we are gone—
as though we had never been here.
17 But the love of the LORD remains forever
with those who fear him.
His salvation extends to the children's
children
18 of those who are faithful to his
covenant,
of those who obey his
commandments!

19 The LORD has made the heavens his
throne;
from there he rules over everything.
20 Praise the LORD, you angels,
you mighty ones who carry out his
plans,
listening for each of his commands.
21 Yes, praise the LORD, you armies of
angels
who serve him and do his will!
22 Praise the LORD, everything he has
created,
everything in all his kingdom.

Let all that I am praise the LORD.

104

1 Let all that I am praise the
LORD.

O LORD my God, how great you are!
You are robed with honor and majesty.
2 You are dressed in a robe of light.
You stretch out the starry curtain of the
heavens;
3 you lay out the rafters of your home
in the rain clouds.
You make the clouds your chariot;
you ride upon the wings of the
wind.
4 The winds are your messengers;
flames of fire are your servants.*

5 You placed the world on its foundation
so it would never be moved.
6 You clothed the earth with floods of
water,
water that covered even the
mountains.
7 At your command, the water fled;
at the sound of your thunder, it
hurried away.
8 Mountains rose and valleys sank
to the levels you decreed.
9 Then you set a firm boundary for the
seas,
so they would never again cover the
earth.

10 You make springs pour water into the
ravines,
so streams gush down from the
mountains.
11 They provide water for all the animals,
and the wild donkeys quench their
thirst.
12 The birds nest beside the streams
and sing among the branches of the
trees.
13 You send rain on the mountains from
your heavenly home,
and you fill the earth with the fruit of
your labor.
14 You cause grass to grow for the livestock
and plants for people to use.
You allow them to produce food from
the earth—
15 wine to make them glad,
olive oil to soothe their skin,
and bread to give them strength.
16 The trees of the LORD are well cared
for—
the cedars of Lebanon that he planted.
17 There the birds make their nests,
and the storks make their homes in
the cypresses.

102:13 Hebrew *Zion;* also in 102:16. **104:4** Greek version reads *He sends his angels like the winds, / his servants like flames of fire.* Compare Heb 1:7.

18 High in the mountains live the wild goats,
and the rocks form a refuge for the hyraxes.*
19 You made the moon to mark the seasons,
and the sun knows when to set.
20 You send the darkness, and it becomes night,
when all the forest animals prowl about.
21 Then the young lions roar for their prey,
stalking the food provided by God.
22 At dawn they slink back
into their dens to rest.
23 Then people go off to their work,
where they labor until evening.

24 O LORD, what a variety of things you have made!
In wisdom you have made them all.
The earth is full of your creatures.
25 Here is the ocean, vast and wide,
teeming with life of every kind,
both large and small.
26 See the ships sailing along,
and Leviathan,* which you made to play in the sea.

27 They all depend on you
to give them food as they need it.
28 When you supply it, they gather it.
You open your hand to feed them,
and they are richly satisfied.
29 But if you turn away from them, they panic.
When you take away their breath,
they die and turn again to dust.
30 When you give them your breath,* life is created,
and you renew the face of the earth.

31 May the glory of the LORD continue forever!
The LORD takes pleasure in all he has made!
32 The earth trembles at his glance;
the mountains smoke at his touch.

33 I will sing to the LORD as long as I live.
I will praise my God to my last breath!
34 May all my thoughts be pleasing to him,
for I rejoice in the LORD.
35 Let all sinners vanish from the face of the earth;
let the wicked disappear forever.

Let all that I am praise the LORD.

Praise the LORD!

105

1 Give thanks to the LORD and proclaim his greatness.
Let the whole world know what he has done.
2 Sing to him; yes, sing his praises.
Tell everyone about his wonderful deeds.
3 Exult in his holy name;
rejoice, you who worship the LORD.
4 Search for the LORD and for his strength;
continually seek him.
5 Remember the wonders he has performed,
his miracles, and the rulings he has given,
6 you children of his servant Abraham,
you descendants of Jacob, his chosen ones.

7 He is the LORD our God.
His justice is seen throughout the land.
8 He always stands by his covenant—
the commitment he made to a thousand generations.
9 This is the covenant he made with Abraham
and the oath he swore to Isaac.
10 He confirmed it to Jacob as a decree,
and to the people of Israel as a never-ending covenant:
11 "I will give you the land of Canaan
as your special possession."

12 He said this when they were few in number,
a tiny group of strangers in Canaan.
13 They wandered from nation to nation,
from one kingdom to another.
14 Yet he did not let anyone oppress them.
He warned kings on their behalf:
15 "Do not touch my chosen people,
and do not hurt my prophets."

16 He called for a famine on the land of Canaan,
cutting off its food supply.
17 Then he sent someone to Egypt ahead of them—
Joseph, who was sold as a slave.
18 They bruised his feet with fetters
and placed his neck in an iron collar.
19 Until the time came to fulfill his dreams,*
the LORD tested Joseph's character.
20 Then Pharaoh sent for him and set him free;

the ruler of the nation opened his
prison door.
21 Joseph was put in charge of all the
king's household;
he became ruler over all the king's
possessions.
22 He could instruct* the king's aides as he
pleased
and teach the king's advisers.
23 Then Israel arrived in Egypt;
Jacob lived as a foreigner in the land
of Ham.
24 And the LORD multiplied the people of
Israel
until they became too mighty for their
enemies.
25 Then he turned the Egyptians against
the Israelites,
and they plotted against the LORD's
servants.
26 But the LORD sent his servant Moses,
along with Aaron, whom he had
chosen.
27 They performed miraculous signs
among the Egyptians,
and wonders in the land of Ham.
28 The LORD blanketed Egypt in darkness,
for they had defied* his commands to
let his people go.
29 He turned their water into blood,
poisoning all the fish.
30 Then frogs overran the land
and even invaded the king's
bedrooms.
31 When the LORD spoke, flies descended
on the Egyptians,
and gnats swarmed across Egypt.
32 He sent them hail instead of rain,
and lightning flashed over the land.
33 He ruined their grapevines and fig trees
and shattered all the trees.
34 He spoke, and hordes of locusts came—
young locusts beyond number.
35 They ate up everything green in the
land,
destroying all the crops in their fields.
36 Then he killed the oldest son in each
Egyptian home,
the pride and joy of each family.
37 The LORD brought his people out of
Egypt, loaded with silver and gold;
and not one among the tribes of Israel
even stumbled.
38 Egypt was glad when they were gone,
for they feared them greatly.
39 The LORD spread a cloud above them as
a covering
and gave them a great fire to light the
darkness.
40 They asked for meat, and he sent them
quail;
he satisfied their hunger with
manna—bread from heaven.
41 He split open a rock, and water gushed
out
to form a river through the dry
wasteland.
42 For he remembered his sacred promise
to his servant Abraham.
43 So he brought his people out of Egypt
with joy,
his chosen ones with rejoicing.
44 He gave his people the lands of pagan
nations,
and they harvested crops that others
had planted.
45 All this happened so they would follow
his decrees
and obey his instructions.

Praise the LORD!

106

1 Praise the LORD!

Give thanks to the LORD, for he
is good!
His faithful love endures forever.
2 Who can list the glorious miracles of the
LORD?
Who can ever praise him enough?
3 There is joy for those who deal justly
with others
and always do what is right.
4 Remember me, LORD, when you show
favor to your people;
come near and rescue me.
5 Let me share in the prosperity of your
chosen ones.
Let me rejoice in the joy of your people;
let me praise you with those who are
your heritage.
6 Like our ancestors, we have sinned.
We have done wrong! We have acted
wickedly!

104:18 Or *coneys*, or *rock badgers*. **104:26** The identification of Leviathan is disputed, ranging from an earthly creature to a mythical sea monster in ancient literature. **104:30** Or *When you send your Spirit*. **105:19** Hebrew *his word*. **105:22** As in Greek and Syriac versions; Hebrew reads *bind* or *imprison*. **105:28** As in Greek and Syriac versions; Hebrew reads *had not defied*.

7 Our ancestors in Egypt
were not impressed by the LORD's
miraculous deeds.
They soon forgot his many acts of
kindness to them.
Instead, they rebelled against him at
the Red Sea.*
8 Even so, he saved them—
to defend the honor of his name
and to demonstrate his mighty power.
9 He commanded the Red Sea* to dry up.
He led Israel across the sea as if it
were a desert.
10 So he rescued them from their enemies
and redeemed them from their foes.
11 Then the water returned and covered
their enemies;
not one of them survived.
12 Then his people believed his promises.
Then they sang his praise.

13 Yet how quickly they forgot what he had
done!
They wouldn't wait for his counsel!
14 In the wilderness their desires ran wild,
testing God's patience in that dry
wasteland.
15 So he gave them what they asked for,
but he sent a plague along with it.
16 The people in the camp were jealous of
Moses
and envious of Aaron, the LORD's holy
priest.
17 Because of this, the earth opened up;
it swallowed Dathan
and buried Abiram and the other
rebels.
18 Fire fell upon their followers;
a flame consumed the wicked.

19 The people made a calf at Mount Sinai*;
they bowed before an image made of
gold.
20 They traded their glorious God
for a statue of a grass-eating bull.
21 They forgot God, their savior,
who had done such great things in
Egypt—
22 such wonderful things in the land of
Ham,
such awesome deeds at the Red Sea.
23 So he declared he would destroy them.
But Moses, his chosen one, stepped
between the LORD and the people.
He begged him to turn from his anger
and not destroy them.

24 The people refused to enter the pleasant
land,
for they wouldn't believe his promise
to care for them.
25 Instead, they grumbled in their tents
and refused to obey the LORD.
26 Therefore, he solemnly swore
that he would kill them in the
wilderness,
27 that he would scatter their descendants*
among the nations,
exiling them to distant lands.

28 Then our ancestors joined in the
worship of Baal at Peor;
they even ate sacrifices offered to the
dead!
29 They angered the LORD with all these
things,
so a plague broke out among them.
30 But Phinehas had the courage to
intervene,
and the plague was stopped.
31 So he has been regarded as a righteous
man
ever since that time.

32 At Meribah, too, they angered the LORD,
causing Moses serious trouble.
33 They made Moses angry,*
and he spoke foolishly.

34 Israel failed to destroy the nations in the
land,
as the LORD had commanded them.
35 Instead, they mingled among the pagans
and adopted their evil customs.
36 They worshiped their idols,
which led to their downfall.
37 They even sacrificed their sons
and their daughters to the demons.
38 They shed innocent blood,
the blood of their sons and daughters.
By sacrificing them to the idols of Canaan,
they polluted the land with murder.
39 They defiled themselves by their evil
deeds,
and their love of idols was adultery in
the LORD's sight.

40 That is why the LORD's anger burned
against his people,
and he abhorred his own special
possession.
41 He handed them over to pagan nations,
and they were ruled by those who
hated them.

42 Their enemies crushed them
and brought them under their cruel power.
43 Again and again he rescued them,
but they chose to rebel against him,
and they were finally destroyed by their sin.
44 Even so, he pitied them in their distress
and listened to their cries.
45 He remembered his covenant with them
and relented because of his unfailing love.
46 He even caused their captors
to treat them with kindness.

47 Save us, O LORD our God!
Gather us back from among the nations,
so we can thank your holy name
and rejoice and praise you.

48 Praise the LORD, the God of Israel,
who lives from everlasting to everlasting!
Let all the people say, "Amen!"

Praise the LORD!

BOOK FIVE (Psalms 107–150)

107

1 Give thanks to the LORD, for he is good!
His faithful love endures forever.
2 Has the LORD redeemed you? Then speak out!
Tell others he has redeemed you from your enemies.
3 For he has gathered the exiles from many lands,
from east and west,
from north and south.*

4 Some wandered in the wilderness,
lost and homeless.
5 Hungry and thirsty,
they nearly died.
6 "LORD, help!" they cried in their trouble,
and he rescued them from their distress.
7 He led them straight to safety,
to a city where they could live.
8 Let them praise the LORD for his great love
and for the wonderful things he has done for them.
9 For he satisfies the thirsty
and fills the hungry with good things.
10 Some sat in darkness and deepest gloom,
imprisoned in iron chains of misery.
11 They rebelled against the words of God,
scorning the counsel of the Most High.
12 That is why he broke them with hard labor;
they fell, and no one was there to help them.
13 "LORD, help!" they cried in their trouble,
and he saved them from their distress.
14 He led them from the darkness and deepest gloom;
he snapped their chains.
15 Let them praise the LORD for his great love
and for the wonderful things he has done for them.
16 For he broke down their prison gates of bronze;
he cut apart their bars of iron.

17 Some were fools; they rebelled
and suffered for their sins.
18 They couldn't stand the thought of food,
and they were knocking on death's door.
19 "LORD, help!" they cried in their trouble,
and he saved them from their distress.
20 He sent out his word and healed them,
snatching them from the door of death.
21 Let them praise the LORD for his great love
and for the wonderful things he has done for them.
22 Let them offer sacrifices of thanksgiving
and sing joyfully about his glorious acts.

23 Some went off to sea in ships,
plying the trade routes of the world.
24 They, too, observed the LORD's power in action,
his impressive works on the deepest seas.
25 He spoke, and the winds rose,
stirring up the waves.

106:7 Hebrew *at the sea, the sea of reeds.* **106:9** Hebrew *sea of reeds;* also in 106:22. **106:19** Hebrew *at Horeb,* another name for Sinai. **106:27** As in Syriac version; Hebrew reads *he would cause their descendants to fall.* **106:33** Hebrew *They embittered his spirit.* **107:3** Hebrew *and sea.*

[26] Their ships were tossed to the heavens
and plunged again to the depths;
the sailors cringed in terror.
[27] They reeled and staggered like drunkards
and were at their wits' end.
[28] "LORD, help!" they cried in their trouble,
and he saved them from their distress.
[29] He calmed the storm to a whisper
and stilled the waves.
[30] What a blessing was that stillness
as he brought them safely into harbor!
[31] Let them praise the LORD for his great love
and for the wonderful things he has done for them.
[32] Let them exalt him publicly before the congregation
and before the leaders of the nation.

[33] He changes rivers into deserts,
and springs of water into dry, thirsty land.
[34] He turns the fruitful land into salty wastelands,
because of the wickedness of those who live there.
[35] But he also turns deserts into pools of water,
the dry land into springs of water.
[36] He brings the hungry to settle there
and to build their cities.
[37] They sow their fields, plant their vineyards,
and harvest their bumper crops.
[38] How he blesses them!
They raise large families there,
and their herds of livestock increase.

[39] When they decrease in number and become impoverished
through oppression, trouble, and sorrow,
[40] the LORD pours contempt on their princes,
causing them to wander in trackless wastelands.
[41] But he rescues the poor from trouble
and increases their families like flocks of sheep.
[42] The godly will see these things and be glad,
while the wicked are struck silent.
[43] Those who are wise will take all this to heart;
they will see in our history the faithful love of the LORD.

108
A song. A psalm of David.

[1] My heart is confident in you, O God;
no wonder I can sing your praises
with all my heart!
[2] Wake up, lyre and harp!
I will wake the dawn with my song.
[3] I will thank you, LORD, among all the people.
I will sing your praises among the nations.
[4] For your unfailing love is higher than the heavens.
Your faithfulness reaches to the clouds.
[5] Be exalted, O God, above the highest heavens.
May your glory shine over all the earth.

[6] Now rescue your beloved people.
Answer and save us by your power.
[7] God has promised this by his holiness*:
"I will divide up Shechem with joy.
I will measure out the valley of Succoth.
[8] Gilead is mine,
and Manasseh, too.
Ephraim, my helmet, will produce my warriors,
and Judah, my scepter, will produce my kings.
[9] But Moab, my washbasin, will become my servant,
and I will wipe my feet on Edom
and shout in triumph over Philistia."

[10] Who will bring me into the fortified city?
Who will bring me victory over Edom?
[11] Have you rejected us, O God?
Will you no longer march with our armies?
[12] Oh, please help us against our enemies,
for all human help is useless.
[13] With God's help we will do mighty things,
for he will trample down our foes.

109
For the choir director: A psalm of David.

[1] O God, whom I praise,
don't stand silent and aloof
[2] while the wicked slander me
and tell lies about me.
[3] They surround me with hateful words
and fight against me for no reason.

4 I love them, but they try to destroy me
with accusations
even as I am praying for them!
5 They repay evil for good,
and hatred for my love.
6 They say,* "Get an evil person to turn
against him.
Send an accuser to bring him to trial.
7 When his case comes up for judgment,
let him be pronounced guilty.
Count his prayers as sins.
8 Let his years be few;
let someone else take his position.
9 May his children become fatherless,
and his wife a widow.
10 May his children wander as beggars
and be driven from* their ruined
homes.
11 May creditors seize his entire estate,
and strangers take all he has earned.
12 Let no one be kind to him;
let no one pity his fatherless children.
13 May all his offspring die.
May his family name be blotted out in
the next generation.
14 May the LORD never forget the sins of his
fathers;
may his mother's sins never be erased
from the record.
15 May the LORD always remember these
sins,
and may his name disappear from
human memory.
16 For he refused all kindness to others;
he persecuted the poor and needy,
and he hounded the brokenhearted
to death.
17 He loved to curse others;
now you curse him.
He never blessed others;
now don't you bless him.
18 Cursing is as natural to him as his
clothing,
or the water he drinks,
or the rich food he eats.
19 Now may his curses return and cling
to him like clothing;
may they be tied around him like a
belt."
20 May those curses become the LORD's
punishment
for my accusers who speak evil of me.
21 But deal well with me, O Sovereign LORD,
for the sake of your own reputation!
Rescue me
because you are so faithful and good.
22 For I am poor and needy,
and my heart is full of pain.
23 I am fading like a shadow at dusk;
I am brushed off like a locust.
24 My knees are weak from fasting,
and I am skin and bones.
25 I am a joke to people everywhere;
when they see me, they shake their
heads in scorn.

26 Help me, O LORD my God!
Save me because of your unfailing love.
27 Let them see that this is your doing,
that you yourself have done it,
LORD.
28 Then let them curse me if they like,
but you will bless me!
When they attack me, they will be
disgraced!
But I, your servant, will go right on
rejoicing!
29 May my accusers be clothed with
disgrace;
may their humiliation cover them like
a cloak.
30 But I will give repeated thanks to the
LORD,
praising him to everyone.
31 For he stands beside the needy,
ready to save them from those who
condemn them.

110 *A psalm of David.*

1 The LORD said to my Lord,*
"Sit in the place of honor at my right
hand
until I humble your enemies,
making them a footstool under your
feet."
2 The LORD will extend your powerful
kingdom from Jerusalem*;
you will rule over your enemies.
3 When you go to war,
your people will serve you willingly.
You are arrayed in holy garments,
and your strength will be renewed
each day like the morning dew.
4 The LORD has taken an oath and will not
break his vow:

108:7 Or *in his sanctuary.* **109:6** Hebrew lacks *They say.* **109:10** As in Greek version; Hebrew reads *and seek.* **110:1** Or *my lord.* **110:2** Hebrew *Zion.*

"You are a priest forever in the order
of Melchizedek."
5 The Lord stands at your right hand to
protect you.
He will strike down many kings when
his anger erupts.
6 He will punish the nations
and fill their lands with corpses;
he will shatter heads over the whole
earth.
7 But he himself will be refreshed from
brooks along the way.
He will be victorious.

111

★ 1 Praise the LORD!

I will thank the LORD with all
my heart
as I meet with his godly people.
2 How amazing are the deeds of the LORD!
All who delight in him should ponder
them.
3 Everything he does reveals his glory and
majesty.
His righteousness never fails.
4 He causes us to remember his wonderful
works.
How gracious and merciful is our
LORD!
5 He gives food to those who fear him;
he always remembers his covenant.
6 He has shown his great power to his
people
by giving them the lands of other
nations.
7 All he does is just and good,
and all his commandments are
trustworthy.
8 They are forever true,
to be obeyed faithfully and with
integrity.
9 He has paid a full ransom for his people.
He has guaranteed his covenant with
them forever.
What a holy, awe-inspiring name he
has!
10 Fear of the LORD is the foundation of
true wisdom.
All who obey his commandments will
grow in wisdom.

Praise him forever!

112

★ 1 Praise the LORD!

How joyful are those who fear
the LORD
and delight in obeying his commands.
2 Their children will be successful
everywhere;
an entire generation of godly people
will be blessed.
3 They themselves will be wealthy,
and their good deeds will last forever.
4 Light shines in the darkness for the
godly.
They are generous, compassionate,
and righteous.
5 Good comes to those who lend money
generously
and conduct their business fairly.

The Messianic King

David probably wrote Psalm 110 for his son's future coronation; but he was writing far more than he understood. The Jews recognized that this psalm was prophetic of the Messiah, who would be both a king and a priest and who would rule over his enemies and establish God's Kingdom. Jesus used this psalm in his debate with the Pharisees to demonstrate that, although descended from David, the Messiah was also David's "Lord," proving he must therefore have been more than merely human (Matthew 22:41-46)—something that he himself was, of course. Peter quoted from the psalm on the day of Pentecost as prophetic of Christ's resurrection, ascension, and exaltation (Acts 2:33-36). And Hebrews uses the psalm to show that Jesus is far greater than not just David but the very angels of heaven (Hebrews 1:13). The promises of a messianic king find all their fulfillment in Christ.

▸ *See also* ***Jesus Christ in the Psalms****, page 614;* ***Prophecies about Christ****, page 806;* ***Prophecies of the Messiah****, page 1044.*

6 Such people will not be overcome by evil.
Those who are righteous will be long remembered.
7 They do not fear bad news;
they confidently trust the LORD to care for them.
8 They are confident and fearless
and can face their foes triumphantly.
9 They share freely and give generously to those in need.
Their good deeds will be remembered forever.
They will have influence and honor.
10 The wicked will see this and be infuriated.
They will grind their teeth in anger;
they will slink away, their hopes thwarted.

113

1 Praise the LORD!
Yes, give praise, O servants of the LORD.
Praise the name of the LORD!
2 Blessed be the name of the LORD
now and forever.
3 Everywhere—from east to west—
praise the name of the LORD.
4 For the LORD is high above the nations;
his glory is higher than the heavens.

5 Who can be compared with the LORD our God,
who is enthroned on high?
6 He stoops to look down
on heaven and on earth.
7 He lifts the poor from the dust
and the needy from the garbage dump.
8 He sets them among princes,
even the princes of his own people!
9 He gives the childless woman a family,
making her a happy mother.

Praise the LORD!

114

1 When the Israelites escaped from Egypt—
when the family of Jacob left that foreign land—
2 the land of Judah became God's sanctuary,
and Israel became his kingdom.

3 The Red Sea* saw them coming and hurried out of their way!
The water of the Jordan River turned away.
4 The mountains skipped like rams,
the hills like lambs!
5 What's wrong, Red Sea, that made you hurry out of their way?
What happened, Jordan River, that you turned away?
6 Why, mountains, did you skip like rams?
Why, hills, like lambs?

7 Tremble, O earth, at the presence of the Lord,
at the presence of the God of Jacob.
8 He turned the rock into a pool of water;
yes, a spring of water flowed from solid rock.

115

1 Not to us, O LORD, not to us,
but to your name goes all the glory
for your unfailing love and faithfulness.
2 Why let the nations say,
"Where is their God?"
3 Our God is in the heavens,
and he does as he wishes.
4 Their idols are merely things of silver and gold,
shaped by human hands.
5 They have mouths but cannot speak,
and eyes but cannot see.
6 They have ears but cannot hear,
and noses but cannot smell.
7 They have hands but cannot feel,
and feet but cannot walk,
and throats but cannot make a sound.
8 And those who make idols are just like them,
as are all who trust in them.

9 O Israel, trust the LORD!
He is your helper and your shield.
10 O priests, descendants of Aaron, trust the LORD!
He is your helper and your shield.
11 All you who fear the LORD, trust the LORD!
He is your helper and your shield.

12 The LORD remembers us and will bless us.
He will bless the people of Israel
and bless the priests, the descendants of Aaron.

111 This psalm is a Hebrew acrostic poem; after the introductory note of praise, each line begins with a successive letter of the Hebrew alphabet. **112** This psalm is a Hebrew acrostic poem; after the introductory note of praise, each line begins with a successive letter of the Hebrew alphabet. **114:3** Hebrew *the sea;* also in 114:5.

13 He will bless those who fear the LORD,
both great and lowly.
14 May the LORD richly bless
both you and your children.
15 May you be blessed by the LORD,
who made heaven and earth.
16 The heavens belong to the LORD,
but he has given the earth to all
humanity.
17 The dead cannot sing praises to the LORD,
for they have gone into the silence of
the grave.
18 But we can praise the LORD
both now and forever!

Praise the LORD!

116 1 I love the LORD because he
hears my voice
and my prayer for mercy.
2 Because he bends down to listen,
I will pray as long as I have breath!
3 Death wrapped its ropes around me;
the terrors of the grave* overtook me.
I saw only trouble and sorrow.
4 Then I called on the name of the LORD:
"Please, LORD, save me!"
5 How kind the LORD is! How good he is!
So merciful, this God of ours!
6 The LORD protects those of childlike faith;
I was facing death, and he saved me.
7 Let my soul be at rest again,
for the LORD has been good to me.
8 He has saved me from death,
my eyes from tears,
my feet from stumbling.
9 And so I walk in the LORD's
presence
as I live here on earth!
10 I believed in you, so I said,
"I am deeply troubled, LORD."
11 In my anxiety I cried out to you,
"These people are all liars!"
12 What can I offer the LORD
for all he has done for me?
13 I will lift up the cup of salvation
and praise the LORD's name for
saving me.
14 I will keep my promises to the LORD
in the presence of all his people.
15 The LORD cares deeply
when his loved ones die.
16 O LORD, I am your servant;
yes, I am your servant, born into your
household;
you have freed me from my chains.
17 I will offer you a sacrifice of
thanksgiving
and call on the name of the LORD.
18 I will fulfill my vows to the LORD
in the presence of all his people—

Resting in God

The psalmists knew life as it really was—often full of struggle, threat, and opposition—as reflected in Psalm 116's opening verses. But they also knew that the answer to such things lay, not in panicking or frantic activity, but in going back to God and trusting in him—the God who is kind, good, and merciful (116:5), just as he revealed to Moses (Exodus 34:6-7). It is in going back to this revelation—God's own revelation of what he is really like—that we find both peace and hope.

Resting in God—trusting wholly in him and not ourselves—is something that we can all too easily lose in the course of life. That is why the psalmist wrote, "Let my soul be at rest *again*" (Psalm 116:7)—that word "again" shows that he had experienced it, lost it, and needed to get it back! Resting in God is what we were made for; so when we recognize we have lost that rest, we need to stop and find it again.

The story of Mary and Martha (Luke 10:38-42) reminds us of the importance of learning how to "stop" and be still in God's presence, listening for his strengthening and directing word. Often we don't hear God simply because we don't take time to stop and listen. But without stopping we will never rest, and without resting we will never hear, and without hearing we will never be reassured that all will be well, no matter what happens.

19 in the house of the LORD
in the heart of Jerusalem.

Praise the LORD!

117

1 Praise the LORD, all you nations.
Praise him, all you people of the earth.
2 For his unfailing love for us is powerful;
the LORD's faithfulness endures forever.

Praise the LORD!

118

1 Give thanks to the LORD, for he is good!
His faithful love endures forever.

2 Let all Israel repeat:
"His faithful love endures forever."
3 Let Aaron's descendants, the priests, repeat:
"His faithful love endures forever."
4 Let all who fear the LORD repeat:
"His faithful love endures forever."
5 In my distress I prayed to the LORD,
and the LORD answered me and set me free.
6 The LORD is for me, so I will have no fear.
What can mere people do to me?
7 Yes, the LORD is for me; he will help me.
I will look in triumph at those who hate me.
8 It is better to take refuge in the LORD
than to trust in people.
9 It is better to take refuge in the LORD
than to trust in princes.

10 Though hostile nations surrounded me,
I destroyed them all with the authority of the LORD.
11 Yes, they surrounded and attacked me,
but I destroyed them all with the authority of the LORD.
12 They swarmed around me like bees;
they blazed against me like a crackling fire.
But I destroyed them all with the authority of the LORD.
13 My enemies did their best to kill me,
but the LORD rescued me.
14 The LORD is my strength and my song;
he has given me victory.
15 Songs of joy and victory are sung in the camp of the godly.
The strong right arm of the LORD has done glorious things!
16 The strong right arm of the LORD is raised in triumph.
The strong right arm of the LORD has done glorious things!
17 I will not die; instead, I will live
to tell what the LORD has done.
18 The LORD has punished me severely,
but he did not let me die.

19 Open for me the gates where the righteous enter,
and I will go in and thank the LORD.
20 These gates lead to the presence of the LORD,
and the godly enter there.
21 I thank you for answering my prayer
and giving me victory!

22 The stone that the builders rejected
has now become the cornerstone.
23 This is the LORD's doing,
and it is wonderful to see.
24 This is the day the LORD has made.
We will rejoice and be glad in it.
25 Please, LORD, please save us.
Please, LORD, please give us success.
26 Bless the one who comes in the name of the LORD.
We bless you from the house of the LORD.
27 The LORD is God, shining upon us.
Take the sacrifice and bind it with cords on the altar.
28 You are my God, and I will praise you!
You are my God, and I will exalt you!

29 Give thanks to the LORD, for he is good!
His faithful love endures forever.

119

Aleph

*1 Joyful are people of integrity,
who follow the instructions of the LORD.
2 Joyful are those who obey his laws
and search for him with all their hearts.
3 They do not compromise with evil,
and they walk only in his paths.
4 You have charged us
to keep your commandments carefully.

116:3 Hebrew *of Sheol.* **119** This psalm is a Hebrew acrostic poem; there are twenty-two stanzas, one for each successive letter of the Hebrew alphabet. Each of the eight verses within each stanza begins with the Hebrew letter named in its heading.

5 Oh, that my actions would consistently
reflect your decrees!
6 Then I will not be ashamed
when I compare my life with your
commands.
7 As I learn your righteous regulations,
I will thank you by living as I should!
8 I will obey your decrees.
Please don't give up on me!

Beth

9 How can a young person stay pure?
By obeying your word.
10 I have tried hard to find you—
don't let me wander from your
commands.
11 I have hidden your word in my heart,
that I might not sin against you.
12 I praise you, O LORD;
teach me your decrees.
13 I have recited aloud
all the regulations you have given us.
14 I have rejoiced in your laws
as much as in riches.
15 I will study your commandments
and reflect on your ways.
16 I will delight in your decrees
and not forget your word.

Gimel

17 Be good to your servant,
that I may live and obey your word.
18 Open my eyes to see
the wonderful truths in your
instructions.
19 I am only a foreigner in the land.
Don't hide your commands from me!
20 I am always overwhelmed
with a desire for your regulations.
21 You rebuke the arrogant;
those who wander from your
commands are cursed.
22 Don't let them scorn and insult me,
for I have obeyed your laws.
23 Even princes sit and speak against me,
but I will meditate on your
decrees.
24 Your laws please me;
they give me wise advice.

Daleth

25 I lie in the dust;
revive me by your word.
26 I told you my plans, and you answered.
Now teach me your decrees.
27 Help me understand the meaning of
your commandments,

Delight in God's Law

Psalm 119 is a magnificent, lengthy reflection on God's word. It is skillfully written: The sections begin with consecutive letters of the Hebrew alphabet, and the psalm uses eight Hebrew words to describe God's word (e.g., "instructions," "laws," "regulations," "commands," "decrees"). Such creativity reflects the psalmist's delight in God's Law.

To us, "law" sounds restrictive. But that is not how we are meant to see it. The Hebrew word often translated "law" (*Torah*) means "direction, instruction, or guidance" (it is usually translated "instructions" in the NLT, including here in Psalm 119). In other words, it is not a long list of dos and don'ts (though clearly there are commands there); rather, it is God sharing with his people his heart and his wise ways for living. Once we see that, we can understand why the psalmist became so excited about it. This is God himself giving us the keys for successful living! Little wonder the psalmist can therefore say, "Your instructions are my delight" (119:77), that "your word is a lamp to guide my feet and a light for my path" (119:105), that "the teaching of your word gives light" (119:130), and that "those who love your instructions have great peace and do not stumble" (119:165).

But of course, we cannot say we truly delight in God's Law (no matter how many Scriptures we can recite) unless we are seeking to live it out. Otherwise we are simply like the person who built a house on the sand (Matthew 7:24-27).

▶ *See also* ***Acrostic psalms****, page 624.*

and I will meditate on your wonderful
deeds.
28 I weep with sorrow;
encourage me by your word.
29 Keep me from lying to myself;
give me the privilege of knowing your
instructions.
30 I have chosen to be faithful;
I have determined to live by your
regulations.
31 I cling to your laws.
LORD, don't let me be put to shame!
32 I will pursue your commands,
for you expand my understanding.

He

33 Teach me your decrees, O LORD;
I will keep them to the end.
34 Give me understanding and I will obey
your instructions;
I will put them into practice with all
my heart.
35 Make me walk along the path of your
commands,
for that is where my happiness is
found.
36 Give me an eagerness for your laws
rather than a love for money!
37 Turn my eyes from worthless things,
and give me life through your word.*
38 Reassure me of your promise,
made to those who fear you.
39 Help me abandon my shameful ways;
for your regulations are good.
40 I long to obey your commandments!
Renew my life with your goodness.

Waw

41 LORD, give me your unfailing love,
the salvation that you promised me.
42 Then I can answer those who taunt me,
for I trust in your word.
43 Do not snatch your word of truth from me,
for your regulations are my only hope.
44 I will keep on obeying your instructions
forever and ever.
45 I will walk in freedom,
for I have devoted myself to your
commandments.
46 I will speak to kings about your laws,
and I will not be ashamed.
47 How I delight in your commands!
How I love them!
48 I honor and love your commands.
I meditate on your decrees.

Zayin

49 Remember your promise to me;
it is my only hope.
50 Your promise revives me;
it comforts me in all my troubles.
51 The proud hold me in utter contempt,
but I do not turn away from your
instructions.
52 I meditate on your age-old regulations;
O LORD, they comfort me.
53 I become furious with the wicked,
because they reject your instructions.
54 Your decrees have been the theme of my
songs
wherever I have lived.
55 I reflect at night on who you are, O LORD;
therefore, I obey your instructions.
56 This is how I spend my life:
obeying your commandments.

Heth

57 LORD, you are mine!
I promise to obey your words!
58 With all my heart I want your blessings.
Be merciful as you promised.
59 I pondered the direction of my life,
and I turned to follow your laws.
60 I will hurry, without delay,
to obey your commands.
61 Evil people try to drag me into sin,
but I am firmly anchored to your
instructions.
62 I rise at midnight to thank you
for your just regulations.
63 I am a friend to anyone who fears you—
anyone who obeys your
commandments.
64 O LORD, your unfailing love fills the
earth;
teach me your decrees.

Teth

65 You have done many good things for me,
LORD,
just as you promised.
66 I believe in your commands;
now teach me good judgment and
knowledge.
67 I used to wander off until you
disciplined me;
but now I closely follow your word.
68 You are good and do only good;
teach me your decrees.

119:37 Some manuscripts read *in your ways.*

69 Arrogant people smear me with lies,
but in truth I obey your
commandments with all my heart.
70 Their hearts are dull and stupid,
but I delight in your instructions.
71 My suffering was good for me,
for it taught me to pay attention to
your decrees.
72 Your instructions are more valuable to me
than millions in gold and silver.

Yodh

73 You made me; you created me.
Now give me the sense to follow your
commands.
74 May all who fear you find in me a cause
for joy,
for I have put my hope in your word.
75 I know, O LORD, that your regulations
are fair;
you disciplined me because I needed it.
76 Now let your unfailing love comfort me,
just as you promised me, your servant.
77 Surround me with your tender mercies
so I may live,
for your instructions are my delight.
78 Bring disgrace upon the arrogant people
who lied about me;
meanwhile, I will concentrate on your
commandments.
79 Let me be united with all who fear you,
with those who know your laws.
80 May I be blameless in keeping your
decrees;
then I will never be ashamed.

Kaph

81 I am worn out waiting for your rescue,
but I have put my hope in your word.
82 My eyes are straining to see your
promises come true.
When will you comfort me?
83 I am shriveled like a wineskin in the
smoke,
but I have not forgotten to obey your
decrees.
84 How long must I wait?
When will you punish those who
persecute me?
85 These arrogant people who hate your
instructions
have dug deep pits to trap me.
86 All your commands are trustworthy.
Protect me from those who hunt me
down without cause.
87 They almost finished me off,
but I refused to abandon your
commandments.
88 In your unfailing love, spare my life;
then I can continue to obey your
laws.

Lamedh

89 Your eternal word, O LORD,
stands firm in heaven.
90 Your faithfulness extends to every
generation,
as enduring as the earth you created.
91 Your regulations remain true to this
day,
for everything serves your plans.
92 If your instructions hadn't sustained me
with joy,
I would have died in my misery.
93 I will never forget your commandments,
for by them you give me life.
94 I am yours; rescue me!
For I have worked hard at obeying
your commandments.
95 Though the wicked hide along the way
to kill me,
I will quietly keep my mind on your
laws.
96 Even perfection has its limits,
but your commands have no limit.

Mem

97 Oh, how I love your instructions!
I think about them all day long.
98 Your commands make me wiser than
my enemies,
for they are my constant guide.
99 Yes, I have more insight than my
teachers,
for I am always thinking of your
laws.
100 I am even wiser than my elders,
for I have kept your commandments.
101 I have refused to walk on any evil path,
so that I may remain obedient to your
word.
102 I haven't turned away from your
regulations,
for you have taught me well.
103 How sweet your words taste to me;
they are sweeter than honey.
104 Your commandments give me
understanding;
no wonder I hate every false way
of life.

Nun

105 Your word is a lamp to guide my feet
and a light for my path.
106 I've promised it once, and I'll promise it again:
I will obey your righteous regulations.
107 I have suffered much, O LORD;
restore my life again as you promised.
108 LORD, accept my offering of praise,
and teach me your regulations.
109 My life constantly hangs in the balance,
but I will not stop obeying your instructions.
110 The wicked have set their traps for me,
but I will not turn from your commandments.
111 Your laws are my treasure;
they are my heart's delight.
112 I am determined to keep your decrees
to the very end.

Samekh

113 I hate those with divided loyalties,
but I love your instructions.
114 You are my refuge and my shield;
your word is my source of hope.
115 Get out of my life, you evil-minded people,
for I intend to obey the commands of my God.
116 LORD, sustain me as you promised, that I may live!
Do not let my hope be crushed.
117 Sustain me, and I will be rescued;
then I will meditate continually on your decrees.
118 But you have rejected all who stray from your decrees.
They are only fooling themselves.
119 You skim off the wicked of the earth like scum;
no wonder I love to obey your laws!
120 I tremble in fear of you;
I stand in awe of your regulations.

Ayin

121 Don't leave me to the mercy of my enemies,
for I have done what is just and right.
122 Please guarantee a blessing for me.
Don't let the arrogant oppress me!
123 My eyes strain to see your rescue,
to see the truth of your promise fulfilled.
124 I am your servant; deal with me in unfailing love,
and teach me your decrees.
125 Give discernment to me, your servant;
then I will understand your laws.
126 LORD, it is time for you to act,
for these evil people have violated your instructions.
127 Truly, I love your commands
more than gold, even the finest gold.
128 Each of your commandments is right.
That is why I hate every false way.

Pe

129 Your laws are wonderful.
No wonder I obey them!
130 The teaching of your word gives light,
so even the simple can understand.
131 I pant with expectation,
longing for your commands.
132 Come and show me your mercy,
as you do for all who love your name.
133 Guide my steps by your word,
so I will not be overcome by evil.
134 Ransom me from the oppression of evil people;
then I can obey your commandments.
135 Look upon me with love;
teach me your decrees.
136 Rivers of tears gush from my eyes
because people disobey your instructions.

Tsadhe

137 O LORD, you are righteous,
and your regulations are fair.
138 Your laws are perfect
and completely trustworthy.
139 I am overwhelmed with indignation,
for my enemies have disregarded your words.
140 Your promises have been thoroughly tested;
that is why I love them so much.
141 I am insignificant and despised,
but I don't forget your commandments.
142 Your justice is eternal,
and your instructions are perfectly true.
143 As pressure and stress bear down on me,
I find joy in your commandments.
144 Your laws are always right;
help me to understand them so I may live.

Qoph

145 I pray with all my heart; answer me, LORD!
I will obey your decrees.
146 I cry out to you; rescue me,
that I may obey your laws.
147 I rise early, before the sun is up;
I cry out for help and put my hope in your words.
148 I stay awake through the night,
thinking about your promise.
149 In your faithful love, O LORD, hear my cry;
let me be revived by following your regulations.
150 Lawless people are coming to attack me;
they live far from your instructions.
151 But you are near, O LORD,
and all your commands are true.
152 I have known from my earliest days
that your laws will last forever.

Resh

153 Look upon my suffering and rescue me,
for I have not forgotten your instructions.
154 Argue my case; take my side!
Protect my life as you promised.
155 The wicked are far from rescue,
for they do not bother with your decrees.
156 LORD, how great is your mercy;
let me be revived by following your regulations.
157 Many persecute and trouble me,
yet I have not swerved from your laws.
158 Seeing these traitors makes me sick at heart,
because they care nothing for your word.
159 See how I love your commandments, LORD.
Give back my life because of your unfailing love.
160 The very essence of your words is truth;
all your just regulations will stand forever.

Shin

161 Powerful people harass me without cause,
but my heart trembles only at your word.
162 I rejoice in your word
like one who discovers a great treasure.
163 I hate and abhor all falsehood,
but I love your instructions.
164 I will praise you seven times a day
because all your regulations are just.
165 Those who love your instructions have great peace
and do not stumble.
166 I long for your rescue, LORD,
so I have obeyed your commands.
167 I have obeyed your laws,
for I love them very much.
168 Yes, I obey your commandments and laws
because you know everything I do.

Taw

169 O LORD, listen to my cry;
give me the discerning mind you promised.
170 Listen to my prayer;
rescue me as you promised.
171 Let praise flow from my lips,
for you have taught me your decrees.
172 Let my tongue sing about your word,
for all your commands are right.
173 Give me a helping hand,
for I have chosen to follow your commandments.
174 O LORD, I have longed for your rescue,
and your instructions are my delight.
175 Let me live so I can praise you,
and may your regulations help me.
176 I have wandered away like a lost sheep;
come and find me,
for I have not forgotten your commands.

120

A song for pilgrims ascending to Jerusalem.

1 I took my troubles to the LORD;
I cried out to him, and he answered my prayer.
2 Rescue me, O LORD, from liars
and from all deceitful people.
3 O deceptive tongue, what will God do to you?
How will he increase your punishment?
4 You will be pierced with sharp arrows
and burned with glowing coals.
5 How I suffer in far-off Meshech.
It pains me to live in distant Kedar.
6 I am tired of living
among people who hate peace.

7 I search for peace;
but when I speak of peace, they want war!

121 *A song for pilgrims ascending to Jerusalem.*

1 I look up to the mountains—
does my help come from there?
2 My help comes from the LORD,
who made heaven and earth!

3 He will not let you stumble;
the one who watches over you will not slumber.
4 Indeed, he who watches over Israel
never slumbers or sleeps.

5 The LORD himself watches over you!
The LORD stands beside you as your protective shade.
6 The sun will not harm you by day,
nor the moon at night.

7 The LORD keeps you from all harm
and watches over your life.
8 The LORD keeps watch over you as you come and go,
both now and forever.

122 *A song for pilgrims ascending to Jerusalem. A psalm of David.*

1 I was glad when they said to me,
"Let us go to the house of the LORD."
2 And now here we are,
standing inside your gates,
O Jerusalem.
3 Jerusalem is a well-built city;
its seamless walls cannot be breached.
4 All the tribes of Israel—the LORD's people—
make their pilgrimage here.
They come to give thanks to the name of the LORD,
as the law requires of Israel.
5 Here stand the thrones where judgment is given,
the thrones of the dynasty of David.

6 Pray for peace in Jerusalem.
May all who love this city prosper.
7 O Jerusalem, may there be peace within your walls
and prosperity in your palaces.
8 For the sake of my family and friends,
I will say,
"May you have peace."
9 For the sake of the house of the LORD our God,
I will seek what is best for you,
O Jerusalem.

123 *A song for pilgrims ascending to Jerusalem.*

1 I lift my eyes to you,
O God, enthroned in heaven.

Preparing for worship

Psalms 120–134 are each titled "A song for pilgrims ascending to Jerusalem" (literally, "A song of ascents"). These fifteen psalms were probably used on the annual religious pilgrimages, which saw worshipers singing as they approached Jerusalem (e.g., Isaiah 30:29). Together with Psalms 135 and 136, this collection became known as "The Great Hallel" ("The Great Praise").

These psalms speak to us of the need to prepare ourselves as we come to enter God's presence. It isn't so much about checking whether we are worthy to come or not—the simple answer is, apart from Christ's righteousness we aren't! Rather it is about stirring our hearts and spirits so we can give God our best offering of praise and prepare our hearts to receive from him. The sheer variety of psalms in this collection—prayer, affirmation, celebration, lament, thanksgiving, anticipation—shows that different people prepare for worship in different ways. Some prefer to sing or pray; others to read Scripture or quietly meditate. The important thing is that, however we do it, we do it, so that when we come together we are ready to give God our best.

▶ *See also **Worship**, page 662.*

2 We keep looking to the LORD our God for
his mercy,
just as servants keep their eyes on
their master,
as a slave girl watches her mistress for
the slightest signal.
3 Have mercy on us, LORD, have mercy,
for we have had our fill of contempt.
4 We have had more than our fill of the
scoffing of the proud
and the contempt of the
arrogant.

124 *A song for pilgrims ascending to Jerusalem. A psalm of David.*

1 What if the LORD had not been on our
side?
Let all Israel repeat:
2 What if the LORD had not been on our
side
when people attacked us?
3 They would have swallowed us alive
in their burning anger.
4 The waters would have engulfed us;
a torrent would have overwhelmed us.
5 Yes, the raging waters of their fury
would have overwhelmed our very
lives.

6 Praise the LORD,
who did not let their teeth tear us apart!
7 We escaped like a bird from a hunter's
trap.
The trap is broken, and we are free!
8 Our help is from the LORD,
who made heaven and earth.

125 *A song for pilgrims ascending to Jerusalem.*

1 Those who trust in the LORD are as
secure as Mount Zion;
they will not be defeated but will
endure forever.
2 Just as the mountains surround
Jerusalem,
so the LORD surrounds his people,
both now and forever.
3 The wicked will not rule the land of the
godly,
for then the godly might be tempted
to do wrong.
4 O LORD, do good to those who are good,
whose hearts are in tune with you.
5 But banish those who turn to crooked
ways, O LORD.
Take them away with those who do
evil.

May Israel have peace!

126 *A song for pilgrims ascending to Jerusalem.*

1 When the LORD brought back his exiles
to Jerusalem,*
it was like a dream!
2 We were filled with laughter,
and we sang for joy.
And the other nations said,
"What amazing things the LORD has
done for them."
3 Yes, the LORD has done amazing things
for us!
What joy!

4 Restore our fortunes, LORD,
as streams renew the desert.
5 Those who plant in tears
will harvest with shouts of joy.
6 They weep as they go to plant their seed,
but they sing as they return with the
harvest.

127 *A song for pilgrims ascending to Jerusalem. A psalm of Solomon.*

1 Unless the LORD builds a house,
the work of the builders is wasted.
Unless the LORD protects a city,
guarding it with sentries will do no
good.
2 It is useless for you to work so hard
from early morning until late at night,
anxiously working for food to eat;
for God gives rest to his loved ones.

3 Children are a gift from the LORD;
they are a reward from him.
4 Children born to a young man
are like arrows in a warrior's hands.
5 How joyful is the man whose quiver is
full of them!
He will not be put to shame when he
confronts his accusers at the city
gates.

128 *A song for pilgrims ascending to Jerusalem.*

1 How joyful are those who fear the
LORD—
all who follow his ways!
2 You will enjoy the fruit of your labor.
How joyful and prosperous you will be!

3 Your wife will be like a fruitful grapevine,
flourishing within your home.
Your children will be like vigorous
young olive trees
as they sit around your table.
4 That is the LORD's blessing
for those who fear him.

5 May the LORD continually bless you
from Zion.
May you see Jerusalem prosper as
long as you live.
6 May you live to enjoy your
grandchildren.
May Israel have peace!

129 *A song for pilgrims ascending to Jerusalem.*

1 From my earliest youth my enemies have
persecuted me.
Let all Israel repeat this:
2 From my earliest youth my enemies have
persecuted me,
but they have never defeated me.
3 My back is covered with cuts,
as if a farmer had plowed long furrows.
4 But the LORD is good;
he has cut me free from the ropes of
the ungodly.

5 May all who hate Jerusalem*
be turned back in shameful defeat.
6 May they be as useless as grass on a
rooftop,
turning yellow when only half grown,
7 ignored by the harvester,
despised by the binder.
8 And may those who pass by
refuse to give them this blessing:
"The LORD bless you;
we bless you in the LORD's name."

130 *A song for pilgrims ascending to Jerusalem.*

1 From the depths of despair, O LORD,
I call for your help.
2 Hear my cry, O Lord.
Pay attention to my prayer.

3 LORD, if you kept a record of our sins,
who, O Lord, could ever survive?
4 But you offer forgiveness,
that we might learn to fear you.

5 I am counting on the LORD;
yes, I am counting on him.
I have put my hope in his word.
6 I long for the Lord
more than sentries long for the dawn,
yes, more than sentries long for the
dawn.

7 O Israel, hope in the LORD;
for with the LORD there is unfailing
love.
His redemption overflows.
8 He himself will redeem Israel
from every kind of sin.

131 *A song for pilgrims ascending to Jerusalem. A psalm of David.*

1 LORD, my heart is not proud;
my eyes are not haughty.
I don't concern myself with matters too
great
or too awesome for me to grasp.
2 Instead, I have calmed and quieted
myself,
like a weaned child who no longer
cries for its mother's milk.
Yes, like a weaned child is my soul
within me.

3 O Israel, put your hope in the LORD—
now and always.

132 *A song for pilgrims ascending to Jerusalem.*

1 LORD, remember David
and all that he suffered.
2 He made a solemn promise to the LORD.
He vowed to the Mighty One of Israel,*
3 "I will not go home;
I will not let myself rest.
4 I will not let my eyes sleep
nor close my eyelids in slumber
5 until I find a place to build a house for
the LORD,
a sanctuary for the Mighty One of
Israel."

6 We heard that the Ark was in Ephrathah;
then we found it in the distant
countryside of Jaar.
7 Let us go to the sanctuary of the LORD;
let us worship at the footstool of his
throne.
8 Arise, O LORD, and enter your resting
place,
along with the Ark, the symbol of your
power.

126:1 Hebrew *Zion.* **129:5** Hebrew *Zion.* **132:2** Hebrew *of Jacob;* also in 132:5. See note on 44:4.

9 May your priests be clothed in godliness;
may your loyal servants sing for joy.
10 For the sake of your servant David,
do not reject the king you have anointed.
11 The LORD swore an oath to David
with a promise he will never take back:
"I will place one of your descendants
on your throne.
12 If your descendants obey the terms of my covenant
and the laws that I teach them,
then your royal line
will continue forever and ever."

13 For the LORD has chosen Jerusalem*;
he has desired it for his home.
14 "This is my resting place forever," he said.
"I will live here, for this is the home I desired.
15 I will bless this city and make it prosperous;
I will satisfy its poor with food.
16 I will clothe its priests with godliness;
its faithful servants will sing for joy.
17 Here I will increase the power of David;
my anointed one will be a light for my people.
18 I will clothe his enemies with shame,
but he will be a glorious king."

133

A song for pilgrims ascending to Jerusalem. A psalm of David.

1 How wonderful and pleasant it is
when brothers live together in harmony!
2 For harmony is as precious as the anointing oil
that was poured over Aaron's head,
that ran down his beard
and onto the border of his robe.
3 Harmony is as refreshing as the dew from Mount Hermon
that falls on the mountains of Zion.
And there the LORD has pronounced his blessing,
even life everlasting.

134

A song for pilgrims ascending to Jerusalem.

1 Oh, praise the LORD, all you servants of the LORD,
you who serve at night in the house of the LORD.
2 Lift your hands toward the sanctuary,
and praise the LORD.
3 May the LORD, who made heaven and earth,
bless you from Jerusalem.*

Unity

Psalm 133 is a short song in praise of unity. Using two images—the precious and costly anointing oil poured over Aaron and the priests, and the refreshing dew that fell on Mount Hermon's dry ground—the psalmist describes how precious and refreshing it is when God's people live in harmony. But unity is not just pleasant; it attracts God's blessing. He *commands* his blessing to fall on people who live in harmony (133:3). So even if we find it hard sometimes to be united with a fellow Christian, because of something they said or did or believe, here is a motivation to be united: Do you want to be blessed? Then live in unity with them!

The fact that God considers unity so highly is reflected in the many exhortations to pursue it in the New Testament (e.g., Romans 15:5-6; 1 Corinthians 10:16-17; 12:12-27; Galatians 3:26-28; Ephesians 2:11-22; 4:1-6; Philippians 1:27; Colossians 3:15). Unity is God's declared goal for his people and his creation (Ephesians 1:9-10).

Unity is not an optional extra in the Christian faith. For "If someone says, 'I love God,' but hates a fellow believer, that person is a liar; for if we don't love people we can see, how can we love God, whom we cannot see? And he has given us this command: Those who love God must also love their fellow believers" (1 John 4:20-21).

135

1 Praise the LORD!

Praise the name of the LORD!
Praise him, you who serve the LORD,
2 you who serve in the house of the LORD,
in the courts of the house of our God.

3 Praise the LORD, for the LORD is good;
celebrate his lovely name with music.
4 For the LORD has chosen Jacob for himself,
Israel for his own special treasure.

5 I know the greatness of the LORD—
that our Lord is greater than any other god.
6 The LORD does whatever pleases him
throughout all heaven and earth,
and on the seas and in their depths.
7 He causes the clouds to rise over the whole earth.
He sends the lightning with the rain
and releases the wind from his storehouses.

8 He destroyed the firstborn in each Egyptian home,
both people and animals.
9 He performed miraculous signs and wonders in Egypt
against Pharaoh and all his people.
10 He struck down great nations
and slaughtered mighty kings—
11 Sihon king of the Amorites,
Og king of Bashan,
and all the kings of Canaan.
12 He gave their land as an inheritance,
a special possession to his people Israel.

13 Your name, O LORD, endures forever;
your fame, O LORD, is known to every generation.
14 For the LORD will give justice to his people
and have compassion on his servants.

15 The idols of the nations are merely things of silver and gold,
shaped by human hands.
16 They have mouths but cannot speak,
and eyes but cannot see.
17 They have ears but cannot hear,
and mouths but cannot breathe.
18 And those who make idols are just like them,
as are all who trust in them.

19 O Israel, praise the LORD!
O priests—descendants of Aaron—praise the LORD!
20 O Levites, praise the LORD!
All you who fear the LORD, praise the LORD!
21 The LORD be praised from Zion,
for he lives here in Jerusalem.

Praise the LORD!

136

1 Give thanks to the LORD, for he is good!
His faithful love endures forever.
2 Give thanks to the God of gods.
His faithful love endures forever.
3 Give thanks to the Lord of lords.
His faithful love endures forever.

4 Give thanks to him who alone does mighty miracles.
His faithful love endures forever.
5 Give thanks to him who made the heavens so skillfully.
His faithful love endures forever.
6 Give thanks to him who placed the earth among the waters.
His faithful love endures forever.
7 Give thanks to him who made the heavenly lights—
His faithful love endures forever.
8 the sun to rule the day,
His faithful love endures forever.
9 and the moon and stars to rule the night.
His faithful love endures forever.

10 Give thanks to him who killed the firstborn of Egypt.
His faithful love endures forever.
11 He brought Israel out of Egypt.
His faithful love endures forever.
12 He acted with a strong hand and powerful arm.
His faithful love endures forever.
13 Give thanks to him who parted the Red Sea.*
His faithful love endures forever.

132:13 Hebrew *Zion.* **134:3** Hebrew *Zion.* **136:13** Hebrew *sea of reeds;* also in 136:15.

▸ **135:6** *See **God's sovereignty**, page 584.*

[14] He led Israel safely through,
His faithful love endures forever.
[15] but he hurled Pharaoh and his army into the Red Sea.
His faithful love endures forever.
[16] Give thanks to him who led his people through the wilderness.
His faithful love endures forever.
[17] Give thanks to him who struck down mighty kings.
His faithful love endures forever.
[18] He killed powerful kings—
His faithful love endures forever.
[19] Sihon king of the Amorites,
His faithful love endures forever.
[20] and Og king of Bashan.
His faithful love endures forever.
[21] God gave the land of these kings as an inheritance—
His faithful love endures forever.
[22] a special possession to his servant Israel.
His faithful love endures forever.

[23] He remembered us in our weakness.
His faithful love endures forever.
[24] He saved us from our enemies.
His faithful love endures forever.
[25] He gives food to every living thing.
His faithful love endures forever.
[26] Give thanks to the God of heaven.
His faithful love endures forever.

137

[1] Beside the rivers of Babylon,
we sat and wept
as we thought of Jerusalem.*
[2] We put away our harps,
hanging them on the branches of poplar trees.
[3] For our captors demanded a song from us.
Our tormentors insisted on a joyful hymn:
"Sing us one of those songs of Jerusalem!"
[4] But how can we sing the songs of the LORD
while in a pagan land?

[5] If I forget you, O Jerusalem,
let my right hand forget how to play the harp.
[6] May my tongue stick to the roof of my mouth
if I fail to remember you,
if I don't make Jerusalem my greatest joy.

[7] O LORD, remember what the Edomites did
on the day the armies of Babylon captured Jerusalem.
"Destroy it!" they yelled.
"Level it to the ground!"
[8] O Babylon, you will be destroyed.
Happy is the one who pays you back
for what you have done to us.
[9] Happy is the one who takes your babies
and smashes them against the rocks!

138

A psalm of David.

[1] I give you thanks, O LORD, with all my heart;
I will sing your praises before the gods.
[2] I bow before your holy Temple as I worship.
I praise your name for your unfailing love and faithfulness;

The rivers of Babylon

Psalm 137 was written to recall the years God's people spent in exile in Babylon. The Jews had settled in communities alongside Babylon's two great rivers, the Euphrates and the Tigris, and some of their tributaries and canals. These rivers, like the Nile in Egypt, provided water not only for drinking but also for irrigation. The Tigris was the shorter yet faster flowing of the two rivers, reflected in its name, which meant "arrow." The Euphrates was longer and more slow-flowing and is often simply called "the River" in the Old Testament, as it marked the boundary between Israel and its enemies (e.g., Exodus 23:31; see footnote). Sadly, the Jews in exile had ended up on the wrong side of that river.

▶ *See also **The Nile**, page 66.*

for your promises are backed
by all the honor of your name.
3 As soon as I pray, you answer me;
you encourage me by giving me
strength.
4 Every king in all the earth will thank
you, LORD,
for all of them will hear your words.
5 Yes, they will sing about the LORD's
ways,
for the glory of the LORD is very great.
6 Though the LORD is great, he cares for
the humble,
but he keeps his distance from the
proud.
7 Though I am surrounded by troubles,
you will protect me from the anger of
my enemies.
You reach out your hand,
and the power of your right hand
saves me.
8 The LORD will work out his plans for my
life—
for your faithful love, O LORD, endures
forever.
Don't abandon me, for you made me.

139

For the choir director: A psalm of David.

1 O LORD, you have examined my heart
and know everything about me.
2 You know when I sit down or stand up.
You know my thoughts even when I'm
far away.
3 You see me when I travel
and when I rest at home.
You know everything I do.
4 You know what I am going to say
even before I say it, LORD.
5 You go before me and follow me.
You place your hand of blessing on
my head.
6 Such knowledge is too wonderful for me,
too great for me to understand!

7 I can never escape from your Spirit!
I can never get away from your
presence!
8 If I go up to heaven, you are there;
if I go down to the grave,* you are
there.
9 If I ride the wings of the morning,
if I dwell by the farthest oceans,
10 even there your hand will guide me,
and your strength will support me.
11 I could ask the darkness to hide me
and the light around me to become
night—
12 but even in darkness I cannot hide
from you.
To you the night shines as bright as day.
Darkness and light are the same to you.

13 You made all the delicate, inner parts of
my body
and knit me together in my mother's
womb.
14 Thank you for making me so
wonderfully complex!

137:1 Hebrew *Zion;* also in 137:3. **139:8** Hebrew *to Sheol.*

The God who is everywhere and knows everything

The delightful and reassuring Psalm 139, attributed to King David, is in praise of the God who knows—a word that recurs throughout the psalm (139:1-4, 6, 23). It begins by affirming God's intimate knowledge of his people (139:1-6). He knows absolutely everything about us: our waking and sleeping, our comings and goings, our thoughts and actions—he knows it all. In light of this, there is no place we can go that lies beyond that knowledge (139:7-16), neither in the heavens nor in the depths, neither in the east nor in the west, neither in daylight nor in darkness, not even back to our mother's womb before we were born. Even there he knew us.

God knows who we are, and God knows where we are; for God is everywhere (he is omnipresent) and knows everything (he is omniscient). This could be frightening—if we did not know what God was like! But David knew that God loves us and is for us. And that is why he could invite such a God to search and test his heart and expose whatever was wrong there in order to bring him into God's life and God's ways.

Your workmanship is marvelous—how well I know it.
15 You watched me as I was being formed in utter seclusion,
as I was woven together in the dark of the womb.
16 You saw me before I was born.
Every day of my life was recorded in your book.
Every moment was laid out
before a single day had passed.

17 How precious are your thoughts about me,* O God.
They cannot be numbered!
18 I can't even count them;
they outnumber the grains of sand!
And when I wake up,
you are still with me!

19 O God, if only you would destroy the wicked!
Get out of my life, you murderers!
20 They blaspheme you;
your enemies misuse your name.
21 O LORD, shouldn't I hate those who hate you?
Shouldn't I despise those who oppose you?
22 Yes, I hate them with total hatred,
for your enemies are my enemies.

23 Search me, O God, and know my heart;
test me and know my anxious thoughts.
24 Point out anything in me that offends you,
and lead me along the path of everlasting life.

140

For the choir director: A psalm of David.

1 O LORD, rescue me from evil people.
Protect me from those who are violent,
2 those who plot evil in their hearts
and stir up trouble all day long.
3 Their tongues sting like a snake;
the venom of a viper drips from their lips. *Interlude*

4 O LORD, keep me out of the hands of the wicked.
Protect me from those who are violent,
for they are plotting against me.
5 The proud have set a trap to catch me;
they have stretched out a net;
they have placed traps all along the way. *Interlude*

6 I said to the LORD, "You are my God!"
Listen, O LORD, to my cries for mercy!
7 O Sovereign LORD, the strong one who rescued me,
you protected me on the day of battle.
8 LORD, do not let evil people have their way.
Do not let their evil schemes succeed,
or they will become proud. *Interlude*

9 Let my enemies be destroyed
by the very evil they have planned for me.
10 Let burning coals fall down on their heads.
Let them be thrown into the fire
or into watery pits from which they can't escape.
11 Don't let liars prosper here in our land.
Cause great disasters to fall on the violent.

12 But I know the LORD will help those they persecute;
he will give justice to the poor.
13 Surely righteous people are praising your name;
the godly will live in your presence.

141

A psalm of David.

1 O LORD, I am calling to you. Please hurry!
Listen when I cry to you for help!
2 Accept my prayer as incense offered to you,
and my upraised hands as an evening offering.

3 Take control of what I say, O LORD,
and guard my lips.
4 Don't let me drift toward evil
or take part in acts of wickedness.
Don't let me share in the delicacies
of those who do wrong.

5 Let the godly strike me!
It will be a kindness!
If they correct me, it is soothing medicine.
Don't let me refuse it.

But I pray constantly
against the wicked and their deeds.

[6] When their leaders are thrown down
from a cliff,
the wicked will listen to my words and
find them true.
[7] Like rocks brought up by a plow,
the bones of the wicked will lie
scattered without burial.*
[8] I look to you for help, O Sovereign LORD.
You are my refuge; don't let them
kill me.
[9] Keep me from the traps they have set
for me,
from the snares of those who do
wrong.
[10] Let the wicked fall into their own nets,
but let me escape.

142 *A psalm* of David, regarding his experience in the cave. A prayer.*

[1] I cry out to the LORD;
I plead for the LORD's mercy.
[2] I pour out my complaints before him
and tell him all my troubles.
[3] When I am overwhelmed,
you alone know the way I should turn.
Wherever I go,
my enemies have set traps for me.
[4] I look for someone to come and help me,
but no one gives me a passing
thought!
No one will help me;
no one cares a bit what happens
to me.
[5] Then I pray to you, O LORD.
I say, "You are my place of refuge.
You are all I really want in life.
[6] Hear my cry,
for I am very low.
Rescue me from my persecutors,
for they are too strong for me.
[7] Bring me out of prison
so I can thank you.
The godly will crowd around me,
for you are good to me."

143 *A psalm of David.*

[1] Hear my prayer, O LORD;
listen to my plea!
Answer me because you are faithful
and righteous.
[2] Don't put your servant on trial,
for no one is innocent before you.
[3] My enemy has chased me.
He has knocked me to the ground
and forces me to live in darkness like
those in the grave.
[4] I am losing all hope;
I am paralyzed with fear.
[5] I remember the days of old.
I ponder all your great works
and think about what you have done.
[6] I lift my hands to you in prayer.
I thirst for you as parched land thirsts
for rain. *Interlude*

[7] Come quickly, LORD, and answer me,
for my depression deepens.
Don't turn away from me,
or I will die.
[8] Let me hear of your unfailing love each
morning,
for I am trusting you.
Show me where to walk,
for I give myself to you.
[9] Rescue me from my enemies, LORD;
I run to you to hide me.
[10] Teach me to do your will,
for you are my God.
May your gracious Spirit lead me
forward
on a firm footing.
[11] For the glory of your name, O LORD,
preserve my life.
Because of your faithfulness, bring me
out of this distress.
[12] In your unfailing love, silence all my
enemies
and destroy all my foes,
for I am your servant.

144 *A psalm of David.*

[1] Praise the LORD, who is my rock.
He trains my hands for war
and gives my fingers skill for battle.
[2] He is my loving ally and my fortress,
my tower of safety, my rescuer.
He is my shield, and I take refuge in him.
He makes the nations* submit to me.

[3] O LORD, what are human beings that
you should notice them,
mere mortals that you should think
about them?
[4] For they are like a breath of air;
their days are like a passing shadow.

139:17 Or *How precious to me are your thoughts.*
141:7 Hebrew *our bones will be scattered at the mouth of Sheol.* **142:TITLE** Hebrew *maskil.* This may be a literary or musical term. **144:2** Some manuscripts read *my people.*

5 Open the heavens, LORD, and come down.
Touch the mountains so they billow smoke.
6 Hurl your lightning bolts and scatter your enemies!
Shoot your arrows and confuse them!
7 Reach down from heaven and rescue me;
rescue me from deep waters,
from the power of my enemies.
8 Their mouths are full of lies;
they swear to tell the truth, but they lie instead.

9 I will sing a new song to you, O God!
I will sing your praises with a ten-stringed harp.
10 For you grant victory to kings!
You rescued your servant David from the fatal sword.
11 Save me!
Rescue me from the power of my enemies.
Their mouths are full of lies;
they swear to tell the truth, but they lie instead.
12 May our sons flourish in their youth
like well-nurtured plants.
May our daughters be like graceful pillars,
carved to beautify a palace.
13 May our barns be filled
with crops of every kind.
May the flocks in our fields multiply by the thousands,
even tens of thousands,
14 and may our oxen be loaded down with produce.
May there be no enemy breaking through our walls,
no going into captivity,
no cries of alarm in our town squares.
15 Yes, joyful are those who live like this!
Joyful indeed are those whose God is the LORD.

145*

A psalm of praise of David.

1 I will exalt you, my God and King,
and praise your name forever and ever.
2 I will praise you every day;
yes, I will praise you forever.
3 Great is the LORD! He is most worthy of praise!
No one can measure his greatness.
4 Let each generation tell its children
of your mighty acts;
let them proclaim your power.
5 I will meditate on your majestic, glorious splendor
and your wonderful miracles.
6 Your awe-inspiring deeds will be on every tongue;
I will proclaim your greatness.
7 Everyone will share the story of your wonderful goodness;
they will sing with joy about your righteousness.

8 The LORD is merciful and compassionate,
slow to get angry and filled with unfailing love.
9 The LORD is good to everyone.
He showers compassion on all his creation.
10 All of your works will thank you, LORD,
and your faithful followers will praise you.
11 They will speak of the glory of your kingdom;
they will give examples of your power.
12 They will tell about your mighty deeds
and about the majesty and glory of your reign.
13 For your kingdom is an everlasting kingdom.
You rule throughout all generations.

The LORD always keeps his promises;
he is gracious in all he does.*
14 The LORD helps the fallen
and lifts those bent beneath their loads.
15 The eyes of all look to you in hope;
you give them their food as they need it.
16 When you open your hand,
you satisfy the hunger and thirst of every living thing.
17 The LORD is righteous in everything he does;
he is filled with kindness.
18 The LORD is close to all who call on him,
yes, to all who call on him in truth.

▸ **145:4** *See* ***From one generation to another****, page 651.*

19 He grants the desires of those who fear him;
he hears their cries for help and rescues them.
20 The LORD protects all those who love him,
but he destroys the wicked.
21 I will praise the LORD,
and may everyone on earth bless his holy name
forever and ever.

146

1 Praise the LORD!

Let all that I am praise the LORD.
2 I will praise the LORD as long as I live.
I will sing praises to my God with my dying breath.
3 Don't put your confidence in powerful people;
there is no help for you there.
4 When they breathe their last, they return to the earth,
and all their plans die with them.
5 But joyful are those who have the God of Israel* as their helper,
whose hope is in the LORD their God.
6 He made heaven and earth,
the sea, and everything in them.
He keeps every promise forever.
7 He gives justice to the oppressed
and food to the hungry.
The LORD frees the prisoners.
8 The LORD opens the eyes of the blind.
The LORD lifts up those who are weighed down.
The LORD loves the godly.
9 The LORD protects the foreigners among us.
He cares for the orphans and widows,
but he frustrates the plans of the wicked.
10 The LORD will reign forever.
He will be your God, O Jerusalem,*
throughout the generations.

Praise the LORD!

147

1 Praise the LORD!

How good to sing praises to our God!
How delightful and how fitting!
2 The LORD is rebuilding Jerusalem
and bringing the exiles back to Israel.
3 He heals the brokenhearted
and bandages their wounds.
4 He counts the stars
and calls them all by name.
5 How great is our Lord! His power is absolute!
His understanding is beyond comprehension!
6 The LORD supports the humble,
but he brings the wicked down into the dust.
7 Sing out your thanks to the LORD;
sing praises to our God with a harp.
8 He covers the heavens with clouds,
provides rain for the earth,

145 This psalm is a Hebrew acrostic poem; each verse (including 13b) begins with a successive letter of the Hebrew alphabet. **145:13** As in Dead Sea Scrolls and Greek and Syriac versions; the Masoretic Text lacks the final two lines of this verse. **146:5** Hebrew *of Jacob*. See note on 44:4. **146:10** Hebrew *Zion*.

Hallelujah!

Psalms 146–150 each begin and end with the expression "Praise the LORD"—in Hebrew, *Hallelujah*—stirring the hearts of worshipers as they reflect on God. This cry of praise was carried over into Christian worship (e.g., Revelation 19:1-6).

Hallelujah is a word that is meant to be shouted out, not whispered. It reflects the nature of Old Testament worship, which was generally noisy and lively, with all sorts of instruments being used and lots of clapping and dancing.

The Hebrew word *Hallelujah* is still used in most Christian traditions around the world. In fact, it has the privilege of being one of the few words that is the same in every language, which is surely appropriate, for the praise of God cuts across "every nation and tribe and people and language" (Revelation 7:9). This one word unites all God's people, whoever and wherever they may be.

▸ *See also* ***The power of praise****, page 501;* ***Worship****, page 662.*

and makes the grass grow in
mountain pastures.
9 He gives food to the wild animals
and feeds the young ravens when they
cry.
10 He takes no pleasure in the strength of
a horse
or in human might.
11 No, the LORD's delight is in those who
fear him,
those who put their hope in his
unfailing love.

12 Glorify the LORD, O Jerusalem!
Praise your God, O Zion!
13 For he has strengthened the bars of your
gates
and blessed your children within your
walls.
14 He sends peace across your nation
and satisfies your hunger with the
finest wheat.
15 He sends his orders to the world—
how swiftly his word flies!
16 He sends the snow like white wool;
he scatters frost upon the ground like
ashes.
17 He hurls the hail like stones.*
Who can stand against his freezing
cold?
18 Then, at his command, it all melts.
He sends his winds, and the ice
thaws.
19 He has revealed his words to Jacob,
his decrees and regulations to
Israel.
20 He has not done this for any other
nation;
they do not know his regulations.

Praise the LORD!

148

1 Praise the LORD!

Praise the LORD from the
heavens!
Praise him from the skies!
2 Praise him, all his angels!
Praise him, all the armies of heaven!
3 Praise him, sun and moon!
Praise him, all you twinkling stars!
4 Praise him, skies above!
Praise him, vapors high above the
clouds!
5 Let every created thing give praise to
the LORD,
for he issued his command, and they
came into being.
6 He set them in place forever and ever.
His decree will never be revoked.

7 Praise the LORD from the earth,
you creatures of the ocean depths,
8 fire and hail, snow and clouds,*
wind and weather that obey him,
9 mountains and all hills,
fruit trees and all cedars,
10 wild animals and all livestock,
small scurrying animals and
birds,
11 kings of the earth and all people,
rulers and judges of the earth,
12 young men and young women,
old men and children.

13 Let them all praise the name of the
LORD.
For his name is very great;
his glory towers over the earth and
heaven!
14 He has made his people strong,
honoring his faithful ones—
the people of Israel who are close
to him.

Praise the LORD!

149

1 Praise the LORD!

Sing to the LORD a new song.
Sing his praises in the assembly of the
faithful.

2 O Israel, rejoice in your Maker.
O people of Jerusalem,* exult in your
King.
3 Praise his name with dancing,
accompanied by tambourine and
harp.
4 For the LORD delights in his people;
he crowns the humble with victory.
5 Let the faithful rejoice that he honors
them.
Let them sing for joy as they lie on
their beds.

6 Let the praises of God be in their
mouths,
and a sharp sword in their hands—
7 to execute vengeance on the nations
and punishment on the peoples,
8 to bind their kings with shackles
and their leaders with iron
chains,

9 to execute the judgment written against
them.
This is the glorious privilege of his
faithful ones.

Praise the LORD!

150

1 Praise the LORD!

Praise God in his sanctuary;
praise him in his mighty heaven!
2 Praise him for his mighty works;
praise his unequaled
greatness!
3 Praise him with a blast of the ram's horn;
praise him with the lyre and harp!
4 Praise him with the tambourine and
dancing;
praise him with strings and flutes!
5 Praise him with a clash of cymbals;
praise him with loud clanging
cymbals.
6 Let everything that breathes sing praises
to the LORD!

Praise the LORD!

147:17 Hebrew *like bread crumbs.* **148:8** Or *mist,* or *smoke.* **149:2** Hebrew *Zion.*

Proverbs *Wisdom for life*

Proverbs—part of the Wisdom Literature in the Bible—is a collection of short sayings that seek to bring God's wisdom to everyday life situations. They highlight what happens when people do not walk in God's ways, and the blessing that follows when they do. There are insights on every aspect of life—family, marriage, home, work, poverty, justice, attitudes. Their message is often driven home by the use of powerful imagery.

What's it all about?

Proverbs contains hundreds of wise sayings for life, in no particular order, though they are grouped by author. Many of them were written or collected by King Solomon, who was renowned for his wisdom (1 Kings 4:29-34), or wise men of his day.

The underlying aim of Proverbs is stated in its opening verses (1:1-7): to describe what true wisdom is like and to seek to instill it into God's people as they realize the importance of "fear of the LORD" (1:7). This wisdom is not theoretical, but rather very practical. Many of the proverbs have to do with ordinary life: money, marriage, work, business matters, words, pleasure, recreation, family life. Others are about our relationship with God and how to follow him. But the underlying theme of them all is that respect for God and his ways is the key to a happy and productive life. In fact, people who don't pay attention to God's ways are, quite simply, "fools."

As well as its many short, individual sayings—some humorous, some shocking, but all powerful in their imagery—Proverbs contains longer poems (especially in chapters 1–9). Chapter 8 contains a long poem about God's use of wisdom in creation—a passage that anticipates Christ's role as the Word (see John 1)—and in chapter 31 there is a long poem about the ideal wife. Her behavior—godly, diligent, gracious, and creative—personifies true wisdom.

OVERVIEW

True wisdom
1:1–9:18

Proverbs of Solomon
10:1–22:16

Thirty sayings of the wise
22:17–24:22

More wise sayings
24:23-34

Hezekiah's collection of Solomon's proverbs · *25:1–29:27*

Sayings of Agur
30:1-33

Sayings of King Lemuel
31:1-9

The ideal wife
31:10-31

What does it mean for us?

With so many different themes in Proverbs we could be forgiven for thinking there is no underlying message to the book. And yet there is. It is the absolute conviction that living life God's way always pays off in the end. God in his wisdom has established wise ways for getting the most out of life, and the truly wise person will follow those ways.

However, we should remember that the blessing of walking in the truth of Proverbs is not always automatic or immediate, for they are not promises but observations. For example, "Lazy people are soon poor; hard workers get rich" (10:4) is generally true. But in a fallen world lazy people sometimes get rich, and hardworking people sometimes become poor. Nevertheless, the underlying principle is still correct and is a wise truth worth following. We should therefore see Proverbs as providing incentives rather than promises.

The Purpose of Proverbs

1 These are the proverbs of Solomon, David's son, king of Israel.

2 Their purpose is to teach people wisdom
and discipline,
to help them understand the insights
of the wise.
3 Their purpose is to teach people to live
disciplined and successful lives,
to help them do what is right, just,
and fair.
4 These proverbs will give insight to the
simple,
knowledge and discernment to the
young.
5 Let the wise listen to these proverbs and
become even wiser.
Let those with understanding receive
guidance
6 by exploring the meaning in these
proverbs and parables,
the words of the wise and their riddles.
7 Fear of the LORD is the foundation of true
knowledge,
but fools despise wisdom and discipline.

A Father's Exhortation: Acquire Wisdom

8 My child,* listen when your father
corrects you.
Don't neglect your mother's instruction.
9 What you learn from them will crown you
with grace
and be a chain of honor around your
neck.

10 My child, if sinners entice you,
turn your back on them!
11 They may say, "Come and join us.
Let's hide and kill someone!
Just for fun, let's ambush the innocent!
12 Let's swallow them alive, like the grave*;
let's swallow them whole, like those
who go down to the pit of death.
13 Think of the great things we'll get!
We'll fill our houses with all the stuff
we take.
14 Come, throw in your lot with us;
we'll all share the loot."

15 My child, don't go along with them!
Stay far away from their paths.
16 They rush to commit evil deeds.
They hurry to commit murder.
17 If a bird sees a trap being set,
it knows to stay away.
18 But these people set an ambush for
themselves;
they are trying to get themselves killed.
19 Such is the fate of all who are greedy for
money;
it robs them of life.

Wisdom Shouts in the Streets

20 Wisdom shouts in the streets.
She cries out in the public square.
21 She calls to the crowds along the main
street,
to those gathered in front of the city
gate:
22 "How long, you simpletons,
will you insist on being simpleminded?
How long will you mockers relish your
mocking?
How long will you fools hate
knowledge?
23 Come and listen to my counsel.
I'll share my heart with you
and make you wise.

24 "I called you so often, but you wouldn't
come.
I reached out to you, but you paid no
attention.
25 You ignored my advice
and rejected the correction I offered.
26 So I will laugh when you are in trouble!
I will mock you when disaster
overtakes you—
27 when calamity overtakes you like a storm,
when disaster engulfs you like a cyclone,
and anguish and distress overwhelm
you.

1:8 Hebrew *My son;* also in 1:10, 15. **1:12** Hebrew *like Sheol.*

28 "When they cry for help, I will not
answer.
Though they anxiously search for me,
they will not find me.
29 For they hated knowledge
and chose not to fear the LORD.
30 They rejected my advice
and paid no attention when I
corrected them.
31 Therefore, they must eat the bitter fruit
of living their own way,
choking on their own schemes.
32 For simpletons turn away from
me—to death.
Fools are destroyed by their own
complacency.
33 But all who listen to me will live in
peace,
untroubled by fear of harm."

The Benefits of Wisdom

2 1 My child,* listen to what I say,
and treasure my commands.
2 Tune your ears to wisdom,
and concentrate on understanding.
3 Cry out for insight,
and ask for understanding.
4 Search for them as you would for silver;
seek them like hidden treasures.
5 Then you will understand what it means
to fear the LORD,
and you will gain knowledge of God.
6 For the LORD grants wisdom!
From his mouth come knowledge and
understanding.
7 He grants a treasure of common sense to
the honest.
He is a shield to those who walk with
integrity.
8 He guards the paths of the just
and protects those who are faithful
to him.
9 Then you will understand what is right,
just, and fair,
and you will find the right way to go.
10 For wisdom will enter your heart,
and knowledge will fill you with joy.
11 Wise choices will watch over you.
Understanding will keep you safe.

12 Wisdom will save you from evil people,
from those whose words are twisted.
13 These men turn from the right way
to walk down dark paths.
14 They take pleasure in doing wrong,
and they enjoy the twisted ways of evil.
15 Their actions are crooked,
and their ways are wrong.

16 Wisdom will save you from the immoral
woman,
from the seductive words of the
promiscuous woman.
17 She has abandoned her husband
and ignores the covenant she made
before God.
18 Entering her house leads to death;
it is the road to the grave.*
19 The man who visits her is doomed.
He will never reach the paths of life.

20 So follow the steps of the good,
and stay on the paths of the righteous.
21 For only the godly will live in the land,
and those with integrity will remain
in it.
22 But the wicked will be removed from the
land,
and the treacherous will be uprooted.

Trusting in the LORD

3 1 My child,* never forget the things
I have taught you.
Store my commands in your heart.
2 If you do this, you will live many years,
and your life will be satisfying.

Who wrote Proverbs?

The association of the book of Proverbs with Solomon is supported by the headings of some of the collections of proverbs (Proverbs 1:1; 10:1), by his reputation for wisdom, and by the record of Scripture itself (1 Kings 4:32). In addition to composing many of the proverbs himself, Solomon may also have collected and edited the proverbs of others (see Ecclesiastes 12:9-10). Other people certainly contributed some of the proverbs in this book (see Proverbs 22:17; 30:1; 31:1).

3 Never let loyalty and kindness leave you!
Tie them around your neck as a reminder.
Write them deep within your heart.
4 Then you will find favor with both God and people,
and you will earn a good reputation.

5 Trust in the LORD with all your heart;
do not depend on your own understanding.
6 Seek his will in all you do,
and he will show you which path to take.

7 Don't be impressed with your own wisdom.
Instead, fear the LORD and turn away from evil.
8 Then you will have healing for your body
and strength for your bones.

9 Honor the LORD with your wealth
and with the best part of everything you produce.
10 Then he will fill your barns with grain,
and your vats will overflow with good wine.

11 My child, don't reject the LORD's discipline,
and don't be upset when he corrects you.
12 For the LORD corrects those he loves,
just as a father corrects a child in whom he delights.*

13 Joyful is the person who finds wisdom,
the one who gains understanding.
14 For wisdom is more profitable than silver,
and her wages are better than gold.
15 Wisdom is more precious than rubies;
nothing you desire can compare with her.
16 She offers you long life in her right hand,
and riches and honor in her left.
17 She will guide you down delightful paths;
all her ways are satisfying.
18 Wisdom is a tree of life to those who embrace her;
happy are those who hold her tightly.

19 By wisdom the LORD founded the earth;
by understanding he created the heavens.
20 By his knowledge the deep fountains of the earth burst forth,
and the dew settles beneath the night sky.

21 My child, don't lose sight of common sense and discernment.
Hang on to them,
22 for they will refresh your soul.
They are like jewels on a necklace.
23 They keep you safe on your way,
and your feet will not stumble.
24 You can go to bed without fear;
you will lie down and sleep soundly.
25 You need not be afraid of sudden disaster
or the destruction that comes upon the wicked,
26 for the LORD is your security.
He will keep your foot from being caught in a trap.

27 Do not withhold good from those who deserve it
when it's in your power to help them.
28 If you can help your neighbor now, don't say,
"Come back tomorrow, and then I'll help you."

29 Don't plot harm against your neighbor,
for those who live nearby trust you.
30 Don't pick a fight without reason,
when no one has done you harm.

31 Don't envy violent people
or copy their ways.
32 Such wicked people are detestable to the LORD,
but he offers his friendship to the godly.

33 The LORD curses the house of the wicked,
but he blesses the home of the upright.

34 The LORD mocks the mockers
but is gracious to the humble.*

35 The wise inherit honor,
but fools are put to shame!

2:1 Hebrew *My son.* **2:18** Hebrew *to the spirits of the dead.* **3:1** Hebrew *My son;* also in 3:11, 21. **3:12** Greek version reads *loves, / and he punishes those he accepts as his children.* Compare Heb 12:6. **3:34** Greek version reads *The LORD opposes the proud / but gives grace to the humble.* Compare Jas 4:6; 1 Pet 5:5.

▸ **3:11-12** *See **God's discipline**, page 1000.*

A Father's Wise Advice

4 [1] My children,* listen when your
father corrects you.
Pay attention and learn good
judgment,
[2] for I am giving you good guidance.
Don't turn away from my instructions.
[3] For I, too, was once my father's son,
tenderly loved as my mother's only
child.

[4] My father taught me,
"Take my words to heart.
Follow my commands, and you will
live.
[5] Get wisdom; develop good judgment.
Don't forget my words or turn away
from them.
[6] Don't turn your back on wisdom, for she
will protect you.
Love her, and she will guard you.
[7] Getting wisdom is the wisest thing you
can do!
And whatever else you do, develop
good judgment.
[8] If you prize wisdom, she will make you
great.
Embrace her, and she will honor you.
[9] She will place a lovely wreath on your
head;
she will present you with a beautiful
crown."

[10] My child,* listen to me and do as I say,
and you will have a long, good life.
[11] I will teach you wisdom's ways
and lead you in straight paths.
[12] When you walk, you won't be held back;
when you run, you won't stumble.
[13] Take hold of my instructions; don't let
them go.
Guard them, for they are the key to life.

[14] Don't do as the wicked do,
and don't follow the path of
evildoers.
[15] Don't even think about it; don't go that
way.
Turn away and keep moving.
[16] For evil people can't sleep until they've
done their evil deed for the day.
They can't rest until they've caused
someone to stumble.
[17] They eat the food of wickedness
and drink the wine of violence!

[18] The way of the righteous is like the first
gleam of dawn,
which shines ever brighter until the
full light of day.
[19] But the way of the wicked is like total
darkness.
They have no idea what they are
stumbling over.

[20] My child, pay attention to what I say.
Listen carefully to my words.
[21] Don't lose sight of them.
Let them penetrate deep into your
heart,
[22] for they bring life to those who find
them,
and healing to their whole body.
[23] Guard your heart above all else,
for it determines the course of your
life.

[24] Avoid all perverse talk;
stay away from corrupt speech.
[25] Look straight ahead,
and fix your eyes on what lies before
you.
[26] Mark out a straight path for your feet;
stay on the safe path.
[27] Don't get sidetracked;
keep your feet from following evil.

Avoid Immoral Women

5 [1] My son, pay attention to my wisdom;
listen carefully to my wise
counsel.
[2] Then you will show discernment,
and your lips will express what you've
learned.
[3] For the lips of an immoral woman are as
sweet as honey,
and her mouth is smoother than oil.
[4] But in the end she is as bitter as poison,
as dangerous as a double-edged sword.
[5] Her feet go down to death;
her steps lead straight to the grave.*
[6] For she cares nothing about the path to
life.
She staggers down a crooked trail and
doesn't realize it.

▸ 4:23 See ***The heart***, page 909.

7 So now, my sons, listen to me.
Never stray from what I am about to say:
8 Stay away from her!
Don't go near the door of her house!
9 If you do, you will lose your honor
and will lose to merciless people all you have achieved.
10 Strangers will consume your wealth,
and someone else will enjoy the fruit of your labor.
11 In the end you will groan in anguish
when disease consumes your body.
12 You will say, "How I hated discipline!
If only I had not ignored all the warnings!
13 Oh, why didn't I listen to my teachers?
Why didn't I pay attention to my instructors?
14 I have come to the brink of utter ruin,
and now I must face public disgrace."

15 Drink water from your own well—
share your love only with your wife.*
16 Why spill the water of your springs in the streets,
having sex with just anyone?*
17 You should reserve it for yourselves.
Never share it with strangers.

18 Let your wife be a fountain of blessing for you.
Rejoice in the wife of your youth.
19 She is a loving deer, a graceful doe.
Let her breasts satisfy you always.
May you always be captivated by her love.
20 Why be captivated, my son, by an immoral woman,
or fondle the breasts of a promiscuous woman?
21 For the LORD sees clearly what a man does,
examining every path he takes.
22 An evil man is held captive by his own sins;
they are ropes that catch and hold him.
23 He will die for lack of self-control;
he will be lost because of his great foolishness.

Lessons for Daily Life

6 1 My child,* if you have put up security for a friend's debt
or agreed to guarantee the debt of a stranger—
2 if you have trapped yourself by your agreement
and are caught by what you said—
3 follow my advice and save yourself,
for you have placed yourself at your friend's mercy.
Now swallow your pride;
go and beg to have your name erased.
4 Don't put it off; do it now!
Don't rest until you do.
5 Save yourself like a gazelle escaping from a hunter,
like a bird fleeing from a net.

6 Take a lesson from the ants, you lazybones.
Learn from their ways and become wise!
7 Though they have no prince
or governor or ruler to make them work,
8 they labor hard all summer,
gathering food for the winter.

4:1 Hebrew *My sons.* **4:10** Hebrew *My son;* also in 4:20. **5:5** Hebrew *to Sheol.* **5:15** Hebrew *Drink water from your own cistern, / flowing water from your own well.* **5:16** Hebrew *Why spill your springs in the streets, / your streams in the city squares?* **6:1** Hebrew *My son.*

Wisdom

Proverbs repeatedly urges us to "get wisdom" (4:5, 7)—in fact its first nine chapters are devoted to wisdom; for, no matter what it costs, it will repay a hundredfold. The importance of wisdom is seen in how many times it is referred to in the book.

Wisdom is not about being clever—accumulating facts or acquiring knowledge—rather it is about getting to know God better, letting that relationship shape our thinking, and then living that out in every aspect of life. It is taking God's wise words and applying them in God's wise ways, pursuing true success through God-centered living.

▶ *See also **Foolishness**, page 609.*

[9] But you, lazybones, how long will you sleep?
When will you wake up?
[10] A little extra sleep, a little more slumber,
a little folding of the hands to rest—
[11] then poverty will pounce on you like a bandit;
scarcity will attack you like an armed robber.

[12] What are worthless and wicked people like?
They are constant liars,
[13] signaling their deceit with a wink of the eye,
a nudge of the foot, or the wiggle of fingers.
[14] Their perverted hearts plot evil,
and they constantly stir up trouble.
[15] But they will be destroyed suddenly,
broken in an instant beyond all hope of healing.

[16] There are six things the LORD hates—
no, seven things he detests:
[17] haughty eyes,
a lying tongue,
hands that kill the innocent,
[18] a heart that plots evil,
feet that race to do wrong,
[19] a false witness who pours out lies,
a person who sows discord in a family.

[20] My son, obey your father's commands,
and don't neglect your mother's instruction.
[21] Keep their words always in your heart.
Tie them around your neck.
[22] When you walk, their counsel will lead you.
When you sleep, they will protect you.
When you wake up, they will advise you.
[23] For their command is a lamp
and their instruction a light;
their corrective discipline
is the way to life.
[24] It will keep you from the immoral woman,
from the smooth tongue of a promiscuous woman.
[25] Don't lust for her beauty.
Don't let her coy glances seduce you.
[26] For a prostitute will bring you to poverty,*
but sleeping with another man's wife will cost you your life.
[27] Can a man scoop a flame into his lap
and not have his clothes catch on fire?
[28] Can he walk on hot coals
and not blister his feet?
[29] So it is with the man who sleeps with another man's wife.
He who embraces her will not go unpunished.

[30] Excuses might be found for a thief
who steals because he is starving.
[31] But if he is caught, he must pay back seven times what he stole,
even if he has to sell everything in his house.

Laziness

Proverbs often warns against the dangers of laziness (e.g., 6:6-11). Of course, it is easy to excuse laziness ("It's not the right moment." "The Lord hasn't spoken yet." "I need to pray about it more."); but this is no different from the person in Proverbs who lazed around because "There's a lion out there!" (22:13). We need to stop excusing our laziness and call it what it is—sin.

First, laziness is a sin against God. God is a God who works (John 5:17), and, since we are made in his image, we are called to reflect that in work too. Second, it is a sin against ourselves, for work is part of how we find fulfillment in life. Third, it is a sin against others, for our laziness inevitably affects others.

Laziness always has consequences, both practical (e.g., Proverbs 19:15; 20:4; 24:30-34) and spiritual (as when King David stayed at home rather than going to battle and then fell into sin with Bathsheba, 2 Samuel 11). The devil will always find work for idle hands!

▶ *See also **Work**, page 1376.*

32 But the man who commits adultery is
an utter fool,
for he destroys himself.
33 He will be wounded and disgraced.
His shame will never be erased.
34 For the woman's jealous husband will
be furious,
and he will show no mercy when he
takes revenge.
35 He will accept no compensation,
nor be satisfied with a payoff of any
size.

Another Warning about Immoral Women

7 1 Follow my advice, my son;
always treasure my commands.
2 Obey my commands and live!
Guard my instructions as you guard
your own eyes.*
3 Tie them on your fingers as a reminder.
Write them deep within your heart.

4 Love wisdom like a sister;
make insight a beloved member of
your family.
5 Let them protect you from an affair with
an immoral woman,
from listening to the flattery of a
promiscuous woman.

6 While I was at the window of my house,
looking through the curtain,
7 I saw some naive young men,
and one in particular who lacked
common sense.
8 He was crossing the street near the
house of an immoral woman,
strolling down the path by her
house.
9 It was at twilight, in the evening,
as deep darkness fell.
10 The woman approached him,
seductively dressed and sly of heart.
11 She was the brash, rebellious type,
never content to stay at home.
12 She is often in the streets and
markets,
soliciting at every corner.
13 She threw her arms around him and
kissed him,
and with a brazen look she said,
14 "I've just made my peace offerings
and fulfilled my vows.
15 You're the one I was looking for!
I came out to find you, and here you
are!
16 My bed is spread with beautiful
blankets,
with colored sheets of Egyptian linen.
17 I've perfumed my bed
with myrrh, aloes, and cinnamon.
18 Come, let's drink our fill of love until
morning.
Let's enjoy each other's caresses,
19 for my husband is not home.
He's away on a long trip.
20 He has taken a wallet full of money with
him
and won't return until later this
month.*"

21 So she seduced him with her pretty
speech
and enticed him with her flattery.
22 He followed her at once,
like an ox going to the slaughter.
He was like a stag caught in a trap,*
23 awaiting the arrow that would pierce
its heart.
He was like a bird flying into a snare,
little knowing it would cost him his
life.

24 So listen to me, my sons,
and pay attention to my words.
25 Don't let your hearts stray away toward
her.
Don't wander down her wayward
path.
26 For she has been the ruin of many;
many men have been her victims.
27 Her house is the road to the grave.*
Her bedroom is the den of death.

Wisdom Calls for a Hearing

8 1 Listen as Wisdom calls out!
Hear as understanding raises her
voice!
2 On the hilltop along the road,
she takes her stand at the crossroads.
3 By the gates at the entrance to the town,
on the road leading in, she cries
aloud,

6:26 Hebrew *to a loaf of bread.* **7:2** Hebrew *as the pupil of your eye.* **7:20** Hebrew *until the moon is full.* **7:22** As in Greek and Syriac versions; Hebrew reads *slaughter, as shackles are for the discipline of a fool.* **7:27** Hebrew *to Sheol.*

▸ **6:32** *See* ***Adultery****, page 353.*

4 "I call to you, to all of you!
I raise my voice to all people.
5 You simple people, use good judgment.
You foolish people, show some understanding.
6 Listen to me! For I have important things to tell you.
Everything I say is right,
7 for I speak the truth
and detest every kind of deception.
8 My advice is wholesome.
There is nothing devious or crooked in it.
9 My words are plain to anyone with understanding,
clear to those with knowledge.
10 Choose my instruction rather than silver,
and knowledge rather than pure gold.
11 For wisdom is far more valuable than rubies.
Nothing you desire can compare with it.

12 "I, Wisdom, live together with good judgment.
I know where to discover knowledge and discernment.
13 All who fear the LORD will hate evil.
Therefore, I hate pride and arrogance,
corruption and perverse speech.
14 Common sense and success belong to me.
Insight and strength are mine.
15 Because of me, kings reign,
and rulers make just decrees.
16 Rulers lead with my help,
and nobles make righteous judgments.*
17 "I love all who love me.
Those who search will surely find me.
18 I have riches and honor,
as well as enduring wealth and justice.
19 My gifts are better than gold, even the purest gold,
my wages better than sterling silver!
20 I walk in righteousness,
in paths of justice.
21 Those who love me inherit wealth.
I will fill their treasuries.

22 "The LORD formed me from the beginning,
before he created anything else.
23 I was appointed in ages past,
at the very first, before the earth began.
24 I was born before the oceans were created,
before the springs bubbled forth their waters.
25 Before the mountains were formed,
before the hills, I was born—
26 before he had made the earth and fields
and the first handfuls of soil.
27 I was there when he established the heavens,
when he drew the horizon on the oceans.

Wisdom personified

In contrast to the short sayings of much of Proverbs, chapter 8 is a lengthy poem in which wisdom is personified—seen as a great lady calling in the street (8:1-4), appealing to all to come and listen and understand wisdom's benefits (8:5-21). In 8:22-31 we see wisdom's divine origin: Wisdom was there long before creation came into being but was then actively involved in it. The poem ends with an appeal to listen to wisdom and a statement of the blessing of doing so (8:32-36). The writer's appeal is simple: If God himself needed wisdom to bring about his creation, how much more do we need it in our daily lives!

While these verses do not directly describe Christ, they are a preparation for the New Testament's teaching of Christ as the Word of God (John 1:1-3, 14) and the wisdom of God (1 Corinthians 1:24, 30; Colossians 2:3), and of his role as agent of creation (Colossians 1:15-17). There are many parallels: "appointed in ages past . . . there when he established the heavens . . . the architect at his side" (Proverbs 8:23, 27, 30); and yet there are differences, for Christ, unlike wisdom, had no beginning. He was not simply with God; he was God.

28 I was there when he set the clouds
above,
when he established springs deep in
the earth.
29 I was there when he set the limits of the
seas,
so they would not spread beyond their
boundaries.
And when he marked off the earth's
foundations,
30 I was the architect at his side.
I was his constant delight,
rejoicing always in his presence.
31 And how happy I was with the world he
created;
how I rejoiced with the human family!
32 "And so, my children,* listen to me,
for all who follow my ways are joyful.
33 Listen to my instruction and be wise.
Don't ignore it.
34 Joyful are those who listen to me,
watching for me daily at my gates,
waiting for me outside my home!
35 For whoever finds me finds life
and receives favor from the LORD.
36 But those who miss me injure themselves.
All who hate me love death."

9 1 Wisdom has built her house;
she has carved its seven columns.
2 She has prepared a great banquet,
mixed the wines, and set the table.
3 She has sent her servants to invite
everyone to come.
She calls out from the heights
overlooking the city.
4 "Come in with me," she urges the
simple.
To those who lack good judgment,
she says,
5 "Come, eat my food,
and drink the wine I have mixed.
6 Leave your simple ways behind, and
begin to live;
learn to use good judgment."
7 Anyone who rebukes a mocker will get
an insult in return.
Anyone who corrects the wicked will
get hurt.
8 So don't bother correcting
mockers;
they will only hate you.
But correct the wise,
and they will love you.
9 Instruct the wise,
and they will be even wiser.
Teach the righteous,
and they will learn even more.
10 Fear of the LORD is the foundation of
wisdom.
Knowledge of the Holy One results
in good judgment.
11 Wisdom will multiply your days
and add years to your life.
12 If you become wise, you will be the one
to benefit.

8:16 Some Hebrew manuscripts and Greek version read *and nobles are judges over the earth.* **8:32** Hebrew *my sons.*

The fear of the LORD

While some fear can be destructive, there is a fear that can only ever do us good: the fear of the LORD (Yahweh), an idea found several times in Proverbs and over one hundred times in the Bible. This is not fear like that of a child who fears their drunken father; rather, it is the fear of due respect that then guides our actions (e.g., Deuteronomy 10:12-13). It is about having reverence for God and recognizing who he is, what he is like, and how he could treat us, if he wished to—with judgment rather than with grace. When we have encountered God as he really is, we will be so in awe, so overwhelmed, that we will not want to offend him and will therefore live accordingly.

The fear of the LORD helps us to hate evil (Proverbs 8:13) and so keeps us from sinning (Exodus 20:20) and from self-deceit (Psalm 36:1-2). It brings to us God's wisdom (Proverbs 9:10), God's insights and blessings (Psalm 25:12-14), God's protection and provision (Psalm 34:7-11), and God's compassion and love (Psalm 103:13-17). A right fear of God ultimately replaces all other fears in life (Luke 12:4-5).

If you scorn wisdom, you will be the
one to suffer.

Folly Calls for a Hearing

13 The woman named Folly is brash.
She is ignorant and doesn't know it.
14 She sits in her doorway
on the heights overlooking the city.
15 She calls out to men going by
who are minding their own business.
16 "Come in with me," she urges the
simple.
To those who lack good judgment,
she says,
17 "Stolen water is refreshing;
food eaten in secret tastes the best!"
18 But little do they know that the dead are
there.
Her guests are in the depths of the
grave.*

The Proverbs of Solomon

10 The proverbs of Solomon:

A wise child* brings joy to a father;
a foolish child brings grief to a mother.

2 Tainted wealth has no lasting value,
but right living can save your life.

3 The LORD will not let the godly go
hungry,
but he refuses to satisfy the craving
of the wicked.

4 Lazy people are soon poor;
hard workers get rich.

5 A wise youth harvests in the summer,
but one who sleeps during harvest is
a disgrace.

6 The godly are showered with blessings;
the words of the wicked conceal
violent intentions.

7 We have happy memories of the godly,
but the name of a wicked person rots
away.

8 The wise are glad to be instructed,
but babbling fools fall flat on their
faces.

9 People with integrity walk safely,
but those who follow crooked paths
will be exposed.

10 People who wink at wrong cause trouble,
but a bold reproof promotes peace.*

11 The words of the godly are a life-giving
fountain;
the words of the wicked conceal
violent intentions.

12 Hatred stirs up quarrels,
but love makes up for all offenses.

13 Wise words come from the lips of people
with understanding,
but those lacking sense will be beaten
with a rod.

14 Wise people treasure knowledge,
but the babbling of a fool invites
disaster.

15 The wealth of the rich is their fortress;
the poverty of the poor is their
destruction.

16 The earnings of the godly enhance their
lives,
but evil people squander their money
on sin.

17 People who accept discipline are on the
pathway to life,
but those who ignore correction will
go astray.

18 Hiding hatred makes you a liar;
slandering others makes you a fool.

19 Too much talk leads to sin.
Be sensible and keep your mouth
shut.

20 The words of the godly are like sterling
silver;
the heart of a fool is worthless.

21 The words of the godly encourage many,
but fools are destroyed by their lack of
common sense.

22 The blessing of the LORD makes a person
rich,
and he adds no sorrow with it.

23 Doing wrong is fun for a fool,
but living wisely brings pleasure to
the sensible.

24 The fears of the wicked will be fulfilled;
the hopes of the godly will be
granted.

25 When the storms of life come, the
wicked are whirled away,
but the godly have a lasting
foundation.

26 Lazy people irritate their employers,
like vinegar to the teeth or smoke in the eyes.

27 Fear of the LORD lengthens one's life,
but the years of the wicked are cut short.

28 The hopes of the godly result in happiness,
but the expectations of the wicked come to nothing.

29 The way of the LORD is a stronghold to those with integrity,
but it destroys the wicked.

30 The godly will never be disturbed,
but the wicked will be removed from the land.

31 The mouth of the godly person gives wise advice,
but the tongue that deceives will be cut off.

32 The lips of the godly speak helpful words,
but the mouth of the wicked speaks perverse words.

11 1 The LORD detests the use of dishonest scales,
but he delights in accurate weights.

2 Pride leads to disgrace,
but with humility comes wisdom.

3 Honesty guides good people;
dishonesty destroys treacherous people.

4 Riches won't help on the day of judgment,
but right living can save you from death.

5 The godly are directed by honesty;
the wicked fall beneath their load of sin.

6 The godliness of good people rescues them;
the ambition of treacherous people traps them.

7 When the wicked die, their hopes die with them,
for they rely on their own feeble strength.

8 The godly are rescued from trouble,
and it falls on the wicked instead.

9 With their words, the godless destroy their friends,
but knowledge will rescue the righteous.

10 The whole city celebrates when the godly succeed;
they shout for joy when the wicked die.

11 Upright citizens are good for a city and make it prosper,
but the talk of the wicked tears it apart.

9:18 Hebrew *in Sheol.* **10:1** Hebrew *son;* also in 10:1b. **10:10** As in Greek version; Hebrew reads *but babbling fools fall flat on their faces.*

Honesty

Honesty is about speaking and living in a way that conveys truth and righteousness. God regards honesty very highly, for it is a reflection of his own character. So whenever we are not honest, we are denying the God who made us.

Here in Proverbs 11:1, honesty in business is commended (see also Deuteronomy 25:13-16; Proverbs 16:11). Elsewhere honesty is called for in speech (e.g., Ephesians 4:25) and leadership (e.g., Titus 1:7; 2:7-8). The delight of getting an honest answer is reflected in Proverbs 24:26: "An honest answer is like a kiss of friendship."

It is easy to try to explain away our lack of honesty—"I didn't want to hurt their feelings"; "I needed to protect myself"; "I might have gotten into trouble if I told the truth"; "You have to be ruthless in business these days." But such answers simply drive us deeper into falsehood, where God can never be found. As Jesus said, "Just say a simple, 'Yes, I will,' or 'No, I won't.' Anything beyond this is from the evil one" (Matthew 5:37).

[12] It is foolish to belittle one's neighbor;
a sensible person keeps quiet.

[13] A gossip goes around telling secrets,
but those who are trustworthy can keep a confidence.

[14] Without wise leadership, a nation falls;
there is safety in having many advisers.

[15] There's danger in putting up security for a stranger's debt;
it's safer not to guarantee another person's debt.

[16] A gracious woman gains respect,
but ruthless men gain only wealth.

[17] Your kindness will reward you,
but your cruelty will destroy you.

[18] Evil people get rich for the moment,
but the reward of the godly will last.

[19] Godly people find life;
evil people find death.

[20] The LORD detests people with crooked hearts,
but he delights in those with integrity.

[21] Evil people will surely be punished,
but the children of the godly will go free.

[22] A beautiful woman who lacks discretion
is like a gold ring in a pig's snout.

[23] The godly can look forward to a reward,
while the wicked can expect only judgment.

[24] Give freely and become more wealthy;
be stingy and lose everything.

[25] The generous will prosper;
those who refresh others will themselves be refreshed.

[26] People curse those who hoard their grain,
but they bless the one who sells in time of need.

[27] If you search for good, you will find favor;
but if you search for evil, it will find you!

[28] Trust in your money and down you go!
But the godly flourish like leaves in spring.

[29] Those who bring trouble on their families inherit the wind.
The fool will be a servant to the wise.

[30] The seeds of good deeds become a tree of life;
a wise person wins friends.*

[31] If the righteous are rewarded here on earth,
what will happen to wicked sinners?*

12

[1] To learn, you must love discipline;
it is stupid to hate correction.

[2] The LORD approves of those who are good,
but he condemns those who plan wickedness.

[3] Wickedness never brings stability,
but the godly have deep roots.

[4] A worthy wife is a crown for her husband,
but a disgraceful woman is like cancer in his bones.

[5] The plans of the godly are just;
the advice of the wicked is treacherous.

[6] The words of the wicked are like a murderous ambush,
but the words of the godly save lives.

[7] The wicked die and disappear,
but the family of the godly stands firm.

[8] A sensible person wins admiration,
but a warped mind is despised.

[9] Better to be an ordinary person with a servant
than to be self-important but have no food.

[10] The godly care for their animals,
but the wicked are always cruel.

[11] A hard worker has plenty of food,
but a person who chases fantasies has no sense.

[12] Thieves are jealous of each other's loot,
but the godly are well rooted and bear their own fruit.

[13] The wicked are trapped by their own words,
but the godly escape such trouble.

14 Wise words bring many benefits,
and hard work brings rewards.

15 Fools think their own way is right,
but the wise listen to others.

16 A fool is quick-tempered,
but a wise person stays calm when insulted.

17 An honest witness tells the truth;
a false witness tells lies.

18 Some people make cutting remarks,
but the words of the wise bring healing.

19 Truthful words stand the test of time,
but lies are soon exposed.

20 Deceit fills hearts that are plotting evil;
joy fills hearts that are planning peace!

21 No harm comes to the godly,
but the wicked have their fill of trouble.

22 The LORD detests lying lips,
but he delights in those who tell the truth.

23 The wise don't make a show of their knowledge,
but fools broadcast their foolishness.

24 Work hard and become a leader;
be lazy and become a slave.

25 Worry weighs a person down;
an encouraging word cheers a person up.

26 The godly give good advice to their friends;*
the wicked lead them astray.

27 Lazy people don't even cook the game they catch,
but the diligent make use of everything they find.

28 The way of the godly leads to life;
that path does not lead to death.

13

1 A wise child accepts a parent's discipline;*
a mocker refuses to listen to correction.

2 Wise words will win you a good meal,
but treacherous people have an appetite for violence.

3 Those who control their tongue will have a long life;
opening your mouth can ruin everything.

4 Lazy people want much but get little,
but those who work hard will prosper.

5 The godly hate lies;
the wicked cause shame and disgrace.

6 Godliness guards the path of the blameless,
but the evil are misled by sin.

7 Some who are poor pretend to be rich;
others who are rich pretend to be poor.

8 The rich can pay a ransom for their lives,
but the poor won't even get threatened.

9 The life of the godly is full of light and joy,
but the light of the wicked will be snuffed out.

10 Pride leads to conflict;
those who take advice are wise.

11 Wealth from get-rich-quick schemes quickly disappears;
wealth from hard work grows over time.

12 Hope deferred makes the heart sick,
but a dream fulfilled is a tree of life.

13 People who despise advice are asking for trouble;
those who respect a command will succeed.

14 The instruction of the wise is like a life-giving fountain;
those who accept it avoid the snares of death.

15 A person with good sense is respected;
a treacherous person is headed for destruction.*

16 Wise people think before they act;
fools don't—and even brag about their foolishness.

11:30 Or *and those who win souls are wise.* **11:31** Greek version reads *If the righteous are barely saved, / what will happen to godless sinners?* Compare 1 Pet 4:18. **12:26** Or *The godly are cautious in friendship;* or *The godly are freed from evil.* The meaning of the Hebrew is uncertain. **13:1** Hebrew *A wise son accepts his father's discipline.* **13:15** As in Greek version; Hebrew reads *the way of the treacherous is lasting.*

17 An unreliable messenger stumbles into
trouble,
but a reliable messenger brings healing.

18 If you ignore criticism, you will end in
poverty and disgrace;
if you accept correction, you will be
honored.

19 It is pleasant to see dreams come true,
but fools refuse to turn from evil to
attain them.

20 Walk with the wise and become wise;
associate with fools and get in
trouble.

21 Trouble chases sinners,
while blessings reward the righteous.

22 Good people leave an inheritance to
their grandchildren,
but the sinner's wealth passes to the
godly.

23 A poor person's farm may produce much
food,
but injustice sweeps it all away.

24 Those who spare the rod of discipline
hate their children.
Those who love their children care
enough to discipline them.

25 The godly eat to their hearts' content,
but the belly of the wicked goes hungry.

14 1 A wise woman builds her home,
but a foolish woman tears it
down with her own hands.

2 Those who follow the right path fear the
LORD;
those who take the wrong path
despise him.

3 A fool's proud talk becomes a rod that
beats him,
but the words of the wise keep them
safe.

4 Without oxen a stable stays clean,
but you need a strong ox for a large
harvest.

5 An honest witness does not lie;
a false witness breathes lies.

6 A mocker seeks wisdom and never
finds it,
but knowledge comes easily to those
with understanding.

7 Stay away from fools,
for you won't find knowledge on their
lips.

8 The prudent understand where they are
going,
but fools deceive themselves.

9 Fools make fun of guilt,
but the godly acknowledge it and seek
reconciliation.

10 Each heart knows its own bitterness,
and no one else can fully share its joy.

11 The house of the wicked will be
destroyed,
but the tent of the godly will flourish.

Oppression

Oppression—the exploitation of the poor, weak, and vulnerable by the rich, powerful, and strong—is repeatedly condemned in the Bible. What lies behind oppression is a desire for power (e.g., Exodus 1:8-11), property (e.g., 1 Kings 21:1-16), or money (e.g., Amos 2:6), and those who suffer at its hands are the weak, the poor, widows, orphans, servants, and foreigners.

Proverbs reaffirms the Law, forbidding the exploitation and oppression of the poor and warning that God himself will take up their cause (Proverbs 22:22-23); for to oppress a fellow human being is to show contempt for God, in whose image they are made (Proverbs 14:31). But not only are we not to oppress others; we are to extend practical help toward those who are oppressed (e.g., Proverbs 31:8-9, 20), and failure to do so will hinder our prayers (Proverbs 21:13). Furthermore, we are not to oppress those who would seek to oppress us (Proverbs 20:22).

▶ *See also **Is God concerned about social justice?**, page 994.*

12 There is a path before each person that seems right,
but it ends in death.

13 Laughter can conceal a heavy heart,
but when the laughter ends, the grief remains.

14 Backsliders get what they deserve;
good people receive their reward.

15 Only simpletons believe everything they're told!
The prudent carefully consider their steps.

16 The wise are cautious* and avoid danger;
fools plunge ahead with reckless confidence.

17 Short-tempered people do foolish things,
and schemers are hated.

18 Simpletons are clothed with foolishness,*
but the prudent are crowned with knowledge.

19 Evil people will bow before good people;
the wicked will bow at the gates of the godly.

20 The poor are despised even by their neighbors,
while the rich have many "friends."

21 It is a sin to belittle one's neighbor;
blessed are those who help the poor.

22 If you plan to do evil, you will be lost;
if you plan to do good, you will receive unfailing love and faithfulness.

23 Work brings profit,
but mere talk leads to poverty!

24 Wealth is a crown for the wise;
the effort of fools yields only foolishness.

25 A truthful witness saves lives,
but a false witness is a traitor.

26 Those who fear the LORD are secure;
he will be a refuge for their children.

27 Fear of the LORD is a life-giving fountain;
it offers escape from the snares of death.

28 A growing population is a king's glory;
a prince without subjects has nothing.

29 People with understanding control their anger;
a hot temper shows great foolishness.

30 A peaceful heart leads to a healthy body;
jealousy is like cancer in the bones.

31 Those who oppress the poor insult their Maker,
but helping the poor honors him.

32 The wicked are crushed by disaster,
but the godly have a refuge when they die.

33 Wisdom is enshrined in an understanding heart;
wisdom is not* found among fools.

34 Godliness makes a nation great,
but sin is a disgrace to any people.

35 A king rejoices in wise servants
but is angry with those who disgrace him.

15

1 A gentle answer deflects anger,
but harsh words make tempers flare.

2 The tongue of the wise makes knowledge appealing,
but the mouth of a fool belches out foolishness.

3 The LORD is watching everywhere,
keeping his eye on both the evil and the good.

4 Gentle words are a tree of life;
a deceitful tongue crushes the spirit.

5 Only a fool despises a parent's* discipline;
whoever learns from correction is wise.

6 There is treasure in the house of the godly,
but the earnings of the wicked bring trouble.

7 The lips of the wise give good advice;
the heart of a fool has none to give.

8 The LORD detests the sacrifice of the wicked,
but he delights in the prayers of the upright.

14:16 Hebrew *The wise fear.* **14:18** Or *inherit foolishness.*
14:33 As in Greek and Syriac versions; Hebrew lacks *not.*
15:5 Hebrew *father's.*

9 The LORD detests the way of the wicked,
but he loves those who pursue godliness.

10 Whoever abandons the right path will be severely disciplined;
whoever hates correction will die.

11 Even Death and Destruction* hold no secrets from the LORD.
How much more does he know the human heart!

12 Mockers hate to be corrected,
so they stay away from the wise.

13 A glad heart makes a happy face;
a broken heart crushes the spirit.

14 A wise person is hungry for knowledge,
while the fool feeds on trash.

15 For the despondent, every day brings trouble;
for the happy heart, life is a continual feast.

16 Better to have little, with fear for the LORD,
than to have great treasure and inner turmoil.

17 A bowl of vegetables with someone you love
is better than steak with someone you hate.

18 A hot-tempered person starts fights;
a cool-tempered person stops them.

19 A lazy person's way is blocked with briers,
but the path of the upright is an open highway.

20 Sensible children bring joy to their father;
foolish children despise their mother.

21 Foolishness brings joy to those with no sense;
a sensible person stays on the right path.

22 Plans go wrong for lack of advice;
many advisers bring success.

23 Everyone enjoys a fitting reply;
it is wonderful to say the right thing at the right time!

24 The path of life leads upward for the wise;
they leave the grave* behind.

25 The LORD tears down the house of the proud,
but he protects the property of widows.

26 The LORD detests evil plans,
but he delights in pure words.

27 Greed brings grief to the whole family,
but those who hate bribes will live.

28 The heart of the godly thinks carefully before speaking;
the mouth of the wicked overflows with evil words.

29 The LORD is far from the wicked,
but he hears the prayers of the righteous.

30 A cheerful look brings joy to the heart;
good news makes for good health.

31 If you listen to constructive criticism,
you will be at home among the wise.

32 If you reject discipline, you only harm yourself;
but if you listen to correction, you grow in understanding.

33 Fear of the LORD teaches wisdom;
humility precedes honor.

16

1 We can make our own plans,
but the LORD gives the right answer.

2 People may be pure in their own eyes,
but the LORD examines their motives.

3 Commit your actions to the LORD,
and your plans will succeed.

4 The LORD has made everything for his own purposes,
even the wicked for a day of disaster.

5 The LORD detests the proud;
they will surely be punished.

6 Unfailing love and faithfulness make atonement for sin.
By fearing the LORD, people avoid evil.

7 When people's lives please the LORD,
even their enemies are at peace with them.

8 Better to have little, with godliness,
than to be rich and dishonest.

9 We can make our plans,
but the LORD determines our steps.

10 The king speaks with divine wisdom;
he must never judge unfairly.

11 The LORD demands accurate scales and balances;
he sets the standards for fairness.

12 A king detests wrongdoing,
for his rule is built on justice.

13 The king is pleased with words from righteous lips;
he loves those who speak honestly.

14 The anger of the king is a deadly threat;
the wise will try to appease it.

15 When the king smiles, there is life;
his favor refreshes like a spring rain.

16 How much better to get wisdom than gold,
and good judgment than silver!

17 The path of the virtuous leads away from evil;
whoever follows that path is safe.

18 Pride goes before destruction,
and haughtiness before a fall.

19 Better to live humbly with the poor
than to share plunder with the proud.

20 Those who listen to instruction will prosper;
those who trust the LORD will be joyful.

21 The wise are known for their understanding,
and pleasant words are persuasive.

22 Discretion is a life-giving fountain to those who possess it,
but discipline is wasted on fools.

23 From a wise mind comes wise speech;
the words of the wise are persuasive.

24 Kind words are like honey—
sweet to the soul and healthy for the body.

25 There is a path before each person that seems right,
but it ends in death.

26 It is good for workers to have an appetite;
an empty stomach drives them on.

27 Scoundrels create trouble;
their words are a destructive blaze.

28 A troublemaker plants seeds of strife;
gossip separates the best of friends.

29 Violent people mislead their companions,
leading them down a harmful path.

30 With narrowed eyes, people plot evil;
with a smirk, they plan their mischief.

31 Gray hair is a crown of glory;
it is gained by living a godly life.

32 Better to be patient than powerful;
better to have self-control than to conquer a city.

33 We may throw the dice,*
but the LORD determines how they fall.

17

1 Better a dry crust eaten in peace
than a house filled with feasting—and conflict.

2 A wise servant will rule over the master's disgraceful son
and will share the inheritance of the master's children.

3 Fire tests the purity of silver and gold,
but the LORD tests the heart.

4 Wrongdoers eagerly listen to gossip;
liars pay close attention to slander.

5 Those who mock the poor insult their Maker;
those who rejoice at the misfortune of others will be punished.

6 Grandchildren are the crowning glory of the aged;
parents* are the pride of their children.

7 Eloquent words are not fitting for a fool;
even less are lies fitting for a ruler.

8 A bribe is like a lucky charm;
whoever gives one will prosper!

9 Love prospers when a fault is forgiven,
but dwelling on it separates close friends.

10 A single rebuke does more for a person of understanding
than a hundred lashes on the back of a fool.

11 Evil people are eager for rebellion,
but they will be severely punished.

15:11 Hebrew *Sheol and Abaddon.* **15:24** Hebrew *Sheol.*
16:33 Hebrew *We may cast lots.* **17:6** Hebrew *fathers.*

12 It is safer to meet a bear robbed of her cubs
than to confront a fool caught in foolishness.

13 If you repay good with evil,
evil will never leave your house.

14 Starting a quarrel is like opening a floodgate,
so stop before a dispute breaks out.

15 Acquitting the guilty and condemning the innocent—
both are detestable to the LORD.

16 It is senseless to pay to educate a fool,
since he has no heart for learning.

17 A friend is always loyal,
and a brother is born to help in time of need.

18 It's poor judgment to guarantee another person's debt
or put up security for a friend.

19 Anyone who loves to quarrel loves sin;
anyone who trusts in high walls invites disaster.

20 The crooked heart will not prosper;
the lying tongue tumbles into trouble.

21 It is painful to be the parent of a fool;
there is no joy for the father of a rebel.

22 A cheerful heart is good medicine,
but a broken spirit saps a person's strength.

23 The wicked take secret bribes
to pervert the course of justice.

24 Sensible people keep their eyes glued on wisdom,
but a fool's eyes wander to the ends of the earth.

25 Foolish children* bring grief to their father
and bitterness to the one who gave them birth.

26 It is wrong to punish the godly for being good
or to flog leaders for being honest.

27 A truly wise person uses few words;
a person with understanding is even-tempered.

28 Even fools are thought wise when they keep silent;
with their mouths shut, they seem intelligent.

Family

Family is the gift of God, reflecting the relational nature of the Trinity, and a key means of our expressing our humanity through committed relationships. At creation, God established family as the setting for men and women to find fulfillment in one another and to provide a safe place for rearing children (Genesis 1:27-28; 2:19-25).

In the Bible, family is never understood in the narrow sense of a father, a mother, and their children. A household included the patriarch, his wife, his sons and daughters, his sons' wives, his grandchildren, and any other relatives dependent on him. This concept of family could make room for all. And beyond the family lay the clan—a grouping of families based on kinship and territory. The clans made up the twelve tribes, which in turn made up Israel. The nation was therefore thoroughly family-based.

Within this context, children are seen as a blessing (Proverbs 17:6), the elderly are to be cared for (1 Timothy 5:4), and any Christian who fails to live like this is seen as worse than an unbeliever (1 Timothy 5:8). Within the framework of a secure family, parents are encouraged to lovingly discipline their children as part of training them for life (Proverbs 22:6; Hebrews 12:7-11) and are warned that leaving them undisciplined is a recipe for disaster (Proverbs 13:24; 29:15).

▶ *See also* ***Children****, page 1100.*

18 [1] Unfriendly people care only
about themselves;
they lash out at common sense.

[2] Fools have no interest in understanding;
they only want to air their own
opinions.

[3] Doing wrong leads to disgrace,
and scandalous behavior brings
contempt.

[4] Wise words are like deep waters;
wisdom flows from the wise like
a bubbling brook.

[5] It is not right to acquit the guilty
or deny justice to the innocent.

[6] Fools' words get them into constant
quarrels;
they are asking for a beating.

[7] The mouths of fools are their ruin;
they trap themselves with their lips.

[8] Rumors are dainty morsels
that sink deep into one's heart.

[9] A lazy person is as bad as
someone who destroys things.

[10] The name of the LORD is a strong fortress;
the godly run to him and are safe.

[11] The rich think of their wealth as a strong
defense;
they imagine it to be a high wall of
safety.

[12] Haughtiness goes before destruction;
humility precedes honor.

[13] Spouting off before listening to the facts
is both shameful and foolish.

[14] The human spirit can endure a sick
body,
but who can bear a crushed spirit?

[15] Intelligent people are always ready to
learn.
Their ears are open for knowledge.

[16] Giving a gift can open doors;
it gives access to important people!

[17] The first to speak in court sounds right—
until the cross-examination begins.

[18] Flipping a coin* can end arguments;
it settles disputes between powerful
opponents.

[19] An offended friend is harder to win back
than a fortified city.
Arguments separate friends like a gate
locked with bars.

[20] Wise words satisfy like a good meal;
the right words bring satisfaction.

[21] The tongue can bring death or life;
those who love to talk will reap the
consequences.

[22] The man who finds a wife finds a
treasure,
and he receives favor from the LORD.

[23] The poor plead for mercy;
the rich answer with insults.

[24] There are "friends" who destroy each
other,
but a real friend sticks closer than
a brother.

19 [1] Better to be poor and honest
than to be dishonest and a fool.

[2] Enthusiasm without knowledge is no
good;
haste makes mistakes.

[3] People ruin their lives by their own
foolishness
and then are angry at the LORD.

[4] Wealth makes many "friends";
poverty drives them all away.

[5] A false witness will not go unpunished,
nor will a liar escape.

[6] Many seek favors from a ruler;
everyone is the friend of a person who
gives gifts!

[7] The relatives of the poor despise them;
how much more will their friends
avoid them!
Though the poor plead with them,
their friends are gone.

[8] To acquire wisdom is to love yourself;
people who cherish understanding
will prosper.

[9] A false witness will not go unpunished,
and a liar will be destroyed.

[10] It isn't right for a fool to live in luxury
or for a slave to rule over princes!

17:25 Hebrew *A foolish son.* **18:18** Hebrew *Casting lots.*

11 Sensible people control their temper;
they earn respect by overlooking wrongs.

12 The king's anger is like a lion's roar,
but his favor is like dew on the grass.

13 A foolish child* is a calamity to a father;
a quarrelsome wife is as annoying as constant dripping.

14 Fathers can give their sons an inheritance of houses and wealth,
but only the LORD can give an understanding wife.

15 Lazy people sleep soundly,
but idleness leaves them hungry.

16 Keep the commandments and keep your life;
despising them leads to death.

17 If you help the poor, you are lending to the LORD—
and he will repay you!

18 Discipline your children while there is hope.
Otherwise you will ruin their lives.

19 Hot-tempered people must pay the penalty.
If you rescue them once, you will have to do it again.

20 Get all the advice and instruction you can,
so you will be wise the rest of your life.

21 You can make many plans,
but the LORD's purpose will prevail.

22 Loyalty makes a person attractive.
It is better to be poor than dishonest.

23 Fear of the LORD leads to life,
bringing security and protection from harm.

24 Lazy people take food in their hand
but don't even lift it to their mouth.

25 If you punish a mocker, the simpleminded will learn a lesson;
if you correct the wise, they will be all the wiser.

26 Children who mistreat their father or chase away their mother
are an embarrassment and a public disgrace.

27 If you stop listening to instruction, my child,
you will turn your back on knowledge.

28 A corrupt witness makes a mockery of justice;
the mouth of the wicked gulps down evil.

29 Punishment is made for mockers,
and the backs of fools are made to be beaten.

20

1 Wine produces mockers; alcohol leads to brawls.
Those led astray by drink cannot be wise.

2 The king's fury is like a lion's roar;
to rouse his anger is to risk your life.

3 Avoiding a fight is a mark of honor;
only fools insist on quarreling.

4 Those too lazy to plow in the right season
will have no food at the harvest.

5 Though good advice lies deep within the heart,
a person with understanding will draw it out.

6 Many will say they are loyal friends,
but who can find one who is truly reliable?

7 The godly walk with integrity;
blessed are their children who follow them.

8 When a king sits in judgment, he weighs all the evidence,
distinguishing the bad from the good.

9 Who can say, "I have cleansed my heart;
I am pure and free from sin"?

10 False weights and unequal measures*—
the LORD detests double standards of every kind.

11 Even children are known by the way they act,
whether their conduct is pure, and whether it is right.

12 Ears to hear and eyes to see—
both are gifts from the LORD.

13 If you love sleep, you will end in poverty.
Keep your eyes open, and there will be plenty to eat!

14 The buyer haggles over the price, saying,
"It's worthless,"
then brags about getting a bargain!

15 Wise words are more valuable
than much gold and many rubies.

16 Get security from someone who
guarantees a stranger's debt.
Get a deposit if he does it for
foreigners.*

17 Stolen bread tastes sweet,
but it turns to gravel in the mouth.

18 Plans succeed through good counsel;
don't go to war without wise advice.

19 A gossip goes around telling secrets,
so don't hang around with
chatterers.

20 If you insult your father or mother,
your light will be snuffed out in total
darkness.

21 An inheritance obtained too early in life
is not a blessing in the end.

22 Don't say, "I will get even for this wrong."
Wait for the LORD to handle the
matter.

23 The LORD detests double standards;
he is not pleased by dishonest scales.

24 The LORD directs our steps,
so why try to understand everything
along the way?

25 Don't trap yourself by making a rash
promise to God
and only later counting the cost.

26 A wise king scatters the wicked like
wheat,
then runs his threshing wheel over
them.

27 The LORD's light penetrates the human
spirit,*
exposing every hidden motive.

28 Unfailing love and faithfulness protect
the king;
his throne is made secure through love.

29 The glory of the young is their strength;
the gray hair of experience is the
splendor of the old.

30 Physical punishment cleanses away evil;*
such discipline purifies the heart.

21

1 The king's heart is like a stream
of water directed by the LORD;
he guides it wherever he pleases.

2 People may be right in their own eyes,
but the LORD examines their heart.

3 The LORD is more pleased when we do
what is right and just
than when we offer him sacrifices.

19:13 Hebrew *son;* also in 19:27. **20:10** Hebrew *A stone and a stone, an ephah and an ephah.* **20:16** An alternate reading in the Masoretic Text is *for a promiscuous woman.* **20:27** Or *The human spirit is the LORD's light.* **20:30** The meaning of the Hebrew is uncertain.

Vows

The Bible urges us not to be rash in making a vow—a solemn promise to God—for, while Scripture does not require us to make vows, once made they are binding (e.g., Deuteronomy 23:21-23). This is why we are urged not to make them hastily. Proverbs warns, "Don't trap yourself by making a rash promise to God and only later counting the cost" (Proverbs 20:25)—advice that could have spared Jephthah from much heartache had he heeded it (Judges 11:30-40).

If we do choose to make a vow, it should be out of loyalty, gratitude, or dedication, and not an attempt to bargain with God. Some examples of those who made appropriate vows include: Jacob, who vowed to serve God alone if he protected him (Genesis 28:20-22); Hannah, who vowed to dedicate her child to God's service if she became pregnant (1 Samuel 1:11); and Paul, who fulfilled a vow before setting sail on a journey (Acts 18:18).

For most of us, one of the most important vows we will ever take is the vow of marriage, which is why breaking that vow is seen as so abhorrent to God (e.g., Malachi 2:13-16).

4 Haughty eyes, a proud heart,
and evil actions are all sin.
5 Good planning and hard work lead to prosperity,
but hasty shortcuts lead to poverty.
6 Wealth created by a lying tongue
is a vanishing mist and a deadly trap.*
7 The violence of the wicked sweeps them away,
because they refuse to do what is just.
8 The guilty walk a crooked path;
the innocent travel a straight road.
9 It's better to live alone in the corner of an attic
than with a quarrelsome wife in a lovely home.
10 Evil people desire evil;
their neighbors get no mercy from them.
11 If you punish a mocker, the simpleminded become wise;
if you instruct the wise, they will be all the wiser.
12 The Righteous One* knows what is going on in the homes of the wicked;
he will bring disaster on them.
13 Those who shut their ears to the cries of the poor
will be ignored in their own time of need.
14 A secret gift calms anger;
a bribe under the table pacifies fury.
15 Justice is a joy to the godly,
but it terrifies evildoers.
16 The person who strays from common sense
will end up in the company of the dead.
17 Those who love pleasure become poor;
those who love wine and luxury will never be rich.
18 The wicked are punished in place of the godly,
and traitors in place of the honest.
19 It's better to live alone in the desert
than with a quarrelsome, complaining wife.
20 The wise have wealth and luxury,
but fools spend whatever they get.
21 Whoever pursues righteousness and unfailing love
will find life, righteousness, and honor.
22 The wise conquer the city of the strong
and level the fortress in which they trust.
23 Watch your tongue and keep your mouth shut,
and you will stay out of trouble.
24 Mockers are proud and haughty;
they act with boundless arrogance.
25 Despite their desires, the lazy will come to ruin,
for their hands refuse to work.
26 Some people are always greedy for more,
but the godly love to give!
27 The sacrifice of an evil person is detestable,
especially when it is offered with wrong motives.
28 A false witness will be cut off,
but a credible witness will be allowed to speak.
29 The wicked bluff their way through,
but the virtuous think before they act.
30 No human wisdom or understanding or plan
can stand against the LORD.
31 The horse is prepared for the day of battle,
but the victory belongs to the LORD.

22

1 Choose a good reputation over great riches;
being held in high esteem is better than silver or gold.
2 The rich and poor have this in common:
The LORD made them both.
3 A prudent person foresees danger and takes precautions.
The simpleton goes blindly on and suffers the consequences.
4 True humility and fear of the LORD
lead to riches, honor, and long life.

5 Corrupt people walk a thorny,
treacherous road;
whoever values life will avoid it.

6 Direct your children onto the right path,
and when they are older, they will not
leave it.

7 Just as the rich rule the poor,
so the borrower is servant to the
lender.

8 Those who plant injustice will harvest
disaster,
and their reign of terror will come to
an end.*

9 Blessed are those who are generous,
because they feed the poor.

10 Throw out the mocker, and fighting
goes, too.
Quarrels and insults will disappear.

11 Whoever loves a pure heart and gracious
speech
will have the king as a friend.

12 The LORD preserves those with
knowledge,
but he ruins the plans of the
treacherous.

13 The lazy person claims, "There's a lion
out there!
If I go outside, I might be killed!"

14 The mouth of an immoral woman is a
dangerous trap;
those who make the LORD angry will
fall into it.

15 A youngster's heart is filled with
foolishness,
but physical discipline will drive it far
away.

16 A person who gets ahead by oppressing
the poor
or by showering gifts on the rich will
end in poverty.

Sayings of the Wise

17 Listen to the words of the wise;
apply your heart to my instruction.

18 For it is good to keep these sayings in
your heart
and always ready on your lips.

19 I am teaching you today—yes, you—
so you will trust in the LORD.

20 I have written thirty sayings* for you,
filled with advice and knowledge.

21 In this way, you may know the truth
and take an accurate report to those
who sent you.

22 Don't rob the poor just because you can,
or exploit the needy in court.

23 For the LORD is their defender.
He will ruin anyone who ruins them.

24 Don't befriend angry people
or associate with hot-tempered
people,

25 or you will learn to be like them
and endanger your soul.

26 Don't agree to guarantee another
person's debt
or put up security for someone else.

27 If you can't pay it,
even your bed will be snatched from
under you.

28 Don't cheat your neighbor by moving
the ancient boundary markers
set up by previous generations.

29 Do you see any truly competent
workers?
They will serve kings
rather than working for ordinary
people.

23 1 While dining with a ruler,
pay attention to what is put
before you.

2 If you are a big eater,
put a knife to your throat;

3 don't desire all the delicacies,
for he might be trying to trick you.

4 Don't wear yourself out trying to get
rich.
Be wise enough to know when to quit.

5 In the blink of an eye wealth disappears,
for it will sprout wings
and fly away like an eagle.

6 Don't eat with people who are stingy;
don't desire their delicacies.

7 They are always thinking about how
much it costs.*

21:6 As in Greek version; Hebrew reads *mist for those who seek death.* **21:12** Or *The righteous man.* **22:8** The Greek version includes an additional proverb: *God blesses a man who gives cheerfully, / but his worthless deeds will come to an end.* Compare 2 Cor 9:7. **22:20** Or *excellent sayings;* the meaning of the Hebrew is uncertain. **23:7** The meaning of the Hebrew is uncertain.

"Eat and drink," they say, but they
don't mean it.
8 You will throw up what little you've
eaten,
and your compliments will be wasted.

9 Don't waste your breath on fools,
for they will despise the wisest advice.

10 Don't cheat your neighbor by moving
the ancient boundary markers;
don't take the land of defenseless
orphans.
11 For their Redeemer* is strong;
he himself will bring their charges
against you.

12 Commit yourself to instruction;
listen carefully to words of knowledge.

13 Don't fail to discipline your children.
The rod of punishment won't kill
them.
14 Physical discipline
may well save them from death.*

15 My child,* if your heart is wise,
my own heart will rejoice!
16 Everything in me will celebrate
when you speak what is right.

17 Don't envy sinners,
but always continue to fear the LORD.
18 You will be rewarded for this;
your hope will not be disappointed.

19 My child, listen and be wise:
Keep your heart on the right course.
20 Do not carouse with drunkards
or feast with gluttons,
21 for they are on their way to poverty,
and too much sleep clothes them
in rags.

22 Listen to your father, who gave you life,
and don't despise your mother when
she is old.
23 Get the truth and never sell it;
also get wisdom, discipline, and good
judgment.
24 The father of godly children has cause
for joy.
What a pleasure to have children who
are wise.*
25 So give your father and mother joy!
May she who gave you birth be happy.

26 O my son, give me your heart.
May your eyes take delight in
following my ways.
27 A prostitute is a dangerous trap;
a promiscuous woman is as
dangerous as falling into a narrow
well.

Listening

It is sometimes said that God gave us two ears and one mouth because he wants us to listen twice as much as we talk. Of course, many people talk twice as much as they listen. But the Bible counsels us, "You must all be quick to listen, slow to speak . . ." (James 1:19), and Jesus urges us to "pay attention to how you hear" (Luke 8:18).

Who do we need to listen to? First and foremost, of course, we should listen to God—not just hearing his word but acting upon it (e.g., James 1:22-25). But then we should be ready to listen to the wisdom of godly people around us. "Get all the advice and instruction you can," Proverbs urges us (Proverbs 19:20), and "listen carefully to words of knowledge" (Proverbs 23:12)—something that Solomon's son Rehoboam failed to do, rejecting wise advice while accepting bad advice because it pandered to his ego. The result of that was disastrous—the division of the kingdom (1 Kings 12:1-20). Children are urged to listen to their parents (Psalm 34:11; Proverbs 1:8-9; Ephesians 6:1-3); the spiritually young are urged to listen to the mature (Proverbs 5:7); and Christians are urged to listen to their leaders (1 John 4:6).

Listening—and acting in light of what we hear—is something that the Bible calls all of us to. Yet in a world where we are so often encouraged to stand up for ourselves and speak up, the call to listen comes as a constant challenge.

28 She hides and waits like a robber,
eager to make more men unfaithful.

29 Who has anguish? Who has sorrow?
Who is always fighting? Who is always complaining?
Who has unnecessary bruises? Who has bloodshot eyes?
30 It is the one who spends long hours in the taverns,
trying out new drinks.
31 Don't gaze at the wine, seeing how red it is,
how it sparkles in the cup, how smoothly it goes down.
32 For in the end it bites like a poisonous snake;
it stings like a viper.
33 You will see hallucinations,
and you will say crazy things.
34 You will stagger like a sailor tossed at sea,
clinging to a swaying mast.
35 And you will say, "They hit me, but I didn't feel it.
I didn't even know it when they beat me up.
When will I wake up
so I can look for another drink?"

24 1 Don't envy evil people
or desire their company.
2 For their hearts plot violence,
and their words always stir up trouble.

3 A house is built by wisdom
and becomes strong through good sense.
4 Through knowledge its rooms are filled
with all sorts of precious riches and valuables.

5 The wise are mightier than the strong,*
and those with knowledge grow stronger and stronger.
6 So don't go to war without wise guidance;
victory depends on having many advisers.

7 Wisdom is too lofty for fools.
Among leaders at the city gate, they have nothing to say.

8 A person who plans evil
will get a reputation as a troublemaker.
9 The schemes of a fool are sinful;
everyone detests a mocker.

10 If you fail under pressure,
your strength is too small.

11 Rescue those who are unjustly sentenced to die;
save them as they stagger to their death.
12 Don't excuse yourself by saying, "Look, we didn't know."
For God understands all hearts, and he sees you.
He who guards your soul knows you knew.
He will repay all people as their actions deserve.

13 My child,* eat honey, for it is good,
and the honeycomb is sweet to the taste.
14 In the same way, wisdom is sweet to your soul.
If you find it, you will have a bright future,
and your hopes will not be cut short.

15 Don't wait in ambush at the home of the godly,
and don't raid the house where the godly live.
16 The godly may trip seven times, but they will get up again.
But one disaster is enough to overthrow the wicked.

17 Don't rejoice when your enemies fall;
don't be happy when they stumble.
18 For the LORD will be displeased with you
and will turn his anger away from them.

19 Don't fret because of evildoers;
don't envy the wicked.
20 For evil people have no future;
the light of the wicked will be snuffed out.

21 My child, fear the LORD and the king.
Don't associate with rebels,
22 for disaster will hit them suddenly.
Who knows what punishment will come
from the LORD and the king?

23:11 Or *redeemer.* **23:14** Hebrew *from Sheol.* **23:15** Hebrew *My son;* also in 23:19. **23:24** Hebrew *to have a wise son.* **24:5** As in Greek version; Hebrew reads *A wise man is strength.* **24:13** Hebrew *My son;* also in 24:21.

More Sayings of the Wise

23 Here are some further sayings of the wise:

It is wrong to show favoritism when
passing judgment.
24 A judge who says to the wicked, "You
are innocent,"
will be cursed by many people and
denounced by the nations.
25 But it will go well for those who convict
the guilty;
rich blessings will be showered on
them.

26 An honest answer
is like a kiss of friendship.

27 Do your planning and prepare your
fields
before building your house.

28 Don't testify against your neighbors
without cause;
don't lie about them.
29 And don't say, "Now I can pay them
back for what they've done to me!
I'll get even with them!"

30 I walked by the field of a lazy person,
the vineyard of one with no common
sense.
31 I saw that it was overgrown with nettles.
It was covered with weeds,
and its walls were broken down.
32 Then, as I looked and thought about it,
I learned this lesson:
33 A little extra sleep, a little more slumber,
a little folding of the hands to rest—
34 then poverty will pounce on you like a
bandit;
scarcity will attack you like an armed
robber.

More Proverbs of Solomon

25 These are more proverbs of Solomon, collected by the advisers of King Hezekiah of Judah.

2 It is God's privilege to conceal things
and the king's privilege to discover
them.

3 No one can comprehend the height of
heaven, the depth of the earth,
or all that goes on in the king's mind!

4 Remove the impurities from silver,
and the sterling will be ready for the
silversmith.
5 Remove the wicked from the king's court,
and his reign will be made secure by
justice.

6 Don't demand an audience with the king
or push for a place among the great.
7 It's better to wait for an invitation to the
head table
than to be sent away in public disgrace.

Just because you've seen something,
8 don't be in a hurry to go to court.
For what will you do in the end
if your neighbor deals you a shameful
defeat?

9 When arguing with your neighbor,
don't betray another person's secret.
10 Others may accuse you of gossip,
and you will never regain your good
reputation.

11 Timely advice is lovely,
like golden apples in a silver basket.

12 To one who listens, valid criticism
is like a gold earring or other gold
jewelry.

13 Trustworthy messengers refresh like
snow in summer.
They revive the spirit of their employer.

14 A person who promises a gift but doesn't
give it
is like clouds and wind that bring no
rain.

15 Patience can persuade a prince,
and soft speech can break bones.

16 Do you like honey?
Don't eat too much, or it will make
you sick!

17 Don't visit your neighbors too often,
or you will wear out your welcome.

18 Telling lies about others
is as harmful as hitting them with
an ax,
wounding them with a sword,
or shooting them with a sharp arrow.

19 Putting confidence in an unreliable
person in times of trouble
is like chewing with a broken tooth or
walking on a lame foot.

20 Singing cheerful songs to a person with
a heavy heart

is like taking someone's coat in cold
weather
or pouring vinegar in a wound.*

21 If your enemies are hungry, give them
food to eat.
If they are thirsty, give them water to
drink.
22 You will heap burning coals of shame on
their heads,
and the LORD will reward you.
23 As surely as a north wind brings rain,
so a gossiping tongue causes anger!
24 It's better to live alone in the corner of
an attic
than with a quarrelsome wife in a
lovely home.
25 Good news from far away
is like cold water to the thirsty.
26 If the godly give in to the wicked,
it's like polluting a fountain or
muddying a spring.
27 It's not good to eat too much honey,
and it's not good to seek honors for
yourself.
28 A person without self-control
is like a city with broken-down walls.

26 1 Honor is no more associated with
fools
than snow with summer or rain with
harvest.
2 Like a fluttering sparrow or a darting
swallow,
an undeserved curse will not land on
its intended victim.
3 Guide a horse with a whip, a donkey
with a bridle,
and a fool with a rod to his back!
4 Don't answer the foolish arguments of
fools,
or you will become as foolish as they
are.
5 Be sure to answer the foolish arguments
of fools,
or they will become wise in their own
estimation.
6 Trusting a fool to convey a message
is like cutting off one's feet or
drinking poison!
7 A proverb in the mouth of a fool
is as useless as a paralyzed leg.
8 Honoring a fool
is as foolish as tying a stone to a
slingshot.
9 A proverb in the mouth of a fool
is like a thorny branch brandished
by a drunk.
10 An employer who hires a fool or a
bystander
is like an archer who shoots at random.

25:20 As in Greek version; Hebrew reads *pouring vinegar on soda.*

Gossip

While we all say we hate gossip (especially if it concerns us), we are probably all guilty of having shared in it, perhaps even disguising it as concern for someone; and we probably even enjoyed it, for "rumors are dainty morsels that sink deep into one's heart" (Proverbs 26:22). Yet God hates gossip (e.g., Psalm 101:5) and clearly forbids it (e.g., Exodus 23:1), listing it with other grievous sins (e.g., Romans 1:28-32). It harms not just others, Proverbs tells us (e.g., 16:27-28; 26:17-28), but also ourselves (e.g., 13:3) and our relationships (17:9).

Although the tongue is so small, it can have powerful effects, for good or bad (James 3:3-12). Rather than use it for gossip—behind which lie other sins like unforgiveness, jealousy, prejudice, pride, and lack of love—the Bible urges us to use it for good. And if we find ourselves at the receiving end of gossip, we should handle it as Nehemiah did: by declaring it to be nonsense and simply getting on with life (Nehemiah 6:5-15).

▶ *See also **Speech**, page 1416.*

11 As a dog returns to its vomit,
so a fool repeats his foolishness.

12 There is more hope for fools
than for people who think they are wise.

13 The lazy person claims, "There's a lion on the road!
Yes, I'm sure there's a lion out there!"

14 As a door swings back and forth on its hinges,
so the lazy person turns over in bed.

15 Lazy people take food in their hand
but don't even lift it to their mouth.

16 Lazy people consider themselves smarter
than seven wise counselors.

17 Interfering in someone else's argument
is as foolish as yanking a dog's ears.

18 Just as damaging
as a madman shooting a deadly weapon
19 is someone who lies to a friend
and then says, "I was only joking."

20 Fire goes out without wood,
and quarrels disappear when gossip stops.

21 A quarrelsome person starts fights
as easily as hot embers light charcoal
or fire lights wood.

22 Rumors are dainty morsels
that sink deep into one's heart.

23 Smooth* words may hide a wicked heart,
just as a pretty glaze covers a clay pot.

24 People may cover their hatred with pleasant words,
but they're deceiving you.
25 They pretend to be kind, but don't believe them.
Their hearts are full of many evils.*
26 While their hatred may be concealed by trickery,
their wrongdoing will be exposed in public.

27 If you set a trap for others,
you will get caught in it yourself.
If you roll a boulder down on others,
it will crush you instead.

28 A lying tongue hates its victims,
and flattering words cause ruin.

27

1 Don't brag about tomorrow,
since you don't know what the day will bring.

2 Let someone else praise you, not your own mouth—
a stranger, not your own lips.

3 A stone is heavy and sand is weighty,
but the resentment caused by a fool is even heavier.

4 Anger is cruel, and wrath is like a flood,
but jealousy is even more dangerous.

5 An open rebuke
is better than hidden love!

6 Wounds from a sincere friend
are better than many kisses from an enemy.

7 A person who is full refuses honey,
but even bitter food tastes sweet to the hungry.

8 A person who strays from home
is like a bird that strays from its nest.

9 The heartfelt counsel of a friend
is as sweet as perfume and incense.

10 Never abandon a friend—
either yours or your father's.
When disaster strikes, you won't have to ask your brother for assistance.
It's better to go to a neighbor than to a brother who lives far away.

11 Be wise, my child,* and make my heart glad.
Then I will be able to answer my critics.

12 A prudent person foresees danger and takes precautions.
The simpleton goes blindly on and suffers the consequences.

13 Get security from someone who guarantees a stranger's debt.
Get a deposit if he does it for foreigners.*

14 A loud and cheerful greeting early in the morning
will be taken as a curse!

15 A quarrelsome wife is as annoying
as constant dripping on a rainy day.
16 Stopping her complaints is like trying to stop the wind

or trying to hold something with
greased hands.

17 As iron sharpens iron,
so a friend sharpens a friend.

18 As workers who tend a fig tree are
allowed to eat the fruit,
so workers who protect their
employer's interests will be
rewarded.

19 As a face is reflected in water,
so the heart reflects the real person.

20 Just as Death and Destruction* are never
satisfied,
so human desire is never satisfied.

21 Fire tests the purity of silver and gold,
but a person is tested by being
praised.*

22 You cannot separate fools from their
foolishness,
even though you grind them like grain
with mortar and pestle.

23 Know the state of your flocks,
and put your heart into caring for your
herds,

24 for riches don't last forever,
and the crown might not be passed to
the next generation.

25 After the hay is harvested and the new
crop appears
and the mountain grasses are
gathered in,

26 your sheep will provide wool for clothing,
and your goats will provide the price
of a field.

27 And you will have enough goats' milk
for yourself,
your family, and your servant girls.

28 1 The wicked run away when no
one is chasing them,
but the godly are as bold as lions.

2 When there is moral rot within a nation,
its government topples easily.
But wise and knowledgeable leaders
bring stability.

3 A poor person who oppresses the poor
is like a pounding rain that destroys
the crops.

4 To reject the law is to praise the wicked;
to obey the law is to fight them.

5 Evil people don't understand justice,
but those who follow the LORD
understand completely.

6 Better to be poor and honest
than to be dishonest and rich.

7 Young people who obey the law are
wise;
those with wild friends bring shame
to their parents.*

8 Income from charging high interest rates
will end up in the pocket of someone
who is kind to the poor.

9 God detests the prayers
of a person who ignores the law.

26:23 As in Greek version; Hebrew reads *Burning.* **26:25** Hebrew *seven evils.* **27:11** Hebrew *my son.* **27:13** As in Greek and Latin versions (see also 20:16); Hebrew reads *for a promiscuous woman.* **27:20** Hebrew *Sheol and Abaddon.* **27:21** Or *by flattery.* **28:7** Hebrew *their father.*

Friendship

The Bible says that good friends can be a great blessing, but bad friends can ruin our character and lives. What characterizes a good friendship? Proverbs says that "a friend is always loyal, and a brother is born to help in time of need" (Proverbs 17:17). This is what Naomi found in Ruth (Ruth 1:8-18), what David found in Jonathan (1 Samuel 18:1; 20:16-17; 23:16), and what Paul found in Timothy (Philippians 2:19-22) and Titus (2 Corinthians 7:6). True friends are always there for us, always supportive, yet never afraid to tell us the truth (Proverbs 27:6). By contrast, bad friends can lead us away from the right path (e.g., Proverbs 22:24-25; 2 Corinthians 6:14-18). We should therefore be very careful how we choose our friends or what friendships we continue with.

▶ *See also **Being there**, page 575.*

10 Those who lead good people along an
evil path
will fall into their own trap,
but the honest will inherit good things.

11 Rich people may think they are wise,
but a poor person with discernment
can see right through them.

12 When the godly succeed, everyone is
glad.
When the wicked take charge, people
go into hiding.

13 People who conceal their sins will not
prosper,
but if they confess and turn from
them, they will receive mercy.

14 Blessed are those who fear to do wrong,*
but the stubborn are headed for
serious trouble.

15 A wicked ruler is as dangerous to the
poor
as a roaring lion or an attacking bear.

16 A ruler with no understanding will
oppress his people,
but one who hates corruption will
have a long life.

17 A murderer's tormented conscience will
drive him into the grave.
Don't protect him!

18 The blameless will be rescued from
harm,
but the crooked will be suddenly
destroyed.

19 A hard worker has plenty of food,
but a person who chases fantasies
ends up in poverty.

20 The trustworthy person will get a rich
reward,
but a person who wants quick riches
will get into trouble.

21 Showing partiality is never good,
yet some will do wrong for a mere
piece of bread.

22 Greedy people try to get rich quick
but don't realize they're headed for
poverty.

23 In the end, people appreciate honest
criticism
far more than flattery.

24 Anyone who steals from his father and
mother
and says, "What's wrong with that?"
is no better than a murderer.

25 Greed causes fighting;
trusting the LORD leads to
prosperity.

26 Those who trust their own insight are
foolish,
but anyone who walks in wisdom is
safe.

27 Whoever gives to the poor will lack
nothing,
but those who close their eyes to
poverty will be cursed.

28 When the wicked take charge, people go
into hiding.
When the wicked meet disaster, the
godly flourish.

29

1 Whoever stubbornly refuses to
accept criticism
will suddenly be destroyed beyond
recovery.

2 When the godly are in authority, the
people rejoice.
But when the wicked are in power,
they groan.

3 The man who loves wisdom brings joy
to his father,
but if he hangs around with
prostitutes, his wealth is wasted.

4 A just king gives stability to his nation,
but one who demands bribes
destroys it.

5 To flatter friends
is to lay a trap for their feet.

6 Evil people are trapped by sin,
but the righteous escape, shouting
for joy.

7 The godly care about the rights of the
poor;
the wicked don't care at all.

8 Mockers can get a whole town
agitated,
but the wise will calm anger.

9 If a wise person takes a fool to court,
there will be ranting and ridicule but
no satisfaction.

10 The bloodthirsty hate blameless people,
but the upright seek to help them.*

11 Fools vent their anger,
but the wise quietly hold it back.

12 If a ruler pays attention to liars,
all his advisers will be wicked.

13 The poor and the oppressor have this in common—
the LORD gives sight to the eyes of both.

14 If a king judges the poor fairly,
his throne will last forever.

15 To discipline a child produces wisdom,
but a mother is disgraced by an undisciplined child.

16 When the wicked are in authority, sin flourishes,
but the godly will live to see their downfall.

17 Discipline your children, and they will give you peace of mind
and will make your heart glad.

18 When people do not accept divine guidance, they run wild.
But whoever obeys the law is joyful.

19 Words alone will not discipline a servant;
the words may be understood, but they are not heeded.

20 There is more hope for a fool
than for someone who speaks without thinking.

21 A servant pampered from childhood
will become a rebel.

22 An angry person starts fights;
a hot-tempered person commits all kinds of sin.

23 Pride ends in humiliation,
while humility brings honor.

24 If you assist a thief, you only hurt yourself.
You are sworn to tell the truth, but you dare not testify.

25 Fearing people is a dangerous trap,
but trusting the LORD means safety.

26 Many seek the ruler's favor,
but justice comes from the LORD.

27 The righteous despise the unjust;
the wicked despise the godly.

The Sayings of Agur

30 The sayings of Agur son of Jakeh contain this message.*

I am weary, O God;
I am weary and worn out, O God.*
2 I am too stupid to be human,
and I lack common sense.
3 I have not mastered human wisdom,
nor do I know the Holy One.

4 Who but God goes up to heaven and comes back down?
Who holds the wind in his fists?
Who wraps up the oceans in his cloak?
Who has created the whole wide world?
What is his name—and his son's name?
Tell me if you know!

5 Every word of God proves true.
He is a shield to all who come to him for protection.
6 Do not add to his words,
or he may rebuke you and expose you as a liar.

7 O God, I beg two favors from you;
let me have them before I die.
8 First, help me never to tell a lie.
Second, give me neither poverty nor riches!
Give me just enough to satisfy my needs.
9 For if I grow rich, I may deny you and say, "Who is the LORD?"
And if I am too poor, I may steal and thus insult God's holy name.

10 Never slander a worker to the employer,
or the person will curse you, and you will pay for it.

11 Some people curse their father
and do not thank their mother.
12 They are pure in their own eyes,
but they are filthy and unwashed.
13 They look proudly around,
casting disdainful glances.
14 They have teeth like swords
and fangs like knives.

28:14 Or *those who fear the LORD;* Hebrew reads *those who fear.* **29:10** Or *The bloodthirsty hate blameless people, / and they seek to kill the upright;* Hebrew reads *The bloodthirsty hate blameless people; / as for the upright, they seek their life.* **30:1a** Or *son of Jakeh from Massa;* or *son of Jakeh, an oracle.* **30:1b** The Hebrew can also be translated *The man declares this to Ithiel, / to Ithiel and to Ucal.*

They devour the poor from the earth
and the needy from among humanity.

15 The leech has two suckers
that cry out, "More, more!"*
There are three things that are never
satisfied—
no, four that never say, "Enough!":
16 the grave,*
the barren womb,
the thirsty desert,
the blazing fire.

17 The eye that mocks a father
and despises a mother's instructions
will be plucked out by ravens of the
valley
and eaten by vultures.

18 There are three things that amaze me—
no, four things that I don't
understand:
19 how an eagle glides through the sky,
how a snake slithers on a rock,
how a ship navigates the ocean,
how a man loves a woman.

20 An adulterous woman consumes a man,
then wipes her mouth and says,
"What's wrong with that?"

21 There are three things that make the
earth tremble—
no, four it cannot endure:
22 a slave who becomes a king,
an overbearing fool who
prospers,
23 a bitter woman who finally gets
a husband,
a servant girl who supplants her
mistress.

24 There are four things on earth that are
small but unusually wise:
25 Ants—they aren't strong,
but they store up food all summer.
26 Hyraxes*—they aren't powerful,
but they make their homes among
the rocks.
27 Locusts—they have no king,
but they march in formation.
28 Lizards—they are easy to catch,
but they are found even in kings'
palaces.

29 There are three things that walk with
stately stride—
no, four that strut about:
30 the lion, king of animals, who won't turn
aside for anything,

Women

Proverbs has much to say about women—both good women and bad. On the one hand, the adulterous woman is warned against and condemned (e.g., Proverbs 5:3-6; 7:6-27), but on the other hand, God's ideal woman (as depicted in 31:10-31) is highly praised—and not just for her domestic skills. This woman is engaged in business (31:16) and trading (31:18), cares for the poor (31:20), and thinks ahead for her family (31:21). Part of the respect in which her husband is held is due to her (31:23). Little wonder she is praised.

This chapter is a healthy corrective to any who think the Bible has too low a view of women. Yes, Genesis 2:18 says that Eve was created as Adam's "helper," but this does not mean she was his servant. The Hebrew expression in Genesis means "a help corresponding to/matching him," and the word translated "helper" is used of God himself elsewhere (e.g., Exodus 18:4; Psalm 70:5). So this is a high view of women.

Many godly women are noted and commended in the Bible—women like Deborah, Ruth, Hannah, and Esther in the Old Testament and Mary, Martha, Dorcas, and Priscilla in the New Testament. And since the New Testament tells us that when we come to Christ, all the old divisions—such as Jew and Gentile, slave and free, and male and female—are abolished (Galatians 3:28), any view of women that belittles them is less than Christian.

▸ *See also* ***Adam and Eve****, page 6.*

31 the strutting rooster,
the male goat,
a king as he leads his army.

32 If you have been a fool by being proud
or plotting evil,
cover your mouth in shame.

33 As the beating of cream yields butter
and striking the nose causes bleeding,
so stirring up anger causes quarrels.

The Sayings of King Lemuel

31 The sayings of King Lemuel contain this message,* which his mother taught him.

2 O my son, O son of my womb,
O son of my vows,
3 do not waste your strength on women,
on those who ruin kings.

4 It is not for kings, O Lemuel, to guzzle
wine.
Rulers should not crave alcohol.
5 For if they drink, they may forget the law
and not give justice to the oppressed.
6 Alcohol is for the dying,
and wine for those in bitter distress.
7 Let them drink to forget their poverty
and remember their troubles no more.

8 Speak up for those who cannot speak for
themselves;
ensure justice for those being crushed.
9 Yes, speak up for the poor and helpless,
and see that they get justice.

A Wife of Noble Character

10*Who can find a virtuous and capable
wife?
She is more precious than rubies.
11 Her husband can trust her,
and she will greatly enrich his life.
12 She brings him good, not harm,
all the days of her life.

13 She finds wool and flax
and busily spins it.
14 She is like a merchant's ship,
bringing her food from afar.
15 She gets up before dawn to prepare
breakfast for her household
and plan the day's work for her
servant girls.

16 She goes to inspect a field and buys it;
with her earnings she plants a
vineyard.
17 She is energetic and strong,
a hard worker.
18 She makes sure her dealings are
profitable;
her lamp burns late into the night.

19 Her hands are busy spinning thread,
her fingers twisting fiber.
20 She extends a helping hand to the poor
and opens her arms to the needy.
21 She has no fear of winter for her
household,
for everyone has warm* clothes.

22 She makes her own bedspreads.
She dresses in fine linen and purple
gowns.
23 Her husband is well known at the city
gates,
where he sits with the other civic
leaders.
24 She makes belted linen garments
and sashes to sell to the merchants.

25 She is clothed with strength and dignity,
and she laughs without fear of the
future.
26 When she speaks, her words are wise,
and she gives instructions with
kindness.
27 She carefully watches everything in her
household
and suffers nothing from laziness.

28 Her children stand and bless her.
Her husband praises her:
29 "There are many virtuous and capable
women in the world,
but you surpass them all!"

30 Charm is deceptive, and beauty does not
last;
but a woman who fears the LORD will
be greatly praised.
31 Reward her for all she has done.
Let her deeds publicly declare her
praise.

30:15 Hebrew *two daughters who cry out, "Give, give!"* **30:16** Hebrew *Sheol.* **30:26** Or *Coneys,* or *Rock badgers.* **31:1** Or *of Lemuel, king of Massa;* or *of King Lemuel, an oracle.* **31:10** Verses 10-31 comprise a Hebrew acrostic poem; each verse begins with a successive letter of the Hebrew alphabet. **31:21** As in Greek and Latin versions; Hebrew reads *scarlet.*

Ecclesiastes *The quest for meaning*

Ecclesiastes (from a Greek word meaning "Teacher") is a book about life. In this book, we are taken on a journey through life, from birth to death, and shown how human accomplishments convinced the writer that life is empty and futile if lived without God.

The book has a timeless flavor. The frustrations and longings of the human heart find their echoes in the book of Ecclesiastes. An outlook that is limited to life "under the sun"—this present world—is without meaning or hope. The pleasures of the world, enjoyable though they might be, do not bring ultimate satisfaction. Life simply does not make sense apart from God.

While the book is anonymous, both Jewish and Christian traditions ascribe its authorship to Solomon.

What's it all about?

In chapters 1 and 2 the writer draws on his own experiences of life. His great wisdom only serves to show him how meaningless life is: Everything on earth is so futile and fleeting (the word translated "meaningless" really means "a breath"—life passes as quickly as breath from your mouth, as wind that blows by). Life is "like chasing the wind." He then offers some general observations on life (chapters 3–5): There is a time for everything (3:1-8), and time passes very quickly, so we need to make the most of it; there is unfairness in the world, and both the good and the bad will die one day; people are always struggling to improve their lot, but it is better to be content with what you have; wealth cannot buy happiness. The only solution is to fear—be in awe of—God (5:1-7) and to put him at the center of everything.

In chapters 6 to 8 the writer gives some practical advice. He reminds us that although good things can happen to bad people, and bad things to good people, God is in control. Ultimately those who respect God will be better off than those who don't. In chapter 9 he writes about the unpredictability of life and the certainty of death for all of us (9:1-12) and urges us therefore to pursue the path of wisdom (9:13-18). In chapter 10 he records some proverbs concerning wisdom and foolishness. In chapter 11 he shares some wise advice in the light of life's unpredictability, and in chapter 12 he urges us to remember and honor our Creator in our youth (12:1-7).

The writer concludes with this observation: "That's the whole story. Here now is my final conclusion: Fear God and obey his commands, for this is everyone's duty. God will judge us for everything we do, including every secret thing, whether good or bad" (12:13-14).

OVERVIEW

The emptiness of life without God
1:1–2:26

A time for everything
3:1-15

The futility of life without God
3:16–8:17

The uncertainty of life without God
9:1–11:10

A call to remember God
12:1-14

What does it mean for us?

Ecclesiastes is a book of contrasts. On the one hand, it highlights the emptiness of human life, as summed up in the phrase "Everything is meaningless, completely meaningless." This refers to the meaningless contradiction of much human activity, and to the irony that death ultimately destroys all human achievements—those of both the rich and the poor, of both the wise and the foolish. But life is only meaningless if we leave God out of the equation! For Ecclesiastes also sees God at work throughout human life—the God who wants us to find satisfaction in the world he has created. But that can only happen when we put him right at the center of everything. Those who trust in God's providence rather than living to please themselves not only are wise but also can enjoy life to the full.

1 These are the words of the Teacher,* King
David's son, who ruled in Jerusalem.

Everything Is Meaningless

2 "Everything is meaningless," says the
Teacher, "completely meaningless!"
3 What do people get for all their hard
work under the sun? 4 Generations come
and generations go, but the earth never
changes. 5 The sun rises and the sun sets,
then hurries around to rise again. 6 The
wind blows south, and then turns north.
Around and around it goes, blowing in
circles. 7 Rivers run into the sea, but the sea
is never full. Then the water returns again
to the rivers and flows out again to the sea.
8 Everything is wearisome beyond description. No matter how much we see, we are
never satisfied. No matter how much we
hear, we are not content.
9 History merely repeats itself. It has all
been done before. Nothing under the sun
is truly new. 10 Sometimes people say, "Here
is something new!" But actually it is old;
nothing is ever truly new. 11 We don't remember what happened in the past, and in future
generations, no one will remember what we
are doing now.

The Teacher Speaks: The Futility of Wisdom

12 I, the Teacher, was king of Israel, and
I lived in Jerusalem. 13 I devoted myself to
search for understanding and to explore
by wisdom everything being done under
heaven. I soon discovered that God has
dealt a tragic existence to the human race.
14 I observed everything going on under the
sun, and really, it is all meaningless—like
chasing the wind.

15 What is wrong cannot be made right.
What is missing cannot be recovered.

16 I said to myself, "Look, I am wiser than
any of the kings who ruled in Jerusalem
before me. I have greater wisdom and knowledge than any of them." 17 So I set out to learn
everything from wisdom to madness and
folly. But I learned firsthand that pursuing
all this is like chasing the wind.

18 The greater my wisdom, the greater my
grief.
To increase knowledge only increases
sorrow.

The Futility of Pleasure

2 I said to myself, "Come on, let's try pleasure. Let's look for the 'good things' in
life." But I found that this, too, was meaningless. 2 So I said, "Laughter is silly. What good
does it do to seek pleasure?" 3 After much
thought, I decided to cheer myself with wine.
And while still seeking wisdom, I clutched at
foolishness. In this way, I tried to experience
the only happiness most people find during
their brief life in this world.
4 I also tried to find meaning by building
huge homes for myself and by planting beautiful vineyards. 5 I made gardens and parks,
filling them with all kinds of fruit trees.
6 I built reservoirs to collect the water to irrigate my many flourishing groves. 7 I bought
slaves, both men and women, and others
were born into my household. I also owned
large herds and flocks, more than any of the
kings who had lived in Jerusalem before me.
8 I collected great sums of silver and gold, the
treasure of many kings and provinces. I hired
wonderful singers, both men and women,
and had many beautiful concubines. I had
everything a man could desire!
9 So I became greater than all who had lived

1:1 Hebrew *Qoheleth;* this term is rendered "the Teacher" throughout this book.

in Jerusalem before me, and my wisdom
never failed me. [10]Anything I wanted,
I would take. I denied myself no pleasure.
I even found great pleasure in hard work,
a reward for all my labors. [11]But as I looked
at everything I had worked so hard to accomplish, it was all so meaningless—like
chasing the wind. There was nothing really
worthwhile anywhere.

The Wise and the Foolish

[12]So I decided to compare wisdom with
foolishness and madness (for who can do
this better than I, the king?*). [13]I thought,
"Wisdom is better than foolishness, just as
light is better than darkness. [14]For the wise
can see where they are going, but fools walk
in the dark." Yet I saw that the wise and the
foolish share the same fate. [15]Both will die.
So I said to myself, "Since I will end up the
same as the fool, what's the value of all my
wisdom? This is all so meaningless!" [16]For
the wise and the foolish both die. The wise
will not be remembered any longer than
the fool. In the days to come, both will be
forgotten.

[17]So I came to hate life because everything
done here under the sun is so troubling.
Everything is meaningless—like chasing
the wind.

The Futility of Work

[18]I came to hate all my hard work here on
earth, for I must leave to others everything
I have earned. [19]And who can tell whether
my successors will be wise or foolish? Yet
they will control everything I have gained
by my skill and hard work under the sun.
How meaningless! [20]So I gave up in despair,
questioning the value of all my hard work
in this world.

[21]Some people work wisely with knowledge and skill, then must leave the fruit of
their efforts to someone who hasn't worked
for it. This, too, is meaningless, a great
tragedy. [22]So what do people get in this life
for all their hard work and anxiety? [23]Their
days of labor are filled with pain and grief;
even at night their minds cannot rest. It is
all meaningless.

[24]So I decided there is nothing better
than to enjoy food and drink and to find
satisfaction in work. Then I realized that
these pleasures are from the hand of God.
[25]For who can eat or enjoy anything apart
from him?* [26]God gives wisdom, knowledge, and joy to those who please him.
But if a sinner becomes wealthy, God takes
the wealth away and gives it to those who
please him. This, too, is meaningless—like
chasing the wind.

A Time for Everything

3 [1]For everything there is a season,
a time for every activity under
heaven.
[2]A time to be born and a time to die.
A time to plant and a time to harvest.

The use of time

The Teacher has already said that life is merely "a breath" (the meaning of the word "meaningless" in Ecclesiastes 1–2). And yet, although life passes so quickly, there is an appointed right time for everything (3:1-8), so it is wise to embrace the time we have as God's gift (3:9-15).

The Bible often encourages us to make wise use of our time, since we do not know what the future holds. Jesus said we should use our time in light of his return, which could happen at any moment (Matthew 24:36–25:13). Paul wrote to his churches to "be careful how you live. Don't live like fools, but like those who are wise. Make the most of every opportunity in these evil days" (Ephesians 5:15-16). James warned people not to base too much on their human plans, but rather to live as people guided by the principle of "if the Lord wants us to" (James 4:13-15).

If we claim to love God and follow Jesus, we will always seek to use the time God gives us wisely. Each moment should be cherished, not wasted.

▶ *See also* ***Waiting****, page 558.*

3 A time to kill and a time to heal.
A time to tear down and a time to build up.
4 A time to cry and a time to laugh.
A time to grieve and a time to dance.
5 A time to scatter stones and a time to gather stones.
A time to embrace and a time to turn away.
6 A time to search and a time to quit searching.
A time to keep and a time to throw away.
7 A time to tear and a time to mend.
A time to be quiet and a time to speak.
8 A time to love and a time to hate.
A time for war and a time for peace.

9 What do people really get for all their
hard work? 10 I have seen the burden God
has placed on us all. 11 Yet God has made
everything beautiful for its own time. He has planted eternity in the human heart, but even so, people cannot see the whole scope of God's work from beginning to end.
12 So I concluded there is nothing better than
to be happy and enjoy ourselves as long as
we can. 13 And people should eat and drink
and enjoy the fruits of their labor, for these are gifts from God.

14 And I know that whatever God does is
final. Nothing can be added to it or taken from it. God's purpose is that people should
fear him. 15 What is happening now has happened before, and what will happen in the future has happened before, because God makes the same things happen over and over again.

The Injustices of Life

16 I also noticed that under the sun there is
evil in the courtroom. Yes, even the courts
of law are corrupt! 17 I said to myself, "In due
season God will judge everyone, both good and bad, for all their deeds."

18 I also thought about the human condition—how God proves to people that they
are like animals. 19 For people and animals
share the same fate—both breathe* and both must die. So people have no real advantage over the animals. How meaningless! 20 Both go to the same place—they
came from dust and they return to dust.
21 For who can prove that the human spirit
goes up and the spirit of animals goes down into the earth? 22 So I saw that there is
nothing better for people than to be happy in their work. That is our lot in life. And no one can bring us back to see what happens after we die.

4 Again, I observed all the oppression that takes place under the sun. I saw the tears of the oppressed, with no one to comfort them. The oppressors have great power, and
their victims are helpless. 2 So I concluded
that the dead are better off than the living.
3 But most fortunate of all are those who are
not yet born. For they have not seen all the evil that is done under the sun.

4 Then I observed that most people are
motivated to success because they envy their neighbors. But this, too, is meaningless—like chasing the wind.

5 "Fools fold their idle hands,
leading them to ruin."

6 And yet,

"Better to have one handful with quietness
than two handfuls with hard work
and chasing the wind."

The Advantages of Companionship

7 I observed yet another example of something meaningless under the sun. 8 This is
the case of a man who is all alone, without a child or a brother, yet who works hard to gain as much wealth as he can. But then he asks himself, "Who am I working for? Why am I giving up so much pleasure now?" It is all so meaningless and depressing.

9 Two people are better off than one, for
they can help each other succeed. 10 If one
person falls, the other can reach out and help. But someone who falls alone is in real
trouble. 11 Likewise, two people lying close
together can keep each other warm. But
how can one be warm alone? 12 A person
standing alone can be attacked and defeated, but two can stand back-to-back and conquer. Three are even better, for a triple-braided cord is not easily broken.

The Futility of Political Power

13 It is better to be a poor but wise youth
than an old and foolish king who refuses

2:12 The meaning of the Hebrew is uncertain. **2:25** As in Greek and Syriac versions; Hebrew reads *apart from me?* **3:19** Or *both have the same spirit*.

all advice. 14Such a youth could rise from
poverty and succeed. He might even
become king, though he has been in
prison. 15But then everyone rushes to the
side of yet another youth* who replaces
him. 16Endless crowds stand around him,*
but then another generation grows up and
rejects him, too. So it is all meaningless—
like chasing the wind.

Approaching God with Care

5 1*As you enter the house of God, keep
your ears open and your mouth shut. It
is evil to make mindless offerings to God.
2*Don't make rash promises, and don't be
hasty in bringing matters before God. After
all, God is in heaven, and you are here on
earth. So let your words be few.

3Too much activity gives you restless
dreams; too many words make you a fool.

4When you make a promise to God, don't
delay in following through, for God takes
no pleasure in fools. Keep all the promises
you make to him. 5It is better to say nothing
than to make a promise and not keep it.
6Don't let your mouth make you sin. And
don't defend yourself by telling the Temple
messenger that the promise you made was
a mistake. That would make God angry,
and he might wipe out everything you have
achieved.

7Talk is cheap, like daydreams and other
useless activities. Fear God instead.

The Futility of Wealth

8Don't be surprised if you see a poor person
being oppressed by the powerful and if
justice is being miscarried throughout the
land. For every official is under orders from
higher up, and matters of justice get lost in
red tape and bureaucracy. 9Even the king
milks the land for his own profit!*

10Those who love money will never have
enough. How meaningless to think that
wealth brings true happiness! 11The more
you have, the more people come to help
you spend it. So what good is wealth—
except perhaps to watch it slip through your
fingers!

12People who work hard sleep well,
whether they eat little or much. But the rich
seldom get a good night's sleep.

13There is another serious problem I have
seen under the sun. Hoarding riches harms
the saver. 14Money is put into risky investments that turn sour, and everything is lost.
In the end, there is nothing left to pass on
to one's children. 15We all come to the end
of our lives as naked and empty-handed as
on the day we were born. We can't take our
riches with us.

16And this, too, is a very serious problem.
People leave this world no better off than
when they came. All their hard work is
for nothing—like working for the wind.
17Throughout their lives, they live under a
cloud—frustrated, discouraged, and angry.

Teamwork

There is nothing worse than being "a man who is all alone" (Ecclesiastes 4:8), for he has no one with whom to share the results of his labor. By contrast, one who works with another is truly blessed (4:9-12). Each can encourage and protect the other, and "they can help each other succeed."

From the beginning, God designed human beings not to function alone but to live in community (Genesis 2:18). That is why marriage is such a blessing, for "two people are better off than one." (Ecclesiastes 4:9-12 is a passage often used at weddings.) But God wants us to learn how to work in teams larger than just the marriage partnership. In a team we can draw on one another's strengths, make up for one another's deficiencies, and encourage one another along the way. This is why Jesus sent out his disciples in pairs (Luke 10:1), and why Paul never traveled alone on his missionary journeys (e.g., Acts 13:4, 13; 14:1; 15:22; 16:6; 17:15; 18:18). The church is a key setting for teamwork, and Paul stressed that no one member of the church ever has all the gifts or abilities needed (1 Corinthians 12:12-31).

The only things that keep us from working in a team are pride and the belief that we can succeed alone.

[18]Even so, I have noticed one thing, at
least, that is good. It is good for people to
eat, drink, and enjoy their work under the
sun during the short life God has given
them, and to accept their lot in life. [19]And it
is a good thing to receive wealth from God
and the good health to enjoy it. To enjoy
your work and accept your lot in life—this
is indeed a gift from God. [20]God keeps such
people so busy enjoying life that they take
no time to brood over the past.

6 There is another serious tragedy I have
seen under the sun, and it weighs
heavily on humanity. [2]God gives some
people great wealth and honor and everything they could ever want, but then he
doesn't give them the chance to enjoy these
things. They die, and someone else, even
a stranger, ends up enjoying their wealth!
This is meaningless—a sickening tragedy.
[3]A man might have a hundred children
and live to be very old. But if he finds no
satisfaction in life and doesn't even get a
decent burial, it would have been better
for him to be born dead. [4]His birth would
have been meaningless, and he would have
ended in darkness. He wouldn't even have
had a name, [5]and he would never have seen
the sun or known of its existence. Yet he
would have had more peace than in growing
up to be an unhappy man. [6]He might live a
thousand years twice over but still not find
contentment. And since he must die like
everyone else—well, what's the use?
[7]All people spend their lives scratching for food, but they never seem to have
enough. [8]So are wise people really better off
than fools? Do poor people gain anything
by being wise and knowing how to act in
front of others?
[9]Enjoy what you have rather than desir-
ing what you don't have. Just dreaming
about nice things is meaningless—like
chasing the wind.

The Future—Determined and Unknown

[10]Everything has already been decided.
It was known long ago what each person
would be. So there's no use arguing with
God about your destiny.
[11]The more words you speak, the less they
mean. So what good are they?
[12]In the few days of our meaningless lives,
who knows how our days can best be spent?
Our lives are like a shadow. Who can tell
what will happen on this earth after we are
gone?

Wisdom for Life

7 [1] A good reputation is more valuable
than costly perfume.
And the day you die is better than the
day you are born.
2 Better to spend your time at funerals
than at parties.
After all, everyone dies—
so the living should take this to heart.
3 Sorrow is better than laughter,
for sadness has a refining influence
on us.
4 A wise person thinks a lot about death,
while a fool thinks only about having
a good time.
5 Better to be criticized by a wise person
than to be praised by a fool.
6 A fool's laughter is quickly gone,
like thorns crackling in a fire.
This also is meaningless.

7 Extortion turns wise people into fools,
and bribes corrupt the heart.
8 Finishing is better than starting.
Patience is better than pride.

9 Control your temper,
for anger labels you a fool.

10 Don't long for "the good old days."
This is not wise.

11 Wisdom is even better when you have
money.
Both are a benefit as you go through
life.
12 Wisdom and money can get you almost
anything,
but only wisdom can save your life.

13 Accept the way God does things,
for who can straighten what he has
made crooked?
14 Enjoy prosperity while you can,
but when hard times strike, realize
that both come from God.
Remember that nothing is certain in
this life.

4:15 Hebrew *the second youth.* **4:16** Hebrew *There is no end to all the people, to all those who are before them.* **5:1** Verse 5:1 is numbered 4:17 in Hebrew text. **5:2** Verses 5:2-20 are numbered 5:1-19 in Hebrew text. **5:9** The meaning of the Hebrew in verses 8 and 9 is uncertain.

The Limits of Human Wisdom

[15]I have seen everything in this meaningless life, including the death of good young people and the long life of wicked people. [16]So don't be too good or too wise! Why destroy yourself? [17]On the other hand, don't be too wicked either. Don't be a fool! Why die before your time? [18]Pay attention to these instructions, for anyone who fears God will avoid both extremes.*

[19]One wise person is stronger than ten leading citizens of a town!

[20]Not a single person on earth is always good and never sins.

[21]Don't eavesdrop on others—you may hear your servant curse you. [22]For you know how often you yourself have cursed others.

[23]I have always tried my best to let wisdom guide my thoughts and actions. I said to myself, "I am determined to be wise." But it didn't work. [24]Wisdom is always distant and difficult to find. [25]I searched everywhere, determined to find wisdom and to understand the reason for things. I was determined to prove to myself that wickedness is stupid and that foolishness is madness.

[26]I discovered that a seductive woman* is a trap more bitter than death. Her passion is a snare, and her soft hands are chains. Those who are pleasing to God will escape her, but sinners will be caught in her snare.

[27]"This is my conclusion," says the Teacher. "I discovered this after looking at the matter from every possible angle. [28]Though I have searched repeatedly, I have not found what I was looking for. Only one out of a thousand men is virtuous, but not one woman! [29]But I did find this: God created people to be virtuous, but they have each turned to follow their own downward path."

8 [1] How wonderful to be wise,
to analyze and interpret things.
Wisdom lights up a person's face,
softening its harshness.

Obedience to the King

[2]Obey the king since you vowed to God that you would. [3]Don't try to avoid doing your duty, and don't stand with those who plot evil, for the king can do whatever he wants. [4]His command is backed by great power. No one can resist or question it. [5]Those who obey him will not be punished. Those who are wise will find a time and a way to do what is right, [6]for there is a time and a way for everything, even when a person is in trouble.

Bribery

Bribery—paying money or giving a gift to get a favorable decision or some other benefit—was widespread in Bible times, as it still is in some parts of the world today. People said that you couldn't get by in life without it. But God detests bribery, for it corrupts the heart of both the giver and the recipient—"bribes corrupt the heart" (Ecclesiastes 7:7); "a bribe makes you ignore something that you clearly see" (Exodus 23:8). This is why offering or accepting a bribe is constantly forbidden in Scripture, and forbidden in very plain words—"Take no bribes" (Exodus 23:8).

It was when Samuel's sons began to accept bribes that they began to drift from God (1 Samuel 8:3), in contrast to their godly father, who never accepted a bribe (1 Samuel 12:3) and whom God used powerfully. Paul refused to offer a bribe even when doing so could have led to his release from a Roman prison (Acts 24:26). God himself "cannot be bribed" (Deuteronomy 10:17), and to engage in bribery is to defile his image within us.

In some parts of the world today it can still seem impossible to survive or get what you need in life without paying a bribe. In the West, bribery is more often associated with powerful businessmen who give "thank yous" to get what they want, though it can also be found at times in more ordinary circumstances. But Christians are called to reject any expression of bribery, choosing instead the way that honors God and his Word and trusting the outcome to the one who knows everything and can provide all we need.

7 Indeed, how can people avoid what they
don't know is going to happen? 8 None of
us can hold back our spirit from departing.
None of us has the power to prevent the day
of our death. There is no escaping that obligation, that dark battle. And in the face of
death, wickedness will certainly not rescue
the wicked.

The Wicked and the Righteous

9 I have thought deeply about all that goes
on here under the sun, where people have
the power to hurt each other. 10 I have seen
wicked people buried with honor. Yet they
were the very ones who frequented the
Temple and are now praised* in the same
city where they committed their crimes!
This, too, is meaningless. 11 When a crime is
not punished quickly, people feel it is safe
to do wrong. 12 But even though a person
sins a hundred times and still lives a long
time, I know that those who fear God will be
better off. 13 The wicked will not prosper, for
they do not fear God. Their days will never
grow long like the evening shadows.

14 And this is not all that is meaningless in
our world. In this life, good people are often
treated as though they were wicked, and
wicked people are often treated as though
they were good. This is so meaningless!

15 So I recommend having fun, because
there is nothing better for people in this
world than to eat, drink, and enjoy life.
That way they will experience some happiness along with all the hard work God gives
them under the sun.

16 In my search for wisdom and in my observation of people's burdens here on earth,
I discovered that there is ceaseless activity,
day and night. 17 I realized that no one can
discover everything God is doing under the
sun. Not even the wisest people discover
everything, no matter what they claim.

Death Comes to All

9 This, too, I carefully explored: Even
though the actions of godly and wise
people are in God's hands, no one knows
whether God will show them favor. 2 The same
destiny ultimately awaits everyone, whether
righteous or wicked, good or bad,* ceremonially clean or unclean, religious or irreligious.
Good people receive the same treatment as
sinners, and people who make promises to
God are treated like people who don't.

3 It seems so wrong that everyone under
the sun suffers the same fate. Already
twisted by evil, people choose their own
mad course, for they have no hope. There
is nothing ahead but death anyway. 4 There
is hope only for the living. As they say, "It's
better to be a live dog than a dead lion!"

5 The living at least know they will die,
but the dead know nothing. They have no
further reward, nor are they remembered.
6 Whatever they did in their lifetime—loving,
hating, envying—is all long gone. They no
longer play a part in anything here on earth.
7 So go ahead. Eat your food with joy, and
drink your wine with a happy heart, for God
approves of this! 8 Wear fine clothes, with a
splash of cologne!

9 Live happily with the woman you love
through all the meaningless days of life
that God has given you under the sun. The
wife God gives you is your reward for all
your earthly toil. 10 Whatever you do, do
well. For when you go to the grave,* there
will be no work or planning or knowledge
or wisdom.

11 I have observed something else under
the sun. The fastest runner doesn't always
win the race, and the strongest warrior
doesn't always win the battle. The wise
sometimes go hungry, and the skillful are
not necessarily wealthy. And those who are
educated don't always lead successful lives.
It is all decided by chance, by being in the
right place at the right time.

12 People can never predict when hard
times might come. Like fish in a net or birds
in a trap, people are caught by sudden
tragedy.

Thoughts on Wisdom and Folly

13 Here is another bit of wisdom that has impressed me as I have watched the way our
world works. 14 There was a small town with
only a few people, and a great king came
with his army and besieged it. 15 A poor, wise
man knew how to save the town, and so it
was rescued. But afterward no one thought
to thank him. 16 So even though wisdom is
better than strength, those who are wise
will be despised if they are poor. What they
say will not be appreciated for long.

7:18 Or *will follow them both.* **7:26** Hebrew *a woman.* **8:10** As in some Hebrew manuscripts and Greek version; many Hebrew manuscripts read *and are forgotten.* **9:2** As in Greek and Syriac versions and Latin Vulgate; Hebrew lacks *or bad.* **9:10** Hebrew *to Sheol.*

17 Better to hear the quiet words of a wise person
than the shouts of a foolish king.
18 Better to have wisdom than weapons of war,
but one sinner can destroy much that is good.

10 1 As dead flies cause even a bottle of perfume to stink,
so a little foolishness spoils great wisdom and honor.

2 A wise person chooses the right road;
a fool takes the wrong one.
3 You can identify fools
just by the way they walk down the street!

4 If your boss is angry at you, don't quit!
A quiet spirit can overcome even great mistakes.

The Ironies of Life

5 There is another evil I have seen under
the sun. Kings and rulers make a grave
mistake 6 when they give great authority to
foolish people and low positions to people
of proven worth. 7 I have even seen servants
riding horseback like princes—and princes
walking like servants!

8 When you dig a well,
you might fall in.
When you demolish an old wall,
you could be bitten by a snake.
9 When you work in a quarry,
stones might fall and crush you.
When you chop wood,
there is danger with each stroke of your ax.

10 Using a dull ax requires great strength,
so sharpen the blade.
That's the value of wisdom;
it helps you succeed.

11 If a snake bites before you charm it,
what's the use of being a snake charmer?

12 Wise words bring approval,
but fools are destroyed by their own words.

13 Fools base their thoughts on foolish assumptions,
so their conclusions will be wicked madness;
14 they chatter on and on.

No one really knows what is going to happen;
no one can predict the future.

15 Fools are so exhausted by a little work
that they can't even find their way home.

16 What sorrow for the land ruled by a servant,*
the land whose leaders feast in the morning.
17 Happy is the land whose king is a noble leader
and whose leaders feast at the proper time
to gain strength for their work, not to get drunk.

18 Laziness leads to a sagging roof;
idleness leads to a leaky house.

19 A party gives laughter,
wine gives happiness,
and money gives everything!

20 Never make light of the king, even in your thoughts.
And don't make fun of the powerful, even in your own bedroom.
For a little bird might deliver your message
and tell them what you said.

The Uncertainties of Life

11 1 Send your grain across the seas,
and in time, profits will flow back to you.*
2 But divide your investments among many places,*
for you do not know what risks might lie ahead.

3 When clouds are heavy, the rains come down.
Whether a tree falls north or south,
it stays where it falls.

4 Farmers who wait for perfect weather never plant.
If they watch every cloud, they never harvest.

5 Just as you cannot understand the path
of the wind or the mystery of a tiny baby

growing in its mother's womb,* so you
cannot understand the activity of God, who
does all things.
6 Plant your seed in the morning and
keep busy all afternoon, for you don't know
if profit will come from one activity or
another—or maybe both.

Advice for Young and Old

7 Light is sweet; how pleasant to see a new
day dawning.
8 When people live to be very old, let them
rejoice in every day of life. But let them also
remember there will be many dark days.
Everything still to come is meaningless.
9 Young people,* it's wonderful to be
young! Enjoy every minute of it. Do everything you want to do; take it all in. But remember that you must give an account to
God for everything you do. 10 So refuse to
worry, and keep your body healthy. But remember that youth, with a whole life before
you, is meaningless.

12 Don't let the excitement of youth
cause you to forget your Creator.
Honor him in your youth before you grow
old and say, "Life is not pleasant anymore."
2 Remember him before the light of the sun,
moon, and stars is dim to your old eyes,
and rain clouds continually darken your
sky. 3 Remember him before your legs—the
guards of your house—start to tremble;
and before your shoulders—the strong
men—stoop. Remember him before your
teeth—your few remaining servants—stop
grinding; and before your eyes—the women
looking through the windows—see dimly.
4 Remember him before the door to life's
opportunities is closed and the sound of
work fades. Now you rise at the first chirp-
ing of the birds, but then all their sounds
will grow faint.
5 Remember him before you become
fearful of falling and worry about danger
in the streets; before your hair turns white
like an almond tree in bloom, and you drag
along without energy like a dying grasshopper, and the caperberry no longer inspires sexual desire. Remember him before
you near the grave, your everlasting home,
when the mourners will weep at your
funeral.
6 Yes, remember your Creator now while
you are young, before the silver cord of life
snaps and the golden bowl is broken. Don't
wait until the water jar is smashed at the
spring and the pulley is broken at the well.
7 For then the dust will return to the earth,
and the spirit will return to God who gave it.

Concluding Thoughts about the Teacher

8 "Everything is meaningless," says the
Teacher, "completely meaningless."
9 Keep this in mind: The Teacher was
considered wise, and he taught the people
everything he knew. He listened carefully
to many proverbs, studying and classifying
them. 10 The Teacher sought to find just the
right words to express truths clearly.*
11 The words of the wise are like cattle
prods—painful but helpful. Their collected
sayings are like a nail-studded stick with
which a shepherd* drives the sheep.
12 But, my child,* let me give you some
further advice: Be careful, for writing books
is endless, and much study wears you out.
13 That's the whole story. Here now is
my final conclusion: Fear God and obey
his commands, for this is everyone's duty.
14 God will judge us for everything we do,
including every secret thing, whether good
or bad.

10:16 Or *a child.* **11:1** Or *Give generously, / for your gifts will return to you later.* Hebrew reads *Throw your bread on the waters, / for after many days you will find it again.* **11:2** Hebrew *among seven or even eight.* **11:5** Some manuscripts read *Just as you cannot understand how breath comes to a tiny baby in its mother's womb.* **11:9** Hebrew *Young man.* **12:10** Or *sought to write what was upright and true.* **12:11** Or *one shepherd.* **12:12** Hebrew *my son.*

Song of Songs *A celebration of love*

The Bible records many great romances, but none can compare with the one recorded in the Song of Songs. This touching collection of love songs features a dialogue between a young Israelite woman and her lover. The Song is a celebration of human love, set in drama, poetry, and the most sensuous language found in the Bible.

Although Song of Songs is often interpreted as an allegory of God's love for Israel or Christ's love for the church, in the mind of the writer it was written as a celebration of human love in all its passion, power, and spontaneity. Such love is one of God's great gifts to us and a wonderful aspect of life in his good creation.

The opening verse attributes authorship of the poem to Solomon, who is referred to seven times.

What's it all about?

The title of the book—the Song of Songs—is a Hebrew way of saying "The Best of Songs"—best, because it deals with one of humanity's deepest sources of joy: the love between a man and a woman. The opening words of the Song set the tone for what follows: "Kiss me and kiss me again, for your love is sweeter than wine" (1:2). We immediately see that this is going to be a very open and honest reflection on romantic love in all its aspects. In turn throughout the poem, the young man and the young woman express their love and remember key moments of their courtship. The woman, a goatherd (1:8), also speaks to the women of Jerusalem about love. With vivid and sensual imagery, the lovers describe each other and the pleasure they find in their mutual love.

In chapter 5 the woman relates a troubling dream and speaks about the shame and humiliation she received while looking for her lover. But the young man and the other young women praise her beauty (chapters 6 and 7), and in chapter 8 she speaks eloquently about the strength of love, which has drawn them together. They have experienced that "love is as strong as death" (8:6)—and they will take this love with them as they continue into life together (8:14).

OVERVIEW

The title
1:1

First meeting of the young man and the young woman · *1:2–2:7*

Second meeting of the young man and the young woman · *2:8–3:5*

Third meeting of the young man and the young woman · *3:6–5:1*

The young woman dreams
5:2–6:3

Fourth meeting of the young man and the young woman · *6:4–8:4*

Conclusion
8:5-14

What does it mean for us?

This book celebrates the joys of romantic love, an appropriate and healthy expression of God's gift of sexuality. But the atmosphere is a world away from that of most modern love songs. Even the most explicit lyrics here never become even slightly unclean. The lovers' intoxication with love might sound up-to-date, but there's an innocence about their feelings that is refreshing. There is also a reminder "not to awaken love until the time is right" (3:5)—that is, until the time is appropriate for it to be expressed, which, for Christians, is always within marriage.

In spite of the many physical images and the passionate nature of the couple's relationship, the love celebrated here is not purely physical, but spiritual too—as all true love, romantic or otherwise, really is. This may be why the book has often been read on two levels: first, at the level it was originally intended, as a superb account of human love; but second, as an allegory of God's love for his people, his "bride" (see Ephesians 5:25-33 and Revelation 19:7).

However we read it, the Song's imagery leaves us convinced that this is love in the way that it is meant to be: rich, full, tender, and unashamed. We feel that God is with the two as they love. This book's inclusion in the Bible reinforces the Christian belief that God created intimacy to be enjoyed, and that these unique and tender feelings are part of his plan for his children.

1 This is Solomon's song of songs, more wonderful than any other.

*Young Woman**

2 Kiss me and kiss me again,
for your love is sweeter than wine.
3 How pleasing is your fragrance;
your name is like the spreading
fragrance of scented oils.
No wonder all the young women love
you!
4 Take me with you; come, let's run!
The king has brought me into his
bedroom.

Young Women of Jerusalem

How happy we are for you, O king.
We praise your love even more than
wine.

Young Woman

How right they are to adore you.
5 I am dark but beautiful,
O women of Jerusalem—
dark as the tents of Kedar,
dark as the curtains of Solomon's tents.
6 Don't stare at me because I am dark—
the sun has darkened my skin.
My brothers were angry with me;
they forced me to care for their
vineyards,
so I couldn't care for myself—my own
vineyard.
7 Tell me, my love, where are you leading
your flock today?
Where will you rest your sheep at noon?
For why should I wander like a prostitute*
among your friends and their flocks?

Young Man

8 If you don't know, O most beautiful
woman,
follow the trail of my flock,
and graze your young goats by the
shepherds' tents.
9 You are as exciting, my darling,
as a mare among Pharaoh's stallions.
10 How lovely are your cheeks;
your earrings set them afire!
How lovely is your neck,
enhanced by a string of jewels.
11 We will make for you earrings of gold
and beads of silver.

Young Woman

12 The king is lying on his couch,
enchanted by the fragrance of my
perfume.
13 My lover is like a sachet of myrrh
lying between my breasts.
14 He is like a bouquet of sweet henna
blossoms
from the vineyards of En-gedi.

Young Man

15 How beautiful you are, my darling,
how beautiful!
Your eyes are like doves.

Young Woman

16 You are so handsome, my love,
pleasing beyond words!
The soft grass is our bed;
17 fragrant cedar branches are the beams
of our house,
and pleasant smelling firs are the rafters.

Young Woman

2 1 I am the spring crocus blooming on
the Sharon Plain,*
the lily of the valley.

1:1 The headings identifying the speakers are not in the original text, though the Hebrew usually gives clues by means of the gender of the person speaking. **1:7** Hebrew *like a veiled woman.* **2:1** Traditionally rendered *I am the rose of Sharon.* Sharon Plain is a region in the coastal plain of Palestine.

Young Man
2 Like a lily among thistles
is my darling among young women.

Young Woman
3 Like the finest apple tree in the orchard
is my lover among other young
men.
I sit in his delightful shade
and taste his delicious fruit.
4 He escorts me to the banquet hall;
it's obvious how much he loves me.
5 Strengthen me with raisin cakes,
refresh me with apples,
for I am weak with love.
6 His left arm is under my head,
and his right arm embraces me.

7 Promise me, O women of Jerusalem,
by the gazelles and wild deer,
not to awaken love until the time is
right.*

8 Ah, I hear my lover coming!
He is leaping over the mountains,
bounding over the hills.
9 My lover is like a swift gazelle
or a young stag.
Look, there he is behind the wall,
looking through the window,
peering into the room.

10 My lover said to me,
"Rise up, my darling!
Come away with me, my fair one!
11 Look, the winter is past,
and the rains are over and gone.
12 The flowers are springing up,
the season of singing birds* has come,
and the cooing of turtledoves fills the
air.
13 The fig trees are forming young fruit,
and the fragrant grapevines are
blossoming.
Rise up, my darling!
Come away with me, my fair one!"

Young Man
14 My dove is hiding behind the rocks,
behind an outcrop on the cliff.
Let me see your face;
let me hear your voice.
For your voice is pleasant,
and your face is lovely.

Young Women of Jerusalem
15 Catch all the foxes,
those little foxes,

Sexuality

The fact that this Song speaks openly about love and intimacy shows that such things have God's blessing. Our sexuality is not something to be ashamed of; it is part of what makes us human.

But like anything else in life, our sexuality needs to be handled in God's way if it is not to become destructive, to us and others. That is why the Bible says that sexual relationships belong only within the lifelong relationship of marriage (e.g., Hebrews 13:4), for sex isn't just a physical act; it is an expression of becoming "united into one" (Genesis 2:24). This physical act strengthens the underlying spiritual bond, which is why Christians cannot sleep around as the world does (1 Corinthians 6:15-20). But within marriage, sex is a wonderful gift.

Sinful human nature challenges God's design for our sexuality through things like masturbation, sex before marriage, adultery, homosexuality, lust, and pornography (a massive problem these days because of its easy availability on the Internet). The world says such things are "normal," but they cannot be normal for us. Such behavior will not receive God's blessing—and who of us would want to live apart from his blessing?

If you are struggling with any of these issues, don't hide them, for the enemy has power over things kept in darkness. Bring them into the light by discussing your difficulties with a more mature Christian and asking them to pray with you for help and victory. God can help you and bring you into blessing.

► *See also **Does marriage still matter to God?**, page 976.*

before they ruin the vineyard of love,
for the grapevines are blossoming!

Young Woman

16 My lover is mine, and I am his.
He browses among the lilies.
17 Before the dawn breezes blow
and the night shadows flee,
return to me, my love, like a gazelle
or a young stag on the rugged
mountains.*

Young Woman

3 1 One night as I lay in bed, I yearned
for my lover.
I yearned for him, but he did not
come.
2 So I said to myself, "I will get up and
roam the city,
searching in all its streets and squares.
I will search for the one I love."
So I searched everywhere but did not
find him.
3 The watchmen stopped me as they made
their rounds,
and I asked, "Have you seen the one
I love?"
4 Then scarcely had I left them
when I found my love!
I caught and held him tightly,
then I brought him to my mother's
house,
into my mother's bed, where I had
been conceived.
5 Promise me, O women of Jerusalem,
by the gazelles and wild deer,
not to awaken love until the time is
right.*

Young Women of Jerusalem

6 Who is this sweeping in from the
wilderness
like a cloud of smoke?
Who is it, fragrant with myrrh and
frankincense
and every kind of spice?
7 Look, it is Solomon's carriage,
surrounded by sixty heroic men,
the best of Israel's soldiers.
8 They are all skilled swordsmen,
experienced warriors.
Each wears a sword on his thigh,
ready to defend the king against an
attack in the night.
9 King Solomon's carriage is built
of wood imported from Lebanon.
10 Its posts are silver,
its canopy gold;
its cushions are purple.
It was decorated with love
by the young women of Jerusalem.

Young Woman

11 Come out to see King Solomon,
young women of Jerusalem.*
He wears the crown his mother gave him
on his wedding day,
his most joyous day.

Young Man

4 1 You are beautiful, my darling,
beautiful beyond words.
Your eyes are like doves
behind your veil.
Your hair falls in waves,
like a flock of goats winding down the
slopes of Gilead.
2 Your teeth are as white as sheep,
recently shorn and freshly washed.
Your smile is flawless,
each tooth matched with its twin.*
3 Your lips are like scarlet ribbon;
your mouth is inviting.
Your cheeks are like rosy pomegranates
behind your veil.
4 Your neck is as beautiful as the tower of
David,
jeweled with the shields of a thousand
heroes.
5 Your breasts are like two fawns,
twin fawns of a gazelle grazing among
the lilies.
6 Before the dawn breezes blow
and the night shadows flee,
I will hurry to the mountain of myrrh
and to the hill of frankincense.
7 You are altogether beautiful, my
darling,
beautiful in every way.
8 Come with me from Lebanon, my bride,
come with me from Lebanon.
Come down* from Mount Amana,
from the peaks of Senir and Hermon,
where the lions have their dens
and leopards live among the hills.
9 You have captured my heart,
my treasure,* my bride.

2:7 Or *not to awaken love until it is ready.* **2:12** Or *the season of pruning vines.* **2:17** Or *on the hills of Bether.* **3:5** Or *not to awaken love until it is ready.* **3:11** Hebrew *of Zion.* **4:2** Hebrew *Not one is missing; each has a twin.* **4:8** Or *Look down.* **4:9** Hebrew *my sister;* also in 4:10, 12.

You hold it hostage with one glance of
your eyes,
with a single jewel of your necklace.
10 Your love delights me,
my treasure, my bride.
Your love is better than wine,
your perfume more fragrant than
spices.
11 Your lips are as sweet as nectar, my
bride.
Honey and milk are under your
tongue.
Your clothes are scented
like the cedars of Lebanon.

12 You are my private garden, my treasure,
my bride,
a secluded spring, a hidden fountain.
13 Your thighs shelter a paradise of
pomegranates
with rare spices—
henna with nard,
14 nard and saffron,
fragrant calamus and cinnamon,
with all the trees of frankincense, myrrh,
and aloes,
and every other lovely spice.
15 You are a garden fountain,
a well of fresh water
streaming down from Lebanon's
mountains.

Young Woman

16 Awake, north wind!
Rise up, south wind!
Blow on my garden
and spread its fragrance all around.
Come into your garden, my love;
taste its finest fruits.

Young Man

5 1 I have entered my garden, my
treasure,* my bride!
I gather myrrh with my spices
and eat honeycomb with my honey.
I drink wine with my milk.

Young Women of Jerusalem

Oh, lover and beloved, eat and drink!
Yes, drink deeply of your love!

Young Woman

2 I slept, but my heart was awake,
when I heard my lover knocking and
calling:
"Open to me, my treasure, my darling,
my dove, my perfect one.
My head is drenched with dew,
my hair with the dampness of the
night."

3 But I responded,
"I have taken off my robe.
Should I get dressed again?
I have washed my feet.
Should I get them soiled?"

4 My lover tried to unlatch the door,
and my heart thrilled within me.
5 I jumped up to open the door for my love,
and my hands dripped with perfume.
My fingers dripped with lovely myrrh
as I pulled back the bolt.
6 I opened to my lover,
but he was gone!
My heart sank.
I searched for him
but could not find him anywhere.
I called to him,
but there was no reply.
7 The night watchmen found me
as they made their rounds.
They beat and bruised me
and stripped off my veil,
those watchmen on the walls.

8 Make this promise, O women of
Jerusalem—
If you find my lover,
tell him I am weak with love.

Young Women of Jerusalem

9 Why is your lover better than all others,
O woman of rare beauty?
What makes your lover so special
that we must promise this?

Young Woman

10 My lover is dark and dazzling,
better than ten thousand others!
11 His head is finest gold,
his wavy hair is black as a raven.
12 His eyes sparkle like doves
beside springs of water;
they are set like jewels
washed in milk.
13 His cheeks are like gardens of spices
giving off fragrance.
His lips are like lilies,
perfumed with myrrh.
14 His arms are like rounded bars of gold,
set with beryl.
His body is like bright ivory,
glowing with lapis lazuli.

15 His legs are like marble pillars
set in sockets of finest gold.
His posture is stately,
like the noble cedars of Lebanon.
16 His mouth is sweetness itself;
he is desirable in every way.
Such, O women of Jerusalem,
is my lover, my friend.

Young Women of Jerusalem

6 1 Where has your lover gone,
O woman of rare beauty?
Which way did he turn
so we can help you find him?

Young Woman

2 My lover has gone down to his garden,
to his spice beds,
to browse in the gardens
and gather the lilies.
3 I am my lover's, and my lover is mine.
He browses among the lilies.

Young Man

4 You are beautiful, my darling,
like the lovely city of Tirzah.
Yes, as beautiful as Jerusalem,
as majestic as an army with billowing banners.
5 Turn your eyes away,
for they overpower me.
Your hair falls in waves,
like a flock of goats winding down the slopes of Gilead.
6 Your teeth are as white as sheep
that are freshly washed.
Your smile is flawless,
each tooth matched with its twin.*
7 Your cheeks are like rosy pomegranates
behind your veil.

8 Even among sixty queens
and eighty concubines
and countless young women,
9 I would still choose my dove, my perfect one—
the favorite of her mother,
dearly loved by the one who bore her.
The young women see her and praise her;
even queens and royal concubines
sing her praises:
10 "Who is this, arising like the dawn,
as fair as the moon,
as bright as the sun,
as majestic as an army with billowing banners?"

Young Woman

11 I went down to the grove of walnut trees
and out to the valley to see the new spring growth,
to see whether the grapevines had budded
or the pomegranates were in bloom.
12 Before I realized it,
my strong desires had taken me to the chariot of a noble man.*

Young Women of Jerusalem

13* Return, return to us, O maid of Shulam.
Come back, come back, that we may see you again.

Young Man

Why do you stare at this young woman of Shulam,
as she moves so gracefully between two lines of dancers?*

7 1* How beautiful are your sandaled feet,
O queenly maiden.
Your rounded thighs are like jewels,
the work of a skilled craftsman.
2 Your navel is perfectly formed
like a goblet filled with mixed wine.
Between your thighs lies a mound of wheat
bordered with lilies.
3 Your breasts are like two fawns,
twin fawns of a gazelle.
4 Your neck is as beautiful as an ivory tower.
Your eyes are like the sparkling pools in Heshbon
by the gate of Bath-rabbim.
Your nose is as fine as the tower of Lebanon
overlooking Damascus.
5 Your head is as majestic as Mount Carmel,
and the sheen of your hair radiates royalty.
The king is held captive by its tresses.
6 Oh, how beautiful you are!
How pleasing, my love, how full of delights!

5:1 Hebrew *my sister;* also in 5:2. **6:6** Hebrew *Not one is missing; each has a twin.* **6:12** Or *to the royal chariots of my people,* or *to the chariots of Amminadab.* The meaning of the Hebrew is uncertain. **6:13a** Verse 6:13 is numbered 7:1 in Hebrew text. **6:13b** Or *as you would at the movements of two armies?* or *as you would at the dance of Mahanaim?* The meaning of the Hebrew is uncertain. **7:1** Verses 7:1-13 are numbered 7:2-14 in Hebrew text.

[7] You are slender like a palm tree,
and your breasts are like its clusters of fruit.
[8] I said, "I will climb the palm tree
and take hold of its fruit."
May your breasts be like grape clusters,
and the fragrance of your breath like apples.
[9] May your kisses be as exciting as the best wine—

Young Woman

Yes, wine that goes down smoothly for my lover,
flowing gently over lips and teeth.*
[10] I am my lover's,
and he claims me as his own.
[11] Come, my love, let us go out to the fields
and spend the night among the wildflowers.*
[12] Let us get up early and go to the vineyards
to see if the grapevines have budded,
if the blossoms have opened,
and if the pomegranates have bloomed.
There I will give you my love.
[13] There the mandrakes give off their fragrance,
and the finest fruits are at our door,
new delights as well as old,
which I have saved for you, my lover.

Young Woman

8

[1] Oh, I wish you were my brother,
who nursed at my mother's breasts.
Then I could kiss you no matter who was watching,
and no one would criticize me.
[2] I would bring you to my childhood home,
and there you would teach me.*
I would give you spiced wine to drink,
my sweet pomegranate wine.
[3] Your left arm would be under my head,
and your right arm would embrace me.
[4] Promise me, O women of Jerusalem,
not to awaken love until the time is right.*

Young Women of Jerusalem

[5] Who is this sweeping in from the desert,
leaning on her lover?

Young Woman

I aroused you under the apple tree,
where your mother gave you birth,
where in great pain she delivered you.
[6] Place me like a seal over your heart,
like a seal on your arm.
For love is as strong as death,
its jealousy* as enduring as the grave.*
Love flashes like fire,
the brightest kind of flame.
[7] Many waters cannot quench love,
nor can rivers drown it.
If a man tried to buy love
with all his wealth,
his offer would be utterly scorned.

The Young Woman's Brothers

[8] We have a little sister
too young to have breasts.
What will we do for our sister
if someone asks to marry her?
[9] If she is a virgin, like a wall,
we will protect her with a silver tower.
But if she is promiscuous, like a swinging door,
we will block her door with a cedar bar.

Young Woman

[10] I was a virgin, like a wall;
now my breasts are like towers.
When my lover looks at me,
he is delighted with what he sees.

[11] Solomon has a vineyard at Baal-hamon,
which he leases out to tenant farmers.
Each of them pays a thousand pieces of silver
for harvesting its fruit.
[12] But my vineyard is mine to give,
and Solomon need not pay a thousand pieces of silver.
But I will give two hundred pieces
to those who care for its vines.

Young Man

[13] O my darling, lingering in the gardens,
your companions are fortunate to hear your voice.
Let me hear it, too!

Young Woman

[14] Come away, my love! Be like a gazelle
or a young stag on the mountains of spices.

7:9 As in Greek and Syriac versions and Latin Vulgate; Hebrew reads *over lips of sleepers.* **7:11** Or *in the villages.* **8:2** Or *there she will teach me.* **8:4** Or *not to awaken love until it is ready.* **8:6a** Or *its passion.* **8:6b** Hebrew *as Sheol.*

Isaiah *Salvation comes from God alone*

With great privilege comes great responsibility. This message lies at the heart of Isaiah's prophecies to the people of Judah. Through increasing prosperity, they had become complacent in their walk with God, despite an outward show of religion. "The children I raised and cared for have rebelled against me. . . . They have despised the Holy One of Israel and turned their backs on him" (1:2-4). Therefore God's judgment was surely coming on them, Isaiah prophesied—not to destroy, but to purge and bring to repentance, so that God's people might become what he had always intended them to be: a light to the nations. At a time of political turmoil, they were not to look to other things or other nations for salvation; God alone is the one who saves, and a glorious future is assured for those who will trust in him, Isaiah announced.

What's it all about?

Isaiah was called to be a prophet in 740 BC, and his prophecies in chapters 1 to 39 cover the next forty years. He was a contemporary of Amos and Hosea (who prophesied to Israel) and Micah (who also prophesied to Judah), and they all addressed similar themes: people's abandoning their respect and love for God, and the impact that had on the very fabric of society. The rich were taking advantage of the poor, and rulers had no faith in God's ability to protect them. So, when Israel and Syria attacked Judah, King Ahaz made an alliance with godless Assyria to try to protect his country. But Assyria was a dangerous ally, and they eventually invaded Judah during the reign of Ahaz's son Hezekiah. Though Judah was miraculously delivered from the Assyrians, largely because of King Hezekiah's faith, Isaiah warned that a greater threat would come in the future from Babylon, the superpower that would supplant Assyria and exile Judah. This would be a sure sign of God's judgment because of Judah's failure to trust him.

Chapters 40 to 55 look ahead to events at the end of the Exile, over 150 years later—events Isaiah could not possibly have known about except by God's Spirit. These chapters offer hope and comfort, not only to the exiles but also to Isaiah's immediate audience. Chapters 56 to 66 look even further ahead to the situation of the exiles who returned to Judah. These are some of the most beautiful and stirring chapters in the Bible. Here Isaiah encouraged the people to leave their sin behind in light of all that God would do, for one day the whole world would see his glory. Isaiah's vision is so specific in parts that some think these long-range future prophecies must have been written later, in exile, by his disciples. However, for those who accept the reality of prophecy, no such suppositions are demanded. And the testimony of both Jewish intertestamental literature and the New Testament is that Isaiah was the book's sole author.

page 748

Isaiah is the longest of the prophetic books, and the one most frequently quoted in the New Testament, for his revelation was foundational to New Testament thinking about Jesus and salvation.

What does it mean for us?

Isaiah paints a big picture of God: glorious, holy, exalted, sovereign, righteous—and therefore utterly overwhelming, as he experienced in his vision of God's throne (chapter 6). It was perhaps this vision that led him to adopt his favorite title for God: "the Holy One of Israel" (used twenty-five times). And yet in that same vision he discovered that this holiness comes to cleanse and commission us, to restore us to God's purposes, making us the light to the nations that he had always planned for his people to be. But will we run from such a God (as Judah was doing) or to such a God (as Isaiah was calling them to do)?

Isaiah shows us that no matter how bad things get, God can, and will, redeem his people—though discipline may be part of that process. He described this restoration as nothing less than a new Exodus (e.g., 43:16-19), proclaiming that God wanted to do "*something new*" for his people (43:19) through a *new experience* of his Spirit (44:3) that would bring them into a *new covenant* (59:21) and result in God's Kingdom being established on the earth. All this would be brought about through the one whom God called "my servant"—one whom the New Testament identified as Jesus.

Isaiah reminds us of God's big plan for the world and invites us to deal with our sin so that we can be part of it.

▶ *See also* ***A timeline of the Bible****, pages A22-A24.*

OVERVIEW

THE BOOK OF THE KING

Judah's sin rebuked but hope promised · *1:1–5:30*

Isaiah's call to be a prophet *6:1-13*

Grace and hope for God's people *7:1–12:6*

God's judgment upon the nations *13:1–23:18*

Judgment and victory at the end of history · *24:1–27:13*

Sorrow announced for God's people *28:1–33:24*

Judgment and salvation *34:1–35:10*

A call to trust God in the face of an attack on Jerusalem · *36:1–38:22*

Hezekiah and the Babylonian envoys *39:1-8*

THE BOOK OF THE SERVANT

The future deliverance of Israel *40:1–48:22*

The Servant's role in Israel's glorious restoration · *49:1–55:13*

THE BOOK OF THE CONQUEROR

A call to come to God and live righteously · *56:1–59:15*

The coming of the anointed conqueror and the new creation · *59:15–66:24*

1 These are the visions that Isaiah son of
Amoz saw concerning Judah and Jerusalem. He saw these visions during the years
when Uzziah, Jotham, Ahaz, and Hezekiah
were kings of Judah.*

A Message for Rebellious Judah

2 Listen, O heavens! Pay attention, earth!
This is what the LORD says:
"The children I raised and cared for
have rebelled against me.
3 Even an ox knows its owner,
and a donkey recognizes its master's care—
but Israel doesn't know its master.
My people don't recognize my care for them."
4 Oh, what a sinful nation they are—
loaded down with a burden of guilt.
They are evil people,
corrupt children who have rejected the LORD.
They have despised the Holy One of Israel
and turned their backs on him.

5 Why do you continue to invite
punishment?
Must you rebel forever?
Your head is injured,
and your heart is sick.
6 You are battered from head to foot—
covered with bruises, welts, and
infected wounds—
without any soothing ointments or
bandages.
7 Your country lies in ruins,
and your towns are burned.
Foreigners plunder your fields before
your eyes
and destroy everything they see.
8 Beautiful Jerusalem* stands abandoned
like a watchman's shelter in a vineyard,
like a lean-to in a cucumber field after
the harvest,
like a helpless city under siege.
9 If the LORD of Heaven's Armies
had not spared a few of us,*
we would have been wiped out like
Sodom,
destroyed like Gomorrah.

10 Listen to the LORD, you leaders of
"Sodom."
Listen to the law of our God, people of
"Gomorrah."
11 "What makes you think I want all your
sacrifices?"
says the LORD.
"I am sick of your burnt offerings of
rams
and the fat of fattened cattle.
I get no pleasure from the blood
of bulls and lambs and goats.
12 When you come to worship me,
who asked you to parade through my
courts with all your ceremony?
13 Stop bringing me your meaningless gifts;
the incense of your offerings
disgusts me!
As for your celebrations of the new
moon and the Sabbath
and your special days for fasting—
they are all sinful and false.
I want no more of your pious meetings.
14 I hate your new moon celebrations and
your annual festivals.
They are a burden to me. I cannot
stand them!
15 When you lift up your hands in prayer,
I will not look.
Though you offer many prayers, I will
not listen,
for your hands are covered with the
blood of innocent victims.
16 Wash yourselves and be clean!
Get your sins out of my sight.
Give up your evil ways.
17 Learn to do good.
Seek justice.
Help the oppressed.
Defend the cause of orphans.
Fight for the rights of widows.

18 "Come now, let's settle this,"
says the LORD.
"Though your sins are like scarlet,
I will make them as white as snow.
Though they are red like crimson,
I will make them as white as wool.
19 If you will only obey me,
you will have plenty to eat.
20 But if you turn away and refuse to listen,
you will be devoured by the sword of
your enemies.
I, the LORD, have spoken!"

Unfaithful Jerusalem

21 See how Jerusalem, once so faithful,
has become a prostitute.
Once the home of justice and
righteousness,
she is now filled with murderers.
22 Once like pure silver,
you have become like worthless slag.
Once so pure,
you are now like watered-down wine.
23 Your leaders are rebels,
the companions of thieves.
All of them love bribes
and demand payoffs,
but they refuse to defend the cause of
orphans
or fight for the rights of widows.

24 Therefore, the Lord, the LORD of
Heaven's Armies,
the Mighty One of Israel, says,
"I will take revenge on my enemies
and pay back my foes!

1:1 These kings reigned from 792 to 686 B.C. **1:8** Hebrew *The daughter of Zion.* **1:9** Greek version reads *a few of our children.* Compare Rom 9:29.

▸ **1:17** *See **Widows**, page 400.*

25 I will raise my fist against you.
I will melt you down and skim off your slag.
I will remove all your impurities.
26 Then I will give you good judges again
and wise counselors like you used to have.
Then Jerusalem will again be called the Home of Justice
and the Faithful City."

27 Zion will be restored by justice;
those who repent will be revived by righteousness.
28 But rebels and sinners will be completely destroyed,
and those who desert the LORD will be consumed.

29 You will be ashamed of your idol worship
in groves of sacred oaks.
You will blush because you worshiped
in gardens dedicated to idols.
30 You will be like a great tree with withered leaves,
like a garden without water.
31 The strongest among you will disappear like straw;
their evil deeds will be the spark that sets it on fire.
They and their evil works will burn up together,
and no one will be able to put out the fire.

The LORD's Future Reign

2 This is a vision that Isaiah son of Amoz saw concerning Judah and Jerusalem:

2 In the last days, the mountain of the LORD's house
will be the highest of all—
the most important place on earth.
It will be raised above the other hills,
and people from all over the world
will stream there to worship.
3 People from many nations will come and say,
"Come, let us go up to the mountain of the LORD,
to the house of Jacob's God.
There he will teach us his ways,
and we will walk in his paths."
For the LORD's teaching will go out from Zion;
his word will go out from Jerusalem.
4 The LORD will mediate between nations
and will settle international disputes.
They will hammer their swords into plowshares
and their spears into pruning hooks.
Nation will no longer fight against nation,
nor train for war anymore.

A Warning of Judgment

5 Come, descendants of Jacob,
let us walk in the light of the LORD!
6 For the LORD has rejected his people,
the descendants of Jacob,
because they have filled their land with practices from the East
and with sorcerers, as the Philistines do.
They have made alliances with pagans.
7 Israel is full of silver and gold;
there is no end to its treasures.
Their land is full of warhorses;
there is no end to its chariots.
8 Their land is full of idols;

The Holy One of Israel

Isaiah's distinctive title for God—"the Holy One of Israel"—is found throughout his prophecy (e.g., Isaiah 1:4), though it occurs only seven times elsewhere in the whole Bible. It seems to have originated from his vision of God in his infinite holiness at his commissioning as a prophet (chapter 6), where the angels worshiped God as "holy, holy, holy"—a Hebrew way of saying "the holiest of all." And yet, here was the wonder: This holy, infinite, transcendent, incomparable God had given himself to little Israel. He was not just the Holy One, but the Holy One of Israel. And this holiness did not just confront Israel's sin; it dealt with it, even as it would deal with Isaiah's (6:6-7). As the one who is sovereign over all things, God is utterly able to do this, and none can resist him—not even his own people.

the people worship things they have made
with their own hands.
9 So now they will be humbled,
and all will be brought low—
do not forgive them.
10 Crawl into caves in the rocks.
Hide in the dust
from the terror of the LORD
and the glory of his majesty.
11 Human pride will be brought down,
and human arrogance will be humbled.
Only the LORD will be exalted
on that day of judgment.

12 For the LORD of Heaven's Armies
has a day of reckoning.
He will punish the proud and mighty
and bring down everything that is exalted.
13 He will cut down the tall cedars of Lebanon
and all the mighty oaks of Bashan.
14 He will level all the high mountains
and all the lofty hills.
15 He will break down every high tower
and every fortified wall.
16 He will destroy all the great trading ships*
and every magnificent vessel.
17 Human pride will be humbled,
and human arrogance will be brought down.
Only the LORD will be exalted
on that day of judgment.

18 Idols will completely disappear.
19 When the LORD rises to shake the earth,
his enemies will crawl into holes in the ground.
They will hide in caves in the rocks
from the terror of the LORD
and the glory of his majesty.
20 On that day of judgment they will
abandon the gold and silver idols
they made for themselves to worship.
They will leave their gods to the rodents and bats,
21 while they crawl away into caverns
and hide among the jagged rocks in the cliffs.
They will try to escape the terror of the LORD
and the glory of his majesty
as he rises to shake the earth.

22 Don't put your trust in mere humans.
They are as frail as breath.
What good are they?

Judgment against Judah

3 1 The Lord, the LORD of Heaven's Armies,
will take away from Jerusalem and Judah
everything they depend on:
every bit of bread
and every drop of water,
2 all their heroes and soldiers,
judges and prophets,
fortune-tellers and elders,
3 army officers and high officials,
advisers, skilled sorcerers, and astrologers.

4 I will make boys their leaders,
and toddlers their rulers.
5 People will oppress each other—
man against man,
neighbor against neighbor.
Young people will insult their elders,
and vulgar people will sneer at the honorable.

6 In those days a man will say to his brother,
"Since you have a coat, you be our leader!
Take charge of this heap of ruins!"
7 But he will reply,
"No! I can't help.
I don't have any extra food or clothes.
Don't put me in charge!"

8 For Jerusalem will stumble,
and Judah will fall,
because they speak out against the LORD
and refuse to obey him.
They provoke him to his face.
9 The very look on their faces gives them away.
They display their sin like the people of Sodom
and don't even try to hide it.
They are doomed!
They have brought destruction upon themselves.

10 Tell the godly that all will be well for them.
They will enjoy the rich reward they have earned!

2:16 Hebrew *every ship of Tarshish.*

11 But the wicked are doomed,
for they will get exactly what they deserve.

12 Childish leaders oppress my people,
and women rule over them.
O my people, your leaders mislead you;
they send you down the wrong road.
13 The LORD takes his place in court
and presents his case against his people.*
14 The LORD comes forward to pronounce judgment
on the elders and rulers of his people:
"You have ruined Israel, my vineyard.
Your houses are filled with things stolen from the poor.
15 How dare you crush my people,
grinding the faces of the poor into the dust?"
demands the Lord, the LORD of Heaven's Armies.

A Warning to Jerusalem

16 The LORD says, "Beautiful Zion* is haughty:
craning her elegant neck,
flirting with her eyes,
walking with dainty steps,
tinkling her ankle bracelets.
17 So the Lord will send scabs on her head;
the LORD will make beautiful Zion bald."

18 On that day of judgment
the Lord will strip away everything that makes her beautiful:
ornaments, headbands, crescent necklaces,
19 earrings, bracelets, and veils;
20 scarves, ankle bracelets, sashes,
perfumes, and charms;
21 rings, jewels,
22 party clothes, gowns, capes, and purses;
23 mirrors, fine linen garments,
head ornaments, and shawls.
24 Instead of smelling of sweet perfume,
she will stink.
She will wear a rope for a sash,
and her elegant hair will fall out.
She will wear rough burlap instead of rich robes.
Shame will replace her beauty.*
25 The men of the city will be killed with the sword,
and her warriors will die in battle.
26 The gates of Zion will weep and mourn.
The city will be like a ravaged woman,
huddled on the ground.

4 In that day so few men will be left that
seven women will fight for each man,
saying, "Let us all marry you! We will
provide our own food and clothing. Only let
us take your name so we won't be mocked
as old maids."

A Promise of Restoration

2 But in that day, the branch* of the LORD
will be beautiful and glorious;
the fruit of the land will be the pride and glory
of all who survive in Israel.
3 All who remain in Zion
will be a holy people—
those who survive the destruction of Jerusalem
and are recorded among the living.
4 The Lord will wash the filth from beautiful Zion*
and cleanse Jerusalem of its bloodstains
with the hot breath of fiery judgment.
5 Then the LORD will provide shade for Mount Zion
and all who assemble there.
He will provide a canopy of cloud during the day
and smoke and flaming fire at night,
covering the glorious land.
6 It will be a shelter from daytime heat
and a hiding place from storms and rain.

A Song about the LORD's Vineyard

5 1 Now I will sing for the one I love
a song about his vineyard:
My beloved had a vineyard
on a rich and fertile hill.
2 He plowed the land, cleared its stones,
and planted it with the best vines.

▸ **3:13-15** *See **Poverty**, page 1142.*
5:1 *See **Prophecy in the Old Testament**, page 903; **Grapevines and vineyards**, page 913.*

In the middle he built a watchtower
and carved a winepress in the nearby rocks.
Then he waited for a harvest of sweet grapes,
but the grapes that grew were bitter.

3 Now, you people of Jerusalem and Judah,
you judge between me and my vineyard.
4 What more could I have done for my vineyard
that I have not already done?
When I expected sweet grapes,
why did my vineyard give me bitter grapes?

5 Now let me tell you
what I will do to my vineyard:
I will tear down its hedges
and let it be destroyed.
I will break down its walls
and let the animals trample it.
6 I will make it a wild place
where the vines are not pruned and the ground is not hoed,
a place overgrown with briers and thorns.
I will command the clouds
to drop no rain on it.

7 The nation of Israel is the vineyard of the LORD of Heaven's Armies.
The people of Judah are his pleasant garden.
He expected a crop of justice,
but instead he found oppression.
He expected to find righteousness,
but instead he heard cries of violence.

Judah's Guilt and Judgment

8 What sorrow for you who buy up house after house and field after field,
until everyone is evicted and you live alone in the land.
9 But I have heard the LORD of Heaven's Armies
swear a solemn oath:
"Many houses will stand deserted;
even beautiful mansions will be empty.
10 Ten acres* of vineyard will not produce
even six gallons* of wine.
Ten baskets of seed will yield only one basket* of grain."

11 What sorrow for those who get up early in the morning
looking for a drink of alcohol
and spend long evenings drinking wine
to make themselves flaming drunk.
12 They furnish wine and lovely music at their grand parties—
lyre and harp, tambourine and flute—
but they never think about the LORD
or notice what he is doing.

13 So my people will go into exile far away
because they do not know me.
Those who are great and honored will starve,
and the common people will die of thirst.
14 The grave* is licking its lips in anticipation,
opening its mouth wide.
The great and the lowly
and all the drunken mob will be swallowed up.
15 Humanity will be destroyed, and people brought down;
even the arrogant will lower their eyes in humiliation.
16 But the LORD of Heaven's Armies will be exalted by his justice.
The holiness of God will be displayed by his righteousness.
17 In that day lambs will find good pastures,
and fattened sheep and young goats* will feed among the ruins.

18 What sorrow for those who drag their sins behind them
with ropes made of lies,
who drag wickedness behind them like a cart!
19 They even mock God and say,
"Hurry up and do something!
We want to see what you can do.
Let the Holy One of Israel carry out his plan,
for we want to know what it is."

3:13 As in Greek and Syriac versions; Hebrew reads *against the peoples.* **3:16** Or *The women of Zion* (with corresponding changes to plural forms through verse 24); Hebrew reads *The daughters of Zion;* also in 3:17. **3:24** As in Dead Sea Scrolls; Masoretic Text reads *robes / because instead of beauty.* **4:2** Or *the Branch.* **4:4** Or *from the women of Zion;* Hebrew reads *from the daughters of Zion.* **5:10a** Hebrew *A ten yoke,* that is, the area of land plowed by ten teams of oxen in one day. **5:10b** Hebrew *a bath* [21 liters]. **5:10c** Hebrew *A homer* [5 bushels or 220 liters] *of seed will yield only an ephah* [20 quarts or 22 liters]. **5:14** Hebrew *Sheol.* **5:17** As in Greek version; Hebrew reads *and strangers.*

20 What sorrow for those who say
that evil is good and good is evil,
that dark is light and light is dark,
that bitter is sweet and sweet is bitter.
21 What sorrow for those who are wise in their own eyes
and think themselves so clever.
22 What sorrow for those who are heroes at drinking wine
and boast about all the alcohol they can hold.
23 They take bribes to let the wicked go free,
and they punish the innocent.

24 Therefore, just as fire licks up stubble
and dry grass shrivels in the flame,
so their roots will rot
and their flowers wither.
For they have rejected the law of the LORD of Heaven's Armies;
they have despised the word of the Holy One of Israel.
25 That is why the LORD's anger burns against his people,
and why he has raised his fist to crush them.
The mountains tremble,
and the corpses of his people litter the streets like garbage.
But even then the LORD's anger is not satisfied.
His fist is still poised to strike!

26 He will send a signal to distant nations far away
and whistle to those at the ends of the earth.
They will come racing toward Jerusalem.
27 They will not get tired or stumble.
They will not stop for rest or sleep.
Not a belt will be loose,
not a sandal strap broken.
28 Their arrows will be sharp
and their bows ready for battle.
Sparks will fly from their horses' hooves,
and the wheels of their chariots will spin like a whirlwind.
29 They will roar like lions,
like the strongest of lions.
Growling, they will pounce on their victims and carry them off,
and no one will be there to rescue them.
30 They will roar over their victims on that day of destruction
like the roaring of the sea.
If someone looks across the land,
only darkness and distress will be seen;
even the light will be darkened by clouds.

The holiness of God

Chapter 6 records Isaiah's call to prophetic ministry. In 740 BC King Uzziah (also called Azariah), a godly and powerful king who had reigned for fifty-two years, died. But God wanted Isaiah to know that although the king of Judah had died, the King of kings was still on his throne and still in control. And this king was unlike any other. What made him different was his holiness. Holiness is that aspect of God's nature that marks him out as utterly different from everyone and everything else, that separates him from anything imperfect or impure, and that drives him to act to put things right. This holiness calls people to be holy (Leviticus 11:45), yet also makes them holy (Leviticus 20:8), as Isaiah discovered that day when, in response to his acknowledgment of his sinfulness, a coal from the altar touched his lips to cleanse him (Isaiah 6:6-7). This encounter with God's holiness led Isaiah to adopt the name for God "the Holy One of Israel" (see *The Holy One of Israel*, page 750).

This incident shows that holiness begins, not with our human efforts to live better lives, but with an encounter with the living God. Only he can make us truly holy.

▸ *See also* ***Holiness****, page 128.*

Isaiah's Cleansing and Call

6 It was in the year King Uzziah died*
that I saw the Lord. He was sitting on a
lofty throne, and the train of his robe filled
the Temple. [2]Attending him were mighty
seraphim, each having six wings. With two
wings they covered their faces, with two
they covered their feet, and with two they
flew. [3]They were calling out to each other,

"Holy, holy, holy is the LORD of Heaven's
Armies!
The whole earth is filled with his
glory!"

[4]Their voices shook the Temple to its foundations, and the entire building was filled
with smoke.
[5]Then I said, "It's all over! I am doomed,
for I am a sinful man. I have filthy lips, and I
live among a people with filthy lips. Yet I have
seen the King, the LORD of Heaven's Armies."
[6]Then one of the seraphim flew to me with
a burning coal he had taken from the altar
with a pair of tongs. [7]He touched my lips
with it and said, "See, this coal has touched
your lips. Now your guilt is removed, and
your sins are forgiven."
[8]Then I heard the Lord asking, "Whom
should I send as a messenger to this people?
Who will go for us?"
I said, "Here I am. Send me."
[9]And he said, "Yes, go, and say to this
people,

'Listen carefully, but do not understand.
Watch closely, but learn nothing.'
10 Harden the hearts of these people.
Plug their ears and shut their eyes.
That way, they will not see with their
eyes,
nor hear with their ears,
nor understand with their hearts
and turn to me for healing."*

[11]Then I said, "Lord, how long will this
go on?"
And he replied,

"Until their towns are empty,
their houses are deserted,
and the whole country is a wasteland;
12 until the LORD has sent everyone away,
and the entire land of Israel lies
deserted.
13 If even a tenth—a remnant—survive,
it will be invaded again and burned.
But as a terebinth or oak tree leaves a
stump when it is cut down,
so Israel's stump will be a holy seed."

A Message for Ahaz

7 When Ahaz, son of Jotham and grandson of Uzziah, was king of Judah, King
Rezin of Syria* and Pekah son of Remaliah,
the king of Israel, set out to attack Jerusalem. However, they were unable to carry out
their plan.
[2]The news had come to the royal court of
Judah: "Syria is allied with Israel* against
us!" So the hearts of the king and his people
trembled with fear, like trees shaking in a
storm.
[3]Then the LORD said to Isaiah, "Take your
son Shear-jashub* and go out to meet King
Ahaz. You will find him at the end of the aqueduct that feeds water into the upper pool,
near the road leading to the field where
cloth is washed.* [4]Tell him to stop worrying.
Tell him he doesn't need to fear the fierce
anger of those two burned-out embers, King
Rezin of Syria and Pekah son of Remaliah.
[5]Yes, the kings of Syria and Israel are plotting against him, saying, [6]'We will attack
Judah and capture it for ourselves. Then
we will install the son of Tabeel as Judah's
king.' [7]But this is what the Sovereign LORD
says:

"This invasion will never happen;
it will never take place;
8 for Syria is no stronger than its capital,
Damascus,
and Damascus is no stronger than its
king, Rezin.
As for Israel, within sixty-five years
it will be crushed and completely
destroyed.
9 Israel is no stronger than its capital,
Samaria,

6:1 King Uzziah died in 740 B.C. **6:9-10** Greek version reads *And he said, "Go and say to this people, / 'When you hear what I say, you will not understand. / When you see what I do, you will not comprehend.' / For the hearts of these people are hardened, / and their ears cannot hear, and they have closed their eyes— / so their eyes cannot see, / and their ears cannot hear, / and their hearts cannot understand, / and they cannot turn to me and let me heal them."* Compare Matt 13:14-15; Mark 4:12; Luke 8:10; Acts 28:26-27. **7:1** Hebrew *Aram;* also in 7:2, 4, 5, 8. **7:2** Hebrew *Ephraim,* referring to the northern kingdom of Israel; also in 7:5, 8, 9, 17. **7:3a** *Shear-jashub* means "A remnant will return." **7:3b** Or *bleached.*

▸ **6:1-5** *See **Glory**, page 946.*

and Samaria is no stronger than its
king, Pekah son of Remaliah.
Unless your faith is firm,
I cannot make you stand firm."

The Sign of Immanuel

10Later, the LORD sent this message to King
Ahaz: 11"Ask the LORD your God for a sign of
confirmation, Ahaz. Make it as difficult as
you want—as high as heaven or as deep as
the place of the dead.*"
12But the king refused. "No," he said, "I
will not test the LORD like that."
13Then Isaiah said, "Listen well, you royal
family of David! Isn't it enough to exhaust
human patience? Must you exhaust the patience of my God as well? 14All right then, the
Lord himself will give you the sign. Look!
The virgin* will conceive a child! She will
give birth to a son and will call him Immanuel (which means 'God is with us'). 15By the
time this child is old enough to choose what
is right and reject what is wrong, he will be
eating yogurt* and honey. 16For before the
child is that old, the lands of the two kings
you fear so much will both be deserted.
17"Then the LORD will bring things on you,
your nation, and your family unlike anything since Israel broke away from Judah.
He will bring the king of Assyria upon you!"
18In that day the LORD will whistle for the
army of southern Egypt and for the army of
Assyria. They will swarm around you like
flies and bees. 19They will come in vast hordes
and settle in the fertile areas and also in the
desolate valleys, caves, and thorny places.
20In that day the Lord will hire a "razor" from
beyond the Euphrates River*—the king of Assyria—and use it to shave off everything: your
land, your crops, and your people.*
21In that day a farmer will be fortunate
to have a cow and two sheep or goats left.
22Nevertheless, there will be enough milk for
everyone because so few people will be left
in the land. They will eat their fill of yogurt
and honey. 23In that day the lush vineyards,
now worth 1,000 pieces of silver,* will
become patches of briers and thorns. 24The
entire land will become a vast expanse of
briers and thorns, a hunting ground overrun
by wildlife. 25No one will go to the fertile
hillsides where the gardens once grew, for
briers and thorns will cover them. Cattle,
sheep, and goats will graze there.

The Coming Assyrian Invasion

8 Then the LORD said to me, "Make a
large signboard and clearly write this
name on it: Maher-shalal-hash-baz.*" 2I
asked Uriah the priest and Zechariah son of
Jeberekiah, both known as honest men, to
witness my doing this.
3Then I slept with my wife, and she
became pregnant and gave birth to a son.
And the LORD said, "Call him Maher-shalal-
hash-baz. 4For before this child is old
enough to say 'Papa' or 'Mama,' the king of
Assyria will carry away both the abundance
of Damascus and the riches of Samaria."
5Then the LORD spoke to me again and
said, 6"My care for the people of Judah is
like the gently flowing waters of Shiloah, but

Immanuel

King Ahaz was afraid when Syria and Israel pressured him to join their coalition against Assyria (Isaiah 7:1-2); but Isaiah told him to trust in God, and offered him a sign of confirmation. Ahaz refused to "test the LORD" (7:12); but Isaiah saw through his sham spirituality and gave him a sign anyway. Pointing to a young woman, he declared, "The virgin will conceive a child! She will give birth to a son and will call him Immanuel (which means 'God is with us')" (7:14). He added that before the child was old enough to discern right and wrong, the threat from Syria and Israel would have passed. And indeed it did; Assyria conquered Syria in 732 BC and Israel in 722 BC.

While Isaiah was prophesying about a young woman at the court and the years ahead (as 7:17-25 shows), the early church quickly saw this as also being prophetic of the birth of Jesus (Matthew 1:22-23).

▶ *See **Prophecies about Christ**, page 806.*

they have rejected it. They are rejoicing over
what will happen to* King Rezin and King
Pekah.* 7 Therefore, the Lord will overwhelm
them with a mighty flood from the Euphrates
River*—the king of Assyria and all his glory.
This flood will overflow all its channels 8 and
sweep into Judah until it is chin deep. It will
spread its wings, submerging your land from
one end to the other, O Immanuel.

9 "Huddle together, you nations, and be terrified.
Listen, all you distant lands.
Prepare for battle, but you will be crushed!
Yes, prepare for battle, but you will be crushed!
10 Call your councils of war, but they will be worthless.
Develop your strategies, but they will not succeed.
For God is with us!*"

A Call to Trust the LORD

11 The LORD has given me a strong warning not to think like everyone else does. He said,

12 "Don't call everything a conspiracy, like they do,
and don't live in dread of what frightens them.
13 Make the LORD of Heaven's Armies holy in your life.
He is the one you should fear.
He is the one who should make you tremble.
14 He will keep you safe.
But to Israel and Judah
he will be a stone that makes people stumble,
a rock that makes them fall.
And for the people of Jerusalem
he will be a trap and a snare.
15 Many will stumble and fall,
never to rise again.
They will be snared and captured."
16 Preserve the teaching of God;
entrust his instructions to those who follow me.
17 I will wait for the LORD,
who has turned away from the descendants of Jacob.
I will put my hope in him.

18 I and the children the LORD has given
me serve as signs and warnings to Israel
from the LORD of Heaven's Armies who
dwells in his Temple on Mount Zion.
19 Someone may say to you, "Let's ask
the mediums and those who consult the
spirits of the dead. With their whisperings
and mutterings, they will tell us what to
do." But shouldn't people ask God for guidance? Should the living seek guidance from
the dead?
20 Look to God's instructions and teachings! People who contradict his word are
completely in the dark. 21 They will go from
one place to another, weary and hungry.
And because they are hungry, they will rage
and curse their king and their God. They
will look up to heaven 22 and down at the
earth, but wherever they look, there will be
trouble and anguish and dark despair. They
will be thrown out into the darkness.

Hope in the Messiah

9 1* Nevertheless, that time of darkness
and despair will not go on forever.
The land of Zebulun and Naphtali will be
humbled, but there will be a time in the
future when Galilee of the Gentiles, which
lies along the road that runs between the
Jordan and the sea, will be filled with glory.

2* The people who walk in darkness
will see a great light.
For those who live in a land of deep darkness,*
a light will shine.
3 You will enlarge the nation of Israel,
and its people will rejoice.
They will rejoice before you
as people rejoice at the harvest
and like warriors dividing the plunder.
4 For you will break the yoke of their slavery
and lift the heavy burden from their shoulders.

7:11 Hebrew *as deep as Sheol.* **7:14** Or *young woman.* **7:15** Or *curds;* also in 7:22. **7:20a** Hebrew *the river.* **7:20b** Hebrew *shave off the head, the hair of the legs, and the beard.* **7:23** Hebrew *1,000 [shekels] of silver,* about 25 pounds or 11.4 kilograms in weight. **8:1** *Maher-shalal-hash-baz* means "Swift to plunder and quick to carry away." **8:6a** Or *They are rejoicing because of.* **8:6b** Hebrew *and the son of Remaliah.* **8:7** Hebrew *the river.* **8:10** Hebrew *Immanuel!* **9:1** Verse 9:1 is numbered 8:23 in Hebrew text. **9:2a** Verses 9:2-21 are numbered 9:1-20 in Hebrew text. **9:2b** Greek version reads *a land where death casts its shadow.* Compare Matt 4:16.

▸ **8:19** *See **The occult**, page 337.*

You will break the oppressor's rod,
just as you did when you destroyed
the army of Midian.
5 The boots of the warrior
and the uniforms bloodstained by war
will all be burned.
They will be fuel for the fire.
6 For a child is born to us,
a son is given to us.
The government will rest on his
shoulders.
And he will be called:
Wonderful Counselor,* Mighty God,
Everlasting Father, Prince of Peace.
7 His government and its peace
will never end.
He will rule with fairness and justice
from the throne of his ancestor
David
for all eternity.
The passionate commitment of the LORD
of Heaven's Armies
will make this happen!

The LORD's Anger against Israel

8 The Lord has spoken out against Jacob;
his judgment has fallen upon Israel.
9 And the people of Israel* and
Samaria,
who spoke with such pride and
arrogance,
will soon know it.
10 They said, "We will replace the broken
bricks of our ruins with finished
stone,
and replant the felled sycamore-fig
trees with cedars."
11 But the LORD will bring Rezin's enemies
against Israel
and stir up all their foes.
12 The Syrians* from the east and the
Philistines from the west
will bare their fangs and devour
Israel.
But even then the LORD's anger will not
be satisfied.
His fist is still poised to strike.
13 For after all this punishment, the people
will still not repent.
They will not seek the LORD of
Heaven's Armies.
14 Therefore, in a single day the LORD will
destroy both the head and the tail,
the noble palm branch and the lowly
reed.
15 The leaders of Israel are the head,
and the lying prophets are the tail.
16 For the leaders of the people have
misled them.
They have led them down the path of
destruction.
17 That is why the Lord takes no pleasure
in the young men
and shows no mercy even to the
widows and orphans.
For they are all wicked hypocrites,
and they all speak foolishness.
But even then the LORD's anger will not
be satisfied.
His fist is still poised to strike.
18 This wickedness is like a brushfire.
It burns not only briers and thorns
but also sets the forests ablaze.
Its burning sends up clouds of smoke.
19 The land will be blackened
by the fury of the LORD of Heaven's
Armies.
The people will be fuel for the fire,
and no one will spare even his own
brother.
20 They will attack their neighbor on the
right
but will still be hungry.
They will devour their neighbor on the
left
but will not be satisfied.
In the end they will even eat their own
children.*
21 Manasseh will feed on Ephraim,
Ephraim will feed on Manasseh,
and both will devour Judah.
But even then the LORD's anger will not
be satisfied.
His fist is still poised to strike.

10 1 What sorrow awaits the unjust
judges
and those who issue unfair laws.
2 They deprive the poor of justice
and deny the rights of the needy
among my people.
They prey on widows
and take advantage of orphans.

▸ **10:1** *See* ***Injustice****, page 811.*

[3] What will you do when I punish you,
when I send disaster upon you from a distant land?
To whom will you turn for help?
Where will your treasures be safe?
[4] You will stumble along as prisoners
or lie among the dead.
But even then the LORD's anger will not be satisfied.
His fist is still poised to strike.

Judgment against Assyria

[5] "What sorrow awaits Assyria, the rod of my anger.
I use it as a club to express my anger.
[6] I am sending Assyria against a godless nation,
against a people with whom I am angry.
Assyria will plunder them,
trampling them like dirt beneath its feet.
[7] But the king of Assyria will not
understand that he is my tool;
his mind does not work that way.
His plan is simply to destroy,
to cut down nation after nation.
[8] He will say,
'Each of my princes will soon be a king.
[9] We destroyed Calno just as we did Carchemish.
Hamath fell before us as Arpad did.
And we destroyed Samaria just as we did Damascus.
[10] Yes, we have finished off many a kingdom
whose gods were greater than those in Jerusalem and Samaria.
[11] So we will defeat Jerusalem and her gods,
just as we destroyed Samaria with hers.'"

[12] After the Lord has used the king of Assyria to accomplish his purposes on Mount Zion and in Jerusalem, he will turn against the king of Assyria and punish him—for he is proud and arrogant. [13] He boasts,

"By my own powerful arm I have done this.
With my own shrewd wisdom I planned it.
I have broken down the defenses of nations
and carried off their treasures.
I have knocked down their kings like a bull.
[14] I have robbed their nests of riches
and gathered up kingdoms as a farmer gathers eggs.
No one can even flap a wing against me
or utter a peep of protest."
[15] But can the ax boast greater power than
the person who uses it?
Is the saw greater than the person who saws?
Can a rod strike unless a hand moves it?
Can a wooden cane walk by itself?
[16] Therefore, the Lord, the LORD of Heaven's Armies,
will send a plague among Assyria's proud troops,
and a flaming fire will consume its glory.
[17] The LORD, the Light of Israel, will be a fire;
the Holy One will be a flame.
He will devour the thorns and briers with fire,
burning up the enemy in a single night.
[18] The LORD will consume Assyria's glory
like a fire consumes a forest in a fruitful land;
it will waste away like sick people in a plague.
[19] Of all that glorious forest, only a few trees will survive—
so few that a child could count them!

Hope for the LORD's People

[20] In that day the remnant left in Israel,
the survivors in the house of Jacob,
will no longer depend on allies
who seek to destroy them.
But they will faithfully trust the LORD,
the Holy One of Israel.
[21] A remnant will return;*
yes, the remnant of Jacob will return
to the Mighty God.
[22] But though the people of Israel are as numerous
as the sand of the seashore,
only a remnant of them will return.
The LORD has rightly decided to destroy his people.

9:6 Or *Wonderful, Counselor.* **9:9** Hebrew *of Ephraim,* referring to the northern kingdom of Israel. **9:12** Hebrew *Arameans.* **9:20** Or *eat their own arms.* **10:21** Hebrew *Shear-jashub;* see 7:3; 8:18.

23 Yes, the Lord, the LORD of Heaven's
Armies,
has already decided to destroy the
entire land.*

24 So this is what the Lord, the LORD of
Heaven's Armies, says: "O my people in
Zion, do not be afraid of the Assyrians when
they oppress you with rod and club as the
Egyptians did long ago.
25 In a little while
my anger against you will end, and then my
anger will rise up to destroy them."
26 The
LORD of Heaven's Armies will lash them
with his whip, as he did when Gideon triumphed over the Midianites at the rock of
Oreb, or when the LORD's staff was raised to
drown the Egyptian army in the sea.

27 In that day the LORD will end the
bondage of his people.
He will break the yoke of slavery
and lift it from their shoulders.*

28 Look, the Assyrians are now at Aiath.
They are passing through Migron
and are storing their equipment at
Micmash.
29 They are crossing the pass
and are camping at Geba.
Fear strikes the town of Ramah.
All the people of Gibeah, the
hometown of Saul,
are running for their lives.
30 Scream in terror,
you people of Gallim!
Shout out a warning to Laishah.
Oh, poor Anathoth!
31 There go the people of Madmenah, all
fleeing.
The citizens of Gebim are trying to
hide.
32 The enemy stops at Nob for the rest of
that day.
He shakes his fist at beautiful Mount
Zion, the mountain of Jerusalem.

33 But look! The Lord, the LORD of Heaven's
Armies,
will chop down the mighty tree of
Assyria with great power!
He will cut down the proud.
That lofty tree will be brought
down.
34 He will cut down the forest trees with
an ax.
Lebanon will fall to the Mighty One.*

A Branch from David's Line

11
1 Out of the stump of David's
family* will grow a shoot—
yes, a new Branch bearing fruit from
the old root.
2 And the Spirit of the LORD will rest on
him—
the Spirit of wisdom and
understanding,
the Spirit of counsel and might,
the Spirit of knowledge and the fear
of the LORD.

The Branch

Having portrayed the destruction of human arrogance as the felling of a mighty forest (Isaiah 10:33-34), Isaiah now inverted the picture (11:1). God's people would soon look like a tree cut down to the point where it could never grow again (a prophecy fulfilled in 586 BC when Babylon invaded and destroyed Jerusalem); yet God would turn things around. Isaiah saw a shoot springing out of the tree stump that was left, and a branch growing from it—the same "beautiful and glorious" branch he had seen spring up in chapter 4 and which led to the restoration of God's people.

What Isaiah was seeing was the restoration of David's kingdom under a Spirit-filled king (11:2) whose reign would bring about righteousness (11:3-5), peace (11:6-16), and joy (12:1-6). But in chapter 53 he saw even more: The branch that would spring up (53:2) would bring this about at the price of his own suffering and death (53:3-12).

Isaiah was seeing nothing less than the person and work of Jesus the Messiah—over seven hundred years before he came to earth.

3 He will delight in obeying the LORD.
He will not judge by appearance
nor make a decision based on hearsay.
4 He will give justice to the poor
and make fair decisions for the exploited.
The earth will shake at the force of his word,
and one breath from his mouth will destroy the wicked.
5 He will wear righteousness like a belt
and truth like an undergarment.

6 In that day the wolf and the lamb will live together;
the leopard will lie down with the baby goat.
The calf and the yearling will be safe with the lion,
and a little child will lead them all.
7 The cow will graze near the bear.
The cub and the calf will lie down together.
The lion will eat hay like a cow.
8 The baby will play safely near the hole of a cobra.
Yes, a little child will put its hand in a nest of deadly snakes without harm.
9 Nothing will hurt or destroy in all my holy mountain,
for as the waters fill the sea,
so the earth will be filled with people who know the LORD.

10 In that day the heir to David's throne*
will be a banner of salvation to all the world.
The nations will rally to him,
and the land where he lives will be a glorious place.*
11 In that day the Lord will reach out his hand a second time
to bring back the remnant of his people—
those who remain in Assyria and northern Egypt;
in southern Egypt, Ethiopia,* and Elam;
in Babylonia,* Hamath, and all the distant coastlands.
12 He will raise a flag among the nations
and assemble the exiles of Israel.
He will gather the scattered people of Judah
from the ends of the earth.
13 Then at last the jealousy between Israel* and Judah will end.
They will not be rivals anymore.
14 They will join forces to swoop down on Philistia to the west.
Together they will attack and plunder the nations to the east.
They will occupy the lands of Edom and Moab,
and Ammon will obey them.
15 The LORD will make a dry path through the gulf of the Red Sea.*
He will wave his hand over the Euphrates River,*
sending a mighty wind to divide it into seven streams
so it can easily be crossed on foot.
16 He will make a highway for the remnant of his people,
the remnant coming from Assyria,
just as he did for Israel long ago
when they returned from Egypt.

Songs of Praise for Salvation

12 1 In that day you will sing:
"I will praise you, O LORD!
You were angry with me, but not any more.
Now you comfort me.
2 See, God has come to save me.
I will trust in him and not be afraid.
The LORD GOD is my strength and my song;
he has given me victory."

3 With joy you will drink deeply
from the fountain of salvation!
4 In that wonderful day you will sing:
"Thank the LORD! Praise his name!
Tell the nations what he has done.
Let them know how mighty he is!
5 Sing to the LORD, for he has done wonderful things.
Make known his praise around the world.

10:22-23 Greek version reads *only a remnant of them will be saved. / For he will carry out his sentence quickly and with finality and righteousness; / for God will carry out his sentence upon all the world with finality.* Compare Rom 9:27-28. **10:27** As in Greek version; Hebrew reads *The yoke will be broken, / for you have grown so fat.* **10:34** Or *with an ax / as even the mighty trees of Lebanon fall.* **11:1** Hebrew *the stump of the line of Jesse.* Jesse was King David's father. **11:10a** Hebrew *the root of Jesse.* **11:10b** Greek version reads *In that day the heir to David's throne* [literally *the root of Jesse*] *will come, / and he will rule over the Gentiles. / They will place their hopes on him.* Compare Rom 15:12. **11:11a** Hebrew *in Pathros, Cush.* **11:11b** Hebrew *in Shinar.* **11:13** Hebrew *Ephraim,* referring to the northern kingdom of Israel. **11:15a** Hebrew *will destroy the tongue of the sea of Egypt.* **11:15b** Hebrew *the river.*

6 Let all the people of Jerusalem* shout
his praise with joy!
For great is the Holy One of Israel who
lives among you."

A Message about Babylon

13 Isaiah son of Amoz received this message concerning the destruction of Babylon:

2 "Raise a signal flag on a bare hilltop.
Call up an army against Babylon.
Wave your hand to encourage them
as they march into the palaces of the
high and mighty.
3 I, the LORD, have dedicated these
soldiers for this task.
Yes, I have called mighty warriors to
express my anger,
and they will rejoice when I am
exalted."
4 Hear the noise on the mountains!
Listen, as the vast armies march!
It is the noise and shouting of many
nations.
The LORD of Heaven's Armies has
called this army together.
5 They come from distant countries,
from beyond the farthest horizons.
They are the LORD's weapons to carry
out his anger.
With them he will destroy the whole
land.

6 Scream in terror, for the day of the LORD
has arrived—
the time for the Almighty to destroy.
7 Every arm is paralyzed with fear.
Every heart melts,
8 and people are terrified.
Pangs of anguish grip them,
like those of a woman in labor.
They look helplessly at one another,
their faces aflame with fear.

9 For see, the day of the LORD is coming—
the terrible day of his fury and fierce
anger.
The land will be made desolate,
and all the sinners destroyed with it.
10 The heavens will be black above
them;
the stars will give no light.
The sun will be dark when it rises,
and the moon will provide no light.
11 "I, the LORD, will punish the world for
its evil
and the wicked for their sin.
I will crush the arrogance of the proud
and humble the pride of the mighty.
12 I will make people scarcer than gold—
more rare than the fine gold of
Ophir.
13 For I will shake the heavens.
The earth will move from its place
when the LORD of Heaven's Armies
displays his wrath
in the day of his fierce anger."

14 Everyone in Babylon will run about like
a hunted gazelle,
like sheep without a shepherd.
They will try to find their own people
and flee to their own land.
15 Anyone who is captured will be cut
down—
run through with a sword.
16 Their little children will be dashed to
death before their eyes.
Their homes will be sacked, and their
wives will be raped.

17 "Look, I will stir up the Medes against
Babylon.
They cannot be tempted by silver
or bribed with gold.
18 The attacking armies will shoot down
the young men with arrows.
They will have no mercy on helpless
babies
and will show no compassion for
children."

19 Babylon, the most glorious of kingdoms,
the flower of Chaldean pride,
will be devastated like Sodom and
Gomorrah
when God destroyed them.
20 Babylon will never be inhabited again.
It will remain empty for generation
after generation.
Nomads will refuse to camp there,
and shepherds will not bed down
their sheep.
21 Desert animals will move into the ruined
city,

▸ **13:6** *See* ***The day of the LORD****, page 988.*

and the houses will be haunted by
howling creatures.
Owls will live among the ruins,
and wild goats will go there to dance.
22 Hyenas will howl in its fortresses,
and jackals will make dens in its
luxurious palaces.
Babylon's days are numbered;
its time of destruction will soon arrive.

A Taunt for Babylon's King

14 But the LORD will have mercy on the
descendants of Jacob. He will choose
Israel as his special people once again. He
will bring them back to settle once again in
their own land. And people from many different nations will come and join them there
and unite with the people of Israel.* 2 The
nations of the world will help the people of
Israel to return, and those who come to live
in the LORD's land will serve them. Those
who captured Israel will themselves be captured, and Israel will rule over its enemies.
3 In that wonderful day when the LORD
gives his people rest from sorrow and fear,
from slavery and chains, 4 you will taunt the
king of Babylon. You will say,

"The mighty man has been destroyed.
Yes, your insolence* is ended.
5 For the LORD has crushed your wicked
power
and broken your evil rule.
6 You struck the people with endless
blows of rage
and held the nations in your angry
grip
with unrelenting tyranny.
7 But finally the earth is at rest and quiet.
Now it can sing again!
8 Even the trees of the forest—
the cypress trees and the cedars of
Lebanon—
sing out this joyous song:
'Since you have been cut down,
no one will come now to cut us down!'

9 "In the place of the dead* there is
excitement
over your arrival.
The spirits of world leaders and mighty
kings long dead
stand up to see you.
10 With one voice they all cry out,
'Now you are as weak as we are!
11 Your might and power were buried with
you.*
The sound of the harp in your palace
has ceased.
Now maggots are your sheet,
and worms your blanket.'

12 "How you are fallen from heaven,
O shining star, son of the morning!
You have been thrown down to the earth,
you who destroyed the nations of the
world.
13 For you said to yourself,
'I will ascend to heaven and set my
throne above God's stars.
I will preside on the mountain of the gods
far away in the north.*
14 I will climb to the highest heavens
and be like the Most High.'
15 Instead, you will be brought down to the
place of the dead,
down to its lowest depths.
16 Everyone there will stare at you and ask,
'Can this be the one who shook the earth
and made the kingdoms of the world
tremble?
17 Is this the one who destroyed the world
and made it into a wasteland?
Is this the king who demolished the
world's greatest cities
and had no mercy on his prisoners?'

18 "The kings of the nations lie in stately
glory,
each in his own tomb,
19 but you will be thrown out of your grave
like a worthless branch.
Like a corpse trampled underfoot,
you will be dumped into a mass grave
with those killed in battle.
You will descend to the pit.
20 You will not be given a proper burial,
for you have destroyed your nation
and slaughtered your people.
The descendants of such an evil person
will never again receive honor.

12:6 Hebrew *Zion.* **14:1** Hebrew *the house of Jacob.* The names "Jacob" and "Israel" are often interchanged throughout the Old Testament, referring sometimes to the individual patriarch and sometimes to the nation. **14:4** As in Dead Sea Scrolls; the meaning of the Masoretic Text is uncertain. **14:9** Hebrew *Sheol;* also in 14:15. **14:11** Hebrew *were brought down to Sheol.* **14:13** Or *on the heights of Zaphon.*

▸ **14:12** *See* ***Satan****, page 566.*

21 Kill this man's children!
Let them die because of their father's sins!
They must not rise and conquer the earth,
filling the world with their cities."

22 This is what the LORD of Heaven's Armies says:
"I, myself, have risen against Babylon!
I will destroy its children and its children's children,"
says the LORD.
23 "I will make Babylon a desolate place of owls,
filled with swamps and marshes.
I will sweep the land with the broom of destruction.
I, the LORD of Heaven's Armies, have spoken!"

A Message about Assyria

24 The LORD of Heaven's Armies has sworn this oath:

"It will all happen as I have planned.
It will be as I have decided.
25 I will break the Assyrians when they are in Israel;
I will trample them on my mountains.
My people will no longer be their slaves
nor bow down under their heavy loads.
26 I have a plan for the whole earth,
a hand of judgment upon all the nations.
27 The LORD of Heaven's Armies has spoken—
who can change his plans?
When his hand is raised,
who can stop him?"

A Message about Philistia

28 This message came to me the year King Ahaz died:*

29 Do not rejoice, you Philistines,
that the rod that struck you is broken—
that the king who attacked you is dead.
For from that snake a more poisonous snake will be born,
a fiery serpent to destroy you!
30 I will feed the poor in my pasture;
the needy will lie down in peace.
But as for you, I will wipe you out with famine
and destroy the few who remain.

31 Wail at the gates! Weep in the cities!
Melt with fear, you Philistines!
A powerful army comes like smoke from the north.
Each soldier rushes forward eager to fight.

32 What should we tell the Philistine messengers? Tell them,

"The LORD has built Jerusalem*;
its walls will give refuge to his oppressed people."

A Message about Moab

15 This message came to me concerning Moab:

In one night the town of Ar will be leveled,
and the city of Kir will be destroyed.
2 Your people will go to their temple in Dibon to mourn.
They will go to their sacred shrines to weep.
They will wail for the fate of Nebo and Medeba,
shaving their heads in sorrow and cutting off their beards.
3 They will wear burlap as they wander the streets.
From every home and public square
will come the sound of wailing.
4 The people of Heshbon and Elealeh will cry out;
their voices will be heard as far away as Jahaz!
The bravest warriors of Moab will cry out in utter terror.
They will be helpless with fear.

5 My heart weeps for Moab.
Its people flee to Zoar and Eglath-shelishiyah.
Weeping, they climb the road to Luhith.
Their cries of distress can be heard all along the road to Horonaim.
6 Even the waters of Nimrim are dried up!
The grassy banks are scorched.
The tender plants are gone;
nothing green remains.
7 The people grab their possessions
and carry them across the Ravine of Willows.
8 A cry of distress echoes through the land of Moab
from one end to the other—
from Eglaim to Beer-elim.

9 The stream near Dibon* runs red with blood,
but I am still not finished with Dibon!
Lions will hunt down the survivors—
both those who try to escape
and those who remain behind.

16 1 Send lambs from Sela as tribute
to the ruler of the land.
Send them through the desert
to the mountain of beautiful Zion.
2 The women of Moab are left like homeless birds
at the shallow crossings of the Arnon River.
3 "Help us," they cry.
"Defend us against our enemies.
Protect us from their relentless attack.
Do not betray us now that we have escaped.
4 Let our refugees stay among you.
Hide them from our enemies until the terror is past."

When oppression and destruction have ended
and enemy raiders have disappeared,
5 then God will establish one of David's descendants as king.
He will rule with mercy and truth.
He will always do what is just
and be eager to do what is right.

6 We have heard about proud Moab—
about its pride and arrogance and rage.
But all that boasting has disappeared.
7 The entire land of Moab weeps.
Yes, everyone in Moab mourns
for the cakes of raisins from Kir-hareseth.
They are all gone now.
8 The farms of Heshbon are abandoned;
the vineyards at Sibmah are deserted.
The rulers of the nations have broken down Moab—
that beautiful grapevine.
Its tendrils spread north as far as the town of Jazer
and trailed eastward into the wilderness.
Its shoots reached so far west
that they crossed over the Dead Sea.*
9 So now I weep for Jazer and the vineyards of Sibmah;
my tears will flow for Heshbon and Elealeh.
There are no more shouts of joy
over your summer fruits and harvest.
10 Gone now is the gladness,
gone the joy of harvest.

14:28 King Ahaz died in 715 B.C. **14:32** Hebrew *Zion.* **15:9** As in Dead Sea Scrolls, some Greek manuscripts, and Latin Vulgate; Masoretic Text reads *Dimon;* also in 15:9b. **16:8** Hebrew *the sea.*

The nations

Isaiah 13–23 speaks of God's judgment on the godless surrounding nations. What Isaiah wanted to show is that God is no local tribal deity, but rather the God of the whole earth who therefore calls all nations to account. His judgment upon them is part of his sovereign plan not just for Israel but also for the whole world.

This is why Isaiah saw hope, and not just judgment, for all these nations. While the Old Testament often speaks of "the nations" as a symbol of those who oppose God, it also looks forward to a time when "the nations will rally to him" (11:10). Isaiah looked toward the climax of human history, seeing how God "will raise a flag among the nations" (11:12) and gather his people "from the ends of the earth." In the messianic kingdom there will be room for both Jew and Gentile who believe in Christ, as John's visions in Revelation make clear (e.g., Revelation 5:9; 7:9-10).

Paul quotes Isaiah 11:10 in Romans 15:12 in support of his goal of reaching the Gentiles with the gospel. For him, this was the beginning of the end time, and so he firmly expected that the nations would turn to God, just as the prophets had promised. Little wonder he was so excited to go among them. The challenge is, are we?

There will be no singing in the
vineyards,
no more happy shouts,
no treading of grapes in the
winepresses.
I have ended all their harvest joys.
11 My heart's cry for Moab is like a lament
on a harp.
I am filled with anguish for
Kir-hareseth.*
12 The people of Moab will worship at their
pagan shrines,
but it will do them no good.
They will cry to the gods in their
temples,
but no one will be able to save them.

13The LORD has already said these things
about Moab in the past. 14But now the LORD
says, "Within three years, counting each
day,* the glory of Moab will be ended. From
its great population, only a feeble few will
be left alive."

A Message about Damascus and Israel

17 This message came to me concerning Damascus:

"Look, the city of Damascus will
disappear!
It will become a heap of ruins.
2 The towns of Aroer will be deserted.
Flocks will graze in the streets and lie
down undisturbed,
with no one to chase them away.
3 The fortified towns of Israel* will also be
destroyed,
and the royal power of Damascus will
end.
All that remains of Syria*
will share the fate of Israel's departed
glory,"
declares the LORD of Heaven's
Armies.

4 "In that day Israel's* glory will grow
dim;
its robust body will waste away.
5 The whole land will look like a
grainfield
after the harvesters have gathered the
grain.
It will be desolate,
like the fields in the valley of Rephaim
after the harvest.
6 Only a few of its people will be left,
like stray olives left on a tree after the
harvest.
Only two or three remain in the highest
branches,
four or five scattered here and there
on the limbs,"
declares the LORD, the God of Israel.

7 Then at last the people will look to their
Creator
and turn their eyes to the Holy One of
Israel.
8 They will no longer look to their idols for
help
or worship what their own hands have
made.
They will never again bow down to their
Asherah poles
or worship at the pagan shrines they
have built.
9 Their largest cities will be like a deserted
forest,
like the land the Hivites and Amorites
abandoned*
when the Israelites came here so long
ago.
It will be utterly desolate.
10 Why? Because you have turned from the
God who can save you.
You have forgotten the Rock who can
hide you.
So you may plant the finest grapevines
and import the most expensive
seedlings.
11 They may sprout on the day you set
them out;
yes, they may blossom on the very
morning you plant them,
but you will never pick any grapes from
them.
Your only harvest will be a load of
grief and unrelieved pain.

12 Listen! The armies of many nations
roar like the roaring of the sea.
Hear the thunder of the mighty
forces
as they rush forward like thundering
waves.
13 But though they thunder like breakers
on a beach,
God will silence them, and they will
run away.
They will flee like chaff scattered by the
wind,

like a tumbleweed whirling before a
storm.
14 In the evening Israel waits in terror,
but by dawn its enemies are dead.
This is the just reward of those who
plunder us,
a fitting end for those who destroy us.

A Message about Ethiopia

18 [1] Listen, Ethiopia*—land of
fluttering sails*
that lies at the headwaters of the
Nile,
[2] that sends ambassadors
in swift boats down the river.

Go, swift messengers!
Take a message to a tall,
smooth-skinned people,
who are feared far and wide
for their conquests and destruction,
and whose land is divided by
rivers.
[3] All you people of the world,
everyone who lives on the earth—
when I raise my battle flag on the
mountain, look!
When I blow the ram's horn, listen!
[4] For the LORD has told me this:
"I will watch quietly from my dwelling
place—
as quietly as the heat rises on a
summer day,
or as the morning dew forms during
the harvest."
[5] Even before you begin your attack,
while your plans are ripening like
grapes,
the LORD will cut off your new growth
with pruning shears.
He will snip off and discard your
spreading branches.
[6] Your mighty army will be left dead in the
fields
for the mountain vultures and wild
animals.
The vultures will tear at the corpses all
summer.
The wild animals will gnaw at the
bones all winter.

[7] At that time the LORD of Heaven's
Armies will receive gifts
from this land divided by rivers,
from this tall, smooth-skinned people,
who are feared far and wide for their
conquests and destruction.
They will bring the gifts to Jerusalem,*
where the LORD of Heaven's Armies
dwells.

A Message about Egypt

19 This message came to me concerning
Egypt:

Look! The LORD is advancing against
Egypt,
riding on a swift cloud.
The idols of Egypt tremble.
The hearts of the Egyptians melt with
fear.

[2] "I will make Egyptian fight against
Egyptian—
brother against brother,
neighbor against neighbor,
city against city,
province against province.
[3] The Egyptians will lose heart,
and I will confuse their plans.
They will plead with their idols for
wisdom
and call on spirits, mediums, and
those who consult the spirits of the
dead.
[4] I will hand Egypt over
to a hard, cruel master.
A fierce king will rule them,"
says the Lord, the LORD of Heaven's
Armies.

[5] The waters of the Nile will fail to rise
and flood the fields.
The riverbed will be parched and dry.
[6] The canals of the Nile will dry up,
and the streams of Egypt will stink
with rotting reeds and rushes.
[7] All the greenery along the riverbank
and all the crops along the river
will dry up and blow away.
[8] The fishermen will lament for lack of
work.
Those who cast hooks into the Nile
will groan,
and those who use nets will lose
heart.

16:11 Hebrew *Kir-heres,* a variant spelling of Kir-hareseth. **16:14** Hebrew *Within three years, as a servant bound by contract would count them.* **17:3a** Hebrew *of Ephraim,* referring to the northern kingdom of Israel. **17:3b** Hebrew *Aram.* **17:4** Hebrew *Jacob's.* See note on 14:1. **17:9** As in Greek version; Hebrew reads *like places of the wood and the highest bough.* **18:1a** Hebrew *Cush.* **18:1b** Or *land of many locusts;* Hebrew reads *land of whirring wings.* **18:7** Hebrew *to Mount Zion.*

9 There will be no flax for the harvesters,
no thread for the weavers.
10 They will be in despair,
and all the workers will be sick at heart.

11 What fools are the officials of Zoan!
Their best counsel to the king of Egypt is stupid and wrong.
Will they still boast to Pharaoh of their wisdom?
Will they dare brag about all their wise ancestors?
12 Where are your wise counselors, Pharaoh?
Let them tell you what God plans,
what the LORD of Heaven's Armies is going to do to Egypt.
13 The officials of Zoan are fools,
and the officials of Memphis* are deluded.
The leaders of the people
have led Egypt astray.
14 The LORD has sent a spirit of foolishness on them,
so all their suggestions are wrong.
They cause Egypt to stagger
like a drunk in his vomit.
15 There is nothing Egypt can do.
All are helpless—
the head and the tail,
the noble palm branch and the lowly reed.

16 In that day the Egyptians will be as
weak as women. They will cower in fear
beneath the upraised fist of the LORD of
Heaven's Armies. 17 Just to speak the name
of Israel will terrorize them, for the LORD
of Heaven's Armies has laid out his plans
against them.

18 In that day five of Egypt's cities will
follow the LORD of Heaven's Armies. They
will even begin to speak Hebrew, the language of Canaan. One of these cities will be
Heliopolis, the City of the Sun.*

19 In that day there will be an altar to the
LORD in the heart of Egypt, and there will
be a monument to the LORD at its border.
20 It will be a sign and a witness that the
LORD of Heaven's Armies is worshiped in
the land of Egypt. When the people cry
to the LORD for help against those who
oppress them, he will send them a savior
who will rescue them. 21 The LORD will make
himself known to the Egyptians. Yes, they
will know the LORD and will give their sacrifices and offerings to him. They will make
a vow to the LORD and will keep it. 22 The
LORD will strike Egypt, and then he will
bring healing. For the Egyptians will turn
to the LORD, and he will listen to their pleas
and heal them.

23 In that day Egypt and Assyria will be
connected by a highway. The Egyptians and
Assyrians will move freely between their
lands, and they will both worship God. 24 In
that day Israel will be the third, along with
Egypt and Assyria, a blessing in the midst of
the earth. 25 For the LORD of Heaven's Armies
will say, "Blessed be Egypt, my people.
Blessed be Assyria, the land I have made.
Blessed be Israel, my special possession!"

Mediums

Like many other ancient peoples, the Egyptians consulted the dead for guidance through mediums, as Isaiah saw them doing in 19:3. But God consistently forbade his people to do this (e.g., Leviticus 19:31; Deuteronomy 18:9-13). The Bible shows that engaging in such practices is not mere harmless fun but dangerous (e.g., 1 Samuel 28:1-20; 31:1-6) and says that God turns against those who engage in them (Leviticus 20:6). As God's people, we don't need to consult the dead when we have the living God as our guide. As Isaiah put it, "Someone may say to you, 'Let's ask the mediums and those who consult the spirits of the dead. With their whisperings and mutterings, they will tell us what to do.' But shouldn't people ask God for guidance? Should the living seek guidance from the dead? Look to God's instructions and teachings!" (Isaiah 8:19-20).

▸ *See also **The occult**, page 337.*

A Message about Egypt and Ethiopia

20 In the year when King Sargon of Assyria sent his commander in chief to capture the Philistine city of Ashdod,* 2 the LORD told Isaiah son of Amoz, "Take off the burlap you have been wearing, and remove your sandals." Isaiah did as he was told and walked around naked and barefoot.

3 Then the LORD said, "My servant Isaiah has been walking around naked and barefoot for the last three years. This is a sign—a symbol of the terrible troubles I will bring upon Egypt and Ethiopia.* 4 For the king of Assyria will take away the Egyptians and Ethiopians* as prisoners. He will make them walk naked and barefoot, both young and old, their buttocks bared, to the shame of Egypt. 5 Then the Philistines will be thrown into panic, for they counted on the power of Ethiopia and boasted of their allies in Egypt! 6 They will say, 'If this can happen to Egypt, what chance do we have? We were counting on Egypt to protect us from the king of Assyria.'"

A Message about Babylon

21 This message came to me concerning Babylon—the desert by the sea*:

Disaster is roaring down on you from the desert,
like a whirlwind sweeping in from the Negev.
2 I see a terrifying vision:
I see the betrayer betraying,
the destroyer destroying.
Go ahead, you Elamites and Medes,
attack and lay siege.
I will make an end
to all the groaning Babylon caused.
3 My stomach aches and burns with pain.
Sharp pangs of anguish are upon me,
like those of a woman in labor.
I grow faint when I hear what God is planning;
I am too afraid to look.
4 My mind reels and my heart races.
I longed for evening to come,
but now I am terrified of the dark.
5 Look! They are preparing a great feast.
They are spreading rugs for people to sit on.
Everyone is eating and drinking.
But quick! Grab your shields and prepare for battle.
You are being attacked!
6 Meanwhile, the Lord said to me,
"Put a watchman on the city wall.
Let him shout out what he sees.
7 He should look for chariots
drawn by pairs of horses,
and for riders on donkeys and camels.
Let the watchman be fully alert."
8 Then the watchman* called out,
"Day after day I have stood on the watchtower, my lord.
Night after night I have remained at my post.
9 Now at last—look!
Here comes a man in a chariot
with a pair of horses!"
Then the watchman said,
"Babylon is fallen, fallen!
All the idols of Babylon
lie broken on the ground!"
10 O my people, threshed and winnowed,
I have told you everything the LORD of Heaven's Armies has said,
everything the God of Israel has told me.

A Message about Edom

11 This message came to me concerning Edom*:

Someone from Edom* keeps calling to me,
"Watchman, how much longer until morning?
When will the night be over?"
12 The watchman replies,
"Morning is coming, but night will soon return.
If you wish to ask again, then come back and ask."

19:13 Hebrew *Noph.* **19:18** Or *will be the City of Destruction.* **20:1** Ashdod was captured by Assyria in 711 B.C. **20:3** Hebrew *Cush;* also in 20:5. **20:4** Hebrew *Cushites.* **21:1** Hebrew *concerning the desert by the sea.* **21:8** As in Dead Sea Scrolls and Syriac version; Masoretic Text reads *a lion.* **21:11a** Hebrew *Dumah,* which means "silence" or "stillness." It is a wordplay on the word *Edom.* **21:11b** Hebrew *Seir,* another name for Edom.

▸ **21:9** *See* ***Babylon****, page 445.*

A Message about Arabia

13This message came to me concerning
Arabia:

O caravans from Dedan,
hide in the deserts of Arabia.
14 O people of Tema,
bring water to these thirsty people,
food to these weary refugees.
15 They have fled from the sword,
from the drawn sword,
from the bent bow
and the terrors of battle.

16The Lord said to me, "Within a year,
counting each day,* all the glory of Kedar
will come to an end. 17Only a few of its courageous archers will survive. I, the LORD,
the God of Israel, have spoken!"

A Message about Jerusalem

22 This message came to me concerning Jerusalem—the Valley of Vision*:

What is happening?
Why is everyone running to the
rooftops?
2 The whole city is in a terrible uproar.
What do I see in this reveling city?
Bodies are lying everywhere,
killed not in battle but by famine and
disease.
3 All your leaders have fled.
They surrendered without resistance.
The people tried to slip away,
but they were captured, too.
4 That's why I said, "Leave me alone to
weep;
do not try to comfort me.
Let me cry for my people
as I watch them being destroyed."

5 Oh, what a day of crushing defeat!
What a day of confusion and terror
brought by the Lord, the LORD of
Heaven's Armies,
upon the Valley of Vision!
The walls of Jerusalem have been
broken,
and cries of death echo from the
mountainsides.
6 Elamites are the archers,
with their chariots and charioteers.
The men of Kir hold up the
shields.
7 Chariots fill your beautiful valleys,
and charioteers storm your gates.
8 Judah's defenses have been stripped
away.
You run to the armory* for your
weapons.
9 You inspect the breaks in the walls of
Jerusalem.*
You store up water in the lower pool.
10 You survey the houses and tear some
down
for stone to strengthen the walls.

The keys of the Kingdom

Isaiah prophesied to Shebna, the worthless administrator of the royal palace (Isaiah 22:15), that he would be replaced by Eliakim. Symbolizing his new authority, Eliakim was given a key, a robe, and a position of honor. But Isaiah saw more: His reference to being a father and holding the key of the house of David shows he saw in him a symbol of the coming Messiah (22:21-22).

Keys today are small, but in Bible times they were large and heavy—sometimes, for important buildings, large enough to be carried on one's shoulder. Such a key therefore served as a symbol of power, authority, and trust. Just as Eliakim had authority to lock and unlock the palace rooms, so Isaiah saw the coming of one who would have power and authority to lock and unlock God's Kingdom.

In the New Testament this image is applied to Jesus. He is the one who "has the key of David. What he opens, no one can close; and what he closes, no one can open" (Revelation 3:7). He is the one who can be trusted, with authority to unlock every situation, even "death and the grave" (Revelation 1:18). And to those who believe in him, like Peter, he delegates "the keys of the Kingdom" (Matthew 16:19)—the ability to open the doors for many to come in.

11 Between the city walls, you build a reservoir
for water from the old pool.
But you never ask for help from the One who did all this.
You never considered the One who planned this long ago.

12 At that time the Lord, the LORD of Heaven's Armies,
called you to weep and mourn.
He told you to shave your heads in sorrow for your sins
and to wear clothes of burlap to show your remorse.
13 But instead, you dance and play;
you slaughter cattle and kill sheep.
You feast on meat and drink wine.
You say, "Let's feast and drink,
for tomorrow we die!"

14The LORD of Heaven's Armies has revealed this to me: "Till the day you die, you will never be forgiven for this sin." That is the judgment of the Lord, the LORD of Heaven's Armies.

A Message for Shebna

15This is what the Lord, the LORD of Heaven's Armies, said to me: "Confront Shebna, the palace administrator, and give him this message:

16 "Who do you think you are,
and what are you doing here,
building a beautiful tomb for yourself—
a monument high up in the rock?
17 For the LORD is about to hurl you away, mighty man.
He is going to grab you,
18 crumple you into a ball,
and toss you away into a distant, barren land.
There you will die,
and your glorious chariots will be broken and useless.
You are a disgrace to your master!

19"Yes, I will drive you out of office," says
the LORD. "I will pull you down from your
high position. 20And then I will call my
servant Eliakim son of Hilkiah to replace you.
21I will dress him in your royal robes and will
give him your title and your authority. And
he will be a father to the people of Jerusalem and Judah. 22I will give him the key to the
house of David—the highest position in the
royal court. When he opens doors, no one
will be able to close them; when he closes
doors, no one will be able to open them.
23He will bring honor to his family name, for
I will drive him firmly in place like a nail in
the wall. 24They will give him great responsibility, and he will bring honor to even the
lowliest members of his family.*"

25But the LORD of Heaven's Armies also
says: "The time will come when I will pull out the nail that seemed so firm. It will come out and fall to the ground. Everything it supports will fall with it. I, the LORD, have spoken!"

A Message about Tyre

23 This message came to me concerning Tyre:

Wail, you trading ships of Tarshish,
for the harbor and houses of Tyre are gone!
The rumors you heard in Cyprus*
are all true.
2 Mourn in silence, you people of the coast
and you merchants of Sidon.
Your traders crossed the sea,*
3 sailing over deep waters.
They brought you grain from Egypt*
and harvests from along the Nile.
You were the marketplace of the world.

4 But now you are put to shame, city of Sidon,
for Tyre, the fortress of the sea, says,*
"Now I am childless;
I have no sons or daughters."
5 When Egypt hears the news about Tyre,
there will be great sorrow.
6 Send word now to Tarshish!
Wail, you people who live in distant lands!
7 Is this silent ruin all that is left of your once joyous city?
What a long history was yours!
Think of all the colonists you sent to distant places.

21:16 Hebrew *Within a year, as a servant bound by contract would count it.* Some ancient manuscripts read *Within three years,* as in 16:14. **22:1** Hebrew *concerning the Valley of Vision.* **22:8** Hebrew *to the House of the Forest;* see 1 Kgs 7:2-5. **22:9** Hebrew *the city of David.* **22:24** Hebrew *They will hang on him all the glory of his father's house: its offspring and offshoots, all its lesser vessels, from the bowls to all the jars.* **23:1** Hebrew *Kittim;* also in 23:12. **23:2** As in Dead Sea Scrolls and Greek version; Masoretic Text reads *Those who have gone over the sea have filled you.* **23:3** Hebrew *from Shihor,* a branch of the Nile River. **23:4** Or *for the god of the sea says;* Hebrew reads *for the sea, the fortress of the sea, says.*

8 Who has brought this disaster on Tyre,
that great creator of kingdoms?
Her traders were all princes,
her merchants were nobles.
9 The LORD of Heaven's Armies has done it
to destroy your pride
and bring low all earth's nobility.
10 Come, people of Tarshish,
sweep over the land like the flooding Nile,
for Tyre is defenseless.*
11 The LORD held out his hand over the sea
and shook the kingdoms of the earth.
He has spoken out against Phoenicia,*
ordering that her fortresses be destroyed.
12 He says, "Never again will you rejoice,
O daughter of Sidon, for you have been crushed.
Even if you flee to Cyprus,
you will find no rest."

13 Look at the land of Babylonia*—
the people of that land are gone!
The Assyrians have handed Babylon over
to the wild animals of the desert.
They have built siege ramps against its walls,
torn down its palaces,
and turned it to a heap of rubble.
14 Wail, you ships of Tarshish,
for your harbor is destroyed!

15 For seventy years, the length of a king's
life, Tyre will be forgotten. But then the city
will come back to life as in the song about
the prostitute:

16 Take a harp and walk the streets,
you forgotten harlot.
Make sweet melody and sing your songs
so you will be remembered again.

17 Yes, after seventy years the LORD will
revive Tyre. But she will be no different than
she was before. She will again be a prostitute to all kingdoms around the world. 18 But
in the end her profits will be given to the
LORD. Her wealth will not be hoarded but
will provide good food and fine clothing for
the LORD's priests.

Destruction of the Earth

24

1 Look! The LORD is about to
destroy the earth
and make it a vast wasteland.
He devastates the surface of the earth
and scatters the people.
2 Priests and laypeople,
servants and masters,
maids and mistresses,
buyers and sellers,
lenders and borrowers,
bankers and debtors—none will be spared.
3 The earth will be completely emptied
and looted.
The LORD has spoken!

4 The earth mourns and dries up,
and the land wastes away and withers.
Even the greatest people on earth
waste away.
5 The earth suffers for the sins of its people,
for they have twisted God's instructions,
violated his laws,
and broken his everlasting covenant.
6 Therefore, a curse consumes the earth.
Its people must pay the price for their sin.
They are destroyed by fire,
and only a few are left alive.
7 The grapevines waste away,
and there is no new wine.
All the merrymakers sigh and mourn.
8 The cheerful sound of tambourines is stilled;
the happy cries of celebration are heard no more.
The melodious chords of the harp are silent.
9 Gone are the joys of wine and song;
alcoholic drink turns bitter in the mouth.
10 The city writhes in chaos;
every home is locked to keep out intruders.
11 Mobs gather in the streets, crying out for wine.
Joy has turned to gloom.
Gladness has been banished from the land.
12 The city is left in ruins,
its gates battered down.
13 Throughout the earth the story is the same—
only a remnant is left,
like the stray olives left on the tree
or the few grapes left on the vine after harvest.

[14] But all who are left shout and sing for joy.
Those in the west praise the LORD's majesty.
[15] In eastern lands, give glory to the LORD.
In the lands beyond the sea, praise the name of the LORD, the God of Israel.
[16] We hear songs of praise from the ends of the earth,
songs that give glory to the Righteous One!

But my heart is heavy with grief.
Weep for me, for I wither away.
Deceit still prevails,
and treachery is everywhere.
[17] Terror and traps and snares will be your lot,
you people of the earth.
[18] Those who flee in terror will fall into a trap,
and those who escape the trap will be caught in a snare.

Destruction falls like rain from the heavens;
the foundations of the earth shake.
[19] The earth has broken up.
It has utterly collapsed;
it is violently shaken.
[20] The earth staggers like a drunk.
It trembles like a tent in a storm.
It falls and will not rise again,
for the guilt of its rebellion is very heavy.

[21] In that day the LORD will punish the gods in the heavens
and the proud rulers of the nations on earth.
[22] They will be rounded up and put in prison.
They will be shut up in prison
and will finally be punished.
[23] Then the glory of the moon will wane,
and the brightness of the sun will fade,
for the LORD of Heaven's Armies will rule on Mount Zion.
He will rule in great glory in Jerusalem,
in the sight of all the leaders of his people.

Praise for Judgment and Salvation

25 [1] O LORD, I will honor and praise your name,
for you are my God.
You do such wonderful things!
You planned them long ago,
and now you have accomplished them.
[2] You turn mighty cities into heaps of ruins.
Cities with strong walls are turned to rubble.
Beautiful palaces in distant lands disappear
and will never be rebuilt.
[3] Therefore, strong nations will declare your glory;
ruthless nations will fear you.

[4] But you are a tower of refuge to the poor, O LORD,
a tower of refuge to the needy in distress.
You are a refuge from the storm
and a shelter from the heat.
For the oppressive acts of ruthless people
are like a storm beating against a wall,
[5] or like the relentless heat of the desert.
But you silence the roar of foreign nations.
As the shade of a cloud cools relentless heat,
so the boastful songs of ruthless people are stilled.

[6] In Jerusalem,* the LORD of Heaven's Armies
will spread a wonderful feast
for all the people of the world.
It will be a delicious banquet
with clear, well-aged wine and choice meat.
[7] There he will remove the cloud of gloom,
the shadow of death that hangs over the earth.
[8] He will swallow up death forever!
The Sovereign LORD will wipe away all tears.
He will remove forever all insults and mockery
against his land and people.
The LORD has spoken!
[9] In that day the people will proclaim,
"This is our God!
We trusted in him, and he saved us!

23:10 The meaning of the Hebrew in this verse is uncertain.
23:11 Hebrew *Canaan.* **23:13** Or *Chaldea.* **25:6** Hebrew *On this mountain;* also in 25:10.

This is the LORD, in whom we trusted.
Let us rejoice in the salvation he brings!"
10 For the LORD's hand of blessing will rest on Jerusalem.
But Moab will be crushed.
It will be like straw trampled down and left to rot.
11 God will push down Moab's people as a swimmer pushes down water with his hands.
He will end their pride and all their evil works.
12 The high walls of Moab will be demolished.
They will be brought down to the ground,
down into the dust.

A Song of Praise to the LORD

26 In that day, everyone in the land of Judah will sing this song:

Our city is strong!
We are surrounded by the walls of God's salvation.
2 Open the gates to all who are righteous;
allow the faithful to enter.
3 You will keep in perfect peace
all who trust in you,
all whose thoughts are fixed on you!
4 Trust in the LORD always,
for the LORD GOD is the eternal Rock.
5 He humbles the proud
and brings down the arrogant city.
He brings it down to the dust.
6 The poor and oppressed trample it underfoot,
and the needy walk all over it.

7 But for those who are righteous,
the way is not steep and rough.
You are a God who does what is right,
and you smooth out the path ahead of them.
8 LORD, we show our trust in you by obeying your laws;
our heart's desire is to glorify your name.
9 In the night I search for you;
in the morning* I earnestly seek you.
For only when you come to judge the earth
will people learn what is right.
10 Your kindness to the wicked
does not make them do good.
Although others do right, the wicked keep doing wrong
and take no notice of the LORD's majesty.
11 O LORD, they pay no attention to your upraised fist.
Show them your eagerness to defend your people.
Then they will be ashamed.
Let your fire consume your enemies.

Peace

People search for peace in all kinds of things, whether religious activities like pilgrimage or meditation, or more worldly things like money, success, or alcohol. In Isaiah's day, people were also looking for peace. Assyria's empire was expanding rapidly, and Israel, to Judah's north, had been conquered in 722 BC. The Assyrian border was now just a few miles north of Jerusalem, which would soon be attacked, spared only through God's intervention (Isaiah 36–37). It was in this context that Isaiah called people to find their peace in God alone—a peace that begins not with feelings, but with the mind (26:3). Why? Because it is in our mind that our fears play havoc. That is why we should fill our mind with Scripture, especially Scriptures that declare God's promises. Those who fix their mind on God will then find they are kept in "perfect peace"—or as it says in the Hebrew text, "peace, peace," a repetition underlining the reality of this peace compared to the shallowness and fleetingness of the so-called peace brought by other things. The Hebrew word for peace is "shalom"—meaning not just the absence of strife but the positive presence of God that transforms everything, making it whole. Such peace comes only as we trust in him (26:3-4).

12 LORD, you will grant us peace;
all we have accomplished is really from you.
13 O LORD our God, others have ruled us,
but you alone are the one we worship.
14 Those we served before are dead and gone.
Their departed spirits will never return!
You attacked them and destroyed them,
and they are long forgotten.
15 O LORD, you have made our nation great;
yes, you have made us great.
You have extended our borders,
and we give you the glory!

16 LORD, in distress we searched for you.
We prayed beneath the burden of your discipline.
17 Just as a pregnant woman
writhes and cries out in pain as she gives birth,
so were we in your presence, LORD.
18 We, too, writhe in agony,
but nothing comes of our suffering.
We have not given salvation to the earth,
nor brought life into the world.
19 But those who die in the LORD will live;
their bodies will rise again!
Those who sleep in the earth
will rise up and sing for joy!
For your life-giving light will fall like dew
on your people in the place of the dead!

Restoration for Israel

20 Go home, my people,
and lock your doors!
Hide yourselves for a little while
until the LORD's anger has passed.
21 Look! The LORD is coming from heaven
to punish the people of the earth for their sins.
The earth will no longer hide those who have been killed.
They will be brought out for all to see.

27 In that day the LORD will take his terrible, swift sword and punish Leviathan,* the swiftly moving serpent, the coiling, writhing serpent. He will kill the dragon of the sea.

2 "In that day,
sing about the fruitful vineyard.
3 I, the LORD, will watch over it,
watering it carefully.
Day and night I will watch so no one can harm it.
4 My anger will be gone.
If I find briers and thorns growing,
I will attack them;
I will burn them up—
5 unless they turn to me for help.
Let them make peace with me;
yes, let them make peace with me."
6 The time is coming when Jacob's descendants will take root.
Israel will bud and blossom
and fill the whole earth with fruit!

7 Has the LORD struck Israel
as he struck her enemies?
Has he punished her
as he punished them?
8 No, but he exiled Israel to call her to account.
She was exiled from her land
as though blown away in a storm from the east.
9 The LORD did this to purge Israel's* wickedness,
to take away all her sin.
As a result, all the pagan altars will be crushed to dust.
No Asherah pole or pagan shrine will be left standing.
10 The fortified towns will be silent and empty,
the houses abandoned, the streets overgrown with weeds.
Calves will graze there,
chewing on twigs and branches.
11 The people are like the dead branches of a tree,
broken off and used for kindling beneath the cooking pots.
Israel is a foolish and stupid nation,
for its people have turned away from God.
Therefore, the one who made them
will show them no pity or mercy.

12 Yet the time will come when the LORD
will gather them together like handpicked
grain. One by one he will gather them—from
the Euphrates River* in the east to the Brook
of Egypt in the west. 13 In that day the great

26:9 Hebrew *within me.* **27:1** The identification of Leviathan is disputed, ranging from an earthly creature to a mythical sea monster in ancient literature. **27:9** Hebrew *Jacob's.* See note on 14:1. **27:12** Hebrew *the river.*

trumpet will sound. Many who were dying in exile in Assyria and Egypt will return to Jerusalem to worship the LORD on his holy mountain.

A Message about Samaria

28 [1] What sorrow awaits the proud
city of Samaria—
the glorious crown of the drunks of
Israel.*
It sits at the head of a fertile valley,
but its glorious beauty will fade like a
flower.
It is the pride of a people
brought down by wine.
[2] For the Lord will send a mighty army
against it.
Like a mighty hailstorm and a
torrential rain,
they will burst upon it like a surging
flood
and smash it to the ground.
[3] The proud city of Samaria—
the glorious crown of the drunks of
Israel*—
will be trampled beneath its enemies'
feet.
[4] It sits at the head of a fertile valley,
but its glorious beauty will fade like a
flower.
Whoever sees it will snatch it up,
as an early fig is quickly picked and
eaten.

[5] Then at last the LORD of Heaven's
Armies
will himself be Israel's glorious
crown.
He will be the pride and joy
of the remnant of his people.
[6] He will give a longing for justice
to their judges.
He will give great courage
to their warriors who stand at the
gates.

[7] Now, however, Israel is led by drunks
who reel with wine and stagger with
alcohol.
The priests and prophets stagger with
alcohol
and lose themselves in wine.
They reel when they see visions
and stagger as they render decisions.
[8] Their tables are covered with vomit;
filth is everywhere.
[9] "Who does the LORD think we are?" they
ask.
"Why does he speak to us like this?
Are we little children,
just recently weaned?
[10] He tells us everything over and over—
one line at a time,
one line at a time,
a little here,
and a little there!"

[11] So now God will have to speak to his
people
through foreign oppressors who speak
a strange language!
[12] God has told his people,
"Here is a place of rest;
let the weary rest here.
This is a place of quiet rest."
But they would not listen.
[13] So the LORD will spell out his message
for them again,
one line at a time,
one line at a time,
a little here,
and a little there,
so that they will stumble and fall.
They will be injured, trapped, and
captured.

[14] Therefore, listen to this message from
the LORD,
you scoffing rulers in Jerusalem.
[15] You boast, "We have struck a bargain to
cheat death
and have made a deal to dodge the
grave.*
The coming destruction can never
touch us,
for we have built a strong refuge made
of lies and deception."

[16] Therefore, this is what the Sovereign
LORD says:
"Look! I am placing a foundation stone
in Jerusalem,*
a firm and tested stone.
It is a precious cornerstone that is safe
to build on.
Whoever believes need never be
shaken.*
[17] I will test you with the measuring line of
justice
and the plumb line of righteousness.
Since your refuge is made of lies,
a hailstorm will knock it down.

Since it is made of deception,
a flood will sweep it away.
18 I will cancel the bargain you made to cheat death,
and I will overturn your deal to dodge the grave.
When the terrible enemy sweeps through,
you will be trampled into the ground.
19 Again and again that flood will come,
morning after morning,
day and night,
until you are carried away."

This message will bring terror to your people.
20 The bed you have made is too short to lie on.
The blankets are too narrow to cover you.
21 The LORD will come as he did against the Philistines at Mount Perazim
and against the Amorites at Gibeon.
He will come to do a strange thing;
he will come to do an unusual deed:
22 For the Lord, the LORD of Heaven's Armies,
has plainly said that he is determined to crush the whole land.
So scoff no more,
or your punishment will be even greater.

23 Listen to me;
listen, and pay close attention.
24 Does a farmer always plow and never sow?
Is he forever cultivating the soil and never planting?
25 Does he not finally plant his seeds—
black cumin, cumin, wheat, barley, and emmer wheat—
each in its proper way,
and each in its proper place?
26 The farmer knows just what to do,
for God has given him understanding.
27 A heavy sledge is never used to thresh black cumin;
rather, it is beaten with a light stick.
A threshing wheel is never rolled on cumin;
instead, it is beaten lightly with a flail.
28 Grain for bread is easily crushed,
so he doesn't keep on pounding it.
He threshes it under the wheels of a cart,
but he doesn't pulverize it.
29 The LORD of Heaven's Armies is a wonderful teacher,
and he gives the farmer great wisdom.

A Message about Jerusalem

29 1 "What sorrow awaits Ariel,* the City of David.
Year after year you celebrate your feasts.
2 Yet I will bring disaster upon you,
and there will be much weeping and sorrow.
For Jerusalem will become what her name Ariel means—
an altar covered with blood.
3 I will be your enemy,
surrounding Jerusalem and attacking its walls.
I will build siege towers
and destroy it.
4 Then deep from the earth you will speak;
from low in the dust your words will come.
Your voice will whisper from the ground
like a ghost conjured up from the grave.

5 "But suddenly, your ruthless enemies will be crushed
like the finest of dust.
Your many attackers will be driven away
like chaff before the wind.
Suddenly, in an instant,
6 I, the LORD of Heaven's Armies, will act for you
with thunder and earthquake and great noise,
with whirlwind and storm and consuming fire.
7 All the nations fighting against Jerusalem*
will vanish like a dream!
Those who are attacking her walls
will vanish like a vision in the night.
8 A hungry person dreams of eating
but wakes up still hungry.

28:1 Hebrew *What sorrow awaits the crowning glory of the drunks of Ephraim,* referring to Samaria, capital of the northern kingdom of Israel. **28:3** Hebrew *The crowning glory of the drunks of Ephraim;* see note on 28:1. **28:15** Hebrew *Sheol;* also in 28:18. **28:16a** Hebrew *in Zion.* **28:16b** Greek version reads *Look! I am placing a stone in the foundation of Jerusalem* [literally *Zion*], */ a precious cornerstone for its foundation, chosen for great honor. / Anyone who trusts in him will never be disgraced.* Compare Rom 9:33; 1 Pet 2:6. **29:1** *Ariel* sounds like a Hebrew term that means "hearth" or "altar." **29:7** Hebrew *Ariel.*

A thirsty person dreams of drinking
but is still faint from thirst when
morning comes.
So it will be with your enemies,
with those who attack Mount Zion."

9 Are you amazed and incredulous?
Don't you believe it?
Then go ahead and be blind.
You are stupid, but not from wine!
You stagger, but not from liquor!
10 For the LORD has poured out on you a
spirit of deep sleep.
He has closed the eyes of your
prophets and visionaries.

11 All the future events in this vision are
like a sealed book to them. When you give
it to those who can read, they will say, "We
can't read it because it is sealed." 12 When
you give it to those who cannot read, they
will say, "We don't know how to read."

13 And so the Lord says,
"These people say they are mine.
They honor me with their lips,
but their hearts are far from me.
And their worship of me
is nothing but man-made rules
learned by rote.*
14 Because of this, I will once again
astound these hypocrites
with amazing wonders.
The wisdom of the wise will pass away,
and the intelligence of the intelligent
will disappear."

15 What sorrow awaits those who try to
hide their plans from the LORD,
who do their evil deeds in the dark!
"The LORD can't see us," they say.
"He doesn't know what's going on!"
16 How foolish can you be?
He is the Potter, and he is certainly
greater than you, the clay!
Should the created thing say of the one
who made it,
"He didn't make me"?
Does a jar ever say,
"The potter who made me is
stupid"?

17 Soon—and it will not be very long—
the forests of Lebanon will become a
fertile field,
and the fertile field will yield
bountiful crops.
18 In that day the deaf will hear words read
from a book,
and the blind will see through the
gloom and darkness.
19 The humble will be filled with fresh joy
from the LORD.
The poor will rejoice in the Holy One
of Israel.
20 The scoffer will be gone,
the arrogant will disappear,
and those who plot evil will be killed.
21 Those who convict the innocent
by their false testimony will
disappear.
A similar fate awaits those who use
trickery to pervert justice
and who tell lies to destroy the
innocent.

22 That is why the LORD, who redeemed
Abraham, says to the people of Israel,*

"My people will no longer be ashamed
or turn pale with fear.
23 For when they see their many children
and all the blessings I have given them,
they will recognize the holiness of the
Holy One of Jacob.
They will stand in awe of the God of
Israel.
24 Then the wayward will gain
understanding,
and complainers will accept
instruction.

Judah's Worthless Treaty with Egypt

30 1 "What sorrow awaits my
rebellious children,"
says the LORD.
"You make plans that are contrary to
mine.
You make alliances not directed by my
Spirit,
thus piling up your sins.
2 For without consulting me,
you have gone down to Egypt for help.
You have put your trust in Pharaoh's
protection.
You have tried to hide in his shade.
3 But by trusting Pharaoh, you will be
humiliated,
and by depending on him, you will be
disgraced.
4 For though his power extends to Zoan
and his officials have arrived in
Hanes,

5 all who trust in him will be ashamed.
He will not help you.
Instead, he will disgrace you."

6 This message came to me concerning the animals in the Negev:

The caravan moves slowly
across the terrible desert to Egypt—
donkeys weighed down with riches
and camels loaded with treasure—
all to pay for Egypt's protection.
They travel through the wilderness,
a place of lionesses and lions,
a place where vipers and poisonous snakes live.
All this, and Egypt will give you nothing in return.
7 Egypt's promises are worthless!
Therefore, I call her Rahab—
the Harmless Dragon.*

A Warning for Rebellious Judah

8 Now go and write down these words.
Write them in a book.
They will stand until the end of time
as a witness
9 that these people are stubborn rebels
who refuse to pay attention to the LORD's instructions.
10 They tell the seers,
"Stop seeing visions!"
They tell the prophets,
"Don't tell us what is right.
Tell us nice things.
Tell us lies.
11 Forget all this gloom.
Get off your narrow path.
Stop telling us about your
'Holy One of Israel.'"

12 This is the reply of the Holy One of Israel:

"Because you despise what I tell you
and trust instead in oppression and lies,
13 calamity will come upon you suddenly—
like a bulging wall that bursts and falls.
In an instant it will collapse
and come crashing down.
14 You will be smashed like a piece of pottery—
shattered so completely that
there won't be a piece big enough
to carry coals from a fireplace
or a little water from the well."

15 This is what the Sovereign LORD,
the Holy One of Israel, says:
"Only in returning to me
and resting in me will you be saved.
In quietness and confidence is your strength.
But you would have none of it.
16 You said, 'No, we will get our help from Egypt.
They will give us swift horses for riding into battle.'
But the only swiftness you are going to see
is the swiftness of your enemies chasing you!
17 One of them will chase a thousand of you.
Five of them will make all of you flee.
You will be left like a lonely flagpole on a hill
or a tattered banner on a distant mountaintop."

Blessings for the LORD's People

18 So the LORD must wait for you to come to him
so he can show you his love and compassion.
For the LORD is a faithful God.
Blessed are those who wait for his help.

19 O people of Zion, who live in Jerusalem,
you will weep no more.
He will be gracious if you ask for help.
He will surely respond to the sound of your cries.
20 Though the Lord gave you adversity for food
and suffering for drink,
he will still be with you to teach you.
You will see your teacher with your own eyes.
21 Your own ears will hear him.
Right behind you a voice will say,
"This is the way you should go,"
whether to the right or to the left.
22 Then you will destroy all your silver idols
and your precious gold images.
You will throw them out like filthy rags,
saying to them, "Good riddance!"

29:13 Greek version reads *Their worship is a farce, / for they teach man-made ideas as commands from God.* Compare Mark 7:7. **29:22** Hebrew *of Jacob.* See note on 14:1. **30:7** Hebrew *Rahab who sits still.* Rahab is the name of a mythical sea monster that represents chaos in ancient literature. The name is used here as a poetic name for Egypt.

23 Then the LORD will bless you with rain
at planting time. There will be wonderful
harvests and plenty of pastureland for your
livestock. 24 The oxen and donkeys that till
the ground will eat good grain, its chaff
blown away by the wind. 25 In that day,
when your enemies are slaughtered and the
towers fall, there will be streams of water
flowing down every mountain and hill.
26 The moon will be as bright as the sun,
and the sun will be seven times brighter—
like the light of seven days in one! So it will
be when the LORD begins to heal his people
and cure the wounds he gave them.

27 Look! The LORD is coming from far away,
burning with anger,
surrounded by thick, rising smoke.
His lips are filled with fury;
his words consume like fire.
28 His hot breath pours out like a flood
up to the neck of his enemies.
He will sift out the proud nations for
destruction.
He will bridle them and lead them
away to ruin.

29 But the people of God will sing a song of
joy,
like the songs at the holy festivals.
You will be filled with joy,
as when a flutist leads a group of
pilgrims
to Jerusalem, the mountain of the
LORD—
to the Rock of Israel.
30 And the LORD will make his majestic
voice heard.
He will display the strength of his
mighty arm.
It will descend with devouring
flames,
with cloudbursts, thunderstorms, and
huge hailstones.
31 At the LORD's command, the Assyrians
will be shattered.
He will strike them down with his
royal scepter.
32 And as the LORD strikes them with his
rod of punishment,*
his people will celebrate with
tambourines and harps.
Lifting his mighty arm, he will fight
the Assyrians.
33 Topheth—the place of burning—
has long been ready for the Assyrian
king;
the pyre is piled high with wood.
The breath of the LORD, like fire from a
volcano,
will set it ablaze.

The Futility of Relying on Egypt

31 1 What sorrow awaits those who
look to Egypt for help,
trusting their horses, chariots, and
charioteers
and depending on the strength of
human armies
instead of looking to the LORD,
the Holy One of Israel.

Depending only on God

Faced with the increasing threat of Assyria, many people in Judah felt they needed to do something. Some thought that making an alliance with Egypt to the south would protect Judah from Assyria. After all, Egypt had many horses and chariots (Isaiah 31:1). But in reality, Egypt was simply using Judah, hoping it would be a buffer between them and the Assyrians.

Isaiah denounced such a strategy, not because it is wrong to ask for help, but because Judah was asking for help from a godless nation and preferring to do this rather than trust only in God (31:1). Addressing the people as "rebellious children," God confronted them with their sin: "You make plans that are contrary to mine. You make alliances not directed by my Spirit" (30:1). And yet, when Hezekiah put his trust in God alone when Assyria surrounded Jerusalem (chapters 36–37), God delivered them in an utterly miraculous way (37:36-38).

God wants us to depend on him alone so that when victory comes, the glory can only be given to him and not to us or others.

[2] In his wisdom, the LORD will send great disaster;
he will not change his mind.
He will rise against the wicked
and against their helpers.
[3] For these Egyptians are mere humans, not God!
Their horses are puny flesh, not mighty spirits!
When the LORD raises his fist against them,
those who help will stumble,
and those being helped will fall.
They will all fall down and die together.

[4]But this is what the LORD has told me:

"When a strong young lion
stands growling over a sheep it has killed,
it is not frightened by the shouts and noise
of a whole crowd of shepherds.
In the same way, the LORD of Heaven's Armies
will come down and fight on Mount Zion.
[5] The LORD of Heaven's Armies will hover over Jerusalem
and protect it like a bird protecting its nest.
He will defend and save the city;
he will pass over it and rescue it."

[6]Though you are such wicked rebels, my
people, come and return to the LORD. [7]I
know the glorious day will come when each
of you will throw away the gold idols and
silver images your sinful hands have made.

[8] "The Assyrians will be destroyed,
but not by the swords of men.
The sword of God will strike them,
and they will panic and flee.
The strong young Assyrians
will be taken away as captives.
[9] Even the strongest will quake with terror,
and princes will flee when they see your battle flags,"
says the LORD, whose fire burns in Zion,
whose flame blazes from Jerusalem.

Israel's Ultimate Deliverance

32 [1] Look, a righteous king is coming!
And honest princes will rule under him.
[2] Each one will be like a shelter from the wind
and a refuge from the storm,
like streams of water in the desert
and the shadow of a great rock in a parched land.

[3] Then everyone who has eyes will be able to see the truth,
and everyone who has ears will be able to hear it.
[4] Even the hotheads will be full of sense and understanding.
Those who stammer will speak out plainly.
[5] In that day ungodly fools will not be heroes.
Scoundrels will not be respected.
[6] For fools speak foolishness
and make evil plans.
They practice ungodliness
and spread false teachings about the LORD.
They deprive the hungry of food
and give no water to the thirsty.
[7] The smooth tricks of scoundrels are evil.
They plot crooked schemes.
They lie to convict the poor,
even when the cause of the poor is just.
[8] But generous people plan to do what is generous,
and they stand firm in their generosity.

[9] Listen, you women who lie around in ease.
Listen to me, you who are so smug.
[10] In a short time—just a little more than a year—
you careless ones will suddenly begin to care.
For your fruit crops will fail,
and the harvest will never take place.
[11] Tremble, you women of ease;
throw off your complacency.
Strip off your pretty clothes,
and put on burlap to show your grief.
[12] Beat your breasts in sorrow for your bountiful farms
and your fruitful grapevines.
[13] For your land will be overgrown with thorns and briers.
Your joyful homes and happy towns will be gone.

30:32 As in some Hebrew manuscripts and Syriac version; Masoretic Text reads *with the founded rod.*

14 The palace and the city will be deserted,
and busy towns will be empty.
Wild donkeys will frolic and flocks will graze
in the empty forts* and watchtowers
15 until at last the Spirit is poured out
on us from heaven.
Then the wilderness will become a fertile field,
and the fertile field will yield bountiful crops.
16 Justice will rule in the wilderness
and righteousness in the fertile field.
17 And this righteousness will bring peace.
Yes, it will bring quietness and confidence forever.
18 My people will live in safety, quietly at home.
They will be at rest.
19 Even if the forest should be destroyed
and the city torn down,
20 the LORD will greatly bless his people.
Wherever they plant seed, bountiful crops will spring up.
Their cattle and donkeys will graze freely.

A Message about Assyria

33 1 What sorrow awaits you
Assyrians, who have destroyed others*
but have never been destroyed yourselves.
You betray others,
but you have never been betrayed.
When you are done destroying,
you will be destroyed.
When you are done betraying,
you will be betrayed.
2 But LORD, be merciful to us,
for we have waited for you.
Be our strong arm each day
and our salvation in times of trouble.
3 The enemy runs at the sound of your voice.
When you stand up, the nations flee!
4 Just as caterpillars and locusts strip the fields and vines,
so the fallen army of Assyria will be stripped!
5 Though the LORD is very great and lives in heaven,
he will make Jerusalem* his home of justice and righteousness.
6 In that day he will be your sure foundation,
providing a rich store of salvation, wisdom, and knowledge.
The fear of the LORD will be your treasure.
7 But now your brave warriors weep in public.
Your ambassadors of peace cry in bitter disappointment.
8 Your roads are deserted;
no one travels them anymore.
The Assyrians have broken their peace treaty
and care nothing for the promises they made before witnesses.*
They have no respect for anyone.
9 The land of Israel wilts in mourning.
Lebanon withers with shame.
The plain of Sharon is now a wilderness.
Bashan and Carmel have been plundered.
10 But the LORD says: "Now I will stand up.
Now I will show my power and might.
11 You Assyrians produce nothing but dry grass and stubble.
Your own breath will turn to fire and consume you.
12 Your people will be burned up completely,
like thornbushes cut down and tossed in a fire.
13 Listen to what I have done, you nations far away!
And you that are near, acknowledge my might!"
14 The sinners in Jerusalem shake with fear.
Terror seizes the godless.
"Who can live with this devouring fire?" they cry.
"Who can survive this all-consuming fire?"
15 Those who are honest and fair,
who refuse to profit by fraud,
who stay far away from bribes,
who refuse to listen to those who plot murder,
who shut their eyes to all enticement to do wrong—
16 these are the ones who will dwell on high.
The rocks of the mountains will be their fortress.

Food will be supplied to them,
and they will have water in
abundance.
17 Your eyes will see the king in all his
splendor,
and you will see a land that stretches
into the distance.
18 You will think back to this time of terror,
asking,
"Where are the Assyrian officers
who counted our towers?
Where are the bookkeepers
who recorded the plunder taken from
our fallen city?"
19 You will no longer see these fierce,
violent people
with their strange, unknown
language.

20 Instead, you will see Zion as a place of
holy festivals.
You will see Jerusalem, a city quiet
and secure.
It will be like a tent whose ropes are taut
and whose stakes are firmly fixed.
21 The LORD will be our Mighty One.
He will be like a wide river of
protection
that no enemy can cross,
that no enemy ship can sail upon.
22 For the LORD is our judge,
our lawgiver, and our king.
He will care for us and save us.
23 The enemies' sails hang loose
on broken masts with useless tackle.
Their treasure will be divided by the
people of God.
Even the lame will take their share!
24 The people of Israel will no longer say,
"We are sick and helpless,"
for the LORD will forgive their sins.

A Message for the Nations

34 1 Come here and listen, O nations
of the earth.
Let the world and everything in it hear
my words.
2 For the LORD is enraged against the
nations.
His fury is against all their armies.
He will completely destroy* them,
dooming them to slaughter.
3 Their dead will be left unburied,
and the stench of rotting bodies will
fill the land.
The mountains will flow with their
blood.
4 The heavens above will melt away
and disappear like a rolled-up scroll.
The stars will fall from the sky
like withered leaves from a grapevine,
or shriveled figs from a fig tree.

5 And when my sword has finished its
work in the heavens,
it will fall upon Edom,
the nation I have marked for
destruction.
6 The sword of the LORD is drenched with
blood
and covered with fat—
with the blood of lambs and goats,
with the fat of rams prepared for
sacrifice.
Yes, the LORD will offer a sacrifice in the
city of Bozrah.
He will make a mighty slaughter in
Edom.
7 Even men as strong as wild oxen will
die—
the young men alongside the
veterans.
The land will be soaked with blood
and the soil enriched with fat.

8 For it is the day of the LORD's revenge,
the year when Edom will be paid back
for all it did to Israel.*
9 The streams of Edom will be filled with
burning pitch,
and the ground will be covered with
fire.
10 This judgment on Edom will never end;
the smoke of its burning will rise
forever.
The land will lie deserted from
generation to generation.
No one will live there anymore.
11 It will be haunted by the desert owl and
the screech owl,
the great owl and the raven.*
For God will measure that land
carefully;
he will measure it for chaos and
destruction.

32:14 Hebrew *the Ophel.* **33:1** Hebrew *What sorrow awaits you, O destroyer.* The Hebrew text does not specifically name Assyria as the object of the prophecy in this chapter. **33:5** Hebrew *Zion;* also in 33:14. **33:8** As in Dead Sea Scrolls; Masoretic Text reads *care nothing for the cities.* **34:2** The Hebrew term used here refers to the complete consecration of things or people to the LORD, either by destroying them or by giving them as an offering; similarly in 34:5. **34:8** Hebrew *to Zion.* **34:11** The identification of some of these birds is uncertain.

12 It will be called the Land of Nothing,
and all its nobles will soon be gone.*
13 Thorns will overrun its palaces;
nettles and thistles will grow in its
forts.
The ruins will become a haunt for jackals
and a home for owls.
14 Desert animals will mingle there with
hyenas,
their howls filling the night.
Wild goats will bleat at one another
among the ruins,
and night creatures* will come there
to rest.
15 There the owl will make her nest and lay
her eggs.
She will hatch her young and cover
them with her wings.
And the buzzards will come,
each one with its mate.

16 Search the book of the LORD,
and see what he will do.
Not one of these birds and animals will
be missing,
and none will lack a mate,
for the LORD has promised this.
His Spirit will make it all come true.
17 He has surveyed and divided the land
and deeded it over to those
creatures.
They will possess it forever,
from generation to generation.

Hope for Restoration

35 1 Even the wilderness and desert
will be glad in those days.
The wasteland will rejoice and
blossom with spring crocuses.
2 Yes, there will be an abundance of
flowers
and singing and joy!
The deserts will become as green as the
mountains of Lebanon,
as lovely as Mount Carmel or the plain
of Sharon.
There the LORD will display his glory,
the splendor of our God.
3 With this news, strengthen those who
have tired hands,
and encourage those who have weak
knees.
4 Say to those with fearful hearts,
"Be strong, and do not fear,
for your God is coming to destroy your
enemies.
He is coming to save you."

5 And when he comes, he will open the
eyes of the blind
and unplug the ears of the deaf.
6 The lame will leap like a deer,
and those who cannot speak will sing
for joy!
Springs will gush forth in the
wilderness,
and streams will water the wasteland.
7 The parched ground will become a pool,
and springs of water will satisfy the
thirsty land.
Marsh grass and reeds and rushes will
flourish
where desert jackals once lived.

8 And a great road will go through that
once deserted land.
It will be named the Highway of
Holiness.

The wilderness

The Hebrew word often translated "wilderness" could refer to any arid region on the margins of civilization where it was difficult to sustain life. Many key Bible stories take place in the wilderness, such as Moses' encounter with God (Exodus 3), Israel's journey to the Promised Land (e.g., Exodus 16:1), and Jesus' struggle against Satan (Matthew 4:1)—probably because life in the wilderness was difficult with the challenges of finding food and water (e.g., Exodus 15:22–17:7) and therefore provided an opportunity to discover God anew and see him provide. Israel didn't always rise to that challenge, however, and then the wilderness became a place of discipline (e.g., Numbers 14). In the prophecy of Isaiah 35, the prophet saw God transforming the wilderness in readiness for his people's going home.

Evil-minded people will never travel
on it.
It will be only for those who walk in
God's ways;
fools will never walk there.
9 Lions will not lurk along its course,
nor any other ferocious beasts.
There will be no other dangers.
Only the redeemed will walk on it.
10 Those who have been ransomed by the
LORD will return.
They will enter Jerusalem* singing,
crowned with everlasting joy.
Sorrow and mourning will disappear,
and they will be filled with joy and
gladness.

Assyria Invades Judah

36 In the fourteenth year of King Hezekiah's reign,* King Sennacherib of
Assyria came to attack the fortified towns
of Judah and conquered them. 2 Then the
king of Assyria sent his chief of staff* from
Lachish with a huge army to confront King
Hezekiah in Jerusalem. The Assyrians took
up a position beside the aqueduct that feeds
water into the upper pool, near the road
leading to the field where cloth is washed.*
3 These are the officials who went out to
meet with them: Eliakim son of Hilkiah,
the palace administrator; Shebna the court
secretary; and Joah son of Asaph, the royal
historian.

Sennacherib Threatens Jerusalem

4 Then the Assyrian king's chief of staff told
them to give this message to Hezekiah:

"This is what the great king of Assyria
says: What are you trusting in that
makes you so confident? 5 Do you think*
that mere words can substitute for
military skill and strength? Who are
you counting on, that you have rebelled
against me? 6 On Egypt? If you lean on
Egypt, it will be like a reed that splinters
beneath your weight and pierces your
hand. Pharaoh, the king of Egypt, is
completely unreliable!
7 "But perhaps you will say to me,
'We are trusting in the LORD our God!'
But isn't he the one who was insulted
by Hezekiah? Didn't Hezekiah tear
down his shrines and altars and make
everyone in Judah and Jerusalem
worship only at the altar here in
Jerusalem?
8 "I'll tell you what! Strike a bargain
with my master, the king of Assyria. I
will give you 2,000 horses if you can
find that many men to ride on them!
9 With your tiny army, how can you
think of challenging even the weakest
contingent of my master's troops, even
with the help of Egypt's chariots and
charioteers? 10 What's more, do you think
we have invaded your land without the
LORD's direction? The LORD himself told
us, 'Attack this land and destroy it!'"

11 Then Eliakim, Shebna, and Joah said to
the Assyrian chief of staff, "Please speak to
us in Aramaic, for we understand it well.
Don't speak in Hebrew,* for the people on
the wall will hear."
12 But Sennacherib's chief of staff replied,
"Do you think my master sent this message
only to you and your master? He wants all
the people to hear it, for when we put this
city under siege, they will suffer along with
you. They will be so hungry and thirsty that
they will eat their own dung and drink their
own urine."
13 Then the chief of staff stood and shouted
in Hebrew to the people on the wall, "Listen
to this message from the great king of
Assyria! 14 This is what the king says: Don't let
Hezekiah deceive you. He will never be able
to rescue you. 15 Don't let him fool you into
trusting in the LORD by saying, 'The LORD
will surely rescue us. This city will never fall
into the hands of the Assyrian king!'
16 "Don't listen to Hezekiah! These are the
terms the king of Assyria is offering: Make
peace with me—open the gates and come
out. Then each of you can continue eating
from your own grapevine and fig tree and
drinking from your own well. 17 Then I will
arrange to take you to another land like this
one—a land of grain and new wine, bread
and vineyards.

34:12 The meaning of the Hebrew is uncertain. **34:14** Hebrew *Lilith*, possibly a reference to a mythical demon of the night. **35:10** Hebrew *Zion.* **36:1** The fourteenth year of Hezekiah's reign was 701 B.C. **36:2a** Or *the rabshakeh;* also in 36:4, 11, 12, 22. **36:2b** Or *bleached.* **36:5** As in Dead Sea Scrolls (see also 2 Kgs 18:20); Masoretic Text reads *Do I think.* **36:11** Hebrew *in the dialect of Judah;* also in 36:13.

▸ **36:1** *See* ***Sennacherib's siege of Jerusalem****, page 514.*

18"Don't let Hezekiah mislead you by
saying, 'The LORD will rescue us!' Have
the gods of any other nations ever saved
their people from the king of Assyria?
19What happened to the gods of Hamath
and Arpad? And what about the gods of
Sepharvaim? Did any god rescue Samaria
from my power? 20What god of any nation
has ever been able to save its people from
my power? So what makes you think that
the LORD can rescue Jerusalem from me?"
21But the people were silent and did not
utter a word because Hezekiah had commanded them, "Do not answer him."
22Then Eliakim son of Hilkiah, the palace
administrator; Shebna the court secretary;
and Joah son of Asaph, the royal historian,
went back to Hezekiah. They tore their
clothes in despair, and they went in to see
the king and told him what the Assyrian
chief of staff had said.

Hezekiah Seeks the LORD's Help

37 When King Hezekiah heard their
report, he tore his clothes and put
on burlap and went into the Temple of the
LORD. 2And he sent Eliakim the palace administrator, Shebna the court secretary, and
the leading priests, all dressed in burlap, to
the prophet Isaiah son of Amoz. 3They told
him, "This is what King Hezekiah says:
Today is a day of trouble, insults, and disgrace. It is like when a child is ready to be
born, but the mother has no strength to
deliver the baby. 4But perhaps the LORD
your God has heard the Assyrian chief of
staff,* sent by the king to defy the living
God, and will punish him for his words. Oh,
pray for those of us who are left!"
5After King Hezekiah's officials delivered
the king's message to Isaiah, 6the prophet
replied, "Say to your master, 'This is what
the LORD says: Do not be disturbed by
this blasphemous speech against me from
the Assyrian king's messengers. 7Listen! I
myself will move against him,* and the king
will receive a message that he is needed at
home. So he will return to his land, where I
will have him killed with a sword.'"
8Meanwhile, the Assyrian chief of staff
left Jerusalem and went to consult the king
of Assyria, who had left Lachish and was
attacking Libnah.
9Soon afterward King Sennacherib received word that King Tirhakah of Ethiopia*
was leading an army to fight against him.
Before leaving to meet the attack, he sent
messengers back to Hezekiah in Jerusalem
with this message:

10"This message is for King Hezekiah of
Judah. Don't let your God, in whom you
trust, deceive you with promises that
Jerusalem will not be captured by the
king of Assyria. 11You know perfectly
well what the kings of Assyria have
done wherever they have gone. They

King Hezekiah

Hezekiah was one of Judah's best kings, ruling for twenty-nine years. He made several important decisions, like strengthening the army and building a tunnel to secure Jerusalem's water supply; but he is commended chiefly for his spiritual reforms—removing paganism and reorganizing Temple worship (2 Kings 18:1-8; 2 Chronicles 29–31). When Assyria marched on Jerusalem in 701 BC, Hezekiah's first response was to pray and send for Isaiah (Isaiah 37:1-2). Encouraged by Isaiah to trust God, Hezekiah spread out the Assyrian king's threatening letter before God and prayed for deliverance (37:14-20). In response to his faith, God sent an angel that night who killed 185,000 Assyrian soldiers, and the remnants of the army withdrew (37:36-37). When Hezekiah contracted a fatal illness, he called out to God, and God extended his life (chapter 38)—another example of his faith. Sadly the faith that resisted Assyrian attack melted before Babylonian flattery, and his pride led him to show his wealth to the Babylonians, who would soon come to take it away.

▸ *See also* ***Assyria****, page 431.*

have completely destroyed everyone
who stood in their way! Why should
you be any different? 12 Have the gods
of other nations rescued them—such
nations as Gozan, Haran, Rezeph,
and the people of Eden who were in
Tel-assar? My predecessors destroyed
them all! 13 What happened to the king
of Hamath and the king of Arpad? What
happened to the kings of Sepharvaim,
Hena, and Ivvah?"

14 After Hezekiah received the letter from
the messengers and read it, he went up
to the LORD's Temple and spread it out
before the LORD. 15 And Hezekiah prayed
this prayer before the LORD: 16 "O LORD of
Heaven's Armies, God of Israel, you are
enthroned between the mighty cherubim!
You alone are God of all the kingdoms of the
earth. You alone created the heavens and
the earth. 17 Bend down, O LORD, and listen!
Open your eyes, O LORD, and see! Listen to
Sennacherib's words of defiance against the
living God.

18 "It is true, LORD, that the kings of Assyria
have destroyed all these nations. 19 And they
have thrown the gods of these nations into
the fire and burned them. But of course
the Assyrians could destroy them! They
were not gods at all—only idols of wood
and stone shaped by human hands. 20 Now,
O LORD our God, rescue us from his power;
then all the kingdoms of the earth will know
that you alone, O LORD, are God.*"

Isaiah Predicts Judah's Deliverance

21 Then Isaiah son of Amoz sent this message
to Hezekiah: "This is what the LORD, the
God of Israel, says: Because you prayed
about King Sennacherib of Assyria, 22 the
LORD has spoken this word against him:

"The virgin daughter of Zion
despises you and laughs at you.
The daughter of Jerusalem
shakes her head in derision as you flee.

23 "Whom have you been defying and ridiculing?
Against whom did you raise your voice?
At whom did you look with such haughty eyes?
It was the Holy One of Israel!
24 By your messengers you have defied the Lord.
You have said, 'With my many chariots
I have conquered the highest mountains—
yes, the remotest peaks of Lebanon.
I have cut down its tallest cedars
and its finest cypress trees.
I have reached its farthest heights
and explored its deepest forests.
25 I have dug wells in many foreign lands*
and refreshed myself with their water.
With the sole of my foot,
I stopped up all the rivers of Egypt!'

26 "But have you not heard?
I decided this long ago.
Long ago I planned it,
and now I am making it happen.
I planned for you to crush fortified cities
into heaps of rubble.
27 That is why their people have so little power
and are so frightened and confused.
They are as weak as grass,
as easily trampled as tender green shoots.
They are like grass sprouting on a housetop,
scorched* before it can grow lush and tall.

28 "But I know you well—
where you stay
and when you come and go.
I know the way you have raged against me.
29 And because of your raging against me
and your arrogance, which I have heard for myself,
I will put my hook in your nose
and my bit in your mouth.
I will make you return
by the same road on which you came."

30 Then Isaiah said to Hezekiah, "Here is the
proof that what I say is true:

"This year you will eat only what grows up by itself,

37:4 Or *the rabshakeh;* also in 37:8. **37:7** Hebrew *I will put a spirit in him.* **37:9** Hebrew *of Cush.* **37:20** As in Dead Sea Scrolls (see also 2 Kgs 19:19); Masoretic Text reads *you alone are the LORD.* **37:25** As in Dead Sea Scrolls (see also 2 Kgs 19:24); Masoretic Text lacks *in many foreign lands.* **37:27** As in Dead Sea Scrolls and some Greek manuscripts (see also 2 Kgs 19:26); most Hebrew manuscripts read *like a terraced field.*

and next year you will eat what
springs up from that.
But in the third year you will plant crops
and harvest them;
you will tend vineyards and eat their
fruit.
31 And you who are left in Judah,
who have escaped the ravages of the
siege,
will put roots down in your own soil
and grow up and flourish.
32 For a remnant of my people will spread
out from Jerusalem,
a group of survivors from Mount Zion.
The passionate commitment of the LORD
of Heaven's Armies
will make this happen!

33 "And this is what the LORD says about the
king of Assyria:

"'His armies will not enter Jerusalem.
They will not even shoot an arrow
at it.
They will not march outside its gates
with their shields
nor build banks of earth against its
walls.
34 The king will return to his own country
by the same road on which he came.
He will not enter this city,'
says the LORD.
35 'For my own honor and for the sake of
my servant David,
I will defend this city and protect it.'"

36 That night the angel of the LORD went
out to the Assyrian camp and killed 185,000
Assyrian soldiers. When the surviving
Assyrians* woke up the next morning, they
found corpses everywhere. 37 Then King
Sennacherib of Assyria broke camp and returned to his own land. He went home to his
capital of Nineveh and stayed there.
38 One day while he was worshiping in the
temple of his god Nisroch, his sons Adrammelech and Sharezer killed him with their
swords. They then escaped to the land
of Ararat, and another son, Esarhaddon,
became the next king of Assyria.

Hezekiah's Sickness and Recovery

38 About that time Hezekiah became
deathly ill, and the prophet Isaiah
son of Amoz went to visit him. He gave the
king this message: "This is what the LORD
says: 'Set your affairs in order, for you are
going to die. You will not recover from this
illness.'"
2 When Hezekiah heard this, he turned
his face to the wall and prayed to the LORD,
3 "Remember, O LORD, how I have always
been faithful to you and have served you
single-mindedly, always doing what pleases
you." Then he broke down and wept bitterly.
4 Then this message came to Isaiah from
the LORD: 5 "Go back to Hezekiah and tell
him, 'This is what the LORD, the God of
your ancestor David, says: I have heard your
prayer and seen your tears. I will add fifteen
years to your life, 6 and I will rescue you and
this city from the king of Assyria. Yes, I will
defend this city.
7 "'And this is the sign from the LORD to
prove that he will do as he promised: 8 I will
cause the sun's shadow to move ten steps
backward on the sundial* of Ahaz!'" So the
shadow on the sundial moved backward
ten steps.

Hezekiah's Poem of Praise

9 When King Hezekiah was well again, he
wrote this poem:

10 I said, "In the prime of my life,
must I now enter the place of the
dead?*
Am I to be robbed of the rest of my
years?"
11 I said, "Never again will I see the LORD
GOD
while still in the land of the living.
Never again will I see my friends
or be with those who live in this
world.
12 My life has been blown away
like a shepherd's tent in a storm.
It has been cut short,
as when a weaver cuts cloth from a
loom.
Suddenly, my life was over.
13 I waited patiently all night,
but I was torn apart as though by lions.
Suddenly, my life was over.
14 Delirious, I chattered like a swallow or a
crane,
and then I moaned like a mourning
dove.
My eyes grew tired of looking to heaven
for help.
I am in trouble, Lord. Help me!"

[15] But what could I say?
For he himself sent this sickness.
Now I will walk humbly throughout my years
because of this anguish I have felt.
[16] Lord, your discipline is good,
for it leads to life and health.
You restore my health
and allow me to live!
[17] Yes, this anguish was good for me,
for you have rescued me from death
and forgiven all my sins.
[18] For the dead* cannot praise you;
they cannot raise their voices in praise.
Those who go down to the grave
can no longer hope in your faithfulness.
[19] Only the living can praise you as I do today.
Each generation tells of your faithfulness to the next.
[20] Think of it—the LORD is ready to heal me!
I will sing his praises with instruments
every day of my life
in the Temple of the LORD.

[21]Isaiah had said to Hezekiah's servants, "Make an ointment from figs and spread it over the boil, and Hezekiah will recover."

[22]And Hezekiah had asked, "What sign will prove that I will go to the Temple of the LORD?"

Envoys from Babylon

39 Soon after this, Merodach-baladan son of Baladan, king of Babylon, sent Hezekiah his best wishes and a gift. He had heard that Hezekiah had been very sick and that he had recovered. [2]Hezekiah was delighted with the Babylonian envoys and showed them everything in his treasure-houses—the silver, the gold, the spices, and the aromatic oils. He also took them to see his armory and showed them everything in his royal treasuries! There was nothing in his palace or kingdom that Hezekiah did not show them.

[3]Then Isaiah the prophet went to King Hezekiah and asked him, "What did those men want? Where were they from?"

Hezekiah replied, "They came from the distant land of Babylon."

[4]"What did they see in your palace?" asked Isaiah.

"They saw everything," Hezekiah replied. "I showed them everything I own—all my royal treasuries."

[5]Then Isaiah said to Hezekiah, "Listen to this message from the LORD of Heaven's Armies: [6]'The time is coming when everything in your palace—all the treasures stored up by your ancestors until now—will be carried off to Babylon. Nothing will be left,' says the LORD. [7]'Some of your very own sons will be taken away into exile. They will become eunuchs who will serve in the palace of Babylon's king.'"

[8]Then Hezekiah said to Isaiah, "This message you have given me from the LORD is good." For the king was thinking, "At least there will be peace and security during my lifetime."

Comfort for God's People

40 [1] "Comfort, comfort my people,"
says your God.
[2] "Speak tenderly to Jerusalem.
Tell her that her sad days are gone
and her sins are pardoned.
Yes, the LORD has punished her twice over
for all her sins."
[3] Listen! It's the voice of someone shouting,
"Clear the way through the wilderness
for the LORD!
Make a straight highway through the wasteland
for our God!
[4] Fill in the valleys,
and level the mountains and hills.
Straighten the curves,
and smooth out the rough places.
[5] Then the glory of the LORD will be revealed,
and all people will see it together.
The LORD has spoken!"*
[6] A voice said, "Shout!"
I asked, "What should I shout?"

"Shout that people are like the grass.
Their beauty fades as quickly
as the flowers in a field.
[7] The grass withers and the flowers fade

37:36 Hebrew *When they.* **38:8** Hebrew *the steps.* **38:10** Hebrew *enter the gates of Sheol?* **38:18** Hebrew *Sheol.* **40:3-5** Greek version reads *He is a voice shouting in the wilderness, / "Prepare the way for the LORD's coming! / Clear a road for our God! / Fill in the valleys, / and level the mountains and hills. / And then the glory of the LORD will be revealed, / and all people will see the salvation sent from God. / The LORD has spoken!"* Compare Matt 3:3; Mark 1:3; Luke 3:4-6.

beneath the breath of the LORD.
And so it is with people.
8 The grass withers and the flowers fade,
but the word of our God stands
forever."

9 O Zion, messenger of good news,
shout from the mountaintops!
Shout it louder, O Jerusalem.*
Shout, and do not be afraid.
Tell the towns of Judah,
"Your God is coming!"
10 Yes, the Sovereign LORD is coming in
power.
He will rule with a powerful arm.
See, he brings his reward with him as
he comes.
11 He will feed his flock like a shepherd.
He will carry the lambs in his arms,
holding them close to his heart.
He will gently lead the mother sheep
with their young.

The LORD Has No Equal

12 Who else has held the oceans in his
hand?
Who has measured off the heavens
with his fingers?
Who else knows the weight of the earth
or has weighed the mountains and
hills on a scale?
13 Who is able to advise the Spirit of the
LORD?*
Who knows enough to give him advice
or teach him?
14 Has the LORD ever needed anyone's
advice?
Does he need instruction about what
is good?
Did someone teach him what is right
or show him the path of justice?
15 No, for all the nations of the world
are but a drop in the bucket.
They are nothing more
than dust on the scales.
He picks up the whole earth
as though it were a grain of sand.
16 All the wood in Lebanon's forests
and all Lebanon's animals would not
be enough
to make a burnt offering worthy of our
God.
17 The nations of the world are worth
nothing to him.
In his eyes they count for less than
nothing—
mere emptiness and froth.

18 To whom can you compare God?
What image can you find to resemble
him?
19 Can he be compared to an idol formed in
a mold,
overlaid with gold, and decorated
with silver chains?
20 Or if people are too poor for that,
they might at least choose wood that
won't decay
and a skilled craftsman
to carve an image that won't fall down!

21 Haven't you heard? Don't you
understand?
Are you deaf to the words of God—
the words he gave before the world
began?
Are you so ignorant?
22 God sits above the circle of the earth.
The people below seem like
grasshoppers to him!
He spreads out the heavens like a
curtain
and makes his tent from them.
23 He judges the great people of the world
and brings them all to nothing.
24 They hardly get started, barely taking
root,
when he blows on them and they
wither.
The wind carries them off like chaff.

25 "To whom will you compare me?
Who is my equal?" asks the Holy One.

26 Look up into the heavens.
Who created all the stars?
He brings them out like an army, one
after another,
calling each by its name.
Because of his great power and
incomparable strength,
not a single one is missing.
27 O Jacob, how can you say the LORD does
not see your troubles?
O Israel, how can you say God ignores
your rights?

▸ **40:11** *See **Shepherds**, page 936.*

28 Have you never heard?
Have you never understood?
The LORD is the everlasting God,
the Creator of all the earth.
He never grows weak or weary.
No one can measure the depths of his understanding.
29 He gives power to the weak
and strength to the powerless.
30 Even youths will become weak and tired,
and young men will fall in exhaustion.
31 But those who trust in the LORD will find new strength.
They will soar high on wings like eagles.
They will run and not grow weary.
They will walk and not faint.

God's Help for Israel

41 1 "Listen in silence before me, you lands beyond the sea.
Bring your strongest arguments.
Come now and speak.
The court is ready for your case.

2 "Who has stirred up this king from the east,
rightly calling him to God's service?
Who gives this man victory over many nations
and permits him to trample their kings underfoot?
With his sword, he reduces armies to dust.
With his bow, he scatters them like chaff before the wind.
3 He chases them away and goes on safely,
though he is walking over unfamiliar ground.
4 Who has done such mighty deeds,
summoning each new generation from the beginning of time?
It is I, the LORD, the First and the Last.
I alone am he."

5 The lands beyond the sea watch in fear.
Remote lands tremble and mobilize for war.
6 The idol makers encourage one another,
saying to each other, "Be strong!"
7 The carver encourages the goldsmith,
and the molder helps at the anvil.
"Good," they say. "It's coming along fine."
Carefully they join the parts together,
then fasten the thing in place so it won't fall over.

40:9 Or *O messenger of good news, shout to Zion from the mountaintops! Shout it louder to Jerusalem.* **40:13** Greek version reads *Who can know the LORD's thoughts?* Compare Rom 11:34; 1 Cor 2:16.

The greatness of God

In chapters 1–39 Isaiah had spoken of the Assyrian threat, which climaxed in Assyria's attack on Jerusalem (chapters 36–38), and the rising power of Babylon, which sought Judah's help against Assyria (chapter 39). Now, from chapter 40 onward, there is a sudden leap forward to a future time when Babylon will have conquered Assyria, established its own kingdom, and exiled Judah. But Isaiah prophesied that God's people should not be discouraged when that happens (40:1-2), for that would be the very moment when God would display his greatness; so even now they should prepare for his coming (40:3-5).

In contrast to the frailty and transience of humanity (40:6-8), God is great, Isaiah declared. He saw him coming "in power" (40:10)—yet also with tenderness (40:11). His greatness is seen in his creation (40:12) and in his wisdom (40:13-14); compared to him, "the nations of the world are but a drop in the bucket" (40:15), "less than nothing" (40:17)—yes, even nations like Assyria and Babylon. God is greater than them all! He rules over rulers (40:21-24), sustains the universe (40:26), and is the everlasting God who never gets weary (40:28).

It is as we remind ourselves how very great God is, Isaiah declared, that everything else seems so small. It is as we trust in this great God that we find our resources strengthened by him (40:30-31).

8 "But as for you, Israel my servant,
Jacob my chosen one,
descended from Abraham my friend,
9 I have called you back from the ends of the earth,
saying, 'You are my servant.'
For I have chosen you
and will not throw you away.
10 Don't be afraid, for I am with you.
Don't be discouraged, for I am your God.
I will strengthen you and help you.
I will hold you up with my victorious right hand.

11 "See, all your angry enemies lie there,
confused and humiliated.
Anyone who opposes you will die
and come to nothing.
12 You will look in vain
for those who tried to conquer you.
Those who attack you
will come to nothing.
13 For I hold you by your right hand—
I, the LORD your God.
And I say to you,
'Don't be afraid. I am here to help you.
14 Though you are a lowly worm, O Jacob,
don't be afraid, people of Israel, for I will help you.
I am the LORD, your Redeemer.
I am the Holy One of Israel.'
15 You will be a new threshing instrument
with many sharp teeth.
You will tear your enemies apart,
making chaff of mountains.
16 You will toss them into the air,
and the wind will blow them all away;
a whirlwind will scatter them.
Then you will rejoice in the LORD.
You will glory in the Holy One of Israel.

17 "When the poor and needy search for water and there is none,
and their tongues are parched from thirst,
then I, the LORD, will answer them.
I, the God of Israel, will never abandon them.
18 I will open up rivers for them on the high plateaus.
I will give them fountains of water in the valleys.
I will fill the desert with pools of water.
Rivers fed by springs will flow across the parched ground.
19 I will plant trees in the barren desert—
cedar, acacia, myrtle, olive, cypress, fir, and pine.
20 I am doing this so all who see this miracle
will understand what it means—
that it is the LORD who has done this,
the Holy One of Israel who created it.

21 "Present the case for your idols,"
says the LORD.
"Let them show what they can do,"
says the King of Israel.*
22 "Let them try to tell us what happened long ago
so that we may consider the evidence.
Or let them tell us what the future holds,
so we can know what's going to happen.
23 Yes, tell us what will occur in the days ahead.
Then we will know you are gods.
In fact, do anything—good or bad!
Do something that will amaze and frighten us.
24 But no! You are less than nothing and can do nothing at all.
Those who choose you pollute themselves.

25 "But I have stirred up a leader who will approach from the north.
From the east he will call on my name.
I will give him victory over kings and princes.
He will trample them as a potter treads on clay.
26 "Who told you from the beginning
that this would happen?
Who predicted this,
making you admit that he was right?
No one said a word!
27 I was the first to tell Zion,
'Look! Help is on the way!'*
I will send Jerusalem a messenger with good news.
28 Not one of your idols told you this.
Not one gave any answer when I asked.
29 See, they are all foolish, worthless things.
All your idols are as empty as the wind.

The LORD's Chosen Servant

42

1 "Look at my servant, whom I strengthen.
He is my chosen one, who pleases me.
I have put my Spirit upon him.
He will bring justice to the nations.
2 He will not shout
or raise his voice in public.
3 He will not crush the weakest reed
or put out a flickering candle.
He will bring justice to all who have been wronged.
4 He will not falter or lose heart
until justice prevails throughout the earth.
Even distant lands beyond the sea will wait for his instruction.*"
5 God, the LORD, created the heavens and stretched them out.
He created the earth and everything in it.
He gives breath to everyone,
life to everyone who walks the earth.
And it is he who says,
6 "I, the LORD, have called you to demonstrate my righteousness.
I will take you by the hand and guard you,
and I will give you to my people, Israel,
as a symbol of my covenant with them.
And you will be a light to guide the nations.
7 You will open the eyes of the blind.
You will free the captives from prison,
releasing those who sit in dark dungeons.
8 "I am the LORD; that is my name!
I will not give my glory to anyone else,
nor share my praise with carved idols.
9 Everything I prophesied has come true,
and now I will prophesy again.
I will tell you the future before it happens."

A Song of Praise to the LORD

10 Sing a new song to the LORD!
Sing his praises from the ends of the earth!
Sing, all you who sail the seas,
all you who live in distant coastlands.
11 Join in the chorus, you desert towns;
let the villages of Kedar rejoice!
Let the people of Sela sing for joy;
shout praises from the mountaintops!
12 Let the whole world glorify the LORD;
let it sing his praise.
13 The LORD will march forth like a mighty hero;
he will come out like a warrior, full of fury.
He will shout his battle cry
and crush all his enemies.

41:21 Hebrew *the King of Jacob.* See note on 14:1. **41:27** Or *'Look! They are coming home.'* **42:4** Greek version reads *And his name will be the hope of all the world.* Compare Matt 12:21.

The Servant Songs

The Servant Songs are poems about someone who would supremely fulfill the role of God's servant. Isaiah recorded four "Servant Songs": 42:1-4; 49:1-6; 50:4-9; 52:13–53:12. Initially, it seems as if the Servant is Israel; but by chapter 53 Isaiah is clearly referring to an individual who would obey God completely and give his life as a sacrifice for sinners.

The New Testament sees these prophecies of the suffering Servant fulfilled in Jesus Christ. Jesus said he had come as a servant (e.g., Mark 10:45) and quoted from the fourth Servant Song (Luke 22:37). Peter referred to him as God's Servant (e.g., Acts 3:13; cf. 1 Peter 2:21-25), and Paul often alluded to this concept of Jesus as the Servant (e.g., Philippians 2:6-11). There are also a number of direct quotations from the Servant Songs in the New Testament, showing how widely this interpretation was accepted (e.g., Matthew 8:17; 12:18-21; John 12:38; Acts 8:32-33; Romans 10:16; 15:21). As you read the Servant Songs, think about how accurately they prophesy about Jesus.

14 He will say, "I have long been silent;
yes, I have restrained myself.
But now, like a woman in labor,
I will cry and groan and pant.
15 I will level the mountains and hills
and blight all their greenery.
I will turn the rivers into dry land
and will dry up all the pools.
16 I will lead blind Israel down a new path,
guiding them along an unfamiliar
way.
I will brighten the darkness before them
and smooth out the road ahead of
them.
Yes, I will indeed do these things;
I will not forsake them.
17 But those who trust in idols,
who say, 'You are our gods,'
will be turned away in shame.

Israel's Failure to Listen and See

18 "Listen, you who are deaf!
Look and see, you blind!
19 Who is as blind as my own people, my
servant?
Who is as deaf as my messenger?
Who is as blind as my chosen people,
the servant of the LORD?
20 You see and recognize what is right
but refuse to act on it.
You hear with your ears,
but you don't really listen."
21 Because he is righteous,
the LORD has exalted his glorious law.
22 But his own people have been robbed
and plundered,
enslaved, imprisoned, and trapped.
They are fair game for anyone
and have no one to protect them,
no one to take them back home.
23 Who will hear these lessons from the
past
and see the ruin that awaits you in the
future?
24 Who allowed Israel to be robbed and
hurt?
It was the LORD, against whom we
sinned,
for the people would not walk in his
path,
nor would they obey his law.
25 Therefore, he poured out his fury on
them
and destroyed them in battle.
They were enveloped in flames,
but they still refused to understand.
They were consumed by fire,
but they did not learn their
lesson.

The Savior of Israel

43 1 But now, O Jacob, listen to the
LORD who created you.
O Israel, the one who formed you
says,
"Do not be afraid, for I have ransomed
you.
I have called you by name; you are
mine.
2 When you go through deep waters,
I will be with you.
When you go through rivers of difficulty,
you will not drown.
When you walk through the fire of
oppression,
you will not be burned up;
the flames will not consume you.
3 For I am the LORD, your God,
the Holy One of Israel, your Savior.
I gave Egypt as a ransom for your
freedom;
I gave Ethiopia* and Seba in your
place.
4 Others were given in exchange for you.
I traded their lives for yours
because you are precious to me.
You are honored, and I love you.
5 "Do not be afraid, for I am with you.
I will gather you and your children
from east and west.
6 I will say to the north and south,
'Bring my sons and daughters back to
Israel
from the distant corners of the earth.
7 Bring all who claim me as their God,
for I have made them for my glory.
It was I who created them.'"
8 Bring out the people who have eyes but
are blind,
who have ears but are deaf.
9 Gather the nations together!
Assemble the peoples of the world!
Which of their idols has ever foretold
such things?
Which can predict what will happen
tomorrow?
Where are the witnesses of such
predictions?

Who can verify that they spoke the truth?

10 "But you are my witnesses, O Israel!" says the LORD.
"You are my servant.
You have been chosen to know me, believe in me,
and understand that I alone am God.
There is no other God—
there never has been, and there never will be.
11 I, yes I, am the LORD,
and there is no other Savior.
12 First I predicted your rescue,
then I saved you and proclaimed it to the world.
No foreign god has ever done this.
You are witnesses that I am the only God,"
says the LORD.
13 "From eternity to eternity I am God.
No one can snatch anyone out of my hand.
No one can undo what I have done."

The LORD's Promise of Victory

14 This is what the LORD says—your Redeemer, the Holy One of Israel:

"For your sakes I will send an army against Babylon,
forcing the Babylonians* to flee in those ships they are so proud of.
15 I am the LORD, your Holy One,
Israel's Creator and King.
16 I am the LORD, who opened a way through the waters,
making a dry path through the sea.
17 I called forth the mighty army of Egypt
with all its chariots and horses.
I drew them beneath the waves, and they drowned,
their lives snuffed out like a smoldering candlewick.

18 "But forget all that—
it is nothing compared to what I am going to do.
19 For I am about to do something new.
See, I have already begun! Do you not see it?
I will make a pathway through the wilderness.
I will create rivers in the dry wasteland.
20 The wild animals in the fields will thank me,
the jackals and owls, too,
for giving them water in the desert.
Yes, I will make rivers in the dry wasteland
so my chosen people can be refreshed.
21 I have made Israel for myself,
and they will someday honor me before the whole world.

22 "But, dear family of Jacob, you refuse to ask for my help.
You have grown tired of me, O Israel!
23 You have not brought me sheep or goats for burnt offerings.
You have not honored me with sacrifices,
though I have not burdened and wearied you
with requests for grain offerings and frankincense.
24 You have not brought me fragrant calamus
or pleased me with the fat from sacrifices.
Instead, you have burdened me with your sins
and wearied me with your faults.

25 "I—yes, I alone—will blot out your sins for my own sake
and will never think of them again.
26 Let us review the situation together,
and you can present your case to prove your innocence.
27 From the very beginning, your first ancestor sinned against me;
all your leaders broke my laws.
28 That is why I have disgraced your priests;
I have decreed complete destruction* for Jacob
and shame for Israel.

44 1 "But now, listen to me, Jacob my servant,
Israel my chosen one.
2 The LORD who made you and helps you says:
Do not be afraid, O Jacob, my servant,
O dear Israel,* my chosen one.

43:3 Hebrew *Cush.* **43:14** Or *Chaldeans.* **43:28** The Hebrew term used here refers to the complete consecration of things or people to the LORD, either by destroying them or by giving them as an offering. **44:2** Hebrew *Jeshurun,* a term of endearment for Israel.

3 For I will pour out water to quench your thirst
and to irrigate your parched fields.
And I will pour out my Spirit on your descendants,
and my blessing on your children.
4 They will thrive like watered grass,
like willows on a riverbank.
5 Some will proudly claim, 'I belong to the LORD.'
Others will say, 'I am a descendant of Jacob.'
Some will write the LORD's name on their hands
and will take the name of Israel as their own."

The Foolishness of Idols

6 This is what the LORD says—Israel's King and Redeemer, the LORD of Heaven's Armies:

"I am the First and the Last;
there is no other God.
7 Who is like me?
Let him step forward and prove to you his power.
Let him do as I have done since ancient times
when I established a people and explained its future.
8 Do not tremble; do not be afraid.
Did I not proclaim my purposes for you long ago?
You are my witnesses—is there any other God?
No! There is no other Rock—not one!"
9 How foolish are those who manufacture idols.
These prized objects are really worthless.
The people who worship idols don't know this,
so they are all put to shame.
10 Who but a fool would make his own god—
an idol that cannot help him one bit?
11 All who worship idols will be disgraced
along with all these craftsmen—mere humans—
who claim they can make a god.
They may all stand together,
but they will stand in terror and shame.
12 The blacksmith stands at his forge to make a sharp tool,
pounding and shaping it with all his might.
His work makes him hungry and weak.
It makes him thirsty and faint.
13 Then the wood-carver measures a block of wood
and draws a pattern on it.
He works with chisel and plane
and carves it into a human figure.
He gives it human beauty
and puts it in a little shrine.
14 He cuts down cedars;
he selects the cypress and the oak;
he plants the pine in the forest
to be nourished by the rain.
15 Then he uses part of the wood to make a fire.
With it he warms himself and bakes his bread.
Then—yes, it's true—he takes the rest of it
and makes himself a god to worship!
He makes an idol
and bows down in front of it!
16 He burns part of the tree to roast his meat
and to keep himself warm.
He says, "Ah, that fire feels good."
17 Then he takes what's left
and makes his god: a carved idol!
He falls down in front of it,
worshiping and praying to it.
"Rescue me!" he says.
"You are my god!"

18 Such stupidity and ignorance!
Their eyes are closed, and they cannot see.
Their minds are shut, and they cannot think.
19 The person who made the idol never stops to reflect,
"Why, it's just a block of wood!
I burned half of it for heat
and used it to bake my bread and roast my meat.
How can the rest of it be a god?
Should I bow down to worship a piece of wood?"
20 The poor, deluded fool feeds on ashes.
He trusts something that can't help him at all.
Yet he cannot bring himself to ask,
"Is this idol that I'm holding in my hand a lie?"

Restoration for Jerusalem

21 "Pay attention, O Jacob,
for you are my servant, O Israel.
I, the LORD, made you,
and I will not forget you.
22 I have swept away your sins like a cloud.
I have scattered your offenses like the morning mist.
Oh, return to me,
for I have paid the price to set you free."

23 Sing, O heavens, for the LORD has done this wondrous thing.
Shout for joy, O depths of the earth!
Break into song,
O mountains and forests and every tree!
For the LORD has redeemed Jacob
and is glorified in Israel.

24 This is what the LORD says—
your Redeemer and Creator:
"I am the LORD, who made all things.
I alone stretched out the heavens.
Who was with me
when I made the earth?
25 I expose the false prophets as liars
and make fools of fortune-tellers.
I cause the wise to give bad advice,
thus proving them to be fools.
26 But I carry out the predictions of my prophets!
By them I say to Jerusalem, 'People will live here again,'
and to the towns of Judah, 'You will be rebuilt;
I will restore all your ruins!'
27 When I speak to the rivers and say, 'Dry up!'
they will be dry.
28 When I say of Cyrus, 'He is my shepherd,'
he will certainly do as I say.
He will command, 'Rebuild Jerusalem';
he will say, 'Restore the Temple.'"

Cyrus, the LORD's Chosen One

45 1 This is what the LORD says to Cyrus, his anointed one,
whose right hand he will empower.
Before him, mighty kings will be paralyzed with fear.
Their fortress gates will be opened,
never to shut again.
2 This is what the LORD says:

"I will go before you, Cyrus,
and level the mountains.*
I will smash down gates of bronze
and cut through bars of iron.
3 And I will give you treasures hidden in the darkness—
secret riches.
I will do this so you may know that I am the LORD,
the God of Israel, the one who calls you by name.

4 "And why have I called you for this work?
Why did I call you by name when you did not know me?
It is for the sake of Jacob my servant,
Israel my chosen one.
5 I am the LORD;
there is no other God.
I have equipped you for battle,
though you don't even know me,
6 so all the world from east to west
will know there is no other God.
I am the LORD, and there is no other.
7 I create the light and make the darkness.
I send good times and bad times.
I, the LORD, am the one who does these things.

8 "Open up, O heavens,
and pour out your righteousness.
Let the earth open wide
so salvation and righteousness can sprout up together.
I, the LORD, created them.

9 "What sorrow awaits those who argue with their Creator.
Does a clay pot argue with its maker?
Does the clay dispute with the one who shapes it, saying,
'Stop, you're doing it wrong!'
Does the pot exclaim,
'How clumsy can you be?'
10 How terrible it would be if a newborn baby said to its father,
'Why was I born?'
or if it said to its mother,
'Why did you make me this way?'"
11 This is what the LORD says—
the Holy One of Israel and your Creator:

45:2 As in Dead Sea Scrolls and Greek version; Masoretic Text reads *the swellings.*

"Do you question what I do for my
children?
Do you give me orders about the work
of my hands?
12 I am the one who made the earth
and created people to live on it.
With my hands I stretched out the
heavens.
All the stars are at my command.
13 I will raise up Cyrus to fulfill my
righteous purpose,
and I will guide his actions.
He will restore my city and free my
captive people—
without seeking a reward!
I, the LORD of Heaven's Armies, have
spoken!"

Future Conversion of Gentiles

14 This is what the LORD says:

"You will rule the Egyptians,
the Ethiopians,* and the Sabeans.
They will come to you with all their
merchandise,
and it will all be yours.
They will follow you as prisoners in
chains.
They will fall to their knees in front of
you and say,
'God is with you, and he is the only God.
There is no other.'"

15 Truly, O God of Israel, our Savior,
you work in mysterious ways.
16 All craftsmen who make idols will be
humiliated.
They will all be disgraced together.
17 But the LORD will save the people of
Israel
with eternal salvation.
Throughout everlasting ages,
they will never again be humiliated
and disgraced.

18 For the LORD is God,
and he created the heavens and earth
and put everything in place.
He made the world to be lived in,
not to be a place of empty chaos.
"I am the LORD," he says,
"and there is no other.
19 I publicly proclaim bold promises.
I do not whisper obscurities in some
dark corner.
I would not have told the people of
Israel* to seek me
if I could not be found.
I, the LORD, speak only what is true
and declare only what is right.

20 "Gather together and come,
you fugitives from surrounding nations.
What fools they are who carry around
their wooden idols
and pray to gods that cannot save!
21 Consult together, argue your case.
Get together and decide what to say.
Who made these things known so long
ago?
What idol ever told you they would
happen?
Was it not I, the LORD?
For there is no other God but me,
a righteous God and Savior.
There is none but me.

King Cyrus

History shows us that every empire—even the greatest—rises and then falls. Babylon was the greatest empire the world had known, but it became internally weak; and a new empire budded right under its nose—Persia. In 539 BC King Cyrus of Persia attacked the Babylonians and conquered Babylon, swallowing up its empire. Cyrus's approach to conquered peoples was very different from that of the Babylonians. He believed that if you treated them well they would serve you well; so in 538 BC he issued a decree allowing conquered peoples, including the Jews, to go back to their homelands (2 Chronicles 36:22-23; Ezra 1:1-4). This in itself was a remarkable event; but even more remarkable is the fact that Isaiah prophesied this would happen, even calling Cyrus by name, over 150 years before it occurred (Isaiah 45:1-13).

▶ *See also* ***Persia****, page 519.*

22 Let all the world look to me for salvation!
For I am God; there is no other.
23 I have sworn by my own name;
I have spoken the truth,
and I will never go back on my word:
Every knee will bend to me,
and every tongue will declare
allegiance to me.*"
24 The people will declare,
"The LORD is the source of all my
righteousness and strength."
And all who were angry with him
will come to him and be ashamed.
25 In the LORD all the generations of Israel
will be justified,
and in him they will boast.

Babylon's False Gods

46 1 Bel and Nebo, the gods of
Babylon,
bow as they are lowered to the
ground.
They are being hauled away on ox carts.
The poor beasts stagger under the
weight.
2 Both the idols and their owners are
bowed down.
The gods cannot protect the people,
and the people cannot protect the gods.
They go off into captivity together.

3 "Listen to me, descendants of Jacob,
all you who remain in Israel.
I have cared for you since you were born.
Yes, I carried you before you were
born.
4 I will be your God throughout your
lifetime—
until your hair is white with age.
I made you, and I will care for you.
I will carry you along and save you.

5 "To whom will you compare me?
Who is my equal?
6 Some people pour out their silver and
gold
and hire a craftsman to make a god
from it.
Then they bow down and worship it!
7 They carry it around on their shoulders,
and when they set it down, it stays
there.
It can't even move!
And when someone prays to it, there is
no answer.
It can't rescue anyone from trouble.

8 "Do not forget this! Keep it in mind!
Remember this, you guilty ones.
9 Remember the things I have done in the
past.
For I alone am God!
I am God, and there is none like me.
10 Only I can tell you the future
before it even happens.
Everything I plan will come to pass,
for I do whatever I wish.
11 I will call a swift bird of prey from the
east—
a leader from a distant land to come
and do my bidding.
I have said what I would do,
and I will do it.

12 "Listen to me, you stubborn people
who are so far from doing right.
13 For I am ready to set things right,
not in the distant future, but right now!
I am ready to save Jerusalem*
and show my glory to Israel.

Prediction of Babylon's Fall

47 1 "Come down, virgin daughter of
Babylon, and sit in the dust.
For your days of sitting on a throne
have ended.
O daughter of Babylonia,* never again
will you be
the lovely princess, tender and
delicate.
2 Take heavy millstones and grind flour.
Remove your veil, and strip off your
robe.
Expose yourself to public view.*
3 You will be naked and burdened with
shame.
I will take vengeance against you
without pity."

4 Our Redeemer, whose name is the LORD
of Heaven's Armies,
is the Holy One of Israel.

5 "O beautiful Babylon, sit now in
darkness and silence.
Never again will you be known as the
queen of kingdoms.
6 For I was angry with my chosen people
and punished them by letting them
fall into your hands.

45:14 Hebrew *Cushites.* **45:19** Hebrew *of Jacob.* See note on 14:1. **45:23** Hebrew *will confess;* Greek version reads *will declare allegiance to God.* Compare Rom 14:11. **46:13** Hebrew *Zion.* **47:1** Or *Chaldea;* also in 47:5. **47:2** Hebrew *Bare your legs; pass through the rivers.*

But you, Babylon, showed them no mercy.
You oppressed even the elderly.
7 You said, 'I will reign forever as queen of the world!'
You did not reflect on your actions or think about their consequences.

8 "Listen to this, you pleasure-loving kingdom,
living at ease and feeling secure.
You say, 'I am the only one, and there is no other.
I will never be a widow or lose my children.'
9 Well, both these things will come upon you in a moment:
widowhood and the loss of your children.
Yes, these calamities will come upon you,
despite all your witchcraft and magic.

10 "You felt secure in your wickedness.
'No one sees me,' you said.
But your 'wisdom' and 'knowledge' have led you astray,
and you said, 'I am the only one, and there is no other.'
11 So disaster will overtake you,
and you won't be able to charm it away.
Calamity will fall upon you,
and you won't be able to buy your way out.
A catastrophe will strike you suddenly,
one for which you are not prepared.

12 "Now use your magical charms!
Use the spells you have worked at all these years!
Maybe they will do you some good.
Maybe they can make someone afraid of you.
13 All the advice you receive has made you tired.
Where are all your astrologers,
those stargazers who make predictions each month?
Let them stand up and save you from what the future holds.
14 But they are like straw burning in a fire;
they cannot save themselves from the flame.
You will get no help from them at all;
their hearth is no place to sit for warmth.
15 And all your friends,
those with whom you've done business since childhood,
will go their own ways,
turning a deaf ear to your cries.

God's Stubborn People

48 1 "Listen to me, O family of Jacob,
you who are called by the name of Israel
and born into the family of Judah.
Listen, you who take oaths in the name of the LORD
and call on the God of Israel.
You don't keep your promises,
2 even though you call yourself the holy city
and talk about depending on the God of Israel,
whose name is the LORD of Heaven's Armies.
3 Long ago I told you what was going to happen.
Then suddenly I took action,
and all my predictions came true.
4 For I know how stubborn and obstinate you are.
Your necks are as unbending as iron.
Your heads are as hard as bronze.
5 That is why I told you what would happen;
I told you beforehand what I was going to do.
Then you could never say, 'My idols did it.
My wooden image and metal god commanded it to happen!'
6 You have heard my predictions and seen them fulfilled,
but you refuse to admit it.
Now I will tell you new things,
secrets you have not yet heard.
7 They are brand new, not things from the past.
So you cannot say, 'We knew that all the time!'

8 "Yes, I will tell you of things that are entirely new,
things you never heard of before.
For I know so well what traitors you are.
You have been rebels from birth.
9 Yet for my own sake and for the honor of my name,
I will hold back my anger and not wipe you out.

10 I have refined you, but not as silver is
refined.
Rather, I have refined you in the
furnace of suffering.
11 I will rescue you for my sake—
yes, for my own sake!
I will not let my reputation be tarnished,
and I will not share my glory with
idols!

Freedom from Babylon

12 "Listen to me, O family of Jacob,
Israel my chosen one!
I alone am God,
the First and the Last.
13 It was my hand that laid the foundations
of the earth,
my right hand that spread out the
heavens above.
When I call out the stars,
they all appear in order."
14 Have any of your idols ever told you
this?
Come, all of you, and listen:
The LORD has chosen Cyrus as his ally.
He will use him to put an end to the
empire of Babylon
and to destroy the Babylonian*
armies.
15 "I have said it: I am calling Cyrus!
I will send him on this errand and will
help him succeed.
16 Come closer, and listen to this.
From the beginning I have told you
plainly what would happen."

And now the Sovereign LORD and his Spirit
have sent me with this message.
17 This is what the LORD says—
your Redeemer, the Holy One of Israel:
"I am the LORD your God,
who teaches you what is good for you
and leads you along the paths you
should follow.
18 Oh, that you had listened to my
commands!
Then you would have had peace
flowing like a gentle river
and righteousness rolling over you
like waves in the sea.
19 Your descendants would have been like
the sands along the seashore—
too many to count!
There would have been no need for your
destruction,
or for cutting off your family name."
20 Yet even now, be free from your captivity!
Leave Babylon and the Babylonians.*
Sing out this message!
Shout it to the ends of the earth!
The LORD has redeemed his servants,
the people of Israel.*
21 They were not thirsty
when he led them through the
desert.
He divided the rock,
and water gushed out for them to
drink.
22 "But there is no peace for the wicked,"
says the LORD.

The LORD's Servant Commissioned

49 1 Listen to me, all you in distant
lands!
Pay attention, you who are far away!
The LORD called me before my birth;
from within the womb he called me
by name.
2 He made my words of judgment as sharp
as a sword.
He has hidden me in the shadow of
his hand.
I am like a sharp arrow in his quiver.
3 He said to me, "You are my servant,
Israel,
and you will bring me glory."
4 I replied, "But my work seems so
useless!
I have spent my strength for nothing
and to no purpose.
Yet I leave it all in the LORD's hand;
I will trust God for my reward."
5 And now the LORD speaks—
the one who formed me in my
mother's womb to be his servant,
who commissioned me to bring Israel
back to him.
The LORD has honored me,
and my God has given me strength.
6 He says, "You will do more than restore
the people of Israel to me.
I will make you a light to the Gentiles,
and you will bring my salvation to the
ends of the earth."

48:14 Or *Chaldean.* **48:20a** Or *the Chaldeans.* **48:20b** Hebrew *his servant, Jacob.* See note on 14:1.

7 The LORD, the Redeemer
and Holy One of Israel,
says to the one who is despised and
rejected by the nations,
to the one who is the servant of rulers:
"Kings will stand at attention when you
pass by.
Princes will also bow low
because of the LORD, the faithful one,
the Holy One of Israel, who has
chosen you."

Promises of Israel's Restoration

8 This is what the LORD says:

"At just the right time, I will respond to
you.*
On the day of salvation I will help you.
I will protect you and give you to the
people
as my covenant with them.
Through you I will reestablish the land
of Israel
and assign it to its own people again.
9 I will say to the prisoners, 'Come out in
freedom,'
and to those in darkness, 'Come into
the light.'
They will be my sheep, grazing in green
pastures
and on hills that were previously bare.
10 They will neither hunger nor thirst.
The searing sun will not reach them
anymore.
For the LORD in his mercy will lead
them;
he will lead them beside cool waters.
11 And I will make my mountains into level
paths for them.
The highways will be raised above the
valleys.
12 See, my people will return from far
away,
from lands to the north and west,
and from as far south as Egypt.*"

13 Sing for joy, O heavens!
Rejoice, O earth!
Burst into song, O mountains!
For the LORD has comforted his people
and will have compassion on them in
their suffering.
14 Yet Jerusalem* says, "The LORD has
deserted us;
the Lord has forgotten us."

15 "Never! Can a mother forget her nursing
child?
Can she feel no love for the child she
has borne?
But even if that were possible,
I would not forget you!
16 See, I have written your name on the
palms of my hands.
Always in my mind is a picture of
Jerusalem's walls in ruins.
17 Soon your descendants will come back,
and all who are trying to destroy you
will go away.
18 Look around you and see,
for all your children will come back
to you.
As surely as I live," says the LORD,
"they will be like jewels or bridal
ornaments for you to display.

19 "Even the most desolate parts of your
abandoned land
will soon be crowded with your
people.
Your enemies who enslaved you
will be far away.
20 The generations born in exile will return
and say,
'We need more room! It's crowded
here!'
21 Then you will think to yourself,
'Who has given me all these
descendants?
For most of my children were killed,
and the rest were carried away into
exile.
I was left here all alone.
Where did all these people come
from?
Who bore these children?
Who raised them for me?'"

22 This is what the Sovereign LORD says:
"See, I will give a signal to the godless
nations.
They will carry your little sons back to
you in their arms;
they will bring your daughters on
their shoulders.
23 Kings and queens will serve you
and care for all your needs.
They will bow to the earth before you
and lick the dust from your feet.
Then you will know that I am the LORD.
Those who trust in me will never be
put to shame."

24 Who can snatch the plunder of war from
the hands of a warrior?
Who can demand that a tyrant* let his
captives go?
25 But the LORD says,
"The captives of warriors will be
released,
and the plunder of tyrants will be
retrieved.
For I will fight those who fight you,
and I will save your children.
26 I will feed your enemies with their own
flesh.
They will be drunk with rivers of their
own blood.
All the world will know that I, the LORD,
am your Savior and your Redeemer,
the Mighty One of Israel.*"

50 This is what the LORD says:
"Was your mother sent away
because I divorced her?
Did I sell you as slaves to my
creditors?
No, you were sold because of your sins.
And your mother, too, was taken
because of your sins.
2 Why was no one there when I came?
Why didn't anyone answer when I
called?
Is it because I have no power to rescue?
No, that is not the reason!
For I can speak to the sea and make it
dry up!
I can turn rivers into deserts covered
with dying fish.
3 I dress the skies in darkness,
covering them with clothes of
mourning."

The LORD's Obedient Servant

4 The Sovereign LORD has given me his
words of wisdom,
so that I know how to comfort the
weary.
Morning by morning he wakens me
and opens my understanding to his
will.
5 The Sovereign LORD has spoken to me,
and I have listened.
I have not rebelled or turned away.
6 I offered my back to those who beat me
and my cheeks to those who pulled
out my beard.
I did not hide my face
from mockery and spitting.
7 Because the Sovereign LORD helps me,
I will not be disgraced.
Therefore, I have set my face like a stone,
determined to do his will.
And I know that I will not be put to
shame.
8 He who gives me justice is near.
Who will dare to bring charges against
me now?
Where are my accusers?
Let them appear!
9 See, the Sovereign LORD is on my side!
Who will declare me guilty?
All my enemies will be destroyed
like old clothes that have been eaten
by moths!

10 Who among you fears the LORD
and obeys his servant?
If you are walking in darkness,
without a ray of light,
trust in the LORD
and rely on your God.
11 But watch out, you who live in your own
light
and warm yourselves by your own
fires.
This is the reward you will receive from
me:
You will soon fall down in great
torment.

A Call to Trust the LORD

51 1 "Listen to me, all who hope for
deliverance—
all who seek the LORD!
Consider the rock from which you were
cut,
the quarry from which you were
mined.
2 Yes, think about Abraham, your
ancestor,
and Sarah, who gave birth to your
nation.
Abraham was only one man when I
called him.
But when I blessed him, he became a
great nation."

49:8 Greek version reads *I heard you*. Compare 2 Cor 6:2. **49:12** As in Dead Sea Scrolls, which read *from the region of Aswan*, which is in southern Egypt. Masoretic Text reads *from the region of Sinim*. **49:14** Hebrew *Zion*. **49:24** As in Dead Sea Scrolls, Syriac version, and Latin Vulgate (also see 49:25); Masoretic Text reads *a righteous person*. **49:26** Hebrew *of Jacob*. See note on 14:1.

[3] The LORD will comfort Israel* again
and have pity on her ruins.
Her desert will blossom like Eden,
her barren wilderness like the garden of the LORD.
Joy and gladness will be found there.
Songs of thanksgiving will fill the air.

[4] "Listen to me, my people.
Hear me, Israel,
for my law will be proclaimed,
and my justice will become a light to the nations.
[5] My mercy and justice are coming soon.
My salvation is on the way.
My strong arm will bring justice to the nations.
All distant lands will look to me
and wait in hope for my powerful arm.
[6] Look up to the skies above,
and gaze down on the earth below.
For the skies will disappear like smoke,
and the earth will wear out like a piece of clothing.
The people of the earth will die like flies,
but my salvation lasts forever.
My righteous rule will never end!

[7] "Listen to me, you who know right from wrong,
you who cherish my law in your hearts.
Do not be afraid of people's scorn,
nor fear their insults.
[8] For the moth will devour them as it devours clothing.
The worm will eat at them as it eats wool.
But my righteousness will last forever.
My salvation will continue from generation to generation."

[9] Wake up, wake up, O LORD! Clothe yourself with strength!
Flex your mighty right arm!
Rouse yourself as in the days of old
when you slew Egypt, the dragon of the Nile.*
[10] Are you not the same today,
the one who dried up the sea,
making a path of escape through the depths
so that your people could cross over?
[11] Those who have been ransomed by the LORD will return.
They will enter Jerusalem* singing,
crowned with everlasting joy.
Sorrow and mourning will disappear,
and they will be filled with joy and gladness.

[12] "I, yes I, am the one who comforts you.
So why are you afraid of mere humans,
who wither like the grass and disappear?
[13] Yet you have forgotten the LORD, your Creator,
the one who stretched out the sky like a canopy
and laid the foundations of the earth.
Will you remain in constant dread of human oppressors?
Will you continue to fear the anger of your enemies?
Where is their fury and anger now?
It is gone!
[14] Soon all you captives will be released!
Imprisonment, starvation, and death will not be your fate!
[15] For I am the LORD your God,
who stirs up the sea, causing its waves to roar.
My name is the LORD of Heaven's Armies.
[16] And I have put my words in your mouth
and hidden you safely in my hand.
I stretched out* the sky like a canopy
and laid the foundations of the earth.
I am the one who says to Israel,
'You are my people!'"

[17] Wake up, wake up, O Jerusalem!
You have drunk the cup of the LORD's fury.
You have drunk the cup of terror,
tipping out its last drops.
[18] Not one of your children is left alive
to take your hand and guide you.
[19] These two calamities have fallen on you:
desolation and destruction, famine and war.
And who is left to sympathize with you?
Who is left to comfort you?*
[20] For your children have fainted and lie in the streets,
helpless as antelopes caught in a net.

▸ **51:17-23** *See **Does God really get angry?**, page 854.*

The LORD has poured out his fury;
God has rebuked them.

21 But now listen to this, you afflicted ones
who sit in a drunken stupor,
though not from drinking wine.
22 This is what the Sovereign LORD,
your God and Defender, says:
"See, I have taken the terrible cup from
your hands.
You will drink no more of my fury.
23 Instead, I will hand that cup to your
tormentors,
those who said, 'We will trample you
into the dust
and walk on your backs.'"

Deliverance for Jerusalem

52 1 Wake up, wake up, O Zion!
Clothe yourself with strength.
Put on your beautiful clothes, O holy
city of Jerusalem,
for unclean and godless people will
enter your gates no longer.
2 Rise from the dust, O Jerusalem.
Sit in a place of honor.
Remove the chains of slavery from your
neck,
O captive daughter of Zion.
3 For this is what the LORD says:
"When I sold you into exile,
I received no payment.
Now I can redeem you
without having to pay for you."

4 This is what the Sovereign LORD says:
"Long ago my people chose to live in Egypt.
Now they are oppressed by Assyria. 5 What
is this?" asks the LORD. "Why are my people
enslaved again? Those who rule them shout
in exultation.* My name is blasphemed all
day long.* 6 But I will reveal my name to
my people, and they will come to know its
power. Then at last they will recognize that
I am the one who speaks to them."

7 How beautiful on the mountains
are the feet of the messenger who
brings good news,
the good news of peace and salvation,
the news that the God of Israel*
reigns!
8 The watchmen shout and sing with joy,
for before their very eyes
they see the LORD returning to
Jerusalem.*
9 Let the ruins of Jerusalem break into
joyful song,
for the LORD has comforted his
people.
He has redeemed Jerusalem.
10 The LORD has demonstrated his holy
power
before the eyes of all the nations.
All the ends of the earth will see
the victory of our God.

11 Get out! Get out and leave your captivity,
where everything you touch is
unclean.
Get out of there and purify yourselves,
you who carry home the sacred
objects of the LORD.
12 You will not leave in a hurry,
running for your lives.
For the LORD will go ahead of you;
yes, the God of Israel will protect you
from behind.

The LORD's Suffering Servant

13 See, my servant will prosper;
he will be highly exalted.
14 But many were amazed when they saw
him.*
His face was so disfigured he seemed
hardly human,
and from his appearance, one would
scarcely know he was a man.
15 And he will startle* many nations.
Kings will stand speechless in his
presence.
For they will see what they had not been
told;
they will understand what they had
not heard about.*

53 1 Who has believed our message?
To whom has the LORD
revealed his powerful arm?
2 My servant grew up in the LORD's
presence like a tender green shoot,
like a root in dry ground.

51:3 Hebrew *Zion;* also in 51:16. **51:9** Hebrew *You slew Rahab; you pierced the dragon.* Rahab is the name of a mythical sea monster that represents chaos in ancient literature. The name is used here as a poetic name for Egypt. **51:11** Hebrew *Zion.* **51:16** As in Syriac version (see also 51:13); Hebrew reads *planted.* **51:19** As in Dead Sea Scrolls and Greek, Latin, and Syriac versions; Masoretic Text reads *How can I comfort you?* **52:5a** As in Dead Sea Scrolls; Masoretic Text reads *Those who rule them wail.* **52:5b** Greek version reads *The Gentiles continually blaspheme my name because of you.* Compare Rom 2:24. **52:7** Hebrew *of Zion.* **52:8** Hebrew *to Zion.* **52:14** As in Syriac version; Hebrew reads *you.* **52:15a** Or *cleanse.* **52:15b** Greek version reads *Those who have never been told about him will see, / and those who have never heard of him will understand.* Compare Rom 15:21.

There was nothing beautiful or majestic
about his appearance,
nothing to attract us to him.
3 He was despised and rejected—
a man of sorrows, acquainted with
deepest grief.
We turned our backs on him and looked
the other way.
He was despised, and we did not care.

4 Yet it was our weaknesses he carried;
it was our sorrows* that weighed him
down.
And we thought his troubles were a
punishment from God,
a punishment for his own sins!
5 But he was pierced for our rebellion,
crushed for our sins.
He was beaten so we could be whole.
He was whipped so we could be
healed.
6 All of us, like sheep, have strayed away.
We have left God's paths to follow our
own.
Yet the LORD laid on him
the sins of us all.

7 He was oppressed and treated harshly,
yet he never said a word.
He was led like a lamb to the slaughter.
And as a sheep is silent before the
shearers,
he did not open his mouth.
8 Unjustly condemned,
he was led away.*
No one cared that he died without
descendants,
that his life was cut short in
midstream.*
But he was struck down
for the rebellion of my people.
9 He had done no wrong
and had never deceived anyone.
But he was buried like a criminal;
he was put in a rich man's grave.

10 But it was the LORD's good plan to crush
him
and cause him grief.
Yet when his life is made an offering for
sin,
he will have many descendants.
He will enjoy a long life,
and the LORD's good plan will prosper
in his hands.
11 When he sees all that is accomplished
by his anguish,
he will be satisfied.
And because of his experience,

Prophecies about Christ

In chapters 53 and 61, two of Isaiah's most famous chapters, Isaiah saw the coming Messiah with amazing clarity, about seven hundred years before he came.

Chapter 53 foresees the Messiah's death—a death that would not only be a sacrifice but also a substitution—it is *our* griefs and sorrows he carried (53:4), *our* rebellion and sins he paid for (53:5-6), not his own. Through this death, people are healed (53:5)—brought into God's wholeness (*shalom*). The prophecy also has many details about Christ's final hours: how he was oppressed, was treated harshly, remained silent, and was buried in a rich man's grave. But Isaiah saw that it would not all end in death; he anticipated Christ's resurrection (53:10-11) and exaltation (53:12), which would enable him to "make it possible for many to be counted righteous" (53:11) because of the way that he "bore the sins of many" (53:12).

Chapter 61 foresees the Spirit-anointed nature of the Messiah's work. Jesus quoted from this passage in the synagogue at the start of his ministry (Luke 4:18-19), declaring that "the Scripture you've just heard has been fulfilled this very day!" (Luke 4:21), thus making it clear that he saw himself as the Servant that Isaiah had prophesied.

▸ *See also* ***Jesus Christ in the Psalms****, page 614;* ***The Messianic King****, page 674;* ***Prophecies of the Messiah****, page 1044;* ***Jesus and the Old Testament****, page 1079;* ***The Old Testament in the New Testament****, page 1403;* ***Prophecies of the Messiah****, Visual Overview Z12.*

my righteous servant will make it
possible
for many to be counted righteous,
for he will bear all their sins.
12 I will give him the honors of a victorious
soldier,
because he exposed himself to death.
He was counted among the rebels.
He bore the sins of many and
interceded for rebels.

Future Glory for Jerusalem

54 1 "Sing, O childless woman,
you who have never given
birth!
Break into loud and joyful song,
O Jerusalem,
you who have never been in labor.
For the desolate woman now has more
children
than the woman who lives with her
husband,"
says the LORD.
2 "Enlarge your house; build an addition.
Spread out your home, and spare no
expense!
3 For you will soon be bursting at the
seams.
Your descendants will occupy other
nations
and resettle the ruined cities.

4 "Fear not; you will no longer live in
shame.
Don't be afraid; there is no more
disgrace for you.
You will no longer remember the shame
of your youth
and the sorrows of widowhood.
5 For your Creator will be your husband;
the LORD of Heaven's Armies is his
name!
He is your Redeemer, the Holy One of
Israel,
the God of all the earth.
6 For the LORD has called you back from
your grief—
as though you were a young wife
abandoned by her husband,"
says your God.
7 "For a brief moment I abandoned you,
but with great compassion I will take
you back.
8 In a burst of anger I turned my face away
for a little while.
But with everlasting love I will have
compassion on you,"
says the LORD, your Redeemer.

9 "Just as I swore in the time of Noah
that I would never again let a flood
cover the earth,
so now I swear
that I will never again be angry and
punish you.
10 For the mountains may move
and the hills disappear,
but even then my faithful love for you
will remain.
My covenant of blessing will never be
broken,"
says the LORD, who has mercy on you.

11 "O storm-battered city,
troubled and desolate!
I will rebuild you with precious jewels
and make your foundations from lapis
lazuli.
12 I will make your towers of sparkling
rubies,
your gates of shining gems,
and your walls of precious stones.
13 I will teach all your children,
and they will enjoy great peace.
14 You will be secure under a government
that is just and fair.
Your enemies will stay far away.
You will live in peace,
and terror will not come near.
15 If any nation comes to fight you,
it is not because I sent them.
Whoever attacks you will go down in
defeat.

16 "I have created the blacksmith
who fans the coals beneath the forge
and makes the weapons of
destruction.
And I have created the armies that
destroy.
17 But in that coming day
no weapon turned against you will
succeed.
You will silence every voice
raised up to accuse you.
These benefits are enjoyed by the
servants of the LORD;

53:4 Or *Yet it was our sicknesses he carried; / it was our diseases.* **53:8a** Greek version reads *He was humiliated and received no justice.* Compare Acts 8:33. **53:8b** Or *As for his contemporaries, / who cared that his life was cut short in midstream?* Greek version reads *Who can speak of his descendants? / For his life was taken from the earth.* Compare Acts 8:33.

their vindication will come from me.
I, the LORD, have spoken!

Invitation to the LORD's Salvation

55 1 "Is anyone thirsty?
Come and drink—
even if you have no money!
Come, take your choice of wine or milk—
it's all free!
2 Why spend your money on food that
does not give you strength?
Why pay for food that does you no
good?
Listen to me, and you will eat what is
good.
You will enjoy the finest food.

3 "Come to me with your ears wide open.
Listen, and you will find life.
I will make an everlasting covenant with
you.
I will give you all the unfailing love I
promised to David.
4 See how I used him to display my power
among the peoples.
I made him a leader among the nations.
5 You also will command nations you do
not know,
and peoples unknown to you will
come running to obey,
because I, the LORD your God,
the Holy One of Israel, have made you
glorious."

6 Seek the LORD while you can find him.
Call on him now while he is near.
7 Let the wicked change their ways
and banish the very thought of doing
wrong.
Let them turn to the LORD that he may
have mercy on them.
Yes, turn to our God, for he will
forgive generously.

8 "My thoughts are nothing like your
thoughts," says the LORD.
"And my ways are far beyond anything
you could imagine.
9 For just as the heavens are higher than
the earth,
so my ways are higher than your ways
and my thoughts higher than your
thoughts.

10 "The rain and snow come down from
the heavens
and stay on the ground to water the
earth.
They cause the grain to grow,
producing seed for the farmer
and bread for the hungry.
11 It is the same with my word.
I send it out, and it always produces
fruit.
It will accomplish all I want it to,
and it will prosper everywhere I
send it.
12 You will live in joy and peace.

Thought

Our thinking is a God-given gift. God wants us to use it for good—for things like exploring the wonders of his world (1 Kings 4:29-34), meditation (Psalm 1:1-2), reflecting on our behavior (e.g., Revelation 2:5), learning from the past (1 Corinthians 10:1-12), or considering what we are living for (Philippians 3:7-11). But thoughts can also be used for evil; they can become proud, fearful, ambitious, or lustful, which is why Scripture tells us to "let God transform you into a new person by changing the way you think" (Romans 12:2).

But no matter how good, clear, or clever we think our thoughts are, they will always fall short of God's thoughts, which are far higher—as high as the heavens above the earth (Isaiah 55:9). Can such a gulf be spanned? Yes it can! Does not rain come from heaven to earth? And is it not effective when it falls? (55:10). If this is the case with rain, is it not conceivable that God's thoughts could also come to us and be effective? Jesus tells us the answer is yes, promising to send the Holy Spirit to reveal the Father's heart (e.g., John 14:26). This calls, not for arrogance, but for humble dependence on God's Spirit, who wants to fill our thoughts with the good things God has for us (e.g., Romans 8:5-11).

The mountains and hills will burst
into song,
and the trees of the field will clap
their hands!
13 Where once there were thorns, cypress
trees will grow.
Where nettles grew, myrtles will
sprout up.
These events will bring great honor to
the LORD's name;
they will be an everlasting sign of his
power and love."

Blessings for All Nations

56 This is what the LORD says:
"Be just and fair to all.
Do what is right and good,
for I am coming soon to rescue you
and to display my righteousness
among you.
2 Blessed are all those
who are careful to do this.
Blessed are those who honor my
Sabbath days of rest
and keep themselves from doing
wrong.

3 "Don't let foreigners who commit
themselves to the LORD say,
'The LORD will never let me be part of
his people.'
And don't let the eunuchs say,
'I'm a dried-up tree with no children
and no future.'
4 For this is what the LORD says:
I will bless those eunuchs
who keep my Sabbath days holy
and who choose to do what pleases me
and commit their lives to me.
5 I will give them—within the walls of my
house—
a memorial and a name
far greater than sons and daughters
could give.
For the name I give them is an
everlasting one.
It will never disappear!

6 "I will also bless the foreigners who
commit themselves to the LORD,
who serve him and love his name,
who worship him and do not desecrate
the Sabbath day of rest,
and who hold fast to my
covenant.
7 I will bring them to my holy mountain of
Jerusalem
and will fill them with joy in my house
of prayer.
I will accept their burnt offerings and
sacrifices,
because my Temple will be called a
house of prayer for all nations.
8 For the Sovereign LORD,
who brings back the outcasts of Israel,
says:
I will bring others, too,
besides my people Israel."

Sinful Leaders Condemned

9 Come, wild animals of the field!
Come, wild animals of the forest!
Come and devour my people!
10 For the leaders of my people—
the LORD's watchmen, his
shepherds—
are blind and ignorant.
They are like silent watchdogs
that give no warning when danger
comes.
They love to lie around, sleeping and
dreaming.
11 Like greedy dogs, they are never
satisfied.
They are ignorant shepherds,
all following their own path
and intent on personal gain.
12 "Come," they say, "let's get some wine
and have a party.
Let's all get drunk.
Then tomorrow we'll do it again
and have an even bigger party!"

57 1 Good people pass away;
the godly often die before their
time.
But no one seems to care or wonder
why.
No one seems to understand
that God is protecting them from the
evil to come.
2 For those who follow godly paths
will rest in peace when they die.

Idolatrous Worship Condemned

3 "But you—come here, you witches'
children,
you offspring of adulterers and
prostitutes!
4 Whom do you mock,

making faces and sticking out your
tongues?
You children of sinners and liars!
5 You worship your idols with great
passion
beneath the oaks and under every
green tree.
You sacrifice your children down in the
valleys,
among the jagged rocks in the cliffs.
6 Your gods are the smooth stones in the
valleys.
You worship them with liquid
offerings and grain offerings.
They, not I, are your inheritance.
Do you think all this makes me happy?
7 You have committed adultery on every
high mountain.
There you have worshiped idols
and have been unfaithful to me.
8 You have put pagan symbols
on your doorposts and behind your
doors.
You have left me
and climbed into bed with these
detestable gods.
You have committed yourselves to them.
You love to look at their naked bodies.
9 You have gone to Molech*
with olive oil and many perfumes,
sending your agents far and wide,
even to the world of the dead.*
10 You grew weary in your search,
but you never gave up.
Desire gave you renewed strength,
and you did not grow weary.

11 "Are you afraid of these idols?
Do they terrify you?
Is that why you have lied to me
and forgotten me and my words?
Is it because of my long silence
that you no longer fear me?
12 Now I will expose your so-called good
deeds.
None of them will help you.
13 Let's see if your idols can save you
when you cry to them for help.
Why, a puff of wind can knock them
down!
If you just breathe on them, they fall
over!
But whoever trusts in me will inherit the
land
and possess my holy mountain."

God Forgives the Repentant

14 God says, "Rebuild the road!
Clear away the rocks and stones
so my people can return from
captivity."
15 The high and lofty one who lives in
eternity,
the Holy One, says this:
"I live in the high and holy place
with those whose spirits are contrite
and humble.
I restore the crushed spirit of the
humble
and revive the courage of those with
repentant hearts.
16 For I will not fight against you forever;
I will not always be angry.
If I were, all people would pass away—
all the souls I have made.
17 I was angry,
so I punished these greedy people.
I withdrew from them,
but they kept going on their own
stubborn way.
18 I have seen what they do,
but I will heal them anyway!
I will lead them.
I will comfort those who mourn,
19 bringing words of praise to their lips.
May they have abundant peace, both
near and far,"
says the LORD, who heals them.
20 "But those who still reject me are like
the restless sea,
which is never still
but continually churns up mud and
dirt.
21 There is no peace for the wicked,"
says my God.

True and False Worship

58 1 "Shout with the voice of a
trumpet blast.
Shout aloud! Don't be timid.
Tell my people Israel* of their sins!
2 Yet they act so pious!
They come to the Temple every day
and seem delighted to learn all
about me.
They act like a righteous nation
that would never abandon the laws
of its God.
They ask me to take action on their
behalf,
pretending they want to be near me.

3 'We have fasted before you!' they say.
'Why aren't you impressed?
We have been very hard on ourselves,
and you don't even notice it!'

"I will tell you why!" I respond.
"It's because you are fasting to please yourselves.
Even while you fast,
you keep oppressing your workers.
4 What good is fasting
when you keep on fighting and quarreling?
This kind of fasting
will never get you anywhere with me.
5 You humble yourselves
by going through the motions of penance,
bowing your heads
like reeds bending in the wind.
You dress in burlap
and cover yourselves with ashes.
Is this what you call fasting?
Do you really think this will please the LORD?

6 "No, this is the kind of fasting I want:
Free those who are wrongly imprisoned;
lighten the burden of those who work for you.
Let the oppressed go free,
and remove the chains that bind people.
7 Share your food with the hungry,
and give shelter to the homeless.
Give clothes to those who need them,
and do not hide from relatives who need your help.

8 "Then your salvation will come like the dawn,
and your wounds will quickly heal.
Your godliness will lead you forward,
and the glory of the LORD will protect you from behind.
9 Then when you call, the LORD will answer.
'Yes, I am here,' he will quickly reply.

"Remove the heavy yoke of oppression.
Stop pointing your finger and spreading vicious rumors!
10 Feed the hungry,
and help those in trouble.
Then your light will shine out from the darkness,

57:9a Or *to the king.* **57:9b** Hebrew *to Sheol.* **58:1** Hebrew *Jacob.* See note on 14:1.

Injustice

Religious practices were abundant in Isaiah's day—praying, fasting, and wearing burlap and covering oneself with ashes (Isaiah 58:2-5). Yet this was all meaningless because of the injustice that God's people were engaging in. Exploitation, fighting, oppression, disregarding the hungry, naked, and homeless (58:3-7)—such injustice offends God, who is just and who demands justice among his people. What he longs for is not more religion but for us to "free those who are wrongly imprisoned; lighten the burden of those who work for you. Let the oppressed go free, and remove the chains that bind people" (58:6).

Injustice—whether deception, dishonesty, fraud, oppression, false accusation, bribery, or cheating, whether in family, business, law, government, or church—is abhorrent to God. It is never hidden from him (Amos 5:11-12), and he detests it (Proverbs 6:16-19), condemns it (Isaiah 10:1-3; James 5:1-6), and warns that it will be punished (Micah 2:1-4). As his people, we are called to hate and expose it too.

What if we are the victims of injustice? If we have opportunity, we should challenge it, as Paul did (e.g., Acts 22:24-29; 25:1-12). But ultimately, entrusting our cause to God is the best course of action (Matthew 5:38-48), just as Jesus modeled for us (1 Peter 2:23).

▸ *See also* ***Crime and punishment****, page 91;* ***Oppression****, page 710;* ***Is God concerned about social justice?****, page 994.*

and the darkness around you will be
as bright as noon.
11 The LORD will guide you continually,
giving you water when you are dry
and restoring your strength.
You will be like a well-watered garden,
like an ever-flowing spring.
12 Some of you will rebuild the deserted
ruins of your cities.
Then you will be known as a rebuilder
of walls
and a restorer of homes.

13 "Keep the Sabbath day holy.
Don't pursue your own interests on
that day,
but enjoy the Sabbath
and speak of it with delight as the
LORD's holy day.
Honor the Sabbath in everything you do
on that day,
and don't follow your own desires or
talk idly.
14 Then the LORD will be your delight.
I will give you great honor
and satisfy you with the inheritance I
promised to your ancestor Jacob.
I, the LORD, have spoken!"

Warnings against Sin

59 1 Listen! The LORD's arm is not too
weak to save you,
nor is his ear too deaf to hear you call.
2 It's your sins that have cut you off from
God.
Because of your sins, he has turned
away
and will not listen anymore.
3 Your hands are the hands of murderers,
and your fingers are filthy with sin.
Your lips are full of lies,
and your mouth spews corruption.

4 No one cares about being fair and
honest.
The people's lawsuits are based on
lies.
They conceive evil deeds
and then give birth to sin.
5 They hatch deadly snakes
and weave spiders' webs.
Whoever eats their eggs will die;
whoever cracks them will hatch a
viper.
6 Their webs can't be made into clothing,
and nothing they do is productive.
All their activity is filled with sin,
and violence is their trademark.
7 Their feet run to do evil,
and they rush to commit murder.
They think only about sinning.
Misery and destruction always follow
them.
8 They don't know where to find peace
or what it means to be just and good.
They have mapped out crooked roads,
and no one who follows them knows a
moment's peace.

9 So there is no justice among us,
and we know nothing about right
living.
We look for light but find only darkness.
We look for bright skies but walk in
gloom.
10 We grope like the blind along a wall,
feeling our way like people without
eyes.
Even at brightest noontime,
we stumble as though it were dark.
Among the living,
we are like the dead.
11 We growl like hungry bears;
we moan like mournful doves.
We look for justice, but it never comes.
We look for rescue, but it is far away
from us.
12 For our sins are piled up before God
and testify against us.
Yes, we know what sinners we are.
13 We know we have rebelled and have
denied the LORD.
We have turned our backs on our God.
We know how unfair and oppressive we
have been,
carefully planning our deceitful lies.
14 Our courts oppose the righteous,
and justice is nowhere to be found.
Truth stumbles in the streets,
and honesty has been outlawed.
15 Yes, truth is gone,
and anyone who renounces evil is
attacked.

The LORD looked and was displeased
to find there was no justice.
16 He was amazed to see that no one
intervened
to help the oppressed.
So he himself stepped in to save them
with his strong arm,
and his justice sustained him.

[17] He put on righteousness as his body
armor
and placed the helmet of salvation on
his head.
He clothed himself with a robe of
vengeance
and wrapped himself in a cloak of
divine passion.
[18] He will repay his enemies for their evil
deeds.
His fury will fall on his foes.
He will pay them back even to the
ends of the earth.
[19] In the west, people will respect the
name of the LORD;
in the east, they will glorify him.
For he will come like a raging flood tide
driven by the breath of the LORD.*

[20] "The Redeemer will come to Jerusalem
to buy back those in Israel
who have turned from their sins,"*
says the LORD.

[21] "And this is my covenant with them," says the LORD. "My Spirit will not leave them, and neither will these words I have given you. They will be on your lips and on the lips of your children and your children's children forever. I, the LORD, have spoken!

Future Glory for Jerusalem

60 [1] "Arise, Jerusalem! Let your light
shine for all to see.
For the glory of the LORD rises to shine
on you.
[2] Darkness as black as night covers all the
nations of the earth,
but the glory of the LORD rises and
appears over you.
[3] All nations will come to your light;
mighty kings will come to see your
radiance.

[4] "Look and see, for everyone is coming
home!
Your sons are coming from distant
lands;
your little daughters will be carried
home.
[5] Your eyes will shine,
and your heart will thrill with joy,
for merchants from around the world
will come to you.
They will bring you the wealth of
many lands.
[6] Vast caravans of camels will converge on
you,
the camels of Midian and Ephah.
The people of Sheba will bring gold and
frankincense
and will come worshiping the LORD.
[7] The flocks of Kedar will be given to you,
and the rams of Nebaioth will be
brought for my altars.
I will accept their offerings,
and I will make my Temple glorious.

[8] "And what do I see flying like clouds to
Israel,
like doves to their nests?
[9] They are ships from the ends of the
earth,
from lands that trust in me,
led by the great ships of Tarshish.
They are bringing the people of Israel
home from far away,
carrying their silver and gold.
They will honor the LORD your God,
the Holy One of Israel,
for he has filled you with splendor.

[10] "Foreigners will come to rebuild your
towns,
and their kings will serve you.
For though I have destroyed you in my
anger,
I will now have mercy on you through
my grace.
[11] Your gates will stay open day and night
to receive the wealth of many lands.
The kings of the world will be led as
captives
in a victory procession.
[12] For the nations that refuse to serve you
will be destroyed.

[13] "The glory of Lebanon will be yours—
the forests of cypress, fir, and pine—
to beautify my sanctuary.
My Temple will be glorious!
[14] The descendants of your tormentors
will come and bow before you.
Those who despised you
will kiss your feet.
They will call you the City of the LORD,
and Zion of the Holy One of Israel.

59:19 Or *When the enemy comes like a raging flood tide, / the Spirit of the LORD will drive him back.* **59:20** Hebrew *The Redeemer will come to Zion / to buy back those in Jacob / who have turned from their sins.* Greek version reads *The one who rescues will come on behalf of Zion, / and he will turn Jacob away from ungodliness.* Compare Rom 11:26.

15 “Though you were once despised and
hated,
with no one traveling through you,
I will make you beautiful forever,
a joy to all generations.
16 Powerful kings and mighty nations
will satisfy your every need,
as though you were a child
nursing at the breast of a queen.
You will know at last that I, the LORD,
am your Savior and your Redeemer,
the Mighty One of Israel.*
17 I will exchange your bronze for gold,
your iron for silver,
your wood for bronze,
and your stones for iron.
I will make peace your leader
and righteousness your ruler.
18 Violence will disappear from your land;
the desolation and destruction of war
will end.
Salvation will surround you like city
walls,
and praise will be on the lips of all
who enter there.

19 “No longer will you need the sun to
shine by day,
nor the moon to give its light by night,
for the LORD your God will be your
everlasting light,
and your God will be your glory.
20 Your sun will never set;
your moon will not go down.
For the LORD will be your everlasting
light.
Your days of mourning will come to
an end.
21 All your people will be righteous.
They will possess their land forever,
for I will plant them there with my own
hands
in order to bring myself glory.
22 The smallest family will become a
thousand people,
and the tiniest group will become a
mighty nation.
At the right time, I, the LORD, will
make it happen.”

Good News for the Oppressed

61 1 The Spirit of the Sovereign LORD
is upon me,
for the LORD has anointed me
to bring good news to the poor.
He has sent me to comfort the
brokenhearted
and to proclaim that captives will be
released
and prisoners will be freed.*
2 He has sent me to tell those who mourn
that the time of the LORD’s favor has
come,*
and with it, the day of God’s anger
against their enemies.
3 To all who mourn in Israel,*
he will give a crown of beauty for
ashes,
a joyous blessing instead of mourning,
festive praise instead of despair.
In their righteousness, they will be like
great oaks
that the LORD has planted for his own
glory.
4 They will rebuild the ancient ruins,
repairing cities destroyed long ago.
They will revive them,
though they have been deserted for
many generations.
5 Foreigners will be your servants.
They will feed your flocks
and plow your fields
and tend your vineyards.
6 You will be called priests of the LORD,
ministers of our God.
You will feed on the treasures of the
nations
and boast in their riches.
7 Instead of shame and dishonor,
you will enjoy a double share of honor.
You will possess a double portion of
prosperity in your land,
and everlasting joy will be yours.

8 “For I, the LORD, love justice.
I hate robbery and wrongdoing.
I will faithfully reward my people for
their suffering
and make an everlasting covenant
with them.
9 Their descendants will be recognized
and honored among the nations.
Everyone will realize that they are a
people
the LORD has blessed.”

10 I am overwhelmed with joy in the LORD
my God!
For he has dressed me with the
clothing of salvation

and draped me in a robe of
righteousness.
I am like a bridegroom dressed for his
wedding
or a bride with her jewels.
11 The Sovereign LORD will show his justice
to the nations of the world.
Everyone will praise him!
His righteousness will be like a garden
in early spring,
with plants springing up everywhere.

Isaiah's Prayer for Jerusalem

62 1 Because I love Zion,
I will not keep still.
Because my heart yearns for Jerusalem,
I cannot remain silent.
I will not stop praying for her
until her righteousness shines like the
dawn,
and her salvation blazes like a
burning torch.
2 The nations will see your righteousness.
World leaders will be blinded by your
glory.
And you will be given a new name
by the LORD's own mouth.
3 The LORD will hold you in his hand for
all to see—
a splendid crown in the hand of God.
4 Never again will you be called "The
Forsaken City"*
or "The Desolate Land."*
Your new name will be "The City of
God's Delight"*
and "The Bride of God,"*
for the LORD delights in you
and will claim you as his bride.
5 Your children will commit themselves to
you, O Jerusalem,
just as a young man commits himself
to his bride.
Then God will rejoice over you
as a bridegroom rejoices over his
bride.

6 O Jerusalem, I have posted watchmen on
your walls;
they will pray day and night,
continually.
Take no rest, all you who pray to the
LORD.
7 Give the LORD no rest until he completes
his work,
until he makes Jerusalem the pride of
the earth.
8 The LORD has sworn to Jerusalem by his
own strength:
"I will never again hand you over to
your enemies.
Never again will foreign warriors come
and take away your grain and new
wine.
9 You raised the grain, and you will eat it,
praising the LORD.
Within the courtyards of the Temple,
you yourselves will drink the wine you
have pressed."

60:16 Hebrew *of Jacob.* See note on 14:1. **61:1** Greek version reads *and the blind will see.* Compare Luke 4:18. **61:2** Or *to proclaim the acceptable year of the LORD.* **61:3** Hebrew *in Zion.* **62:4a** Hebrew *Azubah,* which means "forsaken." **62:4b** Hebrew *Shemamah,* which means "desolate." **62:4c** Hebrew *Hephzibah,* which means "my delight is in her." **62:4d** Hebrew *Beulah,* which means "married."

Watchmen

Watchmen were lookouts, posted on watchtowers. From earliest times watchtowers were built in fields for watchmen to look for thieves or wild animals coming to take the crops or livestock (e.g., Isaiah 5:2; 27:3; Mark 12:1). Later, more complex towers were built into city walls to watch out for approaching enemies (e.g., 2 Samuel 18:24; 2 Kings 9:17). The prophets used the work of watchmen as an image to describe an aspect of their ministry—that of watching and praying. Here, in preparation for the coming great salvation that he had prophesied, Isaiah appointed "watchmen" to pray for this salvation to become a reality (Isaiah 62:6). God appointed Ezekiel as a watchman to pass on his warnings of impending danger (Ezekiel 3:17). Habakkuk saw himself as a watchman waiting on God (Habakkuk 2:1). The New Testament shows that some were still waiting and watching when Jesus came (e.g., Luke 2:25-38), and Jesus urges us all to be alert and keep watch in preparation for his coming again (Matthew 24:42).

10 Go out through the gates!
Prepare the highway for my people to return!
Smooth out the road; pull out the boulders;
raise a flag for all the nations to see.
11 The LORD has sent this message to every land:
"Tell the people of Israel,*
'Look, your Savior is coming.
See, he brings his reward with him as he comes.'"
12 They will be called "The Holy People"
and "The People Redeemed by the LORD."
And Jerusalem will be known as "The Desirable Place"
and "The City No Longer Forsaken."

Judgment against the LORD's Enemies

63 1 Who is this who comes from Edom,
from the city of Bozrah,
with his clothing stained red?
Who is this in royal robes,
marching in his great strength?

"It is I, the LORD, announcing your salvation!
It is I, the LORD, who has the power to save!"

2 Why are your clothes so red,
as if you have been treading out grapes?
3 "I have been treading the winepress alone;
no one was there to help me.
In my anger I have trampled my enemies
as if they were grapes.
In my fury I have trampled my foes.
Their blood has stained my clothes.
4 For the time has come for me to avenge my people,
to ransom them from their oppressors.
5 I was amazed to see that no one intervened
to help the oppressed.
So I myself stepped in to save them with my strong arm,
and my wrath sustained me.
6 I crushed the nations in my anger
and made them stagger and fall to the ground,
spilling their blood upon the earth."

Praise for Deliverance

7 I will tell of the LORD's unfailing love.
I will praise the LORD for all he has done.
I will rejoice in his great goodness to Israel,
which he has granted according to his mercy and love.
8 He said, "They are my very own people.
Surely they will not betray me again."
And he became their Savior.
9 In all their suffering he also suffered,
and he personally* rescued them.
In his love and mercy he redeemed them.
He lifted them up and carried them
through all the years.
10 But they rebelled against him
and grieved his Holy Spirit.
So he became their enemy
and fought against them.

11 Then they remembered those days of old
when Moses led his people out of Egypt.
They cried out, "Where is the one who
brought Israel through the sea,
with Moses as their shepherd?
Where is the one who sent his Holy Spirit
to be among his people?
12 Where is the one whose power was displayed
when Moses lifted up his hand—
the one who divided the sea before them,
making himself famous forever?
13 Where is the one who led them through the bottom of the sea?
They were like fine stallions
racing through the desert, never stumbling.
14 As with cattle going down into a peaceful valley,
the Spirit of the LORD gave them rest.
You led your people, LORD,
and gained a magnificent reputation."

Prayer for Mercy and Pardon

15 LORD, look down from heaven;
look from your holy, glorious home,
and see us.
Where is the passion and the might
you used to show on our behalf?
Where are your mercy and
compassion now?

16 Surely you are still our Father!
Even if Abraham and Jacob* would disown us,
LORD, you would still be our Father.
You are our Redeemer from ages past.
17 LORD, why have you allowed us to turn from your path?
Why have you given us stubborn hearts so we no longer fear you?
Return and help us, for we are your servants,
the tribes that are your special possession.
18 How briefly your holy people possessed your holy place,
and now our enemies have destroyed it.
19 Sometimes it seems as though we never belonged to you,
as though we had never been known as your people.

64

1*Oh, that you would burst from the heavens and come down!
How the mountains would quake in your presence!
2*As fire causes wood to burn
and water to boil,
your coming would make the nations tremble.
Then your enemies would learn the reason for your fame!
3 When you came down long ago,
you did awesome deeds beyond our highest expectations.
And oh, how the mountains quaked!
4 For since the world began,
no ear has heard
and no eye has seen a God like you,
who works for those who wait for him!
5 You welcome those who gladly do good,
who follow godly ways.
But you have been very angry with us,
for we are not godly.
We are constant sinners;
how can people like us be saved?
6 We are all infected and impure with sin.
When we display our righteous deeds,
they are nothing but filthy rags.
Like autumn leaves, we wither and fall,
and our sins sweep us away like the wind.
7 Yet no one calls on your name
or pleads with you for mercy.
Therefore, you have turned away from us
and turned us over* to our sins.
8 And yet, O LORD, you are our Father.
We are the clay, and you are the potter.
We all are formed by your hand.
9 Don't be so angry with us, LORD.
Please don't remember our sins forever.

62:11 Hebrew *Tell the daughter of Zion.* **63:9** Hebrew *and the angel of his presence.* **63:16** Hebrew *Israel.* See note on 14:1. **64:1** In the Hebrew text this verse is included in 63:19. **64:2** Verses 64:2-12 are numbered 64:1-11 in Hebrew text. **64:7** As in Greek, Syriac, and Aramaic versions; Hebrew reads *melted us.*

Revival

Having declared all God's wonderful promises for the future, Isaiah now called out for God to come and do what he had promised. He asked him to rip open the heavens and come down (Isaiah 64:1), to be as fire causing wood to burn (64:2). Here is a cry for revival—the sovereign activity of God in renewing his people.

Yet Isaiah also recognized there were hindrances to this: God's people were walking in sin and disregarding him (64:5-7). Little wonder he had not yet come but had hidden his face (64:7); for the prerequisites of revival are longing (Psalm 80), repentance (2 Chronicles 7:14), and humility (Isaiah 57:15).

But even then, no one can command God. Even if we fulfill the conditions, the timing of God's sending revival is his alone. This is why Isaiah urged the people to wait, for "since the world began, no ear has heard and no eye has seen a God like you, who works for those who wait for him!" (64:4). God acts when we wait.

But revival is more than a renewed sense of God's presence: It demands change, obedience, zeal, generosity, and mission. Such a price is one that Western Christians are ready to discuss and even pray about, but do not fully embrace in reality. So it is hardly surprising that revival does not come.

Look at us, we pray,
and see that we are all your people.
10 Your holy cities are destroyed.
Zion is a wilderness;
yes, Jerusalem is a desolate ruin.
11 The holy and beautiful Temple
where our ancestors praised you
has been burned down,
and all the things of beauty are destroyed.
12 After all this, LORD, must you still refuse to help us?
Will you continue to be silent and punish us?

Judgment and Final Salvation

65 The LORD says,
"I was ready to respond, but no one asked for help.
I was ready to be found, but no one was looking for me.
I said, 'Here I am, here I am!'
to a nation that did not call on my name.*
2 All day long I opened my arms to a rebellious people.*
But they follow their own evil paths
and their own crooked schemes.
3 All day long they insult me to my face
by worshiping idols in their sacred gardens.
They burn incense on pagan altars.
4 At night they go out among the graves,
worshiping the dead.
They eat the flesh of pigs
and make stews with other forbidden foods.
5 Yet they say to each other,
'Don't come too close or you will defile me!
I am holier than you!'
These people are a stench in my nostrils,
an acrid smell that never goes away.

6 "Look, my decree is written out* in front of me:
I will not stand silent;
I will repay them in full!
Yes, I will repay them—
7 both for their own sins
and for those of their ancestors,"
says the LORD.
"For they also burned incense on the mountains
and insulted me on the hills.
I will pay them back in full!

8 "But I will not destroy them all,"
says the LORD.
"For just as good grapes are found among a cluster of bad ones
(and someone will say, 'Don't throw them all away—
some of those grapes are good!'),
so I will not destroy all Israel.
For I still have true servants there.
9 I will preserve a remnant of the people of Israel*
and of Judah to possess my land.
Those I choose will inherit it,
and my servants will live there.
10 The plain of Sharon will again be filled with flocks
for my people who have searched for me,
and the valley of Achor will be a place to pasture herds.

11 "But because the rest of you have forsaken the LORD
and have forgotten his Temple,
and because you have prepared feasts to honor the god of Fate
and have offered mixed wine to the god of Destiny,
12 now I will 'destine' you for the sword.
All of you will bow down before the executioner.
For when I called, you did not answer.
When I spoke, you did not listen.
You deliberately sinned—before my very eyes—
and chose to do what you know I despise."

13 Therefore, this is what the Sovereign LORD says:
"My servants will eat,
but you will starve.
My servants will drink,
but you will be thirsty.
My servants will rejoice,
but you will be sad and ashamed.
14 My servants will sing for joy,
but you will cry in sorrow and despair.
15 Your name will be a curse word among my people,
for the Sovereign LORD will destroy you

and will call his true servants by
another name.
16 All who invoke a blessing or take an
oath
will do so by the God of truth.
For I will put aside my anger
and forget the evil of earlier days.
17 "Look! I am creating new heavens and a
new earth,
and no one will even think about the
old ones anymore.
18 Be glad; rejoice forever in my creation!
And look! I will create Jerusalem as a
place of happiness.
Her people will be a source of joy.
19 I will rejoice over Jerusalem
and delight in my people.
And the sound of weeping and crying
will be heard in it no more.

20 "No longer will babies die when only a
few days old.
No longer will adults die before they
have lived a full life.
No longer will people be considered old
at one hundred!
Only the cursed will die that young!
21 In those days people will live in the
houses they build
and eat the fruit of their own
vineyards.
22 Unlike the past, invaders will not take
their houses
and confiscate their vineyards.
For my people will live as long as trees,
and my chosen ones will have time to
enjoy their hard-won gains.
23 They will not work in vain,
and their children will not be doomed
to misfortune.
For they are people blessed by the LORD,
and their children, too, will be
blessed.
24 I will answer them before they even call
to me.
While they are still talking about their
needs,
I will go ahead and answer their
prayers!
25 The wolf and the lamb will feed together.
The lion will eat hay like a cow.
But the snakes will eat dust.
In those days no one will be hurt or
destroyed on my holy mountain.
I, the LORD, have spoken!"

66 This is what the LORD says:
"Heaven is my throne,
and the earth is my footstool.
Could you build me a temple as good as
that?
Could you build me such a resting
place?
2 My hands have made both heaven and
earth;
they and everything in them are
mine.*
I, the LORD, have spoken!

"I will bless those who have humble and
contrite hearts,
who tremble at my word.
3 But those who choose their own ways—
delighting in their detestable sins—
will not have their offerings accepted.
When such people sacrifice a bull,
it is no more acceptable than a human
sacrifice.
When they sacrifice a lamb,
it's as though they had sacrificed a
dog!
When they bring an offering of grain,
they might as well offer the blood of
a pig.
When they burn frankincense,
it's as if they had blessed an idol.
4 I will send them great trouble—
all the things they feared.
For when I called, they did not answer.
When I spoke, they did not listen.
They deliberately sinned before my very
eyes
and chose to do what they know I
despise."

5 Hear this message from the LORD,
all you who tremble at his words:
"Your own people hate you
and throw you out for being loyal to
my name.
'Let the LORD be honored!' they scoff.
'Be joyful in him!'
But they will be put to shame.
6 What is all the commotion in the city?
What is that terrible noise from the
Temple?

65:1 Or *to a nation that did not bear my name.* **65:1-2** Greek version reads *I was found by people who were not looking for me. / I showed myself to those who were not asking for me. / All day long I opened my arms to them, / but they were disobedient and rebellious.* Compare Rom 10:20-21. **65:6** Or *their sins are written out;* Hebrew reads *it stands written.* **65:9** Hebrew *remnant of Jacob.* See note on 14:1. **66:2** As in Greek, Latin, and Syriac versions; Hebrew reads *these things are.*

It is the voice of the LORD
taking vengeance against his enemies.

7 "Before the birth pains even begin,
Jerusalem gives birth to a son.
8 Who has ever seen anything as strange as this?
Who ever heard of such a thing?
Has a nation ever been born in a single day?
Has a country ever come forth in a mere moment?
But by the time Jerusalem's* birth pains begin,
her children will be born.
9 Would I ever bring this nation to the point of birth
and then not deliver it?" asks the LORD.
"No! I would never keep this nation from being born,"
says your God.

10 "Rejoice with Jerusalem!
Be glad with her, all you who love her
and all you who mourn for her.
11 Drink deeply of her glory
even as an infant drinks at its mother's comforting breasts."

12 This is what the LORD says:
"I will give Jerusalem a river of peace and prosperity.
The wealth of the nations will flow to her.
Her children will be nursed at her breasts,
carried in her arms, and held on her lap.
13 I will comfort you there in Jerusalem
as a mother comforts her child."

14 When you see these things, your heart will rejoice.
You will flourish like the grass!
Everyone will see the LORD's hand of blessing on his servants—
and his anger against his enemies.
15 See, the LORD is coming with fire,
and his swift chariots roar like a whirlwind.
He will bring punishment with the fury of his anger
and the flaming fire of his hot rebuke.
16 The LORD will punish the world by fire
and by his sword.
He will judge the earth,
and many will be killed by him.

17 "Those who 'consecrate' and 'purify'
themselves in a sacred garden with its idol
in the center—feasting on pork and rats and
other detestable meats—will come to a terrible end," says the LORD.
18 "I can see what they are doing, and
I know what they are thinking. So I will
gather all nations and peoples together, and
they will see my glory.
19 I will perform a sign
among them. And I will send those who
survive to be messengers to the nations—
to Tarshish, to the Libyans* and Lydians*
(who are famous as archers), to Tubal and
Greece,* and to all the lands beyond the sea
that have not heard of my fame or seen my
glory. There they will declare my glory to
the nations.
20 They will bring the remnant
of your people back from every nation. They
will bring them to my holy mountain in Jerusalem as an offering to the LORD. They
will ride on horses, in chariots and wagons,
and on mules and camels," says the LORD.
21 "And I will appoint some of them to be
my priests and Levites. I, the LORD, have
spoken!

22 "As surely as my new heavens and earth will remain,
so will you always be my people,
with a name that will never disappear,"
says the LORD.
23 "All humanity will come to worship me
from week to week
and from month to month.
24 And as they go out, they will see
the dead bodies of those who have rebelled against me.
For the worms that devour them will never die,
and the fire that burns them will never go out.
All who pass by
will view them with utter horror."

66:8 Hebrew *Zion's*. **66:19a** As in some Greek manuscripts, which read *Put* [that is, *Libya*]; Hebrew reads *Pul*. **66:19b** Hebrew *Lud*. **66:19c** Hebrew *Javan*.

Jeremiah

God's messenger in a time of spiritual crisis

Jeremiah is a book for those who have wandered away from God. The people of Judah had forsaken God, and Jeremiah warned them of impending judgment if they did not change. But he also encouraged them to amend their ways because God still loved them tenderly.

Jeremiah was a priest who was called to be a prophet at an early age and who prophesied through the reigns of five kings in turbulent times. His prophetic call led him into much trouble: He was rejected by his family; the people of Jerusalem conspired to kill him; he almost lost his life several times; he was imprisoned by unfriendly officials; and when Jerusalem fell, he was forced to leave Judah for Egypt.

Jeremiah was the prophet of the broken heart. He had to deliver a stern message of judgment—but he was also sensitive, tenderhearted, and prone to introspection, and he felt the full force of his words. He was a prophet whose vulnerability shines through.

What's it all about?

While still young and inexperienced, Jeremiah was called to be a prophet, even though he was reluctant to be one. God encouraged him by telling him that he had been chosen before he was born (chapter 1). Jeremiah brought God's messages to the people of Judah, warning them that judgment was imminent, and that they had only themselves to blame. But if they would change their ways, God would forgive them, even at that late stage.

Chapters 2 to 38 record Jeremiah delivering message after message warning God's people to repent. God reproved them for their idolatry and their unfair dealings with one another. Because their prosperity was built on other people's misery, their homes and possessions would be plundered. The people were keeping up their religious observances but refusing to obey God. God had therefore rejected them, loathing their insincerity. But their response was only to persecute Jeremiah.

In chapters 40 to 43, Jeremiah was set free from his imprisonment by the Babylonians, and he then spoke to the people who were left in the land after the fall of Jerusalem. He warned them not to flee to Egypt but to trust God to protect and provide for them in their own land. The people rejected his advice, however, and headed for Egypt, taking Jeremiah with them against his will.

Jeremiah also prophesied to surrounding non-Jewish nations, including Babylon (chapters 46 to 51). The nations prided themselves on their military skill—but they must answer to God for their evil ways. The book ends with

OVERVIEW

Jeremiah's call
1:1-19

Jeremiah's warnings to Judah, before the fall of Jerusalem · *2:1–38:28*

The fall of Jerusalem
39:1-10

Jeremiah's experiences after the fall of Jerusalem · *39:11–45:5*

Messages of judgment to the nations
46:1–51:64

The exile of Judah in retrospect
52:1-34

page 822

an appendix, looking back to see how Jeremiah's message of judgment had indeed been fulfilled (chapter 52). Nebuchadnezzar's army invaded Judah and burned Jerusalem, leading the people away as captives—the judgment of God on them.

What does it mean for us?

Whether it's cooking a meal or making something, we often don't get things right the first time. It's good to get a second chance, and Jeremiah shows us that God is always ready to give us another chance. He is not waiting with a big stick, ready to strike us as soon as we fail. In fact, he is immensely patient. Ultimately, judgment for wrongdoing is a reality, as Jeremiah often underlines; but God longs for us to repent that we may find a new beginning.

Jeremiah reminds us that God can refashion us as he chooses. When we fail to meet his standards, he doesn't reject us. He patiently starts all over again with us. Each of us is special to him.

Jeremiah spoke about a fresh hope. He promised a new and lasting covenant that God would write on people's hearts (31:33-34). This covenant would be marked by forgiveness of sins and knowing God personally. The New Testament sees this being fulfilled through the sacrificial death of Jesus Christ (Luke 22:20).

In Jeremiah, too, we see that ministry for God can be costly. Jeremiah suffered spiritually, socially, and personally because he was obedient to God's call.

▶ *See also* ***A timeline of the Bible****, pages A22-A24.*

1 These are the words of Jeremiah son of
Hilkiah, one of the priests from the town
of Anathoth in the land of Benjamin. [2]The
LORD first gave messages to Jeremiah during
the thirteenth year of the reign of Josiah son
of Amon, king of Judah.* [3]The LORD's messages continued throughout the reign of King
Jehoiakim, Josiah's son, until the eleventh
year of the reign of King Zedekiah, another
of Josiah's sons. In August* of that eleventh
year the people of Jerusalem were taken
away as captives.

Jeremiah's Call and First Visions

[4]The LORD gave me this message:

5 "I knew you before I formed you in your
mother's womb.
Before you were born I set you apart
and appointed you as my prophet to
the nations."

[6]"O Sovereign LORD," I said, "I can't speak
for you! I'm too young!"

[7]The LORD replied, "Don't say, 'I'm too
young,' for you must go wherever I send
you and say whatever I tell you. [8]And don't
be afraid of the people, for I will be with
you and will protect you. I, the LORD, have
spoken!" [9]Then the LORD reached out and
touched my mouth and said,

"Look, I have put my words in your mouth!
10 Today I appoint you to stand up
against nations and kingdoms.
Some you must uproot and tear down,
destroy and overthrow.
Others you must build up
and plant."

[11]Then the LORD said to me, "Look, Jeremiah! What do you see?"

And I replied, "I see a branch from an
almond tree."

[12]And the LORD said, "That's right, and it
means that I am watching,* and I will certainly carry out all my plans."

[13]Then the LORD spoke to me again and
asked, "What do you see now?"

And I replied, "I see a pot of boiling water,
spilling from the north."

[14]"Yes," the LORD said, "for terror from
the north will boil out on the people of this
land. [15]Listen! I am calling the armies of the

▶ **1:4-19** *See* ***The call and cost of ministry****, page 901.*

kingdoms of the north to come to Jerusalem.
I, the LORD, have spoken!

"They will set their thrones
at the gates of the city.
They will attack its walls
and all the other towns of Judah.
16 I will pronounce judgment
on my people for all their evil—
for deserting me and burning incense to
other gods.
Yes, they worship idols made with
their own hands!

17 "Get up and prepare for action.
Go out and tell them everything I tell
you to say.
Do not be afraid of them,
or I will make you look foolish in front
of them.
18 For see, today I have made you strong
like a fortified city that cannot be
captured,
like an iron pillar or a bronze wall.
You will stand against the whole land—
the kings, officials, priests, and
people of Judah.
19 They will fight you, but they will fail.
For I am with you, and I will take care
of you.
I, the LORD, have spoken!"

The LORD's Case against His People

2 The LORD gave me another message. He
said, 2"Go and shout this message to Jerusalem. This is what the LORD says:

"I remember how eager you were to
please me
as a young bride long ago,
how you loved me and followed me
even through the barren wilderness.
3 In those days Israel was holy to the
LORD,
the first of his children.*
All who harmed his people were
declared guilty,
and disaster fell on them.
I, the LORD, have spoken!"

4Listen to the word of the LORD, people
of Jacob—all you families of Israel! 5This is
what the LORD says:

"What did your ancestors find wrong
with me
that led them to stray so far from me?

1:2 The thirteenth year of Josiah's reign was 627 B.C. **1:3** Hebrew *In the fifth month,* of the ancient Hebrew lunar calendar. A number of events in Jeremiah can be cross-checked with dates in surviving Babylonian records and related accurately to our modern calendar. The fifth month in the eleventh year of Zedekiah's reign occurred within the months of August and September 586 B.C. Also see 52:12 and the note there. **1:12** The Hebrew word for "watching" *(shoqed)* sounds like the word for "almond tree" *(shaqed).* **2:3** Hebrew *the firstfruits of his harvest.*

Abortion

God's words to Jeremiah at his call—"I knew you before I formed you in your mother's womb. Before you were born I set you apart" (Jeremiah 1:5)—show that life does not begin at birth, but at the very moment of our conception (see also Psalm 139:13-16). Christians oppose such things as abortion and euthanasia because both violate the sanctity of God-given life and the potential which that life contains.

Abortion—the deliberate termination of pregnancy—was as common in the ancient world as it is today (even in countries where it is illegal or frowned upon). But Christians have always opposed it, believing life is sacred—even life in the womb. Every human being is made in God's image (Genesis 1:27), and the giving and taking of life is God's right alone. While God may delegate permission to take life in limited circumstances as an act of justice (e.g., murder, Genesis 9:6), a fetus has done nothing to deserve death, and abortion is therefore morally bad and always wrong.

However, few women willingly choose abortion. More often they are driven to it by fear or circumstances, or forced into it by a bullying husband or partner. Christians should always be ready to show compassion to those who have had an abortion. Women feel guilty enough without Christians adding to it. Confessed to God, abortion can be forgiven as much as any other act against God.

They worshiped worthless idols,
only to become worthless themselves.
6 They did not ask, 'Where is the LORD
who brought us safely out of Egypt
and led us through the barren
wilderness—
a land of deserts and pits,
a land of drought and death,
where no one lives or even travels?'
7 "And when I brought you into a fruitful
land
to enjoy its bounty and goodness,
you defiled my land and
corrupted the possession I had
promised you.
8 The priests did not ask,
'Where is the LORD?'
Those who taught my word ignored me,
the rulers turned against me,
and the prophets spoke in the name of
Baal,
wasting their time on worthless idols.
9 Therefore, I will bring my case against
you,"
says the LORD.
"I will even bring charges against your
children's children
in the years to come.
10 "Go west and look in the land of Cyprus*;
go east and search through the land
of Kedar.
Has anyone ever heard of anything
as strange as this?
11 Has any nation ever traded its gods for
new ones,
even though they are not gods at all?
Yet my people have exchanged their
glorious God*
for worthless idols!
12 The heavens are shocked at such a thing
and shrink back in horror and dismay,"
says the LORD.
13 "For my people have done two evil
things:
They have abandoned me—
the fountain of living water.
And they have dug for themselves
cracked cisterns
that can hold no water at all!

The Results of Israel's Sin

14 "Why has Israel become a slave?
Why has he been carried away as
plunder?
15 Strong lions have roared against him,
and the land has been destroyed.
The towns are now in ruins,
and no one lives in them anymore.
16 Egyptians, marching from their cities of
Memphis* and Tahpanhes,
have destroyed Israel's glory and
power.
17 And you have brought this upon
yourselves
by rebelling against the LORD your God,
even though he was leading you on
the way!
18 "What have you gained by your
alliances with Egypt
and your covenants with Assyria?
What good to you are the streams of the
Nile*
or the waters of the Euphrates River?*
19 Your wickedness will bring its own
punishment.
Your turning from me will shame you.
You will see what an evil, bitter thing it is
to abandon the LORD your God and
not to fear him.
I, the Lord, the LORD of Heaven's
Armies, have spoken!
20 "Long ago I broke the yoke that
oppressed you
and tore away the chains of your
slavery,
but still you said,
'I will not serve you.'
On every hill and under every green tree,
you have prostituted yourselves by
bowing down to idols.
21 But I was the one who planted you,
choosing a vine of the purest stock—
the very best.
How did you grow into this corrupt
wild vine?
22 No amount of soap or lye can make you
clean.
I still see the stain of your guilt.
I, the Sovereign LORD, have spoken!

Israel, an Unfaithful Wife

23 "You say, 'That's not true!
I haven't worshiped the images of Baal!'
But how can you say that?
Go and look in any valley in the land!
Face the awful sins you have done.
You are like a restless female camel
desperately searching for a mate.

24 You are like a wild donkey,
sniffing the wind at mating time.
Who can restrain her lust?
Those who desire her don't need to search,
for she goes running to them!
25 When will you stop running?
When will you stop panting after other gods?
But you say, 'Save your breath.
I'm in love with these foreign gods,
and I can't stop loving them now!'
26 "Israel is like a thief
who feels shame only when he gets caught.
They, their kings, officials, priests, and prophets—
all are alike in this.
27 To an image carved from a piece of wood
they say,
'You are my father.'
To an idol chiseled from a block of stone
they say,
'You are my mother.'
They turn their backs on me,
but in times of trouble they cry out to me,
'Come and save us!'
28 But why not call on these gods you have made?
When trouble comes, let them save you if they can!
For you have as many gods
as there are towns in Judah.
29 Why do you accuse me of doing wrong?
You are the ones who have rebelled,"
says the LORD.
30 "I have punished your children,
but they did not respond to my discipline.
You yourselves have killed your prophets
as a lion kills its prey.
31 "O my people, listen to the words of the LORD!
Have I been like a desert to Israel?
Have I been to them a land of darkness?
Why then do my people say, 'At last we are free from God!
We don't need him anymore!'
32 Does a young woman forget her jewelry,
or a bride her wedding dress?
Yet for years on end
my people have forgotten me.
33 "How you plot and scheme to win your lovers.
Even an experienced prostitute could learn from you!
34 Your clothing is stained with the blood
of the innocent and the poor,
though you didn't catch them
breaking into your houses!
35 And yet you say,
'I have done nothing wrong.
Surely God isn't angry with me!'
But now I will punish you severely
because you claim you have not sinned.
36 First here, then there—
you flit from one ally to another asking for help.
But your new friends in Egypt will let you down,
just as Assyria did before.
37 In despair, you will be led into exile
with your hands on your heads,
for the LORD has rejected the nations you trust.
They will not help you at all.

3

1 "If a man divorces a woman
and she goes and marries someone else,
he will not take her back again,
for that would surely corrupt the land.
But you have prostituted yourself with many lovers,
so why are you trying to come back to me?"
says the LORD.
2 "Look at the shrines on every hilltop.
Is there any place you have not been defiled
by your adultery with other gods?
You sit like a prostitute beside the road
waiting for a customer.
You sit alone like a nomad in the desert.
You have polluted the land with your prostitution
and your wickedness.
3 That's why even the spring rains have failed.
For you are a brazen prostitute and completely shameless.

2:10 Hebrew *Kittim.* **2:11** Hebrew *their glory.* **2:16** Hebrew *Noph.* **2:18a** Hebrew *of Shihor,* a branch of the Nile River. **2:18b** Hebrew *the river?*

4 Yet you say to me,
'Father, you have been my guide since my youth.
5 Surely you won't be angry forever!
Surely you can forget about it!'
So you talk,
but you keep on doing all the evil you can."

Judah Follows Israel's Example

6During the reign of King Josiah, the LORD
said to me, "Have you seen what fickle
Israel has done? Like a wife who commits
adultery, Israel has worshiped other gods
on every hill and under every green tree.
7I thought, 'After she has done all this, she
will return to me.' But she did not return,
and her faithless sister Judah saw this.
8She saw* that I divorced faithless Israel
because of her adultery. But that treacherous sister Judah had no fear, and now she,
too, has left me and given herself to prostitution. 9Israel treated it all so lightly—she
thought nothing of committing adultery by
worshiping idols made of wood and stone.
So now the land has been polluted. 10But
despite all this, her faithless sister Judah
has never sincerely returned to me. She
has only pretended to be sorry. I, the LORD,
have spoken!"

Hope for Wayward Israel

11Then the LORD said to me, "Even faithless
Israel is less guilty than treacherous Judah!
12Therefore, go and give this message to
Israel.* This is what the LORD says:

"O Israel, my faithless people,
come home to me again,
for I am merciful.
I will not be angry with you forever.
13 Only acknowledge your guilt.
Admit that you rebelled against the LORD your God
and committed adultery against him
by worshiping idols under every green tree.
Confess that you refused to listen to my voice.
I, the LORD, have spoken!

14 "Return home, you wayward children,"
says the LORD,
"for I am your master.
I will bring you back to the land of Israel*—
one from this town and two from that family—
from wherever you are scattered.
15 And I will give you shepherds after my own heart,
who will guide you with knowledge and understanding.

16"And when your land is once more
filled with people," says the LORD, "you
will no longer wish for 'the good old days'
when you possessed the Ark of the LORD's
Covenant. You will not miss those days or
even remember them, and there will be no
need to rebuild the Ark. 17In that day Jerusalem will be known as 'The Throne of the
LORD.' All nations will come there to honor
the LORD. They will no longer stubbornly
follow their own evil desires. 18In those days
the people of Judah and Israel will return
together from exile in the north. They will
return to the land I gave your ancestors as
an inheritance forever.

19 "I thought to myself,
'I would love to treat you as my own children!'
I wanted nothing more than to give you this beautiful land—
the finest possession in the world.
I looked forward to your calling me 'Father,'
and I wanted you never to turn from me.
20 But you have been unfaithful to me, you people of Israel!
You have been like a faithless wife who leaves her husband.
I, the LORD, have spoken."

21 Voices are heard high on the windswept mountains,
the weeping and pleading of Israel's people.
For they have chosen crooked paths
and have forgotten the LORD their God.

22 "My wayward children," says the LORD,
"come back to me, and I will heal your wayward hearts."
"Yes, we're coming," the people reply,
"for you are the LORD our God.
23 Our worship of idols on the hills
and our religious orgies on the mountains
are a delusion.

Only in the LORD our God
will Israel ever find salvation.
24 From childhood we have watched
as everything our ancestors worked for—
their flocks and herds, their sons and daughters—
was squandered on a delusion.
25 Let us now lie down in shame
and cover ourselves with dishonor,
for we and our ancestors have sinned
against the LORD our God.
From our childhood to this day
we have never obeyed him."

4

1 "O Israel," says the LORD,
"if you wanted to return to me, you could.
You could throw away your detestable idols
and stray away no more.
2 Then when you swear by my name, saying,
'As surely as the LORD lives,'
you could do so
with truth, justice, and righteousness.
Then you would be a blessing to the nations of the world,
and all people would come and praise my name."

Coming Judgment against Judah

3This is what the LORD says to the people of Judah and Jerusalem:

"Plow up the hard ground of your hearts!
Do not waste your good seed among thorns.
4 O people of Judah and Jerusalem,
surrender your pride and power.
Change your hearts before the LORD,*
or my anger will burn like an unquenchable fire
because of all your sins.
5 "Shout to Judah, and broadcast to Jerusalem!
Tell them to sound the alarm throughout the land:
'Run for your lives!
Flee to the fortified cities!'
6 Raise a signal flag as a warning for Jerusalem*:
'Flee now! Do not delay!'
For I am bringing terrible destruction upon you
from the north."
7 A lion stalks from its den,
a destroyer of nations.
It has left its lair and is headed your way.
It's going to devastate your land!
Your towns will lie in ruins,
with no one living in them anymore.
8 So put on clothes of mourning
and weep with broken hearts,
for the fierce anger of the LORD
is still upon us.
9 "In that day," says the LORD,
"the king and the officials will tremble in fear.
The priests will be struck with horror,
and the prophets will be appalled."

3:8 As in Dead Sea Scrolls, one Greek manuscript, and Syriac version; Masoretic Text reads *I saw.* **3:12** Hebrew *toward the north.* **3:14** Hebrew *to Zion.* **4:4** Hebrew *Circumcise yourselves to the LORD, and take away the foreskins of your heart.* **4:6** Hebrew *Zion.*

The north

Jeremiah prophesied that destruction would come upon Jerusalem "from the north" (e.g., Jeremiah 1:13-15; 4:6; 6:1). The Babylonian invasions, and the Assyrian one before them, all came from the north, for two reasons. First, the geography of the Fertile Crescent meant that invaders from Mesopotamia followed the flow of its rivers and the roads that went with them rather than trying to cut across empty, arid desert. Second, people attacking Jerusalem had no alternative to attacking from the north. Jerusalem was surrounded by steep valleys to its west, south, and east, so the only way an army could attack in those days was from the north.

▶ *See also **The Exile** map, Visual Overview Z9.*

10 Then I said, "O Sovereign LORD,
the people have been deceived by what you said,
for you promised peace for Jerusalem.
But the sword is held at their throats!"

11 The time is coming when the LORD will say
to the people of Jerusalem,
"My dear people, a burning wind is blowing in from the desert,
and it's not a gentle breeze useful for winnowing grain.
12 It is a roaring blast sent by me!
Now I will pronounce your destruction!"

13 Our enemy rushes down on us like storm clouds!
His chariots are like whirlwinds.
His horses are swifter than eagles.
How terrible it will be, for we are doomed!
14 O Jerusalem, cleanse your heart
that you may be saved.
How long will you harbor
your evil thoughts?
15 Your destruction has been announced
from Dan and the hill country of Ephraim.

16 "Warn the surrounding nations
and announce this to Jerusalem:
The enemy is coming from a distant land,
raising a battle cry against the towns of Judah.
17 They surround Jerusalem like watchmen around a field,
for my people have rebelled against me,"
says the LORD.
18 "Your own actions have brought this upon you.
This punishment is bitter, piercing you to the heart!"

Jeremiah Weeps for His People

19 My heart, my heart—I writhe in pain!
My heart pounds within me! I cannot be still.
For I have heard the blast of enemy trumpets
and the roar of their battle cries.
20 Waves of destruction roll over the land,
until it lies in complete desolation.
Suddenly my tents are destroyed;
in a moment my shelters are crushed.
21 How long must I see the battle flags
and hear the trumpets of war?

22 "My people are foolish
and do not know me," says the LORD.
"They are stupid children
who have no understanding.
They are clever enough at doing wrong,
but they have no idea how to do right!"

Jeremiah's Vision of Coming Disaster

23 I looked at the earth, and it was empty and formless.
I looked at the heavens, and there was no light.
24 I looked at the mountains and hills,
and they trembled and shook.
25 I looked, and all the people were gone.
All the birds of the sky had flown away.
26 I looked, and the fertile fields had become a wilderness.
The towns lay in ruins,
crushed by the LORD's fierce anger.

27 This is what the LORD says:
"The whole land will be ruined,
but I will not destroy it completely.
28 The earth will mourn
and the heavens will be draped in black
because of my decree against my people.
I have made up my mind and will not change it."

29 At the noise of charioteers and archers,
the people flee in terror.
They hide in the bushes
and run for the mountains.
All the towns have been abandoned—
not a person remains!
30 What are you doing,
you who have been plundered?
Why do you dress up in beautiful clothing
and put on gold jewelry?
Why do you brighten your eyes with mascara?
Your primping will do you no good!
The allies who were your lovers
despise you and seek to kill you.

31 I hear a cry, like that of a woman in labor,
the groans of a woman giving birth to her first child.

It is beautiful Jerusalem*
gasping for breath and crying out,
"Help! I'm being murdered!"

The Sins of Judah

5 1 "Run up and down every street in
Jerusalem," says the LORD.
"Look high and low; search
throughout the city!
If you can find even one just and honest
person,
I will not destroy the city.
2 But even when they are under oath,
saying, 'As surely as the LORD lives,'
they are still telling lies!"

3 LORD, you are searching for honesty.
You struck your people,
but they paid no attention.
You crushed them,
but they refused to be corrected.
They are determined, with faces set like
stone;
they have refused to repent.

4 Then I said, "But what can we expect
from the poor?
They are ignorant.
They don't know the ways of the LORD.
They don't understand God's laws.
5 So I will go and speak to their leaders.
Surely they know the ways of the
LORD
and understand God's laws."
But the leaders, too, as one man,
had thrown off God's yoke
and broken his chains.
6 So now a lion from the forest will attack
them;
a wolf from the desert will pounce on
them.
A leopard will lurk near their towns,
tearing apart any who dare to venture
out.
For their rebellion is great,
and their sins are many.

7 "How can I pardon you?
For even your children have turned
from me.
They have sworn by gods that are not
gods at all!
I fed my people until they were full.
But they thanked me by committing
adultery
and lining up at the brothels.
8 They are well-fed, lusty stallions,
each neighing for his neighbor's wife.
9 Should I not punish them for this?" says
the LORD.
"Should I not avenge myself against
such a nation?

10 "Go down the rows of the vineyards and
destroy the grapevines,
leaving a scattered few alive.
Strip the branches from the vines,
for these people do not belong to the
LORD.
11 The people of Israel and Judah
are full of treachery against me,"
says the LORD.
12 "They have lied about the LORD
and said, 'He won't bother us!
No disasters will come upon us.
There will be no war or famine.
13 God's prophets are all windbags
who don't really speak for him.
Let their predictions of disaster fall
on themselves!'"

14 Therefore, this is what the LORD God of
Heaven's Armies says:

"Because the people are talking like this,
my messages will flame out of your
mouth
and burn the people like kindling
wood.
15 O Israel, I will bring a distant nation
against you,"
says the LORD.
"It is a mighty nation,
an ancient nation,
a people whose language you do not
know,
whose speech you cannot understand.
16 Their weapons are deadly;
their warriors are mighty.
17 They will devour the food of your
harvest;
they will devour your sons and
daughters.
They will devour your flocks and herds;
they will devour your grapes and figs.
And they will destroy your fortified
towns,
which you think are so safe.

18 "Yet even in those days I will not blot
you out completely," says the LORD. 19 "And

4:31 Hebrew *the daughter of Zion.*

when your people ask, 'Why did the LORD our God do all this to us?' you must reply, 'You rejected him and gave yourselves to foreign gods in your own land. Now you will serve foreigners in a land that is not your own.'

A Warning for God's People

20 "Make this announcement to Israel,*
and say this to Judah:
21 Listen, you foolish and senseless
people,
with eyes that do not see
and ears that do not hear.
22 Have you no respect for me?
Why don't you tremble in my
presence?
I, the LORD, define the ocean's sandy
shoreline
as an everlasting boundary that the
waters cannot cross.
The waves may toss and roar,
but they can never pass the
boundaries I set.
23 But my people have stubborn and
rebellious hearts.
They have turned away and
abandoned me.
24 They do not say from the heart,
'Let us live in awe of the LORD our God,
for he gives us rain each spring and fall,
assuring us of a harvest when the time
is right.'
25 Your wickedness has deprived you of
these wonderful blessings.
Your sin has robbed you of all these
good things.

26 "Among my people are wicked men
who lie in wait for victims like a
hunter hiding in a blind.
They continually set traps
to catch people.
27 Like a cage filled with birds,
their homes are filled with evil plots.
And now they are great and rich.
28 They are fat and sleek,
and there is no limit to their wicked
deeds.
They refuse to provide justice to orphans
and deny the rights of the poor.
29 Should I not punish them for this?" says
the LORD.
"Should I not avenge myself against
such a nation?
30 A horrible and shocking thing
has happened in this land—
31 the prophets give false prophecies,
and the priests rule with an iron hand.
Worse yet, my people like it that way!
But what will you do when the end
comes?

Jerusalem's Last Warning

6 1 "Run for your lives, you people of
Benjamin!
Get out of Jerusalem!
Sound the alarm in Tekoa!
Send up a signal at Beth-hakkerem!
A powerful army is coming from the
north,
coming with disaster and destruction.
2 O Jerusalem,* you are my beautiful and
delicate daughter—
but I will destroy you!
3 Enemies will surround you, like
shepherds camped around the city.
Each chooses a place for his troops to
devour.
4 They shout, 'Prepare for battle!
Attack at noon!'
'No, it's too late; the day is fading,
and the evening shadows are falling.'
5 'Well then, let's attack at night
and destroy her palaces!'"

6 This is what the LORD of Heaven's
Armies says:
"Cut down the trees for battering rams.
Build siege ramps against the walls of
Jerusalem.
This is the city to be punished,
for she is wicked through and
through.
7 She spouts evil like a fountain.
Her streets echo with the sounds of
violence and destruction.
I always see her sickness and sores.
8 Listen to this warning, Jerusalem,
or I will turn from you in disgust.
Listen, or I will turn you into a heap of
ruins,
a land where no one lives."

9 This is what the LORD of Heaven's
Armies says:
"Even the few who remain in Israel
will be picked over again,
as when a harvester checks each vine a
second time
to pick the grapes that were missed."

Judah's Constant Rebellion

10 To whom can I give warning?
Who will listen when I speak?
Their ears are closed,
and they cannot hear.
They scorn the word of the LORD.
They don't want to listen at all.
11 So now I am filled with the LORD's fury.
Yes, I am tired of holding it in!

"I will pour out my fury on children
playing in the streets
and on gatherings of young men,
on husbands and wives
and on those who are old and gray.
12 Their homes will be turned over to their
enemies,
as will their fields and their wives.
For I will raise my powerful fist
against the people of this land,"
says the LORD.
13 "From the least to the greatest,
their lives are ruled by greed.
From prophets to priests,
they are all frauds.
14 They offer superficial treatments
for my people's mortal wound.
They give assurances of peace
when there is no peace.
15 Are they ashamed of their disgusting
actions?
Not at all—they don't even know how
to blush!
Therefore, they will lie among the
slaughtered.
They will be brought down when I
punish them,"
says the LORD.

Judah Rejects the LORD's Way

16 This is what the LORD says:
"Stop at the crossroads and look around.
Ask for the old, godly way, and walk
in it.
Travel its path, and you will find rest for
your souls.
But you reply, 'No, that's not the road
we want!'
17 I posted watchmen over you who said,
'Listen for the sound of the alarm.'
But you replied,
'No! We won't pay attention!'

18 "Therefore, listen to this, all you
nations.
Take note of my people's situation.
19 Listen, all the earth!
I will bring disaster on my people.
It is the fruit of their own schemes,
because they refuse to listen to me.
They have rejected my word.
20 There's no use offering me sweet
frankincense from Sheba.
Keep your fragrant calamus imported
from distant lands!
I will not accept your burnt offerings.
Your sacrifices have no pleasing
aroma for me."

21 Therefore, this is what the LORD says:
"I will put obstacles in my people's
path.
Fathers and sons will both fall over them.
Neighbors and friends will die
together."

An Invasion from the North

22 This is what the LORD says:
"Look! A great army coming from the
north!
A great nation is rising against you
from far-off lands.
23 They are armed with bows and spears.
They are cruel and show no mercy.
They sound like a roaring sea
as they ride forward on horses.
They are coming in battle formation,
planning to destroy you, beautiful
Jerusalem.*"

24 We have heard reports about the enemy,
and we wring our hands in fright.
Pangs of anguish have gripped us,
like those of a woman in labor.
25 Don't go out to the fields!
Don't travel on the roads!
The enemy's sword is everywhere
and terrorizes us at every turn!
26 Oh, my people, dress yourselves in
burlap
and sit among the ashes.
Mourn and weep bitterly, as for the loss
of an only son.
For suddenly the destroying armies
will be upon you!

27 "Jeremiah, I have made you a tester of
metals,*

5:20 Hebrew *to the house of Jacob.* The names "Jacob" and "Israel" are often interchanged throughout the Old Testament, referring sometimes to the individual patriarch and sometimes to the nation. **6:2** Hebrew *Daughter of Zion.* **6:23** Hebrew *daughter of Zion.* **6:27** As in Greek version; Hebrew reads *a tester of my people a fortress.*

that you may determine the quality
of my people.
28 They are the worst kind of rebel,
full of slander.
They are as hard as bronze and iron,
and they lead others into corruption.
29 The bellows fiercely fan the flames
to burn out the corruption.
But it does not purify them,
for the wickedness remains.
30 I will label them 'Rejected Silver,'
for I, the LORD, am discarding them."

Jeremiah Speaks at the Temple

7 The LORD gave another message to Jeremiah. He said, 2"Go to the entrance of
the LORD's Temple, and give this message to
the people: 'O Judah, listen to this message
from the LORD! Listen to it, all of you who
worship here! 3This is what the LORD of
Heaven's Armies, the God of Israel, says:
"'Even now, if you quit your evil ways,
I will let you stay in your own land. 4But
don't be fooled by those who promise you
safety simply because the LORD's Temple
is here. They chant, "The LORD's Temple
is here! The LORD's Temple is here!" 5But
I will be merciful only if you stop your evil
thoughts and deeds and start treating each
other with justice; 6only if you stop exploiting foreigners, orphans, and widows; only
if you stop your murdering; and only if
you stop harming yourselves by worshiping idols. 7Then I will let you stay in this
land that I gave to your ancestors to keep
forever.
8"'Don't be fooled into thinking that you
will never suffer because the Temple is here.
It's a lie! 9Do you really think you can steal,
murder, commit adultery, lie, and burn
incense to Baal and all those other new
gods of yours, 10and then come here and
stand before me in my Temple and chant,
"We are safe!"—only to go right back to all
those evils again? 11Don't you yourselves
admit that this Temple, which bears my
name, has become a den of thieves? Surely
I see all the evil going on there. I, the LORD,
have spoken!
12"'Go now to the place at Shiloh where
I once put the Tabernacle that bore my
name. See what I did there because of
all the wickedness of my people, the Israelites. 13While you were doing these
wicked things, says the LORD, I spoke to
you about it repeatedly, but you would not
listen. I called out to you, but you refused
to answer. 14So just as I destroyed Shiloh,
I will now destroy this Temple that bears
my name, this Temple that you trust in for
help, this place that I gave to you and your
ancestors. 15And I will send you out of my
sight into exile, just as I did your relatives,
the people of Israel.*'

Buildings for worship

While a building for worship can be very useful, it can also be very dangerous, as Jeremiah exposed. The Temple that Solomon had built was magnificent, and God's glory had filled it at its dedication (2 Chronicles 3–7). But little by little, God's people had come to trust in the Temple of God rather than the God of the Temple. They believed that as long as the Temple stood, they would be safe, for this was God's dwelling place. But Jeremiah warned them this was not the case: "Don't be fooled by those who promise you safety simply because the LORD's Temple is here" (Jeremiah 7:4). For their passion for the Temple was not matched by passion for godly living (7:5-6).

Still today it is easy for us to get our focus wrong, to be more concerned for our building and its appearance than for the life and mission of the church. In the Bible, "church" is never a building; it's always a people. In fact, church buildings didn't develop until after the Roman emperor Constantine's conversion in AD 312.

Buildings are good servants but poor masters. To focus wrongly on buildings is to fall into the same error as in Jeremiah's day, and to risk the same outcome.

▶ *See also* ***Does it matter how our church buildings look?****, page 906.*

Judah's Persistent Idolatry

16“Pray no more for these people, Jeremiah.
Do not weep or pray for them, and don't beg
me to help them, for I will not listen to you.
17Don't you see what they are doing throughout the towns of Judah and in the streets
of Jerusalem? 18No wonder I am so angry!
Watch how the children gather wood and
the fathers build sacrificial fires. See how
the women knead dough and make cakes to
offer to the Queen of Heaven. And they pour
out liquid offerings to their other idol gods!
19Am I the one they are hurting?” asks the
LORD. “Most of all, they hurt themselves, to
their own shame.”
20So this is what the Sovereign LORD says:
“I will pour out my terrible fury on this
place. Its people, animals, trees, and crops
will be consumed by the unquenchable fire
of my anger.”
21This is what the LORD of Heaven's
Armies, the God of Israel, says: “Take your
burnt offerings and your other sacrifices
and eat them yourselves! 22When I led your
ancestors out of Egypt, it was not burnt offerings and sacrifices I wanted from them.
23This is what I told them: ‘Obey me, and I
will be your God, and you will be my people.
Do everything as I say, and all will be well!’
24“But my people would not listen to me.
They kept doing whatever they wanted,
following the stubborn desires of their evil
hearts. They went backward instead of
forward. 25From the day your ancestors left
Egypt until now, I have continued to send
my servants, the prophets—day in and day
out. 26But my people have not listened to
me or even tried to hear. They have been
stubborn and sinful—even worse than their
ancestors.
27“Tell them all this, but do not expect
them to listen. Shout out your warnings,
but do not expect them to respond. 28Say
to them, ‘This is the nation whose people
will not obey the LORD their God and who
refuse to be taught. Truth has vanished
from among them; it is no longer heard on
their lips. 29Shave your head in mourning,
and weep alone on the mountains. For the
LORD has rejected and forsaken this generation that has provoked his fury.’

The Valley of Slaughter

30“The people of Judah have sinned before
my very eyes,” says the LORD. “They have
set up their abominable idols right in the
Temple that bears my name, defiling it.
31They have built pagan shrines at Topheth,
the garbage dump in the valley of Ben-
Hinnom, and there they burn their sons
and daughters in the fire. I have never commanded such a horrible deed; it never even
crossed my mind to command such a thing!
32So beware, for the time is coming,” says
the LORD, “when that garbage dump will
no longer be called Topheth or the valley
of Ben-Hinnom, but the Valley of Slaughter. They will bury the bodies in Topheth
until there is no more room for them. 33The
bodies of my people will be food for the
vultures and wild animals, and no one will
be left to scare them away. 34I will put an
end to the happy singing and laughter in
the streets of Jerusalem. The joyful voices
of bridegrooms and brides will no longer be
heard in the towns of Judah. The land will
lie in complete desolation.

8 “In that day,” says the LORD, “the enemy
will break open the graves of the kings
and officials of Judah, and the graves of
the priests, prophets, and common people
of Jerusalem. 2They will spread out their
bones on the ground before the sun, moon,
and stars—the gods my people have loved,
served, and worshiped. Their bones will not
be gathered up again or buried but will be
scattered on the ground like manure. 3And
the people of this evil nation who survive
will wish to die rather than live where I will
send them. I, the LORD of Heaven's Armies,
have spoken!

Deception by False Prophets

4“Jeremiah, say to the people, ‘This is what
the LORD says:

“‘When people fall down, don't they get
up again?
When they discover they're on the
wrong road, don't they turn back?
5 Then why do these people stay on their
self-destructive path?
Why do the people of Jerusalem refuse
to turn back?
They cling tightly to their lies
and will not turn around.
6 I listen to their conversations
and don't hear a word of truth.

7:15 Hebrew *of Ephraim,* referring to the northern kingdom of Israel.

Is anyone sorry for doing wrong?
Does anyone say, "What a terrible thing I have done"?
No! All are running down the path of sin
as swiftly as a horse galloping into battle!
7 Even the stork that flies across the sky
knows the time of her migration,
as do the turtledove, the swallow, and the crane.*
They all return at the proper time each year.
But not my people!
They do not know the LORD's laws.

8 "'How can you say, "We are wise
because we have the word of the LORD,"
when your teachers have twisted it by writing lies?
9 These wise teachers will fall
into the trap of their own foolishness,
for they have rejected the word of the LORD.
Are they so wise after all?
10 I will give their wives to others
and their farms to strangers.
From the least to the greatest,
their lives are ruled by greed.
Yes, even my prophets and priests are like that.
They are all frauds.
11 They offer superficial treatments
for my people's mortal wound.
They give assurances of peace
when there is no peace.
12 Are they ashamed of these disgusting actions?
Not at all—they don't even know how to blush!
Therefore, they will lie among the slaughtered.
They will be brought down when I punish them,
says the LORD.
13 I will surely consume them.
There will be no more harvests of figs and grapes.
Their fruit trees will all die.
Whatever I gave them will soon be gone.
I, the LORD, have spoken!'

14 "Then the people will say,
'Why should we wait here to die?
Come, let's go to the fortified towns and die there.
For the LORD our God has decreed our destruction
and has given us a cup of poison to drink
because we sinned against the LORD.
15 We hoped for peace, but no peace came.
We hoped for a time of healing, but found only terror.'

16 "The snorting of the enemies' warhorses can be heard
all the way from the land of Dan in the north!
The neighing of their stallions makes the whole land tremble.
They are coming to devour the land
and everything in it—
cities and people alike.
17 I will send these enemy troops among you
like poisonous snakes you cannot charm.
They will bite you, and you will die.
I, the LORD, have spoken!"

Jeremiah Weeps for Sinful Judah

18 My grief is beyond healing;
my heart is broken.
19 Listen to the weeping of my people;
it can be heard all across the land.
"Has the LORD abandoned Jerusalem?*"
the people ask.
"Is her King no longer there?"

"Oh, why have they provoked my anger
with their carved idols
and their worthless foreign gods?"
says the LORD.

20 "The harvest is finished,
and the summer is gone," the people cry,
"yet we are not saved!"

21 I hurt with the hurt of my people.
I mourn and am overcome with grief.
22 Is there no medicine in Gilead?
Is there no physician there?
Why is there no healing
for the wounds of my people?

9 1*If only my head were a pool of water
and my eyes a fountain of tears,
I would weep day and night
for all my people who have been slaughtered.

2*Oh, that I could go away and forget my
people
and live in a travelers' shack in the
desert.
For they are all adulterers—
a pack of treacherous liars.

Judgment for Disobedience

3 "My people bend their tongues like bows
to shoot out lies.
They refuse to stand up for the truth.
They only go from bad to worse.
They do not know me,"
says the LORD.

4 "Beware of your neighbor!
Don't even trust your brother!
For brother takes advantage of brother,
and friend slanders friend.
5 They all fool and defraud each other;
no one tells the truth.
With practiced tongues they tell lies;
they wear themselves out with all
their sinning.
6 They pile lie upon lie
and utterly refuse to acknowledge me,"
says the LORD.

7 Therefore, this is what the LORD of
Heaven's Armies says:
"See, I will melt them down in a
crucible
and test them like metal.
What else can I do with my people?*
8 For their tongues shoot lies like
poisoned arrows.
They speak friendly words to their
neighbors
while scheming in their heart to kill
them.
9 Should I not punish them for this?" says
the LORD.
"Should I not avenge myself against
such a nation?"

10 I will weep for the mountains
and wail for the wilderness pastures.
For they are desolate and empty of life;
the lowing of cattle is heard no more;
the birds and wild animals have all
fled.

11 "I will make Jerusalem into a heap of
ruins," says the LORD.
"It will be a place haunted by jackals.
The towns of Judah will be ghost towns,
with no one living in them."

12 Who is wise enough to understand all
this? Who has been instructed by the LORD
and can explain it to others? Why has the
land been so ruined that no one dares to
travel through it?
13 The LORD replies, "This has happened
because my people have abandoned my instructions; they have refused to obey what
I said. 14 Instead, they have stubbornly followed their own desires and worshiped the
images of Baal, as their ancestors taught
them. 15 So now, this is what the LORD of
Heaven's Armies, the God of Israel, says:
Look! I will feed them with bitterness and
give them poison to drink. 16 I will scatter
them around the world, in places they and
their ancestors never heard of, and even
there I will chase them with the sword until
I have destroyed them completely."

Weeping in Jerusalem

17 This is what the LORD of Heaven's
Armies says:
"Consider all this, and call for the
mourners.
Send for the women who mourn at
funerals.
18 Quick! Begin your weeping!
Let the tears flow from your eyes.
19 Hear the people of Jerusalem* crying in
despair,
'We are ruined! We are completely
humiliated!
We must leave our land,
because our homes have been torn
down.'"

20 Listen, you women, to the words of the
LORD;
open your ears to what he has to say.
Teach your daughters to wail;
teach one another how to lament.
21 For death has crept in through our
windows
and has entered our mansions.
It has killed off the flower of our youth:
Children no longer play in the
streets,
and young men no longer gather in
the squares.

22 This is what the LORD says:

8:7 The identification of some of these birds is uncertain.
8:19 Hebrew *Zion?* **9:1** Verse 9:1 is numbered 8:23 in Hebrew text. **9:2** Verses 9:2-26 are numbered 9:1-25 in Hebrew text.
9:7 Hebrew *with the daughter of my people?* Greek version reads *with the evil daughter of my people?* **9:19** Hebrew *Zion.*

"Bodies will be scattered across the
fields like clumps of manure,
like bundles of grain after the harvest.
No one will be left to bury them."

23 This is what the LORD says:
"Don't let the wise boast in their
wisdom,
or the powerful boast in their power,
or the rich boast in their riches.
24 But those who wish to boast
should boast in this alone:
that they truly know me and understand
that I am the LORD
who demonstrates unfailing love
and who brings justice and
righteousness to the earth,
and that I delight in these things.
I, the LORD, have spoken!

25 "A time is coming," says the LORD,
"when I will punish all those who are circumcised in body but not in spirit—26 the
Egyptians, Edomites, Ammonites, Moabites,
the people who live in the desert in remote
places,* and yes, even the people of Judah.
And like all these pagan nations, the people
of Israel also have uncircumcised hearts."

Idolatry Brings Destruction

10 Hear the word that the LORD speaks
to you, O Israel! 2 This is what the
LORD says:
"Do not act like the other nations,
who try to read their future in the stars.
Do not be afraid of their predictions,
even though other nations are
terrified by them.
3 Their ways are futile and foolish.
They cut down a tree, and a craftsman
carves an idol.
4 They decorate it with gold and silver
and then fasten it securely with
hammer and nails
so it won't fall over.
5 Their gods are like
helpless scarecrows in a cucumber
field!

Idols

Idols—representations of gods—were common in Bible times. However, the Ten Commandments forbade Israel to make any kind of idol, for it was impossible to represent the living God in any meaningful way (Exodus 20:3-6). The prophets constantly mocked the idols of other religions (e.g., Isaiah 44:9-20; Jeremiah 10:1-11), and the psalmist warned that "those who make idols are just like them"—unresponsive and lifeless (Psalm 135:16-18). Nevertheless, once the Israelites entered Canaan, idolatry became very attractive to them, not least because it was associated with highly sexualized practices in Canaanite worship. The northern kingdom of Israel was even founded on idolatry (1 Kings 12:25-33), so it is hardly surprising they were strongly influenced by it, and idol worship is noted as a key factor in Israel's demise and downfall (2 Kings 17:7-12). In Jeremiah's day, the southern kingdom of Judah had also fallen into idolatry (e.g., Jeremiah 11:9-13), despite the presence of the Jerusalem Temple.

In the New Testament, too, idolatry is always condemned. It is an offense to the creator God and invariably leads to other sinful practices (Romans 1:18-25). Moreover, behind the idols, harmless though they themselves might seem, stand demonic powers (1 Corinthians 10:18-21; Revelation 9:20).

Of course, idolatry may not just involve worshiping a representation of a god; increasingly today people are often seen as "idols," seen as something special and so to be "worshiped"—people like film stars, soccer players, politicians, and business executives. But when King Herod Agrippa allowed people to say of him, "It's the voice of a god, not of a man," God immediately struck him dead (Acts 12:21-23). God will share his glory with no one.

▶ *See also **Calf idols**, page 980.*

They cannot speak,
and they need to be carried because they cannot walk.
Do not be afraid of such gods,
for they can neither harm you nor do you any good."

6 LORD, there is no one like you!
For you are great, and your name is full of power.
7 Who would not fear you, O King of nations?
That title belongs to you alone!
Among all the wise people of the earth
and in all the kingdoms of the world,
there is no one like you.

8 People who worship idols are stupid and foolish.
The things they worship are made of wood!
9 They bring beaten sheets of silver from Tarshish
and gold from Uphaz,
and they give these materials to skillful craftsmen
who make their idols.
Then they dress these gods in royal blue
and purple robes
made by expert tailors.
10 But the LORD is the only true God.
He is the living God and the everlasting King!
The whole earth trembles at his anger.
The nations cannot stand up to his wrath.

11 Say this to those who worship other gods: "Your so-called gods, who did not make the heavens and earth, will vanish from the earth and from under the heavens."*

12 But the LORD made the earth by his power,
and he preserves it by his wisdom.
With his own understanding
he stretched out the heavens.
13 When he speaks in the thunder,
the heavens roar with rain.
He causes the clouds to rise over the earth.
He sends the lightning with the rain
and releases the wind from his storehouses.
14 The whole human race is foolish and has no knowledge!
The craftsmen are disgraced by the idols they make,
for their carefully shaped works are a fraud.
These idols have no breath or power.
15 Idols are worthless; they are ridiculous lies!
On the day of reckoning they will all be destroyed.
16 But the God of Israel* is no idol!
He is the Creator of everything that exists,
including Israel, his own special possession.
The LORD of Heaven's Armies is his name!

The Coming Destruction

17 Pack your bags and prepare to leave;
the siege is about to begin.
18 For this is what the LORD says:
"Suddenly, I will fling out
all you who live in this land.
I will pour great troubles upon you,
and at last you will feel my anger."

19 My wound is severe,
and my grief is great.
My sickness is incurable,
but I must bear it.
20 My home is gone,
and no one is left to help me rebuild it.
My children have been taken away,
and I will never see them again.
21 The shepherds of my people have lost their senses.
They no longer seek wisdom from the LORD.
Therefore, they fail completely,
and their flocks are scattered.
22 Listen! Hear the terrifying roar of great armies
as they roll down from the north.
The towns of Judah will be destroyed
and become a haunt for jackals.

Jeremiah's Prayer

23 I know, LORD, that our lives are not our own.
We are not able to plan our own course.
24 So correct me, LORD, but please be gentle.

9:26 Or *in the desert and clip the corners of their hair.* **10:11** The original text of this verse is in Aramaic. **10:16** Hebrew *the Portion of Jacob.* See note on 5:20.

Do not correct me in anger, for I would
die.
25 Pour out your wrath on the nations that
refuse to acknowledge you—
on the peoples that do not call upon
your name.
For they have devoured your people
Israel*;
they have devoured and consumed
them,
making the land a desolate
wilderness.

Judah's Broken Covenant

11 The LORD gave another message to Jeremiah. He said, 2 "Remind the people
of Judah and Jerusalem about the terms of
my covenant with them. 3 Say to them, 'This
is what the LORD, the God of Israel, says:
Cursed is anyone who does not obey the
terms of my covenant! 4 For I said to your ancestors when I brought them out of the iron-
smelting furnace of Egypt, "If you obey me
and do whatever I command you, then you
will be my people, and I will be your God." 5 I
said this so I could keep my promise to your
ancestors to give you a land flowing with
milk and honey—the land you live in today.'"

Then I replied, "Amen, LORD! May it
be so."

6 Then the LORD said, "Broadcast this
message in the streets of Jerusalem. Go
from town to town throughout the land and
say, 'Remember the ancient covenant, and
do everything it requires. 7 For I solemnly
warned your ancestors when I brought them
out of Egypt, "Obey me!" I have repeated
this warning over and over to this day, 8 but
your ancestors did not listen or even pay attention. Instead, they stubbornly followed
their own evil desires. And because they
refused to obey, I brought upon them all the
curses described in this covenant.'"

9 Again the LORD spoke to me and said,
"I have discovered a conspiracy against
me among the people of Judah and Jerusalem. 10 They have returned to the sins of
their ancestors. They have refused to listen
to me and are worshiping other gods. Israel
and Judah have both broken the covenant I
made with their ancestors. 11 Therefore, this
is what the LORD says: I am going to bring
calamity upon them, and they will not
escape. Though they beg for mercy, I will
not listen to their cries. 12 Then the people
of Judah and Jerusalem will pray to their
idols and burn incense before them. But
the idols will not save them when disaster
strikes! 13 Look now, people of Judah; you
have as many gods as you have towns. You
have as many altars of shame—altars for
burning incense to your god Baal—as there
are streets in Jerusalem.

14 "Pray no more for these people, Jeremiah. Do not weep or pray for them, for I
will not listen to them when they cry out to
me in distress.

15 "What right do my beloved people have
to come to my Temple,
when they have done so many
immoral things?
Can their vows and sacrifices prevent
their destruction?
They actually rejoice in doing evil!
16 I, the LORD, once called them a thriving
olive tree,
beautiful to see and full of good fruit.
But now I have sent the fury of their
enemies
to burn them with fire,
leaving them charred and broken.

17 "I, the LORD of Heaven's Armies, who
planted this olive tree, have ordered it destroyed. For the people of Israel and Judah
have done evil, arousing my anger by
burning incense to Baal."

A Plot against Jeremiah

18 Then the LORD told me about the plots my
enemies were making against me. 19 I was
like a lamb being led to the slaughter. I had
no idea that they were planning to kill me!
"Let's destroy this man and all his words,"
they said. "Let's cut him down, so his name
will be forgotten forever."

20 O LORD of Heaven's Armies,
you make righteous judgments,
and you examine the deepest
thoughts and secrets.
Let me see your vengeance against
them,
for I have committed my cause to you.

21 This is what the LORD says about the
men of Anathoth who wanted me dead.
They had said, "We will kill you if you do not
stop prophesying in the LORD's name." 22 So
this is what the LORD of Heaven's Armies
says about them: "I will punish them! Their

young men will die in battle, and their boys
and girls will starve to death. 23 Not one of
these plotters from Anathoth will survive,
for I will bring disaster upon them when
their time of punishment comes."

Jeremiah Questions the LORD's Justice

12 1 LORD, you always give me justice
when I bring a case before you.
So let me bring you this complaint:
Why are the wicked so prosperous?
Why are evil people so happy?
2 You have planted them,
and they have taken root and prospered.
Your name is on their lips,
but you are far from their hearts.
3 But as for me, LORD, you know my heart.
You see me and test my thoughts.
Drag these people away like sheep to be butchered!
Set them aside to be slaughtered!
4 How long must this land mourn?
Even the grass in the fields has withered.
The wild animals and birds have disappeared
because of the evil in the land.
For the people have said,
"The LORD doesn't see what's ahead for us!"

The LORD's Reply to Jeremiah

5 "If racing against mere men makes you tired,
how will you race against horses?
If you stumble and fall on open ground,
what will you do in the thickets near the Jordan?
6 Even your brothers, members of your own family,
have turned against you.
They plot and raise complaints against you.
Do not trust them,
no matter how pleasantly they speak.
7 "I have abandoned my people, my special possession.
I have surrendered my dearest ones to their enemies.
8 My chosen people have roared at me like a lion of the forest,
so I have treated them with contempt.
9 My chosen people act like speckled vultures,*
but they themselves are surrounded by vultures.
Bring on the wild animals to pick their corpses clean!
10 "Many rulers have ravaged my vineyard,
trampling down the vines
and turning all its beauty into a barren wilderness.
11 They have made it an empty wasteland;
I hear its mournful cry.
The whole land is desolate,
and no one even cares.
12 On all the bare hilltops,
destroying armies can be seen.
The sword of the LORD devours people
from one end of the nation to the other.
No one will escape!
13 My people have planted wheat
but are harvesting thorns.
They have worn themselves out,
but it has done them no good.
They will harvest a crop of shame
because of the fierce anger of the LORD."

A Message for Israel's Neighbors

14 Now this is what the LORD says: "I will
uproot from their land all the evil nations
reaching out for the possession I gave my
people Israel. And I will uproot Judah from
among them. 15 But afterward I will return
and have compassion on all of them. I will
bring them home to their own lands again,
each nation to its own possession. 16 And
if these nations truly learn the ways of my
people, and if they learn to swear by my
name, saying, 'As surely as the LORD lives'
(just as they taught my people to swear by
the name of Baal), then they will be given
a place among my people. 17 But any nation
who refuses to obey me will be uprooted
and destroyed. I, the LORD, have spoken!"

Jeremiah's Linen Loincloth

13 This is what the LORD said to me: "Go
and buy a linen loincloth and put it on,
but do not wash it." 2 So I bought the loincloth
as the LORD directed me, and I put it on.
3 Then the LORD gave me another message:
4 "Take the linen loincloth you are wearing,

10:25 Hebrew *devoured Jacob.* See note on 5:20. **12:9** Or *speckled hyenas.*

and go to the Euphrates River.* Hide it there
in a hole in the rocks." 5 So I went and hid
it by the Euphrates as the LORD had instructed me.
6 A long time afterward the LORD said
to me, "Go back to the Euphrates and get
the loincloth I told you to hide there." 7 So I
went to the Euphrates and dug it out of the
hole where I had hidden it. But now it was
rotting and falling apart. The loincloth was
good for nothing.
8 Then I received this message from the
LORD: 9 "This is what the LORD says: This
shows how I will rot away the pride of Judah
and Jerusalem. 10 These wicked people refuse
to listen to me. They stubbornly follow their
own desires and worship other gods. Therefore, they will become like this loincloth—
good for nothing! 11 As a loincloth clings to a
man's waist, so I created Judah and Israel to
cling to me, says the LORD. They were to be
my people, my pride, my glory—an honor to
my name. But they would not listen to me.
12 "So tell them, 'This is what the LORD,
the God of Israel, says: May all your jars be
filled with wine.' And they will reply, 'Of
course! Jars are made to be filled with wine!'
13 "Then tell them, 'No, this is what the
LORD means: I will fill everyone in this land
with drunkenness—from the king sitting on
David's throne to the priests and the prophets,
right down to the common people of Jerusalem. 14 I will smash them against each other,
even parents against children, says the LORD.
I will not let my pity or mercy or compassion
keep me from destroying them.'"

A Warning against Pride

15 Listen and pay attention!
Do not be arrogant, for the LORD has spoken.
16 Give glory to the LORD your God
before it is too late.
Acknowledge him before he brings darkness upon you,
causing you to stumble and fall on the darkening mountains.
For then, when you look for light,
you will find only terrible darkness and gloom.
17 And if you still refuse to listen,
I will weep alone because of your pride.
My eyes will overflow with tears,
because the LORD's flock will be led away into exile.

18 Say to the king and his mother,
"Come down from your thrones
and sit in the dust,
for your glorious crowns
will soon be snatched from your heads."
19 The towns of the Negev will close their gates,
and no one will be able to open them.
The people of Judah will be taken away as captives.
All will be carried into exile.

20 Open up your eyes and see
the armies marching down from the north!
Where is your flock—
your beautiful flock—
that he gave you to care for?
21 What will you say when the LORD takes
the allies you have cultivated
and appoints them as your rulers?
Pangs of anguish will grip you,
like those of a woman in labor!
22 You may ask yourself,
"Why is all this happening to me?"
It is because of your many sins!
That is why you have been stripped
and raped by invading armies.
23 Can an Ethiopian* change the color of his skin?
Can a leopard take away its spots?
Neither can you start doing good,
for you have always done evil.

24 "I will scatter you like chaff
that is blown away by the desert winds.
25 This is your allotment,
the portion I have assigned to you,"
says the LORD,
"for you have forgotten me,
putting your trust in false gods.
26 I myself will strip you
and expose you to shame.
27 I have seen your adultery and lust,
and your disgusting idol worship out in the fields and on the hills.
What sorrow awaits you, Jerusalem!
How long before you are pure?"

Judah's Terrible Drought

14 This message came to Jeremiah from
the LORD, explaining why he was
holding back the rain:

[2] "Judah wilts;
commerce at the city gates grinds to a halt.
All the people sit on the ground in mourning,
and a great cry rises from Jerusalem.
[3] The nobles send servants to get water,
but all the wells are dry.
The servants return with empty pitchers,
confused and desperate,
covering their heads in grief.
[4] The ground is parched
and cracked for lack of rain.
The farmers are deeply troubled;
they, too, cover their heads.
[5] Even the doe abandons her newborn fawn
because there is no grass in the field.
[6] The wild donkeys stand on the bare hills
panting like thirsty jackals.
They strain their eyes looking for grass,
but there is none to be found."

[7] The people say, "Our wickedness has caught up with us, LORD,
but help us for the sake of your own reputation.
We have turned away from you
and sinned against you again and again.
[8] O Hope of Israel, our Savior in times of trouble,
why are you like a stranger to us?
Why are you like a traveler passing through the land,
stopping only for the night?
[9] Are you also confused?
Is our champion helpless to save us?
You are right here among us, LORD.
We are known as your people.
Please don't abandon us now!"

[10] So this is what the LORD says to his people:
"You love to wander far from me
and do not restrain yourselves.
Therefore, I will no longer accept you as my people.
Now I will remember all your wickedness
and will punish you for your sins."

The LORD Forbids Jeremiah to Intercede

[11]Then the LORD said to me, "Do not pray
for these people anymore. [12]When they fast,
I will pay no attention. When they present
their burnt offerings and grain offerings to
me, I will not accept them. Instead, I will
devour them with war, famine, and disease."

13:4 Hebrew *Perath;* also in 13:5, 6, 7. **13:23** Hebrew *a Cushite.*

Backsliding

No one wakes up saying, "I think I will start backsliding today." Backsliding doesn't work like that. It begins with little things: missing Sunday worship because we have had a busy week; rushing out without praying because we are late for work; missing our offering one month because of financial pressure; becoming careless about sin because we are tired. And so, little by little, the passion for God we once had begins to fade. At first we can explain it; later we excuse it; but eventually we no longer care.

This is Judah's situation that Jeremiah confronted in chapter 14. At one level, the people seemed to recognize that they had drifted away. In fact, the word in 14:7 that is translated as "turned away" (or "backsliding" in some English versions) really means "defection"—they had gone over to the other side! And yet despite these words, they didn't seem prepared to change or do anything about it, which is why God spoke so strongly in 14:10. The New Testament also includes strong warnings about the danger of backsliding (e.g., Hebrews 6:4-12).

But we should never give up on backsliders, no matter how far they have drifted. God is faithful, and so there is always hope. For, as Paul wrote to Timothy, "If we are unfaithful, he remains faithful, for he cannot deny who he is" (2 Timothy 2:13).

▶ *See also* ***Can a Christian lose their salvation?****, page 1401.*

13 Then I said, "O Sovereign LORD, their
prophets are telling them, 'All is well—no
war or famine will come. The LORD will
surely send you peace.'"
14 Then the LORD said, "These prophets are
telling lies in my name. I did not send them
or tell them to speak. I did not give them any
messages. They prophesy of visions and revelations they have never seen or heard. They
speak foolishness made up in their own lying
hearts. 15 Therefore, this is what the LORD
says: I will punish these lying prophets, for
they have spoken in my name even though
I never sent them. They say that no war or
famine will come, but they themselves will
die by war and famine! 16 As for the people
to whom they prophesy—their bodies will
be thrown out into the streets of Jerusalem,
victims of famine and war. There will be
no one left to bury them. Husbands, wives,
sons, and daughters—all will be gone. For I
will pour out their own wickedness on them.
17 Now, Jeremiah, say this to them:

"Night and day my eyes overflow with tears.
I cannot stop weeping,
for my virgin daughter—my precious people—
has been struck down
and lies mortally wounded.

18 If I go out into the fields,
I see the bodies of people slaughtered by the enemy.
If I walk the city streets,
I see people who have died of starvation.
The prophets and priests continue with their work,
but they don't know what they're doing."

A Prayer for Healing

19 LORD, have you completely rejected Judah?
Do you really hate Jerusalem?*
Why have you wounded us past all hope of healing?
We hoped for peace, but no peace came.
We hoped for a time of healing, but found only terror.

20 LORD, we confess our wickedness
and that of our ancestors, too.
We all have sinned against you.

21 For the sake of your reputation, LORD,
do not abandon us.
Do not disgrace your own glorious throne.
Please remember us,
and do not break your covenant with us.

22 Can any of the worthless foreign gods send us rain?
Does it fall from the sky by itself?
No, you are the one, O LORD our God!
Only you can do such things.
So we will wait for you to help us.

Judah's Inevitable Doom

15 Then the LORD said to me, "Even if
Moses and Samuel stood before me
pleading for these people, I wouldn't help
them. Away with them! Get them out of my
sight! 2 And if they say to you, 'But where can
we go?' tell them, 'This is what the LORD says:

"'Those who are destined for death, to death;
those who are destined for war, to war;
those who are destined for famine, to famine;
those who are destined for captivity, to captivity.'

3 "I will send four kinds of destroyers
against them," says the LORD. "I will send
the sword to kill, the dogs to drag away, the
vultures to devour, and the wild animals
to finish up what is left. 4 Because of the
wicked things Manasseh son of Hezekiah,
king of Judah, did in Jerusalem, I will make
my people an object of horror to all the kingdoms of the earth.

5 "Who will feel sorry for you, Jerusalem?
Who will weep for you?
Who will even bother to ask how you are?

6 You have abandoned me
and turned your back on me,"
says the LORD.
"Therefore, I will raise my fist to destroy you.
I am tired of always giving you another chance.

7 I will winnow you like grain at the gates of your cities
and take away the children you hold dear.

I will destroy my own people,
because they refuse to change their evil ways.
8 There will be more widows
than the grains of sand on the seashore.
At noontime I will bring a destroyer
against the mothers of young men.
I will cause anguish and terror
to come upon them suddenly.
9 The mother of seven grows faint and gasps for breath;
her sun has gone down while it is still day.
She sits childless now,
disgraced and humiliated.
And I will hand over those who are left
to be killed by the enemy.
I, the LORD, have spoken!"

Jeremiah's Complaint

10 Then I said,

"What sorrow is mine, my mother.
Oh, that I had died at birth!
I am hated everywhere I go.
I am neither a lender who threatens to foreclose
nor a borrower who refuses to pay—
yet they all curse me."

11 The LORD replied,

"I will take care of you, Jeremiah.
Your enemies will ask you to plead on their behalf
in times of trouble and distress.
12 Can a man break a bar of iron from the north,
or a bar of bronze?
13 At no cost to them,
I will hand over your wealth and treasures
as plunder to your enemies,
for sin runs rampant in your land.
14 I will tell your enemies to take you
as captives to a foreign land.
For my anger blazes like a fire
that will burn forever.*"

15 Then I said,

"LORD, you know what's happening to me.
Please step in and help me. Punish my persecutors!
Please give me time; don't let me die young.
It's for your sake that I am suffering.
16 When I discovered your words,
I devoured them.
They are my joy and my heart's delight,
for I bear your name,
O LORD God of Heaven's Armies.
17 I never joined the people in their merry feasts.
I sat alone because your hand was on me.
I was filled with indignation at their sins.
18 Why then does my suffering continue?
Why is my wound so incurable?
Your help seems as uncertain as a seasonal brook,
like a spring that has gone dry."

19 This is how the LORD responds:

"If you return to me, I will restore you
so you can continue to serve me.
If you speak good words rather than worthless ones,
you will be my spokesman.
You must influence them;
do not let them influence you!
20 They will fight against you like an attacking army,
but I will make you as secure as
a fortified wall of bronze.
They will not conquer you,
for I am with you to protect and rescue you.
I, the LORD, have spoken!
21 Yes, I will certainly keep you safe from these wicked men.
I will rescue you from their cruel hands."

Jeremiah Forbidden to Marry

16 The LORD gave me another message.
He said, 2"Do not get married or have
children in this place. 3For this is what the
LORD says about the children born here
in this city and about their mothers and
fathers: 4They will die from terrible diseases. No one will mourn for them or bury
them, and they will lie scattered on the
ground like manure. They will die from war
and famine, and their bodies will be food
for the vultures and wild animals."

14:19 Hebrew *Zion?* **15:14** As in some Hebrew manuscripts (see also 17:4); most Hebrew manuscripts read *will burn against you.*

Judah's Coming Punishment

5 This is what the LORD says: "Do not go to
funerals to mourn and show sympathy for
these people, for I have removed my protection and peace from them. I have taken away
my unfailing love and my mercy. 6 Both the
great and the lowly will die in this land. No
one will bury them or mourn for them. Their
friends will not cut themselves in sorrow or
shave their heads in sadness. 7 No one will
offer a meal to comfort those who mourn for
the dead—not even at the death of a mother
or father. No one will send a cup of wine to
console them.

8 "And do not go to their feasts and parties.
Do not eat and drink with them at all. 9 For
this is what the LORD of Heaven's Armies,
the God of Israel, says: In your own lifetime,
before your very eyes, I will put an end to
the happy singing and laughter in this land.
The joyful voices of bridegrooms and brides
will no longer be heard.

10 "When you tell the people all these things,
they will ask, 'Why has the LORD decreed
such terrible things against us? What have
we done to deserve such treatment? What is
our sin against the LORD our God?'

11 "Then you will give them the LORD's
reply: 'It is because your ancestors were unfaithful to me. They worshiped other gods
and served them. They abandoned me and
did not obey my word. 12 And you are even
worse than your ancestors! You stubbornly
follow your own evil desires and refuse to
listen to me. 13 So I will throw you out of
this land and send you into a foreign land
where you and your ancestors have never
been. There you can worship idols day and
night—and I will grant you no favors!'

Hope despite the Disaster

14 "But the time is coming," says the LORD,
"when people who are taking an oath will
no longer say, 'As surely as the LORD lives,
who rescued the people of Israel from the
land of Egypt.' 15 Instead, they will say, 'As
surely as the LORD lives, who brought the
people of Israel back to their own land from
the land of the north and from all the countries to which he had exiled them.' For I will
bring them back to this land that I gave their
ancestors.

16 "But now I am sending for many fishermen who will catch them," says the LORD.
"I am sending for hunters who will hunt
them down in the mountains, hills, and
caves. 17 I am watching them closely, and
I see every sin. They cannot hope to hide
from me. 18 I will double their punishment
for all their sins, because they have defiled
my land with lifeless images of their detestable gods and have filled my territory with
their evil deeds."

Jeremiah's Prayer of Confidence

19 LORD, you are my strength and fortress,
my refuge in the day of trouble!
Nations from around the world
will come to you and say,
"Our ancestors left us a foolish heritage,
for they worshiped worthless idols.
20 Can people make their own gods?
These are not real gods at all!"

21 The LORD says,
"Now I will show them my power;
now I will show them my might.
At last they will know and understand
that I am the LORD.

Judah's Sin and Punishment

17

1 "The sin of Judah
is inscribed with an iron
chisel—
engraved with a diamond point on their
stony hearts
and on the corners of their altars.
2 Even their children go to worship
at their pagan altars and Asherah
poles,
beneath every green tree
and on every high hill.
3 So I will hand over my holy mountain—
along with all your wealth and
treasures
and your pagan shrines—
as plunder to your enemies,
for sin runs rampant in your land.
4 The wonderful possession I have
reserved for you
will slip from your hands.
I will tell your enemies to take you
as captives to a foreign land.
For my anger blazes like a fire
that will burn forever."

Wisdom from the LORD

5 This is what the LORD says:
"Cursed are those who put their trust
in mere humans,

who rely on human strength
and turn their hearts away from the LORD.
6 They are like stunted shrubs in the desert,
with no hope for the future.
They will live in the barren wilderness,
in an uninhabited salty land.

7 "But blessed are those who trust in the LORD
and have made the LORD their hope and confidence.
8 They are like trees planted along a riverbank,
with roots that reach deep into the water.
Such trees are not bothered by the heat
or worried by long months of drought.
Their leaves stay green,
and they never stop producing fruit.

9 "The human heart is the most deceitful of all things,
and desperately wicked.
Who really knows how bad it is?
10 But I, the LORD, search all hearts
and examine secret motives.
I give all people their due rewards,
according to what their actions deserve."

Jeremiah's Trust in the LORD

11 Like a partridge that hatches eggs she has not laid,
so are those who get their wealth by unjust means.
At midlife they will lose their riches;
in the end, they will become poor old fools.
12 But we worship at your throne—
eternal, high, and glorious!
13 O LORD, the hope of Israel,
all who turn away from you will be disgraced.
They will be buried in the dust of the earth,
for they have abandoned the LORD,
the fountain of living water.

14 O LORD, if you heal me, I will be truly healed;
if you save me, I will be truly saved.
My praises are for you alone!
15 People scoff at me and say,
"What is this 'message from the LORD' you talk about?
Why don't your predictions come true?"
16 LORD, I have not abandoned my job
as a shepherd for your people.
I have not urged you to send disaster.
You have heard everything I've said.
17 LORD, don't terrorize me!
You alone are my hope in the day of disaster.
18 Bring shame and dismay on all who persecute me,
but don't let me experience shame and dismay.
Bring a day of terror on them.
Yes, bring double destruction upon them!

Observing the Sabbath

19This is what the LORD said to me: "Go and
stand in the gates of Jerusalem, first in the
gate where the king goes in and out, and
then in each of the other gates. 20Say to all
the people, 'Listen to this message from the
LORD, you kings of Judah and all you people
of Judah and everyone living in Jerusalem.
21This is what the LORD says: Listen to my
warning! Stop carrying on your trade at Jerusalem's gates on the Sabbath day. 22Do
not do your work on the Sabbath, but make
it a holy day. I gave this command to your
ancestors, 23but they did not listen or obey.
They stubbornly refused to pay attention or
accept my discipline.
24"'But if you obey me, says the LORD, and
do not carry on your trade at the gates or
work on the Sabbath day, and if you keep
it holy, 25then kings and their officials will
go in and out of these gates forever. There
will always be a descendant of David sitting
on the throne here in Jerusalem. Kings and
their officials will always ride in and out
among the people of Judah in chariots and
on horses, and this city will remain forever.
26And from all around Jerusalem, from the
towns of Judah and Benjamin, from the
western foothills* and the hill country and
the Negev, the people will come with their
burnt offerings and sacrifices. They will
bring their grain offerings, frankincense,
and thanksgiving offerings to the LORD's
Temple.
27"'But if you do not listen to me and
refuse to keep the Sabbath holy, and if on

17:26 Hebrew *the Shephelah.*

the Sabbath day you bring loads of merchandise through the gates of Jerusalem just as on other days, then I will set fire to these gates. The fire will spread to the palaces, and no one will be able to put out the roaring flames.'"

The Potter and the Clay

18 The LORD gave another message to Jeremiah. He said, [2]"Go down to the potter's shop, and I will speak to you there." [3]So I did as he told me and found the potter working at his wheel. [4]But the jar he was making did not turn out as he had hoped, so he crushed it into a lump of clay again and started over.

[5]Then the LORD gave me this message: [6]"O Israel, can I not do to you as this potter has done to his clay? As the clay is in the potter's hand, so are you in my hand. [7]If I announce that a certain nation or kingdom is to be uprooted, torn down, and destroyed, [8]but then that nation renounces its evil ways, I will not destroy it as I had planned. [9]And if I announce that I will plant and build up a certain nation or kingdom, [10]but then that nation turns to evil and refuses to obey me, I will not bless it as I said I would.

[11]"Therefore, Jeremiah, go and warn all Judah and Jerusalem. Say to them, 'This is what the LORD says: I am planning disaster for you instead of good. So turn from your evil ways, each of you, and do what is right.'"

[12]But the people replied, "Don't waste your breath. We will continue to live as we want to, stubbornly following our own evil desires."

[13]So this is what the LORD says:

"Has anyone ever heard of such a thing,
even among the pagan nations?
My virgin daughter Israel
has done something terrible!
14 Does the snow ever disappear from the mountaintops of Lebanon?
Do the cold streams flowing from those distant mountains ever run dry?
15 But my people are not so reliable, for they have deserted me;
they burn incense to worthless idols.
They have stumbled off the ancient highways
and walk in muddy paths.
16 Therefore, their land will become desolate,
a monument to their stupidity.
All who pass by will be astonished
and will shake their heads in amazement.
17 I will scatter my people before their enemies
as the east wind scatters dust.
And in all their trouble I will turn my back on them
and refuse to notice their distress."

A Plot against Jeremiah

[18]Then the people said, "Come on, let's plot a way to stop Jeremiah. We have plenty of priests and wise men and prophets. We don't need him to teach the word and give us advice and prophecies. Let's spread rumors about him and ignore what he says."

19 LORD, hear me and help me!
Listen to what my enemies are saying.
20 Should they repay evil for good?
They have dug a pit to kill me,
though I pleaded for them
and tried to protect them from your anger.

God molds his people

Potters make vessels or figures out of clay. Sometimes a piece doesn't work out properly, so the potter has to start all over again, pushing the clay back down into itself. But the final outcome is a beautiful vessel or sculpture that has been created out of ordinary clay. Jeremiah used the picture of the potter to show God's molding of his people into what he wanted them to become: "As the clay is in the potter's hand, so are you in my hand" (Jeremiah 18:6). At times he pulls up the clay, at other times he pushes it down—but all the time he knows what he is doing.

The right response to God is therefore always humble submission into his hands. The challenge comes constantly to us: How moldable, how teachable are we?

21 So let their children starve!
Let them die by the sword!
Let their wives become childless widows.
Let their old men die in a plague,
and let their young men be killed in battle!
22 Let screaming be heard from their homes
as warriors come suddenly upon them.
For they have dug a pit for me
and have hidden traps along my path.
23 LORD, you know all about their murderous plots against me.
Don't forgive their crimes and blot out their sins.
Let them die before you.
Deal with them in your anger.

Jeremiah's Shattered Jar

19 This is what the LORD said to me:
"Go and buy a clay jar. Then ask
some of the leaders of the people and of the
priests to follow you. 2 Go out through the
Gate of Broken Pots to the garbage dump in
the valley of Ben-Hinnom, and give them
this message. 3 Say to them, 'Listen to this
message from the LORD, you kings of Judah
and citizens of Jerusalem! This is what the
LORD of Heaven's Armies, the God of Israel,
says: I will bring a terrible disaster on this
place, and the ears of those who hear about
it will ring!
4 "'For Israel has forsaken me and turned
this valley into a place of wickedness. The
people burn incense to foreign gods—idols
never before acknowledged by this generation, by their ancestors, or by the kings of
Judah. And they have filled this place with
the blood of innocent children. 5 They have
built pagan shrines to Baal, and there they
burn their sons as sacrifices to Baal. I have
never commanded such a horrible deed; it
never even crossed my mind to command
such a thing! 6 So beware, for the time is
coming, says the LORD, when this garbage
dump will no longer be called Topheth or
the valley of Ben-Hinnom, but the Valley of
Slaughter.
7 "'For I will upset the careful plans of
Judah and Jerusalem. I will allow the people
to be slaughtered by invading armies, and I
will leave their dead bodies as food for the
vultures and wild animals. 8 I will reduce
Jerusalem to ruins, making it a monument
to their stupidity. All who pass by will be
astonished and will gasp at the destruction they see there. 9 I will see to it that your
enemies lay siege to the city until all the
food is gone. Then those trapped inside
will eat their own sons and daughters and
friends. They will be driven to utter despair.'
10 "As these men watch you, Jeremiah,
smash the jar you brought. 11 Then say to
them, 'This is what the LORD of Heaven's
Armies says: As this jar lies shattered, so
I will shatter the people of Judah and Jerusalem beyond all hope of repair. They will bury
the bodies here in Topheth, the garbage
dump, until there is no more room for them.
12 This is what I will do to this place and its
people, says the LORD. I will cause this city
to become defiled like Topheth. 13 Yes, all the
houses in Jerusalem, including the palace of
Judah's kings, will become like Topheth—all
the houses where you burned incense on the
rooftops to your star gods, and where liquid
offerings were poured out to your idols.'"
14 Then Jeremiah returned from Topheth,
the garbage dump where he had delivered
this message, and he stopped in front of the
Temple of the LORD. He said to the people
there, 15 "This is what the LORD of Heaven's
Armies, the God of Israel, says: 'I will bring
disaster upon this city and its surrounding towns as I promised, because you have
stubbornly refused to listen to me.'"

Jeremiah and Pashhur

20 Now Pashhur son of Immer, the
priest in charge of the Temple of the
LORD, heard what Jeremiah was prophesying. 2 So he arrested Jeremiah the prophet
and had him whipped and put in stocks at
the Benjamin Gate of the LORD's Temple.
3 The next day, when Pashhur finally released him, Jeremiah said, "Pashhur, the
LORD has changed your name. From now
on you are to be called 'The Man Who Lives
in Terror.'* 4 For this is what the LORD says:
'I will send terror upon you and all your
friends, and you will watch as they are
slaughtered by the swords of the enemy. I
will hand the people of Judah over to the
king of Babylon. He will take them captive
to Babylon or run them through with the
sword. 5 And I will let your enemies plunder

20:3 Hebrew *Magor-missabib,* which means "surrounded by terror"; also in 20:10.

Jerusalem. All the famed treasures of the
city—the precious jewels and gold and silver
of your kings—will be carried off to Babylon. 6 As for you, Pashhur, you and all your
household will go as captives to Babylon.
There you will die and be buried, you and
all your friends to whom you prophesied
that everything would be all right.'"

Jeremiah's Complaint

7 O LORD, you misled me,
and I allowed myself to be misled.
You are stronger than I am,
and you overpowered me.
Now I am mocked every day;
everyone laughs at me.
8 When I speak, the words burst out.
"Violence and destruction!" I shout.
So these messages from the LORD
have made me a household joke.
9 But if I say I'll never mention the LORD
or speak in his name,
his word burns in my heart like a fire.
It's like a fire in my bones!
I am worn out trying to hold it in!
I can't do it!
10 I have heard the many rumors about me.
They call me "The Man Who Lives in
Terror."
They threaten, "If you say anything, we
will report it."
Even my old friends are watching me,
waiting for a fatal slip.
"He will trap himself," they say,
"and then we will get our revenge on
him."
11 But the LORD stands beside me like a
great warrior.
Before him my persecutors will
stumble.
They cannot defeat me.
They will fail and be thoroughly
humiliated.
Their dishonor will never be
forgotten.
12 O LORD of Heaven's Armies,
you test those who are righteous,
and you examine the deepest
thoughts and secrets.
Let me see your vengeance against them,
for I have committed my cause to you.

Does God mind if we are honest with him?

"O LORD, you misled me, and I allowed myself to be misled," Jeremiah complained (Jeremiah 20:7). His accusation is even stronger when one realizes that the word "misled" can also mean "seduced." Jeremiah accused God of having sweet-talked him into becoming a prophet through false promises (see 1:4-19); the reality, he felt, was far from what he had expected. He had had enough—though deep down he knew he couldn't give up (20:9). However, the moment he off-loaded his complaint, something changed in him. It was as if he were free to rise in faith again. So within a few verses we read, "But the LORD stands beside me like a great warrior" (20:11).

Jeremiah wasn't alone in bringing plain speaking, grievances, hurts, disappointments, and anger to God. Other examples in the Bible include Moses complaining that God had made things worse for the Hebrew slaves (Exodus 5:22-23), Elijah complaining that not only had his work been fruitless but also Jezebel was out to kill him for it (1 Kings 19:1-10), and Job complaining that he was suffering without cause and demanding that God show the charges against him (Job 10:1-7).

Through all these examples we see that God is well able to handle our telling him what we really think. We don't need to dress up prayer in religious or unreal language. In fact, the surprising thing about prayer in the Bible is that, unlike in other ancient religions, there are no special words to use. What God wants from us is the open and honest sharing of our hearts. As David put it, "Pour out your heart to him, for God is our refuge" (Psalm 62:8).

▶ *See also* ***Perseverance in prayer****, page 1184.*

13 Sing to the LORD!
Praise the LORD!
For though I was poor and needy,
he rescued me from my oppressors.

14 Yet I curse the day I was born!
May no one celebrate the day of my birth.
15 I curse the messenger who told my father,
"Good news—you have a son!"
16 Let him be destroyed like the cities of old
that the LORD overthrew without mercy.
Terrify him all day long with battle shouts,
17 because he did not kill me at birth.
Oh, that I had died in my mother's womb,
that her body had been my grave!
18 Why was I ever born?
My entire life has been filled
with trouble, sorrow, and shame.

No Deliverance from Babylon

21 The LORD spoke through Jeremiah
when King Zedekiah sent Pashhur
son of Malkijah and Zephaniah son of Maaseiah, the priest, to speak with him. They
begged Jeremiah, 2"Please speak to the
LORD for us and ask him to help us. King
Nebuchadnezzar* of Babylon is attacking
Judah. Perhaps the LORD will be gracious
and do a mighty miracle as he has done in
the past. Perhaps he will force Nebuchadnezzar to withdraw his armies."

3Jeremiah replied, "Go back to King Zedekiah and tell him, 4'This is what the LORD,
the God of Israel, says: I will make your
weapons useless against the king of Babylon and the Babylonians* who are outside
your walls attacking you. In fact, I will bring
your enemies right into the heart of this
city. 5I myself will fight against you with a
strong hand and a powerful arm, for I am
very angry. You have made me furious! 6I
will send a terrible plague upon this city,
and both people and animals will die. 7And
after all that, says the LORD, I will hand over
King Zedekiah, his staff, and everyone else
in the city who survives the disease, war,
and famine. I will hand them over to King
Nebuchadnezzar of Babylon and to their
other enemies. He will slaughter them and
show them no mercy, pity, or compassion.'
8"Tell all the people, 'This is what the
LORD says: Take your choice of life or death!
9Everyone who stays in Jerusalem will die
from war, famine, or disease, but those who
go out and surrender to the Babylonians
will live. Their reward will be life! 10For
I have decided to bring disaster and not
good upon this city, says the LORD. It will
be handed over to the king of Babylon, and
he will reduce it to ashes.'

Judgment on Judah's Kings

11"Say to the royal family of Judah, 'Listen to
this message from the LORD! 12This is what
the LORD says to the dynasty of David:

"'Give justice each morning to the people you judge!
Help those who have been robbed;
rescue them from their oppressors.
Otherwise, my anger will burn like an unquenchable fire
because of all your sins.
13 I will personally fight against the people in Jerusalem,
that mighty fortress—
the people who boast, "No one can touch us here.
No one can break in here."
14 And I myself will punish you for your sinfulness,
says the LORD.
I will light a fire in your forests
that will burn up everything around you."'

A Message for Judah's Kings

22 This is what the LORD said to me:
"Go over and speak directly to the
king of Judah. Say to him, 2'Listen to this
message from the LORD, you king of Judah,
sitting on David's throne. Let your attendants and your people listen, too. 3This is
what the LORD says: Be fair-minded and
just. Do what is right! Help those who have
been robbed; rescue them from their oppressors. Quit your evil deeds! Do not mistreat foreigners, orphans, and widows. Stop
murdering the innocent! 4If you obey me,
there will always be a descendant of David
sitting on the throne here in Jerusalem. The
king will ride through the palace gates in
chariots and on horses, with his parade of
attendants and subjects. 5But if you refuse

21:2 Hebrew *Nebuchadrezzar,* a variant spelling of Nebuchadnezzar; also in 21:7. **21:4** Or *Chaldeans;* also in 21:9.

to pay attention to this warning, I swear by my own name, says the LORD, that this palace will become a pile of rubble.'"

A Message about the Palace

6 Now this is what the LORD says concerning Judah's royal palace:

"I love you as much as fruitful Gilead
and the green forests of Lebanon.
But I will turn you into a desert,
with no one living within your walls.
7 I will call for wreckers,
who will bring out their tools to dismantle you.
They will tear out all your fine cedar beams
and throw them on the fire.

8 "People from many nations will pass by the ruins of this city and say to one another, 'Why did the LORD destroy such a great city?' 9 And the answer will be, 'Because they violated their covenant with the LORD their God by worshiping other gods.'"

A Message about Jehoahaz

10 Do not weep for the dead king or mourn his loss.
Instead, weep for the captive king being led away!
For he will never return to see his native land again.

11 For this is what the LORD says about Jehoahaz,* who succeeded his father, King Josiah, and was taken away as a captive: "He will never return. 12 He will die in a distant land and will never again see his own country."

A Message about Jehoiakim

13 And the LORD says, "What sorrow awaits Jehoiakim,*
who builds his palace with forced labor.*
He builds injustice into its walls,
for he makes his neighbors work for nothing.
He does not pay them for their labor.
14 He says, 'I will build a magnificent palace
with huge rooms and many windows.
I will panel it throughout with fragrant cedar
and paint it a lovely red.'
15 But a beautiful cedar palace does not make a great king!
Your father, Josiah, also had plenty to eat and drink.
But he was just and right in all his dealings.
That is why God blessed him.
16 He gave justice and help to the poor and needy,
and everything went well for him.
Isn't that what it means to know me?"
says the LORD.
17 "But you! You have eyes only for greed and dishonesty!
You murder the innocent,
oppress the poor, and reign ruthlessly."

18 Therefore, this is what the LORD says about Jehoiakim, son of King Josiah:

"The people will not mourn for him,
crying to one another,
'Alas, my brother! Alas, my sister!'
His subjects will not mourn for him,
crying,
'Alas, our master is dead! Alas, his splendor is gone!'
19 He will be buried like a dead donkey—
dragged out of Jerusalem and dumped outside the gates!
20 Weep for your allies in Lebanon.
Shout for them in Bashan.
Search for them in the regions east of the river.*
See, they are all destroyed.
Not one is left to help you.
21 I warned you when you were prosperous,
but you replied, 'Don't bother me.'
You have been that way since childhood—
you simply will not obey me!
22 And now the wind will blow away your allies.
All your friends will be taken away as captives.
Surely then you will see your wickedness and be ashamed.
23 It may be nice to live in a beautiful palace
paneled with wood from the cedars of Lebanon,
but soon you will groan with pangs of anguish—
anguish like that of a woman in labor.

A Message for Jehoiachin

24 "As surely as I live," says the LORD, "I will abandon you, Jehoiachin* son of Jehoiakim, king of Judah. Even if you were the

signet ring on my right hand, I would pull
you off. 25 I will hand you over to those who
seek to kill you, those you so desperately
fear—to King Nebuchadnezzar* of Babylon
and the mighty Babylonian* army. 26 I will
expel you and your mother from this land,
and you will die in a foreign country, not
in your native land. 27 You will never again
return to the land you yearn for.

28 "Why is this man Jehoiachin like a
discarded, broken jar?
Why are he and his children to be
exiled to a foreign land?
29 O earth, earth, earth!
Listen to this message from the LORD!
30 This is what the LORD says:
'Let the record show that this man
Jehoiachin was childless.
He is a failure,
for none of his children will succeed him
on the throne of David
to rule over Judah.'

The Righteous Descendant

23 "What sorrow awaits the leaders of
my people—the shepherds of my
sheep—for they have destroyed and scattered the very ones they were expected to
care for," says the LORD.

2 Therefore, this is what the LORD, the
God of Israel, says to these shepherds:
"Instead of caring for my flock and leading
them to safety, you have deserted them and
driven them to destruction. Now I will pour
out judgment on you for the evil you have
done to them. 3 But I will gather together
the remnant of my flock from the countries
where I have driven them. I will bring them
back to their own sheepfold, and they will
be fruitful and increase in number. 4 Then
I will appoint responsible shepherds who
will care for them, and they will never be
afraid again. Not a single one will be lost or
missing. I, the LORD, have spoken!

5 "For the time is coming,"
says the LORD,
"when I will raise up a righteous
descendant*
from King David's line.
He will be a King who rules with wisdom.
He will do what is just and right
throughout the land.
6 And this will be his name:
'The LORD Is Our Righteousness.'*
In that day Judah will be saved,
and Israel will live in safety.

7 "In that day," says the LORD, "when
people are taking an oath, they will no
longer say, 'As surely as the LORD lives, who
rescued the people of Israel from the land of
Egypt.' 8 Instead, they will say, 'As surely as
the LORD lives, who brought the people of
Israel back to their own land from the land
of the north and from all the countries to
which he had exiled them.' Then they will
live in their own land."

Judgment on False Prophets

9 My heart is broken because of the false
prophets,
and my bones tremble.
I stagger like a drunkard,
like someone overcome by wine,
because of the holy words
the LORD has spoken against them.
10 For the land is full of adultery,
and it lies under a curse.
The land itself is in mourning—
its wilderness pastures are dried up.
For they all do evil
and abuse what power they have.

11 "Even the priests and prophets
are ungodly, wicked men.
I have seen their despicable acts
right here in my own Temple,"
says the LORD.
12 "Therefore, the paths they take
will become slippery.
They will be chased through the dark,
and there they will fall.
For I will bring disaster upon them
at the time fixed for their punishment.
I, the LORD, have spoken!

13 "I saw that the prophets of Samaria were
terribly evil,
for they prophesied in the name of
Baal
and led my people of Israel into sin.
14 But now I see that the prophets of
Jerusalem are even worse!
They commit adultery and love
dishonesty.

22:11 Hebrew *Shallum,* another name for Jehoahaz.
22:13a The brother and successor of the exiled Jehoahaz. See 22:18. **22:13b** Hebrew *by unrighteousness.* **22:20** Or *in Abarim.*
22:24 Hebrew *Coniah,* a variant spelling of Jehoiachin; also in 22:28. **22:25a** Hebrew *Nebuchadrezzar,* a variant spelling of Nebuchadnezzar. **22:25b** Or *Chaldean.* **23:5** Hebrew *a righteous branch.* **23:6** Hebrew *Yahweh Tsidqenu.*

They encourage those who are doing evil
so that no one turns away from their
sins.
These prophets are as wicked
as the people of Sodom and Gomorrah
once were."

15 Therefore, this is what the LORD of Heaven's Armies says concerning the prophets:

"I will feed them with bitterness
and give them poison to drink.
For it is because of Jerusalem's prophets
that wickedness has filled this land."

16 This is what the LORD of Heaven's Armies says to his people:

"Do not listen to these prophets when
they prophesy to you,
filling you with futile hopes.
They are making up everything they say.
They do not speak for the LORD!
17 They keep saying to those who despise
my word,
'Don't worry! The LORD says you will
have peace!'
And to those who stubbornly follow
their own desires,
they say, 'No harm will come your way!'

18 "Have any of these prophets been in the
LORD's presence
to hear what he is really saying?
Has even one of them cared enough
to listen?
19 Look! The LORD's anger bursts out like
a storm,
a whirlwind that swirls down on the
heads of the wicked.
20 The anger of the LORD will not
diminish
until it has finished all he has
planned.
In the days to come
you will understand all this very
clearly.

21 "I have not sent these prophets,
yet they run around claiming to speak
for me.
I have given them no message,
yet they go on prophesying.
22 If they had stood before me and listened
to me,
they would have spoken my words,
and they would have turned my people
from their evil ways and deeds.
23 Am I a God who is only close at hand?"
says the LORD.
"No, I am far away at the same time.
24 Can anyone hide from me in a secret
place?
Am I not everywhere in all the
heavens and earth?"
says the LORD.

25 "I have heard these prophets say, 'Listen
to the dream I had from God last night.'
And then they proceed to tell lies in my
name. 26 How long will this go on? If they
are prophets, they are prophets of deceit,
inventing everything they say. 27 By telling
these false dreams, they are trying to get my
people to forget me, just as their ancestors
did by worshiping the idols of Baal.

28 "Let these false prophets tell their
dreams,
but let my true messengers faithfully
proclaim my every word.
There is a difference between straw
and grain!
29 Does not my word burn like fire?"
says the LORD.
"Is it not like a mighty hammer
that smashes a rock to pieces?

30 "Therefore," says the LORD, "I am
against these prophets who steal messages from each other and claim they are
from me. 31 I am against these smooth-
tongued prophets who say, 'This prophecy
is from the LORD!' 32 I am against these false
prophets. Their imaginary dreams are flagrant lies that lead my people into sin. I did
not send or appoint them, and they have no
message at all for my people. I, the LORD,
have spoken!

False Prophecies and False Prophets

33 "Suppose one of the people or one of the
prophets or priests asks you, 'What prophecy has the LORD burdened you with now?'
You must reply, 'You are the burden!* The
LORD says he will abandon you!'

34 "If any prophet, priest, or anyone else
says, 'I have a prophecy from the LORD,'
I will punish that person along with his
entire family. 35 You should keep asking
each other, 'What is the LORD's answer?' or
'What is the LORD saying?' 36 But stop using
this phrase, 'prophecy from the LORD.' For
people are using it to give authority to their

own ideas, turning upside down the words
of our God, the living God, the LORD of
Heaven's Armies.
37 "This is what you should say to the
prophets: 'What is the LORD's answer?' or
'What is the LORD saying?' 38 But suppose
they respond, 'This is a prophecy from the
LORD!' Then you should say, 'This is what
the LORD says: Because you have used this
phrase, "prophecy from the LORD," even
though I warned you not to use it, 39 I will
forget you completely.* I will expel you from
my presence, along with this city that I gave
to you and your ancestors. 40 And I will make
you an object of ridicule, and your name
will be infamous throughout the ages.'"

Good and Bad Figs

24 After King Nebuchadnezzar* of
Babylon exiled Jehoiachin* son of
Jehoiakim, king of Judah, to Babylon along
with the officials of Judah and all the craftsmen and artisans, the LORD gave me this
vision. I saw two baskets of figs placed in
front of the LORD's Temple in Jerusalem.
2 One basket was filled with fresh, ripe figs,
while the other was filled with bad figs that
were too rotten to eat.
3 Then the LORD said to me, "What do you
see, Jeremiah?"
I replied, "Figs, some very good and some
very bad, too rotten to eat."
4 Then the LORD gave me this message:
5 "This is what the LORD, the God of Israel,
says: The good figs represent the exiles I sent
from Judah to the land of the Babylonians.*
6 I will watch over and care for them, and I
will bring them back here again. I will build
them up and not tear them down. I will plant
them and not uproot them. 7 I will give them
hearts that recognize me as the LORD. They
will be my people, and I will be their God,
for they will return to me wholeheartedly.
8 "But the bad figs," the LORD said, "represent King Zedekiah of Judah, his officials,
all the people left in Jerusalem, and those
who live in Egypt. I will treat them like bad
figs, too rotten to eat. 9 I will make them an
object of horror and a symbol of evil to every
nation on earth. They will be disgraced and
mocked, taunted and cursed, wherever I
scatter them. 10 And I will send war, famine,
and disease until they have vanished from
the land of Israel, which I gave to them and
their ancestors."

Seventy Years of Captivity

25 This message for all the people of
Judah came to Jeremiah from the
LORD during the fourth year of Jehoiakim's
reign over Judah.* This was the year when
King Nebuchadnezzar* of Babylon began
his reign.
2 Jeremiah the prophet said to all the people
in Judah and Jerusalem, 3 "For the past
twenty-three years—from the thirteenth year
of the reign of Josiah son of Amon,* king of
Judah, until now—the LORD has been giving
me his messages. I have faithfully passed
them on to you, but you have not listened.
4 "Again and again the LORD has sent you
his servants, the prophets, but you have
not listened or even paid attention. 5 Each
time the message was this: 'Turn from the
evil road you are traveling and from the
evil things you are doing. Only then will I
let you live in this land that the LORD gave
to you and your ancestors forever. 6 Do not
provoke my anger by worshiping idols you
made with your own hands. Then I will not
harm you.'
7 "But you would not listen to me," says
the LORD. "You made me furious by worshiping idols you made with your own
hands, bringing on yourselves all the disasters you now suffer. 8 And now the LORD
of Heaven's Armies says: Because you have
not listened to me, 9 I will gather together
all the armies of the north under King Nebuchadnezzar of Babylon, whom I have appointed as my deputy. I will bring them all
against this land and its people and against
the surrounding nations. I will completely
destroy* you and make you an object of
horror and contempt and a ruin forever.
10 I will take away your happy singing and
laughter. The joyful voices of bridegrooms
and brides will no longer be heard. Your
millstones will fall silent, and the lights in
your homes will go out. 11 This entire land
will become a desolate wasteland. Israel
and her neighboring lands will serve the
king of Babylon for seventy years.

23:33 As in Greek version and Latin Vulgate; Hebrew reads *What burden?* **23:39** Some Hebrew manuscripts and Greek version read *I will surely lift you up.* **24:1a** Hebrew *Nebuchadrezzar,* a variant spelling of Nebuchadnezzar. **24:1b** Hebrew *Jeconiah,* a variant spelling of Jehoiachin. **24:5** Or *Chaldeans.* **25:1a** The fourth year of Jehoiakim's reign and the accession year of Nebuchadnezzar's reign was 605 B.C. **25:1b** Hebrew *Nebuchadrezzar,* a variant spelling of Nebuchadnezzar; also in 25:9. **25:3** The thirteenth year of Josiah's reign was 627 B.C. **25:9** The Hebrew term used here refers to the complete consecration of things or people to the LORD, either by destroying them or by giving them as an offering.

12 “Then, after the seventy years of captivity are over, I will punish the king of
Babylon and his people for their sins,”
says the LORD. “I will make the country of
the Babylonians* a wasteland forever. 13 I
will bring upon them all the terrors I have
promised in this book—all the penalties announced by Jeremiah against the nations.
14 Many nations and great kings will enslave
the Babylonians, just as they enslaved my
people. I will punish them in proportion to
the suffering they cause my people.”

The Cup of the LORD’s Anger

15 This is what the LORD, the God of Israel,
said to me: “Take from my hand this cup
filled to the brim with my anger, and make
all the nations to whom I send you drink
from it. 16 When they drink from it, they will
stagger, crazed by the warfare I will send
against them.”

17 So I took the cup of anger from the LORD
and made all the nations drink from it—
every nation to which the LORD sent me. 18 I
went to Jerusalem and the other towns of
Judah, and their kings and officials drank
from the cup. From that day until this,
they have been a desolate ruin, an object
of horror, contempt, and cursing. 19 I gave
the cup to Pharaoh, king of Egypt, his attendants, his officials, and all his people,
20 along with all the foreigners living in that
land. I also gave it to all the kings of the land
of Uz and the kings of the Philistine cities of
Ashkelon, Gaza, Ekron, and what remains of
Ashdod. 21 Then I gave the cup to the nations
of Edom, Moab, and Ammon, 22 and the
kings of Tyre and Sidon, and the kings of the
regions across the sea. 23 I gave it to Dedan,
Tema, and Buz, and to the people who live
in distant places.* 24 I gave it to the kings of
Arabia, the kings of the nomadic tribes of
the desert, 25 and to the kings of Zimri, Elam,
and Media. 26 And I gave it to the kings of the
northern countries, far and near, one after
the other—all the kingdoms of the world.
And finally, the king of Babylon* himself
drank from the cup of the LORD’s anger.

27 Then the LORD said to me, “Now tell
them, ‘This is what the LORD of Heaven’s
Armies, the God of Israel, says: Drink from
this cup of my anger. Get drunk and vomit;
fall to rise no more, for I am sending terrible wars against you.’ 28 And if they refuse
to accept the cup, tell them, ‘The LORD
of Heaven’s Armies says: You have no
choice but to drink from it. 29 I have begun
to punish Jerusalem, the city that bears

Does God really get angry?

We probably all recoil when we read about “the wrath of God.” We ask ourselves, isn’t this simply people attributing human emotions to God? Can we really believe that God becomes angry? And doesn’t this conflict with Jesus’ picture of God?

But in speaking of God’s wrath, the Bible isn’t thinking of the human kind of anger, which is *reactive* to something said or done that offends us. God’s anger is not *reactive* in that way, but rather *responsive*. It is like our response when we walk past a drain with a bad smell and instinctively turn away in disgust. God’s wrath is his absolutely right response to human sin because, being holy and perfect, he cannot bear with it, so great is its stench.

Several of the prophets used the image of “the cup of the LORD’s anger” (e.g., Jeremiah 25:15-29; see also Isaiah 51:17-23). The cup symbolized the fullness of God’s holy anger and judgment against sin that was being kept for the moment when sinners would have to drink from it—a truth not only declared by the prophets but also by Jesus. Yes, he spoke of God’s love and mercy, but he also spoke of a Day of Judgment when everyone would have to give account (e.g., Matthew 12:36; 25:31-46). Judgment and mercy are not irreconcilable opposites, therefore, but two sides of the same coin.

▸ *See also* ***The character of God****, page 104.*

my name. Now should I let you go unpunished? No, you will not escape disaster.
I will call for war against all the nations of
the earth. I, the LORD of Heaven's Armies,
have spoken!'

30"Now prophesy all these things, and say
to them,

"'The LORD will roar against his own
land
from his holy dwelling in heaven.
He will shout like those who tread
grapes;
he will shout against everyone on
earth.
31 His cry of judgment will reach the ends
of the earth,
for the LORD will bring his case
against all the nations.
He will judge all the people of the earth,
slaughtering the wicked with the
sword.
I, the LORD, have spoken!'"
32 This is what the LORD of Heaven's
Armies says:
"Look! Disaster will fall upon nation
after nation!
A great whirlwind of fury is rising
from the most distant corners of the
earth!"

33In that day those the LORD has slaughtered will fill the earth from one end to the
other. No one will mourn for them or gather
up their bodies to bury them. They will be
scattered on the ground like manure.

34 Weep and moan, you evil shepherds!
Roll in the dust, you leaders of the
flock!
The time of your slaughter has arrived;
you will fall and shatter like a fragile
vase.
35 You will find no place to hide;
there will be no way to escape.
36 Listen to the frantic cries of the
shepherds.
The leaders of the flock are wailing in
despair,
for the LORD is ruining their pastures.
37 Peaceful meadows will be turned into a
wasteland
by the LORD's fierce anger.
38 He has left his den like a strong lion
seeking its prey,
and their land will be made desolate
by the sword* of the enemy
and the LORD's fierce anger.

Jeremiah's Escape from Death

26 This message came to Jeremiah from
the LORD early in the reign of Jehoiakim son of Josiah,* king of Judah. 2"This is
what the LORD says: Stand in the courtyard
in front of the Temple of the LORD, and make
an announcement to the people who have
come there to worship from all over Judah.
Give them my entire message; include every
word. 3Perhaps they will listen and turn
from their evil ways. Then I will change my
mind about the disaster I am ready to pour
out on them because of their sins.

4"Say to them, 'This is what the LORD
says: If you will not listen to me and obey
my word I have given you, 5and if you will
not listen to my servants, the prophets—for I
sent them again and again to warn you, but
you would not listen to them—6then I will
destroy this Temple as I destroyed Shiloh,
the place where the Tabernacle was located.
And I will make Jerusalem an object of
cursing in every nation on earth.'"

7The priests, the prophets, and all the
people listened to Jeremiah as he spoke in
front of the LORD's Temple. 8But when Jeremiah had finished his message, saying
everything the LORD had told him to say,
the priests and prophets and all the people
at the Temple mobbed him. "Kill him!" they
shouted. 9"What right do you have to prophesy in the LORD's name that this Temple
will be destroyed like Shiloh? What do you
mean, saying that Jerusalem will be destroyed and left with no inhabitants?" And
all the people threatened him as he stood in
front of the Temple.

10When the officials of Judah heard what
was happening, they rushed over from the
palace and sat down at the New Gate of
the Temple to hold court. 11The priests and
prophets presented their accusations to the
officials and the people. "This man should
die!" they said. "You have heard with your
own ears what a traitor he is, for he has
prophesied against this city."

12Then Jeremiah spoke to the officials and
the people in his own defense. "The LORD

25:12 Or *Chaldeans.* **25:23** Or *who clip the corners of their hair.* **25:26** Hebrew *of Sheshach,* a code name for Babylon. **25:38** As in some Hebrew manuscripts and Greek version; Masoretic Text reads *by the anger.* **26:1** The first year of Jehoiakim's reign was 608 B.C.

sent me to prophesy against this Temple
and this city," he said. "The LORD gave me
every word that I have spoken. 13But if you
stop your sinning and begin to obey the
LORD your God, he will change his mind
about this disaster that he has announced
against you. 14As for me, I am in your
hands—do with me as you think best. 15But
if you kill me, rest assured that you will be
killing an innocent man! The responsibility
for such a deed will lie on you, on this city,
and on every person living in it. For it is absolutely true that the LORD sent me to speak
every word you have heard."

16Then the officials and the people said to
the priests and prophets, "This man does
not deserve the death sentence, for he has
spoken to us in the name of the LORD our
God."

17Then some of the wise old men stood
and spoke to all the people assembled
there. 18They said, "Remember when Micah
of Moresheth prophesied during the reign of
King Hezekiah of Judah. He told the people
of Judah,

'This is what the LORD of Heaven's
Armies says:
Mount Zion will be plowed like an open
field;
Jerusalem will be reduced to ruins!
A thicket will grow on the heights
where the Temple now stands.'*

19But did King Hezekiah and the people
kill him for saying this? No, they turned
from their sins and worshiped the LORD.
They begged him for mercy. Then the LORD
changed his mind about the terrible disaster he had pronounced against them. So we
are about to do ourselves great harm."

20At this time Uriah son of Shemaiah from
Kiriath-jearim was also prophesying for
the LORD. And he predicted the same terrible disaster against the city and nation as
Jeremiah did. 21When King Jehoiakim and
the army officers and officials heard what
he was saying, the king sent someone to
kill him. But Uriah heard about the plan
and escaped in fear to Egypt. 22Then King
Jehoiakim sent Elnathan son of Acbor to
Egypt along with several other men to
capture Uriah. 23They took him prisoner
and brought him back to King Jehoiakim.
The king then killed Uriah with a sword and
had him buried in an unmarked grave.

24Nevertheless, Ahikam son of Shaphan
stood up for Jeremiah and persuaded the
court not to turn him over to the mob to be
killed.

Jeremiah Wears an Ox Yoke

27 This message came to Jeremiah from
the LORD early in the reign of Zedekiah* son of Josiah, king of Judah.

2This is what the LORD said to me: "Make a
yoke, and fasten it on your neck with leather
straps. 3Then send messages to the kings
of Edom, Moab, Ammon, Tyre, and Sidon
through their ambassadors who have come
to see King Zedekiah in Jerusalem. 4Give
them this message for their masters: 'This
is what the LORD of Heaven's Armies, the
God of Israel, says: 5With my great strength
and powerful arm I made the earth and all
its people and every animal. I can give these
things of mine to anyone I choose. 6Now I
will give your countries to King Nebuchadnezzar of Babylon, who is my servant. I
have put everything, even the wild animals,
under his control. 7All the nations will serve
him, his son, and his grandson until his
time is up. Then many nations and great
kings will conquer and rule over Babylon.
8So you must submit to Babylon's king and
serve him; put your neck under Babylon's
yoke! I will punish any nation that refuses
to be his slave, says the LORD. I will send
war, famine, and disease upon that nation
until Babylon has conquered it.

9"'Do not listen to your false prophets,
fortune-tellers, interpreters of dreams,
mediums, and sorcerers who say, "The king
of Babylon will not conquer you." 10They
are all liars, and their lies will lead to your
being driven out of your land. I will drive
you out and send you far away to die. 11But
the people of any nation that submits to the
king of Babylon will be allowed to stay in
their own country to farm the land as usual.
I, the LORD, have spoken!'"

12Then I repeated this same message to
King Zedekiah of Judah. "If you want to
live, submit to the yoke of the king of Babylon and his people. 13Why do you insist on
dying—you and your people? Why should
you choose war, famine, and disease, which
the LORD will bring against every nation that
refuses to submit to Babylon's king? 14Do not
listen to the false prophets who keep telling
you, 'The king of Babylon will not conquer

you.' They are liars. [15]This is what the LORD says: 'I have not sent these prophets! They are telling you lies in my name, so I will drive you from this land. You will all die—you and all these prophets, too.'"

[16]Then I spoke to the priests and the people and said, "This is what the LORD says: 'Do not listen to your prophets who claim that soon the gold articles taken from my Temple will be returned from Babylon. It is all a lie! [17]Do not listen to them. Surrender to the king of Babylon, and you will live. Why should this whole city be destroyed? [18]If they really are prophets and speak the LORD's messages, let them pray to the LORD of Heaven's Armies. Let them pray that the articles remaining in the LORD's Temple and in the king's palace and in the palaces of Jerusalem will not be carried away to Babylon!'

[19]"For the LORD of Heaven's Armies has spoken about the pillars in front of the Temple, the great bronze basin called the Sea, the water carts, and all the other ceremonial articles. [20]King Nebuchadnezzar of Babylon left them here when he exiled Jehoiachin* son of Jehoiakim, king of Judah, to Babylon, along with all the other nobles of Judah and Jerusalem. [21]Yes, this is what the LORD of Heaven's Armies, the God of Israel, says about the precious things still in the Temple, in the palace of Judah's king, and in Jerusalem: [22]'They will all be carried away to Babylon and will stay there until I send for them,' says the LORD. 'Then I will bring them back to Jerusalem again.'"

Jeremiah Condemns Hananiah

28 One day in late summer* of that same year—the fourth year of the reign of Zedekiah, king of Judah—Hananiah son of Azzur, a prophet from Gibeon, addressed me publicly in the Temple while all the priests and people listened. He said, [2]"This is what the LORD of Heaven's Armies, the God of Israel, says: 'I will remove the yoke of the king of Babylon from your necks. [3]Within two years I will bring back all the Temple treasures that King Nebuchadnezzar carried off to Babylon. [4]And I will bring back Jehoiachin* son of Jehoiakim, king of Judah, and all the other captives that were taken to Babylon. I will surely break the yoke that the king of Babylon has put on your necks. I, the LORD, have spoken!'"

[5]Jeremiah responded to Hananiah as they stood in front of all the priests and people at the Temple. [6]He said, "Amen! May your prophecies come true! I hope the LORD does everything you say. I hope he does bring back from Babylon the treasures of this Temple and all the captives. [7]But listen now to the solemn words I speak to you in the presence of all these people. [8]The ancient prophets who preceded you and me spoke against many nations, always warning of war, disaster, and disease. [9]So a prophet who predicts peace must show he is right. Only when his predictions come true can we know that he is really from the LORD."

[10]Then Hananiah the prophet took the yoke off Jeremiah's neck and broke it in pieces. [11]And Hananiah said again to the crowd that had gathered, "This is what the LORD says: 'Just as this yoke has been broken, within two years I will break the yoke of oppression from all the nations now subject to King Nebuchadnezzar of Babylon.'" With that, Jeremiah left the Temple area.

[12]Soon after this confrontation with Hananiah, the LORD gave this message to Jeremiah: [13]"Go and tell Hananiah, 'This is what the LORD says: You have broken a wooden yoke, but you have replaced it with a yoke of iron. [14]The LORD of Heaven's Armies, the God of Israel, says: I have put a yoke of iron on the necks of all these nations, forcing them into slavery under King Nebuchadnezzar of Babylon. I have put everything, even the wild animals, under his control.'"

[15]Then Jeremiah the prophet said to Hananiah, "Listen, Hananiah! The LORD has not sent you, but the people believe your lies. [16]Therefore, this is what the LORD says: 'You must die. Your life will end this very year because you have rebelled against the LORD.'"

[17]Two months later* the prophet Hananiah died.

A Letter to the Exiles

29 Jeremiah wrote a letter from Jerusalem to the elders, priests, prophets, and all the people who had been exiled to

26:18 Mic 3:12. **27:1** As in some Hebrew manuscripts and Syriac version (see also 27:3, 12); most Hebrew manuscripts read *Jehoiakim.* **27:20** Hebrew *Jeconiah,* a variant spelling of Jehoiachin. **28:1** Hebrew *In the fifth month,* of the ancient Hebrew lunar calendar. The fifth month in the fourth year of Zedekiah's reign occurred within the months of August and September 593 B.C. Also see note on 1:3. **28:4** Hebrew *Jeconiah,* a variant spelling of Jehoiachin. **28:17** Hebrew *In the seventh month of that same year.* See 28:1 and the note there.

Babylon by King Nebuchadnezzar. 2This
was after King Jehoiachin,* the queen
mother, the court officials, the other officials of Judah, and all the craftsmen and
artisans had been deported from Jerusalem. 3He sent the letter with Elasah son
of Shaphan and Gemariah son of Hilkiah
when they went to Babylon as King Zedekiah's ambassadors to Nebuchadnezzar. This
is what Jeremiah's letter said:

4This is what the LORD of Heaven's
Armies, the God of Israel, says to all the
captives he has exiled to Babylon from
Jerusalem: 5"Build homes, and plan to
stay. Plant gardens, and eat the food
they produce. 6Marry and have children.
Then find spouses for them so that you
may have many grandchildren. Multiply!
Do not dwindle away! 7And work for the
peace and prosperity of the city where
I sent you into exile. Pray to the LORD
for it, for its welfare will determine your
welfare."

8This is what the LORD of Heaven's
Armies, the God of Israel, says: "Do not let
your prophets and fortune-tellers who are
with you in the land of Babylon trick you.
Do not listen to their dreams, 9because
they are telling you lies in my name. I
have not sent them," says the LORD.

10This is what the LORD says: "You will
be in Babylon for seventy years. But then
I will come and do for you all the good
things I have promised, and I will bring
you home again. 11For I know the plans I
have for you," says the LORD. "They are
plans for good and not for disaster, to
give you a future and a hope. 12In those
days when you pray, I will listen. 13If you
look for me wholeheartedly, you will
find me. 14I will be found by you," says
the LORD. "I will end your captivity and
restore your fortunes. I will gather you
out of the nations where I sent you and
will bring you home again to your own
land."

15You claim that the LORD has raised
up prophets for you in Babylon. 16But
this is what the LORD says about the
king who sits on David's throne and
all those still living here in Jerusalem—
your relatives who were not exiled to
Babylon. 17This is what the LORD of
Heaven's Armies says: "I will send war,
famine, and disease upon them and
make them like bad figs, too rotten to
eat. 18Yes, I will pursue them with war,
famine, and disease, and I will scatter
them around the world. In every nation
where I send them, I will make them an

Working for the good of society

Jerusalem's judgment came, not all at once, but in stages. In 605 BC Babylon besieged it, humiliated King Jehoiakim, and took some of the people (including Daniel) into exile. In 597 BC they attacked again, this time exiling his son Jehoiachin and many leading citizens (2 Kings 24). The final destruction and exile would not come until 586 BC; and somewhere in this intervening period, Jeremiah wrote to the exiles, assuring them that God had not abandoned them, still had a purpose for them, and would bring them home within the seventy years prophesied. In the meantime, they were not to lament their fate or give in to life's hardships. They were to start working for the good of Babylon. Yes, Babylon! Why? Because "its welfare will determine your welfare" (Jeremiah 29:7). So they were to build houses and plan to stay, planting gardens, marrying off their children, and multiplying (29:5-6).

God still calls his people to seek the good of the places where he has put them, not to live in a separate world, uncaring about what happens around them. Christians should be the best workers in society and pray for their government, whatever it may be like (e.g., Romans 13:1-7; 1 Timothy 2:1-2). If society is blessed, so will we be.

▶ *See also **Salt and light**, page 1075; **Christians and government**, page 1297.*

object of damnation, horror, contempt,
and mockery. 19 For they refuse to listen
to me, though I have spoken to them
repeatedly through the prophets I sent.
And you who are in exile have not
listened either," says the LORD.

20 Therefore, listen to this message
from the LORD, all you captives there
in Babylon. 21 This is what the LORD of
Heaven's Armies, the God of Israel,
says about your prophets—Ahab son of
Kolaiah and Zedekiah son of Maaseiah—
who are telling you lies in my name: "I
will turn them over to Nebuchadnezzar*
for execution before your eyes. 22 Their
terrible fate will become proverbial,
so that the Judean exiles will curse
someone by saying, 'May the LORD make
you like Zedekiah and Ahab, whom the
king of Babylon burned alive!' 23 For
these men have done terrible things
among my people. They have committed
adultery with their neighbors' wives and
have lied in my name, saying things I
did not command. I am a witness to this.
I, the LORD, have spoken."

A Message for Shemaiah

24 The LORD sent this message to Shemaiah
the Nehelamite in Babylon: 25 "This is what
the LORD of Heaven's Armies, the God of
Israel, says: You wrote a letter on your own
authority to Zephaniah son of Maaseiah,
the priest, and you sent copies to the other
priests and people in Jerusalem. You wrote
to Zephaniah,

26 "The LORD has appointed you to
replace Jehoiada as the priest in charge
of the house of the LORD. You are
responsible to put into stocks and neck
irons any crazy man who claims to be
a prophet. 27 So why have you done
nothing to stop Jeremiah from Anathoth,
who pretends to be a prophet among
you? 28 Jeremiah sent a letter here to
Babylon, predicting that our captivity
will be a long one. He said, 'Build
homes, and plan to stay. Plant gardens,
and eat the food they produce.'"

29 But when Zephaniah the priest received
Shemaiah's letter, he took it to Jeremiah
and read it to him. 30 Then the LORD gave
this message to Jeremiah: 31 "Send an open
letter to all the exiles in Babylon. Tell them,
'This is what the LORD says concerning Shemaiah the Nehelamite: Since he has prophesied to you when I did not send him and
has tricked you into believing his lies, 32 I
will punish him and his family. None of his
descendants will see the good things I will
do for my people, for he has incited you to
rebel against me. I, the LORD, have spoken!'"

Promises of Deliverance

30 The LORD gave another message to
Jeremiah. He said, 2 "This is what the
LORD, the God of Israel, says: Write down for
the record everything I have said to you, Jeremiah. 3 For the time is coming when I will
restore the fortunes of my people of Israel
and Judah. I will bring them home to this land
that I gave to their ancestors, and they will
possess it again. I, the LORD, have spoken!"

4 This is the message the LORD gave concerning Israel and Judah. 5 This is what the
LORD says:

"I hear cries of fear;
there is terror and no peace.
6 Now let me ask you a question:
Do men give birth to babies?
Then why do they stand there,
ashen-faced,
hands pressed against their sides
like a woman in labor?
7 In all history there has never been such
a time of terror.
It will be a time of trouble for my
people Israel.*
Yet in the end they will be saved!
8 For in that day,"
says the LORD of Heaven's Armies,
"I will break the yoke from their necks
and snap their chains.
Foreigners will no longer be their masters.
9 For my people will serve the LORD
their God
and their king descended from David—
the king I will raise up for them.

10 "So do not be afraid, Jacob, my servant;
do not be dismayed, Israel,"
says the LORD.
"For I will bring you home again from
distant lands,
and your children will return from
their exile.

29:2 Hebrew *Jeconiah,* a variant spelling of Jehoiachin. **29:21** Hebrew *Nebuchadrezzar,* a variant spelling of Nebuchadnezzar. **30:7** Hebrew *Jacob;* also in 30:10b, 18. See note on 5:20.

Israel will return to a life of peace and
quiet,
and no one will terrorize them.
11 For I am with you and will save you,"
says the LORD.
"I will completely destroy the nations
where I have scattered you,
but I will not completely destroy you.
I will discipline you, but with justice;
I cannot let you go unpunished."

12 This is what the LORD says:
"Your injury is incurable—
a terrible wound.
13 There is no one to help you
or to bind up your injury.
No medicine can heal you.
14 All your lovers—your allies—have left you
and do not care about you anymore.
I have wounded you cruelly,
as though I were your enemy.
For your sins are many,
and your guilt is great.
15 Why do you protest your punishment—
this wound that has no cure?
I have had to punish you
because your sins are many
and your guilt is great.

16 "But all who devour you will be devoured,
and all your enemies will be sent into
exile.
All who plunder you will be plundered,
and all who attack you will be
attacked.
17 I will give you back your health
and heal your wounds," says the
LORD.
"For you are called an outcast—
'Jerusalem* for whom no one cares.'"

18 This is what the LORD says:
"When I bring Israel home again from
captivity
and restore their fortunes,
Jerusalem will be rebuilt on its ruins,
and the palace reconstructed as before.
19 There will be joy and songs of
thanksgiving,
and I will multiply my people, not
diminish them;
I will honor them, not despise them.
20 Their children will prosper as they did
long ago.
I will establish them as a nation
before me,
and I will punish anyone who hurts
them.
21 They will have their own ruler again,
and he will come from their own
people.
I will invite him to approach me," says
the LORD,
"for who would dare to come unless
invited?
22 You will be my people,
and I will be your God."
23 Look! The LORD's anger bursts out like a
storm,
a driving wind that swirls down on the
heads of the wicked.
24 The fierce anger of the LORD will not
diminish
until it has finished all he has
planned.
In the days to come
you will understand all this.

Hope for Restoration

31 "In that day," says the LORD, "I will
be the God of all the families of Israel,
and they will be my people. 2This is what
the LORD says:

"Those who survive the coming
destruction
will find blessings even in the barren
land,
for I will give rest to the people of
Israel."
3 Long ago the LORD said to Israel:
"I have loved you, my people, with an
everlasting love.
With unfailing love I have drawn you
to myself.
4 I will rebuild you, my virgin Israel.
You will again be happy
and dance merrily with your
tambourines.
5 Again you will plant your vineyards on
the mountains of Samaria
and eat from your own gardens there.
6 The day will come when watchmen will
shout
from the hill country of Ephraim,
'Come, let us go up to Jerusalem*
to worship the LORD our God.'"
7 Now this is what the LORD says:
"Sing with joy for Israel.*
Shout for the greatest of nations!

Shout out with praise and joy:
'Save your people, O LORD,
the remnant of Israel!'
8 For I will bring them from the north
and from the distant corners of the earth.
I will not forget the blind and lame,
the expectant mothers and women in labor.
A great company will return!
9 Tears of joy will stream down their faces,
and I will lead them home with great care.
They will walk beside quiet streams
and on smooth paths where they will not stumble.
For I am Israel's father,
and Ephraim is my oldest child.
10 "Listen to this message from the LORD,
you nations of the world;
proclaim it in distant coastlands:
The LORD, who scattered his people,
will gather them and watch over them
as a shepherd does his flock.
11 For the LORD has redeemed Israel
from those too strong for them.
12 They will come home and sing songs of joy on the heights of Jerusalem.
They will be radiant because of the LORD's good gifts—
the abundant crops of grain, new wine, and olive oil,
and the healthy flocks and herds.
Their life will be like a watered garden,
and all their sorrows will be gone.
13 The young women will dance for joy,
and the men—old and young—will join in the celebration.
I will turn their mourning into joy.
I will comfort them and exchange their sorrow for rejoicing.
14 The priests will enjoy abundance,
and my people will feast on my good gifts.
I, the LORD, have spoken!"

Rachel's Sadness Turns to Joy

15 This is what the LORD says:

"A cry is heard in Ramah—
deep anguish and bitter weeping.
Rachel weeps for her children,
refusing to be comforted—
for her children are gone."

16 But now this is what the LORD says:
"Do not weep any longer,
for I will reward you," says the LORD.
"Your children will come back to you
from the distant land of the enemy.

30:17 Hebrew *Zion.* **31:6** Hebrew *Zion;* also in 31:12.
31:7 Hebrew *Jacob;* also in 31:11. See note on 5:20.

The new covenant

In the high point of his prophesying, Jeremiah looked ahead in 31:31-34 to the new covenant that God would one day make with his people—the one we now know was made through Jesus Christ. The importance of these verses is reflected in the fact that this is the longest continuous Old Testament passage quoted in the New Testament (Hebrews 8:8-12).

Jeremiah saw a time coming when God would make "a new covenant" (the only occurrence of this expression in the Old Testament). Everyone knew that covenants could only be sealed with blood (even as the covenant through Christ would be sealed through his blood), but this one would have a difference. Because God's people had proved incapable of keeping the covenant made through Moses, God would come and make a new kind of covenant—one written not on stone tablets, but on human hearts instead, so they would not have to depend on something outside of themselves telling them what to do, but on something inside themselves leading them into what to do. This would open up the possibility not only of knowing God as never before but also of having their sins dealt with once and for all (Jeremiah 31:34). A fresh start is promised for all!

▶ *See also **Covenant**, page 19.*

17 There is hope for your future," says the
LORD.
"Your children will come again to
their own land.
18 I have heard Israel* saying,
'You disciplined me severely,
like a calf that needs training for the
yoke.
Turn me again to you and restore me,
for you alone are the LORD my God.
19 I turned away from God,
but then I was sorry.
I kicked myself for my stupidity!
I was thoroughly ashamed of all I did
in my younger days.'

20 "Is not Israel still my son,
my darling child?" says the LORD.
"I often have to punish him,
but I still love him.
That's why I long for him
and surely will have mercy on him.
21 Set up road signs;
put up guideposts.
Mark well the path
by which you came.
Come back again, my virgin Israel;
return to your towns here.
22 How long will you wander,
my wayward daughter?
For the LORD will cause something new
to happen—
Israel will embrace her God.*"

23This is what the LORD of Heaven's Armies, the God of Israel, says: "When I bring
them back from captivity, the people of
Judah and its towns will again say, 'The
LORD bless you, O righteous home, O holy
mountain!' 24Townspeople and farmers and
shepherds alike will live together in peace
and happiness. 25For I have given rest to the
weary and joy to the sorrowing."

26At this, I woke up and looked around.
My sleep had been very sweet.

27"The day is coming," says the LORD,
"when I will greatly increase the human
population and the number of animals here
in Israel and Judah. 28In the past I deliberately uprooted and tore down this nation. I
overthrew it, destroyed it, and brought disaster upon it. But in the future I will just
as deliberately plant it and build it up. I, the
LORD, have spoken!

29"The people will no longer quote this
proverb:
'The parents have eaten sour grapes,
but their children's mouths pucker at
the taste.'

30All people will die for their own sins—
those who eat the sour grapes will be the
ones whose mouths will pucker.

31"The day is coming," says the LORD,
"when I will make a new covenant with the
people of Israel and Judah. 32This covenant
will not be like the one I made with their ancestors when I took them by the hand and
brought them out of the land of Egypt. They
broke that covenant, though I loved them as
a husband loves his wife," says the LORD.

33"But this is the new covenant I will
make with the people of Israel after those
days," says the LORD. "I will put my instructions deep within them, and I will write
them on their hearts. I will be their God,
and they will be my people. 34And they will
not need to teach their neighbors, nor will
they need to teach their relatives, saying,
'You should know the LORD.' For everyone,
from the least to the greatest, will know me
already," says the LORD. "And I will forgive
their wickedness, and I will never again remember their sins."

35 It is the LORD who provides the sun to
light the day
and the moon and stars to light the
night,
and who stirs the sea into roaring
waves.
His name is the LORD of Heaven's
Armies,
and this is what he says:
36 "I am as likely to reject my people Israel
as I am to abolish the laws of nature!"
37 This is what the LORD says:
"Just as the heavens cannot be
measured
and the foundations of the earth
cannot be explored,
so I will not consider casting them away
for the evil they have done.
I, the LORD, have spoken!

38"The day is coming," says the LORD,
"when all Jerusalem will be rebuilt for me,
from the Tower of Hananel to the Corner
Gate. 39A measuring line will be stretched
out over the hill of Gareb and across to
Goah. 40And the entire area—including the
graveyard and ash dump in the valley, and

all the fields out to the Kidron Valley on the east as far as the Horse Gate—will be holy to the LORD. The city will never again be captured or destroyed."

Jeremiah's Land Purchase

32 The following message came to Jeremiah from the LORD in the tenth year of the reign of Zedekiah,* king of Judah. This was also the eighteenth year of the reign of King Nebuchadnezzar.* [2]Jerusalem was then under siege from the Babylonian army, and Jeremiah was imprisoned in the courtyard of the guard in the royal palace. [3]King Zedekiah had put him there, asking why he kept giving this prophecy: "This is what the LORD says: 'I am about to hand this city over to the king of Babylon, and he will take it. [4]King Zedekiah will be captured by the Babylonians* and taken to meet the king of Babylon face to face. [5]He will take Zedekiah to Babylon, and I will deal with him there,' says the LORD. 'If you fight against the Babylonians, you will never succeed.'"

[6]At that time the LORD sent me a message. He said, [7]"Your cousin Hanamel son of Shallum will come and say to you, 'Buy my field at Anathoth. By law you have the right to buy it before it is offered to anyone else.'"

[8]Then, just as the LORD had said he would, my cousin Hanamel came and visited me in the prison. He said, "Please buy my field at Anathoth in the land of Benjamin. By law you have the right to buy it before it is offered to anyone else, so buy it for yourself." Then I knew that the message I had heard was from the LORD.

[9]So I bought the field at Anathoth, paying Hanamel seventeen pieces* of silver for it. [10]I signed and sealed the deed of purchase before witnesses, weighed out the silver, and paid him. [11]Then I took the sealed deed and an unsealed copy of the deed, which contained the terms and conditions of the purchase, [12]and I handed them to Baruch son of Neriah and grandson of Mahseiah. I did all this in the presence of my cousin Hanamel, the witnesses who had signed the deed, and all the men of Judah who were there in the courtyard of the guardhouse.

[13]Then I said to Baruch as they all listened, [14]"This is what the LORD of Heaven's Armies, the God of Israel, says: 'Take both this sealed deed and the unsealed copy, and put them into a pottery jar to preserve them for a long time.' [15]For this is what the LORD of Heaven's Armies, the God of Israel, says: 'Someday people will again own property here in this land and will buy and sell houses and vineyards and fields.'"

Jeremiah's Prayer

[16]Then after I had given the papers to Baruch, I prayed to the LORD:

[17]"O Sovereign LORD! You made the heavens and earth by your strong hand and powerful arm. Nothing is too hard for you! [18]You show unfailing love to thousands, but you also bring the consequences of one generation's sin upon the next. You are the great and powerful God, the LORD of Heaven's Armies. [19]You have all wisdom and do great and mighty miracles. You see the conduct of all people, and you give them what they deserve. [20]You performed miraculous signs and wonders in the land of Egypt—things still remembered to this day! And you have continued to do great miracles in Israel and all around the world. You have made your name famous to this day.

[21]"You brought Israel out of Egypt with mighty signs and wonders, with a strong hand and powerful arm, and with overwhelming terror. [22]You gave the people of Israel this land that you had promised their ancestors long before—a land flowing with milk and honey. [23]Our ancestors came and conquered it and lived in it, but they refused to obey you or follow your word. They have not done anything you commanded. That is why you have sent this terrible disaster upon them.

[24]"See how the siege ramps have been built against the city walls! Through war, famine, and disease, the city will be handed over to the Babylonians, who will conquer it. Everything has happened just as you said. [25]And yet, O Sovereign LORD, you have told me to buy the field—paying good money for it before these witnesses—even though

31:18 Hebrew *Ephraim,* referring to the northern kingdom of Israel; also in 31:20. **31:22** Hebrew *a woman will surround a man.* **32:1a** The tenth year of Zedekiah's reign and the eighteenth year of Nebuchadnezzar's reign was 587 B.C. **32:1b** Hebrew *Nebuchadrezzar,* a variant spelling of Nebuchadnezzar; also in 32:28. **32:4** Or *Chaldeans;* also in 32:5, 24, 25, 28, 29, 43. **32:9** Hebrew *17 shekels,* about 7 ounces or 194 grams in weight.

the city will soon be handed over to the
Babylonians."

A Prediction of Jerusalem's Fall

26Then this message came to Jeremiah from
the LORD: 27"I am the LORD, the God of all
the peoples of the world. Is anything too
hard for me? 28Therefore, this is what the
LORD says: I will hand this city over to the
Babylonians and to Nebuchadnezzar, king
of Babylon, and he will capture it. 29The
Babylonians outside the walls will come in
and set fire to the city. They will burn down
all these houses where the people provoked
my anger by burning incense to Baal on the
rooftops and by pouring out liquid offerings
to other gods. 30Israel and Judah have done
nothing but wrong since their earliest days.
They have infuriated me with all their evil
deeds," says the LORD. 31"From the time this
city was built until now, it has done nothing
but anger me, so I am determined to get rid
of it.

32"The sins of Israel and Judah—the sins
of the people of Jerusalem, the kings, the
officials, the priests, and the prophets—
have stirred up my anger. 33My people
have turned their backs on me and have
refused to return. Even though I diligently
taught them, they would not receive instruction or obey. 34They have set up their
abominable idols right in my own Temple,
defiling it. 35They have built pagan shrines
to Baal in the valley of Ben-Hinnom, and
there they sacrifice their sons and daughters to Molech. I have never commanded
such a horrible deed; it never even crossed
my mind to command such a thing. What
an incredible evil, causing Judah to sin so
greatly!

A Promise of Restoration

36"Now I want to say something more about
this city. You have been saying, 'It will fall
to the king of Babylon through war, famine,
and disease.' But this is what the LORD, the
God of Israel, says: 37I will certainly bring
my people back again from all the countries where I will scatter them in my fury.
I will bring them back to this very city and
let them live in peace and safety. 38They will
be my people, and I will be their God. 39And
I will give them one heart and one purpose:
to worship me forever, for their own good
and for the good of all their descendants.
40And I will make an everlasting covenant
with them: I will never stop doing good for
them. I will put a desire in their hearts to
worship me, and they will never leave me.
41I will find joy doing good for them and will
faithfully and wholeheartedly replant them
in this land.

42"This is what the LORD says: Just as I
have brought all these calamities on them,
so I will do all the good I have promised
them. 43Fields will again be bought and
sold in this land about which you now say,
'It has been ravaged by the Babylonians, a
desolate land where people and animals
have all disappeared.' 44Yes, fields will
once again be bought and sold—deeds
signed and sealed and witnessed—in the
land of Benjamin and here in Jerusalem, in
the towns of Judah and in the hill country,
in the foothills of Judah* and in the Negev,
too. For someday I will restore prosperity to
them. I, the LORD, have spoken!"

Promises of Peace and Prosperity

33 While Jeremiah was still confined in
the courtyard of the guard, the LORD
gave him this second message: 2"This is
what the LORD says—the LORD who made
the earth, who formed and established it,
whose name is the LORD: 3Ask me and I will
tell you remarkable secrets you do not know
about things to come. 4For this is what the
LORD, the God of Israel, says: You have torn
down the houses of this city and even the
king's palace to get materials to strengthen
the walls against the siege ramps and
swords of the enemy. 5You expect to fight
the Babylonians,* but the men of this city
are already as good as dead, for I have determined to destroy them in my terrible
anger. I have abandoned them because of
all their wickedness.

6"Nevertheless, the time will come when
I will heal Jerusalem's wounds and give it
prosperity and true peace. 7I will restore
the fortunes of Judah and Israel and rebuild
their towns. 8I will cleanse them of their
sins against me and forgive all their sins of
rebellion. 9Then this city will bring me joy,
glory, and honor before all the nations of
the earth! The people of the world will see
all the good I do for my people, and they
will tremble with awe at the peace and prosperity I provide for them.

10"This is what the LORD says: You have

said, 'This is a desolate land where people
and animals have all disappeared.' Yet in
the empty streets of Jerusalem and Judah's
other towns, there will be heard once more
11the sounds of joy and laughter. The joyful
voices of bridegrooms and brides will be
heard again, along with the joyous songs of
people bringing thanksgiving offerings to
the LORD. They will sing,

'Give thanks to the LORD of Heaven's
Armies,
for the LORD is good.
His faithful love endures forever!'

For I will restore the prosperity of this land
to what it was in the past, says the LORD.
12"This is what the LORD of Heaven's
Armies says: This land—though it is now
desolate and has no people and animals—
will once more have pastures where shepherds can lead their flocks. 13Once again
shepherds will count their flocks in the
towns of the hill country, the foothills of
Judah,* the Negev, the land of Benjamin,
the vicinity of Jerusalem, and all the towns
of Judah. I, the LORD, have spoken!
14"The day will come, says the LORD,
when I will do for Israel and Judah all the
good things I have promised them.

15 "In those days and at that time
I will raise up a righteous descendant*
from King David's line.
He will do what is just and right
throughout the land.
16 In that day Judah will be saved,
and Jerusalem will live in safety.
And this will be its name:
'The LORD Is Our Righteousness.'*

17For this is what the LORD says: David will
have a descendant sitting on the throne of
Israel forever. 18And there will always be
Levitical priests to offer burnt offerings and
grain offerings and sacrifices to me."
19Then this message came to Jeremiah
from the LORD: 20"This is what the LORD
says: If you can break my covenant with the
day and the night so that one does not follow
the other, 21only then will my covenant with
my servant David be broken. Only then will
he no longer have a descendant to reign on
his throne. The same is true for my covenant
with the Levitical priests who minister before
me. 22And as the stars of the sky cannot
be counted and the sand on the seashore
cannot be measured, so I will multiply the
descendants of my servant David and the
Levites who minister before me."
23The LORD gave another message to Jeremiah. He said, 24"Have you noticed what
people are saying?—'The LORD chose Judah
and Israel and then abandoned them!'
They are sneering and saying that Israel is
not worthy to be counted as a nation. 25But
this is what the LORD says: I would no more
reject my people than I would change my
laws that govern night and day, earth and
sky. 26I will never abandon the descendants
of Jacob or David, my servant, or change the
plan that David's descendants will rule the
descendants of Abraham, Isaac, and Jacob.
Instead, I will restore them to their land and
have mercy on them."

A Warning for Zedekiah

34 King Nebuchadnezzar* of Babylon
came with all the armies from the
kingdoms he ruled, and he fought against
Jerusalem and the towns of Judah. At that
time this message came to Jeremiah from
the LORD: 2"Go to King Zedekiah of Judah,
and tell him, 'This is what the LORD, the
God of Israel, says: I am about to hand this
city over to the king of Babylon, and he will
burn it down. 3You will not escape his grasp
but will be captured and taken to meet the
king of Babylon face to face. Then you will
be exiled to Babylon.
4"'But listen to this promise from the
LORD, O Zedekiah, king of Judah. This is
what the LORD says: You will not be killed
in war 5but will die peacefully. People will
burn incense in your memory, just as they
did for your ancestors, the kings who preceded you. They will mourn for you, crying,
"Alas, our master is dead!" This I have
decreed, says the LORD.'"
6So Jeremiah the prophet delivered the
message to King Zedekiah of Judah. 7At this
time the Babylonian army was besieging
Jerusalem, Lachish, and Azekah—the only
fortified cities of Judah not yet captured.

Freedom for Hebrew Slaves

8This message came to Jeremiah from the
LORD after King Zedekiah made a covenant
with the people, proclaiming freedom for

32:44 Hebrew *the Shephelah.* **33:5** Or *Chaldeans.* **33:13** Hebrew *the Shephelah.* **33:15** Hebrew *a righteous branch.* **33:16** Hebrew *Yahweh Tsidqenu.* **34:1** Hebrew *Nebuchadrezzar,* a variant spelling of Nebuchadnezzar.

the slaves. 9He had ordered all the people
to free their Hebrew slaves—both men and
women. No one was to keep a fellow Judean
in bondage. 10The officials and all the people
had obeyed the king's command, 11but later
they changed their minds. They took back
the men and women they had freed, forcing
them to be slaves again.

12So the LORD gave them this message
through Jeremiah: 13"This is what the
LORD, the God of Israel, says: I made a covenant with your ancestors long ago when
I rescued them from their slavery in Egypt.
14I told them that every Hebrew slave must
be freed after serving six years. But your ancestors paid no attention to me. 15Recently
you repented and did what was right, following my command. You freed your slaves
and made a solemn covenant with me in the
Temple that bears my name. 16But now you
have shrugged off your oath and defiled my
name by taking back the men and women
you had freed, forcing them to be slaves
once again.

17"Therefore, this is what the LORD says:
Since you have not obeyed me by setting
your countrymen free, I will set you free to
be destroyed by war, disease, and famine.
You will be an object of horror to all the
nations of the earth. 18Because you have
broken the terms of our covenant, I will cut
you apart just as you cut apart the calf when
you walked between its halves to solem-
nize your vows. 19Yes, I will cut you apart,
whether you are officials of Judah or Jerusalem, court officials, priests, or common
people—for you have broken your oath. 20I
will give you to your enemies, and they will
kill you. Your bodies will be food for the vultures and wild animals.

21"I will hand over King Zedekiah of Judah
and his officials to the army of the king of
Babylon. And although they have left Jerusalem for a while, 22I will call the Babylonian armies back again. They will fight
against this city and will capture it and burn
it down. I will see to it that all the towns
of Judah are destroyed, with no one living
there."

The Faithful Recabites

35 This is the message the LORD gave
Jeremiah when Jehoiakim son of
Josiah was king of Judah: 2"Go to the settlement where the families of the Recabites
live, and invite them to the LORD's Temple.
Take them into one of the inner rooms, and
offer them some wine."

3So I went to see Jaazaniah son of Jeremiah and grandson of Habazziniah and
all his brothers and sons—representing
all the Recabite families. 4I took them to
the Temple, and we went into the room assigned to the sons of Hanan son of Igdaliah,
a man of God. This room was located next
to the one used by the Temple officials, directly above the room of Maaseiah son of
Shallum, the Temple gatekeeper.

5I set cups and jugs of wine before them
and invited them to have a drink, 6but they
refused. "No," they said, "we don't drink
wine, because our ancestor Jehonadab* son
of Recab gave us this command: 'You and
your descendants must never drink wine.
7And do not build houses or plant crops or
vineyards, but always live in tents. If you
follow these commands, you will live long,
good lives in the land.' 8So we have obeyed
him in all these things. We have never had a
drink of wine to this day, nor have our wives,
our sons, or our daughters. 9We haven't
built houses or owned vineyards or farms
or planted crops. 10We have lived in tents
and have fully obeyed all the commands of
Jehonadab, our ancestor. 11But when King
Nebuchadnezzar* of Babylon attacked this
country, we were afraid of the Babylonian
and Syrian* armies. So we decided to move
to Jerusalem. That is why we are here."

12Then the LORD gave this message to Jeremiah: 13"This is what the LORD of Heaven's
Armies, the God of Israel, says: Go and
say to the people in Judah and Jerusalem,
'Come and learn a lesson about how to obey
me. 14The Recabites do not drink wine to
this day because their ancestor Jehonadab
told them not to. But I have spoken to you
again and again, and you refuse to obey me.
15Time after time I sent you prophets, who
told you, "Turn from your wicked ways, and
start doing things right. Stop worshiping
other gods so that you might live in peace
here in the land I have given to you and
your ancestors." But you would not listen
to me or obey me. 16The descendants of Jehonadab son of Recab have obeyed their
ancestor completely, but you have refused
to listen to me.'

17"Therefore, this is what the LORD God
of Heaven's Armies, the God of Israel, says:

'Because you refuse to listen or answer when I call, I will send upon Judah and Jerusalem all the disasters I have threatened.'"

18 Then Jeremiah turned to the Recabites and said, "This is what the LORD of Heaven's Armies, the God of Israel, says: 'You have obeyed your ancestor Jehonadab in every respect, following all his instructions.' 19 Therefore, this is what the LORD of Heaven's Armies, the God of Israel, says: 'Jehonadab son of Recab will always have descendants who serve me.'"

Baruch Reads the LORD's Messages

36 During the fourth year that Jehoiakim son of Josiah was king in Judah,* the LORD gave this message to Jeremiah: 2 "Get a scroll, and write down all my messages against Israel, Judah, and the other nations. Begin with the first message back in the days of Josiah, and write down every message, right up to the present time. 3 Perhaps the people of Judah will repent when they hear again all the terrible things I have planned for them. Then I will be able to forgive their sins and wrongdoings."

4 So Jeremiah sent for Baruch son of Neriah, and as Jeremiah dictated all the prophecies that the LORD had given him, Baruch wrote them on a scroll. 5 Then Jeremiah said to Baruch, "I am a prisoner here and unable to go to the Temple. 6 So you go to the Temple on the next day of fasting, and read the messages from the LORD that I have had you write on this scroll. Read them so the people who are there from all over Judah will hear them. 7 Perhaps even yet they will turn from their evil ways and ask the LORD's forgiveness before it is too late. For the LORD has threatened them with his terrible anger."

8 Baruch did as Jeremiah told him and read these messages from the LORD to the people at the Temple. 9 He did this on a day of sacred fasting held in late autumn,* during the fifth year of the reign of Jehoiakim son of Josiah. People from all over Judah had come to Jerusalem to attend the services at the Temple on that day. 10 Baruch read Jeremiah's words on the scroll to all the people. He stood in front of the Temple room of Gemariah, son of Shaphan the secretary. This room was just off the upper courtyard of the Temple, near the New Gate entrance.

11 When Micaiah son of Gemariah and grandson of Shaphan heard the messages from the LORD, 12 he went down to the secretary's room in the palace where the administrative officials were meeting. Elishama the secretary was there, along with Delaiah son of Shemaiah, Elnathan son of Acbor, Gemariah son of Shaphan, Zedekiah son of Hananiah, and all the other officials. 13 When Micaiah told them about the messages Baruch was reading to the people, 14 the officials sent Jehudi son of Nethaniah, grandson of Shelemiah and great-grandson

35:6 Hebrew *Jonadab,* a variant spelling of Jehonadab; also in 35:10, 19. See 2 Kgs 10:15. **35:11a** Hebrew *Nebuchadrezzar,* a variant spelling of Nebuchadnezzar. **35:11b** Or *Chaldean and Aramean.* **36:1** The fourth year of Jehoiakim's reign was 605 B.C. **36:9** Hebrew *in the ninth month,* of the ancient Hebrew lunar calendar (also in 36:22). The ninth month in the fifth year of Jehoiakim's reign occurred within the months of November and December 604 B.C. Also see note on 1:3.

King Jehoiakim

After the godly King Josiah's death in battle against Egypt, he was succeeded by his son Jehoahaz. But Jehoahaz reigned for only three months before being removed by Egypt and replaced with his brother Jehoiakim (2 Kings 23:31-37). Jehoiakim didn't follow his father's ways but rather "did what was evil in the LORD's sight" (2 Kings 23:37). He killed the prophet Uriah for opposing him (Jeremiah 26:20-23) and destroyed a scroll of Jeremiah's prophecies, cutting it up as it was read to him and throwing it into the fire (Jeremiah 36:21-23). In 605 BC, following Babylon's defeat of Egypt, Babylon forced Jehoiakim to submit to their rule; but when he rebelled three years later, they attacked Judah (2 Kings 24:1-2) and took Jehoiakim into exile (2 Chronicles 36:6). We are not told how he died, but Jeremiah had prophesied he would be "buried like a dead donkey" (Jeremiah 22:18-23), suggesting a sad ending to this godless life.

of Cushi, to ask Baruch to come and read the messages to them, too. So Baruch took the scroll and went to them. 15“Sit down and read the scroll to us,” the officials said, and Baruch did as they requested.

16When they heard all the messages, they looked at one another in alarm. “We must tell the king what we have heard,” they said to Baruch. 17“But first, tell us how you got these messages. Did they come directly from Jeremiah?”

18So Baruch explained, “Jeremiah dictated them, and I wrote them down in ink, word for word, on this scroll.”

19“You and Jeremiah should both hide,” the officials told Baruch. “Don’t tell anyone where you are!” 20Then the officials left the scroll for safekeeping in the room of Elishama the secretary and went to tell the king what had happened.

King Jehoiakim Burns the Scroll

21The king sent Jehudi to get the scroll. Jehudi brought it from Elishama’s room and read it to the king as all his officials stood by. 22It was late autumn, and the king was in a winterized part of the palace, sitting in front of a fire to keep warm. 23Each time Jehudi finished reading three or four columns, the king took a knife and cut off that section of the scroll. He then threw it into the fire, section by section, until the whole scroll was burned up. 24Neither the king nor his attendants showed any signs of fear or repentance at what they heard. 25Even when Elnathan, Delaiah, and Gemariah begged the king not to burn the scroll, he wouldn’t listen.

26Then the king commanded his son Jerahmeel, Seraiah son of Azriel, and Shelemiah son of Abdeel to arrest Baruch and Jeremiah. But the LORD had hidden them.

Jeremiah Rewrites the Scroll

27After the king had burned the scroll on which Baruch had written Jeremiah’s words, the LORD gave Jeremiah another message. He said, 28“Get another scroll, and write everything again just as you did on the scroll King Jehoiakim burned. 29Then say to the king, ‘This is what the LORD says: You burned the scroll because it said the king of Babylon would destroy this land and empty it of people and animals. 30Now this is what the LORD says about King Jehoiakim of Judah: He will have no heirs to sit on the throne of David. His dead body will be thrown out to lie unburied—exposed to the heat of the day and the frost of the night. 31I will punish him and his family and his attendants for their sins. I will pour out on them and on all the people of Jerusalem and Judah all the disasters I promised, for they would not listen to my warnings.’”

32So Jeremiah took another scroll and dictated again to his secretary, Baruch. He wrote everything that had been on the scroll King Jehoiakim had burned in the fire. Only this time he added much more!

Zedekiah Calls for Jeremiah

37 Zedekiah son of Josiah succeeded Jehoiachin* son of Jehoiakim as the king of Judah. He was appointed by King Nebuchadnezzar* of Babylon. 2But neither King Zedekiah nor his attendants nor the people who were left in the land listened to what the LORD said through Jeremiah.

3Nevertheless, King Zedekiah sent Jehucal son of Shelemiah, and Zephaniah the priest, son of Maaseiah, to ask Jeremiah, “Please pray to the LORD our God for us.” 4Jeremiah had not yet been imprisoned, so he could come and go among the people as he pleased.

5At this time the army of Pharaoh Hophra* of Egypt appeared at the southern border of Judah. When the Babylonian* army heard about it, they withdrew from their siege of Jerusalem.

6Then the LORD gave this message to Jeremiah: 7“This is what the LORD, the God of Israel, says: The king of Judah sent you to ask me what is going to happen. Tell him, ‘Pharaoh’s army is about to return to Egypt, though he came here to help you. 8Then the Babylonians* will come back and capture this city and burn it to the ground.’

9“This is what the LORD says: Do not fool yourselves into thinking that the Babylonians are gone for good. They aren’t! 10Even if you were to destroy the entire Babylonian army, leaving only a handful of wounded survivors, they would still stagger from their tents and burn this city to the ground!”

Jeremiah Is Imprisoned

11When the Babylonian army left Jerusalem because of Pharaoh’s approaching army, 12Jeremiah started to leave the city

on his way to the territory of Benjamin, to
claim his share of the property among his
relatives there.* 13But as he was walking
through the Benjamin Gate, a sentry arrested him and said, "You are defecting to
the Babylonians!" The sentry making the
arrest was Irijah son of Shelemiah, grandson of Hananiah.
14"That's not true!" Jeremiah protested.
"I had no intention of doing any such
thing." But Irijah wouldn't listen, and he
took Jeremiah before the officials. 15They
were furious with Jeremiah and had him
flogged and imprisoned in the house of Jonathan the secretary. Jonathan's house had
been converted into a prison. 16Jeremiah
was put into a dungeon cell, where he remained for many days.
17Later King Zedekiah secretly requested
that Jeremiah come to the palace, where the
king asked him, "Do you have any messages
from the LORD?"
"Yes, I do!" said Jeremiah. "You will be
defeated by the king of Babylon."
18Then Jeremiah asked the king, "What
crime have I committed? What have I done
against you, your attendants, or the people
that I should be imprisoned like this?
19Where are your prophets now who told
you the king of Babylon would not attack
you or this land? 20Listen, my lord the king, I
beg you. Don't send me back to the dungeon
in the house of Jonathan the secretary, for I
will die there."
21So King Zedekiah commanded that
Jeremiah not be returned to the dungeon.
Instead, he was imprisoned in the courtyard of the guard in the royal palace. The
king also commanded that Jeremiah be
given a loaf of fresh bread every day as long
as there was any left in the city. So Jeremiah
was put in the palace prison.

Jeremiah in a Cistern

38 Now Shephatiah son of Mattan,
Gedaliah son of Pashhur, Jehucal*
son of Shelemiah, and Pashhur son of Malkijah heard what Jeremiah had been telling
the people. He had been saying, 2"This is
what the LORD says: 'Everyone who stays
in Jerusalem will die from war, famine,
or disease, but those who surrender to
the Babylonians* will live. Their reward
will be life. They will live!' 3The LORD also
says: 'The city of Jerusalem will certainly
be handed over to the army of the king of
Babylon, who will capture it.'"
4So these officials went to the king and
said, "Sir, this man must die! That kind of
talk will undermine the morale of the few
fighting men we have left, as well as that of
all the people. This man is a traitor!"
5King Zedekiah agreed. "All right," he
said. "Do as you like. I can't stop you."
6So the officials took Jeremiah from his
cell and lowered him by ropes into an empty
cistern in the prison yard. It belonged to
Malkijah, a member of the royal family.
There was no water in the cistern, but there
was a thick layer of mud at the bottom, and
Jeremiah sank down into it.
7But Ebed-melech the Ethiopian,* an important court official, heard that Jeremiah
was in the cistern. At that time the king
was holding court at the Benjamin Gate,
8so Ebed-melech rushed from the palace
to speak with him. 9"My lord the king,"
he said, "these men have done a very evil
thing in putting Jeremiah the prophet into
the cistern. He will soon die of hunger, for
almost all the bread in the city is gone."
10So the king told Ebed-melech, "Take
thirty of my men with you, and pull Jeremiah out of the cistern before he dies."
11So Ebed-melech took the men with him
and went to a room in the palace beneath
the treasury, where he found some old rags
and discarded clothing. He carried these to
the cistern and lowered them to Jeremiah on
a rope. 12Ebed-melech called down to Jeremiah, "Put these rags under your armpits
to protect you from the ropes." Then when
Jeremiah was ready, 13they pulled him out.
So Jeremiah was returned to the courtyard
of the guard—the palace prison—where he
remained.

Zedekiah Questions Jeremiah

14One day King Zedekiah sent for Jeremiah
and had him brought to the third entrance
of the LORD's Temple. "I want to ask you
something," the king said. "And don't try to
hide the truth."
15Jeremiah said, "If I tell you the truth,

37:1a Hebrew *Coniah,* a variant spelling of Jehoiachin. **37:1b** Hebrew *Nebuchadrezzar,* a variant spelling of Nebuchadnezzar. **37:5a** Hebrew *army of Pharaoh;* see 44:30. **37:5b** Or *Chaldean;* also in 37:10, 11. **37:8** Or *Chaldeans;* also in 37:9, 13. **37:12** Hebrew *to separate from there in the midst of the people.* **38:1** Hebrew *Jucal,* a variant spelling of Jehucal; see 37:3. **38:2** Or *Chaldeans;* also in 38:18, 19, 23. **38:7** Hebrew *the Cushite.*

you will kill me. And if I give you advice, you won't listen to me anyway."

16So King Zedekiah secretly promised him, "As surely as the LORD our Creator lives, I will not kill you or hand you over to the men who want you dead."

17Then Jeremiah said to Zedekiah, "This is what the LORD God of Heaven's Armies, the God of Israel, says: 'If you surrender to the Babylonian officers, you and your family will live, and the city will not be burned down. 18But if you refuse to surrender, you will not escape! This city will be handed over to the Babylonians, and they will burn it to the ground.'"

19"But I am afraid to surrender," the king said, "for the Babylonians may hand me over to the Judeans who have defected to them. And who knows what they will do to me!"

20Jeremiah replied, "You won't be handed over to them if you choose to obey the LORD. Your life will be spared, and all will go well for you. 21But if you refuse to surrender, this is what the LORD has revealed to me: 22All the women left in your palace will be brought out and given to the officers of the Babylonian army. Then the women will taunt you, saying,

'What fine friends you have!
They have betrayed and misled you.
When your feet sank in the mud,
they left you to your fate!'

23All your wives and children will be led out to the Babylonians, and you will not escape. You will be seized by the king of Babylon, and this city will be burned down."

24Then Zedekiah said to Jeremiah, "Don't tell anyone you told me this, or you will die! 25My officials may hear that I spoke to you, and they may say, 'Tell us what you and the king were talking about. If you don't tell us, we will kill you.' 26If this happens, just tell them you begged me not to send you back to Jonathan's dungeon, for fear you would die there."

27Sure enough, it wasn't long before the king's officials came to Jeremiah and asked him why the king had called for him. But Jeremiah followed the king's instructions, and they left without finding out the truth. No one had overheard the conversation between Jeremiah and the king. 28And Jeremiah remained a prisoner in the courtyard of the guard until the day Jerusalem was captured.

The Fall of Jerusalem

39 In January* of the ninth year of King Zedekiah's reign, King Nebuchadnezzar* of Babylon came with his entire army to besiege Jerusalem. 2Two and a half years later, on July 18* in the eleventh year of Zedekiah's reign, a section of the city wall was broken down. 3All the officers of the Babylonian army came in and sat in triumph at the Middle Gate: Nergal-sharezer of Samgar, and Nebo-sarsekim,* a chief officer, and Nergal-sharezer, the king's adviser, and all the other officers of the king of Babylon.

4When King Zedekiah of Judah and all the soldiers saw that the Babylonians had broken into the city, they fled. They waited for nightfall and then slipped through the gate between the two walls behind the king's garden and headed toward the Jordan Valley.*

5But the Babylonian* troops chased them and overtook Zedekiah on the plains of Jericho. They captured him and took him to King Nebuchadnezzar of Babylon, who was at Riblah in the land of Hamath. There the king of Babylon pronounced judgment upon Zedekiah. 6The king of Babylon made Zedekiah watch as he slaughtered his sons at Riblah. The king of Babylon also slaughtered all the nobles of Judah. 7Then he gouged out Zedekiah's eyes and bound him in bronze chains to lead him away to Babylon.

8Meanwhile, the Babylonians burned Jerusalem, including the royal palace and the houses of the people, and they tore down the walls of the city. 9Then Nebuzaradan, the captain of the guard, took as exiles to Babylon the rest of the people who remained in the city, those who had defected to him, and everyone else who remained. 10But Nebuzaradan allowed some of the poorest people to stay behind in the land of Judah, and he assigned them to care for the vineyards and fields.

Jeremiah Remains in Judah

11King Nebuchadnezzar had told Nebuzaradan, the captain of the guard, to find Jeremiah. 12"See that he isn't hurt," he said. "Look after him well, and give him anything he wants." 13So Nebuzaradan, the captain of the guard; Nebushazban, a chief officer; Nergal-sharezer, the king's adviser; and the

other officers of Babylon's king 14sent messengers to bring Jeremiah out of the prison.
They put him under the care of Gedaliah
son of Ahikam and grandson of Shaphan,
who took him back to his home. So Jeremiah
stayed in Judah among his own people.
15The LORD had given the following
message to Jeremiah while he was still in
prison: 16"Say to Ebed-melech the Ethiopian,* 'This is what the LORD of Heaven's
Armies, the God of Israel, says: I will do
to this city everything I have threatened. I
will send disaster, not prosperity. You will
see its destruction, 17but I will rescue you
from those you fear so much. 18Because
you trusted me, I will give you your life as a
reward. I will rescue you and keep you safe.
I, the LORD, have spoken!'"

40 The LORD gave a message to
Jeremiah after Nebuzaradan, the
captain of the guard, had released him at
Ramah. He had found Jeremiah bound in
chains among all the other captives of Jerusalem and Judah who were being sent to
exile in Babylon.
2The captain of the guard called for Jeremiah and said, "The LORD your God has
brought this disaster on this land, 3just as he
said he would. For these people have sinned
against the LORD and disobeyed him. That
is why it happened. 4But I am going to take
off your chains and let you go. If you want to
come with me to Babylon, you are welcome.
I will see that you are well cared for. But if
you don't want to come, you may stay here.
The whole land is before you—go wherever
you like. 5If you decide to stay, then return
to Gedaliah son of Ahikam and grandson of
Shaphan. He has been appointed governor
of Judah by the king of Babylon. Stay there
with the people he rules. But it's up to you;
go wherever you like."
Then Nebuzaradan, the captain of the
guard, gave Jeremiah some food and money
and let him go. 6So Jeremiah returned to
Gedaliah son of Ahikam at Mizpah, and he
lived in Judah with the few who were still
left in the land.

Gedaliah Governs in Judah

7The leaders of the Judean military groups
in the countryside heard that the king of

39:1a Hebrew *In the tenth month,* of the ancient Hebrew lunar calendar. A number of events in Jeremiah can be cross-checked with dates in surviving Babylonian records and related accurately to our modern calendar. This event occurred on January 15, 588 B.C.; see 52:4a and the note there. **39:1b** Hebrew *Nebuchadrezzar,* a variant spelling of Nebuchadnezzar; also in 39:5, 11. **39:2** Hebrew *On the ninth day of the fourth month.* This day was July 18, 586 B.C.; also see note on 39:1a. **39:3** Or *Nergal-sharezer, Samgar-nebo, Sarsekim.* **39:4** Hebrew *the Arabah.* **39:5** Or *Chaldean;* similarly in 39:8. **39:16** Hebrew *the Cushite.*

The fall of Jerusalem

It is almost impossible to exaggerate the shock among God's people when Jerusalem was conquered by the Babylonians. Everything they had ever believed in was now gone: The city of God's dwelling was crushed; the Davidic line, promised to endure forever, was ended; the Temple, where God dwelled, was destroyed and looted; the priesthood was rendered useless. What now of God's blessing, God's promises—even God himself?

Yet all this was exactly what the prophets had said would happen. And the signs had been obvious for anyone who would look. Babylon had been getting increasingly frustrated with Jerusalem. It had deported some leading citizens (including Daniel) in 605 BC, and more in 597 BC, including King Jehoiachin and Ezekiel. But when Zedekiah, whom the Babylonians had imposed as ruler, rebelled, it was the final straw. In 588 BC, Babylon marched on Jerusalem and besieged it for two years until it fell in 586 BC. The walls were broken down, the Temple and every important building were destroyed, and the population was exiled (2 Kings 25:1-21; 2 Chronicles 36:17-21; Jeremiah 39:1-10; 52:1-30). Zedekiah was captured, and his sons were killed before him; then his eyes were gouged out, and he was taken to Babylon. The devastation was complete, and Judah's history seemed over.

Many years would pass before the exiles would see what God was going to do.

Babylon had appointed Gedaliah son of Ahikam as governor over the poor people who were left behind in Judah—the men, women, and children who hadn't been exiled to Babylon. 8So they went to see Gedaliah at Mizpah. These included: Ishmael son of Nethaniah, Johanan and Jonathan sons of Kareah, Seraiah son of Tanhumeth, the sons of Ephai the Netophathite, Jezaniah son of the Maacathite, and all their men.

9Gedaliah vowed to them that the Babylonians* meant them no harm. "Don't be afraid to serve them. Live in the land and serve the king of Babylon, and all will go well for you," he promised. 10"As for me, I will stay at Mizpah to represent you before the Babylonians who come to meet with us. Settle in the towns you have taken, and live off the land. Harvest the grapes and summer fruits and olives, and store them away."

11When the Judeans in Moab, Ammon, Edom, and the other nearby countries heard that the king of Babylon had left a few people in Judah and that Gedaliah was the governor, 12they began to return to Judah from the places to which they had fled. They stopped at Mizpah to meet with Gedaliah and then went into the Judean countryside to gather a great harvest of grapes and other crops.

A Plot against Gedaliah

13Soon after this, Johanan son of Kareah and the other military leaders came to Gedaliah at Mizpah. 14They said to him, "Did you know that Baalis, king of Ammon, has sent Ishmael son of Nethaniah to assassinate you?" But Gedaliah refused to believe them.

15Later Johanan had a private conference with Gedaliah and volunteered to kill Ishmael secretly. "Why should we let him come and murder you?" Johanan asked. "What will happen then to the Judeans who have returned? Why should the few of us who are still left be scattered and lost?"

16But Gedaliah said to Johanan, "I forbid you to do any such thing, for you are lying about Ishmael."

The Murder of Gedaliah

41 But in midautumn of that year,* Ishmael son of Nethaniah and grandson of Elishama, who was a member of the royal family and had been one of the king's high officials, went to Mizpah with ten men to meet Gedaliah. While they were eating together, 2Ishmael and his ten men suddenly jumped up, drew their swords, and killed Gedaliah, whom the king of Babylon had appointed governor. 3Ishmael also killed all the Judeans and the Babylonian* soldiers who were with Gedaliah at Mizpah.

4The next day, before anyone had heard about Gedaliah's murder, 5eighty men arrived from Shechem, Shiloh, and Samaria to worship at the Temple of the LORD. They had shaved off their beards, torn their clothes, and cut themselves, and had brought along grain offerings and frankincense. 6Ishmael left Mizpah to meet them, weeping as he went. When he reached them, he said, "Oh, come and see what has happened to Gedaliah!"

7But as soon as they were all inside the town, Ishmael and his men killed all but ten of them and threw their bodies into a cistern. 8The other ten had talked Ishmael into letting them go by promising to bring him their stores of wheat, barley, olive oil, and honey that they had hidden away. 9The cistern where Ishmael dumped the bodies of the men he murdered was the large one* dug by King Asa when he fortified Mizpah to protect himself against King Baasha of Israel. Ishmael son of Nethaniah filled it with corpses.

10Then Ishmael made captives of the king's daughters and the other people who had been left under Gedaliah's care in Mizpah by Nebuzaradan, the captain of the guard. Taking them with him, he started back toward the land of Ammon.

11But when Johanan son of Kareah and the other military leaders heard about Ishmael's crimes, 12they took all their men and set out to stop him. They caught up with him at the large pool near Gibeon. 13The people Ishmael had captured shouted for joy when they saw Johanan and the other military leaders. 14And all the captives from Mizpah escaped and began to help Johanan. 15Meanwhile, Ishmael and eight of his men escaped from Johanan into the land of Ammon.

16Then Johanan son of Kareah and the other military leaders took all the people they had rescued in Gibeon—the soldiers, women, children, and court officials* whom Ishmael had captured after he killed Gedaliah. 17They took them all to the village of Geruth-kimham near Bethlehem, where

they prepared to leave for Egypt. [18]They
were afraid of what the Babylonians* would
do when they heard that Ishmael had killed
Gedaliah, the governor appointed by the
Babylonian king.

Warning to Stay in Judah

42 Then all the military leaders, including Johanan son of Kareah and Jezaniah* son of Hoshaiah, and all the people,
from the least to the greatest, approached
[2]Jeremiah the prophet. They said, "Please
pray to the LORD your God for us. As you can
see, we are only a tiny remnant compared
to what we were before. [3]Pray that the LORD
your God will show us what to do and where
to go."
[4]"All right," Jeremiah replied. "I will pray
to the LORD your God, as you have asked,
and I will tell you everything he says. I will
hide nothing from you."
[5]Then they said to Jeremiah, "May the
LORD your God be a faithful witness against
us if we refuse to obey whatever he tells us
to do! [6]Whether we like it or not, we will
obey the LORD our God to whom we are
sending you with our plea. For if we obey
him, everything will turn out well for us."
[7]Ten days later the LORD gave his reply
to Jeremiah. [8]So he called for Johanan son
of Kareah and the other military leaders,
and for all the people, from the least to the
greatest. [9]He said to them, "You sent me
to the LORD, the God of Israel, with your
request, and this is his reply: [10]'Stay here
in this land. If you do, I will build you up
and not tear you down; I will plant you and
not uproot you. For I am sorry about all the
punishment I have had to bring upon you.
[11]Do not fear the king of Babylon anymore,'
says the LORD. 'For I am with you and will
save you and rescue you from his power. [12]I
will be merciful to you by making him kind,
so he will let you stay here in your land.'
[13]"But if you refuse to obey the LORD your
God, and if you say, 'We will not stay here;
[14]instead, we will go to Egypt where we
will be free from war, the call to arms, and
hunger,' [15]then hear the LORD's message
to the remnant of Judah. This is what the
LORD of Heaven's Armies, the God of Israel,
says: 'If you are determined to go to Egypt
and live there, [16]the very war and famine
you fear will catch up to you, and you will
die there. [17]That is the fate awaiting every
one of you who insists on going to live in
Egypt. Yes, you will die from war, famine,
and disease. None of you will escape the disaster I will bring upon you there.'
[18]"This is what the LORD of Heaven's
Armies, the God of Israel, says: 'Just as my
anger and fury have been poured out on the
people of Jerusalem, so they will be poured
out on you when you enter Egypt. You will
be an object of damnation, horror, cursing,
and mockery. And you will never see your
homeland again.'
[19]"Listen, you remnant of Judah. The
LORD has told you: 'Do not go to Egypt!'
Don't forget this warning I have given you
today. [20]For you were not being honest
when you sent me to pray to the LORD your
God for you. You said, 'Just tell us what the
LORD our God says, and we will do it!' [21]And
today I have told you exactly what he said,
but you will not obey the LORD your God
any better now than you have in the past.
[22]So you can be sure that you will die from
war, famine, and disease in Egypt, where
you insist on going."

Jeremiah Taken to Egypt

43 When Jeremiah had finished giving
this message from the LORD their
God to all the people, [2]Azariah son of Hoshaiah and Johanan son of Kareah and all
the other proud men said to Jeremiah, "You
lie! The LORD our God hasn't forbidden us
to go to Egypt! [3]Baruch son of Neriah has
convinced you to say this, because he wants
us to stay here and be killed by the Babylonians* or be carried off into exile."
[4]So Johanan and the other military leaders
and all the people refused to obey the LORD's
command to stay in Judah. [5]Johanan and the
other leaders took with them all the people
who had returned from the nearby countries to which they had fled. [6]In the crowd
were men, women, and children, the king's
daughters, and all those whom Nebuzaradan, the captain of the guard, had left with
Gedaliah. The prophet Jeremiah and Baruch
were also included. [7]The people refused
to obey the voice of the LORD and went to
Egypt, going as far as the city of Tahpanhes.

40:9 Or *Chaldeans;* also in 40:10. **41:1** Hebrew *in the seventh month,* of the ancient Hebrew lunar calendar. This month occurred within the months of October and November 586 B.C.; also see note on 39:1a. **41:3** Or *Chaldean.* **41:9** As in Greek version; Hebrew reads *murdered because of Gedaliah was one.* **41:16** Or *eunuchs.* **41:18** Or *Chaldeans.* **42:1** Greek version reads *Azariah;* compare 43:2. **43:3** Or *Chaldeans.*

8Then at Tahpanhes, the LORD gave
another message to Jeremiah. He said,
9"While the people of Judah are watching,
take some large rocks and bury them under
the pavement stones at the entrance of
Pharaoh's palace here in Tahpanhes. 10Then
say to the people of Judah, 'This is what the
LORD of Heaven's Armies, the God of Israel,
says: I will certainly bring my servant Nebuchadnezzar,* king of Babylon, here to
Egypt. I will set his throne over these stones
that I have hidden. He will spread his royal
canopy over them. 11And when he comes, he
will destroy the land of Egypt. He will bring
death to those destined for death, captivity
to those destined for captivity, and war to
those destined for war. 12He will set fire to
the temples of Egypt's gods; he will burn the
temples and carry the idols away as plunder.
He will pick clean the land of Egypt as a
shepherd picks fleas from his cloak. And
he himself will leave unharmed. 13He will
break down the sacred pillars standing in
the temple of the sun* in Egypt, and he will
burn down the temples of Egypt's gods.'"

Judgment for Idolatry

44 This is the message Jeremiah received concerning the Judeans
living in northern Egypt in the cities of
Migdol, Tahpanhes, and Memphis,* and in
southern Egypt* as well: 2"This is what the
LORD of Heaven's Armies, the God of Israel,
says: You saw the calamity I brought on Jerusalem and all the towns of Judah. They
now lie deserted and in ruins. 3They provoked my anger with all their wickedness.
They burned incense and worshiped other
gods—gods that neither they nor you nor
any of your ancestors had ever even known.
4"Again and again I sent my servants,
the prophets, to plead with them, 'Don't do
these horrible things that I hate so much.'
5But my people would not listen or turn
back from their wicked ways. They kept
on burning incense to these gods. 6And so
my fury boiled over and fell like fire on the
towns of Judah and into the streets of Jerusalem, and they are still a desolate ruin
today.
7"And now the LORD God of Heaven's
Armies, the God of Israel, asks you: Why
are you destroying yourselves? For not one
of you will survive—not a man, woman, or
child among you who has come here from
Judah, not even the babies in your arms.
8Why provoke my anger by burning incense
to the idols you have made here in Egypt?
You will only destroy yourselves and make
yourselves an object of cursing and mockery
for all the nations of the earth. 9Have you
forgotten the sins of your ancestors, the sins
of the kings and queens of Judah, and the
sins you and your wives committed in Judah
and Jerusalem? 10To this very hour you have
shown no remorse or reverence. No one has

Worshiping other gods

At the beginning of the Ten Commandments lie the commands to have no other god but the one true living God and not to make any idols, lest they lead people away from him (see *Idols*, page 836). Failure to obey would lead to judgment, God had said (Exodus 20:3-6). And yet God's people had failed to heed his commands again and again. After the division of the kingdom following Solomon's death, both Israel and Judah repeatedly fell into idolatry and worshiped other gods—or at least had tried to mix the worship of the LORD (Yahweh) with the worship of other gods—forgetting that, to God, these were "horrible things" (Jeremiah 44:4). And so, because they had ignored the repeated warnings of the prophets, judgment had now come upon them. Jerusalem was conquered and its Temple destroyed (chapter 39), and its people were now heading for exile.

Today it is not just an idol that can become another god in our lives. Work, family, playing or watching sports, using the Internet—in fact, anything that demands the best of our time, energy, and attention—can be another god to which we give our worship, that is, the best of our lives. If we see this happening, Jeremiah's challenge to us is to change while there is still time.

chosen to follow my word and the decrees I
gave to you and your ancestors before you.
11 "Therefore, this is what the LORD of
Heaven's Armies, the God of Israel, says: I
am determined to destroy every one of you!
12 I will take this remnant of Judah—those
who were determined to come here and live
in Egypt—and I will consume them. They will
fall here in Egypt, killed by war and famine.
All will die, from the least to the greatest.
They will be an object of damnation, horror,
cursing, and mockery. 13 I will punish them
in Egypt just as I punished them in Jerusalem, by war, famine, and disease. 14 Of that
remnant who fled to Egypt, hoping someday
to return to Judah, there will be no survivors.
Even though they long to return home, only
a handful will do so."
15 Then all the women present and all the
men who knew that their wives had burned
incense to idols—a great crowd of all the
Judeans living in northern Egypt and southern Egypt*—answered Jeremiah, 16 "We will
not listen to your messages from the LORD!
17 We will do whatever we want. We will burn
incense and pour out liquid offerings to the
Queen of Heaven just as much as we like—
just as we, and our ancestors, and our kings
and officials have always done in the towns
of Judah and in the streets of Jerusalem. For
in those days we had plenty to eat, and we
were well off and had no troubles! 18 But ever
since we quit burning incense to the Queen
of Heaven and stopped worshiping her with
liquid offerings, we have been in great trouble
and have been dying from war and famine."
19 "Besides," the women added, "do you
suppose that we were burning incense and
pouring out liquid offerings to the Queen
of Heaven, and making cakes marked with
her image, without our husbands knowing
it and helping us? Of course not!"
20 Then Jeremiah said to all of them, men
and women alike, who had given him that
answer, 21 "Do you think the LORD did not
know that you and your ancestors, your
kings and officials, and all the people were
burning incense to idols in the towns of
Judah and in the streets of Jerusalem? 22 It
was because the LORD could no longer bear
all the disgusting things you were doing that
he made your land an object of cursing—a
desolate ruin without inhabitants—as it is
today. 23 All these terrible things happened
to you because you have burned incense to
idols and sinned against the LORD. You have
refused to obey him and have not followed
his instructions, his decrees, and his laws."
24 Then Jeremiah said to them all, including the women, "Listen to this message from
the LORD, all you citizens of Judah who live
in Egypt. 25 This is what the LORD of Heav-
en's Armies, the God of Israel, says: 'You
and your wives have said, "We will keep
our promises to burn incense and pour out
liquid offerings to the Queen of Heaven,"
and you have proved by your actions that
you meant it. So go ahead and carry out
your promises and vows to her!'
26 "But listen to this message from the
LORD, all you Judeans now living in Egypt:
'I have sworn by my great name,' says the
LORD, 'that my name will no longer be
spoken by any of the Judeans in the land
of Egypt. None of you may invoke my name
or use this oath: "As surely as the Sovereign
LORD lives." 27 For I will watch over you to
bring you disaster and not good. Everyone
from Judah who is now living in Egypt will
suffer war and famine until all of you are
dead. 28 Only a small number will escape
death and return to Judah from Egypt. Then
all those who came to Egypt will find out
whose words are true—mine or theirs!
29 "'And this is the proof I give you,' says
the LORD, 'that all I have threatened will
happen to you and that I will punish you
here.' 30 This is what the LORD says: 'I will
turn Pharaoh Hophra, king of Egypt, over to
his enemies who want to kill him, just as I
turned King Zedekiah of Judah over to King
Nebuchadnezzar* of Babylon.'"

A Message for Baruch

45 The prophet Jeremiah gave a
message to Baruch son of Neriah in
the fourth year of the reign of Jehoiakim son
of Josiah,* after Baruch had written down
everything Jeremiah had dictated to him.
He said, 2 "This is what the LORD, the God of
Israel, says to you, Baruch: 3 You have said,
'I am overwhelmed with trouble! Haven't
I had enough pain already? And now the
LORD has added more! I am worn out from
sighing and can find no rest.'

43:10 Hebrew *Nebuchadrezzar,* a variant spelling of Nebuchadnezzar. **43:13** Or *in Heliopolis.* **44:1a** Hebrew *Noph.* **44:1b** Hebrew *in Pathros.* **44:15** Hebrew *in Egypt, in Pathros.* **44:30** Hebrew *Nebuchadrezzar,* a variant spelling of Nebuchadnezzar. **45:1** The fourth year of Jehoiakim's reign was 605 B.C.

[4]"Baruch, this is what the LORD says: 'I
will destroy this nation that I built. I will
uproot what I planted. [5]Are you seeking
great things for yourself? Don't do it! I will
bring great disaster upon all these people;
but I will give you your life as a reward wherever you go. I, the LORD, have spoken!'"

Messages for the Nations

46 The following messages were given to Jeremiah the prophet from the LORD concerning foreign nations.

Messages about Egypt

[2]This message concerning Egypt was given in the fourth year of the reign of Jehoiakim son of Josiah, the king of Judah, on the occasion of the battle of Carchemish* when Pharaoh Neco, king of Egypt, and his army were defeated beside the Euphrates River by King Nebuchadnezzar* of Babylon.

3 "Prepare your shields,
and advance into battle!
4 Harness the horses,
and mount the stallions.
Take your positions.
Put on your helmets.
Sharpen your spears,
and prepare your armor.
5 But what do I see?
The Egyptian army flees in terror.
The bravest of its fighting men run
without a backward glance.
They are terrorized at every turn,"
says the LORD.
6 "The swiftest runners cannot flee;
the mightiest warriors cannot escape.
By the Euphrates River to the north,
they stumble and fall.

7 "Who is this, rising like the Nile at floodtime,
overflowing all the land?
8 It is the Egyptian army,
overflowing all the land,
boasting that it will cover the earth like a flood,
destroying cities and their people.
9 Charge, you horses and chariots;
attack, you mighty warriors of Egypt!
Come, all you allies from Ethiopia,
Libya, and Lydia*
who are skilled with the shield and bow!
10 For this is the day of the Lord, the LORD of Heaven's Armies,
a day of vengeance on his enemies.
The sword will devour until it is satisfied,
yes, until it is drunk with your blood!
The Lord, the LORD of Heaven's Armies,
will receive a sacrifice today
in the north country beside the Euphrates River.

11 "Go up to Gilead to get medicine,
O virgin daughter of Egypt!
But your many treatments
will bring you no healing.
12 The nations have heard of your shame.
The earth is filled with your cries of despair.
Your mightiest warriors will run into each other
and fall down together."

[13]Then the LORD gave the prophet Jeremiah this message about King Nebuchadnezzar's plans to attack Egypt.

14 "Shout it out in Egypt!
Publish it in the cities of Migdol,
Memphis,* and Tahpanhes!
Mobilize for battle,
for the sword will devour everyone around you.
15 Why have your warriors fallen?
They cannot stand, for the LORD has knocked them down.
16 They stumble and fall over each other
and say among themselves,
'Come, let's go back to our people,
to the land of our birth.
Let's get away from the sword of the enemy!'
17 There they will say,
'Pharaoh, the king of Egypt, is a loudmouth
who missed his opportunity!'

18 "As surely as I live," says the King,
whose name is the LORD of Heaven's Armies,
"one is coming against Egypt
who is as tall as Mount Tabor,
or as Mount Carmel by the sea!
19 Pack up! Get ready to leave for exile,
you citizens of Egypt!
The city of Memphis will be destroyed,
without a single inhabitant.

20 Egypt is as sleek as a beautiful heifer,
but a horsefly from the north is on its way!
21 Egypt's mercenaries have become like fattened calves.
They, too, will turn and run,
for it is a day of great disaster for Egypt,
a time of great punishment.
22 Egypt flees, silent as a serpent gliding away.
The invading army marches in;
they come against her with axes like woodsmen.
23 They will cut down her people like trees," says the LORD,
"for they are more numerous than locusts.
24 Egypt will be humiliated;
she will be handed over to people from the north."

25The LORD of Heaven's Armies, the God
of Israel, says: "I will punish Amon, the god
of Thebes,* and all the other gods of Egypt.
I will punish its rulers and Pharaoh, too,
and all who trust in him. 26I will hand them
over to those who want them killed—to
King Nebuchadnezzar of Babylon and his
army. But afterward the land will recover
from the ravages of war. I, the LORD, have
spoken!

27 "But do not be afraid, Jacob, my servant;
do not be dismayed, Israel.
For I will bring you home again from distant lands,
and your children will return from their exile.
Israel* will return to a life of peace and quiet,
and no one will terrorize them.
28 Do not be afraid, Jacob, my servant,
for I am with you," says the LORD.
"I will completely destroy the nations to which I have exiled you,
but I will not completely destroy you.
I will discipline you, but with justice;
I cannot let you go unpunished."

A Message about Philistia

47 This is the LORD's message to the
prophet Jeremiah concerning the
Philistines of Gaza, before it was captured
by the Egyptian army. 2This is what the
LORD says:

"A flood is coming from the north
to overflow the land.
It will destroy the land and everything in it—
cities and people alike.
People will scream in terror,
and everyone in the land will wail.
3 Hear the clatter of stallions' hooves
and the rumble of wheels as the chariots rush by.
Terrified fathers run madly,
without a backward glance at their helpless children.

4 "The time has come for the Philistines to be destroyed,
along with their allies from Tyre and Sidon.
Yes, the LORD is destroying the remnant of the Philistines,
those colonists from the island of Crete.*
5 Gaza will be humiliated, its head shaved bald;
Ashkelon will lie silent.
You remnant from the Mediterranean coast,*
how long will you cut yourselves in mourning?

6 "Now, O sword of the LORD,
when will you be at rest again?
Go back into your sheath;
rest and be still.

7 "But how can it be still
when the LORD has sent it on a mission?
For the city of Ashkelon
and the people living along the sea
must be destroyed."

A Message about Moab

48 This message was given concerning Moab. This is what the LORD of
Heaven's Armies, the God of Israel, says:

"What sorrow awaits the city of Nebo;
it will soon lie in ruins.
The city of Kiriathaim will be humiliated and captured;

46:2a This event occurred in 605 B.C., during the fourth year of Jehoiakim's reign (according to the calendar system in which the new year begins in the spring). **46:2b** Hebrew *Nebuchadrezzar,* a variant spelling of Nebuchadnezzar; also in 46:13, 26. **46:9** Hebrew *from Cush, Put, and Lud.* **46:14** Hebrew *Noph;* also in 46:19. **46:25** Hebrew *of No.* **46:27** Hebrew *Jacob.* See note on 5:20. **47:4** Hebrew *from Caphtor.* **47:5** Hebrew *the plain.*

the fortress will be humiliated and
broken down.
2 No one will ever brag about Moab
again,
for in Heshbon there is a plot to
destroy her.
'Come,' they say, 'we will cut her off
from being a nation.'
The town of Madmen,* too, will be
silenced;
the sword will follow you there.
3 Listen to the cries from Horonaim,
cries of devastation and great
destruction.
4 All Moab is destroyed.
Her little ones will cry out.*
5 Her refugees weep bitterly,
climbing the slope to Luhith.
They cry out in terror,
descending the slope to Horonaim.
6 Flee for your lives!
Hide* in the wilderness!
7 Because you have trusted in your wealth
and skill,
you will be taken captive.
Your god Chemosh, with his priests and
officials,
will be hauled off to distant lands!

8 "All the towns will be destroyed,
and no one will escape—
either on the plateaus or in the valleys,
for the LORD has spoken.
9 Oh, that Moab had wings
so she could fly away,*
for her towns will be left empty,
with no one living in them.
10 Cursed are those who refuse to do the
LORD's work,
who hold back their swords from
shedding blood!

11 "From his earliest history, Moab has
lived in peace,
never going into exile.
He is like wine that has been allowed to
settle.
He has not been poured from flask to
flask,
and he is now fragrant and smooth.
12 But the time is coming soon," says the
LORD,
"when I will send men to pour him
from his jar.
They will pour him out,
then shatter the jar!

13 At last Moab will be ashamed of his idol
Chemosh,
as the people of Israel were ashamed
of their gold calf at Bethel.*

14 "You used to boast, 'We are heroes,
mighty men of war.'
15 But now Moab and his towns will be
destroyed.
His most promising youth are doomed
to slaughter,"
says the King, whose name is the
LORD of Heaven's Armies.
16 "Destruction is coming fast for Moab;
calamity threatens ominously.
17 You friends of Moab,
weep for him and cry!
See how the strong scepter is broken,
how the beautiful staff is shattered!

18 "Come down from your glory
and sit in the dust, you people of
Dibon,
for those who destroy Moab will shatter
Dibon, too.
They will tear down all your towers.
19 You people of Aroer,
stand beside the road and watch.
Shout to those who flee from Moab,
'What has happened there?'
20 "And the reply comes back,
'Moab lies in ruins, disgraced;
weep and wail!
Tell it by the banks of the Arnon River:
Moab has been destroyed!'
21 Judgment has been poured out on the
towns of the plateau—
on Holon and Jahaz* and Mephaath,
22 on Dibon and Nebo and Beth-diblathaim,
23 on Kiriathaim and Beth-gamul and
Beth-meon,
24 on Kerioth and Bozrah—
all the towns of Moab, far and near.
25 "The strength of Moab has ended.
His arm has been broken," says the
LORD.
26 "Let him stagger and fall like a drunkard,
for he has rebelled against the LORD.
Moab will wallow in his own vomit,
ridiculed by all.
27 Did you not ridicule the people of Israel?
Were they caught in the company of
thieves
that you should despise them as
you do?

28 "You people of Moab,
flee from your towns and live in the caves.
Hide like doves that nest
in the clefts of the rocks.
29 We have all heard of the pride of Moab,
for his pride is very great.
We know of his lofty pride,
his arrogance, and his haughty heart.
30 I know about his insolence,"
says the LORD,
"but his boasts are empty—
as empty as his deeds.
31 So now I wail for Moab;
yes, I will mourn for Moab.
My heart is broken for the men of Kir-hareseth.*

32 "You people of Sibmah, rich in vineyards,
I will weep for you even more than I did for Jazer.
Your spreading vines once reached as far as the Dead Sea,*
but the destroyer has stripped you bare!
He has harvested your grapes and summer fruits.
33 Joy and gladness are gone from fruitful Moab.
The presses yield no wine.
No one treads the grapes with shouts of joy.
There is shouting, yes, but not of joy.

34 "Instead, their awful cries of terror
can be heard from Heshbon clear across to
Elealeh and Jahaz; from Zoar all the way to
Horonaim and Eglath-shelishiyah. Even the
waters of Nimrim are dried up now.
35 "I will put an end to Moab," says the
LORD, "for the people offer sacrifices at the
pagan shrines and burn incense to their
false gods. 36 My heart moans like a flute for
Moab and Kir-hareseth, for all their wealth
has disappeared. 37 The people shave their
heads and beards in mourning. They slash
their hands and put on clothes made of
burlap. 38 There is crying and sorrow in every
Moabite home and on every street. For I
have smashed Moab like an old, unwanted
jar. 39 How it is shattered! Hear the wailing!
See the shame of Moab! It has become an
object of ridicule, an example of ruin to all
its neighbors."
40 This is what the LORD says:

"Look! The enemy swoops down like an eagle,
spreading his wings over Moab.
41 Its cities will fall,
and its strongholds will be seized.
Even the mightiest warriors will be in anguish
like a woman in labor.
42 Moab will no longer be a nation,
for it has boasted against the LORD.

43 "Terror and traps and snares will be your lot,
O Moab," says the LORD.
44 "Those who flee in terror will fall into a trap,
and those who escape the trap will step into a snare.
I will see to it that you do not get away,
for the time of your judgment has come,"
says the LORD.
45 "The people flee as far as Heshbon
but are unable to go on.
For a fire comes from Heshbon,
King Sihon's ancient home,
to devour the entire land
with all its rebellious people.
46 "What sorrow awaits you, O people of Moab!
The people of the god Chemosh are destroyed!
Your sons and your daughters
have been taken away as captives.
47 But I will restore the fortunes of Moab
in days to come.
I, the LORD, have spoken!"

This is the end of Jeremiah's prophecy concerning Moab.

A Message about Ammon

49 This message was given concerning the Ammonites. This is what the LORD says:

"Are there no descendants of Israel
to inherit the land of Gad?

48:2 *Madmen* sounds like the Hebrew word for "silence"; it should not be confused with the English word *madmen*. **48:4** Greek version reads *Her cries are heard as far away as Zoar.* **48:6** Or *Hide like a wild donkey;* or *Hide like a juniper shrub;* or *Be like* [the town of] *Aroer.* The meaning of the Hebrew is uncertain. **48:9** Or *Put salt on Moab, / for she will be laid waste.* **48:13** Hebrew *ashamed when they trusted in Bethel.* **48:21** Hebrew *Jahzah,* a variant spelling of Jahaz. **48:31** Hebrew *Kir-heres,* a variant spelling of Kir-hareseth; also in 48:36. **48:32** Hebrew *the sea of Jazer.*

Why are you, who worship Molech,*
living in its towns?
2 In the days to come," says the LORD,
"I will sound the battle cry against
your city of Rabbah.
It will become a desolate heap of ruins,
and the neighboring towns will be
burned.
Then Israel will take back the land
you took from her," says the LORD.

3 "Cry out, O Heshbon,
for the town of Ai is destroyed.
Weep, O people of Rabbah!
Put on your clothes of mourning.
Weep and wail, hiding in the hedges,
for your god Molech, with his priests
and officials,
will be hauled off to distant lands.
4 You are proud of your fertile valleys,
but they will soon be ruined.
You trusted in your wealth,
you rebellious daughter,
and thought no one could ever harm
you.
5 But look! I will bring terror upon you,"
says the Lord, the LORD of Heaven's
Armies.
"Your neighbors will chase you from
your land,
and no one will help your exiles as
they flee.
6 But I will restore the fortunes of the
Ammonites
in days to come.
I, the LORD, have spoken."

Messages about Edom

7 This message was given concerning Edom. This is what the LORD of Heaven's Armies says:

"Is there no wisdom in Teman?
Is no one left to give wise counsel?
8 Turn and flee!
Hide in deep caves, you people of
Dedan!
For when I bring disaster on Edom,*
I will punish you, too!
9 Those who harvest grapes
always leave a few for the poor.
If thieves came at night,
they would not take everything.
10 But I will strip bare the land of Edom,
and there will be no place left to
hide.
Its children, its brothers, and its
neighbors
will all be destroyed,
and Edom itself will be no more.
11 But I will protect the orphans who
remain among you.
Your widows, too, can depend on me
for help."

12 And this is what the LORD says: "If the innocent must suffer, how much more must you! You will not go unpunished! You must drink this cup of judgment! 13 For I have sworn by my own name," says the LORD, "that Bozrah will become an object of horror and a heap of ruins; it will be mocked and cursed. All its towns and villages will be desolate forever."

14 I have heard a message from the LORD
that an ambassador was sent to the
nations to say,
"Form a coalition against Edom,
and prepare for battle!"
15 The LORD says to Edom,
"I will cut you down to size among the
nations.
You will be despised by all.
16 You have been deceived
by the fear you inspire in others
and by your own pride.
You live in a rock fortress
and control the mountain heights.
But even if you make your nest among
the peaks with the eagles,
I will bring you crashing
down,"
says the LORD.
17 "Edom will be an object of horror.
All who pass by will be appalled
and will gasp at the destruction they
see there.
18 It will be like the destruction of Sodom
and Gomorrah
and their neighboring towns," says
the LORD.
"No one will live there;
no one will inhabit it.
19 I will come like a lion from the thickets
of the Jordan,
leaping on the sheep in the
pasture.
I will chase Edom from its land,
and I will appoint the leader of my
choice.

For who is like me, and who can
challenge me?
What ruler can oppose my will?"
20 Listen to the LORD's plans against Edom
and the people of Teman.
Even the little children will be dragged
off like sheep,
and their homes will be destroyed.
21 The earth will shake with the noise of
Edom's fall,
and its cry of despair will be heard all
the way to the Red Sea.*
22 Look! The enemy swoops down like an
eagle,
spreading his wings over Bozrah.
Even the mightiest warriors will be in
anguish
like a woman in labor.

A Message about Damascus

23 This message was given concerning Damascus. This is what the LORD says:

"The towns of Hamath and Arpad are
struck with fear,
for they have heard the news of their
destruction.
Their hearts are troubled
like a wild sea in a raging storm.
24 Damascus has become feeble,
and all her people turn to flee.
Fear, anguish, and pain have gripped her
as they grip a woman in labor.
25 That famous city, a city of joy,
will be forsaken!
26 Her young men will fall in the streets
and die.
Her soldiers will all be killed,"
says the LORD of Heaven's Armies.
27 "And I will set fire to the walls of
Damascus
that will burn up the palaces of
Ben-hadad."

A Message about Kedar and Hazor

28 This message was given concerning Kedar and the kingdoms of Hazor, which were attacked by King Nebuchadnezzar* of Babylon. This is what the LORD says:

"Advance against Kedar!
Destroy the warriors from the East!
29 Their flocks and tents will be captured,
and their household goods and
camels will be taken away.
Everywhere shouts of panic will be
heard:
'We are terrorized at every turn!'
30 Run for your lives," says the LORD.
"Hide yourselves in deep caves, you
people of Hazor,
for King Nebuchadnezzar of Babylon
has plotted against you
and is preparing to destroy you.
31 "Go up and attack that complacent
nation,"
says the LORD.
"Its people live alone in the desert
without walls or gates.
32 Their camels and other livestock will all
be yours.
I will scatter to the winds these people
who live in remote places.*
I will bring calamity upon them
from every direction," says the LORD.
33 "Hazor will be inhabited by jackals,
and it will be desolate forever.
No one will live there;
no one will inhabit it."

A Message about Elam

34 This message concerning Elam came to
the prophet Jeremiah from the LORD at the
beginning of the reign of King Zedekiah of
Judah. 35 This is what the LORD of Heaven's
Armies says:

"I will destroy the archers of Elam—
the best of their forces.
36 I will bring enemies from all directions,
and I will scatter the people of Elam to
the four winds.
They will be exiled to countries
around the world.
37 I myself will go with Elam's enemies to
shatter it.
In my fierce anger, I will bring great
disaster
upon the people of Elam," says the
LORD.
"Their enemies will chase them with the
sword
until I have destroyed them
completely.
38 I will set my throne in Elam," says the
LORD,

49:1 Hebrew *Malcam*, a variant spelling of Molech; also in 49:3. **49:8** Hebrew *Esau;* also in 49:10. **49:21** Hebrew *sea of reeds.* **49:28** Hebrew *Nebuchadrezzar*, a variant spelling of Nebuchadnezzar; also in 49:30. **49:32** Or *who clip the corners of their hair.*

"and I will destroy its king and
officials.
39 But I will restore the fortunes of Elam
in days to come.
I, the LORD, have spoken!"

A Message about Babylon

50 The LORD gave Jeremiah the prophet
this message concerning Babylon
and the land of the Babylonians.* 2 This is
what the LORD says:

"Tell the whole world,
and keep nothing back.
Raise a signal flag
to tell everyone that Babylon will fall!
Her images and idols* will be shattered.
Her gods Bel and Marduk will be
utterly disgraced.
3 For a nation will attack her from the
north
and bring such destruction that no
one will live there again.
Everything will be gone;
both people and animals will flee.

Hope for Israel and Judah

4 "In those coming days,"
says the LORD,
"the people of Israel will return home
together with the people of Judah.
They will come weeping
and seeking the LORD their God.
5 They will ask the way to Jerusalem*
and will start back home again.
They will bind themselves to the LORD
with an eternal covenant that will
never be forgotten.

6 "My people have been lost sheep.
Their shepherds have led them astray
and turned them loose in the
mountains.
They have lost their way
and can't remember how to get back
to the sheepfold.
7 All who found them devoured them.
Their enemies said,
'We did nothing wrong in attacking
them,
for they sinned against the LORD,
their true place of rest,
and the hope of their ancestors.'

8 "But now, flee from Babylon!
Leave the land of the Babylonians.
Like male goats at the head of the flock,
lead my people home again.
9 For I am raising up an army
of great nations from the north.
They will join forces to attack
Babylon,
and she will be captured.
The enemies' arrows will go straight
to the mark;
they will not miss!
10 Babylonia* will be looted
until the attackers are glutted with
loot.
I, the LORD, have spoken!

Babylon's Sure Fall

11 "You rejoice and are glad,
you who plundered my chosen
people.
You frisk about like a calf in a meadow
and neigh like a stallion.
12 But your homeland* will be
overwhelmed
with shame and disgrace.
You will become the least of nations—
a wilderness, a dry and desolate land.
13 Because of the LORD's anger,
Babylon will become a deserted
wasteland.
All who pass by will be horrified
and will gasp at the destruction they
see there.

14 "Yes, prepare to attack Babylon,
all you surrounding nations.
Let your archers shoot at her; spare no
arrows.
For she has sinned against the LORD.
15 Shout war cries against her from every
side.
Look! She surrenders!
Her walls have fallen.
It is the LORD's vengeance,
so take vengeance on her.
Do to her as she has done to others!
16 Take from Babylon all those who plant
crops;
send all the harvesters away.
Because of the sword of the enemy,
everyone will run away and rush back
to their own lands.

Hope for God's People

17 "The Israelites are like sheep
that have been scattered by lions.

First the king of Assyria ate them up.
Then King Nebuchadnezzar* of Babylon cracked their bones."
18 Therefore, this is what the LORD of Heaven's Armies,
the God of Israel, says:
"Now I will punish the king of Babylon and his land,
just as I punished the king of Assyria.
19 And I will bring Israel home again to its own land,
to feed in the fields of Carmel and Bashan,
and to be satisfied once more
in the hill country of Ephraim and Gilead.
20 In those days," says the LORD,
"no sin will be found in Israel or in Judah,
for I will forgive the remnant I preserve.

The LORD's Judgment on Babylon

21 "Go up, my warriors, against the land of Merathaim
and against the people of Pekod.
Pursue, kill, and completely destroy* them,
as I have commanded you," says the LORD.
22 "Let the battle cry be heard in the land,
a shout of great destruction.
23 Babylon, the mightiest hammer in all the earth,
lies broken and shattered.
Babylon is desolate among the nations!
24 Listen, Babylon, for I have set a trap for you.
You are caught, for you have fought against the LORD.
25 The LORD has opened his armory
and brought out weapons to vent his fury.
The terror that falls upon the Babylonians
will be the work of the Sovereign LORD of Heaven's Armies.
26 Yes, come against her from distant lands.
Break open her granaries.
Crush her walls and houses into heaps of rubble.
Destroy her completely, and leave nothing!
27 Destroy even her young bulls—
it will be terrible for them, too!
Slaughter them all!
For Babylon's day of reckoning has come.
28 Listen to the people who have escaped from Babylon,
as they tell in Jerusalem
how the LORD our God has taken vengeance
against those who destroyed his Temple.

29 "Send out a call for archers to come to Babylon.
Surround the city so none can escape.
Do to her as she has done to others,
for she has defied the LORD, the Holy One of Israel.
30 Her young men will fall in the streets and die.
Her soldiers will all be killed,"
says the LORD.

31 "See, I am your enemy, you arrogant people,"
says the Lord, the LORD of Heaven's Armies.
"Your day of reckoning has arrived—
the day when I will punish you.
32 O land of arrogance, you will stumble and fall,
and no one will raise you up.
For I will light a fire in the cities of Babylon
that will burn up everything around them."

33 This is what the LORD of Heaven's Armies says:
"The people of Israel and Judah have been wronged.
Their captors hold them and refuse to let them go.
34 But the one who redeems them is strong.
His name is the LORD of Heaven's Armies.
He will defend them
and give them rest again in Israel.
But for the people of Babylon
there will be no rest!

50:1 Or *Chaldeans;* also in 50:8, 25, 35, 45. **50:2** The Hebrew term (literally *round things*) probably alludes to dung. **50:5** Hebrew *Zion;* also in 50:28. **50:10** Or *Chaldea.* **50:12** Hebrew *your mother.* **50:17** Hebrew *Nebuchadrezzar,* a variant spelling of Nebuchadnezzar. **50:21** The Hebrew term used here refers to the complete consecration of things or people to the LORD, either by destroying them or by giving them as an offering.

35 "The sword of destruction will strike the
Babylonians,"
says the LORD.
"It will strike the people of Babylon—
her officials and wise men, too.
36 The sword will strike her wise counselors,
and they will become fools.
The sword will strike her mightiest
warriors,
and panic will seize them.
37 The sword will strike her horses and
chariots
and her allies from other lands,
and they will all become like women.
The sword will strike her treasures,
and they all will be plundered.
38 A drought* will strike her water supply,
causing it to dry up.
And why? Because the whole land is
filled with idols,
and the people are madly in love with
them.

39 "Soon Babylon will be inhabited by
desert animals and hyenas.
It will be a home for owls.
Never again will people live there;
it will lie desolate forever.
40 I will destroy it as I* destroyed Sodom
and Gomorrah
and their neighboring towns," says
the LORD.
"No one will live there;
no one will inhabit it.

41 "Look! A great army is coming from the
north.
A great nation and many kings
are rising against you from far-off
lands.
42 They are armed with bows and spears.
They are cruel and show no mercy.
As they ride forward on horses,
they sound like a roaring sea.
They are coming in battle formation,
planning to destroy you, Babylon.
43 The king of Babylon has heard reports
about the enemy,
and he is weak with fright.
Pangs of anguish have gripped him,
like those of a woman in labor.

44 "I will come like a lion from the thickets
of the Jordan,
leaping on the sheep in the pasture.
I will chase Babylon from its land,
and I will appoint the leader of my
choice.
For who is like me, and who can
challenge me?
What ruler can oppose my will?"

45 Listen to the LORD's plans against
Babylon
and the land of the Babylonians.
Even the little children will be dragged
off like sheep,
and their homes will be destroyed.
46 The earth will shake with the shout,
"Babylon has been taken!"
and its cry of despair will be heard
around the world.

51

1 This is what the LORD says:
"I will stir up a destroyer against
Babylon
and the people of Babylonia.*
2 Foreigners will come and winnow her,
blowing her away as chaff.
They will come from every side
to rise against her in her day of
trouble.
3 Don't let the archers put on their
armor
or draw their bows.
Don't spare even her best soldiers!
Let her army be completely
destroyed.*
4 They will fall dead in the land of the
Babylonians,*
slashed to death in her streets.
5 For the LORD of Heaven's Armies
has not abandoned Israel and Judah.
He is still their God,
even though their land was filled with
sin
against the Holy One of Israel."

6 Flee from Babylon! Save yourselves!
Don't get trapped in her punishment!
It is the LORD's time for vengeance;
he will repay her in full.
7 Babylon has been a gold cup in the
LORD's hands,
a cup that made the whole earth
drunk.
The nations drank Babylon's wine,
and it drove them all mad.
8 But suddenly Babylon, too, has fallen.
Weep for her.
Give her medicine.
Perhaps she can yet be healed.

9 We would have helped her if we could,
but nothing can save her now.
Let her go; abandon her.
Return now to your own land.
For her punishment reaches to the heavens;
it is so great it cannot be measured.
10 The LORD has vindicated us.
Come, let us announce in Jerusalem*
everything the LORD our God has done.
11 Sharpen the arrows!
Lift up the shields!*
For the LORD has inspired the kings of the Medes
to march against Babylon and destroy her.
This is his vengeance against those
who desecrated his Temple.
12 Raise the battle flag against Babylon!
Reinforce the guard and station the watchmen.
Prepare an ambush,
for the LORD will fulfill all his plans against Babylon.
13 You are a city by a great river,
a great center of commerce,
but your end has come.
The thread of your life is cut.
14 The LORD of Heaven's Armies has taken this vow
and has sworn to it by his own name:
"Your cities will be filled with enemies,
like fields swarming with locusts,
and they will shout in triumph over you."

A Hymn of Praise to the LORD

15 The LORD made the earth by his power,
and he preserves it by his wisdom.
With his own understanding
he stretched out the heavens.
16 When he speaks in the thunder,
the heavens roar with rain.
He causes the clouds to rise over the earth.
He sends the lightning with the rain
and releases the wind from his storehouses.
17 The whole human race is foolish and has no knowledge!
The craftsmen are disgraced by the idols they make,
for their carefully shaped works are a fraud.
These idols have no breath or power.
18 Idols are worthless; they are ridiculous lies!
On the day of reckoning they will all be destroyed.
19 But the God of Israel* is no idol!
He is the Creator of everything that exists,
including his people, his own special possession.
The LORD of Heaven's Armies is his name!

Babylon's Great Punishment

20 "You* are my battle-ax and sword,"
says the LORD.
"With you I will shatter nations
and destroy many kingdoms.
21 With you I will shatter armies—
destroying the horse and rider,
the chariot and charioteer.
22 With you I will shatter men and women,
old people and children,
young men and young women.
23 With you I will shatter shepherds and flocks,
farmers and oxen,
captains and officers.

24 "I will repay Babylon
and the people of Babylonia*
for all the wrong they have done
to my people in Jerusalem," says the LORD.

25 "Look, O mighty mountain, destroyer of the earth!
I am your enemy," says the LORD.
"I will raise my fist against you,
to knock you down from the heights.
When I am finished,
you will be nothing but a heap of burnt rubble.

50:38 Or *sword;* the Hebrew words for *drought* and *sword* are very similar. **50:40** Hebrew *as God.* **51:1** Hebrew *of Leb-kamai,* a code name for Babylonia. **51:3** The Hebrew term used here refers to the complete consecration of things or people to the LORD, either by destroying them or by giving them as an offering. **51:4** Or *Chaldeans;* also in 51:54. **51:10** Hebrew *Zion;* also in 51:24. **51:11** Greek version reads *Fill up the quivers.* **51:19** Hebrew *the Portion of Jacob.* See note on 5:20. **51:20** Possibly Cyrus, whom God used to conquer Babylon. Compare Isa 44:28; 45:1. **51:24** Or *Chaldea;* also in 51:35.

▸ **51:8** *See **Babylon**, page 445.*

26 You will be desolate forever.
Even your stones will never again be used for building.
You will be completely wiped out,"
says the LORD.

27 Raise a signal flag to the nations.
Sound the battle cry!
Mobilize them all against Babylon.
Prepare them to fight against her!
Bring out the armies of Ararat, Minni, and Ashkenaz.
Appoint a commander,
and bring a multitude of horses like swarming locusts!
28 Bring against her the armies of the nations—
led by the kings of the Medes
and all their captains and officers.

29 The earth trembles and writhes in pain,
for everything the LORD has planned against Babylon stands unchanged.
Babylon will be left desolate without a single inhabitant.
30 Her mightiest warriors no longer fight.
They stay in their barracks, their courage gone.
They have become like women.
The invaders have burned the houses
and broken down the city gates.
31 The news is passed from one runner to the next
as the messengers hurry to tell the king
that his city has been captured.
32 All the escape routes are blocked.
The marshes have been set aflame,
and the army is in a panic.

33 This is what the LORD of Heaven's Armies,
the God of Israel, says:
"Babylon is like wheat on a threshing floor,
about to be trampled.
In just a little while
her harvest will begin."

34 "King Nebuchadnezzar* of Babylon has eaten and crushed us
and drained us of strength.
He has swallowed us like a great monster
and filled his belly with our riches.
He has thrown us out of our own country.
35 Make Babylon suffer as she made us suffer,"
say the people of Zion.
"Make the people of Babylonia pay for spilling our blood,"
says Jerusalem.

The LORD's Vengeance on Babylon

36 This is what the LORD says to Jerusalem:

"I will be your lawyer to plead your case,
and I will avenge you.
I will dry up her river,
as well as her springs,
37 and Babylon will become a heap of ruins,
haunted by jackals.
She will be an object of horror and contempt,
a place where no one lives.
38 Her people will roar together like strong lions.
They will growl like lion cubs.
39 And while they lie inflamed with all their wine,
I will prepare a different kind of feast for them.
I will make them drink until they fall asleep,
and they will never wake up again,"
says the LORD.
40 "I will bring them down
like lambs to the slaughter,
like rams and goats to be sacrificed.

41 "How Babylon* is fallen—
great Babylon, praised throughout the earth!
Now she has become an object of horror among the nations.
42 The sea has risen over Babylon;
she is covered by its crashing waves.
43 Her cities now lie in ruins;
she is a dry wasteland
where no one lives or even passes by.
44 And I will punish Bel, the god of Babylon,
and make him vomit up all he has eaten.
The nations will no longer come and worship him.
The wall of Babylon has fallen!

A Message for the Exiles

45 "Come out, my people, flee from Babylon.

Save yourselves! Run from the LORD's
fierce anger.
46 But do not panic; don't be afraid
when you hear the first rumor of
approaching forces.
For rumors will keep coming year by
year.
Violence will erupt in the land
as the leaders fight against each other.
47 For the time is surely coming
when I will punish this great city and
all her idols.
Her whole land will be disgraced,
and her dead will lie in the streets.
48 Then the heavens and earth will
rejoice,
for out of the north will come
destroying armies
against Babylon," says the LORD.
49 "Just as Babylon killed the people of
Israel
and others throughout the world,
so must her people be killed.
50 Get out, all you who have escaped the
sword!
Do not stand and watch—flee while
you can!
Remember the LORD, though you are
in a far-off land,
and think about your home in
Jerusalem."

51 "We are ashamed," the people say.
"We are insulted and disgraced
because the LORD's Temple
has been defiled by foreigners."

52 "Yes," says the LORD, "but the time is
coming
when I will destroy Babylon's idols.
The groans of her wounded people
will be heard throughout the land.
53 Though Babylon reaches as high as the
heavens
and makes her fortifications
incredibly strong,
I will still send enemies to plunder her.
I, the LORD, have spoken!

Babylon's Complete Destruction

54 "Listen! Hear the cry of Babylon,
the sound of great destruction from
the land of the Babylonians.
55 For the LORD is destroying Babylon.
He will silence her loud voice.
Waves of enemies pound against her;
the noise of battle rings through the
city.
56 Destroying armies come against Babylon.
Her mighty men are captured,
and their weapons break in their
hands.
For the LORD is a God who gives just
punishment;
he always repays in full.
57 I will make her officials and wise men
drunk,
along with her captains, officers, and
warriors.
They will fall asleep
and never wake up again!"
says the King, whose name is
the LORD of Heaven's Armies.

58 This is what the LORD of Heaven's
Armies says:
"The thick walls of Babylon will be
leveled to the ground,
and her massive gates will be burned.
The builders from many lands have
worked in vain,
for their work will be destroyed by fire!"

Jeremiah's Message Sent to Babylon

59 The prophet Jeremiah gave this message to
Seraiah son of Neriah and grandson of Mahseiah, a staff officer, when Seraiah went to
Babylon with King Zedekiah of Judah. This
was during the fourth year of Zedekiah's
reign.* 60 Jeremiah had recorded on a scroll
all the terrible disasters that would soon
come upon Babylon—all the words written
here. 61 He said to Seraiah, "When you get to
Babylon, read aloud everything on this scroll.
62 Then say, 'LORD, you have said that you will
destroy Babylon so that neither people nor
animals will remain here. She will lie empty
and abandoned forever.' 63 When you have
finished reading the scroll, tie it to a stone
and throw it into the Euphrates River. 64 Then
say, 'In this same way Babylon and her
people will sink, never again to rise, because
of the disasters I will bring upon her.'"
This is the end of Jeremiah's messages.

The Fall of Jerusalem

52 Zedekiah was twenty-one years
old when he became king, and he
reigned in Jerusalem eleven years. His

51:34 Hebrew *Nebuchadrezzar,* a variant spelling of Nebuchadnezzar. **51:41** Hebrew *Sheshach,* a code name for Babylon. **51:59** The fourth year of Zedekiah's reign was 593 B.C.

mother was Hamutal, the daughter of Jeremiah from Libnah. 2But Zedekiah did what was evil in the LORD's sight, just as Jehoiakim had done. 3These things happened because of the LORD's anger against the people of Jerusalem and Judah, until he finally banished them from his presence and sent them into exile.

Zedekiah rebelled against the king of Babylon. 4So on January 15,* during the ninth year of Zedekiah's reign, King Nebuchadnezzar* of Babylon led his entire army against Jerusalem. They surrounded the city and built siege ramps against its walls. 5Jerusalem was kept under siege until the eleventh year of King Zedekiah's reign.

6By July 18 in the eleventh year of Zedekiah's reign,* the famine in the city had become very severe, and the last of the food was entirely gone. 7Then a section of the city wall was broken down, and all the soldiers fled. Since the city was surrounded by the Babylonians,* they waited for nightfall. Then they slipped through the gate between the two walls behind the king's garden and headed toward the Jordan Valley.*

8But the Babylonian troops chased King Zedekiah and overtook him on the plains of Jericho, for his men had all deserted him and scattered. 9They captured the king and took him to the king of Babylon at Riblah in the land of Hamath. There the king of Babylon pronounced judgment upon Zedekiah. 10The king of Babylon made Zedekiah watch as he slaughtered his sons. He also slaughtered all the officials of Judah at Riblah. 11Then he gouged out Zedekiah's eyes and bound him in bronze chains, and the king of Babylon led him away to Babylon. Zedekiah remained there in prison until the day of his death.

The Temple Destroyed

12On August 17 of that year,* which was the nineteenth year of King Nebuchadnezzar's reign, Nebuzaradan, the captain of the guard and an official of the Babylonian king, arrived in Jerusalem. 13He burned down the Temple of the LORD, the royal palace, and all the houses of Jerusalem. He destroyed all the important buildings* in the city. 14Then he supervised the entire Babylonian* army as they tore down the walls of Jerusalem on every side. 15Then Nebuzaradan, the captain of the guard, took as exiles some of the poorest of the people, the rest of the people who remained in the city, the defectors who had declared their allegiance to the king of Babylon, and the rest of the craftsmen. 16But Nebuzaradan allowed some of the poorest people to stay behind to care for the vineyards and fields.

17The Babylonians broke up the bronze pillars in front of the LORD's Temple, the bronze water carts, and the great bronze basin called the Sea, and they carried all the bronze away to Babylon. 18They also took all the ash buckets, shovels, lamp snuffers, basins, dishes, and all the other bronze articles used for making sacrifices at the Temple. 19The captain of the guard also took the small bowls, incense burners, basins, pots, lampstands, ladles, bowls used for liquid offerings, and all the other articles made of pure gold or silver.

20The weight of the bronze from the two pillars, the Sea with the twelve bronze oxen beneath it, and the water carts was too great to be measured. These things had been made for the LORD's Temple in the days of King Solomon. 21Each of the pillars was 27 feet tall and 18 feet in circumference.* They were hollow, with walls 3 inches thick.* 22The bronze capital on top of each pillar was 7½ feet* high and was decorated with a network of bronze pomegranates all the way around. 23There were 96 pomegranates on the sides, and a total of 100 pomegranates on the network around the top.

24Nebuzaradan, the captain of the guard, took with him as prisoners Seraiah the high priest, Zephaniah the priest of the second rank, and the three chief gatekeepers. 25And from among the people still hiding in the city, he took an officer who had been in charge of the Judean army; seven of the king's personal advisers; the army commander's chief secretary, who was in charge of recruitment; and sixty other citizens. 26Nebuzaradan, the captain of the guard, took them all to the king of Babylon at Riblah. 27And there at Riblah, in the land of Hamath, the king of Babylon had them

▸ **52:1-30** *See* ***The fall of Jerusalem,*** *page 871.*

all put to death. So the people of Judah were
sent into exile from their land.
[28]The number of captives taken to Babylon
in the seventh year of Nebuchadnezzar's
reign* was 3,023. [29]Then in Nebuchadnezzar's eighteenth year* he took 832 more.
[30]In Nebuchadnezzar's twenty-third year*
he sent Nebuzaradan, the captain of the
guard, who took 745 more—a total of 4,600
captives in all.

Hope for Israel's Royal Line

[31]In the thirty-seventh year of the exile of
King Jehoiachin of Judah, Evil-merodach
ascended to the Babylonian throne. He
was kind to* Jehoiachin and released him
from prison on March 31 of that year.* [32]He
spoke kindly to Jehoiachin and gave him a
higher place than all the other exiled kings
in Babylon. [33]He supplied Jehoiachin with
new clothes to replace his prison garb and
allowed him to dine in the king's presence
for the rest of his life. [34]So the Babylonian
king gave him a regular food allowance as
long as he lived. This continued until the
day of his death.

52:4a Hebrew *on the tenth day of the tenth month,* of the ancient Hebrew lunar calendar. A number of events in Jeremiah can be cross-checked with dates in surviving Babylonian records and related accurately to our modern calendar. This day was January 15, 588 B.C. **52:4b** Hebrew *Nebuchadrezzar,* a variant spelling of Nebuchadnezzar; also in 52:12, 28, 29, 30. **52:6** Hebrew *By the ninth day of the fourth month* [in the eleventh year of Zedekiah's reign]. This day was July 18, 586 B.C.; also see note on 52:4a. **52:7a** Or *the Chaldeans;* similarly in 52:8, 17. **52:7b** Hebrew *the Arabah.* **52:12** Hebrew *On the tenth day of the fifth month,* of the ancient Hebrew lunar calendar. This day was August 17, 586 B.C.; also see note on 52:4a. **52:13** Or *destroyed the houses of all the important people.* **52:14** Or *Chaldean.* **52:21a** Hebrew *18 cubits* [8.3 meters] *tall and 12 cubits* [5.5 meters] *in circumference.* **52:21b** Hebrew *4 fingers thick* [8 centimeters]. **52:22** Hebrew *5 cubits* [2.3 meters]. **52:28** This exile in the seventh year of Nebuchadnezzar's reign occurred in 597 B.C. **52:29** This exile in the eighteenth year of Nebuchadnezzar's reign occurred in 586 B.C. **52:30** This exile in the twenty-third year of Nebuchadnezzar's reign occurred in 581 B.C. **52:31a** Hebrew *He raised the head of.* **52:31b** Hebrew *on the twenty-fifth day of the twelfth month,* of the ancient Hebrew lunar calendar. This day was March 31, 561 B.C.; also see note on 52:4a.

Lamentations *A city in mourning*

Lamentations is a collection of five poems that mourn the capture and destruction of Jerusalem, written soon after the event. The poems' author—the prophet Jeremiah, according to ancient Jewish and Christian tradition (though in fact the work is anonymous)—was an eyewitness of all the terrible suffering of those days. The city had been destroyed by the Babylonian army, and its inhabitants had been carried away into exile. The writer's sorrow reflects that of God himself. God's heart had always been to bless his people, but their disobedience had made judgment inevitable, and all the author could do, therefore, was to lament.

What's it all about?

Five poems, each made up of twenty-two verses—except the third, which has sixty-six verses (three times twenty-two)—review the punishment that God's people had to bear because of their persistent wrongdoing. The author alternately comments on Jerusalem, speaks as the city itself, and offers words of hope.

In chapter 1, the city is represented as a desolate widow, sitting alone in the night and crying for her children. She appealed to friends and passersby, but no one comforted her. This despair that the city found itself in was not some accident; it was the just punishment that God had warned his people about and had now brought upon her.

Chapter 2 describes the siege of Jerusalem and the resultant ruin of a once happy, bustling city as "the Lord in his anger" (2:1) came upon them. The enemy that attacked them was not Babylon, but God himself: "The Lord has vanquished Israel like an enemy" (2:5). The prophet lamented for the city, but others simply scoffed: "Is this the city called 'Most Beautiful in All the World' and 'Joy of All the Earth'?" (2:15).

In chapter 3, the prophet reflects on his own misery. He identified with his people; their sorrows were his. But in spite of all the suffering, he was convinced that God could still be trusted, and in a surge of faith he calls out, "The faithful love of the LORD never ends! His mercies never cease. Great is his faithfulness; his mercies begin afresh each morning" (3:22-23). He then appeals to the nation to return to God and ask for forgiveness.

Chapter 4 recounts how Jerusalem had suffered devastation, degradation, and hunger as a result of the Babylonian onslaught. Truly "the gold has lost its luster" (4:1)—Jerusalem's splendor was now gone. Nevertheless the prophet could confidently say, "O beautiful Jerusalem, your punishment will end" (4:22).

In the final chapter, the prophet speaks on behalf of the nation, calling upon God to see their misery and pleading for restoration. Affirming God's eternal kingship, he appeals, "Restore us, O LORD, and bring us back to you again! Give us back the joys we once had!" (5:21).

OVERVIEW

What does it mean for us?

Lamentations brings us face-to-face with the misery that sin inevitably brings, as Jerusalem was now experiencing. The writer does not try to cover up what had gone wrong: Jerusalem, and especially its religious leaders (4:13), had sinned grievously and repeatedly, and they utterly deserved God's judgment. Yet at the heart of the book stands the affirmation that, even then, God remains faithful toward his people (3:21-23). This is why the author's cry of hope triumphs over his cry of despair, even in the midst of devastation.

Recognizing where we have gone wrong is always the first step in coming back to God. God does not violate our wills; he lets us make wrong choices if that is what we want to do. But he is always there, waiting for us to turn around, eager to bring us back.

The last word is never with sin. It is always with *God* and his love, faithfulness, salvation, and hope, which are the basis of comfort even when sin's consequences overwhelm us.

Sorrow in Jerusalem

1* 1 Jerusalem, once so full of people,
is now deserted.
She who was once great among the nations
now sits alone like a widow.
Once the queen of all the earth,
she is now a slave.

2 She sobs through the night;
tears stream down her cheeks.
Among all her lovers,
there is no one left to comfort her.
All her friends have betrayed her
and become her enemies.

3 Judah has been led away into captivity,
oppressed with cruel slavery.
She lives among foreign nations
and has no place of rest.
Her enemies have chased her down,
and she has nowhere to turn.

4 The roads to Jerusalem* are in mourning,
for crowds no longer come to celebrate the festivals.
The city gates are silent,
her priests groan,
her young women are crying—
how bitter is her fate!

5 Her oppressors have become her masters,
and her enemies prosper,
for the LORD has punished Jerusalem
for her many sins.
Her children have been captured
and taken away to distant lands.

6 All the majesty of beautiful Jerusalem*
has been stripped away.
Her princes are like starving deer
searching for pasture.
They are too weak to run
from the pursuing enemy.

7 In the midst of her sadness and wandering,
Jerusalem remembers her ancient splendor.
But now she has fallen to her enemy,
and there is no one to help her.
Her enemy struck her down
and laughed as she fell.

8 Jerusalem has sinned greatly,
so she has been tossed away like a filthy rag.
All who once honored her now despise her,
for they have seen her stripped naked and humiliated.
All she can do is groan
and hide her face.

9 She defiled herself with immorality
and gave no thought to her future.
Now she lies in the gutter
with no one to lift her out.
"LORD, see my misery," she cries.
"The enemy has triumphed."

10 The enemy has plundered her completely,
taking every precious thing she owns.
She has seen foreigners violate her sacred Temple,
the place the LORD had forbidden them to enter.

1 Each of the first four chapters of this book is an acrostic, laid out in the order of the Hebrew alphabet. The first word of each verse begins with a successive Hebrew letter. Chapters 1, 2, and 4 have one verse for each of the 22 Hebrew letters. Chapter 3 contains 22 stanzas of three verses each. Though chapter 5 has 22 verses, it is not an acrostic. **1:4** Hebrew *Zion;* also in 1:17. **1:6** Hebrew *of the daughter of Zion.*

11 Her people groan as they search for bread.
They have sold their treasures for food to stay alive.
"O LORD, look," she mourns, "and see how I am despised.

12 "Does it mean nothing to you, all you who pass by?
Look around and see if there is any suffering like mine,
which the LORD brought on me when he erupted in fierce anger.

13 "He has sent fire from heaven that burns in my bones.
He has placed a trap in my path and turned me back.
He has left me devastated, racked with sickness all day long.

14 "He wove my sins into ropes to hitch me to a yoke of captivity.
The Lord sapped my strength and turned me over to my enemies;
I am helpless in their hands.

15 "The Lord has treated my mighty men with contempt.
At his command a great army has come to crush my young warriors.
The Lord has trampled his beloved city* like grapes are trampled in a winepress.

16 "For all these things I weep; tears flow down my cheeks.
No one is here to comfort me; any who might encourage me are far away.
My children have no future, for the enemy has conquered us."

17 Jerusalem reaches out for help, but no one comforts her.
Regarding his people Israel,* the LORD has said,
"Let their neighbors be their enemies!
Let them be thrown away like a filthy rag!"

18 "The LORD is right," Jerusalem says, "for I rebelled against him.
Listen, people everywhere; look upon my anguish and despair,
for my sons and daughters have been taken captive to distant lands.

19 "I begged my allies for help, but they betrayed me.
My priests and leaders starved to death in the city,
even as they searched for food to save their lives.

20 "LORD, see my anguish! My heart is broken
and my soul despairs, for I have rebelled against you.
In the streets the sword kills, and at home there is only death.

Mourning

Mourning is a natural expression of the loss of something precious. Lamentations opens with a lament over the loss of Jerusalem, precious to God and to his people, after the city was devastated by the Babylonians. Laments—songs of mourning or sorrow—were common in ancient times, either to express grief at a time of bereavement or tragedy, or to express repentance.

Mourning is expressed differently in different cultures. In Bible times common expressions of mourning included weeping, tearing one's clothes, wearing burlap and ashes, beating one's head or chest, tearing one's beard, removing one's head covering, singing songs of lament, and even silence.

The Bible's inclusion of so many examples of mourning shows that God does not want us to cover up our feelings or pretend they are not there. Even the most spiritual people mourn the loss of a loved one, and trying to remain unmoved does little to help. However, there is also a time for mourning to end (Ecclesiastes 3:4). David grieved over the loss of his and Bathsheba's child; but he knew there was also a time to turn and face life again, confident that God still had plans for his future (2 Samuel 12:19-25).

21 "Others heard my groans,
but no one turned to comfort me.
When my enemies heard about my troubles,
they were happy to see what you had done.
Oh, bring the day you promised,
when they will suffer as I have suffered.

22 "Look at all their evil deeds, LORD.
Punish them,
as you have punished me
for all my sins.
My groans are many,
and I am sick at heart."

God's Anger at Sin

2 1 The Lord in his anger
has cast a dark shadow over
beautiful Jerusalem.*
The fairest of Israel's cities lies in the dust,
thrown down from the heights of heaven.
In his day of great anger,
the Lord has shown no mercy even to his Temple.*

2 Without mercy the Lord has destroyed
every home in Israel.*
In his anger he has broken down
the fortress walls of beautiful Jerusalem.*
He has brought them to the ground,
dishonoring the kingdom and its rulers.

3 All the strength of Israel
vanishes beneath his fierce anger.
The Lord has withdrawn his protection
as the enemy attacks.
He consumes the whole land of Israel
like a raging fire.

4 He bends his bow against his people,
as though he were their enemy.
His strength is used against them
to kill their finest youth.
His fury is poured out like fire
on beautiful Jerusalem.*

5 Yes, the Lord has vanquished Israel
like an enemy.
He has destroyed her palaces
and demolished her fortresses.
He has brought unending sorrow and tears
upon beautiful Jerusalem.

6 He has broken down his Temple
as though it were merely a garden shelter.
The LORD has blotted out all memory
of the holy festivals and Sabbath days.
Kings and priests fall together
before his fierce anger.

7 The Lord has rejected his own altar;
he despises his own sanctuary.
He has given Jerusalem's palaces
to her enemies.
They shout in the LORD's Temple
as though it were a day of celebration.

8 The LORD was determined
to destroy the walls of beautiful Jerusalem.
He made careful plans for their destruction,
then did what he had planned.
Therefore, the ramparts and walls
have fallen down before him.

9 Jerusalem's gates have sunk into the ground.
He has smashed their locks and bars.
Her kings and princes have been exiled
to distant lands;
her law has ceased to exist.
Her prophets receive
no more visions from the LORD.

10 The leaders of beautiful Jerusalem
sit on the ground in silence.
They are clothed in burlap
and throw dust on their heads.
The young women of Jerusalem
hang their heads in shame.

11 I have cried until the tears no longer come;
my heart is broken.
My spirit is poured out in agony
as I see the desperate plight of my people.
Little children and tiny babies
are fainting and dying in the streets.

12 They cry out to their mothers,
"We need food and drink!"
Their lives ebb away in the streets

1:15 Hebrew *the virgin daughter of Judah.* **1:17** Hebrew *Jacob.* The names "Jacob" and "Israel" are often interchanged throughout the Old Testament, referring sometimes to the individual patriarch and sometimes to the nation. **2:1a** Hebrew *the daughter of Zion;* also in 2:8, 10, 18. **2:1b** Hebrew *his footstool.* **2:2a** Hebrew *Jacob;* also in 2:3b. See note on 1:17. **2:2b** Hebrew *the daughter of Judah;* also in 2:5. **2:4** Hebrew *on the tent of the daughter of Zion.*

like the life of a warrior wounded in
battle.
They gasp for life
as they collapse in their mothers' arms.

13 What can I say about you?
Who has ever seen such sorrow?
O daughter of Jerusalem,
to what can I compare your anguish?
O virgin daughter of Zion,
how can I comfort you?
For your wound is as deep as the sea.
Who can heal you?

14 Your prophets have said
so many foolish things, false to the
core.
They did not save you from exile
by pointing out your sins.
Instead, they painted false pictures,
filling you with false hope.

15 All who pass by jeer at you.
They scoff and insult beautiful
Jerusalem,* saying,
"Is this the city called 'Most Beautiful in
All the World'
and 'Joy of All the Earth'?"

16 All your enemies mock you.
They scoff and snarl and say,
"We have destroyed her at last!
We have long waited for this day,
and it is finally here!"

17 But it is the LORD who did just as he
planned.
He has fulfilled the promises of
disaster
he made long ago.
He has destroyed Jerusalem without
mercy.
He has caused her enemies to gloat
over her
and has given them power over her.

18 Cry aloud* before the Lord,
O walls of beautiful Jerusalem!
Let your tears flow like a river
day and night.
Give yourselves no rest;
give your eyes no relief.

19 Rise during the night and cry out.
Pour out your hearts like water to the
Lord.
Lift up your hands to him in prayer,
pleading for your children,
for in every street
they are faint with hunger.

20 "O LORD, think about this!
Should you treat your own people this
way?
Should mothers eat their own children,
those they once bounced on their
knees?
Should priests and prophets be killed
within the Lord's Temple?

21 "See them lying in the streets—
young and old,
boys and girls,
killed by the swords of the enemy.
You have killed them in your anger,
slaughtering them without mercy.

22 "You have invited terrors from all around,
as though you were calling them to a
day of feasting.
In the day of the LORD's anger,
no one has escaped or survived.
The enemy has killed all the children
whom I carried and raised."

Hope in the LORD's Faithfulness

3 1 I am the one who has seen the
afflictions
that come from the rod of the LORD's
anger.
2 He has led me into darkness,
shutting out all light.
3 He has turned his hand against me
again and again, all day long.

4 He has made my skin and flesh grow old.
He has broken my bones.
5 He has besieged and surrounded me
with anguish and distress.
6 He has buried me in a dark place,
like those long dead.

7 He has walled me in, and I cannot
escape.
He has bound me in heavy chains.
8 And though I cry and shout,
he has shut out my prayers.
9 He has blocked my way with a high
stone wall;
he has made my road crooked.

10 He has hidden like a bear or a lion,
waiting to attack me.
11 He has dragged me off the path and torn
me in pieces,
leaving me helpless and devastated.

12 He has drawn his bow
and made me the target for his
arrows.
13 He shot his arrows
deep into my heart.
14 My own people laugh at me.
All day long they sing their mocking
songs.
15 He has filled me with bitterness
and given me a bitter cup of sorrow to
drink.
16 He has made me chew on gravel.
He has rolled me in the dust.
17 Peace has been stripped away,
and I have forgotten what prosperity is.
18 I cry out, "My splendor is gone!
Everything I had hoped for from the
LORD is lost!"
19 The thought of my suffering and
homelessness
is bitter beyond words.*
20 I will never forget this awful time,
as I grieve over my loss.
21 Yet I still dare to hope
when I remember this:
22 The faithful love of the LORD never ends!*
His mercies never cease.
23 Great is his faithfulness;
his mercies begin afresh each morning.
24 I say to myself, "The LORD is my
inheritance;
therefore, I will hope in him!"
25 The LORD is good to those who depend
on him,
to those who search for him.
26 So it is good to wait quietly
for salvation from the LORD.
27 And it is good for people to submit at an
early age
to the yoke of his discipline:
28 Let them sit alone in silence
beneath the LORD's demands.
29 Let them lie face down in the dust,
for there may be hope at last.
30 Let them turn the other cheek to those
who strike them
and accept the insults of their
enemies.
31 For no one is abandoned
by the Lord forever.
32 Though he brings grief, he also shows
compassion
because of the greatness of his
unfailing love.
33 For he does not enjoy hurting people
or causing them sorrow.

2:15 Hebrew *the daughter of Jerusalem.* **2:18** Hebrew *Their heart cried.* **3:19** Or *is wormwood and gall.* **3:22** As in Syriac version; Hebrew reads *of the LORD keeps us from destruction.*

Hope

The author of Lamentations had seen great misery and suffering when Jerusalem was destroyed (the Babylonian army was notoriously cruel), and this is apparent in the first two laments. But now, in a surge of faith, the hope that he had lost (Lamentations 3:18) returned; and what stirred his hope was nothing about himself, or Jerusalem, or God's people, but God himself: "The faithful love of the LORD never ends! His mercies never cease. Great is his faithfulness; his mercies begin afresh each morning" (3:22-23).

Our hope lies in knowing that God is faithful! Once we grasp this, it will take us through anything, and we can put our hope in God (3:24), waiting on him to act—waiting, not out of resignation, but in confidence that he will indeed do what he has promised to do, even if he does so in a way that is different from the one we had expected.

Hope lies at the heart of Jesus' message—not just hope for a better future (that if we believe in him, we will go to heaven one day), but hope for a better present (for the Kingdom of Heaven has already come to us in him). Christians have every reason, therefore, whatever their circumstances, to be a people of hope.

▶ *See also* ***The character of God****, page 104;* ***Faithfulness****, page 1307.*

34 If people crush underfoot
all the prisoners of the land,
35 if they deprive others of their rights
in defiance of the Most High,
36 if they twist justice in the courts—
doesn't the Lord see all these things?

37 Who can command things to happen
without the Lord's permission?
38 Does not the Most High
send both calamity and good?
39 Then why should we, mere humans, complain
when we are punished for our sins?

40 Instead, let us test and examine our ways.
Let us turn back to the LORD.
41 Let us lift our hearts and hands
to God in heaven and say,
42 "We have sinned and rebelled,
and you have not forgiven us.

43 "You have engulfed us with your anger,
chased us down,
and slaughtered us without mercy.
44 You have hidden yourself in a cloud
so our prayers cannot reach you.
45 You have discarded us as refuse and garbage
among the nations.

46 "All our enemies
have spoken out against us.
47 We are filled with fear,
for we are trapped, devastated, and ruined."
48 Tears stream from my eyes
because of the destruction of my people!

49 My tears flow endlessly;
they will not stop
50 until the LORD looks down
from heaven and sees.
51 My heart is breaking
over the fate of all the women of Jerusalem.

52 My enemies, whom I have never harmed,
hunted me down like a bird.
53 They threw me into a pit
and dropped stones on me.
54 The water rose over my head,
and I cried out, "This is the end!"

55 But I called on your name, LORD,
from deep within the pit.
56 You heard me when I cried, "Listen to my pleading!
Hear my cry for help!"
57 Yes, you came when I called;
you told me, "Do not fear."

58 Lord, you have come to my defense;
you have redeemed my life.
59 You have seen the wrong they have done to me, LORD.
Be my judge, and prove me right.
60 You have seen the vengeful plots
my enemies have laid against me.

61 LORD, you have heard the vile names they call me.
You know all about the plans they have made.
62 My enemies whisper and mutter
as they plot against me all day long.
63 Look at them! Whether they sit or stand,
I am the object of their mocking songs.

64 Pay them back, LORD,
for all the evil they have done.
65 Give them hard and stubborn hearts,
and then let your curse fall on them!
66 Chase them down in your anger,
destroying them beneath the LORD's heavens.

God's Anger Satisfied

4 1 How the gold has lost its luster!
Even the finest gold has become dull.
The sacred gemstones
lie scattered in the streets!

2 See how the precious children of Jerusalem,*
worth their weight in fine gold,
are now treated like pots of clay
made by a common potter.

3 Even the jackals feed their young,
but not my people Israel.
They ignore their children's cries,
like ostriches in the desert.

4 The parched tongues of their little ones
stick to the roofs of their mouths in thirst.
The children cry for bread,
but no one has any to give them.

5 The people who once ate the richest foods
now beg in the streets for anything they can get.

Those who once wore the finest clothes
now search the garbage dumps for
food.

6 The guilt* of my people
is greater than that of Sodom,
where utter disaster struck in a moment
and no hand offered help.

7 Our princes once glowed with health—
brighter than snow, whiter than milk.
Their faces were as ruddy as rubies,
their appearance like fine jewels.*

8 But now their faces are blacker than soot.
No one recognizes them in the streets.
Their skin sticks to their bones;
it is as dry and hard as wood.

9 Those killed by the sword are better off
than those who die of hunger.
Starving, they waste away
for lack of food from the fields.

10 Tenderhearted women
have cooked their own children.
They have eaten them
to survive the siege.

11 But now the anger of the LORD is satisfied.
His fierce anger has been poured out.
He started a fire in Jerusalem*
that burned the city to its
foundations.

12 Not a king in all the earth—
no one in all the world—
would have believed that an enemy
could march through the gates of
Jerusalem.

13 Yet it happened because of the sins of
her prophets
and the sins of her priests,
who defiled the city
by shedding innocent blood.

14 They wandered blindly
through the streets,
so defiled by blood
that no one dared touch them.

15 "Get away!" the people shouted at them.
"You're defiled! Don't touch us!"
So they fled to distant lands
and wandered among foreign nations,
but none would let them stay.

16 The LORD himself has scattered them,
and he no longer helps them.
People show no respect for the priests
and no longer honor the leaders.

17 We looked in vain for our allies
to come and save us,
but we were looking to nations
that could not help us.

18 We couldn't go into the streets
without danger to our lives.
Our end was near; our days were
numbered.
We were doomed!

19 Our enemies were swifter than eagles in
flight.
If we fled to the mountains, they
found us.
If we hid in the wilderness,
they were waiting for us there.

20 Our king—the LORD's anointed, the very
life of our nation—
was caught in their snares.
We had thought that his shadow
would protect us against any nation
on earth!

21 Are you rejoicing in the land of Uz,
O people of Edom?
But you, too, must drink from the cup of
the LORD's anger.
You, too, will be stripped naked in
your drunkenness.

22 O beautiful Jerusalem,* your
punishment will end;
you will soon return from exile.
But Edom, your punishment is just
beginning;
soon your many sins will be exposed.

Prayer for Restoration

5 1 LORD, remember what has happened
to us.
See how we have been disgraced!
2 Our inheritance has been turned over to
strangers,
our homes to foreigners.
3 We are orphaned and fatherless.
Our mothers are widowed.
4 We have to pay for water to drink,
and even firewood is expensive.
5 Those who pursue us are at our heels;
we are exhausted but are given no rest.

4:2 Hebrew *precious sons of Zion.* **4:6** Or *punishment.* **4:7** Hebrew *like lapis lazuli.* **4:11** Hebrew *in Zion.* **4:22** Hebrew *O daughter of Zion.*

6 We submitted to Egypt and Assyria
to get enough food to survive.
7 Our ancestors sinned, but they have died—
and we are suffering the punishment they deserved!

8 Slaves have now become our masters;
there is no one left to rescue us.
9 We hunt for food at the risk of our lives,
for violence rules the countryside.
10 The famine has blackened our skin
as though baked in an oven.
11 Our enemies rape the women in Jerusalem*
and the young girls in all the towns of Judah.
12 Our princes are being hanged by their thumbs,
and our elders are treated with contempt.
13 Young men are led away to work at millstones,
and boys stagger under heavy loads of wood.
14 The elders no longer sit in the city gates;
the young men no longer dance and sing.
15 Joy has left our hearts;
our dancing has turned to mourning.
16 The garlands have* fallen from our heads.
Weep for us because we have sinned.
17 Our hearts are sick and weary,
and our eyes grow dim with tears.
18 For Jerusalem* is empty and desolate,
a place haunted by jackals.

19 But LORD, you remain the same forever!
Your throne continues from generation to generation.
20 Why do you continue to forget us?
Why have you abandoned us for so long?
21 Restore us, O LORD, and bring us back to you again!
Give us back the joys we once had!
22 Or have you utterly rejected us?
Are you angry with us still?

5:11 Hebrew *in Zion.* **5:16** Or *The crown has.* **5:18** Hebrew *Mount Zion.*

Ezekiel *The watchman's message*

Ezekiel was a priest who, in 597 BC while in his mid-twenties, was deported to Babylon. This second deportation happened eight years after the first (which had included Daniel). The final deportation, which would take almost everyone else in Judah, was still eleven years away. Ezekiel was now far removed from his beloved Temple in Jerusalem, so his work as a priest was over; but in 593 BC, when he was thirty (1:1), God appeared to him in a dramatic vision and called him to be "a watchman" (3:17; 33:7)—a prophet warning his fellow exiles.

The early years of Ezekiel's ministry saw him bringing no reassurance: Jerusalem would indeed fall as the judgment of God (chapters 1–24). But once he received news that Jerusalem had fallen, symbolized in the death of his wife, his message completely changed; he began to prophesy that God would come to revive and restore his people and to establish his kingdom on earth (chapters 33–48).

What's it all about?

Ezekiel is one of the longest books in the Old Testament. It has four main blocks.

The first block (chapters 1–24) contains prophecies predicting the fall of Jerusalem. Ezekiel acted out many of these prophecies, sometimes rather strangely. On one occasion he lay on his left side for 390 days and then on his right side for 40 days; on another he shaved his head and beard, burned some of the hair, and scattered some of it around the city. His actions attracted the people's attention, which was, of course, the point; he wanted them to know how certain and how imminent God's punishment on Jerusalem was.

The second block (chapters 25–32) contains Ezekiel's prophecies of judgment on the surrounding nations, showing that the destiny of every nation (not just Judah) lay in God's hands.

The third block (chapters 33–39) was delivered after the fall of Jerusalem in 586 BC. With Jerusalem's judgment now clear and all false hopes shattered, Ezekiel now began to offer hope. He reminded the exiles that God was still their shepherd (chapter 34) and called them to repent, encouraging them that they could once again become a new community committed to God. In a vision, he saw a valley filled with dry bones. When God breathed life into them, they turned into a vast army of living people—a picture of how much God wanted to renew his people.

OVERVIEW

Ezekiel's vision and call
1:1–3:27

Symbolic acts prophesying the coming destruction of Jerusalem
4:1–5:17

Prophecies of God's judgment on Jerusalem and Judah · *6:1–12:28*

God's judgment on Judah explained
13:1–24:27

Prophecies of judgment on other nations · *25:1–32:32*

Prophecies of consolation and God's intentions · *33:1–39:29*

A vision of restoration: new Temple and new worship · *40:1–48:35*

page 900

The final block (chapters 40–48) looks forward to a gloriously restored Temple and land filled with God's glory. Christians differ in how they interpret these chapters. Some believe they will be fulfilled literally and that sacrifices will again be offered in a restored Temple in a future millennial age. Others, however, see it as a prophetic picture of the renewal that Christ would bring in the new-covenant age.

Although Ezekiel's words were addressed to the people of Judah, he refers to them as "the people of Israel," for Judah was now all that was left of "Israel" and the historic promises made to it.

What does it mean for us?

Ezekiel's visions remind us that God is awesome, holy, and beyond human comprehension, as we see from his very first vision. And yet this God who is transcendent, all-powerful, and utterly sovereign over creation and human history also comes down to meet us at our level. He speaks in words and images we can grasp (the use of so much Temple imagery is exactly because Ezekiel, as a former priest, could understand that). He both warns us and offers us hope for the future. Ezekiel's God may have brought judgment, but he is also a God of love who is waiting to turn his spectacular power and glory to our benefit. He repeats his ultimate goal throughout the book: "Then they will know that I am the LORD."

Ezekiel reminds us that the community of God's people is a renewed community, made up of those whose hearts have been transformed and cleansed by God's Spirit; a community that is his holy temple, refreshed by life-giving water that flows out from us to those in the world around us; and a community whose distinguishing feature is the glorious presence of the LORD—hence its new name, "The LORD Is There" (48:35).

▶ *See also* ***A timeline of the Bible****, pages A22-A24.*

A Vision of Living Beings

1 On July 31* of my thirtieth year,* while
I was with the Judean exiles beside the
Kebar River in Babylon, the heavens were
opened and I saw visions of God. 2 This
happened during the fifth year of King Jehoiachin's captivity. 3 (The LORD gave this
message to Ezekiel son of Buzi, a priest,
beside the Kebar River in the land of the Babylonians,* and he felt the hand of the LORD
take hold of him.)
4 As I looked, I saw a great storm coming
from the north, driving before it a huge
cloud that flashed with lightning and shone
with brilliant light. There was fire inside the
cloud, and in the middle of the fire glowed
something like gleaming amber.* 5 From the
center of the cloud came four living beings
that looked human, 6 except that each had
four faces and four wings. 7 Their legs were
straight, and their feet had hooves like those
of a calf and shone like burnished bronze.
8 Under each of their four wings I could see
human hands. So each of the four beings had
four faces and four wings. 9 The wings of each
living being touched the wings of the beings
beside it. Each one moved straight forward
in any direction without turning around.
10 Each had a human face in the front, the
face of a lion on the right side, the face of an
ox on the left side, and the face of an eagle
at the back. 11 Each had two pairs of outstretched wings—one pair stretched out to
touch the wings of the living beings on either
side of it, and the other pair covered its body.
12 They went in whatever direction the spirit
chose, and they moved straight forward in
any direction without turning around.
13 The living beings looked like bright coals
of fire or brilliant torches, and lightning
seemed to flash back and forth among them.
14 And the living beings darted to and fro like
flashes of lightning.
15 As I looked at these beings, I saw four
wheels touching the ground beside them,
one wheel belonging to each. 16 The wheels
sparkled as if made of beryl. All four wheels
looked alike and were made the same; each
wheel had a second wheel turning crosswise
within it. 17 The beings could move in any
of the four directions they faced, without
turning as they moved. 18 The rims of the four

wheels were tall and frightening, and they were covered with eyes all around.

[19]When the living beings moved, the wheels moved with them. When they flew upward, the wheels went up, too. [20]The spirit of the living beings was in the wheels. So wherever the spirit went, the wheels and the living beings also went. [21]When the beings moved, the wheels moved. When the beings stopped, the wheels stopped. When the beings flew upward, the wheels rose up, for the spirit of the living beings was in the wheels.

[22]Spread out above them was a surface like the sky, glittering like crystal. [23]Beneath this surface the wings of each living being stretched out to touch the others' wings, and each had two wings covering its body. [24]As they flew, their wings sounded to me like waves crashing against the shore or like the voice of the Almighty* or like the shouting of a mighty army. When they stopped, they let down their wings. [25]As they stood with wings lowered, a voice spoke from beyond the crystal surface above them.

[26]Above this surface was something that looked like a throne made of blue lapis lazuli. And on this throne high above was a figure whose appearance resembled a man. [27]From what appeared to be his waist up, he looked like gleaming amber, flickering like a fire. And from his waist down, he looked like a burning flame, shining with splendor. [28]All around him was a glowing halo, like a rainbow shining in the clouds on a rainy day. This is what the glory of the LORD looked like to me. When I saw it, I fell face down on the ground, and I heard someone's voice speaking to me.

Ezekiel's Call and Commission

2 "Stand up, son of man," said the voice. "I want to speak with you." [2]The Spirit came into me as he spoke, and he set me on my feet. I listened carefully to his words. [3]"Son of man," he said, "I am sending you to the nation of Israel, a rebellious nation that has rebelled against me. They and their ancestors have been rebelling against me to this very day. [4]They are a stubborn and hard-hearted people. But I am sending you to say to them, 'This is what the Sovereign LORD says!' [5]And whether they listen or refuse to listen—for remember, they are rebels—at least they will know they have had a prophet among them.

[6]"Son of man, do not fear them or their words. Don't be afraid even though their threats surround you like nettles and briers and stinging scorpions. Do not be dismayed by their dark scowls, even though they are rebels. [7]You must give them my messages whether they listen or not. But they won't listen, for they are completely rebellious! [8]Son of man, listen to what I say to you. Do

1:1a Hebrew *On the fifth day of the fourth month,* of the ancient Hebrew lunar calendar. A number of dates in Ezekiel can be cross-checked with dates in surviving Babylonian records and related accurately to our modern calendar. This event occurred on July 31, 593 B.C. **1:1b** Or *in the thirtieth year.* **1:3** Or *Chaldeans.* **1:4** Or *like burnished metal;* also in 1:27. **1:24** Hebrew *Shaddai.*

The call and cost of ministry

We don't know how long Ezekiel's vision lasted. It may have been over in a few minutes or it may have taken hours. But in comparison to his years of ministry, it only took a moment. Many times the Bible shows that God's calling to ministry takes only moments, but the outworking of that call—with all its costs—takes a lifetime.

The strange things that God called Ezekiel to do (lying on his side, cutting off his hair, building a miniature city) and the forthrightness of his message would lead many to reject him, God warned him; but he must continue anyway, for such is the cost of being God's servant (Ezekiel 2:5). Jeremiah's call came quickly (Jeremiah 1:4-19), but he then experienced years of mockery, rejection, false accusation, and imprisonment. David was called as Israel's king in a moment (1 Samuel 16:12-13), but he then spent some ten years on the run from Saul.

The call may be quick, but the cost is high; for it is through the cost that God shapes us into what he wants us to be. Little wonder that Jesus warned people to count the cost before following him (Luke 14:25-33).

not join them in their rebellion. Open your mouth, and eat what I give you."

9Then I looked and saw a hand reaching out to me. It held a scroll, 10which he unrolled. And I saw that both sides were covered with funeral songs, words of sorrow, and pronouncements of doom.

3 The voice said to me, "Son of man, eat what I am giving you—eat this scroll! Then go and give its message to the people of Israel." 2So I opened my mouth, and he fed me the scroll. 3"Fill your stomach with this," he said. And when I ate it, it tasted as sweet as honey in my mouth.

4Then he said, "Son of man, go to the people of Israel and give them my messages. 5I am not sending you to a foreign people whose language you cannot understand. 6No, I am not sending you to people with strange and difficult speech. If I did, they would listen! 7But the people of Israel won't listen to you any more than they listen to me! For the whole lot of them are hard-hearted and stubborn. 8But look, I have made you as obstinate and hard-hearted as they are. 9I have made your forehead as hard as the hardest rock! So don't be afraid of them or fear their angry looks, even though they are rebels."

10Then he added, "Son of man, let all my words sink deep into your own heart first. Listen to them carefully for yourself. 11Then go to your people in exile and say to them, 'This is what the Sovereign LORD says!' Do this whether they listen to you or not."

12Then the Spirit lifted me up, and I heard a loud rumbling sound behind me. (May the glory of the LORD be praised in his place!)* 13It was the sound of the wings of the living beings as they brushed against each other and the rumbling of their wheels beneath them.

14The Spirit lifted me up and took me away. I went in bitterness and turmoil, but the LORD's hold on me was strong. 15Then I came to the colony of Judean exiles in Tel-abib, beside the Kebar River. I was overwhelmed and sat among them for seven days.

A Watchman for Israel

16After seven days the LORD gave me a message. He said, 17"Son of man, I have appointed you as a watchman for Israel. Whenever you receive a message from me, warn people immediately. 18If I warn the wicked, saying, 'You are under the penalty of death,' but you fail to deliver the warning, they will die in their sins. And I will hold you responsible for their deaths. 19If you warn them and they refuse to repent and keep on sinning, they will die in their sins. But you will have saved yourself because you obeyed me.

20"If righteous people turn away from their righteous behavior and ignore the obstacles I put in their way, they will die. And if you do not warn them, they will die in their sins. None of their righteous acts will be remembered, and I will hold you responsible for their deaths. 21But if you warn righteous people not to sin and they listen to you and do not sin, they will live, and you will have saved yourself, too."

22Then the LORD took hold of me and said, "Get up and go out into the valley, and I will speak to you there." 23So I got up and went, and there I saw the glory of the LORD, just as I had seen in my first vision by the Kebar River. And I fell face down on the ground.

24Then the Spirit came into me and set me on my feet. He spoke to me and said, "Go to your house and shut yourself in. 25There, son of man, you will be tied with ropes so you cannot go out among the people. 26And I will make your tongue stick to the roof of your mouth so that you will be speechless and unable to rebuke them, for they are rebels. 27But when I give you a message, I will loosen your tongue and let you speak. Then you will say to them, 'This is what the Sovereign LORD says!' Those who choose to listen will listen, but those who refuse will refuse, for they are rebels.

A Sign of the Coming Siege

4 "And now, son of man, take a large clay brick and set it down in front of you. Then draw a map of the city of Jerusalem on it. 2Show the city under siege. Build a wall around it so no one can escape. Set up the enemy camp, and surround the city with siege ramps and battering rams. 3Then take an iron griddle and place it between you and the city. Turn toward the city and

▸ **3:17** *See* ***Watchmen****, page 815.*

demonstrate how harsh the siege will be against Jerusalem. This will be a warning to the people of Israel.

4"Now lie on your left side and place the sins of Israel on yourself. You are to bear their sins for the number of days you lie there on your side. 5I am requiring you to bear Israel's sins for 390 days—one day for each year of their sin. 6After that, turn over and lie on your right side for 40 days—one day for each year of Judah's sin.

7"Meanwhile, keep staring at the siege of Jerusalem. Lie there with your arm bared and prophesy her destruction. 8I will tie you up with ropes so you won't be able to turn from side to side until the days of your siege have been completed.

9"Now go and get some wheat, barley, beans, lentils, millet, and emmer wheat, and mix them together in a storage jar. Use them to make bread for yourself during the 390 days you will be lying on your side. 10Ration this out to yourself, eight ounces* of food for each day, and eat it at set times. 11Then measure out a jar* of water for each day, and drink it at set times. 12Prepare and eat this food as you would barley cakes. While all the people are watching, bake it over a fire using dried human dung as fuel and then eat the bread." 13Then the LORD said, "This is how Israel will eat defiled bread in the Gentile lands to which I will banish them!"

14Then I said, "O Sovereign LORD, must I be defiled by using human dung? For I have never been defiled before. From the time I was a child until now I have never eaten any animal that died of sickness or was killed by other animals. I have never eaten any meat forbidden by the law."

15"All right," the LORD said. "You may bake your bread with cow dung instead of human dung." 16Then he told me, "Son of man, I will make food very scarce in Jerusalem. It will be weighed out with great care and eaten fearfully. The water will be rationed out drop by drop, and the people will drink it with dismay. 17Lacking food and water, people will look at one another in terror, and they will waste away under their punishment.

A Sign of the Coming Judgment

5 "Son of man, take a sharp sword and use it as a razor to shave your head and beard. Use a scale to weigh the hair into three equal parts. 2Place a third of it at the center of your map of Jerusalem. After

3:12 A possible reading for this verse is *Then the Spirit lifted me up, and as the glory of the LORD rose from its place, I heard a loud rumbling sound behind me.* **4:10** Hebrew *20 shekels* [228 grams]. **4:11** Hebrew *1/6 of a hin* [about 1 pint or 0.6 liters].

Prophecy in the Old Testament

Although Israel had asked for a king, it remained a theocracy (a nation ruled by God). The role of the prophets, therefore, was not so much to predict the future as to ensure that God's nation lived in line with God's Law.

The prophets did this in many different ways, often reflecting their background or character. Isaiah was very educated, so his language is grand and poetic; Ezekiel was a priest, so he often spoke of holiness and the Temple. And just as their character and language were different, so was their delivery. While most prophecies were delivered by declaring words, Ezekiel acted out some of his prophecies (Ezekiel 4–5); Jeremiah wrote a letter (Jeremiah 29); Isaiah sang a song (Isaiah 5); Nathan told a parable (2 Samuel 12); Elijah performed miracles (1 Kings 17–18); and Hosea married an unfaithful woman as a prophetic action (Hosea 1–3). Prophecy came in many different ways, through all kinds of people, showing that the prophets were not "overtaken" by God, but real people whom God's Spirit filled and used in different ways.

In New Testament times the role of prophet changed, for the church is not a theocratic nation. The prophet became one who "strengthens others, encourages them, and comforts them" (1 Corinthians 14:3).

▶ *See also* ***Samuel****, page 309;* ***Elijah****, page 402;* ***Elisha****, page 413;* ***Prophecy in the New Testament****, page 1318.*

acting out the siege, burn it there. Scatter another third across your map and chop it with a sword. Scatter the last third to the wind, for I will scatter my people with the sword. [3]Keep just a bit of the hair and tie it up in your robe. [4]Then take some of these hairs out and throw them into the fire, burning them up. A fire will then spread from this remnant and destroy all of Israel.

[5]"This is what the Sovereign LORD says: This is an illustration of what will happen to Jerusalem. I placed her at the center of the nations, [6]but she has rebelled against my regulations and decrees and has been even more wicked than the surrounding nations. She has refused to obey the regulations and decrees I gave her to follow.

[7]"Therefore, this is what the Sovereign LORD says: You people have behaved worse than your neighbors and have refused to obey my decrees and regulations. You have not even lived up to the standards of the nations around you. [8]Therefore, I myself, the Sovereign LORD, am now your enemy. I will punish you publicly while all the nations watch. [9]Because of your detestable idols, I will punish you like I have never punished anyone before or ever will again. [10]Parents will eat their own children, and children will eat their parents. I will punish you and scatter to the winds the few who survive.

[11]"As surely as I live, says the Sovereign LORD, I will cut you off completely. I will show you no pity at all because you have defiled my Temple with your vile images and detestable sins. [12]A third of your people will die in the city from disease and famine. A third of them will be slaughtered by the enemy outside the city walls. And I will scatter a third to the winds, chasing them with my sword. [13]Then at last my anger will be spent, and I will be satisfied. And when my fury against them has subsided, all Israel will know that I, the LORD, have spoken to them in my jealous anger.

[14]"So I will turn you into a ruin, a mockery in the eyes of the surrounding nations and to all who pass by. [15]You will become an object of mockery and taunting and horror. You will be a warning to all the nations around you. They will see what happens when the LORD punishes a nation in anger and rebukes it, says the LORD.

[16]"I will shower you with the deadly arrows of famine to destroy you. The famine will become more and more severe until every crumb of food is gone. [17]And along with the famine, wild animals will attack you and rob you of your children. Disease and war will stalk your land, and I will bring the sword of the enemy against you. I, the LORD, have spoken!"

Judgment against Israel's Mountains

6 Again a message came to me from the LORD: [2]"Son of man, turn and face the mountains of Israel and prophesy against them. [3]Proclaim this message from the Sovereign LORD against the mountains of Israel. This is what the Sovereign LORD says to the mountains and hills and to the ravines and valleys: I am about to bring war upon you, and I will smash your pagan shrines. [4]All your altars will be demolished, and your places of worship will be destroyed. I will kill your people in front of your idols.* [5]I will lay your corpses in front of your idols and scatter your bones around your altars. [6]Wherever you live there will be desolation, and I will destroy your pagan shrines. Your altars will be demolished, your idols will be smashed, your places of worship will be torn down, and all the religious objects you have made will be destroyed. [7]The place will be littered with corpses, and you will know that I alone am the LORD.

[8]"But I will let a few of my people escape destruction, and they will be scattered among the nations of the world. [9]Then when they are exiled among the nations, they will remember me. They will recognize how hurt I am by their unfaithful hearts and lustful eyes that long for their idols. Then at last they will hate themselves for all their detestable sins. [10]They will know that I alone am the LORD and that I was serious when I said I would bring this calamity on them.

[11]"This is what the Sovereign LORD says: Clap your hands in horror, and stamp your feet. Cry out because of all the detestable sins the people of Israel have committed. Now they are going to die from war and famine and disease. [12]Disease will strike down those who are far away in exile. War will destroy those who are nearby. And anyone who survives will be killed by famine. So at last I will spend my fury on them. [13]They will know that I am the LORD when their dead lie scattered among their idols and altars on every hill and mountain and under every green

tree and every great shade tree—the places
where they offered sacrifices to their idols.
14 I will crush them and make their cities
desolate from the wilderness in the south to
Riblah* in the north. Then they will know
that I am the LORD."

The Coming of the End

7 Then this message came to me from the
LORD: 2 "Son of man, this is what the
Sovereign LORD says to Israel:

"The end is here!
Wherever you look—
east, west, north, or south—
your land is finished.
3 No hope remains,
for I will unleash my anger against you.
I will call you to account
for all your detestable sins.
4 I will turn my eyes away and show no pity.
I will repay you for all your detestable sins.
Then you will know that I am the LORD.

5 "This is what the Sovereign LORD says:
Disaster after disaster
is coming your way!
6 The end has come.
It has finally arrived.
Your final doom is waiting!
7 O people of Israel, the day of your destruction is dawning.
The time has come; the day of trouble is near.
Shouts of anguish will be heard on the mountains,
not shouts of joy.
8 Soon I will pour out my fury on you
and unleash my anger against you.
I will call you to account
for all your detestable sins.
9 I will turn my eyes away and show no pity.
I will repay you for all your detestable sins.
Then you will know that it is I, the LORD,
who is striking the blow.

10 "The day of judgment is here;
your destruction awaits!
The people's wickedness and pride
have blossomed to full flower.
11 Their violence has grown into a rod
that will beat them for their wickedness.
None of these proud and wicked people will survive.
All their wealth and prestige will be swept away.
12 Yes, the time has come;
the day is here!
Buyers should not rejoice over bargains,
nor sellers grieve over losses,
for all of them will fall
under my terrible anger.
13 Even if the merchants survive,
they will never return to their business.
For what God has said applies to everyone—
it will not be changed!
Not one person whose life is twisted by sin
will ever recover.

The Desolation of Israel

14 "The trumpet calls Israel's army to mobilize,
but no one listens,
for my fury is against them all.
15 There is war outside the city
and disease and famine within.
Those outside the city walls
will be killed by enemy swords.
Those inside the city
will die of famine and disease.
16 The survivors who escape to the mountains
will moan like doves, weeping for their sins.
17 Their hands will hang limp,
their knees will be weak as water.
18 They will dress themselves in burlap;
horror and shame will cover them.
They will shave their heads
in sorrow and remorse.

19 "They will throw their money in the streets,
tossing it out like worthless trash.
Their silver and gold won't save them
on that day of the LORD's anger.
It will neither satisfy nor feed them,
for their greed can only trip them up.
20 They were proud of their beautiful jewelry
and used it to make detestable idols
and vile images.
Therefore, I will make all their wealth
disgusting to them.

6:4 The Hebrew term (literally *round things*) probably alludes to dung; also in 6:5, 6, 9, 13. **6:14** As in some Hebrew manuscripts; most Hebrew manuscripts read *Diblah*.

[21] I will give it as plunder to foreigners,
to the most wicked of nations,
and they will defile it.
[22] I will turn my eyes from them
as these robbers invade and defile my
treasured land.

[23] "Prepare chains for my people,
for the land is bloodied by terrible
crimes.
Jerusalem is filled with violence.
[24] I will bring the most ruthless of nations
to occupy their homes.
I will break down their proud fortresses
and defile their sanctuaries.
[25] Terror and trembling will overcome my
people.
They will look for peace but not
find it.
[26] Calamity will follow calamity;
rumor will follow rumor.
They will look in vain
for a vision from the prophets.
They will receive no teaching from the
priests
and no counsel from the leaders.
[27] The king and the prince will stand
helpless,
weeping in despair,
and the people's hands
will tremble with fear.
I will bring on them
the evil they have done to others,
and they will receive the punishment
they so richly deserve.
Then they will know that I am the
LORD."

Idolatry in the Temple

8 Then on September 17,* during the
sixth year of King Jehoiachin's captivity,
while the leaders of Judah were in my home,
the Sovereign LORD took hold of me. [2]I saw
a figure that appeared to be a man.* From
what appeared to be his waist down, he
looked like a burning flame. From the waist
up he looked like gleaming amber.* [3]He
reached out what seemed to be a hand and
took me by the hair. Then the Spirit lifted
me up into the sky and transported me to
Jerusalem in a vision from God. I was taken
to the north gate of the inner courtyard of
the Temple, where there is a large idol that
has made the LORD very jealous. [4]Suddenly,
the glory of the God of Israel was there, just
as I had seen it before in the valley.
[5]Then the LORD said to me, "Son of man,

Does it matter how our church buildings look?

Christian buildings have taken many shapes, styles, and sizes over the centuries. Some have been simple huts, others grand venues seating thousands; some have been plain and without decoration, while others have had millions of dollars spent on decorating them. But passages like Ezekiel 8 have caused some Christians to think we should not decorate our buildings at all. After all, isn't this what other religions do? And doesn't God describe the decoration of the Temple here as "detestable" (Ezekiel 8:9-10)?

It is important to take these verses in context. What was happening here was that the leaders had allowed pagan symbols to be used in decorating God's Temple. "Crawling animals" were described in the Law as "unclean" along with certain other types of animals (e.g., Leviticus 11); yet what God called unclean was now being portrayed in his holy Temple, as though it were no different from a pagan sanctuary. The objection therefore is not to decoration itself, but to decoration with things that God had said were unacceptable to him. By contrast, God was very happy to have decoration on the Tabernacle's curtains (Exodus 26:1) and on the Ark of the Covenant (Exodus 37:1-9), and Solomon had richly decorated the Temple when it was first built (1 Kings 6).

It seems therefore that God does not care how our buildings look, as long as what is in them helps us to worship him and does not detract from that.

▶ *See also* ***Buildings for worship****, page 832.*

look toward the north." So I looked, and there to the north, beside the entrance to the gate near the altar, stood the idol that had made the LORD so jealous.

6 "Son of man," he said, "do you see what they are doing? Do you see the detestable sins the people of Israel are committing to drive me from my Temple? But come, and you will see even more detestable sins than these!" 7 Then he brought me to the door of the Temple courtyard, where I could see a hole in the wall. 8 He said to me, "Now, son of man, dig into the wall." So I dug into the wall and found a hidden doorway.

9 "Go in," he said, "and see the wicked and detestable sins they are committing in there!" 10 So I went in and saw the walls covered with engravings of all kinds of crawling animals and detestable creatures. I also saw the various idols* worshiped by the people of Israel. 11 Seventy leaders of Israel were standing there with Jaazaniah son of Shaphan in the center. Each of them held an incense burner, from which a cloud of incense rose above their heads.

12 Then the LORD said to me, "Son of man, have you seen what the leaders of Israel are doing with their idols in dark rooms? They are saying, 'The LORD doesn't see us; he has deserted our land!'" 13 Then the LORD added, "Come, and I will show you even more detestable sins than these!"

14 He brought me to the north gate of the LORD's Temple, and some women were sitting there, weeping for the god Tammuz. 15 "Have you seen this?" he asked. "But I will show you even more detestable sins than these!"

16 Then he brought me into the inner courtyard of the LORD's Temple. At the entrance to the sanctuary, between the entry room and the bronze altar, there were about twenty-five men with their backs to the sanctuary of the LORD. They were facing east, bowing low to the ground, worshiping the sun!

17 "Have you seen this, son of man?" he asked. "Is it nothing to the people of Judah that they commit these detestable sins, leading the whole nation into violence, thumbing their noses at me, and provoking my anger? 18 Therefore, I will respond in fury. I will neither pity nor spare them. And though they cry for mercy, I will not listen."

The Slaughter of Idolaters

9 Then the LORD thundered, "Bring on the men appointed to punish the city! Tell them to bring their weapons with them!" 2 Six men soon appeared from the upper gate that faces north, each carrying a deadly weapon in his hand. With them was a man dressed in linen, who carried a writer's case at his side. They all went into the Temple courtyard and stood beside the bronze altar.

3 Then the glory of the God of Israel rose up from between the cherubim, where it had rested, and moved to the entrance of the Temple. And the LORD called to the man dressed in linen who was carrying the writer's case. 4 He said to him, "Walk through the streets of Jerusalem and put a mark on the foreheads of all who weep and sigh because of the detestable sins being committed in their city."

5 Then I heard the LORD say to the other men, "Follow him through the city and kill everyone whose forehead is not marked. Show no mercy; have no pity! 6 Kill them all—old and young, girls and women and little children. But do not touch anyone with the mark. Begin right here at the Temple." So they began by killing the seventy leaders.

7 "Defile the Temple!" the LORD commanded. "Fill its courtyards with corpses. Go!" So they went and began killing throughout the city.

8 While they were out killing, I was all alone. I fell face down on the ground and cried out, "O Sovereign LORD! Will your fury against Jerusalem wipe out everyone left in Israel?"

9 Then he said to me, "The sins of the people of Israel and Judah are very, very great. The entire land is full of murder; the city is filled with injustice. They are saying, 'The LORD doesn't see it! The LORD has abandoned the land!' 10 So I will not spare them or have any pity on them. I will fully repay them for all they have done."

11 Then the man in linen clothing, who carried the writer's case, reported back and said, "I have done as you commanded."

8:1 Hebrew *on the fifth [day] of the sixth month,* of the ancient Hebrew lunar calendar. This event occurred on September 17, 592 B.C.; also see note on 1:1. **8:2a** As in Greek version; Hebrew reads *appeared to be fire.* **8:2b** Or *like burnished metal.* **8:10** The Hebrew term (literally *round things*) probably alludes to dung.

The LORD's Glory Leaves the Temple

10 In my vision I saw what appeared to
be a throne of blue lapis lazuli above
the crystal surface over the heads of the
cherubim. 2Then the LORD spoke to the man
in linen clothing and said, "Go between the
whirling wheels beneath the cherubim, and
take a handful of burning coals and scatter
them over the city." He did this as I watched.
3The cherubim were standing at the south
end of the Temple when the man went in,
and the cloud of glory filled the inner courtyard. 4Then the glory of the LORD rose up
from above the cherubim and went over
to the entrance of the Temple. The Temple
was filled with this cloud of glory, and the
courtyard glowed brightly with the glory
of the LORD. 5The moving wings of the
cherubim sounded like the voice of God
Almighty* and could be heard even in the
outer courtyard.
6The LORD said to the man in linen clothing, "Go between the cherubim and take
some burning coals from between the
wheels." So the man went in and stood
beside one of the wheels. 7Then one of the
cherubim reached out his hand and took
some live coals from the fire burning among
them. He put the coals into the hands of the
man in linen clothing, and the man took
them and went out. 8(All the cherubim had
what looked like human hands under their
wings.)
9I looked, and each of the four cherubim
had a wheel beside him, and the wheels
sparkled like beryl. 10All four wheels looked
alike and were made the same; each wheel
had a second wheel turning crosswise
within it. 11The cherubim could move in any
of the four directions they faced, without
turning as they moved. They went straight
in the direction they faced, never turning
aside. 12Both the cherubim and the wheels
were covered with eyes. The cherubim
had eyes all over their bodies, including
their hands, their backs, and their wings.
13I heard someone refer to the wheels as
"the whirling wheels." 14Each of the four
cherubim had four faces: the first was the
face of an ox,* the second was a human
face, the third was the face of a lion, and
the fourth was the face of an eagle.
15Then the cherubim rose upward.
These were the same living beings I had
seen beside the Kebar River. 16When the
cherubim moved, the wheels moved with
them. When they lifted their wings to fly,
the wheels stayed beside them. 17When the
cherubim stopped, the wheels stopped.
When they flew upward, the wheels rose
up, for the spirit of the living beings was in
the wheels.
18Then the glory of the LORD moved out
from the entrance of the Temple and hovered
above the cherubim. 19And as I watched, the
cherubim flew with their wheels to the east
gate of the LORD's Temple. And the glory of
the God of Israel hovered above them.
20These were the same living beings
I had seen beneath the God of Israel when
I was by the Kebar River. I knew they were
cherubim, 21for each had four faces and four
wings and what looked like human hands
under their wings. 22And their faces were
just like the faces of the beings I had seen at
the Kebar, and they traveled straight ahead,
just as the others had.

Judgment on Israel's Leaders

11 Then the Spirit lifted me and brought
me to the east gateway of the LORD's
Temple, where I saw twenty-five prominent
men of the city. Among them were Jaazaniah
son of Azzur and Pelatiah son of Benaiah,
who were leaders among the people.
2The Spirit said to me, "Son of man, these
are the men who are planning evil and
giving wicked counsel in this city. 3They
say to the people, 'Is it not a good time to
build houses? This city is like an iron pot.
We are safe inside it like meat in a pot.*'
4Therefore, son of man, prophesy against
them loudly and clearly."
5Then the Spirit of the LORD came upon
me, and he told me to say, "This is what the
LORD says to the people of Israel: I know
what you are saying, for I know every
thought that comes into your minds. 6You
have murdered many in this city and filled
its streets with the dead.
7"Therefore, this is what the Sovereign
LORD says: This city is an iron pot all right,
but the pieces of meat are the victims of
your injustice. As for you, I will soon drag
you from this pot. 8I will bring on you the
sword of war you so greatly fear, says the
Sovereign LORD. 9I will drive you out of Jerusalem and hand you over to foreigners, who
will carry out my judgments against you.
10You will be slaughtered all the way to the

borders of Israel. I will execute judgment on
you, and you will know that I am the LORD.
11 No, this city will not be an iron pot for you,
and you will not be like meat safe inside it.
I will judge you even to the borders of Israel,
12 and you will know that I am the LORD. For
you have refused to obey my decrees and
regulations; instead, you have copied the
standards of the nations around you."

13 While I was still prophesying, Pelatiah
son of Benaiah suddenly died. Then I fell
face down on the ground and cried out,
"O Sovereign LORD, are you going to kill
everyone in Israel?"

Hope for Exiled Israel

14 Then this message came to me from the
LORD: 15 "Son of man, the people still left in
Jerusalem are talking about you and your
relatives and all the people of Israel who
are in exile. They are saying, 'Those people
are far away from the LORD, so now he has
given their land to us!'

16 "Therefore, tell the exiles, 'This is what
the Sovereign LORD says: Although I have
scattered you in the countries of the world,
I will be a sanctuary to you during your time
in exile. 17 I, the Sovereign LORD, will gather
you back from the nations where you have
been scattered, and I will give you the land
of Israel once again.'

18 "When the people return to their homeland, they will remove every trace of their
vile images and detestable idols. 19 And
I will give them singleness of heart and put
a new spirit within them. I will take away
their stony, stubborn heart and give them
a tender, responsive heart,* 20 so they will
obey my decrees and regulations. Then
they will truly be my people, and I will be
their God. 21 But as for those who long for
vile images and detestable idols, I will repay
them fully for their sins. I, the Sovereign
LORD, have spoken!"

The LORD's Glory Leaves Jerusalem

22 Then the cherubim lifted their wings and
rose into the air with their wheels beside
them, and the glory of the God of Israel
hovered above them. 23 Then the glory of
the LORD went up from the city and stopped
above the mountain to the east.

24 Afterward the Spirit of God carried me
back again to Babylonia,* to the people in
exile there. And so ended the vision of my
visit to Jerusalem. 25 And I told the exiles
everything the LORD had shown me.

Signs of the Coming Exile

12 Again a message came to me from the
LORD: 2 "Son of man, you live among
rebels who have eyes but refuse to see. They
have ears but refuse to hear. For they are a
rebellious people.

3 "So now, son of man, pretend you are
being sent into exile. Pack the few items an
exile could carry, and leave your home to go
somewhere else. Do this right in front of the
people so they can see you. For perhaps they

10:5 Hebrew *El-Shaddai*. **10:14** Hebrew *the face of a cherub*; compare 1:10. **11:3** Hebrew *This city is the pot, and we are the meat*. **11:19** Hebrew *a heart of flesh*. **11:24** Or *Chaldea*.

The heart

Nowadays we use the heart as an image of affection ("I love you with all my heart"). But in Bible times the heart spoke of something different. It was seen as the governing center of the whole of life—your character, personality, mind, will, everything. That is why Proverbs says, "Guard your heart above all else, for it determines the course of your life" (Proverbs 4:23). The heart was what made you "you." And that is why God promised here, "I will give them singleness of heart and put a new spirit within them. I will take away their stony, stubborn heart and give them a tender, responsive heart" (Ezekiel 11:19)—in other words, he promised to remake people from the inside out. Later, Ezekiel prophesied how God would do this: It would be by the work of his Spirit (36:25-27)—something Jeremiah saw would only be possible when God made his new covenant with people (Jeremiah 31:31-33), which the New Testament tells us happened in Jesus.

▸ *See also* ***Hardness of heart****, page 1132;* ***The new birth****, page 1203.*

will pay attention to this, even though they
are such rebels. 4Bring your baggage outside
during the day so they can watch you. Then
in the evening, as they are watching, leave
your house as captives do when they begin
a long march to distant lands. 5Dig a hole
through the wall while they are watching
and go out through it. 6As they watch, lift
your pack to your shoulders and walk away
into the night. Cover your face so you cannot
see the land you are leaving. For I have made
you a sign for the people of Israel."

7So I did as I was told. In broad daylight
I brought my pack outside, filled with the
things I might carry into exile. Then in the
evening while the people looked on, I dug
through the wall with my hands and went
out into the night with my pack on my
shoulder.

8The next morning this message came
to me from the LORD: 9"Son of man, these
rebels, the people of Israel, have asked you
what all this means. 10Say to them, 'This
is what the Sovereign LORD says: These
actions contain a message for King Zedekiah in Jerusalem* and for all the people of
Israel.' 11Explain that your actions are a sign
to show what will soon happen to them, for
they will be driven into exile as captives.

12"Even Zedekiah will leave Jerusalem at
night through a hole in the wall, taking only
what he can carry with him. He will cover his
face, and his eyes will not see the land he is
leaving. 13Then I will throw my net over him
and capture him in my snare. I will bring him
to Babylon, the land of the Babylonians,*
though he will never see it, and he will die
there. 14I will scatter his servants and warriors
to the four winds and send the sword after
them. 15And when I scatter them among the
nations, they will know that I am the LORD.
16But I will spare a few of them from death by
war, famine, or disease, so they can confess
all their detestable sins to their captors. Then
they will know that I am the LORD."

17Then this message came to me from
the LORD: 18"Son of man, tremble as you
eat your food. Shake with fear as you
drink your water. 19Tell the people, 'This is
what the Sovereign LORD says concerning
those living in Israel and Jerusalem: They
will eat their food with trembling and sip
their water in despair, for their land will
be stripped bare because of their violence.
20The cities will be destroyed and the farmland made desolate. Then you will know
that I am the LORD.'"

A New Proverb for Israel

21Again a message came to me from the LORD:
22"Son of man, you've heard that proverb they
quote in Israel: 'Time passes, and prophecies
come to nothing.' 23Tell the people, 'This is
what the Sovereign LORD says: I will put an
end to this proverb, and you will soon stop
quoting it.' Now give them this new proverb
to replace the old one: 'The time has come for
every prophecy to be fulfilled!'

24"There will be no more false visions and
flattering predictions in Israel. 25For I am the
LORD! If I say it, it will happen. There will be
no more delays, you rebels of Israel. I will
fulfill my threat of destruction in your own
lifetime. I, the Sovereign LORD, have spoken!"

26Then this message came to me from the
LORD: 27"Son of man, the people of Israel
are saying, 'He's talking about the distant
future. His visions won't come true for a
long, long time.' 28Therefore, tell them, 'This
is what the Sovereign LORD says: No more
delay! I will now do everything I have threatened. I, the Sovereign LORD, have spoken!'"

Judgment against False Prophets

13 Then this message came to me from
the LORD: 2"Son of man, prophesy
against the false prophets of Israel who
are inventing their own prophecies. Say to
them, 'Listen to the word of the LORD. 3This
is what the Sovereign LORD says: What
sorrow awaits the false prophets who are
following their own imaginations and have
seen nothing at all!'

4"O people of Israel, these prophets of
yours are like jackals digging in the ruins.
5They have done nothing to repair the
breaks in the walls around the nation. They
have not helped it to stand firm in battle
on the day of the LORD. 6Instead, they have
told lies and made false predictions. They
say, 'This message is from the LORD,' even
though the LORD never sent them. And yet
they expect him to fulfill their prophecies!
7Can your visions be anything but false if

▸ **13:5** *See **The day of the LORD**, page 988.*

you claim, ‘This message is from the LORD,’
when I have not even spoken to you?
[8]“Therefore, this is what the Sovereign
LORD says: Because what you say is false
and your visions are a lie, I will stand
against you, says the Sovereign LORD. [9]I will
raise my fist against all the prophets who
see false visions and make lying predictions, and they will be banished from the
community of Israel. I will blot their names
from Israel’s record books, and they will
never again set foot in their own land. Then
you will know that I am the Sovereign LORD.
[10]“This will happen because these evil
prophets deceive my people by saying, ‘All is
peaceful’ when there is no peace at all! It’s
as if the people have built a flimsy wall, and
these prophets are trying to reinforce it by
covering it with whitewash! [11]Tell these white-
washers that their wall will soon fall down. A
heavy rainstorm will undermine it; great hailstones and mighty winds will knock it down.
[12]And when the wall falls, the people will cry
out, ‘What happened to your whitewash?’
[13]“Therefore, this is what the Sovereign
LORD says: I will sweep away your whitewashed wall with a storm of indignation,
with a great flood of anger, and with hailstones of fury. [14]I will break down your wall
right to its foundation, and when it falls, it
will crush you. Then you will know that I
am the LORD. [15]At last my anger against the
wall and those who covered it with whitewash will be satisfied. Then I will say to
you: ‘The wall and those who whitewashed
it are both gone. [16]They were lying prophets
who claimed peace would come to Jerusalem when there was no peace. I, the Sovereign LORD, have spoken!’

Judgment against False Women Prophets

[17]“Now, son of man, speak out against the
women who prophesy from their own imaginations. [18]This is what the Sovereign LORD
says: What sorrow awaits you women who
are ensnaring the souls of my people, young
and old alike. You tie magic charms on their
wrists and furnish them with magic veils. Do
you think you can trap others without bringing destruction on yourselves? [19]You bring
shame on me among my people for a few
handfuls of barley or a piece of bread. By
lying to my people who love to listen to lies,
you kill those who should not die, and you
promise life to those who should not live.
[20]“This is what the Sovereign LORD says:
I am against all your magic charms, which
you use to ensnare my people like birds.
I will tear them from your arms, setting
my people free like birds set free from a

12:10 Hebrew *the prince in Jerusalem;* similarly in 12:12. **12:13** Or *Chaldeans.*

False prophecy

The Old Testament prophets often attacked other so-called prophets who were not called by God (e.g., Ezekiel 13:10). These false prophets lulled people into a false sense of security, saying only what people wanted to hear. Their messages offended no one, and they scorned the true prophets for upsetting people with their warnings of judgment. Of course, this meant that the people were faced with conflicting messages and voices. Inevitably, most of them took the easier message, which seemed to allow them to continue living as they were. But the message of true prophets like Ezekiel was, “Get real! You will reap what you sow unless you change.” A true messenger of God will always disturb us when we’re in the wrong.

Moses had given very clear and simple guidelines for discerning true and false prophets (Deuteronomy 18:17-22): The words of a true prophet will come to pass, while those of a false prophet won’t. The false prophet is characterized by making up his prophecy or speaking it in the name of another god, and such prophets were to be stoned to death. But prophets whose word was not intentionally misleading but simply wrong were not to be stoned; their word was simply to be ignored.

▶ *See also* ***Prophecy in the Old Testament****, page 903.*

cage. 21I will tear off the magic veils and save my people from your grasp. They will no longer be your victims. Then you will know that I am the LORD. 22You have discouraged the righteous with your lies, but I didn't want them to be sad. And you have encouraged the wicked by promising them life, even though they continue in their sins. 23Because of all this, you will no longer talk of seeing visions that you never saw, nor will you make predictions. For I will rescue my people from your grasp. Then you will know that I am the LORD."

The Idolatry of Israel's Leaders

14 Then some of the leaders of Israel visited me, and while they were sitting with me, 2this message came to me from the LORD: 3"Son of man, these leaders have set up idols* in their hearts. They have embraced things that will make them fall into sin. Why should I listen to their requests? 4Tell them, 'This is what the Sovereign LORD says: The people of Israel have set up idols in their hearts and fallen into sin, and then they go to a prophet asking for a message. So I, the LORD, will give them the kind of answer their great idolatry deserves. 5I will do this to capture the minds and hearts of all my people who have turned from me to worship their detestable idols.'

6"Therefore, tell the people of Israel, 'This is what the Sovereign LORD says: Repent and turn away from your idols, and stop all your detestable sins. 7I, the LORD, will answer all those, both Israelites and foreigners, who reject me and set up idols in their hearts and so fall into sin, and who then come to a prophet asking for my advice. 8I will turn against such people and make a terrible example of them, eliminating them from among my people. Then you will know that I am the LORD.

9"'And if a prophet is deceived into giving a message, it is because I, the LORD, have deceived that prophet. I will lift my fist against such prophets and cut them off from the community of Israel. 10False prophets and those who seek their guidance will all be punished for their sins. 11In this way, the people of Israel will learn not to stray from me, polluting themselves with sin. They will be my people, and I will be their God. I, the Sovereign LORD, have spoken!'"

The Certainty of the LORD's Judgment

12Then this message came to me from the LORD: 13"Son of man, suppose the people of a country were to sin against me, and I lifted my fist to crush them, cutting off their food supply and sending a famine to destroy both people and animals. 14Even if Noah, Daniel, and Job were there, their righteousness would save no one but themselves, says the Sovereign LORD.

15"Or suppose I were to send wild animals to invade the country, kill the people, and make the land too desolate and dangerous to pass through. 16As surely as I live, says the Sovereign LORD, even if those three men were there, they wouldn't be able to save their own sons or daughters. They alone would be saved, but the land would be made desolate.

17"Or suppose I were to bring war against the land, and I sent enemy armies to destroy both people and animals. 18As surely as I live, says the Sovereign LORD, even if those three men were there, they wouldn't be able to save their own sons or daughters. They alone would be saved.

19"Or suppose I were to pour out my fury by sending an epidemic into the land, and the disease killed people and animals alike. 20As surely as I live, says the Sovereign LORD, even if Noah, Daniel, and Job were there, they wouldn't be able to save their own sons or daughters. They alone would be saved by their righteousness.

21"Now this is what the Sovereign LORD says: How terrible it will be when all four of these dreadful punishments fall upon Jerusalem—war, famine, wild animals, and disease—destroying all her people and animals. 22Yet there will be survivors, and they will come here to join you as exiles in Babylon. You will see with your own eyes how wicked they are, and then you will feel better about what I have done to Jerusalem. 23When you meet them and see their behavior, you will understand that these things are not being done to Israel without cause. I, the Sovereign LORD, have spoken!"

Jerusalem—a Useless Vine

15 Then this message came to me from the LORD: 2"Son of man, how does a grapevine compare to a tree? Is a vine's wood as useful as the wood of a tree? 3Can its wood be used for making things, like pegs to hang up pots and pans? 4No, it can only be used for fuel, and even as fuel, it burns too quickly. 5Vines are useless both before and after being put into the fire!

6"And this is what the Sovereign LORD says: The people of Jerusalem are like grapevines growing among the trees of the forest. Since they are useless, I have thrown them on the fire to be burned. 7And I will see to it that if they escape from one fire, they will fall into another. When I turn against them, you will know that I am the LORD. 8And I will make the land desolate because my people have been unfaithful to me. I, the Sovereign LORD, have spoken!"

Jerusalem—an Unfaithful Wife

16 Then another message came to me from the LORD: 2"Son of man, confront Jerusalem with her detestable sins. 3Give her this message from the Sovereign LORD: You are nothing but a Canaanite! Your father was an Amorite and your mother a Hittite. 4On the day you were born, no one cared about you. Your umbilical cord was not cut, and you were never washed, rubbed with salt, and wrapped in cloth. 5No one had the slightest interest in you; no one pitied you or cared for you. On the day you were born, you were unwanted, dumped in a field and left to die.

6"But I came by and saw you there, helplessly kicking about in your own blood. As you lay there, I said, 'Live!' 7And I helped you to thrive like a plant in the field. You grew up and became a beautiful jewel. Your breasts became full, and your body hair grew, but you were still naked. 8And when I passed by again, I saw that you were old enough for love. So I wrapped my cloak around you to cover your nakedness and declared my marriage vows. I made a covenant with you, says the Sovereign LORD, and you became mine.

9"Then I bathed you and washed off your blood, and I rubbed fragrant oils into your skin. 10I gave you expensive clothing of fine linen and silk, beautifully embroidered, and sandals made of fine goatskin leather. 11I gave you lovely jewelry, bracelets, beautiful necklaces, 12a ring for your nose, earrings for your ears, and a lovely crown for your head. 13And so you were adorned with gold and silver. Your clothes were made of fine linen and costly fabric and were beautifully embroidered. You ate the finest foods—choice flour, honey, and olive oil—and became more beautiful than ever. You looked like a queen, and so you were! 14Your fame soon spread throughout the world because of your beauty. I dressed you in my splendor and perfected your beauty, says the Sovereign LORD.

15"But you thought your fame and beauty were your own. So you gave yourself as a prostitute to every man who came along. Your beauty was theirs for the asking. 16You used the lovely things I gave you to make shrines for idols, where you played the prostitute. Unbelievable! How could such a thing

14:3 The Hebrew term (literally *round things*) probably alludes to dung; also in 14:4, 5, 6, 7.

Grapevines and vineyards

Grapevines were a precious crop, sometimes grown alone alongside the home and sometimes in vineyards. Their grapes were either pressed to produce wine or dried in the sun to produce raisins. With its sunny slopes, Israel was an ideal place for vine cultivation, and one of the first things that Moses' scouts brought back from the Promised Land was a branch so heavy with grapes that it needed two men to carry it (Numbers 13:17-24).

The vine quickly became one of Israel's national symbols, and God often spoke of Israel as his vine or vineyard that he lovingly tended (see Isaiah 5:1-7; Jeremiah 12:10; Ezekiel 19:10-14). But here in Ezekiel 15, the image is turned on its head: Instead of a fruitful, cultivated vine, Jerusalem is like a wild vine in the forest, useless even for fuel—a picture of the failure of God's people to live out the identity he intended for them. Jesus saw himself as "the true grapevine"—the true Israel—and called his followers to stay close to him and draw life from him just as a vine branch does from its stem, assuring us that if we do, we will produce much fruit (John 15:1-8).

ever happen? [17]You took the very jewels and gold and silver ornaments I had given you and made statues of men and worshiped them. This is adultery against me! [18]You used the beautifully embroidered clothes I gave you to dress your idols. Then you used my special oil and my incense to worship them. [19]Imagine it! You set before them as a sacrifice the choice flour, olive oil, and honey I had given you, says the Sovereign LORD.

[20]"Then you took your sons and daughters—the children you had borne to me—and sacrificed them to your gods. Was your prostitution not enough? [21]Must you also slaughter my children by sacrificing them to idols? [22]In all your years of adultery and detestable sin, you have not once remembered the days long ago when you lay naked in a field, kicking about in your own blood.

[23]"What sorrow awaits you, says the Sovereign LORD. In addition to all your other wickedness, [24]you built a pagan shrine and put altars to idols in every town square. [25]On every street corner you defiled your beauty, offering your body to every passerby in an endless stream of prostitution. [26]Then you added lustful Egypt to your lovers, provoking my anger with your increasing promiscuity. [27]That is why I struck you with my fist and reduced your boundaries. I handed you over to your enemies, the Philistines, and even they were shocked by your lewd conduct. [28]You have prostituted yourself with the Assyrians, too. It seems you can never find enough new lovers! And after your prostitution there, you still were not satisfied. [29]You added to your lovers by embracing Babylonia,* the land of merchants, but you still weren't satisfied.

[30]"What a sick heart you have, says the Sovereign LORD, to do such things as these, acting like a shameless prostitute. [31]You build your pagan shrines on every street corner and your altars to idols in every square. In fact, you have been worse than a prostitute, so eager for sin that you have not even demanded payment. [32]Yes, you are an adulterous wife who takes in strangers instead of her own husband. [33]Prostitutes charge for their services—but not you! You give gifts to your lovers, bribing them to come and have sex with you. [34]So you are the opposite of other prostitutes. You pay your lovers instead of their paying you!

Judgment on Jerusalem's Prostitution

[35]"Therefore, you prostitute, listen to this message from the LORD! [36]This is what the Sovereign LORD says: Because you have poured out your lust and exposed yourself in prostitution to all your lovers, and because you have worshiped detestable idols,* and because you have slaughtered your children as sacrifices to your gods, [37]this is what I am going to do. I will gather together all your allies—the lovers with whom you have sinned, both those you loved and those you hated—and I will strip you naked in front of them so they can stare at you. [38]I will punish you for your murder and adultery. I will cover you with blood in my jealous fury. [39]Then I will give you to these many nations who are your lovers, and they will destroy you. They will knock down your pagan shrines and the altars to your idols. They will strip you and take your beautiful jewels, leaving you stark naked. [40]They will band together in a mob to stone you and cut you up with swords. [41]They will burn your homes and punish you in front of many women. I will stop your prostitution and end your payments to your many lovers.

[42]"Then at last my fury against you will be spent, and my jealous anger will subside. I will be calm and will not be angry with you anymore. [43]But first, because you have not remembered your youth but have angered me by doing all these evil things, I will fully repay you for all of your sins, says the Sovereign LORD. For you have added lewd acts to all your detestable sins. [44]Everyone who makes up proverbs will say of you, 'Like mother, like daughter.' [45]For your mother loathed her husband and her children, and so do you. And you are exactly like your sisters, for they despised their husbands and their children. Truly your mother was a Hittite and your father an Amorite.

[46]"Your older sister was Samaria, who lived with her daughters in the north. Your younger sister was Sodom, who lived with her daughters in the south. [47]But you have not merely sinned as they did. You quickly surpassed them in corruption. [48]As surely as I live, says the Sovereign LORD, Sodom and her daughters were never as wicked

as you and your daughters. 49 Sodom's sins
were pride, gluttony, and laziness, while the
poor and needy suffered outside her door.
50 She was proud and committed detestable
sins, so I wiped her out, as you have seen.*
51 "Even Samaria did not commit half your
sins. You have done far more detestable
things than your sisters ever did. They seem
righteous compared to you. 52 Shame on
you! Your sins are so terrible that you make
your sisters seem righteous, even virtuous.
53 "But someday I will restore the fortunes
of Sodom and Samaria, and I will restore
you, too. 54 Then you will be truly ashamed
of everything you have done, for your sins
make them feel good in comparison. 55 Yes,
your sisters, Sodom and Samaria, and all
their people will be restored, and at that
time you also will be restored. 56 In your
proud days you held Sodom in contempt.
57 But now your greater wickedness has been
exposed to all the world, and you are the
one who is scorned—by Edom* and all her
neighbors and by Philistia. 58 This is your
punishment for all your lewdness and detestable sins, says the LORD.
59 "Now this is what the Sovereign LORD
says: I will give you what you deserve, for
you have taken your solemn vows lightly by
breaking your covenant. 60 Yet I will remember the covenant I made with you when you
were young, and I will establish an everlasting covenant with you. 61 Then you will
remember with shame all the evil you have
done. I will make your sisters, Samaria and
Sodom, to be your daughters, even though
they are not part of our covenant. 62 And
I will reaffirm my covenant with you, and
you will know that I am the LORD. 63 You will
remember your sins and cover your mouth
in silent shame when I forgive you of all that
you have done. I, the Sovereign LORD, have
spoken!"

A Story of Two Eagles

17 Then this message came to me from
the LORD: 2 "Son of man, give this
riddle, and tell this story to the people of
Israel. 3 Give them this message from the
Sovereign LORD:

"A great eagle with broad wings and
long feathers,
covered with many-colored plumage,
came to Lebanon.
He seized the top of a cedar tree
4 and plucked off its highest branch.
He carried it away to a city filled with
merchants.
He planted it in a city of traders.
5 He also took a seedling from the land
and planted it in fertile soil.
He placed it beside a broad river,
where it could grow like a willow tree.
6 It took root there and
grew into a low, spreading vine.
Its branches turned up toward the
eagle,
and its roots grew down into the
ground.
It produced strong branches
and put out shoots.
7 But then another great eagle came
with broad wings and full plumage.
So the vine now sent its roots and
branches
toward him for water,
8 even though it was already planted in
good soil
and had plenty of water
so it could grow into a splendid vine
and produce rich leaves and luscious
fruit.
9 "So now the Sovereign LORD asks:
Will this vine grow and prosper?
No! I will pull it up, roots and all!
I will cut off its fruit
and let its leaves wither and die.
I will pull it up easily
without a strong arm or a large army.
10 But when the vine is transplanted,
will it thrive?
No, it will wither away
when the east wind blows against it.
It will die in the same good soil
where it had grown so well."

The Riddle Explained

11 Then this message came to me from the
LORD: 12 "Say to these rebels of Israel: Don't
you understand the meaning of this riddle
of the eagles? The king of Babylon came to
Jerusalem, took away her king and princes,
and brought them to Babylon. 13 He made
a treaty with a member of the royal family

16:29 Or *Chaldea*. **16:36** The Hebrew term (literally *round things*) probably alludes to dung. **16:50** As in a few Hebrew manuscripts and Greek version; Masoretic Text reads *as I have seen*. **16:57** As in many Hebrew manuscripts and Syriac version; Masoretic Text reads *Aram*.

and forced him to take an oath of loyalty. He
also exiled Israel's most influential leaders,
14so Israel would not become strong again
and revolt. Only by keeping her treaty with
Babylon could Israel survive.

15"Nevertheless, this man of Israel's royal
family rebelled against Babylon, sending
ambassadors to Egypt to request a great
army and many horses. Can Israel break her
sworn treaties like that and get away with it?
16No! For as surely as I live, says the Sovereign
LORD, the king of Israel will die in Babylon,
the land of the king who put him in power
and whose treaty he disregarded and broke.
17Pharaoh and all his mighty army will fail
to help Israel when the king of Babylon lays
siege to Jerusalem again and destroys many
lives. 18For the king of Israel disregarded his
treaty and broke it after swearing to obey;
therefore, he will not escape.

19"So this is what the Sovereign LORD
says: As surely as I live, I will punish him for
breaking my covenant and disregarding the
solemn oath he made in my name. 20I will
throw my net over him and capture him in
my snare. I will bring him to Babylon and
put him on trial for this treason against me.
21And all his best warriors* will be killed in
battle, and those who survive will be scattered to the four winds. Then you will know
that I, the LORD, have spoken.

22"This is what the Sovereign LORD says:
I will take a branch from the top of a tall
cedar, and I will plant it on the top of
Israel's highest mountain. 23It will become
a majestic cedar, sending forth its branches
and producing seed. Birds of every sort will
nest in it, finding shelter in the shade of
its branches. 24And all the trees will know
that it is I, the LORD, who cuts the tall tree
down and makes the short tree grow tall.
It is I who makes the green tree wither and
gives the dead tree new life. I, the LORD,
have spoken, and I will do what I said!"

The Justice of a Righteous God

18 Then another message came to me
from the LORD: 2"Why do you quote
this proverb concerning the land of Israel:
'The parents have eaten sour grapes, but
their children's mouths pucker at the taste'?
3As surely as I live, says the Sovereign LORD,
you will not quote this proverb anymore in
Israel. 4For all people are mine to judge—
both parents and children alike. And this
is my rule: The person who sins is the one
who will die.

5"Suppose a certain man is righteous and
does what is just and right. 6He does not feast
in the mountains before Israel's idols* or
worship them. He does not commit adultery
or have intercourse with a woman during her
menstrual period. 7He is a merciful creditor,
not keeping the items given as security by
poor debtors. He does not rob the poor but
instead gives food to the hungry and provides clothes for the needy. 8He grants loans
without interest, stays away from injustice,
is honest and fair when judging others, 9and
faithfully obeys my decrees and regulations.
Anyone who does these things is just and
will surely live, says the Sovereign LORD.

10"But suppose that man has a son who
grows up to be a robber or murderer and
refuses to do what is right. 11And that son
does all the evil things his father would
never do—he worships idols on the mountains, commits adultery, 12oppresses the
poor and helpless, steals from debtors by
refusing to let them redeem their security,
worships idols, commits detestable sins,
13and lends money at excessive interest.
Should such a sinful person live? No! He
must die and must take full blame.

14"But suppose that sinful son, in turn,
has a son who sees his father's wickedness
and decides against that kind of life. 15This
son refuses to worship idols on the mountains and does not commit adultery. 16He
does not exploit the poor, but instead is fair
to debtors and does not rob them. He gives
food to the hungry and provides clothes for
the needy. 17He helps the poor,* does not
lend money at interest, and obeys all my
regulations and decrees. Such a person will
not die because of his father's sins; he will
surely live. 18But the father will die for his
many sins—for being cruel, robbing people,
and doing what was clearly wrong among
his people.

19"'What?' you ask. 'Doesn't the child pay
for the parent's sins?' No! For if the child
does what is just and right and keeps my
decrees, that child will surely live. 20The
person who sins is the one who will die. The
child will not be punished for the parent's
sins, and the parent will not be punished
for the child's sins. Righteous people will
be rewarded for their own righteous behavior, and wicked people will be punished

for their own wickedness. [21]But if wicked
people turn away from all their sins and
begin to obey my decrees and do what is
just and right, they will surely live and not
die. [22]All their past sins will be forgotten,
and they will live because of the righteous
things they have done.

[23]"Do you think that I like to see wicked
people die? says the Sovereign LORD. Of
course not! I want them to turn from their
wicked ways and live. [24]However, if righteous people turn from their righteous behavior and start doing sinful things and act
like other sinners, should they be allowed
to live? No, of course not! All their righteous
acts will be forgotten, and they will die for
their sins.

[25]"Yet you say, 'The Lord isn't doing
what's right!' Listen to me, O people of
Israel. Am I the one not doing what's right,
or is it you? [26]When righteous people turn
from their righteous behavior and start
doing sinful things, they will die for it. Yes,
they will die because of their sinful deeds.
[27]And if wicked people turn from their wickedness, obey the law, and do what is just
and right, they will save their lives. [28]They
will live because they thought it over and
decided to turn from their sins. Such people
will not die. [29]And yet the people of Israel
keep saying, 'The Lord isn't doing what's
right!' O people of Israel, it is you who are
not doing what's right, not I.

[30]"Therefore, I will judge each of you,
O people of Israel, according to your actions,
says the Sovereign LORD. Repent, and turn
from your sins. Don't let them destroy you!
[31]Put all your rebellion behind you, and find
yourselves a new heart and a new spirit.
For why should you die, O people of Israel?
[32]I don't want you to die, says the Sovereign
LORD. Turn back and live!

A Funeral Song for Israel's Kings

19 "Sing this funeral song for the princes of Israel:

[2] "What is your mother?
  A lioness among lions!
She lay down among the young lions
  and reared her cubs.
[3] She raised one of her cubs
  to become a strong young lion.
He learned to hunt and devour prey,
  and he became a man-eater.
[4] Then the nations heard about him,
  and he was trapped in their pit.
They led him away with hooks
  to the land of Egypt.

[5] "When the lioness saw
  that her hopes for him were gone,
she took another of her cubs
  and taught him to be a strong young lion.
[6] He prowled among the other lions
  and stood out among them in his strength.
He learned to hunt and devour prey,
  and he, too, became a man-eater.
[7] He demolished fortresses*
  and destroyed their towns and cities.
Their farms were desolated,
  and their crops were destroyed.
The land and its people trembled in fear
  when they heard him roar.
[8] Then the armies of the nations attacked him,
  surrounding him from every direction.
They threw a net over him
  and captured him in their pit.
[9] With hooks, they dragged him into a cage
  and brought him before the king of Babylon.
They held him in captivity,
  so his voice could never again be heard
  on the mountains of Israel.

[10] "Your mother was like a vine
  planted by the water's edge.
It had lush, green foliage
  because of the abundant water.
[11] Its branches became strong—
  strong enough to be a ruler's scepter.
It grew very tall,
  towering above all others.
It stood out because of its height
  and its many lush branches.
[12] But the vine was uprooted in fury
  and thrown down to the ground.
The desert wind dried up its fruit
  and tore off its strong branches,
so that it withered
  and was destroyed by fire.
[13] Now the vine is transplanted to the wilderness,
  where the ground is hard and dry.

17:21 As in many Hebrew manuscripts; Masoretic Text reads *his fleeing warriors.* The meaning is uncertain. **18:6** The Hebrew term (literally *round things*) probably alludes to dung; also in 18:12, 15. **18:17** Greek version reads *He refuses to do evil.* **19:7** As in Greek version; Hebrew reads *He knew widows.*

[14] A fire has burst out from its branches
and devoured its fruit.
Its remaining limbs are not
strong enough to be a ruler's scepter.

"This is a funeral song, and it will be used
in a funeral."

The Rebellion of Israel

20 On August 14,* during the seventh
year of King Jehoiachin's captivity,
some of the leaders of Israel came to request
a message from the LORD. They sat down in
front of me to wait for his reply. [2]Then this
message came to me from the LORD: [3]"Son
of man, tell the leaders of Israel, 'This is
what the Sovereign LORD says: How dare
you come to ask me for a message? As surely
as I live, says the Sovereign LORD, I will tell
you nothing!'

[4]"Son of man, bring charges against them
and condemn them. Make them realize how
detestable the sins of their ancestors really
were. [5]Give them this message from the Sovereign LORD: When I chose Israel—when I revealed myself to the descendants of Jacob in
Egypt—I took a solemn oath that I, the LORD,
would be their God. [6]I took a solemn oath
that day that I would bring them out of Egypt
to a land I had discovered and explored for
them—a good land, a land flowing with milk
and honey, the best of all lands anywhere.
[7]Then I said to them, 'Each of you, get rid
of the vile images you are so obsessed with.
Do not defile yourselves with the idols* of
Egypt, for I am the LORD your God.'

[8]"But they rebelled against me and would
not listen. They did not get rid of the vile
images they were obsessed with, or forsake
the idols of Egypt. Then I threatened to pour
out my fury on them to satisfy my anger
while they were still in Egypt. [9]But I didn't
do it, for I acted to protect the honor of
my name. I would not allow shame to be
brought on my name among the surrounding nations who saw me reveal myself by
bringing the Israelites out of Egypt. [10]So
I brought them out of Egypt and led them
into the wilderness. [11]There I gave them my
decrees and regulations so they could find
life by keeping them. [12]And I gave them my
Sabbath days of rest as a sign between them
and me. It was to remind them that I am the
LORD, who had set them apart to be holy.

[13]"But the people of Israel rebelled against
me, and they refused to obey my decrees
there in the wilderness. They wouldn't
obey my regulations even though obedience would have given them life. They also

The Sabbath

God reminded his people that the Sabbath was both *a gift* and *a sign* (Ezekiel 20:12). At creation when God "rested from all his work," he "blessed the seventh day and declared it holy" (Genesis 2:2-3)—long before he instructed his people to observe the Sabbath day in the Ten Commandments (Exodus 20:8-11). The word "rested" comes from the Hebrew root for "Sabbath." Thus God established the divine pattern for healthy living: six days of work, followed by one day of rest.

But besides being a gift to humanity, the Sabbath was also a *sign* for Israel. "Be careful to keep my Sabbath day, for the Sabbath is a sign of the covenant between me and you from generation to generation. It is given so you may know that I am the LORD" (Exodus 31:13). The Sabbath was one of the external signs that marked Israel out as God's people, and as such it was to be honored. But by Ezekiel's day, people were dishonoring the Sabbath (and therefore dishonoring God) in how they were using it (e.g., Ezekiel 22:8, 26).

By New Testament times, Sabbath-keeping had become burdensome, due to the addition of endless human rules defining what could and couldn't be done. But Jesus reminded people that "the Sabbath was made to meet the needs of people, and not people to meet the requirements of the Sabbath" (Mark 2:27). God's appointed day of rest is meant to bless us, not curse us.

▶ *See also **Sunday**, page 1121.*

violated my Sabbath days. So I threatened to pour out my fury on them, and I made plans to utterly consume them in the wilderness. [14]But again I held back in order to protect the honor of my name before the nations who had seen my power in bringing Israel out of Egypt. [15]But I took a solemn oath against them in the wilderness. I swore I would not bring them into the land I had given them, a land flowing with milk and honey, the most beautiful place on earth. [16]For they had rejected my regulations, refused to follow my decrees, and violated my Sabbath days. Their hearts were given to their idols. [17]Nevertheless, I took pity on them and held back from destroying them in the wilderness.

[18]"Then I warned their children not to follow in their parents' footsteps, defiling themselves with their idols. [19]'I am the LORD your God,' I told them. 'Follow my decrees, pay attention to my regulations, [20]and keep my Sabbath days holy, for they are a sign to remind you that I am the LORD your God.'

[21]"But their children, too, rebelled against me. They refused to keep my decrees and follow my regulations, even though obedience would have given them life. And they also violated my Sabbath days. So again I threatened to pour out my fury on them in the wilderness. [22]Nevertheless, I withdrew my judgment against them to protect the honor of my name before the nations that had seen my power in bringing them out of Egypt. [23]But I took a solemn oath against them in the wilderness. I swore I would scatter them among all the nations [24]because they did not obey my regulations. They scorned my decrees by violating my Sabbath days and longing for the idols of their ancestors. [25]I gave them over to worthless decrees and regulations that would not lead to life. [26]I let them pollute themselves* with the very gifts I had given them, and I allowed them to give their firstborn children as offerings to their gods—so I might devastate them and remind them that I alone am the LORD.

Judgment and Restoration

[27]"Therefore, son of man, give the people of Israel this message from the Sovereign LORD: Your ancestors continued to blaspheme and betray me, [28]for when I brought them into the land I had promised them, they offered sacrifices on every high hill and under every green tree they saw! They roused my fury as they offered up sacrifices to their gods. They brought their perfumes and incense and poured out their liquid offerings to them. [29]I said to them, 'What is this high place where you are going?' (This kind of pagan shrine has been called Bamah—'high place'—ever since.)

[30]"Therefore, give the people of Israel this message from the Sovereign LORD: Do you plan to pollute yourselves just as your ancestors did? Do you intend to keep prostituting yourselves by worshiping vile images? [31]For when you offer gifts to them and give your little children to be burned as sacrifices,* you continue to pollute yourselves with idols to this day. Should I allow you to ask for a message from me, O people of Israel? As surely as I live, says the Sovereign LORD, I will tell you nothing.

[32]"You say, 'We want to be like the nations all around us, who serve idols of wood and stone.' But what you have in mind will never happen. [33]As surely as I live, says the Sovereign LORD, I will rule over you with an iron fist in great anger and with awesome power. [34]And in anger I will reach out with my strong hand and powerful arm, and I will bring you back* from the lands where you are scattered. [35]I will bring you into the wilderness of the nations, and there I will judge you face to face. [36]I will judge you there just as I did your ancestors in the wilderness after bringing them out of Egypt, says the Sovereign LORD. [37]I will examine you carefully and hold you to the terms of the covenant. [38]I will purge you of all those who rebel and revolt against me. I will bring them out of the countries where they are in exile, but they will never enter the land of Israel. Then you will know that I am the LORD.

[39]"As for you, O people of Israel, this is what the Sovereign LORD says: Go right ahead and worship your idols, but sooner or later you will obey me and will stop bringing shame on my holy name by worshiping idols. [40]For on my holy mountain, the great mountain of Israel, says the Sovereign LORD, the people of Israel will someday worship me, and I will accept them. There I will require that

20:1 Hebrew *In the fifth month, on the tenth day,* of the ancient Hebrew lunar calendar. This day was August 14, 591 B.C.; also see note on 1:1. **20:7** The Hebrew term (literally *round things*) probably alludes to dung; also in 20:8, 16, 18, 24, 31, 39. **20:25-26** Or *I gave them worthless decrees and regulations. . . . I polluted them.* **20:31** Or *and make your little children pass through the fire.* **20:34** Greek version reads *I will welcome you.* Compare 2 Cor 6:17.

you bring me all your offerings and choice
gifts and sacrifices. 41When I bring you home
from exile, you will be like a pleasing sacrifice to me. And I will display my holiness
through you as all the nations watch. 42Then
when I have brought you home to the land
I promised with a solemn oath to give to your
ancestors, you will know that I am the LORD.
43You will look back on all the ways you
defiled yourselves and will hate yourselves
because of the evil you have done. 44You will
know that I am the LORD, O people of Israel,
when I have honored my name by treating
you mercifully in spite of your wickedness.
I, the Sovereign LORD, have spoken!"

Judgment against the Negev

45*Then this message came to me from the
LORD: 46"Son of man, turn and face the south*
and speak out against it; prophesy against
the brushlands of the Negev. 47Tell the southern wilderness, 'This is what the Sovereign
LORD says: Hear the word of the LORD! I will
set you on fire, and every tree, both green and
dry, will be burned. The terrible flames will
not be quenched and will scorch everything
from south to north. 48And everyone in the
world will see that I, the LORD, have set this
fire. It will not be put out.'"
49Then I said, "O Sovereign LORD, they are
saying of me, 'He only talks in riddles!'"

The LORD's Sword of Judgment

21 1*Then this message came to me from
the LORD: 2"Son of man, turn and
face Jerusalem and prophesy against Israel
and her sanctuaries. 3Tell her, 'This is what
the LORD says: I am your enemy, O Israel,
and I am about to unsheath my sword to
destroy your people—the righteous and the
wicked alike. 4Yes, I will cut off both the
righteous and the wicked! I will draw my
sword against everyone in the land from
south to north. 5Everyone in the world will
know that I am the LORD. My sword is in my
hand, and it will not return to its sheath
until its work is finished.'
6"Son of man, groan before the people!
Groan before them with bitter anguish and
a broken heart. 7When they ask why you are
groaning, tell them, 'I groan because of the
terrifying news I have heard. When it comes
true, the boldest heart will melt with fear;
all strength will disappear. Every spirit will
faint; strong knees will become as weak as
water. And the Sovereign LORD says: It is
coming! It's on its way!'"
8Then the LORD said to me, 9"Son of man,
give the people this message from the Lord:

"A sword, a sword
  is being sharpened and polished.
10 It is sharpened for terrible slaughter
  and polished to flash like lightning!
Now will you laugh?
  Those far stronger than you have
    fallen beneath its power!*
11 Yes, the sword is now being sharpened
    and polished;
  it is being prepared for the executioner.

12 "Son of man, cry out and wail;
  pound your thighs in anguish,
for that sword will slaughter my people
    and their leaders—
  everyone will die!
13 It will put them all to the test.
  What chance do they have?*
  says the Sovereign LORD.

14 "Son of man, prophesy to them
  and clap your hands.
Then take the sword and brandish
    it twice,
  even three times,
to symbolize the great massacre,
  the great massacre facing them on
    every side.
15 Let their hearts melt with terror,
  for the sword glitters at every gate.
It flashes like lightning
  and is polished for slaughter!
16 O sword, slash to the right,
  then slash to the left,
wherever you will,
  wherever you want.
17 I, too, will clap my hands,
  and I will satisfy my fury.
  I, the LORD, have spoken!"

Omens for Babylon's King

18Then this message came to me from the
LORD: 19"Son of man, make a map and trace
two routes on it for the sword of Babylon's
king to follow. Put a signpost on the road
that comes out of Babylon where the road
forks into two—20one road going to Ammon
and its capital, Rabbah, and the other to
Judah and fortified Jerusalem. 21The king of
Babylon now stands at the fork, uncertain
whether to attack Jerusalem or Rabbah.

He calls his magicians to look for omens.
They cast lots by shaking arrows from the
quiver. They inspect the livers of animal
sacrifices. 22 The omen in his right hand
says, 'Jerusalem!' With battering rams his
soldiers will go against the gates, shouting
for the kill. They will put up siege towers
and build ramps against the walls. 23 The
people of Jerusalem will think it is a false
omen, because of their treaty with the
Babylonians. But the king of Babylon will
remind the people of their rebellion. Then
he will attack and capture them.

24 "Therefore, this is what the Sovereign
LORD says: Again and again you remind me
of your sin and your guilt. You don't even
try to hide it! In everything you do, your sins
are obvious for all to see. So now the time of
your punishment has come!

25 "O you corrupt and wicked prince of
Israel, your final day of reckoning is here!
26 This is what the Sovereign LORD says:

"Take off your jeweled crown,
for the old order changes.
Now the lowly will be exalted,
and the mighty will be brought down.
27 Destruction! Destruction!
I will surely destroy the kingdom.
And it will not be restored until the one appears
who has the right to judge it.
Then I will hand it over to him.

A Message for the Ammonites

28 "And now, son of man, prophesy concerning the Ammonites and their mockery. Give them this message from the Sovereign LORD:

"A sword, a sword
is drawn for your slaughter.
It is polished to destroy,
flashing like lightning!
29 Your prophets have given false visions,
and your fortune-tellers have told lies.
The sword will fall on the necks of the wicked
for whom the day of final reckoning has come.
30 "Now return the sword to its sheath,
for in your own country,
the land of your birth,
I will pass judgment upon you.
31 I will pour out my fury on you
and blow on you with the fire of my anger.
I will hand you over to cruel men
who are skilled in destruction.
32 You will be fuel for the fire,
and your blood will be spilled in your own land.
You will be utterly wiped out,
your memory lost to history,
for I, the LORD, have spoken!"

The Sins of Jerusalem

22 Now this message came to me from
the LORD: 2 "Son of man, are you
ready to judge Jerusalem? Are you ready to
judge this city of murderers? Publicly denounce her detestable sins, 3 and give her
this message from the Sovereign LORD:
O city of murderers, doomed and damned—
city of idols,* filthy and foul—4 you are guilty
because of the blood you have shed. You are
defiled because of the idols you have made.
Your day of destruction has come! You have
reached the end of your years. I will make you
an object of mockery throughout the world.
5 O infamous city, filled with confusion, you
will be mocked by people far and near.

6 "Every leader in Israel who lives within
your walls is bent on murder. 7 Fathers and
mothers are treated with contempt. Foreigners are forced to pay for protection.
Orphans and widows are wronged and oppressed among you. 8 You despise my holy
things and violate my Sabbath days of rest.
9 People accuse others falsely and send
them to their death. You are filled with idol
worshipers and people who do obscene
things. 10 Men sleep with their fathers' wives
and force themselves on women who are
menstruating. 11 Within your walls live men
who commit adultery with their neighbors'
wives, who defile their daughters-in-law, or
who rape their own sisters. 12 There are hired
murderers, loan racketeers, and extortioners everywhere. They never even think of
me and my commands, says the Sovereign
LORD.

13 "But now I clap my hands in indignation
over your dishonest gain and bloodshed.

20:45 Verses 20:45-49 are numbered 21:1-5 in Hebrew text. **20:46** Hebrew *toward Teman.* **21:1** Verses 21:1-32 are numbered 21:6-37 in Hebrew text. **21:10** The meaning of the Hebrew is uncertain. **21:13** The meaning of the Hebrew is uncertain. **22:3** The Hebrew term (literally *round things*) probably alludes to dung; also in 22:4.

14 How strong and courageous will you be
in my day of reckoning? I, the LORD, have
spoken, and I will do what I said. 15 I will
scatter you among the nations and purge
you of your wickedness. 16 And when I have
been dishonored among the nations because
of you,* you will know that I am the LORD."

The LORD's Refining Furnace

17 Then this message came to me from the
LORD: 18 "Son of man, the people of Israel are
the worthless slag that remains after silver is
smelted. They are the dross that is left over—
a useless mixture of copper, tin, iron, and
lead. 19 So tell them, 'This is what the Sovereign LORD says: Because you are all worthless
slag, I will bring you to my crucible in Jerusalem. 20 Just as silver, copper, iron, lead, and tin
are melted down in a furnace, I will melt you
down in the heat of my fury. 21 I will gather
you together and blow the fire of my anger
upon you, 22 and you will melt like silver in
fierce heat. Then you will know that I, the
LORD, have poured out my fury on you.'"

The Sins of Israel's Leaders

23 Again a message came to me from the LORD:
24 "Son of man, give the people of Israel this
message: In the day of my indignation, you
will be like a polluted land, a land without
rain. 25 Your princes* plot conspiracies just
as lions stalk their prey. They devour innocent people, seizing treasures and extorting
wealth. They make many widows in the land.
26 Your priests have violated my instructions
and defiled my holy things. They make no
distinction between what is holy and what is
not. And they do not teach my people the difference between what is ceremonially clean
and unclean. They disregard my Sabbath
days so that I am dishonored among them.
27 Your leaders are like wolves who tear apart
their victims. They actually destroy people's
lives for money! 28 And your prophets cover
up for them by announcing false visions
and making lying predictions. They say,
'My message is from the Sovereign LORD,'
when the LORD hasn't spoken a single word
to them. 29 Even common people oppress the
poor, rob the needy, and deprive foreigners
of justice.

30 "I looked for someone who might rebuild
the wall of righteousness that guards the
land. I searched for someone to stand in the
gap in the wall so I wouldn't have to destroy
the land, but I found no one. 31 So now I will
pour out my fury on them, consuming them
with the fire of my anger. I will heap on their
heads the full penalty for all their sins. I, the
Sovereign LORD, have spoken!"

Prayer as intercession

Part of the prophet's task was to intercede with God on behalf of his people (e.g., Genesis 20:7; 1 Samuel 12:23; Jeremiah 37:3). But rather than do this, Israel's leaders had both sinned and led God's people into sin (Ezekiel 22:24-29). God could not even find one man who would stand in the gap—like a soldier might stand in a breached wall and fight—to defend Judah through prayer (22:30).

Intercession is not praying for ourselves; it is lifting up other people or situations before God in prayer. It is often associated with fasting, which can then lead to a breakthrough—an answer to our prayer and fasting where seemingly unconquerable obstacles suddenly give way. Notable prayers of intercession in the Bible include Moses' prayer for Israel to be spared (Exodus 32:9-14); Hezekiah's prayer for Jerusalem's deliverance (2 Kings 19:14-19); Nehemiah's intercession for Jerusalem (Nehemiah 1); Daniel's intercession for the exile to be ended (Daniel 9:1-19); Jesus' intercession for his disciples (John 17:6-26); and Paul's intercession for the church (Ephesians 1:15-23).

Common topics of intercession in the Bible include family, friends, health and healing, deliverance, spiritual growth, protection, for opportunities to open up, for growth and breakthroughs in the church, and for revival in our nation.

▸ *See also* ***The Lord's Prayer***, *page 1077;* ***Perseverance in prayer***, *page 1184.*

The Adultery of Two Sisters

23 This message came to me from the LORD: 2"Son of man, once there were two sisters who were daughters of the same mother. 3They became prostitutes in Egypt. Even as young girls, they allowed men to fondle their breasts. 4The older girl was named Oholah, and her sister was Oholibah. I married them, and they bore me sons and daughters. I am speaking of Samaria and Jerusalem, for Oholah is Samaria and Oholibah is Jerusalem.

5"Then Oholah lusted after other lovers instead of me, and she gave her love to the Assyrian officers. 6They were all attractive young men, captains and commanders dressed in handsome blue, charioteers driving their horses. 7And so she prostituted herself with the most desirable men of Assyria, worshiping their idols* and defiling herself. 8For when she left Egypt, she did not leave her spirit of prostitution behind. She was still as lewd as in her youth, when the Egyptians slept with her, fondled her breasts, and used her as a prostitute.

9"And so I handed her over to her Assyrian lovers, whom she desired so much. 10They stripped her, took away her children as their slaves, and then killed her. After she received her punishment, her reputation was known to every woman in the land.

11"Yet even though Oholibah saw what had happened to Oholah, her sister, she followed right in her footsteps. And she was even more depraved, abandoning herself to her lust and prostitution. 12She fawned over all the Assyrian officers—those captains and commanders in handsome uniforms, those charioteers driving their horses—all of them attractive young men. 13I saw the way she was going, defiling herself just like her older sister.

14"Then she carried her prostitution even further. She fell in love with pictures that were painted on a wall—pictures of Babylonian* military officers, outfitted in striking red uniforms. 15Handsome belts encircled their waists, and flowing turbans crowned their heads. They were dressed like chariot officers from the land of Babylonia.* 16When she saw these paintings, she longed to give herself to them, so she sent messengers to Babylonia to invite them to come to her. 17So they came and committed adultery with her, defiling her in the bed of love. After being defiled, however, she rejected them in disgust.

18"In the same way, I became disgusted with Oholibah and rejected her, just as I had rejected her sister, because she flaunted herself before them and gave herself to satisfy their lusts. 19Yet she turned to even greater prostitution, remembering her youth when she was a prostitute in Egypt. 20She lusted after lovers with genitals as large as a donkey's and emissions like those of a horse. 21And so, Oholibah, you relived your former days as a young girl in Egypt, when you first allowed your breasts to be fondled.

The LORD's Judgment of Oholibah

22"Therefore, Oholibah, this is what the Sovereign LORD says: I will send your lovers against you from every direction—those very nations from which you turned away in disgust. 23For the Babylonians will come with all the Chaldeans from Pekod and Shoa and Koa. And all the Assyrians will come with them—handsome young captains, commanders, chariot officers, and other high-ranking officers, all riding their horses. 24They will all come against you from the north* with chariots, wagons, and a great army prepared for attack. They will take up positions on every side, surrounding you with men armed with shields and helmets. And I will hand you over to them for punishment so they can do with you as they please. 25I will turn my jealous anger against you, and they will deal harshly with you. They will cut off your nose and ears, and any survivors will then be slaughtered by the sword. Your children will be taken away as captives, and everything that is left will be burned. 26They will strip you of your beautiful clothes and jewels. 27In this way, I will put a stop to the lewdness and prostitution you brought from Egypt. You will never again cast longing eyes on those things or fondly remember your time in Egypt.

28"For this is what the Sovereign LORD says: I will surely hand you over to your enemies, to those you loathe, those you rejected. 29They will treat you with hatred and rob you of all you own, leaving you stark

22:16 As in one Hebrew manuscript and Greek and Syriac versions; Masoretic Text reads *when you have been dishonored among the nations.* **22:25** As in Greek version; Hebrew reads *prophets.* **23:7** The Hebrew term (literally *round things*) probably alludes to dung; also in 23:30, 37, 39, 49. **23:14** Or *Chaldean.* **23:15** Or *Chaldea;* also in 23:16. **23:24** As in Greek version; the meaning of the Hebrew is uncertain.

naked. The shame of your prostitution will
be exposed to all the world. 30 You brought
all this on yourself by prostituting yourself
to other nations, defiling yourself with all
their idols. 31 Because you have followed in
your sister's footsteps, I will force you to
drink the same cup of terror she drank.

32 "Yes, this is what the Sovereign LORD
says:

"You will drink from your sister's cup
of terror,
a cup that is large and deep.
It is filled to the brim
with scorn and derision.
33 Drunkenness and anguish will fill you,
for your cup is filled to the brim with
distress and desolation,
the same cup your sister Samaria
drank.
34 You will drain that cup of terror
to the very bottom.
Then you will smash it to pieces
and beat your breast in anguish.
I, the Sovereign LORD, have spoken!

35 "And because you have forgotten me
and turned your back on me, this is what
the Sovereign LORD says: You must bear
the consequences of all your lewdness and
prostitution."

The LORD's Judgment on Both Sisters

36 The LORD said to me, "Son of man, you
must accuse Oholah and Oholibah of all
their detestable sins. 37 They have committed both adultery and murder—adultery by
worshiping idols and murder by burning
as sacrifices the children they bore to
me. 38 Furthermore, they have defiled my
Temple and violated my Sabbath day! 39 On
the very day that they sacrificed their children to their idols, they boldly came into
my Temple to worship! They came in and
defiled my house.

40 "You sisters sent messengers to distant
lands to get men. Then when they arrived,
you bathed yourselves, painted your eyelids,
and put on your finest jewels for them. 41 You
sat with them on a beautifully embroidered
couch and put my incense and my special
oil on a table that was spread before you.
42 From your room came the sound of many
men carousing. They were lustful men
and drunkards* from the wilderness, who
put bracelets on your wrists and beautiful
crowns on your heads. 43 Then I said, 'If they
really want to have sex with old worn-out
prostitutes like these, let them!' 44 And that
is what they did. They had sex with Oholah
and Oholibah, these shameless prostitutes.
45 But righteous people will judge these sister
cities for what they really are—adulterers
and murderers.

46 "Now this is what the Sovereign LORD
says: Bring an army against them and hand
them over to be terrorized and plundered.
47 For their enemies will stone them and kill
them with swords. They will butcher their
sons and daughters and burn their homes.
48 In this way, I will put an end to lewdness
and idolatry in the land, and my judgment will be a warning to all women not to
follow your wicked example. 49 You will be
fully repaid for all your prostitution—your
worship of idols. Yes, you will suffer the full
penalty. Then you will know that I am the
Sovereign LORD."

The Sign of the Cooking Pot

24 On January 15,* during the ninth
year of King Jehoiachin's captivity,
this message came to me from the LORD:
2 "Son of man, write down today's date,
because on this very day the king of Babylon
is beginning his attack against Jerusalem.
3 Then give these rebels an illustration with
this message from the Sovereign LORD:

"Put a pot on the fire,
and pour in some water.
4 Fill it with choice pieces of meat—
the rump and the shoulder
and all the most tender cuts.
5 Use only the best sheep from the flock,
and heap fuel on the fire beneath the
pot.
Bring the pot to a boil,
and cook the bones along with the
meat.

6 "Now this is what the Sovereign LORD
says:
What sorrow awaits Jerusalem,
the city of murderers!
She is a cooking pot
whose corruption can't be cleaned
out.
Take the meat out in random order,
for no piece is better than another.
7 For the blood of her murders
is splashed on the rocks.

It isn't even spilled on the ground,
where the dust could cover it!
8 So I will splash her blood on a rock
for all to see,
an expression of my anger
and vengeance against her.

9 "This is what the Sovereign LORD says:
What sorrow awaits Jerusalem,
the city of murderers!
I myself will pile up the fuel beneath
her.
10 Yes, heap on the wood!
Let the fire roar to make the pot boil.
Cook the meat with many spices,
and afterward burn the bones.
11 Now set the empty pot on the coals.
Heat it red hot!
Burn away the filth and corruption.
12 But it's hopeless;
the corruption can't be cleaned out.
So throw it into the fire.
13 Your impurity is your lewdness
and the corruption of your idolatry.
I tried to cleanse you,
but you refused.
So now you will remain in your filth
until my fury against you has been
satisfied.

14 "I, the LORD, have spoken! The time has
come, and I won't hold back. I will not change
my mind, and I will have no pity on you. You
will be judged on the basis of all your wicked
actions, says the Sovereign LORD."

The Death of Ezekiel's Wife

15 Then this message came to me from the
LORD: 16 "Son of man, with one blow I will
take away your dearest treasure. Yet you
must not show any sorrow at her death.
Do not weep; let there be no tears. 17 Groan
silently, but let there be no wailing at her
grave. Do not uncover your head or take
off your sandals. Do not perform the usual
rituals of mourning or accept any food
brought to you by consoling friends."

18 So I proclaimed this to the people the
next morning, and in the evening my wife
died. The next morning I did everything
I had been told to do. 19 Then the people
asked, "What does all this mean? What are
you trying to tell us?"

20 So I said to them, "A message came to
me from the LORD, 21 and I was told to give
this message to the people of Israel. This is
what the Sovereign LORD says: I will defile
my Temple, the source of your security and
pride, the place your heart delights in. Your
sons and daughters whom you left behind
in Judah will be slaughtered by the sword.
22 Then you will do as Ezekiel has done. You
will not mourn in public or console yourselves
by eating the food brought by friends. 23 Your
heads will remain covered, and your sandals
will not be taken off. You will not mourn or
weep, but you will waste away because of
your sins. You will groan among yourselves
for all the evil you have done. 24 Ezekiel is an
example for you; you will do just as he has
done. And when that time comes, you will
know that I am the Sovereign LORD."

25 Then the LORD said to me, "Son of man,
on the day I take away their stronghold—
their joy and glory, their heart's desire, their
dearest treasure—I will also take away their
sons and daughters. 26 And on that day a
survivor from Jerusalem will come to you in
Babylon and tell you what has happened.
27 And when he arrives, your voice will suddenly return so you can talk to him, and you
will be a symbol for these people. Then they
will know that I am the LORD."

A Message for Ammon

25 Then this message came to me from
the LORD: 2 "Son of man, turn and
face the land of Ammon and prophesy
against its people. 3 Give the Ammonites
this message from the Sovereign LORD:
Hear the word of the Sovereign LORD!
Because you cheered when my Temple was
defiled, mocked Israel in her desolation,
and laughed at Judah as she went away into
exile, 4 I will allow nomads from the eastern
deserts to overrun your country. They will
set up their camps among you and pitch
their tents on your land. They will harvest
all your fruit and drink the milk from your
livestock. 5 And I will turn the city of Rabbah
into a pasture for camels, and all the land
of the Ammonites into a resting place for
sheep and goats. Then you will know that
I am the LORD.

6 "This is what the Sovereign LORD says:
Because you clapped and danced and
cheered with glee at the destruction of my
people, 7 I will raise my fist of judgment

23:42 Or *Sabeans.* **24:1** Hebrew *On the tenth day of the tenth month,* of the ancient Hebrew lunar calendar. This event occurred on January 15, 588 B.C.; also see note on 1:1.

against you. I will give you as plunder to
many nations. I will cut you off from being
a nation and destroy you completely. Then
you will know that I am the LORD.

A Message for Moab

8“This is what the Sovereign LORD says:
Because the people of Moab* have said
that Judah is just like all the other nations,
9I will open up their eastern flank and wipe
out their glorious frontier towns—Beth-
jeshimoth, Baal-meon, and Kiriathaim.
10And I will hand Moab over to nomads from
the eastern deserts, just as I handed over
Ammon. Yes, the Ammonites will no longer
be counted among the nations. 11In the same
way, I will bring my judgment down on the
Moabites. Then they will know that I am the
LORD.

A Message for Edom

12“This is what the Sovereign LORD says:
The people of Edom have sinned greatly
by avenging themselves against the people
of Judah. 13Therefore, says the Sovereign
LORD, I will raise my fist of judgment
against Edom. I will wipe out its people
and animals with the sword. I will make
a wasteland of everything from Teman to
Dedan. 14I will accomplish this by the hand
of my people of Israel. They will carry out
my vengeance with anger, and Edom will
know that this vengeance is from me. I, the
Sovereign LORD, have spoken!

A Message for Philistia

15“This is what the Sovereign LORD says:
The people of Philistia have acted against
Judah out of bitter revenge and long-
standing contempt. 16Therefore, this is
what the Sovereign LORD says: I will raise
my fist of judgment against the land of the
Philistines. I will wipe out the Kerethites
and utterly destroy the people who live by
the sea. 17I will execute terrible vengeance
against them to punish them for what
they have done. And when I have inflicted
my revenge, they will know that I am the
LORD.”

A Message for Tyre

26 On February 3, during the twelfth
year of King Jehoiachin’s captivity,*
this message came to me from the LORD:
2“Son of man, Tyre has rejoiced over the fall
of Jerusalem, saying, ‘Ha! She who was the
gateway to the rich trade routes to the east
has been broken, and I am the heir! Because
she has been made desolate, I will become
wealthy!’

3“Therefore, this is what the Sovereign
LORD says: I am your enemy, O Tyre, and
I will bring many nations against you, like
the waves of the sea crashing against your
shoreline. 4They will destroy the walls of
Tyre and tear down its towers. I will scrape
away its soil and make it a bare rock! 5It
will be just a rock in the sea, a place for
fishermen to spread their nets, for I have
spoken, says the Sovereign LORD. Tyre will
become the prey of many nations, 6and its
mainland villages will be destroyed by the
sword. Then they will know that I am the
LORD.

7“This is what the Sovereign LORD says:
From the north I will bring King Nebuchadnezzar* of Babylon against Tyre. He is
king of kings and brings his horses, chariots, charioteers, and great army. 8First he
will destroy your mainland villages. Then
he will attack you by building a siege wall,
constructing a ramp, and raising a roof of
shields against you. 9He will pound your
walls with battering rams and demolish
your towers with sledgehammers. 10The
hooves of his horses will choke the city
with dust, and the noise of the charioteers
and chariot wheels will shake your walls as
they storm through your broken gates. 11His
horsemen will trample through every street
in the city. They will butcher your people,
and your strong pillars will topple.

12“They will plunder all your riches and
merchandise and break down your walls.
They will destroy your lovely homes and
dump your stones and timbers and even your
dust into the sea. 13I will stop the music of
your songs. No more will the sound of harps
be heard among your people. 14I will make
your island a bare rock, a place for fishermen to spread their nets. You will never be
rebuilt, for I, the LORD, have spoken. Yes, the
Sovereign LORD has spoken!

The Effect of Tyre’s Destruction

15“This is what the Sovereign LORD says to
Tyre: The whole coastline will tremble at
the sound of your fall, as the screams of the
wounded echo in the continuing slaughter. 16All the seaport rulers will step down

from their thrones and take off their royal
robes and beautiful clothing. They will sit
on the ground trembling with horror at your
destruction. 17 Then they will wail for you,
singing this funeral song:

"O famous island city,
once ruler of the sea,
how you have been destroyed!
Your people, with their naval power,
once spread fear around the world.
18 Now the coastlands tremble at your fall.
The islands are dismayed as you
disappear.

19 "This is what the Sovereign LORD says:
I will make Tyre an uninhabited ruin, like
many others. I will bury you beneath the
terrible waves of enemy attack. Great seas
will swallow you. 20 I will send you to the pit
to join those who descended there long ago.
Your city will lie in ruins, buried beneath
the earth, like those in the pit who have
entered the world of the dead. You will
have no place of respect here in the land
of the living. 21 I will bring you to a terrible
end, and you will exist no more. You will
be looked for, but you will never again be
found. I, the Sovereign LORD, have spoken!"

The End of Tyre's Glory

27 Then this message came to me from
the LORD: 2 "Son of man, sing a
funeral song for Tyre, 3 that mighty gateway
to the sea, the trading center of the world.
Give Tyre this message from the Sovereign
LORD:

"You boasted, O Tyre,
'My beauty is perfect!'
4 You extended your boundaries into the
sea.
Your builders made your beauty
perfect.
5 You were like a great ship
built of the finest cypress from Senir.*
They took a cedar from Lebanon
to make a mast for you.
6 They carved your oars
from the oaks of Bashan.
Your deck of pine from the coasts of
Cyprus*
was inlaid with ivory.
7 Your sails were made of Egypt's finest
linen,
and they flew as a banner above you.
You stood beneath blue and purple
awnings
made bright with dyes from the coasts
of Elishah.
8 Your oarsmen came from Sidon and
Arvad;
your helmsmen were skilled men from
Tyre itself.
9 Wise old craftsmen from Gebal did the
caulking.
Ships from every land came with
goods to barter for your trade.

10 "Men from distant Persia, Lydia, and
Libya* served in your great army. They hung
their shields and helmets on your walls,
giving you great honor. 11 Men from Arvad and
Helech stood on your walls. Your towers were
manned by men from Gammad. Their shields
hung on your walls, completing your beauty.

12 "Tarshish sent merchants to buy your
wares in exchange for silver, iron, tin, and
lead. 13 Merchants from Greece,* Tubal, and
Meshech brought slaves and articles of
bronze to trade with you.

14 "From Beth-togarmah came riding
horses, chariot horses, and mules, all in
exchange for your goods. 15 Merchants came
to you from Dedan.* Numerous coastlands
were your captive markets; they brought
payment in ivory tusks and ebony wood.

16 "Syria* sent merchants to buy your rich
variety of goods. They traded turquoise,
purple dyes, embroidery, fine linen, and
jewelry of coral and rubies. 17 Judah and Israel
traded for your wares, offering wheat from
Minnith, figs,* honey, olive oil, and balm.

18 "Damascus sent merchants to buy your
rich variety of goods, bringing wine from
Helbon and white wool from Zahar. 19 Greeks
from Uzal* came to trade for your merchandise. Wrought iron, cassia, and fragrant
calamus were bartered for your wares.

20 "Dedan sent merchants to trade their
expensive saddle blankets with you. 21 The
Arabians and the princes of Kedar sent merchants to trade lambs and rams and male

25:8 As in Greek version; Hebrew reads *Moab and Seir.* **26:1** Hebrew *In the eleventh year, on the first day of the month,* of the ancient Hebrew lunar calendar year. Since an element is missing in the date formula here, scholars have reconstructed this probable reading: *In the eleventh [month of the twelfth] year, on the first day of the month.* This reading would put this message on February 3, 585 B.C.; also see note on 1:1. **26:7** Hebrew *Nebuchadrezzar,* a variant spelling of Nebuchadnezzar. **27:5** Or *Hermon.* **27:6** Hebrew *Kittim.* **27:10** Hebrew *Paras, Lud, and Put.* **27:13** Hebrew *Javan.* **27:15** Greek version reads *Rhodes.* **27:16** Hebrew *Aram;* some manuscripts read *Edom.* **27:17** The meaning of the Hebrew is uncertain. **27:19** Hebrew *Vedan and Javan from Uzal.* The meaning of the Hebrew is uncertain.

goats in exchange for your goods. [22]The
merchants of Sheba and Raamah came with all kinds of spices, jewels, and gold in exchange for your wares.

[23]"Haran, Canneh, Eden, Sheba, Asshur, and Kilmad came with their merchandise, too. [24]They brought choice fabrics to trade—blue cloth, embroidery, and multicolored carpets rolled up and bound with cords.
[25]The ships of Tarshish were your ocean caravans. Your island warehouse was filled to the brim!

The Destruction of Tyre

26 "But look! Your oarsmen
have taken you into stormy seas!
A mighty eastern gale
has wrecked you in the heart of the sea!
27 Everything is lost—
your riches and wares,
your sailors and pilots,
your ship builders, merchants, and warriors.
On the day of your ruin,
everyone on board sinks into the depths of the sea.
28 Your cities by the sea tremble
as your pilots cry out in terror.
29 All the oarsmen abandon their ships;
the sailors and pilots stand on the shore.
30 They cry aloud over you
and weep bitterly.
They throw dust on their heads
and roll in ashes.
31 They shave their heads in grief for you
and dress themselves in burlap.
They weep for you with bitter anguish
and deep mourning.
32 As they wail and mourn over you,
they sing this sad funeral song:
'Was there ever such a city as Tyre,
now silent at the bottom of the sea?
33 The merchandise you traded
satisfied the desires of many nations.
Kings at the ends of the earth
were enriched by your trade.
34 Now you are a wrecked ship,
broken at the bottom of the sea.
All your merchandise and crew
have gone down with you.
35 All who live along the coastlands
are appalled at your terrible fate.
Their kings are filled with horror
and look on with twisted faces.
36 The merchants among the nations
shake their heads at the sight of you,*
for you have come to a horrible end
and will exist no more.'"

A Message for Tyre's King

28 Then this message came to me from the LORD: [2]"Son of man, give the prince of Tyre this message from the Sovereign LORD:

"In your great pride you claim, 'I am a god!
I sit on a divine throne in the heart of the sea.'

The origins of Satan

Where did Satan come from? After all, if everything God created at the beginning was good, where did evil come from? The short answer is—the Bible doesn't tell us (and whenever it doesn't tell us something, we are wise not to be too dogmatic about it!). But from early times, many Christians have felt that three passages give us some insights into this question. In chapter 28, Ezekiel is prophesying against the king of Tyre when suddenly he moves from describing the king and his pride (Ezekiel 28:1-10) to what seems to be the spiritual power behind him (28:11-19)—one who was "in Eden, the garden of God . . . the mighty angelic guardian . . . blameless in all you did from the day you were created until the day evil was found in you." If this was indeed Satan, then we are being told that, although one of the highest angels, he became proud and rebelled against God. A similar picture is found in Isaiah 14:12-15 and Revelation 12:1-9.

▶ *See also* ***Pride****, page 559;* ***Satan****, page 566.*

But you are only a man and not a god,
though you boast that you are a god.
3 You regard yourself as wiser than Daniel
and think no secret is hidden from you.
4 With your wisdom and understanding
you have amassed great wealth—
gold and silver for your treasuries.
5 Yes, your wisdom has made you very rich,
and your riches have made you very proud.

6 "Therefore, this is what the Sovereign LORD says:
Because you think you are as wise as a god,
7 I will now bring against you a foreign army,
the terror of the nations.
They will draw their swords against your marvelous wisdom
and defile your splendor!
8 They will bring you down to the pit,
and you will die in the heart of the sea,
pierced with many wounds.
9 Will you then boast, 'I am a god!'
to those who kill you?
To them you will be no god
but merely a man!
10 You will die like an outcast*
at the hands of foreigners.
I, the Sovereign LORD, have spoken!"

11 Then this further message came to me
from the LORD: 12 "Son of man, sing this
funeral song for the king of Tyre. Give him
this message from the Sovereign LORD:

"You were the model of perfection,
full of wisdom and exquisite in beauty.
13 You were in Eden,
the garden of God.
Your clothing was adorned with every precious stone*—
red carnelian, pale-green peridot, white moonstone,
blue-green beryl, onyx, green jasper,
blue lapis lazuli, turquoise, and emerald—
all beautifully crafted for you
and set in the finest gold.
They were given to you
on the day you were created.
14 I ordained and anointed you
as the mighty angelic guardian.*
You had access to the holy mountain of God
and walked among the stones of fire.

15 "You were blameless in all you did
from the day you were created
until the day evil was found in you.
16 Your rich commerce led you to violence,
and you sinned.
So I banished you in disgrace
from the mountain of God.
I expelled you, O mighty guardian,
from your place among the stones of fire.
17 Your heart was filled with pride
because of all your beauty.
Your wisdom was corrupted
by your love of splendor.
So I threw you to the ground
and exposed you to the curious gaze of kings.
18 You defiled your sanctuaries
with your many sins and your dishonest trade.
So I brought fire out from within you,
and it consumed you.
I reduced you to ashes on the ground
in the sight of all who were watching.
19 All who knew you are appalled at your fate.
You have come to a terrible end,
and you will exist no more."

A Message for Sidon

20 Then another message came to me from
the LORD: 21 "Son of man, turn and face the
city of Sidon and prophesy against it. 22 Give
the people of Sidon this message from the
Sovereign LORD:

"I am your enemy, O Sidon,
and I will reveal my glory by what I do to you.
When I bring judgment against you
and reveal my holiness among you,
everyone watching will know
that I am the LORD.
23 I will send a plague against you,
and blood will be spilled in your streets.
The attack will come from every direction,

27:36 Hebrew *hiss at you.* **28:10** Hebrew *will die the death of the uncircumcised.* **28:13** The identification of some of these gemstones is uncertain. **28:14** Hebrew *guardian cherub;* similarly in 28:16.

and your people will lie slaughtered
within your walls.
Then everyone will know
that I am the LORD.
24 No longer will Israel's scornful neighbors
prick and tear at her like briers and
thorns.
For then they will know
that I am the Sovereign LORD.

Restoration for Israel

25“This is what the Sovereign LORD says:
The people of Israel will again live in their
own land, the land I gave my servant Jacob.
For I will gather them from the distant lands
where I have scattered them. I will reveal to
the nations of the world my holiness among
my people. 26They will live safely in Israel
and build homes and plant vineyards. And
when I punish the neighboring nations that
treated them with contempt, they will know
that I am the LORD their God.”

A Message for Egypt

29 On January 7,* during the tenth year
of King Jehoiachin's captivity, this
message came to me from the LORD: 2“Son
of man, turn and face Egypt and prophesy
against Pharaoh the king and all the people
of Egypt. 3Give them this message from the
Sovereign LORD:

“I am your enemy, O Pharaoh, king of
Egypt—
you great monster, lurking in the
streams of the Nile.
For you have said, ‘The Nile River is mine;
I made it for myself.’
4 I will put hooks in your jaws
and drag you out on the land
with fish sticking to your scales.
5 I will leave you and all your fish
stranded in the wilderness to die.
You will lie unburied on the open ground,
for I have given you as food to the wild
animals and birds.
6 All the people of Egypt will know that
I am the LORD,
for to Israel you were just a staff made
of reeds.
7 When Israel leaned on you,
you splintered and broke
and stabbed her in the armpit.
When she put her weight on you,
you collapsed, and her legs gave way.

8“Therefore, this is what the Sovereign
LORD says: I will bring an army against
you, O Egypt, and destroy both people and
animals. 9The land of Egypt will become a
desolate wasteland, and the Egyptians will
know that I am the LORD.

“Because you said, ‘The Nile River is
mine; I made it,’ 10I am now the enemy of
both you and your river. I will make the
land of Egypt a totally desolate wasteland,
from Migdol to Aswan, as far south as the
border of Ethiopia.* 11For forty years not a
soul will pass that way, neither people nor
animals. It will be completely uninhabited.
12I will make Egypt desolate, and it will be
surrounded by other desolate nations. Its
cities will be empty and desolate for forty
years, surrounded by other ruined cities.
I will scatter the Egyptians to distant lands.

13“But this is what the Sovereign LORD
also says: At the end of the forty years I will
bring the Egyptians home again from the
nations to which they have been scattered.
14I will restore the prosperity of Egypt and
bring its people back to the land of Pathros
in southern Egypt from which they came.
But Egypt will remain an unimportant,
minor kingdom. 15It will be the lowliest of
all the nations, never again great enough to
rise above its neighbors.

16“Then Israel will no longer be tempted to
trust in Egypt for help. Egypt's shattered condition will remind Israel of how sinful she
was to trust Egypt in earlier days. Then Israel
will know that I am the Sovereign LORD.”

Nebuchadnezzar to Conquer Egypt

17On April 26, the first day of the new year,*
during the twenty-seventh year of King Jehoiachin's captivity, this message came to
me from the LORD: 18“Son of man, the army
of King Nebuchadnezzar* of Babylon fought
so hard against Tyre that the warriors'
heads were rubbed bare and their shoulders
were raw and blistered. Yet Nebuchadnezzar and his army won no plunder to compensate them for all their work. 19Therefore,
this is what the Sovereign LORD says: I will
give the land of Egypt to Nebuchadnezzar,
king of Babylon. He will carry off its wealth,
plundering everything it has so he can pay
his army. 20Yes, I have given him the land
of Egypt as a reward for his work, says the
Sovereign LORD, because he was working
for me when he destroyed Tyre.

[21]"And the day will come when I will cause the ancient glory of Israel to revive,* and then, Ezekiel, your words will be respected. Then they will know that I am the LORD."

A Sad Day for Egypt

30 This is another message that came to me from the LORD: [2]"Son of man, prophesy and give this message from the Sovereign LORD:

"Weep and wail
for that day,
[3] for the terrible day is almost here—
the day of the LORD!
It is a day of clouds and gloom,
a day of despair for the nations.
[4] A sword will come against Egypt,
and those who are slaughtered will
cover the ground.
Its wealth will be carried away
and its foundations destroyed.
The land of Ethiopia* will be ravished.
[5] Ethiopia, Libya, Lydia, all Arabia,*
and all their other allies
will be destroyed in that war.

[6] "For this is what the LORD says:
All of Egypt's allies will fall,
and the pride of her power will end.
From Migdol to Aswan*
they will be slaughtered by the
sword,
says the Sovereign LORD.
[7] Egypt will be desolate,
surrounded by desolate nations,
and its cities will be in ruins,
surrounded by other ruined cities.
[8] And the people of Egypt will know that
I am the LORD
when I have set Egypt on fire
and destroyed all their allies.
[9] At that time I will send swift messengers
in ships
to terrify the complacent Ethiopians.
Great panic will come upon them
on that day of Egypt's certain
destruction.
Watch for it!
It is sure to come!

[10] "For this is what the Sovereign LORD
says:
By the power of King Nebuchadnezzar*
of Babylon,
I will destroy the hordes of Egypt.
[11] He and his armies—the most ruthless of
all—
will be sent to demolish the land.
They will make war against Egypt
until slaughtered Egyptians cover the
ground.
[12] I will dry up the Nile River
and sell the land to wicked men.
I will destroy the land of Egypt and
everything in it
by the hands of foreigners.
I, the LORD, have spoken!

[13] "This is what the Sovereign LORD says:
I will smash the idols* of Egypt
and the images at Memphis.*
There will be no rulers left in Egypt;
terror will sweep the land.
[14] I will destroy southern Egypt,*
set fire to Zoan,
and bring judgment against
Thebes.*
[15] I will pour out my fury on Pelusium,*
the strongest fortress of Egypt,
and I will stamp out
the hordes of Thebes.
[16] Yes, I will set fire to all Egypt!
Pelusium will be racked with pain;
Thebes will be torn apart;
Memphis will live in constant terror.
[17] The young men of Heliopolis and
Bubastis* will die in battle,
and the women* will be taken away
as slaves.
[18] When I come to break the proud
strength of Egypt,
it will be a dark day for Tahpanhes,
too.
A dark cloud will cover Tahpanhes,
and its daughters will be led away as
captives.
[19] And so I will greatly punish Egypt,
and they will know that I am the
LORD."

29:1 Hebrew *On the twelfth day of the tenth month,* of the ancient Hebrew lunar calendar. This event occurred on January 7, 587 B.C.; also see note on 1:1. **29:10** Hebrew *from Migdol to Syene as far as the border of Cush.* **29:17** Hebrew *On the first day of the first month,* of the ancient Hebrew lunar calendar. This event occurred on April 26, 571 B.C.; also see note on 1:1. **29:18** Hebrew *Nebuchadrezzar,* a variant spelling of Nebuchadnezzar; also in 29:19. **29:21** Hebrew *I will cause a horn to sprout for the house of Israel.* **30:4** Hebrew *Cush;* similarly in 30:9. **30:5** Hebrew *Cush, Put, Lud, all Arabia, Cub. Cub* is otherwise unknown and may be another spelling for *Lub* (Libya). **30:6** Hebrew *to Syene.* **30:10** Hebrew *Nebuchadrezzar,* a variant spelling of Nebuchadnezzar. **30:13a** The Hebrew term (literally *round things*) probably alludes to dung. **30:13b** Hebrew *Noph;* also in 30:16. **30:14a** Hebrew *Pathros.* **30:14b** Hebrew *No;* also in 30:15, 16. **30:15** Hebrew *Sin;* also in 30:16. **30:17a** Hebrew *of Awen and Pi-beseth.* **30:17b** Or *and her cities.*

The Broken Arms of Pharaoh

20On April 29,* during the eleventh year of
King Jehoiachin's captivity, this message
came to me from the LORD: 21"Son of man, I
have broken the arm of Pharaoh, the king of
Egypt. His arm has not been put in a cast so
that it may heal. Neither has it been bound
up with a splint to make it strong enough
to hold a sword. 22Therefore, this is what
the Sovereign LORD says: I am the enemy of
Pharaoh, the king of Egypt! I will break both
of his arms—the good arm along with the
broken one—and I will make his sword clatter
to the ground. 23I will scatter the Egyptians
to many lands throughout the world. 24I will
strengthen the arms of Babylon's king and
put my sword in his hand. But I will break
the arms of Pharaoh, king of Egypt, and he
will lie there mortally wounded, groaning
in pain. 25I will strengthen the arms of the
king of Babylon, while the arms of Pharaoh
fall useless to his sides. And when I put my
sword in the hand of Babylon's king and he
brings it against the land of Egypt, Egypt
will know that I am the LORD. 26I will scatter
the Egyptians among the nations, dispers-
ing them throughout the earth. Then they
will know that I am the LORD."

Egypt Compared to Fallen Assyria

31 On June 21,* during the eleventh year
of King Jehoiachin's captivity, this
message came to me from the LORD: 2"Son
of man, give this message to Pharaoh, king
of Egypt, and all his hordes:

"To whom would you compare your
greatness?
3 You are like mighty Assyria,
which was once like a cedar of
Lebanon,
with beautiful branches that cast deep
forest shade
and with its top high among the clouds.
4 Deep springs watered it
and helped it to grow tall and
luxuriant.
The water flowed around it like a river,
streaming to all the trees nearby.
5 This great tree towered high,
higher than all the other trees
around it.
It prospered and grew long thick
branches
because of all the water at its roots.
6 The birds nested in its branches,
and in its shade all the wild animals
gave birth.
All the great nations of the world
lived in its shadow.
7 It was strong and beautiful,
with wide-spreading branches,
for its roots went deep
into abundant water.
8 No other cedar in the garden of God
could rival it.
No cypress had branches to equal it;
no plane tree had boughs to compare.
No tree in the garden of God
came close to it in beauty.
9 Because I made this tree so beautiful,
and gave it such magnificent foliage,
it was the envy of all the other trees of
Eden,
the garden of God.

10"Therefore, this is what the Sovereign
LORD says: Because Egypt* became proud
and arrogant, and because it set itself so
high above the others, with its top reaching
to the clouds, 11I will hand it over to a mighty
nation that will destroy it as its wickedness deserves. I have already discarded it.
12A foreign army—the terror of the nations—
has cut it down and left it fallen on the
ground. Its branches are scattered across
the mountains and valleys and ravines of
the land. All those who lived in its shadow
have gone away and left it lying there.

13 "The birds roost on its fallen trunk,
and the wild animals lie among its
branches.
14 Let the tree of no other nation
proudly exult in its own prosperity,
though it be higher than the clouds
and it be watered from the depths.
For all are doomed to die,
to go down to the depths of the earth.
They will land in the pit
along with everyone else on earth.

15"This is what the Sovereign LORD says:
When Assyria went down to the grave,*
I made the deep springs mourn. I stopped
its rivers and dried up its abundant water.
I clothed Lebanon in black and caused the
trees of the field to wilt. 16I made the nations
shake with fear at the sound of its fall, for
I sent it down to the grave with all the others
who descend to the pit. And all the other

proud trees of Eden, the most beautiful and
the best of Lebanon, the ones whose roots
went deep into the water, took comfort to
find it there with them in the depths of the
earth. 17Its allies, too, were all destroyed and
had passed away. They had gone down to
the grave—all those nations that had lived
in its shade.

18"O Egypt, to which of the trees of Eden
will you compare your strength and glory?
You, too, will be brought down to the
depths with all these other nations. You
will lie there among the outcasts* who have
died by the sword. This will be the fate of
Pharaoh and all his hordes. I, the Sovereign
LORD, have spoken!"

A Warning for Pharaoh

32 On March 3,* during the twelfth year
of King Jehoiachin's captivity, this
message came to me from the LORD: 2"Son
of man, mourn for Pharaoh, king of Egypt,
and give him this message:

"You think of yourself as a strong young
lion among the nations,
but you are really just a sea monster,
heaving around in your own rivers,
stirring up mud with your feet.
3 Therefore, this is what the Sovereign
LORD says:
I will send many people
to catch you in my net
and haul you out of the water.
4 I will leave you stranded on the land to
die.
All the birds of the heavens will land
on you,
and the wild animals of the whole
earth
will gorge themselves on you.
5 I will scatter your flesh on the hills
and fill the valleys with your bones.
6 I will drench the earth with your
gushing blood
all the way to the mountains,
filling the ravines to the brim.
7 When I blot you out,
I will veil the heavens and darken the
stars.
I will cover the sun with a cloud,
and the moon will not give you its light.
8 I will darken the bright stars overhead
and cover your land in darkness.
I, the Sovereign LORD, have spoken!

9"I will disturb many hearts when I bring
news of your downfall to distant nations
you have never seen. 10Yes, I will shock
many lands, and their kings will be terrified at your fate. They will shudder in fear
for their lives as I brandish my sword before
them on the day of your fall. 11For this is
what the Sovereign LORD says:

"The sword of the king of Babylon
will come against you.
12 I will destroy your hordes with the
swords of mighty warriors—
the terror of the nations.
They will shatter the pride of Egypt,
and all its hordes will be destroyed.
13 I will destroy all your flocks and herds
that graze beside the streams.
Never again will people or animals
muddy those waters with their feet.
14 Then I will let the waters of Egypt
become calm again,
and they will flow as smoothly as
olive oil,
says the Sovereign LORD.
15 And when I destroy Egypt
and strip you of everything you own
and strike down all your people,
then you will know that I am the
LORD.
16 Yes, this is the funeral song
they will sing for Egypt.
Let all the nations mourn.
Let them mourn for Egypt and its
hordes.
I, the Sovereign LORD, have spoken!"

Egypt Falls into the Pit

17On March 17,* during the twelfth year,
another message came to me from the
LORD: 18"Son of man, weep for the hordes of
Egypt and for the other mighty nations.* For
I will send them down to the world below in
company with those who descend to the pit.
19Say to them,

30:20 Hebrew *On the seventh day of the first month,* of the ancient Hebrew lunar calendar. This event occurred on April 29, 587 B.C.; also see note on 1:1. **31:1** Hebrew *On the first day of the third month,* of the ancient Hebrew lunar calendar. This event occurred on June 21, 587 B.C.; also see note on 1:1. **31:10** Hebrew *you.* **31:15** Hebrew *to Sheol;* also in 31:16, 17. **31:18** Hebrew *among the uncircumcised.* **32:1** Hebrew *On the first day of the twelfth month,* of the ancient Hebrew lunar calendar. This event occurred on March 3, 585 B.C.; also see note on 1:1. **32:17** Hebrew *On the fifteenth day of the month,* presumably in the twelfth month of the ancient Hebrew lunar calendar (see 32:1). This would put this message at the end of King Jehoiachin's twelfth year of captivity, on March 17, 585 B.C.; also see note on 1:1. Greek version reads *On the fifteenth day of the first month,* which would put this message on April 27, 586 B.C., at the beginning of Jehoiachin's twelfth year. **32:18** The meaning of the Hebrew is uncertain.

'O Egypt, are you lovelier than the other
nations?
No! So go down to the pit and lie there
among the outcasts.*'

20The Egyptians will fall with the many
who have died by the sword, for the sword
is drawn against them. Egypt and its hordes
will be dragged away to their judgment.
21Down in the grave* mighty leaders will
mockingly welcome Egypt and its allies,
saying, 'They have come down; they lie
among the outcasts, hordes slaughtered by
the sword.'

22"Assyria lies there surrounded by the
graves of its army, those who were slaughtered by the sword. 23Their graves are in the
depths of the pit, and they are surrounded
by their allies. They struck terror in the
hearts of people everywhere, but now they
have been slaughtered by the sword.

24"Elam lies there surrounded by the
graves of all its hordes, those who were
slaughtered by the sword. They struck
terror in the hearts of people everywhere,
but now they have descended as outcasts to
the world below. Now they lie in the pit and
share the shame of those who have gone
before them. 25They have a resting place
among the slaughtered, surrounded by the
graves of all their hordes. Yes, they terrorized the nations while they lived, but now
they lie in shame with others in the pit, all
of them outcasts, slaughtered by the sword.

26"Meshech and Tubal are there, surrounded by the graves of all their hordes.
They once struck terror in the hearts of
people everywhere. But now they are outcasts, all slaughtered by the sword. 27They
are not buried in honor like their fallen
heroes, who went down to the grave* with
their weapons—their shields covering their
bodies* and their swords beneath their
heads. Their guilt rests upon them because
they brought terror to everyone while they
were still alive.

28"You too, Egypt, will lie crushed and
broken among the outcasts, all slaughtered
by the sword.

29"Edom is there with its kings and
princes. Mighty as they were, they also lie
among those slaughtered by the sword, with
the outcasts who have gone down to the pit.

30"All the princes of the north and the
Sidonians are there with others who have
died. Once a terror, they have been put
to shame. They lie there as outcasts with
others who were slaughtered by the sword.
They share the shame of all who have descended to the pit.

31"When Pharaoh and his entire army
arrive, he will take comfort that he is not
alone in having his hordes killed, says the
Sovereign LORD. 32Although I have caused
his terror to fall upon all the living, Pharaoh
and his hordes will lie there among the outcasts who were slaughtered by the sword.
I, the Sovereign LORD, have spoken!"

Ezekiel as Israel's Watchman

33 Once again a message came to me
from the LORD: 2"Son of man, give
your people this message: 'When I bring an
army against a country, the people of that
land choose one of their own to be a watchman. 3When the watchman sees the enemy
coming, he sounds the alarm to warn the
people. 4Then if those who hear the alarm
refuse to take action, it is their own fault if
they die. 5They heard the alarm but ignored
it, so the responsibility is theirs. If they had
listened to the warning, they could have
saved their lives. 6But if the watchman sees
the enemy coming and doesn't sound the
alarm to warn the people, he is responsible
for their captivity. They will die in their sins,
but I will hold the watchman responsible
for their deaths.'

7"Now, son of man, I am making you a
watchman for the people of Israel. Therefore, listen to what I say and warn them for
me. 8If I announce that some wicked people
are sure to die and you fail to tell them to
change their ways, then they will die in their
sins, and I will hold you responsible for their
deaths. 9But if you warn them to repent and
they don't repent, they will die in their sins,
but you will have saved yourself.

The Watchman's Message

10"Son of man, give the people of Israel
this message: You are saying, 'Our sins are
heavy upon us; we are wasting away! How
can we survive?' 11As surely as I live, says
the Sovereign LORD, I take no pleasure in
the death of wicked people. I only want
them to turn from their wicked ways so they
can live. Turn! Turn from your wickedness,
O people of Israel! Why should you die?

12"Son of man, give your people this

message: The righteous behavior of righteous people will not save them if they turn to sin, nor will the wicked behavior of wicked people destroy them if they repent and turn from their sins. 13When I tell righteous people that they will live, but then they sin, expecting their past righteousness to save them, then none of their righteous acts will be remembered. I will destroy them for their sins. 14And suppose I tell some wicked people that they will surely die, but then they turn from their sins and do what is just and right. 15For instance, they might give back a debtor's security, return what they have stolen, and obey my life-giving laws, no longer doing what is evil. If they do this, then they will surely live and not die. 16None of their past sins will be brought up again, for they have done what is just and right, and they will surely live.

17"Your people are saying, 'The Lord isn't doing what's right,' but it is they who are not doing what's right. 18For again I say, when righteous people turn away from their righteous behavior and turn to evil, they will die. 19But if wicked people turn from their wickedness and do what is just and right, they will live. 20O people of Israel, you are saying, 'The Lord isn't doing what's right.' But I judge each of you according to your deeds."

Explanation of Jerusalem's Fall

21On January 8,* during the twelfth year of our captivity, a survivor from Jerusalem came to me and said, "The city has fallen!" 22The previous evening the LORD had taken hold of me and given me back my voice. So I was able to speak when this man arrived the next morning.

23Then this message came to me from the LORD: 24"Son of man, the scattered remnants of Israel living among the ruined cities keep saying, 'Abraham was only one man, yet he gained possession of the entire land. We are many; surely the land has been given to us as a possession.' 25So tell these people, 'This is what the Sovereign LORD says: You eat meat with blood in it, you worship idols,* and you murder the innocent. Do you really think the land should be yours? 26Murderers! Idolaters! Adulterers! Should the land belong to you?'

27"Say to them, 'This is what the Sovereign LORD says: As surely as I live, those living in the ruins will die by the sword. And I will send wild animals to eat those living in the open fields. Those hiding in the forts and caves will die of disease. 28I will completely destroy the land and demolish her pride. Her arrogant power will come to an end. The mountains of Israel will be so desolate that no one will even travel through them. 29When I have completely destroyed the land because of their detestable sins, then they will know that I am the LORD.'

30"Son of man, your people talk about you in their houses and whisper about you at the doors. They say to each other, 'Come on, let's go hear the prophet tell us what the LORD is saying!' 31So my people come pretending to be sincere and sit before you. They listen to your words, but they have no intention of doing what you say. Their mouths are full of lustful words, and their hearts seek only after money. 32You are very entertaining to them, like someone who sings love songs with a beautiful voice or plays fine music on an instrument. They hear what you say, but they don't act on it! 33But when all these terrible things happen to them—as they certainly will—then they will know a prophet has been among them."

The Shepherds of Israel

34 Then this message came to me from the LORD: 2"Son of man, prophesy against the shepherds, the leaders of Israel. Give them this message from the Sovereign LORD: What sorrow awaits you shepherds who feed yourselves instead of your flocks. Shouldn't shepherds feed their sheep? 3You drink the milk, wear the wool, and butcher the best animals, but you let your flocks starve. 4You have not taken care of the weak. You have not tended the sick or bound up the injured. You have not gone looking for those who have wandered away and are lost. Instead, you have ruled them with harshness and cruelty. 5So my sheep have been scattered without a shepherd, and they are easy prey for any wild animal. 6They have wandered through all the mountains and all the hills, across the face of the earth, yet no one has gone to search for them.

32:19 Hebrew *the uncircumcised;* also in 32:21, 24, 25, 26, 28, 29, 30, 32. **32:21** Hebrew *in Sheol.* **32:27a** Hebrew *to Sheol.* **32:27b** The meaning of the Hebrew is uncertain. **33:21** Hebrew *On the fifth day of the tenth month,* of the ancient Hebrew lunar calendar. This event occurred on January 8, 585 B.C.; also see note on 1:1. **33:25** The Hebrew term (literally *round things*) probably alludes to dung.

7“Therefore, you shepherds, hear the
word of the LORD: 8As surely as I live, says
the Sovereign LORD, you abandoned my
flock and left them to be attacked by every
wild animal. And though you were my shepherds, you didn’t search for my sheep when
they were lost. You took care of yourselves
and left the sheep to starve. 9Therefore, you
shepherds, hear the word of the LORD. 10This
is what the Sovereign LORD says: I now
consider these shepherds my enemies, and
I will hold them responsible for what has
happened to my flock. I will take away their
right to feed the flock, and I will stop them
from feeding themselves. I will rescue my
flock from their mouths; the sheep will no
longer be their prey.

The Good Shepherd

11“For this is what the Sovereign LORD says:
I myself will search and find my sheep.
12I will be like a shepherd looking for his
scattered flock. I will find my sheep and
rescue them from all the places where they
were scattered on that dark and cloudy
day. 13I will bring them back home to their
own land of Israel from among the peoples
and nations. I will feed them on the mountains of Israel and by the rivers and in all
the places where people live. 14Yes, I will
give them good pastureland on the high
hills of Israel. There they will lie down in
pleasant places and feed in the lush pastures of the hills. 15I myself will tend my
sheep and give them a place to lie down
in peace, says the Sovereign LORD. 16I will
search for my lost ones who strayed away,
and I will bring them safely home again.
I will bandage the injured and strengthen
the weak. But I will destroy those who are
fat and powerful. I will feed them, yes—
feed them justice!

17“And as for you, my flock, this is what
the Sovereign LORD says to his people: I
will judge between one animal of the flock
and another, separating the sheep from the
goats. 18Isn’t it enough for you to keep the
best of the pastures for yourselves? Must
you also trample down the rest? Isn’t it
enough for you to drink clear water for yourselves? Must you also muddy the rest with
your feet? 19Why must my flock eat what you
have trampled down and drink water you
have fouled?

20“Therefore, this is what the Sovereign
LORD says: I will surely judge between the
fat sheep and the scrawny sheep. 21For you
fat sheep pushed and butted and crowded
my sick and hungry flock until you scattered them to distant lands. 22So I will
rescue my flock, and they will no longer be
abused. I will judge between one animal of
the flock and another. 23And I will set over
them one shepherd, my servant David. He
will feed them and be a shepherd to them.
24And I, the LORD, will be their God, and
my servant David will be a prince among
my people. I, the LORD, have spoken!

Shepherds

Shepherds and their flocks were very common in Bible times. Sheep were kept for their wool, though some were used for food or sacrifices; goats were kept for milk. Sheep were kept out on the hills, which meant a shepherd’s life was hard, as Jacob discovered (Genesis 31:40-41). Good shepherds took their work seriously, seeking the sheep when they got lost (Luke 15:4-6) and risking their life for them (John 10:11). Their main tools were the rod (for chasing away wild animals) and the staff (longer, with a curved end) for guiding sheep or rescuing them.

The Bible pictures God as the good shepherd who cares for his sheep (Genesis 48:15; Psalm 23; Isaiah 40:11; Ezekiel 34:7-31), and Jesus used this picture of himself (John 10:1-18), an image the early church retained (Hebrews 13:20; 1 Peter 5:4).

But the great Shepherd of the sheep had also called under-shepherds to care for his people. Their complete failure to reflect God’s heart in this way led Ezekiel to utterly condemn them, but also to prophesy that what they would not do, God himself would one day come and do (Ezekiel 34:11-16).

The LORD's Covenant of Peace

25"I will make a covenant of peace with my
people and drive away the dangerous animals
from the land. Then they will be able to camp
safely in the wildest places and sleep in the
woods without fear. 26I will bless my people
and their homes around my holy hill. And
in the proper season I will send the showers
they need. There will be showers of blessing.
27The orchards and fields of my people will
yield bumper crops, and everyone will live
in safety. When I have broken their chains
of slavery and rescued them from those who
enslaved them, then they will know that
I am the LORD. 28They will no longer be prey
for other nations, and wild animals will no
longer devour them. They will live in safety,
and no one will frighten them.
29"And I will make their land famous for
its crops, so my people will never again
suffer from famines or the insults of foreign
nations. 30In this way, they will know that I,
the LORD their God, am with them. And they
will know that they, the people of Israel, are
my people, says the Sovereign LORD. 31You
are my flock, the sheep of my pasture. You
are my people, and I am your God. I, the
Sovereign LORD, have spoken!"

A Message for Edom

35 Again a message came to me from
the LORD: 2"Son of man, turn and
face Mount Seir, and prophesy against its
people. 3Give them this message from the
Sovereign LORD:

"I am your enemy, O Mount Seir,
and I will raise my fist against you
to destroy you completely.
4 I will demolish your cities
and make you desolate.
Then you will know that I am the LORD.

5"Your eternal hatred for the people of
Israel led you to butcher them when they
were helpless, when I had already punished
them for all their sins. 6As surely as I live,
says the Sovereign LORD, since you show no
distaste for blood, I will give you a blood-
bath of your own. Your turn has come! 7I will
make Mount Seir utterly desolate, killing off
all who try to escape and any who return.
8I will fill your mountains with the dead.
Your hills, your valleys, and your ravines
will be filled with people slaughtered by
the sword. 9I will make you desolate forever.
Your cities will never be rebuilt. Then you
will know that I am the LORD.
10"For you said, 'The lands of Israel and
Judah will be ours. We will take possession
of them. What do we care that the LORD is
there!' 11Therefore, as surely as I live, says
the Sovereign LORD, I will pay back your
angry deeds with my own. I will punish you
for all your acts of anger, envy, and hatred.
And I will make myself known to Israel* by
what I do to you. 12Then you will know that
I, the LORD, have heard every contemptuous
word you spoke against the mountains of
Israel. For you said, 'They are desolate; they
have been given to us as food to eat!' 13In
saying that, you boasted proudly against
me, and I have heard it all!
14"This is what the Sovereign LORD says:
The whole world will rejoice when I make
you desolate. 15You rejoiced at the desolation of Israel's territory. Now I will rejoice at
yours! You will be wiped out, you people of
Mount Seir and all who live in Edom! Then
you will know that I am the LORD.

Restoration for Israel

36 "Son of man, prophesy to Israel's
mountains. Give them this message:
O mountains of Israel, hear the word of the
LORD! 2This is what the Sovereign LORD says:
Your enemies have taunted you, saying,
'Aha! Now the ancient heights belong to us!'
3Therefore, son of man, give the mountains of
Israel this message from the Sovereign LORD:
Your enemies have attacked you from all directions, making you the property of many
nations and the object of much mocking and
slander. 4Therefore, O mountains of Israel,
hear the word of the Sovereign LORD. He
speaks to the hills and mountains, ravines
and valleys, and to ruined wastes and long-
deserted cities that have been destroyed and
mocked by the surrounding nations. 5This is
what the Sovereign LORD says: My jealous
anger burns against these nations, especially
Edom, because they have shown utter contempt for me by gleefully taking my land for
themselves as plunder.
6"Therefore, prophesy to the hills and
mountains, the ravines and valleys of Israel.
This is what the Sovereign LORD says: I am
furious that you have suffered shame before
the surrounding nations. 7Therefore, this is
what the Sovereign LORD says: I have taken

35:11 Hebrew *to them;* Greek version reads *to you.*

a solemn oath that those nations will soon
have their own shame to endure.
8"But the mountains of Israel will produce
heavy crops of fruit for my people—for they
will be coming home again soon! 9See, I care
about you, and I will pay attention to you.
Your ground will be plowed and your crops
planted. 10I will greatly increase the population of Israel, and the ruined cities will be
rebuilt and filled with people. 11I will increase
not only the people, but also your animals.
O mountains of Israel, I will bring people to
live on you once again. I will make you even
more prosperous than you were before. Then
you will know that I am the LORD. 12I will
cause my people to walk on you once again,
and you will be their territory. You will never
again rob them of their children.
13"This is what the Sovereign LORD says:
The other nations taunt you, saying, 'Israel
is a land that devours its own people and
robs them of their children!' 14But you will
never again devour your people or rob
them of their children, says the Sovereign
LORD. 15I will not let you hear those other
nations insult you, and you will no longer
be mocked by them. You will not be a land
that causes its nation to fall, says the Sovereign LORD."
16Then this further message came to me
from the LORD: 17"Son of man, when the
people of Israel were living in their own
land, they defiled it by the evil way they
lived. To me their conduct was as unclean
as a woman's menstrual cloth. 18They polluted the land with murder and the worship
of idols,* so I poured out my fury on them.
19I scattered them to many lands to punish
them for the evil way they had lived. 20But
when they were scattered among the
nations, they brought shame on my holy
name. For the nations said, 'These are the
people of the LORD, but he couldn't keep
them safe in his own land!' 21Then I was
concerned for my holy name, on which my
people brought shame among the nations.
22"Therefore, give the people of Israel
this message from the Sovereign LORD: I am
bringing you back, but not because you
deserve it. I am doing it to protect my holy
name, on which you brought shame while
you were scattered among the nations.
23I will show how holy my great name is—
the name on which you brought shame
among the nations. And when I reveal my
holiness through you before their very eyes,
says the Sovereign LORD, then the nations
will know that I am the LORD. 24For I will
gather you up from all the nations and bring
you home again to your land.
25"Then I will sprinkle clean water on
you, and you will be clean. Your filth will be
washed away, and you will no longer worship
idols. 26And I will give you a new heart, and I
will put a new spirit in you. I will take out your
stony, stubborn heart and give you a tender,
responsive heart.* 27And I will put my Spirit
in you so that you will follow my decrees and
be careful to obey my regulations.
28"And you will live in Israel, the land
I gave your ancestors long ago. You will be
my people, and I will be your God. 29I will
cleanse you of your filthy behavior. I will give
you good crops of grain, and I will send no
more famines on the land. 30I will give you
great harvests from your fruit trees and fields,
and never again will the surrounding nations
be able to scoff at your land for its famines.
31Then you will remember your past sins
and despise yourselves for all the detestable
things you did. 32But remember, says the Sovereign LORD, I am not doing this because you
deserve it. O my people of Israel, you should
be utterly ashamed of all you have done!
33"This is what the Sovereign LORD says:
When I cleanse you from your sins, I will
repopulate your cities, and the ruins will be
rebuilt. 34The fields that used to lie empty
and desolate in plain view of everyone will
again be farmed. 35And when I bring you
back, people will say, 'This former wasteland is now like the Garden of Eden! The
abandoned and ruined cities now have
strong walls and are filled with people!'
36Then the surrounding nations that survive
will know that I, the LORD, have rebuilt the
ruins and replanted the wasteland. For I,
the LORD, have spoken, and I will do what
I say.
37"This is what the Sovereign LORD says:
I am ready to hear Israel's prayers and to
increase their numbers like a flock. 38They
will be as numerous as the sacred flocks
that fill Jerusalem's streets at the time of her

▸ **36:25-27** *See **Covenant**, page 19; **The heart**, page 909.*

festivals. The ruined cities will be crowded
with people once more, and everyone will
know that I am the LORD."

A Valley of Dry Bones

37 The LORD took hold of me, and
I was carried away by the Spirit of
the LORD to a valley filled with bones. 2He
led me all around among the bones that
covered the valley floor. They were scattered everywhere across the ground and
were completely dried out. 3Then he asked
me, "Son of man, can these bones become
living people again?"

"O Sovereign LORD," I replied, "you alone
know the answer to that."

4Then he said to me, "Speak a prophetic
message to these bones and say, 'Dry bones,
listen to the word of the LORD! 5This is what
the Sovereign LORD says: Look! I am going
to put breath into you and make you live
again! 6I will put flesh and muscles on you
and cover you with skin. I will put breath
into you, and you will come to life. Then you
will know that I am the LORD.'"

7So I spoke this message, just as he told
me. Suddenly as I spoke, there was a rattling noise all across the valley. The bones
of each body came together and attached
themselves as complete skeletons. 8Then
as I watched, muscles and flesh formed
over the bones. Then skin formed to cover
their bodies, but they still had no breath
in them.

9Then he said to me, "Speak a prophetic
message to the winds, son of man. Speak
a prophetic message and say, 'This is what
the Sovereign LORD says: Come, O breath,
from the four winds! Breathe into these
dead bodies so they may live again.'"

10So I spoke the message as he commanded me, and breath came into their
bodies. They all came to life and stood up
on their feet—a great army.

11Then he said to me, "Son of man, these
bones represent the people of Israel. They
are saying, 'We have become old, dry
bones—all hope is gone. Our nation is
finished.' 12Therefore, prophesy to them
and say, 'This is what the Sovereign LORD
says: O my people, I will open your graves
of exile and cause you to rise again. Then
I will bring you back to the land of Israel.
13When this happens, O my people, you will
know that I am the LORD. 14I will put my
Spirit in you, and you will live again and
return home to your own land. Then you
will know that I, the LORD, have spoken,
and I have done what I said. Yes, the LORD
has spoken!'"

36:18 The Hebrew term (literally *round things*) probably alludes to dung; also in 36:25. **36:26** Hebrew *a heart of flesh.*

Renewal

In chapters 36 and 37, Ezekiel anticipates two aspects of renewal—the recovery of spiritual life that was once experienced but has now been lost and the renewing of the people of God. Israel had become like a pile of dry bones in a desert, scattered and lifeless, and Ezekiel could not even answer when God asked if they could live again (Ezekiel 37:3). Yet when God's Spirit came upon them, they rattled, moved, formed bodies, and lived again—and then formed a mighty army. Unlikely though it seemed, this was what God would do with his people.

But first a more fundamental renewal needed to take place, as Ezekiel saw in chapter 36—a renewal that would be in people's hearts, a renewal of cleansing and empowering, which would start on the inside and work outward (36:26-27). Ezekiel was seeing nothing less than the promised coming of the fullness of baptism in the Holy Spirit on the day of Pentecost (Acts 1:8; 2:1-4, 16-21). Sadly, Israel's rejection of this inner renewal by the Holy Spirit through faith in Jesus Christ would mean that the renewal of the nation would be shallow and short-lived: The initial positive response to the gospel by Jews (e.g., Acts 2:41; 4:4; 5:12-16) quickly gave way, under pressure from their leaders, to outright opposition (e.g., Acts 4:1-22; 5:17-42; 7:1–8:3). Renewal of our own lives must always precede any longing for renewal in our nation.

Reunion of Israel and Judah

[15]Again a message came to me from the
LORD: [16]"Son of man, take a piece of wood
and carve on it these words: 'This represents Judah and its allied tribes.' Then take
another piece and carve these words on it:
'This represents Ephraim and the northern
tribes of Israel.'* [17]Now hold them together
in your hand as if they were one piece of
wood. [18]When your people ask you what
your actions mean, [19]say to them, 'This is
what the Sovereign LORD says: I will take
Ephraim and the northern tribes and join
them to Judah. I will make them one piece
of wood in my hand.'

[20]"Then hold out the pieces of wood you
have inscribed, so the people can see them.
[21]And give them this message from the
Sovereign LORD: I will gather the people
of Israel from among the nations. I will
bring them home to their own land from
the places where they have been scattered.
[22]I will unify them into one nation on the
mountains of Israel. One king will rule them
all; no longer will they be divided into two
nations or into two kingdoms. [23]They will
never again pollute themselves with their
idols* and vile images and rebellion, for I
will save them from their sinful apostasy.*
I will cleanse them. Then they will truly be
my people, and I will be their God.

[24]"My servant David will be their king,
and they will have only one shepherd. They
will obey my regulations and be careful to
keep my decrees. [25]They will live in the land
I gave my servant Jacob, the land where
their ancestors lived. They and their children and their grandchildren after them
will live there forever, generation after
generation. And my servant David will be
their prince forever. [26]And I will make a covenant of peace with them, an everlasting
covenant. I will give them their land and
increase their numbers,* and I will put my
Temple among them forever. [27]I will make
my home among them. I will be their God,
and they will be my people. [28]And when my
Temple is among them forever, the nations
will know that I am the LORD, who makes
Israel holy."

A Message for Gog

38 This is another message that came
to me from the LORD: [2]"Son of man,
turn and face Gog of the land of Magog,
the prince who rules over the nations of
Meshech and Tubal, and prophesy against
him. [3]Give him this message from the Sovereign LORD: Gog, I am your enemy! [4]I will
turn you around and put hooks in your jaws
to lead you out with your whole army—your
horses and charioteers in full armor and a
great horde armed with shields and swords.
[5]Persia, Ethiopia, and Libya* will join you,
too, with all their weapons. [6]Gomer and all
its armies will also join you, along with the
armies of Beth-togarmah from the distant
north, and many others.

[7]"Get ready; be prepared! Keep all the
armies around you mobilized, and take
command of them. [8]A long time from now
you will be called into action. In the distant
future you will swoop down on the land of
Israel, which will be enjoying peace after recovering from war and after its people have
returned from many lands to the mountains
of Israel. [9]You and all your allies—a vast and
awesome army—will roll down on them like
a storm and cover the land like a cloud.

[10]"This is what the Sovereign LORD says:
At that time evil thoughts will come to your
mind, and you will devise a wicked scheme.
[11]You will say, 'Israel is an unprotected land
filled with unwalled villages! I will march
against her and destroy these people
who live in such confidence! [12]I will go to
those formerly desolate cities that are now
filled with people who have returned from
exile in many nations. I will capture vast
amounts of plunder, for the people are rich
with livestock and other possessions now.
They think the whole world revolves around
them!' [13]But Sheba and Dedan and the merchants of Tarshish will ask, 'Do you really
think the armies you have gathered can
rob them of silver and gold? Do you think
you can drive away their livestock and seize
their goods and carry off plunder?'

[14]"Therefore, son of man, prophesy
against Gog. Give him this message from
the Sovereign LORD: When my people are
living in peace in their land, then you will
rouse yourself.* [15]You will come from your
homeland in the distant north with your
vast cavalry and your mighty army, [16]and
you will attack my people Israel, covering
their land like a cloud. At that time in the
distant future, I will bring you against my
land as everyone watches, and my holiness
will be displayed by what happens to you,

Gog. Then all the nations will know that
I am the LORD.
17“This is what the Sovereign LORD asks:
Are you the one I was talking about long
ago, when I announced through Israel's
prophets that in the future I would bring
you against my people? 18But this is what
the Sovereign LORD says: When Gog invades
the land of Israel, my fury will boil over! 19In
my jealousy and blazing anger, I promise a
mighty shaking in the land of Israel on that
day. 20All living things—the fish in the sea,
the birds of the sky, the animals of the field,
the small animals that scurry along the
ground, and all the people on earth—will
quake in terror at my presence. Mountains
will be thrown down; cliffs will crumble;
walls will fall to the earth. 21I will summon
the sword against you on all the hills of
Israel, says the Sovereign LORD. Your men
will turn their swords against each other.
22I will punish you and your armies with
disease and bloodshed; I will send torrential rain, hailstones, fire, and burning
sulfur! 23In this way, I will show my greatness and holiness, and I will make myself
known to all the nations of the world. Then
they will know that I am the LORD.

The Slaughter of Gog's Hordes

39 “Son of man, prophesy against Gog.
Give him this message from the Sovereign LORD: I am your enemy, O Gog, ruler
of the nations of Meshech and Tubal. 2I will
turn you around and drive you toward the
mountains of Israel, bringing you from the
distant north. 3I will knock the bow from
your left hand and the arrows from your
right hand, and I will leave you helpless.
4You and your army and your allies will all
die on the mountains. I will feed you to the
vultures and wild animals. 5You will fall in
the open fields, for I have spoken, says the
Sovereign LORD. 6And I will rain down fire
on Magog and on all your allies who live
safely on the coasts. Then they will know
that I am the LORD.
7“In this way, I will make known my holy
name among my people of Israel. I will
not let anyone bring shame on it. And the
nations, too, will know that I am the LORD,
the Holy One of Israel. 8That day of judgment will come, says the Sovereign LORD.
Everything will happen just as I have declared it.
9“Then the people in the towns of Israel
will go out and pick up your small and
large shields, bows and arrows, javelins
and spears, and they will use them for fuel.
There will be enough to last them seven
years! 10They won't need to cut wood from
the fields or forests, for these weapons will
give them all the fuel they need. They will
plunder those who planned to plunder
them, and they will rob those who planned
to rob them, says the Sovereign LORD.
11“And I will make a vast graveyard for
Gog and his hordes in the Valley of the Travelers, east of the Dead Sea.* It will block the
way of those who travel there, and they will
change the name of the place to the Valley
of Gog's Hordes. 12It will take seven months
for the people of Israel to bury the bodies
and cleanse the land. 13Everyone in Israel
will help, for it will be a glorious victory for
Israel when I demonstrate my glory on that
day, says the Sovereign LORD.
14“After seven months, teams of men will
be appointed to search the land for skeletons to bury, so the land will be made
clean again. 15Whenever bones are found,
a marker will be set up so the burial crews
will take them to be buried in the Valley of
Gog's Hordes. 16(There will be a town there
named Hamonah, which means ‘horde.’)
And so the land will finally be cleansed.
17“And now, son of man, this is what the
Sovereign LORD says: Call all the birds and
wild animals. Say to them: Gather together
for my great sacrificial feast. Come from far
and near to the mountains of Israel, and
there eat flesh and drink blood! 18Eat the
flesh of mighty men and drink the blood of
princes as though they were rams, lambs,
goats, and bulls—all fattened animals from
Bashan! 19Gorge yourselves with flesh until
you are glutted; drink blood until you are
drunk. This is the sacrificial feast I have prepared for you. 20Feast at my banquet table—
feast on horses and charioteers, on mighty
men and all kinds of valiant warriors, says
the Sovereign LORD.
21“In this way, I will demonstrate my glory

37:16 Hebrew *This is Ephraim's wood, representing Joseph and all the house of Israel;* similarly in 37:19. **37:23a** The Hebrew term (literally *round things*) probably alludes to dung. **37:23b** As in many Hebrew manuscripts and Greek version; Masoretic Text reads *from all their dwelling places where they sinned.* **37:26** Hebrew reads *I will give them and increase their numbers;* Greek version lacks the entire phrase. **38:5** Hebrew *Paras, Cush, and Put.* **38:14** As in Greek version; Hebrew reads *then you will know.* **39:11** Hebrew *the sea.*

to the nations. Everyone will see the punishment I have inflicted on them and the power of my fist when I strike. [22]And from that time on the people of Israel will know that I am the LORD their God. [23]The nations will then know why Israel was sent away to exile—it was punishment for sin, for they were unfaithful to their God. Therefore, I turned away from them and let their enemies destroy them. [24]I turned my face away and punished them because of their defilement and their sins.

Restoration for God's People

[25]"So now, this is what the Sovereign LORD says: I will end the captivity of my people*; I will have mercy on all Israel, for I jealously guard my holy reputation! [26]They will accept responsibility for* their past shame and unfaithfulness after they come home to live in peace in their own land, with no one to bother them. [27]When I bring them home from the lands of their enemies, I will display my holiness among them for all the nations to see. [28]Then my people will know that I am the LORD their God, because I sent them away to exile and brought them home again. I will leave none of my people behind. [29]And I will never again turn my face from them, for I will pour out my Spirit upon the people of Israel. I, the Sovereign LORD, have spoken!"

The New Temple Area

40 On April 28,* during the twenty-fifth year of our captivity—fourteen years after the fall of Jerusalem—the LORD took hold of me. [2]In a vision from God he took me to the land of Israel and set me down on a very high mountain. From there I could see toward the south what appeared to be a city. [3]As he brought me nearer, I saw a man whose face shone like bronze standing beside a gateway entrance. He was holding in his hand a linen measuring cord and a measuring rod.

[4]He said to me, "Son of man, watch and listen. Pay close attention to everything I show you. You have been brought here so I can show you many things. Then you will return to the people of Israel and tell them everything you have seen."

The East Gateway

[5]I could see a wall completely surrounding the Temple area. The man took a measuring rod that was 10½ feet* long and measured the wall, and the wall was 10½ feet* thick and 10½ feet high.

[6]Then he went over to the eastern gateway. He climbed the steps and measured the threshold of the gateway; it was 10½ feet front to back.* [7]There were guard alcoves on each side built into the gateway passage. Each of these alcoves was 10½ feet square, with a distance between them of 8¾ feet* along the passage wall. The gateway's inner threshold, which led to the entry room at the inner end of the gateway passage, was 10½ feet front to back. [8]He also measured the entry room of the gateway.* [9]It was 14 feet* across, with supporting columns 3½ feet* thick. This entry room was at the inner end of the gateway structure, facing toward the Temple.

[10]There were three guard alcoves on each side of the gateway passage. Each had the same measurements, and the dividing walls separating them were also identical. [11]The man measured the gateway entrance, which was 17½ feet* wide at the opening and 22¾ feet* wide in the gateway passage. [12]In front of each of the guard alcoves was a 21-inch* curb. The alcoves themselves were 10½ feet* on each side.

[13]Then he measured the entire width of the gateway, measuring the distance between the back walls of facing guard alcoves; this distance was 43¾ feet.* [14]He measured the dividing walls all along the inside of the gateway up to the entry room of the gateway; this distance was 105 feet.* [15]The full length of the gateway passage was 87½ feet* from one end to the other. [16]There were recessed windows that narrowed inward through the walls of the guard alcoves and their dividing walls. There were also windows in the entry room. The surfaces of the dividing walls were decorated with carved palm trees.

The Outer Courtyard

[17]Then the man brought me through the gateway into the outer courtyard of the Temple. A stone pavement ran along the walls of the courtyard, and thirty rooms were built against the walls, opening onto the pavement. [18]This pavement flanked the gates and extended out from the walls into the courtyard the same distance as the gateway entrance. This was the lower

pavement. 19 Then the man measured across the Temple's outer courtyard between the outer and inner gateways; the distance was 175 feet.*

The North Gateway

20 The man measured the gateway on the north just like the one on the east. 21 Here, too, there were three guard alcoves on each side, with dividing walls and an entry room. All the measurements matched those of the east gateway. The gateway passage was 87½ feet long and 43¾ feet wide between the back walls of facing guard alcoves. 22 The windows, the entry room, and the palm tree decorations were identical to those in the east gateway. There were seven steps leading up to the gateway entrance, and the entry room was at the inner end of the gateway passage. 23 Here on the north side, just as on the east, there was another gateway leading to the Temple's inner courtyard directly opposite this outer gateway. The distance between the two gateways was 175 feet.

The South Gateway

24 Then the man took me around to the south gateway and measured its various parts, and they were exactly the same as in the others. 25 It had windows along the walls as the others did, and there was an entry room where the gateway passage opened into the outer courtyard. And like the others, the gateway passage was 87½ feet long and 43¾ feet wide between the back walls of facing guard alcoves. 26 This gateway also had a stairway of seven steps leading up to it, and an entry room at the inner end, and palm tree decorations along the dividing walls. 27 And here again, directly opposite the outer gateway, was another gateway that led into the inner courtyard. The distance between the two gateways was 175 feet.

Gateways to the Inner Courtyard

28 Then the man took me to the south gateway leading into the inner courtyard. He measured it, and it had the same measurements as the other gateways. 29 Its guard alcoves, dividing walls, and entry room were the same size as those in the others. It also had windows along its walls and in the entry room. And like the others, the gateway passage was 87½ feet long and 43¾ feet wide. 30 (The entry rooms of the gateways leading into the inner courtyard were 14 feet* across and 43¾ feet wide.) 31 The entry room to the south gateway faced into the outer courtyard. It had palm tree decorations on its columns, and there were eight steps leading to its entrance.

32 Then he took me to the east gateway leading to the inner courtyard. He measured it, and it had the same measurements as the other gateways. 33 Its guard alcoves, dividing walls, and entry room were the same size as those of the others, and there were windows along the walls and in the entry room. The gateway passage measured 87½ feet long and 43¾ feet wide. 34 Its entry room faced into the outer courtyard. It had palm tree decorations on its columns, and there were eight steps leading to its entrance.

35 Then he took me around to the north gateway leading to the inner courtyard. He measured it, and it had the same measurements as the other gateways. 36 The guard alcoves, dividing walls, and entry room of this gateway had the same measurements as in the others and the same window arrangements. The gateway passage measured 87½ feet long and 43¾ feet wide. 37 Its entry room* faced into the outer courtyard, and it had palm tree decorations on the columns. There were eight steps leading to its entrance.

Rooms for Preparing Sacrifices

38 A door led from the entry room of one of the inner gateways into a side room,

39:25 Hebrew *of Jacob.* **39:26** A few Hebrew manuscripts read *They will forget.* **40:1** Hebrew *At the beginning of the year, on the tenth day of the month,* of the ancient Hebrew lunar calendar. This event occurred on April 28, 573 B.C.; also see note on 1:1. **40:5a** Hebrew *6 long cubits* [3.2 meters], *each being a cubit* [18 inches or 45 centimeters] *and a handbreadth* [3 inches or 8 centimeters] *in length.* **40:5b** Hebrew *1 rod* [3.2 meters]; also in 40:5c, 7. **40:6** As in Greek version, which reads *1 rod* [3.2 meters] *deep;* Hebrew reads *1 rod deep, and 1 threshold, 1 rod deep.* **40:7** Hebrew *5 cubits* [2.7 meters]; also in 40:48. **40:8** As in many Hebrew manuscripts and Syriac version; other Hebrew manuscripts add *which faced inward toward the Temple; it was 1 rod* [10.5 feet or 3.2 meters] *deep. 9 Then he measured the entry room of the gateway.* **40:9a** Hebrew *8 cubits* [4.2 meters]. **40:9b** Hebrew *2 cubits* [1.1 meters]. **40:11a** Hebrew *10 cubits* [5.3 meters]. **40:11b** Hebrew *13 cubits* [6.9 meters]. **40:12a** Hebrew *1 cubit* [53 centimeters]. **40:12b** Hebrew *6 cubits* [3.2 meters]. **40:13** Hebrew *25 cubits* [13.3 meters]; also in 40:21, 25, 29, 30, 33, 36. **40:14** Hebrew *60 cubits* [31.8 meters]. Greek version reads *20 cubits* [35 feet or 10.6 meters]. The meaning of the Hebrew in this verse is uncertain. **40:15** Hebrew *50 cubits* [26.5 meters]; also in 40:21, 25, 29, 33, 36. **40:19** Hebrew *100 cubits* [53 meters]; also in 40:23, 27, 47. **40:30** As in 40:9, which reads *8 cubits* [14 feet or 4.2 meters]; here the Hebrew reads *5 cubits* [8¾ feet or 2.7 meters]. Some Hebrew manuscripts and the Greek version lack this entire verse. **40:37** As in Greek version (compare parallels at 40:26, 31, 34); Hebrew reads *Its dividing wall.*

where the meat for sacrifices was washed.
[39]On each side of this entry room were two
tables, where the sacrificial animals were
slaughtered for the burnt offerings, sin offerings, and guilt offerings. [40]Outside the
entry room, on each side of the stairs going
up to the north entrance, were two more
tables. [41]So there were eight tables in all—
four inside and four outside—where the
sacrifices were cut up and prepared. [42]There
were also four tables of finished stone for
preparation of the burnt offerings, each
31½ inches square and 21 inches high.* On
these tables were placed the butchering
knives and other implements for slaughtering the sacrificial animals. [43]There were
hooks, each 3 inches* long, fastened all
around the foyer walls. The sacrificial meat
was laid on the tables.

Rooms for the Priests

[44]Inside the inner courtyard were two
rooms,* one beside the north gateway,
facing south, and the other beside the
south* gateway, facing north. [45]And the
man said to me, "The room beside the north
inner gate is for the priests who supervise the Temple maintenance. [46]The room
beside the south inner gate is for the priests
in charge of the altar—the descendants of
Zadok—for they alone of all the Levites may
approach the LORD to minister to him."

The Inner Courtyard and Temple

[47]Then the man measured the inner courtyard, and it was a square, 175 feet wide
and 175 feet across. The altar stood in the
courtyard in front of the Temple. [48]Then he
brought me to the entry room of the Temple.
He measured the walls on either side of the
opening to the entry room, and they were
8¾ feet thick. The entrance itself was 24½
feet wide, and the walls on each side of the
entrance were an additional 5¼ feet long.*
[49]The entry room was 35 feet* wide and
21 feet* deep. There were ten steps* leading
up to it, with a column on each side.

41
After that, the man brought me into
the sanctuary of the Temple. He
measured the walls on either side of its
doorway,* and they were 10½ feet* thick.
[2]The doorway was 17½ feet* wide, and the
walls on each side of it were 8¾ feet* long.
The sanctuary itself was 70 feet long and
35 feet wide.*
[3]Then he went beyond the sanctuary into
the inner room. He measured the walls on
either side of its entrance, and they were 3½
feet* thick. The entrance was 10½ feet wide,
and the walls on each side of the entrance
were 12¼ feet* long. [4]The inner room of the
sanctuary was 35 feet* long and 35 feet wide.
"This," he told me, "is the Most Holy Place."
[5]Then he measured the wall of the Temple,
and it was 10½ feet thick. There was a row of
rooms along the outside wall; each room was
7 feet* wide. [6]These side rooms were built in
three levels, one above the other, with thirty
rooms on each level. The supports for these
side rooms rested on exterior ledges on the
Temple wall; they did not extend into the
wall. [7]Each level was wider than the one
below it, corresponding to the narrowing of
the Temple wall as it rose higher. A stairway
led up from the bottom level through the
middle level to the top level.
[8]I saw that the Temple was built on a
terrace, which provided a foundation for
the side rooms. This terrace was 10½ feet*
high. [9]The outer wall of the Temple's side
rooms was 8¾ feet thick. This left an open
area between these side rooms [10]and the row
of rooms along the outer wall of the inner
courtyard. This open area was 35 feet wide,
and it went all the way around the Temple.
[11]Two doors opened from the side rooms into
the terrace yard, which was 8¾ feet wide.
One door faced north and the other south.
[12]A large building stood on the west,
facing the Temple courtyard. It was 122½
feet wide and 157½ feet long, and its walls
were 8¾ feet* thick. [13]Then the man measured the Temple, and it was 175 feet* long.
The courtyard around the building, including its walls, was an additional 175 feet in
length. [14]The inner courtyard to the east
of the Temple was also 175 feet wide. [15]The
building to the west, including its two
walls, was also 175 feet wide.
The sanctuary, the inner room, and the
entry room of the Temple [16]were all paneled
with wood, as were the frames of the recessed windows. The inner walls of the
Temple were paneled with wood above and
below the windows. [17]The space above the
door leading into the inner room, and its
walls inside and out, were also paneled.
[18]All the walls were decorated with carvings

of cherubim, each with two faces, and
there was a carving of a palm tree between
each of the cherubim. [19]One face—that of a
man—looked toward the palm tree on one
side. The other face—that of a young lion—
looked toward the palm tree on the other
side. The figures were carved all along the
inside of the Temple, [20]from the floor to the
top of the walls, including the outer wall of
the sanctuary.
[21]There were square columns at the entrance to the sanctuary, and the ones at
the entrance of the Most Holy Place were
similar. [22]There was an altar made of
wood, 5¼ feet high and 3½ feet across.* Its
corners, base, and sides were all made of
wood. "This," the man told me, "is the table
that stands in the LORD's presence."
[23]Both the sanctuary and the Most Holy
Place had double doorways, [24]each with two
swinging doors. [25]The doors leading into the
sanctuary were decorated with carved cherubim and palm trees, just as on the walls. And
there was a wooden roof at the front of the
entry room to the Temple. [26]On both sides of
the entry room were recessed windows decorated with carved palm trees. The side rooms
along the outside wall also had roofs.

Rooms for the Priests

42 Then the man led me out of the
Temple courtyard by way of the
north gateway. We entered the outer courtyard and came to a group of rooms against
the north wall of the inner courtyard. [2]This
structure, whose entrance opened toward
the north, was 175 feet* long and 87½ feet*
wide. [3]One block of rooms overlooked the 35-
foot* width of the inner courtyard. Another
block of rooms looked out onto the pavement of the outer courtyard. The two blocks
were built three levels high and stood across
from each other. [4]Between the two blocks of
rooms ran a walkway 17½ feet* wide. It extended the entire 175 feet of the complex,*
and all the doors faced north. [5]Each of the
two upper levels of rooms was narrower
than the one beneath it because the upper
levels had to allow space for walkways in
front of them. [6]Since there were three levels
and they did not have supporting columns
as in the courtyards, each of the upper
levels was set back from the level beneath
it. [7]There was an outer wall that separated
the rooms from the outer courtyard; it was
87½ feet long. [8]This wall added length to
the outer block of rooms, which extended
for only 87½ feet, while the inner block—
the rooms toward the Temple—extended
for 175 feet. [9]There was an eastern entrance
from the outer courtyard to these rooms.
[10]On the south* side of the Temple there
were two blocks of rooms just south of the
inner courtyard between the Temple and
the outer courtyard. These rooms were arranged just like the rooms on the north.
[11]There was a walkway between the two
blocks of rooms just like the complex on
the north side of the Temple. This complex
of rooms was the same length and width
as the other one, and it had the same entrances and doors. The dimensions of each
were identical. [12]So there was an entrance in
the wall facing the doors of the inner block
of rooms, and another on the east at the end
of the interior walkway.
[13]Then the man told me, "These rooms
that overlook the Temple from the north
and south are holy. Here the priests who
offer sacrifices to the LORD will eat the most
holy offerings. And because these rooms are
holy, they will be used to store the sacred
offerings—the grain offerings, sin offerings,
and guilt offerings. [14]When the priests leave
the sanctuary, they must not go directly
to the outer courtyard. They must first take
off the clothes they wore while ministering,
because these clothes are holy. They must
put on other clothes before entering the parts
of the building complex open to the public."
[15]When the man had finished measuring

40:42 Hebrew *1½ cubits* [80 centimeters] *long and 1½ cubits wide and 1 cubit* [53 centimeters] *high.* **40:43** Hebrew *a handbreadth* [8 centimeters]. **40:44a** As in Greek version; Hebrew reads *rooms for singers.* **40:44b** As in Greek version; Hebrew reads *east.* **40:48** As in Greek version, which reads *The entrance was 14 cubits* [7.4 meters] *wide, and the walls of the entrance were 3 cubits* [1.6 meters] *on each side;* Hebrew lacks *14 cubits wide, and the walls of the entrance were.* **40:49a** Hebrew *20 cubits* [10.6 meters]. **40:49b** As in Greek version, which reads *12 cubits* [21 feet or 6.4 meters]; Hebrew reads *11 cubits* [19¼ feet or 5.8 meters]. **40:49c** As in Greek version; Hebrew reads *There were steps that were.* **41:1a** As in Greek version; the meaning of the Hebrew is uncertain. **41:1b** Hebrew *6 cubits* [3.2 meters]; also in 41:3, 5. **41:2a** Hebrew *10 cubits* [5.3 meters]. **41:2b** Hebrew *5 cubits* [2.7 meters]; also in 41:9, 11. **41:2c** Hebrew *40 cubits* [21.2 meters] *long and 20 cubits* [10.6 meters] *wide.* **41:3a** Hebrew *2 cubits* [1.1 meters]. **41:3b** Hebrew *7 cubits* [3.7 meters]. **41:4** Hebrew *20 cubits* [10.6 meters]; also in 41:4b, 10. **41:5** Hebrew *4 cubits* [2.1 meters]. **41:8** Hebrew *1 rod, 6 cubits* [3.2 meters]. **41:12** Hebrew *70 cubits* [37.1 meters] *wide and 90 cubits* [47.7 meters] *long, and its walls were 5 cubits* [2.7 meters] *thick.* **41:13** Hebrew *100 cubits* [53 meters]; also in 41:13b, 14, 15. **41:22** Hebrew *3 cubits* [1.6 meters] *high and 2 cubits* [1.1 meters] *across.* **42:2a** Hebrew *100 cubits* [53 meters]; also in 42:8. **42:2b** Hebrew *50 cubits* [26.5 meters]; also in 42:7, 8. **42:3** Hebrew *20[-cubit]* [10.6-meter]. **42:4a** Hebrew *10 cubits* [5.3 meters]. **42:4b** As in Greek and Syriac versions, which read *Its length was 100 cubits* [53 meters]; Hebrew reads *and a passage 1 cubit* [21 inches or 53 centimeters] *wide.* **42:10** As in Greek version; Hebrew reads *east.*

the inside of the Temple area, he led me
out through the east gateway to measure
the entire perimeter. [16]He measured the
east side with his measuring rod, and it
was 875 feet long.* [17]Then he measured the
north side, and it was also 875 feet. [18]The
south side was also 875 feet, [19]and the west
side was also 875 feet. [20]So the area was
875 feet on each side with a wall all around
it to separate what was holy from what was
common.

The LORD's Glory Returns

43 After this, the man brought me back
around to the east gateway. [2]Sud-
denly, the glory of the God of Israel appeared
from the east. The sound of his coming was
like the roar of rushing waters, and the whole
landscape shone with his glory. [3]This vision
was just like the others I had seen, first by
the Kebar River and then when he came* to
destroy Jerusalem. I fell face down on the
ground. [4]And the glory of the LORD came into
the Temple through the east gateway.

[5]Then the Spirit took me up and brought
me into the inner courtyard, and the glory
of the LORD filled the Temple. [6]And I heard
someone speaking to me from within the
Temple, while the man who had been measuring stood beside me. [7]The LORD said
to me, "Son of man, this is the place of
my throne and the place where I will rest
my feet. I will live here forever among the
people of Israel. They and their kings will
not defile my holy name any longer by their
adulterous worship of other gods or by
honoring the relics of their kings who have
died.* [8]They put their idol altars right next
to mine with only a wall between them and
me. They defiled my holy name by such
detestable sin, so I consumed them in my
anger. [9]Now let them stop worshiping other
gods and honoring the relics of their kings,
and I will live among them forever.

[10]"Son of man, describe to the people of
Israel the Temple I have shown you, so they
will be ashamed of all their sins. Let them
study its plan, [11]and they will be ashamed*
of what they have done. Describe to them all
the specifications of the Temple—including
its entrances and exits—and everything else
about it. Tell them about its decrees and
laws. Write down all these specifications
and decrees as they watch so they will be
sure to remember and follow them. [12]And
this is the basic law of the Temple: absolute
holiness! The entire top of the mountain
where the Temple is built is holy. Yes, this
is the basic law of the Temple.

Glory

In chapter 10, Ezekiel had seen God's glory leave the Temple because it was defiled (Ezekiel 10:18); but now that the Temple had been renewed in his vision, he saw that glory returning (43:2).

The root of the Hebrew word for glory means "heaviness." It refers to the heaviness of God's worthiness and splendor. Whenever God revealed his glory, it was accompanied by manifestations such as a cloud or fire (e.g., Exodus 16:10; 24:15-17), and its presence was always overwhelming (e.g., Exodus 40:34-35; Isaiah 6:1-5). Those who experienced it found it almost impossible to describe, as we see in Ezekiel's opening vision (Ezekiel 1). When Moses asked to see God's glorious presence, he was only allowed to see God from behind, lest he die from God's overwhelming glory (Exodus 33:18-23).

For Ezekiel, God's glory was not static, something simply to be gazed upon; it was active, always going out from God, transforming what it touched (e.g., Ezekiel 1:28; 9:3-4; 10:4; 43:4-5). While that glory already fills the earth (Numbers 14:21; Isaiah 6:3), not all recognize it; but the day will surely come when "as the waters fill the sea, the earth will be filled with an awareness of the glory of the LORD" (Habakkuk 2:14).

▸ *See also* ***The glory of God****, page 115.*

The Altar

13“These are the measurements of the
altar*: There is a gutter all around the
altar 21 inches deep and 21 inches wide,*
with a curb 9 inches* wide around its
edge. And this is the height* of the altar:
14From the gutter the altar rises 3½ feet*
to a lower ledge that surrounds the altar
and is 21 inches* wide. From the lower
ledge the altar rises 7 feet* to the upper
ledge that is also 21 inches wide. 15The top
of the altar, the hearth, rises another 7 feet
higher, with a horn rising up from each of
the four corners. 16The top of the altar is
square, measuring 21 feet by 21 feet.* 17The
upper ledge also forms a square, measuring 24½ feet by 24½ feet,* with a 21-inch
gutter and a 10½-inch curb* all around the
edge. There are steps going up the east side
of the altar.”

18Then he said to me, “Son of man, this is
what the Sovereign LORD says: These will be
the regulations for the burning of offerings
and the sprinkling of blood when the altar
is built. 19At that time, the Levitical priests
of the family of Zadok, who minister before
me, are to be given a young bull for a sin offering, says the Sovereign LORD. 20You will
take some of its blood and smear it on the
four horns of the altar, the four corners of the
upper ledge, and the curb that runs around
that ledge. This will cleanse and make atonement for the altar. 21Then take the young bull
for the sin offering and burn it at the appointed place outside the Temple area.

22“On the second day, sacrifice as a sin
offering a young male goat that has no
physical defects. Then cleanse and make
atonement for the altar again, just as you
did with the young bull. 23When you have
finished the cleansing ceremony, offer
another young bull that has no defects and
a perfect ram from the flock. 24You are to
present them to the LORD, and the priests
are to sprinkle salt on them and offer them
as a burnt offering to the LORD.

25“Every day for seven days a male goat,
a young bull, and a ram from the flock will
be sacrificed as a sin offering. None of these
animals may have physical defects of any
kind. 26Do this each day for seven days to
cleanse and make atonement for the altar,
thus setting it apart for holy use. 27On the
eighth day, and on each day afterward, the
priests will sacrifice on the altar the burnt
offerings and peace offerings of the people.
Then I will accept you. I, the Sovereign
LORD, have spoken!”

The Prince, Levites, and Priests

44 Then the man brought me back to
the east gateway in the outer wall of
the Temple area, but it was closed. 2And the
LORD said to me, “This gate must remain
closed; it will never again be opened. No
one will ever open it and pass through, for
the LORD, the God of Israel, has entered
here. Therefore, it must always remain shut.
3Only the prince himself may sit inside this
gateway to feast in the LORD’s presence. But
he may come and go only through the entry
room of the gateway.”

4Then the man brought me through the
north gateway to the front of the Temple.
I looked and saw that the glory of the LORD
filled the Temple of the LORD, and I fell face
down on the ground.

5And the LORD said to me, “Son of man,
take careful notice. Use your eyes and ears,
and listen to everything I tell you about the
regulations concerning the LORD’s Temple.
Take careful note of the procedures for using
the Temple’s entrances and exits. 6And
give these rebels, the people of Israel, this
message from the Sovereign LORD: O people
of Israel, enough of your detestable sins!
7You have brought uncircumcised foreigners into my sanctuary—people who have no
heart for God. In this way, you defiled my
Temple even as you offered me my food, the
fat and blood of sacrifices. In addition to all
your other detestable sins, you have broken
my covenant. 8Instead of safeguarding my
sacred rituals, you have hired foreigners to
take charge of my sanctuary.

9“So this is what the Sovereign LORD says:
No foreigners, including those who live
among the people of Israel, will enter my
sanctuary if they have not been circumcised

42:16 As in 45:2 and in Greek version at 42:17, which reads *500 cubits* [265 meters]; Hebrew reads *500 rods* [5,250 feet or 1,590 meters]; similarly in 42:17, 18, 19, 20. **43:3** As in some Hebrew manuscripts and Latin Vulgate; Masoretic Text reads *I came.* **43:7** Or *kings on their high places.* **43:11** As in Greek version; Hebrew reads *if they are ashamed.* **43:13a** Hebrew *measurements of the altar in long cubits, each being a cubit* [18 inches or 45 centimeters] *and a handbreadth* [3 inches or 8 centimeters] *in length.* **43:13b** Hebrew *a cubit* [53 centimeters] *deep and a cubit wide.* **43:13c** Hebrew *1 span* [23 centimeters]. **43:13d** As in Greek version; Hebrew reads *base.* **43:14a** Hebrew *2 cubits* [1.1 meters]. **43:14b** Hebrew *1 cubit* [53 centimeters]; also in 43:14d. **43:14c** Hebrew *4 cubits* [2.1 meters]; also in 43:15. **43:16** Hebrew *12 [cubits]* [6.4 meters] *long and 12 [cubits] wide.* **43:17a** Hebrew *14 [cubits]* [7.4 meters] *long and 14 [cubits] wide.* **43:17b** Hebrew *a gutter of 1 cubit* [53 centimeters] *and a curb of ½ a cubit* [27 centimeters].

and have not surrendered themselves to
the LORD. 10 And the men of the tribe of Levi
who abandoned me when Israel strayed
away from me to worship idols* must bear
the consequences of their unfaithfulness.
11 They may still be Temple guards and
gatekeepers, and they may slaughter the
animals brought for burnt offerings and
be present to help the people. 12 But they
encouraged my people to worship idols,
causing Israel to fall into deep sin. So I have
taken a solemn oath that they must bear the
consequences for their sins, says the Sovereign LORD. 13 They may not approach me to
minister as priests. They may not touch any
of my holy things or the holy offerings, for
they must bear the shame of all the detestable sins they have committed. 14 They are
to serve as the Temple caretakers, taking
charge of the maintenance work and performing general duties.

15 "However, the Levitical priests of the
family of Zadok continued to minister faithfully in the Temple when Israel abandoned
me for idols. These men will serve as my
ministers. They will stand in my presence
and offer the fat and blood of the sacrifices,
says the Sovereign LORD. 16 They alone
will enter my sanctuary and approach my
table to serve me. They will fulfill all my
requirements.

17 "When they enter the gateway to the
inner courtyard, they must wear only linen
clothing. They must wear no wool while on
duty in the inner courtyard or in the Temple
itself. 18 They must wear linen turbans and
linen undergarments. They must not wear
anything that would cause them to perspire.
19 When they return to the outer courtyard
where the people are, they must take off the
clothes they wear while ministering to me.
They must leave them in the sacred rooms
and put on other clothes so they do not endanger anyone by transmitting holiness to
them through this clothing.

20 "They must neither shave their heads
nor let their hair grow too long. Instead,
they must trim it regularly. 21 The priests
must not drink wine before entering the
inner courtyard. 22 They may choose their
wives only from among the virgins of Israel
or the widows of the priests. They may not
marry other widows or divorced women.
23 They will teach my people the difference between what is holy and what is
common, what is ceremonially clean and
unclean.

24 "They will serve as judges to resolve any
disagreements among my people. Their decisions must be based on my regulations.
And the priests themselves must obey my
instructions and decrees at all the sacred
festivals, and see to it that the Sabbaths are
set apart as holy days.

25 "A priest must not defile himself by
being in the presence of a dead person
unless it is his father, mother, child,
brother, or unmarried sister. In such cases
it is permitted. 26 Even then, he can return to
his Temple duties only after being ceremonially cleansed and then waiting for seven
days. 27 The first day he returns to work and
enters the inner courtyard and the sanctuary, he must offer a sin offering for himself,
says the Sovereign LORD.

28 "The priests will not have any property
or possession of land, for I alone am their
special possession. 29 Their food will come
from the gifts and sacrifices brought to
the Temple by the people—the grain offerings, the sin offerings, and the guilt offerings. Whatever anyone sets apart* for the
LORD will belong to the priests. 30 The first
of the ripe fruits and all the gifts brought
to the LORD will go to the priests. The first
batch of dough must also be given to the
priests so the LORD will bless your homes.
31 The priests may not eat meat from any
bird or animal that dies a natural death or
that dies after being attacked by another
animal.

Division of the Land

45 "When you divide the land among
the tribes of Israel, you must set aside
a section for the LORD as his holy portion.
This piece of land will be $8\frac{1}{3}$ miles long and
$6\frac{2}{3}$ miles wide.* The entire area will be holy.
2 A section of this land, measuring 875 feet by
875 feet,* will be set aside for the Temple.
An additional strip of land $87\frac{1}{2}$ feet* wide
is to be left empty all around it. 3 Within the
larger sacred area, measure out a portion
of land $8\frac{1}{3}$ miles long and $3\frac{1}{3}$ miles wide.*
Within it the sanctuary of the Most Holy
Place will be located. 4 This area will be holy,
set aside for the priests who minister to the
LORD in the sanctuary. They will use it for
their homes, and my Temple will be located
within it. 5 The strip of sacred land next to it,

also 8⅓ miles long and 3⅓ miles wide, will be a living area for the Levites who work at the Temple. It will be their possession and a place for their towns.*

6"Adjacent to the larger sacred area will be a section of land 8⅓ miles long and 1⅔ miles wide.* This will be set aside for a city where anyone in Israel can live.

7"Two special sections of land will be set apart for the prince. One section will share a border with the east side of the sacred lands and city, and the second section will share a border on the west side. Then the far eastern and western borders of the prince's lands will line up with the eastern and western boundaries of the tribal areas. 8These sections of land will be the prince's allotment. Then my princes will no longer oppress and rob my people; they will assign the rest of the land to the people, giving an allotment to each tribe.

Rules for the Princes

9"For this is what the Sovereign LORD says: Enough, you princes of Israel! Stop your violence and oppression and do what is just and right. Quit robbing and cheating my people out of their land. Stop expelling them from their homes, says the Sovereign LORD. 10Use only honest weights and scales and honest measures, both dry and liquid.* 11The homer* will be your standard unit for measuring volume. The ephah and the bath* will each measure one-tenth of a homer. 12The standard unit for weight will be the silver shekel.* One shekel will consist of twenty gerahs, and sixty shekels will be equal to one mina.*

Special Offerings and Celebrations

13"You must give this tax to the prince: one bushel of wheat or barley for every 60* you harvest, 14one percent of your olive oil,* 15and one sheep or goat for every 200 in your flocks in Israel. These will be the grain offerings, burnt offerings, and peace offerings that will make atonement for the people who bring them, says the Sovereign LORD. 16All the people of Israel must join in bringing these offerings to the prince. 17The prince will be required to provide offerings that are given at the religious festivals, the new moon celebrations, the Sabbath days, and all other similar occasions. He will provide the sin offerings, burnt offerings, grain offerings, liquid offerings, and peace offerings to purify the people of Israel, making them right with the LORD.*

18"This is what the Sovereign LORD says: In early spring, on the first day of each new year,* sacrifice a young bull with no defects to purify the Temple. 19The priest will take blood from this sin offering and put it on the doorposts of the Temple, the four corners of the upper ledge of the altar, and the gateposts at the entrance to the inner courtyard. 20Do this also on the seventh day of the new year for anyone who has sinned through error or ignorance. In this way, you will purify* the Temple.

21"On the fourteenth day of the first month,* you must celebrate the Passover. This festival will last for seven days. The bread you eat during that time must be made without yeast. 22On the day of Passover the prince will provide a young bull as a sin offering for himself and the people of Israel. 23On each of the seven days of the feast he will prepare a burnt offering to the LORD, consisting of seven young bulls and seven rams without defects. A male goat will also be given each day for a sin offering. 24The prince will provide a basket of flour as a grain offering and a gallon of olive oil* with each young bull and ram.

25"During the seven days of the Festival of Shelters, which occurs every year in early autumn,* the prince will provide

44:10 The Hebrew term (literally *round things*) probably alludes to dung; also in 44:12. **44:29** The Hebrew term used here refers to the complete consecration of things or people to the LORD, either by destroying them or by giving them as an offering. **45:1** As in Greek version, which reads *25,000 [cubits]* [13.3 kilometers] *long and 20,000 [cubits]* [10.6 kilometers] *wide;* Hebrew reads *25,000 [cubits] long and 10,000 [cubits]* [3⅓ miles or 5.3 kilometers] *wide.* Compare 45:3, 5; 48:9. **45:2a** Hebrew *500 [cubits]* [265 meters] *by 500 [cubits], a square.* **45:2b** Hebrew *50 cubits* [26.5 meters]. **45:3** Hebrew *25,000 [cubits]* [13.3 kilometers] *long and 10,000 [cubits]* [5.3 kilometers] *wide;* also in 45:5. **45:5** As in Greek version; Hebrew reads *They will have as their possession 20 rooms.* **45:6** Hebrew *25,000 [cubits]* [13.3 kilometers] *long and 5,000 [cubits]* [2.65 kilometers] *wide.* **45:10** Hebrew *Use honest scales, an honest ephah, and an honest bath.* **45:11a** The *homer* measures about 50 gallons or 220 liters. **45:11b** The *ephah* is a dry measure; the *bath* is a liquid measure. **45:12a** The *shekel* weighs about 0.4 ounces or 11 grams. **45:12b** Elsewhere the *mina* is equated to 50 shekels. **45:13** Hebrew *⅙ of an ephah from each homer of wheat and ⅙ of an ephah from each homer of barley.* **45:14** Hebrew *the portion of oil, measured by the bath, is ⅒ of a bath from each cor, which consists of 10 baths or 1 homer, for 10 baths are equivalent to a homer.* **45:17** Or *to make atonement for the people of Israel.* **45:18** Hebrew *On the first day of the first month,* of the Hebrew calendar. This day in the ancient Hebrew lunar calendar occurred in March or April. **45:20** Or *will make atonement for.* **45:21** This day in the ancient Hebrew lunar calendar occurred in late March, April, or early May. **45:24** Hebrew *an ephah* [20 quarts or 22 liters] *of flour . . . and a hin* [3.8 liters] *of olive oil.* **45:25** Hebrew *the festival which begins on the fifteenth day of the seventh month* (see Lev 23:34). This day in the ancient Hebrew lunar calendar occurred in late September, October, or early November.

these same sacrifices for the sin offering, the burnt offering, and the grain offering, along with the required olive oil.

46 "This is what the Sovereign LORD says: The east gateway of the inner courtyard will be closed during the six workdays each week, but it will be open on Sabbath days and the days of new moon celebrations. [2]The prince will enter the entry room of the gateway from the outside. Then he will stand by the gatepost while the priest offers his burnt offering and peace offering. He will bow down in worship inside the gateway passage and then go back out the way he came. The gateway will not be closed until evening. [3]The common people will bow down and worship the LORD in front of this gateway on Sabbath days and the days of new moon celebrations.

[4]"Each Sabbath day the prince will present to the LORD a burnt offering of six lambs and one ram, all with no defects. [5]He will present a grain offering of a basket of choice flour to go with the ram and whatever amount of flour he chooses to go with each lamb, and he is to offer one gallon of olive oil* for each basket of flour. [6]At the new moon celebrations, he will bring one young bull, six lambs, and one ram, all with no defects. [7]With the young bull he must bring a basket of choice flour for a grain offering. With the ram he must bring another basket of flour. And with each lamb he is to bring whatever amount of flour he chooses to give. With each basket of flour he must offer one gallon of olive oil.

[8]"The prince must enter the gateway through the entry room, and he must leave the same way. [9]But when the people come in through the north gateway to worship the LORD during the religious festivals, they must leave by the south gateway. And those who entered through the south gateway must leave by the north gateway. They must never leave by the same gateway they came in, but must always use the opposite gateway. [10]The prince will enter and leave with the people on these occasions.

[11]"So at the special feasts and sacred festivals, the grain offering will be a basket of choice flour with each young bull, another basket of flour with each ram, and as much flour as the worshiper chooses to give with each lamb. Give one gallon of olive oil with each basket of flour. [12]When the prince offers a voluntary burnt offering or peace offering to the LORD, the east gateway to the inner courtyard will be opened for him, and he will offer his sacrifices as he does on Sabbath days. Then he will leave, and the gateway will be shut behind him.

[13]"Each morning you must sacrifice a one-year-old lamb with no defects as a burnt offering to the LORD. [14]With the lamb, a grain offering must also be given to the LORD—about three quarts of flour with a third of a gallon of olive oil* to moisten the choice flour. This will be a permanent law for you. [15]The lamb, the grain offering, and the olive oil must be given as a daily sacrifice every morning without fail.

[16]"This is what the Sovereign LORD says: If the prince gives a gift of land to one of his sons as his inheritance, it will belong to him and his descendants forever. [17]But if the prince gives a gift of land from his inheritance to one of his servants, the servant may keep it only until the Year of Jubilee, which comes every fiftieth year.* At that time the land will return to the prince. But when the prince gives gifts to his sons, those gifts will be permanent. [18]And the prince may never take anyone's property by force. If he gives property to his sons, it must be from his own land, for I do not want any of my people unjustly evicted from their property."

The Temple Kitchens

[19]In my vision, the man brought me through the entrance beside the gateway and led me to the sacred rooms assigned to the priests, which faced toward the north. He showed me a place at the extreme west end of these rooms. [20]He explained, "This is where the priests will cook the meat from the guilt offerings and sin offerings and bake the flour from the grain offerings into bread. They will do it here to avoid carrying the sacrifices through the outer courtyard and endangering the people by transmitting holiness to them."

[21]Then he brought me back to the outer courtyard and led me to each of its four corners. In each corner I saw an enclosure. [22]Each of these enclosures was 70 feet long and 52½ feet wide,* surrounded by walls. [23]Along the inside of these walls was a

ledge of stone with fireplaces under the ledge all the way around. [24]The man said to me, "These are the kitchens to be used by the Temple assistants to boil the sacrifices offered by the people."

The River of Healing

47 In my vision, the man brought me back to the entrance of the Temple. There I saw a stream flowing east from beneath the door of the Temple and passing to the right of the altar on its south side. [2]The man brought me outside the wall through the north gateway and led me around to the eastern entrance. There I could see the water flowing out through the south side of the east gateway.

[3]Measuring as he went, he took me along the stream for 1,750 feet* and then led me across. The water was up to my ankles. [4]He measured off another 1,750 feet and led me across again. This time the water was up to my knees. After another 1,750 feet, it was up to my waist. [5]Then he measured another 1,750 feet, and the river was too deep to walk across. It was deep enough to swim in, but too deep to walk through.

[6]He asked me, "Have you been watching, son of man?" Then he led me back along the riverbank. [7]When I returned, I was surprised by the sight of many trees growing on both sides of the river. [8]Then he said to me, "This river flows east through the desert into the valley of the Dead Sea.* The waters of this stream will make the salty waters of the Dead Sea fresh and pure. [9]There will be swarms of living things wherever the water of this river flows.* Fish will abound in the Dead Sea, for its waters will become fresh. Life will flourish wherever this water flows. [10]Fishermen will stand along the shores of the Dead Sea. All the way from En-gedi to En-eglaim, the shores will be covered with nets drying in the sun. Fish of every kind will fill the Dead Sea, just as they fill the Mediterranean.* [11]But the marshes and swamps will not be purified; they will still be salty. [12]Fruit trees of all kinds will grow along both sides of the river. The leaves of these trees will never turn brown and fall, and there will always be fruit on their branches. There will be a new crop every month, for they are watered by the river flowing from the Temple. The fruit will be for food and the leaves for healing."

Boundaries for the Land

[13]This is what the Sovereign LORD says: "Divide the land in this way for the twelve tribes of Israel: The descendants of Joseph will be given two shares of land.* [14]Otherwise each tribe will receive an equal share. I took a solemn oath and swore that I would give this land to your ancestors, and it will now come to you as your possession.

46:5 Hebrew *an ephah* [20 quarts or 22 liters] *of choice flour . . . a hin* [3.8 liters] *of olive oil;* similarly in 46:7, 11. **46:14** Hebrew *⅙ of an ephah* [3.7 liters] *of flour with ⅓ of a hin* [1.3 liters] *of olive oil.* **46:17** Hebrew *until the Year of Release;* see Lev 25:8-17. **46:22** Hebrew *40 [cubits]* [21.2 meters] *long and 30 [cubits]* [15.9 meters] *wide.* **47:3** Hebrew *1,000 cubits* [530 meters]; also in 47:4, 5. **47:8** Hebrew *the sea.* **47:9** As in Greek and Syriac versions; Hebrew reads *of these two rivers flow.* **47:10** Hebrew *the Great Sea;* also in 47:15, 17, 19, 20. **47:13** It was important to retain twelve portions of land. Since Levi had no portion, the descendants of Joseph's sons, Ephraim and Manasseh, received land as two tribes.

Going deeper with God

The prophetic vision of Ezekiel 47 is a powerful invitation to us all to keep going deeper with God. Ezekiel saw water—a common symbol in the Bible for God's Spirit—flowing in ever-increasing breadth and depth from the renewed Temple that had just been filled with God's glory. But for Ezekiel, the invitation was not just to watch this river from the safety of the bank, but to enter it; and not just to paddle or wade in it, but to throw himself deep into it. Such is God's invitation to his people concerning his Spirit: to be "filled with the Holy Spirit" (Ephesians 5:18).

But the Spirit's work is not there simply to do us good; it is meant to flow out into the desert of life, transforming things and bringing fruitfulness wherever it goes. If we are truly filled with God's Spirit, we will not keep him to ourselves but will share the fruits of his life wherever we go, taking his resources of refreshment and encouragement to all those around us.

15“These are the boundaries of the land: The northern border will run from the Mediterranean toward Hethlon, then on through Lebo-hamath to Zedad; 16then it will run to Berothah and Sibraim,* which are on the border between Damascus and Hamath, and finally to Hazer-hatticon, on the border of Hauran. 17So the northern border will run from the Mediterranean to Hazar-enan, on the border between Hamath to the north and Damascus to the south.

18“The eastern border starts at a point between Hauran and Damascus and runs south along the Jordan River between Israel and Gilead, past the Dead Sea* and as far south as Tamar.* This will be the eastern border.

19“The southern border will go west from Tamar to the waters of Meribah at Kadesh* and then follow the course of the Brook of Egypt to the Mediterranean. This will be the southern border.

20“On the west side, the Mediterranean itself will be your border from the southern border to the point where the northern border begins, opposite Lebo-hamath.

21“Divide the land within these boundaries among the tribes of Israel. 22Distribute the land as an allotment for yourselves and for the foreigners who have joined you and are raising their families among you. They will be like native-born Israelites to you and will receive an allotment among the tribes. 23These foreigners are to be given land within the territory of the tribe with whom they now live. I, the Sovereign LORD, have spoken!

Division of the Land

48 “Here is the list of the tribes of Israel and the territory each is to receive. The territory of Dan is in the extreme north. Its boundary line follows the Hethlon road to Lebo-hamath and then runs on to Hazar-enan on the border of Damascus, with Hamath to the north. Dan’s territory extends all the way across the land of Israel from east to west.

2“Asher’s territory lies south of Dan’s and also extends from east to west. 3Naphtali’s land lies south of Asher’s, also extending from east to west. 4Then comes Manasseh south of Naphtali, and its territory also extends from east to west. 5South of Manasseh is Ephraim, 6and then Reuben, 7and then Judah, all of whose boundaries extend from east to west.

8“South of Judah is the land set aside for a special purpose. It will be 8⅓ miles* wide and will extend as far east and west as the tribal territories, with the Temple at the center.

9“The area set aside for the LORD’s Temple will be 8⅓ miles long and 6⅔ miles wide.* 10For the priests there will be a strip of land measuring 8⅓ miles long by 3⅓ miles wide,* with the LORD’s Temple at the center. 11This area is set aside for the ordained priests, the descendants of Zadok who served me faithfully and did not go astray with the people of Israel and the rest of the Levites. 12It will be their special portion when the land is distributed, the most sacred land of all. Next to the priests’ territory will lie the land where the other Levites will live.

13“The land allotted to the Levites will be the same size and shape as that belonging to the priests—8⅓ miles long and 3⅓ miles wide. Together these portions of land will measure 8⅓ miles long by 6⅔ miles wide.* 14None of this special land may ever be sold or traded or used by others, for it belongs to the LORD; it is set apart as holy.

15“An additional strip of land 8⅓ miles long by 1⅔ miles wide,* south of the sacred Temple area, will be allotted for public use—homes, pasturelands, and common lands, with a city at the center. 16The city will measure 1½ miles* on each side—north, south, east, and west. 17Open lands will surround the city for 150 yards* in every direction. 18Outside the city there will be a farming area that stretches 3⅓ miles to the east and 3⅓ miles to the west* along the border of the sacred area. This farmland will produce food for the people working in the city. 19Those who come from the various tribes to work in the city may farm it. 20This entire area—including the sacred lands and the city—is a square that measures 8⅓ miles* on each side.

21“The areas that remain, to the east and to the west of the sacred lands and the city, will belong to the prince. Each of these areas will be 8⅓ miles wide, extending in opposite directions to the eastern and western borders of Israel, with the sacred lands and the sanctuary of the Temple in the center. 22So the prince’s land will include everything between the territories allotted to Judah and Benjamin, except for the areas set aside for the sacred lands and the city.

[23]"These are the territories allotted to the rest of the tribes. Benjamin's territory lies just south of the prince's lands, and it extends across the entire land of Israel from east to west. [24]South of Benjamin's territory lies that of Simeon, also extending across the land from east to west. [25]Next is the territory of Issachar with the same eastern and western boundaries.

[26]"Then comes the territory of Zebulun, which also extends across the land from east to west. [27]The territory of Gad is just south of Zebulun with the same borders to the east and west. [28]The southern border of Gad runs from Tamar to the waters of Meribah at Kadesh* and then follows the Brook of Egypt to the Mediterranean.*

[29]"These are the allotments that will be set aside for each tribe's exclusive possession. I, the Sovereign LORD, have spoken!

The Gates of the City

[30]"These will be the exits to the city: On the north wall, which is 1½ miles long, [31]there will be three gates, each one named after a tribe of Israel. The first will be named for Reuben, the second for Judah, and the third for Levi. [32]On the east wall, also 1½ miles long, the gates will be named for Joseph, Benjamin, and Dan. [33]The south wall, also 1½ miles long, will have gates named for Simeon, Issachar, and Zebulun. [34]And on the west wall, also 1½ miles long, the gates will be named for Gad, Asher, and Naphtali.

[35]"The distance around the entire city will be 6 miles.* And from that day the name of the city will be 'The LORD Is There.'*"

47:15-16 As in Greek version; Masoretic Text reads *then on through Lebo to Zedad;* [16]*then it will run to Hamath, Berothah, and Sibraim.* **47:18a** Hebrew *the eastern sea.* **47:18b** As in Greek version; Hebrew reads *you will measure.* **47:19** Hebrew *waters of Meribath-kadesh.* **48:8** Hebrew *25,000 [cubits]* [13.3 kilometers]. **48:9** As in one Greek manuscript and the Greek reading in 45:1: *25,000 [cubits]* [13.3 kilometers] *long and 20,000 [cubits]* [10.6 kilometers] *wide;* Hebrew reads *25,000 [cubits] long and 10,000 [cubits]* [3⅓ miles or 5.3 kilometers] *wide.* Similarly in 48:13b. Compare 45:1-5; 48:10-13. **48:10** Hebrew *25,000 [cubits]* [13.3 kilometers] *long by 10,000 [cubits]* [5.3 kilometers] *wide;* also in 48:13a. **48:13** See note on 48:9. **48:15** Hebrew *25,000 [cubits]* [13.3 kilometers] *long by 5,000 [cubits]* [2.65 kilometers] *wide.* **48:16** Hebrew *4,500 [cubits]* [2.4 kilometers]; also in 48:30, 32, 33, 34. **48:17** Hebrew *250 [cubits]* [133 meters]. **48:18** Hebrew *10,000 [cubits]* [5.3 kilometers] *to the east and 10,000 [cubits] to the west.* **48:20** Hebrew *25,000 [cubits]* [13.3 kilometers]; also in 48:21. **48:28a** Hebrew *waters of Meribath-kadesh.* **48:28b** Hebrew *the Great Sea.* **48:35a** Hebrew *18,000 [cubits]* [9.6 kilometers]. **48:35b** Hebrew *Yahweh Shammah.*

Daniel *Faithful to God*

Daniel was a young Jewish man, educated and of high rank, whose life offered a model for Jews living in a foreign, pagan environment. Deported with the first batch of Jewish exiles in 605 BC, he spent the rest of his life in Babylon, where he lived an exemplary life in the corrupt royal court. Through maintaining his faith rather than hiding it, he rose to the highest position in the state and exercised political influence in both the Babylonian and Persian Empires. God gave him the gifts of interpreting dreams and predicting future events, some of which lay many years in the future. The book named after him contains gripping stories and strange visions, and the combination of history and prophecy makes for exciting—and sometimes even rather frightening—reading.

What's it all about?

Daniel and three other Jewish young men, exiled to Babylon in 605 BC, were assigned to serve in the court of King Nebuchadnezzar (chapter 1). When no one could interpret one of the king's dreams, Daniel offered to do so, and when he did, he was given a position of authority (chapter 2). But when the king ordered everyone to bow down to a gold statue, Daniel's three friends refused. They were thrown into a furnace, but God kept them safe. When they came out, they were unburned, not even smelling of smoke. Nebuchadnezzar was amazed and issued a decree honoring the God of the Jews and forbidding anything to be spoken against him (chapter 3).

In chapter 4, Daniel interpreted another of Nebuchadnezzar's dreams, foretelling his temporary madness and fall from power. When his sanity was eventually restored, the king praised Daniel's God for humbling and restoring him. In chapter 5, at a royal banquet given by King Belshazzar, strange writing appeared on the wall, and Daniel was called upon to interpret it. He warned of the coming end of the Babylonian Empire and was again rewarded for his insight. Later, after the Medes and Persians had conquered Babylon, fulfilling Daniel's words, King Darius the Mede decreed that no one should pray to anyone except the king. Daniel refused to stop praying to God and was thrown into a den of lions, but God protected him, which led Darius to issue a decree that all should worship the God of Daniel (chapter 6).

Chapters 7 to 12 contain Daniel's own visions. This material is known as *apocalyptic*: symbolic, visionary literature (not meant to be taken literally) that looked to the future, was concerned with the supernatural world and its impact on this world, and brought reassurance to God's suffering people. The visions

OVERVIEW

reveal God's perspective on Israel's role among the nations at that time; but they also point to the *end* of time when God will finally reveal his power, all empires will fall before him, and "someone like a son of man" (interpreted by Jesus as a reference to himself) will rule God's kingdom (7:13-14). In the meantime, God is in control of history.

What does it mean for us?

Daniel was written to inspire God's people during their time of exile and to give them fresh hope. They were under pressure to give up their faith; but Daniel shows that, if we remain faithful, God is able to keep us safe, as Daniel himself experienced. We too should maintain a faithful witness, confident in God's deliverance—but prepared to continue trusting him whatever happens (see 3:17-18).

Daniel prayed long and hard, confessing the sins of his people and seeking God. Sometimes he would fast (go without food) so he could give God his full attention. While the answer to his prayer always came, it did not always come quickly, and sometimes there was huge spiritual resistance (10:12-14); but this book shows us we should not give up when our prayers are not answered immediately. The angel assured Daniel that *as soon as* he made up his mind to seek God, God answered him (10:12), but the answer took a while to come for reasons only God understands. Even when nothing seems to be happening, we need to trust God. This was a message that the Jews needed to hear at that time.

The book of Daniel also demonstrates that, whatever human rulers may do, God remains in control and continues to work out his purposes. Every other kingdom will one day fail, but his will last forever. That is why seeking his Kingdom above all else (Matthew 6:33) should always be our priority.

▸ *See also* ***A timeline of the Bible****, pages A22-A24.*

Daniel in Nebuchadnezzar's Court

1 During the third year of King Jehoiakim's
reign in Judah,* King Nebuchadnezzar of
Babylon came to Jerusalem and besieged it.
2The Lord gave him victory over King Jehoiakim of Judah and permitted him to take some
of the sacred objects from the Temple of God.
So Nebuchadnezzar took them back to the
land of Babylonia* and placed them in the
treasure-house of his god.
3Then the king ordered Ashpenaz, his
chief of staff, to bring to the palace some of
the young men of Judah's royal family and
other noble families, who had been brought
to Babylon as captives. 4"Select only strong,
healthy, and good-looking young men," he
said. "Make sure they are well versed in every
branch of learning, are gifted with knowledge
and good judgment, and are suited to serve
in the royal palace. Train these young men
in the language and literature of Babylon.*"
5The king assigned them a daily ration of food
and wine from his own kitchens. They were
to be trained for three years, and then they
would enter the royal service.
6Daniel, Hananiah, Mishael, and Azariah
were four of the young men chosen, all from
the tribe of Judah. 7The chief of staff renamed
them with these Babylonian names:

Daniel was called Belteshazzar.
Hananiah was called Shadrach.
Mishael was called Meshach.
Azariah was called Abednego.

8But Daniel was determined not to defile
himself by eating the food and wine given to
them by the king. He asked the chief of staff
for permission not to eat these unacceptable foods. 9Now God had given the chief of
staff both respect and affection for Daniel.
10But he responded, "I am afraid of my lord
the king, who has ordered that you eat this
food and wine. If you become pale and thin
compared to the other youths your age, I am
afraid the king will have me beheaded."
11Daniel spoke with the attendant who
had been appointed by the chief of staff to
look after Daniel, Hananiah, Mishael, and
Azariah. 12"Please test us for ten days on a

1:1 This event occurred in 605 B.C., during the third year of Jehoiakim's reign (according to the calendar system in which the new year begins in the spring). **1:2** Hebrew *the land of Shinar.* **1:4** Or *of the Chaldeans.*

diet of vegetables and water," Daniel said. 13"At the end of the ten days, see how we look compared to the other young men who are eating the king's food. Then make your decision in light of what you see." 14The attendant agreed to Daniel's suggestion and tested them for ten days.

15At the end of the ten days, Daniel and his three friends looked healthier and better nourished than the young men who had been eating the food assigned by the king. 16So after that, the attendant fed them only vegetables instead of the food and wine provided for the others.

17God gave these four young men an unusual aptitude for understanding every aspect of literature and wisdom. And God gave Daniel the special ability to interpret the meanings of visions and dreams.

18When the training period ordered by the king was completed, the chief of staff brought all the young men to King Nebuchadnezzar. 19The king talked with them, and no one impressed him as much as Daniel, Hananiah, Mishael, and Azariah. So they entered the royal service. 20Whenever the king consulted them in any matter requiring wisdom and balanced judgment, he found them ten times more capable than any of the magicians and enchanters in his entire kingdom.

21Daniel remained in the royal service until the first year of the reign of King Cyrus.*

Nebuchadnezzar's Dream

2 One night during the second year of his reign,* Nebuchadnezzar had such disturbing dreams that he couldn't sleep. 2He called in his magicians, enchanters, sorcerers, and astrologers,* and he demanded that they tell him what he had dreamed. As they stood before the king, 3he said, "I have had a dream that deeply troubles me, and I must know what it means."

4Then the astrologers answered the king in Aramaic,* "Long live the king! Tell us the dream, and we will tell you what it means."

5But the king said to the astrologers, "I am serious about this. If you don't tell me what my dream was and what it means, you will be torn limb from limb, and your houses will be turned into heaps of rubble! 6But if you tell me what I dreamed and what the dream means, I will give you many wonderful gifts and honors. Just tell me the dream and what it means!"

7They said again, "Please, Your Majesty. Tell us the dream, and we will tell you what it means."

8The king replied, "I know what you are doing! You're stalling for time because you know I am serious when I say, 9'If you don't

Serving God in our work

Most Christians spend most of their time, not in church, but in the workplace; and Daniel is an excellent role model for them.

Note that Daniel initially made no mention of God in his new surroundings. He didn't begin by preaching; instead, he lived out his faith, showing that a life with God was better than one without him. He started by giving himself to everything required of him, learning the Babylonians' language and literature (Daniel 1:4), which would have included many myths about their gods. But he did not fear becoming contaminated by such things, because his faith was strong. Even being renamed after a pagan god (1:7) didn't trouble him, for his heart was secure. And when he was required to eat the palace's fine food—much of which was forbidden to him as a Jew—he did not make a fuss; he simply asked—graciously—that he and his friends be tested on their own diet for ten days to see which worked best, confident of the outcome (1:11-16). At the end of their training, Daniel and his friends were far brighter than their fellow students because God had helped them with their secular work and learning (1:17-20). The quality of Daniel's life was preparing the way for the quality of his words to come.

▶ *See also* ***Working for the glory of God****, page 1265;* ***Work****, page 1376.*

tell me the dream, you are doomed.' So you have conspired to tell me lies, hoping I will change my mind. But tell me the dream, and then I'll know that you can tell me what it means."

[10]The astrologers replied to the king, "No one on earth can tell the king his dream! And no king, however great and powerful, has ever asked such a thing of any magician, enchanter, or astrologer! [11]The king's demand is impossible. No one except the gods can tell you your dream, and they do not live here among people."

[12]The king was furious when he heard this, and he ordered that all the wise men of Babylon be executed. [13]And because of the king's decree, men were sent to find and kill Daniel and his friends.

[14]When Arioch, the commander of the king's guard, came to kill them, Daniel handled the situation with wisdom and discretion. [15]He asked Arioch, "Why has the king issued such a harsh decree?" So Arioch told him all that had happened. [16]Daniel went at once to see the king and requested more time to tell the king what the dream meant.

[17]Then Daniel went home and told his friends Hananiah, Mishael, and Azariah what had happened. [18]He urged them to ask the God of heaven to show them his mercy by telling them the secret, so they would not be executed along with the other wise men of Babylon. [19]That night the secret was revealed to Daniel in a vision. Then Daniel praised the God of heaven. [20]He said,

"Praise the name of God forever and
ever,
for he has all wisdom and power.
21 He controls the course of world events;
he removes kings and sets up other
kings.
He gives wisdom to the wise
and knowledge to the scholars.
22 He reveals deep and mysterious
things
and knows what lies hidden in
darkness,
though he is surrounded by light.
23 I thank and praise you, God of my
ancestors,
for you have given me wisdom and
strength.
You have told me what we asked of you
and revealed to us what the king
demanded."

Daniel Interprets the Dream

[24]Then Daniel went in to see Arioch, whom the king had ordered to execute the wise men of Babylon. Daniel said to him, "Don't kill the wise men. Take me to the king, and I will tell him the meaning of his dream."

[25]Arioch quickly took Daniel to the king and said, "I have found one of the captives from Judah who will tell the king the meaning of his dream!"

[26]The king said to Daniel (also known as

1:21 Cyrus began his reign (over Babylon) in 539 B.C. **2:1** The second year of Nebuchadnezzar's reign was 603 B.C. **2:2** Or *Chaldeans;* also in 2:4, 5, 10. **2:4** The original text from this point through chapter 7 is in Aramaic.

King Nebuchadnezzar

When Daniel said he could interpret King Nebuchadnezzar's dream (Daniel 2:24), he was taking his life in his hands, for Nebuchadnezzar was not a man to be messed with. He had led the army that defeated the Assyrian-Egyptian alliance in 605 BC, which led to Babylon swallowing up the Assyrian Empire. He had attacked Judah and enforced several deportations—including the first one of 605 BC, when Daniel had been exiled and forced to serve him. Nebuchadnezzar used the wealth from his conquests to enrich his empire and undertake great building projects, determined to make Babylon the greatest city in the world. He was an intelligent (1:18-20), ruthless (2:12; 3:13), and proud despot (4:29-30); and yet, when he recognized the living God at work, he was ready to humble himself, which always pleases God (2:46-49; 3:28-30; 4:34-37).

▶ *See also **Babylon**, page 445.*

Belteshazzar), "Is this true? Can you tell me
what my dream was and what it means?"
[27]Daniel replied, "There are no wise men,
enchanters, magicians, or fortune-tellers
who can reveal the king's secret. [28]But there
is a God in heaven who reveals secrets, and
he has shown King Nebuchadnezzar what
will happen in the future. Now I will tell you
your dream and the visions you saw as you
lay on your bed.
[29]"While Your Majesty was sleeping, you
dreamed about coming events. He who
reveals secrets has shown you what is going
to happen. [30]And it is not because I am wiser
than anyone else that I know the secret of
your dream, but because God wants you to
understand what was in your heart.
[31]"In your vision, Your Majesty, you saw
standing before you a huge, shining statue
of a man. It was a frightening sight. [32]The
head of the statue was made of fine gold.
Its chest and arms were silver, its belly and
thighs were bronze, [33]its legs were iron,
and its feet were a combination of iron and
baked clay. [34]As you watched, a rock was
cut from a mountain,* but not by human
hands. It struck the feet of iron and clay,
smashing them to bits. [35]The whole statue
was crushed into small pieces of iron, clay,
bronze, silver, and gold. Then the wind blew
them away without a trace, like chaff on a
threshing floor. But the rock that knocked
the statue down became a great mountain
that covered the whole earth.
[36]"That was the dream. Now we will tell
the king what it means. [37]Your Majesty, you
are the greatest of kings. The God of heaven
has given you sovereignty, power, strength,
and honor. [38]He has made you the ruler over
all the inhabited world and has put even the
wild animals and birds under your control.
You are the head of gold.
[39]"But after your kingdom comes to an
end, another kingdom, inferior to yours,
will rise to take your place. After that
kingdom has fallen, yet a third kingdom,
represented by bronze, will rise to rule the
world. [40]Following that kingdom, there
will be a fourth one, as strong as iron. That
kingdom will smash and crush all previous
empires, just as iron smashes and crushes
everything it strikes. [41]The feet and toes you
saw were a combination of iron and baked
clay, showing that this kingdom will be
divided. Like iron mixed with clay, it will
have some of the strength of iron. [42]But
while some parts of it will be as strong as
iron, other parts will be as weak as clay.
[43]This mixture of iron and clay also shows
that these kingdoms will try to strengthen
themselves by forming alliances with each
other through intermarriage. But they will
not hold together, just as iron and clay do
not mix.
[44]"During the reigns of those kings, the
God of heaven will set up a kingdom that
will never be destroyed or conquered. It
will crush all these kingdoms into nothing-
ness, and it will stand forever. [45]That is the
meaning of the rock cut from the mountain, though not by human hands, that
crushed to pieces the statue of iron, bronze,
clay, silver, and gold. The great God was
showing the king what will happen in the
future. The dream is true, and its meaning
is certain."

Nebuchadnezzar Rewards Daniel

[46]Then King Nebuchadnezzar threw himself
down before Daniel and worshiped him,
and he commanded his people to offer sacrifices and burn sweet incense before him.
[47]The king said to Daniel, "Truly, your God
is the greatest of gods, the Lord over kings,
a revealer of mysteries, for you have been
able to reveal this secret."
[48]Then the king appointed Daniel to a
high position and gave him many valuable
gifts. He made Daniel ruler over the whole
province of Babylon, as well as chief over all
his wise men. [49]At Daniel's request, the king
appointed Shadrach, Meshach, and Abednego to be in charge of all the affairs of the
province of Babylon, while Daniel remained
in the king's court.

Nebuchadnezzar's Gold Statue

3 King Nebuchadnezzar made a gold
statue ninety feet tall and nine feet
wide* and set it up on the plain of Dura
in the province of Babylon. [2]Then he sent
messages to the high officers, officials,
governors, advisers, treasurers, judges,
magistrates, and all the provincial officials
to come to the dedication of the statue he
had set up. [3]So all these officials* came and
stood before the statue King Nebuchadnezzar had set up.
[4]Then a herald shouted out, "People of
all races and nations and languages, listen

to the king's command! [5]When you hear the
sound of the horn, flute, zither, lyre, harp,
pipes, and other musical instruments,* bow
to the ground to worship King Nebuchadnezzar's gold statue. [6]Anyone who refuses
to obey will immediately be thrown into a
blazing furnace."

[7]So at the sound of the musical instruments,* all the people, whatever their race
or nation or language, bowed to the ground
and worshiped the gold statue that King
Nebuchadnezzar had set up.

[8]But some of the astrologers* went to
the king and informed on the Jews. [9]They
said to King Nebuchadnezzar, "Long live
the king! [10]You issued a decree requiring
all the people to bow down and worship
the gold statue when they hear the sound
of the horn, flute, zither, lyre, harp, pipes,
and other musical instruments. [11]That
decree also states that those who refuse to
obey must be thrown into a blazing furnace.
[12]But there are some Jews—Shadrach,
Meshach, and Abednego—whom you have
put in charge of the province of Babylon.
They pay no attention to you, Your Majesty.
They refuse to serve your gods and do not
worship the gold statue you have set up."

[13]Then Nebuchadnezzar flew into a rage
and ordered that Shadrach, Meshach,
and Abednego be brought before him.
When they were brought in, [14]Nebuchad-
nezzar said to them, "Is it true, Shadrach,
Meshach, and Abednego, that you refuse to
serve my gods or to worship the gold statue
I have set up? [15]I will give you one more
chance to bow down and worship the statue
I have made when you hear the sound of the
musical instruments.* But if you refuse, you
will be thrown immediately into the blazing
furnace. And then what god will be able to
rescue you from my power?"

[16]Shadrach, Meshach, and Abednego
replied, "O Nebuchadnezzar, we do not
need to defend ourselves before you. [17]If
we are thrown into the blazing furnace,
the God whom we serve is able to save us.
He will rescue us from your power, Your
Majesty. [18]But even if he doesn't, we want to
make it clear to you, Your Majesty, that we
will never serve your gods or worship the
gold statue you have set up."

2:34 As in Greek version (see also 2:45); Hebrew lacks *from a mountain.* **3:1** Aramaic *60 cubits* [27 meters] *tall and 6 cubits* [2.7 meters] *wide.* **3:3** Aramaic *the high officers, officials, governors, advisers, treasurers, judges, magistrates, and all the provincial officials.* **3:5** The identification of some of these musical instruments is uncertain. **3:7** Aramaic *the horn, flute, zither, lyre, harp, and other musical instruments.* **3:8** Aramaic *Chaldeans.* **3:15** Aramaic *the horn, flute, zither, lyre, harp, pipes, and other musical instruments.*

Trusting God whatever happens

In his sermons on the book of Daniel, the nineteenth-century British preacher C. H. Spurgeon said, "Your duty is to do the right! Consequences are with God!" and "It is yours and mine to do the right, though the heavens fall—and follow the command of Christ whatever the consequences may be."

Shadrach, Meshach, and Abednego, Daniel's three friends, certainly lived by this principle. Even under threat of death, they refused to worship Nebuchadnezzar's gold statue. They were determined to remain faithful to God, no matter what happened. "If we are thrown into the blazing furnace, the God whom we serve is able to save us," they stated confidently (Daniel 3:17). And even if he didn't, they declared, "We will never serve your gods or worship the gold statue you have set up" (3:18).

Many Christians today want to serve God only for what they can get out of it; and if things do not go their way, they drift away. But these three friends demonstrate what true faith is like: resolving to trust God whatever happens, whether things work out our way or not, knowing that God has a bigger purpose than our comfort or the answering of our prayers. For those who make this decision, there is always a glorious outcome—even if it may not come in the way we expected.

▶ *See also* ***Trusting God when we cannot see the way ahead****, page 57;* ***Why doesn't God always answer prayer?****, page 641;* ***Why do bad things happen in life?****, page 1025.*

The Blazing Furnace

19 Nebuchadnezzar was so furious with Shadrach, Meshach, and Abednego that his face became distorted with rage. He commanded that the furnace be heated seven times hotter than usual. 20 Then he ordered some of the strongest men of his army to bind Shadrach, Meshach, and Abednego and throw them into the blazing furnace. 21 So they tied them up and threw them into the furnace, fully dressed in their pants, turbans, robes, and other garments. 22 And because the king, in his anger, had demanded such a hot fire in the furnace, the flames killed the soldiers as they threw the three men in. 23 So Shadrach, Meshach, and Abednego, securely tied, fell into the roaring flames.

24 But suddenly, Nebuchadnezzar jumped up in amazement and exclaimed to his advisers, "Didn't we tie up three men and throw them into the furnace?"

"Yes, Your Majesty, we certainly did," they replied.

25 "Look!" Nebuchadnezzar shouted. "I see four men, unbound, walking around in the fire unharmed! And the fourth looks like a god*!"

26 Then Nebuchadnezzar came as close as he could to the door of the flaming furnace and shouted: "Shadrach, Meshach, and Abednego, servants of the Most High God, come out! Come here!"

So Shadrach, Meshach, and Abednego stepped out of the fire. 27 Then the high officers, officials, governors, and advisers crowded around them and saw that the fire had not touched them. Not a hair on their heads was singed, and their clothing was not scorched. They didn't even smell of smoke!

28 Then Nebuchadnezzar said, "Praise to the God of Shadrach, Meshach, and Abednego! He sent his angel to rescue his servants who trusted in him. They defied the king's command and were willing to die rather than serve or worship any god except their own God. 29 Therefore, I make this decree: If any people, whatever their race or nation or language, speak a word against the God of Shadrach, Meshach, and Abednego, they will be torn limb from limb, and their houses will be turned into heaps of rubble. There is no other god who can rescue like this!"

30 Then the king promoted Shadrach, Meshach, and Abednego to even higher positions in the province of Babylon.

Nebuchadnezzar's Dream about a Tree

4 1* King Nebuchadnezzar sent this message to the people of every race and nation and language throughout the world:

"Peace and prosperity to you!

2 "I want you all to know about the miraculous signs and wonders the Most High God has performed for me.

3 How great are his signs,
  how powerful his wonders!
His kingdom will last forever,
  his rule through all generations.

4* "I, Nebuchadnezzar, was living in my palace in comfort and prosperity. 5 But one night I had a dream that frightened me; I saw visions that terrified me as I lay in my bed. 6 So I issued an order calling in all the wise men of Babylon, so they could tell me what my dream meant. 7 When all the magicians, enchanters, astrologers,* and fortune-tellers came in, I told them the dream, but they could not tell me what it meant. 8 At last Daniel came in before me, and I told him the dream. (He was named Belteshazzar after my god, and the spirit of the holy gods is in him.)

9 "I said to him, 'Belteshazzar, chief of the magicians, I know that the spirit of the holy gods is in you and that no mystery is too great for you to solve. Now tell me what my dream means.

10 "'While I was lying in my bed, this is what I dreamed. I saw a large tree in the middle of the earth. 11 The tree grew very tall and strong, reaching high into the heavens for all the world to see. 12 It had fresh green leaves, and it was loaded with fruit for all to eat. Wild animals lived in its shade, and birds nested in its branches. All the world was fed from this tree.

13 "'Then as I lay there dreaming, I saw a messenger,* a holy one, coming down from heaven. 14 The messenger shouted,

"Cut down the tree and lop off its
  branches!
Shake off its leaves and scatter its
  fruit!

Chase the wild animals from its shade
and the birds from its branches.
15 But leave the stump and the roots in
the ground,
bound with a band of iron and
bronze
and surrounded by tender grass.
Now let him be drenched with the
dew of heaven,
and let him live with the wild
animals among the plants of the
field.
16 For seven periods of time,
let him have the mind of a wild
animal
instead of the mind of a human.
17 For this has been decreed by the
messengers*;
it is commanded by the holy ones,
so that everyone may know
that the Most High rules over the
kingdoms of the world.
He gives them to anyone he chooses—
even to the lowliest of people.”

18“‘Belteshazzar, that was the dream
that I, King Nebuchadnezzar, had. Now
tell me what it means, for none of the
wise men of my kingdom can do so. But
you can tell me because the spirit of the
holy gods is in you.’

Daniel Explains the Dream

19“Upon hearing this, Daniel (also
known as Belteshazzar) was overcome
for a time, frightened by the meaning
of the dream. Then the king said to him,
‘Belteshazzar, don’t be alarmed by the
dream and what it means.’

“Belteshazzar replied, ‘I wish the
events foreshadowed in this dream would
happen to your enemies, my lord, and not
to you! 20The tree you saw was growing
very tall and strong, reaching high into
the heavens for all the world to see. 21It
had fresh green leaves and was loaded
with fruit for all to eat. Wild animals
lived in its shade, and birds nested in its
branches. 22That tree, Your Majesty, is
you. For you have grown strong and great;
your greatness reaches up to heaven, and
your rule to the ends of the earth.

23“‘Then you saw a messenger, a holy
one, coming down from heaven and
saying, “Cut down the tree and destroy
it. But leave the stump and the roots in
the ground, bound with a band of iron
and bronze and surrounded by tender
grass. Let him be drenched with the dew
of heaven. Let him live with the animals
of the field for seven periods of time.”

24“‘This is what the dream means,
Your Majesty, and what the Most High
has declared will happen to my lord the
king. 25You will be driven from human
society, and you will live in the fields
with the wild animals. You will eat grass
like a cow, and you will be drenched
with the dew of heaven. Seven periods
of time will pass while you live this way,
until you learn that the Most High rules
over the kingdoms of the world and
gives them to anyone he chooses. 26But
the stump and roots of the tree were left
in the ground. This means that you will
receive your kingdom back again when
you have learned that heaven rules.

27“‘King Nebuchadnezzar, please
accept my advice. Stop sinning and do
what is right. Break from your wicked
past and be merciful to the poor. Perhaps
then you will continue to prosper.’

The Dream’s Fulfillment

28“But all these things did happen to
King Nebuchadnezzar. 29Twelve months
later he was taking a walk on the flat
roof of the royal palace in Babylon. 30As
he looked out across the city, he said,
‘Look at this great city of Babylon! By
my own mighty power, I have built this
beautiful city as my royal residence to
display my majestic splendor.’

31“While these words were still in his
mouth, a voice called down from heaven,
‘O King Nebuchadnezzar, this message
is for you! You are no longer ruler of
this kingdom. 32You will be driven from
human society. You will live in the fields
with the wild animals, and you will eat
grass like a cow. Seven periods of time
will pass while you live this way, until
you learn that the Most High rules over
the kingdoms of the world and gives
them to anyone he chooses.’

33“That same hour the judgment was
fulfilled, and Nebuchadnezzar was

3:25 Aramaic *like a son of the gods.* **4:1** Verses 4:1-3 are numbered 3:31-33 in Aramaic text. **4:4** Verses 4:4-37 are numbered 4:1-34 in Aramaic text. **4:7** Or *Chaldeans.* **4:13** Aramaic *a watcher;* also in 4:23. **4:17** Aramaic *the watchers.*

driven from human society. He ate grass
like a cow, and he was drenched with the
dew of heaven. He lived this way until
his hair was as long as eagles' feathers
and his nails were like birds' claws.

Nebuchadnezzar Praises God

34 "After this time had passed, I,
Nebuchadnezzar, looked up to heaven.
My sanity returned, and I praised and
worshiped the Most High and honored
the one who lives forever.

His rule is everlasting,
  and his kingdom is eternal.
35 All the people of the earth
  are nothing compared to him.
He does as he pleases
  among the angels of heaven
  and among the people of the earth.
No one can stop him or say to him,
  'What do you mean by doing these
    things?'

36 "When my sanity returned to me, so
did my honor and glory and kingdom. My
advisers and nobles sought me out, and
I was restored as head of my kingdom,
with even greater honor than before.
37 "Now I, Nebuchadnezzar, praise and
glorify and honor the King of heaven. All
his acts are just and true, and he is able
to humble the proud."

The Writing on the Wall

5 Many years later King Belshazzar gave
a great feast for 1,000 of his nobles,
and he drank wine with them. 2 While Belshazzar was drinking the wine, he gave
orders to bring in the gold and silver cups
that his predecessor,* Nebuchadnezzar,
had taken from the Temple in Jerusalem.
He wanted to drink from them with his
nobles, his wives, and his concubines. 3 So
they brought these gold cups taken from
the Temple, the house of God in Jerusalem,
and the king and his nobles, his wives, and
his concubines drank from them. 4 While
they drank from them they praised their
idols made of gold, silver, bronze, iron,
wood, and stone.
5 Suddenly, they saw the fingers of a
human hand writing on the plaster wall of
the king's palace, near the lampstand. The
king himself saw the hand as it wrote, 6 and
his face turned pale with fright. His knees
knocked together in fear and his legs gave
way beneath him.
7 The king shouted for the enchanters, astrologers,* and fortune-tellers to be brought
before him. He said to these wise men of
Babylon, "Whoever can read this writing
and tell me what it means will be dressed
in purple robes of royal honor and will have
a gold chain placed around his neck. He
will become the third highest ruler in the
kingdom!"
8 But when all the king's wise men had
come in, none of them could read the writing
or tell him what it meant. 9 So the king grew
even more alarmed, and his face turned
pale. His nobles, too, were shaken.
10 But when the queen mother heard what
was happening, she hurried to the banquet
hall. She said to Belshazzar, "Long live
the king! Don't be so pale and frightened.
11 There is a man in your kingdom who
has within him the spirit of the holy gods.
During Nebuchadnezzar's reign, this man
was found to have insight, understanding,
and wisdom like that of the gods. Your predecessor, the king—your predecessor King
Nebuchadnezzar—made him chief over all
the magicians, enchanters, astrologers,
and fortune-tellers of Babylon. 12 This man
Daniel, whom the king named Belteshazzar, has exceptional ability and is filled with
divine knowledge and understanding. He
can interpret dreams, explain riddles, and
solve difficult problems. Call for Daniel, and
he will tell you what the writing means."

Daniel Explains the Writing

13 So Daniel was brought in before the king.
The king asked him, "Are you Daniel, one
of the exiles brought from Judah by my predecessor, King Nebuchadnezzar? 14 I have
heard that you have the spirit of the gods
within you and that you are filled with
insight, understanding, and wisdom. 15 My
wise men and enchanters have tried to
read the words on the wall and tell me their
meaning, but they cannot do it. 16 I am told
that you can give interpretations and solve
difficult problems. If you can read these
words and tell me their meaning, you will
be clothed in purple robes of royal honor,
and you will have a gold chain placed
around your neck. You will become the
third highest ruler in the kingdom."
17 Daniel answered the king, "Keep your

gifts or give them to someone else, but I will
tell you what the writing means. 18Your
Majesty, the Most High God gave sovereignty, majesty, glory, and honor to your predecessor, Nebuchadnezzar. 19He made him
so great that people of all races and nations
and languages trembled before him in fear.
He killed those he wanted to kill and spared
those he wanted to spare. He honored those
he wanted to honor and disgraced those he
wanted to disgrace. 20But when his heart
and mind were puffed up with arrogance, he
was brought down from his royal throne and
stripped of his glory. 21He was driven from
human society. He was given the mind of a
wild animal, and he lived among the wild
donkeys. He ate grass like a cow, and he was
drenched with the dew of heaven, until he
learned that the Most High God rules over
the kingdoms of the world and appoints
anyone he desires to rule over them.

22"You are his successor,* O Belshazzar,
and you knew all this, yet you have not
humbled yourself. 23For you have proudly
defied the Lord of heaven and have had
these cups from his Temple brought before
you. You and your nobles and your wives
and concubines have been drinking wine
from them while praising gods of silver,
gold, bronze, iron, wood, and stone—gods
that neither see nor hear nor know anything
at all. But you have not honored the God
who gives you the breath of life and controls
your destiny! 24So God has sent this hand to
write this message.

25"This is the message that was written:
MENE, MENE, TEKEL, and PARSIN. 26This is
what these words mean:

Mene means 'numbered'—God has
numbered the days of your reign and
has brought it to an end.

27 *Tekel* means 'weighed'—you have been
weighed on the balances and have not
measured up.

28 *Parsin** means 'divided'—your kingdom
has been divided and given to the
Medes and Persians."

29Then at Belshazzar's command, Daniel
was dressed in purple robes, a gold chain
was hung around his neck, and he was
proclaimed the third highest ruler in the
kingdom.

30That very night Belshazzar, the Babylonian* king, was killed.*

31*And Darius the Mede took over the
kingdom at the age of sixty-two.

Daniel in the Lions' Den

6 1*Darius the Mede decided to divide
the kingdom into 120 provinces, and he
appointed a high officer to rule over each
province. 2The king also chose Daniel and
two others as administrators to supervise
the high officers and protect the king's interests. 3Daniel soon proved himself more
capable than all the other administrators
and high officers. Because of Daniel's great
ability, the king made plans to place him
over the entire empire.

4Then the other administrators and high
officers began searching for some fault in
the way Daniel was handling government
affairs, but they couldn't find anything to
criticize or condemn. He was faithful, always
responsible, and completely trustworthy.
5So they concluded, "Our only chance of
finding grounds for accusing Daniel will be
in connection with the rules of his religion."

6So the administrators and high officers
went to the king and said, "Long live King
Darius! 7We are all in agreement—we administrators, officials, high officers, advisers, and governors—that the king should
make a law that will be strictly enforced.
Give orders that for the next thirty days
any person who prays to anyone, divine
or human—except to you, Your Majesty—
will be thrown into the den of lions. 8And
now, Your Majesty, issue and sign this law
so it cannot be changed, an official law of
the Medes and Persians that cannot be
revoked." 9So King Darius signed the law.

10But when Daniel learned that the law
had been signed, he went home and knelt
down as usual in his upstairs room, with its
windows open toward Jerusalem. He prayed
three times a day, just as he had always
done, giving thanks to his God. 11Then the
officials went together to Daniel's house
and found him praying and asking for God's
help. 12So they went straight to the king
and reminded him about his law. "Did you
not sign a law that for the next thirty days
any person who prays to anyone, divine or

5:2 Aramaic *father;* also in 5:11, 13, 18. **5:7** Or *Chaldeans;* also in 5:11. **5:22** Aramaic *son.* **5:28** Aramaic *Peres,* the singular of *Parsin.* **5:30a** Or *Chaldean.* **5:30b** The Persians and Medes conquered Babylon in October 539 B.C. **5:31** Verse 5:31 is numbered 6:1 in Aramaic text. **6:1** Verses 6:1-28 are numbered 6:2-29 in Aramaic text.

human—except to you, Your Majesty—will
be thrown into the den of lions?"
"Yes," the king replied, "that decision
stands; it is an official law of the Medes and
Persians that cannot be revoked."
13Then they told the king, "That man
Daniel, one of the captives from Judah, is
ignoring you and your law. He still prays to
his God three times a day."
14Hearing this, the king was deeply
troubled, and he tried to think of a way to
save Daniel. He spent the rest of the day
looking for a way to get Daniel out of this
predicament.
15In the evening the men went together to
the king and said, "Your Majesty, you know
that according to the law of the Medes and
the Persians, no law that the king signs can
be changed."
16So at last the king gave orders for Daniel
to be arrested and thrown into the den of
lions. The king said to him, "May your God,
whom you serve so faithfully, rescue you."
17A stone was brought and placed over the
mouth of the den. The king sealed the stone
with his own royal seal and the seals of his
nobles, so that no one could rescue Daniel.
18Then the king returned to his palace and
spent the night fasting. He refused his usual
entertainment and couldn't sleep at all that
night.
19Very early the next morning, the king
got up and hurried out to the lions' den.
20When he got there, he called out in
anguish, "Daniel, servant of the living God!
Was your God, whom you serve so faithfully, able to rescue you from the lions?"
21Daniel answered, "Long live the king!
22My God sent his angel to shut the lions'
mouths so that they would not hurt me, for
I have been found innocent in his sight. And
I have not wronged you, Your Majesty."
23The king was overjoyed and ordered
that Daniel be lifted from the den. Not
a scratch was found on him, for he had
trusted in his God.
24Then the king gave orders to arrest the
men who had maliciously accused Daniel.
He had them thrown into the lions' den,
along with their wives and children. The
lions leaped on them and tore them apart
before they even hit the floor of the den.
25Then King Darius sent this message to
the people of every race and nation and language throughout the world:

"Peace and prosperity to you!
26"I decree that everyone throughout
my kingdom should tremble with fear
before the God of Daniel.

For he is the living God,
and he will endure forever.
His kingdom will never be destroyed,
and his rule will never end.
27 He rescues and saves his people;
he performs miraculous signs and
wonders
in the heavens and on earth.
He has rescued Daniel
from the power of the lions."

28So Daniel prospered during the reign of
Darius and the reign of Cyrus the Persian.*

Daniel's Vision of Four Beasts

7 Earlier, during the first year of King Belshazzar's reign in Babylon,* Daniel had
a dream and saw visions as he lay in his
bed. He wrote down the dream, and this is
what he saw.
2In my vision that night, I, Daniel, saw a
great storm churning the surface of a great
sea, with strong winds blowing from every direction. 3Then four huge beasts came up out
of the water, each different from the others.
4The first beast was like a lion with
eagles' wings. As I watched, its wings were
pulled off, and it was left standing with its
two hind feet on the ground, like a human
being. And it was given a human mind.
5Then I saw a second beast, and it looked
like a bear. It was rearing up on one side,
and it had three ribs in its mouth between
its teeth. And I heard a voice saying to it,
"Get up! Devour the flesh of many people!"
6Then the third of these strange beasts
appeared, and it looked like a leopard. It
had four bird's wings on its back, and it
had four heads. Great authority was given
to this beast.
7Then in my vision that night, I saw a
fourth beast—terrifying, dreadful, and very
strong. It devoured and crushed its victims
with huge iron teeth and trampled their
remains beneath its feet. It was different
from any of the other beasts, and it had ten
horns.
8As I was looking at the horns, suddenly
another small horn appeared among them.
Three of the first horns were torn out by the
roots to make room for it. This little horn

had eyes like human eyes and a mouth that
was boasting arrogantly.

9 I watched as thrones were put in place
and the Ancient One* sat down to
judge.
His clothing was as white as snow,
his hair like purest wool.
He sat on a fiery throne
with wheels of blazing fire,
10 and a river of fire was pouring out,
flowing from his presence.
Millions of angels ministered to him;
many millions stood to attend him.
Then the court began its session,
and the books were opened.

11 I continued to watch because I could
hear the little horn's boastful speech. I kept
watching until the fourth beast was killed
and its body was destroyed by fire. 12 The
other three beasts had their authority taken
from them, but they were allowed to live a
while longer.*

13 As my vision continued that night, I saw
someone like a son of man* coming with
the clouds of heaven. He approached the
Ancient One and was led into his presence.
14 He was given authority, honor, and sovereignty over all the nations of the world,
so that people of every race and nation
and language would obey him. His rule is
eternal—it will never end. His kingdom will
never be destroyed.

The Vision Is Explained

15 I, Daniel, was troubled by all I had seen, and
my visions terrified me. 16 So I approached one
of those standing beside the throne and asked
him what it all meant. He explained it to me
like this: 17 "These four huge beasts represent
four kingdoms that will arise from the earth.
18 But in the end, the holy people of the Most
High will be given the kingdom, and they will
rule forever and ever."

19 Then I wanted to know the true meaning
of the fourth beast, the one so different from
the others and so terrifying. It had devoured
and crushed its victims with iron teeth and
bronze claws, trampling their remains
beneath its feet. 20 I also asked about the
ten horns on the fourth beast's head and
the little horn that came up afterward and
destroyed three of the other horns. This
horn had seemed greater than the others,
and it had human eyes and a mouth that
was boasting arrogantly. 21 As I watched, this
horn was waging war against God's holy

6:28 Or *of Darius, that is, the reign of Cyrus the Persian.*
7:1 The first year of Belshazzar's reign (who was co-regent with his father, Nabonidus) was 556 B.C. (or perhaps as late as 553 B.C.).
7:9 Aramaic *an Ancient of Days;* also in 7:13, 22. **7:12** Aramaic *for a season and a time.* **7:13** Or *like a Son of Man.*

▸ **7:13** *See **The Son of Man**, page 1101.*

Daniel's visions

Chapter 7 opens by telling us that Daniel "had a dream and saw visions." Dreams normally happen when one is asleep and visions when awake, but often the Bible uses these terms interchangeably. Dreams and visions were seen as important means of divine revelation in the ancient world.

Up to this point, Daniel had interpreted the dreams of others; but now, so deep was the revelation that his own dreams and visions contained, Daniel needed someone to interpret them to him (e.g., Daniel 7:16; 8:15-16; 9:21-23; 10:11-14). In these visions—a vision of four beasts (chapter 7), two animals (chapter 8), an angel (chapter 9), a man (chapter 10), and a panorama of history to the end times (chapters 11–12)—God revealed to him, through apocalyptic imagery—imagery that was generally well-understood at the time, even if Daniel needed the overall meaning explained—the rise of succeeding empires and the ultimate triumph of the kingdom of God over them all. And right at the heart of these revelations stands "someone like a son of man" (7:13)—the one whom the New Testament reveals to be Jesus. Daniel was shown that, despite all the chaos around, God knows where he is taking history.

people and was defeating them, [22]until the Ancient One—the Most High—came and judged in favor of his holy people. Then the time arrived for the holy people to take over the kingdom.

[23]Then he said to me, "This fourth beast is the fourth world power that will rule the earth. It will be different from all the others. It will devour the whole world, trampling and crushing everything in its path. [24]Its ten horns are ten kings who will rule that empire. Then another king will arise, different from the other ten, who will subdue three of them. [25]He will defy the Most High and oppress the holy people of the Most High. He will try to change their sacred festivals and laws, and they will be placed under his control for a time, times, and half a time.

[26]"But then the court will pass judgment, and all his power will be taken away and completely destroyed. [27]Then the sovereignty, power, and greatness of all the kingdoms under heaven will be given to the holy people of the Most High. His kingdom will last forever, and all rulers will serve and obey him."

[28]That was the end of the vision. I, Daniel, was terrified by my thoughts and my face was pale with fear, but I kept these things to myself.

Daniel's Vision of a Ram and Goat

8 [1]*During the third year of King Belshazzar's reign, I, Daniel, saw another vision, following the one that had already appeared to me. [2]In this vision I was at the fortress of Susa, in the province of Elam, standing beside the Ulai River.*

[3]As I looked up, I saw a ram with two long horns standing beside the river.* One of the horns was longer than the other, even though it had grown later than the other one. [4]The ram butted everything out of his way to the west, to the north, and to the south, and no one could stand against him or help his victims. He did as he pleased and became very great.

[5]While I was watching, suddenly a male goat appeared from the west, crossing the land so swiftly that he didn't even touch the ground. This goat, which had one very large horn between its eyes, [6]headed toward the two-horned ram that I had seen standing beside the river, rushing at him in a rage. [7]The goat charged furiously at the ram and struck him, breaking off both his horns. Now the ram was helpless, and the goat knocked him down and trampled him. No one could rescue the ram from the goat's power.

[8]The goat became very powerful. But at the height of his power, his large horn was broken off. In the large horn's place grew four prominent horns pointing in the four directions of the earth. [9]Then from one of the prominent horns came a small horn whose power grew very great. It extended toward the south and the east and toward the glorious land of Israel. [10]Its power reached to the heavens, where it attacked the heavenly army, throwing some of the heavenly beings and some of the stars to the ground and trampling them. [11]It even challenged the

Identification of the four kingdoms

Chapter 2	Chapter 7	Chapter 8	Empire	Dates
Statue's head of gold	Lion		Babylon	625–539 BC
Chest and arms of silver	Bear	Ram	Medo-Persia	539–331 BC
Belly and thighs of bronze	Leopard	Goat	Greece	331–63 BC
Legs of iron, feet of clay	Terrifying beast		Rome	63 BC–AD 476

Commander of heaven's army by canceling
the daily sacrifices offered to him and by
destroying his Temple. 12 The army of heaven
was restrained from responding to this rebellion. So the daily sacrifice was halted, and
truth was overthrown. The horn succeeded
in everything it did.*

13 Then I heard two holy ones talking to
each other. One of them asked, "How long
will the events of this vision last? How long
will the rebellion that causes desecration
stop the daily sacrifices? How long will the
Temple and heaven's army be trampled on?"

14 The other replied, "It will take 2,300 evenings and mornings; then the Temple will
be made right again."

Gabriel Explains the Vision

15 As I, Daniel, was trying to understand
the meaning of this vision, someone who
looked like a man stood in front of me.
16 And I heard a human voice calling out
from the Ulai River, "Gabriel, tell this man
the meaning of his vision."

17 As Gabriel approached the place where
I was standing, I became so terrified that
I fell with my face to the ground. "Son of
man," he said, "you must understand that
the events you have seen in your vision
relate to the time of the end."

18 While he was speaking, I fainted and
lay there with my face to the ground. But
Gabriel roused me with a touch and helped
me to my feet.

19 Then he said, "I am here to tell you what
will happen later in the time of wrath. What
you have seen pertains to the very end of
time. 20 The two-horned ram represents the
kings of Media and Persia. 21 The shaggy
male goat represents the king of Greece,*
and the large horn between his eyes represents the first king of the Greek Empire.
22 The four prominent horns that replaced
the one large horn show that the Greek
Empire will break into four kingdoms, but
none as great as the first.

23 "At the end of their rule, when their sin
is at its height, a fierce king, a master of intrigue, will rise to power. 24 He will become
very strong, but not by his own power. He
will cause a shocking amount of destruction and succeed in everything he does. He
will destroy powerful leaders and devastate the holy people. 25 He will be a master
of deception and will become arrogant; he
will destroy many without warning. He will
even take on the Prince of princes in battle,
but he will be broken, though not by human
power.

26 "This vision about the 2,300 evenings
and mornings* is true. But none of these
things will happen for a long time, so keep
this vision a secret."

27 Then I, Daniel, was overcome and lay
sick for several days. Afterward I got up and
performed my duties for the king, but I was
greatly troubled by the vision and could not
understand it.

8:1 The original text from this point through chapter 12 is in Hebrew. See note at 2:4. **8:2** Or *the Ulai Gate;* also in 8:16. **8:3** Or *the gate;* also in 8:6. **8:11-12** The meaning of the Hebrew for these verses is uncertain. **8:21** Hebrew *of Javan.* **8:26** Hebrew *about the evenings and mornings;* compare 8:14.

Gabriel

Daniel's vision of the ram and the goat was interpreted to him by Gabriel (Daniel 8:15-26). He would appear to Daniel again to predict Jerusalem's future and the coming of the Anointed One or Messiah (9:20-27). We don't meet Gabriel again until the New Testament, where he announces the birth of John the Baptist to Zechariah (Luke 1:8-20) and the birth of Jesus to Mary (Luke 1:26-38). The fearful responses of Daniel (Daniel 8:17), Zechariah (Luke 1:11-13), and Mary (Luke 1:30) reflect what an awesome angelic being Gabriel must be. In Jewish intertestamental literature—that is, literature written in the period between the end of the Old Testament and the beginning of the New Testament—Gabriel is seen as an archangel who stands in God's presence to serve him and present the prayers of God's people. Gabriel and Michael are the only two angels referred to by name in the Bible.

▶ *See also* ***The archangel Michael****, page 972;* ***Angels****, page 1397.*

Daniel's Prayer for His People

9 It was the first year of the reign of Darius
the Mede, the son of Ahasuerus, who
became king of the Babylonians.* 2During
the first year of his reign, I, Daniel, learned
from reading the word of the LORD, as revealed to Jeremiah the prophet, that Jerusalem must lie desolate for seventy years.*
3So I turned to the Lord God and pleaded
with him in prayer and fasting. I also wore
rough burlap and sprinkled myself with
ashes.

4I prayed to the LORD my God and
confessed:

"O Lord, you are a great and awesome
God! You always fulfill your covenant
and keep your promises of unfailing
love to those who love you and obey your
commands. 5But we have sinned and
done wrong. We have rebelled against
you and scorned your commands and
regulations. 6We have refused to listen
to your servants the prophets, who
spoke on your authority to our kings
and princes and ancestors and to all
the people of the land.

7"Lord, you are in the right; but
as you see, our faces are covered
with shame. This is true of all of us,
including the people of Judah and
Jerusalem and all Israel, scattered
near and far, wherever you have driven
us because of our disloyalty to you.
8O LORD, we and our kings, princes,
and ancestors are covered with shame
because we have sinned against you.
9But the Lord our God is merciful and
forgiving, even though we have rebelled
against him. 10We have not obeyed the
LORD our God, for we have not followed
the instructions he gave us through
his servants the prophets. 11All Israel
has disobeyed your instruction and
turned away, refusing to listen to your
voice.

"So now the solemn curses and
judgments written in the Law of Moses,
the servant of God, have been poured
down on us because of our sin. 12You
have kept your word and done to us
and our rulers exactly as you warned.
Never has there been such a disaster as
happened in Jerusalem. 13Every curse
written against us in the Law of Moses
has come true. Yet we have refused to
seek mercy from the LORD our God by
turning from our sins and recognizing
his truth. 14Therefore, the LORD has
brought upon us the disaster he
prepared. The LORD our God was right
to do all of these things, for we did not
obey him.

15"O Lord our God, you brought lasting
honor to your name by rescuing your
people from Egypt in a great display
of power. But we have sinned and are
full of wickedness. 16In view of all your
faithful mercies, Lord, please turn
your furious anger away from your city
Jerusalem, your holy mountain. All the
neighboring nations mock Jerusalem
and your people because of our sins and
the sins of our ancestors.

17"O our God, hear your servant's
prayer! Listen as I plead. For your own
sake, Lord, smile again on your desolate
sanctuary.

18"O my God, lean down and listen to
me. Open your eyes and see our despair.
See how your city—the city that bears
your name—lies in ruins. We make this
plea, not because we deserve help, but
because of your mercy.

19"O Lord, hear. O Lord, forgive.
O Lord, listen and act! For your own
sake, do not delay, O my God, for your
people and your city bear your name."

Gabriel's Message about the Anointed One

20I went on praying and confessing my sin
and the sin of my people, pleading with the
LORD my God for Jerusalem, his holy mountain. 21As I was praying, Gabriel, whom I had
seen in the earlier vision, came swiftly to me
at the time of the evening sacrifice. 22He explained to me, "Daniel, I have come here to
give you insight and understanding. 23The
moment you began praying, a command
was given. And now I am here to tell you
what it was, for you are very precious to
God. Listen carefully so that you can understand the meaning of your vision.

24"A period of seventy sets of seven* has
been decreed for your people and your holy

▸ **9:1-19** See ***Prayer as intercession***, *page 922.* **9:3** See ***Does fasting have any value?***, *page 1042.*

city to finish their rebellion, to put an end to their sin, to atone for their guilt, to bring in everlasting righteousness, to confirm the prophetic vision, and to anoint the Most Holy Place.* [25]Now listen and understand! Seven sets of seven plus sixty-two sets of seven* will pass from the time the command is given to rebuild Jerusalem until a ruler—the Anointed One*—comes. Jerusalem will be rebuilt with streets and strong defenses,* despite the perilous times.

[26]"After this period of sixty-two sets of seven,* the Anointed One will be killed, appearing to have accomplished nothing, and a ruler will arise whose armies will destroy the city and the Temple. The end will come with a flood, and war and its miseries are decreed from that time to the very end. [27]The ruler will make a treaty with the people for a period of one set of seven,* but after half this time, he will put an end to the sacrifices and offerings. And as a climax to all his terrible deeds,* he will set up a sacrilegious object that causes desecration,* until the fate decreed for this defiler is finally poured out on him."

Daniel's Vision of a Messenger

10 In the third year of the reign of King Cyrus of Persia,* Daniel (also known as Belteshazzar) had another vision. He understood that the vision concerned events certain to happen in the future—times of war and great hardship.

[2]When this vision came to me, I, Daniel, had been in mourning for three whole weeks. [3]All that time I had eaten no rich food. No meat or wine crossed my lips, and I used no fragrant lotions until those three weeks had passed.

[4]On April 23,* as I was standing on the bank of the great Tigris River, [5]I looked up and saw a man dressed in linen clothing, with a belt of pure gold around his waist. [6]His body looked like a precious gem. His face flashed like lightning, and his eyes flamed like torches. His arms and feet shone like polished bronze, and his voice roared like a vast multitude of people.

[7]Only I, Daniel, saw this vision. The men with me saw nothing, but they were suddenly terrified and ran away to hide. [8]So I was left there all alone to see this amazing

9:1 Or *the Chaldeans.* **9:2** See Jer 25:11-12; 29:10. **9:24a** Hebrew *seventy sevens.* **9:24b** Or *the Most Holy One.* **9:25a** Hebrew *Seven sevens plus sixty-two sevens.* **9:25b** Or *an anointed one;* similarly in 9:26. Hebrew reads *a messiah.* **9:25c** Or *and a moat,* or *and trenches.* **9:26** Hebrew *After sixty-two sevens.* **9:27a** Hebrew *for one seven.* **9:27b** Hebrew *And on the wing;* the meaning of the Hebrew is uncertain. **9:27c** Hebrew *an abomination of desolation.* **10:1** The third year of Cyrus's reign was 536 B.C. **10:4** Hebrew *On the twenty-fourth day of the first month,* of the ancient Hebrew lunar calendar. This date in the book of Daniel can be cross-checked with dates in surviving Persian records and can be related accurately to our modern calendar. This event occurred on April 23, 536 B.C.

Principalities and powers

Daniel had been praying and fasting for three weeks (Daniel 10:3), seeking understanding. When God's messenger came in response, he explained that he had been delayed because "the spirit prince of the kingdom of Persia" blocked his way (10:13) and that he was able to break through only because Michael, the archangel, came to his aid in response to Daniel's prayer. Daniel was experiencing what Paul would write about many centuries later: "For we are not fighting against flesh-and-blood enemies, but against evil rulers and authorities of the unseen world, against mighty powers in this dark world, and against evil spirits in the heavenly places" (Ephesians 6:12). He learned not only that spiritual warfare is real but also that we have the weapons to overcome when faced with it.

Note, however, that Daniel was unaware of this battle at the time; he only understood it later. There is no suggestion that there were territorial spirits at work that he had to identify, bind, and overcome before his prayer could be answered; there was indeed a territorial spirit, but overcoming it was God's work alone. Daniel's part was not to engage with demons but to engage with God, to simply be faithful in praying and fasting until God himself broke through the opposition and came with his answer. Our focus should never be on demons, but always on Christ.

▶ *See also **Demons**, page 1126.*

vision. My strength left me, my face grew
deathly pale, and I felt very weak. [9]Then
I heard the man speak, and when I heard
the sound of his voice, I fainted and lay
there with my face to the ground.
[10]Just then a hand touched me and lifted
me, still trembling, to my hands and knees.
[11]And the man said to me, "Daniel, you are
very precious to God, so listen carefully
to what I have to say to you. Stand up, for
I have been sent to you." When he said this
to me, I stood up, still trembling.
[12]Then he said, "Don't be afraid, Daniel.
Since the first day you began to pray for
understanding and to humble yourself
before your God, your request has been
heard in heaven. I have come in answer
to your prayer. [13]But for twenty-one days
the spirit prince* of the kingdom of Persia
blocked my way. Then Michael, one of the
archangels,* came to help me, and I left him
there with the spirit prince of the kingdom
of Persia.* [14]Now I am here to explain what
will happen to your people in the future, for
this vision concerns a time yet to come."
[15]While he was speaking to me, I looked
down at the ground, unable to say a word.
[16]Then the one who looked like a man*
touched my lips, and I opened my mouth
and began to speak. I said to the one standing in front of me, "I am filled with anguish
because of the vision I have seen, my lord,
and I am very weak. [17]How can someone
like me, your servant, talk to you, my
lord? My strength is gone, and I can hardly
breathe."
[18]Then the one who looked like a man
touched me again, and I felt my strength
returning. [19]"Don't be afraid," he said, "for
you are very precious to God. Peace! Be encouraged! Be strong!"

As he spoke these words to me, I suddenly
felt stronger and said to him, "Please speak to
me, my lord, for you have strengthened me."
[20]He replied, "Do you know why I have
come? Soon I must return to fight against
the spirit prince of the kingdom of Persia,
and after that the spirit prince of the
kingdom of Greece* will come. [21]Meanwhile,
I will tell you what is written in the Book of
Truth. (No one helps me against these spirit
princes except Michael, your spirit prince.*
[11:1]I have been standing beside Michael* to
support and strengthen him since the first
year of the reign of Darius the Mede.)

Kings of the South and North

11 [2]"Now then, I will reveal the truth to
you. Three more Persian kings will
reign, to be succeeded by a fourth, far richer
than the others. He will use his wealth to stir
up everyone to fight against the kingdom of
Greece.*
[3]"Then a mighty king will rise to power
who will rule with great authority and accomplish everything he sets out to do. [4]But
at the height of his power, his kingdom
will be broken apart and divided into four
parts. It will not be ruled by the king's descendants, nor will the kingdom hold the
authority it once had. For his empire will
be uprooted and given to others.
[5]"The king of the south will increase in
power, but one of his own officials will
become more powerful than he and will
rule his kingdom with great strength.
[6]"Some years later an alliance will be
formed between the king of the north and
the king of the south. The daughter of the
king of the south will be given in marriage to
the king of the north to secure the alliance,
but she will lose her influence over him, and
so will her father. She will be abandoned
along with her supporters. [7]But when one of
her relatives* becomes king of the south, he
will raise an army and enter the fortress of
the king of the north and defeat him. [8]When
he returns to Egypt, he will carry back their
idols with him, along with priceless articles
of gold and silver. For some years afterward
he will leave the king of the north alone.
[9]"Later the king of the north will invade the
realm of the king of the south but will soon
return to his own land. [10]However, the sons of
the king of the north will assemble a mighty
army that will advance like a flood and carry
the battle as far as the enemy's fortress.
[11]"Then, in a rage, the king of the south
will rally against the vast forces assembled
by the king of the north and will defeat
them. [12]After the enemy army is swept away,
the king of the south will be filled with pride
and will execute many thousands of his
enemies. But his success will be short lived.
[13]"A few years later the king of the north
will return with a fully equipped army far
greater than before. [14]At that time there will
be a general uprising against the king of the
south. Violent men among your own people
will join them in fulfillment of this vision,
but they will not succeed. [15]Then the king of

the north will come and lay siege to a fortified city and capture it. The best troops of
the south will not be able to stand in the
face of the onslaught.
16 "The king of the north will march onward
unopposed; none will be able to stop him.
He will pause in the glorious land of Israel,*
intent on destroying it. 17 He will make plans
to come with the might of his entire kingdom
and will form an alliance with the king of
the south. He will give him a daughter in
marriage in order to overthrow the kingdom
from within, but his plan will fail.
18 "After this, he will turn his attention to
the coastland and conquer many cities. But
a commander from another land will put
an end to his insolence and cause him to
retreat in shame. 19 He will take refuge in his
own fortresses but will stumble and fall and
be seen no more.
20 "His successor will send out a tax collector to maintain the royal splendor. But
after a very brief reign, he will die, though
not from anger or in battle.
21 "The next to come to power will be a
despicable man who is not in line for royal
succession. He will slip in when least expected and take over the kingdom by flattery and intrigue. 22 Before him great armies
will be swept away, including a covenant
prince. 23 With deceitful promises, he will
make various alliances. He will become
strong despite having only a handful of
followers. 24 Without warning he will enter
the richest areas of the land. Then he will
distribute among his followers the plunder
and wealth of the rich—something his predecessors had never done. He will plot the
overthrow of strongholds, but this will last
for only a short while.
25 "Then he will stir up his courage and
raise a great army against the king of the
south. The king of the south will go to battle
with a mighty army, but to no avail, for there
will be plots against him. 26 His own household will cause his downfall. His army will
be swept away, and many will be killed.
27 Seeking nothing but each other's harm,
these kings will plot against each other at
the conference table, attempting to deceive
each other. But it will make no difference,
for the end will come at the appointed time.
28 "The king of the north will then return
home with great riches. On the way he will
set himself against the people of the holy
covenant, doing much damage before continuing his journey.
29 "Then at the appointed time he will
once again invade the south, but this time
the result will be different. 30 For warships
from western coastlands* will scare him off,
and he will withdraw and return home. But
he will vent his anger against the people of
the holy covenant and reward those who
forsake the covenant.
31 "His army will take over the Temple fortress, pollute the sanctuary, put a stop to the
daily sacrifices, and set up the sacrilegious
object that causes desecration.* 32 He will
flatter and win over those who have violated
the covenant. But the people who know
their God will be strong and will resist him.
33 "Wise leaders will give instruction to
many, but these teachers will die by fire and
sword, or they will be jailed and robbed.
34 During these persecutions, little help will
arrive, and many who join them will not
be sincere. 35 And some of the wise will fall
victim to persecution. In this way, they will
be refined and cleansed and made pure
until the time of the end, for the appointed
time is still to come.
36 "The king will do as he pleases, exalt-
ing himself and claiming to be greater than
every god, even blaspheming the God of
gods. He will succeed, but only until the
time of wrath is completed. For what has
been determined will surely take place. 37 He
will have no respect for the gods of his ancestors, or for the god loved by women, or
for any other god, for he will boast that he is
greater than them all. 38 Instead of these, he
will worship the god of fortresses—a god his
ancestors never knew—and lavish on him
gold, silver, precious stones, and expensive
gifts. 39 Claiming this foreign god's help, he
will attack the strongest fortresses. He will
honor those who submit to him, appointing
them to positions of authority and dividing
the land among them as their reward.*
40 "Then at the time of the end, the king of
the south will attack the king of the north.

10:13a Hebrew *the prince;* also in 10:13c, 20. **10:13b** Hebrew *the chief princes.* **10:13c** As in one Greek version; Hebrew reads *and I was left there with the kings of Persia.* The meaning of the Hebrew is uncertain. **10:16** As in most manuscripts of the Masoretic Text; one manuscript of the Masoretic Text and one Greek version read *Then something that looked like a human hand.* **10:20** Hebrew *of Javan.* **10:21** Hebrew *against these except Michael, your prince.* **11:1** Hebrew *him.* **11:2** Hebrew *of Javan.* **11:7** Hebrew *a branch from her roots.* **11:16** Hebrew *the glorious land.* **11:30** Hebrew *from Kittim.* **11:31** Hebrew *the abomination of desolation.* **11:39** Or *at a price.*

The king of the north will storm out with
chariots, charioteers, and a vast navy. He
will invade various lands and sweep through
them like a flood. 41He will enter the glorious land of Israel,* and many nations will
fall, but Moab, Edom, and the best part of
Ammon will escape. 42He will conquer many
countries, and even Egypt will not escape.
43He will gain control over the gold, silver,
and treasures of Egypt, and the Libyans and
Ethiopians* will be his servants.

44"But then news from the east and the
north will alarm him, and he will set out in
great anger to destroy and obliterate many.
45He will stop between the glorious holy
mountain and the sea and will pitch his royal
tents. But while he is there, his time will suddenly run out, and no one will help him.

The Time of the End

12 "At that time Michael, the archangel*
who stands guard over your nation,
will arise. Then there will be a time of
anguish greater than any since nations first
came into existence. But at that time every
one of your people whose name is written
in the book will be rescued. 2Many of those
whose bodies lie dead and buried will rise
up, some to everlasting life and some to
shame and everlasting disgrace. 3Those
who are wise will shine as bright as the sky,
and those who lead many to righteousness
will shine like the stars forever. 4But you,
Daniel, keep this prophecy a secret; seal
up the book until the time of the end, when
many will rush here and there, and knowledge will increase."

5Then I, Daniel, looked and saw two
others standing on opposite banks of the
river. 6One of them asked the man dressed
in linen, who was now standing above the
river, "How long will it be until these shocking events are over?"

7The man dressed in linen, who was
standing above the river, raised both his
hands toward heaven and took a solemn
oath by the One who lives forever, saying,
"It will go on for a time, times, and half
a time. When the shattering of the holy
people has finally come to an end, all these
things will have happened."

8I heard what he said, but I did not understand what he meant. So I asked, "How will
all this finally end, my lord?"

9But he said, "Go now, Daniel, for what
I have said is kept secret and sealed until
the time of the end. 10Many will be purified,
cleansed, and refined by these trials. But the
wicked will continue in their wickedness,
and none of them will understand. Only
those who are wise will know what it means.

11"From the time the daily sacrifice is
stopped and the sacrilegious object that
causes desecration* is set up to be worshiped, there will be 1,290 days. 12And
blessed are those who wait and remain until
the end of the 1,335 days!

13"As for you, go your way until the end.
You will rest, and then at the end of the
days, you will rise again to receive the inheritance set aside for you."

11:41 Hebrew *the glorious land.* **11:43** Hebrew *Cushites.*
12:1 Hebrew *the great prince.* **12:11** Hebrew *the abomination of desolation.*

The archangel Michael

The book of Daniel comes to a climax as God reveals to Daniel something of his plans for the end time. He is told about Michael, whom the New Testament calls an archangel or "one of the mightiest of the angels" (Jude 1:9), and one of whose roles is to stand guard over God's people (Daniel 12:1). Daniel had already experienced something of this—though without knowing it at the time—when an angel sent with the answers to Daniel's prayers had been resisted by spiritual opposition, and it had been Michael who had come to the rescue (10:12-14). In Revelation we find Michael and his angels defeating Satan in heavenly warfare so he can no longer accuse God's people (Revelation 12:7-12).

▶ *See also **Angels**, page 1397.*

Hosea *Unfaithful people, faithful God*

Hosea prophesied to the northern kingdom of Israel during the prosperous, but corrupt and idolatrous, reign of King Jeroboam II in the middle of the eighth century BC, shortly before the nation was invaded by Assyria. He was one of the two writing prophets to come from the northern kingdom (the other was Jonah). The first three chapters record the tragedy of his personal life. Hosea's wife was unfaithful to him, and God used their sad marriage as a living example of his own relationship with Israel. Israel had been unfaithful to him, as many rich images in the prophecy show; but Hosea shows us that no matter how unfaithful they were, God would remain faithful, for his covenant love cannot let his people go.

Hosea is the first of a series of twelve short prophetic books sometimes called "the Minor Prophets."

What's it all about?

God told Hosea to take a wife, yet warned him in advance that she would be unfaithful (chapter 1). The purpose behind this was that she would become a living symbol of God's wayward people and their unfaithfulness to him. When Gomer had children, Hosea was instructed to give each one a specific, meaningful name that signified the way Israel had drifted from God.

As predicted, Gomer quickly left Hosea to pursue other lovers, which must have been incredibly painful to Hosea. But God told him to find her and bring her back home again as his wife (chapter 3), a picture of how God was ready to receive Israel back, in spite of all her idolatry. (Israel was steeped in the worship of Baal, a nature and fertility god, at this time.)

From chapter 4 onward God then presented his case against faithless Israel, highlighting their sin and idolatry, and their refusal to repent. He declared, "There is no faithfulness, no kindness, no knowledge of God in your land" (4:1) and told Israel, "You are a prostitute through and through" (5:4). Their shallow pretense at repentance (6:1-3) was quickly exposed by God, who told them, "Your love vanishes like the morning mist and disappears like dew in the sunlight" (6:4). They would therefore be punished for their sins and could expect destruction at any moment (chapters 8–9). And yet, God is merciful and loves his people. In chapter 11, he recalled how he saved them from Egypt and "led Israel along with . . . ropes of kindness and love" (11:4). No matter what they had done, he could not give up on them (11:8-9). His love for his people is infinite, and, when they eventually repented, they would be blessed again.

OVERVIEW

Hosea is told to marry Gomer
1:1–2:1

Hosea's unfaithful wife pictures Israel's fall and restoration · *2:2-23*

God commands Hosea to be reconciled to his wife · *3:1-5*

God rebukes Israel for its sin
4:1–5:15

Israel's unwillingness to repent
6:1–7:16

Israel's punishment
8:1–10:15

God's love for Israel and anger at her sin · *11:1–13:16*

Promise of blessing and restoration
14:1-9

page 974

What does it mean for us?

Hosea is brimming with images that show all that God wants to be for his people. God is depicted as a husband, a father, a doctor, a fruitful tree—in other words, as one who can fulfill all his people's needs. But in order for those needs to be fulfilled, we have to draw close to him.

Even though we often follow our own ways instead of God's, God has a heart of love: He is slow to anger and does not want to abandon us. He longs to draw us back to himself and will not give up on us. But we must return to him.

God's love is constant—but it is also demanding. People can only enjoy his blessings if they are willing to live exclusively for him, just as spouses can only benefit from marriage if they are willing to give the marriage their all. Hosea invites us to see our relationship with God as something life-changing, permanent, and exclusive, and to reflect on the pain God feels when our commitment runs low and our vows are broken.

▶ *See also* ***A timeline of the Bible****, pages A22-A24.*

1 The LORD gave this message to Hosea son
of Beeri during the years when Uzziah,
Jotham, Ahaz, and Hezekiah were kings of
Judah, and Jeroboam son of Jehoash* was
king of Israel.

Hosea's Wife and Children

[2]When the LORD first began speaking to
Israel through Hosea, he said to him, "Go
and marry a prostitute,* so that some of her
children will be conceived in prostitution.
This will illustrate how Israel has acted like
a prostitute by turning against the LORD and
worshiping other gods."
[3]So Hosea married Gomer, the daughter of
Diblaim, and she became pregnant and gave
Hosea a son. [4]And the LORD said, "Name the
child Jezreel, for I am about to punish King
Jehu's dynasty to avenge the murders he
committed at Jezreel. In fact, I will bring an
end to Israel's independence. [5]I will break its
military power in the Jezreel Valley."
[6]Soon Gomer became pregnant again
and gave birth to a daughter. And the
LORD said to Hosea, "Name your daughter Lo-ruhamah—'Not loved'—for I will no
longer show love to the people of Israel or
forgive them. [7]But I will show love to the
people of Judah. I will free them from their
enemies—not with weapons and armies or
horses and charioteers, but by my power as
the LORD their God."
[8]After Gomer had weaned Lo-ruhamah,
she again became pregnant and gave birth
to a second son. [9]And the LORD said, "Name
him Lo-ammi—'Not my people'—for Israel is
not my people, and I am not their God.
[10]*"Yet the time will come when Israel's
people will be like the sands of the seashore—
too many to count! Then, at the place where
they were told, 'You are not my people,' it
will be said, 'You are children of the living
God.' [11]Then the people of Judah and Israel
will unite together. They will choose one
leader for themselves, and they will return
from exile together. What a day that will
be—the day of Jezreel*—when God will again
plant his people in his land.
[2:1]*"In that day you will call your brothers
Ammi—'My people.' And you will call your
sisters Ruhamah—'The ones I love.'

Charges against an Unfaithful Wife

2 [2] "But now bring charges against
Israel—your mother—
for she is no longer my wife,
and I am no longer her husband.
Tell her to remove the prostitute's
makeup from her face
and the clothing that exposes her
breasts.
[3] Otherwise, I will strip her as naked
as she was on the day she was born.
I will leave her to die of thirst,
as in a dry and barren wilderness.
[4] And I will not love her children,
for they were conceived in
prostitution.

▶ **1:2** *See* ***Prophecy in the Old Testament****, page 903.*

5 Their mother is a shameless prostitute
and became pregnant in a shameful way.
She said, 'I'll run after other lovers
and sell myself to them for food and water,
for clothing of wool and linen,
and for olive oil and drinks.'

6 "For this reason I will fence her in with thornbushes.
I will block her path with a wall
to make her lose her way.
7 When she runs after her lovers,
she won't be able to catch them.
She will search for them
but not find them.
Then she will think,
'I might as well return to my husband,
for I was better off with him than I am now.'
8 She doesn't realize it was I who gave her everything she has—
the grain, the new wine, the olive oil;
I even gave her silver and gold.
But she gave all my gifts to Baal.

9 "But now I will take back the ripened grain and new wine
I generously provided each harvest season.
I will take away the wool and linen clothing
I gave her to cover her nakedness.
10 I will strip her naked in public,
while all her lovers look on.
No one will be able
to rescue her from my hands.
11 I will put an end to her annual festivals,
her new moon celebrations, and her Sabbath days—
all her appointed festivals.
12 I will destroy her grapevines and fig trees,
things she claims her lovers gave her.
I will let them grow into tangled thickets,
where only wild animals will eat the fruit.
13 I will punish her for all those times
when she burned incense to her images of Baal,
when she put on her earrings and jewels
and went out to look for her lovers
but forgot all about me,"
says the LORD.

The LORD's Love for Unfaithful Israel

14 "But then I will win her back once again.
I will lead her into the desert
and speak tenderly to her there.
15 I will return her vineyards to her
and transform the Valley of Trouble*
into a gateway of hope.
She will give herself to me there,
as she did long ago when she was young,
when I freed her from her captivity in Egypt.

1:1 Hebrew *Joash,* a variant spelling of Jehoash. **1:2** Or *a promiscuous woman.* **1:10** Verses 1:10-11 are numbered 2:1-2 in Hebrew text. **1:11** *Jezreel* means "God plants." **2:1** Verses 2:1-23 are numbered 2:3-25 in Hebrew text. **2:15** Hebrew *valley of Achor.*

Gomer's children

Like his contemporary Isaiah (Isaiah 8:1-18), Hosea was told to give his children specific names that had prophetic significance. Gomer's firstborn, a son, he named *Jezreel* (meaning "God scatters" or "God plants")—the name of the place where King Jehu had come to power amid great bloodshed (2 Kings 9–10). The king's descendants would now be judged and scattered at the very same place (Hosea 1:4-5)—though they would also one day be replanted in hope (1:10-11).

Gomer had two more children. The second, a daughter, was named *Lo-ruhamah* (meaning "not loved"). She would symbolize the change in God's attitude toward his people Israel; in place of the compassion with which he had called and led them, there would now be no pity for them, no forgiveness (1:6-7).

By the time Gomer bore her third child, a son, things had deteriorated so badly that Hosea named him *Lo-ammi* (meaning "not my people"), to portray how the covenant relationship between God and Israel was now utterly broken (1:8-9). And yet, despite all this, with God there is always hope (1:10-11; 2:22-23).

16 When that day comes," says the
LORD,
"you will call me 'my husband'
instead of 'my master.'*
17 O Israel, I will wipe the many names
of Baal from your lips,
and you will never mention them
again.
18 On that day I will make a covenant
with all the wild animals and the
birds of the sky
and the animals that scurry along the
ground
so they will not harm you.
I will remove all weapons of war from
the land,
all swords and bows,
so you can live unafraid
in peace and safety.
19 I will make you my wife forever,
showing you righteousness and justice,
unfailing love and compassion.
20 I will be faithful to you and make you
mine,
and you will finally know me as the
LORD.
21 "In that day, I will answer,"
says the LORD.
"I will answer the sky as it pleads for
clouds.
And the sky will answer the earth with
rain.
22 Then the earth will answer the thirsty
cries
of the grain, the grapevines, and the
olive trees.
And they in turn will answer,
'Jezreel'—'God plants!'
23 At that time I will plant a crop of
Israelites
and raise them for myself.
I will show love
to those I called 'Not loved.'*

Does marriage still matter to God?

In days when there is often great diversity in domestic and family arrangements, does marriage still matter? If two people (of whatever sex) love each other, isn't it enough for them just to live together?

While not wishing to judge others' lifestyles, Christians are called to follow the Bible's teaching about relationships. The Bible makes clear that God's intention for intimate relationships is for one man to live faithfully with one woman in marriage throughout their lives, the two becoming one (Genesis 2:24), something both Jesus and Paul reaffirmed (Matthew 19:4-6; Ephesians 5:31), and something Hosea was determined to live out. When Jewish leaders looked to find ways around this, Jesus made the challenge of marriage even more demanding, such was his high esteem of it (Matthew 19:1-12).

Of course, Adam and Eve didn't have a wedding ceremony; and throughout the biblical period the actual way of getting married seems to have varied. But at the heart of marriage always lay the concept of *covenant*—a binding commitment to relationship. This is the word that the Bible uses of God's relationship with people—one he has no intention of breaking and in which he gives himself fully and permanently. And this is what he calls a man and woman to in marriage: a lifelong, binding, committed relationship, declared in public, with both parties resolved to make it work, no matter what happens. Any relationship without such a covenant at its heart is therefore a pale reflection of what God intends for marriage, and we cannot expect his blessing on it.

The Bible's high view of marriage is reflected in the New Testament's describing the church as the bride of Christ (2 Corinthians 11:2; Ephesians 5:25-32; Revelation 19:7; 21:2, 9), a powerful image of the union between Jesus and his church, and a model for every married couple.

► *See also* ***Can a Christian marry a non-Christian?****, page 1329.*

And to those I called 'Not my people,'*
I will say, 'Now you are my people.'
And they will reply, 'You are our God!'"

Hosea's Wife Is Redeemed

3 Then the LORD said to me, "Go and
love your wife again, even though
she* commits adultery with another lover.
This will illustrate that the LORD still loves
Israel, even though the people have turned
to other gods and love to worship them.*"
2 So I bought her back for fifteen pieces
of silver* and five bushels of barley and a
measure of wine.*
3 Then I said to her, "You
must live in my house for many days and
stop your prostitution. During this time, you
will not have sexual relations with anyone,
not even with me.*"
4 This shows that Israel will go a long time
without a king or prince, and without sacrifices, sacred pillars, priests,* or even idols!
5 But afterward the people will return and
devote themselves to the LORD their God
and to David's descendant, their king.* In
the last days, they will tremble in awe of the
LORD and of his goodness.

The LORD's Case against Israel

4 1 Hear the word of the LORD, O people
of Israel!
The LORD has brought charges against
you, saying:
"There is no faithfulness, no kindness,
no knowledge of God in your land.
2 You make vows and break them;
you kill and steal and commit
adultery.
There is violence everywhere—
one murder after another.
3 That is why your land is in mourning,
and everyone is wasting away.
Even the wild animals, the birds of the
sky,
and the fish of the sea are
disappearing.
4 "Don't point your finger at someone
else
and try to pass the blame!
My complaint, you priests,
is with you.*
5 So you will stumble in broad daylight,
and your false prophets will fall with
you in the night.
And I will destroy Israel, your mother.
6 My people are being destroyed
because they don't know me.
Since you priests refuse to know me,
I refuse to recognize you as my priests.
Since you have forgotten the laws of
your God,
I will forget to bless your children.
7 The more priests there are,
the more they sin against me.
They have exchanged the glory of God
for the shame of idols.*
8 "When the people bring their sin
offerings, the priests get fed.
So the priests are glad when the
people sin!
9 'And what the priests do, the people
also do.'
So now I will punish both priests and
people
for their wicked deeds.
10 They will eat and still be hungry.
They will play the prostitute and gain
nothing from it,
for they have deserted the LORD
11 to worship other gods.

"Wine has robbed my people
of their understanding.
12 They ask a piece of wood for advice!
They think a stick can tell them the
future!
Longing after idols
has made them foolish.
They have played the prostitute,
serving other gods and deserting their
God.
13 They offer sacrifices to idols on the
mountaintops.
They go up into the hills to burn
incense
in the pleasant shade of oaks,
poplars, and terebinth trees.

"That is why your daughters turn to
prostitution,
and your daughters-in-law commit
adultery.

2:16 Hebrew *'my baal.'* **2:23a** Hebrew *Lo-ruhamah;* see 1:6. **2:23b** Hebrew *Lo-ammi;* see 1:9. **3:1a** Or *Go and love a woman who.* **3:1b** Hebrew *love their raisin cakes.* **3:2a** Hebrew *15 [shekels] of silver,* about 6 ounces or 171 grams in weight. **3:2b** As in Greek version, which reads *a homer of barley and a wineskin full of wine;* Hebrew reads *a homer* [5 bushels or 220 liters] *of barley and a lethek* [2.5 bushels or 110 liters] *of barley.* **3:3** Or *and I will live with you.* **3:4** Hebrew *ephod,* the vest worn by the priest. **3:5** Hebrew *to David their king.* **4:4** Hebrew *Your people are like those with a complaint against the priests.* **4:7** As in Syriac version and an ancient Hebrew tradition; Masoretic Text reads *I will turn their glory into shame.*

14 But why should I punish them
for their prostitution and adultery?
For your men are doing the same thing,
sinning with whores and shrine
prostitutes.
O foolish people! You refuse to
understand,
so you will be destroyed.

15 "Though you, Israel, are a prostitute,
may Judah not be guilty of such
things.
Do not join the false worship at Gilgal
or Beth-aven,*
and do not take oaths there in the
LORD's name.
16 Israel is stubborn,
like a stubborn heifer.
So should the LORD feed her
like a lamb in a lush pasture?
17 Leave Israel* alone,
because she is married to idolatry.
18 When the rulers of Israel finish their
drinking,
off they go to find some prostitutes.
They love shame more than honor.*
19 So a mighty wind will sweep them away.
Their sacrifices to idols will bring
them shame.

The Failure of Israel's Leaders

5 1 "Hear this, you priests.
Pay attention, you leaders of
Israel.
Listen, you members of the royal family.
Judgment has been handed down
against you.
For you have led the people into a snare
by worshiping the idols at Mizpah and
Tabor.
2 You have dug a deep pit to trap them at
Acacia Grove.*
But I will settle with you for what you
have done.
3 I know what you are like, O Ephraim.
You cannot hide yourself from me,
O Israel.
You have left me as a prostitute leaves
her husband;
you are utterly defiled.
4 Your deeds won't let you return to your
God.
You are a prostitute through and
through,
and you do not know the LORD.

5 "The arrogance of Israel testifies against
her;
Israel and Ephraim will stumble
under their load of guilt.
Judah, too, will fall with them.
6 When they come with their flocks and
herds
to offer sacrifices to the LORD,
they will not find him,
because he has withdrawn from them.
7 They have betrayed the honor of the
LORD,
bearing children that are not his.
Now their false religion will devour
them
along with their wealth.*

8 "Sound the alarm in Gibeah!
Blow the trumpet in Ramah!
Raise the battle cry in Beth-aven*!
Lead on into battle, O warriors of
Benjamin!
9 One thing is certain, Israel*:
On your day of punishment,
you will become a heap of rubble.

10 "The leaders of Judah have become like
thieves.*
So I will pour my anger on them like a
waterfall.
11 The people of Israel will be crushed and
broken by my judgment
because they are determined to
worship idols.*
12 I will destroy Israel as a moth consumes
wool.
I will make Judah as weak as rotten
wood.

13 "When Israel and Judah saw how sick
they were,
Israel turned to Assyria—
to the great king there—
but he could neither help nor cure
them.
14 I will be like a lion to Israel,
like a strong young lion to Judah.
I will tear them to pieces!
I will carry them off,
and no one will be left to rescue
them.
15 Then I will return to my place
until they admit their guilt and turn
to me.
For as soon as trouble comes,
they will earnestly search for me."

A Call to Repentance

6 [1] "Come, let us return to the LORD.
He has torn us to pieces;
now he will heal us.
He has injured us;
now he will bandage our wounds.
[2] In just a short time he will restore us,
so that we may live in his presence.
[3] Oh, that we might know the LORD!
Let us press on to know him.
He will respond to us as surely as the arrival of dawn
or the coming of rains in early spring."
[4] "O Israel* and Judah,
what should I do with you?" asks the LORD.
"For your love vanishes like the morning mist
and disappears like dew in the sunlight.
[5] I sent my prophets to cut you to pieces—
to slaughter you with my words,
with judgments as inescapable as light.
[6] I want you to show love,*
not offer sacrifices.
I want you to know me*
more than I want burnt offerings.
[7] But like Adam,* you broke my covenant
and betrayed my trust.
[8] "Gilead is a city of sinners,
tracked with footprints of blood.
[9] Priests form bands of robbers,
waiting in ambush for their victims.
They murder travelers along the road to Shechem
and practice every kind of sin.
[10] Yes, I have seen something horrible in Ephraim and Israel:
My people are defiled by prostituting themselves with other gods!
[11] "O Judah, a harvest of punishment is also waiting for you,
though I wanted to restore the fortunes of my people.

Israel's Love for Wickedness

7 [1] "I want to heal Israel, but its* sins are too great.
Samaria is filled with liars.
Thieves are on the inside
and bandits on the outside!
[2] Its people don't realize
that I am watching them.
Their sinful deeds are all around them,
and I see them all.
[3] "The people entertain the king with their wickedness,
and the princes laugh at their lies.
[4] They are all adulterers,
always aflame with lust.
They are like an oven that is kept hot
while the baker is kneading the dough.
[5] On royal holidays, the princes get drunk with wine,
carousing with those who mock them.
[6] Their hearts are like an oven
blazing with intrigue.
Their plot smolders* through the night,
and in the morning it breaks out like a raging fire.
[7] Burning like an oven,
they consume their leaders.
They kill their kings one after another,
and no one cries to me for help.
[8] "The people of Israel mingle with godless foreigners,
making themselves as worthless as a half-baked cake!
[9] Worshiping foreign gods has sapped their strength,
but they don't even know it.
Their hair is gray,
but they don't realize they're old and weak.
[10] Their arrogance testifies against them,
yet they don't return to the LORD their God
or even try to find him.
[11] "The people of Israel have become like silly, witless doves,
first calling to Egypt, then flying to Assyria for help.
[12] But as they fly about,
I will throw my net over them
and bring them down like a bird from the sky.

4:15 *Beth-aven* means "house of wickedness"; it is being used as another name for Bethel, which means "house of God." **4:17** Hebrew *Ephraim,* referring to the northern kingdom of Israel. **4:18** As in Greek version; the meaning of the Hebrew is uncertain. **5:2** Hebrew *at Shittim.* The meaning of the Hebrew for this sentence is uncertain. **5:7** The meaning of the Hebrew is uncertain. **5:8** *Beth-aven* means "house of wickedness"; it is being used as another name for Bethel, which means "house of God." **5:9** Hebrew *Ephraim,* referring to the northern kingdom of Israel; also in 5:11, 12, 13, 14. **5:10** Hebrew *like those who move a boundary marker.* **5:11** Or *determined to follow human commands.* The meaning of the Hebrew is uncertain. **6:4** Hebrew *Ephraim,* referring to the northern kingdom of Israel. **6:6a** Greek version translates this Hebrew term as *to show mercy.* Compare Matt 9:13; 12:7. **6:6b** Hebrew *to know God.* **6:7** Or *But at Adam.* **7:1** Hebrew *Ephraim's,* referring to the northern kingdom of Israel; similarly in 7:8, 11. **7:6** Hebrew *Their baker sleeps.*

I will punish them for all the evil
they do.*
13 "What sorrow awaits those who have
deserted me!
Let them die, for they have rebelled
against me.
I wanted to redeem them,
but they have told lies about me.
14 They do not cry out to me with sincere
hearts.
Instead, they sit on their couches and
wail.
They cut themselves,* begging foreign
gods for grain and new wine,
and they turn away from me.
15 I trained them and made them strong,
yet now they plot evil against me.
16 They look everywhere except to the Most
High.
They are as useless as a crooked bow.
Their leaders will be killed by their
enemies
because of their insolence toward me.
Then the people of Egypt
will laugh at them.

Israel Harvests the Whirlwind

8
1 "Sound the alarm!
The enemy descends like an eagle
on the people of the LORD,
for they have broken my covenant
and revolted against my law.
2 Now Israel pleads with me,
'Help us, for you are our God!'
3 But it is too late.
The people of Israel have rejected what
is good,
and now their enemies will chase
after them.
4 The people have appointed kings
without my consent,
and princes without my approval.
By making idols for themselves from
their silver and gold,
they have brought about their own
destruction.
5 "O Samaria, I reject this calf—
this idol you have made.
My fury burns against you.
How long will you be incapable
of innocence?
6 This calf you worship, O Israel,
was crafted by your own hands!
It is not God!
Therefore, it must be smashed to bits.
7 "They have planted the wind
and will harvest the whirlwind.
The stalks of grain wither
and produce nothing to eat.
And even if there is any grain,
foreigners will eat it.
8 The people of Israel have been
swallowed up;
they lie among the nations like an old
discarded pot.
9 Like a wild donkey looking for a mate,
they have gone up to Assyria.

Calf idols

One of the ancient Near East's most common idols was the calf or bull. Israel had encountered such idols in Egypt, where the bull-god Apis was worshiped. This was why Moses was so angry when he came down Mount Sinai and found Israel worshiping a gold calf (Exodus 32)—it was as good as abandoning the LORD (Yahweh), who had freed them. When Israel entered Canaan, they encountered bull idols as symbols of the fertility god Baal, whose sexualized worship was a constant snare to them. When Israel broke away from Judah, Jeroboam set up two gold calves as centers of worship in rivalry to Jerusalem (1 Kings 12:26-30). This reduction of the LORD to the level of a mere nature god brought constant opposition from the prophets; and here, Hosea states clearly, "This calf you worship, O Israel, was crafted by your own hands! It is not God!" (Hosea 8:6). The Ten Commandments tell us not to make idols of any kind, for God cannot tolerate such worship (Exodus 20:4-6).

▶ *See also **Idols**, page 836.*

The people of Israel* have sold themselves—
sold themselves to many lovers.
10 But though they have sold themselves to many allies,
I will now gather them together for judgment.
Then they will writhe
under the burden of the great king.

11 "Israel has built many altars to take away sin,
but these very altars became places for sinning!
12 Even though I gave them all my laws,
they act as if those laws don't apply to them.
13 The people love to offer sacrifices to me,
feasting on the meat,
but I do not accept their sacrifices.
I will hold my people accountable for their sins,
and I will punish them.
They will return to Egypt.
14 Israel has forgotten its Maker and built great palaces,
and Judah has fortified its cities.
Therefore, I will send down fire on their cities
and will burn up their fortresses."

Hosea Announces Israel's Punishment

9 1 O people of Israel,
do not rejoice as other nations do.
For you have been unfaithful to your God,
hiring yourselves out like prostitutes,
worshiping other gods on every threshing floor.
2 So now your harvests will be too small to feed you.
There will be no grapes for making new wine.
3 You may no longer stay here in the LORD's land.
Instead, you will return to Egypt,
and in Assyria you will eat food
that is ceremonially unclean.
4 There you will make no offerings of wine to the LORD.
None of your sacrifices there will please him.
They will be unclean, like food touched by a person in mourning.
All who present such sacrifices will be defiled.
They may eat this food themselves,
but they may not offer it to the LORD.
5 What then will you do on festival days?
How will you observe the LORD's festivals?
6 Even if you escape destruction from Assyria,
Egypt will conquer you, and Memphis* will bury you.
Nettles will take over your treasures of silver;
thistles will invade your ruined homes.

7 The time of Israel's punishment has come;
the day of payment is here.
Soon Israel will know this all too well.
Because of your great sin and hostility,
you say, "The prophets are crazy
and the inspired men are fools!"
8 The prophet is a watchman over Israel* for my God,
yet traps are laid for him wherever he goes.
He faces hostility even in the house of God.
9 The things my people do are as depraved
as what they did in Gibeah long ago.
God will not forget.
He will surely punish them for their sins.

10 The LORD says, "O Israel, when I first found you,
it was like finding fresh grapes in the desert.
When I saw your ancestors,
it was like seeing the first ripe figs of the season.
But then they deserted me for Baal-peor,
giving themselves to that shameful idol.
Soon they became vile,
as vile as the god they worshiped.
11 The glory of Israel will fly away like a bird,
for your children will not be born
or grow in the womb
or even be conceived.

7:12 Hebrew *I will punish them because of what was reported against them in the assembly.* **7:14** As in Greek version; Hebrew reads *They gather together.* **8:9** Hebrew *Ephraim,* referring to the northern kingdom of Israel; also in 8:11. **9:6** Memphis was the capital of northern Egypt. **9:8** Hebrew *Ephraim,* referring to the northern kingdom of Israel; also in 9:11, 13, 16.

12 Even if you do have children who
grow up,
I will take them from you.
It will be a terrible day when I turn away
and leave you alone.
13 I have watched Israel become as
beautiful as Tyre.
But now Israel will bring out her
children for slaughter."

14 O LORD, what should I request for your
people?
I will ask for wombs that don't give
birth
and breasts that give no milk.

15 The LORD says, "All their wickedness
began at Gilgal;
there I began to hate them.
I will drive them from my land
because of their evil actions.
I will love them no more
because all their leaders are rebels.
16 The people of Israel are struck down.
Their roots are dried up,
and they will bear no more fruit.
And if they give birth,
I will slaughter their beloved
children."

17 My God will reject the people of Israel
because they will not listen or obey.
They will be wanderers,
homeless among the nations.

The LORD's Judgment against Israel

10 1 How prosperous Israel is—
a luxuriant vine loaded with
fruit.
But the richer the people get,
the more pagan altars they build.
The more bountiful their harvests,
the more beautiful their sacred pillars.
2 The hearts of the people are fickle;
they are guilty and must be punished.
The LORD will break down their altars
and smash their sacred pillars.
3 Then they will say, "We have no king
because we didn't fear the LORD.
But even if we had a king,
what could he do for us anyway?"
4 They spout empty words
and make covenants they don't intend
to keep.
So injustice springs up among them
like poisonous weeds in a farmer's
field.

5 The people of Samaria tremble in fear
for their calf idol at Beth-aven,*
and they mourn for it.
Though its priests rejoice over it,
its glory will be stripped away.*
6 This idol will be carted away to Assyria,
a gift to the great king there.
Ephraim will be ridiculed and Israel will
be shamed,
because its people have trusted in this
idol.
7 Samaria and its king will be cut off;
they will float away like driftwood on
an ocean wave.
8 And the pagan shrines of Aven,* the
place of Israel's sin, will crumble.
Thorns and thistles will grow up
around their altars.
They will beg the mountains, "Bury us!"
and plead with the hills, "Fall on us!"

9 The LORD says, "O Israel, ever since
Gibeah,
there has been only sin and more sin!
You have made no progress whatsoever.
Was it not right that the wicked men
of Gibeah were attacked?
10 Now whenever it fits my plan,
I will attack you, too.
I will call out the armies of the nations
to punish you for your multiplied sins.

11 "Israel* is like a trained heifer treading
out the grain—
an easy job she loves.
But I will put a heavy yoke on her
tender neck.
I will force Judah to pull the plow
and Israel* to break up the hard
ground.
12 I said, 'Plant the good seeds of
righteousness,
and you will harvest a crop of love.
Plow up the hard ground of your hearts,
for now is the time to seek the LORD,
that he may come
and shower righteousness upon you.'

13 "But you have cultivated wickedness
and harvested a thriving crop of sins.
You have eaten the fruit of lies—
trusting in your military might,
believing that great armies
could make your nation safe.
14 Now the terrors of war
will rise among your people.

All your fortifications will fall,
just as when Shalman destroyed
Beth-arbel.
Even mothers and children
were dashed to death there.
15 You will share that fate, Bethel,
because of your great wickedness.
When the day of judgment dawns,
the king of Israel will be completely
destroyed.

The LORD's Love for Israel

11 1 "When Israel was a child, I loved
him,
and I called my son out of Egypt.
2 But the more I called to him,
the farther he moved from me,*
offering sacrifices to the images of Baal
and burning incense to idols.
3 I myself taught Israel* how to walk,
leading him along by the hand.
But he doesn't know or even care
that it was I who took care of him.
4 I led Israel along
with my ropes of kindness and love.
I lifted the yoke from his neck,
and I myself stooped to feed him.

5 "But since my people refuse to return
to me,
they will return to Egypt
and will be forced to serve Assyria.
6 War will swirl through their cities;
their enemies will crash through their
gates.
They will destroy them,
trapping them in their own evil
plans.
7 For my people are determined to
desert me.
They call me the Most High,
but they don't truly honor me.

8 "Oh, how can I give you up, Israel?
How can I let you go?
How can I destroy you like Admah
or demolish you like Zeboiim?
My heart is torn within me,
and my compassion overflows.
9 No, I will not unleash my fierce anger.
I will not completely destroy Israel,
for I am God and not a mere mortal.
I am the Holy One living among you,
and I will not come to destroy.
10 For someday the people will follow me.
I, the LORD, will roar like a lion.
And when I roar,

10:5a *Beth-aven* means "house of wickedness"; it is being used as another name for Bethel, which means "house of God." **10:5b** Or *will be taken away into exile.* **10:8** *Aven* is a reference to Beth-aven; see 10:5a and the note there. **10:11a** Hebrew *Ephraim,* referring to the northern kingdom of Israel. **10:11b** Hebrew *Jacob.* The names "Jacob" and "Israel" are often interchanged throughout the Old Testament, referring sometimes to the individual patriarch and sometimes to the nation. **11:2** As in Greek version; Hebrew reads *the more they called to him, the farther he moved from them.* **11:3** Hebrew *Ephraim,* referring to the northern kingdom of Israel; also in 11:8, 9, 12.

Compassion

Despite Gomer's unfaithfulness, God commanded Hosea to take her back as his wife, a picture of God's own faithfulness and compassion toward Israel (Hosea 3). Compassion is a deep feeling of sympathy, care, and kindness toward those in need that leads to action—even for those who (like Gomer and Israel) don't deserve it. God himself reveals that compassion is one of his fundamental qualities (Exodus 34:6-7), and the Bible often describes him in this way (e.g., Psalm 103:8-18; Joel 2:13).

God's compassion is seen throughout Hosea's prophecies as he declares his resolve to care for Israel, despite her willful sinfulness and rejection of him, and despite the increasing difficulties she found herself in. Despite everything, God promised that Israel would come through the discipline of his judgment and be blessed once again (Hosea 11:8-11).

Christ's whole life modeled compassion—healing the sick, feeding the hungry, welcoming the rejected, caring for the needy. His followers are called to reflect that compassion in the way they care for one another and for others (e.g., Colossians 3:12), even when people don't deserve it (e.g., Luke 6:27-36), for God showed us compassion when we did not deserve it (Ephesians 4:32).

my people will return trembling from
the west.
11 Like a flock of birds, they will come from
Egypt.
Trembling like doves, they will return
from Assyria.
And I will bring them home again,"
says the LORD.

Charges against Israel and Judah

12*Israel surrounds me with lies and deceit,
but Judah still obeys God
and is faithful to the Holy One.*

12

1*The people of Israel* feed on the
wind;
they chase after the east wind all day
long.
They pile up lies and violence;
they are making an alliance with
Assyria
while sending olive oil to buy support
from Egypt.
2 Now the LORD is bringing charges
against Judah.
He is about to punish Jacob* for all his
deceitful ways,
and pay him back for all he has done.
3 Even in the womb,
Jacob struggled with his brother;
when he became a man,
he even fought with God.
4 Yes, he wrestled with the angel and won.
He wept and pleaded for a blessing
from him.
There at Bethel he met God face to face,
and God spoke to him*—
5 the LORD God of Heaven's Armies,
the LORD is his name!
6 So now, come back to your God.
Act with love and justice,
and always depend on him.
7 But no, the people are like crafty
merchants
selling from dishonest scales—
they love to cheat.
8 Israel boasts, "I am rich!
I've made a fortune all by myself!
No one has caught me cheating!
My record is spotless!"
9 "But I am the LORD your God,
who rescued you from slavery in Egypt.
And I will make you live in tents again,
as you do each year at the Festival of
Shelters.*
10 I sent my prophets to warn you
with many visions and parables."
11 But the people of Gilead are worthless
because of their idol worship.
And in Gilgal, too, they sacrifice bulls;
their altars are lined up like the heaps
of stone
along the edges of a plowed field.
12 Jacob fled to the land of Aram,
and there he* earned a wife by
tending sheep.
13 Then by a prophet
the LORD brought Jacob's
descendants* out of Egypt;
and by that prophet
they were protected.
14 But the people of Israel
have bitterly provoked the LORD,
so their Lord will now sentence them to
death
in payment for their sins.

The LORD's Anger against Israel

13

1 When the tribe of Ephraim spoke,
the people shook with fear,
for that tribe was important in
Israel.
But the people of Ephraim sinned by
worshiping Baal
and thus sealed their destruction.
2 Now they continue to sin by making
silver idols,
images shaped skillfully with human
hands.
"Sacrifice to these," they cry,
"and kiss the calf idols!"
3 Therefore, they will disappear like the
morning mist,
like dew in the morning sun,
like chaff blown by the wind,
like smoke from a chimney.

4 "I have been the LORD your God
ever since I brought you out of Egypt.
You must acknowledge no God but me,
for there is no other savior.
5 I took care of you in the wilderness,
in that dry and thirsty land.
6 But when you had eaten and were
satisfied,
you became proud and forgot me.
7 So now I will attack you like a lion,
like a leopard that lurks along the road.

8 Like a bear whose cubs have been taken
away,
I will tear out your heart.
I will devour you like a hungry lioness
and mangle you like a wild animal.

9 "You are about to be destroyed, O Israel—
yes, by me, your only helper.
10 Now where is* your king?
Let him save you!
Where are all the leaders of the land,
the king and the officials you
demanded of me?
11 In my anger I gave you kings,
and in my fury I took them away.

12 "Ephraim's guilt has been collected,
and his sin has been stored up for
punishment.
13 Pain has come to the people
like the pain of childbirth,
but they are like a child
who resists being born.
The moment of birth has arrived,
but they stay in the womb!

14 "Should I ransom them from the grave*?
Should I redeem them from death?
O death, bring on your terrors!
O grave, bring on your plagues!*
For I will not take pity on them.
15 Ephraim was the most fruitful of all his
brothers,
but the east wind—a blast from the
LORD—
will arise in the desert.
All their flowing springs will run dry,
and all their wells will disappear.
Every precious thing they own
will be plundered and carried away.
16*The people of Samaria
must bear the consequences of their
guilt
because they rebelled against their God.
They will be killed by an invading army,
their little ones dashed to death
against the ground,
their pregnant women ripped open by
swords."

Healing for the Repentant

14 1*Return, O Israel, to the LORD your
God,
for your sins have brought you down.
2 Bring your confessions, and return to
the LORD.
Say to him,
"Forgive all our sins and graciously
receive us,
so that we may offer you our praises.*
3 Assyria cannot save us,
nor can our warhorses.
Never again will we say to the idols we
have made,
'You are our gods.'
No, in you alone
do the orphans find mercy."

4 The LORD says,
"Then I will heal you of your
faithlessness;
my love will know no bounds,
for my anger will be gone forever.
5 I will be to Israel
like a refreshing dew from heaven.
Israel will blossom like the lily;
it will send roots deep into the soil
like the cedars in Lebanon.
6 Its branches will spread out like
beautiful olive trees,
as fragrant as the cedars of Lebanon.
7 My people will again live under my shade.
They will flourish like grain and
blossom like grapevines.
They will be as fragrant as the wines
of Lebanon.

8 "O Israel,* stay away from idols!
I am the one who answers your
prayers and cares for you.
I am like a tree that is always green;
all your fruit comes from me."

9 Let those who are wise understand these
things.
Let those with discernment listen
carefully.
The paths of the LORD are true and right,
and righteous people live by walking
in them.
But in those paths sinners stumble
and fall.

11:12a Verse 11:12 is numbered 12:1 in Hebrew text. **11:12b** Or *and Judah is unruly against God, the faithful Holy One.* The meaning of the Hebrew is uncertain. **12:1a** Verses 12:1-14 are numbered 12:2-15 in Hebrew text. **12:1b** Hebrew *Ephraim,* referring to the northern kingdom of Israel; also in 12:8, 14. **12:2** *Jacob* sounds like the Hebrew word for "deceiver." **12:4** As in Greek and Syriac versions; Hebrew reads *to us.* **12:9** Hebrew *as in the days of your appointed feast.* **12:12** Hebrew *Israel.* See note on 10:11b. **12:13** Hebrew *brought Israel.* See note on 10:11b. **13:10** As in Greek and Syriac versions and Latin Vulgate; Hebrew reads *I will be.* **13:14a** Hebrew *Sheol;* also in 13:14b. **13:14b** Greek version reads *O death, where is your punishment? / O grave* [Hades], *where is your sting?* Compare 1 Cor 15:55. **13:16** Verse 16 is numbered 14:1 in Hebrew text. **14:1** Verses 14:1-9 are numbered 14:2-10 in Hebrew text. **14:2** As in Greek and Syriac versions, which read *may repay the fruit of our lips;* Hebrew reads *may repay the bulls of our lips.* **14:8** Hebrew *Ephraim,* referring to the northern kingdom of Israel.

Joel *The day of the LORD*

Confronted with God's judgment in the form of a plague of locusts that had swept through the land, Joel called on all God's people to repent, for only this would avert even greater judgment on the coming "day of the LORD." Some interpret the locust invasion as a prophetic glimpse of an enemy coming to devastate everything in its path. If this is the case, then the army concerned probably belonged to Assyria, or possibly Babylon, though it is difficult to date the book or even to see whether it is set in Israel or Judah, which makes it difficult to locate historically. But whether the devastation of the locusts is real or symbolic, beyond it there is hope: God would gather his people again and restore their fortunes.

What's it all about?

Joel began by describing the terrible plague of locusts that had invaded the land like a great army, destroying all the crops. This devastation was a foretaste of God's coming judgment, he warned, a foretaste of "the day of the LORD" (1:15; 2:1, 11, 31; 3:14)—the day when God would both judge his enemies and fulfill his promises. He urged the people to repent therefore: "Don't tear your clothing in your grief, but tear your hearts instead" (2:13). Joel repeatedly reminded the people that God was kind—"merciful and compassionate, slow to get angry and filled with unfailing love" (2:13)—and called them to return to him, saying, "Who knows? Perhaps he will give you a reprieve, sending you a blessing instead of this curse" (2:14). He assured them that God would receive them back so that they could enjoy his blessings again and receive far more than he had recently taken away (2:18-27). But above all, they would know God's presence: "Then you will know that I am among my people Israel, that I am the LORD your God, and there is no other" (2:27). It is never too late, and no one is so deep in wrongdoing that they can't turn around and find God's blessing again.

But then Joel looked further ahead—much further—to a time in the future when God would pour out his Spirit on all people (2:28). In the past, God's Spirit had been available only to kings, prophets, and judges, but Joel saw a time coming when the Spirit would be available to everyone who believed, no matter what their role or position in life. These promises, the apostle Peter claimed, were fulfilled on the day of Pentecost (Acts 2:16-21).

Joel then announced that the coming day of the LORD would bring judgment upon God's enemies (Joel 3). He saw "thousands upon thousands . . . waiting

OVERVIEW

GOD'S JUDGMENT UPON HIS PEOPLE

A plague of locusts has invaded the land · *1:1-12*

A call to repentance
1:13-20

The coming "day of the LORD"
2:1-17

GOD'S MERCY UPON HIS PEOPLE

God's restoration of his people
2:18-27

God's renewal of his people
2:28-32

The nations are judged
3:1-16

God's people are blessed
3:17-21

in the valley of decision" (3:14)—the whole world gathered before God for his final verdict upon them. But that same day would bring blessing for those who trust in him, and at last God would make his home with his people (3:21).

What does it mean for us?

Joel is a reminder that when catastrophes strike in life, the first person we need to turn to is God. In fact, this particular crisis had come about as a result of God's people's own sinful behavior, for God had warned them that if they did not keep his covenant, then one of the consequences would be swarms of insects devouring the land (Deuteronomy 28:42). And yet, despite their foolishness and sin, God was still ready to welcome them back, as he always is. God would always prefer to encounter us with mercy rather than with judgment (and Joel's "day of the LORD" included both), but the choice of which it is lies with us.

While Joel's prophecy was about real locusts, it reminds us that the most devastating kind of "locust" is sin. If tolerated for long enough, sin will mercilessly spoil everything we value, just as those locusts had devastated the nation's fields. But Joel brings the refreshing news that God can and will restore what we lost to the locusts (Joel 2:25). What the locusts have devoured, God can give back, even though that may seem impossible. When we turn to God, he can restore our lives to what they were meant to be. He pardons those who turn back to him. This is true restoration.

▸ *See also* ***A timeline of the Bible****, pages A22-A24.*

1 The LORD gave this message to Joel son of Pethuel.

Mourning over the Locust Plague

2 Hear this, you leaders of the people.
Listen, all who live in the land.
In all your history,
has anything like this happened before?
3 Tell your children about it in the years to come,
and let your children tell their children.
Pass the story down from generation to generation.
4 After the cutting locusts finished eating the crops,
the swarming locusts took what was left!
After them came the hopping locusts,
and then the stripping locusts,* too!
5 Wake up, you drunkards, and weep!
Wail, all you wine-drinkers!
All the grapes are ruined,
and all your sweet wine is gone.
6 A vast army of locusts* has invaded my land,
a terrible army too numerous to count.
Its teeth are like lions' teeth,
its fangs like those of a lioness.
7 It has destroyed my grapevines
and ruined my fig trees,
stripping their bark and destroying it,
leaving the branches white and bare.
8 Weep like a bride dressed in black,
mourning the death of her husband.
9 For there is no grain or wine
to offer at the Temple of the LORD.
So the priests are in mourning.
The ministers of the LORD are weeping.
10 The fields are ruined,
the land is stripped bare.
The grain is destroyed,
the grapes have shriveled,
and the olive oil is gone.
11 Despair, all you farmers!
Wail, all you vine growers!
Weep, because the wheat and barley—
all the crops of the field—are ruined.
12 The grapevines have dried up,
and the fig trees have withered.
The pomegranate trees, palm trees, and apple trees—
all the fruit trees—have dried up.
And the people's joy has dried up with them.
13 Dress yourselves in burlap and weep, you priests!
Wail, you who serve before the altar!

1:4 The precise identification of the four kinds of locusts mentioned here is uncertain. **1:6** Hebrew *A nation.*

Come, spend the night in burlap,
you ministers of my God.
For there is no grain or wine
to offer at the Temple of your God.
14 Announce a time of fasting;
call the people together for a solemn meeting.
Bring the leaders
and all the people of the land
into the Temple of the LORD your God,
and cry out to him there.
15 The day of the LORD is near,
the day when destruction comes from the Almighty.
How terrible that day will be!
16 Our food disappears before our very eyes.
No joyful celebrations are held in the house of our God.
17 The seeds die in the parched ground,
and the grain crops fail.
The barns stand empty,
and granaries are abandoned.
18 How the animals moan with hunger!
The herds of cattle wander about confused,
because they have no pasture.
The flocks of sheep and goats bleat in misery.
19 LORD, help us!
The fire has consumed the wilderness pastures,
and flames have burned up all the trees.
20 Even the wild animals cry out to you
because the streams have dried up,
and fire has consumed the wilderness pastures.

Locusts Invade like an Army

2 1 Sound the trumpet in Jerusalem*!
Raise the alarm on my holy mountain!
Let everyone tremble in fear
because the day of the LORD is upon us.
2 It is a day of darkness and gloom,
a day of thick clouds and deep blackness.
Suddenly, like dawn spreading across the mountains,
a great and mighty army appears.
Nothing like it has been seen before
or will ever be seen again.
3 Fire burns in front of them,
and flames follow after them.
Ahead of them the land lies
as beautiful as the Garden of Eden.
Behind them is nothing but desolation;
not one thing escapes.

The day of the LORD

The day of the LORD is a major theme in Joel—the phrase occurs five times in this short book (e.g., Joel 1:15). Seven other prophets (Isaiah, Ezekiel, Amos, Obadiah, Zephaniah, Zechariah, and Malachi) also speak of it, showing it was a common theme. The term initially referred to any decisive intervention of God in human history (e.g., Joel 2:1), but the prophets saw such interventions as anticipations of the last great day when God would finally judge the nations (e.g., Joel 3:14) and establish his reign on the earth (e.g., Joel 2:31-32; 3:17-18). God's people eagerly looked forward to that day and often spoke about it, believing it would bring Israel's vindication; but the prophets warned them that, unless they repented, there was nothing to look forward to; they too would be judged along with everyone else.

The New Testament picks up this expression, applying it to the return of Christ (e.g., 1 Thessalonians 5:4; 2 Peter 3:10).

The day of the LORD reminds us that neither our lives nor time itself will last forever, and that we should therefore turn to God while there is still time, knowing that a day of accounting is surely coming for all of us.

▶ *See also* ***The return of Jesus Christ****, page 1372.*

4 They look like horses;
they charge forward like warhorses.*
5 Look at them as they leap along the mountaintops.
Listen to the noise they make—like the rumbling of chariots,
like the roar of fire sweeping across a field of stubble,
or like a mighty army moving into battle.

6 Fear grips all the people;
every face grows pale with terror.
7 The attackers march like warriors
and scale city walls like soldiers.
Straight forward they march,
never breaking rank.
8 They never jostle each other;
each moves in exactly the right position.
They break through defenses
without missing a step.
9 They swarm over the city
and run along its walls.
They enter all the houses,
climbing like thieves through the windows.
10 The earth quakes as they advance,
and the heavens tremble.
The sun and moon grow dark,
and the stars no longer shine.

11 The LORD is at the head of the column.
He leads them with a shout.
This is his mighty army,
and they follow his orders.
The day of the LORD is an awesome, terrible thing.
Who can possibly survive?

A Call to Repentance

12 That is why the LORD says,
"Turn to me now, while there is time.
Give me your hearts.
Come with fasting, weeping, and mourning.
13 Don't tear your clothing in your grief,
but tear your hearts instead."
Return to the LORD your God,
for he is merciful and compassionate,
slow to get angry and filled with unfailing love.
He is eager to relent and not punish.
14 Who knows? Perhaps he will give you a reprieve,
sending you a blessing instead of this curse.
Perhaps you will be able to offer grain and wine
to the LORD your God as before.

15 Blow the ram's horn in Jerusalem!
Announce a time of fasting;
call the people together
for a solemn meeting.
16 Gather all the people—
the elders, the children, and even the babies.
Call the bridegroom from his quarters
and the bride from her private room.
17 Let the priests, who minister in the LORD's presence,
stand and weep between the entry room to the Temple and the altar.
Let them pray, "Spare your people, LORD!
Don't let your special possession
become an object of mockery.
Don't let them become a joke for
unbelieving foreigners who say,
'Has the God of Israel left them?'"

The LORD's Promise of Restoration

18 Then the LORD will pity his people
and jealously guard the honor of his land.
19 The LORD will reply,
"Look! I am sending you grain and new wine and olive oil,
enough to satisfy your needs.
You will no longer be an object of mockery
among the surrounding nations.
20 I will drive away these armies from the north.
I will send them into the parched wastelands.
Those in the front will be driven into the Dead Sea,
and those at the rear into the Mediterranean.*
The stench of their rotting bodies will rise over the land."

Surely the LORD has done great things!
21 Don't be afraid, O land.
Be glad now and rejoice,
for the LORD has done great things.

2:1 Hebrew *Zion;* also in 2:15, 23. **2:4** Or *like charioteers.* **2:20** Hebrew *into the eastern sea, . . . into the western sea.*

22 Don't be afraid, you animals of the field,
for the wilderness pastures will soon be green.
The trees will again be filled with fruit;
fig trees and grapevines will be loaded down once more.
23 Rejoice, you people of Jerusalem!
Rejoice in the LORD your God!
For the rain he sends demonstrates his faithfulness.
Once more the autumn rains will come,
as well as the rains of spring.
24 The threshing floors will again be piled high with grain,
and the presses will overflow with new wine and olive oil.

25 The LORD says, "I will give you back what you lost
to the swarming locusts, the hopping locusts,
the stripping locusts, and the cutting locusts.*
It was I who sent this great destroying army against you.
26 Once again you will have all the food you want,
and you will praise the LORD your God,
who does these miracles for you.
Never again will my people be disgraced.
27 Then you will know that I am among my people Israel,
that I am the LORD your God, and there is no other.
Never again will my people be disgraced.

The LORD's Promise of His Spirit

28*"Then, after doing all those things,
I will pour out my Spirit upon all people.
Your sons and daughters will prophesy.
Your old men will dream dreams,
and your young men will see visions.
29 In those days I will pour out my Spirit
even on servants—men and women alike.
30 And I will cause wonders in the heavens and on the earth—
blood and fire and columns of smoke.
31 The sun will become dark,
and the moon will turn blood red
before that great and terrible* day of the LORD arrives.
32 But everyone who calls on the name of the LORD
will be saved,
for some on Mount Zion in Jerusalem will escape,
just as the LORD has said.
These will be among the survivors
whom the LORD has called.

Judgment against Enemy Nations

3 1*"At the time of those events," says the LORD,
"when I restore the prosperity of Judah and Jerusalem,
2 I will gather the armies of the world
into the valley of Jehoshaphat.*
There I will judge them
for harming my people, my special possession,
for scattering my people among the nations,
and for dividing up my land.
3 They threw dice* to decide which of my people
would be their slaves.
They traded boys to obtain prostitutes
and sold girls for enough wine to get drunk.

4"What do you have against me, Tyre and
Sidon and you cities of Philistia? Are you
trying to take revenge on me? If you are,
then watch out! I will strike swiftly and pay
you back for everything you have done.
5You have taken my silver and gold and all
my precious treasures, and have carried
them off to your pagan temples. 6You have
sold the people of Judah and Jerusalem to
the Greeks,* so they could take them far
from their homeland.

7"But I will bring them back from all the
places to which you sold them, and I will
pay you back for everything you have done.
8I will sell your sons and daughters to the
people of Judah, and they will sell them to
the people of Arabia,* a nation far away.
I, the LORD, have spoken!"

9 Say to the nations far and wide:
"Get ready for war!
Call out your best warriors.
Let all your fighting men advance for the attack.
10 Hammer your plowshares into swords
and your pruning hooks into spears.

Train even your weaklings to be
warriors.
11 Come quickly, all you nations
everywhere.
Gather together in the valley."

And now, O LORD, call out your
warriors!

12 "Let the nations be called to arms.
Let them march to the valley of
Jehoshaphat.
There I, the LORD, will sit
to pronounce judgment on them all.
13 Swing the sickle,
for the harvest is ripe.*
Come, tread the grapes,
for the winepress is full.
The storage vats are overflowing
with the wickedness of these
people."

14 Thousands upon thousands are waiting
in the valley of decision.
There the day of the LORD will soon
arrive.
15 The sun and moon will grow dark,
and the stars will no longer shine.
16 The LORD's voice will roar from Zion
and thunder from Jerusalem,
and the heavens and the earth will
shake.
But the LORD will be a refuge for his
people,
a strong fortress for the people of
Israel.

Blessings for God's People

17 "Then you will know that I, the LORD
your God,
live in Zion, my holy mountain.
Jerusalem will be holy forever,
and foreign armies will never conquer
her again.
18 In that day the mountains will drip with
sweet wine,
and the hills will flow with milk.
Water will fill the streambeds of Judah,
and a fountain will burst forth from
the LORD's Temple,
watering the arid valley of acacias.*
19 But Egypt will become a wasteland
and Edom will become a wilderness,
because they attacked the people of
Judah
and killed innocent people in their
land.

20 "But Judah will be filled with people
forever,
and Jerusalem will endure through all
generations.
21 I will pardon my people's crimes,
which I have not yet pardoned;
and I, the LORD, will make my home
in Jerusalem* with my people."

2:25 The precise identification of the four kinds of locusts mentioned here is uncertain. **2:28** Verses 2:28-32 are numbered 3:1-5 in Hebrew text. **2:31** Greek version reads *glorious.* **3:1** Verses 3:1-21 are numbered 4:1-21 in Hebrew text. **3:2** *Jehoshaphat* means "the LORD judges." **3:3** Hebrew *They cast lots.* **3:6** Hebrew *to the peoples of Javan.* **3:8** Hebrew *to the Sabeans.* **3:13** Greek version reads *for the harvest time has come.* Compare Mark 4:29. **3:18** Hebrew *valley of Shittim.* **3:21** Hebrew *Zion.*

Amos *A call for social justice*

Amos was a shepherd from Tekoa, twelve miles south of Jerusalem, who lived about the same time as Hosea. Although he came from the southern kingdom of Judah, God sent him to preach in the northern kingdom of Israel, which immediately made him unwelcome. His message, challenging Israel for the superficiality of their religion and their mistreatment of the poor, was deeply resented. But he continued to challenge them that being God's chosen people was a privilege and a responsibility, not an excuse for living an easy life or a reason for thinking they could do whatever they liked because they believed God was with them. They believed that "the day of the LORD" would see their enemies judged, but Amos warned them that judgment would come on them too unless they changed.

What's it all about?

The book opens with Amos's vision of coming judgment as God roars out like a lion (1:2). It begins with words of condemnation for Israel's neighbors who had done wrong: Syria, Philistia, Phoenicia, Edom, Ammon, and Moab (chapters 1–2). Even Judah to the south would not be spared (2:4-5). But before the people of Israel could shout their "Amen!" (for they would have been delighted to hear all these nations being denounced), Amos turned on them, too. *Their* sins—social, sexual, and spiritual (2:6-8)—surpassed those of any other nation, he said, as the nations he summoned as witnesses would agree (3:9). And lest they be tempted to take all this lightly, he then declared, "The lion has roared—so who isn't frightened?" (3:8). God's judgment was surely coming.

Amos then went on to rebuke the people for their self-centered living, their disregard of the poor, their perversion of justice, their hypocrisy, and the shallowness of their religion, which was all about externals rather than the heart. In spite of many warnings, Israel had not repented (chapter 4), so Amos declared to them, "Prepare to meet your God in judgment, you people of Israel!" (4:12). He warned them that the "day of the LORD" would spell disaster and gloom for them (chapter 5) and that the complacent and uncaring rich would be brought low (chapter 6). While in the past God had overlooked their wrongdoings, Amos now saw through a series of visions that time had run out and judgment was inevitable (chapters 7–8): Israel would be destroyed (chapter 9). But the book ends on a note of hope: God would not completely annihilate his people. He would rebuild the deserted cities and prosper his people once again (9:11-15).

OVERVIEW

What does it mean for us?

Amos's message, challenging the wealthy for their disregard of the poor, has resounded throughout history and inspired many calls for social justice. He reminds us that the all-powerful God loves the poor and weak and sees what is happening to them. God will make sure justice comes their way, and he calls us to be part of that.

At the time that Amos was preaching, many people were optimistic. Business was booming, life was good, and people were happy—all except the poor, that is. Amos reminds us that complacency can lead to disaster. We constantly need to be on our guard, regularly taking stock of our spiritual state. When we are satisfied and have everything we need, it is all too easy to forget God, or at least to keep up a veneer of religion but not let him challenge and change our lives. Amos calls for religion that truly makes a difference, not just to us but also to the society in which we live. Still today we need to remember that our faith is meaningless if it does not find practical expression toward those who are in need.

▶ *See also* ***A timeline of the Bible**, pages A22-A24.*

1 This message was given to Amos, a shepherd from the town of Tekoa in Judah. He
received this message in visions two years
before the earthquake, when Uzziah was
king of Judah and Jeroboam II, the son of
Jehoash,* was king of Israel.
2 This is what he saw and heard:

"The LORD's voice will roar from Zion
and thunder from Jerusalem!
The lush pastures of the shepherds will dry up;
the grass on Mount Carmel will wither and die."

God's Judgment on Israel's Neighbors

3 This is what the LORD says:

"The people of Damascus have sinned again and again,*
and I will not let them go unpunished!
They beat down my people in Gilead
as grain is threshed with iron sledges.
4 So I will send down fire on King Hazael's palace,
and the fortresses of King Ben-hadad will be destroyed.
5 I will break down the gates of Damascus
and slaughter the people in the valley of Aven.
I will destroy the ruler in Beth-eden,
and the people of Aram will go as captives to Kir,"
says the LORD.

6 This is what the LORD says:

"The people of Gaza have sinned again and again,
and I will not let them go unpunished!
They sent whole villages into exile,
selling them as slaves to Edom.
7 So I will send down fire on the walls of Gaza,
and all its fortresses will be destroyed.
8 I will slaughter the people of Ashdod
and destroy the king of Ashkelon.
Then I will turn to attack Ekron,
and the few Philistines still left will be killed,"
says the Sovereign LORD.

9 This is what the LORD says:

"The people of Tyre have sinned again and again,
and I will not let them go unpunished!
They broke their treaty of brotherhood with Israel,
selling whole villages as slaves to Edom.
10 So I will send down fire on the walls of Tyre,
and all its fortresses will be destroyed."

11 This is what the LORD says:

"The people of Edom have sinned again and again,
and I will not let them go unpunished!

1:1 Hebrew *Joash,* a variant spelling of Jehoash. **1:3** Hebrew *have committed three sins, even four;* also in 1:6, 9, 11, 13.

They chased down their relatives, the
Israelites, with swords,
showing them no mercy.
In their rage, they slashed them
continually
and were unrelenting in their anger.
12 So I will send down fire on Teman,
and the fortresses of Bozrah will be
destroyed."

13 This is what the LORD says:
"The people of Ammon have sinned
again and again,
and I will not let them go
unpunished!
When they attacked Gilead to extend
their borders,
they ripped open pregnant women
with their swords.
14 So I will send down fire on the walls of
Rabbah,
and all its fortresses will be
destroyed.
The battle will come upon them with
shouts,
like a whirlwind in a mighty storm.
15 And their king* and his princes will go
into exile together,"
says the LORD.

2 This is what the LORD says:
"The people of Moab have sinned
again and again,*
and I will not let them go unpunished!
They desecrated the bones of Edom's
king,
burning them to ashes.
2 So I will send down fire on the land of
Moab,
and all the fortresses in Kerioth will
be destroyed.
The people will fall in the noise of
battle,
as the warriors shout and the ram's
horn sounds.
3 And I will destroy their king
and slaughter all their
princes,"
says the LORD.

God's Judgment on Judah and Israel

4 This is what the LORD says:
"The people of Judah have sinned again
and again,
and I will not let them go unpunished!
They have rejected the instruction of the
LORD,
refusing to obey his decrees.

Is God concerned about social justice?

Although many religions separate the sacred and the secular, the Bible sees no such separation. All of life is given by God and is therefore to be enjoyed and stewarded, in the knowledge that one day we will be accountable to him.

This is why prophets like Amos had no doubt that God was concerned with social justice. They fearlessly confronted lack of compassion and unjust social structures (e.g., Isaiah 3:13-15; Amos 4:1-3; 5:10-17; 8:4-14). Here in chapter 2, Amos challenges not just sexual and spiritual sin (2:7-8) but also social sin (2:6-7)—it is all offensive to God. He refused to let people think they could be religious yet neglect justice, and he said that God could not stand their worship any longer (5:21-24). Meanwhile, in the south, Micah was reminding people that God wanted people "to do what is right, to love mercy, and to walk humbly with your God" (Micah 6:8). In speaking like this, the prophets were simply calling God's people back to the Law, which required justice for the poor (Exodus 23:6), care for widows and orphans (Deuteronomy 14:28-29), and generous lending without interest (Leviticus 25:35-38).

Social justice and care for the poor was a key aspect of apostolic Christianity too (Acts 2:45; 4:34-35; Galatians 2:9-10). Being a Christian is not just about "getting saved." It also requires a fundamental commitment to social justice.

▶ *See also **Injustice**, page 811; **Oppression**, page 710.*

They have been led astray by the same
lies
that deceived their ancestors.
5 So I will send down fire on Judah,
and all the fortresses of Jerusalem will
be destroyed."

6 This is what the LORD says:

"The people of Israel have sinned again
and again,
and I will not let them go unpunished!
They sell honorable people for silver
and poor people for a pair of sandals.
7 They trample helpless people in the dust
and shove the oppressed out of the
way.
Both father and son sleep with the same
woman,
corrupting my holy name.
8 At their religious festivals,
they lounge in clothing their debtors
put up as security.
In the house of their gods,*
they drink wine bought with unjust
fines.

9 "But as my people watched,
I destroyed the Amorites,
though they were as tall as cedars
and as strong as oaks.
I destroyed the fruit on their branches
and dug out their roots.
10 It was I who rescued you from Egypt
and led you through the desert for
forty years,
so you could possess the land of the
Amorites.
11 I chose some of your sons to be prophets
and others to be Nazirites.
Can you deny this, my people of Israel?"
asks the LORD.
12 "But you caused the Nazirites to sin by
making them drink wine,
and you commanded the prophets,
'Shut up!'

13 "So I will make you groan
like a wagon loaded down with
sheaves of grain.
14 Your fastest runners will not get away.
The strongest among you will become
weak.
Even mighty warriors will be unable to
save themselves.
15 The archers will not stand their
ground.
The swiftest runners won't be fast
enough to escape.
Even those riding horses won't be able
to save themselves.
16 On that day the most courageous of your
fighting men
will drop their weapons and run for
their lives,"
says the LORD.

3 Listen to this message that the LORD
has spoken against you, O people of
Israel—against the entire family I rescued
from Egypt:

2 "From among all the families on the
earth,
I have been intimate with you alone.
That is why I must punish you
for all your sins."

Witnesses against Guilty Israel

3 Can two people walk together
without agreeing on the direction?
4 Does a lion ever roar in a thicket
without first finding a victim?
Does a young lion growl in its den
without first catching its prey?
5 Does a bird ever get caught in a trap
that has no bait?
Does a trap spring shut
when there's nothing to catch?
6 When the ram's horn blows a warning,
shouldn't the people be alarmed?
Does disaster come to a city
unless the LORD has planned it?
7 Indeed, the Sovereign LORD never does
anything
until he reveals his plans to his
servants the prophets.

8 The lion has roared—
so who isn't frightened?
The Sovereign LORD has spoken—
so who can refuse to proclaim his
message?
9 Announce this to the leaders of
Philistia*
and to the great ones of Egypt:
"Take your seats now on the hills
around Samaria,
and witness the chaos and oppression
in Israel."

1:15 Hebrew *malcam,* possibly referring to their god Molech.
2:1 Hebrew *have committed three sins, even four;* also in 2:4, 6.
2:8 Or *their God.* **3:9** Hebrew *Ashdod.*

10 "My people have forgotten how to do
right,"
says the LORD.
"Their fortresses are filled with
wealth
taken by theft and violence.
11 Therefore," says the Sovereign LORD,
"an enemy is coming!
He will surround them and shatter their
defenses.
Then he will plunder all their
fortresses."

12 This is what the LORD says:

"A shepherd who tries to rescue a sheep
from a lion's mouth
will recover only two legs or a piece of
an ear.
So it will be for the Israelites in Samaria
lying on luxurious beds,
and for the people of Damascus
reclining on couches.*

13 "Now listen to this, and announce it
throughout all Israel,*" says the Lord, the
LORD God of Heaven's Armies.

14 "On the very day I punish Israel for its
sins,
I will destroy the pagan altars at
Bethel.
The horns of the altar will be cut off
and fall to the ground.
15 And I will destroy the beautiful homes
of the wealthy—
their winter mansions and their
summer houses, too—
all their palaces filled with ivory,"
says the LORD.

Israel's Failure to Learn

4 1 Listen to me, you fat cows*
living in Samaria,
you women who oppress the poor
and crush the needy,
and who are always calling to your
husbands,
"Bring us another drink!"
2 The Sovereign LORD has sworn this by
his holiness:
"The time will come when you will be
led away
with hooks in your noses.
Every last one of you will be dragged
away
like a fish on a hook!
3 You will be led out through the ruins of
the wall;
you will be thrown from your
fortresses,*"
says the LORD.

4 "Go ahead and offer sacrifices to the
idols at Bethel.
Keep on disobeying at Gilgal.
Offer sacrifices each morning,
and bring your tithes every three days.
5 Present your bread made with yeast
as an offering of thanksgiving.
Then give your extra voluntary offerings
so you can brag about it everywhere!
This is the kind of thing you Israelites
love to do,"
says the Sovereign LORD.

6 "I brought hunger to every city
and famine to every town.
But still you would not return to me,"
says the LORD.

7 "I kept the rain from falling
when your crops needed it the
most.
I sent rain on one town
but withheld it from another.
Rain fell on one field,
while another field withered away.
8 People staggered from town to town
looking for water,
but there was never enough.
But still you would not return to me,"
says the LORD.

9 "I struck your farms and vineyards with
blight and mildew.
Locusts devoured all your fig and
olive trees.
But still you would not return to me,"
says the LORD.

10 "I sent plagues on you
like the plagues I sent on Egypt long
ago.
I killed your young men in war
and led all your horses away.*
The stench of death filled the air!
But still you would not return to me,"
says the LORD.

▸ **4:1** *See **Poverty**, page 1142.*

11 "I destroyed some of your cities,
as I destroyed* Sodom and Gomorrah.
Those of you who survived
were like charred sticks pulled from a fire.
But still you would not return to me,"
says the LORD.

12 "Therefore, I will bring upon you all the disasters I have announced.
Prepare to meet your God in judgment, you people of Israel!"

13 For the LORD is the one who shaped the mountains,
stirs up the winds, and reveals his thoughts to mankind.
He turns the light of dawn into darkness
and treads on the heights of the earth.
The LORD God of Heaven's Armies is his name!

A Call to Repentance

5 Listen, you people of Israel! Listen to this funeral song I am singing:

2 "The virgin Israel has fallen,
never to rise again!
She lies abandoned on the ground,
with no one to help her up."

3 The Sovereign LORD says:

"When a city sends a thousand men to battle,
only a hundred will return.
When a town sends a hundred,
only ten will come back alive."

4 Now this is what the LORD says to the family of Israel:

"Come back to me and live!
5 Don't worship at the pagan altars at Bethel;
don't go to the shrines at Gilgal or Beersheba.
For the people of Gilgal will be dragged off into exile,
and the people of Bethel will be reduced to nothing."
6 Come back to the LORD and live!
Otherwise, he will roar through Israel*
like a fire,
devouring you completely.
Your gods in Bethel
won't be able to quench the flames.
7 You twist justice, making it a bitter pill for the oppressed.
You treat the righteous like dirt.

8 It is the LORD who created the stars,
the Pleiades and Orion.
He turns darkness into morning
and day into night.
He draws up water from the oceans
and pours it down as rain on the land.
The LORD is his name!
9 With blinding speed and power he destroys the strong,
crushing all their defenses.

10 How you hate honest judges!
How you despise people who tell the truth!

3:12 The meaning of the Hebrew in this sentence is uncertain. **3:13** Hebrew *the house of Jacob.* The names "Jacob" and "Israel" are often interchanged throughout the Old Testament, referring sometimes to the individual patriarch and sometimes to the nation. **4:1** Hebrew *you cows of Bashan.* **4:3** Or *thrown out toward Harmon,* possibly a reference to Mount Hermon. **4:10** Or *and slaughtered your captured horses.* **4:11** Hebrew *as when God destroyed.* **5:6** Hebrew *the house of Joseph.*

Beersheba

Beersheba, like Bethel and Gilgal, had become a place of idolatry by Amos's time, which is why he called people to return to God instead of worshiping at these empty centers of religion that were now doomed (Amos 5:4-6). Situated in the Negev, Beersheba was Israel's southernmost town; hence the expression "from Dan to Beersheba" meant from north to south. It stood on an important trade route to Egypt and had played a key role in the lives of Israel's patriarchs (e.g., Genesis 21:32-34; 22:19; 26:23-33; 28:10; 46:1-5), which is why it became a center of pilgrimage. Its demise stands as a reminder that no place in itself is sacred, no matter how much God might have done there. Such a place stays holy only when the holy God is continually and rightly honored there.

▶ *See also* ***"From Dan to Beersheba,"*** *page 345;* ***Pilgrimage,*** *page 656.*

11 You trample the poor,
stealing their grain through taxes and unfair rent.
Therefore, though you build beautiful stone houses,
you will never live in them.
Though you plant lush vineyards,
you will never drink wine from them.
12 For I know the vast number of your sins
and the depth of your rebellions.
You oppress good people by taking bribes
and deprive the poor of justice in the courts.
13 So those who are smart keep their mouths shut,
for it is an evil time.

14 Do what is good and run from evil
so that you may live!
Then the LORD God of Heaven's Armies
will be your helper,
just as you have claimed.
15 Hate evil and love what is good;
turn your courts into true halls of justice.
Perhaps even yet the LORD God of Heaven's Armies
will have mercy on the remnant of his people.*

16Therefore, this is what the Lord, the LORD God of Heaven's Armies, says:

"There will be crying in all the public squares
and mourning in every street.
Call for the farmers to weep with you,
and summon professional mourners to wail.
17 There will be wailing in every vineyard,
for I will destroy them all,"
says the LORD.

Warning of Coming Judgment

18 What sorrow awaits you who say,
"If only the day of the LORD were here!"
You have no idea what you are wishing for.
That day will bring darkness, not light.
19 In that day you will be like a man who runs from a lion—
only to meet a bear.
Escaping from the bear, he leans his hand against a wall in his house—
and he's bitten by a snake.
20 Yes, the day of the LORD will be dark and hopeless,
without a ray of joy or hope.

21 "I hate all your show and pretense—
the hypocrisy of your religious festivals and solemn assemblies.
22 I will not accept your burnt offerings
and grain offerings.
I won't even notice all your choice
peace offerings.
23 Away with your noisy hymns of praise!
I will not listen to the music of your harps.
24 Instead, I want to see a mighty flood of justice,
an endless river of righteous living.

25"Was it to me you were bringing sacrifices and offerings during the forty years
in the wilderness, Israel? 26No, you served
your pagan gods—Sakkuth your king god
and Kaiwan your star god—the images you
made for yourselves. 27So I will send you
into exile, to a land east of Damascus,*"
says the LORD, whose name is the God of
Heaven's Armies.

6 1 What sorrow awaits you who lounge in luxury in Jerusalem,*
and you who feel secure in Samaria!
You are famous and popular in Israel,
and people go to you for help.
2 But go over to Calneh
and see what happened there.
Then go to the great city of Hamath
and down to the Philistine city of Gath.
You are no better than they were,
and look at how they were destroyed.
3 You push away every thought of coming disaster,
but your actions only bring the day of judgment closer.
4 How terrible for you who sprawl on ivory beds
and lounge on your couches,
eating the meat of tender lambs from the flock
and of choice calves fattened in the stall.

▸ **5:18** *See* ***The day of the LORD****, page 988.*

5 You sing trivial songs to the sound of the harp
and fancy yourselves to be great musicians like David.
6 You drink wine by the bowlful
and perfume yourselves with fragrant lotions.
You care nothing about the ruin of your nation.*
7 Therefore, you will be the first to be led away as captives.
Suddenly, all your parties will end.

8 The Sovereign LORD has sworn by his own
name, and this is what he, the LORD God of
Heaven's Armies, says:

"I despise the arrogance of Israel,*
and I hate their fortresses.
I will give this city
and everything in it to their enemies."

9 (If there are ten men left in one house, they
will all die. 10 And when a relative who is responsible to dispose of the dead* goes into
the house to carry out the bodies, he will ask
the last survivor, "Is anyone else with you?"
When the person begins to swear, "No,
by . . . ," he will interrupt and say, "Stop!
Don't even mention the name of the LORD.")

11 When the LORD gives the command,
homes both great and small will be smashed to pieces.

12 Can horses gallop over boulders?
Can oxen be used to plow them?
But that's how foolish you are when you turn justice into poison
and the sweet fruit of righteousness into bitterness.
13 And you brag about your conquest of Lo-debar.*
You boast, "Didn't we take Karnaim* by our own strength?"

14 "O people of Israel, I am about to bring an enemy nation against you,"
says the LORD God of Heaven's Armies.
"They will oppress you throughout your land—
from Lebo-hamath in the north
to the Arabah Valley in the south."

A Vision of Locusts

7 The Sovereign LORD showed me a
vision. I saw him preparing to send
a vast swarm of locusts over the land.
This was after the king's share had been
harvested from the fields and as the main
crop was coming up. 2 In my vision the
locusts ate every green plant in sight. Then
I said, "O Sovereign LORD, please forgive
us or we will not survive, for Israel* is so
small."
3 So the LORD relented from this plan.
"I will not do it," he said.

A Vision of Fire

4 Then the Sovereign LORD showed me
another vision. I saw him preparing to
punish his people with a great fire. The fire
had burned up the depths of the sea and
was devouring the entire land. 5 Then I said,
"O Sovereign LORD, please stop or we will
not survive, for Israel is so small."
6 Then the LORD relented from this plan,
too. "I will not do that either," said the Sovereign LORD.

A Vision of a Plumb Line

7 Then he showed me another vision. I saw
the Lord standing beside a wall that had
been built using a plumb line. He was using
a plumb line to see if it was still straight.
8 And the LORD said to me, "Amos, what do
you see?"

I answered, "A plumb line."

And the Lord replied, "I will test my
people with this plumb line. I will no longer
ignore all their sins. 9 The pagan shrines of
your ancestors* will be ruined, and the
temples of Israel will be destroyed; I will
bring the dynasty of King Jeroboam to a
sudden end."

Amos and Amaziah

10 Then Amaziah, the priest of Bethel, sent a
message to Jeroboam, king of Israel: "Amos
is hatching a plot against you right here on
your very doorstep! What he is saying is intolerable. 11 He is saying, 'Jeroboam will soon
be killed, and the people of Israel will be
sent away into exile.'"
12 Then Amaziah sent orders to Amos:
"Get out of here, you prophet! Go on back

5:15 Hebrew *the remnant of Joseph.* **5:26-27** Greek version reads *No, you carried your pagan gods—the shrine of Molech, the star of your god Rephan, and the images you made for yourselves. So I will send you into exile, to a land east of Damascus.* Compare Acts 7:43. **6:1** Hebrew *in Zion.* **6:6** Hebrew *of Joseph.* **6:8** Hebrew *Jacob.* See note on 3:13. **6:10** Or *to burn the dead.* The meaning of the Hebrew is uncertain. **6:13a** *Lo-debar* means "nothing." **6:13b** *Karnaim* means "horns," a term that symbolizes strength. **7:2** Hebrew *Jacob;* also in 7:5. See note on 3:13. **7:9** Hebrew *of Isaac.*

to the land of Judah, and earn your living
by prophesying there! [13]Don't bother us with
your prophecies here in Bethel. This is the
king's sanctuary and the national place of
worship!"
[14]But Amos replied, "I'm not a professional prophet, and I was never trained
to be one.* I'm just a shepherd, and I take
care of sycamore-fig trees. [15]But the LORD
called me away from my flock and told me,
'Go and prophesy to my people in Israel.'
[16]Now then, listen to this message from the
LORD:

"You say,
'Don't prophesy against Israel.
Stop preaching against my
people.*'
17 But this is what the LORD says:
'Your wife will become a prostitute in
this city,
and your sons and daughters will be
killed.
Your land will be divided up,
and you yourself will die in a foreign
land.
And the people of Israel will certainly
become captives in exile,
far from their homeland.'"

A Vision of Ripe Fruit

8 Then the Sovereign LORD showed me
another vision. In it I saw a basket filled
with ripe fruit. [2]"What do you see, Amos?"
he asked.
I replied, "A basket full of ripe fruit."
Then the LORD said, "Like this fruit, Israel
is ripe for punishment! I will not delay their
punishment again. [3]In that day the singing
in the temple will turn to wailing. Dead
bodies will be scattered everywhere. They
will be carried out of the city in silence.
I, the Sovereign LORD, have spoken!"

4 Listen to this, you who rob the poor
and trample down the needy!
5 You can't wait for the Sabbath day to be
over
and the religious festivals to end
so you can get back to cheating the
helpless.
You measure out grain with dishonest
measures
and cheat the buyer with dishonest
scales.*
6 And you mix the grain you sell
with chaff swept from the
floor.
Then you enslave poor people

God's discipline

"Who ever heard of a child who is never disciplined by its father?" asks the writer of Hebrews (Hebrews 12:7). Good, loving discipline is a sign we are true children, he goes on to say; and it is no different with God. He too disciplines us, and that discipline is good for us because it shows that God is treating us "as his own children." That is why Proverbs says, "My child, don't reject the LORD's discipline, and don't be upset when he corrects you. For the LORD corrects those he loves, just as a father corrects a child in whom he delights" (Proverbs 3:11-12).

Discipline is designed to bring us to a place of maturity and responsibility, whether exercised by our parents or by God. Israel had failed to heed God's repeated warnings through the prophets and was continuing in its immature behavior, so now God's discipline was about to come in the form of conquest by Assyria. But this discipline wasn't because he didn't love them; it was because he did. He simply couldn't let them get away with how they were behaving any longer; they were like ripe fruit that demanded attention immediately (Amos 8:2).

While "no discipline is enjoyable while it is happening—it's painful!" (Hebrews 12:11), God's discipline is always meant for our good. But we need to respond to it and learn from it if we are not to face the same discipline again.

The Bible urges parents to imitate God by exercising loving and purposeful discipline with their children (e.g., Proverbs 13:24; Ephesians 6:4) and shows us what happens when discipline is neglected (e.g., 1 Samuel 2:12-17; 3:12-13).

for one piece of silver or a pair of
sandals.
7 Now the LORD has sworn this oath
by his own name, the Pride of Israel*:
"I will never forget
the wicked things you have done!
8 The earth will tremble for your deeds,
and everyone will mourn.
The ground will rise like the Nile River at
floodtime;
it will heave up, then sink again.
9 "In that day," says the Sovereign LORD,
"I will make the sun go down at
noon
and darken the earth while it is still
day.
10 I will turn your celebrations into times
of mourning
and your singing into weeping.
You will wear funeral clothes
and shave your heads to show your
sorrow—
as if your only son had died.
How very bitter that day will be!

11 "The time is surely coming," says the
Sovereign LORD,
"when I will send a famine on the
land—
not a famine of bread or water
but of hearing the words of the LORD.
12 People will stagger from sea to sea
and wander from border to border*
searching for the word of the LORD,
but they will not find it.
13 Beautiful girls and strong young men
will grow faint in that day,
thirsting for the LORD's word.
14 And those who swear by the shameful
idols of Samaria—
who take oaths in the name of the god
of Dan
and make vows in the name of the god
of Beersheba*—
they will all fall down,
never to rise again."

A Vision of God at the Altar

9 Then I saw a vision of the Lord standing
beside the altar. He said,

"Strike the tops of the Temple columns,
so that the foundation will shake.
Bring down the roof
on the heads of the people below.
I will kill with the sword those who
survive.
No one will escape!
2 "Even if they dig down to the place of
the dead,*
I will reach down and pull them up.
Even if they climb up into the
heavens,
I will bring them down.
3 Even if they hide at the very top of
Mount Carmel,
I will search them out and capture
them.
Even if they hide at the bottom of the
ocean,
I will send the sea serpent after them
to bite them.
4 Even if their enemies drive them into
exile,
I will command the sword to kill them
there.
I am determined to bring disaster upon
them
and not to help them."

5 The Lord, the LORD of Heaven's Armies,
touches the land and it melts,
and all its people mourn.
The ground rises like the Nile River at
floodtime,
and then it sinks again.
6 The LORD's home reaches up to the
heavens,
while its foundation is on the earth.
He draws up water from the oceans
and pours it down as rain on the
land.
The LORD is his name!

7 "Are you Israelites more important to me
than the Ethiopians?*" asks the LORD.
"I brought Israel out of Egypt,
but I also brought the Philistines from
Crete*
and led the Arameans out of Kir.

8 "I, the Sovereign LORD,
am watching this sinful nation of
Israel.
I will destroy it
from the face of the earth.

7:14 Or *I'm not a prophet nor the son of a prophet.* **7:16** Hebrew *against the house of Isaac.* **8:5** Hebrew *You make the ephah* [a unit for measuring grain] *small and the shekel* [a unit of weight] *great, and you deal falsely by using deceitful balances.* **8:7** Hebrew *the pride of Jacob.* See note on 3:13. **8:12** Hebrew *from north to east.* **8:14** Hebrew *the way of Beersheba.* **9:2** Hebrew *to Sheol.* **9:7a** Hebrew *the Cushites?* **9:7b** Hebrew *Captor.*

But I will never completely destroy the
family of Israel,*"
says the LORD.
9 "For I will give the command
and will shake Israel along with the
other nations
as grain is shaken in a sieve,
yet not one true kernel will be lost.
10 But all the sinners will die by the sword—
all those who say, 'Nothing bad will
happen to us.'

A Promise of Restoration

11 "In that day I will restore the fallen
house* of David.
I will repair its damaged walls.
From the ruins I will rebuild it
and restore its former glory.
12 And Israel will possess what is left of
Edom
and all the nations I have called to be
mine.*"
The LORD has spoken,
and he will do these things.

13 "The time will come," says the LORD,
"when the grain and grapes will grow
faster
than they can be harvested.
Then the terraced vineyards on the hills
of Israel
will drip with sweet wine!
14 I will bring my exiled people of Israel
back from distant lands,
and they will rebuild their ruined cities
and live in them again.
They will plant vineyards and
gardens;
they will eat their crops and drink
their wine.
15 I will firmly plant them there
in their own land.
They will never again be uprooted
from the land I have given them,"
says the LORD your God.

9:8 Hebrew *the house of Jacob.* See note on 3:13. **9:11a** Or *kingdom;* Hebrew reads *tent.* **9:11b-12** Greek version reads *and restore its former glory, / so that the rest of humanity, including the Gentiles— / all those I have called to be mine—might seek me.* Compare Acts 15:16-17.

Obadiah

Announcement of God's punishment on Edom

Although Obadiah's identity is uncertain, he was probably a contemporary of Jeremiah. His name means "servant of the LORD," and the focus of his prophecies is Edom, a nation to the southeast of Judah, whose people were the descendants of Esau. Obadiah denounced them for the way they had gloated over Judah's devastation by foreign powers, rather than coming to her aid, and declared that they would therefore experience God's judgment. And what is true of Edom would be true of all who oppose God and his people. By contrast, however, God's own covenant people who had already experienced God's judgment would be restored.

What's it all about?

Obadiah's short prophecy, only twenty-one verses long, predicts how the neighboring nation of Edom would be punished for its pride and for the way it had gloated over Judah's misfortune. When Judah was invaded by Babylon, Edom "stood aloof, refusing to help them" (1:11). The Edomites, as the descendants of Esau, Jacob's older brother, were related to the Israelites (see 1:12); but relations between the two nations were often hostile. Now, Obadiah accused the Edomites of gloating and rejoicing over their relatives' misfortune (1:12) and of making the most of Judah's tragic situation (1:12-14).

They would not get away with their behavior, Obadiah declared: "As you have done to Israel, so it will be done to you" (1:15). The coming day of the LORD would bring justice: punishment for the Edomites (1:15-18) but restoration for God's people (1:19-21).

OVERVIEW

Edom's pride and downfall
1:1-14

Edom's punishment and Israel's restoration · *1:15-21*

What does it mean for us?

There is nothing so soul-destroying as a sense of injustice—especially when we are at the receiving end of it, as Judah was here. We all react badly to people who are full of pride, greed, cunning, cruelty, and insincerity and who gloat over others' misfortune, especially when such people seem to go unpunished while others suffer instead. Obadiah tackles this issue. He reminds us that the apparent success enjoyed by wicked people is only temporary. God sees everything and will, in his own time, act to restore justice swiftly and convincingly as a sign of the ultimate success of his kingdom.

Obadiah challenges us to have God's perspective on injustice and disloyalty. We need to exercise faith and hope in times of despair, trusting that though injustice might last for a time, God's Kingdom will last forever.

▶ *See also **A timeline of the Bible**, pages A22-A24.*

This is the vision that the Sovereign LORD revealed to Obadiah concerning the land of Edom.

Edom's Judgment Announced

We have heard a message from the LORD
that an ambassador was sent to the nations to say,
"Get ready, everyone!
Let's assemble our armies and attack Edom!"

2 The LORD says to Edom,
"I will cut you down to size among the nations;
you will be greatly despised.
3 You have been deceived by your own pride
because you live in a rock fortress
and make your home high in the mountains.
'Who can ever reach us way up here?'
you ask boastfully.
4 But even if you soar as high as eagles
and build your nest among the stars,
I will bring you crashing down,"
says the LORD.

5 "If thieves came at night and robbed you
(what a disaster awaits you!),
they would not take everything.
Those who harvest grapes
always leave a few for the poor.
But your enemies will wipe you out completely!
6 Every nook and cranny of Edom*
will be searched and looted.
Every treasure will be found and taken.

7 "All your allies will turn against you.
They will help to chase you from your land.
They will promise you peace
while plotting to deceive and destroy you.
Your trusted friends will set traps for you,
and you won't even know about it.
8 At that time not a single wise person
will be left in the whole land of Edom,"
says the LORD.
"For on the mountains of Edom
I will destroy everyone who has understanding.
9 The mightiest warriors of Teman
will be terrified,
and everyone on the mountains of Edom
will be cut down in the slaughter.

Reasons for Edom's Punishment

10 "Because of the violence you did
to your close relatives in Israel,*
you will be filled with shame
and destroyed forever.

What you sow you reap

It is easy to think that people get away with things in life. Those who cheat, lie, and steal never seem to get caught; those who break promises seem to get away with it; those who do shady business deals seem only to prosper. That's how people in Obadiah's day were thinking about Edom. Although the Edomites were related to the people of Judah by ancestry (they were descendants of Esau, Jacob's older brother), they had not only failed to come to Judah's aid when they were attacked by Babylon but had even taken advantage of the situation (Obadiah 1:10-14). And now they were rejoicing! It all seemed so unfair.

But Obadiah assured God's people that what had happened to Judah would also one day happen to Edom (1:15-21). Edom had failed to understand the principle that we reap whatever we sow—if not in this life, then certainly in the next. If we sow wickedness, we will reap wickedness; if we sow goodness, we will reap goodness. And while people may be fooled, God never is. "Don't be misled—you cannot mock the justice of God. You will always harvest what you plant," wrote Paul (Galatians 6:7). So "let's not get tired of doing what is good. At just the right time we will reap a harvest of blessing if we don't give up" (Galatians 6:9).

11 When they were invaded,
you stood aloof, refusing to help them.
Foreign invaders carried off their wealth
and cast lots to divide up Jerusalem,
but you acted like one of Israel's enemies.

12 "You should not have gloated
when they exiled your relatives to distant lands.
You should not have rejoiced
when the people of Judah suffered such misfortune.
You should not have spoken arrogantly
in that terrible time of trouble.
13 You should not have plundered the land of Israel
when they were suffering such calamity.
You should not have gloated over their destruction
when they were suffering such calamity.
You should not have seized their wealth
when they were suffering such calamity.
14 You should not have stood at the crossroads,
killing those who tried to escape.
You should not have captured the survivors
and handed them over in their terrible time of trouble.

Edom Destroyed, Israel Restored

15 "The day is near when I, the LORD,
will judge all godless nations!
As you have done to Israel,
so it will be done to you.
All your evil deeds
will fall back on your own heads.
16 Just as you swallowed up my people
on my holy mountain,
so you and the surrounding nations
will swallow the punishment I pour out on you.
Yes, all you nations will drink and stagger
and disappear from history.

17 "But Jerusalem* will become a refuge for those who escape;
it will be a holy place.
And the people of Israel* will come back
to reclaim their inheritance.
18 The people of Israel will be a raging fire,
and Edom a field of dry stubble.
The descendants of Joseph will be a flame
roaring across the field, devouring everything.
There will be no survivors in Edom.
I, the LORD, have spoken!

19 "Then my people living in the Negev
will occupy the mountains of Edom.
Those living in the foothills of Judah*
will possess the Philistine plains
and take over the fields of Ephraim and Samaria.
And the people of Benjamin
will occupy the land of Gilead.
20 The exiles of Israel will return to their land
and occupy the Phoenician coast as far north as Zarephath.
The captives from Jerusalem exiled in the north*
will return home and resettle the towns of the Negev.
21 Those who have been rescued* will go up to* Mount Zion in Jerusalem
to rule over the mountains of Edom.
And the LORD himself will be king!"

6 Hebrew *Esau;* also in 8b, 9, 18, 19, 21. **10** Hebrew *your brother Jacob.* The names "Jacob" and "Israel" are often interchanged throughout the Old Testament, referring sometimes to the individual patriarch and sometimes to the nation. **17a** Hebrew *Mount Zion.* **17b** Hebrew *house of Jacob;* also in 18. See note on 10. **19** Hebrew *the Shephelah.* **20** Hebrew *in Sepharad.* **21a** As in Greek and Syriac versions; Hebrew reads *Rescuers.* **21b** Or *from.*

▸ **1:15** *See* ***The day of the LORD****, page 988.*

Jonah *The reluctant prophet*

Jonah prophesied during the reign of Jeroboam II, who ruled the northern kingdom of Israel from 793 to 753 BC (2 Kings 14:25). Jeroboam capitalized on temporary Assyrian weakness by expanding Israel's borders to its ancient limits, which made people proud and complacent. But the Assyrian threat was still very real; and since Jonah came from Gath-hepher in Zebulun, his region would have been among the first to be conquered if the Assyrians attacked. It was little wonder he hated them!

His hatred was exposed when, sent by God to Nineveh, Assyria's capital, to give it the opportunity to repent, Jonah preferred to run away from God rather than be obedient. But he learned two big lessons: First, you can never run away from God, and it is always better to obey him the first time; and second, God loves everyone, even our enemies.

What's it all about?

The book opens with God's call to Jonah to go and preach in Nineveh, one of Assyria's great cities, in order to warn the people about their wicked lifestyles. Fearing that the Assyrians might actually repent (4:2), Jonah tried to run away from God. He boarded a ship heading in the opposite direction from Nineveh—west instead of east. When a fierce storm hit the boat, the sailors cast lots (a method of choosing or deciding similar to throwing dice) to discover who was responsible for their misfortune. When it became clear it was Jonah, they reluctantly threw him overboard, hoping the storm would then stop.

Jonah was swallowed by some sort of great sea creature, sent by God for this very task (1:17). He remained in its belly three days, and it was only when he called out to God that the sea creature spit him out onto the beach. God then gave him a second chance, again telling him to go to Nineveh, and this time he obeyed. The people heeded his warnings, and even the king repented. As a result, God forgave them; but Jonah became very angry. He clearly was unwilling to accept the nature and depth of God's love and forgiveness, and he probably did not want to forgive the Assyrians for their earlier opposition to God's people.

Sitting down in a deserted spot, he became so depressed that he asked God to take his life. God caused a plant to grow over Jonah's head to shelter him from the burning sun, but the next morning a worm attacked the tree and it withered, robbing him of the shade. Jonah again said that he really would prefer to die. But God used the tree to teach Jonah about mercy: If he felt sad about a plant, couldn't God feel sad about sinners? The book ends with this open-ended question, demanding a response from its readers.

OVERVIEW

God calls Jonah to go to Nineveh, but Jonah runs away · *1:1-16*

Jonah is swallowed by a big fish *1:17–2:10*

God calls Jonah a second time, and Jonah obeys · *3:1-10*

Jonah gets angry at God's forgiveness of Nineveh · *4:1-11*

What does it mean for us?

Can God bless people who are wicked? The answer, this book makes clear, is yes. The Assyrians were renowned for their cruelty, and in Jonah's day they still remained a real threat to God's people, despite internal problems back home. It is no wonder that Jonah was reluctant to go to their capital city.

But God always forgives people who repent, and the people of Nineveh were quick to do so. Their ready response to God's message takes Jonah—and us—by surprise. Sometimes it is the people whom we least expect to change who do. The book of Jonah teaches us never to dismiss anyone as beyond God's love or power to save. *Everyone* has the right to hear God's good news, whatever nation, people group, or social group they come from; and only God knows who will or will not respond. God makes his offer of forgiveness available to everyone, and so should we. Jonah's big lesson was that God's love is not just for "us," but also for "them."

The good news of God's love must be proclaimed to all, irrespective of nationality or race or background. We must never exclude people from the possibility of God's blessing.

▸ *See also* ***A timeline of the Bible****, pages A22–A24.*

Jonah Runs from the LORD

1 The LORD gave this message to Jonah son of Amittai: 2"Get up and go to the great city of Nineveh. Announce my judgment against it because I have seen how wicked its people are."

3But Jonah got up and went in the opposite direction to get away from the LORD. He went down to the port of Joppa, where he found a ship leaving for Tarshish. He bought a ticket and went on board, hoping to escape from the LORD by sailing to Tarshish.

4But the LORD hurled a powerful wind over the sea, causing a violent storm that threatened to break the ship apart. 5Fearing for their lives, the desperate sailors shouted to their gods for help and threw the cargo overboard to lighten the ship.

But all this time Jonah was sound asleep down in the hold. 6So the captain went down after him. "How can you sleep at a time like this?" he shouted. "Get up and pray to your god! Maybe he will pay attention to us and spare our lives."

7Then the crew cast lots to see which of them had offended the gods and caused the terrible storm. When they did this, the lots identified Jonah as the culprit. 8"Why has this awful storm come down on us?" they demanded. "Who are you? What is your line of work? What country are you from? What is your nationality?"

9Jonah answered, "I am a Hebrew, and I worship the LORD, the God of heaven, who made the sea and the land."

10The sailors were terrified when they heard this, for he had already told them he was running away from the LORD. "Oh, why did you do it?" they groaned. 11And since the storm was getting worse all the time, they asked him, "What should we do to you to stop this storm?"

12"Throw me into the sea," Jonah said, "and it will become calm again. I know that this terrible storm is all my fault."

13Instead, the sailors rowed even harder to get the ship to the land. But the stormy sea was too violent for them, and they couldn't make it. 14Then they cried out to the LORD, Jonah's God. "O LORD," they pleaded, "don't make us die for this man's sin. And don't hold us responsible for his death. O LORD, you have sent this storm upon him for your own good reasons."

15Then the sailors picked Jonah up and threw him into the raging sea, and the storm stopped at once! 16The sailors were awestruck by the LORD's great power, and they offered him a sacrifice and vowed to serve him.

17*Now the LORD had arranged for a great fish to swallow Jonah. And Jonah was inside the fish for three days and three nights.

1:17 Verse 1:17 is numbered 2:1 in Hebrew text.

▸ **1:2** *See* ***Nineveh****, page 1021.*

Jonah's Prayer

2 1*Then Jonah prayed to the LORD his
God from inside the fish. 2He said,

"I cried out to the LORD in my great
trouble,
and he answered me.
I called to you from the land of the
dead,*
and LORD, you heard me!
3 You threw me into the ocean depths,
and I sank down to the heart of the
sea.
The mighty waters engulfed me;
I was buried beneath your wild and
stormy waves.
4 Then I said, 'O LORD, you have driven
me from your presence.
Yet I will look once more toward your
holy Temple.'

5 "I sank beneath the waves,
and the waters closed over me.
Seaweed wrapped itself around my
head.
6 I sank down to the very roots of the
mountains.
I was imprisoned in the earth,
whose gates lock shut forever.
But you, O LORD my God,
snatched me from the jaws of death!
7 As my life was slipping away,
I remembered the LORD.
And my earnest prayer went out to you
in your holy Temple.
8 Those who worship false gods
turn their backs on all God's
mercies.
9 But I will offer sacrifices to you with
songs of praise,
and I will fulfill all my vows.
For my salvation comes from the LORD
alone."

10Then the LORD ordered the fish to spit
Jonah out onto the beach.

Jonah Goes to Nineveh

3 Then the LORD spoke to Jonah a second
time: 2"Get up and go to the great city
of Nineveh, and deliver the message I have
given you."

3This time Jonah obeyed the LORD's command and went to Nineveh, a city so large
that it took three days to see it all.* 4On the
day Jonah entered the city, he shouted to
the crowds: "Forty days from now Nineveh
will be destroyed!" 5The people of Nineveh
believed God's message, and from the greatest to the least, they declared a fast and put
on burlap to show their sorrow.

6When the king of Nineveh heard what
Jonah was saying, he stepped down from
his throne and took off his royal robes. He
dressed himself in burlap and sat on a heap
of ashes. 7Then the king and his nobles sent
this decree throughout the city:

"No one, not even the animals from
your herds and flocks, may eat or drink
anything at all. 8People and animals
alike must wear garments of mourning,
and everyone must pray earnestly to
God. They must turn from their evil ways
and stop all their violence. 9Who can
tell? Perhaps even yet God will change

Was it a whale?

Was it really a whale that swallowed Jonah, as we see so often in pictures of this story? Actually, the Bible simply calls it "a great fish" (Jonah 1:17), so we do not really know what it was. But the fish is not the center of the story; Jonah is.

Some Christians think that the book of Jonah is a sort of parable, rather than a factual story, and that it is the message that matters, not whether the fish was real or not. But there is no real reason to dismiss the story as unhistorical. Yes, it involves an unusual miracle; but then, many of the miracles of Elijah and Elisha, who were prophets shortly before Jonah's time, were unusual too. The nature of Israel's faith at this time was such that something very special was needed to get through to them. Moreover, Jesus seemed to treat this story as historical, comparing his own death and resurrection to the three days and three nights that Jonah spent in the fish's belly (Matthew 12:39-40).

his mind and hold back his fierce anger
from destroying us."

10When God saw what they had done and
how they had put a stop to their evil ways,
he changed his mind and did not carry out
the destruction he had threatened.

Jonah's Anger at the Lord's Mercy

4 This change of plans greatly upset
Jonah, and he became very angry. 2So
he complained to the Lord about it: "Didn't
I say before I left home that you would do
this, Lord? That is why I ran away to Tarshish! I knew that you are a merciful and
compassionate God, slow to get angry and
filled with unfailing love. You are eager to
turn back from destroying people. 3Just kill
me now, Lord! I'd rather be dead than alive
if what I predicted will not happen."
4The Lord replied, "Is it right for you to
be angry about this?"
5Then Jonah went out to the east side of
the city and made a shelter to sit under as
he waited to see what would happen to the
city. 6And the Lord God arranged for a leafy
plant to grow there, and soon it spread its
broad leaves over Jonah's head, shading him
from the sun. This eased his discomfort, and
Jonah was very grateful for the plant.
7But God also arranged for a worm! The
next morning at dawn the worm ate through
the stem of the plant so that it withered away.
8And as the sun grew hot, God arranged for
a scorching east wind to blow on Jonah. The
sun beat down on his head until he grew
faint and wished to die. "Death is certainly
better than living like this!" he exclaimed.
9Then God said to Jonah, "Is it right for
you to be angry because the plant died?"

"Yes," Jonah retorted, "even angry
enough to die!"
10Then the Lord said, "You feel sorry
about the plant, though you did nothing to
put it there. It came quickly and died quickly.
11But Nineveh has more than 120,000 people
living in spiritual darkness,* not to mention
all the animals. Shouldn't I feel sorry for
such a great city?"

2:1 Verses 2:1-10 are numbered 2:2-11 in Hebrew text. **2:2** Hebrew *from Sheol.* **3:3** Hebrew *a great city to God, of three days' journey.* **4:11** Hebrew *people who don't know their right hand from their left.*

Does God change his mind?

"I am the Lord, and I do not change" (Malachi 3:6). This saying, frequently quoted out of context, is often used to prove that God never changes his mind. But Jonah's story shows us that he does! In fact, the Bible has many examples of this happening. For example, God changed his mind about blessing the human race once sin became rampant on the earth (contrast Genesis 1:27-28 with Genesis 6:6-7); he also changed his mind about destroying Israel after hearing Moses' prayer (contrast Exodus 32:9-10 with Exodus 32:14). In the first example, blessing is turned into curse, and in the second, curse is turned into blessing.

However, this possibility of change does not mean that God is unreliable; rather, it proves the very opposite. For while God is unchanging in his character, he is not always unchanging in his actions. In fact, sometimes he has to change his declared actions in order to be faithful to his character. So, because his essential nature is one of righteousness, he gladly changes his mind when, threatened with judgment, sinners then repent, just as the Ninevites did (Jonah 3:10). God clearly changed his mind, but only to be consistent with what he is like and what he wants.

Changing his mind does not mean that God is unreliable or fickle; it means his purposes will surely come to pass.

▶ *See also* ***The character of God****, page 104.*

Micah *Judgment, but hope*

Micah was a prophet who preached during the reigns of Jotham (750–735 BC), Ahaz (735–715 BC), and Hezekiah (715–686 BC), all kings of Judah, the southern kingdom. He was therefore a contemporary of Isaiah.

At the heart of Micah's prophecies lie the key themes of judgment and forgiveness. The book contains prophecies about God's punishment of both Israel and Judah for their sins. He challenged their idolatry, injustice, and empty religious rituals. And yet this judgment is mixed with hope. Assyria would soon invade and wreak havoc; but, one day, God would restore his people—for the Judge who scatters his people is also the Shepherd who gathers them. Micah comforted the people with the thought that punishment did not mean rejection.

What's it all about?

Micah preached during a time of crisis. The nation of Judah was prosperous at this time, but politically unstable; and the two superpowers of the day, Egypt and Assyria, were battling for supremacy, with Judah stuck between them. Within Judah, the rich were becoming richer by cheating the poor, judges were corrupt, and even prophets and priests put money before God. There were idols everywhere. And yet, despite all this, the people still thought that God would protect them. Their consciences were being suppressed by false prophets and corrupt priests.

Like a lawyer in a court, Micah presented God's case against the capitals of both Judah and Israel (Jerusalem and Samaria; chapters 1–2), as well as their leaders and prophets (chapter 3). Because of their sin, judgment would surely come. But Micah also promised a golden future when God himself would be king, ruling from Zion (Jerusalem), to which all nations would flock (chapters 4–5). He also promised that a king would one day come from Bethlehem (5:2), the place where Jesus would be born. The trial is resumed in chapter 6 when God presented a complaint against his people. He had looked for justice, kindness, and humility, but found only unjustly gained riches and false business dealings, despite having made clear to his people what he desires: "to do what is right, to love mercy, and to walk humbly with your God" (6:8). But the book ends with a promise that God would shepherd his people again one day. He would forgive all their sins because he is merciful and there is no one like him (7:18).

Micah saw signs of hope in two places: Jerusalem and Bethlehem. In chapter 4, Mount Zion (Jerusalem) is presented as the religious focal point of the world, as Micah looked forward to a day when people of all nations would worship God there and when peace and blessing would flow from it to other nations. In chapter 5, Micah prophesied that God's chosen ruler would one day come from Bethlehem, bringing hope to the whole world. Christians believe that this prophecy was fulfilled in Jesus Christ (see Matthew 2:6).

OVERVIEW

What does it mean for us?

Micah's great theme is that God is a God of justice and forgiveness. How people behave toward one another—not what they *say* they believe—is the real test of how much they respect God. Religion is not about keeping outward appearances or external observances, any more than true friendships or real family life are. Micah drives home how uninterested God is in routine, empty worship; he wants worship from the heart—but worship that is also expressed in the way we deal with others. In one of the book's key passages, Micah says that God is not really interested in our offerings and sacrifices (6:6-7); but rather, "the LORD has told you what is good, and this is what he requires of you: to do what is right, to love mercy, and to walk humbly with your God" (6:8). These three key virtues—living in a godly, merciful, and humble way—still remain a good test of how real our faith in God is.

▶ *See also* ***A timeline of the Bible****, pages A22-A24.*

1 The LORD gave this message to Micah of Moresheth during the years when Jotham, Ahaz, and Hezekiah were kings of Judah. The visions he saw concerned both Samaria and Jerusalem.

Grief over Samaria and Jerusalem

2 Attention! Let all the people of the world
listen!
Let the earth and everything in it hear.
The Sovereign LORD is making
accusations against you;
the Lord speaks from his holy Temple.
3 Look! The LORD is coming!
He leaves his throne in heaven
and tramples the heights of the earth.
4 The mountains melt beneath his feet
and flow into the valleys
like wax in a fire,
like water pouring down a hill.
5 And why is this happening?
Because of the rebellion of Israel*—
yes, the sins of the whole nation.
Who is to blame for Israel's rebellion?
Samaria, its capital city!
Where is the center of idolatry in Judah?
In Jerusalem, its capital!

6 "So I, the LORD, will make the city of
Samaria
a heap of ruins.
Her streets will be plowed up
for planting vineyards.
I will roll the stones of her walls into the
valley below,
exposing her foundations.
7 All her carved images will be smashed.
All her sacred treasures will be burned.
These things were bought with the money
earned by her prostitution,
and they will now be carried away
to pay prostitutes elsewhere."

8 Therefore, I will mourn and lament.
I will walk around barefoot and naked.
I will howl like a jackal
and moan like an owl.
9 For my people's wound
is too deep to heal.
It has reached into Judah,
even to the gates of Jerusalem.

10 Don't tell our enemies in Gath*;
don't weep at all.
You people in Beth-leaphrah,*
roll in the dust to show your despair.
11 You people in Shaphir,*
go as captives into exile—naked and
ashamed.
The people of Zaanan*
dare not come outside their walls.
The people of Beth-ezel* mourn,
for their house has no support.
12 The people of Maroth* anxiously wait for
relief,
but only bitterness awaits them
as the LORD's judgment reaches
even to the gates of Jerusalem.

13 Harness your chariot horses and flee,
you people of Lachish.*

1:5 Hebrew *Jacob;* also in 1:5b. The names "Jacob" and "Israel" are often interchanged throughout the Old Testament, referring sometimes to the individual patriarch and sometimes to the nation. **1:10a** *Gath* sounds like the Hebrew term for "tell." **1:10b** *Beth-leaphrah* means "house of dust." **1:11a** *Shaphir* means "pleasant." **1:11b** *Zaanan* sounds like the Hebrew term for "come out." **1:11c** *Beth-ezel* means "adjoining house." **1:12** *Maroth* sounds like the Hebrew term for "bitter." **1:13a** *Lachish* sounds like the Hebrew term for "team of horses."

You were the first city in Judah
to follow Israel in her rebellion,
and you led Jerusalem* into sin.
14 Send farewell gifts to Moresheth-gath*;
there is no hope of saving it.
The town of Aczib*
has deceived the kings of Israel.
15 O people of Mareshah,*
I will bring a conqueror to capture
your town.
And the leaders* of Israel
will go to Adullam.

16 Oh, people of Judah, shave your heads
in sorrow,
for the children you love will be
snatched away.
Make yourselves as bald as a vulture,
for your little ones will be exiled to
distant lands.

Judgment against Wealthy Oppressors

2
1 What sorrow awaits you who lie
awake at night,
thinking up evil plans.
You rise at dawn and hurry to carry
them out,
simply because you have the power
to do so.
2 When you want a piece of land,
you find a way to seize it.
When you want someone's house,
you take it by fraud and violence.
You cheat a man of his property,
stealing his family's inheritance.

3 But this is what the LORD says:
"I will reward your evil with evil;
you won't be able to pull your neck
out of the noose.
You will no longer walk around proudly,
for it will be a terrible time."

4 In that day your enemies will make fun
of you
by singing this song of despair about
you:
"We are finished,
completely ruined!
God has confiscated our land,
taking it from us.
He has given our fields
to those who betrayed us.*"
5 Others will set your boundaries then,
and the LORD's people will have no say
in how the land is divided.

True and False Prophets

6 "Don't say such things,"
the people respond.*
"Don't prophesy like that.
Such disasters will never come our
way!"

7 Should you talk that way, O family of
Israel?*
Will the LORD's Spirit have patience
with such behavior?
If you would do what is right,
you would find my words comforting.
8 Yet to this very hour
my people rise against me like an
enemy!
You steal the shirts right off the backs
of those who trusted you,
making them as ragged as men
returning from battle.
9 You have evicted women from their
pleasant homes
and forever stripped their children of
all that God would give them.
10 Up! Begone!
This is no longer your land and home,
for you have filled it with sin
and ruined it completely.

11 Suppose a prophet full of lies would say
to you,
"I'll preach to you the joys of wine
and alcohol!"
That's just the kind of prophet you
would like!

Hope for Restoration

12 "Someday, O Israel, I will gather you;
I will gather the remnant who are left.
I will bring you together again like sheep
in a pen,
like a flock in its pasture.
Yes, your land will again
be filled with noisy crowds!
13 Your leader will break out
and lead you out of exile,
out through the gates of the enemy
cities,
back to your own land.
Your king will lead you;
the LORD himself will guide you."

Judgment against Israel's Leaders

3
1 I said, "Listen, you leaders of Israel!
You are supposed to know right
from wrong,

2 but you are the very ones
who hate good and love evil.
You skin my people alive
and tear the flesh from their bones.
3 Yes, you eat my people's flesh,
strip off their skin,
and break their bones.
You chop them up
like meat for the cooking pot.
4 Then you beg the LORD for help in times of trouble!
Do you really expect him to answer?
After all the evil you have done,
he won't even look at you!"

5 This is what the LORD says:
"You false prophets are leading my people astray!
You promise peace for those who give you food,
but you declare war on those who refuse to feed you.
6 Now the night will close around you,
cutting off all your visions.
Darkness will cover you,
putting an end to your predictions.
The sun will set for you prophets,
and your day will come to an end.
7 Then you seers will be put to shame,
and you fortune-tellers will be disgraced.
And you will cover your faces
because there is no answer from God."
8 But as for me, I am filled with power—
with the Spirit of the LORD.
I am filled with justice and strength
to boldly declare Israel's sin and rebellion.
9 Listen to me, you leaders of Israel!
You hate justice and twist all that is right.
10 You are building Jerusalem
on a foundation of murder and corruption.
11 You rulers make decisions based on bribes;
you priests teach God's laws only for a price;
you prophets won't prophesy unless you are paid.
Yet all of you claim to depend on the LORD.
"No harm can come to us," you say,
"for the LORD is here among us."
12 Because of you, Mount Zion will be
plowed like an open field;
Jerusalem will be reduced to ruins!
A thicket will grow on the heights
where the Temple now stands.

The LORD's Future Reign

4 1 In the last days, the mountain of the LORD's house
will be the highest of all—
the most important place on earth.
It will be raised above the other hills,
and people from all over the world
will stream there to worship.
2 People from many nations will come and say,
"Come, let us go up to the mountain of the LORD,
to the house of Jacob's God.
There he will teach us his ways,
and we will walk in his paths."
For the LORD's teaching will go out from Zion;
his word will go out from Jerusalem.
3 The LORD will mediate between peoples
and will settle disputes between strong nations far away.
They will hammer their swords into plowshares
and their spears into pruning hooks.
Nation will no longer fight against nation,
nor train for war anymore.
4 Everyone will live in peace and prosperity,
enjoying their own grapevines and fig trees,
for there will be nothing to fear.
The LORD of Heaven's Armies
has made this promise!
5 Though the nations around us follow their idols,
we will follow the LORD our God
forever and ever.

Israel's Return from Exile

6 "In that coming day," says the LORD,
"I will gather together those who are lame,
those who have been exiles,
and those whom I have filled with grief.
7 Those who are weak will survive as a remnant;

1:13b Hebrew *the daughter of Zion.* **1:14a** *Moresheth* sounds like the Hebrew term for "gift" or "dowry." **1:14b** *Aczib* means "deception." **1:15a** *Mareshah* sounds like the Hebrew term for "conqueror." **1:15b** Hebrew *the glory.* **2:4** Or *to those who took us captive.* **2:6** Or *the prophets respond;* Hebrew reads *they prophesy.* **2:7** Hebrew *O house of Jacob?* See note on 1:5a.

those who were exiles will become
a strong nation.
Then I, the LORD, will rule from
Jerusalem*
as their king forever."
8 As for you, Jerusalem,
the citadel of God's people,*
your royal might and power
will come back to you again.
The kingship will be restored
to my precious Jerusalem.
9 But why are you now screaming in terror?
Have you no king to lead you?
Have your wise people all died?
Pain has gripped you like a woman in
childbirth.
10 Writhe and groan like a woman in labor,
you people of Jerusalem,*
for now you must leave this city
to live in the open country.
You will soon be sent in exile
to distant Babylon.
But the LORD will rescue you there;
he will redeem you from the grip
of your enemies.
11 Now many nations have gathered
against you.
"Let her be desecrated," they say.
"Let us see the destruction of
Jerusalem.*"
12 But they do not know the LORD's thoughts
or understand his plan.
These nations don't know
that he is gathering them together
to be beaten and trampled
like sheaves of grain on a threshing
floor.
13 "Rise up and crush the nations,
O Jerusalem!"*
says the LORD.
"For I will give you iron horns and
bronze hooves,
so you can trample many nations to
pieces.
You will present their stolen riches to
the LORD,
their wealth to the Lord of all the
earth."

5 1*Mobilize! Marshal your troops!
The enemy is laying siege to
Jerusalem.
They will strike Israel's leader
in the face with a rod.

A Ruler from Bethlehem

2*But you, O Bethlehem Ephrathah,

Nothing is too insignificant to God

If anyone had said that Bethlehem would become significant in God's plans, people would have laughed. A small town—too small to even be noted in Joshua's long list of towns (Joshua 15)—in the district of Ephrathah in Judah, Bethlehem seemed to be associated with tragedy: Rachel, Jacob's wife, was buried here after dying in childbirth (Genesis 35:17-19), and Elimelech and Naomi abandoned it because of famine (Ruth 1:1). It was indeed "only a small village among all the people of Judah" (Micah 5:2). And yet this insignificant, tragic town became the birthplace of King David (1 Samuel 17:12) and, centuries later, of Jesus, Israel's Messiah (Matthew 2:1-6)—though even that was tinged with tragedy (Matthew 2:16-18).

God rarely chooses what we see as significant. Abraham was a pagan; Moses couldn't speak properly; Gideon was fearful; Ruth was an outsider; David was young; Amos was a farmer; Peter was a fisherman—none had what we might see as the "right" qualifications. And Jesus himself not only was born in Bethlehem but also grew up in the similarly humble town of Nazareth, a town that was often despised (John 1:46).

Insignificant people and insignificant places are often chosen by God. Why? To make it clear that "our great power is from God, not from ourselves" (2 Corinthians 4:7).

▶ *See **Bethlehem**, page 1154.*

are only a small village among all the
people of Judah.
Yet a ruler of Israel,
whose origins are in the distant past,
will come from you on my behalf.
3 The people of Israel will be abandoned
to their enemies
until the woman in labor gives birth.
Then at last his fellow countrymen
will return from exile to their own land.
4 And he will stand to lead his flock with
the LORD's strength,
in the majesty of the name of the LORD
his God.
Then his people will live there
undisturbed,
for he will be highly honored around
the world.
5 And he will be the source of peace.

When the Assyrians invade our land
and break through our defenses,
we will appoint seven rulers to watch
over us,
eight princes to lead us.
6 They will rule Assyria with drawn
swords
and enter the gates of the land of
Nimrod.
He will rescue us from the Assyrians
when they pour over the borders to
invade our land.

The Remnant Purified

7 Then the remnant left in Israel*
will take their place among the nations.
They will be like dew sent by the LORD
or like rain falling on the grass,
which no one can hold back
and no one can restrain.
8 The remnant left in Israel
will take their place among the
nations.
They will be like a lion among the
animals of the forest,
like a strong young lion among flocks
of sheep and goats,
pouncing and tearing as they go
with no rescuer in sight.
9 The people of Israel will stand up to
their foes,
and all their enemies will be wiped out.

10 "In that day," says the LORD,
"I will slaughter your horses
and destroy your chariots.
11 I will tear down your walls
and demolish your defenses.
12 I will put an end to all witchcraft,
and there will be no more
fortune-tellers.
13 I will destroy all your idols and sacred
pillars,
so you will never again worship the
work of your own hands.
14 I will abolish your idol shrines with their
Asherah poles
and destroy your pagan cities.
15 I will pour out my vengeance
on all the nations that refuse to
obey me."

The LORD's Case against Israel

6 Listen to what the LORD is saying:
"Stand up and state your case
against me.
Let the mountains and hills be called
to witness your complaints.
2 And now, O mountains,
listen to the LORD's complaint!
He has a case against his people.
He will bring charges against
Israel.

3 "O my people, what have I done to you?
What have I done to make you tired
of me?
Answer me!
4 For I brought you out of Egypt
and redeemed you from slavery.
I sent Moses, Aaron, and Miriam to
help you.
5 Don't you remember, my people,
how King Balak of Moab tried to have
you cursed
and how Balaam son of Beor blessed
you instead?
And remember your journey from Acacia
Grove* to Gilgal,
when I, the LORD, did everything I
could
to teach you about my faithfulness."

6 What can we bring to the LORD?
Should we bring him burnt offerings?
Should we bow before God Most High
with offerings of yearling calves?

4:7 Hebrew *Mount Zion.* **4:8** Hebrew *As for you, Migdal-eder, / the Ophel of the daughter of Zion.* **4:10** Hebrew *O daughter of Zion.* **4:11** Hebrew *of Zion.* **4:13** Hebrew *"Rise up and thresh, O daughter of Zion."* **5:1** Verse 5:1 is numbered 4:14 in Hebrew text. **5:2** Verses 5:2-15 are numbered 5:1-14 in Hebrew text. **5:7** Hebrew *in Jacob;* also in 5:8. See note on 1:5a. **6:5** Hebrew *Shittim.*

7 Should we offer him thousands of rams
and ten thousand rivers of olive oil?
Should we sacrifice our firstborn children
to pay for our sins?

8 No, O people, the LORD has told you
what is good,
and this is what he requires of you:
to do what is right, to love mercy,
and to walk humbly with your God.

Israel's Guilt and Punishment

9 Fear the LORD if you are wise!
His voice calls to everyone in
Jerusalem:
"The armies of destruction are coming;
the LORD is sending them.*
10 What shall I say about the homes of the
wicked
filled with treasures gained by
cheating?
What about the disgusting practice
of measuring out grain with dishonest
measures?*
11 How can I tolerate your merchants
who use dishonest scales and
weights?
12 The rich among you have become
wealthy
through extortion and violence.
Your citizens are so used to lying
that their tongues can no longer tell
the truth.

13 "Therefore, I will wound you!
I will bring you to ruin for all your sins.
14 You will eat but never have enough.
Your hunger pangs and emptiness will
remain.
And though you try to save your money,
it will come to nothing in the end.
You will save a little,
but I will give it to those who conquer
you.
15 You will plant crops
but not harvest them.
You will press your olives
but not get enough oil to anoint
yourselves.
You will trample the grapes
but get no juice to make your wine.
16 You keep only the laws of evil King
Omri;
you follow only the example of wicked
King Ahab!
Therefore, I will make an example of
you,
bringing you to complete ruin.
You will be treated with contempt,
mocked by all who see you."

Misery Turned to Hope

7 1 How miserable I am!
I feel like the fruit picker after the
harvest
who can find nothing to eat.
Not a cluster of grapes or a single early
fig
can be found to satisfy my hunger.
2 The godly people have all disappeared;
not one honest person is left on the
earth.
They are all murderers,
setting traps even for their own
brothers.
3 Both their hands are equally skilled at
doing evil!
Officials and judges alike demand
bribes.
The people with influence get what they
want,
and together they scheme to twist
justice.
4 Even the best of them is like a brier;
the most honest is as dangerous as a
hedge of thorns.
But your judgment day is coming swiftly
now.
Your time of punishment is here, a
time of confusion.
5 Don't trust anyone—
not your best friend or even your wife!
6 For the son despises his father.
The daughter defies her mother.
The daughter-in-law defies her
mother-in-law.
Your enemies are right in your own
household!
7 As for me, I look to the LORD for help.
I wait confidently for God to save me,
and my God will certainly hear me.
8 Do not gloat over me, my enemies!
For though I fall, I will rise again.
Though I sit in darkness,
the LORD will be my light.

▸ **6:8** *See* ***Is God concerned about social justice?***, *page 994.*

9 I will be patient as the LORD punishes me,
for I have sinned against him.
But after that, he will take up my case
and give me justice for all I have
suffered from my enemies.
The LORD will bring me into the light,
and I will see his righteousness.
10 Then my enemies will see that the LORD
is on my side.
They will be ashamed that they
taunted me, saying,
"So where is the LORD—
that God of yours?"
With my own eyes I will see their
downfall;
they will be trampled like mud in the
streets.

11 In that day, Israel, your cities will be
rebuilt,
and your borders will be extended.
12 People from many lands will come and
honor you—
from Assyria all the way to the towns
of Egypt,
from Egypt all the way to the Euphrates
River,*
and from distant seas and mountains.
13 But the land* will become empty and
desolate
because of the wickedness of those
who live there.

The LORD's Compassion on Israel

14 O LORD, protect your people with your
shepherd's staff;
lead your flock, your special possession.
Though they live alone in a thicket
on the heights of Mount Carmel,*
let them graze in the fertile pastures of
Bashan and Gilead
as they did long ago.

15 "Yes," says the LORD,
"I will do mighty miracles for you,
like those I did when I rescued you
from slavery in Egypt."

16 All the nations of the world will stand
amazed
at what the LORD will do for you.
They will be embarrassed
at their feeble power.
They will cover their mouths in silent
awe,
deaf to everything around them.
17 Like snakes crawling from their holes,
they will come out to meet the LORD
our God.
They will fear him greatly,
trembling in terror at his
presence.

18 Where is another God like you,
who pardons the guilt of the
remnant,
overlooking the sins of his special
people?
You will not stay angry with your people
forever,
because you delight in showing
unfailing love.
19 Once again you will have compassion
on us.
You will trample our sins under your
feet
and throw them into the depths of the
ocean!
20 You will show us your faithfulness and
unfailing love
as you promised to our ancestors
Abraham and Jacob long ago.

6:9 Hebrew *"Listen to the rod. / Who appointed it?"* **6:10** Hebrew *of using the short ephah?* The ephah was a unit for measuring grain. **7:12** Hebrew *the river.* **7:13** Or *earth.* **7:14** Or *surrounded by a fruitful land.*

Nahum

Announcement of God's punishment on Nineveh

We know nothing about Nahum except that he was a native of Elkosh (1:1), and we don't even know where that was! His name means "comfort," reflecting the comfort he would bring to Judah through announcing God's punishment against Nineveh, the capital of Assyria, the enemy of God's people. The Neo-Assyrian Empire was the greatest world power in its day. Since Nineveh fell in 612 BC, and Thebes (referred to in 3:8) fell in 663 BC, Nahum's message was given sometime between those two dates. Nineveh, however, does not simply represent the Assyrian Empire, but all those who set themselves up against God.

OVERVIEW

God's anger against Nineveh
1:1-15

Nineveh will be destroyed
2:1–3:19

What's it all about?

Nahum's message stands in stark contrast to that of Jonah. When Jonah was sent to Nineveh to warn them of God's coming judgment, the city had repented. But their repentance did not last. As Assyria became more and more powerful and grew in size, it became increasingly cruel and arrogant. It had conquered and exiled Israel, Judah's northern neighbor, in 722 BC; and so now God's message to the Assyrians through Nahum was that his judgment on them was certain and sure.

Nahum began by focusing on God's good and righteous character (1:1-7); God is "good, a strong refuge when trouble comes" (1:7). But Assyria's cruelty had reached such heights that now God would "sweep away his enemies in an overwhelming flood" (1:8), which would bring great joy to Judah (1:15). In chapter 2, Nahum saw in vivid detail the city of Nineveh being attacked and plundered (2:1-10), and he sang a taunting song over it (2:11-13). In chapter 3, he saw more details of the onslaught against Nineveh and declared the reasons for God's judgment on it. Such was the certainty of that judgment that there would be no hope for the city: "There is no healing for your wound; your injury is fatal" (3:19). And everyone who heard the news would rejoice, Nahum said.

History would eventually prove Nahum right; Nineveh was so completely destroyed in 612 BC that it was never rebuilt.

What does it mean for us?

Nahum confronts us with the inevitable consequences of sin: Punishment (chapter 1) is inevitable when the God who is described in chapter 1 meets the evil described in chapter 3. God may be "slow to get angry" (1:3), but he is also "a jealous God, filled with vengeance and rage" (1:2). He may be kind, but he is also just. He may be "slow to get angry," but he also "never lets the guilty go unpunished" (1:3). These aspects of his character are not contradictory but complementary, like the two sides of a coin. This means that while God may bear with people's sinful ways for a time, there comes a point when his righteous judgment must come in order for him to be true to his own character. We should never think that just because we seem to be getting away with things now, God does not notice or will not one day call us to account. Sin always gets its just deserts.

But Nahum also reminds us that when we are on the receiving end of other people's sins, the final word is always with the LORD (Yahweh). For God's people, he is both "a strong refuge when trouble comes" (1:7) and a guarantee that evil will not ultimately succeed.

▶ *See also* ***A timeline of the Bible****, pages A22-A24.*

1 This message concerning Nineveh came as a vision to Nahum, who lived in Elkosh.

The LORD's Anger against Nineveh

2 The LORD is a jealous God,
filled with vengeance and rage.
He takes revenge on all who oppose him
and continues to rage against his enemies!
3 The LORD is slow to get angry, but his power is great,
and he never lets the guilty go unpunished.
He displays his power in the whirlwind and the storm.
The billowing clouds are the dust beneath his feet.
4 At his command the oceans dry up,
and the rivers disappear.
The lush pastures of Bashan and Carmel fade,
and the green forests of Lebanon wither.
5 In his presence the mountains quake,
and the hills melt away;
the earth trembles,
and its people are destroyed.
6 Who can stand before his fierce anger?
Who can survive his burning fury?
His rage blazes forth like fire,
and the mountains crumble to dust in his presence.

7 The LORD is good,
a strong refuge when trouble comes.
He is close to those who trust in him.
8 But he will sweep away his enemies*
in an overwhelming flood.
He will pursue his foes
into the darkness of night.

9 Why are you scheming against the LORD?
He will destroy you with one blow;
he won't need to strike twice!
10 His enemies, tangled like thornbushes
and staggering like drunks,
will be burned up like dry stubble in a field.
11 Who is this wicked counselor of yours
who plots evil against the LORD?

12 This is what the LORD says:
"Though the Assyrians have many allies,
they will be destroyed and disappear.
O my people, I have punished you before,
but I will not punish you again.
13 Now I will break the yoke of bondage from your neck
and tear off the chains of Assyrian oppression."

14 And this is what the LORD says
concerning the Assyrians in Nineveh:
"You will have no more children to carry on your name.
I will destroy all the idols in the temples of your gods.
I am preparing a grave for you
because you are despicable!"

15*Look! A messenger is coming over the mountains with good news!
He is bringing a message of peace.
Celebrate your festivals, O people of Judah,
and fulfill all your vows,
for your wicked enemies will never invade your land again.
They will be completely destroyed!

The Fall of Nineveh

2 1*Your enemy is coming to crush you, Nineveh.
Man the ramparts! Watch the roads!
Prepare your defenses! Call out your forces!

1:8 As in Greek version; Hebrew reads *sweep away her place.*
1:15 Verse 1:15 is numbered 2:1 in Hebrew text. **2:1** Verses 2:1-13 are numbered 2:2-14 in Hebrew text.

[2] Even though the destroyer has destroyed
Judah,
the LORD will restore its honor.
Israel's vine has been stripped of
branches,
but he will restore its splendor.

[3] Shields flash red in the sunlight!
See the scarlet uniforms of the valiant
troops!
Watch as their glittering chariots move
into position,
with a forest of spears waving above
them.*
[4] The chariots race recklessly along the
streets
and rush wildly through the squares.
They flash like firelight
and move as swiftly as lightning.
[5] The king shouts to his officers;
they stumble in their haste,
rushing to the walls to set up their
defenses.
[6] The river gates have been torn open!
The palace is about to collapse!
[7] Nineveh's exile has been decreed,
and all the servant girls mourn its
capture.
They moan like doves
and beat their breasts in sorrow.
[8] Nineveh is like a leaking water reservoir!
The people are slipping away.
"Stop, stop!" someone shouts,
but no one even looks back.
[9] Loot the silver!
Plunder the gold!
There's no end to Nineveh's treasures—
its vast, uncounted wealth.
[10] Soon the city is plundered, empty, and
ruined.
Hearts melt and knees shake.
The people stand aghast,
their faces pale and trembling.

[11] Where now is that great Nineveh,
that den filled with young lions?
It was a place where people—like lions
and their cubs—
walked freely and without fear.
[12] The lion tore up meat for his cubs
and strangled prey for his mate.
He filled his den with prey,
his caverns with his plunder.

[13] "I am your enemy!"
says the LORD of Heaven's Armies.
"Your chariots will soon go up in smoke.
Your young men* will be killed in
battle.
Never again will you plunder conquered
nations.
The voices of your proud messengers
will be heard no more."

The LORD's Judgment against Nineveh

3 [1] What sorrow awaits Nineveh,
the city of murder and lies!
She is crammed with wealth
and is never without victims.

God our refuge

Nahum's prophecy begins with two contrasts. Whereas Nineveh was about to experience divine anger (Nahum 1:1-6), Judah could know God as "good" (1:7); and while an "overwhelming flood" was about to sweep over Nineveh (1:8)—a picture of the Babylonian army that would soon sweep through Assyria—God's people would find God to be "a strong refuge when trouble comes" (1:7). The God who brings judgment upon the wicked is the same God who brings protection to his people.

Seeing God as the never-failing protector of his people, especially in times of trouble, is very common in the Scriptures. He is often described as a refuge or fortress—evoking the image of an impregnable place in the rocks from which any enemy can be held back and defeated and where the Lord's servant can therefore feel utterly secure (e.g., Psalms 9:9; 18:1-3; 27:1-3; 144:2; Jeremiah 16:19; Joel 3:16).

When we are faced with trials, troubles, or opposition, we can still run to God, "our refuge and strength, always ready to help in times of trouble" (Psalm 46:1).

2 Hear the crack of whips,
the rumble of wheels!
Horses' hooves pound,
and chariots clatter wildly.
3 See the flashing swords and glittering spears
as the charioteers charge past!
There are countless casualties,
heaps of bodies—
so many bodies that
people stumble over them.
4 All this because Nineveh,
the beautiful and faithless city,
mistress of deadly charms,
enticed the nations with her beauty.
She taught them all her magic,
enchanting people everywhere.

5 "I am your enemy!"
says the LORD of Heaven's Armies.
"And now I will lift your skirts
and show all the earth your nakedness and shame.
6 I will cover you with filth
and show the world how vile you really are.
7 All who see you will shrink back and say,
'Nineveh lies in ruins.
Where are the mourners?'
Does anyone regret your destruction?"

8 Are you any better than the city of Thebes,*
situated on the Nile River, surrounded by water?
She was protected by the river on all sides,
walled in by water.
9 Ethiopia* and the land of Egypt
gave unlimited assistance.
The nations of Put and Libya
were among her allies.
10 Yet Thebes fell,
and her people were led away as captives.
Her babies were dashed to death
against the stones of the streets.
Soldiers threw dice* to get Egyptian officers as servants.
All their leaders were bound in chains.

11 And you, Nineveh, will also stagger like a drunkard.
You will hide for fear of the attacking enemy.
12 All your fortresses will fall.
They will be devoured like the ripe figs
that fall into the mouths
of those who shake the trees.
13 Your troops will be as weak
and helpless as women.
The gates of your land will be opened wide to the enemy
and set on fire and burned.
14 Get ready for the siege!
Store up water!
Strengthen the defenses!
Go into the pits to trample clay,
and pack it into molds,
making bricks to repair the walls.

2:3 Greek and Syriac versions read *into position, / the horses whipped into a frenzy.* **2:13** Hebrew *young lions.* **3:8** Hebrew *No-amon;* also in 3:10. **3:9** Hebrew *Cush.* **3:10** Hebrew *They cast lots.*

Nineveh

Nineveh had been given its chance to repent through Jonah, but its response had been shallow and short-lived, and the city had become even more heartless and cruel. So now Nahum declared that God's judgment was coming upon it. Nineveh, standing on the banks of the Tigris River, had been founded by Nimrod, a descendant of Noah's son Ham (Genesis 10:8-12). Around 700 BC Sennacherib made it the capital of Assyria in place of Asshur. He undertook an extensive building program there, constructing extensive city walls and a water supply system. He built a beautiful palace with walls lined with low reliefs of the king at leisure and at war, along with huge sculptures and elaborate furnishings. Nineveh survived until it was destroyed by Babylon in 612 BC, just as Nahum prophesied, never to be rebuilt again.

▶ *See also* ***Assyria****, page 431.*

15 But the fire will devour you;
the sword will cut you down.
The enemy will consume you like
locusts,
devouring everything they see.
There will be no escape,
even if you multiply like swarming
locusts.
16 Your merchants have multiplied
until they outnumber the stars.
But like a swarm of locusts,
they strip the land and fly away.
17 Your guards* and officials are also like
swarming locusts
that crowd together in the hedges on
a cold day.
But like locusts that fly away when the
sun comes up,
all of them will fly away and
disappear.

18 Your shepherds are asleep, O Assyrian
king;
your princes lie dead in the dust.
Your people are scattered across the
mountains
with no one to gather them together.
19 There is no healing for your
wound;
your injury is fatal.
All who hear of your destruction
will clap their hands for joy.
Where can anyone be found
who has not suffered from your
continual cruelty?

3:17 Or *princes*.

Habakkuk *The eternal question: "Why?"*

We know nothing about Habakkuk, though his prediction of the coming Babylonian invasion (1:6) suggests he lived in Judah, probably during King Josiah's reign (640–609 BC), or possibly during King Jehoiakim's reign (609–598 BC), but sometime before the collapse of the Assyrian Empire in 605 BC.

Although Habakkuk is a prophetic book, at times it reads like a psalm, especially chapter 3, which even has some of the musical directions associated with the psalms. This has led some to think that Habakkuk may have been a Levite who worked in the Jerusalem Temple.

This book is unusual among the prophetic books in that it is not addressed to God's people. Much of it is a conversation between the prophet and God. Habakkuk tried to reconcile his beliefs with the facts of life as he saw them. He was perplexed by the "why?" of what was happening all around him, but he knew that God ultimately held the answer.

What's it all about?

The book begins with Habakkuk complaining to God that not only had he not yet answered his prayers, but he was also still tolerating injustice in Judah (1:2-4). God's answer is surprising: He was raising up Babylon to be the instrument of his judgment (1:5-11). This answer was just too much for Habakkuk: How could such a holy God, who cannot even look upon evil (1:13), use a wicked nation like Babylon to punish Judah, his chosen people? So he set himself up like a watchman in a watchtower (2:1), waiting for God's answer.

God's answer did come—though not in the way Habakkuk expected. God would use Babylon, as he had said; but then his judgment would come on Babylon, too. There would be a delay before this happened, so Habakkuk was told to write down the message and to wait for "a future time" (2:2-3). It would take faith to wait for this moment, but God assured him that the righteous would be preserved through it all by remaining faithful (2:4). God was well aware of the Babylonians' wickedness and would punish them, but at the right time and according to his reckoning. He told Habakkuk to write this answer plainly so that all would see and understand this message. God wanted everyone to know that while it may seem, initially, that the wicked are not punished for their plans and actions, they will indeed be judged in the end. And the purpose of that judgment and the removal of sin is so that one day "as the waters fill the sea, the earth will be filled with an awareness of the glory of the LORD" (2:14).

OVERVIEW

Habakkuk's first complaint: Why does wickedness in Judah go unpunished? · *1:1-4*

God's answer: Babylon will bring God's judgment · *1:5-11*

Habakkuk's second complaint: How can a righteous God use sinful Babylon? · *1:12–2:1*

God's answer: Babylon itself will be punished, and God's glory will be revealed · *2:2-20*

Habakkuk's prayer *3:1-19*

In chapter 3, Habakkuk's questions are stilled, and he offers a thrilling hymn of praise. He put his confidence in God and in everything that God would do, even when things looked their worst and there seemed to be no hope (3:17-18).

What does it mean for us?

God wants us to be real and not pretend that we don't have questions. Habakkuk shows that God *wants* us to come to him with our struggles, questions, and doubts. And he *wants* to reveal himself to us so that we can carry on with joy and hope, not with bitter resignation. If we don't bring God any questions, we won't receive any answers.

Habakkuk could ask "why?"—why do the righteous suffer and the wicked apparently prosper?—because he had a tender, trusting relationship with God. In spite of the contradictions that perplexed him, he *knew* that God was in control. His questions sprang from faith, not from a lack of it. This book shows that we don't need to hide our questions from God. In fact, God even responds to our questions when our trust in him is limited. But we do need to stay close to him, believing that he will speak to us as we do so. The answer may not be what we expect, but it *will* be good to hear, and it will cause us to keep trusting in him.

▸ *See also **A timeline of the Bible**, pages A22-A24.*

1 This is the message that the prophet Habakkuk received in a vision.

Habakkuk's Complaint

2 How long, O LORD, must I call for help?
But you do not listen!
"Violence is everywhere!" I cry,
but you do not come to save.
3 Must I forever see these evil deeds?
Why must I watch all this misery?
Wherever I look,
I see destruction and violence.
I am surrounded by people
who love to argue and fight.
4 The law has become paralyzed,
and there is no justice in the courts.
The wicked far outnumber the righteous,
so that justice has become perverted.

The LORD's Reply

5 The LORD replied,

"Look around at the nations;
look and be amazed!*
For I am doing something in your own day,
something you wouldn't believe
even if someone told you about it.
6 I am raising up the Babylonians,*
a cruel and violent people.
They will march across the world
and conquer other lands.
7 They are notorious for their cruelty
and do whatever they like.
8 Their horses are swifter than cheetahs*
and fiercer than wolves at dusk.
Their charioteers charge from far away.
Like eagles, they swoop down to
devour their prey.

9 "On they come, all bent on violence.
Their hordes advance like a desert wind,
sweeping captives ahead of them like
sand.
10 They scoff at kings and princes
and scorn all their fortresses.
They simply pile ramps of earth
against their walls and capture
them!
11 They sweep past like the wind
and are gone.
But they are deeply guilty,
for their own strength is their god."

Habakkuk's Second Complaint

12 O LORD my God, my Holy One, you who
are eternal—
surely you do not plan to wipe us out?
O LORD, our Rock, you have sent these
Babylonians to correct us,
to punish us for our many sins.
13 But you are pure and cannot stand the
sight of evil.
Will you wink at their treachery?
Should you be silent while the wicked
swallow up people more righteous
than they?
14 Are we only fish to be caught and killed?
Are we only sea creatures that have no
leader?

15 Must we be strung up on their hooks
and caught in their nets while they
rejoice and celebrate?
16 Then they will worship their nets
and burn incense in front of them.
"These nets are the gods who have made
us rich!"
they will claim.
17 Will you let them get away with this
forever?
Will they succeed forever in their
heartless conquests?

2 1 I will climb up to my watchtower
and stand at my guardpost.
There I will wait to see what the LORD
says
and how he* will answer my
complaint.

The LORD's Second Reply

2 Then the LORD said to me,

"Write my answer plainly on tablets,
so that a runner can carry the correct
message to others.
3 This vision is for a future time.
It describes the end, and it will be
fulfilled.
If it seems slow in coming, wait patiently,
for it will surely take place.
It will not be delayed.
4 "Look at the proud!
They trust in themselves, and their
lives are crooked.
But the righteous will live by their
faithfulness to God.*
5 Wealth* is treacherous,
and the arrogant are never at rest.
They open their mouths as wide as the
grave,*
and like death, they are never
satisfied.
In their greed they have gathered up
many nations
and swallowed many peoples.
6 "But soon their captives will taunt them.
They will mock them, saying,
'What sorrow awaits you thieves!
Now you will get what you deserve!
You've become rich by extortion,
but how much longer can this go on?'
7 Suddenly, your debtors will take action.
They will turn on you and take all you
have,
while you stand trembling and
helpless.

1:5 Greek version reads *Look, you mockers; / look and be amazed and die.* Compare Acts 13:41. **1:6** Or *Chaldeans.* **1:8** Or *leopards.* **2:1** As in Syriac version; Hebrew reads *I.* **2:3b-4** Greek version reads *If the vision is delayed, wait patiently, / for it will surely come and not delay. / [4]I will take no pleasure in anyone who turns away. / But the righteous person will live by my faith.* Compare Rom 1:17; Gal 3:11; Heb 10:37-38. **2:5a** As in Dead Sea Scroll 1QpHab; other Hebrew manuscripts read *Wine.* **2:5b** Hebrew *as Sheol.*

Why do bad things happen in life?

If there is a good God, why do bad things happen? Habakkuk didn't really get an answer to this age-old question; but he did get a fresh revelation of God in light of which he was content to wait, trust God, and see what happened.

Many have tried to propose answers, however. Some suggest that evil is not real, only an illusion from which we need to be freed; others, that it is a punishment for sin (something Jesus clearly denied in John 9:1-3); and yet others, that God permits it to purify our character or show us our need. But there always remains the nagging question "*why*?"

Actually, the Bible never fully answers this question. It certainly roots evil in the Fall, which led to pain, toil, and death (Genesis 3:14-19), and it recognizes the devil's activity in opposing God's plans. But most of all, it tells us that God doesn't leave us alone in our pain. In Christ, he entered our world and shared our suffering to redeem us. One day all evil and suffering *will* be removed, and "there will be no more death or sorrow or crying or pain" (Revelation 21:4). But in the meantime, God walks with us, giving us courage and confidence as we trust in him.

▶ *See also* ***Trusting God when we cannot see the way ahead****, page 57;* ***God intended it all for good****, page 62;* ***Suffering: Why do bad things happen to good people?****, page 567.*

8 Because you have plundered many nations,
now all the survivors will plunder you.
You committed murder throughout the countryside
and filled the towns with violence.

9 "What sorrow awaits you who build big houses
with money gained dishonestly!
You believe your wealth will buy security,
putting your family's nest beyond the reach of danger.
10 But by the murders you committed,
you have shamed your name and forfeited your lives.
11 The very stones in the walls cry out against you,
and the beams in the ceilings echo the complaint.
12 "What sorrow awaits you who build cities
with money gained through murder and corruption!
13 Has not the LORD of Heaven's Armies promised
that the wealth of nations will turn to ashes?
They work so hard,
but all in vain!
14 For as the waters fill the sea,
the earth will be filled with an awareness
of the glory of the LORD.

15 "What sorrow awaits you who make your neighbors drunk!
You force your cup on them
so you can gloat over their shameful nakedness.
16 But soon it will be your turn to be disgraced.
Come, drink and be exposed!*
Drink from the cup of the LORD's judgment,
and all your glory will be turned to shame.
17 You cut down the forests of Lebanon.
Now you will be cut down.
You destroyed the wild animals,
so now their terror will be yours.
You committed murder throughout the countryside
and filled the towns with violence.

18 "What good is an idol carved by man,
or a cast image that deceives you?
How foolish to trust in your own creation—
a god that can't even talk!
19 What sorrow awaits you who say to wooden idols,
'Wake up and save us!'
To speechless stone images you say,
'Rise up and teach us!'
Can an idol tell you what to do?
They may be overlaid with gold and silver,
but they are lifeless inside.
20 But the LORD is in his holy Temple.
Let all the earth be silent before him."

Habakkuk's Prayer

3 This prayer was sung by the prophet Habakkuk*:

2 I have heard all about you, LORD.
I am filled with awe by your amazing works.
In this time of our deep need,
help us again as you did in years gone by.
And in your anger,
remember your mercy.

3 I see God moving across the deserts from Edom,*
the Holy One coming from Mount Paran.*
His brilliant splendor fills the heavens,
and the earth is filled with his praise.
4 His coming is as brilliant as the sunrise.
Rays of light flash from his hands,
where his awesome power is hidden.
5 Pestilence marches before him;
plague follows close behind.
6 When he stops, the earth shakes.
When he looks, the nations tremble.
He shatters the everlasting mountains
and levels the eternal hills.
He is the Eternal One!*
7 I see the people of Cushan in distress,
and the nation of Midian trembling in terror.

8 Was it in anger, LORD, that you struck the rivers
and parted the sea?
Were you displeased with them?
No, you were sending your chariots of salvation!

9 You brandished your bow
and your quiver of arrows.
You split open the earth with flowing rivers.
10 The mountains watched and trembled.
Onward swept the raging waters.
The mighty deep cried out,
lifting its hands in submission.
11 The sun and moon stood still in the sky
as your brilliant arrows flew
and your glittering spear flashed.

12 You marched across the land in anger
and trampled the nations in your fury.
13 You went out to rescue your chosen people,
to save your anointed ones.
You crushed the heads of the wicked
and stripped their bones from head to toe.
14 With his own weapons,
you destroyed the chief of those
who rushed out like a whirlwind,
thinking Israel would be easy prey.
15 You trampled the sea with your horses,
and the mighty waters piled high.

16 I trembled inside when I heard this;
my lips quivered with fear.
My legs gave way beneath me,*
and I shook in terror.
I will wait quietly for the coming day
when disaster will strike the people who invade us.
17 Even though the fig trees have no blossoms,
and there are no grapes on the vines;
even though the olive crop fails,
and the fields lie empty and barren;
even though the flocks die in the fields,
and the cattle barns are empty,
18 yet I will rejoice in the LORD!
I will be joyful in the God of my salvation!
19 The Sovereign LORD is my strength!
He makes me as surefooted as a deer,*
able to tread upon the heights.

(For the choir director: This prayer is to be accompanied by stringed instruments.)

2:16 Dead Sea Scrolls and Greek and Syriac versions read *and stagger!* **3:1** Hebrew adds *according to shigionoth,* probably indicating the musical setting for the prayer. **3:3a** Hebrew *Teman.* **3:3b** Hebrew adds *selah;* also in 3:9, 13. The meaning of this Hebrew term is uncertain; it is probably a musical or literary term. **3:6** Or *The ancient paths belong to him.* **3:16** Hebrew *Decay entered my bones.* **3:19** Or *He gives me the speed of a deer.*

Zephaniah *Judgment and salvation*

Zephaniah was a prophet in Judah during the reign of the reformer-king Josiah (640–609 BC). He was a fourth-generation descendant of the godly King Hezekiah (1:1) and so was a man of considerable social standing, as reflected in his prophecies, which show an awareness of political issues and events in the royal court. A contemporary of Jeremiah, he tried to shake the people of Judah out of their complacency, warning that a day of judgment was coming. He warned that corrupt rulers would be destroyed and the land given to the poor, and he looked forward to the coming "day of the LORD," when God would establish his reign on the earth.

What's it all about?

Zephaniah preached when the godly King Josiah was embarking on religious reformation in Judah—a reform that was desperately needed because of the actions of a previous, wicked king, Manasseh. His very name—Zephaniah, which means "the LORD has hidden (me)"—suggests that his parents may have had to hide him from Manasseh.

Josiah himself was a good king who was probably influenced by Zephaniah's preaching. But by contrast, the people of Judah, and especially Jerusalem, had advanced too far toward spiritual ruin, and Zephaniah warned that God's judgment was now close: "That terrible day of the LORD is near. Swiftly it comes" (1:14). Chapter 1 is filled with terror as the prophet vividly describes God's judgment coming upon the land as that great "day of the LORD" approaches. But chapter 2 opens with an invitation, for there was still time to repent and avoid this disaster, if the people were willing: "Seek the LORD. . . . Seek to do what is right and to live humbly. Perhaps even yet the LORD will protect you—protect you from his anger on that day of destruction" (2:3). The prophet then went on to proclaim God's judgment on the nations around Judah (2:4-15), before returning to denounce Judah and Jerusalem, who were just as sinful as those nations and so could not expect to escape (3:3-8). This section concludes with God announcing his intention to gather all peoples before him—not for blessing, but for judgment (3:8).

But judgment is not the last word; hope is! For Zephaniah foresaw a time when the nations would turn and worship the LORD (Yahweh; 3:9-10), as would his own people (3:11-13). He foresaw the joy that this would bring as his people realized that the LORD had removed "his hand of judgment" and that he, their "mighty savior," was living among them (3:15-17). The fortunes of God's people would be restored at last.

OVERVIEW

God's coming judgment on Judah
1:1-18

A call to repentance and humility
2:1-3

God's coming judgment on the nations and on Jerusalem · *2:4–3:8*

Hope for the future for both the nations and Judah · *3:9-20*

What does it mean for us?

Against a background of a faithless nation, surrounded by wicked nations, Zephaniah spoke about a remnant—a small group of people who would remain faithful to God (2:7-9; 3:9-13) and form the core of a new, renewed nation, free from the wrongdoing that had resulted in God's punishment. They were humble and knew how very much they needed God, so they were spared the judgment of the day of the LORD (2:3).

The book of Zephaniah reminds us how important it is to stay humble in all our dealings with God. In the Bible, humility—not moral perfection—is the way to a secure future. Zephaniah warned that God cannot work with people who are proud and boastful. They may look good on the outside, but they cannot be used by God. And just relying on the past spiritual history of our ancestors won't be sufficient either; each generation has to walk humbly with God themselves.

But Zephaniah also reminds us that God's people are not just called to look to their own spiritual condition; they are also called to take God's message to those who do not yet know him, for he longs to "purify the speech of all people, so that everyone can worship the LORD together" (3:9).

▶ *See also **A timeline of the Bible**, pages A22-A24.*

1 The LORD gave this message to Zephaniah when Josiah son of Amon was king of Judah. Zephaniah was the son of Cushi, son of Gedaliah, son of Amariah, son of Hezekiah.

Coming Judgment against Judah

2 "I will sweep away everything
from the face of the earth," says the LORD.
3 "I will sweep away people and animals alike.
I will sweep away the birds of the sky
and the fish in the sea.
I will reduce the wicked to heaps of rubble,*
and I will wipe humanity from the face of the earth," says the LORD.
4 "I will crush Judah and Jerusalem with my fist
and destroy every last trace of their Baal worship.
I will put an end to all the idolatrous priests,
so that even the memory of them will disappear.
5 For they go up to their roofs
and bow down to the sun, moon, and stars.
They claim to follow the LORD,
but then they worship Molech,* too.
6 And I will destroy those who used to worship me
but now no longer do.
They no longer ask for the LORD's guidance
or seek my blessings."

7 Stand in silence in the presence of the Sovereign LORD,
for the awesome day of the LORD's judgment is near.
The LORD has prepared his people for a great slaughter
and has chosen their executioners.*
8 "On that day of judgment,"
says the LORD,
"I will punish the leaders and princes of Judah
and all those following pagan customs.
9 Yes, I will punish those who participate
in pagan worship ceremonies,
and those who fill their masters'
houses with violence and deceit.

10 "On that day," says the LORD,
"a cry of alarm will come from the Fish Gate
and echo throughout the New Quarter of the city.*
And a great crash will sound from the hills.
11 Wail in sorrow, all you who live in the market area,*
for all the merchants and traders will be destroyed.

1:3 The meaning of the Hebrew is uncertain. **1:5** Hebrew *Malcam,* a variant spelling of Molech; or it could possibly mean *their king.* **1:7** Hebrew *has prepared a sacrifice and sanctified his guests.* **1:10** Or *the Second Quarter,* a newer section of Jerusalem. Hebrew reads *the Mishneh.* **1:11** Or *in the valley,* a lower section of Jerusalem. Hebrew reads *the Maktesh.*

▶ **1:7** *See **The day of the LORD**, page 988.*

12 "I will search with lanterns in
Jerusalem's darkest corners
to punish those who sit complacent in
their sins.
They think the LORD will do nothing to
them,
either good or bad.
13 So their property will be plundered,
their homes will be ransacked.
They will build new homes
but never live in them.
They will plant vineyards
but never drink wine from them.

14 "That terrible day of the LORD is near.
Swiftly it comes—
a day of bitter tears,
a day when even strong men will cry
out.
15 It will be a day when the LORD's anger is
poured out—
a day of terrible distress and anguish,
a day of ruin and desolation,
a day of darkness and gloom,
a day of clouds and blackness,
16 a day of trumpet calls and battle cries.
Down go the walled cities
and the strongest battlements!

17 "Because you have sinned against the
LORD,
I will make you grope around like the
blind.
Your blood will be poured into the dust,
and your bodies will lie rotting on the
ground."
18 Your silver and gold will not save you
on that day of the LORD's anger.
For the whole land will be devoured
by the fire of his jealousy.
He will make a terrifying end
of all the people on earth.*

A Call to Repentance

2 [1] Gather together—yes, gather together,
you shameless nation.
2 Gather before judgment begins,
before your time to repent is blown
away like chaff.
Act now, before the fierce fury of the
LORD falls
and the terrible day of the LORD's
anger begins.
3 Seek the LORD, all who are humble,
and follow his commands.
Seek to do what is right
and to live humbly.
Perhaps even yet the LORD will protect
you—
protect you from his anger on that day
of destruction.

Judgment against Philistia

4 Gaza and Ashkelon will be abandoned,
Ashdod and Ekron torn down.
5 And what sorrow awaits you Philistines*
who live along the coast and in the
land of Canaan,
for this judgment is against you, too!
The LORD will destroy you
until not one of you is left.
6 The Philistine coast will become a
wilderness pasture,
a place of shepherd camps
and enclosures for sheep and goats.
7 The remnant of the tribe of Judah will
pasture there.
They will rest at night in the
abandoned houses in Ashkelon.
For the LORD their God will visit his
people in kindness
and restore their prosperity again.

Judgment against Moab and Ammon

8 "I have heard the taunts of the Moabites
and the insults of the Ammonites,
mocking my people
and invading their borders.
9 Now, as surely as I live,"
says the LORD of Heaven's Armies, the
God of Israel,
"Moab and Ammon will be destroyed—
destroyed as completely as Sodom
and Gomorrah.
Their land will become a place of
stinging nettles,
salt pits, and eternal desolation.
The remnant of my people will plunder
them
and take their land."
10 They will receive the wages of their
pride,
for they have scoffed at the people of
the LORD of Heaven's Armies.
11 The LORD will terrify them
as he destroys all the gods in the land.
Then nations around the world will
worship the LORD,
each in their own land.

Judgment against Ethiopia and Assyria

12 "You Ethiopians* will also be
slaughtered
by my sword," says the LORD.

13 And the LORD will strike the lands of the
north with his fist,
destroying the land of Assyria.
He will make its great capital, Nineveh,
a desolate wasteland,
parched like a desert.
14 The proud city will become a pasture for
flocks and herds,
and all sorts of wild animals will
settle there.
The desert owl and screech owl will
roost on its ruined columns,
their calls echoing through the gaping
windows.
Rubble will block all the doorways,
and the cedar paneling will be
exposed to the weather.
15 This is the boisterous city,
once so secure.
"I am the greatest!" it boasted.
"No other city can compare
with me!"
But now, look how it has become
an utter ruin,
a haven for wild animals.
Everyone passing by will laugh in
derision
and shake a defiant fist.

Jerusalem's Rebellion and Redemption

3 1 What sorrow awaits rebellious,
polluted Jerusalem,
the city of violence and crime!
2 No one can tell it anything;
it refuses all correction.
It does not trust in the LORD
or draw near to its God.
3 Its leaders are like roaring lions
hunting for their victims.
Its judges are like ravenous wolves at
evening time,
who by dawn have left no trace of
their prey.
4 Its prophets are arrogant liars seeking
their own gain.
Its priests defile the Temple by
disobeying God's instructions.
5 But the LORD is still there in the city,
and he does no wrong.
Day by day he hands down justice,
and he does not fail.
But the wicked know no shame.

6 "I have wiped out many nations,
devastating their fortress walls and
towers.
Their streets are now deserted;
their cities lie in silent ruin.
There are no survivors—
none at all.

1:18 Or *the people living in the land.* **2:5** Hebrew *Kerethites.* **2:12** Hebrew *Cushites.*

The presence of God

Time and time again in the Bible we see the presence of God transforming things, whether situations or people. In Zephaniah 3:17, the prophet looks beyond the coming judgment to the restoration of God's people, not only delivered by his victory but also transformed by his presence. The image in 3:17 is first of a victorious warrior, but then of a caring mother whose very presence settles the child she is nursing as she sings over it with joy. Such is the transforming presence of God among his people.

It was the presence of God that allayed Moses' fears (Exodus 33:12-17), that answered Job's questions (Job 38:1; 42:1-5), that overcame Isaiah's unworthiness (Isaiah 6:1-8), that settled Paul's frustrations (2 Corinthians 12:7-10), and that reassured John in exile (Revelation 1:9-18). God's presence is the answer to all our needs—and we don't need some kind of special mystical experience to know that presence. We can have confidence that he is there for the simple reason that he has promised to never fail us or abandon us (Deuteronomy 31:6; Joshua 1:5; Hebrews 13:5).

▶ *See also* ***Moses, the man who loved God's presence****, page 69.*

7 I thought, 'Surely they will have
reverence for me now!
Surely they will listen to my warnings.
Then I won't need to strike again,
destroying their homes.'
But no, they get up early
to continue their evil deeds.
8 Therefore, be patient," says the LORD.
"Soon I will stand and accuse these
evil nations.
For I have decided to gather the
kingdoms of the earth
and pour out my fiercest anger and
fury on them.
All the earth will be devoured
by the fire of my jealousy.

9 "Then I will purify the speech of all
people,
so that everyone can worship the
LORD together.
10 My scattered people who live beyond the
rivers of Ethiopia*
will come to present their offerings.
11 On that day you will no longer need to
be ashamed,
for you will no longer be rebels
against me.
I will remove all proud and arrogant
people from among you.
There will be no more haughtiness on
my holy mountain.
12 Those who are left will be the lowly and
humble,
for it is they who trust in the name of
the LORD.
13 The remnant of Israel will do no wrong;
they will never tell lies or deceive one
another.
They will eat and sleep in safety,
and no one will make them afraid."

14 Sing, O daughter of Zion;
shout aloud, O Israel!
Be glad and rejoice with all your heart,
O daughter of Jerusalem!
15 For the LORD will remove his hand of
judgment
and will disperse the armies of your
enemy.
And the LORD himself, the King of Israel,
will live among you!
At last your troubles will be over,
and you will never again fear
disaster.
16 On that day the announcement to
Jerusalem will be,
"Cheer up, Zion! Don't be afraid!
17 For the LORD your God is living among
you.
He is a mighty savior.
He will take delight in you with
gladness.
With his love, he will calm all your
fears.*
He will rejoice over you with joyful
songs."
18 "I will gather you who mourn for the
appointed festivals;
you will be disgraced no more.*
19 And I will deal severely with all who
have oppressed you.
I will save the weak and helpless
ones;
I will bring together
those who were chased away.
I will give glory and fame to my former
exiles,
wherever they have been mocked and
shamed.
20 On that day I will gather you together
and bring you home again.
I will give you a good name, a name of
distinction,
among all the nations of the earth,
as I restore your fortunes before their
very eyes.
I, the LORD, have spoken!"

3:10 Hebrew *Cush.* **3:17** Or *He will be silent in his love.* Greek and Syriac versions read *He will renew you with his love.* **3:18** The meaning of the Hebrew for this verse is uncertain.

Haggai *Putting God first*

Haggai was a prophet to those who had returned to Judah from exile in Babylon after Babylon was conquered by King Cyrus of Persia. After their initial enthusiasm, during which they started to rebuild the Temple in Jerusalem, many had become discouraged and were neglecting God's house in order to focus on their homes and fields. Prophesying for just under four months—August 29 to December 18, 520 BC (1:1; 2:20)—Haggai encouraged them to not become distracted but rather to put God first. If they did, all the other blessings they longed for would then follow.

What's it all about?

When the exiles returned from Babylon, they immediately set to work rebuilding the Temple (see Ezra 3). But before long they encountered problems, in the shape of opposition from the non-Jewish local residents. These opponents hindered the work in every way they could, and the exiles soon became discouraged; as a result, the building work came to a standstill (Ezra 4). About fifteen years after the building work stopped, Haggai delivered a message to encourage the people to start building again (Haggai 1). He was soon joined by the prophet Zechariah (Ezra 5:1).

OVERVIEW

Through Haggai, God challenged the people for saying it wasn't time to rebuild the Temple yet (Haggai 1:2) and then rebuked them for living in luxury while his house lay in ruins. Because they were putting their own comfort before God, everything was going wrong for them. In spite of their hard work, they suffered from poor harvests and droughts, and their money never stretched far enough (1:5-6). God was a low priority in their lives. They had forgotten that without his blessing on their work they would always lack what they needed. A drought was his way of getting their attention (1:10-11). Led by Zerubbabel, the governor, and Jeshua, the high priest, the people heeded Haggai's warnings and started rebuilding (1:12-15).

In chapter 2, we read of how God promised to strengthen the people for the building work and to fill the Temple with his glory once again, just as at the dedication of the first Temple (2 Chronicles 7:1-3). In another message, Haggai challenged the priests to think about holiness, for it was not simply being back in the Holy Land that made people holy, but rather living in holy ways (Haggai 2:10-14). And now that the people were putting God first again, things would start to go better for them (2:15-19). The book ends with a personal message of affirmation for Zerubbabel, the governor.

What does it mean for us?

Haggai reminds us that, if we will use our resources to further God's concerns, rather than just our own, then those resources will always go much further. We

page 1034

will be blessed, because God never leaves himself in debt to anyone who gives. If we will honor him with our income, he will always work on our behalf.

Haggai pointed out that the people had been working hard, but for little profit; and even what prosperity they had never seemed to stretch far enough. Haggai told them to get God involved in their work by investing something of themselves in his work—especially the building of his Temple. When we put him first in our lives, we will have more than enough, and the ability to enjoy it.

The prophets often brought personal messages to individuals. In this book, God addressed Zerubbabel and Jeshua. Sometimes we forget that God knows us by name. We are not just tiny specks in a mass of humanity; we are marked out. Since God calls us individually, it should come as no surprise that he will sometimes speak to us personally. In his final words to Zerubbabel (2:20-23) lay the hope for the nation's future. The prophets encourage us to expect to hear God's voice, disciplining, calling, and affirming us.

▶ *See also* ***A timeline of the Bible****, pages A22-A24;* ***Prosperity****, page 1176.*

A Call to Rebuild the Temple

1 On August 29* of the second year of King
Darius's reign, the LORD gave a message
through the prophet Haggai to Zerubbabel
son of Shealtiel, governor of Judah, and to
Jeshua* son of Jehozadak, the high priest.
2 "This is what the LORD of Heaven's
Armies says: The people are saying, 'The
time has not yet come to rebuild the house
of the LORD.'"
3 Then the LORD sent this message through
the prophet Haggai: 4 "Why are you living
in luxurious houses while my house lies in
ruins? 5 This is what the LORD of Heaven's
Armies says: Look at what's happening to
you! 6 You have planted much but harvest
little. You eat but are not satisfied. You drink
but are still thirsty. You put on clothes but
cannot keep warm. Your wages disappear
as though you were putting them in pockets
filled with holes!
7 "This is what the LORD of Heaven's Armies
says: Look at what's happening to you! 8 Now
go up into the hills, bring down timber, and
rebuild my house. Then I will take pleasure
in it and be honored, says the LORD. 9 You
hoped for rich harvests, but they were poor.
And when you brought your harvest home,
I blew it away. Why? Because my house lies
in ruins, says the LORD of Heaven's Armies,
while all of you are busy building your own
fine houses. 10 It's because of you that the
heavens withhold the dew and the earth produces no crops. 11 I have called for a drought
on your fields and hills—a drought to wither
the grain and grapes and olive trees and all
your other crops, a drought to starve you and
your livestock and to ruin everything you
have worked so hard to get."

Obedience to God's Call

12 Then Zerubbabel son of Shealtiel, and
Jeshua son of Jehozadak, the high priest, and
the whole remnant of God's people began to
obey the message from the LORD their God.
When they heard the words of the prophet
Haggai, whom the LORD their God had sent,
the people feared the LORD. 13 Then Haggai,
the LORD's messenger, gave the people this
message from the LORD: "I am with you, says
the LORD!"
14 So the LORD sparked the enthusiasm
of Zerubbabel son of Shealtiel, governor of
Judah, and the enthusiasm of Jeshua son
of Jehozadak, the high priest, and the enthusiasm of the whole remnant of God's
people. They began to work on the house
of their God, the LORD of Heaven's Armies,
15 on September 21* of the second year of King
Darius's reign.

The New Temple's Diminished Splendor

2 Then on October 17 of that same year,*
the LORD sent another message through
the prophet Haggai. 2 "Say this to Zerubbabel son of Shealtiel, governor of Judah, and
to Jeshua* son of Jehozadak, the high priest,
and to the remnant of God's people there

▶ **1:1** *See* ***Zerubbabel****, page 525.*

in the land: [3]'Does anyone remember this house—this Temple—in its former splendor? How, in comparison, does it look to you now? It must seem like nothing at all! [4]But now the LORD says: Be strong, Zerubbabel. Be strong, Jeshua son of Jehozadak, the high priest. Be strong, all you people still left in the land. And now get to work, for I am with you, says the LORD of Heaven's Armies. [5]My Spirit remains among you, just as I promised when you came out of Egypt. So do not be afraid.'

[6]"For this is what the LORD of Heaven's Armies says: In just a little while I will again shake the heavens and the earth, the oceans and the dry land. [7]I will shake all the nations, and the treasures of all the nations will be brought to this Temple. I will fill this place with glory, says the LORD of Heaven's Armies. [8]The silver is mine, and the gold is mine, says the LORD of Heaven's Armies. [9]The future glory of this Temple will be greater than its past glory, says the LORD of Heaven's Armies. And in this place I will bring peace. I, the LORD of Heaven's Armies, have spoken!"

Blessings Promised for Obedience

[10]On December 18* of the second year of King Darius's reign, the LORD sent this message to the prophet Haggai: [11]"This is what the LORD of Heaven's Armies says. Ask the priests this question about the law: [12]'If one of you is carrying some meat from a holy sacrifice in his robes and his robe happens to brush against some bread or stew, wine or olive oil, or any other kind of food, will it also become holy?'"

The priests replied, "No."

[13]Then Haggai asked, "If someone becomes ceremonially unclean by touching a dead person and then touches any of these foods, will the food be defiled?"

And the priests answered, "Yes."

[14]Then Haggai responded, "That is how it is with this people and this nation, says the LORD. Everything they do and everything they offer is defiled by their sin. [15]Look at what was happening to you before you began to lay the foundation of the LORD's Temple. [16]When you hoped for a twenty-bushel crop, you harvested only ten. When you expected to draw fifty gallons from the winepress, you found only twenty. [17]I sent blight and mildew and hail to destroy everything you worked so hard to produce. Even so, you refused to return to me, says the LORD.

1:1a Hebrew *On the first day of the sixth month,* of the ancient Hebrew lunar calendar. A number of dates in Haggai can be cross-checked with dates in surviving Persian records and related accurately to our modern calendar. This event occurred on August 29, 520 B.C. **1:1b** Hebrew *Joshua,* a variant spelling of Jeshua; also in 1:12, 14. **1:15** Hebrew *on the twenty-fourth day of the sixth month,* of the ancient Hebrew lunar calendar. This event occurred on September 21, 520 B.C.; also see note on 1:1a. **2:1** Hebrew *on the twenty-first day of the seventh month,* of the ancient Hebrew lunar calendar. This event (in the second year of Darius's reign) occurred on October 17, 520 B.C.; also see note on 1:1a. **2:2** Hebrew *Joshua,* a variant spelling of Jeshua; also in 2:4. **2:10** Hebrew *On the twenty-fourth day of the ninth month,* of the ancient Hebrew lunar calendar (similarly in 2:18). This event occurred on December 18, 520 B.C.; also see note on 1:1a.

Giving God our best

Haggai's central challenge was that the returning exiles simply weren't giving God their best. Of course they needed to build homes and plant fields, but this had become the sole object of their attention. They weren't content with simple homes but wanted luxurious houses (Haggai 1:4). These personal projects had consumed their resources, leaving little to give to God's work, meaning that his house (the Temple) remained a ruin (1:4). So God challenged them to bring timber and rebuild his house; then he would "take pleasure in it and be honored" (1:8). Only then could he lift the curse they had brought upon themselves (1:10-11; see also Deuteronomy 28:38-40).

It is always easy to rationalize not giving God our best. Here the people were saying that the time wasn't right (Haggai 1:2). But this was just an excuse. God is realistic—he knows we need a home, clothes, and food (Matthew 6:25-32)—but Jesus said our priority is to "seek the Kingdom of God above all else, and live righteously," promising that "he will give you everything you need" (Matthew 6:33). When we get our priorities right, God's provision is always released to us.

18"Think about this eighteenth day of December, the day* when the foundation of the LORD's Temple was laid. Think carefully. 19I am giving you a promise now while the seed is still in the barn.* You have not yet harvested your grain, and your grapevines, fig trees, pomegranates, and olive trees have not yet produced their crops. But from this day onward I will bless you."

Promises for Zerubbabel

20On that same day, December 18,* the LORD sent this second message to Haggai: 21"Tell Zerubbabel, the governor of Judah, that I am about to shake the heavens and the earth. 22I will overthrow royal thrones and destroy the power of foreign kingdoms. I will overturn their chariots and riders. The horses will fall, and their riders will kill each other.

23"But when this happens, says the LORD of Heaven's Armies, I will honor you, Zerubbabel son of Shealtiel, my servant. I will make you like a signet ring on my finger, says the LORD, for I have chosen you. I, the LORD of Heaven's Armies, have spoken!"

2:18 Or *On this eighteenth day of December, think about the day.* **2:19** Hebrew *Is the seed yet in the barn?* **2:20** Hebrew *On the twenty-fourth day of the [ninth] month;* see note on 2:10.

Zechariah *God is coming!*

Zechariah was both a prophet and a priest. He was a contemporary of Haggai but continued to minister long after him. Born in exile, Zechariah returned to his native homeland when a small group of exiles returned to Jerusalem. In writings full of spectacular imagery and graphic detail, he sought to encourage the returning exiles, who had become discouraged when things didn't work out as they had hoped. He assured them that God was still with them and that great things lay ahead. While he wrote primarily to encourage this small group of returning Jews, his visions of restoration and glory reached far into the future, to a time when God would cleanse his people once and for all.

What's it all about?

The first part of the book (chapters 1–8) contains Zechariah's call to be a prophet and his first prophetic word, followed by eight striking visions given during the night. An angelic guide led him through each scene and interpreted it for him. Through these visions, Zechariah was shown that God was still in control and still had a plan for his people. In fact, the Temple that was being rebuilt and the priests serving in it were signs of his commitment to his people. Of course, Satan wanted to hinder all this, as we see in his accusations against the high priest (3:1-3). But God's cleansing of the high priest had far-reaching implications, for God's ultimate plan was to "remove the sins of this land in a single day" (3:9) through his servant, the Branch (3:8)—a prophecy of what Jesus would do when he died on the cross on Good Friday. Of course, none of this could happen by merely human effort, which is why Zechariah was reminded that "it is not by force nor by strength, but by my Spirit, says the LORD of Heaven's Armies" (4:6). In light of all this, God's people needed to give themselves again to him and his work and to live out their faith with justice and mercy (chapter 7) so that God could bless them again (chapter 8).

The second part of the book (chapters 9–14) contains messages given after the rebuilding of the Temple was completed. Zechariah warned that God's kingdom would not be established just yet: Difficult times still lay ahead, but Israel's enemies would surely be punished. God would send a descendant of King David to be their ruler—a king who was humble and would bring peace (9:9-11), a good shepherd (13:7) who would be the means of their cleansing (13:1). Christians look back to these passages and see clear prophesying about Jesus.

OVERVIEW

Zechariah's commission and first prophecy · *1:1-6*

Eight visions
1:7–6:8

The symbolic crowning of Jeshua the high priest · *6:9-15*

True fasting
7:1-14

Future blessing for God's people
8:1-23

The coming of the messianic king
9:1–10:12

The rejection of the messianic shepherd-king · *11:1-17*

The restoration and renewal of God's people · *12:1–13:9*

The Messiah's coming and his kingdom · *14:1-21*

page 1038

What does it mean for us?

Zechariah challenges God's people by calling us to integrity. Spiritual integrity brings together outward signs of devotion to God and inner purity. Such integrity is all about God and his work—his special presence and his work of forgiveness. Zechariah's vision of Jeshua wearing dirty clothes shows that God not only forgives sin; he also lavishes us with dignity, honor, and happiness. He transforms us from the inside out. The new clothes Jeshua was given to wear symbolize the new person he became. God's forgiveness is not a temporary way of solving a problem; it means a new start in life. Such a new start for God's people would have a number of results: Outward signs of devotion to God would be transformed (fasts would become festivals of joy; Zechariah 7–8); nations would turn to God (8:20-23); God's people would know victory and forgiveness (chapters 9–13); deep cleansing would be experienced (13:1); and God's universal kingship would be known (14:9). What challenge and encouragement we find in Zechariah! Here we encounter a God who displays his glory by bringing his people peace, forgiveness, and victory through his chosen shepherd-king.

▶ *See also* ***A timeline of the Bible**, pages A22-A24.*

A Call to Return to the LORD

1 In November* of the second year of
King Darius's reign, the LORD gave this
message to the prophet Zechariah son of Berekiah and grandson of Iddo:
2"I, the LORD, was very angry with your ancestors. 3Therefore, say to the people, 'This
is what the LORD of Heaven's Armies says:
Return to me, and I will return to you, says
the LORD of Heaven's Armies.' 4Don't be like
your ancestors who would not listen or pay
attention when the earlier prophets said to
them, 'This is what the LORD of Heaven's
Armies says: Turn from your evil ways, and
stop all your evil practices.'
5"Where are your ancestors now? They and
the prophets are long dead. 6But everything
I said through my servants the prophets happened to your ancestors, just as I said. As a
result, they repented and said, 'We have received what we deserved from the LORD of
Heaven's Armies. He has done what he said
he would do.'"

A Man among the Myrtle Trees

7Three months later, on February 15,* the LORD
sent another message to the prophet Zechariah son of Berekiah and grandson of Iddo.
8In a vision during the night, I saw a man
sitting on a red horse that was standing
among some myrtle trees in a small valley.
Behind him were riders on red, brown, and
white horses. 9I asked the angel who was
talking with me, "My lord, what do these
horses mean?"
"I will show you," the angel replied.
10The rider standing among the myrtle
trees then explained, "They are the ones the
LORD has sent out to patrol the earth."
11Then the other riders reported to the
angel of the LORD, who was standing among
the myrtle trees, "We have been patrolling
the earth, and the whole earth is at peace."
12Upon hearing this, the angel of the LORD
prayed this prayer: "O LORD of Heaven's
Armies, for seventy years now you have
been angry with Jerusalem and the towns of
Judah. How long until you again show mercy
to them?" 13And the LORD spoke kind and
comforting words to the angel who talked
with me.
14Then the angel said to me, "Shout this
message for all to hear: 'This is what the
LORD of Heaven's Armies says: My love for
Jerusalem and Mount Zion is passionate
and strong. 15But I am very angry with the
other nations that are now enjoying peace
and security. I was only a little angry with
my people, but the nations inflicted harm on
them far beyond my intentions.
16"'Therefore, this is what the LORD says:
I have returned to show mercy to Jerusalem.
My Temple will be rebuilt, says the LORD of
Heaven's Armies, and measurements will be
taken for the reconstruction of Jerusalem.*'
17"Say this also: 'This is what the LORD of
Heaven's Armies says: The towns of Israel
will again overflow with prosperity, and the
LORD will again comfort Zion and choose Jerusalem as his own.'"

Four Horns and Four Blacksmiths

18*Then I looked up and saw four animal
horns. 19"What are these?" I asked the angel
who was talking with me.
He replied, "These horns represent the
nations that scattered Judah, Israel, and
Jerusalem."
20Then the LORD showed me four blacksmiths. 21"What are these men coming to
do?" I asked.
The angel replied, "These four horns—
these nations—scattered and humbled
Judah. Now these blacksmiths have come to
terrify those nations and throw them down
and destroy them."

Future Prosperity of Jerusalem

2 1*When I looked again, I saw a man with
a measuring line in his hand. 2"Where
are you going?" I asked.
He replied, "I am going to measure Jerusalem, to see how wide and how long it is."
3Then the angel who was with me went
to meet a second angel who was coming
toward him. 4The other angel said, "Hurry,
and say to that young man, 'Jerusalem will
someday be so full of people and livestock
that there won't be room enough for everyone! Many will live outside the city walls.
5Then I, myself, will be a protective wall of
fire around Jerusalem, says the LORD. And
I will be the glory inside the city!'"

The Exiles Are Called Home

6The LORD says, "Come away! Flee from
Babylon in the land of the north, for I have
scattered you to the four winds. 7Come
away, people of Zion, you who are exiled in
Babylon!"
8After a period of glory, the LORD of
Heaven's Armies sent me* against the
nations who plundered you. For he said,
"Anyone who harms you harms my most
precious possession.* 9I will raise my fist
to crush them, and their own slaves will
plunder them." Then you will know that
the LORD of Heaven's Armies has sent me.
10The LORD says, "Shout and rejoice,
O beautiful Jerusalem,* for I am coming
to live among you. 11Many nations will
join themselves to the LORD on that day,
and they, too, will be my people. I will

1:1 Hebrew *In the eighth month.* A number of dates in Zechariah can be cross-checked with dates in surviving Persian records and related accurately to our modern calendar. This month of the ancient Hebrew lunar calendar occurred within the months of October and November 520 B.C. **1:7** Hebrew *On the twenty-fourth day of the eleventh month, the month of Shebat, in the second year of Darius.* This event occurred on February 15, 519 B.C.; also see note on 1:1. **1:16** Hebrew *and the measuring line will be stretched out over Jerusalem.* **1:18** Verses 1:18-21 are numbered 2:1-4 in Hebrew text. **2:1** Verses 2:1-13 are numbered 2:5-17 in Hebrew text. **2:8a** The meaning of the Hebrew is uncertain. **2:8b** Hebrew *Anyone who touches you touches the pupil of his eye.* **2:10** Hebrew *O daughter of Zion.*

Prophetic imagery

Today, businesses understand the power of using imagery or logos because they know it communicates quickly and clearly. If we see a certain logo, we know instantly which company it represents. And that's how it was with the imagery used by the prophets. For us, their imagery often seems strange and removed from our way of thinking; but for those who first heard it, they knew exactly what it meant—and what it didn't. For example, a horn was a symbol of strength, whether of God, an individual, or a nation (as in Zechariah 1:18); eyes were a symbol of God's ability to see everything; the vine, a symbol of Israel; oil, a symbol of God's Spirit; fire, a symbol of God's holy presence; the flock, a symbol of God's people; a beast, a symbol of a nation or power opposed to God.

Understanding that these symbols had well-understood meanings is important; otherwise, if we impose our own meanings on them—meanings that would have been meaningless to the first hearers—then we are in danger of misinterpreting God's word. Nowhere is this more important to remember than when we come to a book like Revelation, where John uses many Old Testament prophetic images. Take care not to give symbols your own meanings that were irrelevant in Bible times.

▸ *See also* ***Identification of the four kingdoms****, page 966;* ***The use of numbers in Revelation****, page 1453.*

live among you, and you will know that
the LORD of Heaven's Armies sent me to
you. 12The land of Judah will be the LORD's
special possession in the holy land, and he
will once again choose Jerusalem to be his
own city. 13Be silent before the LORD, all humanity, for he is springing into action from
his holy dwelling."

Cleansing for the High Priest

3 Then the angel showed me Jeshua* the
high priest standing before the angel of
the LORD. The Accuser, Satan,* was there
at the angel's right hand, making accusations against Jeshua. 2And the LORD said
to Satan, "I, the LORD, reject your accusations, Satan. Yes, the LORD, who has chosen
Jerusalem, rebukes you. This man is like a
burning stick that has been snatched from
the fire."

3Jeshua's clothing was filthy as he stood
there before the angel. 4So the angel said
to the others standing there, "Take off his
filthy clothes." And turning to Jeshua he
said, "See, I have taken away your sins, and
now I am giving you these fine new clothes."

5Then I said, "They should also place
a clean turban on his head." So they put
a clean priestly turban on his head and
dressed him in new clothes while the angel
of the LORD stood by.

6Then the angel of the LORD spoke very
solemnly to Jeshua and said, 7"This is what
the LORD of Heaven's Armies says: If you
follow my ways and carefully serve me, then
you will be given authority over my Temple
and its courtyards. I will let you walk among
these others standing here.

8"Listen to me, O Jeshua the high priest,
and all you other priests. You are symbols of
things to come. Soon I am going to bring my
servant, the Branch. 9Now look at the jewel
I have set before Jeshua, a single stone with
seven facets.* I will engrave an inscription
on it, says the LORD of Heaven's Armies, and
I will remove the sins of this land in a single
day.

10"And on that day, says the LORD of
Heaven's Armies, each of you will invite
your neighbor to sit with you peacefully
under your own grapevine and fig tree."

A Lampstand and Two Olive Trees

4 Then the angel who had been talking
with me returned and woke me, as
though I had been asleep. 2"What do you
see now?" he asked.

I answered, "I see a solid gold lampstand
with a bowl of oil on top of it. Around the
bowl are seven lamps, each having seven
spouts with wicks. 3And I see two olive
trees, one on each side of the bowl." 4Then
I asked the angel, "What are these, my lord?
What do they mean?"

5"Don't you know?" the angel asked.

"No, my lord," I replied.

6Then he said to me, "This is what the
LORD says to Zerubbabel: It is not by force
nor by strength, but by my Spirit, says the
LORD of Heaven's Armies. 7Nothing, not
even a mighty mountain, will stand in Zerubbabel's way; it will become a level plain
before him! And when Zerubbabel sets
the final stone of the Temple in place, the
people will shout: 'May God bless it! May
God bless it!'*"

8Then another message came to me from
the LORD: 9"Zerubbabel is the one who laid
the foundation of this Temple, and he will
complete it. Then you will know that the
LORD of Heaven's Armies has sent me. 10Do
not despise these small beginnings, for the
LORD rejoices to see the work begin, to see
the plumb line in Zerubbabel's hand."

(The seven lamps* represent the eyes of
the LORD that search all around the world.)

The Holy Land

It surprises many to discover that, while the expression "the Holy Land" is a common name for Israel among Christians today, Zechariah 2:12 is in fact the only place in the Bible where it is given that name—and even then it is more of a description than a name. The usual term in the Bible for Israel is "the Promised Land" or even simply "the land." "The Holy Land" only came into common Christian usage in the Middle Ages.

11Then I asked the angel, "What are these
two olive trees on each side of the lampstand, 12and what are the two olive branches
that pour out golden oil through two gold
tubes?"
13"Don't you know?" he asked.
"No, my lord," I replied.
14Then he said to me, "They represent the
two anointed ones* who stand in the court
of the Lord of all the earth."

A Flying Scroll

5 I looked up again and saw a scroll flying
through the air.
2"What do you see?" the angel asked.
"I see a flying scroll," I replied. "It appears
to be about 30 feet long and 15 feet wide.*"
3Then he said to me, "This scroll contains
the curse that is going out over the entire
land. One side of the scroll says that those
who steal will be banished from the land;
the other side says that those who swear
falsely will be banished from the land. 4And
this is what the LORD of Heaven's Armies
says: I am sending this curse into the house
of every thief and into the house of everyone who swears falsely using my name.
And my curse will remain in that house and
completely destroy it—even its timbers and
stones."

A Woman in a Basket

5Then the angel who was talking with me
came forward and said, "Look up and see
what's coming."
6"What is it?" I asked.
He replied, "It is a basket for measuring
grain,* and it's filled with the sins* of everyone throughout the land."
7Then the heavy lead cover was lifted off
the basket, and there was a woman sitting
inside it. 8The angel said, "The woman's
name is Wickedness," and he pushed her
back into the basket and closed the heavy
lid again.
9Then I looked up and saw two women
flying toward us, gliding on the wind. They
had wings like a stork, and they picked up
the basket and flew into the sky.
10"Where are they taking the basket?"
I asked the angel.
11He replied, "To the land of Babylonia,*
where they will build a temple for the
basket. And when the temple is ready, they
will set the basket there on its pedestal."

Four Chariots

6 Then I looked up again and saw four
chariots coming from between two
bronze mountains. 2The first chariot was
pulled by red horses, the second by black
horses, 3the third by white horses, and the
fourth by powerful dappled-gray horses.
4"And what are these, my lord?" I asked the
angel who was talking with me.
5The angel replied, "These are the four
spirits* of heaven who stand before the
Lord of all the earth. They are going out to
do his work. 6The chariot with black horses
is going north, the chariot with white
horses is going west,* and the chariot with
dappled-gray horses is going south."
7The powerful horses were eager to set
out to patrol the earth. And the LORD said,
"Go and patrol the earth!" So they left at
once on their patrol.
8Then the LORD summoned me and said,
"Look, those who went north have vented
the anger of my Spirit* there in the land of
the north."

The Crowning of Jeshua

9Then I received another message from the
LORD: 10"Heldai, Tobijah, and Jedaiah will
bring gifts of silver and gold from the Jews
exiled in Babylon. As soon as they arrive,
meet them at the home of Josiah son of
Zephaniah. 11Accept their gifts, and make
a crown from the silver and gold. Then
put the crown on the head of Jeshua* son
of Jehozadak, the high priest. 12Tell him,
'This is what the LORD of Heaven's Armies
says: Here is the man called the Branch.
He will branch out from where he is and
build the Temple of the LORD. 13Yes, he
will build the Temple of the LORD. Then
he will receive royal honor and will rule as
king from his throne. He will also serve as
priest from his throne,* and there will be
perfect harmony between his two roles.'
14"The crown will be a memorial in the
Temple of the LORD to honor those who

3:1a Hebrew *Joshua,* a variant spelling of Jeshua; also in 3:3, 4, 6, 8, 9. **3:1b** Hebrew *The satan;* similarly in 3:2. **3:9** Hebrew *seven eyes.* **4:7** Hebrew *'Grace, grace to it.'* **4:10** Or *The seven facets* (see 3:9); Hebrew reads *These seven.* **4:14** Or *two heavenly beings;* Hebrew reads *two sons of fresh oil.* **5:2** Hebrew *20 cubits* [9.2 meters] *long and 10 cubits* [4.6 meters] *wide.* **5:6a** Hebrew *an ephah* [20 quarts or 22 liters]; also in 5:7, 8, 9, 10, 11. **5:6b** As in Greek version; Hebrew reads *the appearance.* **5:11** Hebrew *the land of Shinar.* **6:5** Or *the four winds.* **6:6** Hebrew *is going after them.* **6:8** Hebrew *have given my Spirit rest.* **6:11** Hebrew *Joshua,* a variant spelling of Jeshua. **6:13** Or *There will be a priest by his throne.*

gave it—Heldai,* Tobijah, Jedaiah, and
Josiah* son of Zephaniah."
15 People will come from distant lands to
rebuild the Temple of the LORD. And when
this happens, you will know that my messages have been from the LORD of Heaven's
Armies. All this will happen if you carefully
obey what the LORD your God says.

A Call to Justice and Mercy

7 On December 7* of the fourth year of
King Darius's reign, another message
came to Zechariah from the LORD. 2 The
people of Bethel had sent Sharezer and Regemmelech,* along with their attendants,
to seek the LORD's favor. 3 They were to ask
this question of the prophets and the priests
at the Temple of the LORD of Heaven's
Armies: "Should we continue to mourn and
fast each summer on the anniversary of the
Temple's destruction,* as we have done for
so many years?"
4 The LORD of Heaven's Armies sent me
this message in reply: 5 "Say to all your
people and your priests, 'During these
seventy years of exile, when you fasted
and mourned in the summer and in early
autumn,* was it really for me that you were
fasting? 6 And even now in your holy festivals, aren't you eating and drinking just
to please yourselves? 7 Isn't this the same
message the LORD proclaimed through the
prophets in years past when Jerusalem
and the towns of Judah were bustling with
people, and the Negev and the foothills of
Judah* were well populated?'"
8 Then this message came to Zechariah
from the LORD: 9 "This is what the LORD
of Heaven's Armies says: Judge fairly, and
show mercy and kindness to one another.
10 Do not oppress widows, orphans, foreigners, and the poor. And do not scheme
against each other.
11 "Your ancestors refused to listen to this
message. They stubbornly turned away and
put their fingers in their ears to keep from
hearing. 12 They made their hearts as hard
as stone, so they could not hear the instructions or the messages that the LORD of
Heaven's Armies had sent them by his Spirit
through the earlier prophets. That is why the
LORD of Heaven's Armies was so angry with
them.
13 "Since they refused to listen when
I called to them, I would not listen when
they called to me, says the LORD of
Heaven's Armies. 14 As with a whirlwind, I
scattered them among the distant nations,
where they lived as strangers. Their land
became so desolate that no one even traveled through it. They turned their pleasant
land into a desert."

Does fasting have any value?

At first sight Zechariah's words in 7:5 look like God is not interested in fasting—abstaining from food, partially or totally, for a period to devote oneself more fully to God. But Zechariah was not attacking fasting, but those who thought the mere practice of fasting, rather than the heart behind it, would achieve the desired result. Fasting is in fact commended in the Bible. It varied in kind (partial or complete) and length (one, three, or seven days were the norm) and was used to express grief (2 Samuel 1:12) or repentance (1 Samuel 7:5-6), to seek guidance (Acts 13:1-3), to express dependence on God (Ezra 8:21-23), and to pray for a breakthrough in some seemingly impossible situation (Nehemiah 1:1-5; Esther 4:1-3; Daniel 9:1-3).

Fasting was almost always voluntary—only one fast was commanded, on the Day of Atonement (Leviticus 16:29-31). But after the Exile other fasts were introduced, like those here in Zechariah 7:5, linked with Jerusalem's destruction. By New Testament times fasting was a twice-weekly requirement for pious Jews (Luke 18:12), and its outward show was condemned by Jesus (Matthew 6:16). Nevertheless Jesus still fasted (Matthew 4:1-2) and expected his followers would do so (Mark 2:19-20), though in a different spirit (Matthew 6:17-18). The early church continued the practice (Acts 13:2-3; 14:23), and many Christians still fast today.

Promised Blessings for Jerusalem

8 Then another message came to me from
the LORD of Heaven's Armies: 2"This is
what the LORD of Heaven's Armies says:
My love for Mount Zion is passionate and
strong; I am consumed with passion for
Jerusalem!

3"And now the LORD says: I am returning
to Mount Zion, and I will live in Jerusalem.
Then Jerusalem will be called the Faithful
City; the mountain of the LORD of Heaven's
Armies will be called the Holy Mountain.

4"This is what the LORD of Heaven's
Armies says: Once again old men and
women will walk Jerusalem's streets with
their canes and will sit together in the city
squares. 5And the streets of the city will be
filled with boys and girls at play.

6"This is what the LORD of Heaven's
Armies says: All this may seem impossible to you now, a small remnant of God's
people. But is it impossible for me? says the
LORD of Heaven's Armies.

7"This is what the LORD of Heaven's
Armies says: You can be sure that I will
rescue my people from the east and from the
west. 8I will bring them home again to live
safely in Jerusalem. They will be my people,
and I will be faithful and just toward them
as their God.

9"This is what the LORD of Heaven's
Armies says: Be strong and finish the
task! Ever since the laying of the foundation of the Temple of the LORD of Heaven's
Armies, you have heard what the prophets
have been saying about completing the
building. 10Before the work on the Temple
began, there were no jobs and no money
to hire people or animals. No traveler was
safe from the enemy, for there were enemies
on all sides. I had turned everyone against
each other.

11"But now I will not treat the remnant
of my people as I treated them before, says
the LORD of Heaven's Armies. 12For I am
planting seeds of peace and prosperity
among you. The grapevines will be heavy
with fruit. The earth will produce its crops,
and the heavens will release the dew. Once
more I will cause the remnant in Judah and
Israel to inherit these blessings. 13Among
the other nations, Judah and Israel became
symbols of a cursed nation. But no longer!
Now I will rescue you and make you both a
symbol and a source of blessing. So don't be
afraid. Be strong, and get on with rebuilding the Temple!

14"For this is what the LORD of Heaven's
Armies says: I was determined to punish
you when your ancestors angered me, and
I did not change my mind, says the LORD
of Heaven's Armies. 15But now I am determined to bless Jerusalem and the people of
Judah. So don't be afraid. 16But this is what
you must do: Tell the truth to each other.
Render verdicts in your courts that are
just and that lead to peace. 17Don't scheme
against each other. Stop your love of telling
lies that you swear are the truth. I hate all
these things, says the LORD."

18Here is another message that came to me
from the LORD of Heaven's Armies. 19"This is
what the LORD of Heaven's Armies says: The
traditional fasts and times of mourning you
have kept in early summer, midsummer,
autumn, and winter* are now ended. They
will become festivals of joy and celebration
for the people of Judah. So love truth and
peace.

20"This is what the LORD of Heaven's
Armies says: People from nations and
cities around the world will travel to Jerusalem. 21The people of one city will say
to the people of another, 'Come with us
to Jerusalem to ask the LORD to bless us.
Let's worship the LORD of Heaven's Armies.
I'm determined to go.' 22Many peoples and
powerful nations will come to Jerusalem to
seek the LORD of Heaven's Armies and to
ask for his blessing.

23"This is what the LORD of Heaven's
Armies says: In those days ten men from different nations and languages of the world
will clutch at the sleeve of one Jew. And they
will say, 'Please let us walk with you, for we
have heard that God is with you.'"

6:14a As in Syriac version (compare 6:10); Hebrew reads *Helem.* **6:14b** As in Syriac version (compare 6:10); Hebrew reads *Hen.* **7:1** Hebrew *On the fourth day of the ninth month, the month of Kislev,* of the ancient Hebrew lunar calendar. This event occurred on December 7, 518 B.C.; also see note on 1:1. **7:2** Or *Bethel-sharezer had sent Regemmelech.* **7:3** Hebrew *mourn and fast in the fifth month.* The Temple had been destroyed in the fifth month of the ancient Hebrew lunar calendar (August 586 B.C.); see 2 Kgs 25:8. **7:5** Hebrew *fasted and mourned in the fifth and seventh months.* The fifth month of the ancient Hebrew lunar calendar usually occurs within the months of July and August. The seventh month usually occurs within the months of September and October; both the Day of Atonement and the Festival of Shelters were celebrated in the seventh month. **7:7** Hebrew *the Shephelah.* **8:19** Hebrew *in the fourth, fifth, seventh, and tenth months.* The fourth month of the ancient Hebrew lunar calendar usually occurs within the months of June and July. The fifth month usually occurs within the months of July and August. The seventh month usually occurs within the months of September and October. The tenth month usually occurs within the months of December and January.

Judgment against Israel's Enemies

9 This is the message* from the LORD against the land of Aram* and the city of Damascus, for the eyes of humanity, including all the tribes of Israel, are on the LORD.

2 Doom is certain for Hamath,
near Damascus,
and for the cities of Tyre and Sidon,
though they are so clever.
3 Tyre has built a strong fortress
and has made silver and gold
as plentiful as dust in the streets!
4 But now the Lord will strip away Tyre's
possessions
and hurl its fortifications into the sea,
and it will be burned to the ground.
5 The city of Ashkelon will see Tyre fall
and will be filled with fear.
Gaza will shake with terror,
as will Ekron, for their hopes will be
dashed.
Gaza's king will be killed,
and Ashkelon will be deserted.
6 Foreigners will occupy the city of Ashdod.
I will destroy the pride of the
Philistines.
7 I will grab the bloody meat from their
mouths
and snatch the detestable sacrifices
from their teeth.
Then the surviving Philistines will
worship our God
and become like a clan in Judah.*
The Philistines of Ekron will join my
people,
as the ancient Jebusites once did.
8 I will guard my Temple
and protect it from invading armies.
I am watching closely to ensure
that no more foreign oppressors
overrun my people's land.

Zion's Coming King

9 Rejoice, O people of Zion!*
Shout in triumph, O people of
Jerusalem!
Look, your king is coming to you.
He is righteous and victorious,*
yet he is humble, riding on a donkey—
riding on a donkey's colt.
10 I will remove the battle chariots from
Israel*
and the warhorses from Jerusalem.
I will destroy all the weapons used in
battle,
and your king will bring peace to the
nations.
His realm will stretch from sea to sea
and from the Euphrates River* to the
ends of the earth.*
11 Because of the covenant I made with you,
sealed with blood,
I will free your prisoners
from death in a waterless dungeon.
12 Come back to the place of safety,
all you prisoners who still have hope!
I promise this very day
that I will repay two blessings for each
of your troubles.
13 Judah is my bow,
and Israel is my arrow.
Jerusalem* is my sword,
and like a warrior, I will brandish it
against the Greeks.*

Prophecies of the Messiah

Zechariah contains a number of prophecies about the coming Messiah, including

- his triumphal entry as king into Jerusalem (Zechariah 9:9; see Matthew 21:5);
- his betrayal for thirty pieces of silver (Zechariah 11:12; see Matthew 26:15);
- his being pierced (Zechariah 12:10; see John 19:34, 37); and
- the scattering of his followers (Zechariah 13:7; see Matthew 26:31).

Such detailed prophecies show the amazing level of inspiration of the Holy Spirit upon the prophets.

▶ *See also **Jesus Christ in the Psalms**, page 614; **The Messianic King**, page 674; **Prophecies about Christ**, page 806; **Jesus and the Old Testament**, page 1079; **The Old Testament in the New Testament**, page 1403; **Prophecies of the Messiah**, Visual Overview Z12.*

14 The LORD will appear above his people;
his arrows will fly like lightning!
The Sovereign LORD will sound the ram's horn
and attack like a whirlwind from the southern desert.
15 The LORD of Heaven's Armies will protect his people,
and they will defeat their enemies by hurling great stones.
They will shout in battle as though drunk with wine.
They will be filled with blood like a bowl,
drenched with blood like the corners of the altar.
16 On that day the LORD their God will rescue his people,
just as a shepherd rescues his sheep.
They will sparkle in his land
like jewels in a crown.
17 How wonderful and beautiful they will be!
The young men will thrive on abundant grain,
and the young women will flourish on new wine.

The LORD Will Restore His People

10 [1] Ask the LORD for rain in the spring,
for he makes the storm clouds.
And he will send showers of rain
so every field becomes a lush pasture.
2 Household gods give worthless advice,
fortune-tellers predict only lies,
and interpreters of dreams pronounce falsehoods that give no comfort.
So my people are wandering like lost sheep;
they are attacked because they have no shepherd.

3 "My anger burns against your shepherds,
and I will punish these leaders.*
For the LORD of Heaven's Armies has arrived
to look after Judah, his flock.
He will make them strong and glorious,
like a proud warhorse in battle.
4 From Judah will come the cornerstone,
the tent peg,
the bow for battle,
and all the rulers.
5 They will be like mighty warriors in battle,
trampling their enemies in the mud under their feet.
Since the LORD is with them as they fight,
they will overthrow even the enemy's horsemen.

6 "I will strengthen Judah and save Israel*;
I will restore them because of my compassion.
It will be as though I had never rejected them,
for I am the LORD their God, who will hear their cries.
7 The people of Israel* will become like mighty warriors,
and their hearts will be made happy as if by wine.
Their children, too, will see it and be glad;
their hearts will rejoice in the LORD.
8 When I whistle to them, they will come running,
for I have redeemed them.
From the few who are left,
they will grow as numerous as they were before.
9 Though I have scattered them like seeds among the nations,
they will still remember me in distant lands.
They and their children will survive
and return again to Israel.
10 I will bring them back from Egypt
and gather them from Assyria.
I will resettle them in Gilead and Lebanon
until there is no more room for them all.
11 They will pass safely through the sea of distress,*
for the waves of the sea will be held back,
and the waters of the Nile will dry up.
The pride of Assyria will be crushed,
and the rule of Egypt will end.

9:1a Hebrew *An Oracle: The message.* **9:1b** Hebrew *land of Hadrach.* **9:7** Hebrew *like a leader in Judah.* **9:9a** Hebrew *O daughter of Zion!* **9:9b** Hebrew *and is being vindicated.* **9:10a** Hebrew *Ephraim,* referring to the northern kingdom of Israel; also in 9:13. **9:10b** Hebrew *the river.* **9:10c** Or *the end of the land.* **9:13a** Hebrew *Zion.* **9:13b** Hebrew *the sons of Javan.* **10:3** Or *these male goats.* **10:6** Hebrew *save the house of Joseph.* **10:7** Hebrew *of Ephraim.* **10:11** Or *the sea of Egypt,* referring to the Red Sea.

12 By my power* I will make my people
strong,
and by my authority they will go
wherever they wish.
I, the LORD, have spoken!"

11 1 Open your doors, Lebanon,
so that fire may devour your
cedar forests.
2 Weep, you cypress trees, for all the
ruined cedars;
the most majestic ones have fallen.
Weep, you oaks of Bashan,
for the thick forests have been cut
down.
3 Listen to the wailing of the shepherds,
for their rich pastures are destroyed.
Hear the young lions roaring,
for their thickets in the Jordan Valley
are ruined.

The Good and Evil Shepherds

4 This is what the LORD my God says: "Go
and care for the flock that is intended for
slaughter. 5 The buyers slaughter their sheep
without remorse. The sellers say, 'Praise the
LORD! Now I'm rich!' Even the shepherds
have no compassion for them. 6 Likewise,
I will no longer have pity on the people of
the land," says the LORD. "I will let them fall
into each other's hands and into the hands
of their king. They will turn the land into
a wilderness, and I will not rescue them."

7 So I cared for the flock intended for
slaughter—the flock that was oppressed.
Then I took two shepherd's staffs and named
one Favor and the other Union. 8 I got rid of
their three evil shepherds in a single month.

But I became impatient with these sheep,
and they hated me, too. 9 So I told them,
"I won't be your shepherd any longer. If
you die, you die. If you are killed, you are
killed. And let those who remain devour
each other!"

10 Then I took my staff called Favor and
cut it in two, showing that I had revoked the
covenant I had made with all the nations.
11 That was the end of my covenant with
them. The suffering flock was watching me,
and they knew that the LORD was speaking
through my actions.

12 And I said to them, "If you like, give me
my wages, whatever I am worth; but only if
you want to." So they counted out for my
wages thirty pieces of silver.

13 And the LORD said to me, "Throw it
to the potter*"—this magnificent sum at
which they valued me! So I took the thirty
coins and threw them to the potter in the
Temple of the LORD.

14 Then I took my other staff, Union, and
cut it in two, showing that the bond of unity
between Judah and Israel was broken.

15 Then the LORD said to me, "Go again
and play the part of a worthless shepherd.
16 This illustrates how I will give this nation
a shepherd who will not care for those who
are dying, nor look after the young, nor heal
the injured, nor feed the healthy. Instead,
this shepherd will eat the meat of the fattest
sheep and tear off their hooves.

17 "What sorrow awaits this worthless
shepherd
who abandons the flock!
The sword will cut his arm
and pierce his right eye.
His arm will become useless,
and his right eye completely blind."

Future Deliverance for Jerusalem

12 This* message concerning the fate
of Israel came from the LORD: "This
message is from the LORD, who stretched
out the heavens, laid the foundations of the
earth, and formed the human spirit. 2 I will
make Jerusalem like an intoxicating drink
that makes the nearby nations stagger when
they send their armies to besiege Jerusalem
and Judah. 3 On that day I will make Jerusalem an immovable rock. All the nations will
gather against it to try to move it, but they
will only hurt themselves.

4 "On that day," says the LORD, "I will
cause every horse to panic and every rider to
lose his nerve. I will watch over the people
of Judah, but I will blind all the horses of
their enemies. 5 And the clans of Judah will
say to themselves, 'The people of Jerusalem
have found strength in the LORD of Heaven's
Armies, their God.'

6 "On that day I will make the clans of
Judah like a flame that sets a woodpile
ablaze or like a burning torch among
sheaves of grain. They will burn up all the
neighboring nations right and left, while the
people living in Jerusalem remain secure.

7 "The LORD will give victory to the rest
of Judah first, before Jerusalem, so that
the people of Jerusalem and the royal line

of David will not have greater honor than the rest of Judah. 8On that day the LORD will defend the people of Jerusalem; the weakest among them will be as mighty as King David! And the royal descendants will be like God, like the angel of the LORD who goes before them! 9For on that day I will begin to destroy all the nations that come against Jerusalem.

10"Then I will pour out a spirit* of grace and prayer on the family of David and on the people of Jerusalem. They will look on me whom they have pierced and mourn for him as for an only son. They will grieve bitterly for him as for a firstborn son who has died. 11The sorrow and mourning in Jerusalem on that day will be like the great mourning for Hadad-rimmon in the valley of Megiddo.

12"All Israel will mourn, each clan by itself, and with the husbands separate from their wives. The clan of David will mourn alone, as will the clan of Nathan, 13the clan of Levi, and the clan of Shimei. 14Each of the surviving clans from Judah will mourn separately, and with the husbands separate from their wives.

A Fountain of Cleansing

13 "On that day a fountain will be opened for the dynasty of David and for the people of Jerusalem, a fountain to cleanse them from all their sins and impurity.

2"And on that day," says the LORD of Heaven's Armies, "I will erase idol worship throughout the land, so that even the names of the idols will be forgotten. I will remove from the land both the false prophets and the spirit of impurity that came with them. 3If anyone continues to prophesy, his own father and mother will tell him, 'You must die, for you have prophesied lies in the name of the LORD.' And as he prophesies, his own father and mother will stab him.

4"On that day people will be ashamed to claim the prophetic gift. No one will pretend to be a prophet by wearing prophet's clothes. 5He will say, 'I'm no prophet; I'm a farmer. I began working for a farmer as a boy.' 6And if someone asks, 'Then what about those wounds on your chest?*' he will say, 'I was wounded at my friends' house!'

The Scattering of the Sheep

7 "Awake, O sword, against my shepherd,
the man who is my partner,"
says the LORD of Heaven's Armies.
"Strike down the shepherd,
and the sheep will be scattered,
and I will turn against the lambs.
8 Two-thirds of the people in the land
will be cut off and die," says the LORD.
"But one-third will be left in the land.
9 I will bring that group through the fire
and make them pure.
I will refine them like silver
and purify them like gold.
They will call on my name,
and I will answer them.
I will say, 'These are my people,'
and they will say, 'The LORD is our
God.'"

The LORD Will Rule the Earth

14 Watch, for the day of the LORD is coming when your possessions will be plundered right in front of you! 2I will gather all the nations to fight against Jerusalem. The city will be taken, the houses looted, and the women raped. Half the population will be taken into captivity, and the rest will be left among the ruins of the city.

3Then the LORD will go out to fight against those nations, as he has fought in times past. 4On that day his feet will stand on the Mount of Olives, east of Jerusalem. And the Mount of Olives will split apart, making a wide valley running from east to west. Half the mountain will move toward the north and half toward the south. 5You will flee through this valley, for it will reach across to Azal.* Yes, you will flee as you did from the earthquake in the days of King Uzziah of Judah. Then the LORD my God will come, and all his holy ones with him.*

6On that day the sources of light will no longer shine,* 7yet there will be continuous day! Only the LORD knows how this could happen. There will be no normal day and night, for at evening time it will still be light.

10:12 Hebrew *In the LORD.* **11:13** Syriac version reads *into the treasury;* also in 11:13b. Compare Matt 27:6-10. **12:1** Hebrew *An Oracle: This.* **12:10** Or *the Spirit.* **13:6** Hebrew *wounds between your hands?* **14:5a** The meaning of the Hebrew is uncertain. **14:5b** As in Greek version; Hebrew reads *with you.* **14:6** Hebrew *the precious ones shall diminish;* or *the precious ones and frost.* The meaning of the Hebrew is uncertain.

▸ **14:1** *See* ***The day of the LORD**, page 988.*

8 On that day life-giving waters will flow out from Jerusalem, half toward the Dead Sea and half toward the Mediterranean,* flowing continuously in both summer and winter.

9 And the LORD will be king over all the earth. On that day there will be one LORD—his name alone will be worshiped.

10 All the land from Geba, north of Judah, to Rimmon, south of Jerusalem, will become one vast plain. But Jerusalem will be raised up in its original place and will be inhabited all the way from the Benjamin Gate over to the site of the old gate, then to the Corner Gate, and from the Tower of Hananel to the king's winepresses. 11 And Jerusalem will be filled, safe at last, never again to be cursed and destroyed.

12 And the LORD will send a plague on all the nations that fought against Jerusalem. Their people will become like walking corpses, their flesh rotting away. Their eyes will rot in their sockets, and their tongues will rot in their mouths. 13 On that day they will be terrified, stricken by the LORD with great panic. They will fight their neighbors hand to hand. 14 Judah, too, will be fighting at Jerusalem. The wealth of all the neighboring nations will be captured—great quantities of gold and silver and fine clothing. 15 This same plague will strike the horses, mules, camels, donkeys, and all the other animals in the enemy camps.

16 In the end, the enemies of Jerusalem who survive the plague will go up to Jerusalem each year to worship the King, the LORD of Heaven's Armies, and to celebrate the Festival of Shelters. 17 Any nation in the world that refuses to come to Jerusalem to worship the King, the LORD of Heaven's Armies, will have no rain. 18 If the people of Egypt refuse to attend the festival, the LORD will punish* them with the same plague that he sends on the other nations who refuse to go. 19 Egypt and the other nations will all be punished if they don't go to celebrate the Festival of Shelters.

20 On that day even the harness bells of the horses will be inscribed with these words: HOLY TO THE LORD. And the cooking pots in the Temple of the LORD will be as sacred as the basins used beside the altar. 21 In fact, every cooking pot in Jerusalem and Judah will be holy to the LORD of Heaven's Armies. All who come to worship will be free to use any of these pots to boil their sacrifices. And on that day there will no longer be traders* in the Temple of the LORD of Heaven's Armies.

14:8 Hebrew *half toward the eastern sea and half toward the western sea.* **14:18** As in some Hebrew manuscripts and Greek and Syriac versions; Masoretic Text reads *will not punish.* **14:21** Hebrew *Canaanites.*

Malachi *Getting ready for God's messenger*

Only four chapters long, Malachi is the last of the prophetic books and the last book in the Old Testament. In his prophetic messages, Malachi, whose name means "my messenger," challenged the emptiness of religious ritual and dead orthodoxy. Both priests and people were trying to get away with the bare minimum rather than giving God their best, whether in the way they worshiped or in how they lived. And yet God still reaffirmed his covenant love for them. Malachi looked forward to the "day of the LORD," when God would come to both judge his people and prepare them for something better.

What's it all about?

Malachi was a contemporary of Ezra and Nehemiah, and his work dates from around 430 BC. This was some eighty to ninety years after Haggai and Zechariah had urged the people to finish rebuilding the Temple, promising blessing and the return of God's presence if they did so. The Temple was completed, but the years had passed by and none of the promised blessings had come. In fact, rather than blessing, all the people experienced was hardship (e.g., 3:9-11), and even fulfilling God's requirements, they felt, was pointless (e.g., 3:14). And so they had become weary and disheartened.

Against this background of weariness and dead tradition, the book opens with the assurance that God still loved his people, in spite of their failure to honor him as their Father (1:2-6). Priests were offering substandard sacrifices and neglecting their duty to teach God's people how to live, yet they thought this was all right (1:7-14). They failed to see that they were dishonoring the covenant God had made with their ancestor Levi and that their behavior was more likely to bring curse than blessing (2:1-9). The people were then challenged for breaking the covenant with God by marrying non-Israelites and tolerating divorce, forgetting that God hates divorce (2:10-16).

But Malachi promised that God would demonstrate the justice his people claimed was lacking (2:17)—though not in the way they thought. He promised to send his messenger (3:1), who would both judge the wicked and refine God's own people (3:2-5). In light of this, they needed to get ready—beginning with no longer cheating God by withholding their tithes (3:6-12). While some continued to complain (3:13-15), "those who feared the LORD spoke with each other, and the LORD listened to what they said" (3:16). God promised that such people would be spared on the coming "day of the LORD" (3:17–4:3). The book closes with an appeal to remember the Law God gave through Moses and to be ready

OVERVIEW

page 1050

for another Elijah, who would come before that great day (4:4-6). The New Testament sees this prophecy as fulfilled in John the Baptist (e.g., Luke 1:17).

What does it mean for us?

In Malachi, God brings many complaints about what his people had been *saying*. God has listened and kept a record of what he has heard. But the book notes that God also hears and takes notice of good conversation (3:16). It reminds us that our unintentional comments are remembered long after we have forgotten them and, one day, we will be reminded of them, for better or worse.

The people's complaining arose from weariness and the fact that God wasn't doing things according to their timetable. But real faith is about holding onto God's promises, even if they seem slow in coming. Ultimately God always does what he said he would do.

In Malachi, God rebuked his people for their spiritual indifference and their attitude of heart. They were bringing substandard animals for their sacrifices and withholding their tithes. It is rather like if we found the smallest bill we could for the offering on Sunday but made a big show of giving it. Such behavior reflects our inner state: that our hearts and minds are not committed to what we are doing.

Is God greedy? No, says Malachi. But by neglecting to honor him with their income, the people were forfeiting his blessings. In the only place in the Bible where God invites people to test him, he says that heaven is bursting with blessing for people who give their offerings to him because they trust him (3:10-12). So put God to the test: Give him your best, and watch him do the same for you.

▶ *See also **A timeline of the Bible**, pages A22-A24.*

1 This is the message* that the LORD gave to
Israel through the prophet Malachi.*

The LORD's Love for Israel

2 "I have always loved you," says the LORD.
But you retort, "Really? How have you
loved us?"
And the LORD replies, "This is how
I showed my love for you: I loved your an-
cestor Jacob, 3 but I rejected his brother, Esau,
and devastated his hill country. I turned
Esau's inheritance into a desert for jackals."
4 Esau's descendants in Edom may say,
"We have been shattered, but we will rebuild
the ruins."
But the LORD of Heaven's Armies replies,
"They may try to rebuild, but I will demolish
them again. Their country will be known as
'The Land of Wickedness,' and their people
will be called 'The People with Whom the
LORD Is Forever Angry.' 5 When you see the
destruction for yourselves, you will say,
'Truly, the LORD's greatness reaches far
beyond Israel's borders!'"

Unworthy Sacrifices

6 The LORD of Heaven's Armies says to the
priests: "A son honors his father, and a
servant respects his master. If I am your
father and master, where are the honor and
respect I deserve? You have shown contempt
for my name!
"But you ask, 'How have we ever shown
contempt for your name?'
7 "You have shown contempt by offering
defiled sacrifices on my altar.
"Then you ask, 'How have we defiled the
sacrifices?*'
"You defile them by saying the altar of the
LORD deserves no respect. 8 When you give
blind animals as sacrifices, isn't that wrong?
And isn't it wrong to offer animals that are
crippled and diseased? Try giving gifts like
that to your governor, and see how pleased
he is!" says the LORD of Heaven's Armies.
9 "Go ahead, beg God to be merciful to you!
But when you bring that kind of offering,
why should he show you any favor at all?"
asks the LORD of Heaven's Armies.
10 "How I wish one of you would shut the
Temple doors so that these worthless sacrifices could not be offered! I am not pleased
with you," says the LORD of Heaven's Armies,
"and I will not accept your offerings. 11 But my
name is honored* by people of other nations
from morning till night. All around the world

they offer* sweet incense and pure offerings in honor of my name. For my name is
great among the nations," says the LORD of
Heaven's Armies.
12"But you dishonor my name with your
actions. By bringing contemptible food, you
are saying it's all right to defile the Lord's
table. 13You say, 'It's too hard to serve the
LORD,' and you turn up your noses at my
commands," says the LORD of Heaven's
Armies. "Think of it! Animals that are stolen
and crippled and sick are being presented
as offerings! Should I accept from you such
offerings as these?" asks the LORD.
14"Cursed is the cheat who promises to
give a fine ram from his flock but then sacrifices a defective one to the Lord. For I am
a great king," says the LORD of Heaven's
Armies, "and my name is feared among the
nations!

A Warning to the Priests

2 "Listen, you priests—this command
is for you! 2Listen to me and make up
your minds to honor my name," says the
LORD of Heaven's Armies, "or I will bring a
terrible curse against you. I will curse even
the blessings you receive. Indeed, I have
already cursed them, because you have not
taken my warning to heart. 3I will punish
your descendants and splatter your faces
with the manure from your festival sacrifices, and I will throw you on the manure
pile. 4Then at last you will know it was I who
sent you this warning so that my covenant
with the Levites can continue," says the
LORD of Heaven's Armies.
5"The purpose of my covenant with the
Levites was to bring life and peace, and that
is what I gave them. This required reverence
from them, and they greatly revered me and
stood in awe of my name. 6They passed on
to the people the truth of the instructions
they received from me. They did not lie or
cheat; they walked with me, living good
and righteous lives, and they turned many
from lives of sin.
7"The words of a priest's lips should preserve knowledge of God, and people should
go to him for instruction, for the priest is the
messenger of the LORD of Heaven's Armies.
8But you priests have left God's paths. Your
instructions have caused many to stumble
into sin. You have corrupted the covenant
I made with the Levites," says the LORD
of Heaven's Armies. 9"So I have made you
despised and humiliated in the eyes of all
the people. For you have not obeyed me but
have shown favoritism in the way you carry
out my instructions."

A Call to Faithfulness

10Are we not all children of the same Father?
Are we not all created by the same God?
Then why do we betray each other, violating the covenant of our ancestors?
11Judah has been unfaithful, and a detestable thing has been done in Israel and in
Jerusalem. The men of Judah have defiled
the LORD's beloved sanctuary by marrying
women who worship idols. 12May the LORD
cut off from the nation of Israel* every last
man who has done this and yet brings an
offering to the LORD of Heaven's Armies.
13Here is another thing you do. You cover
the LORD's altar with tears, weeping and
groaning because he pays no attention to
your offerings and doesn't accept them with
pleasure. 14You cry out, "Why doesn't the
LORD accept my worship?" I'll tell you why!
Because the LORD witnessed the vows you
and your wife made when you were young.
But you have been unfaithful to her, though
she remained your faithful partner, the wife
of your marriage vows.
15Didn't the LORD make you one with your
wife? In body and spirit you are his.* And
what does he want? Godly children from
your union. So guard your heart; remain
loyal to the wife of your youth. 16"For I hate
divorce!"* says the LORD, the God of Israel.
"To divorce your wife is to overwhelm her
with cruelty,*" says the LORD of Heaven's
Armies. "So guard your heart; do not be
unfaithful to your wife."
17You have wearied the LORD with your
words.

1:1a Hebrew *An Oracle: The message.* **1:1b** *Malachi* means "my messenger." **1:7** As in Greek version; Hebrew reads *defiled you?* **1:11a** Or *will be honored.* **1:11b** Or *will offer.* **2:12** Hebrew *from the tents of Jacob.* The names "Jacob" and "Israel" are often interchanged throughout the Old Testament, referring sometimes to the individual patriarch and sometimes to the nation. **2:15** Or *Didn't the one LORD make us and preserve our life and breath?* or *Didn't the one LORD make her, both flesh and spirit?* The meaning of the Hebrew is uncertain. **2:16a** Hebrew *For he hates divorcing.* **2:16b** Hebrew *to cover one's garment with violence.*

▸ **2:14** *See **Faithfulness**, page 1307.*

"How have we wearied him?" you ask.
You have wearied him by saying that all
who do evil are good in the LORD's sight,
and he is pleased with them. You have
wearied him by asking, "Where is the God
of justice?"

The Coming Day of Judgment

3 "Look! I am sending my messenger,
and he will prepare the way before me.
Then the Lord you are seeking will suddenly
come to his Temple. The messenger of the
covenant, whom you look for so eagerly, is
surely coming," says the LORD of Heaven's
Armies.
2"But who will be able to endure it when
he comes? Who will be able to stand and
face him when he appears? For he will be
like a blazing fire that refines metal, or like
a strong soap that bleaches clothes. 3He
will sit like a refiner of silver, burning away
the dross. He will purify the Levites, refining them like gold and silver, so that they
may once again offer acceptable sacrifices
to the LORD. 4Then once more the LORD will
accept the offerings brought to him by the
people of Judah and Jerusalem, as he did
in the past.
5"At that time I will put you on trial. I am
eager to witness against all sorcerers and
adulterers and liars. I will speak against
those who cheat employees of their wages,
who oppress widows and orphans, or who
deprive the foreigners living among you of
justice, for these people do not fear me,"
says the LORD of Heaven's Armies.

A Call to Repentance

6"I am the LORD, and I do not change. That
is why you descendants of Jacob are not
already destroyed. 7Ever since the days
of your ancestors, you have scorned my
decrees and failed to obey them. Now return
to me, and I will return to you," says the
LORD of Heaven's Armies.
"But you ask, 'How can we return when
we have never gone away?'
8"Should people cheat God? Yet you have
cheated me!
"But you ask, 'What do you mean? When
did we ever cheat you?'
"You have cheated me of the tithes and
offerings due to me. 9You are under a curse,
for your whole nation has been cheating me.
10Bring all the tithes into the storehouse so
there will be enough food in my Temple. If

Should Christians still tithe?

The Jewish Law said that one-tenth of people's income belonged to God (Leviticus 27:30). Not to give that tithe, therefore, was to cheat God, Malachi said (Malachi 3:9). But should Christians, who do not live under the Law, still tithe?

A good starting point is to remember that the Patriarchs tithed long before the Law was given (Genesis 14:18-20; 28:20-22)—a spontaneous expression of worship and thanksgiving. In the Law, the tithe was used for various purposes: supporting the Levites' ministry, providing for the poor, even being enjoyed by the worshipers (Deuteronomy 14:22-29). By New Testament times, however, the rabbis had added many rules about tithing, which became opportunities for self-righteousness. It was this, rather than tithing as such, that Jesus attacked. As a Jew, he would have tithed, and he never abolished tithing, simply saying it should be done with right attitudes (Matthew 23:23-24).

While Acts and the New Testament letters do not command tithing, they stress the importance of generous giving (e.g., Acts 11:29; Romans 12:13; 1 Corinthians 16:1-2; 2 Corinthians 8–9; Galatians 2:10; Philippians 4:14-17; 1 Timothy 5:17-18). While we cannot prove that the early Christians tithed, it is hard to imagine them understanding "generous giving" as *less* than what was required by the Law. Ultimately, giving, at whatever level, requires faith; but that is what being a Christian is all about.

▶ *See also* ***Giving****, page 1331.*

you do," says the LORD of Heaven's Armies,
"I will open the windows of heaven for you.
I will pour out a blessing so great you won't
have enough room to take it in! Try it! Put
me to the test! 11"Your crops will be abundant, for I will guard them from insects and
disease.* Your grapes will not fall from the
vine before they are ripe," says the LORD of
Heaven's Armies. 12"Then all nations will
call you blessed, for your land will be such a
delight," says the LORD of Heaven's Armies.
13"You have said terrible things about
me," says the LORD.

"But you say, 'What do you mean? What
have we said against you?'

14"You have said, 'What's the use of
serving God? What have we gained by
obeying his commands or by trying to show
the LORD of Heaven's Armies that we are
sorry for our sins? 15From now on we will
call the arrogant blessed. For those who
do evil get rich, and those who dare God to
punish them suffer no harm.'"

The LORD's Promise of Mercy

16Then those who feared the LORD spoke
with each other, and the LORD listened to
what they said. In his presence, a scroll
of remembrance was written to record the
names of those who feared him and always
thought about the honor of his name.

17"They will be my people," says the LORD
of Heaven's Armies. "On the day when I act
in judgment, they will be my own special
treasure. I will spare them as a father spares
an obedient child. 18Then you will again see
the difference between the righteous and
the wicked, between those who serve God
and those who do not."

The Coming Day of Judgment

4 1*The LORD of Heaven's Armies says,
"The day of judgment is coming,
burning like a furnace. On that day the arrogant and the wicked will be burned up
like straw. They will be consumed—roots,
branches, and all.

2"But for you who fear my name, the Sun
of Righteousness will rise with healing in
his wings.* And you will go free, leaping
with joy like calves let out to pasture. 3On
the day when I act, you will tread upon
the wicked as if they were dust under your
feet," says the LORD of Heaven's Armies.

4"Remember to obey the Law of Moses,
my servant—all the decrees and regulations that I gave him on Mount Sinai* for
all Israel.

5"Look, I am sending you the prophet
Elijah before the great and dreadful day
of the LORD arrives. 6His preaching will
turn the hearts of fathers to their children,
and the hearts of children to their fathers.
Otherwise I will come and strike the land
with a curse."

3:11 Hebrew *from the devourer.* **4:1** Verses 4:1-6 are numbered 3:19-24 in Hebrew text. **4:2** Or *the sun of righteousness will rise with healing in its wings.* **4:4** Hebrew *Horeb,* another name for Sinai.

▸ **4:5** *See* ***The day of the LORD****, page 988;* ***John the Baptist****, page 1156.*

Between the two Testaments

While turning from Malachi to Matthew takes just a moment, the reality is that over four hundred years have just sped by. The Bible is silent about those years. It is as if God's people had stopped listening, so God had stopped speaking. But he had not stopped working, for through changes in the world, he was preparing for the coming of the promised Messiah.

History

Ever since Babylon had conquered it, Judah (all that then remained of God's people) had ceased to be an independent nation. Persia had allowed the Jews to return home, but Judah still remained part of their empire. But things were about to change again.

The Greek Empire

A new empire was arising to the west—Greece. In 334 BC, Alexander the Great marched east, conquering everything before him: Asia Minor, Syria, Egypt, Persia, even reaching India—thus establishing the greatest empire the world had ever known.

But Alexander's aim wasn't simply to create an empire, but a way of life. He imposed Greek culture—art, architecture, sport, customs, beliefs—and Greek became the international language. However, much Greek culture violated Jewish standards of holiness—for example, athletes performed naked, theater plays were often sexually explicit, and religion was polytheistic and idolatrous—and this produced many tensions.

The empire divides

After Alexander's death, his empire was divided among his generals: two minor nations in Greece's heartland and two major empires across the bulk of its lands—the Ptolemaic Empire in north Africa and the Seleucid Empire in western Asia. Once again, Israel lay sandwiched between two opposing empires.

Initially, Judea (as the Jewish nation was now called) was part of the Ptolemaic Empire, and the Jews experienced considerable tolerance. Then the Seleucids gained control of the region, and when King Antiochus IV Epiphanes came to the throne, everything changed. He firmly imposed Greek culture and practices on the Jews. In 167 BC, he destroyed Jerusalem and tried to exterminate Judaism, forbidding sacrifices, circumcision, and Sabbath observance, forcing Jews to eat pork, destroying their Scriptures, and erecting pagan altars. But when he placed a statue of Zeus in the Temple and sacrificed a pig on its altar, the Jews had had enough.

The Maccabean War and the Hasmoneans

Inspired by an old priest, Mattathias, who killed a Seleucid officer rather than offer a pagan sacrifice, a revolt erupted. After Mattathias's death, his son Judas Maccabeus (after whom the revolt was named) became leader, recapturing Jerusalem and purifying the Temple in 164 BC, an event commemorated in the festival of Hanukkah (meaning "Dedication").

The war continued, with the Seleucids gradually giving the Jews increasing independence. This led to the establishment of the Hasmonean dynasty (named after Hasmon, Mattathias's father). But there was little difference between the Hasmoneans and the Seleucids, and sometimes they even persecuted their own people.

The Roman Empire

But everything was about to change again. Another empire was arising in the west—Rome. As Rome expanded, defeating Carthage and Corinth in 146 BC and Athens in

86 BC, the Greek Empire collapsed. In 63 BC, General Pompey conquered Syria and Palestine, making them a Roman province. Most Jews resented Roman rule, and after Herod the Great's death in 4 BC there were many uprisings over the next seventy years.

Preparation for the gospel

As we review this period, it is clear that God was at work behind the scenes. Through the rise of Greece, God had given the world an international language. By New Testament times, if you spoke Greek, you could be understood anywhere—an invaluable asset for preachers of the gospel. Moreover, in the third century BC the Old Testament had been translated into Greek (a version called the *Septuagint*, from the Greek word for "seventy," because, according to tradition, seventy scholars translated it). This translation enabled Jews who had been dispersed far from Israel and who had lost the ability to read Hebrew to now understand their own Scriptures again—also invaluable for Christian preachers, who appealed to those Scriptures as proof of who Jesus was.

Rome had also contributed much that prepared for the spread of the gospel. While Rome's iron rule was fearsome, it made for widespread peace. Excellent roads linked every city, and the army ensured that attacks by robbers or pirates were rare, thus making travel safer. Again, this would be extremely helpful in ensuring the rapid spread of the gospel.

Developments in Judaism itself also helped. Denied their Temple during the Exile, Jews had developed the practice of gathering locally to pray and read Scripture—the foundation of future synagogues, which by New Testament times were found in Jewish communities throughout the world. These synagogues would become the favorite starting point for the Christian mission.

Through all these events it is clear that, while God had been silent, he had not been inactive. He had been guiding and shaping circumstances to prepare the way for the coming of his Son, Jesus.

The Apocrypha

What is the Apocrypha?

The Apocrypha is a collection of sixteen books (or parts of books) mainly written between about 300 BC and AD 100. While never seen as Scripture by the Jews, these works were nevertheless highly esteemed by them and so were included in the first-ever translation of the Bible, the Septuagint, which was the Greek version of the Old Testament (with the exception of the book of 2 Esdras, which was written later).

These sixteen books are in addition to the sixty-six books in the Bible that all branches of the church accept. Because these sixteen books were never seen as Scripture by Jews, Protestant churches do not recognize them as authoritative, though occasionally a Protestant Bible will include them in a separate section between the two Testaments. However, other churches (Roman Catholic, Coptic, Eastern Orthodox) accept some or all of these books as authoritative and include them within the Old Testament.

All sixteen books are heavily influenced by the Old Testament. They are Jewish books, and they illustrate how Jewish ideas developed during the period after the writing of the Old Testament was completed. Many of them were originally written in Hebrew, the main language of the Old Testament.

The books of the Apocrypha

Tobit (c. 200–180 BC) A romantic story describing the adventures of a blind and poor Jewish exile named Tobit, his son Tobias, and Sarah, the woman Tobias eventually married. Tobias delivered Sarah from a demon that had afflicted her and her seven previous husbands, and Tobit's sight and his wealth were restored to him. The book aims to show that the righteous are ultimately rewarded.

Judith (c. 150–100 BC) A historical novel which tells the story of Judith, a beautiful and godly Jewish woman, who delivered the Jews by deceiving and then killing Holofernes, the commander of Nebuchadnezzar's army. Although its historical details are generally unreliable, its aim was to strengthen faith in God.

Greek Additions to the Book of Esther (second century BC) Six passages that were added to the book of Esther to give it a more religious tone (the book was renowned for not mentioning God) and to show that piety lay behind the Jews' deliverance.

Wisdom of Solomon (c. 100–50 BC) Written as Solomon's testimony, this book seeks to stir a love for wisdom as it reflects on life.

Ecclesiasticus (c. 175 BC in Hebrew; c. 130 BC in Greek) Originally called The Wisdom of Jesus ben Sira, but renamed in the Vulgate (the Latin translation of the Bible). Written in Hebrew by Ben Sira (or "Sirach," the Greek spelling of Sira), the book was translated into Greek by his grandson. It is a collection of traditional wisdom similar to that found in Proverbs. Ecclesiasticus is a Latin word based on the Greek term *ekklēsia*, "church." The name means "church book" and indicates the book's popularity in the early church.

Baruch (c. mid-second century BC) Claiming to be written in exile by Baruch, Jeremiah's scribe, this book calls Israel back to faithfulness to God in the hope of restoration. Its true aim was to encourage second-century-BC Jews, who by then felt permanently exiled.

Letter of Jeremiah (third century BC) Written as a letter from Jeremiah to the exiles in Babylon, it urged them not to worship idols. It is sometimes printed as chapter 6 of Baruch.

Additions to Daniel (second century BC) Three passages are added to the book of Daniel: (1) *The Prayer of Azariah and the Song of the Three Young Men*, inserted between Daniel 3:23 and 3:24, celebrates God's deliverance of the three young men from the burning fiery furnace and other dangers (Azariah was the Hebrew name of Abednego). It contains a poem that may have been two separate hymns, known in the Western church as the "Benedictus es" and the "Benedicite" from the Latin opening words of each; (2) The stories of Susanna, who, after resisting the advances of two elders, was falsely accused by them of committing adultery with a young man, but who was spared through Daniel's wisdom; (3) *Bel and the Dragon*, which illustrates Daniel's faith and wisdom and provides explanations of events in the Old Testament book of Daniel.

1 Maccabees (c. 100 BC) An account of the Maccabean revolt that occurred between 167 and 164 BC, and of the eventual achievement of Jewish independence in 142 BC. It was written to show how the Jews were faithful to God's Law and is an important historical source for the period.

2 Maccabees (c. 100 BC) Recounts the same events as 1 Maccabees, but from a theological perspective.

1 Esdras (c. 150–100 BC) A compilation of events from passages in 2 Chronicles, Ezra, and Nehemiah, recounting Judah's history from Josiah to Ezra. It says that it was Zerubbabel's wise answer in a debate that led to him being sent to Jerusalem to rebuild the city.

Prayer of Manasseh (first century BC) Written as the prayer of the repentant King Manasseh when he was briefly exiled to Babylon.

Psalm 151 (date uncertain) A psalm attributed to David, reflecting on God's call of him and his victory over Goliath.

3 Maccabees (first century BC) This book's only link with 1–2 Maccabees is its theme—that of resisting Gentile rulers who wanted to impose Gentile traditions on the Jews. It recalls God's deliverance of Jews who lived in late third-century-BC Egypt through their prayer and obedience.

4 Maccabees (date uncertain) A reflection on the power of pious reason over passions and suffering.

2 Esdras (late first century AD) Written as Ezra's reflections on the destruction of the Temple (which happened in 586 BC), its true audience was those Jews who were troubled by its destruction once again, this time by the Romans in AD 70.

There is no common theme or message in these books, nor are they all the same kind of writing. They do, however, contain the same kind of books as we find in the main canon of the Bible. They include historical books such as 1 and 2 Maccabees, wisdom books such as Ecclesiasticus, a prophetic book (Baruch), and various prayers and sermons.

Why only some Bibles include books from the Apocrypha

Because these books were never included in the Hebrew canon (the accepted list of authoritative books) of the Old Testament, there has always been some uncertainty about them. They are sometimes called "deuterocanonical books," meaning a second canon, from the Greek word *deuteros*, meaning "second"—second in order, not in importance, in the eyes of those who see these books as Scripture. The word "Apocrypha" comes from another Greek word and means "hidden" or "secret"—a strange title since there is nothing hidden or secret about these works.

After the Temple was destroyed by Rome in AD 70, and with Christianity's rapid growth threatening Judaism's survival, the Jews closed their canon of Scripture, rejecting the Septuagint's additional books. It was their way of saying "The Christian Bible is false." Many Christians—though by no means all—had accepted them because the Greek version of the Old Testament (the Septuagint), which included the books of the Apocrypha, was widely used in the early church alongside the New Testament, also written in Greek. When Jerome was asked to produce a definitive Latin translation of the Bible in the fourth century AD (the Vulgate), he excluded these deuterocanonical books, convinced that only the Hebrew text was authoritative. However, his view did not prevail, and the Western Catholic Church soon added them (in Latin), recognizing this expanded collection as canonical Scripture.

During the Reformation in the sixteenth century, however, the Protestant churches, keen to return to the Bible's original Hebrew text, decided these books should be excluded from the Bible. They followed Jerome's view that the authoritative books were limited to those in the Hebrew canon, though they did permit the continuing use of the apocryphal books for private edification. The Roman Catholic Church, on the other hand, continued to include seven of these books in its Bible (Tobit, Judith, Wisdom of Solomon, Ecclesiasticus, 1 and 2 Maccabees, and Baruch), as well as some additions to Esther and Daniel. The other books are included in the canon of the various Orthodox churches.

Today, the apocryphal books are printed in some Bibles, though it is still unusual to find them in Bibles produced in the Protestant traditions. Where they do appear in Protestant Bibles, they are usually in a separate section between the Old and New Testaments. In Catholic and Orthodox Bibles, they are dispersed among the books of the Old Testament. But even if we do not accept them as Scripture, they are still of value for their insights into the period between the Testaments and their emphasis on faith, wisdom, and enduring suffering in difficult times.

New Testament

Four Gospels, one story

These days we are very familiar with how various media outlets may report the same event but, while all reports agree on the core facts, one may emphasize one aspect more than another or draw different conclusions. It's exactly the same with the four Gospels—Matthew, Mark, Luke, and John. The four clearly have the same one story—the story of Jesus' life (with his encounters, teaching, and miracles), death, and resurrection. But each Gospel has a slightly different emphasis in how it tells that story. This means that sometimes a particular incident or teaching might be omitted by one or more Gospels, or might be emphasized more, or commented on in a different way, depending on the author's purpose.

That's why, from earliest Christian times, many attempts have been made to try to "harmonize" the four Gospels—either to try to draw them all together to produce a single account of Jesus' life, or to show the relationship between the different Gospel passages. This latter kind of harmonization is called a "synopsis."

While it is impossible to be 100 percent certain about every detail of Jesus' life, or the order in which events happened, the chart below gives a broad picture of how his life probably unfolded. But the main value of this chart is that it will help you to see how the different Gospel writers narrate the same event. As you compare each writer's account of the same event or teaching, you will find many similarities, but sometimes a little detail will be added or a particular comment made. At such times, it's good to stop and ask yourself, I wonder why the writer included that? The answer will serve toward building up a picture of what each Gospel writer wanted to emphasize while still telling the one story: the story of the Son of God who came into the world to save us.

		Matthew	Mark	Luke	John
1.	The Prologue to John's Gospel				1:1-18
2.	The Preface to Luke's Gospel			1:1-4	
3.	The Record of Jesus' Ancestors	1:1-17		3:23-38	
4.	The Birth of John the Baptist Foretold			1:5-25	
5.	The Birth of Jesus Foretold			1:26-38	
6.	Mary Visits Elizabeth			1:39-45	
7.	Mary's Song of Praise			1:46-56	
8.	The Birth of John the Baptist			1:57-66	
9.	Zechariah's Prophecy			1:67-79	
10.	The Growth of John the Baptist			1:80	
11.	The Birth of Jesus	1:18-25		2:1-7	
12.	Shepherds Visit Jesus			2:8-20	
13.	Jesus Is Circumcised			2:21	
14.	Jesus Is Presented in the Temple			2:21-24	
15.	The Prophecy of Simeon			2:25-35	
16.	The Prophecy of Anna			2:36-38	
17.	The Visit of the Wise Men	2:1-12			
18.	The Escape to Egypt	2:13-18			
19.	The Return to Nazareth	2:19-23		2:39	
20.	Jesus' Childhood			2:40	
21.	Jesus Speaks with the Teachers			2:41-50	

		Matthew	Mark	Luke	John
22.	Jesus Grows in Wisdom and Stature			2:51-52	
23.	John the Baptist Prepares the Way for Jesus	3:1-12	1:1-8	3:1-18	1:19-28
24.	The Baptism of Jesus	3:13-17	1:9-11	3:21-22	
25.	Satan Tempts Jesus in the Wilderness	4:1-11	1:12-13	4:1-13	
26.	John the Baptist's Testimony about Jesus				1:29-34
27.	The First Disciples				1:35-51
28.	The Wedding at Cana				2:1-12
29.	Jesus Clears the Temple (cp. #163)				2:13-22
30.	Jesus Ministers in Jerusalem				2:23-25
31.	Jesus and Nicodemus				3:1-21
32.	John the Baptist Exalts Jesus				3:22-36
33.	Jesus Leaves for Galilee after Herod Arrests John	4:12	1:14	3:19-20	4:1-3
34.	Jesus Passes through Samaria				4:4-38
35.	Many Samaritans Believe				4:39-42
36.	Jesus Preaches in Galilee	4:13-17	1:14-15	4:14-15	4:43-45
37.	Jesus Heals an Official's Son				4:46-54
38.	Jesus Is Rejected at Nazareth (cp. #79)			4:16-30	
39.	Fishermen Follow Jesus	4:18-22	1:16-20	5:1-11	
40.	Jesus Exorcises a Demon and Teaches with Authority		1:21-28	4:31-37	
41.	Jesus Heals Peter's Mother-in-Law and Others	8:14-17	1:29-34	4:38-41	
42.	Jesus Preaches throughout Galilee	4:23-25	1:35-39	4:42-44	
43.	Jesus Heals a Man with Leprosy	8:1-4	1:40-45	5:12-16	
44.	Jesus Forgives and Heals a Paralyzed Man	9:1-8	2:1-12	5:17-26	
45.	Jesus Calls Matthew and Dines at His House	9:9-13	2:13-17	5:27-32	
46.	A Discussion about Fasting	9:14-17	2:18-22	5:33-39	
47.	Jesus Heals a Lame Man				5:1-15
48.	The Disciples Pick Wheat on the Sabbath	12:1-8	2:23-28	6:1-5	
49.	Jesus Heals on the Sabbath	12:9-15a	3:1-6	6:6-11	
50.	Large Crowds Follow Jesus	12:15-21	3:7-12	6:17-19	
51.	Jesus Selects the Twelve Disciples		3:13-19	6:12-16	
52.	Jesus' Sermon	5:1–7:29		cp. 6:20-49	
53.	The Faith of a Roman Officer	8:5-13		7:1-10	
54.	Jesus Raises a Widow's Son from the Dead			7:11-17	
55.	Jesus Eases John the Baptist's Doubts	11:1-19		7:18-35	
56.	Judgment for the Unbelievers	11:20-24			
57.	Jesus' Prayer of Thanksgiving	11:25-30			
58.	A Sinful Woman Anoints Jesus			7:36-50	
59.	The Women Who Traveled with Jesus			8:1-3	
60.	Jesus Is Accused of Being Empowered by Satan	12:22-37	3:20-30	cp. 11:14-23	
61.	The Sign of Jonah	12:38-45		cp. 11:27-32	

		Matthew	Mark	Luke	John
62.	Jesus' True Family	12:46-50	3:31-35	8:19-21	
63.	The Parable of the Farmer Scattering Seed	13:1-9	4:1-9	8:4-8	
64.	Jesus Explains the Parable of the Farmer Scattering Seed	13:10-23	4:10-20	8:9-15	
65.	The Parable of the Lamp		4:21-25	8:16-18	
66.	The Parable of the Growing Seed		4:26-29		
67.	The Parable of the Wheat and Weeds	13:24-30			
68.	The Parable of the Mustard Seed	13:31-32	4:30-32	13:18-19	
69.	The Parable of the Yeast	13:33		13:20-21	
70.	Comment on Jesus' Use of Parables	13:34-35	4:33-34		
71.	Jesus Explains the Parable of the Wheat and Weeds	13:36-43			
72.	The Parable of the Hidden Treasure	13:44			
73.	The Parable of the Pearl Merchant	13:45-46			
74.	The Parable of the Fishing Net	13:47-52			
75.	Jesus Calms the Storm	8:23-27	4:35-41	8:22-25	
76.	Jesus Heals a Demon-Possessed Man	8:29-34	5:1-20	8:26-39	
77.	Jesus Heals a Woman and Raises a Girl from the Dead	9:18-26	5:21-43	8:40-56	
78.	Jesus Heals the Blind and Mute	9:27-34			
79.	Jesus Is Rejected at Nazareth (cp. #38)	13:53-58	6:1-6a		
80.	Prayer for More Workers	9:35-38			
81.	Jesus Sends Out the Twelve Disciples	10:1-15	6:6-13	9:1-6	
82.	Jesus Warns the Disciples of Persecution	10:16-42			
83.	Herod Mistakes Jesus for John the Baptist Back from the Dead	14:1-2	6:14-16		
84.	Herod Executes John the Baptist	14:3-12	6:14-29	9:7-9	
85.	Jesus Miraculously Feeds 5,000	14:13-21	6:30-44	9:10-17	6:1-15
86.	Jesus Walks on Water	14:22-33	6:45-52		6:16-21
87.	All Who Touch Jesus Are Healed	14:34-36	6:53-56		
88.	Jesus Is the True Bread of Heaven				6:22-59
89.	Many Disciples Desert Jesus				6:60-71
90.	Jesus Teaches about Inner Purity	15:1-20	7:1-23		
91.	A Woman from Phoenicia Believes in Jesus	15:21-28	7:24-30		
92.	Jesus Heals Many People	15:29-31	7:31-37		
93.	Jesus Miraculously Feeds 4,000	15:32-39	8:1-10		
94.	Religious Leaders Demand a Sign	16:1-4	8:11-13		
95.	Jesus Warns the Disciples about Corrupt Teachings	16:5-12	8:14-21		
96.	Jesus Heals a Blind Man		8:22-26		
97.	Peter Declares Jesus Is the Christ	16:13-20	8:27-30	9:18-21	
98.	Jesus Predicts His Death and Resurrection the First Time	16:21-28	8:31–9:1	9:22-27	
99.	The Transfiguration of Jesus	17:1-13	9:2-13	9:28-36	
100.	Jesus Heals a Demon-Possessed Boy	17:14-21	9:14-29	9:37-43a	

		Matthew	Mark	Luke	John
101.	Jesus Predicts His Death and Resurrection the Second Time	17:22-23	9:30-32	9:43-45	
102.	Jesus Is Questioned about the Temple Tax	17:24-27			
103.	Argument about Who Is the Greatest	18:1-5	9:33-37	9:46-48	
104.	The Disciples Forbid Another Man from Using Jesus' Name		9:38-41	9:49-50	
105.	Jesus Warns against Temptation	18:6-10	9:42-50		
106.	Correcting Another Believer	18:15-20			
107.	The Parable of the Unforgiving Debtor	18:21-35			
108.	Jesus' Brothers Ridicule Him				7:1-9
109.	The Mistaken Zeal of James and John			9:51-56	
110.	The Cost of Following Jesus	8:18-22		9:57-62	
111.	Jesus Teaches Openly at the Temple				7:10-39
112.	Division and Unbelief				7:40-52
113.	Jesus Forgives an Adulterous Woman				7:53–8:11
114.	Jesus Is the Light of the World				8:12-20
115.	Jesus Warns the Unbelieving				8:21-30
116.	Jesus Identifies God's True Children and Claims Deity				8:31-59
117.	Jesus Heals a Man Born Blind				9:1-34
118.	Spiritual Blindness				9:35-41
119.	Jesus Is the Good Shepherd				10:1-21
120.	Jesus Sends Out Seventy-Two Disciples			10:1-24	
121.	The Parable of the Good Samaritan			10:25-37	
122.	Jesus Visits Mary and Martha			10:38-42	
123.	Jesus Teaches about Prayer			11:1-13	
124.	Jesus Is Accused of Being in League with Satan			11:14-28	
125.	The Sign of Jonah			11:29-32	
126.	The Light Within			11:33-36	
127.	Jesus Criticizes the Religious Leaders			11:37–12:12	
128.	Jesus Speaks about Worldliness and Spiritual Alertness			12:13-59	
129.	Jesus Calls the People to Repent			13:1-9	
130.	Jesus Heals a Crippled Woman			13:10-21	
131.	Jesus Claims to Be God's Son				10:22-38
132.	Jesus Departs Jerusalem				10:39-42
133.	The Narrow Door into the Kingdom			13:22-30	
134.	Jesus Grieves over Jerusalem	23:37-39		13:31-35	
135.	Jesus Heals on the Sabbath			14:1-6	
136.	Jesus Teaches about Humility			14:7-14	
137.	The Parable of the Great Feast (cp. #169)			14:15-24	
138.	The Cost of Being a Disciple			14:25-35	
139.	The Parable of the Lost Sheep	18:12-14		15:1-7	

		Matthew	Mark	Luke	John
140.	The Parable of the Lost Coin			15:8-10	
141.	The Parable of the Lost Son			15:11-32	
142.	The Parable of the Shrewd Manager			16:1-13	
143.	Jesus Confronts Scoffing Pharisees			16:14-18	
144.	The Parable of the Rich Man and Lazarus			16:19-31	
145.	Jesus Teaches about Forgiveness and Faith			17:1-10	
146.	Jesus Raises Lazarus from the Dead				11:1-44
147.	The Religious Leaders Plot to Murder Jesus				11:45-57
148.	Jesus Heals Ten Men with Leprosy			17:11-19	
149.	The Coming of the Kingdom			17:20-37	
150.	The Parable of the Persistent Widow			18:1-8	
151.	The Parable of the Pharisee and Tax Collector			18:9-14	
152.	Jesus Teaches about Marriage and Divorce	19:1-12	10:1-12		
153.	Jesus Blesses the Children	19:13-15	10:13-16	18:15-17	
154.	The Rich Young Ruler	19:16-30	10:17-31	18:18-30	
155.	The Parable of the Vineyard Workers	20:1-16			
156.	Jesus Predicts His Death and Resurrection the Third Time	20:17-19	10:32-34	18:31-34	
157.	Jesus Teaches about Service	20:20-28	10:35-45		
158.	Jesus Heals the Blind	20:29-34	10:46-52	18:35-43	
159.	Jesus Brings Salvation to Zacchaeus			19:1-10	
160.	The Parable of the Ten Servants			19:11-27	
161.	A Woman Anoints Jesus	26:6-13	14:3-9		cp. 12:1-11
162.	Jesus Rides Triumphantly into Jerusalem [Sunday]	21:1-11	11:1-11	19:28-44	12:12-19
163.	Jesus Clears the Temple (cp. #29) [Tuesday]	21:12-17	11:15-19	19:45-48	
164.	The Significance of Jesus' Approaching Death				12:20-50
165.	A Lesson from the Fig Tree [Wednesday]	21:18-22	11:12-14, 20-25		
166.	Religious Leaders Challenge Jesus' Authority	21:23-27	11:27-33	20:1-8	
167.	The Parable of the Two Sons	21:28-32			
168.	The Parable of the Evil Farmers	21:33-46	12:1-12	20:9-19	
169.	The Parable of the Wedding Feast (cp. #137)	22:1-14			
170.	Taxes for Caesar	22:15-22	12:13-17	20:20-26	
171.	Discussion about the Resurrection	22:23-33	12:18-27	20:27-40	
172.	Discussion about the Greatest Commandment	22:34-40	12:28-34		
173.	A Question about the Messiah	22:41-46	12:35-37	20:41-44	
174.	Jesus Denounces the Religious Leaders	23:1-36	12:38-40	20:45-47	
175.	The Widow's Offering		12:41-44	21:1-4	
176.	Jesus Foretells the Future	24:1-51	13:1-37	21:5-38	
177.	The Parable of the Ten Bridesmaids	25:1-13			
178.	The Parable of the Three Servants	25:14-30			
179.	The Final Judgment	25:31-46			

		Matthew	Mark	Luke	John
180.	The Religious Leaders Continue Their Plot to Murder Jesus	26:1-5	14:1-2	22:1-2	
181.	Judas Agrees to Betray Jesus	26:14-16	14:10-11	22:3-6	
182.	Preparation for the Passover [Thursday]	26:17-19	14:12-16	22:7-13	
183.	Jesus Washes the Disciples' Feet				13:1-20
184.	The Last Supper	26:20-30	14:17-26	22:14-30	13:21-30
185.	Jesus Predicts Peter's Denial	26:31-35	14:27-31	22:31-38	13:31-38
186.	Jesus' Farewell Discourse				14:1–16:33
187.	Jesus' Intercessory Prayer				17:1-26
188.	Jesus Agonizes in the Garden	26:36-46	14:32-42	22:39-46	
189.	Jesus Is Betrayed and Arrested [Friday]	26:47-56	14:43-52	22:47-53	18:1-11
190.	Annas Questions Jesus				18:12-23
191.	Jesus Is Brought before Caiaphas	26:57-68	14:53-65	22:54, 63-65	18:24
192.	Peter Denies Knowing Jesus	26:69-75	14:66-72	22:54-62	18:25-27
193.	Religious Leaders Condemn Jesus	27:1-2	15:1	22:66-71	
194.	Judas Hangs Himself	27:3-10			
195.	Jesus' Trial before Pilate	27:11-14	15:2-5	23:1-7	18:28-37
196.	Jesus' Trial before Herod			23:8-12	
197.	Pilate Hands Jesus over to Be Crucified	27:15-26	15:6-15	23:13-25	18:38–19:16a
198.	Roman Soldiers Mock Jesus	27:27-31	15:16-19		
199.	Jesus Is Led Away to Be Crucified	27:32-34	15:20-23	23:26-32	19:16-17
200.	Jesus Is Crucified	27:35-56	15:24-41	23:33-49	19:18-37
201.	Jesus Is Laid in the Tomb	27:57-61	15:42-47	23:50-56	19:38-42
202.	Guards Are Posted Outside the Tomb [Saturday]	27:62-66			
203.	Women Come to the Empty Tomb and Report This to the Disciples [Sunday]	28:1-8	16:1-8	24:1-11	20:1-2
204.	Peter and John See the Empty Tomb and John Believes			24:12	20:3-10
205.	Jesus Appears to Mary Magdalene and Another Mary	28:9-10	16:9		20:11-17
206.	Mary Magdalene Tells the Disciples She Has Seen Jesus		16:10-11		20:18
207.	The Guards Report to the Sanhedrin	28:11-15			
208.	Jesus Appears to Cleopas and His Companion		16:12-13	24:13-35	
209.	Jesus Appears to the Disciples in Jerusalem		16:14	24:36-49	20:19-23
210.	Jesus Appears to the Disciples with Thomas				20:24-29
211.	Jesus Appears to Seven Disciples				21:1-23
212.	Jesus Gives the Great Commission	28:16-20	16:15-18		
213.	Jesus Ascends into Heaven		16:14	24:50-53	
214.	The Reason John Wrote His Gospel				20:30-31
215.	The Epilogue of John's Gospel				21:24-25

page 1066

Matthew *Jesus: the Messiah king*

Matthew's well-ordered story about Jesus shows that Jesus was the expected Messiah, Israel's long-awaited king, and demonstrates how he fulfilled many Old Testament Scriptures that prophesied his coming. This king welcomed all people, especially those on the margins of society—even non-Jews (Gentiles), much to the annoyance of the Jewish religious elite. He laughed with them and enjoyed their company. And he exposed the emptiness of outdated norms that locked people out of God's friendship rather than helping them to know it. In Jesus, a new day had dawned: The Kingdom of Heaven was already among them because he was among them.

What's it all about?

Matthew's Gospel opens with a genealogy, preparing us for his claims: Jesus was indeed the promised "descendant of David" (1:1), the Messiah (1:16). His story opens with Jesus' birth in Bethlehem, focusing on the homage of visiting Gentiles and the wrath of Herod—both pictures of what was to come. After fleeing to Egypt to avoid Herod's infanticide, Jesus' parents eventually returned to Nazareth, where Jesus grew up.

Jumping ahead thirty years, Matthew records the work of John the Baptist, Jesus' forerunner (chapter 3). After being baptized by John, Jesus was tempted by the devil in the wilderness (chapter 4). Victorious, he returned to Galilee and began preaching, "Repent of your sins and turn to God, for the Kingdom of Heaven is near" (4:17), proving this by healing people from all kinds of diseases. He called his first followers, four fishermen—Andrew and Peter, James and John—and others soon joined him.

Vast crowds began to gather, as at the Sermon on the Mount (chapters 5–7). Jesus explained to them what God's Kingdom was like—a kingdom that turns accepted ways of behavior upside down and that is built around a loving Father who knows our needs. More and more people came to him, and he healed them all, as Isaiah foretold (8:17). But he not only healed; he also claimed he could forgive sins (9:6). This claim, together with his rejecting the traditions of the Jewish leaders and mixing

OVERVIEW

Jesus' birth and early years
1:1–2:23

Preparation for ministry
3:1–4:11

Jesus' message and ministry
4:12–25:46

Jesus begins his ministry
4:12-25

Jesus preaches his Sermon on the Mount · *5:1–7:29*

Jesus demonstrates the power of the Kingdom · *8:1–9:38*

Jesus commissions the twelve apostles · *10:1-42*

Jesus teaches about the Kingdom of Heaven · *11:1–13:58*

Reactions to the ministry of Jesus
14:1–16:28

The Transfiguration and final ministry in Galilee · *17:1–18:35*

Conflicts with religious leaders
19:1–23:39

Jesus teaches on the Mount of Olives · *24:1–25:46*

Jesus' last supper, arrest, death, and resurrection · *26:1–28:20*

with those they deemed to be outcasts (including Matthew himself; 9:9), brought him into fierce conflict with those leaders (9:10-13). But what Jesus was bringing demanded an utterly new framework (9:16-17).

Jesus commissioned twelve apostles (from a Greek word meaning "sent ones"; chapter 10), chosen from his wider group of disciples to be his special representatives, sending them out to preach and heal. When John the Baptist, now in prison, began to doubt if Jesus was truly the Messiah, Jesus sent word of his miracles as authentication (chapter 11)—miracles he continued to perform despite being accused of doing them by Satan's power (12:22-24).

In chapter 13 Matthew collects some of Jesus' parables about God's Kingdom and the mysterious way in which it operates. In chapters 14 to 18, after John's execution, we see not only more miracles but also people's reactions to them. Many views of Jesus were developing, but Peter acknowledged that he was the expected Messiah and Son of God (16:16). From that point, Jesus started speaking more plainly about his death (16:21), and conflicts with the religious leaders increased. By the time he entered Jerusalem on a donkey (chapter 21), fulfilling Zechariah's prophecy, they were already conspiring against him. His parables spoke of their rejection of him and alluded to his coming death (chapters 21–22). He also warned the religious leaders that they would not escape God's judgment (chapter 23).

On the Mount of Olives, Jesus taught his disciples about the future of Jerusalem and of the world itself, promising he would return (chapter 24) and calling them to stay alert (chapters 24–25). In Bethany, he shared a final supper with them, preparing them for his death, which would introduce God's new covenant and be the means of forgiveness (26:28). Then, in the garden of Gethsemane, he was betrayed, arrested, taken away to be tried, and condemned to death by crucifixion (chapters 26–27).

But death didn't have the final word. On the third day—Sunday—Mary Magdalene found his tomb empty. "He isn't here! He is risen," the angel at the tomb said (28:6). Jesus later appeared to his followers, commissioning them for their task and assuring them of his ongoing presence with them (28:20).

What does it mean for us?

Matthew stresses that Jesus was everything the prophets had hoped for. The opening genealogy demonstrates that he came as the climax of God's purpose that began with Abraham; and throughout his Gospel, Matthew comments on incidents in Jesus' life with the words, "This fulfilled what the Lord had spoken through the prophet" (e.g., 2:15).

Yet Jesus is not simply good news for Jews, but for all people. Even though his focus is the Jews, Matthew concludes with "the Great Commission," in which the risen Jesus sends his followers to "make disciples of all the nations" (28:19).

To help us remember Jesus' teaching, Matthew organizes it into five great "blocks" of material, reflecting the five books of the Pentateuch (the first five books of the Bible), as though he were saying, "Here is God's new 'Law.'" Each block (chapters 5–7; 10; 13; 18; 24–25) has its own clear theme to help us grasp the point. One of those blocks of teaching—the Sermon on the Mount (chapters 5–7)—shows how Jesus wanted his followers to live.

This emphasis on the new lifestyle and the mission to which God calls us can often make us feel inadequate. But Matthew constantly reminds us of the presence of Jesus with us. In the first chapter, Jesus is called Immanuel ("God is with us"), and in the final chapter the risen Christ promises, "I am with you always, even to the end of the age." His presence is what enables us to live as he calls us to.

▶ *See also **Four Gospels, one story**, pages 1060-1065; **Matthew**, page 1081; **The Ministry of Jesus** map, Visual Overview Z10.*

The Ancestors of Jesus the Messiah

1 This is a record of the ancestors of Jesus the Messiah, a descendant of David and of Abraham*:

2 Abraham was the father of Isaac.
Isaac was the father of Jacob.
Jacob was the father of Judah and his brothers.
3 Judah was the father of Perez and Zerah (whose mother was Tamar).
Perez was the father of Hezron.
Hezron was the father of Ram.*
4 Ram was the father of Amminadab.
Amminadab was the father of Nahshon.
Nahshon was the father of Salmon.
5 Salmon was the father of Boaz (whose mother was Rahab).
Boaz was the father of Obed (whose mother was Ruth).
Obed was the father of Jesse.
6 Jesse was the father of King David.
David was the father of Solomon (whose mother was Bathsheba, the widow of Uriah).
7 Solomon was the father of Rehoboam.
Rehoboam was the father of Abijah.
Abijah was the father of Asa.*
8 Asa was the father of Jehoshaphat.
Jehoshaphat was the father of Jehoram.*
Jehoram was the father* of Uzziah.
9 Uzziah was the father of Jotham.
Jotham was the father of Ahaz.
Ahaz was the father of Hezekiah.
10 Hezekiah was the father of Manasseh.
Manasseh was the father of Amon.*
Amon was the father of Josiah.
11 Josiah was the father of Jehoiachin* and his brothers (born at the time of the exile to Babylon).
12 After the Babylonian exile:
Jehoiachin was the father of Shealtiel.
Shealtiel was the father of Zerubbabel.
13 Zerubbabel was the father of Abiud.
Abiud was the father of Eliakim.
Eliakim was the father of Azor.
14 Azor was the father of Zadok.
Zadok was the father of Akim.
Akim was the father of Eliud.
15 Eliud was the father of Eleazar.
Eleazar was the father of Matthan.
Matthan was the father of Jacob.
16 Jacob was the father of Joseph, the husband of Mary.
Mary gave birth to Jesus, who is called the Messiah.

17 All those listed above include fourteen generations from Abraham to David, fourteen from David to the Babylonian exile, and fourteen from the Babylonian exile to the Messiah.

The Birth of Jesus the Messiah

18 This is how Jesus the Messiah was born. His mother, Mary, was engaged to be married to

▸ **1:1** *See* ***Genealogies****, page 454.*

Joseph of Nazareth

Joseph and Mary were "engaged to be married" (Matthew 1:18)—or "betrothed." Betrothal had some significant differences from modern engagement. It began with the boy's parents choosing his wife (normally while both were teenagers), and a legal contract was then made, as binding as marriage itself. This is why Mary is called Joseph's wife (1:20). When Joseph discovered she was pregnant, he assumed she had been unfaithful; and sexual unfaithfulness during betrothal was considered adultery. But rather than create a fuss, Joseph decided to quietly break the engagement (literally, "divorce her"; 1:19). When an angel told him what had really happened, he responded with faith and immediately turned the betrothal into marriage (1:24). He again responded in faith when an angel warned him of Herod's plans (2:13). We only hear of Joseph once more—the family visit to Jerusalem when Jesus was twelve (Luke 2:41-50). It seems likely therefore that Joseph died while Jesus was young.

▸ *See also* ***Does marriage still matter to God?****, page 976;* ***Mary, the mother of Jesus****, page 1153.*

Joseph. But before the marriage took place,
while she was still a virgin, she became pregnant through the power of the Holy Spirit.
19 Joseph, to whom she was engaged, was a
righteous man and did not want to disgrace
her publicly, so he decided to break the engagement* quietly.
20 As he considered this, an angel of the
Lord appeared to him in a dream. "Joseph,
son of David," the angel said, "do not be
afraid to take Mary as your wife. For the
child within her was conceived by the Holy
Spirit. 21 And she will have a son, and you
are to name him Jesus,* for he will save his
people from their sins."
22 All of this occurred to fulfill the Lord's
message through his prophet:

23 "Look! The virgin will conceive a child!
She will give birth to a son,
and they will call him Immanuel,*
which means 'God is with us.'"

24 When Joseph woke up, he did as the
angel of the Lord commanded and took
Mary as his wife. 25 But he did not have
sexual relations with her until her son was
born. And Joseph named him Jesus.

Visitors from the East

2 Jesus was born in Bethlehem in Judea,
during the reign of King Herod. About
that time some wise men* from eastern lands
arrived in Jerusalem, asking, 2 "Where is the
newborn king of the Jews? We saw his star as
it rose,* and we have come to worship him."
3 King Herod was deeply disturbed when
he heard this, as was everyone in Jerusalem.
4 He called a meeting of the leading priests
and teachers of religious law and asked,
"Where is the Messiah supposed to be born?"
5 "In Bethlehem in Judea," they said, "for
this is what the prophet wrote:

6 'And you, O Bethlehem in the land of
Judah,
are not least among the ruling cities*
of Judah,
for a ruler will come from you
who will be the shepherd for my
people Israel.'*"

7 Then Herod called for a private meeting
with the wise men, and he learned from
them the time when the star first appeared.
8 Then he told them, "Go to Bethlehem and
search carefully for the child. And when
you find him, come back and tell me so that
I can go and worship him, too!"
9 After this interview the wise men went
their way. And the star they had seen in
the east guided them to Bethlehem. It went
ahead of them and stopped over the place
where the child was. 10 When they saw
the star, they were filled with joy! 11 They
entered the house and saw the child with
his mother, Mary, and they bowed down
and worshiped him. Then they opened their
treasure chests and gave him gifts of gold,
frankincense, and myrrh.

1:1 Greek *Jesus the Messiah, Son of David and son of Abraham.* **1:3** Greek *Aram,* a variant spelling of Ram; also in 1:4. See 1 Chr 2:9-10. **1:7** Greek *Asaph,* a variant spelling of Asa; also in 1:8. See 1 Chr 3:10. **1:8a** Greek *Joram,* a variant spelling of Jehoram; also in 1:8b. See 1 Kgs 22:50 and note at 1 Chr 3:11. **1:8b** Or *ancestor;* also in 1:11. **1:10** Greek *Amos,* a variant spelling of Amon; also in 1:10b. See 1 Chr 3:14. **1:11** Greek *Jeconiah,* a variant spelling of Jehoiachin; also in 1:12. See 2 Kgs 24:6 and note at 1 Chr 3:16. **1:19** Greek *to divorce her.* **1:21** *Jesus* means "The LORD saves." **1:23** Isa 7:14; 8:8, 10 (Greek version). **2:1** Or *royal astrologers;* Greek reads *magi;* also in 2:7, 16. **2:2** Or *star in the east.* **2:6a** Greek *the rulers.* **2:6b** Mic 5:2; 2 Sam 5:2.

The wise men

While countless nativity plays portray the visitors of Matthew 2:1-12 as kings, they were in fact "magi"—Persian court officials whose role was a mix of priest, astronomer, and royal adviser—a role Daniel had fulfilled in exile (Daniel 1:17-20; 2:46-48). It was probably during that exile that magi became familiar with the Jewish Scriptures that spoke of a coming Messiah. This, together with their astrology—a practice forbidden to God's people (e.g., Jeremiah 10:2)—had led them to discern the arrival of the promised king, something Herod immediately saw as a threat to himself. Their expensive gifts symbolized Jesus' future: Gold represented his kingship; frankincense, his priestly role; myrrh, his death for all. The three gifts led to the tradition that there were three visitors, though the actual number is unknown.

[12]When it was time to leave, they returned to their own country by another route, for God had warned them in a dream not to return to Herod.

The Escape to Egypt

[13]After the wise men were gone, an angel of the Lord appeared to Joseph in a dream. "Get up! Flee to Egypt with the child and his mother," the angel said. "Stay there until I tell you to return, because Herod is going to search for the child to kill him."

[14]That night Joseph left for Egypt with the child and Mary, his mother, [15]and they stayed there until Herod's death. This fulfilled what the Lord had spoken through the prophet: "I called my Son out of Egypt."*

[16]Herod was furious when he realized that the wise men had outwitted him. He sent soldiers to kill all the boys in and around Bethlehem who were two years old and under, based on the wise men's report of the star's first appearance. [17]Herod's brutal action fulfilled what God had spoken through the prophet Jeremiah:

[18] "A cry was heard in Ramah—
weeping and great mourning.
Rachel weeps for her
children,
refusing to be comforted,
for they are dead."*

The Return to Nazareth

[19]When Herod died, an angel of the Lord appeared in a dream to Joseph in Egypt. [20]"Get up!" the angel said. "Take the child and his mother back to the land of Israel, because those who were trying to kill the child are dead."

[21]So Joseph got up and returned to the land of Israel with Jesus and his mother. [22]But when he learned that the new ruler of Judea was Herod's son Archelaus, he was afraid to go there. Then, after being warned in a dream, he left for the region of Galilee. [23]So the family went and lived in a town called Nazareth. This fulfilled what the prophets had said: "He will be called a Nazarene."

John the Baptist Prepares the Way

3 In those days John the Baptist came to the Judean wilderness and began preaching. His message was, [2]"Repent of your sins and turn to God, for the Kingdom of Heaven is near.*" [3]The prophet Isaiah was speaking about John when he said,

"He is a voice shouting in the wilderness,
'Prepare the way for the LORD's
coming!
Clear the road for him!'"*

2:15 Hos 11:1. **2:18** Jer 31:15. **3:2** Or *has come*, or *is coming soon.* **3:3** Isa 40:3 (Greek version).

▸ **2:23** *See **Nazareth**, page 1155.*

Names and titles of Jesus

In the first of forty-seven quotations from the Old Testament, Matthew sees the incarnation of Jesus as the fulfillment of Isaiah's prophecy that one day a virgin would give birth to a son who would be "Immanuel"—"God is with us" (Matthew 1:23). Matthew uses several names and titles for Jesus, but among his favorite are "Son of God," "the Son," "Son of Man," "Son of David," "Lord," and "Messiah" (Christ). Names and titles of Jesus mentioned in the Bible are listed on the facing page.

The New Testament sees Jesus as no less than God himself, come to earth in human form; and it sees the Holy Spirit, whom Jesus sent, to be the continuance of his presence with us. Father, Son, and Holy Spirit are therefore all fully and equally God. Yet the Bible is clear that this does not mean there are three gods; rather, the one true God is so complex and wonderful that he exists simultaneously in three different persons. This mystery of the faith is known as the doctrine of the Trinity.

▸ *See also **Immanuel**, page 756; **The Son of Man**, page 1101; **The deity of Jesus Christ**, page 1364; **Savior**, page 1428.*

Name or title	Example verse
Great Shepherd	1 Peter 5:4
Christ	John 1:17
Everlasting Father	Isaiah 9:6
Faithful witness	Revelation 3:14
Head of the church	Colossians 1:18
High Priest	Hebrews 2:17
Immanuel	Matthew 1:23
King of all kings	Revelation 17:14
King of the Jews	Luke 23:38
Lamb of God	John 1:29
Last Adam	1 Corinthians 15:45
Lion of the tribe of Judah	Revelation 5:5
Lord	Matthew 20:30
Lord of all lords	Revelation 17:14
Mediator	1 Timothy 2:5
Messiah	John 1:41
Mighty God	Isaiah 9:6
Prince of Peace	Isaiah 9:6
Rabbi	Mark 9:5
Rock	1 Corinthians 10:4
Savior	2 Peter 1:1
Son	Matthew 11:27
Son of David	Matthew 9:27
Son of God	Matthew 14:33
Son of Man	Matthew 9:6
Son of the Most High	Luke 1:32
Teacher	John 13:13
True light	John 1:9
Wonderful Counselor	Isaiah 9:6
Word	John 1:1
Word of God	Revelation 19:13

4John's clothes were woven from coarse
camel hair, and he wore a leather belt
around his waist. For food he ate locusts
and wild honey. 5People from Jerusalem
and from all of Judea and all over the Jordan
Valley went out to see and hear John. 6And
when they confessed their sins, he baptized
them in the Jordan River.

7But when he saw many Pharisees and
Sadducees coming to watch him baptize,*
he denounced them. "You brood of snakes!"
he exclaimed. "Who warned you to flee
the coming wrath? 8Prove by the way you
live that you have repented of your sins
and turned to God. 9Don't just say to each
other, 'We're safe, for we are descendants
of Abraham.' That means nothing, for I tell
you, God can create children of Abraham
from these very stones. 10Even now the ax
of God's judgment is poised, ready to sever
the roots of the trees. Yes, every tree that
does not produce good fruit will be chopped
down and thrown into the fire.

11"I baptize with* water those who repent
of their sins and turn to God. But someone
is coming soon who is greater than I am—
so much greater that I'm not worthy even to
be his slave and carry his sandals. He will
baptize you with the Holy Spirit and with
fire.* 12He is ready to separate the chaff from
the wheat with his winnowing fork. Then
he will clean up the threshing area, gathering the wheat into his barn but burning the
chaff with never-ending fire."

The Baptism of Jesus

13Then Jesus went from Galilee to the Jordan
River to be baptized by John. 14But John tried
to talk him out of it. "I am the one who
needs to be baptized by you," he said, "so
why are you coming to me?"

15But Jesus said, "It should be done, for
we must carry out all that God requires.*"
So John agreed to baptize him.

16After his baptism, as Jesus came up out
of the water, the heavens were opened* and
he saw the Spirit of God descending like a
dove and settling on him. 17And a voice from

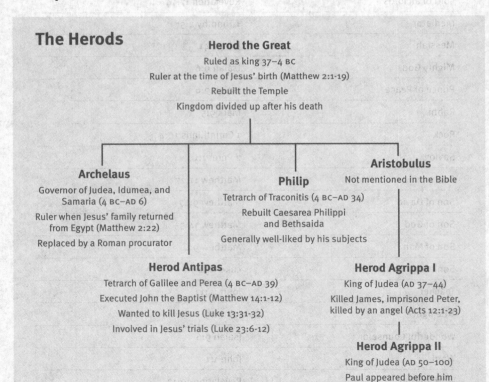

The Herods

Herod the Great

Ruled as king 37–4 BC

Ruler at the time of Jesus' birth (Matthew 2:1-19)

Rebuilt the Temple

Kingdom divided up after his death

Archelaus

Governor of Judea, Idumea, and Samaria (4 BC–AD 6)

Ruler when Jesus' family returned from Egypt (Matthew 2:22)

Replaced by a Roman procurator

Herod Antipas

Tetrarch of Galilee and Perea (4 BC–AD 39)

Executed John the Baptist (Matthew 14:1-12)

Wanted to kill Jesus (Luke 13:31-32)

Involved in Jesus' trials (Luke 23:6-12)

Philip

Tetrarch of Traconitis (4 BC–AD 34)

Rebuilt Caesarea Philippi and Bethsaida

Generally well-liked by his subjects

Aristobulus

Not mentioned in the Bible

Herod Agrippa I

King of Judea (AD 37–44)

Killed James, imprisoned Peter, killed by an angel (Acts 12:1-23)

Herod Agrippa II

King of Judea (AD 50–100)

Paul appeared before him (Acts 25:13–26:32).

heaven said, "This is my dearly loved Son,
who brings me great joy."

The Temptation of Jesus

4 Then Jesus was led by the Spirit into the
wilderness to be tempted there by the
devil. [2]For forty days and forty nights he
fasted and became very hungry.
[3]During that time the devil* came and
said to him, "If you are the Son of God, tell
these stones to become loaves of bread."
[4]But Jesus told him, "No! The Scriptures
say,

'People do not live by bread alone,
but by every word that comes from the
mouth of God.'*"

[5]Then the devil took him to the holy
city, Jerusalem, to the highest point of the
Temple, [6]and said, "If you are the Son of
God, jump off! For the Scriptures say,

'He will order his angels to protect
you.
And they will hold you up with their
hands
so you won't even hurt your foot on a
stone.'*"

[7]Jesus responded, "The Scriptures also
say, 'You must not test the LORD your God.'*"
[8]Next the devil took him to the peak of a
very high mountain and showed him all the
kingdoms of the world and their glory. [9]"I
will give it all to you," he said, "if you will
kneel down and worship me."
[10]"Get out of here, Satan," Jesus told him.
"For the Scriptures say,

'You must worship the LORD your God
and serve only him.'*"

[11]Then the devil went away, and angels
came and took care of Jesus.

The Ministry of Jesus Begins

[12]When Jesus heard that John had been arrested, he left Judea and returned to Galilee.
[13]He went first to Nazareth, then left there
and moved to Capernaum, beside the Sea of
Galilee, in the region of Zebulun and Naphtali. [14]This fulfilled what God said through
the prophet Isaiah:

3:7 Or *coming to be baptized.* **3:11a** Or *in.* **3:11b** Or *in the Holy Spirit and in fire.* **3:15** Or *for we must fulfill all righteousness.* **3:16** Some manuscripts read *opened to him.* **4:3** Greek *the tempter.* **4:4** Deut 8:3. **4:6** Ps 91:11-12. **4:7** Deut 6:16. **4:10** Deut 6:13.

▶ **4:1** *See **The wilderness**, page 784; **Temptation**, page 1313.* **4:4** *See **Jesus and the Old Testament**, page 1079.*

Jesus' baptism

Jesus' first step of preparation for ministry was to go to the Jordan River to be baptized by John (see also Mark 1:9-11; Luke 3:21-22; John 1:29-34). John's message had been a call for repentance (Matthew 3:1-2) and a changed lifestyle (3:8), yet here was God's Son, who needed neither to repent nor to change his lifestyle. Little wonder, then, that John did not want to baptize Jesus (3:14). But despite John's reluctance, Jesus insisted on going ahead and was baptized, humbly identifying himself with sinners and modeling the need for us to turn to God afresh. Above all, he said that being baptized was necessary, "for we must carry out all that God requires" (3:15). If Jesus was baptized to mark the beginning of his ministry, how much more do we need to be baptized to show we have begun a new life with him, burying our old life and leaving it behind (see Romans 6:3-7).

As Jesus was baptized, God confirmed his calling by sending his Holy Spirit on him and confirming with a voice from heaven that he was indeed his Son. Passages such as this one, which closely link the persons of the Father, the Son, and the Holy Spirit, led the early church to grasp that, although God is one (e.g., Deuteronomy 6:4; see footnote), this one God exists simultaneously in three persons—the doctrine of the Trinity.

▶ *See also **John the Baptist**, page 1156; **Baptism**, page 1238.*

[15] "In the land of Zebulun and of Naphtali,
beside the sea, beyond the Jordan River,
in Galilee where so many Gentiles live,
[16] the people who sat in darkness
have seen a great light.
And for those who lived in the land
where death casts its shadow,
a light has shined."*

[17]From then on Jesus began to preach, "Repent of your sins and turn to God, for the Kingdom of Heaven is near.*"

The First Disciples

[18]One day as Jesus was walking along the shore of the Sea of Galilee, he saw two brothers—Simon, also called Peter, and Andrew—throwing a net into the water, for they fished for a living. [19]Jesus called out to them, "Come, follow me, and I will show you how to fish for people!" [20]And they left their nets at once and followed him.

[21]A little farther up the shore he saw two other brothers, James and John, sitting in a boat with their father, Zebedee, repairing their nets. And he called them to come, too. [22]They immediately followed him, leaving the boat and their father behind.

Crowds Follow Jesus

[23]Jesus traveled throughout the region of Galilee, teaching in the synagogues and announcing the Good News about the Kingdom. And he healed every kind of disease and illness. [24]News about him spread as far as Syria, and people soon began bringing to him all who were sick. And whatever their sickness or disease, or if they were demon possessed or epileptic or paralyzed—he healed them all. [25]Large crowds followed him wherever he went—people from Galilee, the Ten Towns,* Jerusalem, from all over Judea, and from east of the Jordan River.

The Sermon on the Mount

5 One day as he saw the crowds gathering, Jesus went up on the mountainside and sat down. His disciples gathered around him, [2]and he began to teach them.

The Beatitudes

[3] "God blesses those who are poor and
realize their need for him,*
for the Kingdom of Heaven is theirs.
[4] God blesses those who mourn,
for they will be comforted.
[5] God blesses those who are humble,
for they will inherit the whole earth.

God's Kingdom

At the heart of Jesus' preaching lay this simple message: "the Kingdom of Heaven is near" (Matthew 4:17)—a shocking message to his fellow Jews. They too believed in God's Kingdom, but only as something future—when the Messiah would come and defeat God's enemies so God could establish his Kingdom on earth. But how could that Kingdom be here when the Romans were still there?

But their understanding of God's Kingdom was wrong. They were thinking of it as a place, and while it would be a place one day, that's not how it would begin. The Greek word for "kingdom" means "the act of ruling," not "a place ruled"; and Jesus declared that God's act of ruling had begun even now, through him, as his victory over sin, sickness, and circumstances demonstrated. Yes, God's Kingdom had a future aspect, as the parables in Matthew 25 show; but through Jesus, God's rule was starting to break in and come right now, and it would continue to grow (as the parables in Matthew 13 show) until it was all that remained.

Some have tried to distinguish between "Kingdom of Heaven" and "Kingdom of God," but this is to misunderstand Jewish thinking. By Jesus' day, Jews did not use the name "God," seeing it as too holy; instead, they spoke of "heaven." The Kingdom of Heaven is therefore simply another way of speaking about the Kingdom of God.

6 God blesses those who hunger and thirst
for justice,*
for they will be satisfied.
7 God blesses those who are merciful,
for they will be shown mercy.
8 God blesses those whose hearts are
pure,
for they will see God.
9 God blesses those who work for peace,
for they will be called the children of
God.
10 God blesses those who are persecuted
for doing right,
for the Kingdom of Heaven is theirs.

11 "God blesses you when people mock you
and persecute you and lie about you and say
all sorts of evil things against you because
you are my followers. 12 Be happy about
it! Be very glad! For a great reward awaits
you in heaven. And remember, the ancient
prophets were persecuted in the same way.

Teaching about Salt and Light

13 "You are the salt of the earth. But what
good is salt if it has lost its flavor? Can you
make it salty again? It will be thrown out
and trampled underfoot as worthless.
14 "You are the light of the world—like a
city on a hilltop that cannot be hidden. 15 No
one lights a lamp and then puts it under
a basket. Instead, a lamp is placed on a
stand, where it gives light to everyone in
the house. 16 In the same way, let your good
deeds shine out for all to see, so that everyone will praise your heavenly Father.

Teaching about the Law

17 "Don't misunderstand why I have come.
I did not come to abolish the law of Moses
or the writings of the prophets. No, I came
to accomplish their purpose. 18 I tell you the
truth, until heaven and earth disappear, not
even the smallest detail of God's law will disappear until its purpose is achieved. 19 So if
you ignore the least commandment and teach
others to do the same, you will be called the
least in the Kingdom of Heaven. But anyone
who obeys God's laws and teaches them will
be called great in the Kingdom of Heaven.
20 "But I warn you—unless your righteousness is better than the righteousness of the
teachers of religious law and the Pharisees,
you will never enter the Kingdom of Heaven!

Teaching about Anger

21 "You have heard that our ancestors were
told, 'You must not murder. If you commit
murder, you are subject to judgment.'* 22 But I
say, if you are even angry with someone,* you
are subject to judgment! If you call someone
an idiot,* you are in danger of being brought

4:15-16 Isa 9:1-2 (Greek version). **4:17** Or *has come,* or *is coming soon.* **4:25** Greek *Decapolis.* **5:3** Greek *poor in spirit.* **5:6** Or *for righteousness.* **5:21** Exod 20:13; Deut 5:17. **5:22a** Some manuscripts add *without cause.* **5:22b** Greek uses an Aramaic term of contempt: *If you say to your brother, 'Raca.'*

Salt and light

Much of Jesus' teaching came in the form of simple images or stories from everyday life. In Matthew 5:13-16, he used two very common pictures to show the effects that his followers are to have on the world around them.

First, they should be like salt. While today we mainly use salt for flavoring food, in Bible times its main function was as a preservative—to stop fish or meat from going rotten. That's what I want you to be like, Jesus told his followers—involved in society both to stop it from decaying and to bring wholesome flavor to it. But if salt loses its saltiness—that is, if salt becomes weakened by being corrupted with impurities—it can't do its job. So it is with Christians.

Second, Christians should be like light. No one lights a lamp to put it under a bowl; the light is there to be seen—not for its own sake, but to help people see clearly and to expose what is dark and hidden. That's how Christians should live in society.

Through these two images Jesus teaches that he doesn't want Christians withdrawing from society, but rather to be deeply involved in it and influencing it, exposing what is evil, revealing God's light, and adding what is good.

before the court. And if you curse someone,*
you are in danger of the fires of hell.*
23"So if you are presenting a sacrifice* at
the altar in the Temple and you suddenly
remember that someone has something
against you, 24leave your sacrifice there at the
altar. Go and be reconciled to that person.
Then come and offer your sacrifice to God.
25"When you are on the way to court
with your adversary, settle your differences
quickly. Otherwise, your accuser may hand
you over to the judge, who will hand you
over to an officer, and you will be thrown
into prison. 26And if that happens, you
surely won't be free again until you have
paid the last penny.*

Teaching about Adultery

27"You have heard the commandment that
says, 'You must not commit adultery.'* 28But I
say, anyone who even looks at a woman with
lust has already committed adultery with her
in his heart. 29So if your eye—even your good
eye*—causes you to lust, gouge it out and
throw it away. It is better for you to lose one
part of your body than for your whole body
to be thrown into hell. 30And if your hand—
even your stronger hand*—causes you to sin,
cut it off and throw it away. It is better for you
to lose one part of your body than for your
whole body to be thrown into hell.

Teaching about Divorce

31"You have heard the law that says, 'A man
can divorce his wife by merely giving her a
written notice of divorce.'* 32But I say that a
man who divorces his wife, unless she has
been unfaithful, causes her to commit adultery. And anyone who marries a divorced
woman also commits adultery.

Teaching about Vows

33"You have also heard that our ancestors
were told, 'You must not break your vows;
you must carry out the vows you make to
the LORD.'* 34But I say, do not make any
vows! Do not say, 'By heaven!' because
heaven is God's throne. 35And do not say,
'By the earth!' because the earth is his footstool. And do not say, 'By Jerusalem!' for
Jerusalem is the city of the great King. 36Do
not even say, 'By my head!' for you can't
turn one hair white or black. 37Just say a
simple, 'Yes, I will,' or 'No, I won't.' Anything beyond this is from the evil one.

Teaching about Revenge

38"You have heard the law that says the
punishment must match the injury: 'An eye
for an eye, and a tooth for a tooth.'* 39But I
say, do not resist an evil person! If someone
slaps you on the right cheek, offer the other
cheek also. 40If you are sued in court and
your shirt is taken from you, give your coat,
too. 41If a soldier demands that you carry his
gear for a mile,* carry it two miles. 42Give
to those who ask, and don't turn away from
those who want to borrow.

Teaching about Love for Enemies

43"You have heard the law that says, 'Love
your neighbor'* and hate your enemy. 44But
I say, love your enemies!* Pray for those
who persecute you! 45In that way, you will
be acting as true children of your Father in
heaven. For he gives his sunlight to both
the evil and the good, and he sends rain on
the just and the unjust alike. 46If you love
only those who love you, what reward is
there for that? Even corrupt tax collectors
do that much. 47If you are kind only to your
friends,* how are you different from anyone
else? Even pagans do that. 48But you are to
be perfect, even as your Father in heaven
is perfect.

Teaching about Giving to the Needy

6 "Watch out! Don't do your good deeds
publicly, to be admired by others, for
you will lose the reward from your Father in
heaven. 2When you give to someone in need,
don't do as the hypocrites do—blowing
trumpets in the synagogues and streets to
call attention to their acts of charity! I tell
you the truth, they have received all the
reward they will ever get. 3But when you
give to someone in need, don't let your left
hand know what your right hand is doing.
4Give your gifts in private, and your Father,
who sees everything, will reward you.

Teaching about Prayer and Fasting

5"When you pray, don't be like the hypocrites who love to pray publicly on street

▸ **5:28** *See **Lust**, page 589.* **5:43** *See **Love your neighbor as yourself**, page 139.*

corners and in the synagogues where everyone can see them. I tell you the truth, that is
all the reward they will ever get. 6 But when
you pray, go away by yourself, shut the
door behind you, and pray to your Father in
private. Then your Father, who sees everything, will reward you.
7 "When you pray, don't babble on and on
as the Gentiles do. They think their prayers
are answered merely by repeating their
words again and again. 8 Don't be like them,
for your Father knows exactly what you need
even before you ask him! 9 Pray like this:

Our Father in heaven,
  may your name be kept holy.
10 May your Kingdom come soon.
May your will be done on earth,
  as it is in heaven.
11 Give us today the food we need,*
12 and forgive us our sins,
  as we have forgiven those who sin
    against us.
13 And don't let us yield to temptation,*
  but rescue us from the evil one.*

14 "If you forgive those who sin against
you, your heavenly Father will forgive you.
15 But if you refuse to forgive others, your
Father will not forgive your sins.
16 "And when you fast, don't make it
obvious, as the hypocrites do, for they try
to look miserable and disheveled so people
will admire them for their fasting. I tell you
the truth, that is the only reward they will
ever get. 17 But when you fast, comb your
hair* and wash your face. 18 Then no one
will notice that you are fasting, except your
Father, who knows what you do in private.
And your Father, who sees everything, will
reward you.

Teaching about Money and Possessions

19 "Don't store up treasures here on earth,
where moths eat them and rust destroys
them, and where thieves break in and steal.

5:22c Greek *if you say, 'You fool.'* **5:22d** Greek *Gehenna;* also in 5:29, 30. **5:23** Greek *gift;* also in 5:24. **5:26** Greek *the last kodrantes* [i.e., quadrans]. **5:27** Exod 20:14; Deut 5:18. **5:29** Greek *your right eye.* **5:30** Greek *your right hand.* **5:31** Deut 24:1. **5:33** Num 30:2. **5:38** Greek *the law that says: 'An eye for an eye and a tooth for a tooth.'* Exod 21:24; Lev 24:20; Deut 19:21. **5:41** Greek *milion* [4,854 feet or 1,478 meters]. **5:43** Lev 19:18. **5:44** Some manuscripts add *Bless those who curse you. Do good to those who hate you.* Compare Luke 6:27-28. **5:47** Greek *your brothers.* **6:11** Or *Give us today our food for the day;* or *Give us today our food for tomorrow.* **6:13a** Or *And keep us from being tested.* **6:13b** Or *from evil.* Some manuscripts add *For yours is the kingdom and the power and the glory forever. Amen.* **6:17** Greek *anoint your head.*

▸ **6:16** *See* ***Does fasting have any value?****, page 1042.*

The Lord's Prayer

In contrast to the long, showy prayers of the hypocrites of his day (Matthew 6:5-8), Jesus taught his disciples to pray simply. The Lord's Prayer, as it is known, occurs twice, here and in Luke 11:2-4, in slightly different forms, perhaps reflecting different occasions when Jesus taught it. Matthew presents it as a model to be followed (Matthew 6:9), while Luke presents it as a prayer to be recited (Luke 11:2)—though however we use it, we should avoid the mindless repetition that Jesus rebuked (Matthew 6:5-8).

The prayer falls into clear sections that can help us in our own praying. First comes prayer about God—honoring him (6:9), praying for his Kingdom to come and his will to be done (6:10). Only then comes prayer about us. (Why think about God first? Because that puts everything in perspective!) Jesus encourages us to pray about our present needs (6:11), our past sins (6:12), and our future welfare (6:13).

But this is not just a prayer; it is an expression of relationship. It is heart-to-heart sharing between child and father—a perfect, heavenly Father who is limitless in the power and resources he wants to give us and who would never abuse us or trick us (7:9-11). This is why we can trust him when we pray.

▸ *See also* ***Praying in the moment****, page 537;* ***Longing for God****, page 628;* ***Why doesn't God always answer prayer?****, page 641;* ***Does God mind if we are honest with him?****, page 848;* ***Prayer as intercession****, page 922;* ***Perseverance in prayer****, page 1184.*

20 Store your treasures in heaven, where
moths and rust cannot destroy, and thieves
do not break in and steal. 21 Wherever your
treasure is, there the desires of your heart
will also be.

22 "Your eye is like a lamp that provides
light for your body. When your eye is
healthy, your whole body is filled with light.
23 But when your eye is unhealthy, your
whole body is filled with darkness. And
if the light you think you have is actually
darkness, how deep that darkness is!

24 "No one can serve two masters. For you
will hate one and love the other; you will
be devoted to one and despise the other.
You cannot serve God and be enslaved to
money.

25 "That is why I tell you not to worry about
everyday life—whether you have enough
food and drink, or enough clothes to wear.
Isn't life more than food, and your body
more than clothing? 26 Look at the birds.
They don't plant or harvest or store food in
barns, for your heavenly Father feeds them.
And aren't you far more valuable to him
than they are? 27 Can all your worries add a
single moment to your life?

28 "And why worry about your clothing?
Look at the lilies of the field and how they
grow. They don't work or make their clothing, 29 yet Solomon in all his glory was not
dressed as beautifully as they are. 30 And if
God cares so wonderfully for wildflowers
that are here today and thrown into the fire
tomorrow, he will certainly care for you.
Why do you have so little faith?

31 "So don't worry about these things,
saying, 'What will we eat? What will we
drink? What will we wear?' 32 These things
dominate the thoughts of unbelievers, but
your heavenly Father already knows all
your needs. 33 Seek the Kingdom of God*
above all else, and live righteously, and he
will give you everything you need.

34 "So don't worry about tomorrow, for tomorrow will bring its own worries. Today's
trouble is enough for today.

Do Not Judge Others

7 "Do not judge others, and you will not
be judged. 2 For you will be treated as
you treat others.* The standard you use in
judging is the standard by which you will
be judged.*

3 "And why worry about a speck in your
friend's eye* when you have a log in your
own? 4 How can you think of saying to
your friend,* 'Let me help you get rid of that
speck in your eye,' when you can't see past
the log in your own eye? 5 Hypocrite! First
get rid of the log in your own eye; then you
will see well enough to deal with the speck
in your friend's eye.

6 "Don't waste what is holy on people who
are unholy.* Don't throw your pearls to pigs!
They will trample the pearls, then turn and
attack you.

Effective Prayer

7 "Keep on asking, and you will receive what
you ask for. Keep on seeking, and you will
find. Keep on knocking, and the door will
be opened to you. 8 For everyone who asks,
receives. Everyone who seeks, finds. And
to everyone who knocks, the door will be
opened.

9 "You parents—if your children ask for
a loaf of bread, do you give them a stone
instead? 10 Or if they ask for a fish, do you give
them a snake? Of course not! 11 So if you sinful
people know how to give good gifts to your
children, how much more will your heavenly
Father give good gifts to those who ask him.

The Golden Rule

12 "Do to others whatever you would like
them to do to you. This is the essence of all
that is taught in the law and the prophets.

The Narrow Gate

13 "You can enter God's Kingdom only
through the narrow gate. The highway
to hell* is broad, and its gate is wide for
the many who choose that way. 14 But the
gateway to life is very narrow and the road
is difficult, and only a few ever find it.

The Tree and Its Fruit

15 "Beware of false prophets who come disguised as harmless sheep but are really
vicious wolves. 16 You can identify them by
their fruit, that is, by the way they act. Can you
pick grapes from thornbushes, or figs from
thistles? 17 A good tree produces good fruit,

▸ **6:27** *See **Worry**, page 1189.*

and a bad tree produces bad fruit. [18]A good tree can't produce bad fruit, and a bad tree can't produce good fruit. [19]So every tree that does not produce good fruit is chopped down and thrown into the fire. [20]Yes, just as you can identify a tree by its fruit, so you can identify people by their actions.

True Disciples

[21]"Not everyone who calls out to me, 'Lord! Lord!' will enter the Kingdom of Heaven. Only those who actually do the will of my Father in heaven will enter. [22]On judgment day many will say to me, 'Lord! Lord! We prophesied in your name and cast out demons in your name and performed many miracles in your name.' [23]But I will reply, 'I never knew you. Get away from me, you who break God's laws.'

Building on a Solid Foundation

[24]"Anyone who listens to my teaching and follows it is wise, like a person who builds a house on solid rock. [25]Though the rain comes in torrents and the floodwaters rise and the winds beat against that house, it won't collapse because it is built on bedrock. [26]But anyone who hears my teaching and doesn't obey it is foolish, like a person who builds a house on sand. [27]When the rains and floods come and the winds beat against that house, it will collapse with a mighty crash."

[28]When Jesus had finished saying these things, the crowds were amazed at his teaching, [29]for he taught with real authority—quite unlike their teachers of religious law.

Jesus Heals a Man with Leprosy

8 Large crowds followed Jesus as he came down the mountainside. [2]Suddenly, a man with leprosy approached him and knelt before him. "Lord," the man said, "if you are willing, you can heal me and make me clean."

[3]Jesus reached out and touched him. "I am willing," he said. "Be healed!" And instantly the leprosy disappeared. [4]Then Jesus said to him, "Don't tell anyone about this. Instead,

6:33 Some manuscripts do not include *of God*. **7:2a** Or *For God will judge you as you judge others.* **7:2b** Or *The measure you give will be the measure you get back.* **7:3** Greek *your brother's eye;* also in 7:5. **7:4** Greek *your brother.* **7:6** Greek *Don't give the sacred to dogs.* **7:13** Greek *The road that leads to destruction.*

▸ **8:2-3** *See* ***Jesus' miracles****, page 1128.*

Jesus and the Old Testament

Matthew knew his Scriptures well. He quotes from what we now call the Old Testament (though to him, of course, those were the only Scriptures he knew) some forty-seven times to show how Jesus fulfilled messianic prophecy (e.g., Matthew 8:17). But in doing this, he was following Jesus' example. Jesus turned to the Old Testament for guidance and encouragement (e.g., 4:4, 7, 10), quoted it in his teaching (e.g., 13:14-15), referred to its stories (e.g., 12:40), used quotations from it to settle arguments (e.g., 22:31-32) or reply to questions (e.g., 19:16-19), and frequently used its imagery (e.g., 24:31).

But not only did Jesus quote the Old Testament, he also said that he was the fulfillment of it: "I did not come to abolish the law of Moses or the writings of the prophets. No, I came to accomplish their purpose" (5:17)—that is, to give the Old Testament its full meaning and bring to pass all that it could only point to. When he then said that "not even the smallest detail of God's law will disappear until its purpose is achieved" (5:18), he emphasized its abiding importance and his total commitment to it.

Christians therefore cannot dismiss the Old Testament—though they must take care to interpret all it says in light of Christ's coming, to which it pointed and for which it prepared.

▸ *See also* ***Jesus Christ in the Psalms****, page 614;* ***Prophecies about Christ****, page 806;* ***Prophecies of the Messiah****, page 1044;* ***The Old Testament in the New Testament****, page 1403;* ***Prophecies of the Messiah****, Visual Overview Z12.*

go to the priest and let him examine you.
Take along the offering required in the law
of Moses for those who have been healed of
leprosy.* This will be a public testimony that
you have been cleansed."

The Faith of a Roman Officer

5 When Jesus returned to Capernaum, a
Roman officer* came and pleaded with
him, 6 "Lord, my young servant* lies in bed,
paralyzed and in terrible pain."
7 Jesus said, "I will come and heal him."
8 But the officer said, "Lord, I am not
worthy to have you come into my home. Just
say the word from where you are, and my
servant will be healed. 9 I know this because
I am under the authority of my superior
officers, and I have authority over my soldiers. I only need to say, 'Go,' and they go,
or 'Come,' and they come. And if I say to my
slaves, 'Do this,' they do it."
10 When Jesus heard this, he was amazed.
Turning to those who were following him,
he said, "I tell you the truth, I haven't seen
faith like this in all Israel! 11 And I tell you
this, that many Gentiles will come from all
over the world—from east and west—and sit
down with Abraham, Isaac, and Jacob at the
feast in the Kingdom of Heaven. 12 But many
Israelites—those for whom the Kingdom
was prepared—will be thrown into outer
darkness, where there will be weeping and
gnashing of teeth."
13 Then Jesus said to the Roman officer,
"Go back home. Because you believed, it
has happened." And the young servant was
healed that same hour.

Jesus Heals Many People

14 When Jesus arrived at Peter's house,
Peter's mother-in-law was sick in bed with
a high fever. 15 But when Jesus touched her
hand, the fever left her. Then she got up and
prepared a meal for him.
16 That evening many demon-possessed
people were brought to Jesus. He cast out
the evil spirits with a simple command,
and he healed all the sick. 17 This fulfilled
the word of the Lord through the prophet
Isaiah, who said,

"He took our sicknesses
and removed our diseases."*

The Cost of Following Jesus

18 When Jesus saw the crowd around him, he
instructed his disciples to cross to the other
side of the lake.
19 Then one of the teachers of religious
law said to him, "Teacher, I will follow you
wherever you go."
20 But Jesus replied, "Foxes have dens to
live in, and birds have nests, but the Son
of Man* has no place even to lay his head."
21 Another of his disciples said, "Lord, first
let me return home and bury my father."
22 But Jesus told him, "Follow me now. Let
the spiritually dead bury their own dead.*"

Jesus Calms the Storm

23 Then Jesus got into the boat and started
across the lake with his disciples. 24 Suddenly, a fierce storm struck the lake, with
waves breaking into the boat. But Jesus was
sleeping. 25 The disciples went and woke
him up, shouting, "Lord, save us! We're
going to drown!"
26 Jesus responded, "Why are you afraid?
You have so little faith!" Then he got up and
rebuked the wind and waves, and suddenly
there was a great calm.
27 The disciples were amazed. "Who is this
man?" they asked. "Even the winds and
waves obey him!"

Jesus Heals Two Demon-Possessed Men

28 When Jesus arrived on the other side of the
lake, in the region of the Gadarenes,* two
men who were possessed by demons met
him. They came out of the tombs and were
so violent that no one could go through that
area.
29 They began screaming at him, "Why are
you interfering with us, Son of God? Have
you come here to torture us before God's appointed time?"
30 There happened to be a large herd
of pigs feeding in the distance. 31 So the
demons begged, "If you cast us out, send
us into that herd of pigs."
32 "All right, go!" Jesus commanded
them. So the demons came out of the men
and entered the pigs, and the whole herd
plunged down the steep hillside into the
lake and drowned in the water.
33 The herdsmen fled to the nearby town,

▸ **8:28** *See **Demons**, page 1126.*

telling everyone what happened to the demon-possessed men. 34Then the entire town
came out to meet Jesus, but they begged
him to go away and leave them alone.

Jesus Heals a Paralyzed Man

9 Jesus climbed into a boat and went back
across the lake to his own town. 2Some
people brought to him a paralyzed man on
a mat. Seeing their faith, Jesus said to the
paralyzed man, "Be encouraged, my child!
Your sins are forgiven."
3But some of the teachers of religious
law said to themselves, "That's blasphemy!
Does he think he's God?"
4Jesus knew* what they were thinking, so
he asked them, "Why do you have such evil
thoughts in your hearts? 5Is it easier to say
'Your sins are forgiven,' or 'Stand up and
walk'? 6So I will prove to you that the Son
of Man* has the authority on earth to forgive
sins." Then Jesus turned to the paralyzed
man and said, "Stand up, pick up your mat,
and go home!"
7And the man jumped up and went home!
8Fear swept through the crowd as they saw
this happen. And they praised God for
giving humans such authority.

Jesus Calls Matthew

9As Jesus was walking along, he saw a man
named Matthew sitting at his tax collector's
booth. "Follow me and be my disciple,"
Jesus said to him. So Matthew got up and
followed him.
10Later, Matthew invited Jesus and his disciples to his home as dinner guests, along
with many tax collectors and other disreputable sinners. 11But when the Pharisees saw
this, they asked his disciples, "Why does
your teacher eat with such scum?*"
12When Jesus heard this, he said, "Healthy
people don't need a doctor—sick people
do." 13Then he added, "Now go and learn
the meaning of this Scripture: 'I want you
to show mercy, not offer sacrifices.'* For I
have come to call not those who think they
are righteous, but those who know they are
sinners."

A Discussion about Fasting

14One day the disciples of John the Baptist
came to Jesus and asked him, "Why don't
your disciples fast* like we do and the Pharisees do?"
15Jesus replied, "Do wedding guests
mourn while celebrating with the groom?
Of course not. But someday the groom will
be taken away from them, and then they will
fast.
16"Besides, who would patch old clothing
with new cloth? For the new patch would
shrink and rip away from the old cloth,
leaving an even bigger tear than before.

8:4 See Lev 14:2-32. **8:5** Greek *a centurion;* similarly in 8:8, 13. **8:6** Or *child;* also in 8:13. **8:17** Isa 53:4. **8:20** "Son of Man" is a title Jesus used for himself. **8:22** Greek *Let the dead bury their own dead.* **8:28** Other manuscripts read *Gerasenes;* still others read *Gergesenes.* Compare Mark 5:1; Luke 8:26. **9:4** Some manuscripts read *saw.* **9:6** "Son of Man" is a title Jesus used for himself. **9:11** Greek *with tax collectors and sinners?* **9:13** Hos 6:6 (Greek version). **9:14** Some manuscripts read *fast often.*

Matthew

When Jesus called Matthew to be a disciple (Matthew 9:9-13), he called one of the most hated members of society in those days. Tax collectors were seen as collaborators with Rome, for they generally bought the right to collect taxes for Rome for a particular region. They would pay a lump sum up front and were then free to recoup their investment by setting taxes at whatever level they saw as appropriate, and all this was backed up by Roman swords. Tax collectors were therefore considered cheats as well as collaborators. Matthew's tax district was particularly lucrative. Capernaum was close to a major trading highway and was located on the lakeside—and Herod Antipas also taxed fishermen. The change in Matthew that motivated him to leave all this behind was therefore profound. Matthew's work as a tax collector, which involved writing, organization, and attention to detail, would serve him well when he later came to write this Gospel.

▶ *See also* ***Apostles of Jesus****, page 1122.*

17"And no one puts new wine into old
wineskins. For the old skins would burst
from the pressure, spilling the wine and
ruining the skins. New wine is stored in new
wineskins so that both are preserved."

Jesus Heals in Response to Faith

18As Jesus was saying this, the leader of a
synagogue came and knelt before him. "My
daughter has just died," he said, "but you
can bring her back to life again if you just
come and lay your hand on her."
19So Jesus and his disciples got up and
went with him. 20Just then a woman who
had suffered for twelve years with constant
bleeding came up behind him. She touched
the fringe of his robe, 21for she thought, "If
I can just touch his robe, I will be healed."
22Jesus turned around, and when he saw
her he said, "Daughter, be encouraged! Your
faith has made you well." And the woman
was healed at that moment.
23When Jesus arrived at the official's home,
he saw the noisy crowd and heard the funeral
music. 24"Get out!" he told them. "The girl
isn't dead; she's only asleep." But the crowd
laughed at him. 25After the crowd was put
outside, however, Jesus went in and took
the girl by the hand, and she stood up! 26The
report of this miracle swept through the
entire countryside.

Jesus Heals the Blind

27After Jesus left the girl's home, two blind
men followed along behind him, shouting,
"Son of David, have mercy on us!"
28They went right into the house where he
was staying, and Jesus asked them, "Do you
believe I can make you see?"
"Yes, Lord," they told him, "we do."
29Then he touched their eyes and said,
"Because of your faith, it will happen." 30Then
their eyes were opened, and they could see!
Jesus sternly warned them, "Don't tell anyone
about this." 31But instead, they went out and
spread his fame all over the region.
32When they left, a demon-possessed
man who couldn't speak was brought to
Jesus. 33So Jesus cast out the demon, and
then the man began to speak. The crowds
were amazed. "Nothing like this has ever
happened in Israel!" they exclaimed.

Mission

Mission is all about being sent and going. God is a sending God, which is why the story of redemption begins with God calling Abraham to go, promising that his going would one day affect every nation (Genesis 12:1-3). But sadly, rather than "go," Abraham's descendants, the nation of Israel, preferred to "stay," keeping God's blessing for themselves rather than taking it to others.

So when Israel would not go, God did the "going" himself, coming in the person of his Son, Jesus. Jesus not only spoke about going with the Good News, he also modeled it by going to people that the religious leaders felt weren't worth going to—outcasts like sinners, tax collectors, and prostitutes. And then he told his disciples to go—at first just to Jews (Matthew 10:1-6), but then to every nation (28:19). The book of Acts is the account of how the church put this "going" into practice.

Still today the church is called to "go." The problem is never with the harvest—two thousand years ago Jesus said that "the harvest is great" (Matthew 9:37). The problem is there are not enough workers, which is why we should pray for more (9:38). But praying for workers is never an excuse for not going ourselves. Our God is a going God, and he calls us to go with him. For some, that may simply mean starting to see your workplace as your "mission field" and not just where you earn money; for others, it may involve moving to a different part of your nation or even to another nation. Regardless, Christians should always be ready to go wherever Jesus leads.

▶ *See also **Being a witness**, page 1456.*

34But the Pharisees said, "He can cast out
demons because he is empowered by the
prince of demons."

The Need for Workers

35Jesus traveled through all the towns and
villages of that area, teaching in the synagogues and announcing the Good News
about the Kingdom. And he healed every
kind of disease and illness. 36When he saw
the crowds, he had compassion on them
because they were confused and helpless,
like sheep without a shepherd. 37He said to
his disciples, "The harvest is great, but the
workers are few. 38So pray to the Lord who
is in charge of the harvest; ask him to send
more workers into his fields."

Jesus Sends Out the Twelve Apostles

10 Jesus called his twelve disciples together and gave them authority to
cast out evil* spirits and to heal every kind
of disease and illness. 2Here are the names
of the twelve apostles:

first, Simon (also called Peter),
then Andrew (Peter's brother),
James (son of Zebedee),
John (James's brother),
3 Philip,
Bartholomew,
Thomas,
Matthew (the tax collector),
James (son of Alphaeus),
Thaddaeus,*
4 Simon (the zealot*),
Judas Iscariot (who later betrayed him).

5Jesus sent out the twelve apostles with
these instructions: "Don't go to the Gentiles
or the Samaritans, 6but only to the people of
Israel—God's lost sheep. 7Go and announce
to them that the Kingdom of Heaven is
near.* 8Heal the sick, raise the dead, cure
those with leprosy, and cast out demons.
Give as freely as you have received!

9"Don't take any money in your money
belts—no gold, silver, or even copper coins.
10Don't carry a traveler's bag with a change
of clothes and sandals or even a walking
stick. Don't hesitate to accept hospitality,
because those who work deserve to be fed.

11"Whenever you enter a city or village,
search for a worthy person and stay in his
home until you leave town. 12When you
enter the home, give it your blessing. 13If
it turns out to be a worthy home, let your
blessing stand; if it is not, take back the
blessing. 14If any household or town refuses
to welcome you or listen to your message,
shake its dust from your feet as you leave.
15I tell you the truth, the wicked cities of
Sodom and Gomorrah will be better off than
such a town on the judgment day.

16"Look, I am sending you out as sheep
among wolves. So be as shrewd as snakes
and harmless as doves. 17But beware! For
you will be handed over to the courts
and will be flogged with whips in the
synagogues. 18You will stand trial before
governors and kings because you are my
followers. But this will be your opportunity to tell the rulers and other unbelievers
about me.* 19When you are arrested, don't
worry about how to respond or what to
say. God will give you the right words at
the right time. 20For it is not you who will
be speaking—it will be the Spirit of your
Father speaking through you.

21"A brother will betray his brother
to death, a father will betray his own
child, and children will rebel against their
parents and cause them to be killed. 22And
all nations will hate you because you are
my followers.* But everyone who endures
to the end will be saved. 23When you are
persecuted in one town, flee to the next.
I tell you the truth, the Son of Man* will
return before you have reached all the
towns of Israel.

24"Students* are not greater than their
teacher, and slaves are not greater than
their master. 25Students are to be like their
teacher, and slaves are to be like their
master. And since I, the master of the
household, have been called the prince of
demons,* the members of my household
will be called by even worse names!

26"But don't be afraid of those who
threaten you. For the time is coming when

10:1 Greek *unclean.* **10:3** Other manuscripts read *Lebbaeus;* still others read *Lebbaeus who is called Thaddaeus.* **10:4** Greek *the Cananean,* an Aramaic term for Jewish nationalists. **10:7** Or *has come,* or *is coming soon.* **10:18** Or *But this will be your testimony against the rulers and other unbelievers.* **10:22** Greek *on account of my name.* **10:23** "Son of Man" is a title Jesus used for himself. **10:24** Or *Disciples.* **10:25** Greek *Beelzeboul;* other manuscripts read *Beezeboul;* Latin version reads *Beelzebub.*

▸ **10:2** *See* ***Apostles of Jesus,*** *page 1122.* **10:17** *See* ***Persecution,*** *page 1452.*

everything that is covered will be revealed,
and all that is secret will be made known to
all. 27What I tell you now in the darkness,
shout abroad when daybreak comes. What
I whisper in your ear, shout from the housetops for all to hear!
28"Don't be afraid of those who want to
kill your body; they cannot touch your
soul. Fear only God, who can destroy both
soul and body in hell.* 29What is the price
of two sparrows—one copper coin*? But
not a single sparrow can fall to the ground
without your Father knowing it. 30And the
very hairs on your head are all numbered.
31So don't be afraid; you are more valuable
to God than a whole flock of sparrows.
32"Everyone who acknowledges me publicly here on earth, I will also acknowledge
before my Father in heaven. 33But everyone
who denies me here on earth, I will also
deny before my Father in heaven.
34"Don't imagine that I came to bring
peace to the earth! I came not to bring
peace, but a sword.

35 'I have come to set a man against his
    father,
  a daughter against her mother,
and a daughter-in-law against her
    mother-in-law.
36 Your enemies will be right in your
    own household!'*

37"If you love your father or mother more
than you love me, you are not worthy of
being mine; or if you love your son or
daughter more than me, you are not worthy
of being mine. 38If you refuse to take up your
cross and follow me, you are not worthy of
being mine. 39If you cling to your life, you
will lose it; but if you give up your life for
me, you will find it.
40"Anyone who receives you receives
me, and anyone who receives me receives
the Father who sent me. 41If you receive
a prophet as one who speaks for God,*
you will be given the same reward as a
prophet. And if you receive righteous
people because of their righteousness, you
will be given a reward like theirs. 42And if
you give even a cup of cold water to one of
the least of my followers, you will surely
be rewarded."

Jesus and John the Baptist

11 When Jesus had finished giving these
instructions to his twelve disciples,
he went out to teach and preach in towns
throughout the region.
2John the Baptist, who was in prison,
heard about all the things the Messiah
was doing. So he sent his disciples to ask
Jesus, 3"Are you the Messiah we've been
expecting,* or should we keep looking for
someone else?"
4Jesus told them, "Go back to John and
tell him what you have heard and seen—5the
blind see, the lame walk, those with leprosy
are cured, the deaf hear, the dead are raised
to life, and the Good News is being preached
to the poor." 6And he added, "God blesses
those who do not fall away because of me.*"
7As John's disciples were leaving, Jesus
began talking about him to the crowds.
"What kind of man did you go into the
wilderness to see? Was he a weak reed,
swayed by every breath of wind? 8Or were
you expecting to see a man dressed in expensive clothes? No, people with expensive
clothes live in palaces. 9Were you looking
for a prophet? Yes, and he is more than a
prophet. 10John is the man to whom the
Scriptures refer when they say,

'Look, I am sending my messenger
    ahead of you,
  and he will prepare your way before
    you.'*

11"I tell you the truth, of all who have ever
lived, none is greater than John the Baptist.
Yet even the least person in the Kingdom of
Heaven is greater than he is! 12And from the
time John the Baptist began preaching until
now, the Kingdom of Heaven has been forcefully advancing,* and violent people are attacking it. 13For before John came, all the
prophets and the law of Moses looked forward
to this present time. 14And if you are willing
to accept what I say, he is Elijah, the one the
prophets said would come.* 15Anyone with
ears to hear should listen and understand!
16"To what can I compare this generation?
It is like children playing a game in the public
square. They complain to their friends,

17 'We played wedding songs,
  and you didn't dance,

▸ **11:1-3** *See **Doubt**, page 1414.* **11:2** *See **John the Baptist**, page 1156.*

so we played funeral songs,
and you didn't mourn.'

[18]For John didn't spend his time eating and
drinking, and you say, 'He's possessed by
a demon.' [19]The Son of Man,* on the other
hand, feasts and drinks, and you say, 'He's
a glutton and a drunkard, and a friend of tax
collectors and other sinners!' But wisdom is
shown to be right by its results."

Judgment for the Unbelievers

[20]Then Jesus began to denounce the towns
where he had done so many of his miracles,
because they hadn't repented of their sins
and turned to God. [21]"What sorrow awaits
you, Korazin and Bethsaida! For if the miracles I did in you had been done in wicked
Tyre and Sidon, their people would have
repented of their sins long ago, clothing
themselves in burlap and throwing ashes
on their heads to show their remorse. [22]I tell
you, Tyre and Sidon will be better off on
judgment day than you.

[23]"And you people of Capernaum, will
you be honored in heaven? No, you will go
down to the place of the dead.* For if the
miracles I did for you had been done in
wicked Sodom, it would still be here today.
[24]I tell you, even Sodom will be better off on
judgment day than you."

Jesus' Prayer of Thanksgiving

[25]At that time Jesus prayed this prayer:
"O Father, Lord of heaven and earth, thank
you for hiding these things from those who
think themselves wise and clever, and
for revealing them to the childlike. [26]Yes,
Father, it pleased you to do it this way!

[27]"My Father has entrusted everything to
me. No one truly knows the Son except the
Father, and no one truly knows the Father
except the Son and those to whom the Son
chooses to reveal him."

[28]Then Jesus said, "Come to me, all of you
who are weary and carry heavy burdens,
and I will give you rest. [29]Take my yoke upon
you. Let me teach you, because I am humble
and gentle at heart, and you will find rest
for your souls. [30]For my yoke is easy to bear,
and the burden I give you is light."

A Discussion about the Sabbath

12 At about that time Jesus was walking
through some grainfields on the
Sabbath. His disciples were hungry, so they
began breaking off some heads of grain and

10:28 Greek *Gehenna.* **10:29** Greek *one assarion* [i.e., one "as," a Roman coin equal to 1/16 of a denarius]. **10:35-36** Mic 7:6. **10:41** Greek *receive a prophet in the name of a prophet.* **11:3** Greek *Are you the one who is coming?* **11:6** Or *who are not offended by me.* **11:10** Mal 3:1. **11:12** Or *the Kingdom of Heaven has suffered from violence.* **11:14** See Mal 4:5. **11:19** "Son of Man" is a title Jesus used for himself. **11:23** Greek *to Hades.*

Taking Christ's yoke

Sometimes Jesus' sayings seem strange. In Matthew 11:28-30, he invites those who are burdened to come to him, and he promises them rest. Yet then he invites them to take his yoke upon them. How can you get rid of a burden and pick one up at the same time? Very easily, once we understand the background.

The teachers of religious law (or scribes) and the Pharisees spoke of carrying "the yoke of God's Law," by which they meant taking on oneself the obligation to keep his commandments. The trouble is that they had added so many of their own laws to his Law, in their attempt to explain and apply it, that their yoke had become heavier than God's and everyone struggled to carry it. (We see an example of this in the story that follows in chapter 12, where they complained that Jesus' disciples were "working" on the Sabbath because they picked some grain to satisfy their hunger, an argument Jesus rejected.)

In contrast to their heavy yoke, Jesus says, "My yoke is easy to bear (literally, "kind"), and the burden I give you is light." In other words, taking up the obligation to live his way does not weigh us down but rather lifts us up, for he gives us his Spirit to help us from within. Being a Christian is not about obedience to a list of rules; it is a liberating loyalty to a person.

▶ *See also* ***Discipleship and the cross****, page 1095.*

eating them. 2But some Pharisees saw them
do it and protested, "Look, your disciples
are breaking the law by harvesting grain on
the Sabbath."
3Jesus said to them, "Haven't you read
in the Scriptures what David did when he
and his companions were hungry? 4He went
into the house of God, and he and his companions broke the law by eating the sacred
loaves of bread that only the priests are
allowed to eat. 5And haven't you read in the
law of Moses that the priests on duty in the
Temple may work on the Sabbath? 6I tell
you, there is one here who is even greater
than the Temple! 7But you would not have
condemned my innocent disciples if you
knew the meaning of this Scripture: 'I want
you to show mercy, not offer sacrifices.'*
8For the Son of Man* is Lord, even over the
Sabbath!"

Jesus Heals on the Sabbath

9Then Jesus went over to their synagogue,
10where he noticed a man with a deformed
hand. The Pharisees asked Jesus, "Does the
law permit a person to work by healing on
the Sabbath?" (They were hoping he would
say yes, so they could bring charges against
him.)
11And he answered, "If you had a sheep
that fell into a well on the Sabbath, wouldn't
you work to pull it out? Of course you
would. 12And how much more valuable is a
person than a sheep! Yes, the law permits a
person to do good on the Sabbath."
13Then he said to the man, "Hold out your
hand." So the man held out his hand, and it
was restored, just like the other one! 14Then
the Pharisees called a meeting to plot how
to kill Jesus.

Jesus, God's Chosen Servant

15But Jesus knew what they were planning.
So he left that area, and many people followed him. He healed all the sick among
them, 16but he warned them not to reveal
who he was. 17This fulfilled the prophecy of
Isaiah concerning him:

18 "Look at my Servant, whom I have
chosen.
He is my Beloved, who pleases me.
I will put my Spirit upon him,
and he will proclaim justice to the
nations.
19 He will not fight or shout
or raise his voice in public.
20 He will not crush the weakest reed
or put out a flickering candle.
Finally he will cause justice to be
victorious.
21 And his name will be the hope
of all the world."*

▸ **12:1** *See **Sunday**, page 1121.*

The Pharisees

Some of Jesus' most vociferous opponents were the Pharisees. Being a Pharisee wasn't a job (most were middle-class merchants), but a lifestyle. Pharisees lived in scrupulous obedience to both the Jewish Law and all the oral traditions based on it that had developed over the generations. While often seen today as hypocrites concerned only with externals, they never in fact saw obedience and purity as an end in itself, but rather as essential to preparing for God's coming to liberate his people. They clashed with Jesus so much because they saw his teaching and lifestyle as undermining the Law and therefore keeping God from coming—ironic, since God was there in person before their eyes, yet their traditions kept them from seeing it. Jesus said that their traditions and interpretations undermined God's original intentions (e.g., Matthew 5:21-48) and that their teaching one thing but doing another made them hypocrites (e.g., 23:1-39). For Jesus, real holiness was not about avoiding wrongdoers but taking hold of them and transforming them into something good and powerful.

▸ *See also **The Sadducees**, page 1104.*

Jesus and the Prince of Demons

[22]Then a demon-possessed man, who was blind and couldn't speak, was brought to Jesus. He healed the man so that he could both speak and see. [23]The crowd was amazed and asked, "Could it be that Jesus is the Son of David, the Messiah?"

[24]But when the Pharisees heard about the miracle, they said, "No wonder he can cast out demons. He gets his power from Satan,* the prince of demons."

[25]Jesus knew their thoughts and replied, "Any kingdom divided by civil war is doomed. A town or family splintered by feuding will fall apart. [26]And if Satan is casting out Satan, he is divided and fighting against himself. His own kingdom will not survive. [27]And if I am empowered by Satan, what about your own exorcists? They cast out demons, too, so they will condemn you for what you have said. [28]But if I am casting out demons by the Spirit of God, then the Kingdom of God has arrived among you. [29]For who is powerful enough to enter the house of a strong man and plunder his goods? Only someone even stronger—someone who could tie him up and then plunder his house.

[30]"Anyone who isn't with me opposes me, and anyone who isn't working with me is actually working against me.

[31]"So I tell you, every sin and blasphemy can be forgiven—except blasphemy against the Holy Spirit, which will never be forgiven. [32]Anyone who speaks against the Son of Man can be forgiven, but anyone who speaks against the Holy Spirit will never be forgiven, either in this world or in the world to come.

[33]"A tree is identified by its fruit. If a tree is good, its fruit will be good. If a tree is bad, its fruit will be bad. [34]You brood of snakes! How could evil men like you speak what is good and right? For whatever is in your heart determines what you say. [35]A good person produces good things from the treasury of a good heart, and an evil person produces evil things from the treasury of an evil heart. [36]And I tell you this, you must give an account on judgment day for every idle word you speak. [37]The words you say will either acquit you or condemn you."

The Sign of Jonah

[38]One day some teachers of religious law and Pharisees came to Jesus and said, "Teacher, we want you to show us a miraculous sign to prove your authority."

[39]But Jesus replied, "Only an evil, adulterous generation would demand a miraculous sign; but the only sign I will give them is the sign of the prophet Jonah. [40]For as Jonah was in the belly of the great fish for three days and three nights, so will the Son of Man be in the heart of the earth for three days and three nights.

[41]"The people of Nineveh will stand up against this generation on judgment day and condemn it, for they repented of their sins at the preaching of Jonah. Now someone greater than Jonah is here—but you refuse to repent. [42]The queen of Sheba* will also stand up against this generation on judgment day and condemn it, for she came from a distant land to hear the wisdom of Solomon. Now someone greater than Solomon is here—but you refuse to listen.

[43]"When an evil* spirit leaves a person, it goes into the desert, seeking rest but finding none. [44]Then it says, 'I will return to the person I came from.' So it returns and finds its former home empty, swept, and in order. [45]Then the spirit finds seven other spirits more evil than itself, and they all enter the person and live there. And so that person is worse off than before. That will be the experience of this evil generation."

The True Family of Jesus

[46]As Jesus was speaking to the crowd, his mother and brothers stood outside, asking to speak to him. [47]Someone told Jesus, "Your mother and your brothers are standing outside, and they want to speak to you."*

[48]Jesus asked, "Who is my mother? Who are my brothers?" [49]Then he pointed to his disciples and said, "Look, these are my mother and brothers. [50]Anyone who does the will of my Father in heaven is my brother and sister and mother!"

12:7 Hos 6:6 (Greek version). **12:8** "Son of Man" is a title Jesus used for himself. **12:18-21** Isa 42:1-4 (Greek version for 42:4). **12:24** Greek *Beelzeboul;* also in 12:27. Other manuscripts read *Beezeboul;* Latin version reads *Beelzebub.* **12:42** Greek *The queen of the south.* **12:43** Greek *unclean.* **12:47** Some manuscripts do not include verse 47. Compare Mark 3:32 and Luke 8:20.

▸ **12:32** *See* ***Is there anything God won't forgive?****, page 633.* **12:34** *See* ***Speech****, page 1416.*

Parable of the Farmer Scattering Seed

13 Later that same day Jesus left the
house and sat beside the lake. [2]A
large crowd soon gathered around him, so
he got into a boat. Then he sat there and
taught as the people stood on the shore. [3]He
told many stories in the form of parables,
such as this one:

"Listen! A farmer went out to plant
some seeds. [4]As he scattered them across
his field, some seeds fell on a footpath,
and the birds came and ate them. [5]Other
seeds fell on shallow soil with underlying
rock. The seeds sprouted quickly because
the soil was shallow. [6]But the plants soon
wilted under the hot sun, and since they
didn't have deep roots, they died. [7]Other
seeds fell among thorns that grew up and
choked out the tender plants. [8]Still other
seeds fell on fertile soil, and they produced a crop that was thirty, sixty, and
even a hundred times as much as had been
planted! [9]Anyone with ears to hear should
listen and understand."

[10]His disciples came and asked him, "Why
do you use parables when you talk to the
people?"

[11]He replied, "You are permitted to
understand the secrets* of the Kingdom
of Heaven, but others are not. [12]To those
who listen to my teaching, more understanding will be given, and they will have
an abundance of knowledge. But for those
who are not listening, even what little
understanding they have will be taken
away from them. [13]That is why I use these
parables,

> For they look, but they don't really see.
> They hear, but they don't really listen
> or understand.

[14]This fulfills the prophecy of Isaiah that
says,

> 'When you hear what I say,
> you will not understand.
> When you see what I do,
> you will not comprehend.
> [15] For the hearts of these people are
> hardened,
> and their ears cannot hear,
> and they have closed their eyes—
> so their eyes cannot see,
> and their ears cannot hear,
> and their hearts cannot
> understand,
> and they cannot turn to me
> and let me heal them.'*

13:11 Greek *the mysteries.* **13:14-15** Isa 6:9-10 (Greek version).

The parables of Jesus

Stories communicate powerfully and memorably (we often remember a story when we can't remember a list of points). While Jesus wasn't the first to use stories (prophets and rabbis had done so), he did not use them as mere illustrations, but as the essence of what he wanted to teach. In fact, one-third of his teaching is in parables—sometimes long stories, sometimes short sayings; sometimes serious, sometimes hilarious (e.g., a man walking around with a log in his eye!). All of them were rooted in everyday life—like sowing seed or catching fish (Matthew 13)—or recent events, like Herod going to Rome to be appointed king (Luke 19:12).

However, his stories rarely unfolded as you would expect. Workers who only worked for part of the day received a full-day's wage (Matthew 20:1-16). A Samaritan, not the religious leaders, helped the man who was robbed (Luke 10:30-37). What Jesus was doing was getting people to stop and think. But although parables helped some to understand, they also blinded others to the truth—which is why he used them (Matthew 13:10-17). The parables called for faith.

When reading parables, remember that they have one main point, as the context normally shows—e.g., the parable of the unforgiving debtor (18:22-35) was told in response to a question (18:21). The whole parable is the answer. If we try to interpret every detail of the story, then we will miss Jesus' point completely.

▶ *See also* ***Hardness of heart****, page 1132.*

Jesus' parables

Parable	Matthew	Mark	Luke
A lamp under a basket	5:14-15	4:21-22	8:16; 11:33
The wise and foolish builders	7:24-27		6:47-49
New cloth on old clothing	9:16	2:21	5:36
New wine in old wineskins	9:17	2:22	5:37-38
The farmer and the soils	13:3-8	4:2-20	8:4-8
The weeds	13:24-30		
The mustard seed	13:31-32	4:30-32	13:18-19
The yeast	13:33		13:20-21
The hidden treasure	13:44		
The valuable pearl	13:45-46		
The net	13:47-48		
A homeowner	13:52		
The lost sheep	18:12-13		15:4-6
The unforgiving debtor	18:23-34		
The vineyard workers	20:1-16		
The two sons	21:28-31		
The evil farmers	21:33-41	12:1-9	20:9-16
The wedding feast	22:2-14		
The fig tree	24:32-33	13:28-29	21:29-32
The ten bridesmaids	25:1-13		
The bags of silver (talents)	25:14-30		cp. 19:12-27
The sheep and the goats	25:31-46		
The growing seed		4:26-29	
A moneylender			7:41-43
The good Samaritan			10:30-37
A friend in need			11:5-8
The rich fool			12:16-21
Watchful servants			12:35-40
The unfruitful fig tree			13:6-9
The lowest place at the feast			14:7-14
The great feast			14:16-24
The cost of discipleship			14:28-33
A lost coin			15:8-10
The lost son			15:11-32
The shrewd manager			16:1-8
A rich man and Lazarus			16:19-31
A master and his servant			17:7-10
A persistent widow			18:2-8
A Pharisee and a tax collector			18:10-14

16“But blessed are your eyes, because they see; and your ears, because they hear. 17I tell you the truth, many prophets and righteous people longed to see what you see, but they didn’t see it. And they longed to hear what you hear, but they didn’t hear it.

18“Now listen to the explanation of the parable about the farmer planting seeds: 19The seed that fell on the footpath represents those who hear the message about the Kingdom and don’t understand it. Then the evil one comes and snatches away the seed that was planted in their hearts. 20The seed on the rocky soil represents those who hear the message and immediately receive it with joy. 21But since they don’t have deep roots, they don’t last long. They fall away as soon as they have problems or are persecuted for believing God’s word. 22The seed that fell among the thorns represents those who hear God’s word, but all too quickly the message is crowded out by the worries of this life and the lure of wealth, so no fruit is produced. 23The seed that fell on good soil represents those who truly hear and understand God’s word and produce a harvest of thirty, sixty, or even a hundred times as much as had been planted!”

Parable of the Wheat and Weeds

24Here is another story Jesus told: “The Kingdom of Heaven is like a farmer who planted good seed in his field. 25But that night as the workers slept, his enemy came and planted weeds among the wheat, then slipped away. 26When the crop began to grow and produce grain, the weeds also grew.

27“The farmer’s workers went to him and said, ‘Sir, the field where you planted that good seed is full of weeds! Where did they come from?’

28“‘An enemy has done this!’ the farmer exclaimed.

“‘Should we pull out the weeds?’ they asked.

29“‘No,’ he replied, ‘you’ll uproot the wheat if you do. 30Let both grow together until the harvest. Then I will tell the harvesters to sort out the weeds, tie them into bundles, and burn them, and to put the wheat in the barn.’”

Parable of the Mustard Seed

31Here is another illustration Jesus used: “The Kingdom of Heaven is like a mustard seed planted in a field. 32It is the smallest of all seeds, but it becomes the largest of garden plants; it grows into a tree, and birds come and make nests in its branches.”

Parable of the Yeast

33Jesus also used this illustration: “The Kingdom of Heaven is like the yeast a woman used in making bread. Even though she put only a little yeast in three measures of flour, it permeated every part of the dough.”

34Jesus always used stories and illustrations like these when speaking to the crowds. In fact, he never spoke to them without using such parables. 35This fulfilled what God had spoken through the prophet:

“I will speak to you in parables.
  I will explain things hidden since the
    creation of the world.*”

Parable of the Wheat and Weeds Explained

36Then, leaving the crowds outside, Jesus went into the house. His disciples said, “Please explain to us the story of the weeds in the field.”

37Jesus replied, “The Son of Man* is the farmer who plants the good seed. 38The field is the world, and the good seed represents the people of the Kingdom. The weeds are the people who belong to the evil one. 39The enemy who planted the weeds among the wheat is the devil. The harvest is the end of the world,* and the harvesters are the angels.

40“Just as the weeds are sorted out and burned in the fire, so it will be at the end of the world. 41The Son of Man will send his angels, and they will remove from his Kingdom everything that causes sin and all who do evil. 42And the angels will throw them into the fiery furnace, where there will be weeping and gnashing of teeth. 43Then the righteous will shine like the sun in their Father’s Kingdom. Anyone with ears to hear should listen and understand!

Parables of the Hidden Treasure and the Pearl

44“The Kingdom of Heaven is like a treasure that a man discovered hidden in a field. In his excitement, he hid it again and sold everything he owned to get enough money to buy the field.

45“Again, the Kingdom of Heaven is like a merchant on the lookout for choice pearls.

46 When he discovered a pearl of great value,
he sold everything he owned and bought it!

Parable of the Fishing Net

47 "Again, the Kingdom of Heaven is like a
fishing net that was thrown into the water
and caught fish of every kind. 48 When the
net was full, they dragged it up onto the
shore, sat down, and sorted the good fish
into crates, but threw the bad ones away.
49 That is the way it will be at the end of the
world. The angels will come and separate the
wicked people from the righteous, 50 throwing the wicked into the fiery furnace, where
there will be weeping and gnashing of teeth.
51 Do you understand all these things?"

"Yes," they said, "we do."

52 Then he added, "Every teacher of religious law who becomes a disciple in the
Kingdom of Heaven is like a homeowner
who brings from his storeroom new gems
of truth as well as old."

Jesus Rejected at Nazareth

53 When Jesus had finished telling these
stories and illustrations, he left that part
of the country. 54 He returned to Nazareth,
his hometown. When he taught there in the
synagogue, everyone was amazed and said,
"Where does he get this wisdom and the
power to do miracles?" 55 Then they scoffed,
"He's just the carpenter's son, and we know
Mary, his mother, and his brothers—James,
Joseph,* Simon, and Judas. 56 All his sisters
live right here among us. Where did he learn
all these things?" 57 And they were deeply offended and refused to believe in him.

Then Jesus told them, "A prophet is
honored everywhere except in his own
hometown and among his own family."
58 And so he did only a few miracles there
because of their unbelief.

The Death of John the Baptist

14 When Herod Antipas, the ruler of
Galilee,* heard about Jesus, 2 he said
to his advisers, "This must be John the
Baptist raised from the dead! That is why
he can do such miracles."

3 For Herod had arrested and imprisoned
John as a favor to his wife Herodias (the
former wife of Herod's brother Philip). 4 John
had been telling Herod, "It is against God's
law for you to marry her." 5 Herod wanted to
kill John, but he was afraid of a riot, because
all the people believed John was a prophet.

6 But at a birthday party for Herod, Herodias's daughter performed a dance that
greatly pleased him, 7 so he promised with
a vow to give her anything she wanted. 8 At
her mother's urging, the girl said, "I want
the head of John the Baptist on a tray!"
9 Then the king regretted what he had said;
but because of the vow he had made in
front of his guests, he issued the necessary orders. 10 So John was beheaded in the
prison, 11 and his head was brought on a
tray and given to the girl, who took it to her
mother. 12 Later, John's disciples came for his
body and buried it. Then they went and told
Jesus what had happened.

Jesus Feeds Five Thousand

13 As soon as Jesus heard the news, he left
in a boat to a remote area to be alone. But
the crowds heard where he was headed and
followed on foot from many towns. 14 Jesus
saw the huge crowd as he stepped from the
boat, and he had compassion on them and
healed their sick.

15 That evening the disciples came to him
and said, "This is a remote place, and it's
already getting late. Send the crowds away
so they can go to the villages and buy food
for themselves."

16 But Jesus said, "That isn't necessary—
you feed them."

17 "But we have only five loaves of bread
and two fish!" they answered.

18 "Bring them here," he said. 19 Then he
told the people to sit down on the grass.
Jesus took the five loaves and two fish,
looked up toward heaven, and blessed
them. Then, breaking the loaves into pieces,
he gave the bread to the disciples, who distributed it to the people. 20 They all ate as
much as they wanted, and afterward, the
disciples picked up twelve baskets of leftovers. 21 About 5,000 men were fed that day,
in addition to all the women and children!

13:35 Some manuscripts do not include *of the world.* Ps 78:2. **13:37** "Son of Man" is a title Jesus used for himself. **13:39** Or *the age;* also in 13:40, 49. **13:55** Other manuscripts read *Joses;* still others read *John.* **14:1** Greek *Herod the tetrarch.* Herod Antipas was a son of King Herod and was ruler over Galilee.

▸ **14:1-2** *See **John the Baptist**, page 1156.*

Jesus Walks on Water

22 Immediately after this, Jesus insisted that
his disciples get back into the boat and
cross to the other side of the lake, while
he sent the people home. 23 After sending
them home, he went up into the hills by
himself to pray. Night fell while he was
there alone.
24 Meanwhile, the disciples were in trouble
far away from land, for a strong wind had
risen, and they were fighting heavy waves.
25 About three o'clock in the morning* Jesus
came toward them, walking on the water.
26 When the disciples saw him walking on
the water, they were terrified. In their fear,
they cried out, "It's a ghost!"
27 But Jesus spoke to them at once. "Don't
be afraid," he said. "Take courage. I am
here!*"
28 Then Peter called to him, "Lord, if it's
really you, tell me to come to you, walking
on the water."
29 "Yes, come," Jesus said.
So Peter went over the side of the boat
and walked on the water toward Jesus.
30 But when he saw the strong* wind and the
waves, he was terrified and began to sink.
"Save me, Lord!" he shouted.
31 Jesus immediately reached out and
grabbed him. "You have so little faith,"
Jesus said. "Why did you doubt me?"
32 When they climbed back into the boat,
the wind stopped. 33 Then the disciples worshiped him. "You really are the Son of God!"
they exclaimed.
34 After they had crossed the lake, they
landed at Gennesaret. 35 When the people
recognized Jesus, the news of his arrival
spread quickly throughout the whole area,
and soon people were bringing all their sick
to be healed. 36 They begged him to let the
sick touch at least the fringe of his robe, and
all who touched him were healed.

Jesus Teaches about Inner Purity

15 Some Pharisees and teachers of religious law now arrived from Jerusalem
to see Jesus. They asked him, 2 "Why do your
disciples disobey our age-old tradition? For
they ignore our tradition of ceremonial
hand washing before they eat."
3 Jesus replied, "And why do you, by
your traditions, violate the direct commandments of God? 4 For instance, God
says, 'Honor your father and mother,'*
and 'Anyone who speaks disrespectfully
of father or mother must be put to death.'*
5 But you say it is all right for people to say

Galilee

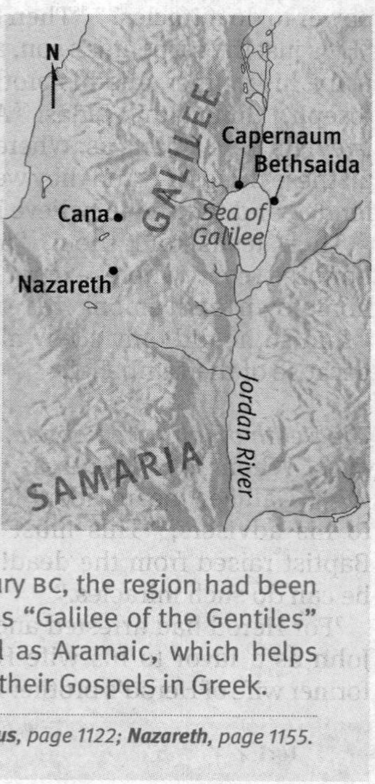

Galilee, which was ruled by Herod Antipas (Matthew 14:1), was a hilly, fertile region lying west of the Jordan River and the Sea of Galilee and north of Samaria. Several major roads passed through it, bringing with them trade and prosperity. Its lake—called the Sea of Kinnereth in Old Testament times and the Sea of Galilee, Sea of Tiberias, and Lake Gennesaret in New Testament times—supported a vibrant fishing industry, which added to its general prosperity. Several of Jesus' disciples had fished these waters. The region had a population of around 300,000 people, who lived in some two hundred small towns and villages. One such town was Nazareth, Jesus' hometown, whose population was no more than a few hundred. After Assyria's invasion in the eighth century BC, the region had been settled by non-Jewish immigrants and became known as "Galilee of the Gentiles" (see 4:15). People there generally spoke Greek as well as Aramaic, which helps explain why the Galileans Matthew and John could write their Gospels in Greek.

▸ *See also* ***The Herods****, page 1072;* ***Capernaum****, page 1096;* ***Apostles of Jesus****, page 1122;* ***Nazareth****, page 1155.*

to their parents, 'Sorry, I can't help you. For
I have vowed to give to God what I would
have given to you.' [6]In this way, you say they
don't need to honor their parents.* And so
you cancel the word of God for the sake of
your own tradition. [7]You hypocrites! Isaiah
was right when he prophesied about you,
for he wrote,

[8] 'These people honor me with their lips,
but their hearts are far from me.
[9] Their worship is a farce,
for they teach man-made ideas as
commands from God.'*"

[10]Then Jesus called to the crowd to
come and hear. "Listen," he said, "and try
to understand. [11]It's not what goes into your
mouth that defiles you; you are defiled by
the words that come out of your mouth."
[12]Then the disciples came to him and
asked, "Do you realize you offended the
Pharisees by what you just said?"
[13]Jesus replied, "Every plant not planted
by my heavenly Father will be uprooted, [14]so
ignore them. They are blind guides leading
the blind, and if one blind person guides
another, they will both fall into a ditch."
[15]Then Peter said to Jesus, "Explain to us
the parable that says people aren't defiled
by what they eat."
[16]"Don't you understand yet?" Jesus
asked. [17]"Anything you eat passes through
the stomach and then goes into the sewer.
[18]But the words you speak come from the
heart—that's what defiles you. [19]For from
the heart come evil thoughts, murder, adultery, all sexual immorality, theft, lying,
and slander. [20]These are what defile you.
Eating with unwashed hands will never
defile you."

The Faith of a Gentile Woman

[21]Then Jesus left Galilee and went north to
the region of Tyre and Sidon. [22]A Gentile*
woman who lived there came to him, pleading, "Have mercy on me, O Lord, Son of
David! For my daughter is possessed by a
demon that torments her severely."
[23]But Jesus gave her no reply, not even a
word. Then his disciples urged him to send
her away. "Tell her to go away," they said.
"She is bothering us with all her begging."
[24]Then Jesus said to the woman, "I was
sent only to help God's lost sheep—the
people of Israel."
[25]But she came and worshiped him,
pleading again, "Lord, help me!"
[26]Jesus responded, "It isn't right to take
food from the children and throw it to the
dogs."
[27]She replied, "That's true, Lord, but even
dogs are allowed to eat the scraps that fall
beneath their masters' table."
[28]"Dear woman," Jesus said to her, "your

14:25 Greek *In the fourth watch of the night.* **14:27** Or *The 'I AM' is here;* Greek reads *I am.* See Exod 3:14. **14:30** Some manuscripts do not include *strong.* **15:4a** Exod 20:12; Deut 5:16. **15:4b** Exod 21:17 (Greek version); Lev 20:9 (Greek version). **15:6** Greek *their father;* other manuscripts read *their father or their mother.* **15:8-9** Isa 29:13 (Greek version). **15:22** Greek *Canaanite.*

Tyre and Sidon

In contrast to the Pharisees, who rejected Jesus' message because he wouldn't keep their traditions (Matthew 15:1-20), Matthew tells us of a Gentile woman who was so desperate for her daughter to be healed that she broke all traditions—including that of a woman not speaking to a male stranger in public. She came from "the region of Tyre and Sidon" (15:21), two important seaports of Phoenicia (modern Lebanon), to the northwest of Galilee. Notorious to Jews for both its godless lifestyle and its Canaanite religion since the time of Jezebel (1 Kings 16:30-31), the region had been heavily influenced by Greek culture, which only made it worse in Jewish eyes. Yet no nation or people group is beyond God's reach, as this story shows. While Jesus' mission was first to the Jews, it didn't stop there, as he would later make very clear (e.g., Matthew 28:18-20), and the woman's faith found healing for her daughter.

▶ *See also* ***Mission****, page 1082;* ***The mission of Jesus****, page 1159.*

faith is great. Your request is granted." And her daughter was instantly healed.

Jesus Heals Many People

29 Jesus returned to the Sea of Galilee and climbed a hill and sat down. 30 A vast crowd brought to him people who were lame, blind, crippled, those who couldn't speak, and many others. They laid them before Jesus, and he healed them all. 31 The crowd was amazed! Those who hadn't been able to speak were talking, the crippled were made well, the lame were walking, and the blind could see again! And they praised the God of Israel.

Jesus Feeds Four Thousand

32 Then Jesus called his disciples and told them, "I feel sorry for these people. They have been here with me for three days, and they have nothing left to eat. I don't want to send them away hungry, or they will faint along the way."

33 The disciples replied, "Where would we get enough food here in the wilderness for such a huge crowd?"

34 Jesus asked, "How much bread do you have?"

They replied, "Seven loaves, and a few small fish."

35 So Jesus told all the people to sit down on the ground. 36 Then he took the seven loaves and the fish, thanked God for them, and broke them into pieces. He gave them to the disciples, who distributed the food to the crowd.

37 They all ate as much as they wanted. Afterward, the disciples picked up seven large baskets of leftover food. 38 There were 4,000 men who were fed that day, in addition to all the women and children. 39 Then Jesus sent the people home, and he got into a boat and crossed over to the region of Magadan.

Leaders Demand a Miraculous Sign

16 One day the Pharisees and Sadducees came to test Jesus, demanding that he show them a miraculous sign from heaven to prove his authority.

2 He replied, "You know the saying, 'Red sky at night means fair weather tomorrow; 3 red sky in the morning means foul weather all day.' You know how to interpret the weather signs in the sky, but you don't know how to interpret the signs of the times!* 4 Only an evil, adulterous generation would demand a miraculous sign, but the only sign I will give them is the sign of the prophet Jonah.*" Then Jesus left them and went away.

Yeast of the Pharisees and Sadducees

5 Later, after they crossed to the other side of the lake, the disciples discovered they had forgotten to bring any bread. 6 "Watch out!" Jesus warned them. "Beware of the yeast of the Pharisees and Sadducees."

7 At this they began to argue with each other because they hadn't brought any bread. 8 Jesus knew what they were saying, so he said, "You have so little faith! Why are you arguing with each other about having no bread? 9 Don't you understand even yet? Don't you remember the 5,000 I fed with five loaves, and the baskets of leftovers you

Caesarea Philippi

Jesus could not have picked a better place than Caesarea Philippi to ask his disciples who they thought he was. Caesarea Philippi had been rebuilt on the site of Paneas by Philip, son of Herod the Great, in honor of Tiberius Caesar. It lay twenty-five miles north of the Sea of Galilee at the foot of Mount Hermon, by the source of the Jordan River. In earlier times it had been a place of Baal worship and was now renowned for its shrines to the nature-god Pan and its temple honoring Caesar Augustus. In a place steeped in religious alternatives, Jesus asked his disciples to decide, for he could not be just one among many. Peter chose rightly when he declared that Jesus (not Pan, Caesar, or any other religious figure) was "the Messiah, the Son of the living God" (Matthew 16:16). Such a clear answer is always blessed (16:17-19).

▶ *See also **Peter**, page 1421.*

picked up? [10]Or the 4,000 I fed with seven loaves, and the large baskets of leftovers you picked up? [11]Why can't you understand that I'm not talking about bread? So again I say, 'Beware of the yeast of the Pharisees and Sadducees.'"

[12]Then at last they understood that he wasn't speaking about the yeast in bread, but about the deceptive teaching of the Pharisees and Sadducees.

Peter's Declaration about Jesus

[13]When Jesus came to the region of Caesarea Philippi, he asked his disciples, "Who do people say that the Son of Man is?"*

[14]"Well," they replied, "some say John the Baptist, some say Elijah, and others say Jeremiah or one of the other prophets."

[15]Then he asked them, "But who do you say I am?"

[16]Simon Peter answered, "You are the Messiah,* the Son of the living God."

[17]Jesus replied, "You are blessed, Simon son of John,* because my Father in heaven has revealed this to you. You did not learn this from any human being. [18]Now I say to you that you are Peter (which means 'rock'),* and upon this rock I will build my church, and all the powers of hell* will not conquer it. [19]And I will give you the keys of the Kingdom of Heaven. Whatever you forbid* on earth will be forbidden in heaven, and whatever you permit* on earth will be permitted in heaven."

[20]Then he sternly warned the disciples not to tell anyone that he was the Messiah.

Jesus Predicts His Death

[21]From then on Jesus* began to tell his disciples plainly that it was necessary for him to go to Jerusalem, and that he would suffer many terrible things at the hands of the elders, the leading priests, and the teachers of religious law. He would be killed, but on the third day he would be raised from the dead.

[22]But Peter took him aside and began to reprimand him* for saying such things. "Heaven forbid, Lord," he said. "This will never happen to you!"

16:2-3 Several manuscripts do not include any of the words in 16:2-3 after *He replied.* **16:4** Greek *the sign of Jonah.* **16:13** "Son of Man" is a title Jesus used for himself. **16:16** Or *the Christ. Messiah* (a Hebrew term) and *Christ* (a Greek term) both mean "anointed one." **16:17** Greek *Simon bar-Jonah;* see John 1:42; 21:15-17. **16:18a** Greek *that you are Peter.* **16:18b** Greek *and the gates of Hades.* **16:19a** Or *bind,* or *lock.* **16:19b** Or *loose,* or *open.* **16:21** Some manuscripts read *Jesus the Messiah.* **16:22** Or *began to correct him.*

▸ **16:19** *See* ***The keys of the Kingdom****, page 770.*

Discipleship and the cross

Two and a half years of amazing teaching and stunning miracles had caused many people to think that Jesus must be John the Baptist raised from the dead, or maybe Elijah or another prophet. But Jesus asked Peter the most important question anyone must answer in life: "But who do you say I am?" (Matthew 16:15). By now, Peter had got it!—"You are the Messiah, the Son of the living God" (16:16). On such a confession, Jesus could build his church (16:18).

But when Jesus then started talking about being killed, Peter rebuked him (16:21-22). In Peter's mind (like everyone else's in those days), the Messiah was expected to expel the Romans and establish God's Kingdom. But this was so far from the truth that Jesus called him "Satan." God's Kingdom would not come through violence, but through suffering, as the prophets had foretold (e.g., Isaiah 53). But Jesus hadn't finished, for not only did a cross lie ahead for him, but also for everyone who wants to be his disciple (Matthew 16:24). And trying to avoid it would only lead to losing one's life, not saving it (16:25-26).

Today, some preachers teach only victory, health, and prosperity for Christians, but this is not how Jesus saw things. Discipleship will always involve a cross, in one way or another.

▸ *See also* ***Counting the cost****, page 1180;* ***Life from death****, page 1219;* ***Mentoring****, page 1385.*

23 Jesus turned to Peter and said, "Get away
from me, Satan! You are a dangerous trap
to me. You are seeing things merely from a
human point of view, not from God's."
24 Then Jesus said to his disciples, "If any of
you wants to be my follower, you must give
up your own way, take up your cross, and
follow me. 25 If you try to hang on to your life,
you will lose it. But if you give up your life for
my sake, you will save it. 26 And what do you
benefit if you gain the whole world but lose
your own soul?* Is anything worth more than
your soul? 27 For the Son of Man will come
with his angels in the glory of his Father and
will judge all people according to their deeds.
28 And I tell you the truth, some standing here
right now will not die before they see the Son
of Man coming in his Kingdom."

The Transfiguration

17 Six days later Jesus took Peter and the
two brothers, James and John, and led
them up a high mountain to be alone. 2 As
the men watched, Jesus' appearance was
transformed so that his face shone like the
sun, and his clothes became as white as
light. 3 Suddenly, Moses and Elijah appeared
and began talking with Jesus.
4 Peter exclaimed, "Lord, it's wonderful
for us to be here! If you want, I'll make three
shelters as memorials*—one for you, one
for Moses, and one for Elijah."
5 But even as he spoke, a bright cloud
overshadowed them, and a voice from the
cloud said, "This is my dearly loved Son,
who brings me great joy. Listen to him."
6 The disciples were terrified and fell face
down on the ground.
7 Then Jesus came over and touched them.
"Get up," he said. "Don't be afraid." 8 And
when they looked up, Moses and Elijah
were gone, and they saw only Jesus.
9 As they went back down the mountain,
Jesus commanded them, "Don't tell anyone
what you have seen until the Son of Man*
has been raised from the dead."
10 Then his disciples asked him, "Why do
the teachers of religious law insist that Elijah
must return before the Messiah comes?*"
11 Jesus replied, "Elijah is indeed coming
first to get everything ready. 12 But I tell you,
Elijah has already come, but he wasn't recognized, and they chose to abuse him. And
in the same way they will also make the Son
of Man suffer." 13 Then the disciples realized
he was talking about John the Baptist.

Jesus Heals a Demon-Possessed Boy

14 At the foot of the mountain, a large crowd
was waiting for them. A man came and knelt
before Jesus and said, 15 "Lord, have mercy
on my son. He has seizures and suffers terribly. He often falls into the fire or into the
water. 16 So I brought him to your disciples,
but they couldn't heal him."
17 Jesus said, "You faithless and corrupt

▸ **17:2** *See **The Transfiguration**, page 1169.*

Capernaum

In Matthew 17:24, Jesus and his disciples returned to Capernaum (Kephar Nahum, "the village of Nahum"). Jesus had relocated to Capernaum after being rejected by his hometown of Nazareth (Luke 4:16-31). Capernaum, a small town of around 1,500 inhabitants, was on the northern shore of the Sea of Galilee, one of several towns that had developed around the lake because of the fishing industry it supported. Jesus' relocation here was very strategic. The main north–south highway ran just outside the town and generated a lot of business. So although Capernaum was relatively affluent, it was also fairly quiet and therefore an ideal place to which Jesus could retreat. He saw coming here as coming back home (Mark 2:1)—especially Peter's house. But despite the many miracles he performed here, Jesus condemned Capernaum's and other neighboring towns' unbelief (Matthew 11:20-24).

▸ *See also **Galilee**, page 1092.*

people! How long must I be with you? How
long must I put up with you? Bring the
boy here to me." 18 Then Jesus rebuked the
demon in the boy, and it left him. From that
moment the boy was well.
19 Afterward the disciples asked Jesus
privately, "Why couldn't we cast out that
demon?"
20 "You don't have enough faith," Jesus
told them. "I tell you the truth, if you had
faith even as small as a mustard seed, you
could say to this mountain, 'Move from here
to there,' and it would move. Nothing would
be impossible.*"

Jesus Again Predicts His Death

22 After they gathered again in Galilee, Jesus
told them, "The Son of Man is going to be
betrayed into the hands of his enemies. 23 He
will be killed, but on the third day he will
be raised from the dead." And the disciples
were filled with grief.

Payment of the Temple Tax

24 On their arrival in Capernaum, the collectors of the Temple tax* came to Peter and
asked him, "Doesn't your teacher pay the
Temple tax?"
25 "Yes, he does," Peter replied. Then he
went into the house.

But before he had a chance to speak, Jesus
asked him, "What do you think, Peter?* Do
kings tax their own people or the people
they have conquered?*"
26 "They tax the people they have conquered," Peter replied.

"Well, then," Jesus said, "the citizens are
free! 27 However, we don't want to offend
them, so go down to the lake and throw in
a line. Open the mouth of the first fish you
catch, and you will find a large silver coin.*
Take it and pay the tax for both of us."

The Greatest in the Kingdom

18 About that time the disciples came to
Jesus and asked, "Who is greatest in
the Kingdom of Heaven?"
2 Jesus called a little child to him and put
the child among them. 3 Then he said, "I tell
you the truth, unless you turn from your sins
and become like little children, you will never
get into the Kingdom of Heaven. 4 So anyone
who becomes as humble as this little child is
the greatest in the Kingdom of Heaven.
5 "And anyone who welcomes a little child
like this on my behalf* is welcoming me.
6 But if you cause one of these little ones
who trusts in me to fall into sin, it would
be better for you to have a large millstone
tied around your neck and be drowned in
the depths of the sea.
7 "What sorrow awaits the world, because
it tempts people to sin. Temptations are inevitable, but what sorrow awaits the person
who does the tempting. 8 So if your hand or
foot causes you to sin, cut it off and throw it
away. It's better to enter eternal life with only
one hand or one foot than to be thrown into
eternal fire with both of your hands and feet.
9 And if your eye causes you to sin, gouge it
out and throw it away. It's better to enter
eternal life with only one eye than to have
two eyes and be thrown into the fire of hell.*
10 "Beware that you don't look down on
any of these little ones. For I tell you that in
heaven their angels are always in the presence of my heavenly Father.*

Parable of the Lost Sheep

12 "If a man has a hundred sheep and one of
them wanders away, what will he do? Won't
he leave the ninety-nine others on the hills
and go out to search for the one that is lost?
13 And if he finds it, I tell you the truth, he
will rejoice over it more than over the ninety-
nine that didn't wander away! 14 In the same
way, it is not my heavenly Father's will that
even one of these little ones should perish.

Correcting Another Believer

15 "If another believer* sins against you,* go
privately and point out the offense. If the
other person listens and confesses it, you
have won that person back. 16 But if you are
unsuccessful, take one or two others with
you and go back again, so that everything
you say may be confirmed by two or three
witnesses. 17 If the person still refuses to
listen, take your case to the church. Then if
he or she won't accept the church's decision,
treat that person as a pagan or a corrupt tax
collector.

16:26 Or *your self?* also in 16:26b. **17:4** Greek *three tabernacles.* **17:9** "Son of Man" is a title Jesus used for himself. **17:10** Greek *that Elijah must come first?* **17:20** Some manuscripts add verse 21, *But this kind of demon won't leave except by prayer and fasting.* Compare Mark 9:29. **17:24** Greek *the two-drachma [tax];* also in 17:24b. See Exod 30:13-16; Neh 10:32-33. **17:25a** Greek *Simon?* **17:25b** Greek *their sons or others?* **17:27** Greek *a stater* [a Greek coin equivalent to four drachmas]. **18:5** Greek *in my name.* **18:9** Greek *the Gehenna of fire.* **18:10** Some manuscripts add verse 11, *And the Son of Man came to save those who are lost.* Compare Luke 19:10. **18:15a** Greek *If your brother.* **18:15b** Some manuscripts do not include *against you.*

18“I tell you the truth, whatever you forbid*
on earth will be forbidden in heaven, and
whatever you permit* on earth will be permitted in heaven.
19“I also tell you this: If two of you agree
here on earth concerning anything you ask,
my Father in heaven will do it for you. 20For
where two or three gather together as my
followers,* I am there among them.”

Parable of the Unforgiving Debtor

21Then Peter came to him and asked, “Lord,
how often should I forgive someone* who
sins against me? Seven times?”
22“No, not seven times,” Jesus replied,
“but seventy times seven!*
23“Therefore, the Kingdom of Heaven
can be compared to a king who decided
to bring his accounts up to date with servants who had borrowed money from
him. 24In the process, one of his debtors
was brought in who owed him millions of
dollars.* 25He couldn’t pay, so his master
ordered that he be sold—along with his
wife, his children, and everything he
owned—to pay the debt.
26“But the man fell down before his
master and begged him, ‘Please, be patient
with me, and I will pay it all.’ 27Then his
master was filled with pity for him, and he
released him and forgave his debt.
28“But when the man left the king, he
went to a fellow servant who owed him a
few thousand dollars.* He grabbed him by
the throat and demanded instant payment.
29“His fellow servant fell down before him
and begged for a little more time. ‘Be patient
with me, and I will pay it,’ he pleaded. 30But
his creditor wouldn’t wait. He had the man
arrested and put in prison until the debt
could be paid in full.
31“When some of the other servants saw
this, they were very upset. They went to the
king and told him everything that had happened. 32Then the king called in the man he
had forgiven and said, ‘You evil servant! I
forgave you that tremendous debt because
you pleaded with me. 33Shouldn’t you have
mercy on your fellow servant, just as I had
mercy on you?’ 34Then the angry king sent
the man to prison to be tortured until he
had paid his entire debt.
35“That’s what my heavenly Father will do
to you if you refuse to forgive your brothers
and sisters* from your heart.”

Discussion about Divorce and Marriage

19 When Jesus had finished saying these
things, he left Galilee and went down
to the region of Judea east of the Jordan
River. 2Large crowds followed him there,
and he healed their sick.

Forgiven and forgiving

The assurance that we can know God’s forgiveness—no matter what we have been or done—lay at the heart of Jesus’ message. Of course, the religious leaders also knew that God forgives, but for them, forgiveness was only for those people who, like them, kept God’s Law. What offended them was Jesus’ proclaiming forgiveness for the wrong kind of people—sinners, tax collectors, prostitutes, lawbreakers, even a dying criminal on a cross. Even worse, he claimed to offer God’s forgiveness himself—and then healed people to prove it (Mark 2:1-12).

But Jesus also taught that the forgiven must be forgiving. In Matthew 18:23-35, he used a parable to teach that unforgiveness not only demonstrates ungratefulness to God, who has freely forgiven us, but also becomes a prison that traps and torments us—us, not the person we won’t forgive!—not to mention that it brings God’s judgment upon us. That’s why forgiving others is so important, even more important than going to worship (5:23-26). And if ever we are tempted to think Jesus doesn’t know how hard it is to forgive, we should remember that, even as he was nailed to the cross, he prayed, “Father, forgive them” (Luke 23:34). Such is the forgiveness that Jesus’ disciples are called to give.

▶ *See also **Is there anything God won’t forgive?**, page 633; **How can I be sure God has forgiven me?**, page 1433.*

3Some Pharisees came and tried to trap
him with this question: "Should a man
be allowed to divorce his wife for just any
reason?"
4"Haven't you read the Scriptures?" Jesus
replied. "They record that from the beginning
'God made them male and female.'*" 5And he
said, "'This explains why a man leaves his
father and mother and is joined to his wife,
and the two are united into one.'* 6Since they
are no longer two but one, let no one split
apart what God has joined together."
7"Then why did Moses say in the law that
a man could give his wife a written notice of
divorce and send her away?"* they asked.
8Jesus replied, "Moses permitted divorce
only as a concession to your hard hearts,
but it was not what God had originally
intended. 9And I tell you this, whoever divorces his wife and marries someone else
commits adultery—unless his wife has been
unfaithful.*"
10Jesus' disciples then said to him, "If this
is the case, it is better not to marry!"
11"Not everyone can accept this statement,"
Jesus said. "Only those whom God helps.
12Some are born as eunuchs, some have been
made eunuchs by others, and some choose
not to marry* for the sake of the Kingdom of
Heaven. Let anyone accept this who can."

Jesus Blesses the Children

13One day some parents brought their children to Jesus so he could lay his hands on
them and pray for them. But the disciples
scolded the parents for bothering him.
14But Jesus said, "Let the children come
to me. Don't stop them! For the Kingdom
of Heaven belongs to those who are like
these children." 15And he placed his hands
on their heads and blessed them before he
left.

The Rich Man

16Someone came to Jesus with this question: "Teacher,* what good deed must I do
to have eternal life?"
17"Why ask me about what is good?"
Jesus replied. "There is only One who is
good. But to answer your question—if
you want to receive eternal life, keep* the
commandments."
18"Which ones?" the man asked.
And Jesus replied: "'You must not murder.
You must not commit adultery. You must not
steal. You must not testify falsely. 19Honor
your father and mother. Love your neighbor
as yourself.'*"
20"I've obeyed all these commandments,"
the young man replied. "What else must
I do?"
21Jesus told him, "If you want to be perfect,
go and sell all your possessions and give the
money to the poor, and you will have treasure in heaven. Then come, follow me."
22But when the young man heard this, he
went away sad, for he had many possessions.
23Then Jesus said to his disciples, "I tell
you the truth, it is very hard for a rich person
to enter the Kingdom of Heaven. 24I'll say it
again—it is easier for a camel to go through
the eye of a needle than for a rich person to
enter the Kingdom of God!"
25The disciples were astounded. "Then
who in the world can be saved?" they asked.
26Jesus looked at them intently and said,
"Humanly speaking, it is impossible. But
with God everything is possible."
27Then Peter said to him, "We've given
up everything to follow you. What will we
get?"
28Jesus replied, "I assure you that when
the world is made new* and the Son of
Man* sits upon his glorious throne, you
who have been my followers will also sit
on twelve thrones, judging the twelve
tribes of Israel. 29And everyone who has
given up houses or brothers or sisters or
father or mother or children or property,
for my sake, will receive a hundred times
as much in return and will inherit eternal
life. 30But many who are the greatest now
will be least important then, and those
who seem least important now will be the
greatest then.*"

18:18a Or *bind,* or *lock.* **18:18b** Or *loose,* or *open.* **18:20** Greek *gather together in my name.* **18:21** Greek *my brother.* **18:22** Or *seventy-seven times.* **18:24** Greek *10,000 talents* [375 tons or 340 metric tons of silver]. **18:28** Greek *100 denarii.* A denarius was equivalent to a laborer's full day's wage. **18:35** Greek *your brother.* **19:4** Gen 1:27; 5:2. **19:5** Gen 2:24. **19:7** See Deut 24:1. **19:9** Some manuscripts add *And anyone who marries a divorced woman commits adultery.* Compare Matt 5:32. **19:12** Greek *and some make themselves eunuchs.* **19:16** Some manuscripts read *Good Teacher.* **19:17** Some manuscripts read *continue to keep.* **19:18-19** Exod 20:12-16; Deut 5:16-20; Lev 19:18. **19:28a** Or *in the regeneration.* **19:28b** "Son of Man" is a title Jesus used for himself. **19:30** Greek *But many who are first will be last; and the last, first.*

▸ **19:1-12** *See **Does marriage still matter to God?**, page 976.*

Parable of the Vineyard Workers

20 "For the Kingdom of Heaven is like
the landowner who went out early
one morning to hire workers for his vineyard. [2]He agreed to pay the normal daily
wage* and sent them out to work.
[3]"At nine o'clock in the morning he was
passing through the marketplace and
saw some people standing around doing
nothing. [4]So he hired them, telling them he
would pay them whatever was right at the
end of the day. [5]So they went to work in the
vineyard. At noon and again at three o'clock
he did the same thing.
[6]"At five o'clock that afternoon he was
in town again and saw some more people
standing around. He asked them, 'Why
haven't you been working today?'
[7]"They replied, 'Because no one hired us.'
"The landowner told them, 'Then go out
and join the others in my vineyard.'
[8]"That evening he told the foreman to
call the workers in and pay them, beginning with the last workers first. [9]When
those hired at five o'clock were paid, each
received a full day's wage. [10]When those
hired first came to get their pay, they
assumed they would receive more. But
they, too, were paid a day's wage. [11]When
they received their pay, they protested to
the owner, [12]'Those people worked only
one hour, and yet you've paid them just as
much as you paid us who worked all day in
the scorching heat.'
[13]"He answered one of them, 'Friend, I
haven't been unfair! Didn't you agree to work
all day for the usual wage? [14]Take your money
and go. I wanted to pay this last worker the
same as you. [15]Is it against the law for me to
do what I want with my money? Should you
be jealous because I am kind to others?'
[16]"So those who are last now will be first
then, and those who are first will be last."

Jesus Again Predicts His Death

[17]As Jesus was going up to Jerusalem, he
took the twelve disciples aside privately
and told them what was going to happen
to him. [18]"Listen," he said, "we're going up
to Jerusalem, where the Son of Man* will
be betrayed to the leading priests and the
teachers of religious law. They will sentence
him to die. [19]Then they will hand him over
to the Romans* to be mocked, flogged with
a whip, and crucified. But on the third day
he will be raised from the dead."

Jesus Teaches about Serving Others

[20]Then the mother of James and John, the
sons of Zebedee, came to Jesus with her

Children

The disciples no doubt thought they were helping Jesus when they tried to prevent people from bringing their children to him for him to bless them; after all, Jesus was far too important, they thought, to waste his time on such matters. But by making room for these children and blessing them, Jesus showed the importance of children—which was especially significant in a society where they were often seen as having little value until they came of age—and he made clear that there was a place in God's Kingdom for them.

Jews had always seen children as a blessing from God, and having many children was seen as a special blessing (e.g., Psalm 127:3-5). Sons were particularly important, because they would continue the family name and lead the extended family. So when a son was born, his mother became known as "Mother of . . . ," like "Mary the mother of Jesus" (Acts 1:14). Sons provided for their parents in their old age and, in days when there was little concept of an afterlife, the sense of living on through one's sons was crucial. Childlessness was seen as a great misfortune.

Jesus loved children, even though he never had any of his own. He enjoyed spending time with them, refused to exclude them, and told his disciples they could learn from them (e.g., Matthew 19:13-15; 21:14-16; Mark 9:14-27).

▶ *See also* ***Childlessness****, page 25;* ***Family****, page 714.*

sons. She knelt respectfully to ask a favor.
21 "What is your request?" he asked.
She replied, "In your Kingdom, please
let my two sons sit in places of honor next
to you, one on your right and the other on
your left."
22 But Jesus answered by saying to them,
"You don't know what you are asking! Are
you able to drink from the bitter cup of suffering I am about to drink?"
"Oh yes," they replied, "we are able!"
23 Jesus told them, "You will indeed drink
from my bitter cup. But I have no right to
say who will sit on my right or my left. My
Father has prepared those places for the
ones he has chosen."
24 When the ten other disciples heard
what James and John had asked, they were
indignant. 25 But Jesus called them together
and said, "You know that the rulers in this
world lord it over their people, and officials
flaunt their authority over those under
them. 26 But among you it will be different.
Whoever wants to be a leader among you
must be your servant, 27 and whoever wants
to be first among you must become your
slave. 28 For even the Son of Man came not
to be served but to serve others and to give
his life as a ransom for many."

Jesus Heals Two Blind Men

29 As Jesus and the disciples left the town
of Jericho, a large crowd followed behind.
30 Two blind men were sitting beside the
road. When they heard that Jesus was
coming that way, they began shouting,
"Lord, Son of David, have mercy on us!"
31 "Be quiet!" the crowd yelled at them.
But they only shouted louder, "Lord, Son
of David, have mercy on us!"
32 When Jesus heard them, he stopped
and called, "What do you want me to do for
you?"
33 "Lord," they said, "we want to see!"
34 Jesus felt sorry for them and touched their
eyes. Instantly they could see! Then they
followed him.

Jesus' Triumphant Entry

21 As Jesus and the disciples approached Jerusalem, they came to
the town of Bethphage on the Mount of
Olives. Jesus sent two of them on ahead.
2 "Go into the village over there," he said.
"As soon as you enter it, you will see a
donkey tied there, with its colt beside

20:2 Greek *a denarius*, the payment for a full day's labor; similarly in 20:9, 10, 13. **20:18** "Son of Man" is a title Jesus used for himself. **20:19** Greek *the Gentiles*.

▸ **20:28** *See* ***Redemption****, page 1136.*

The Son of Man

One of Jesus' favorite titles for himself was "Son of Man" (e.g., Matthew 20:28). He chose this title because it enabled him to lay claims to being the Messiah without using the actual word. He took this approach because current Jewish expectation was that the Messiah would be a military deliverer who would raise an army and free Israel from Rome's power. But this was far from Jesus' thinking. He had come to free them, not with a sword but with a cross. He therefore used "Son of Man," a rather enigmatic title, yet one which—for those who thought about it—had an obvious meaning. For "Son of Man" drew together two strands of Jewish thinking: first, that of man as frail and human (e.g., Psalm 8:3-5, where "son of man" is used in the Hebrew); but second, the expectation of a man who one day would rule in glory and power (Daniel 7:13-14). Jesus brought these two aspects together: He came into this world as a frail human being who would die, yet he would also rise from the dead and at the end of the age receive his Kingdom from his Father. The title "Son of Man" therefore spoke of both the means and the end—humility and glory.

▸ *See also* ***Names and titles of Jesus****, page 1070.*

it. Untie them and bring them to me. 3If
anyone asks what you are doing, just say,
'The Lord needs them,' and he will immediately let you take them."
4This took place to fulfill the prophecy
that said,

5 "Tell the people of Jerusalem,*
'Look, your King is coming to you.
He is humble, riding on a donkey—
riding on a donkey's colt.'"*

6The two disciples did as Jesus commanded. 7They brought the donkey and the
colt to him and threw their garments over
the colt, and he sat on it.*
8Most of the crowd spread their garments
on the road ahead of him, and others cut
branches from the trees and spread them
on the road. 9Jesus was in the center of the
procession, and the people all around him
were shouting,

"Praise God* for the Son of David!
Blessings on the one who comes in
the name of the LORD!
Praise God in highest heaven!"*

10The entire city of Jerusalem was in an
uproar as he entered. "Who is this?" they
asked.
11And the crowds replied, "It's Jesus, the
prophet from Nazareth in Galilee."

Jesus Clears the Temple

12Jesus entered the Temple and began to
drive out all the people buying and selling
animals for sacrifice. He knocked over the
tables of the money changers and the chairs
of those selling doves. 13He said to them,
"The Scriptures declare, 'My Temple will
be called a house of prayer,' but you have
turned it into a den of thieves!'"*
14The blind and the lame came to him
in the Temple, and he healed them. 15The
leading priests and the teachers of religious law saw these wonderful miracles
and heard even the children in the Temple
shouting, "Praise God for the Son of David."
But the leaders were indignant. 16They
asked Jesus, "Do you hear what these children are saying?"
"Yes," Jesus replied. "Haven't you ever
read the Scriptures? For they say, 'You have
taught children and infants to give you
praise.'*" 17Then he returned to Bethany,
where he stayed overnight.

Jesus Curses the Fig Tree

18In the morning, as Jesus was returning to
Jerusalem, he was hungry, 19and he noticed
a fig tree beside the road. He went over to
see if there were any figs, but there were
only leaves. Then he said to it, "May you
never bear fruit again!" And immediately
the fig tree withered up.
20The disciples were amazed when they
saw this and asked, "How did the fig tree
wither so quickly?"
21Then Jesus told them, "I tell you the
truth, if you have faith and don't doubt, you
can do things like this and much more. You
can even say to this mountain, 'May you be
lifted up and thrown into the sea,' and it
will happen. 22You can pray for anything,
and if you have faith, you will receive it."

The Authority of Jesus Challenged

23When Jesus returned to the Temple and
began teaching, the leading priests and
elders came up to him. They demanded,
"By what authority are you doing all these
things? Who gave you the right?"
24"I'll tell you by what authority I do
these things if you answer one question,"
Jesus replied. 25"Did John's authority to
baptize come from heaven, or was it merely
human?"
They talked it over among themselves.
"If we say it was from heaven, he will ask
us why we didn't believe John. 26But if we
say it was merely human, we'll be mobbed
because the people believe John was a
prophet." 27So they finally replied, "We
don't know."
And Jesus responded, "Then I won't tell
you by what authority I do these things.

Parable of the Two Sons

28"But what do you think about this? A man
with two sons told the older boy, 'Son, go
out and work in the vineyard today.' 29The
son answered, 'No, I won't go,' but later he
changed his mind and went anyway. 30Then
the father told the other son, 'You go,' and
he said, 'Yes, sir, I will.' But he didn't go.

▸ **21:23** *See **Authority**, page 1187.*

31“Which of the two obeyed his father?”
They replied, “The first.”*

Then Jesus explained his meaning: “I tell you the truth, corrupt tax collectors and prostitutes will get into the Kingdom of God before you do. 32For John the Baptist came and showed you the right way to live, but you didn't believe him, while tax collectors and prostitutes did. And even when you saw this happening, you refused to believe him and repent of your sins.

Parable of the Evil Farmers

33“Now listen to another story. A certain landowner planted a vineyard, built a wall around it, dug a pit for pressing out the grape juice, and built a lookout tower. Then he leased the vineyard to tenant farmers and moved to another country. 34At the time of the grape harvest, he sent his servants to collect his share of the crop. 35But the farmers grabbed his servants, beat one, killed one, and stoned another. 36So the landowner sent a larger group of his servants to collect for him, but the results were the same.

37“Finally, the owner sent his son, thinking, ‘Surely they will respect my son.’

38“But when the tenant farmers saw his son coming, they said to one another, ‘Here comes the heir to this estate. Come on, let's kill him and get the estate for ourselves!’ 39So they grabbed him, dragged him out of the vineyard, and murdered him.

40“When the owner of the vineyard returns,” Jesus asked, “what do you think he will do to those farmers?”

41The religious leaders replied, “He will put the wicked men to a horrible death and lease the vineyard to others who will give him his share of the crop after each harvest.”

42Then Jesus asked them, “Didn't you ever read this in the Scriptures?

‘The stone that the builders rejected
has now become the cornerstone.
This is the Lord's doing,
and it is wonderful to see.’*

43I tell you, the Kingdom of God will be taken away from you and given to a nation that will produce the proper fruit. 44Anyone who stumbles over that stone will be broken to pieces, and it will crush anyone it falls on.*”

45When the leading priests and Pharisees heard this parable, they realized he was telling the story against them—they were the wicked farmers. 46They wanted to arrest him, but they were afraid of the crowds, who considered Jesus to be a prophet.

Parable of the Great Feast

22 Jesus also told them other parables. He said, 2“The Kingdom of Heaven can be illustrated by the story of a king who prepared a great wedding feast for his son. 3When the banquet was ready, he sent his servants to notify those who were invited. But they all refused to come!

4“So he sent other servants to tell them, ‘The feast has been prepared. The bulls and fattened cattle have been killed, and everything is ready. Come to the banquet!’ 5But the guests he had invited ignored them and went their own way, one to his farm, another to his business. 6Others seized his messengers and insulted them and killed them.

7“The king was furious, and he sent out his army to destroy the murderers and burn their town. 8And he said to his servants, ‘The wedding feast is ready, and the guests I invited aren't worthy of the honor. 9Now go out to the street corners and invite everyone you see.’ 10So the servants brought in everyone they could find, good and bad alike, and the banquet hall was filled with guests.

11“But when the king came in to meet the guests, he noticed a man who wasn't wearing the proper clothes for a wedding. 12‘Friend,’ he asked, ‘how is it that you are here without wedding clothes?’ But the man had no reply. 13Then the king said to his aides, ‘Bind his hands and feet and throw him into the outer darkness, where there will be weeping and gnashing of teeth.’

14“For many are called, but few are chosen.”

Taxes for Caesar

15Then the Pharisees met together to plot how to trap Jesus into saying something for which he could be arrested. 16They sent some of their disciples, along with the supporters of Herod, to meet with him.

21:5a Greek *Tell the daughter of Zion*. Isa 62:11. **21:5b** Zech 9:9. **21:7** Greek *over them, and he sat on them.* **21:9a** Greek *Hosanna*, an exclamation of praise that literally means “save now”; also in 21:9b, 15. **21:9b** Pss 118:25-26; 148:1. **21:13** Isa 56:7; Jer 7:11. **21:16** Ps 8:2 (Greek version). **21:29-31** Other manuscripts read “*The second.*” In still other manuscripts the first son says “Yes” but does nothing, the second son says “No” but then repents and goes, and the answer to Jesus' question is that the second son obeyed his father. **21:42** Ps 118:22-23. **21:44** This verse is not included in some early manuscripts. Compare Luke 20:18.

"Teacher," they said, "we know how honest
you are. You teach the way of God truthfully.
You are impartial and don't play favorites.
17 Now tell us what you think about this: Is it
right to pay taxes to Caesar or not?"
18 But Jesus knew their evil motives. "You
hypocrites!" he said. "Why are you trying to
trap me? 19 Here, show me the coin used for
the tax." When they handed him a Roman
coin,* 20 he asked, "Whose picture and title
are stamped on it?"
21 "Caesar's," they replied.
"Well, then," he said, "give to Caesar
what belongs to Caesar, and give to God
what belongs to God."
22 His reply amazed them, and they went
away.

Discussion about Resurrection

23 That same day Jesus was approached by
some Sadducees—religious leaders who say
there is no resurrection from the dead. They
posed this question: 24 "Teacher, Moses said,
'If a man dies without children, his brother
should marry the widow and have a child
who will carry on the brother's name.'*
25 Well, suppose there were seven brothers. The oldest one married and then died
without children, so his brother married the
widow. 26 But the second brother also died,
and the third brother married her. This continued with all seven of them. 27 Last of all,
the woman also died. 28 So tell us, whose
wife will she be in the resurrection? For all
seven were married to her."
29 Jesus replied, "Your mistake is that you
don't know the Scriptures, and you don't
know the power of God. 30 For when the
dead rise, they will neither marry nor be
given in marriage. In this respect they will
be like the angels in heaven.
31 "But now, as to whether there will be a
resurrection of the dead—haven't you ever
read about this in the Scriptures? Long after
Abraham, Isaac, and Jacob had died, God
said,* 32 'I am the God of Abraham, the God
of Isaac, and the God of Jacob.'* So he is the
God of the living, not the dead."
33 When the crowds heard him, they were
astounded at his teaching.

The Most Important Commandment

34 But when the Pharisees heard that he had
silenced the Sadducees with his reply, they
met together to question him again. 35 One
of them, an expert in religious law, tried
to trap him with this question: 36 "Teacher,
which is the most important commandment
in the law of Moses?"
37 Jesus replied, "'You must love the
LORD your God with all your heart, all your
soul, and all your mind.'* 38 This is the first
and greatest commandment. 39 A second
is equally important: 'Love your neighbor

▸ **22:17** *See* ***Paying taxes****, page 1139.*

Saddučees

Although a much smaller group than the Pharisees, the Sadducees were in many ways far more significant, for they were the aristocratic families that controlled the high priesthood and the Temple. Their name probably derives from Zadok, Solomon's high priest, and this ancestry gave them cause for much pride. They stood out from the Pharisees in two key ways: First, they accepted only the Torah (the first five books of the Scriptures) as God's word, so they excluded any doctrines not found in it—including the resurrection of the dead (Matthew 22:23); second, they believed that strict purity was only incumbent on priests, not on everyone. Yet they found themselves allying with the Pharisees against Jesus, whom they saw as a troublemaker who threatened the political status quo. Any turmoil might cause Rome to clamp down, meaning the Sadducees would lose their influence. It was a leading Sadducee—Caiaphas, the high priest—who pressed for Jesus' execution (John 18:14).

▸ *See also* ***The Pharisees****, page 1086.*

as yourself.'* 40 The entire law and all the
demands of the prophets are based on these
two commandments."

Whose Son Is the Messiah?

41 Then, surrounded by the Pharisees, Jesus
asked them a question: 42 "What do you
think about the Messiah? Whose son is he?"

They replied, "He is the son of David."

43 Jesus responded, "Then why does David,
speaking under the inspiration of the Spirit,
call the Messiah 'my Lord'? For David said,

44 'The LORD said to my Lord,
Sit in the place of honor at my right
hand
until I humble your enemies beneath
your feet.'*

45 Since David called the Messiah 'my Lord,'
how can the Messiah be his son?"

46 No one could answer him. And after
that, no one dared to ask him any more
questions.

Jesus Criticizes the Religious Leaders

23 Then Jesus said to the crowds and
to his disciples, 2 "The teachers of
religious law and the Pharisees are the official interpreters of the law of Moses.* 3 So
practice and obey whatever they tell you,
but don't follow their example. For they
don't practice what they teach. 4 They crush
people with unbearable religious demands
and never lift a finger to ease the burden.

5 "Everything they do is for show. On their
arms they wear extra wide prayer boxes
with Scripture verses inside, and they wear
robes with extra long tassels.* 6 And they
love to sit at the head table at banquets and
in the seats of honor in the synagogues.
7 They love to receive respectful greetings
as they walk in the marketplaces, and to be
called 'Rabbi.'*

8 "Don't let anyone call you 'Rabbi,' for
you have only one teacher, and all of you are
equal as brothers and sisters.* 9 And don't
address anyone here on earth as 'Father,'
for only God in heaven is your Father. 10 And
don't let anyone call you 'Teacher,' for you
have only one teacher, the Messiah. 11 The
greatest among you must be a servant.
12 But those who exalt themselves will be
humbled, and those who humble themselves will be exalted.

13 "What sorrow awaits you teachers of religious law and you Pharisees. Hypocrites! For
you shut the door of the Kingdom of Heaven
in people's faces. You won't go in yourselves,
and you don't let others enter either.*

15 "What sorrow awaits you teachers of religious law and you Pharisees. Hypocrites!
For you cross land and sea to make one
convert, and then you turn that person into
twice the child of hell* you yourselves are!

16 "Blind guides! What sorrow awaits you!
For you say that it means nothing to swear
'by God's Temple,' but that it is binding to
swear 'by the gold in the Temple.' 17 Blind
fools! Which is more important—the gold
or the Temple that makes the gold sacred?
18 And you say that to swear 'by the altar' is
not binding, but to swear 'by the gifts on
the altar' is binding. 19 How blind! For which
is more important—the gift on the altar or
the altar that makes the gift sacred? 20 When
you swear 'by the altar,' you are swearing by
it and by everything on it. 21 And when you
swear 'by the Temple,' you are swearing by
it and by God, who lives in it. 22 And when
you swear 'by heaven,' you are swearing by
the throne of God and by God, who sits on
the throne.

23 "What sorrow awaits you teachers of
religious law and you Pharisees. Hypocrites! For you are careful to tithe even the
tiniest income from your herb gardens,*
but you ignore the more important aspects
of the law—justice, mercy, and faith. You
should tithe, yes, but do not neglect the
more important things. 24 Blind guides! You
strain your water so you won't accidentally
swallow a gnat, but you swallow a camel!*

25 "What sorrow awaits you teachers of

22:19 Greek *a denarius.* **22:24** Deut 25:5-6. **22:31** Greek *read about this? God said.* **22:32** Exod 3:6. **22:37** Deut 6:5. **22:39** Lev 19:18. **22:44** Ps 110:1. **23:2** Greek *and the Pharisees sit in the seat of Moses.* **23:5** Greek *They enlarge their phylacteries and lengthen their tassels.* **23:7** *Rabbi,* from Aramaic, means "master" or "teacher." **23:8** Greek *brothers.* **23:13** Some manuscripts add verse 14, *What sorrow awaits you teachers of religious law and you Pharisees. Hypocrites! You shamelessly cheat widows out of their property and then pretend to be pious by making long prayers in public. Because of this, you will be severely punished.* Compare Mark 12:40 and Luke 20:47. **23:15** Greek *of Gehenna;* also in 23:33. **23:23** Greek *tithe the mint, the dill, and the cumin.* **23:24** See Lev 11:4, 23, where gnats and camels are both forbidden as food.

▸ **22:39** *See **Love your neighbor as yourself**, page 139.* **23:12** *See **Pride**, page 559.*
23:23 *See **Should Christians still tithe?**, page 1052.*

religious law and you Pharisees. Hypocrites!
For you are so careful to clean the outside
of the cup and the dish, but inside you are
filthy—full of greed and self-indulgence!
26 You blind Pharisee! First wash the inside
of the cup and the dish,* and then the
outside will become clean, too.

27 "What sorrow awaits you teachers of religious law and you Pharisees. Hypocrites!
For you are like whitewashed tombs—beautiful on the outside but filled on the inside
with dead people's bones and all sorts of
impurity. 28 Outwardly you look like righteous people, but inwardly your hearts are
filled with hypocrisy and lawlessness.

29 "What sorrow awaits you teachers of religious law and you Pharisees. Hypocrites!
For you build tombs for the prophets your
ancestors killed, and you decorate the monuments of the godly people your ancestors
destroyed. 30 Then you say, 'If we had lived
in the days of our ancestors, we would never
have joined them in killing the prophets.'

31 "But in saying that, you testify against
yourselves that you are indeed the descendants of those who murdered the prophets.
32 Go ahead and finish what your ancestors
started. 33 Snakes! Sons of vipers! How will
you escape the judgment of hell?

34 "Therefore, I am sending you prophets
and wise men and teachers of religious
law. But you will kill some by crucifixion,
and you will flog others with whips in your
synagogues, chasing them from city to city.
35 As a result, you will be held responsible
for the murder of all godly people of all
time—from the murder of righteous Abel to
the murder of Zechariah son of Berekiah,
whom you killed in the Temple between
the sanctuary and the altar. 36 I tell you the
truth, this judgment will fall on this very
generation.

Jesus Grieves over Jerusalem

37 "O Jerusalem, Jerusalem, the city that kills
the prophets and stones God's messengers!
How often I have wanted to gather your children together as a hen protects her chicks
beneath her wings, but you wouldn't let me.
38 And now, look, your house is abandoned
and desolate.* 39 For I tell you this, you will
never see me again until you say, 'Blessings
on the one who comes in the name of the
LORD!'*"

Jesus Speaks about the Future

24 As Jesus was leaving the Temple
grounds, his disciples pointed out to
him the various Temple buildings. 2 But he
responded, "Do you see all these buildings?

Hypocrisy

In Matthew 23 Jesus shows no mercy toward the Pharisees, calling them "hypocrites" (e.g., 23:13). The word originally came from Greek theater, where it meant "actor." In those days, actors held masks before their faces with big smiles or frowns on them to depict their feelings. So "hypocrite" gradually came to mean anyone who (metaphorically) wore a mask, hiding their true face and feelings from others, pretending to be something different from what they were.

That is what Jesus accused the Pharisees of: on the surface, pretending to be one thing (religious zealots, eager to fulfill God's Law), but underneath, trying to make life easy for themselves and hard for others, excusing their own faults while highlighting others'. Some of Jesus' harshest words are reserved, not for "sinners," but for hypocrites, describing them here as children of hell (23:15), "blind guides" (23:16), "whitewashed tombs" (23:27), and "snakes" (23:33). Such language leaves us in no doubt about what he thought of those whose inner reality didn't match the outward show.

There was no hint of hypocrisy in Jesus (e.g., 1 Peter 2:22), and his followers are called to live the same way (1 Peter 2:1; see also 2 Corinthians 1:12-14; 1 Thessalonians 2:3-6).

▶ *See also* ***Honesty****, page 707;* ***The Pharisees****, page 1086.*

I tell you the truth, they will be completely demolished. Not one stone will be left on top of another!"

[3]Later, Jesus sat on the Mount of Olives. His disciples came to him privately and said, "Tell us, when will all this happen? What sign will signal your return and the end of the world?*"

[4]Jesus told them, "Don't let anyone mislead you, [5]for many will come in my name, claiming, 'I am the Messiah.' They will deceive many. [6]And you will hear of wars and threats of wars, but don't panic. Yes, these things must take place, but the end won't follow immediately. [7]Nation will go to war against nation, and kingdom against kingdom. There will be famines and earthquakes in many parts of the world. [8]But all this is only the first of the birth pains, with more to come.

[9]"Then you will be arrested, persecuted, and killed. You will be hated all over the world because you are my followers.* [10]And many will turn away from me and betray and hate each other. [11]And many false prophets will appear and will deceive many people. [12]Sin will be rampant everywhere, and the love of many will grow cold. [13]But the one who endures to the end will be saved. [14]And the Good News about the Kingdom will be preached throughout the whole world, so that all nations* will hear it; and then the end will come.

[15]"The day is coming when you will see what Daniel the prophet spoke about—the sacrilegious object that causes desecration* standing in the Holy Place." (Reader, pay attention!) [16]"Then those in Judea must flee to the hills. [17]A person out on the deck of a roof must not go down into the house to pack. [18]A person out in the field must not return even to get a coat. [19]How terrible it will be for pregnant women and for nursing mothers in those days. [20]And pray that your flight will not be in winter or on the Sabbath. [21]For there will be greater anguish than at any time since the world began. And it will never be so great again. [22]In fact, unless that time of calamity is shortened, not a single person will survive. But it will be shortened for the sake of God's chosen ones.

[23]"Then if anyone tells you, 'Look, here is the Messiah,' or 'There he is,' don't believe it. [24]For false messiahs and false prophets will rise up and perform great signs and wonders so as to deceive, if possible, even God's chosen ones. [25]See, I have warned you about this ahead of time.

[26]"So if someone tells you, 'Look, the Messiah is out in the desert,' don't bother to go and look. Or, 'Look, he is hiding here,' don't believe it! [27]For as the lightning flashes in the east and shines to the west, so it will be when the Son of Man* comes. [28]Just as the gathering of vultures shows there is a carcass nearby, so these signs indicate that the end is near.*

[29]"Immediately after the anguish of those days,

the sun will be darkened,
    the moon will give no light,
the stars will fall from the sky,
    and the powers in the heavens will
        be shaken.*

[30]And then at last, the sign that the Son of Man is coming will appear in the heavens, and there will be deep mourning among all the peoples of the earth. And they will see the Son of Man coming on the clouds of heaven with power and great glory.* [31]And he will send out his angels with the mighty blast of a trumpet, and they will gather his chosen ones from all over the world*—from the farthest ends of the earth and heaven.

[32]"Now learn a lesson from the fig tree. When its branches bud and its leaves begin to sprout, you know that summer is near. [33]In the same way, when you see all these things, you can know his return is very near, right at the door. [34]I tell you the truth, this generation* will not pass from the scene until all these things take place. [35]Heaven and earth will disappear, but my words will never disappear.

[36]"However, no one knows the day or hour when these things will happen, not even the angels in heaven or the Son himself.* Only the Father knows.

[37]"When the Son of Man returns, it will be like it was in Noah's day. [38]In those days before the flood, the people were enjoying banquets and parties and weddings right up to the time Noah entered his boat. [39]People

23:26 Some manuscripts do not include *and the dish.* **23:38** Some manuscripts do not include *and desolate.* **23:39** Ps 118:26. **24:3** Or *the age?* **24:9** Greek *on account of my name.* **24:14** Or *all peoples.* **24:15** Greek *the abomination of desolation.* See Dan 9:27; 11:31; 12:11. **24:27** "Son of Man" is a title Jesus used for himself. **24:28** Greek *Wherever the carcass is, the vultures gather.* **24:29** See Isa 13:10; 34:4; Joel 2:10. **24:30** See Dan 7:13. **24:31** Greek *from the four winds.* **24:34** Or *this age,* or *this nation.* **24:36** Some manuscripts do not include *or the Son himself.*

didn't realize what was going to happen until the flood came and swept them all away. That is the way it will be when the Son of Man comes.

40 "Two men will be working together in the field; one will be taken, the other left. 41 Two women will be grinding flour at the mill; one will be taken, the other left.

42 "So you, too, must keep watch! For you don't know what day your Lord is coming. 43 Understand this: If a homeowner knew exactly when a burglar was coming, he would keep watch and not permit his house to be broken into. 44 You also must be ready all the time, for the Son of Man will come when least expected.

45 "A faithful, sensible servant is one to whom the master can give the responsibility of managing his other household servants and feeding them. 46 If the master returns and finds that the servant has done a good job, there will be a reward. 47 I tell you the truth, the master will put that servant in charge of all he owns. 48 But what if the servant is evil and thinks, 'My master won't be back for a while,' 49 and he begins beating the other servants, partying, and getting drunk? 50 The master will return unannounced and unexpected, 51 and he will cut the servant to pieces and assign him a place with the hypocrites. In that place there will be weeping and gnashing of teeth.

Parable of the Ten Bridesmaids

25 "Then the Kingdom of Heaven will be like ten bridesmaids* who took their lamps and went to meet the bridegroom. 2 Five of them were foolish, and five were wise. 3 The five who were foolish didn't take enough olive oil for their lamps, 4 but the other five were wise enough to take along extra oil. 5 When the bridegroom was delayed, they all became drowsy and fell asleep.

6 "At midnight they were roused by the shout, 'Look, the bridegroom is coming! Come out and meet him!'

7 "All the bridesmaids got up and prepared their lamps. 8 Then the five foolish ones asked the others, 'Please give us some of your oil because our lamps are going out.'

9 "But the others replied, 'We don't have enough for all of us. Go to a shop and buy some for yourselves.'

10 "But while they were gone to buy oil, the bridegroom came. Then those who were ready went in with him to the marriage feast, and the door was locked. 11 Later, when the other five bridesmaids returned, they stood outside, calling, 'Lord! Lord! Open the door for us!'

12 "But he called back, 'Believe me, I don't know you!'

13 "So you, too, must keep watch! For you do not know the day or hour of my return.

Hell

The "eternal fire" that Jesus speaks of in Matthew 25:41 is what he refers to elsewhere as "hell" (e.g., 5:29-30; 10:28; 23:33)—the destiny of those who reject him and live godless lives. "Hell" in Greek is *Gehenna*, meaning "Valley of Hinnom," the place where children were sacrificed by fire by wicked kings in Old Testament times (e.g., 2 Kings 23:10). It was seen as such a godless place that it became Jerusalem's rubbish dump, and from that, a symbol of the place of sinners' punishment.

This view of the destiny of the wicked was reaffirmed by Jesus; in fact no one in the Bible speaks about hell more than he. He described its fire as eternal (Matthew 18:8) and unquenchable (Mark 9:43). Some think this language is metaphorical rather than literal since the New Testament uses other imagery too, describing it as a place of darkness and misery (Matthew 25:30), of everlasting destruction and exclusion from God's presence (2 Thessalonians 1:9), as a second death (Revelation 2:11), and as a lake of fire (Revelation 20:15). Whatever the exact nature of hell, Jesus said it should be avoided at all costs (Matthew 5:29-30).

▶ *See also* ***Repentance****, page 1253;* ***Heaven****, page 1451.*

Parable of the Three Servants

[14]“Again, the Kingdom of Heaven can be illustrated by the story of a man going on a
long trip. He called together his servants and
entrusted his money to them while he was
gone. [15]He gave five bags of silver* to one,
two bags of silver to another, and one bag of
silver to the last—dividing it in proportion to
their abilities. He then left on his trip.

[16]“The servant who received the five
bags of silver began to invest the money
and earned five more. [17]The servant with
two bags of silver also went to work and
earned two more. [18]But the servant who received the one bag of silver dug a hole in the
ground and hid the master’s money.

[19]“After a long time their master returned
from his trip and called them to give an
account of how they had used his money.
[20]The servant to whom he had entrusted the
five bags of silver came forward with five
more and said, ‘Master, you gave me five
bags of silver to invest, and I have earned
five more.’

[21]“The master was full of praise. ‘Well
done, my good and faithful servant. You
have been faithful in handling this small
amount, so now I will give you many more
responsibilities. Let’s celebrate together!*’

[22]“The servant who had received the
two bags of silver came forward and said,
‘Master, you gave me two bags of silver to
invest, and I have earned two more.’

[23]“The master said, ‘Well done, my good
and faithful servant. You have been faithful in handling this small amount, so now
I will give you many more responsibilities.
Let’s celebrate together!’

[24]“Then the servant with the one bag of
silver came and said, ‘Master, I knew you
were a harsh man, harvesting crops you
didn’t plant and gathering crops you didn’t
cultivate. [25]I was afraid I would lose your
money, so I hid it in the earth. Look, here is
your money back.’

[26]“But the master replied, ‘You wicked
and lazy servant! If you knew I harvested
crops I didn’t plant and gathered crops I
didn’t cultivate, [27]why didn’t you deposit
my money in the bank? At least I could have
gotten some interest on it.’

[28]“Then he ordered, ‘Take the money
from this servant, and give it to the one
with the ten bags of silver. [29]To those who
use well what they are given, even more will
be given, and they will have an abundance.
But from those who do nothing, even what
little they have will be taken away. [30]Now
throw this useless servant into outer darkness, where there will be weeping and
gnashing of teeth.’

The Final Judgment

[31]“But when the Son of Man* comes in his
glory, and all the angels with him, then he
will sit upon his glorious throne. [32]All the
nations* will be gathered in his presence,
and he will separate the people as a shepherd separates the sheep from the goats.
[33]He will place the sheep at his right hand
and the goats at his left.

[34]“Then the King will say to those on
his right, ‘Come, you who are blessed by
my Father, inherit the Kingdom prepared
for you from the creation of the world.
[35]For I was hungry, and you fed me. I was
thirsty, and you gave me a drink. I was
a stranger, and you invited me into your
home. [36]I was naked, and you gave me
clothing. I was sick, and you cared for me.
I was in prison, and you visited me.’

[37]“Then these righteous ones will reply,
‘Lord, when did we ever see you hungry and
feed you? Or thirsty and give you something
to drink? [38]Or a stranger and show you hospitality? Or naked and give you clothing?
[39]When did we ever see you sick or in prison
and visit you?’

[40]“And the King will say, ‘I tell you the
truth, when you did it to one of the least of
these my brothers and sisters,* you were
doing it to me!’

[41]“Then the King will turn to those on the
left and say, ‘Away with you, you cursed
ones, into the eternal fire prepared for the
devil and his demons.* [42]For I was hungry,
and you didn’t feed me. I was thirsty, and you
didn’t give me a drink. [43]I was a stranger, and
you didn’t invite me into your home. I was
naked, and you didn’t give me clothing. I was
sick and in prison, and you didn’t visit me.’

[44]“Then they will reply, ‘Lord, when
did we ever see you hungry or thirsty or a
stranger or naked or sick or in prison, and
not help you?’

25:1 Or *virgins;* also in 25:7, 11. **25:15** Greek *talents;* also throughout the story. A talent is equal to 75 pounds or 34 kilograms. **25:21** Greek *Enter into the joy of your master* [or *your Lord*]; also in 25:23. **25:31** “Son of Man” is a title Jesus used for himself. **25:32** Or *peoples.* **25:40** Greek *my brothers.* **25:41** Greek *his angels.*

45 “And he will answer, ‘I tell you the truth,
when you refused to help the least of these
my brothers and sisters, you were refusing
to help me.’
46 “And they will go away into eternal
punishment, but the righteous will go into
eternal life.”

The Plot to Kill Jesus

26 When Jesus had finished saying all
these things, he said to his disciples,
2 “As you know, Passover begins in two days,
and the Son of Man* will be handed over to
be crucified.”
3 At that same time the leading priests
and elders were meeting at the residence
of Caiaphas, the high priest, 4 plotting how
to capture Jesus secretly and kill him. 5 “But
not during the Passover celebration,” they
agreed, “or the people may riot.”

Jesus Anointed at Bethany

6 Meanwhile, Jesus was in Bethany at the
home of Simon, a man who had previously had leprosy. 7 While he was eating,* a
woman came in with a beautiful alabaster
jar of expensive perfume and poured it over
his head.
8 The disciples were indignant when they
saw this. “What a waste!” they said. 9 “It
could have been sold for a high price and
the money given to the poor.”
10 But Jesus, aware of this, replied, “Why
criticize this woman for doing such a
good thing to me? 11 You will always have
the poor among you, but you will not
always have me. 12 She has poured this
perfume on me to prepare my body for
burial. 13 I tell you the truth, wherever the
Good News is preached throughout the
world, this woman’s deed will be remembered and discussed.”

Judas Agrees to Betray Jesus

14 Then Judas Iscariot, one of the twelve
disciples, went to the leading priests 15 and
asked, “How much will you pay me to
betray Jesus to you?” And they gave him
thirty pieces of silver. 16 From that time on,
Judas began looking for an opportunity to
betray Jesus.

The Last Supper

17 On the first day of the Festival of Unleavened Bread, the disciples came to
Jesus and asked, “Where do you want us to
prepare the Passover meal for you?”
18 “As you go into the city,” he told them,
“you will see a certain man. Tell him, ‘The
Teacher says: My time has come, and I will

▸ **26:14-16** *See* ***Why did Judas betray Jesus?****, page 1191.*

The Last Supper

Knowing he would die the next day, Jesus shared the Passover meal with his disciples (Matthew 26:17-30). This annual festival celebrated the Exodus (e.g., Exodus 12:14-20; Deuteronomy 16:1-8); but by Jesus’ time it also looked forward to God’s freeing his people once again, this time from Roman rule.

But Jesus gave a new meaning to the meal. He changed the traditional wording over the bread and wine, saying that the bread now symbolized his body and the wine his blood, both of which would shortly be offered up. In doing this, he was placing himself at the center of Israel’s story, claiming to be the one who would bring about not only the new exodus for which Israel longed but also the new covenant that Jeremiah had prophesied (Jeremiah 31:31-34), a covenant bringing forgiveness of sins (Matthew 26:28).

Jesus’ command to “do this in remembrance of me” (Luke 22:19) led to the sharing of bread and wine becoming a key part of Christian worship, initially in the context of a meal (Acts 2:46). Today Christians still remember Christ’s death this way, calling it by different names (Mass, the Eucharist, Holy Communion, the Lord’s Supper, Breaking of Bread) and celebrating it in very different styles.

eat the Passover meal with my disciples at
your house.'" 19 So the disciples did as Jesus
told them and prepared the Passover meal
there.
20 When it was evening, Jesus sat down
at the table* with the Twelve. 21 While they
were eating, he said, "I tell you the truth,
one of you will betray me."
22 Greatly distressed, each one asked in
turn, "Am I the one, Lord?"
23 He replied, "One of you who has just
eaten from this bowl with me will betray
me. 24 For the Son of Man must die, as the
Scriptures declared long ago. But how terrible it will be for the one who betrays him.
It would be far better for that man if he had
never been born!"
25 Judas, the one who would betray him,
also asked, "Rabbi, am I the one?"
And Jesus told him, "You have said it."
26 As they were eating, Jesus took some
bread and blessed it. Then he broke it in
pieces and gave it to the disciples, saying,
"Take this and eat it, for this is my body."
27 And he took a cup of wine and gave
thanks to God for it. He gave it to them and
said, "Each of you drink from it, 28 for this
is my blood, which confirms the covenant*
between God and his people. It is poured
out as a sacrifice to forgive the sins of many.
29 Mark my words—I will not drink wine
again until the day I drink it new with you
in my Father's Kingdom."
30 Then they sang a hymn and went out to
the Mount of Olives.

Jesus Predicts Peter's Denial

31 On the way, Jesus told them, "Tonight all
of you will desert me. For the Scriptures say,

'God will strike* the Shepherd,
and the sheep of the flock will
be scattered.'

32 But after I have been raised from the dead,
I will go ahead of you to Galilee and meet
you there."
33 Peter declared, "Even if everyone else
deserts you, I will never desert you."
34 Jesus replied, "I tell you the truth,
Peter—this very night, before the rooster
crows, you will deny three times that you
even know me."
35 "No!" Peter insisted. "Even if I have to
die with you, I will never deny you!" And all
the other disciples vowed the same.

Jesus Prays in Gethsemane

36 Then Jesus went with them to the olive
grove called Gethsemane, and he said, "Sit
here while I go over there to pray." 37 He took
Peter and Zebedee's two sons, James and
John, and he became anguished and distressed. 38 He told them, "My soul is crushed
with grief to the point of death. Stay here
and keep watch with me."
39 He went on a little farther and bowed
with his face to the ground, praying, "My
Father! If it is possible, let this cup of suffering be taken away from me. Yet I want your
will to be done, not mine."
40 Then he returned to the disciples
and found them asleep. He said to Peter,
"Couldn't you watch with me even one
hour? 41 Keep watch and pray, so that you
will not give in to temptation. For the spirit
is willing, but the body is weak!"

26:2 "Son of Man" is a title Jesus used for himself. **26:7** Or *reclining*. **26:20** Or *Jesus reclined*. **26:28** Some manuscripts read *the new covenant*. **26:31** Greek *I will strike*. Zech 13:7.

Gethsemane

All of us have our favorite places to which we like to retreat when we need some rest or time to think, and Jesus was no different. A garden called Gethsemane on the slopes of the Mount of Olives, overlooking Jerusalem, was one of Jesus' favorite spots (John 18:1-2). "Gethsemane" means "oil press," indicating there was at least one oil press there, for in Jesus' day the hillside was covered with olive groves. It is tragic that a place of intimacy with his disciples became the very place that one of them, Judas, betrayed him (Matthew 26:47-56). Since it was night, Jesus would have easily seen the flames of the crowd's torches as they left the city and made their way down the Kidron Valley and up the slopes of the Mount of Olives; yet he chose not to run but to await what he knew was his God-given destiny.

42 Then Jesus left them a second time and prayed, "My Father! If this cup cannot be taken away* unless I drink it, your will be done." 43 When he returned to them again, he found them sleeping, for they couldn't keep their eyes open.

44 So he went to pray a third time, saying the same things again. 45 Then he came to the disciples and said, "Go ahead and sleep. Have your rest. But look—the time has come. The Son of Man is betrayed into the hands of sinners. 46 Up, let's be going. Look, my betrayer is here!"

Jesus Is Betrayed and Arrested

47 And even as Jesus said this, Judas, one of the twelve disciples, arrived with a crowd of men armed with swords and clubs. They had been sent by the leading priests and elders of the people. 48 The traitor, Judas, had given them a prearranged signal: "You will know which one to arrest when I greet him with a kiss." 49 So Judas came straight to Jesus. "Greetings, Rabbi!" he exclaimed and gave him the kiss.

50 Jesus said, "My friend, go ahead and do what you have come for."

Then the others grabbed Jesus and arrested him. 51 But one of the men with Jesus pulled out his sword and struck the high priest's slave, slashing off his ear.

52 "Put away your sword," Jesus told him. "Those who use the sword will die by the sword. 53 Don't you realize that I could ask my Father for thousands* of angels to protect us, and he would send them instantly? 54 But if I did, how would the Scriptures be fulfilled that describe what must happen now?"

55 Then Jesus said to the crowd, "Am I some dangerous revolutionary, that you come with swords and clubs to arrest me? Why didn't you arrest me in the Temple? I was there teaching every day. 56 But this is all happening to fulfill the words of the prophets as recorded in the Scriptures." At that point, all the disciples deserted him and fled.

Jesus before the Council

57 Then the people who had arrested Jesus led him to the home of Caiaphas, the high priest, where the teachers of religious law and the elders had gathered. 58 Meanwhile, Peter followed him at a distance and came to the high priest's courtyard. He went in and sat with the guards and waited to see how it would all end.

59 Inside, the leading priests and the entire high council* were trying to find witnesses who would lie about Jesus, so they could put him to death. 60 But even though they found many who agreed to give false witness, they could not use anyone's testimony. Finally, two men came forward 61 who declared, "This man said, 'I am able to destroy the Temple of God and rebuild it in three days.'"

62 Then the high priest stood up and said to Jesus, "Well, aren't you going to answer these charges? What do you have to say for yourself?" 63 But Jesus remained silent. Then the high priest said to him, "I demand in the name of the living God—tell us if you are the Messiah, the Son of God."

64 Jesus replied, "You have said it. And in the future you will see the Son of Man seated in the place of power at God's right hand* and coming on the clouds of heaven."*

65 Then the high priest tore his clothing to show his horror and said, "Blasphemy! Why do we need other witnesses? You have all heard his blasphemy. 66 What is your verdict?"

"Guilty!" they shouted. "He deserves to die!"

67 Then they began to spit in Jesus' face and beat him with their fists. And some slapped him, 68 jeering, "Prophesy to us, you Messiah! Who hit you that time?"

Peter Denies Jesus

69 Meanwhile, Peter was sitting outside in the courtyard. A servant girl came over and said to him, "You were one of those with Jesus the Galilean."

70 But Peter denied it in front of everyone. "I don't know what you're talking about," he said.

71 Later, out by the gate, another servant girl noticed him and said to those standing around, "This man was with Jesus of Nazareth.*"

72 Again Peter denied it, this time with an oath. "I don't even know the man," he said.

73 A little later some of the other bystanders

▸ **26:57** *See **Annas and Caiaphas**, page 1227.*

came over to Peter and said, "You must be one of them; we can tell by your Galilean accent."

[74]Peter swore, "A curse on me if I'm lying—I don't know the man!" And immediately the rooster crowed.

[75]Suddenly, Jesus' words flashed through Peter's mind: "Before the rooster crows, you will deny three times that you even know me." And he went away, weeping bitterly.

Judas Hangs Himself

27 Very early in the morning the leading priests and the elders of the people met again to lay plans for putting Jesus to death. [2]Then they bound him, led him away, and took him to Pilate, the Roman governor.

[3]When Judas, who had betrayed him, realized that Jesus had been condemned to die, he was filled with remorse. So he took the thirty pieces of silver back to the leading priests and the elders. [4]"I have sinned," he declared, "for I have betrayed an innocent man."

"What do we care?" they retorted. "That's your problem."

[5]Then Judas threw the silver coins down in the Temple and went out and hanged himself.

[6]The leading priests picked up the coins. "It wouldn't be right to put this money in the Temple treasury," they said, "since it was payment for murder."* [7]After some discussion they finally decided to buy the potter's field, and they made it into a cemetery for foreigners. [8]That is why the field is still called the Field of Blood. [9]This fulfilled the prophecy of Jeremiah that says,

"They took* the thirty pieces of silver—
the price at which he was valued by
the people of Israel,
10 and purchased the potter's field,
as the LORD directed.*"

Jesus' Trial before Pilate

[11]Now Jesus was standing before Pilate, the Roman governor. "Are you the king of the Jews?" the governor asked him.

Jesus replied, "You have said it."

[12]But when the leading priests and the elders made their accusations against him, Jesus remained silent. [13]"Don't you hear all these charges they are bringing against you?" Pilate demanded. [14]But Jesus made no response to any of the charges, much to the governor's surprise.

[15]Now it was the governor's custom each year during the Passover celebration to release one prisoner to the crowd—anyone they wanted. [16]This year there was a notorious prisoner, a man named Barabbas.* [17]As the crowds gathered before Pilate's house that morning, he asked them, "Which one do you want me to release to you—Barabbas, or Jesus who is called the Messiah?" [18](He knew very well that the religious leaders had arrested Jesus out of envy.)

[19]Just then, as Pilate was sitting on the judgment seat, his wife sent him this message: "Leave that innocent man alone. I suffered through a terrible nightmare about him last night."

[20]Meanwhile, the leading priests and the elders persuaded the crowd to ask for Barabbas to be released and for Jesus to be put to death. [21]So the governor asked again, "Which of these two do you want me to release to you?"

The crowd shouted back, "Barabbas!"

[22]Pilate responded, "Then what should I do with Jesus who is called the Messiah?"

They shouted back, "Crucify him!"

[23]"Why?" Pilate demanded. "What crime has he committed?"

But the mob roared even louder, "Crucify him!"

[24]Pilate saw that he wasn't getting anywhere and that a riot was developing. So he sent for a bowl of water and washed his hands before the crowd, saying, "I am innocent of this man's blood. The responsibility is yours!"

[25]And all the people yelled back, "We will take responsibility for his death—we and our children!"*

[26]So Pilate released Barabbas to them. He ordered Jesus flogged with a lead-tipped whip, then turned him over to the Roman soldiers to be crucified.

26:42 Greek *If this cannot pass.* **26:53** Greek *twelve legions.* **26:59** Greek *the Sanhedrin.* **26:64a** Greek *seated at the right hand of the power.* See Ps 110:1. **26:64b** See Dan 7:13. **26:71** Or *Jesus the Nazarene.* **27:6** Greek *since it is the price for blood.* **27:9** Or *I took.* **27:9-10** Greek *as the LORD directed me.* Zech 11:12-13; Jer 32:6-9. **27:16** Some manuscripts read *Jesus Barabbas;* also in 27:17. **27:25** Greek *"His blood be on us and on our children."*

▸ **27:11** *See* ***Pilate,*** *page 1145.*

The Soldiers Mock Jesus

27 Some of the governor's soldiers took
Jesus into their headquarters* and called
out the entire regiment. 28 They stripped
him and put a scarlet robe on him. 29 They
wove thorn branches into a crown and put
it on his head, and they placed a reed stick
in his right hand as a scepter. Then they
knelt before him in mockery and taunted,
"Hail! King of the Jews!" 30 And they spit
on him and grabbed the stick and struck
him on the head with it. 31 When they were
finally tired of mocking him, they took
off the robe and put his own clothes on
him again. Then they led him away to be
crucified.

The Crucifixion

32 Along the way, they came across a man
named Simon, who was from Cyrene,* and
the soldiers forced him to carry Jesus' cross.
33 And they went out to a place called Golgotha (which means "Place of the Skull").
34 The soldiers gave Jesus wine mixed with
bitter gall, but when he had tasted it, he
refused to drink it.

35 After they had nailed him to the cross,
the soldiers gambled for his clothes by
throwing dice.* 36 Then they sat around and
kept guard as he hung there. 37 A sign was
fastened above Jesus' head, announcing the
charge against him. It read: "This is Jesus,
the King of the Jews." 38 Two revolutionaries* were crucified with him, one on his
right and one on his left.

39 The people passing by shouted abuse,
shaking their heads in mockery. 40 "Look
at you now!" they yelled at him. "You said
you were going to destroy the Temple and
rebuild it in three days. Well then, if you
are the Son of God, save yourself and come
down from the cross!"

41 The leading priests, the teachers of religious law, and the elders also mocked Jesus.
42 "He saved others," they scoffed, "but
he can't save himself! So he is the King of
Israel, is he? Let him come down from the
cross right now, and we will believe in him!

▸ **27:33** *See **Golgotha, Place of the Skull**, page 1193.*

The death of Jesus

While tradition makes much of Jesus' crucifixion, the Gospels say very little about the details of it. Matthew simply notes, "After they had nailed him to the cross . . ." (27:35). And yet crucifixion was horrific, designed to instill fear. The victim was flogged and stripped naked, and his wrists were nailed to the crossbar, which was lifted onto a stake. The legs were pushed up and sideways and the ankles nailed to the upright so the arms had to carry the weight, making breathing almost impossible. Victims could remain conscious for days before finally dying, their bodies left for the birds.

But it was not just pain that caused Jesus to cry, "My God, my God, why have you abandoned me?" (27:46); it was the weight of humanity's sin that he was carrying, which separated him from his Father. Unusually, he survived only three hours. As he died, "the curtain in the sanctuary of the Temple was torn in two" (27:51)—the curtain of the Most Holy Place where God was believed to dwell—symbolizing that the way to God was now open.

In those days, crucifixion was despised—by Romans, because it was reserved for the worst offenders; by Jews, because the Law said that anyone who was hung on a tree was cursed in the sight of God (Deuteronomy 21:23). When Jesus died on the cross, therefore, he experienced not just death, but a death despised by all. Yet this death was what God would use to deal with our sin and put us in a right relationship with himself.

▸ *See also **Redemption**, page 1136; **Justification**, page 1288; **Christ's resurrection and ours**, page 1320; **Reconciliation**, page 1328.*

43He trusted God, so let God rescue him now if he wants him! For he said, 'I am the Son of God.'" 44Even the revolutionaries who were crucified with him ridiculed him in the same way.

The Death of Jesus

45At noon, darkness fell across the whole land until three o'clock. 46At about three o'clock, Jesus called out with a loud voice, *"Eli, Eli,* lema sabachthani?"* which means "My God, my God, why have you abandoned me?"*

47Some of the bystanders misunderstood and thought he was calling for the prophet Elijah. 48One of them ran and filled a sponge with sour wine, holding it up to him on a reed stick so he could drink. 49But the rest said, "Wait! Let's see whether Elijah comes to save him."*

50Then Jesus shouted out again, and he released his spirit. 51At that moment the curtain in the sanctuary of the Temple was torn in two, from top to bottom. The earth shook, rocks split apart, 52and tombs opened. The bodies of many godly men and women who had died were raised from the dead. 53They left the cemetery after Jesus' resurrection, went into the holy city of Jerusalem, and appeared to many people.

54The Roman officer* and the other soldiers at the crucifixion were terrified by the earthquake and all that had happened. They said, "This man truly was the Son of God!"

55And many women who had come from Galilee with Jesus to care for him were watching from a distance. 56Among them were Mary Magdalene, Mary (the mother of James and Joseph), and the mother of James and John, the sons of Zebedee.

The Burial of Jesus

57As evening approached, Joseph, a rich man from Arimathea who had become a follower of Jesus, 58went to Pilate and asked for Jesus' body. And Pilate issued an order to release it to him. 59Joseph took the body and wrapped it in a long sheet of clean linen cloth. 60He placed it in his own new tomb, which had been carved out of the rock. Then he rolled a great stone across the entrance and left. 61Both Mary Magdalene and the other Mary were sitting across from the tomb and watching.

The Guard at the Tomb

62The next day, on the Sabbath,* the leading priests and Pharisees went to see Pilate. 63They told him, "Sir, we remember what that deceiver once said while he was still alive: 'After three days I will rise from the dead.' 64So we request that you seal the tomb until the third day. This will prevent his disciples from coming and stealing his body and then telling everyone he was raised from the dead! If that happens, we'll be worse off than we were at first."

65Pilate replied, "Take guards and secure it the best you can." 66So they sealed the tomb and posted guards to protect it.

The Resurrection

28 Early on Sunday morning,* as the new day was dawning, Mary Magdalene and the other Mary went out to visit the tomb.

2Suddenly there was a great earthquake! For an angel of the Lord came down from heaven, rolled aside the stone, and sat on it. 3His face shone like lightning, and his clothing was as white as snow. 4The guards shook with fear when they saw him, and they fell into a dead faint.

5Then the angel spoke to the women. "Don't be afraid!" he said. "I know you are looking for Jesus, who was crucified. 6He isn't here! He is risen from the dead, just as he said would happen. Come, see where his body was lying. 7And now, go quickly and tell his disciples that he has risen from the dead, and he is going ahead of you to Galilee. You will see him there. Remember what I have told you."

8The women ran quickly from the tomb. They were very frightened but also filled with great joy, and they rushed to give the disciples the angel's message. 9And as they

27:27 Or *into the Praetorium.* **27:32** *Cyrene* was a city in northern Africa. **27:35** Greek *by casting lots.* A few late manuscripts add *This fulfilled the word of the prophet: "They divided my garments among themselves and cast lots for my robe."* See Ps 22:18. **27:38** Or *criminals;* also in 27:44. **27:46a** Some manuscripts read *Eloi, Eloi.* **27:46b** Ps 22:1. **27:49** Some manuscripts add *And another took a spear and pierced his side, and out flowed water and blood.* Compare John 19:34. **27:54** Greek *The centurion.* **27:62** Or *On the next day, which is after the Preparation.* **28:1** Greek *After the Sabbath, on the first day of the week.*

▸ **27:46** *See **Jesus' seven sayings from the cross**, page 1229.* **28:1** *See **Mary Magdalene**, page 1166.*

went, Jesus met them and greeted them.
And they ran to him, grasped his feet, and
worshiped him. 10Then Jesus said to them,
"Don't be afraid! Go tell my brothers to leave
for Galilee, and they will see me there."

The Report of the Guard

11As the women were on their way, some of
the guards went into the city and told the
leading priests what had happened. 12A
meeting with the elders was called, and
they decided to give the soldiers a large
bribe. 13They told the soldiers, "You must
say, 'Jesus' disciples came during the night
while we were sleeping, and they stole
his body.' 14If the governor hears about it,
we'll stand up for you so you won't get in
trouble." 15So the guards accepted the bribe
and said what they were told to say. Their
story spread widely among the Jews, and
they still tell it today.

The Great Commission

16Then the eleven disciples left for Galilee,
going to the mountain where Jesus had told
them to go. 17When they saw him, they worshiped him—but some of them doubted!
18Jesus came and told his disciples,
"I have been given all authority in heaven
and on earth. 19Therefore, go and make disciples of all the nations,* baptizing them in
the name of the Father and the Son and the
Holy Spirit. 20Teach these new disciples to
obey all the commands I have given you.
And be sure of this: I am with you always,
even to the end of the age."

28:19 Or *all peoples.*

▸ **28:19-20** *See* ***Being a witness****, page 1456.*

Mark *Jesus, the suffering Son*

Mark's Gospel is a fast-moving account of Jesus' life, emphasizing miracles rather than teaching. However, Jesus is no mere miracle-worker; from the outset Mark makes clear he is "Jesus the Messiah, the Son of God" (1:1), a theme that recurs at key points (e.g., 8:29; 15:39). But this divine Jesus is also utterly human, falling asleep after exhausting ministry and exasperated at his disciples for their slowness to understand. The Messiah is truly both "Son of God" and "Son of Man," Mark's two favorite titles for him.

Mark underlines to his mainly Gentile readers—we know they were Gentiles because even simple Jewish words and customs are explained—that this Messiah is a suffering Messiah (e.g., 8:31), and that suffering is part of the call to all who want to be his disciples (e.g., 8:34-35). This emphasis on discipleship—a major theme for Mark—was particularly relevant because he was writing this in Rome when Christians were beginning to face severe persecution under Emperor Nero. Mark wanted to encourage them to follow the example of their Lord and not to give up.

What's it all about?

Omitting the story of Jesus' birth, Mark begins his Gospel with the preaching of John the Baptist and how it fulfilled Isaiah's prophecy. He then quickly narrates Jesus' baptism, temptation, and call of the disciples to take us to the beginning of Jesus' ministry (1:14). There is a sense of urgency about Jesus' mission. Jesus healed and delivered people from demons at every turn; we can almost feel the excitement as we see people thronging around him. Whole towns and villages were stirring, trying to work out who this man was (1:27); but Mark shows that Jesus revealed who he really was by what he did and what he taught.

When Jesus called Levi (Matthew), an unpopular tax collector, to follow him and then ate in his house, the religious leaders took offense (2:13-17)—the beginning of much future antagonism.

In chapter 4, Mark gives us a taste of Jesus' teaching through parables, collecting together some of his parables of the Kingdom. But he can't wait to get back to Jesus' miracles, and in chapters 4 and 5 we find Jesus calming the storm, driving out demons, healing disease, and raising a little girl to life.

But back in Nazareth, his hometown, Jesus was rejected (chapter 6), so he traveled from village to village, teaching, and sent out his twelve disciples to preach as well. Even when Herod had John the Baptist beheaded, Jesus was undeterred. He continued to do miracles of healing for everyone who came to him, including a non-Jewish woman (chapter 7), showing his message was not just for Jews. He was concerned for the crowds and miraculously fed them, though he refused the religious leaders' demand for a special sign (chapter 8).

Then, it was time for Jesus to confront his disciples with his true identity. "Who do you say I am?" he asked them (8:29). Although Peter acknowledged him as the Messiah, he didn't truly understand Jesus' mission. So when Jesus explained that he would be a *suffering* Messiah, Peter wanted to correct him; but from then on Jesus began to prepare his disciples for his death (8:31). While Jesus continued to preach and heal people, the disciples' lack of understanding and faith is brought into sharp relief (chapters 9–10).

From chapter 11 onward, events move even more rapidly. Jesus entered Jerusalem to the delight of the crowds, but attracted more criticism from the religious leaders. They saw him as a dangerous breaker of their traditions, especially through his healings on the Sabbath. And they suspected that the healings, which made him so popular, were done through the devil's power. Mark records more of Jesus' teaching, including warnings about coming events, both for Jerusalem and the whole world (chapter 13), before turning to the final events of Jesus' life: his last supper with his followers, his betrayal, and his crucifixion. These were dark days for the disciples. Their failures reached a climax when Peter denied ever having known Jesus (chapter 14). Jesus was crucified and then buried in a tomb belonging to one of his followers.

Mark concludes with the story of the empty tomb and the promise that the risen Jesus would appear to the disciples—including Peter, who denied him (16:1-8). A concluding section, added a little later by someone other than Mark, summarizes the appearances of the risen Jesus (16:9-20).

What does it mean for us?

In Mark's story, Jesus is a man of action—constantly on the move, healing the sick and preaching the Good News of God's Kingdom. His miracles show him acting with God-given authority that stirred people's excitement and expectation.

But as the story develops, the focus on Jesus' power and authority gives way to suffering and death. From chapter 8—where Peter at last recognizes that Jesus is the Messiah—onward, Jesus' path is set toward the cross. Only one more miracle story occurs; the rest is an account of Jesus' journey toward his destiny in Jerusalem—to die and give up his life for the sake of the world.

Mark's portrayal of the disciples shows how all followers of Jesus are called to mirror both the power and the suffering of Jesus. In their witness to God's Kingdom, they share his power, but they must also learn that the way of discipleship is a way of self-denial, suffering, and learning through our mistakes. Mark never covers up the disciples' failures—even Peter's denial of Jesus. And yet after his resurrection Jesus promises forgiveness to Peter (see 16:7). Nothing is more encouraging in our discipleship than to know that Jesus' first disciples fell far short of perfection—and yet he worked with them, was patient with them, and built his church through them.

▶ *See also **Four Gospels, one story**, pages 1060-1065; **Mark**, page 1388; **The Ministry of Jesus** map, Visual Overview Z10.*

OVERVIEW

John the Baptist Prepares the Way

1 This is the Good News about Jesus the Messiah, the Son of God.* It began 2 just as the prophet Isaiah had written:

> "Look, I am sending my messenger
> ahead of you,
> and he will prepare your way.*
> 3 He is a voice shouting in the wilderness,
> 'Prepare the way for the LORD's coming!
> Clear the road for him!'*"

4 This messenger was John the Baptist. He was in the wilderness and preached that people should be baptized to show that they had repented of their sins and turned to God to be forgiven. 5 All of Judea, including all the people of Jerusalem, went out to see and hear John. And when they confessed their sins, he baptized them in the Jordan River. 6 His clothes were woven from coarse camel hair, and he wore a leather belt around his waist. For food he ate locusts and wild honey.

7 John announced: "Someone is coming soon who is greater than I am—so much greater that I'm not even worthy to stoop down like a slave and untie the straps of his sandals. 8 I baptize you with* water, but he will baptize you with the Holy Spirit!"

The Baptism and Temptation of Jesus

9 One day Jesus came from Nazareth in Galilee, and John baptized him in the Jordan River. 10 As Jesus came up out of the water, he saw the heavens splitting apart and the Holy Spirit descending on him* like a dove. 11 And a voice from heaven said, "You are my dearly loved Son, and you bring me great joy."

12 The Spirit then compelled Jesus to go into the wilderness, 13 where he was tempted by Satan for forty days. He was out among the wild animals, and angels took care of him.

14 Later on, after John was arrested, Jesus went into Galilee, where he preached God's Good News.* 15 "The time promised by God has come at last!" he announced. "The Kingdom of God is near! Repent of your sins and believe the Good News!"

The First Disciples

16 One day as Jesus was walking along the shore of the Sea of Galilee, he saw Simon* and his brother Andrew throwing a net into the water, for they fished for a living. 17 Jesus called out to them, "Come, follow me, and I will show you how to fish for people!" 18 And they left their nets at once and followed him.

19 A little farther up the shore Jesus saw Zebedee's sons, James and John, in a boat repairing their nets. 20 He called them at once, and they also followed him, leaving their father, Zebedee, in the boat with the hired men.

Jesus Casts Out an Evil Spirit

21 Jesus and his companions went to the town of Capernaum. When the Sabbath day came, he went into the synagogue and began to teach. 22 The people were amazed at his teaching, for he taught with real authority—quite unlike the teachers of religious law.

23 Suddenly, a man in the synagogue who was possessed by an evil* spirit cried out, 24 "Why are you interfering with us, Jesus of Nazareth? Have you come to destroy us? I know who you are—the Holy One of God!"

25 But Jesus reprimanded him. "Be quiet! Come out of the man," he ordered. 26 At that, the evil spirit screamed, threw the man into a convulsion, and then came out of him.

27 Amazement gripped the audience, and they began to discuss what had happened. "What sort of new teaching is this?" they asked excitedly. "It has such authority! Even evil spirits obey his orders!" 28 The news about Jesus spread quickly throughout the entire region of Galilee.

Jesus Heals Many People

29 After Jesus left the synagogue with James and John, they went to Simon and Andrew's home. 30 Now Simon's mother-in-law was sick in bed with a high fever. They told Jesus about her right away. 31 So he went to her bedside, took her by the hand, and helped her sit up. Then the fever left her, and she prepared a meal for them.

32 That evening after sunset, many sick

1:1 Some manuscripts do not include *the Son of God.* **1:2** Mal 3:1. **1:3** Isa 40:3 (Greek version). **1:8** Or *in;* also in 1:8b. **1:10** Or *toward him,* or *into him.* **1:14** Some manuscripts read *the Good News of the Kingdom of God.* **1:16** *Simon* is called "Peter" in 3:16 and thereafter. **1:23** Greek *unclean;* also in 1:26, 27.

▸ **1:4** *See* ***John the Baptist****, page 1156.* **1:9** *See* ***Jesus' baptism****, page 1073.*
1:15 *See* ***God's Kingdom****, page 1074.*

and demon-possessed people were brought to Jesus. 33The whole town gathered at the door to watch. 34So Jesus healed many people who were sick with various diseases, and he cast out many demons. But because the demons knew who he was, he did not allow them to speak.

Jesus Preaches in Galilee

35Before daybreak the next morning, Jesus got up and went out to an isolated place to pray. 36Later Simon and the others went out to find him. 37When they found him, they said, "Everyone is looking for you."

38But Jesus replied, "We must go on to other towns as well, and I will preach to them, too. That is why I came." 39So he traveled throughout the region of Galilee, preaching in the synagogues and casting out demons.

Jesus Heals a Man with Leprosy

40A man with leprosy came and knelt in front of Jesus, begging to be healed. "If you are willing, you can heal me and make me clean," he said.

41Moved with compassion,* Jesus reached out and touched him. "I am willing," he said. "Be healed!" 42Instantly the leprosy disappeared, and the man was healed. 43Then Jesus sent him on his way with a stern warning: 44"Don't tell anyone about this. Instead, go to the priest and let him examine you. Take along the offering required in the law of Moses for those who have been healed of leprosy.* This will be a public testimony that you have been cleansed."

45But the man went and spread the word, proclaiming to everyone what had happened. As a result, large crowds soon surrounded Jesus, and he couldn't publicly enter a town anywhere. He had to stay out in the secluded places, but people from everywhere kept coming to him.

Jesus Heals a Paralyzed Man

2 When Jesus returned to Capernaum several days later, the news spread quickly that he was back home. 2Soon the house where he was staying was so packed with visitors that there was no more room, even outside the door. While he was preaching God's word to them, 3four men arrived carrying a paralyzed man on a mat. 4They couldn't bring him to Jesus because of the crowd, so they dug a hole through the roof above his head. Then they lowered the man on his mat, right down in front of Jesus.

▸ **2:1** *See* ***Capernaum****, page 1096.*

The gospel

Mark tells us what his book is all about in his opening sentence: "This is the Good News about Jesus the Messiah, the Son of God" (1:1). "Good News," or "gospel," translates the Greek word *euangelion,* from which our word "evangelism" comes. Prior to the writing of Mark, no written work had ever been called a *euangelion*. Rather, the word was used by messengers of the Roman emperor who were dispatched across the empire bearing news. They went to key places in cities and shouted, "*Euangelion!* . . . Good news!" and then, as the crowd gathered, shared with them the news that the emperor had sent.

Mark is saying that's what we have here: good news! It is the good news that God's Kingdom is here (1:15) because Jesus, God's Son, is here (1:1). Jesus is both the bringer of the good news and the good news itself: the good news that through him, the Messiah (Christ), God is intervening to save people—though, as the reader will see, in a very different way from what was expected.

When we speak about Jesus today, we should ensure that what we share is good news, not bad news. There is indeed bad news for those who reject Christ, but that is never where Jesus began.

▸ *See also* ***The power of the gospel****, page 1279.*

[5]Seeing their faith, Jesus said to the paralyzed man, "My child, your sins are forgiven."

[6]But some of the teachers of religious law who were sitting there thought to themselves, [7]"What is he saying? This is blasphemy! Only God can forgive sins!"

[8]Jesus knew immediately what they were thinking, so he asked them, "Why do you question this in your hearts? [9]Is it easier to say to the paralyzed man 'Your sins are forgiven,' or 'Stand up, pick up your mat, and walk'? [10]So I will prove to you that the Son of Man* has the authority on earth to forgive sins." Then Jesus turned to the paralyzed man and said, [11]"Stand up, pick up your mat, and go home!"

[12]And the man jumped up, grabbed his mat, and walked out through the stunned onlookers. They were all amazed and praised God, exclaiming, "We've never seen anything like this before!"

Jesus Calls Levi (Matthew)

[13]Then Jesus went out to the lakeshore again and taught the crowds that were coming to him. [14]As he walked along, he saw Levi son of Alphaeus sitting at his tax collector's booth. "Follow me and be my disciple," Jesus said to him. So Levi got up and followed him.

[15]Later, Levi invited Jesus and his disciples to his home as dinner guests, along with many tax collectors and other disreputable sinners. (There were many people of this kind among Jesus' followers.) [16]But when the teachers of religious law who were Pharisees* saw him eating with tax collectors and other sinners, they asked his disciples, "Why does he eat with such scum?*"

[17]When Jesus heard this, he told them, "Healthy people don't need a doctor—sick people do. I have come to call not those who think they are righteous, but those who know they are sinners."

A Discussion about Fasting

[18]Once when John's disciples and the Pharisees were fasting, some people came to Jesus and asked, "Why don't your disciples fast like John's disciples and the Pharisees do?"

[19]Jesus replied, "Do wedding guests fast while celebrating with the groom? Of course not. They can't fast while the groom is with them. [20]But someday the groom will be taken away from them, and then they will fast.

1:41 Some manuscripts read *Moved with anger.* **1:44** See Lev 14:2-32. **2:10** "Son of Man" is a title Jesus used for himself. **2:16a** Greek *the scribes of the Pharisees.* **2:16b** Greek *with tax collectors and sinners?*

▸ **2:13-17** See ***Matthew***, page 1081.

Sunday

Although given as God's gift to do people good (see *The Sabbath*, page 918), by New Testament times the Sabbath had become a burden, as the teachers of religious law added countless additions and interpretations to God's command. As a result, Jesus reminded them that "the Sabbath was made to meet the needs of people, and not people to meet the requirements of the Sabbath" (Mark 2:27).

Christians no longer need to keep Sabbath (Saturday), of course, as we do not live under the Jewish Law that commanded it, and Paul challenged those who wanted to make a law of keeping it (Colossians 2:16-17). But since God modeled the principle of six days of labor followed by one day of rest, and then blessed that day (Genesis 2:2-3), it would seem wise to follow that principle today. Very early on, however, the church moved its day of celebration (though not necessarily a day of "rest," especially for slaves) from Saturday to Sunday to commemorate the Resurrection, which happened on a Sunday (Matthew 28:1; Mark 16:2; Luke 24:1; John 20:1). So, "on the first day of the week," they came together to break bread (Acts 20:7) and make their offerings (1 Corinthians 16:2).

Whenever we can, Christians should seek to make Sunday different from the rest of the week, enjoying physical rest and spiritual refreshment.

[21]"Besides, who would patch old clothing
with new cloth? For the new patch would
shrink and rip away from the old cloth,
leaving an even bigger tear than before.
[22]"And no one puts new wine into old
wineskins. For the wine would burst the
wineskins, and the wine and the skins
would both be lost. New wine calls for new
wineskins."

A Discussion about the Sabbath

[23]One Sabbath day as Jesus was walking
through some grainfields, his disciples
began breaking off heads of grain to eat.
[24]But the Pharisees said to Jesus, "Look,
why are they breaking the law by harvesting grain on the Sabbath?"
[25]Jesus said to them, "Haven't you ever
read in the Scriptures what David did when
he and his companions were hungry? [26]He
went into the house of God (during the days
when Abiathar was high priest) and broke
the law by eating the sacred loaves of bread
that only the priests are allowed to eat. He
also gave some to his companions."
[27]Then Jesus said to them, "The Sabbath
was made to meet the needs of people, and
not people to meet the requirements of the
Sabbath. [28]So the Son of Man is Lord, even
over the Sabbath!"

Jesus Heals on the Sabbath

3 Jesus went into the synagogue again
and noticed a man with a deformed
hand. [2]Since it was the Sabbath, Jesus'
enemies watched him closely. If he healed
the man's hand, they planned to accuse him
of working on the Sabbath.
[3]Jesus said to the man with the deformed
hand, "Come and stand in front of everyone." [4]Then he turned to his critics and
asked, "Does the law permit good deeds on
the Sabbath, or is it a day for doing evil? Is
this a day to save life or to destroy it?" But
they wouldn't answer him.
[5]He looked around at them angrily and
was deeply saddened by their hard hearts.
Then he said to the man, "Hold out your
hand." So the man held out his hand, and
it was restored! [6]At once the Pharisees went
away and met with the supporters of Herod
to plot how to kill Jesus.

Crowds Follow Jesus

[7]Jesus went out to the lake with his disciples, and a large crowd followed him.
They came from all over Galilee, Judea, [8]Je-
rusalem, Idumea, from east of the Jordan
River, and even from as far north as Tyre
and Sidon. The news about his miracles had
spread far and wide, and vast numbers of
people came to see him.
[9]Jesus instructed his disciples to have a
boat ready so the crowd would not crush
him. [10]He had healed many people that
day, so all the sick people eagerly pushed
forward to touch him. [11]And whenever those
possessed by evil* spirits caught sight of
him, the spirits would throw them to the

3:11 Greek *unclean;* also in 3:30.

Apostles of Jesus

From among his many followers, Jesus chose just twelve to be his "apostles" (Mark 3:14)—twelve to recall the twelve patriarchs (the sons of Jacob), and to symbolize his reestablishing of Israel around himself. These apostles would both travel with Jesus and go out to preach and cast out demons (3:14-15).

- ***Andrew*** Fisherman from Bethsaida, Simon Peter's brother, and former disciple of John the Baptist (John 1:35-40); known for introducing others to Jesus (John 1:41-42; 6:8-9; 12:22).
- ***Bartholomew*** Also known as Nathanael, from Cana (John 21:2), who was brought to Jesus by Philip, with whom he is often linked (Matthew 10:3; John 1:45). He quickly recognized Jesus for who he was and was blessed by Jesus because of it (John 1:45-51).
- ***James, son of Alphaeus*** Little is known about him; he may be the "James the younger" mentioned in Mark 15:40.

- ***James, son of Zebedee*** Fisherman from Capernaum, John's brother (Matthew 4:21-22; Mark 1:19-20), and one of Jesus' three closest friends, with him on key occasions (e.g., Mark 5:37; 14:32-33), yet whose mother sought for more (Matthew 20:20-28). He was killed by Herod Agrippa (Acts 12:1-2) in AD 44, the first apostle to be martyred.
- ***John*** Fisherman, James's brother, both called "Sons of Thunder" (Mark 3:17). Transformed into "the disciple Jesus loved" (John 13:23), he was one of Jesus' three closest friends and the only one of the apostles known to have witnessed Jesus' crucifixion—where Mary was entrusted to his care—and the first apostle to see Jesus' empty tomb (John 19:26-27; 20:3-5). He became a leader in the Jerusalem church (Acts 1-4; 8:14; Galatians 2:9) and later, according to tradition, in Ephesus. He wrote the fourth Gospel, three letters, and Revelation.
- ***Judas Iscariot*** The group's treasurer, who often stole their money for himself (John 12:6). His love of money led him to betray Jesus for thirty pieces of silver, four months' wages (Matthew 26:14-16, 47-49; Mark 14:10-11, 43-45; Luke 22:3-6, 47-48), and he then committed suicide out of remorse over Jesus' death (Matthew 27:3-10; Acts 1:16-19). He would thereafter be identified as the one who betrayed Jesus (e.g., Mark 3:19).
- ***Matthew*** Also called Levi, a tax collector, who introduced his fellow tax collectors to Jesus (Matthew 9:9-13; Mark 2:14-17; Luke 5:27-32) and who wrote the Gospel named after him.
- ***Peter*** Fisherman from Capernaum, Andrew's brother, and one of Jesus' three closest friends. He was originally called Simon, but Jesus renamed him Peter—Cephas in Aramaic, meaning "rock"—saying that on this rock (probably the rock of Peter's confession) he would build his church (Matthew 16:16-18). He sometimes acted as a spokesman for the other apostles (e.g., Matthew 15:15; John 6:68). Peter had to get the better of his natural impulsiveness, as seen especially in his denial of Jesus (Mark 14:27-31, 66-72) and later restoration (John 21:15-19). He became a leader in the Jerusalem church (e.g., Acts 1:15; 2:14; 4:1-3), a bold proclaimer of the gospel (e.g., Acts 2:14-41), and initiated taking the gospel to Gentiles (Acts 10). According to tradition, he ended up in Rome, where he was martyred during Nero's persecution.
- ***Philip*** From Bethsaida, a friend of Andrew, probably (as his name reflects) from a Greek background, which is why he was the one to introduce some Greeks to Jesus (John 12:20-22). He introduced Nathanael to Jesus (John 1:43-45).
- ***Simon the Zealot*** A former member of the Jewish revolutionary party committed to violently overthrowing Roman rule (Matthew 10:4; Mark 3:18; Luke 6:15).
- ***Thaddaeus*** Mentioned only in the list in Matthew 10:3 and Mark 3:18, but also called Judas, son of James (Luke 6:16; Acts 1:13). He probably changed his name to avoid association with Judas Iscariot (see John 14:22, where John has to make clear which Judas he means).
- ***Thomas*** Also called Didymus or "the Twin" (e.g., John 11:16), Thomas is best known for his doubting of the claims of Jesus' resurrection by the other disciples (John 20:24-25)—though his confession, "My Lord and my God!" when he encountered the risen Christ earned Jesus' commendation (John 20:26-29).

▸ *See also **Matthew**, page 1081; **Why did Judas betray Jesus?**, page 1191; **Andrew**, page 1200; **John**, page 1224; **Thomas**, page 1231; **Peter**, page 1421.*

ground in front of him shrieking, "You are
the Son of God!" [12]But Jesus sternly commanded the spirits not to reveal who he
was.

Jesus Chooses the Twelve Apostles

[13]Afterward Jesus went up on a mountain
and called out the ones he wanted to go
with him. And they came to him. [14]Then he
appointed twelve of them and called them
his apostles.* They were to accompany him,
and he would send them out to preach,
[15]giving them authority to cast out demons.
[16]These are the twelve he chose:

Simon (whom he named Peter),
[17] James and John (the sons of Zebedee,
but Jesus nicknamed them "Sons of
Thunder"*),
[18] Andrew,
Philip,
Bartholomew,
Matthew,
Thomas,
James (son of Alphaeus),
Thaddaeus,
Simon (the zealot*),
[19] Judas Iscariot (who later betrayed him).

Jesus and the Prince of Demons

[20]One time Jesus entered a house, and the
crowds began to gather again. Soon he and
his disciples couldn't even find time to eat.
[21]When his family heard what was happening, they tried to take him away. "He's out
of his mind," they said.

[22]But the teachers of religious law who
had arrived from Jerusalem said, "He's possessed by Satan,* the prince of demons.
That's where he gets the power to cast out
demons."

[23]Jesus called them over and responded
with an illustration. "How can Satan cast
out Satan?" he asked. [24]"A kingdom divided
by civil war will collapse. [25]Similarly, a
family splintered by feuding will fall apart.
[26]And if Satan is divided and fights against
himself, how can he stand? He would never
survive. [27]Let me illustrate this further. Who
is powerful enough to enter the house of a
strong man and plunder his goods? Only
someone even stronger—someone who
could tie him up and then plunder his
house.

[28]"I tell you the truth, all sin and blasphemy can be forgiven, [29]but anyone who
blasphemes the Holy Spirit will never be
forgiven. This is a sin with eternal consequences." [30]He told them this because they
were saying, "He's possessed by an evil
spirit."

The True Family of Jesus

[31]Then Jesus' mother and brothers came to
see him. They stood outside and sent word
for him to come out and talk with them.
[32]There was a crowd sitting around Jesus,
and someone said, "Your mother and your
brothers* are outside asking for you."

[33]Jesus replied, "Who is my mother? Who
are my brothers?" [34]Then he looked at those
around him and said, "Look, these are my
mother and brothers. [35]Anyone who does
God's will is my brother and sister and
mother."

Parable of the Farmer Scattering Seed

4 Once again Jesus began teaching by
the lakeshore. A very large crowd soon
gathered around him, so he got into a boat.
Then he sat in the boat while all the people
remained on the shore. [2]He taught them by
telling many stories in the form of parables,
such as this one:

[3]"Listen! A farmer went out to plant some
seed. [4]As he scattered it across his field,
some of the seed fell on a footpath, and
the birds came and ate it. [5]Other seed fell
on shallow soil with underlying rock. The
seed sprouted quickly because the soil was
shallow. [6]But the plant soon wilted under the
hot sun, and since it didn't have deep roots,
it died. [7]Other seed fell among thorns that
grew up and choked out the tender plants
so they produced no grain. [8]Still other seeds
fell on fertile soil, and they sprouted, grew,
and produced a crop that was thirty, sixty,
and even a hundred times as much as had
been planted!" [9]Then he said, "Anyone with
ears to hear should listen and understand."

[10]Later, when Jesus was alone with the
twelve disciples and with the others who
were gathered around, they asked him what
the parables meant.

▸ **3:29** *See **Is there anything God won't forgive?**, page 633.* **3:31-35** *See **Mary, the mother of Jesus**, page 1153.* **4:2** *See **The parables of Jesus**, page 1088.*

11 He replied, "You are permitted to understand the secret* of the Kingdom of God. But I use parables for everything I say to outsiders, 12 so that the Scriptures might be fulfilled:

'When they see what I do,
they will learn nothing.
When they hear what I say,
they will not understand.
Otherwise, they will turn to me
and be forgiven.'*"

13 Then Jesus said to them, "If you can't understand the meaning of this parable, how will you understand all the other parables? 14 The farmer plants seed by taking God's word to others. 15 The seed that fell on the footpath represents those who hear the message, only to have Satan come at once and take it away. 16 The seed on the rocky soil represents those who hear the message and immediately receive it with joy. 17 But since they don't have deep roots, they don't last long. They fall away as soon as they have problems or are persecuted for believing God's word. 18 The seed that fell among the thorns represents others who hear God's word, 19 but all too quickly the message is crowded out by the worries of this life, the lure of wealth, and the desire for other things, so no fruit is produced. 20 And the seed that fell on good soil represents those who hear and accept God's word and produce a harvest of thirty, sixty, or even a hundred times as much as had been planted!"

Parable of the Lamp

21 Then Jesus asked them, "Would anyone light a lamp and then put it under a basket or under a bed? Of course not! A lamp is placed on a stand, where its light will shine. 22 For everything that is hidden will eventually be brought into the open, and every secret will be brought to light. 23 Anyone with ears to hear should listen and understand."

24 Then he added, "Pay close attention to what you hear. The closer you listen, the more understanding you will be given*—and you will receive even more. 25 To those who listen to my teaching, more understanding will be given. But for those who are not listening, even what little understanding they have will be taken away from them."

Parable of the Growing Seed

26 Jesus also said, "The Kingdom of God is like a farmer who scatters seed on the ground. 27 Night and day, while he's asleep or awake, the seed sprouts and grows, but he does not understand how it happens. 28 The earth produces the crops on its own. First a leaf blade pushes through, then the heads of wheat are formed, and finally the grain ripens. 29 And as soon as the grain is ready, the farmer comes and harvests it with a sickle, for the harvest time has come."

Parable of the Mustard Seed

30 Jesus said, "How can I describe the Kingdom of God? What story should I use to illustrate it? 31 It is like a mustard seed planted in the ground. It is the smallest of all seeds, 32 but it becomes the largest of all garden plants; it grows long branches, and birds can make nests in its shade."

33 Jesus used many similar stories and illustrations to teach the people as much as they could understand. 34 In fact, in his public ministry he never taught without using parables; but afterward, when he was alone with his disciples, he explained everything to them.

Jesus Calms the Storm

35 As evening came, Jesus said to his disciples, "Let's cross to the other side of the lake." 36 So they took Jesus in the boat and started out, leaving the crowds behind (although other boats followed). 37 But soon a fierce storm came up. High waves were breaking into the boat, and it began to fill with water.

38 Jesus was sleeping at the back of the boat with his head on a cushion. The disciples woke him up, shouting, "Teacher, don't you care that we're going to drown?"

39 When Jesus woke up, he rebuked the wind and said to the waves, "Silence! Be still!" Suddenly the wind stopped, and there was a great calm. 40 Then he asked them, "Why are you afraid? Do you still have no faith?"

41 The disciples were absolutely terrified.

3:14 Some manuscripts do not include *and called them his apostles.* **3:17** Greek *whom he named Boanerges, which means Sons of Thunder.* **3:18** Greek *the Cananean,* an Aramaic term for Jewish nationalists. **3:22** Greek *Beelzeboul;* other manuscripts read *Beezeboul;* Latin version reads *Beelzebub.* **3:32** Some manuscripts add *and sisters.* **4:11** Greek *mystery.* **4:12** Isa 6:9-10 (Greek version). **4:24** Or *The measure you give will be the measure you get back.*

"Who is this man?" they asked each other.
"Even the wind and waves obey him!"

Jesus Heals a Demon-Possessed Man

5 So they arrived at the other side of the
lake, in the region of the Gerasenes.*
2When Jesus climbed out of the boat, a man
possessed by an evil* spirit came out from
the tombs to meet him. 3This man lived in
the burial caves and could no longer be restrained, even with a chain. 4Whenever he
was put into chains and shackles—as he
often was—he snapped the chains from his
wrists and smashed the shackles. No one
was strong enough to subdue him. 5Day
and night he wandered among the burial
caves and in the hills, howling and cutting
himself with sharp stones.
6When Jesus was still some distance
away, the man saw him, ran to meet him,
and bowed low before him. 7With a shriek,
he screamed, "Why are you interfering with me, Jesus, Son of the Most High
God? In the name of God, I beg you, don't
torture me!" 8For Jesus had already said to
the spirit, "Come out of the man, you evil
spirit."
9Then Jesus demanded, "What is your
name?"
And he replied, "My name is Legion,
because there are many of us inside this
man." 10Then the evil spirits begged him
again and again not to send them to some
distant place.
11There happened to be a large herd of
pigs feeding on the hillside nearby. 12"Send
us into those pigs," the spirits begged. "Let
us enter them."
13So Jesus gave them permission. The evil
spirits came out of the man and entered the
pigs, and the entire herd of about 2,000 pigs
plunged down the steep hillside into the
lake and drowned in the water.
14The herdsmen fled to the nearby town
and the surrounding countryside, spreading the news as they ran. People rushed
out to see what had happened. 15A crowd
soon gathered around Jesus, and they
saw the man who had been possessed by
the legion of demons. He was sitting there
fully clothed and perfectly sane, and they
were all afraid. 16Then those who had seen
what happened told the others about the
demon-possessed man and the pigs. 17And
the crowd began pleading with Jesus to go
away and leave them alone.
18As Jesus was getting into the boat,
the man who had been demon possessed

Demons

Jesus didn't see "evil" as something impersonal, but personal, rooted in Satan and expressed through demons (evil spirits) who serve him. A key aspect of Jesus' demonstrating that God's Kingdom had truly come, therefore, was to free people from the grip of such powers, plundering Satan's house and reclaiming what he had stolen (Matthew 12:29; John 10:10). And although the demons were strong—manifesting their presence through screaming, convulsions, wild behavior, and unusual strength—Jesus was stronger (Luke 11:21-22).

While the Gospels refer to many exorcisms, only four are described at length, all in Mark's Gospel: the man in the synagogue (1:21-28), the man who lived among tombs (5:1-20), the Syro-Phoenician woman's daughter (7:24-30), and the boy with a spirit that made him unable to hear and speak (9:14-29). While exorcists were common in Bible times (e.g., 9:38-40), Jesus differed greatly from them; first, because he never used set methods or complicated formulas—he simply commanded demons to leave; and second, because he drove them out by his own authority, not in the name of some deity. And when he spoke, they left.

Jesus not only "went around doing good and healing all who were oppressed by the devil" (Acts 10:38), he sent his disciples out to do the same (Mark 3:14-15). However, our focus should not be the demons, but Jesus.

▶ *See also **Satan**, page 566.*

begged to go with him. 19But Jesus said, "No, go home to your family, and tell them everything the Lord has done for you and how merciful he has been." 20So the man started off to visit the Ten Towns* of that region and began to proclaim the great things Jesus had done for him; and everyone was amazed at what he told them.

Jesus Heals in Response to Faith

21Jesus got into the boat again and went back to the other side of the lake, where a large crowd gathered around him on the shore. 22Then a leader of the local synagogue, whose name was Jairus, arrived. When he saw Jesus, he fell at his feet, 23pleading fervently with him. "My little daughter is dying," he said. "Please come and lay your hands on her; heal her so she can live."

24Jesus went with him, and all the people followed, crowding around him. 25A woman in the crowd had suffered for twelve years with constant bleeding. 26She had suffered a great deal from many doctors, and over the years she had spent everything she had to pay them, but she had gotten no better. In fact, she had gotten worse. 27She had heard about Jesus, so she came up behind him through the crowd and touched his robe. 28For she thought to herself, "If I can just touch his robe, I will be healed." 29Immediately the bleeding stopped, and she could feel in her body that she had been healed of her terrible condition.

30Jesus realized at once that healing power had gone out from him, so he turned around in the crowd and asked, "Who touched my robe?"

31His disciples said to him, "Look at this crowd pressing around you. How can you ask, 'Who touched me?'"

32But he kept on looking around to see who had done it. 33Then the frightened woman, trembling at the realization of what had happened to her, came and fell to her knees in front of him and told him what she had done. 34And he said to her, "Daughter, your faith has made you well. Go in peace. Your suffering is over."

35While he was still speaking to her, messengers arrived from the home of Jairus, the leader of the synagogue. They told him, "Your daughter is dead. There's no use troubling the Teacher now."

36But Jesus overheard* them and said to Jairus, "Don't be afraid. Just have faith."

37Then Jesus stopped the crowd and wouldn't let anyone go with him except Peter, James, and John (the brother of James). 38When they came to the home of the synagogue leader, Jesus saw much commotion and weeping and wailing. 39He went inside and asked, "Why all this commotion and weeping? The child isn't dead; she's only asleep."

40The crowd laughed at him. But he made them all leave, and he took the girl's father and mother and his three disciples into the room where the girl was lying. 41Holding her hand, he said to her, *"Talitha koum,"* which means "Little girl, get up!" 42And the girl, who was twelve years old, immediately stood up and walked around! They were overwhelmed and totally amazed. 43Jesus gave them strict orders not to tell anyone what had happened, and then he told them to give her something to eat.

Jesus Rejected at Nazareth

6 Jesus left that part of the country and returned with his disciples to Nazareth, his hometown. 2The next Sabbath he began teaching in the synagogue, and many who heard him were amazed. They asked, "Where did he get all this wisdom and the power to perform such miracles?" 3Then they scoffed, "He's just a carpenter, the son of Mary* and the brother of James, Joseph,* Judas, and Simon. And his sisters live right here among us." They were deeply offended and refused to believe in him.

4Then Jesus told them, "A prophet is honored everywhere except in his own hometown and among his relatives and his own family." 5And because of their unbelief, he couldn't do any miracles among them except to place his hands on a few sick people and heal them. 6And he was amazed at their unbelief.

Jesus Sends Out the Twelve Disciples

Then Jesus went from village to village, teaching the people. 7And he called his twelve disciples together and began sending them out two by two, giving them

5:1 Other manuscripts read *Gadarenes;* still others read *Gergesenes.* See Matt 8:28; Luke 8:26. **5:2** Greek *unclean;* also in 5:8, 13. **5:20** Greek *Decapolis.* **5:36** Or *ignored.* **6:3a** Some manuscripts read *He's just the son of the carpenter and of Mary.* **6:3b** Most manuscripts read *Joses;* see Matt 13:55.

Jesus' miracles

	Matthew	Mark	Luke	John
Miracles of healing				
A man with leprosy	8:2-3	1:40-42	5:12-13	
A Roman officer's servant	8:5-13		7:1-10	
Peter's mother-in-law	8:14-15	1:30-31	4:38-39	
Demon-possessed men/man	8:28-34	5:1-15	8:27-35	
A paralyzed man	9:2-7	2:3-12	5:18-25	
A woman with bleeding	9:20-22	5:25-29	8:43-48	
Two blind men	9:27-31			
A mute, demon-possessed man	9:32-33			
A man with a deformed hand	12:10-13	3:1-5	6:6-10	
A blind, mute, demon-possessed man	12:22		11:14	
A Gentile woman's daughter	15:21-28	7:24-30		
A demon-possessed boy	17:14-18	9:17-29	9:38-43	
Bartimaeus and another blind man	20:29-34	10:46-52	18:35-43	
A deaf man		7:31-37		
A demon-possessed man at the synagogue		1:23-26	4:33-35	
A blind man at Bethsaida		8:22-26		
A crippled woman			13:11-13	
A man with an abnormal swelling			14:1-4	
Ten men with leprosy			17:11-19	
The high priest's servant			22:50-51	
An official's son at Capernaum				4:46-54
A sick man at the pool of Bethesda				5:1-9
A man born blind				9:1-7
Miracles over nature				
Calming the storm	8:23-27	4:37-41	8:22-25	
Walking on water	14:25	6:48-51		6:19-21
Feeding the five thousand	14:15-21	6:35-44	9:12-17	6:5-13
Feeding the four thousand	15:32-38	8:1-9		
Coin in a fish's mouth	17:24-27			
A fig tree withered	21:18-22	11:12-26		
Catches of fish			5:1-11	21:1-11
Water turned into wine				2:1-11
Miracles of raising the dead				
Jairus's daughter	9:18-25	5:22-42	8:41-56	
A widow's son at Nain			7:11-15	
Lazarus				11:1-44

authority to cast out evil* spirits. 8He told
them to take nothing for their journey
except a walking stick—no food, no traveler's bag, no money.* 9He allowed them
to wear sandals but not to take a change of
clothes.
10"Wherever you go," he said, "stay in
the same house until you leave town. 11But
if any place refuses to welcome you or listen
to you, shake its dust from your feet as you
leave to show that you have abandoned
those people to their fate."
12So the disciples went out, telling everyone they met to repent of their sins and turn
to God. 13And they cast out many demons
and healed many sick people, anointing
them with olive oil.

The Death of John the Baptist

14Herod Antipas, the king, soon heard about
Jesus, because everyone was talking about
him. Some were saying,* "This must be
John the Baptist raised from the dead. That
is why he can do such miracles." 15Others
said, "He's the prophet Elijah." Still others
said, "He's a prophet like the other great
prophets of the past."
16When Herod heard about Jesus, he said,
"John, the man I beheaded, has come back
from the dead."
17For Herod had sent soldiers to arrest
and imprison John as a favor to Herodias.
She had been his brother Philip's wife, but
Herod had married her. 18John had been
telling Herod, "It is against God's law for you
to marry your brother's wife." 19So Herodias
bore a grudge against John and wanted to
kill him. But without Herod's approval she
was powerless, 20for Herod respected John;
and knowing that he was a good and holy
man, he protected him. Herod was greatly
disturbed whenever he talked with John,
but even so, he liked to listen to him.
21Herodias's chance finally came on
Herod's birthday. He gave a party for his high
government officials, army officers, and the
leading citizens of Galilee. 22Then his daughter, also named Herodias,* came in and performed a dance that greatly pleased Herod
and his guests. "Ask me for anything you
like," the king said to the girl, "and I will give
it to you." 23He even vowed, "I will give you
whatever you ask, up to half my kingdom!"
24She went out and asked her mother,
"What should I ask for?"

Her mother told her, "Ask for the head of
John the Baptist!"
25So the girl hurried back to the king
and told him, "I want the head of John the
Baptist, right now, on a tray!"
26Then the king deeply regretted what he
had said; but because of the vows he had
made in front of his guests, he couldn't
refuse her. 27So he immediately sent an executioner to the prison to cut off John's head
and bring it to him. The soldier beheaded
John in the prison, 28brought his head on
a tray, and gave it to the girl, who took it to
her mother. 29When John's disciples heard
what had happened, they came to get his
body and buried it in a tomb.

Jesus Feeds Five Thousand

30The apostles returned to Jesus from their
ministry tour and told him all they had
done and taught. 31Then Jesus said, "Let's
go off by ourselves to a quiet place and rest
awhile." He said this because there were so
many people coming and going that Jesus
and his apostles didn't even have time to
eat.
32So they left by boat for a quiet place,
where they could be alone. 33But many
people recognized them and saw them
leaving, and people from many towns ran
ahead along the shore and got there ahead
of them. 34Jesus saw the huge crowd as he
stepped from the boat, and he had compassion on them because they were like sheep
without a shepherd. So he began teaching
them many things.
35Late in the afternoon his disciples came
to him and said, "This is a remote place, and
it's already getting late. 36Send the crowds
away so they can go to the nearby farms and
villages and buy something to eat."
37But Jesus said, "You feed them."
"With what?" they asked. "We'd have to
work for months to earn enough money* to
buy food for all these people!"
38"How much bread do you have?" he
asked. "Go and find out."
They came back and reported, "We have
five loaves of bread and two fish."
39Then Jesus told the disciples to have
the people sit down in groups on the green

6:7 Greek *unclean.* **6:8** Greek *no copper coins in their money belts.* **6:14** Some manuscripts read *He was saying.* **6:22** Some manuscripts read *the daughter of Herodias herself.* **6:37** Greek *It would take 200 denarii.* A denarius was equivalent to a laborer's full day's wage.

grass. 40 So they sat down in groups of fifty
or a hundred.
41 Jesus took the five loaves and two fish,
looked up toward heaven, and blessed
them. Then, breaking the loaves into pieces,
he kept giving the bread to the disciples so
they could distribute it to the people. He
also divided the fish for everyone to share.
42 They all ate as much as they wanted, 43 and
afterward, the disciples picked up twelve
baskets of leftover bread and fish. 44 A total
of 5,000 men and their families were fed.*

Jesus Walks on Water

45 Immediately after this, Jesus insisted that
his disciples get back into the boat and
head across the lake to Bethsaida, while he
sent the people home. 46 After telling everyone good-bye, he went up into the hills by
himself to pray.
47 Late that night, the disciples were in
their boat in the middle of the lake, and
Jesus was alone on land. 48 He saw that
they were in serious trouble, rowing hard
and struggling against the wind and waves.
About three o'clock in the morning* Jesus
came toward them, walking on the water.
He intended to go past them, 49 but when
they saw him walking on the water, they
cried out in terror, thinking he was a ghost.
50 They were all terrified when they saw him.
But Jesus spoke to them at once. "Don't
be afraid," he said. "Take courage! I am
here!*" 51 Then he climbed into the boat,
and the wind stopped. They were totally
amazed, 52 for they still didn't understand
the significance of the miracle of the loaves.
Their hearts were too hard to take it in.
53 After they had crossed the lake, they
landed at Gennesaret. They brought the
boat to shore 54 and climbed out. The people
recognized Jesus at once, 55 and they ran
throughout the whole area, carrying sick
people on mats to wherever they heard he
was. 56 Wherever he went—in villages, cities,
or the countryside—they brought the sick
out to the marketplaces. They begged him
to let the sick touch at least the fringe of his
robe, and all who touched him were healed.

Jesus Teaches about Inner Purity

7 One day some Pharisees and teachers
of religious law arrived from Jerusalem
to see Jesus. 2 They noticed that some of his
disciples failed to follow the Jewish ritual of
hand washing before eating. 3 (The Jews, especially the Pharisees, do not eat until they
have poured water over their cupped hands,*
as required by their ancient traditions. 4 Similarly, they don't eat anything from the market
until they immerse their hands* in water.
This is but one of many traditions they have
clung to—such as their ceremonial washing
of cups, pitchers, and kettles.*)
5 So the Pharisees and teachers of religious law asked him, "Why don't your disciples follow our age-old tradition? They eat
without first performing the hand-washing
ceremony."
6 Jesus replied, "You hypocrites! Isaiah
was right when he prophesied about you,
for he wrote,

'These people honor me with their lips,
but their hearts are far from me.
7 Their worship is a farce,
for they teach man-made ideas as
commands from God.'*

8 For you ignore God's law and substitute
your own tradition."
9 Then he said, "You skillfully sidestep
God's law in order to hold on to your own
tradition. 10 For instance, Moses gave you
this law from God: 'Honor your father and

The Ten Towns

The Ten Towns (Mark 7:31), or Decapolis, was an association of ten free Greek cities that lay to the southeast of the Sea of Galilee. They had a strongly Greek culture and most of their residents were Gentiles, though many Jews had also migrated there. So Jesus was almost certainly ministering to both Jews and Gentiles here, and news of his earlier ministry in the region had already spread far and wide (5:20). It was to the city of Pella in this region that many Jewish Christians fled just before Jerusalem's fall in AD 70.

mother,'* and 'Anyone who speaks disrespectfully of father or mother must be put to
death.'* 11But you say it is all right for people
to say to their parents, 'Sorry, I can't help
you. For I have vowed to give to God what
I would have given to you.'* 12In this way,
you let them disregard their needy parents.
13And so you cancel the word of God in order
to hand down your own tradition. And this
is only one example among many others."
14Then Jesus called to the crowd to come
and hear. "All of you listen," he said, "and
try to understand. 15It's not what goes into
your body that defiles you; you are defiled
by what comes from your heart.*"
17Then Jesus went into a house to get
away from the crowd, and his disciples
asked him what he meant by the parable
he had just used. 18"Don't you understand
either?" he asked. "Can't you see that the
food you put into your body cannot defile
you? 19Food doesn't go into your heart, but
only passes through the stomach and then
goes into the sewer." (By saying this, he declared that every kind of food is acceptable
in God's eyes.)
20And then he added, "It is what comes
from inside that defiles you. 21For from
within, out of a person's heart, come evil
thoughts, sexual immorality, theft, murder,
22adultery, greed, wickedness, deceit,
lustful desires, envy, slander, pride, and
foolishness. 23All these vile things come
from within; they are what defile you."

The Faith of a Gentile Woman

24Then Jesus left Galilee and went north to
the region of Tyre.* He didn't want anyone
to know which house he was staying in, but
he couldn't keep it a secret. 25Right away a
woman who had heard about him came and
fell at his feet. Her little girl was possessed
by an evil* spirit, 26and she begged him to
cast out the demon from her daughter.

Since she was a Gentile, born in Syrian
Phoenicia, 27Jesus told her, "First I should
feed the children—my own family, the
Jews.* It isn't right to take food from the
children and throw it to the dogs."
28She replied, "That's true, Lord, but even
the dogs under the table are allowed to eat
the scraps from the children's plates."
29"Good answer!" he said. "Now go home,
for the demon has left your daughter."
30And when she arrived home, she found
her little girl lying quietly in bed, and the
demon was gone.

Jesus Heals a Deaf Man

31Jesus left Tyre and went up to Sidon before
going back to the Sea of Galilee and the
region of the Ten Towns.* 32A deaf man
with a speech impediment was brought to
him, and the people begged Jesus to lay his
hands on the man to heal him.
33Jesus led him away from the crowd
so they could be alone. He put his fingers
into the man's ears. Then, spitting on his
own fingers, he touched the man's tongue.
34Looking up to heaven, he sighed and said,
"Ephphatha," which means, "Be opened!"
35Instantly the man could hear perfectly,
and his tongue was freed so he could speak
plainly!
36Jesus told the crowd not to tell anyone,
but the more he told them not to, the more
they spread the news. 37They were completely amazed and said again and again,
"Everything he does is wonderful. He even
makes the deaf to hear and gives speech to
those who cannot speak."

Jesus Feeds Four Thousand

8 About this time another large crowd
had gathered, and the people ran out
of food again. Jesus called his disciples and
told them, 2"I feel sorry for these people.
They have been here with me for three days,
and they have nothing left to eat. 3If I send
them home hungry, they will faint along the
way. For some of them have come a long
distance."
4His disciples replied, "How are we supposed to find enough food to feed them out
here in the wilderness?"

6:44 Some manuscripts read *fed from the loaves.* **6:48** Greek *About the fourth watch of the night.* **6:50** Or *The 'I AM' is here;* Greek reads *I am.* See Exod 3:14. **7:3** Greek *have washed with the fist.* **7:4a** Some manuscripts read *sprinkle themselves.* **7:4b** Some manuscripts add *and dining couches.* **7:7** Isa 29:13 (Greek version). **7:10a** Exod 20:12; Deut 5:16. **7:10b** Exod 21:17 (Greek version); Lev 20:9 (Greek version). **7:11** Greek *'What I would have given to you is Corban' (that is, a gift).* **7:15** Some manuscripts add verse 16, *Anyone with ears to hear should listen and understand.* Compare 4:9, 23. **7:24** Some manuscripts add *and Sidon.* **7:25** Greek *unclean.* **7:27** Greek *Let the children eat first.* **7:31** Greek *Decapolis.*

▸**7:24** *See* ***Tyre and Sidon****, page 1093.*

5Jesus asked, "How much bread do you
have?"
"Seven loaves," they replied.
6So Jesus told all the people to sit down on
the ground. Then he took the seven loaves,
thanked God for them, and broke them into
pieces. He gave them to his disciples, who
distributed the bread to the crowd. 7A few
small fish were found, too, so Jesus also
blessed these and told the disciples to distribute them.
8They ate as much as they wanted. Afterward, the disciples picked up seven large
baskets of leftover food. 9There were about
4,000 men in the crowd that day, and Jesus
sent them home after they had eaten. 10Im-
mediately after this, he got into a boat with
his disciples and crossed over to the region
of Dalmanutha.

Pharisees Demand a Miraculous Sign

11When the Pharisees heard that Jesus had
arrived, they came and started to argue with
him. Testing him, they demanded that he
show them a miraculous sign from heaven
to prove his authority.
12When he heard this, he sighed deeply
in his spirit and said, "Why do these people
keep demanding a miraculous sign? I tell
you the truth, I will not give this generation
any such sign." 13So he got back into the
boat and left them, and he crossed to the
other side of the lake.

Yeast of the Pharisees and Herod

14But the disciples had forgotten to bring
any food. They had only one loaf of bread
with them in the boat. 15As they were crossing the lake, Jesus warned them, "Watch
out! Beware of the yeast of the Pharisees
and of Herod."
16At this they began to argue with each
other because they hadn't brought any
bread. 17Jesus knew what they were saying,
so he said, "Why are you arguing about
having no bread? Don't you know or understand even yet? Are your hearts too hard to
take it in? 18'You have eyes—can't you see?
You have ears—can't you hear?'* Don't you
remember anything at all? 19When I fed
the 5,000 with five loaves of bread, how
many baskets of leftovers did you pick up
afterward?"
"Twelve," they said.

Hardness of heart

No one wakes up one day and decides to make their heart hard. It is something that creeps up on us slowly, as we neglect the promptings of our conscience or ignore God's word. Left unchallenged, our hearts eventually become so hardened that we cannot hear, even if we want to. This is why Paul said keeping a clear conscience is so important (1 Timothy 1:19; see *Conscience,* page 333).

But hardness of heart can even happen to those who are actively following God, like Jesus' disciples (Mark 8:17). They weren't like the Pharisees, always looking for signs (8:11-12); but they still lacked understanding, despite all they had experienced (8:17-21). This too was a kind of hardness of heart.

This was why Jesus taught the parable of the sower (4:1-20), which underlines the importance of receptiveness. It asks, How ready are our hearts to receive God's word—not just when we first hear the gospel, but *every* time we hear God's word? In Matthew's version (Matthew 13:1-23) Jesus explains that the seed is "the message about the Kingdom" (Matthew 13:19). In other words, the parable is about how we respond every time God challenges us about life in his Kingdom. If our hearts are hard, the devil will snatch the word away; if our hearts are shallow, the word will grow but shrivel when problems come; if our hearts are cluttered with worries, the word will be unfruitful; only if our hearts are like good soil will the word take root and bear fruit (Matthew 13:23). Keeping our hearts soft is therefore a key to Christian growth.

▶ *See also **The heart**, page 909.*

[20]“And when I fed the 4,000 with seven
loaves, how many large baskets of leftovers
did you pick up?”
“Seven,” they said.
[21]“Don’t you understand yet?” he asked
them.

Jesus Heals a Blind Man

[22]When they arrived at Bethsaida, some
people brought a blind man to Jesus, and
they begged him to touch the man and heal
him. [23]Jesus took the blind man by the hand
and led him out of the village. Then, spitting
on the man’s eyes, he laid his hands on him
and asked, “Can you see anything now?”
[24]The man looked around. “Yes,” he said,
“I see people, but I can’t see them very clearly.
They look like trees walking around.”
[25]Then Jesus placed his hands on the
man’s eyes again, and his eyes were
opened. His sight was completely restored,
and he could see everything clearly. [26]Jesus
sent him away, saying, “Don’t go back into
the village on your way home.”

Peter’s Declaration about Jesus

[27]Jesus and his disciples left Galilee and
went up to the villages near Caesarea Philippi. As they were walking along, he asked
them, “Who do people say I am?”
[28]“Well,” they replied, “some say John the
Baptist, some say Elijah, and others say you
are one of the other prophets.”
[29]Then he asked them, “But who do you
say I am?”
Peter replied, “You are the Messiah.*”
[30]But Jesus warned them not to tell
anyone about him.

Jesus Predicts His Death

[31]Then Jesus began to tell them that the Son
of Man* must suffer many terrible things
and be rejected by the elders, the leading
priests, and the teachers of religious law.
He would be killed, but three days later he
would rise from the dead. [32]As he talked
about this openly with his disciples, Peter
took him aside and began to reprimand him
for saying such things.*
[33]Jesus turned around and looked at his
disciples, then reprimanded Peter. “Get
away from me, Satan!” he said. “You are
seeing things merely from a human point
of view, not from God’s.”
[34]Then, calling the crowd to join his disciples, he said, “If any of you wants to be my
follower, you must give up your own way,
take up your cross, and follow me. [35]If you
try to hang on to your life, you will lose it.
But if you give up your life for my sake and
for the sake of the Good News, you will save
it. [36]And what do you benefit if you gain the
whole world but lose your own soul?* [37]Is
anything worth more than your soul? [38]If
anyone is ashamed of me and my message
in these adulterous and sinful days, the Son
of Man will be ashamed of that person when
he returns in the glory of his Father with the
holy angels.”

9 Jesus went on to say, “I tell you the
truth, some standing here right now will
not die before they see the Kingdom of God
arrive in great power!”

The Transfiguration

[2]Six days later Jesus took Peter, James, and
John, and led them up a high mountain to
be alone. As the men watched, Jesus’ appearance was transformed, [3]and his clothes
became dazzling white, far whiter than any
earthly bleach could ever make them. [4]Then
Elijah and Moses appeared and began
talking with Jesus.
[5]Peter exclaimed, “Rabbi, it’s wonderful
for us to be here! Let’s make three shelters
as memorials*—one for you, one for Moses,
and one for Elijah.” [6]He said this because he
didn’t really know what else to say, for they
were all terrified.
[7]Then a cloud overshadowed them, and a
voice from the cloud said, “This is my dearly
loved Son. Listen to him.” [8]Suddenly, when
they looked around, Moses and Elijah were
gone, and they saw only Jesus with them.
[9]As they went back down the mountain, he told them not to tell anyone what
they had seen until the Son of Man* had
risen from the dead. [10]So they kept it to

8:18 Jer 5:21. **8:29** Or *the Christ. Messiah* (a Hebrew term) and *Christ* (a Greek term) both mean “anointed one.” **8:31** “Son of Man” is a title Jesus used for himself. **8:32** Or *began to correct him.* **8:36** Or *your self?* also in 8:37. **9:5** Greek *three tabernacles.* **9:9** “Son of Man” is a title Jesus used for himself.

▸ **8:27** *See **Caesarea Philippi**, page 1094.* **8:29** *See **Peter**, page 1421.* **8:31-38** *See **Discipleship and the cross**, page 1095.* **9:2** *See **The Transfiguration**, page 1169.*

themselves, but they often asked each other
what he meant by "rising from the dead."
11 Then they asked him, "Why do the
teachers of religious law insist that Elijah
must return before the Messiah comes?*"
12 Jesus responded, "Elijah is indeed
coming first to get everything ready. Yet why
do the Scriptures say that the Son of Man
must suffer greatly and be treated with utter
contempt? 13 But I tell you, Elijah has already
come, and they chose to abuse him, just as
the Scriptures predicted."

Jesus Heals a Demon-Possessed Boy

14 When they returned to the other disciples,
they saw a large crowd surrounding them,
and some teachers of religious law were
arguing with them. 15 When the crowd saw
Jesus, they were overwhelmed with awe,
and they ran to greet him.
16 "What is all this arguing about?" Jesus
asked.
17 One of the men in the crowd spoke up
and said, "Teacher, I brought my son so you
could heal him. He is possessed by an evil
spirit that won't let him talk. 18 And whenever this spirit seizes him, it throws him violently to the ground. Then he foams at the
mouth and grinds his teeth and becomes
rigid.* So I asked your disciples to cast out
the evil spirit, but they couldn't do it."
19 Jesus said to them,* "You faithless
people! How long must I be with you? How
long must I put up with you? Bring the boy
to me."
20 So they brought the boy. But when the
evil spirit saw Jesus, it threw the child into
a violent convulsion, and he fell to the
ground, writhing and foaming at the mouth.
21 "How long has this been happening?"
Jesus asked the boy's father.
He replied, "Since he was a little boy.
22 The spirit often throws him into the fire or
into water, trying to kill him. Have mercy on
us and help us, if you can."
23 "What do you mean, 'If I can'?" Jesus
asked. "Anything is possible if a person
believes."

Humility

Even followers of Jesus get into arguments sometimes—and not always for the best of reasons! But Jesus always notices such things, just as he did in Mark 9:33; and when he asked his disciples about it, they were embarrassed "because they had been arguing about which of them was the greatest" (9:34). The desire for status was as big an issue then as now; and they were almost certainly arguing about who would have the greatest status in God's coming Kingdom, for this incident happens in the midst of Jesus' revealing more about the messianic kingdom. Ever since Peter had acknowledged Jesus as the Messiah (8:29), Jesus had explained that his messiahship would be characterized by suffering, not by political liberation, as people expected. Yet the Transfiguration (9:3-13) probably stirred their hopes that something glorious was about to happen. So the disciples were probably thinking of the status and power that would be theirs when Jesus acted.

Jesus therefore takes this opportunity to explain that he does want them to be "first" (that is, to be leaders), but that leadership in God's Kingdom comes not through ruling over others but through serving them, through taking "last place"—the humble place—as children had to in those days. In contrast to the disciples' desire for status, following Jesus means being ready to be a "servant of everyone else" (9:35).

Paul defines humility in this way: "Don't think you are better than you really are. Be honest in your evaluation of yourselves" (Romans 12:3). He reminds us that Christ's humility, as seen in the Incarnation, should always be our model (Philippians 2:5-11). True humility is always marked by putting others first.

▸ *See also **The humility of Christ**, page 1358.*

24The father instantly cried out, "I do
believe, but help me overcome my unbelief!"
25When Jesus saw that the crowd of onlookers was growing, he rebuked the evil*
spirit. "Listen, you spirit that makes this
boy unable to hear and speak," he said. "I
command you to come out of this child and
never enter him again!"
26Then the spirit screamed and threw the
boy into another violent convulsion and
left him. The boy appeared to be dead. A
murmur ran through the crowd as people
said, "He's dead." 27But Jesus took him by
the hand and helped him to his feet, and
he stood up.
28Afterward, when Jesus was alone in the
house with his disciples, they asked him,
"Why couldn't we cast out that evil spirit?"
29Jesus replied, "This kind can be cast out
only by prayer.*"

Jesus Again Predicts His Death

30Leaving that region, they traveled through
Galilee. Jesus didn't want anyone to know
he was there, 31for he wanted to spend more
time with his disciples and teach them. He
said to them, "The Son of Man is going to
be betrayed into the hands of his enemies.
He will be killed, but three days later he will
rise from the dead." 32They didn't understand what he was saying, however, and
they were afraid to ask him what he meant.

The Greatest in the Kingdom

33After they arrived at Capernaum and
settled in a house, Jesus asked his disciples,
"What were you discussing out on the
road?" 34But they didn't answer, because
they had been arguing about which of them
was the greatest. 35He sat down, called the
twelve disciples over to him, and said,
"Whoever wants to be first must take last
place and be the servant of everyone else."
36Then he put a little child among them.
Taking the child in his arms, he said to
them, 37"Anyone who welcomes a little child
like this on my behalf* welcomes me, and
anyone who welcomes me welcomes not
only me but also my Father who sent me."

Using the Name of Jesus

38John said to Jesus, "Teacher, we saw
someone using your name to cast out
demons, but we told him to stop because he
wasn't in our group."
39"Don't stop him!" Jesus said. "No one
who performs a miracle in my name will
soon be able to speak evil of me. 40Anyone
who is not against us is for us. 41If anyone
gives you even a cup of water because you
belong to the Messiah, I tell you the truth,
that person will surely be rewarded.
42"But if you cause one of these little ones
who trusts in me to fall into sin, it would
be better for you to be thrown into the sea
with a large millstone hung around your
neck. 43If your hand causes you to sin, cut it
off. It's better to enter eternal life with only
one hand than to go into the unquenchable fires of hell* with two hands.* 45If your
foot causes you to sin, cut it off. It's better
to enter eternal life with only one foot than
to be thrown into hell with two feet.* 47And
if your eye causes you to sin, gouge it out.
It's better to enter the Kingdom of God with
only one eye than to have two eyes and
be thrown into hell, 48'where the maggots
never die and the fire never goes out.'*
49"For everyone will be tested with fire.*
50Salt is good for seasoning. But if it loses its
flavor, how do you make it salty again? You
must have the qualities of salt among yourselves and live in peace with each other."

Discussion about Divorce and Marriage

10 Then Jesus left Capernaum and went
down to the region of Judea and into
the area east of the Jordan River. Once again
crowds gathered around him, and as usual
he was teaching them.
2Some Pharisees came and tried to trap
him with this question: "Should a man be
allowed to divorce his wife?"
3Jesus answered them with a question:
"What did Moses say in the law about
divorce?"
4"Well, he permitted it," they replied. "He
said a man can give his wife a written notice
of divorce and send her away."*
5But Jesus responded, "He wrote this
commandment only as a concession to your
hard hearts. 6But 'God made them male and
female'* from the beginning of creation.

9:11 Greek *that Elijah must come first?* **9:18** Or *becomes weak.* **9:19** Or *said to his disciples.* **9:25** Greek *unclean.* **9:29** Some manuscripts read *by prayer and fasting.* **9:37** Greek *in my name.* **9:43a** Greek *Gehenna;* also in 9:45, 47. **9:43b** Some manuscripts add verse 44, *'where the maggots never die and the fire never goes out.'* See 9:48. **9:45** Some manuscripts add verse 46, *'where the maggots never die and the fire never goes out.'* See 9:48. **9:48** Isa 66:24. **9:49** Greek *salted with fire;* other manuscripts add *and every sacrifice will be salted with salt.* **10:4** See Deut 24:1. **10:6** Gen 1:27; 5:2.

7‘This explains why a man leaves his father
and mother and is joined to his wife,* 8and
the two are united into one.’* Since they
are no longer two but one, 9let no one split
apart what God has joined together.”
10Later, when he was alone with his disciples in the house, they brought up the
subject again. 11He told them, “Whoever
divorces his wife and marries someone else
commits adultery against her. 12And if a
woman divorces her husband and marries
someone else, she commits adultery.”

Jesus Blesses the Children

13One day some parents brought their children to Jesus so he could touch and bless
them. But the disciples scolded the parents
for bothering him.
14When Jesus saw what was happening,
he was angry with his disciples. He said to
them, “Let the children come to me. Don’t
stop them! For the Kingdom of God belongs
to those who are like these children. 15I tell
you the truth, anyone who doesn’t receive
the Kingdom of God like a child will never
enter it.” 16Then he took the children in his
arms and placed his hands on their heads
and blessed them.

The Rich Man

17As Jesus was starting out on his way to Jerusalem, a man came running up to him,
knelt down, and asked, “Good Teacher,
what must I do to inherit eternal life?”
18“Why do you call me good?” Jesus
asked. “Only God is truly good. 19But to
answer your question, you know the commandments: ‘You must not murder. You
must not commit adultery. You must not
steal. You must not testify falsely. You must
not cheat anyone. Honor your father and
mother.’*”
20“Teacher,” the man replied, “I’ve
obeyed all these commandments since I
was young.”
21Looking at the man, Jesus felt genuine
love for him. “There is still one thing you
haven’t done,” he told him. “Go and sell all
your possessions and give the money to the
poor, and you will have treasure in heaven.
Then come, follow me.”
22At this the man’s face fell, and he went
away sad, for he had many possessions.
23Jesus looked around and said to his disciples, “How hard it is for the rich to enter
the Kingdom of God!” 24This amazed them.
But Jesus said again, “Dear children, it is
very hard* to enter the Kingdom of God. 25In

▶ **10:13** *See **Children**, page 1100.*

Redemption

Redemption is one of the Bible’s key themes. The word means “paying a price (a ransom) to get something back” or “rescue from oppression.” Mark’s Jewish readers would immediately think of God’s great intervention when he redeemed Israel from slavery in Egypt (e.g., Exodus 6:6-8). But Mark’s Gentile readers would have understood the concept too, though for different reasons: For them, a “ransom” (in Greek, *lutron*) was paid to redeem property pledged against a loan or to buy freedom from slavery. So both Jewish and Greek readers understood this idea of ransom: It was about paying a price to get back something that had been lost.

In Mark 10:45, Jesus said that this was exactly what he was about to do: give his own life as a ransom (*lutron*) to free, not him, but us—the word “for” in the last phrase of 10:45 means “in place of.” Through Jesus’ death he would pay the price that we should pay—but couldn’t because of our sin—to free us from slavery to sin, death, and judgment. This substitutionary sacrifice lies at the heart of the New Testament’s understanding of his death. Jesus died as our Savior so we could be free!

▶ *See also **The death of Jesus**, page 1114; **Justification**, page 1288.*

fact, it is easier for a camel to go through the eye of a needle than for a rich person to enter the Kingdom of God!"

[26]The disciples were astounded. "Then who in the world can be saved?" they asked.

[27]Jesus looked at them intently and said, "Humanly speaking, it is impossible. But not with God. Everything is possible with God."

[28]Then Peter began to speak up. "We've given up everything to follow you," he said.

[29]"Yes," Jesus replied, "and I assure you that everyone who has given up house or brothers or sisters or mother or father or children or property, for my sake and for the Good News, [30]will receive now in return a hundred times as many houses, brothers, sisters, mothers, children, and property—along with persecution. And in the world to come that person will have eternal life. [31]But many who are the greatest now will be least important then, and those who seem least important now will be the greatest then.*"

Jesus Again Predicts His Death

[32]They were now on the way up to Jerusalem, and Jesus was walking ahead of them. The disciples were filled with awe, and the people following behind were overwhelmed with fear. Taking the twelve disciples aside, Jesus once more began to describe everything that was about to happen to him. [33]"Listen," he said, "we're going up to Jerusalem, where the Son of Man* will be betrayed to the leading priests and the teachers of religious law. They will sentence him to die and hand him over to the Romans.* [34]They will mock him, spit on him, flog him with a whip, and kill him, but after three days he will rise again."

Jesus Teaches about Serving Others

[35]Then James and John, the sons of Zebedee, came over and spoke to him. "Teacher," they said, "we want you to do us a favor."

[36]"What is your request?" he asked.

[37]They replied, "When you sit on your glorious throne, we want to sit in places of honor next to you, one on your right and the other on your left."

[38]But Jesus said to them, "You don't know what you are asking! Are you able to drink from the bitter cup of suffering I am about to drink? Are you able to be baptized with the baptism of suffering I must be baptized with?"

[39]"Oh yes," they replied, "we are able!"

Then Jesus told them, "You will indeed drink from my bitter cup and be baptized with my baptism of suffering. [40]But I have no right to say who will sit on my right or my left. God has prepared those places for the ones he has chosen."

[41]When the ten other disciples heard what James and John had asked, they were indignant. [42]So Jesus called them together and said, "You know that the rulers in this world lord it over their people, and officials flaunt their authority over those under them. [43]But among you it will be different. Whoever wants to be a leader among you must be your servant, [44]and whoever wants to be first among you must be the slave of everyone else. [45]For even the Son of Man came not to be served but to serve others and to give his life as a ransom for many."

Jesus Heals Blind Bartimaeus

[46]Then they reached Jericho, and as Jesus and his disciples left town, a large crowd followed him. A blind beggar named Bartimaeus (son of Timaeus) was sitting beside the road. [47]When Bartimaeus heard that Jesus of Nazareth was nearby, he began to shout, "Jesus, Son of David, have mercy on me!"

[48]"Be quiet!" many of the people yelled at him.

But he only shouted louder, "Son of David, have mercy on me!"

[49]When Jesus heard him, he stopped and said, "Tell him to come here."

So they called the blind man. "Cheer up," they said. "Come on, he's calling you!" [50]Bartimaeus threw aside his coat, jumped up, and came to Jesus.

[51]"What do you want me to do for you?" Jesus asked.

"My Rabbi,*" the blind man said, "I want to see!"

[52]And Jesus said to him, "Go, for your

10:7 Some manuscripts do not include *and is joined to his wife.* **10:7-8** Gen 2:24. **10:19** Exod 20:12-16; Deut 5:16-20. **10:24** Some manuscripts read *very hard for those who trust in riches.* **10:31** Greek *But many who are first will be last; and the last, first.* **10:33a** "Son of Man" is a title Jesus used for himself. **10:33b** Greek *the Gentiles.* **10:51** Greek uses the Hebrew term *Rabboni.*

▸ **10:45** *See **The Son of Man**, page 1101.*

faith has healed you." Instantly the man
could see, and he followed Jesus down the
road.*

Jesus' Triumphant Entry

11 As Jesus and his disciples approached
Jerusalem, they came to the towns of
Bethphage and Bethany on the Mount of
Olives. Jesus sent two of them on ahead.
2"Go into that village over there," he told
them. "As soon as you enter it, you will see
a young donkey tied there that no one has
ever ridden. Untie it and bring it here. 3If
anyone asks, 'What are you doing?' just say,
'The Lord needs it and will return it soon.'"
4The two disciples left and found the colt
standing in the street, tied outside the front
door. 5As they were untying it, some bystanders demanded, "What are you doing,
untying that colt?" 6They said what Jesus
had told them to say, and they were permitted to take it. 7Then they brought the colt to
Jesus and threw their garments over it, and
he sat on it.
8Many in the crowd spread their garments on the road ahead of him, and others
spread leafy branches they had cut in the
fields. 9Jesus was in the center of the procession, and the people all around him were
shouting,

"Praise God!*
Blessings on the one who comes in
the name of the LORD!
10 Blessings on the coming Kingdom of our
ancestor David!
Praise God in highest heaven!"*

11So Jesus came to Jerusalem and went
into the Temple. After looking around carefully at everything, he left because it was
late in the afternoon. Then he returned to
Bethany with the twelve disciples.

Jesus Curses the Fig Tree

12The next morning as they were leaving
Bethany, Jesus was hungry. 13He noticed a
fig tree in full leaf a little way off, so he went
over to see if he could find any figs. But there
were only leaves because it was too early in
the season for fruit. 14Then Jesus said to the
tree, "May no one ever eat your fruit again!"
And the disciples heard him say it.

Jesus Clears the Temple

15When they arrived back in Jerusalem,
Jesus entered the Temple and began to drive
out the people buying and selling animals
for sacrifices. He knocked over the tables of
the money changers and the chairs of those
selling doves, 16and he stopped everyone
from using the Temple as a marketplace.*
17He said to them, "The Scriptures declare,
'My Temple will be called a house of prayer
for all nations,' but you have turned it into
a den of thieves."*
18When the leading priests and teachers
of religious law heard what Jesus had done,
they began planning how to kill him. But
they were afraid of him because the people
were so amazed at his teaching.
19That evening Jesus and the disciples
left* the city.
20The next morning as they passed by the
fig tree he had cursed, the disciples noticed
it had withered from the roots up. 21Peter
remembered what Jesus had said to the tree
on the previous day and exclaimed, "Look,
Rabbi! The fig tree you cursed has withered
and died!"
22Then Jesus said to the disciples, "Have
faith in God. 23I tell you the truth, you can say
to this mountain, 'May you be lifted up and
thrown into the sea,' and it will happen. But
you must really believe it will happen and
have no doubt in your heart. 24I tell you, you
can pray for anything, and if you believe that
you've received it, it will be yours. 25But when
you are praying, first forgive anyone you are
holding a grudge against, so that your Father
in heaven will forgive your sins, too.*"

The Authority of Jesus Challenged

27Again they entered Jerusalem. As Jesus was
walking through the Temple area, the leading
priests, the teachers of religious law, and the
elders came up to him. 28They demanded,
"By what authority are you doing all these
things? Who gave you the right to do them?"
29"I'll tell you by what authority I do these
things if you answer one question," Jesus
replied. 30"Did John's authority to baptize
come from heaven, or was it merely human?
Answer me!"
31They talked it over among themselves.
"If we say it was from heaven, he will ask

▸ **11:28** *See **Authority**, page 1187.*

why we didn't believe John. [32]But do we dare
say it was merely human?" For they were
afraid of what the people would do, because
everyone believed that John was a prophet.
[33]So they finally replied, "We don't know."
And Jesus responded, "Then I won't tell
you by what authority I do these things."

Parable of the Evil Farmers

12 Then Jesus began teaching them with
stories: "A man planted a vineyard.
He built a wall around it, dug a pit for pressing out the grape juice, and built a lookout
tower. Then he leased the vineyard to tenant
farmers and moved to another country. [2]At
the time of the grape harvest, he sent one of
his servants to collect his share of the crop.
[3]But the farmers grabbed the servant, beat
him up, and sent him back empty-handed.
[4]The owner then sent another servant, but
they insulted him and beat him over the
head. [5]The next servant he sent was killed.
Others he sent were either beaten or killed,
[6]until there was only one left—his son whom
he loved dearly. The owner finally sent him,
thinking, 'Surely they will respect my son.'
[7]"But the tenant farmers said to one
another, 'Here comes the heir to this estate.
Let's kill him and get the estate for ourselves!' [8]So they grabbed him and murdered
him and threw his body out of the vineyard.
[9]"What do you suppose the owner of the
vineyard will do?" Jesus asked. "I'll tell
you—he will come and kill those farmers
and lease the vineyard to others. [10]Didn't
you ever read this in the Scriptures?

'The stone that the builders rejected
has now become the cornerstone.
11 This is the LORD's doing,
and it is wonderful to see.'*"

[12]The religious leaders* wanted to arrest
Jesus because they realized he was telling
the story against them—they were the
wicked farmers. But they were afraid of the
crowd, so they left him and went away.

Taxes for Caesar

[13]Later the leaders sent some Pharisees
and supporters of Herod to trap Jesus into
saying something for which he could be
arrested. [14]"Teacher," they said, "we know
how honest you are. You are impartial and
don't play favorites. You teach the way of
God truthfully. Now tell us—is it right to
pay taxes to Caesar or not? [15]Should we pay
them, or shouldn't we?"
Jesus saw through their hypocrisy and
said, "Why are you trying to trap me? Show
me a Roman coin,* and I'll tell you." [16]When

10:52 Or *on the way.* **11:9** Greek *Hosanna,* an exclamation of praise that literally means "save now"; also in 11:10. **11:9-10** Pss 118:25-26; 148:1. **11:16** Or *from carrying merchandise through the Temple.* **11:17** Isa 56:7; Jer 7:11. **11:19** Greek *they left;* other manuscripts read *he left.* **11:25** Some manuscripts add verse 26, *But if you refuse to forgive, your Father in heaven will not forgive your sins.* Compare Matt 6:15. **12:10-11** Ps 118:22-23. **12:12** Greek *They.* **12:15** Greek *a denarius.*

Paying taxes

No one likes paying taxes, and it was no different in New Testament times. But paying taxes then was far more significant because of what it said about you. When the Jewish leaders asked, "Is it right to pay taxes to Caesar or not?" (Mark 12:14), they were referring to taxes that the Roman occupiers had imposed on them, which were thus seen as the work of an oppressive regime. To reject paying taxes was to declare yourself a rebel against Rome; to pay them meant you accepted Rome's rule and were willing to compromise. In whichever way Jesus answered, he was cornered, which was why they asked the question (12:13).

Jesus' answer both cut through their hypocrisy and gave guidelines on how believers should live in an unbelieving world: "Give to Caesar what belongs to Caesar, and give to God what belongs to God" (12:17). That is, pay both your taxes and your tithes. There are obligations to the state that do not infringe on our obligations to God, so we should support the state unless it cuts across our duty to God—a message the New Testament, written at a time when rulers could not be voted out, repeats many times (e.g., Romans 13:1-7; 1 Timothy 2:1-2; Titus 3:1-2; 1 Peter 2:13-17).

they handed it to him, he asked, “Whose
picture and title are stamped on it?”
“Caesar’s,” they replied.
17 “Well, then,” Jesus said, “give to Caesar
what belongs to Caesar, and give to God
what belongs to God.”
His reply completely amazed them.

Discussion about Resurrection

18 Then Jesus was approached by some Sadducees—religious leaders who say there is no
resurrection from the dead. They posed this
question: 19 “Teacher, Moses gave us a law
that if a man dies, leaving a wife without
children, his brother should marry the
widow and have a child who will carry on the
brother’s name.* 20 Well, suppose there were
seven brothers. The oldest one married and
then died without children. 21 So the second
brother married the widow, but he also died
without children. Then the third brother
married her. 22 This continued with all seven
of them, and still there were no children.
Last of all, the woman also died. 23 So tell us,
whose wife will she be in the resurrection?
For all seven were married to her.”
24 Jesus replied, “Your mistake is that you
don’t know the Scriptures, and you don’t
know the power of God. 25 For when the dead
rise, they will neither marry nor be given in
marriage. In this respect they will be like the
angels in heaven.
26 “But now, as to whether the dead will
be raised—haven’t you ever read about this
in the writings of Moses, in the story of the
burning bush? Long after Abraham, Isaac,
and Jacob had died, God said to Moses,* ‘I
am the God of Abraham, the God of Isaac,
and the God of Jacob.’* 27 So he is the God of
the living, not the dead. You have made a
serious error.”

The Most Important Commandment

28 One of the teachers of religious law was
standing there listening to the debate. He
realized that Jesus had answered well, so he
asked, “Of all the commandments, which is
the most important?”
29 Jesus replied, “The most important
commandment is this: ‘Listen, O Israel!
The LORD our God is the one and only LORD.
30 And you must love the LORD your God
with all your heart, all your soul, all your
mind, and all your strength.’* 31 The second
is equally important: ‘Love your neighbor
as yourself.’* No other commandment is
greater than these.”
32 The teacher of religious law replied,
“Well said, Teacher. You have spoken the
truth by saying that there is only one God
and no other. 33 And I know it is important to
love him with all my heart and all my understanding and all my strength, and to love
my neighbor as myself. This is more important than to offer all of the burnt offerings
and sacrifices required in the law.”
34 Realizing how much the man understood, Jesus said to him, “You are not far
from the Kingdom of God.” And after that,
no one dared to ask him any more questions.

Whose Son Is the Messiah?

35 Later, as Jesus was teaching the people in
the Temple, he asked, “Why do the teachers of religious law claim that the Messiah
is the son of David? 36 For David himself,
speaking under the inspiration of the Holy
Spirit, said,

‘The LORD said to my Lord,
Sit in the place of honor at my right
hand
until I humble your enemies beneath
your feet.’*

37 Since David himself called the Messiah
‘my Lord,’ how can the Messiah be his son?”
The large crowd listened to him with great
delight.
38 Jesus also taught: “Beware of these
teachers of religious law! For they like to
parade around in flowing robes and receive
respectful greetings as they walk in the
marketplaces. 39 And how they love the seats
of honor in the synagogues and the head
table at banquets. 40 Yet they shamelessly
cheat widows out of their property and then
pretend to be pious by making long prayers
in public. Because of this, they will be more
severely punished.”

The Widow’s Offering

41 Jesus sat down near the collection box
in the Temple and watched as the crowds
dropped in their money. Many rich people

▸ **12:18** *See **Sadducees**, page 1104.*

put in large amounts. 42 Then a poor widow
came and dropped in two small coins.*
43 Jesus called his disciples to him and
said, "I tell you the truth, this poor widow
has given more than all the others who are
making contributions. 44 For they gave a tiny
part of their surplus, but she, poor as she
is, has given everything she had to live on."

Jesus Speaks about the Future

13 As Jesus was leaving the Temple that
day, one of his disciples said, "Teacher,
look at these magnificent buildings! Look at
the impressive stones in the walls."
2 Jesus replied, "Yes, look at these great
buildings. But they will be completely demolished. Not one stone will be left on top
of another!"
3 Later, Jesus sat on the Mount of Olives
across the valley from the Temple. Peter,
James, John, and Andrew came to him privately and asked him, 4 "Tell us, when will
all this happen? What sign will show us that
these things are about to be fulfilled?"
5 Jesus replied, "Don't let anyone mislead
you, 6 for many will come in my name, claiming, 'I am the Messiah.'* They will deceive
many. 7 And you will hear of wars and threats
of wars, but don't panic. Yes, these things
must take place, but the end won't follow
immediately. 8 Nation will go to war against
nation, and kingdom against kingdom.
There will be earthquakes in many parts of
the world, as well as famines. But this is only
the first of the birth pains, with more to come.
9 "When these things begin to happen,
watch out! You will be handed over to the
local councils and beaten in the synagogues.
You will stand trial before governors and
kings because you are my followers. But
this will be your opportunity to tell them
about me.* 10 For the Good News must first
be preached to all nations.* 11 But when you
are arrested and stand trial, don't worry in
advance about what to say. Just say what
God tells you at that time, for it is not you
who will be speaking, but the Holy Spirit.
12 "A brother will betray his brother to
death, a father will betray his own child,
and children will rebel against their parents
and cause them to be killed. 13 And everyone
will hate you because you are my followers.* But the one who endures to the end
will be saved.
14 "The day is coming when you will see
the sacrilegious object that causes desecration* standing where he* should not be."
(Reader, pay attention!) "Then those in
Judea must flee to the hills. 15 A person out
on the deck of a roof must not go down into
the house to pack. 16 A person out in the field
must not return even to get a coat. 17 How
terrible it will be for pregnant women and
for nursing mothers in those days. 18 And
pray that your flight will not be in winter.
19 For there will be greater anguish in those
days than at any time since God created the
world. And it will never be so great again.
20 In fact, unless the Lord shortens that time
of calamity, not a single person will survive.
But for the sake of his chosen ones he has
shortened those days.
21 "Then if anyone tells you, 'Look, here is
the Messiah,' or 'There he is,' don't believe
it. 22 For false messiahs and false prophets
will rise up and perform signs and wonders
so as to deceive, if possible, even God's
chosen ones. 23 Watch out! I have warned
you about this ahead of time!
24 "At that time, after the anguish of those
days,

the sun will be darkened,
  the moon will give no light,
25 the stars will fall from the sky,
  and the powers in the heavens will
    be shaken.*

26 Then everyone will see the Son of Man*
coming on the clouds with great power and
glory.* 27 And he will send out his angels to
gather his chosen ones from all over the
world*—from the farthest ends of the earth
and heaven.
28 "Now learn a lesson from the fig tree.
When its branches bud and its leaves begin
to sprout, you know that summer is near.
29 In the same way, when you see all these
things taking place, you can know that his
return is very near, right at the door. 30 I tell
you the truth, this generation* will not pass
from the scene before all these things take
place. 31 Heaven and earth will disappear,
but my words will never disappear.

12:19 See Deut 25:5-6. **12:26a** Greek *in the story of the bush? God said to him.* **12:26b** Exod 3:6. **12:29-30** Deut 6:4-5. **12:31** Lev 19:18. **12:36** Ps 110:1. **12:42** Greek *two lepta, which is a kodrantes* [i.e., a quadrans]. **13:6** Greek *claiming, 'I am.'* **13:9** Or *But this will be your testimony against them.* **13:10** Or *all peoples.* **13:13** Greek *on account of my name.* **13:14a** Greek *the abomination of desolation.* See Dan 9:27; 11:31; 12:11. **13:14b** Or *it.* **13:24-25** See Isa 13:10; 34:4; Joel 2:10. **13:26a** "Son of Man" is a title Jesus used for himself. **13:26b** See Dan 7:13. **13:27** Greek *from the four winds.* **13:30** Or *this age,* or *this nation.*

32“However, no one knows the day or hour
when these things will happen, not even the
angels in heaven or the Son himself. Only
the Father knows. 33And since you don’t
know when that time will come, be on
guard! Stay alert*!
34“The coming of the Son of Man can be
illustrated by the story of a man going on
a long trip. When he left home, he gave
each of his slaves instructions about the
work they were to do, and he told the gatekeeper to watch for his return. 35You, too,
must keep watch! For you don’t know when
the master of the household will return—in
the evening, at midnight, before dawn, or at
daybreak. 36Don’t let him find you sleeping
when he arrives without warning. 37I say to
you what I say to everyone: Watch for him!”

Jesus Anointed at Bethany

14 It was now two days before Passover and the Festival of Unleavened
Bread. The leading priests and the teachers
of religious law were still looking for an opportunity to capture Jesus secretly and kill
him. 2“But not during the Passover celebration,” they agreed, “or the people may riot.”
3Meanwhile, Jesus was in Bethany at the
home of Simon, a man who had previously
had leprosy. While he was eating,* a woman
came in with a beautiful alabaster jar of
expensive perfume made from essence of
nard. She broke open the jar and poured
the perfume over his head.
4Some of those at the table were indignant.
“Why waste such expensive perfume?” they
asked. 5“It could have been sold for a year’s
wages* and the money given to the poor!”
So they scolded her harshly.
6But Jesus replied, “Leave her alone. Why
criticize her for doing such a good thing to
me? 7You will always have the poor among
you, and you can help them whenever you
want to. But you will not always have me.
8She has done what she could and has
anointed my body for burial ahead of time.
9I tell you the truth, wherever the Good
News is preached throughout the world,
this woman’s deed will be remembered and
discussed.”

Judas Agrees to Betray Jesus

10Then Judas Iscariot, one of the twelve disciples, went to the leading priests to arrange
to betray Jesus to them. 11They were delighted
when they heard why he had come, and they

▸ **14:10** *See* ***Why did Judas betray Jesus?****, page 1191.*

Poverty

Jesus’ reply to those who rebuked an action that they saw as a waste of money (Mark 14:4-9) has sometimes been misused to support lack of care for the poor. But when Jesus said, “You will always have the poor among you,” he didn’t mean, “There will always be poverty, and there’s nothing you can do about it”; in context he meant that while there would always be an opportunity to help the poor, there would not always be an opportunity to do what this woman did: anoint his body for burial.

In fact, the Bible has much to say about the poor. The Law commanded generous giving and lending, and forbade exploiting the poor (e.g., Leviticus 25:35-43; Deuteronomy 15:1-11). Jesus himself modeled care for the poor and needy (e.g., Matthew 15:32; Luke 4:18; John 13:29), and this concern was continued in the early church, where it was not an optional extra but a foundational apostolic principle (Galatians 2:9-10). Yes, poverty can result from foolishness or laziness (Proverbs 6:9-11), but the Bible sees the greatest cause of poverty as the result of others’ greed and lust for power and denounces those who oppress the poor (e.g., Isaiah 3:13-15; Amos 4:1; 8:4). If we have resources, they should be used for the good of others and not just ourselves.

▸ *See also* ***Prosperity****, page 1176.*

promised to give him money. So he began
looking for an opportunity to betray Jesus.

The Last Supper

12 On the first day of the Festival of Unleavened Bread, when the Passover lamb
is sacrificed, Jesus' disciples asked him,
"Where do you want us to go to prepare the
Passover meal for you?"
13 So Jesus sent two of them into Jerusalem with these instructions: "As you go into
the city, a man carrying a pitcher of water
will meet you. Follow him. 14 At the house he
enters, say to the owner, 'The Teacher asks:
Where is the guest room where I can eat
the Passover meal with my disciples?' 15 He
will take you upstairs to a large room that
is already set up. That is where you should
prepare our meal." 16 So the two disciples
went into the city and found everything
just as Jesus had said, and they prepared
the Passover meal there.
17 In the evening Jesus arrived with the
Twelve. 18 As they were at the table* eating,
Jesus said, "I tell you the truth, one of you
eating with me here will betray me."
19 Greatly distressed, each one asked in
turn, "Am I the one?"
20 He replied, "It is one of you twelve who is
eating from this bowl with me. 21 For the Son
of Man* must die, as the Scriptures declared
long ago. But how terrible it will be for the
one who betrays him. It would be far better
for that man if he had never been born!"
22 As they were eating, Jesus took some
bread and blessed it. Then he broke it in
pieces and gave it to the disciples, saying,
"Take it, for this is my body."
23 And he took a cup of wine and gave
thanks to God for it. He gave it to them, and
they all drank from it. 24 And he said to them,
"This is my blood, which confirms the covenant* between God and his people. It is
poured out as a sacrifice for many. 25 I tell you
the truth, I will not drink wine again until the
day I drink it new in the Kingdom of God."
26 Then they sang a hymn and went out to
the Mount of Olives.

Jesus Predicts Peter's Denial

27 On the way, Jesus told them, "All of you
will desert me. For the Scriptures say,

'God will strike* the Shepherd,
and the sheep will be scattered.'

28 But after I am raised from the dead, I will
go ahead of you to Galilee and meet you
there."
29 Peter said to him, "Even if everyone else
deserts you, I never will."
30 Jesus replied, "I tell you the truth,
Peter—this very night, before the rooster
crows twice, you will deny three times that
you even know me."
31 "No!" Peter declared emphatically. "Even
if I have to die with you, I will never deny
you!" And all the others vowed the same.

Jesus Prays in Gethsemane

32 They went to the olive grove called Gethsemane, and Jesus said, "Sit here while I go
and pray." 33 He took Peter, James, and John
with him, and he became deeply troubled
and distressed. 34 He told them, "My soul
is crushed with grief to the point of death.
Stay here and keep watch with me."
35 He went on a little farther and fell to the
ground. He prayed that, if it were possible,
the awful hour awaiting him might pass him
by. 36 "Abba, Father,"* he cried out, "everything is possible for you. Please take this
cup of suffering away from me. Yet I want
your will to be done, not mine."
37 Then he returned and found the disciples asleep. He said to Peter, "Simon, are
you asleep? Couldn't you watch with me
even one hour? 38 Keep watch and pray, so
that you will not give in to temptation. For
the spirit is willing, but the body is weak."
39 Then Jesus left them again and prayed
the same prayer as before. 40 When he returned to them again, he found them sleeping, for they couldn't keep their eyes open.
And they didn't know what to say.
41 When he returned to them the third
time, he said, "Go ahead and sleep. Have
your rest. But no—the time has come. The
Son of Man is betrayed into the hands of
sinners. 42 Up, let's be going. Look, my betrayer is here!"

13:33 Some manuscripts add *and pray*. **14:3** Or *reclining*. **14:5** Greek *for 300 denarii*. A denarius was equivalent to a laborer's full day's wage. **14:18** Or *As they reclined*. **14:21** "Son of Man" is a title Jesus used for himself. **14:24** Some manuscripts read *the new covenant*. **14:27** Greek *I will strike*. Zech 13:7. **14:36** *Abba* is an Aramaic term for "father."

▸ **14:12-26** *See **The Last Supper**, page 1110.* **14:32** *See **Gethsemane**, page 1111.*

Jesus Is Betrayed and Arrested

43 And immediately, even as Jesus said this, Judas, one of the twelve disciples, arrived with a crowd of men armed with swords and clubs. They had been sent by the leading priests, the teachers of religious law, and the elders. 44 The traitor, Judas, had given them a prearranged signal: "You will know which one to arrest when I greet him with a kiss. Then you can take him away under guard." 45 As soon as they arrived, Judas walked up to Jesus. "Rabbi!" he exclaimed, and gave him the kiss.

46 Then the others grabbed Jesus and arrested him. 47 But one of the men with Jesus pulled out his sword and struck the high priest's slave, slashing off his ear.

48 Jesus asked them, "Am I some dangerous revolutionary, that you come with swords and clubs to arrest me? 49 Why didn't you arrest me in the Temple? I was there among you teaching every day. But these things are happening to fulfill what the Scriptures say about me."

50 Then all his disciples deserted him and ran away. 51 One young man following behind was clothed only in a long linen shirt. When the mob tried to grab him, 52 he slipped out of his shirt and ran away naked.

Jesus before the Council

53 They took Jesus to the high priest's home where the leading priests, the elders, and the teachers of religious law had gathered. 54 Meanwhile, Peter followed him at a distance and went right into the high priest's courtyard. There he sat with the guards, warming himself by the fire.

55 Inside, the leading priests and the entire high council* were trying to find evidence against Jesus, so they could put him to death. But they couldn't find any. 56 Many false witnesses spoke against him, but they contradicted each other. 57 Finally, some men stood up and gave this false testimony: 58 "We heard him say, 'I will destroy this Temple made with human hands, and in three days I will build another, made without human hands.'" 59 But even then they didn't get their stories straight!

60 Then the high priest stood up before the others and asked Jesus, "Well, aren't you going to answer these charges? What do you have to say for yourself?" 61 But Jesus was silent and made no reply. Then the high priest asked him, "Are you the Messiah, the Son of the Blessed One?"

62 Jesus said, "I Am.* And you will see the Son of Man seated in the place of power at God's right hand* and coming on the clouds of heaven.*"

63 Then the high priest tore his clothing to show his horror and said, "Why do we need other witnesses? 64 You have all heard his blasphemy. What is your verdict?"

"Guilty!" they all cried. "He deserves to die!"

65 Then some of them began to spit at him, and they blindfolded him and beat him with their fists. "Prophesy to us," they jeered. And the guards slapped him as they took him away.

Abba

At the moment of deepest testing, Jesus expressed his deepest trust in his Father. He called him "Abba" (Mark 14:36)—an Aramaic word meaning "daddy" (Aramaic was the everyday language of ordinary people and was the language that Jesus used). It was the word used by children of their fathers; but Jesus took it and unashamedly used it of his heavenly Father, something that there is no record of any Jew ever having done before. It is a word that expresses intimacy, dependence, and trust, and a word that the early church quickly picked up. They realized that through faith in Jesus we have been adopted into God's family, so we too can call God our Father by the Holy Spirit who lives within us (see Romans 8:15-16; Galatians 4:6). Jesus has not just cleansed us from our sin; he has brought us close to almighty God, whom we can now know as our Father, our Daddy.

▸ *See also* ***Life in the Spirit****, page 1291;* ***Living by the Spirit****, page 1342;* ***The Christian's relationship with the Holy Spirit****, page 1350.*

Peter Denies Jesus

66 Meanwhile, Peter was in the courtyard below. One of the servant girls who worked for the high priest came by 67 and noticed Peter warming himself at the fire. She looked at him closely and said, "You were one of those with Jesus of Nazareth.*"

68 But Peter denied it. "I don't know what you're talking about," he said, and he went out into the entryway. Just then, a rooster crowed.*

69 When the servant girl saw him standing there, she began telling the others, "This man is definitely one of them!" 70 But Peter denied it again.

A little later some of the other bystanders confronted Peter and said, "You must be one of them, because you are a Galilean."

71 Peter swore, "A curse on me if I'm lying—I don't know this man you're talking about!" 72 And immediately the rooster crowed the second time.

Suddenly, Jesus' words flashed through Peter's mind: "Before the rooster crows twice, you will deny three times that you even know me." And he broke down and wept.

Jesus' Trial before Pilate

15 Very early in the morning the leading priests, the elders, and the teachers of religious law—the entire high council*—met to discuss their next step. They bound Jesus, led him away, and took him to Pilate, the Roman governor.

2 Pilate asked Jesus, "Are you the king of the Jews?"

Jesus replied, "You have said it."

3 Then the leading priests kept accusing him of many crimes, 4 and Pilate asked him, "Aren't you going to answer them? What about all these charges they are bringing against you?" 5 But Jesus said nothing, much to Pilate's surprise.

6 Now it was the governor's custom each year during the Passover celebration to release one prisoner—anyone the people requested. 7 One of the prisoners at that time was Barabbas, a revolutionary who had committed murder in an uprising. 8 The crowd went to Pilate and asked him to release a prisoner as usual.

9 "Would you like me to release to you this 'King of the Jews'?" Pilate asked. 10 (For he realized by now that the leading priests had arrested Jesus out of envy.) 11 But at this point the leading priests stirred up the crowd to demand the release of Barabbas instead of Jesus. 12 Pilate asked them, "Then what should I do with this man you call the king of the Jews?"

13 They shouted back, "Crucify him!"

14 "Why?" Pilate demanded. "What crime has he committed?"

But the mob roared even louder, "Crucify him!"

14:55 Greek *the Sanhedrin.* **14:62a** Or *The 'I AM' is here;* or *I am the LORD.* See Exod 3:14. **14:62b** Greek *seated at the right hand of the power.* See Ps 110:1. **14:62c** See Dan 7:13. **14:67** Or *Jesus the Nazarene.* **14:68** Some manuscripts do not include *Just then, a rooster crowed.* **15:1** Greek *the Sanhedrin;* also in 15:43.

Pilate

Since only Rome could impose the death penalty, the Jewish high council took Jesus to Pilate, the Roman governor, changing their accusation from blasphemy to treason. Pilate, governor of Judea from AD 26 to 36, lived in Caesarea on the coast but had come to Jerusalem for Passover to ensure that no trouble erupted. He would have stayed in Herod's palace, which is where Jesus' trial took place. Jewish sources describe him as a harsh, greedy, and cruel man who had taken Temple funds to build an aqueduct. But, like many bullies, he was also weak underneath. He was well aware of what the Jewish leaders were up to (Mark 15:10), yet he wanted to pass the buck. So he asked the crowd whom they wanted released for the Passover amnesty and, sensing a riot in the making, quickly handed Jesus over for execution (15:6-15). He then tried to wash his hands of the whole affair (Matthew 27:24). Pilate appeared to have gotten himself out of trouble, but his power was short-lived—he was soon removed from office as a result of mishandling a riot in Samaria.

15So to pacify the crowd, Pilate released Barabbas to them. He ordered Jesus flogged with a lead-tipped whip, then turned him over to the Roman soldiers to be crucified.

The Soldiers Mock Jesus

16The soldiers took Jesus into the courtyard of the governor's headquarters (called the Praetorium) and called out the entire regiment. 17They dressed him in a purple robe, and they wove thorn branches into a crown and put it on his head. 18Then they saluted him and taunted, "Hail! King of the Jews!" 19And they struck him on the head with a reed stick, spit on him, and dropped to their knees in mock worship. 20When they were finally tired of mocking him, they took off the purple robe and put his own clothes on him again. Then they led him away to be crucified.

The Crucifixion

21A passerby named Simon, who was from Cyrene,* was coming in from the countryside just then, and the soldiers forced him to carry Jesus' cross. (Simon was the father of Alexander and Rufus.) 22And they brought Jesus to a place called Golgotha (which means "Place of the Skull"). 23They offered him wine drugged with myrrh, but he refused it.

24Then the soldiers nailed him to the cross. They divided his clothes and threw dice* to decide who would get each piece. 25It was nine o'clock in the morning when they crucified him. 26A sign announced the charge against him. It read, "The King of the Jews." 27Two revolutionaries* were crucified with him, one on his right and one on his left.*

29The people passing by shouted abuse, shaking their heads in mockery. "Ha! Look at you now!" they yelled at him. "You said you were going to destroy the Temple and rebuild it in three days. 30Well then, save yourself and come down from the cross!"

31The leading priests and teachers of religious law also mocked Jesus. "He saved others," they scoffed, "but he can't save himself! 32Let this Messiah, this King of Israel, come down from the cross so we can see it and believe him!" Even the men who were crucified with Jesus ridiculed him.

The Death of Jesus

33At noon, darkness fell across the whole land until three o'clock. 34Then at three o'clock Jesus called out with a loud voice, *"Eloi, Eloi, lema sabachthani?"* which means "My God, my God, why have you abandoned me?"*

35Some of the bystanders misunderstood and thought he was calling for the prophet Elijah. 36One of them ran and filled a sponge with sour wine, holding it up to him on a reed stick so he could drink. "Wait!" he said. "Let's see whether Elijah comes to take him down!"

37Then Jesus uttered another loud cry and breathed his last. 38And the curtain in the sanctuary of the Temple was torn in two, from top to bottom.

39When the Roman officer* who stood facing him* saw how he had died, he exclaimed, "This man truly was the Son of God!"

40Some women were there, watching from a distance, including Mary Magdalene, Mary (the mother of James the younger and of Joseph*), and Salome. 41They had been followers of Jesus and had cared for him while he was in Galilee. Many other women who had come with him to Jerusalem were also there.

The Burial of Jesus

42This all happened on Friday, the day of preparation,* the day before the Sabbath. As evening approached, 43Joseph of Arimathea took a risk and went to Pilate and asked for Jesus' body. (Joseph was an honored member of the high council, and he was waiting for the Kingdom of God to come.) 44Pilate couldn't believe that Jesus was already dead, so he called for the Roman officer and asked if he had died yet. 45The officer confirmed that Jesus was dead, so Pilate told Joseph he could have the body. 46Joseph bought a long sheet of linen cloth. Then he took Jesus' body down from the cross, wrapped it in the cloth, and laid it in a tomb that had been carved out of the rock. Then he rolled a stone in front of the entrance. 47Mary Magdalene and Mary the mother of Joseph saw where Jesus' body was laid.

▸ **15:22** See ***The death of Jesus***, *page 1114*; ***Golgotha, Place of the Skull***, *page 1193*.

The Resurrection

16 Saturday evening, when the Sabbath
ended, Mary Magdalene, Mary the
mother of James, and Salome went out
and purchased burial spices so they could
anoint Jesus' body. [2]Very early on Sunday
morning,* just at sunrise, they went to the
tomb. [3]On the way they were asking each
other, "Who will roll away the stone for us
from the entrance to the tomb?" [4]But as they
arrived, they looked up and saw that the
stone, which was very large, had already
been rolled aside.
[5]When they entered the tomb, they saw a
young man clothed in a white robe sitting
on the right side. The women were shocked,
[6]but the angel said, "Don't be alarmed. You
are looking for Jesus of Nazareth,* who was
crucified. He isn't here! He is risen from
the dead! Look, this is where they laid his
body. [7]Now go and tell his disciples, including Peter, that Jesus is going ahead of you
to Galilee. You will see him there, just as he
told you before he died."
[8]The women fled from the tomb, trembling
and bewildered, and they said nothing to
anyone because they were too frightened.*

[The most ancient manuscripts of Mark conclude with verse 16:8. Later manuscripts add one or both of the following endings.]

[*Shorter Ending of Mark*]

Then they briefly reported all this to Peter and his companions. Afterward Jesus himself sent them out from east to west with the sacred and unfailing message of salvation that gives eternal life. Amen.

[*Longer Ending of Mark*]

[9]After Jesus rose from the dead early on
Sunday morning, the first person who saw
him was Mary Magdalene, the woman from
whom he had cast out seven demons. [10]She

15:21 *Cyrene* was a city in northern Africa. **15:24** Greek *cast lots.* See Ps 22:18. **15:27a** Or *Two criminals.* **15:27b** Some manuscripts add verse 28, *And the Scripture was fulfilled that said, "He was counted among those who were rebels."* See Isa 53:12; also compare Luke 22:37. **15:34** Ps 22:1. **15:39a** Greek *the centurion;* similarly in 15:44, 45. **15:39b** Some manuscripts add *heard his cry and.* **15:40** Greek *Joses;* also in 15:47. See Matt 27:56. **15:42** Greek *It was the day of preparation.* **16:2** Greek *on the first day of the week;* also in 16:9. **16:6** Or *Jesus the Nazarene.* **16:8** The most reliable early manuscripts of the Gospel of Mark end at verse 8. Other manuscripts include various endings to the Gospel. A few include both the "shorter ending" and the "longer ending." The majority of manuscripts include the "longer ending" immediately after verse 8.

▸ **16:1** *See **Mary Magdalene**, page 1166.* **16:6** *See **Christ's resurrection and ours**, page 1320.*

Signs that follow

While many scholars question whether Mark 16:9-20 is part of Mark's original Gospel—the vocabulary, style, and content are quite different from the rest of Mark, and many ancient manuscripts don't contain the passage—nevertheless, it summarizes concisely the post-Resurrection events and the mission of the church. Even if someone else added these verses, perhaps trying to round off Mark's abrupt ending, they still reflect how the early church saw its mission: going out with the message of the risen Jesus, confident that he was with them and would authenticate their message. And as they did so "the Lord worked through them, confirming what they said by many miraculous signs" (16:20).

Signs accompanying the word were a consistent feature of the early church's life (Acts 2:42-43; 3:1-26; 4:30; 5:12-16; 6:8; 8:4-8; 9:32-43; 14:1-3, 8-18; 16:16-40; 19:11-20; 20:7-12; 28:1-10). It was the norm, not something unusual or exceptional. Today, in a world full of religion on the one hand, and full of skepticism on the other, miracles are still an excellent door-opener for the gospel message, and Scripture itself nowhere indicates that such things were intended to cease.

The unusual signs here (picking up snakes and drinking deadly poison) are not, in context, intended to be demonstrations of faith, but are assurances of protection for those who go out with the message of the gospel.

▸ *See also **Miracles and healing**, page 1243.*

went to the disciples, who were grieving and weeping, and told them what had happened. [11]But when she told them that Jesus was alive and she had seen him, they didn't believe her.

[12]Afterward he appeared in a different form to two of his followers who were walking from Jerusalem into the country. [13]They rushed back to tell the others, but no one believed them.

[14]Still later he appeared to the eleven disciples as they were eating together. He rebuked them for their stubborn unbelief because they refused to believe those who had seen him after he had been raised from the dead.*

[15]And then he told them, "Go into all the world and preach the Good News to everyone. [16]Anyone who believes and is baptized will be saved. But anyone who refuses to believe will be condemned. [17]These miraculous signs will accompany those who believe: They will cast out demons in my name, and they will speak in new languages.* [18]They will be able to handle snakes with safety, and if they drink anything poisonous, it won't hurt them. They will be able to place their hands on the sick, and they will be healed."

[19]When the Lord Jesus had finished talking with them, he was taken up into heaven and sat down in the place of honor at God's right hand. [20]And the disciples went everywhere and preached, and the Lord worked through them, confirming what they said by many miraculous signs.

16:14 Some early manuscripts add: *And they excused themselves, saying, "This age of lawlessness and unbelief is under Satan, who does not permit God's truth and power to conquer the evil [unclean] spirits. Therefore, reveal your justice now." This is what they said to Christ. And Christ replied to them, "The period of years of Satan's power has been fulfilled, but other dreadful things will happen soon. And I was handed over to death for those who have sinned, so that they may return to the truth and sin no more, and so they may inherit the spiritual, incorruptible, and righteous glory in heaven."*
16:17 Or *new tongues;* some manuscripts do not include *new.*

▸ **16:19** *See* ***Jesus' ascension,*** *page 1196.*

Luke *Jesus: good news for everyone*

Luke's Gospel, the longest of the four Gospels, was written to reassure believers that the Christian message was true and well-founded (1:3-4) and was indeed for everyone. It is "good news that will bring great joy to all people" (2:10)—especially "outsiders," whether marginalized Jews or even Gentiles, as reflected in Luke's careful choice of stories. His all-embracing account, stretching from Jesus' conception to his ascension, provides details not found in the other Gospels, such as Jesus' birth and childhood, and incidents reflecting his true humanity. This Jesus is one that everyone can identify with, no matter what their background, and who through the cross offers salvation to all, which is the focus of this Gospel.

Luke, the only non-Jewish author in the New Testament, continues his story in the book of Acts (see Acts 1:1) to show how Jesus' message did indeed go out to everyone.

What's it all about?

Luke's story begins with angels announcing the coming births of John the Baptist and Jesus. Mary, Jesus' mother, was told that her son would be the Son of God and would be named Jesus (which means "the LORD saves").

A Roman census compelled Mary and Joseph to travel to Bethlehem, Joseph's ancestral town, where Jesus was born (chapter 2). Angels announced his birth and its significance to shepherds, and eight days later Jesus was circumcised. Luke then moves forward twelve years, when we find the young Jesus debating with the Jewish teachers at Passover in Jerusalem, while his worried parents searched the city for him (2:41-52). Luke notes how, over the coming years, "Jesus grew in wisdom and in stature and in favor with God and all the people" (2:52). He then jumps ahead once again to when Jesus, now about thirty years old (3:23), began his public ministry by reading from the prophet Isaiah, declaring that this was his manifesto and mission statement (4:16-21).

Jesus began to preach and heal the sick (chapter 4), and he called his first disciples (chapter 5), later adding others (6:12-16). Through miracles, conversations, and parables he revealed the message of the Kingdom that those disciples would preach, demonstrating its authority and power. He then sent them on a preaching tour, and when they returned, he began to prepare them for the unexpected: his death (chapter 9).

Most of chapters 10 to 18, not found in the other Gospels, focuses on Jesus' teaching—about prayer, relationships, and the Holy Spirit—and his tender relationships with people, like his friends, Martha and Mary. Jesus accepted people whom the religious leaders regarded as sinners and outcasts. He told parables—including the story of the lost son (chapter 15), the poor man who was received into glory (chapter 16), and the tax collector (another outcast in Jewish society) who was put right with God (chapter 18)—to show what God was really like. In the midst of all this he healed ten men with leprosy, only one of whom (a Samaritan) thanked him (chapter 17), and he showed kindness to both a wealthy ruler and a blind beggar (chapter 18). All of this shows the breadth of the message he had come to bring.

Chapters 19 to 23 record Jesus' final week in Jerusalem. He entered the city on a colt to the welcome of cheering crowds (chapter 19). But the jubilation soon turned to sorrow as Jesus cried over the city, foreseeing its future destruction by the Romans. He taught in the Temple and continued to prepare his disciples for his death. After sharing a last meal with them, he went to the garden of Gethsemane, where he was arrested and taken away to be tried. He was crucified along with two criminals, one of whom sought his forgiveness. Jesus died and was buried in a tomb belonging to one of his followers.

Once the Sabbath was over, some women visited the tomb and found it empty (chapter 24), but the other disciples dismissed their story as nonsense. Jesus then appeared to two of his followers on the road to Emmaus, but the disciples refused to believe their account. Eventually Jesus appeared to the eleven disciples and challenged them for their unbelief. He commissioned them to take the good news "to all the nations, beginning in Jerusalem" (24:47) and told them to wait in the city until they received the power that they needed for their mission.

What does it mean for us?

Luke's passion was for everyone, both Jew and Gentile, to know that they could be saved. In fact he uses the words *salvation*, *save*, and *Savior* more than any other Gospel writer. But this salvation isn't just about going to heaven when we die; it's about being made whole—deliverance from danger, healing of sickness, and forgiveness of sins are all seen as "salvation" by Luke. He wants us to know that Jesus is concerned for our physical, mental, and spiritual well-being, and he wants us to both experience this salvation and to share it with others. There is no hindrance to anyone receiving this salvation: Jew or Gentile, rich or poor, man or woman, elite or outcast—all are welcomed by Jesus in Luke's Gospel. By believing in him, all can be forgiven and receive God's Holy Spirit.

The book of Acts, the second volume of Luke's two-part work, shows how the early church took Jesus' message of salvation far and wide, bringing together people of all nationalities, backgrounds, and professions to share their new lives in a new community. Both his Gospel and Acts emphasize the truthfulness and historicity of the Christian message (Luke 1:1-4; Acts 1:1-3) as a sound basis for building our lives upon.

▶ *See also **Four Gospels, one story**, pages 1060-1065; **Luke**, page 1278; **The Ministry of Jesus** map, Visual Overview Z10.*

OVERVIEW

Introduction

1 Many people have set out to write accounts about the events that have been fulfilled among us. 2 They used the eyewitness reports circulating among us from the early disciples.* 3 Having carefully investigated everything from the beginning, I also have decided to write an accurate account for you, most honorable Theophilus, 4 so you can be certain of the truth of everything you were taught.

The Birth of John the Baptist Foretold

5 When Herod was king of Judea, there was a Jewish priest named Zechariah. He was a member of the priestly order of Abijah, and his wife, Elizabeth, was also from the priestly line of Aaron. 6 Zechariah and Elizabeth were righteous in God's eyes, careful to obey all of the Lord's commandments and regulations. 7 They had no children because Elizabeth was unable to conceive, and they were both very old.

8 One day Zechariah was serving God in the Temple, for his order was on duty that week. 9 As was the custom of the priests, he was chosen by lot to enter the sanctuary of the Lord and burn incense. 10 While the incense was being burned, a great crowd stood outside, praying.

11 While Zechariah was in the sanctuary, an angel of the Lord appeared to him, standing to the right of the incense altar. 12 Zechariah was shaken and overwhelmed with fear when he saw him. 13 But the angel said, "Don't be afraid, Zechariah! God has heard your prayer. Your wife, Elizabeth, will give you a son, and you are to name him John. 14 You will have great joy and gladness, and many will rejoice at his birth, 15 for he will be great in the eyes of the Lord. He must never touch wine or other alcoholic drinks. He will be filled with the Holy Spirit, even before his birth.* 16 And he will turn many Israelites to the Lord their God. 17 He will be a man with the spirit and power of Elijah. He will prepare the people for the coming of the Lord. He will turn the hearts of the fathers to their children,* and he will cause those who are rebellious to accept the wisdom of the godly."

18 Zechariah said to the angel, "How can I be sure this will happen? I'm an old man now, and my wife is also well along in years."

19 Then the angel said, "I am Gabriel! I stand in the very presence of God. It was he who sent me to bring you this good news! 20 But now, since you didn't believe what I said, you will be silent and unable to speak until the child is born. For my words will certainly be fulfilled at the proper time."

21 Meanwhile, the people were waiting for Zechariah to come out of the sanctuary, wondering why he was taking so long. 22 When he finally did come out, he couldn't speak to them. Then they realized from his gestures and his silence that he must have seen a vision in the sanctuary.

23 When Zechariah's week of service in the Temple was over, he returned home. 24 Soon afterward his wife, Elizabeth, became pregnant and went into seclusion for five months. 25 "How kind the Lord is!" she exclaimed. "He has taken away my disgrace of having no children."

1:2 Greek *from those who from the beginning were servants of the word.* **1:15** Or *even from birth.* **1:17** See Mal 4:5-6.

▸ **1:13** *See* ***John the Baptist****, page 1156.*

Theophilus

Because publishing in the ancient world was expensive (since every copy was written by hand on costly parchment), most writers needed a sponsor—and that's probably who Theophilus ("Lover of God") was. Luke refers to him as "most honorable" (1:3), using exactly the same word in the original Greek as he does when describing the Roman governors Felix (Acts 23:26; 24:3) and Festus (Acts 26:25). This at the very least shows that Theophilus was a man of some wealth and social standing; but as to who exactly he was, we have no idea—though we have much to be grateful to him for. Without him we probably wouldn't have Luke's Gospel or Acts (Acts 1:1).

The Birth of Jesus Foretold

26 In the sixth month of Elizabeth's pregnancy, God sent the angel Gabriel to Nazareth, a village in Galilee, 27 to a virgin named Mary. She was engaged to be married to a man named Joseph, a descendant of King David. 28 Gabriel appeared to her and said, "Greetings,* favored woman! The Lord is with you!*"

29 Confused and disturbed, Mary tried to think what the angel could mean. 30 "Don't be afraid, Mary," the angel told her, "for you have found favor with God! 31 You will conceive and give birth to a son, and you will name him Jesus. 32 He will be very great and will be called the Son of the Most High. The Lord God will give him the throne of his ancestor David. 33 And he will reign over Israel* forever; his Kingdom will never end!"

34 Mary asked the angel, "But how can this happen? I am a virgin."

35 The angel replied, "The Holy Spirit will come upon you, and the power of the Most High will overshadow you. So the baby to be born will be holy, and he will be called the Son of God. 36 What's more, your relative Elizabeth has become pregnant in her old age! People used to say she was barren, but she has conceived a son and is now in her sixth month. 37 For the word of God will never fail.*"

38 Mary responded, "I am the Lord's servant. May everything you have said about me come true." And then the angel left her.

Mary Visits Elizabeth

39 A few days later Mary hurried to the hill country of Judea, to the town 40 where Zechariah lived. She entered the house and greeted Elizabeth. 41 At the sound of Mary's greeting, Elizabeth's child leaped within her, and Elizabeth was filled with the Holy Spirit.

42 Elizabeth gave a glad cry and exclaimed to Mary, "God has blessed you above all women, and your child is blessed. 43 Why am I so honored, that the mother of my Lord should visit me? 44 When I heard your greeting, the baby in my womb jumped for joy. 45 You are blessed because you believed that the Lord would do what he said."

▸ **1:26** *See **Angels**, page 1397.*

The Virgin Birth

People in the first century knew as well as us how pregnancy happened. That's why, when Gabriel told Mary she would become pregnant and give birth to God's Son, she said, "But how can this happen? I am a virgin" (Luke 1:34). It's also why Joseph needed a miraculous revelation to convince him that Mary was telling the truth (Matthew 1:20-25). Like most people today, they both thought it was impossible. Yet the fact of it is central to understanding who Jesus is and why he came.

Through the Virgin Birth, God did two things. First, he made it possible for his Son to become human—what is called "the Incarnation." Jesus wasn't merely a prophet, a holy man, or half-God, half-man; he was God in human form—both fully God and fully human. Second, God was starting the human race afresh in Jesus, who would deal with human sin and so be the firstborn of a new creation (see Romans 8:29) so that all who are "in him" through faith can be part of that new creation too. Through his Spirit, God created in Mary's womb a brand-new, perfect human nature for Jesus, just like Adam's nature before he sinned. This meant Jesus was free of the sin that had infected all humanity, and so, having maintained that sinlessness throughout his life through dependence on the Holy Spirit, he could die in our place—not paying the price of his own sin (for he had none), but ours. The Virgin Birth made possible the seeming impossibility of God becoming man.

▸ *See also* ***Mary, the mother of Jesus**, page 1153;* ***The Incarnation**, page 1199.*

The Magnificat: Mary's Song of Praise

46 Mary responded,

"Oh, how my soul praises the Lord.
47 How my spirit rejoices in God my Savior!
48 For he took notice of his lowly servant girl,
and from now on all generations will call me blessed.
49 For the Mighty One is holy,
and he has done great things for me.
50 He shows mercy from generation to generation
to all who fear him.
51 His mighty arm has done tremendous things!
He has scattered the proud and haughty ones.
52 He has brought down princes from their thrones
and exalted the humble.
53 He has filled the hungry with good things
and sent the rich away with empty hands.
54 He has helped his servant Israel
and remembered to be merciful.
55 For he made this promise to our ancestors,
to Abraham and his children forever."

56 Mary stayed with Elizabeth about three months and then went back to her own home.

The Birth of John the Baptist

57 When it was time for Elizabeth's baby to
be born, she gave birth to a son. 58 And when
her neighbors and relatives heard that the Lord had been very merciful to her, everyone rejoiced with her.

59 When the baby was eight days old, they all came for the circumcision ceremony. They wanted to name him Zechariah, after his
father. 60 But Elizabeth said, "No! His name is John!"

61 "What?" they exclaimed. "There is no one in all your family by that name."
62 So they used gestures to ask the baby's
father what he wanted to name him. 63 He
motioned for a writing tablet, and to everyone's surprise he wrote, "His name is John."
64 Instantly Zechariah could speak again, and he began praising God.

65 Awe fell upon the whole neighborhood, and the news of what had happened spread
throughout the Judean hills. 66 Everyone
who heard about it reflected on these events and asked, "What will this child turn out to be?" For the hand of the Lord was surely upon him in a special way.

1:28a Or *Rejoice.* **1:28b** Some manuscripts add *Blessed are you among women.* **1:33** Greek *over the house of Jacob.* **1:37** Some manuscripts read *For nothing is impossible with God.*

Mary, the mother of Jesus

Luke's opening chapter reveals Mary's faith and humility as she hears she is about to become pregnant by the work of the Holy Spirit and will be the means of God's Son coming into this world. Little wonder Elizabeth said, "God has blessed you above all women" (Luke 1:42). Mary's song (often called the Magnificat from its opening word in the Latin Bible) not only reflects her praise but recalls God's promise to Abraham, a promise about to be fulfilled in a completely new way. But after these birth stories, there are few references to her in the rest of the New Testament, and what we do hear highlights her humanness: anxiety at losing Jesus (2:41-51); prompting Jesus to act when the wine ran out at a wedding, leading to Jesus' rebuke (John 2:1-11); worrying about Jesus when she thought he was working too hard (Mark 3:20-21, 31-35); being commended to John's care by Jesus as he was crucified (John 19:25-27); praying with the disciples in the upper room (Acts 1:14). It was perhaps what the angel revealed to her that day that helped her get through all of these experiences.

▸ *See also* ***Joseph of Nazareth****, page 1068;* ***The Virgin Birth****, page 1152.*

Zechariah's Prophecy

67 Then his father, Zechariah, was filled with
the Holy Spirit and gave this prophecy:

68 "Praise the Lord, the God of Israel,
because he has visited and redeemed
his people.
69 He has sent us a mighty Savior*
from the royal line of his servant
David,
70 just as he promised
through his holy prophets long ago.
71 Now we will be saved from our
enemies
and from all who hate us.
72 He has been merciful to our ancestors
by remembering his sacred covenant—
73 the covenant he swore with an oath
to our ancestor Abraham.
74 We have been rescued from our enemies
so we can serve God without fear,
75 in holiness and righteousness
for as long as we live.

76 "And you, my little son,
will be called the prophet of the Most
High,
because you will prepare the way for
the Lord.
77 You will tell his people how to find
salvation
through forgiveness of their sins.
78 Because of God's tender mercy,
the morning light from heaven is
about to break upon us,*
79 to give light to those who sit in darkness
and in the shadow of death,
and to guide us to the path of
peace."

80 John grew up and became strong in
spirit. And he lived in the wilderness until
he began his public ministry to Israel.

The Birth of Jesus

2 At that time the Roman emperor, Augustus, decreed that a census should
be taken throughout the Roman Empire.
2 (This was the first census taken when Qui-
rinius was governor of Syria.) 3 All returned
to their own ancestral towns to register for
this census. 4 And because Joseph was a
descendant of King David, he had to go to
Bethlehem in Judea, David's ancient home.
He traveled there from the village of Nazareth in Galilee. 5 He took with him Mary, to
whom he was engaged, who was now expecting a child.

6 And while they were there, the time came
for her baby to be born. 7 She gave birth to
her firstborn son. She wrapped him snugly
in strips of cloth and laid him in a manger,
because there was no lodging available for
them.

The Shepherds and Angels

8 That night there were shepherds staying
in the fields nearby, guarding their flocks
of sheep. 9 Suddenly, an angel of the Lord
appeared among them, and the radiance
of the Lord's glory surrounded them. They
were terrified, 10 but the angel reassured
them. "Don't be afraid!" he said. "I bring
you good news that will bring great joy to
all people. 11 The Savior—yes, the Messiah,
the Lord—has been born today in Bethlehem, the city of David! 12 And you will recognize him by this sign: You will find a baby

▸ **2:4** *See **Joseph of Nazareth**, page 1068.*

Bethlehem

The fact that Jesus was born in Bethlehem rather than in his parents' hometown of Nazareth was due to Caesar's call for a census. This required everyone to go back to their ancestral town to register—which for Joseph meant Bethlehem (Luke 2:4). Bethlehem (meaning "House of Bread") lay five miles southwest of Jerusalem and 2,654 feet above sea level, so it would have been a three-day journey from Nazareth—not easy for Mary in her heavily pregnant condition. Its significance lay in being King David's home (1 Samuel 16), and Micah had prophesied that the Messiah would come from here (Micah 5:2; Matthew 2:1-6). From a human point of view, an inconvenient political incident ensured God's word was fulfilled.

wrapped snugly in strips of cloth, lying in a
manger."
13 Suddenly, the angel was joined by a vast
host of others—the armies of heaven—praising God and saying,

14 "Glory to God in highest heaven,
and peace on earth to those with
whom God is pleased."

15 When the angels had returned to heaven,
the shepherds said to each other, "Let's go to
Bethlehem! Let's see this thing that has happened, which the Lord has told us about."
16 They hurried to the village and found
Mary and Joseph. And there was the baby,
lying in the manger. 17 After seeing him,
the shepherds told everyone what had
happened and what the angel had said to
them about this child. 18 All who heard the
shepherds' story were astonished, 19 but
Mary kept all these things in her heart
and thought about them often. 20 The shepherds went back to their flocks, glorifying
and praising God for all they had heard
and seen. It was just as the angel had told
them.

Jesus Is Presented in the Temple

21 Eight days later, when the baby was circumcised, he was named Jesus, the name
given him by the angel even before he was
conceived.
22 Then it was time for their purification
offering, as required by the law of Moses
after the birth of a child; so his parents took
him to Jerusalem to present him to the Lord.
23 The law of the Lord says, "If a woman's
first child is a boy, he must be dedicated to
the LORD."* 24 So they offered the sacrifice
required in the law of the Lord—"either a
pair of turtledoves or two young pigeons."*

The Prophecy of Simeon

25 At that time there was a man in Jerusalem named Simeon. He was righteous and
devout and was eagerly waiting for the
Messiah to come and rescue Israel. The Holy
Spirit was upon him 26 and had revealed to
him that he would not die until he had seen
the Lord's Messiah. 27 That day the Spirit
led him to the Temple. So when Mary and
Joseph came to present the baby Jesus to
the Lord as the law required, 28 Simeon was
there. He took the child in his arms and
praised God, saying,

29 "Sovereign Lord, now let your servant
die in peace,
as you have promised.
30 I have seen your salvation,
31 which you have prepared for all
people.
32 He is a light to reveal God to the nations,
and he is the glory of your people
Israel!"

33 Jesus' parents were amazed at what was
being said about him. 34 Then Simeon blessed

1:69 Greek *has raised up a horn of salvation for us.* **1:78** Or *the Morning Light from Heaven is about to visit us.* **2:23** Exod 13:2. **2:24** Lev 12:8.

Nazareth

It was in Nazareth (Luke 2:51), a small town of just a few hundred people in the lower hills of Galilee, that Jesus grew up and spent most of his life, working in the family carpentry business and becoming known as "the carpenter's son" (Matthew 13:55)—though a carpenter was more like today's construction worker. There was probably not a great deal of work in such a small place, but just a few miles down the road Herod Antipas was constructing a new city called Sepphoris (not mentioned in the New Testament, probably because Jesus avoided it during his ministry), and Joseph and Jesus probably worked on projects there. But Nazareth was seen as a backwater, and Nathanael couldn't believe Philip would think the Messiah could come from such a place (John 1:46), especially since it wasn't even mentioned in the Old Testament. Jesus was often called "Jesus of Nazareth" (e.g., Mark 10:47), even though he left here for good and relocated to Capernaum when Nazareth decisively rejected him (Luke 4:24-31).

▸ *See also* ***Galilee****, page 1092;* ***Capernaum****, page 1096.*

them, and he said to Mary, the baby's mother,
"This child is destined to cause many in
Israel to fall, and many others to rise. He
has been sent as a sign from God, but many
will oppose him. 35As a result, the deepest
thoughts of many hearts will be revealed.
And a sword will pierce your very soul."

The Prophecy of Anna

36Anna, a prophet, was also there in the
Temple. She was the daughter of Phanu-
el from the tribe of Asher, and she was
very old. Her husband died when they
had been married only seven years. 37Then
she lived as a widow to the age of eighty-
four.* She never left the Temple but stayed
there day and night, worshiping God with
fasting and prayer. 38She came along just
as Simeon was talking with Mary and
Joseph, and she began praising God. She
talked about the child to everyone who had
been waiting expectantly for God to rescue
Jerusalem.

39When Jesus' parents had fulfilled all the
requirements of the law of the Lord, they returned home to Nazareth in Galilee. 40There
the child grew up healthy and strong. He
was filled with wisdom, and God's favor
was on him.

Jesus Speaks with the Teachers

41Every year Jesus' parents went to Jerusalem for the Passover festival. 42When Jesus
was twelve years old, they attended the
festival as usual. 43After the celebration
was over, they started home to Nazareth,
but Jesus stayed behind in Jerusalem. His
parents didn't miss him at first, 44because
they assumed he was among the other
travelers. But when he didn't show up
that evening, they started looking for him
among their relatives and friends.

45When they couldn't find him, they went
back to Jerusalem to search for him there.
46Three days later they finally discovered
him in the Temple, sitting among the religious teachers, listening to them and asking
questions. 47All who heard him were amazed
at his understanding and his answers.

48His parents didn't know what to think.
"Son," his mother said to him, "why have
you done this to us? Your father and I have
been frantic, searching for you everywhere."

49"But why did you need to search?" he
asked. "Didn't you know that I must be
in my Father's house?"* 50But they didn't
understand what he meant.

51Then he returned to Nazareth with them
and was obedient to them. And his mother
stored all these things in her heart.

52Jesus grew in wisdom and in stature and
in favor with God and all the people.

John the Baptist Prepares the Way

3 It was now the fifteenth year of the reign
of Tiberius, the Roman emperor. Pontius
Pilate was governor over Judea; Herod
Antipas was ruler* over Galilee; his brother

John the Baptist

The Old Testament prophet Malachi had promised that God would send his messenger prior to the Messiah's coming in order to prepare the way (Malachi 4:5-6), and an angel had told Zechariah, John's father, that John would be that messenger (Luke 1:13-17). Once called by God, John immediately began preaching, calling people to repent and to demonstrate that repentance through being baptized (3:3) and living differently (3:7-14). When people started thinking he might be the Messiah, he quickly made clear he wasn't but was merely the one preparing the way for him (3:15-17), which is why he was hesitant to baptize Jesus (Matthew 3:13-15). His preaching won over many ordinary Jews but offended the religious leaders, and his opposition to Herod's marriage to Herodias (Herod's sister-in-law) led to his imprisonment (Matthew 14:3-5). While in prison, he began to have doubts, wondering whether he had got it wrong about Jesus; but Jesus quickly reassured him (Luke 7:18-23) and said that "of all who have ever lived, none is greater than John" (7:28). John was eventually beheaded by Herod Antipas (Matthew 14:1-12).

Philip was ruler* over Iturea and Traconitis; Lysanias was ruler over Abilene. 2 Annas
and Caiaphas were the high priests. At this
time a message from God came to John son
of Zechariah, who was living in the wilderness. 3 Then John went from place to place
on both sides of the Jordan River, preaching
that people should be baptized to show that
they had repented of their sins and turned
to God to be forgiven. 4 Isaiah had spoken of
John when he said,

"He is a voice shouting in the wilderness,
'Prepare the way for the LORD's coming!
Clear the road for him!
5 The valleys will be filled,
and the mountains and hills made
level.
The curves will be straightened,
and the rough places made smooth.
6 And then all people will see
the salvation sent from God.'"*

7 When the crowds came to John for
baptism, he said, "You brood of snakes!
Who warned you to flee the coming wrath?
8 Prove by the way you live that you have repented of your sins and turned to God. Don't
just say to each other, 'We're safe, for we
are descendants of Abraham.' That means
nothing, for I tell you, God can create children of Abraham from these very stones.
9 Even now the ax of God's judgment is
poised, ready to sever the roots of the trees.
Yes, every tree that does not produce good
fruit will be chopped down and thrown into
the fire."

10 The crowds asked, "What should we do?"

11 John replied, "If you have two shirts,
give one to the poor. If you have food, share
it with those who are hungry."

12 Even corrupt tax collectors came to be
baptized and asked, "Teacher, what should
we do?"

13 He replied, "Collect no more taxes than
the government requires."

14 "What should we do?" asked some
soldiers.

John replied, "Don't extort money or
make false accusations. And be content
with your pay."

15 Everyone was expecting the Messiah
to come soon, and they were eager to
know whether John might be the Messiah.
16 John answered their questions by saying,
"I baptize you with* water; but someone
is coming soon who is greater than I am—
so much greater that I'm not even worthy
to be his slave and untie the straps of
his sandals. He will baptize you with the
Holy Spirit and with fire.* 17 He is ready to
separate the chaff from the wheat with his
winnowing fork. Then he will clean up the
threshing area, gathering the wheat into
his barn but burning the chaff with never-
ending fire." 18 John used many such warnings as he announced the Good News to
the people.

19 John also publicly criticized Herod
Antipas, the ruler of Galilee,* for marrying
Herodias, his brother's wife, and for many
other wrongs he had done. 20 So Herod put
John in prison, adding this sin to his many
others.

The Baptism of Jesus

21 One day when the crowds were being
baptized, Jesus himself was baptized. As
he was praying, the heavens opened, 22 and
the Holy Spirit, in bodily form, descended
on him like a dove. And a voice from heaven
said, "You are my dearly loved Son, and you
bring me great joy.*"

The Ancestors of Jesus

23 Jesus was about thirty years old when he
began his public ministry.

Jesus was known as the son of Joseph.
Joseph was the son of Heli.
24 Heli was the son of Matthat.
Matthat was the son of Levi.
Levi was the son of Melki.
Melki was the son of Jannai.
Jannai was the son of Joseph.
25 Joseph was the son of Mattathias.
Mattathias was the son of Amos.
Amos was the son of Nahum.
Nahum was the son of Esli.
Esli was the son of Naggai.
26 Naggai was the son of Maath.

2:37 Or *She had been a widow for eighty-four years.* **2:49** Or *"Didn't you realize that I should be involved with my Father's affairs?"* **3:1a** Greek *Herod was tetrarch.* Herod Antipas was a son of King Herod. **3:1b** Greek *tetrarch;* also in 3:1c. **3:4-6** Isa 40:3-5 (Greek version). **3:16a** Or *in.* **3:16b** Or *in the Holy Spirit and in fire.* **3:19** Greek *Herod the tetrarch.* **3:22** Some manuscripts read *my Son, and today I have become your Father.*

▸ **3:21** *See **Jesus' baptism**, page 1073.* **3:23** *See **Genealogies**, page 454.*

Maath was the son of Mattathias.
Mattathias was the son of Semein.
Semein was the son of Josech.
Josech was the son of Joda.
27 Joda was the son of Joanan.
Joanan was the son of Rhesa.
Rhesa was the son of Zerubbabel.
Zerubbabel was the son of Shealtiel.
Shealtiel was the son of Neri.
28 Neri was the son of Melki.
Melki was the son of Addi.
Addi was the son of Cosam.
Cosam was the son of Elmadam.
Elmadam was the son of Er.
29 Er was the son of Joshua.
Joshua was the son of Eliezer.
Eliezer was the son of Jorim.
Jorim was the son of Matthat.
Matthat was the son of Levi.
30 Levi was the son of Simeon.
Simeon was the son of Judah.
Judah was the son of Joseph.
Joseph was the son of Jonam.
Jonam was the son of Eliakim.
31 Eliakim was the son of Melea.
Melea was the son of Menna.
Menna was the son of Mattatha.
Mattatha was the son of Nathan.
Nathan was the son of David.
32 David was the son of Jesse.
Jesse was the son of Obed.
Obed was the son of Boaz.
Boaz was the son of Salmon.*
Salmon was the son of Nahshon.
33 Nahshon was the son of Amminadab.
Amminadab was the son of Admin.
Admin was the son of Arni.*
Arni was the son of Hezron.
Hezron was the son of Perez.
Perez was the son of Judah.
34 Judah was the son of Jacob.
Jacob was the son of Isaac.
Isaac was the son of Abraham.
Abraham was the son of Terah.
Terah was the son of Nahor.
35 Nahor was the son of Serug.
Serug was the son of Reu.
Reu was the son of Peleg.
Peleg was the son of Eber.
Eber was the son of Shelah.
36 Shelah was the son of Cainan.
Cainan was the son of Arphaxad.
Arphaxad was the son of Shem.
Shem was the son of Noah.
Noah was the son of Lamech.
37 Lamech was the son of Methuselah.
Methuselah was the son of Enoch.
Enoch was the son of Jared.
Jared was the son of Mahalalel.
Mahalalel was the son of Kenan.
38 Kenan was the son of Enosh.*
Enosh was the son of Seth.
Seth was the son of Adam.
Adam was the son of God.

The Temptation of Jesus

4 Then Jesus, full of the Holy Spirit, returned from the Jordan River. He was
led by the Spirit in the wilderness,* 2where
he was tempted by the devil for forty days.
Jesus ate nothing all that time and became
very hungry.

3Then the devil said to him, "If you are the
Son of God, tell this stone to become a loaf
of bread."

4But Jesus told him, "No! The Scriptures
say, 'People do not live by bread alone.'*"

5Then the devil took him up and revealed
to him all the kingdoms of the world in a
moment of time. 6"I will give you the glory of
these kingdoms and authority over them,"
the devil said, "because they are mine to
give to anyone I please. 7I will give it all to
you if you will worship me."

8Jesus replied, "The Scriptures say,

'You must worship the LORD your
God
and serve only him.'*"

9Then the devil took him to Jerusalem, to
the highest point of the Temple, and said,
"If you are the Son of God, jump off! 10For
the Scriptures say,

'He will order his angels to protect and
guard you.
11 And they will hold you up with their
hands
so you won't even hurt your foot on a
stone.'*"

12Jesus responded, "The Scriptures also
say, 'You must not test the LORD your God.'*"

13When the devil had finished tempting
Jesus, he left him until the next opportunity
came.

Jesus Rejected at Nazareth

14Then Jesus returned to Galilee, filled with
the Holy Spirit's power. Reports about him
spread quickly through the whole region.

15 He taught regularly in their synagogues
and was praised by everyone.
16 When he came to the village of Nazareth, his boyhood home, he went as usual to
the synagogue on the Sabbath and stood up
to read the Scriptures. 17 The scroll of Isaiah
the prophet was handed to him. He unrolled the scroll and found the place where
this was written:

18 "The Spirit of the LORD is upon me,
for he has anointed me to bring Good
News to the poor.
He has sent me to proclaim that captives
will be released,
that the blind will see,
that the oppressed will be set free,
19 and that the time of the LORD's favor
has come.*"

20 He rolled up the scroll, handed it back
to the attendant, and sat down. All eyes
in the synagogue looked at him intently.
21 Then he began to speak to them. "The
Scripture you've just heard has been fulfilled this very day!"
22 Everyone spoke well of him and was
amazed by the gracious words that came
from his lips. "How can this be?" they asked.
"Isn't this Joseph's son?"
23 Then he said, "You will undoubtedly
quote me this proverb: 'Physician, heal
yourself'—meaning, 'Do miracles here in
your hometown like those you did in Capernaum.' 24 But I tell you the truth, no prophet
is accepted in his own hometown.
25 "Certainly there were many needy
widows in Israel in Elijah's time, when the
heavens were closed for three and a half
years, and a severe famine devastated the
land. 26 Yet Elijah was not sent to any of
them. He was sent instead to a foreigner—a
widow of Zarephath in the land of Sidon.
27 And many in Israel had leprosy in the
time of the prophet Elisha, but the only one
healed was Naaman, a Syrian."
28 When they heard this, the people in the
synagogue were furious. 29 Jumping up, they
mobbed him and forced him to the edge of
the hill on which the town was built. They

3:32 Greek *Sala*, a variant spelling of Salmon; also in 3:32b. See Ruth 4:20-21. **3:33** Some manuscripts read *Amminadab was the son of Aram. Arni* and *Aram* are alternate spellings of Ram. See 1 Chr 2:9-10. **3:38** Greek *Enos*, a variant spelling of Enosh; also in 3:38b. See Gen 5:6. **4:1** Some manuscripts read *into the wilderness*. **4:4** Deut 8:3. **4:8** Deut 6:13. **4:10-11** Ps 91:11-12. **4:12** Deut 6:16. **4:18-19** Or *and to proclaim the acceptable year of the LORD*. Isa 61:1-2 (Greek version); 58:6.

▸ **4:16** *See **Nazareth**, page 1155.*

The mission of Jesus

After his baptism and temptations, Jesus "returned to Galilee, filled with the Holy Spirit's power" (Luke 4:14). While his ministry led to initial popularity (4:15), things quickly changed. Invited to read the Scriptures in Nazareth's synagogue, he turned to that day's reading—Isaiah's prophecy of the Messiah bringing God's new age of freedom (Isaiah 61:1-2). Everyone was eager to hear his comments, but he simply said, "The Scripture you've just heard has been fulfilled this very day!" (Luke 4:21). Isaiah's prophecy was starting to be fulfilled, he was claiming! This sounded exciting, but then he reminded them that, whenever people had rejected the prophets, God had sent them to minister elsewhere, even to Gentiles (4:26-27). This was not the kind of new age they wanted nor the kind of Messiah they wanted, so, driving him out of town, they tried to kill him. He miraculously escaped and left Nazareth, never to return.

He moved to Capernaum, from where he exercised the messianic ministry that Isaiah had prophesied: preaching good news to the poor, proclaiming freedom for those imprisoned (whether by sickness, sin, demons, or circumstances), restoring sight to the blind (physically and spiritually), and freeing the oppressed, thus showing that God's promised time of favor had arrived. His mission was never merely one of words, but words and action, just as ours should be.

intended to push him over the cliff, 30but he
passed right through the crowd and went on
his way.

Jesus Casts Out a Demon

31Then Jesus went to Capernaum, a town in
Galilee, and taught there in the synagogue
every Sabbath day. 32There, too, the people
were amazed at his teaching, for he spoke
with authority.

33Once when he was in the synagogue,
a man possessed by a demon—an evil*
spirit—cried out, shouting, 34"Go away! Why
are you interfering with us, Jesus of Nazareth? Have you come to destroy us? I know
who you are—the Holy One of God!"

35But Jesus reprimanded him. "Be quiet!
Come out of the man," he ordered. At that,
the demon threw the man to the floor as
the crowd watched; then it came out of him
without hurting him further.

36Amazed, the people exclaimed, "What
authority and power this man's words
possess! Even evil spirits obey him, and
they flee at his command!" 37The news
about Jesus spread through every village in
the entire region.

Jesus Heals Many People

38After leaving the synagogue that day, Jesus
went to Simon's home, where he found
Simon's mother-in-law very sick with a high
fever. "Please heal her," everyone begged.
39Standing at her bedside, he rebuked the
fever, and it left her. And she got up at once
and prepared a meal for them.

40As the sun went down that evening,
people throughout the village brought sick
family members to Jesus. No matter what
their diseases were, the touch of his hand
healed every one. 41Many were possessed
by demons; and the demons came out at
his command, shouting, "You are the Son
of God!" But because they knew he was the
Messiah, he rebuked them and refused to
let them speak.

Jesus Continues to Preach

42Early the next morning Jesus went out
to an isolated place. The crowds searched
everywhere for him, and when they finally
found him, they begged him not to leave
them. 43But he replied, "I must preach the
Good News of the Kingdom of God in other
towns, too, because that is why I was sent."
44So he continued to travel around, preaching in synagogues throughout Judea.*

The First Disciples

5 One day as Jesus was preaching on the
shore of the Sea of Galilee,* great crowds
pressed in on him to listen to the word of
God. 2He noticed two empty boats at the
water's edge, for the fishermen had left them
and were washing their nets. 3Stepping into
one of the boats, Jesus asked Simon,* its
owner, to push it out into the water. So he sat
in the boat and taught the crowds from there.

4When he had finished speaking, he said
to Simon, "Now go out where it is deeper,
and let down your nets to catch some fish."

5"Master," Simon replied, "we worked
hard all last night and didn't catch a thing.
But if you say so, I'll let the nets down
again." 6And this time their nets were so full
of fish they began to tear! 7A shout for help
brought their partners in the other boat,
and soon both boats were filled with fish
and on the verge of sinking.

8When Simon Peter realized what had happened, he fell to his knees before Jesus and
said, "Oh, Lord, please leave me—I'm such
a sinful man." 9For he was awestruck by the
number of fish they had caught, as were the
others with him. 10His partners, James and
John, the sons of Zebedee, were also amazed.

Jesus replied to Simon, "Don't be afraid!
From now on you'll be fishing for people!"
11And as soon as they landed, they left
everything and followed Jesus.

Jesus Heals a Man with Leprosy

12In one of the villages, Jesus met a man
with an advanced case of leprosy. When the
man saw Jesus, he bowed with his face to
the ground, begging to be healed. "Lord,"
he said, "if you are willing, you can heal me
and make me clean."

13Jesus reached out and touched him.
"I am willing," he said. "Be healed!" And instantly the leprosy disappeared. 14Then Jesus
instructed him not to tell anyone what had

▸ **4:31** *See **Capernaum**, page 1096.* **4:33-35** *See **Jesus' miracles**, page 1128.* **4:43** *See **God's Kingdom**, page 1074.*

happened. He said, "Go to the priest and let
him examine you. Take along the offering required in the law of Moses for those who have
been healed of leprosy.* This will be a public
testimony that you have been cleansed."
15 But despite Jesus' instructions, the
report of his power spread even faster, and
vast crowds came to hear him preach and to
be healed of their diseases. 16 But Jesus often
withdrew to the wilderness for prayer.

Jesus Heals a Paralyzed Man

17 One day while Jesus was teaching, some
Pharisees and teachers of religious law
were sitting nearby. (It seemed that these
men showed up from every village in all
Galilee and Judea, as well as from Jerusalem.) And the Lord's healing power was
strongly with Jesus.
18 Some men came carrying a paralyzed
man on a sleeping mat. They tried to take
him inside to Jesus, 19 but they couldn't
reach him because of the crowd. So they
went up to the roof and took off some tiles.
Then they lowered the sick man on his mat
down into the crowd, right in front of Jesus.
20 Seeing their faith, Jesus said to the man,
"Young man, your sins are forgiven."
21 But the Pharisees and teachers of religious law said to themselves, "Who does
he think he is? That's blasphemy! Only God
can forgive sins!"
22 Jesus knew what they were thinking, so
he asked them, "Why do you question this
in your hearts? 23 Is it easier to say 'Your sins
are forgiven,' or 'Stand up and walk'? 24 So I
will prove to you that the Son of Man* has
the authority on earth to forgive sins." Then
Jesus turned to the paralyzed man and said,
"Stand up, pick up your mat, and go home!"
25 And immediately, as everyone watched,
the man jumped up, picked up his mat, and
went home praising God. 26 Everyone was
gripped with great wonder and awe, and
they praised God, exclaiming, "We have
seen amazing things today!"

Jesus Calls Levi (Matthew)

27 Later, as Jesus left the town, he saw a tax
collector named Levi sitting at his tax collector's booth. "Follow me and be my disciple," Jesus said to him. 28 So Levi got up,
left everything, and followed him.
29 Later, Levi held a banquet in his home
with Jesus as the guest of honor. Many of
Levi's fellow tax collectors and other guests

4:33 Greek *unclean;* also in 4:36. **4:44** Some manuscripts read *Galilee.* **5:1** Greek *Lake Gennesaret,* another name for the Sea of Galilee. **5:3** *Simon* is called "Peter" in 6:14 and thereafter. **5:14** See Lev 14:2-32. **5:24** "Son of Man" is a title Jesus used for himself.

Conviction

Conviction is the sense we have when our innermost being sees the truth of something and it overwhelms us. That's what happened to Peter (Luke 5:8), and through an unlikely event. Despite his many years' experience, the night's fishing had produced nothing. So when Jesus, a carpenter, told him what to do, it was ridiculous; yet there was something about Jesus' teaching that he had been hearing which stirred his heart to obey. And when he did, he caught one of his biggest catches ever.

It was through a simple, everyday—yet unexpected—event that God touched Peter's heart. Suddenly aware of being in the presence of someone special (even if he didn't know who at that moment), he became deeply aware of his own sinfulness—even though Jesus had said nothing about sin. He was discovering that God's kindness is intended to turn us from sin (Romans 2:4). The more we see of God, the more we should be convicted of our shortcomings—but also of God's ability to meet those shortcomings through Jesus.

Whenever we feel convicted, we should take care not to harden our hearts (see *Hardness of heart*, page 1132) but should respond quickly, for we do not know what miracle of change God will bring out of it.

▶ *See also* ***Repentance****, page 1253.*

also ate with them. 30But the Pharisees and their teachers of religious law complained bitterly to Jesus' disciples, "Why do you eat and drink with such scum?*"

31Jesus answered them, "Healthy people don't need a doctor—sick people do. 32I have come to call not those who think they are righteous, but those who know they are sinners and need to repent."

A Discussion about Fasting

33One day some people said to Jesus, "John the Baptist's disciples fast and pray regularly, and so do the disciples of the Pharisees. Why are your disciples always eating and drinking?"

34Jesus responded, "Do wedding guests fast while celebrating with the groom? Of course not. 35But someday the groom will be taken away from them, and then they will fast."

36Then Jesus gave them this illustration: "No one tears a piece of cloth from a new garment and uses it to patch an old garment. For then the new garment would be ruined, and the new patch wouldn't even match the old garment.

37"And no one puts new wine into old wineskins. For the new wine would burst the wineskins, spilling the wine and ruining the skins. 38New wine must be stored in new wineskins. 39But no one who drinks the old wine seems to want the new wine. 'The old is just fine,' they say."

A Discussion about the Sabbath

6 One Sabbath day as Jesus was walking through some grainfields, his disciples broke off heads of grain, rubbed off the husks in their hands, and ate the grain. 2But some Pharisees said, "Why are you breaking the law by harvesting grain on the Sabbath?"

3Jesus replied, "Haven't you read in the Scriptures what David did when he and his companions were hungry? 4He went into the house of God and broke the law by eating the sacred loaves of bread that only the priests can eat. He also gave some to his companions." 5And Jesus added, "The Son of Man* is Lord, even over the Sabbath."

Jesus Heals on the Sabbath

6On another Sabbath day, a man with a deformed right hand was in the synagogue while Jesus was teaching. 7The teachers of religious law and the Pharisees watched Jesus closely. If he healed the man's hand, they planned to accuse him of working on the Sabbath.

8But Jesus knew their thoughts. He said to the man with the deformed hand, "Come and stand in front of everyone." So the man came forward. 9Then Jesus said to his critics, "I have a question for you. Does the law permit good deeds on the Sabbath, or is it a day for doing evil? Is this a day to save life or to destroy it?"

10He looked around at them one by one and then said to the man, "Hold out your hand." So the man held out his hand, and it was restored! 11At this, the enemies of Jesus were wild with rage and began to discuss what to do with him.

Jesus Chooses the Twelve Apostles

12One day soon afterward Jesus went up on a mountain to pray, and he prayed to God all night. 13At daybreak he called together all of his disciples and chose twelve of them to be apostles. Here are their names:

14 Simon (whom he named Peter),
Andrew (Peter's brother),
James,
John,
Philip,
Bartholomew,
15 Matthew,
Thomas,
James (son of Alphaeus),
Simon (who was called the zealot),
16 Judas (son of James),
Judas Iscariot (who later betrayed him).

Crowds Follow Jesus

17When they came down from the mountain, the disciples stood with Jesus on a large, level area, surrounded by many of his followers and by the crowds. There were people from all over Judea and from Jerusalem and from as far north as the seacoasts of Tyre and Sidon. 18They had come to hear him and to be healed of their diseases; and

▸ **5:27-32** *See **Matthew**, page 1081.* **6:1** *See **Sunday**, page 1121.* **6:13** *See **Apostles of Jesus**, page 1122.*

those troubled by evil* spirits were healed.
[19]Everyone tried to touch him, because
healing power went out from him, and he
healed everyone.

The Beatitudes

[20]Then Jesus turned to his disciples and
said,

"God blesses you who are poor,
for the Kingdom of God is yours.
[21] God blesses you who are hungry now,
for you will be satisfied.
God blesses you who weep now,
for in due time you will laugh.

[22]What blessings await you when people
hate you and exclude you and mock you
and curse you as evil because you follow
the Son of Man. [23]When that happens, be
happy! Yes, leap for joy! For a great reward
awaits you in heaven. And remember, their
ancestors treated the ancient prophets that
same way.

Sorrows Foretold

[24] "What sorrow awaits you who are rich,
for you have your only happiness now.
[25] What sorrow awaits you who are fat and
prosperous now,
for a time of awful hunger awaits you.
What sorrow awaits you who laugh now,
for your laughing will turn to
mourning and sorrow.
[26] What sorrow awaits you who are praised
by the crowds,
for their ancestors also praised false
prophets.

Love for Enemies

[27]"But to you who are willing to listen, I say,
love your enemies! Do good to those who
hate you. [28]Bless those who curse you. Pray
for those who hurt you. [29]If someone slaps
you on one cheek, offer the other cheek
also. If someone demands your coat, offer
your shirt also. [30]Give to anyone who asks;
and when things are taken away from you,
don't try to get them back. [31]Do to others as
you would like them to do to you.

[32]"If you love only those who love you,
why should you get credit for that? Even
sinners love those who love them! [33]And
if you do good only to those who do
good to you, why should you get credit?
Even sinners do that much! [34]And if you
lend money only to those who can repay
you, why should you get credit? Even
sinners will lend to other sinners for a full
return.

[35]"Love your enemies! Do good to them.
Lend to them without expecting to be
repaid. Then your reward from heaven will
be very great, and you will truly be acting
as children of the Most High, for he is kind
to those who are unthankful and wicked.
[36]You must be compassionate, just as your
Father is compassionate.

Do Not Judge Others

[37]"Do not judge others, and you will not be
judged. Do not condemn others, or it will
all come back against you. Forgive others,
and you will be forgiven. [38]Give, and you
will receive. Your gift will return to you in
full—pressed down, shaken together to
make room for more, running over, and
poured into your lap. The amount you
give will determine the amount you get
back.*"

[39]Then Jesus gave the following illustration: "Can one blind person lead another?
Won't they both fall into a ditch? [40]Stu-
dents* are not greater than their teacher.
But the student who is fully trained will
become like the teacher.

[41]"And why worry about a speck in
your friend's eye* when you have a log in
your own? [42]How can you think of saying,
'Friend,* let me help you get rid of that
speck in your eye,' when you can't see past
the log in your own eye? Hypocrite! First get
rid of the log in your own eye; then you will
see well enough to deal with the speck in
your friend's eye.

The Tree and Its Fruit

[43]"A good tree can't produce bad fruit, and
a bad tree can't produce good fruit. [44]A
tree is identified by its fruit. Figs are never
gathered from thornbushes, and grapes are
not picked from bramble bushes. [45]A good
person produces good things from the treasury of a good heart, and an evil person
produces evil things from the treasury of an
evil heart. What you say flows from what is
in your heart.

5:30 Greek *with tax collectors and sinners?* **6:5** "Son of Man" is a title Jesus used for himself. **6:18** Greek *unclean.* **6:38** Or *The measure you give will be the measure you get back.* **6:40** Or *Disciples.* **6:41** Greek *your brother's eye;* also in 6:42. **6:42** Greek *Brother.*

Building on a Solid Foundation

46 "So why do you keep calling me 'Lord,
Lord!' when you don't do what I say? 47 I
will show you what it's like when someone
comes to me, listens to my teaching, and
then follows it. 48 It is like a person building
a house who digs deep and lays the foundation on solid rock. When the floodwaters
rise and break against that house, it stands
firm because it is well built. 49 But anyone
who hears and doesn't obey is like a person
who builds a house right on the ground,
without a foundation. When the floods
sweep down against that house, it will collapse into a heap of ruins."

The Faith of a Roman Officer

7 When Jesus had finished saying all
this to the people, he returned to Capernaum. 2 At that time the highly valued
slave of a Roman officer* was sick and near
death. 3 When the officer heard about Jesus,
he sent some respected Jewish elders to ask
him to come and heal his slave. 4 So they
earnestly begged Jesus to help the man. "If
anyone deserves your help, he does," they
said, 5 "for he loves the Jewish people and
even built a synagogue for us."
6 So Jesus went with them. But just before
they arrived at the house, the officer sent
some friends to say, "Lord, don't trouble
yourself by coming to my home, for I am
not worthy of such an honor. 7 I am not even
worthy to come and meet you. Just say the
word from where you are, and my servant
will be healed. 8 I know this because I am
under the authority of my superior officers,
and I have authority over my soldiers. I only
need to say, 'Go,' and they go, or 'Come,' and
they come. And if I say to my slaves, 'Do this,'
they do it."
9 When Jesus heard this, he was amazed.
Turning to the crowd that was following
him, he said, "I tell you, I haven't seen faith
like this in all Israel!" 10 And when the officer's friends returned to his house, they
found the slave completely healed.

Jesus Raises a Widow's Son

11 Soon afterward Jesus went with his disciples
to the village of Nain, and a large crowd followed him. 12 A funeral procession was coming
out as he approached the village gate. The
young man who had died was a widow's only
son, and a large crowd from the village was
with her. 13 When the Lord saw her, his heart
overflowed with compassion. "Don't cry!" he
said. 14 Then he walked over to the coffin and
touched it, and the bearers stopped. "Young
man," he said, "I tell you, get up." 15 Then the
dead boy sat up and began to talk! And Jesus
gave him back to his mother.

Jesus: good news for all

Luke shows how Jesus often turned social conventions upside down by mixing with people seen as "outsiders" in some way—women, children, the poor, tax collectors, people with leprosy, Samaritans, and non-Jews (Gentiles). While for the Pharisees, such interaction was impossible for the truly godly, for Jesus it was his sheer delight. *Women*, seen as second-class citizens, were accepted equally with men, included among his disciples (Luke 8:1-3), taught in ways relevant to them (15:8-10), not condemned for the life they had fallen into (7:36-50), and blessed by being the first to witness his resurrection (24:1-12). *Children*, seen as insignificant, were welcomed and esteemed (9:46-48). *The poor*, ignored in society, had a special place in his heart (4:18; 6:20; 7:22). *Tax collectors*, hated for colluding with Rome and defrauding fellow Jews, were often his companions (5:27-31; 19:1-10). *People with leprosy*, avoided at all costs, were not only befriended but touched by him (5:12-13). *Samaritans*, despised by Jews, were recipients of his ministry (17:11-19) and illustrations in his teaching (10:25-37). Even *Gentiles* received his healing (7:1-10).

Jesus loved spending time with those whom the religious purists saw as being of doubtful character, behavior, and background. When questioned about it, he said, "Healthy people don't need a doctor—sick people do" (5:31).

[16]Great fear swept the crowd, and they
praised God, saying, "A mighty prophet has
risen among us," and "God has visited his
people today." [17]And the news about Jesus
spread throughout Judea and the surrounding countryside.

Jesus and John the Baptist

[18]The disciples of John the Baptist told John
about everything Jesus was doing. So John
called for two of his disciples, [19]and he sent
them to the Lord to ask him, "Are you the
Messiah we've been expecting,* or should
we keep looking for someone else?"
[20]John's two disciples found Jesus and said
to him, "John the Baptist sent us to ask, 'Are
you the Messiah we've been expecting, or
should we keep looking for someone else?'"
[21]At that very time, Jesus cured many
people of their diseases, illnesses, and evil
spirits, and he restored sight to many who
were blind. [22]Then he told John's disciples,
"Go back to John and tell him what you have
seen and heard—the blind see, the lame
walk, those with leprosy are cured, the deaf
hear, the dead are raised to life, and the
Good News is being preached to the poor."
[23]And he added, "God blesses those who do
not fall away because of me.*"
[24]After John's disciples left, Jesus began
talking about him to the crowds. "What
kind of man did you go into the wilderness
to see? Was he a weak reed, swayed by every
breath of wind? [25]Or were you expecting to
see a man dressed in expensive clothes? No,
people who wear beautiful clothes and live
in luxury are found in palaces. [26]Were you
looking for a prophet? Yes, and he is more
than a prophet. [27]John is the man to whom
the Scriptures refer when they say,

'Look, I am sending my messenger
ahead of you,
and he will prepare your way before
you.'*

[28]I tell you, of all who have ever lived, none
is greater than John. Yet even the least
person in the Kingdom of God is greater
than he is!"
[29]When they heard this, all the people—
even the tax collectors—agreed that God's
way was right,* for they had been baptized
by John. [30]But the Pharisees and experts in
religious law rejected God's plan for them,
for they had refused John's baptism.
[31]"To what can I compare the people of
this generation?" Jesus asked. "How can
I describe them? [32]They are like children
playing a game in the public square. They
complain to their friends,

'We played wedding songs,
and you didn't dance,
so we played funeral songs,
and you didn't weep.'

[33]For John the Baptist didn't spend his time
eating bread or drinking wine, and you say,
'He's possessed by a demon.' [34]The Son of
Man,* on the other hand, feasts and drinks,
and you say, 'He's a glutton and a drunkard, and a friend of tax collectors and other
sinners!' [35]But wisdom is shown to be right
by the lives of those who follow it.*"

Jesus Anointed by a Sinful Woman

[36]One of the Pharisees asked Jesus to have
dinner with him, so Jesus went to his home
and sat down to eat.* [37]When a certain
immoral woman from that city heard he
was eating there, she brought a beautiful
alabaster jar filled with expensive perfume.
[38]Then she knelt behind him at his feet,
weeping. Her tears fell on his feet, and she
wiped them off with her hair. Then she kept
kissing his feet and putting perfume on
them.
[39]When the Pharisee who had invited him
saw this, he said to himself, "If this man
were a prophet, he would know what kind
of woman is touching him. She's a sinner!"
[40]Then Jesus answered his thoughts.
"Simon," he said to the Pharisee, "I have
something to say to you."
"Go ahead, Teacher," Simon replied.
[41]Then Jesus told him this story: "A man
loaned money to two people—500 pieces
of silver* to one and 50 pieces to the other.
[42]But neither of them could repay him, so
he kindly forgave them both, canceling

7:2 Greek *a centurion;* similarly in 7:6. **7:19** Greek *Are you the one who is coming?* Also in 7:20. **7:23** Or *who are not offended by me.* **7:27** Mal 3:1. **7:29** Or *praised God for his justice.* **7:34** "Son of Man" is a title Jesus used for himself. **7:35** Or *But wisdom is justified by all her children.* **7:36** Or *and reclined.* **7:41** Greek *500 denarii.* A denarius was equivalent to a laborer's full day's wage.

▸ **7:18** *See* ***John the Baptist****, page 1156.*

their debts. Who do you suppose loved him
more after that?"
43Simon answered, "I suppose the one for
whom he canceled the larger debt."
"That's right," Jesus said. 44Then he
turned to the woman and said to Simon,
"Look at this woman kneeling here. When
I entered your home, you didn't offer me
water to wash the dust from my feet, but she
has washed them with her tears and wiped
them with her hair. 45You didn't greet me
with a kiss, but from the time I first came in,
she has not stopped kissing my feet. 46You
neglected the courtesy of olive oil to anoint
my head, but she has anointed my feet with
rare perfume.
47"I tell you, her sins—and they are many—
have been forgiven, so she has shown me
much love. But a person who is forgiven
little shows only little love." 48Then Jesus
said to the woman, "Your sins are forgiven."
49The men at the table said among themselves, "Who is this man, that he goes
around forgiving sins?"
50And Jesus said to the woman, "Your
faith has saved you; go in peace."

Women Who Followed Jesus

8 Soon afterward Jesus began a tour of
the nearby towns and villages, preaching and announcing the Good News about
the Kingdom of God. He took his twelve disciples with him, 2along with some women
who had been cured of evil spirits and diseases. Among them were Mary Magdalene,
from whom he had cast out seven demons;
3Joanna, the wife of Chuza, Herod's business manager; Susanna; and many others
who were contributing from their own resources to support Jesus and his disciples.

Parable of the Farmer Scattering Seed

4One day Jesus told a story in the form of a
parable to a large crowd that had gathered
from many towns to hear him: 5"A farmer
went out to plant his seed. As he scattered
it across his field, some seed fell on a footpath, where it was stepped on, and the birds
ate it. 6Other seed fell among rocks. It began
to grow, but the plant soon wilted and died
for lack of moisture. 7Other seed fell among
thorns that grew up with it and choked out
the tender plants. 8Still other seed fell on
fertile soil. This seed grew and produced a
crop that was a hundred times as much as
had been planted!" When he had said this,
he called out, "Anyone with ears to hear
should listen and understand."
9His disciples asked him what this parable
meant. 10He replied, "You are permitted to
understand the secrets* of the Kingdom of
God. But I use parables to teach the others
so that the Scriptures might be fulfilled:

'When they look, they won't really see.
When they hear, they won't
understand.'*

11"This is the meaning of the parable: The
seed is God's word. 12The seeds that fell on
the footpath represent those who hear the
message, only to have the devil come and
take it away from their hearts and prevent
them from believing and being saved. 13The
seeds on the rocky soil represent those who
hear the message and receive it with joy.
But since they don't have deep roots, they

Mary Magdalene

Mary Magdalene has often received bad press due to being identified by some as the sinful woman who anointed Jesus' feet (Luke 7:36-50), but there are no grounds for this. We don't know much about her, other than that she came from Magdala on the western shore of the Sea of Galilee (as her name shows) and that she was delivered from seven demons by Jesus (8:2). She was part of a group of women who supported Jesus' ministry financially (8:2-3), was still with them at the cross (Matthew 27:55-56), and was one of the first to witness the Resurrection (Matthew 28:1-9; John 20:1-2, 11-18). Unorthodox Gnostic writers in the second century AD promoted their own interpretation of Mary, claiming she had secret knowledge (*gnōsis*) that Jesus had shared with her—a theme still repeated in some modern novels.

believe for a while, then they fall away when
they face temptation. 14 The seeds that fell
among the thorns represent those who hear
the message, but all too quickly the message
is crowded out by the cares and riches and
pleasures of this life. And so they never grow
into maturity. 15 And the seeds that fell on the
good soil represent honest, good-hearted
people who hear God's word, cling to it, and
patiently produce a huge harvest.

Parable of the Lamp

16 "No one lights a lamp and then covers it
with a bowl or hides it under a bed. A lamp
is placed on a stand, where its light can be
seen by all who enter the house. 17 For all that
is secret will eventually be brought into the
open, and everything that is concealed will
be brought to light and made known to all.

18 "So pay attention to how you hear. To
those who listen to my teaching, more understanding will be given. But for those who
are not listening, even what they think they
understand will be taken away from them."

The True Family of Jesus

19 Then Jesus' mother and brothers came
to see him, but they couldn't get to him
because of the crowd. 20 Someone told Jesus,
"Your mother and your brothers are standing outside, and they want to see you."

21 Jesus replied, "My mother and my brothers are all those who hear God's word and
obey it."

Jesus Calms the Storm

22 One day Jesus said to his disciples, "Let's
cross to the other side of the lake." So they
got into a boat and started out. 23 As they
sailed across, Jesus settled down for a nap.
But soon a fierce storm came down on the
lake. The boat was filling with water, and
they were in real danger.

24 The disciples went and woke him up,
shouting, "Master, Master, we're going to
drown!"

When Jesus woke up, he rebuked the
wind and the raging waves. Suddenly the
storm stopped and all was calm. 25 Then he
asked them, "Where is your faith?"

The disciples were terrified and amazed.
"Who is this man?" they asked each other.
"When he gives a command, even the wind
and waves obey him!"

Jesus Heals a Demon-Possessed Man

26 So they arrived in the region of the Gerasenes,* across the lake from Galilee. 27 As
Jesus was climbing out of the boat, a man
who was possessed by demons came out
to meet him. For a long time he had been
homeless and naked, living in the tombs
outside the town.

28 As soon as he saw Jesus, he shrieked and
fell down in front of him. Then he screamed,
"Why are you interfering with me, Jesus,
Son of the Most High God? Please, I beg you,
don't torture me!" 29 For Jesus had already
commanded the evil* spirit to come out of
him. This spirit had often taken control of
the man. Even when he was placed under
guard and put in chains and shackles, he
simply broke them and rushed out into the
wilderness, completely under the demon's
power.

30 Jesus demanded, "What is your name?"

"Legion," he replied, for he was filled
with many demons. 31 The demons kept
begging Jesus not to send them into the
bottomless pit.*

32 There happened to be a large herd of
pigs feeding on the hillside nearby, and the
demons begged him to let them enter into
the pigs.

So Jesus gave them permission. 33 Then the
demons came out of the man and entered
the pigs, and the entire herd plunged down
the steep hillside into the lake and drowned.

34 When the herdsmen saw it, they fled
to the nearby town and the surrounding
countryside, spreading the news as they
ran. 35 People rushed out to see what had
happened. A crowd soon gathered around
Jesus, and they saw the man who had been
freed from the demons. He was sitting at
Jesus' feet, fully clothed and perfectly sane,
and they were all afraid. 36 Then those who
had seen what happened told the others
how the demon-possessed man had been
healed. 37 And all the people in the region of
the Gerasenes begged Jesus to go away and

8:10a Greek *mysteries.* **8:10b** Isa 6:9 (Greek version).
8:26 Other manuscripts read *Gadarenes;* still others read
Gergesenes; also in 8:37. See Matt 8:28; Mark 5:1. **8:29** Greek
unclean. **8:31** Or *the abyss,* or *the underworld.*

▸ **8:14** *See* ***Hardness of heart,*** *page 1132.*

leave them alone, for a great wave of fear
swept over them.
So Jesus returned to the boat and left,
crossing back to the other side of the lake.
38The man who had been freed from the
demons begged to go with him. But Jesus
sent him home, saying, 39"No, go back to
your family, and tell them everything God
has done for you." So he went all through
the town proclaiming the great things Jesus
had done for him.

Jesus Heals in Response to Faith

40On the other side of the lake the crowds
welcomed Jesus, because they had been
waiting for him. 41Then a man named Jairus,
a leader of the local synagogue, came and
fell at Jesus' feet, pleading with him to come
home with him. 42His only daughter,* who
was about twelve years old, was dying.
As Jesus went with him, he was surrounded by the crowds. 43A woman in the
crowd had suffered for twelve years with
constant bleeding,* and she could find
no cure. 44Coming up behind Jesus, she
touched the fringe of his robe. Immediately,
the bleeding stopped.
45"Who touched me?" Jesus asked.
Everyone denied it, and Peter said,
"Master, this whole crowd is pressing up
against you."
46But Jesus said, "Someone deliberately
touched me, for I felt healing power go
out from me." 47When the woman realized
that she could not stay hidden, she began
to tremble and fell to her knees in front of
him. The whole crowd heard her explain
why she had touched him and that she had
been immediately healed. 48"Daughter," he
said to her, "your faith has made you well.
Go in peace."
49While he was still speaking to her, a
messenger arrived from the home of Jairus,
the leader of the synagogue. He told him,
"Your daughter is dead. There's no use troubling the Teacher now."
50But when Jesus heard what had happened, he said to Jairus, "Don't be afraid.
Just have faith, and she will be healed."
51When they arrived at the house, Jesus
wouldn't let anyone go in with him except
Peter, John, James, and the little girl's father
and mother. 52The house was filled with
people weeping and wailing, but he said,
"Stop the weeping! She isn't dead; she's
only asleep."
53But the crowd laughed at him because
they all knew she had died. 54Then Jesus took
her by the hand and said in a loud voice,
"My child, get up!" 55And at that moment
her life* returned, and she immediately
stood up! Then Jesus told them to give her
something to eat. 56Her parents were overwhelmed, but Jesus insisted that they not
tell anyone what had happened.

Jesus Sends Out the Twelve Disciples

9 One day Jesus called together his twelve
disciples* and gave them power and authority to cast out all demons and to heal
all diseases. 2Then he sent them out to tell
everyone about the Kingdom of God and
to heal the sick. 3"Take nothing for your
journey," he instructed them. "Don't take
a walking stick, a traveler's bag, food,
money,* or even a change of clothes. 4Wher-
ever you go, stay in the same house until
you leave town. 5And if a town refuses to
welcome you, shake its dust from your feet
as you leave to show that you have abandoned those people to their fate."
6So they began their circuit of the villages,
preaching the Good News and healing the
sick.

Herod's Confusion

7When Herod Antipas, the ruler of Galilee,*
heard about everything Jesus was doing, he
was puzzled. Some were saying that John
the Baptist had been raised from the dead.
8Others thought Jesus was Elijah or one of
the other prophets risen from the dead.
9"I beheaded John," Herod said, "so who
is this man about whom I hear such stories?"
And he kept trying to see him.

Jesus Feeds Five Thousand

10When the apostles returned, they told
Jesus everything they had done. Then he
slipped quietly away with them toward the
town of Bethsaida. 11But the crowds found
out where he was going, and they followed
him. He welcomed them and taught them
about the Kingdom of God, and he healed
those who were sick.

▸ **8:26-39** *See* ***Demons****, page 1126.*

[12]Late in the afternoon the twelve disciples came to him and said, "Send the crowds away to the nearby villages and farms, so they can find food and lodging for the night. There is nothing to eat here in this remote place."

[13]But Jesus said, "You feed them."

"But we have only five loaves of bread and two fish," they answered. "Or are you expecting us to go and buy enough food for this whole crowd?" [14]For there were about 5,000 men there.

Jesus replied, "Tell them to sit down in groups of about fifty each." [15]So the people all sat down. [16]Jesus took the five loaves and two fish, looked up toward heaven, and blessed them. Then, breaking the loaves into pieces, he kept giving the bread and fish to the disciples so they could distribute it to the people. [17]They all ate as much as they wanted, and afterward, the disciples picked up twelve baskets of leftovers!

Peter's Declaration about Jesus

[18]One day Jesus left the crowds to pray alone. Only his disciples were with him, and he asked them, "Who do people say I am?"

[19]"Well," they replied, "some say John the Baptist, some say Elijah, and others say you are one of the other ancient prophets risen from the dead."

[20]Then he asked them, "But who do you say I am?"

Peter replied, "You are the Messiah* sent from God!"

Jesus Predicts His Death

[21]Jesus warned his disciples not to tell anyone who he was. [22]"The Son of Man* must suffer many terrible things," he said. "He will be rejected by the elders, the leading priests, and the teachers of religious law. He will be killed, but on the third day he will be raised from the dead."

[23]Then he said to the crowd, "If any of you wants to be my follower, you must give up your own way, take up your cross daily, and follow me. [24]If you try to hang on to your life,

8:42 Or *His only child, a daughter.* **8:43** Some manuscripts add *having spent everything she had on doctors.* **8:55** Or *her spirit.* **9:1** Greek *the Twelve;* other manuscripts read *the twelve apostles.* **9:3** Or *silver coins.* **9:7** Greek *Herod the tetrarch.* Herod Antipas was a son of King Herod and was ruler over Galilee. **9:20** Or *the Christ. Messiah* (a Hebrew term) and *Christ* (a Greek term) both mean "anointed one." **9:22** "Son of Man" is a title Jesus used for himself.

▸ **9:20** *See* ***Peter****, page 1421.*

The Transfiguration

A week after Peter acknowledged Jesus as Messiah (Luke 9:20), Jesus took Peter, James, and John up a mountain where his "appearance was transformed" (Matthew 17:2; Mark 9:2). There, Moses and Elijah appeared and discussed "his exodus from this world" (Luke 9:31)—an allusion to the great deliverance that his coming death would bring. Then a cloud enveloped them, and God confirmed that Jesus was his Son (9:35). The experience terrified the disciples (Matthew 17:6-7), and Peter never forgot it (2 Peter 1:16-18).

At the Transfiguration, Jesus' glory, left in heaven at his incarnation, momentarily broke through into this world—a revelation to the disciples of who he was, and a confirmation to Jesus of the Father's love. The incident is rich in Old Testament imagery. Moses and Elijah, representing the Law and the Prophets, honor the one whose revelation theirs had prepared for. It was on a mountain (Sinai) that Moses had encountered God's glory and received the first covenant; now Jesus encountered that same glory on this mountain in preparation for the better covenant his death would bring. Clouds often symbolized God's presence (Exodus 13:21-22; 19:16-19; 40:34-35); now here was that same cloud, speaking of God's glory in Jesus. The whole Old Testament pointed to Jesus; that is why the disciples should "listen to him" (Luke 9:35).

▸ *See also* ***The Incarnation****, page 1199.*

you will lose it. But if you give up your life
for my sake, you will save it. 25 And what do
you benefit if you gain the whole world but
are yourself lost or destroyed? 26 If anyone is
ashamed of me and my message, the Son of
Man will be ashamed of that person when
he returns in his glory and in the glory of
the Father and the holy angels. 27 I tell you
the truth, some standing here right now will
not die before they see the Kingdom of God."

The Transfiguration

28 About eight days later Jesus took Peter,
John, and James up on a mountain to pray.
29 And as he was praying, the appearance of
his face was transformed, and his clothes
became dazzling white. 30 Suddenly, two
men, Moses and Elijah, appeared and
began talking with Jesus. 31 They were glorious to see. And they were speaking about
his exodus from this world, which was
about to be fulfilled in Jerusalem.

32 Peter and the others had fallen asleep.
When they woke up, they saw Jesus' glory
and the two men standing with him. 33 As
Moses and Elijah were starting to leave,
Peter, not even knowing what he was saying,
blurted out, "Master, it's wonderful for us to
be here! Let's make three shelters as memorials*—one for you, one for Moses, and
one for Elijah." 34 But even as he was saying
this, a cloud overshadowed them, and terror
gripped them as the cloud covered them.

35 Then a voice from the cloud said, "This
is my Son, my Chosen One.* Listen to him."
36 When the voice finished, Jesus was there
alone. They didn't tell anyone at that time
what they had seen.

Jesus Heals a Demon-Possessed Boy

37 The next day, after they had come down
the mountain, a large crowd met Jesus.
38 A man in the crowd called out to him,
"Teacher, I beg you to look at my son, my
only child. 39 An evil spirit keeps seizing
him, making him scream. It throws him into
convulsions so that he foams at the mouth.
It batters him and hardly ever leaves him
alone. 40 I begged your disciples to cast out
the spirit, but they couldn't do it."

41 Jesus said, "You faithless and corrupt
people! How long must I be with you and
put up with you?" Then he said to the man,
"Bring your son here."

42 As the boy came forward, the demon
knocked him to the ground and threw him
into a violent convulsion. But Jesus rebuked
the evil* spirit and healed the boy. Then he
gave him back to his father. 43 Awe gripped
the people as they saw this majestic display
of God's power.

Jesus Again Predicts His Death

While everyone was marveling at everything he was doing, Jesus said to his disciples, 44 "Listen to me and remember what
I say. The Son of Man is going to be betrayed
into the hands of his enemies." 45 But they
didn't know what he meant. Its significance
was hidden from them, so they couldn't
understand it, and they were afraid to ask
him about it.

The Greatest in the Kingdom

46 Then his disciples began arguing about
which of them was the greatest. 47 But
Jesus knew their thoughts, so he brought
a little child to his side. 48 Then he said to
them, "Anyone who welcomes a little child
like this on my behalf* welcomes me, and
anyone who welcomes me also welcomes
my Father who sent me. Whoever is the
least among you is the greatest."

Using the Name of Jesus

49 John said to Jesus, "Master, we saw
someone using your name to cast out
demons, but we told him to stop because
he isn't in our group."

50 But Jesus said, "Don't stop him! Anyone
who is not against you is for you."

Opposition from Samaritans

51 As the time drew near for him to ascend to
heaven, Jesus resolutely set out for Jerusalem. 52 He sent messengers ahead to a Samaritan village to prepare for his arrival. 53 But
the people of the village did not welcome
Jesus because he was on his way to Jerusalem. 54 When James and John saw this, they
said to Jesus, "Lord, should we call down
fire from heaven to burn them up*?" 55 But
Jesus turned and rebuked them.* 56 So they
went on to another village.

▸ **9:23-26** *See* ***Discipleship and the cross****, page 1095.*

The Cost of Following Jesus

57As they were walking along, someone
said to Jesus, "I will follow you wherever
you go."
58But Jesus replied, "Foxes have dens to
live in, and birds have nests, but the Son
of Man has no place even to lay his head."
59He said to another person, "Come,
follow me."

The man agreed, but he said, "Lord, first
let me return home and bury my father."
60But Jesus told him, "Let the spiritually
dead bury their own dead!* Your duty is to
go and preach about the Kingdom of God."
61Another said, "Yes, Lord, I will follow
you, but first let me say good-bye to my
family."
62But Jesus told him, "Anyone who puts a
hand to the plow and then looks back is not
fit for the Kingdom of God."

Jesus Sends Out His Disciples

10 The Lord now chose seventy-two*
other disciples and sent them ahead
in pairs to all the towns and places he
planned to visit. 2These were his instructions to them: "The harvest is great, but
the workers are few. So pray to the Lord
who is in charge of the harvest; ask him to
send more workers into his fields. 3Now go,
and remember that I am sending you out
as lambs among wolves. 4Don't take any
money with you, nor a traveler's bag, nor
an extra pair of sandals. And don't stop to
greet anyone on the road.
5"Whenever you enter someone's home,
first say, 'May God's peace be on this
house.' 6If those who live there are peaceful, the blessing will stand; if they are
not, the blessing will return to you. 7Don't
move around from home to home. Stay in
one place, eating and drinking what they
provide. Don't hesitate to accept hospitality,
because those who work deserve their pay.
8"If you enter a town and it welcomes
you, eat whatever is set before you. 9Heal
the sick, and tell them, 'The Kingdom of
God is near you now.' 10But if a town refuses
to welcome you, go out into its streets and
say, 11'We wipe even the dust of your town
from our feet to show that we have abandoned you to your fate. And know this—the
Kingdom of God is near!' 12I assure you,
even wicked Sodom will be better off than
such a town on judgment day.
13"What sorrow awaits you, Korazin and
Bethsaida! For if the miracles I did in you
had been done in wicked Tyre and Sidon,
their people would have repented of their
sins long ago, clothing themselves in burlap
and throwing ashes on their heads to show
their remorse. 14Yes, Tyre and Sidon will be
better off on judgment day than you. 15And
you people of Capernaum, will you be

9:33 Greek *three tabernacles.* **9:35** Some manuscripts read *This is my dearly loved Son.* **9:42** Greek *unclean.* **9:48** Greek *in my name.* **9:54** Some manuscripts add *as Elijah did.* **9:55** Some manuscripts add an expanded conclusion to verse 55 and an additional sentence in verse 56: *And he said, "You don't realize what your hearts are like. [56]For the Son of Man has not come to destroy people's lives, but to save them."* **9:60** Greek *Let the dead bury their own dead.* **10:1** Some manuscripts read *seventy;* also in 10:17.

Martha and Mary

Martha and Mary were the sisters of Lazarus, whom Jesus raised from the dead (John 11). They lived in the little village of Bethany on the eastern slopes of the Mount of Olives, just two miles from Jerusalem. Martha is often criticized for her apparent lack of spirituality, busying herself preparing the meal rather than sitting at Jesus' feet like Mary, and then complaining to Jesus because he hadn't told Mary to help her (Luke 10:38-40). While this story indeed carries warnings of the danger of busyness, the truth is that Martha too was a deeply spiritual woman. It was she, rather than Mary, who affirmed her faith in Jesus as the resurrection and the life, a confession that was vindicated through the raising of Lazarus. But Mary also demonstrated great faith when, on another occasion at their home, she anointed Jesus' feet with precious ointment, which Jesus interpreted as preparation for his impending burial (Matthew 26:6-13; Mark 14:3-9; John 12:1-8).

▶ *See also* ***Lazarus****, page 1217.*

honored in heaven? No, you will go down to the place of the dead.*"

16 Then he said to the disciples, "Anyone who accepts your message is also accepting me. And anyone who rejects you is rejecting me. And anyone who rejects me is rejecting God, who sent me."

17 When the seventy-two disciples returned, they joyfully reported to him, "Lord, even the demons obey us when we use your name!"

18 "Yes," he told them, "I saw Satan fall from heaven like lightning! 19 Look, I have given you authority over all the power of the enemy, and you can walk among snakes and scorpions and crush them. Nothing will injure you. 20 But don't rejoice because evil spirits obey you; rejoice because your names are registered in heaven."

Jesus' Prayer of Thanksgiving

21 At that same time Jesus was filled with the joy of the Holy Spirit, and he said, "O Father, Lord of heaven and earth, thank you for hiding these things from those who think themselves wise and clever, and for revealing them to the childlike. Yes, Father, it pleased you to do it this way.

22 "My Father has entrusted everything to me. No one truly knows the Son except the Father, and no one truly knows the Father except the Son and those to whom the Son chooses to reveal him."

23 Then when they were alone, he turned to the disciples and said, "Blessed are the eyes that see what you have seen. 24 I tell you, many prophets and kings longed to see what you see, but they didn't see it. And they longed to hear what you hear, but they didn't hear it."

The Most Important Commandment

25 One day an expert in religious law stood up to test Jesus by asking him this question: "Teacher, what should I do to inherit eternal life?"

26 Jesus replied, "What does the law of Moses say? How do you read it?"

27 The man answered, "'You must love the LORD your God with all your heart, all your soul, all your strength, and all your mind.' And, 'Love your neighbor as yourself.'"*

28 "Right!" Jesus told him. "Do this and you will live!"

29 The man wanted to justify his actions, so he asked Jesus, "And who is my neighbor?"

Parable of the Good Samaritan

30 Jesus replied with a story: "A Jewish man was traveling from Jerusalem down to Jericho, and he was attacked by bandits. They stripped him of his clothes, beat him up, and left him half dead beside the road.

31 "By chance a priest came along. But when he saw the man lying there, he crossed to the other side of the road and passed him by. 32 A Temple assistant* walked over and looked at him lying there, but he also passed by on the other side.

33 "Then a despised Samaritan came along, and when he saw the man, he felt compassion for him. 34 Going over to him, the Samaritan soothed his wounds with olive oil and wine and bandaged them. Then he put the man on his own donkey and took him to an inn, where he took care of him. 35 The next day he handed the innkeeper two silver coins,* telling him, 'Take care of this man. If his bill runs higher than this, I'll pay you the next time I'm here.'

36 "Now which of these three would you say was a neighbor to the man who was attacked by bandits?" Jesus asked.

37 The man replied, "The one who showed him mercy."

Then Jesus said, "Yes, now go and do the same."

Jesus Visits Martha and Mary

38 As Jesus and the disciples continued on their way to Jerusalem, they came to a certain village where a woman named Martha welcomed him into her home. 39 Her sister, Mary, sat at the Lord's feet, listening to what he taught. 40 But Martha was distracted by the big dinner she was preparing. She came to Jesus and said, "Lord, doesn't it seem unfair to you that my sister just sits here while I do all the work? Tell her to come and help me."

41 But the Lord said to her, "My dear Martha, you are worried and upset over all these details! 42 There is only one thing worth being concerned about. Mary has discovered it, and it will not be taken away from her."

▸ **10:30-37** See ***The parables of Jesus***, *page 1088*; ***The Samaritans***, *page 1204*.

Teaching about Prayer

11 Once Jesus was in a certain place
praying. As he finished, one of his disciples came to him and said, "Lord, teach us
to pray, just as John taught his disciples."
2 Jesus said, "This is how you should
pray:*

"Father, may your name be kept holy.
May your Kingdom come soon.
3 Give us each day the food we need,*
4 and forgive us our sins,
as we forgive those who sin
against us.
And don't let us yield to temptation.*"

5 Then, teaching them more about
prayer, he used this story: "Suppose you
went to a friend's house at midnight,
wanting to borrow three loaves of bread.
You say to him, 6 'A friend of mine has just
arrived for a visit, and I have nothing for
him to eat.' 7 And suppose he calls out from
his bedroom, 'Don't bother me. The door is
locked for the night, and my family and I are
all in bed. I can't help you.' 8 But I tell you
this—though he won't do it for friendship's
sake, if you keep knocking long enough, he
will get up and give you whatever you need
because of your shameless persistence.*
9 "And so I tell you, keep on asking, and
you will receive what you ask for. Keep on
seeking, and you will find. Keep on knocking, and the door will be opened to you.
10 For everyone who asks, receives. Everyone who seeks, finds. And to everyone who
knocks, the door will be opened.
11 "You fathers—if your children ask* for
a fish, do you give them a snake instead?
12 Or if they ask for an egg, do you give them
a scorpion? Of course not! 13 So if you sinful
people know how to give good gifts to your
children, how much more will your heavenly Father give the Holy Spirit to those who
ask him."

Jesus and the Prince of Demons

14 One day Jesus cast out a demon from a man
who couldn't speak, and when the demon
was gone, the man began to speak. The
crowds were amazed, 15 but some of them
said, "No wonder he can cast out demons.
He gets his power from Satan,* the prince
of demons." 16 Others, trying to test Jesus,

10:15 Greek *to Hades.* **10:27** Deut 6:5; Lev 19:18. **10:32** Greek *A Levite.* **10:35** Greek *two denarii.* A denarius was equivalent to a laborer's full day's wage. **11:2** Some manuscripts add additional phrases from the Lord's Prayer as it reads in Matt 6:9-13. **11:3** Or *Give us each day our food for the day;* or *Give us each day our food for tomorrow.* **11:4** Or *And keep us from being tested.* **11:8** Or *in order to avoid shame,* or *so his reputation won't be damaged.* **11:11** Some manuscripts add *for bread, do you give them a stone? Or [if they ask].* **11:15** Greek *Beelzeboul;* also in 11:18, 19. Other manuscripts read *Beezeboul;* Latin version reads *Beelzebub.*

▸ **11:2-4** *See **The Lord's Prayer**, page 1077.*

Asking for the Holy Spirit

It is impossible to become a Christian or live as a Christian without the Holy Spirit's help. When Jesus told his disciples, "I will not abandon you as orphans—I will come to you" (John 14:18), he was thinking about their need of the Holy Spirit. He also said, "You know him, because he lives *with* you now and later will be *in* you" (John 14:17)—the one who was "with" had to become the one who was "in." The Holy Spirit is *with* us, leading us to faith in Jesus, but we all then need more of his presence and power *in* us in an ongoing way (see Acts 1:8; 2:4; Ephesians 5:18).

This is why Jesus encouraged his disciples to ask for the Holy Spirit (Luke 11:13), the climax of his teaching on prayer (11:1-13). God is so good that we can ask him, not only for our daily needs (11:2-4), but also for the gift of the Spirit. We need not fear that God will deny us our request (11:5-8), nor that he will give us something nasty or permit us to be tricked or deceived (11:11-12). We never need to fear asking for more of God's Holy Spirit in our lives. After all, this is what Jesus promised us.

▸ *See also **The Christian's relationship with the Holy Spirit**, page 1350.*

demanded that he show them a miraculous sign from heaven to prove his authority.

17He knew their thoughts, so he said, "Any kingdom divided by civil war is doomed. A family splintered by feuding will fall apart. 18You say I am empowered by Satan. But if Satan is divided and fighting against himself, how can his kingdom survive? 19And if I am empowered by Satan, what about your own exorcists? They cast out demons, too, so they will condemn you for what you have said. 20But if I am casting out demons by the power of God,* then the Kingdom of God has arrived among you. 21For when a strong man is fully armed and guards his palace, his possessions are safe—22until someone even stronger attacks and overpowers him, strips him of his weapons, and carries off his belongings.

23"Anyone who isn't with me opposes me, and anyone who isn't working with me is actually working against me.

24"When an evil* spirit leaves a person, it goes into the desert, searching for rest. But when it finds none, it says, 'I will return to the person I came from.' 25So it returns and finds that its former home is all swept and in order. 26Then the spirit finds seven other spirits more evil than itself, and they all enter the person and live there. And so that person is worse off than before."

27As he was speaking, a woman in the crowd called out, "God bless your mother—the womb from which you came, and the breasts that nursed you!"

28Jesus replied, "But even more blessed are all who hear the word of God and put it into practice."

The Sign of Jonah

29As the crowd pressed in on Jesus, he said, "This evil generation keeps asking me to show them a miraculous sign. But the only sign I will give them is the sign of Jonah. 30What happened to him was a sign to the people of Nineveh that God had sent him. What happens to the Son of Man* will be a sign to these people that he was sent by God.

31"The queen of Sheba* will stand up against this generation on judgment day and condemn it, for she came from a distant land to hear the wisdom of Solomon. Now someone greater than Solomon is here—but you refuse to listen. 32The people of Nineveh will also stand up against this generation on judgment day and condemn it, for they repented of their sins at the preaching of Jonah. Now someone greater than Jonah is here—but you refuse to repent.

Receiving the Light

33"No one lights a lamp and then hides it or puts it under a basket.* Instead, a lamp is placed on a stand, where its light can be seen by all who enter the house.

34"Your eye is like a lamp that provides light for your body. When your eye is healthy, your whole body is filled with light. But when it is unhealthy, your body is filled with darkness. 35Make sure that the light you think you have is not actually darkness. 36If you are filled with light, with no dark corners, then your whole life will be radiant, as though a floodlight were filling you with light."

Jesus Criticizes the Religious Leaders

37As Jesus was speaking, one of the Pharisees invited him home for a meal. So he went in and took his place at the table.* 38His host was amazed to see that he sat down to eat without first performing the hand-washing ceremony required by Jewish custom. 39Then the Lord said to him, "You Pharisees are so careful to clean the outside of the cup and the dish, but inside you are filthy—full of greed and wickedness! 40Fools! Didn't God make the inside as well as the outside? 41So clean the inside by giving gifts to the poor, and you will be clean all over.

42"What sorrow awaits you Pharisees! For you are careful to tithe even the tiniest income from your herb gardens,* but you ignore justice and the love of God. You should tithe, yes, but do not neglect the more important things.

43"What sorrow awaits you Pharisees! For you love to sit in the seats of honor in the synagogues and receive respectful greetings as you walk in the marketplaces. 44Yes, what sorrow awaits you! For you are like hidden graves in a field. People walk over them without knowing the corruption they are stepping on."

45"Teacher," said an expert in religious law, "you have insulted us, too, in what you just said."

46"Yes," said Jesus, "what sorrow also awaits you experts in religious law! For you crush people with unbearable religious

demands, and you never lift a finger to
ease the burden. 47What sorrow awaits you!
For you build monuments for the prophets
your own ancestors killed long ago. 48But
in fact, you stand as witnesses who agree
with what your ancestors did. They killed
the prophets, and you join in their crime by
building the monuments! 49This is what God
in his wisdom said about you:* 'I will send
prophets and apostles to them, but they will
kill some and persecute the others.'

50"As a result, this generation will be
held responsible for the murder of all God's
prophets from the creation of the world—
51from the murder of Abel to the murder of
Zechariah, who was killed between the altar
and the sanctuary. Yes, it will certainly be
charged against this generation.

52"What sorrow awaits you experts in
religious law! For you remove the key to
knowledge from the people. You don't enter
the Kingdom yourselves, and you prevent
others from entering."

53As Jesus was leaving, the teachers of
religious law and the Pharisees became
hostile and tried to provoke him with many
questions. 54They wanted to trap him into
saying something they could use against
him.

A Warning against Hypocrisy

12 Meanwhile, the crowds grew until
thousands were milling about and
stepping on each other. Jesus turned first to
his disciples and warned them, "Beware of
the yeast of the Pharisees—their hypocrisy.
2The time is coming when everything that
is covered up will be revealed, and all that
is secret will be made known to all. 3What-
ever you have said in the dark will be heard
in the light, and what you have whispered
behind closed doors will be shouted from
the housetops for all to hear!

4"Dear friends, don't be afraid of those
who want to kill your body; they cannot do
any more to you after that. 5But I'll tell you
whom to fear. Fear God, who has the power
to kill you and then throw you into hell.*
Yes, he's the one to fear.

6"What is the price of five sparrows—two
copper coins*? Yet God does not forget a
single one of them. 7And the very hairs on
your head are all numbered. So don't be
afraid; you are more valuable to God than
a whole flock of sparrows.

8"I tell you the truth, everyone who acknowledges me publicly here on earth,
the Son of Man* will also acknowledge in
the presence of God's angels. 9But anyone
who denies me here on earth will be denied
before God's angels. 10Anyone who speaks
against the Son of Man can be forgiven, but
anyone who blasphemes the Holy Spirit will
not be forgiven.

11"And when you are brought to trial in the
synagogues and before rulers and authorities, don't worry about how to defend yourself or what to say, 12for the Holy Spirit will
teach you at that time what needs to be said."

Parable of the Rich Fool

13Then someone called from the crowd,
"Teacher, please tell my brother to divide
our father's estate with me."

14Jesus replied, "Friend, who made me
a judge over you to decide such things as
that?" 15Then he said, "Beware! Guard
against every kind of greed. Life is not measured by how much you own."

16Then he told them a story: "A rich man
had a fertile farm that produced fine crops.
17He said to himself, 'What should I do? I don't
have room for all my crops.' 18Then he said,
'I know! I'll tear down my barns and build
bigger ones. Then I'll have room enough to
store all my wheat and other goods. 19And I'll
sit back and say to myself, "My friend, you
have enough stored away for years to come.
Now take it easy! Eat, drink, and be merry!"'

20"But God said to him, 'You fool! You will
die this very night. Then who will get everything you worked for?'

21"Yes, a person is a fool to store up
earthly wealth but not have a rich relationship with God."

Teaching about Money and Possessions

22Then, turning to his disciples, Jesus said,
"That is why I tell you not to worry about
everyday life—whether you have enough
food to eat or enough clothes to wear. 23For
life is more than food, and your body more
than clothing. 24Look at the ravens. They
don't plant or harvest or store food in barns,

11:20 Greek *by the finger of God.* **11:24** Greek *unclean.* **11:30** "Son of Man" is a title Jesus used for himself. **11:31** Greek *The queen of the south.* **11:33** Some manuscripts do not include *or puts it under a basket.* **11:37** Or *and reclined.* **11:42** Greek *tithe the mint, the rue, and every herb.* **11:49** Greek *Therefore, the wisdom of God said.* **12:5** Greek *Gehenna.* **12:6** Greek *two assaria* [Roman coins equal to 1/16 of a denarius]. **12:8** "Son of Man" is a title Jesus used for himself.

for God feeds them. And you are far more
valuable to him than any birds! 25 Can all
your worries add a single moment to your
life? 26 And if worry can't accomplish a little
thing like that, what's the use of worrying
over bigger things?
27 "Look at the lilies and how they grow.
They don't work or make their clothing, yet
Solomon in all his glory was not dressed as
beautifully as they are. 28 And if God cares so
wonderfully for flowers that are here today
and thrown into the fire tomorrow, he will
certainly care for you. Why do you have so
little faith?
29 "And don't be concerned about what to
eat and what to drink. Don't worry about
such things. 30 These things dominate the
thoughts of unbelievers all over the world,
but your Father already knows your needs.
31 Seek the Kingdom of God above all else,
and he will give you everything you need.
32 "So don't be afraid, little flock. For it
gives your Father great happiness to give
you the Kingdom.
33 "Sell your possessions and give to those
in need. This will store up treasure for you
in heaven! And the purses of heaven never
get old or develop holes. Your treasure
will be safe; no thief can steal it and no
moth can destroy it. 34 Wherever your treasure is, there the desires of your heart will
also be.

Be Ready for the Lord's Coming

35 "Be dressed for service and keep your
lamps burning, 36 as though you were
waiting for your master to return from the
wedding feast. Then you will be ready to
open the door and let him in the moment
he arrives and knocks. 37 The servants who
are ready and waiting for his return will be
rewarded. I tell you the truth, he himself
will seat them, put on an apron, and serve
them as they sit and eat! 38 He may come in
the middle of the night or just before dawn.*
But whenever he comes, he will reward the
servants who are ready.
39 "Understand this: If a homeowner
knew exactly when a burglar was coming,
he would not permit his house to be broken
into. 40 You also must be ready all the time,
for the Son of Man will come when least
expected."
41 Peter asked, "Lord, is that illustration
just for us or for everyone?"
42 And the Lord replied, "A faithful, sensible

Prosperity

God undoubtedly wants us to prosper, but in our materialistic times we too quickly think of prosperity as wealth and possessions. Indeed the recent "prosperity gospel" movement claims that if only we have faith or give enough we will automatically prosper financially. But as Jesus said in Luke 12:15, "Life is not measured by how much you own."

The Bible indeed records many who prospered under God's hand. In the Old Testament, prosperity was a blessing of the covenant linked to the land of Israel and a sign of God's approval. But the New Testament completely reverses this, expressed supremely in Jesus who "though he was rich, yet for your sakes he became poor" (2 Corinthians 8:9). He had "no place even to lay his head" (Luke 9:58) and had to borrow a donkey when he needed one (19:30-31)—hardly signs of material prosperity. He blessed those who were poor (e.g., 6:20) and declared woes on the rich (e.g., 6:24), and his teaching focused on the cost of discipleship rather than its benefits (e.g., Matthew 10:21-39). Material prosperity has clearly ceased to be an indicator of spiritual blessing.

God wants us to prosper, but that prosperity may or may not include material prosperity. He promises to provide all we need, not all we want (Matthew 6:25-34), and to give to us so we can give, not keep (2 Corinthians 8–9). Prosperity takes on new dimensions in Christ.

▸ *See also **Poverty**, page 1142; **Money**, page 1417.*

servant is one to whom the master can give
the responsibility of managing his other
household servants and feeding them. 43 If
the master returns and finds that the servant
has done a good job, there will be a reward.
44 I tell you the truth, the master will put that
servant in charge of all he owns. 45 But what
if the servant thinks, 'My master won't be
back for a while,' and he begins beating the
other servants, partying, and getting drunk?
46 The master will return unannounced and
unexpected, and he will cut the servant in
pieces and banish him with the unfaithful.

47 "And a servant who knows what the
master wants, but isn't prepared and
doesn't carry out those instructions, will
be severely punished. 48 But someone who
does not know, and then does something
wrong, will be punished only lightly. When
someone has been given much, much will
be required in return; and when someone
has been entrusted with much, even more
will be required.

Jesus Causes Division

49 "I have come to set the world on fire, and
I wish it were already burning! 50 I have a
terrible baptism of suffering ahead of me,
and I am under a heavy burden until it is
accomplished. 51 Do you think I have come
to bring peace to the earth? No, I have come
to divide people against each other! 52 From
now on families will be split apart, three
in favor of me, and two against—or two in
favor and three against.

53 'Father will be divided against
son
and son against father;
mother against daughter
and daughter against mother;
and mother-in-law against
daughter-in-law
and daughter-in-law against
mother-in-law.'*"

54 Then Jesus turned to the crowd and said,
"When you see clouds beginning to form in
the west, you say, 'Here comes a shower.'
And you are right. 55 When the south wind
blows, you say, 'Today will be a scorcher.'
And it is. 56 You fools! You know how to interpret the weather signs of the earth and
sky, but you don't know how to interpret the
present times.

57 "Why can't you decide for yourselves
what is right? 58 When you are on the way
to court with your accuser, try to settle the
matter before you get there. Otherwise, your
accuser may drag you before the judge,
who will hand you over to an officer, who
will throw you into prison. 59 And if that
happens, you won't be free again until you
have paid the very last penny.*"

A Call to Repentance

13 About this time Jesus was informed
that Pilate had murdered some
people from Galilee as they were offering
sacrifices at the Temple. 2 "Do you think
those Galileans were worse sinners than all
the other people from Galilee?" Jesus asked.
"Is that why they suffered? 3 Not at all! And
you will perish, too, unless you repent of
your sins and turn to God. 4 And what about
the eighteen people who died when the
tower in Siloam fell on them? Were they the
worst sinners in Jerusalem? 5 No, and I tell
you again that unless you repent, you will
perish, too."

Parable of the Barren Fig Tree

6 Then Jesus told this story: "A man planted
a fig tree in his garden and came again and
again to see if there was any fruit on it,
but he was always disappointed. 7 Finally,
he said to his gardener, 'I've waited three
years, and there hasn't been a single fig!
Cut it down. It's just taking up space in the
garden.'

8 "The gardener answered, 'Sir, give it one
more chance. Leave it another year, and I'll
give it special attention and plenty of fer-
tilizer. 9 If we get figs next year, fine. If not,
then you can cut it down.'"

Jesus Heals on the Sabbath

10 One Sabbath day as Jesus was teaching in a
synagogue, 11 he saw a woman who had been
crippled by an evil spirit. She had been bent
double for eighteen years and was unable
to stand up straight. 12 When Jesus saw her,
he called her over and said, "Dear woman,
you are healed of your sickness!" 13 Then he
touched her, and instantly she could stand
straight. How she praised God!

14 But the leader in charge of the synagogue was indignant that Jesus had healed
her on the Sabbath day. "There are six days

12:38 Greek *in the second or third watch.* **12:53** Mic 7:6.
12:59 Greek *last lepton* [the smallest Jewish coin].

of the week for working," he said to the crowd. "Come on those days to be healed, not on the Sabbath."
[15]But the Lord replied, "You hypocrites! Each of you works on the Sabbath day! Don't you untie your ox or your donkey from its stall on the Sabbath and lead
it out for water? [16]This dear woman, a
daughter of Abraham, has been held in bondage by Satan for eighteen years. Isn't it right that she be released, even on the Sabbath?"
[17]This shamed his enemies, but all the people rejoiced at the wonderful things he did.

Parable of the Mustard Seed

[18]Then Jesus said, "What is the Kingdom of
God like? How can I illustrate it? [19]It is like
a tiny mustard seed that a man planted in a garden; it grows and becomes a tree, and the birds make nests in its branches."

Parable of the Yeast

[20]He also asked, "What else is the Kingdom
of God like? [21]It is like the yeast a woman
used in making bread. Even though she put only a little yeast in three measures of flour, it permeated every part of the dough."

The Narrow Door

[22]Jesus went through the towns and villages, teaching as he went, always pressing on toward Jerusalem. [23]Someone asked
him, "Lord, will only a few be saved?"
He replied, [24]"Work hard to enter the
narrow door to God's Kingdom, for many
will try to enter but will fail. [25]When the
master of the house has locked the door, it will be too late. You will stand outside knocking and pleading, 'Lord, open the door for us!' But he will reply, 'I don't know
you or where you come from.' [26]Then you
will say, 'But we ate and drank with you,
and you taught in our streets.' [27]And he will
reply, 'I tell you, I don't know you or where you come from. Get away from me, all you who do evil.'
[28]"There will be weeping and gnashing
of teeth, for you will see Abraham, Isaac, Jacob, and all the prophets in the Kingdom
of God, but you will be thrown out. [29]And
people will come from all over the world—from east and west, north and south—to take their places in the Kingdom of God.
[30]And note this: Some who seem least im-
portant now will be the greatest then, and some who are the greatest now will be least important then.*"

Tragic events

When things go wrong, it is natural to ask "why?" The traditional Jewish answer had always been the same: sin. That's what Job's friends had tried to convince him of when so many things went wrong for him (see *Suffering: Why do bad things happen to good people?*, page 567), and it's what those who informed Jesus about the people killed by Pilate assumed (Luke 13:1). Such an approach was well-intentioned: to protect God from the accusation that he himself sends evil onto people. The only alternative therefore was that the fault must lie with humans.

But Jesus says here that life isn't that simple. It is not the case that disaster only comes to the sinful (see also John 9:1-3). These Galileans weren't worse sinners than others; they were just unfortunate in being picked out by Pilate. And the people on whom the tower fell were just unfortunate in being at the wrong place at the wrong time. The victims' sin, quite simply, had nothing to do with it.

So what does lie behind tragedies and natural disasters? The Bible says that it is the result of living in a fallen world. Whatever we may understand about the natural causes of things like earthquakes and tsunamis, there is something spiritual going on behind that. Sin has gotten into the very fabric of creation, messing it up to the point that it is now longing for the return of Jesus to redeem it and put it right again (Romans 8:19-22).

Compassion, not judgment, should therefore be our response in such situations.

Jesus Grieves over Jerusalem

31 At that time some Pharisees said to him, "Get away from here if you want to live! Herod Antipas wants to kill you!"

32 Jesus replied, "Go tell that fox that I will keep on casting out demons and healing people today and tomorrow; and the third day I will accomplish my purpose. 33 Yes, today, tomorrow, and the next day I must proceed on my way. For it wouldn't do for a prophet of God to be killed except in Jerusalem!

34 "O Jerusalem, Jerusalem, the city that kills the prophets and stones God's messengers! How often I have wanted to gather your children together as a hen protects her chicks beneath her wings, but you wouldn't let me. 35 And now, look, your house is abandoned. And you will never see me again until you say, 'Blessings on the one who comes in the name of the LORD!'*"

Jesus Heals on the Sabbath

14 One Sabbath day Jesus went to eat dinner in the home of a leader of the Pharisees, and the people were watching him closely. 2 There was a man there whose arms and legs were swollen.* 3 Jesus asked the Pharisees and experts in religious law, "Is it permitted in the law to heal people on the Sabbath day, or not?" 4 When they refused to answer, Jesus touched the sick man and healed him and sent him away. 5 Then he turned to them and said, "Which of you doesn't work on the Sabbath? If your son* or your cow falls into a pit, don't you rush to get him out?" 6 Again they could not answer.

Jesus Teaches about Humility

7 When Jesus noticed that all who had come to the dinner were trying to sit in the seats of honor near the head of the table, he gave them this advice: 8 "When you are invited to a wedding feast, don't sit in the seat of honor. What if someone who is more distinguished than you has also been invited? 9 The host will come and say, 'Give this person your seat.' Then you will be embarrassed, and you will have to take whatever seat is left at the foot of the table!

10 "Instead, take the lowest place at the foot of the table. Then when your host sees you, he will come and say, 'Friend, we have a better place for you!' Then you will be honored in front of all the other guests. 11 For those who exalt themselves will be humbled, and those who humble themselves will be exalted."

12 Then he turned to his host. "When you put on a luncheon or a banquet," he said, "don't invite your friends, brothers, relatives, and rich neighbors. For they will invite you back, and that will be your only reward. 13 Instead, invite the poor, the crippled, the lame, and the blind. 14 Then at the resurrection of the righteous, God will reward you for inviting those who could not repay you."

Parable of the Great Feast

15 Hearing this, a man sitting at the table with Jesus exclaimed, "What a blessing it will be to attend a banquet* in the Kingdom of God!"

16 Jesus replied with this story: "A man prepared a great feast and sent out many invitations. 17 When the banquet was ready, he sent his servant to tell the guests, 'Come, the banquet is ready.' 18 But they all began making excuses. One said, 'I have just bought a field and must inspect it. Please excuse me.' 19 Another said, 'I have just bought five pairs of oxen, and I want to try them out. Please excuse me.' 20 Another said, 'I just got married, so I can't come.'

21 "The servant returned and told his master what they had said. His master was furious and said, 'Go quickly into the streets and alleys of the town and invite the poor, the crippled, the blind, and the lame.' 22 After the servant had done this, he reported, 'There is still room for more.' 23 So his master said, 'Go out into the country lanes and behind the hedges and urge anyone you find to come, so that the house will be full. 24 For none of those I first invited will get even the smallest taste of my banquet.'"

The Cost of Being a Disciple

25 A large crowd was following Jesus. He turned around and said to them, 26 "If you want to be my disciple, you must, by comparison, hate everyone else—your father and mother, wife and children, brothers and sisters—yes, even your own life. Otherwise,

13:30 Greek *Some are last who will be first, and some are first who will be last.* **13:35** Ps 118:26. **14:2** Or *who had dropsy.* **14:5** Some manuscripts read *donkey.* **14:15** Greek *to eat bread.*

▸ **13:31** *See **The Herods**, page 1072.*

you cannot be my disciple. 27And if you do
not carry your own cross and follow me, you
cannot be my disciple.
28"But don't begin until you count the cost.
For who would begin construction of a building without first calculating the cost to see if
there is enough money to finish it? 29Other-
wise, you might complete only the foundation before running out of money, and then
everyone would laugh at you. 30They would
say, 'There's the person who started that
building and couldn't afford to finish it!'
31"Or what king would go to war against
another king without first sitting down with
his counselors to discuss whether his army
of 10,000 could defeat the 20,000 soldiers
marching against him? 32And if he can't, he
will send a delegation to discuss terms of
peace while the enemy is still far away. 33So
you cannot become my disciple without
giving up everything you own.
34"Salt is good for seasoning. But if it loses
its flavor, how do you make it salty again?
35Flavorless salt is good neither for the soil
nor for the manure pile. It is thrown away.
Anyone with ears to hear should listen and
understand!"

Parable of the Lost Sheep

15 Tax collectors and other notorious
sinners often came to listen to Jesus
teach. 2This made the Pharisees and teachers of religious law complain that he was
associating with such sinful people—even
eating with them!
3So Jesus told them this story: 4"If a man
has a hundred sheep and one of them gets
lost, what will he do? Won't he leave the
ninety-nine others in the wilderness and
go to search for the one that is lost until
he finds it? 5And when he has found it, he
will joyfully carry it home on his shoulders.
6When he arrives, he will call together his
friends and neighbors, saying, 'Rejoice with
me because I have found my lost sheep.' 7In
the same way, there is more joy in heaven
over one lost sinner who repents and returns
to God than over ninety-nine others who are
righteous and haven't strayed away!

Parable of the Lost Coin

8"Or suppose a woman has ten silver coins*
and loses one. Won't she light a lamp and
sweep the entire house and search carefully
until she finds it? 9And when she finds it,

Counting the cost

Healings, miracles, demons fleeing—it was all so exciting! Little wonder "a large crowd was following Jesus" (Luke 14:25) as his fame spread (4:37; 5:15, 17; 7:17). So now was the time for Jesus to show that being his follower wasn't just about blessing; there was a cost—a cost that may impact family relationships (14:26; see also Matthew 10:37-39) and even life itself (Luke 14:26-27), a cost that calls for readiness to give up everything for Jesus' sake (14:33). (Note: Jesus' reference to "hating" your family in 14:26 is simply a Jewish way of saying "loving less." The key issue here, as in Matthew 10, is the challenge to put Christ first, even before those we love and honor, including our family members.)

To reinforce the point, Jesus told two parables about the importance of counting the cost: the first about a man building a tower, the second about a king going to war. Both must decide at the beginning whether they can finish what they start—at the beginning, not halfway through when they risk facing mockery or defeat. Becoming Jesus' disciple means deciding right at the beginning if you are ready to give up everything to gain what he offers. Sometimes today the gospel is preached in ways that make it all about blessing; then, when difficulties come, people get disheartened and fall away. But Jesus says: Count the cost *before* you start following. If you decide at the beginning, it will be so much easier later.

We must make up our minds now that nothing is worth more to us—nothing has a more important place in our lives—than our relationship with Jesus.

▶ *See also* ***Discipleship and the cross****, page 1095;* ***Life from death****, page 1219.*

she will call in her friends and neighbors
and say, 'Rejoice with me because I have
found my lost coin.' [10]In the same way, there
is joy in the presence of God's angels when
even one sinner repents."

Parable of the Lost Son

[11]To illustrate the point further, Jesus told
them this story: "A man had two sons. [12]The
younger son told his father, 'I want my
share of your estate now before you die.'
So his father agreed to divide his wealth
between his sons.

[13]"A few days later this younger son packed
all his belongings and moved to a distant
land, and there he wasted all his money in
wild living. [14]About the time his money ran
out, a great famine swept over the land, and
he began to starve. [15]He persuaded a local
farmer to hire him, and the man sent him
into his fields to feed the pigs. [16]The young
man became so hungry that even the pods
he was feeding the pigs looked good to him.
But no one gave him anything.

[17]"When he finally came to his senses,
he said to himself, 'At home even the hired
servants have food enough to spare, and
here I am dying of hunger! [18]I will go home
to my father and say, "Father, I have sinned
against both heaven and you, [19]and I am
no longer worthy of being called your son.
Please take me on as a hired servant."'

[20]"So he returned home to his father.
And while he was still a long way off, his
father saw him coming. Filled with love and
compassion, he ran to his son, embraced
him, and kissed him. [21]His son said to him,
'Father, I have sinned against both heaven
and you, and I am no longer worthy of being
called your son.*'

[22]"But his father said to the servants,
'Quick! Bring the finest robe in the house
and put it on him. Get a ring for his finger
and sandals for his feet. [23]And kill the calf
we have been fattening. We must celebrate
with a feast, [24]for this son of mine was dead
and has now returned to life. He was lost,
but now he is found.' So the party began.

[25]"Meanwhile, the older son was in the
fields working. When he returned home, he
heard music and dancing in the house, [26]and
he asked one of the servants what was going
on. [27]'Your brother is back,' he was told, 'and
your father has killed the fattened calf. We
are celebrating because of his safe return.'

[28]"The older brother was angry and
wouldn't go in. His father came out and
begged him, [29]but he replied, 'All these years
I've slaved for you and never once refused to
do a single thing you told me to. And in all
that time you never gave me even one young
goat for a feast with my friends. [30]Yet when
this son of yours comes back after squandering your money on prostitutes, you celebrate by killing the fattened calf!'

[31]"His father said to him, 'Look, dear son,
you have always stayed by me, and everything I have is yours. [32]We had to celebrate
this happy day. For your brother was dead
and has come back to life! He was lost, but
now he is found!'"

Parable of the Shrewd Manager

16 Jesus told this story to his disciples:
"There was a certain rich man who
had a manager handling his affairs. One
day a report came that the manager was
wasting his employer's money. [2]So the employer called him in and said, 'What's this
I hear about you? Get your report in order,
because you are going to be fired.'

[3]"The manager thought to himself, 'Now
what? My boss has fired me. I don't have the
strength to dig ditches, and I'm too proud to
beg. [4]Ah, I know how to ensure that I'll have
plenty of friends who will give me a home
when I am fired.'

[5]"So he invited each person who owed
money to his employer to come and discuss
the situation. He asked the first one, 'How
much do you owe him?' [6]The man replied,
'I owe him 800 gallons of olive oil.' So the
manager told him, 'Take the bill and quickly
change it to 400 gallons.*'

[7]"'And how much do you owe my employer?' he asked the next man. 'I owe him
1,000 bushels of wheat,' was the reply.
'Here,' the manager said, 'take the bill and
change it to 800 bushels.*'

[8]"The rich man had to admire the dishonest rascal for being so shrewd. And it
is true that the children of this world are
more shrewd in dealing with the world
around them than are the children of the
light. [9]Here's the lesson: Use your worldly
resources to benefit others and make
friends. Then, when your possessions are

15:8 Greek *ten drachmas.* A drachma was the equivalent of a full day's wage. **15:21** Some manuscripts add *Please take me on as a hired servant.* **16:6** Greek *100 baths . . . 50 [baths].* **16:7** Greek *100 korous . . . 80 [korous].*

gone, they will welcome you to an eternal home.*

10“If you are faithful in little things, you will be faithful in large ones. But if you are dishonest in little things, you won’t be honest with greater responsibilities. 11And if you are untrustworthy about worldly wealth, who will trust you with the true riches of heaven? 12And if you are not faithful with other people’s things, why should you be trusted with things of your own?

13“No one can serve two masters. For you will hate one and love the other; you will be devoted to one and despise the other. You cannot serve God and be enslaved to money.”

14The Pharisees, who dearly loved their money, heard all this and scoffed at him. 15Then he said to them, “You like to appear righteous in public, but God knows your hearts. What this world honors is detestable in the sight of God.

16“Until John the Baptist, the law of Moses and the messages of the prophets were your guides. But now the Good News of the Kingdom of God is preached, and everyone is eager to get in.* 17But that doesn’t mean that the law has lost its force. It is easier for heaven and earth to disappear than for the smallest point of God’s law to be overturned.

18“For example, a man who divorces his wife and marries someone else commits adultery. And anyone who marries a woman divorced from her husband commits adultery.”

Parable of the Rich Man and Lazarus

19Jesus said, “There was a certain rich man who was splendidly clothed in purple and fine linen and who lived each day in luxury. 20At his gate lay a poor man named Lazarus who was covered with sores. 21As Lazarus lay there longing for scraps from the rich man’s table, the dogs would come and lick his open sores.

22“Finally, the poor man died and was carried by the angels to sit beside Abraham at the heavenly banquet.* The rich man also died and was buried, 23and he went to the place of the dead.* There, in torment, he saw Abraham in the far distance with Lazarus at his side.

24“The rich man shouted, ‘Father Abraham, have some pity! Send Lazarus over here to dip the tip of his finger in water and cool my tongue. I am in anguish in these flames.’

25“But Abraham said to him, ‘Son, remember that during your lifetime you had everything you wanted, and Lazarus had nothing. So now he is here being comforted, and you are in anguish. 26And besides, there is a great chasm separating us. No one can cross over to you from here, and no one can cross over to us from there.’

27“Then the rich man said, ‘Please, Father Abraham, at least send him to my father’s home. 28For I have five brothers, and I want him to warn them so they don’t end up in this place of torment.’

29“But Abraham said, ‘Moses and the prophets have warned them. Your brothers can read what they wrote.’

30“The rich man replied, ‘No, Father Abraham! But if someone is sent to them from the dead, then they will repent of their sins and turn to God.’

31“But Abraham said, ‘If they won’t listen to Moses and the prophets, they won’t be persuaded even if someone rises from the dead.’”

Teachings about Forgiveness and Faith

17 One day Jesus said to his disciples, “There will always be temptations to sin, but what sorrow awaits the person who does the tempting! 2It would be better to be thrown into the sea with a millstone hung around your neck than to cause one of these little ones to fall into sin. 3So watch yourselves!

“If another believer* sins, rebuke that person; then if there is repentance, forgive. 4Even if that person wrongs you seven times a day and each time turns again and asks forgiveness, you must forgive.”

5The apostles said to the Lord, “Show us how to increase our faith.”

6The Lord answered, “If you had faith even as small as a mustard seed, you could say to this mulberry tree, ‘May you be uprooted and be planted in the sea,’ and it would obey you!

7“When a servant comes in from plowing or taking care of sheep, does his master say, ‘Come in and eat with me’? 8No, he says, ‘Prepare my meal, put on your apron, and serve me while I eat. Then you can eat later.’ 9And does the master thank the servant for doing what he was told to do? Of course not.

[10]In the same way, when you obey me you
should say, 'We are unworthy servants who
have simply done our duty.'"

Ten Healed of Leprosy

[11]As Jesus continued on toward Jerusalem,
he reached the border between Galilee and
Samaria. [12]As he entered a village there, ten
men with leprosy stood at a distance, [13]crying
out, "Jesus, Master, have mercy on us!"
[14]He looked at them and said, "Go show
yourselves to the priests."* And as they
went, they were cleansed of their leprosy.
[15]One of them, when he saw that he was
healed, came back to Jesus, shouting,
"Praise God!" [16]He fell to the ground at
Jesus' feet, thanking him for what he had
done. This man was a Samaritan.
[17]Jesus asked, "Didn't I heal ten men?
Where are the other nine? [18]Has no one returned to give glory to God except this foreigner?" [19]And Jesus said to the man, "Stand
up and go. Your faith has healed you.*"

The Coming of the Kingdom

[20]One day the Pharisees asked Jesus, "When
will the Kingdom of God come?"
Jesus replied, "The Kingdom of God can't
be detected by visible signs.* [21]You won't be
able to say, 'Here it is!' or 'It's over there!' For
the Kingdom of God is already among you.*"
[22]Then he said to his disciples, "The time
is coming when you will long to see the day
when the Son of Man returns,* but you won't
see it. [23]People will tell you, 'Look, there is
the Son of Man,' or 'Here he is,' but don't go
out and follow them. [24]For as the lightning
flashes and lights up the sky from one end
to the other, so it will be on the day* when
the Son of Man comes. [25]But first the Son of
Man must suffer terribly* and be rejected by
this generation.
[26]"When the Son of Man returns, it will be
like it was in Noah's day. [27]In those days, the
people enjoyed banquets and parties and
weddings right up to the time Noah entered
his boat and the flood came and destroyed
them all.
[28]"And the world will be as it was in the
days of Lot. People went about their daily
business—eating and drinking, buying
and selling, farming and building—[29]until
the morning Lot left Sodom. Then fire and
burning sulfur rained down from heaven
and destroyed them all. [30]Yes, it will be
'business as usual' right up to the day when
the Son of Man is revealed. [31]On that day a
person out on the deck of a roof must not go
down into the house to pack. A person out
in the field must not return home. [32]Remem-
ber what happened to Lot's wife! [33]If you
cling to your life, you will lose it, and if you
let your life go, you will save it. [34]That night
two people will be asleep in one bed; one
will be taken, the other left. [35]Two women
will be grinding flour together at the mill;
one will be taken, the other left.*"
[37]"Where will this happen, Lord?"* the
disciples asked.
Jesus replied, "Just as the gathering of
vultures shows there is a carcass nearby, so
these signs indicate that the end is near."*

Parable of the Persistent Widow

18 One day Jesus told his disciples
a story to show that they should
always pray and never give up. [2]"There was
a judge in a certain city," he said, "who
neither feared God nor cared about people.
[3]A widow of that city came to him repeatedly, saying, 'Give me justice in this dispute
with my enemy.' [4]The judge ignored her for a
while, but finally he said to himself, 'I don't
fear God or care about people, [5]but this
woman is driving me crazy. I'm going to see
that she gets justice, because she is wearing
me out with her constant requests!'"
[6]Then the Lord said, "Learn a lesson from
this unjust judge. [7]Even he rendered a just
decision in the end. So don't you think God
will surely give justice to his chosen people
who cry out to him day and night? Will he
keep putting them off? [8]I tell you, he will
grant justice to them quickly! But when the
Son of Man* returns, how many will he find
on the earth who have faith?"

Parable of the Pharisee and Tax Collector

[9]Then Jesus told this story to some who had
great confidence in their own righteousness and scorned everyone else: [10]"Two
men went to the Temple to pray. One was a

16:9 Or *you will be welcomed into eternal homes.* **16:16** Or *everyone is urged to enter in.* **16:22** Greek *to Abraham's bosom.* **16:23** Greek *to Hades.* **17:3** Greek *If your brother.* **17:14** See Lev 14:2-32. **17:19** Or *Your faith has saved you.* **17:20** Or *by your speculations.* **17:21** Or *is within you,* or *is in your grasp.* **17:22** Or *long for even one day with the Son of Man.* "Son of Man" is a title Jesus used for himself. **17:24** Some manuscripts do not include *on the day.* **17:25** Or *suffer many things.* **17:35** Some manuscripts add verse 36, *Two men will be working in the field; one will be taken, the other left.* Compare Matt 24:40. **17:37a** Greek *"Where, Lord?"* **17:37b** Greek *"Wherever the carcass is, the vultures gather."* **18:8** "Son of Man" is a title Jesus used for himself.

Pharisee, and the other was a despised tax collector. [11]The Pharisee stood by himself and prayed this prayer*: 'I thank you, God, that I am not like other people—cheaters, sinners, adulterers. I'm certainly not like that tax collector! [12]I fast twice a week, and I give you a tenth of my income.'

[13]"But the tax collector stood at a distance and dared not even lift his eyes to heaven as he prayed. Instead, he beat his chest in sorrow, saying, 'O God, be merciful to me, for I am a sinner.' [14]I tell you, this sinner, not the Pharisee, returned home justified before God. For those who exalt themselves will be humbled, and those who humble themselves will be exalted."

Jesus Blesses the Children

[15]One day some parents brought their little children to Jesus so he could touch and bless them. But when the disciples saw this, they scolded the parents for bothering him.

[16]Then Jesus called for the children and said to the disciples, "Let the children come to me. Don't stop them! For the Kingdom of God belongs to those who are like these children. [17]I tell you the truth, anyone who doesn't receive the Kingdom of God like a child will never enter it."

The Rich Man

[18]Once a religious leader asked Jesus this question: "Good Teacher, what should I do to inherit eternal life?"

[19]"Why do you call me good?" Jesus asked him. "Only God is truly good. [20]But to answer your question, you know the commandments: 'You must not commit adultery. You must not murder. You must not steal. You must not testify falsely. Honor your father and mother.'*"

[21]The man replied, "I've obeyed all these commandments since I was young."

[22]When Jesus heard his answer, he said, "There is still one thing you haven't done. Sell all your possessions and give the money to the poor, and you will have treasure in heaven. Then come, follow me."

[23]But when the man heard this he became very sad, for he was very rich.

[24]When Jesus saw this,* he said, "How hard it is for the rich to enter the Kingdom of God! [25]In fact, it is easier for a camel to go through the eye of a needle than for a rich person to enter the Kingdom of God!"

[26]Those who heard this said, "Then who in the world can be saved?"

[27]He replied, "What is impossible for people is possible with God."

▸ **18:15** *See **Children**, page 1100.*

Perseverance in prayer

Prayer is a key theme in Luke's Gospel (e.g., 3:21; 5:16; 6:12, 28; 9:18, 28; 11:1-13; 18:1-14; 19:46; 21:36; 22:32, 39-46). Here in Luke 18:1-8, Jesus teaches about prayer in the context of the coming of God's Kingdom (17:20-37). Knowing that difficult times lay ahead for his disciples, Jesus was aware that they could become discouraged if they prayed for the coming of God's Kingdom, as he had instructed (11:2), yet didn't see it. So he used this opportunity to encourage them to "stick with it" when praying—not just for the coming of God's Kingdom but for anything. His parable teaches that if an unjust judge will finally grant a widow's request—a widow who means nothing to him—how much more will God, who is completely just, answer his children's prayers and intervene on their behalf.

If we ever wonder why our prayers aren't answered immediately, sometimes (like with the coming of the Kingdom) it has to do with God's timing. Sometimes it is because God wants us to spend time with him, listening to his voice and gaining his perspective. As we do, we often find that what we are praying for changes. Whether it is our prayers that are answered or our hearts that are changed, persistence in prayer is always effective in the end.

▸ *See also **Why doesn't God always answer prayer?**, page 641; **The Lord's Prayer**, page 1077.*

28 Peter said, "We've left our homes to follow you."

29 "Yes," Jesus replied, "and I assure you that everyone who has given up house or wife or brothers or parents or children, for the sake of the Kingdom of God, 30 will be repaid many times over in this life, and will have eternal life in the world to come."

Jesus Again Predicts His Death

31 Taking the twelve disciples aside, Jesus said, "Listen, we're going up to Jerusalem, where all the predictions of the prophets concerning the Son of Man will come true. 32 He will be handed over to the Romans,* and he will be mocked, treated shamefully, and spit upon. 33 They will flog him with a whip and kill him, but on the third day he will rise again."

34 But they didn't understand any of this. The significance of his words was hidden from them, and they failed to grasp what he was talking about.

Jesus Heals a Blind Beggar

35 As Jesus approached Jericho, a blind beggar was sitting beside the road. 36 When he heard the noise of a crowd going past, he asked what was happening. 37 They told him that Jesus the Nazarene* was going by. 38 So he began shouting, "Jesus, Son of David, have mercy on me!"

39 "Be quiet!" the people in front yelled at him.

But he only shouted louder, "Son of David, have mercy on me!"

40 When Jesus heard him, he stopped and ordered that the man be brought to him. As the man came near, Jesus asked him, 41 "What do you want me to do for you?"

"Lord," he said, "I want to see!"

42 And Jesus said, "All right, receive your sight! Your faith has healed you." 43 Instantly the man could see, and he followed Jesus, praising God. And all who saw it praised God, too.

Jesus and Zacchaeus

19 Jesus entered Jericho and made his way through the town. 2 There was a man there named Zacchaeus. He was the chief tax collector in the region, and he had become very rich. 3 He tried to get a look at Jesus, but he was too short to see over the crowd. 4 So he ran ahead and climbed a sycamore-fig tree beside the road, for Jesus was going to pass that way.

5 When Jesus came by, he looked up at Zacchaeus and called him by name. "Zacchaeus!" he said. "Quick, come down! I must be a guest in your home today."

6 Zacchaeus quickly climbed down and took Jesus to his house in great excitement and joy. 7 But the people were displeased. "He has gone to be the guest of a notorious sinner," they grumbled.

8 Meanwhile, Zacchaeus stood before the Lord and said, "I will give half my wealth to the poor, Lord, and if I have cheated people on their taxes, I will give them back four times as much!"

9 Jesus responded, "Salvation has come to this home today, for this man has shown himself to be a true son of Abraham. 10 For the Son of Man* came to seek and save those who are lost."

Parable of the Ten Servants

11 The crowd was listening to everything Jesus said. And because he was nearing Jerusalem, he told them a story to correct the impression that the Kingdom of God would begin right away. 12 He said, "A nobleman was called away to a distant empire to be crowned king and then return. 13 Before he left, he called together ten of his servants and divided among them ten pounds of silver,* saying, 'Invest this for me while I am gone.' 14 But his people hated him and sent a delegation after him to say, 'We do not want him to be our king.'

15 "After he was crowned king, he returned and called in the servants to whom he had given the money. He wanted to find out what their profits were. 16 The first servant reported, 'Master, I invested your money and made ten times the original amount!'

17 "'Well done!' the king exclaimed. 'You are a good servant. You have been faithful with the little I entrusted to you, so you will be governor of ten cities as your reward.'

18 "The next servant reported, 'Master, I invested your money and made five times the original amount.'

19 "'Well done!' the king said. 'You will be governor over five cities.'

18:11 Some manuscripts read *stood and prayed this prayer to himself.* **18:20** Exod 20:12-16; Deut 5:16-20. **18:24** Some manuscripts read *When Jesus saw how sad the man was.* **18:32** Greek *the Gentiles.* **18:37** Or *Jesus of Nazareth.* **19:10** "Son of Man" is a title Jesus used for himself. **19:13** Greek *ten minas;* one mina was worth about three months' wages.

20“But the third servant brought back
only the original amount of money and
said, ‘Master, I hid your money and kept it
safe. 21I was afraid because you are a hard
man to deal with, taking what isn’t yours
and harvesting crops you didn’t plant.’

22“‘You wicked servant!’ the king roared.
‘Your own words condemn you. If you knew
that I’m a hard man who takes what isn’t
mine and harvests crops I didn’t plant,
23why didn’t you deposit my money in the
bank? At least I could have gotten some interest on it.’

24“Then, turning to the others standing
nearby, the king ordered, ‘Take the money
from this servant, and give it to the one who
has ten pounds.’

25“‘But, master,’ they said, ‘he already
has ten pounds!’

26“‘Yes,’ the king replied, ‘and to those
who use well what they are given, even
more will be given. But from those who do
nothing, even what little they have will be
taken away. 27And as for these enemies of
mine who didn’t want me to be their king—
bring them in and execute them right here
in front of me.’”

Jesus’ Triumphant Entry

28After telling this story, Jesus went on toward
Jerusalem, walking ahead of his disciples.
29As he came to the towns of Bethphage and
Bethany on the Mount of Olives, he sent
two disciples ahead. 30“Go into that village
over there,” he told them. “As you enter it,
you will see a young donkey tied there that
no one has ever ridden. Untie it and bring it
here. 31If anyone asks, ‘Why are you untying
that colt?’ just say, ‘The Lord needs it.’”

32So they went and found the colt, just as
Jesus had said. 33And sure enough, as they
were untying it, the owners asked them,
“Why are you untying that colt?”

34And the disciples simply replied, “The
Lord needs it.” 35So they brought the colt to
Jesus and threw their garments over it for
him to ride on.

36As he rode along, the crowds spread out
their garments on the road ahead of him.
37When he reached the place where the
road started down the Mount of Olives, all
of his followers began to shout and sing as
they walked along, praising God for all the
wonderful miracles they had seen.

38 “Blessings on the King who comes in the
name of the LORD!
Peace in heaven, and glory in highest
heaven!”*

39But some of the Pharisees among the
crowd said, “Teacher, rebuke your followers for saying things like that!”

40He replied, “If they kept quiet, the stones
along the road would burst into cheers!”

Jesus Weeps over Jerusalem

41But as he came closer to Jerusalem and saw
the city ahead, he began to weep. 42“How I
wish today that you of all people would
understand the way to peace. But now it
is too late, and peace is hidden from your
eyes. 43Before long your enemies will build

Restitution

Restitution—making amends for something lost, damaged, or stolen—was a fundamental principle of Jewish law (e.g., Exodus 22:1-15). It required not just the return of what was lost or stolen, but an additional payment as a penalty. For example, if livestock was stolen and slaughtered or sold, it had to be replaced fivefold (Exodus 22:1), though if recovered only twofold (Exodus 22:4), just as with stolen goods (Exodus 22:7). If the thief couldn’t make restitution, he was sold into slavery (limited to seven years) to pay off the debt (Exodus 22:3), reflecting how fundamental this principle of restitution was among God’s people.

When Zacchaeus pledged to repay fourfold what he had cheated people out of (Luke 19:8), he was taking upon himself almost the most extreme requirement, reflecting the sincerity of his repentance. If we wrong someone today, restitution is still a good principle to follow, both to show others the depth of our repentance and to remind ourselves of the cost of wronging others.

ramparts against your walls and encircle you
and close in on you from every side. 44They
will crush you into the ground, and your
children with you. Your enemies will not
leave a single stone in place, because you
did not recognize it when God visited you.*"

Jesus Clears the Temple

45Then Jesus entered the Temple and began
to drive out the people selling animals for
sacrifices. 46He said to them, "The Scriptures declare, 'My Temple will be a house
of prayer,' but you have turned it into a den
of thieves."*

47After that, he taught daily in the
Temple, but the leading priests, the teachers of religious law, and the other leaders of
the people began planning how to kill him.
48But they could think of nothing, because
all the people hung on every word he said.

The Authority of Jesus Challenged

20 One day as Jesus was teaching the
people and preaching the Good
News in the Temple, the leading priests,
the teachers of religious law, and the elders
came up to him. 2They demanded, "By what
authority are you doing all these things?
Who gave you the right?"

3"Let me ask you a question first," he
replied. 4"Did John's authority to baptize
come from heaven, or was it merely human?"

5They talked it over among themselves.
"If we say it was from heaven, he will ask
why we didn't believe John. 6But if we say
it was merely human, the people will stone
us because they are convinced John was a
prophet." 7So they finally replied that they
didn't know.

8And Jesus responded, "Then I won't tell
you by what authority I do these things."

Parable of the Evil Farmers

9Now Jesus turned to the people again
and told them this story: "A man planted a
vineyard, leased it to tenant farmers, and
moved to another country to live for several
years. 10At the time of the grape harvest, he
sent one of his servants to collect his share
of the crop. But the farmers attacked the
servant, beat him up, and sent him back
empty-handed. 11So the owner sent another
servant, but they also insulted him, beat
him up, and sent him away empty-handed.
12A third man was sent, and they wounded
him and chased him away.

13"'What will I do?' the owner asked
himself. 'I know! I'll send my cherished son.
Surely they will respect him.'

14"But when the tenant farmers saw his
son, they said to each other, 'Here comes
the heir to this estate. Let's kill him and get
the estate for ourselves!' 15So they dragged
him out of the vineyard and murdered him.

19:38 Pss 118:26; 148:1. **19:44** Greek *did not recognize the time of your visitation,* a reference to the Messiah's coming. **19:46** Isa 56:7; Jer 7:11.

Authority

Fallen human beings love authority. It satisfies something within us when we can set ourselves above others and tell them what to do or think. That's what Israel's religious leaders loved. It made them feel important and kept others in their proper place. Yet here was Jesus, a man with no proper religious or secular authority, gathering crowds. Hence their question, "By what authority are you doing all these things?" (Luke 20:2)—referring not just to his miracles but also to the cleansing of the Temple that had just happened (19:45-48). They wanted to discredit Jesus in the eyes of the people and of Rome. But, apart from asking them a question they dared not answer, Jesus wouldn't respond (20:3-8). True authority speaks for itself, and God backs it up, just as with Jesus' miracles.

The early church leaders never tried to enforce their authority, and those who did were rebuked (3 John 1:9-10). They didn't make demands or appeal to their position but rather appealed as spiritual parents and proved their authority by their lifestyle and ministry (e.g., 1 Corinthians 9:1-15; 1 Thessalonians 2:1-12), leaving it to God to authenticate their authority (2 Corinthians 12:12). Still today, true authority comes from a godly life and a self-effacing ministry that God alone authenticates.

“What do you suppose the owner of the
vineyard will do to them?” Jesus asked.
16“I’ll tell you—he will come and kill those
farmers and lease the vineyard to others.”

“How terrible that such a thing should
ever happen,” his listeners protested.
17Jesus looked at them and said, “Then
what does this Scripture mean?

‘The stone that the builders rejected
has now become the cornerstone.’*

18Everyone who stumbles over that stone
will be broken to pieces, and it will crush
anyone it falls on.”

19The teachers of religious law and the
leading priests wanted to arrest Jesus immediately because they realized he was
telling the story against them—they were
the wicked farmers. But they were afraid of
the people’s reaction.

Taxes for Caesar

20Watching for their opportunity, the leaders
sent spies pretending to be honest men.
They tried to get Jesus to say something
that could be reported to the Roman governor so he would arrest Jesus. 21“Teacher,”
they said, “we know that you speak and
teach what is right and are not influenced
by what others think. You teach the way of
God truthfully. 22Now tell us—is it right for
us to pay taxes to Caesar or not?”

23He saw through their trickery and said,
24“Show me a Roman coin.* Whose picture
and title are stamped on it?”

“Caesar’s,” they replied.

25“Well then,” he said, “give to Caesar
what belongs to Caesar, and give to God
what belongs to God.”

26So they failed to trap him by what he
said in front of the people. Instead, they
were amazed by his answer, and they
became silent.

Discussion about Resurrection

27Then Jesus was approached by some Sadducees—religious leaders who say there is
no resurrection from the dead. 28They posed
this question: “Teacher, Moses gave us a
law that if a man dies, leaving a wife but
no children, his brother should marry the
widow and have a child who will carry on
the brother’s name.* 29Well, suppose there
were seven brothers. The oldest one married
and then died without children. 30So the
second brother married the widow, but he
also died. 31Then the third brother married
her. This continued with all seven of them,
who died without children. 32Finally, the
woman also died. 33So tell us, whose wife
will she be in the resurrection? For all seven
were married to her!”

34Jesus replied, “Marriage is for people
here on earth. 35But in the age to come, those
worthy of being raised from the dead will
neither marry nor be given in marriage. 36And
they will never die again. In this respect they
will be like angels. They are children of God
and children of the resurrection.

37“But now, as to whether the dead will
be raised—even Moses proved this when he
wrote about the burning bush. Long after
Abraham, Isaac, and Jacob had died, he referred to the Lord* as ‘the God of Abraham,
the God of Isaac, and the God of Jacob.’*
38So he is the God of the living, not the dead,
for they are all alive to him.”

39“Well said, Teacher!” remarked some
of the teachers of religious law who were
standing there. 40And then no one dared to
ask him any more questions.

Whose Son Is the Messiah?

41Then Jesus presented them with a ques-
tion. “Why is it,” he asked, “that the
Messiah is said to be the son of David? 42For
David himself wrote in the book of Psalms:

‘The LORD said to my Lord,
Sit in the place of honor at my right
hand
43 until I humble your enemies,
making them a footstool under your
feet.’*

44Since David called the Messiah ‘Lord,’
how can the Messiah be his son?”

45Then, with the crowds listening, he
turned to his disciples and said, 46“Beware
of these teachers of religious law! For they
like to parade around in flowing robes and
love to receive respectful greetings as they
walk in the marketplaces. And how they
love the seats of honor in the synagogues
and the head table at banquets. 47Yet they

▸ **20:22** *See **Paying taxes**, page 1139.* **20:27** *See **Sadducees**, page 1104.*

shamelessly cheat widows out of their property and then pretend to be pious by making
long prayers in public. Because of this, they
will be severely punished."

The Widow's Offering

21 While Jesus was in the Temple, he
watched the rich people dropping
their gifts in the collection box. 2 Then a poor
widow came by and dropped in two small
coins.*
3 "I tell you the truth," Jesus said, "this
poor widow has given more than all the rest
of them. 4 For they have given a tiny part of
their surplus, but she, poor as she is, has
given everything she has."

Jesus Speaks about the Future

5 Some of his disciples began talking about
the majestic stonework of the Temple and
the memorial decorations on the walls.
But Jesus said, 6 "The time is coming when
all these things will be completely demolished. Not one stone will be left on top of
another!"
7 "Teacher," they asked, "when will all
this happen? What sign will show us that
these things are about to take place?"
8 He replied, "Don't let anyone mislead
you, for many will come in my name,
claiming, 'I am the Messiah,'* and saying,
'The time has come!' But don't believe them.
9 And when you hear of wars and insurrec-
tions, don't panic. Yes, these things must
take place first, but the end won't follow
immediately." 10 Then he added, "Nation
will go to war against nation, and kingdom
against kingdom. 11 There will be great
earthquakes, and there will be famines and
plagues in many lands, and there will be
terrifying things and great miraculous signs
from heaven.
12 "But before all this occurs, there will
be a time of great persecution. You will be
dragged into synagogues and prisons, and
you will stand trial before kings and governors because you are my followers. 13 But this
will be your opportunity to tell them about
me.* 14 So don't worry in advance about how
to answer the charges against you, 15 for I will
give you the right words and such wisdom
that none of your opponents will be able to
reply or refute you! 16 Even those closest to
you—your parents, brothers, relatives, and
friends—will betray you. They will even kill
some of you. 17 And everyone will hate you

20:17 Ps 118:22. **20:24** Greek *a denarius.* **20:28** See Deut 25:5-6. **20:37a** Greek *when he wrote about the bush. He referred to the Lord.* **20:37b** Exod 3:6. **20:42-43** Ps 110:1. **21:2** Greek *two lepta* [the smallest of Jewish coins]. **21:8** Greek *claiming, 'I am.'* **21:13** Or *This will be your testimony against them.*

Worry

Worry—deep unease about the future and how things will turn out—is one of the devil's two main weapons for trying to choke God's life within us, Jesus said (Matthew 13:22). And there are certainly many things to worry about if we choose to—health, family, studies, work, relationships, money, the future . . . But not only is worry profitless (Matthew 6:27), it actually harms us, making our hearts heavy (Proverbs 12:25), our spirits dull (Luke 21:34), and our bodies and minds exhausted (1 Kings 19:3-5) as we needlessly think, "What if . . . ?"

But Jesus says his followers need not worry, for we have a loving heavenly Father who is committed to caring for us. If he feeds birds and makes grass grow (Matthew 6:26-30), can we not see that he will care for us? That is why Paul said, "Don't worry about anything; instead, pray about everything. Tell God what you need, and thank him for all he has done," assuring us that as we do so we "will experience God's peace, which exceeds anything we can understand. His peace will guard your hearts and minds as you live in Christ Jesus" (Philippians 4:6-7).

Jesus promised that if we seek God's Kingdom above all else, then God will always provide for us (Matthew 6:33). This is not a promise we will be rich—but it is a promise that we will be okay!

▶ *See also* ***Trusting God when we cannot see the way ahead****, page 57;* ***Trusting God whatever happens****, page 959.*

because you are my followers.* 18But not a
hair of your head will perish! 19By standing
firm, you will win your souls.
20"And when you see Jerusalem surrounded by armies, then you will know
that the time of its destruction has arrived.
21Then those in Judea must flee to the hills.
Those in Jerusalem must get out, and those
out in the country should not return to the
city. 22For those will be days of God's vengeance, and the prophetic words of the
Scriptures will be fulfilled. 23How terrible it
will be for pregnant women and for nursing
mothers in those days. For there will be disaster in the land and great anger against
this people. 24They will be killed by the
sword or sent away as captives to all the
nations of the world. And Jerusalem will
be trampled down by the Gentiles until the
period of the Gentiles comes to an end.
25"And there will be strange signs in the
sun, moon, and stars. And here on earth
the nations will be in turmoil, perplexed by
the roaring seas and strange tides. 26People
will be terrified at what they see coming
upon the earth, for the powers in the heavens
will be shaken. 27Then everyone will see the
Son of Man* coming on a cloud with power
and great glory.* 28So when all these things
begin to happen, stand and look up, for your
salvation is near!"
29Then he gave them this illustration:
"Notice the fig tree, or any other tree. 30When
the leaves come out, you know without being
told that summer is near. 31In the same way,
when you see all these things taking place,
you can know that the Kingdom of God is
near. 32I tell you the truth, this generation will
not pass from the scene until all these things
have taken place. 33Heaven and earth will disappear, but my words will never disappear.
34"Watch out! Don't let your hearts be
dulled by carousing and drunkenness, and
by the worries of this life. Don't let that day
catch you unaware, 35like a trap. For that
day will come upon everyone living on the
earth. 36Keep alert at all times. And pray
that you might be strong enough to escape
these coming horrors and stand before the
Son of Man."
37Every day Jesus went to the Temple to
teach, and each evening he returned to
spend the night on the Mount of Olives.
38The crowds gathered at the Temple early
each morning to hear him.

Judas Agrees to Betray Jesus

22 The Festival of Unleavened Bread,
which is also called Passover, was
approaching. 2The leading priests and teachers of religious law were plotting how to kill
Jesus, but they were afraid of the people's
reaction.
3Then Satan entered into Judas Iscariot,
who was one of the twelve disciples, 4and he
went to the leading priests and captains of
the Temple guard to discuss the best way to
betray Jesus to them. 5They were delighted,
and they promised to give him money. 6So
he agreed and began looking for an opportunity to betray Jesus so they could arrest
him when the crowds weren't around.

The Last Supper

7Now the Festival of Unleavened Bread
arrived, when the Passover lamb is sacrificed. 8Jesus sent Peter and John ahead and
said, "Go and prepare the Passover meal, so
we can eat it together."
9"Where do you want us to prepare it?"
they asked him.
10He replied, "As soon as you enter Jerusalem, a man carrying a pitcher of water
will meet you. Follow him. At the house he
enters, 11say to the owner, 'The Teacher asks:
Where is the guest room where I can eat
the Passover meal with my disciples?' 12He
will take you upstairs to a large room that
is already set up. That is where you should
prepare our meal." 13They went off to the city
and found everything just as Jesus had said,
and they prepared the Passover meal there.
14When the time came, Jesus and the
apostles sat down together at the table.*
15Jesus said, "I have been very eager to eat
this Passover meal with you before my suffering begins. 16For I tell you now that I
won't eat this meal again until its meaning
is fulfilled in the Kingdom of God."
17Then he took a cup of wine and gave
thanks to God for it. Then he said, "Take this
and share it among yourselves. 18For I will
not drink wine again until the Kingdom of
God has come."
19He took some bread and gave thanks to
God for it. Then he broke it in pieces and
gave it to the disciples, saying, "This is my
body, which is given for you. Do this in remembrance of me."
20After supper he took another cup of wine
and said, "This cup is the new covenant

between God and his people—an agreement
confirmed with my blood, which is poured
out as a sacrifice for you.*
21“But here at this table, sitting among us
as a friend, is the man who will betray me.
22For it has been determined that the Son
of Man* must die. But what sorrow awaits
the one who betrays him.” 23The disciples
began to ask each other which of them
would ever do such a thing.
24Then they began to argue among themselves about who would be the greatest
among them. 25Jesus told them, “In this
world the kings and great men lord it over
their people, yet they are called ‘friends of
the people.’ 26But among you it will be different. Those who are the greatest among
you should take the lowest rank, and the
leader should be like a servant. 27Who is
more important, the one who sits at the
table or the one who serves? The one who
sits at the table, of course. But not here! For
I am among you as one who serves.
28“You have stayed with me in my time of
trial. 29And just as my Father has granted
me a Kingdom, I now grant you the right 30to
eat and drink at my table in my Kingdom.
And you will sit on thrones, judging the
twelve tribes of Israel.

Jesus Predicts Peter's Denial

31“Simon, Simon, Satan has asked to sift
each of you like wheat. 32But I have pleaded
in prayer for you, Simon, that your faith
should not fail. So when you have repented
and turned to me again, strengthen your
brothers.”
33Peter said, “Lord, I am ready to go to
prison with you, and even to die with you.”
34But Jesus said, “Peter, let me tell you
something. Before the rooster crows tomorrow morning, you will deny three times that
you even know me.”
35Then Jesus asked them, “When I sent you
out to preach the Good News and you did not
have money, a traveler's bag, or an extra pair
of sandals, did you need anything?”
“No,” they replied.
36“But now,” he said, “take your money
and a traveler's bag. And if you don't have
a sword, sell your cloak and buy one! 37For
the time has come for this prophecy about
me to be fulfilled: ‘He was counted among
the rebels.’* Yes, everything written about
me by the prophets will come true.”
38“Look, Lord,” they replied, “we have
two swords among us.”
“That's enough,” he said.

Jesus Prays on the Mount of Olives

39Then, accompanied by the disciples, Jesus
left the upstairs room and went as usual to

21:17 Greek *on account of my name.* **21:27a** “Son of Man” is a title Jesus used for himself. **21:27b** See Dan 7:13. **22:14** Or *reclined together.* **22:19-20** Some manuscripts do not include 22:19b-20, *which is given for you . . . which is poured out as a sacrifice for you.* **22:22** “Son of Man” is a title Jesus used for himself. **22:37** Isa 53:12.

▸ **22:7-30** *See* ***The Last Supper****, page 1110.*

Why did Judas betray Jesus?

While many explanations have been suggested for why Judas betrayed Jesus—for example, that he wanted Jesus to be a messiah who would fight the Romans and thought that if he handed him over to them it would force him to act—the only motive the Gospels offer is that he simply did it for the money (Luke 22:4-5), outraged by what he saw as the extravagant waste of the anointing of Jesus' feet (Matthew 26:8-16; John 12:1-7). Not that he gained much, for the thirty pieces of silver he was paid was only about four months' wages.

Judas seemed to have a weakness for money; yet interestingly, Jesus made him the group's treasurer (John 12:6). Jesus surely knew what Judas was like; so in giving him this role he was giving him an opportunity to change, to face up to his weakness and let Jesus free him from it. But Judas's continued feeding of that weakness eventually opened a door to Satan, who now “entered into Judas” (Luke 22:3). Judas's tragic end—he committed suicide (Matthew 27:1-5)—is a warning to us all to bring our character weaknesses into the light and let Jesus deal with them.

the Mount of Olives. 40There he told them,
"Pray that you will not give in to temptation."
41He walked away, about a stone's throw,
and knelt down and prayed, 42"Father, if
you are willing, please take this cup of suffering away from me. Yet I want your will to
be done, not mine." 43Then an angel from
heaven appeared and strengthened him.
44He prayed more fervently, and he was in
such agony of spirit that his sweat fell to the
ground like great drops of blood.*
45At last he stood up again and returned
to the disciples, only to find them asleep,
exhausted from grief. 46"Why are you sleeping?" he asked them. "Get up and pray, so
that you will not give in to temptation."

Jesus Is Betrayed and Arrested

47But even as Jesus said this, a crowd approached, led by Judas, one of the twelve disciples. Judas walked over to Jesus to greet him
with a kiss. 48But Jesus said, "Judas, would
you betray the Son of Man with a kiss?"
49When the other disciples saw what was
about to happen, they exclaimed, "Lord,
should we fight? We brought the swords!"
50And one of them struck at the high priest's
slave, slashing off his right ear.
51But Jesus said, "No more of this." And
he touched the man's ear and healed him.
52Then Jesus spoke to the leading priests,
the captains of the Temple guard, and the
elders who had come for him. "Am I some
dangerous revolutionary," he asked, "that
you come with swords and clubs to arrest me?
53Why didn't you arrest me in the Temple? I
was there every day. But this is your moment,
the time when the power of darkness reigns."

Peter Denies Jesus

54So they arrested him and led him to the
high priest's home. And Peter followed at a
distance. 55The guards lit a fire in the middle
of the courtyard and sat around it, and Peter
joined them there. 56A servant girl noticed
him in the firelight and began staring at
him. Finally she said, "This man was one
of Jesus' followers!"
57But Peter denied it. "Woman," he said,
"I don't even know him!"
58After a while someone else looked at
him and said, "You must be one of them!"
"No, man, I'm not!" Peter retorted.
59About an hour later someone else insisted, "This must be one of them, because
he is a Galilean, too."
60But Peter said, "Man, I don't know what
you are talking about." And immediately,
while he was still speaking, the rooster
crowed.
61At that moment the Lord turned and
looked at Peter. Suddenly, the Lord's words
flashed through Peter's mind: "Before the
rooster crows tomorrow morning, you will
deny three times that you even know me."
62And Peter left the courtyard, weeping
bitterly.
63The guards in charge of Jesus began
mocking and beating him. 64They blindfolded him and said, "Prophesy to us! Who
hit you that time?" 65And they hurled all
sorts of terrible insults at him.

Jesus before the Council

66At daybreak all the elders of the people assembled, including the leading priests and
the teachers of religious law. Jesus was led
before this high council,* 67and they said,
"Tell us, are you the Messiah?"
But he replied, "If I tell you, you won't
believe me. 68And if I ask you a question,
you won't answer. 69But from now on the
Son of Man will be seated in the place of
power at God's right hand.*"
70They all shouted, "So, are you claiming
to be the Son of God?"
And he replied, "You say that I am."
71"Why do we need other witnesses?"
they said. "We ourselves heard him say it."

Jesus' Trial before Pilate

23 Then the entire council took Jesus to
Pilate, the Roman governor. 2They
began to state their case: "This man has been
leading our people astray by telling them not
to pay their taxes to the Roman government
and by claiming he is the Messiah, a king."
3So Pilate asked him, "Are you the king
of the Jews?"
Jesus replied, "You have said it."
4Pilate turned to the leading priests and
to the crowd and said, "I find nothing wrong
with this man!"
5Then they became insistent. "But he

▸ **22:39** *See* ***Gethsemane****, page 1111.* **23:1** *See* ***Pilate****, page 1145.*

is causing riots by his teaching wherever he goes—all over Judea, from Galilee to Jerusalem!"

6 "Oh, is he a Galilean?" Pilate asked. 7 When they said that he was, Pilate sent him to Herod Antipas, because Galilee was under Herod's jurisdiction, and Herod happened to be in Jerusalem at the time.

8 Herod was delighted at the opportunity to see Jesus, because he had heard about him and had been hoping for a long time to see him perform a miracle. 9 He asked Jesus question after question, but Jesus refused to answer. 10 Meanwhile, the leading priests and the teachers of religious law stood there shouting their accusations. 11 Then Herod and his soldiers began mocking and ridiculing Jesus. Finally, they put a royal robe on him and sent him back to Pilate. 12 (Herod and Pilate, who had been enemies before, became friends that day.)

13 Then Pilate called together the leading priests and other religious leaders, along with the people, 14 and he announced his verdict. "You brought this man to me, accusing him of leading a revolt. I have examined him thoroughly on this point in your presence and find him innocent. 15 Herod came to the same conclusion and sent him back to us. Nothing this man has done calls for the death penalty. 16 So I will have him flogged, and then I will release him."*

18 Then a mighty roar rose from the crowd, and with one voice they shouted, "Kill him, and release Barabbas to us!" 19 (Barabbas was in prison for taking part in an insurrection in Jerusalem against the government, and for murder.) 20 Pilate argued with them, because he wanted to release Jesus. 21 But they kept shouting, "Crucify him! Crucify him!"

22 For the third time he demanded, "Why? What crime has he committed? I have found no reason to sentence him to death. So I will have him flogged, and then I will release him."

23 But the mob shouted louder and louder, demanding that Jesus be crucified, and their voices prevailed. 24 So Pilate sentenced Jesus to die as they demanded. 25 As they had requested, he released Barabbas, the man in prison for insurrection and murder. But he turned Jesus over to them to do as they wished.

The Crucifixion

26 As they led Jesus away, a man named Simon, who was from Cyrene,* happened to be coming in from the countryside. The soldiers seized him and put the cross on him and made him carry it behind Jesus. 27 A large crowd trailed behind, including many grief-stricken women. 28 But Jesus turned and said to them, "Daughters of Jerusalem, don't weep for me, but weep for

22:43-44 Verses 43 and 44 are not included in the most ancient manuscripts. **22:66** Greek *before their Sanhedrin.* **22:69** See Ps 110:1. **23:16** Some manuscripts add verse 17, *Now it was necessary for him to release one prisoner to them during the Passover celebration.* Compare Matt 27:15; Mark 15:6; John 18:39. **23:26** *Cyrene* was a city in northern Africa.

▸ **23:7** See **The Herods**, page 1072.

Golgotha, Place of the Skull

Having been rushed through mockeries of religious and secular trials, Jesus was taken away to the place of execution and crucified. Such places were normally just outside the city walls so that everyone coming in would see the executions and the list of crimes on the cross in the hope it would serve as a deterrent. Jerusalem's place of execution at this time lay outside the northwestern city walls. It was called The Skull—in Greek, *Kranion*, or in Aramaic, *Golgotha* (Matthew 27:33; John 19:17). In the Latin Bible the word was translated as *Calvariae*, from which the word "Calvary" comes. The tradition that Jesus was crucified on a hill comes from the assumption that "The Skull" must have been hill-shaped, though the Gospels say nothing of a hill. The name is more likely to be a reference to the deathly things that were committed there.

▸ *See also* ***The death of Jesus****, page 1114.*

yourselves and for your children. 29For the
days are coming when they will say, 'Fortunate indeed are the women who are childless, the wombs that have not borne a child
and the breasts that have never nursed.'
30People will beg the mountains, 'Fall on
us,' and plead with the hills, 'Bury us.'*
31For if these things are done when the tree
is green, what will happen when it is dry?*"
32Two others, both criminals, were led out
to be executed with him. 33When they came to
a place called The Skull,* they nailed him to
the cross. And the criminals were also crucified—one on his right and one on his left.
34Jesus said, "Father, forgive them, for
they don't know what they are doing."*
And the soldiers gambled for his clothes by
throwing dice.*
35The crowd watched and the leaders
scoffed. "He saved others," they said,
"let him save himself if he is really God's
Messiah, the Chosen One." 36The soldiers
mocked him, too, by offering him a drink
of sour wine. 37They called out to him, "If
you are the King of the Jews, save yourself!"
38A sign was fastened above him with these
words: "This is the King of the Jews."
39One of the criminals hanging beside him
scoffed, "So you're the Messiah, are you?
Prove it by saving yourself—and us, too,
while you're at it!"
40But the other criminal protested, "Don't
you fear God even when you have been sentenced to die? 41We deserve to die for our
crimes, but this man hasn't done anything
wrong." 42Then he said, "Jesus, remember
me when you come into your Kingdom."
43And Jesus replied, "I assure you, today
you will be with me in paradise."

The Death of Jesus

44By this time it was about noon, and darkness fell across the whole land until three
o'clock. 45The light from the sun was gone.
And suddenly, the curtain in the sanctuary
of the Temple was torn down the middle.
46Then Jesus shouted, "Father, I entrust my
spirit into your hands!"* And with those
words he breathed his last.
47When the Roman officer* overseeing
the execution saw what had happened, he
worshiped God and said, "Surely this man
was innocent.*" 48And when all the crowd
that came to see the crucifixion saw what
had happened, they went home in deep
sorrow.* 49But Jesus' friends, including the
women who had followed him from Galilee,
stood at a distance watching.

The Burial of Jesus

50Now there was a good and righteous man
named Joseph. He was a member of the
Jewish high council, 51but he had not agreed
with the decision and actions of the other
religious leaders. He was from the town of
Arimathea in Judea, and he was waiting
for the Kingdom of God to come. 52He went
to Pilate and asked for Jesus' body. 53Then
he took the body down from the cross and
wrapped it in a long sheet of linen cloth and

▸ **23:34, 43, 46** *See* ***Jesus' seven sayings from the cross****, page 1229.*

Paradise

In the ancient Greek edition of the Old Testament, "paradise" (*paradeisos*) was often used to translate Hebrew words meaning "garden" or "park" (e.g., in the Greek text of Genesis 2:8, 10; Nehemiah 2:8; Ecclesiastes 2:5; Song of Songs 4:12). In later (nonbiblical) Jewish literature it came to mean the place where the souls of the righteous went until the coming of the messianic kingdom.
In the New Testament the word is used three times: by Jesus in his assurance to the criminal crucified alongside him, but who put his trust in him, that this was where they would both go after death (Luke 23:43); by Paul in his description of his heavenly experience (2 Corinthians 12:2-4); and in Revelation as God's gift to those who overcome (Revelation 2:7).

▸ *See also* ***The return of Jesus Christ****, page 1372;* ***Heaven****, page 1451.*

laid it in a new tomb that had been carved out of rock. 54 This was done late on Friday afternoon, the day of preparation,* as the Sabbath was about to begin.

55 As his body was taken away, the women from Galilee followed and saw the tomb where his body was placed. 56 Then they went home and prepared spices and ointments to anoint his body. But by the time they were finished the Sabbath had begun, so they rested as required by the law.

The Resurrection

24 But very early on Sunday morning* the women went to the tomb, taking the spices they had prepared. 2 They found that the stone had been rolled away from the entrance. 3 So they went in, but they didn't find the body of the Lord Jesus. 4 As they stood there puzzled, two men suddenly appeared to them, clothed in dazzling robes.

5 The women were terrified and bowed with their faces to the ground. Then the men asked, "Why are you looking among the dead for someone who is alive? 6 He isn't here! He is risen from the dead! Remember what he told you back in Galilee, 7 that the Son of Man* must be betrayed into the hands of sinful men and be crucified, and that he would rise again on the third day."

8 Then they remembered that he had said this. 9 So they rushed back from the tomb to tell his eleven disciples—and everyone else—what had happened. 10 It was Mary Magdalene, Joanna, Mary the mother of James, and several other women who told the apostles what had happened. 11 But the story sounded like nonsense to the men, so they didn't believe it. 12 However, Peter jumped up and ran to the tomb to look. Stooping, he peered in and saw the empty linen wrappings; then he went home again, wondering what had happened.

The Walk to Emmaus

13 That same day two of Jesus' followers were walking to the village of Emmaus, seven miles* from Jerusalem. 14 As they walked along they were talking about everything that had happened. 15 As they talked and discussed these things, Jesus himself suddenly came and began walking with them. 16 But God kept them from recognizing him.

17 He asked them, "What are you discussing so intently as you walk along?"

They stopped short, sadness written across their faces. 18 Then one of them, Cleopas, replied, "You must be the only person in Jerusalem who hasn't heard about all the things that have happened there the last few days."

19 "What things?" Jesus asked.

"The things that happened to Jesus, the man from Nazareth," they said. "He was a prophet who did powerful miracles, and he was a mighty teacher in the eyes of God and all the people. 20 But our leading priests and other religious leaders handed him over to be condemned to death, and they crucified him. 21 We had hoped he was the Messiah who had come to rescue Israel. This all happened three days ago.

22 "Then some women from our group of his followers were at his tomb early this morning, and they came back with an amazing report. 23 They said his body was missing, and they had seen angels who told them Jesus is alive! 24 Some of our men ran out to see, and sure enough, his body was gone, just as the women had said."

25 Then Jesus said to them, "You foolish people! You find it so hard to believe all that the prophets wrote in the Scriptures. 26 Wasn't it clearly predicted that the Messiah would have to suffer all these things before entering his glory?" 27 Then Jesus took them through the writings of Moses and all the prophets, explaining from all the Scriptures the things concerning himself.

28 By this time they were nearing Emmaus and the end of their journey. Jesus acted as if he were going on, 29 but they begged him, "Stay the night with us, since it is getting late." So he went home with them. 30 As they sat down to eat,* he took the bread and blessed it. Then he broke it and gave it to them. 31 Suddenly, their eyes were opened,

23:30 Hos 10:8. **23:31** Or *If these things are done to me, the living tree, what will happen to you, the dry tree?* **23:33** Sometimes rendered *Calvary,* which comes from the Latin word for "skull." **23:34a** This sentence is not included in many ancient manuscripts. **23:34b** Greek *by casting lots.* See Ps 22:18. **23:46** Ps 31:5. **23:47a** Greek *the centurion.* **23:47b** Or *righteous.* **23:48** Greek *went home beating their breasts.* **23:54** Greek *It was the day of preparation.* **24:1** Greek *But on the first day of the week, very early in the morning.* **24:7** "Son of Man" is a title Jesus used for himself. **24:13** Greek *60 stadia* [11.1 kilometers]. **24:30** Or *As they reclined.*

▸ **24:6** See ***Christ's resurrection and ours,*** page 1320. **24:10** See ***Mary Magdalene,*** page 1166.

and they recognized him. And at that moment he disappeared!

32They said to each other, "Didn't our hearts burn within us as he talked with us on the road and explained the Scriptures to us?" 33And within the hour they were on their way back to Jerusalem. There they found the eleven disciples and the others who had gathered with them, 34who said, "The Lord has really risen! He appeared to Peter.*"

Jesus Appears to the Disciples

35Then the two from Emmaus told their story of how Jesus had appeared to them as they were walking along the road, and how they had recognized him as he was breaking the bread. 36And just as they were telling about it, Jesus himself was suddenly standing there among them. "Peace be with you," he said. 37But the whole group was startled and frightened, thinking they were seeing a ghost!

38"Why are you frightened?" he asked. "Why are your hearts filled with doubt? 39Look at my hands. Look at my feet. You can see that it's really me. Touch me and make sure that I am not a ghost, because ghosts don't have bodies, as you see that I do." 40As he spoke, he showed them his hands and his feet.

41Still they stood there in disbelief, filled with joy and wonder. Then he asked them, "Do you have anything here to eat?" 42They gave him a piece of broiled fish, 43and he ate it as they watched.

44Then he said, "When I was with you before, I told you that everything written about me in the law of Moses and the prophets and in the Psalms must be fulfilled." 45Then he opened their minds to understand the Scriptures. 46And he said, "Yes, it was written long ago that the Messiah would suffer and die and rise from the dead on the third day. 47It was also written that this message would be proclaimed in the authority of his name to all the nations,* beginning in Jerusalem: 'There is forgiveness of sins for all who repent.' 48You are witnesses of all these things.

49"And now I will send the Holy Spirit, just as my Father promised. But stay here in the city until the Holy Spirit comes and fills you with power from heaven."

The Ascension

50Then Jesus led them to Bethany, and lifting his hands to heaven, he blessed them. 51While he was blessing them, he left them and was taken up to heaven. 52So they worshiped him and then returned to Jerusalem filled with great joy. 53And they spent all of their time in the Temple, praising God.

24:34 Greek *Simon.* **24:47** Or *all peoples.*

Jesus' ascension

Forty days after his resurrection (Acts 1:3), Jesus took his disciples to a spot near Bethany on the Mount of Olives where he took his final leave of them. Unlike his previous disappearances—for it seems clear he hadn't stayed permanently with them but had come and gone over those forty days—this time his departure was both obvious and final. "He left them and was taken up to heaven" (Luke 24:51), enveloped by a cloud (Acts 1:9). Since clouds frequently symbolized God's presence (e.g., Exodus 13:21; 24:15-16; Numbers 9:15-23; 11:25; 2 Chronicles 5:13-14), here was the Father coming to take Jesus home.

This return of Jesus to heaven—"the Ascension"—completed his mission as he took his rightful place at God's right hand, exalted because of his willing submission (Philippians 2:5-11). But he returned different from how he came, for he took his humanity with him, showing that there is indeed a place in heaven for humanity.

The Ascension convinced Christians that Jesus was now exalted in heaven, seated on his throne, reigning over his enemies (Acts 2:32-33; 5:30-31; Ephesians 4:7-10; Colossians 3:1; Hebrews 4:14; 1 Peter 3:22; Revelation 1:12-18; 5:1-10; 7:9-17), and praying for us (Romans 8:34; Hebrews 7:25). Such a truth can only cause us to worship (Luke 24:52).

John *Jesus: the Son of God*

John's story of Jesus is unique. In the Gospels of Matthew, Mark, and Luke, we see Jesus preaching about the Kingdom of God; but in the Gospel of John, Jesus teaches about himself. In Matthew, Mark, and Luke, we read all about Jesus' ministry and many miracles; but in John, we read more about who Jesus is. Selected miracles—which John calls "signs"—point to Jesus' true significance. The messenger takes precedence over the message. These are not contradictory accounts, however, but rather complementary. John is writing with a different purpose. What matters to him is our response to the person of Jesus. He writes "so that you may continue to believe that Jesus is the Messiah, the Son of God, and that by believing in him you will have life by the power of his name" (20:31).

What's it all about?

John's opening words—"In the beginning the Word already existed"—deliberately echo the opening words of Genesis: "In the beginning God . . ." John wants us to know that this story is about someone who has been with God from the beginning, indeed who is God himself (1:1-2). That is why Jesus could bring revelation as no one else could, why his words are trustworthy and life-giving—though many rejected them in the drama that unfolded.

The story begins with John the Baptist announcing the Messiah's coming and being questioned by Jerusalem's religious leaders. When Jesus arrived, John saw God's Spirit descending on him, confirming him as the Messiah, and disciples began to gather to him. Soon afterward Jesus was invited to a wedding (chapter 2) where he performed the first of his miraculous signs (2:11), which led his disciples to believe in him. But confrontation wasn't far away. When he drove out money changers and merchants from the Temple, the religious leaders challenged him, demanding a sign to prove his authority to do this. But not all the leaders responded negatively: Nicodemus wanted to know more (chapter 3), and Jesus spoke to him of the importance of being "born again" (3:3).

Jesus then headed north for Galilee (4:3), meeting a Samaritan woman on the way. He revealed details about her life that convinced her he was a prophet. Refusing to be deflected by her questions about the right way to worship, he told her that "God is Spirit, so those who worship him must worship in spirit and in truth" (4:24). Many Samaritans believed because of her testimony. Later, he returned to Cana where he healed an official's son. On his return to Jerusalem (chapter 5), he aroused more hostility from the Jewish leaders, not only by healing a man on the Sabbath, but by claiming equality with God. Back in Galilee (chapter 6), he fed a crowd of thousands and then taught them not to seek earthly bread but heavenly bread. When he identified this bread with his own flesh (6:55), many decided they could no longer follow him. But when Jesus asked if the Twelve wanted to leave, Peter replied, "Lord, to whom would we go? You have the words that give eternal life" (6:68).

The remaining chapters record the growing hostility of the Jewish leaders toward Jesus. He antagonized them with his claims, accusing them of being slaves rather than free children of Abraham, and of having the devil as their father (chapter 8).

Their unbelief reached a climax when Jesus healed a man blind from birth (chapter 9), something they could neither explain away nor believe. Jesus said it was because they were not part of his flock, the flock of the good shepherd who lays down his life for his sheep (chapter 10). When he raised Lazarus from the dead (chapter 11), this was too much. They resolved to kill him (11:53).

At his final meal (chapter 13) Jesus prepared his disciples for his death. He washed their feet and gave them a new commandment: to love each other as he had loved them (13:34). He encouraged them to trust God and promised to send the Holy Spirit to be with them (chapter 14), calling them to abide in him and be fruitful (chapter 15), and praying for them (chapter 17).

Betrayed by Judas, Jesus was arrested and tried before Pontius Pilate (chapters 18–19). On his cross, Pilate posted the very title the Jewish leaders refused to accept: "Jesus of Nazareth, the King of the Jews" (19:19). Jesus died and was buried in a borrowed tomb. On the third day his followers found the tomb empty, and many appearances of the risen Jesus followed (chapters 20–21), including one where he commissioned Peter to shepherd his flock.

OVERVIEW

- **Jesus is introduced as the Word and true light** · *1:1-18*
- **Jesus' baptism by John and the calling of the disciples** · *1:19-51*
- **Jesus turns water into wine and clears out the Temple** · *2:1-25*
- **Jesus' conversation with Nicodemus** *3:1-21*
- **John the Baptist's testimony** *3:22-36*
- **Jesus' conversation with a Samaritan woman and its results** · *4:1-54*
- **Jesus heals a paralyzed man and speaks about himself** · *5:1-47*
- **Jesus feeds the five thousand and teaches about the "bread of life"** *6:1-71*
- **Jesus' teaching causes division among the Jews** · *7:1–8:59*
- **Jesus heals a blind man** *9:1-41*
- **Jesus presents himself as the good shepherd** · *10:1-42*
- **Jesus raises Lazarus from the dead** *11:1-57*
- **Jesus enters Jerusalem and teaches about his death** · *12:1-50*
- **Jesus shares the Passover meal with his disciples** · *13:1-38*
- **Jesus' farewell teaching and prayer** *14:1–17:26*
- **Jesus' arrest and crucifixion** *18:1–19:42*
- **The appearances of the resurrected Jesus** · *20:1–21:25*

What does it mean for us?

By the end of John's Gospel, we have to make a decision about Jesus Christ. One way or the other, the Jesus whom John presents demands a response. We must decide whether or not we will believe in him and follow him forever.

Responses to Jesus are not always black and white. Certainly, we can choose to reject his claims outright, or become wholehearted followers. But in this Gospel there are others who fall into neither category. Some, like the disciples at the Sea of Galilee, followed him up to a point and then decided to leave (6:60-66). Others, like the parents of the man born blind, were afraid of the consequences of believing (9:18-23). Some Jewish leaders, like Nicodemus, believed but remained secret believers (3:1-2). Still others, like Pilate, felt they had too much to lose (19:12-16). Thomas believed, but then seemed to lose his faith when things appeared to go wrong (20:24-25), and Peter even denied that he was a disciple of Jesus (18:17, 25-27)—though these disciples both found a way back to strong faith again (John 20:24-29; 21:15-19).

However we choose to respond, John makes it clear that indifference is not an option. When a light goes on in a dark room, it's impossible to ignore it. We either have to run for cover if we want to continue living in darkness, or adjust our eyes to the brightness—and what it reveals. But John underlines that each of us has a decision to make.

▶ *See also* ***Four Gospels, one story****, pages 1060-1065;* ***John****, page 1224;* ***The Ministry of Jesus*** *map, Visual Overview Z10.*

Prologue: Christ, the Eternal Word

1 1 In the beginning the Word already
existed.
The Word was with God,
and the Word was God.
2 He existed in the beginning with God.
3 God created everything through him,
and nothing was created except
through him.
4 The Word gave life to everything that
was created,*
and his life brought light to
everyone.
5 The light shines in the darkness,
and the darkness can never
extinguish it.*

6 God sent a man, John the Baptist,* 7 to
tell about the light so that everyone might
believe because of his testimony. 8 John
himself was not the light; he was simply a
witness to tell about the light. 9 The one who
is the true light, who gives light to everyone,
was coming into the world.

10 He came into the very world he created,
but the world didn't recognize him. 11 He came
to his own people, and even they rejected
him. 12 But to all who believed him and accepted him, he gave the right to become children of God. 13 They are reborn—not with a
physical birth resulting from human passion
or plan, but a birth that comes from God.

14 So the Word became human* and made
his home among us. He was full of unfailing
love and faithfulness.* And we have seen
his glory, the glory of the Father's one and
only Son.

15 John testified about him when he
shouted to the crowds, "This is the one I
was talking about when I said, 'Someone is
coming after me who is far greater than I
am, for he existed long before me.'"

16 From his abundance we have all received one gracious blessing after another.*
17 For the law was given through Moses, but
God's unfailing love and faithfulness came
through Jesus Christ. 18 No one has ever seen
God. But the unique One, who is himself
God,* is near to the Father's heart. He has
revealed God to us.

The Testimony of John the Baptist

19 This was John's testimony when the Jewish
leaders sent priests and Temple assistants*
from Jerusalem to ask John, "Who are you?"
20 He came right out and said, "I am not the
Messiah."

21 "Well then, who are you?" they asked.
"Are you Elijah?"

1:3-4 Or *and nothing that was created was created except through him. The Word gave life to everything.* **1:5** Or *and the darkness has not understood it.* **1:6** Greek *a man named John.* **1:14a** Greek *became flesh.* **1:14b** Or *grace and truth;* also in 1:17. **1:16** Or *received the grace of Christ rather than the grace of the law;* Greek reads *received grace upon grace.* **1:18** Some manuscripts read *But the one and only Son.* **1:19** Greek *and Levites.*

The Incarnation

Unlike everyone else who has ever lived, the beginning of Jesus' earthly life was not the beginning of him; he has always been the Son of God. Jesus was not merely a prophet or holy man but none other than God himself in human flesh, the second person of the Trinity come to us in human form. Jesus did this, not by pretending to be human, nor by becoming some sort of half-man, half-god, but by humbling himself to take a real human nature, being fully divine and fully human. He became a real human being, just like you and me—but with one difference: He was without sin. Jesus was God-become-man, fully God and fully human, the same eternal being he had always been, but now in a different form of existence. Look at Jesus, John says, and you are looking at God himself (John 1:18).

The reality of the Incarnation is reflected in how Jesus, though he was God, is seen as utterly human in the Gospels. He experienced normal human development (Luke 2:40, 52), became tired (John 4:6) and hungry and thirsty (Matthew 4:2; John 19:28), and ultimately bled and died (John 19:32-34). God really had become a man.

▶ *See also* ***Names and titles of Jesus****, page 1070;* ***The Virgin Birth****, page 1152;* ***The deity of Jesus Christ****, page 1364.*

"No," he replied.
"Are you the Prophet we are expecting?"*
"No."
[22]"Then who are you? We need an answer
for those who sent us. What do you have to
say about yourself?"
[23]John replied in the words of the prophet
Isaiah:

"I am a voice shouting in the wilderness,
'Clear the way for the LORD's coming!'"*

[24]Then the Pharisees who had been sent
[25]asked him, "If you aren't the Messiah or
Elijah or the Prophet, what right do you
have to baptize?"
[26]John told them, "I baptize with* water,
but right here in the crowd is someone you
do not recognize. [27]Though his ministry
follows mine, I'm not even worthy to be his
slave and untie the straps of his sandal."
[28]This encounter took place in Bethany,
an area east of the Jordan River, where John
was baptizing.

Jesus, the Lamb of God

[29]The next day John saw Jesus coming
toward him and said, "Look! The Lamb of
God who takes away the sin of the world!
[30]He is the one I was talking about when I
said, 'A man is coming after me who is far
greater than I am, for he existed long before
me.' [31]I did not recognize him as the Messiah,
but I have been baptizing with water so that
he might be revealed to Israel."
[32]Then John testified, "I saw the Holy
Spirit descending like a dove from heaven
and resting upon him. [33]I didn't know he
was the one, but when God sent me to
baptize with water, he told me, 'The one on
whom you see the Spirit descend and rest
is the one who will baptize with the Holy
Spirit.' [34]I saw this happen to Jesus, so I
testify that he is the Chosen One of God.*"

The First Disciples

[35]The following day John was again standing with two of his disciples. [36]As Jesus
walked by, John looked at him and declared, "Look! There is the Lamb of God!"
[37]When John's two disciples heard this, they
followed Jesus.
[38]Jesus looked around and saw them following. "What do you want?" he asked them.
They replied, "Rabbi" (which means
"Teacher"), "where are you staying?"
[39]"Come and see," he said. It was about
four o'clock in the afternoon when they
went with him to the place where he was
staying, and they remained with him the
rest of the day.
[40]Andrew, Simon Peter's brother, was one
of these men who heard what John said and
then followed Jesus. [41]Andrew went to find
his brother, Simon, and told him, "We have
found the Messiah" (which means "Christ"*).
[42]Then Andrew brought Simon to meet
Jesus. Looking intently at Simon, Jesus
said, "Your name is Simon, son of John—but
you will be called Cephas" (which means
"Peter"*).
[43]The next day Jesus decided to go to
Galilee. He found Philip and said to him,
"Come, follow me." [44]Philip was from Bethsaida, Andrew and Peter's hometown.

▸ **1:42** *See* ***Peter****, page 1421.*

Andrew

Andrew was a fisherman from Bethsaida and a disciple of John the Baptist. But when John directed Andrew and his unnamed companion (who from earliest times was identified as John, the author of this Gospel) to Jesus as the Lamb of God, they were quick to follow Jesus and to start listening to him (John 1:35-39). What Andrew heard convinced him he had found the promised Messiah, and he immediately went and told his brother Simon Peter (1:40-42)—an excellent example of the value of sharing our newfound faith with others. He would continue to have a role of introducing others to Jesus (6:8-9; 12:20-22).

▸ *See also* ***Apostles of Jesus****, page 1122.*

45 Philip went to look for Nathanael and told
him, "We have found the very person Moses*
and the prophets wrote about! His name is
Jesus, the son of Joseph from Nazareth."
46 "Nazareth!" exclaimed Nathanael. "Can
anything good come from Nazareth?"
"Come and see for yourself," Philip replied.
47 As they approached, Jesus said, "Now
here is a genuine son of Israel—a man of
complete integrity."
48 "How do you know about me?" Nathanael asked.
Jesus replied, "I could see you under the
fig tree before Philip found you."
49 Then Nathanael exclaimed, "Rabbi, you
are the Son of God—the King of Israel!"
50 Jesus asked him, "Do you believe this
just because I told you I had seen you under
the fig tree? You will see greater things than
this." 51 Then he said, "I tell you the truth,
you will all see heaven open and the angels
of God going up and down on the Son of
Man, the one who is the stairway between
heaven and earth.*"

The Wedding at Cana

2 The next day* there was a wedding celebration in the village of Cana in Galilee.
Jesus' mother was there, 2 and Jesus and his

1:21 Greek *Are you the Prophet?* See Deut 18:15, 18; Mal 4:5-6. **1:23** Isa 40:3. **1:26** Or *in;* also in 1:31, 33. **1:34** Some manuscripts read *the Son of God.* **1:41** *Messiah* (a Hebrew term) and *Christ* (a Greek term) both mean "anointed one." **1:42** The names *Cephas* (from Aramaic) and *Peter* (from Greek) both mean "rock." **1:45** Greek *Moses in the law.* **1:51** Greek *going up and down on the Son of Man;* see Gen 28:10-17. "Son of Man" is a title Jesus used for himself. **2:1** Greek *On the third day;* see 1:35, 43.

▸ **1:46** *See **Nazareth**, page 1155.* **2:1** *See **Mary, the mother of Jesus**, page 1153.*

John's seven signs

John described Jesus' miracles as "signs" because he wanted us to look beyond the miraculous event itself to what it pointed to. While John knew of many more miracles of Jesus (John 20:30), he chose just seven—the number that signified in Judaism perfection or completeness—to help us see who Jesus was and to respond to him in faith (e.g., 2:11). In contrast to the signs performed by Moses that produced only judgment (Exodus 7–12), Jesus' signs brought only blessing.

Sign	Significance
Water turned into wine at a wedding (2:1-11)	The old "wine" of Judaism with all its rituals can no longer satisfy; only Jesus can.
Healing of an official's son (4:46-54)	Jesus has authority over all things and all people; faith in him transforms things.
Healing of the crippled man (5:1-18)	Jesus' authority comes from his relationship with his Father (5:17) and works even when unbelief (5:7, 13-15) and religion (5:9-10) get in the way.
Feeding of the five thousand (6:1-15)	Jesus is a greater provider than Moses, who provided food in the wilderness for forty years; he provides the bread of life for eternity (6:25-59).
Walking on water (6:16-21)	Jesus is the sovereign ruler over the world he created; nothing is beyond his control.
Healing of the man born blind (9:1-41)	Jesus has power to deal with not just physical but also spiritual blindness.
Raising Lazarus from the dead (11:1-57)	Jesus showed he is "the resurrection and the life" (11:25) in preparation for his own resurrection.

disciples were also invited to the celebration. [3]The wine supply ran out during the festivities, so Jesus' mother told him, "They have no more wine."

[4]"Dear woman, that's not our problem," Jesus replied. "My time has not yet come."

[5]But his mother told the servants, "Do whatever he tells you."

[6]Standing nearby were six stone water jars, used for Jewish ceremonial washing. Each could hold twenty to thirty gallons.* [7]Jesus told the servants, "Fill the jars with water." When the jars had been filled, [8]he said, "Now dip some out, and take it to the master of ceremonies." So the servants followed his instructions.

[9]When the master of ceremonies tasted the water that was now wine, not knowing where it had come from (though, of course, the servants knew), he called the bridegroom over. [10]"A host always serves the best wine first," he said. "Then, when everyone has had a lot to drink, he brings out the less expensive wine. But you have kept the best until now!"

[11]This miraculous sign at Cana in Galilee was the first time Jesus revealed his glory. And his disciples believed in him.

[12]After the wedding he went to Capernaum for a few days with his mother, his brothers, and his disciples.

Jesus Clears the Temple

[13]It was nearly time for the Jewish Passover celebration, so Jesus went to Jerusalem. [14]In the Temple area he saw merchants selling cattle, sheep, and doves for sacrifices; he also saw dealers at tables exchanging foreign money. [15]Jesus made a whip from some ropes and chased them all out of the Temple. He drove out the sheep and cattle, scattered the money changers' coins over the floor, and turned over their tables. [16]Then, going over to the people who sold doves, he told them, "Get these things out of here. Stop turning my Father's house into a marketplace!"

[17]Then his disciples remembered this prophecy from the Scriptures: "Passion for God's house will consume me."*

[18]But the Jewish leaders demanded, "What are you doing? If God gave you authority to do this, show us a miraculous sign to prove it."

[19]"All right," Jesus replied. "Destroy this temple, and in three days I will raise it up."

[20]"What!" they exclaimed. "It has taken forty-six years to build this Temple, and you can rebuild it in three days?" [21]But when Jesus said "this temple," he meant his own body. [22]After he was raised from the dead, his disciples remembered he had said this, and they believed both the Scriptures and what Jesus had said.

Jesus and Nicodemus

[23]Because of the miraculous signs Jesus did in Jerusalem at the Passover celebration, many began to trust in him. [24]But Jesus didn't trust them, because he knew all about people. [25]No one needed to tell him about human nature, for he knew what was in each person's heart.

3 There was a man named Nicodemus, a Jewish religious leader who was a Pharisee. [2]After dark one evening, he came to speak with Jesus. "Rabbi," he said, "we all know that God has sent you to teach us. Your miraculous signs are evidence that God is with you."

[3]Jesus replied, "I tell you the truth, unless you are born again,* you cannot see the Kingdom of God."

[4]"What do you mean?" exclaimed Nicodemus. "How can an old man go back into his mother's womb and be born again?"

[5]Jesus replied, "I assure you, no one can enter the Kingdom of God without being born of water and the Spirit.* [6]Humans can reproduce only human life, but the Holy Spirit gives birth to spiritual life.* [7]So don't be surprised when I say, 'You* must be born again.' [8]The wind blows wherever it wants. Just as you can hear the wind but can't tell where it comes from or where it is going, so you can't explain how people are born of the Spirit."

[9]"How are these things possible?" Nicodemus asked.

[10]Jesus replied, "You are a respected Jewish teacher, and yet you don't understand these things? [11]I assure you, we tell you what we know and have seen, and yet you won't believe our testimony. [12]But if you don't believe me when I tell you about earthly things, how can you possibly believe if I tell you about heavenly things? [13]No one has ever gone to heaven and returned. But the Son of Man* has come down from heaven. [14]And as Moses lifted up the

bronze snake on a pole in the wilderness, so the Son of Man must be lifted up, [15]so that everyone who believes in him will have eternal life.*

[16]"For this is how God loved the world: He gave* his one and only Son, so that everyone who believes in him will not perish but have eternal life. [17]God sent his Son into the world not to judge the world, but to save the world through him.

[18]"There is no judgment against anyone who believes in him. But anyone who does not believe in him has already been judged for not believing in God's one and only Son. [19]And the judgment is based on this fact: God's light came into the world, but people loved the darkness more than the light, for their actions were evil. [20]All who do evil hate the light and refuse to go near it for fear their sins will be exposed. [21]But those who do what is right come to the light so others can see that they are doing what God wants.*"

John the Baptist Exalts Jesus

[22]Then Jesus and his disciples left Jerusalem and went into the Judean countryside. Jesus spent some time with them there, baptizing people.

[23]At this time John the Baptist was baptizing at Aenon, near Salim, because there was plenty of water there; and people kept coming to him for baptism. [24](This was before John was thrown into prison.) [25]A debate broke out between John's disciples and a certain Jew* over ceremonial cleansing. [26]So John's disciples came to him and said, "Rabbi, the man you met on the other side of the Jordan River, the one you identified as the Messiah, is also baptizing people. And everybody is going to him instead of coming to us."

[27]John replied, "No one can receive anything unless God gives it from heaven. [28]You yourselves know how plainly I told you, 'I am not the Messiah. I am only here to prepare the way for him.' [29]It is the bridegroom who marries the bride, and the bridegroom's friend is simply glad to stand with him and hear his vows. Therefore, I am filled with joy at his success. [30]He must become greater and greater, and I must become less and less.

[31]"He has come from above and is greater than anyone else. We are of the earth, and we

2:6 Greek *2 or 3 measures* [75 to 113 liters]. **2:17** Or *"Concern for God's house will be my undoing."* Ps 69:9. **3:3** Or *born from above;* also in 3:7. **3:5** Or *and spirit.* The Greek word for *Spirit* can also be translated *wind;* see 3:8. **3:6** Greek *what is born of the Spirit is spirit.* **3:7** The Greek word for *you* is plural; also in 3:12. **3:13** Some manuscripts add *who lives in heaven.* "Son of Man" is a title Jesus used for himself. **3:15** Or *everyone who believes will have eternal life in him.* **3:16** Or *For God loved the world so much that he gave.* **3:21** Or *can see God at work in what he is doing.* **3:25** Some manuscripts read *some Jews.*

The new birth

While the religious leaders opposed Jesus—the teachers of religious law and the Pharisees said he undermined the Scriptures, and the priests contended that he undermined the Temple's importance—Nicodemus felt he should be given a fair hearing, especially in light of all he was doing (John 3:2). Jesus said the only way Nicodemus could see God's Kingdom was not by following the old Jewish rituals, which had become lifeless, but by being "born again" (3:3). When Nicodemus failed to understand, Jesus explained that he meant a brand-new birth—not birth as a Jew or as a human being, but a birth by the work of the Holy Spirit (3:5-6).

Being a Christian isn't about following a set of religious rules or moral code, or trying to be good, or being born into a Christian family; it involves a personal and radical transformation of our hearts. This occurs when we face up to our sinfulness, believe Christ died to pay the price of our sins, ask for his forgiveness, and invite his Spirit to come and live inside us to transform us from within. This regeneration is entirely God's work and grace (e.g., 1:12-13), made possible by Christ's resurrection (1 Peter 1:3-5) and brought about by God's Spirit (Titus 3:4-7), and it is available to all.

▶ *See also* ***Nicodemus****, page 1230.*

speak of earthly things, but he has come from heaven and is greater than anyone else.* [32]He testifies about what he has seen and heard, but how few believe what he tells them! [33]Anyone who accepts his testimony can affirm that God is true. [34]For he is sent by God. He speaks God's words, for God gives him the Spirit without limit. [35]The Father loves his Son and has put everything into his hands. [36]And anyone who believes in God's Son has eternal life. Anyone who doesn't obey the Son will never experience eternal life but remains under God's angry judgment."

Jesus and the Samaritan Woman

4 Jesus* knew the Pharisees had heard that he was baptizing and making more disciples than John [2](though Jesus himself didn't baptize them—his disciples did). [3]So he left Judea and returned to Galilee.

[4]He had to go through Samaria on the way. [5]Eventually he came to the Samaritan village of Sychar, near the field that Jacob gave to his son Joseph. [6]Jacob's well was there; and Jesus, tired from the long walk, sat wearily beside the well about noontime. [7]Soon a Samaritan woman came to draw water, and Jesus said to her, "Please give me a drink." [8]He was alone at the time because his disciples had gone into the village to buy some food.

[9]The woman was surprised, for Jews refuse to have anything to do with Samaritans.* She said to Jesus, "You are a Jew, and I am a Samaritan woman. Why are you asking me for a drink?"

[10]Jesus replied, "If you only knew the gift God has for you and who you are speaking to, you would ask me, and I would give you living water."

[11]"But sir, you don't have a rope or a bucket," she said, "and this well is very deep. Where would you get this living water? [12]And besides, do you think you're greater than our ancestor Jacob, who gave us this well? How can you offer better water than he and his sons and his animals enjoyed?"

[13]Jesus replied, "Anyone who drinks this water will soon become thirsty again. [14]But those who drink the water I give will never be thirsty again. It becomes a fresh, bubbling spring within them, giving them eternal life."

[15]"Please, sir," the woman said, "give me this water! Then I'll never be thirsty again, and I won't have to come here to get water."

[16]"Go and get your husband," Jesus told her.

[17]"I don't have a husband," the woman replied.

Jesus said, "You're right! You don't have a husband—[18]for you have had five husbands, and you aren't even married to the man you're living with now. You certainly spoke the truth!"

The Samaritans

When Jesus engaged in conversation with a Samaritan woman (John 4:7), he was breaking two Jewish taboos—first, because she was a woman (rabbis didn't speak to women in public), and second, because she was a Samaritan. For Jews, Samaritans were unclean, so drinking her water was contaminating, which is why she was surprised (4:9). Like most prejudices, this one was deep-rooted and long-standing. It went back to the northern kingdom of Israel's exile in 722 BC when Assyria not only deported most Israelites but also forcibly relocated other people to the area that became known as Samaria, resulting in a mixed population. Such racial impurity was despised by orthodox Jews, and they did all they could to avoid Samaritans, even taking the longer route east of the Jordan to reach Galilee instead of passing through Samaria. This is why Jesus' parable of a *good* Samaritan (Luke 10:25-37) would have been so striking. But Jesus rejected such prejudices. He preached the good news to the Samaritans (John 4:39-42) and commanded his disciples to include Samaria when sending them out to preach (Acts 1:8). The early church found considerable evangelistic success here (e.g., Acts 8:4-25).

▶ *See also* ***The Exile****, page 433.*

19“Sir,” the woman said, “you must be
a prophet. 20So tell me, why is it that you
Jews insist that Jerusalem is the only place
of worship, while we Samaritans claim it is
here at Mount Gerizim,* where our ancestors worshiped?”
21Jesus replied, “Believe me, dear woman,
the time is coming when it will no longer
matter whether you worship the Father on
this mountain or in Jerusalem. 22You Samaritans know very little about the one
you worship, while we Jews know all about
him, for salvation comes through the Jews.
23But the time is coming—indeed it’s here
now—when true worshipers will worship
the Father in spirit and in truth. The Father
is looking for those who will worship him
that way. 24For God is Spirit, so those who
worship him must worship in spirit and in
truth.”
25The woman said, “I know the Messiah is
coming—the one who is called Christ. When
he comes, he will explain everything to us.”
26Then Jesus told her, “I AM the Messiah!”*
27Just then his disciples came back.
They were shocked to find him talking to a
woman, but none of them had the nerve to
ask, “What do you want with her?” or “Why
are you talking to her?” 28The woman left
her water jar beside the well and ran back
to the village, telling everyone, 29“Come and
see a man who told me everything I ever
did! Could he possibly be the Messiah?”
30So the people came streaming from the
village to see him.
31Meanwhile, the disciples were urging
Jesus, “Rabbi, eat something.”
32But Jesus replied, “I have a kind of food
you know nothing about.”
33“Did someone bring him food while we
were gone?” the disciples asked each other.
34Then Jesus explained: “My nourishment
comes from doing the will of God, who sent
me, and from finishing his work. 35You know
the saying, ‘Four months between planting and harvest.’ But I say, wake up and
look around. The fields are already ripe*
for harvest. 36The harvesters are paid good
wages, and the fruit they harvest is people
brought to eternal life. What joy awaits both
the planter and the harvester alike! 37You
know the saying, ‘One plants and another
harvests.’ And it’s true. 38I sent you to
harvest where you didn’t plant; others had
already done the work, and now you will get
to gather the harvest.”

Many Samaritans Believe

39Many Samaritans from the village believed
in Jesus because the woman had said, “He
told me everything I ever did!” 40When they

3:31 Some manuscripts do not include *and is greater than anyone else.* **4:1** Some manuscripts read *The Lord.* **4:9** Some manuscripts do not include this sentence. **4:20** Greek *on this mountain.* **4:26** Or *“The ‘I AM’ is here”*; or *“I am the LORD”*; Greek reads *“I am, the one speaking to you.”* See Exod 3:14. **4:35** Greek *white.*

Forms of worship

While some claim that the way they worship is the only “right” way, Jesus made clear that it isn’t the externals of worship that matter, but the heart behind it. Trying to deflect Jesus, the Samaritan woman had raised the issue of the right way to worship (John 4:16-20). Samaritans believed Mount Gerizim in Samaria (where Abraham and Jacob had built altars and where the covenant blessings were proclaimed over Israel at the time of Joshua) was the right place to worship God, and they had even once built a temple there. For Jews the Temple in Jerusalem was the right place to worship.

Jesus did not say that the Jews were right and the Samaritans wrong, even though salvation came through the Jews (4:22). Both were wrong, because God wanted those who would worship “in spirit” (or, “in the Holy Spirit”) and in truth (4:23-24). The place and form of worship are now irrelevant, because we no longer need to go to a particular place. We can worship God anywhere and in any way, because God’s people are now God’s temple, filled with his Spirit. This means we can worship him in any way that is pleasing to his Spirit and consistent with his truth. To insist there is a “right” way is to return to the old covenant.

came out to see him, they begged him to stay in their village. So he stayed for two days, 41long enough for many more to hear his message and believe. 42Then they said to the woman, "Now we believe, not just because of what you told us, but because we have heard him ourselves. Now we know that he is indeed the Savior of the world."

Jesus Heals an Official's Son

43At the end of the two days, Jesus went on to Galilee. 44He himself had said that a prophet is not honored in his own hometown. 45Yet the Galileans welcomed him, for they had been in Jerusalem at the Passover celebration and had seen everything he did there.

46As he traveled through Galilee, he came to Cana, where he had turned the water into wine. There was a government official in nearby Capernaum whose son was very sick. 47When he heard that Jesus had come from Judea to Galilee, he went and begged Jesus to come to Capernaum to heal his son, who was about to die.

48Jesus asked, "Will you never believe in me unless you see miraculous signs and wonders?"

49The official pleaded, "Lord, please come now before my little boy dies."

50Then Jesus told him, "Go back home. Your son will live!" And the man believed what Jesus said and started home.

51While the man was on his way, some of his servants met him with the news that his son was alive and well. 52He asked them when the boy had begun to get better, and they replied, "Yesterday afternoon at one o'clock his fever suddenly disappeared!" 53Then the father realized that that was the very time Jesus had told him, "Your son will live." And he and his entire household believed in Jesus. 54This was the second miraculous sign Jesus did in Galilee after coming from Judea.

Jesus Heals a Lame Man

5 Afterward Jesus returned to Jerusalem for one of the Jewish holy days. 2Inside the city, near the Sheep Gate, was the pool of Bethesda,* with five covered porches. 3Crowds of sick people—blind, lame, or paralyzed—lay on the porches.* 5One of the men lying there had been sick for thirty-eight years. 6When Jesus saw him and knew he had been ill for a long time, he asked him, "Would you like to get well?"

7"I can't, sir," the sick man said, "for I have no one to put me into the pool when the water bubbles up. Someone else always gets there ahead of me."

8Jesus told him, "Stand up, pick up your mat, and walk!"

9Instantly, the man was healed! He rolled up his sleeping mat and began walking! But this miracle happened on the Sabbath, 10so the Jewish leaders objected. They said to the man who was cured, "You can't work on the Sabbath! The law doesn't allow you to carry that sleeping mat!"

11But he replied, "The man who healed me told me, 'Pick up your mat and walk.'"

12"Who said such a thing as that?" they demanded.

13The man didn't know, for Jesus had disappeared into the crowd. 14But afterward Jesus found him in the Temple and told him, "Now you are well; so stop sinning, or something even worse may happen to you." 15Then the man went and told the Jewish leaders that it was Jesus who had healed him.

Jesus Claims to Be the Son of God

16So the Jewish leaders began harassing* Jesus for breaking the Sabbath rules. 17But Jesus replied, "My Father is always working, and so am I." 18So the Jewish leaders tried all the harder to find a way to kill him. For he not only broke the Sabbath, he called God his Father, thereby making himself equal with God.

19So Jesus explained, "I tell you the truth, the Son can do nothing by himself. He does only what he sees the Father doing. Whatever the Father does, the Son also does. 20For the Father loves the Son and shows him everything he is doing. In fact, the Father will show him how to do even greater works than healing this man. Then you will truly be astonished. 21For just as the Father gives life to those he raises from the dead, so the Son gives life to anyone he wants. 22In addition, the Father judges no one. Instead, he has given the Son absolute authority to judge, 23so that everyone will honor the Son, just as they honor the Father. Anyone

▸ **4:46-54** *See* ***Jesus' miracles****, page 1128.*

who does not honor the Son is certainly not
honoring the Father who sent him.
24"I tell you the truth, those who listen to
my message and believe in God who sent
me have eternal life. They will never be condemned for their sins, but they have already
passed from death into life.
25"And I assure you that the time is
coming, indeed it's here now, when the
dead will hear my voice—the voice of the
Son of God. And those who listen will live.
26The Father has life in himself, and he has
granted that same life-giving power to his
Son. 27And he has given him authority to
judge everyone because he is the Son of
Man.* 28Don't be so surprised! Indeed, the
time is coming when all the dead in their
graves will hear the voice of God's Son,
29and they will rise again. Those who have
done good will rise to experience eternal
life, and those who have continued in evil
will rise to experience judgment. 30I can do
nothing on my own. I judge as God tells me.
Therefore, my judgment is just, because I
carry out the will of the one who sent me,
not my own will.

Witnesses to Jesus

31"If I were to testify on my own behalf,
my testimony would not be valid. 32But
someone else is also testifying about me,
and I assure you that everything he says
about me is true. 33In fact, you sent investi-
gators to listen to John the Baptist, and his
testimony about me was true. 34Of course,
I have no need of human witnesses, but I
say these things so you might be saved.
35John was like a burning and shining lamp,
and you were excited for a while about his
message. 36But I have a greater witness than
John—my teachings and my miracles. The
Father gave me these works to accomplish,
and they prove that he sent me. 37And the
Father who sent me has testified about me
himself. You have never heard his voice or
seen him face to face, 38and you do not have
his message in your hearts, because you do
not believe me—the one he sent to you.
39"You search the Scriptures because
you think they give you eternal life. But the
Scriptures point to me! 40Yet you refuse to
come to me to receive this life.
41"Your approval means nothing to me,
42because I know you don't have God's love
within you. 43For I have come to you in my
Father's name, and you have rejected me.
Yet if others come in their own name, you
gladly welcome them. 44No wonder you
can't believe! For you gladly honor each
other, but you don't care about the honor
that comes from the one who alone is God.*
45"Yet it isn't I who will accuse you before
the Father. Moses will accuse you! Yes,
Moses, in whom you put your hopes. 46If you
really believed Moses, you would believe
me, because he wrote about me. 47But since
you don't believe what he wrote, how will
you believe what I say?"

Jesus Feeds Five Thousand

6 After this, Jesus crossed over to the far
side of the Sea of Galilee, also known
as the Sea of Tiberias. 2A huge crowd kept
following him wherever he went, because
they saw his miraculous signs as he healed
the sick. 3Then Jesus climbed a hill and sat
down with his disciples around him. 4(It was
nearly time for the Jewish Passover celebration.) 5Jesus soon saw a huge crowd of people
coming to look for him. Turning to Philip, he
asked, "Where can we buy bread to feed all
these people?" 6He was testing Philip, for he
already knew what he was going to do.
7Philip replied, "Even if we worked for
months, we wouldn't have enough money*
to feed them!"
8Then Andrew, Simon Peter's brother,
spoke up. 9"There's a young boy here with
five barley loaves and two fish. But what
good is that with this huge crowd?"
10"Tell everyone to sit down," Jesus said.
So they all sat down on the grassy slopes.
(The men alone numbered about 5,000.)
11Then Jesus took the loaves, gave thanks
to God, and distributed them to the people.
Afterward he did the same with the fish.
And they all ate as much as they wanted.
12After everyone was full, Jesus told his disciples, "Now gather the leftovers, so that
nothing is wasted." 13So they picked up the
pieces and filled twelve baskets with scraps
left by the people who had eaten from the
five barley loaves.

5:2 Other manuscripts read *Beth-zatha;* still others read *Bethsaida.* **5:3** Some manuscripts add an expanded conclusion to verse 3 and all of verse 4: *waiting for a certain movement of the water, 4for an angel of the Lord came from time to time and stirred up the water. And the first person to step in after the water was stirred was healed of whatever disease he had.* **5:16** Or *persecuting.* **5:27** "Son of Man" is a title Jesus used for himself. **5:44** Some manuscripts read *from the only One.* **6:7** Greek *Two hundred denarii would not be enough.* A denarius was equivalent to a laborer's full day's wage.

The "I am" sayings of Jesus

John loved the symbols and imagery that Jesus used to convey who he was, all of it rooted in the Old Testament. Some of the most powerful are linked with his "I am" sayings. This was the name God had revealed to Moses when he first encountered him—"I AM WHO I AM" or simply "I AM" (Exodus 3:14). By using this term Jesus was claiming to be none other than God himself. John records seven "I am" sayings, all revealing something about the nature of God himself:

Saying	Significance
"I am the bread of life. Whoever comes to me will never be hungry again. Whoever believes in me will never be thirsty." (John 6:35)	Jesus himself provides lasting spiritual nourishment to satisfy our deepest human longings. When we receive him into our lives, we will never need to look anywhere else for spiritual satisfaction.
"I am the light of the world. If you follow me, you won't have to walk in darkness, because you will have the light that leads to life." (8:12)	Jesus brings God's light into this dark world to help us see things as they really are. That light helps us to avoid stumbling or taking the wrong path.
"I am the gate for the sheep. . . . Those who come in through me will be saved." (10:7, 9)	Jesus is the only way into God's salvation and God's family. Whoever trusts in him can be assured of being eternally saved and of finding all that their soul longs for.
"I am the good shepherd. The good shepherd sacrifices his life for the sheep." (10:11)	Unlike Israel's faithless shepherds (see Ezekiel 34), Jesus cares for his sheep, even to the point of giving his life for them. He constantly provides for, protects, and cares for his people.
"I am the resurrection and the life. Anyone who believes in me will live, even after dying. Everyone who lives in me and believes in me will never ever die." (11:25-26)	Because Jesus himself is both the resurrection and the life, he gives us resurrection and life. Through faith in him we begin to experience new life right now, life that not even death can end.
"I am the way, the truth, and the life. No one can come to the Father except through me." (14:6)	Unlike other religious leaders, Jesus does not show the way to God; he *is* the way. Through putting our trust in him we can know God as Father and find both truth and life.
"I am the true grapevine, and my Father is the gardener." (15:1).	Israel (often symbolized as a vine) had failed in its mission of being a light to the world; but Jesus is the true vine, who invites all to become part of God's great family and purposes.

In addition to these seven examples, there are two unqualified uses of the term. The first is when Jesus says, "Before Abraham was even born, I AM!" (8:58). The crowd's reaction—they were ready to stone him (8:59)—shows they understood the claim he was making and saw this as blasphemy. The second is when Jesus is arrested in the garden of Gethsemane. In response to the soldiers' and officials' saying they are looking for Jesus the Nazarene, Jesus replies, "I AM he" (18:5). Their response of falling to the ground indicates that, at that moment, they sensed they were encountering someone who was more than a mere man.

14 When the people saw him* do this miraculous sign, they exclaimed, "Surely, he
is the Prophet we have been expecting!"*
15 When Jesus saw that they were ready to
force him to be their king, he slipped away
into the hills by himself.

Jesus Walks on Water

16 That evening Jesus' disciples went down
to the shore to wait for him. 17 But as darkness fell and Jesus still hadn't come back,
they got into the boat and headed across
the lake toward Capernaum. 18 Soon a gale
swept down upon them, and the sea grew
very rough. 19 They had rowed three or
four miles* when suddenly they saw Jesus
walking on the water toward the boat. They
were terrified, 20 but he called out to them,
"Don't be afraid. I am here!*" 21 Then they
were eager to let him in the boat, and immediately they arrived at their destination!

Jesus, the Bread of Life

22 The next day the crowd that had stayed
on the far shore saw that the disciples
had taken the only boat, and they realized
Jesus had not gone with them. 23 Several
boats from Tiberias landed near the place
where the Lord had blessed the bread and
the people had eaten. 24 So when the crowd
saw that neither Jesus nor his disciples
were there, they got into the boats and went
across to Capernaum to look for him. 25 They
found him on the other side of the lake and
asked, "Rabbi, when did you get here?"
26 Jesus replied, "I tell you the truth, you
want to be with me because I fed you, not
because you understood the miraculous
signs. 27 But don't be so concerned about
perishable things like food. Spend your
energy seeking the eternal life that the Son
of Man* can give you. For God the Father
has given me the seal of his approval."
28 They replied, "We want to perform
God's works, too. What should we do?"
29 Jesus told them, "This is the only work
God wants from you: Believe in the one he
has sent."
30 They answered, "Show us a miraculous
sign if you want us to believe in you. What
can you do? 31 After all, our ancestors ate
manna while they journeyed through the
wilderness! The Scriptures say, 'Moses gave
them bread from heaven to eat.'*"
32 Jesus said, "I tell you the truth, Moses
didn't give you bread from heaven. My
Father did. And now he offers you the true
bread from heaven. 33 The true bread of God
is the one who comes down from heaven
and gives life to the world."
34 "Sir," they said, "give us that bread every
day."
35 Jesus replied, "I am the bread of life.
Whoever comes to me will never be hungry
again. Whoever believes in me will never be
thirsty. 36 But you haven't believed in me even
though you have seen me. 37 However, those
the Father has given me will come to me, and
I will never reject them. 38 For I have come
down from heaven to do the will of God who
sent me, not to do my own will. 39 And this is
the will of God, that I should not lose even
one of all those he has given me, but that I
should raise them up at the last day. 40 For it
is my Father's will that all who see his Son
and believe in him should have eternal life. I
will raise them up at the last day."
41 Then the people* began to murmur in
disagreement because he had said, "I am the
bread that came down from heaven." 42 They
said, "Isn't this Jesus, the son of Joseph? We
know his father and mother. How can he
say, 'I came down from heaven'?"
43 But Jesus replied, "Stop complaining
about what I said. 44 For no one can come
to me unless the Father who sent me draws
them to me, and at the last day I will raise
them up. 45 As it is written in the Scriptures,*
'They will all be taught by God.' Everyone
who listens to the Father and learns from
him comes to me. 46 (Not that anyone has
ever seen the Father; only I, who was sent
from God, have seen him.)
47 "I tell you the truth, anyone who believes
has eternal life. 48 Yes, I am the bread of life!
49 Your ancestors ate manna in the wilderness, but they all died. 50 Anyone who eats
the bread from heaven, however, will never
die. 51 I am the living bread that came down
from heaven. Anyone who eats this bread
will live forever; and this bread, which I will
offer so the world may live, is my flesh."
52 Then the people began arguing with
each other about what he meant. "How can
this man give us his flesh to eat?" they asked.

6:14a Some manuscripts read *Jesus*. **6:14b** See Deut 18:15, 18; Mal 4:5-6. **6:19** Greek *25 or 30 stadia* [4.6 or 5.5 kilometers]. **6:20** Or *The 'I Am' is here;* Greek reads *I am.* See Exod 3:14. **6:27** "Son of Man" is a title Jesus used for himself. **6:31** Exod 16:4; Ps 78:24. **6:41** Greek *Jewish people;* also in 6:52. **6:45** Greek *in the prophets.* Isa 54:13.

53 So Jesus said again, "I tell you the truth,
unless you eat the flesh of the Son of Man
and drink his blood, you cannot have eternal
life within you. 54 But anyone who eats my
flesh and drinks my blood has eternal life,
and I will raise that person at the last day.
55 For my flesh is true food, and my blood
is true drink. 56 Anyone who eats my flesh
and drinks my blood remains in me, and I
in him. 57 I live because of the living Father
who sent me; in the same way, anyone who
feeds on me will live because of me. 58 I am
the true bread that came down from heaven.
Anyone who eats this bread will not die as
your ancestors did (even though they ate the
manna) but will live forever."
59 He said these things while he was teaching in the synagogue in Capernaum.

Many Disciples Desert Jesus

60 Many of his disciples said, "This is very
hard to understand. How can anyone
accept it?"
61 Jesus was aware that his disciples were
complaining, so he said to them, "Does this
offend you? 62 Then what will you think if you
see the Son of Man ascend to heaven again?
63 The Spirit alone gives eternal life. Human
effort accomplishes nothing. And the very
words I have spoken to you are spirit and
life. 64 But some of you do not believe me."
(For Jesus knew from the beginning which
ones didn't believe, and he knew who would
betray him.) 65 Then he said, "That is why I
said that people can't come to me unless the
Father gives them to me."
66 At this point many of his disciples
turned away and deserted him. 67 Then Jesus
turned to the Twelve and asked, "Are you
also going to leave?"
68 Simon Peter replied, "Lord, to whom
would we go? You have the words that give
eternal life. 69 We believe, and we know you
are the Holy One of God.*"
70 Then Jesus said, "I chose the twelve of
you, but one is a devil." 71 He was speaking
of Judas, son of Simon Iscariot, one of the
Twelve, who would later betray him.

Jesus and His Brothers

7 After this, Jesus traveled around Galilee.
He wanted to stay out of Judea, where
the Jewish leaders were plotting his death.
2 But soon it was time for the Jewish Festival of Shelters, 3 and Jesus' brothers said to
him, "Leave here and go to Judea, where
your followers can see your miracles! 4 You
can't become famous if you hide like this!
If you can do such wonderful things, show
yourself to the world!" 5 For even his brothers didn't believe in him.
6 Jesus replied, "Now is not the right time
for me to go, but you can go anytime. 7 The
world can't hate you, but it does hate me
because I accuse it of doing evil. 8 You go on.
I'm not going* to this festival, because my
time has not yet come." 9 After saying these
things, Jesus remained in Galilee.

Jesus Teaches Openly at the Temple

10 But after his brothers left for the festival,
Jesus also went, though secretly, staying
out of public view. 11 The Jewish leaders
tried to find him at the festival and kept
asking if anyone had seen him. 12 There was
a lot of grumbling about him among the
crowds. Some argued, "He's a good man,"
but others said, "He's nothing but a fraud
who deceives the people." 13 But no one had
the courage to speak favorably about him
in public, for they were afraid of getting in
trouble with the Jewish leaders.
14 Then, midway through the festival,
Jesus went up to the Temple and began to
teach. 15 The people* were surprised when
they heard him. "How does he know so
much when he hasn't been trained?" they
asked.
16 So Jesus told them, "My message is not
my own; it comes from God who sent me.
17 Anyone who wants to do the will of God
will know whether my teaching is from God
or is merely my own. 18 Those who speak for
themselves want glory only for themselves,
but a person who seeks to honor the one
who sent him speaks truth, not lies. 19 Moses
gave you the law, but none of you obeys it!
In fact, you are trying to kill me."
20 The crowd replied, "You're demon possessed! Who's trying to kill you?"
21 Jesus replied, "I did one miracle on the
Sabbath, and you were amazed. 22 But you
work on the Sabbath, too, when you obey
Moses' law of circumcision. (Actually, this
tradition of circumcision began with the patriarchs, long before the law of Moses.) 23 For
if the correct time for circumcising your son
falls on the Sabbath, you go ahead and do it
so as not to break the law of Moses. So why
should you be angry with me for healing a

man on the Sabbath? 24 Look beneath the
surface so you can judge correctly."

Is Jesus the Messiah?

25 Some of the people who lived in Jerusalem
started to ask each other, "Isn't this the man
they are trying to kill? 26 But here he is, speaking in public, and they say nothing to him.
Could our leaders possibly believe that he
is the Messiah? 27 But how could he be? For
we know where this man comes from. When
the Messiah comes, he will simply appear;
no one will know where he comes from."

28 While Jesus was teaching in the Temple,
he called out, "Yes, you know me, and you
know where I come from. But I'm not here
on my own. The one who sent me is true,
and you don't know him. 29 But I know him
because I come from him, and he sent me to
you." 30 Then the leaders tried to arrest him;
but no one laid a hand on him, because his
time* had not yet come.

31 Many among the crowds at the Temple
believed in him. "After all," they said,
"would you expect the Messiah to do more
miraculous signs than this man has done?"

32 When the Pharisees heard that the
crowds were whispering such things, they
and the leading priests sent Temple guards
to arrest Jesus. 33 But Jesus told them,
"I will be with you only a little longer.
Then I will return to the one who sent me.
34 You will search for me but not find me.
And you cannot go where I am going."

35 The Jewish leaders were puzzled by
this statement. "Where is he planning to
go?" they asked. "Is he thinking of leaving
the country and going to the Jews in other
lands?* Maybe he will even teach the
Greeks! 36 What does he mean when he says,
'You will search for me but not find me,' and
'You cannot go where I am going'?"

Jesus Promises Living Water

37 On the last day, the climax of the festival,
Jesus stood and shouted to the crowds,
"Anyone who is thirsty may come to me!
38 Anyone who believes in me may come and
drink! For the Scriptures declare, 'Rivers
of living water will flow from his heart.'"*
39 (When he said "living water," he was
speaking of the Spirit, who would be given
to everyone believing in him. But the Spirit
had not yet been given,* because Jesus had
not yet entered into his glory.)

Division and Unbelief

40 When the crowds heard him say this, some
of them declared, "Surely this man is the
Prophet we've been expecting."* 41 Others
said, "He is the Messiah." Still others said,
"But he can't be! Will the Messiah come
from Galilee? 42 For the Scriptures clearly
state that the Messiah will be born of the
royal line of David, in Bethlehem, the
village where King David was born."* 43 So
the crowd was divided about him. 44 Some
even wanted him arrested, but no one laid
a hand on him.

45 When the Temple guards returned
without having arrested Jesus, the leading
priests and Pharisees demanded, "Why
didn't you bring him in?"

46 "We have never heard anyone speak like
this!" the guards responded.

47 "Have you been led astray, too?" the
Pharisees mocked. 48 "Is there a single one of
us rulers or Pharisees who believes in him?
49 This foolish crowd follows him, but they are
ignorant of the law. God's curse is on them!"

50 Then Nicodemus, the leader who had
met with Jesus earlier, spoke up. 51 "Is it
legal to convict a man before he is given a
hearing?" he asked.

52 They replied, "Are you from Galilee, too?
Search the Scriptures and see for yourself—
no prophet ever comes* from Galilee!"

[*The most ancient Greek manuscripts do not include John 7:53–8:11.*]

53 Then the meeting broke up, and everybody went home.

A Woman Caught in Adultery

8 Jesus returned to the Mount of Olives,
2 but early the next morning he was
back again at the Temple. A crowd soon
gathered, and he sat down and taught
them. 3 As he was speaking, the teachers of
religious law and the Pharisees brought a
woman who had been caught in the act of
adultery. They put her in front of the crowd.

6:69 Other manuscripts read *you are the Christ, the Holy One of God;* still others read *you are the Christ, the Son of God;* and still others read *you are the Christ, the Son of the living God.* **7:8** Some manuscripts read *not yet going.* **7:15** Greek *Jewish people.* **7:30** Greek *his hour.* **7:35** Or *the Jews who live among the Greeks?* **7:37-38** Or *"Let anyone who is thirsty come to me and drink. 38 For the Scriptures declare, 'Rivers of living water will flow from the heart of anyone who believes in me.'"* **7:39** Several early manuscripts read *But as yet there was no Spirit.* Still others read *But as yet there was no Holy Spirit.* **7:40** See Deut 18:15, 18; Mal 4:5-6. **7:42** See Mic 5:2. **7:52** Some manuscripts read *the prophet does not come.*

4"Teacher," they said to Jesus, "this woman was caught in the act of adultery. 5The law of Moses says to stone her. What do you say?"

6They were trying to trap him into saying something they could use against him, but Jesus stooped down and wrote in the dust with his finger. 7They kept demanding an answer, so he stood up again and said, "All right, but let the one who has never sinned throw the first stone!" 8Then he stooped down again and wrote in the dust.

9When the accusers heard this, they slipped away one by one, beginning with the oldest, until only Jesus was left in the middle of the crowd with the woman. 10Then Jesus stood up again and said to the woman, "Where are your accusers? Didn't even one of them condemn you?"

11"No, Lord," she said.

And Jesus said, "Neither do I. Go and sin no more."

Jesus, the Light of the World

12Jesus spoke to the people once more and said, "I am the light of the world. If you follow me, you won't have to walk in darkness, because you will have the light that leads to life."

13The Pharisees replied, "You are making those claims about yourself! Such testimony is not valid."

14Jesus told them, "These claims are valid even though I make them about myself. For I know where I came from and where I am going, but you don't know this about me. 15You judge me by human standards, but I do not judge anyone. 16And if I did, my judgment would be correct in every respect because I am not alone. The Father* who sent me is with me. 17Your own law says that if two people agree about something, their witness is accepted as fact.* 18I am one witness, and my Father who sent me is the other."

19"Where is your father?" they asked.

Jesus answered, "Since you don't know who I am, you don't know who my Father is. If you knew me, you would also know my Father." 20Jesus made these statements while he was teaching in the section of the Temple known as the Treasury. But he was not arrested, because his time* had not yet come.

The Unbelieving People Warned

21Later Jesus said to them again, "I am going away. You will search for me but will die in your sin. You cannot come where I am going."

22The people* asked, "Is he planning to commit suicide? What does he mean, 'You cannot come where I am going'?"

23Jesus continued, "You are from below; I am from above. You belong to this world; I do not. 24That is why I said that you will die in your sins; for unless you believe that I AM who I claim to be,* you will die in your sins."

25"Who are you?" they demanded.

Jesus replied, "The one I have always claimed to be.* 26I have much to say about you and much to condemn, but I won't. For I say only what I have heard from the one who sent me, and he is completely truthful." 27But they still didn't understand that he was talking about his Father.

28So Jesus said, "When you have lifted up the Son of Man on the cross, then you will understand that I AM he.* I do nothing on

The Mount of Olives

The Mount of Olives (John 8:1) was a hill that lay on the east side of the Kidron Valley, overlooking the city of Jerusalem. The garden of Gethsemane, one of Jesus' favorite retreat spots, was located here on its western slope, while the village of Bethany lay just over the hill on the other side. It was from the Mount of Olives that Jesus entered Jerusalem on Palm Sunday (Matthew 21:1-17), and he spent his final night here before his arrest (John 18:1-12). Roman soldiers camped here during their siege of Jerusalem in AD 70, destroying most of the olive trees, according to the Jewish historian Josephus. Today it is the location of an ancient Jewish cemetery, with 150,000 graves on its hillside, for many devout Jews believe this is the spot to which the Messiah will one day come.

▶ *See also **Gethsemane**, page 1111.*

my own but say only what the Father taught me. 29And the one who sent me is with me—he has not deserted me. For I always do what pleases him." 30Then many who heard him say these things believed in him.

Jesus and Abraham

31Jesus said to the people who believed in him, "You are truly my disciples if you remain faithful to my teachings. 32And you will know the truth, and the truth will set you free."

33"But we are descendants of Abraham," they said. "We have never been slaves to anyone. What do you mean, 'You will be set free'?"

34Jesus replied, "I tell you the truth, everyone who sins is a slave of sin. 35A slave is not a permanent member of the family, but a son is part of the family forever. 36So if the Son sets you free, you are truly free. 37Yes, I realize that you are descendants of Abraham. And yet some of you are trying to kill me because there's no room in your hearts for my message. 38I am telling you what I saw when I was with my Father. But you are following the advice of your father."

39"Our father is Abraham!" they declared.

"No," Jesus replied, "for if you were really the children of Abraham, you would follow his example.* 40Instead, you are trying to kill me because I told you the truth, which I heard from God. Abraham never did such a thing. 41No, you are imitating your real father."

They replied, "We aren't illegitimate children! God himself is our true Father."

42Jesus told them, "If God were your Father, you would love me, because I have come to you from God. I am not here on my own, but he sent me. 43Why can't you understand what I am saying? It's because you can't even hear me! 44For you are the children of your father the devil, and you love to do the evil things he does. He was a murderer from the beginning. He has always hated the truth, because there is no truth in him. When he lies, it is consistent with his character; for he is a liar and the father of lies. 45So when I tell the truth, you just naturally don't believe me! 46Which of you can truthfully accuse me of sin? And since I am telling you the truth, why don't you believe me? 47Anyone who belongs to God listens gladly to the words of God. But you don't listen because you don't belong to God."

48The people retorted, "You Samaritan devil! Didn't we say all along that you were possessed by a demon?"

49"No," Jesus said, "I have no demon in me. For I honor my Father—and you dishonor me. 50And though I have no wish to glorify myself, God is going to glorify me. He is the true judge. 51I tell you the truth, anyone who obeys my teaching will never die!"

52The people said, "Now we know you are possessed by a demon. Even Abraham and the prophets died, but you say, 'Anyone who obeys my teaching will never die!' 53Are you greater than our father Abraham? He died, and so did the prophets. Who do you think you are?"

54Jesus answered, "If I want glory for myself, it doesn't count. But it is my Father who will glorify me. You say, 'He is our God,'* 55but you don't even know him. I know him. If I said otherwise, I would be as great a liar as you! But I do know him and obey him. 56Your father Abraham rejoiced as he looked forward to my coming. He saw it and was glad."

57The people said, "You aren't even fifty years old. How can you say you have seen Abraham?*"

58Jesus answered, "I tell you the truth, before Abraham was even born, I AM!*" 59At that point they picked up stones to throw at him. But Jesus was hidden from them and left the Temple.

Jesus Heals a Man Born Blind

9 As Jesus was walking along, he saw a man who had been blind from birth. 2"Rabbi," his disciples asked him, "why was this man born blind? Was it because of his own sins or his parents' sins?"

3"It was not because of his sins or his

8:16 Some manuscripts read *The One.* **8:17** See Deut 19:15. **8:20** Greek *his hour.* **8:22** Greek *Jewish people;* also in 8:31, 48, 52, 57. **8:24** Greek *unless you believe that I am.* See Exod 3:14. **8:25** Or *Why do I speak to you at all?* **8:28** Greek *When you have lifted up the Son of Man, then you will know that I am.* "Son of Man" is a title Jesus used for himself. **8:39** Some manuscripts read *if you are really the children of Abraham, follow his example.* **8:54** Some manuscripts read *You say he is your God.* **8:57** Some manuscripts read *How can you say Abraham has seen you?* **8:58** Or *before Abraham was even born, I have always been alive;* Greek reads *before Abraham was, I am.* See Exod 3:14.

▸ **8:44** *See **False teaching**, page 1443.*

parents' sins," Jesus answered. "This happened so the power of God could be seen in him. 4We must quickly carry out the tasks assigned us by the one who sent us.* The night is coming, and then no one can work. 5But while I am here in the world, I am the light of the world."

6Then he spit on the ground, made mud with the saliva, and spread the mud over the blind man's eyes. 7He told him, "Go wash yourself in the pool of Siloam" (Siloam means "sent"). So the man went and washed and came back seeing!

8His neighbors and others who knew him as a blind beggar asked each other, "Isn't this the man who used to sit and beg?" 9Some said he was, and others said, "No, he just looks like him!"

But the beggar kept saying, "Yes, I am the same one!"

10They asked, "Who healed you? What happened?"

11He told them, "The man they call Jesus made mud and spread it over my eyes and told me, 'Go to the pool of Siloam and wash yourself.' So I went and washed, and now I can see!"

12"Where is he now?" they asked.

"I don't know," he replied.

13Then they took the man who had been blind to the Pharisees, 14because it was on the Sabbath that Jesus had made the mud and healed him. 15The Pharisees asked the man all about it. So he told them, "He put the mud over my eyes, and when I washed it away, I could see!"

16Some of the Pharisees said, "This man Jesus is not from God, for he is working on the Sabbath." Others said, "But how could an ordinary sinner do such miraculous signs?" So there was a deep division of opinion among them.

17Then the Pharisees again questioned the man who had been blind and demanded, "What's your opinion about this man who healed you?"

The man replied, "I think he must be a prophet."

18The Jewish leaders still refused to believe the man had been blind and could now see, so they called in his parents. 19They asked them, "Is this your son? Was he born blind? If so, how can he now see?"

20His parents replied, "We know this is our son and that he was born blind, 21but we don't know how he can see or who healed him. Ask him. He is old enough to speak for himself." 22His parents said this because they were afraid of the Jewish leaders, who had announced that anyone saying Jesus

▸ **9:1-3** *See* ***Suffering: Why do bad things happen to good people?****, page 567.*

Lying

Most of us have acquired the ability to lie. It starts while we are very young, when parents ask us if we did something and we say no, knowing full well that we did. As we get older, we become more skilled in lying, using it not only to get out of trouble but also to gain advantage. Convinced that everyone else does it and that we can't get through life without it, lying becomes normal for us.

What a shock then to hear Jesus saying that the devil is "the father of lies" (John 8:44) and to discover that lying aligns ourselves with him. When we first encounter the devil in Scripture, we find him lying, telling Eve that God's command was unreasonable and his motives suspect (Genesis 3:1-5). Lying is demonic, which is why the Bible condemns it (e.g., Exodus 20:16; Proverbs 6:16-19) and urges us to avoid it and pursue truth instead (e.g., Psalm 34:12-14; Ephesians 4:25).

Lying gradually dulls our conscience. The more we lie, the less it troubles us, and we end up among those whose "consciences are dead" (1 Timothy 4:2). As children of the God of truth, our passion should always be to pursue truth, whatever the cost.

▸ *See also* ***Honesty****, page 707;* ***Hardness of heart****, page 1132.*

was the Messiah would be expelled from
the synagogue. [23]That's why they said, "He
is old enough. Ask him."
[24]So for the second time they called in
the man who had been blind and told him,
"God should get the glory for this,* because
we know this man Jesus is a sinner."
[25]"I don't know whether he is a sinner,"
the man replied. "But I know this: I was
blind, and now I can see!"
[26]"But what did he do?" they asked. "How
did he heal you?"
[27]"Look!" the man exclaimed. "I told you
once. Didn't you listen? Why do you want
to hear it again? Do you want to become his
disciples, too?"
[28]Then they cursed him and said, "You are
his disciple, but we are disciples of Moses!
[29]We know God spoke to Moses, but we don't
even know where this man comes from."
[30]"Why, that's very strange!" the man
replied. "He healed my eyes, and yet you
don't know where he comes from? [31]We know
that God doesn't listen to sinners, but he is
ready to hear those who worship him and do
his will. [32]Ever since the world began, no one
has been able to open the eyes of someone
born blind. [33]If this man were not from God,
he couldn't have done it."
[34]"You were born a total sinner!" they answered.
"Are you trying to teach us?" And
they threw him out of the synagogue.

Spiritual Blindness

[35]When Jesus heard what had happened, he
found the man and asked, "Do you believe
in the Son of Man?*"
[36]The man answered, "Who is he, sir? I
want to believe in him."
[37]"You have seen him," Jesus said, "and
he is speaking to you!"
[38]"Yes, Lord, I believe!" the man said.
And he worshiped Jesus.
[39]Then Jesus told him,* "I entered this
world to render judgment—to give sight to
the blind and to show those who think they
see* that they are blind."
[40]Some Pharisees who were standing
nearby heard him and asked, "Are you
saying we're blind?"
[41]"If you were blind, you wouldn't be
guilty," Jesus replied. "But you remain
guilty because you claim you can see.

The Good Shepherd and His Sheep

10 "I tell you the truth, anyone who
sneaks over the wall of a sheepfold,
rather than going through the gate, must
surely be a thief and a robber! [2]But the one
who enters through the gate is the shepherd
of the sheep. [3]The gatekeeper opens
the gate for him, and the sheep recognize
his voice and come to him. He calls his
own sheep by name and leads them out.
[4]After he has gathered his own flock, he
walks ahead of them, and they follow him
because they know his voice. [5]They won't
follow a stranger; they will run from him
because they don't know his voice."
[6]Those who heard Jesus use this illustration
didn't understand what he meant, [7]so
he explained it to them: "I tell you the truth,

9:4 Other manuscripts read *I must quickly carry out the tasks assigned me by the one who sent me;* still others read *We must quickly carry out the tasks assigned us by the one who sent me.* **9:24** Or *Give glory to God, not to Jesus;* Greek reads *Give glory to God.* **9:35** Some manuscripts read *the Son of God?* "Son of Man" is a title Jesus used for himself. **9:38-39a** Some manuscripts do not include *"Yes, Lord, I believe!" the man said. And he worshiped Jesus. Then Jesus told him.* **9:39b** Greek *those who see.*

The Pool of Siloam

For many centuries the pool to which Jesus sent the blind man to bathe (John 9:7) was thought to have been the pool to the south of the Temple Mount at the end of Hezekiah's tunnel, which brought water from the Gihon Spring. However, recent archaeological excavations have unearthed an even larger pool to the southeast of this traditional site that clearly dates from the time before and during the New Testament. It seems likely that this was the pool to which Jesus sent the man—not because he saw the pool as having healing properties in itself but because it gave the man an opportunity to express his faith in a tangible way.

▶ *See also* ***King Hezekiah****, page 786;* ***John's seven signs****, page 1201.*

I am the gate for the sheep. 8All who came
before me* were thieves and robbers. But the
true sheep did not listen to them. 9Yes, I am
the gate. Those who come in through me will
be saved.* They will come and go freely and
will find good pastures. 10The thief's purpose
is to steal and kill and destroy. My purpose is
to give them a rich and satisfying life.
11"I am the good shepherd. The good shepherd sacrifices his life for the sheep. 12A hired
hand will run when he sees a wolf coming.
He will abandon the sheep because they
don't belong to him and he isn't their shepherd. And so the wolf attacks them and scatters the flock. 13The hired hand runs away
because he's working only for the money
and doesn't really care about the sheep.
14"I am the good shepherd; I know my
own sheep, and they know me, 15just as my
Father knows me and I know the Father. So I
sacrifice my life for the sheep. 16I have other
sheep, too, that are not in this sheepfold.
I must bring them also. They will listen to
my voice, and there will be one flock with
one shepherd.
17"The Father loves me because I sacrifice my life so I may take it back again. 18No
one can take my life from me. I sacrifice it
voluntarily. For I have the authority to lay
it down when I want to and also to take it
up again. For this is what my Father has
commanded."
19When he said these things, the people*
were again divided in their opinions about
him. 20Some said, "He's demon possessed
and out of his mind. Why listen to a man
like that?" 21Others said, "This doesn't
sound like a man possessed by a demon!
Can a demon open the eyes of the blind?"

Jesus Claims to Be the Son of God

22It was now winter, and Jesus was in Jerusalem at the time of Hanukkah, the Festival of Dedication. 23He was in the Temple,
walking through the section known as
Solomon's Colonnade. 24The people surrounded him and asked, "How long are you
going to keep us in suspense? If you are the
Messiah, tell us plainly."
25Jesus replied, "I have already told you,
and you don't believe me. The proof is the
work I do in my Father's name. 26But you
don't believe me because you are not my
sheep. 27My sheep listen to my voice; I know
them, and they follow me. 28I give them
eternal life, and they will never perish. No
one can snatch them away from me, 29for
my Father has given them to me, and he is
more powerful than anyone else.* No one
can snatch them from the Father's hand.
30The Father and I are one."
31Once again the people picked up stones
to kill him. 32Jesus said, "At my Father's direction I have done many good works. For
which one are you going to stone me?"
33They replied, "We're stoning you not for
any good work, but for blasphemy! You, a
mere man, claim to be God."
34Jesus replied, "It is written in your own
Scriptures* that God said to certain leaders
of the people, 'I say, you are gods!'* 35And
you know that the Scriptures cannot be
altered. So if those people who received
God's message were called 'gods,' 36why
do you call it blasphemy when I say, 'I am
the Son of God'? After all, the Father set me
apart and sent me into the world. 37Don't
believe me unless I carry out my Father's
work. 38But if I do his work, believe in the
evidence of the miraculous works I have
done, even if you don't believe me. Then
you will know and understand that the
Father is in me, and I am in the Father."
39Once again they tried to arrest him, but
he got away and left them. 40He went beyond
the Jordan River near the place where John
was first baptizing and stayed there awhile.
41And many followed him. "John didn't
perform miraculous signs," they remarked
to one another, "but everything he said
about this man has come true." 42And many
who were there believed in Jesus.

The Raising of Lazarus

11 A man named Lazarus was sick. He
lived in Bethany with his sisters,
Mary and Martha. 2This is the Mary who
later poured the expensive perfume on the
Lord's feet and wiped them with her hair.*
Her brother, Lazarus, was sick. 3So the two
sisters sent a message to Jesus telling him,
"Lord, your dear friend is very sick."
4But when Jesus heard about it he said,
"Lazarus's sickness will not end in death.

▸ **10:1-18** *See* ***Shepherds****, page 936.*

No, it happened for the glory of God so that
the Son of God will receive glory from this."
5 So although Jesus loved Martha, Mary, and
Lazarus, 6 he stayed where he was for the
next two days. 7 Finally, he said to his disciples, "Let's go back to Judea."
8 But his disciples objected. "Rabbi," they
said, "only a few days ago the people* in
Judea were trying to stone you. Are you
going there again?"
9 Jesus replied, "There are twelve hours of
daylight every day. During the day people
can walk safely. They can see because they
have the light of this world. 10 But at night
there is danger of stumbling because they
have no light." 11 Then he said, "Our friend
Lazarus has fallen asleep, but now I will go
and wake him up."
12 The disciples said, "Lord, if he is sleeping, he will soon get better!" 13 They thought
Jesus meant Lazarus was simply sleeping,
but Jesus meant Lazarus had died.
14 So he told them plainly, "Lazarus is
dead. 15 And for your sakes, I'm glad I wasn't
there, for now you will really believe. Come,
let's go see him."
16 Thomas, nicknamed the Twin,* said to
his fellow disciples, "Let's go, too—and die
with Jesus."
17 When Jesus arrived at Bethany, he was
told that Lazarus had already been in his
grave for four days. 18 Bethany was only
a few miles* down the road from Jerusalem, 19 and many of the people had come
to console Martha and Mary in their loss.
20 When Martha got word that Jesus was
coming, she went to meet him. But Mary
stayed in the house. 21 Martha said to Jesus,
"Lord, if only you had been here, my brother
would not have died. 22 But even now I know
that God will give you whatever you ask."
23 Jesus told her, "Your brother will rise
again."
24 "Yes," Martha said, "he will rise when
everyone else rises, at the last day."
25 Jesus told her, "I am the resurrection
and the life.* Anyone who believes in me
will live, even after dying. 26 Everyone who
lives in me and believes in me will never
ever die. Do you believe this, Martha?"
27 "Yes, Lord," she told him. "I have always
believed you are the Messiah, the Son of God,
the one who has come into the world from

10:8 Some manuscripts do not include *before me.* **10:9** Or *will find safety.* **10:19** Greek *Jewish people;* also in 10:24, 31. **10:29** Other manuscripts read *for what my Father has given me is more powerful than anything;* still others read *for regarding that which my Father has given me, he is greater than all.* **10:34a** Greek *your own law.* **10:34b** Ps 82:6. **11:2** This incident is recorded in chapter 12. **11:8** Greek *Jewish people;* also in 11:19, 31, 33, 36, 45, 54. **11:16** Greek *Thomas, who was called Didymus.* **11:18** Greek *was about 15 stadia* [about 2.8 kilometers]. **11:25** Some manuscripts do not include *and the life.*

▸ **11:16** *See **Thomas**, page 1231.*

Lazarus

Lazarus is best known not for his life, but for his death. Brother of Martha and Mary, Lazarus lived in the tiny village of Bethany on the eastern slopes of the Mount of Olives, two miles from Jerusalem. Jesus visited often (e.g., Luke 10:38-42; John 11:1–12:11), and Lazarus was his "dear friend" (John 11:3). Jesus' initial response to news of his illness seems strange—he stayed where he was, east of the Jordan (10:39-40), for another two days (11:6). By the time he reached Bethany, Lazarus had been dead four days (11:17). But Jesus knew all along of God's plan to bring glory from this (11:4). When Jesus arrived, Martha expressed her disappointment, but also her faith (11:21-22), and Jesus invited her to believe he was "the resurrection and the life" (11:25). Jesus went to the tomb, wept with the mourners, and then after ordering the stone to be removed, prayed and called Lazarus to come out. When Lazarus did just that, the onlookers were so shocked that Jesus needed to tell them to remove the graveclothes (11:40-45). The miracle led some to believe in Jesus (11:45), but it also hardened the religious leaders' belief that Jesus had to go (11:46-53).

▸ *See also **Martha and Mary**, page 1171; **John's seven signs**, page 1201; **Life from death**, page 1219.*

God." 28Then she returned to Mary. She called Mary aside from the mourners and told her, "The Teacher is here and wants to see you." 29So Mary immediately went to him.

30Jesus had stayed outside the village, at the place where Martha met him. 31When the people who were at the house consoling Mary saw her leave so hastily, they assumed she was going to Lazarus's grave to weep. So they followed her there. 32When Mary arrived and saw Jesus, she fell at his feet and said, "Lord, if only you had been here, my brother would not have died."

33When Jesus saw her weeping and saw the other people wailing with her, a deep anger welled up within him,* and he was deeply troubled. 34"Where have you put him?" he asked them.

They told him, "Lord, come and see." 35Then Jesus wept. 36The people who were standing nearby said, "See how much he loved him!" 37But some said, "This man healed a blind man. Couldn't he have kept Lazarus from dying?"

38Jesus was still angry as he arrived at the tomb, a cave with a stone rolled across its entrance. 39"Roll the stone aside," Jesus told them.

But Martha, the dead man's sister, protested, "Lord, he has been dead for four days. The smell will be terrible."

40Jesus responded, "Didn't I tell you that you would see God's glory if you believe?" 41So they rolled the stone aside. Then Jesus looked up to heaven and said, "Father, thank you for hearing me. 42You always hear me, but I said it out loud for the sake of all these people standing here, so that they will believe you sent me." 43Then Jesus shouted, "Lazarus, come out!" 44And the dead man came out, his hands and feet bound in graveclothes, his face wrapped in a headcloth. Jesus told them, "Unwrap him and let him go!"

The Plot to Kill Jesus

45Many of the people who were with Mary believed in Jesus when they saw this happen. 46But some went to the Pharisees and told them what Jesus had done. 47Then the leading priests and Pharisees called the high council* together. "What are we going to do?" they asked each other. "This man certainly performs many miraculous signs. 48If we allow him to go on like this, soon everyone will believe in him. Then the Roman army will come and destroy both our Temple* and our nation."

49Caiaphas, who was high priest at that time,* said, "You don't know what you're talking about! 50You don't realize that it's better for you that one man should die for the people than for the whole nation to be destroyed."

51He did not say this on his own; as high priest at that time he was led to prophesy that Jesus would die for the entire nation. 52And not only for that nation, but to bring together and unite all the children of God scattered around the world.

53So from that time on, the Jewish leaders began to plot Jesus' death. 54As a result, Jesus stopped his public ministry among the people and left Jerusalem. He went to a place near the wilderness, to the village of Ephraim, and stayed there with his disciples.

55It was now almost time for the Jewish Passover celebration, and many people from all over the country arrived in Jerusalem several days early so they could go through the purification ceremony before Passover began. 56They kept looking for Jesus, but as they stood around in the Temple, they said to each other, "What do you think? He won't come for Passover, will he?" 57Meanwhile, the leading priests and Pharisees had publicly ordered that anyone seeing Jesus must report it immediately so they could arrest him.

Jesus Anointed at Bethany

12 Six days before the Passover celebration began, Jesus arrived in Bethany, the home of Lazarus—the man he had raised from the dead. 2A dinner was prepared in Jesus' honor. Martha served, and Lazarus was among those who ate* with him. 3Then Mary took a twelve-ounce jar* of expensive perfume made from essence of nard, and she anointed Jesus' feet with it, wiping his feet with her hair. The house was filled with the fragrance.

4But Judas Iscariot, the disciple who would soon betray him, said, 5"That perfume was

▸ **11:49** *See **Annas and Caiaphas**, page 1227.*

worth a year's wages.* It should have been
sold and the money given to the poor." [6]Not
that he cared for the poor—he was a thief,
and since he was in charge of the disciples'
money, he often stole some for himself.
[7]Jesus replied, "Leave her alone. She did
this in preparation for my burial. [8]You will
always have the poor among you, but you
will not always have me."
[9]When all the people* heard of Jesus'
arrival, they flocked to see him and also to
see Lazarus, the man Jesus had raised from
the dead. [10]Then the leading priests decided
to kill Lazarus, too, [11]for it was because of
him that many of the people had deserted
them* and believed in Jesus.

Jesus' Triumphant Entry

[12]The next day, the news that Jesus was on
the way to Jerusalem swept through the city.
A large crowd of Passover visitors [13]took
palm branches and went down the road to
meet him. They shouted,

"Praise God!*
Blessings on the one who comes in the
name of the LORD!
Hail to the King of Israel!"*

[14]Jesus found a young donkey and rode on
it, fulfilling the prophecy that said:

[15] "Don't be afraid, people of Jerusalem.*
Look, your King is coming,
riding on a donkey's colt."*

[16]His disciples didn't understand at the
time that this was a fulfillment of prophecy. But after Jesus entered into his glory,
they remembered what had happened and
realized that these things had been written
about him.
[17]Many in the crowd had seen Jesus call
Lazarus from the tomb, raising him from the
dead, and they were telling others* about
it. [18]That was the reason so many went out
to meet him—because they had heard about
this miraculous sign. [19]Then the Pharisees
said to each other, "There's nothing we can
do. Look, everyone* has gone after him!"

Jesus Predicts His Death

[20]Some Greeks who had come to Jerusalem
for the Passover celebration [21]paid a visit to
Philip, who was from Bethsaida in Galilee.

11:33 Or *he was angry in his spirit.* **11:47** Greek *the Sanhedrin.* **11:48** Or *our position;* Greek reads *our place.* **11:49** Greek *that year;* also in 11:51. **12:2** Or *who reclined.* **12:3** Greek *took 1 litra* [327 grams]. **12:5** Greek *worth 300 denarii.* A denarius was equivalent to a laborer's full day's wage. **12:9** Greek *Jewish people;* also in 12:11. **12:11** Or *had deserted their traditions;* Greek reads *had deserted.* **12:13a** Greek *Hosanna,* an exclamation of praise adapted from a Hebrew expression that means "save now." **12:13b** Ps 118:25-26; Zeph 3:15. **12:15a** Greek *daughter of Zion.* **12:15b** Zech 9:9. **12:17** Greek *were testifying.* **12:19** Greek *the world.*

Life from death

It was only five days before Jesus would be crucified (John 12:1, 12), and he wanted to prepare his disciples. Although he said, "Now the time has come for the Son of Man to enter into his glory" (12:23), what would happen would look anything but glorifying. Arrested, tried, flogged, mocked, and crucified—what could this have to do with glory? But it revealed a principle of how God's world and Kingdom operate: "Unless a kernel of wheat is planted in the soil and dies, it remains alone. But its death will produce many new kernels" (12:24).

Nature shows us that any plant that clings onto its fruit or seed will not endure, but if that plant yields its seed to "die"—to fall and be buried—a miracle happens: The seed, apparently dead, starts to spring into life as the rain and heat nurture it, and it becomes fruitful. That's how it would be for Jesus. He would die, yet from that death, resurrection life would spring forth, benefiting not just him but us: true glory.

God often calls his children to walk this way of denying ourselves, requiring us to give up some hope or ambition. It is often only when we let these things go and trust and obey God that life can spring forth more wonderfully than we could ever have imagined.

▸ *See also* ***Discipleship and the cross****, page 1095;* ***Counting the cost****, page 1180.*

They said, "Sir, we want to meet Jesus."
[22]Philip told Andrew about it, and they went
together to ask Jesus.
[23]Jesus replied, "Now the time has come
for the Son of Man* to enter into his glory.
[24]I tell you the truth, unless a kernel of
wheat is planted in the soil and dies, it
remains alone. But its death will produce
many new kernels—a plentiful harvest of
new lives. [25]Those who love their life in this
world will lose it. Those who care nothing
for their life in this world will keep it for
eternity. [26]Anyone who wants to serve me
must follow me, because my servants must
be where I am. And the Father will honor
anyone who serves me.
[27]"Now my soul is deeply troubled.
Should I pray, 'Father, save me from this
hour'? But this is the very reason I came!
[28]Father, bring glory to your name."
Then a voice spoke from heaven, saying,
"I have already brought glory to my name,
and I will do so again." [29]When the crowd
heard the voice, some thought it was
thunder, while others declared an angel
had spoken to him.
[30]Then Jesus told them, "The voice was
for your benefit, not mine. [31]The time for
judging this world has come, when Satan,
the ruler of this world, will be cast out.
[32]And when I am lifted up from the earth,
I will draw everyone to myself." [33]He said
this to indicate how he was going to die.
[34]The crowd responded, "We understood
from Scripture* that the Messiah would live
forever. How can you say the Son of Man will
die? Just who is this Son of Man, anyway?"
[35]Jesus replied, "My light will shine for you
just a little longer. Walk in the light while
you can, so the darkness will not overtake
you. Those who walk in the darkness cannot
see where they are going. [36]Put your trust in
the light while there is still time; then you
will become children of the light."
After saying these things, Jesus went
away and was hidden from them.

The Unbelief of the People

[37]But despite all the miraculous signs Jesus
had done, most of the people still did not
believe in him. [38]This is exactly what Isaiah
the prophet had predicted:

"LORD, who has believed our message?
To whom has the LORD revealed his
powerful arm?"*

[39]But the people couldn't believe, for as
Isaiah also said,

[40] "The Lord has blinded their eyes
and hardened their hearts—
so that their eyes cannot see,
and their hearts cannot understand,

Loving others

It is impossible to love Jesus without loving others, Jesus teaches in these chapters (John 13:34-35; 14:15-24; 15:9-17). It made such a profound impression on John that it became a key theme of his first letter. Many Christians love the verse from John, "For this is how God loved the world: He gave his one and only Son . . ." (3:16), but far fewer remember what John says in 1 John 3:16: "We know what real love is because Jesus gave up his life for us. So we also ought to give up our lives for our brothers and sisters."

Loving others, even giving up our lives for them, should be the most natural consequence for followers of Christ. If we don't love others, people may rightly doubt whether we are truly Christians. "For if we don't love people we can see, how can we love God, whom we cannot see?" (1 John 4:20). Paul describes in 1 Corinthians 13:4-7 the kind of self-sacrificial love we are to show. Of course, it is easy to love those whose interests, social background, or people group are like ours. But Jesus loved everyone, especially those whom others rejected. We are called to do the same. When we do, it is a powerful testimony (John 13:35); if we don't, how can we truly be sure we are Jesus' friends (15:13-14)?

▶ *See also **Love your neighbor as yourself**, page 139.*

and they cannot turn to me
and have me heal them."*

[41]Isaiah was referring to Jesus when he said
this, because he saw the future and spoke
of the Messiah's glory. [42]Many people did
believe in him, however, including some
of the Jewish leaders. But they wouldn't
admit it for fear that the Pharisees would
expel them from the synagogue. [43]For they
loved human praise more than the praise
of God.

[44]Jesus shouted to the crowds, "If you
trust me, you are trusting not only me, but
also God who sent me. [45]For when you see
me, you are seeing the one who sent me. [46]I
have come as a light to shine in this dark
world, so that all who put their trust in me
will no longer remain in the dark. [47]I will not
judge those who hear me but don't obey me,
for I have come to save the world and not
to judge it. [48]But all who reject me and my
message will be judged on the day of judgment by the truth I have spoken. [49]I don't
speak on my own authority. The Father who
sent me has commanded me what to say
and how to say it. [50]And I know his commands lead to eternal life; so I say whatever
the Father tells me to say."

Jesus Washes His Disciples' Feet

13 Before the Passover celebration,
Jesus knew that his hour had come
to leave this world and return to his Father.
He had loved his disciples during his ministry on earth, and now he loved them to the
very end.* [2]It was time for supper, and the
devil had already prompted Judas,* son of
Simon Iscariot, to betray Jesus. [3]Jesus knew
that the Father had given him authority over
everything and that he had come from God
and would return to God. [4]So he got up from
the table, took off his robe, wrapped a towel
around his waist, [5]and poured water into a
basin. Then he began to wash the disciples'
feet, drying them with the towel he had
around him.

[6]When Jesus came to Simon Peter, Peter
said to him, "Lord, are you going to wash
my feet?"

[7]Jesus replied, "You don't understand
now what I am doing, but someday you
will."

[8]"No," Peter protested, "you will never
ever wash my feet!"

Jesus replied, "Unless I wash you, you
won't belong to me."

[9]Simon Peter exclaimed, "Then wash my
hands and head as well, Lord, not just my
feet!"

[10]Jesus replied, "A person who has bathed
all over does not need to wash, except for
the feet,* to be entirely clean. And you disciples are clean, but not all of you." [11]For
Jesus knew who would betray him. That is
what he meant when he said, "Not all of you
are clean."

[12]After washing their feet, he put on his
robe again and sat down and asked, "Do
you understand what I was doing? [13]You
call me 'Teacher' and 'Lord,' and you are
right, because that's what I am. [14]And since
I, your Lord and Teacher, have washed your
feet, you ought to wash each other's feet.
[15]I have given you an example to follow. Do
as I have done to you. [16]I tell you the truth,
slaves are not greater than their master. Nor
is the messenger more important than the
one who sends the message. [17]Now that you
know these things, God will bless you for
doing them.

Jesus Predicts His Betrayal

[18]"I am not saying these things to all of you;
I know the ones I have chosen. But this
fulfills the Scripture that says, 'The one
who eats my food has turned against me.'*
[19]I tell you this beforehand, so that when
it happens you will believe that I Am the
Messiah.* [20]I tell you the truth, anyone who
welcomes my messenger is welcoming me,
and anyone who welcomes me is welcoming the Father who sent me."

[21]Now Jesus was deeply troubled,* and he
exclaimed, "I tell you the truth, one of you
will betray me!"

[22]The disciples looked at each other, wondering whom he could mean. [23]The disciple
Jesus loved was sitting next to Jesus at the
table.* [24]Simon Peter motioned to him to
ask, "Who's he talking about?" [25]So that disciple leaned over to Jesus and asked, "Lord,
who is it?"

[26]Jesus responded, "It is the one to whom

12:23 "Son of Man" is a title Jesus used for himself. **12:34** Greek *from the law.* **12:38** Isa 53:1. **12:40** Isa 6:10. **13:1** Or *he showed them the full extent of his love.* **13:2** Or *the devil had already intended for Judas.* **13:10** Some manuscripts do not include *except for the feet.* **13:18** Ps 41:9. **13:19** Or *that the 'I Am' has come;* or *that I am the Lord;* Greek reads *that I am.* See Exod 3:14. **13:21** Greek *was troubled in his spirit.* **13:23** Greek *was reclining on Jesus' bosom.* The "disciple Jesus loved" was probably John.

I give the bread I dip in the bowl." And
when he had dipped it, he gave it to Judas,
son of Simon Iscariot. 27 When Judas had
eaten the bread, Satan entered into him.
Then Jesus told him, "Hurry and do what
you're going to do." 28 None of the others at
the table knew what Jesus meant. 29 Since
Judas was their treasurer, some thought
Jesus was telling him to go and pay for the
food or to give some money to the poor. 30 So
Judas left at once, going out into the night.

Jesus Predicts Peter's Denial

31 As soon as Judas left the room, Jesus said,
"The time has come for the Son of Man* to
enter into his glory, and God will be glorified because of him. 32 And since God receives glory because of the Son,* he will
give his own glory to the Son, and he will
do so at once. 33 Dear children, I will be with
you only a little longer. And as I told the
Jewish leaders, you will search for me, but
you can't come where I am going. 34 So now
I am giving you a new commandment: Love
each other. Just as I have loved you, you
should love each other. 35 Your love for one
another will prove to the world that you are
my disciples."
36 Simon Peter asked, "Lord, where are
you going?"
And Jesus replied, "You can't go with me
now, but you will follow me later."
37 "But why can't I come now, Lord?" he
asked. "I'm ready to die for you."
38 Jesus answered, "Die for me? I tell you
the truth, Peter—before the rooster crows
tomorrow morning, you will deny three
times that you even know me.

Jesus, the Way to the Father

14 "Don't let your hearts be troubled.
Trust in God, and trust also in me.
2 There is more than enough room in my
Father's home.* If this were not so, would
I have told you that I am going to prepare a
place for you?* 3 When everything is ready,
I will come and get you, so that you will
always be with me where I am. 4 And you
know the way to where I am going."
5 "No, we don't know, Lord," Thomas said.
"We have no idea where you are going, so
how can we know the way?"
6 Jesus told him, "I am the way, the truth,
and the life. No one can come to the Father
except through me. 7 If you had really known
me, you would know who my Father is.*
From now on, you do know him and have
seen him!"
8 Philip said, "Lord, show us the Father,
and we will be satisfied."

▸ **14:6** *See* ***Jesus: the only way to God,*** *page 1241.*

The help of the Holy Spirit

As part of preparing his disciples for what was coming, Jesus wanted them to know that he wasn't about to abandon them—neither after his death nor, later, after his ascension. "I will not abandon you as orphans—I will come to you" (John 14:18). The context makes clear he was talking about the Holy Spirit.

All that he had been to the disciples while he was with them, the Spirit would be when he was no longer there. This comes out in Jesus' promise, "I will ask the Father, and he will give you *another* Advocate, who will never leave you" (14:16). There are two Greek words for "another"—one meaning "another of a different sort" and the other "another of the same sort." It is the latter that is used here. Jesus was saying that the Holy Spirit would be exactly the same sort of helper, encourager, and guide that he himself had been. The Spirit would be their "advocate" or "counselor." For us, a counselor means an adviser, such as a therapist or a lawyer. But the Greek word means "someone called alongside to help." That's what the Holy Spirit would be and do. If we are filled with the Holy Spirit, his help is always there, whatever the situation. We simply need to ask.

▸ *See also* ***The Christian's relationship with the Holy Spirit,*** *page 1350.*

9 Jesus replied, "Have I been with you all this time, Philip, and yet you still don't know who I am? Anyone who has seen me has seen the Father! So why are you asking me to show him to you? 10 Don't you believe that I am in the Father and the Father is in me? The words I speak are not my own, but my Father who lives in me does his work through me. 11 Just believe that I am in the Father and the Father is in me. Or at least believe because of the work you have seen me do.

12 "I tell you the truth, anyone who believes in me will do the same works I have done, and even greater works, because I am going to be with the Father. 13 You can ask for anything in my name, and I will do it, so that the Son can bring glory to the Father. 14 Yes, ask me for anything in my name, and I will do it!

Jesus Promises the Holy Spirit

15 "If you love me, obey* my commandments. 16 And I will ask the Father, and he will give you another Advocate,* who will never leave you. 17 He is the Holy Spirit, who leads into all truth. The world cannot receive him, because it isn't looking for him and doesn't recognize him. But you know him, because he lives with you now and later will be in you.* 18 No, I will not abandon you as orphans—I will come to you. 19 Soon the world will no longer see me, but you will see me. Since I live, you also will live. 20 When I am raised to life again, you will know that I am in my Father, and you are in me, and I am in you. 21 Those who accept my commandments and obey them are the ones who love me. And because they love me, my Father will love them. And I will love them and reveal myself to each of them."

22 Judas (not Judas Iscariot, but the other disciple with that name) said to him, "Lord, why are you going to reveal yourself only to us and not to the world at large?"

23 Jesus replied, "All who love me will do what I say. My Father will love them, and we will come and make our home with each of them. 24 Anyone who doesn't love me will not obey me. And remember, my words are not my own. What I am telling you is from the Father who sent me. 25 I am telling you these things now while I am still with you. 26 But when the Father sends the Advocate as my representative—that is, the Holy Spirit—he will teach you everything and will remind you of everything I have told you.

27 "I am leaving you with a gift—peace of mind and heart. And the peace I give is a gift the world cannot give. So don't be troubled or afraid. 28 Remember what I told you: I am going away, but I will come back to you again. If you really loved me, you would be happy that I am going to the Father, who is greater than I am. 29 I have told you these things before they happen so that when they do happen, you will believe.

30 "I don't have much more time to talk to you, because the ruler of this world approaches. He has no power over me, 31 but I will do what the Father requires of me, so that the world will know that I love the Father. Come, let's be going.

Jesus, the True Vine

15 "I am the true grapevine, and my Father is the gardener. 2 He cuts off every branch of mine that doesn't produce fruit, and he prunes the branches that do bear fruit so they will produce even more. 3 You have already been pruned and purified by the message I have given you. 4 Remain in me, and I will remain in you. For a branch cannot produce fruit if it is severed from the vine, and you cannot be fruitful unless you remain in me.

5 "Yes, I am the vine; you are the branches. Those who remain in me, and I in them, will produce much fruit. For apart from me you can do nothing. 6 Anyone who does not remain in me is thrown away like a useless branch and withers. Such branches are gathered into a pile to be burned. 7 But if you remain in me and my words remain in you, you may ask for anything you want, and it will be granted! 8 When you produce much fruit, you are my true disciples. This brings great glory to my Father.

9 "I have loved you even as the Father has loved me. Remain in my love. 10 When you obey my commandments, you remain in my love, just as I obey my Father's commandments and remain in his love. 11 I have told you these things so that you will be filled

13:31 "Son of Man" is a title Jesus used for himself. **13:32** Several early manuscripts do not include *And since God receives glory because of the Son.* **14:2a** Or *There are many rooms in my Father's house.* **14:2b** Or *If this were not so, I would have told you that I am going to prepare a place for you.* Some manuscripts read *If this were not so, I would have told you. I am going to prepare a place for you.* **14:7** Some manuscripts read *If you have really known me, you will know who my Father is.* **14:15** Other manuscripts read *you will obey;* still others read *you should obey.* **14:16** Or *Comforter,* or *Encourager,* or *Counselor.* Greek reads *Paraclete;* also in 14:26. **14:17** Some manuscripts read *and is in you.*

with my joy. Yes, your joy will overflow!
12This is my commandment: Love each other
in the same way I have loved you. 13There is
no greater love than to lay down one's life for
one's friends. 14You are my friends if you do
what I command. 15I no longer call you slaves,
because a master doesn't confide in his
slaves. Now you are my friends, since I have
told you everything the Father told me. 16You
didn't choose me. I chose you. I appointed
you to go and produce lasting fruit, so that
the Father will give you whatever you ask for,
using my name. 17This is my command: Love
each other.

The World's Hatred

18"If the world hates you, remember that
it hated me first. 19The world would love
you as one of its own if you belonged to it,
but you are no longer part of the world. I
chose you to come out of the world, so it
hates you. 20Do you remember what I told
you? 'A slave is not greater than the master.'
Since they persecuted me, naturally they
will persecute you. And if they had listened
to me, they would listen to you. 21They will
do all this to you because of me, for they
have rejected the one who sent me. 22They
would not be guilty if I had not come and
spoken to them. But now they have no
excuse for their sin. 23Anyone who hates
me also hates my Father. 24If I hadn't done
such miraculous signs among them that no
one else could do, they would not be guilty.
But as it is, they have seen everything I did,
yet they still hate me and my Father. 25This
fulfills what is written in their Scriptures*:
'They hated me without cause.'

26"But I will send you the Advocate*—the
Spirit of truth. He will come to you from the
Father and will testify all about me. 27And
you must also testify about me because you
have been with me from the beginning of
my ministry.

16 "I have told you these things so that
you won't abandon your faith. 2For
you will be expelled from the synagogues,
and the time is coming when those who kill
you will think they are doing a holy service
for God. 3This is because they have never
known the Father or me. 4Yes, I'm telling
you these things now, so that when they
happen, you will remember my warning. I
didn't tell you earlier because I was going
to be with you for a while longer.

The Work of the Holy Spirit

5"But now I am going away to the one who
sent me, and not one of you is asking where
I am going. 6Instead, you grieve because of
what I've told you. 7But in fact, it is best
for you that I go away, because if I don't,
the Advocate* won't come. If I do go away,
then I will send him to you. 8And when
he comes, he will convict the world of its
sin, and of God's righteousness, and of the
coming judgment. 9The world's sin is that it
refuses to believe in me. 10Righteousness is
available because I go to the Father, and you

John

While Jesus called all his disciples "friends" (John 15:15), John was one of three with whom Jesus had a particularly close friendship and whom he often took aside (e.g., Matthew 17:1; 26:37; Mark 5:37). He gave both him and his brother James, who had both been fishermen (Luke 5:1-11), the nickname "Sons of Thunder" (Mark 3:17), probably reflecting their fiery character (e.g., Luke 9:52-55). But the process of discipleship transformed John into "the disciple Jesus loved" (John 13:23), and it was into his hands that Jesus entrusted his mother, Mary, when he was dying on the cross (19:25-27). John witnessed some amazing events, like the raising of Jairus's daughter (Mark 5:37-43) and Jesus' transfiguration (Mark 9:2-13), and he was the first apostle to see Jesus' empty tomb (John 20:1-5). He became a key leader in the Jerusalem church (Acts 1–4; 8:14; Galatians 2:9) and later, according to tradition, in Ephesus. He wrote the fourth Gospel, the letters that bear his name and, in his old age, the book of Revelation when Jesus appeared to him one last time.

will see me no more. 11 Judgment will come
because the ruler of this world has already
been judged.

12 "There is so much more I want to tell
you, but you can't bear it now. 13 When the
Spirit of truth comes, he will guide you into
all truth. He will not speak on his own but
will tell you what he has heard. He will tell
you about the future. 14 He will bring me
glory by telling you whatever he receives
from me. 15 All that belongs to the Father is
mine; this is why I said, 'The Spirit will tell
you whatever he receives from me.'

Sadness Will Be Turned to Joy

16 "In a little while you won't see me
anymore. But a little while after that, you
will see me again."

17 Some of the disciples asked each other,
"What does he mean when he says, 'In a
little while you won't see me, but then you
will see me,' and 'I am going to the Father'?
18 And what does he mean by 'a little while'?
We don't understand."

19 Jesus realized they wanted to ask him
about it, so he said, "Are you asking yourselves what I meant? I said in a little while
you won't see me, but a little while after
that you will see me again. 20 I tell you the
truth, you will weep and mourn over what
is going to happen to me, but the world will
rejoice. You will grieve, but your grief will
suddenly turn to wonderful joy. 21 It will be like
a woman suffering the pains of labor. When
her child is born, her anguish gives way to
joy because she has brought a new baby into
the world. 22 So you have sorrow now, but I
will see you again; then you will rejoice, and
no one can rob you of that joy. 23 At that time
you won't need to ask me for anything. I tell
you the truth, you will ask the Father directly,
and he will grant your request because you
use my name. 24 You haven't done this before.
Ask, using my name, and you will receive,
and you will have abundant joy.

25 "I have spoken of these matters in
figures of speech, but soon I will stop speaking figuratively and will tell you plainly all
about the Father. 26 Then you will ask in my
name. I'm not saying I will ask the Father on
your behalf, 27 for the Father himself loves
you dearly because you love me and believe
that I came from God.* 28 Yes, I came from
the Father into the world, and now I will
leave the world and return to the Father."

29 Then his disciples said, "At last you are
speaking plainly and not figuratively. 30 Now
we understand that you know everything,
and there's no need to question you. From
this we believe that you came from God."

31 Jesus asked, "Do you finally believe?
32 But the time is coming—indeed it's here
now—when you will be scattered, each one
going his own way, leaving me alone. Yet
I am not alone because the Father is with
me. 33 I have told you all this so that you
may have peace in me. Here on earth you
will have many trials and sorrows. But take
heart, because I have overcome the world."

The Prayer of Jesus

17 After saying all these things, Jesus
looked up to heaven and said, "Father,
the hour has come. Glorify your Son so he can
give glory back to you. 2 For you have given
him authority over everyone. He gives eternal
life to each one you have given him. 3 And this
is the way to have eternal life—to know you,
the only true God, and Jesus Christ, the one
you sent to earth. 4 I brought glory to you here
on earth by completing the work you gave me
to do. 5 Now, Father, bring me into the glory
we shared before the world began.

6 "I have revealed you* to the ones you
gave me from this world. They were always
yours. You gave them to me, and they have
kept your word. 7 Now they know that everything I have is a gift from you, 8 for I have
passed on to them the message you gave
me. They accepted it and know that I came
from you, and they believe you sent me.

9 "My prayer is not for the world, but for
those you have given me, because they
belong to you. 10 All who are mine belong to
you, and you have given them to me, so they
bring me glory. 11 Now I am departing from
the world; they are staying in this world, but
I am coming to you. Holy Father, you have
given me your name;* now protect them by
the power of your name so that they will be
united just as we are. 12 During my time here,
I protected them by the power of the name
you gave me.* I guarded them so that not
one was lost, except the one headed for destruction, as the Scriptures foretold.

15:25 Greek *in their law.* Pss 35:19; 69:4. **15:26** Or *Comforter,* or *Encourager,* or *Counselor.* Greek reads *Paraclete.* **16:7** Or *Comforter,* or *Encourager,* or *Counselor.* Greek reads *Paraclete.* **16:27** Some manuscripts read *from the Father.* **17:6** Greek *have revealed your name;* also in 17:26. **17:11** Some manuscripts read *you have given me these [disciples].* **17:12** Some manuscripts read *I protected those you gave me, by the power of your name.*

13“Now I am coming to you. I told them
many things while I was with them in this
world so they would be filled with my joy.
14I have given them your word. And the
world hates them because they do not
belong to the world, just as I do not belong
to the world. 15I'm not asking you to take
them out of the world, but to keep them
safe from the evil one. 16They do not belong
to this world any more than I do. 17Make
them holy by your truth; teach them your
word, which is truth. 18Just as you sent me
into the world, I am sending them into the
world. 19And I give myself as a holy sacrifice for them so they can be made holy by
your truth.

20“I am praying not only for these disciples but also for all who will ever believe
in me through their message. 21I pray that
they will all be one, just as you and I are
one—as you are in me, Father, and I am in
you. And may they be in us so that the world
will believe you sent me.

22“I have given them the glory you gave
me, so they may be one as we are one. 23I am
in them and you are in me. May they experience such perfect unity that the world will
know that you sent me and that you love
them as much as you love me. 24Father, I
want these whom you have given me to be
with me where I am. Then they can see all
the glory you gave me because you loved me
even before the world began!

25“O righteous Father, the world doesn't
know you, but I do; and these disciples
know you sent me. 26I have revealed you
to them, and I will continue to do so. Then
your love for me will be in them, and I will
be in them.”

Jesus Is Betrayed and Arrested

18 After saying these things, Jesus
crossed the Kidron Valley with his
disciples and entered a grove of olive trees.
2Judas, the betrayer, knew this place, because
Jesus had often gone there with his disciples.
3The leading priests and Pharisees had given
Judas a contingent of Roman soldiers and
Temple guards to accompany him. Now with
blazing torches, lanterns, and weapons, they
arrived at the olive grove.

4Jesus fully realized all that was going to
happen to him, so he stepped forward to
meet them. “Who are you looking for?” he
asked.

5“Jesus the Nazarene,”* they replied.

“I AM he,”* Jesus said. (Judas, who betrayed him, was standing with them.) 6As
Jesus said “I AM he,” they all drew back
and fell to the ground! 7Once more he asked
them, “Who are you looking for?”

And again they replied, “Jesus the
Nazarene.”

8“I told you that I AM he,” Jesus said.
“And since I am the one you want, let these
others go.” 9He did this to fulfill his own

▸ **17:6-26** *See* ***Prayer as intercession****, page 922.* **18:2** *See* ***Why did Judas betray Jesus?****, page 1191.*

The world

Jesus uses the word “world” (*kosmos* in Greek) repeatedly in his prayer in John 17. It is a word that is used in the New Testament in three distinct ways: first, in the sense of “creation,” the world that God made (e.g., John 17:5; Acts 17:24); second, in the sense of “the people of the world” (e.g., John 3:16; 17:18); and third, in the sense of “the world system that lives life without reference to God” (e.g., John 17:14; 1 John 2:15). Jesus does not want us to leave “the world” in the first two senses, but he does want us to leave “the world” in the third sense. It is in this last sense that John tells us, “Do not love this world nor the things it offers you, for when you love the world, you do not have the love of the Father in you” (1 John 2:15) and that James says, “Don't you realize that friendship with the world makes you an enemy of God?” (James 4:4). Jesus wants us in “the world” and reaching “the world,” but he does not want “the world” in us, which is why he prays for his disciples to be protected from it.

statement: "I did not lose a single one of
those you have given me."*
10 Then Simon Peter drew a sword and
slashed off the right ear of Malchus, the
high priest's slave. 11 But Jesus said to Peter,
"Put your sword back into its sheath. Shall
I not drink from the cup of suffering the
Father has given me?"

Jesus at the High Priest's House

12 So the soldiers, their commanding officer,
and the Temple guards arrested Jesus and
tied him up. 13 First they took him to Annas,
since he was the father-in-law of Caiaphas,
the high priest at that time.* 14 Caiaphas
was the one who had told the other Jewish
leaders, "It's better that one man should die
for the people."

Peter's First Denial

15 Simon Peter followed Jesus, as did another
of the disciples. That other disciple was acquainted with the high priest, so he was
allowed to enter the high priest's courtyard
with Jesus. 16 Peter had to stay outside the
gate. Then the disciple who knew the high
priest spoke to the woman watching at the
gate, and she let Peter in. 17 The woman
asked Peter, "You're not one of that man's
disciples, are you?"

"No," he said, "I am not."

18 Because it was cold, the household servants and the guards had made a charcoal
fire. They stood around it, warming themselves, and Peter stood with them, warming
himself.

The High Priest Questions Jesus

19 Inside, the high priest began asking Jesus
about his followers and what he had been
teaching them. 20 Jesus replied, "Everyone
knows what I teach. I have preached regularly
in the synagogues and the Temple, where the
people* gather. I have not spoken in secret.
21 Why are you asking me this question? Ask
those who heard me. They know what I said."
22 Then one of the Temple guards standing nearby slapped Jesus across the face. "Is
that the way to answer the high priest?" he
demanded.

23 Jesus replied, "If I said anything wrong,
you must prove it. But if I'm speaking the
truth, why are you beating me?"

24 Then Annas bound Jesus and sent him
to Caiaphas, the high priest.

Peter's Second and Third Denials

25 Meanwhile, as Simon Peter was standing
by the fire warming himself, they asked him
again, "You're not one of his disciples, are
you?"

He denied it, saying, "No, I am not."

26 But one of the household slaves of the

18:5a Or *Jesus of Nazareth;* also in 18:7. **18:5b** Or *"The 'I AM' is here"*; or *"I am the LORD"*; Greek reads *I am;* also in 18:6, 8. See Exod 3:14. **18:9** See John 6:39 and 17:12. **18:13** Greek *that year.* **18:20** Greek *Jewish people;* also in 18:38.

Annas and Caiaphas

Eager to give Jesus' trial a semblance of legality, his accusers had the charges against him confirmed by two high priests. Annas was high priest from AD 6–15 but was deposed by Rome and replaced by a succession of his sons, as well as his son-in-law Caiaphas (AD 18–36); but many Jews still saw Annas as the rightful high priest, so Luke rightly speaks of both Annas and Caiaphas as high priests (Luke 3:2; Acts 4:6). Therefore, holding trials before both Annas (John 18:13, 19-23) and Caiaphas (John 18:24; Matthew 26:57-67) was making things doubly sure. They were Sadducees, members of one of the three wealthiest priestly families who lived in the affluent upper city of Jerusalem. Their interrogations focused on Jesus' teaching (John 18:19), and they ultimately charged him with blasphemy (Matthew 26:59-67), though they changed the charge to treason (claiming to be king of the Jews when only Caesar was king) when they brought him before Pilate (Luke 23:1-5). Ironically, Caiaphas had unwittingly prophesied the outcome of Jesus' death (John 11:49-52).

▸ *See also **Sadducees**, page 1104.*

high priest, a relative of the man whose ear
Peter had cut off, asked, "Didn't I see you
out there in the olive grove with Jesus?"
27 Again Peter denied it. And immediately a
rooster crowed.

Jesus' Trial before Pilate

28 Jesus' trial before Caiaphas ended in the
early hours of the morning. Then he was
taken to the headquarters of the Roman
governor.* His accusers didn't go inside
because it would defile them, and they
wouldn't be allowed to celebrate the Passover. 29 So Pilate, the governor, went out
to them and asked, "What is your charge
against this man?"

30 "We wouldn't have handed him over to
you if he weren't a criminal!" they retorted.

31 "Then take him away and judge him by
your own law," Pilate told them.

"Only the Romans are permitted to
execute someone," the Jewish leaders
replied. 32 (This fulfilled Jesus' prediction
about the way he would die.*)

33 Then Pilate went back into his headquarters and called for Jesus to be brought
to him. "Are you the king of the Jews?" he
asked him.

34 Jesus replied, "Is this your own question, or did others tell you about me?"

35 "Am I a Jew?" Pilate retorted. "Your own
people and their leading priests brought you
to me for trial. Why? What have you done?"

36 Jesus answered, "My Kingdom is not an
earthly kingdom. If it were, my followers
would fight to keep me from being handed
over to the Jewish leaders. But my Kingdom
is not of this world."

37 Pilate said, "So you are a king?"

Jesus responded, "You say I am a king.
Actually, I was born and came into the
world to testify to the truth. All who love
the truth recognize that what I say is true."

38 "What is truth?" Pilate asked. Then he
went out again to the people and told them,
"He is not guilty of any crime. 39 But you
have a custom of asking me to release one
prisoner each year at Passover. Would you
like me to release this 'King of the Jews'?"

40 But they shouted back, "No! Not this
man. We want Barabbas!" (Barabbas was a
revolutionary.)

Jesus Sentenced to Death

19 Then Pilate had Jesus flogged with a
lead-tipped whip. 2 The soldiers wove
a crown of thorns and put it on his head,
and they put a purple robe on him. 3 "Hail!
King of the Jews!" they mocked, as they
slapped him across the face.

4 Pilate went outside again and said to the
people, "I am going to bring him out to you
now, but understand clearly that I find him
not guilty." 5 Then Jesus came out wearing
the crown of thorns and the purple robe.
And Pilate said, "Look, here is the man!"

6 When they saw him, the leading priests
and Temple guards began shouting,
"Crucify him! Crucify him!"

"Take him yourselves and crucify him,"
Pilate said. "I find him not guilty."

7 The Jewish leaders replied, "By our law
he ought to die because he called himself
the Son of God."

8 When Pilate heard this, he was more
frightened than ever. 9 He took Jesus back
into the headquarters* again and asked him,
"Where are you from?" But Jesus gave no
answer. 10 "Why don't you talk to me?" Pilate
demanded. "Don't you realize that I have the
power to release you or crucify you?"

11 Then Jesus said, "You would have no
power over me at all unless it were given to
you from above. So the one who handed me
over to you has the greater sin."

12 Then Pilate tried to release him, but the
Jewish leaders shouted, "If you release this
man, you are no 'friend of Caesar.'* Anyone
who declares himself a king is a rebel
against Caesar."

13 When they said this, Pilate brought
Jesus out to them again. Then Pilate sat
down on the judgment seat on the platform that is called the Stone Pavement (in
Hebrew, *Gabbatha*). 14 It was now about
noon on the day of preparation for the Passover. And Pilate said to the people,* "Look,
here is your king!"

15 "Away with him," they yelled. "Away
with him! Crucify him!"

"What? Crucify your king?" Pilate asked.

"We have no king but Caesar," the leading
priests shouted back.

16 Then Pilate turned Jesus over to them to
be crucified.

▸ **18:29** *See* ***Pilate****, page 1145.*

The Crucifixion
So they took Jesus away. [17]Carrying the cross by himself, he went to the place called Place of the Skull (in Hebrew, *Golgotha*). [18]There they nailed him to the cross. Two others were crucified with him, one on either side, with Jesus between them. [19]And Pilate posted a sign on the cross that read, "Jesus of Nazareth,* the King of the Jews." [20]The place where Jesus was crucified was near the city, and the sign was written in Hebrew, Latin, and Greek, so that many people could read it.

[21]Then the leading priests objected and said to Pilate, "Change it from 'The King of the Jews' to 'He said, I am King of the Jews.'"

[22]Pilate replied, "No, what I have written, I have written."

[23]When the soldiers had crucified Jesus,

18:28 Greek *to the Praetorium;* also in 18:33. **18:32** See John 12:32-33. **19:9** Greek *the Praetorium.* **19:12** "Friend of Caesar" is a technical term that refers to an ally of the emperor. **19:14** Greek *Jewish people;* also in 19:20. **19:19** Or *Jesus the Nazarene.*

▸ **19:17** *See **The death of Jesus**, page 1114; **Golgotha, Place of the Skull**, page 1193.*

Jesus' seven sayings from the cross

The Gospels record seven different sayings spoken by Jesus on the cross. Often used as a focus for reflection on Good Friday, they are traditionally seen as having been spoken in the following order:

	Traditional title	Saying	Significance
1	Words of forgiveness	"Father, forgive them, for they don't know what they are doing." (Luke 23:34)	Jesus fulfills his own teaching about loving one's enemies and shows that the cross is the basis on which divine forgiveness can be given.
2	Words of salvation	"I assure you, today you will be with me in paradise." (Luke 23:43)	Jesus shows that it is never too late to ask to be saved and find the assurance of eternal life.
3	Words of relationship	"Dear woman, here is your son. . . . Here is your mother." (John 19:26-27)	Jesus, still thinking of others even in his agony, remembers the fifth commandment—honor your parents.
4	Words of abandonment	"My God, my God, why have you abandoned me?" (Matthew 27:46)	Quoting from Psalm 22, Jesus expresses his sense of complete desertion, even by his Father (because of the sin he was bearing).
5	Words of distress	"I am thirsty." (John 19:28)	His body weakened by pain, blood loss, and dehydration, Jesus shows his true humanity.
6	Words of reunion	"Father, I entrust my spirit into your hands!" (Luke 23:46)	Quoting from Psalm 31:5, Jesus entrusts himself to the Father, for what follows now lies entirely in his hands.
7	Words of triumph	"It is finished!" (John 19:30)	Jesus proclaims victory at the moment of apparent defeat, declaring, "It is all accomplished!" or even "It is all paid for!"

they divided his clothes among the four of
them. They also took his robe, but it was
seamless, woven in one piece from top to
bottom. [24]So they said, "Rather than tearing
it apart, let's throw dice* for it." This fulfilled the Scripture that says, "They divided
my garments among themselves and threw
dice for my clothing."* So that is what they
did.

[25]Standing near the cross were Jesus'
mother, and his mother's sister, Mary (the
wife of Clopas), and Mary Magdalene.
[26]When Jesus saw his mother standing there
beside the disciple he loved, he said to her,
"Dear woman, here is your son." [27]And he
said to this disciple, "Here is your mother."
And from then on this disciple took her into
his home.

The Death of Jesus

[28]Jesus knew that his mission was now finished, and to fulfill Scripture he said, "I am
thirsty."* [29]A jar of sour wine was sitting
there, so they soaked a sponge in it, put it
on a hyssop branch, and held it up to his
lips. [30]When Jesus had tasted it, he said, "It
is finished!" Then he bowed his head and
gave up his spirit.

[31]It was the day of preparation, and the
Jewish leaders didn't want the bodies
hanging there the next day, which was
the Sabbath (and a very special Sabbath,
because it was Passover week). So they
asked Pilate to hasten their deaths by
ordering that their legs be broken. Then
their bodies could be taken down. [32]So the
soldiers came and broke the legs of the two
men crucified with Jesus. [33]But when they
came to Jesus, they saw that he was already
dead, so they didn't break his legs. [34]One
of the soldiers, however, pierced his side
with a spear, and immediately blood and
water flowed out. [35](This report is from an
eyewitness giving an accurate account. He
speaks the truth so that you also may continue to believe.*) [36]These things happened
in fulfillment of the Scriptures that say, "Not
one of his bones will be broken,"* [37]and
"They will look on the one they pierced."*

The Burial of Jesus

[38]Afterward Joseph of Arimathea, who had
been a secret disciple of Jesus (because he
feared the Jewish leaders), asked Pilate for
permission to take down Jesus' body. When
Pilate gave permission, Joseph came and
took the body away. [39]With him came Nicodemus, the man who had come to Jesus at night.
He brought about seventy-five pounds* of
perfumed ointment made from myrrh and
aloes. [40]Following Jewish burial custom,
they wrapped Jesus' body with the spices
in long sheets of linen cloth. [41]The place of
crucifixion was near a garden, where there
was a new tomb, never used before. [42]And
so, because it was the day of preparation for
the Jewish Passover* and since the tomb was
close at hand, they laid Jesus there.

▸ **19:25** *See **Mary, the mother of Jesus**, page 1153.*

Nicodemus

People rarely respond to the gospel the first time they hear it, especially in our culture today; but we never know what happens to the seed we sow, as the story of Nicodemus shows. Jesus' challenge to Nicodemus that religion wasn't enough to save him and that he needed to be "born again" had ended with Nicodemus seemingly confused (John 3:1-21). But the message slowly got through to his heart. By chapter 7 we find him arguing against condemning Jesus without a fair trial (7:50-51), and here at the end of Jesus' life, we find him joining Joseph of Arimathea, "a secret disciple" (19:38), in giving Jesus a decent burial. Nicodemus contributed seventy-five pounds of perfumed spices for anointing the body—an amount that would have been fabulously expensive, reflecting that, even if he was not yet a believer in Jesus, he was surely well on the way.

▸ *See also **The new birth**, page 1203.*

The Resurrection

20 Early on Sunday morning,* while
it was still dark, Mary Magdalene
came to the tomb and found that the stone
had been rolled away from the entrance.
[2]She ran and found Simon Peter and the
other disciple, the one whom Jesus loved.
She said, "They have taken the Lord's body
out of the tomb, and we don't know where
they have put him!"
[3]Peter and the other disciple started out
for the tomb. [4]They were both running, but
the other disciple outran Peter and reached
the tomb first. [5]He stooped and looked in
and saw the linen wrappings lying there, but
he didn't go in. [6]Then Simon Peter arrived
and went inside. He also noticed the linen
wrappings lying there, [7]while the cloth that
had covered Jesus' head was folded up and
lying apart from the other wrappings. [8]Then
the disciple who had reached the tomb first
also went in, and he saw and believed—[9]for
until then they still hadn't understood the
Scriptures that said Jesus must rise from the
dead. [10]Then they went home.

Jesus Appears to Mary Magdalene

[11]Mary was standing outside the tomb
crying, and as she wept, she stooped and
looked in. [12]She saw two white-robed angels,
one sitting at the head and the other at the
foot of the place where the body of Jesus
had been lying. [13]"Dear woman, why are you
crying?" the angels asked her.
"Because they have taken away my Lord,"
she replied, "and I don't know where they
have put him."
[14]She turned to leave and saw someone
standing there. It was Jesus, but she didn't
recognize him. [15]"Dear woman, why are
you crying?" Jesus asked her. "Who are you
looking for?"
She thought he was the gardener. "Sir,"
she said, "if you have taken him away, tell
me where you have put him, and I will go
and get him."
[16]"Mary!" Jesus said.
She turned to him and cried out,
"Rabboni!" (which is Hebrew for "Teacher").
[17]"Don't cling to me," Jesus said, "for I
haven't yet ascended to the Father. But go
find my brothers and tell them, 'I am ascending to my Father and your Father, to
my God and your God.'"
[18]Mary Magdalene found the disciples
and told them, "I have seen the Lord!" Then
she gave them his message.

Jesus Appears to His Disciples

[19]That Sunday evening* the disciples were
meeting behind locked doors because they
were afraid of the Jewish leaders. Suddenly,
Jesus was standing there among them!
"Peace be with you," he said. [20]As he spoke,
he showed them the wounds in his hands
and his side. They were filled with joy when

19:24a Greek *cast lots.* **19:24b** Ps 22:18. **19:28** See Pss 22:15; 69:21. **19:35** Some manuscripts read *that you also may believe.* **19:36** Exod 12:46; Num 9:12; Ps 34:20. **19:37** Zech 12:10. **19:39** Greek *100 litras* [32.7 kilograms]. **19:42** Greek *because of the Jewish day of preparation.* **20:1** Greek *On the first day of the week.* **20:19** Greek *In the evening of that day, the first day of the week.*

▸ **20:1** See ***Mary Magdalene,*** *page 1166.* **20:8-9** See ***Christ's resurrection and ours,*** *page 1320.*

Thomas

Names have a way of sticking, and sadly for Thomas, the one that has stuck with him through the centuries is "doubting." "Doubting Thomas" has become a common expression for anyone who is skeptical about something. Yet John 20:24-29 shows us that Thomas—also called Didymus ("the Twin"; 11:16)—was as believing as he was doubting. While he found it hard, if not impossible, to believe in the Resurrection (and who of us wouldn't have done so?), once he saw the risen Jesus he came out with an amazing confession (without even putting his fingers in the hands that were offered to him)—"My Lord and my God!"—and he was promptly commended by Jesus for it (20:28-29). It is not what we have doubted that matters, but what we end up believing.

▸ *See also* ***Apostles of Jesus,*** *page 1122.*

they saw the Lord! 21Again he said, "Peace be
with you. As the Father has sent me, so I am
sending you." 22Then he breathed on them
and said, "Receive the Holy Spirit. 23If you
forgive anyone's sins, they are forgiven. If you
do not forgive them, they are not forgiven."

Jesus Appears to Thomas

24One of the twelve disciples, Thomas (nicknamed the Twin),* was not with the others
when Jesus came. 25They told him, "We
have seen the Lord!"

But he replied, "I won't believe it unless
I see the nail wounds in his hands, put my
fingers into them, and place my hand into
the wound in his side."

26Eight days later the disciples were together again, and this time Thomas was
with them. The doors were locked; but suddenly, as before, Jesus was standing among
them. "Peace be with you," he said. 27Then
he said to Thomas, "Put your finger here,
and look at my hands. Put your hand into
the wound in my side. Don't be faithless any
longer. Believe!"

28"My Lord and my God!" Thomas
exclaimed.

29Then Jesus told him, "You believe
because you have seen me. Blessed are
those who believe without seeing me."

Purpose of the Book

30The disciples saw Jesus do many other
miraculous signs in addition to the ones recorded in this book. 31But these are written
so that you may continue to believe* that
Jesus is the Messiah, the Son of God, and
that by believing in him you will have life
by the power of his name.

Epilogue: Jesus Appears to Seven Disciples

21 Later, Jesus appeared again to the
disciples beside the Sea of Galilee.*
This is how it happened. 2Several of the
disciples were there—Simon Peter, Thomas
(nicknamed the Twin),* Nathanael from
Cana in Galilee, the sons of Zebedee, and
two other disciples.

3Simon Peter said, "I'm going fishing."

"We'll come, too," they all said. So they
went out in the boat, but they caught
nothing all night.

4At dawn Jesus was standing on the
beach, but the disciples couldn't see who
he was. 5He called out, "Fellows,* have you
caught any fish?"

"No," they replied.

6Then he said, "Throw out your net on the
right-hand side of the boat, and you'll get
some!" So they did, and they couldn't haul in
the net because there were so many fish in it.

Handling failure

Peter must have felt incredibly bad as Jesus stood before him. After all, he had boldly declared, "Even if everyone else deserts you, I never will" (Mark 14:29). Yet, when challenged about being one of Jesus' followers, he had denied it three times (John 18:15-18, 25-27), just as Jesus had prophesied (Mark 14:30). His fear had been stronger than his desire. And now, he felt useless. But Jesus hadn't finished with him yet!

To cancel out his three denials, Jesus gave him three opportunities to affirm his love for him. But Peter's affirmation of that love was no longer the brash declaration of previous days; rather, it now came out in the humble words of one who had learned his lesson and had discovered what he was really like. And Jesus not only forgave him, he recommissioned him—three times!—for his service (John 21:15-17). He called him to take care of his sheep, prophesying what this would one day cost him (21:18-19) and taking him back to the heart of a relationship with Jesus: "Follow me!" (21:19).

Satan always tries to convince us that our failure disqualifies us, both from friendship with Jesus and from being able to serve him. But this incident, like so many others in the Bible, shows that failure does not disqualify us—*providing* we handle that failure rightly, by confessing it and learning from it. When we do, we are ready to start again.

[7]Then the disciple Jesus loved said to Peter,
"It's the Lord!" When Simon Peter heard that
it was the Lord, he put on his tunic (for he had
stripped for work), jumped into the water,
and headed to shore. [8]The others stayed with
the boat and pulled the loaded net to the
shore, for they were only about a hundred
yards* from shore. [9]When they got there,
they found breakfast waiting for them—fish
cooking over a charcoal fire, and some bread.
[10]"Bring some of the fish you've just
caught," Jesus said. [11]So Simon Peter went
aboard and dragged the net to the shore.
There were 153 large fish, and yet the net
hadn't torn.
[12]"Now come and have some breakfast!"
Jesus said. None of the disciples dared
to ask him, "Who are you?" They knew it
was the Lord. [13]Then Jesus served them the
bread and the fish. [14]This was the third time
Jesus had appeared to his disciples since he
had been raised from the dead.
[15]After breakfast Jesus asked Simon Peter,
"Simon son of John, do you love me more
than these?*"
"Yes, Lord," Peter replied, "you know I
love you."
"Then feed my lambs," Jesus told him.
[16]Jesus repeated the question: "Simon son
of John, do you love me?"
"Yes, Lord," Peter said, "you know I love
you."
"Then take care of my sheep," Jesus said.
[17]A third time he asked him, "Simon son
of John, do you love me?"
Peter was hurt that Jesus asked the question a third time. He said, "Lord, you know
everything. You know that I love you."
Jesus said, "Then feed my sheep.
[18]"I tell you the truth, when you were
young, you were able to do as you liked;
you dressed yourself and went wherever you wanted to go. But when you are
old, you will stretch out your hands, and
others* will dress you and take you where
you don't want to go." [19]Jesus said this to
let him know by what kind of death he
would glorify God. Then Jesus told him,
"Follow me."
[20]Peter turned around and saw behind
them the disciple Jesus loved—the one who
had leaned over to Jesus during supper
and asked, "Lord, who will betray you?"
[21]Peter asked Jesus, "What about him,
Lord?"
[22]Jesus replied, "If I want him to remain
alive until I return, what is that to you? As
for you, follow me." [23]So the rumor spread
among the community of believers* that
this disciple wouldn't die. But that isn't
what Jesus said at all. He only said, "If I
want him to remain alive until I return,
what is that to you?"
[24]This disciple is the one who testifies to
these events and has recorded them here.
And we know that his account of these
things is accurate.
[25]Jesus also did many other things. If they
were all written down, I suppose the whole
world could not contain the books that
would be written.

20:24 Greek *Thomas, who was called Didymus.* **20:31** Some manuscripts read *that you may believe.* **21:1** Greek *Sea of Tiberias,* another name for the Sea of Galilee. **21:2** Greek *Thomas, who was called Didymus.* **21:5** Greek *Children.* **21:8** Greek *200 cubits* [90 meters]. **21:15** Or *more than these others do?* **21:18** Some manuscripts read *and another one.* **21:23** Greek *the brothers.*

Acts of the Apostles

Into all the world

Acts is the second part of Luke's two-volume work, as reflected in the fact that both Luke and Acts are dedicated to Theophilus (Luke 1:3; Acts 1:1). Continuing the account begun in Luke's Gospel, it records the beginnings of the Christian church. From its birth at Pentecost, the church was filled and guided by the Holy Spirit, just as Jesus had promised. It grew rapidly as the disciples went out with the message of Jesus.

Luke's heroes in Acts are the apostles Peter and Paul, and he draws many parallels between them. Paul, in particular, dominates the book. We read about the dramatic conversion of this persecutor-turned-apostle and see how his missionary journeys helped bring the gospel message to the Gentile world across Asia Minor and into Europe. The picture we get is of a gospel message that just cannot be stopped.

What's it all about?

Acts records the rapid spread of the gospel "in Jerusalem, throughout Judea, in Samaria, and to the ends of the earth" (1:8), just as Jesus promised. Chapters 1 to 11 record events in Jerusalem soon after Jesus' death. On the Day of Pentecost, the believers received the promised gift of the Holy Spirit. Pentecost was one of the three occasions each year when all Jewish men had to visit the Temple in Jerusalem, so Jerusalem was overflowing with visitors. Filled with God's Spirit, the disciples began to speak in other languages. Miraculously, people in the crowd—regardless of their native language—understood what they were saying in their own language. Some cynics accused the disciples of drunkenness, but Peter quickly explained. Using the Old Testament, he interpreted the meaning of these strange events, and three thousand people were converted that day. The church was born.

Following the Day of Pentecost, the apostles performed amazing healing miracles as they continued to preach the gospel. Clashes with the authorities came early on. In the persecution that followed, Stephen was stoned to death. His death was witnessed by a young man named Saul who was a fanatical persecutor of Christians (8:1-3). But on his way to Damascus, planning to arrest more Christians there, Saul had a vision of Jesus, who changed him and commissioned him to take the gospel to non-Jews (chapter 9).

Chapter 10 describes the conversion of Cornelius, a Roman army officer—hence a non-Jew. Because of a vision, he had invited Peter to his house. When Peter arrived, he presented the gospel to Cornelius and his whole household, and they were converted and received the Holy Spirit, to Peter's great surprise. Jewish Christians in Jerusalem questioned Peter's actions but soon recognized that God wanted non-Jews to be saved too (chapter 11).

Elsewhere, other non-Jews were coming to faith in Christ. The Jerusalem church sent Barnabas to Antioch to monitor events and he, in turn, invited Saul (now renamed Paul) to join him there. Back in Jerusalem, the clampdown on the church continued. Peter was imprisoned but was miraculously released while the disciples were praying (chapter 12).

Chapters 13 to 28 focus on Paul and his travels from his base in Antioch. The influx of non-Jews into the church created new challenges, and in chapter 15 the apostles resolved not to require them to be circumcised (as many Jewish Christians expected), but to call on them to observe some basic Jewish dietary laws (for the sake of fellowship) and to avoid sexual sin. Paul continued his missionary journeys, encountering frequent hostility from Jewish leaders (e.g., 17:5-9). But when he was rejected by Jews, he preached to Gentiles (18:6). He preached in Antioch, Philippi, Athens, Corinth, and Ephesus—all the most prominent cities of that region. When he returned to Jerusalem, he was arrested when a riot broke out on account of his preaching. As a Roman citizen, he was tried before the governor at Caesarea, and again before King Agrippa. But he exercised his right to be tried before Caesar in Rome. His ship was shipwrecked, but the passengers survived, and Paul finally reached Rome. Acts closes with Paul living under house arrest, where he openly preached the gospel for two years. Luke wanted us to know that nothing could stop the spread of the Good News of Jesus.

OVERVIEW

What does it mean for us?

In Acts, Luke continues his presentation of the Good News that he had begun in his Gospel. He records the preaching of the apostles, especially Peter and Paul, and shows the triumphant advance of the Christian message despite bitter opposition and persecution.

This message focused on Jesus, the Messiah and Son of God, who was put to death by sinful humanity but was raised from the dead by the Father, in fulfillment of Scripture. The message that the apostles proclaimed—that through repentance and faith in Jesus our sins can be forgiven and we can make a fresh start as the Holy Spirit comes to live within us—is still as relevant today. The gospel is still God's means of transforming individuals and society.

But we also see different responses to this message. Some, like Lydia and the jailor at Philippi, believed it; others, like Demetrius the silversmith, rejected it; and yet others, like Governor Felix, simply postponed the decision. We too will experience different responses whenever we share the Good News of Jesus; but wherever people accept the message, lives can be powerfully transformed, just as they were in Acts.

Acts shows us that, despite the worst that Jewish opponents and the Roman state could do, the gospel spread powerfully, as it is still doing to this day. Acts serves as a great encouragement to us not to give up when our Christian witness seems hard or is resisted, for ultimately the Good News always triumphs.

▶ *See also **Luke**, page 1278.*

The Promise of the Holy Spirit

1 In my first book* I told you, Theophilus, about everything Jesus began to do and teach [2]until the day he was taken up to heaven after giving his chosen apostles further instructions through the Holy Spirit. [3]During the forty days after he suffered and died, he appeared to the apostles from time to time, and he proved to them in many ways that he was actually alive. And he talked to them about the Kingdom of God.

[4]Once when he was eating with them, he commanded them, "Do not leave Jerusalem until the Father sends you the gift he promised, as I told you before. [5]John baptized with* water, but in just a few days you will be baptized with the Holy Spirit."

The Ascension of Jesus

[6]So when the apostles were with Jesus, they kept asking him, "Lord, has the time come for you to free Israel and restore our kingdom?"

[7]He replied, "The Father alone has the authority to set those dates and times, and they are not for you to know. [8]But you will receive power when the Holy Spirit comes upon you. And you will be my witnesses, telling people about me everywhere—in Jerusalem, throughout Judea, in Samaria, and to the ends of the earth."

[9]After saying this, he was taken up into a cloud while they were watching, and they could no longer see him. [10]As they strained to see him rising into heaven, two white-robed men suddenly stood among them. [11]"Men of Galilee," they said, "why are you standing here staring into heaven? Jesus has been taken from you into heaven, but someday he will return from heaven in the same way you saw him go!"

Matthias Replaces Judas

[12]Then the apostles returned to Jerusalem from the Mount of Olives, a distance of half a mile.* [13]When they arrived, they went to the upstairs room of the house where they were staying.

Here are the names of those who were

▸ **1:1** *See **Theophilus**, page 1151.* **1:8** *See **Being a witness**, page 1456.* **1:9** *See **Jesus' ascension**, page 1196.*

The Holy Spirit in Acts

From the beginning of Acts, Luke wants us to see the key role that the Holy Spirit had in the life and growth of the church (Acts 1:4-5, 8). The coming of the Holy Spirit empowered the disciples to be effective witnesses and lead transformed lives. When the Spirit came at Pentecost, the disciples were changed from timid people, hiding in the upper room, into bold witnesses to Jesus Christ. Neither opposition (e.g., 4:1-31; 12:1-24) nor persecution (e.g., 6:8–7:60; 19:23–20:6) could stop them.

But the Spirit came not only to empower but also to transform, increasing holiness in the lives of Jesus' followers. When Ananias and Sapphira tried to deceive the apostles in financial matters, they paid a heavy price for their dishonesty. As Peter denounced them for lying to the Holy Spirit, they dropped dead, bringing a holy awe upon the church (5:1-11).

Throughout Acts, the Spirit is constantly at work, initiating events (e.g., 8:29; 13:2, 4), empowering the disciples (e.g., 4:8; 6:5), backing up their words with miracles of healing (e.g., 3:6–4:20; 14:3), and impressing people with the truth of their message (e.g., 2:1-41; 10:34-48). His coming was part of God's plan that all people everywhere should know God, just as Joel, quoted by Peter at Pentecost, had prophesied (Acts 2:16-21). The exalted Jesus had now sent the Spirit, just as the crowd at Pentecost witnessed (2:33).

▸ *See also **Life in the Spirit**, page 1291; **Living by the Spirit**, page 1342; **The Christian's relationship with the Holy Spirit**, page 1350.*

present: Peter, John, James, Andrew, Philip, Thomas, Bartholomew, Matthew, James (son of Alphaeus), Simon (the zealot), and Judas (son of James). 14They all met together and were constantly united in prayer, along with Mary the mother of Jesus, several other women, and the brothers of Jesus.

15During this time, when about 120 believers* were together in one place, Peter stood up and addressed them. 16"Brothers," he said, "the Scriptures had to be fulfilled concerning Judas, who guided those who arrested Jesus. This was predicted long ago by the Holy Spirit, speaking through King David. 17Judas was one of us and shared in the ministry with us."

18(Judas had bought a field with the money he received for his treachery. Falling headfirst there, his body split open, spilling out all his intestines. 19The news of his death spread to all the people of Jerusalem, and they gave the place the Aramaic name *Akeldama,* which means "Field of Blood.")

20Peter continued, "This was written in the book of Psalms, where it says, 'Let his home become desolate, with no one living in it.' It also says, 'Let someone else take his position.'*

21"So now we must choose a replacement for Judas from among the men who were with us the entire time we were traveling with the Lord Jesus—22from the time he was baptized by John until the day he was taken from us. Whoever is chosen will join us as a witness of Jesus' resurrection."

23So they nominated two men: Joseph called Barsabbas (also known as Justus) and Matthias. 24Then they all prayed, "O Lord, you know every heart. Show us which of these men you have chosen 25as an apostle to replace Judas in this ministry, for he has deserted us and gone where he belongs." 26Then they cast lots, and Matthias was selected to become an apostle with the other eleven.

The Holy Spirit Comes

2 On the day of Pentecost* all the believers were meeting together in one place. 2Suddenly, there was a sound from heaven like the roaring of a mighty windstorm, and it filled the house where they were sitting. 3Then, what looked like flames or tongues of fire appeared and settled on each of them. 4And everyone present was filled with the Holy Spirit and began speaking in other languages,* as the Holy Spirit gave them this ability.

5At that time there were devout Jews from every nation living in Jerusalem. 6When they heard the loud noise, everyone came running, and they were bewildered to hear

1:1 The reference is to the Gospel of Luke. **1:5** Or *in;* also in 1:5b. **1:12** Greek *a Sabbath day's journey.* **1:15** Greek *brothers.* **1:20** Pss 69:25; 109:8. **2:1** The Festival of Pentecost came 50 days after Passover (when Jesus was crucified). **2:4** Or *in other tongues.*

▸ **1:14** *See* ***Mary, the mother of Jesus,*** *page 1153.* **2:1-4** *See* ***Renewal,*** *page 939.*

Matthias

While Jesus had had many disciples and followers, he had chosen just twelve to be apostles (Mark 3:13-19). At first it probably wasn't clear to them why; but gradually they saw that Jesus was recreating Israel around himself, created not around twelve tribes as in the Old Testament, but around twelve apostles. But one of those twelve, Judas, had betrayed him (Acts 1:15-19), which meant there was now a vacancy. So using the only method of guidance they knew at this time, after they had prayed, they cast lots, and Matthias was chosen (1:20-26). And with that, the story of Matthias begins and ends, for we never hear anything about him again. While other apostles would eventually be called—like Paul and Barnabas (Acts 14:1-4, 14) and James, the brother of Jesus (Galatians 1:19)—these twelve remained foundational apostles in early church thinking (e.g., 1 Corinthians 15:5; Revelation 21:14).

▸ *See also* ***Apostles of Jesus,*** *page 1122;* ***Guidance,*** *page 1261.*

their own languages being spoken by the
believers.
[7]They were completely amazed. "How
can this be?" they exclaimed. "These
people are all from Galilee, [8]and yet we
hear them speaking in our own native languages! [9]Here we are—Parthians, Medes,
Elamites, people from Mesopotamia,
Judea, Cappadocia, Pontus, the province
of Asia, [10]Phrygia, Pamphylia, Egypt, and
the areas of Libya around Cyrene, visitors
from Rome [11](both Jews and converts to
Judaism), Cretans, and Arabs. And we all
hear these people speaking in our own languages about the wonderful things God has
done!" [12]They stood there amazed and perplexed. "What can this mean?" they asked
each other.
[13]But others in the crowd ridiculed them,
saying, "They're just drunk, that's all!"

Peter Preaches to the Crowd

[14]Then Peter stepped forward with the
eleven other apostles and shouted to the
crowd, "Listen carefully, all of you, fellow
Jews and residents of Jerusalem! Make no
mistake about this. [15]These people are not
drunk, as some of you are assuming. Nine
o'clock in the morning is much too early for
that. [16]No, what you see was predicted long
ago by the prophet Joel:

[17] 'In the last days,' God says,
'I will pour out my Spirit upon all people.
Your sons and daughters will prophesy.
Your young men will see visions,
and your old men will dream dreams.
[18] In those days I will pour out my Spirit
even on my servants—men and women alike—
and they will prophesy.
[19] And I will cause wonders in the heavens above
and signs on the earth below—
blood and fire and clouds of smoke.
[20] The sun will become dark,
and the moon will turn blood red
before that great and glorious day of the LORD arrives.
[21] But everyone who calls on the name of the LORD
will be saved.'*

[22]"People of Israel, listen! God publicly
endorsed Jesus the Nazarene* by doing
powerful miracles, wonders, and signs
through him, as you well know. [23]But God
knew what would happen, and his prearranged plan was carried out when Jesus
was betrayed. With the help of lawless
Gentiles, you nailed him to a cross and
killed him. [24]But God released him from
the horrors of death and raised him back to

Baptism

Just as circumcision had been the outward sign of relationship with God under the old covenant, so baptism became that outward sign in the church. When people responded to Peter's message, his immediate call was for them to repent of their sins and be baptized (Acts 2:38). In demanding baptism as the sign of repentance, Peter was obeying Jesus' command to "go and make disciples of all the nations, baptizing them in the name of the Father and the Son and the Holy Spirit" (Matthew 28:19). Baptism symbolizes the beginning of the Christian life, recalling Jesus' death, burial, and resurrection (e.g., Romans 6:1-11) and his washing us clean (e.g., Titus 3:5). Its importance is reflected in the fact that Jesus himself was baptized, to identify with sinners. Even though he was without sin, he did it to "carry out all that God requires" (Matthew 3:15).

Churches today differ in their baptismal practice. Some immerse the candidate in water, while others sprinkle water on their head. Some reserve it for those who have made a conscious decision to follow Jesus, while others baptize the infants of believers. All agree, however, that baptism is a central mark of the Christian life.

▶ *See also **Jesus' baptism**, page 1073; **Repentance**, page 1253.*

life, for death could not keep him in its grip.
25 King David said this about him:

'I see that the LORD is always with me.
I will not be shaken, for he is right
beside me.
26 No wonder my heart is glad,
and my tongue shouts his praises!
My body rests in hope.
27 For you will not leave my soul among
the dead*
or allow your Holy One to rot in the
grave.
28 You have shown me the way of life,
and you will fill me with the joy of
your presence.'*

29 "Dear brothers, think about this! You can
be sure that the patriarch David wasn't referring to himself, for he died and was buried,
and his tomb is still here among us. 30 But he
was a prophet, and he knew God had promised with an oath that one of David's own
descendants would sit on his throne. 31 David
was looking into the future and speaking of
the Messiah's resurrection. He was saying
that God would not leave him among the
dead or allow his body to rot in the grave.

32 "God raised Jesus from the dead, and we
are all witnesses of this. 33 Now he is exalted
to the place of highest honor in heaven, at
God's right hand. And the Father, as he had
promised, gave him the Holy Spirit to pour
out upon us, just as you see and hear today.
34 For David himself never ascended into
heaven, yet he said,

'The LORD said to my Lord,
"Sit in the place of honor at my right
hand
35 until I humble your enemies,
making them a footstool under your
feet."'*

36 "So let everyone in Israel know for
certain that God has made this Jesus, whom
you crucified, to be both Lord and Messiah!"

37 Peter's words pierced their hearts, and
they said to him and to the other apostles,
"Brothers, what should we do?"

38 Peter replied, "Each of you must repent
of your sins and turn to God, and be baptized
in the name of Jesus Christ for the forgiveness
of your sins. Then you will receive the gift of
the Holy Spirit. 39 This promise is to you, to
your children, and to those far away*—all
who have been called by the Lord our God."
40 Then Peter continued preaching for a long
time, strongly urging all his listeners, "Save
yourselves from this crooked generation!"

41 Those who believed what Peter said
were baptized and added to the church that
day—about 3,000 in all.

The Believers Form a Community

42 All the believers devoted themselves to the
apostles' teaching, and to fellowship, and
to sharing in meals (including the Lord's
Supper*), and to prayer.

43 A deep sense of awe came over them
all, and the apostles performed many miraculous signs and wonders. 44 And all the
believers met together in one place and
shared everything they had. 45 They sold
their property and possessions and shared
the money with those in need. 46 They worshiped together at the Temple each day, met
in homes for the Lord's Supper, and shared
their meals with great joy and generosity*—47 all the while praising God and enjoying the goodwill of all the people. And each
day the Lord added to their fellowship those
who were being saved.

Peter Heals a Crippled Beggar

3 Peter and John went to the Temple
one afternoon to take part in the three
o'clock prayer service. 2 As they approached
the Temple, a man lame from birth was
being carried in. Each day he was put beside
the Temple gate, the one called the Beautiful Gate, so he could beg from the people
going into the Temple. 3 When he saw Peter
and John about to enter, he asked them for
some money.

4 Peter and John looked at him intently,
and Peter said, "Look at us!" 5 The lame man
looked at them eagerly, expecting some
money. 6 But Peter said, "I don't have any
silver or gold for you. But I'll give you what
I have. In the name of Jesus Christ the Nazarene,* get up and* walk!"

2:17-21 Joel 2:28-32. **2:22** Or *Jesus of Nazareth.* **2:27** Greek *in Hades;* also in 2:31. **2:25-28** Ps 16:8-11 (Greek version). **2:34-35** Ps 110:1. **2:39** Or *and to people far in the future,* or *and to the Gentiles.* **2:42** Greek *the breaking of bread;* also in 2:46. **2:46** Or *and sincere hearts.* **3:6a** Or *Jesus Christ of Nazareth.* **3:6b** Some manuscripts do not include *get up and.*

▸ **2:42** *See **Fellowship**, page 1357; **Growing as a Christian**, page 1430.*

7 Then Peter took the lame man by the right hand and helped him up. And as he did, the man's feet and ankles were instantly healed and strengthened. 8 He jumped up, stood on his feet, and began to walk! Then, walking, leaping, and praising God, he went into the Temple with them.

9 All the people saw him walking and heard him praising God. 10 When they realized he was the lame beggar they had seen so often at the Beautiful Gate, they were absolutely astounded! 11 They all rushed out in amazement to Solomon's Colonnade, where the man was holding tightly to Peter and John.

Peter Preaches in the Temple

12 Peter saw his opportunity and addressed the crowd. "People of Israel," he said, "what is so surprising about this? And why stare at us as though we had made this man walk by our own power or godliness? 13 For it is the God of Abraham, Isaac, and Jacob—the God of all our ancestors—who has brought glory to his servant Jesus by doing this. This is the same Jesus whom you handed over and rejected before Pilate, despite Pilate's decision to release him. 14 You rejected this holy, righteous one and instead demanded the release of a murderer. 15 You killed the author of life, but God raised him from the dead. And we are witnesses of this fact!

16 "Through faith in the name of Jesus, this man was healed—and you know how crippled he was before. Faith in Jesus' name has healed him before your very eyes.

17 "Friends,* I realize that what you and your leaders did to Jesus was done in ignorance. 18 But God was fulfilling what all the prophets had foretold about the Messiah—that he must suffer these things. 19 Now repent of your sins and turn to God, so that your sins may be wiped away. 20 Then times of refreshment will come from the presence of the Lord, and he will again send you Jesus, your appointed Messiah. 21 For he must remain in heaven until the time for the final restoration of all things, as God promised long ago through his holy prophets. 22 Moses said, 'The LORD your God will raise up for you a Prophet like me from among your own people. Listen carefully to everything he tells you.'* 23 Then Moses said, 'Anyone who will not listen to that Prophet will be completely cut off from God's people.'*

24 "Starting with Samuel, every prophet spoke about what is happening today. 25 You are the children of those prophets, and you are included in the covenant God promised to your ancestors. For God said to Abraham, 'Through your descendants* all the families on earth will be blessed.' 26 When God raised up his servant, Jesus, he sent him first to you people of Israel, to bless you by turning each of you back from your sinful ways."

Peter and John before the Council

4 While Peter and John were speaking to the people, they were confronted by the priests, the captain of the Temple guard, and some of the Sadducees. 2 These leaders were very disturbed that Peter and John were teaching the people that through Jesus there is a resurrection of the dead. 3 They arrested them and, since it was already evening, put them in jail until morning. 4 But many of the people who heard their message believed it, so the number of men who believed now totaled about 5,000.

5 The next day the council of all the rulers and elders and teachers of religious law met in Jerusalem. 6 Annas the high priest was there, along with Caiaphas, John, Alexander, and other relatives of the high priest. 7 They brought in the two disciples and demanded, "By what power, or in whose name, have you done this?"

8 Then Peter, filled with the Holy Spirit, said to them, "Rulers and elders of our people, 9 are we being questioned today because we've done a good deed for a crippled man? Do you want to know how he was healed? 10 Let me clearly state to all of you and to all the people of Israel that he was healed by the powerful name of Jesus Christ the Nazarene,* the man you crucified but whom God raised from the dead. 11 For Jesus is the one referred to in the Scriptures, where it says,

'The stone that you builders rejected
  has now become the cornerstone.'*

▸ **3:1-26** *See* ***Signs that follow****, page 1147.* **4:6** *See* ***Annas and Caiaphas****, page 1227.*

12 There is salvation in no one else! God
has given no other name under heaven by
which we must be saved."
13 The members of the council were
amazed when they saw the boldness of
Peter and John, for they could see that they
were ordinary men with no special training in the Scriptures. They also recognized
them as men who had been with Jesus. 14 But
since they could see the man who had been
healed standing right there among them,
there was nothing the council could say.
15 So they ordered Peter and John out of the
council chamber* and conferred among
themselves.
16 "What should we do with these men?"
they asked each other. "We can't deny that
they have performed a miraculous sign,
and everybody in Jerusalem knows about
it. 17 But to keep them from spreading their
propaganda any further, we must warn
them not to speak to anyone in Jesus' name
again." 18 So they called the apostles back in
and commanded them never again to speak
or teach in the name of Jesus.
19 But Peter and John replied, "Do you
think God wants us to obey you rather than
him? 20 We cannot stop telling about everything we have seen and heard."
21 The council then threatened them
further, but they finally let them go because
they didn't know how to punish them
without starting a riot. For everyone was
praising God 22 for this miraculous sign—the
healing of a man who had been lame for
more than forty years.

The Believers Pray for Courage

23 As soon as they were freed, Peter and John
returned to the other believers and told
them what the leading priests and elders
had said. 24 When they heard the report, all
the believers lifted their voices together in
prayer to God: "O Sovereign Lord, Creator of
heaven and earth, the sea, and everything
in them— 25 you spoke long ago by the Holy
Spirit through our ancestor David, your
servant, saying,

'Why were the nations so angry?
Why did they waste their time with
futile plans?
26 The kings of the earth prepared for
battle;
the rulers gathered together
against the LORD
and against his Messiah.'*

27 "In fact, this has happened here in this
very city! For Herod Antipas, Pontius Pilate
the governor, the Gentiles, and the people
of Israel were all united against Jesus, your
holy servant, whom you anointed. 28 But
everything they did was determined beforehand according to your will. 29 And now,
O Lord, hear their threats, and give us, your

3:17 Greek *Brothers.* **3:22** Deut 18:15. **3:23** Deut 18:19; Lev 23:29. **3:25** Greek *your seed;* see Gen 12:3; 22:18. **4:10** Or *Jesus Christ of Nazareth.* **4:11** Ps 118:22. **4:15** Greek *the Sanhedrin.* **4:25-26** Or *his anointed one;* or *his Christ.* Ps 2:1-2.

Jesus: the only way to God

For many people, Peter's declaration that salvation can be found only through Jesus Christ (Acts 4:12) sounds arrogant, especially when there are so many religions, all claiming to be valid paths to God. Yet it is impossible to be faithful to Jesus and not believe this. After all, Jesus himself said, "No one truly knows the Father except the Son" (Matthew 11:27) and "I am the way, the truth, and the life. No one can come to the Father except through me" (John 14:6). Peter was simply agreeing with what his master had said, and the other apostles did the same. Paul wrote that "there is one God and one Mediator who can reconcile God and humanity—the man Christ Jesus" (1 Timothy 2:5), and John wrote that "whoever has the Son has life; whoever does not have God's Son does not have life" (1 John 5:12).

Such a bold claim has implications. It means we have a duty to share the gospel with everyone, for to believe that Christ is the only way and not tell others is outrageous. But we should do so "in a gentle and respectful way" (1 Peter 3:16), not with aggression or violence. Our lives should be the first proof that the gospel is true.

servants, great boldness in preaching your word. 30 Stretch out your hand with healing power; may miraculous signs and wonders be done through the name of your holy servant Jesus."

31 After this prayer, the meeting place shook, and they were all filled with the Holy Spirit. Then they preached the word of God with boldness.

The Believers Share Their Possessions

32 All the believers were united in heart and mind. And they felt that what they owned was not their own, so they shared everything they had. 33 The apostles testified powerfully to the resurrection of the Lord Jesus, and God's great blessing was upon them all. 34 There were no needy people among them, because those who owned land or houses would sell them 35 and bring the money to the apostles to give to those in need.

36 For instance, there was Joseph, the one the apostles nicknamed Barnabas (which means "Son of Encouragement"). He was from the tribe of Levi and came from the island of Cyprus. 37 He sold a field he owned and brought the money to the apostles.

Ananias and Sapphira

5 But there was a certain man named Ananias who, with his wife, Sapphira, sold some property. 2 He brought part of the money to the apostles, claiming it was the full amount. With his wife's consent, he kept the rest.

3 Then Peter said, "Ananias, why have you let Satan fill your heart? You lied to the Holy Spirit, and you kept some of the money for yourself. 4 The property was yours to sell or not sell, as you wished. And after selling it, the money was also yours to give away. How could you do a thing like this? You weren't lying to us but to God!"

5 As soon as Ananias heard these words, he fell to the floor and died. Everyone who heard about it was terrified. 6 Then some young men got up, wrapped him in a sheet, and took him out and buried him.

7 About three hours later his wife came in, not knowing what had happened. 8 Peter asked her, "Was this the price you and your husband received for your land?"

"Yes," she replied, "that was the price."

9 And Peter said, "How could the two of you even think of conspiring to test the Spirit of the Lord like this? The young men who buried your husband are just outside the door, and they will carry you out, too."

10 Instantly, she fell to the floor and died. When the young men came in and saw that she was dead, they carried her out and buried her beside her husband. 11 Great fear gripped the entire church and everyone else who heard what had happened.

The Apostles Heal Many

12 The apostles were performing many miraculous signs and wonders among the people. And all the believers were meeting regularly at the Temple in the area known

Barnabas

Many of us have been given a nickname in life—some affectionate, some not quite so welcome. But the nickname given to Joseph, a Levite from Cyprus, was an incredible honor. His life was so full of encouragement that the apostles nicknamed him "Barnabas" ("Son of Encouragement"—or perhaps in our language, Mr. Encourager). Here in Acts 4:36-37, we find him engaging in extravagant practical support for needy Christians; later we find him welcoming the newly converted Paul when others were afraid of him (9:26-27), then introducing him to the Antioch church (11:25-26). He and Paul were called by the Holy Spirit to lead a significant missionary expansion from Antioch (13:1-3). Initially Barnabas was the "senior partner" of the team, for his name comes first (e.g., 13:2, 7); but it isn't long before Paul is being named first (e.g., 13:14, 42-43, 45-46, 50). That Barnabas had the grace to move from the leading role to a supporting one says much about this bighearted man.

▸ *See also* ***The power of encouragement****, page 578;* ***Mentoring****, page 1385.*

as Solomon's Colonnade. [13]But no one else dared to join them, even though all the people had high regard for them. [14]Yet more and more people believed and were brought to the Lord—crowds of both men and women. [15]As a result of the apostles' work, sick people were brought out into the streets on beds and mats so that Peter's shadow might fall across some of them as he went by. [16]Crowds came from the villages around Jerusalem, bringing their sick and those possessed by evil* spirits, and they were all healed.

The Apostles Meet Opposition

[17]The high priest and his officials, who were Sadducees, were filled with jealousy. [18]They arrested the apostles and put them in the public jail. [19]But an angel of the Lord came at night, opened the gates of the jail, and brought them out. Then he told them, [20]"Go to the Temple and give the people this message of life!"

[21]So at daybreak the apostles entered the Temple, as they were told, and immediately began teaching.

When the high priest and his officials arrived, they convened the high council*—the full assembly of the elders of Israel. Then they sent for the apostles to be brought from the jail for trial. [22]But when the Temple guards went to the jail, the men were gone. So they returned to the council and reported, [23]"The jail was securely locked, with the guards standing outside, but when we opened the gates, no one was there!"

[24]When the captain of the Temple guard and the leading priests heard this, they were perplexed, wondering where it would all end. [25]Then someone arrived with startling news: "The men you put in jail are standing in the Temple, teaching the people!"

[26]The captain went with his Temple guards and arrested the apostles, but without violence, for they were afraid the people would stone them. [27]Then they brought the apostles before the high council, where the high priest confronted them. [28]"We gave you strict orders never again to teach in this man's name!" he said. "Instead, you have filled all Jerusalem with your teaching about him, and you want to make us responsible for his death!"

[29]But Peter and the apostles replied, "We must obey God rather than any human authority. [30]The God of our ancestors raised Jesus from the dead after you killed him by

5:16 Greek *unclean.* **5:21** Greek *Sanhedrin;* also in 5:27, 41.

Miracles and healing

For the early church, just as for Jesus, sharing the gospel wasn't just about words but also involved "many miraculous signs and wonders" (Acts 5:12). Several specific healings are recorded in Acts (e.g., 3:1-10; 9:32-43; 14:8-10; 20:7-12), though it is clear there were many others, all seen as a normal part of Christian witness (e.g., 5:12-16; 8:4-8). Not all the miracles were healings, however: Ananias and Sapphira dropping dead (5:1-11), visitations from angels (10:1-8), and miraculous release from prison (12:1-19; 16:16-40) all played their part in spreading the Good News.

What is the purpose of miracles? First, they demonstrate the reality and superiority of the living God, especially in polytheistic cultures (e.g., 19:11-20). Second, they draw attention to the gospel. Peter's healing of the lame man (3:1-10) led to an opportunity to explain about Jesus, who had brought about the healing (3:11-26; 4:5-12). Third, they are a tangible manifestation of God's care. Peter was following the example of Jesus, who healed the sick because "he had compassion on them" (Matthew 14:14).

Of course, not everyone appreciated these miracles, and they often led to persecution (e.g., Acts 5:17-20; 14:8-20)—a reminder that miracles in themselves cannot bring about belief.

▶ *See also **Signs that follow**, page 1147.*

hanging him on a cross.* 31Then God put
him in the place of honor at his right hand
as Prince and Savior. He did this so the
people of Israel would repent of their sins
and be forgiven. 32We are witnesses of these
things and so is the Holy Spirit, who is given
by God to those who obey him."
33When they heard this, the high council
was furious and decided to kill them. 34But
one member, a Pharisee named Gamaliel,
who was an expert in religious law and
respected by all the people, stood up and
ordered that the men be sent outside the
council chamber for a while. 35Then he
said to his colleagues, "Men of Israel, take
care what you are planning to do to these
men! 36Some time ago there was that fellow
Theudas, who pretended to be someone
great. About 400 others joined him, but he
was killed, and all his followers went their
various ways. The whole movement came
to nothing. 37After him, at the time of the
census, there was Judas of Galilee. He got
people to follow him, but he was killed, too,
and all his followers were scattered.
38"So my advice is, leave these men alone.
Let them go. If they are planning and doing
these things merely on their own, it will
soon be overthrown. 39But if it is from God,
you will not be able to overthrow them. You
may even find yourselves fighting against
God!"
40The others accepted his advice. They
called in the apostles and had them flogged.
Then they ordered them never again to
speak in the name of Jesus, and they let
them go.
41The apostles left the high council rejoicing that God had counted them worthy to
suffer disgrace for the name of Jesus.* 42And
every day, in the Temple and from house to
house, they continued to teach and preach
this message: "Jesus is the Messiah."

Seven Men Chosen to Serve

6 But as the believers* rapidly multiplied,
there were rumblings of discontent. The
Greek-speaking believers complained about
the Hebrew-speaking believers, saying that
their widows were being discriminated
against in the daily distribution of food.
2So the Twelve called a meeting of all
the believers. They said, "We apostles
should spend our time teaching the word
of God, not running a food program. 3And
so, brothers, select seven men who are
well respected and are full of the Spirit and
wisdom. We will give them this responsibility. 4Then we apostles can spend our time in
prayer and teaching the word."
5Everyone liked this idea, and they chose
the following: Stephen (a man full of faith
and the Holy Spirit), Philip, Procorus,
Nicanor, Timon, Parmenas, and Nicolas of
Antioch (an earlier convert to the Jewish
faith). 6These seven were presented to the
apostles, who prayed for them as they laid
their hands on them.
7So God's message continued to spread.
The number of believers greatly increased
in Jerusalem, and many of the Jewish priests
were converted, too.

Stephen Is Arrested

8Stephen, a man full of God's grace and
power, performed amazing miracles and
signs among the people. 9But one day some
men from the Synagogue of Freed Slaves,
as it was called, started to debate with him.
They were Jews from Cyrene, Alexandria,
Cilicia, and the province of Asia. 10None of
them could stand against the wisdom and
the Spirit with which Stephen spoke.
11So they persuaded some men to lie
about Stephen, saying, "We heard him blaspheme Moses, and even God." 12This roused
the people, the elders, and the teachers of
religious law. So they arrested Stephen and
brought him before the high council.*
13The lying witnesses said, "This man is
always speaking against the holy Temple
and against the law of Moses. 14We have
heard him say that this Jesus of Nazareth*
will destroy the Temple and change the
customs Moses handed down to us."
15At this point everyone in the high
council stared at Stephen, because his face
became as bright as an angel's.

Stephen Addresses the Council

7 Then the high priest asked Stephen,
"Are these accusations true?"
2This was Stephen's reply: "Brothers and
fathers, listen to me. Our glorious God appeared to our ancestor Abraham in Mesopotamia before he settled in Haran.* 3God
told him, 'Leave your native land and your
relatives, and come into the land that I will
show you.'* 4So Abraham left the land of
the Chaldeans and lived in Haran until his

father died. Then God brought him here to
the land where you now live.
5“But God gave him no inheritance here,
not even one square foot of land. God did
promise, however, that eventually the
whole land would belong to Abraham and
his descendants—even though he had no
children yet. 6God also told him that his
descendants would live in a foreign land,
where they would be oppressed as slaves
for 400 years. 7‘But I will punish the nation
that enslaves them,’ God said, ‘and in the
end they will come out and worship me here
in this place.’*

8“God also gave Abraham the covenant
of circumcision at that time. So when
Abraham became the father of Isaac, he
circumcised him on the eighth day. And the
practice was continued when Isaac became
the father of Jacob, and when Jacob became
the father of the twelve patriarchs of the Israelite nation.

9“These patriarchs were jealous of their
brother Joseph, and they sold him to be a
slave in Egypt. But God was with him 10and
rescued him from all his troubles. And
God gave him favor before Pharaoh, king
of Egypt. God also gave Joseph unusual
wisdom, so that Pharaoh appointed him
governor over all of Egypt and put him in
charge of the palace.

11“But a famine came upon Egypt and
Canaan. There was great misery, and our
ancestors ran out of food. 12Jacob heard that
there was still grain in Egypt, so he sent his
sons—our ancestors—to buy some. 13The
second time they went, Joseph revealed
his identity to his brothers,* and they were
introduced to Pharaoh. 14Then Joseph sent
for his father, Jacob, and all his relatives to
come to Egypt, seventy-five persons in all.
15So Jacob went to Egypt. He died there,
as did our ancestors. 16Their bodies were
taken to Shechem and buried in the tomb
Abraham had bought for a certain price
from Hamor’s sons in Shechem.

17“As the time drew near when God would
fulfill his promise to Abraham, the number
of our people in Egypt greatly increased.
18But then a new king came to the throne
of Egypt who knew nothing about Joseph.
19This king exploited our people and oppressed them, forcing parents to abandon
their newborn babies so they would die.

20“At that time Moses was born—a
beautiful child in God’s eyes. His parents
cared for him at home for three months.
21When they had to abandon him, Pharaoh’s daughter adopted him and raised
him as her own son. 22Moses was taught all
the wisdom of the Egyptians, and he was
powerful in both speech and action.

23“One day when Moses was forty years
old, he decided to visit his relatives, the
people of Israel. 24He saw an Egyptian mis-
treating an Israelite. So Moses came to the
man’s defense and avenged him, killing the
Egyptian. 25Moses assumed his fellow Israelites would realize that God had sent him
to rescue them, but they didn’t.

26“The next day he visited them again and
saw two men of Israel fighting. He tried to
be a peacemaker. ‘Men,’ he said, ‘you are
brothers. Why are you fighting each other?’

27“But the man in the wrong pushed
Moses aside. ‘Who made you a ruler and
judge over us?’ he asked. 28‘Are you going to
kill me as you killed that Egyptian yesterday?’ 29When Moses heard that, he fled the
country and lived as a foreigner in the land
of Midian. There his two sons were born.

30“Forty years later, in the desert near
Mount Sinai, an angel appeared to Moses in
the flame of a burning bush. 31When Moses
saw it, he was amazed at the sight. As he
went to take a closer look, the voice of the
LORD called out to him, 32‘I am the God of
your ancestors—the God of Abraham, Isaac,
and Jacob.’ Moses shook with terror and did
not dare to look.

33“Then the LORD said to him, ‘Take off
your sandals, for you are standing on holy
ground. 34I have certainly seen the oppression of my people in Egypt. I have heard
their groans and have come down to rescue
them. Now go, for I am sending you back
to Egypt.’*

35“So God sent back the same man his
people had previously rejected when they
demanded, ‘Who made you a ruler and
judge over us?’ Through the angel who appeared to him in the burning bush, God sent
Moses to be their ruler and savior. 36And by
means of many wonders and miraculous
signs, he led them out of Egypt, through

5:30 Greek *on a tree.* **5:41** Greek *for the name.* **6:1** Greek *disciples;* also in 6:2, 7. **6:12** Greek *Sanhedrin;* also in 6:15. **6:14** Or *Jesus the Nazarene.* **7:2** *Mesopotamia* was the region now called Iraq. *Haran* was a city in what is now called Syria. **7:3** Gen 12:1. **7:5-7** Gen 12:7; 15:13-14; Exod 3:12. **7:13** Other manuscripts read *Joseph was recognized by his brothers.* **7:31-34** Exod 3:5-10.

the Red Sea, and through the wilderness for
forty years.
37 "Moses himself told the people of Israel,
'God will raise up for you a Prophet like me
from among your own people.'* 38 Moses
was with our ancestors, the assembly of
God's people in the wilderness, when the
angel spoke to him at Mount Sinai. And
there Moses received life-giving words to
pass on to us.*
39 "But our ancestors refused to listen to
Moses. They rejected him and wanted to
return to Egypt. 40 They told Aaron, 'Make
us some gods who can lead us, for we don't
know what has become of this Moses, who
brought us out of Egypt.' 41 So they made an
idol shaped like a calf, and they sacrificed
to it and celebrated over this thing they had
made. 42 Then God turned away from them
and abandoned them to serve the stars of
heaven as their gods! In the book of the
prophets it is written,

'Was it to me you were bringing
  sacrifices and offerings
 during those forty years in the
  wilderness, Israel?
43 No, you carried your pagan gods—
 the shrine of Molech,
 the star of your god Rephan,
 and the images you made to worship
  them.
So I will send you into exile
 as far away as Babylon.'*

44 "Our ancestors carried the Tabernacle*
with them through the wilderness. It was
constructed according to the plan God had
shown to Moses. 45 Years later, when Joshua
led our ancestors in battle against the
nations that God drove out of this land, the
Tabernacle was taken with them into their
new territory. And it stayed there until the
time of King David.
46 "David found favor with God and asked
for the privilege of building a permanent
Temple for the God of Jacob.* 47 But it was
Solomon who actually built it. 48 However,
the Most High doesn't live in temples made
by human hands. As the prophet says,

49 'Heaven is my throne,
  and the earth is my footstool.
 Could you build me a temple as good as
  that?'
  asks the LORD.
 'Could you build me such a resting
  place?
50 Didn't my hands make both heaven
  and earth?'*

51 "You stubborn people! You are heathen*
at heart and deaf to the truth. Must you
forever resist the Holy Spirit? That's what
your ancestors did, and so do you! 52 Name
one prophet your ancestors didn't persecute!
They even killed the ones who predicted the
coming of the Righteous One—the Messiah
whom you betrayed and murdered. 53 You deliberately disobeyed God's law, even though
you received it from the hands of angels."
54 The Jewish leaders were infuriated by
Stephen's accusation, and they shook their
fists at him in rage.* 55 But Stephen, full of the

Stephen

Stephen had been one of the seven men chosen to run the church's food program (Acts 6:1-6). But he wasn't just a practical server; he also "performed amazing miracles and signs among the people" (6:8) and was a powerful preacher (6:10). Opponents therefore accused him of blasphemy and brought him before the Jewish high council (6:11-12). In his defense (7:2-53, the longest speech in Acts) Stephen recalled Israel's history, showing how the people had often rejected God, and applied that to the Jewish leaders' present rejection of Jesus the Messiah. He accused his audience of being "stubborn . . . heathen at heart and deaf to the truth" and resisting the Holy Spirit (7:51). Their growing anger erupted when he claimed to see "the Son of Man standing in the place of honor at God's right hand" (7:56). They dragged him outside the city and stoned him. He died praying for both himself and them (7:57-60). His martyrdom unleashed a great outbreak of persecution against the church (8:1-3).

Holy Spirit, gazed steadily into heaven and
saw the glory of God, and he saw Jesus standing in the place of honor at God's right hand.
56 And he told them, "Look, I see the heavens
opened and the Son of Man standing in the
place of honor at God's right hand!"
57 Then they put their hands over their
ears and began shouting. They rushed at
him 58 and dragged him out of the city and
began to stone him. His accusers took off
their coats and laid them at the feet of a
young man named Saul.*
59 As they stoned him, Stephen prayed,
"Lord Jesus, receive my spirit." 60 He fell to
his knees, shouting, "Lord, don't charge
them with this sin!" And with that, he died.

8 Saul was one of the witnesses, and he
agreed completely with the killing of
Stephen.

Persecution Scatters the Believers

A great wave of persecution began that day,
sweeping over the church in Jerusalem;
and all the believers except the apostles
were scattered through the regions of Judea
and Samaria. 2 (Some devout men came
and buried Stephen with great mourning.)
3 But Saul was going everywhere to destroy
the church. He went from house to house,
dragging out both men and women to throw
them into prison.

Philip Preaches in Samaria

4 But the believers who were scattered
preached the Good News about Jesus wherever they went. 5 Philip, for example, went
to the city of Samaria and told the people
there about the Messiah. 6 Crowds listened
intently to Philip because they were eager
to hear his message and see the miraculous
signs he did. 7 Many evil* spirits were cast
out, screaming as they left their victims. And
many who had been paralyzed or lame were
healed. 8 So there was great joy in that city.
9 A man named Simon had been a sorcerer
there for many years, amazing the people of
Samaria and claiming to be someone great.
10 Everyone, from the least to the greatest,
often spoke of him as "the Great One—the
Power of God." 11 They listened closely to
him because for a long time he had astounded them with his magic.
12 But now the people believed Philip's
message of Good News concerning the
Kingdom of God and the name of Jesus
Christ. As a result, many men and women
were baptized. 13 Then Simon himself believed and was baptized. He began following Philip wherever he went, and he was

7:37 Deut 18:15. **7:38** Some manuscripts read *to you.* **7:42-43** Amos 5:25-27 (Greek version). **7:44** Greek *the tent of witness.* **7:46** Some manuscripts read *the house of Jacob.* **7:49-50** Isa 66:1-2. **7:51** Greek *uncircumcised.* **7:54** Greek *they were grinding their teeth against him.* **7:58** *Saul* is later called Paul; see 13:9. **8:7** Greek *unclean.*

Philip

Philip, called "Philip the Evangelist" to distinguish him from Philip the apostle, was one of the seven men who ran the church's food program (Acts 6:1-6). When persecution erupted after Stephen's martyrdom (chapter 7), he went to Samaria—home of the Samaritans, who were hated by Jews—where he performed many miracles of healing, and many responded to the gospel (8:4-13). His ministry was so effective that Peter and John came to see what was happening and to pray for the new believers (8:14-17). An angel then told Philip to head for the desert road to Gaza, but didn't tell him why. There he met an Ethiopian eunuch who was reading from Isaiah. Starting from the passage the eunuch had been reading (it's always good to start from what people are already interested in when seeking to share the Good News), Philip shared the gospel with him, and the eunuch was immediately baptized (8:26-38). A miracle then occurred as "the Spirit of the Lord snatched Philip away" (8:39). He suddenly found himself farther north, where he continued to evangelize (8:40). He finally moved to Caesarea, where we find him twenty years later (21:8).

▸ *See also **Samaria**, page 399; **The Samaritans**, page 1204; **Baptism**, page 1238; **The First Journeys of Christian Leaders** maps, Visual Overview Z14.*

amazed by the signs and great miracles Philip performed.

[14]When the apostles in Jerusalem heard that the people of Samaria had accepted God's message, they sent Peter and John there. [15]As soon as they arrived, they prayed for these new believers to receive the Holy Spirit. [16]The Holy Spirit had not yet come upon any of them, for they had only been baptized in the name of the Lord Jesus. [17]Then Peter and John laid their hands upon these believers, and they received the Holy Spirit.

[18]When Simon saw that the Spirit was given when the apostles laid their hands on people, he offered them money to buy this power. [19]"Let me have this power, too," he exclaimed, "so that when I lay my hands on people, they will receive the Holy Spirit!"

[20]But Peter replied, "May your money be destroyed with you for thinking God's gift can be bought! [21]You can have no part in this, for your heart is not right with God. [22]Repent of your wickedness and pray to the Lord. Perhaps he will forgive your evil thoughts, [23]for I can see that you are full of bitter jealousy and are held captive by sin."

[24]"Pray to the Lord for me," Simon exclaimed, "that these terrible things you've said won't happen to me!"

[25]After testifying and preaching the word of the Lord in Samaria, Peter and John returned to Jerusalem. And they stopped in many Samaritan villages along the way to preach the Good News.

Philip and the Ethiopian Eunuch

[26]As for Philip, an angel of the Lord said to him, "Go south* down the desert road that runs from Jerusalem to Gaza." [27]So he started out, and he met the treasurer of Ethiopia, a eunuch of great authority under the Kandake, the queen of Ethiopia. The eunuch had gone to Jerusalem to worship, [28]and he was now returning. Seated in his carriage, he was reading aloud from the book of the prophet Isaiah.

[29]The Holy Spirit said to Philip, "Go over and walk along beside the carriage."

[30]Philip ran over and heard the man reading from the prophet Isaiah. Philip asked, "Do you understand what you are reading?"

[31]The man replied, "How can I, unless someone instructs me?" And he urged Philip to come up into the carriage and sit with him.

[32]The passage of Scripture he had been reading was this:

"He was led like a sheep to the
    slaughter.
  And as a lamb is silent before the
    shearers,
  he did not open his mouth.
[33] He was humiliated and received no
    justice.
  Who can speak of his descendants?
  For his life was taken from the
    earth."*

[34]The eunuch asked Philip, "Tell me, was the prophet talking about himself or someone else?" [35]So beginning with this same Scripture, Philip told him the Good News about Jesus.

[36]As they rode along, they came to some water, and the eunuch said, "Look! There's some water! Why can't I be baptized?"* [38]He ordered the carriage to stop, and they went down into the water, and Philip baptized him.

[39]When they came up out of the water, the Spirit of the Lord snatched Philip away. The eunuch never saw him again but went on his way rejoicing. [40]Meanwhile, Philip found himself farther north at the town of Azotus. He preached the Good News there and in every town along the way until he came to Caesarea.

Saul's Conversion

9 Meanwhile, Saul was uttering threats with every breath and was eager to kill the Lord's followers.* So he went to the high priest. [2]He requested letters addressed to the synagogues in Damascus, asking for their cooperation in the arrest of any followers of the Way he found there. He wanted to bring them—both men and women—back to Jerusalem in chains.

[3]As he was approaching Damascus on this mission, a light from heaven suddenly shone down around him. [4]He fell to the ground and heard a voice saying to him, "Saul! Saul! Why are you persecuting me?"

[5]"Who are you, lord?" Saul asked.

And the voice replied, "I am Jesus, the one you are persecuting! [6]Now get up and go into the city, and you will be told what you must do."

[7]The men with Saul stood speechless, for
they heard the sound of someone's voice
but saw no one! [8]Saul picked himself up off
the ground, but when he opened his eyes
he was blind. So his companions led him by
the hand to Damascus. [9]He remained there
blind for three days and did not eat or drink.

[10]Now there was a believer* in Damascus
named Ananias. The Lord spoke to him in a
vision, calling, "Ananias!"

"Yes, Lord!" he replied.

[11]The Lord said, "Go over to Straight
Street, to the house of Judas. When you get
there, ask for a man from Tarsus named
Saul. He is praying to me right now. [12]I
have shown him a vision of a man named
Ananias coming in and laying hands on
him so he can see again."

[13]"But Lord," exclaimed Ananias, "I've
heard many people talk about the terrible
things this man has done to the believers*
in Jerusalem! [14]And he is authorized by the
leading priests to arrest everyone who calls
upon your name."

[15]But the Lord said, "Go, for Saul is my
chosen instrument to take my message to
the Gentiles and to kings, as well as to the
people of Israel. [16]And I will show him how
much he must suffer for my name's sake."

[17]So Ananias went and found Saul. He
laid his hands on him and said, "Brother
Saul, the Lord Jesus, who appeared to you
on the road, has sent me so that you might
regain your sight and be filled with the Holy
Spirit." [18]Instantly something like scales fell
from Saul's eyes, and he regained his sight.
Then he got up and was baptized. [19]After-
ward he ate some food and regained his
strength.

Saul in Damascus and Jerusalem

Saul stayed with the believers* in Damascus
for a few days. [20]And immediately he began
preaching about Jesus in the synagogues,
saying, "He is indeed the Son of God!"

[21]All who heard him were amazed. "Isn't
this the same man who caused such devastation among Jesus' followers in Jerusalem?" they asked. "And didn't he come here
to arrest them and take them in chains to
the leading priests?"

[22]Saul's preaching became more and
more powerful, and the Jews in Damascus
couldn't refute his proofs that Jesus was
indeed the Messiah. [23]After a while some of
the Jews plotted together to kill him. [24]They
were watching for him day and night at the
city gate so they could murder him, but Saul
was told about their plot. [25]So during the
night, some of the other believers* lowered
him in a large basket through an opening in
the city wall.

[26]When Saul arrived in Jerusalem, he tried
to meet with the believers, but they were all
afraid of him. They did not believe he had
truly become a believer! [27]Then Barnabas
brought him to the apostles and told them
how Saul had seen the Lord on the way to Damascus and how the Lord had spoken to Saul.
He also told them that Saul had preached
boldly in the name of Jesus in Damascus.

[28]So Saul stayed with the apostles and
went all around Jerusalem with them,
preaching boldly in the name of the Lord.

8:26 Or *Go at noon.* **8:32-33** Isa 53:7-8 (Greek version). **8:36** Some manuscripts add verse 37, *"You can," Philip answered, "if you believe with all your heart." And the eunuch replied, "I believe that Jesus Christ is the Son of God."* **9:1** Greek *disciples.* **9:10** Greek *disciple;* also in 9:26, 36. **9:13** Greek *God's holy people;* also in 9:32, 41. **9:19** Greek *disciples;* also in 9:26, 38. **9:25** Greek *his disciples.*

Damascus

When Saul, later called Paul, headed for Damascus (Acts 9:1-2), he was targeting one of the most strategic cities of the region. Damascus was the capital of Syria (in Old Testament times, Aram), 135 miles north of Jerusalem. It was strategically located at the crossroads of the main trade routes—Mesopotamia lay to the east, Egypt and Arabia to the south, and Asia Minor (modern Turkey) to the north. Saul knew that if Christianity took hold in Damascus, it could spread everywhere; so he was determined to nip it in the bud. But in his attempts to conquer Christianity, he found instead that it conquered him. The risen Jesus revealed himself to him, and his life would never be the same again.

▶ *See also* ***The apostle Paul****, page 1272.*

29He debated with some Greek-speaking
Jews, but they tried to murder him. 30When
the believers* heard about this, they took
him down to Caesarea and sent him away
to Tarsus, his hometown.
31The church then had peace throughout
Judea, Galilee, and Samaria, and it became
stronger as the believers lived in the fear of
the Lord. And with the encouragement of
the Holy Spirit, it also grew in numbers.

Peter Heals Aeneas and Raises Dorcas

32Meanwhile, Peter traveled from place to
place, and he came down to visit the believers in the town of Lydda. 33There he met a
man named Aeneas, who had been paralyzed and bedridden for eight years. 34Peter
said to him, "Aeneas, Jesus Christ heals you!
Get up, and roll up your sleeping mat!" And
he was healed instantly. 35Then the whole
population of Lydda and Sharon saw Aeneas
walking around, and they turned to the Lord.
36There was a believer in Joppa named
Tabitha (which in Greek is Dorcas*). She
was always doing kind things for others
and helping the poor. 37About this time she
became ill and died. Her body was washed
for burial and laid in an upstairs room.
38But the believers had heard that Peter was
nearby at Lydda, so they sent two men to
beg him, "Please come as soon as possible!"
39So Peter returned with them; and as
soon as he arrived, they took him to the
upstairs room. The room was filled with
widows who were weeping and showing
him the coats and other clothes Dorcas had
made for them. 40But Peter asked them all to
leave the room; then he knelt and prayed.
Turning to the body he said, "Get up, Tabitha." And she opened her eyes! When she
saw Peter, she sat up! 41He gave her his hand
and helped her up. Then he called in the
widows and all the believers, and he presented her to them alive.
42The news spread through the whole
town, and many believed in the Lord. 43And
Peter stayed a long time in Joppa, living
with Simon, a tanner of hides.

Cornelius Calls for Peter

10 In Caesarea there lived a Roman army
officer* named Cornelius, who was a
captain of the Italian Regiment. 2He was a
devout, God-fearing man, as was everyone
in his household. He gave generously to the
poor and prayed regularly to God. 3One afternoon about three o'clock, he had a vision
in which he saw an angel of God coming
toward him. "Cornelius!" the angel said.
4Cornelius stared at him in terror. "What
is it, sir?" he asked the angel.
And the angel replied, "Your prayers
and gifts to the poor have been received by
God as an offering! 5Now send some men to
Joppa, and summon a man named Simon
Peter. 6He is staying with Simon, a tanner
who lives near the seashore."
7As soon as the angel was gone, Cornelius
called two of his household servants and a
devout soldier, one of his personal attendants. 8He told them what had happened
and sent them off to Joppa.

Peter Visits Cornelius

9The next day as Cornelius's messengers
were nearing the town, Peter went up on the

Synagogues

As a Jew, it was natural for Paul to begin his evangelism in the synagogues (e.g., Acts 9:20; 13:5, 14; 14:1; 17:2, 10, 17; 18:4, 19), for he believed that the Jews should be the first to hear about the Messiah (Romans 1:16). The synagogue (from a Greek word meaning "gathering") had developed as an institution during the Exile. With the Temple in Jerusalem almost one thousand miles away and lying in ruins, the Jews could no longer offer sacrifices; so they had to develop new ways of worshiping. They therefore began to simply "gather" wherever they could—often under trees by Babylon's rivers (e.g., Psalm 137:1), where they would read the Law, listen to sermons, pray, and share friendship. By New Testament times, synagogues were a key social and religious meeting place, and Paul made use of this fact by always beginning his preaching there.

flat roof to pray. It was about noon, 10and
he was hungry. But while a meal was being
prepared, he fell into a trance. 11He saw the
sky open, and something like a large sheet
was let down by its four corners. 12In the
sheet were all sorts of animals, reptiles, and
birds. 13Then a voice said to him, "Get up,
Peter; kill and eat them."

14"No, Lord," Peter declared. "I have
never eaten anything that our Jewish laws
have declared impure and unclean.*"

15But the voice spoke again: "Do not
call something unclean if God has made
it clean." 16The same vision was repeated
three times. Then the sheet was suddenly
pulled up to heaven.

17Peter was very perplexed. What could
the vision mean? Just then the men sent
by Cornelius found Simon's house. Standing outside the gate, 18they asked if a man
named Simon Peter was staying there.

19Meanwhile, as Peter was puzzling over
the vision, the Holy Spirit said to him, "Three
men have come looking for you. 20Get up, go
downstairs, and go with them without hesitation. Don't worry, for I have sent them."

21So Peter went down and said, "I'm the
man you are looking for. Why have you
come?"

22They said, "We were sent by Cornelius,
a Roman officer. He is a devout and God-
fearing man, well respected by all the Jews.
A holy angel instructed him to summon
you to his house so that he can hear your
message." 23So Peter invited the men to stay
for the night. The next day he went with
them, accompanied by some of the brothers from Joppa.

24They arrived in Caesarea the following
day. Cornelius was waiting for them and
had called together his relatives and close
friends. 25As Peter entered his home, Cornelius fell at his feet and worshiped him.
26But Peter pulled him up and said, "Stand
up! I'm a human being just like you!" 27So
they talked together and went inside, where
many others were assembled.

28Peter told them, "You know it is against
our laws for a Jewish man to enter a Gentile
home like this or to associate with you. But
God has shown me that I should no longer
think of anyone as impure or unclean. 29So
I came without objection as soon as I was
sent for. Now tell me why you sent for me."

30Cornelius replied, "Four days ago I was
praying in my house about this same time,

9:30 Greek *brothers.* **9:36** The names *Tabitha* in Aramaic and *Dorcas* in Greek both mean "gazelle." **10:1** Greek *a centurion;* similarly in 10:22. **10:14** Greek *anything common and unclean.*

Goodness

The world today can be remarkably critical of those who do good. Perhaps it is because others' good deeds expose our own lack of them, so we look for reasons why they can't be good, dismissing people who do good as self-serving or hypocritical. Despite this, Christians should be unashamed do-gooders. After all, God himself is good, and that goodness flows into his creation (Genesis 1:4, 10, 12, 18, 21, 25, 31). But it is not only creation that is designed to show God's goodness; so are God's people. Paul wrote that Christians are "God's masterpiece" and that God has "created us anew in Christ Jesus, so we can do the good things he planned for us long ago" (Ephesians 2:10). That's what Dorcas had become known for—"always doing kind things for others and helping the poor" (Acts 9:36). Such good works not only have value in themselves, treating others with the dignity God gives them; they also build platforms for the gospel. As Jesus said, "Let your good deeds shine out for all to see, so that everyone will praise your heavenly Father" (Matthew 5:16).

The New Testament not only calls believers to do good works (e.g., Galatians 6:9-10; 1 Peter 3:8-17); it also casts doubt on the reality of the salvation of those who claim to be saved but do not do good works (e.g., James 2:14-26). Good works cannot save us, but they can show we are saved.

▸ *See also **Faith and works**, page 1415.*

three o'clock in the afternoon. Suddenly,
a man in dazzling clothes was standing in
front of me. 31He told me, 'Cornelius, your
prayer has been heard, and your gifts to
the poor have been noticed by God! 32Now
send messengers to Joppa, and summon a
man named Simon Peter. He is staying in
the home of Simon, a tanner who lives near
the seashore.' 33So I sent for you at once,
and it was good of you to come. Now we
are all here, waiting before God to hear the
message the Lord has given you."

The Gentiles Hear the Good News

34Then Peter replied, "I see very clearly that
God shows no favoritism. 35In every nation
he accepts those who fear him and do what
is right. 36This is the message of Good News
for the people of Israel—that there is peace
with God through Jesus Christ, who is Lord
of all. 37You know what happened throughout Judea, beginning in Galilee, after John
began preaching his message of baptism.
38And you know that God anointed Jesus
of Nazareth with the Holy Spirit and with
power. Then Jesus went around doing good
and healing all who were oppressed by the
devil, for God was with him.

39"And we apostles are witnesses of all
he did throughout Judea and in Jerusalem.
They put him to death by hanging him on
a cross,* 40but God raised him to life on the
third day. Then God allowed him to appear,
41not to the general public,* but to us whom
God had chosen in advance to be his witnesses. We were those who ate and drank
with him after he rose from the dead. 42And
he ordered us to preach everywhere and to
testify that Jesus is the one appointed by
God to be the judge of all—the living and
the dead. 43He is the one all the prophets
testified about, saying that everyone who
believes in him will have their sins forgiven
through his name."

The Gentiles Receive the Holy Spirit

44Even as Peter was saying these things, the
Holy Spirit fell upon all who were listening
to the message. 45The Jewish believers* who
came with Peter were amazed that the gift of
the Holy Spirit had been poured out on the
Gentiles, too. 46For they heard them speaking in other tongues* and praising God.

Then Peter asked, 47"Can anyone object
to their being baptized, now that they have
received the Holy Spirit just as we did?" 48So
he gave orders for them to be baptized in
the name of Jesus Christ. Afterward Cornelius asked him to stay with them for several
days.

Peter Explains His Actions

11 Soon the news reached the apostles
and other believers* in Judea that
the Gentiles had received the word of God.
2But when Peter arrived back in Jerusalem,

Prejudice

When Peter resisted God's command (Acts 10:14), he was revealing not just his traditions—after all, in the Law Jews were forbidden to eat unclean foods—but also his prejudice. His attitude was so ingrained that even when God, who had given that Law, told him to act differently, he struggled. But Peter was about to find his prejudices challenged and changed. He was led to enter the home of a Gentile, a big step for a Jew (10:28); but remembering his vision, and finding Gentiles hungry to hear God's word, he finally realized what God was doing: "I see very clearly that God shows no favoritism. In every nation he accepts those who fear him and do what is right" (10:34-35). He had worked through his prejudice, and the church would never be the same again.

Prejudice—a built-in dislike of people (e.g., John 7:49), ethnic groups (e.g., Esther 3:5-6), places (e.g., John 1:46) or ideas (e.g., Matthew 22:23)—is deeply rooted in fallen humanity. Yet God himself is without prejudice (e.g., Matthew 5:45; Acts 10:34; Romans 2:11), and he calls his people to be without prejudice too (e.g., Leviticus 19:15; James 2:8-9). To have prejudice in our lives is not to live as a Christian.

the Jewish believers* criticized him. 3“You
entered the home of Gentiles* and even ate
with them!” they said.
4Then Peter told them exactly what had
happened. 5“I was in the town of Joppa,” he
said, “and while I was praying, I went into
a trance and saw a vision. Something like a
large sheet was let down by its four corners
from the sky. And it came right down to me.
6When I looked inside the sheet, I saw all
sorts of tame and wild animals, reptiles,
and birds. 7And I heard a voice say, ‘Get up,
Peter; kill and eat them.’
8“‘No, Lord,’ I replied. ‘I have never eaten
anything that our Jewish laws have declared
impure or unclean.*’
9“But the voice from heaven spoke again:
‘Do not call something unclean if God has
made it clean.’ 10This happened three times
before the sheet and all it contained was
pulled back up to heaven.
11“Just then three men who had been
sent from Caesarea arrived at the house
where we were staying. 12The Holy Spirit
told me to go with them and not to worry
that they were Gentiles. These six brothers
here accompanied me, and we soon entered
the home of the man who had sent for us.
13He told us how an angel had appeared to
him in his home and had told him, ‘Send
messengers to Joppa, and summon a man
named Simon Peter. 14He will tell you how
you and everyone in your household can be
saved!’
15“As I began to speak,” Peter continued,
“the Holy Spirit fell on them, just as he fell
on us at the beginning. 16Then I thought of
the Lord’s words when he said, ‘John baptized with* water, but you will be baptized
with the Holy Spirit.’ 17And since God gave
these Gentiles the same gift he gave us
when we believed in the Lord Jesus Christ,
who was I to stand in God’s way?”
18When the others heard this, they
stopped objecting and began praising God.
They said, “We can see that God has also
given the Gentiles the privilege of repenting
of their sins and receiving eternal life.”

10:39 Greek *on a tree.* **10:41** Greek *the people.* **10:45** Greek *The faithful ones of the circumcision.* **10:46** Or *in other languages.* **11:1** Greek *brothers.* **11:2** Greek *those of the circumcision.* **11:3** Greek *of uncircumcised men.* **11:8** Greek *anything common or unclean.* **11:16** Or *in*; also in 11:16b.

Repentance

Repentance is a common theme in the preaching of the apostles in Acts (e.g., 2:38; 3:19; 5:31; 8:22; 11:18; 13:24; 17:30; 19:4; 20:21; 26:20). Repentance is about recognizing that the way we have been thinking and living is wrong, that it falls short of God’s standards and God’s ways. But simply recognizing this is not enough; we then have to do something about it. This is why Peter, after healing the crippled beggar at the Temple, told the crowd, “Now repent of your sins and turn to God” (Acts 3:19; see also 26:20). Once we see we are in the wrong, we need to make a conscious decision to stop living that way, to seek God’s forgiveness and cleansing for what is past on the basis of Christ’s sacrifice for us, and to turn and follow him from then on. Repentance therefore involves a turning *from* sin and a turning *to* God in faith. Faith is simply trusting God, his word, and his promises, and choosing to rely completely on him from now on.

But Acts 11:18 reminds us that repentance is not just a decision that *we* make; repentance is also the gift of God (see also Romans 2:4)—a gift that he longs for all to find (2 Peter 3:9). Without God opening our eyes to see ourselves as we really are, we would never turn to him.

Repentance is crucial to opening the door to a relationship with God. But it is also crucial to maintaining that relationship with him, which is why we often find calls to God’s own people to repent—not to find salvation again, but to restore the relationship with God that has been broken and to put faith in him afresh (e.g., 2 Chronicles 7:13-14; Psalm 51:1-13; 2 Corinthians 7:8-11; Revelation 2:4-6).

▸ *See also **Faith**, page 1286.*

The Church in Antioch of Syria

[19]Meanwhile, the believers who had been
scattered during the persecution after
Stephen's death traveled as far as Phoenicia, Cyprus, and Antioch of Syria. They
preached the word of God, but only to Jews.
[20]However, some of the believers who went
to Antioch from Cyprus and Cyrene began
preaching to the Gentiles* about the Lord
Jesus. [21]The power of the Lord was with
them, and a large number of these Gentiles
believed and turned to the Lord.

[22]When the church at Jerusalem heard
what had happened, they sent Barnabas
to Antioch. [23]When he arrived and saw this
evidence of God's blessing, he was filled
with joy, and he encouraged the believers
to stay true to the Lord. [24]Barnabas was a
good man, full of the Holy Spirit and strong
in faith. And many people were brought to
the Lord.

[25]Then Barnabas went on to Tarsus to
look for Saul. [26]When he found him, he
brought him back to Antioch. Both of them
stayed there with the church for a full year,
teaching large crowds of people. (It was at
Antioch that the believers* were first called
Christians.)

[27]During this time some prophets traveled from Jerusalem to Antioch. [28]One of
them named Agabus stood up in one of the
meetings and predicted by the Spirit that a
great famine was coming upon the entire
Roman world. (This was fulfilled during
the reign of Claudius.) [29]So the believers
in Antioch decided to send relief to the
brothers and sisters* in Judea, everyone
giving as much as they could. [30]This they
did, entrusting their gifts to Barnabas and
Saul to take to the elders of the church in
Jerusalem.

James Is Killed and Peter Is Imprisoned

12 About that time King Herod Agrippa*
began to persecute some believers
in the church. [2]He had the apostle James
(John's brother) killed with a sword. [3]When
Herod saw how much this pleased the
Jewish people, he also arrested Peter. (This
took place during the Passover celebration.*) [4]Then he imprisoned him, placing
him under the guard of four squads of four
soldiers each. Herod intended to bring
Peter out for public trial after the Passover.
[5]But while Peter was in prison, the church
prayed very earnestly for him.

Peter's Miraculous Escape from Prison

[6]The night before Peter was to be placed
on trial, he was asleep, fastened with two
chains between two soldiers. Others stood
guard at the prison gate. [7]Suddenly, there
was a bright light in the cell, and an angel
of the Lord stood before Peter. The angel
struck him on the side to awaken him and
said, "Quick! Get up!" And the chains fell
off his wrists. [8]Then the angel told him, "Get
dressed and put on your sandals." And he
did. "Now put on your coat and follow me,"
the angel ordered.

[9]So Peter left the cell, following the angel.
But all the time he thought it was a vision.
He didn't realize it was actually happening.
[10]They passed the first and second guard

▸ **11:27-30** *See **Prophecy in the New Testament**, page 1318.* **12:1** *See **The Herods**, page 1072.*

Christian

While today "Christian" is the most common term for a follower of Jesus, it didn't start out that way. In fact, it was first used of them by outsiders as a nickname—created in the same way as "Herodian" or "Caesarian," but almost certainly with a derogatory tone, for Antiochans were notorious for making fun of people. The word only occurs three times in the New Testament (Acts 11:26; 26:28; 1 Peter 4:16), in each case in the context of sneering unbelievers. The far more common word for a follower of Jesus was "disciple," which occurs 282 times in the New Testament; but in the second century AD the church adopted the term "Christian" with pride, and it has stuck ever since. Sadly, in many places today it is identified with a certain culture rather than a real relationship with Jesus Christ.

posts and came to the iron gate leading to
the city, and this opened for them all by
itself. So they passed through and started
walking down the street, and then the angel
suddenly left him.
11 Peter finally came to his senses. "It's
really true!" he said. "The Lord has sent his
angel and saved me from Herod and from
what the Jewish leaders* had planned to do
to me!"
12 When he realized this, he went to the
home of Mary, the mother of John Mark,
where many were gathered for prayer.
13 He knocked at the door in the gate, and
a servant girl named Rhoda came to open
it. 14 When she recognized Peter's voice, she
was so overjoyed that, instead of opening
the door, she ran back inside and told everyone, "Peter is standing at the door!"
15 "You're out of your mind!" they said.
When she insisted, they decided, "It must
be his angel."
16 Meanwhile, Peter continued knocking.
When they finally opened the door and saw
him, they were amazed. 17 He motioned for
them to quiet down and told them how the
Lord had led him out of prison. "Tell James
and the other brothers what happened," he
said. And then he went to another place.
18 At dawn there was a great commotion
among the soldiers about what had happened to Peter. 19 Herod Agrippa ordered a
thorough search for him. When he couldn't
be found, Herod interrogated the guards and
sentenced them to death. Afterward Herod
left Judea to stay in Caesarea for a while.

The Death of Herod Agrippa

20 Now Herod was very angry with the people
of Tyre and Sidon. So they sent a delegation to make peace with him because their
cities were dependent upon Herod's country
for food. The delegates won the support of
Blastus, Herod's personal assistant, 21 and an
appointment with Herod was granted. When
the day arrived, Herod put on his royal robes,
sat on his throne, and made a speech to them.
22 The people gave him a great ovation, shouting, "It's the voice of a god, not of a man!"
23 Instantly, an angel of the Lord struck
Herod with a sickness, because he accepted
the people's worship instead of giving the
glory to God. So he was consumed with
worms and died.
24 Meanwhile, the word of God continued to spread, and there were many new
believers.
25 When Barnabas and Saul had finished
their mission to Jerusalem, they returned,*
taking John Mark with them.

Barnabas and Saul Are Commissioned

13 Among the prophets and teachers
of the church at Antioch of Syria
were Barnabas, Simeon (called "the black
man"*), Lucius (from Cyrene), Manaen

11:20 Greek *the Hellenists* (i.e., those who speak Greek); other manuscripts read *the Greeks.* **11:26** Greek *disciples;* also in 11:29. **11:29** Greek *the brothers.* **12:1** Greek *Herod the king.* He was the nephew of Herod Antipas and a grandson of Herod the Great. **12:3** Greek *the days of unleavened bread.* **12:11** Or *the Jewish people.* **12:25** Or *mission, they returned to Jerusalem.* Other manuscripts read *mission, they returned from Jerusalem;* still others read *mission, they returned from Jerusalem to Antioch.* **13:1a** Greek *who was called Niger.*

Antioch

The persecution that followed Stephen's martyrdom caused Christians to flee, taking the gospel with them (Acts 8:1-4). Some fled north to Antioch in Syria, where they began to preach effectively to Gentiles as well as Jews (11:19-21). Antioch (modern Antakya in Turkey) was a key city, with a population of half a million people. It lay on the Orontes River, so it had access to the sea, and it was the capital of the Roman province of Syria. Only Alexandria and Rome were larger in ancient times. It became a major base for the expansion of Christianity, and all Paul's missionary journeys were based out of the church here. Eventually the Antioch church would overtake Jerusalem in significance because the Jerusalem church became stuck in its Jewish ways while Antioch was open to the fresh things that the Holy Spirit was leading them into—a salutary warning about not remaining stuck in the past.

▸ *See also* ***Paul's Missionary Journeys*** *map, Visual Overview Z15.*

(the childhood companion of King Herod Antipas*), and Saul. 2One day as these men were worshiping the Lord and fasting, the Holy Spirit said, "Appoint Barnabas and Saul for the special work to which I have called them." 3So after more fasting and prayer, the men laid their hands on them and sent them on their way.

Paul's First Missionary Journey

4So Barnabas and Saul were sent out by the Holy Spirit. They went down to the seaport of Seleucia and then sailed for the island of Cyprus. 5There, in the town of Salamis, they went to the Jewish synagogues and preached the word of God. John Mark went with them as their assistant.

6Afterward they traveled from town to town across the entire island until finally they reached Paphos, where they met a Jewish sorcerer, a false prophet named Bar-Jesus. 7He had attached himself to the governor, Sergius Paulus, who was an intelligent man. The governor invited Barnabas and Saul to visit him, for he wanted to hear the word of God. 8But Elymas, the sorcerer (as his name means in Greek), interfered and urged the governor to pay no attention to what Barnabas and Saul said. He was trying to keep the governor from believing.

9Saul, also known as Paul, was filled with the Holy Spirit, and he looked the sorcerer in the eye. 10Then he said, "You son of the devil, full of every sort of deceit and fraud, and enemy of all that is good! Will you never stop perverting the true ways of the Lord? 11Watch now, for the Lord has laid his hand of punishment upon you, and you will be struck blind. You will not see the sunlight for some time." Instantly mist and darkness came over the man's eyes, and he began groping around begging for someone to take his hand and lead him.

12When the governor saw what had happened, he became a believer, for he was astonished at the teaching about the Lord.

Paul Preaches in Antioch of Pisidia

13Paul and his companions then left Paphos by ship for Pamphylia, landing at the port town of Perga. There John Mark left them and returned to Jerusalem. 14But Paul and Barnabas traveled inland to Antioch of Pisidia.*

On the Sabbath they went to the synagogue for the services. 15After the usual readings from the books of Moses* and the prophets, those in charge of the service sent them this message: "Brothers, if you have any word of encouragement for the people, come and give it."

16So Paul stood, lifted his hand to quiet them, and started speaking. "Men of Israel," he said, "and you God-fearing Gentiles, listen to me.

17"The God of this nation of Israel chose our ancestors and made them multiply and grow strong during their stay in Egypt. Then with a powerful arm he led them out of their slavery. 18He put up with them* through forty years of wandering in the wilderness. 19Then he destroyed seven nations in Canaan and gave their land to Israel as an inheritance. 20All this took about 450 years.

"After that, God gave them judges to rule until the time of Samuel the prophet. 21Then the people begged for a king, and God gave them Saul son of Kish, a man of the tribe of Benjamin, who reigned for forty years. 22But God removed Saul and replaced him with David, a man about whom God said, 'I have found David son of Jesse, a man after my own heart. He will do everything I want him to do.'*

23"And it is one of King David's descendants, Jesus, who is God's promised Savior of Israel! 24Before he came, John the Baptist preached that all the people of Israel needed to repent of their sins and turn to God and be baptized. 25As John was finishing his ministry he asked, 'Do you think I am the Messiah? No, I am not! But he is coming soon—and I'm not even worthy to be his slave and untie the sandals on his feet.'

26"Brothers—you sons of Abraham, and also you God-fearing Gentiles—this message of salvation has been sent to us! 27The people in Jerusalem and their leaders did not recognize Jesus as the one the prophets had spoken about. Instead, they condemned him, and in doing this they fulfilled the prophets' words that are read every Sabbath. 28They found no legal reason to execute him, but they asked Pilate to have him killed anyway.

▸ **13:2** *See **Does fasting have any value?**, page 1042.*

29“When they had done all that the prophecies said about him, they took him down
from the cross* and placed him in a tomb.
30But God raised him from the dead! 31And
over a period of many days he appeared to
those who had gone with him from Galilee
to Jerusalem. They are now his witnesses to
the people of Israel.
32“And now we are here to bring you this
Good News. The promise was made to our
ancestors, 33and God has now fulfilled it
for us, their descendants, by raising Jesus.
This is what the second psalm says about
Jesus:

> ‘You are my Son.
> Today I have become your Father.*’

34For God had promised to raise him from
the dead, not leaving him to rot in the grave.
He said, ‘I will give you the sacred blessings
I promised to David.’* 35Another psalm explains it more fully: ‘You will not allow your
Holy One to rot in the grave.’* 36This is not a
reference to David, for after David had done
the will of God in his own generation, he
died and was buried with his ancestors, and
his body decayed. 37No, it was a reference to
someone else—someone whom God raised
and whose body did not decay.
38*“Brothers, listen! We are here to proclaim that through this man Jesus there is
forgiveness for your sins. 39Everyone who
believes in him is made right in God’s sight—
something the law of Moses could never do.
40Be careful! Don’t let the prophets’ words
apply to you. For they said,

> 41 ‘Look, you mockers,
> be amazed and die!
> For I am doing something in your own
> day,
> something you wouldn’t believe
> even if someone told you about it.’*”

42As Paul and Barnabas left the synagogue that day, the people begged them
to speak about these things again the next
week. 43Many Jews and devout converts to
Judaism followed Paul and Barnabas, and
the two men urged them to continue to rely
on the grace of God.

Paul Turns to the Gentiles

44The following week almost the entire city
turned out to hear them preach the word of
the Lord. 45But when some of the Jews saw the
crowds, they were jealous; so they slandered
Paul and argued against whatever he said.
46Then Paul and Barnabas spoke out
boldly and declared, “It was necessary that

13:1b Greek *Herod the tetrarch.* **13:13-14** *Pamphylia* and *Pisidia* were districts in what is now Turkey. **13:15** Greek *from the law.* **13:18** Some manuscripts read *He cared for them;* compare Deut 1:31. **13:22** 1 Sam 13:14. **13:29** Greek *from the tree.* **13:33** Or *Today I reveal you as my Son.* Ps 2:7. **13:34** Isa 55:3. **13:35** Ps 16:10. **13:38** English translations divide verses 38 and 39 in various ways. **13:41** Hab 1:5 (Greek version).

Election

“All who were chosen for eternal life became believers” (Acts 13:48). In this short statement, Luke sums up how salvation involves both divine appointment and human faith. On the one hand, God elects (chooses) people (e.g., Deuteronomy 7:7-8; John 15:16; Romans 8:33; 1 Peter 2:9), for we cannot save ourselves—and he does so even before our lives (Jeremiah 1:5) and the world itself (Ephesians 1:4) began. Yet on the other hand, people are constantly called to repent and choose God: This is our responsibility (Mark 1:15; John 1:12; Acts 2:38; 3:19; 16:31; 17:30). Both aspects—God’s election and human response—are vital. How these fit together is a mystery, though Paul tries hard to explain it in Romans 9–11.

There is nothing arbitrary about election, however, nor is it an end in itself. It is part of God’s overall plan, a means of bringing about his will. It should not make us arrogant (“God has chosen us and not others”)—though sadly this happened with Israel. Rather, the doctrine of election should restrain our pride (1 Corinthians 1:26-31), bring encouragement in hardship (Romans 8:28-39), be a provocation to holy living (Colossians 3:12-14), stir worship to God for the privilege of being his children (Ephesians 1:3-12), and be a stimulus to preach the gospel (2 Timothy 2:10). Election is for a purpose, not an end in itself.

we first preach the word of God to you Jews.
But since you have rejected it and judged
yourselves unworthy of eternal life, we will
offer it to the Gentiles. 47 For the Lord gave us
this command when he said,

'I have made you a light to the Gentiles,
to bring salvation to the farthest
corners of the earth.'*"

48 When the Gentiles heard this, they
were very glad and thanked the Lord for
his message; and all who were chosen for
eternal life became believers. 49 So the Lord's
message spread throughout that region.
50 Then the Jews stirred up the influential religious women and the leaders of the
city, and they incited a mob against Paul
and Barnabas and ran them out of town.
51 So they shook the dust from their feet as
a sign of rejection and went to the town of
Iconium. 52 And the believers* were filled
with joy and with the Holy Spirit.

Paul and Barnabas in Iconium

14 The same thing happened in Iconium.* Paul and Barnabas went to the
Jewish synagogue and preached with such
power that a great number of both Jews
and Greeks became believers. 2 Some of the
Jews, however, spurned God's message and
poisoned the minds of the Gentiles against
Paul and Barnabas. 3 But the apostles stayed
there a long time, preaching boldly about
the grace of the Lord. And the Lord proved
their message was true by giving them
power to do miraculous signs and wonders.
4 But the people of the town were divided in
their opinion about them. Some sided with
the Jews, and some with the apostles.
5 Then a mob of Gentiles and Jews, along
with their leaders, decided to attack and
stone them. 6 When the apostles learned of
it, they fled to the region of Lycaonia—to
the towns of Lystra and Derbe and the surrounding area. 7 And there they preached
the Good News.

Paul and Barnabas in Lystra and Derbe

8 While they were at Lystra, Paul and Barnabas came upon a man with crippled feet.
He had been that way from birth, so he had
never walked. He was sitting 9 and listening
as Paul preached. Looking straight at him,
Paul realized he had faith to be healed. 10 So
Paul called to him in a loud voice, "Stand
up!" And the man jumped to his feet and
started walking.
11 When the crowd saw what Paul had
done, they shouted in their local dialect,
"These men are gods in human form!"
12 They decided that Barnabas was the Greek
god Zeus and that Paul was Hermes, since

Accountability

There is something in our sinful human hearts that reacts negatively to the idea of accountability. While we know we have to live with it in our workplace, many reject it in the church. Yet God wants us to be accountable—to be responsible to others for our actions. In fact, it was when Adam and Eve didn't want to be accountable to God that things started to go wrong (Genesis 2:15-17; 3:1-24).

Jesus himself believed in accountability, both teaching its importance (e.g., Matthew 25:19-30) and implementing it with his disciples (e.g., Luke 9:1-2, 10). He strongly commended the Roman officer for his understanding of accountability, saying he had never seen such great faith (Matthew 8:5-10). Above all, he lived a life of complete accountability to his Father (e.g., John 8:28).

It is not surprising therefore that accountability operated at every level of the early church's life. It was put into practice concerning what they believed (Galatians 2:2) and how they lived with one another (James 5:16). Even the apostles were ready to give an account of their ministry. So, having been sent out by the church at Antioch (Acts 13:1-3), Paul and Barnabas reported back to them upon their return (14:26-27).

Accountability is a good principle, calling us to be faithful and trustworthy servants.

he was the chief speaker. 13Now the temple
of Zeus was located just outside the town.
So the priest of the temple and the crowd
brought bulls and wreaths of flowers to the
town gates, and they prepared to offer sacrifices to the apostles.
14But when the apostles Barnabas and
Paul heard what was happening, they tore
their clothing in dismay and ran out among
the people, shouting, 15"Friends,* why
are you doing this? We are merely human
beings—just like you! We have come to
bring you the Good News that you should
turn from these worthless things and turn to
the living God, who made heaven and earth,
the sea, and everything in them. 16In the
past he permitted all the nations to go their
own ways, 17but he never left them without
evidence of himself and his goodness. For
instance, he sends you rain and good crops
and gives you food and joyful hearts." 18But
even with these words, Paul and Barnabas
could scarcely restrain the people from sacrificing to them.
19Then some Jews arrived from Antioch
and Iconium and won the crowds to their
side. They stoned Paul and dragged him out
of town, thinking he was dead. 20But as the
believers* gathered around him, he got up
and went back into the town. The next day
he left with Barnabas for Derbe.

Paul and Barnabas Return to Antioch of Syria

21After preaching the Good News in Derbe
and making many disciples, Paul and Barnabas returned to Lystra, Iconium, and
Antioch of Pisidia, 22where they strengthened the believers. They encouraged them
to continue in the faith, reminding them
that we must suffer many hardships to enter
the Kingdom of God. 23Paul and Barnabas
also appointed elders in every church. With
prayer and fasting, they turned the elders
over to the care of the Lord, in whom they
had put their trust. 24Then they traveled
back through Pisidia to Pamphylia. 25They
preached the word in Perga, then went
down to Attalia.
26Finally, they returned by ship to Antioch
of Syria, where their journey had begun. The
believers there had entrusted them to the
grace of God to do the work they had now
completed. 27Upon arriving in Antioch, they
called the church together and reported
everything God had done through them and
how he had opened the door of faith to the
Gentiles, too. 28And they stayed there with
the believers for a long time.

The Council at Jerusalem

15 While Paul and Barnabas were at
Antioch of Syria, some men from
Judea arrived and began to teach the believers*: "Unless you are circumcised as
required by the law of Moses, you cannot
be saved." 2Paul and Barnabas disagreed
with them, arguing vehemently. Finally, the
church decided to send Paul and Barnabas
to Jerusalem, accompanied by some local
believers, to talk to the apostles and elders
about this question. 3The church sent the
delegates to Jerusalem, and they stopped
along the way in Phoenicia and Samaria to
visit the believers. They told them—much to
everyone's joy—that the Gentiles, too, were
being converted.
4When they arrived in Jerusalem, Barnabas and Paul were welcomed by the whole
church, including the apostles and elders.
They reported everything God had done
through them. 5But then some of the believers who belonged to the sect of the Pharisees stood up and insisted, "The Gentile
converts must be circumcised and required
to follow the law of Moses."
6So the apostles and elders met together
to resolve this issue. 7At the meeting, after a
long discussion, Peter stood and addressed
them as follows: "Brothers, you all know
that God chose me from among you some
time ago to preach to the Gentiles so that
they could hear the Good News and believe.
8God knows people's hearts, and he confirmed that he accepts Gentiles by giving
them the Holy Spirit, just as he did to us.
9He made no distinction between us and
them, for he cleansed their hearts through
faith. 10So why are you now challenging God
by burdening the Gentile believers* with
a yoke that neither we nor our ancestors
were able to bear? 11We believe that we are
all saved the same way, by the undeserved
grace of the Lord Jesus."
12Everyone listened quietly as Barnabas
and Paul told about the miraculous signs

13:47 Isa 49:6. **13:52** Greek *the disciples.* **14:1** *Iconium,* as well as *Lystra* and *Derbe* (14:6), were towns in what is now Turkey. **14:15** Greek *Men.* **14:20** Greek *disciples;* also in 14:22, 28. **15:1** Greek *brothers;* also in 15:3, 23, 32, 33, 36, 40. **15:10** Greek *disciples.*

and wonders God had done through them among the Gentiles.

13 When they had finished, James stood and said, "Brothers, listen to me. 14 Peter* has told you about the time God first visited the Gentiles to take from them a people for himself. 15 And this conversion of Gentiles is exactly what the prophets predicted. As it is written:

16 'Afterward I will return
and restore the fallen house* of David.
I will rebuild its ruins
and restore it,
17 so that the rest of humanity might seek
the LORD,
including the Gentiles—
all those I have called to be mine.
The LORD has spoken—
18 he who made these things known so
long ago.'*

19 "And so my judgment is that we should not make it difficult for the Gentiles who are turning to God. 20 Instead, we should write and tell them to abstain from eating food offered to idols, from sexual immorality, from eating the meat of strangled animals, and from consuming blood. 21 For these laws of Moses have been preached in Jewish synagogues in every city on every Sabbath for many generations."

The Letter for Gentile Believers

22 Then the apostles and elders together with the whole church in Jerusalem chose delegates, and they sent them to Antioch of Syria with Paul and Barnabas to report on this decision. The men chosen were two of the church leaders*—Judas (also called Barsabbas) and Silas. 23 This is the letter they took with them:

"This letter is from the apostles and elders, your brothers in Jerusalem. It is written to the Gentile believers in Antioch, Syria, and Cilicia. Greetings!

24 "We understand that some men from here have troubled you and upset you with their teaching, but we did not send them! 25 So we decided, having come to complete agreement, to send you official representatives, along with our beloved Barnabas and Paul, 26 who have risked their lives for the name of our Lord Jesus Christ. 27 We are sending Judas and Silas to confirm what we have decided concerning your question.

28 "For it seemed good to the Holy Spirit and to us to lay no greater burden on you than these few requirements: 29 You must abstain from eating food offered to idols, from consuming blood or the meat of strangled animals, and from sexual immorality. If you do this, you will do well. Farewell."

30 The messengers went at once to Antioch, where they called a general meeting of the believers and delivered the letter. 31 And there was great joy throughout the church that day as they read this encouraging message.

32 Then Judas and Silas, both being prophets, spoke at length to the believers,

▸ **15:13** *See **James**, page 1413.*

The Council of Jerusalem

When Paul and Barnabas excitedly shared all God had done among the Gentiles (Acts 14:26-27), not everyone was happy. Some Jewish Christians came to Antioch and said the new converts weren't real Christians unless they were circumcised and kept the Jewish Law—in other words, they needed to become Jews to be "real" Christians. Not for the last time in his life, Paul argued against this fiercely, and he and Barnabas were sent to a special meeting of the apostles and elders in Jerusalem—the first church council. After much debate, Peter reminded the council how he had seen the Holy Spirit fall on uncircumcised Gentiles (15:6-11; see 11:1-18), and Paul and Barnabas shared their mission experiences (15:12). It was finally agreed that the Jewish Law was not binding on Gentile Christians but that they should observe some basic Jewish dietary laws (for the sake of fellowship) and avoid all sexual sin. In this way, a division was averted.

encouraging and strengthening their faith.
33 They stayed for a while, and then the believers sent them back to the church in Jerusalem with a blessing of peace.*
35 Paul and Barnabas stayed in Antioch. They and many others taught and preached the word of the Lord there.

Paul and Barnabas Separate

36 After some time Paul said to Barnabas, "Let's go back and visit each city where we previously preached the word of the Lord, to see how the new believers are doing."
37 Barnabas agreed and wanted to take along John Mark.
38 But Paul disagreed strongly, since John Mark had deserted them in Pamphylia and had not continued with them in their work.
39 Their disagreement was so sharp that they separated. Barnabas took John Mark with him and sailed for Cyprus.
40 Paul chose Silas, and as he left, the believers entrusted him to the Lord's gracious care.
41 Then he traveled throughout Syria and Cilicia, strengthening the churches there.

Paul's Second Missionary Journey

16 Paul went first to Derbe and then to Lystra, where there was a young disciple named Timothy. His mother was a Jewish believer, but his father was a Greek.
2 Timothy was well thought of by the believers* in Lystra and Iconium,
3 so Paul wanted him to join them on their journey. In deference to the Jews of the area, he arranged for Timothy to be circumcised before they left, for everyone knew that his father was a Greek.
4 Then they went from town to town, instructing the believers to follow the decisions made by the apostles and elders in Jerusalem.
5 So the churches were strengthened in their faith and grew larger every day.

A Call from Macedonia

6 Next Paul and Silas traveled through the area of Phrygia and Galatia, because the Holy Spirit had prevented them from preaching the word in the province of Asia at that time.
7 Then coming to the borders of Mysia, they headed north for the province of Bithynia,* but again the Spirit of Jesus did not allow them to go there.
8 So instead, they went on through Mysia to the seaport of Troas.
9 That night Paul had a vision: A man from Macedonia in northern Greece was standing there, pleading with him, "Come over to

15:14 Greek *Simeon.* **15:16** Or *kingdom;* Greek reads *tent.* **15:16-18** Amos 9:11-12 (Greek version); Isa 45:21. **15:22** Greek *were leaders among the brothers.* **15:33** Some manuscripts add verse 34, *But Silas decided to stay there.* **16:2** Greek *brothers;* also in 16:40. **16:6-7** *Phrygia, Galatia, Asia, Mysia,* and *Bithynia* were all districts in what is now Turkey.

▸ **15:37** See ***Mark***, page 1388. **16:1-3** See ***Timothy***, page 1380; ***Mentoring***, page 1385. **16:6** See ***Galatia***, page 1338.

Guidance

The Bible assures us often that God wants to guide us, as surely as a shepherd guides his sheep (Psalm 23). Sometimes that guidance is very obvious, as when Paul had a vision of a man pleading for him to come to Macedonia (Acts 16:9-10); sometimes it only becomes clear with hindsight (e.g., Genesis 50:20). But whether it is obvious or not, Christians have the tremendous reassurance of knowing that their heavenly Father is committed to guiding them.

Guidance finds many expressions. A key one is Scripture: "Your word is a lamp to guide my feet and a light for my path" (Psalm 119:105). If we read God's word regularly, we will find him guiding us again and again through what we read. Other means include prophecy (e.g., Acts 11:27-30); prayer (e.g., Acts 13:1-3, where the Holy Spirit brought strategic guidance for the church out of their prayer); dreams and visions (e.g., Acts 10:9-20; 16:9-10); circumstances, as doors open or close before us (e.g., Acts 16:6-8); conviction—a stirring of the Holy Spirit to do something or go somewhere (e.g., Acts 8:29); and the counsel of godly friends (e.g., Proverbs 15:22). When several of these come together, the guidance is all the surer.

Macedonia and help us!" [10]So we* decided to leave for Macedonia at once, having concluded that God was calling us to preach the Good News there.

Lydia of Philippi Believes in Jesus

[11]We boarded a boat at Troas and sailed straight across to the island of Samothrace, and the next day we landed at Neapolis. [12]From there we reached Philippi, a major city of that district of Macedonia and a Roman colony. And we stayed there several days.

[13]On the Sabbath we went a little way outside the city to a riverbank, where we thought people would be meeting for prayer, and we sat down to speak with some women who had gathered there. [14]One of them was Lydia from Thyatira, a merchant of expensive purple cloth, who worshiped God. As she listened to us, the Lord opened her heart, and she accepted what Paul was saying. [15]She and her household were baptized, and she asked us to be her guests. "If you agree that I am a true believer in the Lord," she said, "come and stay at my home." And she urged us until we agreed.

Paul and Silas in Prison

[16]One day as we were going down to the place of prayer, we met a slave girl who had a spirit that enabled her to tell the future. She earned a lot of money for her masters by telling fortunes. [17]She followed Paul and the rest of us, shouting, "These men are servants of the Most High God, and they have come to tell you how to be saved."

[18]This went on day after day until Paul got so exasperated that he turned and said to the demon within her, "I command you in the name of Jesus Christ to come out of her." And instantly it left her.

[19]Her masters' hopes of wealth were now shattered, so they grabbed Paul and Silas and dragged them before the authorities at the marketplace. [20]"The whole city is in an uproar because of these Jews!" they shouted to the city officials. [21]"They are teaching customs that are illegal for us Romans to practice."

[22]A mob quickly formed against Paul and Silas, and the city officials ordered them stripped and beaten with wooden rods. [23]They were severely beaten, and then they were thrown into prison. The jailer was ordered to make sure they didn't escape. [24]So the jailer put them into the inner dungeon and clamped their feet in the stocks.

[25]Around midnight Paul and Silas were praying and singing hymns to God, and the other prisoners were listening. [26]Suddenly, there was a massive earthquake, and the prison was shaken to its foundations. All the doors immediately flew open, and the chains of every prisoner fell off! [27]The jailer woke up to see the prison doors wide open. He assumed the prisoners had escaped, so he drew his sword to kill himself. [28]But Paul

▶ **16:12** *See **Philippi**, page 1356.* **16:16** *See **The occult**, page 337.*

Lydia

Lydia shows us that not everyone who played a significant role in the early church was what we would call today a "full-time" church worker, pastor, or priest. Lydia was a businesswoman from Philippi, a significant Roman city. She was a dealer in purple cloth—an expensive fabric that was worn only by the very rich—so in our terms she was in "high-end" fashion. She is described as someone who "worshiped God" (Acts 16:14)—that is, she believed in the one true God but hadn't converted to Judaism. She responded quickly to the gospel and was baptized. She then opened her home, which was no doubt extensive since she would have been a wealthy woman, to become the base for the church in Philippi (16:15, 40).

▶ *See also **Working for the glory of God**, page 1265; **Hospitality**, page 1410.*

shouted to him, "Stop! Don't kill yourself!
We are all here!"
29The jailer called for lights and ran to the
dungeon and fell down trembling before
Paul and Silas. 30Then he brought them
out and asked, "Sirs, what must I do to be
saved?"
31They replied, "Believe in the Lord Jesus
and you will be saved, along with everyone
in your household." 32And they shared the
word of the Lord with him and with all who
lived in his household. 33Even at that hour
of the night, the jailer cared for them and
washed their wounds. Then he and everyone in his household were immediately
baptized. 34He brought them into his house
and set a meal before them, and he and his
entire household rejoiced because they all
believed in God.
35The next morning the city officials sent
the police to tell the jailer, "Let those men
go!" 36So the jailer told Paul, "The city officials have said you and Silas are free to
leave. Go in peace."
37But Paul replied, "They have publicly
beaten us without a trial and put us in
prison—and we are Roman citizens. So now
they want us to leave secretly? Certainly not!
Let them come themselves to release us!"
38When the police reported this, the city
officials were alarmed to learn that Paul and
Silas were Roman citizens. 39So they came to
the jail and apologized to them. Then they
brought them out and begged them to leave
the city. 40When Paul and Silas left the prison,
they returned to the home of Lydia. There
they met with the believers and encouraged
them once more. Then they left town.

Paul Preaches in Thessalonica

17 Paul and Silas then traveled through
the towns of Amphipolis and Apollo-
nia and came to Thessalonica, where there
was a Jewish synagogue. 2As was Paul's
custom, he went to the synagogue service,
and for three Sabbaths in a row he used the
Scriptures to reason with the people. 3He explained the prophecies and proved that the
Messiah must suffer and rise from the dead.
He said, "This Jesus I'm telling you about
is the Messiah." 4Some of the Jews who listened were persuaded and joined Paul and
Silas, along with many God-fearing Greek
men and quite a few prominent women.*
5But some of the Jews were jealous, so
they gathered some troublemakers from the
marketplace to form a mob and start a riot.
They attacked the home of Jason, searching for Paul and Silas so they could drag
them out to the crowd.* 6Not finding them
there, they dragged out Jason and some of
the other believers* instead and took them
before the city council. "Paul and Silas have
caused trouble all over the world," they
shouted, "and now they are here disturbing our city, too. 7And Jason has welcomed
them into his home. They are all guilty of
treason against Caesar, for they profess allegiance to another king, named Jesus."
8The people of the city, as well as the city
council, were thrown into turmoil by these
reports. 9So the officials forced Jason and
the other believers to post bond, and then
they released them.

16:10 Luke, the writer of this book, here joined Paul and accompanied him on his journey. **17:4** Some manuscripts read *quite a few of the wives of the leading men.* **17:5** Or *the city council.* **17:6** Greek *brothers;* also in 17:10, 14.

▸ **17:1** *See* ***Thessalonica****, page 1370.*

Silas

Silas was a leader in the church at Jerusalem, and he was one of the two men chosen to accompany Paul and Barnabas with the letter from the council of Jerusalem to the church in Antioch (Acts 15:22). He must have struck up a friendship with Paul, for after Paul's disagreement with Barnabas regarding John Mark, Paul chose Silas to accompany him on his second missionary journey, in which Silas played a significant role (15:36-41). He is associated with two of Paul's letters (1 Thessalonians 1:1; 2 Thessalonians 1:1) and one of Peter's (1 Peter 5:12).

▸ *See also* ***Paul's Missionary Journeys*** *map, Visual Overview Z15.*

Paul and Silas in Berea

10That very night the believers sent Paul
and Silas to Berea. When they arrived
there, they went to the Jewish synagogue.
11And the people of Berea were more open-
minded than those in Thessalonica, and
they listened eagerly to Paul's message.
They searched the Scriptures day after day
to see if Paul and Silas were teaching the
truth. 12As a result, many Jews believed, as
did many of the prominent Greek women
and men.

13But when some Jews in Thessalonica
learned that Paul was preaching the word
of God in Berea, they went there and stirred
up trouble. 14The believers acted at once,
sending Paul on to the coast, while Silas
and Timothy remained behind. 15Those es-
corting Paul went with him all the way to
Athens; then they returned to Berea with
instructions for Silas and Timothy to hurry
and join him.

Paul Preaches in Athens

16While Paul was waiting for them in
Athens, he was deeply troubled by all the
idols he saw everywhere in the city. 17He
went to the synagogue to reason with the
Jews and the God-fearing Gentiles, and
he spoke daily in the public square to all
who happened to be there.

18He also had a debate with some of the
Epicurean and Stoic philosophers. When
he told them about Jesus and his resurrection, they said, "What's this babbler trying
to say with these strange ideas he's picked
up?" Others said, "He seems to be preaching about some foreign gods."

19Then they took him to the high council
of the city.* "Come and tell us about this
new teaching," they said. 20"You are saying
some rather strange things, and we want
to know what it's all about." 21(It should be
explained that all the Athenians as well as
the foreigners in Athens seemed to spend
all their time discussing the latest ideas.)

22So Paul, standing before the council,*
addressed them as follows: "Men of Athens,
I notice that you are very religious in every
way, 23for as I was walking along I saw
your many shrines. And one of your altars
had this inscription on it: 'To an Unknown
God.' This God, whom you worship without
knowing, is the one I'm telling you about.

24"He is the God who made the world and
everything in it. Since he is Lord of heaven
and earth, he doesn't live in man-made
temples, 25and human hands can't serve
his needs—for he has no needs. He himself
gives life and breath to everything, and
he satisfies every need. 26From one man*
he created all the nations throughout the
whole earth. He decided beforehand when
they should rise and fall, and he determined their boundaries.

27"His purpose was for the nations to seek
after God and perhaps feel their way toward
him and find him—though he is not far from
any one of us. 28For in him we live and move
and exist. As some of your* own poets have
said, 'We are his offspring.' 29And since this
is true, we shouldn't think of God as an idol
designed by craftsmen from gold or silver
or stone.

30"God overlooked people's ignorance
about these things in earlier times, but
now he commands everyone everywhere to
repent of their sins and turn to him. 31For

Athens

While Athens' glory days were now past, the city remained the great symbol of Greek philosophy. As Greece's capital, it was filled with beautiful buildings and temples, and its streets were lined with statues of famous men and Greek gods, which troubled Paul deeply (Acts 17:16). His evangelism took several approaches—reasoning with Jews and God-fearing Gentiles in the synagogues, preaching in the streets, and debating with the philosophers (17:16-18). He even got to speak to the influential city council (the Areopagus), where he interacted with them by looking for points of contact and quoting their own authors, yet ultimately calling upon them to repent (17:29-31). While some sneered when he spoke of the Resurrection, at least some of these influential intellectuals believed (17:32-34).

he has set a day for judging the world with
justice by the man he has appointed, and
he proved to everyone who this is by raising
him from the dead."
[32]When they heard Paul speak about the
resurrection of the dead, some laughed in
contempt, but others said, "We want to hear
more about this later." [33]That ended Paul's
discussion with them, [34]but some joined
him and became believers. Among them
were Dionysius, a member of the council,*
a woman named Damaris, and others with
them.

Paul Meets Priscilla and Aquila in Corinth

18 Then Paul left Athens and went
to Corinth.* [2]There he became acquainted with a Jew named Aquila, born in
Pontus, who had recently arrived from Italy
with his wife, Priscilla. They had left Italy
when Claudius Caesar deported all Jews from
Rome. [3]Paul lived and worked with them, for
they were tentmakers* just as he was.
[4]Each Sabbath found Paul at the synagogue, trying to convince the Jews and
Greeks alike. [5]And after Silas and Timothy
came down from Macedonia, Paul spent all
his time preaching the word. He testified to
the Jews that Jesus was the Messiah. [6]But
when they opposed and insulted him, Paul
shook the dust from his clothes and said,
"Your blood is upon your own heads—I am
innocent. From now on I will go preach to
the Gentiles."
[7]Then he left and went to the home of
Titius Justus, a Gentile who worshiped
God and lived next door to the synagogue.
[8]Crispus, the leader of the synagogue,
and everyone in his household believed
in the Lord. Many others in Corinth also
heard Paul, became believers, and were
baptized.
[9]One night the Lord spoke to Paul in a
vision and told him, "Don't be afraid! Speak
out! Don't be silent! [10]For I am with you, and
no one will attack and harm you, for many
people in this city belong to me." [11]So Paul
stayed there for the next year and a half,
teaching the word of God.
[12]But when Gallio became governor of

17:19 Or *the most learned society of philosophers in the city.* Greek reads *the Areopagus.* **17:22** Traditionally rendered *standing in the middle of Mars Hill;* Greek reads *standing in the middle of the Areopagus.* **17:26** Greek *From one;* other manuscripts read *From one blood.* **17:28** Some manuscripts read *our.* **17:34** Greek *an Areopagite.* **18:1** *Athens* and *Corinth* were major cities in Achaia, the region in the southern portion of the Greek peninsula. **18:3** Or *leatherworkers.*

▸ **18:1** *See **Corinth**, page 1304.* **18:2** *See **Aquila and Priscilla**, page 1321.*

Working for the glory of God

For many Christians, becoming a "full-time" Christian leader is life's highest goal. Yet this is not a goal we find in the Bible. Serving God in this way is indeed a high calling, but most people who served God in the Bible weren't priests or pastors, but people engaged in secular work. In fact, Luke goes out of his way in Acts to note the wide-ranging professions of some key individuals in the early church: Dorcas, a dressmaker (9:39); Simon, a tanner (9:43); Lydia, a textile merchant (16:14); Priscilla and Aquila, tentmakers (18:2-3). Luke himself was a doctor (Colossians 4:14). And even Paul, the great apostle, maintained his trade as a tentmaker (Acts 18:3), using this as a means of supporting his missionary endeavors (1 Corinthians 9:1-18; 1 Thessalonians 2:9). We find a similar picture in the Old Testament.

God didn't call these people out of their workplaces to serve him; he used them in and through those workplaces—and not simply to earn money to give to the church or as an opportunity to witness. Rather, work is an opportunity to reflect what it means to be made in God's image, for God himself works (Genesis 2:2; John 5:17). We therefore need to see our work not as just a duty but as God's vocation for our lives.

▸ *See also **Serving God in our work**, page 956; **Work**, page 1376.*

Achaia, some Jews rose up together against
Paul and brought him before the governor
for judgment. 13They accused Paul of "per-
suading people to worship God in ways that
are contrary to our law."
14But just as Paul started to make his
defense, Gallio turned to Paul's accusers
and said, "Listen, you Jews, if this were a
case involving some wrongdoing or a serious
crime, I would have a reason to accept your
case. 15But since it is merely a question of
words and names and your Jewish law, take
care of it yourselves. I refuse to judge such
matters." 16And he threw them out of the
courtroom.
17The crowd* then grabbed Sosthenes,
the leader of the synagogue, and beat him
right there in the courtroom. But Gallio paid
no attention.

Paul Returns to Antioch of Syria

18Paul stayed in Corinth for some time after
that, then said good-bye to the brothers and
sisters* and went to nearby Cenchrea. There
he shaved his head according to Jewish
custom, marking the end of a vow. Then he
set sail for Syria, taking Priscilla and Aquila
with him.
19They stopped first at the port of Ephesus,
where Paul left the others behind. While
he was there, he went to the synagogue to
reason with the Jews. 20They asked him to
stay longer, but he declined. 21As he left,
however, he said, "I will come back later,*
God willing." Then he set sail from Ephesus.
22The next stop was at the port of Caesarea. From there he went up and visited the
church at Jerusalem* and then went back
to Antioch.
23After spending some time in Antioch,
Paul went back through Galatia and
Phrygia, visiting and strengthening all the
believers.*

Apollos Instructed at Ephesus

24Meanwhile, a Jew named Apollos, an eloquent speaker who knew the Scriptures
well, had arrived in Ephesus from Alexandria in Egypt. 25He had been taught the
way of the Lord, and he taught others about
Jesus with an enthusiastic spirit* and with
accuracy. However, he knew only about
John's baptism. 26When Priscilla and Aquila
heard him preaching boldly in the synagogue, they took him aside and explained
the way of God even more accurately.
27Apollos had been thinking about going
to Achaia, and the brothers and sisters in
Ephesus encouraged him to go. They wrote
to the believers in Achaia, asking them to
welcome him. When he arrived there, he
proved to be of great benefit to those who,
by God's grace, had believed. 28He refuted
the Jews with powerful arguments in public
debate. Using the Scriptures, he explained
to them that Jesus was the Messiah.

Paul's Third Missionary Journey

19 While Apollos was in Corinth, Paul
traveled through the interior regions
until he reached Ephesus, on the coast,
where he found several believers.* 2"Did
you receive the Holy Spirit when you believed?" he asked them.
"No," they replied, "we haven't even
heard that there is a Holy Spirit."
3"Then what baptism did you experience?" he asked.
And they replied, "The baptism of John."
4Paul said, "John's baptism called for
repentance from sin. But John himself told
the people to believe in the one who would
come later, meaning Jesus."
5As soon as they heard this, they were
baptized in the name of the Lord Jesus.
6Then when Paul laid his hands on them,
the Holy Spirit came on them, and they
spoke in other tongues* and prophesied.
7There were about twelve men in all.

Paul Ministers in Ephesus

8Then Paul went to the synagogue and
preached boldly for the next three months,
arguing persuasively about the Kingdom
of God. 9But some became stubborn, rejecting his message and publicly speaking
against the Way. So Paul left the synagogue
and took the believers with him. Then he
held daily discussions at the lecture hall of
Tyrannus. 10This went on for the next two
years, so that people throughout the province of Asia—both Jews and Greeks—heard
the word of the Lord.
11God gave Paul the power to perform

▸ **19:1** *See **Ephesus**, page 1347.*

unusual miracles. 12 When handkerchiefs or aprons that had merely touched his skin were placed on sick people, they were healed of their diseases, and evil spirits were expelled.

13 A group of Jews was traveling from town to town casting out evil spirits. They tried to use the name of the Lord Jesus in their incantation, saying, "I command you in the name of Jesus, whom Paul preaches, to come out!" 14 Seven sons of Sceva, a leading priest, were doing this. 15 But one time when they tried it, the evil spirit replied, "I know Jesus, and I know Paul, but who are you?" 16 Then the man with the evil spirit leaped on them, overpowered them, and attacked them with such violence that they fled from the house, naked and battered.

17 The story of what happened spread quickly all through Ephesus, to Jews and Greeks alike. A solemn fear descended on the city, and the name of the Lord Jesus was greatly honored. 18 Many who became believers confessed their sinful practices. 19 A number of them who had been practicing sorcery brought their incantation books and burned them at a public bonfire. The value of the books was several million dollars.* 20 So the message about the Lord spread widely and had a powerful effect.

21 Afterward Paul felt compelled by the Spirit* to go over to Macedonia and Achaia before going to Jerusalem. "And after that," he said, "I must go on to Rome!" 22 He sent his two assistants, Timothy and Erastus, ahead to Macedonia while he stayed awhile longer in the province of Asia.

The Riot in Ephesus

23 About that time, serious trouble developed in Ephesus concerning the Way. 24 It began with Demetrius, a silversmith who had a large business manufacturing silver shrines of the Greek goddess Artemis.* He kept many craftsmen busy. 25 He called them together, along with others employed in similar trades, and addressed them as follows:

"Gentlemen, you know that our wealth comes from this business. 26 But as you have seen and heard, this man Paul has persuaded many people that handmade gods aren't really gods at all. And he's done this not only here in Ephesus but throughout the entire province! 27 Of course, I'm not just talking about the loss of public respect for our business. I'm also concerned that the temple of the great goddess Artemis will lose its influence and that Artemis—this magnificent goddess worshiped throughout the province of Asia and all around the world—will be robbed of her great prestige!"

18:17 Greek *Everyone;* other manuscripts read *All the Greeks.* **18:18** Greek *brothers;* also in 18:27. **18:21** Some manuscripts read *"I must by all means be at Jerusalem for the upcoming festival, but I will come back later."* **18:22** Greek *the church.* **18:23** Greek *disciples;* also in 18:27. **18:25** Or *with enthusiasm in the Spirit.* **19:1** Greek *disciples;* also in 19:9, 30. **19:6** Or *in other languages.* **19:19** Greek *50,000 pieces of silver,* each of which was the equivalent of a day's wage. **19:21** Or *decided in his spirit.* **19:24** *Artemis* is otherwise known as Diana.

▸ **19:21** *See **Rome**, page 1283.*

The riot over Artemis

Paul's successful preaching in Ephesus meant that many abandoned their idolatry (Acts 19:1-20), which had a huge economic impact (19:23-27). The local guilds were disturbed that sales of their idols, shrines, and amulets would be affected, so they stirred up a riot in opposition to "the Way"—an early term for Christianity (9:2; 19:9; 22:4; 24:14, 22). Artemis (or Diana to the Romans), whose statues were made in Ephesus, was a famous Greek goddess, worshiped across the ancient world. But Ephesus was special because her "image" (19:35)—probably a meteorite—fell to earth here. Her temple here was 350 feet long and 150 feet wide and was one of the seven wonders of the ancient world. It served not only as a place of worship but also as a bank, with deposits from across the world. The gospel was challenging status-quo economics—something as unwelcome in those days as in our own.

▸ *See also **Idols**, page 836; **Ephesus**, page 1347.*

28 At this their anger boiled, and they
began shouting, "Great is Artemis of the
Ephesians!" 29 Soon the whole city was filled
with confusion. Everyone rushed to the
amphitheater, dragging along Gaius and
Aristarchus, who were Paul's traveling companions from Macedonia. 30 Paul wanted to
go in, too, but the believers wouldn't let
him. 31 Some of the officials of the province,
friends of Paul, also sent a message to him,
begging him not to risk his life by entering
the amphitheater.

32 Inside, the people were all shouting,
some one thing and some another. Everything was in confusion. In fact, most of
them didn't even know why they were there.
33 The Jews in the crowd pushed Alexander
forward and told him to explain the situation. He motioned for silence and tried to
speak. 34 But when the crowd realized he
was a Jew, they started shouting again and
kept it up for about two hours: "Great is
Artemis of the Ephesians! Great is Artemis
of the Ephesians!"

35 At last the mayor was able to quiet
them down enough to speak. "Citizens of
Ephesus," he said. "Everyone knows that
Ephesus is the official guardian of the temple
of the great Artemis, whose image fell down
to us from heaven. 36 Since this is an undeniable fact, you should stay calm and not
do anything rash. 37 You have brought these
men here, but they have stolen nothing from
the temple and have not spoken against our
goddess.

38 "If Demetrius and the craftsmen have a
case against them, the courts are in session
and the officials can hear the case at once.
Let them make formal charges. 39 And if
there are complaints about other matters,
they can be settled in a legal assembly. 40 I
am afraid we are in danger of being charged
with rioting by the Roman government,
since there is no cause for all this commotion. And if Rome demands an explanation,
we won't know what to say." 41 *Then he dismissed them, and they dispersed.

Paul Goes to Macedonia and Greece

20 When the uproar was over, Paul
sent for the believers* and encouraged them. Then he said good-bye and left
for Macedonia. 2 While there, he encouraged
the believers in all the towns he passed
through. Then he traveled down to Greece,
3 where he stayed for three months. He was

Teaching God's word

Teaching God's word, both in public and in homes, played a big part in Paul's life (Acts 20:20). As a young man he had trained under Gamaliel, a leading rabbi (22:3), and did well in his studies (Galatians 1:14). It was here that his love for God's word and teaching developed. But when he met the risen Christ, his eyes were opened to understand Scripture as never before.

His passion for teaching and preaching is clear both from Acts and his letters, and he saw teachers and preachers as gifts given by Christ to equip believers for their ministry (Ephesians 4:11-12). From the very beginning, Christians had "devoted themselves to the apostles' teaching" (Acts 2:42), and Luke commends the Bereans who "searched the Scriptures day after day to see if Paul and Silas were teaching the truth" (Acts 17:11).

Ezra, the scribe who ministered to the Jews who returned from exile, sets an excellent example for teachers. He "had determined to study and obey the Law of the LORD and to teach those decrees and regulations to the people of Israel" (Ezra 7:10). Teachers and preachers should first study God's word carefully, then put it into practice themselves, before daring to teach others. James warns that "we who teach will be judged more strictly" (James 3:1)—a good caution against being overambitious in this area.

▸ *See also* ***Bible teaching****, page 529;* ***The Scriptures in public worship****, page 544;* ***Studying God's word****, page 1387.*

preparing to sail back to Syria when he discovered a plot by some Jews against his life,
so he decided to return through Macedonia.
4 Several men were traveling with him.
They were Sopater son of Pyrrhus from
Berea; Aristarchus and Secundus from
Thessalonica; Gaius from Derbe; Timothy;
and Tychicus and Trophimus from the
province of Asia. 5 They went on ahead and
waited for us at Troas. 6 After the Passover*
ended, we boarded a ship at Philippi in
Macedonia and five days later joined them
in Troas, where we stayed a week.

Paul's Final Visit to Troas

7 On the first day of the week, we gathered
with the local believers to share in the Lord's
Supper.* Paul was preaching to them, and
since he was leaving the next day, he kept
talking until midnight. 8 The upstairs room
where we met was lighted with many flickering lamps. 9 As Paul spoke on and on, a
young man named Eutychus, sitting on the
windowsill, became very drowsy. Finally,
he fell sound asleep and dropped three
stories to his death below. 10 Paul went
down, bent over him, and took him into his
arms. "Don't worry," he said, "he's alive!"
11 Then they all went back upstairs, shared
in the Lord's Supper,* and ate together. Paul
continued talking to them until dawn, and
then he left. 12 Meanwhile, the young man
was taken home alive and well, and everyone was greatly relieved.

Paul Meets the Ephesian Elders

13 Paul went by land to Assos, where he had
arranged for us to join him, while we traveled by ship. 14 He joined us there, and we
sailed together to Mitylene. 15 The next day
we sailed past the island of Kios. The following day we crossed to the island of Samos,
and* a day later we arrived at Miletus.
16 Paul had decided to sail on past Ephesus,
for he didn't want to spend any more time
in the province of Asia. He was hurrying to
get to Jerusalem, if possible, in time for the
Festival of Pentecost. 17 But when we landed
at Miletus, he sent a message to the elders of
the church at Ephesus, asking them to come
and meet him.
18 When they arrived he declared, "You
know that from the day I set foot in the
province of Asia until now 19 I have done the
Lord's work humbly and with many tears.
I have endured the trials that came to me
from the plots of the Jews. 20 I never shrank
back from telling you what you needed to
hear, either publicly or in your homes. 21 I
have had one message for Jews and Greeks
alike—the necessity of repenting from sin
and turning to God, and of having faith in
our Lord Jesus.
22 "And now I am bound by the Spirit* to
go to Jerusalem. I don't know what awaits
me, 23 except that the Holy Spirit tells me
in city after city that jail and suffering lie
ahead. 24 But my life is worth nothing to
me unless I use it for finishing the work
assigned me by the Lord Jesus—the work
of telling others the Good News about the
wonderful grace of God.
25 "And now I know that none of you to
whom I have preached the Kingdom will
ever see me again. 26 I declare today that I
have been faithful. If anyone suffers eternal
death, it's not my fault,* 27 for I didn't shrink
from declaring all that God wants you to
know.
28 "So guard yourselves and God's people.
Feed and shepherd God's flock—his church,
purchased with his own blood*—over
which the Holy Spirit has appointed you as
leaders.* 29 I know that false teachers, like
vicious wolves, will come in among you
after I leave, not sparing the flock. 30 Even
some men from your own group will rise
up and distort the truth in order to draw a
following. 31 Watch out! Remember the three
years I was with you—my constant watch
and care over you night and day, and my
many tears for you.
32 "And now I entrust you to God and the
message of his grace that is able to build
you up and give you an inheritance with all
those he has set apart for himself.
33 "I have never coveted anyone's silver or
gold or fine clothes. 34 You know that these
hands of mine have worked to supply my
own needs and even the needs of those who
were with me. 35 And I have been a constant
example of how you can help those in need
by working hard. You should remember the
words of the Lord Jesus: 'It is more blessed
to give than to receive.'"

19:41 Some translations include verse 41 as part of verse 40. **20:1** Greek *disciples.* **20:6** Greek *the days of unleavened bread.* **20:7** Greek *to break bread.* **20:11** Greek *broke the bread.* **20:15** Some manuscripts read *and having stayed at Trogyllium.* **20:22** Or *by my spirit,* or by an inner compulsion; Greek reads *by the spirit.* **20:26** Greek *I am innocent of the blood of all.* **20:28a** Or *with the blood of his own [Son].* **20:28b** Or *overseers,* or *bishops.*

36 When he had finished speaking, he
knelt and prayed with them. 37 They all cried
as they embraced and kissed him good-bye.
38 They were sad most of all because he had
said that they would never see him again.
Then they escorted him down to the ship.

Paul's Journey to Jerusalem

21 After saying farewell to the Ephesian
elders, we sailed straight to the island
of Cos. The next day we reached Rhodes and
then went to Patara. 2 There we boarded a
ship sailing for Phoenicia. 3 We sighted the
island of Cyprus, passed it on our left, and
landed at the harbor of Tyre, in Syria, where
the ship was to unload its cargo.

4 We went ashore, found the local believers,* and stayed with them a week. These
believers prophesied through the Holy Spirit
that Paul should not go on to Jerusalem.
5 When we returned to the ship at the end of
the week, the entire congregation, including women* and children, left the city and
came down to the shore with us. There we
knelt, prayed, 6 and said our farewells. Then
we went aboard, and they returned home.

7 The next stop after leaving Tyre was Ptolemais, where we greeted the brothers and
sisters* and stayed for one day. 8 The next
day we went on to Caesarea and stayed at
the home of Philip the Evangelist, one of the
seven men who had been chosen to distribute food. 9 He had four unmarried daughters
who had the gift of prophecy.

10 Several days later a man named Agabus,
who also had the gift of prophecy, arrived
from Judea. 11 He came over, took Paul's belt,
and bound his own feet and hands with it.
Then he said, "The Holy Spirit declares, 'So
shall the owner of this belt be bound by the
Jewish leaders in Jerusalem and turned over
to the Gentiles.'" 12 When we heard this, we
and the local believers all begged Paul not
to go on to Jerusalem.

13 But he said, "Why all this weeping? You
are breaking my heart! I am ready not only
to be jailed at Jerusalem but even to die for
the sake of the Lord Jesus." 14 When it was
clear that we couldn't persuade him, we
gave up and said, "The Lord's will be done."

Paul Arrives at Jerusalem

15 After this we packed our things and left
for Jerusalem. 16 Some believers from Caesarea accompanied us, and they took us
to the home of Mnason, a man originally
from Cyprus and one of the early believers.
17 When we arrived, the brothers and sisters
in Jerusalem welcomed us warmly.

18 The next day Paul went with us to meet
with James, and all the elders of the Jerusalem church were present. 19 After greeting
them, Paul gave a detailed account of the
things God had accomplished among the
Gentiles through his ministry.

20 After hearing this, they praised God.
And then they said, "You know, dear
brother, how many thousands of Jews have
also believed, and they all follow the law
of Moses very seriously. 21 But the Jewish
believers here in Jerusalem have been told
that you are teaching all the Jews who live
among the Gentiles to turn their backs on
the laws of Moses. They've heard that you
teach them not to circumcise their children
or follow other Jewish customs. 22 What
should we do? They will certainly hear that
you have come.

Tarsus

When Paul was arrested by the Romans, he explained that he was not the Egyptian terrorist the Roman commander mistook him for, but rather a Jew from Tarsus (Acts 21:33-39). Tarsus was the principal city of Cilicia in southeast Asia Minor, and it was an important and strategically located commercial center, a university city, and a home to schools of Stoic philosophy. Paul rightly describes it as "an important city" (21:39). It served as a base for both Alexander the Great and Pompey and was the location of Antony's first meeting with Cleopatra. Hair from the region's goats was famous and was used for tentmaking, which became a specialized occupation in Cilicia—one that Paul himself had learned and would continue to use to support his ministry (Acts 18:3; 20:34; 1 Corinthians 4:12).

23“Here’s what we want you to do. We have four men here who have completed their vow. 24Go with them to the Temple and join them in the purification ceremony, paying for them to have their heads ritually shaved. Then everyone will know that the rumors are all false and that you yourself observe the Jewish laws.

25“As for the Gentile believers, they should do what we already told them in a letter: They should abstain from eating food offered to idols, from consuming blood or the meat of strangled animals, and from sexual immorality.”

Paul Is Arrested

26So Paul went to the Temple the next day with the other men. They had already started the purification ritual, so he publicly announced the date when their vows would end and sacrifices would be offered for each of them.

27The seven days were almost ended when some Jews from the province of Asia saw Paul in the Temple and roused a mob against him. They grabbed him, 28yelling, “Men of Israel, help us! This is the man who preaches against our people everywhere and tells everybody to disobey the Jewish laws. He speaks against the Temple—and even defiles this holy place by bringing in Gentiles.*” 29(For earlier that day they had seen him in the city with Trophimus, a Gentile from Ephesus,* and they assumed Paul had taken him into the Temple.)

30The whole city was rocked by these accusations, and a great riot followed. Paul was grabbed and dragged out of the Temple, and immediately the gates were closed behind him. 31As they were trying to kill him, word reached the commander of the Roman regiment that all Jerusalem was in an uproar. 32He immediately called out his soldiers and officers* and ran down among the crowd. When the mob saw the commander and the troops coming, they stopped beating Paul.

33Then the commander arrested him and ordered him bound with two chains. He asked the crowd who he was and what he had done. 34Some shouted one thing and some another. Since he couldn’t find out the truth in all the uproar and confusion, he ordered that Paul be taken to the fortress. 35As Paul reached the stairs, the mob grew so violent the soldiers had to lift him to their shoulders to protect him. 36And the crowd followed behind, shouting, “Kill him, kill him!”

Paul Speaks to the Crowd

37As Paul was about to be taken inside, he said to the commander, “May I have a word with you?”

“Do you know Greek?” the commander asked, surprised. 38“Aren’t you the Egyptian who led a rebellion some time ago and took 4,000 members of the Assassins out into the desert?”

39“No,” Paul replied, “I am a Jew and a citizen of Tarsus in Cilicia, which is an important city. Please, let me talk to these people.” 40The commander agreed, so Paul stood on the stairs and motioned to the people to be quiet. Soon a deep silence enveloped the crowd, and he addressed them in their own language, Aramaic.*

22 “Brothers and esteemed fathers,” Paul said, “listen to me as I offer my defense.” 2When they heard him speaking in their own language,* the silence was even greater.

3Then Paul said, “I am a Jew, born in Tarsus, a city in Cilicia, and I was brought up and educated here in Jerusalem under Gamaliel. As his student, I was carefully trained in our Jewish laws and customs. I became very zealous to honor God in everything I did, just like all of you today. 4And I persecuted the followers of the Way, hounding some to death, arresting both men and women and throwing them in prison. 5The high priest and the whole council of elders can testify that this is so. For I received letters from them to our Jewish brothers in Damascus, authorizing me to bring the followers of the Way from there to Jerusalem, in chains, to be punished.

6“As I was on the road, approaching Damascus about noon, a very bright light from heaven suddenly shone down around me. 7I fell to the ground and heard a voice saying to me, ‘Saul, Saul, why are you persecuting me?’

8“‘Who are you, lord?’ I asked.

“And the voice replied, ‘I am Jesus the Nazarene,* the one you are persecuting.’ 9The people with me saw the light but didn’t understand the voice speaking to me.

21:4 Greek *disciples;* also in 21:16. **21:5** Or *wives.* **21:7** Greek *brothers;* also in 21:17. **21:28** Greek *Greeks.* **21:29** Greek *Trophimus, the Ephesian.* **21:32** Greek *centurions.* **21:40** Or *Hebrew.* **22:2** Greek *in Aramaic,* or *in Hebrew.* **22:8** Or *Jesus of Nazareth.*

10“I asked, ‘What should I do, Lord?’
“And the Lord told me, ‘Get up and go
into Damascus, and there you will be told
everything you are to do.’
11“I was blinded by the intense light and
had to be led by the hand to Damascus by
my companions. 12A man named Ananias
lived there. He was a godly man, deeply
devoted to the law, and well regarded by all
the Jews of Damascus. 13He came and stood
beside me and said, ‘Brother Saul, regain
your sight.’ And that very moment I could
see him!
14“Then he told me, ‘The God of our ancestors has chosen you to know his will
and to see the Righteous One and hear him
speak. 15For you are to be his witness, telling
everyone what you have seen and heard.
16What are you waiting for? Get up and be
baptized. Have your sins washed away by
calling on the name of the Lord.’
17“After I returned to Jerusalem, I was
praying in the Temple and fell into a trance.
18I saw a vision of Jesus* saying to me,
‘Hurry! Leave Jerusalem, for the people here
won’t accept your testimony about me.’
19“‘But Lord,’ I argued, ‘they certainly
know that in every synagogue I imprisoned and beat those who believed in you.
20And I was in complete agreement when
your witness Stephen was killed. I stood by
and kept the coats they took off when they
stoned him.’
21“But the Lord said to me, ‘Go, for I will
send you far away to the Gentiles!’”
22The crowd listened until Paul said that
word. Then they all began to shout, “Away
with such a fellow! He isn’t fit to live!”
23They yelled, threw off their coats, and
tossed handfuls of dust into the air.

Paul Reveals His Roman Citizenship

24The commander brought Paul inside and
ordered him lashed with whips to make
him confess his crime. He wanted to find
out why the crowd had become so furious.
25When they tied Paul down to lash him,
Paul said to the officer* standing there, “Is
it legal for you to whip a Roman citizen who
hasn’t even been tried?”
26When the officer heard this, he went to
the commander and asked, “What are you
doing? This man is a Roman citizen!”
27So the commander went over and asked
Paul, “Tell me, are you a Roman citizen?”
“Yes, I certainly am,” Paul replied.
28“I am, too,” the commander muttered,
“and it cost me plenty!”
Paul answered, “But I am a citizen by
birth!”
29The soldiers who were about to inter-
rogate Paul quickly withdrew when they

The apostle Paul

Much of the second half of Acts is taken up by the adventures of Paul. When we first meet him, he was a most unlikely candidate for becoming a leading apostle. Formerly a young Pharisee from Tarsus who was fiercely proud of his Jewish heritage (Philippians 3:4-6) and exceptionally zealous to defend “the traditions of [his] ancestors” (Galatians 1:14), he was committed to destroying the church (Acts 8:1-3). But a dramatic encounter with the risen Jesus utterly transformed his life (9:1-22), and he became the church’s most successful missionary and theologian. If Paul could be converted, then anyone can.

Although not one of the original Twelve, Paul was quickly recognized as an apostle because of the special call on his life by the risen Jesus to take the gospel to the Gentile world (e.g., Galatians 2:7-9). The rest of his life was spent doing exactly that. His call as the apostle to the Gentiles was reinforced by him changing his Jewish name, Saul, to a Greek name, Paul. However, he always retained his longing for his own people, the Jews (Romans 9:1-5), to discover Jesus as Messiah; and he always preached to them first (e.g., Acts 14:1-3; 17:1-4; 19:8-10), seeking to show how Jesus had fulfilled all the promises made to Abraham.

▸ *See also* ***Mentoring****, page 1385;* ***The First Journeys of Christian Leaders*** *maps, Visual Overview Z14;* ***Paul’s Missionary Journeys*** *map, Visual Overview Z15.*

heard he was a Roman citizen, and the
commander was frightened because he had
ordered him bound and whipped.

Paul before the High Council

30 The next day the commander ordered the
leading priests into session with the Jewish
high council.* He wanted to find out what
the trouble was all about, so he released
Paul to have him stand before them.

23 Gazing intently at the high council,*
Paul began: "Brothers, I have always
lived before God with a clear conscience!"
2 Instantly Ananias the high priest commanded those close to Paul to slap him on
the mouth. 3 But Paul said to him, "God will
slap you, you corrupt hypocrite!* What kind
of judge are you to break the law yourself by
ordering me struck like that?"
4 Those standing near Paul said to him,
"Do you dare to insult God's high priest?"
5 "I'm sorry, brothers. I didn't realize he
was the high priest," Paul replied, "for the
Scriptures say, 'You must not speak evil of
any of your rulers.'*"
6 Paul realized that some members of the
high council were Sadducees and some
were Pharisees, so he shouted, "Brothers, I
am a Pharisee, as were my ancestors! And I
am on trial because my hope is in the resurrection of the dead!"
7 This divided the council—the Pharisees
against the Sadducees—8 for the Sadducees
say there is no resurrection or angels or
spirits, but the Pharisees believe in all of
these. 9 So there was a great uproar. Some
of the teachers of religious law who were
Pharisees jumped up and began to argue
forcefully. "We see nothing wrong with
him," they shouted. "Perhaps a spirit or an
angel spoke to him." 10 As the conflict grew
more violent, the commander was afraid
they would tear Paul apart. So he ordered
his soldiers to go and rescue him by force
and take him back to the fortress.
11 That night the Lord appeared to Paul and
said, "Be encouraged, Paul. Just as you have
been a witness to me here in Jerusalem, you
must preach the Good News in Rome as well."

The Plan to Kill Paul

12 The next morning a group of Jews* got together and bound themselves with an oath
not to eat or drink until they had killed
Paul. 13 There were more than forty of them
in the conspiracy. 14 They went to the leading
priests and elders and told them, "We have
bound ourselves with an oath to eat nothing
until we have killed Paul. 15 So you and the
high council should ask the commander
to bring Paul back to the council again.
Pretend you want to examine his case more
fully. We will kill him on the way."
16 But Paul's nephew—his sister's son—
heard of their plan and went to the fortress
and told Paul. 17 Paul called for one of the
Roman officers* and said, "Take this young
man to the commander. He has something
important to tell him."
18 So the officer did, explaining, "Paul, the
prisoner, called me over and asked me to
bring this young man to you because he has
something to tell you."
19 The commander took his hand, led him
aside, and asked, "What is it you want to
tell me?"
20 Paul's nephew told him, "Some Jews
are going to ask you to bring Paul before
the high council tomorrow, pretending they
want to get some more information. 21 But
don't do it! There are more than forty men
hiding along the way ready to ambush him.
They have vowed not to eat or drink anything until they have killed him. They are
ready now, just waiting for your consent."
22 "Don't let anyone know you told me
this," the commander warned the young
man.

Paul Is Sent to Caesarea

23 Then the commander called two of his officers and ordered, "Get 200 soldiers ready
to leave for Caesarea at nine o'clock tonight.
Also take 200 spearmen and 70 mounted
troops. 24 Provide horses for Paul to ride, and
get him safely to Governor Felix." 25 Then he
wrote this letter to the governor:

> 26 "From Claudius Lysias, to his
> Excellency, Governor Felix: Greetings!
> 27 "This man was seized by some Jews,
> and they were about to kill him when I
> arrived with the troops. When I learned
> that he was a Roman citizen, I removed
> him to safety. 28 Then I took him to their
> high council to try to learn the basis of

22:18 Greek *him.* **22:25** Greek *the centurion;* also in 22:26.
22:30 Greek *Sanhedrin.* **23:1** Greek *Sanhedrin;* also in 23:6, 15,
20, 28. **23:3** Greek *you whitewashed wall.* **23:5** Exod 22:28.
23:12 Greek *the Jews.* **23:17** Greek *centurions;* also in 23:23.

the accusations against him. [29]I soon discovered the charge was something regarding their religious law—certainly nothing worthy of imprisonment or death. [30]But when I was informed of a plot to kill him, I immediately sent him on to you. I have told his accusers to bring their charges before you."

[31]So that night, as ordered, the soldiers took Paul as far as Antipatris. [32]They returned to the fortress the next morning, while the mounted troops took him on to Caesarea. [33]When they arrived in Caesarea, they presented Paul and the letter to Governor Felix. [34]He read it and then asked Paul what province he was from. "Cilicia," Paul answered.

[35]"I will hear your case myself when your accusers arrive," the governor told him. Then the governor ordered him kept in the prison at Herod's headquarters.*

Paul Appears before Felix

24 Five days later Ananias, the high priest, arrived with some of the Jewish elders and the lawyer* Tertullus, to present their case against Paul to the governor. [2]When Paul was called in, Tertullus presented the charges against Paul in the following address to the governor:

"You have provided a long period of peace for us Jews and with foresight have enacted reforms for us. [3]For all of this, Your Excellency, we are very grateful to you. [4]But I don't want to bore you, so please give me your attention for only a moment. [5]We have found this man to be a troublemaker who is constantly stirring up riots among the Jews all over the world. He is a ringleader of the cult known as the Nazarenes. [6]Furthermore, he was trying to desecrate the Temple when we arrested him.* [8]You can find out the truth of our accusations by examining him yourself." [9]Then the other Jews chimed in, declaring that everything Tertullus said was true.

[10]The governor then motioned for Paul to speak. Paul said, "I know, sir, that you have been a judge of Jewish affairs for many years, so I gladly present my defense before you. [11]You can quickly discover that I arrived in Jerusalem no more than twelve days ago to worship at the Temple. [12]My accusers never found me arguing with anyone in the Temple, nor stirring up a riot in any synagogue or on the streets of the city. [13]These men cannot prove the things they accuse me of doing.

[14]"But I admit that I follow the Way, which they call a cult. I worship the God of our ancestors, and I firmly believe the Jewish law and everything written in the prophets. [15]I have the same hope in God that these men have, that he will raise both the righteous and the unrighteous. [16]Because of this, I always try to maintain a clear conscience before God and all people.

[17]"After several years away, I returned to Jerusalem with money to aid my people and to offer sacrifices to God. [18]My accusers saw me in the Temple as I was completing a purification ceremony. There was no crowd around me and no rioting. [19]But some Jews from the province of Asia were there—and they ought to be here to bring charges if they have anything against me! [20]Ask these men here what crime the Jewish high council* found me guilty of, [21]except for the one time I shouted out, 'I am on trial before you today because I believe in the resurrection of the dead!'"

[22]At that point Felix, who was quite familiar with the Way, adjourned the hearing and said, "Wait until Lysias, the garrison commander, arrives. Then I will decide the case." [23]He ordered an officer* to keep Paul in custody but to give him some freedom and allow his friends to visit him and take care of his needs.

[24]A few days later Felix came back with his wife, Drusilla, who was Jewish. Sending for Paul, they listened as he told them about faith in Christ Jesus. [25]As he reasoned with them about righteousness and self-control and the coming day of judgment, Felix became frightened. "Go away for now," he replied. "When it is more convenient, I'll call for you again." [26]He also hoped that Paul would bribe him, so he sent for him quite often and talked with him.

[27]After two years went by in this way, Felix was succeeded by Porcius Festus. And because Felix wanted to gain favor with the Jewish people, he left Paul in prison.

Paul Appears before Festus

25 Three days after Festus arrived in Caesarea to take over his new responsibilities, he left for Jerusalem, [2]where

the leading priests and other Jewish leaders
met with him and made their accusations
against Paul. 3They asked Festus as a favor
to transfer Paul to Jerusalem (planning
to ambush and kill him on the way). 4But
Festus replied that Paul was at Caesarea and
he himself would be returning there soon.
5So he said, "Those of you in authority can
return with me. If Paul has done anything
wrong, you can make your accusations."

6About eight or ten days later Festus returned to Caesarea, and on the following
day he took his seat in court and ordered
that Paul be brought in. 7When Paul arrived,
the Jewish leaders from Jerusalem gathered
around and made many serious accusations
they couldn't prove.

8Paul denied the charges. "I am not guilty
of any crime against the Jewish laws or the
Temple or the Roman government," he said.

9Then Festus, wanting to please the Jews,
asked him, "Are you willing to go to Jerusalem and stand trial before me there?"

10But Paul replied, "No! This is the official Roman court, so I ought to be tried
right here. You know very well I am not
guilty of harming the Jews. 11If I have done
something worthy of death, I don't refuse to
die. But if I am innocent, no one has a right
to turn me over to these men to kill me. I
appeal to Caesar!"

12Festus conferred with his advisers and
then replied, "Very well! You have appealed
to Caesar, and to Caesar you will go!"

13A few days later King Agrippa arrived
with his sister, Bernice,* to pay their respects to Festus. 14During their stay of
several days, Festus discussed Paul's case
with the king. "There is a prisoner here,"
he told him, "whose case was left for me by
Felix. 15When I was in Jerusalem, the leading
priests and Jewish elders pressed charges
against him and asked me to condemn him.
16I pointed out to them that Roman law does
not convict people without a trial. They
must be given an opportunity to confront
their accusers and defend themselves.

17"When his accusers came here for the
trial, I didn't delay. I called the case the very
next day and ordered Paul brought in. 18But
the accusations made against him weren't
any of the crimes I expected. 19Instead, it
was something about their religion and a

23:35 Greek *Herod's Praetorium.* **24:1** Greek *some elders and an orator.* **24:6** Some manuscripts add an expanded conclusion to verse 6, all of verse 7, and an additional phrase in verse 8: *We would have judged him by our law, 7but Lysias, the commander of the garrison, came and violently took him away from us, 8commanding his accusers to come before you.* **24:20** Greek *Sanhedrin.* **24:23** Greek *a centurion.* **25:13** Greek *Agrippa the king and Bernice arrived.*

▸ **25:13** *See **The Herods**, page 1072.*

When is it right to stand up for your rights?

While God's people are called to be humble (e.g., Micah 6:8; James 4:10; 1 Peter 5:5-7), the wrong kind of humility can hinder the gospel rather than help it. Paul had been arrested and was on trial before the Roman governor, Festus. Festus's predecessor, Felix, had delayed justice, hoping Paul would give him a bribe to free him (Acts 24:26), though Paul refused. But two years had now passed (24:27), and Paul decided it was time to assert his rights as a Roman citizen, just as he had done previously (16:37-39; 22:25-29). This time, however, he made the ultimate claim: "I appeal to Caesar!" (25:11)—the right of every Roman citizen. While this carried risks, Paul knew that if he won his case, it would lead not just to his acquittal but to the opportunity to preach about Jesus in Rome, as he had hoped to do for some time (Romans 1:15). Perhaps he even hoped that it might lead to the acceptance of Christianity as an official religion in the Roman Empire. This was not just about Paul's personal future, then, but about the future of the gospel.

While as Christians we should always be humble and submissive to those in authority over us (e.g., Romans 13:1-7; Ephesians 6:5-9), there comes a point when it is right before God to claim our rights, especially when doing so can further the gospel.

dead man named Jesus, who Paul insists is
alive. [20]I was at a loss to know how to investigate these things, so I asked him whether
he would be willing to stand trial on these
charges in Jerusalem. [21]But Paul appealed
to have his case decided by the emperor. So
I ordered that he be held in custody until I
could arrange to send him to Caesar."
[22]"I'd like to hear the man myself," Agrippa
said.

And Festus replied, "You will—tomorrow!"

Paul Speaks to Agrippa

[23]So the next day Agrippa and Bernice
arrived at the auditorium with great pomp,
accompanied by military officers and
prominent men of the city. Festus ordered
that Paul be brought in. [24]Then Festus said,
"King Agrippa and all who are here, this is
the man whose death is demanded by all
the Jews, both here and in Jerusalem. [25]But
in my opinion he has done nothing deserving death. However, since he appealed his
case to the emperor, I have decided to send
him to Rome.
[26]"But what shall I write the emperor?
For there is no clear charge against him. So
I have brought him before all of you, and
especially you, King Agrippa, so that after
we examine him, I might have something
to write. [27]For it makes no sense to send a
prisoner to the emperor without specifying
the charges against him!"

26 Then Agrippa said to Paul, "You may
speak in your defense."

So Paul, gesturing with his hand, started
his defense: [2]"I am fortunate, King Agrippa,
that you are the one hearing my defense
today against all these accusations made
by the Jewish leaders, [3]for I know you are
an expert on all Jewish customs and controversies. Now please listen to me patiently!
[4]"As the Jewish leaders are well aware,
I was given a thorough Jewish training
from my earliest childhood among my own
people and in Jerusalem. [5]If they would
admit it, they know that I have been a
member of the Pharisees, the strictest sect
of our religion. [6]Now I am on trial because of
my hope in the fulfillment of God's promise
made to our ancestors. [7]In fact, that is why
the twelve tribes of Israel zealously worship
God night and day, and they share the same
hope I have. Yet, Your Majesty, they accuse
me for having this hope! [8]Why does it seem
incredible to any of you that God can raise
the dead?
[9]"I used to believe that I ought to do
everything I could to oppose the very name
of Jesus the Nazarene.* [10]Indeed, I did
just that in Jerusalem. Authorized by the
leading priests, I caused many believers*
there to be sent to prison. And I cast my vote
against them when they were condemned to
death. [11]Many times I had them punished in
the synagogues to get them to curse Jesus.*
I was so violently opposed to them that I
even chased them down in foreign cities.
[12]"One day I was on such a mission to
Damascus, armed with the authority and
commission of the leading priests. [13]About
noon, Your Majesty, as I was on the road,
a light from heaven brighter than the sun
shone down on me and my companions.
[14]We all fell down, and I heard a voice
saying to me in Aramaic,* 'Saul, Saul, why
are you persecuting me? It is useless for you
to fight against my will.*'
[15]"'Who are you, lord?' I asked.

"And the Lord replied, 'I am Jesus, the one
you are persecuting. [16]Now get to your feet!
For I have appeared to you to appoint you
as my servant and witness. Tell people that
you have seen me, and tell them what I will
show you in the future. [17]And I will rescue
you from both your own people and the
Gentiles. Yes, I am sending you to the Gentiles [18]to open their eyes, so they may turn
from darkness to light and from the power
of Satan to God. Then they will receive forgiveness for their sins and be given a place
among God's people, who are set apart by
faith in me.'
[19]"And so, King Agrippa, I obeyed that
vision from heaven. [20]I preached first to
those in Damascus, then in Jerusalem and
throughout all Judea, and also to the Gentiles, that all must repent of their sins and
turn to God—and prove they have changed
by the good things they do. [21]Some Jews arrested me in the Temple for preaching this,
and they tried to kill me. [22]But God has protected me right up to this present time so I

▸ **26:5** *See **The apostle Paul**, page 1272.*

can testify to everyone, from the least to the
greatest. I teach nothing except what the
prophets and Moses said would happen—
23 that the Messiah would suffer and be the
first to rise from the dead, and in this way
announce God's light to Jews and Gentiles
alike."
24 Suddenly, Festus shouted, "Paul, you
are insane. Too much study has made you
crazy!"
25 But Paul replied, "I am not insane,
Most Excellent Festus. What I am saying is
the sober truth. 26 And King Agrippa knows
about these things. I speak boldly, for I am
sure these events are all familiar to him,
for they were not done in a corner! 27 King
Agrippa, do you believe the prophets? I
know you do—"
28 Agrippa interrupted him. "Do you think
you can persuade me to become a Christian
so quickly?"*
29 Paul replied, "Whether quickly or not,
I pray to God that both you and everyone
here in this audience might become the
same as I am, except for these chains."
30 Then the king, the governor, Bernice,
and all the others stood and left. 31 As they
went out, they talked it over and agreed,
"This man hasn't done anything to deserve
death or imprisonment."
32 And Agrippa said to Festus, "He could
have been set free if he hadn't appealed to
Caesar."

Paul Sails for Rome

27 When the time came, we set sail for
Italy. Paul and several other prisoners were placed in the custody of a Roman
officer* named Julius, a captain of the Imperial Regiment. 2 Aristarchus, a Macedonian from Thessalonica, was also with us.
We left on a ship whose home port was
Adramyttium on the northwest coast of the
province of Asia;* it was scheduled to make
several stops at ports along the coast of the
province.
3 The next day when we docked at Sidon,
Julius was very kind to Paul and let him go
ashore to visit with friends so they could
provide for his needs. 4 Putting out to sea
from there, we encountered strong head-
winds that made it difficult to keep the ship
on course, so we sailed north of Cyprus
between the island and the mainland.
5 Keeping to the open sea, we passed along
the coast of Cilicia and Pamphylia, landing
at Myra, in the province of Lycia. 6 There
the commanding officer found an Egyptian
ship from Alexandria that was bound for
Italy, and he put us on board.
7 We had several days of slow sailing,
and after great difficulty we finally neared
Cnidus. But the wind was against us, so we
sailed across to Crete and along the sheltered coast of the island, past the cape of
Salmone. 8 We struggled along the coast
with great difficulty and finally arrived at
Fair Havens, near the town of Lasea. 9 We
had lost a lot of time. The weather was becoming dangerous for sea travel because it
was so late in the fall,* and Paul spoke to
the ship's officers about it.
10 "Men," he said, "I believe there is
trouble ahead if we go on—shipwreck, loss
of cargo, and danger to our lives as well."
11 But the officer in charge of the prisoners
listened more to the ship's captain and the
owner than to Paul. 12 And since Fair Havens
was an exposed harbor—a poor place to
spend the winter—most of the crew wanted
to go on to Phoenix, farther up the coast of
Crete, and spend the winter there. Phoenix
was a good harbor with only a southwest
and northwest exposure.

The Storm at Sea

13 When a light wind began blowing from
the south, the sailors thought they could
make it. So they pulled up anchor and
sailed close to the shore of Crete. 14 But the
weather changed abruptly, and a wind of
typhoon strength (called a "northeaster")
burst across the island and blew us out
to sea. 15 The sailors couldn't turn the ship
into the wind, so they gave up and let it run
before the gale.
16 We sailed along the sheltered side of a
small island named Cauda,* where with
great difficulty we hoisted aboard the lifeboat
being towed behind us. 17 Then the sailors
bound ropes around the hull of the ship
to strengthen it. They were afraid of being
driven across to the sandbars of Syrtis off the

26:9 Or *Jesus of Nazareth.* **26:10** Greek *many of God's holy people.* **26:11** Greek *to blaspheme.* **26:14a** Or *Hebrew.* **26:14b** Greek *It is hard for you to kick against the oxgoads.* **26:28** Or *"A little more, and your arguments would make me a Christian."* **27:1** Greek *centurion;* similarly in 27:6, 11, 31, 43. **27:2** *Asia* was a Roman province in what is now western Turkey. **27:9** Greek *because the fast was now already gone by.* This fast was associated with the Day of Atonement (*Yom Kippur*), which occurred in late September or early October. **27:16** Some manuscripts read *Claude.*

African coast, so they lowered the sea anchor to slow the ship and were driven before the wind.

18The next day, as gale-force winds continued to batter the ship, the crew began throwing the cargo overboard. 19The following day they even took some of the ship's gear and threw it overboard. 20The terrible storm raged for many days, blotting out the sun and the stars, until at last all hope was gone.

21No one had eaten for a long time. Finally, Paul called the crew together and said, "Men, you should have listened to me in the first place and not left Crete. You would have avoided all this damage and loss. 22But take courage! None of you will lose your lives, even though the ship will go down. 23For last night an angel of the God to whom I belong and whom I serve stood beside me, 24and he said, 'Don't be afraid, Paul, for you will surely stand trial before Caesar! What's more, God in his goodness has granted safety to everyone sailing with you.' 25So take courage! For I believe God. It will be just as he said. 26But we will be shipwrecked on an island."

The Shipwreck

27About midnight on the fourteenth night of the storm, as we were being driven across the Sea of Adria,* the sailors sensed land was near. 28They dropped a weighted line and found that the water was 120 feet deep. But a little later they measured again and found it was only 90 feet deep.* 29At this rate they were afraid we would soon be driven against the rocks along the shore, so they threw out four anchors from the back of the ship and prayed for daylight.

30Then the sailors tried to abandon the ship; they lowered the lifeboat as though they were going to put out anchors from the front of the ship. 31But Paul said to the commanding officer and the soldiers, "You will all die unless the sailors stay aboard." 32So the soldiers cut the ropes to the lifeboat and let it drift away.

33Just as day was dawning, Paul urged everyone to eat. "You have been so worried that you haven't touched food for two weeks," he said. 34"Please eat something now for your own good. For not a hair of your heads will perish." 35Then he took some bread, gave thanks to God before them all, and broke off a piece and ate it. 36Then everyone was encouraged and began to eat—37all 276 of us who were on board. 38After eating, the crew lightened the ship further by throwing the cargo of wheat overboard.

39When morning dawned, they didn't recognize the coastline, but they saw a bay with a beach and wondered if they could get to shore by running the ship aground. 40So they cut off the anchors and left them in the sea. Then they lowered the rudders, raised the foresail, and headed toward shore. 41But they hit a shoal and ran the ship aground too soon. The bow of the ship stuck fast, while the stern was repeatedly smashed by the force of the waves and began to break apart.

Luke

From Acts 16:10 onward, the narrative often switches from the third person ("he" or "they") to the first person ("we"), as in chapter 27. The "we" included Luke, author of both Acts and the Gospel of Luke and one of Paul's co-workers at this time (Philemon 1:24). Luke was a doctor (Colossians 4:14)—hence his interest in the details of illness (e.g., Luke 4:38; 6:6; 8:43; Acts 28:8) and his Gospel's emphasis on Jesus' compassion. He was almost certainly a Gentile (therefore the only non-Jew to write a book of the Bible) and, according to early tradition, he came from Antioch, which may explain why Antioch often features in Acts (6:5; 11:19-30; 13:1-3; 14:26-28; 15:22-35). He was well educated, as reflected in his good Greek writing style and the attention he pays to historical, political, and geographical details. He accompanied Paul at various times from his second missionary journey onward to his first imprisonment in Rome, with which Acts ends, and he was a loyal friend even when others deserted Paul (2 Timothy 4:10-11).

[42]The soldiers wanted to kill the prisoners to make sure they didn't swim ashore and escape. [43]But the commanding officer wanted to spare Paul, so he didn't let them carry out their plan. Then he ordered all who could swim to jump overboard first and make for land. [44]The others held on to planks or debris from the broken ship.* So everyone escaped safely to shore.

Paul on the Island of Malta

28 Once we were safe on shore, we learned that we were on the island of Malta. [2]The people of the island were very kind to us. It was cold and rainy, so they built a fire on the shore to welcome us.

[3]As Paul gathered an armful of sticks and was laying them on the fire, a poisonous snake, driven out by the heat, bit him on the hand. [4]The people of the island saw it hanging from his hand and said to each other, "A murderer, no doubt! Though he escaped the sea, justice will not permit him to live." [5]But Paul shook off the snake into the fire and was unharmed. [6]The people waited for him to swell up or suddenly drop dead. But when they had waited a long time and saw that he wasn't harmed, they changed their minds and decided he was a god.

[7]Near the shore where we landed was an estate belonging to Publius, the chief official of the island. He welcomed us and treated us kindly for three days. [8]As it happened, Publius's father was ill with fever and dysentery. Paul went in and prayed for him, and laying his hands on him, he healed him. [9]Then all the other sick people on the island came and were healed. [10]As a result we were showered with honors, and when the time came to sail, people supplied us with everything we would need for the trip.

Paul Arrives at Rome

[11]It was three months after the shipwreck that we set sail on another ship that had wintered at the island—an Alexandrian ship with the twin gods* as its figurehead. [12]Our first stop was Syracuse,* where we stayed three days. [13]From there we sailed across to Rhegium.* A day later a south wind began blowing, so the following day we sailed up the coast to Puteoli. [14]There we found some believers,* who invited us to spend a week with them. And so we came to Rome.

[15]The brothers and sisters* in Rome had heard we were coming, and they came to

27:27 The *Sea of Adria* includes the central portion of the Mediterranean. **27:28** Greek *20 fathoms . . . 15 fathoms* [37 meters . . . 27 meters]. **27:44** Or *or were helped by members of the ship's crew.* **28:11** The *twin gods* were the Roman gods Castor and Pollux. **28:12** *Syracuse* was on the island of Sicily. **28:13** *Rhegium* was on the southern tip of Italy. **28:14** Greek *brothers.* **28:15a** Greek *brothers.*

The power of the gospel

Luke ends his account of the church's early days just as he began: with the power of the gospel. He began by describing the coming of the Holy Spirit and his empowering of believers to preach the gospel boldly, leading to three thousand people being saved. He then showed us how that gospel pushed across geographical and social barriers. Nothing could stop it—not persecution, or opposition, or mockery. The gospel simply kept advancing. Now, at the end of Luke's account, we find Paul under house arrest, but not even that can stop the gospel. Over this two-year period, while Paul awaited his trial, he "welcomed all who visited him, boldly proclaiming the Kingdom of God and teaching about the Lord Jesus Christ. And no one tried to stop him" (Acts 28:30-31). And it was while he was here that he wrote Ephesians, Philippians, Colossians, and Philemon. Nothing could stop the power of the gospel. After all, the gospel is "the power of God at work, saving everyone who believes" (Romans 1:16).

Although Luke tells us no more, we can work out from Paul's letters, reinforced by early church tradition, that he was eventually released and made more journeys, probably reaching Spain, before he was finally arrested again and executed around AD 67. But not even that could stop the power of the gospel, as the church around the world today still testifies.

meet us at the Forum* on the Appian Way.
Others joined us at The Three Taverns.*
When Paul saw them, he was encouraged
and thanked God.
[16]When we arrived in Rome, Paul was
permitted to have his own private lodging,
though he was guarded by a soldier.

Paul Preaches at Rome under Guard

[17]Three days after Paul's arrival, he called
together the local Jewish leaders. He said to
them, "Brothers, I was arrested in Jerusalem
and handed over to the Roman government,
even though I had done nothing against
our people or the customs of our ancestors. [18]The Romans tried me and wanted to
release me, because they found no cause for
the death sentence. [19]But when the Jewish
leaders protested the decision, I felt it necessary to appeal to Caesar, even though I
had no desire to press charges against my
own people. [20]I asked you to come here
today so we could get acquainted and so I
could explain to you that I am bound with
this chain because I believe that the hope
of Israel—the Messiah—has already come."
[21]They replied, "We have had no letters
from Judea or reports against you from
anyone who has come here. [22]But we want
to hear what you believe, for the only thing
we know about this movement is that it is
denounced everywhere."
[23]So a time was set, and on that day a
large number of people came to Paul's
lodging. He explained and testified about
the Kingdom of God and tried to persuade
them about Jesus from the Scriptures. Using
the law of Moses and the books of the
prophets, he spoke to them from morning
until evening. [24]Some were persuaded
by the things he said, but others did not
believe. [25]And after they had argued back
and forth among themselves, they left with
this final word from Paul: "The Holy Spirit
was right when he said to your ancestors
through Isaiah the prophet,

[26] 'Go and say to this people:
When you hear what I say,
you will not understand.
When you see what I do,
you will not comprehend.
[27] For the hearts of these people are
hardened,
and their ears cannot hear,
and they have closed their eyes—
so their eyes cannot see,
and their ears cannot hear,
and their hearts cannot understand,
and they cannot turn to me
and let me heal them.'*

[28]So I want you to know that this salvation
from God has also been offered to the Gentiles, and they will accept it."*
[30]For the next two years, Paul lived in
Rome at his own expense.* He welcomed
all who visited him, [31]boldly proclaiming
the Kingdom of God and teaching about
the Lord Jesus Christ. And no one tried to
stop him.

28:15b *The Forum* was about 43 miles (70 kilometers) from Rome. **28:15c** *The Three Taverns* was about 35 miles (57 kilometers) from Rome. **28:26-27** Isa 6:9-10 (Greek version). **28:28** Some manuscripts add verse 29, *And when he had said these words, the Jews departed, greatly disagreeing with each other.* **28:30** Or *in his own rented quarters.*

Romans *The good news of the gospel*

Never having visited the church in Rome, Paul writes in anticipation of a future visit. Hoping they will support him in his plans to evangelize Spain, he wants them to be reassured about the gospel he preaches: how it is the faithful fulfillment of all that God promised in the Old Testament, beginning with the promise to Abraham, and brought to fruition by Christ's death. Through faith in Christ, we can live a new life by the power of the Holy Spirit, and this life is now fully available to Jews and Gentiles alike. Both can be part of God's one big family that is called to take the Good News to all nations.

What's it all about?

Paul begins by setting the scene for the Good News he is about to outline. The backdrop is human sin. He argues that everyone—Jew and Gentile alike—is affected by sin's power, because everyone has sinned (chapters 1–3). God gave the Jews his Law; but they failed to live by it, so that couldn't help them. But God has now provided the complete remedy, for Jew and Gentile alike: his own Son. Christ has done what the Law could not do: He has broken sin's power and made it possible for people to be put in a right relationship with God. Moreover, this provision of God is available to everyone—both Jew and Gentile—on exactly the same basis: through faith in Jesus Christ.

Anticipating that the Roman believers might think this was some new idea, Paul reminds them that this was how God began his plan for humanity—through faith. He reminds them of Abraham who "believed God, and God counted him as righteous because of his faith" (4:3). The same still applies. Through faith in Christ we are "made right" with God—brought into a new relationship with him and given a new legal standing before him, which brings many blessings (chapter 5). No longer do we have to live as slaves to sin (chapters 6–7), for God has given us his Holy Spirit to transform us (chapter 8).

In chapters 9 to 11, Paul addresses the issue of Israel. A few years earlier all the Jews (including Jewish Christians) had been expelled from Rome, leaving behind a largely Gentile church. It seems likely that many Gentile Christians thought this was God's judgment on the Jews, his way of saying he had no further plan for them because of their unbelief. As Jews began to return, Jewish Christians came back into the church there, and this caused tensions. Paul says that, although Israel indeed rejected their Messiah, something good

OVERVIEW

came out of it: The gospel came to the Gentiles. Nevertheless, the Jews' stumbling is temporary, for God will not abandon his promise to them; in the end, faithful Israel will be saved.

The remaining chapters deal with how Christians should relate to each other and to society at large. In particular, Paul urges Jewish and Gentile believers to accept one another and respect differences between the groups. He concludes by greeting friends and co-workers.

What does it mean for us?

At the heart of Romans lies Paul's conviction that God never gives up on his plans. Neither human sin nor Israel's disobedience can stop his plan from being worked out—this plan of having a people who know and love him filling the whole earth, just as he promised to Abraham. Even the most religious person in the world—whether Jew or Gentile—has fallen short of what God requires, but God has intervened in Christ to save those who put their trust in him and to draw them back into his plan. Through faith in Christ we can be put into a right relationship with God (be justified), be renewed by his Spirit, and live in a right relationship with him and with others, becoming part of his one people. This is all part of God's righteousness—his faithfulness to his own character and plans, and his ability to make us righteous before him as we trust in his Son.

If we want salvation to be in our own hands—to try to come to God on our own terms—we will always end up missing it. The answer is always to take God's remedy, and not try to invent our own.

Greetings from Paul

1 This letter is from Paul, a slave of Christ
Jesus, chosen by God to be an apostle
and sent out to preach his Good News. 2God
promised this Good News long ago through
his prophets in the holy Scriptures. 3The
Good News is about his Son. In his earthly
life he was born into King David's family
line, 4and he was shown to be* the Son of
God when he was raised from the dead by the
power of the Holy Spirit.* He is Jesus Christ
our Lord. 5Through Christ, God has given us
the privilege* and authority as apostles to
tell Gentiles everywhere what God has done
for them, so that they will believe and obey
him, bringing glory to his name.
6And you are included among those Gentiles who have been called to belong to Jesus
Christ. 7I am writing to all of you in Rome
who are loved by God and are called to be
his own holy people.

May God our Father and the Lord Jesus
Christ give you grace and peace.

God's Good News

8Let me say first that I thank my God through
Jesus Christ for all of you, because your faith
in him is being talked about all over the world.
9God knows how often I pray for you. Day and
night I bring you and your needs in prayer
to God, whom I serve with all my heart* by
spreading the Good News about his Son.
10One of the things I always pray for is the
opportunity, God willing, to come at last to
see you. 11For I long to visit you so I can bring
you some spiritual gift that will help you
grow strong in the Lord. 12When we get together, I want to encourage you in your faith,
but I also want to be encouraged by yours.
13I want you to know, dear brothers and
sisters,* that I planned many times to visit
you, but I was prevented until now. I want to
work among you and see spiritual fruit, just
as I have seen among other Gentiles. 14For I
have a great sense of obligation to people in
both the civilized world and the rest of the
world,* to the educated and uneducated
alike. 15So I am eager to come to you in Rome,
too, to preach the Good News.
16For I am not ashamed of this Good News
about Christ. It is the power of God at work,
saving everyone who believes—the Jew first
and also the Gentile.* 17This Good News tells
us how God makes us right in his sight. This

▸ **1:16** *See **The power of the gospel**, page 1279.*

is accomplished from start to finish by faith.
As the Scriptures say, "It is through faith
that a righteous person has life."*

God's Anger at Sin

18 But God shows his anger from heaven
against all sinful, wicked people who sup-
press the truth by their wickedness.* 19 They
know the truth about God because he has
made it obvious to them. 20 For ever since
the world was created, people have seen
the earth and sky. Through everything God
made, they can clearly see his invisible qualities—his eternal power and divine nature.
So they have no excuse for not knowing God.
21 Yes, they knew God, but they wouldn't
worship him as God or even give him
thanks. And they began to think up foolish
ideas of what God was like. As a result, their
minds became dark and confused. 22 Claiming to be wise, they instead became utter
fools. 23 And instead of worshiping the glorious, ever-living God, they worshiped idols
made to look like mere people and birds
and animals and reptiles.
24 So God abandoned them to do whatever
shameful things their hearts desired. As a
result, they did vile and degrading things
with each other's bodies. 25 They traded the
truth about God for a lie. So they worshiped
and served the things God created instead of
the Creator himself, who is worthy of eternal
praise! Amen. 26 That is why God abandoned
them to their shameful desires. Even the
women turned against the natural way to
have sex and instead indulged in sex with
each other. 27 And the men, instead of having
normal sexual relations with women,
burned with lust for each other. Men did
shameful things with other men, and as a
result of this sin, they suffered within themselves the penalty they deserved.
28 Since they thought it foolish to acknowledge God, he abandoned them to their
foolish thinking and let them do things that
should never be done. 29 Their lives became
full of every kind of wickedness, sin, greed,
hate, envy, murder, quarreling, deception,
malicious behavior, and gossip. 30 They
are backstabbers, haters of God, insolent,
proud, and boastful. They invent new ways
of sinning, and they disobey their parents.
31 They refuse to understand, break their
promises, are heartless, and have no mercy.
32 They know God's justice requires that
those who do these things deserve to die,
yet they do them anyway. Worse yet, they
encourage others to do them, too.

God's Judgment of Sin

2 You may think you can condemn such
people, but you are just as bad, and
you have no excuse! When you say they are

1:4a Or *and was designated.* **1:4b** Or *by the Spirit of holiness;* or *in the new realm of the Spirit.* **1:5** Or *the grace.* **1:9** Or *in my spirit.* **1:13** Greek *brothers.* **1:14** Greek *to Greeks and barbarians.* **1:16** Greek *also the Greek.* **1:17** Or *"The righteous will live by faith."* Hab 2:4. **1:18** Or *who, by their wickedness, prevent the truth from being known.*

▸ **1:20** *See **Revelation**, page 612.*

Rome

By New Testament times, Rome had grown from a city to a vast empire, covering Italy, Greece, Macedonia, and parts of North Africa, the Middle East, and Europe. Rome had great temples, theaters, arenas, gymnasiums, forums, public buildings, and baths (all of which were replicated in cities across its empire); but there was also widespread poverty, with the poor living in tenement slums and frequently rioting over food shortages. Many gods were worshiped, and by later New Testament times, Caesar himself was seen as a god, with everyone required to acknowledge him as such once a year—something Christians clearly could not do, which led to fierce persecution. The church in Rome was probably started by converted Jews returning from Jerusalem after Pentecost (Acts 2:10), so its initial makeup would have been predominantly Jewish Christian. But since Rome was a mainly Gentile city, future converts were Gentiles; so it is unsurprising that tensions arose, some of which are dealt with in this letter.

wicked and should be punished, you are
condemning yourself, for you who judge
others do these very same things. 2 And we
know that God, in his justice, will punish
anyone who does such things. 3 Since you
judge others for doing these things, why do
you think you can avoid God's judgment
when you do the same things? 4 Don't you
see how wonderfully kind, tolerant, and
patient God is with you? Does this mean
nothing to you? Can't you see that his kindness is intended to turn you from your sin?

5 But because you are stubborn and
refuse to turn from your sin, you are
storing up terrible punishment for yourself. For a day of anger is coming, when
God's righteous judgment will be revealed.
6 He will judge everyone according to what
they have done. 7 He will give eternal life
to those who keep on doing good, seeking
after the glory and honor and immortality that God offers. 8 But he will pour out
his anger and wrath on those who live for
themselves, who refuse to obey the truth
and instead live lives of wickedness. 9 There
will be trouble and calamity for everyone
who keeps on doing what is evil—for the
Jew first and also for the Gentile.* 10 But
there will be glory and honor and peace
from God for all who do good—for the Jew
first and also for the Gentile. 11 For God does
not show favoritism.

12 When the Gentiles sin, they will be destroyed, even though they never had God's
written law. And the Jews, who do have
God's law, will be judged by that law when
they fail to obey it. 13 For merely listening to
the law doesn't make us right with God. It
is obeying the law that makes us right in
his sight. 14 Even Gentiles, who do not have
God's written law, show that they know his
law when they instinctively obey it, even
without having heard it. 15 They demonstrate
that God's law is written in their hearts, for
their own conscience and thoughts either
accuse them or tell them they are doing
right. 16 And this is the message I proclaim—
that the day is coming when God, through
Christ Jesus, will judge everyone's secret
life.

What about people who have never heard the gospel?

If faith in Christ is the only means of salvation, what about those who haven't heard the gospel? Paul says such people will be judged in light of what they have heard, not what they haven't (Romans 2:12-15). Gentiles will not be condemned for failing to keep God's Law, which they did not have—though Jews will be because they do have it. In fact sometimes, he says, Gentiles do the good required by God's Law without even knowing it because of their conscience, God's law "written in their hearts" (2:15); and this will be their judge: Did they live up to what they knew God required? However, Paul says our conscience is as likely to accuse as excuse us (2:15), for who can claim to have always followed their conscience? And anyway, conscience is marred by sin; for while God's presence is evident in the world around us, we deliberately turned away from him (1:18-25). So can we really trust our conscience to make us choose what is right? Paul doubts it. Indeed, where he is heading in this argument—that "everyone has sinned; we all fall short of God's glorious standard" (3:23)—suggests that this is extremely unlikely.

While Paul probably does not answer our question as clearly as we would like him to, what we should always remember is that only God—who alone knows all things and alone is full of both justice and mercy—knows what is truly in someone's heart. His mercy and justice may end up reaching many that we didn't expect to see in heaven, and excluding many that we did. Whatever is the right decision to make about such people, God will make it. In the meantime, our responsibility is to share the Good News with everyone we can.

▸ *See also **Conscience**, page 333.*

The Jews and the Law

17 You who call yourselves Jews are relying
on God's law, and you boast about your
special relationship with him. 18 You know
what he wants; you know what is right
because you have been taught his law.
19 You are convinced that you are a guide
for the blind and a light for people who
are lost in darkness. 20 You think you can
instruct the ignorant and teach children
the ways of God. For you are certain that
God's law gives you complete knowledge
and truth.

21 Well then, if you teach others, why don't
you teach yourself? You tell others not to
steal, but do you steal? 22 You say it is wrong
to commit adultery, but do you commit adultery? You condemn idolatry, but do you use
items stolen from pagan temples?* 23 You are
so proud of knowing the law, but you dishonor God by breaking it. 24 No wonder the
Scriptures say, "The Gentiles blaspheme the
name of God because of you."*

25 The Jewish ceremony of circumcision
has value only if you obey God's law. But
if you don't obey God's law, you are no
better off than an uncircumcised Gentile.
26 And if the Gentiles obey God's law, won't
God declare them to be his own people?
27 In fact, uncircumcised Gentiles who keep
God's law will condemn you Jews who are
circumcised and possess God's law but
don't obey it.

28 For you are not a true Jew just because
you were born of Jewish parents or because
you have gone through the ceremony of circumcision. 29 No, a true Jew is one whose
heart is right with God. And true circumcision is not merely obeying the letter of the
law; rather, it is a change of heart produced
by the Spirit. And a person with a changed
heart seeks praise* from God, not from
people.

God Remains Faithful

3 Then what's the advantage of being a
Jew? Is there any value in the ceremony
of circumcision? 2 Yes, there are great benefits! First of all, the Jews were entrusted
with the whole revelation of God.*

3 True, some of them were unfaithful; but
just because they were unfaithful, does that
mean God will be unfaithful? 4 Of course
not! Even if everyone else is a liar, God is
true. As the Scriptures say about him,

"You will be proved right in what you
say,
and you will win your case in
court."*

5 "But," some might say, "our sinfulness
serves a good purpose, for it helps people
see how righteous God is. Isn't it unfair,
then, for him to punish us?" (This is merely
a human point of view.) 6 Of course not! If
God were not entirely fair, how would he
be qualified to judge the world? 7 "But,"
someone might still argue, "how can God
condemn me as a sinner if my dishonesty
highlights his truthfulness and brings him
more glory?" 8 And some people even slander
us by claiming that we say, "The more we
sin, the better it is!" Those who say such
things deserve to be condemned.

All People Are Sinners

9 Well then, should we conclude that we
Jews are better than others? No, not at all,
for we have already shown that all people,
whether Jews or Gentiles,* are under the
power of sin. 10 As the Scriptures say,

"No one is righteous—
not even one.
11 No one is truly wise;
no one is seeking God.
12 All have turned away;
all have become useless.
No one does good,
not a single one."*
13 "Their talk is foul, like the stench from
an open grave.
Their tongues are filled with lies."
"Snake venom drips from their lips."*
14 "Their mouths are full of cursing and
bitterness."*
15 "They rush to commit murder.
16 Destruction and misery always follow
them.
17 They don't know where to find peace."*
18 "They have no fear of God at all."*

19 Obviously, the law applies to those to
whom it was given, for its purpose is to keep
people from having excuses, and to show
that the entire world is guilty before God.
20 For no one can ever be made right with

2:9 Greek *also for the Greek;* also in 2:10. **2:22** Greek *do you steal from temples?* **2:24** Isa 52:5 (Greek version). **2:29** Or *receives praise.* **3:2** Greek *the oracles of God.* **3:4** Ps 51:4 (Greek version). **3:9** Greek *or Greeks.* **3:10-12** Pss 14:1-3; 53:1-3 (Greek version). **3:13** Pss 5:9 (Greek version); 140:3. **3:14** Ps 10:7 (Greek version). **3:15-17** Isa 59:7-8. **3:18** Ps 36:1.

God by doing what the law commands. The law simply shows us how sinful we are.

Christ Took Our Punishment

[21]But now God has shown us a way to be made right with him without keeping the requirements of the law, as was promised in the writings of Moses* and the prophets long ago. [22]We are made right with God by placing our faith in Jesus Christ. And this is true for everyone who believes, no matter who we are.

[23]For everyone has sinned; we all fall short of God's glorious standard. [24]Yet God, in his grace, freely makes us right in his sight. He did this through Christ Jesus when he freed us from the penalty for our sins. [25]For God presented Jesus as the sacrifice for sin. People are made right with God when they believe that Jesus sacrificed his life, shedding his blood. This sacrifice shows that God was being fair when he held back and did not punish those who sinned in times past, [26]for he was looking ahead and including them in what he would do in this present time. God did this to demonstrate his righteousness, for he himself is fair and just, and he makes sinners right in his sight when they believe in Jesus.

[27]Can we boast, then, that we have done anything to be accepted by God? No, because our acquittal is not based on obeying the law. It is based on faith. [28]So we are made right with God through faith and not by obeying the law.

[29]After all, is God the God of the Jews only? Isn't he also the God of the Gentiles? Of course he is. [30]There is only one God, and he makes people right with himself only by faith, whether they are Jews or Gentiles.* [31]Well then, if we emphasize faith, does this mean that we can forget about the law? Of course not! In fact, only when we have faith do we truly fulfill the law.

The Faith of Abraham

4 Abraham was, humanly speaking, the founder of our Jewish nation. What did he discover about being made right with God? [2]If his good deeds had made him acceptable to God, he would have had something to boast about. But that was not God's way. [3]For the Scriptures tell us, "Abraham believed God, and God counted him as righteous because of his faith."*

[4]When people work, their wages are not a gift, but something they have earned. [5]But people are counted as righteous, not because of their work, but because of their faith in God who forgives sinners. [6]David also spoke of this when he described the

▸ **3:23-28** *See* ***Sin****, page 387;* ***Redemption****, page 1136;* ***Faith****, page 1286;* ***Justification****, page 1288.*

Faith

It is a common misunderstanding that people were saved in Old Testament times by keeping the Law instead of by faith as in New Testament times, but nothing could be further from the truth. Paul has already shown that "we are made right with God through faith and not by obeying the law" (Romans 3:28), and in chapter 4 he goes on to prove it by going back to the founder of both the Jewish and the Christian faith—Abraham. How did he get right with God? Not by keeping the Law, but by faith (4:1-3; see Genesis 15:1-6). This message—that we are put right with God through trusting him, not by religion, good works, or trying our best—is constant throughout both the Old and the New Testament. Those who struggle with this message are those who feel we surely need to *do* something to get right with God, or who feel that their good life should earn them more favor than wicked sinners. But this is the grace of God: He makes his forgiveness and friendship available to all on the same basis, the simplest basis of all—simply believing in him and what he says.

▸ *See also* ***Abraham****, page 16;* ***Trusting God when we cannot see the way ahead****, page 57;* ***Repentance****, page 1253;* ***Justification****, page 1288;* ***Faith and works****, page 1415.*

happiness of those who are declared righteous without working for it:

7 "Oh, what joy for those
whose disobedience is forgiven,
whose sins are put out of sight.
8 Yes, what joy for those
whose record the LORD has cleared of
sin."*

9 Now, is this blessing only for the Jews,
or is it also for uncircumcised Gentiles?*
Well, we have been saying that Abraham
was counted as righteous by God because
of his faith. 10 But how did this happen? Was
he counted as righteous only after he was
circumcised, or was it before he was circumcised? Clearly, God accepted Abraham
before he was circumcised!

11 Circumcision was a sign that Abraham
already had faith and that God had already
accepted him and declared him to be righteous—even before he was circumcised. So
Abraham is the spiritual father of those who
have faith but have not been circumcised.
They are counted as righteous because
of their faith. 12 And Abraham is also the
spiritual father of those who have been circumcised, but only if they have the same
kind of faith Abraham had before he was
circumcised.

13 Clearly, God's promise to give the whole
earth to Abraham and his descendants was
based not on his obedience to God's law, but
on a right relationship with God that comes
by faith. 14 If God's promise is only for those
who obey the law, then faith is not necessary
and the promise is pointless. 15 For the law
always brings punishment on those who try
to obey it. (The only way to avoid breaking
the law is to have no law to break!)

16 So the promise is received by faith. It is
given as a free gift. And we are all certain to
receive it, whether or not we live according
to the law of Moses, if we have faith like
Abraham's. For Abraham is the father of
all who believe. 17 That is what the Scriptures mean when God told him, "I have
made you the father of many nations."*
This happened because Abraham believed
in the God who brings the dead back to
life and who creates new things out of
nothing.

18 Even when there was no reason for
hope, Abraham kept hoping—believing
that he would become the father of many
nations. For God had said to him, "That's
how many descendants you will have!"*
19 And Abraham's faith did not weaken, even
though, at about 100 years of age, he figured
his body was as good as dead—and so was
Sarah's womb.

20 Abraham never wavered in believing
God's promise. In fact, his faith grew stronger, and in this he brought glory to God.
21 He was fully convinced that God is able to
do whatever he promises. 22 And because of
Abraham's faith, God counted him as righteous. 23 And when God counted him as righteous, it wasn't just for Abraham's benefit. It
was recorded 24 for our benefit, too, assuring
us that God will also count us as righteous if
we believe in him, the one who raised Jesus
our Lord from the dead. 25 He was handed
over to die because of our sins, and he was
raised to life to make us right with God.

Faith Brings Joy

5 Therefore, since we have been made
right in God's sight by faith, we have
peace* with God because of what Jesus
Christ our Lord has done for us. 2 Because
of our faith, Christ has brought us into this
place of undeserved privilege where we
now stand, and we confidently and joyfully
look forward to sharing God's glory.

3 We can rejoice, too, when we run into
problems and trials, for we know that they
help us develop endurance. 4 And endurance develops strength of character, and
character strengthens our confident hope
of salvation. 5 And this hope will not lead to
disappointment. For we know how dearly
God loves us, because he has given us the
Holy Spirit to fill our hearts with his love.

6 When we were utterly helpless, Christ
came at just the right time and died for
us sinners. 7 Now, most people would not
be willing to die for an upright person,
though someone might perhaps be willing
to die for a person who is especially good.
8 But God showed his great love for us by
sending Christ to die for us while we were
still sinners. 9 And since we have been made
right in God's sight by the blood of Christ,
he will certainly save us from God's condemnation. 10 For since our friendship with

3:21 Greek *in the law.* **3:30** Greek *whether they are circumcised or uncircumcised.* **4:3** Gen 15:6. **4:7-8** Ps 32:1-2 (Greek version). **4:9** Greek *is this blessing only for the circumcised, or is it also for the uncircumcised?* **4:17** Gen 17:5. **4:18** Gen 15:5. **5:1** Some manuscripts read *let us have peace.*

God was restored by the death of his Son
while we were still his enemies, we will certainly be saved through the life of his Son.
11 So now we can rejoice in our wonderful
new relationship with God because our
Lord Jesus Christ has made us friends of
God.

Adam and Christ Contrasted

12 When Adam sinned, sin entered the
world. Adam's sin brought death, so death
spread to everyone, for everyone sinned.
13 Yes, people sinned even before the law
was given. But it was not counted as sin
because there was not yet any law to break.
14 Still, everyone died—from the time of
Adam to the time of Moses—even those
who did not disobey an explicit commandment of God, as Adam did. Now Adam is
a symbol, a representation of Christ, who
was yet to come. 15 But there is a great difference between Adam's sin and God's
gracious gift. For the sin of this one man,
Adam, brought death to many. But even
greater is God's wonderful grace and his
gift of forgiveness to many through this
other man, Jesus Christ. 16 And the result
of God's gracious gift is very different from
the result of that one man's sin. For Adam's
sin led to condemnation, but God's free gift
leads to our being made right with God,
even though we are guilty of many sins.
17 For the sin of this one man, Adam, caused
death to rule over many. But even greater is
God's wonderful grace and his gift of righteousness, for all who receive it will live in
triumph over sin and death through this
one man, Jesus Christ.
18 Yes, Adam's one sin brings condemnation for everyone, but Christ's one act of righteousness brings a right relationship with
God and new life for everyone. 19 Because
one person disobeyed God, many became
sinners. But because one other person
obeyed God, many will be made righteous.
20 God's law was given so that all people
could see how sinful they were. But as people
sinned more and more, God's wonderful
grace became more abundant. 21 So just as
sin ruled over all people and brought them
to death, now God's wonderful grace rules
instead, giving us right standing with God
and resulting in eternal life through Jesus
Christ our Lord.

Justification

The careful argument Paul has been making up to this point now reaches its climax in this bold statement: "We have been made right in God's sight by faith" (Romans 5:1). Everything that follows flows from this central truth.

The theological term for being made right with God is *justification*. Justification is a legal concept—the picture of someone appearing before a judge who declares them "Not guilty." Justification is the affirmation of God the righteous judge that we are now righteous, not because of anything we have done—how could we, for "everyone has sinned; we all fall short of God's glorious standard" (3:23)?—but because of what his Son has done. When Christ died on the cross, he died as the sacrifice for our sin (3:25). Our sin meant that we should have died, for "the wages of sin is death" (6:23); but Christ took the penalty of that sin upon himself and died as our substitute, as our Savior, paying for our sin and freeing us from condemnation as a result. All this is an expression of the righteousness of God—God's righteous act, because he is righteous, to make us righteous before him (see 1:17; 3:21).

Paul's Jewish opponents agreed that God alone can justify people, but they believed he justified good people, those who kept the Law. However, Paul says that God justifies bad people: "God showed his great love for us by sending Christ to die for us while we were still sinners" (5:8). We simply need to receive his work on our behalf by faith.

▸ *See also* ***The death of Jesus****, page 1114;* ***Redemption****, page 1136;* ***Faith****, page 1286.*

Sin's Power Is Broken

6 Well then, should we keep on sinning so
that God can show us more and more of
his wonderful grace? 2 Of course not! Since
we have died to sin, how can we continue to
live in it? 3 Or have you forgotten that when
we were joined with Christ Jesus in baptism,
we joined him in his death? 4 For we died
and were buried with Christ by baptism.
And just as Christ was raised from the dead
by the glorious power of the Father, now we
also may live new lives.

5 Since we have been united with him in
his death, we will also be raised to life as
he was. 6 We know that our old sinful selves
were crucified with Christ so that sin might
lose its power in our lives. We are no longer
slaves to sin. 7 For when we died with Christ
we were set free from the power of sin. 8 And
since we died with Christ, we know we will
also live with him. 9 We are sure of this
because Christ was raised from the dead,
and he will never die again. Death no longer
has any power over him. 10 When he died, he
died once to break the power of sin. But now
that he lives, he lives for the glory of God.
11 So you also should consider yourselves to
be dead to the power of sin and alive to God
through Christ Jesus.

12 Do not let sin control the way you live;*
do not give in to sinful desires. 13 Do not let
any part of your body become an instrument
of evil to serve sin. Instead, give yourselves
completely to God, for you were dead, but
now you have new life. So use your whole
body as an instrument to do what is right
for the glory of God. 14 Sin is no longer your
master, for you no longer live under the
requirements of the law. Instead, you live
under the freedom of God's grace.

15 Well then, since God's grace has set us
free from the law, does that mean we can
go on sinning? Of course not! 16 Don't you
realize that you become the slave of whatever you choose to obey? You can be a slave
to sin, which leads to death, or you can
choose to obey God, which leads to righteous living. 17 Thank God! Once you were
slaves of sin, but now you wholeheartedly
obey this teaching we have given you. 18 Now
you are free from your slavery to sin, and
you have become slaves to righteous living.

19 Because of the weakness of your human
nature, I am using the illustration of slavery
to help you understand all this. Previously,
you let yourselves be slaves to impurity and
lawlessness, which led ever deeper into sin.
Now you must give yourselves to be slaves to
righteous living so that you will become holy.

20 When you were slaves to sin, you were
free from the obligation to do right. 21 And

6:12 Or *Do not let sin reign in your body, which is subject to death.*

Does it matter if I sin?

Paul imagines a question arising from all that he has been saying. If Christ has truly paid the price of sin at the cross, then doesn't logic say that it doesn't matter if we keep on sinning, since that sin is already paid for? And if it's true that "as people sinned more and more, God's wonderful grace became more abundant" (Romans 5:20), shouldn't we sin more to receive more grace?

To such questions Paul's answer is a very strong "No!" (6:2). "Since we have died to sin, how can we continue to live in it?" he continues. This "death" was expressed in our baptism, where our old life was buried (6:3-14) so we could rise to a new life with Jesus (6:4). How could we possibly think of returning to that old life of sin therefore? It would be like a freed slave choosing to go back to slavery (6:15-23).

Becoming a Christian doesn't mean you suddenly stop struggling with sin (7:7-25), but it does mean you recognize it is no longer your friend but your enemy. Sin will not rob you of your relationship with God, but it will rob you of intimacy with God and fruitfulness for him. To think we can carelessly go on sinning is therefore foolish.

▸ *See also **Baptism**, page 1238; **Growing as a Christian**, page 1430; **Becoming like Christ**, page 1435.*

what was the result? You are now ashamed of the things you used to do, things that end in eternal doom. 22But now you are free from the power of sin and have become slaves of God. Now you do those things that lead to holiness and result in eternal life. 23For the wages of sin is death, but the free gift of God is eternal life through Christ Jesus our Lord.

No Longer Bound to the Law

7 Now, dear brothers and sisters*—you who are familiar with the law—don't you know that the law applies only while a person is living? 2For example, when a woman marries, the law binds her to her husband as long as he is alive. But if he dies, the laws of marriage no longer apply to her. 3So while her husband is alive, she would be committing adultery if she married another man. But if her husband dies, she is free from that law and does not commit adultery when she remarries.

4So, my dear brothers and sisters, this is the point: You died to the power of the law when you died with Christ. And now you are united with the one who was raised from the dead. As a result, we can produce a harvest of good deeds for God. 5When we were controlled by our old nature,* sinful desires were at work within us, and the law aroused these evil desires that produced a harvest of sinful deeds, resulting in death. 6But now we have been released from the law, for we died to it and are no longer captive to its power. Now we can serve God, not in the old way of obeying the letter of the law, but in the new way of living in the Spirit.

God's Law Reveals Our Sin

7Well then, am I suggesting that the law of God is sinful? Of course not! In fact, it was the law that showed me my sin. I would never have known that coveting is wrong if the law had not said, "You must not covet."* 8But sin used this command to arouse all kinds of covetous desires within me! If there were no law, sin would not have that power. 9At one time I lived without understanding the law. But when I learned the command not to covet, for instance, the power of sin came to life, 10and I died. So I discovered that the law's commands, which were supposed to bring life, brought spiritual death instead. 11Sin took advantage of those commands and deceived me; it used the commands to kill me. 12But still, the law itself is holy, and its commands are holy and right and good.

13But how can that be? Did the law, which is good, cause my death? Of course not! Sin used what was good to bring about my condemnation to death. So we can see how terrible sin really is. It uses God's good commands for its own evil purposes.

Struggling with Sin

14So the trouble is not with the law, for it is spiritual and good. The trouble is with me, for I am all too human, a slave to sin. 15I don't really understand myself, for I want to do what is right, but I don't do it. Instead, I do what I hate. 16But if I know that what I am doing is wrong, this shows that I agree that the law is good. 17So I am not the one doing wrong; it is sin living in me that does it.

18And I know that nothing good lives in me, that is, in my sinful nature.* I want to do what is right, but I can't. 19I want to do what is good, but I don't. I don't want to do what is wrong, but I do it anyway. 20But if I do what I don't want to do, I am not really the one doing wrong; it is sin living in me that does it.

21I have discovered this principle of life—that when I want to do what is right, I inevitably do what is wrong. 22I love God's law with all my heart. 23But there is another power* within me that is at war with my mind. This power makes me a slave to the sin that is still within me. 24Oh, what a miserable person I am! Who will free me from this life that is dominated by sin and death? 25Thank God! The answer is in Jesus Christ our Lord. So you see how it is: In my mind I really want to obey God's law, but because of my sinful nature I am a slave to sin.

Life in the Spirit

8 So now there is no condemnation for those who belong to Christ Jesus. 2And because you belong to him, the power* of the life-giving Spirit has freed you* from the power of sin that leads to death. 3The law of Moses was unable to save us because of the weakness of our sinful nature.* So God did what the law could not do. He sent his own Son in a body like the bodies we sinners have. And in that body God declared an end to sin's control over us by giving his Son as a sacrifice for our sins. 4He did this so that the just requirement of the law would be fully satisfied for us, who no longer follow our sinful nature but instead follow the Spirit.

[5]Those who are dominated by the sinful nature think about sinful things, but those who are controlled by the Holy Spirit think about things that please the Spirit. [6]So letting your sinful nature control your mind leads to death. But letting the Spirit control your mind leads to life and peace. [7]For the sinful nature is always hostile to God. It never did obey God's laws, and it never will. [8]That's why those who are still under the control of their sinful nature can never please God.

[9]But you are not controlled by your sinful nature. You are controlled by the Spirit if you have the Spirit of God living in you. (And remember that those who do not have the Spirit of Christ living in them do not belong to him at all.) [10]And Christ lives within you, so even though your body will die because of sin, the Spirit gives you life* because you have been made right with God. [11]The Spirit of God, who raised Jesus from the dead, lives in you. And just as God raised Christ Jesus from the dead, he will give life to your mortal bodies by this same Spirit living within you.

[12]Therefore, dear brothers and sisters,* you have no obligation to do what your sinful nature urges you to do. [13]For if you live by its dictates, you will die. But if through the power of the Spirit you put to death the deeds of your sinful nature,* you will live. [14]For all who are led by the Spirit of God are children* of God.

[15]So you have not received a spirit that makes you fearful slaves. Instead, you received God's Spirit when he adopted you as his own children.* Now we call him, "Abba, Father."* [16]For his Spirit joins with our spirit to affirm that we are God's children. [17]And since we are his children, we are his heirs. In fact, together with Christ we are heirs of God's glory. But if we are to share his glory, we must also share his suffering.

The Future Glory

[18]Yet what we suffer now is nothing compared to the glory he will reveal to us later. [19]For all creation is waiting eagerly for that future day when God will reveal who his children really are. [20]Against its will, all creation was subjected to God's curse. But with eager hope, [21]the creation looks forward to the day when it will join God's children in

7:1 Greek *brothers;* also in 7:4. **7:5** Greek *When we were in the flesh.* **7:7** Exod 20:17; Deut 5:21. **7:18** Greek *my flesh;* also in 7:25. **7:23** Greek *law;* also in 7:23b. **8:2a** Greek *the law;* also in 8:2b. **8:2b** Some manuscripts read *me.* **8:3** Greek *our flesh;* similarly in 8:4, 5, 6, 7, 8, 9, 12. **8:10** Or *your spirit is alive.* **8:12** Greek *brothers;* also in 8:29. **8:13** Greek *deeds of the body.* **8:14** Greek *sons;* also in 8:19. **8:15a** Greek *you received a spirit of sonship.* **8:15b** *Abba* is an Aramaic term for "father."

▸ **8:15** See ***Abba***, *page 1144.*

Life in the Spirit

Having explained the great salvation God has given us in Christ, Paul affirms that "now there is no condemnation" for us (Romans 8:1). But being a Christian isn't just about avoiding condemnation; it's about being freed to live a new life in the power of the Holy Spirit. Paul says that "the power of the life-giving Spirit" has overcome "the power of sin that leads to death" (8:2). How can one power overcome another power? Only if it is more powerful! That's why the power of the Spirit could overcome the power of sin—it was far more powerful. Why? Because the Spirit is God himself at work.

This is why continually being filled with the Spirit is so important; without him we simply cannot live the Christian life. So, while the disciples were "filled with the Holy Spirit" (Acts 2:4) at Pentecost, they were filled with him again just a short time later (Acts 4:31). Paul wrote, "Be filled with the Holy Spirit" (Ephesians 5:18). The Greek means "go on being filled with the Holy Spirit"—not just once, but again and again. It is the Spirit who helps us overcome and become more like Christ.

▸ *See also* ***Living by the Spirit****, page 1342;* ***The Christian's relationship with the Holy Spirit****, page 1350.*

glorious freedom from death and decay.
22For we know that all creation has been
groaning as in the pains of childbirth right
up to the present time. 23And we believers
also groan, even though we have the Holy
Spirit within us as a foretaste of future glory,
for we long for our bodies to be released
from sin and suffering. We, too, wait with
eager hope for the day when God will give
us our full rights as his adopted children,*
including the new bodies he has promised
us. 24We were given this hope when we were
saved. (If we already have something, we
don't need to hope* for it. 25But if we look
forward to something we don't yet have, we
must wait patiently and confidently.)

26And the Holy Spirit helps us in our weakness. For example, we don't know what God
wants us to pray for. But the Holy Spirit
prays for us with groanings that cannot be
expressed in words. 27And the Father who
knows all hearts knows what the Spirit is
saying, for the Spirit pleads for us believers*
in harmony with God's own will. 28And we
know that God causes everything to work together* for the good of those who love God
and are called according to his purpose for
them. 29For God knew his people in advance,
and he chose them to become like his Son, so
that his Son would be the firstborn* among
many brothers and sisters. 30And having
chosen them, he called them to come to him.
And having called them, he gave them right
standing with himself. And having given
them right standing, he gave them his glory.

Nothing Can Separate Us from God's Love

31What shall we say about such wonderful
things as these? If God is for us, who can
ever be against us? 32Since he did not spare
even his own Son but gave him up for us all,
won't he also give us everything else? 33Who
dares accuse us whom God has chosen for
his own? No one—for God himself has given
us right standing with himself. 34Who then
will condemn us? No one—for Christ Jesus
died for us and was raised to life for us, and
he is sitting in the place of honor at God's
right hand, pleading for us.

35Can anything ever separate us from
Christ's love? Does it mean he no longer
loves us if we have trouble or calamity, or
are persecuted, or hungry, or destitute, or
in danger, or threatened with death? 36(As
the Scriptures say, "For your sake we are
killed every day; we are being slaughtered
like sheep."*) 37No, despite all these things,
overwhelming victory is ours through
Christ, who loved us.

38And I am convinced that nothing can
ever separate us from God's love. Neither
death nor life, neither angels nor demons,*
neither our fears for today nor our worries
about tomorrow—not even the powers of
hell can separate us from God's love. 39No
power in the sky above or in the earth
below—indeed, nothing in all creation will
ever be able to separate us from the love of
God that is revealed in Christ Jesus our Lord.

God's Selection of Israel

9 With Christ as my witness, I speak with
utter truthfulness. My conscience and
the Holy Spirit confirm it. 2My heart is filled
with bitter sorrow and unending grief 3for
my people, my Jewish brothers and sisters.*
I would be willing to be forever cursed—cut
off from Christ!—if that would save them.
4They are the people of Israel, chosen to
be God's adopted children.* God revealed
his glory to them. He made covenants with
them and gave them his law. He gave them
the privilege of worshiping him and receiving his wonderful promises. 5Abraham,
Isaac, and Jacob are their ancestors, and
Christ himself was an Israelite as far as his
human nature is concerned. And he is God,
the one who rules over everything and is
worthy of eternal praise! Amen.*

6Well then, has God failed to fulfill his
promise to Israel? No, for not all who are
born into the nation of Israel are truly
members of God's people! 7Being descendants of Abraham doesn't make them truly
Abraham's children. For the Scriptures say,
"Isaac is the son through whom your descendants will be counted,"* though Abraham
had other children, too. 8This means that
Abraham's physical descendants are not
necessarily children of God. Only the children of the promise are considered to be
Abraham's children. 9For God had promised,
"I will return about this time next year, and
Sarah will have a son."*

▸ **8:19-22** See ***Suffering: Why do bad things happen to good people?***, *page 567.*

10 This son was our ancestor Isaac. When
he married Rebekah, she gave birth to
twins.* 11 But before they were born, before
they had done anything good or bad, she received a message from God. (This message
shows that God chooses people according
to his own purposes; 12 he calls people, but
not according to their good or bad works.)
She was told, "Your older son will serve your
younger son."* 13 In the words of the Scriptures, "I loved Jacob, but I rejected Esau."*
14 Are we saying, then, that God was
unfair? Of course not! 15 For God said to
Moses,

"I will show mercy to anyone I choose,
and I will show compassion to anyone
I choose."*

16 So it is God who decides to show mercy.
We can neither choose it nor work for it.
17 For the Scriptures say that God told
Pharaoh, "I have appointed you for the very
purpose of displaying my power in you and
to spread my fame throughout the earth."*
18 So you see, God chooses to show mercy to
some, and he chooses to harden the hearts
of others so they refuse to listen.
19 Well then, you might say, "Why does
God blame people for not responding?
Haven't they simply done what he makes
them do?"
20 No, don't say that. Who are you, a mere
human being, to argue with God? Should the
thing that was created say to the one who
created it, "Why have you made me like this?"
21 When a potter makes jars out of clay, doesn't
he have a right to use the same lump of clay
to make one jar for decoration and another to
throw garbage into? 22 In the same way, even
though God has the right to show his anger
and his power, he is very patient with those
on whom his anger falls, who are destined for
destruction. 23 He does this to make the riches
of his glory shine even brighter on those to
whom he shows mercy, who were prepared in
advance for glory. 24 And we are among those
whom he selected, both from the Jews and
from the Gentiles.
25 Concerning the Gentiles, God says in the
prophecy of Hosea,

"Those who were not my people,
I will now call my people.
And I will love those
whom I did not love before."*

26 And,

"Then, at the place where they were told,
'You are not my people,'
there they will be called
'children of the living God.'"*

27 And concerning Israel, Isaiah the prophet
cried out,

"Though the people of Israel are as
numerous as the sand of the
seashore,
only a remnant will be saved.
28 For the LORD will carry out his sentence
upon the earth
quickly and with finality."*

29 And Isaiah said the same thing in another
place:

"If the LORD of Heaven's Armies
had not spared a few of our children,
we would have been wiped out like
Sodom,
destroyed like Gomorrah."*

Israel's Unbelief

30 What does all this mean? Even though
the Gentiles were not trying to follow God's
standards, they were made right with God.
And it was by faith that this took place.
31 But the people of Israel, who tried so hard
to get right with God by keeping the law,
never succeeded. 32 Why not? Because they
were trying to get right with God by keeping
the law* instead of by trusting in him. They
stumbled over the great rock in their path.
33 God warned them of this in the Scriptures
when he said,

"I am placing a stone in Jerusalem* that
makes people stumble,
a rock that makes them fall.
But anyone who trusts in him
will never be disgraced."*

10 Dear brothers and sisters,* the longing
of my heart and my prayer to God is
for the people of Israel to be saved. 2 I know

8:23 Greek *wait anxiously for sonship.* **8:24** Some manuscripts read *wait.* **8:27** Greek *for God's holy people.* **8:28** Some manuscripts read *And we know that everything works together.* **8:29** Or *would be supreme.* **8:36** Ps 44:22. **8:38** Greek *nor rulers.* **9:3** Greek *my brothers.* **9:4** Greek *chosen for sonship.* **9:5** Or *May God, the one who rules over everything, be praised forever. Amen.* **9:7** Gen 21:12. **9:9** Gen 18:10, 14. **9:10** Greek *she conceived children through this one man.* **9:12** Gen 25:23. **9:13** Mal 1:2-3. **9:15** Exod 33:19. **9:17** Exod 9:16 (Greek version). **9:25** Hos 2:23. **9:26** Greek *sons of the living God.* Hos 1:10. **9:27-28** Isa 10:22-23 (Greek version). **9:29** Isa 1:9 (Greek version). **9:32** Greek *by works.* **9:33a** Greek *in Zion.* **9:33b** Isa 8:14; 28:16 (Greek version). **10:1** Greek *Brothers.*

what enthusiasm they have for God, but it
is misdirected zeal. 3For they don't understand God's way of making people right with
himself. Refusing to accept God's way, they
cling to their own way of getting right with
God by trying to keep the law. 4For Christ
has already accomplished the purpose for
which the law was given.* As a result, all
who believe in him are made right with God.

Salvation Is for Everyone

5For Moses writes that the law's way of
making a person right with God requires
obedience to all of its commands.* 6But
faith's way of getting right with God says,
"Don't say in your heart, 'Who will go up
to heaven?' (to bring Christ down to earth).
7And don't say, 'Who will go down to the
place of the dead?' (to bring Christ back to
life again)." 8In fact, it says,

> "The message is very close at hand;
> it is on your lips and in your heart."*

And that message is the very message about
faith that we preach: 9If you openly declare
that Jesus is Lord and believe in your heart
that God raised him from the dead, you
will be saved. 10For it is by believing in your
heart that you are made right with God,
and it is by openly declaring your faith that
you are saved. 11As the Scriptures tell us,
"Anyone who trusts in him will never be disgraced."* 12Jew and Gentile* are the same in
this respect. They have the same Lord, who
gives generously to all who call on him.
13For "Everyone who calls on the name of
the LORD will be saved."*

14But how can they call on him to save
them unless they believe in him? And how
can they believe in him if they have never
heard about him? And how can they hear
about him unless someone tells them? 15And
how will anyone go and tell them without
being sent? That is why the Scriptures say,
"How beautiful are the feet of messengers
who bring good news!"*

16But not everyone welcomes the Good
News, for Isaiah the prophet said, "LORD,
who has believed our message?"* 17So faith
comes from hearing, that is, hearing the
Good News about Christ. 18But I ask, have
the people of Israel actually heard the
message? Yes, they have:

> "The message has gone throughout the
> earth,
> and the words to all the world."*

19But I ask, did the people of Israel really
understand? Yes, they did, for even in the
time of Moses, God said,

What about Israel?

If all Paul has said so far is true, then why did the Jews reject Jesus as the Messiah? And was there still a place for them in God's plan? Paul says an emphatic "yes," which is why he prayed for them (Romans 10:1). His explanation (chapters 9–11) has four key points.

First, being Jewish and being a member of God's people aren't the same thing (9:6-13). Salvation has never been a matter of nationality; God has always worked on the basis of call and faith: "Not all who are born into the nation of Israel are truly members of God's people!" (9:6). Second, being saved isn't about our works, but about God's grace (9:14-29). No one is entitled to that grace, but it is available to everyone, Jew or Gentile. Third, believing is our own responsibility (9:30–10:21). Israel rejected Jesus because they made the wrong choice, while Gentiles made the right choice (9:30-33). Fourth, God still has a plan for Israel (11:1-36). While their unbelief has, in God's sovereignty, opened a door for the Gentiles (11:11-15), a day will come when "all Israel will be saved" (11:26). By this Paul cannot mean "every Jew"—he has already ruled this out in 9:6. Rather, many see this as referring to a great turning of Jews to Christ as their Messiah at the end time. Others see it as a reference to "all God's true people—Jew *and* Gentile"—who, through faith in Christ, have become part of the one united people of God. Either way, it is something that causes Paul to rejoice (11:33-36).

"I will rouse your jealousy through
people who are not even a nation.
I will provoke your anger through the
foolish Gentiles."*

20 And later Isaiah spoke boldly for God,
saying,

"I was found by people who were not
looking for me.
I showed myself to those who were
not asking for me."*

21 But regarding Israel, God said,

"All day long I opened my arms to
them,
but they were disobedient and
rebellious."*

God's Mercy on Israel

11 I ask, then, has God rejected his own
people, the nation of Israel? Of course
not! I myself am an Israelite, a descendant
of Abraham and a member of the tribe of
Benjamin.
2 No, God has not rejected his own people,
whom he chose from the very beginning. Do
you realize what the Scriptures say about
this? Elijah the prophet complained to God
about the people of Israel and said, 3 "LORD,
they have killed your prophets and torn
down your altars. I am the only one left, and
now they are trying to kill me, too."*
4 And do you remember God's reply? He
said, "No, I have 7,000 others who have
never bowed down to Baal!"*
5 It is the same today, for a few of the
people of Israel* have remained faithful
because of God's grace—his undeserved
kindness in choosing them. 6 And since it
is through God's kindness, then it is not by
their good works. For in that case, God's
grace would not be what it really is—free
and undeserved.
7 So this is the situation: Most of the
people of Israel have not found the favor of
God they are looking for so earnestly. A few
have—the ones God has chosen—but the
hearts of the rest were hardened. 8 As the
Scriptures say,

"God has put them into a deep sleep.
To this day he has shut their eyes so they
do not see,
and closed their ears so they do not
hear."*

9 Likewise, David said,

"Let their bountiful table become a snare,
a trap that makes them think all is well.
Let their blessings cause them to stumble,
and let them get what they deserve.
10 Let their eyes go blind so they cannot see,
and let their backs be bent forever."*

11 Did God's people stumble and fall
beyond recovery? Of course not! They were
disobedient, so God made salvation available to the Gentiles. But he wanted his own
people to become jealous and claim it for
themselves. 12 Now if the Gentiles were enriched because the people of Israel turned
down God's offer of salvation, think how
much greater a blessing the world will share
when they finally accept it.
13 I am saying all this especially for you
Gentiles. God has appointed me as the
apostle to the Gentiles. I stress this, 14 for I
want somehow to make the people of Israel
jealous of what you Gentiles have, so I might
save some of them. 15 For since their rejection
meant that God offered salvation to the rest
of the world, their acceptance will be even
more wonderful. It will be life for those who
were dead! 16 And since Abraham and the
other patriarchs were holy, their descendants will also be holy—just as the entire
batch of dough is holy because the portion
given as an offering is holy. For if the roots of
the tree are holy, the branches will be, too.
17 But some of these branches from Abraham's tree—some of the people of Israel—
have been broken off. And you Gentiles, who
were branches from a wild olive tree, have
been grafted in. So now you also receive the
blessing God has promised Abraham and his
children, sharing in the rich nourishment
from the root of God's special olive tree. 18 But
you must not brag about being grafted in to
replace the branches that were broken off.
You are just a branch, not the root.
19 "Well," you may say, "those branches
were broken off to make room for me." 20 Yes,
but remember—those branches were broken
off because they didn't believe in Christ, and
you are there because you do believe. So
don't think highly of yourself, but fear what

10:4 Or *For Christ is the end of the law.* **10:5** See Lev 18:5. **10:6-8** Deut 30:12-14. **10:11** Isa 28:16 (Greek version). **10:12** Greek *and Greek.* **10:13** Joel 2:32. **10:15** Isa 52:7. **10:16** Isa 53:1. **10:18** Ps 19:4. **10:19** Deut 32:21. **10:20** Isa 65:1 (Greek version). **10:21** Isa 65:2 (Greek version). **11:3** 1 Kgs 19:10, 14. **11:4** 1 Kgs 19:18. **11:5** Greek *for a remnant.* **11:8** Isa 29:10; Deut 29:4. **11:9-10** Ps 69:22-23 (Greek version).

could happen. [21]For if God did not spare the
original branches, he won't* spare you either.
[22]Notice how God is both kind and severe.
He is severe toward those who disobeyed, but
kind to you if you continue to trust in his kindness. But if you stop trusting, you also will be
cut off. [23]And if the people of Israel turn from
their unbelief, they will be grafted in again,
for God has the power to graft them back into
the tree. [24]You, by nature, were a branch cut
from a wild olive tree. So if God was willing
to do something contrary to nature by graft-
ing you into his cultivated tree, he will be
far more eager to graft the original branches
back into the tree where they belong.

God's Mercy Is for Everyone

[25]I want you to understand this mystery,
dear brothers and sisters,* so that you will
not feel proud about yourselves. Some of
the people of Israel have hard hearts, but
this will last only until the full number of
Gentiles comes to Christ. [26]And so all Israel
will be saved. As the Scriptures say,

"The one who rescues will come from
Jerusalem,*
and he will turn Israel* away from
ungodliness.
[27] And this is my covenant with them,
that I will take away their sins."*

[28]Many of the people of Israel are now
enemies of the Good News, and this benefits
you Gentiles. Yet they are still the people
he loves because he chose their ancestors
Abraham, Isaac, and Jacob. [29]For God's gifts
and his call can never be withdrawn. [30]Once,
you Gentiles were rebels against God, but
when the people of Israel rebelled against
him, God was merciful to you instead. [31]Now
they are the rebels, and God's mercy has
come to you so that they, too, will share* in
God's mercy. [32]For God has imprisoned everyone in disobedience so he could have mercy
on everyone.
[33]Oh, how great are God's riches and
wisdom and knowledge! How impossible
it is for us to understand his decisions and
his ways!

[34] For who can know the LORD's thoughts?
Who knows enough to give him
advice?*
[35] And who has given him so much
that he needs to pay it back?*

[36]For everything comes from him and
exists by his power and is intended for his
glory. All glory to him forever! Amen.

A Living Sacrifice to God

12 And so, dear brothers and sisters,*
I plead with you to give your bodies
to God because of all he has done for you.
Let them be a living and holy sacrifice—the
kind he will find acceptable. This is truly
the way to worship him.* [2]Don't copy the
behavior and customs of this world, but let
God transform you into a new person by
changing the way you think. Then you will
learn to know God's will for you, which is
good and pleasing and perfect.
[3]Because of the privilege and authority*
God has given me, I give each of you this
warning: Don't think you are better than
you really are. Be honest in your evaluation
of yourselves, measuring yourselves by the
faith God has given us.* [4]Just as our bodies
have many parts and each part has a special
function, [5]so it is with Christ's body. We are
many parts of one body, and we all belong
to each other.
[6]In his grace, God has given us different
gifts for doing certain things well. So if God
has given you the ability to prophesy, speak
out with as much faith as God has given you.
[7]If your gift is serving others, serve them well.
If you are a teacher, teach well. [8]If your gift is
to encourage others, be encouraging. If it is
giving, give generously. If God has given you
leadership ability, take the responsibility
seriously. And if you have a gift for showing
kindness to others, do it gladly.
[9]Don't just pretend to love others. Really
love them. Hate what is wrong. Hold tightly
to what is good. [10]Love each other with
genuine affection,* and take delight in honoring each other. [11]Never be lazy, but work
hard and serve the Lord enthusiastically.*
[12]Rejoice in our confident hope. Be patient in
trouble, and keep on praying. [13]When God's
people are in need, be ready to help them.
Always be eager to practice hospitality.
[14]Bless those who persecute you. Don't
curse them; pray that God will bless them.

▸ **12:2** *See **Thought**, page 808.* **12:4-8** *See **Gifts of the Holy Spirit**, page 1316; **Service**, page 1424.* **12:13** *See **Hospitality**, page 1410.*

15 Be happy with those who are happy, and
weep with those who weep. 16 Live in harmony
with each other. Don't be too proud to enjoy
the company of ordinary people. And don't
think you know it all!
17 Never pay back evil with more evil. Do
things in such a way that everyone can see
you are honorable. 18 Do all that you can to
live in peace with everyone.
19 Dear friends, never take revenge. Leave
that to the righteous anger of God. For the
Scriptures say,

"I will take revenge;
I will pay them back,"*
says the LORD.

20 Instead,

"If your enemies are hungry, feed them.
If they are thirsty, give them
something to drink.
In doing this, you will heap
burning coals of shame on their heads."*

21 Don't let evil conquer you, but conquer
evil by doing good.

Respect for Authority

13 Everyone must submit to governing
authorities. For all authority comes
from God, and those in positions of authority
have been placed there by God. 2 So anyone
who rebels against authority is rebelling
against what God has instituted, and they
will be punished. 3 For the authorities do not
strike fear in people who are doing right, but
in those who are doing wrong. Would you
like to live without fear of the authorities?
Do what is right, and they will honor you.
4 The authorities are God's servants, sent for
your good. But if you are doing wrong, of
course you should be afraid, for they have
the power to punish you. They are God's
servants, sent for the very purpose of punishing those who do what is wrong. 5 So you
must submit to them, not only to avoid punishment, but also to keep a clear conscience.
6 Pay your taxes, too, for these same
reasons. For government workers need to be
paid. They are serving God in what they do.
7 Give to everyone what you owe them: Pay
your taxes and government fees to those
who collect them, and give respect and
honor to those who are in authority.

11:21 Some manuscripts read *perhaps he won't.* **11:25** Greek *brothers.* **11:26a** Greek *from Zion.* **11:26b** Greek *Jacob.* **11:26-27** Isa 59:20-21; 27:9 (Greek version). **11:31** Other manuscripts read *will now share;* still others read *will someday share.* **11:34** Isa 40:13 (Greek version). **11:35** See Job 41:11. **12:1a** Greek *brothers.* **12:1b** Or *This is your spiritual worship;* or *This is your reasonable service.* **12:3a** Or *Because of the grace;* compare 1:5. **12:3b** Or *by the faith God has given you;* or *by the standard of our God-given faith.* **12:10** Greek *with brotherly love.* **12:11** Or *but serve the Lord with a zealous spirit;* or *but let the Spirit excite you as you serve the Lord.* **12:19** Deut 32:35. **12:20** Prov 25:21-22.

Christians and government

Some Christians were obviously thinking, "Why should I submit to pagan rulers? They persecute us! My allegiance is to Christ alone!" But Paul knew that God, in his sovereignty, had established these rulers (Romans 13:1) and that rebellion against them is therefore rebellion against God (13:2). While they might not recognize it, the rulers are actually God's servants (13:4), there to establish law and order. And if we are good citizens, we have nothing to fear from them.

This teaching—repeated by the apostle Peter (1 Peter 2:13-25)—is all the more remarkable considering that the early church didn't live under a democratic government but under a totalitarian state that persecuted them. But Paul understood that bad government is better than no government, which leads to utter chaos. So Christians should submit to authorities (Romans 13:5), pay taxes (13:6-7), and respect rulers (13:5-7). Of course, if we live in a democracy, we should take the opportunity to vote for our leaders; but once they are established, we should submit to them, whether we voted for them or not.

Are there exceptions to this rule? Yes—if the authorities require us to do something contrary to God's will. In such cases, as Peter told the Jewish high council, "We must obey God rather than any human authority" (Acts 5:29).

▸ *See also **Paying taxes**, page 1139.*

Love Fulfills God's Requirements

8 Owe nothing to anyone—except for your obligation to love one another. If you love your neighbor, you will fulfill the requirements of God's law. 9 For the commandments say, "You must not commit adultery. You must not murder. You must not steal. You must not covet."* These—and other such commandments—are summed up in this one commandment: "Love your neighbor as yourself."* 10 Love does no wrong to others, so love fulfills the requirements of God's law.

11 This is all the more urgent, for you know how late it is; time is running out. Wake up, for our salvation is nearer now than when we first believed. 12 The night is almost gone; the day of salvation will soon be here. So remove your dark deeds like dirty clothes, and put on the shining armor of right living. 13 Because we belong to the day, we must live decent lives for all to see. Don't participate in the darkness of wild parties and drunkenness, or in sexual promiscuity and immoral living, or in quarreling and jealousy. 14 Instead, clothe yourself with the presence of the Lord Jesus Christ. And don't let yourself think about ways to indulge your evil desires.

The Danger of Criticism

14 Accept other believers who are weak in faith, and don't argue with them about what they think is right or wrong. 2 For instance, one person believes it's all right to eat anything. But another believer with a sensitive conscience will eat only vegetables. 3 Those who feel free to eat anything must not look down on those who don't. And those who don't eat certain foods must not condemn those who do, for God has accepted them. 4 Who are you to condemn someone else's servants? Their own master will judge whether they stand or fall. And with the Lord's help, they will stand and receive his approval.

5 In the same way, some think one day is more holy than another day, while others think every day is alike. You should each be fully convinced that whichever day you choose is acceptable. 6 Those who worship the Lord on a special day do it to honor him. Those who eat any kind of food do so to honor the Lord, since they give thanks to God before eating. And those who refuse to eat certain foods also want to please the Lord and give thanks to God. 7 For we don't live for ourselves or die for ourselves. 8 If we live, it's to honor the Lord. And if we die, it's to honor the Lord. So whether we live or die, we belong to the Lord. 9 Christ died and rose again for this very purpose—to be Lord both of the living and of the dead.

10 So why do you condemn another believer*? Why do you look down on another believer? Remember, we will all stand before the judgment seat of God. 11 For the Scriptures say,

> "'As surely as I live,' says the LORD,
> 'every knee will bend to me,
> and every tongue will declare
> allegiance to God.*'"

12 Yes, each of us will give a personal account to God. 13 So let's stop condemning each other. Decide instead to live in such a way that you will not cause another believer to stumble and fall.

14 I know and am convinced on the authority of the Lord Jesus that no food, in and of itself, is wrong to eat. But if someone believes it is wrong, then for that person it is wrong. 15 And if another believer is distressed by what you eat, you are not acting in love if you eat it. Don't let your eating ruin someone for whom Christ died. 16 Then you will not be criticized for doing something you believe is good. 17 For the Kingdom of God is not a matter of what we eat or drink, but of living a life of goodness and peace and joy in the Holy Spirit. 18 If you serve Christ with this attitude, you will please God, and others will approve of you, too. 19 So then, let us aim for harmony in the church and try to build each other up.

20 Don't tear apart the work of God over what you eat. Remember, all foods are acceptable, but it is wrong to eat something if it makes another person stumble. 21 It is better not to eat meat or drink wine or do anything else if it might cause another believer to stumble.* 22 You may believe there's nothing wrong with what you are doing, but keep it between yourself and God. Blessed

▸ **13:9** *See **Love your neighbor as yourself**, page 139.*

are those who don't feel guilty for doing something they have decided is right. 23 But if you have doubts about whether or not you should eat something, you are sinning if you go ahead and do it. For you are not following your convictions. If you do anything you believe is not right, you are sinning.*

Living to Please Others

15 We who are strong must be considerate of those who are sensitive about things like this. We must not just please ourselves. 2 We should help others do what is right and build them up in the Lord. 3 For even Christ didn't live to please himself. As the Scriptures say, "The insults of those who insult you, O God, have fallen on me."* 4 Such things were written in the Scriptures long ago to teach us. And the Scriptures give us hope and encouragement as we wait patiently for God's promises to be fulfilled.

5 May God, who gives this patience and encouragement, help you live in complete harmony with each other, as is fitting for followers of Christ Jesus. 6 Then all of you can join together with one voice, giving praise and glory to God, the Father of our Lord Jesus Christ.

7 Therefore, accept each other just as Christ has accepted you so that God will be given glory. 8 Remember that Christ came as a servant to the Jews* to show that God is true to the promises he made to their ancestors. 9 He also came so that the Gentiles might give glory to God for his mercies to them. That is what the psalmist meant when he wrote:

"For this, I will praise you among the
  Gentiles;
I will sing praises to your name."*

10 And in another place it is written,

"Rejoice with his people,
you Gentiles."*

11 And yet again,

"Praise the LORD, all you Gentiles.
Praise him, all you people of the
  earth."*

12 And in another place Isaiah said,

"The heir to David's throne* will come,
and he will rule over the Gentiles.
They will place their hope on him."*

13 I pray that God, the source of hope, will fill you completely with joy and peace because you trust in him. Then you will overflow with confident hope through the power of the Holy Spirit.

Paul's Reason for Writing

14 I am fully convinced, my dear brothers and sisters,* that you are full of goodness. You know these things so well you can teach each other all about them. 15 Even so, I have been bold enough to write about some of these points, knowing that all you need is this reminder. For by God's grace, 16 I am a special messenger from Christ Jesus to you Gentiles. I bring you the Good News so that I might present you as an acceptable offering to God, made holy by the Holy Spirit. 17 So I have reason to be enthusiastic about all Christ Jesus has done through me in my service to God. 18 Yet I dare not boast about anything except what Christ has done through me, bringing the Gentiles to God by my message and by the way I worked among them. 19 They were convinced by the power of miraculous signs and wonders and by the power of God's Spirit.* In this way, I have fully presented the Good News of Christ from Jerusalem all the way to Illyricum.*

20 My ambition has always been to preach the Good News where the name of Christ has never been heard, rather than where a church has already been started by someone else. 21 I have been following the plan spoken of in the Scriptures, where it says,

"Those who have never been told about
  him will see,
and those who have never heard of
  him will understand."*

22 In fact, my visit to you has been delayed so long because I have been preaching in these places.

Paul's Travel Plans

23 But now I have finished my work in these regions, and after all these long years of

13:9a Exod 20:13-15, 17. **13:9b** Lev 19:18. **14:10** Greek *your brother;* also in 14:10b, 13, 15, 21. **14:11** Or *declare praise for God.* Isa 49:18; 45:23 (Greek version). **14:21** Some manuscripts read *to stumble or be offended or be weakened.* **14:23** Some manuscripts place the text of 16:25-27 here. **15:3** Greek *who insult you have fallen on me.* Ps 69:9. **15:8** Greek *servant of circumcision.* **15:9** Ps 18:49. **15:10** Deut 32:43. **15:11** Ps 117:1. **15:12a** Greek *The root of Jesse.* David was the son of Jesse. **15:12b** Isa 11:10 (Greek version). **15:14** Greek *brothers;* also in 15:30. **15:19a** Other manuscripts read *the Spirit;* still others read *the Holy Spirit.* **15:19b** *Illyricum* was a region northeast of Italy. **15:21** Isa 52:15 (Greek version).

waiting, I am eager to visit you. [24]I am planning to go to Spain, and when I do, I will stop off in Rome. And after I have enjoyed your fellowship for a little while, you can provide for my journey.

[25]But before I come, I must go to Jerusalem to take a gift to the believers* there. [26]For you see, the believers in Macedonia and Achaia* have eagerly taken up an offering for the poor among the believers in Jerusalem. [27]They were glad to do this because they feel they owe a real debt to them. Since the Gentiles received the spiritual blessings of the Good News from the believers in Jerusalem, they feel the least they can do in return is to help them financially. [28]As soon as I have delivered this money and completed this good deed of theirs, I will come to see you on my way to Spain. [29]And I am sure that when I come, Christ will richly bless our time together.

[30]Dear brothers and sisters, I urge you in the name of our Lord Jesus Christ to join in my struggle by praying to God for me. Do this because of your love for me, given to you by the Holy Spirit. [31]Pray that I will be rescued from those in Judea who refuse to obey God. Pray also that the believers there will be willing to accept the donation* I am taking to Jerusalem. [32]Then, by the will of God, I will be able to come to you with a joyful heart, and we will be an encouragement to each other.

[33]And now may God, who gives us his peace, be with you all. Amen.*

Paul Greets His Friends

16 I commend to you our sister Phoebe, who is a deacon in the church in Cenchrea. [2]Welcome her in the Lord as one who is worthy of honor among God's people. Help her in whatever she needs, for she has been helpful to many, and especially to me.

[3]Give my greetings to Priscilla and Aquila, my co-workers in the ministry of Christ Jesus. [4]In fact, they once risked their lives for me. I am thankful to them, and so are all the Gentile churches. [5]Also give my greetings to the church that meets in their home.

Greet my dear friend Epenetus. He was the first person from the province of Asia to become a follower of Christ. [6]Give my greetings to Mary, who has worked so hard for your benefit. [7]Greet Andronicus and Junia,* my fellow Jews,* who were in prison with me. They are highly respected among the apostles and became followers of Christ before I did. [8]Greet Ampliatus, my dear friend in the Lord. [9]Greet Urbanus,

What kind of church does God want?

Paul's reference to "the church that meets in their home" (Romans 16:5) is a reminder that the early Christians did not have special buildings to meet in, but rather met in the homes of their members (see also Acts 2:46; 18:7; 1 Corinthians 16:19; Colossians 4:15; Philemon 1:2). In fact, church buildings didn't appear until after the Roman emperor Constantine's conversion in AD 312 and his legalization of Christianity the following year. The first Christians met for fellowship in homes, and the church in a particular city was made up of several such "house churches," overseen by a group of church leaders in that city (e.g., Philippians 1:1).

Today there are different views on the best model for church. Some argue we should meet in homes, as in the New Testament; others believe God wants megachurches that can impact a city. Both can have their place, but the key matter is asking God what he wants for us—and then not imposing our model on others or claiming it is the only model. In fact, the New Testament never says churches should be a certain size or follow a certain pattern or meet in a certain kind of place; rather, it simply gives principles, values, and motives for bringing God's people together. After all, that is what the word "church" means—not a building, but "God's gathered people."

▸ *See also **The church**, page 1348; **Belonging to a church**, page 1406.*

our co-worker in Christ, and my dear friend
Stachys.
10 Greet Apelles, a good man whom Christ
approves. And give my greetings to the believers from the household of Aristobulus.
11 Greet Herodion, my fellow Jew.* Greet the
Lord's people from the household of Nar-
cissus. 12 Give my greetings to Tryphena and
Tryphosa, the Lord's workers, and to dear
Persis, who has worked so hard for the Lord.
13 Greet Rufus, whom the Lord picked out to
be his very own; and also his dear mother,
who has been a mother to me.
14 Give my greetings to Asyncritus,
Phlegon, Hermes, Patrobas, Hermas, and
the brothers and sisters* who meet with
them. 15 Give my greetings to Philologus,
Julia, Nereus and his sister, and to
Olympas and all the believers* who meet
with them. 16 Greet each other with a sacred
kiss. All the churches of Christ send you
their greetings.

Paul's Final Instructions

17 And now I make one more appeal, my dear
brothers and sisters. Watch out for people
who cause divisions and upset people's
faith by teaching things contrary to what
you have been taught. Stay away from
them. 18 Such people are not serving Christ
our Lord; they are serving their own personal interests. By smooth talk and glowing
words they deceive innocent people. 19 But
everyone knows that you are obedient to the
Lord. This makes me very happy. I want you
to be wise in doing right and to stay innocent of any wrong. 20 The God of peace will
soon crush Satan under your feet. May the
grace of our Lord Jesus* be with you.
21 Timothy, my fellow worker, sends you
his greetings, as do Lucius, Jason, and So-
sipater, my fellow Jews.
22 I, Tertius, the one writing this letter for
Paul, send my greetings, too, as one of the
Lord's followers.
23 Gaius says hello to you. He is my host
and also serves as host to the whole church.
Erastus, the city treasurer, sends you his
greetings, and so does our brother Quartus.*
25 Now all glory to God, who is able to
make you strong, just as my Good News
says. This message about Jesus Christ has
revealed his plan for you Gentiles, a plan
kept secret from the beginning of time. 26 But
now as the prophets* foretold and as the
eternal God has commanded, this message
is made known to all Gentiles everywhere,
so that they too might believe and obey him.
27 All glory to the only wise God, through
Jesus Christ, forever. Amen.*

15:25 Greek *God's holy people;* also in 15:26, 31. **15:26** *Macedonia* and *Achaia* were the northern and southern regions of Greece. **15:31** Greek *the ministry;* other manuscripts read *the gift.* **15:33** Some manuscripts do not include *Amen.* One very early manuscript places 16:25-27 here. **16:7a** *Junia* is a feminine name. Some late manuscripts accent the word so it reads *Junias,* a masculine name; still others read *Julia* (feminine). **16:7b** Or *compatriots;* also in 16:21. **16:11** Or *compatriot.* **16:14** Greek *brothers;* also in 16:17. **16:15** Greek *all of God's holy people.* **16:20** Some manuscripts read *Lord Jesus Christ.* **16:23** Some manuscripts add verse 24, *May the grace of our Lord Jesus Christ be with you all. Amen.* Still others add this sentence after verse 27. **16:26** Greek *the prophetic writings.* **16:25-27** Various manuscripts place the doxology (shown here as 16:25-27) after 14:23 or after 15:33 or after 16:23.

1 Corinthians

Letter to a problem church

First Corinthians is a letter written by the apostle Paul to a church with big problems. The Corinthian Christians were enthusiastic, but immature, believers; and the church was troubled by quarreling, immorality, and disunity. They exercised many gifts of the Holy Spirit, which Paul was pleased about, but they used them in a very immature and arrogant way, which he most definitely was not pleased about. We are meant to use the Spirit's gifts for the good of others, not just for our own benefit, he reminds them. Paul had founded this church (Acts 18:1-18), and he knew it was his responsibility as their founding apostle to set them straight. In this letter he corrects them, disciplines them, clarifies some misunderstandings, and answers their questions.

What's it all about?

Knowledge was a fashionable word in the busy and cosmopolitan city of Corinth. All sorts of religious groups there claimed to have "knowledge" of spiritual truths that others didn't have. And the church there was no different. Different groups were claiming superior knowledge of one kind or another and were becoming arrogant because of it. Paul therefore opens his letter by addressing the issue of real knowledge, or wisdom. This has nothing to do with intelligence or worldly values. Real wisdom, he says, is found only in the cross of Christ (chapters 1–2).

Paul then reprimands them for their ungodly attitudes and behavior. They were dividing into opposing factions based on their preferences for different apostles (chapters 3–4). There were examples of immorality (including the case of a man having an affair with his mother-in-law—which some in the church were actually proud about), strange ideas about marriage, and confusion over eating meat offered to idols (chapters 5–10). The Corinthians were abusing their freedom because of their idea that in Christ they were free and so could live however they wanted to. It was even affecting the way that they shared the Lord's Supper. Paul warns them that true freedom is about living in love and caring for others, not ignoring them.

In chapters 12 to 14, Paul reminds the Corinthians that they form one body, the body of Christ. It is only when the various parts are working in harmony

OVERVIEW

Introduction and greeting
1:1-9

Divisions over the nature of true wisdom · *1:10–2:16*

Divisions over favorite apostles
3:1–4:21

Moral and legal problems within the church · *5:1–6:20*

Answers to their questions about marriage · *7:1-40*

Answers to their questions about food offered to idols · *8:1-13*

The meaning of true freedom
9:1–11:1

Divisions over worship
11:2-34

Using spiritual gifts
12:1–14:40

Christ's resurrection and ours
15:1-58

Personal requests and greetings
16:1-24

that the body is healthy. In worshiping together, they should recognize their different gifts and value those who contribute to the common good. Right at the heart of this section is a passage on the meaning of true love (chapter 13), which reinforces Paul's point that the Spirit's gifts should be used for the good of the whole church, not for selfish enjoyment.

Paul ends by considering the resurrection (chapter 15). Apparently, some Christians believed they were so spiritual that their "resurrection" had already taken place. Paul tells them that they are wrong. There is a "not yet" aspect to the Christian life; as Christians we are waiting for the final resurrection of the dead, when our physical bodies will be changed. Only then will death be defeated forever.

What does it mean for us?

This letter reminds us that being a Christian is not simply about "Jesus and me"; it is about "Jesus and me and you." When we become Christians, we become part of God's big family—or to use the picture Paul uses in this letter, part of Christ's body here on earth. We therefore need our brothers and sisters—and they in turn need us. That's why we cannot live our Christian life without regard for one another; and that's why divisions, arrogance, unholy living, and so on harm both our Christian brothers and sisters and us. We are truly free when we put the concerns and needs of others before our own.

The letter also reminds us about what it means to be truly spiritual. Being spiritual is not just about praying, meditating, or worshiping; it is about *everything* we do in everyday life. We often tend to think of "the spirit" as something detached from everyday life, but Paul reminds us that true spirituality is as much about what we say and do as about what we believe. It is about how we use and misuse our bodies. A truly spiritual person is someone who can both hold their tongue in a quarrel and contain their appetites for food and sex. So to be truly spiritual is to use physical, material things for God's glory and for the blessing of others.

Greetings from Paul

1 This letter is from Paul, chosen by the will
of God to be an apostle of Christ Jesus,
and from our brother Sosthenes.
2 I am writing to God's church in Corinth,*
to you who have been called by God to be
his own holy people. He made you holy by
means of Christ Jesus,* just as he did for all
people everywhere who call on the name of
our Lord Jesus Christ, their Lord and ours.
3 May God our Father and the Lord Jesus
Christ give you grace and peace.

Paul Gives Thanks to God

4 I always thank my God for you and for the
gracious gifts he has given you, now that you
belong to Christ Jesus. 5 Through him, God
has enriched your church in every way—with
all of your eloquent words and all of your
knowledge. 6 This confirms that what I told
you about Christ is true. 7 Now you have every
spiritual gift you need as you eagerly wait for
the return of our Lord Jesus Christ. 8 He will
keep you strong to the end so that you will
be free from all blame on the day when our
Lord Jesus Christ returns. 9 God will do this,
for he is faithful to do what he says, and he
has invited you into partnership with his
Son, Jesus Christ our Lord.

Divisions in the Church

10 I appeal to you, dear brothers and sisters,*
by the authority of our Lord Jesus Christ, to
live in harmony with each other. Let there be
no divisions in the church. Rather, be of one
mind, united in thought and purpose. 11 For
some members of Chloe's household have
told me about your quarrels, my dear brothers and sisters. 12 Some of you are saying,
"I am a follower of Paul." Others are saying,
"I follow Apollos," or "I follow Peter,*" or "I
follow only Christ."
13 Has Christ been divided into factions?
Was I, Paul, crucified for you? Were any of
you baptized in the name of Paul? Of course
not! 14 I thank God that I did not baptize any
of you except Crispus and Gaius, 15 for now no
one can say they were baptized in my name.
16 (Oh yes, I also baptized the household of
Stephanas, but I don't remember baptizing

1:2a *Corinth* was the capital city of Achaia, the southern region of the Greek peninsula. **1:2b** Or *because you belong to Christ Jesus.* **1:10** Greek *brothers;* also in 1:11, 26. **1:12** Greek *Cephas.*

anyone else.) 17For Christ didn't send me to
baptize, but to preach the Good News—and
not with clever speech, for fear that the
cross of Christ would lose its power.

The Wisdom of God

18The message of the cross is foolish to those
who are headed for destruction! But we who
are being saved know it is the very power of
God. 19As the Scriptures say,

"I will destroy the wisdom of the wise
and discard the intelligence of the
intelligent."*

20So where does this leave the philosophers, the scholars, and the world's brilliant debaters? God has made the wisdom
of this world look foolish. 21Since God in his
wisdom saw to it that the world would never
know him through human wisdom, he has
used our foolish preaching to save those
who believe. 22It is foolish to the Jews, who
ask for signs from heaven. And it is foolish
to the Greeks, who seek human wisdom.
23So when we preach that Christ was crucified, the Jews are offended and the Gentiles
say it's all nonsense.

24But to those called by God to salvation,
both Jews and Gentiles,* Christ is the power
of God and the wisdom of God. 25This foolish
plan of God is wiser than the wisest of
human plans, and God's weakness is stronger than the greatest of human strength.

26Remember, dear brothers and sisters,
that few of you were wise in the world's
eyes or powerful or wealthy* when God
called you. 27Instead, God chose things the
world considers foolish in order to shame
those who think they are wise. And he
chose things that are powerless to shame
those who are powerful. 28God chose things
despised by the world,* things counted as
nothing at all, and used them to bring to
nothing what the world considers important. 29As a result, no one can ever boast in
the presence of God.

30God has united you with Christ Jesus.
For our benefit God made him to be wisdom
itself. Christ made us right with God; he
made us pure and holy, and he freed us
from sin. 31Therefore, as the Scriptures say,
"If you want to boast, boast only about the
LORD."*

Paul's Message of Wisdom

2 When I first came to you, dear brothers
and sisters,* I didn't use lofty words and
impressive wisdom to tell you God's secret
plan.* 2For I decided that while I was with
you I would forget everything except Jesus
Christ, the one who was crucified. 3I came
to you in weakness—timid and trembling.
4And my message and my preaching were
very plain. Rather than using clever and
persuasive speeches, I relied only on the
power of the Holy Spirit. 5I did this so you

Corinth

Corinth, a city of 650,000 people (two-thirds of them slaves) stood on the narrow strip of land connecting the Greek mainland and the Peloponnesian peninsula. It had two ports, one a mile-and-a-half to the west on the Mediterranean Sea and the other six miles to the east on the Aegean Sea. They were joined by a rolling roadway across which goods or even small ships could be dragged. It was therefore a major commercial city, with all the immorality that sailors and travelers brought. Immorality also played a part in religion, for among the twelve temples in Corinth was one to Aphrodite, the goddess of love, where religious prostitution was practiced. Corinth was so notorious for immorality that a word was created based on it—"to Corinthianize," meaning to practice sexual immorality. Religion was closely linked with civic and business affairs, and sacrifices to seal business deals were common. All this explains why Paul devotes much of this letter, written to a church that he himself had founded (Acts 18), to the dangers of idolatry and immorality, which were the atmosphere in which they lived.

▸ *See also **Idols**, page 836; **Worldliness**, page 1306; **Paul's Missionary Journeys** map, Visual Overview Z15.*

would trust not in human wisdom but in the power of God.

6Yet when I am among mature believers, I do speak with words of wisdom, but not the kind of wisdom that belongs to this world or to the rulers of this world, who are soon forgotten. 7No, the wisdom we speak of is the mystery of God*—his plan that was previously hidden, even though he made it for our ultimate glory before the world began. 8But the rulers of this world have not understood it; if they had, they would not have crucified our glorious Lord. 9That is what the Scriptures mean when they say,

"No eye has seen, no ear has heard,
  and no mind has imagined
what God has prepared
  for those who love him."*

10But* it was to us that God revealed these things by his Spirit. For his Spirit searches out everything and shows us God's deep secrets. 11No one can know a person's thoughts except that person's own spirit, and no one can know God's thoughts except God's own Spirit. 12And we have received God's Spirit (not the world's spirit), so we can know the wonderful things God has freely given us.

13When we tell you these things, we do not use words that come from human wisdom. Instead, we speak words given to us by the Spirit, using the Spirit's words to explain spiritual truths.* 14But people who aren't spiritual* can't receive these truths from God's Spirit. It all sounds foolish to them and they can't understand it, for only those who are spiritual can understand what the Spirit means. 15Those who are spiritual can evaluate all things, but they themselves cannot be evaluated by others. 16For,

"Who can know the LORD's thoughts?
  Who knows enough to teach him?"*

But we understand these things, for we have the mind of Christ.

Paul and Apollos, Servants of Christ

3 Dear brothers and sisters,* when I was with you I couldn't talk to you as I would to spiritual people.* I had to talk as though you belonged to this world or as

1:19 Isa 29:14. **1:24** Greek *and Greeks.* **1:26** Or *high born.* **1:28** Or *God chose those who are low born.* **1:31** Jer 9:24. **2:1a** Greek *brothers.* **2:1b** Greek *God's mystery;* other manuscripts read *God's testimony.* **2:7** Greek *But we speak God's wisdom in a mystery.* **2:9** Isa 64:4. **2:10** Some manuscripts read *For.* **2:13** Or *explaining spiritual truths in spiritual language,* or *explaining spiritual truths to spiritual people.* **2:14** Or *who don't have the Spirit;* or *who have only physical life.* **2:16** Isa 40:13 (Greek version). **3:1a** Greek *Brothers.* **3:1b** Or *to people who have the Spirit.*

Divisions in the church

News of growing divisions in the church, reported to him by members of the church (1 Corinthians 1:11), deeply troubled Paul. After all, he had planted this church and had spent eighteen months with them (Acts 18:1-11), so he deeply felt the pain of these divisions. But even more troubling was the Corinthians' failure to understand what the church is: the body of Christ on earth (1 Corinthians 12:12-31). To divide from other Christians is therefore to rip his body apart. That is why Paul speaks so strongly against disunity, exposing its foolishness (1:12-17) and immaturity (3:1-23), saying its roots lie in arrogance (3:21; 4:6-8, 18-19) and in people's desire to have their own way (e.g., 6:12; 8:9; 10:23). To live with divisions, whatever their root—race, gender, or opinion—is to deny the cross of Christ, who died to bring about unity (Ephesians 2:14-18).

But because the church is made up of people who aren't perfect yet, there will inevitably be times when disagreements arise. So Jesus himself told us what to do in such situations: Talk to the person concerned—not *about* them—and if harmony cannot be reached, then draw in the church leaders to help bring about reconciliation (Matthew 18:15-20). As Paul exhorts the Ephesians, "keep yourselves united in the Spirit, binding yourselves together with peace" (Ephesians 4:3).

▶ *See also* ***Unity****, page 686;* ***The church****, page 1348.*

though you were infants in Christ. 2 I had
to feed you with milk, not with solid food,
because you weren't ready for anything
stronger. And you still aren't ready, 3 for you
are still controlled by your sinful nature.
You are jealous of one another and quarrel
with each other. Doesn't that prove you are
controlled by your sinful nature? Aren't you
living like people of the world? 4 When one
of you says, "I am a follower of Paul," and
another says, "I follow Apollos," aren't you
acting just like people of the world?
5 After all, who is Apollos? Who is Paul?
We are only God's servants through whom
you believed the Good News. Each of us did
the work the Lord gave us. 6 I planted the
seed in your hearts, and Apollos watered
it, but it was God who made it grow. 7 It's
not important who does the planting, or
who does the watering. What's important
is that God makes the seed grow. 8 The one
who plants and the one who waters work
together with the same purpose. And both
will be rewarded for their own hard work.
9 For we are both God's workers. And you are
God's field. You are God's building.
10 Because of God's grace to me, I have
laid the foundation like an expert builder.
Now others are building on it. But whoever
is building on this foundation must be very
careful. 11 For no one can lay any foundation
other than the one we already have—Jesus
Christ.
12 Anyone who builds on that foundation
may use a variety of materials—gold, silver,
jewels, wood, hay, or straw. 13 But on the
judgment day, fire will reveal what kind of
work each builder has done. The fire will
show if a person's work has any value. 14 If
the work survives, that builder will receive
a reward. 15 But if the work is burned up, the
builder will suffer great loss. The builder
will be saved, but like someone barely escaping through a wall of flames.
16 Don't you realize that all of you together
are the temple of God and that the Spirit of
God lives in* you? 17 God will destroy anyone
who destroys this temple. For God's temple
is holy, and you are that temple.
18 Stop deceiving yourselves. If you think
you are wise by this world's standards, you
need to become a fool to be truly wise. 19 For
the wisdom of this world is foolishness to
God. As the Scriptures say,

Worldliness

Paul says he had to talk to the Corinthians as though they "belonged to this world" (1 Corinthians 3:1)—as though they lived like the non-Christians of the world around them. Yet throughout the Bible God's people are called to be different from those around them: "Come out from among unbelievers, and separate yourselves from them" (2 Corinthians 6:17). This does not mean cutting ourselves off from them, for that is not what Jesus did or taught, but living among them while remaining distinct in belief and action.

Yet the behavior of these Christians was little different from their non-Christian neighbors. As a busy port and commercial center, Corinth had developed a reputation as a highly immoral city, even leading to the expression "to Corinthianize," meaning to indulge in sexual immorality. Corinth also had many pagan temples whose meat, sacrificed to idols, was then sold in markets and restaurants. But rather than standing apart from such cultural practices, the church had participated in them; and some were even proud of it (1 Corinthians 5:1-2; 6:12-13).

It is always easy to rationalize worldliness—to say we need to identify with our friends, or that God understands our weakness. But Paul warns that such behavior is not a minor matter; it is dangerous, striking at the very root of our relationship with Christ and defiling our bodies, which the Holy Spirit has made his temple (6:18-20).

▶ *See also* ***Becoming like Christ****, page 1435.*

"He traps the wise
in the snare of their own cleverness."*

[20]And again,

"The LORD knows the thoughts of the wise;
he knows they are worthless."*

[21]So don't boast about following a particular human leader. For everything belongs to you—[22]whether Paul or Apollos or Peter,* or the world, or life and death, or the present and the future. Everything belongs to you, [23]and you belong to Christ, and Christ belongs to God.

Paul's Relationship with the Corinthians

4 So look at Apollos and me as mere servants of Christ who have been put in
charge of explaining God's mysteries. [2]Now,
a person who is put in charge as a manager
must be faithful. [3]As for me, it matters very
little how I might be evaluated by you or by
any human authority. I don't even trust my
own judgment on this point. [4]My conscience
is clear, but that doesn't prove I'm right. It is
the Lord himself who will examine me and
decide.
[5]So don't make judgments about anyone
ahead of time—before the Lord returns. For
he will bring our darkest secrets to light and
will reveal our private motives. Then God
will give to each one whatever praise is due.
[6]Dear brothers and sisters,* I have used
Apollos and myself to illustrate what I've
been saying. If you pay attention to what
I have quoted from the Scriptures,* you
won't be proud of one of your leaders at the
expense of another. [7]For what gives you the
right to make such a judgment? What do
you have that God hasn't given you? And if
everything you have is from God, why boast
as though it were not a gift?
[8]You think you already have everything
you need. You think you are already rich.
You have begun to reign in God's kingdom
without us! I wish you really were reigning
already, for then we would be reigning with
you. [9]Instead, I sometimes think God has put
us apostles on display, like prisoners of war
at the end of a victor's parade, condemned
to die. We have become a spectacle to the
entire world—to people and angels alike.
[10]Our dedication to Christ makes us look
like fools, but you claim to be so wise in
Christ! We are weak, but you are so powerful!
You are honored, but we are ridiculed.

3:16 Or *among.* **3:19** Job 5:13. **3:20** Ps 94:11. **3:22** Greek *Cephas.* **4:6a** Greek *Brothers.* **4:6b** Or *If you learn not to go beyond "what is written."*

Faithfulness

Paul's commendation of his spiritual son Timothy as a "faithful child in the Lord" (1 Corinthians 4:17) brings home to us the importance of faithfulness in the Christian life. Faithfulness is one of God's own characteristics, noted in Scripture again and again (e.g., Exodus 34:6; Deuteronomy 7:9; 32:4; Psalm 89:8; 1 Corinthians 1:9; 10:13; 1 Thessalonians 5:24; 2 Timothy 2:13). It is not surprising therefore that God calls his children to demonstrate this same kind of faithfulness, both to him (e.g., Joshua 24:14) and to one another (e.g., Hebrews 13:4).

Faithfulness is about being loyal and true in all we say and do. It finds expression in things like keeping our promises, fulfilling our obligations, telling the truth, serving others even when it costs us, being honest and reliable in the workplace, and handling money with absolute integrity (especially when we are handling it on behalf of others). The story of Ruth is a wonderful example of selfless faithfulness to others, demonstrated even at cost to herself (e.g., Ruth 1:16-17). Faithfulness in marriage—something often neglected in our modern world—is particularly demanded of God's people (e.g., Malachi 2:13-16; Hebrews 13:4).

If we do not live as faithful people in every part of our lives, it seriously undermines our message that God is faithful and is always there for people. If they cannot see faithfulness in us, whom they can see, why should they believe in a faithful God whom they cannot see?

11Even now we go hungry and thirsty, and we don't have enough clothes to keep warm. We are often beaten and have no home. 12We work wearily with our own hands to earn our living. We bless those who curse us. We are patient with those who abuse us. 13We appeal gently when evil things are said about us. Yet we are treated like the world's garbage, like everybody's trash—right up to the present moment.

14I am not writing these things to shame you, but to warn you as my beloved children. 15For even if you had ten thousand others to teach you about Christ, you have only one spiritual father. For I became your father in Christ Jesus when I preached the Good News to you. 16So I urge you to imitate me.

17That's why I have sent Timothy, my beloved and faithful child in the Lord. He will remind you of how I follow Christ Jesus, just as I teach in all the churches wherever I go.

18Some of you have become arrogant, thinking I will not visit you again. 19But I will come—and soon—if the Lord lets me, and then I'll find out whether these arrogant people just give pretentious speeches or whether they really have God's power. 20For the Kingdom of God is not just a lot of talk; it is living by God's power. 21Which do you choose? Should I come with a rod to punish you, or should I come with love and a gentle spirit?

Paul Condemns Spiritual Pride

5 I can hardly believe the report about the sexual immorality going on among you—something that even pagans don't do. I am told that a man in your church is living in sin with his stepmother.* 2You are so proud of yourselves, but you should be mourning in sorrow and shame. And you should remove this man from your fellowship.

3Even though I am not with you in person, I am with you in the Spirit.* And as though I were there, I have already passed judgment on this man 4in the name of the Lord Jesus. You must call a meeting of the church.* I will be present with you in spirit, and so will the power of our Lord Jesus. 5Then you must throw this man out and hand him over to Satan so that his sinful nature will be destroyed* and he himself* will be saved on the day the Lord* returns.

6Your boasting about this is terrible. Don't you realize that this sin is like a little yeast that spreads through the whole batch of dough? 7Get rid of the old "yeast" by removing this wicked person from among you. Then you will be like a fresh batch of dough made without yeast, which is what you really are. Christ, our Passover Lamb, has been sacrificed for us.* 8So let us celebrate the festival, not with the old bread* of wickedness and evil, but with the new bread* of sincerity and truth.

9When I wrote to you before, I told you not to associate with people who indulge in sexual sin. 10But I wasn't talking about unbelievers who indulge in sexual sin, or are greedy, or cheat people, or worship idols. You would have to leave this world to avoid people like that. 11I meant that you are not to associate with anyone who claims to be a believer* yet indulges in sexual sin, or is greedy, or worships idols, or is abusive, or is a drunkard, or cheats people. Don't even eat with such people.

12It isn't my responsibility to judge outsiders, but it certainly is your responsibility to judge those inside the church who are sinning. 13God will judge those on the outside; but as the Scriptures say, "You must remove the evil person from among you."*

Avoiding Lawsuits with Christians

6 When one of you has a dispute with another believer, how dare you file a lawsuit and ask a secular court to decide the matter instead of taking it to other believers*! 2Don't you realize that someday we believers will judge the world? And since you are going to judge the world, can't you decide even these little things among yourselves? 3Don't you realize that we will judge angels? So you should surely be able to resolve ordinary disputes in this life. 4If you have legal disputes about such matters, why go to outside judges who are not respected by the church? 5I am saying this to shame you. Isn't there anyone in all

▸ **5:7** *See **The Passover**, page 80.*

the church who is wise enough to decide
these issues? 6But instead, one believer*
sues another—right in front of unbelievers!
7Even to have such lawsuits with one
another is a defeat for you. Why not just
accept the injustice and leave it at that? Why
not let yourselves be cheated? 8Instead, you
yourselves are the ones who do wrong and
cheat even your fellow believers.*
9Don't you realize that those who do
wrong will not inherit the Kingdom of God?
Don't fool yourselves. Those who indulge in
sexual sin, or who worship idols, or commit
adultery, or are male prostitutes, or practice
homosexuality, 10or are thieves, or greedy
people, or drunkards, or are abusive, or
cheat people—none of these will inherit the
Kingdom of God. 11Some of you were once
like that. But you were cleansed; you were
made holy; you were made right with God
by calling on the name of the Lord Jesus
Christ and by the Spirit of our God.

Avoiding Sexual Sin

12You say, "I am allowed to do anything"—
but not everything is good for you. And
even though "I am allowed to do anything,"
I must not become a slave to anything. 13You
say, "Food was made for the stomach, and
the stomach for food." (This is true, though
someday God will do away with both of
them.) But you can't say that our bodies
were made for sexual immorality. They were
made for the Lord, and the Lord cares about
our bodies. 14And God will raise us from the
dead by his power, just as he raised our
Lord from the dead.
15Don't you realize that your bodies are
actually parts of Christ? Should a man take
his body, which is part of Christ, and join
it to a prostitute? Never! 16And don't you
realize that if a man joins himself to a prostitute, he becomes one body with her? For
the Scriptures say, "The two are united into
one."* 17But the person who is joined to the
Lord is one spirit with him.

5:1 Greek *his father's wife.* **5:3** Or *in spirit.* **5:4** Or *In the name of the Lord Jesus, you must call a meeting of the church.* **5:5a** Or *so that his body will be destroyed;* Greek reads *for the destruction of the flesh.* **5:5b** Greek *and the spirit.* **5:5c** Other manuscripts read *the Lord Jesus;* still others read *our Lord Jesus Christ.* **5:7** Greek *has been sacrificed.* **5:8a** Greek *not with old leaven.* **5:8b** Greek *but with unleavened [bread].* **5:11** Greek *a brother.* **5:13** Deut 17:7. **6:1** Greek *God's holy people;* also in 6:2. **6:6** Greek *one brother.* **6:8** Greek *even the brothers.* **6:16** Gen 2:24.

Casual sex

For many people nowadays, sex is simply something you do, a recreational pastime—harmless fun, provided you take precautions and "don't hurt anybody." That may have been your own view in the past; but now that you are a Christian, it's important you understand what God thinks about sex. God invented sex, and he planned that it should take place within the loving relationship of the marriage of one man to one woman, to strengthen that relationship (Genesis 2:24). Jesus challenged those who didn't live this way—forgiving them, but also telling them to "go and sin no more" (John 8:11). And the New Testament letters constantly call Christians to live a holy life in this area (e.g., 1 Corinthians 6:9-20; Galatians 5:19-25; Ephesians 5:3-14; 1 Thessalonians 4:1-5; Hebrews 13:4).

The Bible tells us why avoiding sexual immorality is important. It is because, in the sexual act, something actually happens at a spiritual level: Two people become "one" (1 Corinthians 6:16), just like God said at the beginning (Genesis 2:24). Any kind of casual sex therefore makes you "one" with the other person, linking you in some way. It also abuses your body, which now belongs to God and is the temple of the Holy Spirit (1 Corinthians 6:15-20). That's why there is no place in God's Kingdom for such behavior (6:9-10) and why we are told to "run from sexual sin!" (6:18). It affects not just our life but also our relationship with God.

But if you have failed in this area, don't despair! There is as much forgiveness for sexual sin as anything else, as the Corinthians themselves discovered (6:9-11). Confess what you have done and then "go and sin no more."

▶ *See also* ***Prostitution****, page 285;* ***Sexuality****, page 742.*

18 Run from sexual sin! No other sin so
clearly affects the body as this one does.
For sexual immorality is a sin against your
own body. 19 Don't you realize that your body
is the temple of the Holy Spirit, who lives in
you and was given to you by God? You do
not belong to yourself, 20 for God bought you
with a high price. So you must honor God
with your body.

Instruction on Marriage

7 Now regarding the questions you asked
in your letter. Yes, it is good to abstain
from sexual relations.* 2 But because there
is so much sexual immorality, each man
should have his own wife, and each woman
should have her own husband.

3 The husband should fulfill his wife's
sexual needs, and the wife should fulfill
her husband's needs. 4 The wife gives authority over her body to her husband, and
the husband gives authority over his body
to his wife.

5 Do not deprive each other of sexual relations, unless you both agree to refrain
from sexual intimacy for a limited time so
you can give yourselves more completely
to prayer. Afterward, you should come together again so that Satan won't be able
to tempt you because of your lack of self-
control. 6 I say this as a concession, not as a
command. 7 But I wish everyone were single,
just as I am. Yet each person has a special
gift from God, of one kind or another.

8 So I say to those who aren't married and
to widows—it's better to stay unmarried,
just as I am. 9 But if they can't control themselves, they should go ahead and marry. It's
better to marry than to burn with lust.

10 But for those who are married, I have
a command that comes not from me, but
from the Lord.* A wife must not leave her
husband. 11 But if she does leave him, let her
remain single or else be reconciled to him.
And the husband must not leave his wife.

12 Now, I will speak to the rest of you,
though I do not have a direct command
from the Lord. If a fellow believer* has a
wife who is not a believer and she is willing
to continue living with him, he must not
leave her. 13 And if a believing woman has
a husband who is not a believer and he
is willing to continue living with her, she
must not leave him. 14 For the believing
wife brings holiness to her marriage, and
the believing husband* brings holiness
to his marriage. Otherwise, your children
would not be holy, but now they are holy.
15 (But if the husband or wife who isn't a
believer insists on leaving, let them go. In
such cases the believing husband or wife*
is no longer bound to the other, for God has
called you* to live in peace.) 16 Don't you
wives realize that your husbands might
be saved because of you? And don't you
husbands realize that your wives might be
saved because of you?

17 Each of you should continue to live in
whatever situation the Lord has placed
you, and remain as you were when God
first called you. This is my rule for all the
churches. 18 For instance, a man who was
circumcised before he became a believer
should not try to reverse it. And the man
who was uncircumcised when he became
a believer should not be circumcised now.
19 For it makes no difference whether or not
a man has been circumcised. The important
thing is to keep God's commandments.

20 Yes, each of you should remain as you
were when God called you. 21 Are you a slave?
Don't let that worry you—but if you get a
chance to be free, take it. 22 And remember,
if you were a slave when the Lord called you,
you are now free in the Lord. And if you were
free when the Lord called you, you are now
a slave of Christ. 23 God paid a high price for
you, so don't be enslaved by the world.*
24 Each of you, dear brothers and sisters,*
should remain as you were when God first
called you.

25 Now regarding your question about
the young women who are not yet married.
I do not have a command from the Lord for
them. But the Lord in his mercy has given
me wisdom that can be trusted, and I will
share it with you. 26 Because of the present crisis,* I think it is best to remain as
you are. 27 If you have a wife, do not seek
to end the marriage. If you do not have a
wife, do not seek to get married. 28 But if
you do get married, it is not a sin. And if a
young woman gets married, it is not a sin.
However, those who get married at this time
will have troubles, and I am trying to spare
you those problems.

29 But let me say this, dear brothers and
sisters: The time that remains is very short.
So from now on, those with wives should
not focus only on their marriage. 30 Those

who weep or who rejoice or who buy things
should not be absorbed by their weeping
or their joy or their possessions. 31Those
who use the things of the world should not
become attached to them. For this world as
we know it will soon pass away.

32I want you to be free from the concerns
of this life. An unmarried man can spend
his time doing the Lord's work and thinking how to please him. 33But a married man
has to think about his earthly responsibilities and how to please his wife. 34His interests are divided. In the same way, a woman
who is no longer married or has never been
married can be devoted to the Lord and holy
in body and in spirit. But a married woman
has to think about her earthly responsibilities and how to please her husband. 35I am
saying this for your benefit, not to place restrictions on you. I want you to do whatever
will help you serve the Lord best, with as
few distractions as possible.

36But if a man thinks that he's treating his
fiancée improperly and will inevitably give
in to his passion, let him marry her as he
wishes. It is not a sin. 37But if he has decided
firmly not to marry and there is no urgency
and he can control his passion, he does well
not to marry. 38So the person who marries
his fiancée does well, and the person who
doesn't marry does even better.

39A wife is bound to her husband as long
as he lives. If her husband dies, she is free
to marry anyone she wishes, but only if
he loves the Lord.* 40But in my opinion it
would be better for her to stay single, and
I think I am giving you counsel from God's
Spirit when I say this.

Food Sacrificed to Idols

8 Now regarding your question about
food that has been offered to idols.
Yes, we know that "we all have knowledge" about this issue. But while knowledge makes us feel important, it is love

7:1 Or *to live a celibate life;* Greek reads *It is good for a man not to touch a woman.* **7:10** See Matt 5:32; 19:9; Mark 10:11-12; Luke 16:18. **7:12** Greek *a brother.* **7:14** Greek *the brother.* **7:15a** Greek *the brother or sister.* **7:15b** Some manuscripts read *us.* **7:23** Greek *don't become slaves of people.* **7:24** Greek *brothers;* also in 7:29. **7:26** Or *the pressures of life.* **7:39** Greek *but only in the Lord.*

Freedom and responsibility

In 1 Corinthians 8–10, Paul replies to another question from the Corinthians (the first was at 7:1). It concerned "food that has been offered to idols" (8:1). Corinth had many temples; and since sacrifices involved only part of the animal, the rest was eaten by worshipers at the temple or sold in markets. Division had arisen over whether Christians could eat such meat. Since it had been offered to idols, some rejected it; but others ate it, saying idols had no power. Such disagreements had led to both offense and arrogance.

Paul says idols indeed have no power (8:4-6), but eating meat in a temple might undermine a weaker Christian's faith (8:7). So stronger Christians should put weaker Christians' interests first (8:9-13), not insisting on their rights (chapter 9), and therefore avoid eating in temples (10:14-24). But meat from the temples that had been bought in the marketplace can be eaten (10:25-33) since it has now lost its idolatrous associations.

The principle behind this issue is still relevant today: How do we deal with issues that we don't feel strongly about but that other Christians do? (In Romans 14, Paul deals with the opposite side of the same coin: How do we deal with issues that we ourselves feel strongly about but that other Christians don't?) It is easy to look down on others we feel aren't as strong or enlightened as us, or to dismiss as "weak" those who don't feel free to do what we do—and equally to dismiss as "unspiritual" those who do things that we don't. But Christians are called to understand one other and live together harmoniously. So stronger Christians should always put weaker Christians' interests first, and not insist on their rights.

▸ *See also* ***Living with differences****, page 1365.*

that strengthens the church. 2Anyone who claims to know all the answers doesn't really know very much. 3But the person who loves God is the one whom God recognizes.*

4So, what about eating meat that has been offered to idols? Well, we all know that an idol is not really a god and that there is only one God. 5There may be so-called gods both in heaven and on earth, and some people actually worship many gods and many lords. 6But for us,

There is one God, the Father,
by whom all things were created,
and for whom we live.
And there is one Lord, Jesus Christ,
through whom all things were created,
and through whom we live.

7However, not all believers know this. Some are accustomed to thinking of idols as being real, so when they eat food that has been offered to idols, they think of it as the worship of real gods, and their weak consciences are violated. 8It's true that we can't win God's approval by what we eat. We don't lose anything if we don't eat it, and we don't gain anything if we do.

9But you must be careful so that your freedom does not cause others with a weaker conscience to stumble. 10For if others see you—with your "superior knowledge"—eating in the temple of an idol, won't they be encouraged to violate their conscience by eating food that has been offered to an idol? 11So because of your superior knowledge, a weak believer* for whom Christ died will be destroyed. 12And when you sin against other believers* by encouraging them to do something they believe is wrong, you are sinning against Christ. 13So if what I eat causes another believer to sin, I will never eat meat again as long as I live—for I don't want to cause another believer to stumble.

Paul Gives Up His Rights

9 Am I not as free as anyone else? Am I not an apostle? Haven't I seen Jesus our Lord with my own eyes? Isn't it because of my work that you belong to the Lord? 2Even if others think I am not an apostle, I certainly am to you. You yourselves are proof that I am the Lord's apostle.

3This is my answer to those who question my authority.* 4Don't we have the right to live in your homes and share your meals? 5Don't we have the right to bring a believing wife* with us as the other apostles and the Lord's brothers do, and as Peter* does? 6Or is it only Barnabas and I who have to work to support ourselves?

7What soldier has to pay his own expenses? What farmer plants a vineyard and doesn't have the right to eat some of its fruit? What shepherd cares for a flock of sheep and isn't allowed to drink some of the milk? 8Am I expressing merely a human opinion, or does the law say the same thing? 9For the law of Moses says, "You must not muzzle an ox to keep it from eating as it treads out the grain."* Was God thinking only about oxen when he said this? 10Wasn't he actually speaking to us? Yes, it was written for us, so that the one who plows and the one who threshes the grain might both expect a share of the harvest.

11Since we have planted spiritual seed among you, aren't we entitled to a harvest of physical food and drink? 12If you support others who preach to you, shouldn't we have an even greater right to be supported? But we have never used this right. We would rather put up with anything than be an obstacle to the Good News about Christ.

13Don't you realize that those who work in the temple get their meals from the offerings brought to the temple? And those who serve at the altar get a share of the sacrificial offerings. 14In the same way, the Lord ordered that those who preach the Good News should be supported by those who benefit from it. 15Yet I have never used any of these rights. And I am not writing this to suggest that I want to start now. In fact, I would rather die than lose my right to boast about preaching without charge. 16Yet preaching the Good News is not something I can boast about. I am compelled by God to do it. How terrible for me if I didn't preach the Good News!

17If I were doing this on my own initiative, I would deserve payment. But I have no choice, for God has given me this sacred trust. 18What then is my pay? It is the opportunity to preach the Good News without charging anyone. That's why I never demand my rights when I preach the Good News.

19Even though I am a free man with no master, I have become a slave to all people to bring many to Christ. 20When I was with the Jews, I lived like a Jew to bring the Jews to Christ. When I was with those who follow the Jewish law, I too lived under that law. Even though I am not subject to the law, I did this so I could bring to Christ those who are under the law. [21]When I am with the Gentiles who do not follow the Jewish law,* I too live apart from that law so I can bring them to Christ. But I do not ignore the law of God; I obey the law of Christ.

[22]When I am with those who are weak, I share their weakness, for I want to bring the weak to Christ. Yes, I try to find common ground with everyone, doing everything I can to save some. [23]I do everything to spread the Good News and share in its blessings.

[24]Don't you realize that in a race everyone runs, but only one person gets the prize? So run to win! [25]All athletes are disciplined in their training. They do it to win a prize that will fade away, but we do it for an eternal prize. [26]So I run with purpose in every step. I am not just shadowboxing. [27]I discipline my body like an athlete, training it to do what it should. Otherwise, I fear that after preaching to others I myself might be disqualified.

Lessons from Israel's Idolatry

10 I don't want you to forget, dear brothers and sisters,* about our ancestors in the wilderness long ago. All of them were guided by a cloud that moved ahead of them, and all of them walked through the sea on dry ground. [2]In the cloud and in the sea, all of them were baptized as followers of Moses. [3]All of them ate the same spiritual food, [4]and all of them drank the same spiritual water. For they drank from the spiritual rock that traveled with them, and that rock was Christ. [5]Yet God was not pleased with most of them, and their bodies were scattered in the wilderness.

[6]These things happened as a warning to us, so that we would not crave evil things as they did, [7]or worship idols as some of them did. As the Scriptures say, "The people celebrated with feasting and drinking, and they indulged in pagan revelry."* [8]And we must not engage in sexual immorality as some of them did, causing 23,000 of them to die in one day.

[9]Nor should we put Christ* to the test, as some of them did and then died from snakebites. [10]And don't grumble as some of them did, and then were destroyed by the angel of death. [11]These things happened to them as examples for us. They were written down to warn us who live at the end of the age.

[12]If you think you are standing strong, be careful not to fall. [13]The temptations in your life are no different from what others experience. And God is faithful. He will not allow the temptation to be more than you

8:3 Some manuscripts read *the person who loves has full knowledge.* **8:11** Greek *brother;* also in 8:13. **8:12** Greek *brothers.* **9:3** Greek *those who examine me.* **9:5a** Greek *a sister a wife.* **9:5b** Greek *Cephas.* **9:9** Deut 25:4. **9:21** Greek *those without the law.* **10:1** Greek *brothers.* **10:7** Exod 32:6. **10:9** Some manuscripts read *the Lord.*

Temptation

Temptation—the incitement to do wrong—is as old as the Garden of Eden (Genesis 3:1) and is therefore something that everyone experiences. No temptation is unique to us (1 Corinthians 10:13), though the devil tries to get us to think it is. To deal with it requires two things.

First, remember that temptation is not the same thing as sin. Jesus was tempted (Matthew 4:1-11), yet he was without sin (Hebrews 4:15), for he refused to say yes to it. It is not temptation itself but giving in to temptation that is sin. Second, be aware of the devil's strategies against us. He sends temptation when we are weak, or discouraged, or tired, or alone, often reminding us of things that were important to us in the past, hoping to draw us into them. He lies to us, saying we will feel better if we do it, when really we know we will feel worse.

Paul therefore gives us both an assurance and a challenge: an assurance that God will sustain us and provide an escape (1 Corinthians 10:13); and a challenge to "flee from the worship of idols" (10:14)—flee, not entertain in our thoughts. When Joseph fled temptation (Genesis 39:1-12), he was ultimately blessed; but when David yielded to temptation (2 Samuel 11), it led to disaster.

can stand. When you are tempted, he will
show you a way out so that you can endure.
14So, my dear friends, flee from the worship
of idols. 15You are reasonable people. Decide
for yourselves if what I am saying is true.
16When we bless the cup at the Lord's Table,
aren't we sharing in the blood of Christ? And
when we break the bread, aren't we sharing
in the body of Christ? 17And though we are
many, we all eat from one loaf of bread,
showing that we are one body. 18Think about
the people of Israel. Weren't they united by
eating the sacrifices at the altar?

19What am I trying to say? Am I saying that
food offered to idols has some significance,
or that idols are real gods? 20No, not at all. I
am saying that these sacrifices are offered to
demons, not to God. And I don't want you to
participate with demons. 21You cannot drink
from the cup of the Lord and from the cup
of demons, too. You cannot eat at the Lord's
Table and at the table of demons, too. 22What?
Do we dare to rouse the Lord's jealousy? Do
you think we are stronger than he is?

23You say, "I am allowed to do anything"*—but not everything is good for you.
You say, "I am allowed to do anything"—but
not everything is beneficial. 24Don't be concerned for your own good but for the good
of others.

25So you may eat any meat that is sold in
the marketplace without raising questions
of conscience. 26For "the earth is the LORD's,
and everything in it."*

27If someone who isn't a believer asks
you home for dinner, accept the invitation
if you want to. Eat whatever is offered to you
without raising questions of conscience.
28(But suppose someone tells you, "This
meat was offered to an idol." Don't eat it,
out of consideration for the conscience of
the one who told you. 29It might not be a
matter of conscience for you, but it is for the
other person.) For why should my freedom
be limited by what someone else thinks? 30If
I can thank God for the food and enjoy it,
why should I be condemned for eating it?

31So whether you eat or drink, or whatever
you do, do it all for the glory of God. 32Don't
give offense to Jews or Gentiles* or the
church of God. 33I, too, try to please everyone in everything I do. I don't just do what
is best for me; I do what is best for others so
that many may be saved. 11:1And you should
imitate me, just as I imitate Christ.

Instructions for Public Worship

11 2I am so glad that you always keep
me in your thoughts, and that you are
following the teachings I passed on to you.
3But there is one thing I want you to know:
The head of every man is Christ, the head
of woman is man, and the head of Christ
is God.* 4A man dishonors his head* if he
covers his head while praying or prophesying. 5But a woman dishonors her head* if
she prays or prophesies without a covering
on her head, for this is the same as shaving
her head. 6Yes, if she refuses to wear a head
covering, she should cut off all her hair! But
since it is shameful for a woman to have
her hair cut or her head shaved, she should
wear a covering.*

7A man should not wear anything on his
head when worshiping, for man is made in
God's image and reflects God's glory. And
woman reflects man's glory. 8For the first
man didn't come from woman, but the first
woman came from man. 9And man was not
made for woman, but woman was made
for man. 10For this reason, and because the
angels are watching, a woman should wear
a covering on her head to show she is under
authority.*

11But among the Lord's people, women
are not independent of men, and men are
not independent of women. 12For although
the first woman came from man, every other
man was born from a woman, and everything comes from God.

13Judge for yourselves. Is it right for a
woman to pray to God in public without covering her head? 14Isn't it obvious that it's disgraceful for a man to have long hair? 15And
isn't long hair a woman's pride and joy? For
it has been given to her as a covering. 16But
if anyone wants to argue about this, I simply
say that we have no other custom than this,
and neither do God's other churches.

Order at the Lord's Supper

17But in the following instructions, I cannot
praise you. For it sounds as if more harm
than good is done when you meet together.
18First, I hear that there are divisions among
you when you meet as a church, and to some
extent I believe it. 19But, of course, there
must be divisions among you so that you
who have God's approval will be recognized!
20When you meet together, you are not
really interested in the Lord's Supper. 21For

some of you hurry to eat your own meal
without sharing with others. As a result,
some go hungry while others get drunk.
22 What? Don't you have your own homes
for eating and drinking? Or do you really
want to disgrace God's church and shame
the poor? What am I supposed to say? Do
you want me to praise you? Well, I certainly
will not praise you for this!

23 For I pass on to you what I received
from the Lord himself. On the night when
he was betrayed, the Lord Jesus took some
bread 24 and gave thanks to God for it. Then
he broke it in pieces and said, "This is my
body, which is given for you.* Do this in remembrance of me." 25 In the same way, he
took the cup of wine after supper, saying,
"This cup is the new covenant between God
and his people—an agreement confirmed
with my blood. Do this in remembrance of
me as often as you drink it." 26 For every time
you eat this bread and drink this cup, you
are announcing the Lord's death until he
comes again.

27 So anyone who eats this bread or drinks
this cup of the Lord unworthily is guilty of
sinning against* the body and blood of the
Lord. 28 That is why you should examine
yourself before eating the bread and drinking the cup. 29 For if you eat the bread or
drink the cup without honoring the body of
Christ,* you are eating and drinking God's
judgment upon yourself. 30 That is why
many of you are weak and sick and some
have even died.

31 But if we would examine ourselves, we
would not be judged by God in this way.
32 Yet when we are judged by the Lord, we
are being disciplined so that we will not be
condemned along with the world.

33 So, my dear brothers and sisters,* when
you gather for the Lord's Supper, wait for
each other. 34 If you are really hungry, eat
at home so you won't bring judgment upon
yourselves when you meet together. I'll give
you instructions about the other matters
after I arrive.

Spiritual Gifts

12 Now, dear brothers and sisters,*
regarding your question about the
special abilities the Spirit gives us. I don't
want you to misunderstand this. 2 You know
that when you were still pagans, you were
led astray and swept along in worshiping
speechless idols. 3 So I want you to know
that no one speaking by the Spirit of God
will curse Jesus, and no one can say Jesus
is Lord, except by the Holy Spirit.

4 There are different kinds of spiritual
gifts, but the same Spirit is the source
of them all. 5 There are different kinds of
service, but we serve the same Lord. 6 God
works in different ways, but it is the same
God who does the work in all of us.

7 A spiritual gift is given to each of us so
we can help each other. 8 To one person the
Spirit gives the ability to give wise advice*;
to another the same Spirit gives a message of
special knowledge.* 9 The same Spirit gives
great faith to another, and to someone else
the one Spirit gives the gift of healing. 10 He
gives one person the power to perform miracles, and another the ability to prophesy.
He gives someone else the ability to discern
whether a message is from the Spirit of God
or from another spirit. Still another person
is given the ability to speak in unknown
languages,* while another is given the
ability to interpret what is being said. 11 It is
the one and only Spirit who distributes all
these gifts. He alone decides which gift each
person should have.

One Body with Many Parts

12 The human body has many parts, but the
many parts make up one whole body. So it
is with the body of Christ. 13 Some of us are
Jews, some are Gentiles,* some are slaves,
and some are free. But we have all been
baptized into one body by one Spirit, and
we all share the same Spirit.*

14 Yes, the body has many different parts,
not just one part. 15 If the foot says, "I am not
a part of the body because I am not a hand,"

10:23 Greek *All things are lawful;* also in 10:23b. **10:26** Ps 24:1. **10:32** Greek *or Greeks.* **11:3** Or *to know: The source of every man is Christ, the source of woman is man, and the source of Christ is God.* Or *to know: Every man is responsible to Christ, a woman is responsible to her husband, and Christ is responsible to God.* **11:4** Or *dishonors Christ.* **11:5** Or *dishonors her husband.* **11:6** Or *should have long hair.* **11:10** Greek *should have an authority on her head.* **11:24** Greek *which is for you;* other manuscripts read *which is broken for you.* **11:27** Or *is responsible for.* **11:29** Greek *the body;* other manuscripts read *the Lord's body.* **11:33** Greek *brothers.* **12:1** Greek *brothers.* **12:8a** Or *gives a word of wisdom.* **12:8b** Or *gives a word of knowledge.* **12:10** Or *in various tongues;* also in 12:28, 30. **12:13a** Greek *some are Greeks.* **12:13b** Greek *we were all given one Spirit to drink.*

▸ **12:7-11** *See* ***Service***, *page 1424.*

that does not make it any less a part of the
body. 16 And if the ear says, "I am not part of
the body because I am not an eye," would
that make it any less a part of the body? 17 If
the whole body were an eye, how would you
hear? Or if your whole body were an ear,
how would you smell anything?
18 But our bodies have many parts, and
God has put each part just where he wants
it. 19 How strange a body would be if it had
only one part! 20 Yes, there are many parts,
but only one body. 21 The eye can never say
to the hand, "I don't need you." The head
can't say to the feet, "I don't need you."
22 In fact, some parts of the body that
seem weakest and least important are actually the most necessary. 23 And the parts
we regard as less honorable are those we
clothe with the greatest care. So we carefully protect those parts that should not be
seen, 24 while the more honorable parts do
not require this special care. So God has put
the body together such that extra honor and
care are given to those parts that have less
dignity. 25 This makes for harmony among
the members, so that all the members care
for each other. 26 If one part suffers, all
the parts suffer with it, and if one part is
honored, all the parts are glad.
27 All of you together are Christ's body,
and each of you is a part of it. 28 Here are
some of the parts God has appointed for the
church:

first are apostles,
second are prophets,
third are teachers,
then those who do miracles,
those who have the gift of healing,
those who can help others,
those who have the gift of leadership,
those who speak in unknown languages.

29 Are we all apostles? Are we all prophets?
Are we all teachers? Do we all have the
power to do miracles? 30 Do we all have the
gift of healing? Do we all have the ability
to speak in unknown languages? Do we all
have the ability to interpret unknown languages? Of course not! 31 So you should earnestly desire the most helpful gifts.
But now let me show you a way of life that
is best of all.

Love Is the Greatest

13 If I could speak all the languages of
earth and of angels, but didn't love
others, I would only be a noisy gong or a
clanging cymbal. 2 If I had the gift of prophecy, and if I understood all of God's secret
plans and possessed all knowledge, and if
I had such faith that I could move mountains, but didn't love others, I would be

Gifts of the Holy Spirit

The fact that Paul devotes three chapters (1 Corinthians 12–14) to gifts of the Holy Spirit indicates that this was an important issue in Corinth. Clearly some Corinthians were using these gifts selfishly or seeing them as signs of spiritual superiority. Yet Paul's answer is not to tell them to stop using these gifts, but rather to tell them how to use the gifts correctly.

He begins by reminding them of their purpose: to bring honor to Jesus (12:1-6). Then he says that the Spirit's gifts are for everyone (12:7), not just those who think they are more spiritual. These gifts are characterized by variety and unity (12:12-31)—variety in the many types of gifts given (12:7-11), none of which is more important than another (12:12-26); unity in their purpose of building up the church (14:1-12). Right at the heart of everything stands Paul's reminder that all the gifts must be exercised in love; otherwise they are meaningless (chapter 13).

Sometimes in discussing these gifts, Christians make a distinction between "spiritual" gifts and "practical" gifts, often implying a sense of hierarchy. But in all its lists of spiritual gifts (Romans 12:6-8; 1 Corinthians 12:7-10, 28-30; Ephesians 4:11-12; 1 Peter 4:10-11), the New Testament never distinguishes between "spiritual" and "practical" gifts. This is fitting, because "it is the one and only Spirit who distributes all these gifts" (1 Corinthians 12:11).

nothing. 3If I gave everything I have to the
poor and even sacrificed my body, I could
boast about it;* but if I didn't love others,
I would have gained nothing.
4Love is patient and kind. Love is not
jealous or boastful or proud 5or rude. It does
not demand its own way. It is not irritable,
and it keeps no record of being wronged. 6It
does not rejoice about injustice but rejoices
whenever the truth wins out. 7Love never
gives up, never loses faith, is always hopeful,
and endures through every circumstance.
8Prophecy and speaking in unknown languages* and special knowledge will become
useless. But love will last forever! 9Now our
knowledge is partial and incomplete, and
even the gift of prophecy reveals only part
of the whole picture! 10But when the time of
perfection comes, these partial things will
become useless.
11When I was a child, I spoke and thought
and reasoned as a child. But when I grew
up, I put away childish things. 12Now we see
things imperfectly, like puzzling reflections
in a mirror, but then we will see everything
with perfect clarity.* All that I know now
is partial and incomplete, but then I will
know everything completely, just as God
now knows me completely.
13Three things will last forever—faith,
hope, and love—and the greatest of these
is love.

Tongues and Prophecy

14 Let love be your highest goal! But you
should also desire the special abilities the Spirit gives—especially the ability
to prophesy. 2For if you have the ability
to speak in tongues,* you will be talking
only to God, since people won't be able
to understand you. You will be speaking
by the power of the Spirit,* but it will all
be mysterious. 3But one who prophesies
strengthens others, encourages them, and
comforts them. 4A person who speaks in
tongues is strengthened personally, but one
who speaks a word of prophecy strengthens
the entire church.
5I wish you could all speak in tongues,
but even more I wish you could all prophesy. For prophecy is greater than speaking
in tongues, unless someone interprets what
you are saying so that the whole church will
be strengthened.
6Dear brothers and sisters,* if I should
come to you speaking in an unknown language,* how would that help you? But if
I bring you a revelation or some special
knowledge or prophecy or teaching, that
will be helpful. 7Even lifeless instruments
like the flute or the harp must play the notes
clearly, or no one will recognize the melody.
8And if the bugler doesn't sound a clear call,
how will the soldiers know they are being
called to battle?
9It's the same for you. If you speak to
people in words they don't understand, how
will they know what you are saying? You
might as well be talking into empty space.
10There are many different languages in
the world, and every language has meaning.
11But if I don't understand a language, I will
be a foreigner to someone who speaks it,
and the one who speaks it will be a foreigner to me. 12And the same is true for you.
Since you are so eager to have the special
abilities the Spirit gives, seek those that will
strengthen the whole church.
13So anyone who speaks in tongues
should pray also for the ability to interpret what has been said. 14For if I pray in
tongues, my spirit is praying, but I don't
understand what I am saying.
15Well then, what shall I do? I will pray
in the spirit,* and I will also pray in words
I understand. I will sing in the spirit, and I
will also sing in words I understand. 16For if
you praise God only in the spirit, how can
those who don't understand you praise God
along with you? How can they join you in
giving thanks when they don't understand
what you are saying? 17You will be giving
thanks very well, but it won't strengthen
the people who hear you.
18I thank God that I speak in tongues more
than any of you. 19But in a church meeting
I would rather speak five understandable
words to help others than ten thousand
words in an unknown language.
20Dear brothers and sisters, don't be

13:3 Some manuscripts read *sacrificed my body to be burned.* **13:8** Or *in tongues.* **13:12** Greek *see face to face.* **14:2a** Or *in unknown languages;* also in 14:4, 5, 13, 14, 18, 22, 26, 27, 28, 39. **14:2b** Or *speaking in your spirit.* **14:6a** Greek *brothers;* also in 14:20, 26, 39. **14:6b** Or *in tongues;* also in 14:19, 23. **14:15** Or *in the Spirit;* also in 14:15b, 16.

▸ **13:4-7** *See* ***Loving others****, page 1220.*

childish in your understanding of these things. Be innocent as babies when it comes to evil, but be mature in understanding matters of this kind. 21It is written in the Scriptures*:

"I will speak to my own people
through strange languages
and through the lips of foreigners.
But even then, they will not listen to me,"*
says the LORD.

22So you see that speaking in tongues is a sign, not for believers, but for unbelievers. Prophecy, however, is for the benefit of believers, not unbelievers. 23Even so, if unbelievers or people who don't understand these things come into your church meeting and hear everyone speaking in an unknown language, they will think you are crazy. 24But if all of you are prophesying, and unbelievers or people who don't understand these things come into your meeting, they will be convicted of sin and judged by what you say. 25As they listen, their secret thoughts will be exposed, and they will fall to their knees and worship God, declaring, "God is truly here among you."

A Call to Orderly Worship

26Well, my brothers and sisters, let's summarize. When you meet together, one will sing, another will teach, another will tell some special revelation God has given, one will speak in tongues, and another will interpret what is said. But everything that is done must strengthen all of you.

27No more than two or three should speak in tongues. They must speak one at a time, and someone must interpret what they say. 28But if no one is present who can interpret, they must be silent in your church meeting and speak in tongues to God privately.

29Let two or three people prophesy, and let the others evaluate what is said. 30But if someone is prophesying and another person receives a revelation from the Lord, the one who is speaking must stop. 31In this way, all who prophesy will have a turn to speak, one after the other, so that everyone will learn and be encouraged. 32Remember that people who prophesy are in control of their spirit and can take turns. 33For God is not a God of disorder but of peace, as in all the meetings of God's holy people.*

34Women should be silent during the church meetings. It is not proper for them to speak. They should be submissive, just as the law says. 35If they have any questions, they should ask their husbands at home, for it is improper for women to speak in church meetings.*

36Or do you think God's word originated with you Corinthians? Are you the only ones to whom it was given? 37If you claim to be

Prophecy in the New Testament

Despite the Corinthians' misuse of spiritual gifts, Paul does not try to stop their use but rather encourages them to seek the gifts all the more (1 Corinthians 14:1)—especially prophecy. Prophecy is not a sermon. As in Old Testament times, it is a word brought directly from God. But its purpose has changed. In the Old Testament, the prophet's role was to call Israel's king and people to live in line with the covenant God had made with them (see *Prophecy in the Old Testament*, page 903). But the church is not a theocratic nation, so prophecy's purpose is now different. While it may still involve predicting future events at times (e.g., Acts 11:27-30; 21:10-11), its main purpose now is to strengthen, encourage, and comfort others (1 Corinthians 14:3) in order to strengthen (or "build up") the church (14:4-5, 12, 17). While only some will become recognized as "prophets" (e.g., 12:28-29), all should desire to prophesy (14:1)—at least at this level of strengthening, encouraging, and comforting others. And just as in the Old Testament (Deuteronomy 18:17-22), prophecy should always be tested (1 Corinthians 14:29).

The need for prophecy will only disappear "when the time of perfection comes" (13:10)—the perfected order at Christ's return—for once he is in our midst, there will be no need of prophecy or any other gift of the Holy Spirit.

a prophet or think you are spiritual, you should recognize that what I am saying is a command from the Lord himself. 38 But if you do not recognize this, you yourself will not be recognized.*

39 So, my dear brothers and sisters, be eager to prophesy, and don't forbid speaking in tongues. 40 But be sure that everything is done properly and in order.

The Resurrection of Christ

15 Let me now remind you, dear brothers and sisters,* of the Good News I preached to you before. You welcomed it then, and you still stand firm in it. 2 It is this Good News that saves you if you continue to believe the message I told you—unless, of course, you believed something that was never true in the first place.*

3 I passed on to you what was most important and what had also been passed on to me. Christ died for our sins, just as the Scriptures said. 4 He was buried, and he was raised from the dead on the third day, just as the Scriptures said. 5 He was seen by Peter* and then by the Twelve. 6 After that, he was seen by more than 500 of his followers* at one time, most of whom are still alive, though some have died. 7 Then he was seen by James and later by all the apostles. 8 Last of all, as though I had been born at the wrong time, I also saw him. 9 For I am the least of all the apostles. In fact, I'm not even worthy to be called an apostle after the way I persecuted God's church.

10 But whatever I am now, it is all because God poured out his special favor on me—and not without results. For I have worked harder than any of the other apostles; yet it was not I but God who was working through me by his grace. 11 So it makes no difference whether I preach or they preach, for we all preach the same message you have already believed.

The Resurrection of the Dead

12 But tell me this—since we preach that Christ rose from the dead, why are some of you saying there will be no resurrection of the dead? 13 For if there is no resurrection of the dead, then Christ has not been raised either. 14 And if Christ has not been raised, then all our preaching is useless, and your faith is useless. 15 And we apostles would all be lying about God—for we have said that God raised Christ from the grave. But that can't be true if there is no resurrection of the dead. 16 And if there is no resurrection of the dead, then Christ has not been raised. 17 And if Christ has not been raised, then your faith is useless and you are still guilty of your sins. 18 In that case, all who have died believing in Christ are lost! 19 And if our hope in Christ is only for this life, we are more to be pitied than anyone in the world.

20 But in fact, Christ has been raised from the dead. He is the first of a great harvest of all who have died.

21 So you see, just as death came into the world through a man, now the resurrection from the dead has begun through another man. 22 Just as everyone dies because we all belong to Adam, everyone who belongs to Christ will be given new life. 23 But there is an order to this resurrection: Christ was raised as the first of the harvest; then all who belong to Christ will be raised when he comes back.

24 After that the end will come, when he will turn the Kingdom over to God the Father, having destroyed every ruler and authority and power. 25 For Christ must reign until he humbles all his enemies beneath his feet. 26 And the last enemy to be destroyed is death. 27 For the Scriptures say, "God has put all things under his authority."* (Of course, when it says "all things are under his authority," that does not include God himself, who gave Christ his authority.) 28 Then, when all things are under his authority, the Son will put himself under God's authority, so that God, who gave his Son authority over all things, will be utterly supreme over everything everywhere.

29 If the dead will not be raised, what point is there in people being baptized for those who are dead? Why do it unless the dead will someday rise again?

30 And why should we ourselves risk our lives hour by hour? 31 For I swear, dear brothers and sisters, that I face death daily. This is as certain as my pride in what Christ Jesus our Lord has done in you. 32 And what value was there in fighting wild beasts—those people of Ephesus*—if there will be no resurrection

14:21a Greek *in the law.* **14:21b** Isa 28:11-12. **14:33** The phrase *as in all the meetings of God's holy people* could instead be joined to the beginning of 14:34. **14:35** Some manuscripts place verses 34-35 after 14:40. **14:38** Some manuscripts read *If you are ignorant of this, stay in your ignorance.* **15:1** Greek *brothers;* also in 15:31, 50, 58. **15:2** Or *unless you never believed it in the first place.* **15:5** Greek *Cephas.* **15:6** Greek *the brothers.* **15:27** Ps 8:6. **15:32a** Greek *fighting wild beasts in Ephesus.*

from the dead? And if there is no resurrection, "Let's feast and drink, for tomorrow
we die!"* 33Don't be fooled by those who say
such things, for "bad company corrupts good
character." 34Think carefully about what is
right, and stop sinning. For to your shame I
say that some of you don't know God at all.

The Resurrection Body

35But someone may ask, "How will the dead
be raised? What kind of bodies will they
have?" 36What a foolish question! When
you put a seed into the ground, it doesn't
grow into a plant unless it dies first. 37And
what you put in the ground is not the plant
that will grow, but only a bare seed of wheat
or whatever you are planting. 38Then God
gives it the new body he wants it to have.
A different plant grows from each kind of
seed. 39Similarly there are different kinds
of flesh—one kind for humans, another for
animals, another for birds, and another for
fish.

40There are also bodies in the heavens
and bodies on the earth. The glory of the
heavenly bodies is different from the glory
of the earthly bodies. 41The sun has one kind
of glory, while the moon and stars each have
another kind. And even the stars differ from
each other in their glory.

42It is the same way with the resurrection
of the dead. Our earthly bodies are planted
in the ground when we die, but they will
be raised to live forever. 43Our bodies are
buried in brokenness, but they will be
raised in glory. They are buried in weakness, but they will be raised in strength.
44They are buried as natural human bodies,
but they will be raised as spiritual bodies.
For just as there are natural bodies, there
are also spiritual bodies.

45The Scriptures tell us, "The first man,
Adam, became a living person."* But the
last Adam—that is, Christ—is a life-giving
Spirit. 46What comes first is the natural
body, then the spiritual body comes later.
47Adam, the first man, was made from the
dust of the earth, while Christ, the second
man, came from heaven. 48Earthly people
are like the earthly man, and heavenly
people are like the heavenly man. 49Just as
we are now like the earthly man, we will
someday be like* the heavenly man.

50What I am saying, dear brothers and
sisters, is that our physical bodies cannot
inherit the Kingdom of God. These dying
bodies cannot inherit what will last forever.

51But let me reveal to you a wonderful
secret. We will not all die, but we will all be
transformed! 52It will happen in a moment,
in the blink of an eye, when the last trumpet
is blown. For when the trumpet sounds,
those who have died will be raised to live
forever. And we who are living will also be
transformed. 53For our dying bodies must be
transformed into bodies that will never die;

Christ's resurrection and ours

Christ's resurrection from the dead is so foundational to Christian faith that Paul says, "If Christ has not been raised, then all our preaching is useless, and your faith is useless. . . . And you are still guilty of your sins" (1 Corinthians 15:14, 17). But the Resurrection did in fact take place, as Paul makes clear in introducing this section (15:1-9). And it is through Christ's resurrection that we can be sure that death is conquered, sin is forgiven, new life is given, and victory is assured (15:12-28).

Paul describes Christ as "the first of a great harvest of all who have died" (15:20). The first part of the harvest, or firstfruits, assured that the rest of the crop would follow, and it was dedicated to God as a sign of thanksgiving and faith (e.g., Exodus 23:19; Leviticus 23:9-14). In describing Christ as "the first of a great harvest," Paul sees his resurrection as God's pledge that the rest will follow; that is, that those who believe in him will also be raised from the dead. When we die, our spirits will go to be with Christ in heaven (e.g., John 14:1-3), but when Christ returns, there will be a great resurrection. We will be given transformed, glorious, immortal bodies, just like Christ's resurrection body (1 Corinthians 15:35-49), so we can live in God's Kingdom in all its fullness (15:50-57).

our mortal bodies must be transformed into
immortal bodies.
54 Then, when our dying bodies have been
transformed into bodies that will never
die,* this Scripture will be fulfilled:

"Death is swallowed up in victory.*
55 O death, where is your victory?
O death, where is your sting?*"

56 For sin is the sting that results in death,
and the law gives sin its power. 57 But thank
God! He gives us victory over sin and death
through our Lord Jesus Christ.
58 So, my dear brothers and sisters, be
strong and immovable. Always work enthusiastically for the Lord, for you know
that nothing you do for the Lord is ever
useless.

The Collection for Jerusalem

16 Now regarding your question about
the money being collected for God's
people in Jerusalem. You should follow
the same procedure I gave to the churches
in Galatia. 2 On the first day of each week,
you should each put aside a portion of the
money you have earned. Don't wait until I
get there and then try to collect it all at once.
3 When I come, I will write letters of recommendation for the messengers you choose
to deliver your gift to Jerusalem. 4 And if it
seems appropriate for me to go along, they
can travel with me.

Paul's Final Instructions

5 I am coming to visit you after I have been
to Macedonia,* for I am planning to travel
through Macedonia. 6 Perhaps I will stay
awhile with you, possibly all winter, and
then you can send me on my way to my next
destination. 7 This time I don't want to make
just a short visit and then go right on. I want
to come and stay awhile, if the Lord will let
me. 8 In the meantime, I will be staying here
at Ephesus until the Festival of Pentecost.
9 There is a wide-open door for a great work
here, although many oppose me.
10 When Timothy comes, don't intimidate
him. He is doing the Lord's work, just as I
am. 11 Don't let anyone treat him with contempt. Send him on his way with your blessing when he returns to me. I expect him to
come with the other believers.*
12 Now about our brother Apollos—I urged
him to visit you with the other believers, but
he was not willing to go right now. He will
see you later when he has the opportunity.
13 Be on guard. Stand firm in the faith. Be
courageous.* Be strong. 14 And do everything with love.
15 You know that Stephanas and his
household were the first of the harvest of
believers in Greece,* and they are spending their lives in service to God's people.
I urge you, dear brothers and sisters,* 16 to
submit to them and others like them who
serve with such devotion. 17 I am very glad
that Stephanas, Fortunatus, and Achaicus
have come here. They have been providing

15:32b Isa 22:13. **15:45** Gen 2:7. **15:49** Some manuscripts read *let us be like.* **15:54a** Some manuscripts add *and our mortal bodies have been transformed into immortal bodies.* **15:54b** Isa 25:8. **15:55** Hos 13:14 (Greek version). **16:5** *Macedonia* was in the northern region of Greece. **16:11** Greek *with the brothers;* also in 16:12. **16:13** Greek *Be men.* **16:15a** Greek *in Achaia,* the southern region of the Greek peninsula. **16:15b** Greek *brothers;* also in 16:20.

Aquila and Priscilla

In his concluding comments, Paul sends greetings from Aquila and Priscilla, a married couple who helped him found the church in Corinth (Acts 18:1-3). They were tentmakers like Paul and had ended up in Corinth when the Emperor Claudius had expelled all Jews (including Jewish Christians) from Rome. Since the three of them were newly arrived in a strange city, they linked up and formed a partnership, in both tentmaking and sharing the gospel. After eighteen months in Corinth, they accompanied Paul to Ephesus (Acts 18:18-19), where they became key workers in the church there (Acts 18:24-26). In Ephesus they opened up their home for church meetings (1 Corinthians 16:19). Aquila and Priscilla show that it isn't necessary to be in "full-time" ministry to play an extremely effective part in the church's life.

▶ *See also **Serving God in our work**, page 956.*

the help you weren't here to give me. [18]They
have been a wonderful encouragement to
me, as they have been to you. You must
show your appreciation to all who serve so
well.

Paul's Final Greetings

[19]The churches here in the province of
Asia* send greetings in the Lord, as do
Aquila and Priscilla* and all the others who
gather in their home for church meetings.
[20]All the brothers and sisters here send
greetings to you. Greet each other with a
sacred kiss.

[21]HERE IS MY GREETING IN MY OWN
HANDWRITING—PAUL.

[22]If anyone does not love the Lord, that
person is cursed. Our Lord, come!*

[23]May the grace of the Lord Jesus be with
you.

[24]My love to all of you in Christ Jesus.*

16:19a *Asia* was a Roman province in what is now western Turkey. **16:19b** Greek *Prisca*. **16:22** From Aramaic, *Marana tha*. Some manuscripts read *Maran atha*, "Our Lord has come." **16:24** Some manuscripts add *Amen*.

2 Corinthians *Weakness and strength*

When Paul left Corinth, he left behind a thriving church. But it wasn't long before some opponents arrived, questioning Paul's integrity and authority as an apostle and presenting themselves as "super apostles." How could Paul be a real apostle, they asked, when he suffered so much? But they failed to understand that suffering and weakness were what God used to reveal his glory, as the cross itself demonstrates. To reject this was to preach "a different kind of gospel" (11:4). A visit to resolve the problems had proved painful (2:1-11), and Paul had left. He later sent Titus with a severe letter, and Titus returned with news that the church had had a change of heart (7:5-13), which gave Paul much joy. He then wrote this letter to prepare the way for a personal visit, revealing much of what he had gone through as an apostle.

What's it all about?

Paul opens his letter with a series of references to comfort. He knew from personal experience that God comforts us in all our difficulties, for God had been with him throughout the painful disagreement between him and the Corinthian church. Paul then invites the church to forgive someone—perhaps the man referred to in 1 Corinthians 5, whose sexual sin had created so many problems for the church and for Paul—and to receive him back into fellowship (chapter 2).

In chapters 3 and 4, Paul reminds them that he needs no letter of recommendation, for they themselves are that letter; and both they and he are servants of the new covenant. He compares the glory of this covenant with that of the old covenant, concluding that Christians experience far more glory than the Israelites ever did. Every day Christians are being changed by the Spirit to reflect more and more of God's glory. But they still live in the world and have to endure problems and hardships. Their bodies are like "fragile clay jars" (4:7). They contain a great treasure, but they will only be completely transformed at the final resurrection (chapter 5). Until then, they must press on, live by the Spirit, and live each day to please God.

In chapter 6, Paul warns the Corinthians not to associate in unhelpful ways with non-Christians. They must remember that God lives in and among them and that he has set them apart to be his own people. He then commends them for taking his previous reprimands to heart (chapter 7).

OVERVIEW

Greetings and introduction
1:1-11

The history of the dispute
1:12–2:13

The new covenant and its servants
2:14–4:18

Reasons for courage and confidence
5:1–6:2

Paul defends himself and his co-workers · *6:3-13*

Relationships with nonbelievers
6:14–7:4

Paul's joy over the repentant Corinthians · *7:5-16*

Encouragements about money and giving · *8:1–9:15*

Paul's vindication of his ministry
10:1–12:21

Final greetings and encouragements
13:1-14

In chapters 8 and 9, Paul discusses the offering that was being organized for the poor Christians in Judea. Because of a famine, the Jerusalem church was in distress, and Paul wanted his churches to have the privilege of contributing to their needs. The Corinthians' generosity was to reflect the generosity of God himself.

A discontented minority had still been complaining about Paul, saying that he was bold in his letters but weak in person (10:1). So Paul defends his authority, which is God-given, given to "build up" and not to "tear down" (10:8; see also 13:10). He reminds them of all the hardships he had suffered while preaching the gospel. These sufferings, rather than eloquence or good looks, were his true credentials.

What does it mean for us?

The Corinthians had been deceived by the eloquent teachers who had arrived after Paul had left. In the bustling metropolis of Corinth, appearance was everything; and in spite of their Christian beliefs, the Corinthians brought the world's values to church with them. And they were impressed by what they saw in these self-styled "super apostles."

Paul reminds us that we need to be impressed only by what impresses God. Faithfulness in serving him, especially when that involves weakness, suffering, and tears, is far more worthy of our attention than eloquence or appearance. Outward impressions alone are not an indicator of who is or isn't a follower of Christ. If we keep this in mind, we will not be so easily deceived, as the Corinthians were.

Paul had not enjoyed disciplining this church he had founded, but discipline is sometimes necessary and is really an expression of love. If we are to mature spiritually and emotionally, then we too need to accept correction from those we trust.

Greetings from Paul

1 This letter is from Paul, chosen by the will
of God to be an apostle of Christ Jesus,
and from our brother Timothy.
I am writing to God's church in Corinth and
to all of his holy people throughout Greece.*
2May God our Father and the Lord Jesus
Christ give you grace and peace.

God Offers Comfort to All

3All praise to God, the Father of our Lord
Jesus Christ. God is our merciful Father and
the source of all comfort. 4He comforts us
in all our troubles so that we can comfort
others. When they are troubled, we will be
able to give them the same comfort God has
given us. 5For the more we suffer for Christ,
the more God will shower us with his comfort
through Christ. 6Even when we are weighed
down with troubles, it is for your comfort and
salvation! For when we ourselves are comforted, we will certainly comfort you. Then
you can patiently endure the same things we
suffer. 7We are confident that as you share
in our sufferings, you will also share in the
comfort God gives us.
8We think you ought to know, dear brothers and sisters,* about the trouble we went
through in the province of Asia. We were
crushed and overwhelmed beyond our
ability to endure, and we thought we would
never live through it. 9In fact, we expected
to die. But as a result, we stopped relying on
ourselves and learned to rely only on God,
who raises the dead. 10And he did rescue
us from mortal danger, and he will rescue
us again. We have placed our confidence in
him, and he will continue to rescue us. 11And
you are helping us by praying for us. Then
many people will give thanks because God
has graciously answered so many prayers for
our safety.

Paul's Change of Plans

12We can say with confidence and a clear conscience that we have lived with a God-given
holiness* and sincerity in all our dealings.
We have depended on God's grace, not on
our own human wisdom. That is how we
have conducted ourselves before the world,
and especially toward you. 13Our letters have
been straightforward, and there is nothing
written between the lines and nothing you
can't understand. I hope someday you will
fully understand us, 14even if you don't
understand us now. Then on the day when

the Lord Jesus* returns, you will be proud
of us in the same way we are proud of you.
[15]Since I was so sure of your understanding and trust, I wanted to give you a
double blessing by visiting you twice—[16]first
on my way to Macedonia and again when I
returned from Macedonia.* Then you could
send me on my way to Judea.
[17]You may be asking why I changed my
plan. Do you think I make my plans carelessly? Do you think I am like people of
the world who say "Yes" when they really
mean "No"? [18]As surely as God is faithful,
our word to you does not waver between
"Yes" and "No." [19]For Jesus Christ, the Son
of God, does not waver between "Yes" and
"No." He is the one whom Silas,* Timothy,
and I preached to you, and as God's ultimate "Yes," he always does what he says.
[20]For all of God's promises have been fulfilled in Christ with a resounding "Yes!"
And through Christ, our "Amen" (which
means "Yes") ascends to God for his glory.
[21]It is God who enables us, along with
you, to stand firm for Christ. He has commissioned us, [22]and he has identified us as
his own by placing the Holy Spirit in our
hearts as the first installment that guarantees everything he has promised us.
[23]Now I call upon God as my witness that
I am telling the truth. The reason I didn't
return to Corinth was to spare you from a
severe rebuke. [24]But that does not mean we
want to dominate you by telling you how to
put your faith into practice. We want to work
together with you so you will be full of joy,
for it is by your own faith that you stand firm.

2 So I decided that I would not bring you
grief with another painful visit. [2]For if
I cause you grief, who will make me glad?
Certainly not someone I have grieved. [3]That
is why I wrote to you as I did, so that when
I do come, I won't be grieved by the very
ones who ought to give me the greatest
joy. Surely you all know that my joy comes
from your being joyful. [4]I wrote that letter
in great anguish, with a troubled heart and
many tears. I didn't want to grieve you, but
I wanted to let you know how much love
I have for you.

Forgiveness for the Sinner

[5]I am not overstating it when I say that
the man who caused all the trouble hurt
all of you more than he hurt me. [6]Most of
you opposed him, and that was punishment enough. [7]Now, however, it is time to
forgive and comfort him. Otherwise he may

1:1 Greek *Achaia,* the southern region of the Greek peninsula. **1:8** Greek *brothers.* **1:12** Some manuscripts read *honesty.* **1:14** Some manuscripts read *our Lord Jesus.* **1:16** *Macedonia* was in the northern region of Greece. **1:19** Greek *Silvanus.*

Integrity

No sooner has Paul begun his letter than he launches into a defense of his integrity, for he had been accused of serious shortcomings in this area. Urged on by the arrival of self-styled "super apostles," the church had accused Paul, first, of constantly changing his plans to visit them (1 Corinthians 16:5; 2 Corinthians 1:15–2:4) and, second, of mishandling the offering for the Jerusalem church (2 Corinthians 2:17; 8:18-21). As proof of his integrity, Paul could appeal not only to his conscience before God but also to what they knew of him (1:12). He had always taken practical steps not only to do what was right but also to be seen to do what is right—for example, by ensuring he was always accompanied by others when the offering was collected or conveyed to others (8:18-24).

It takes a lifetime to build a reputation, but only a moment to lose it. Christians—especially Christian leaders—should therefore take great pains to walk in integrity, ensuring that our words and our deeds are true and in harmony. To fail to do so is to open oneself to temptation and disaster. Money, position, fame, wrong relationships, abuse of authority—such things are temptations to us all, so we need to be both watchful and accountable, no matter who we are.

▶ *See also* ***Becoming like Christ****, page 1435;* ***Living according to the truth****, page 1439.*

be overcome by discouragement. 8So I urge you now to reaffirm your love for him.

9I wrote to you as I did to test you and see if you would fully comply with my instructions. 10When you forgive this man, I forgive him, too. And when I forgive whatever needs to be forgiven, I do so with Christ's authority for your benefit, 11so that Satan will not outsmart us. For we are familiar with his evil schemes.

12When I came to the city of Troas to preach the Good News of Christ, the Lord opened a door of opportunity for me. 13But I had no peace of mind because my dear brother Titus hadn't yet arrived with a report from you. So I said good-bye and went on to Macedonia to find him.

Ministers of the New Covenant

14But thank God! He has made us his captives and continues to lead us along in Christ's triumphal procession. Now he uses us to spread the knowledge of Christ everywhere, like a sweet perfume. 15Our lives are a Christ-like fragrance rising up to God. But this fragrance is perceived differently by those who are being saved and by those who are perishing. 16To those who are perishing, we are a dreadful smell of death and doom. But to those who are being saved, we are a life-giving perfume. And who is adequate for such a task as this?

17You see, we are not like the many hucksters* who preach for personal profit. We preach the word of God with sincerity and with Christ's authority, knowing that God is watching us.

3 Are we beginning to praise ourselves again? Are we like others, who need to bring you letters of recommendation, or who ask you to write such letters on their behalf? Surely not! 2The only letter of recommendation we need is you yourselves. Your lives are a letter written in our* hearts; everyone can read it and recognize our good work among you. 3Clearly, you are a letter from Christ showing the result of our ministry among you. This "letter" is written not with pen and ink, but with the Spirit of the living God. It is carved not on tablets of stone, but on human hearts.

4We are confident of all this because of our great trust in God through Christ. 5It is not that we think we are qualified to do anything on our own. Our qualification comes from God. 6He has enabled us to be ministers of his new covenant. This is a covenant not of written laws, but of the Spirit. The old written covenant ends in death; but under the new covenant, the Spirit gives life.

The Glory of the New Covenant

7The old way,* with laws etched in stone, led to death, though it began with such glory that the people of Israel could not bear to look at Moses' face. For his face shone with the glory of God, even though the brightness was already fading away. 8Shouldn't we expect far greater glory under the new way, now that the Holy Spirit is giving life? 9If the old way, which brings condemnation, was glorious, how much more glorious is the new way, which makes us right with God! 10In fact, that first glory was not glorious at all compared with the overwhelming glory of the new way. 11So if the old way, which has been replaced, was glorious, how much more glorious is the new, which remains forever!

12Since this new way gives us such confidence, we can be very bold. 13We are not like Moses, who put a veil over his face so the people of Israel would not see the glory, even though it was destined to fade away. 14But the people's minds were hardened, and to this day whenever the old covenant is being read, the same veil covers their minds so they cannot understand the truth. And this veil can be removed only by believing in Christ. 15Yes, even today when they read Moses' writings, their hearts are covered with that veil, and they do not understand.

16But whenever someone turns to the Lord, the veil is taken away. 17For the Lord is the Spirit, and wherever the Spirit of the Lord is, there is freedom. 18So all of us who have had that veil removed can see and reflect the glory of the Lord. And the Lord—who is the Spirit—makes us more and more like him as we are changed into his glorious image.

▸ **3:18** *See **Becoming like Christ**, page 1435.*

Treasure in Fragile Clay Jars

4 Therefore, since God in his mercy has
given us this new way,* we never give
up. [2]We reject all shameful deeds and un-
derhanded methods. We don't try to trick
anyone or distort the word of God. We tell
the truth before God, and all who are honest
know this.
[3]If the Good News we preach is hidden
behind a veil, it is hidden only from people
who are perishing. [4]Satan, who is the god of
this world, has blinded the minds of those
who don't believe. They are unable to see the
glorious light of the Good News. They don't
understand this message about the glory of
Christ, who is the exact likeness of God.
[5]You see, we don't go around preaching
about ourselves. We preach that Jesus Christ
is Lord, and we ourselves are your servants
for Jesus' sake. [6]For God, who said, "Let
there be light in the darkness," has made
this light shine in our hearts so we could
know the glory of God that is seen in the
face of Jesus Christ.
[7]We now have this light shining in our
hearts, but we ourselves are like fragile clay
jars containing this great treasure.* This
makes it clear that our great power is from
God, not from ourselves.
[8]We are pressed on every side by troubles,
but we are not crushed. We are perplexed,
but not driven to despair. [9]We are hunted
down, but never abandoned by God. We get
knocked down, but we are not destroyed.
[10]Through suffering, our bodies continue to
share in the death of Jesus so that the life of
Jesus may also be seen in our bodies.
[11]Yes, we live under constant danger of
death because we serve Jesus, so that the
life of Jesus will be evident in our dying
bodies. [12]So we live in the face of death, but
this has resulted in eternal life for you.
[13]But we continue to preach because we
have the same kind of faith the psalmist
had when he said, "I believed in God, so I
spoke."* [14]We know that God, who raised
the Lord Jesus,* will also raise us with Jesus
and present us to himself together with you.
[15]All of this is for your benefit. And as God's
grace reaches more and more people, there
will be great thanksgiving, and God will
receive more and more glory.
[16]That is why we never give up. Though
our bodies are dying, our spirits are*
being renewed every day. [17]For our present
troubles are small and won't last very long.
Yet they produce for us a glory that vastly
outweighs them and will last forever! [18]So
we don't look at the troubles we can see
now; rather, we fix our gaze on things that
cannot be seen. For the things we see now
will soon be gone, but the things we cannot
see will last forever.

New Bodies

5 For we know that when this earthly
tent we live in is taken down (that is,
when we die and leave this earthly body),
we will have a house in heaven, an eternal
body made for us by God himself and not
by human hands. [2]We grow weary in our
present bodies, and we long to put on our
heavenly bodies like new clothing. [3]For we
will put on heavenly bodies; we will not be
spirits without bodies.* [4]While we live in
these earthly bodies, we groan and sigh, but
it's not that we want to die and get rid of
these bodies that clothe us. Rather, we want
to put on our new bodies so that these dying
bodies will be swallowed up by life. [5]God
himself has prepared us for this, and as a
guarantee he has given us his Holy Spirit.
[6]So we are always confident, even though
we know that as long as we live in these
bodies we are not at home with the Lord.
[7]For we live by believing and not by seeing.
[8]Yes, we are fully confident, and we would
rather be away from these earthly bodies,
for then we will be at home with the Lord.
[9]So whether we are here in this body or
away from this body, our goal is to please
him. [10]For we must all stand before Christ to
be judged. We will each receive whatever we
deserve for the good or evil we have done in
this earthly body.

We Are God's Ambassadors

[11]Because we understand our fearful responsibility to the Lord, we work hard to
persuade others. God knows we are sincere,
and I hope you know this, too. [12]Are we commending ourselves to you again? No, we are
giving you a reason to be proud of us,* so you
can answer those who brag about having a
spectacular ministry rather than having a

2:17 Some manuscripts read *the rest of the hucksters.* **3:2** Some manuscripts read *your.* **3:7** Or *ministry;* also in 3:8, 9, 10, 11, 12. **4:1** Or *ministry.* **4:7** Greek *We now have this treasure in clay jars.* **4:13** Ps 116:10. **4:14** Some manuscripts read *who raised Jesus.* **4:16** Greek *our inner being is.* **5:3** Greek *we will not be naked.* **5:12** Some manuscripts read *proud of yourselves.*

sincere heart. [13]If it seems we are crazy, it is to bring glory to God. And if we are in our right minds, it is for your benefit. [14]Either way, Christ's love controls us.* Since we believe that Christ died for all, we also believe that we have all died to our old life.* [15]He died for everyone so that those who receive his new life will no longer live for themselves. Instead, they will live for Christ, who died and was raised for them.

[16]So we have stopped evaluating others from a human point of view. At one time we thought of Christ merely from a human point of view. How differently we know him now! [17]This means that anyone who belongs to Christ has become a new person. The old life is gone; a new life has begun!

[18]And all of this is a gift from God, who brought us back to himself through Christ. And God has given us this task of reconciling people to him. [19]For God was in Christ, reconciling the world to himself, no longer counting people's sins against them. And he gave us this wonderful message of reconciliation. [20]So we are Christ's ambassadors; God is making his appeal through us. We speak for Christ when we plead, "Come back to God!" [21]For God made Christ, who never sinned, to be the offering for our sin,* so that we could be made right with God through Christ.

6 As God's partners,* we beg you not to accept this marvelous gift of God's kindness and then ignore it. [2]For God says,

"At just the right time, I heard you.
On the day of salvation, I helped you."*

Indeed, the "right time" is now. Today is the day of salvation.

Paul's Hardships

[3]We live in such a way that no one will stumble because of us, and no one will find fault with our ministry. [4]In everything we do, we show that we are true ministers of God. We patiently endure troubles and hardships and calamities of every kind. [5]We have been beaten, been put in prison, faced angry mobs, worked to exhaustion, endured sleepless nights, and gone without food. [6]We prove ourselves by our purity, our understanding, our patience, our kindness, by the Holy Spirit within us,* and by our sincere love. [7]We faithfully preach the truth. God's power is working in us. We use the weapons of righteousness in the right hand for attack and the left hand for defense. [8]We serve God whether people honor us or despise us, whether they slander us or praise us. We are honest, but they call us impostors. [9]We are ignored, even though we are well known. We live close to death, but

Reconciliation

Reconciliation—the restoration of broken relationship—was a deep need at Corinth. Paul's first letter revealed that factions had developed in the church (1 Corinthians 1:11-12), and now there was even a rift between the church and its founding apostle. But Paul's appeal for them to be reconciled is not rooted in emotion or practical needs, but in the very heart of the gospel, the cross. For the cross is all about reconciliation.

Because of sin, our relationship with God was broken, and a great gulf appeared between us and him. But at the cross, Christ took our sin upon himself, paying the price for it and washing us clean, thus removing all barriers to our friendship with God (see 2 Corinthians 5:18-21). So as Christ hung on the cross, he reached out to God with one hand, as it were, and to us with the other and drew us back together in his own body.

But reconciliation cannot stop there. Once we have been reconciled to God, we find ourselves alongside others who are reconciled to him too, including many with whom we wouldn't normally associate, or maybe whom we avoided or even hated in the past. But to come to Christ is to come to one another. We cannot say we have been reconciled to God if we are unwilling to be reconciled to one another.

we are still alive. We have been beaten, but
we have not been killed. [10]Our hearts ache,
but we always have joy. We are poor, but
we give spiritual riches to others. We own
nothing, and yet we have everything.
[11]Oh, dear Corinthian friends! We have
spoken honestly with you, and our hearts are
open to you. [12]There is no lack of love on our
part, but you have withheld your love from
us. [13]I am asking you to respond as if you were
my own children. Open your hearts to us!

The Temple of the Living God

[14]Don't team up with those who are unbelievers. How can righteousness be a
partner with wickedness? How can light
live with darkness? [15]What harmony can
there be between Christ and the devil*?
How can a believer be a partner with an
unbeliever? [16]And what union can there be
between God's temple and idols? For we are
the temple of the living God. As God said:

"I will live in them
  and walk among them.
I will be their God,
  and they will be my people.*
[17] Therefore, come out from among
  unbelievers,
  and separate yourselves from them,
  says the LORD.
Don't touch their filthy things,
  and I will welcome you.*
[18] And I will be your Father,
  and you will be my sons and
  daughters,
  says the LORD Almighty.*"

7 Because we have these promises, dear
friends, let us cleanse ourselves from
everything that can defile our body or spirit.
And let us work toward complete holiness
because we fear God.
[2]Please open your hearts to us. We have
not done wrong to anyone, nor led anyone
astray, nor taken advantage of anyone. [3]I'm
not saying this to condemn you. I said before
that you are in our hearts, and we live or die
together with you. [4]I have the highest confidence in you, and I take great pride in you.
You have greatly encouraged me and made
me happy despite all our troubles.

Paul's Joy at the Church's Repentance

[5]When we arrived in Macedonia, there was
no rest for us. We faced conflict from every
direction, with battles on the outside and

5:14a Or *urges us on.* **5:14b** Greek *Since one died for all, then all died.* **5:21** Or *to become sin itself.* **6:1** Or *As we work together.* **6:2** Isa 49:8 (Greek version). **6:6** Or *by our holiness of spirit.* **6:15** Greek *Beliar;* various other manuscripts render this proper name of the devil as *Belian, Beliab,* or *Belial.* **6:16** Lev 26:12; Ezek 37:27. **6:17** Isa 52:11; Ezek 20:34 (Greek version). **6:18** 2 Sam 7:14.

Can a Christian marry a non-Christian?

Finding a spouse is one of life's biggest issues. But alongside natural longings, Christians can often experience pressure from friends or family members who steer them toward marriage with a non-Christian. The Bible, however, forbids this. If you are a committed Christian, your relationship with Jesus is the most fundamental aspect of life; marrying a non-Christian excludes this from the marriage—hardly a good basis for a happy life. While Paul said that someone who became a Christian should not divorce their unbelieving spouse but pray for them to be saved (1 Corinthians 7:12-16), this is wholly different from choosing to marry an unbeliever. To do this—even with evangelistic intentions—is to disobey God. The one criterion governing a Christian's choice of spouse is that he or she must love the Lord (1 Corinthians 7:39), and we are commanded, "Don't team up with those who are unbelievers" (2 Corinthians 6:14). Just before the Israelites entered the Promised Land, where they would encounter peoples of many beliefs, Moses said, "Do not let your daughters and sons marry their sons and daughters, for they will lead your children away from me to worship other gods" (Deuteronomy 7:3-4). The wise Christian therefore resolves that marrying a non-Christian is not an option and trusts God to provide the right partner.

▶ *See also* ***Does marriage still matter to God?****, page 976.*

fear on the inside. 6But God, who encourages
those who are discouraged, encouraged us
by the arrival of Titus. 7His presence was a
joy, but so was the news he brought of the
encouragement he received from you. When
he told us how much you long to see me, and
how sorry you are for what happened, and
how loyal you are to me, I was filled with joy!
8I am not sorry that I sent that severe letter
to you, though I was sorry at first, for I know
it was painful to you for a little while. 9Now
I am glad I sent it, not because it hurt you,
but because the pain caused you to repent
and change your ways. It was the kind of
sorrow God wants his people to have, so
you were not harmed by us in any way. 10For
the kind of sorrow God wants us to experience leads us away from sin and results in
salvation. There's no regret for that kind of
sorrow. But worldly sorrow, which lacks repentance, results in spiritual death.

11Just see what this godly sorrow produced
in you! Such earnestness, such concern to
clear yourselves, such indignation, such
alarm, such longing to see me, such zeal,
and such a readiness to punish wrong. You
showed that you have done everything necessary to make things right. 12My purpose,
then, was not to write about who did the
wrong or who was wronged. I wrote to you
so that in the sight of God you could see for
yourselves how loyal you are to us. 13We
have been greatly encouraged by this.

In addition to our own encouragement,
we were especially delighted to see how
happy Titus was about the way all of you
welcomed him and set his mind* at ease. 14I
had told him how proud I was of you—and
you didn't disappoint me. I have always told
you the truth, and now my boasting to Titus
has also proved true! 15Now he cares for you
more than ever when he remembers the way
all of you obeyed him and welcomed him
with such fear and deep respect. 16I am very
happy now because I have complete confidence in you.

A Call to Generous Giving

8 Now I want you to know, dear brothers
and sisters,* what God in his kindness
has done through the churches in Macedonia. 2They are being tested by many
troubles, and they are very poor. But they
are also filled with abundant joy, which has
overflowed in rich generosity.

3For I can testify that they gave not only
what they could afford, but far more. And
they did it of their own free will. 4They
begged us again and again for the privilege
of sharing in the gift for the believers in
Jerusalem.* 5They even did more than we
had hoped, for their first action was to give
themselves to the Lord and to us, just as
God wanted them to do.

6So we have urged Titus, who encouraged
your giving in the first place, to return to
you and encourage you to finish this ministry of giving. 7Since you excel in so many
ways—in your faith, your gifted speakers,
your knowledge, your enthusiasm, and
your love from us*—I want you to excel also
in this gracious act of giving.

8I am not commanding you to do this.
But I am testing how genuine your love is
by comparing it with the eagerness of the
other churches.

9You know the generous grace of our Lord
Jesus Christ. Though he was rich, yet for
your sakes he became poor, so that by his
poverty he could make you rich.

10Here is my advice: It would be good for
you to finish what you started a year ago.
Last year you were the first who wanted to
give, and you were the first to begin doing
it. 11Now you should finish what you started.
Let the eagerness you showed in the beginning be matched now by your giving. Give
in proportion to what you have. 12Whatever
you give is acceptable if you give it eagerly.
And give according to what you have, not
what you don't have. 13Of course, I don't
mean your giving should make life easy for
others and hard for yourselves. I only mean
that there should be some equality. 14Right
now you have plenty and can help those
who are in need. Later, they will have plenty
and can share with you when you need it.
In this way, things will be equal. 15As the
Scriptures say,

> "Those who gathered a lot had nothing
> left over,
> and those who gathered only a little
> had enough."*

Titus and His Companions

16But thank God! He has given Titus the
same enthusiasm for you that I have.
17Titus welcomed our request that he visit
you again. In fact, he himself was very eager

to go and see you. 18 We are also sending
another brother with Titus. All the churches
praise him as a preacher of the Good News.
19 He was appointed by the churches to accompany us as we take the offering to Jerusalem*—a service that glorifies the Lord and
shows our eagerness to help.
20 We are traveling together to guard
against any criticism for the way we are handling this generous gift. 21 We are careful to be
honorable before the Lord, but we also want
everyone else to see that we are honorable.
22 We are also sending with them another
of our brothers who has proven himself
many times and has shown on many occasions how eager he is. He is now even
more enthusiastic because of his great confidence in you. 23 If anyone asks about Titus,
say that he is my partner who works with
me to help you. And the brothers with him
have been sent by the churches,* and they
bring honor to Christ. 24 So show them your
love, and prove to all the churches that our
boasting about you is justified.

The Collection for Christians in Jerusalem

9 I really don't need to write to you about
this ministry of giving for the believers
in Jerusalem.* 2 For I know how eager you
are to help, and I have been boasting to the
churches in Macedonia that you in Greece*
were ready to send an offering a year ago. In
fact, it was your enthusiasm that stirred up
many of the Macedonian believers to begin
giving.
3 But I am sending these brothers to be sure
you really are ready, as I have been telling
them, and that your money is all collected.
I don't want to be wrong in my boasting
about you. 4 We would be embarrassed—not
to mention your own embarrassment—if
some Macedonian believers came with me
and found that you weren't ready after all I
had told them! 5 So I thought I should send
these brothers ahead of me to make sure the
gift you promised is ready. But I want it to be
a willing gift, not one given grudgingly.
6 Remember this—a farmer who plants
only a few seeds will get a small crop. But
the one who plants generously will get a
generous crop. 7 You must each decide in
your heart how much to give. And don't give
reluctantly or in response to pressure. "For
God loves a person who gives cheerfully."*
8 And God will generously provide all you
need. Then you will always have everything
you need and plenty left over to share with
others. 9 As the Scriptures say,

> "They share freely and give generously
> to the poor.

7:13 Greek *his spirit.* **8:1** Greek *brothers.* **8:4** Greek *for God's holy people.* **8:7** Some manuscripts read *your love for us.* **8:15** Exod 16:18. **8:19** See 1 Cor 16:3-4. **8:23** Greek *are apostles of the churches.* **9:1** Greek *about the offering for God's holy people.* **9:2** Greek *in Achaia,* the southern region of the Greek peninsula. *Macedonia* was in the northern region of Greece. **9:7** See footnote on Prov 22:8.

Giving

Paul urges the Corinthians to show the genuineness of their repentance for the breakdown of relationship with him by giving—not to him, but to the poor and suffering Jerusalem church. He holds up the generous Macedonians as both example and provocation (2 Corinthians 8:1-5).

Four principles undergird Paul's encouragements about giving. First, God loves a *giver*, for when we give, we reflect our giving God who gave us his Son (8:9). Second, God loves a *generous* giver, and when we sow generously with our resources we always reap a harvest (9:6-11). Third, God loves a *willing* giver (9:7), for giving out of a sense of duty is not true giving. Fourth, God loves a *cheerful* giver (9:7)—though cheerfulness alone can be a false indicator, for it is easy to be cheerful if our giving costs us nothing. Of course, we should never give in order to receive, as some preachers encourage. But if we give as God prompts us, he will meet our needs in the way he knows is best.

Paul does not give guidelines about how much the Corinthians should give—that is between the giver and God. But his Jewish traditions would certainly have led him to tithe as a starting point (see *Should Christians still tithe?*, page 1052).

Their good deeds will be remembered
forever."*

10 For God is the one who provides seed for the farmer and then bread to eat. In the same way, he will provide and increase your resources and then produce a great harvest of generosity* in you.

11 Yes, you will be enriched in every way so that you can always be generous. And when we take your gifts to those who need them, they will thank God. 12 So two good things will result from this ministry of giving—the needs of the believers in Jerusalem* will be met, and they will joyfully express their thanks to God.

13 As a result of your ministry, they will give glory to God. For your generosity to them and to all believers will prove that you are obedient to the Good News of Christ. 14 And they will pray for you with deep affection because of the overflowing grace God has given to you. 15 Thank God for this gift* too wonderful for words!

Paul Defends His Authority

10 Now I, Paul, appeal to you with the gentleness and kindness of Christ—though I realize you think I am timid in person and bold only when I write from far away. 2 Well, I am begging you now so that when I come I won't have to be bold with those who think we act from human motives.

3 We are human, but we don't wage war as humans do. 4 *We use God's mighty weapons, not worldly weapons, to knock down the strongholds of human reasoning and to destroy false arguments. 5 We destroy every proud obstacle that keeps people from knowing God. We capture their rebellious thoughts and teach them to obey Christ. 6 And after you have become fully obedient, we will punish everyone who remains disobedient.

7 Look at the obvious facts.* Those who say they belong to Christ must recognize that we belong to Christ as much as they do. 8 I may seem to be boasting too much about the authority given to us by the Lord. But our authority builds you up; it doesn't tear you down. So I will not be ashamed of using my authority.

9 I'm not trying to frighten you by my letters. 10 For some say, "Paul's letters are demanding and forceful, but in person he is weak, and his speeches are worthless!" 11 Those people should realize that our actions when we arrive in person will be as forceful as what we say in our letters from far away.

12 Oh, don't worry; we wouldn't dare say that we are as wonderful as these other men who tell you how important they are! But they are only comparing themselves with each other, using themselves as the standard of measurement. How ignorant!

13 We will not boast about things done outside our area of authority. We will boast only about what has happened within the boundaries of the work God has given us, which includes our working with you. 14 We are not reaching beyond these boundaries when we claim authority over you, as if we had never visited you. For we were the first to travel all the way to Corinth with the Good News of Christ.

15 Nor do we boast and claim credit for the work someone else has done. Instead, we hope that your faith will grow so that the boundaries of our work among you will be extended. 16 Then we will be able to go and preach the Good News in other places far beyond you, where no one else is working. Then there will be no question of our boasting about work done in someone else's territory. 17 As the Scriptures say, "If you want to boast, boast only about the LORD."*

18 When people commend themselves, it doesn't count for much. The important thing is for the Lord to commend them.

Paul and the False Apostles

11 I hope you will put up with a little more of my foolishness. Please bear with me. 2 For I am jealous for you with the jealousy of God himself. I promised you as a pure bride* to one husband—Christ. 3 But I fear that somehow your pure and undivided devotion to Christ will be corrupted, just as Eve was deceived by the cunning ways of the serpent. 4 You happily put up with whatever anyone tells you, even if they preach a different Jesus than the one we preach, or a different kind of Spirit than the one you received, or a different kind of gospel than the one you believed.

5 But I don't consider myself inferior in any way to these "super apostles" who teach such things. 6 I may be unskilled as a

speaker, but I'm not lacking in knowledge.
We have made this clear to you in every possible way.
7 Was I wrong when I humbled myself
and honored you by preaching God's Good
News to you without expecting anything in
return? 8 I "robbed" other churches by accepting their contributions so I could serve
you at no cost. 9 And when I was with you
and didn't have enough to live on, I did not
become a financial burden to anyone. For
the brothers who came from Macedonia
brought me all that I needed. I have never
been a burden to you, and I never will be.
10 As surely as the truth of Christ is in me, no
one in all of Greece* will ever stop me from
boasting about this. 11 Why? Because I don't
love you? God knows that I do.
12 But I will continue doing what I have
always done. This will undercut those who
are looking for an opportunity to boast
that their work is just like ours. 13 These
people are false apostles. They are deceitful workers who disguise themselves as
apostles of Christ. 14 But I am not surprised!
Even Satan disguises himself as an angel of
light. 15 So it is no wonder that his servants
also disguise themselves as servants of righteousness. In the end they will get the punishment their wicked deeds deserve.

Paul's Many Trials

16 Again I say, don't think that I am a fool
to talk like this. But even if you do, listen
to me, as you would to a foolish person,
while I also boast a little. 17 Such boasting
is not from the Lord, but I am acting like a
fool. 18 And since others boast about their
human achievements, I will, too. 19 After all,
you think you are so wise, but you enjoy
putting up with fools! 20 You put up with it
when someone enslaves you, takes everything you have, takes advantage of you,
takes control of everything, and slaps you
in the face. 21 I'm ashamed to say that we've
been too "weak" to do that!

But whatever they dare to boast about—
I'm talking like a fool again—I dare to boast
about it, too. 22 Are they Hebrews? So am I.
Are they Israelites? So am I. Are they descendants of Abraham? So am I. 23 Are they
servants of Christ? I know I sound like a
madman, but I have served him far more!
I have worked harder, been put in prison
more often, been whipped times without
number, and faced death again and again.
24 Five different times the Jewish leaders
gave me thirty-nine lashes. 25 Three times
I was beaten with rods. Once I was stoned.
Three times I was shipwrecked. Once I spent
a whole night and a day adrift at sea. 26 I have
traveled on many long journeys. I have faced
danger from rivers and from robbers. I have
faced danger from my own people, the Jews,
as well as from the Gentiles. I have faced
danger in the cities, in the deserts, and
on the seas. And I have faced danger from
men who claim to be believers but are not.*
27 I have worked hard and long, enduring
many sleepless nights. I have been hungry
and thirsty and have often gone without
food. I have shivered in the cold, without
enough clothing to keep me warm.
28 Then, besides all this, I have the daily
burden of my concern for all the churches.
29 Who is weak without my feeling that
weakness? Who is led astray, and I do not
burn with anger?
30 If I must boast, I would rather boast
about the things that show how weak I am.
31 God, the Father of our Lord Jesus, who is
worthy of eternal praise, knows I am not
lying. 32 When I was in Damascus, the governor under King Aretas kept guards at the
city gates to catch me. 33 I had to be lowered
in a basket through a window in the city
wall to escape from him.

Paul's Vision and His Thorn in the Flesh

12 This boasting will do no good, but
I must go on. I will reluctantly tell
about visions and revelations from the
Lord. 2 I* was caught up to the third heaven
fourteen years ago. Whether I was in my
body or out of my body, I don't know—only
God knows. 3 Yes, only God knows whether
I was in my body or outside my body. But I
do know 4 that I was caught up* to paradise
and heard things so astounding that they

9:9 Ps 112:9. **9:10** Greek *righteousness.* **9:12** Greek *of God's holy people.* **9:15** Greek *his gift.* **10:4** English translations divide verses 4 and 5 in various ways. **10:7** Or *You look at things only on the basis of appearance.* **10:17** Jer 9:24. **11:2** Greek *a virgin.* **11:10** Greek *Achaia,* the southern region of the Greek peninsula. **11:26** Greek *from false brothers.* **12:2** Greek *I know a man in Christ who.* **12:3-4** Greek *But I know such a man, 4that he was caught up.*

▸ **11:13-15** *See* ***False teaching****, page 1443.*

cannot be expressed in words, things no
human is allowed to tell.
[5]That experience is worth boasting about,
but I'm not going to do it. I will boast only
about my weaknesses. [6]If I wanted to boast,
I would be no fool in doing so, because I
would be telling the truth. But I won't do
it, because I don't want anyone to give me
credit beyond what they can see in my life
or hear in my message, [7]even though I have
received such wonderful revelations from
God. So to keep me from becoming proud,
I was given a thorn in my flesh, a messenger
from Satan to torment me and keep me from
becoming proud.
[8]Three different times I begged the Lord
to take it away. [9]Each time he said, "My
grace is all you need. My power works best
in weakness." So now I am glad to boast
about my weaknesses, so that the power of
Christ can work through me. [10]That's why
I take pleasure in my weaknesses, and in
the insults, hardships, persecutions, and
troubles that I suffer for Christ. For when
I am weak, then I am strong.

Paul's Concern for the Corinthians

[11]You have made me act like a fool. You
ought to be writing commendations for me,
for I am not at all inferior to these "super
apostles," even though I am nothing at all.
[12]When I was with you, I certainly gave you
proof that I am an apostle. For I patiently
did many signs and wonders and miracles
among you. [13]The only thing I failed to do,
which I do in the other churches, was to
become a financial burden to you. Please
forgive me for this wrong!
[14]Now I am coming to you for the third
time, and I will not be a burden to you.
I don't want what you have—I want you.
After all, children don't provide for their
parents. Rather, parents provide for their
children. [15]I will gladly spend myself and all
I have for you, even though it seems that the
more I love you, the less you love me.
[16]Some of you admit I was not a burden
to you. But others still think I was sneaky
and took advantage of you by trickery. [17]But
how? Did any of the men I sent to you take
advantage of you? [18]When I urged Titus to
visit you and sent our other brother with
him, did Titus take advantage of you? No!
For we have the same spirit and walk in each
other's steps, doing things the same way.
[19]Perhaps you think we're saying these
things just to defend ourselves. No, we
tell you this as Christ's servants, and with

▸ **12:9** *See **The presence of God**, page 1031.*

Weakness

Few of us like to be weak, and even fewer like to admit our weakness to others. Yet the cross proves that God demonstrates his power through weakness, not through strength. And though this is foolish to human ways of thinking, it is the wisdom of God (1 Corinthians 1:18–2:5).

Weakness was not just a theological idea for Paul; he experienced it personally. He writes here of "a thorn in my flesh" (2 Corinthians 12:7) that clearly made life difficult. We have no idea what this was. Some think it was a physical condition, perhaps an eye disease since he mentions needing to write in large letters (Galatians 6:11); others think it may have been particular people, for while sickness is never described as a "thorn" in the Bible, people are (Numbers 33:55; Joshua 23:13). Perhaps Paul was thinking of opponents who constantly dogged his footsteps. Whatever it was, Paul saw it as "a messenger from Satan" (2 Corinthians 12:7). Yet despite much prayer, God hadn't removed this "thorn," and Paul came to see why: It forced him to depend on God and to learn the truth of Jesus' words to him—"My grace is all you need. My power works best in weakness" (12:9). Mature disciples, Paul came to understand, don't boast of their strength but of their weakness (12:9-10).

God as our witness. Everything we do, dear
friends, is to strengthen you. [20]For I am
afraid that when I come I won't like what I
find, and you won't like my response. I am
afraid that I will find quarreling, jealousy,
anger, selfishness, slander, gossip, arrogance, and disorderly behavior. [21]Yes, I am
afraid that when I come again, God will
humble me in your presence. And I will be
grieved because many of you have not given
up your old sins. You have not repented of
your impurity, sexual immorality, and eagerness for lustful pleasure.

Paul's Final Advice

13 This is the third time I am coming
to visit you (and as the Scriptures
say, "The facts of every case must be established by the testimony of two or three
witnesses"*). [2]I have already warned those
who had been sinning when I was there on
my second visit. Now I again warn them and
all others, just as I did before, that next time
I will not spare them.

[3]I will give you all the proof you want that
Christ speaks through me. Christ is not weak
when he deals with you; he is powerful
among you. [4]Although he was crucified in
weakness, he now lives by the power of
God. We, too, are weak, just as Christ was,
but when we deal with you we will be alive
with him and will have God's power.

[5]Examine yourselves to see if your faith is
genuine. Test yourselves. Surely you know
that Jesus Christ is among you*; if not, you
have failed the test of genuine faith. [6]As you
test yourselves, I hope you will recognize
that we have not failed the test of apostolic
authority.

[7]We pray to God that you will not do what
is wrong by refusing our correction. I hope
we won't need to demonstrate our authority
when we arrive. Do the right thing before
we come—even if that makes it look like we
have failed to demonstrate our authority.
[8]For we cannot oppose the truth, but must
always stand for the truth. [9]We are glad to
seem weak if it helps show that you are actually strong. We pray that you will become
mature.

[10]I am writing this to you before I come,
hoping that I won't need to deal severely
with you when I do come. For I want to
use the authority the Lord has given me to
strengthen you, not to tear you down.

Paul's Final Greetings

[11]Dear brothers and sisters,* I close my
letter with these last words: Be joyful. Grow
to maturity. Encourage each other. Live in
harmony and peace. Then the God of love
and peace will be with you.

[12]Greet each other with a sacred kiss.
[13]All of God's people here send you their
greetings.

[14]*May the grace of the Lord Jesus Christ,
the love of God, and the fellowship of the
Holy Spirit be with you all.

13:1 Deut 19:15. **13:5** Or *in you.* **13:11** Greek *Brothers.*
13:14 Some English translations include verse 13 as part of verse 12, and then verse 14 becomes verse 13.

Galatians *True freedom*

A crisis had hit the churches in Galatia (part of Asia Minor, or modern Turkey) that Paul had started. Soon after his departure, they had been visited by Jewish Christian teachers who were insisting that Paul's Gentile converts should be circumcised and observe the Jewish Law, and that unless they did so, they weren't real Christians. And because Paul didn't insist on such things, they said he wasn't a proper apostle. Paul's outrage can be seen throughout the letter as he passionately defends his apostolic calling and authority and strongly stresses that to insist on keeping the Jewish Law is to undermine the gospel of grace that can be received by faith alone.

What's it all about?

Paul's first missionary journey had taken him to Galatia, where he had preached a message of salvation for all, Jew and Gentile, based on faith in Jesus Christ and nothing else. But Jewish Christians arrived soon after, insisting that Gentiles needed to become Jews before they could truly regard themselves as Abraham's children. So Paul wrote this letter to correct this fundamental error.

Paul is amazed that his converts have so quickly accepted "a different way that pretends to be the Good News" (1:6) from these "Judaizers." He reminds them that God called him to preach the one true gospel to the Gentiles. The church leaders in Jerusalem had acknowledged this call and had given his message their approval (2:1-10). But even Peter had withdrawn from fellowship with Gentile Christians under pressure from these Judaizers, such was their power, and Paul had confronted him about this hypocrisy (2:11-14).

Paul insists that the days of thinking that observing the Jewish Law could make it possible to get right with God or win his favor are over. Jew and Gentile alike are accepted by God on equal terms: through faith in Jesus. And if God accepts Gentiles on the basis of their faith, then it is foolish to expect them to follow the Jewish Law. He reminds them that *all* the blessings they have received came through faith (3:2-5) and reassures them they are already children of Abraham, whose faith also put him right with God (3:6-7). The Jewish Law was merely a guardian, keeping people in check until Christ came and leading them to him. Its days are now over (3:25).

Paul affirms that Christ has abolished every division between people. We can all now be children of God and through his Spirit know him as our Father (4:6). We are now free, and Paul defends this freedom to the utmost. But freedom

OVERVIEW

Paul's gospel and authority come from God · *1:1-24*

Paul and other apostles: agreement and disagreement · *2:1-21*

Law versus faith and promise *3:1-22*

Living as children, not slaves *3:23–4:7*

Paul's love for his converts *4:8-20*

Lessons from Abraham's sons *4:21-31*

Freedom in Christ *5:1-15*

A call to live by the Spirit, not the sinful nature · *5:16–6:18*

does not mean freedom to do wrong: Christians are free to love and serve one another—and such love fulfills the Law (5:13-14).

Paul concludes his letter by reminding the Galatians that the Holy Spirit, not human nature or human traditions, is what really matters, for it is he who has brought about the "new creation" in our lives.

What does it mean for us?

When we hear of people being held hostage by terrorists, we all hold our breath until they are free, for we all value freedom. When Christ died on the cross, he died to set us free. How foolish then to abandon that freedom and hand ourselves over to spiritual terrorists! Paul identifies three such terrorists that seek to deprive us of our freedom: the Old Testament Law, which even if we try to keep, we constantly break; religious observances imposed on us by others; and our inward sinful desires and the failures they lead to. But Christ came to give us the freedom we cannot achieve ourselves.

Now that we are free, we must stand our ground to remain free. First, we must resist the subtle temptation to try to win God's favor by making external rules more important than they are, assuming they can win God's favor; and second, we must resist the temptation to try to win other people's favor by conforming to what they feel is important in the Christian life. Only Christ's death on the cross both puts us right and keeps us right with God, and the power of his Holy Spirit is what helps us to reject our old sinful ways and live a life that is pleasing to the Father and a blessing to others.

Greetings from Paul

1 This letter is from Paul, an apostle. I was
not appointed by any group of people or
any human authority, but by Jesus Christ
himself and by God the Father, who raised
Jesus from the dead.
2 All the brothers and sisters* here join
me in sending this letter to the churches of
Galatia.
3 May God the Father and our Lord Jesus
Christ* give you grace and peace. 4 Jesus gave
his life for our sins, just as God our Father
planned, in order to rescue us from this evil
world in which we live. 5 All glory to God
forever and ever! Amen.

There Is Only One Good News

6 I am shocked that you are turning away so
soon from God, who called you to himself
through the loving mercy of Christ.* You
are following a different way that pretends
to be the Good News 7 but is not the Good
News at all. You are being fooled by those
who deliberately twist the truth concerning
Christ.
8 Let God's curse fall on anyone, including
us or even an angel from heaven, who
preaches a different kind of Good News
than the one we preached to you. 9 I say
again what we have said before: If anyone
preaches any other Good News than the one
you welcomed, let that person be cursed.
10 Obviously, I'm not trying to win the approval
of people, but of God. If pleasing
people were my goal, I would not be Christ's
servant.

Paul's Message Comes from Christ

11 Dear brothers and sisters, I want you to
understand that the gospel message I preach
is not based on mere human reasoning. 12 I
received my message from no human source,
and no one taught me. Instead, I received it
by direct revelation from Jesus Christ.*
13 You know what I was like when I followed
the Jewish religion—how I violently
persecuted God's church. I did my best to
destroy it. 14 I was far ahead of my fellow Jews
in my zeal for the traditions of my ancestors.
15 But even before I was born, God chose me
and called me by his marvelous grace. Then
it pleased him 16 to reveal his Son to me* so
that I would proclaim the Good News about
Jesus to the Gentiles.
When this happened, I did not rush out to
consult with any human being.* 17 Nor did I
go up to Jerusalem to consult with those who

1:2 Greek *brothers;* also in 1:11. **1:3** Some manuscripts read *God our Father and the Lord Jesus Christ.* **1:6** Some manuscripts read *through loving mercy.* **1:12** Or *by the revelation of Jesus Christ.* **1:16a** Or *in me.* **1:16b** Greek *with flesh and blood.*

were apostles before I was. Instead, I went
away into Arabia, and later I returned to the
city of Damascus.
18 Then three years later I went to Jerusalem to get to know Peter,* and I stayed
with him for fifteen days. 19 The only other
apostle I met at that time was James, the
Lord's brother. 20 I declare before God that
what I am writing to you is not a lie.
21 After that visit I went north into the
provinces of Syria and Cilicia. 22 And still
the churches in Christ that are in Judea
didn't know me personally. 23 All they knew
was that people were saying, "The one who
used to persecute us is now preaching the
very faith he tried to destroy!" 24 And they
praised God because of me.

The Apostles Accept Paul

2 Then fourteen years later I went back
to Jerusalem again, this time with Barnabas; and Titus came along, too. 2 I went
there because God revealed to me that
I should go. While I was there I met privately with those considered to be leaders
of the church and shared with them the
message I had been preaching to the Gentiles. I wanted to make sure that we were in
agreement, for fear that all my efforts had
been wasted and I was running the race for
nothing. 3 And they supported me and did
not even demand that my companion Titus
be circumcised, though he was a Gentile.*
4 Even that question came up only because
of some so-called believers there—false
ones, really*—who were secretly brought in.
They sneaked in to spy on us and take away
the freedom we have in Christ Jesus. They
wanted to enslave us and force us to follow
their Jewish regulations. 5 But we refused
to give in to them for a single moment. We
wanted to preserve the truth of the gospel
message for you.
6 And the leaders of the church had
nothing to add to what I was preaching. (By
the way, their reputation as great leaders
made no difference to me, for God has no
favorites.) 7 Instead, they saw that God had
given me the responsibility of preaching
the gospel to the Gentiles, just as he had
given Peter the responsibility of preaching
to the Jews. 8 For the same God who worked
through Peter as the apostle to the Jews
also worked through me as the apostle to
the Gentiles.
9 In fact, James, Peter,* and John, who were
known as pillars of the church, recognized
the gift God had given me, and they accepted
Barnabas and me as their co-workers. They
encouraged us to keep preaching to the Gentiles, while they continued their work with
the Jews. 10 Their only suggestion was that
we keep on helping the poor, which I have
always been eager to do.

Paul Confronts Peter

11 But when Peter came to Antioch, I had to
oppose him to his face, for what he did was
very wrong. 12 When he first arrived, he ate
with the Gentile believers, who were not

▸ **2:10** *See **Poverty**, page 1142.*

Galatia

Paul's addressing of this letter to "the churches of Galatia" (Galatians 1:2) shows that it was written as a *circular letter*, designed to be passed from one church to another. What we are not really sure about is what Paul meant by "Galatia"—though it was definitely in modern Turkey. There was a people group called Galatians (descended from the Gauls who had invaded in the third century BC) in northern Turkey, but there was also a Roman province called Galatia in southern Turkey. Paul visited the latter during his first missionary journey (Acts 13:3–14:28), prior to the Council of Jerusalem; but there is no mention of the former in Acts. While scholars are divided in their opinion about which "Galatians" Paul was writing to, it really makes no difference to the interpretation of the letter.

▸ *See also **Paul's Missionary Journeys** map, Visual Overview Z15.*

circumcised. But afterward, when some friends of James came, Peter wouldn't eat with the Gentiles anymore. He was afraid of criticism from these people who insisted on the necessity of circumcision. [13]As a result, other Jewish believers followed Peter's hypocrisy, and even Barnabas was led astray by their hypocrisy.

[14]When I saw that they were not following the truth of the gospel message, I said to Peter in front of all the others, "Since you, a Jew by birth, have discarded the Jewish laws and are living like a Gentile, why are you now trying to make these Gentiles follow the Jewish traditions?

[15]"You and I are Jews by birth, not 'sinners' like the Gentiles. [16]Yet we know that a person is made right with God by faith in Jesus Christ, not by obeying the law. And we have believed in Christ Jesus, so that we might be made right with God because of our faith in Christ, not because we have obeyed the law. For no one will ever be made right with God by obeying the law."*

[17]But suppose we seek to be made right with God through faith in Christ and then we are found guilty because we have abandoned the law. Would that mean Christ has led us into sin? Absolutely not! [18]Rather, I am a sinner if I rebuild the old system of law I already tore down. [19]For when I tried to keep the law, it condemned me. So I died to the law—I stopped trying to meet all its requirements—so that I might live for God. [20]My old self has been crucified with Christ.* It is no longer I who live, but Christ lives in me. So I live in this earthly body by trusting in the Son of God, who loved me and gave himself for me. [21]I do not treat the grace of God as meaningless. For if keeping the law could make us right with God, then there was no need for Christ to die.

The Law and Faith in Christ

3 Oh, foolish Galatians! Who has cast an evil spell on you? For the meaning of Jesus Christ's death was made as clear to you as if you had seen a picture of his death on the cross. [2]Let me ask you this one question: Did you receive the Holy Spirit by obeying the law of Moses? Of course not! You received the Spirit because you believed the message you heard about Christ. [3]How foolish can you be? After starting your new lives in the Spirit, why are you now trying

1:18 Greek *Cephas.* **2:3** Greek *a Greek.* **2:4** Greek *some false brothers.* **2:9** Greek *Cephas;* also in 2:11, 14. **2:16** Some translators hold that the quotation extends through verse 14; others through verse 16; and still others through verse 21. **2:20** Some English translations put this sentence in verse 19.

▸ **2:16** *See **Justification**, page 1288.*

Legalism

As the gospel spread beyond Israel, the question of whether Gentiles needed to become Jews in order to become Christians became a significant issue (e.g., Acts 15:1). The final answer, given at the Council of Jerusalem (AD 49), would be a firm no (see Acts 15:23-29); but for now, Paul was struggling with Jewish Christian teachers who insisted that Gentiles must be circumcised and keep the Jewish Law if they hoped to be saved. Paul fiercely opposed this viewpoint, describing it as "a different way that pretends to be the Good News" (Galatians 1:6). He asks the Galatians to consider whether they received God's Spirit through keeping the Law or through faith (3:2-4), and he appeals to Abraham's faith as an example (3:6-29). Jesus has brought us freedom from the Jewish Law and legalism; to go back to keeping the Law is to return to slavery (5:1).

Insisting that people live by our rules and way of doing things in addition to faith in Jesus is still a temptation in the church today. This finds expression in things like imposing rules about behavior or dress or traditions, or insisting that our own interpretations of particular Scriptures are foundational to being a "real" Christian. To all who add anything to faith in Christ alone as the basis of salvation, Paul would say, "Oh, foolish Christians!" (see 3:1).

to become perfect by your own human
effort? 4Have you experienced* so much for
nothing? Surely it was not in vain, was it?
5I ask you again, does God give you the
Holy Spirit and work miracles among you
because you obey the law? Of course not!
It is because you believe the message you
heard about Christ.
6In the same way, "Abraham believed
God, and God counted him as righteous
because of his faith."* 7The real children
of Abraham, then, are those who put their
faith in God.
8What's more, the Scriptures looked
forward to this time when God would make
the Gentiles right in his sight because of
their faith. God proclaimed this good news
to Abraham long ago when he said, "All
nations will be blessed through you."* 9So
all who put their faith in Christ share the
same blessing Abraham received because
of his faith.
10But those who depend on the law to
make them right with God are under his
curse, for the Scriptures say, "Cursed is
everyone who does not observe and obey
all the commands that are written in God's
Book of the Law."* 11So it is clear that no
one can be made right with God by trying
to keep the law. For the Scriptures say, "It
is through faith that a righteous person
has life."* 12This way of faith is very different from the way of law, which says, "It is
through obeying the law that a person has
life."*
13But Christ has rescued us from the curse
pronounced by the law. When he was hung
on the cross, he took upon himself the curse
for our wrongdoing. For it is written in the
Scriptures, "Cursed is everyone who is hung
on a tree."* 14Through Christ Jesus, God has
blessed the Gentiles with the same blessing
he promised to Abraham, so that we who
are believers might receive the promised*
Holy Spirit through faith.

The Law and God's Promise

15Dear brothers and sisters,* here's an
example from everyday life. Just as no
one can set aside or amend an irrevocable
agreement, so it is in this case. 16God gave
the promises to Abraham and his child.*
And notice that the Scripture doesn't say
"to his children,*" as if it meant many descendants. Rather, it says "to his child"—
and that, of course, means Christ. 17This is
what I am trying to say: The agreement God
made with Abraham could not be canceled

▸ **3:6-9** *See **Abraham**, page 16.*

Equality

The ancient world was full of divisions, just like today—divisions based on nationality (Roman versus non-Roman), ethnicity (Jew versus Gentile), social standing (free citizen versus slave), and gender (male versus female). But in Christ, all such divisions are abolished, for "you are all children of God through faith in Christ Jesus" (Galatians 3:26). Whatever our background, we all came to God the same way: through Jesus Christ. And in him we become part of one great family (Ephesians 2:19).

The church should therefore be the greatest advocate of equality; indeed, to retain attitudes that look down on others is to deny the gospel. At the cross, Christ broke down every dividing barrier (Ephesians 2:11-22), and to rebuild them is to deny his work. Of course, this doesn't mean all distinctions are obliterated in everyday life. The servant is still a servant and the master is still a master—though their relationship with Christ will transform how they relate to one another (Ephesians 6:5-9); and the same is true of a husband and wife (Ephesians 5:21-33). But to think of others as somehow less than ourselves and to treat them as such, whether on the basis of their race, ethnicity, gender, or social standing, is unacceptable behavior for a Christian.

430 years later when God gave the law to Moses. God would be breaking his promise. [18]For if the inheritance could be received by keeping the law, then it would not be the result of accepting God's promise. But God graciously gave it to Abraham as a promise.

[19]Why, then, was the law given? It was given alongside the promise to show people their sins. But the law was designed to last only until the coming of the child who was promised. God gave his law through angels to Moses, who was the mediator between God and the people. [20]Now a mediator is helpful if more than one party must reach an agreement. But God, who is one, did not use a mediator when he gave his promise to Abraham.

[21]Is there a conflict, then, between God's law and God's promises?* Absolutely not! If the law could give us new life, we could be made right with God by obeying it. [22]But the Scriptures declare that we are all prisoners of sin, so we receive God's promise of freedom only by believing in Jesus Christ.

God's Children through Faith

[23]Before the way of faith in Christ was available to us, we were placed under guard by the law. We were kept in protective custody, so to speak, until the way of faith was revealed.

[24]Let me put it another way. The law was our guardian until Christ came; it protected us until we could be made right with God through faith. [25]And now that the way of faith has come, we no longer need the law as our guardian.

[26]For you are all children* of God through faith in Christ Jesus. [27]And all who have been united with Christ in baptism have put on Christ, like putting on new clothes.* [28]There is no longer Jew or Gentile,* slave or free, male and female. For you are all one in Christ Jesus. [29]And now that you belong to Christ, you are the true children* of Abraham. You are his heirs, and God's promise to Abraham belongs to you.

4 Think of it this way. If a father dies and leaves an inheritance for his young children, those children are not much better off than slaves until they grow up, even though they actually own everything their father had. [2]They have to obey their guardians until they reach whatever age their father set. [3]And that's the way it was with us before Christ came. We were like children; we were slaves to the basic spiritual principles* of this world.

[4]But when the right time came, God sent his Son, born of a woman, subject to the law. [5]God sent him to buy freedom for us who were slaves to the law, so that he could adopt us as his very own children.* [6]And because we* are his children, God has sent the Spirit of his Son into our hearts, prompting us to call out, "Abba, Father."* [7]Now you are no longer a slave but God's own child.* And since you are his child, God has made you his heir.

Paul's Concern for the Galatians

[8]Before you Gentiles knew God, you were slaves to so-called gods that do not even exist. [9]So now that you know God (or should I say, now that God knows you), why do you want to go back again and become slaves once more to the weak and useless spiritual principles of this world? [10]You are trying to earn favor with God by observing certain days or months or seasons or years. [11]I fear for you. Perhaps all my hard work with you was for nothing. [12]Dear brothers and sisters,* I plead with you to live as I do in freedom from these things, for I have become like you Gentiles—free from those laws.

You did not mistreat me when I first preached to you. [13]Surely you remember that I was sick when I first brought you the Good News. [14]But even though my condition tempted you to reject me, you did not despise me or turn me away. No, you took me in and cared for me as though I were an angel from God or even Christ Jesus himself. [15]Where is that joyful and grateful spirit you felt then? I am sure you would have taken out your own

3:4 Or *Have you suffered.* **3:6** Gen 15:6. **3:8** Gen 12:3; 18:18; 22:18. **3:10** Deut 27:26. **3:11** Hab 2:4. **3:12** Lev 18:5. **3:13** Deut 21:23 (Greek version). **3:14** Some manuscripts read *the blessing of the.* **3:15** Greek *Brothers.* **3:16a** Greek *seed;* also in 3:16c, 19. See notes on Gen 12:7 and 13:15. **3:16b** Greek *seeds.* **3:21** Some manuscripts read *and the promises?* **3:26** Greek *sons.* **3:27** Greek *have put on Christ.* **3:28** Greek *Jew or Greek.* **3:29** Greek *seed.* **4:3** Or *powers;* also in 4:9. **4:5** Greek *sons;* also in 4:6. **4:6a** Greek *you.* **4:6b** *Abba* is an Aramaic term for "father." **4:7** Greek *son;* also in 4:7b. **4:12** Greek *brothers;* also in 4:28, 31.

▸ **4:6** *See **Abba**, page 1144.*

eyes and given them to me if it had been possible. 16 Have I now become your enemy because I am telling you the truth?

17 Those false teachers are so eager to win your favor, but their intentions are not good. They are trying to shut you off from me so that you will pay attention only to them. 18 If someone is eager to do good things for you, that's all right; but let them do it all the time, not just when I'm with you.

19 Oh, my dear children! I feel as if I'm going through labor pains for you again, and they will continue until Christ is fully developed in your lives. 20 I wish I were with you right now so I could change my tone. But at this distance I don't know how else to help you.

Abraham's Two Children

21 Tell me, you who want to live under the law, do you know what the law actually says? 22 The Scriptures say that Abraham had two sons, one from his slave wife and one from his freeborn wife.* 23 The son of the slave wife was born in a human attempt to bring about the fulfillment of God's promise. But the son of the freeborn wife was born as God's own fulfillment of his promise.

24 These two women serve as an illustration of God's two covenants. The first woman, Hagar, represents Mount Sinai where people received the law that enslaved them. 25 And now Jerusalem is just like Mount Sinai in Arabia,* because she and her children live in slavery to the law. 26 But the other woman, Sarah, represents the heavenly Jerusalem. She is the free woman, and she is our mother. 27 As Isaiah said,

> "Rejoice, O childless woman,
> you who have never given birth!
> Break into a joyful shout,
> you who have never been in labor!
> For the desolate woman now has more
> children
> than the woman who lives with her
> husband!"*

28 And you, dear brothers and sisters, are children of the promise, just like Isaac. 29 But you are now being persecuted by those who want you to keep the law, just as Ishmael, the child born by human effort, persecuted Isaac, the child born by the power of the Spirit.

30 But what do the Scriptures say about that? "Get rid of the slave and her son, for the son of the slave woman will not share the inheritance with the free woman's son."* 31 So, dear brothers and sisters, we are not children of the slave woman; we are children of the free woman.

Living by the Spirit

Throughout this letter, Paul has been arguing that trying to obey the Jewish Law only leads to slavery (Galatians 4:8-31). But Christ has set us free (5:1), and the way to maintain that freedom is to "let the Holy Spirit guide [our] lives" (5:16), to be "directed by the Spirit" (5:18), and to "follow the Spirit's leading in every part of our lives" (5:25). After all, it was the Holy Spirit, not religious rules, that brought us to Christ, and it is he who helps us see God as our "Abba"—our daddy (4:6).

That is why, no matter what experiences of the Spirit we may have had, we all need to "be filled with the Holy Spirit"—literally, to "go on being filled with the Spirit" (Ephesians 5:18). We need to "let the Holy Spirit guide [our] lives" (Galatians 5:16)—that is, to follow his leadings and be filled with his power. As we do, his fruit grows in us—"love, joy, peace, patience, kindness, goodness, faithfulness, gentleness, and self-control" (5:22-23). These are not his fruits (plural), but his fruit (singular); it is as if nine different fruits were all found on one tree. All of them (not just those we like or find easy) should be growing in us. No matter how gifted someone is, lack of this fruit is a serious indicator that they are not living by the Spirit.

▸ *See also* ***Life in the Spirit****, page 1291;* ***The Christian's relationship with the Holy Spirit****, page 1350.*

Freedom in Christ

5 So Christ has truly set us free. Now make
sure that you stay free, and don't get tied
up again in slavery to the law.
[2]Listen! I, Paul, tell you this: If you are
counting on circumcision to make you right
with God, then Christ will be of no benefit to
you. [3]I'll say it again. If you are trying to find
favor with God by being circumcised, you
must obey every regulation in the whole
law of Moses. [4]For if you are trying to make
yourselves right with God by keeping the
law, you have been cut off from Christ! You
have fallen away from God's grace.
[5]But we who live by the Spirit eagerly wait
to receive by faith the righteousness God has
promised to us. [6]For when we place our faith
in Christ Jesus, there is no benefit in being
circumcised or being uncircumcised. What
is important is faith expressing itself in love.
[7]You were running the race so well. Who
has held you back from following the truth?
[8]It certainly isn't God, for he is the one who
called you to freedom. [9]This false teaching
is like a little yeast that spreads through the
whole batch of dough! [10]I am trusting the
Lord to keep you from believing false teachings. God will judge that person, whoever
he is, who has been confusing you.
[11]Dear brothers and sisters,* if I were still
preaching that you must be circumcised—
as some say I do—why am I still being
persecuted? If I were no longer preaching
salvation through the cross of Christ, no one
would be offended. [12]I just wish that those
troublemakers who want to mutilate you by
circumcision would mutilate themselves.*
[13]For you have been called to live in
freedom, my brothers and sisters. But don't
use your freedom to satisfy your sinful
nature. Instead, use your freedom to serve
one another in love. [14]For the whole law can
be summed up in this one command: "Love
your neighbor as yourself."* [15]But if you are
always biting and devouring one another,
watch out! Beware of destroying one another.

Living by the Spirit's Power

[16]So I say, let the Holy Spirit guide your lives.
Then you won't be doing what your sinful
nature craves. [17]The sinful nature wants to
do evil, which is just the opposite of what
the Spirit wants. And the Spirit gives us
desires that are the opposite of what the
sinful nature desires. These two forces are
constantly fighting each other, so you are
not free to carry out your good intentions.
[18]But when you are directed by the Spirit,
you are not under obligation to the law of
Moses.
[19]When you follow the desires of your
sinful nature, the results are very clear:
sexual immorality, impurity, lustful pleasures, [20]idolatry, sorcery, hostility, quarreling, jealousy, outbursts of anger, selfish
ambition, dissension, division, [21]envy,
drunkenness, wild parties, and other sins
like these. Let me tell you again, as I have
before, that anyone living that sort of life
will not inherit the Kingdom of God.
[22]But the Holy Spirit produces this kind
of fruit in our lives: love, joy, peace, patience, kindness, goodness, faithfulness,
[23]gentleness, and self-control. There is no
law against these things!
[24]Those who belong to Christ Jesus have
nailed the passions and desires of their
sinful nature to his cross and crucified them
there. [25]Since we are living by the Spirit, let
us follow the Spirit's leading in every part
of our lives. [26]Let us not become conceited,
or provoke one another, or be jealous of one
another.

We Harvest What We Plant

6 Dear brothers and sisters, if another
believer* is overcome by some sin, you
who are godly* should gently and humbly
help that person back onto the right path.
And be careful not to fall into the same
temptation yourself. [2]Share each other's
burdens, and in this way obey the law of
Christ. [3]If you think you are too important
to help someone, you are only fooling yourself. You are not that important.

4:22 See Gen 16:15; 21:2-3. **4:25** Greek *And Hagar, which is Mount Sinai in Arabia, is now like Jerusalem;* other manuscripts read *And Mount Sinai in Arabia is now like Jerusalem.* **4:27** Isa 54:1. **4:30** Gen 21:10. **5:11** Greek *Brothers;* similarly in 5:13. **5:12** Or *castrate themselves,* or *cut themselves off from you;* Greek reads *cut themselves off.* **5:14** Lev 19:18. **6:1a** Greek *Brothers, if a man.* **6:1b** Greek *spiritual.*

▸ **5:14** *See* ***Love your neighbor as yourself****, page 139.* **5:22-23** *See* ***Peace****, page 774;* ***Compassion****, page 983;* ***Loving others****, page 1220;* ***Goodness****, page 1251;* ***Faithfulness****, page 1307;* ***Joy****, page 1360.*

[4]Pay careful attention to your own work, for then you will get the satisfaction of a job well done, and you won't need to compare yourself to anyone else. [5]For we are each responsible for our own conduct.

[6]Those who are taught the word of God should provide for their teachers, sharing all good things with them.

[7]Don't be misled—you cannot mock the justice of God. You will always harvest what you plant. [8]Those who live only to satisfy their own sinful nature will harvest decay and death from that sinful nature. But those who live to please the Spirit will harvest everlasting life from the Spirit. [9]So let's not get tired of doing what is good. At just the right time we will reap a harvest of blessing if we don't give up. [10]Therefore, whenever we have the opportunity, we should do good to everyone—especially to those in the family of faith.

Paul's Final Advice

[11]NOTICE WHAT LARGE LETTERS I USE AS I WRITE THESE CLOSING WORDS IN MY OWN HANDWRITING.

[12]Those who are trying to force you to be circumcised want to look good to others. They don't want to be persecuted for teaching that the cross of Christ alone can save. [13]And even those who advocate circumcision don't keep the whole law themselves. They only want you to be circumcised so they can boast about it and claim you as their disciples.

[14]As for me, may I never boast about anything except the cross of our Lord Jesus Christ. Because of that cross,* my interest in this world has been crucified, and the world's interest in me has also died. [15]It doesn't matter whether we have been circumcised or not. What counts is whether we have been transformed into a new creation. [16]May God's peace and mercy be upon all who live by this principle; they are the new people of God.*

[17]From now on, don't let anyone trouble me with these things. For I bear on my body the scars that show I belong to Jesus.

[18]Dear brothers and sisters,* may the grace of our Lord Jesus Christ be with your spirit. Amen.

6:14 Or *Because of him.* **6:16** Greek *this principle, and upon the Israel of God.* **6:18** Greek *Brothers.*

▸ **6:7** *See **What you sow you reap**, page 1004.*

Ephesians *God's plan for the church*

Written by Paul while in prison in Rome, Ephesians seeks to remind believers of God's great purposes for his church. Although addressed to the church in Ephesus—an important commercial center on the coast of western Asia Minor (modern Turkey) with a population of about half a million in Paul's day—it was probably also intended to be circulated among other churches in that region. Paul had started the church in Ephesus and had spent two to three years there, and the warmth of his love for the Ephesians comes out in the letter as he encourages them to be the church that God wants them to be—a people reconciled to God and to one another.

What's it all about?

Paul opens his letter with a lavish review of God's blessings that are ours in Christ. He highlights God's wisdom and planning, reminding the church that believers have been showered with God's kindness, adopted as his children, formed into his own people, and filled with his Holy Spirit. He prays that the Ephesians may understand these blessings more and more fully and realize what God's plan in Christ for the church is—and play their part in it (chapter 1).

Paul then outlines the steps in this plan. First, God reconciled each of them as individuals to himself (2:1-10) so that, second, he could reconcile them to one another. He broke down every human barrier in Christ—even that greatest of barriers, the one between Jew and Gentile—and formed them into one new body, the church, the place where God now dwells by his Spirit (2:11-22). Paul describes this as God's "mysterious plan," and it leads him to an outburst of praise (chapter 3).

But now the church has to live out that life in practical ways here on earth (chapters 4–6). Believers must guard their unity (4:1-16) and live as people of light (4:17–5:20), paying particular attention to relationships both in the family and in work settings (5:21–6:9). These are all ways of letting people see how life is transformed when we come to understand God's plan and our place in it. But we will not achieve all this without a fight: We have spiritual enemies who want us, and God, to fail and who are constantly waging battle. However, we do not face these forces unarmed. God has provided us with spiritual weapons that can bring about victory (6:10-20).

OVERVIEW

page 1346

Paul concludes with greetings, mentioning Tychicus, a faithful fellow-worker (6:21) who probably carried this letter to the church.

What does it mean for us?

Ephesians is full of reminders of both God's kindness and God's plan. His kindness is shown in his choosing us even before the world began, making us his own children and giving us his Spirit (chapter 1). We are indeed privileged to now have access to God and to have a firm hope for the future—though such privilege needs not only to be appreciated but also to be lived out in our daily lives. God's children cannot live as they used to live!

But God's kindness does not stand alone; it is part of his plan. We cannot choose to enjoy his kindness but stand apart from that plan. To have the first we must embrace the second. When God called each of us to himself, he called us to one another too, irrespective of the spiritual, ethnic, or social background from which we came. And that is what the church is all about: It is the community where we experience this kindness and live out these privileges together. To be a Christian but not to be part of the church would be impossible in Paul's thinking; the two belong inextricably together. It is impossible to be a solitary Christian! And it is equally impossible to be a Christian who does not have room in their heart for people from different backgrounds, of whatever kind.

Greetings from Paul

1 This letter is from Paul, chosen by the will
of God to be an apostle of Christ Jesus.
I am writing to God's holy people in
Ephesus,* who are faithful followers of
Christ Jesus.
2 May God our Father and the Lord Jesus
Christ give you grace and peace.

Spiritual Blessings

3 All praise to God, the Father of our Lord
Jesus Christ, who has blessed us with every
spiritual blessing in the heavenly realms
because we are united with Christ. 4 Even
before he made the world, God loved us and
chose us in Christ to be holy and without
fault in his eyes. 5 God decided in advance
to adopt us into his own family by bringing
us to himself through Jesus Christ. This is
what he wanted to do, and it gave him great
pleasure. 6 So we praise God for the glorious
grace he has poured out on us who belong to
his dear Son.* 7 He is so rich in kindness and
grace that he purchased our freedom with
the blood of his Son and forgave our sins. 8 He
has showered his kindness on us, along with
all wisdom and understanding.
9 God has now revealed to us his mysterious
will regarding Christ—which is to fulfill his
own good plan. 10 And this is the plan: At the
right time he will bring everything together
under the authority of Christ—everything in
heaven and on earth. 11 Furthermore, because
we are united with Christ, we have received
an inheritance from God,* for he chose us in
advance, and he makes everything work out
according to his plan.
12 God's purpose was that we Jews who
were the first to trust in Christ would bring
praise and glory to God. 13 And now you Gentiles have also heard the truth, the Good
News that God saves you. And when you
believed in Christ, he identified you as his
own* by giving you the Holy Spirit, whom
he promised long ago. 14 The Spirit is God's
guarantee that he will give us the inheritance
he promised and that he has purchased us to
be his own people. He did this so we would
praise and glorify him.

Paul's Prayer for Spiritual Wisdom

15 Ever since I first heard of your strong faith
in the Lord Jesus and your love for God's
people everywhere,* 16 I have not stopped
thanking God for you. I pray for you constantly, 17 asking God, the glorious Father of
our Lord Jesus Christ, to give you spiritual
wisdom* and insight so that you might grow
in your knowledge of God. 18 I pray that your
hearts will be flooded with light so that you
can understand the confident hope he has
given to those he called—his holy people
who are his rich and glorious inheritance.*
19 I also pray that you will understand the
incredible greatness of God's power for us
who believe him. This is the same mighty

power [20]that raised Christ from the dead
and seated him in the place of honor at
God's right hand in the heavenly realms.
[21]Now he is far above any ruler or authority or power or leader or anything else—not
only in this world but also in the world to
come. [22]God has put all things under the
authority of Christ and has made him head
over all things for the benefit of the church.
[23]And the church is his body; it is made full
and complete by Christ, who fills all things
everywhere with himself.

Made Alive with Christ

2 Once you were dead because of your
disobedience and your many sins. [2]You
used to live in sin, just like the rest of the
world, obeying the devil—the commander
of the powers in the unseen world.* He is
the spirit at work in the hearts of those who
refuse to obey God. [3]All of us used to live
that way, following the passionate desires
and inclinations of our sinful nature. By our
very nature we were subject to God's anger,
just like everyone else.

[4]But God is so rich in mercy, and he loved
us so much, [5]that even though we were dead
because of our sins, he gave us life when he
raised Christ from the dead. (It is only by
God's grace that you have been saved!) [6]For
he raised us from the dead along with Christ
and seated us with him in the heavenly
realms because we are united with Christ
Jesus. [7]So God can point to us in all future
ages as examples of the incredible wealth of
his grace and kindness toward us, as shown
in all he has done for us who are united with
Christ Jesus.

[8]God saved you by his grace when you believed. And you can't take credit for this; it
is a gift from God. [9]Salvation is not a reward
for the good things we have done, so none
of us can boast about it. [10]For we are God's
masterpiece. He has created us anew in
Christ Jesus, so we can do the good things
he planned for us long ago.

Oneness and Peace in Christ

[11]Don't forget that you Gentiles used to be
outsiders. You were called "uncircumcised
heathens" by the Jews, who were proud of
their circumcision, even though it affected
only their bodies and not their hearts.
[12]In those days you were living apart from
Christ. You were excluded from citizenship
among the people of Israel, and you did not
know the covenant promises God had made
to them. You lived in this world without God
and without hope. [13]But now you have been
united with Christ Jesus. Once you were far

1:1 The most ancient manuscripts do not include *in Ephesus.* **1:6** Greek *to us in the beloved.* **1:11** Or *we have become God's inheritance.* **1:13** Or *he put his seal on you.* **1:15** Some manuscripts read *your faithfulness to the Lord Jesus and to God's people everywhere.* **1:17** Or *to give you the Spirit of wisdom.* **1:18** Or *called, and the rich and glorious inheritance he has given to his holy people.* **2:2** Greek *obeying the commander of the power of the air.*

▸ **1:19-21** *See* ***God's power****, page 596.*

Ephesus

Ephesus was the leading city of western Asia Minor (modern Turkey). Standing at the intersection of major trade routes and with a link to the Aegean Sea via the Cayster River, it was an important commercial center with a population of about five hundred thousand. It had wonderful buildings, including a theater seating twenty-five thousand and a temple to the goddess Diana (in Greek, Artemis), which was one of the seven wonders of the ancient world. There was also a huge fascination with magic and the occult at Ephesus, and Paul's preaching had led many to burn their books of spells and incantations (Acts 19:17-20). But when his preaching started to affect the economy based on the worship of Artemis, it had led to a riot (Acts 19:23-41). All this helps explain why Paul had to emphasize that Christ alone is "far above any ruler or authority or power or leader or anything else" (Ephesians 1:21).

▸ *See also* ***The riot over Artemis****, page 1267;* ***Paul's Missionary Journeys*** *map, Visual Overview Z15.*

away from God, but now you have been brought near to him through the blood of Christ.

14 For Christ himself has brought peace to us. He united Jews and Gentiles into one people when, in his own body on the cross, he broke down the wall of hostility that separated us. 15 He did this by ending the system of law with its commandments and regulations. He made peace between Jews and Gentiles by creating in himself one new people from the two groups. 16 Together as one body, Christ reconciled both groups to God by means of his death on the cross, and our hostility toward each other was put to death.

17 He brought this Good News of peace to you Gentiles who were far away from him, and peace to the Jews who were near. 18 Now all of us can come to the Father through the same Holy Spirit because of what Christ has done for us.

A Temple for the Lord

19 So now you Gentiles are no longer strangers and foreigners. You are citizens along with all of God's holy people. You are members of God's family. 20 Together, we are his house, built on the foundation of the apostles and the prophets. And the cornerstone is Christ Jesus himself. 21 We are carefully joined together in him, becoming a holy temple for the Lord. 22 Through him you Gentiles are also being made part of this dwelling where God lives by his Spirit.

God's Mysterious Plan Revealed

3 When I think of all this, I, Paul, a prisoner of Christ Jesus for the benefit of you Gentiles* . . . 2 assuming, by the way, that you know God gave me the special responsibility of extending his grace to you Gentiles. 3 As I briefly wrote earlier, God himself revealed his mysterious plan to me. 4 As you read what I have written, you will understand my insight into this plan regarding Christ. 5 God did not reveal it to previous generations, but now by his Spirit he has revealed it to his holy apostles and prophets.

6 And this is God's plan: Both Gentiles and Jews who believe the Good News share equally in the riches inherited by God's children. Both are part of the same body, and both enjoy the promise of blessings because they belong to Christ Jesus.* 7 By God's grace and mighty power, I have been given the privilege of serving him by spreading this Good News.

▸ **2:14** *See* ***Equality****, page 1340.*

The church

Paul's central theme in Ephesians—the church—is clear even from his greeting: "To God's holy people in Ephesus" (Ephesians 1:1), or "God's consecrated people"—in other words, the church. And the importance of the church is seen in his declaration that everything God did through Christ, he did for the church (1:22). Clearly the church is no optional or peripheral matter.

The Greek word for "church"—*ekklēsia*—means "called-out ones"—those called out of their old life into a new life through faith in Christ. While this faith must be personal, it cannot be private. For when we believe in him, we are born again into a new family, and we discover other "called-out ones" who have believed too. It is therefore impossible to be a true Christian without being part of God's family, the church.

Besides this picture of the church as God's family (2:19), Paul uses other pictures in Ephesians, such as God's building (2:20-22), Christ's body (1:23; 4:15-16), and God's army (6:10-20)—all images that speak of the importance of togetherness and solidarity, and the impossibility of isolation.

▸ *See also* ***What kind of church does God want?****, page 1300;* ***Divisions in the church****, page 1305;* ***Belonging to a church****, page 1406;* ***The seven churches of Revelation****, page 1448.*

8 Though I am the least deserving of all
God's people, he graciously gave me the
privilege of telling the Gentiles about the
endless treasures available to them in Christ.
9 I was chosen to explain to everyone* this
mysterious plan that God, the Creator of all
things, had kept secret from the beginning.
10 God's purpose in all this was to use the
church to display his wisdom in its rich
variety to all the unseen rulers and authorities in the heavenly places. 11 This was his
eternal plan, which he carried out through
Christ Jesus our Lord.
12 Because of Christ and our faith in him,*
we can now come boldly and confidently
into God's presence. 13 So please don't lose
heart because of my trials here. I am suffering for you, so you should feel honored.

Paul's Prayer for Spiritual Growth

14 When I think of all this, I fall to my knees
and pray to the Father,* 15 the Creator of
everything in heaven and on earth.* 16 I pray
that from his glorious, unlimited resources
he will empower you with inner strength
through his Spirit. 17 Then Christ will make
his home in your hearts as you trust in
him. Your roots will grow down into God's
love and keep you strong. 18 And may you
have the power to understand, as all God's
people should, how wide, how long, how
high, and how deep his love is. 19 May you
experience the love of Christ, though it is
too great to understand fully. Then you will
be made complete with all the fullness of
life and power that comes from God.
20 Now all glory to God, who is able,
through his mighty power at work within
us, to accomplish infinitely more than we
might ask or think. 21 Glory to him in the
church and in Christ Jesus through all generations forever and ever! Amen.

Unity in the Body

4 Therefore I, a prisoner for serving the
Lord, beg you to lead a life worthy of
your calling, for you have been called by
God. 2 Always be humble and gentle. Be
patient with each other, making allowance
for each other's faults because of your love.

3:1 Paul resumes this thought in verse 14: "When I think of all this, I fall to my knees and pray to the Father." **3:6** Or *because they are united with Christ Jesus.* **3:9** Some manuscripts do not include *to everyone.* **3:12** Or *Because of Christ's faithfulness.* **3:14** Some manuscripts read *the Father of our Lord Jesus Christ.* **3:15** Or *from whom every family in heaven and on earth takes its name.*

Access to God

In New Testament times, the Greek word for "access" (translated "come" in Ephesians 2:18) was used of introducing someone into the presence of a king. Obviously you couldn't just come into his presence. You needed an introduction from someone who knew you, someone who could vouch for you and explain what you wanted and why the king should give you his time. Then, if you were fortunate, you might be granted an audience. And that is exactly what Jesus has done for us, Paul says. Through his death on the cross, Jesus has introduced us into the royal presence of God. Now all of us, whatever our backgrounds, can enter without fear—and whenever we like.

But all this has nothing to do with what we ourselves have done; it is all about God's grace and kindness from start to finish, as Paul has already made clear (2:4-9). Grace—God's undeserved kindness and favor toward sinners—is a consistent theme of Scripture (e.g., Exodus 34:6; Psalm 103:8-18; Joel 2:13; John 1:16-17) and undergirds Paul's writings. It is God's own grace that brings us into his presence. And this grace is not something that comes and goes; it is "where we now stand" (Romans 5:2).

But just because we have free access into God's presence doesn't mean we should take that privilege lightly. Rather, we should come before God in an attitude of dedicating our lives to him, trusting he will use us in fruitful service as we do so.

▶ *See also **Faith and works**, page 1415.*

[3]Make every effort to keep yourselves united in the Spirit, binding yourselves together with peace. [4]For there is one body and one Spirit, just as you have been called to one glorious hope for the future.

[5] There is one Lord, one faith, one
baptism,
[6] one God and Father of all,
who is over all, in all, and living through
all.

[7]However, he has given each one of us a special gift* through the generosity of Christ. [8]That is why the Scriptures say,

"When he ascended to the heights,
he led a crowd of captives
and gave gifts to his people."*

[9]Notice that it says "he ascended." This clearly means that Christ also descended to our lowly world.* [10]And the same one who descended is the one who ascended higher than all the heavens, so that he might fill the entire universe with himself.

[11]Now these are the gifts Christ gave to the church: the apostles, the prophets, the evangelists, and the pastors and teachers. [12]Their responsibility is to equip God's people to do his work and build up the church, the body of Christ. [13]This will continue until we all come to such unity in our faith and knowledge of God's Son that we will be mature in the Lord, measuring up to the full and complete standard of Christ.

[14]Then we will no longer be immature like children. We won't be tossed and blown about by every wind of new teaching. We will not be influenced when people try to trick us with lies so clever they sound like the truth. [15]Instead, we will speak the truth in love, growing in every way more and more like Christ, who is the head of his body, the church. [16]He makes the whole body fit together perfectly. As each part does its own special work, it helps the other parts grow, so that the whole body is healthy and growing and full of love.

Living as Children of Light

[17]With the Lord's authority I say this: Live no longer as the Gentiles do, for they are hopelessly confused. [18]Their minds are full of darkness; they wander far from the life God gives because they have closed their minds and hardened their hearts against him. [19]They have no sense of shame. They

▸ **4:1-6** *See* ***Unity****, page 686.*

The Christian's relationship with the Holy Spirit

If we are going to live the Christian life as God intends, then we need the Holy Spirit. Without him, we will end up frustrated, weary, and defeated, which is why Paul tells us we need to "be filled with the Holy Spirit" (Ephesians 5:18)—literally, "go on being filled with the Spirit."

The imagery of being filled makes it easy to think of the Spirit as a "thing"; and indeed, many of the images of him are things: wind, fire, water, oil. But the Spirit is not a "thing"; he is a person. In fact, along with the Father and the Son, he is one of the three persons of the Trinity, and therefore God himself. That is why we read that the Holy Spirit can experience sorrow as the result of our actions (4:30)—only a person can experience sorrow. Elsewhere we read that the Spirit prays on our behalf (Romans 8:26-27) and can make decisions (1 Corinthians 12:11); he can be lied to (Acts 5:3-4) and resisted (Acts 7:51)—all characteristics of a person.

It is because the Holy Spirit is a person that we can have a relationship with him, and this relationship therefore needs developing. One way to do this is to avoid the kinds of things that offend him, such as those Paul mentions here (Ephesians 4:31; 5:3-7), and to pursue what pleases him (4:32; 5:8-20). After all, the Holy Spirit needs a holy temple (1 Corinthians 6:19).

▸ *See also* ***Life in the Spirit****, page 1291;* ***Living by the Spirit****, page 1342.*

live for lustful pleasure and eagerly practice
every kind of impurity.
[20]But that isn't what you learned about
Christ. [21]Since you have heard about Jesus
and have learned the truth that comes from
him, [22]throw off your old sinful nature and
your former way of life, which is corrupted
by lust and deception. [23]Instead, let the
Spirit renew your thoughts and attitudes.
[24]Put on your new nature, created to be like
God—truly righteous and holy.
[25]So stop telling lies. Let us tell our neighbors the truth, for we are all parts of the
same body. [26]And "don't sin by letting anger
control you."* Don't let the sun go down
while you are still angry, [27]for anger gives a
foothold to the devil.
[28]If you are a thief, quit stealing. Instead,
use your hands for good hard work, and
then give generously to others in need.
[29]Don't use foul or abusive language. Let
everything you say be good and helpful, so
that your words will be an encouragement
to those who hear them.
[30]And do not bring sorrow to God's Holy
Spirit by the way you live. Remember, he
has identified you as his own,* guaranteeing that you will be saved on the day of
redemption.
[31]Get rid of all bitterness, rage, anger,
harsh words, and slander, as well as all types
of evil behavior. [32]Instead, be kind to each
other, tenderhearted, forgiving one another,
just as God through Christ has forgiven you.

Living in the Light

5 Imitate God, therefore, in everything
you do, because you are his dear children. [2]Live a life filled with love, following
the example of Christ. He loved us* and
offered himself as a sacrifice for us, a pleasing aroma to God.
[3]Let there be no sexual immorality, impurity, or greed among you. Such sins have
no place among God's people. [4]Obscene
stories, foolish talk, and coarse jokes—
these are not for you. Instead, let there be
thankfulness to God. [5]You can be sure that
no immoral, impure, or greedy person will
inherit the Kingdom of Christ and of God.
For a greedy person is an idolater, worshiping the things of this world.
[6]Don't be fooled by those who try to
excuse these sins, for the anger of God will
fall on all who disobey him. [7]Don't participate in the things these people do. [8]For
once you were full of darkness, but now you
have light from the Lord. So live as people
of light! [9]For this light within you produces
only what is good and right and true.
[10]Carefully determine what pleases the
Lord. [11]Take no part in the worthless deeds
of evil and darkness; instead, expose them.
[12]It is shameful even to talk about the things
that ungodly people do in secret. [13]But their
evil intentions will be exposed when the
light shines on them, [14]for the light makes
everything visible. This is why it is said,

"Awake, O sleeper,
rise up from the dead,
and Christ will give you light."

Living by the Spirit's Power

[15]So be careful how you live. Don't live like
fools, but like those who are wise. [16]Make
the most of every opportunity in these evil
days. [17]Don't act thoughtlessly, but understand what the Lord wants you to do. [18]Don't
be drunk with wine, because that will ruin
your life. Instead, be filled with the Holy
Spirit, [19]singing psalms and hymns and
spiritual songs among yourselves, and
making music to the Lord in your hearts.
[20]And give thanks for everything to God the
Father in the name of our Lord Jesus Christ.

Spirit-Guided Relationships: Wives and Husbands

[21]And further, submit to one another out of
reverence for Christ.
[22]For wives, this means submit to your
husbands as to the Lord. [23]For a husband is
the head of his wife as Christ is the head of
the church. He is the Savior of his body, the
church. [24]As the church submits to Christ,
so you wives should submit to your husbands in everything.
[25]For husbands, this means love your
wives, just as Christ loved the church. He
gave up his life for her [26]to make her holy
and clean, washed by the cleansing of God's

4:7 Greek *a grace.* **4:8** Ps 68:18. **4:9** Some manuscripts read *to the lower parts of the earth.* **4:26** Ps 4:4. **4:30** Or *has put his seal on you.* **5:2** Some manuscripts read *loved you.*

▸ **4:25** *See **Honesty**, page 707.* **5:16** *See **The use of time**, page 732.*

word.* 27He did this to present her to himself
as a glorious church without a spot or wrinkle
or any other blemish. Instead, she will be
holy and without fault. 28In the same way,
husbands ought to love their wives as they
love their own bodies. For a man who loves
his wife actually shows love for himself. 29No
one hates his own body but feeds and cares
for it, just as Christ cares for the church.
30And we are members of his body.
31As the Scriptures say, "A man leaves his
father and mother and is joined to his wife,
and the two are united into one."* 32This is
a great mystery, but it is an illustration of
the way Christ and the church are one. 33So
again I say, each man must love his wife as
he loves himself, and the wife must respect
her husband.

Children and Parents

6 Children, obey your parents because
you belong to the Lord,* for this is the
right thing to do. 2"Honor your father and
mother." This is the first commandment
with a promise: 3If you honor your father
and mother, "things will go well for you,
and you will have a long life on the earth."*
4Fathers,* do not provoke your children
to anger by the way you treat them. Rather,
bring them up with the discipline and instruction that comes from the Lord.

Slaves and Masters

5Slaves, obey your earthly masters with deep
respect and fear. Serve them sincerely as you
would serve Christ. 6Try to please them all
the time, not just when they are watching
you. As slaves of Christ, do the will of God
with all your heart. 7Work with enthusiasm,
as though you were working for the Lord
rather than for people. 8Remember that the
Lord will reward each one of us for the good
we do, whether we are slaves or free.
9Masters, treat your slaves in the same
way. Don't threaten them; remember, you
both have the same Master in heaven, and
he has no favorites.

The Whole Armor of God

10A final word: Be strong in the Lord and in
his mighty power. 11Put on all of God's armor
so that you will be able to stand firm against
all strategies of the devil. 12For we* are not
fighting against flesh-and-blood enemies,
but against evil rulers and authorities of
the unseen world, against mighty powers
in this dark world, and against evil spirits
in the heavenly places.
13Therefore, put on every piece of God's
armor so you will be able to resist the enemy
in the time of evil. Then after the battle you
will still be standing firm. 14Stand your
ground, putting on the belt of truth and the

▸ **5:31** *See* ***Does marriage still matter to God?****, page 976.*

Submission and relationships

Submission isn't an easy idea to most of us. It brings to mind pictures of letting others trample over us and tell us what to do. But this is not the vision of submission that Paul teaches in Ephesians 5. He starts by saying that submission is a mark of the Spirit-filled life, for 5:21 continues the idea that began in 5:18. The signs of being Spirit-filled include singing (5:19), thanking (5:20), *and* submitting (5:21). And this submission is mutual: All should submit to one another (5:21). Paul goes on to illustrate submission in various everyday relationships. Wives should submit to their husbands, but husbands must love their wives as Christ loves the church (5:22-33); children should submit to parents, but parents must not provoke them (6:1-4); slaves should submit to masters, but masters must remember they too have a master, in heaven (6:5-9). However we seek to work out such relationships practically in our modern world—and different Christians come up with different ways of doing this—willing, mutual submission should always characterize them, for it is a powerful sign of the Spirit-filled life and a powerful testimony to unbelievers.

body armor of God's righteousness. [15]For
shoes, put on the peace that comes from
the Good News so that you will be fully prepared.* [16]In addition to all of these, hold up
the shield of faith to stop the fiery arrows
of the devil.* [17]Put on salvation as your
helmet, and take the sword of the Spirit,
which is the word of God.

[18]Pray in the Spirit at all times and on
every occasion. Stay alert and be persistent in your prayers for all believers
everywhere.*

[19]And pray for me, too. Ask God to give
me the right words so I can boldly explain
God's mysterious plan that the Good News
is for Jews and Gentiles alike.* [20]I am in
chains now, still preaching this message as
God's ambassador. So pray that I will keep
on speaking boldly for him, as I should.

Final Greetings

[21]To bring you up to date, Tychicus will give
you a full report about what I am doing and
how I am getting along. He is a beloved
brother and faithful helper in the Lord's
work. [22]I have sent him to you for this very
purpose—to let you know how we are doing
and to encourage you.

[23]Peace be with you, dear brothers and
sisters,* and may God the Father and the
Lord Jesus Christ give you love with faithfulness. [24]May God's grace be eternally upon
all who love our Lord Jesus Christ.

5:26 Greek *washed by water with the word.* **5:31** Gen 2:24. **6:1** Or *Children, obey your parents who belong to the Lord;* some manuscripts read simply *Children, obey your parents.* **6:2-3** Exod 20:12; Deut 5:16. **6:4** Or *Parents.* **6:12** Some manuscripts read *you.* **6:15** Or *For shoes, put on the readiness to preach the Good News of peace with God.* **6:16** Greek *the evil one.* **6:18** Greek *all of God's holy people.* **6:19** Greek *explain the mystery of the Good News;* some manuscripts read simply *explain the mystery.* **6:23** Greek *brothers.*

Spiritual warfare

Paul has shown throughout Ephesians that God's plan is to bring glory to himself "in the church and in Christ Jesus" (Ephesians 3:21). It is because of this that both Christ and the church are opposed. Christ was endlessly opposed by the devil (e.g., Matthew 4:1-11); and while he utterly defeated him and every demon at the cross (Colossians 2:15), the devil still keeps trying to fight back. Not until the end will he finally be destroyed (Revelation 20:7-10). In the meantime, he fights against the other instrument of God's glory, the church, which is therefore in constant warfare—not against people, but against the spiritual powers at work behind them (Ephesians 6:12).

Yet God gives us armor for this battle (6:11); in fact, the Greek word means the armor of a fully equipped Roman soldier, ready for battle. But the items Paul lists aren't things we are meant to put on in a crisis; we are to put them on *now* so that *when* the devil attacks we are not caught unprepared (6:11). Things like truth, righteousness, peace, faith, salvation, the word of God, and Spirit-inspired prayer (6:14-18)—these are things that should *always* characterize our lives. When we have such things in place, the devil will not be victorious, no matter how hard he fights.

▶ *See also* ***Principalities and powers,*** *page 969.*

Philippians *Real joy*

Although written while Paul was in prison because of his faith, Philippians is a letter full of joy. He writes to a church with whom he has a particularly close relationship, thanking them for the gift they had sent him and telling them about his hardships. In it he shares with them the secret of true contentment, which is not dependent on outward circumstances. Because of Jesus, he says, Christians can be joyful whether or not things seem to be going their way.

Philippi was in Macedonia (modern northeastern Greece), the first place in Europe where Paul established a church (Acts 16).

What's it all about?

Paul begins by giving thanks to God for the church in Philippi and for their partnership with him in spreading the gospel (1:3-11). This was a church that he himself had founded (Acts 16:11-40), so he felt particularly close to them. He tells them about his imprisonment but doesn't want them to feel sorry for him, for it had given him many opportunities to preach the gospel (Philippians 1:12-18). Although he believes he will be released soon, he urges them, whatever happens, to stand firm and to think and act like Jesus (1:18-29). Using what was probably an early Christian hymn, he reminds them how Jesus chose the way of humiliation, suffering, and death but was exalted by God because of this (2:1-11). This way of living is God's will for all Christians, and he is constantly at work within us to enable us to work out our faith (2:12-13). Paul writes of Timothy and Epaphroditus, both of whom are excellent examples of selfless service for others (2:19-30).

Paul then urges the Philippians to rejoice in their Lord and warns them of those who would rob them of this joy—the Judaizers, who wanted to impose the requirements of the old Jewish Law on them (3:1-4). These things were once important to him, but he had sacrificed them all for Christ's sake (3:4-10). He encourages them to be mature, letting go of the past and constantly striving for God's best (3:12-16). But it wasn't just the Judaizers who were a danger; so were those who took the opposite line, insisting that, since Christians were absolutely free, it didn't matter what they did with their bodies anymore (3:17-19). The Philippians should remember that their true home is in heaven, the hope of which should fill their thoughts (3:20-21).

Paul's letter ends with some exhortations (4:2-9) and with an expression of thanks for the gift they had just sent him, for which God would richly bless them (4:10-19).

Throughout this letter, themes of joy and rejoicing appear many times, culminating in Paul's invitation to "always be full of joy in the Lord. I say it again—rejoice!" (4:4).

OVERVIEW

Greetings and thanksgiving for the Philippians · *1:1-11*

How God used Paul's imprisonment for good · *1:12-30*

An exhortation to humble service *2:1-30*

Warnings against those who undermine the gospel, and encouragement to press on · *3:1–4:1*

Final exhortations and thanks for the Philippians' gift · *4:2-23*

What does it mean for us?

Paul's letter is full of confidence that real joy is always possible. He writes from a prison cell, awaiting trial, probably in Rome. From a natural point of view, this is not the sort of situation that evokes confidence or joy in any form. But Paul knew that joy is different from happiness. Happiness is based on happenings, but joy comes from relationships. Paul experienced Christ's friendship when no one else was around, and he knew that nothing could ever take that away. Paul invites us to get to know Jesus and find out what real joy means.

Joy is not a momentary expression of happiness because things have gone well. Rather, it is a deep sense of well-being that comes from our relationship with God through Jesus Christ and the consequent conviction that, whatever happens, God is in control and things will therefore turn out all right eventually. We can know the life of Christ welling up from within us because the Holy Spirit lives in us. As we grow as Christians, we can increasingly experience joy in Jesus Christ, even in all life's ups and downs.

Greetings from Paul

1 This letter is from Paul and Timothy,
slaves of Christ Jesus.
I am writing to all of God's holy people in
Philippi who belong to Christ Jesus, including the church leaders* and deacons.
2 May God our Father and the Lord Jesus
Christ give you grace and peace.

Paul's Thanksgiving and Prayer

3 Every time I think of you, I give thanks to my
God. 4 Whenever I pray, I make my requests
for all of you with joy, 5 for you have been my
partners in spreading the Good News about
Christ from the time you first heard it until
now. 6 And I am certain that God, who began
the good work within you, will continue his
work until it is finally finished on the day
when Christ Jesus returns.
7 So it is right that I should feel as I do
about all of you, for you have a special place
in my heart. You share with me the special
favor of God, both in my imprisonment and
in defending and confirming the truth of the
Good News. 8 God knows how much I love
you and long for you with the tender compassion of Christ Jesus.
9 I pray that your love will overflow
more and more, and that you will keep on
growing in knowledge and understanding.
10 For I want you to understand what really
matters, so that you may live pure and
blameless lives until the day of Christ's
return. 11 May you always be filled with the
fruit of your salvation—the righteous character produced in your life by Jesus Christ*—for
this will bring much glory and praise to God.

Paul's Joy That Christ Is Preached

12 And I want you to know, my dear brothers
and sisters,* that everything that has happened to me here has helped to spread the
Good News. 13 For everyone here, including
the whole palace guard,* knows that I am
in chains because of Christ. 14 And because
of my imprisonment, most of the believers*
here have gained confidence and boldly
speak God's message* without fear.
15 It's true that some are preaching out of
jealousy and rivalry. But others preach about
Christ with pure motives. 16 They preach
because they love me, for they know I have
been appointed to defend the Good News.
17 Those others do not have pure motives as
they preach about Christ. They preach with
selfish ambition, not sincerely, intending to
make my chains more painful to me. 18 But
that doesn't matter. Whether their motives
are false or genuine, the message about
Christ is being preached either way, so
I rejoice. And I will continue to rejoice. 19 For
I know that as you pray for me and the Spirit
of Jesus Christ helps me, this will lead to my
deliverance.

Paul's Life for Christ

20 For I fully expect and hope that I will never
be ashamed, but that I will continue to be
bold for Christ, as I have been in the past.
And I trust that my life will bring honor to
Christ, whether I live or die. 21 For to me,
living means living for Christ, and dying is

1:1 Or *overseers*, or *bishops*. **1:11** Greek *with the fruit of righteousness through Jesus Christ*. **1:12** Greek *brothers*. **1:13** Greek *including all the Praetorium*. **1:14a** Greek *brothers in the Lord*. **1:14b** Some manuscripts read *speak the message*.

even better. 22But if I live, I can do more
fruitful work for Christ. So I really don't
know which is better. 23I'm torn between
two desires: I long to go and be with Christ,
which would be far better for me. 24But for
your sakes, it is better that I continue to live.
25Knowing this, I am convinced that I will
remain alive so I can continue to help all
of you grow and experience the joy of your
faith. 26And when I come to you again, you
will have even more reason to take pride
in Christ Jesus because of what he is doing
through me.

Live as Citizens of Heaven

27Above all, you must live as citizens
of heaven, conducting yourselves in a
manner worthy of the Good News about
Christ. Then, whether I come and see you
again or only hear about you, I will know
that you are standing together with one
spirit and one purpose, fighting together
for the faith, which is the Good News.
28Don't be intimidated in any way by your
enemies. This will be a sign to them that
they are going to be destroyed, but that
you are going to be saved, even by God
himself. 29For you have been given not
only the privilege of trusting in Christ but
also the privilege of suffering for him. 30We
are in this struggle together. You have seen
my struggle in the past, and you know that
I am still in the midst of it.

Have the Attitude of Christ

2 Is there any encouragement from belonging to Christ? Any comfort from his
love? Any fellowship together in the Spirit?
Are your hearts tender and compassionate? 2Then make me truly happy by agreeing wholeheartedly with each other, loving
one another, and working together with one
mind and purpose.
3Don't be selfish; don't try to impress
others. Be humble, thinking of others as
better than yourselves. 4Don't look out only
for your own interests, but take an interest
in others, too.
5You must have the same attitude that
Christ Jesus had.

6 Though he was God,*
he did not think of equality with God
as something to cling to.
7 Instead, he gave up his divine privileges*;
he took the humble position of a slave*
and was born as a human being.
When he appeared in human form,*
8 he humbled himself in obedience to
God
and died a criminal's death on a cross.

9 Therefore, God elevated him to the place
of highest honor
and gave him the name above all
other names,
10 that at the name of Jesus every knee
should bow,

▸ **1:23** *See* ***Heaven****, page 1451.*

Philippi

Philippi was a leading city of Macedonia (modern northeastern Greece), the first place where Paul established a church in Europe (Acts 16:6-40) and therefore a place he felt much affection for, as is clear throughout the letter to the Philippians. Philippi was located on the main highway (the Via Egnatia) that ran from the eastern provinces to Rome, and this had brought much prosperity. The city was named after Philip II, father of Alexander the Great, so it was proud of its history. But it was even more proud to have been granted the status of a Roman colony, which meant its citizens had legal rights and privileges just like those of Rome itself (e.g., Acts 16:20-21). They were exempt from certain taxes and had better land rights, so many former soldiers settled there. Philippi was almost entirely Gentile; in fact, there weren't even enough Jews for a synagogue (Acts 16:13), which explains why there are no quotations from the Old Testament in this letter.

▸ *See also* ***Lydia****, page 1262;* ***Paul's Missionary Journeys*** *map, Visual Overview Z15.*

in heaven and on earth and under the
earth,
11 and every tongue declare that Jesus
Christ is Lord,
to the glory of God the Father.

Shine Brightly for Christ

12 Dear friends, you always followed my instructions when I was with you. And now that
I am away, it is even more important. Work
hard to show the results of your salvation,
obeying God with deep reverence and fear.
13 For God is working in you, giving you the
desire and the power to do what pleases him.
14 Do everything without complaining
and arguing, 15 so that no one can criticize
you. Live clean, innocent lives as children
of God, shining like bright lights in a world
full of crooked and perverse people. 16 Hold
firmly to the word of life; then, on the day
of Christ's return, I will be proud that I did
not run the race in vain and that my work
was not useless. 17 But I will rejoice even if I
lose my life, pouring it out like a liquid offering to God,* just like your faithful service
is an offering to God. And I want all of you
to share that joy. 18 Yes, you should rejoice,
and I will share your joy.

Paul Commends Timothy

19 If the Lord Jesus is willing, I hope to send
Timothy to you soon for a visit. Then he
can cheer me up by telling me how you
are getting along. 20 I have no one else like
Timothy, who genuinely cares about your
welfare. 21 All the others care only for themselves and not for what matters to Jesus
Christ. 22 But you know how Timothy has
proved himself. Like a son with his father,
he has served with me in preaching the
Good News. 23 I hope to send him to you
just as soon as I find out what is going to
happen to me here. 24 And I have confidence
from the Lord that I myself will come to see
you soon.

Paul Commends Epaphroditus

25 Meanwhile, I thought I should send
Epaphroditus back to you. He is a true
brother, co-worker, and fellow soldier. And
he was your messenger to help me in my
need. 26 I am sending him because he has
been longing to see you, and he was very
distressed that you heard he was ill. 27 And
he certainly was ill; in fact, he almost died.
But God had mercy on him—and also on
me, so that I would not have one sorrow
after another.
28 So I am all the more anxious to send
him back to you, for I know you will be glad
to see him, and then I will not be so worried

2:6 Or *Being in the form of God.* **2:7a** Greek *he emptied himself.* **2:7b** Or *the form of a slave.* **2:7c** Some English translations put this phrase in verse 8. **2:17** Greek *I will rejoice even if I am to be poured out as a liquid offering.*

Fellowship

When Christians speak of "having fellowship" nowadays, they often simply mean "sharing friendship," perhaps over a cup of coffee or a meal after a church service. But in the New Testament "fellowship" is something much more powerful. The Greek word for fellowship (*koinōnia*) originally meant "partnership"—like a business partnership where two or more parties invest time, energy, and resources for a common purpose. And that's what being a Christian is all about: not just believing the same things as others, but together with them investing everything we are and have for the adventure that God has called us into.

In Philippians 1:5, when Paul expresses gratitude that the Philippians have been his partners (translating *koinōnia*) in spreading the Good News, he is not just thinking about happy meetings, but rather the tangible ways in which they partnered in the gospel with him since he first took the gospel to Philippi (Acts 16). When the church was born at Pentecost in Jerusalem, "All the believers devoted themselves to the apostles' teaching, and to fellowship (*koinōnia*)"—not just meetings, but sharing their lives and resources, with powerful consequences (Acts 2:42-47). True fellowship will always have practical outcomes.

about you. [29]Welcome him in the Lord's
love* and with great joy, and give him the
honor that people like him deserve. [30]For
he risked his life for the work of Christ,
and he was at the point of death while
doing for me what you couldn't do from far
away.

The Priceless Value of Knowing Christ

3 Whatever happens, my dear brothers
and sisters,* rejoice in the Lord. I never
get tired of telling you these things, and I do
it to safeguard your faith.

[2]Watch out for those dogs, those people
who do evil, those mutilators who say you
must be circumcised to be saved. [3]For we
who worship by the Spirit of God* are the
ones who are truly circumcised. We rely on
what Christ Jesus has done for us. We put
no confidence in human effort, [4]though I
could have confidence in my own effort if
anyone could. Indeed, if others have reason
for confidence in their own efforts, I have
even more!

[5]I was circumcised when I was eight days
old. I am a pure-blooded citizen of Israel
and a member of the tribe of Benjamin—a
real Hebrew if there ever was one! I was a
member of the Pharisees, who demand the
strictest obedience to the Jewish law. [6]I was
so zealous that I harshly persecuted the
church. And as for righteousness, I obeyed
the law without fault.

[7]I once thought these things were
valuable, but now I consider them worthless because of what Christ has done. [8]Yes,
everything else is worthless when compared with the infinite value of knowing
Christ Jesus my Lord. For his sake I have
discarded everything else, counting it all
as garbage, so that I could gain Christ [9]and
become one with him. I no longer count on
my own righteousness through obeying the
law; rather, I become righteous through
faith in Christ.* For God's way of making
us right with himself depends on faith.
[10]I want to know Christ and experience
the mighty power that raised him from the
dead. I want to suffer with him, sharing
in his death, [11]so that one way or another
I will experience the resurrection from the
dead!

Pressing toward the Goal

[12]I don't mean to say that I have already
achieved these things or that I have already
reached perfection. But I press on to possess
that perfection for which Christ Jesus first
possessed me. [13]No, dear brothers and
sisters, I have not achieved it,* but I focus

The humility of Christ

For Paul, unity in the church was of prime importance. But unity is impossible without humility—the kind of humility that puts oneself last and others first. And Paul knows no better place to find an example of the kind of humility he means than in Christ himself. This humility is the subject of the early Christian hymn in Philippians 2:6-11—a hymn Paul may have written himself, or it may have been written by someone else and used by him. The hymn covers Christ's pre-existence (2:6), incarnation (2:7), crucifixion (2:8), resurrection and ascension (2:9), and exaltation (2:10-11). And running through it all is his humility—the humility of the one who was God-become-man, with all the limitations that involved. And in becoming a man, he did not choose to become some great king or ruler but constantly took the lowest place in life, always ready to serve others rather than to be served—so much so that the hymn describes him metaphorically as "a slave." From the heights of being God to the depths of being "a slave"! Such was the humility that Christ willingly demonstrated—not to gain anything for his own sake (after all, he was God, so he could achieve nothing higher), but for ours. Such humility always attracts God's blessing; and such humility is the attitude that Christians should adopt toward one another (2:5).

▶ *See also **Humility**, page 1134.*

on this one thing: Forgetting the past and
looking forward to what lies ahead, 14I press
on to reach the end of the race and receive
the heavenly prize for which God, through
Christ Jesus, is calling us.
15Let all who are spiritually mature agree
on these things. If you disagree on some
point, I believe God will make it plain to
you. 16But we must hold on to the progress
we have already made.
17Dear brothers and sisters, pattern your
lives after mine, and learn from those who
follow our example. 18For I have told you
often before, and I say it again with tears in
my eyes, that there are many whose conduct
shows they are really enemies of the cross
of Christ. 19They are headed for destruction. Their god is their appetite, they brag
about shameful things, and they think only
about this life here on earth. 20But we are
citizens of heaven, where the Lord Jesus
Christ lives. And we are eagerly waiting for
him to return as our Savior. 21He will take
our weak mortal bodies and change them
into glorious bodies like his own, using the
same power with which he will bring everything under his control.

4 Therefore, my dear brothers and
sisters,* stay true to the Lord. I love you
and long to see you, dear friends, for you
are my joy and the crown I receive for my
work.

Words of Encouragement

2Now I appeal to Euodia and Syntyche.
Please, because you belong to the Lord,
settle your disagreement. 3And I ask you,
my true partner,* to help these two women,
for they worked hard with me in telling
others the Good News. They worked along
with Clement and the rest of my co-workers,
whose names are written in the Book of Life.
4Always be full of joy in the Lord. I say
it again—rejoice! 5Let everyone see that you
are considerate in all you do. Remember,
the Lord is coming soon.*
6Don't worry about anything; instead,
pray about everything. Tell God what you
need, and thank him for all he has done.
7Then you will experience God's peace,

2:29 Greek *in the Lord*. **3:1** Greek *brothers;* also in 3:13, 17. **3:3** Some manuscripts read *worship God in spirit;* one early manuscript reads *worship in spirit*. **3:9** Or *through the faithfulness of Christ*. **3:13** Some manuscripts read *not yet achieved it*. **4:1** Greek *brothers;* also in 4:8. **4:3** Or *loyal Syzygus*. **4:5** Greek *the Lord is near*.

▸**4:7** *See **Peace**, page 774.*

Pressing on

No one ever achieved anything by just starting; we have to see our undertakings through to the end. And the Christian life is no different. Believing in Jesus is a great beginning; but if that is where it ends, our faith will never grow, and discouragements will quickly wear us down. That's why the Bible often encourages us to press on in our walk with God.

In Philippians 3:13-14, Paul uses imagery that would have been familiar to his readers. Greeks were passionate about sport, especially competitive games (like our modern Olympics); so he likens the Christian faith to being in a race. He imagines himself as a runner forgetting the track already covered (for constantly thinking about that would make him lose focus) and looking straight ahead, straining for "the end of the race"—the Greek word used here meant "the finish line." That's what Christians should be like, he says: runners in a race, constantly pressing on, determined to win the prize.

Just as there are things that help or hinder an athlete's training, so there are things that help or hinder us, too. The following help us: prayer, Bible reading, fellowship, and worship. The following hinder us and need to be discarded: laziness, sin, and mixing with the wrong people (Hebrews 12:1). But we are not left to our own efforts; God is constantly working within us to bring about his purposes (Philippians 2:12-13).

which exceeds anything we can understand. His peace will guard your hearts and
minds as you live in Christ Jesus.
8 And now, dear brothers and sisters, one
final thing. Fix your thoughts on what is
true, and honorable, and right, and pure,
and lovely, and admirable. Think about
things that are excellent and worthy of
praise. 9 Keep putting into practice all you
learned and received from me—everything
you heard from me and saw me doing. Then
the God of peace will be with you.

Paul's Thanks for Their Gifts

10 How I praise the Lord that you are concerned about me again. I know you have
always been concerned for me, but you didn't
have the chance to help me. 11 Not that I was
ever in need, for I have learned how to be
content with whatever I have. 12 I know how
to live on almost nothing or with everything.
I have learned the secret of living in every
situation, whether it is with a full stomach
or empty, with plenty or little. 13 For I can do
everything through Christ,* who gives me
strength. 14 Even so, you have done well to
share with me in my present difficulty.
15 As you know, you Philippians were
the only ones who gave me financial help
when I first brought you the Good News
and then traveled on from Macedonia. No
other church did this. 16 Even when I was in
Thessalonica you sent help more than once.
17 I don't say this because I want a gift from
you. Rather, I want you to receive a reward
for your kindness.
18 At the moment I have all I need—and
more! I am generously supplied with the
gifts you sent me with Epaphroditus.
They are a sweet-smelling sacrifice that
is acceptable and pleasing to God. 19 And
this same God who takes care of me will
supply all your needs from his glorious
riches, which have been given to us in
Christ Jesus.
20 Now all glory to God our Father forever
and ever! Amen.

Paul's Final Greetings

21 Give my greetings to each of God's holy
people—all who belong to Christ Jesus. The
brothers who are with me send you their
greetings. 22 And all the rest of God's people
send you greetings, too, especially those in
Caesar's household.
23 May the grace of the Lord Jesus Christ be
with your spirit.*

4:13 Greek *through the one.* **4:23** Some manuscripts add *Amen.*

Joy

It's easy to be joyful when things go well. But, from a human perspective, things weren't going well for Paul; he was in chains, imprisoned in Rome (Philippians 1:13). And yet joy is a constant theme of this letter (1:4, 18, 25; 2:2, 17-18, 29; 3:1; 4:1, 4, 10). Why could Paul be so joyful when things were so difficult? Because he knew that true joy was not a happiness that depended on circumstances, but rather was the deep contentment that came from knowing God was in control and that therefore things would always turn out well in the end (e.g., 1:12-14). That is why he writes, "*Always* be full of joy in the Lord"—and lest they misunderstood, he adds, "I say it again—rejoice!" (4:4). Yes, God's people can rejoice, even in the face of opposition or persecution (e.g., James 1:2-4; 1 Peter 4:12-16).

The opposite of joy is worry—fear that things won't work out as we had hoped. So Paul says, "Don't worry about anything" (Philippians 4:6). Why? Because while things may not work out as we had hoped, they will always work out as God has ordained, which is far better. Joy, part of the fruit of the Spirit (Galatians 5:22), should characterize God's people, for his kingdom is about "living a life of goodness and peace and joy in the Holy Spirit" (Romans 14:17).

Colossians *Christ is supreme over all things*

Paul wrote Colossians from prison in Rome to a church he had never visited. It seems to have been founded by Epaphras (1:7), who was probably converted during the time Paul spent in nearby Ephesus (Acts 19:1-10). In this letter, Paul tackles some ideas that had trickled into the church from other religions and philosophies of the day and that had led to confused thinking. He demonstrates the supremacy of Christ over all things, thus showing that in him believers have everything they need; so they do not need to look to anything or anyone else. He wrote this letter around the same time as Ephesians, while in prison (or more accurately, house arrest) in Rome.

What's it all about?

Pagan ideas, secular philosophies, and folk religion had all flourished in Colosse in Asia Minor (modern Turkey). Some of the church members had taken various parts of all these and tried to blend them with their Christian faith. Some were claiming the importance of particular ceremonies or holy days (2:16-17); others, the importance of angel-worship (2:18) or asceticism (2:20-21); still others the importance of philosophy and human wisdom (2:8). But for Paul, all these were distractions from Christ, in whom, he says, "lie hidden all the treasures of wisdom and knowledge" (2:3). He alone is all they need.

Paul begins by launching into a review of all that Christ is and has done (1:13-20). When we see Christ, he says, we see God. Christ is the creator of everything and is the "head" of the church. And because of his death on the cross, we can now be reconciled to God (1:20, 22).

Paul then turns to the practical implications of Christ's death and its consequences. Christians must draw their life from Christ, not from other things. He alone is all they need, so they do not need to go looking elsewhere for so-called spiritual insights. If believers hold closely to him, they will not be deceived.

Paul urges them to set their minds on things above—but warns them not to be so heavenly minded that they are no earthly good. Love for God should spill over into love for others—fellow believers, spouses, children, parents, slaves, and masters (chapter 3). They should constantly pray and make the most of every opportunity to share the Good News and to live godly lives.

He concludes by sending greetings from some of his co-workers (4:7-18): Tychicus, who delivered both this letter and Ephesians; Onesimus, a runaway slave (see the letter to Philemon); Aristarchus, a fellow prisoner; Mark, who

OVERVIEW

wrote the Gospel bearing his name; Epaphras, the founder of the church at Colosse (1:7); Luke, who also wrote a Gospel; Demas, who would later desert Paul (2 Timothy 4:10); and Archippus, a "fellow soldier" (Philemon 1:2). This shows us that Paul didn't operate alone in his ministry but always worked in a team.

What does it mean for us?

Most of us are fascinated by what's new, whether it is a new idea or a new product; and if we are one of the first to see or obtain it, we can easily become proud. The Colossians certainly became proud of what they thought were their new discoveries; but in fact, all this had done was to take them away from Christ, God's ultimate revelation. Their so-called discoveries had simply misled them. This is why Paul spends so much time focusing on Christ and his superiority over all things (in fact, Colossians is one of the most Christ-centered books in the New Testament).

When we are tempted to embrace some preacher's latest idea that sounds so good and promises so much, or when we read the latest Christian book with its promises of success if only we will follow the model it proposes, we should stop and ask ourselves, Is this adding to Jesus, like the Colossians did? Does it actually push Jesus to one side rather than exalt him alone? The Colossians certainly didn't set out to do that, but that's where their embracing of all these so-called deeper spiritual ideas led them. And the same can happen to us unless we keep Jesus—the Jesus of the Bible—central in all our thinking and living.

Greetings from Paul

1 This letter is from Paul, chosen by the will of God to be an apostle of Christ Jesus, and from our brother Timothy.

2 We are writing to God's holy people in the city of Colosse, who are faithful brothers and sisters* in Christ.

May God our Father give you grace and peace.

Paul's Thanksgiving and Prayer

3 We always pray for you, and we give thanks to God, the Father of our Lord Jesus Christ.
4 For we have heard of your faith in Christ Jesus and your love for all of God's people,
5 which come from your confident hope of what God has reserved for you in heaven. You have had this expectation ever since you first heard the truth of the Good News.

6 This same Good News that came to you is going out all over the world. It is bearing fruit everywhere by changing lives, just as it changed your lives from the day you first heard and understood the truth about God's wonderful grace.

7 You learned about the Good News from Epaphras, our beloved co-worker. He is Christ's faithful servant, and he is helping us on your behalf.*
8 He has told us about the love for others that the Holy Spirit has given you.

9 So we have not stopped praying for you since we first heard about you. We ask God to give you complete knowledge of his will and to give you spiritual wisdom and understanding.
10 Then the way you live will always honor and please the Lord, and your lives will produce every kind of good fruit. All the while, you will grow as you learn to know God better and better.

11 We also pray that you will be strengthened with all his glorious power so you will have all the endurance and patience you need. May you be filled with joy,*
12 always thanking the Father. He has enabled you to share in the inheritance that belongs to his people, who live in the light.
13 For he has rescued us from the kingdom of darkness and transferred us into the Kingdom of his dear Son,
14 who purchased our freedom* and forgave our sins.

Christ Is Supreme

15 Christ is the visible image of the invisible
God.
He existed before anything was created
and is supreme over all creation,*
16 for through him God created everything
in the heavenly realms and on earth.
He made the things we can see
and the things we can't see—
such as thrones, kingdoms, rulers, and
authorities in the unseen world.

Everything was created through him
and for him.
17 He existed before anything else,
and he holds all creation together.
18 Christ is also the head of the church,
which is his body.
He is the beginning,
supreme over all who rise from the
dead.*
So he is first in everything.
19 For God in all his fullness
was pleased to live in Christ,
20 and through him God reconciled
everything to himself.
He made peace with everything in
heaven and on earth
by means of Christ's blood on the
cross.

21 This includes you who were once far
away from God. You were his enemies, separated from him by your evil thoughts and
actions. 22 Yet now he has reconciled you to
himself through the death of Christ in his
physical body. As a result, he has brought
you into his own presence, and you are
holy and blameless as you stand before him
without a single fault.
23 But you must continue to believe this
truth and stand firmly in it. Don't drift away
from the assurance you received when you
heard the Good News. The Good News has
been preached all over the world, and I,
Paul, have been appointed as God's servant
to proclaim it.

Paul's Work for the Church

24 I am glad when I suffer for you in my
body, for I am participating in the sufferings of Christ that continue for his
body, the church. 25 God has given me the
responsibility of serving his church by proclaiming his entire message to you. 26 This
message was kept secret for centuries and
generations past, but now it has been revealed to God's people. 27 For God wanted
them to know that the riches and glory of
Christ are for you Gentiles, too. And this is
the secret: Christ lives in you. This gives you
assurance of sharing his glory.
28 So we tell others about Christ, warning
everyone and teaching everyone with all
the wisdom God has given us. We want
to present them to God, perfect* in their
relationship to Christ. 29 That's why I work
and struggle so hard, depending on Christ's
mighty power that works within me.

2 I want you to know how much I have
agonized for you and for the church
at Laodicea, and for many other believers
who have never met me personally. 2 I want
them to be encouraged and knit together
by strong ties of love. I want them to have
complete confidence that they understand
God's mysterious plan, which is Christ
himself. 3 In him lie hidden all the treasures
of wisdom and knowledge.
4 I am telling you this so no one will deceive
you with well-crafted arguments. 5 For though
I am far away from you, my heart is with you.
And I rejoice that you are living as you should
and that your faith in Christ is strong.

Freedom from Rules and New Life in Christ

6 And now, just as you accepted Christ Jesus
as your Lord, you must continue to follow

1:2 Greek *faithful brothers.* **1:7** Or *he is ministering on your behalf;* some manuscripts read *he is ministering on our behalf.* **1:11** Or *all the patience and endurance you need with joy.* **1:14** Some manuscripts add *with his blood.* **1:15** Or *He is the firstborn of all creation.* **1:18** Or *the firstborn from the dead.* **1:28** Or *mature.*

Colosse

By New Testament times, Colosse's glory days were past. It had once been a leading city in Asia Minor (modern Turkey), located in the Lycus valley on the great east-west trade route that ran from Mesopotamia in the east to Ephesus on the Aegean Sea, one hundred miles to the west of Colosse. But by the time of this letter it was now a second-rate market town, overshadowed by its neighbors Laodicea and Hierapolis (see Colossians 4:13) that lay further down the valley. Archaeological evidence shows that, besides the worship of the main Roman gods, there were also many "mystery cults" (with their supposed secret knowledge and secret practices) in Colosse, as well as a Jewish presence.

him. [7]Let your roots grow down into him,
and let your lives be built on him. Then
your faith will grow strong in the truth you
were taught, and you will overflow with
thankfulness.

[8]Don't let anyone capture you with empty
philosophies and high-sounding nonsense
that come from human thinking and from
the spiritual powers* of this world, rather
than from Christ. [9]For in Christ lives all the
fullness of God in a human body.* [10]So you
also are complete through your union with
Christ, who is the head over every ruler and
authority.

[11]When you came to Christ, you were
"circumcised," but not by a physical procedure. Christ performed a spiritual circumcision—the cutting away of your sinful
nature.* [12]For you were buried with Christ
when you were baptized. And with him you
were raised to new life because you trusted
the mighty power of God, who raised Christ
from the dead.

[13]You were dead because of your sins
and because your sinful nature was not yet
cut away. Then God made you alive with
Christ, for he forgave all our sins. [14]He canceled the record of the charges against us
and took it away by nailing it to the cross.
[15]In this way, he disarmed* the spiritual
rulers and authorities. He shamed them
publicly by his victory over them on the
cross.

[16]So don't let anyone condemn you for
what you eat or drink, or for not celebrating certain holy days or new moon ceremonies or Sabbaths. [17]For these rules are
only shadows of the reality yet to come.
And Christ himself is that reality. [18]Don't
let anyone condemn you by insisting on
pious self-denial or the worship of angels,*
saying they have had visions about these
things. Their sinful minds have made
them proud, [19]and they are not connected
to Christ, the head of the body. For he
holds the whole body together with its
joints and ligaments, and it grows as God
nourishes it.

[20]You have died with Christ, and he has
set you free from the spiritual powers of
this world. So why do you keep on following the rules of the world, such as, [21]"Don't
handle! Don't taste! Don't touch!"? [22]Such
rules are mere human teachings about
things that deteriorate as we use them.
[23]These rules may seem wise because they
require strong devotion, pious self-denial,
and severe bodily discipline. But they
provide no help in conquering a person's
evil desires.

The deity of Jesus Christ

Jesus isn't merely another prophet or holy man; he is none other than God himself, come among us in human form (see *The Incarnation*, page 1199). Paul says he is "the visible image of the invisible God" (Colossians 1:15). The word translated "image" means "exact replica," just as a rubber stamp produces an exact replica of itself on paper. Look at Jesus, and you are looking at God himself (see also Hebrews 1:3)—a fact underlined by Paul's ascribing the role of creator (Colossians 1:16; see Genesis 1:1) and sustainer of everything (Colossians 1:17) to him. He reinforces this by saying that "he existed before anything was created" (1:15)—literally, that he was "the firstborn of all creation" (1:15, see footnote). This phrase in the original Greek doesn't mean that Jesus was created, however, for he "existed before anything else" (1:17); rather, Paul is thinking of the rights and privileges which only the firstborn son had. And, making his point even clearer, he concludes by saying that "God in all his fullness was pleased to live in Christ" (1:19).

John's Gospel begins by affirming the same truth: "In the beginning the Word already existed. The Word was with God, and the Word was God. . . . The Word became human and made his home among us" (John 1:1, 14). The deity of Jesus was not a later idea imposed by the church, as some claim, for even Jesus' opponents understood clearly who he himself claimed to be (e.g., John 5:18).

Living the New Life

3 Since you have been raised to new life
with Christ, set your sights on the realities of heaven, where Christ sits in the place
of honor at God's right hand. 2Think about
the things of heaven, not the things of earth.
3For you died to this life, and your real life
is hidden with Christ in God. 4And when
Christ, who is your* life, is revealed to the
whole world, you will share in all his glory.
5So put to death the sinful, earthly things
lurking within you. Have nothing to do
with sexual immorality, impurity, lust, and
evil desires. Don't be greedy, for a greedy
person is an idolater, worshiping the things
of this world. 6Because of these sins, the
anger of God is coming.* 7You used to do
these things when your life was still part of
this world. 8But now is the time to get rid
of anger, rage, malicious behavior, slander,
and dirty language. 9Don't lie to each other,
for you have stripped off your old sinful
nature and all its wicked deeds. 10Put on
your new nature, and be renewed as you
learn to know your Creator and become
like him. 11In this new life, it doesn't matter
if you are a Jew or a Gentile,* circumcised
or uncircumcised, barbaric, uncivilized,*
slave, or free. Christ is all that matters, and
he lives in all of us.
12Since God chose you to be the holy
people he loves, you must clothe yourselves with tenderhearted mercy, kindness, humility, gentleness, and patience.
13Make allowance for each other's faults,
and forgive anyone who offends you. Remember, the Lord forgave you, so you
must forgive others. 14Above all, clothe
yourselves with love, which binds us all
together in perfect harmony. 15And let the
peace that comes from Christ rule in your
hearts. For as members of one body you
are called to live in peace. And always be
thankful.
16Let the message about Christ, in all its
richness, fill your lives. Teach and counsel
each other with all the wisdom he gives.
Sing psalms and hymns and spiritual songs
to God with thankful hearts. 17And whatever
you do or say, do it as a representative of
the Lord Jesus, giving thanks through him
to God the Father.

Instructions for Christian Households

18Wives, submit to your husbands, as is
fitting for those who belong to the Lord.

2:8 Or *the spiritual principles;* also in 2:20. **2:9** Or *in him dwells all the completeness of the Godhead bodily.* **2:11** Greek *the cutting away of the body of the flesh.* **2:15** Or *he stripped off.* **2:18** Or *or worshiping with angels.* **3:4** Some manuscripts read *our.* **3:6** Some manuscripts read *is coming on all who disobey him.* **3:11a** Greek *a Greek.* **3:11b** Greek *Barbarian, Scythian.*

Living with differences

There is something in the heart of sinful human beings that constantly leads each one of us to think that we are right and everyone else is wrong. Even among Christians this can be a problem, and we can be quick to despise or cut off those who think or live differently from us.

That's what the Colossians were doing. Some insisted that certain festivals and holy days should be kept (Colossians 2:16) and looked down on those who didn't observe them. Some promoted asceticism or angel worship, claiming to have received special revelations (2:18). And some wanted a Christianity full of rules (2:20-21). But Paul would have none of this, as he makes plain in 2:16-23; for while it is one thing to say that something helps you in your walk with Jesus, it is quite another to impose it on a fellow Christian and to look down on them if they don't embrace it too. We have to learn to live with differences. What does it matter if they choose to fast regularly and you don't? If they kneel to pray and you sit or stand? If they have a different view on some aspect of Christ's return? As long as we hold to fundamental biblical teaching on who Jesus is and what he did, then there is room for diversity on other things. Christians should be bighearted toward one another, remembering that we are called to build up the body, not tear it apart (see 2:19).

▸ *See also* ***Freedom and responsibility****, page 1311.*

19 Husbands, love your wives and never treat them harshly.

20 Children, always obey your parents, for this pleases the Lord. 21 Fathers, do not aggravate your children, or they will become discouraged.

22 Slaves, obey your earthly masters in everything you do. Try to please them all the time, not just when they are watching you. Serve them sincerely because of your reverent fear of the Lord. 23 Work willingly at whatever you do, as though you were working for the Lord rather than for people. 24 Remember that the Lord will give you an inheritance as your reward, and that the Master you are serving is Christ.* 25 But if you do what is wrong, you will be paid back for the wrong you have done. For God has no favorites.

4 Masters, be just and fair to your slaves. Remember that you also have a Master—in heaven.

An Encouragement for Prayer

2 Devote yourselves to prayer with an alert mind and a thankful heart. 3 Pray for us, too, that God will give us many opportunities to speak about his mysterious plan concerning Christ. That is why I am here in chains. 4 Pray that I will proclaim this message as clearly as I should.

5 Live wisely among those who are not believers, and make the most of every opportunity. 6 Let your conversation be gracious and attractive* so that you will have the right response for everyone.

Paul's Final Instructions and Greetings

7 Tychicus will give you a full report about how I am getting along. He is a beloved brother and faithful helper who serves with me in the Lord's work. 8 I have sent him to you for this very purpose—to let you know how we are doing and to encourage you. 9 I am also sending Onesimus, a faithful and beloved brother, one of your own people. He and Tychicus will tell you everything that's happening here.

10 Aristarchus, who is in prison with me, sends you his greetings, and so does Mark, Barnabas's cousin. As you were instructed before, make Mark welcome if he comes your way. 11 Jesus (the one we call Justus) also sends his greetings. These are the only Jewish believers among my co-workers; they are working with me here for the Kingdom of God. And what a comfort they have been!

12 Epaphras, a member of your own fellowship and a servant of Christ Jesus,

▸ **3:18–4:1** *See **Submission and relationships**, page 1352.*

Thankfulness

Thankfulness is a recurring theme in Colossians—Paul reminds his readers five times to be thankful (Colossians 1:12; 2:7; 3:15, 17; 4:2). Why is there a need for so many reminders? Because people so easily forget to be grateful, and often, what we at first see as a privilege quickly becomes a right.

At the head of our list of those to whom we should be thankful is, of course, God himself. If our prayers seldom contain much thanksgiving, there is clearly something wrong. But there are others to whom we should be thankful too: our parents, our teachers, our church leaders, our employer, to name just a few. In some cultures, people are reluctant to express gratitude, especially when it involves thanking those who are perceived as being of lower social standing, such as servants. But Christians of whatever culture are called to be different. Our whole lives should be full of thanksgiving, not just to God but to all who serve us in any way, even—no, especially—those we feel are lower down the social ladder. And if it is not the cultural norm to do this in our own nation, then we are proclaiming that there is a higher and better culture: that of the Kingdom of God.

▸ *See also **Thanksgiving**, page 665.*

sends you his greetings. He always prays
earnestly for you, asking God to make you
strong and perfect, fully confident that
you are following the whole will of God. 13I
can assure you that he prays hard for you
and also for the believers in Laodicea and
Hierapolis.
14Luke, the beloved doctor, sends his
greetings, and so does Demas. 15Please give
my greetings to our brothers and sisters* at
Laodicea, and to Nympha and the church
that meets in her house.
16After you have read this letter, pass it
on to the church at Laodicea so they can
read it, too. And you should read the letter
I wrote to them.
17And say to Archippus, "Be sure to carry
out the ministry the Lord gave you."
18HERE IS MY GREETING IN MY OWN
HANDWRITING—PAUL.

Remember my chains.
May God's grace be with you.

3:24 Or *and serve Christ as your Master.* **4:6** Greek *and seasoned with salt.* **4:15** Greek *brothers.*

The power of technology

Advances in technology are almost a daily occurrence these days. While many welcome such advances with open arms, others can be suspicious of them. So is there an appropriate Christian response to technology?

Technology goes back to the earliest times of human existence. In Genesis 4 we read, without any note of disapproval, of how Cain's descendants developed metalworking and the use of tools (Genesis 4:22). And Paul certainly wasn't afraid to use the technology of his day. He used letters, even though parchment was extremely expensive, because he knew it was important to write down what needed to be heard. If he hadn't, we wouldn't have much of the New Testament. He used messengers to carry news to and from churches (e.g., Colossians 4:7-9). If he hadn't, we wouldn't have known about the problems the early church faced (e.g., 1 Corinthians 5:1). He used ships to hasten his journeys, thus speeding the spread of the gospel when most people felt it was safer to travel by land and avoided sailing on the open seas. He certainly wasn't afraid of the technology of his day.

Over the centuries, the church has often used technology to spread the gospel, whether through the printing of Bibles in fifteenth-century Europe or through the use of radio, TV, and the Internet for broadcasting the gospel and sharing Christian resources in the twenty-first century. So technology can definitely be a blessing.

But perhaps the challenge for many of us today is not hesitancy in using technology, but the danger of it becoming all-consuming in our lives. If we read something on the Internet or see something on YouTube, we often assume it is true, without really checking it out. If a preacher has a TV show, we may think that their teaching must be true, or why else would God be blessing them with the finances to produce it. And some of us get consumed with the latest gizmo, app, or website, not seeing that we are in danger of becoming distracted and making the messenger more important than the message.

Technology is a great gift to humankind and to the church. But as Christians we must always ensure it stays our servant and doesn't become our master.

1 & 2 Thessalonians

Living in light of Christ's return

Paul's two letters to the church at Thessalonica, the capital of the Roman province of Macedonia (modern Greece), are some of the earliest New Testament documents (only James, and possibly Galatians, were written earlier). Written some six months apart, probably around AD 50 or 51 while Paul was in Corinth, they seek to encourage the new converts in their faith, for Paul had had to leave them abruptly (Acts 17:5-10). He writes to encourage them in the trials they were facing, to provide practical teaching on how to live the Christian life, and to give assurance concerning Christ's return and what will happen then.

What's it all about?

In 1 Thessalonians, Paul looks back to his short but—thanks to the Holy Spirit—successful time working with Silas in Thessalonica. He says how proud he is of the church's reputation (chapters 1–2) and how, in spite of persecutions and setbacks, they persevered. His failure to return, he reassures them, was not because of a lack of concern but because of obstacles and opposition (2:18). Now, unable to bear the lack of news any longer, he sent Timothy to find out how they were. The news of their faith made him happy, and he looked forward to visiting them again (chapter 3).

Meanwhile, they should continue to lead lives that please God (chapter 4). They should avoid sexual sins and exercise self-control, in stark contrast to those who don't know God. And they should keep working to provide themselves with an honest income.

Paul then tells them not to grieve too much for people who have died, for Christ will soon return—along with those who have died trusting in him—and then all Christians will be together again with him forever. He outlines how events will unfold at that time, but he emphasizes that they must not become preoccupied with looking for signs of Christ's return; for when he comes, he will come quickly, unmistakably, and unannounced. Their task is to remain alert and to lead holy lives. They can be confident that God will keep them safe and blameless until that day (5:23).

OVERVIEW

1 THESSALONIANS

Thanksgiving for the Thessalonians' faith · *1:1-10*

Paul's work in Thessalonica
2:1–3:13

A life that pleases God
4:1-12

Teaching on the return of Christ
4:13–5:11

Final instructions
5:12-28

2 THESSALONIANS

Thanksgiving and prayer
1:1-12

What will happen before Christ returns · *2:1-12*

Reassurance and a call to stand firm
2:13-17

Paul's request for prayer
3:1-5

Encouragement not to give up working
3:6-15

Final greetings
3:16-18

In 2 Thessalonians, Paul looks once again at what will happen before Christ returns, seeking to correct some misunderstandings that had arisen—especially the thought that "the day of the Lord has already begun" (2:2). The world is ripe for judgment but, before that can come, certain events must unfold. The evil at work in the world will increase until it culminates in the appearance of "the man of lawlessness," whom Christ will eventually destroy (chapter 2). In light of this, they should stand firm.

Some of Paul's converts were so fixated on these future events that they had forgotten the here and now and had even given up work. While this could sound very spiritual, Paul was not impressed. He had no sympathy for people who had no time for work but had plenty of time for "meddling in other people's business" (3:11). He reminds them of the example he and his fellow workers set while among them in Thessalonica and says that those unwilling to work have given up their right to support (3:6-10).

What does it mean for us?

The early church expected Christ to return at any moment, and Paul himself expected to live to see the day. That happy prospect spurred him on to achieve great things in a short span of time. But his converts in Thessalonica saw no point in starting something when the completion date might never come. Why waste time working when Christ might return at any moment? they thought.

But Paul reminds us that how we live in the present matters greatly to God. Work has great value in itself, and our attitude toward it can express a lot about our attitude to life in general. Paul believed that the best way to prepare for a heavenly future is to live a productive life here on earth right now. Moreover, Christians can more easily share the Good News with nonbelievers if they live a life those nonbelievers can respect. And diligence and integrity at work win respect in every age.

The sure fact that Christ will one day return is meant to encourage and inspire us and to provoke us to share the gospel with others, not to get us to sit back in happy contentment that everything will be all right for us while we lack concern for others.

1 Thessalonians

Greetings from Paul

1 This letter is from Paul, Silas,* and
Timothy.

We are writing to the church in Thessalonica, to you who belong to God the Father and the Lord Jesus Christ.

May God give you grace and peace.

The Faith of the Thessalonian Believers

[2]We always thank God for all of you and
pray for you constantly. [3]As we pray to our
God and Father about you, we think of your
faithful work, your loving deeds, and the enduring hope you have because of our Lord
Jesus Christ.
[4]We know, dear brothers and sisters,* that
God loves you and has chosen you to be his
own people. [5]For when we brought you the
Good News, it was not only with words but
also with power, for the Holy Spirit gave you
full assurance* that what we said was true.
And you know of our concern for you from
the way we lived when we were with you.
[6]So you received the message with joy from
the Holy Spirit in spite of the severe suffering it brought you. In this way, you imitated
both us and the Lord. [7]As a result, you have
become an example to all the believers in
Greece—throughout both Macedonia and
Achaia.*
[8]And now the word of the Lord is ringing

1:1 Greek *Silvanus,* the Greek form of the name. **1:4** Greek *brothers.* **1:5** Or *with the power of the Holy Spirit, so you can have full assurance.* **1:7** *Macedonia* and *Achaia* were the northern and southern regions of Greece.

out from you to people everywhere, even
beyond Macedonia and Achaia, for wherever
we go we find people telling us about your
faith in God. We don't need to tell them about
it, 9 for they keep talking about the wonderful
welcome you gave us and how you turned
away from idols to serve the living and
true God. 10 And they speak of how you are
looking forward to the coming of God's Son
from heaven—Jesus, whom God raised from
the dead. He is the one who has rescued us
from the terrors of the coming judgment.

Paul Remembers His Visit

2 You yourselves know, dear brothers and
sisters,* that our visit to you was not a
failure. 2 You know how badly we had been
treated at Philippi just before we came to you
and how much we suffered there. Yet our
God gave us the courage to declare his Good
News to you boldly, in spite of great opposition. 3 So you can see we were not preaching
with any deceit or impure motives or trickery.

4 For we speak as messengers approved
by God to be entrusted with the Good News.
Our purpose is to please God, not people.
He alone examines the motives of our
hearts. 5 Never once did we try to win you
with flattery, as you well know. And God is
our witness that we were not pretending to
be your friends just to get your money! 6 As
for human praise, we have never sought it
from you or anyone else.

7 As apostles of Christ we certainly had
a right to make some demands of you, but
instead we were like children* among you.
Or we were like a mother feeding and caring
for her own children. 8 We loved you so much
that we shared with you not only God's
Good News but our own lives, too.

9 Don't you remember, dear brothers and
sisters, how hard we worked among you?
Night and day we toiled to earn a living so
that we would not be a burden to any of you
as we preached God's Good News to you.
10 You yourselves are our witnesses—and so
is God—that we were devout and honest and
faultless toward all of you believers. 11 And
you know that we treated each of you as a
father treats his own children. 12 We pleaded
with you, encouraged you, and urged you
to live your lives in a way that God would
consider worthy. For he called you to share
in his Kingdom and glory.

13 Therefore, we never stop thanking God
that when you received his message from
us, you didn't think of our words as mere
human ideas. You accepted what we said as
the very word of God—which, of course, it
is. And this word continues to work in you
who believe.

14 And then, dear brothers and sisters, you
suffered persecution from your own countrymen. In this way, you imitated the believers
in God's churches in Judea who, because
of their belief in Christ Jesus, suffered from
their own people, the Jews. 15 For some of
the Jews killed the prophets, and some even
killed the Lord Jesus. Now they have persecuted us, too. They fail to please God and
work against all humanity 16 as they try to
keep us from preaching the Good News of
salvation to the Gentiles. By doing this, they
continue to pile up their sins. But the anger
of God has caught up with them at last.

Timothy's Good Report about the Church

17 Dear brothers and sisters, after we were
separated from you for a little while (though
our hearts never left you), we tried very

Thessalonica

Thessalonica was the capital of the Roman province of Macedonia (the northern part of modern Greece), with a population variously estimated at between one hundred thousand and two hundred thousand. Its location on the coast at the crossroads of the Via Egnatia (which ran from the eastern provinces to Rome) and the road leading north to the River Danube gave it particular significance as a commercial and communications center. Once again, Paul had chosen an immensely strategic location for starting a church—though his preaching stirred up much opposition from the Jews (Acts 17:1-10). Persecution would continue to characterize the life of this church.

hard to come back because of our intense
longing to see you again. 18 We wanted very
much to come to you, and I, Paul, tried
again and again, but Satan prevented us.
19 After all, what gives us hope and joy, and
what will be our proud reward and crown
as we stand before our Lord Jesus when he
returns? It is you! 20 Yes, you are our pride
and joy.

3 Finally, when we could stand it no
longer, we decided to stay alone in
Athens, 2 and we sent Timothy to visit you.
He is our brother and God's co-worker* in
proclaiming the Good News of Christ. We
sent him to strengthen you, to encourage
you in your faith, 3 and to keep you from
being shaken by the troubles you were
going through. But you know that we are
destined for such troubles. 4 Even while we
were with you, we warned you that troubles
would soon come—and they did, as you well
know. 5 That is why, when I could bear it no
longer, I sent Timothy to find out whether
your faith was still strong. I was afraid that
the tempter had gotten the best of you and
that our work had been useless.

6 But now Timothy has just returned,
bringing us good news about your faith and
love. He reports that you always remember
our visit with joy and that you want to see
us as much as we want to see you. 7 So we
have been greatly encouraged in the midst
of our troubles and suffering, dear brothers
and sisters,* because you have remained
strong in your faith. 8 It gives us new life to
know that you are standing firm in the Lord.

9 How we thank God for you! Because of
you we have great joy as we enter God's
presence. 10 Night and day we pray earnestly
for you, asking God to let us see you again
to fill the gaps in your faith.

11 May God our Father and our Lord Jesus
bring us to you very soon. 12 And may the
Lord make your love for one another and
for all people grow and overflow, just as
our love for you overflows. 13 May he, as a
result, make your hearts strong, blameless,
and holy as you stand before God our Father
when our Lord Jesus comes again with all
his holy people. Amen.

Live to Please God

4 Finally, dear brothers and sisters,* we
urge you in the name of the Lord Jesus
to live in a way that pleases God, as we have

2:1 Greek *brothers;* also in 2:9, 14, 17. **2:7** Some manuscripts read *we were gentle.* **3:2** Other manuscripts read *and God's servant;* still others read *and a co-worker,* or *and a servant and co-worker for God,* or *and God's servant and our co-worker.* **3:7** Greek *brothers.* **4:1** Greek *brothers;* also in 4:10, 13.

Conversion

Becoming a Christian is not about choosing to practice a religion, or to live a certain lifestyle, or to follow a certain path. It is about a change that happens in your heart. It means deciding that the way you have been going in life is completely wrong and making a whole change of direction to follow Jesus Christ from now on. It is about stopping, leaving some things behind, turning around to walk the opposite way, and starting all over again. This is called "conversion." It is a decision on our part that is matched by an action on God's part: an inner renewing of us that only he can give. Through this experience we find forgiveness, new life, and a relationship with God that will last forever.

This is what had happened to the Thessalonians (1 Thessalonians 1:9-10). They had turned away from their idol worship and had committed themselves to serve only the living God as they waited for the return of Jesus Christ and the Kingdom that he would bring. In this letter, Paul calls on them not to sit around speculating on all this, but to live out their newfound faith in godly living. Godly living in the present and godly hope for the future are marks of true conversion.

▶ *See also* ***Repentance****, page 1253.*

taught you. You live this way already, and
we encourage you to do so even more. [2]For
you remember what we taught you by the
authority of the Lord Jesus.
[3]God's will is for you to be holy, so stay
away from all sexual sin. [4]Then each of you
will control his own body* and live in holiness and honor—[5]not in lustful passion
like the pagans who do not know God and
his ways. [6]Never harm or cheat a fellow believer in this matter by violating his wife,*
for the Lord avenges all such sins, as we
have solemnly warned you before. [7]God has
called us to live holy lives, not impure lives.
[8]Therefore, anyone who refuses to live by
these rules is not disobeying human teaching but is rejecting God, who gives his Holy
Spirit to you.
[9]But we don't need to write to you about
the importance of loving each other,* for
God himself has taught you to love one
another. [10]Indeed, you already show your
love for all the believers* throughout
Macedonia. Even so, dear brothers and
sisters, we urge you to love them even
more.
[11]Make it your goal to live a quiet life,
minding your own business and working
with your hands, just as we instructed you
before. [12]Then people who are not believers
will respect the way you live, and you will
not need to depend on others.

The Hope of the Resurrection

[13]And now, dear brothers and sisters,
we want you to know what will happen
to the believers who have died* so you
will not grieve like people who have no
hope. [14]For since we believe that Jesus
died and was raised to life again, we also
believe that when Jesus returns, God will
bring back with him the believers who
have died.
[15]We tell you this directly from the Lord:
We who are still living when the Lord returns
will not meet him ahead of those who have
died.* [16]For the Lord himself will come down
from heaven with a commanding shout,
with the voice of the archangel, and with
the trumpet call of God. First, the believers
who have died* will rise from their graves.
[17]Then, together with them, we who are still
alive and remain on the earth will be caught
up in the clouds to meet the Lord in the air.
Then we will be with the Lord forever. [18]So
encourage each other with these words.

5 Now concerning how and when all this
will happen, dear brothers and sisters,*
we don't really need to write you. [2]For you

▶ **4:3** *See **Sexuality**, page 742.* **4:11-12** *See **Work**, page 1376.*

The return of Jesus Christ

The return of Jesus at the end of the age is one of the most glorious and encouraging truths of the New Testament. When he comes this time (in contrast to the obscurity of his first coming), no one will miss it, Paul says; for his return will be public, visible, and glorious (1 Thessalonians 4:16). Moreover, he will be accompanied by "the believers who have died" (4:14)—who are at present safe with Jesus in heaven. And at that moment, believers who are alive on that day "will be caught up in the clouds to meet the Lord in the air. Then we will be with the Lord forever" (4:17).

This glorious hope is not meant to lead to arguments over details, timing, or the order of events. Rather, it is meant to encourage us and to provoke us to holiness, right living (5:6-11; see also 2 Peter 3:10-14), and sharing the gospel with others while there is still opportunity (see Matthew 24:14), for after his return there is no hope for those who have not believed in him (Revelation 20:11-15). His return will be sudden, "like a thief in the night" (1 Thessalonians 5:2); we should therefore be living in constant readiness.

▶ *See also **Hell**, page 1108; **Heaven**, page 1451; **The Last Judgment**, page 1465; **The new Jerusalem**, page 1466.*

know quite well that the day of the Lord's
return will come unexpectedly, like a thief
in the night. 3When people are saying,
"Everything is peaceful and secure," then
disaster will fall on them as suddenly as a
pregnant woman's labor pains begin. And
there will be no escape.

4But you aren't in the dark about these
things, dear brothers and sisters, and you
won't be surprised when the day of the Lord
comes like a thief.* 5For you are all children
of the light and of the day; we don't belong
to darkness and night. 6So be on your
guard, not asleep like the others. Stay alert
and be clearheaded. 7Night is the time when
people sleep and drinkers get drunk. 8But
let us who live in the light be clearheaded,
protected by the armor of faith and love,
and wearing as our helmet the confidence
of our salvation.

9For God chose to save us through our
Lord Jesus Christ, not to pour out his anger
on us. 10Christ died for us so that, whether
we are dead or alive when he returns, we
can live with him forever. 11So encourage
each other and build each other up, just as
you are already doing.

Paul's Final Advice

12Dear brothers and sisters, honor those who
are your leaders in the Lord's work. They
work hard among you and give you spiritual
guidance. 13Show them great respect and
wholehearted love because of their work.
And live peacefully with each other.

14Brothers and sisters, we urge you to
warn those who are lazy. Encourage those
who are timid. Take tender care of those
who are weak. Be patient with everyone.

15See that no one pays back evil for evil,
but always try to do good to each other and
to all people.

16Always be joyful. 17Never stop praying.
18Be thankful in all circumstances, for this is
God's will for you who belong to Christ Jesus.

19Do not stifle the Holy Spirit. 20Do not
scoff at prophecies, 21but test everything
that is said. Hold on to what is good. 22Stay
away from every kind of evil.

4:4 Or *will know how to take a wife for himself;* or *will learn to live with his own wife;* Greek reads *will know how to possess his own vessel.* **4:6** Greek *Never harm or cheat a brother in this matter.* **4:9** Greek *about brotherly love.* **4:10** Greek *the brothers.* **4:13** Greek *those who have fallen asleep;* also in 4:14. **4:15** Greek *those who have fallen asleep.* **4:16** Greek *the dead in Christ.* **5:1** Greek *brothers;* also in 5:4, 12, 14, 25, 26, 27. **5:4** Some manuscripts read *comes upon you as if you were thieves.*

Spirit, soul, and body

While some use 1 Thessalonians 5:23 to support the belief that humans are tripartite (comprising a spirit, a soul, and a body), Paul was in fact simply using a Jewish way of saying "your whole being." Unlike Greeks, whose philosophy separated human beings into different parts, the Jews had a holistic view of what it meant to be a person. People were not like machines, made up of different "bits" (whether three or any other number); they were one whole being, with every aspect made by God and capable of being submitted to God for his use. By contrast, Greeks saw the body as a prison or tomb that trapped the spirit, leaving the spirit longing to escape and be free.

This is why, for us as Christians, just being concerned with "saving souls" or only meeting people's spiritual needs can never be enough. Yes, our souls are supremely important, as Jesus underlined (Matthew 16:26); but this is not a reason for neglecting the needs of people's bodies (Matthew 25:31-46). God is concerned for our whole being!

We should take care therefore not to fall into the trap of overemphasizing the different aspects of our being. After all, in Matthew 10:28, Jesus speaks about our having a body and soul; in Matthew 22:37 of a heart, soul, and mind; and in Mark 12:30 of heart, soul, mind, and strength; and in 1 Corinthians 7:34, Paul speaks of body and spirit. This rich diversity of terminology shows that there is not a defined number of parts to our humanity; these are simply different ways of speaking about "the whole of us"—even if particular aspects are sometimes emphasized—and it is the whole of us that God cares for.

Paul's Final Greetings

23Now may the God of peace make you holy
in every way, and may your whole spirit and
soul and body be kept blameless until our
Lord Jesus Christ comes again. 24God will
make this happen, for he who calls you is
faithful.
25Dear brothers and sisters, pray for us.
26Greet all the brothers and sisters with a
sacred kiss.
27I command you in the name of the Lord to
read this letter to all the brothers and sisters.
28May the grace of our Lord Jesus Christ
be with you.

2 Thessalonians

Greetings from Paul

1 This letter is from Paul, Silas,* and
Timothy.
We are writing to the church in Thessalonica, to you who belong to God our Father
and the Lord Jesus Christ.
2May God our Father* and the Lord Jesus
Christ give you grace and peace.

Encouragement during Persecution

3Dear brothers and sisters,* we can't help
but thank God for you, because your faith
is flourishing and your love for one another
is growing. 4We proudly tell God's other
churches about your endurance and faithfulness in all the persecutions and hardships you are suffering. 5And God will use
this persecution to show his justice and to
make you worthy of his Kingdom, for which
you are suffering. 6In his justice he will pay
back those who persecute you.
7And God will provide rest for you who
are being persecuted and also for us when
the Lord Jesus appears from heaven. He will
come with his mighty angels, 8in flaming
fire, bringing judgment on those who don't
know God and on those who refuse to obey
the Good News of our Lord Jesus. 9They
will be punished with eternal destruction,
forever separated from the Lord and from
his glorious power. 10When he comes on
that day, he will receive glory from his holy
people—praise from all who believe. And
this includes you, for you believed what we
told you about him.
11So we keep on praying for you, asking our
God to enable you to live a life worthy of his
call. May he give you the power to accomplish all the good things your faith prompts
you to do. 12Then the name of our Lord Jesus
will be honored because of the way you live,
and you will be honored along with him. This
is all made possible because of the grace of
our God and Lord, Jesus Christ.*

Events prior to the Lord's Second Coming

2 Now, dear brothers and sisters,* let us
clarify some things about the coming of
our Lord Jesus Christ and how we will be
gathered to meet him. 2Don't be so easily
shaken or alarmed by those who say that
the day of the Lord has already begun. Don't
believe them, even if they claim to have had
a spiritual vision, a revelation, or a letter
supposedly from us. 3Don't be fooled by
what they say. For that day will not come
until there is a great rebellion against God
and the man of lawlessness* is revealed—
the one who brings destruction.* 4He will
exalt himself and defy everything that
people call god and every object of worship.
He will even sit in the temple of God, claiming that he himself is God.
5Don't you remember that I told you
about all this when I was with you? 6And
you know what is holding him back, for he
can be revealed only when his time comes.
7For this lawlessness is already at work secretly, and it will remain secret until the
one who is holding it back steps out of the
way. 8Then the man of lawlessness will be
revealed, but the Lord Jesus will slay him

▸ *For introduction to **1 & 2 Thessalonians**, see page 1368.*
2:1 *See **The return of Jesus Christ**, page 1372.*

with the breath of his mouth and destroy him by the splendor of his coming.

[9]This man will come to do the work of Satan with counterfeit power and signs and miracles. [10]He will use every kind of evil deception to fool those on their way to destruction, because they refuse to love and accept the truth that would save them. [11]So God will cause them to be greatly deceived, and they will believe these lies. [12]Then they will be condemned for enjoying evil rather than believing the truth.

Believers Should Stand Firm

[13]As for us, we can't help but thank God for you, dear brothers and sisters loved by the Lord. We are always thankful that God chose you to be among the first* to experience salvation—a salvation that came through the Spirit who makes you holy and through your belief in the truth. [14]He called you to salvation when we told you the Good News; now you can share in the glory of our Lord Jesus Christ.

[15]With all these things in mind, dear brothers and sisters, stand firm and keep a strong grip on the teaching we passed on to you both in person and by letter.

[16]Now may our Lord Jesus Christ himself and God our Father, who loved us and by his grace gave us eternal comfort and a wonderful hope, [17]comfort you and strengthen you in every good thing you do and say.

Paul's Request for Prayer

3 Finally, dear brothers and sisters,* we ask you to pray for us. Pray that the Lord's message will spread rapidly and be honored wherever it goes, just as when it came to you. [2]Pray, too, that we will be rescued from wicked and evil people, for not everyone is a believer. [3]But the Lord is faithful; he will strengthen you and guard you from the evil one.* [4]And we are confident in the Lord that you are doing and will continue to do the things we commanded you. [5]May the Lord lead your hearts into a full understanding and expression of the love of God and the patient endurance that comes from Christ.

An Exhortation to Proper Living

[6]And now, dear brothers and sisters, we give you this command in the name of our

1:1 Greek *Silvanus,* the Greek form of the name. **1:2** Some manuscripts read *God the Father.* **1:3** Greek *Brothers.* **1:12** Or *of our God and our Lord Jesus Christ.* **2:1** Greek *brothers;* also in 2:13, 15. **2:3a** Some manuscripts read *the man of sin.* **2:3b** Greek *the son of destruction.* **2:13** Some manuscripts read *chose you from the very beginning.* **3:1** Greek *brothers;* also in 3:6, 13. **3:3** Or *from evil.*

The man of lawlessness

Paul had previously written about Christ's return and the day of the Lord (1 Thessalonians 4:13–5:11), but some of the Thessalonians had gotten confused, thinking that day had already come, or at least begun (2 Thessalonians 2:1-2). However, Paul says it cannot have happened, for two things must happen before it does: first, a great rebellion, when many will abandon the faith (see Matthew 24:10-13); and second, the appearance of "the man of lawlessness" (2 Thessalonians 2:3)—a term used only in this chapter. Elsewhere he is called "the Antichrist" (e.g., 1 John 2:18). This mysterious figure—who is clearly not Satan himself, for Paul distinguishes between the two (2 Thessalonians 2:9)—will personify the increasing hostility toward God, even trying to set himself up in God's place (2:4) and performing miracles (2:9). He will be the ultimate expression of the lawlessness that is at work in the world even now, but Christ will overthrow him (2:6-8).

In light of this reassurance, Christians do not need to fear but should simply "stand firm" (2:15). Things will get very dark before Christ's return, but that means the light can shine all the brighter; and the Bible's teaching that God's Kingdom cannot be overcome (e.g., Daniel 2:31-45; Matthew 13) should give us much hope.

▶ *See also **The Antichrist**, page 1434.*

Lord Jesus Christ: Stay away from all believers* who live idle lives and don't follow the tradition they received* from us. [7]For you know that you ought to imitate us. We were not idle when we were with you. [8]We never accepted food from anyone without paying for it. We worked hard day and night so we would not be a burden to any of you. [9]We certainly had the right to ask you to feed us, but we wanted to give you an example to follow. [10]Even while we were with you, we gave you this command: "Those unwilling to work will not get to eat."

[11]Yet we hear that some of you are living idle lives, refusing to work and meddling in other people's business. [12]We command such people and urge them in the name of the Lord Jesus Christ to settle down and work to earn their own living. [13]As for the rest of you, dear brothers and sisters, never get tired of doing good.

[14]Take note of those who refuse to obey what we say in this letter. Stay away from them so they will be ashamed. [15]Don't think of them as enemies, but warn them as you would a brother or sister.*

Paul's Final Greetings

[16]Now may the Lord of peace himself give you his peace at all times and in every situation. The Lord be with you all.

[17]HERE IS MY GREETING IN MY OWN HANDWRITING—PAUL. I DO THIS IN ALL MY LETTERS TO PROVE THEY ARE FROM ME.

[18]May the grace of our Lord Jesus Christ be with you all.

3:6a Greek *from every brother.* **3:6b** Some manuscripts read *you received.* **3:15** Greek *as a brother.*

Work

Some Thessalonians, expecting that Christ's return was imminent, had stopped working. At one level this seemed so "spiritual," but Paul exposed it for what it was: idleness (2 Thessalonians 3:6). He had already addressed this issue in his first letter to them (1 Thessalonians 4:11-12), but things had gotten worse, so now he speaks even more plainly: "Those unwilling to work will not get to eat" (2 Thessalonians 3:10). As proof that work is "spiritual," Paul reminds them of his own example. When he was among them, he hadn't been ashamed to work for his living (3:7-9). Jesus too wasn't afraid to work, spending most of his life as a carpenter (Matthew 13:55), and he said that his Father was "always working" (John 5:17). In fact, when we first meet God in the Bible, he is working on creation; and he gave work as a gift to Adam (Genesis 2:15), part of being created in God's image. When sin entered the world, it was the ground that was cursed, not work (Genesis 3:17-18). Work is something through which we are meant to glorify God and find fulfillment (Ecclesiastes 2:24; 3:22). All who work—not just pastors, priests, or church leaders—are serving God.

Of course, sometimes people find themselves out of work through no fault of their own, and this can be soul-destroying. So when we can help such people, we should, like the employer in Jesus' parable (Matthew 20:1-16). We should show compassion to them and provide practical help wherever possible, just as Boaz did. He not only allowed Ruth to pick up the leftover crops when his field was being harvested but also went far beyond the requirements of the Jewish Law in providing for her (Ruth 2:8-9, 15-16).

▶ *See also* ***Serving God in our work****, page 956;* ***Working for the glory of God****, page 1265.*

1 & 2 Timothy, Titus

Letters of advice to church leaders

All three of these letters were sent to individual church leaders, offering advice and encouragement. Paul had left Timothy in charge of the church at Ephesus (1 Timothy 1:3), but when he realized he might not be able to return soon (3:14-15) he sent his first letter (dated somewhere between AD 63 and 65) to refute false teaching and give counsel on how to organize the growing church. His second letter, written a year or so later as Paul neared the end of his life (2 Timothy 4:6-8), reflects the increasing persecution of those days. He expresses his deep affection and concern for Timothy and encourages him to stand firm. He urges him to guard the truth of the gospel (e.g., 1:13-14) and to keep on preaching it (4:2). Titus, written around the same time as 1 Timothy, is a letter of encouragement and direction to Titus, who led the church on the island of Crete (Titus 1:5). Paul especially encourages him to stand against the false teaching that was so prevalent.

Because these letters provide advice on the local church, they are sometimes referred to as the "Pastoral Letters."

What's it all about?

In 1 Timothy, Paul offers some fatherly advice to his "true son in the faith" (1:2)—an indication that he had probably led Timothy to faith in Christ when he first met him at Lystra (Acts 14:6-20) during his first missionary journey. Paul met him again when he returned during his second missionary journey and, clearly seeing potential in him, took Timothy with him as he continued his journey (Acts 16:1-5). While Timothy was a devoted companion (he was with Paul during his first imprisonment; see Philippians 1:1), he seems to have been somewhat timid, which explains Paul's encouragements and direct instructions in this letter. He warns Timothy about the dangers of false teachings in the church at Ephesus that were distracting people from what is real and important, and he encourages him to hold closely to his faith in Christ—Christ who can save even the worst of sinners, such as Paul himself used to be (1 Timothy 1:15-16).

Paul encourages Timothy to fight the spiritual battle well (1:18) and continue to do what he knows is right. He gives Timothy instructions for leading the church well. He urges him to get the church to pray for rulers (chapter 2) and outlines the high qualifications for those who are appointed leaders in it (chapter 3). In chapter 4 he again warns Timothy against false teachings and calls on him to set an example to the church in both his life and his teaching. In chapters 5 and 6 he offers practical advice on how to handle various needs within the church and how to live the Christian life, including a warning about the love of money.

Second Timothy is a farewell letter, written as Paul anticipated his approaching death. In chapters 1 and 2 he reminds Timothy of the qualities necessary for a faithful minister of Christ. Timothy should be bold, hold to the truth, be disciplined, and be prepared for hardship. Paul urges him to leave religious controversies alone and to keep his life pure. Paul then warns him in chapter 3 about opposition that Christians will experience in the "last days" (the time before Christ's return). He encourages Timothy to follow his example and to stay faithful to the tried and tested teachings of God's word. Paul concludes with greetings and some personal requests (4:9-22).

Titus reads like a shortened version of 1 Timothy (it was written around the same time), but it is tailored to events in Crete, where Paul had left Titus to structure the life of the church (Titus 1:5), institute proper leadership (1:6-9), and deal with false teaching (1:10-16). God's grace should lead us to live good and godly lives—something that Cretans were not known for (1:12)—for there is an inseparable link between belief and behavior (2:1–3:11). The letter includes succinct summaries of the gospel in 2:14 and 3:4-7.

What does it mean for us?

In 1 Timothy, Paul has a lot to say about the Christian's responsibility to church, family, and society. It seems as if false teaching, a major concern of this letter, was undermining proper Christian behavior in all those areas of life. Paul therefore shows how right relationships are crucial and how family life provides the setting within which those relationships grow and mature, allowing us to both give and receive, and to care for one another.

Right relationships both in the home and with others are seen as a fundamental requirement for church leadership in 1 Timothy 3, for leadership skills are developed at home long before they ever reach church. And no one should ever underestimate the effect a Christian home can have on family members. Timothy's mother, Eunice, and his grandmother Lois were both Jewish believers who had helped Timothy to grow spiritually (2 Timothy 1:5).

These letters also speak strongly about the power of the gospel. Sometimes people can feel so guilty about their past that they think God could never forgive or accept them. While writing 1 Timothy, Paul was reminded of his own past. He had rejected Jesus' teachings, and even hunted down and murdered Christians before becoming a Christian himself; and yet God forgave and used him. Paul didn't forget his past. Instead, he put it to good effect, using it to illustrate God's mercy toward him. Then he got on with the business of living in that mercy day by day. Paul's experience is a clear call for any one of us who struggles with our past to let God's love for us *today*, not our past, determine our future.

Some have dismissed Paul's apparent attitude to women in these letters as very old-fashioned—for example, his call for women to be submissive to their husbands and not teach, or for them to avoid elaborate hairdos and expensive clothing (1 Timothy 2:9-15; Titus 2:4-5). But when we understand Paul's context, it throws a different light on these teachings. Women in the first century were denied education and were effectively treated as second-class citizens. So when Paul says that a woman should "learn quietly"

OVERVIEW

1 TIMOTHY

Advice to Timothy about false teaching · *1:1-20*

Instructions about prayer *2:1-15*

Qualifications for church leadership *3:1-16*

Dealing with false teaching *4:1-16*

Dealing with various practical needs in the church · *5:1–6:2*

False teaching and the call to be a good example · *6:3-21*

2 TIMOTHY

Encouragements to Timothy to remain faithful · *1:1-18*

A call to bold and godly leadership *2:1-26*

Standing firm in godless times *3:1–4:8*

Final instructions in light of Paul's impending death · *4:9-22*

TITUS

Qualifications for church leadership *1:1-16*

Characteristics of true godliness *2:1–3:15*

but not teach, he's acknowledging an opportunity for learning, which was quite new. But he was still concerned that Christians shouldn't be seen to be needlessly flouting society's norms—he wanted the young church to win respect, not censure. Elsewhere in his letters and in Acts we clearly see that Paul had great respect for women's leadership and influence (e.g., Acts 16:13-15, 40; 18:24-26; 21:8-9; Romans 16:1-16; Philippians 4:2-3; Colossians 4:15).

1 Timothy

Greetings from Paul

1 This letter is from Paul, an apostle of Christ Jesus, appointed by the command of God our Savior and Christ Jesus, who gives us hope.

[2]I am writing to Timothy, my true son in the faith.

May God the Father and Christ Jesus our Lord give you grace, mercy, and peace.

Warnings against False Teachings

[3]When I left for Macedonia, I urged you to stay there in Ephesus and stop those whose teaching is contrary to the truth. [4]Don't let them waste their time in endless discussion of myths and spiritual pedigrees. These things only lead to meaningless speculations,* which don't help people live a life of faith in God.*

[5]The purpose of my instruction is that all believers would be filled with love that comes from a pure heart, a clear conscience, and genuine faith. [6]But some people have missed this whole point. They have turned away from these things and spend their time in meaningless discussions. [7]They want to be known as teachers of the law of Moses, but they don't know what they are talking about, even though they speak so confidently.

[8]We know that the law is good when used correctly. [9]For the law was not intended for people who do what is right. It is for people who are lawless and rebellious, who are ungodly and sinful, who consider nothing sacred and defile what is holy, who kill their father or mother or commit other murders. [10]The law is for people who are sexually immoral, or who practice homosexuality, or are slave traders,* liars, promise breakers, or who do anything else that contradicts the wholesome teaching [11]that comes from the glorious Good News entrusted to me by our blessed God.

Paul's Gratitude for God's Mercy

[12]I thank Christ Jesus our Lord, who has given me strength to do his work. He considered me trustworthy and appointed me to serve him, [13]even though I used to blaspheme the name of Christ. In my insolence, I persecuted his people. But God had mercy on me because I did it in ignorance and unbelief. [14]Oh, how generous and gracious our Lord was! He filled me with the faith and love that come from Christ Jesus.

[15]This is a trustworthy saying, and everyone should accept it: "Christ Jesus came into the world to save sinners"—and I am the worst of them all. [16]But God had mercy on me so that Christ Jesus could use me as a prime example of his great patience with even the worst sinners. Then others will realize that they, too, can believe in him and receive eternal life. [17]All honor and glory to God forever and ever! He is the eternal King, the unseen one who never dies; he alone is God. Amen.

Timothy's Responsibility

[18]Timothy, my son, here are my instructions for you, based on the prophetic words spoken about you earlier. May they help you fight well in the Lord's battles. [19]Cling to your faith in Christ, and keep your conscience clear. For some people have deliberately violated their consciences; as a result, their faith has been shipwrecked. [20]Hymenaeus

1:4a Greek *in myths and endless genealogies, which cause speculation.* **1:4b** Greek *a stewardship of God in faith.*
1:10 Or *kidnappers.*

and Alexander are two examples. I threw
them out and handed them over to Satan
so they might learn not to blaspheme God.

Instructions about Worship

2 I urge you, first of all, to pray for all
people. Ask God to help them; intercede
on their behalf, and give thanks for them.
2Pray this way for kings and all who are in
authority so that we can live peaceful and
quiet lives marked by godliness and dignity.
3This is good and pleases God our Savior,
4who wants everyone to be saved and to
understand the truth. 5For,

> There is one God and one Mediator who
> can reconcile God and humanity—the
> man Christ Jesus. 6He gave his life to
> purchase freedom for everyone.

This is the message God gave to the world at
just the right time. 7And I have been chosen
as a preacher and apostle to teach the Gentiles this message about faith and truth. I'm
not exaggerating—just telling the truth.
8In every place of worship, I want men to
pray with holy hands lifted up to God, free
from anger and controversy.
9And I want women to be modest in their
appearance.* They should wear decent
and appropriate clothing and not draw attention to themselves by the way they fix
their hair or by wearing gold or pearls or
expensive clothes. 10For women who claim
to be devoted to God should make themselves attractive by the good things they do.
11Women should learn quietly and submissively. 12I do not let women teach men
or have authority over them.* Let them
listen quietly. 13For God made Adam first,
and afterward he made Eve. 14And it was
not Adam who was deceived by Satan.
The woman was deceived, and sin was the
result. 15But women will be saved through
childbearing,* assuming they continue to
live in faith, love, holiness, and modesty.

Leaders in the Church

3 This is a trustworthy saying: "If someone
aspires to be a church leader,* he desires
an honorable position." 2So a church leader
must be a man whose life is above reproach.
He must be faithful to his wife.* He must
exercise self-control, live wisely, and have
a good reputation. He must enjoy having
guests in his home, and he must be able to
teach. 3He must not be a heavy drinker* or
be violent. He must be gentle, not quarrelsome, and not love money. 4He must manage
his own family well, having children who
respect and obey him. 5For if a man cannot
manage his own household, how can he
take care of God's church?
6A church leader must not be a new believer, because he might become proud, and

Timothy

It is likely that Timothy was just a teenager when Paul first met him at Lystra, probably during his first visit there as part of his first missionary journey (Acts 14:6-20). Whether it was Paul who had led him to faith in Christ at that time, or whether it was his mother and his grandmother who had done so later (2 Timothy 1:5), is unclear. But something clearly "clicked" between Paul and Timothy when Paul returned (Acts 16:1-3), so much so that Paul calls him "my true son in the faith" (1 Timothy 1:2). Paul took Timothy with him on his second missionary journey and must have discipled him well, for he sent him as his personal representative to Thessalonica (1 Thessalonians 3:1-6), Macedonia (Acts 19:22), and Corinth (1 Corinthians 4:17). He eventually sent him to lead the church in Ephesus (1 Timothy 1:3), where there were many challenges. He was clearly still young at this time, for Paul tells him, "Don't let anyone think less of you because you are young" (4:12); and he needed much encouragement. He was perhaps in his early thirties when 1 Timothy was written, showing we don't have to wait till we are old to serve God fruitfully.

▶ *See also* ***Mentoring****, page 1385.*

the devil would cause him to fall.* 7 Also, people outside the church must speak well of him so that he will not be disgraced and fall into the devil's trap.

8 In the same way, deacons must be well respected and have integrity. They must not be heavy drinkers or dishonest with money. 9 They must be committed to the mystery of the faith now revealed and must live with a clear conscience. 10 Before they are appointed as deacons, let them be closely examined. If they pass the test, then let them serve as deacons.

11 In the same way, their wives* must be respected and must not slander others. They must exercise self-control and be faithful in everything they do.

12 A deacon must be faithful to his wife, and he must manage his children and household well. 13 Those who do well as deacons will be rewarded with respect from others and will have increased confidence in their faith in Christ Jesus.

The Truths of Our Faith

14 I am writing these things to you now, even though I hope to be with you soon, 15 so that if I am delayed, you will know how people must conduct themselves in the household of God. This is the church of the living God, which is the pillar and foundation of the truth.

16 Without question, this is the great mystery of our faith*:

Christ* was revealed in a human body
  and vindicated by the Spirit.*
He was seen by angels
  and announced to the nations.
He was believed in throughout the world
  and taken to heaven in glory.

Warnings against False Teachers

4 Now the Holy Spirit tells us clearly that in the last times some will turn away from the true faith; they will follow deceptive spirits and teachings that come from demons. 2 These people are hypocrites and liars, and their consciences are dead.*

3 They will say it is wrong to be married

2:9 Or *to pray in modest apparel.* **2:12** Or *teach men or usurp their authority.* **2:15** Or *will be saved by accepting their role as mothers,* or *will be saved by the birth of the Child.* **3:1** Or *an overseer,* or *a bishop;* also in 3:2, 6. **3:2** Or *must have only one wife,* or *must be married only once;* Greek reads *must be the husband of one wife;* also in 3:12. **3:3** Greek *must not drink too much wine;* similarly in 3:8. **3:6** Or *he might fall into the same judgment as the devil.* **3:11** Or *the women deacons.* The Greek word can be translated *women* or *wives.* **3:16a** Or *of godliness.* **3:16b** Greek *He who;* other manuscripts read *God.* **3:16c** Or *in his spirit.* **4:2** Greek *are seared.*

▸ **3:1-13** *See **Leaders in the church**, page 1390.* **4:2** *See **Conscience**, page 333.*

How should we dress?

Paul's words in 1 Timothy 2:9 (like those of Peter in 1 Peter 3:1-6) are sometimes used to suggest God opposes fine clothing and jewelry. But this cannot be the case; after all, jewelry was used as a marriage gift (e.g., Genesis 24:52-53) and fine clothing as a mark of honor (e.g., Genesis 37:3). And God commanded the Israelites to take both from the Egyptians (Exodus 12:35-36).

What lay behind Paul's and Peter's words was their cultural context. Elaborate hair braiding and wearing ostentatious jewelry were common among Roman women, a way of showing their importance and wealth. Some of the Christian women in Ephesus had fallen into this trap of needing to "look good"—still a powerful force today, when advertising suggests our lives can only be complete if we wear particular styles or brands or this year's fashions.

What matters much more than what we wear, Paul and Peter underline, is what our hearts and lives are like. Neither apostle actually gives instruction on what *is* appropriate to wear (an important reminder for the older generation, who often look down on younger Christians because of the fashions they choose); their real point is that true adornment is never external. Both women and men should give their best energies and resources to serving God and others, not to looking good.

and wrong to eat certain foods. But God
created those foods to be eaten with thanks
by faithful people who know the truth.
4Since everything God created is good, we
should not reject any of it but receive it with
thanks. 5For we know it is made acceptable*
by the word of God and prayer.

A Good Servant of Christ Jesus

6If you explain these things to the brothers and sisters,* Timothy, you will be a
worthy servant of Christ Jesus, one who is
nourished by the message of faith and the
good teaching you have followed. 7Do not
waste time arguing over godless ideas and
old wives' tales. Instead, train yourself to be
godly. 8"Physical training is good, but training for godliness is much better, promising
benefits in this life and in the life to come."
9This is a trustworthy saying, and everyone
should accept it. 10This is why we work hard
and continue to struggle,* for our hope is
in the living God, who is the Savior of all
people and particularly of all believers.

11Teach these things and insist that everyone learn them. 12Don't let anyone think
less of you because you are young. Be an
example to all believers in what you say, in
the way you live, in your love, your faith,
and your purity. 13Until I get there, focus
on reading the Scriptures to the church,
encouraging the believers, and teaching
them.

14Do not neglect the spiritual gift you received through the prophecy spoken over
you when the elders of the church laid their
hands on you. 15Give your complete attention to these matters. Throw yourself into
your tasks so that everyone will see your
progress. 16Keep a close watch on how you
live and on your teaching. Stay true to what
is right for the sake of your own salvation
and the salvation of those who hear you.

Advice about Widows, Elders, and Slaves

5 Never speak harshly to an older man,*
but appeal to him respectfully as you
would to your own father. Talk to younger
men as you would to your own brothers.
2Treat older women as you would your
mother, and treat younger women with all
purity as you would your own sisters.

3Take care of* any widow who has no one
else to care for her. 4But if she has children
or grandchildren, their first responsibility is to show godliness at home and repay
their parents by taking care of them. This is
something that pleases God.

5Now a true widow, a woman who is truly
alone in this world, has placed her hope in
God. She prays night and day, asking God for
his help. 6But the widow who lives only for

Young people

Timothy was probably in his late twenties or early thirties, which, in the culture of his time, was seen as surprisingly young to hold such an influential position of leadership. But many young people had been used by God. Samuel was a young boy when God called him as one of Israel's greatest prophets (1 Samuel 3); David was a young teenager, dismissed by his brothers, when God called him to be king (1 Samuel 16); Daniel was a young man (Daniel 1:4-6) when God began to use him to bring powerful words to pagan kings; and Jesus' disciples were probably in their twenties. Clearly, age is not a barrier to God.

Sadly, age can sometimes be a barrier in the church, however. Some were looking down on Timothy, calling his leadership into question (see 1 Timothy 4:12), which is why Paul reminds him that leadership has nothing to do with age but rather with God's call and gifting (4:14). Older people should be ready to make space for younger leaders, training them and releasing them into ministry, just as Paul did with Timothy (see *Mentoring*, page 1385). Indeed, leaders are not successful unless they have trained up the next generation of leaders and are making plans for passing on the baton to them. But equally, younger people should remember that there is much wisdom in the older generation and that they neglect that wisdom to their loss (e.g., 1 Kings 12:1-20).

pleasure is spiritually dead even while she
lives. 7Give these instructions to the church
so that no one will be open to criticism.
8But those who won't care for their relatives, especially those in their own household, have denied the true faith. Such
people are worse than unbelievers.
9A widow who is put on the list for support
must be a woman who is at least sixty years
old and was faithful to her husband.* 10She
must be well respected by everyone because
of the good she has done. Has she brought up
her children well? Has she been kind to strangers and served other believers humbly?* Has
she helped those who are in trouble? Has she
always been ready to do good?
11The younger widows should not be on
the list, because their physical desires will
overpower their devotion to Christ and they
will want to remarry. 12Then they would be
guilty of breaking their previous pledge.
13And if they are on the list, they will learn to
be lazy and will spend their time gossiping
from house to house, meddling in other people's business and talking about things they
shouldn't. 14So I advise these younger widows
to marry again, have children, and take care
of their own homes. Then the enemy will not
be able to say anything against them. 15For
I am afraid that some of them have already
gone astray and now follow Satan.
16If a woman who is a believer has relatives who are widows, she must take care
of them and not put the responsibility on
the church. Then the church can care for the
widows who are truly alone.
17Elders who do their work well should be
respected and paid well,* especially those
who work hard at both preaching and teaching. 18For the Scripture says, "You must not
muzzle an ox to keep it from eating as it
treads out the grain." And in another place,
"Those who work deserve their pay!"*
19Do not listen to an accusation against an
elder unless it is confirmed by two or three
witnesses. 20Those who sin should be reprimanded in front of the whole church; this
will serve as a strong warning to others.
21I solemnly command you in the presence of God and Christ Jesus and the highest
angels to obey these instructions without
taking sides or showing favoritism to anyone.
22Never be in a hurry about appointing a
church leader.* Do not share in the sins of
others. Keep yourself pure.
23Don't drink only water. You ought to
drink a little wine for the sake of your
stomach because you are sick so often.
24Remember, the sins of some people are
obvious, leading them to certain judgment.
But there are others whose sins will not be
revealed until later. 25In the same way, the
good deeds of some people are obvious.
And the good deeds done in secret will
someday come to light.

6 All slaves should show full respect for
their masters so they will not bring
shame on the name of God and his teaching.
2If the masters are believers, that is no excuse
for being disrespectful. Those slaves should
work all the harder because their efforts are
helping other believers* who are well loved.

False Teaching and True Riches

Teach these things, Timothy, and encourage everyone to obey them. 3Some people
may contradict our teaching, but these are
the wholesome teachings of the Lord Jesus
Christ. These teachings promote a godly life.
4Anyone who teaches something different is
arrogant and lacks understanding. Such a
person has an unhealthy desire to quibble
over the meaning of words. This stirs up
arguments ending in jealousy, division,
slander, and evil suspicions. 5These people
always cause trouble. Their minds are
corrupt, and they have turned their backs
on the truth. To them, a show of godliness
is just a way to become wealthy.
6Yet true godliness with contentment is
itself great wealth. 7After all, we brought
nothing with us when we came into the
world, and we can't take anything with us
when we leave it. 8So if we have enough food
and clothing, let us be content.
9But people who long to be rich fall into
temptation and are trapped by many foolish
and harmful desires that plunge them into
ruin and destruction. 10For the love of

4:5 Or *made holy.* **4:6** Greek *brothers.* **4:10** Some manuscripts read *continue to suffer.* **5:1** Or *an elder.* **5:3** Or *Honor.* **5:9** Greek *was the wife of one husband.* **5:10** Greek *and washed the feet of God's holy people?* **5:17** Greek *should be worthy of double honor.* **5:18** Deut 25:4; Luke 10:7. **5:22** Greek *about the laying on of hands.* **6:2** Greek *brothers.*

▸ **5:3-16** *See **Widows**, page 400.*

money is the root of all kinds of evil. And some people, craving money, have wandered from the true faith and pierced themselves with many sorrows.

Paul's Final Instructions

[11]But you, Timothy, are a man of God; so run from all these evil things. Pursue righteousness and a godly life, along with faith, love, perseverance, and gentleness. [12]Fight the good fight for the true faith. Hold tightly to the eternal life to which God has called you, which you have declared so well before many witnesses. [13]And I charge you before God, who gives life to all, and before Christ Jesus, who gave a good testimony before Pontius Pilate, [14]that you obey this command without wavering. Then no one can find fault with you from now until our Lord Jesus Christ comes again. [15]For,

> At just the right time Christ will be
> revealed from heaven by the blessed
> and only almighty God, the King of all
> kings and Lord of all lords. [16]He alone
> can never die, and he lives in light so
> brilliant that no human can approach
> him. No human eye has ever seen him,
> nor ever will. All honor and power to
> him forever! Amen.

[17]Teach those who are rich in this world not to be proud and not to trust in their money, which is so unreliable. Their trust should be in God, who richly gives us all we need for our enjoyment. [18]Tell them to use their money to do good. They should be rich in good works and generous to those in need, always being ready to share with others. [19]By doing this they will be storing up their treasure as a good foundation for the future so that they may experience true life.

[20]Timothy, guard what God has entrusted to you. Avoid godless, foolish discussions with those who oppose you with their so-called knowledge. [21]Some people have wandered from the faith by following such foolishness.

May God's grace be with you all.

▸ **6:9-10** *See* ***Money****, page 1417.*

2 Timothy

Greetings from Paul

1 This letter is from Paul, chosen by the will of God to be an apostle of Christ Jesus. I have been sent out to tell others about the life he has promised through faith in Christ Jesus.

[2]I am writing to Timothy, my dear son.

May God the Father and Christ Jesus our Lord give you grace, mercy, and peace.

Encouragement to Be Faithful

[3]Timothy, I thank God for you—the God I serve with a clear conscience, just as my ancestors did. Night and day I constantly remember you in my prayers. [4]I long to see you again, for I remember your tears as we parted. And I will be filled with joy when we are together again.

[5]I remember your genuine faith, for you share the faith that first filled your grandmother Lois and your mother, Eunice. And I know that same faith continues strong in you. [6]This is why I remind you to fan into flames the spiritual gift God gave you when I laid my hands on you. [7]For God has not given us a spirit of fear and timidity, but of power, love, and self-discipline.

[8]So never be ashamed to tell others about our Lord. And don't be ashamed of me, either, even though I'm in prison for him. With the strength God gives you, be ready to suffer with me for the sake of the Good News. [9]For God saved us and called us to live a holy life. He did this, not because we deserved it, but because that was his plan

▸ *For introduction to* ***1 & 2 Timothy, Titus****, see page 1377.*

from before the beginning of time—to show
us his grace through Christ Jesus. 10 And now
he has made all of this plain to us by the appearing of Christ Jesus, our Savior. He broke
the power of death and illuminated the way
to life and immortality through the Good
News. 11 And God chose me to be a preacher,
an apostle, and a teacher of this Good News.
12 That is why I am suffering here in prison.
But I am not ashamed of it, for I know the
one in whom I trust, and I am sure that he is
able to guard what I have entrusted to him*
until the day of his return.
13 Hold on to the pattern of wholesome
teaching you learned from me—a pattern
shaped by the faith and love that you have
in Christ Jesus. 14 Through the power of the
Holy Spirit who lives within us, carefully
guard the precious truth that has been entrusted to you.
15 As you know, everyone from the province of Asia has deserted me—even Phyge-
lus and Hermogenes.
16 May the Lord show special kindness
to Onesiphorus and all his family because
he often visited and encouraged me. He
was never ashamed of me because I was
in chains. 17 When he came to Rome, he
searched everywhere until he found me.
18 May the Lord show him special kindness on
the day of Christ's return. And you know very
well how helpful he was in Ephesus.

A Good Soldier of Christ Jesus

2 Timothy, my dear son, be strong through
the grace that God gives you in Christ
Jesus. 2 You have heard me teach things
that have been confirmed by many reliable
witnesses. Now teach these truths to other
trustworthy people who will be able to pass
them on to others.
3 Endure suffering along with me, as a
good soldier of Christ Jesus. 4 Soldiers don't
get tied up in the affairs of civilian life, for
then they cannot please the officer who enlisted them. 5 And athletes cannot win the
prize unless they follow the rules. 6 And
hardworking farmers should be the first to
enjoy the fruit of their labor. 7 Think about
what I am saying. The Lord will help you
understand all these things.

1:12 Or *what has been entrusted to me.*

Mentoring

Paul's calling Timothy "my dear son" (2 Timothy 1:2) reflects the close bond that had developed between them. They had perhaps first met during Paul's first visit to Lystra, Timothy's hometown, as part of Paul's first missionary journey (Acts 14:6-20). When Paul returned to Lystra during his second missionary journey, he saw great potential in Timothy and took him with him as he continued his journey (Acts 16:1-3). As a good mentor, Paul gave him increasing responsibilities as he proved himself, and slowly he grew from being an "assistant" (Acts 19:22), to serving as Paul's representative (e.g., 1 Corinthians 4:17), to overseeing the church in Ephesus on Paul's behalf (1 Timothy 1:3). He worked alongside Paul "like a son with his father" (Philippians 2:22), not just being taught, but having his character shaped as they labored together. He learned "on the job," just as the disciples had done with Jesus. Paul was clearly strategic in making plans for passing on the baton of leadership.

Paul had received mentoring himself. As a young Jew, he had been mentored by Gamaliel, a leading rabbi (Acts 22:3). When Paul (then Saul) was a new Christian, Barnabas had taken him under his wing (Acts 9:27) and remained the senior figure for some time, as the order of names shows (Acts 13:2-4). But "Barnabas and Saul" soon became "Saul/Paul and Barnabas" (e.g., Acts 13:42-50), showing that Barnabas was ready to yield to what he saw God doing. The best mentors are always those who want their spiritual "children" to advance further than they have gone themselves.

▸ *See also **Barnabas**, page 1242; **Timothy**, page 1380; **Leaders in the church**, page 1390.*

8 Always remember that Jesus Christ, a descendant of King David, was raised from the
dead. This is the Good News I preach. 9 And
because I preach this Good News, I am suffering and have been chained like a criminal. But the word of God cannot be chained.
10 So I am willing to endure anything if it will
bring salvation and eternal glory in Christ
Jesus to those God has chosen.
11 This is a trustworthy saying:

If we die with him,
    we will also live with him.
12 If we endure hardship,
    we will reign with him.
If we deny him,
    he will deny us.
13 If we are unfaithful,
    he remains faithful,
    for he cannot deny who he is.

14 Remind everyone about these things,
and command them in God's presence to
stop fighting over words. Such arguments
are useless, and they can ruin those who
hear them.

An Approved Worker

15 Work hard so you can present yourself to God and receive his approval. Be a
good worker, one who does not need to be
ashamed and who correctly explains the
word of truth. 16 Avoid worthless, foolish talk
that only leads to more godless behavior.
17 This kind of talk spreads like cancer,* as in
the case of Hymenaeus and Philetus. 18 They
have left the path of truth, claiming that
the resurrection of the dead has already occurred; in this way, they have turned some
people away from the faith.
19 But God's truth stands firm like a foundation stone with this inscription: "The
LORD knows those who are his,"* and "All
who belong to the LORD must turn away
from evil."*
20 In a wealthy home some utensils are
made of gold and silver, and some are made
of wood and clay. The expensive utensils
are used for special occasions, and the
cheap ones are for everyday use. 21 If you
keep yourself pure, you will be a special
utensil for honorable use. Your life will be
clean, and you will be ready for the Master
to use you for every good work.
22 Run from anything that stimulates
youthful lusts. Instead, pursue righteous
living, faithfulness, love, and peace. Enjoy
the companionship of those who call on the
Lord with pure hearts.
23 Again I say, don't get involved in foolish,
ignorant arguments that only start fights.
24 A servant of the Lord must not quarrel but
must be kind to everyone, be able to teach,
and be patient with difficult people. 25 Gently
instruct those who oppose the truth. Perhaps
God will change those people's hearts, and
they will learn the truth. 26 Then they will
come to their senses and escape from the
devil's trap. For they have been held captive
by him to do whatever he wants.

The Dangers of the Last Days

3 You should know this, Timothy, that in
the last days there will be very difficult
times. 2 For people will love only themselves
and their money. They will be boastful and
proud, scoffing at God, disobedient to their
parents, and ungrateful. They will consider
nothing sacred. 3 They will be unloving and
unforgiving; they will slander others and
have no self-control. They will be cruel
and hate what is good. 4 They will betray
their friends, be reckless, be puffed up with
pride, and love pleasure rather than God.
5 They will act religious, but they will reject
the power that could make them godly. Stay
away from people like that!
6 They are the kind who work their way into
people's homes and win the confidence of*
vulnerable women who are burdened with
the guilt of sin and controlled by various
desires. 7 (Such women are forever following new teachings, but they are never able
to understand the truth.) 8 These teachers
oppose the truth just as Jannes and Jambres
opposed Moses. They have depraved minds
and a counterfeit faith. 9 But they won't get
away with this for long. Someday everyone
will recognize what fools they are, just as
with Jannes and Jambres.

Paul's Charge to Timothy

10 But you, Timothy, certainly know what
I teach, and how I live, and what my
purpose in life is. You know my faith, my
patience, my love, and my endurance. 11 You
know how much persecution and suffering
I have endured. You know all about how I
was persecuted in Antioch, Iconium, and
Lystra—but the Lord rescued me from all of
it. 12 Yes, and everyone who wants to live a

godly life in Christ Jesus will suffer persecution. 13But evil people and impostors will
flourish. They will deceive others and will
themselves be deceived.
14But you must remain faithful to the
things you have been taught. You know they
are true, for you know you can trust those
who taught you. 15You have been taught the
holy Scriptures from childhood, and they
have given you the wisdom to receive the
salvation that comes by trusting in Christ
Jesus. 16All Scripture is inspired by God and
is useful to teach us what is true and to make
us realize what is wrong in our lives. It corrects us when we are wrong and teaches us
to do what is right. 17God uses it to prepare
and equip his people to do every good work.

4 I solemnly urge you in the presence of
God and Christ Jesus, who will someday
judge the living and the dead when he
comes to set up his Kingdom: 2Preach the
word of God. Be prepared, whether the
time is favorable or not. Patiently correct,
rebuke, and encourage your people with
good teaching.
3For a time is coming when people will
no longer listen to sound and wholesome
teaching. They will follow their own desires
and will look for teachers who will tell them
whatever their itching ears want to hear.
4They will reject the truth and chase after
myths.
5But you should keep a clear mind in
every situation. Don't be afraid of suffering
for the Lord. Work at telling others the Good
News, and fully carry out the ministry God
has given you.
6As for me, my life has already been poured
out as an offering to God. The time of my
death is near. 7I have fought the good fight, I
have finished the race, and I have remained
faithful. 8And now the prize awaits me—the
crown of righteousness, which the Lord, the
righteous Judge, will give me on the day of
his return. And the prize is not just for me
but for all who eagerly look forward to his
appearing.

Paul's Final Words

9Timothy, please come as soon as you can.
10Demas has deserted me because he loves
the things of this life and has gone to Thessalonica. Crescens has gone to Galatia, and

2:17 Greek *gangrene*. **2:19a** Num 16:5. **2:19b** See Isa 52:11.
3:6 Greek *and take captive*.

▸ **3:12** *See **Persecution**, page 1452.* **4:6-8** *See **Heaven**, page 1451.*

Studying God's word

Christians often wish they knew the Bible like some great preacher or author. They can, of course; but it demands time, effort, and hard work—like that of a good worker (2 Timothy 2:15). We need to read it, meditate on it, study it, consult others if we don't understand it, and consider it as essential as daily food.

That's what Paul had done. His studying Scripture as a young man under Gamaliel (Acts 22:3) bore much fruit when he became a Christian leader, as he mined the Old Testament to find Christ in it. Timothy, too, had been taught the Scriptures from childhood (2 Timothy 1:5; 3:15). By contrast, a lack of studying Scripture had led the Ephesian church to be led astray by every new idea that came along. So Paul urges Timothy to keep studying Scripture so he can use it to correct error and explain the truth (4:2-5).

We need this book because it is not like any other book, secular or sacred. It is "inspired by God" (3:16). That is, God's Spirit directed the thoughts of its writers so that what they wrote was exactly what God wanted written. The Bible is therefore God's revelation to us—revealing his nature, heart, and purposes—and his invitation to join in his story.

▸ *See also **Bible teaching**, page 529; **The Scriptures in public worship**, page 544; **Meditation**, page 603; **Teaching God's word**, page 1268.*

Titus has gone to Dalmatia. 11 Only Luke is
with me. Bring Mark with you when you
come, for he will be helpful to me in my ministry. 12 I sent Tychicus to Ephesus. 13 When
you come, be sure to bring the coat I left with
Carpus at Troas. Also bring my books, and
especially my papers.*

14 Alexander the coppersmith did me
much harm, but the Lord will judge him for
what he has done. 15 Be careful of him, for he
fought against everything we said.

16 The first time I was brought before
the judge, no one came with me. Everyone abandoned me. May it not be counted
against them. 17 But the Lord stood with
me and gave me strength so that I might
preach the Good News in its entirety for
all the Gentiles to hear. And he rescued me
from certain death.* 18 Yes, and the Lord will
deliver me from every evil attack and will
bring me safely into his heavenly Kingdom.
All glory to God forever and ever! Amen.

Paul's Final Greetings

19 Give my greetings to Priscilla and Aquila
and those living in the household of Onesiphorus. 20 Erastus stayed at Corinth, and
I left Trophimus sick at Miletus.

21 Do your best to get here before winter.
Eubulus sends you greetings, and so do
Pudens, Linus, Claudia, and all the broth-
ers and sisters.*

22 May the Lord be with your spirit. And
may his grace be with all of you.

4:13 Greek *especially the parchments.* **4:17** Greek *from the mouth of a lion.* **4:21** Greek *brothers.*

Mark

The Mark whom Paul refers to in 2 Timothy 4:11 is none other than the Mark who wrote the Gospel bearing his name—though his early life would not lead us to think this possible. Mark—also called John (Acts 12:12)—was Barnabas's cousin (Colossians 4:10), and he accompanied Barnabas and Paul on their first missionary journey. However, halfway through, he pulled out, leaving Paul unimpressed and refusing to take Mark with him again (Acts 13:13; 15:36-40). But Barnabas, ever the encourager, didn't give up on Mark and took him to Cyprus with him (Acts 15:39). Later Paul and Mark were reconciled, and Paul, now nearing the end of his life, tells Timothy to "bring Mark with you when you come, for he will be helpful to me in my ministry" (2 Timothy 4:11). Peter describes Mark as "my son" (1 Peter 5:13), and early church tradition closely associates the two. In fact, Mark's Gospel seems to be based around Peter's memoirs. Mark's life shows us that we should never write anyone off, even after we feel they have let us down.

▸ *See also* ***Barnabas****, page 1242.*

Titus

Greetings from Paul

1 This letter is from Paul, a slave of God
and an apostle of Jesus Christ. I have
been sent to proclaim faith to* those God
has chosen and to teach them to know the
truth that shows them how to live godly
lives. 2 This truth gives them confidence
that they have eternal life, which God—
who does not lie—promised them before the
world began. 3 And now at just the right time
he has revealed this message, which we announce to everyone. It is by the command
of God our Savior that I have been entrusted
with this work for him.
4 I am writing to Titus, my true son in the
faith that we share.

May God the Father and Christ Jesus our
Savior give you grace and peace.

Titus's Work in Crete

5 I left you on the island of Crete so you could
complete our work there and appoint elders
in each town as I instructed you. 6 An elder
must live a blameless life. He must be faithful to his wife,* and his children must be
believers who don't have a reputation for
being wild or rebellious. 7 A church leader*
is a manager of God's household, so he must
live a blameless life. He must not be arrogant
or quick-tempered; he must not be a heavy
drinker,* violent, or dishonest with money.
8 Rather, he must enjoy having guests in
his home, and he must love what is good. He
must live wisely and be just. He must live a
devout and disciplined life. 9 He must have a
strong belief in the trustworthy message he
was taught; then he will be able to encourage
others with wholesome teaching and show
those who oppose it where they are wrong.
10 For there are many rebellious people
who engage in useless talk and deceive
others. This is especially true of those who
insist on circumcision for salvation. 11 They
must be silenced, because they are turning
whole families away from the truth by their
false teaching. And they do it only for money.

1:1 Or *to strengthen the faith of.* **1:6** Or *must have only one wife,* or *must be married only once;* Greek reads *must be the husband of one wife.* **1:7a** Or *An overseer,* or *A bishop.* **1:7b** Greek *must not drink too much wine.*

▶ *For introduction to* ***1 & 2 Timothy, Titus,*** *see page 1377.*

Titus

Paul had sailed along the coast of Crete while under arrest and on his way to Rome, but we have no record of him going ashore there at the time (see Acts 27:7-12). After his release in Rome, he must have returned there with Titus at some point, for he writes, "I left you on the island of Crete so you could complete our work there and appoint elders in each town as I instructed you" (Titus 1:5). Paul describes Titus as "my true son in the faith that we share" (1:4)—suggesting he was probably converted under Paul's ministry—and "my partner who works with me" (2 Corinthians 8:23). He had accompanied Paul and Barnabas on their visit to Jerusalem to meet with the apostles (Galatians 2:1-3); had been sent by Paul to Corinth to deal with difficulties in the church there, eventually returning with good news (2 Corinthians 7:5-15); and had organized the offering from Corinth for Jerusalem (2 Corinthians 8:16–9:15). Paul's leaving him to lead the work in Crete is a measure of Paul's strong confidence in this young man.

▶ *See also* ***Paul's Missionary Journeys*** *map, Visual Overview Z15.*

12 Even one of their own men, a prophet from
Crete, has said about them, "The people of
Crete are all liars, cruel animals, and lazy
gluttons."* 13 This is true. So reprimand them
sternly to make them strong in the faith.
14 They must stop listening to Jewish myths
and the commands of people who have
turned away from the truth.

15 Everything is pure to those whose hearts
are pure. But nothing is pure to those who
are corrupt and unbelieving, because their
minds and consciences are corrupted.
16 Such people claim they know God, but
they deny him by the way they live. They
are detestable and disobedient, worthless
for doing anything good.

Promote Right Teaching

2 As for you, Titus, promote the kind of
living that reflects wholesome teaching. 2 Teach the older men to exercise self-
control, to be worthy of respect, and to live
wisely. They must have sound faith and be
filled with love and patience.

3 Similarly, teach the older women to
live in a way that honors God. They must
not slander others or be heavy drinkers.*
Instead, they should teach others what is
good. 4 These older women must train the
younger women to love their husbands and
their children, 5 to live wisely and be pure,
to work in their homes,* to do good, and
to be submissive to their husbands. Then
they will not bring shame on the word of
God.

6 In the same way, encourage the young
men to live wisely. 7 And you yourself must
be an example to them by doing good works
of every kind. Let everything you do reflect
the integrity and seriousness of your teaching. 8 Teach the truth so that your teaching
can't be criticized. Then those who oppose
us will be ashamed and have nothing bad
to say about us.

9 Slaves must always obey their masters
and do their best to please them. They must
not talk back 10 or steal, but must show themselves to be entirely trustworthy and good.
Then they will make the teaching about God
our Savior attractive in every way.

11 For the grace of God has been revealed,
bringing salvation to all people. 12 And we
are instructed to turn from godless living
and sinful pleasures. We should live in
this evil world with wisdom, righteousness, and devotion to God, 13 while we look

▸ **1:15** *See **Conscience**, page 333.* **2:2** *See **Respect for those who are older**, page 415.*

Leaders in the church

While there are many different leadership structures in churches today, things were simpler in New Testament times. There were, it seems, two categories of local church leadership: elders (also called "church leaders"), who had responsibility for the spiritual life of the church; and deacons, who concerned themselves with its practical affairs. The requirements for both, however, were high (see 1 Timothy 3:1-13).

It was Paul's practice to install elders wherever he started churches (Acts 14:23); but he had no time to do so in Crete, so he instructs Titus to do it (Titus 1:5). Of all the qualities he tells him to seek in potential elders (1:6-9), all but one—a good grasp of doctrine—have to do with character and family life. For if someone cannot care for their own life and family well, they cannot care for God's church well. The same pattern is found in 1 Timothy 3:1-7, where all but one quality—an ability to teach—are again related to character and home life.

Interestingly, what is not mentioned is the issue of age. Timothy was probably only in his late twenties or early thirties, and Titus was a young man too. So eligibility for leadership does not seem to depend on age or worldly experience, but suitability of character and God's call.

▸ *See also **The kind of leaders God wants**, page 170; **Mentoring**, page 1385.*

forward with hope to that wonderful day when the glory of our great God and Savior, Jesus Christ, will be revealed. [14]He gave his life to free us from every kind of sin, to cleanse us, and to make us his very own people, totally committed to doing good deeds.

[15]You must teach these things and encourage the believers to do them. You have the authority to correct them when necessary, so don't let anyone disregard what you say.

Do What Is Good

3 Remind the believers to submit to the government and its officers. They should be obedient, always ready to do what is good. [2]They must not slander anyone and must avoid quarreling. Instead, they should be gentle and show true humility to everyone.

[3]Once we, too, were foolish and disobedient. We were misled and became slaves to many lusts and pleasures. Our lives were full of evil and envy, and we hated each other. [4]But—

When God our Savior revealed his
kindness and love, [5]he saved us, not
because of the righteous things we
had done, but because of his mercy.
He washed away our sins, giving us
a new birth and new life through the
Holy Spirit.* [6]He generously poured out
the Spirit upon us through Jesus Christ
our Savior. [7]Because of his grace he
made us right in his sight and gave us
confidence that we will inherit eternal
life.

[8]This is a trustworthy saying, and I want you to insist on these teachings so that all who trust in God will devote themselves to doing good. These teachings are good and beneficial for everyone.

[9]Do not get involved in foolish discussions about spiritual pedigrees* or in quarrels and fights about obedience to Jewish laws. These things are useless and a waste of time. [10]If people are causing divisions among you, give a first and second warning. After that, have nothing more to do with them. [11]For people like that have turned away from the truth, and their own sins condemn them.

Paul's Final Remarks and Greetings

[12]I am planning to send either Artemas or Tychicus to you. As soon as one of them arrives, do your best to meet me at Nicopolis, for I have decided to stay there for the winter. [13]Do everything you can to help Zenas the lawyer and Apollos with their trip. See that they are given everything they need. [14]Our people must learn to do good by meeting the urgent needs of others; then they will not be unproductive.

[15]Everybody here sends greetings. Please give my greetings to the believers—all who love us.

May God's grace be with you all.

1:12 This quotation is from Epimenides of Knossos. **2:3** Greek *be enslaved to much wine.* **2:5** Some manuscripts read *to care for their homes.* **3:5** Greek *He saved us through the washing of regeneration and renewing of the Holy Spirit.* **3:9** Or *spiritual genealogies.*

Philemon *Receive him as a brother*

In this short personal letter to his friend Philemon, who lived in Colosse, Paul writes about a slave named Onesimus, who had stolen from his master and run away—an offense punishable by death under Roman law. Onesimus had met Paul in Rome, had become a Christian, and had been useful to Paul in his missionary work; so Paul now appeals to Philemon on his behalf. The one whom Philemon once saw as not of much use had now become "useful" (the meaning of the name *Onesimus*) to Paul (1:11).

Some years later there was a bishop of Ephesus called Onesimus, to whom Ignatius, the bishop of Antioch, wrote a letter, making the same pun on the meaning of his name "Useful." It is therefore possible that this runaway slave eventually became a bishop.

What's it all about?

Paul begins by commending Philemon as "our beloved co-worker" (1:1) and by praising him for his kindness toward fellow Christians (1:5). He then raises the matter of his appeal for Onesimus, Philemon's runaway slave, telling Philemon how useful he has been to him while in prison. He has grown very fond of Onesimus and refers to him as "my child" (1:10), which suggests that he became a Christian through Paul's ministry. Paul says he is sending the runaway back home and appeals to Philemon to welcome him warmly, as a Christian brother, when he gets back. Now that they are fellow believers, this should affect the master-slave relationship between them. Paul offers to repay any losses that Philemon may have experienced (after all, Philemon had probably had to buy a replacement slave)—though he also reminds him that he owes his very existence as a Christian to Paul (1:19). The implication of what he is asking for is clear: nothing less than giving Onesimus his freedom.

Paul asks Philemon to prepare a guest room for him so he will have somewhere to stay upon his release from prison (1:22) and ends by sending various greetings.

OVERVIEW

What does it mean for us?

From heaven's perspective, the two main subjects of this letter were both free, and both used their freedom to serve other people. But in practical terms, their circumstances were quite different. Philemon was a wealthy and influential businessman in Colosse, and master of his own destiny. But Onesimus was the very opposite. He had nothing, and his future was linked to his master's.

Paul's very short letter reveals how, whatever people's social standing, God's love reaches out to meet them and accept them where they are. And the church—in this case the church that met in Philemon's house—is meant to be a microcosm of heaven, where there will be no divisions. We need to start living that out right now.

While Paul didn't attack the social evil of slavery as such—for he could do nothing to change it—he did provide a basis from which it would eventually be attacked and destroyed, declaring that all, slaves and free alike, are equal in the family of God.

Greetings from Paul

This letter is from Paul, a prisoner for preaching the Good News about Christ Jesus, and from our brother Timothy.

I am writing to Philemon, our beloved coworker, [2]and to our sister Apphia, and to our fellow soldier Archippus, and to the church that meets in your* house.

[3]May God our Father and the Lord Jesus Christ give you grace and peace.

Paul's Thanksgiving and Prayer

[4]I always thank my God when I pray for you, Philemon, [5]because I keep hearing about your faith in the Lord Jesus and your love for all of God's people. [6]And I am praying that you will put into action the generosity that comes from your faith as you understand and experience all the good things we have in Christ. [7]Your love has given me much joy and comfort, my brother, for your kindness has often refreshed the hearts of God's people.

Paul's Appeal for Onesimus

[8]That is why I am boldly asking a favor of you. I could demand it in the name of Christ because it is the right thing for you to do. [9]But because of our love, I prefer simply to ask you. Consider this as a request from me—Paul, an old man and now also a prisoner for the sake of Christ Jesus.*

[10]I appeal to you to show kindness to my child, Onesimus. I became his father in the faith while here in prison. [11]Onesimus* hasn't been of much use to you in the past, but now he is very useful to both of us. [12]I am sending him back to you, and with him comes my own heart.

[13]I wanted to keep him here with me while I am in these chains for preaching the Good News, and he would have helped me on your behalf. [14]But I didn't want to do anything without your consent. I wanted you to

2 Throughout this letter, *you* and *your* are singular except in verses 3, 22, and 25. **9** Or *a prisoner of Christ Jesus.* **11** *Onesimus* means "useful."

Slavery

Paul was in a real dilemma. As a Roman citizen, he was obliged to hand over Onesimus, this runaway slave, for slaves were their master's property, and absconding was a capital offense. But as a Christian, he had a duty to care for Onesimus, who had become a Christian through Paul (Philemon 1:10), and he was obliged to give him sanctuary (Deuteronomy 23:15-16). But Philemon too was in a dilemma, as Paul reminds him. As a master, he had absolute rights over Onesimus; but as a Christian, he and Onesimus were now brothers in Christ. Paul therefore appeals to him to forgive Onesimus, just as Jesus had forgiven Philemon himself.

While Paul doesn't attack slavery (it was so deeply entrenched in society that he knew he couldn't change it), he does start to undermine it. Elsewhere we find him encouraging slaves to gain their freedom whenever possible (1 Corinthians 7:21), denouncing slave trading as incompatible with Christianity (1 Timothy 1:9-11) and calling on Christian masters and slaves alike to function in light of their relationship to Christ (Ephesians 6:5-9; Colossians 3:22-25). Above all, he insisted that "there is no longer Jew or Gentile, slave or free, male and female. For you are all one in Christ Jesus" (Galatians 3:28). Such teaching sowed the seeds of the destruction of slavery in due course.

help because you were willing, not because
you were forced. [15]It seems you lost Onesimus for a little while so that you could have
him back forever. [16]He is no longer like a
slave to you. He is more than a slave, for he
is a beloved brother, especially to me. Now
he will mean much more to you, both as a
man and as a brother in the Lord.

[17]So if you consider me your partner,
welcome him as you would welcome me. [18]If
he has wronged you in any way or owes you
anything, charge it to me. [19]I, PAUL, WRITE
THIS WITH MY OWN HAND: I WILL REPAY IT.
AND I WON'T MENTION THAT YOU OWE ME
YOUR VERY SOUL!

[20]Yes, my brother, please do me this
favor* for the Lord's sake. Give me this encouragement in Christ.

[21]I am confident as I write this letter that
you will do what I ask and even more! [22]One
more thing—please prepare a guest room for
me, for I am hoping that God will answer
your prayers and let me return to you soon.

Paul's Final Greetings

[23]Epaphras, my fellow prisoner in Christ
Jesus, sends you his greetings. [24]So do
Mark, Aristarchus, Demas, and Luke, my
co-workers.

[25]May the grace of the Lord Jesus Christ be
with your spirit.

20 Greek *onaimen*, a play on the name Onesimus.

Hebrews *Jesus Christ above all*

Written to encourage Christians from a Jewish background who were being persecuted and thus were tempted to revert to their old Judaism, this letter seeks to show that Jesus is better than anything the old covenant had to offer. It lifts Jesus up as a far better priest and sacrifice, the perfect model and leader, and presents many reasons to remain faithful. It contains many allusions and references to the Old Testament and shows how Jesus brought about a new covenant between God and humanity that was far better than the old one. In Jesus, God meets us and we meet God.

While Paul has traditionally been seen by many as the author of Hebrews, the style of writing and method of argument make this unlikely. The truth is that we do not know who wrote it; we only know that the writer was a Jewish Christian writing to other Jewish Christians. It was probably written before AD 70, when the Jerusalem Temple was destroyed.

What's it all about?

The writer's opening words (1:1-2) sum up the heart of his message: how unique the revelation through God's Son really is. Jesus is utterly greater than any messenger who came before him, so we should take the gospel seriously, remembering the miracles and signs that confirmed it (2:4).

Chapter 2 outlines the lengths to which God has gone to save us. He sent his Son as a human being to identify with us and destroy the devil and his works. Through his sacrifice for sins, we can now become part of God's family.

In chapters 3 to 5, the writer encourages his readers to stay focused on Jesus, who is greater even than Moses and who brings a rest greater than that which Joshua gave to Israel when they entered the Promised Land. The temptation to revert to sin is always there; but Jesus is there to help us in temptation, trials, and weaknesses. Through him, our "great High Priest" (4:14), we can boldly approach God, knowing we will receive the help we need. Unlike the priests of the old covenant, Jesus was sinless, so his prayers on our behalf are always effective. Therefore, we should press on and not fall back, for God has promised to be with us (chapter 6). The writer then compares Jesus' priesthood with that of Melchizedek, who, like Jesus, was both a priest and a king (Genesis 14:18-20). But even this comparison is limited, for Jesus is unique—and uniquely suited to meeting our needs (chapters 7–8).

Chapters 8 to 10 consider the new covenant that Jesus our High Priest has brought about between God and humanity. The old covenant required blood sacrifices for sin, but it could never really get to the root of the problem. Jesus' once-for-all sacrifice on the cross, however, is the ultimate and final remedy for sin.

Chapter 11 encourages the readers to live by faith, reminding them of heroes of faith from Israel's history. All these examples encourage us to keep going as we keep our eyes on Jesus (12:1-2). The concluding chapters teach us how to live out our faith in practical ways; and the letter ends with a reminder that, when we suffer abuse and persecution, we share in the sufferings of Christ.

What does it mean for us?

While not all of us will face persecution for being a Christian, all of us will certainly face challenging times and pressures in life. It is at such times that Satan tempts us to go back to our old way of life, telling us it was so much easier then. At such times we, like the recipients of Hebrews, have a decision to make: Do we go back to our old way of life, which we left because we realized it wasn't fulfilling and saw that Jesus offered something far better? Or do we press on and trust God to bring us through? Hebrews encourages us to keep trusting in Christ and all he has done for us, and to not give up (3:6, 14; 10:23, 35-36; 12:1).

Being a Christian is like canoeing upstream. The moment we lift our paddles, the current effortlessly sweeps the boat downstream. So we can't stop paddling! Hebrews tells us that the same is true in life. Keeping the flame of God's love glowing in our lives requires attention, consistency, and, usually, effort. Nobody feels spiritual all of the time; we don't always "feel" like getting up for church services any more than we always "feel" like being nice! Christians often need to go against the flow, as it were, to do the opposite of the general way of life around us, and sometimes that can feel like hard work. But with a clear focus on Jesus, and the support of other Christians, we will keep going to the end.

OVERVIEW

The supremacy of God's Son
1:1-14

Warnings about neglecting Christ and his salvation · *2:1-18*

Jesus, greater than Moses
3:1-19

Jesus, greater than Israel's rest in the Promised Land · *4:1-13*

Jesus, our High Priest
4:14–5:10

Warnings against turning away from the faith · *5:11–6:12*

The certainty of God's promise
6:13-20

Jesus, the priest like King Melchizedek · *7:1-28*

Jesus, High Priest of a better covenant · *8:1-13*

Jesus, the bringer of a better sanctuary · *9:1-10*

Jesus, the better sacrifice
9:11–10:18

A call to persevere and live by faith
10:19–11:40

A call to embrace God's discipline and Kingdom · *12:1-29*

Exhortations to live out the faith, and conclusion · *13:1-25*

Jesus Christ Is God's Son

1 Long ago God spoke many times and in
many ways to our ancestors through the
prophets. 2 And now in these final days, he
has spoken to us through his Son. God promised everything to the Son as an inheritance,
and through the Son he created the universe.
3 The Son radiates God's own glory and expresses the very character of God, and he
sustains everything by the mighty power
of his command. When he had cleansed us
from our sins, he sat down in the place of
honor at the right hand of the majestic God
in heaven. 4 This shows that the Son is far
greater than the angels, just as the name God
gave him is greater than their names.

The Son Is Greater Than the Angels

5 For God never said to any angel what he said
to Jesus:

"You are my Son.
Today I have become your
Father.*"

God also said,

"I will be his Father,
and he will be my Son."*

6 And when he brought his supreme* Son into
the world, God said,*

"Let all of God's angels worship him."*

7 Regarding the angels, he says,

"He sends his angels like the winds,
his servants like flames of fire."*

8 But to the Son he says,

"Your throne, O God, endures forever
and ever.
You rule with a scepter of justice.
9 You love justice and hate evil.
Therefore, O God, your God has
anointed you,
pouring out the oil of joy on you more
than on anyone else."*

10 He also says to the Son,

"In the beginning, Lord, you laid the
foundation of the earth
and made the heavens with your
hands.
11 They will perish, but you remain forever.
They will wear out like old clothing.
12 You will fold them up like a cloak
and discard them like old
clothing.
But you are always the same;
you will live forever."*

13 And God never said to any of the angels,

"Sit in the place of honor at my right
hand
until I humble your enemies,
making them a footstool under your
feet."*

14 Therefore, angels are only servants—spirits sent to care for people who will inherit salvation.

A Warning against Drifting Away

2 So we must listen very carefully to the
truth we have heard, or we may drift
away from it. 2 For the message God delivered through angels has always stood
firm, and every violation of the law and
every act of disobedience was punished.
3 So what makes us think we can escape if
we ignore this great salvation that was first
announced by the Lord Jesus himself and
then delivered to us by those who heard him
speak? 4 And God confirmed the message
by giving signs and wonders and various

1:5a Or *Today I reveal you as my Son.* Ps 2:7. **1:5b** 2 Sam 7:14. **1:6a** Or *firstborn.* **1:6b** Or *when he again brings his supreme Son* [or *firstborn Son*] *into the world, God will say.* **1:6c** Deut 32:43. **1:7** Ps 104:4 (Greek version). **1:8-9** Ps 45:6-7. **1:10-12** Ps 102:25-27. **1:13** Ps 110:1.

Angels

Angels are spiritual beings created to serve God. Although often portrayed in art with white robes and wings, in the Bible itself they are described in much more "human" ways and are sometimes even mistaken for people at first (e.g., Genesis 19:1-3). They do not have wings, although some heavenly beings—some kinds of cherubim (Ezekiel 10:3-5) and seraphim (Isaiah 6:2)—do.

The word "angel" means "messenger," for one of their chief roles is to take God's message to people (e.g., Luke 1:26-38). But they also convey his blessing (Genesis 24:40), intervention (Genesis 22:9-12), help (Daniel 6:22), protection (Psalm 91:11), direction (Acts 8:26), and even judgment (Genesis 19:1-29).

Despite the importance of angels, they are merely created beings and so are not to be worshiped or prayed to. When angel-worship crept into the church in Colosse—possibly the result of thinking that God was too transcendent, too otherworldly, to be approached directly—Paul quickly corrected this error (Colossians 2:18). And the writer of Hebrews emphasized Jesus' complete superiority to angels (Hebrews 1:5-14). Nor are angels' evil counterparts—demons—to gain our attention. Demons are fallen angels who rebelled with Satan, but they are vastly outnumbered by God's angels. When Satan rebelled, he took only one-third of the angels with him (Revelation 12:3-4, where the stars symbolize angels), meaning there are two angels for every demon. We therefore have nothing to fear!

▸ *See also **The angel of the LORD**, page 271; **Gabriel**, page 967; **The archangel Michael**, page 972.*

miracles and gifts of the Holy Spirit whenever he chose.

Jesus, the Man

5 And furthermore, it is not angels who will
control the future world we are talking
about. 6 For in one place the Scriptures say,

> "What are mere mortals that you should
> think about them,
> or a son of man* that you should care
> for him?
> 7 Yet for a little while you made them a
> little lower than the angels
> and crowned them with glory and
> honor.*
> 8 You gave them authority over all
> things."*

Now when it says "all things," it means
nothing is left out. But we have not yet seen
all things put under their authority. 9 What
we do see is Jesus, who for a little while
was given a position "a little lower than
the angels"; and because he suffered death
for us, he is now "crowned with glory and
honor." Yes, by God's grace, Jesus tasted
death for everyone. 10 God, for whom and
through whom everything was made, chose
to bring many children into glory. And it
was only right that he should make Jesus,
through his suffering, a perfect leader, fit to
bring them into their salvation.

11 So now Jesus and the ones he makes
holy have the same Father. That is why
Jesus is not ashamed to call them his brothers and sisters.* 12 For he said to God,

> "I will proclaim your name to my
> brothers and sisters.
> I will praise you among your
> assembled people."*

13 He also said,

> "I will put my trust in him,"
> that is, "I and the children God has
> given me."*

14 Because God's children are human
beings—made of flesh and blood—the Son
also became flesh and blood. For only as
a human being could he die, and only by
dying could he break the power of the devil,
who had* the power of death. 15 Only in this
way could he set free all who have lived
their lives as slaves to the fear of dying.

16 We also know that the Son did not come
to help angels; he came to help the descendants of Abraham. 17 Therefore, it was necessary for him to be made in every respect
like us, his brothers and sisters,* so that
he could be our merciful and faithful High
Priest before God. Then he could offer a sacrifice that would take away the sins of the
people. 18 Since he himself has gone through
suffering and testing, he is able to help us
when we are being tested.

Jesus Is Greater Than Moses

3 And so, dear brothers and sisters who
belong to God and* are partners with
those called to heaven, think carefully
about this Jesus whom we declare to be
God's messenger* and High Priest. 2 For he
was faithful to God, who appointed him,
just as Moses served faithfully when he was
entrusted with God's entire* house.

3 But Jesus deserves far more glory than
Moses, just as a person who builds a house
deserves more praise than the house itself.
4 For every house has a builder, but the one
who built everything is God.

5 Moses was certainly faithful in God's
house as a servant. His work was an illustration of the truths God would reveal later.
6 But Christ, as the Son, is in charge of God's
entire house. And we are God's house, if we
keep our courage and remain confident in
our hope in Christ.*

7 That is why the Holy Spirit says,

> "Today when you hear his voice,
> 8 don't harden your hearts
> as Israel did when they rebelled,
> when they tested me in the
> wilderness.
> 9 There your ancestors tested and tried my
> patience,
> even though they saw my miracles for
> forty years.
> 10 So I was angry with them, and I said,
> 'Their hearts always turn away from me.
> They refuse to do what I tell them.'
> 11 So in my anger I took an oath:
> 'They will never enter my place of
> rest.'"*

12 Be careful then, dear brothers and sisters.*
Make sure that your own hearts are not evil
and unbelieving, turning you away from the
living God. 13 You must warn each other every
day, while it is still "today," so that none of
you will be deceived by sin and hardened

against God. [14]For if we are faithful to the
end, trusting God just as firmly as when
we first believed, we will share in all that
belongs to Christ. [15]Remember what it says:

"Today when you hear his voice,
don't harden your hearts
as Israel did when they rebelled."*

[16]And who was it who rebelled against
God, even though they heard his voice?
Wasn't it the people Moses led out of Egypt?
[17]And who made God angry for forty years?
Wasn't it the people who sinned, whose
corpses lay in the wilderness? [18]And to
whom was God speaking when he took an
oath that they would never enter his rest?
Wasn't it the people who disobeyed him?
[19]So we see that because of their unbelief
they were not able to enter his rest.

Promised Rest for God's People

4 God's promise of entering his rest still
stands, so we ought to tremble with
fear that some of you might fail to experience it. [2]For this good news—that God has
prepared this rest—has been announced to
us just as it was to them. But it did them
no good because they didn't share the faith
of those who listened to God.* [3]For only we
who believe can enter his rest. As for the
others, God said,

"In my anger I took an oath:
'They will never enter my place of
rest,'"*

even though this rest has been ready since
he made the world. [4]We know it is ready
because of the place in the Scriptures
where it mentions the seventh day: "On the
seventh day God rested from all his work."*
[5]But in the other passage God said, "They
will never enter my place of rest."*

[6]So God's rest is there for people to enter,
but those who first heard this good news
failed to enter because they disobeyed God.
[7]So God set another time for entering his
rest, and that time is today. God announced
this through David much later in the words
already quoted:

"Today when you hear his voice,
don't harden your hearts."*

[8]Now if Joshua had succeeded in giving
them this rest, God would not have spoken
about another day of rest still to come. [9]So
there is a special rest* still waiting for the
people of God. [10]For all who have entered
into God's rest have rested from their labors,
just as God did after creating the world. [11]So
let us do our best to enter that rest. But if
we disobey God, as the people of Israel did,
we will fall.

2:6 Or *the Son of Man.* **2:7** Some manuscripts add *You gave them charge of everything you made.* **2:6-8** Ps 8:4-6 (Greek version). **2:11** Greek *brothers;* also in 2:12. **2:12** Ps 22:22. **2:13** Isa 8:17-18. **2:14** Or *has.* **2:17** Greek *like the brothers.* **3:1a** Greek *And so, holy brothers who.* **3:1b** Greek *God's apostle.* **3:2** Some manuscripts do not include *entire.* **3:6** Some manuscripts add *faithful to the end.* **3:7-11** Ps 95:7-11. **3:12** Greek *brothers.* **3:15** Ps 95:7-8. **4:2** Some manuscripts read *they didn't combine what they heard with faith.* **4:3** Ps 95:11. **4:4** Gen 2:2. **4:5** Ps 95:11. **4:7** Ps 95:7-8. **4:9** Or *a Sabbath rest.*

Confidence

Confidence—the assurance we can do or say something—is a valuable asset. When we know we have the ability or resources to do a task, or that right is on our side, we can face the toughest challenges. Of course, some of us are naturally more confident than others; and our confidence can be challenged when we encounter someone who is just as confident as us but takes a different viewpoint.

Hebrews, however, speaks of an entirely different kind of confidence, one that isn't based on our abilities and knowledge—which will ultimately fail in some situation or other—but rather, one that is based on Christ alone. Such confidence means we can approach God boldly (Hebrews 4:16)—yes, boldly! For it is not dependent on us—our efforts or goodness—but on Christ our great High Priest alone (4:14-15), who not only acted as our priest but who also offered himself as a perfect sacrifice for us (9:11-14, 24-28). It was through this sacrifice that he removed every trace of sin from us, thus cleansing our conscience (9:14) and removing any barrier to our being able to enter God's presence and know him as our friend. Because of Christ, God is now utterly approachable (10:19-22).

12For the word of God is alive and powerful. It is sharper than the sharpest two-edged sword, cutting between soul and spirit, between joint and marrow. It exposes our innermost thoughts and desires. 13Nothing in all creation is hidden from God. Everything is naked and exposed before his eyes, and he is the one to whom we are accountable.

Christ Is Our High Priest

14So then, since we have a great High Priest who has entered heaven, Jesus the Son of God, let us hold firmly to what we believe. 15This High Priest of ours understands our weaknesses, for he faced all of the same testings we do, yet he did not sin. 16So let us come boldly to the throne of our gracious God. There we will receive his mercy, and we will find grace to help us when we need it most.

5 Every high priest is a man chosen to represent other people in their dealings with God. He presents their gifts to God and offers sacrifices for their sins. 2And he is able to deal gently with ignorant and wayward people because he himself is subject to the same weaknesses. 3That is why he must offer sacrifices for his own sins as well as theirs.

4And no one can become a high priest simply because he wants such an honor. He must be called by God for this work, just as Aaron was. 5That is why Christ did not honor himself by assuming he could become High Priest. No, he was chosen by God, who said to him,

"You are my Son.
Today I have become your Father.*"

6And in another passage God said to him,

"You are a priest forever in the order of
Melchizedek."*

7While Jesus was here on earth, he offered prayers and pleadings, with a loud cry and tears, to the one who could rescue him from death. And God heard his prayers because of his deep reverence for God. 8Even though Jesus was God's Son, he learned obedience from the things he suffered. 9In this way, God qualified him as a perfect High Priest, and he became the source of eternal salvation for all those who obey him. 10And God designated him to be a High Priest in the order of Melchizedek.

A Call to Spiritual Growth

11There is much more we would like to say about this, but it is difficult to explain, especially since you are spiritually dull and don't seem to listen. 12You have been believers so long now that you ought to be teaching others. Instead, you need someone to teach you again the basic things about God's word.* You are like babies who need milk and cannot eat solid food. 13For someone who lives on milk is still an infant and doesn't know how to do what is right. 14Solid food is for those who are mature, who through training have the skill to recognize the difference between right and wrong.

6 So let us stop going over the basic teachings about Christ again and again. Let us go on instead and become mature in our understanding. Surely we don't need to start again with the fundamental importance of repenting from evil deeds* and placing our faith in God. 2You don't need further instruction about baptisms, the laying on of hands, the resurrection of the dead, and eternal judgment. 3And so, God willing, we will move forward to further understanding.

4For it is impossible to bring back to repentance those who were once enlightened—those who have experienced the good things of heaven and shared in the Holy Spirit, 5who have tasted the goodness of the word of God and the power of the age to come—6and who then turn away from God. It is impossible to bring such people back to repentance; by rejecting the Son of God, they themselves are nailing him to the cross once again and holding him up to public shame.

7When the ground soaks up the falling rain and bears a good crop for the farmer, it has God's blessing. 8But if a field bears thorns and thistles, it is useless. The farmer will soon condemn that field and burn it.

9Dear friends, even though we are talking this way, we really don't believe it applies to you. We are confident that you are meant for better things, things that come with salvation. 10For God is not unjust. He will not forget how hard you have worked for him and how you have shown your love to him by caring for other believers,* as you still do. 11Our great desire is that you will keep on

loving others as long as life lasts, in order
to make certain that what you hope for will
come true. 12Then you will not become spiritually dull and indifferent. Instead, you will
follow the example of those who are going
to inherit God's promises because of their
faith and endurance.

God's Promises Bring Hope

13For example, there was God's promise to
Abraham. Since there was no one greater
to swear by, God took an oath in his own
name, saying:

14 "I will certainly bless you,
and I will multiply your descendants
beyond number."*

15Then Abraham waited patiently, and he
received what God had promised.
16Now when people take an oath, they call
on someone greater than themselves to hold
them to it. And without any question that
oath is binding. 17God also bound himself
with an oath, so that those who received
the promise could be perfectly sure that he
would never change his mind. 18So God has
given both his promise and his oath. These
two things are unchangeable because it is
impossible for God to lie. Therefore, we who
have fled to him for refuge can have great
confidence as we hold to the hope that
lies before us. 19This hope is a strong and
trustworthy anchor for our souls. It leads us
through the curtain into God's inner sanctuary. 20Jesus has already gone in there for
us. He has become our eternal High Priest in
the order of Melchizedek.

Melchizedek Is Greater Than Abraham

7 This Melchizedek was king of the city
of Salem and also a priest of God Most
High. When Abraham was returning home
after winning a great battle against the
kings, Melchizedek met him and blessed
him. 2Then Abraham took a tenth of all
he had captured in battle and gave it to
Melchizedek. The name Melchizedek means
"king of justice," and king of Salem means
"king of peace." 3There is no record of his
father or mother or any of his ancestors—no
beginning or end to his life. He remains a
priest forever, resembling the Son of God.
4Consider then how great this Melchizedek was. Even Abraham, the great patriarch
of Israel, recognized this by giving him a
tenth of what he had taken in battle. 5Now

5:5 Or *Today I reveal you as my Son.* Ps 2:7. **5:6** Ps 110:4. **5:12** Or *about the oracles of God.* **6:1** Greek *from dead works.* **6:10** Greek *for God's holy people.* **6:14** Gen 22:17.

Can a Christian lose their salvation?

Hebrews 6:4-6 is a difficult passage that has sometimes caused some Christians to doubt their salvation. But we must remember for whom it was written: Jewish Christians who, under persecution, were considering reverting to Judaism. If Jesus is superior to everything from the old covenant (chapters 1–5), how can they hope to be saved if they abandon him and return to what they discovered couldn't save them? the author asks. But his going on to speak of God's justice and faithfulness (6:6-20) suggests he believes this will not—indeed, could not—happen. For the New Testament often speaks of God's faithfulness and ability to keep his people. Jesus promised that his sheep "will never perish. No one can snatch them away from me" (John 10:28). And Paul promised that "God, who began the good work within you, will continue his work until it is finally finished on the day when Christ Jesus returns" (Philippians 1:6).

Of course, the Bible challenges Christians to not become faithless, careless, or lazy; but such passages are not meant to discourage us. Rather, they are meant to provoke us to press on with God in challenging and hard times so that we do not miss out on what he wants to do in us through them. Ultimately, the Bible assures us that "if we are unfaithful, he remains faithful, for he cannot deny who he is" (2 Timothy 2:13).

▶ *See also* ***Backsliding****, page 841;* ***Pressing on****, page 1359.*

the law of Moses required that the priests,
who are descendants of Levi, must collect a
tithe from the rest of the people of Israel,*
who are also descendants of Abraham. [6]But
Melchizedek, who was not a descendant
of Levi, collected a tenth from Abraham.
And Melchizedek placed a blessing upon
Abraham, the one who had already received
the promises of God. [7]And without question,
the person who has the power to give a blessing is greater than the one who is blessed.
[8]The priests who collect tithes are men
who die, so Melchizedek is greater than they
are, because we are told that he lives on.
[9]In addition, we might even say that these
Levites—the ones who collect the tithe—paid
a tithe to Melchizedek when their ancestor
Abraham paid a tithe to him. [10]For although
Levi wasn't born yet, the seed from which
he came was in Abraham's body when
Melchizedek collected the tithe from him.
[11]So if the priesthood of Levi, on which
the law was based, could have achieved the
perfection God intended, why did God need
to establish a different priesthood, with a
priest in the order of Melchizedek instead
of the order of Levi and Aaron?*
[12]And if the priesthood is changed, the
law must also be changed to permit it. [13]For
the priest we are talking about belongs to a
different tribe, whose members have never
served at the altar as priests. [14]What I mean
is, our Lord came from the tribe of Judah,
and Moses never mentioned priests coming
from that tribe.

Jesus Is like Melchizedek

[15]This change has been made very clear
since a different priest, who is like Melchizedek, has appeared. [16]Jesus became a
priest, not by meeting the physical requirement of belonging to the tribe of Levi, but
by the power of a life that cannot be destroyed. [17]And the psalmist pointed this out
when he prophesied,

> "You are a priest forever in the order of
> Melchizedek."*

[18]Yes, the old requirement about the priesthood was set aside because it was weak and
useless. [19]For the law never made anything
perfect. But now we have confidence in a
better hope, through which we draw near
to God.
[20]This new system was established with a
solemn oath. Aaron's descendants became
priests without such an oath, [21]but there was
an oath regarding Jesus. For God said to him,

> "The LORD has taken an oath and will
> not break his vow:
> 'You are a priest forever.'"*

[22]Because of this oath, Jesus is the one who
guarantees this better covenant with God.

Melchizedek

Wanting to show that Jesus' priesthood is utterly different from that of old-covenant priests, the writer of Hebrews once again uses an Old Testament illustration. He reminds his readers of Melchizedek, "king of the city of Salem and also a priest of God Most High" (Hebrews 7:1; see Genesis 14:18)—someone who was both a king and a priest, just like Jesus. His argument goes like this: Abraham was blessed by Melchizedek and tithed the spoils of battle to him (Genesis 14:17-20). Levi, the founder of Israel's priesthood, was descended from Abraham; so that means he too, indirectly, was blessed by Melchizedek and gave him his tithe (while he was still in Abraham's genes as it were). So, since the greater always blesses the lesser, that means Melchizedek must have been a greater priest than all Levi's descendants. And since Jesus is a priest like Melchizedek (a priest-king), that means he too is greater than all the priests of the old covenant. The writer isn't saying that Melchizedek really was Jesus, appearing in the Old Testament, but rather simply seeing him as a foreshadowing or "type" of Jesus.

▶ *See also* ***The Old Testament in the New Testament****, page 1403.*

23 There were many priests under the old
system, for death prevented them from remaining in office. 24 But because Jesus lives
forever, his priesthood lasts forever. 25 Therefore he is able, once and forever, to save*
those who come to God through him. He lives
forever to intercede with God on their behalf.
26 He is the kind of high priest we need
because he is holy and blameless, unstained
by sin. He has been set apart from sinners
and has been given the highest place of
honor in heaven.* 27 Unlike those other high
priests, he does not need to offer sacrifices
every day. They did this for their own sins
first and then for the sins of the people. But
Jesus did this once for all when he offered
himself as the sacrifice for the people's sins.
28 The law appointed high priests who were
limited by human weakness. But after the
law was given, God appointed his Son with
an oath, and his Son has been made the
perfect High Priest forever.

Christ Is Our High Priest

8 Here is the main point: We have a
High Priest who sat down in the place
of honor beside the throne of the majestic
God in heaven. 2 There he ministers in the
heavenly Tabernacle,* the true place of
worship that was built by the Lord and not
by human hands.
3 And since every high priest is required
to offer gifts and sacrifices, our High Priest
must make an offering, too. 4 If he were here
on earth, he would not even be a priest, since
there already are priests who offer the gifts
required by the law. 5 They serve in a system
of worship that is only a copy, a shadow of
the real one in heaven. For when Moses was
getting ready to build the Tabernacle, God
gave him this warning: "Be sure that you
make everything according to the pattern
I have shown you here on the mountain."*
6 But now Jesus, our High Priest, has been
given a ministry that is far superior to the
old priesthood, for he is the one who mediates for us a far better covenant with God,
based on better promises.
7 If the first covenant had been faultless,
there would have been no need for a second
covenant to replace it. 8 But when God found
fault with the people, he said:

"The day is coming, says the LORD,
when I will make a new covenant
with the people of Israel and Judah.

7:5 Greek *from their brothers.* **7:11** Greek *the order of Aaron?* **7:17** Ps 110:4. **7:21** Ps 110:4. **7:25** Or *is able to save completely.* **7:26** Or *has been exalted higher than the heavens.* **8:2** Or *tent;* also in 8:5. **8:5** Exod 25:40; 26:30.

The Old Testament in the New Testament

The first Christians' "Bible" wasn't our Bible, for the New Testament was yet to be written. Their Bible consisted simply of what we call "the Old Testament," which they saw not only as the record of God's dealings with Israel but also as preparation for the coming of the Messiah, Jesus. That is why the New Testament often looks back to the Old Testament, showing that it both anticipated and prepared for his coming—something Jesus himself did as he explained "from all the Scriptures the things concerning himself" (Luke 24:27).

It was natural therefore that Hebrews, written to Christians from a Jewish background, should make much use of the Old Testament, quoting it and referring to its practices and stories. It sees all these as "shadows" (Hebrews 8:5; 10:1)—things whose primary purpose was to point beyond themselves to a reality elsewhere, that is, to Jesus. So, we find references to the high priest, sacrifices, covenant, the Tabernacle, and Sabbath rest, all of which pointed to Jesus Christ. Even the mysterious character Melchizedek, someone who was both a priest and a king, was a shadow or "type" of Jesus, who was himself both a priest and a king. And yet, while Jesus is like all these shadows, he is also better than them all.

▶ *See also* ***Jesus Christ in the Psalms,*** *page 614;* ***Prophecies about Christ,*** *page 806;* ***Prophecies of the Messiah,*** *page 1044;* ***Jesus and the Old Testament,*** *page 1079;* ***The Old Testament in the New Testament Letters,*** *Visual Overview Z16.*

9 This covenant will not be like the one
I made with their ancestors
when I took them by the hand
and led them out of the land of Egypt.
They did not remain faithful to my
covenant,
so I turned my back on them, says the
LORD.
10 But this is the new covenant I will make
with the people of Israel on that day,*
says the LORD:
I will put my laws in their minds,
and I will write them on their hearts.
I will be their God,
and they will be my people.
11 And they will not need to teach their
neighbors,
nor will they need to teach their
relatives,*
saying, 'You should know the LORD.'
For everyone, from the least to the
greatest,
will know me already.
12 And I will forgive their wickedness,
and I will never again remember their
sins."*

[13]When God speaks of a "new" covenant, it means he has made the first one obsolete. It is now out of date and will soon disappear.

Old Rules about Worship

9 That first covenant between God and Israel had regulations for worship and a place of worship here on earth. [2]There were two rooms in that Tabernacle.* In the first room were a lampstand, a table, and sacred loaves of bread on the table. This room was called the Holy Place. [3]Then there was a curtain, and behind the curtain was the second room* called the Most Holy Place. [4]In that room were a gold incense altar and a wooden chest called the Ark of the Covenant, which was covered with gold on all sides. Inside the Ark were a gold jar containing manna, Aaron's staff that sprouted leaves, and the stone tablets of the covenant. [5]Above the Ark were the cherubim of divine glory, whose wings stretched out over the Ark's cover, the place of atonement. But we cannot explain these things in detail now.

[6]When these things were all in place, the priests regularly entered the first room* as they performed their religious duties. [7]But only the high priest ever entered the Most Holy Place, and only once a year. And he always offered blood for his own sins and for the sins the people had committed in ignorance. [8]By these regulations the Holy Spirit revealed that the entrance to the Most Holy Place was not freely open as long as the Tabernacle* and the system it represented were still in use.

[9]This is an illustration pointing to the present time. For the gifts and sacrifices that the priests offer are not able to cleanse the consciences of the people who bring them. [10]For that old system deals only with food and drink and various cleansing ceremonies—physical regulations that were in effect only until a better system could be established.

Christ Is the Perfect Sacrifice

[11]So Christ has now become the High Priest over all the good things that have come.* He has entered that greater, more perfect Tabernacle in heaven, which was not made by human hands and is not part of this created world. [12]With his own blood—not the blood of goats and calves—he entered the Most Holy Place once for all time and secured our redemption forever.

[13]Under the old system, the blood of goats and bulls and the ashes of a heifer could cleanse people's bodies from ceremonial impurity. [14]Just think how much more the blood of Christ will purify our consciences from sinful deeds* so that we can worship the living God. For by the power of the eternal Spirit, Christ offered himself to God as a perfect sacrifice for our sins. [15]That is why he is the one who mediates a new covenant between God and people, so that all who are called can receive the eternal inheritance God has promised them. For Christ died to set them free from the penalty of the sins they had committed under that first covenant.

[16]Now when someone leaves a will,* it is necessary to prove that the person who made it is dead.* [17]The will goes into effect only after the person's death. While the person who made it is still alive, the will cannot be put into effect.

[18]That is why even the first covenant was put into effect with the blood of an animal. [19]For after Moses had read each of God's commandments to all the people, he took the blood of calves and goats,* along

with water, and sprinkled both the book of
God's law and all the people, using hyssop
branches and scarlet wool. 20 Then he said,
"This blood confirms the covenant God
has made with you."* 21 And in the same
way, he sprinkled blood on the Tabernacle
and on everything used for worship. 22 In
fact, according to the law of Moses, nearly
everything was purified with blood. For
without the shedding of blood, there is no
forgiveness.

23 That is why the Tabernacle and everything in it, which were copies of things in
heaven, had to be purified by the blood of
animals. But the real things in heaven had
to be purified with far better sacrifices than
the blood of animals.

24 For Christ did not enter into a holy place
made with human hands, which was only a
copy of the true one in heaven. He entered
into heaven itself to appear now before God
on our behalf. 25 And he did not enter heaven
to offer himself again and again, like the high
priest here on earth who enters the Most Holy
Place year after year with the blood of an
animal. 26 If that had been necessary, Christ
would have had to die again and again, ever
since the world began. But now, once for all
time, he has appeared at the end of the age*
to remove sin by his own death as a sacrifice.

27 And just as each person is destined to
die once and after that comes judgment,
28 so also Christ was offered once for all time
as a sacrifice to take away the sins of many
people. He will come again, not to deal with
our sins, but to bring salvation to all who
are eagerly waiting for him.

Christ's Sacrifice Once for All

10 The old system under the law of
Moses was only a shadow, a dim
preview of the good things to come, not
the good things themselves. The sacrifices
under that system were repeated again and
again, year after year, but they were never
able to provide perfect cleansing for those
who came to worship. 2 If they could have
provided perfect cleansing, the sacrifices
would have stopped, for the worshipers would have been purified once for all
time, and their feelings of guilt would have
disappeared.

3 But instead, those sacrifices actually reminded them of their sins year after year.
4 For it is not possible for the blood of bulls
and goats to take away sins. 5 That is why,
when Christ* came into the world, he said
to God,

> "You did not want animal sacrifices or
> sin offerings.
> But you have given me a body to offer.
> 6 You were not pleased with burnt
> offerings
> or other offerings for sin.
> 7 Then I said, 'Look, I have come to do
> your will, O God—
> as is written about me in the
> Scriptures.'"*

8 First, Christ said, "You did not want
animal sacrifices or sin offerings or burnt
offerings or other offerings for sin, nor were
you pleased with them" (though they are
required by the law of Moses). 9 Then he
said, "Look, I have come to do your will."
He cancels the first covenant in order to put
the second into effect. 10 For God's will was
for us to be made holy by the sacrifice of the
body of Jesus Christ, once for all time.

11 Under the old covenant, the priest
stands and ministers before the altar day
after day, offering the same sacrifices again
and again, which can never take away sins.
12 But our High Priest offered himself to
God as a single sacrifice for sins, good for
all time. Then he sat down in the place of
honor at God's right hand. 13 There he waits
until his enemies are humbled and made a
footstool under his feet. 14 For by that one
offering he forever made perfect those who
are being made holy.

15 And the Holy Spirit also testifies that
this is so. For he says,

> 16 "This is the new covenant I will make
> with my people on that day,* says the
> LORD:
> I will put my laws in their hearts,
> and I will write them on their
> minds."*

17 Then he says,

> "I will never again remember
> their sins and lawless deeds."*

8:10 Greek *after those days.* **8:11** Greek *their brother.* **8:8-12** Jer 31:31-34. **9:2** Or *tent;* also in 9:11, 21. **9:3** Greek *second tent.* **9:6** Greek *first tent.* **9:8** Or *the first room;* Greek reads *the first tent.* **9:11** Some manuscripts read *that are about to come.* **9:14** Greek *from dead works.* **9:16a** Or *covenant;* also in 9:17. **9:16b** Or *Now when someone makes a covenant, it is necessary to ratify it with the death of a sacrifice.* **9:19** Some manuscripts do not include *and goats.* **9:20** Exod 24:8. **9:26** Greek *the ages.* **10:5** Greek *he;* also in 10:8. **10:5-7** Ps 40:6-8 (Greek version). **10:16a** Greek *after those days.* **10:16b** Jer 31:33a. **10:17** Jer 31:34b.

18And when sins have been forgiven, there is
no need to offer any more sacrifices.

A Call to Persevere

19And so, dear brothers and sisters,* we
can boldly enter heaven's Most Holy Place
because of the blood of Jesus. 20By his
death,* Jesus opened a new and life-giving
way through the curtain into the Most Holy
Place. 21And since we have a great High
Priest who rules over God's house, 22let us go
right into the presence of God with sincere
hearts fully trusting him. For our guilty consciences have been sprinkled with Christ's
blood to make us clean, and our bodies have
been washed with pure water.
23Let us hold tightly without wavering to
the hope we affirm, for God can be trusted
to keep his promise. 24Let us think of ways
to motivate one another to acts of love and
good works. 25And let us not neglect our
meeting together, as some people do, but
encourage one another, especially now that
the day of his return is drawing near.
26Dear friends, if we deliberately continue
sinning after we have received knowledge of
the truth, there is no longer any sacrifice that
will cover these sins. 27There is only the terrible expectation of God's judgment and the
raging fire that will consume his enemies.
28For anyone who refused to obey the law
of Moses was put to death without mercy
on the testimony of two or three witnesses.
29Just think how much worse the punishment will be for those who have trampled
on the Son of God, and have treated the
blood of the covenant, which made us holy,
as if it were common and unholy, and have
insulted and disdained the Holy Spirit who
brings God's mercy to us. 30For we know the
one who said,

> "I will take revenge.
>   I will pay them back."*

He also said,

> "The LORD will judge his own people."*

31It is a terrible thing to fall into the hands
of the living God.
32Think back on those early days when
you first learned about Christ.* Remember
how you remained faithful even though it
meant terrible suffering. 33Sometimes you
were exposed to public ridicule and were
beaten, and sometimes you helped others
who were suffering the same things. 34You
suffered along with those who were thrown
into jail, and when all you owned was taken
from you, you accepted it with joy. You
knew there were better things waiting for
you that will last forever.
35So do not throw away this confident

Belonging to a church

The writer of Hebrews knew that his readers, believers pressured into abandoning their Christian faith, desperately needed encouragement and support. That is why he urges them not to neglect meeting together, as some were doing (Hebrews 10:25). Being together—praying for one another, sharing testimonies of what God has done, hearing God's word, and declaring in worship that God is greater than anything we are facing—encourages us to keep going. And that is what these believers needed.

But this message is not just for them; it is also for us today. It may not be persecution that makes us wonder if we have time or energy to be part of the church. It can be things like the pressures of family, work, or finances; or weariness at the end of the week; or friends who invite us to something that seems more fun. But belonging to a church isn't just about attending occasional services; it's about committed participation to its life in an ongoing way. God didn't design us to live out our faith at a purely individual level; he wants us to be part of his church, which provides the fellowship and encouragement that all of us need. No one can live the Christian life in isolation.

▶ *See also **The church**, page 1348.*

trust in the Lord. Remember the great
reward it brings you! 36 Patient endurance is
what you need now, so that you will continue to do God's will. Then you will receive
all that he has promised.

37 "For in just a little while,
the Coming One will come and not
delay.
38 And my righteous ones will live by faith.*
But I will take no pleasure in anyone
who turns away."*

39 But we are not like those who turn away
from God to their own destruction. We are
the faithful ones, whose souls will be saved.

Great Examples of Faith

11 Faith shows the reality of what we
hope for; it is the evidence of things we
cannot see. 2 Through their faith, the people
in days of old earned a good reputation.
3 By faith we understand that the entire
universe was formed at God's command,
that what we now see did not come from
anything that can be seen.
4 It was by faith that Abel brought a more
acceptable offering to God than Cain did.
Abel's offering gave evidence that he was a
righteous man, and God showed his approval
of his gifts. Although Abel is long dead, he
still speaks to us by his example of faith.
5 It was by faith that Enoch was taken up
to heaven without dying—"he disappeared,
because God took him."* For before he was
taken up, he was known as a person who
pleased God. 6 And it is impossible to please
God without faith. Anyone who wants to
come to him must believe that God exists
and that he rewards those who sincerely
seek him.
7 It was by faith that Noah built a large boat
to save his family from the flood. He obeyed
God, who warned him about things that had
never happened before. By his faith Noah
condemned the rest of the world, and he received the righteousness that comes by faith.
8 It was by faith that Abraham obeyed
when God called him to leave home and go
to another land that God would give him as
his inheritance. He went without knowing
where he was going. 9 And even when he
reached the land God promised him, he
lived there by faith—for he was like a foreigner, living in tents. And so did Isaac and
Jacob, who inherited the same promise.
10 Abraham was confidently looking forward
to a city with eternal foundations, a city designed and built by God.
11 It was by faith that even Sarah was able
to have a child, though she was barren and
was too old. She believed* that God would
keep his promise. 12 And so a whole nation
came from this one man who was as good as
dead—a nation with so many people that,
like the stars in the sky and the sand on the
seashore, there is no way to count them.
13 All these people died still believing what
God had promised them. They did not receive
what was promised, but they saw it all from
a distance and welcomed it. They agreed
that they were foreigners and nomads here
on earth. 14 Obviously people who say such
things are looking forward to a country they
can call their own. 15 If they had longed for
the country they came from, they could
have gone back. 16 But they were looking for
a better place, a heavenly homeland. That is
why God is not ashamed to be called their
God, for he has prepared a city for them.
17 It was by faith that Abraham offered Isaac
as a sacrifice when God was testing him.
Abraham, who had received God's promises,
was ready to sacrifice his only son, Isaac,
18 even though God had told him, "Isaac is the
son through whom your descendants will be
counted."* 19 Abraham reasoned that if Isaac
died, God was able to bring him back to life
again. And in a sense, Abraham did receive
his son back from the dead.
20 It was by faith that Isaac promised
blessings for the future to his sons, Jacob
and Esau.
21 It was by faith that Jacob, when he was
old and dying, blessed each of Joseph's sons
and bowed in worship as he leaned on his
staff.
22 It was by faith that Joseph, when he

10:19 Greek *brothers.* **10:20** Greek *Through his flesh.* **10:30a** Deut 32:35. **10:30b** Deut 32:36. **10:32** Greek *when you were first enlightened.* **10:38** Or *my righteous ones will live by their faithfulness;* Greek reads *my righteous one will live by faith.* **10:37-38** Hab 2:3-4. **11:5** Gen 5:24. **11:11** Or *It was by faith that he [Abraham] was able to have a child, even though Sarah was barren and he was too old. He believed.* **11:18** Gen 21:12.

▸ **11:4** *See **Cain and Abel**, page 8.* **11:7** *See **Noah**, page 12.* **11:8** *See **Abraham**, page 16.* **11:9** *See **Isaac and Rebekah**, page 28; **Jacob and Esau**, page 40.* **11:11** *See **Sarah**, page 27.*

was about to die, said confidently that the
people of Israel would leave Egypt. He even
commanded them to take his bones with
them when they left.

[23]It was by faith that Moses' parents hid
him for three months when he was born.
They saw that God had given them an
unusual child, and they were not afraid to
disobey the king's command.

[24]It was by faith that Moses, when he grew
up, refused to be called the son of Pharaoh's
daughter. [25]He chose to share the oppression of God's people instead of enjoying the
fleeting pleasures of sin. [26]He thought it was
better to suffer for the sake of Christ than
to own the treasures of Egypt, for he was
looking ahead to his great reward. [27]It was
by faith that Moses left the land of Egypt,
not fearing the king's anger. He kept right
on going because he kept his eyes on the
one who is invisible. [28]It was by faith that
Moses commanded the people of Israel to
keep the Passover and to sprinkle blood
on the doorposts so that the angel of death
would not kill their firstborn sons.

[29]It was by faith that the people of Israel
went right through the Red Sea as though
they were on dry ground. But when the Egyptians tried to follow, they were all drowned.

[30]It was by faith that the people of Israel
marched around Jericho for seven days, and
the walls came crashing down.

[31]It was by faith that Rahab the prostitute
was not destroyed with the people in her
city who refused to obey God. For she had
given a friendly welcome to the spies.

[32]How much more do I need to say? It
would take too long to recount the stories
of the faith of Gideon, Barak, Samson, Jephthah, David, Samuel, and all the prophets.
[33]By faith these people overthrew kingdoms,
ruled with justice, and received what God
had promised them. They shut the mouths
of lions, [34]quenched the flames of fire, and
escaped death by the edge of the sword.
Their weakness was turned to strength.
They became strong in battle and put whole
armies to flight. [35]Women received their
loved ones back again from death.

But others were tortured, refusing to turn
from God in order to be set free. They placed
their hope in a better life after the resurrection. [36]Some were jeered at, and their backs
were cut open with whips. Others were
chained in prisons. [37]Some died by stoning,
some were sawed in half,* and others were
killed with the sword. Some went about
wearing skins of sheep and goats, destitute
and oppressed and mistreated. [38]They were
too good for this world, wandering over
deserts and mountains, hiding in caves and
holes in the ground.

[39]All these people earned a good reputation because of their faith, yet none of
them received all that God had promised.
[40]For God had something better in mind for
us, so that they would not reach perfection
without us.

God's Discipline Proves His Love

12 Therefore, since we are surrounded
by such a huge crowd of witnesses to
the life of faith, let us strip off every weight
that slows us down, especially the sin that so
easily trips us up. And let us run with endurance the race God has set before us. [2]We do
this by keeping our eyes on Jesus, the champion who initiates and perfects our faith.*
Because of the joy* awaiting him, he endured
the cross, disregarding its shame. Now he is
seated in the place of honor beside God's
throne. [3]Think of all the hostility he endured
from sinful people;* then you won't become
weary and give up. [4]After all, you have not yet
given your lives in your struggle against sin.

[5]And have you forgotten the encouraging
words God spoke to you as his children?*
He said,

> "My child,* don't make light of the
> LORD's discipline,
> and don't give up when he corrects you.
> [6] For the LORD disciplines those he loves,
> and he punishes each one he accepts
> as his child."*

[7]As you endure this divine discipline, remember that God is treating you as his own
children. Who ever heard of a child who
is never disciplined by its father? [8]If God
doesn't discipline you as he does all of his
children, it means that you are illegitimate
and are not really his children at all. [9]Since

▸ **11:22** *See* ***Joseph****, page 47.* **11:24** *See* ***Moses, the man who loved God's presence****, page 69;* ***Moses, the faithful servant****, page 239.* **11:31** *See* ***Prostitution****, page 285.* **11:32** *See* ***Gideon****, page 279;* ***Samuel****, page 309;* ***King David****, page 323.*

we respected our earthly fathers who disciplined us, shouldn't we submit even more
to the discipline of the Father of our spirits,
and live forever?*
[10]For our earthly fathers disciplined us for
a few years, doing the best they knew how.
But God's discipline is always good for us,
so that we might share in his holiness. [11]No
discipline is enjoyable while it is happening—it's painful! But afterward there will be
a peaceful harvest of right living for those
who are trained in this way.
[12]So take a new grip with your tired hands
and strengthen your weak knees. [13]Mark out
a straight path for your feet so that those
who are weak and lame will not fall but
become strong.

A Call to Listen to God

[14]Work at living in peace with everyone,
and work at living a holy life, for those who
are not holy will not see the Lord. [15]Look
after each other so that none of you fails
to receive the grace of God. Watch out that
no poisonous root of bitterness grows up to
trouble you, corrupting many. [16]Make sure
that no one is immoral or godless like Esau,
who traded his birthright as the firstborn
son for a single meal. [17]You know that afterward, when he wanted his father's blessing, he was rejected. It was too late for
repentance, even though he begged with
bitter tears.
[18]You have not come to a physical mountain,* to a place of flaming fire, darkness,
gloom, and whirlwind, as the Israelites did
at Mount Sinai. [19]For they heard an awesome
trumpet blast and a voice so terrible that
they begged God to stop speaking. [20]They
staggered back under God's command: "If
even an animal touches the mountain, it
must be stoned to death."* [21]Moses himself
was so frightened at the sight that he said,
"I am terrified and trembling."*
[22]No, you have come to Mount Zion, to the
city of the living God, the heavenly Jerusalem, and to countless thousands of angels
in a joyful gathering. [23]You have come to the
assembly of God's firstborn children, whose
names are written in heaven. You have come
to God himself, who is the judge over all
things. You have come to the spirits of the
righteous ones in heaven who have now been
made perfect. [24]You have come to Jesus, the
one who mediates the new covenant between
God and people, and to the sprinkled blood,
which speaks of forgiveness instead of crying
out for vengeance like the blood of Abel.
[25]Be careful that you do not refuse to
listen to the One who is speaking. For if
the people of Israel did not escape when
they refused to listen to Moses, the earthly
messenger, we will certainly not escape if
we reject the One who speaks to us from
heaven! [26]When God spoke from Mount
Sinai his voice shook the earth, but now he
makes another promise: "Once again I will
shake not only the earth but the heavens
also."* [27]This means that all of creation will
be shaken and removed, so that only unshakable things will remain.
[28]Since we are receiving a Kingdom that is
unshakable, let us be thankful and please
God by worshiping him with holy fear and
awe. [29]For our God is a devouring fire.

Concluding Words

13 Keep on loving each other as brothers and sisters.* [2]Don't forget to show
hospitality to strangers, for some who have
done this have entertained angels without
realizing it! [3]Remember those in prison, as
if you were there yourself. Remember also
those being mistreated, as if you felt their
pain in your own bodies.
[4]Give honor to marriage, and remain
faithful to one another in marriage. God will
surely judge people who are immoral and
those who commit adultery.
[5]Don't love money; be satisfied with what
you have. For God has said,

"I will never fail you.
I will never abandon you."*

[6]So we can say with confidence,

"The LORD is my helper,
so I will have no fear.
What can mere people do to me?"*

11:37 Some manuscripts add *some were tested.* **12:2a** Or *Jesus, the originator and perfecter of our faith.* **12:2b** Or *Instead of the joy.* **12:3** Some manuscripts read *Think of how people hurt themselves by opposing him.* **12:5a** Greek *sons;* also in 12:7, 8. **12:5b** Greek *son;* also in 12:6, 7. **12:5-6** Prov 3:11-12 (Greek version). **12:9** Or *and really live?* **12:18** Greek *to something that can be touched.* **12:20** Exod 19:13. **12:21** Deut 9:19. **12:26** Hag 2:6. **13:1** Greek *Continue in brotherly love.* **13:5** Deut 31:6, 8. **13:6** Ps 118:6.

▸ **12:5-11** *See* ***God's discipline****, page 1000.* **13:4** *See* ***Faithfulness****, page 1307.*

7Remember your leaders who taught you
the word of God. Think of all the good that
has come from their lives, and follow the
example of their faith.
8Jesus Christ is the same yesterday,
today, and forever. 9So do not be attracted
by strange, new ideas. Your strength comes
from God's grace, not from rules about food,
which don't help those who follow them.
10We have an altar from which the priests in
the Tabernacle* have no right to eat. 11Under
the old system, the high priest brought the
blood of animals into the Holy Place as a sacrifice for sin, and the bodies of the animals
were burned outside the camp. 12So also Jesus
suffered and died outside the city gates to
make his people holy by means of his own
blood. 13So let us go out to him, outside the
camp, and bear the disgrace he bore. 14For
this world is not our permanent home; we
are looking forward to a home yet to come.
15Therefore, let us offer through Jesus a continual sacrifice of praise to God, proclaiming
our allegiance to his name. 16And don't forget
to do good and to share with those in need.
These are the sacrifices that please God.
17Obey your spiritual leaders, and do
what they say. Their work is to watch over
your souls, and they are accountable to
God. Give them reason to do this with joy
and not with sorrow. That would certainly
not be for your benefit.
18Pray for us, for our conscience is clear
and we want to live honorably in everything
we do. 19And especially pray that I will be
able to come back to you soon.

20 Now may the God of peace—
who brought up from the dead our
Lord Jesus,
the great Shepherd of the sheep,
and ratified an eternal covenant with
his blood—
21 may he equip you with all you need
for doing his will.
May he produce in you,*
through the power of Jesus Christ,
every good thing that is pleasing to him.
All glory to him forever and ever!
Amen.

22I urge you, dear brothers and sisters,* to
pay attention to what I have written in this
brief exhortation.
23I want you to know that our brother
Timothy has been released from jail. If he
comes here soon, I will bring him with me
to see you.
24Greet all your leaders and all the believers there.* The believers from Italy send you
their greetings.
25May God's grace be with you all.

13:10 Or *tent.* **13:21** Some manuscripts read *in us.* **13:22** Greek *brothers.* **13:24** Greek *all of God's holy people.*

Hospitality

Hospitality was very much a part of Middle Eastern culture, and we find many examples of it in the Bible (e.g., Genesis 18:1-8; 19:1-3; Exodus 2:18-20; 2 Samuel 17:27-29; 1 Kings 17:7-16; Job 31:32). Jesus himself was the recipient of hospitality (e.g., Matthew 9:10; Mark 1:29-31; Luke 10:38-42; John 2:1-2), and he anticipated that hospitality would be extended to his disciples (Matthew 10:11-14) and that they would exercise hospitality too (Luke 14:12-14). Christians' opening up of their homes was crucial to the early Christian mission, providing both a place for traveling missionaries (e.g., Acts 16:15; 18:2-3) and a base for the church (e.g., Romans 16:5; 1 Corinthians 16:19).

Yet the New Testament's repeated commands to exercise hospitality (e.g., Romans 12:13; 1 Timothy 3:2; 5:10; Hebrews 13:2; 1 Peter 4:9; 3 John 1:5-8) suggest this was not something that could be taken for granted. For some, the lack of hospitality may have been rooted in selfishness, preferring to keep their home and food for themselves and their family; for others, in embarrassment that their home was humble or their food simple. But Christian hospitality is not about what is offered, but how it is offered. And if God has welcomed us into his home, then we should be willing to welcome others into ours.

James *Faith works*

This letter (one of the earliest writings of the New Testament) is addressed not to a particular church but to what James calls "the 'twelve tribes'—Jewish believers scattered abroad" (1:1). These Jewish Christians living outside of Palestine were experiencing various "troubles" (1:2). The pressure from these troubles—probably hardships and persecution—had spilled over into the life of the church, producing various kinds of conflicts. The letter is therefore full of practical teaching on how to live out the Christian faith, and it stresses that "faith is dead without good works" (2:26). It was written by James—almost certainly the James who was the brother of Jesus (Matthew 13:55) and leader of the church in Jerusalem (Acts 15).

What's it all about?

James is a collection of teachings about how Christians should work out what they believe in everyday life. The letter opens with a reference to the troubles God's people were facing, and it reminds believers of how God will generously give everyone the wisdom and patience they need to come through them. Indeed, these troubles will be used by God to strengthen them in their faith. God will help them get through their trials and temptations and will reward them at the end. They therefore need to ensure that they obey God's word and not merely hear it.

In chapter 2, James rebukes favoritism within the church, especially that which favors the rich over the poor. Favoritism violates what he calls "the royal law"—that is, to love our neighbor as ourselves. To fail to do so is as bad as breaking the whole Jewish Law. He goes on to speak powerfully about the link between faith and action, giving two examples from the Old Testament of people whose faith was worked out in action—Abraham and Rahab.

In chapter 3, James writes about the importance of our words. Our tongues may be small, but they are very powerful! And since Christian teachers exercise such a great influence with their words, James advises restraint in the appointment of teachers. He praises consistency in speech and says our words should match our intentions. He then contrasts worldly and spiritual wisdom, encouraging us to give ourselves completely to God and warning us not to judge one another. Rather than fighting, we should submit to God and his will; rather than boasting of our ambitions, we should let God plan our lives (chapter 4).

The final chapter includes warnings to the rich, an encouragement to wait patiently for Christ's return, and some stirring reflections on the power of prayer.

OVERVIEW

page 1412

What does it mean for us?

The Christians addressed by James clearly included some very wealthy people—but also some who were incredibly poor. But he warns believers not to let social status influence how they treat people, for God has no favorites—though he does show a special regard for the poor. If we're going to serve anyone, it should be the ones who are poor. After all, the poor have nothing to give to us in return; so there can be no chance of our giving to them with mixed motives, in the hope of getting something in return.

James presupposes that all Christians have faith and that God expects such faith to result in practical action. We will know if we are real followers of Jesus by the way we treat people (2:8-9), control our tongues (3:1-12), suspend our judgments (4:11-12), involve God in our decision-making (4:13-17), and use our money (5:1-6). Some people have only an intellectual faith in God. That kind of faith won't save us, any more than it saves demons (2:19)! According to James, it is good for nothing. But real faith both makes a difference in lives and sees amazing answers to prayer (5:13-18).

Greetings from James

1 This letter is from James, a slave of God
and of the Lord Jesus Christ.
I am writing to the "twelve tribes"—Jewish
believers scattered abroad.
Greetings!

Faith and Endurance

2Dear brothers and sisters,* when troubles of
any kind come your way, consider it an opportunity for great joy. 3For you know that
when your faith is tested, your endurance has
a chance to grow. 4So let it grow, for when
your endurance is fully developed, you will
be perfect and complete, needing nothing.
5If you need wisdom, ask our generous
God, and he will give it to you. He will not
rebuke you for asking. 6But when you ask
him, be sure that your faith is in God alone.
Do not waver, for a person with divided
loyalty is as unsettled as a wave of the sea
that is blown and tossed by the wind. 7Such
people should not expect to receive anything from the Lord. 8Their loyalty is divided
between God and the world, and they are unstable in everything they do.
9Believers who are* poor have something
to boast about, for God has honored them.
10And those who are rich should boast that
God has humbled them. They will fade away
like a little flower in the field. 11The hot sun
rises and the grass withers; the little flower
droops and falls, and its beauty fades away.
In the same way, the rich will fade away with
all of their achievements.
12God blesses those who patiently endure
testing and temptation. Afterward they will
receive the crown of life that God has promised to those who love him. 13And remember,
when you are being tempted, do not say, "God
is tempting me." God is never tempted to do
wrong,* and he never tempts anyone else.
14Temptation comes from our own desires,
which entice us and drag us away. 15These
desires give birth to sinful actions. And when
sin is allowed to grow, it gives birth to death.
16So don't be misled, my dear brothers and
sisters. 17Whatever is good and perfect is a
gift coming down to us from God our Father,
who created all the lights in the heavens.* He
never changes or casts a shifting shadow.*
18He chose to give birth to us by giving us
his true word. And we, out of all creation,
became his prized possession.*

Listening and Doing

19Understand this, my dear brothers and
sisters: You must all be quick to listen, slow
to speak, and slow to get angry. 20Human
anger* does not produce the righteousness*
God desires. 21So get rid of all the filth and
evil in your lives, and humbly accept the
word God has planted in your hearts, for it
has the power to save your souls.
22But don't just listen to God's word. You
must do what it says. Otherwise, you are only
fooling yourselves. 23For if you listen to the
word and don't obey, it is like glancing at
your face in a mirror. 24You see yourself, walk
away, and forget what you look like. 25But if

▸ **1:2** *See **Joy**, page 1360.*

you look carefully into the perfect law that
sets you free, and if you do what it says and
don't forget what you heard, then God will
bless you for doing it.
26 If you claim to be religious but don't
control your tongue, you are fooling yourself, and your religion is worthless. 27 Pure
and genuine religion in the sight of God
the Father means caring for orphans and
widows in their distress and refusing to let
the world corrupt you.

A Warning against Prejudice

2 My dear brothers and sisters,* how can
you claim to have faith in our glorious
Lord Jesus Christ if you favor some people
over others?
2 For example, suppose someone comes
into your meeting* dressed in fancy clothes
and expensive jewelry, and another comes
in who is poor and dressed in dirty clothes.
3 If you give special attention and a good
seat to the rich person, but you say to the
poor one, "You can stand over there, or else
sit on the floor"—well, 4 doesn't this discrimination show that your judgments are
guided by evil motives?
5 Listen to me, dear brothers and sisters.
Hasn't God chosen the poor in this world to
be rich in faith? Aren't they the ones who
will inherit the Kingdom he promised to
those who love him? 6 But you dishonor the
poor! Isn't it the rich who oppress you and
drag you into court? 7 Aren't they the ones
who slander Jesus Christ, whose noble
name* you bear?
8 Yes indeed, it is good when you obey
the royal law as found in the Scriptures:
"Love your neighbor as yourself."* 9 But if
you favor some people over others, you are
committing a sin. You are guilty of breaking
the law.
10 For the person who keeps all of the laws
except one is as guilty as a person who has
broken all of God's laws. 11 For the same God
who said, "You must not commit adultery,"
also said, "You must not murder."* So if you
murder someone but do not commit adultery, you have still broken the law.
12 So whatever you say or whatever you
do, remember that you will be judged by
the law that sets you free. 13 There will be no
mercy for those who have not shown mercy
to others. But if you have been merciful,
God will be merciful when he judges you.

Faith without Good Deeds Is Dead

14 What good is it, dear brothers and sisters,
if you say you have faith but don't show
it by your actions? Can that kind of faith
save anyone? 15 Suppose you see a brother
or sister who has no food or clothing, 16 and
you say, "Good-bye and have a good day;
stay warm and eat well"—but then you
don't give that person any food or clothing.
What good does that do?

1:2 Greek *brothers;* also in 1:16, 19. **1:9** Greek *The brother who is.* **1:13** Or *God should not be put to a test by evil people.* **1:17a** Greek *from above, from the Father of lights.* **1:17b** Some manuscripts read *He never changes, as a shifting shadow does.* **1:18** Greek *we became a kind of firstfruit of his creatures.* **1:20a** Greek *A man's anger.* **1:20b** Or *the justice.* **2:1** Greek *brothers;* also in 2:5, 14. **2:2** Greek *your synagogue.* **2:7** Greek *slander the noble name.* **2:8** Lev 19:18. **2:11** Exod 20:13-14; Deut 5:17-18.

▸ **1:22-25** *See* ***Listening****, page 720.* **1:27** *See* ***Widows****, page 400.* **2:8** *See* ***Love your neighbor as yourself****, page 139.*

James

The James who wrote this letter was not the apostle James, for he had been martyred in AD 44 (Acts 12:1-2), before this letter was written. Rather, it was written by "James the Just," as he came to be known—the leader of the church in Jerusalem and the one who came up with the solution for the Jewish-Gentile problem (Acts 15:12-31). He was also the brother of Jesus, one of several sons born to Joseph and Mary after Jesus' birth (Matthew 13:55—though some church traditions, wishing to maintain Mary's perpetual virginity, interpret "brothers" as "cousins"). James never spoke of himself as Jesus' brother, probably because it would have seemed like he was trying to "pull rank." He simply speaks of himself in James 1:1 as "a slave of God and of the Lord Jesus Christ."

17 So you see, faith by itself isn't enough.
Unless it produces good deeds, it is dead
and useless.
18 Now someone may argue, "Some people
have faith; others have good deeds." But I
say, "How can you show me your faith if you
don't have good deeds? I will show you my
faith by my good deeds."
19 You say you have faith, for you believe
that there is one God.* Good for you! Even
the demons believe this, and they tremble
in terror.
20 How foolish! Can't you see that
faith without good deeds is useless?
21 Don't you remember that our ancestor
Abraham was shown to be right with God by
his actions when he offered his son Isaac on
the altar?
22 You see, his faith and his actions
worked together. His actions made his faith
complete.
23 And so it happened just as the
Scriptures say: "Abraham believed God,
and God counted him as righteous because
of his faith."* He was even called the friend
of God.*
24 So you see, we are shown to be
right with God by what we do, not by faith
alone.
25 Rahab the prostitute is another
example. She was shown to be right with
God by her actions when she hid those
messengers and sent them safely away
by a different road.
26 Just as the body is
dead without breath,* so also faith is dead
without good works.

▸ **2:25** *See **Prostitution**, page 285.*

Doubt

Doubt can be both good and bad. In James 1:5-8, which speaks of "wavering" and "divided loyalty," it is clearly bad. James's point is that when we ask God for things, there is no point doubting—otherwise we might just as well not pray! If we have understood that God is generous (1:5) and loves to answer prayer (5:13-18), then we won't doubt when we pray, with part of us thinking that God wants to answer our prayer and another part thinking that he won't. That sort of double-mindedness is useless, says James. God may not always give us exactly what we ask for, for his wisdom is greater than ours. But can we not trust him that he always wants our good, and so ask in faith, knowing he will adjust our requests as he sees best? To doubt is to completely undermine our prayers.

But there is another kind of doubt than can be good, especially if we handle it correctly. We may be tempted to doubt God's word, truth, or promises, or even our relationship with him. Undealt with, this kind of doubt is destructive. But if we use such doubts to press on further with God, to dig deeper into his word, and to be honest in our praying, then they can be helpful. Many of the Bible's great figures had times of doubt—people like Abraham (Genesis 15:1-8), Moses (Exodus 4:1-17), Elijah (1 Kings 19:1-18), and John the Baptist (Matthew 11:1-3). These doubts did not lead them to turn from God, however, but to turn to him. They honestly shared with God their doubts, worries, or concerns and found their faith strengthened as a result, not weakened.

What is interesting is that in all the cases above—Abraham, Moses, Elijah, and John the Baptist—while God listened to their doubts and encouraged them, he also provoked them not to sit in their doubt forever but to "get on with it." Adopting our modern world's love of "being on a journey" can leave us in a constant state of indecision or unwillingness to commit, something that is far removed from the decisive action that Jesus calls us to as disciples. All good doubt leads to action.

Doubt can be helpful—but we have to handle it properly.

▸ *See also **Does God mind if we are honest with him?**, page 848.*

Controlling the Tongue

3 Dear brothers and sisters,* not many
of you should become teachers in the
church, for we who teach will be judged
more strictly. 2 Indeed, we all make many
mistakes. For if we could control our
tongues, we would be perfect and could
also control ourselves in every other way.
3 We can make a large horse go wherever we want by means of a small bit in its
mouth. 4 And a small rudder makes a huge
ship turn wherever the pilot chooses to go,
even though the winds are strong. 5 In the
same way, the tongue is a small thing that
makes grand speeches.

But a tiny spark can set a great forest on
fire. 6 And among all the parts of the body,
the tongue is a flame of fire. It is a whole
world of wickedness, corrupting your entire
body. It can set your whole life on fire, for it
is set on fire by hell itself.*
7 People can tame all kinds of animals,
birds, reptiles, and fish, 8 but no one can
tame the tongue. It is restless and evil, full
of deadly poison. 9 Sometimes it praises our
Lord and Father, and sometimes it curses
those who have been made in the image of
God. 10 And so blessing and cursing come
pouring out of the same mouth. Surely, my
brothers and sisters, this is not right! 11 Does
a spring of water bubble out with both fresh
water and bitter water? 12 Does a fig tree
produce olives, or a grapevine produce figs?
No, and you can't draw fresh water from a
salty spring.*

True Wisdom Comes from God

13 If you are wise and understand God's
ways, prove it by living an honorable life,
doing good works with the humility that
comes from wisdom. 14 But if you are bitterly
jealous and there is selfish ambition in your
heart, don't cover up the truth with boasting and lying. 15 For jealousy and selfishness
are not God's kind of wisdom. Such things
are earthly, unspiritual, and demonic. 16 For
wherever there is jealousy and selfish ambition, there you will find disorder and evil of
every kind.
17 But the wisdom from above is first of
all pure. It is also peace loving, gentle at
all times, and willing to yield to others. It is
full of mercy and the fruit of good deeds. It
shows no favoritism and is always sincere.
18 And those who are peacemakers will
plant seeds of peace and reap a harvest of
righteousness.*

2:19 Some manuscripts read *that God is one;* see Deut 6:4. **2:23a** Gen 15:6. **2:23b** See Isa 41:8. **2:26** Or *without spirit.* **3:1** Greek *brothers;* also in 3:10. **3:6** Or *for it will burn in hell* (Greek *Gehenna*). **3:12** Greek *from salt.* **3:18** Or *of good things,* or *of justice.*

Faith and works

Some people read what James writes about faith and works in 2:14-26 and jump to the conclusion that he is contradicting Paul. After all, Paul says again and again things like, "God saved you by his grace when you believed. . . . Salvation is not a reward for the good things we have done, so none of us can boast about it" (Ephesians 2:8-9). Isn't that clearly the opposite of what James says here?

Because the Bible is God's word, it does not contradict itself; and if it seems to, then we have failed to read the relevant passages in their proper context. When we consider the contexts of Paul and James, we can immediately see that what they are saying is not contradictory but complementary. To people who thought that works could make them right with God or win his favor, Paul says: "No they can't! Only faith can save you!" And to people who were saved and thought they didn't need to bother with doing good works, James says, "Yes you do! Good works won't save you, but they will show that you are saved!"

Both faith and works are needed—faith to save us and works to show we are truly saved—and different writers emphasize different aspects in different situations. If we truly believe that God is good, how can we fail to express that belief by doing good?

▶ *See also **Goodness**, page 1251; **Faith**, page 1286.*

Drawing Close to God

4 What is causing the quarrels and fights
among you? Don't they come from the
evil desires at war within you? 2You want
what you don't have, so you scheme and
kill to get it. You are jealous of what others
have, but you can't get it, so you fight and
wage war to take it away from them. Yet
you don't have what you want because you
don't ask God for it. 3And even when you
ask, you don't get it because your motives
are all wrong—you want only what will give
you pleasure.
4You adulterers!* Don't you realize that
friendship with the world makes you an
enemy of God? I say it again: If you want to
be a friend of the world, you make yourself
an enemy of God. 5Do you think the Scriptures have no meaning? They say that God
is passionate that the spirit he has placed
within us should be faithful to him.* 6And
he gives grace generously. As the Scriptures
say,

"God opposes the proud
but gives grace to the humble."*

7So humble yourselves before God. Resist
the devil, and he will flee from you. 8Come
close to God, and God will come close to
you. Wash your hands, you sinners; purify
your hearts, for your loyalty is divided
between God and the world. 9Let there be
tears for what you have done. Let there be
sorrow and deep grief. Let there be sadness
instead of laughter, and gloom instead of
joy. 10Humble yourselves before the Lord,
and he will lift you up in honor.

Warning against Judging Others

11Don't speak evil against each other, dear
brothers and sisters.* If you criticize and
judge each other, then you are criticizing
and judging God's law. But your job is to
obey the law, not to judge whether it applies
to you. 12God alone, who gave the law, is the
Judge. He alone has the power to save or to
destroy. So what right do you have to judge
your neighbor?

Warning about Self-Confidence

13Look here, you who say, "Today or tomorrow we are going to a certain town and will
stay there a year. We will do business there
and make a profit." 14How do you know
what your life will be like tomorrow? Your
life is like the morning fog—it's here a little
while, then it's gone. 15What you ought to
say is, "If the Lord wants us to, we will live
and do this or that." 16Otherwise you are
boasting about your own pretentious plans,
and all such boasting is evil.
17Remember, it is sin to know what you
ought to do and then not do it.

Warning to the Rich

5 Look here, you rich people: Weep and
groan with anguish because of all the
terrible troubles ahead of you. 2Your wealth
is rotting away, and your fine clothes are
moth-eaten rags. 3Your gold and silver are

Speech

The smallest things in life, James writes, can have the biggest effects: A tiny bit can steer a strong horse; a small rudder can steer a large ship; a match can cause a whole forest fire (James 3:3-6). And that's how it is with our tongue; it is such a small part of our body but can have a huge effect—especially when we use it carelessly and end up saying something we wish we hadn't.

Jesus said that what comes out of our mouths shows what is really going on in our hearts (Matthew 12:34-35). James says that if what comes out is favoritism (James 2:1-13), cursing (3:10), quarrels (4:1-3), slander (4:11-12), or arrogance (4:13-17), this isn't true Christian faith; in fact, failing to control our tongue in such ways makes our faith worthless (1:26).

Since Jesus said we will be judged one day for every word we have spoken (Matthew 12:36-37), a true Christian will want to learn how to submit their tongue (along with every other part of their life) to Jesus. On our own, we can't do this (James 3:8); but God will help us if we ask him.

corroded. The very wealth you were counting on will eat away your flesh like fire.
This corroded treasure you have hoarded
will testify against you on the day of judgment. [4]For listen! Hear the cries of the field
workers whom you have cheated of their
pay. The cries of those who harvest your
fields have reached the ears of the LORD of
Heaven's Armies.
[5]You have spent your years on earth in
luxury, satisfying your every desire. You
have fattened yourselves for the day of
slaughter. [6]You have condemned and killed
innocent people,* who do not resist you.*

Patience and Endurance

[7]Dear brothers and sisters,* be patient as
you wait for the Lord's return. Consider the
farmers who patiently wait for the rains
in the fall and in the spring. They eagerly
look for the valuable harvest to ripen. [8]You,
too, must be patient. Take courage, for the
coming of the Lord is near.
[9]Don't grumble about each other, brothers and sisters, or you will be judged. For
look—the Judge is standing at the door!
[10]For examples of patience in suffering, dear brothers and sisters, look at the
prophets who spoke in the name of the
Lord. [11]We give great honor to those who
endure under suffering. For instance, you
know about Job, a man of great endurance.
You can see how the Lord was kind to him
at the end, for the Lord is full of tenderness
and mercy.
[12]But most of all, my brothers and sisters,
never take an oath, by heaven or earth or
anything else. Just say a simple yes or no,
so that you will not sin and be condemned.

The Power of Prayer

[13]Are any of you suffering hardships? You
should pray. Are any of you happy? You
should sing praises. [14]Are any of you sick?
You should call for the elders of the church
to come and pray over you, anointing you
with oil in the name of the Lord. [15]Such a
prayer offered in faith will heal the sick,
and the Lord will make you well. And if
you have committed any sins, you will be
forgiven.
[16]Confess your sins to each other and pray
for each other so that you may be healed.

4:4 Greek *You adulteresses!* **4:5** Or *They say that the spirit God has placed within us is filled with envy;* or *They say that the Holy Spirit, whom God has placed within us, opposes our envy.* **4:6** Prov 3:34 (Greek version). **4:11** Greek *brothers.* **5:6a** Or *killed the Righteous One.* **5:6b** Or *Don't they resist you?* or *Doesn't God oppose you?* or *Aren't they now accusing you before God?* **5:7** Greek *brothers;* also in 5:9, 10, 12, 19.

▸ **5:1-6** *See **Injustice**, page 811.*

Money

Jesus said, "It is easier for a camel to go through the eye of a needle than for a rich person to enter the Kingdom of God!" (Matthew 19:24)—and history has proved him right. For the more materialistic a society becomes, the more God gets pushed into the background and the less people feel a need of him. Little wonder Jesus said, "You cannot serve God and be enslaved to money" (Matthew 6:24).

God is not against money (after all, there are people in the Bible who were blessed with considerable wealth), and the Bible claims no spiritual benefit to poverty in its own right. But the gospel is not about making us prosperous; it is about making us holy. It is all too easy for money and possessions to make us greedy and blind to the needs of others (James 5:1-6) and to turn our hearts away from God (e.g., Deuteronomy 8:10-14; 1 Timothy 6:9-10). The Bible therefore calls us to guard our hearts against materialism (e.g., Luke 12:13-21).

God calls us to invest our resources for the work of his Kingdom, not just for our own benefit (e.g., 1 Timothy 6:17-19), and to not love money (Hebrews 13:5). The so-called "Prosperity Gospel" is a product of twenty-first-century Western culture, not the Bible.

▸ *See also **Prosperity**, page 1176; **Giving**, page 1331.*

The earnest prayer of a righteous person has great power and produces wonderful results. 17Elijah was as human as we are, and yet when he prayed earnestly that no rain would fall, none fell for three and a half years! 18Then, when he prayed again, the sky sent down rain and the earth began to yield its crops.

Restore Wandering Believers

19My dear brothers and sisters, if someone among you wanders away from the truth and is brought back, 20you can be sure that whoever brings the sinner back from wandering will save that person from death and bring about the forgiveness of many sins.

1 Peter *Encouragement to suffering Christians*

Written by the apostle Peter (1:1), one of Jesus' twelve disciples and a leading figure in the early church, this letter seeks to encourage persecuted Christians in Asia Minor (1:1). Peter urges them to stand firm in God's grace (5:12), for not only would this grace take them through the difficult times they were experiencing, but the very life they were experiencing was itself part of God's grace to them. Although at first Peter had concentrated on the mission to Jews in Judea, he later traveled in the Gentile world, ending up in Rome. It was while he was here that a particularly severe persecution broke out against Christians under the emperor Nero in AD 64. Peter himself was executed sometime after that, between AD 64 and 67.

What's it all about?

Peter writes to Christians in various parts of Asia Minor (modern-day Turkey) who were starting to experience persecution from the state. He therefore begins by reminding them that they are special and chosen by God. They can "live with great expectation" because Christ has been raised from the dead and the inheritance Christ has won for them is "pure and undefiled, beyond the reach of change and decay" (1:3-4). Peter wants them to know they can come through their trials, not worn out and compromised, but confident in who they are.

In light of all this, Peter calls upon his readers to "prepare your minds for action" (1:13) and to be holy, remembering the precious price God has paid for each one of them (1:18-21). The only proper response to this is for them to love one another (1:22-25), to grow in their faith (2:1-3), and to let themselves be built into the spiritual temple that God is building, confident that they are indeed his holy people (2:4-10).

He then reminds them of their responsibilities in society—even a society that is against them. In spite of opposition and hostility, believers must live as good citizens, living godly lives and setting a good example so that no one has just grounds for accusing them (2:12). Submission is important, and he teaches masters and slaves, and husbands and wives, about their respective roles and responsibilities, warning them not to conform to worldly patterns of behavior. All believers should use their lives and their gifts wisely and handle suffering as Christ himself did (chapter 4). He concludes by appealing to church leaders, calling on them to lead their flock as Christ himself did, and appealing to the church to submit to their leadership. He reminds them that the devil is always on the prowl, looking to destroy God's people, and that the present persecution is one example of that; so he calls them to stand firm, reminding them that God is able to protect them and bring them safely through this difficult time (5:8-11).

OVERVIEW

The believer's priceless inheritance and new status · *1:1–2:10*

Living as Christians in a hostile world *2:11–3:12*

Understanding suffering and persevering through it · *3:13–4:19*

Final instructions on how to behave, and greetings · *5:1-14*

What does it mean for us?

From the beginning, Christians had faced arbitrary persecution (e.g., Acts 4:1-21; 5:17-40; 6:8–7:60); but now, across the Roman Empire, state-sponsored opposition and persecution was breaking out. So it was a difficult time to be a Christian. At such times we need to remember who we are as Christians—"God's chosen people" (1 Peter 1:1) who have an inheritance that is "pure and undefiled, beyond the reach of change and decay" (1:4); "living stones" (2:5) in God's temple; and "a chosen people . . . royal priests, a holy nation, God's very own possession" (2:9). That's why we shouldn't get discouraged; and that's why we should stand firm, resisting the pressure to adapt and conform—a very real temptation when that would mean our persecutors would leave us alone.

When the world is against us, we should remember that this world isn't our real home anyway. Remembering we are only "living as foreigners" (1:1) passing through helps us to keep things in perspective. But at the same time, Peter warns us not to opt out of society: Christians should live as good, respectful citizens, giving no one grounds for accusing us of disloyalty or of not caring about our nation.

Peter shows us that one of the first strategies in dealing with potential attack is preparation. As believers we know our faith will be tested, so we should always be alert. The trial will not last forever, and difficulties make us depend on Christ even more. This letter shows that it's possible to come through the worst situations with a strong, unshaken faith in God's love.

▸ *See also* ***Peter****, page 1421.*

Greetings from Peter

1 This letter is from Peter, an apostle of
Jesus Christ.
I am writing to God's chosen people who
are living as foreigners in the provinces
of Pontus, Galatia, Cappadocia, Asia, and
Bithynia.* 2God the Father knew you and
chose you long ago, and his Spirit has made
you holy. As a result, you have obeyed him
and have been cleansed by the blood of Jesus
Christ.

May God give you more and more grace
and peace.

The Hope of Eternal Life

3All praise to God, the Father of our Lord
Jesus Christ. It is by his great mercy that
we have been born again, because God
raised Jesus Christ from the dead. Now we
live with great expectation, 4and we have a
priceless inheritance—an inheritance that is
kept in heaven for you, pure and undefiled,
beyond the reach of change and decay. 5And
through your faith, God is protecting you by
his power until you receive this salvation,
which is ready to be revealed on the last day
for all to see.

6So be truly glad.* There is wonderful joy
ahead, even though you must endure many
trials for a little while. 7These trials will show
that your faith is genuine. It is being tested
as fire tests and purifies gold—though your
faith is far more precious than mere gold.
So when your faith remains strong through
many trials, it will bring you much praise
and glory and honor on the day when Jesus
Christ is revealed to the whole world.

8You love him even though you have
never seen him. Though you do not see him
now, you trust him; and you rejoice with a
glorious, inexpressible joy. 9The reward for
trusting him will be the salvation of your
souls.

10This salvation was something even the
prophets wanted to know more about when
they prophesied about this gracious salvation prepared for you. 11They wondered what
time or situation the Spirit of Christ within
them was talking about when he told them
in advance about Christ's suffering and his
great glory afterward.

12They were told that their messages were
not for themselves, but for you. And now this
Good News has been announced to you by
those who preached in the power of the Holy
Spirit sent from heaven. It is all so wonderful

that even the angels are eagerly watching these things happen.

A Call to Holy Living

13 So prepare your minds for action and exercise self-control. Put all your hope in the gracious salvation that will come to you when Jesus Christ is revealed to the world.
14 So you must live as God's obedient children. Don't slip back into your old ways of living to satisfy your own desires. You didn't know any better then.
15 But now you must be holy in everything you do, just as God who chose you is holy.
16 For the Scriptures say, "You must be holy because I am holy."*
17 And remember that the heavenly Father to whom you pray has no favorites. He will judge or reward you according to what you do. So you must live in reverent fear of him during your time here as "temporary residents."
18 For you know that God paid a ransom to save you from the empty life you inherited from your ancestors. And it was not paid with mere gold or silver, which lose their value.
19 It was the precious blood of Christ, the sinless, spotless Lamb of God.
20 God chose him as your ransom long before the world began, but now in these last days he has been revealed for your sake.
21 Through Christ you have come to trust in God. And you have placed your faith and hope in God because he raised Christ from the dead and gave him great glory.
22 You were cleansed from your sins when you obeyed the truth, so now you must show sincere love to each other as brothers and sisters.* Love each other deeply with all your heart.*
23 For you have been born again, but not to a life that will quickly end. Your new life will last forever because it comes from the eternal, living word of God.
24 As the Scriptures say,

"People are like grass;
their beauty is like a flower in the field.
The grass withers and the flower fades.
25 But the word of the Lord remains forever."*

And that word is the Good News that was preached to you.

2 So get rid of all evil behavior. Be done with all deceit, hypocrisy, jealousy, and all unkind speech.
2 Like newborn babies, you must crave pure spiritual milk so that you will grow into a full experience of salvation. Cry out for this nourishment,
3 now that you have had a taste of the Lord's kindness.

1:1 *Pontus, Galatia, Cappadocia, Asia,* and *Bithynia* were Roman provinces in what is now Turkey. **1:6** Or *So you are truly glad.* **1:16** Lev 11:44-45; 19:2; 20:7. **1:22a** Greek *must have brotherly love.* **1:22b** Some manuscripts read *with a pure heart.* **1:24-25** Isa 40:6-8.

▸ **1:16** *See* ***Holiness****, page 128.*

Peter

Peter, also called Simon, had been one of Jesus' original twelve apostles (Matthew 4:18-20; John 1:35-42). Formerly a Galilean fisherman, Peter was a working man who was used to plain speaking. In the Gospels we see his initial struggles with discipleship—on the one hand, he exercised great faith, as when he attempted to walk on water (Matthew 14:25-33) and declared whom he understood Jesus to be (Matthew 16:16); but on the other hand he had times of great weakness, as when he struggled with the issue of forgiveness (Matthew 18:21), or had unrealistic views about himself (Matthew 26:33-35), or denied Jesus (Mark 14:66-72). But once he was filled with the Holy Spirit at Pentecost, he changed. He played a key role in the church's life in Judea and Samaria, fulfilling the name "Rock" that Jesus had given him (Matthew 16:18). He eventually overcame his old Jewish prejudices and took the gospel to Gentiles (Acts 10), ending up in Rome, where he was martyred around AD 65–67.

▸ *See also* ***Apostles of Jesus****, page 1122;* ***The First Journeys of Christian Leaders*** *maps, Visual Overview Z14.*

Living Stones for God's House

4You are coming to Christ, who is the living cornerstone of God's temple. He was rejected by people, but he was chosen by God for great honor.

5And you are living stones that God is
building into his spiritual temple. What's
more, you are his holy priests.* Through
the mediation of Jesus Christ, you offer
spiritual sacrifices that please God. 6As the
Scriptures say,

"I am placing a cornerstone in
Jerusalem,*
chosen for great honor,
and anyone who trusts in him
will never be disgraced."*

7Yes, you who trust him recognize the honor
God has given him.* But for those who
reject him,

"The stone that the builders rejected
has now become the cornerstone."*

8And,

"He is the stone that makes people
stumble,
the rock that makes them fall."*

They stumble because they do not obey God's word, and so they meet the fate that was planned for them.

9But you are not like that, for you are a chosen people. You are royal priests,* a holy nation, God's very own possession. As a result, you can show others the goodness of God, for he called you out of the darkness into his wonderful light.

10 "Once you had no identity as a people;
now you are God's people.
Once you received no mercy;
now you have received God's mercy."*

11Dear friends, I warn you as "temporary
residents and foreigners" to keep away
from worldly desires that wage war against
your very souls. 12Be careful to live properly
among your unbelieving neighbors. Then
even if they accuse you of doing wrong,
they will see your honorable behavior, and
they will give honor to God when he judges
the world.*

Respecting People in Authority

13For the Lord's sake, submit to all human
authority—whether the king as head of
state, 14or the officials he has appointed. For
the king has sent them to punish those who
do wrong and to honor those who do right.
15It is God's will that your honorable
lives should silence those ignorant people
who make foolish accusations against you.
16For you are free, yet you are God's slaves,
so don't use your freedom as an excuse to

▸ **2:13-17** *See* ***Christians and government****, page 1297.*

Every Christian is a priest

The early church had no special priesthood. In fact, the New Testament goes out of its way to avoid using any special "priestly" words (of which there were many in those days) for church leaders. What it stresses, by contrast, is that in Christ all true believers are now priests. Hence Peter writes that God's people are "holy priests" (1 Peter 2:5) and "royal priests" (2:9), and John refers to believers as a "Kingdom of priests" in Revelation (Revelation 1:6; 5:10). While Paul does not use the language of priesthood, he clearly saw every church member as equal with every other and expected all to play their part in church life (e.g., 1 Corinthians 12:12-27).

One of the main roles of priests under the old covenant was to offer sacrifices; but this is now no longer needed, for Christ offered himself as the once-for-all, never to be repeated sacrifice (see Hebrews 9:24–10:14). But other roles of the priest remain as a calling for us all—for example, intercession, worship, and service. Even if the church you belong to does have a particular priesthood with certain functions restricted to priests, we should nevertheless remember that we are all called to be priests in these ways.

do evil. [17]Respect everyone, and love the
family of believers.* Fear God, and respect
the king.

Slaves

[18]You who are slaves must submit to your
masters with all respect.* Do what they tell
you—not only if they are kind and reasonable, but even if they are cruel. [19]For God is
pleased when, conscious of his will, you patiently endure unjust treatment. [20]Of course,
you get no credit for being patient if you are
beaten for doing wrong. But if you suffer for
doing good and endure it patiently, God is
pleased with you.

[21]For God called you to do good, even if
it means suffering, just as Christ suffered*
for you. He is your example, and you must
follow in his steps.

[22] He never sinned,
 nor ever deceived anyone.*
[23] He did not retaliate when he was
 insulted,
 nor threaten revenge when he
 suffered.
He left his case in the hands of God,
 who always judges fairly.
[24] He personally carried our sins
 in his body on the cross
so that we can be dead to sin
 and live for what is right.
By his wounds
 you are healed.
[25] Once you were like sheep
 who wandered away.
But now you have turned to your
 Shepherd,
 the Guardian of your souls.

Wives

3 In the same way, you wives must accept
the authority of your husbands. Then,
even if some refuse to obey the Good News,
your godly lives will speak to them without
any words. They will be won over [2]by observing your pure and reverent lives.

[3]Don't be concerned about the outward
beauty of fancy hairstyles, expensive
jewelry, or beautiful clothes. [4]You should
clothe yourselves instead with the beauty
that comes from within, the unfading
beauty of a gentle and quiet spirit, which
is so precious to God. [5]This is how the holy
women of old made themselves beautiful.
They put their trust in God and accepted the
authority of their husbands. [6]For instance,
Sarah obeyed her husband, Abraham, and
called him her master. You are her daughters when you do what is right without fear
of what your husbands might do.

Husbands

[7]In the same way, you husbands must give
honor to your wives. Treat your wife with
understanding as you live together. She
may be weaker than you are, but she is your
equal partner in God's gift of new life. Treat
her as you should so your prayers will not
be hindered.

All Christians

[8]Finally, all of you should be of one mind.
Sympathize with each other. Love each
other as brothers and sisters.* Be tenderhearted, and keep a humble attitude.
[9]Don't repay evil for evil. Don't retaliate with
insults when people insult you. Instead,
pay them back with a blessing. That is what
God has called you to do, and he will grant
you his blessing. [10]For the Scriptures say,

"If you want to enjoy life
 and see many happy days,
keep your tongue from speaking evil
 and your lips from telling lies.
[11] Turn away from evil and do good.
 Search for peace, and work to
 maintain it.
[12] The eyes of the LORD watch over those
 who do right,
 and his ears are open to their prayers.
But the LORD turns his face
 against those who do evil."*

Suffering for Doing Good

[13]Now, who will want to harm you if you are
eager to do good? [14]But even if you suffer
for doing what is right, God will reward you
for it. So don't worry or be afraid of their
threats. [15]Instead, you must worship Christ
as Lord of your life. And if someone asks
about your hope as a believer, always be
ready to explain it. [16]But do this in a gentle
and respectful way.* Keep your conscience

2:5 Greek *holy priesthood.* **2:6a** Greek *in Zion.* **2:6b** Isa 28:16 (Greek version). **2:7a** Or *Yes, for you who believe, there is honor.* **2:7b** Ps 118:22. **2:8** Isa 8:14. **2:9** Greek *a royal priesthood.* **2:10** Hos 1:6, 9; 2:23. **2:12** Or *on the day of visitation.* **2:17** Greek *love the brotherhood.* **2:18** Or *because you fear God;* Greek reads *in all fear.* **2:21** Some manuscripts read *died.* **2:22** Isa 53:9. **3:8** Greek *Show brotherly love.* **3:10-12** Ps 34:12-16. **3:16** Some English translations put this sentence in verse 15.

clear. Then if people speak against you,
they will be ashamed when they see what
a good life you live because you belong to
Christ. 17 Remember, it is better to suffer for
doing good, if that is what God wants, than
to suffer for doing wrong!

18 Christ suffered* for our sins once for
all time. He never sinned, but he died for
sinners to bring you safely home to God. He
suffered physical death, but he was raised
to life in the Spirit.*

19 So he went and preached to the spirits in
prison—20 those who disobeyed God long ago
when God waited patiently while Noah was
building his boat. Only eight people were
saved from drowning in that terrible flood.*
21 And that water is a picture of baptism,
which now saves you, not by removing dirt
from your body, but as a response to God
from* a clean conscience. It is effective
because of the resurrection of Jesus Christ.

22 Now Christ has gone to heaven. He is
seated in the place of honor next to God,
and all the angels and authorities and
powers accept his authority.

Living for God

4 So then, since Christ suffered physical
pain, you must arm yourselves with
the same attitude he had, and be ready to
suffer, too. For if you have suffered physically for Christ, you have finished with
sin.* 2 You won't spend the rest of your
lives chasing your own desires, but you
will be anxious to do the will of God. 3 You
have had enough in the past of the evil
things that godless people enjoy—their
immorality and lust, their feasting and
drunkenness and wild parties, and their
terrible worship of idols.

4 Of course, your former friends are surprised when you no longer plunge into the
flood of wild and destructive things they do.
So they slander you. 5 But remember that they
will have to face God, who stands ready to
judge everyone, both the living and the dead.
6 That is why the Good News was preached to
those who are now dead*—so although they
were destined to die like all people,* they
now live forever with God in the Spirit.*

7 The end of the world is coming soon.
Therefore, be earnest and disciplined in
your prayers. 8 Most important of all, continue to show deep love for each other, for
love covers a multitude of sins. 9 Cheerfully
share your home with those who need a
meal or a place to stay.

10 God has given each of you a gift from
his great variety of spiritual gifts. Use them
well to serve one another. 11 Do you have the
gift of speaking? Then speak as though
God himself were speaking through you.
Do you have the gift of helping others?
Do it with all the strength and energy that
God supplies. Then everything you do will

Service

Since service lay at the very heart of Christ's incarnation (Philippians 2:6-7) and ministry (Matthew 20:28), it should not surprise us to find that service is a repeated call on Christians' lives throughout the New Testament. In 1 Peter 4:10-11, Peter reminds us that any gift we have is something that we have received from God, and that therefore we should be faithful in how we use it, remembering that its sole purpose is that God—not us—should receive glory through it. Paul teaches the same thing in Romans 12:4-8 and 1 Corinthians 12:7-11.

No matter what our role may be in society or in the church, all of us are called to have an attitude and heart of service. Even if we are leaders in the church or managers in business, we should never lord it over others (1 Peter 5:3) but rather seek their good and not our own (Philippians 2:3-4), even being ready to lay down our lives for others as Christ laid down his life for us (1 John 3:16). Servanthood lies at the heart of God's Kingdom.

Whatever we do, our response should always be, "We are unworthy servants who have simply done our duty" (Luke 17:10).

▶ *See also* ***Gifts of the Holy Spirit**, page 1316.*

bring glory to God through Jesus Christ. All glory and power to him forever and ever! Amen.

Suffering for Being a Christian

[12]Dear friends, don't be surprised at the fiery trials you are going through, as if something strange were happening to you. [13]Instead, be very glad—for these trials make you partners with Christ in his suffering, so that you will have the wonderful joy of seeing his glory when it is revealed to all the world.

[14]If you are insulted because you bear the name of Christ, you will be blessed, for the glorious Spirit of God* rests upon you.* [15]If you suffer, however, it must not be for murder, stealing, making trouble, or prying into other people's affairs. [16]But it is no shame to suffer for being a Christian. Praise God for the privilege of being called by his name! [17]For the time has come for judgment, and it must begin with God's household. And if judgment begins with us, what terrible fate awaits those who have never obeyed God's Good News? [18]And also,

"If the righteous are barely saved,
what will happen to godless
sinners?"*

[19]So if you are suffering in a manner that pleases God, keep on doing what is right, and trust your lives to the God who created you, for he will never fail you.

Advice for Elders and Young Men

5 And now, a word to you who are elders in the churches. I, too, am an elder and a witness to the sufferings of Christ. And I, too, will share in his glory when he is revealed to the whole world. As a fellow elder, I appeal to you: [2]Care for the flock that God has entrusted to you. Watch over it willingly, not grudgingly—not for what you will get out of it, but because you are eager to serve God. [3]Don't lord it over the people assigned to your care, but lead them by your own good example. [4]And when the Great Shepherd appears, you will receive a crown of never-ending glory and honor.

[5]In the same way, you who are younger must accept the authority of the elders. And all of you, dress yourselves in humility as you relate to one another, for

"God opposes the proud
but gives grace to the humble."*

[6]So humble yourselves under the mighty power of God, and at the right time he will lift you up in honor. [7]Give all your worries and cares to God, for he cares about you.

[8]Stay alert! Watch out for your great enemy, the devil. He prowls around like a roaring lion, looking for someone to devour. [9]Stand firm against him, and be strong in your faith. Remember that your family of believers* all over the world is going through the same kind of suffering you are.

[10]In his kindness God called you to share in his eternal glory by means of Christ Jesus. So after you have suffered a little while, he will restore, support, and strengthen you, and he will place you on a firm foundation. [11]All power to him forever! Amen.

Peter's Final Greetings

[12]I have written and sent this short letter to you with the help of Silas,* whom I commend to you as a faithful brother. My purpose in writing is to encourage you and assure you that what you are experiencing is truly part of God's grace for you. Stand firm in this grace.

[13]Your sister church here in Babylon* sends you greetings, and so does my son Mark. [14]Greet each other with a kiss of love.

Peace be with all of you who are in Christ.

3:18a Some manuscripts read *died.* **3:18b** Or *in spirit.* **3:20** Greek *saved through water.* **3:21** Or *as an appeal to God for.* **4:1** Or *For the one* [or *One*] *who has suffered physically has finished with sin.* **4:6a** Greek *preached even to the dead.* **4:6b** Or *so although people had judged them worthy of death.* **4:6c** Or *in spirit.* **4:14a** Or *for the glory of God, which is his Spirit.* **4:14b** Some manuscripts add *On their part he is blasphemed, but on your part he is glorified.* **4:18** Prov 11:31 (Greek version). **5:5** Prov 3:34 (Greek version). **5:9** Greek *your brotherhood.* **5:12** Greek *Silvanus.* **5:13** Greek *The elect one in Babylon.* Babylon was probably symbolic for Rome.

▸ **4:12-14** *See **Joy**, page 1360.*

2 Peter *Holding firm to what we know*

Written toward the end of Peter's life (1:13-15), this letter encourages its readers to stand firm in the face of opposition—this time, not from outside the church as in 1 Peter, but from inside the church through false teaching. In light of the coming day of the Lord, believers should hold on to what they have received and live righteously, for God has given us everything we need to do so.

What's it all about?

Second Peter opens with the bold reminder that everything the believer needs to live a godly life has already been provided by God (1:3). But we should not take these things for granted; believers have a part to play too in developing their spiritual lives. So faith has to work closely together with other qualities like moral excellence, knowledge, self-control, patient endurance, godliness, brotherly affection, and love. Giving ourselves to such things will make us increasingly "productive and useful" (1:8) and ensure we never fall (1:10).

Peter knew that his death was rapidly approaching (1:13-14), so he reminds believers to trust the message they had heard from people who could be trusted—people who, like Peter himself, had not made up stories about Jesus (1:16-18), but who spoke the truth that was in line with all that the prophets had foretold (1:19-21). In chapter 2, he warns about false teachers who lead people astray—not just into wrong beliefs, but into wrong lifestyles. Such teachers can seem attractive, promising all kinds of things; but they are only in it for their own gain. When Christ returns, they will be severely punished by God for the harm they have done.

And if people scoff at the idea of future judgment at Jesus' return, then believers should be patient, Peter writes in chapter 3. Christ will come again, and Peter outlines some of the events that will accompany this. If his return seems delayed, it is only because God is being patient, wanting to give everyone the opportunity to repent (3:8-9). But the day of the Lord will certainly come, and this prospect should spur them on to living good lives. He then concludes with remarks about Paul's letters which, interestingly, he ranks along with "other parts of Scripture" (3:15-16)—suggesting that Paul's letters were already starting to be seen as "Scripture"—and which some people were misinterpreting.

Although this letter claims to be written by the apostle Peter (1:1) and clearly reflects an eyewitness account of the Transfiguration (1:16-18), some doubt Peter's authorship because its style and content are very different from 1 Peter. However, 1 Peter was written "with the help of Silas" (1 Peter 5:12), which may help explain the differences.

OVERVIEW

God's blessings and the apostle's trustworthy message · *1:1-21*

Warnings against false teachers
2:1-22

Living in light of Jesus' return
3:1-18

What does it mean for us?

At a time when different religious ideas were vying for people's attention, Peter urged believers to stick to two guideposts they could trust: God's word and the teaching of the apostles. Unlike the message brought by false teachers, the Christian gospel is not someone's invention: It is the word of God himself. That word was announced beforehand by the Old Testament prophets and faithfully brought to them by Jesus' own disciples, eyewitnesses to his life and teaching whose own lives lived up to his message (chapter 1). By contrast, these false teachers were inventing their own stories (2:3) and living lives that were not a reflection of the true gospel (2:13-22). Peter urges his readers to reject their teachings and hold on to the truth they have received in the certainty that God will reward them when Christ returns.

Still today there are those who want to add to the gospel or shape it in their own way, usually to obtain some personal gain from it (2:3); but we should constantly test their teachings, and the lives of the teachers themselves, by the truth of Scripture. And if we are tempted to become discouraged by all that is going on around us, we should remember again the sure and certain promise of Christ's return at the end of the age, when he will judge the guilty and reward the faithful.

▸ *See also* ***Peter****, page 1421.*

Greetings from Peter

1 This letter is from Simon* Peter, a slave and apostle of Jesus Christ.

I am writing to you who share the same precious faith we have. This faith was given to you because of the justice and fairness* of Jesus Christ, our God and Savior.

2 May God give you more and more grace and peace as you grow in your knowledge of God and Jesus our Lord.

Growing in Faith

3 By his divine power, God has given us everything we need for living a godly life. We have received all of this by coming to know him, the one who called us to himself by means of his marvelous glory and excellence. 4 And because of his glory and excellence, he has given us great and precious promises. These are the promises that enable you to share his divine nature and escape the world's corruption caused by human desires.

5 In view of all this, make every effort to respond to God's promises. Supplement your faith with a generous provision of moral excellence, and moral excellence with knowledge, 6 and knowledge with self-control, and self-control with patient endurance, and patient endurance with godliness, 7 and godliness with brotherly affection, and brotherly affection with love for everyone.

8 The more you grow like this, the more productive and useful you will be in your knowledge of our Lord Jesus Christ. 9 But those who fail to develop in this way are shortsighted or blind, forgetting that they have been cleansed from their old sins.

10 So, dear brothers and sisters,* work hard to prove that you really are among those God has called and chosen. Do these things, and you will never fall away. 11 Then God will give you a grand entrance into the eternal Kingdom of our Lord and Savior Jesus Christ.

Paying Attention to Scripture

12 Therefore, I will always remind you about these things—even though you already know them and are standing firm in the truth you have been taught. 13 And it is only right that I should keep on reminding you as long as I live.* 14 For our Lord Jesus Christ has shown me that I must soon leave this earthly life,* 15 so I will work hard to make sure you always remember these things after I am gone.

16 For we were not making up clever stories when we told you about the powerful coming of our Lord Jesus Christ. We saw his majestic splendor with our own eyes 17 when he received honor and glory from God the Father. The voice from the majestic glory of God said to him, "This is my dearly loved Son, who brings me great joy."* 18 We ourselves heard

1:1a Greek *Simeon.* **1:1b** Or *to you in the righteousness.* **1:10** Greek *brothers.* **1:13** Greek *as long as I am in this tent* [or *tabernacle*]. **1:14** Greek *I must soon put off my tent* [or *tabernacle*]. **1:17** Matt 17:5; Mark 9:7; Luke 9:35.

▸ **1:13-15** *See* ***Heaven****, page 1451.*

that voice from heaven when we were with
him on the holy mountain.
[19]Because of that experience, we have
even greater confidence in the message
proclaimed by the prophets. You must
pay close attention to what they wrote,
for their words are like a lamp shining in
a dark place—until the Day dawns, and
Christ the Morning Star shines* in your
hearts. [20]Above all, you must realize that no
prophecy in Scripture ever came from the
prophet's own understanding,* [21]or from
human initiative. No, those prophets were
moved by the Holy Spirit, and they spoke
from God.

The Danger of False Teachers

2 But there were also false prophets in
Israel, just as there will be false teachers among you. They will cleverly teach destructive heresies and even deny the Master
who bought them. In this way, they will
bring sudden destruction on themselves.
[2]Many will follow their evil teaching and
shameful immorality. And because of these
teachers, the way of truth will be slandered.
[3]In their greed they will make up clever lies
to get hold of your money. But God condemned them long ago, and their destruction will not be delayed.
[4]For God did not spare even the angels
who sinned. He threw them into hell,* in
gloomy pits of darkness,* where they are
being held until the day of judgment. [5]And
God did not spare the ancient world—except
for Noah and the seven others in his family.
Noah warned the world of God's righteous
judgment. So God protected Noah when he
destroyed the world of ungodly people with
a vast flood. [6]Later, God condemned the
cities of Sodom and Gomorrah and turned
them into heaps of ashes. He made them an
example of what will happen to ungodly
people. [7]But God also rescued Lot out of
Sodom because he was a righteous man
who was sick of the shameful immorality
of the wicked people around him. [8]Yes, Lot
was a righteous man who was tormented
in his soul by the wickedness he saw and
heard day after day. [9]So you see, the Lord
knows how to rescue godly people from
their trials, even while keeping the wicked
under punishment until the day of final
judgment. [10]He is especially hard on those
who follow their own twisted sexual desire,
and who despise authority.
These people are proud and arrogant,
daring even to scoff at supernatural beings*
without so much as trembling. [11]But the
angels, who are far greater in power and
strength, do not dare to bring from the
Lord* a charge of blasphemy against those
supernatural beings.
[12]These false teachers are like unthinking
animals, creatures of instinct, born to be
caught and destroyed. They scoff at things
they do not understand, and like animals,
they will be destroyed. [13]Their destruction is
their reward for the harm they have done.
They love to indulge in evil pleasures in
broad daylight. They are a disgrace and a
stain among you. They delight in deception*
even as they eat with you in your fellowship
meals. [14]They commit adultery with their
eyes, and their desire for sin is never satisfied. They lure unstable people into sin,

Savior

The word "Savior" was used of Jesus initially in the context of describing his work of saving people (e.g., Acts 5:30-31; 13:23-39), just as God himself had done in the Old Testament (e.g., Psalm 18:2; 38:21-22; 42:5-11; Isaiah 43:1-13). However, because salvation was so intimately tied up with both who Jesus was (the name Jesus means "Yahweh saves") and what Jesus had come to bring, the word quickly became part of his title (2 Peter 1:1; see also, e.g., 2 Timothy 1:10; Titus 1:4). In his second letter, Peter links the title Savior once with "God" (2 Peter 1:1) and three times with "Lord" (1:11; 2:20; 3:18). This underlines that we cannot claim that Jesus is our Savior unless we are truly living with him as our God and our Lord—living a life of obedience to him and not just looking for a ticket to heaven.

▸ *See also **Names and titles of Jesus**, page 1070; **The death of Jesus**, page 1114.*

and they are well trained in greed. They live
under God's curse. 15 They have wandered
off the right road and followed the footsteps of Balaam son of Beor,* who loved to
earn money by doing wrong. 16 But Balaam
was stopped from his mad course when his
donkey rebuked him with a human voice.
17 These people are as useless as dried-up
springs or as mist blown away by the wind.
They are doomed to blackest darkness.
18 They brag about themselves with empty,
foolish boasting. With an appeal to twisted
sexual desires, they lure back into sin those
who have barely escaped from a lifestyle of
deception. 19 They promise freedom, but they
themselves are slaves of sin and corruption.
For you are a slave to whatever controls you.
20 And when people escape from the wickedness of the world by knowing our Lord and
Savior Jesus Christ and then get tangled up
and enslaved by sin again, they are worse off
than before. 21 It would be better if they had
never known the way to righteousness than
to know it and then reject the command they
were given to live a holy life. 22 They prove
the truth of this proverb: "A dog returns to its
vomit."* And another says, "A washed pig
returns to the mud."

The Day of the Lord Is Coming

3 This is my second letter to you, dear
friends, and in both of them I have tried
to stimulate your wholesome thinking and
refresh your memory. 2 I want you to remember what the holy prophets said long ago
and what our Lord and Savior commanded
through your apostles.
3 Most importantly, I want to remind you
that in the last days scoffers will come,
mocking the truth and following their own
desires. 4 They will say, "What happened
to the promise that Jesus is coming again?
From before the times of our ancestors,
everything has remained the same since the
world was first created."
5 They deliberately forget that God made
the heavens long ago by the word of his
command, and he brought the earth out
from the water and surrounded it with
water. 6 Then he used the water to destroy
the ancient world with a mighty flood. 7 And
by the same word, the present heavens and
earth have been stored up for fire. They are
being kept for the day of judgment, when
ungodly people will be destroyed.
8 But you must not forget this one thing,
dear friends: A day is like a thousand years
to the Lord, and a thousand years is like a
day. 9 The Lord isn't really being slow about
his promise, as some people think. No, he is
being patient for your sake. He does not want
anyone to be destroyed, but wants everyone

1:19 Or *rises.* **1:20** Or *is a matter of one's own interpretation.* **2:4a** Greek *Tartarus.* **2:4b** Some manuscripts read *in chains of gloom.* **2:10** Greek *at glorious ones,* which are probably evil angels. **2:11** Other manuscripts read *to the Lord;* still others do not include this phrase at all. **2:13** Some manuscripts read *in fellowship meals.* **2:15** Some manuscripts read *Bosor.* **2:22** Prov 26:11.

Addiction

Addiction is any compulsive behavior that continues despite knowledge of the outcome. It is slavery to something that has mastered you and from which you cannot escape. The particular addiction Peter was thinking of in 2 Peter 2:19 seems to have been sexual (2:18), though greed and money were also involved (2:13-15). But we can become addicted to anything, even things that in themselves are good, like food or the Internet. A good test is, Can I live without this? If we can't, then it is an addiction.

Addictions never satisfy (Romans 6:21); no matter how much we feed them, they always demand more. And even if we promise to do it just one more time and then stop, we find we can't. Addictions are a god; but as Christians we can only have one God. So if we recognize some addiction in our life, we need to call out to Jesus to set us free. He can break the devil's stronghold and give us the ongoing self-control through the Holy Spirit to live in freedom (see Romans 6:11–7:25; Galatians 5:16-25). If we have prayed and not seen a breakthrough, then we need to humble ourselves and ask some more mature Christians to pray with us, for Christ wants to set us free. To doubt this is to believe the devil rather than him.

to repent. [10]But the day of the Lord will come
as unexpectedly as a thief. Then the heavens
will pass away with a terrible noise, and the
very elements themselves will disappear in
fire, and the earth and everything on it will
be found to deserve judgment.*
[11]Since everything around us is going to
be destroyed like this, what holy and godly
lives you should live, [12]looking forward to
the day of God and hurrying it along. On
that day, he will set the heavens on fire, and
the elements will melt away in the flames.
[13]But we are looking forward to the new
heavens and new earth he has promised, a
world filled with God's righteousness.
[14]And so, dear friends, while you are
waiting for these things to happen, make
every effort to be found living peaceful lives
that are pure and blameless in his sight.
[15]And remember, our Lord's patience
gives people time to be saved. This is what
our beloved brother Paul also wrote to you
with the wisdom God gave him—[16]speaking
of these things in all of his letters. Some of
his comments are hard to understand, and
those who are ignorant and unstable have
twisted his letters to mean something quite
different, just as they do with other parts
of Scripture. And this will result in their
destruction.

Peter's Final Words

[17]You already know these things, dear friends.
So be on guard; then you will not be carried
away by the errors of these wicked people
and lose your own secure footing. [18]Rather,
you must grow in the grace and knowledge
of our Lord and Savior Jesus Christ.

All glory to him, both now and forever!
Amen.

3:10 Other manuscripts read *will be burned up;* one early manuscript reads *will be found destroyed.*

Growing as a Christian

The birth of a baby always brings excitement to a family, but how worried that family would be if the baby always stayed a baby! After all, babies are born for one thing: to grow up. And that's exactly how it is when we become Christians. God does not want us to stay spiritual babies; he wants us to grow up, in both our knowledge and experience, as Peter encourages in 2 Peter 3:18.

Acts 2:42 lists four key practices that helped the first Christians to grow: "All the believers devoted themselves to the apostles' teaching, and to fellowship, and to sharing in meals (including the Lord's Supper), and to prayer." We can follow their example, first, by studying the Bible—for if we do not read it, how can we know what God is like and what he wants?—second, by sharing fellowship with other Christians to encourage one another; third, by sharing the Lord's Supper together to remind us of Christ's sacrifice and to keep him central in our lives; and fourth, by praying—talking to God—both alone and with others. Note that these four things weren't occasional occurrences; rather, the first Christians devoted themselves to them. Doing the same today will help us grow and mature, not just intellectually, but in a living experience of God's grace.

1, 2 & 3 John *Truth and love*

Earliest church tradition ascribed all three of these letters to John the apostle, author of the Gospel that bears his name and possibly a cousin of Jesus. John moved from Jerusalem before its destruction by the Romans in AD 70 and settled in Ephesus, where he spent most of the rest of his life. These three letters were written by him to Christians in that region. Written in his old age, John's letters call their recipients back to the fundamentals of the Christian faith: how we should live and how we should love in light of the One who was the Word become human. If they trust in Christ, they will overcome all obstacles and opponents, John assures them. The second and third letters are personal letters to friends and are the shortest letters in the Bible. The second letter reminds its readers that while they are to love, they are also to be wise and discerning. The third letter is full of encouragement to a fellow Christian.

What's it all about?

In all three letters one word really stands out: love. In 1 John—which opens with words reminiscent of John's Gospel—love is seen as the essential quality of God. Since believers are God's children, they now share in this quality. But John urges them to keep loving one another more and more and to deal with anything that threatens their love, especially sin. That is why he urges them to confess sin quickly and find the forgiveness that comes through Christ's atoning sacrifice (1:5–2:2). If we don't love one another, we are still living in darkness (2:3-14). The one thing we are not to love is "the world" (2:15)—not referring to the people of this world, but the lifestyle of this world, which is full of "antichrists" (2:18-27).

In chapters 3 and 4, John reminds believers that true love is costly, just as it cost Jesus. He laid down his life for us, and we should be ready to lay down our lives for one another (3:16). Love always leads to practical action. So Christians must meet each other's practical and spiritual needs (3:17; 5:16).

In the midst of these exhortations to love, John returns to a major problem his readers were facing: false teachers who were creating confusion with their conflicting claims to know "the truth." John urges them to trust the gift they have received from God—the Holy Spirit—and to remain true to those who first brought them the message of eternal life.

John ends his first letter on a confident note. He assures his readers that they have defeated the world, can lead lives free from fear, and can know that they have eternal life and that God will always hear their prayers.

In 2 John, addressed to an unknown lady and her children, John says that love has to make hard choices sometimes. Members of the church were in a quandary as to when to offer hospitality and when to refuse it. The source of the problem was the false teachers again. Was it ever right to refuse hospitality, church members were asking themselves, to someone claiming to be a messenger of God? Yes, John says, for love sometimes means saying "No." He advises the lady not to receive such people into her home.

Third John is a personal letter to a dear friend, Gaius. Gaius is warned about an autocratic leader in the church named Diotrephes, who was not only out of fellowship with John and his companions but also out of line in his treatment of other Christians. His preoccupation with his own status led him to break the most important commandment of all—to love. John rebukes him and warns Gaius to avoid him.

2 JOHN

Greetings to "the chosen lady"
1:1-3

The commandment to love
1:4-6

Warnings against deceivers
1:7-13

3 JOHN

Greetings to Gaius
1:1-4

Commendation of Gaius
1:5-8

Contrasts between a bad leader and a good leader
1:9-12

Greetings to friends
1:13-15

What does it mean for us?

The letters of John were written to reassure and guide churches that had been troubled by false teaching and false leaders. They can speak powerfully to us today as we try to maintain our Christian life and faith in a world where many beliefs and lifestyles compete for our attention.

In his first letter in particular, John emphasizes the importance of believing the right things about Jesus, especially concerning who he is. Jesus was no mere man, he stresses, nor merely a divine or angelic figure. He was God in human form, "the Word of life" (1 John 1:1) come among us. Only the God-man could bring humanity into true relationship and fellowship with God.

John also stresses the importance of love, for "God is love" (4:8). When a group is disturbed as a result of false teaching or argument as John's churches were, it is easy to become bitter and to look for someone to blame; but maintaining love toward one another is crucial. It is impossible to love and yet think only of ourselves. Love is about putting other people first and caring for them in very practical ways.

Truth and love are things that God holds perfectly in balance. Sadly, Christians can often be keen on truth but short of love, or generous in love but not too concerned about questions of truth. True discipleship, however, means taking both love and truth seriously, as John makes plain in these writings.

▶ *See also **John**, page 1224.*

1 John

Introduction

1 We proclaim to you the one who existed
from the beginning,* whom we have
heard and seen. We saw him with our own
eyes and touched him with our own hands.
He is the Word of life. 2This one who is life
itself was revealed to us, and we have seen
him. And now we testify and proclaim to
you that he is the one who is eternal life.
He was with the Father, and then he was
revealed to us. 3We proclaim to you what
we ourselves have actually seen and heard
so that you may have fellowship with us.
And our fellowship is with the Father and
with his Son, Jesus Christ. 4We are writing
these things so that you may fully share
our joy.*

Living in the Light

5This is the message we heard from Jesus*
and now declare to you: God is light, and
there is no darkness in him at all. 6So we
are lying if we say we have fellowship with
God but go on living in spiritual darkness;
we are not practicing the truth. 7But if we
are living in the light, as God is in the light,
then we have fellowship with each other,
and the blood of Jesus, his Son, cleanses us
from all sin.

8If we claim we have no sin, we are only
fooling ourselves and not living in the truth.
9But if we confess our sins to him, he is
faithful and just to forgive us our sins and to
cleanse us from all wickedness. 10If we claim
we have not sinned, we are calling God a
liar and showing that his word has no place
in our hearts.

2 My dear children, I am writing this
to you so that you will not sin. But if
anyone does sin, we have an advocate who
pleads our case before the Father. He is
Jesus Christ, the one who is truly righteous.

1:1 Greek *What was from the beginning.* **1:4** Or *so that our joy may be complete;* some manuscripts read *your joy.* **1:5** Greek *from him.*

▸ **1:8-9** *See **Sin**, page 387.*

How can I be sure God has forgiven me?

There are few Christians who have not doubted God's forgiveness—especially after committing some particularly bad sin, or after falling into the same old sin yet again. That's the situation John's friends were in, having embraced false teaching. Could God really forgive them now, they wondered. John's reply—a confident "Yes!"—has nothing to do with them, but everything to do with God—the God who is faithful and just (1 John 1:9).

First, God is faithful, he reminds them. Countless Bible stories reveal this: Abraham, forgiven though he lied; David, forgiven though he committed adultery; Peter, forgiven though he denied Jesus; Paul, forgiven though he formerly helped kill Christians. God didn't give up on any of them.

But not only is God faithful; he is also just. He always does what is right. And what is right is to forgive those who trust in Christ, for through his death on the cross he has paid the price of our sin—all of it, past, present, and future—so now there remains no penalty for us to pay.

It is because God is "faithful and just" that we can be confident of forgiveness—a forgiveness that has nothing to do with us, but everything to do with him.

[2]He himself is the sacrifice that atones for our sins—and not only our sins but the sins of all the world.

[3]And we can be sure that we know him if we obey his commandments. [4]If someone claims, "I know God," but doesn't obey God's commandments, that person is a liar and is not living in the truth. [5]But those who obey God's word truly show how completely they love him. That is how we know we are living in him. [6]Those who say they live in God should live their lives as Jesus did.

A New Commandment

[7]Dear friends, I am not writing a new commandment for you; rather it is an old one you have had from the very beginning. This old commandment—to love one another—is the same message you heard before. [8]Yet it is also new. Jesus lived the truth of this commandment, and you also are living it. For the darkness is disappearing, and the true light is already shining.

[9]If anyone claims, "I am living in the light," but hates a fellow believer,* that person is still living in darkness. [10]Anyone who loves a fellow believer* is living in the light and does not cause others to stumble. [11]But anyone who hates a fellow believer is still living and walking in darkness. Such a person does not know the way to go, having been blinded by the darkness.

12 I am writing to you who are God's
children
because your sins have been forgiven
through Jesus.*
13 I am writing to you who are mature in
the faith*
because you know Christ, who existed
from the beginning.
I am writing to you who are young in the
faith
because you have won your battle
with the evil one.
14 I have written to you who are God's
children
because you know the Father.
I have written to you who are mature in
the faith
because you know Christ, who existed
from the beginning.
I have written to you who are young in
the faith
because you are strong.
God's word lives in your hearts,
and you have won your battle with the
evil one.

Do Not Love This World

[15]Do not love this world nor the things it offers you, for when you love the world, you do not have the love of the Father in you. [16]For the world offers only a craving for physical pleasure, a craving for everything we see, and pride in our achievements and

The Antichrist

In 1 John 2:18-27, John warns his readers about the Antichrist who is coming. Despite the many fantasies of movies and novels, the New Testament actually tells us little about him (in fact, the term is only used four times). The Greek preposition "anti" means "against"; so the Antichrist stands against Christ and opposes him, rather than making false claims to be him. Similar ideas are found elsewhere in the New Testament. Paul calls this figure "the man of lawlessness," who will personify increasing rebellion against God, seeking to defy him, performing counterfeit signs, and trying to deceive people (2 Thessalonians 2:1-11). In Revelation, John sees him as a great beast, ruling with false power and fighting God's people (Revelation 13). But John's interest in his letters lies not in the end-time Antichrist, but in the fact that the spirit of Antichrist is already at work and that "already many such antichrists have appeared" (1 John 2:18), leading people astray and causing them to deny God and Christ (2:18-22). For John, Antichrist is anyone working against Christ and his Kingdom.

▶ *See also **The return of Jesus Christ**, page 1372; **The man of lawlessness**, page 1375.*

possessions. These are not from the Father, but are from this world. [17]And this world is fading away, along with everything that people crave. But anyone who does what pleases God will live forever.

Warning about Antichrists

[18]Dear children, the last hour is here. You have heard that the Antichrist is coming, and already many such antichrists have appeared. From this we know that the last hour has come. [19]These people left our churches, but they never really belonged with us; otherwise they would have stayed with us. When they left, it proved that they did not belong with us.

[20]But you are not like that, for the Holy One has given you his Spirit,* and all of you know the truth. [21]So I am writing to you not because you don't know the truth but because you know the difference between truth and lies. [22]And who is a liar? Anyone who says that Jesus is not the Christ.* Anyone who denies the Father and the Son is an antichrist.* [23]Anyone who denies the Son doesn't have the Father, either. But anyone who acknowledges the Son has the Father also.

[24]So you must remain faithful to what you have been taught from the beginning. If you do, you will remain in fellowship with the Son and with the Father. [25]And in this fellowship we enjoy the eternal life he promised us.

[26]I am writing these things to warn you about those who want to lead you astray. [27]But you have received the Holy Spirit,* and he lives within you, so you don't need anyone to teach you what is true. For the Spirit* teaches you everything you need to know, and what he teaches is true—it is not a lie. So just as he has taught you, remain in fellowship with Christ.

Living as Children of God

[28]And now, dear children, remain in fellowship with Christ so that when he returns, you will be full of courage and not shrink back from him in shame.

[29]Since we know that Christ is righteous, we also know that all who do what is right are God's children.

3 See how very much our Father loves us, for he calls us his children, and that is what we are! But the people who belong to this world don't recognize that we are God's children because they don't know him. [2]Dear friends, we are already God's

2:9 Greek *hates his brother;* also in 2:11. **2:10** Greek *loves his brother.* **2:12** Greek *through his name.* **2:13** Or *to you fathers;* also in 2:14. **2:20** Greek *But you have an anointing from the Holy One.* **2:22a** Or *not the Messiah.* **2:22b** Or *the antichrist.* **2:27a** Greek *the anointing from him.* **2:27b** Greek *the anointing.*

Becoming like Christ

We live in a world where people constantly imitate others—their favorite football player, movie star, or business guru. They wear the same clothes as them and imitate their behavior; but their attempts to be like them are doomed to failure, for they have neither the wealth, good looks, nor skills to achieve what they did. And some Christians' attempts to be like Jesus are equally doomed to failure. They try so hard, putting so much effort into becoming like Christ; but it doesn't work. In fact, they are left disappointed and frustrated. And yet, God's goal is for us to become like Christ (1 John 3:2).

What we must realize is this: We cannot become like Christ simply by our own human effort—praying harder, reading the Bible more, giving more, or fasting (valuable though these things are). We become more like Christ as "the Lord—who is the Spirit—makes us more and more like him as we are changed into his glorious image" (2 Corinthians 3:18). This is the Spirit's work, not ours! And yet, for that to happen, we have to yield to him. This means making right choices—choices to forgive, serve, sacrifice, love, give. For it is as we make these choices that the Spirit enables us to live them out; and as we do, we discover that—little by little—we are becoming less like our old selves and more like our Savior.

▶ *See also* ***Holiness****, page 128.*

children, but he has not yet shown us what
we will be like when Christ appears. But we
do know that we will be like him, for we will
see him as he really is. [3]And all who have
this eager expectation will keep themselves
pure, just as he is pure.
[4]Everyone who sins is breaking God's law,
for all sin is contrary to the law of God. [5]And
you know that Jesus came to take away our
sins, and there is no sin in him. [6]Anyone
who continues to live in him will not sin.
But anyone who keeps on sinning does not
know him or understand who he is.
[7]Dear children, don't let anyone deceive
you about this: When people do what is
right, it shows that they are righteous, even
as Christ is righteous. [8]But when people keep
on sinning, it shows that they belong to the
devil, who has been sinning since the beginning. But the Son of God came to destroy
the works of the devil. [9]Those who have
been born into God's family do not make
a practice of sinning, because God's life*
is in them. So they can't keep on sinning,
because they are children of God. [10]So now
we can tell who are children of God and who
are children of the devil. Anyone who does
not live righteously and does not love other
believers* does not belong to God.

Love One Another

[11]This is the message you have heard from
the beginning: We should love one another.
[12]We must not be like Cain, who belonged
to the evil one and killed his brother. And
why did he kill him? Because Cain had been
doing what was evil, and his brother had
been doing what was righteous. [13]So don't
be surprised, dear brothers and sisters,* if
the world hates you.
[14]If we love our brothers and sisters who
are believers,* it proves that we have passed
from death to life. But a person who has
no love is still dead. [15]Anyone who hates
another brother or sister* is really a murderer at heart. And you know that murderers don't have eternal life within them.
[16]We know what real love is because Jesus
gave up his life for us. So we also ought to
give up our lives for our brothers and sisters.
[17]If someone has enough money to live well
and sees a brother or sister* in need but
shows no compassion—how can God's love
be in that person?
[18]Dear children, let's not merely say that
we love each other; let us show the truth by
our actions. [19]Our actions will show that we
belong to the truth, so we will be confident
when we stand before God. [20]Even if we feel
guilty, God is greater than our feelings, and
he knows everything.
[21]Dear friends, if we don't feel guilty, we
can come to God with bold confidence.
[22]And we will receive from him whatever we
ask because we obey him and do the things
that please him.
[23]And this is his commandment: We must
believe in the name of his Son, Jesus Christ,
and love one another, just as he commanded us. [24]Those who obey God's commandments remain in fellowship with him,
and he with them. And we know he lives in
us because the Spirit he gave us lives in us.

Discerning False Prophets

4 Dear friends, do not believe everyone
who claims to speak by the Spirit. You
must test them to see if the spirit they have
comes from God. For there are many false
prophets in the world. [2]This is how we know
if they have the Spirit of God: If a person
claiming to be a prophet* acknowledges that
Jesus Christ came in a real body, that person
has the Spirit of God. [3]But if someone claims
to be a prophet and does not acknowledge
the truth about Jesus, that person is not from
God. Such a person has the spirit of the Antichrist, which you heard is coming into the
world and indeed is already here.
[4]But you belong to God, my dear children.
You have already won a victory over those
people, because the Spirit who lives in you is
greater than the spirit who lives in the world.
[5]Those people belong to this world, so they
speak from the world's viewpoint, and the
world listens to them. [6]But we belong to
God, and those who know God listen to us. If
they do not belong to God, they do not listen
to us. That is how we know if someone has
the Spirit of truth or the spirit of deception.

Loving One Another

[7]Dear friends, let us continue to love one
another, for love comes from God. Anyone

▸ **3:16** *See **Loving others**, page 1220.*

who loves is a child of God and knows God.
8 But anyone who does not love does not
know God, for God is love.

9 God showed how much he loved us by
sending his one and only Son into the world
so that we might have eternal life through
him. 10 This is real love—not that we loved
God, but that he loved us and sent his Son
as a sacrifice to take away our sins.

11 Dear friends, since God loved us that
much, we surely ought to love each other.
12 No one has ever seen God. But if we love
each other, God lives in us, and his love is
brought to full expression in us.

13 And God has given us his Spirit as proof
that we live in him and he in us. 14 Furthermore, we have seen with our own eyes and
now testify that the Father sent his Son to
be the Savior of the world. 15 All who declare
that Jesus is the Son of God have God living
in them, and they live in God. 16 We know
how much God loves us, and we have put
our trust in his love.

God is love, and all who live in love live
in God, and God lives in them. 17 And as we
live in God, our love grows more perfect.
So we will not be afraid on the day of judgment, but we can face him with confidence
because we live like Jesus here in this world.

18 Such love has no fear, because perfect
love expels all fear. If we are afraid, it is for
fear of punishment, and this shows that we
have not fully experienced his perfect love.
19 We love each other* because he loved us
first.

20 If someone says, "I love God," but hates
a fellow believer,* that person is a liar; for
if we don't love people we can see, how can
we love God, whom we cannot see? 21 And he
has given us this command: Those who love
God must also love their fellow believers.*

Faith in the Son of God

5 Everyone who believes that Jesus is the
Christ* has become a child of God. And
everyone who loves the Father loves his
children, too. 2 We know we love God's children if we love God and obey his commandments. 3 Loving God means keeping his
commandments, and his commandments
are not burdensome. 4 For every child of God
defeats this evil world, and we achieve this
victory through our faith. 5 And who can win
this battle against the world? Only those
who believe that Jesus is the Son of God.

6 And Jesus Christ was revealed as God's
Son by his baptism in water and by shedding
his blood on the cross*—not by water only,
but by water and blood. And the Spirit, who

3:9 Greek *because his seed.* **3:10** Greek *does not love his brother.* **3:13** Greek *brothers.* **3:14** Greek *the brothers;* similarly in 3:16. **3:15** Greek *hates his brother.* **3:17** Greek *sees his brother.* **4:2** Greek *If a spirit;* similarly in 4:3. **4:19** Greek *We love.* Other manuscripts read *We love God;* still others read *We love him.* **4:20** Greek *hates his brother.* **4:21** Greek *The one who loves God must also love his brother.* **5:1** Or *the Messiah.* **5:6** Greek *This is he who came by water and blood.*

The love of God

When John wrote "God is love" (1 John 4:8), he didn't mean this is all there is to say about God, any more than when he wrote "God is Spirit" in his Gospel (John 4:24). What he meant was that when we think about love, it's impossible to think of a better example of what love is than God himself.

Love is one of the most fundamental revelations that God gives us of himself in Scripture. Everything he is and does is characterized by love, and discovering this is life-transforming. This is a love that is eternal (Jeremiah 31:3) and lavish (Exodus 34:6-7), that seeks out the unlovely and binds itself to them in covenant (Deuteronomy 7:7-9), that will never let us go and never be overcome (John 10:27-30), and that makes us confident in his presence (1 John 4:17-18).

John had been so overwhelmed by God's love—a love he experienced firsthand (1:1-4)—that he knows it has to overflow to others. If we are truly children of this God, then love will flow out of us too; if it doesn't, we may question whether we have truly encountered this God of love (4:7-8). Such love is not an optional extra; it is an essential part of what it means to be a Christian (4:19-21).

▸ *See also* ***The character of God****, page 104;* ***The compassionate God****, page 666;* ***Compassion****, page 983.*

is truth, confirms it with his testimony. [7]So we have these three witnesses*—[8]the Spirit, the water, and the blood—and all three agree. [9]Since we believe human testimony, surely we can believe the greater testimony that comes from God. And God has testified about his Son. [10]All who believe in the Son of God know in their hearts that this testimony is true. Those who don't believe this are actually calling God a liar because they don't believe what God has testified about his Son.

[11]And this is what God has testified: He has given us eternal life, and this life is in his Son. [12]Whoever has the Son has life; whoever does not have God's Son does not have life.

Conclusion

[13]I have written this to you who believe in the name of the Son of God, so that you may know you have eternal life. [14]And we are confident that he hears us whenever we ask for anything that pleases him. [15]And since we know he hears us when we make our requests, we also know that he will give us what we ask for.

[16]If you see a fellow believer* sinning in a way that does not lead to death, you should pray, and God will give that person life. But there is a sin that leads to death, and I am not saying you should pray for those who commit it. [17]All wicked actions are sin, but not every sin leads to death.

[18]We know that God's children do not make a practice of sinning, for God's Son holds them securely, and the evil one cannot touch them. [19]We know that we are children of God and that the world around us is under the control of the evil one.

[20]And we know that the Son of God has come, and he has given us understanding so that we can know the true God.* And now we live in fellowship with the true God because we live in fellowship with his Son, Jesus Christ. He is the only true God, and he is eternal life.

[21]Dear children, keep away from anything that might take God's place in your hearts.*

5:7 A few very late manuscripts add *in heaven—the Father, the Word, and the Holy Spirit, and these three are one. And we have three witnesses on earth.* **5:16** Greek *a brother.* **5:20** Greek *the one who is true.* **5:21** Greek *keep yourselves from idols.*

2 John

Greetings

This letter is from John, the elder.*

I am writing to the chosen lady and to her children,* whom I love in the truth—as does everyone else who knows the truth—[2]because the truth lives in us and will be with us forever.

[3]Grace, mercy, and peace, which come from God the Father and from Jesus Christ—the Son of the Father—will continue to be with us who live in truth and love.

Live in the Truth

[4]How happy I was to meet some of your children and find them living according to the truth, just as the Father commanded.

[5]I am writing to remind you, dear friends,* that we should love one another. This is not a new commandment, but one we have had from the beginning. [6]Love means doing what God has commanded us, and he has commanded us to love one another, just as you heard from the beginning.

[7]I say this because many deceivers have gone out into the world. They deny that Jesus Christ came* in a real body. Such a person is a deceiver and an antichrist. [8]Watch out that you do not lose what we* have worked so hard to achieve. Be diligent so that you receive your full reward. [9]Anyone who wanders away from this teaching has no relationship with God. But anyone who remains in the teaching of Christ has a relationship with both the Father and the Son.

[10]If anyone comes to your meeting and does not teach the truth about Christ, don't invite that person into your home or give any kind of encouragement. [11]Anyone who

▸ *For introduction to **1, 2, & 3 John**, see page 1431.*

encourages such people becomes a partner in their evil work.

Conclusion

[12]I have much more to say to you, but I don't want to do it with paper and ink. For I hope to visit you soon and talk with you face to face. Then our joy will be complete.

[13]Greetings from the children of your sister,* chosen by God.

1a Greek *From the elder.* **1b** Or *the church God has chosen and its members.* **5** Greek *I urge you, lady.* **7** Or *will come.* **8** Some manuscripts read *you.* **13** Or *from the members of your sister church.*

3 John

Greetings

This letter is from John, the elder.*

I am writing to Gaius, my dear friend, whom I love in the truth.

[2]Dear friend, I hope all is well with you and that you are as healthy in body as you are strong in spirit. [3]Some of the traveling teachers* recently returned and made me very happy by telling me about your faithfulness and that you are living according to the truth. [4]I could have no greater joy than to hear that my children are following the truth.

Caring for the Lord's Workers

[5]Dear friend, you are being faithful to God when you care for the traveling teachers who pass through, even though they are strangers to you. [6]They have told the church here of your loving friendship. Please continue providing for such teachers in a manner that pleases God. [7]For they are traveling for the Lord,* and they accept nothing from people who are not believers.* [8]So we ourselves

1 Greek *From the elder.* **3** Greek *the brothers;* also in verses 5 and 10. **7a** Greek *They went out on behalf of the Name.* **7b** Greek *from Gentiles.*

▸ *For introduction to* ***1, 2, & 3 John****, see page 1431.*

Living according to the truth

False teachers had infiltrated the churches for which John had responsibility. Some were even denying that Jesus had truly come in a real body (2 John 1:7)—a denial of the heart of the Christian faith. But not everyone had been deceived, and John commends the chosen lady and her children (1:1) for "living according to the truth" (1:4).

Living according to the truth is about holding firm to the Jesus revealed in the four Gospels and in the teaching of the apostles, which is based upon his life, death, and resurrection. It was this apostolic teaching that the first Christians devoted themselves to (Acts 2:42) and that we too should seek out—by reading the Bible on our own, participating in small groups where it can be discussed and applied, and listening eagerly to sermons in worship services.

But living according to the truth isn't just about what we know; it is also about how we act. We may know many Bible doctrines and be able to quote many Bible verses; but if we aren't actively seeking to live it out, then we are like the man who built his house on sand rather than on rock (Matthew 7:24-27) or someone who looked in the mirror, only to forget what they looked like (James 1:22-25). Living according to the truth means both knowing it and demonstrating it in our actions.

▸ *See also* ***Integrity****, page 1325.*

should support them so that we can be their
partners as they teach the truth.
[9]I wrote to the church about this, but Diotrephes, who loves to be the leader, refuses
to have anything to do with us. [10]When I
come, I will report some of the things he is
doing and the evil accusations he is making
against us. Not only does he refuse to
welcome the traveling teachers, he also tells
others not to help them. And when they do
help, he puts them out of the church.
[11]Dear friend, don't let this bad example
influence you. Follow only what is good. Remember that those who do good prove that
they are God's children, and those who do
evil prove that they do not know God.*
[12]Everyone speaks highly of Demetrius, as
does the truth itself. We ourselves can say
the same for him, and you know we speak
the truth.

Conclusion

[13]I have much more to say to you, but I don't
want to write it with pen and ink. [14]For I
hope to see you soon, and then we will talk
face to face.
[15]*Peace be with you.

Your friends here send you their greetings. Please give my personal greetings to each of our friends there.

11 Greek *they have not seen God.* **15** Some English translations combine verses 14 and 15 into verse 14.

How not to be a leader

When Jesus taught his disciples about leadership, he gave himself as an example, reminding them that "the Son of Man came not to be served but to serve others" (Matthew 20:28). What a contrast this was to the church leader Diotrephes, "who loves to be the leader" (3 John 1:9). John was so shocked by his behavior that he invented a word to describe him—the Greek really means "who loves to be at the front" or "who loves to be noticed." Diotrephes was clearly ambitious, for he refused to acknowledge John's authority (1:9). Moreover, he was gossiping, refusing hospitality to traveling preachers, and abusing his position by putting people out of the church for doing good (1:10). Eager to make the most of his leadership position, he had forgotten that servanthood lies at the heart of leadership in God's Kingdom.

Servant leadership is about being willing to be the last (Mark 9:33-37) and the least (Matthew 20:20-28). The moment we forget this and start wanting to push ourselves forward and rule over others, we have forgotten what it means to be a servant. By contrast, when we are secure in who we are as leaders, then nothing is beneath us (see John 13:1-5).

▶ *See also* ***The kind of leaders God wants****, page 170;* ***Humility****, page 1134;* ***Leaders in the church****, page 1390.*

Jude *Defending the faith*

Jude wrote this letter to urge its unnamed recipients to "defend the faith that God has entrusted once for all time to his holy people" (1:3). False teachers were causing havoc through promoting various errors, and Jude calls on the church to not be complacent but to resist them and their teaching and to stand firm in the truth they had received.

Jude describes himself as "a brother of James" (1:1), who was a leader in the church at Jerusalem. But since James was also the brother of Jesus (Matthew 13:55; Galatians 1:19), this means that Jude was also Jesus' brother. His referring to himself as "a slave of Jesus Christ" (1:1) probably reflects an unwillingness to draw any benefit or authority from this close family tie.

What's it all about?

This short letter is addressed to all Christians (1:1), reminding them of the need to "defend the faith"—a faith that "God has entrusted once for all time to his holy people" (1:3)—by rejecting false teachings. The false teachers Jude writes of were spreading two main errors: First, they were "saying that God's marvelous grace allows us to live immoral lives" (1:4)—in other words, saying that God's grace and forgiveness were so abundant that it really didn't matter if they sinned, since God would forgive them anyway—and second, they were denying the sovereignty and lordship of Jesus Christ (1:4).

Jude therefore reminds his readers not only of God's mighty acts of intervention on behalf of his people in Old Testament times but also of his mighty acts of judgment on those—both people and angels—who rejected his truth (1:5-7). These false teachers can expect nothing different (1:8-11). Using a variety of images, he portrays the emptiness of their lives and teaching (1:12-13) and declares that judgment will come upon them (1:14-16).

He then urges his readers to be utterly different from these false teachers, whom he describes as "shameless shepherds who care only for themselves" (1:12), who promise much but deliver nothing. He calls on them to remember the teaching of the apostles (1:17-18) and to build each other up in their faith, praying in the power of the Spirit, living in light of Christ's return, keeping themselves in God's love, and helping rescue others from sin (1:20-23). He closes with a confident and joyful prayer, declaring God's absolute ability to keep them, both now and forever (1:24-25).

OVERVIEW

Warnings against false teachers and their heresies · *1:1-16*

Encouragements to continue in the faith · *1:17-23*

A closing doxology
1:24-25

What does it mean for us?

Jude reminds us of the need in every generation to be on our guard against error creeping into the church. False teachers do not stand up in church one Sunday and announce, "I am going to lead you into error." It happens far more subtly, just as it did here, where these teachers "wormed their way into" the churches (1:4). We should therefore always be watchful and on our guard.

page 1442

But being watchful does not mean becoming heresy-hunters (as some Christians try to be, taking delight in searching out even the slightest errors of those they disagree with). Rather, we should ensure that we are building each other up in our faith (1:20), encouraging each other to be holy and faithful through prayer, and remaining in the love of God. Pursuing positives is always much better than seeking out negatives.

Greetings from Jude

This letter is from Jude, a slave of Jesus Christ and a brother of James.

I am writing to all who have been called by God the Father, who loves you and keeps you safe in the care of Jesus Christ.*

2May God give you more and more mercy, peace, and love.

The Danger of False Teachers

3Dear friends, I had been eagerly planning to write to you about the salvation we all share. But now I find that I must write about something else, urging you to defend the faith that God has entrusted once for all time to his holy people. 4I say this because some ungodly people have wormed their way into your churches, saying that God's marvelous grace allows us to live immoral lives. The condemnation of such people was recorded long ago, for they have denied our only Master and Lord, Jesus Christ.

5So I want to remind you, though you already know these things, that Jesus* first rescued the nation of Israel from Egypt, but later he destroyed those who did not remain faithful. 6And I remind you of the angels who did not stay within the limits of authority God gave them but left the place where they belonged. God has kept them securely chained in prisons of darkness, waiting for the great day of judgment. 7And don't forget Sodom and Gomorrah and their neighboring towns, which were filled with immorality and every kind of sexual perversion. Those cities were destroyed by fire and serve as a warning of the eternal fire of God's judgment.

8In the same way, these people—who claim authority from their dreams—live immoral lives, defy authority, and scoff at supernatural beings.* 9But even Michael, one of the mightiest of the angels,* did not dare accuse the devil of blasphemy, but simply said, "The Lord rebuke you!" (This took place when Michael was arguing with the devil about Moses' body.) 10But these people scoff at things they do not understand. Like unthinking animals, they do whatever their instincts tell them, and so they bring about their own destruction. 11What sorrow awaits them! For they follow in the footsteps of Cain, who killed his brother. Like Balaam, they deceive people for money. And like Korah, they perish in their rebellion.

12When these people eat with you in your fellowship meals commemorating the Lord's love, they are like dangerous reefs that can shipwreck you.* They are like shameless shepherds who care only for themselves. They are like clouds blowing over the land without giving any rain. They are like trees in autumn that are doubly dead, for they bear no fruit and have been pulled up by the roots. 13They are like wild waves of the sea, churning up the foam of their shameful deeds. They are like wandering stars, doomed forever to blackest darkness.

14Enoch, who lived in the seventh generation after Adam, prophesied about these people. He said, "Listen! The Lord is coming with countless thousands of his holy ones 15to execute judgment on the people of the world. He will convict every person of all the ungodly things they have done and for all the insults that ungodly sinners have spoken against him."*

16These people are grumblers and complainers, living only to satisfy their desires. They brag loudly about themselves, and they flatter others to get what they want.

A Call to Remain Faithful

17But you, my dear friends, must remember what the apostles of our Lord Jesus Christ predicted. 18They told you that in the last times there would be scoffers whose purpose in life is to satisfy their ungodly desires. 19These people are the ones who are creating

1 Or *keeps you for Jesus Christ.* **5** Other manuscripts read *[the] Lord,* or *God,* or *God Christ.* **8** Greek *at glorious ones,* which are probably evil angels. **9** Greek *Michael, the archangel.* **12** Or *they are contaminants among you;* or *they are stains.* **14-15** The quotation comes from intertestamental literature: 1 Enoch 1:9.

divisions among you. They follow their natural instincts because they do not have God's Spirit in them.

[20]But you, dear friends, must build each other up in your most holy faith, pray in the power of the Holy Spirit,* [21]and await the mercy of our Lord Jesus Christ, who will bring you eternal life. In this way, you will keep yourselves safe in God's love.

[22]And you must show mercy to* those whose faith is wavering. [23]Rescue others by snatching them from the flames of judgment. Show mercy to still others,* but do so with great caution, hating the sins that contaminate their lives.*

A Prayer of Praise

[24]Now all glory to God, who is able to keep you from falling away and will bring you with great joy into his glorious presence without a single fault. [25]All glory to him who alone is God, our Savior through Jesus Christ our Lord. All glory, majesty, power, and authority are his before all time, and in the present, and beyond all time! Amen.

20 Greek *pray in the Holy Spirit.* **22** Some manuscripts read *must reprove.* **22-23a** Some manuscripts have only two categories of people: (1) those whose faith is wavering and therefore need to be snatched from the flames of judgment, and (2) those who need to be shown mercy. **23b** Greek *with fear, hating even the clothing stained by the flesh.*

False teaching

False teaching is anything that denies or distorts some aspect of biblical truth. As Jude notes, it creeps in gradually (Jude 1:4) rather than announcing its arrival. It slowly gains acceptance because it usually appeals to some selfish human interest—perhaps the promise of revelation that others haven't seen, or the assurance of increased wealth if we follow certain principles, or the reassurance that sexual sin doesn't matter to God. But such wrong teachings are dangerous, not just because of their effects but because of their origins—for behind them lies the work of Satan and his deceiving spirits (John 8:44; 2 Corinthians 11:13-15; 1 John 4:1-3). That is why false teaching is destructive (2 Peter 2:1) and valueless (Jude 1:12-13).

The New Testament gives three key guidelines for discerning false teaching. First, we should examine the teachers and ask if their lifestyle reflects that of Christ or seeks selfish gain (e.g., 1:4); second, we should examine the teaching itself to see if it is in line with the basic truths of the gospel (e.g., 1 John 2:20-24; 4:2-3); third, we should examine the fruit that comes from the teaching (e.g., Matthew 7:15-20; 1 Timothy 6:3-5). If all three line up in a positive way, we may confidently give ourselves to the teaching; if they don't, we should take great care.

▶ *See also* ***Integrity****, page 1325.*

Revelation

The sovereignty and triumph of God

Revelation is a letter written by the apostle John to persecuted Christians in churches in Asia Minor (modern Turkey), probably during the period when the Roman emperor Domitian demanded to be worshiped as a god (AD 90–95). Its key message, revealed in a series of visions to John, is that, no matter what evil might be going on in the world, God is still on his throne and is still the Lord of history. The book's key focus is Jesus, risen and glorious, who will one day come again, conquer evil, and establish his Kingdom.

Revelation is an exciting but puzzling book, full of spectacular and mysterious images. It is written in a style of literature known as *apocalyptic* (from the Greek word meaning "revelation"). While its images and symbolic language may be strange to us—and therefore often misunderstood—they would have been readily understood by John's intended readers, who would have been very familiar with Jewish literature of this type.

What's it all about?

The book opens with John seeing a vision of Jesus, standing in the midst of his churches and telling John to write what he sees. Jesus has a message for seven churches, five of which are rebuked for serious failings. Yes, they were facing great problems as a result of persecution; but their greatest problems were internal: apathy, lukewarmness, and sexual immorality. Jesus therefore calls them to repent (chapters 2–3).

John is then shown heaven's perspective on events—events that seemed wild and out of control from the church's perspective. He sees the unseen spiritual warfare in which the church is engaged and that has been going on behind the scenes throughout history between God and Satan and their followers. Yet through it all, God is still firmly on his throne; and Christ, who has already won the decisive victory through his sacrificial death, is seated alongside him (chapters 4–5). The things that are happening in the world are not just wild events, but God's judgment, symbolized by the opening of seals and the blowing of trumpets (chapters 6–11). Yet Christians need not fear, for through all of this, God's people are kept safe, marked with a seal of protection (7:1-17; 14:1-5). The conflict will get worse before it gets better: "beasts" (chapter 13), symbolic of empires or power structures (though some equate the first beast with the Antichrist and

OVERVIEW

John's vision of Jesus and his commission to write · *1:1-20*

Letters to seven churches
2:1–3:22

A vision of heaven
4:1–5:14

Visions of God's judgments in history
6:1–16:21

The destruction of God's enemy, Babylon · *17:1–19:10*

Christ's victory over the beast, Satan, and death; the Last Judgment
19:11–20:15

The new heaven and the new earth
21:1–22:21

the second beast with the false prophet of 16:13), and "Babylon" (chapter 17), symbolic of godlessness, will fight against God and his people. In fact, an "unholy trinity" of the dragon (Satan), the beast, and the false prophet will come against them. But the final day of judgment is surely coming when God will overcome Satan and his hosts and judge the wicked (20:7-15). God will then create "a new heaven and a new earth" (21:1), where his people will enjoy him in peace and prosperity forever (chapters 21–22). The Bible, which began with the story of God's creation, fittingly ends with the promise of his new creation.

The book closes with a warning not to add to what is revealed in "this book"—certainly referring to the book of Revelation, but since this is the closing book of the Bible, probably a reference also to the whole of Scripture as it was brought together. And then there is a final promise from Jesus: "I am coming soon!" "Amen!" John replies. "Come, Lord Jesus!"

What does it mean for us?

Written by John during his exile on the island of Patmos, a Roman penal colony, Revelation can be difficult to read. At first sight, it seems like a book of secret codes waiting to be cracked, but attempts to read it in this way are doomed. In fact, as apocalyptic literature, its imagery was well understood in John's day; so we must interpret that imagery in the way it would have been understood then, not as we might want to interpret it now. We therefore shouldn't get too bogged down in the details, or we will lose the thrust of its basic message: It might look like evil is triumphing now, but God will triumph in the end! Revelation is exactly what it says: a revelation. It was written to *reveal* Jesus and to encourage Christians to keep going, not to confuse us with incomprehensible images that only an enlightened few can understand.

While Revelation is first and foremost a book about events in the first century, it is also about the final victory of good over evil. John believed that behind Rome's persecution lay a spiritual battle between good and evil and that the Christian's real enemy was not any human power but the devil. Revelation predicts not only the fall of Rome but also the fall of the evil that inspired Rome, and that inspires every evil structure in human history. At the center of history is Jesus, the sacrificed Lamb of God, who by his death conquered evil and opened the way to salvation. For those who believe in him the future holds no terrors. John's vision of a new world in which God will wipe away every tear resonates in the heart and imagination of everyone who reads it.

The persecution that John addressed did not end with the fall of the Roman Empire. More Christians have been martyred for their faith in the last hundred years than in the previous nineteen hundred years; so wherever Christians are persecuted, Revelation speaks with fresh power. Jesus, not Satan or any dictator or state, is Lord of history; so Christians can be certain that God will ultimately triumph.

▶ *See also* ***John****, page 1224;* ***The Old Testament in the New Testament Letters****, Visual Overview Z16.*

Prologue

1 This is a revelation from* Jesus Christ,
which God gave him to show his servants
the events that must soon* take place. He
sent an angel to present this revelation to
his servant John, [2]who faithfully reported
everything he saw. This is his report of the
word of God and the testimony of Jesus
Christ.

[3]God blesses the one who reads the words
of this prophecy to the church, and he blesses
all who listen to its message and obey what it
says, for the time is near.

John's Greeting to the Seven Churches

[4]This letter is from John to the seven churches
in the province of Asia.*

Grace and peace to you from the one who is,
who always was, and who is still to come; from
the sevenfold Spirit* before his throne; [5]and
from Jesus Christ. He is the faithful witness
to these things, the first to rise from the dead,
and the ruler of all the kings of the world.

All glory to him who loves us and has freed
us from our sins by shedding his blood for

1:1a Or *of.* **1:1b** Or *suddenly,* or *quickly.* **1:4a** *Asia* was a Roman province in what is now western Turkey. **1:4b** Greek *the seven spirits.*

us. 6He has made us a Kingdom of priests
for God his Father. All glory and power to
him forever and ever! Amen.

7 Look! He comes with the clouds of
heaven.
And everyone will see him—
even those who pierced him.
And all the nations of the world
will mourn for him.
Yes! Amen!

8"I am the Alpha and the Omega—the
beginning and the end,"* says the Lord God.
"I am the one who is, who always was, and
who is still to come—the Almighty One."

Vision of the Son of Man

9I, John, am your brother and your partner in
suffering and in God's Kingdom and in the
patient endurance to which Jesus calls us. I
was exiled to the island of Patmos for preaching the word of God and for my testimony
about Jesus. 10It was the Lord's Day, and I was
worshiping in the Spirit.* Suddenly, I heard
behind me a loud voice like a trumpet blast.
11It said, "Write in a book* everything you see,
and send it to the seven churches in the cities
of Ephesus, Smyrna, Pergamum, Thyatira,
Sardis, Philadelphia, and Laodicea."

12When I turned to see who was speaking
to me, I saw seven gold lampstands. 13And
standing in the middle of the lampstands
was someone like the Son of Man.* He was
wearing a long robe with a gold sash across
his chest. 14His head and his hair were white
like wool, as white as snow. And his eyes
were like flames of fire. 15His feet were like
polished bronze refined in a furnace, and
his voice thundered like mighty ocean
waves. 16He held seven stars in his right
hand, and a sharp two-edged sword came
from his mouth. And his face was like the
sun in all its brilliance.

17When I saw him, I fell at his feet as if I
were dead. But he laid his right hand on me
and said, "Don't be afraid! I am the First and
the Last. 18I am the living one. I died, but
look—I am alive forever and ever! And I hold
the keys of death and the grave.*

19"Write down what you have seen—both
the things that are now happening and
the things that will happen.* 20This is the
meaning of the mystery of the seven stars
you saw in my right hand and the seven
gold lampstands: The seven stars are the
angels* of the seven churches, and the
seven lampstands are the seven churches.

The Message to the Church in Ephesus

2 "Write this letter to the angel* of the
church in Ephesus. This is the message
from the one who holds the seven stars in
his right hand, the one who walks among
the seven gold lampstands:

2"I know all the things you do. I have
seen your hard work and your patient
endurance. I know you don't tolerate evil
people. You have examined the claims
of those who say they are apostles but

Patmos

John received his revelation on Patmos, a tiny island some thirty-five miles off the coast of Asia Minor (modern Turkey) in the Aegean Sea (Revelation 1:9). The island was rocky and largely treeless and was used, like similar islands, by the Romans as a prison colony, especially for political prisoners. John may have simply been living here in exile, or he may have been a prisoner, set to work in the Roman quarries. It was in this place of apparent abandonment that Jesus appeared to him and spoke to him, for no place is beyond God's reach and no circumstance beyond his knowledge (see Psalm 139:1-18). The last time John had heard that voice was sixty years before, but he would have recognized it anywhere. As he turned around, he saw "someone like the Son of Man" (Revelation 1:13)—clearly referring to Jesus, for this was his favorite title for himself—whose revelation not only encouraged first-century churches that were experiencing persecution but which still inspires and challenges us today.

▶ *See also **The Son of Man**, page 1101.*

are not. You have discovered they are
liars. [3]You have patiently suffered for me
without quitting.
[4]"But I have this complaint against
you. You don't love me or each other as
you did at first!* [5]Look how far you have
fallen! Turn back to me and do the works
you did at first. If you don't repent, I will
come and remove your lampstand from
its place among the churches. [6]But this is
in your favor: You hate the evil deeds of
the Nicolaitans, just as I do.
[7]"Anyone with ears to hear must listen
to the Spirit and understand what he is
saying to the churches. To everyone who
is victorious I will give fruit from the tree
of life in the paradise of God.

The Message to the Church in Smyrna

[8]"Write this letter to the angel of the church
in Smyrna. This is the message from the one
who is the First and the Last, who was dead
but is now alive:

[9]"I know about your suffering and
your poverty—but you are rich! I know
the blasphemy of those opposing you.
They say they are Jews, but they are
not, because their synagogue belongs
to Satan. [10]Don't be afraid of what you
are about to suffer. The devil will throw
some of you into prison to test you. You
will suffer for ten days. But if you remain
faithful even when facing death, I will
give you the crown of life.
[11]"Anyone with ears to hear must
listen to the Spirit and understand what
he is saying to the churches. Whoever
is victorious will not be harmed by the
second death.

The Message to the Church in Pergamum

[12]"Write this letter to the angel of the church
in Pergamum. This is the message from the
one with the sharp two-edged sword:

[13]"I know that you live in the city where
Satan has his throne, yet you have
remained loyal to me. You refused to
deny me even when Antipas, my faithful
witness, was martyred among you there
in Satan's city.
[14]"But I have a few complaints against

1:8 Greek *I am the Alpha and the Omega,* referring to the first and last letters of the Greek alphabet. **1:10** Or *in spirit.* **1:11** Or *on a scroll.* **1:13** Or *like a son of man.* See Dan 7:13. "Son of Man" is a title Jesus used for himself. **1:18** Greek *and Hades.* **1:19** Or *what you have seen and what they mean—the things that have already begun to happen.* **1:20** Or *the messengers.* **2:1** Or *the messenger;* also in 2:8, 12, 18. **2:4** Greek *You have lost your first love.*

The dangers of drifting

John's Revelation was directed to seven churches, most of which had become halfhearted. Ephesus had lost the love it had at first (Revelation 2:4), Pergamum had drifted into false teaching (2:14-15), Thyatira had accepted immorality in its midst (2:20), Sardis was living on its past reputation (3:1-2), and Laodicea had become lukewarm and complacent (3:15-17). These churches hadn't set out to become like this; they had simply drifted into it, perhaps through pressure and persecution, but more likely through simply failing to keep a close watch on how they lived and on their teaching (see 1 Timothy 4:16). They were therefore called to "listen to the Spirit and understand what he is saying to the churches" (Revelation 2:7, 11, 17, 29; 3:6, 13, 22)—and change while there was still time.

It is still easy to drift—perhaps not because of persecution, but because of complacency, temptation, or wanting to be like those around us who seem to have such a good time. The Bible calls us to persevere in our walk with Jesus—and while he helps us in that, it is not something he can do for us. So if we find we have drifted, then Jesus' invitation is still available: "I stand at the door and knock. If you hear my voice and open the door, I will come in, and we will share a meal together as friends" (3:20). While often used in evangelistic preaching, this verse is in fact addressed to Christians—Christians who had become lukewarm and were drifting. Its call—and its promise—is still as real today.

▶ *See also* ***Pressing on****, page 1359.*

The seven churches of Revelation

Although some interpret these seven churches as symbolic of the church's history, they were in fact real churches for which John had responsibility from his base in Ephesus. Many of the rebukes given allude to life in the culture around them.

Ephesus (2:1-7)

City: thriving commercial center where there was a great temple to Artemis, one of the seven wonders of the world
Church: commended for persevering; rebuked for losing the love it had at first

Smyrna (2:8-11)

City: leading center of emperor-worship, with a large Jewish community—both of which made it hard to be a Christian here
Church: commended for holding on; not rebuked

Pergamum (2:12-17)

City: official center of emperor-worship in Asia and hence described as "Satan's city" (2:13)
Church: commended for staying faithful to Jesus; rebuked for tolerating false teaching

Thyatira (2:18-29)

City: important producer of dye, clothes, pottery, and brass work; hometown of Lydia, who became a Christian in Philippi (Acts 16:14)
Church: commended for its growing love and service; rebuked for its toleration of idolatry and false teaching about sexuality

Sardis (3:1-6)

City: commercial center with a thriving wool and dyeing industry and gold mines that had made it very wealthy
Church: commended for the few that held on; rebuked for resting solely on their past reputation

Philadelphia (3:7-13)

City: important commercial city and wine-producing area, whose name means "brotherly love" and which was a center of emperor-worship
Church: commended for obedience and not denying Jesus; not rebuked, but reminded there is an open door before them despite all opposition

Laodicea (3:14-22)

City: wealthy from trade, banking, and producing textiles and medicines—especially eye ointments—but with a notoriously poor water supply
Church: the only church not commended for anything; rebuked for being lukewarm, wretched, miserable, poor, blind, and naked; urged to let Jesus back in through the door

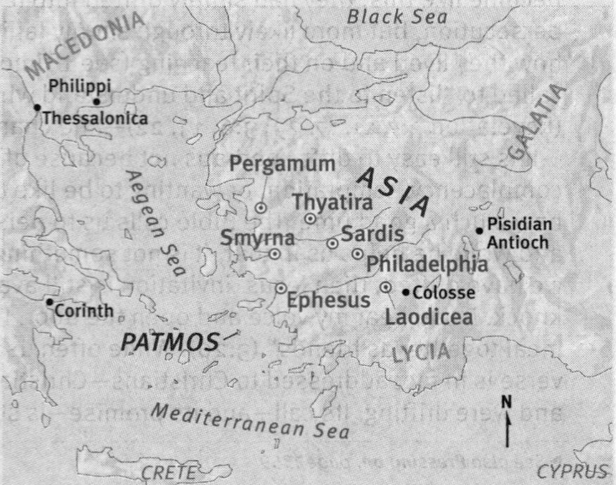

you. You tolerate some among you
whose teaching is like that of Balaam,
who showed Balak how to trip up the
people of Israel. He taught them to sin
by eating food offered to idols and by
committing sexual sin. [15]In a similar
way, you have some Nicolaitans among
you who follow the same teaching.
[16]Repent of your sin, or I will come to
you suddenly and fight against them
with the sword of my mouth.

[17]"Anyone with ears to hear must listen
to the Spirit and understand what he is
saying to the churches. To everyone who
is victorious I will give some of the manna
that has been hidden away in heaven.
And I will give to each one a white stone,
and on the stone will be engraved a new
name that no one understands except the
one who receives it.

The Message to the Church in Thyatira

[18]"Write this letter to the angel of the
church in Thyatira. This is the message
from the Son of God, whose eyes are like
flames of fire, whose feet are like polished
bronze:

[19]"I know all the things you do. I have
seen your love, your faith, your service,
and your patient endurance. And I can
see your constant improvement in all
these things.

[20]"But I have this complaint against
you. You are permitting that woman—
that Jezebel who calls herself a
prophet—to lead my servants astray. She
teaches them to commit sexual sin and
to eat food offered to idols. [21]I gave her
time to repent, but she does not want to
turn away from her immorality.

[22]"Therefore, I will throw her on a bed
of suffering,* and those who commit
adultery with her will suffer greatly
unless they repent and turn away from
her evil deeds. [23]I will strike her children
dead. Then all the churches will know
that I am the one who searches out the
thoughts and intentions of every person.
And I will give to each of you whatever
you deserve.

[24]"But I also have a message for the
rest of you in Thyatira who have not
followed this false teaching ('deeper
truths,' as they call them—depths of
Satan, actually). I will ask nothing more
of you [25]except that you hold tightly to
what you have until I come. [26]To all who
are victorious, who obey me to the very
end,

To them I will give authority over all
the nations.
[27] They will rule the nations with an iron
rod
and smash them like clay pots.*

[28]They will have the same authority I
received from my Father, and I will also
give them the morning star!

[29]"Anyone with ears to hear must
listen to the Spirit and understand what
he is saying to the churches.

The Message to the Church in Sardis

3 "Write this letter to the angel* of the
church in Sardis. This is the message
from the one who has the sevenfold Spirit*
of God and the seven stars:

"I know all the things you do, and that
you have a reputation for being alive—
but you are dead. [2]Wake up! Strengthen
what little remains, for even what is left
is almost dead. I find that your actions
do not meet the requirements of my God.
[3]Go back to what you heard and believed
at first; hold to it firmly. Repent and turn
to me again. If you don't wake up, I will
come to you suddenly, as unexpected as
a thief.

[4]"Yet there are some in the church in
Sardis who have not soiled their clothes
with evil. They will walk with me in
white, for they are worthy. [5]All who are
victorious will be clothed in white. I
will never erase their names from the
Book of Life, but I will announce before
my Father and his angels that they are
mine.

[6]"Anyone with ears to hear must listen
to the Spirit and understand what he is
saying to the churches.

The Message to the Church in Philadelphia

[7]"Write this letter to the angel of the church
in Philadelphia.

This is the message from the one who is
holy and true,

2:22 Greek *a bed.* **2:26-27** Ps 2:8-9 (Greek version). **3:1a** Or *the messenger;* also in 3:7, 14. **3:1b** Greek *the seven spirits.*

the one who has the key of David.
What he opens, no one can close;
and what he closes, no one can open:*

8“I know all the things you do, and I have opened a door for you that no one can close. You have little strength, yet you obeyed my word and did not deny me. 9Look, I will force those who belong to Satan’s synagogue—those liars who say they are Jews but are not—to come and bow down at your feet. They will acknowledge that you are the ones I love.

10“Because you have obeyed my command to persevere, I will protect you from the great time of testing that will come upon the whole world to test those who belong to this world. 11I am coming soon.* Hold on to what you have, so that no one will take away your crown. 12All who are victorious will become pillars in the Temple of my God, and they will never have to leave it. And I will write on them the name of my God, and they will be citizens in the city of my God—the new Jerusalem that comes down from heaven from my God. And I will also write on them my new name.

13“Anyone with ears to hear must listen to the Spirit and understand what he is saying to the churches.

The Message to the Church in Laodicea

14“Write this letter to the angel of the church in Laodicea. This is the message from the one who is the Amen—the faithful and true witness, the beginning* of God’s new creation:

15“I know all the things you do, that you are neither hot nor cold. I wish that you were one or the other! 16But since you are like lukewarm water, neither hot nor cold, I will spit you out of my mouth! 17You say, ‘I am rich. I have everything I want. I don’t need a thing!’ And you don’t realize that you are wretched and miserable and poor and blind and naked. 18So I advise you to buy gold from me—gold that has been purified by fire. Then you will be rich. Also buy white garments from me so you will not be shamed by your nakedness, and ointment for your eyes so you will be able to see. 19I correct and discipline everyone I love. So be diligent and turn from your indifference.

20“Look! I stand at the door and knock. If you hear my voice and open the door, I will come in, and we will share a meal together as friends. 21Those who are victorious will sit with me on my throne, just as I was victorious and sat with my Father on his throne.

22“Anyone with ears to hear must listen to the Spirit and understand what he is saying to the churches.”

Worship in Heaven

4 Then as I looked, I saw a door standing open in heaven, and the same voice I had heard before spoke to me like a trumpet blast. The voice said, “Come up here, and I will show you what must happen after this.” 2And instantly I was in the Spirit,* and I saw a throne in heaven and someone sitting on it. 3The one sitting on the throne was as brilliant as gemstones—like jasper and carnelian. And the glow of an emerald circled his throne like a rainbow. 4Twenty-four thrones surrounded him, and twenty-four elders sat on them. They were all clothed in white and had gold crowns on their heads. 5From the throne came flashes of lightning and the rumble of thunder. And in front of the throne were seven torches with burning flames. This is the sevenfold Spirit* of God. 6In front of the throne was a shiny sea of glass, sparkling like crystal.

In the center and around the throne were four living beings, each covered with eyes, front and back. 7The first of these living beings was like a lion; the second was like an ox; the third had a human face; and the fourth was like an eagle in flight. 8Each of these living beings had six wings, and their wings were covered all over with eyes, inside and out. Day after day and night after night they keep on saying,

“Holy, holy, holy is the Lord God, the Almighty—
the one who always was, who is, and who is still to come.”

9Whenever the living beings give glory and honor and thanks to the one sitting on

▸ **3:7** *See **The keys of the Kingdom**, page 770.*

the throne (the one who lives forever and
ever), 10the twenty-four elders fall down and
worship the one sitting on the throne (the
one who lives forever and ever). And they
lay their crowns before the throne and say,

11 "You are worthy, O Lord our God,
to receive glory and honor and power.
For you created all things,
and they exist because you created
what you pleased."

The Lamb Opens the Scroll

5 Then I saw a scroll* in the right hand of the
one who was sitting on the throne. There
was writing on the inside and the outside of
the scroll, and it was sealed with seven seals.
2And I saw a strong angel, who shouted with
a loud voice: "Who is worthy to break the
seals on this scroll and open it?" 3But no one
in heaven or on earth or under the earth was
able to open the scroll and read it.

4Then I began to weep bitterly because
no one was found worthy to open the scroll
and read it. 5But one of the twenty-four
elders said to me, "Stop weeping! Look, the
Lion of the tribe of Judah, the heir to David's
throne,* has won the victory. He is worthy
to open the scroll and its seven seals."

6Then I saw a Lamb that looked as if it
had been slaughtered, but it was now
standing between the throne and the four
living beings and among the twenty-four
elders. He had seven horns and seven eyes,
which represent the sevenfold Spirit* of
God that is sent out into every part of the
earth. 7He stepped forward and took the
scroll from the right hand of the one sitting
on the throne. 8And when he took the scroll,
the four living beings and the twenty-four
elders fell down before the Lamb. Each one
had a harp, and they held gold bowls filled
with incense, which are the prayers of God's
people. 9And they sang a new song with
these words:

"You are worthy to take the scroll
and break its seals and open it.
For you were slaughtered, and your
blood has ransomed people for God
from every tribe and language and
people and nation.
10 And you have caused them to become
a Kingdom of priests for our God.
And they will reign* on the earth."

11Then I looked again, and I heard the
voices of thousands and millions of angels
around the throne and of the living beings
and the elders. 12And they sang in a mighty
chorus:

3:7 Isa 22:22. **3:11** Or *suddenly*, or *quickly*. **3:14** Or *the ruler*, or *the source*. **4:2** Or *in spirit*. **4:5** Greek *They are the seven spirits*. **5:1** Or *book;* also in 5:2, 3, 4, 5, 7, 8, 9. **5:5** Greek *the root of David*. See Isa 11:10. **5:6** Greek *which are the seven spirits*. **5:10** Some manuscripts read *they are reigning*.

Heaven

The Bible uses the word "heaven(s)" in a number of ways: first, to mean "the sky" or "universe" (e.g., Nehemiah 9:6); second, to mean "God's dwelling place" (e.g., Deuteronomy 26:15; Matthew 6:9); third, as a substitute for God's name (hence, "the Kingdom of Heaven"); and fourth, as the dwelling place of Christians after death (e.g., John 14:1-6; Philippians 1:21-23; 3:12-14; 1 Thessalonians 4:13-14; 1 Peter 1:3-5). In Revelation 4 and 5, it is God's dwelling place that is in mind. But God is not alone; heaven is full of those who have believed in him (e.g., Revelation 7:9-17), as well as angelic beings eager to worship and serve him.

This is why Christians need not fear death (see Philippians 1:23; 2 Timothy 4:6-8; 2 Peter 1:13-15). At death, we will leave our bodies behind and immediately enter God's presence—hence Jesus' promise to the man crucified alongside him, "*Today* you will be with me in paradise" (Luke 23:43). But heaven is not our ultimate home. It is only a glorious waiting room where believers are safe with Christ until his return; for the Bible closes, not with believers spending eternity in heaven, but rather with believers spending eternity on a renewed and glorious earth where "God's home is now among his people" (Revelation 21:1-3).

▶ *See also* ***Paradise****, page 1194;* ***The new Jerusalem****, page 1466.*

"Worthy is the Lamb who was
slaughtered—
to receive power and riches
and wisdom and strength
and honor and glory and blessing."

13 And then I heard every creature in heaven and on earth and under the earth and in the sea. They sang:

"Blessing and honor and glory and
power
belong to the one sitting on the throne
and to the Lamb forever and ever."

14 And the four living beings said, "Amen!" And the twenty-four elders fell down and worshiped the Lamb.

The Lamb Breaks the First Six Seals

6 As I watched, the Lamb broke the first
of the seven seals on the scroll.* Then I
heard one of the four living beings say with
a voice like thunder, "Come!" 2 I looked up
and saw a white horse standing there. Its
rider carried a bow, and a crown was placed
on his head. He rode out to win many battles
and gain the victory.
3 When the Lamb broke the second seal,
I heard the second living being say, "Come!"
4 Then another horse appeared, a red one.
Its rider was given a mighty sword and the
authority to take peace from the earth. And
there was war and slaughter everywhere.
5 When the Lamb broke the third seal,
I heard the third living being say, "Come!"
I looked up and saw a black horse, and its
rider was holding a pair of scales in his hand.
6 And I heard a voice from among the four
living beings say, "A loaf of wheat bread or
three loaves of barley will cost a day's pay.*
And don't waste* the olive oil and wine."
7 When the Lamb broke the fourth seal,
I heard the fourth living being say, "Come!"
8 I looked up and saw a horse whose color
was pale green. Its rider was named Death,
and his companion was the Grave.* These
two were given authority over one-fourth of
the earth, to kill with the sword and famine
and disease* and wild animals.

Persecution

"'A slave is not greater than the master.' Since they persecuted me, naturally they will persecute you" (John 15:20)—these are words of Jesus that most of us probably wish he had not said. But Jesus never promised that following him would be easy, and many have experienced just how difficult it can be. Even today, millions of Christians around the world are persecuted for their faith, whether by atheistic states or fanatical followers of other religions. Sometimes that persecution is subtle—through negative comments, ridicule, or the blocking of employment or promotion. Sometimes it is overt—physical abuse, imprisonment, torture, or even death. We are often surprised when such things happen; but for the early church, this was a normal part of life (e.g., Acts 7:54-60; 2 Corinthians 12:10), just as Jesus foretold (e.g., Matthew 10:17-31; 24:9). In fact, Paul wrote that "everyone who wants to live a godly life in Christ Jesus will suffer persecution" (2 Timothy 3:12). Persecution does not mean that God is not with us, but rather the opposite. It is a sign that God is so with us that people hate us for it.

In times of persecution, Christians are encouraged to adopt certain attitudes: to forgive their persecutors (e.g., Luke 23:34; Romans 12:17-21), trust in God's presence and promises (e.g., 2 Corinthians 4:7-11), pray (e.g., Matthew 5:44; Luke 18:7; Ephesians 6:10-18), and even rejoice that they have been privileged to share in Christ's sufferings (e.g., Colossians 1:24; 1 Peter 4:12-19). And if they take our lives, John sees, we still win. In Revelation 6:9, he sees the souls of the martyrs under heaven's altar, the place where sacrificial blood was poured (see Exodus 29:12). Their lives have been a sacrifice, but that sacrifice is not in vain. Though they must wait a little longer (Revelation 6:10-11), ultimately they will be vindicated (e.g., 7:13-17; 12:10-12; 21:1-7).

9When the Lamb broke the fifth seal,
I saw under the altar the souls of all who
had been martyred for the word of God and
for being faithful in their testimony. 10They
shouted to the Lord and said, "O Sovereign
Lord, holy and true, how long before you
judge the people who belong to this world
and avenge our blood for what they have
done to us?" 11Then a white robe was given
to each of them. And they were told to rest
a little longer until the full number of their
brothers and sisters*—their fellow servants
of Jesus who were to be martyred—had
joined them.
12I watched as the Lamb broke the sixth
seal, and there was a great earthquake. The
sun became as dark as black cloth, and
the moon became as red as blood. 13Then
the stars of the sky fell to the earth like
green figs falling from a tree shaken by a
strong wind. 14The sky was rolled up like a
scroll, and all of the mountains and islands
were moved from their places.
15Then everyone—the kings of the earth,
the rulers, the generals, the wealthy, the
powerful, and every slave and free person—all
hid themselves in the caves and among the
rocks of the mountains. 16And they cried to
the mountains and the rocks, "Fall on us and
hide us from the face of the one who sits on
the throne and from the wrath of the Lamb.
17For the great day of their wrath has come,
and who is able to survive?"

God's People Will Be Preserved

7 Then I saw four angels standing at the
four corners of the earth, holding back
the four winds so they did not blow on the
earth or the sea, or even on any tree. 2And
I saw another angel coming up from the
east, carrying the seal of the living God.
And he shouted to those four angels, who
had been given power to harm land and sea,
3"Wait! Don't harm the land or the sea or the
trees until we have placed the seal of God on
the foreheads of his servants."
4And I heard how many were marked
with the seal of God—144,000 were sealed
from all the tribes of Israel:

6:1 Or *book.* **6:6a** Greek *A choinix* [1 quart or 1 liter] *of wheat for a denarius, and 3 choinix of barley for a denarius.* A denarius was equivalent to a laborer's full day's wage. **6:6b** Or *harm.* **6:8a** Greek *was Hades.* **6:8b** Greek *death.* **6:11** Greek *their brothers.*

The use of numbers in Revelation

Numbers were used in well-understood symbolic ways in Jewish thought and literature—so we are not free to give them our own meaning. For example, the number one symbolized uniqueness (e.g., Deuteronomy 6:4, see footnote); two, unity (e.g., Matthew 18:19); three, God's power or powerful involvement (key events often happened on the third day, e.g., Luke 24:46); four, the whole of creation (e.g., Revelation 7:1); five, half-completion, and ten, completion (e.g., Matthew 25:1-4); six, humankind (created on the sixth day; see Genesis 1:26-31); seven, God and his perfection (for he rested on the seventh day; see Genesis 2:2-3); twelve, God's people (the twelve tribes of Israel, e.g., Genesis 49:28).

Revelation has many "sevens" to symbolize completion—for example, seven churches, letters, seals, trumpets, and plagues—and uses certain key words seven times each (e.g., blessed, coming, persevere). Six falls one short of seven and perfection; so John gives the beast the number, not just six, but 666—that is, no matter how hard he tries, he will never reach seven. He will never be God; he will only ever be a six, a man—so do not fear him.

Sometimes numbers are compounded. One thousand years (Revelation 20:1-6) is ten times ten times ten; so if ten is completion, then ten times ten times ten is absolute completion, the complete time appointed by God. The number of people marked with God's seal in 7:4, 144,000, is twelve times twelve (all God's people) times one thousand (ten times ten times ten—that is, absolutely complete)—John's way of saying that, despite persecution, not a single believer is lost or missing.

John's numbers are symbols, not statistics; to miss this is to misread Revelation.

5 from Judah 12,000
from Reuben 12,000
from Gad 12,000
6 from Asher 12,000
from Naphtali 12,000
from Manasseh 12,000
7 from Simeon 12,000
from Levi 12,000
from Issachar 12,000
8 from Zebulun 12,000
from Joseph 12,000
from Benjamin 12,000

Praise from the Great Crowd

9 After this I saw a vast crowd, too great
to count, from every nation and tribe and
people and language, standing in front
of the throne and before the Lamb. They
were clothed in white robes and held palm
branches in their hands. 10 And they were
shouting with a great roar,

"Salvation comes from our God who sits
on the throne
and from the Lamb!"

11 And all the angels were standing around
the throne and around the elders and the
four living beings. And they fell before the
throne with their faces to the ground and
worshiped God. 12 They sang,

"Amen! Blessing and glory and wisdom
and thanksgiving and honor
and power and strength belong to our
God
forever and ever! Amen."

13 Then one of the twenty-four elders asked
me, "Who are these who are clothed in
white? Where did they come from?"
14 And I said to him, "Sir, you are the one
who knows."
Then he said to me, "These are the ones
who died in* the great tribulation.* They
have washed their robes in the blood of the
Lamb and made them white.

15 "That is why they stand in front of God's
throne
and serve him day and night in his
Temple.
And he who sits on the throne
will give them shelter.
16 They will never again be hungry or
thirsty;
they will never be scorched by the
heat of the sun.
17 For the Lamb on the throne*
will be their Shepherd.
He will lead them to springs of
life-giving water.
And God will wipe every tear from
their eyes."

The Lamb Breaks the Seventh Seal

8 When the Lamb broke the seventh
seal on the scroll,* there was silence
throughout heaven for about half an hour.
2 I saw the seven angels who stand before
God, and they were given seven trumpets.
3 Then another angel with a gold incense
burner came and stood at the altar. And a
great amount of incense was given to him to
mix with the prayers of God's people as an
offering on the gold altar before the throne.
4 The smoke of the incense, mixed with the
prayers of God's holy people, ascended up
to God from the altar where the angel had
poured them out. 5 Then the angel filled the
incense burner with fire from the altar and
threw it down upon the earth; and thunder
crashed, lightning flashed, and there was a
terrible earthquake.

The First Four Trumpets

6 Then the seven angels with the seven trumpets prepared to blow their mighty blasts.
7 The first angel blew his trumpet, and
hail and fire mixed with blood were thrown
down on the earth. One-third of the earth
was set on fire, one-third of the trees were
burned, and all the green grass was burned.
8 Then the second angel blew his trumpet,
and a great mountain of fire was thrown
into the sea. One-third of the water in the
sea became blood, 9 one-third of all things
living in the sea died, and one-third of all
the ships on the sea were destroyed.
10 Then the third angel blew his trumpet,
and a great star fell from the sky, burning
like a torch. It fell on one-third of the rivers
and on the springs of water. 11 The name of
the star was Bitterness.* It made one-third
of the water bitter, and many people died
from drinking the bitter water.
12 Then the fourth angel blew his trumpet,
and one-third of the sun was struck, and
one-third of the moon, and one-third of the
stars, and they became dark. And one-third
of the day was dark, and also one-third of
the night.
13 Then I looked, and I heard a single eagle

crying loudly as it flew through the air, "Terror, terror, terror to all who belong to this world because of what will happen when the last three angels blow their trumpets."

The Fifth Trumpet Brings the First Terror

9 Then the fifth angel blew his trumpet, and I saw a star that had fallen to earth from the sky, and he was given the key to the shaft of the bottomless pit.* 2When he opened it, smoke poured out as though from a huge furnace, and the sunlight and air turned dark from the smoke.

3Then locusts came from the smoke and descended on the earth, and they were given power to sting like scorpions. 4They were told not to harm the grass or plants or trees, but only the people who did not have the seal of God on their foreheads. 5They were told not to kill them but to torture them for five months with pain like the pain of a scorpion sting. 6In those days people will seek death but will not find it. They will long to die, but death will flee from them!

7The locusts looked like horses prepared for battle. They had what looked like gold crowns on their heads, and their faces looked like human faces. 8They had hair like women's hair and teeth like the teeth of a lion. 9They wore armor made of iron, and their wings roared like an army of chariots rushing into battle. 10They had tails that stung like scorpions, and for five months they had the power to torment people. 11Their king is the angel from the bottomless pit; his name in Hebrew is *Abaddon*, and in Greek, *Apollyon*—the Destroyer.

12The first terror is past, but look, two more terrors are coming!

The Sixth Trumpet Brings the Second Terror

13Then the sixth angel blew his trumpet, and I heard a voice speaking from the four horns of the gold altar that stands in the presence of God. 14And the voice said to the sixth angel who held the trumpet, "Release the four angels who are bound at the great Euphrates River." 15Then the four angels who had been prepared for this hour and day and month and year were turned loose to kill one-third of all the people on earth. 16I heard the size of their army, which was 200 million mounted troops.

17And in my vision, I saw the horses and the riders sitting on them. The riders wore armor that was fiery red and dark blue and yellow. The horses had heads like lions, and fire and smoke and burning sulfur billowed from their mouths. 18One-third of all the people on earth were killed by these three plagues—by the fire and smoke and burning sulfur that came from the mouths of the horses. 19Their power was in their mouths and in their tails. For their tails had heads like snakes, with the power to injure people.

20But the people who did not die in these plagues still refused to repent of their evil deeds and turn to God. They continued to worship demons and idols made of gold, silver, bronze, stone, and wood—idols that can neither see nor hear nor walk! 21And they did not repent of their murders or their witchcraft or their sexual immorality or their thefts.

The Angel and the Small Scroll

10 Then I saw another mighty angel coming down from heaven, surrounded by a cloud, with a rainbow over his head. His face shone like the sun, and his feet were like pillars of fire. 2And in his hand was a small scroll* that had been opened. He stood with his right foot on the sea and his left foot on the land. 3And he gave a great shout like the roar of a lion. And when he shouted, the seven thunders answered.

4When the seven thunders spoke, I was about to write. But I heard a voice from heaven saying, "Keep secret* what the seven thunders said, and do not write it down."

5Then the angel I saw standing on the sea and on the land raised his right hand toward heaven. 6He swore an oath in the name of the one who lives forever and ever, who created the heavens and everything in them, the earth and everything in it, and the sea and everything in it. He said, "There will be no more delay. 7When the seventh angel blows his trumpet, God's mysterious plan will be fulfilled. It will happen just as he announced it to his servants the prophets."

8Then the voice from heaven spoke to me again: "Go and take the open scroll from the hand of the angel who is standing on the sea and on the land."

7:14a Greek *who came out of.* **7:14b** Or *the great suffering.* **7:17** Greek *on the center of the throne.* **8:1** Or *book.* **8:11** Greek *Wormwood.* **9:1** Or *the abyss,* or *the underworld;* also in 9:11. **10:2** Or *book;* also in 10:8, 9, 10. **10:4** Greek *Seal up.*

9So I went to the angel and told him to
give me the small scroll. "Yes, take it and
eat it," he said. "It will be sweet as honey
in your mouth, but it will turn sour in your
stomach!" 10So I took the small scroll from
the hand of the angel, and I ate it! It was
sweet in my mouth, but when I swallowed
it, it turned sour in my stomach.
11Then I was told, "You must prophesy
again about many peoples, nations, languages, and kings."

The Two Witnesses

11 Then I was given a measuring stick,
and I was told, "Go and measure the
Temple of God and the altar, and count the
number of worshipers. 2But do not measure
the outer courtyard, for it has been turned
over to the nations. They will trample the
holy city for 42 months. 3And I will give
power to my two witnesses, and they will be
clothed in burlap and will prophesy during
those 1,260 days."
4These two prophets are the two olive
trees and the two lampstands that stand
before the Lord of all the earth. 5If anyone
tries to harm them, fire flashes from their
mouths and consumes their enemies. This
is how anyone who tries to harm them must
die. 6They have power to shut the sky so that
no rain will fall for as long as they prophesy. And they have the power to turn the
rivers and oceans into blood, and to strike
the earth with every kind of plague as often
as they wish.
7When they complete their testimony,
the beast that comes up out of the bottomless pit* will declare war against them, and
he will conquer them and kill them. 8And
their bodies will lie in the main street of Jerusalem,* the city that is figuratively called
"Sodom" and "Egypt," the city where their
Lord was crucified. 9And for three and a
half days, all peoples, tribes, languages,
and nations will stare at their bodies. No
one will be allowed to bury them. 10All the
people who belong to this world will gloat
over them and give presents to each other to
celebrate the death of the two prophets who
had tormented them.
11But after three and a half days, God
breathed life into them, and they stood up!
Terror struck all who were staring at them.
12Then a loud voice from heaven called to
the two prophets, "Come up here!" And they
rose to heaven in a cloud as their enemies
watched.
13At the same time there was a terrible
earthquake that destroyed a tenth of the
city. Seven thousand people died in that

Being a witness

Six of the scroll's seals have been opened, leading to conquest, war, famine, death, martyrdom, and creation's disintegration (Revelation 6)—the result of humanity rejecting God. Reassured that God's people are protected through all this (chapter 7), John then saw the seventh seal opened—the sounding of seven trumpets, serving as a wake-up call to the world (chapters 8–9). But what is needed now is someone to explain what is happening and to call people to repent, which is where the two witnesses (chapter 11) come in—two, for this was the number required to confirm a testimony (Deuteronomy 19:15). Some think these are two individuals who will testify powerfully to Christ in the end time but will be martyred and resurrected (Revelation 11:3-12); but in a book so full of symbolism it seems more likely they symbolize *all* God's people throughout time who are called to be witnesses to Jesus. John sees that, even amid all this chaos and persecution, Christians can be sure that God will help them be a witness, by both word and deed, to his truth; and not even the worst "the beast" can do can stop them (11:7-18).

We may not all be evangelists; but all are called to be witnesses, as Jesus both commanded (Matthew 28:19-20) and promised (Acts 1:8).

▶ *See also* ***Mission****, page 1082.*

earthquake, and everyone else was terrified
and gave glory to the God of heaven.
14 The second terror is past, but look, the
third terror is coming quickly.

The Seventh Trumpet Brings the Third Terror

15 Then the seventh angel blew his trumpet,
and there were loud voices shouting in
heaven:

"The world has now become the
Kingdom of our Lord and of his
Christ,*
and he will reign forever and ever."

16 The twenty-four elders sitting on their
thrones before God fell with their faces to
the ground and worshiped him. 17 And they
said,

"We give thanks to you, Lord God, the
Almighty,
the one who is and who always was,
for now you have assumed your great
power
and have begun to reign.
18 The nations were filled with wrath,
but now the time of your wrath has
come.
It is time to judge the dead
and reward your servants the
prophets,
as well as your holy people,
and all who fear your name,
from the least to the greatest.
It is time to destroy
all who have caused destruction on
the earth."

19 Then, in heaven, the Temple of God was
opened and the Ark of his covenant could be
seen inside the Temple. Lightning flashed,
thunder crashed and roared, and there was
an earthquake and a terrible hailstorm.

The Woman and the Dragon

12 Then I witnessed in heaven an event
of great significance. I saw a woman
clothed with the sun, with the moon
beneath her feet, and a crown of twelve
stars on her head. 2 She was pregnant, and
she cried out because of her labor pains and
the agony of giving birth.
3 Then I witnessed in heaven another
significant event. I saw a large red dragon
with seven heads and ten horns, with seven
crowns on his heads. 4 His tail swept away
one-third of the stars in the sky, and he threw
them to the earth. He stood in front of the
woman as she was about to give birth, ready
to devour her baby as soon as it was born.
5 She gave birth to a son who was to rule
all nations with an iron rod. And her child
was snatched away from the dragon and
was caught up to God and to his throne.
6 And the woman fled into the wilderness,
where God had prepared a place to care for
her for 1,260 days.
7 Then there was war in heaven. Michael
and his angels fought against the dragon
and his angels. 8 And the dragon lost the
battle, and he and his angels were forced out
of heaven. 9 This great dragon—the ancient
serpent called the devil, or Satan, the one
deceiving the whole world—was thrown
down to the earth with all his angels.
10 Then I heard a loud voice shouting
across the heavens,

"It has come at last—
salvation and power
and the Kingdom of our God,
and the authority of his Christ.*
For the accuser of our brothers and
sisters*
has been thrown down to earth—
the one who accuses them
before our God day and night.
11 And they have defeated him by the
blood of the Lamb
and by their testimony.
And they did not love their lives so
much
that they were afraid to die.
12 Therefore, rejoice, O heavens!
And you who live in the heavens,
rejoice!
But terror will come on the earth and
the sea,
for the devil has come down to you in
great anger,
knowing that he has little time."

13 When the dragon realized that he had
been thrown down to the earth, he pursued
the woman who had given birth to the male
child. 14 But she was given two wings like
those of a great eagle so she could fly to the
place prepared for her in the wilderness.

11:7 Or *the abyss*, or *the underworld*. **11:8** Greek *the great city*. **11:15** Or *his Messiah*. **12:10a** Or *his Messiah*. **12:10b** Greek *brothers*.

There she would be cared for and protected
from the dragon* for a time, times, and half
a time.
15 Then the dragon tried to drown the
woman with a flood of water that flowed
from his mouth. 16 But the earth helped her
by opening its mouth and swallowing the
river that gushed out from the mouth of
the dragon. 17 And the dragon was angry at
the woman and declared war against the
rest of her children—all who keep God's
commandments and maintain their testimony for Jesus.
18 Then the dragon took his stand* on the
shore beside the sea.

The Beast out of the Sea

13 Then I saw a beast rising up out of the
sea. It had seven heads and ten horns,
with ten crowns on its horns. And written
on each head were names that blasphemed
God. 2 This beast looked like a leopard, but
it had the feet of a bear and the mouth of a
lion! And the dragon gave the beast his own
power and throne and great authority.
3 I saw that one of the heads of the beast
seemed wounded beyond recovery—but
the fatal wound was healed! The whole
world marveled at this miracle and gave allegiance to the beast. 4 They worshiped the
dragon for giving the beast such power, and
they also worshiped the beast. "Who is as
great as the beast?" they exclaimed. "Who
is able to fight against him?"
5 Then the beast was allowed to speak
great blasphemies against God. And he was
given authority to do whatever he wanted
for forty-two months. 6 And he spoke terrible
words of blasphemy against God, slandering his name and his dwelling—that is,
those who dwell in heaven.* 7 And the beast
was allowed to wage war against God's holy
people and to conquer them. And he was
given authority to rule over every tribe and
people and language and nation. 8 And all
the people who belong to this world worshiped the beast. They are the ones whose
names were not written in the Book of Life
that belongs to the Lamb who was slaughtered before the world was made.*

9 Anyone with ears to hear
should listen and understand.
10 Anyone who is destined for prison
will be taken to prison.
Anyone destined to die by the sword
will die by the sword.

This means that God's holy people must
endure persecution patiently and remain
faithful.

The Beast out of the Earth

11 Then I saw another beast come up out
of the earth. He had two horns like those
of a lamb, but he spoke with the voice of
a dragon. 12 He exercised all the authority
of the first beast. And he required all the
earth and its people to worship the first
beast, whose fatal wound had been healed.
13 He did astounding miracles, even making
fire flash down to earth from the sky while
everyone was watching. 14 And with all the
miracles he was allowed to perform on
behalf of the first beast, he deceived all
the people who belong to this world. He
ordered the people to make a great statue
of the first beast, who was fatally wounded
and then came back to life. 15 He was then
permitted to give life to this statue so that
it could speak. Then the statue of the
beast commanded that anyone refusing to
worship it must die.
16 He required everyone—small and great,
rich and poor, free and slave—to be given a
mark on the right hand or on the forehead.
17 And no one could buy or sell anything
without that mark, which was either the
name of the beast or the number representing his name. 18 Wisdom is needed here.
Let the one with understanding solve the
meaning of the number of the beast, for it is
the number of a man.* His number is 666.*

The Lamb and the 144,000

14 Then I saw the Lamb standing on
Mount Zion, and with him were
144,000 who had his name and his Father's
name written on their foreheads. 2 And I
heard a sound from heaven like the roar of
mighty ocean waves or the rolling of loud
thunder. It was like the sound of many harp-
ists playing together.
3 This great choir sang a wonderful new
song in front of the throne of God and before
the four living beings and the twenty-four

▸ **12:1-18** *See **Satan**, page 566.*

elders. No one could learn this song except
the 144,000 who had been redeemed from
the earth. 4They have kept themselves as
pure as virgins,* following the Lamb wherever he goes. They have been purchased
from among the people on the earth as a
special offering* to God and to the Lamb.
5They have told no lies; they are without
blame.

The Three Angels

6And I saw another angel flying through
the sky, carrying the eternal Good News to
proclaim to the people who belong to this
world—to every nation, tribe, language,
and people. 7"Fear God," he shouted. "Give
glory to him. For the time has come when
he will sit as judge. Worship him who made
the heavens, the earth, the sea, and all the
springs of water."

8Then another angel followed him
through the sky, shouting, "Babylon is
fallen—that great city is fallen—because she
made all the nations of the world drink the
wine of her passionate immorality."

9Then a third angel followed them, shouting, "Anyone who worships the beast and
his statue or who accepts his mark on the
forehead or on the hand 10must drink the
wine of God's anger. It has been poured full
strength into God's cup of wrath. And they
will be tormented with fire and burning
sulfur in the presence of the holy angels and
the Lamb. 11The smoke of their torment will
rise forever and ever, and they will have no
relief day or night, for they have worshiped
the beast and his statue and have accepted
the mark of his name."

12This means that God's holy people must
endure persecution patiently, obeying his
commands and maintaining their faith in
Jesus.

13And I heard a voice from heaven saying,
"Write this down: Blessed are those who
die in the Lord from now on. Yes, says the
Spirit, they are blessed indeed, for they will
rest from their hard work; for their good
deeds follow them!"

The Harvest of the Earth

14Then I saw a white cloud, and seated on
the cloud was someone like the Son of
Man.* He had a gold crown on his head and
a sharp sickle in his hand.

12:14 Greek *the serpent;* also in 12:15. See 12:9. **12:18** Greek *Then he took his stand;* some manuscripts read *Then I took my stand.* Some translations put this entire sentence into 13:1. **13:6** Some manuscripts read *and his dwelling and all who dwell in heaven.* **13:8** Or *not written in the Book of Life before the world was made—the Book that belongs to the Lamb who was slaughtered.* **13:18a** Or *of humanity.* **13:18b** Some manuscripts read *616.* **14:4a** Greek *They are virgins who have not defiled themselves with women.* **14:4b** Greek *as firstfruits.* **14:14** Or *like a son of man.* See Dan 7:13. "Son of Man" is a title Jesus used for himself.

Babylon in Revelation

John refers to "Babylon" several times in Revelation (14:8; 16:19; 17:5; 18:2, 10, 21), though in a book so full of imagery it is very unlikely he was thinking of literal Babylon. In Old Testament times, Babylon had been the political, economic, and religious center of a great empire; but it—and the rulers behind it—was wicked. It was the Babylonians who had ransacked Jerusalem and exiled God's people, forcing them to live under its power; but the prophets had announced its future fall (e.g., Isaiah 21:9; Jeremiah 51:8) in words that John picks up in Revelation 14:8.

John uses "Babylon" as an image of everything that opposes the one true God, just as Babylon itself had done in history. Some think he was thinking, like some contemporary Jewish writers, of Rome and its empire, which had destroyed Jerusalem's Temple in AD 70 and was now persecuting Christians fiercely, but that he didn't want to name the empire directly. Others, however, think he uses "Babylon" to symbolize the totality of the political and religious systems of the world that oppose God, not just then but throughout history. It may include the former, but it certainly extends to the latter, since the fall of "Babylon" awaits the end of human history (chapter 18).

▸ *See also* ***Babylon****, page 445.*

15Then another angel came from the Temple
and shouted to the one sitting on the cloud,
"Swing the sickle, for the time of harvest has
come; the crop on earth is ripe." 16So the one
sitting on the cloud swung his sickle over the
earth, and the whole earth was harvested.
17After that, another angel came from the
Temple in heaven, and he also had a sharp
sickle. 18Then another angel, who had
power to destroy with fire, came from the
altar. He shouted to the angel with the sharp
sickle, "Swing your sickle now to gather
the clusters of grapes from the vines of the
earth, for they are ripe for judgment." 19So
the angel swung his sickle over the earth
and loaded the grapes into the great winepress of God's wrath. 20The grapes were
trampled in the winepress outside the city,
and blood flowed from the winepress in a
stream about 180 miles* long and as high
as a horse's bridle.

The Song of Moses and of the Lamb

15 Then I saw in heaven another marvelous event of great significance. Seven
angels were holding the seven last plagues,
which would bring God's wrath to completion. 2I saw before me what seemed to be a
glass sea mixed with fire. And on it stood all
the people who had been victorious over the
beast and his statue and the number representing his name. They were all holding
harps that God had given them. 3And they
were singing the song of Moses, the servant
of God, and the song of the Lamb:

"Great and marvelous are your works,
O Lord God, the Almighty.
Just and true are your ways,
O King of the nations.*
4 Who will not fear you, Lord,
and glorify your name?
For you alone are holy.
All nations will come and worship
before you,
for your righteous deeds have been
revealed."

The Seven Bowls of the Seven Plagues

5Then I looked and saw that the Temple in
heaven, God's Tabernacle, was thrown wide
open. 6The seven angels who were holding
the seven plagues came out of the Temple.
They were clothed in spotless white linen*
with gold sashes across their chests. 7Then
one of the four living beings handed each of
the seven angels a gold bowl filled with the
wrath of God, who lives forever and ever.
8The Temple was filled with smoke from
God's glory and power. No one could enter
the Temple until the seven angels had completed pouring out the seven plagues.

16 Then I heard a mighty voice from the
Temple say to the seven angels, "Go
your ways and pour out on the earth the
seven bowls containing God's wrath."
2So the first angel left the Temple and
poured out his bowl on the earth, and horrible, malignant sores broke out on everyone who had the mark of the beast and who
worshiped his statue.
3Then the second angel poured out his
bowl on the sea, and it became like the blood
of a corpse. And everything in the sea died.
4Then the third angel poured out his bowl
on the rivers and springs, and they became
blood. 5And I heard the angel who had authority over all water saying,

"You are just, O Holy One, who is and
who always was,
because you have sent these
judgments.
6 Since they shed the blood
of your holy people and your
prophets,
you have given them blood to drink.
It is their just reward."

7And I heard a voice from the altar,* saying,

"Yes, O Lord God, the Almighty,
your judgments are true and just."

8Then the fourth angel poured out his
bowl on the sun, causing it to scorch everyone with its fire. 9Everyone was burned
by this blast of heat, and they cursed the
name of God, who had control over all these
plagues. They did not repent of their sins
and turn to God and give him glory.
10Then the fifth angel poured out his bowl
on the throne of the beast, and his kingdom
was plunged into darkness. His subjects
ground their teeth* in anguish, 11and they
cursed the God of heaven for their pains and
sores. But they did not repent of their evil
deeds and turn to God.
12Then the sixth angel poured out his
bowl on the great Euphrates River, and
it dried up so that the kings from the east

could march their armies toward the west
without hindrance. 13 And I saw three evil*
spirits that looked like frogs leap from the
mouths of the dragon, the beast, and the
false prophet. 14 They are demonic spirits
who work miracles and go out to all the
rulers of the world to gather them for battle
against the Lord on that great judgment day
of God the Almighty.

15 "Look, I will come as unexpectedly as
a thief! Blessed are all who are watching
for me, who keep their clothing ready so
they will not have to walk around naked
and ashamed."

16 And the demonic spirits gathered all the
rulers and their armies to a place with the
Hebrew name *Armageddon.**
17 Then the seventh angel poured out his
bowl into the air. And a mighty shout came
from the throne in the Temple, saying, "It is
finished!" 18 Then the thunder crashed and
rolled, and lightning flashed. And a great
earthquake struck—the worst since people
were placed on the earth. 19 The great city
of Babylon split into three sections, and
the cities of many nations fell into heaps of
rubble. So God remembered all of Babylon's
sins, and he made her drink the cup that
was filled with the wine of his fierce wrath.
20 And every island disappeared, and all the
mountains were leveled. 21 There was a terrible hailstorm, and hailstones weighing
as much as seventy-five pounds* fell from
the sky onto the people below. They cursed
God because of the terrible plague of the
hailstorm.

The Great Prostitute

17 One of the seven angels who had
poured out the seven bowls came over
and spoke to me. "Come with me," he said,
"and I will show you the judgment that is
going to come on the great prostitute, who
rules over many waters. 2 The kings of the
world have committed adultery with her,
and the people who belong to this world
have been made drunk by the wine of her
immorality."
3 So the angel took me in the Spirit* into
the wilderness. There I saw a woman sitting
on a scarlet beast that had seven heads and
ten horns, and blasphemies against God
were written all over it. 4 The woman wore

14:20 Greek *1,600 stadia* [300 kilometers]. **15:3** Some manuscripts read *King of the ages.* **15:6** Other manuscripts read *white stone;* still others read *white [garments] made of linen.* **16:7** Greek *I heard the altar.* **16:10** Greek *gnawed their tongues.* **16:13** Greek *unclean.* **16:16** Or *Harmagedon.* **16:21** Greek *1 talent* [34 kilograms]. **17:3** Or *in spirit.*

Armageddon

Armageddon is the setting for the final battle at the end of time between good and evil. It is a Hebrew word meaning "Mountain of Megiddo"; but since Megiddo was not a mountain but a huge plain where many battles had been fought in ancient times (e.g., 2 Kings 23:29), it seems highly likely that, once again, John was using symbolic rather than literal language. He uses this ancient battle site to symbolize the last great battle between Christ and Satan, whose demonic spirits have gone out "to all the rulers of the world to gather them for battle against the Lord on that great judgment day of God the Almighty" (Revelation 16:14). But he also uses it to recall Old Testament events (for John knew the Scriptures well): the defeat of those who oppressed God's people (e.g., Judges 5:19-21); the destruction of false prophets (1 Kings 18:40—the Kishon Valley ran through the Plain of Megiddo); the defeat of kings who wouldn't listen to God (2 Chronicles 35:20-24); and the destruction of all who come against God's people and his people's turning to him in repentance (Zechariah 12:9–13:1).

But here is the interesting thing: This battle is never fought! While evil forces amass against Christ and his people, God himself intervenes, sending fire from heaven to devour them all (Revelation 20:9). The battle is his, not ours. God himself will overcome evil without our help.

▶ *See also* ***Hazor, Megiddo, and Gezer****, page 388.*

purple and scarlet clothing and beautiful
jewelry made of gold and precious gems
and pearls. In her hand she held a gold
goblet full of obscenities and the impurities
of her immorality. 5A mysterious name
was written on her forehead: "Babylon the
Great, Mother of All Prostitutes and Obscenities in the World." 6I could see that she
was drunk—drunk with the blood of God's
holy people who were witnesses for Jesus.
I stared at her in complete amazement.

7"Why are you so amazed?" the angel
asked. "I will tell you the mystery of this
woman and of the beast with seven heads
and ten horns on which she sits. 8The beast
you saw was once alive but isn't now. And
yet he will soon come up out of the bottomless pit* and go to eternal destruction. And
the people who belong to this world, whose
names were not written in the Book of Life
before the world was made, will be amazed at
the reappearance of this beast who had died.

9"This calls for a mind with understanding: The seven heads of the beast
represent the seven hills where the woman
rules. They also represent seven kings.
10Five kings have already fallen, the sixth
now reigns, and the seventh is yet to come,
but his reign will be brief.

11"The scarlet beast that was, but is no
longer, is the eighth king. He is like the
other seven, and he, too, is headed for destruction. 12The ten horns of the beast are
ten kings who have not yet risen to power.
They will be appointed to their kingdoms
for one brief moment to reign with the
beast. 13They will all agree to give him their
power and authority. 14Together they will go
to war against the Lamb, but the Lamb will
defeat them because he is Lord of all lords
and King of all kings. And his called and
chosen and faithful ones will be with him."

15Then the angel said to me, "The waters
where the prostitute is ruling represent
masses of people of every nation and language. 16The scarlet beast and his ten horns
all hate the prostitute. They will strip her
naked, eat her flesh, and burn her remains
with fire. 17For God has put a plan into their
minds, a plan that will carry out his purposes. They will agree to give their authority
to the scarlet beast, and so the words of God
will be fulfilled. 18And this woman you saw
in your vision represents the great city that
rules over the kings of the world."

The Fall of Babylon

18 After all this I saw another angel
come down from heaven with great
authority, and the earth grew bright with
his splendor. 2He gave a mighty shout:

"Babylon is fallen—that great city is
fallen!
She has become a home for demons.
She is a hideout for every foul* spirit,
a hideout for every foul vulture
and every foul and dreadful animal.*
3 For all the nations have fallen*
because of the wine of her passionate
immorality.
The kings of the world
have committed adultery with her.
Because of her desires for extravagant
luxury,
the merchants of the world have
grown rich."

4Then I heard another voice calling from
heaven,

"Come away from her, my people.
Do not take part in her sins,
or you will be punished with her.
5 For her sins are piled as high as heaven,
and God remembers her evil deeds.
6 Do to her as she has done to others.
Double her penalty* for all her evil
deeds.
She brewed a cup of terror for others,
so brew twice as much* for her.
7 She glorified herself and lived in luxury,
so match it now with torment and
sorrow.
She boasted in her heart,
'I am queen on my throne.
I am no helpless widow,
and I have no reason to mourn.'
8 Therefore, these plagues will overtake
her in a single day—
death and mourning and famine.
She will be completely consumed by
fire,
for the Lord God who judges her is
mighty."

9And the kings of the world who committed adultery with her and enjoyed her
great luxury will mourn for her as they see
the smoke rising from her charred remains.
10They will stand at a distance, terrified by
her great torment. They will cry out,

"How terrible, how terrible for you,
O Babylon, you great city!
In a single moment
God's judgment came on you."

11 The merchants of the world will weep
and mourn for her, for there is no one left to
buy their goods. 12 She bought great quantities of gold, silver, jewels, and pearls; fine
linen, purple, silk, and scarlet cloth; things
made of fragrant thyine wood, ivory goods,
and objects made of expensive wood; and
bronze, iron, and marble. 13 She also bought
cinnamon, spice, incense, myrrh, frankincense, wine, olive oil, fine flour, wheat,
cattle, sheep, horses, wagons, and bodies—
that is, human slaves.

14 "The fancy things you loved so much
are gone," they cry.
"All your luxuries and splendor
are gone forever,
never to be yours again."

15 The merchants who became wealthy by
selling her these things will stand at a distance, terrified by her great torment. They
will weep and cry out,

16 "How terrible, how terrible for that great
city!
She was clothed in finest purple and
scarlet linens,
decked out with gold and precious
stones and pearls!
17 In a single moment
all the wealth of the city is gone!"

And all the captains of the merchant ships
and their passengers and sailors and crews
will stand at a distance. 18 They will cry out as
they watch the smoke ascend, and they will
say, "Where is there another city as great as
this?" 19 And they will weep and throw dust
on their heads to show their grief. And they
will cry out,

"How terrible, how terrible for that great
city!
The shipowners became wealthy
by transporting her great wealth on
the seas.
In a single moment it is all gone."
20 Rejoice over her fate, O heaven
and people of God and apostles and
prophets!
For at last God has judged her
for your sakes.

21 Then a mighty angel picked up a boulder
the size of a huge millstone. He threw it into
the ocean and shouted,

"Just like this, the great city Babylon
will be thrown down with violence
and will never be found again.
22 The sound of harps, singers, flutes, and
trumpets
will never be heard in you again.
No craftsmen and no trades
will ever be found in you again.
The sound of the mill
will never be heard in you again.
23 The light of a lamp
will never shine in you again.
The happy voices of brides and
grooms
will never be heard in you again.
For your merchants were the greatest in
the world,
and you deceived the nations with
your sorceries.
24 In your* streets flowed the blood of the
prophets and of God's holy people
and the blood of people slaughtered
all over the world."

Songs of Victory in Heaven

19 After this, I heard what sounded like
a vast crowd in heaven shouting,

"Praise the LORD!*
Salvation and glory and power belong
to our God.
2 His judgments are true and just.
He has punished the great prostitute
who corrupted the earth with her
immorality.
He has avenged the murder of his
servants."

3 And again their voices rang out:

"Praise the LORD!
The smoke from that city ascends
forever and ever!"

4 Then the twenty-four elders and the four
living beings fell down and worshiped God,
who was sitting on the throne. They cried
out, "Amen! Praise the LORD!"

17:8 Or *the abyss,* or *the underworld.* **18:2a** Greek *unclean;* also in each of the two following phrases. **18:2b** Some manuscripts condense the last two lines to read *a hideout for every foul [unclean] and dreadful vulture.* **18:3** Some manuscripts read *have drunk.* **18:6a** Or *Give her an equal penalty.* **18:6b** Or *brew just as much.* **18:24** Greek *her.* **19:1** Greek *Hallelujah;* also in 19:3, 4, 6. *Hallelujah* is the transliteration of a Hebrew term that means "Praise the LORD."

5 And from the throne came a voice that
said,

"Praise our God,
all his servants,
all who fear him,
from the least to the greatest."

6 Then I heard again what sounded like
the shout of a vast crowd or the roar of
mighty ocean waves or the crash of loud
thunder:

"Praise the LORD!
For the Lord our God,* the Almighty,
reigns.
7 Let us be glad and rejoice,
and let us give honor to him.
For the time has come for the wedding
feast of the Lamb,
and his bride has prepared herself.
8 She has been given the finest of pure
white linen to wear."
For the fine linen represents the good
deeds of God's holy people.

9 And the angel said to me, "Write this:
Blessed are those who are invited to the
wedding feast of the Lamb." And he added,
"These are true words that come from God."
10 Then I fell down at his feet to worship
him, but he said, "No, don't worship me. I am
a servant of God, just like you and your brothers and sisters* who testify about their faith
in Jesus. Worship only God. For the essence of
prophecy is to give a clear witness for Jesus.*"

The Rider on the White Horse

11 Then I saw heaven opened, and a white
horse was standing there. Its rider was
named Faithful and True, for he judges fairly
and wages a righteous war. 12 His eyes were
like flames of fire, and on his head were many
crowns. A name was written on him that no
one understood except himself. 13 He wore a
robe dipped in blood, and his title was the
Word of God. 14 The armies of heaven, dressed
in the finest of pure white linen, followed
him on white horses. 15 From his mouth came
a sharp sword to strike down the nations.
He will rule them with an iron rod. He will
release the fierce wrath of God, the Almighty,
like juice flowing from a winepress. 16 On his
robe at his thigh* was written this title: King
of all kings and Lord of all lords.
17 Then I saw an angel standing in the sun,
shouting to the vultures flying high in the
sky: "Come! Gather together for the great
banquet God has prepared. 18 Come and eat
the flesh of kings, generals, and strong warriors; of horses and their riders; and of all humanity, both free and slave, small and great."
19 Then I saw the beast and the kings of
the world and their armies gathered together to fight against the one sitting on
the horse and his army. 20 And the beast was
captured, and with him the false prophet
who did mighty miracles on behalf of the
beast—miracles that deceived all who had
accepted the mark of the beast and who
worshiped his statue. Both the beast and
his false prophet were thrown alive into the
fiery lake of burning sulfur. 21 Their entire
army was killed by the sharp sword that
came from the mouth of the one riding the
white horse. And the vultures all gorged
themselves on the dead bodies.

The Thousand Years

20 Then I saw an angel coming down
from heaven with the key to the
bottomless pit* and a heavy chain in his
hand. 2 He seized the dragon—that old
serpent, who is the devil, Satan—and
bound him in chains for a thousand years.
3 The angel threw him into the bottomless
pit, which he then shut and locked so Satan
could not deceive the nations anymore until
the thousand years were finished. Afterward he must be released for a little while.
4 Then I saw thrones, and the people
sitting on them had been given the authority to judge. And I saw the souls of those
who had been beheaded for their testimony
about Jesus and for proclaiming the word of
God. They had not worshiped the beast or
his statue, nor accepted his mark on their
foreheads or their hands. They all came to
life again, and they reigned with Christ for
a thousand years.
5 This is the first resurrection. (The rest of
the dead did not come back to life until the
thousand years had ended.) 6 Blessed and
holy are those who share in the first resurrection. For them the second death holds no
power, but they will be priests of God and of
Christ and will reign with him a thousand
years.

The Defeat of Satan

7 When the thousand years come to an end,
Satan will be let out of his prison. 8 He will

go out to deceive the nations—called Gog and Magog—in every corner of the earth. He will gather them together for battle—a mighty army, as numberless as sand along the seashore. 9 And I saw them as they went up on the broad plain of the earth and surrounded God's people and the beloved city. But fire from heaven came down on the attacking armies and consumed them.

10 Then the devil, who had deceived them, was thrown into the fiery lake of burning sulfur, joining the beast and the false prophet. There they will be tormented day and night forever and ever.

The Final Judgment

11 And I saw a great white throne and the one sitting on it. The earth and sky fled from his presence, but they found no place to hide. 12 I saw the dead, both great and small, standing before God's throne. And the books were opened, including the Book of Life. And the dead were judged according to what they had done, as recorded in the books. 13 The sea gave up its dead, and death and the grave* gave up their dead. And all were judged according to their deeds. 14 Then death and the grave were thrown into the lake of fire. This lake of fire is the second death. 15 And anyone whose name was not found recorded in the Book of Life was thrown into the lake of fire.

The New Jerusalem

21 Then I saw a new heaven and a new earth, for the old heaven and the old earth had disappeared. And the sea was also gone. 2 And I saw the holy city, the new Jerusalem, coming down from God out of heaven like a bride beautifully dressed for her husband.

3 I heard a loud shout from the throne, saying, "Look, God's home is now among his people! He will live with them, and they will be his people. God himself will be with them.* 4 He will wipe every tear from their eyes, and there will be no more death or sorrow or crying or pain. All these things are gone forever."

5 And the one sitting on the throne said, "Look, I am making everything new!" And then he said to me, "Write this down, for what I tell you is trustworthy and true." 6 And he also said, "It is finished! I am the Alpha and the Omega—the Beginning and

19:6 Some manuscripts read *the Lord God*. **19:10a** Greek *brothers*. **19:10b** Or *is the message confirmed by Jesus*. **19:16** Or *On his robe and thigh*. **20:1** Or *the abyss*, or *the underworld;* also in 20:3. **20:13** Greek *and Hades;* also in 20:14. **21:3** Some manuscripts read *God himself will be with them, their God*.

The Last Judgment

In Revelation 20, human history as we have known it is about to end. After a period of one thousand years (which some interpret literally and others symbolically), Satan gathers God's enemies for battle against God's people (Revelation 20:7-9). But the battle never takes place; fire from heaven destroys them, and the devil is cast into the lake of burning sulfur to join the beast and the false prophet (20:9-10). Satan is at last overthrown!

It is at this point that the Last Judgment takes place (20:11-15). Everyone—great and small, living and dead—is called before God's throne to be "judged according to what they had done, as recorded in the books" (20:12). But Christians need not fear, for their names have been written in the Book of Life (20:12; see also Exodus 32:32-33; Psalm 69:28; Daniel 12:1; Luke 10:20; Philippians 4:3; Revelation 3:5). So while unbelievers are condemned and thrown into "the lake of fire" (Revelation 20:15), believers enter the new Jerusalem (chapter 21) that God has prepared for them, where they receive the rewards for their service (1 Corinthians 3:13-15; 2 Corinthians 5:10).

Through faith in Christ and because of his sacrifice for our sins, Christians need never fear this Last Judgment; but its solemnness should certainly spur us on to share the gospel with others.

▶ *See also* ***Hell****, page 1108;* ***Heaven****, page 1451;* ***The new Jerusalem****, page 1466.*

the End. To all who are thirsty I will give
freely from the springs of the water of life.
7 All who are victorious will inherit all these
blessings, and I will be their God, and they
will be my children.

8 "But cowards, unbelievers, the corrupt,
murderers, the immoral, those who practice
witchcraft, idol worshipers, and all liars—
their fate is in the fiery lake of burning
sulfur. This is the second death."

9 Then one of the seven angels who held
the seven bowls containing the seven last
plagues came and said to me, "Come with
me! I will show you the bride, the wife of
the Lamb."

10 So he took me in the Spirit* to a great,
high mountain, and he showed me the holy
city, Jerusalem, descending out of heaven
from God. 11 It shone with the glory of God
and sparkled like a precious stone—like
jasper as clear as crystal. 12 The city wall
was broad and high, with twelve gates
guarded by twelve angels. And the names
of the twelve tribes of Israel were written
on the gates. 13 There were three gates on
each side—east, north, south, and west.
14 The wall of the city had twelve foundation
stones, and on them were written the names
of the twelve apostles of the Lamb.

15 The angel who talked to me held in his
hand a gold measuring stick to measure
the city, its gates, and its wall. 16 When he
measured it, he found it was a square, as
wide as it was long. In fact, its length and
width and height were each 1,400 miles.*
17 Then he measured the walls and found
them to be 216 feet thick* (according to the
human standard used by the angel).

18 The wall was made of jasper, and the
city was pure gold, as clear as glass. 19 The
wall of the city was built on foundation
stones inlaid with twelve precious stones:*
the first was jasper, the second sapphire,
the third agate, the fourth emerald, 20 the
fifth onyx, the sixth carnelian, the seventh
chrysolite, the eighth beryl, the ninth topaz,
the tenth chrysoprase, the eleventh jacinth,
the twelfth amethyst.

21 The twelve gates were made of pearls—
each gate from a single pearl! And the main
street was pure gold, as clear as glass.

22 I saw no temple in the city, for the Lord
God Almighty and the Lamb are its temple.
23 And the city has no need of sun or moon,
for the glory of God illuminates the city,
and the Lamb is its light. 24 The nations will
walk in its light, and the kings of the world
will enter the city in all their glory. 25 Its
gates will never be closed at the end of day
because there is no night there. 26 And all
the nations will bring their glory and honor
into the city. 27 Nothing evil* will be allowed
to enter, nor anyone who practices shameful idolatry and dishonesty—but only those

The new Jerusalem

It surprises many to discover that the Bible doesn't end where they thought it ended: with us in heaven, worshiping God forever. Revelation 21 shows that heaven is not our final home at all; it has simply been a beautiful waiting room for believers who died before Christ's return. Our ultimate destiny, this passage shows, is not heaven but a renewed earth (21:1–22:6). John sees "the new Jerusalem" coming down *from* heaven *to* earth, so that "God's home is now among his people! He will live with them" (21:2-3). There follows a description of a beautiful city—as with almost everything else in Revelation, symbolic not literal. There is nothing to spoil this beautiful environment, for "the old heaven and the old earth" (i.e., our present cosmos), where sin and suffering have taken root and done so much damage, have now disappeared (21:1).

The Bible's story began with one man and one woman in a garden, enjoying fellowship with God; it ends with a whole people, now not in a garden but in a city—in those days, a symbol of security—with God again in their midst. Fellowship with him has been restored, and life is back to how it was intended to be.

▸ *See also* ***Jerusalem****, page 347;* ***Zion****, page 649;* ***Heaven****, page 1451.*

whose names are written in the Lamb's Book of Life.

22 Then the angel showed me a river with the water of life, clear as crystal, flowing from the throne of God and of the Lamb. 2It flowed down the center of the main street. On each side of the river grew a tree of life, bearing twelve crops of fruit,* with a fresh crop each month. The leaves were used for medicine to heal the nations.

3No longer will there be a curse upon anything. For the throne of God and of the Lamb will be there, and his servants will worship him. 4And they will see his face, and his name will be written on their foreheads. 5And there will be no night there—no need for lamps or sun—for the Lord God will shine on them. And they will reign forever and ever.

6Then the angel said to me, "Everything you have heard and seen is trustworthy and true. The Lord God, who inspires his prophets,* has sent his angel to tell his servants what will happen soon.*"

Jesus Is Coming

7"Look, I am coming soon! Blessed are
those who obey the words of prophecy
written in this book.*"

8I, John, am the one who heard and saw all these things. And when I heard and saw them, I fell down to worship at the feet of the angel who showed them to me. 9But he said, "No, don't worship me. I am a servant of God, just like you and your brothers the prophets, as well as all who obey what is written in this book. Worship only God!"

10Then he instructed me, "Do not seal up the prophetic words in this book, for the time is near. 11Let the one who is doing harm continue to do harm; let the one who is vile continue to be vile; let the one who is righteous continue to live righteously; let the one who is holy continue to be holy."

12"Look, I am coming soon, bringing
my reward with me to repay all people
according to their deeds. 13I am the
Alpha and the Omega, the First and the
Last, the Beginning and the End."

14Blessed are those who wash their robes. They will be permitted to enter through the gates of the city and eat the fruit from the tree of life. 15Outside the city are the dogs—the sorcerers, the sexually immoral, the murderers, the idol worshipers, and all who love to live a lie.

16"I, Jesus, have sent my angel to give you
this message for the churches. I am both
the source of David and the heir to his
throne.* I am the bright morning star."

17The Spirit and the bride say, "Come." Let anyone who hears this say, "Come." Let anyone who is thirsty come. Let anyone who desires drink freely from the water of life. 18And I solemnly declare to everyone who hears the words of prophecy written in this book: If anyone adds anything to what is written here, God will add to that person the plagues described in this book. 19And if anyone removes any of the words from this book of prophecy, God will remove that person's share in the tree of life and in the holy city that are described in this book.

20He who is the faithful witness to all these things says, "Yes, I am coming soon!"

Amen! Come, Lord Jesus!

21May the grace of the Lord Jesus be with God's holy people.*

21:10 Or *in spirit.* **21:16** Greek *12,000 stadia* [2,220 kilometers]. **21:17** Greek *144 cubits* [65 meters]. **21:19** The identification of some of these gemstones is uncertain. **21:27** Or *ceremonially unclean.* **22:2** Or *twelve kinds of fruit.* **22:6a** Or *The Lord, the God of the spirits of the prophets.* **22:6b** Or *suddenly*, or *quickly;* also in 22:7, 12, 20. **22:7** Or *scroll*; also in 22:9, 10, 18, 19. **22:16** Greek *I am the root and offspring of David.* **22:21** Other manuscripts read *be with all;* still others read *be with all of God's holy people.* Some manuscripts add *Amen.*

Bible Reading Plans

Plan 1: An introduction to the Bible

Time needed: Four weeks

If you're new to the Bible, then this is a great place to begin! This four-week reading plan will take you through some basics of the Christian message, showing you who God is, what he has done for you, and how he wants you to respond.

THE OLD TESTAMENT *(7 Days)*

The Old Testament shows us how God carefully prepared for the coming of Jesus.

- ☐ **Genesis 1–2** Creation: how God created everything perfectly
- ☐ **Genesis 3** Sin: human disobedience and its consequences
- ☐ **Genesis 12:1-9; 15:1-6** Faith: God puts people back into relationship with him through our faith
- ☐ **Exodus 20:1-20** The Ten Commandments: instructions for godly living
- ☐ **Exodus 32:1–34:8** Knowing God: Moses discovers what God is really like
- ☐ **Psalm 23** The God who cares: King David's experience of God's provision and protection
- ☐ **Isaiah 7:14; 9:1-7** Salvation: More than seven hundred years before Jesus' birth, God promises to send a Savior

THE GOSPELS *(7 Days)*

The four Gospels tell us about the coming, ministry, death, and resurrection of Jesus, God's promised Savior.

- ☐ **Luke 2** The Savior's arrival: Jesus' birth and early years
- ☐ **Matthew 3:1–4:11** Baptism and beginnings: Jesus obeys his Father and overcomes the devil
- ☐ **John 1:35-51** Disciples: Jesus calls his first followers
- ☐ **Matthew 5–7** A new way of living: the Sermon on the Mount, the heart of Jesus' teaching
- ☐ **Matthew 8:1-17; 11:1-6** Miracles: a sign that God's Kingdom is breaking into this world through Jesus
- ☐ **Mark 14:1-52** The time has come: preparations for Jesus' death
- ☐ **Mark 14:53–16:20** Defeat and victory: Jesus is tried and crucified, but rises again

THE FIRST CHRISTIANS *(7 Days)*

The book of Acts shows us how the church was born and how the first Christians lived and witnessed.

- ☐ **Acts 1:1-11; 2:1-21** A new season: Jesus leaves, but the Holy Spirit comes
- ☐ **Acts 2:42-47; 4:32-37; 5:12-16** A new way of living: life in the early church
- ☐ **Acts 5:17-42; 7:54–8:3** Opposition: Not everyone is happy with the message of the gospel
- ☐ **Acts 9:1-31** New beginnings: the conversion of Saul (who becomes the apostle Paul)

- ☐ **Acts 10** A gospel for everyone: Peter sees that Christianity is for all peoples and nations
- ☐ **Acts 15:1-35** A gospel of grace: The church agrees that we are saved by Jesus' grace alone and not by what we do
- ☐ **Acts 27–28** The unstoppable gospel: No matter what happens, the gospel's power cannot be stopped

NEW TESTAMENT LETTERS *(7 Days)*

The letters, written by apostles or those closely associated with them, show Christians what they should believe and how they should live.

- ☐ **Romans 3:21–4:8** The foundation of faith: Faith, not works, is what makes us right with God and keeps us in relationship with him
- ☐ **Romans 8:1-39** Conquered and conquering: the blessing of living life in the power of the Holy Spirit
- ☐ **1 Corinthians 13:1-13; 1 John 3:11-20** The power of love: Christ's love changes the way we relate to others
- ☐ **Galatians 5:1-26** Free and fruitful: Christ has freed us to bear good fruit for him
- ☐ **Ephesians 1:15-23; 4:1-16** The body of Christ: the importance of the church
- ☐ **1 Thessalonians 4:13–5:11** He's coming again! Living in light of Christ's promised return
- ☐ **Revelation 21:1-8; 22:1-5** Hope for the future: the assurance that we will be with God forever

Plan 2: An overview of the Bible's story

Time needed: Six months

This Bible reading plan provides readings for 180 days. If you follow it in order, it will take you through the whole Bible, helping you to understand the flow of its overall story and to see its key themes. If you want more variety in your reading, however, you can alternate between sections of the Old Testament and sections of the New Testament.

THE OLD TESTAMENT *(90 Days)*

Creation and the Fall

- ☐ **Genesis 1–2** The creation of the world and humanity
- ☐ **Genesis 3** The origins of sin
- ☐ **Genesis 6:9–7:24; 9:1-17** God punishes human sin through a great flood

God begins to build a family through whom his plan will be worked out

- ☐ **Genesis 12:1-9; 15:1-20; 17:1-27** God calls Abraham and promises to give him descendants and the land of Canaan
- ☐ **Genesis 21:1-7; 22:1-19** God gives Abraham a son but then tests his faith
- ☐ **Genesis 25:19-34; 27:1–28:5** Abraham's son Isaac has two sons, Jacob and Esau, who quarrel
- ☐ **Genesis 29:1–30:24; 35:16-18** Jacob flees Canaan but finds a wife and has twelve sons
- ☐ **Genesis 32:1–33:20** Jacob returns home and is reconciled to his brother
- ☐ **Genesis 37** How Jacob's son Joseph ended up in Egypt
- ☐ **Genesis 41:1-57; 46:1-7; 50:15-21** Joseph gains prominence in Egypt and brings his family there to avoid famine in Canaan

God calls Moses to lead his people out of slavery in Egypt

- ☐ **Exodus 1–2** How the Israelites ended up in slavery, and the birth of Moses
- ☐ **Exodus 3–4** Moses' encounter with the living God
- ☐ **Exodus 12:1-40; 13:17–14:31** God's judgment on wicked Egypt and Israel's miraculous escape
- ☐ **Exodus 19:1–20:21** God makes the Israelites his holy nation and gives them his commandments at Mount Sinai
- ☐ **Exodus 33:1–34:8** God reveals what he is really like to Moses
- ☐ **Leviticus 9** The priests begin their work of offering sacrifices to God
- ☐ **Numbers 13:25–14:45** Grumbling and unbelief lead to forty years in the wilderness
- ☐ **Deuteronomy 31:1-8; 34:1-12** Moses dies and is succeeded by Joshua

God's people enter the Promised Land of Canaan

- ☐ **Joshua 3–4** The Israelites cross the Jordan and enter the Promised Land
- ☐ **Joshua 5:13–6:27** The miraculous conquest of Jericho
- ☐ **Joshua 24** God renews the covenant with his people, and Joshua dies
- ☐ **Judges 6–7** Gideon learns to trust God and defeats the Midianites
- ☐ **Judges 16** Samson, one of Israel's leaders, is undermined by his own weaknesses
- ☐ **Ruth 1** Ruth, a foreigner, finds a home among God's people

God gives his people a king

- ☐ **1 Samuel 1; 3** God gives his people a prophet, Samuel
- ☐ **1 Samuel 9–10** Samuel anoints Saul as Israel's first king
- ☐ **1 Samuel 13; 15** Saul is rejected as king because of his disobedience to God
- ☐ **1 Samuel 16** Samuel anoints David as king
- ☐ **1 Samuel 17** David shows his trust in God as he defeats Goliath
- ☐ **1 Samuel 31; 2 Samuel 2:1-7; 5:1-4** Saul dies in battle, and David replaces him as king
- ☐ **2 Samuel 7** God promises David that one of his descendants will always be on the throne
- ☐ **2 Samuel 11–12** David's sin and restoration
- ☐ **1 Chronicles 29** David encourages people to bring their gifts for building God's Temple
- ☐ **1 Kings 2–3** David's son Solomon succeeds him as king and asks God for wisdom
- ☐ **1 Kings 8** Solomon dedicates the great Temple he built
- ☐ **2 Chronicles 7** God appears to Solomon
- ☐ **1 Kings 11** Solomon's foolishness and death

The nation divides in two (Israel in the north, Judah in the south)

- ☐ **1 Kings 12** The nation divides because of the foolishness of Solomon's son
- ☐ **1 Kings 18** The prophet Elijah challenges Ahab, king of Israel, and the prophets of Baal
- ☐ **2 Kings 2** Elijah is succeeded as prophet by Elisha
- ☐ **2 Kings 4–5** Elisha demonstrates God's power by performing miracles
- ☐ **2 Chronicles 20:1-30** King Jehoshaphat of Judah discovers the power of praise

- ☐ **2 Kings 17** Assyria conquers the wicked northern kingdom of Israel—the judgment of God
- ☐ **2 Kings 19** God spares Jerusalem because of King Hezekiah's faith
- ☐ **2 Kings 22:1–23:3** The young King Josiah renews the covenant with God
- ☐ **2 Kings 25** Jerusalem is conquered by Babylon because of disobedience and is exiled

Life after the Exile

- ☐ **Ezra 1:1-8; 2:68–3:13** God's people return to Judah after a seventy-year exile and rebuild the Temple
- ☐ **Ezra 7** Ezra returns to Jerusalem
- ☐ **Nehemiah 1–2** Nehemiah returns to Jerusalem and rebuilds its walls
- ☐ **Nehemiah 5** Nehemiah's concern for the poor
- ☐ **Nehemiah 8** Ezra teaches the word of God
- ☐ **Esther 3–4; 7** A plot to wipe out God's people is foiled in Persia

Readings from Israel's poetry and wisdom literature
Many of the psalms and "wisdom books" were written during the reigns of Israel's and Judah's kings.

- ☐ **Job 1** Trusting God when things go wrong
- ☐ **Psalm 1:1-6; 119:1-16** The benefits of reading God's word
- ☐ **Psalm 23; 46** Trust in God's provision and protection
- ☐ **Psalm 51** David's prayer of confession
- ☐ **Psalm 103** Praise for God's love and compassion
- ☐ **Psalm 139** God's perfect knowledge of us
- ☐ **Proverbs 3–4** The value of growing in God's wisdom
- ☐ **Ecclesiastes 3** Trusting in God's timing
- ☐ **Song of Songs 2** A love song

Readings from the prophets

- ☐ **Isaiah 6** Isaiah is called to be a prophet in Judah
- ☐ **Isaiah 9:1-7; 11:1-9** Prophecies of the coming of the Messiah
- ☐ **Isaiah 30** Encouragements to trust in God alone as Judah is being attacked by Assyria
- ☐ **Isaiah 40** Isaiah foresees God's coming to rescue his people in the future
- ☐ **Isaiah 53** Isaiah foresees the crucifixion of Christ
- ☐ **Isaiah 61** The coming of God's anointed servant
- ☐ **Jeremiah 1** Jeremiah's call to be a prophet
- ☐ **Jeremiah 7** The worthlessness of the false religion that was practiced by many in Jeremiah's day
- ☐ **Jeremiah 29:1-14** Encouragement to the exiles to seek blessing on the place where God had put them
- ☐ **Jeremiah 31:23-37** God promises a new covenant to his people
- ☐ **Lamentations 3:1-33** Despite his sufferings, the poet declares his confidence in God's faithfulness
- ☐ **Ezekiel 34** Ezekiel, a prophet in exile, prophesies that God will come as the Good Shepherd

- ☐ **Ezekiel 37** God's promise to restore and renew his people
- ☐ **Daniel 1** Daniel learns how to succeed in exile under foreign rulers
- ☐ **Daniel 3** Daniel's friends put their trust in God
- ☐ **Daniel 6** Daniel experiences God's protection
- ☐ **Daniel 7** Daniel sees a vision of the coming of God's Kingdom in Jesus
- ☐ **Hosea 1–2** Hosea's experience of unfaithfulness mirrors that experienced by God with his people Israel
- ☐ **Joel 2:12-32** An appeal to return to God and a prophecy about the Holy Spirit
- ☐ **Amos 5** Amos denounces empty religion among God's people
- ☐ **Obadiah 1** Judgment is proclaimed on the nation of Edom for the way it opposed God's people
- ☐ **Jonah 1–4** Jonah struggles with the fact that God loves people of every nation
- ☐ **Micah 4:1–5:5** God promises to restore his people and give them favor among the nations
- ☐ **Nahum 1** God promises to judge Nineveh, Assyria's capital, for its treatment of his people
- ☐ **Habakkuk 3** Habakkuk's trust in God
- ☐ **Zephaniah 3** God's promise of judgment on his people is followed by a promise of restoration
- ☐ **Haggai 1:1–2:9** A challenge to God's people to put him first in their lives
- ☐ **Zechariah 3–4** Jeshua the high priest and Zerubbabel the governor symbolize God's coming Servant, Jesus
- ☐ **Malachi 3** A call for God's people to honor him, for his coming is close

THE NEW TESTAMENT *(90 Days)*

The life of Jesus

- ☐ **Luke 1** The births of John the Baptist and Jesus are foretold
- ☐ **Luke 2** The birth and childhood of Jesus (1)
- ☐ **Matthew 1:18–2:23** The birth and childhood of Jesus (2)
- ☐ **John 1:1-18** The miracle of Jesus' coming
- ☐ **Matthew 3** John the Baptist prepares the way for Jesus
- ☐ **Luke 4:1-13** Jesus overcomes the devil's temptations
- ☐ **Luke 4:14-44** Jesus is rejected by his hometown and begins his ministry
- ☐ **Mark 1:14-20; Luke 5:1-11** Jesus calls his first disciples
- ☐ **John 2:1-12** Jesus' first miracle
- ☐ **Mark 1:21–2:12** A summary of Jesus' early miracles, showing his power over everything
- ☐ **John 3:1-21** Jesus teaches about the need to be born again
- ☐ **Matthew 5** Jesus' Sermon on the Mount (1)
- ☐ **Matthew 6** Jesus' Sermon on the Mount (2)
- ☐ **Matthew 7** Jesus' Sermon on the Mount (3)
- ☐ **Matthew 10** Jesus sends out his twelve disciples
- ☐ **Matthew 13** Parables about God's Kingdom
- ☐ **Mark 6:30-56** Jesus demonstrates his power by feeding five thousand and walking on water

- ☐ **John 6:25-70** Jesus, the bread of life
- ☐ **Luke 15** Three parables on God's love for the lost
- ☐ **Matthew 18:15-35** Jesus' teaching about forgiveness
- ☐ **Luke 19:1-10; John 4:1-42** Jesus welcomes outsiders
- ☐ **John 11** The raising of Lazarus from the dead and its consequences
- ☐ **Matthew 16:13-28** Jesus predicts his death
- ☐ **Matthew 21** Jesus' Triumphal Entry into Jerusalem and conflicts with the religious leaders
- ☐ **Mark 12:28-34** The greatest commandment
- ☐ **Matthew 24** Jesus teaches about troubles to come and his return at the end of the age
- ☐ **Matthew 25** Jesus teaches about the importance of always being ready for his return
- ☐ **John 13:1-30** Jesus washes his disciples' feet and predicts his betrayal
- ☐ **Mark 14:12-31** The Last Supper and Jesus' prediction of Peter's denial
- ☐ **John 14** Jesus warns the disciples he is leaving but promises that the Holy Spirit will come in his place
- ☐ **John 17** Jesus prays
- ☐ **Mark 14:32-72** Jesus is arrested, and Peter denies knowing him
- ☐ **Matthew 27** Jesus is put on trial, crucified, and buried
- ☐ **Luke 24** The risen Jesus appears to his followers
- ☐ **John 20:19–21:25** More resurrection appearances
- ☐ **Acts 1:1-11** Jesus returns to his Father in heaven

The story of the early church

- ☐ **Acts 2** The coming of the Spirit and the birth of the church
- ☐ **Acts 4** Despite opposition, the church continues to be blessed
- ☐ **Acts 6:8–7:60** The church's first martyr
- ☐ **Acts 8** The gospel begins to spread
- ☐ **Acts 9:1-31** The conversion of Saul (Paul)
- ☐ **Acts 10** Peter realizes that the gospel is for people of all nations and backgrounds
- ☐ **Acts 12** Peter's miraculous escape from prison
- ☐ **Acts 15** The apostles and elders affirm that following the Jewish Law is not necessary for salvation
- ☐ **Acts 16:6-40** Paul takes the gospel to Europe
- ☐ **Acts 19** Paul's preaching provokes severe opposition
- ☐ **Acts 21–22** Paul's arrest is prophesied and takes place
- ☐ **Acts 27–28** Paul is taken as a prisoner to Rome but still keeps preaching about Jesus

Letters from early church leaders

- ☐ **Romans 3:21–4:25** Getting right with God through faith
- ☐ **Romans 5–6** The blessing of being right with God
- ☐ **Romans 8** Life in the Holy Spirit
- ☐ **Romans 14:1–15:13** Learning to accept other Christians who do things differently from us

- ☐ **1 Corinthians 3** The foolishness of divisions in the church
- ☐ **1 Corinthians 12** Using God's gifts for the good of one another in the church
- ☐ **1 Corinthians 13** The importance of love
- ☐ **1 Corinthians 15** Teaching about the resurrection
- ☐ **2 Corinthians 4:1–5:10** God's treasure in clay jars
- ☐ **2 Corinthians 8–9** Teaching about generous giving
- ☐ **2 Corinthians 11:1–12:10** Suffering: the mark of a true servant of Jesus
- ☐ **Galatians 3:1–4:7** Living by the Spirit and not by the Law
- ☐ **Galatians 5** Freedom and fruit
- ☐ **Ephesians 2** Reconciled to God and one another through Christ
- ☐ **Ephesians 4:17–5:20** The importance of living a holy life
- ☐ **Ephesians 6:10-20** Putting on all of God's armor
- ☐ **Philippians 2:1-18** A call to imitate Christ
- ☐ **Philippians 3:1–4:1** A call to press on in our walk with Jesus
- ☐ **Colossians 1:9-23** The supremacy of Christ
- ☐ **Colossians 3:1–4:6** A call to holy living
- ☐ **1 Thessalonians 4:13–5:24** Living in light of Christ's return
- ☐ **2 Thessalonians 3:1-18** A challenge not to be idle
- ☐ **1 Timothy 4** The value of spiritual training
- ☐ **2 Timothy 1:1–2:13** Encouragements to be faithful
- ☐ **Titus 2:1–3:11** Teaching about godly Christian living
- ☐ **Philemon 1** Paul appeals for mercy on behalf of a runaway slave
- ☐ **Hebrews 4:14–5:10; 7:1–8:2** Jesus, our great High Priest, gives us free access to God
- ☐ **Hebrews 11:1–12:3** Examples of faith that encourage us
- ☐ **James 2:1-13** There is no room for favoritism in the church
- ☐ **James 3** Learning to control our words
- ☐ **1 Peter 1:3–2:3** Christians should be characterized by hope and holiness
- ☐ **1 Peter 3:8–4:19** Christians should be ready to suffer for their faith
- ☐ **2 Peter 3** Teaching about the return of Jesus
- ☐ **1 John 1:5–2:17** Walking in the light
- ☐ **1 John 4:7-21** Since we are loved, we should be loving
- ☐ **2 John 1** Living in truth and love
- ☐ **3 John 1** A call to stay faithful even in the face of difficulties and opposition
- ☐ **Jude 1** The importance of standing firm in your faith
- ☐ **Revelation 2–3** Jesus both encourages and challenges the church
- ☐ **Revelation 4–5** A vision of heaven
- ☐ **Revelation 19:11–20:15** Jesus' final victory over evil
- ☐ **Revelation 21:1–22:6** A vision of God's new creation

Basic Truths
OF THE CHRISTIAN FAITH

Christians look to the Bible to provide answers to the basic questions they have about life and faith, but often it seems difficult to find the key places where God's word speaks about a particular question or topic. This section will provide a good starting point to help you find those key places and engage with God's word on many of those basic questions and ideas.

Abandonment

Many of us have times when our circumstances are so overwhelming that we feel utterly alone and think that no one else knows, understands, or cares about our situation. But the Bible reminds us that, no matter what the situation or circumstance might be, God is always with us and will never abandon us.

> *"Do not be afraid or discouraged, for the LORD will personally go ahead of you. He will be with you; he will neither fail you nor abandon you." – Deuteronomy 31:8, page 234*

God promises to never abandon his people Deuteronomy 4:30-31, *page 206* • Joshua 1:1-9, *page 242* • Isaiah 49:14-16, *page 802* • Hebrews 13:5-6, *page 1409*

God himself knows what it feels like to be abandoned Deuteronomy 32:15-18, *page 236* • Judges 10:6-14, *page 283* • Isaiah 65:1-5, *page 818* • Jeremiah 2:4-13, *page 823*

Circumstances can make us feel—wrongly—abandoned by God Judges 6:1-14, *page 276* • 1 Kings 19:1-18, *page 404* • Psalm 44:1-26, *page 628*

Prayers that God would never abandon us 1 Kings 8:54-61, *page 387* • Psalm 27:7-10, *page 617* • Psalm 71:1-24, *page 645*

We can trust God even when everything has gone wrong Job 1:6-22, *page 565* • Habakkuk 3:17-18, *page 1027* • 2 Corinthians 4:7-18, *page 1327*

The Bible assures us that God will be with us in the dark times Psalm 18:1-24, *page 610* • Psalm 23:1-6, *page 615* • Psalm 46:1-11, *page 630* • Isaiah 41:10-14, *page 792*

Honest prayers of some who felt abandoned Psalm 22:1-31, *page 614* • Psalm 38:1-22, *page 625* • Lamentations 5:1-22, *page 897*

Jesus felt abandoned on the cross Matthew 27:45-46, *page 1115*

Jesus promised he would never abandon us Matthew 28:18-20, *page 1116* • John 14:18, *page 1223*

Abortion

The Bible teaches that life does not begin at birth but at the moment of conception. Abortion therefore violates the sanctity of God-given life and the potential which that life contains. Confessed to God, however, abortion can be forgiven, just like any other sin.

> *You made all the delicate, inner parts of my body and knit me together in my mother's womb. Thank you for making me so wonderfully complex! Your workmanship is marvelous—how well I know it. You watched me as I was being formed in utter seclusion, as I was woven together in the dark of the womb. You saw me before I was born. Every day of my life was recorded in your book. Every moment was laid out before a single day had passed. – Psalm 139:13-16, page 689*

BASIC TRUTHS • *page 1478*

Every human being is made in God's image Genesis 1:26-27, *page 5* • Genesis 5:1-2, *page 9*

God forbids the taking of life Genesis 9:5-7, *page 12* • Exodus 20:13, *page 90* • Matthew 19:16-19, *page 1099*

God cares for those not yet born Exodus 21:22-25, *page 91* • Job 10:8-12, *page 573* • Psalm 139:13-18, *page 689*

We should protect all those who are helpless Psalm 82:3-4, *page 655* • Proverbs 31:8-9, *page 729* • Isaiah 58:6-10, *page 811*

Children are a gift from God Psalm 127:3-5, *page 684*

God plans the future of every child Psalm 139:13-16, *page 689* • Isaiah 49:1-3, *page 801* • Jeremiah 1:4-8, *page 822*

Abortion, like every other sin, can be forgiven if confessed 1 John 1:8-9, *page 1433*

▸ *See **Abortion**, page 823.*

Abuse

The Bible forbids people from abusing others—using our position or power to harm them, control them, or exploit them in order to gain advantage for ourselves. It warns of God's judgment on those who do and says that God is always on the side of those who are abused.

> *"The cry of the people of Israel has reached me, and I have seen how harshly the Egyptians abuse them." – Exodus 3:9, page 68*

Abuse of others can arise from our uncontrolled anger Genesis 4:1-15, *page 8* • 1 Kings 21:1-14, *page 407* • Matthew 2:16-18, *page 1070* • Mark 6:14-29, *page 1129*

Every act of abuse is seen by God Genesis 31:38-42, *page 39*

The abuse of power brings God's judgment and curse Exodus 7:14–12:30, *page 73* • Jeremiah 23:1-2, 9-24, *page 851* • Acts 12:1-23, *page 1254*

God forbids abuse of minorities or the underprivileged Exodus 22:21-24, *page 93* • Leviticus 25:35-46, *page 148* • Deuteronomy 24:10-15, 17-18, *page 226*

God promises to protect those who are helpless Deuteronomy 10:17-23, *page 213* • Psalm 12:1-8, *page 608*

God wants his people to care for the needy, not abuse them Deuteronomy 15:1-11, *page 218* • Proverbs 14:31, *page 711* • James 1:27, *page 1413*

Examples of abuse and exploitation Job 24:2-17, *page 584* • Isaiah 3:13-15, *page 752* • Isaiah 58:1-10, *page 810* • Amos 4:1-3, *page 996*

Jesus experienced abuse Matthew 26:67-68, *page 1112* • Matthew 27:26-44, *page 1113* • Luke 4:14-30, *page 1158* • John 8:48, *page 1213*

Family relationships should be marked by love and respect, not abuse Ephesians 5:21–6:4, *page 1351*

▸ *See **Oppression**, page 710.*

Access to God *see Coming into God's presence*

Accountability *see also Responsibility*

Accountability is about recognizing that we are not free to live just for ourselves; rather, we need to be answerable to others for what we think and do. As Christians, we are first and foremost accountable to God, to whom we will one day have to give an account of our lives. But we are also called to be accountable to one another in a local church, just as the first Christians were.

> *One day Jesus called together his twelve disciples and gave them power and authority to cast out all demons and to heal all diseases. Then he sent them out to tell everyone about the Kingdom of God and to heal the sick. . . . When the apostles returned, they told Jesus everything they had done. – Luke 9:1-2, 10, page 1168*

All we do should be done in light of the fact that God will judge our work one day 2 Chronicles 19:5-10, *page 500* • 2 Corinthians 5:6-10, *page 1327*

God will hold us accountable for our actions Ezekiel 18:30-32, *page 917* • Luke 12:42-48, *page 1176* • Romans 2:16, *page 1284* • Revelation 20:11-15, *page 1465*

Church leaders are accountable to God and fellow leaders Ezekiel 34:1-10, *page 935* • Galatians 2:11-14, *page 1338*

We are accountable for every word that we speak Matthew 12:33-37, *page 1087*

We should be held accountable in our Christian ministry Luke 10:1-20, *page 1171*

We should hold each other accountable Luke 17:3-4, *page 1182* • Galatians 6:1-5, *page 1343*

The importance of being accountable to a local church Acts 14:27-28, *page 1259*

God holds us accountable for our attitudes Romans 14:10-12, *page 1298*

We should be willing to be accountable to one another James 5:13-16, *page 1417*

▶ *See **Accountability**, page 1258.*

Accusations

God tells us not to falsely accuse others, for it undermines justice and harmony. The Bible records many examples of people who were falsely accused—with Jesus himself as the greatest example—and shows the unjust outcomes of false accusations.

"Be sure never to charge anyone falsely with evil." – Exodus 23:7, page 93

Examples of false accusations Genesis 39:6-18, *page 49* • Nehemiah 6:1-9, *page 541* • Acts 6:8-15, *page 1244* • Acts 16:16-40, *page 1262*

God forbids false accusations Exodus 20:16, *page 90* • Exodus 23:1, *7*, *page 93* • Luke 3:12-14, *page 1157*

Satan accuses God's people Job 1:6-22, *page 565* • Zechariah 3:1-10, *page 1040*

No one can accuse us regarding our standing before God Isaiah 50:8-9, *page 803* • Romans 8:31-39, *page 1292* • Colossians 1:22, *page 1363*

Jesus was falsely accused Matthew 10:24-25, *page 1083* • Matthew 26:59-60, *page 1112* • Mark 3:20-30, *page 1124* • Luke 23:1-5, *page 1192*

Accusations against church leaders must come from more than one person 1 Timothy 5:19, *page 1383*

Satan, the Accuser, is already overthrown Revelation 12:10-11, *page 1457*

Addiction *see also Desires; Greed*

Any addiction—whether it be to drugs, alcohol, money, sex, or food—creates a dependence that pulls us away from God and other people. These addictions continually demand more, but they are never satisfied. Ultimately, only Jesus can set us free from addictions and help us to control every aspect of our lives through the help of the Holy Spirit.

For you are a slave to whatever controls you. – 2 Peter 2:19, page 1429

Warnings against addiction to food and drink Proverbs 23:1-8, 19-21, 29-35, *page 719* • 1 Corinthians 6:9-10, *page 1309* • Philippians 3:17-21, *page 1359*

Warnings against addiction to money Ecclesiastes 5:10-15, *page 734* • Mark 10:17-27, *page 1136* • Luke 12:13-21, *page 1175*

Warnings against addiction to sexual sin Jeremiah 3:1-5, *page 825* • 1 Corinthians 6:9-20, *page 1309*

Addictions can keep people from loving Jesus fully Mark 10:17-31, *page 1136* • 1 Timothy 6:6-10, *page 1383*

Jesus wants to help set us free from addictions Romans 6:1-23, *page 1289* • Titus 2:11-15

We are addicted to anything that controls us Romans 6:16, *page 1289* • 2 Peter 2:19, *page 1429*

We should not become slaves to anything 1 Corinthians 6:9-20, *page 1309* •

Galatians 4:4-7, *page 1341* • Galatians 5:1, *page 1343* • 2 Peter 2:17-22, *page 1429*

Self-control is part of the Holy Spirit's provision to deal with addiction Galatians 5:13-26, *page 1343*

Any addiction is opposed to the true transformation Jesus wants to perform in our lives Philippians 3:1-21, *page 1358*

Adolescence *see Youth*

Adoption, Spiritual

The Bible tells us that when we turn to Jesus and trust him, we are adopted into God's family. From that point on we can know God as our Father and be sure that he loves us and that all his resources are now at our disposal.

> *For all who are led by the Spirit of God are children of God. So you have not received a spirit that makes you fearful slaves. Instead, you received God's Spirit when he adopted you as his own children. Now we call him, "Abba, Father." For his Spirit joins with our spirit to affirm that we are God's children. And since we are his children, we are his heirs. In fact, together with Christ we are heirs of God's glory. – Romans 8:14-17, page 1291*

God's children should obey him Exodus 19:3-8, *page 88* • Deuteronomy 26:16-19, *page 228* • 1 John 2:3-6, *page 1434* • 1 John 5:1-5, *page 1437*

God lovingly disciplines his children for their good Deuteronomy 8:1-5, *page 211* • Psalm 119:75-76, *page 680* • Hebrews 12:5-11, *page 1408*

We should not reject God's fatherly discipline Job 5:17, *page 569* • Proverbs 3:11-12, *page 699* • Hebrews 12:5-13, *page 1408* • Revelation 3:15-19, *page 1450*

God is our heavenly Father Malachi 2:10, *page 1051* • Matthew 6:9-18, *page 1077* • Romans 8:15-16, *page 1291* • 1 John 3:1, *page 1435*

God our Father will provide for all our needs Matthew 6:28-33, *page 1078* • 2 Corinthians 9:6-10, *page 1331* • Philippians 4:19, *page 1360*

Christians are God's children John 1:12-13, *page 1199* • Galatians 3:26-29, *page 1341* • 1 John 3:1-2, *page 1435*

God's children are his heirs Romans 8:15-17, *page 1291* • Galatians 4:6-7, *page 1341*

God chose us to be adopted as his children Romans 8:22-23, *page 1292* • Ephesians 1:3-5, *page 1346*

God's children should have nothing to do with worldly living 2 Corinthians 6:14-18, *page 1329* • Ephesians 5:1-20, *page 1351*

All of God's children are equal in God's eyes Galatians 3:26-28, *page 1341* • Colossians 3:10-11, *page 1365*

Jesus is our spiritual brother Hebrews 2:11-15, *page 1398*

We should love our Christian brothers and sisters 1 John 3:14-19, *page 1436* • 1 John 4:20-21, *page 1437*

▶ *See* ***Now that you are a Christian****, page A13;* ***Abba****, page 1144;* ***Life in the Spirit****, page 1291;* ***Living by the Spirit****, page 1342;* ***The Christian's relationship with the Holy Spirit****, page 1350.*

Adultery *see also Marriage*

Adultery—the violation of the marriage bond through a sexual relationship with someone who is not one's spouse—is seen by God as something detestable, for it breaks the principle of covenant faithfulness. The Bible both forbids adultery and shows the consequences when it happens. Like any other sin, however, adultery can be forgiven.

> *But the man who commits adultery is an utter fool, for he destroys himself. He will be wounded and disgraced. His shame will never be erased. – Proverbs 6:32-33, page 703*

We should run from situations that might lead to adultery Genesis 39:1-21, *page 49* • 1 Corinthians 6:9-20, *page 1309*

God forbids adultery in the Ten Commandments Exodus 20:14, *page 90*

David's adultery had terrible consequences 2 Samuel 11:1–12:25, *page 352*

David realized that he needed to repent of his adultery 2 Samuel 12:13, *page 354* • Psalm 51:1-19, *page 633*

Enjoyment of our own marriage is the best safeguard against adultery Proverbs 5:15-23, *page 701* • 1 Corinthians 7:1-5 *page 1310*

Adultery is foolish Proverbs 6:32-34, *page 703* • Proverbs 7:7-27, *page 703*

Jesus said that lust is as sinful as adultery Matthew 5:27-28, *page 1076*

Jesus said that remarriage, in some circumstances, is adultery Matthew 5:31-32, *page 1076* • Mark 10:1-12, *page 1135*

God can forgive the adulterer John 8:1-11, *page 1211*

▶ *See* ***Adultery****, page 353;* ***Does marriage still matter to God?****, page 976.*

Advice

The Bible encourages us to be ready to seek advice from others. An unwillingness to seek advice is seen as arrogant, obstinate, and even stupid; but a willingness to seek and follow advice is seen as wise. We should also be ready to offer prayerful advice to others—though ultimately everyone is responsible before God for their own decisions.

Those who take advice are wise. – Proverbs 13:10, page 709

Wise leaders will consider the advice of others Exodus 18:13-26, *page 87* • Proverbs 24:3-6, *page 721*

Advice should always be evaluated Numbers 13:25-30, *page 169* • 2 Samuel 16:15–17:14, *page 360*

Older people often give wise advice 1 Kings 12:1-11, *page 392* • Acts 15:1-35, *page 1259*

Rejecting wise advice invariably leads to disaster 1 Kings 12:1-19, *page 392* • Acts 27:3-26, *page 1277*

Following God's advice always leads to success Psalm 32:8-11, *page 621* • Psalm 73:24, *page 647*

Wise people will always seek advice Proverbs 1:2-9, *page 697* • Proverbs 12:15, *page 709*

We are foolish if we reject advice Proverbs 1:24-33, *page 697*

Good advice helps ensure success Proverbs 11:14, *page 708* • Proverbs 15:22, *page 712* • Proverbs 20:18, *page 717*

Jesus promised that the Holy Spirit would give us advice and counsel John 14:15-26, *page 1223* • John 16:12-15, *page 1225*

▶ *See* ***Wisdom****, page 701.*

Alcohol

The drinking of alcohol is often a matter of considerable debate among Christians. The Bible itself does not prohibit God's people from drinking—apart from Old Testament priests who were about to go on duty (Leviticus 10:8-9, page 127). However, it consistently warns against the dangers of overdrinking and forbids drunkenness, showing the consequences that can follow.

Wine produces mockers; alcohol leads to brawls. Those led astray by drink cannot be wise. – Proverbs 20:1, page 716

Drinking alcohol excessively can lead us to do foolish things Genesis 9:20-25, *page 12* • Genesis 19:30-38, *page 23*

Used properly, wine is seen as a gift from God Deuteronomy 7:12-13, *page 210* • Psalm 104:13-15, *page 667* • Isaiah 25:6-8, *page 773* • 1 Timothy 5:23, *page 1383*

Getting drunk takes us off our guard 2 Samuel 13:28-29, *page 356* • 1 Kings 16:8-10, *page 399* • Proverbs 23:29-35, *page 721* • Luke 21:34-36, *page 1190*

Drinking binges are foolish Proverbs 23:19-21, *page 720* • Isaiah 5:11-13, *page 753*

Jesus produced excellent wine for a wedding John 2:1-11, *page 1201*

We are commanded not to get drunk Romans 13:11-14, *page 1298* • Ephesians 5:18-20, *page 1351* • 1 Thessalonians 5:4-8, *page 1373* • 1 Peter 4:1-5, *page 1424*

Even if we feel free to drink, we should not do so if it will cause others to stumble Romans 14:20-23, *page 1298*

Drunkenness can keep us from God's Kingdom 1 Corinthians 6:9-11, *page 1309* • Galatians 5:19-21, *page 1343*

Church leaders in particular must be moderate in their drinking 1 Timothy 3:1-8, *page 1380* • Titus 2:1-3, *page 1390*

Paul encouraged Timothy to drink a little wine to help with health problems 1 Timothy 5:23, *page 1383*

▶ *See **Addiction**, page 1429.*

Ambition

Ambitions can be both good and bad. The Bible encourages us to put to death the bad ambitions in our lives and to pursue only the good ones—those that serve God and his Kingdom and that put others' interests before our own. Pursuing proper godly ambition means we will keep following Jesus.

> *Everything else is worthless when compared with the infinite value of knowing Christ Jesus my Lord. For his sake I have discarded everything else, counting it all as garbage, so that I could gain Christ and become one with him. – Philippians 3:8-9, page 1358*

Wrong ambitions can lead us to behave deceptively 2 Samuel 15:1-12, *page 358* • Acts 5:1-11, *page 1242*

Wrong ambitions can become a trap Esther 5:9–7:10, *page 558* • Proverbs 11:6, *page 707*

The best ambition is to want to know God more Psalm 27:4-8, *page 617* • Philippians 3:7-14, *page 1358*

The ambition to get rich can take us away from God Matthew 6:24, *page 1078* • 1 Timothy 6:6-10, *page 1383*

The ambition for prestige or position is not in keeping with being a follower of Jesus Mark 9:33-37, *page 1135* • Mark 10:35-45, *page 1137*

We should have the godly ambition to share the Good News Romans 15:20-21, *page 1299*

Selfish ambition is wrong Galatians 5:19-26, *page 1343* • Philippians 3:3-11, *page 1358* • James 3:16-18, *page 1415*

The Christian's ambition should be to live a good life 1 Thessalonians 4:11, *page 1372*

Even church leaders can have ungodly ambition 3 John 1:5-11, *page 1439*

▶ *See **The Absalom spirit**, page 358.*

Angels

Angels are spiritual beings who act as God's messengers. They bring his help, convey his blessing, protect his people, and carry out his judgment. But while they are important, the Bible shows that they are only created beings and so are not to be worshiped or to become the object of too much interest from us.

> *Angels are only servants—spirits sent to care for people who will inherit salvation. – Hebrews 1:14, page 1397*

Angels often look just like people Genesis 19:1-5, *page 22* • Mark 16:5-6, *page 1147* • Hebrews 13:1-2, *page 1409*

Angels sometimes carry out God's judgment Genesis 19:12-29, *page 23* • 2 Samuel 24:15-17, *page 371* • 2 Kings 19:35-36, *page 438*

Angels protect God's people Exodus 23:20-22, *page 94* • Psalm 34:6-7, *page 622* • Psalm 91:9-16, *page 661* • Daniel 6:21-22, *page 964*

Angels delight to worship God Psalm 89:5-8, *page 658* • Revelation 5:6-14, *page 1451*

Angels serve God and do his will Psalm 103:20-21, *page 667* • Hebrews 1:14, *page 1397*

Angels are God's messengers Daniel 8:15-27, *page 967* • Matthew 28:1-8, *page 1115* • Luke 1:5-38, *page 1151* • Luke 2:8-20, *page 1154*

Angels played key roles at the coming of Jesus Matthew 1:18-25, *page 1068* • Matthew 2:19-23, *page 1070* • Luke 1:5-38, *page 1151* • Luke 2:8-15, *page 1154*

Angels will have a role at Christ's return Matthew 13:37-43, *page 1090* • Matthew 24:30-31, *page 1107* • Revelation 19:11-18, *page 1464*

Angels neither marry nor die Matthew 22:29-32, *page 1104* • Luke 20:34-38, *page 1188*

Angels are holy Mark 8:38, *page 1133* • Jude 1:14, *page 1442*

Angels should not be worshiped Colossians 2:16-23, *page 1364* • Revelation 22:8-9, *page 1467*

Jesus is far superior to any angel Hebrews 1:1–2:13, *page 1396*

▸ *See **Angels**, page 1397.*

Anger *see also Bitterness*

Anger is something that all of us fall into at times. But the Bible warns us of the dangers of human anger. Since we never know the whole picture and always see things from our own perspective, our anger tends to be self-serving and is often directed at those who don't deserve it. Only God's anger can be truly righteous, which is why he encourages us to deal with our anger quickly.

> *Stop being angry! Turn from your rage! Do not lose your temper—it only leads to harm. – Psalm 37:8, page 624*

Anger can lead to jealousy, rivalry, and even murder Genesis 4:3-8, *page 8* • 1 Samuel 18:5-9, *page 326*

Gentle words can deal with people's anger 1 Kings 12:1-7, *page 392* • Proverbs 15:1-4, 18, *page 711* • Proverbs 25:15, *page 722*

Anger can lead us to do foolish things Psalm 37:8, *page 624* • Proverbs 14:17, *page 711*

If we get angry, we should exercise self-control Proverbs 16:32, *page 713* • Proverbs 29:11, *page 727* • Ephesians 4:26, *page 1351*

It is wise to avoid angry people Proverbs 22:24-25, *page 719*

People can get angry because of God's grace to others Jonah 4:1-11, *page 1009*

Anger is like murdering someone Matthew 5:21-22, *page 1075* • 1 John 3:14-15, *page 1436*

Jesus showed righteous anger at greed and ungodliness John 2:13-17, *page 1202*

Anger belongs to our old way of life, and it needs to go Galatians 5:19-25, *page 1343* • Colossians 3:8-10, *page 1365*

Anger can give Satan a foothold in our lives Ephesians 4:25-27, *page 1351*

Our anger can never bring about God's righteous purpose James 1:19-21, *page 1412*

We are called to control our tongues James 3:1-12, *page 1415*

▸ *See **Cain and Abel**, page 8.*

Anxiety *see Worry*

Appearance

In a culture where there is so much emphasis on our appearance, it is important to remember that God is far more interested in what we are like on the inside than in how we look on the outside. He looks beyond our outward appearance to our hearts and wants us to be more concerned with our inner spiritual well-being than with our outward physical appearance.

> *"The LORD doesn't see things the way you see them. People judge by outward appearance, but the LORD looks at the heart." – 1 Samuel 16:7, page 323*

BASIC TRUTHS • *page 1484*

God looks at our hearts, not our appearance 1 Samuel 16:1-7, *page 323*

We should remember that physical beauty doesn't last forever Proverbs 31:30-31, *page 729*

Jesus does not want us to worry about things like clothes Matthew 6:25-34, *page 1078*

Appearances can be deceiving Matthew 7:15-20, *page 1078* • Matthew 23:27-28, *page 1106*

We should care more about our hearts than about our appearance 1 Timothy 2:9-10, *page 1380*

We shouldn't judge others by their appearance James 2:2-4, *page 1413*

Inner beauty is more important than physical beauty 1 Peter 3:1-6, *page 1423*

▶ *See **Keeping up appearances**, page 494.*

Approval

While all of us like to be accepted by our friends and colleagues, we should not seek acceptance at any price. Ultimately as Christians, we are called to seek approval from God rather than from other people.

For we speak as messengers approved by God to be entrusted with the Good News. Our purpose is to please God, not people. He alone examines the motives of our hearts. Never once did we try to win you with flattery, as you well know. And God is our witness that we were not pretending to be your friends just to get your money! As for human praise, we have never sought it from you or anyone else. – 1 Thessalonians 2:4-6, page 1370

People often want our approval only while it suits them Job 29:21–30:1, *page 588*

The Father gave his Son unconditional approval Matthew 3:17, *page 1072*

We must sometimes lose human approval in order to gain God's approval Matthew 14:1-12, *page 1091* • John 9:13-38, *page 1214* • Acts 7:51-60, *page 1246*

Our ultimate aim in life should be to win God's approval at the end Matthew 25:14-30, *page 1109* • 2 Corinthians 5:9-10, *page 1327* • 2 Corinthians 10:13-18, *page 1332* • 2 Timothy 2:15, *page 1386*

Jesus did not seek human approval John 5:41-44, *page 1207*

We have God's approval because of our faith in Jesus Romans 3:21-28, *page 1286* • Romans 5:1-5, *page 1287*

God's approval of us and the way we live and serve is what matters, not what others may think of us Romans 14:1-4, *page 1298* • Galatians 1:8-10, *page 1337*

Arguments *see Disagreement*

Armor *see Spiritual warfare*

Ashamed, Being *see Embarrassment*

Assurance

God wants us to be sure about our relationship with him and the fact that we have really become his children. That relationship rests on the facts of Jesus' life, death, and resurrection, not on anything we have done or not done, or on our feelings as to whether we have had a good day or a bad day. If we have truly come to Jesus, he welcomes us and keeps us. His Holy Spirit within us affirms that we belong to him and that nothing can now separate us from him.

"My sheep listen to my voice; I know them, and they follow me. I give them eternal life, and they will never perish. No one can snatch them away from me, for my Father has given them to me, and he is more powerful than anyone else. No one can snatch them from the Father's hand." – John 10:27-29, page 1216

God promises to always be with his people Joshua 1:5-9, *page 242* • Isaiah 41:8-14, *page 792* • Hebrews 13:5-6, *page 1409*

We can be sure we have eternal life through Jesus John 3:16, *page 1203* • John 5:24-26, *page 1207* • John 20:30-31, *page 1232* • 1 John 5:13, *page 1438*

Jesus will never reject anyone who comes to him John 6:37-40, *page 1209* • John 17:1-3, *page 1225*

We can be sure God will keep us to the end John 10:27-30, *page 1216* • Philippians 1:6, *page 1355* • 2 Timothy 1:12, *page 1385*

We can be sure we are God's friends because Jesus died for us Romans 5:6-11, *page 1287* • Colossians 1:21-22, *page 1363*

God's Holy Spirit within us is the assurance we have become God's children Romans 8:15-16, *page 1291* • Ephesians 1:11-14, *page 1346*

Nothing can ever separate us from God's love Romans 8:35-39, *page 1292*

Our salvation was guaranteed before creation Ephesians 1:4-5, *page 1346*

We are assured that we can always boldly enter God's presence Hebrews 4:14-16, *page 1400* • Hebrews 10:19-25, *page 1406*

We can be assured that we are completely forgiven through Jesus Hebrews 9:11-15, *page 1404* • 1 John 1:7-9, *page 1433*

We have the certainty of knowing that we are already God's children 1 John 3:1-3, *page 1435*

▶ *See* ***Confidence****, page 1399;* ***How can I be sure God has forgiven me?****, page 1433.*

Astrology *see Occult*

Atonement *see Jesus Christ: his death*

Attitudes

Our attitudes are important to God, for they reveal what is going on in our hearts. As Christians we are called to imitate the attitudes of Jesus in everything. Part of the work of the Holy Spirit is to expose our bad attitudes and to develop Christlike attitudes in us so that when people encounter us they encounter something of Jesus.

> *You must have the same attitude that Christ Jesus had. Though he was God, he did not think of equality with God as something to cling to. Instead, he gave up his divine privileges; he took the humble position of a slave and was born as a human being. When he appeared in human form, he humbled himself in obedience to God and died a criminal's death on a cross. – Philippians 2:5-8, page 1356*

Bad attitudes affect our relationship with God, not just other people, so they need to be dealt with quickly Genesis 4:6-7, *page 8* • Matthew 5:23-24, *page 1076*

Bad attitudes can lead to poor decisions Numbers 14:1-4, *page 169*

Good attitudes lead to God's blessing Numbers 14:24, *page 171* • Matthew 5:2-12, *page 1074*

Our attitudes should arise from a decision to trust God in everything Proverbs 3:5-6, *page 699*

We can choose our attitudes even when everything has gone wrong or people are against us Habakkuk 3:17-18, *page 1027* • Luke 23:32-34, *page 1194* • Acts 7:54-60, *page 1246* • Acts 16:22-34, *page 1262*

Bad attitudes incur God's judgment Matthew 5:21-22, *page 1075*

Good attitudes please both God and others Luke 2:51-52, *page 1156* • Romans 14:17-18, *page 1298*

The Holy Spirit wants to help develop good attitudes within us Galatians 5:22-26, *page 1343*

Being a Christian involves developing Christlike attitudes Ephesians 4:21-32, *page 1351* • 1 Peter 4:1, *page 1424*

Our attitudes should be characterized by humility and forgiveness, not retaliation Philippians 2:5-15, *page 1356* • 1 Peter 2:21-25, *page 1423* • 1 Peter 3:8-12, *page 1423*

▶ *See* ***Cain and Abel****, page 8;* ***Conscience****, page 333;* ***Pride****, page 559;* ***Hardness of heart****, page 1132;* ***Prejudice****, page 1252.*

Authority *see also Government; Respect*

Authority can be a mixed blessing. Used wisely and received well, it can bring much blessing; but used badly, it can cause much harm. The Bible says that all authority ultimately comes from God and that he delegates it to people called to serve him in both society and church. Those entrusted with authority are called to use it wisely and responsibly—serving others, not themselves—and those under authority are called to receive it as coming from God himself and to trust him through submitting to it.

> *Everyone must submit to governing authorities. For all authority comes from God, and those in positions of authority have been placed there by God. So anyone who rebels against authority is rebelling against what God has instituted, and they will be punished. For the authorities do not strike fear in people who are doing right, but in those who are doing wrong. Would you like to live without fear of the authorities? Do what is right, and they will honor you. The authorities are God's servants, sent for your good. But if you are doing wrong, of course you should be afraid, for they have the power to punish you. They are God's servants, sent for the very purpose of punishing those who do what is wrong. So you must submit to them, not only to avoid punishment, but also to keep a clear conscience. – Romans 13:1-5, page 1297*

Moses delegated his God-given authority to others Deuteronomy 1:9-18, *page 201*

The coming Messiah would have God's authority Psalm 2:1-12, *page 602* • Psalm 110:1-7, *page 673* • Isaiah 9:6-7, *page 758* • Isaiah 11:1-9, *page 760*

People recognized the authority of Jesus Matthew 7:28-29, *page 1079* • Matthew 9:1-8, *page 1081*

Jesus marveled at the Roman officer who understood that to exercise authority we need to be under authority Matthew 8:8-13, *page 1080*

Jesus gave authority to the apostles Matthew 10:1-20, *page 1083* • Matthew 28:18-20, *page 1116*

All authority is given to Jesus Matthew 28:18-20, *page 1116* • John 5:26-27, *page 1207*

There is a time to stand up for our rights when authority is being abused Acts 16:35-39, *page 1263* • Acts 25:1-12, *page 1274*

Church leaders have authority in the church Acts 20:28, *page 1269* • Hebrews 13:17, *page 1410* • 1 Peter 5:1-6, *page 1425*

Christians should recognize the government's authority and submit to it Romans 13:1-7, *page 1297* • Titus 3:1, *page 1391* • 1 Peter 2:13-17, *page 1422*

There is a proper godly order and authority within relationships 1 Corinthians 11:2-12, *page 1314* • Ephesians 5:21–6:4, *page 1351*

The church should submit to Jesus' authority, for he is its head Ephesians 1:19-23, *page 1346* • Ephesians 5:23-24, *page 1351* • Colossians 1:18, *page 1363*

We are called to pray for those in authority 1 Timothy 2:1-2, *page 1380*

The Bible has God's authority 2 Timothy 3:16-17, *page 1387*

▶ *See* ***Authority****, page 1187.*

Backsliding *see also Perseverance*

Backsliding means turning away or drifting away from God. It is often characterized by a gradual cooling in our relationship with him, a decreasing desire to engage in spiritual activities (things like reading our Bible or going to church), and an explaining away of behavior that we would once have seen as wrong. If we see we are starting to backslide, we need to take action quickly, dealing with whatever has gotten in the way and renewing our commitment to Jesus. Putting it off will only make things worse.

> *Be careful then, dear brothers and sisters. Make sure that your own hearts are not evil and unbelieving, turning you away from the living God. You must warn each other every day, while it is still "today," so that none of you will be deceived by sin and hardened against God. For if we are faithful to the end, trusting God just as firmly as when we first believed, we will share in all that belongs to Christ. Remember what it says: "Today when you hear his voice, don't harden your hearts as Israel did when they rebelled." – Hebrews 3:12-15, page 1398*

Pride and self-reliance can lead to backsliding Deuteronomy 8:10-18, *page 211* • Nehemiah 9:16-18, *page 546* • Hosea 13:4-6, *page 984* • 1 Corinthians 5:1-8, *page 1308*

The way out of backsliding is to return to God Jeremiah 3:22, *page 826* • Revelation 3:14-22, *page 1450*

Backsliding can result from not listening to God Jeremiah 7:24-28, *page 833* • Hebrews 2:1-3, *page 1397*

We should remember the challenge that it is those who endure to the end who will be saved Matthew 10:21-22, *page 1083* • Matthew 24:9-13, *page 1107*

The worries of life can choke our newfound faith unless we deal with them Mark 4:18-19, *page 1125* • 1 Timothy 6:6-10, *page 1383*

Being a disciple means following Jesus every day Luke 9:23-27, *page 1169*

We can drift away when other things become more important to us than Jesus Luke 9:57-62, *page 1171*

Backsliding puts us on dangerous ground that we need to get off quickly Hebrews 6:4-12, *page 1400*

We need to patiently endure, not just give in Hebrews 10:35-39, *page 1406* • Hebrews 12:1-3, *page 1408* • James 1:2-4, *page 1412*

Backsliding is any expression of our not loving or serving Jesus as we used to do Revelation 2:4-5, *page 1447* • Revelation 3:1-4, *page 1449*

No matter how faithless we have been, God will always welcome us back Revelation 3:19-20, *page 1450*

▶ *See **Backsliding**, page 841; **Pressing on**, page 1359; **Perseverance in prayer**, page 1184; **Can a Christian lose their salvation?**, page 1401; **The dangers of drifting**, page 1447.*

Bad things: Why do they happen in life? *see also Suffering*

When we go through difficult times, it is natural to ask why they are happening to us. The Bible shows that much of the suffering we experience has its roots in the Fall, when sin entered the world. Sin not only leads people to do bad, foolish, and selfish things, often resulting directly in much suffering, but has also even affected creation itself, resulting in suffering that is beyond human control. But when things do go wrong, we are encouraged to continue to trust God and remember that he can use even bad things for our good.

> *Can anything ever separate us from Christ's love? Does it mean he no longer loves us if we have trouble or calamity, or are persecuted, or hungry, or destitute, or in danger, or threatened with death? (As the Scriptures say, "For your sake we are killed every day; we are being slaughtered like sheep.") No, despite all these things, overwhelming victory is ours through Christ, who loved us. – Romans 8:35-37, page 1292*

Some hardships and suffering are simply the result of living in a fallen world Genesis 3:18-19, *page 7* • Luke 13:1-5, *page 1177* • John 9:1-3, *page 1213*

God can make bad things turn out for our good Genesis 50:19-21, *page 63* • Romans 8:28-39, *page 1292* • Hebrews 12:5-13, *page 1408* • James 1:2-4, *page 1412*

Some hardships and suffering are the direct result of Satan's activity Job 1:1–2:13, *page 565* • 2 Corinthians 12:6-7, *page 1334*

It is natural to ask "why?" when we are going through difficulties or when bad things happen Psalm 22:1-31, *page 614* • Psalm 42:4-11, *page 627* • Psalm 73:1-28, *page 646* • Jeremiah 12:1-4, *page 839*

We can always trust God even when things go wrong Proverbs 3:5-6, *page 699* • Habakkuk 3:17-19, *page 1027* • Philippians 4:4-9, *page 1359*

We can face difficulties boldly when we know that God is with us Daniel 3:1-30, *page 958* • Daniel 6:1-28, *page 963* • Acts 4:1-31, *page 1240*

Jesus experienced bad things happening to him Matthew 2:13-18, *page 1070* • Luke 4:28-30, *page 1159* • John 10:19-20, *page 1216* • John 19:1-30, *page 1228*

Jesus calls us to embrace suffering when it comes and rejoice in it Matthew 5:10-12, *page 1075* • Matthew 16:24-26, *page 1096*

Jesus embraced suffering, confident that God's glory would be revealed through it Luke 24:25-27, *page 1195* • Hebrews 12:1-4, *page 1408*

Any bad things we experience now are nothing compared to the wonderful things we will experience in the life to come Romans 8:18-25, *page 1291* • 2 Corinthians 4:16-18, *page 1327* • 1 Peter 4:12-19, *page 1425*

Christians should sometimes expect hardships and suffering because of their faith 2 Corinthians 1:3-11, *page 1324* • Philippians 1:27-30, *page 1356* • 2 Timothy 1:6-12, *page 1384*

There will be no more sin, suffering, or bad things in God's new creation Revelation 21:1-7, *page 1465*

▶ *See **Trusting God when we cannot see the way ahead**, page 57; **God intended it all for good**, page 62; **Suffering: Why do bad things happen to good people?**, page 567; **Why do bad things happen in life?**, page 1025; **Tragic events**, page 1178.*

Baptism

From the beginning of the church's existence, baptism was the way someone expressed their newfound faith in Jesus. Although adopted from Judaism, it was given new significance, no longer simply symbolizing cleansing but also speaking of the person's identification with Jesus' death and resurrection. Jesus commanded his disciples to baptize all who believed in him. Baptism serves as a sign of repentance, faith, and the desire to start life again.

> *Jesus came and told his disciples, "I have been given all authority in heaven and on earth. Therefore, go and make disciples of all the nations, baptizing them in the name of the Father and the Son and the Holy Spirit. Teach these new disciples to obey all the commands I have given you. And be sure of this: I am with you always, even to the end of the age." – Matthew 28:18-20, page 1116*

Jesus himself was baptized Matthew 3:13-17, *page 1072* • Mark 1:9-11, *page 1119* • Luke 3:21-22, *page 1157*

Jesus commanded that all his followers should be baptized Matthew 28:18-20, *page 1116*

Baptism signifies repentance of our sins and the start of a changed way of life Acts 2:37-41, *page 1239* • Acts 9:1-22, *page 1248*

The early church expected all new Christians to be baptized Acts 8:26-39, *page 1248* • Acts 9:18, *page 1249* • Acts 10:47-48, *page 1252* • Acts 16:13-15, *page 1262* • Acts 16:29-34, *page 1263* • Acts 19:1-7, *page 1266*

Baptism symbolizes our sins being washed away Acts 22:6-16, *page 1271* • Titus 3:3-7, *page 1391*

Baptism unites us with Jesus Romans 6:1-3, 5, *page 1289*

Baptism symbolizes death to our old life and resurrection to a new life with Jesus Romans 6:1-14, *page 1289* • Colossians 2:11-13, *page 1364*

Baptism unites all Christians, no matter our background 1 Corinthians 12:12-13, *page 1315*

▶ *See **Baptism**, page 1238.*

Battle *see Spiritual warfare*

Beauty *see Appearance*

Belief *see Faith*

Bereavement *see also Death; Grief*

Bereavement is something that all of us will have to face at some point in life. The Bible recognizes that the death of a loved one is something profoundly sad, but it also reminds us of God's comforting presence and support at such times. It also reassures us that those who have trusted in Jesus are now in a much better place, safe with him in heaven.

> *And now, dear brothers and sisters, we want you to know what will happen to the believers who have died so you will not grieve like people who have no hope. For since we believe that Jesus died*

and was raised to life again, we also believe that when Jesus returns, God will bring back with him the believers who have died. . . . First, the believers who have died will rise from their graves. Then, together with them, we who are still alive and remain on the earth will be caught up in the clouds to meet the Lord in the air. Then we will be with the Lord forever. So encourage each other with these words. – 1 Thessalonians 4:13-14, 16-18, page 1372

Sadness and weeping at times of grief are natural Genesis 23:1-2, *page 27* • 2 Samuel 1:23-27, *page 343* • 2 Samuel 18:29-33, *page 363* • Acts 9:36-39, *page 1250*

God's presence can be known even in the darkest valley Psalm 23:1-6, *page 615*

God promises his comfort and strength in times of loss or trouble Isaiah 61:1-3, *page 814* • 2 Corinthians 1:3-7, *page 1324*

Jesus promises a blessing on those who mourn Matthew 6:4, *page 1076*

Those who have believed in Jesus are assured of eternal life John 3:16, *page 1203* • John 11:25-26, *page 1217* • 1 John 5:11-13, *page 1438*

Even Jesus wept at the death of his friend Lazarus John 11:31-36, *page 1218*

Not even death can separate us from God's love Romans 8:38-39, *page 1292*

Jesus' resurrection is the assurance that we, too, will one day be raised to new life 1 Corinthians 15:1-58, *page 1319*

Although Christians grieve, it is not the grief of those who have no hope 1 Thessalonians 4:13, *page 1372*

We are called to care for those who have been bereaved 1 Timothy 5:3-4, *page 1382* • James 1:27, *page 1413*

▶ *See **Mourning**, page 892; **Hope**, page 895.*

Bible

"The Bible" (from a Greek word meaning "books") refers to the collection of the books of the Old and New Testaments, the sacred text of Christianity. Though written by human authors, the Bible is the inspired and authoritative word of God, for God's Spirit moved in such a way that what the authors wrote was exactly what God wanted written. The Bible reveals God's heart, plan, and purposes, which is why we need to read it regularly and build our lives upon its teaching.

All Scripture is inspired by God and is useful to teach us what is true and to make us realize what is wrong in our lives. It corrects us when we are wrong and teaches us to do what is right. God uses it to prepare and equip his people to do every good work. – 2 Timothy 3:16-17, page 1387

Studying God's word is a key to our spiritual growth Ezra 7:10, *page 529* • Acts 17:11, *page 1264* • 2 Timothy 3:14-17, *page 1387*

We sometimes need God's word to be read and explained Nehemiah 8:1-8, *page 544* • Acts 8:26-35, *page 1248*

God's word is something we can delight in Psalm 1:2-3, *page 602* • Psalm 119:1-24, *page 677*

God's word is good and does us good Psalm 19:7-14, *page 613*

God's word will last for eternity Psalm 119: 89-96, *page 680* • Matthew 5:18-19, *page 1075*

God's word can be trusted Psalm 119:138-140, *page 681* • Proverbs 30:5-6, *page 727*

We need to respond to Scripture and not just read it Matthew 7:24-29, *page 1079* • John 5:39-40, *page 1207* • Revelation 22:7, *page 1467*

Jesus himself had a high view of Scripture's authority and power Matthew 22:29, *page 1104* • John 10:34-36, *page 1216*

The Holy Spirit helps us understand God's word John 14:26, *page 1223* • John 16:13-15, *page 1225* • 1 Corinthians 2:12-16, *page 1305*

God's word is a Christian's spiritual weapon Ephesians 6:17, *page 1353*

God's word is to be taught and preached 2 Timothy 2:2, 15, *page 1385* • 2 Timothy 4:1-4, *page 1387*

We are warned against adding to or removing from Scripture Revelation 22:17-19, *page 1467*

▶ *See **What is the Bible?**, page A15; see also **Bible teaching**, page 529; **The Scriptures in public worship**, page 544; **Teaching God's word**, page 1268.*

Birth *see also Abortion*

The arrival of a new baby is always an exciting time. The Bible sees every new life as precious and full of potential and calls us to rejoice in the gift of it. But human birth in itself is not all that matters; God also calls us to experience new birth through the power of his Holy Spirit so that when this life ends, we might live with him forever.

> *You made all the delicate, inner parts of my body and knit me together in my mother's womb. Thank you for making me so wonderfully complex! Your workmanship is marvelous—how well I know it. You watched me as I was being formed in utter seclusion, as I was woven together in the dark of the womb. You saw me before I was born. Every day of my life was recorded in your book. Every moment was laid out before a single day had passed. – Psalm 139:13-16, page 689*

God alone is the giver of life Genesis 2:7, *page 5* • Isaiah 42:5, *page 793*

God planned the time of our birth Genesis 21:1-2, *page 24* • Ecclesiastes 3:1-2, *page 732* • Galatians 4:4, *page 1341*

A birth should be a time of rejoicing Genesis 21:1-7, *page 24* • Ruth 4:13-17, *page 303* • Isaiah 54:1, *page 807* • Luke 1:11-14, *page 1151* • Luke 2:8-20, *page 1154*

Sin is something we are born with, not just something we acquire Psalm 51:5, *page 633* • Psalm 58:3, *page 636*

Children are a blessing from God Psalm 127:3-5, *page 684*

God plans our life before we are born Psalm 139:13-16, *page 689* • Isaiah 49:1, *page 801* • Jeremiah 1:5, *page 822*

Although conceived supernaturally, Jesus was born in the normal way Matthew 1:22-25, *page 1069* • Luke 2:1-7, *page 1154*

We need to experience a spiritual rebirth to enter God's Kingdom John 1:12-13, *page 1199* • John 3:3-7, *page 1202*

Jesus identified himself with us in becoming human Galatians 4:4, *page 1341* • Philippians 2:5-8, *page 1356*

Whatever our nationality or status by human birth, we can all equally become God's children Ephesians 2:11-13, *page 1347*

▶ *See **Childlessness**, page 25; **Abortion**, page 823; **Children**, page 1100; **The new birth**, page 1203.*

Bitterness *see also Anger*

Bitterness is a feeling of anger and resentment against others. While it may sometimes be understandable, perhaps because of some troubling life events, it is often irrational, perhaps arising from resentment at the success of others. But whatever its cause, the Bible shows that bitterness is always destructive, not least for the one who experiences it. Bitterness always harms us more than the person we feel bitter about, so the Bible encourages us to seek God when we are tempted to feel bitter and to put our trust in him and his ability to resolve things. It also encourages us to be kind and forgiving to those who have wronged us.

> *Watch out that no poisonous root of bitterness grows up to trouble you, corrupting many. – Hebrews 12:15, page 1409*

Bitterness and resentment need to be dealt with quickly or they grow into something worse Genesis 4:3-8, *page 8* • Genesis 27:1-41, *page 32* • 2 Samuel 13:1-39, *page 355* • Hebrews 12:14-15, *page 1409*

Bitterness can arise as a result of disappointment Genesis 27:30-38, *page 33* • Ruth 1:1-22, *page 299* • 1 Samuel 1:1-11, *page 305*

Bitterness can be overcome through a choice to forgive and be kind Genesis 33:1-11, *page 41* • Ephesians 4:31-32, *page 1351*

Bitterness can arise as a result of life's difficulties Ruth 1:20-21, *page 299* • 1 Samuel 1:10-11, *page 305* • Job 10:1, *page 572*

Rather than become bitter we should trust in God's faithfulness and mercy Psalm 142:1-7, *page 691* • Lamentations 3:1-26, *page 894*

All of us face situations where we could get bitter, but we all have a choice to become bitter or better Proverbs 14:10, *page 710*

Bitterness can come from sin and lead to sin Acts 8:23, *page 1248* • Romans 3:10-18, *page 1285*

Bitterness undermines God's call to be reconciled with others 2 Corinthians 5:17-21, *page 1328*

Since bitterness doesn't just affect us but spreads to others, we should be on our guard against it Hebrews 12:14-17, *page 1409*

Bitterness is unspiritual and demonic James 3:13-18, *page 1415*

▶ *See **Cain and Abel**, page 8; **Jacob and Esau**, page 40.*

Blasphemy

Blasphemy is the use of any speech or action that abuses or dishonors the name of God or Jesus, including using their names as swear words or curses. Claiming to be God is also seen as blasphemy in the Bible.

> *"You must not misuse the name of the LORD your God. The LORD will not let you go unpunished if you misuse his name." – Exodus 20:7, page 90*

Blasphemy was taken so seriously in the Old Testament that its penalty was death Leviticus 24:10-16, *page 146*

Blasphemy is anything that insults or dishonors God, his name, or his word 2 Kings 19:6, *page 436* • Psalm 74:18, *page 648* • Isaiah 52:4-5, *page 805* • Acts 6:11, *page 1244* • Romans 2:21-24, *page 1285*

The Jewish leaders saw Jesus' claims as blasphemy Matthew 9:1-8, *page 1081* • Matthew 26:62-66, *page 1112*

Jesus saw rejection of the Holy Spirit's work as unforgivable blasphemy Matthew 12:24-32, *page 1087* • Mark 3:20-30, *page 1124*

Paul was ashamed that, as a non-Christian, he had gotten people to curse Jesus Acts 26:9-11, *page 1276*

Blasphemy is the hallmark of those who oppose God 2 Thessalonians 2:1-4, *page 1374* • Revelation 13:1-6, *page 1458*

The New Testament sees blasphemy against God as a serious matter that leads to judgment 1 Timothy 1:20, *page 1379*

Blessing

Blessing is seen as something very powerful in the Bible. It can be expressed as a prayer, a declaration, or a gift reflecting the kindness of the one who gives it. God himself loves to bless people so that we can enjoy life to the full, and he calls on us to bless others too. The New Testament sees Jesus as God's ultimate blessing.

> *All praise to God, the Father of our Lord Jesus Christ, who has blessed us with every spiritual blessing in the heavenly realms because we are united with Christ. – Ephesians 1:3, page 1346*

God created people to know his blessing Genesis 1:28, *page 5*

God chose to bring his blessing upon humanity through Abraham and his descendants Genesis 12:1-3, *page 15* • Genesis 22:15-18, *page 26* • Acts 3:25, *page 1240* • Galatians 3:6-9, *page 1340*

God calls his people to bless others Numbers 6:23-27, *page 161* • Luke 6:27-36, *page 1163*

The Bible warns us not to let times of blessing make us forget God Deuteronomy 6:10-12, *page 209*

God blesses those who obey him and his word Deuteronomy 11:26-28, *page 214* • Deuteronomy 28:1-14, *page 229* • Joshua 1:6-9, *page 242* • James 1:22-25, *page 1412*

Those who bless others will themselves be blessed Proverbs 11:24-25, *page 708* • 2 Corinthians 9:6-11, *page 1331*

God blesses us when we put him first Matthew 6:33, *page 1078*

We should bless those who curse us Luke 6:28, *page 1163* • Romans 12:14-18, *page 1296* • 1 Peter 3:8-12, *page 1423*

We obtain more blessing from giving than receiving Acts 20:35, *page 1269*

Christians share in the blessing God gave to Abraham Galatians 3:8-9, *page 1340*

There is blessing for being faithful in challenging times 1 Peter 4:12-19, *page 1425*

▶ *See* ***The power of blessing***, *page 160.*

Blood

For Israel, blood represented life, and under the old covenant, animals were sacrificed so their blood could make atonement for sin. However, all the blood of the Old Testament sacrifices could never really deal with sin. Rather, these sacrifices served simply as a shadow pointing people to Jesus, the perfect sacrifice who would come and shed his blood as the price for all sin.

For without the shedding of blood, there is no forgiveness. – Hebrews 9:22, page 1405

God hates the shedding of an innocent person's blood Genesis 4:10-11, *page 8*

The Old Testament forbade people from consuming blood in food or drink Genesis 9:1-4, *page 12* • Leviticus 3:17, *page 120* • Leviticus 17:10-11, *page 137* • Deuteronomy 12:15-16, *page 215*

The blood of animals was used to seal a covenant in the Old Testament Genesis 15:1-20, *page 18* • Exodus 24:5-8, *page 94* • Jeremiah 34:17-18, *page 866*

The blood of animals played a key part in Old Testament sacrifices Leviticus 1:1-5, *page 117* • Leviticus 16:1-22, *page 135*

Jesus' blood shed on the cross confirms God's new covenant with people Matthew 26:28, *page 1111* • Hebrews 13:20-21, *page 1410*

Only Jesus' shed blood was a sufficient sacrifice for our sins Romans 3:23-26, *page 1286* • Hebrews 9:11-15, *page 1404* • Hebrews 10:1-10, *page 1405*

The shedding of Jesus' blood is remembered in the Lord's Supper 1 Corinthians 11:23-26, *page 1315*

We are redeemed by Jesus' blood Ephesians 1:5-7, *page 1346* • 1 Peter 1:18-20, *page 1421* • Revelation 5:9-10, *page 1451*

▶ *See* ***The importance of blood***, *page 136;* ***The death of Jesus***, *page 1114.*

Boasting *see Pride*

Body of Christ

"The body of Christ" is a term used both of Jesus Christ's physical body, offered on the cross for our salvation, and as an image of the church—the tangible expression of Jesus now on earth. Jesus is the head of that body, and Christians are its "parts," called to serve one another.

The human body has many parts, but the many parts make up one whole body. So it is with the body of Christ. Some of us are Jews, some are Gentiles, some are slaves, and some are free. But we have all been baptized into one body by one Spirit, and we all share the same Spirit. Yes, the body has many different parts, not just one part. – 1 Corinthians 12:12-14, page 1315

Jesus had a real human body, just like ours John 1:14, *page 1199* • John 19:31-37, *page 1230* • John 20:26-27, *page 1232*

The bread and wine shared at Communion are reminders of Christ's body broken and blood shed for our salvation 1 Corinthians 11:23-29, *page 1315*

Jesus carried our sins in his body to the cross 1 Peter 2:24, *page 1423*

The body of Christ, the church, has been given many gifts Romans 12:4-8, *page 1296* • 1 Corinthians 12:12-31, *page 1315* • 1 Peter 4:10-11, *page 1424*

There are many different parts in Christ's body, but there is still only one body 1 Corinthians 12:12-31, *page 1315*

Jesus is the head of the body Ephesians 1:21-23, *page 1347* • Ephesians 4:14-16, *page 1350* • Colossians 1:18, *page 1363* • Colossians 2:18-19, *page 1364*

Christians of different ethnic groups form one body Ephesians 2:11-18, *page 1347* • Ephesians 3:6, *page 1348*

We need to preserve unity in the body of Christ Ephesians 4:3, *page 1350*

Leaders in the body of Christ help the whole body to grow Ephesians 4:11-12, *page 1350*

▸ See **The church**, *page 1348*.

Boldness *see Confidence*

Born again *see Birth*

Bravery *see Courage*

Bribery

Bribery—the paying of money or giving of a gift to get a favorable decision or some other benefit—is something that God detests, for it is an abuse of justice and corrupts the heart of both the giver and the recipient. Offering or accepting a bribe is therefore always forbidden in the Bible.

> *"Take no bribes, for a bribe makes you ignore something that you clearly see. A bribe makes even a righteous person twist the truth." – Exodus 23:8, page 93*

God himself cannot be bribed Deuteronomy 10:17-20, *page 213*

We should not pervert the course of justice by accepting bribes Deuteronomy 16:19-20, *page 220* • Proverbs 17:23, *page 714*

Integrity is the antidote to bribery 1 Samuel 12:1-5, *page 317*

God hates bribery 2 Chronicles 19:5-7, *page 500* • Amos 5:10-15, *page 997*

Bribery should be avoided because it brings corruption and destruction upon both individuals and society Proverbs 29:4, *page 726* • Ecclesiastes 7:7, *page 735*

God will judge those who engage in bribery Isaiah 1:23-28, *page 749* • Micah 3:9-12, *page 1013*

▸ See **Bribery**, *page 736*.

Bullying *see Intimidation*

Business *see also Work*

God expects his people to work well and honestly. Honest business dealings draw God's blessing, but deceitful practices ultimately lead to judgment. The Bible warns against undue confidence in our own abilities and skills and invites us to bring God into all our work, whatever it may be.

> *She goes to inspect a field and buys it; with her earnings she plants a vineyard. She is energetic and strong, a hard worker. She makes sure her dealings are profitable; her lamp burns late into the night. – Proverbs 31:16-18, page 729*

God gives us the ability to work Genesis 2:15, *page 5* • Exodus 35:30-35, *page 108*

While work became harder after the Fall, work itself was not cursed and so is still a blessing Genesis 3:17-19, *page 7*

Everyone needs to take a rest day from their business or work Exodus 20:8-11, *page 90* • Exodus 31:12-17, *page 103* • Leviticus 23:3, *page 143* • Jeremiah 17:19-27, *page 845*

God wants us to be honest in our business deals Leviticus 19:35-36, *page 140* • Proverbs 11:1, *page 707* • Amos 8:4-7, *page 1000*

Success in business can lead to forgetting God Deuteronomy 8:10-18, *page 211*

There is wisdom in being busy and not lazy Proverbs 6:6-11, *page 701*

No matter how successful we are in business, we cannot take our money with us when we die Ecclesiastes 5:12-15, *page 734* • Luke 12:13-21, *page 1175* • 1 Timothy 6:6-10, *page 1383*

The blessings of successful business can be used for the church Acts 16:13-15, *page 1262*

BASIC TRUTHS • *page 1494*

Christian faith will sometimes disrupt traditional business practices Acts 19:23-41, *page 1267*

We should all work as though Jesus were our boss Ephesians 6:5-9, *page 1352*

A warning against overconfidence in business James 4:13-16, *page 1416*

▶ *See **Serving God in our work**, page 956; **Working for the glory of God**, page 1265; **Work**, page 1376.*

Caring *see also Kindness; Love*

Just as God cares for us, so his people are called to care for others. His love and compassion toward us should be reflected in the way we treat others. An uncaring Christianity is not real Christianity.

> *"Give justice to the poor and the orphan; uphold the rights of the oppressed and the destitute. Rescue the poor and helpless; deliver them from the grasp of evil people." – Psalm 82:3-4, page 655*

God cares for the underprivileged Exodus 22:21-24, *page 93* • Deuteronomy 10:17-19, *page 213* • 1 Samuel 2:8, *page 307* • Psalm 68:5-6, *page 642*

God cares for his people Deuteronomy 7:9, *page 210* • Psalm 23:1-6, *page 615* • Psalm 95:6-7, *page 663* • Psalm 121:1-8, *page 683* • 1 Peter 5:7, *page 1425*

We should care for those in need Deuteronomy 24:17-22, *page 227* • Isaiah 1:17, *page 749* • Luke 14:12-14, *page 1179* • Galatians 2:9-10, *page 1338* • James 2:14-17, *page 1413*

Those who do not care for others are rebuked Ezekiel 34:1-24, *page 935* • Matthew 25:31-46, *page 1109*

Jesus said that we should love and care for even those who are our enemies Luke 6:27, *page 1163*

Jesus calls us to care for those who are different from us Luke 10:25-37, *page 1172*

God's care should be reflected in our care for others John 13:34-35, *page 1222* • John 15:12, *page 1224*

We should follow the example of those who care for others Philippians 2:20-21, *page 1357*

Leaders should set the example in caring 1 Thessalonians 2:7-11, *page 1370* • 1 Peter 5:1-3, *page 1425*

We should care especially for the elderly and widowed 1 Timothy 5:3-4, *page 1382* • James 1:27, *page 1413*

▶ *See **Love your neighbor as yourself**, page 139; **The compassionate God**, page 666; **Loving others**, page 1220.*

Character

Through the Holy Spirit, God wants to shape our character—that which expresses who we truly are—and to make that character more and more like Jesus' character so we can reflect him in our daily lives. Even the hard things in life are used by God to bring this about.

> *We can rejoice, too, when we run into problems and trials, for we know that they help us develop endurance. And endurance develops strength of character, and character strengthens our confident hope of salvation. And this hope will not lead to disappointment. For we know how dearly God loves us, because he has given us the Holy Spirit to fill our hearts with his love. – Romans 5:3-5, page 1287*

Challenges in life develop our character Genesis 39:1-23, *page 49* • Romans 5:3-5, *page 1287* • 2 Corinthians 4:8-18, *page 1327* • 1 Peter 1:6-7, *page 1420*

An example of a woman of noble character Proverbs 31:10-31, *page 729*

The character of the truly godly person Micah 6:8, *page 1016*

Jesus summed up in the Sermon on the Mount the sort of character he wants us to have Matthew 5:1–7:29, *page 1074*

Our true inner character is reflected in our actions Matthew 7:17-20, *page 1078* • Matthew 23:25-26, *page 1105* • Mark 7:20-23, *page 1131*

As we grow as Christians, our character should develop in certain ways Romans 12:9-21, *page 1296* • Ephesians 4:17–5:21, *page 1350* • 2 Peter 1:3-11, *page 1427*

The Holy Spirit helps us develop our character 2 Corinthians 3:18, *page 1326* • Galatians 5:22-23, *page 1343*

We are urged to imitate Jesus' character, especially his humility Philippians 2:3-8, *page 1356*

▸ *See* ***Becoming like Christ****, page 1435;* ***Integrity****, page 1325.*

Cheating *see Dishonesty*

Children *see also Youth*

The Bible sees children as a gift from God, and it encourages parents to love, nurture, and train them. In return, children should honor, respect, and obey their parents. Jesus had a big heart for children and said we need to be as humble as they are if we want to enter God's Kingdom.

> *Children are a gift from the LORD; they are a reward from him. Children born to a young man are like arrows in a warrior's hands. How joyful is the man whose quiver is full of them! – Psalm 127:3-5, page 684*

Children are God's gift to bless us Genesis 21:1-7, *page 24* • Deuteronomy 7:12-14, *page 210* • Psalm 127:3-5, *page 684* • Psalm 128:1-6, *page 684*

Children should honor their parents Exodus 20:12, *page 90* • Ephesians 6:1-3, *page 1352* • Colossians 3:20, *page 1366*

Parents should teach their children to follow God and his ways Deuteronomy 6:6-7, *page 208* • Proverbs 22:6, *page 719* • Ephesians 6:4, *page 1352*

Children need to listen to their parents' wisdom Proverbs 1:8-9, *page 697* • Proverbs 5:1-23, *page 700* • Proverbs 23:22-26, *page 720*

Children need to be lovingly disciplined Proverbs 13:24, *page 710* • Proverbs 19:18, *page 716* • Proverbs 29:15, 17, *page 727* • Hebrews 12:5-9, *page 1408*

We need to become childlike to enter God's Kingdom Matthew 11:25-26, *page 1085* • Matthew 18:2-4, *page 1097*

Children are important to Jesus Mark 9:14-27, *page 1134* • Mark 10:13-16, *page 1136*

Christians are children of God John 1:12, *page 1199* • Ephesians 5:1, *page 1351*

Parents should bring up their children well Ephesians 6:4, *page 1352*

We should teach children the Bible from an early age 2 Timothy 3:14-17, *page 1387*

▸ *See* ***Children****, page 1100.*

Christ *see Jesus Christ*

Christian, Becoming a *see Becoming a Christian, page A11*

Christian, Now that you are a *see Now that You Are a Christian, page A13*

Church *see also Worship*

The church is not a building or a denomination but rather all those who are true followers of Jesus. The Bible gives many pictures of the church, such as God's family and the body of Christ. These images underline how we belong both to him and to one another, and how we are called to be united to serve him in the world. The New Testament sees the church as central to God's plans.

> *God has put all things under the authority of Christ and has made him head over all things for the benefit of the church. And the church is his body; it is made full and complete by Christ, who fills all things everywhere with himself. – Ephesians 1:22-23, page 1347*

Jesus promised to build his church despite all opposition Matthew 16:18, *page 1095*

The priorities of the early church Acts 2:42-47, *page 1239* • Acts 4:32-37, *page 1242*

The church is called to engage in mission Acts 13:1-3, *page 1255*

The church is God's temple 1 Corinthians 3:16-17, *page 1306* • 2 Corinthians 6:16, *page 1329* • Ephesians 2:21-22, *page 1348*

The church is the body of Christ 1 Corinthians 12:12-31, *page 1315*

The church is called to be united through the Holy Spirit Galatians 3:26-28, *page 1341* • Ephesians 2:11-18, *page 1347* • Colossians 3:11, *page 1365*

The church is God's family Galatians 6:10, *page 1344* • Ephesians 2:19-22, *page 1348*

Jesus is the head of the church Ephesians 1:22, *page 1347* • Ephesians 5:23-27, *page 1351* • Colossians 1:18, *page 1363*

Jesus gives leaders to the church as a gift Ephesians 4:11, *page 1350*

The importance of meeting together as church members Hebrews 10:25, *page 1406*

The privileges of being God's own people 1 Peter 2:9-10, *page 1422*

The church is the bride of Christ Revelation 19:7-8, *page 1464* • Revelation 21:1-2, *page 1465*

▶ *See **The church**, page 1348; **Belonging to a church**, page 1406.*

Comfort

The Bible reassures us that God is always eager to comfort his people. Through the Holy Spirit who lives within us, God brings us his strength, reassurance, and support in times of difficulty or challenge. He then calls us, having been comforted, to comfort others in their time of need.

> *God is our merciful Father and the source of all comfort. He comforts us in all our troubles so that we can comfort others. When they are troubled, we will be able to give them the same comfort God has given us. For the more we suffer for Christ, the more God will shower us with his comfort through Christ. Even when we are weighed down with troubles, it is for your comfort and salvation! For when we ourselves are comforted, we will certainly comfort you. Then you can patiently endure the same things we suffer. We are confident that as you share in our sufferings, you will also share in the comfort God gives us. – 2 Corinthians 1:3-7, page 1324*

True friends comfort each other 1 Samuel 23:13-18, *page 332* • Job 2:11-13, *page 566* • 2 Corinthians 7:5-7, *page 1329*

We can be comforted by remembering God's love and presence Psalm 42:5, *page 627* • Lamentations 3:20-23, *page 895* • Romans 8:28-29, *page 1292*

God wants to comfort us when we are tired or weak Isaiah 40:28-31, *page 791* • Matthew 11:28-30, *page 1085* • 2 Corinthians 12:9-10, *page 1334*

We can know God's comforting presence when lonely Isaiah 41:10, *page 792* • Isaiah 49:14-16, *page 802* • John 14:18-23, *page 1223*

Jesus promises to comfort those who mourn Matthew 5:4, *page 1074*

We can know God's comfort when suffering 2 Corinthians 4:16-18, *page 1327*

Jesus comforts us in our time of need 2 Timothy 4:9-18, *page 1387* • Revelation 1:9-19, *page 1446*

Everything that disturbs our comfort will be removed at the End Revelation 21:3-4, *page 1465*

▶ *See **Being there**, page 575.*

Coming into God's presence

We have the privilege of being able to come into God's presence because of Jesus and his death on the cross. It is God's grace alone that makes this possible, not our own efforts or successes. This means that no matter how bad we might feel, how much we might have let God down, or how far away from him we might have been, nothing is able to prevent us from coming into his presence.

> *And so, dear brothers and sisters, we can boldly enter heaven's Most Holy Place because of the blood of Jesus. By his death, Jesus opened a new and life-giving way through the curtain into the Most Holy Place. And since we have a great High Priest who rules over God's house, let us go right into the presence of God with sincere hearts fully trusting him. – Hebrews 10:19-22, page 1406*

God's unfailing love, kindness, and favor are the basis of our coming into his presence Exodus 34:5-11, *page 106* • Psalm 103:8-18, *page 667*

In many ways we are always in God's presence Psalm 139:7-12, *page 689* • Jeremiah 23:23-24, *page 852*

We can come into God's presence simply, without ritual and show Matthew 6:5-18, *page 1076*

Jesus promised he would be present where just two or three of his followers gathered Matthew 18:19-20, *page 1098*

We can come into God's presence anywhere, not just in special places John 4:19-24, *page 1205*

Jesus is the only way into the Father's presence John 10:1-10, *page 1215* • John 14:1-6, *page 1222* • Acts 4:8-12, *page 1240*

We have access to God because of Jesus' death on the cross Romans 5:1-11, *page 1287* • Ephesians 2:13-18, *page 1347*

When we come together as believers, we are God's temple where his presence can be found 1 Corinthians 3:16, *page 1306*

We can boldly come into God's presence through Jesus Ephesians 3:12, *page 1349* • Hebrews 10:19-23, *page 1406* • Hebrews 12:18-24, *page 1409*

As we come into God's presence we can always find his mercy, grace, and help Hebrews 4:14-16, *page 1400*

▶ *See* ***Access to God****, page 1349;* ***Confidence****, page 1399.*

Commitment *see also Faithfulness*

Christian commitment is about dedicating our lives to Jesus in response to God's great commitment to us. As Christians we are called to show our commitment by a life of love, obedience, and service.

> *Then [Jesus] said to the crowd, "If any of you wants to be my follower, you must turn from your selfish ways, take up your cross daily, and follow me. If you try to hang on to your life, you will lose it. But if you give up your life for my sake, you will save it. And what do you benefit if you gain the whole world but are yourself lost or destroyed?" – Luke 9:23-25, page 1169*

Commitment to love us and be faithful is within God's very nature Exodus 34:6-7, *page 106* • Psalm 86:15, *page 657* • Psalm 103:1-18, *page 666*

Wholehearted commitment to God is called for Deuteronomy 6:4-25, *page 208* • Joshua 24:14-15, *page 268* • Mark 12:28-30, *page 1140*

God wants us to be committed to the place where he has put us Jeremiah 29:4-7, *page 858*

We show our commitment to Jesus by obeying him Matthew 7:24-27, *page 1079* • John 14:15-27, *page 1223* • Romans 6:17, *page 1289*

We show our commitment to Jesus by following him and becoming disciples Mark 1:16-20, *page 1119* • John 21:18-19, *page 1233*

Jesus urges us to count the cost of commitment Luke 14:25-35, *page 1179*

God's commitment is shown in his giving his Son to the world John 3:16-17, *page 1203* • Romans 5:6-11, *page 1287*

We show our commitment to Jesus through our love for him John 21:15-19, *page 1233*

We should be committed to a Christian community Acts 2:42, *page 1239* • Hebrews 10:24-25, *page 1406*

▶ *See* ***Consecration****, page 267;* ***Discipleship and the cross****, page 1095;* ***Counting the cost****, page 1180.*

Communion

Almost all churches remember Jesus' death for us through sharing bread and wine (or grape juice) together—variously called Communion, the Lord's Supper, the Eucharist, or Mass. The bread represents his body broken for us, and the wine his blood poured out for us as the perfect sacrifice for sin.

> *For I pass on to you what I received from the Lord himself. On the night when he was betrayed, the Lord Jesus took some bread and gave thanks to God for it. Then he broke it in pieces and said, "This is my body, which is given for you. Do this to remember me." In the same way, he took the*

cup of wine after supper, saying, "This cup is the new covenant between God and his people—an agreement confirmed with my blood. Do this to remember me as often as you drink it." For every time you eat this bread and drink this cup, you are announcing the Lord's death until he comes again. – *1 Corinthians 11:23-26, page 1315*

The Lord's Supper is rooted in the Passover, the annual celebration of God's freeing his people from slavery Exodus 12:1-42, *page 78* • Deuteronomy 16:1-8, *page 218* • Matthew 26:17-19, *page 1110*

Jesus himself reinterpreted the Passover meal, focusing on himself as God's new means of bringing freedom Matthew 26:20-30, *page 1111* • Mark 14:12-26, *page 1143* • Luke 22:7-23, *page 1190* • 1 Corinthians 11:23-34, *page 1315*

The Lord's Supper looks forward to the Kingdom of God coming in its fullness Luke 22:17-18, *page 1190* • 1 Corinthians 11:23-26, *page 1315*

Communion reminds us of the new covenant Jesus has established Luke 22:20, *page 1190*

When we share in this meal, we are sharing in Jesus' life John 6:35-58, *page 1209* • 1 Corinthians 10:16-17, *page 1314*

This celebration was a key part of early Christian worship Acts 2:42-47, *page 1239* • Acts 20:7-11, *page 1269*

By sharing in Christ's body and blood we demonstrate we are all part of one body 1 Corinthians 10:16-17, *page 1314*

Communion is a time for remembering the death of Jesus for us 1 Corinthians 11:23-25, *page 1315*

▸ *See **The Last Supper**, page 1110.*

Compassion *see Caring; Kindness; Love*

Complaining *see also Criticism; Ungratefulness*

The Bible sees complaining and grumbling as an expression of lack of trust in God. If we do have concerns, the Bible tells us to share them openly and quickly with both God and others so that bitterness and unbelief do not get a chance to grow and cause untold harm.

Do everything without complaining and arguing, so that no one can criticize you. Live clean, innocent lives as children of God, shining like bright lights in a world full of crooked and perverse people. – *Philippians 2:14-15, page 1357*

To complain about our leaders is to complain about God, who gave those leaders to us Exodus 16:1-12, *page 84*

Justified complaints should be resolved quickly Exodus 18:13-26, *page 87* • Acts 6:1-7, *page 1244*

Complaining can bring God's judgment on us Numbers 11:1-3, *page 167* • Numbers 14:1-24, *page 169* • Numbers 16:1-50, *page 173*

Unresolved complaints always lead to trouble 2 Samuel 15:1-12, *page 358*

The Bible encourages us to bring our complaints openly to God Psalm 142:1-2, *page 691*

Instead of complaining, we should trust God Isaiah 40:27-31, *page 790*

If we have a genuine complaint, we should handle it properly Matthew 18:15-17, *page 1097* • 1 Timothy 5:19-20, *page 1383*

Jesus' challenging teaching sometimes caused people to complain Luke 5:29-32, *page 1161* • John 6:60-69, *page 1210*

The Bible warns us of the dangers of complaining 1 Corinthians 10:1-11, *page 1313* • James 5:9, *page 1417*

Christians are urged not to complain or grumble Philippians 2:13-15, *page 1357* • James 5:7-9, *page 1417*

People often complain because they simply want their own way Jude 1:12-16, *page 1442*

▸ *See **Speech**, page 1416.*

Compromise

While we all have to find ways of living and working peaceably with others, the Bible warns Christians not to compromise the heart of their faith.

> *Don't team up with those who are unbelievers. How can righteousness be a partner with wickedness? How can light live with darkness? What harmony can there be between Christ and the devil? How can a believer be a partner with an unbeliever? And what union can there be between God's temple and idols? For we are the temple of the living God. – 2 Corinthians 6:14-16, page 1329*

Certain kinds of compromise, when key issues of faith are not at stake, are helpful to keep the peace Genesis 13:5-9, *page 16* • Acts 15:1-29, *page 1259* • 1 Corinthians 10:23-33, *page 1314*

Bad compromise is generally rooted in fear Genesis 26:1-9, *page 31* • Galatians 2:11-14, *page 1338*

We should not compromise our convictions in order to make life easier 1 Kings 11:1-13, *page 390* • Daniel 1:4-16, *page 955* • Matthew 6:24, *page 1078*

We cannot compromise on who or what is truly God of our life 1 Kings 18:20-21, *page 402* • Matthew 6:24, *page 1078* • James 4:4-8, *page 1416*

Compromise can keep us from doing what is right Mark 15:6-15, *page 1145*

Compromise over nonessentials can be wise for the sake of the Good News Acts 15:1-29, *page 1259* • Romans 14:1-23, *page 1298* • 1 Corinthians 9:19-23, *page 1312*

Compromise in relationships can weaken our faith 2 Corinthians 6:14-18, *page 1329*

We are not to compromise on the fundamentals of the Good News of Jesus Galatians 1:6-10, *page 1337* • Galatians 2:11-16, *page 1338*

We are not to compromise on our loyalty to God James 4:4-10, *page 1416*

▶ *See **King Solomon**, page 377.*

Confession *see also Repentance*

The Bible assures us that, no matter what we might have done, if we confess our sin—that is, own up to it—and ask for God's forgiveness, he will surely forgive us. This is not because of anything we have done but because of Jesus' death on the cross for us.

> *If we claim to be without sin, we deceive ourselves and the truth is not in us. If we confess our sins to him, he is faithful and just to forgive us our sins and to cleanse us from all wickedness. – 1 John 1:8-9, page 1433*

Sometimes God corners us to bring us to a place of confession Genesis 3:8-11, *page 6* • 2 Samuel 12:1-13, *page 354*

We should not try to hide our sin but rather confess it quickly 2 Samuel 11:26–12:25, *page 354* • Proverbs 28:13, *page 726*

God promises to forgive those who confess their sin 2 Chronicles 7:14, *page 489* • Psalm 32:1-7, *page 620* • Psalm 51:1-12, *page 633*

Our confession should be matched by our actions Ezra 10:1-17, *page 533* • Matthew 3:1-10, *page 1070* • Luke 19:1-10, *page 1185*

When we don't confess our sin, it eats away at us inside Psalm 32:3-5, *page 620*

Jesus' sacrificial death is the basis of our forgiveness, not anything that we might do Romans 3:21-26, *page 1286* • Hebrews 9:24–10:13, *page 1405* • 1 Peter 3:18-22, *page 1424* • 1 John 2:1-2, *page 1433*

We don't confess sin because God doesn't already know about it, but because it humbles us and helps us acknowledge our need of him James 4:6-10, *page 1416* • 1 Peter 5:5-6, *page 1425*

We are urged to pray for one another and confess our sins to one another James 5:13-16, *page 1417*

▶ *See **Is there anything God won't forgive?**, page 633.*

Confidence *see also Courage*

As Christians we can come confidently into God's presence and be sure that he listens to our prayers. The basis for this confidence is not anything we have done, but simply who Jesus is and what he has done for us at the cross.

> *So then, since we have a great High Priest who has entered heaven, Jesus the Son of God, let us hold firmly to what we believe. This High Priest of ours understands our weaknesses, for he faced all of the same testings we do, yet he did not sin. So let us come boldly to the throne of our gracious God. There we will receive his mercy, and we will find grace to help us when we need it most.*
> *– Hebrews 4:14-16, page 1400*

Our confidence comes from knowing that God is unchanging and faithful Numbers 23:18-19, *page 183* • Malachi 3:6, *page 1052* • James 1:12-18, *page 1412*

We can be confident that God is always with us and will never abandon us Deuteronomy 31:7-8, *page 234* • Isaiah 41:8-14, *page 792* • Hebrews 13:5-6, *page 1409*

Confidence in God enables us to face difficulties Habakkuk 3:16-18, *page 1027* • Philippians 4:10-13, *page 1360* • Hebrews 12:1-13, *page 1408*

We can be confident that Jesus will always be with us Matthew 28:18-20, *page 1116* • John 14:18, *page 1223*

We can be confident the Holy Spirit will be with us when we share the Good News John 16:5-15, *page 1224* • Acts 4:8-22, *page 1240* • Acts 9:26-31, *page 1249*

We can be confident that God is working in our circumstances for our good Romans 8:28-39, *page 1292*

We can come confidently into God's presence Hebrews 4:14-16, *page 1400* • Hebrews 10:19-25, *page 1406*

We can be confident God will hear our prayers 1 John 3:21-24, *page 1436* • 1 John 5:13-15, *page 1438*

We can look forward with confidence to the day of judgment 1 John 4:17, *page 1437*

▸ *See* ***Confidence****, page 1399.*

Conscience *see also Guilt; Heart*

Our conscience helps us discern right from wrong, and we need to do all we can to keep it clean before God and other people. When we do wrong, our conscience lets us know it by making us feel bad; but when we confess what we have done wrong, our conscience can be made clean again by Jesus.

> *And since we have a great High Priest who rules over God's house, let us go right into the presence of God with sincere hearts fully trusting him. For our guilty consciences have been sprinkled with Christ's blood to make us clean, and our bodies have been washed with pure water. – Hebrews 10:21-22, page 1406*

Doing wrong affects our conscience 1 Samuel 24:1-7, *page 333* • Matthew 27:1-5, *page 1113*

We should always aim to keep a clear conscience Acts 23:1-5, *page 1273* • Acts 24:10-16, *page 1274* • 2 Corinthians 1:12, *page 1324* • 1 Timothy 1:18-20, *page 1379*

Conscience is built into every person Romans 2:12-15, *page 1284*

We should be sensitive to the consciences of others Romans 14:1-23, *page 1298* • 1 Corinthians 10:23-33, *page 1314*

We should take care not to cause those with weaker consciences to stumble 1 Corinthians 8:1-13, *page 1311*

If we violate our conscience, we are in danger of wrecking our faith 1 Timothy 1:18-20, *page 1379*

Consciences can be destroyed by bad choices 1 Timothy 4:1-3, *page 1381*

Jesus' forgiveness clears our conscience Hebrews 9:11-14, *page 1404* • Hebrews 10:19-22, *page 1406*

A clear conscience helps us live a God-honoring life 1 Peter 3:13-16, *page 1423*

▸ *See* ***Conscience****, page 333.*

Consulting mediums *see Occult*

Continuing in the faith *see Perseverance*

Conversion *see Becoming a Christian, page A11*

Courage *see also Confidence*

God promises to give us the strength and courage we need to face difficult or challenging situations, especially those in which we are naturally fearful. Courage comes from our relationship with God through Jesus. We should show courage in obeying God, standing up for what is right, and boldly telling others about Jesus.

> *"Be strong and courageous, for you are the one who will lead these people to possess all the land I swore to their ancestors I would give them. Be strong and very courageous. Be careful to obey all the instructions Moses gave you. Do not deviate from them, turning either to the right or to the left. Then you will be successful in everything you do. Study this Book of Instruction continually. Meditate on it day and night so you will be sure to obey everything written in it. Only then will you prosper and succeed in all you do. This is my command—be strong and courageous! Do not be afraid or discouraged. For the LORD your God is with you wherever you go." – Joshua 1:6-9, page 242*

We should be courageous in standing up for what is right Exodus 1:15-22, *page 66* • 1 Kings 18:16-46, *page 402*

We are commanded to be strong and courageous Joshua 1:1-9, *page 242* • 1 Corinthians 16:13, *page 1321*

Courage comes from having confidence in God 1 Samuel 17:26-50, *page 325*

We can help one another find courage from God 1 Samuel 23:15-18, *page 332* • 2 Chronicles 32:1-8, *page 514*

We can be courageous and bold in the face of difficulties when we know that God is with us Daniel 3:1-30, *page 958* • Daniel 6:1-28, *page 963* • Micah 3:8, *page 1013*

We can know courage from the presence of Jesus Matthew 14:22-33, *page 1092*

Remembering Jesus' victory should give us courage John 16:33, *page 1225*

God gives us courage to tell others about Jesus Acts 2:1-41, *page 1237* • Acts 4:31, *page 1242*

We can pray for courage and boldness Acts 4:23-31, *page 1241* • Ephesians 6:19-20, *page 1353*

▶ *See* ***Courage****, page 243.*

Covenant

God doesn't just establish a relationship with us; he makes a covenant—a binding, unbreakable commitment—to be our God. In return he calls on us to love and obey him and to join him in his mission. The Old Testament's covenants (with people like Abraham, Moses, and David) simply prepared the way for the new covenant—one that is based on Jesus' death and brings complete forgiveness to all who trust in him.

> *If the first covenant had been faultless, there would have been no need for a second covenant to replace it. But when God found fault with the people, he said: "The day is coming, says the LORD, when I will make a new covenant with the people of Israel and Judah. This covenant will not be like the one I made with their ancestors when I took them by the hand and led them out of the land of Egypt. They did not remain faithful to my covenant, so I turned my back on them, says the LORD. But this is the new covenant I will make with the people of Israel on that day, says the LORD: I will put my laws in their minds, and I will write them on their hearts. I will be their God, and they will be my people. And they will not need to teach their neighbors, nor will they need to teach their relatives, saying, 'You should know the LORD.' For everyone, from the least to the greatest, will know me already. And I will forgive their wickedness, and I will never again remember their sins." When God speaks of a "new" covenant, it means he has made the first one obsolete. It is now out of date and will soon disappear. – Hebrews 8:7-13, page 1403*

BASIC TRUTHS • *page 1502*

Key covenants in the Old Testament Genesis 9:1-17, *page 12* • Genesis 17:1-27, *page 20* • Exodus 24:1-18, *page 94* • 2 Samuel 7:1-29, *page 349*

God's covenants were accompanied by signs Genesis 9:12-17, *page 12* • Genesis 17:9-14, *page 20* • Exodus 24:1-12, *page 94* • 2 Samuel 7:12-16, *page 349* • Matthew 26:26-28, *page 1111*

The Old Testament promised a new covenant that would be inner and spiritual Jeremiah 31:31-34, *page 862* • Ezekiel 36:25-27, *page 938*

Jesus established a new covenant based on his death Matthew 26:26-29, *page 1111* • Hebrews 9:11-15, *page 1404* • Hebrews 13:20, *page 1410*

God's new covenant brings life 2 Corinthians 3:4-6, *page 1326*

The new covenant is vastly superior to the old covenant Hebrews 8:1-6, *page 1403*

The old covenant foreshadowed the new covenant Hebrews 10:1, *page 1405*

▶ *See* ***Covenant****, page 19;* ***The Davidic covenant****, page 468;* ***The new covenant****, page 861.*

Creation *see also Earth*

The Bible tells us that the universe did not come about by accident but as the direct result of God's word and work. As such, it is to be both admired and cared for. Human sin and disobedience has spoiled God's perfect creation, but one day Jesus will return to renew it.

> *O LORD, our Lord, your majestic name fills the earth! Your glory is higher than the heavens. You have taught children and infants to tell of your strength, silencing your enemies and all who oppose you. When I look at the night sky and see the work of your fingers—the moon and the stars you set in place—what are mere mortals that you should think about them, human beings that you should care for them? Yet you made them only a little lower than God and crowned them with glory and honor. You gave them charge of everything you made, putting all things under their authority—the flocks and the herds and all the wild animals, the birds in the sky, the fish in the sea, and everything that swims the ocean currents. O LORD, our Lord, your majestic name fills the earth!*
> *– Psalm 8:1-9, page 605*

Everything that exists was created by God Genesis 1:1-2, *page 4* • Hebrews 11:1-3, *page 1407*

The Holy Spirit played a role in creation Genesis 1:2, *page 4* • Psalm 104:24-30, *page 668*

God created people in his own image Genesis 1:26-27, *page 5* • Genesis 5:1-2, *page 9*

God wants humanity to take care of creation Genesis 1:28, *page 5* • Exodus 23:10-12, *page 93* • Deuteronomy 20:19-20, *page 223*

When God created the world it was very good Genesis 1:31, *page 5*

The creation has been spoiled by sin Genesis 3:17-19, *page 7* • Romans 8:19-22, *page 1291*

Creation displays God's greatness Job 38:1–42:3, *page 595* • Psalm 19:1-6, *page 612* • Isaiah 40:12-31, *page 790* • Romans 1:18-25, *page 1283*

God's wisdom was at work in creation Proverbs 8:22-36, *page 704*

The Creator cares not only for people but also for all of creation Isaiah 40:26-31, *page 790*

Jesus had a role in creation John 1:1-14, *page 1199* • Colossians 1:15-17, *page 1362*

Jesus sustains all creation Colossians 1:15-17, *page 1362* • Hebrews 1:3, *page 1396*

God will make a new heaven and a new earth when Christ returns 2 Peter 3:10-13, *page 1430* • Revelation 21:1-5, *page 1465* • Revelation 22:1-5, *page 1467*

▶ *See* ***Was the world really made in six days?****, page 5;* ***The environment****, page 606;* ***The world****, page 1226.*

Criticism *see also Complaining*

While positive criticism can be helpful and constructive, the Bible challenges us to deal with our own issues before criticizing others. Unjust criticism of others can be immensely destructive and is something God hates.

"And why worry about a speck in your friend's eye when you have a log in your own? How can you think of saying to your friend, 'Let me help you get rid of that speck in your eye,' when you can't see past the log in your own eye? Hypocrite! First get rid of the log in your own eye; then you will see well enough to deal with the speck in your friend's eye." – Matthew 7:3-5, page 1078

We should simply ignore groundless criticism Nehemiah 4:1-6, *page 539* • Nehemiah 6:1-9, *page 541*

We ignore constructive criticism to our loss Proverbs 13:18, *page 710* • Proverbs 15:31-32, *page 712*

Honest criticism is more valuable than flattery Proverbs 28:23, *page 726* • Ecclesiastes 7:5, *page 735*

Having integrity helps safeguard against criticism Daniel 6:1-5, *page 963* • 2 Corinthians 1:12, *page 1324* • 2 Corinthians 8:18-21, *page 1331* • Philippians 2:14-15, *page 1357*

Jesus was often criticized Mark 3:1-4, 20-22, *page 1122* • John 6:41-42, *page 1209*

When we are falsely criticized, we should remember that God knows the truth Mark 14:1-9, *page 1142* • Luke 23:32-43, *page 1194* • 1 Peter 4:1-19, *page 1424*

We shouldn't criticize others by our actions or our words Romans 2:1-11, *page 1283* • James 4:11-12, *page 1416*

Harsh criticism can destroy rather than help Galatians 5:13-15, *page 1343*

Criticism should always be given with a loving and constructive attitude Ephesians 4:15, *page 1350*

▸ *See **Speech**, page 1416.*

Cross *see Jesus Christ: his death*

Day of rest

At the beginning, God said that one day a week should be a day of rest. For Jews, this was the last day of the week and was called the Sabbath; but Christians moved this day of rest from the last day of the week to the first day of the week (Sunday) to commemorate the Resurrection, and they called it "the Lord's Day." Whatever day we use, we should all ensure we set aside one day a week to enjoy the rest and refreshment God has provided.

So the creation of the heavens and the earth and everything in them was completed. On the seventh day God had finished his work of creation, so he rested from all his work. And God blessed the seventh day and declared it holy, because it was the day when he rested from all his work of creation. – Genesis 2:1-3, page 5

A day of rest reminds us that God rested after his work of creation Genesis 2:1-3, *page 5* • Exodus 31:15-17, *page 103* • Ezekiel 20:12, *page 918*

God commands a weekly day of rest Exodus 20:8-11, *page 90* • Exodus 31:12-17, *page 103*

We should not work on the day of rest Leviticus 23:3, *page 143* • Nehemiah 13:15-22, *page 552* • Jeremiah 17:19-27, *page 845* • Luke 23:56, *page 1195*

Keeping the day of rest brings blessing Isaiah 56:2, *page 809* • Isaiah 58:13-14, *page 812*

We should not get legalistic about how people use the weekly day of rest Matthew 12:1-8, *page 1085* • Romans 14:5-12, *page 1298* • Colossians 2:16-17, *page 1364*

We should still help others on the day of rest Matthew 12:9-13, *page 1086* • Luke 13:10-17, *page 1177* • Luke 14:1-6, *page 1179* • John 5:1-18, *page 1206*

Christians moved the weekly day of rest to Sunday to remember Jesus' rising from the dead Matthew 28:1-10, *page 1115* • Mark 16:1-2, *page 1147* • Luke 24:1-12, *page 1195* • John 20:1-10, *page 1231*

Jesus kept the Sabbath, even if not legalistically Luke 4:16-21, *page 1159*

The first Christians met together on the first day of the week, Sunday Acts 20:7-12, *page 1269* • 1 Corinthians 16:1-2, *page 1321*

▸ *See **The Sabbath**, page 918; **Sunday**, page 1121.*

Death *see also Bereavement; Life; Jesus Christ: his death*

Death is not something we need to be afraid of as Christians because Jesus has conquered death. If we trust in him, we can be sure that, even though we will one day die—and none of us knows when that will be—we will live again and be with him forever. When Jesus returns at the end of the age, he will destroy death once and for all. He will give us new resurrection bodies for life in his new Kingdom.

For the wages of sin is death, but the free gift of God is eternal life through Christ Jesus our Lord.
– Romans 6:23, page 1290

Death is a result of sin Genesis 3:17-19, *page 7* • Romans 5:12-21, *page 1288* • Romans 6:23, *page 1290*

Every person will face death followed by judgment Psalm 89:48, *page 659* • 2 Corinthians 5:6-10, *page 1327* • Hebrews 9:27-28, *page 1405* • Revelation 20:11-15, *page 1465*

God is saddened by death Ezekiel 18:30-32, *page 917* • John 11:30-44, *page 1218*

Death comes suddenly and unexpectedly, so we should prepare for it and what follows Luke 12:13-21, *page 1175* • Luke 16:19-31, *page 1182*

If we follow Jesus, death will not be the end of our lives John 8:51, *page 1213* • 1 Thessalonians 4:13-18, *page 1372*

In baptism we identify with Jesus' death so that we can be assured of new life Romans 6:1-11, *page 1289*

At the end of the age Jesus will raise the dead 1 Corinthians 15:50-57, *page 1320*

When we became Christians, we were brought from death to life Ephesians 2:1-10, *page 1347*

We need not fear death, for it simply means going to be with Jesus Philippians 1:20-23, *page 1355* • 2 Timothy 4:6-8, *page 1387*

None of us knows how long we will live, so we should live humbly and in dependence on God James 4:13-17, *page 1416*

At the end of the age God will destroy death forever Revelation 21:1-4, *page 1465*

▶ *See* ***Mourning****, page 892;* ***Hope****, page 895;* ***Life from death****, page 1219;* ***Hell****, page 1108;* ***Christ's resurrection and ours****, page 1320;* ***The return of Jesus Christ****, page 1372;* ***Heaven****, page 1451.*

Debt

The Bible warns of the danger of debt and encourages us to get out of it as quickly as we can. It also calls us to be merciful to those in debt to us, for God has graciously forgiven us all our debts to him.

"If you lend money to any of my people who are in need, do not charge interest as a money lender would. If you take your neighbor's cloak as security for a loan, you must return it before sunset. This coat may be the only blanket your neighbor has. How can a person sleep without it? If you do not return it and your neighbor cries out to me for help, then I will hear, for I am merciful."
– Exodus 22:25-27, page 93

Debt was taken seriously, so any debt that could not be repaid by normal means had to be repaid by up to six years' service instead Exodus 21:1-11, *page 90* • Leviticus 25:35-43, *page 148* • 2 Kings 4:1, *page 415*

We should show compassion toward debtors Exodus 22:25-27, *page 93* • Leviticus 25:35-43, *page 148* • Matthew 18:21-35, *page 1098* • Luke 7:41-43, *page 1165*

All outstanding debts among God's people were canceled after seven years Deuteronomy 15:1-11, *page 218* • Nehemiah 10:31, *page 547*

Security against loans should never rob the debtor of their livelihood Deuteronomy 24:6, 10-13, *page 226*

Wages are to be paid promptly so that people won't get into debt Deuteronomy 24:14-15, *page 226*

The Bible shows the terrible consequences of debt 2 Kings 4:1-7, *page 415* • Nehemiah 5:1-5, *page 540* • Job 24:1-12, *page 584*

We are warned of the dangers of putting up security for other people's debts Proverbs 6:1-5, *page 701* • Proverbs 11:15, *page 708* •

Proverbs 17:18, *page 714* • Proverbs 22:16, *page 719*

We should settle any debts promptly Romans 13:6-7, *page 1297*

The only debt we should have is the obligation to love one another Romans 13:8-10, *page 1298*

▸ *See* ***Debt****, page 219.*

Decisions *see Guidance*

Demons *see also Satan*

Demons are evil spirit-beings that serve Satan and his purposes and that oppose God's people. While the Gospels show they are both real and powerful, we do not need to be afraid of them, for they are subject to Jesus' authority. He came to break the hold of such evil powers and gave his followers authority to do the same in his name.

That evening after sunset, many sick and demon-possessed people were brought to Jesus. The whole town gathered at the door to watch. So Jesus healed many people who were sick with various diseases, and he cast out many demons. But because the demons knew who he was, he did not allow them to speak. – Mark 1:32-34, page 1119

To worship idols and false gods is to worship the demons that lie behind them Deuteronomy 32:15-18, *page 236* • Psalm 106:34-40, *page 670* • 1 Corinthians 10:14-21, *page 1314*

Demons try to hinder God's plan but cannot do so Daniel 10:12-14, *page 970*

Demons were repeatedly defeated by Jesus Matthew 8:16-17, *page 1080* • Matthew 9:32-33, *page 1082* • Mark 5:1-20, *page 1126* • Mark 9:14-20, *page 1134* • Luke 4:31-37, *page 1160* • Colossians 2:15, *page 1364*

Jesus said that casting out demons was a sign of the presence of God's Kingdom Matthew 12:22-29, *page 1087*

Demons are powerful, but not more powerful than Jesus Mark 5:1-13, *page 1126* • Acts 19:13-16, *page 1267*

Jesus gave his followers authority to cast out demons Mark 16:15-18, *page 1148* • Luke 9:1-2, *page 1168* • Luke 10:17-20, *page 1172* • Acts 16:16-18, *page 1262*

God's love is more powerful than demons Romans 8:35-39, *page 1292*

Demons love to deceive people 2 Corinthians 11:13-15, *page 1333* • 1 Timothy 4:1-2, *page 1381*

We are in a battle against the devil's strategies and his army of demons Ephesians 6:10-18, *page 1352*

Demons are angels that have sinned and rebelled and that were expelled from heaven 2 Peter 2:4, *page 1428* • Revelation 12:1-9, *page 1457*

Satan and his demons will one day be bound and judged by God Jude 1:6, *page 1442* • Revelation 20:1-3, 7-10, *page 1464*

▸ *See* ***Demons****, page 1126;* ***Angels****, page 1397.*

Depression

There is nothing worse for someone who is depressed than being told, "Pull yourself together and get on with life." Depression is a deep-rooted despondency accompanied by an inability to do anything about it. Besides clinical causes (for example, an imbalance of body chemistry), depression can also have its roots in fear, circumstances, exhaustion, or even—sometimes—sin. The Bible points to different ways of dealing with it, both spiritual (such as trusting God in it) and practical (such as drawing help and strength from supportive friends).

As the deer longs for streams of water, so I long for you, O God. I thirst for God, the living God. When can I go and stand before him? Day and night I have only tears for food, while my enemies continually taunt me, saying, "Where is this God of yours?" My heart is breaking as I remember how it used to be: I walked among the crowds of worshipers, leading a great procession to the house of God, singing for joy and giving thanks amid the sound of a great celebration! Why am I discouraged? Why is my heart so sad? I will put my hope in God! I will praise him again—my Savior and my God! – Psalm 42:1-5, page 627

Depression can be caused by exhaustion, whether physical, emotional, or spiritual Numbers 11:11-15, *page 167* • 1 Kings 19:1-5, *page 404*

We should never forget that God is always with us and protecting us, no matter what our circumstances or feelings Deuteronomy 31:8, *page 234* • Psalm 3:1-8, *page 603* • Psalm 32:6-10, *page 620* • Isaiah 41:8-10, *page 792*

Depression can be caused by adverse circumstances 1 Kings 19:1-2, *page 404* • Job 6:1-13, *page 569*

Rest, sleep, and good food can help us when we are depressed 1 Kings 19:1-8, *page 404*

While supportive friendship helps those who are depressed, endless advice doesn't Job 16:1-6, *page 577*

We can be absolutely honest with God about how we feel Psalm 22:1-11, *page 614* • Psalm 38:1-22, *page 625* • Psalm 142:1-7, *page 691*

God helps those who feel crushed Psalm 34:17-20, *page 622* • Psalm 147:3, *page 693* • Isaiah 40:28-31, *page 791* • Isaiah 61:1-3, *page 814* • Luke 4:16-19, *page 1159*

Remembering God's acts in the past can help us get through hard times Psalm 42:1-11, *page 627* • Psalm 143:1-12, *page 691*

We should remember that God is always a God of hope Romans 5:1-5, *page 1287* • Romans 15:13, *page 1299* • 2 Thessalonians 2:16-17, *page 1375*

Praying with others can help strengthen us in hard times James 5:13-18, *page 1417*

God will one day remove all causes of sadness and depression Revelation 21:1-5, *page 1465*

▸ *See **Depression**, page 404; **Being there**, page 575.*

Desires *see also Addiction; Greed*

Desires can be good or bad, as all of us have experienced. The Bible tells us to do all we can to run from bad desires and to pursue good desires with the help of the Holy Spirit. Bad desires pull us away from God, but good desires help us keep pressing on with him.

Don't worry about the wicked or envy those who do wrong. For like grass, they soon fade away. Like spring flowers, they soon wither. Trust in the LORD and do good. Then you will live safely in the land and prosper. Take delight in the LORD, and he will give you your heart's desires. – Psalm 37:1-4, page 623

Giving in to desires for what God forbids will always lead to trouble and take us away from God Genesis 3:1-24, *page 6* • 2 Samuel 13:1-39, *page 355* • 2 Timothy 4:10, *page 1387* • 1 John 2:15-17, *page 1434*

We should avoid all evil desires Exodus 20:13-17, *page 90* • Ephesians 4:17-24, *page 1350* • 2 Timothy 2:20-22, *page 1386*

We should especially desire wisdom 2 Chronicles 1:7-12, *page 483* • Proverbs 2:1-22, *page 698* • Proverbs 4:4-13, *page 700* • Proverbs 8:1-36, *page 703* • James 1:2-8, *page 1412*

We should desire to do God's will Psalm 40:1-8, *page 626* • 1 Peter 4:1-3, *page 1424*

We should desire to know God better Psalm 42:1-11, *page 627* • Psalm 84:1-8, *page 655* • Psalm 86:11-13, *page 657*

The desire for money is never satisfied Ecclesiastes 5:10-15, *page 734* • 1 Timothy 6:6-12, *page 1383*

Bad desires come from sin within our own hearts Mark 7:17-23, *page 1131* • James 1:13-15, *page 1412*

Our greatest desire should be to live for God and to obey him Romans 6:12-14, *page 1289* • 1 John 2:15-17, *page 1434*

Christians still struggle with conflicting desires, but Jesus can help us Romans 7:14-25, *page 1290*

We should desire to grow in love 1 Corinthians 13:1-13, *page 1316*

We should put to death our old selfish desires and grow in the fruit of the Spirit Galatians 5:16-26, *page 1343*

Determination *see also Commitment*

Determination can be either good or bad. Determination to go our own way, to ignore the Bible's teaching, or to make selfish decisions will always be unhelpful to us and lead to problems. But good determination can help us keep going in our Christian life, make us resolved not to compromise, and enable us to see something through for God.

> *"Fear the LORD and serve him wholeheartedly. . . . As for me and my family, we will serve the LORD." – Joshua 24:14-15, page 268*

God is determined to bless his people Numbers 24:1-10, *page 183* • Zechariah 8:15, *page 1043*

We should be determined to serve and obey God and God alone Joshua 24:14-24, *page 268* • Psalm 17:3-8, *page 610* • Isaiah 50:5-7, *page 803* • Daniel 6:1-28, *page 963*

Determination can help us make the right choices Ruth 1:6-18, *page 299* • Esther 4:1-16, *page 557* • Daniel 1:6-17, *page 955*

We can determine to stand firm in challenging situations 2 Chronicles 20:15-24, *page 501* • Nehemiah 6:1-9, *page 541* • Isaiah 7:3-9, *page 755* • Acts 16:16-40, *page 1262* • Revelation 3:7-13, *page 1449*

We can determine not to sin Job 31:1, *page 589*

God helps us be determined Isaiah 50:7, *page 803* • Luke 12:11-12, *page 1175* • 2 Timothy 4:16-18, *page 1388*

We have to determine to follow Jesus whatever the cost Mark 8:34-38, *page 1133* • Luke 9:57-62, *page 1171*

We should be determined to put God first, whatever people might think or do Acts 4:1-20, *page 1240*

Devil, The *see Demons; Satan*

Devotion *see also Commitment*

People are devoted to all sorts of things today—their football team, social media, a favorite singer, a hobby—but as Christians our first devotion should be to God. This devotion will express itself in many different ways, such as spending time with him in prayer and worship, reading his word, and wanting to get to know him better. But our devotion to him will also be expressed in our devotion to his people, through loving and serving our Christian brothers and sisters.

> *All the believers devoted themselves to the apostles' teaching, and to fellowship, and to sharing in meals (including the Lord's Supper), and to prayer. – Acts 2:42, page 1239*

We are challenged to be fully devoted to God Deuteronomy 6:4-10, *page 208* • Joshua 24:14-18, *page 268* • 1 Chronicles 28:9, *page 479*

God wants us to be devoted to others in our relationships Ruth 1:16-18, *page 299* • 1 Samuel 18:1-4, *page 326* • Matthew 19:4-6, *page 1099*

Devotion to God should be reflected in wholehearted worship 2 Samuel 6:1-23, *page 348* • Psalm 27:1-14, *page 617* • Revelation 5:6-14, *page 1451*

We should beware of things that seek to turn our devotion from God to other things 1 Kings 11:1-6, *page 390* • 2 Corinthians 11:1-3, *page 1332*

We should be devoted to eager reading of the Scriptures Ezra 7:8-10, *page 529* • Psalm 119:97-112, *page 680* • Acts 17:11-12, *page 1264* • 2 Timothy 3:14-17, *page 1387*

We cannot be devoted to two masters in life Matthew 6:24, *page 1078*

We should be devoted to the practice of prayer Luke 18:1, *page 1183* • Colossians 4:2-4, *page 1366*

We should be devoted to our Christian brothers and sisters Romans 12:9-13, *page 1296* • Hebrews 10:23-25, *page 1406*

We should be devoted to knowing Jesus better Philippians 3:8-11, *page 1358*

Die, What happens when I? *see Death*

Disagreement

As Christians we are called to avoid disagreements as much as possible and to try to settle any disputes quickly before they develop into something worse. When we disagree because of personal opinions, we are wise to keep our thoughts to ourselves and not make an issue of them. Above all, we should remember that it is always better to be kind than to be right.

> *Don't get involved in foolish, ignorant arguments that only start fights. A servant of the Lord must not quarrel but must be kind to everyone . . . and be patient with difficult people. – 2 Timothy 2:23-24, page 1386*

When disagreements arise, God blesses those who take a humble approach Genesis 13:1-18, *page 16* • Genesis 26:12-25, *page 31* • Acts 6:1-7, *page 1244* • James 4:1-10, *page 1416*

Arguments can be avoided by choosing our words carefully Proverbs 15:1-4, *page 711* • Proverbs 25:15, *page 722*

We shouldn't interfere in others' arguments Proverbs 26:17, *page 724*

Those who seek to make peace are blessed by God Matthew 5:9, *page 1075* • James 3:17-18, *page 1415*

We are called to settle disagreements quickly when they occur Matthew 18:15-17, *page 1097* • Philippians 4:2-3, *page 1359*

Action was always taken to quickly resolve disagreements in the church Acts 6:1-7, *page 1244* • Acts 15:1-35, *page 1259*

We should do everything we can to avoid arguments Romans 12:17-21, *page 1297* • Philippians 2:14-16, *page 1357* • 2 Timothy 2:14, *page 1386*

Disagreements over secondary issues should be handled with grace on all sides Romans 14:1-23, *page 1298*

As Christians, we should do everything we can to maintain unity among ourselves 1 Corinthians 1:10-17, *page 1303* • Ephesians 4:1-16, *page 1349* • Philippians 2:1-4, *page 1356*

Loving others should take the place of arguing with them Galatians 5:17-26, *page 1343*

Disappointment

All of us experience disappointment at times, whether that be because our expectations were unrealistic or simply because things didn't turn out as we had hoped. But at such times the Bible encourages us not to get downhearted or to fall into self-pity but to continue to trust in God, whose plans are never thwarted.

> *Even though the fig trees have no blossoms, and there are no grapes on the vines; even though the olive crop fails, and the fields lie empty and barren; even though the flocks die in the fields, and the cattle barns are empty, yet I will rejoice in the LORD! I will be joyful in the God of my salvation! The Sovereign LORD is my strength! He makes me as surefooted as a deer, able to tread upon the heights. – Habakkuk 3:17-19, page 1027*

Many people in the Bible experienced disappointments Genesis 15:1-3, *page 18* • Genesis 27:1-40, *page 32* • Genesis 39:1–40:23, *page 49* • Job 30:26-31, *page 589* • 2 Timothy 4:9-18, *page 1387*

We can grieve over our disappointments, but then we need to move on Ruth 1:1-22, *page 299* • 1 Samuel 1:1-20, *page 305* • Lamentations 3:19-26, *page 895*

We should allow others to encourage us in times of disappointment 1 Samuel 23:13-18, *page 332* • 2 Corinthians 7:5-7, *page 1329*

We should put our trust in God even when things go wrong Job 1:6-22, *page 565* • Psalm 42:11, *page 628* • Habakkuk 3:17-18, *page 1027* • 2 Corinthians 4:7-18, *page 1327*

We can be honest with God about our disappointment Psalm 62:1-8, *page 639* • Jeremiah 15:10-21, *page 843* • Jeremiah 20:7-18, *page 848*

Some of our disappointments come because we are not thinking as God thinks Isaiah 55:1-9, *page 808* • Jonah 4:1-11, *page 1009*

God still has a plan for us even when things have gone wrong Jeremiah 29:10-14, *page 858* • Romans 8:28-39, *page 1292*

We should remember that God always has a resurrection plan in mind Luke 24:1-34, *page 1195* • 2 Corinthians 1:8-9, *page 1324*

We can experience the Lord's presence and strength in our difficulties 2 Corinthians 12:7-10, *page 1334* • 2 Timothy 4:9-18, *page 1387*

We should seek to grow by not complaining about things and instead trusting them to God Philippians 2:14-16, *page 1357* • Philippians 4:6-7, *page 1359*

▶ See ***Trusting God when we cannot see the way ahead***, *page 57;* ***Pressing on***, *page 1359.*

Discernment *see also Wisdom*

God wants us all to grow in discernment, that is, in the wise understanding, insight, and judgment that help us to distinguish between right and wrong. The Bible urges us to pray for such discernment, which is an important part of knowing how God wants us to live in the world.

> *Dear brothers and sisters, I plead with you to give your bodies to God because of all he has done for you. Let them be a living and holy sacrifice—the kind he will find acceptable. This is truly the way to worship him. Don't copy the behavior and customs of this world, but let God transform you into a new person by changing the way you think. Then you will learn to know God's will for you, which is good and pleasing and perfect. – Romans 12:1-2, page 1296*

We should always look beyond outward appearances 1 Samuel 16:1-13, *page 323* • Proverbs 28:11, *page 726* • Isaiah 11:1-3, *page 760* • John 7:24, *page 1211*

We should ask for God's wisdom, especially in difficult decisions 1 Kings 3:5-28, *page 378* • Proverbs 2:1-7, *page 698* • James 1:5-6, *page 1412*

Discernment involves seeing others' motives Nehemiah 6:1-9, *page 541*

We can pray for discernment and should grow in it Psalm 119:124-128, *page 681* • Proverbs 2:1-15, *page 698* • Philippians 1:9-11, *page 1355*

Jesus told us to be discerning about the times we are living in Luke 12:54-59, *page 1177*

We need discernment when we are seeking God's guidance Acts 16:6-10, *page 1261*

We should be discerning in our use of the gifts of the Holy Spirit 1 Corinthians 12:1-3, *page 1315* • 1 Corinthians 14:26-33, *page 1318* • 1 John 4:1-3, *page 1436*

Some people are given a special gift of discernment 1 Corinthians 12:7-11, *page 1315*

We should not be gullible about things or people but rather be ready to test them 1 Thessalonians 5:19-21, *page 1373* • 1 John 4:1-6, *page 1436*

Our aim should be to grow in discerning right and wrong Hebrews 5:11-14, *page 1400*

▶ See ***Wisdom***, *page 701.*

Discipleship

Discipleship is fundamental to being a follower of Jesus. In fact, it's so fundamental that the word "Christian" is only used three times in the New Testament, while the word "disciple" (sometimes translated "believer") is used over 280 times. Discipleship is a lifelong process of learning how to live and serve differently as we allow Jesus to reshape our thinking by his Spirit and his word. Discipleship can be costly, but it is always worth it and is ultimately richly rewarded.

> *"If any of you wants to be my follower, you must turn from your selfish ways, take up your cross daily, and follow me. If you try to hang on to your life, you will lose it. But if you give up your life for my sake, you will save it. And what do you benefit if you gain the whole world but are yourself lost or destroyed? If anyone is ashamed of me and my message, the Son of Man will be ashamed of that person when he returns in his glory and in the glory of the Father and the holy angels." – Luke 9:23-26, page 1169*

BASIC TRUTHS • *page 1510*

Disciples learn from their master Matthew 10:24-25, *page 1083* • Matthew 11:29-30, *page 1085*

We are called to make disciples, not just "Christians" Matthew 28:18-20, *page 1116*

If we follow Jesus as his disciples, we will be truly rewarded Mark 10:24-31, *page 1136*

Discipleship involves being trained for mission Luke 9:1-6, *page 1168* • Luke 10:1-20, *page 1171*

Being a follower of Jesus means putting him first Luke 9:57-62, *page 1171* • Luke 14:25-27, *page 1179* • Philippians 3:7-11, *page 1358*

Being a follower of Jesus means being faithful to him and obeying his teaching John 8:31-32, *page 1213* • John 14:15, *page 1223*

We should be recognized as Jesus' disciples by our love for one another John 13:34-35, *page 1222* • 1 John 4:7-21, *page 1436*

Following Jesus means depending on his resources John 15:1-17, *page 1223*

Love for Jesus is the basis of true discipleship John 21:15-19, *page 1233*

As disciples, we should help other disciples grow Acts 14:21-23, *page 1259*

The goal of discipleship is to become more like Jesus 2 Corinthians 3:16-18, *page 1326* • Ephesians 4:20-24, *page 1351*

Following Jesus means not living for ourselves 2 Corinthians 5:15-17, *page 1328*

▶ *See **Now that you are a Christian**, page A13; **Counting the cost**, page 1180; **Life from death**, page 1219; **Mentoring**, page 1385.*

Discipline *see also Self-control*

None of us instinctively likes discipline. Yet correction given in love—whether by our parents, our bosses, or God—is designed to help bring us to a place of maturity and responsibility. God's discipline is always for our good, even though it can seem painful or unpleasant at the time. We need to learn from God's loving correction and let it help us become more like Jesus.

> *And have you forgotten the encouraging words God spoke to you as his children? He said, "My child, don't make light of the LORD's discipline, and don't give up when he corrects you. For the LORD disciplines those he loves, and he punishes each one he accepts as his child." As you endure this divine discipline, remember that God is treating you as his own children. Who ever heard of a child who is never disciplined by its father? If God doesn't discipline you as he does all of his children, it means that you are illegitimate and are not really his children at all. Since we respected our earthly fathers who disciplined us, shouldn't we submit even more to the discipline of the Father of our spirits, and live forever? For our earthly fathers disciplined us for a few years, doing the best they knew how. But God's discipline is always good for us, so that we might share in his holiness. No discipline is enjoyable while it is happening—it's painful! But afterward there will be a peaceful harvest of right living for those who are trained in this way. – Hebrews 12:5-11, page 1408*

Life's hardships are part of God's training and discipline Deuteronomy 8:1-5, *page 211* • 2 Corinthians 4:1-12, *page 1327*

We neglect discipline to our loss 1 Samuel 2:12-17, *page 307* • 1 Samuel 3:12-13, *page 308* • Proverbs 10:17, *page 706*

God's discipline does not change his love for us Psalm 89:30-34, *page 659*

Parents are responsible for disciplining their children Proverbs 1:8-9, *page 697* • Proverbs 13:24, *page 710* • Ephesians 6:1-4, *page 1352*

The Lord disciplines those he loves Proverbs 3:11-12, *page 699* • Hebrews 12:4-13, *page 1408*

We should not reject God's discipline Proverbs 3:11-12, *page 699*

The church sometimes needs to discipline its members for unacceptable behavior 1 Corinthians 5:1-5, *page 1308*

God's discipline is preparing us for heaven 2 Corinthians 4:16-18, *page 1327*

God's word is his gift to correct us 2 Timothy 3:14-17, *page 1387* • Hebrews 4:12-13, *page 1400*

▶ *See **God's discipline**, page 1000.*

Discrimination

While discrimination is common in society today, whether on the grounds of social, racial, ethnic, or religious background, the Bible shows that it is something God hates. We cannot claim to be followers of Jesus and live at peace with discrimination. God does not discriminate against anyone and neither should we.

Then Peter replied, "I see very clearly that God shows no favoritism. In every nation he accepts those who fear him and do what is right." – Acts 10:34-35, page 1252

We should not discriminate against the disadvantaged Exodus 22:21-27, *page 93* • Malachi 3:5, *page 1052* • James 5:1-4, *page 1416*

We are called to be fair in our judgment of others Leviticus 19:15, *page 139* • Deuteronomy 1:16-17, *page 202*

God commands us to love our neighbor as ourselves Leviticus 19:18, *page 139* • Matthew 22:34-40, *page 1104* • Luke 10:25-37, *page 1172* • Romans 13:8-10, *page 1298*

God himself shows no partiality Deuteronomy 10:17-19, *page 213* • 2 Chronicles 19:4-10, *page 500*

We should not discriminate against other people groups Esther 3:5-6, *page 556* • John 1:45-46, *page 1201* • John 4:4-9, *page 1204*

There is no place for discrimination in the church Acts 6:1-7, *page 1244* • Acts 10:1-48, *page 1250* • Ephesians 2:11-22, *page 1347* • James 2:1-13, *page 1413*

All Christians are equal in God's eyes, so the basis of any discrimination is removed Galatians 3:26-29, *page 1341* • Ephesians 2:11-18, *page 1347* • Colossians 3:10-15, *page 1365*

God has no favorites Colossians 3:25, *page 1366*

Jesus died for people from every nation and background Revelation 5:9-10, *page 1451*

People from every background will all be together in heaven Revelation 7:9, *page 1454*

▶ *See **Prejudice**, page 1252; **Equality**, page 1340.*

Dishonesty *see also Integrity; Stealing*

Because God is truth, he hates dishonesty of every kind. The Bible says that he finds it detestable and urges us therefore to always pursue truth, integrity, and honesty in all our dealings with others, whether in relationships or business.

"You must use accurate scales when you weigh out merchandise, and you must use full and honest measures. Yes, always use honest weights and measures, so that you may enjoy a long life in the land the LORD your God is giving you. All who cheat with dishonest weights and measures are detestable to the LORD your God." – Deuteronomy 25:13-16, page 227

Dishonesty is condemned in the Ten Commandments Exodus 20:15-16, *page 90*

God wants us to be honest in all our business dealings Leviticus 19:35-37, *page 140* • Deuteronomy 25:13-16, *page 227* • Proverbs 11:1, *page 707* • Amos 8:4-10, *page 1000* • Micah 6:9-16, *page 1016*

God hates it when lack of integrity leads to injustice, and he will judge it Job 24:1-25, *page 584* • Isaiah 59:1-21, *page 812* • Zechariah 7:8-14, *page 1042*

We should not lie but rather pursue truth Psalm 34:12-14, *page 622* • Proverbs 6:16-19, *page 702* • Ephesians 4:25, *page 1351*

God does not welcome those who deceive Psalm 101:7, *page 665*

God hates all deception Proverbs 12:22, *page 709* • Acts 5:1-11, *page 1242*

Becoming a Christian will affect our business practices Luke 19:1-10, *page 1185* • Acts 19:17-27, *page 1267* • Ephesians 6:9, *page 1352*

We should not cheat others 1 Corinthians 6:7-8, *page 1309*

▶ *See **Cheating**, page 33; **Honesty**, page 707; **Lying**, page 1214; **Integrity**, page 1325.*

Divination *see Occult*

Divorce *see Marriage*

Doctrine *see also Faith*

"Doctrine" doesn't always get a good press. Some see it as heavy and boring, with no practical value for the Christian life; others use it as a weapon to forcefully argue with other Christians who disagree with them. Neither approach is correct! Doctrine should be a delight to us, for it is the summary of Christian beliefs and teachings that help us both to know God better and to live faithfully and fruitfully for him.

> *The instructions of the LORD are perfect, reviving the soul. The decrees of the LORD are trustworthy, making wise the simple. The commandments of the LORD are right, bringing joy to the heart. The commands of the LORD are clear, giving insight for living. Reverence for the LORD is pure, lasting forever. The laws of the LORD are true; each one is fair. They are more desirable than gold, even the finest gold. They are sweeter than honey, even honey dripping from the comb. They are a warning to your servant, a great reward for those who obey them. – Psalm 19:7-11, page 613*

Knowing, loving, and passing on the teachings of God's word should be a priority for us Deuteronomy 6:4-9, *page 208* • Deuteronomy 11:18-22, *page 214*

We come to know doctrine through being taught God's word Ezra 7:10, *page 529* • Matthew 4:23, *page 1074* • Acts 2:42-47, *page 1239*

We should study the teachings of God's word Proverbs 4:1-4, *page 700* • Acts 17:11, *page 1264*

Doctrine without the Spirit and without love brings legalism like that of the Pharisees Matthew 9:10-13, *page 1081* • Matthew 15:1-20, *page 1092* • Matthew 23:1-39, *page 1105*

Sound doctrine helps us grow and become mature Ephesians 4:11-16, *page 1350* • Colossians 1:28-29, *page 1363*

We are called to protect sound doctrine and expose false doctrine 1 Timothy 1:3-7, *page 1379* • 2 Timothy 1:13-14, *page 1385* • 2 Timothy 4:1-5, *page 1387* • Jude 1:3, *page 1442*

We are called to watch both our life and our doctrine 1 Timothy 4:16, *page 1382*

We should ensure that sound doctrine is passed on 2 Timothy 2:1-2, *page 1385*

Leaders in the church must have and teach sound doctrine Titus 1:6-9, *page 1389* • Titus 2:1-8, *page 1390*

We should hold firmly to the foundational teaching we received Revelation 3:1-3, *page 1449*

Doubt *see also Faith*

All of us have doubts at times; what is crucial is what we do with them. If we simply brood over them and don't share them with others, they have a way of getting bigger and stronger. But the Bible encourages us to be honest about our doubts, seeking help from others and even bringing them to God. Wrestling with doubts ultimately helps us find answers and makes us stronger. And God is still with us, even in the doubting process.

> *O Jacob, how can you say the LORD does not see your troubles? O Israel, how can you say God ignores your rights? Have you never heard? Have you never understood? The LORD is the everlasting God, the Creator of all the earth. He never grows weak or weary. No one can measure the depths of his understanding. He gives power to the weak and strength to the powerless. Even youths will become weak and tired, and young men will fall in exhaustion. But those who trust in the LORD will find new strength. They will soar high on wings like eagles. They will run and not grow weary. They will walk and not faint. – Isaiah 40:27-31, page 790*

We can be honest with God about our doubts Genesis 15:1-8, *page 18* • Mark 9:14-29, *page 1134*

God is happy to meet us in our doubts Exodus 4:1-17, *page 68* • 1 Kings 19:1-21, *page 404* • Matthew 11:2-6, *page 1084*

When we have doubts about moving ahead, we should remember that God is with us Joshua 1:6-9, *page 242*

Doubt and faith are often intertwined Psalm 42:5-11, *page 627*

When we have doubts, we should remember God's faithfulness to us in the past Psalm 77:7-20, *page 650*

In times of doubt or difficulty, we should remember God's promises and trust in God's power Isaiah 41:8-10, *page 792* • 2 Corinthians 12:7-10, *page 1334*

Doubt inhibits our prayers Matthew 21:18-22, *page 1102* • James 1:5-8, *page 1412*

Those with doubt need help and encouragement Mark 9:14-24, *page 1134* • Jude 1:22-23, *page 1443*

A fresh encounter with Jesus dispels doubt John 21:15-19, *page 1233*

If we start doubting our salvation, we should go back to what God did for us through Jesus at the cross Romans 3:23-26, *page 1286* • Romans 5:1-11, *page 1287* • Romans 8:1-2, *page 1290*

The answer to our doubt is to remember the faithfulness of God Hebrews 10:23, *page 1406*

▶ *See **Trusting God when we cannot see the way ahead**, page 57; **Faith**, page 1286; **Doubt**, page 1414.*

Drinking *see Alcohol*

Earth *see also Creation*

When God created the world, it was "very good" (Genesis 1:31), and he gave the human race responsibility for caring for it on his behalf. Although human sin and selfishness have increasingly spoiled the earth, God has not abandoned it; it is still his, which is why Christians should show care and concern for it. Although the earth will one day be judged and cleansed, it will also be renewed and become like Eden once again.

"He is the God who made the world and everything in it. Since he is Lord of heaven and earth, he doesn't live in man-made temples, and human hands can't serve his needs—for he has no needs. He himself gives life and breath to everything, and he satisfies every need. From one man he created all the nations throughout the whole earth. He decided beforehand when they should rise and fall, and he determined their boundaries. His purpose was for the nations to seek after God and perhaps feel their way toward him and find him—though he is not far from any one of us. For in him we live and move and exist. As some of your own poets have said, 'We are his offspring.'" – Acts 17:24-28, page 1264

God created the heavens and the earth Genesis 1:1-31, *page 4* • Nehemiah 9:6, *page 545* • Isaiah 42:5, *page 793* • Acts 14:15, *page 1259* • Revelation 10:5-6, *page 1455* • Psalm 89:11-14, *page 658* • Psalm 95:4-5, *page 663*

People are called to take care of the earth and everything in it Genesis 1:26-28, *page 5* • Genesis 2:15, *page 5* • Exodus 23:10-12, *page 93* • Proverbs 12:10, *page 708*

God made a covenant to protect the earth and all life upon it Genesis 9:1-17, *page 12*

We can defile the earth by our behavior Leviticus 18:24-25, *page 138* • Jeremiah 2:7, *page 824* • Jeremiah 3:2-5, *page 825*

The earth belongs to God 1 Chronicles 29:10-12, *page 480* • Psalm 24:1-2, *page 615*

God sustains the earth and all life on it Job 38:1–42:3, *page 595* • Psalm 104:13-14, *page 667* • Matthew 6:25-30, *page 1078* • Matthew 10:29-31, *page 1084* • Hebrews 1:3, *page 1396*

The present earth will one day be set free from death and decay Romans 8:18-25, *page 1291*

Everything was created through Jesus and for Jesus Colossians 1:15-20, *page 1362*

God will one day create a new earth 2 Peter 3:11-13, *page 1430* • Revelation 21:1-5, *page 1465*

▶ *See **The environment**, page 606; **The world**, page 1226.*

Education *see Teaching*

Election

It is an amazing privilege to have been chosen by God, and it brings huge reassurance. However, this "election," as this choice is often called, should not become a matter of pride, as it often did for Israel. Rather it calls for a response of humility and gratitude, along with a compulsion to go and find others that God is calling, for the Bible says that God's calling of us does not diminish human responsibility to respond to him. How God's choosing and our responding come together remains one of God's mysteries.

When the Gentiles heard this, they were very glad and thanked the Lord for his message; and all who were chosen for eternal life became believers. So the Lord's message spread throughout that region. – Acts 13:48-49, page 1258

Abraham and his descendants, Israel, were chosen by God to carry out his purposes for the world Genesis 12:1-4, *page 15* • Genesis 17:1-6, *page 20* • Exodus 19:3-6, *page 88* • Isaiah 42:1-7, *page 793*

God chooses people as his own out of love Deuteronomy 7:7-11, *page 210* • John 15:15-16, *page 1224* • Ephesians 1:3-8, *page 1346*

The idea of God's people being chosen runs throughout the Bible Deuteronomy 14:2, *page 217* • Psalm 33:12, *page 621* • Isaiah 41:8-10, *page 792* • Mark 13:24-27, *page 1141* • 1 Thessalonians 1:4, *page 1369* • 1 Peter 2:4-10, *page 1422*

God's people are chosen to show others what God is like Isaiah 49:3-6, *page 801* • Matthew 5:13-16, *page 1075* • 1 Peter 2:9-12, *page 1422*

The doctrine of election can encourage us to get through hard times Romans 8:28-39, *page 1292*

Israel's election was not based on physical descent from Abraham, but only on God's mercy Romans 9:6-16, *page 1292*

Israel's election means that, before the end, many Jews will turn in faith to Jesus as Messiah Romans 11:1-12, 25-36, *page 1295*

No one deserves to be chosen by God Ephesians 2:1-10, *page 1347* • 2 Timothy 1:9-11, *page 1384*

The teaching about election is not to make us proud but to encourage us to become more like God Colossians 3:12-15, *page 1365*

The teaching of election should motivate us to share the gospel with others 2 Timothy 2:10, *page 1386*

▶ *See* ***Repentance****, page 1253;* ***Election****, page 1257;* ***Faith****, page 1286.*

Embarrassment

Embarrassment is the sense of shame or awkwardness we feel when we are put on the spot. The Bible encourages us not to be embarrassed because of our Christian faith, but to look to God, who wants to help us stand up for what we believe.

For I am not ashamed of this Good News about Christ. It is the power of God at work, saving everyone who believes—the Jew first and also the Gentile. – Romans 1:16, page 1282

Sometimes our embarrassment might be caused by sin Genesis 3:1-10, *page 6* • 1 Samuel 15:24-31, *page 322* • Ezra 9:1-6, *page 531*

We can sometimes be embarrassed or shamed into doing the right thing 2 Samuel 19:1-8, *page 364* • Ezra 8:21-23, *page 531*

Embarrassment is often caused by what we think people will think of us Matthew 14:1-12, *page 1091* • John 12:42-43, *page 1221*

If we are ashamed of Jesus now, he will be ashamed of us when he returns Mark 8:34-38, *page 1133*

Doing the right thing may sometimes cause embarrassment for us Acts 10:28-35, *page 1251*

We should not be embarrassed about the Good News Romans 1:16, *page 1282* • 2 Timothy 1:8-12, *page 1384*

If we stop being ashamed of sin, it should be a warning sign to us that we are walking a godless path Romans 1:18-22, *page 1283*

We need not be ashamed of our past, for when we become Christians we are forgiven and become brand new people 1 Corinthians 15:9-10, *page 1319* • 2 Corinthians 5:17, *page 1328* • Philippians 3:6-9, *page 1358*

We should not be embarrassed about sharing our testimony 2 Timothy 1:8, *page 1384*

▶ *See* ***Guilt****, page 620.*

Emotions *see also Heart*

Emotions are part of our God-given nature, but they can be one of our best friends or one of our worst enemies! Emotions help us to express our joy, including the joy of our relationship with God; but they can also lie to us, making us feel that something is okay when God's word says it isn't, drag us down when things haven't gone well, and even make us doubt whether God really loves us. Emotions therefore need to be handled wisely, so that we rule them rather than letting them rule us.

Guard your heart above all else, for it determines the course of your life. – Proverbs 4:23, page 700

Our emotions can deceive us, making us feel that something is good when God has said it isn't Genesis 3:1-7, *page 6* • 2 Samuel 13:1-22, *page 355* • Proverbs 14:12, *page 711* • Jeremiah 17:9-10, *page 845*

Not handled properly, our emotions can lead us to sin Genesis 4:2-16, *page 8* • Numbers 14:1-35, *page 169* • 2 Samuel 11:1-27, *page 352* • 2 Samuel 13:1-22, *page 355* • John 18:1-11, *page 1226*

God himself has emotions Genesis 6:5-6, *page 9* • 2 Kings 17:18, *page 432* • Jeremiah 31:3, *page 860* • Zephaniah 3:16-17, *page 1032*

Expressing emotions is a valid aspect of worship 2 Samuel 6:12-22, *page 348* • Ezra 3:8-13, *page 524* • Nehemiah 8:1-12, *page 544* • Psalm 47:1-9, *page 631*

Not handled properly, our emotions can lead to illness 2 Samuel 13:1-4, *page 355* • Proverbs 15:13, *page 712* • Proverbs 17:22, *page 714*

God heals those with broken hearts and emotions Psalm 34:17-18, *page 622* • Isaiah 61:1-3, *page 814*

We should carefully guard our emotions Proverbs 4:23, *page 700*

Emotional excitement alone can mislead us Proverbs 19:2, *page 715*

Jesus experienced emotions Matthew 26:36-38, *page 1111* • John 11:33-38, *page 1218*

We need to let God's Spirit teach us how to control our emotions Galatians 5:16-25, *page 1343* • 2 Timothy 1:7, *page 1384*

Some emotions are sinful and need to be gotten rid of Ephesians 4:29-32, *page 1351* • Colossians 3:5-10, *page 1365* • 1 Peter 2:1-3, *page 1421*

▸ *See **Cain and Abel**, page 8; **The heart**, page 909; **Joy**, page 1360.*

Employment *see Work*

Encouragement

All of us need encouragement. This is not a sign of weakness but simply a reflection of how God has made us to be dependent on one another. But in addition to needing encouragement, we also need to be encouragers, so we can give as well as receive. God himself is the greatest encourager of all.

Let us hold tightly without wavering to the hope we affirm, for God can be trusted to keep his promise. Let us think of ways to motivate one another to acts of love and good works. And let us not neglect our meeting together, as some people do, but encourage one another, especially now that the day of his return is drawing near. – Hebrews 10:23-25, page 1406

God himself encourages us Genesis 15:1-5, *page 18* • Isaiah 40:28-31, *page 791* • Isaiah 41:10, *page 792* • Romans 15:5-6, *page 1299* • 2 Corinthians 7:5-6, *page 1329*

We should encourage those who are weak and afraid Deuteronomy 31:7-8, *page 234* • Isaiah 35:3-4, *page 784* • 1 Thessalonians 5:14, *page 1373*

Encouragement helps us to keep going Judges 20:19-22, *page 295* • 1 Samuel 23:15-18, *page 332* • Acts 11:22-23, *page 1254*

Jesus' ministry brought encouragement to those burdened and in need Matthew 11:28-30, *page 1085* • Luke 4:16-21, *page 1159*

BASIC TRUTHS • *page 1516*

Jesus' presence brings us encouragement Matthew 14:22-33, *page 1092* • 2 Timothy 4:16-18, *page 1388* • Revelation 1:9-18, *page 1446*

The Holy Spirit encourages us Acts 9:31, *page 1250* • Romans 8:15-27, *page 1291*

We should encourage other believers to remain faithful Acts 11:22-24, *page 1254* • Acts 14:21-23, *page 1259* • 1 Thessalonians 2:9-12, *page 1370*

Remembering that we belong to Jesus should encourage us Romans 5:1-2, *page 1287* • Philippians 2:1, *page 1356*

We are called to encourage one another Romans 12:6-8, *page 1296* • Romans 15:1-6, *page 1299* • 2 Corinthians 13:11, *page 1335* • 1 Thessalonians 5:11, *page 1373*

The Bible gives us encouragement as we learn from its lessons Romans 15:4, *page 1299* • Hebrews 11:1–12:3, *page 1407*

Thinking about Jesus' resurrection and second coming should encourage us 1 Thessalonians 4:13-18, *page 1372*

▶ *See **Courage**, page 243; **The power of encouragement**, page 578; **Being there**, page 575; **Barnabas**, page 1242.*

End times *see Jesus Christ: his return*

Endurance *see Perseverance*

Enemies *see also Relationships*

Even the best people in life end up with enemies (think of Jesus!). But the Bible tells us to do all we can to win over our enemies and, even if we can't, to still love them and to leave them to God.

> *"You have heard the law that says, 'Love your neighbor' and hate your enemy. But I say, love your enemies! Pray for those who persecute you! In that way, you will be acting as true children of your Father in heaven. For he gives his sunlight to both the evil and the good, and he sends rain on the just and the unjust alike. If you love only those who love you, what reward is there for that? Even corrupt tax collectors do that much. If you are kind only to your friends, how are you different from anyone else? Even pagans do that. But you are to be perfect, even as your Father in heaven is perfect." – Matthew 5:43-48, page 1076*

God tells us to love our enemies Exodus 23:4-5, *page 93* • Matthew 5:38-48, *page 1076* • Romans 12:9-21, *page 1296*

We should not retaliate but simply trust God Psalm 37:1-9, *page 623* • Acts 7:54-60, *page 1246* • 1 Peter 2:21-23, *page 1423*

A godly life affects even our enemies Proverbs 16:7, *page 712*

We should not be happy when our enemies fail Proverbs 24:17-18, *page 721* • Obadiah 1:12-15, *page 1005*

We should overcome our enemies with kindness, not hatred Proverbs 25:21-22, *page 723* • Romans 12:17-21, *page 1297* • 1 Peter 3:9-11, *page 1423*

Jesus tells us to forgive our enemies Matthew 6:12-15, *page 1077* • Luke 6:27-36, *page 1163* • Luke 23:33-34, *page 1194*

Being a Christian will lead to some becoming our enemies Mark 13:9-13, *page 1141* • John 15:18-21, *page 1224* • 1 John 3:11-13, *page 1436*

Jesus changed us from being God's enemies to becoming his friends Romans 5:6-11, *page 1287*

As Christians, we overcome Satan, our greatest enemy, through the blood of Jesus and our testimony Revelation 12:7-12, *page 1457*

Environment, The *see Creation; Earth*

Envy *see also Jealousy*

Envy is the feeling of discontent that arises within us when we want to have something that someone else has. Envy shows a lack of trust in God and his plans for our life, for he has promised to provide us with everything that we need. Therefore, we do not need to look at others and wish we were like them or wish we had what they had.

> *Truly God is good to Israel, to those whose hearts are pure. But as for me, I almost lost my footing. My feet were slipping, and I was almost gone. For I envied the proud when I saw them prosper despite their wickedness. They seem to live such painless lives; their bodies are so healthy and strong. They don't have troubles like other people; they're not plagued with problems like everyone else. They wear pride like a jeweled necklace and clothe themselves with cruelty. These fat cats have everything their hearts could ever wish for! They scoff and speak only evil; in their pride they seek to crush others. They boast against the very heavens, and their words strut throughout the earth. And so the people are dismayed and confused, drinking in all their words. "What does God know?" they ask. "Does the Most High even know what's happening?" Look at these wicked people—enjoying a life of ease while their riches multiply.* – *Psalm 73:1-12, page 646*

Our behavior should not provoke others to be envious Genesis 37:3-11, *page 46* • Galatians 5:25-26, *page 1343*

God commands us not to desire what belongs to others Exodus 20:17, *page 90*

We should not envy those who do wrong, even if they seem to be blessed Psalm 37:1-7, *page 623* • Proverbs 3:31-33, *page 699* • Proverbs 23:17-18, *page 720* • Proverbs 24:19-20, *page 721*

A prayer of someone struggling with envy Psalm 73:1-20, *page 646*

Envy can eat away at us Proverbs 14:30, *page 711*

Envy can lead us to take foolish, godless steps Matthew 27:15-18, *page 1113*

Envy is part of our old way of living Mark 7:14-23, *page 1131* • Galatians 5:19-26, *page 1343* • Titus 3:3-8, *page 1391*

Wanting what others have destroys our perspective Luke 12:13-21, *page 1175*

We should not be envious when others are blessed Luke 15:11-32, *page 1181*

Envy can cause us to act rashly Acts 7:9-10, *page 1245*

Envy is sin Romans 1:28-32, *page 1283* • Galatians 5:19-21, *page 1343*

Envy leads to other kinds of sin James 3:13-16, *page 1415* • James 4:1-3, *page 1416*

Equality *see Discrimination*

Eschatology *see Jesus Christ: his return*

Eternal life *see also Life*

Through Jesus we can have eternal life—not just life that lasts forever, but life that has all the hallmarks of God's future Kingdom and that we can start to experience right now. None of us can do anything to earn eternal life; it is simply God's gift to us through faith in Jesus. As we believe in him, we are born again by God's Spirit, and our eternal life begins.

> *"For this is how God loved the world: He gave his one and only Son, so that everyone who believes in him will not perish but have eternal life. God sent his Son into the world not to judge the world, but to save the world through him."* – *John 3:16-17, page 1203*

Eternal life is demonstrated in our lives through bearing good fruit and doing God's will Matthew 7:15-27, *page 1078* • Matthew 19:16-26, *page 1099*

Eternal life is worth making any sacrifice for Matthew 18:7-9, *page 1097* • Matthew 19:27-29, *page 1099*

It is those whom God sees as righteous who will receive eternal life Matthew 25:31-46, *page 1109*

Jesus is life itself John 1:1-4, *page 1199* • John 14:6, *page 1222*

We must be reborn spiritually to receive eternal life John 3:1-17, *page 1202*

Eternal life is like fresh water springing up from within us John 4:4-14, *page 1204*

Faith in Jesus assures us that we are not condemned and that we have eternal life John 5:24-30, *page 1207* • John 11:25-26, *page 1217* • 1 John 5:11-13, *page 1438*

Only God's Spirit can give eternal life John 6:63, *page 1210* • 2 Corinthians 3:6, *page 1326*

Eternal life starts with knowing God through Jesus John 17:2-3, *page 1225*

Eternal life is God's free gift and cannot be earned Romans 6:20-23, *page 1289* • Ephesians 2:4-9, *page 1347*

Eternal life will one day be experienced in a new resurrection body 1 Corinthians 15:35-57, *page 1320*

Knowing we have eternal life through Jesus gives us great hope Titus 3:3-7, *page 1391*

▸ *See **The new birth**, page 1203; **Jesus: the only way to God**, page 1241; **Justification**, page 1288; **Christ's resurrection and ours**, page 1320.*

Ethnicity *see Discrimination*

Eucharist *see Communion*

Evangelism *see Witnessing*

Evil *see also Demons; Satan*

Evil is the very opposite of all that God is. If God is truth, evil is lies; if God is love, evil is hate; if God is life, evil is death. This is why God hates evil so much, and why he does so much to keep humanity from experiencing it. Evil will remain in this world until Jesus comes again; but in the meantime, God calls us to expose it and oppose it, replacing it with good. And because God is sovereign, he can always bring good out of evil.

> *Never pay back evil with more evil. Do things in such a way that everyone can see you are honorable. Do all that you can to live in peace with everyone. Dear friends, never take revenge. Leave that to the righteous anger of God. For the Scriptures say, "I will take revenge; I will pay them back," says the LORD. Instead, "If your enemies are hungry, feed them. If they are thirsty, give them something to drink. In doing this, you will heap burning coals of shame on their heads." Don't let evil conquer you, but conquer evil by doing good. – Romans 12:17-21, page 1297*

God did not want people to know what evil was, for he knew what it would do to them Genesis 2:15-17, *page 5* • Genesis 3:1-24, *page 6*

Evil's rapid spread caused God much heartache Genesis 6:5-7, *page 9*

God has always been able to bring good out of evil Genesis 50:19-20, *page 63* • Acts 2:22-36, *page 1238* • Romans 8:28-39, *page 1292*

Worshiping other gods is seen as one of the greatest evils because of what it leads to Exodus 20:3-6, *page 89* • Exodus 32:1-10, *page 103* • Judges 2:1-23, *page 271* • 2 Kings 21:1-16, *page 439*

Although evil often seems to triumph, evildoers will one day be destroyed Job 4:8-9, *page 568* • Psalm 37:8-13, *page 624* • Proverbs 6:12-15, *page 702*

We should avoid those who do evil Psalm 1:1-6, *page 602* • Psalm 26:5, *page 616* • Proverbs 4:14-19, 23-27, *page 700*

God cannot stand the sight of evil Psalm 34:15-16, *page 622* • Habakkuk 1:12-13, *page 1024*

We should pray to be saved from the evil one Matthew 6:9-13, *page 1077*

God permits evil to show us how bad humanity has become Romans 1:24-32, *page 1283*

God's Law exposes evil for what it really is Romans 3:19-20, *page 1285* • Romans 7:7-13, *page 1290*

Christians should not be evildoers Ephesians 4:17-32, *page 1350* • 1 Thessalonians 5:22, *page 1373*

There are spiritual forces at work behind evil Ephesians 6:10-12, *page 1352*

At the end of the age, all evil will be excluded from God's new creation, and only beauty will remain Revelation 20:7-10, *page 1464* • Revelation 21:1-27, *page 1465*

▸ *See **Satan**, page 566; **Demons**, page 1126; **Spiritual warfare**, page 1353.*

Failure, How to handle

We all make mistakes: saying or doing the wrong thing, or not doing or saying the right thing. Rather than trying to excuse ourselves or blame others, the Bible encourages us to accept responsibility, turn back to the Lord, and honestly confess our sin and failure before him. As we do so, he promises to forgive us and restore us so that we can make a fresh start. Failure never disqualifies us, as long as we handle it rightly.

> *If we claim we have no sin, we are only fooling ourselves and not living in the truth. But if we confess our sins to him, he is faithful and just to forgive us our sins and to cleanse us from all wickedness. If we claim we have not sinned, we are calling God a liar and showing that his word has no place in our hearts. – 1 John 1:8-10, page 1433*

We should not shift the blame for our failures or mistakes onto others Genesis 3:1-19, *page 6* • Exodus 32:1-28, *page 103* • 1 Samuel 13:5-14, *page 318* • James 1:12-15, *page 1412*

God is always ready to forgive our failures Exodus 34:6-7, *page 106* • 2 Samuel 12:1-25, *page 354* • Psalm 86:1-5, *page 656* • 1 John 1:8-10, *page 1433*

We sometimes fail because we didn't take advice 1 Kings 12:1-24, *page 392* • Proverbs 15:22, *page 712*

We should deal with failure by repenting and turning back to God Psalm 32:1-5, *page 620* • Psalm 51:1-15, *page 633* • Luke 18:9-14, *page 1183*

We should learn from past failures and mistakes Proverbs 24:16, *page 721* • 1 Corinthians 10:1-11, *page 1313*

The Good News of Jesus is for those who acknowledge their failures and know their need Luke 5:27-32, *page 1161*

No matter how badly we have failed, Jesus will always forgive us when we come back to him John 8:1-11, *page 1211* • John 21:15-19, *page 1233*

▶ *See* ***Is there anything God won't forgive?****, page 633;* ***Hope****, page 895;* ***Handling failure****, page 1232;* ***Pressing on****, page 1359;* ***How can I be sure God has forgiven me?****, page 1433.*

Faith

Faith is simply trusting God. It has nothing to do with how "pumped up" we might feel any given day, and likewise it is not negated by any mistakes we may have made. Faith focuses on God, trusting him both to save us and to help us through life.

> *Faith shows the reality of what we hope for; it is the evidence of things we cannot see. – Hebrews 11:1, page 1407*

Faith is simply trusting God Genesis 15:1-6, *page 18* • Psalm 37:1-6, *page 623* • Proverbs 3:5-6, *page 699*

God is pleased when we trust him Genesis 22:1-18, *page 26* • Psalm 147:10-11, *page 694*

Faith involves trusting Jesus' authority Matthew 8:5-13, *page 1080* • Mark 5:21-43, *page 1127*

Even a little faith goes a long way if it is genuine Matthew 17:14-21, *page 1096* • Luke 17:1-6, *page 1182*

We need to have faith when we pray Matthew 21:21-22, *page 1102* • James 1:5-8, *page 1412* • James 5:13-18, *page 1417*

Jesus encourages us to let our faith grow Mark 9:14-24, *page 1134* • Mark 11:20-24, *page 1138*

Faith is expressed in obedience Luke 6:46-49, *page 1164* • Hebrews 11:7-12, *page 1407*

Faith is needed for salvation John 1:1-13, *page 1199* • John 3:1-21, *page 1202* • Romans 3:21-31, *page 1286* • Galatians 3:5-9, *page 1340* • Ephesians 2:8-9, *page 1347*

Faith comes from hearing the word of God Romans 10:14-18, *page 1294*

Faith is part of the spiritual armor God gives us Ephesians 6:13-18, *page 1352*

Faith is believing what we cannot yet see Hebrews 11:1-3, 13-16, *page 1407* • 1 Peter 1:8-9, *page 1420*

We cannot please God without faith Hebrews 11:6, *page 1407*

Faith needs to be worked out through what we do in life James 2:14-26, *page 1413*

▸ *See **Trusting God when we cannot see the way ahead**, page 57; **Repentance**, page 1253; **Faith**, page 1286; **Justification**, page 1288; **Faith and works**, page 1415.*

Faithfulness *see also Commitment*

One of God's most fundamental qualities is his faithfulness—his unswerving commitment to his purposes and his people. God remains faithful even when others don't, and he calls us as his people to develop this quality in our own lives too.

> *The faithful love of the LORD never ends! His mercies never cease. Great is his faithfulness; his mercies begin afresh each morning. I say to myself, "The LORD is my inheritance; therefore, I will hope in him!" The LORD is good to those who depend on him, to those who search for him. So it is good to wait quietly for salvation from the LORD. And it is good for people to submit at an early age to the yoke of his discipline. – Lamentations 3:22-27, page 895*

God is always faithful Exodus 34:6-7, *page 106* • Psalm 89:1-8, *page 658* • 1 Corinthians 1:4-9, *page 1303* • Hebrews 10:23, *page 1406*

We should be faithful to the promises we make Numbers 30:1-2, *page 192* • Ecclesiastes 5:1-7, *page 734* • Matthew 5:33-37, *page 1076*

Christians should remain faithful in their marriage relationships Deuteronomy 5:18, *page 208* • Malachi 2:13-16, *page 1051* • Matthew 19:1-9, *page 1098* • Hebrews 13:4, *page 1409*

God wants us to be faithful to him and blesses those who are Joshua 24:14-28, *page 268* • Daniel 6:1-28, *page 963* • Hebrews 3:12-15, *page 1398* • Revelation 2:8-10, *page 1447*

We should remain faithful in our relationships Ruth 1:6-18, *page 299* • Proverbs 17:17, *page 714* • Philippians 2:19-22, *page 1357*

We should be faithful in handling money honestly 2 Kings 12:9-15, *page 426* • 2 Kings 22:3-7, *page 440* • Luke 16:10-13, *page 1182*

We should be faithful in handling the resources and gifts entrusted to us Matthew 25:14-30, *page 1109* • Luke 19:11-27, *page 1185* • 1 Corinthians 4:1-2, *page 1307* • 1 Peter 4:10-11, *page 1424*

We need to be faithful in prayer Romans 1:9, *page 1282* • Ephesians 1:15-20, *page 1346* • Colossians 4:2-4, 12-13, *page 1366*

Even when we are faithless, God remains faithful Romans 3:1-4, *page 1285* • 2 Timothy 2:11-13, *page 1386*

God is faithful when we are tempted 1 Corinthians 10:12-13, *page 1313* • 2 Peter 2:4-9, *page 1428*

Faithfulness should be growing in us as part of the fruit of the Spirit Galatians 5:22-23, *page 1343*

We should be faithful concerning the content of the gospel and should pass it on faithfully to others 2 Timothy 1:13-14, *page 1385* • 2 Timothy 2:1-2, *page 1385*

▸ *See **Faithfulness**, page 1307.*

Family *see also Children; Marriage*

The family is hugely important to God, for it is meant to reflect what he himself is like as a relational God. In Bible times, the family was much wider than just a father and mother and their children. It embraced more distant relatives and others in need, so it challenges our modern notion of the nuclear family. God wants his church to be a family in which there is a place and a function for all.

> *Jesus and the ones he makes holy have the same Father. That is why Jesus is not ashamed to call them his brothers and sisters. For he said to God, "I will proclaim your name to my brothers and sisters. I will praise you among your assembled people." He also said, "I will put my trust in him," that is, "I and the children God has given me." – Hebrews 2:11-13, page 1398*

Marriage lies at the heart of the family Genesis 1:26-28, *page 5* • Matthew 19:1-9, *page 1098* • Ephesians 5:21–6:4, *page 1351*

Favoritism and jealousy spoil family life Genesis 16:1-16, *page 19* • Genesis 27:41-45, *page 34* • Genesis 37:2-36, *page 46*

Teaching about God needs to begin in the family Deuteronomy 6:4-9, *page 208* • Proverbs 22:6, *page 719* • Ephesians 6:4, *page 1352*

Integrity needs to begin in the family home Psalm 101:2, *page 664*

Jesus experienced the pressures of family life Mark 3:31-35, *page 1124* • Luke 2:41-52, *page 1156* • John 7:1-5, *page 1210*

Our relationship with God takes priority even over our relationship with our family Luke 9:57-62, *page 1171* • Luke 12:51-53, *page 1177* • Luke 14:25-33, *page 1179*

Christians should help other members of God's family Acts 6:1-7, *page 1244* • Acts 11:27-30, *page 1254* • 2 Corinthians 8:1-15, *page 1330*

Whole families can come to faith together Acts 10:23-48, *page 1251* • Acts 16:25-34, *page 1262*

Christians are members of God's family Galatians 6:10, *page 1344* • Ephesians 2:19-22, *page 1348* • 1 Peter 5:9, *page 1425*

Husbands and wives loving each other is the foundation of family life Ephesians 5:21-33, *page 1351* • Colossians 3:18-19, *page 1365*

Children should obey their parents, and parents are to encourage their children Ephesians 6:1-4, *page 1352* • Colossians 3:20-21, *page 1366*

Church leaders must have a good family life, for they cannot lead a church if they cannot lead their own families 1 Timothy 3:1-5, *page 1380* • Titus 1:6-9, *page 1389*

▶ *See* ***Family****, page 714;* ***Does marriage still matter to God?****, page 976;* ***Children****, page 1100.*

Fasting

Fasting is the practice of going without food, and sometimes drink, for a period of time in order to devote ourselves to God, to pray, or to seek a breakthrough in some seemingly impossible situation. It demonstrates that nothing is more important than getting close to God, not even food. In Bible times, it was practiced both routinely and at times of special need.

> *"And when you fast, don't make it obvious, as the hypocrites do, for they try to look miserable and disheveled so people will admire them for their fasting. I tell you the truth, that is the only reward they will ever get. But when you fast, comb your hair and wash your face. Then no one will notice that you are fasting, except your Father, who knows what you do in private. And your Father, who sees everything, will reward you." – Matthew 6:16-18, page 1077*

Fasting expresses devotion to God and his purposes Exodus 34:27-30, *page 107* • Luke 2:36-37, *page 1156* • Luke 4:1-13, *page 1158*

Fasting can be for various lengths of time Exodus 34:28, *page 107* • 1 Samuel 7:5-6, *page 312* • 1 Samuel 31:11-13, *page 340* • Esther 4:16, *page 558* • Matthew 4:1-2, *page 1073*

Fasting can be total or partial (that is, abstaining from certain types of food) Exodus 34:28, *page 107* • Esther 4:15-16, *page 558* • Daniel 1:8-17, *page 955*

Fasting can express repentance Deuteronomy 9:18-21, *page 212* • 1 Samuel 7:5-6, *page 312* • Nehemiah 9:1-3, *page 545*

Fasting can express grief Judges 20:24-26, *page 295* • 2 Samuel 1:11-12, *page 342*

Fasting can be turned to in times of national crisis 2 Chronicles 20:1-24, *page 500* • Esther 4:1-3, *page 557*

Fasting demonstrates that we are completely dependent on God 2 Chronicles 20:3-4, 12, *page 500* • Ezra 8:21-23, *page 531*

Fasting often leads to a breakthrough in prayer Nehemiah 1:1-11, *page 536* • Esther 4:1-17, *page 557* • Psalm 69:9-18, *page 644* • Daniel 9:1-19, *page 968*

Fasting must be sincere and not just a religious exercise Isaiah 58:1-14, *page 810* • Joel 2:12-14, *page 989* • Zechariah 7:4-12, *page 1042* • Matthew 6:16-18, *page 1077*

Fasting helps us to seek God's insight and guidance Daniel 10:1-14, *page 969* • Acts 13:1-3, *page 1255*

Jesus fasted and expected his followers to do so too Matthew 4:1-2, *page 1073* • Mark 2:19-20, *page 1121*

Fasting can be used to seek God's blessing and mark a new stage in life Acts 14:21-23, *page 1259*

▸ *See* ***Does fasting have any value?***, *page 1042.*

Fatherhood *see Adoption, Spiritual; Children*

Favoritism *see Discrimination*

Fear

Almost all of us have moments in life when we are afraid. At such times, the Bible encourages us to look to God and to draw on the strength and protection that he has promised to give. He does not promise that he will always remove the object of our fear, but he does promise to give us courage to press on.

> *"Don't be afraid of those who want to kill your body; they cannot touch your soul. Fear only God, who can destroy both soul and body in hell. What is the price of two sparrows—one copper coin? But not a single sparrow can fall to the ground without your Father knowing it. And the very hairs on your head are all numbered. So don't be afraid; you are more valuable to God than a whole flock of sparrows." – Matthew 10:28-31, page 1084*

God promises to protect and bless us when we are afraid Genesis 26:23-25, *page 32* • Joshua 1:1-9, *page 242* • Isaiah 43:1-4, *page 794*

Fear is an opportunity to trust God Deuteronomy 1:19-29, *page 202* • Psalm 23:1-6, *page 615* • Matthew 8:23-27, *page 1080*

Having a proper fear of God is the foundation of a wise, godly life Deuteronomy 10:12-16, *page 213* • Proverbs 1:7, *page 697* • Proverbs 9:10-12, *page 705*

Courage comes by putting our confidence in God Deuteronomy 31:7-8, *page 234* • Joshua 1:6-9, *page 242* • Mark 6:47-51, *page 1130*

We can help one another not to be afraid 1 Samuel 23:15-18, *page 332* • 2 Chronicles 32:1-8, *page 514*

A sense of God's presence relieves our fears 1 Kings 19:1-17, *page 404* • Isaiah 41:10, *page 792*

We can send up "arrow prayers" when we are afraid Nehemiah 2:1-5, *page 536*

We should focus on God and trust in him when we are afraid Psalm 27:1-10, *page 617* • Psalm 34:1-10, *page 621* • Psalm 46:1-7, *page 630* • Psalm 91:1-16, *page 660*

We do not need to fear coming into God's presence Romans 8:15-17, *page 1291* • Hebrews 10:19-22, *page 1406* • Hebrews 12:18-24, *page 1409*

God wants to help us share the Good News without fear Ephesians 6:18-20, *page 1353*

God's love drives away fear 1 John 4:16-18, *page 1437*

▸ *See* ***Courage***, *page 243;* ***Praying in the moment***, *page 537;* ***Fear***, *page 630;* ***The fear of the LORD***, *page 705;* ***Peace***, *page 774;* ***Thought***, *page 808.*

Fellowship

"Fellowship" is sometimes used to simply mean "Christians getting together." But the word means something far better and stronger than this. The Greek word for "fellowship" means "partnership," reflecting the strong bond and common purpose that binds Christians together. That fellowship flows out of the fellowship we have with God himself, so it should be energizing, dynamic, and life-changing.

> *We proclaim to you what we ourselves have actually seen and heard so that you may have fellowship with us. And our fellowship is with the Father and with his Son, Jesus Christ. We are writing these things so that you may fully share our joy. This is the message we heard from Jesus and now*

declare to you: God is light, and there is no darkness in him at all. So we are lying if we say we have fellowship with God but go on living in spiritual darkness; we are not practicing the truth. But if we are living in the light, as God is in the light, then we have fellowship with each other, and the blood of Jesus, his Son, cleanses us from all sin. – 1 John 1:3-7, page 1433

We have fellowship with the Father and the Son John 14:23, *page 1223* • 1 John 1:1-4, *page 1433*

Fellowship involves deep and active participation in the life of the Christian community Acts 2:42-47, *page 1239* • Acts 4:32-35, *page 1242*

Our fellowship with one another is based on our fellowship with God through Jesus 1 Corinthians 1:9, *page 1303* • 1 Corinthians 10:16-17, *page 1314*

We have fellowship with the Holy Spirit 1 Corinthians 12:12-13, *page 1315* • 2 Corinthians 13:14, *page 1335* • Philippians 2:1-2, *page 1356*

We can have fellowship in spreading the Good News of Jesus Philippians 1:3-6, *page 1355*

We have fellowship in Jesus' suffering Philippians 3:10-11, *page 1358* • Colossians 1:24, *page 1363* • 1 Peter 4:12-19, *page 1425*

Real fellowship depends on how we live with God and one another 1 John 1:5-7, *page 1433*

▸ *See **Fellowship**, page 1357.*

Followers of Christ *see Discipleship*

Forgiveness

The Christian life is all about forgiveness. It begins with receiving God's forgiveness through faith in Jesus and his death on the cross; it continues as we then live in that forgiveness, receiving it daily from our heavenly Father and sharing it freely with others. We are called to forgive others; and if we do not, then it is doubtful that we have really understood how very much God has forgiven us.

"Forgive us our sins, as we have forgiven those who sin against us. And don't let us yield to temptation, but rescue us from the evil one. If you forgive those who sin against you, your heavenly Father will forgive you. But if you refuse to forgive others, your Father will not forgive your sins." – Matthew 6:12-15, page 1077

God's nature is to forgive Exodus 34:6-7, *page 106* • Psalm 86:5, *page 657* • Psalm 103:1-5, *page 666* • Micah 7:18-20, *page 1017*

Blood has to be shed to bring about forgiveness Leviticus 17:11, *page 137* • Matthew 26:26-28, *page 1111* • Hebrews 9:18-22, *page 1404*

There is great joy in knowing forgiveness Psalm 32:1-5, *page 620* • Acts 8:26-39, *page 1248* • Romans 4:4-8, *page 1286*

We need to pray for forgiveness when we have done wrong Psalm 51:1-19, *page 633* • Hosea 14:1-2, *page 985* • Matthew 6:12, *page 1077*

When we are forgiven, our sins are completely taken away Psalm 103:8-18, *page 667* • Isaiah 6:1-7, *page 755* • John 1:29, *page 1200* • Hebrews 9:24-28, *page 1405*

When God forgives us, he makes us absolutely clean Isaiah 1:18, *page 749* • Ezekiel 36:25-27, *page 938* • 1 Corinthians 6:9-11, *page 1309* • Ephesians 5:25-27, *page 1351*

Confessing our sin is the key to finding forgiveness Jeremiah 36:1-3, *page 867* • Acts 2:38-41, *page 1239* • 1 John 1:8-9, *page 1433*

Jesus has God's authority to forgive sins Matthew 1:20-21, *page 1069* • Mark 2:1-12, *page 1120* • Luke 23:32-34, *page 1194*

Because we are forgiven, we must forgive others too Matthew 6:14-15, *page 1077* • Matthew 18:21-35, *page 1098* • Ephesians 4:31-32, *page 1351* • Colossians 3:12-15, *page 1365*

Jesus can forgive every sin that is brought to him Luke 7:36-50, *page 1165* • John 8:1-11, *page 1211* • 1 John 1:5-10, *page 1433*

Our forgiveness is rooted in the sacrifice of Jesus on the cross Romans 3:23-26, *page 1286* • Ephesians 1:3-8, *page 1346* • Hebrews 9:11-28, *page 1404* • Revelation 5:6-10, *page 1451*

▸ *See **Is there anything God won't forgive?**, page 633; **Forgiven and forgiving**, page 1098; **How can I be sure God has forgiven me?**, page 1433.*

Freedom

The Bible says that Jesus came to set us free—not free to do whatever we please (which is how most people today interpret freedom), but free to be who we were created to be and to do what is right. Religion—trying to gain God's favor through our own achievements—binds us up, but Jesus sets us free in increasing measure to become more and more like him.

"I tell you the truth, everyone who sins is a slave of sin. A slave is not a permanent member of the family, but a son is part of the family forever. So if the Son sets you free, you are truly free." – John 8:34-36, page 1213

God wants to free people Exodus 6:1-8, *page 72* • Psalm 124:6-8, *page 684*

We can pray for freedom Psalm 69:16-18, *page 644* • Psalm 71:1-6, *page 645*

Jesus brings freedom Isaiah 61:1-3, *page 814* • Luke 4:14-21, *page 1158* • John 8:31-36, *page 1213*

Christians are free from sin's controlling power Romans 5:20–6:11, *page 1288* • Romans 8:1-11

The Holy Spirit brings freedom Romans 8:1-2, *page 1290* • 2 Corinthians 3:16-18, *page 1326*

Christians are free not for their own sake but so that they can serve others Galatians 5:13-15, *page 1343*

Christians are set free from the fear of dying Hebrews 2:14-15, *page 1398*

We are not to abuse our freedom 1 Peter 2:15-16, *page 1422*

▶ *See **Legalism**, page 1339.*

Friendship *see also Relationships*

All of us need friends—friends who not only remain loyal and committed to us through difficult times, giving us support and encouragement, but also are not afraid to tell us the truth. Such friendships can be life-giving and are a real gift from God. But equally, the wrong friends can be dangerous, because they can lead us away from the right path. The Bible tells us that the best friend of all is God.

A friend is always loyal, and a brother is born to help in time of need. – Proverbs 17:17, page 714

We can be friends with God Exodus 33:8-11, *page 105* • Psalm 25:14-15, *page 616* • James 2:21-23, *page 1414*

We should beware of bad friends who influence us to do wrong Deuteronomy 13:6-8, *page 216* • Proverbs 22:24-25, *page 719* • 1 Corinthians 15:33, *page 1320*

Good friends always remain loyal 1 Samuel 18:1-4, *page 326* • 1 Samuel 19:1-6, *page 328* • 1 Samuel 20:1-42, *page 328* • Proverbs 17:17, *page 714*

Good friends will not be afraid to tell us the truth 2 Samuel 12:1-14, *page 354* • 2 Samuel 19:1-8, *page 364* • Matthew 16:21-23, *page 1095* • Galatians 2:11-16, *page 1338*

True friends bring comfort and encouragement when we need it Job 2:11-13, *page 566* • Ecclesiastes 4:9-10, *page 733* • 2 Corinthians 7:5-7, *page 1329*

Friends can sometimes cause us pain Psalm 55:12-14, 20-21, *page 635* • 2 Corinthians 2:5, *page 1325*

Real friends stick by us whatever happens Proverbs 18:24, *page 715*

Friends can provide us with honest assessments Proverbs 27:5-6, 9, 17, *page 724* • Proverbs 28:23, *page 726*

Friends love us during difficult times Proverbs 27:10, *page 724* • Ecclesiastes 4:7-12, *page 733*

True friendship is marked by sacrifice John 15:12-13, *page 1224* • Romans 5:6-11, *page 1287*

Jesus saw his disciples as friends not colleagues John 15:15, *page 1224*

True friends support us in tough times Philippians 2:19-30, *page 1357*

▶ *See **Being there**, page 575; **Friendship**, page 725.*

Fruitfulness

Creation itself shows that God delights in fruitfulness. And just as fruit trees bear fruit naturally, so the Holy Spirit wants us to bear fruit that shows what we are and to whom we belong. Good people, like good trees, will always bear good fruit; and Jesus promised that, if we stay close to him and draw on his resources, then we will bear much fruit.

> *But the Holy Spirit produces this kind of fruit in our lives: love, joy, peace, patience, kindness, goodness, faithfulness, gentleness, and self-control. There is no law against these things! – Galatians 5:22-23, page 1343*

God's creation was designed to be fruitful Genesis 1:9-12, *page 4* • Genesis 8:13-17, *page 11*

Human beings were designed to be fruitful Genesis 1:27-28, *page 5* • Genesis 9:1-7, *page 12*

Abraham was called to be spiritually fruitful Genesis 12:1-3, *page 15* • Genesis 15:1-6, *page 18* • Genesis 17:1-8, *page 20*

Israel was destined to be fruitful but often failed to be so Leviticus 26:3-13, *page 149* • Isaiah 5:1-7, *page 752* • Isaiah 27:2-6, *page 775* • Matthew 3:1-10, *page 1070*

Delighting in God and his word will lead to a fruitful life Psalm 1:1-6, *page 602* • Psalm 92:12-15, *page 661* • Jeremiah 17:5-8, *page 844*

God's word is always fruitful Isaiah 55:8-11, *page 808* • Colossians 1:6, *page 1362*

Fruitfulness is a mark of the Spirit's work Ezekiel 36:22-30, *page 938* • Ezekiel 47:1-12, *page 951* • Galatians 5:22-23, *page 1343* • Revelation 22:1-2, *page 1467*

The fruit we bear shows what kind of people we are Matthew 3:7-10, *page 1072* • Matthew 7:15-20, *page 1078*

Jesus rebuked Israel for failing to bear fruit Matthew 21:33-46, *page 1103*

Denying ourselves will lead to a fruitful life John 12:24-26, *page 1220*

Jesus promises that we will be fruitful as long as we stay dependent on him John 15:1-16, *page 1223*

The fruit we receive depends on the seed we sow 2 Corinthians 9:6-10, *page 1331* • Galatians 6:7-10, *page 1344*

Future *see also Jesus Christ: his return*

Wanting to know what lies ahead of us is a natural human inclination, but the reality is that none of us knows—apart from God. This is why the Bible tells us not to waste our time trying to work out the future but rather to trust God, who holds the future in his hands. We may not know what the future holds, but we can know who holds the future.

> *"For I know the plans I have for you," says the LORD. "They are plans for good and not for disaster, to give you a future and a hope. In those days when you pray, I will listen. If you look for me wholeheartedly, you will find me. I will be found by you," says the LORD. – Jeremiah 29:11-14, page 858*

The best way to plan for our future is by being obedient to God Deuteronomy 5:29, *page 208* • Deuteronomy 28:1-14, *page 229*

We should not try to discover the future through horoscopes, astrology, or fortune-telling Deuteronomy 18:9-14, *page 221* • Isaiah 47:12-15, *page 800* • Acts 16:16-18, *page 1262*

God gives us hope for our future Psalm 37:35-38, *page 625* • Proverbs 23:17-18, *page 720* • Jeremiah 31:17, *page 862*

We may try to plan our future, but it is God who leads us Proverbs 16:9, *page 712* • James 4:13-16, *page 1416*

None of us knows what our future holds, and certainly not the moment of our death Ecclesiastes 8:2-8, *page 736*

God has plans for our future, both as individuals and as his people Isaiah 46:9-10, *page 799* • Jeremiah 1:4-5, *page 822* • Jeremiah 29:11-14, *page 858* • 1 Corinthians 2:9, *page 1305*

We can trust God our heavenly Father for our future Matthew 6:25-34, *page 1078* • James 4:13-16, *page 1416*

The climax of the future is the return of Jesus to this world Matthew 24:29-51, *page 1107* • Matthew 25:31-46, *page 1109* • 1 Thessalonians 4:13–5:3, *page 1372* • Revelation 19:11–21:5, *page 1464*

▶ *See **The return of Jesus Christ**, page 1372.*

Generosity *see Giving*

Gentleness

Gentleness is not always a quality that is admired in a world that tells us to be tough and stand up for ourselves; but it is a quality that God greatly esteems, for it is a reflection of his own character. Gentleness is about being kind and considerate, and not dealing with others roughly or harshly.

> *Pursue righteousness and a godly life, along with faith, love, perseverance, and gentleness.*
> *– 1 Timothy 6:11, page 1383*

God is gentle and tender toward his people 1 Kings 19:11-13, *page 404* • Job 15:11, *page 577* • Isaiah 40:1-2, 9-11, *page 789*

God wants us to make our words gentle Proverbs 15:1-4, *page 711* • Proverbs 25:15, *page 722*

Jesus is gentle in dealing with us Matthew 11:28-30, *page 1085* • Mark 10:13-16, *page 1136* • John 8:1-11, *page 1211* • 2 Corinthians 10:1, *page 1332*

Gentleness doesn't mean you can't stand up for your rights Acts 16:35-40, *page 1263* • Acts 22:22-29, *page 1272* • Acts 25:1-12, *page 1274*

Church leaders should lead with gentleness 1 Corinthians 4:10-16, *page 1307* • 1 Thessalonians 2:7-8, *page 1370* • 1 Timothy 3:3, *page 1380*

Gentleness is part of the fruit of the Spirit Galatians 5:22-23, *page 1343* • Colossians 3:12-15, *page 1365*

We should be gentle in restoring fellow believers who are struggling Galatians 6:1-3, *page 1343*

We should be gentle in our dealing with others 1 Timothy 6:11, *page 1383* • 2 Timothy 2:23-26, *page 1386* • Titus 3:1-2, *page 1391*

Godly wisdom is always gentle James 3:17-18, *page 1415*

We should share the Good News of Jesus gently and respectfully 1 Peter 3:13-16, *page 1423*

Giving

The Bible tells us that God is a God who gives generously to us and therefore calls us to be generous givers too, both in our offerings to him and in our support of those in need. If our wallets have not been touched, then our hearts probably haven't been touched either.

> *Remember this—a farmer who plants only a few seeds will get a small crop. But the one who plants generously will get a generous crop. You must each decide in your heart how much to give. And don't give reluctantly or in response to pressure. "For God loves a person who gives cheerfully." And God will generously provide all you need. Then you will always have everything you need and plenty left over to share with others. – 2 Corinthians 9:6-8, page 1331*

The Jewish Law required a tenth of all income to be given to God Leviticus 27:30-32, *page 151* • Malachi 3:10-12, *page 1052*

We give to God because we acknowledge that all we have comes from him 1 Chronicles 29:1-17, *page 480*

Our giving should not be done to attract the attention or admiration of others Matthew 6:1-4, *page 1076* • Acts 5:1-11, *page 1242*

Giving helps us store treasure in heaven Matthew 6:19-21, *page 1077* • 1 Timothy 6:17-19, *page 1383*

We need not fear to give, for God has promised to provide for all our needs Matthew 6:25-34, *page 1078* • Philippians 4:18-20, *page 1360*

God will reward us for giving to others Mark 9:41, *page 1135* • Luke 6:38, *page 1163* • 2 Corinthians 9:6-15, *page 1331*

Jesus commended the widow who gave all that she had Mark 12:41-44, *page 1140*

Giving helps others who are in need Acts 2:44-45, *page 1239* • Acts 4:32-35, *page 1242* • Acts 11:27-30, *page 1254* • Hebrews 13:15-16, *page 1410*

We should support Christian workers through our giving Acts 28:10, *page 1279* • Philippians 4:15-19, *page 1360* • 1 Timothy 5:17-18, *page 1383*

We should give regularly 1 Corinthians 16:1-2, *page 1321*

Giving is not dependent on our wealth but on our hearts 2 Corinthians 8:1-15, *page 1330*

God's gift of his Son to us is what should motivate all our giving 2 Corinthians 8:9, *page 1330* • 2 Corinthians 9:13-15, *page 1332*

God loves for his people to give generously and joyfully 2 Corinthians 9:13-15, *page 1332*

▸ *See **Should Christians still tithe?**, page 1052; **Giving**, page 1331.*

Giving up *see Perseverance*

God *see also Jesus Christ; Holy Spirit*

God is revealed in the Bible as a personal God who is both Creator and Redeemer and who can be known. He has always existed, and he brought everything into being. And when humanity began to spoil not only their own lives but also God's world, God took action to begin a plan of redemption that culminated in the coming of Jesus. Through Jesus, God invites us to know him and become part of his plan that will stretch into eternity.

> *"Yahweh! The LORD! The God of compassion and mercy! I am slow to anger and filled with unfailing love and faithfulness. I lavish unfailing love to a thousand generations. I forgive iniquity, rebellion, and sin." – Exodus 34:6-7, page 106*

God created everything Genesis 1:1–2:3, *page 4* • John 1:1-3, *page 1199* • Colossians 1:15-17, *page 1362* • Hebrews 11:3, *page 1407*

God makes people right with himself through faith Genesis 15:1-6, *page 18* • Romans 3:21-26, *page 1286* • Romans 4:18-25, *page 1287*

God is almighty Genesis 17:1, *page 20* • Job 42:1-2, *page 599* • Mark 10:27, *page 1137* • Revelation 19:5-6, *page 1464*

God is always righteous and just Genesis 18:25, *page 22* • Deuteronomy 32:1-4, *page 235* • Acts 17:30-31, *page 1264* • 1 John 1:8-9, *page 1433*

God is the provider Genesis 22:1-14, *page 26* • Psalm 68:7-10, *page 642* • 2 Corinthians 9:10, *page 1332* • Philippians 4:18-19, *page 1360*

God helps his people when they are in trouble Exodus 2:23-25, *page 67* • Deuteronomy 33:26-29, *page 239* • Psalm 46:1-11, *page 630* • Luke 1:46-55, *page 1153*

God reveals his personal name as Yahweh (the LORD/I AM) Exodus 3:13-15, *page 68*

God redeems and saves his people Exodus 6:1-8, *page 72* • 2 Samuel 7:22-24, *page 350* • Isaiah 54:4-8, *page 807* • Luke 1:67-79, *page 1154*

God is gracious and merciful Exodus 34:6-7, *page 106* • Nehemiah 9:29-31, *page 546* • Psalm 145:8-13, *page 692* • Ephesians 2:4-10, *page 1347*

God is holy Leviticus 11:44-45, *page 129* • Isaiah 6:1-6, *page 755* • Habakkuk 1:12-13, *page 1024* • 1 Peter 1:15-16, *page 1421* • Revelation 4:1-8, *page 1450*

God never changes Numbers 23:19, *page 183* • Malachi 3:6, *page 1052* • James 1:17, *page 1412*

God is one Deuteronomy 6:4 (see footnote), *page 208* • 1 Corinthians 8:6, *page 1312* • Ephesians 4:4-6, *page 1350*

God is loving Deuteronomy 7:7-9, *page 210* • John 3:16-17, *page 1203* • Romans 5:6-8, *page 1287* • 1 John 4:9-19, *page 1437*

God is faithful Deuteronomy 7:9, *page 210* • Psalm 136:1-26, *page 687* • Lamentations 3:22-23, *page 895* • 2 Timothy 2:11-13, *page 1386*

He is the living God 1 Samuel 17:22-26, *page 325* • Psalm 84:1-4, *page 655* • Matthew 16:13-16, *page 1095* • 1 Timothy 4:10, *page 1382*

God is infinite 1 Kings 8:27, *page 386* • Isaiah 57:15, *page 810* • Revelation 1:8, *page 1446*

God is sovereign Job 23:13-14, *page 584* • Jeremiah 18:1-10, *page 846* • Romans 8:28-39, *page 1292*

God sustains creation Job 38:1–42:6, *page 595* • Colossians 1:15-17, *page 1362* • Hebrews 1:1-3, *page 1396*

God cares for and guides his people Psalm 23:1-6, *page 615* • Isaiah 58:11, *page 812* • Jeremiah 23:1-8, *page 851* • John 10:1-18, *page 1215*

God forgives us Psalm 32:1-5, *page 620* • Psalm 103:1-22, *page 666* • Matthew 6:12-15, *page 1077* • 1 John 1:8-9, *page 1433*

God is good Psalm 34:8-10, *page 622* • Psalm 116:1-7, *page 676* • Mark 10:17-18, *page 1136*

God is eternal Psalm 90:1-2, *page 659* • 1 Timothy 1:17, *page 1379* • 1 Timothy 6:15-16, *page 1383* • Revelation 1:8, *page 1446*

God is wise Psalm 104:24, *page 668* • Daniel 2:20-23, *page 957* • Romans 16:27, *page 1301* • 1 Corinthians 1:18-31, *page 1304*

God knows all things Psalm 139:1-18, *page 689* • Isaiah 46:8-10, *page 799* • Matthew 10:29-30, *page 1084* • Romans 11:33-36, *page 1296*

God is present everywhere Psalm 139:7-10, *page 689* • Jeremiah 23:23-24, *page 852* • Jonah 1:1–2:10, *page 1007* • Ephesians 1:19-23, *page 1346*

We can know God as our Father Malachi 2:10, *page 1051* • Matthew 6:9, *page 1077* • Ephesians 3:14-18, *page 1349* • 1 John 3:1-2, *page 1435*

God is spirit and invisible John 4:23-24, *page 1205* • Colossians 1:15, *page 1362* • 1 Timothy 1:17, *page 1379*

▸ *See* ***Names and titles of God****, page 70;* ***The character of God****, page 104;* ***The glory of God****, page 115;* ***The one true God****, page 209;* ***God's sovereignty****, page 584;* ***God's power****, page 596;* ***The God who is everywhere and knows everything****, page 689;* ***The holiness of God****, page 754;* ***The greatness of God****, page 791;* ***Does God really get angry?****, page 854;* ***Does God change his mind?****, page 1009;* ***Abba****, page 1144;* ***Jesus: the only way to God****, page 1241;* ***The love of God****, page 1437.*

God's will *see also Guidance*

God's will is not just his plan and purpose, but also his ability to bring that about. The Bible urges us to seek God's will for our lives and to do all we can to pursue it, just as Jesus himself did. In finding God's will, we are finding what is best for us.

> *"May your Kingdom come soon. May your will be done on earth, as it is in heaven." – Matthew 6:10, page 1077*

God works everything out according to his will and plan Exodus 9:13-16, *page 76* • Proverbs 16:4, *page 712*

Discovering God's will is a joyful thing Psalm 16:5-11, *page 610* • Psalm 40:6-8, *page 626*

God wants to guide us into his will Psalm 48:14, *page 631* • Isaiah 30:19-21, *page 779*

We should gladly submit to God's will, even if it looks challenging, for it is always best Jeremiah 18:1-6, *page 846* • Matthew 26:36-42, *page 1111*

We should pray for God's will to be done Matthew 6:10, *page 1077*

God's will rules over even the small details of life Matthew 10:29-31, *page 1084*

Jesus always fulfilled God's will completely John 4:32-34, *page 1205* • John 6:38-40, *page 1209* • Hebrews 10:4-7, *page 1405*

God takes everything in life, even bad stuff, and works it into his will Romans 8:28-39, *page 1292*

God wants us to understand what his will is Romans 12:1-2, *page 1296* • Ephesians 5:17, *page 1351*

God reveals his will in Jesus Ephesians 1:9-11, *page 1346*

God's will is for us to live holy lives 1 Thessalonians 4:3-8, *page 1372* • 1 Peter 1:13-16, *page 1421* • 1 Peter 2:9-12, *page 1422*

God's will is that all will be saved 1 Timothy 2:3-6, *page 1380* • 2 Peter 3:8-10, *page 1429*

▸ *See* ***Trusting God when we cannot see the way ahead****, page 57;* ***God's sovereignty****, page 584;* ***Why do bad things happen in life?****, page 1025.*

Good News *see Gospel*

Goodness

The Bible shows us that God is good, though the devil often tries to get us to doubt it, especially when things go wrong in our lives. But grasping that God is good—all the time—fundamentally changes how we look at life. And because God is good, we, as his people, are also called to be good.

> *So let's not get tired of doing what is good. At just the right time we will reap a harvest of blessing if we don't give up. Therefore, whenever we have the opportunity, we should do good to everyone—especially to those in the family of faith. – Galatians 6:9-10, page 1344*

God's creation is good Genesis 1:4, 10, 12, 18, 21, 25, 31, *page 4* • 1 Timothy 4:3-4, *page 1382*

God himself is good 2 Chronicles 5:13, *page 487* • Psalm 86:5, *page 657* • Mark 10:17-22, *page 1136*

Jesus always did good Matthew 4:23-25, *page 1074* • Acts 10:37-38, *page 1252*

Our lives should be characterized by goodness Matthew 5:13-16, *page 1075* • Luke 6:27-36, *page 1163* • Galatians 6:9-10, *page 1344* • 1 Peter 3:8-17, *page 1423*

God's gifts are characterized by goodness Matthew 7:7-11, *page 1078* • James 1:16-17, *page 1412*

God's word is good Romans 7:7-13, *page 1290* • 2 Timothy 3:14-17, *page 1387* • Hebrews 6:5, *page 1400*

There is nothing fundamentally good in sinful human nature Romans 7:18-25, *page 1290*

God works everything together for good Romans 8:28-30, *page 1292*

God wants to change our thinking to show us what goodness really is Romans 12:1-2, *page 1296*

Goodness is part of the fruit of the Spirit Galatians 5:22-23, *page 1343*

God has planned good things for us to do Ephesians 2:8-10, *page 1347*

Real faith has to be worked out in goodness Titus 2:11-14, *page 1390* • James 2:14-26, *page 1413*

▸ *See **Goodness**, page 1251; **Faith and works**, page 1415.*

Gospel

The word gospel means "good news." It is the good news of how God acted to rescue us from our sin and its consequences by sending his son Jesus into the world. Jesus both shows what God's Kingdom is like and makes it possible for us to enter that Kingdom through his death on the cross. As we put our trust in Jesus, he forgives our sin and gives us a brand-new start.

> *Jesus traveled throughout the region of Galilee, teaching in the synagogues and announcing the Good News about the Kingdom. And he healed every kind of disease and illness. – Matthew 4:23, page 1074*

Jesus came preaching the Good News of the Kingdom Matthew 4:23, *page 1074* • Matthew 9:35, *page 1083* • Matthew 11:1-6, *page 1084*

Jesus promised that the gospel would be preached throughout the world before his return Matthew 24:13-14, *page 1107*

Christians are commanded to tell others about the gospel Matthew 28:18-20, *page 1116* • Luke 24:46-47, *page 1196* • Acts 1:4-8, *page 1236*

People need to respond to the gospel by repenting and turning back to God Mark 1:14-15, *page 1119* • Acts 20:21, *page 1269*

Jesus said that the gospel is not just about believing things but about the complete transformation of our lives Luke 4:16-21, *page 1159*

People should respond to the gospel with faith John 1:12, *page 1199* • John 3:16-17, 35-36, *page 1203* • Acts 2:37-41, *page 1239* • Romans 1:16, *page 1282*

We can pray for boldness to share the gospel Acts 4:23-31, *page 1241* • Ephesians 6:18-20, *page 1353*

We should always remember that the gospel is powerful Romans 1:16-17, *page 1282*

The gospel is fundamentally about getting into a right relationship with God Romans 3:21-26, *page 1286* • Romans 5:1-11, *page 1287* • 2 Corinthians 5:11-21, *page 1327*

BASIC TRUTHS • *page 1530*

The gospel message focuses on Christ, his death for sins, and his resurrection 1 Corinthians 15:1-8, *page 1319*

The gospel is God's message, not ours Galatians 1:11-12, *page 1337*

Our whole lifestyle should reflect the gospel Ephesians 4:1, *page 1349* • Philippians 1:27-28, *page 1356*

▶ *See **The gospel**, page 1120; **The power of the gospel**, page 1279.*

Gossip

Gossip is one of the curses of modern culture, often encouraged by TV, news websites, and social media. But the Bible tells us that God hates gossip, for it can be deeply damaging to relationships; so as God's people we are called to avoid all gossip and exercise self-control in what we say.

> *A gossip goes around telling secrets, but those who are trustworthy can keep a confidence.*
> *– Proverbs 11:13, page 708*

God's people should not gossip Exodus 23:1, *page 93* • Leviticus 19:16, *page 139* • 1 Timothy 5:13, *page 1383* • James 3:1-12, *page 1415*

We should not be intimidated by gossip Nehemiah 6:5-9, *page 541*

We need to restrain our speech and not gossip Psalm 141:3-4, *page 690* • Proverbs 13:3, *page 709*

Gossip separates friends Proverbs 11:13, *page 708* • Proverbs 16:27-28, *page 713*

There is something about gossip that satisfies our sinful nature Proverbs 18:8, *page 715* • Proverbs 26:20-22, *page 724*

Gossip is harmful Proverbs 25:18, *page 722* • Proverbs 26:17-28, *page 724*

Gossip is part of a sinful way of life Romans 1:29, *page 1283* • 2 Corinthians 12:20, *page 1335*

▶ *See **Gossip**, page 723; **Speech**, page 1416.*

Government *see also Authority*

All of us probably have times when we resent our government, especially when it comes to paying our taxes. But the Bible encourages us to receive our government as something given by God for our protection and blessing—and it even said this under a government led by godless Caesars who were persecuting the church. Even bad government or government we do not like is better than anarchy.

> *Everyone must submit to governing authorities. For all authority comes from God, and those in positions of authority have been placed there by God. So anyone who rebels against authority is rebelling against what God has instituted, and they will be punished. For the authorities do not strike fear in people who are doing right, but in those who are doing wrong. Would you like to live without fear of the authorities? Do what is right, and they will honor you. The authorities are God's servants, sent for your good. But if you are doing wrong, of course you should be afraid, for they have the power to punish you. They are God's servants, sent for the very purpose of punishing those who do what is wrong. So you must submit to them, not only to avoid punishment, but also to keep a clear conscience. Pay your taxes, too, for these same reasons. For government workers need to be paid. They are serving God in what they do. Give to everyone what you owe them: Pay your taxes and government fees to those who collect them, and give respect and honor to those who are in authority. – Romans 13:1-7, page 1297*

God holds all those in government accountable Deuteronomy 17:16-20, *page 220* • 2 Samuel 7:11-14, *page 349* • Hebrews 13:17, *page 1410*

The coming Messiah would exercise God's righteous government Psalm 2:1-12, *page 602* • Psalm 110:1-7, *page 673* • Isaiah 9:6, *page 758* • Isaiah 32:1-2, *page 781*

God rules over the nations Psalm 9:7-8, *page 606* • Psalm 22:27-28, *page 615* • Psalm 47:1-9, *page 631* • Daniel 4:28-37, *page 961*

God has appointed governments to rule wisely Proverbs 8:15-16, *page 704* • Proverbs 28:1-2, *page 725* • Proverbs 29:4, *page 726*

God uses even governments that do not acknowledge him Isaiah 45:1-7, *page 797* • Jeremiah 25:7-14, *page 853*

Even those who don't acknowledge God have received their power from him John 19:8-11, *page 1228* • Romans 13:1, *page 1297*

The first allegiance of God's people is always to God rather than to any government Acts 5:27-29, *page 1243*

God gives authority to those in government Romans 13:1-7, *page 1297*

Christians should obey the government Romans 13:1-7, *page 1297* • Titus 3:1-8, *page 1391* • 1 Peter 2:13-17, *page 1422*

▶ *See* ***Christians and government****, page 1297.*

Grace *see also Mercy*

Grace is God's undeserved love and kindness toward sinners, seen supremely in his sending his Son, Jesus, to be our Savior. As grace has been extended to us, so we are called to extend grace to others.

God is so rich in mercy, and he loved us so much, that even though we were dead because of our sins, he gave us life when he raised Christ from the dead. (It is only by God's grace that you have been saved!) For he raised us from the dead along with Christ and seated us with him in the heavenly realms because we are united with Christ Jesus. So God can point to us in all future ages as examples of the incredible wealth of his grace and kindness toward us, as shown in all he has done for us who are united with Christ Jesus. God saved you by his grace when you believed. And you can't take credit for this; it is a gift from God. Salvation is not a reward for the good things we have done, so none of us can boast about it. For we are God's masterpiece. He has created us anew in Christ Jesus, so we can do the good things he planned for us long ago. – Ephesians 2:4-10, page 1347

God's nature is full of grace Exodus 34:5-7, *page 106* • Deuteronomy 7:7-9, *page 210* • Nehemiah 9:16-21, *page 546* • Psalm 145:8-13, *page 692*

The Old Testament priestly blessing was one of grace Numbers 6:22-27, *page 161*

God loves to be gracious to his people 2 Kings 13:22-23, *page 428* • Ezra 7:8-9, 27-28, *page 529*

Jesus is full of grace John 1:14-18, *page 1199* • 2 Corinthians 8:9, *page 1330*

We are saved by God's grace Romans 3:21-26, *page 1286* • Romans 5:1-11, *page 1287* • Ephesians 1:3-8, *page 1346* • Ephesians 2:4-10, *page 1347*

We should not take God's grace for granted Romans 6:1-23, *page 1289*

Grace is something we can pray for Romans 16:20, *page 1301* • 2 Corinthians 13:14, *page 1335*

God's grace will help us in our need 2 Corinthians 12:6-10, *page 1334* • Hebrews 4:14-16, *page 1400*

God accepts us by his grace Ephesians 2:8-9, *page 1347* • 2 Timothy 1:8-10, *page 1384* • Titus 3:3-7, *page 1391*

Our words should be gracious Colossians 4:5-6, *page 1366*

God's grace gives us hope 1 Peter 1:13, *page 1421*

We should grow in grace 2 Peter 3:18, *page 1430*

▶ *See* ***The character of God****, page 104;* ***The compassionate God****, page 666;* ***Access to God****, page 1349;* ***Faith and works****, page 1415;* ***The love of God****, page 1437.*

Gratitude *see Thankfulness*

Greed *see also Addiction; Desires*

Greed is something that is easier to recognize in others than in ourselves. Yet whenever we have unrestrained desires for more—whether for food, money, or material possessions—that is greed. The Bible warns us of the dangers of greed, in terms of both our life and our eternal destiny.

He [Jesus] said, "Beware! Guard against every kind of greed. Life is not measured by how much you own." Then he told them a story: "A rich man had a fertile farm that produced fine crops.

He said to himself, 'What should I do? I don't have room for all my crops.' Then he said, 'I know! I'll tear down my barns and build bigger ones. Then I'll have room enough to store all my wheat and other goods. And I'll sit back and say to myself, "My friend, you have enough stored away for years to come. Now take it easy! Eat, drink, and be merry!"' But God said to him, 'You fool! You will die this very night. Then who will get everything you worked for?' Yes, a person is a fool to store up earthly wealth but not have a rich relationship with God." – Luke 12:15-21, page 1175

Greed may all too easily accompany prosperity Deuteronomy 8:6-14, *page 211* • Proverbs 30:7-9, *page 727* • Luke 12:13-21, *page 1175*

Greed perverts honesty, justice, and integrity 1 Samuel 8:1-3, *page 313* • Jeremiah 6:13-14, *page 831* • Jeremiah 22:13-17, *page 850* • 2 Peter 2:3, *page 1428*

Greed leads us to do things we wouldn't otherwise do 2 Kings 5:20-27, *page 418* • Mark 14:10-11, *page 1142*

Greed brings trouble Proverbs 15:27, *page 712* • Proverbs 28:25, *page 726*

Those who are greedy never have enough Habakkuk 2:5-14, *page 1025* • Luke 12:15-21, *page 1175*

Greed spoils our lives Mark 7:20-23, *page 1131* • Romans 1:29, *page 1283*

We should learn to be content with what we have Luke 3:12-14, *page 1157* • Philippians 4:10-13, *page 1360* • Hebrews 13:5, *page 1409*

God's people should not be greedy 1 Corinthians 5:9-13, *page 1308* • Ephesians 5:3-5, *page 1351* • Colossians 3:5, *page 1365*

Greedy people will not inherit God's Kingdom Ephesians 5:5, *page 1351*

Church leaders must not be greedy 1 Timothy 3:1-3, *page 1380* • Titus 1:7, *page 1389*

The love of money is the root of all kinds of evil 1 Timothy 6:9-10, *page 1383*

Grief *see also Comfort*

Grief is part of the cost of love. When we lose someone whom we loved and who meant a lot to us, we grieve their loss. Jesus experienced grief when he was among us, and God grieves over people who wander away from him. We can also grieve when we recognize what we have lost because of our sinfulness.

When Jesus saw her [Mary, Lazarus's sister] weeping and saw the other people wailing with her, a deep anger welled up within him, and he was deeply troubled. "Where have you put him?" he asked them. They told him, "Lord, come and see." Then Jesus wept. The people who were standing nearby said, "See how much he loved him!" – John 11:33-36, page 1218

God is always with us, even in our darkest valleys Psalm 23:1-6, *page 615*

Grief is often a necessary part of repentance Psalm 51:1-19, *page 633* • Isaiah 6:1-7, *page 755* • 2 Corinthians 7:10, *page 1330*

Grieving is part of the rhythm of life Ecclesiastes 3:1-8, *page 732*

Isaiah prophesied that God's servant (seen in the New Testament as Jesus) would experience grief Isaiah 53:2-12, *page 805*

God promises to comfort those who grieve Isaiah 61:1-3, *page 814* • Matthew 5:4, *page 1074*

Jesus said that hell is a place of great grief Matthew 8:11-12, *page 1080* • Matthew 13:40-42, 49-50, *page 1090* • Matthew 22:1-13, *page 1103*

Jesus knew deep personal grief Matthew 26:36-38, *page 1111* • Luke 19:41-44, *page 1186*

Jesus experienced grief at the death of his friend Lazarus John 11:1-37, *page 1216*

We can be strengthened in our grief over a lost loved one by remembering the Christian hope John 14:1-6, *page 1222* • 1 Thessalonians 4:13-18, *page 1372* • 1 Peter 1:3-9, *page 1420* • Revelation 21:1-4, *page 1465*

We can cause ourselves grief by bad choices 1 Timothy 6:9-10, *page 1383*

Grief will no longer exist in God's new Kingdom Revelation 21:1-4, *page 1465*

▶ *See **Being there**, page 575.*

Growth *see also Fruitfulness; Perseverance*

When babies are born, everything within them is geared up for growth. Indeed, to stay the same would be to die. And that's how it is when we become Christians. We have started a brand-new life that is designed to experience growth. God does not want us to stay as spiritual babies; he wants us to grow in both our knowledge and our experience of him, and not to stop growing until the day we die.

You must grow in the grace and knowledge of our Lord and Savior Jesus Christ. All glory to him, both now and forever! Amen. – 2 Peter 3:18, page 1430

God's word helps us to grow and be fruitful Psalm 1:1-6, *page 602* • Colossians 3:16, *page 1365* • 2 Timothy 3:14-17, *page 1387* • 1 Peter 2:2, *page 1421*

We grow and are fruitful by maintaining our relationship with Jesus John 15:1-8, 16, *page 1223*

Being part of a vibrant church helps us grow Acts 2:42-47, *page 1239* • Acts 4:32-36, *page 1242*

The goal of growth is to become mature and more like Jesus Romans 8:29-30, *page 1292* • Ephesians 4:14-16, *page 1350*

God wants to produce fruit in our lives by his Spirit Galatians 5:22-23, *page 1343*

Growth is about continually getting to know God better Philippians 3:7-14, *page 1358* • Colossians 1:9-12, *page 1362*

God wants us to grow in Christian characteristics, especially love Colossians 3:12-15, *page 1365* • 1 Thessalonians 3:11-13, *page 1371* • 2 Peter 1:3-11, *page 1427*

We are called to grow in the grace and knowledge of Jesus 2 Peter 3:17-18, *page 1430*

▶ *See **Now that you are a Christian**, page A13; **Growing as a Christian**, page 1430.*

Grumbling *see Complaining*

Guidance

As our loving heavenly Father, God always wants the best for us. We can therefore bring every aspect of our lives to him in prayer, confident that he will guide us onto the right paths, whether through the Bible, the Holy Spirit's witness within us, the counsel of wise friends, or his overruling of circumstances.

Trust in the LORD with all your heart; do not depend on your own understanding. Seek his will in all you do, and he will show you which path to take. – Proverbs 3:5-6, page 699

Guidance sometimes comes through our circumstances Genesis 29:1-14, *page 35* • Ruth 2:1-23, *page 300* • Acts 16:6-10, *page 1261*

Guidance sometimes comes through dreams Genesis 41:1-49, *page 51* • Acts 10:9-23, *page 1250* • Acts 16:6-10, *page 1261*

We should pray for God's direction before making decisions 2 Kings 19:14-19, *page 437* • Nehemiah 1:1-11, *page 536* • Psalm 25:4-5, *page 616* • Acts 13:1-3, *page 1255*

We should remain humble as we seek guidance Psalm 25:9, *page 616* • James 4:13-15, *page 1416* • 1 Peter 5:5-7, *page 1425*

We can trust God to guide us Psalm 32:8-10, *page 621* • Psalm 37:3-5, *page 623* • Proverbs 3:5-6, *page 699* • Isaiah 30:19-21, *page 779* • Jeremiah 29:11, *page 858* • Romans 8:28, *page 1292*

The Bible gives us guidance Psalm 119:97-98, 105, 133, *page 680* • 2 Timothy 3:15-16, *page 1387*

We should seek good advice before making decisions Proverbs 15:22, *page 712* • Proverbs 18:15, *page 715*

The Holy Spirit guides us John 14:15-17, 25-26, *page 1223* • John 16:12-15, *page 1225* • Acts 8:26-29, *page 1248* • Acts 15:28, *page 1260*

We should test different forms of guidance 1 Thessalonians 5:19-22, *page 1373*

▶ *See **Can God still speak through "fleeces"?**, page 277; **Guidance**, page 1261.*

Guilt *see also Confession; Conscience; Repentance*

Guilt is what we feel when we have done wrong, leading to feelings of shame, disgrace, despair, unworthiness, or uncleanness. As such, guilt is good—but only as long as it drives us back to God, who waits, longing to forgive and cleanse us. Unresolved guilt, however, eats away at us, accusing us and even affecting our health. That is why, when we feel guilty, it is so important to confess things quickly.

> *Oh, what joy for those whose disobedience is forgiven, whose sin is put out of sight! Yes, what joy for those whose record the LORD has cleared of guilt, whose lives are lived in complete honesty! When I refused to confess my sin, my body wasted away, and I groaned all day long. Day and night your hand of discipline was heavy on me. My strength evaporated like water in the summer heat. Finally, I confessed all my sins to you and stopped trying to hide my guilt. I said to myself, "I will confess my rebellion to the LORD." And you forgave me! All my guilt is gone. – Psalm 32:1-5, page 620*

Guilt causes us to hide from God Genesis 3:7-11, *page 6*

We need to recognize our sin and admit our guilt in order to be forgiven Leviticus 5:2-6, *page 121* • Numbers 15:27-31, *page 172* • 1 Chronicles 21:7-8, *page 471*

God forgives sin and removes guilt Psalm 32:1-5, *page 620* • Isaiah 6:1-7, *page 755*

The guilt of unconfessed sin separates us from God Psalm 32:3, *page 620* • Isaiah 59:1-3, *page 812*

God can cleanse us from all sin and guilt Psalm 51:1-19, *page 633* • Hebrews 10:19-39, *page 1406*

When God declares us "not guilty!" no one can condemn us Isaiah 50:7-9, *page 803* • Romans 8:1-4, 31-39, *page 1290*

It is the Holy Spirit's role, not ours, to convict people of their guilt and sin John 16:5-11, *page 1224*

Everyone is guilty of sin Romans 1:18–2:10, *page 1283* • Romans 3:9-23, *page 1285*

Jesus takes away all guilt Romans 3:23-24, *page 1286* • Romans 8:1-4, *page 1290*

God can cleanse our guilty consciences Hebrews 9:13-14, *page 1404* • Hebrews 10:19-22, *page 1406*

If we confess our sin, we can know God's forgiveness 1 John 1:8-9, *page 1433*

Freedom from guilt lets us come into God's presence boldly 1 John 3:21-22, *page 1436*

▶ *See* ***Guilt****, page 620.*

Happiness *see Joy*

Hatred

While the Bible calls us to hate all evil, just as God himself does, it also warns us that hatred can be a dangerous emotion. We often end up hating people unjustly or unreasonably, and hatred can destroy us. Love is always better than hatred.

> *"To you who are willing to listen, I say, love your enemies! Do good to those who hate you. Bless those who curse you. Pray for those who hurt you. If someone slaps you on one cheek, offer the other cheek also. If someone demands your coat, offer your shirt also. Give to anyone who asks; and when things are taken away from you, don't try to get them back. Do to others as you would like them to do to you." – Luke 6:27-31, page 1163*

God hates evil Deuteronomy 12:29-31, *page 216* • Psalm 5:4-6, *page 604* • Proverbs 6:16-19, *page 702* • Habakkuk 1:12-13, *page 1024* • Romans 1:18-32, *page 1283*

Hatred causes trouble 2 Samuel 13:22-39, *page 356* • Proverbs 10:12, *page 706*

God's people should hate evil and love good Psalm 97:10-12, *page 664* • Amos 5:14-15, *page 998* • Romans 12:9, *page 1296*

Followers of Jesus will often be hated Matthew 10:21-22, *page 1083* • John 17:14-18, *page 1226*

We should do good to those who hate us Luke 6:27-36, *page 1163* • Romans 12:14-21, *page 1296*

Many in the world hate Jesus John 7:6-7, *page 1210* • John 15:18-19, *page 1224*

We need to get rid of all hatred in our lives Galatians 5:19-23, *page 1343* • 1 John 2:7-11, *page 1434* • 1 John 3:14-19, *page 1436* • 1 John 4:20-21, *page 1437*

Heart *see also Conscience; Emotions; Mind; Soul; Spirit*

The Bible uses the heart as a symbol of our inner being. It includes our personality, character, intellect, and emotions—in short, it is "what makes us tick." That is why Scripture calls us to guard our hearts above everything else and why God wants to renew and transform them by his Spirit.

Guard your heart above all else, for it determines the course of your life. – Proverbs 4:23, page 700

Our hearts can be hard and resistant toward God Exodus 7:8–9:35, *page 73* • Exodus 8:16-19, *page 75* • Ezekiel 2:1-5, *page 901* • Zechariah 7:8-13, *page 1042* • Hebrews 3:7-19, *page 1398*

God can further harden the hard hearts of those who will not yield to him Exodus 9:12, *page 76* • Isaiah 6:8-10, *page 755* • Matthew 13:10-17, *page 1088* • John 12:37-41, *page 1220*

We are called to love God with all of our heart Deuteronomy 6:4-5, *page 208* • Mark 12:28-31, *page 1140*

We are not to be hard-hearted toward those in need Deuteronomy 15:7-11, *page 218* • Jeremiah 5:20-29, *page 830* • James 2:14-17, *page 1413* • 1 John 3:17-18, *page 1436*

God is looking for people with hearts like his own heart 1 Samuel 13:13-14, *page 318* • Acts 13:22, *page 1256*

God wants us to have clean and humble hearts Psalm 24:1-6, *page 615* • Psalm 51:7-17, *page 633* • Isaiah 66:1-2, *page 819* • Jeremiah 4:14, *page 828*

God calls us to soften our hearts when they become hard Jeremiah 4:3-4, *page 827* • Hosea 10:12, *page 982*

The human heart can often be deceitful Jeremiah 17:9-10, *page 845*

God makes our hard hearts responsive to him Jeremiah 31:31-34, *page 862* • Ezekiel 36:25-27, *page 938*

Our words and actions reveal what is truly in our hearts Matthew 12:33-37, *page 1087* • Mark 7:1-23, *page 1130* • Luke 6:45, *page 1163*

Hard hearts stop us from hearing spiritual truth Mark 6:47-52, *page 1130* • Mark 8:14-21, *page 1132*

▶ *See **Hardness of heart**, page 1132.*

Heaven

While the Bible uses the word "heaven" in several ways (including to refer to the sky or universe, or to God's own dwelling place), most Christians use it to speak of our home after death. Jesus assured us that not even death could separate us from him and that we would one day be with him in heaven. However, Revelation makes clear that heaven is not our ultimate home; a renewed and glorified earth is.

For we know that when this earthly tent we live in is taken down (that is, when we die and leave this earthly body), we will have a house in heaven, an eternal body made for us by God himself and not by human hands. – 2 Corinthians 5:1, page 1327

Heaven is God's home Psalm 73:25, *page 647* • Isaiah 66:1-2, *page 819* • Matthew 6:9, *page 1077* • Philippians 3:20, *page 1359*

There will not be any loss, death, or sadness in heaven Isaiah 25:8, *page 773* • Revelation 7:13-17, *page 1454* • Revelation 21:1-4, *page 1465*

God will one day create a new heaven and a new earth Isaiah 65:17-25, *page 819* • Revelation 21:1–22:5, *page 1465*

Believers who have died are now safe with Jesus in heaven Luke 23:42-43, *page 1194* • 1 Thessalonians 4:13-14, *page 1372* • Revelation 7:9-10, *page 1454*

Jesus went ahead of us to prepare heaven for his followers John 14:1-3, *page 1222*

Jesus is now in heaven praying for us Romans 8:34, *page 1292* • Hebrews 7:23-25, *page 1403*

Christians should look forward to heaven 2 Corinthians 5:1-8, *page 1327* • Colossians 3:1-5, *page 1365*

Anticipation of the joys of heaven can keep us going in times of suffering Philippians 1:21-23, *page 1355* • 1 Peter 1:6, *page 1420*

Our inheritance in heaven is safe 1 Peter 1:3-5, *page 1420*

All heaven worships God Revelation 5:6-14, *page 1451* • Revelation 7:9-12, *page 1454* • Revelation 19:1-8, *page 1463*

People from every nation and ethnic group will be in heaven Revelation 7:9-17, *page 1454*

At the End, heaven will come down to earth, and God will renew the earth as our new, eternal home Revelation 21:15, *page 1466*

▸ *See **Heaven**, page 1451; **The new Jerusalem**, page 1466.*

Hell

The Bible uses many different images to describe hell—the place of eternal separation from God for those who have rejected him. Jesus underlined the awfulness of hell and said that we should take all steps necessary to avoid it.

> *"So if your eye—even your good eye—causes you to lust, gouge it out and throw it away. It is better for you to lose one part of your body than for your whole body to be thrown into hell. And if your hand—even your stronger hand—causes you to sin, cut it off and throw it away. It is better for you to lose one part of your body than for your whole body to be thrown into hell."* – *Matthew 5:29-30, page 1076*

Jesus said hell should be avoided at all costs Matthew 5:29-30, *page 1076* • Matthew 18:7-9, *page 1097* • Luke 12:4-5, *page 1175*

The path to hell is comfortable and well populated Matthew 7:13-14, *page 1078*

Hell is a place of darkness and misery Matthew 8:10-12, *page 1080* • Matthew 25:30, *page 1109* • 2 Peter 2:4, *page 1428*

Hell is a place of grief and weeping Matthew 8:11-12, *page 1080* • Matthew 13:37-43, *page 1090* • Matthew 22:1-14, *page 1103* • Matthew 24:45-51, *page 1108*

Hell is a place of eternal fire Matthew 18:7-9, *page 1097* • Matthew 25:41-46, *page 1109* • Mark 9:42-48, *page 1135* • Hebrews 10:27-28, *age 1406* • Revelation 20:11-15, *page 1465*

Hell is a place prepared for Satan and his demons Matthew 25:41-46, *page 1109* • 2 Peter 2:4, *page 1428* • Revelation 20:7-10, *page 1464*

Hell is a place of eternal destruction and exclusion from God's presence 2 Thessalonians 1:7-9, *page 1374* • 2 Peter 3:3-7, *page 1429*

Hell is the destiny of those who do not turn from their sin 2 Peter 2:4-9, *page 1428* • Revelation 20:11-15, *page 1465* • Revelation 21:6-8, *page 1465*

We should do all we can to keep others from hell Jude 1:17-23, *page 1442*

▸ *See **Hell**, page 1108.*

Help of the Holy Spirit *see also Holy Spirit*

If it is impossible to become a Christian without the help of the Holy Spirit, it is even more impossible to live as a Christian without his help. That is why Jesus encouraged us to ask our heavenly Father to give us his Holy Spirit. We can know his presence and power, not just as a one-off experience, but in an ongoing way that makes a difference in our lives.

> *"If you sinful people know how to give good gifts to your children, how much more will your heavenly Father give the Holy Spirit to those who ask him."* – *Luke 11:13, page 1173*

Jesus promised to send the Holy Spirit to help his followers Luke 24:45-49, *page 1196* • John 14:17-18, *page 1223* • Acts 1:8, *page 1236*

We need the Holy Spirit in order to be born again John 3:5-8, *page 1202*

We need the power of the Holy Spirit in order to express our faith effectively Acts 1:8, *page 1236* • Acts 2:1-21, *page 1237* • Acts 4:1-12, *page 1240*

Examples of people being filled with the Spirit in the early church Acts 2:1-4, *page 1237* • Acts 4:31, *page 1242* • Acts 8:4-25, *page 1247* • Acts 9:1-18, *page 1248* • Acts 19:1-7, *page 1266*

The Holy Spirit helps us to know God as a true father Romans 8:15, *page 1291* • Galatians 4:6, *page 1341*

We need the help of the Holy Spirit to pray Romans 8:26-27, *page 1292*

The Holy Spirit wants to help us bear good fruit in life Galatians 5:16, 22-23, *page 1343*

We need to be constantly filled with the Holy Spirit Ephesians 5:18, *page 1351*

▶ *See **Asking for the Holy Spirit**, page 1173; **The help of the Holy Spirit**, page 1222; **Life in the Spirit**, page 1291; **Living by the Spirit**, page 1342; **The Christian's relationship with the Holy Spirit**, page 1350.*

Holiness

Holiness is what makes God different, what separates him from everything else in his creation. As his people, we too are called to be holy, leading lives that are distinct from those of the people around us, in order to reflect what God himself is like.

> *Put all your hope in the gracious salvation that will come to you when Jesus Christ is revealed to the world. So you must live as God's obedient children. Don't slip back into your old ways of living to satisfy your own desires. You didn't know any better then. But now you must be holy in everything you do, just as God who chose you is holy. For the Scriptures say, "You must be holy because I am holy." – 1 Peter 1:13-16, page 1421*

The presence of God is holy Exodus 3:1-6, *page 68* • Isaiah 6:1-5, *page 755* • Revelation 4:1-8, *page 1450*

No one is holy as God is Exodus 15:11, *page 83* • 1 Samuel 2:2, *page 306*

God gave his people a holy day—the Sabbath—on which to rest Exodus 20:8-11, *page 90* • Exodus 31:12-17, *page 103* • Deuteronomy 5:12-15, *page 208* • Nehemiah 13:15-22, *page 552*

Because God is holy, we too are to be holy Leviticus 11:44-45, *page 129* • Leviticus 19:1-2, *page 138* • 1 Peter 1:13-16, *page 1421*

Only God can make us holy, not we ourselves Leviticus 20:8, *page 140* • Psalm 51:1-11, *page 633* • Isaiah 6:1-7, *page 755* • 1 Corinthians 1:30-31, *page 1304*

God is worthy of being worshiped because of his holiness Psalm 99:1-5, *page 664* • Isaiah 6:1-3, *page 755* • Revelation 4:1-11, *page 1450*

Holiness begins in the heart, not in external acts Matthew 5:27-30, *page 1076* • Matthew 23:1-39, *page 1105* • Mark 7:1-23, *page 1130*

God uses his word of truth to make us holy John 17:17, *page 1226*

God wants us to pursue increasing holiness in our lives Romans 6:19-22, *page 1289* • 2 Corinthians 7:1, *page 1329* • Ephesians 4:17–5:20, *page 1350* • 1 Thessalonians 4:3-8, *page 1372* • Hebrews 12:1-4, *page 1408* • 1 Peter 2:9-12, *page 1422*

Our holiness before God is rooted in the once-for-all sacrifice of Jesus on the cross for us 1 Corinthians 1:30, *page 1304* • Hebrews 10:1-14, *page 1405* • 1 Peter 2:21-24, *page 1423*

▶ *See **Holiness**, page 128; **Integrity**, page 1325; **Becoming like Christ**, page 1435.*

Holy Spirit *see also Help of the Holy Spirit; Spiritual gifts*

Christians believe that the Holy Spirit is the third person of the Trinity—the one God who exists simultaneously in three persons: God the Father, God the Son, and God the Holy Spirit. As such, the Holy Spirit is not a mere power or influence but a person, through whom God engages with us and his world. Thus, the Holy Spirit is to be honored as God himself.

> *"But you will receive power when the Holy Spirit comes upon you. And you will be my witnesses, telling people about me everywhere—in Jerusalem, throughout Judea, in Samaria, and to the ends of the earth." – Acts 1:8, page 1236*

BASIC TRUTHS • *page 1538*

The Holy Spirit was involved in Creation Genesis 1:1-2, *page 4* • Psalm 104:24-30 (see footnote on 104:30), *page 668*

The Holy Spirit gives skills and abilities Exodus 31:1-5, *page 102* • 1 Corinthians 12:4-11, *page 1315*

The Holy Spirit was given to empower leaders Numbers 11:21-30, *page 167* • Judges 3:9-10, *page 273* • 1 Samuel 10:1-10, *page 314* • 1 Samuel 16:1-13, *page 323*

The Holy Spirit would anoint the coming Messiah Isaiah 11:1-5, *page 760* • Isaiah 61:1-3, *page 814* • Luke 4:14-21, *page 1158*

God promised to put his Holy Spirit within his people to renew them Isaiah 44:1-4, *page 795* • Ezekiel 36:25-27, *page 938*

God promised to give his Holy Spirit to all his people one day Joel 2:28-29, *page 990* • Acts 2:1-21, *page 1237*

God promised that his Spirit would enable his people Zechariah 4:6, *page 1040*

The Holy Spirit anointed Jesus for his ministry Matthew 3:13-17, *page 1072* • Luke 3:21-22, *page 1157* • John 3:34, *page 1204*

The Holy Spirit led Jesus into the wilderness for his time of testing Matthew 4:1

The Holy Spirit brings about the new birth John 3:3-8, *page 1202* • Titus 3:4-7, *page 1391*

Jesus promised to send the Holy Spirit to his followers John 14:15-18, 26, *page 1223* • John 15:26, *page 1224*

The Holy Spirit is the one who convicts people John 16:5-15, *page 1224*

The Holy Spirit empowers us to be witnesses for Jesus Acts 1:8, *page 1236* • Acts 2:1-41, *page 1237* • Acts 6:8-10, *page 1244* • Acts 7:54-60, *page 1246*

The Holy Spirit gives boldness and strength Acts 4:23-31, *page 1241* • Ephesians 3:14-19, *page 1349*

The Holy Spirit is God himself Acts 5:1-4, *page 1242* • 2 Corinthians 3:16-18, *page 1326*

We are not to resist, bring sorrow to, or stifle the Holy Spirit Acts 7:51, *page 1246* • Ephesians 4:30, *page 1351* • 1 Thessalonians 5:16-22, *page 1373*

The Holy Spirit leads the church in its mission Acts 13:1-3, *page 1255* • Acts 16:6-10, *page 1261*

The Holy Spirit fills our hearts with God's love Romans 5:1-5, *page 1287*

The Holy Spirit frees us to live a completely different way Romans 8:1-27, *page 1290*

The Holy Spirit assures us we are God's children Romans 8:15-16, *page 1291* • Galatians 3:26–4:7, *page 1341* • Ephesians 1:11-14, *page 1346* • 1 John 4:13-16, *page 1437*

The Holy Spirit gives us a foretaste of what is to come Romans 8:18-25, *page 1291* • 2 Corinthians 5:1-5, *page 1327*

The Holy Spirit prays for us and helps us to pray Romans 8:26-27, *page 1292* • Ephesians 6:18, *page 1353*

The Holy Spirit opens our spiritual eyes 1 Corinthians 2:10-12, *page 1305*

The Holy Spirit gives his gifts to the church 1 Corinthians 12:4-11, *page 1315* • 1 Corinthians 14:1-25, *page 1317*

The Holy Spirit brings us freedom 2 Corinthians 3:16-18, *page 1326*

The Holy Spirit makes us more like Jesus 2 Corinthians 3:17-18, *page 1326*

We can live by the power of the Holy Spirit Galatians 5:16-25, *page 1343*

The Holy Spirit forges unity among Christians Ephesians 4:1-6, *page 1349*

We are to be filled with the Holy Spirit Ephesians 5:18, *page 1351*

The people who wrote the Bible were inspired by the Holy Spirit 2 Peter 1:20-21, *page 1428*

▸ *See **Asking for the Holy Spirit**, page 1173; **The help of the Holy Spirit**, page 1222; **The Holy Spirit in Acts**, page 1236; **Life in the Spirit**, page 1291; **Living by the Spirit**, page 1342; **The Christian's relationship with the Holy Spirit**, page 1350.*

Homicide *see Murder*

Homosexuality

In most Western cultures, homosexuality is now seen as normal and completely acceptable. But while Christians should be careful not to be unloving toward gay people in any way, the Bible is clear in its teaching that God's design for intimacy is a lifelong marriage relationship between one man and one woman, meant to reflect Jesus' love for his church. Sexual intimacy in any other context falls short of God's best for people, which is why the Bible sees it as sin.

Don't you realize that those who do wrong will not inherit the Kingdom of God? Don't fool yourselves. Those who indulge in sexual sin, or who worship idols, or commit adultery, or are male prostitutes, or practice homosexuality, or are thieves, or greedy people, or drunkards, or are abusive, or cheat people—none of these will inherit the Kingdom of God. Some of you were once like that. But you were cleansed; you were made holy; you were made right with God by calling on the name of the Lord Jesus Christ and by the Spirit of our God. – 1 Corinthians 6:9-11, page 1309

It is in male and female together that God's image is fully revealed Genesis 1:26-27, *page 5*

God designed sexual intimacy to be between one man and one woman in a lifelong marriage relationship Genesis 2:21-25, *page 6* • Matthew 19:4-6, *page 1099*

Rampant homosexuality brought God's judgment upon Sodom and Gomorrah Genesis 19:1-29, *page 22* • 2 Peter 2:4-10, *page 1428* • Jude 1:7, *page 1442*

The Bible says that God finds same-sex sexual relationships detestable Leviticus 18:22, *page 138*

It is possible to have close same-sex friendships without sexual intimacy 1 Samuel 18:1-4, *page 326*

Homosexual activity is a lifestyle that comes under God's judgment Romans 1:18-32, *page 1283*

The Bible says that homosexual activity is incompatible with being a Christian and that it is possible to change this way of living 1 Corinthians 6:9-11, *page 1309*

▶ *See **Sexuality**, page 742.*

Honesty *see Integrity*

Hope

As Christians, we should be the most hopeful people in the world, for our hope is based on confidence in God's faithfulness and his promises for the future. This hope is for our life both in this world and in the world to come, and as such it is what can keep us going when life gets tough.

We look forward with hope to that wonderful day when the glory of our great God and Savior, Jesus Christ, will be revealed. – Titus 2:13, page 1390

God gives hope to all those in need Psalm 9:18, *page 607* • Psalm 25:1-3, *page 616*

Our hope encourages us to be godly Psalm 25:21, *page 616* • 1 Peter 1:13-16, *page 1421* • 2 Peter 3:8-14, *page 1429*

We can continue to hope in God's promises in hopeless situations Psalm 46:1-11, *page 630* • Lamentations 3:22-26, *page 895* • Romans 4:18-24, *page 1287* • Romans 8:28-39, *page 1292*

We have hope that we will one day be raised from the dead John 11:17-27, *page 1217* • Acts 23:6-11, *page 1273* • 1 Corinthians 15:12-28, *page 1319* • 1 Thessalonians 4:13-18, *page 1372*

Hope is what keeps us going Romans 4:18-21, *page 1287* • 2 Corinthians 4:8-18, *page 1327* • Hebrews 11:1–12:13, *page 1407*

God's promises bring hope Romans 4:20-21, *page 1287* • Hebrews 6:13-20, *page 1401*

Knowing we have been made right with God through Jesus gives us great hope Romans 5:1-11, *page 1287*

We have hope of future glory Romans 8:18-25, *page 1291* • Titus 2:11-13, *page 1390*

Hope encourages us to be bold 2 Corinthians 3:12-18, *page 1326*

Those who are not Christians have no hope Ephesians 2:12-13, *page 1347*

We have hope in God's salvation and eternal life Colossians 1:5, *page 1362* • Titus 1:1-2, *page 1389*

▶ *See **Hope**, page 895.*

Hospitality

Christians should be some of the best providers of hospitality in the world. Since God has welcomed us into his home and family, the Bible tells us that we should do the same for others, generously sharing our love, food, and shelter with them. If we are not hospitable, there is something about the gospel that we have not understood.

> *Keep on loving each other as brothers and sisters. Don't forget to show hospitality to strangers, for some who have done this have entertained angels without realizing it! – Hebrews 13:1-2, page 1409*

Hospitality played an important role in the lives of God's people in the Old Testament Genesis 18:1-8, *page 21* • Exodus 2:18-20, *page 67* • 1 Kings 17:7-16, *page 401*

Jesus received hospitality Matthew 9:10, *page 1081* • Mark 1:29-31, *page 1119* • Luke 10:38-42, *page 1172*

Jesus expected that his disciples would receive hospitality Matthew 10:11-14, *page 1083* • Luke 10:1-12, *page 1171*

Hospitality brings heavenly reward Matthew 10:40-42, *page 1084* • Mark 9:41, *page 1135* • Hebrews 13:1-2, *page 1409*

Jesus expected that his disciples would exercise hospitality Matthew 25:34-36, *page 1109* • Luke 14:12-14, *page 1179*

The first Christians opened up their homes to help traveling missionaries Acts 16:13-15, *page 1262* • Acts 18:1-3, *page 1265* • 3 John 1:5-8, *page 1439*

Christians should be eager to practice hospitality Romans 12:13, *page 1296* • Hebrews 13:1-2, *page 1409*

The first Christians used their homes for church meetings Romans 16:3-5, *page 1300* • 1 Corinthians 16:19, *page 1322*

Christian leaders should be hospitable 1 Timothy 3:1-2, *page 1380*

We should be cheerful about being hospitable 1 Peter 4:9-11, *page 1424*

▶ *See **Hospitality**, page 1410.*

Human race *see Humanity*

Humanity *see also Discrimination*

The Bible says that the human race is the crown of God's creation. Humanity is incomplete without its two different yet complementary aspects, male and female. Together they express the image of God. God created men and women to know him, but the relationship between them and him was spoiled by sin and is only restored through Jesus.

> *When I look at the night sky and see the work of your fingers—the moon and the stars you set in place—what are mere mortals that you should think about them, human beings that you should care for them? Yet you made them only a little lower than God and crowned them with glory and honor. You gave them charge of everything you made, putting all things under their authority—the flocks and the herds and all the wild animals, the birds in the sky, the fish in the sea, and everything that swims the ocean currents. – Psalm 8:3-8, page 605*

The human race is linked to the animal world, yet distinct from it—created on the same day but by a separate act of creation—and given dominion over it Genesis 1:24-28, *page 4*

God's image is shared equally by men and women Genesis 1:26-27, *page 5* • Genesis 5:1-2, *page 9*

The first people disobeyed God and brought sin into the human race, thus breaking relationship with God Genesis 3:1-24, *page 6* • Romans 5:12-19, *page 1288*

Loving and obeying God is the best basis for human life Deuteronomy 10:12-16, *page 213* • Proverbs 1:7, *page 697* • Proverbs 9:10-12, *page 705* • Matthew 22:34-38, *page 1104*

Human life on earth is short and fragile Psalm 90:1-12, *page 659* • Psalm 103:15-16, *page 667* • Ecclesiastes 12:6-7, *page 739*

Human life is intricately made by God Psalm 139:13-18, *page 689*

God calls people to do right and walk humbly before him Micah 6:8, *page 1016*

Jesus became a real human being Matthew 1:18-25, *page 1068* • John 1:1-14, *page 1199* • Hebrews 2:14-15, *page 1398* • 1 John 1:1-4, *page 1433*

Both men and women found a place in the ministry of Jesus Matthew 10:1-4, *page 1083* • Luke 8:1-3, *page 1166* • Acts 1:12-14, *page 1236*

Jesus is the only mediator between God and humanity John 14:6-8, *page 1222* • Acts 4:10-12, *page 1240* • 1 Timothy 2:3-6, *page 1380*

Both men and women were part of Paul's mission teams Acts 16:1-15, *page 1261* • Acts 18:18-28, *page 1266* • Romans 16:1-3, *page 1300*

Men and women are fully equal before God Galatians 3:26-29, *page 1341*

▶ *See **Women**, page 728.*

Humility *see also Self-denial*

Humility is not always greatly admired in our world today. We are encouraged to promote ourselves, to push ourselves forward, for we are told that if we do not do so, no one else will. But the Bible says that humility is a quality God regards highly and that it was something Jesus modeled when he was here on earth.

> *Don't be selfish; don't try to impress others. Be humble, thinking of others as better than yourselves. Don't look out only for your own interests, but take an interest in others, too. You must have the same attitude that Christ Jesus had. Though he was God, he did not think of equality with God as something to cling to. Instead, he gave up his divine privileges; he took the humble position of a slave and was born as a human being. When he appeared in human form, he humbled himself in obedience to God and died a criminal's death on a cross. – Philippians 2:3-8, page 1356*

God himself sometimes humbles us Leviticus 26:14-41, *page 149* • Deuteronomy 8:1-3, *page 211* • Daniel 4:34-37, *page 962*

God wants us to stay humble when we have been successful Deuteronomy 8:11-18, *page 211* • Proverbs 30:7-9, *page 727* • Luke 17:7-10, *page 1182*

God saves those who are humble 2 Samuel 22:26-28, *page 368* • Psalm 18:27, *page 611*

God hears the prayers of the humble 2 Kings 22:8-20, *page 440* • 2 Chronicles 7:12-15, *page 489* • Ezra 8:21-23, *page 531* • Daniel 10:2-12, *page 969*

Those who are humble become wise because they are always ready to learn Proverbs 11:2, *page 707*

God blesses and restores the humble Isaiah 57:15, *page 810* • Isaiah 66:2, *page 819* • Matthew 5:3-5, *page 1074*

God wants us to be humble Micah 6:8, *page 1016* • Matthew 18:1-4, *page 1097* • 2 Corinthians 12:1-10, *page 1333* • James 4:6-10, *page 1416* • 1 Peter 5:5-7, *page 1425*

Jesus came as a humble servant Matthew 11:28-30, *page 1085* • Mark 10:42-45, *page 1137* • 2 Corinthians 8:9, *page 1330* • Philippians 2:3-11, *page 1356*

God will exalt the humble Matthew 23:8-12, *page 1105* • Luke 18:9-14, *page 1183* • James 4:10, *page 1416* • 1 Peter 5:5-6, *page 1425*

We should have a humble and realistic view of ourselves Romans 12:1-3, *page 1296*

We should be humble in dealing with others Philippians 2:1-11, *page 1356* • Colossians 3:12-17, *page 1365*

▶ *See **Humility**, page 1134; **The humility of Christ**, page 1358.*

Husbands and wives *see Marriage*

Hypocrisy

As a God of truth, God hates all hypocrisy. The Old Testament prophets fearlessly exposed it, and Jesus constantly confronted the hypocrisy of the Pharisees, who pretended to be one thing on the outside but were something quite different underneath. We are guilty of hypocrisy whenever our words and actions do not match up.

"Watch out! Don't do your good deeds publicly, to be admired by others, for you will lose the reward from your Father in heaven. When you give to someone in need, don't do as the hypocrites do—blowing trumpets in the synagogues and streets to call attention to their acts of charity! I tell you the truth, they have received all the reward they will ever get. But when you give to someone in need, don't let your left hand know what your right hand is doing. Give your gifts in private, and your Father, who sees everything, will reward you. When you pray, don't be like the hypocrites who love to pray publicly on street corners and in the synagogues where everyone can see them. I tell you the truth, that is all the reward they will ever get. But when you pray, go away by yourself, shut the door behind you, and pray to your Father in private. Then your Father, who sees everything, will reward you." – Matthew 6:1-6, page 1076

God hates hypocrisy in worship Isaiah 29:13-21, *page 778* • Isaiah 58:1-4, *page 810* • Amos 5:21-24, *page 998* • Matthew 15:3-9, *page 1092*

Hypocrites make a great show of their devotion to God Ezekiel 33:31-32, *page 935* • Matthew 6:1-18, *page 1076*

Jesus exposed the hypocrisy of the Pharisees Matthew 6:2, 5, 16, *page 1076* • Matthew 15:1-9, *page 1092* • Matthew 22:15-22, *page 1103* • Matthew 23:1-36, *page 1105*

Jesus warned us to beware of hypocrisy in our own lives Luke 12:1-3, *page 1175* • Luke 20:41-47, *page 1188*

Christian leaders especially should not be hypocrites 1 Corinthians 4:1-5, *page 1307* • 1 Timothy 3:1-8, *page 1380*

We must get rid of all hypocrisy in our lives 2 Corinthians 1:12-14, *page 1324* • 1 Thessalonians 2:1-6, *page 1370* • 1 Peter 2:1-3, *page 1421*

There was no hint of hypocrisy in Jesus' life 1 Peter 2:21-22, *page 1423*

The way we live will show what we really believe 1 John 3:16-19, *page 1436*

▶ *See* ***Hypocrisy****, page 1106.*

Idols

An idol is anything that takes the place of God in our hearts, seeking the love and devotion that belong to him alone. In Bible times, idols were statues of other gods; but these days they are just as likely to take the form of possessions, desires, or other people. There can be no room for idolatry in the Christian life.

Dear children, keep away from anything that might take God's place in your hearts. – 1 John 5:21, page 1438

We should have no other gods but God alone Exodus 20:3, *page 89* • Leviticus 19:1-4, *page 138* • Joshua 24:14-24, *page 268*

God tells us not to have any kind of idol Exodus 20:4-6, *page 89* • Deuteronomy 4:15-24, *page 206*

We give in to idolatry when we start to forget God Exodus 32:1-35, *page 103* • Psalm 106:19-22, *page 670* • Jonah 2:8, *page 1008*

Idols were to be destroyed Deuteronomy 7:25-26, *page 211* • Judges 6:25-32, *page 278*

Idols are completely incapable of helping us in any way 1 Samuel 12:20-21, *page 317* • Psalm 115:3-8, *page 675* • Psalm 135:15-21, *page 687*

Following worthless idols leads to us becoming worthless too 2 Kings 17:14-15, *page 432*

Idolatry was a key factor that led to Israel's exile 2 Kings 17:7-23, *page 432*

God will not share his glory with anyone or anything else Isaiah 42:8, *page 793*

Worshiping idols is foolish and of no value Isaiah 44:9-20, *page 796* • Habakkuk 2:18-20, *page 1026*

Money can become an idol Luke 12:13-21, *page 1175* • Luke 16:13, *page 1182*

An idol is a foolish substitute for the living God Romans 1:20-23, *page 1283*

Though idols may seem harmless, behind them stand demonic powers 1 Corinthians 10:18-21, *page 1314* • Revelation 9:20, *page 1455*

▶ *See* ***Idols****, page 836.*

Illness *see Suffering*

Impatience *see Patience*

Incarnation *see Jesus Christ: his identity and character; Jesus Christ: his life*

Influence in society

While God wants us as his people to be different from those around us, he does not want us to withdraw from the world and stay in a holy huddle. He wants us to exert a positive influence on the world around us, in every sphere where he has placed us.

"You are the salt of the earth. But what good is salt if it has lost its flavor? Can you make it salty again? It will be thrown out and trampled underfoot as worthless. You are the light of the world—like a city on a hilltop that cannot be hidden. No one lights a lamp and then puts it under a basket. Instead, a lamp is placed on a stand, where it gives light to everyone in the house. In the same way, let your good deeds shine out for all to see, so that everyone will praise your heavenly Father." – Matthew 5:13-16, page 1075

God put some of his people in key places of influence Genesis 41:37-44, *page 52* • Esther 4:14, *page 558* • Esther 10:1-3, *page 563* • Daniel 1:1-21, *page 955* • Daniel 2:46-48, *page 958* • Philippians 4:22, *page 1360*

God wants us to serve him where we are Jeremiah 29:4-7, *page 858*

Jesus wants us to have a positive effect on the world around us Matthew 5:13-16, *page 1075*

God wants us to influence society by doing good to those in need Matthew 25:31-46, *page 1109* • Luke 10:25-37, *page 1172* • James 1:26-27, *page 1413*

Christians should not withdraw from the world but rather remain active in it John 17:9-19, *page 1225* • 1 Corinthians 5:9-11, *page 1308*

Our Christian faith should be evident in the way we work Ephesians 6:5-9, *page 1352* • Colossians 3:22-25, *page 1366*

We can influence society by praying for our leaders 1 Timothy 2:1-4, *page 1380*

▶ *See **Serving God in our work**, page 956; **Salt and light**, page 1075; **Working for the glory of God**, page 1265.*

Ingratitude *see Ungratefulness*

Injustice *see Justice*

Insecurity

People can feel insecure for all kinds of reasons—their looks, their education, their job, their personality, their abilities. Insecurity convinces us that we do not have what it takes to tackle what lies ahead of us. But the Bible is full of stories of people who found their insecurities transformed as they trusted in God and followed him. Real security comes from a relationship with him and believing he has a purpose for our lives.

"Do not be afraid or discouraged, for the LORD will personally go ahead of you. He will be with you; he will neither fail you nor abandon you." – Deuteronomy 31:8, page 234

Insecurity can cause us to doubt God's call on our lives Exodus 4:1-17, *page 68* • Judges 6:1-24, *page 276* • Jeremiah 1:4-10, *page 822*

True security is found in God alone Deuteronomy 33:26-29, *page 239* • Psalm 37:1-40, *page 623* • Psalm 46:1-11, *page 630* • Psalm 91:1-16, *page 660* • Proverbs 14:26-27, *page 711* • Matthew 6:31-33, *page 1078* • Luke 12:16-21, *page 1175* • John 10:27-30, *page 1216*

Acting out of insecurity never has a good outcome Judges 9:1-57, *page 281* • 1 Samuel 18:1-16, *page 326* • 2 Kings 11:1-16, *page 425* • Matthew 27:11-26, *page 1113*

BASIC TRUTHS • *page 1544*

Life itself is insecure, which is why we need to trust in God Ecclesiastes 12:1-7, *page 739* • Isaiah 40:6-8, *page 789* • Luke 12:13-20, *page 1175* • 1 Peter 1:23-25, *page 1421*

Insecure people are always looking for weaknesses or faults in others Matthew 7:1-5, *page 1078* • Matthew 9:10-13, *page 1081* • Matthew 15:1-4, *page 1092*

We are insecure if we are trusting in our money and our own resources Luke 12:16-21, *page 1175* • 1 Timothy 6:17-19, *page 1383*

Those who are secure in their relationship with God can take the lowest place and serve John 13:1-17, *page 1221*

Insecure people always compare themselves with others 2 Corinthians 10:12, *page 1332*

▸ *See* ***Trusting God when we cannot see the way ahead****, page 57;* ***Keeping up appearances****, page 494;* ***Rejection****, page 617;* ***Trusting God whatever happens****, page 959.*

Insults

Many people in the Bible experienced the humiliation and pain of insults in one form or another. But when insults come, God calls his people not to retaliate but rather to turn the other cheek and to bless those who insult and hurt them.

> *Don't repay evil for evil. Don't retaliate with insults when people insult you. Instead, pay them back with a blessing. That is what God has called you to do, and he will grant you his blessing. – 1 Peter 3:9, page 1423*

Many of God's people experienced insults 2 Samuel 16:5-13, *page 360* • Psalm 44:13-16, *page 629* • Psalm 69:1-9, *page 644* • Psalm 123:1-4, *page 683* • Jeremiah 20:7-8, *page 848* • 2 Corinthians 12:10, *page 1334*

We should not be affected by insults but simply take them to God in prayer and get on with life Nehemiah 4:1-6, *page 539* • Nehemiah 6:1-9, *page 541*

Even close friends can turn on us Psalm 55:12-14, *page 635*

We should neither react to insults nor fear them Proverbs 12:16, *page 709* • Isaiah 51:7-8, *page 804* • 1 Peter 2:21-23, *page 1423*

We should resolve to conquer evil by doing good Proverbs 25:21-22, *page 723* • Romans 12:14-21, *page 1296* • 1 Peter 3:9-12, *page 1423*

We should not retaliate when insulted Lamentations 3:25-30, *page 895* • Proverbs 12:16, *page 709* • Matthew 5:38-42, *page 1076* • 1 Peter 3:9-12, *page 1423*

God will bless Christians who are insulted or persecuted because of their faith Matthew 5:11-12, *page 1075* • 2 Corinthians 12:10, *page 1334* • Hebrews 10:32-39, *page 1406* • 1 Peter 4:12-14, *page 1425*

Even Jesus experienced insults Luke 22:63-65, *page 1192* • Romans 15:3, *page 1299*

We should take care not to insult the Holy Spirit by our words or actions Hebrews 10:26-31, *page 1406*

▸ *See* ***Speech****, page 1416.*

Integrity *see also Truth*

As a God of truth, God delights in his people's demonstrating truth and integrity, for this reflects his own character. Integrity should characterize every aspect of our lives, and there should be no area that we see as being beyond its reach, whether that be in our personal, social, or business life.

> *I will be careful to live a blameless life—when will you come to help me? I will lead a life of integrity in my own home. I will refuse to look at anything vile and vulgar. I hate all who deal crookedly; I will have nothing to do with them. I will reject perverse ideas and stay away from every evil. I will not tolerate people who slander their neighbors. I will not endure conceit and pride. I will search for faithful people to be my companions. Only those who are above reproach will be allowed to serve me. I will not allow deceivers to serve in my house, and liars will not stay*

in my presence. My daily task will be to ferret out the wicked and free the city of the LORD from their grip. – Psalm 101:2-8, page 664

God blesses integrity in our place of work Genesis 39:1-6, 20-23, *page 49* • Nehemiah 2:1-9, *page 536* • Daniel 1:1-21, *page 955* • Daniel 2:24-49, *page 957*

Honesty is commanded by God Exodus 20:15-16, *page 90*

God is truth and desires truth Numbers 23:19, *page 183* • Psalm 51:6-12, *page 633*

Integrity in business is commended Deuteronomy 25:13-16, *page 227* • Proverbs 11:1-5, *page 707* • Proverbs 16:11, *page 713*

Integrity releases God's blessing 1 Kings 9:4-5, *page 388* • Psalm 101:1-8, *page 664*

Satan hates integrity Job 2:1-10, *page 566*

Integrity begins at home Psalm 101:1-2, *page 664*

We should work hard at integrity Psalm 101:1-8, *page 664* • 2 Corinthians 8:20-21, *page 1331* • Hebrews 13:18, *page 1410*

God hates lies Proverbs 6:16-19, *page 702* • Proverbs 12:22, *page 709*

We should have integrity in how we live Proverbs 19:1, *page 715* • Isaiah 59:9-15, *page 812* • Matthew 5:33-37, *page 1076* • Ephesians 4:25-32, *page 1351*

Lying is one of the things that make us unclean before God Matthew 15:15-20, *page 1093*

Leaders in the church should be full of integrity 2 Corinthians 1:12-23, *page 1324* • 1 Timothy 3:1-10, *page 1380* • Titus 1:6-9, *page 1389* • Titus 2:7, *page 1390*

▸ *See* ***Honesty****, page 707;* ***Integrity****, page 1325;* ***Living according to the truth****, page 1439.*

Intercession *see Prayer*

Intimidation

Intimidation is the use of threatening words or actions to try to get people to do something they don't want to do, or not to do something that they do want to do. God promises to be with us and to help us stand firm whenever we are intimidated.

Later I went to visit Shemaiah son of Delaiah and grandson of Mehetabel, who was confined to his home. He said, "Let us meet together inside the Temple of God and bolt the doors shut. Your enemies are coming to kill you tonight." But I replied, "Should someone in my position run from danger? Should someone in my position enter the Temple to save his life? No, I won't do it!" I realized that God had not spoken to him, but that he had uttered this prophecy against me because Tobiah and Sanballat had hired him. They were hoping to intimidate me and make me sin. Then they would be able to accuse and discredit me. – Nehemiah 6:10-13, page 542

Many people in the Bible experienced intimidation Genesis 19:1-9, *page 22* • 1 Samuel 17:1-11, *page 324* • 2 Kings 18:19-25, *page 435* • Nehemiah 6:5-7, *page 541* • Acts 4:1-31, *page 1240* • Acts 16:16-24, *page 1262*

We should trust God when we are intimidated 1 Samuel 17:32-51, *page 325* • Acts 4:19-22, *page 1241* • Philippians 1:27-30, *page 1356*

We should pray when we are intimidated 2 Kings 19:1-19, *page 436* • Nehemiah 4:4-9, *page 539* • Nehemiah 6:11-14, *page 542* • Psalm 55:9-16, *page 635* • Psalm 64:1-10, *page 640*

We should simply get on with what we are doing Nehemiah 4:1-9, *page 539* • Nehemiah 6:1-9, *page 541*

We do not need to fear, for God is always with us Psalm 27:1-3, *page 617* • Daniel 3:1-30, *page 958* • Acts 16:25-40, *page 1262*

▸ *See* ***Oppression****, page 710.*

Involvement in society *see Influence in society*

Jealousy *see also Envy*

Although "jealousy" is often used negatively nowadays as the equivalent of "envy"—wanting what belongs to someone else—it can also refer to a passionately protective attitude toward something that is ours. That is why the Bible says that God is "jealous," for he wants us to have our lives centered only on him, knowing this is what is best for us.

> *"You must worship no other gods, for the LORD, whose very name is Jealous, is a God who is jealous about his relationship with you." – Exodus 34:14, page 106*

Jealousy can arise from others' good fortune Genesis 26:12-14, *page 31* • 1 Samuel 18:5-8, *page 326*

God doesn't want us to share our devotion with anyone or anything else Exodus 20:4-6, *page 89* • Exodus 34:14, *page 106* • Deuteronomy 32:15-21, *page 236*

One of God's names is Jealous, for he is jealous of his relationship with us Exodus 34:14, *page 106*

We should not be jealous of others' achievements or abilities Numbers 11:26-30, *page 168* • 1 Samuel 18:1-16, *page 326*

Jealousy can destroy us and rob us of peace Job 5:2, *page 568* • Proverbs 14:30, *page 711*

Jealousy can affect our motives Acts 5:17-28, *page 1243* • Acts 13:43-45, *page 1257* • Acts 17:1-7, *page 1263* • Philippians 1:15-19, *page 1355*

God wants the Jews to be jealous of Gentiles who responded to the gospel so that it might provoke them to accept the gospel themselves Romans 10:16-21, *page 1294* • Romans 11:11-14, *page 1295*

Jealousy is part of our old, godless life Romans 13:12-14, *page 1298* • Galatians 5:19-26, *page 1343* • James 3:13-18, *page 1415*

We should not be jealous of other Christians 1 Corinthians 3:1-11, *page 1305* • 2 Corinthians 12:19-21, *page 1334* • Galatians 5:24-26, *page 1343*

Real love is never jealous 1 Corinthians 13:4-7, *page 1317*

We should get rid of all jealousy James 3:14-16, *page 1415* • 1 Peter 2:1, *page 1421*

Jesus Christ: his death

Jesus' death on the cross is the central fact of the Christian gospel. Because the wages of sin is death, Jesus died as our substitute. Through his sacrificial death our sins are atoned for—that is, the price of our sin is paid and we are cleansed so that the righteous anger and judgment of God against sin can be turned away and we can be forgiven. All this becomes ours simply through faith in Jesus.

> *God showed his great love for us by sending Christ to die for us while we were still sinners. And since we have been made right in God's sight by the blood of Christ, he will certainly save us from God's condemnation. For since our friendship with God was restored by the death of his Son while we were still his enemies, we will certainly be saved through the life of his Son. – Romans 5:8-10, page 1287*

The Messiah's death on our behalf, and many of its details, was prophesied long before it happened Psalm 22:1-31, *page 614* • Isaiah 53:3-11, *page 806*

Jesus prophesied his death clearly and in increasing detail Matthew 12:38-40, *page 1087* • Matthew 16:21, *page 1095* • Matthew 17:22-23, *page 1097* • Matthew 20:17-19, *page 1100*

Jesus saw his death as the means of God's establishing his new covenant Matthew 26:26-29, *page 1111*

Jesus' death was a ransom paid to free us Mark 10:35-45, *page 1137* • Ephesians 1:3-7, *page 1346* • Colossians 1:13-14, *page 1362* • 1 Peter 1:18-20, *page 1421*

Jesus laid down his life for us willingly John 10:17-18, *page 1216*

Jesus' death was not an accident or inevitable, but part of God's plan Acts 2:23-24, *page 1238*

Jesus' death was a sacrifice for sin Romans 3:23-25, *page 1286* • Hebrews 9:11-28, *page 1404* • 1 Peter 2:24-25, *page 1423* • 1 John 2:2, *page 1434*

We become identified with Jesus in his death through baptism Romans 6:1-11, *page 1289* • Galatians 2:20, *page 1339*

Jesus' death is remembered in the Lord's Supper 1 Corinthians 11:23-26, *page 1315*

In his death, Jesus took upon himself the curse that was on us Galatians 3:13, *page 1340*

Jesus' death brings freedom and forgiveness Ephesians 1:7-8, *page 1346* • 1 John 1:7-9, *page 1433*

Jesus' death was the means through which he was exalted Philippians 2:6-11, *page 1356* • 1 Peter 1:21, *page 1421*

▶ *See* ***The death of Jesus****, page 1114;* ***Redemption****, page 1136;* ***Justification****, page 1288.*

Jesus Christ: his identity and character *see also Messiah*

The Bible makes clear that Jesus was not just a good man, a holy man, or a prophet, but none other than God himself come into the world. It was through the miracle of the Virgin Birth that he could be both fully man and fully God.

> *In the beginning the Word already existed. The Word was with God, and the Word was God. He existed in the beginning with God. God created everything through him, and nothing was created except through him. The Word gave life to everything that was created, and his life brought light to everyone. . . . So the Word became human and made his home among us. He was full of unfailing love and faithfulness. And we have seen his glory, the glory of the Father's one and only Son. – John 1:1-4, 14, page 1199*

Jesus is God with us Matthew 1:18-23, *page 1068* • Luke 1:26-33, *page 1152* • John 1:1-18, *page 1199*

Jesus is the Savior Matthew 1:20-21, *page 1069* • Luke 2:8-11, *page 1154* • John 4:39-42, *page 1205* • Acts 5:29-32, *page 1243* • 2 Timothy 1:9-10, *page 1384*

Jesus is Lord Matthew 8:1-2, *page 1079* • Luke 6:1-5, *page 1162* • John 20:24-29, *page 1232* • Acts 2:32-36, *page 1239* • Philippians 2:5-11, *page 1356*

Jesus is humble Matthew 11:28-30, *page 1085* • Mark 10:35-45, *page 1137* • Philippians 2:6-8, *page 1356*

Jesus is the Messiah Matthew 16:13-18, *page 1095* • Luke 24:25-27, *page 1195* • John 4:25-29, *page 1205* • John 20:31, *page 1232*

Jesus is the Son of Man Matthew 16:27-28, *page 1096* • Mark 2:1-12, *page 1120* • Mark 10:42-45, *page 1137* • Luke 19:10, *page 1185* • Acts 7:55-56, *page 1246*

Jesus was an obedient Son to his Father Matthew 26:36-42, *page 1111* • John 4:34, *page 1205* • John 8:28-29, *page 1212* • Philippians 2:6-8, *page 1356* • Hebrews 5:7-8, *page 1400*

Jesus is the Son of God Matthew 26:62-65, *page 1112* • Luke 1:30-35, *page 1152* • John 3:35-36, *page 1204* • John 5:16-23, *page 1206* • Hebrews 1:1-14, *page 1396*

Jesus had authority over sin, sickness, and demons Mark 1:21-34, *page 1119* • Mark 1:40–2:12, *page 1120* • Luke 9:1-6, *page 1168*

Jesus is the Servant Mark 10:42-45, *page 1137* • John 13:1-17, *page 1221* • Acts 4:23-30, *page 1241* • Philippians 2:6-8, *page 1356*

Jesus was born as a real human being Luke 2:1-7, *page 1154* • John 1:14, *page 1199* • Galatians 4:4, *page 1341* • Philippians 2:5-11, *page 1356* • Hebrews 2:14-15, *page 1398*

Jesus is God himself John 1:1-5, *page 1199* • John 8:54-59, *page 1213* • Colossians 1:15-20, *page 1362* • Colossians 2:9, *page 1364*

Jesus is the Creator John 1:3-4, *page 1199* • Colossians 1:15-16, *page 1362*

Jesus is the Lamb of God John 1:29-34, *page 1200* • 1 Peter 1:18-19, *page 1421* • Revelation 7:17, *page 1454* • Revelation 21:22-27, *page 1466*

Jesus is the Judge John 5:22-23, *page 1206* • Acts 10:39-43, *page 1252* • Acts 17:30-31, *page 1264*

Jesus is holy and sinless John 8:46, *page 1213* • Hebrews 4:14-15, *page 1400* • Hebrews 7:23-26, *page 1403* • 1 Peter 2:22-23, *page 1423*

Jesus is the good shepherd John 10:1-18, *page 1215* • Hebrews 13:20-21, *page 1410* • 1 Peter 2:21-25, *page 1423* • 1 Peter 5:1-4, *page 1425*

Jesus is the only way to God John 14:1-6, *page 1222* • Acts 4:12, *page 1241* • 1 Timothy 2:3-6, *page 1380*

Jesus is the King John 18:36-37, *page 1228* • John 19:17-22, *page 1229* • Revelation 19:11-16, *page 1464*

Jesus is the head of the church Ephesians 1:22-23, *page 1347* • Ephesians 5:23-32, *page 1351*

Jesus is our High Priest Hebrews 4:14–5:10, *page 1400* • Hebrews 7:23-27, *page 1403* • Hebrews 9:11-15, *page 1404* • Hebrews 10:11-22, *page 1405*

▸ See ***Names and titles of Jesus***, *page 1070;* ***Jesus: the only way to God***, *page 1241;* ***The deity of Jesus Christ***, *page 1364.*

Jesus Christ: his life *see also Jesus Christ: his death*

Although Jesus was God, the miracle of the Virgin Birth enabled him to be born as a perfect man. Jesus shared all the normal experiences of human life—growing up, having a job, facing challenges—yet lived in constant and perfect obedience to his heavenly Father. His teaching about the Kingdom of God, backed up by his miracles, antagonized the Jewish leaders, who conspired to have him executed. But three days later he rose from the dead, just as he had promised. He spent a further forty days with his followers before ascending to heaven and taking his rightful place at his Father's side.

> *"You know what happened throughout Judea, beginning in Galilee, after John began preaching his message of baptism. And you know that God anointed Jesus of Nazareth with the Holy Spirit and with power. Then Jesus went around doing good and healing all who were oppressed by the devil, for God was with him. And we apostles are witnesses of all he did throughout Judea and in Jerusalem. They put him to death by hanging him on a cross, but God raised him to life on the third day. Then God allowed him to appear, not to the general public, but to us whom God had chosen in advance to be his witnesses. We were those who ate and drank with him after he rose from the dead. And he ordered us to preach everywhere and to testify that Jesus is the one appointed by God to be the judge of all—the living and the dead."* – *Acts 10:37-42, page 1252*

Jesus was a descendant of both Abraham and David Matthew 1:1-17, *page 1068* • Luke 3:23-38, *page 1157*

Jesus was miraculously conceived Matthew 1:18-23, *page 1068* • Luke 1:26-38, *page 1152*

Jesus was born like every other human being Matthew 1:24-25, *page 1069* • Luke 2:1-7, *page 1154*

Jesus' family had to flee as refugees to Egypt for a time to avoid persecution, in fulfillment of Scripture Matthew 2:1-23, *page 1069*

Jesus grew up and developed as a normal human being Luke 2:39-52, *page 1156*

Jesus was baptized before beginning his ministry Matthew 3:13-17, *page 1072* • Luke 3:21-22, *page 1157*

Jesus was tempted as we are but did not sin Matthew 4:1-11, *page 1073* • Hebrews 2:14-18, *page 1398* • Hebrews 4:14-16, *page 1400*

Jesus' ministry fulfilled the promise of Isaiah Luke 4:14-21, *page 1158* (see Isaiah 61:1-4, *page 1158*)

Jesus called disciples to be trained by him Matthew 4:18-22, *page 1074* • Mark 1:14-20, *page 1119* • Luke 5:1-11, *page 1160* • John 1:35-51, *page 1200*

Jesus healed the sick Matthew 4:23-24, *page 1074* • Matthew 8:1-17, *page 1079* • Mark 1:29–2:12, *page 1119* • Luke 8:40-56, *page 1168* • John 20:30-31, *page 1232*

Jesus cast out demons Matthew 4:23-24, *page 1074* • Mark 1:21-28, *page 1119* • Luke 8:26-39, *page 1167*

Jesus came to help people on the margins of society Luke 5:24-30, *page 1161* • Luke 7:36-50, *page 1165* • Luke 18:15-17, *page 1184* • Luke 23:40-43, *page 1194*

Jesus taught about God's Kingdom Matthew 5:1–7:29, *page 1074* • Matthew 13:1-52, *page 1088* • Matthew 18:1-35, *page 1097* • Matthew 23:1–25:46, *page 1105* • Mark 1:14-15, *page 1119*

Jesus performed miracles that overruled the normal powers and laws of nature Matthew 8:23-27, *page 1080* • Matthew 14:13-36, *page 1091* • Mark 5:21-43, *page 1127* • Luke 5:4-11, *page 1160* • John 11:1-45, *page 1216*

Jesus was compassionate Matthew 9:35-38, *page 1083* • Matthew 14:13-21, *page 1091* • Mark 1:40-42, *page 1120* • Luke 7:11-17, *page 1164*

Jesus often taught in parables Matthew 13:1-48, *page 1088* • Matthew 25:1-36, *page 1108* • Mark 12:1-12, *page 1139* • Luke 15:1–16:15, *page 1180*

Jesus called people to respond to him Matthew 16:13-19, *page 1095* • Mark 10:46-52, *page*

1137 • Luke 19:1-10, *page 1185* • John 6:61-69, *page 1210*

Jesus was transfigured as God's glory broke through in his life Matthew 17:1-13, *page 1096* • Mark 9:2-13, *page 1133* • Luke 9:28-36, *page 1170*

Jesus shared the Last Supper with his disciples Matthew 26:17-30, *page 1110* • Mark 14:12-26, *page 1143* • Luke 22:7-38, *page 1190* • 1 Corinthians 11:23-26, *page 1315*

Jesus was betrayed, arrested, and tried Matthew 26:47–27:26, *page 1112* • Mark 14:43–15:15, *page 1144* • Luke 22:47–23:25, *page 1192* • John 18:2–19:16, *page 1226*

Jesus was executed by crucifixion Matthew 27:27-56, *page 1114* • Mark 15:16-41, *page 1146* • Luke 23:26-43, *page 1193* • John 19:17-37, *page 1229*

Jesus was buried Matthew 27:57-66, *page 1115* • Mark 15:42-47, *page 1146* • Luke 23:50-56, *page 1194* • John 19:38-42, *page 1230*

Jesus was raised again on the third day Matthew 28:1-15, *page 1115* • Mark 16:1-20, *page 1147* • Luke 24:1-49, *page 1195* • John 20:1-29, *page 1231* • Acts 2:22-32, *page 1238*

Jesus ascended to heaven to his Father's right hand Luke 24:50-53, *page 1196* • Acts 1:1-11, *page 1236* • Acts 2:32-36, *page 1239*

▸ *See **God's Kingdom**, page 1074; **Jesus' baptism**, page 1073; **The parables of Jesus**, page 1088; **Jesus' parables**, page 1089; **Jesus' miracles**, page 1128; **The Virgin Birth**, page 1152; **Jesus: good news for all**, page 1164; **The Incarnation**, page 1199.*

Jesus Christ: his resurrection *see Resurrection*

Jesus Christ: his return

Probably no doctrine causes greater disagreement among Christians than the return of Jesus. This is because there is no systematic teaching on it in the Bible; rather we get isolated teachings, like jigsaw pieces in a box, which different Christians put together in slightly different ways and so end up with a slightly different picture. What all agree on, however, is that at the end of human history, Jesus will return in person and in great glory to conquer evil, judge sinners, transform the redeemed, and establish God's new age. The New Testament sees this as grounds for great hope and as an incentive both to share the gospel with others and to live godly lives in preparation for it.

> *"The coming of the Son of Man can be illustrated by the story of a man going on a long trip. When he left home, he gave each of his slaves instructions about the work they were to do, and he told the gatekeeper to watch for his return. You, too, must keep watch! For you don't know when the master of the household will return—in the evening, at midnight, before dawn, or at daybreak. Don't let him find you sleeping when he arrives without warning. I say to you what I say to everyone: Watch for him!" – Mark 13:34-37, page 1142*

No one knows the date of Jesus' return Matthew 24:36-44, *page 1107* • Acts 1:7, *page 1236*

The return of Jesus will be a time of judgment for unbelievers Matthew 25:31-46, *page 1109* • 2 Thessalonians 1:7-10, *page 1374* • Revelation 20:11-15, *page 1465*

Although we cannot know the date of his return, signs will indicate when it is getting closer Mark 13:1-37, *page 1141* • 2 Thessalonians 2:1-12, *page 1374* • 2 Timothy 3:1-5, *page 1386*

Jesus' return will be unexpected, so we should always be ready Luke 12:35-48, *page 1176* • 1 Thessalonians 5:1-11, *page 1372*

Jesus' return will happen while life is carrying on as usual Luke 17:20-37, *page 1183*

Jesus' return was clearly promised John 14:1-3, *page 1222* • Acts 1:10-11, *page 1236*

Jesus' return will be public, visible, and glorious Acts 1:9-11, *page 1236* • 1 Thessalonians 4:13-18, *page 1372*

Our lives will never be fully complete until Jesus returns and we receive resurrection bodies and live with him on a new earth 1 Corinthians 15:12-58, *page 1319* • 2 Corinthians 5:1-10, *page 1327* • Philippians 3:20-21, *page 1359*

Believers will be resurrected and given glorious bodies 1 Corinthians 15:50-58, *page 1320* • 1 Thessalonians 4:15-18, *page 1372*

Jesus' return will be preceded by the rise of great opposition to God and his people 2 Thessalonians 2:1-12, *page 1374* • Revelation 13:1-18, *page 1458*

The return of Jesus gives us hope Titus 2:11-14, *page 1390* • James 5:7-8, *page 1417* • 2 Peter 3:8-13, *page 1429*

Jesus' return will complete the salvation we have begun to experience now Hebrews 9:27-28, *page 1405*

The return of Jesus should motivate us to continue to serve God 1 Peter 4:7-11, *page 1424*

No matter what period we live in, we should always remember that Jesus is coming "soon" Revelation 22:20-21, *page 1467*

▸ *See **The return of Jesus Christ**, page 1372.*

Joy

Religion that makes people miserable has little to do with the Bible, where faith is constantly seen—in both Old and New Testaments—as a reason for being joyful. Joy is part of the fruit of the Holy Spirit that is inevitably found in our lives when we understand how much God has done for us in Jesus and know that God is constantly with us and for us.

Always be full of joy in the Lord. I say it again—rejoice! – Philippians 4:4, page 1359

Worshiping God should be joyful 2 Samuel 6:12-23, *page 348* • Psalm 47:1-9, *page 631* • Psalm 150:1-6, *page 695*

The joy of God himself can replace our sadness and strengthen us Nehemiah 8:9-10, *page 544* • John 16:16-33, *page 1225*

There is joy in being in God's presence Psalm 16:11, *page 610* • John 15:9-17, *page 1223*

There is joy in discovering treasure in God's word Psalm 119:162, *page 682* • Jeremiah 15:16, *page 843*

God's people can rejoice even in difficult circumstances Habakkuk 3:17-18, *page 1027* • Hebrews 10:32-35, *page 1406* • James 1:2-4, *page 1412*

News of the birth of Jesus brought great joy Luke 2:8-12, *page 1154*

There is great joy when someone finds God's salvation Luke 15:1-7, *page 1180* • Acts 16:25-34, *page 1262*

Joy should be a characteristic of the Christian life Acts 13:44-52, *page 1257* • Philippians 4:4-7, *page 1359* • 1 Peter 1:6-9, *page 1420*

Faith in God through Jesus brings joy Romans 5:1-11, *page 1287* • Romans 15:5-13, *page 1299*

Joy is evidence of the Holy Spirit at work in our lives Galatians 5:22, *page 1343* • 1 Thessalonians 1:4-6, *page 1369*

God gives us all we need for our enjoyment in life 1 Timothy 6:17-19, *page 1383*

Jesus endured the suffering of the cross in anticipation of future joy Hebrews 12:1-4, *page 1408*

▸ *See **Joy**, page 1360.*

Judgment

The Bible speaks solemnly about the reality of judgment—the expression of God's justice that calls everyone to account for their lives. This judgment may begin to be experienced during our lifetimes, but it is particularly associated with the Last Judgment, when all will stand before God and be judged—though those who trust in Jesus need not fear this judgment. God's judgment is always right, considering motives as well as actions, and so will be seen to be fair. He is also slow to bring judgment.

And I saw a great white throne and the one sitting on it. The earth and sky fled from his presence, but they found no place to hide. I saw the dead, both great and small, standing before God's throne. And the books were opened, including the Book of Life. And the dead were judged according to what they had done, as recorded in the books. The sea gave up its dead, and death and the grave gave up their dead. And all were judged according to their deeds. Then death and the grave were thrown into the lake of fire. This lake of fire is the second death. And anyone whose name was not found recorded in the Book of Life was thrown into the lake of fire. – Revelation 20:11-15, page 1465

God always judges righteously and fairly Genesis 18:20-32, *page 22* • 2 Chronicles 19:4-7, *page 500* • Isaiah 11:1-5, *page 760* • Romans 2:5-11, *page 1284* • Revelation 19:11-16, *page 1464*

God is slow to bring judgment, giving time for us to change Psalm 103:8-18, *page 667* • Romans 2:1-4, *page 1283* • 2 Peter 3:3-10, *page 1429*

God will judge all people Ecclesiastes 3:17, *page 733* • Ecclesiastes 11:9, *page 739* • Acts 17:30-31, *page 1264* • Romans 14:10-12, *page 1298* • 2 Timothy 4:1, *page 1387* • Hebrews 9:27-28, *page 1405* • 1 Peter 4:4-5, *page 1424* • Revelation 20:11-15, *page 1465*

God will judge our motives and secrets Ecclesiastes 12:13-14, *page 739* • Romans 2:16, *page 1284*

God delegates his final judgment to Jesus his Son Matthew 16:27, *page 1096* • Matthew 25:31-46, *page 1109* • John 5:22-30, *page 1206*

Those who trust in Jesus need not fear the Last Judgment, for they have already been declared not guilty Romans 5:1-2, *page 1287* • Romans 8:1, *page 1290*

▶ *See* ***Justification****, page 1288;* ***The Last Judgment****, page 1465.*

Justice *see also Judgment*

Because God himself is just, he is always concerned with justice. He therefore calls his people to pursue justice, especially on behalf of those who are unable to secure it themselves, and his prophets constantly challenged those who showed no concern for justice.

> *"Learn to do good. Seek justice. Help the oppressed. Defend the cause of orphans. Fight for the rights of widows." – Isaiah 1:17, page 749*

God himself is just and therefore loves justice Genesis 18:20-32, *page 22* • Deuteronomy 32:3-4, *page 235* • Psalm 11:4-7, *page 608* • Luke 18:1-8, *page 1183* • Revelation 15:3-4, *page 1460*

We can cry out to God for justice Exodus 2:23-25, *page 67* • Luke 18:7-8, *page 1183* • Revelation 6:9-10, *page 1453*

God demands justice in society Exodus 23:1-12, *page 93* • Isaiah 59:1-21, *page 812* • Amos 8:4-10, *page 1000* • Romans 13:1-7, *page 1297* • Colossians 4:1, *page 1366*

Rulers and judges should govern justly Deuteronomy 16:18-20, *page 220* • 1 Kings 10:9, *page 390* • Proverbs 8:15, *page 704* • 1 Peter 2:13-14, *page 1422*

God commands justice for those in need Deuteronomy 24:17-22, *page 227* • Psalm 82:1-4, *page 654* • Proverbs 22:22-23, *page 719* • Proverbs 31:8-9, *page 729* • James 1:26-27, *page 1413*

God condemns injustice Deuteronomy 27:19, *page 229* • Proverbs 6:16-19, *page 702* • Isaiah 10:1-4, *page 758* • Isaiah 58:3-7, *page 811* • Micah 2:1-2, *page 1012* • Malachi 3:5, *page 1052* • James 5:1-6, *page 1416*

We should challenge injustice 1 Kings 21:1-29, *page 407* • Jeremiah 22:1-9, *page 849* • Ezekiel 45:9-10, *page 949* • Amos 4:1-3, *page 996* • Amos 5:11-24, *page 998* • Micah 3:8-12, *page 1013* • Acts 22:22-29, *page 1272* • Acts 25:1-12, *page 1274*

God is more concerned with our just actions than our religious acts Proverbs 21:3, *page 717* • Isaiah 1:10-17, *page 749* • Isaiah 58:1-14, *page 810* • Amos 5:21-24, *page 998* • Micah 6:6-8, *page 1015* • James 1:26-27, *page 1413* • James 2:14-26, *page 1413*

The church is particularly called to care for the poor and those in need Acts 2:45, *page 1239* • Acts 4:34-35, *page 1242* • Acts 11:27-30, *page 1254* • Galatians 2:10, *page 1338* • James 2:14-17, *page 1413*

▶ *See* ***Oppression****, page 710;* ***Is God concerned about social justice?****, page 994.*

Justification

The doctrine of justification is about how the righteous God stays faithful to his purposes and makes sinners right with himself. The Bible tells us that this is all God's doing, from start to finish. God took the initiative to send Jesus to die in our place and pay the price of our sins—death—so that his justice could be satisfied and we could receive his forgiveness through putting our faith in Jesus. Since our sins have been paid for by Jesus, now God's only verdict over us can be "Not guilty," or "Justified!"

> *We are made right with God by placing our faith in Jesus Christ. And this is true for everyone who believes, no matter who we are. For everyone has sinned; we all fall short of God's glorious standard. Yet God, in his grace, freely makes us right in his sight. He did this through Christ Jesus when he freed us from the penalty for our sins. For God presented Jesus as the sacrifice for sin. People are made right with God when they believe that Jesus sacrificed his life, shedding his blood. This sacrifice shows that God was being fair when he held back and did not punish those who sinned in times past, for he was looking ahead and including them in what he would do in this present time. God did this to demonstrate his righteousness, for he himself is fair and just, and he makes sinners right in his sight when they believe in Jesus. – Romans 3:22-26, page 1286*

We get right with God, not by keeping the Jewish Law or by what we do, but simply by trusting God Genesis 15:1-6, *page 18* • Acts 13:38-39, *page 1257* • Romans 1:16-17, *page 1282* • Romans 4:1-25, *page 1286* • Galatians 2:15-21, *page 1339* • Galatians 3:10-12, *page 1340*

When we are made right with God, he forgives all our sins Psalm 32:1-2, *page 620* • Acts 13:38-39, *page 1257* • Romans 3:22-26, *page 1286* • Romans 5:6-11, *page 1287* • 1 John 1:8-9, *page 1433*

Only the humble can be made right with God Luke 18:9-14, *page 1183*

Jesus' death on the cross is the means of our being made right with God Romans 3:21-28, *page 1286* • Romans 4:23-25, *page 1287* • Romans 5:6-11, *page 1287* • Galatians 3:10-13, *page 1340*

When we are made right with God, he credits Jesus' righteousness to us Romans 4:1-8, 20-25, *page 1286* • 1 Corinthians 1:30, *page 1304* • 2 Corinthians 5:18-21, *page 1328*

Getting right with God brings many blessings Romans 5:1-11, *page 1287* • Romans 8:1-39, *page 1290*

Jesus' death fulfills the righteous demands of God's Law Romans 8:1-4, *page 1290*

Good deeds are not the cause of our being made right but rather the consequences of it James 2:14-26, *page 1413*

▸ *See* ***The death of Jesus****, page 1114;* ***Redemption****, page 1136;* ***Justification****, page 1288;* ***Christ's resurrection and ours****, page 1320;* ***Reconciliation****, page 1328.*

Keeping going *see Perseverance*

Kindness *see also Caring; Hospitality; Love*

Throughout the Bible, God is shown to be kind to people—gentle, thoughtful, compassionate, and caring, always showing unfailing love. He calls his people to reflect these qualities in their own lives, leaving judgment to him alone.

> *"Love your enemies! Do good to them. Lend to them without expecting to be repaid. Then your reward from heaven will be very great, and you will truly be acting as children of the Most High, for he is kind to those who are unthankful and wicked. You must be compassionate, just as your Father is compassionate." – Luke 6:35-36, page 1163*

God is kind to all Exodus 34:6-7, *page 106* • Psalm 138:1-8, *page 688* • Luke 6:35-36, *page 1163* • Acts 14:15-17, *page 1259*

We should be kind to those in need Deuteronomy 24:10-22, *page 226* • Ruth 2:1-23, *page 300* • Isaiah 1:17, *page 749* • Luke 10:25-37, *page 1172*

Kindness to the poor is particularly noted by God Deuteronomy 24:19, *page 227* • Proverbs 19:17, *page 716* • Matthew 10:42, *page 1084* • Luke 14:12-13, *page 1179*

We should be kind to our enemies Luke 6:27-36, *page 1163* • Romans 12:9-21, *page 1296* • 1 Thessalonians 5:15, *page 1373*

We should cultivate kindness as part of the fruit of the Spirit 1 Corinthians 13:4-7, *page 1317* • Galatians 5:22-23, *page 1343* • Colossians 3:1-15, *page 1365*

We should be kind to one another Ephesians 4:31-32, *page 1351* • 1 Peter 3:8-12, *page 1423*

It is better to be kind than to be right 2 Timothy 2:23-24, *page 1386*

▶ See ***Love your neighbor as yourself,*** *page 139;* ***The compassionate God,*** *page 666;* ***Loving others,*** *page 1220.*

Kingdom of God/Kingdom of Heaven

At the heart of Jesus' ministry was the message that the Kingdom of God (or Kingdom of Heaven) was breaking into our world, as his authority over sickness, sin, and circumstances demonstrated. The Greek word for "kingdom" means "rule," so God's Kingdom was not a geographical place but a dynamic spiritual entity—though one day it will have a geographical location as it fills the whole earth. Jesus' followers are called to pursue the Kingdom before anything else and to share its Good News with others.

> *Jesus went into Galilee, where he preached God's Good News. "The time promised by God has come at last!" he announced. "The Kingdom of God is near! Repent of your sins and believe the Good News!" – Mark 1:14-15, page 1119*

God's coming Kingdom had been foreseen by the prophets Isaiah 9:1-7, *page 757* • Isaiah 11:1-9, *page 760* • Isaiah 61:1-11, *page 814* • Micah 4:1-5, *page 1013*

Jesus came as the promised messianic king of the Kingdom Matthew 2:1-2, *page 1069* • Matthew 21:1-11, *page 1101* • Matthew 27:11, *page 1113* • Luke 23:36-42, *page 1194* • Revelation 19:11-16, *page 1464*

God's Kingdom is near and has already started to break into our world Matthew 4:17, *page 1074* • Matthew 11:2-11, *page 1084* • Mark 1:14-15, *page 1119* • Luke 10:8-11, *page 1171* • Luke 17:20-21, *page 1183*

Jesus' message focused on God's Kingdom Matthew 4:17, 23-25, *page 1074* • Luke 8:1, *page 1166* • Luke 9:1-6, *page 1168* • Luke 10:1-9, *page 1171* • John 3:1-5, *page 1202* • Acts 1:3, *page 1236*

We should pray for God's Kingdom to come Matthew 6:10, *page 1077*

We should seek God's Kingdom as our priority Matthew 6:28-34, *page 1078* • Matthew 19:16-30, *page 1099* • Luke 9:57-62, *page 1171*

Only through faith, new birth, and obedience will we enter God's Kingdom Matthew 7:21-23, *page 1079* • Mark 10:13-16, *page 1136* • John 3:1-17, *page 1202*

Jesus' miracles were a tangible demonstration of the Kingdom's presence and power Matthew 12:22-28, *page 1087* • Luke 7:18-23, *page 1165* • Luke 11:14-22, *page 1173* • Acts 2:22, *page 1238* • Acts 10:37-43, *page 1252*

God's Kingdom may have small beginnings and be opposed, but its triumph is certain Matthew 13:1-52, *page 1088*

Entering God's Kingdom costs us everything Matthew 13:44-46, *page 1090* • Matthew 19:16-30, *page 1099* • Philippians 3:5-11, *page 1358*

God's Kingdom will come in all its fullness when Jesus returns Matthew 24:1–25:30, *page 1106* • Luke 21:25-36, *page 1190* • 1 Corinthians 15:21-28, *page 1319* • Revelation 11:15-18, *page 1457* • Revelation 19:11–21:5, *page 1464*

The Christian message is about not just salvation but also the Kingdom of God Luke 9:2, 60, *page 1168* • Acts 8:12, *page 1247* • Acts 14:21-22, *page 1259* • Acts 19:8, *page 1266* • Acts 20:25, *page 1269* • Acts 28:23-31, *page 1280*

▶ See ***God's Kingdom,*** *page 1074.*

Labor *see Work*

Language *see Speech*

Larceny *see Stealing*

Last days *see Jesus Christ: his return*

Law

The term "Law" (in Hebrew, "Torah") is used in various ways in the Bible: to describe all the commandments God gave to Moses as part of his covenant with Israel, to denote the Ten Commandments, or to refer to God's word more broadly. Keeping the Law was not a condition for Israel's acceptance by God, but rather a consequence of his already having accepted them. The New Testament is clear that Christians do not have to keep this Law to be put right with God, for God's new covenant is based on faith in Jesus alone.

> *The law applies to those to whom it was given, for its purpose is to keep people from having excuses, and to show that the entire world is guilty before God. For no one can ever be made right with God by doing what the law commands. The law simply shows us how sinful we are. But now God has shown us a way to be made right with him without keeping the requirements of the law, as was promised in the writings of Moses and the prophets long ago. We are made right with God by placing our faith in Jesus Christ. And this is true for everyone who believes, no matter who we are. – Romans 3:19-22, page 1285*

The Law stood at the heart of God's covenant with Israel, governing all aspects of its life Exodus 19:1–24:18, *page 88*

The Ten Commandments stood at the very heart of God's Law Exodus 19:1–20:17, *page 88* • Deuteronomy 5:1-22, *page 207*

God's Law is something his people can delight in Psalm 119:97-104, *page 680* • Romans 7:22, *page 1290*

God promised that a day would come when he would write his Law on people's hearts Jeremiah 31:33-34, *page 862* • Ezekiel 36:25-28, *page 938* • Hebrews 8:7-12, *page 1403*

Jesus came to fulfill God's Law Matthew 5:17-19, *page 1075*

The Law reveals our sin Romans 3:19-20, *page 1285* • Romans 5:20-21, *page 1288* • Romans 7:1-13, *page 1290*

Faith in Jesus, not keeping the Law, is what makes us right with God Romans 3:21-28, *page 1286* • Galatians 2:11-21, *page 1338* • Galatians 3:10-26, *page 1340* • Hebrews 10:1-25, *page 1405*

Jesus fulfilled God's Law for us so that we no longer have to Romans 8:1-4, *page 1290*

The Holy Spirit now helps us from within to do what pleases God Romans 8:1-17, *page 1290* • Galatians 5:16-25, *page 1343*

Love fulfills all the requirements of the Law Romans 13:8-10, *page 1298* • Galatians 5:13-15, *page 1343*

We should take care not to fall into a new kind of law-keeping through being legalistic Romans 14:1-23, *page 1298* • Colossians 2:16-23, *page 1364*

▶ *See **Are the Ten Commandments still relevant today?**, page 89; **Legalism**, page 1339.*

Laziness

Laziness—a resistance to hard work or a tendency to continually put things off—destroys something of God's image in us, for God himself is a worker. The Bible often warns us against laziness, saying that it can destroy our character and ruin our lives. But equally it warns us against overworking and not knowing how to rest.

> *Take a lesson from the ants, you lazybones. Learn from their ways and become wise! Though they have no prince or governor or ruler to make them work, they labor hard all summer, gathering food for the winter. But you, lazybones, how long will you sleep? When will you wake up? A little extra sleep, a little more slumber, a little folding of the hands to rest—then poverty will pounce on you like a bandit; scarcity will attack you like an armed robber. – Proverbs 6:6-11, page 701*

Laziness can ruin our lives Proverbs 6:6-11, *page 701* • Ecclesiastes 10:18, *page 738*

Laziness can make us poor Proverbs 10:4-5, *page 706* • Proverbs 13:4, *page 709* • Proverbs 20:4, 13, *page 716* • Proverbs 24:30-34, *page 722*

Our laziness can irritate others Proverbs 10:26, *page 707*

Lazy people always give in to difficulties Proverbs 15:19, *page 712* • Proverbs 24:30-34, *page 722*

Lazy people prefer sleep to work Proverbs 19:15, *page 716* • Proverbs 26:14-16, *page 724*

Lazy people always make excuses Proverbs 22:13, *page 719* • Proverbs 26:13, *page 724*

The wise know that there is a time to rest and a time to work Ecclesiastes 3:1-13, *page 732*

Laziness will one day be judged Matthew 25:14-30, *page 1109*

Christians should work hard and not be lazy Romans 12:11, *page 1296* • 2 Thessalonians 3:6-15, *page 1375*

Lazy people should not be allowed to sponge off other people 2 Thessalonians 3:6-13, *page 1375*

Our care for others should not encourage laziness 1 Timothy 5:9-15, *page 1383*

▶ *See* ***Laziness****, page 702;* ***Work****, page 1376.*

Leadership

Because God cares for his people, he gives them leaders to care for them on his behalf. Christian leadership is about servanthood, not domination or insisting on our own way. It inspires rather than demands. The Bible tells us that Christian leaders are therefore to be humble, full of faith, and trustworthy. Above all, they must listen to God.

> *This is a trustworthy saying: "If someone aspires to be a church leader, he desires an honorable position." So a church leader must be a man whose life is above reproach. He must be faithful to his wife. He must exercise self-control, live wisely, and have a good reputation. He must enjoy having guests in his home, and he must be able to teach. He must not be a heavy drinker or be violent. He must be gentle, not quarrelsome, and not love money. He must manage his own family well, having children who respect and obey him. For if a man cannot manage his own household, how can he take care of God's church? A church leader must not be a new believer, because he might become proud, and the devil would cause him to fall. Also, people outside the church must speak well of him so that he will not be disgraced and fall into the devil's trap.* – 1 Timothy 3:1-7, *page 1380*

Good leaders are utterly dependent upon God Genesis 15:1-6, *page 18* • Exodus 14:1-31, *page 81* • 2 Kings 19:1-19, *page 436* • 2 Chronicles 20:1-12, *page 500* • 2 Corinthians 1:8-9, *page 1324*

Good leaders learn how to delegate Exodus 18:13-26, *page 87* • 2 Chronicles 8:7-10, *page 490* • Luke 9:1-6, *page 1168* • Acts 15:22-35, *page 1260*

Leaders need to be trustworthy Exodus 18:21, *page 87* • 2 Kings 12:4-16, *page 426* • Acts 6:1-7, *page 1244* • 2 Timothy 2:2, *page 1385*

We should honor our leaders Numbers 12:1-15, *page 168* • 1 Thessalonians 5:12-13, *page 1373* • 1 Timothy 5:17-18, *page 1383* • Hebrews 13:17, *page 1410*

Good leaders identify and mentor their successors Numbers 27:15-23, *page 188* • Mark 3:13-15, *page 1124* • Philippians 2:19-22, *page 1357*

Leaders should represent God in their decisions 2 Chronicles 19:5-7, *page 500* • Acts 15:22-31, *page 1260*

Leaders look out for the interests of others not themselves Ezekiel 34:1-31, *page 935* • John 10:1-18, *page 1215* • 1 Peter 5:1-4, *page 1425*

Leaders will have to give an account to God for their actions Ezekiel 34:9-10, *page 936* • Hebrews 13:17, *page 1410*

Leaders must serve others, not dominate them Matthew 20:20-28, *page 1100* • 1 Peter 5:1-4, *page 1425*

Leaders in the church should watch over God's flock John 21:15-19, *page 1233* • Acts 20:28-32, *page 1269* • 1 Peter 5:1-6, *page 1425*

Leaders should be people of integrity 1 Timothy 3:1-13, *page 1380* • Titus 1:6-9, *page 1389*

Any kind of dictatorial leadership in the church is condemned 3 John 1:9-11, *page 1440*

▶ *See* ***The kind of leaders God wants****, page 170;* ***Mentoring****, page 1385;* ***Leaders in the church****, page 1390;* ***How not to be a leader****, page 1440.*

Learning *see Teaching*

Legalism *see Law*

Leisure *see also Rest*

The Christian life does not consist of endless meetings! Jesus knew how to enjoy ordinary life—sharing meals with people, resting, spending time with children, going to weddings—often much to the irritation of the religious leaders of his day. He believed that God had blessed the whole of life, not just the religious aspects of it. Leisure is something we can therefore enjoy and bring God into.

What do people get in this life for all their hard work and anxiety? Their days of labor are filled with pain and grief; even at night their minds cannot rest. It is all meaningless. So I decided there is nothing better than to enjoy food and drink and to find satisfaction in work. Then I realized that these pleasures are from the hand of God. For who can eat or enjoy anything apart from him? – Ecclesiastes 2:22-25, page 732

Leisure is the gift of God to humanity Genesis 2:1-3, *page 5*

Leisure activities are found throughout the Bible Genesis 4:21, *page 8* • 1 Samuel 16:23, *page 324* • Ecclesiastes 2:5-6, *page 731* • Matthew 11:16-19, *page 1084*

Hospitality should be an important part of our leisure time Genesis 18:1-8, *page 21* • Exodus 2:16-20, *page 67* • Luke 10:38, *page 1172* • Luke 14:12-14, *page 1179* • Romans 12:13, *page 1296* • 1 Peter 4:9, *page 1424*

All work and no play makes for a dull life Psalm 127:2, *page 684*

A life of leisure alone does not satisfy Ecclesiastes 2:1-26, *page 731*

There is a time for everything, including leisure Ecclesiastes 3:1-13, *page 732*

Jesus took time out from his work Mark 6:31-32, *page 1129* • Luke 19:1-6, *page 1185* • John 2:1-12, *page 1201*

Leisure comes after work Luke 17:7-8, *page 1182*

▶ *See* ***Resting in God****, page 676.*

Liberty *see Freedom*

Life *see also Eternal life; Lifestyle*

Life is the gift of God and is therefore precious. God wants us to enjoy life, and life shared with Jesus—found through being born again—is life at its best. Because life is God's gift to us, he wants us to honor and respect it. But he also wants us to live with a proper perspective on it, not making this life the be-all and end-all of everything, but being ready to deny ourselves and even to lay down our lives if necessary. By depending on the Holy Spirit, who lives in us, we can lead lives worthy of our Christian calling.

"The thief's purpose is to steal and kill and destroy. My purpose is to give them a rich and satisfying life." – John 10:10, page 1216

Life comes from God Genesis 2:4-7, *page 5* • Psalm 104:27-30, *page 668*

We should remember that life is short Psalm 39:4-13, *page 626* • Psalm 90:1-12, *page 659* • Isaiah 40:6-8, *page 789* • James 4:13-16, *page 1416*

Each life is precious, for it is carefully created by God Psalm 139:13-16, *page 689* • Jeremiah 1:4-5, *page 822*

Life can be wearisome, but with God it can be enjoyed Ecclesiastes 2:18-24, *page 732* • Ecclesiastes 8:15, *page 737* • Ecclesiastes 9:9, *page 737*

Jesus urges us to have a proper perspective on life Matthew 6:25-33, *page 1078* • Mark 8:34-38, *page 1133*

People must be born again to find eternal life John 3:1-15, *page 1202* • Titus 3:3-7, *page 1391*

Jesus himself is the source of provision for a satisfying life John 6:35-40, *page 1209* • John 7:37-39, *page 1211* • John 14:6-11, *page 1222*

God wants us to live our lives in the power of the Spirit Romans 8:9-14, *page 1291* • Galatians 5:16-25, *page 1343*

Jesus lives in us through his Spirit, so we—both corporately and individually—are now God's temple 1 Corinthians 3:16-17, *page 1306* • 1 Corinthians 6:19-20, *page 1310*

We should live lives worthy of our Christian calling Ephesians 4:1-10, *page 1349* • Colossians 3:1-17, *page 1365*

Our goal should be to live for Jesus Philippians 1:21, *page 1355*

▶ *See* ***Abortion****, page 823;* ***Life from death****, page 1219;* ***Life in the Spirit****, page 1291;* ***Living by the Spirit****, page 1342.*

Lifestyle *see also Life*

When we become Christians, something happens to us: God's Holy Spirit comes to live within us. And as we follow his promptings, we increasingly find that there are things from our old life that we aren't comfortable with anymore; and as we read the Bible, we discover that there are certain attitudes and behaviors that make God unhappy. Our lifestyle will therefore begin to change—and if it doesn't, we may rightly wonder whether we have truly encountered God. A changed lifestyle can never help us find God, but it will certainly show that we have found him.

And so, dear brothers and sisters, I plead with you to give your bodies to God because of all he has done for you. Let them be a living and holy sacrifice—the kind he will find acceptable. This is truly the way to worship him. Don't copy the behavior and customs of this world, but let God transform you into a new person by changing the way you think. Then you will learn to know God's will for you, which is good and pleasing and perfect. – Romans 12:1-2, page 1296

At the heart of our lifestyle should be a desire to love God with all that we are and have Deuteronomy 6:4-9, *page 208* • Matthew 22:34-40, *page 1104*

In the Sermon on the Mount, Jesus taught about the kind of things that should characterize the lifestyle of his followers Matthew 5:1–7:29, *page 1074*

A Christian lifestyle involves loving others Matthew 5:38-48, *page 1076* • Matthew 22:36-40, *page 1104* • Luke 10:25-37, *page 1172* • 1 Corinthians 13:1-13, *page 1316* • Ephesians 5:1-2, *page 1351*

A Christian lifestyle shows concern for the poor and needy Matthew 25:31-40, *page 1109* • Luke 4:14-21, *page 1158* • Acts 11:27-30, *page 1254* • Galatians 2:9-10, *page 1338*

Following Jesus will be reflected in a new lifestyle Luke 19:1-10, *page 1185* • Acts 2:42-47, *page 1239* • Acts 19:13-20, *page 1267* • Ephesians 4:17-32, *page 1350*

We should always imitate Jesus' example of a life of humility John 13:1-17, *page 1221* • Philippians 2:1-11, *page 1356*

The heart of a Christian lifestyle is maintaining a relationship with Jesus John 15:1-8, *page 1223* • Colossians 2:6-7, *page 1363*

God's Spirit within us will show us things from our old life that need to go and new things that need to start growing in us Romans 8:5-17, *page 1291* • Galatians 5:13-26, *page 1343* • Ephesians 4:17-32, *page 1350* • Colossians 3:1-17, *page 1365*

When we become Christians, we become new people and a new way of living begins 2 Corinthians 5:17-20, *page 1328*

A Christian lifestyle involves remaining faithful to Jesus in all circumstances 2 Timothy 3:10-14, *page 1386* • Revelation 2:8-11, *page 1447*

▶ *See* ***Now that you are a Christian****, page A13;* ***Counting the cost****, page 1180;* ***Life from death****, page 1219.*

Light

God is the source of all light. When Jesus came into the world, he came to be its light, and he calls us as his followers to reflect that light. Our light is to be seen, not for its own sake or to try to make us look good, but to help others see clearly. We should expose what is dark and hidden and put what is good into the spotlight.

BASIC TRUTHS • *page 1558*

"You are the light of the world—like a city on a hilltop that cannot be hidden. No one lights a lamp and then puts it under a basket. Instead, a lamp is placed on a stand, where it gives light to everyone in the house. In the same way, let your good deeds shine out for all to see, so that everyone will praise your heavenly Father." – Matthew 5:14-16, page 1075

Light comes from God Genesis 1:3-5, *page 4*

God is light Psalm 27:1-3, *page 617* • 1 John 1:5-7, *page 1433*

God's word gives light to guide us on our path Psalm 119:105, 130, *page 681* • 2 Peter 1:16-19, *page 1427*

God's light penetrates and exposes everything Proverbs 20:27, *page 717* • Hebrews 4:13, *page 1400*

Everything that is hidden will one day be brought into the light Luke 8:16-17, *page 1167* • Ephesians 5:10-16, *page 1351*

Jesus is the light of the world John 1:1-9, *page 1199* • John 8:12-18, *page 1212* • John 9:1-5, *page 1213* • John 12:44-46, *page 1221* • 1 John 2:7-8, *page 1434*

Darkness can never extinguish God's light John 1:5, *page 1199*

People without Jesus love darkness rather than light John 3:19-21, *page 1203* • Ephesians 5:10-14, *page 1351*

God calls us to turn from darkness to light Acts 26:12-18, *page 1276* • Ephesians 5:6-9, *page 1351* • 1 Peter 2:9, *page 1422*

God put his light in our hearts when we became Christians 2 Corinthians 4:3-7, *page 1327*

Christians are called to live as people of light Ephesians 5:3-14, *page 1351* • Philippians 2:14-16, *page 1357* • 1 John 1:5-7, *page 1433*

God's light will one day flood his new creation Revelation 22:1-5, *page 1467*

▶ *See **Salt and light**, page 1075.*

Loneliness

Even in a world where there is more communication than ever, it is still possible to feel incredibly lonely at times. At such moments we should remember that Jesus himself experienced loneliness and therefore understands how we feel and can help us. We should remember too that, no matter how lonely we might feel, God is always with us, and he can use even our loneliness and the feelings that go with it for his good purpose.

Even if my father and mother abandon me, the LORD will hold me close. – Psalm 27:10, page 618

God does not want us to be alone Genesis 2:18, *page 6*

Being alone can sometimes have its benefits Genesis 32:22-32, *page 41* • Exodus 3:1-10, *page 68* • Matthew 6:6, *page 1077* • Mark 1:35, *page 1120*

God never forgets or abandons his people Joshua 1:1-9, *page 242* • Isaiah 41:10-14, *page 792* • Isaiah 49:14-17, *page 802* • Matthew 28:18-20, *page 1116* • John 14:18, *page 1223* • 2 Timothy 4:16-18, *page 1388* • Hebrews 13:5-6, *page 1409*

We should beware of falling into self-pity when we feel lonely 1 Kings 19:1-18, *page 404*

Many leaders in the Bible experienced loneliness at times 1 Kings 19:1-18, *page 404* • 2 Timothy 1:15-18, *page 1385* • 2 Timothy 4:9-18, *page 1387* • Revelation 1:9, *page 1446*

We can ask God to help us in our loneliness Psalm 22:1-31, *page 614* • Psalm 25:14-20, *page 616*

God takes care of the lonely Psalm 68:4-6, *page 642* • Isaiah 61:1-7, *page 814*

Jesus himself experienced loneliness Matthew 26:36-56, *page 1111* • Matthew 27:45-46, *page 1115*

▶ *See **Loneliness**, page 580.*

Longing for God *see Worship*

Lord's Day *see Day of rest*

Lord's Supper *see Communion*

Lost

Even in our busy world, which is more connected than ever because of things like the Internet, it is still possible to feel "lost"—alone, isolated, cut off, empty. But there is an even greater lostness: that of being spiritually lost, cut off from God and not knowing where we are or where we need to go. The good news is that God delights in seeking out the lost, bringing them home, and making them part of his family.

"The Son of Man came to seek and save those who are lost." – Luke 19:10, page 1185

Without God we are lost and have no hope and no home Psalm 107:4-7, *page 671* • Ephesians 2:11-12, *page 1347*

Without God we are like lost sheep wandering around Psalm 119:176, *page 682* • Isaiah 53:6, *page 806* • Jeremiah 50:6, *page 882* • 1 Peter 2:25, *page 1423*

Those who are lost are so valuable to God that he comes looking for them Ezekiel 34:1-16, *page 935* • Luke 15:1-32, *page 1180*

God will go to any lengths to find the lost Matthew 18:12-14, *page 1097*

Having everything in life, but being lost, is one of the saddest and most dangerous conditions Luke 9:24-25, *page 1169* • Luke 12:13-21, *page 1175*

There is rejoicing in heaven when the lost are found Luke 15:7, 10, 32, *page 1180*

God is patient with the lost Luke 15:11-32, *page 1181* • Romans 2:4, *page 1284* • 2 Peter 3:8-9, *page 1429*

Jesus came to seek and save the lost Luke 19:1-10, *page 1185* • John 3:16-17, *page 1203*

▶ *See **Becoming a Christian**, page A11.*

Love

Love is one of the greatest qualities that God wants us to pursue, for he himself is love. The sort of love we are called to cuts across our own desires, rights, and comfort and seeks to put others first, just as Jesus modeled for us. Love that doesn't cost us anything is rarely true love.

Love is patient and kind. Love is not jealous or boastful or proud or rude. It does not demand its own way. It is not irritable, and it keeps no record of being wronged. It does not rejoice about injustice but rejoices whenever the truth wins out. Love never gives up, never loses faith, is always hopeful, and endures through every circumstance. – 1 Corinthians 13:4-7, page 1317

God loves people Exodus 34:6-7, *page 106* • Deuteronomy 7:7-8, *page 210* • John 3:16-17, *page 1203* • Ephesians 3:18-19, *page 1349* • 1 John 4:16, *page 1437*

We should love our neighbor as ourselves Leviticus 19:18, *page 139* • Matthew 19:16-22, *page 1099* • Romans 13:8-10, *page 1298* • Galatians 5:14, *page 1343* • James 2:8, *page 1413*

We should love God with all of our being Deuteronomy 6:4-5, *page 208* • Joshua 22:1-6, *page 265* • Matthew 22:34-40, *page 1104*

Love helps us deal with past offenses Proverbs 10:12, *page 706* • Proverbs 17:9, *page 713* • 1 Peter 4:8, *page 1424*

We should love our enemies Matthew 5:43-48, *page 1076* • Luke 6:27-36, *page 1163* • Acts 7:54-60, *page 1246* • Romans 12:14-21, *page 1296*

God showed his love by sending Jesus to die for us John 3:16-17, *page 1203* • Romans 5:6-11, *page 1287* • Romans 8:31-32, *page 1292*

Christians must love one another John 13:34-35, *page 1222* • 1 Thessalonians 4:9-10, *page 1372* • 1 Peter 1:22, *page 1421* • 2 John 1:5-6, *page 1438*

We show we love Jesus by keeping his commands John 14:15-21, *page 1223* • John 15:9-10, *page 1223* • 1 John 2:3-6, *page 1434*

The Holy Spirit fills our hearts with God's love Romans 5:1-5, *page 1287*

Nothing can ever separate us from God's love Romans 8:31-39, *page 1292*

Love never gives up, despite all the challenges 1 Corinthians 13:4-8, *page 1317*

Love should be continually growing in us as part of the fruit of the Spirit Galatians 5:16-26, *page 1343*

▶ See **Love your neighbor as yourself**, page 139; **Loving others**, page 1220; **Sexuality**, page 742; **The love of God**, page 1437.

Loyalty *see also Commitment; Faithfulness*

Loyalty is about faithful commitment and devotion to other people through good times and bad. God has shown himself to be constantly loyal to his people, and he calls us to reflect such loyalty to others.

> *Never let loyalty and kindness leave you! Tie them around your neck as a reminder. Write them deep within your heart. Then you will find favor with both God and people, and you will earn a good reputation. – Proverbs 3:3-4, page 699*

God is faithfully committed to his people in a covenant Genesis 17:1-8, *page 20* • Exodus 19:1-6, *page 88* • Deuteronomy 7:7-15, *page 210* • Isaiah 55:1-7, *page 808*

We should be loyal to our leaders Numbers 14:1-45, *page 169* • Numbers 16:1-50, *page 173* • Joshua 1:16-17, *page 242* • 2 Corinthians 7:5-7, *page 1329*

We should remain loyal to God Deuteronomy 6:10-25, *page 209* • Deuteronomy 10:12-16, *page 213* • Joshua 24:14-27, *page 268*

There should be strong loyalty in family relationships Ruth 1:16-17, *page 299*

True friends are always loyal 1 Samuel 18:1-4, *page 326* • 1 Samuel 20:1-42, *page 328* • Proverbs 17:17, *page 714* • 2 Corinthians 7:5-7, *page 1329*

We cannot divide our loyalty 1 Kings 18:21, *page 402* • Matthew 6:19-24, *page 1077* • James 1:5-8, *page 1412*

Loyalty attracts God's blessing Proverbs 3:3-4, *page 699*

Loyalty is an essential foundation in marriage Malachi 2:15-16, *page 1051* • Hebrews 13:4, *page 1409*

▶ See **Faithfulness**, page 1307.

Lukewarmness *see Backsliding*

Lust

Lust is an overpowering desire for sexual fulfillment that can cause people to forget boundaries, make unwise choices, and break their promises. That is why the Bible calls us to deal seriously with lust, for God knows the damage it can do, not just to us but to others too.

> *"You have heard the commandment that says, 'You must not commit adultery.' But I say, anyone who even looks at a woman with lust has already committed adultery with her in his heart. So if your eye—even your good eye—causes you to lust, gouge it out and throw it away. It is better for you to lose one part of your body than for your whole body to be thrown into hell. And if your hand—even your stronger hand—causes you to sin, cut it off and throw it away. It is better for you to lose one part of your body than for your whole body to be thrown into hell." – Matthew 5:27-30, page 1076*

Lust can lead to serious consequences Genesis 19:1-29, *page 22* • 2 Samuel 11:1-27, *page 352* • 2 Samuel 13:1-29, *page 355* • Romans 1:18-32, *page 1283*

We should run from situations where lust could develop Genesis 39:1-12, *page 49* • 1 Corinthians 6:15-20, *page 1309*

Lust may begin just with looking 2 Samuel 11:1-5, *page 352* • Job 31:1, *page 589* • Proverbs 6:24-25, *page 702* • Matthew 5:27-28, *page 1076*

We should remember that God will judge the sexually immoral Proverbs 6:20-29, *page 702* • 1 Peter 4:1-5, *page 1424* • 2 Peter 2:12-22, *page 1428* • Revelation 21:5-8, *page 1465*

Lustful thoughts should be killed off quickly Matthew 5:27-30, *page 1076* • 1 Corinthians 6:15-20, *page 1309* • Colossians 3:5-10, *page 1365* • 1 Thessalonians 4:3-5, *page 1372*

Lust begins in the heart and mind Matthew 15:16-20, *page 1093* • James 1:14-15, *page 1412*

The enjoyment of immorality is a sign of godlessness Romans 1:21-27, *page 1283* • 1 Peter 4:1-3, *page 1424*

The Holy Spirit can help us deal with sinful desires Galatians 5:16-26, *page 1343*

▶ *See **Lust**, page 589; **Sexuality**, page 742.*

Lying *see Dishonesty*

Magic *see Occult*

Man *see Humanity*

Marriage *see also Family*

God created people to be in relationship with one another, and a key relationship that he provides is marriage. The Bible sees marriage as a faithful relationship between one man and one woman for life. Marriage is also a picture of God's enduring and sacrificial love for his people.

> *As the Scriptures say, "A man leaves his father and mother and is joined to his wife, and the two are united into one." This is a great mystery, but it is an illustration of the way Christ and the church are one. – Ephesians 5:31-32, page 1352*

Marriage was one of God's first gifts to humanity Genesis 2:4-25, *page 5*

A man and a woman become one through marriage Genesis 2:24, *page 6* • Mark 10:2-12, *page 1135*

Marriage is the proper place for sexual intimacy Proverbs 5:15-23, *page 701* • Song of Songs 4:9-15, *page 743* • 1 Corinthians 7:1-5, *page 1310*

God's love for his people is often illustrated through marriage Isaiah 54:4-8, *page 807* • Jeremiah 2:1-2, *page 823* • Hosea 2:1-20, *page 974* • Hosea 3:1-5, *page 977*

Jesus upheld marriage and opposed the easy divorce practices of his day Matthew 5:31-32, *page 1076* • Matthew 19:1-11, *page 1098* • Mark 10:2-12, *page 1135*

The New Testament provides limited grounds for divorce Matthew 19:8-9, *page 1099* • 1 Corinthians 7:12-16, *page 1310*

Jesus blessed marriage by his presence at a wedding John 2:1-11, *page 1201*

While marriage is a blessing from God, it is not essential for living a fulfilled and godly life 1 Corinthians 7:1-40, *page 1310*

A Christian should not marry a non-Christian 2 Corinthians 6:14-18, *page 1329*

Marriage is a picture of Jesus' love for the church Ephesians 5:21-33, *page 1351*

There must be faithfulness in marriage Hebrews 13:4, *page 1409*

▶ *See **Mixed marriages**, page 532; **Family**, page 714; **Sexuality**, page 742; **Does marriage still matter to God?**, page 976; **Can a Christian marry a non-Christian?**, page 1329.*

Mass *see Communion*

Materialism *see Money*

Maturity *see Growth*

Men *see Humanity; Marriage*

Mercy *see also Grace*

Mercy is God's compassion and patience toward us, his holding back from us the just and righteous anger that our sins deserve. That mercy, his not giving us what we deserve, is matched by his grace—his giving us more than we could ever deserve. Because we have received mercy, we should show mercy toward others too.

BASIC TRUTHS • *page 1562*

The LORD is compassionate and merciful, slow to get angry and filled with unfailing love. He will not constantly accuse us, nor remain angry forever. He does not punish us for all our sins; he does not deal harshly with us, as we deserve. For his unfailing love toward those who fear him is as great as the height of the heavens above the earth. He has removed our sins as far from us as the east is from the west. The LORD is like a father to his children, tender and compassionate to those who fear him. – Psalm 103:8-13, page 667

God is merciful by nature Exodus 34:5-7, *page 106* • 2 Samuel 24:14, *page 371* • Psalm 86:15, *page 657* • Psalm 103:7-8, *page 667* • Ephesians 2:4-5, *page 1347*

God is merciful toward his people Exodus 34:5-7, *page 106* • Nehemiah 9:1-31, *page 545* • Psalm 103:1-18, *page 666* • Luke 1:46-50, *page 1153* • Ephesians 2:4-10, *page 1347* • Hebrews 4:14-16, *page 1400*

God's mercy is never-ending 2 Chronicles 7:1-3, *page 488* • Lamentations 3:22-23, *page 895*

We can pray for God's mercy Psalm 28:1-9, *page 618* • Psalm 31:9-22, *page 619* • Psalm 51:1-19, *page 633* • Psalm 123:1-4, *page 683* • Isaiah 33:2, *page 782*

God's people are called to show mercy to others Micah 6:8, *page 1016* • Zechariah 7:8-10, *page 1042* • Matthew 9:9-13, *page 1081* • Matthew 18:21-35, *page 1098* • James 2:12-13, *page 1413* • Jude 1:22-23, *page 1443*

God blesses those who show mercy to others Matthew 5:7, *page 1075*

If we do not show mercy, we cannot expect to receive mercy Matthew 6:14-15, *page 1077* • Matthew 18:21-35, *page 1098* • James 2:13, *page 1413*

God is merciful toward sinners Luke 18:9-14, *page 1183* • Ephesians 2:4-10, *page 1347* • 1 Timothy 1:15-17, *page 1379*

▸ *See **The character of God**, page 104; **The compassionate God**, page 666; **The love of God**, page 1437.*

Messiah *see also Jesus Christ*

While we don't use the word "Messiah" very much these days, we use its Greek equivalent—Christ—often. Messiah means "anointed one" (not Savior, as often wrongly thought), and it was used of Israel's expected deliverer-king who would save them from their enemies and establish God's Kingdom on earth. Jesus came as this Messiah, but not in the way Israel expected, which is why he often avoided the title. When we speak of Jesus Christ, we are really saying "Jesus the Messiah"—Jesus, God's promised deliverer-king.

John the Baptist, who was in prison, heard about all the things the Messiah was doing. So he sent his disciples to ask Jesus, "Are you the Messiah we've been expecting, or should we keep looking for someone else?" Jesus told them, "Go back to John and tell him what you have heard and seen—the blind see, the lame walk, those with leprosy are cured, the deaf hear, the dead are raised to life, and the Good News is being preached to the poor." And he added, "God blesses those who do not fall away because of me." – Matthew 11:2-6, page 1084

The promise of one who would come to undo Satan's work goes back to earliest times Genesis 3:14-15, *page 7*

God would use the Messiah to establish his glorious Kingdom Psalm 2:1-12, *page 602* • Isaiah 4:2-6, *page 752* • Isaiah 32:1-20, *page 781* • Jeremiah 23:1-6, *page 851* • Zechariah 9:9-10, *page 1044*

The Messiah would be a great king, a descendant of King David Isaiah 9:6-7, *page 758* • Isaiah 11:1-2, *page 760* • Matthew 1:1, *page 1068* • Matthew 21:1-11, *page 1101*

The Messiah would have to suffer and die Isaiah 52:13–53:12, *page 805* • Zechariah 12:10, *page 1047* • Matthew 16:13-28, *page 1095* • Luke 24:25-27, *page 1195* • John 19:31-37, *page 1230*

The Messiah would heal broken lives Isaiah 61:1-3, *page 814* • Luke 4:14-21, *page 1158*

The Messiah would be born in Bethlehem Micah 5:2, *page 1014* • Matthew 2:1-6, *page 1069* • Luke 2:1-7, *page 1154* • John 7:40-42, *page 1211*

Jesus said his actions revealed that he was the Messiah Matthew 11:2-6, *page 1084* • Luke 4:14-21, *page 1158* • John 10:22-26, *page 1216*

Simon Peter acknowledged that Jesus was the Messiah, though Jesus had to correct his understanding of what that meant Matthew 16:13-23, *page 1095*

Jesus often told people not to tell what he had done, for he knew they misunderstood what kind of Messiah he had come to be Matthew 16:13-20, *page 1095* • Mark 1:40-45, *page 1120* • Luke 5:12-16, *page 1160* • John 7:1-4, *page 1210*

Sometimes Jesus openly claimed to be the Messiah Matthew 26:62-68, *page 1112* • John 4:21-30, *page 1205*

The early church boldly proclaimed that Jesus was the Messiah, especially in Jewish contexts Acts 2:32-36, *page 1239* • Acts 3:12-19, *page 1240* • Acts 5:42, *page 1244* • Acts 8:4-12, *page 1247* • Acts 9:17-22, *page 1249* • Acts 18:4-6, 24-28, *page 1265*

▸ *See **Jesus Christ in the Psalms**, page 614; **The Branch**, page 760; **Prophecies of the Messiah**, page 1044.*

Mind *see also Heart; Soul; Spirit*

Today we associate the mind with the brain and thinking, but in Bible times people saw things differently. In fact, Hebrew (the language of the Old Testament) has no word for "mind," and its functions were attributed to "the heart." In the New Testament, "mind" sometimes refers to the seat of our thinking or that which guides us, which is why we are told as Christians to constantly let it be renewed by the Holy Spirit.

> *Don't copy the behavior and customs of this world, but let God transform you into a new person by changing the way you think. Then you will learn to know God's will for you, which is good and pleasing and perfect. – Romans 12:2, page 1296*

We should keep our thoughts fixed on God and the things of God Deuteronomy 4:39-40, *page 207* • Isaiah 26:3-4, *page 774* • Philippians 4:6-9, *page 1359* • Colossians 3:1-2, *page 1365*

We should seek to keep our thoughts clean Psalm 101:2-5, *page 664* • Matthew 5:27-30, *page 1076*

God knows all the thoughts of our minds Psalm 139:1-6, *page 689* • Ezekiel 11:5, *page 908*

Without the Spirit's help, our minds cannot conceive how big God's thoughts and plans are Isaiah 55:6-9, *page 808* • 1 Corinthians 2:6-16, *page 1305*

We should love God with all our mind Matthew 22:34-38, *page 1104* • Luke 10:25-28, *page 1172*

God wants us to have peace in our minds John 14:27, *page 1223* • Philippians 4:6-7, *page 1359*

God wants us to be one in heart and mind with other Christians Acts 4:32-33, *page 1242* • 1 Corinthians 1:10-17, *page 1303* • Philippians 4:2-3, *page 1359*

Without God our thinking remains in darkness Romans 1:21-22, *page 1283* • Ephesians 4:17-24, *page 1350*

There is a battle going on in our minds, but Jesus and his Spirit can help us Romans 7:21-25, *page 1290* • Romans 8:5-17, *page 1291*

God wants to transform the way we think Romans 12:1-2, *page 1296* • Ephesians 4:21-24, *page 1351*

Satan seeks to blind people's minds 2 Corinthians 4:3-4, *page 1327*

▸ *See **Meditation**, page 603; **Thought**, page 808.*

Mission *see Witnessing*

Modesty *see also Humility*

Unlike some other religions, Christianity does not have a list of rules governing how we should dress or behave in front of others; but the Bible does call us as Christians to be modest—unassuming about our abilities and appearance and constantly thinking of how our lives might affect others. Particularly in the Western world, we need to ensure that the way we dress is not provocative or oversexualized. We constantly need to bring our appearance and behavior to Jesus and check with him—through things like prayer, God's word, and accountability to other believers—that he is pleased with us.

> *And all of you, dress yourselves in humility as you relate to one another, for "God opposes the proud but gives grace to the humble." – 1 Peter 5:5, page 1425*

Nakedness is meant to be shared only between a husband and wife Genesis 2:25, *page 6*

After the Fall, nakedness before others is seen as a mark of shame in the Bible Genesis 9:20-27, *page 12* • Isaiah 47:1-3, *page 799* • Habakkuk 2:15-16, *page 1026*

A lack of modesty can lead people into sexual sin 2 Samuel 11:2-5, *page 352* • Proverbs 5:1-6, *page 700* • Proverbs 7:6-27, *page 703*

Immodest dress is a sign of godlessness Isaiah 3:16-24, *page 752* • Revelation 17:3-4, *page 1461*

We should be modest about our achievements, boasting only in God and what he has done Jeremiah 9:23-24, *page 836* • 1 Corinthians 1:26-31, *page 1304* • 1 Corinthians 4:6-16, *page 1307* • 2 Corinthians 10:7-18, *page 1332* • Galatians 6:14, *page 1344*

We should always have a modest assessment of ourselves Romans 12:1-3, *page 1296* • Philippians 2:3-5, *page 1356*

We should be modest with our bodies, especially the sexual parts 1 Corinthians 12:22-24, *page 1316*

While the Bible does not specifically tell us how to dress, it does tell us to dress modestly 1 Timothy 2:9-10, *page 1380* • 1 Peter 3:3-4, *page 1423*

We should be modest in our lifestyle James 5:1-5, *page 1416*

Money *see also Bribery; Giving*

The Bible does not say that money is the root of all evil (as commonly thought), but rather, "the love of money is the root of all kinds of evil" (1 Timothy 6:10). Money in itself is therefore neither good nor bad; it is how we use it that makes the difference. But while the Bible does not condemn having wealth, it does warn us to not let it make us hard-hearted or turn us from God.

> *True godliness with contentment is itself great wealth. After all, we brought nothing with us when we came into the world, and we can't take anything with us when we leave it. So if we have enough food and clothing, let us be content. But people who long to be rich fall into temptation and are trapped by many foolish and harmful desires that plunge them into ruin and destruction. For the love of money is the root of all kinds of evil. And some people, craving money, have wandered from the true faith and pierced themselves with many sorrows. – 1 Timothy 6:6-10, page 1383*

We should take care that money and possessions do not make us neglect God Deuteronomy 8:10-18, *page 211* • Proverbs 30:7-9, *page 727* • Mark 10:17-31, *page 1136* • Luke 12:13-21, *page 1175*

Money and possessions alone do not satisfy Ecclesiastes 5:10-20, *page 734* • Isaiah 55:1-3, *page 808*

We should not make money and possessions the most important things in our lives Matthew 6:19-24, *page 1077* • Luke 12:13-21, *page 1175*

We should pay our taxes on the money we earn Matthew 22:15-21, *page 1103* • Romans 13:6-7, *page 1297*

We should be content with what we have Luke 3:10-14, *page 1157* • 1 Timothy 6:6-10, *page 1383*

Money can make us blind to others' needs Luke 16:19-31, *page 1182* • James 5:1-5, *page 1416*

Christians should share their resources with those in need Acts 2:42-45, *page 1239* • Acts 4:32-37, *page 1242* • Acts 11:27-30, *page 1254* • 2 Corinthians 8:1-15, *page 1330*

We should not be lovers of money 1 Timothy 3:3, *page 1380* • 1 Timothy 6:9-10, *page 1383* • Hebrews 13:5, *page 1409*

We should look to God, not money, for security 1 Timothy 6:17-19, *page 1383*

▸ *See **Prosperity**, page 1176; **Giving**, page 1331; **Money**, page 1417.*

Morals *see Holiness; Integrity*

Motives *see also Conscience; Heart*

Motives—the underlying reasons for what we say or do—are important to God. In fact, the Bible says they are more important than the actual action itself. We can do the right thing from a wrong motive, but God sees straight through this. As Christians we should always want to act from right motives.

People may be pure in their own eyes, but the LORD examines their motives. – Proverbs 16:2, page 712

God always sees the motives in our hearts Genesis 4:1-7, *page 8* • 1 Samuel 15:1-23, *page 321* • Proverbs 20:27, *page 717* • Acts 5:1-11, *page 1242*

Our motives can sometimes be misunderstood Joshua 22:10-31, *page 265* • 2 Corinthians 1:12-24, *page 1324*

God looks at our hearts and motives, not external things 1 Samuel 16:1-7, *page 323* • Psalm 44:21-22, *page 629* • Romans 8:26-27, *page 1292*

How we react often reveals our true motives 2 Samuel 3:6-11, *page 344* • 2 Chronicles 26:16-21, *page 508* • Matthew 26:6-15, *page 1110* • John 11:45-53, *page 1218*

God examines our motives Proverbs 16:2, *page 712* • 1 Thessalonians 2:3-6, *page 1370*

The motive for right behavior should be a desire to please God Isaiah 26:8, *page 774* • 2 Corinthians 5:9-10, *page 1327* • Colossians 3:22-25, *page 1366*

Right motives are essential in every expression of worship Matthew 6:1-18, *page 1076*

Everything we do should have the motive of honoring God 1 Corinthians 10:31, *page 1314* • Colossians 3:17, 23-24, *page 1365*

Right actions can sometimes come from wrong motives Philippians 1:15-18, *page 1355*

Wrong motives hinder our prayers James 1:5-8, *page 1412* • James 4:1-3, *page 1416*

▶ *See* ***Conscience****, page 333;* ***Why was David wrong to take a census?****, page 371;* ***Lying****, page 1214.*

Mourning *see Bereavement; Death; Grief*

Murder

Because everyone is made in God's image, all life is precious. To take someone's life unlawfully is to violate that image. God therefore forbids murder, and in the Old Testament it was punishable by death.

"You must not murder." – Exodus 20:13, page 90

God punished the first murderer Genesis 4:1-16, *page 8*

In the Old Testament, capital punishment was the penalty for murder Genesis 9:5-6, *page 12* • Exodus 21:12-14, *page 91* • Numbers 35:30-34, *page 198*

God forbids murder in the Ten Commandments Exodus 20:13, *page 90*

Those accused of murder must receive a fair trial Deuteronomy 17:8-13, *page 220*

Those guilty of unintentional killing were protected from revenge attacks through cities of refuge to which they could flee while awaiting trial Deuteronomy 19:1-13, *page 221*

Unsolved murders had to be atoned for by the community to cleanse it Deuteronomy 21:1-9, *page 223*

In God's eyes, hateful anger is the same as murder Matthew 5:21-26, *page 1075* • 1 John 3:11-15, *page 1436*

Music

Music, both singing and playing musical instruments, played a big part in worshiping God in Bible times. There is no one style of music that has God's blessing more than another; all can be used for his glory.

Praise the LORD! Praise God in his sanctuary; praise him in his mighty heaven! Praise him for his mighty works; praise his unequaled greatness! Praise him with a blast of the ram's horn; praise him with the lyre and harp! Praise him with the tambourine and dancing; praise him with strings and flutes! Praise him with a clash of cymbals; praise him with loud clanging cymbals. Let everything that breathes sing praises to the LORD! – *Psalm 150:1-6, page 695*

Music was created in the earliest times Genesis 4:21, *page 8*

Music was used at feasts and in celebrations Genesis 31:25-27, *page 39* • Judges 11:34, *page 286* • Luke 15:20-32, *page 1181*

Music can be used to worship God Exodus 15:1, *page 83* • 2 Samuel 6:1-5, *page 348* • 2 Chronicles 5:2-14, *page 486* • Nehemiah 12:27-43, *page 550* • Psalm 33:1-5, *page 621* • Psalm 98:1-9, *page 664* • Psalm 150:1-6, *page 695*

Music can comfort us 1 Samuel 16:14-23, *page 324*

The withdrawal of music was seen as a curse Ezekiel 26:12-13, *page 926* • Revelation 18:21-24, *page 1463*

Music played a part in the early church's worship Ephesians 5:18-20, *page 1351* • Colossians 3:16, *page 1365*

There is music in heaven Revelation 5:6-14, *page 1451*

▶ *See* ***Singing****, page 236;* ***The ministry of music and singing****, page 475.*

Nations

The Bible often uses the term "the nations" to speak of all those who oppose God. But it also looks forward to the end of the age, when people of all nations will know God and become true descendants of Abraham, just as God promised him. The church is called to play its part in that by taking the gospel to the nations.

In the last days, the mountain of the LORD's house will be the highest of all—the most important place on earth. It will be raised above the other hills, and people from all over the world will stream there to worship. People from many nations will come and say, "Come, let us go up to the mountain of the LORD, to the house of Jacob's God. There he will teach us his ways, and we will walk in his paths." – *Micah 4:1-2, page 1013*

The different nations were created by God as part of his plan for filling the earth Genesis 10:32, *page 14* • Genesis 11:1-9, *page 14* • Deuteronomy 32:8, *page 235* • Acts 17:24-27, *page 1264*

Abraham was promised he would become the father of many nations and a means of blessing every nation Genesis 12:1-3, *page 15* • Genesis 17:1-6, *page 20* • Genesis 22:9-18, *page 26* • Acts 3:24-25, *page 1240* • Galatians 3:6-9, *page 1340*

In the Old Testament the nations are often seen as God's enemies Deuteronomy 9:1-6, *page 211* • 2 Samuel 22:47-51, *page 369* • Psalm 2:1-6, *page 602* • Isaiah 17:12-14, *page 766* • Ezekiel 36:1-7, *page 937*

God is sovereign over all the nations 2 Kings 19:14-19, *page 437* • 2 Chronicles 20:1-12, *page 500* • Psalm 47:1-9, *page 631* • Isaiah 40:12-17, *page 790* • Isaiah 41:2-4, *page 791*

One day all the nations will know and worship God Psalm 22:27-28, *page 615* • Psalm 46:10, *page 631* • Isaiah 2:1-4, *page 750* • Isaiah 56:6-8 • Mark 11:15-17, *page 1138* • Revelation 15:1-4, *page 1460* • Revelation 21:22-26, *page 1466*

The nations will one day see God's victory Isaiah 11:10-12, *page 761* • Isaiah 25:1-3, *page 773* • Isaiah 29:5-8, *page 777* • Isaiah 52:4-15, *page 805* • Isaiah 62:1-12, *page 815* • Joel 3:1-16, *page 990* • Obadiah 1:15-16, *page 1005*

No nation lasts forever, only God's Kingdom Daniel 2:24-45, *page 957* • Daniel 7:1-27, *page 964* • Revelation 11:15, *page 1457*

Christians are commanded to take the gospel to the nations Matthew 24:14, *page 1107* • Matthew 28:18-20, *page 1116* • Luke 24:44-49, *page 1196* • Acts 1:6-8, *page 1236*

Jesus came and died for people of all nations Luke 2:25-32, *page 1155* • Acts 10:34-36, *page 1252* • Romans 1:1-6, *page 1282* • Romans 15:7-12, *page 1299* • Revelation 5:6-10, *page 1451*

All barriers of nationality and race are removed in Jesus Acts 10:1-48, *page 1250* • Galatians 3:26-29, *page 1341* • Ephesians 2:11-22, *page 1347*

Mission to the nations was at the heart of the early church's program Acts 11:19-26, *page 1254* • Acts 13:1–14:28, *page 1255* • Acts 15:36-41, *page 1261* • Romans 15:23-24, *page 1299*

Heaven is already populated with Christians from all nations Revelation 7:9-10, *page 1454*

▶ *See **The nations**, page 765.*

Nature *see Creation*

Neighbor *see Love*

New birth *see Birth*

Obedience

Many people see Christianity as simply obedience to a set of religious rules. However, it is anything but that. Yes, Christians are called to obedience—but not to a set of rules. Rather, we are called to liberating loyalty to a person, the Lord Jesus Christ. Obeying him always leads to fulfillment in life.

> *"What is more pleasing to the LORD: your burnt offerings and sacrifices or your obedience to his voice? Listen! Obedience is better than sacrifice, and submission is better than offering the fat of rams."* – 1 Samuel 15:22, page 322

People who obey God will be blessed Genesis 22:15-18, *page 26* • Exodus 19:5-6, *page 88* • Deuteronomy 4:1-8, *page 205* • Deuteronomy 28:1-14, *page 229* • Luke 11:27-28, *page 1174*

Obeying is better than offering sacrifices or constantly saying, "I'm sorry" 1 Samuel 15:10-23, *page 321* • Psalm 40:6-8, *page 626* • Proverbs 21:3, *page 717* • Mark 12:28-33, *page 1140*

Obeying God should be a delight Psalm 40:6-8, *page 626* • Hebrews 10:4-7, *page 1405*

We need to obey God's word, not just listen to it Matthew 7:24-27, *page 1079* • James 1:22-27, *page 1412* • 1 John 2:4, *page 1434*

Obeying God means trusting him Matthew 26:36-46, *page 1111* • Hebrews 11:8-10, *page 1407*

A key aspect of discipleship is learning how to obey Jesus Matthew 28:18-20, *page 1116*

If we say we love God, then we should obey him John 14:15-24, *page 1223* • 1 John 2:3-6, *page 1434* • 1 John 5:3-6, *page 1437* • 2 John 1:6, *page 1438*

Jesus' death broke the power of sin in our lives, so now we can want to obey God Romans 6:1-23, *page 1289* • Romans 7:14-25, *page 1290*

The Holy Spirit helps us to obey God Romans 8:1-17, *page 1290* • 1 Peter 1:1-2, *page 1420*

Christians should obey the government Romans 13:1-7, *page 1297* • Titus 3:1, *page 1391* • 1 Peter 2:13-17, *page 1422*

Children should obey their parents Ephesians 6:1, *page 1352* • Colossians 3:20, *page 1366*

We should follow Jesus' example of humble obedience to the Father Philippians 2:5-11, *page 1356*

▶ *See **Taking Christ's yoke**, page 1085; **Discipleship and the cross**, page 1095; **Counting the cost**, page 1180; **Life from death**, page 1219.*

Occult

The Bible forbids God's people from any involvement with the occult—that is, attempting to communicate with the dead or manipulate supernatural powers. Such powers are real but dangerous; they bring deception not hope, lies not truth. God gives us his Holy Spirit to provide all the guidance we need.

> *"Do not practice fortune-telling or witchcraft. . . . Do not defile yourselves by turning to mediums or to those who consult the spirits of the dead. I am the LORD your God."* – Leviticus 19:26, 31, page 140

God's people should not engage in astrology Deuteronomy 4:19, *page 206* • 2 Kings 21:1-15, *page 439* • Isaiah 47:13-15, *page 800*

God forbids all occult practices Deuteronomy 18:9-14, *page 221* • Jeremiah 10:1-5, *page 836*

The Bible shows us the folly of spiritism and consulting mediums 1 Samuel 28:1-25, *page 337* • Isaiah 8:19-22, *page 757* • Ezekiel 13:8-9, *page 911*

God hates all occult practices and judges those engaged in them 2 Kings 17:16-18, *page 432* • 2 Kings 21:1-15, *page 439* • Isaiah 47:10-15, *page 800*

Astrologers cannot help us Isaiah 47:13-14, *page 800*

People who have been involved in the occult can be converted Acts 8:9-13, *page 1247* • Acts 19:17-20, *page 1267*

Fortune-telling is demonic Acts 16:16-18, *page 1262*

The spirit world is real but dangerous Acts 19:13-16, *page 1267*

Those who engage in occult practices are excluded from God's future Kingdom Revelation 21:5-8, *page 1465* • Revelation 22:14-15, *page 1467*

▶ *See **The occult**, page 337; **False prophecy**, page 911; **Mediums**, page 768; **False teaching**, page 1443.*

Old age

Old age is a part of life that few of us like to think about, yet one that will come to almost all of us. While old age can be frustrating at times, as our bodies get frailer, it can be a time of great usefulness in God's Kingdom, for much wisdom has by then been acquired. That is why the Bible sees old age as a blessing, and why younger people are urged to respect the elderly and listen to their wisdom.

> *"Listen to me, descendants of Jacob, all you who remain in Israel. I have cared for you since you were born. Yes, I carried you before you were born. I will be your God throughout your lifetime—until your hair is white with age. I made you, and I will care for you. I will carry you along and save you." – Isaiah 46:3-4, page 799*

Attaining old age is a blessing from God Genesis 15:15, *page 18* • Deuteronomy 5:32-33, *page 208* • Proverbs 16:31, *page 713* • Ephesians 6:2-3, *page 1352*

Old age can be marked by declining health Genesis 27:1-4, *page 32* • 1 Kings 1:1-4, *page 374* • 2 Corinthians 5:1-5, *page 1327*

We can still be fruitful for God in old age Exodus 7:1-7, *page 73* • Joshua 14:10-14, *page 257* • Psalm 92:11-15, *page 661* • Luke 2:25-38, *page 1155*

We should respect those who are old Leviticus 19:32, *page 140* • Job 32:4, *page 591* • Matthew 15:3-9, *page 1092* • 1 Timothy 5:1-4, *page 1382*

Grandchildren are a blessing to older people Ruth 4:13-17, *page 303* • Job 5:25-27, *page 569* • Psalm 128:5-6, *page 685* • Proverbs 17:6, *page 713*

Older people have acquired wisdom in life 1 Kings 12:1-17, *page 392* • Job 12:12, *page 574* • Job 32:7, *page 591* • Proverbs 20:29, *page 717*

We can expect God to strengthen us in old age Psalm 71:7-18, *page 645* • Isaiah 46:4, *page 799*

We should never forget that this life will end one day Psalm 90:1-12, *page 659* • Ecclesiastes 12:1-7, *page 739*

Society should see the elderly as a blessing, not a burden Isaiah 65:17-20, *page 819* • Zechariah 8:3-5, *page 1043*

The old can receive God's Spirit as much as the young Joel 2:28-29, *page 990* • Acts 2:14-18, *page 1238*

Older people can set an example and mentor younger people Titus 2:1-5, *page 1390*

▶ *See **Respect for those who are older**, page 415; **From one generation to another**, page 651; **Old age**, page 660; **Mentoring**, page 1385.*

Opportunities, Making the most of *see Time*

Opposition *see also Insults; Intimidation; Persecution; Perseverance*

As soon as we decide to follow Jesus, there will be opposition in some form or other. It may come as gentle mocking from friends or colleagues who don't understand why we have become Christians; or it may come as more outright opposition—practical, psychological, or physical—from those who hate God and his people. Through all of this opposition, Satan is at work; but God has given us resources—such as prayer, fasting, fellowship, the encouragement of his Spirit, and his word—to help us press on and be victorious.

You know how badly we had been treated at Philippi just before we came to you and how much we suffered there. Yet our God gave us the courage to declare his Good News to you boldly, in spite of great opposition. – 1 Thessalonians 2:2, page 1370

Opposition to God and his people ultimately comes from Satan Genesis 3:1-7, *page 6* • Ephesians 6:10-12, *page 1352*

When opposed, we should both pray and take what practical steps we can Exodus 17:8-13, *page 86* • Nehemiah 4:1-9, *page 539* • Acts 4:1-31, *page 1240*

We should keep trusting God when we are opposed 1 Samuel 17:32-51, *page 325* • Acts 4:19-22, *page 1241* • Philippians 1:27-30, *page 1356*

We should persevere when opposed and not just give in Nehemiah 6:1-9, *page 541* • Mark 13:9-13, *page 1141* • Hebrews 10:32-39, *page 1406* • Revelation 2:8-11, *page 1447*

We should remember that God is always with us, so we do not need to fear Psalm 27:1-3, *page 617* • Psalm 91:1-16, *page 660* • Daniel 3:1-30, *page 958* • Acts 16:16-40, *page 1262*

God can overcome all opposition Daniel 10:4-19, *page 969* • Romans 8:35-39, *page 1292* • Revelation 12:1-12, *page 1457* • Revelation 19:11–20:10, *page 1464*

Jesus himself was opposed Matthew 4:1-11, *page 1073* • Matthew 13:55-58, *page 1091* • Luke 4:14-30, *page 1158* • John 11:45-54, *page 1218* • Hebrews 12:1-3, *page 1408*

We should not be surprised by opposition Matthew 10:16-22, *page 1083* • John 16:1-4, *page 1224* • 2 Timothy 3:12-14, *page 1386* • 1 Peter 4:12-19, *page 1425*

We should seize the opportunities that opposition provides Mark 13:1-11, *page 1141* • Acts 4:1-22, *page 1240* • Acts 16:25-40, *page 1262* • 1 Corinthians 16:9, *page 1321*

Opposition can help develop our character Romans 5:3-5, *page 1287* • James 1:2-4, *page 1412*

We should remember that nothing can separate us from God's love Romans 8:31-39, *page 1292*

God has given us spiritual weapons to overcome opposition 2 Corinthians 10:3-5, *page 1332* • Ephesians 6:10-18, *page 1352*

▶ *See **Courage**, page 243; **Pressing on**, page 1359.*

Oppression *see Intimidation*

Pain *see Suffering*

Pardon *see Forgiveness*

Parents *see Family; Marriage*

Past

Our past might have shaped who we are, but it does not limit who we can become. Whatever our past—and for all of us it contains good things of which we are proud and bad things of which we are ashamed—when we become Christians, a brand-new life begins. We now see that the good things from the past were not that good in comparison to God's greatness, and that the bad things from the past were not so bad that God cannot forgive them. We have become new people, leaving the past behind and pursuing God's exciting plan ahead of us.

Forgetting the past and looking forward to what lies ahead, I press on to reach the end of the race and receive the heavenly prize for which God, through Christ Jesus, is calling us. – Philippians 3:13-14, page 1358

With God, our future is not limited by our past life or circumstances Genesis 15:1-6, *page 18* • Exodus 3:7-17, *page 68* • Judges 6:11-16, *page 277* • 1 Samuel 16:1-13, *page 323* • Acts 9:1-22, *page 1248*

We should not long for the past, for it is rarely as we remember it Exodus 16:1-3, *page 84* • Numbers 11:4-6, *page 167* • Numbers 14:1-4, *page 169*

We should not forget lessons learned in the past Deuteronomy 4:9-10, *page 206* • Romans 15:1-4, *page 1299* • 1 Corinthians 10:1-11, *page 1313*

God's people should not forget the good things he has done for them in the past Deuteronomy 6:10-12, *page 209* • Joshua 4:1-7, *page 245* • Isaiah 46:8-10, *page 799* • 2 Timothy 2:8, *page 1386*

Our past sin can be forgiven no matter how bad it has been 2 Samuel 11:1–12:13, *page 352* • 2 Chronicles 33:1-13, *page 515* • Luke 15:11-32, *page 1181* • John 8:1-11, *page 1211* • 1 Timothy 1:12-17, *page 1379*

There are things from our past that we simply have to leave behind when we follow Jesus Mark 8:34-38, *page 1133* • Luke 9:57-62, *page 1171* • Ephesians 4:17-32, *page 1350*

We should never forget what Jesus did for us in the past at the cross Luke 22:14-20, *page 1190* • 1 Corinthians 11:23-26, *page 1315*

When we become Christians, we are born again and become brand new people John 1:10-13, *page 1199* • Romans 6:1-4, *page 1289* • 2 Corinthians 5:17, *page 1328* • Galatians 2:20, *page 1339* • Galatians 6:14-16, *page 1344*

We should always take care not to fall into past sins Galatians 4:8-9, *page 1341* • Hebrews 6:1-6, *page 1400*

We should not be preoccupied with our past but rather look to Jesus and the future Philippians 3:1-14, *page 1358* • Hebrews 12:1-2, *page 1408*

▶ *See **Is there anything God won't forgive?**, page 633; **Hope**, page 895; **Handling failure**, page 1232; **Pressing on**, page 1359; **How can I be sure God has forgiven me?**, page 1433.*

Patience *see also Perseverance; Waiting*

The Bible shows us that God himself is patient, so it is not surprising that he calls his people to be patient too. Patience is not always easy, but when we are patient, we give God time to work rather than trying to make things happen ourselves.

> *Rejoice in our confident hope. Be patient in trouble, and keep on praying. – Romans 12:12, page 1296*

God is always patient with us Exodus 34:6-7, *page 106* • Nehemiah 9:29-31, *page 546* • Romans 2:4, *page 1284* • 1 Timothy 1:15-17, *page 1379* • 2 Peter 3:9-15, *page 1429*

We can wait patiently for God to act Psalm 27:1-14, *page 617* • Psalm 37:1-9, *page 623* • Psalm 40:1-17, *page 626* • Isaiah 64:1-4, *page 817* • Habakkuk 2:1-3, *page 1025*

Patience eventually produces a harvest Luke 8:11-15, *page 1166* • Galatians 6:7-9, *page 1344* • 2 Peter 1:5-8, *page 1427*

We should be patient in difficulties Romans 12:12, *page 1296* • 2 Corinthians 6:3-6, *page 1328* • 1 Peter 2:18-25, *page 1423*

Patience demonstrates our love for people 1 Corinthians 13:4-7, *page 1317*

Patience is evidence of the Holy Spirit working in our lives Galatians 5:22-23, *page 1343*

We should be patient with each other Ephesians 4:1-2, *page 1349* • Colossians 3:12-15, *page 1365* • 1 Thessalonians 5:14, *page 1373*

We should be patient in teaching God's word to others 2 Timothy 4:1-5, *page 1387*

Patience helps us receive what God has promised Hebrews 6:11-15, *page 1400*

We should be patient as we wait for Jesus to return James 5:7-11, *page 1417*

Peace *see also Reconciliation; Rest*

God wants us to know peace, both in our hearts and in our relationships. This peace is not simply the absence of strife and tension, but the positive presence of God in our lives that transforms everything.

> *"I am leaving you with a gift—peace of mind and heart. And the peace I give is a gift the world cannot give. So don't be troubled or afraid. Remember what I told you: I am going away, but I will*

come back to you again. If you really loved me, you would be happy that I am going to the Father, who is greater than I am. I have told you these things before they happen so that when they do happen, you will believe." – John 14:27-29, page 1223

A prayer for peace upon others Numbers 6:24-26, *page 161*

We should seek peace and the blessing it brings Psalm 34:11-14, *page 622* • Jeremiah 29:4-7, *page 858* • Colossians 3:12-15, *page 1365* • 1 Peter 3:8-12, *page 1423*

God promises there will be peace in his new Kingdom Isaiah 2:1-4, *page 750* • Ezekiel 34:25-31, *page 937* • Revelation 21:1-4, *page 1465*

Jesus brings God's peace to people Isaiah 9:6-7, *page 758* • Luke 2:8-14, *page 1154* • Romans 5:1-2, *page 1287*

Peace comes as we trust God Isaiah 26:3-4, *page 774* • Romans 15:13, *page 1299* • Philippians 4:6-7, *page 1359*

God blesses those who work for peace Matthew 5:9, *page 1075* • James 3:18, *page 1415*

We should make peace with others quickly Matthew 5:21-26, *page 1075*

Jesus said that his message would sometimes lead to hostility not peace Matthew 10:32-39, *page 1084*

Peace is evidence of the Holy Spirit working in our lives Romans 8:5-6, *page 1291* • Galatians 5:22-23, *page 1343*

We should work hard at living in peace with others Romans 12:17-21, *page 1297* • Hebrews 12:14-15, *page 1409*

God is called "the God of peace" Romans 16:20, *page 1301* • Philippians 4:9, *page 1360* • 1 Thessalonians 5:23, *page 1374* • Hebrews 13:20, *page 1410*

We receive peace from God when we pray Philippians 4:4-7, *page 1359*

▶ *See **Peace**, page 774.*

Peer pressure

While peer pressure has always been a problem, its challenge has grown significantly in recent years through the expansion of social media. Now everything we do, or don't do, can be commented upon, and rapidly; and the pressure to conform to the norms of our friends or colleagues is greater than ever before. But following Jesus means being ready to put him first always and to be led by his Spirit, not by what others think or say.

But when Peter came to Antioch, I had to oppose him to his face, for what he did was very wrong. When he first arrived, he ate with the Gentile believers, who were not circumcised. But afterward, when some friends of James came, Peter wouldn't eat with the Gentiles anymore. He was afraid of criticism from these people who insisted on the necessity of circumcision. As a result, other Jewish believers followed Peter's hypocrisy, and even Barnabas was led astray by their hypocrisy. – Galatians 2:11-13, page 1338

Peer pressure can make us do what is popular rather than what is right Exodus 32:1-29, *page 103* • 2 Chronicles 13:4-7, *page 495* • Matthew 14:1-12, *page 1091* • Matthew 27:11-26, *page 1113* • John 12:37-43, *page 1220* • Galatians 2:11-13, *page 1338*

Mixing with the wrong people produces pressure to go along with the crowd Psalm 1:1-6, *page 602* • Proverbs 13:20, *page 710* • 1 Corinthians 15:30-33, *page 1319* • 2 Corinthians 6:14-18, *page 1329*

We should not succumb to peer pressure that would lead us to do wrong Proverbs 1:10-15, *page 697* • Proverbs 4:14-27, *page 700* • Proverbs 22:24-25, *page 719*

Jesus himself faced peer pressure to do things differently Matthew 16:21-23, *page 1095* • Mark 3:20-21, *page 1124*

Our goal should always be to please God, not others Acts 5:17-29, *page 1243* • 2 Corinthians 6:7-8, *page 1328* • Galatians 1:10, *page 1337*

We can deal with peer pressure by training ourselves to think differently Romans 12:1-2, *page 1296* • 1 Peter 1:13-25, *page 1421*

We should ensure that we get positive peer pressure from having fellowship with like-minded Christians Galatians 6:1-10, *page 1343* • Colossians 2:1-7, *page 1363* • Hebrews 10:23-25, *page 1406*

We should remember that we are only "temporary residents and foreigners" in this world 1 Peter 2:9-12, *page 1422*

▶ See ***Keeping up appearances***, *page 494*; ***Mixed marriages***, *page 532*; ***Friendship***, *page 725*; ***Can a Christian marry a non-Christian?***, *page 1329*.

Persecution *see also Opposition*

We are foolish if we go looking for persecution; but Jesus said that, sometimes, being faithful to him will attract persecution from those who hate him and his message. He promises to be with us at such times and urges us to continue to be faithful.

> *"God blesses those who are persecuted for doing right, for the Kingdom of Heaven is theirs. God blesses you when people mock you and persecute you and lie about you and say all sorts of evil things against you because you are my followers. Be happy about it! Be very glad! For a great reward awaits you in heaven. And remember, the ancient prophets were persecuted in the same way." – Matthew 5:10-12, page 1075*

Many Old Testament prophets were persecuted for their faithfulness to God 1 Kings 19:1-4, *page 404* • Jeremiah 20:1-2, *page 847* • Jeremiah 37:1–38:28, *page 868* • Acts 7:51-52, *page 1246*

God promises to bless those who are persecuted Matthew 5:10-12, *page 1075*

We should pray for, bless, and forgive those who persecute us Matthew 5:43-48, *page 1076* • Luke 23:34, *page 1194* • Romans 12:14-21, *page 1296*

We should remain faithful to God even in persecution Matthew 10:16-28, *page 1083* • 2 Thessalonians 1:3-10, *page 1374* • Revelation 2:8-11, *page 1447*

A time of persecution will come in the end times, but God will preserve his people Luke 21:8-19, *page 1189* • Revelation 7:9-17, *page 1454*

Some form of persecution is inevitable for true disciples John 15:18-21, *page 1224* • Galatians 6:17, *page 1344* • 2 Timothy 3:10-12, *page 1386*

Persecution can strengthen our character Romans 5:3-5, *page 1287* • 2 Corinthians 4:16-18, *page 1327* • 1 Peter 1:3-9, *page 1420*

Persecution can never separate us from God's love Romans 8:31-39, *page 1292*

We should remain patient in persecution Hebrews 10:32-39, *page 1406* • James 5:7-11, *page 1417*

We should maintain our integrity even in persecution 1 Peter 2:11-20, *page 1422*

We should follow Jesus' example in persecution 1 Peter 2:21-25, *page 1423* • 1 Peter 3:8-18, *page 1423*

▶ See ***Persecution***, *page 1452*.

Perseverance *see also Growth, Spiritual*

When we become Christians we are "born again" (John 3:3); but now, like any newborn baby, we need to grow. There are many things we can do to help that growth; but the most important is simply to persevere—to keep going—especially when life gets tough or the devil seems to oppose us. We should remember that God is always with us, helping us through his Holy Spirit, and that he is resolved to bring us into all the purposes he has for us.

> *I want to know Christ and experience the mighty power that raised him from the dead. I want to suffer with him, sharing in his death, so that one way or another I will experience the resurrection from the dead! I don't mean to say that I have already achieved these things or that I have already reached perfection. But I press on to possess that perfection for which Christ Jesus first possessed me. No, dear brothers and sisters, I have not achieved it, but I focus on this one thing: Forgetting the past and looking forward to what lies ahead, I press on to reach the end of the race and receive the heavenly prize for which God, through Christ Jesus, is calling us. – Philippians 3:10-14, page 1358*

Worrying about life can hinder us from persevering Matthew 6:25-34, *page 1078* • Matthew 13:18-23, *page 1090*

Persevering to the end will ensure we are saved Mark 13:13, *page 1141*

We should persevere in prayer Luke 11:1-13, *page 1173* • Luke 18:1-8, *page 1183*

Our motivation for keeping going is knowing that God keeps going with us John 10:27-30, *page 1216* • Philippians 1:4-6, *page 1355* • Philippians 2:12-13, *page 1357* • Jude 1:24-25, *page 1443*

Maintaining our relationship with Jesus is crucial to persevering and being fruitful John 15:1-17, *page 1223*

We should persevere even through difficulties, knowing that God is with us and for us Romans 5:1-5, *page 1287* • Hebrews 12:1-13, *page 1408* • James 1:2-4, *page 1412*

The Holy Spirit is at work within us to help us persevere Romans 8:5-17, *page 1291* • 1 John 4:4, *page 1436*

We should keep working at growing in Christ-like qualities Galatians 5:16-26, *page 1343* • 2 Peter 1:3-11, *page 1427*

Drawing on God's strength helps us keep going Ephesians 6:10-18, *page 1352*

Even when we fail, Jesus is faithful 2 Timothy 2:8-13, *page 1386*

We are urged to keep persevering with Jesus Hebrews 2:1-4, *page 1397* • Revelation 3:14-20, *page 1450*

We should encourage one another to keep going Hebrews 10:23-25, *page 1406*

▶ *See* ***Now that you are a Christian****, page A13;* ***Trusting God when we cannot see the way ahead****, page 57;* ***Pressing on****, page 1359;* ***Perseverance in prayer****, page 1184;* ***Can a Christian lose their salvation?****, page 1401;* ***The dangers of drifting****, page 1447.*

Persistence *see Perseverance*

Philanthropy *see Giving*

Poor *see Poverty*

Popularity *see Peer pressure*

Pornography *see also Lust; Sexuality*

Because of the Internet, pornography—the explicit depiction of sexual acts for the enjoyment of others—is easier to access today than ever before, and therefore easier to be deceitful about. But if we claim to follow a God of purity and truth, pornography should find no place in our lives. It degrades God's image expressed in humanity, reducing people to mere objects, and fosters wrong views of sexual pleasure, often ruining marriages and families as a result. The New Testament tells us to flee *porneia*—the Greek word for "sexual immorality," from which our word *pornography* comes. Accountability to a discipleship partner or more mature Christian can be a great practical help in breaking free from this addiction.

> *So put to death the sinful, earthly things lurking within you. Have nothing to do with sexual immorality, impurity, lust, and evil desires. – Colossians 3:5, page 1365*

Nakedness is something to be enjoyed only between a husband and a wife Genesis 2:25, *page 6*

Lustful looking can often lead to more serious situations 2 Samuel 11:1-27, *page 352* • 2 Samuel 13:1-39, *page 355*

God's people should take care what they let into their lives through their eyes Job 31:1-4, *page 589* • Proverbs 6:25-29, *page 702* • Matthew 5:27-30, *page 1076*

Bad things come from what we let grow in our hearts Mark 7:14-23, *page 1131*

Even if we fail in this area, we should remember that all sins, including sexual sins, can be forgiven John 8:1-11, *page 1211* • 1 John 1:8-9, *page 1433*

Jesus wants to free us all from all addictions that enslave us John 8:33-36, *page 1213*

The enjoyment of immorality is a sign of godlessness Romans 1:21-27, *page 1283* • 1 Peter 4:1-3, *page 1424*

Christians should flee from every kind of immorality Romans 13:8-14, *page 1298* • 1 Corinthians 6:18-20, *page 1310* • 2 Timothy 2:22, *page 1386* • 1 Peter 4:3-5, *page 1424*

Sexual immorality defiles our own body, which is the temple of the Holy Spirit 1 Corinthians 6:15-20, *page 1309*

A healthy sex life between a husband and a wife is one of the best prescriptions against immorality 1 Corinthians 7:1-5, *page 1310*

Christians should avoid lust Ephesians 5:3-5, *page 1351* • Colossians 3:5, *page 1365* • 1 Thessalonians 4:3-5, *page 1372*

Sexual relationships belong exclusively within the bounds of marriage Hebrews 13:4, *page 1409*

▶ *See **Sexuality**, page 742.*

Possessions *see Money*

Poverty

The Bible shows that God has a big heart for the poor, and this was reflected both in his Law and in the challenges the prophets brought to his people. It is because God cares for the poor that we as his people should care too. The Bible urges us to be mindful of them and to be generous in our support of them.

> *Those who oppress the poor insult their Maker, but helping the poor honors him. – Proverbs 14:31, page 711*

The Old Testament Law protected the rights of the poor Leviticus 25:35-43, *page 148* • Deuteronomy 15:1-18, *page 218* • Deuteronomy 24:19-22, *page 227*

God treats poor people with special kindness 1 Samuel 2:8, *page 307* • Psalm 35:10, *page 622* • Matthew 5:3, *page 1074* • James 2:5-6, *page 1413*

God's people are urged to help the poor Psalm 82:3-4, *page 655* • Proverbs 14:31, *page 711* • Matthew 25:31-46, *page 1109* • Luke 14:12-14, *page 1179* • Luke 18:18-24, *page 1184* • James 2:15-16, *page 1413*

God will punish those who oppress the poor Isaiah 3:13-15, *page 752* • Jeremiah 22:13-19, *page 850* • Ezekiel 18:5-13, *page 916* • Amos 2:6-7, *page 995* • Amos 4:1-3, *page 996*

Jesus came to bring Good News to the poor Matthew 11:4-5, *page 1084* • Luke 4:16-21, *page 1159* • 2 Corinthians 8:9, *page 1330*

Jesus himself was poor and needed the support of others Luke 8:1-3, *page 1166* • Luke 9:57-58, *page 1171*

Jesus gave to the poor John 13:29, *page 1222*

Helping the poor was a priority for the apostles and the early church Romans 15:23-29, *page 1299* • 2 Corinthians 8:1–9:15, *page 1330* • Galatians 2:9-10, *page 1338*

We are not to discriminate against the poor James 2:1-13, *page 1413*

▶ *See **Poverty**, page 1142; **Money**, page 1417.*

Power

The Bible tells us that, when the Holy Spirit comes to live within us, we have available to us the same power of God that raised Jesus from the dead. However, this power is not there for selfish purposes or to make us look good; it is to help us become more like Jesus and do the sort of things that he himself would do. It is power to oppose evil and do good, power to share the news of God's love with others.

> *I also pray that you will understand the incredible greatness of God's power for us who believe him. This is the same mighty power that raised Christ from the dead and seated him in the place of honor at God's right hand in the heavenly realms. – Ephesians 1:19-20, page 1346*

God is all-powerful Genesis 17:1, *page 20* • Job 42:1-2, *page 599* • Jeremiah 32:27, *page 864* • Mark 10:27, *page 1137* • Ephesians 3:20, *page 1349*

God gives power and strength to those who trust in him Psalm 68:35, *page 643* • Isaiah 40:28-31, *page 791*

Jesus ministered in power Mark 5:24-30, *page 1127* • Luke 4:14, *page 1158* • Luke 5:17-26, *page 1161* • Acts 2:22-24, *page 1238* • Acts 10:37-38, *page 1252* • 1 Corinthians 1:24, *page 1304*

Jesus' disciples experienced his power when he sent them out to minister Mark 6:7-13,

Prayer *see also Worship*

Prayer is, quite simply, conversation with our heavenly Father. It requires no special words, times, places, or rituals; it is simply about telling him what is on our hearts, thanking him for what he has done, and bringing our needs and concerns to him, knowing that he listens.

> *"Pray like this: Our Father in heaven, may your name be kept holy. May your Kingdom come soon. May your will be done on earth, as it is in heaven. Give us today the food we need and forgive us our sins, as we have forgiven those who sin against us. And don't let us yield to temptation, but rescue us from the evil one." – Matthew 6:9-13, page 1077*

1 Timothy 2:1-4, *page 1380* • James 5:16, *page 1417*

▸ See **Praying in the moment**, page 537; **Longing for God**, page 628; **Why doesn't God always answer prayer?**, page 641; **Does God mind if we are honest with him?**, page 848; **Prayer as intercession**, page 922; **The Lord's Prayer**, page 1077; **Perseverance in prayer**, page 1184.

Preaching *see Bible; Doctrine; Teaching*

Prejudice *see Discrimination*

Pride *see also Humility*

Pride has many different expressions, from boasting of our achievements to imagining that we are something we are not. Pride takes the glory for ourselves, rather than giving it to God; therefore God says that he will always humble the proud.

> *Pride goes before destruction, and haughtiness before a fall. Better to live humbly with the poor than to share plunder with the proud. – Proverbs 16:18-19, page 713*

We should beware of pride in times of success Deuteronomy 8:11-20, *page 211* • Jeremiah 9:23-24, *page 836* • Revelation 3:14-22, *page 1450*

Pride prevents God from hearing and answering our prayers Job 35:9-12, *page 593* • Luke 18:9-14, *page 1183*

God hates pride Proverbs 6:16-19, *page 702* • Proverbs 8:13, *page 704* • Proverbs 16:5, *page 712* • James 4:4-10, *page 1416*

Pride leads to disgrace, shame, and destruction Proverbs 11:2, *page 707* • Proverbs 16:18, *page 713* • Isaiah 2:11-17, *page 751*

Pride can lead to arguments Proverbs 13:10, *page 709*

Pride is sin Proverbs 21:4, *page 718* • Mark 7:20-23, *page 1131* • James 4:13-16, *page 1416*

Proud people will be humbled Isaiah 2:12-17, *page 751* • Matthew 23:8-12, *page 1105* • Luke 1:51-52, *page 1153*

Pride lay behind Satan's downfall Isaiah 14:12-17, *page 763* • Ezekiel 28:12-19, *page 929*

There is no place for pride in the Christian life Romans 3:27, *page 1286* • Romans 12:16, *page 1297* • 1 John 2:15-16, *page 1434*

God reveals himself to the humble, not the proud 1 Corinthians 1:26-31, *page 1304*

Pride is not compatible with love or the fruit of the Spirit 1 Corinthians 13:4-7, *page 1317* • Galatians 5:19-26, *page 1343*

God opposes the proud James 4:6-10, *page 1416* • 1 Peter 5:1-7, *page 1425*

▸ See **Pride**, page 559; **Humility**, page 1134; **The humility of Christ**, page 1358.

Problems *see Stress; Suffering; Testing*

Promises *see also Covenant; Faithfulness*

The Bible shows that, because God is faithful, he always keeps his promises. However, if we are going to appeal to those promises, then it is important that we both trust God and seek to walk in his ways. As his people, God expects us to keep our promises, both to him and to others.

> *By his divine power, God has given us everything we need for living a godly life. We have received all of this by coming to know him, the one who called us to himself by means of his marvelous glory and excellence. And because of his glory and excellence, he has given us great and precious promises. These are the promises that enable you to share his divine nature and escape the world's corruption caused by human desires. – 2 Peter 1:3-4, page 1427*

God's covenant promises were often accompanied by a sign to serve as a reminder Genesis 9:8-17, *page 12* • Genesis 15:1-21, *page 18* • Genesis 17:1-14, *page 20* • Exodus 12:1-20, *page 78* • Matthew 26:17-29, *page 1110*

God promised that Abraham's family would grow and bless all the nations—a promise we share in by faith Genesis 12:1-3, *page 15* • Genesis 17:1-6, *page 20* • Romans 4:13-25, *page 1287*

God is faithful to keep his promises Genesis 21:1-7, *page 24* • Exodus 2:23-25, *page 67* • Numbers 23:19, *page 183* • Joshua 21:43-45, *page 265* • 1 Kings 8:12-26, *page 385* • Psalm 71:19-22, *page 646* • Hebrews 10:23, *page 1406*

God expects us, as his people, to keep our promises Numbers 30:1-2, *page 192* • Deuteronomy 23:21-23, *page 226* • Ecclesiastes 5:1-7, *page 734* • Matthew 5:33-37, *page 1076*

God promises never to leave his people Deuteronomy 31:6-8, *page 234* • Joshua 1:1-9, *page 242* • Hebrews 13:5-6, *page 1409*

God promised to send his Holy Spirit to us Joel 2:28-32, *page 990* • Luke 24:49, *page 1196* • Acts 2:1-21, *page 1237* • Ephesians 1:12-14, *page 1346*

Jesus promised that the Father would hear and answer our prayers Matthew 6:5-8, *page 1076* • Matthew 7:7-11, *page 1078*

Jesus promised eternal life to those who follow him John 5:24-29, *page 1207* • John 11:25-26, *page 1217*

The New Testament promises that Jesus will return John 14:1-3, *page 1222* • Acts 1:10-11, *page 1236* • 1 Thessalonians 5:1-11, *page 1372*

We need to keep hold of God's promises, no matter what happens Romans 4:20-22, *page 1287* • Hebrews 11:1-40, *page 1407*

All God's promises are fulfilled in Jesus 2 Corinthians 1:20, *page 1325*

▶ *See* ***Covenant****, page 19;* ***The new covenant****, page 861;* ***Faithfulness****, page 1307.*

Prophecy *see also Teaching*

Prophecy is sharing a word from God that speaks directly into some specific situation, need, or hope. In the Old Testament, it was a gift that was restricted to anointed and accepted prophets, for it operated at a national level, calling both king and nation back to God's covenant. In the New Testament, it takes on a wider role of encouragement and so is a gift that is available to all God's people.

> *Let love be your highest goal! But you should also desire the special abilities the Spirit gives—especially the ability to prophesy. For if you have the ability to speak in tongues, you will be talking only to God, since people won't be able to understand you. You will be speaking by the power of the Spirit, but it will all be mysterious. But one who prophesies strengthens others, encourages them, and comforts them. – 1 Corinthians 14:1-3, page 1317*

It was the Holy Spirit who enabled people to prophesy Numbers 11:24-29, *page 168* • 1 Samuel 10:5-11, *page 315* • 1 Samuel 19:18-24, *page 328* • Ezekiel 2:1-5, *page 901*

Prophecy reveals a message from God Deuteronomy 18:17-18, *page 221* • 2 Samuel 23:2, *page 369* • 2 Chronicles 24:20, *page 506* • 1 Peter 1:10-11, *page 1420* • 2 Peter 1:20-21, *page 1428*

Prophecy should always be tested Deuteronomy 18:21-22, *page 221* • 1 Corinthians 14:29, *page 1318* • 1 Thessalonians 5:19-22, *page 1373* • 1 John 4:1-3, *page 1436*

God's people often refused to listen to his prophets and brought judgment on themselves 2 Kings 17:13-20, *page 432* • Jeremiah 7:22-29, *page 833* • Matthew 5:11-12, *page 1075* • Matthew 23:29-36, *page 1106*

True prophecy comes from God, not our own thoughts or imaginations Jeremiah 23:25-32, *page 852* • Ezekiel 13:1-12, *page 910*

Prophecy is a gift of the Holy Spirit Acts 2:17-18, *page 1238* • Acts 19:1-6, *page 1266* • Romans 12:6, *page 1296* • 1 Corinthians 12:7-11, *page 1315* • 1 Corinthians 14:1-5, 29-33, *page 1317*

Prophecy was used regularly in the early church to bring encouragement or direction Acts 11:27-30, *page 1254* • Acts 13:1-3, *page 1255* • Acts 15:32, *page 1260* • Acts 21:4-14, *page 1270* • Romans 12:4-6, *page 1296* • 1 Corinthians 12:10, 27-28, *page 1315* • 1 Corinthians 14:29-33, *page 1318* • Ephesians 4:11-13, *page 1350*

Paul encouraged Christians to seek the gift of prophecy 1 Corinthians 14:1, 39, *page 1317*

We should not make light of prophecy 1 Thessalonians 5:20, *page 1373*

▶ *See* ***Prophecies about Christ****, page 806;* ***Prophecy in the Old Testament****, page 903;* ***False prophecy****, page 911;* ***Prophetic imagery****, page 1039;* ***Prophecies of the Messiah****, page 1044;* ***Prophecy in the New Testament****, page 1318.*

Prosperity *see Money*

Purity *see Holiness; Integrity*

Racism *see Discrimination*

Rapture *see Jesus Christ: his return*

Reconciliation *see also Peace*

Reconciliation—the restoration of broken relationship—is the consequence of being made right with God through faith in Jesus and his death on the cross. This reconciliation is first and foremost with God, who now becomes our heavenly Father; but it is also with everyone else who has been reconciled to him, of whatever race or background. Every barrier has now been broken down, and that must be reflected in the way we live.

> *This means that anyone who belongs to Christ has become a new person. The old life is gone; a new life has begun! And all of this is a gift from God, who brought us back to himself through Christ. And God has given us this task of reconciling people to him. For God was in Christ, reconciling the world to himself, no longer counting people's sins against them. And he gave us this wonderful message of reconciliation. So we are Christ's ambassadors; God is making his appeal through us. We speak for Christ when we plead, "Come back to God!" For God made Christ, who never sinned, to be the offering for our sin, so that we could be made right with God through Christ. – 2 Corinthians 5:17-21, page 1328*

Reconciliation is about becoming God's friend Romans 5:6-11, *page 1287* • James 2:21-23, *page 1414*

It was God who took the initiative in reconciliation Romans 5:10-11, *page 1287* • 2 Corinthians 5:18-19, *page 1328* • Colossians 1:20-22, *page 1363*

Reconciliation is about becoming not just God's friends but also God's children Romans 8:14-17, *page 1291* • Galatians 3:26–4:7, *page 1341* • Hebrews 2:11-13, *page 1398*

Creation itself, which has been ruined by human sin, will be reconciled to God at the End Romans 8:19-21, *page 1291* • Revelation 21:1-27, *page 1465*

Christians have the privilege of sharing with others the message of reconciliation with God 2 Corinthians 5:18-20, *page 1328*

Reconciliation means there can be no barriers between God's children, no matter their background Galatians 3:28-29, *page 1341* • Ephesians 2:11-22, *page 1347*

Reconciliation was brought about through Jesus' death on the cross Ephesians 2:14-16, *page 1348* • Colossians 1:15-20, *page 1362*

Even those who are far away from God can be reconciled Ephesians 2:11-13, *page 1347* • Colossians 1:19-22, *page 1363*

As Christians, when we face differences and disagreements with others, we should seek reconciliation quickly Matthew 5:23-24, *page 1076* • Philippians 4:2-3, *page 1359*

▶ *See* ***The death of Jesus****, page 1114;* ***Redemption****, page 1136;* ***Justification****, page 1288;* ***Christ's resurrection and ours****, page 1320;* ***Reconciliation****, page 1328.*

Redemption *see also Freedom*

Redemption is all about paying a price—a ransom—to get something back or set something free. Because people are so precious to God, there is no price he will not pay to get them back from their slavery to sin—even the death of his own Son, Jesus, on the cross. This was foreshadowed in the Old Testament in Israel's great redemption from slavery in Egypt.

> *"Whoever wants to be a leader among you must be your servant, and whoever wants to be first among you must be the slave of everyone else. For even the Son of Man came not to be served but to serve others and to give his life as a ransom for many." – Mark 10:43-45, page 1137*

God redeemed Israel from slavery in Egypt because he loved them Exodus 6:1-8, *page 72* • Deuteronomy 7:7-8, *page 210* • 2 Samuel 7:22-24, *page 350*

The principle of redemption was written into Israel's Law so they would never forget God's redemption of them Exodus 13:11-16, *page 81* • Leviticus 25:25-55, *page 147* • Ruth 2:17–4:12, *page 301*

We can know God as our Redeemer Job 19:25-27, *page 580* • Psalm 19:14, *page 613* • Isaiah 43:1-4, *page 794* • Isaiah 48:17-18, *page 801* • Isaiah 54:1-8, *page 807* • Isaiah 63:15-16, *page 816*

The prophets looked forward to God's coming great redemption Isaiah 35:8-10, *page 784* • Isaiah 40:1-11, *page 789* • Isaiah 61:1-11, *page 814* • Jeremiah 31:7-14, *page 860* • Zechariah 10:6-12, *page 1045*

Jesus' death brings redemption and forgiveness Mark 10:45, *page 1137* • Romans 3:23-24, *page 1286* • Galatians 3:13, *page 1340* • Ephesians 1:3-7, *page 1346* • Colossians 1:13-14, *page 1362* • 1 Peter 1:18-20, *page 1421*

Redemption frees us from the consequences of sin Romans 8:1-2, *page 1290* • Galatians 3:13-14, *page 1340* • Colossians 1:13-14, *page 1362* • Titus 2:14, *page 1391* • Hebrews 9:13-15, *page 1404*

Redemption will be completed when Jesus returns Romans 8:18-25, *page 1291*

Because we have been redeemed, we should honor God in how we live 1 Corinthians 6:18-20, *page 1310*

▸ *See **The death of Jesus**, page 1114; **Redemption**, page 1136; **Justification**, page 1288; **Christ's resurrection and ours**, page 1320; **Reconciliation**, page 1328.*

Regeneration *see Birth*

Regrets *see Past*

Relationships *see also Family; Friendship; Marriage; Submission*

God is a God of relationship; even his own being (the Trinity) speaks of loving and committed relationships. It should not surprise us, therefore, that he wants us to have both a relationship with him and good relationships with one another.

Do all that you can to live in peace with everyone. – Romans 12:18, page 1297

Godly relationships always put others first Ruth 1:1-18, *page 299* • 1 Samuel 18:1-4, *page 326* • 1 Samuel 19:1-7, *page 328* • 1 Samuel 20:1-42, *page 328*

We should maintain good relationships with other believers Matthew 5:23-24, *page 1076* • Matthew 18:15-17, *page 1097* • Romans 12:18, *page 1297* • Romans 14:1-19, *page 1298* • Ephesians 4:1-4, *page 1349*

Our relationship with Jesus should take priority over all other relationships Luke 9:57-62, *page 1171*

Our relationship with God is made possible through faith in Jesus John 1:12-13, *page 1199* • John 14:19-21, *page 1223*

Relationships in the church are meant to be so strong and real that we can be described as a body Romans 12:3-5, *page 1296* • 1 Corinthians 12:12-27, *page 1315* • Ephesians 4:3-4, 25, *page 1350* • Colossians 3:12-15, *page 1365*

Our relationships should not compromise our faith 2 Corinthians 6:14-18, *page 1329* • Ephesians 5:3-14, *page 1351*

We are united with all believers in God's family, no matter their background Galatians 3:26-29, *page 1341* • Ephesians 2:11-22, *page 1347*

A willingness to submit to others is the foundation of all good relationships Ephesians 5:21–6:9, *page 1351*

Our relationships should be pure and not self-serving Philippians 2:1-11, *page 1356*

▸ *See **Submission and relationships**, page 1352.*

Renewal

Whenever we sense that the life of God within us—individually or corporately—is not what it once was, we need to experience renewal. God has promised to renew us by his Holy Spirit; but first, we need to recognize our need and ask God to change us and fill us afresh. The ultimate renewal will happen when Jesus returns.

Create in me a clean heart, O God. Renew a loyal spirit within me. Do not banish me from your presence, and don't take your Holy Spirit from me. Restore to me the joy of your salvation, and make me willing to obey you. – Psalm 51:10-12, page 634

God promises to renew those who humble themselves and trust in him 2 Chronicles 7:12-14, *page 489* • Isaiah 40:27-31, *page 790* • Isaiah 57:14-15, *page 810* • Revelation 3:14-22, *page 1450*

God's word can reveal the need for renewal 2 Chronicles 34:14-33, *page 517* • Nehemiah 8:1–9:38, *page 544*

God's word renews us inwardly Psalm 19:7-14, *page 613* • Hebrews 4:12, *page 1400*

Some prayers for renewal Psalm 51:1-19, *page 633* • Psalm 80:14-19, *page 654* • Psalm 85:1-7, *page 656*

One day, creation itself will be renewed Isaiah 65:17-25, *page 819* • Matthew 19:28, *page 1099* • Romans 8:18-21, *page 1291* • Revelation 21:1-27, *page 1465*

God renews us by his Spirit Ezekiel 36:16-27, *page 938* • Ezekiel 37:1-14, *page 939* • Ephesians 4:21-23, *page 1351*

Religious structures and practices sometimes need renewal Matthew 9:14-17, *page 1081*

Renewal often starts in our thinking Romans 12:1-2, *page 1296* • Ephesians 4:21-24, *page 1351*

Renewal is an ongoing process 2 Corinthians 4:16-18, *page 1327* • Colossians 3:5-10, *page 1365*

Renewal is centered in Jesus 2 Corinthians 5:17, *page 1328* • Titus 3:4-7, *page 1391*

Churches sometimes need renewal Revelation 2:1–3:22, *page 1446*

▶ *See **Renewal**, page 939.*

Repentance *see also Confession*

Repentance is about recognizing that we have done wrong and making a decision to change. No matter what we might have said, thought, or done, the Bible assures us that, when we repent, we can and will be forgiven.

You do not desire a sacrifice, or I would offer one. You do not want a burnt offering. The sacrifice you desire is a broken spirit. You will not reject a broken and repentant heart, O God. – Psalm 51:16-17, page 634

Repentance opens the door to forgiveness, no matter how badly we have sinned 2 Samuel 11:1–12:25, *page 352* • 2 Chronicles 33:1-13, *page 515* • Luke 15:11-32, *page 1181* • Acts 9:1-22, *page 1248*

Repentance opens the door to God's blessing 2 Chronicles 7:12-16, *page 489* • Nehemiah 1:5-9, *page 536* • Hosea 14:1-7, *page 985* • Acts 2:37-39, *page 1239* • Acts 3:19-20, *page 1240*

Repentance brings us freedom Psalm 32:1-7, *page 620*

David's prayer of repentance after his sin with Bathsheba Psalm 51:1-19, *page 633*

God calls on us to repent and promises to forgive us if we do Isaiah 55:6-13, *page 808* • Ezekiel 18:30-32, *page 917* • Acts 2:37-39, *page 1239* • Acts 3:17-20, *page 1240* • Acts 17:24-31, *page 1264*

True repentance is reflected in a changed way of living Isaiah 58:1-14, *page 810* • Luke 3:1-14, *page 1156* • Luke 19:1-10, *page 1185* • Acts 19:17-20, *page 1267* • Acts 26:19-20, *page 1276* • Ephesians 4:17-32, *page 1350*

Repentance must be sincere Jeremiah 29:10-14, *page 858* • Joel 2:12-13, *page 989* • 2 Corinthians 7:8-11, *page 1330*

The call to repentance was part of Jesus' message Matthew 4:17, *page 1074* • Luke 5:27-32, *page 1161* • Luke 13:1-5, *page 1177*

Seeing our need of God will lead us to repent Luke 5:31-32, *page 1162*

There is rejoicing in heaven when a sinner repents Luke 15:1-10, *page 1180*

God's kindness is intended to bring us to repentance Romans 2:1-4, *page 1283* • 2 Peter 3:3-9, *page 1429*

Sometimes whole churches need to repent Revelation 2:1-7, 12-17, *page 1446* • Revelation 3:1-6, *page 1449*

▶ See **Repentance**, page 1253; **Faith**, page 1286.

Reputation *see also Character*

Although God wants us to have a good reputation, it is not an end in itself. Some people seek to build a reputation in areas like business, politics, sports, or entertainment (and even the church!) so that people will think well of them and they will become rich or famous. By contrast, God wants his people to have a good reputation so that it reflects well on him and the sort of God he is.

Choose a good reputation over great riches; being held in high esteem is better than silver or gold. – Proverbs 22:1, page 718

It is good to have a reputation for being godly Genesis 6:9, *page 10* • Joshua 6:27, *page 248* • Job 1:1-22, *page 565* • Hebrews 11:1-2, 39, *page 1407*

A bad reputation is always remembered and will follow us Genesis 18:20-21, *page 22* • Proverbs 25:9-10, *page 722* • Jeremiah 23:13-14, *page 851* • Jude 1:6-7, *page 1442*

A good reputation can be built by obeying God's word Deuteronomy 4:1-8, *page 205*

A good reputation is built through integrity and hard work Ruth 2:1-12, *page 300* • Daniel 1:6-20, *page 955* • Daniel 5:8-16, *page 962* • Acts 9:36, *page 1250*

Outward reputation cannot hide from God what is in the heart 1 Samuel 16:1-7, *page 323* • Acts 5:1-11, *page 1242* • Revelation 3:1-3, *page 1449*

Having a good reputation is a valuable asset Proverbs 22:1, *page 718* • Ecclesiastes 7:1, *page 735*

We can sometimes gain a reputation for doing good things yet having wrong motives Matthew 6:1-18, *page 1076* • Matthew 23:1-33, *page 1105*

Christians should have a reputation for faith and love John 13:34-35, *page 1222* • 2 Corinthians 8:16-24, *page 1330* • Colossians 1:3-6, *page 1362* • 1 Thessalonians 1:8-10, *page 1369*

Christian leaders should be well thought of by non-Christians Acts 5:12-13, *page 1242* • 1 Timothy 3:1-7, *page 1380*

Christians should seek to keep a good reputation with others, especially non-Christians Acts 5:12-16, *page 1242* • 2 Corinthians 6:3-7, *page 1328* • Colossians 4:5-6, *page 1366* • 1 Peter 2:12-17, *page 1422*

We should not seek to boost our reputation as an end in itself 2 Corinthians 10:12-18, *page 1332* • Philippians 3:2-14, *page 1358*

▶ See **Integrity**, page 1325.

Resentment *see Anger; Bitterness*

Respect *see also Authority*

Society encourages us to respect those who have done something great, who hold a significant position, or who are worthy of our admiration. But the Bible calls us to treat all people with respect, both in our words and in our actions, for they are all made in the image of God. Our greatest respect, of course, should be for God himself.

Respect everyone, and love the family of believers. Fear God, and respect the king. – 1 Peter 2:17, page 1423

God calls us to respect human life Genesis 9:5-6, *page 12* • Exodus 20:13, *page 90* • Deuteronomy 27:25, *page 229*

God is worthy of our greatest respect Exodus 3:1-6, *page 68* • 1 Samuel 2:12-17, *page 307* • Psalm 29:1-2, *page 618* • Jeremiah 5:20-25, *page 830* • Malachi 1:6-8, *page 1050*

Our parents are worthy of respect Exodus 20:12, *page 90* • Leviticus 19:3, *page 138* • Proverbs 23:22-25, *page 720* • Matthew 15:1-6, *page 1092* • Ephesians 6:1-3, *page 1352*

Employers and employees should respect one another Leviticus 19:13, *page 139* • Deuteronomy 24:14-15, *page 226* • Ephesians

6:5-9, *page 1352* • Colossians 3:22–4:1, *page 1366*

We should respect the elderly Leviticus 19:32, *page 140* • Job 32:4, *page 591* • Proverbs 23:22-25, *page 720* • 1 Timothy 5:1-2, *page 1382*

Leaders should be those who have earned our respect Deuteronomy 1:9-15, *page 201* • Acts 6:1-7, *page 1244* • 1 Timothy 3:1-13, *page 1380*

We should respect God's word Deuteronomy 4:1-2, *page 205* • Nehemiah 8:4-5, *page 544* • Proverbs 30:5-6, *page 727* • Matthew 5:17-19, *page 1075* • Revelation 22:17-19, *page 1467*

Rulers and those in authority should have our respect 1 Samuel 24:1-22, *page 333* • 1 Samuel 26:1-25, *page 335* • Romans 13:1-7, *page 1297*

Husbands and wives should respect each other Ephesians 5:21-33, *page 1351*

We should respect our Christian leaders 1 Thessalonians 5:12-13, *page 1373* • 1 Timothy 5:17-18, *page 1383* • Hebrews 13:17, *page 1410* • 1 Peter 5:5, *page 1425*

We should show respect to all people 1 Peter 2:17, *page 1423*

▶ *See **Respect for those who are older**, page 415; **Authority**, page 1187; **Submission and relationships**, page 1352.*

Responsibility *see also Accountability*

In our modern world, so many people want their rights, but without responsibilities. But God wants us to grow in our sense of responsibility, both to him for how we live our lives, and to others for how we carry out our duties. God will reward those who carry out their responsibilities well.

> *"The master said, 'Well done, my good and faithful servant. You have been faithful in handling this small amount, so now I will give you many more responsibilities. Let's celebrate together!'"*
> *– Matthew 25:23, page 1109*

We are all responsible for caring for God's world Genesis 1:26-28, *page 5* • Exodus 23:10-12, *page 93*

We are all responsible to God for how we live and will one day have to give an account Ecclesiastes 12:13-14, *page 739* • 2 Corinthians 5:10, *page 1327* • Revelation 20:11-15, *page 1465*

We are each responsible to God for our own decisions and actions Jeremiah 31:29-30, *page 862* • Romans 14:1-13, *page 1298* • Galatians 6:4-5, *page 1344* • James 1:13-16, *page 1412*

Responsibility means being faithful with the gifts we have been given Matthew 25:14-30, *page 1109* • Romans 12:6-8, *page 1296*

We are responsible for the well-being of our neighbor Luke 10:25-37, *page 1172* • Romans 13:8-10, *page 1298*

Ignorance does not absolve us from responsibility Luke 12:39-48, *page 1176* • Romans 1:18-20, *page 1283*

We should not make excuses but accept our responsibility to respond to God Luke 14:15-24, *page 1179*

Everyone has a responsibility to turn back to God Acts 2:32-40, *page 1239* • Acts 17:30-31, *page 1264* • Titus 2:11-14, *page 1390*

We are responsible for how our behavior affects others Romans 14:14-23, *page 1298* • 1 Corinthians 8:1-13, *page 1311* • 2 Corinthians 6:3, *page 1328*

We are responsible for earning a living Ephesians 4:28, *page 1351* • 1 Thessalonians 4:11-12, *page 1372* • 2 Thessalonians 3:6-15, *page 1375*

We should take responsibility for our families 1 Timothy 5:8, *page 1383*

▶ *See **Accountability**, page 1258.*

Rest *see also Day of rest; Leisure; Peace*

Most of us lead busy lives these days, which is why it is more important than ever to know how to rest. At Creation, God modeled rest for us, and he commanded a weekly day of rest. But the greatest rest of all comes from knowing him and trusting in his ability to bring things about, rather than merely relying on our own efforts and activity.

> *Jesus said, "Come to me, all of you who are weary and carry heavy burdens, and I will give you rest. Take my yoke upon you. Let me teach you, because I am humble and gentle at heart, and you will*

find rest for your souls. For my yoke is easy to bear, and the burden I give you is light." – Matthew 11:28-30, page 1085

God modeled the importance of rest for us at Creation Genesis 2:1-3, *page 5*

God tells us to rest one day each week Exodus 20:8-11, *page 90* • Exodus 23:12, *page 93* • Deuteronomy 5:12-15, *page 208*

God offers his people a place of rest Exodus 33:14, *page 106* • Job 11:13-20, *page 573* • Isaiah 28:12, *page 776* • Jeremiah 6:16-19, *page 831*

Trusting in God brings rest Psalm 116:1-9, *page 676* • Isaiah 30:15-18, *page 779* • Isaiah 40:28-31, *page 791*

Too much rest and too little work leads to trouble Proverbs 6:9-11, *page 702* • Proverbs 24:30-34, *page 722*

Jesus promised to give us rest from our burdens Matthew 11:28-30, *page 1085*

Jesus wants us to rest sometimes Mark 6:30-31, *page 1129* • Luke 10:38-42, *page 1172*

Rest is a gift of God Hebrews 4:1-11, *page 1399*

Heaven will be a place of rest and reward Revelation 14:13, *page 1459*

▶ *See **Resting in God**, page 676.*

Resurrection

The resurrection of Jesus Christ is the foundation of the Christian faith. It is because of his resurrection that believers can know new life right now. But his resurrection also assures us that one day we too will be raised, when Jesus returns. For both of these reasons, the Resurrection should affect the way we live in the present.

Christ died for our sins, just as the Scriptures said. He was buried, and he was raised from the dead on the third day, just as the Scriptures said. He was seen by Peter and then by the Twelve. After that, he was seen by more than 500 of his followers at one time, most of whom are still alive, though some have died. Then he was seen by James and later by all the apostles. Last of all, as though I had been born at the wrong time, I also saw him. – 1 Corinthians 15:3-8, page 1319

The Messiah's resurrection was prophesied in the Old Testament Psalm 16:10-11, *page 610* • Isaiah 53:10-12, *page 806*

Resurrection of God's people was promised in the Old Testament Daniel 12:1-3, *page 972*

Jesus prophesied he would be raised from the dead Matthew 12:38-40, *page 1087* • Matthew 16:21, *page 1095* • Matthew 17:22-23, *page 1097*

Jesus' resurrection is a historical fact Matthew 28:1-20, *page 1115* • Mark 16:1-20, *page 1147* • Luke 24:1-49, *page 1195* • John 20:1-29, *page 1231* • 1 Corinthians 15:1-8, *page 1319*

At the End, all people will be resurrected, either to eternal life or to judgment John 5:24-30, *page 1207*

Jesus promised to raise his followers on the last day John 6:35-40, *page 1209* • John 11:23-26, *page 1217*

Forgiven through Jesus' death, we are assured through his resurrection that we are now made right with God (justified) Romans 4:25, *page 1287*

Through baptism, we are united with Jesus in his resurrection Romans 6:1-11, *page 1289*

After his resurrection, Jesus returned to heaven, where he is praying for us now Romans 8:34, *page 1292* • Hebrews 7:25, *page 1403*

Jesus' resurrection is the very foundation of Christianity 1 Corinthians 15:12-21, *page 1319*

Our resurrected bodies will be eternal bodies 1 Corinthians 15:51-53, *page 1320*

Jesus' resurrection demonstrates God's incredible power Ephesians 1:19-20, *page 1346* • Ephesians 2:4-7, *page 1347*

The end-time resurrection of all humanity will be followed by God's judgment Revelation 20:11-15, *page 1465*

▶ *See **Christ's resurrection and ours**, page 1320.*

Revenge

When someone harms us or a person who is close to us, it is natural to want to get revenge. Yet the Bible shows us the danger of revenge and warns us that only God has all the facts needed to be able to judge justly. We should therefore trust him and leave judgment in his hands.

Dear friends, never take revenge. Leave that to the righteous anger of God. For the Scriptures say, "I will take revenge; I will pay them back," says the LORD. Instead, "If your enemies are hungry, feed them. If they are thirsty, give them something to drink. In doing this, you will heap burning coals of shame on their heads." Don't let evil conquer you, but conquer evil by doing good.
– Romans 12:19-21, page 1297

God's people should not seek revenge Genesis 4:1-16, *page 8* • Leviticus 19:18, *page 139* • Romans 12:19, *page 1297*

Plotting revenge never has a good outcome, and events invariably snowball Genesis 4:23-24, page 8 • Judges 15:1-17, *page 288* • 2 Samuel 3:22-39, *page 345* • 2 Samuel 13:1-38, *page 355* • Esther 5:9–7:10, *page 558*

God provided cities of refuge to which accused people could flee for a fair trial and not be subject to revenge Deuteronomy 19:1-10, *page 221*

God promises to avenge where it is needed, and he will do it justly Deuteronomy 32:35-43, *page 237* • Hebrews 10:26-31, *page 1406*

We should leave our desire for revenge in God's hands Proverbs 20:22, *page 717* • Proverbs 24:29, *page 722* • Romans 12:19-21, *page 1297*

Rather than seek revenge, Christians should seek to bless Matthew 5:38-42, *page 1076* • Luke 6:27-36, *page 1163* • 1 Thessalonians 5:15, *page 1373* • 1 Peter 3:9-12, *page 1423*

Jesus is our example of how to not seek revenge Luke 23:32-34, *page 1194* • 1 Peter 2:21-23, *page 1423*

▶ *See* ***What does the Bible teach about revenge?****, page 193;* ***Vengeance in the Psalms****, page 637.*

Riches *see Money*

Right with God, How do I get? *see Justification*

Righteousness *see Justification*

Sabbath *see Day of rest*

Sadness *see Depression; Grief*

Salvation *see also Justification; Reconciliation; Redemption*

God is a God of salvation—a God who has a plan to save his people when their sin and stupidity lead them the wrong way. This plan of salvation is revealed increasingly throughout the Bible's story, climaxing in God's sending of his own Son, Jesus, to be the Savior of the world, and culminating in his making all things new at the End and restoring them to how he planned them to be.

"There is no other God but me, a righteous God and Savior. There is none but me. Let all the world look to me for salvation! For I am God; there is no other." – Isaiah 45:21-22, page 798

In the Old Testament, God is frequently seen as the God of salvation Genesis 49:18, *page 61* • 2 Samuel 22:47-51, *page 369* • Psalm 27:1-14, *page 617* • Psalm 85:1-7, *page 656* • Psalm 91:1-16, *page 660* • Isaiah 25:1-9, *page 773* • Isaiah 63:1-5, *page 816* • Jeremiah 3:22-23, *page 826* • Habakkuk 3:1-19, *page 1026*

Israel's greatest moment of salvation was the exodus from slavery in Egypt Exodus 3:7-17, *page 68* • Exodus 12:31-42 • Exodus 14:1–15:21, *page 81* • Deuteronomy 26:1-10, *page 227* • Joshua 24:14-18, *page 268* • 1 Samuel 12:6-15, *page 317* • Daniel 9:15-19, *page 968* • Acts 7:12-36, *page 1245*

Salvation is about coming out of our slavery and into God's freedom Exodus 20:2, *page 89* • Luke 4:16-21, *page 1159* • Romans 6:20-23, *page 1289* • Galatians 5:1, 13-14, *page 1343* • Colossians 1:13-14, *page 1362*

God often saved Israel from its enemies or individuals from their troubles 2 Kings 19:14-36, *page 437* • 2 Chronicles 18:28-31, *page 500* • Psalm 18:1-50, *page 610* • Psalm 34:1-10, *page 621* • Psalm 46:1-11, *page 630* • Isaiah 12:1-2, *page 761*

Salvation is about being transformed within Psalm 51:10-12, *page 634* • Jeremiah 31:31-34, *page 862* • Ezekiel 36:22-27, *page*

938 • John 3:1-17, *page 1202* • 2 Corinthians 5:17-21, *page 1328* • 1 Peter 1:23, *page 1421*

The coming Messiah would bring God's salvation Isaiah 11:1-16, *page 760* • Isaiah 53:1-12, *page 805* • Isaiah 61:1-9, *page 814* • Matthew 1:18-23, *page 1068* • Luke 1:67-79, *page 1154*

Jesus came to save people from their sin Matthew 1:21, *page 1069* • Luke 2:8-14, *page 1154* • Luke 19:1-10, *page 1185* • John 3:16-17, *page 1203* • Acts 2:22-40, *page 1238* • Titus 2:11-14, *page 1390*

Our salvation needs to be demonstrated in the way we live Luke 19:1-10, *page 1185* • Galatians 5:16-25, *page 1343* • Philippians 2:12-13, *page 1357* • 2 Timothy 2:15-22, *page 1386*

Salvation comes through Jesus alone John 14:1-6, *page 1222* • Acts 2:36-41, *page 1239* • Acts 4:8-12, *page 1240* • Acts 16:25-34, *page 1262*

Salvation comes through Jesus' death on the cross Romans 3:23-28, *page 1286* • Ephesians 1:3-7, *page 1346* • Hebrews 9:11-12, *page 1404* • 1 Peter 1:18-25, *page 1421*

Salvation cannot be earned; it is God's free gift Romans 6:23, *page 1290* • Ephesians 2:1-9, *page 1347* • Titus 3:3-7, *page 1391*

God wants everyone to be saved 1 Timothy 2:1-6, *page 1380* • 2 Peter 3:8-9, *page 1429*

▶ *See **The death of Jesus**, page 1114; **Redemption**, page 1136; **The new birth**, page 1203; **Jesus: the only way to God**, page 1241; **Justification**, page 1288; **Christ's resurrection and ours**, page 1320; **Reconciliation**, page 1328; **Can a Christian lose their salvation?**, page 1401.*

Sanctification *see Holiness*

Satan *see also Demons*

Christians often fall into one of two extremes concerning Satan, God's archenemy: either showing too much interest in him and ascribing too much power to him, or ignoring him completely as if he did not exist. While Satan is real, our focus should not be on him, but on God. Satan's power is limited, for he is only a created being and can do no more than God permits; and one day he will be completely conquered. In the meantime, we should be alert to his major tactics of deceit and temptation.

> *Stay alert! Watch out for your great enemy, the devil. He prowls around like a roaring lion, looking for someone to devour. Stand firm against him, and be strong in your faith. Remember that your family of believers all over the world is going through the same kind of suffering you are.* – 1 Peter 5:8-9, page 1425

Satan tempted Adam and Eve Genesis 3:1-19, *page 6*

Satan is ultimately under God's authority Job 1:6-12, *page 565* • Job 2:1-7, *page 566*

Satan tempted Jesus, but Jesus triumphed Matthew 4:1-11, *page 1073*

God can protect us from Satan Matthew 6:13, *page 1077* • 2 Thessalonians 3:3, *page 1375*

Satan opposes God and his purposes Matthew 13:3-4, 19, *page 1088* • Matthew 16:21-23, *page 1095* • 1 Thessalonians 3:5, *page 1371*

Satan is evil John 8:42-44, *page 1213* • John 10:6-10, *page 1215*

Satan tries to deceive people 2 Corinthians 2:9-11, *page 1326* • 2 Corinthians 11:13-15, *page 1333* • Revelation 12:7-9, *page 1457*

Satan tries to blind people to God's truth 2 Corinthians 4:1-4, *page 1327* • 2 Corinthians 11:3, *page 1332*

We should stand against Satan and his demons with the spiritual weapons God supplies Ephesians 6:10-18, *page 1352*

Jesus destroyed Satan's work by his death on the cross Colossians 2:15, *page 1364* • 1 John 3:7-8, *page 1436*

Believers have the authority to resist Satan James 4:7-10, *page 1416*

Satan accuses believers but can be overcome by our testimony Revelation 12:10-12, *page 1457*

Satan is ultimately a defeated enemy Revelation 20:7-10, *page 1464*

▶ *See **Satan**, page 566; **The origins of Satan**, page 928; **Spiritual warfare**, page 1353.*

Scripture *see Bible*

Second coming of Christ *see Jesus Christ: his return*

Self-control *see also Discipline*

Many people like to control others; but the Bible tells us that the only thing we should be seeking to control is ourselves. God wants us to be in command of our emotions, desires, behavior, and reactions, and he has put his Holy Spirit within us as a resource to help us do this.

> *Better to be patient than powerful; better to have self-control than to conquer a city. – Proverbs 16:32, page 713*

Failure to control our emotions can lead to disastrous results Genesis 4:1-16, *page 8* • 2 Samuel 11:1-27, *page 352* • 2 Samuel 13:1-39, *page 355* • Matthew 14:1-11, *page 1091* • Romans 1:24-32, *page 1283*

We need to control ourselves sexually 2 Samuel 13:1-22, *page 355* • Matthew 5:27-30, *page 1076* • 1 Corinthians 6:18-20, *page 1310* • 1 Corinthians 7:1-9, *page 1310* • 1 Thessalonians 4:1-8, *page 1371*

We can help to keep our thoughts clean by letting our minds be renewed Psalm 101:2-5, *page 664* • Romans 12:1-2, *page 1296* • Ephesians 4:17-24, *page 1350*

We need to control our speech Psalm 141:3-4, *page 690* • James 3:1-12, *page 1415*

Wise people control their anger Proverbs 15:18, *page 712* • Proverbs 29:11, *page 727* • Ephesians 4:25-27, *page 1351* • James 1:19-21, *page 1412*

Discipline and training are important parts of self-control 1 Corinthians 9:24-27, *page 1313* • 1 Timothy 4:7-10, *page 1382* • 2 Peter 1:5-11, *page 1427*

Self-control should be a growing characteristic of the Christian life Galatians 5:16-26, *page 1343* • 2 Peter 1:3-11, *page 1427*

Being filled with the Holy Spirit enables us to be self-controlled Ephesians 5:15-18, *page 1351*

Christian leaders especially must exercise self-control 1 Timothy 3:1-5, *page 1380* • Titus 1:6-8, *page 1389*

Self-denial *see also Fasting; Humility*

We live in a world where we are surrounded by advertisements, all telling us what we cannot live without or what we need more of to make life better. By contrast, Jesus said that the real way to discover fullness of life is to deny ourselves—learning how to say no to the wrong things and the unhelpful or unneeded things in order to say yes to the right things.

> *He [Jesus] said to the crowd, "If any of you wants to be my follower, you must give up your own way, take up your cross daily, and follow me. If you try to hang on to your life, you will lose it. But if you give up your life for my sake, you will save it." – Luke 9:23-24, page 1169*

We sometimes have to deny ourselves for the sake of others Ruth 2:8-12, *page 300* • Esther 4:13-16, *page 558* • Romans 14:14-22, *page 1298* • Philippians 2:3-8, *page 1356*

Putting God first will sometimes mean saying no to things Daniel 1:1-20, *page 955* • Luke 1:11-17, *page 1151* • Hebrews 11:24-26, *page 1408*

Fasting is an opportunity for self-denial in order to seek God in prayer Daniel 10:1-3, *page 969* • Matthew 4:1-11, *page 1073* • Acts 13:1-3, *page 1255*

Denying ourselves is part of following Jesus Matthew 16:24-28, *page 1096* • Luke 9:23-26, *page 1169* • Acts 21:10-13, *page 1270* • Philippians 3:7-11, *page 1358*

Jesus denied himself for our sake Matthew 26:36-39, *page 1111* • 2 Corinthians 8:9, *page 1330* • Philippians 2:5-8, *page 1356*

Jesus promised that any sacrifices we make for him will be more than made up for in the life to come Mark 10:23-31, *page 1136*

Self-denial helps prepare us for eternity John 12:24-25, *page 1220*

Self-denial is about saying no to our old way of life Romans 8:12-14, *page 1291* • Galatians 5:24-25, *page 1343* •

Colossians 3:5-15, *page 1365* • Titus 2:1-14, *page 1390*

We sometimes have to deny ourselves for the sake of the gospel 1 Corinthians 9:19-27, *page 1312*

▶ See **Does fasting have any value?**, page 1042; **Discipleship and the cross**, page 1095; **Life from death**, page 1219.

Self-esteem

God wants us to have a proper sense of our personal worth and dignity, for we are all created in his image. However, our self-respect should be rooted in who we are in Christ, not in the opinion of others, whose judgments can be fickle, partial, or simply wrong. Equally, God does not want us to think of ourselves so highly that we become arrogant.

> *Because of the privilege and authority God has given me, I give each of you this warning: Don't think you are better than you really are. Be honest in your evaluation of yourselves, measuring yourselves by the faith God has given us. – Romans 12:3, page 1296*

We are made in God's image, and he took special care over creating each of us Genesis 1:26-27, *page 5* • Genesis 5:1-2, *page 9* • Psalm 139:1-18, *page 689* • Isaiah 64:8, *page 817* • Jeremiah 1:4-5, *page 822*

Our circumstances and others' attitudes can undermine our self-esteem Exodus 3:1-11, *page 68* • Exodus 4:1-17, *page 68* • Judges 6:1-15, *page 276* • Ruth 1:1-21, *page 299*

Our self-esteem should not be based on external appearances 1 Samuel 16:6-7, *page 323* • Matthew 23:1-12, *page 1105* • 1 Peter 3:3-4, *page 1423*

Our self-esteem should be rooted primarily in our relationship with God 2 Samuel 7:18-29, *page 349* • Jeremiah 9:23-24, *page 836* • John 13:2-5, *page 1221* • 1 Corinthians 1:30-31, *page 1304* • 2 Corinthians 5:1-5, *page 1327*

Having a proper self-esteem means we will not overestimate ourselves or our abilities Job 38:1–42:6, *page 595* • Proverbs 27:2, *page 724* • Romans 12:1-3, *page 1296* • 2 Corinthians 10:12, 18, *page 1332* • Galatians 6:3-5, *page 1343*

God places great value on us, and we are precious to him Psalm 8:3-5, *page 605* • Isaiah 43:1-4, *page 794* • Daniel 10:19, *page 970* • Matthew 6:25-34, *page 1078* • Matthew 10:29-31, *page 1084*

We should remember that anything that is good about us comes from God Psalm 16:1-2, *page 609* • 2 Corinthians 11:16-30, *page 1333*

We should never forget we are sinners saved solely by God's grace Isaiah 6:1-7, *page 755* • Romans 3:23-26, *page 1286* • 1 Corinthians 15:3-10, *page 1319* • 1 Timothy 1:15-17, *page 1379*

God wants us to have a proper self-esteem Matthew 22:34-39, *page 1104* • Ephesians 5:29, *page 1352*

We should respect our body and treat it properly, remembering it is God's temple Romans 6:12-14, *page 1289* • 1 Corinthians 6:18-20, *page 1310*

When we have healthy self-esteem, we are free to esteem others and not put them down 1 Corinthians 12:22-26, *page 1316* • Galatians 6:1-3, *page 1343* • Philippians 2:3-5, *page 1356*

▶ See **Abba**, page 1144; **Handling failure**, page 1232; **Confidence**, page 1399.

Selfishness *see also Ambition*

There is something within us all that veers toward selfishness at times—making life comfortable for us even at the expense of others. But for us as Christians, God, not "self," is meant to be at the center of our lives, which is why the Bible sees selfishness as sin and urges us to increasingly think of ourselves less and think of others more.

> *Don't be selfish; don't try to impress others. Be humble, thinking of others as better than yourselves. Don't look out only for your own interests, but take an interest in others, too. You must have the same attitude that Christ Jesus had. – Philippians 2:3-5, page 1356*

BASIC TRUTHS • *page 1588*

Selfishness causes us to think only of ourselves Genesis 4:8-9, *page 8* • Genesis 13:5-13, *page 16* • Judges 21:24-25, *page 297* • Philippians 2:19-21, *page 1357*

Selfishness makes us forget God Deuteronomy 8:11-18, *page 211* • Haggai 1:2-11, *page 1034* • Malachi 1:6-14, *page 1050* • Romans 1:18-32, *page 1283*

God cannot bless selfishness and ultimately brings his judgment on it Proverbs 21:13, *page 718* • Amos 6:1-7, *page 998* • Matthew 25:31-46, *page 1109*

Selfishness causes us to break the second great commandment Matthew 22:34-40, *page 1104* • John 13:34, *page 1222*

Selfishness leads us to ignore the needs of others Matthew 25:41-43, *page 1109* • Luke 16:19-31, *page 1182* • Galatians 6:7-10, *page 1344*

We should not be selfish with our resources Luke 12:13-21, *page 1175* • Acts 2:42-47, *page 1239* • Acts 4:32-37, *page 1242* • Hebrews 13:15-16, *page 1410*

We should not be selfish with our money Acts 5:1-11, *page 1242* • 2 Corinthians 8:1–9:15, *page 1330* • 1 Timothy 6:17-19, *page 1383*

Generous giving helps us deal with our selfishness Acts 20:35, *page 1269* • 2 Corinthians 9:6-15, *page 1331*

We should look out for the needs of others and not just our own needs 1 Corinthians 10:23-24, *page 1314* • Galatians 6:2-3, *page 1343* • Philippians 2:3-11, *page 1356*

Selfishness undermines the very heart of the gospel 2 Corinthians 5:14-15, *page 1328*

Selfishness is an expression of sin Galatians 5:19-21, *page 1343* • 2 Timothy 3:1-5, *page 1386*

Selfishness leads to other sins James 3:13-16, *page 1415*

▶ *See **The Absalom spirit**, page 358; **Unity**, page 686; **Teamwork**, page 734; **What you sow you reap**, page 1004.*

Self-pity

It's very easy to fall into self-pity. All it takes is a change in circumstances or some personal loss or disappointment—real or perceived—and we can quickly find ourselves thinking, "Poor me!" The Bible encourages us to focus on God at such times, remembering that our lives are in his hands and that nothing gets past him without his knowledge and permission. If something has come our way, then God ultimately means it for our good. Self-pity often prevents us from seeing what that good is.

> *This change of plans greatly upset Jonah, and he became very angry. So he complained to the LORD about it: "Didn't I say before I left home that you would do this, LORD? That is why I ran away to Tarshish! I knew that you are a merciful and compassionate God, slow to get angry and filled with unfailing love. You are eager to turn back from destroying people. Just kill me now, LORD! I'd rather be dead than alive if what I predicted will not happen." The LORD replied, "Is it right for you to be angry about this?" – Jonah 4:1-4, page 1009*

Self-pity can sometimes blind us to our own sin Genesis 4:8-14, *page 8* • 1 Kings 21:1-7, *page 407* • 2 Corinthians 7:8-10, *page 1330*

Remembering that God works everything together for good can help us deal with self-pity Genesis 50:14-20, *page 63* • Jeremiah 29:10-14, *page 858* • Romans 8:28-39, *page 1292*

God does not let his servants sit in self-pity but leads them on to the next step Exodus 4:10-17, *page 69* • 1 Kings 19:1-18, *page 404* • Jonah 1:1–2:10, *page 1007* • John 21:15-19, *page 1233*

Things not working out as we wanted can lead to self-pity Numbers 14:1-12, *page 169* • 2 Kings 20:1-3, *page 438* • Job 3:1-26, *page 567* • Job 6:1-13, *page 569* • Jonah 4:1-11, *page 1009*

Envy of others can lead to self-pity Psalm 73:1-14, *page 646*

Understanding that we are called to a life of self-denial and not comfort helps us deal with self-pity Matthew 10:29-39, *page 1084* • Matthew 16:24-26, *page 1096* • Luke 14:25-33, *page 1179*

Getting over-busy can lead to self-pity Luke 10:38-42, *page 1172*

Indulging in self-pity means we are elevating self to the most important place, rather than having a humble opinion of ourselves Romans 12:1-3, *page 1296* • Philippians 2:4-11, *page 1356*

Learning to give thanks in every situation can help us deal with self-pity Ephesians 5:18-20, *page 1351* • 1 Thessalonians 5:15-18, *page 1373*

▶ See ***Trusting God when we cannot see the way ahead***, *page 57;* ***God intended it all for good***, *page 62;* ***Suffering: Why do bad things happen to good people?***, *page 567;* ***Why do bad things happen in life?***, *page 1025;* ***Handling failure***, *page 1232.*

Service

Serving is often looked down on in the world today, but it is something that God esteems highly. He modeled its importance for us in the life of Jesus, who came as the promised faithful Servant of God and who constantly served others in their need, even to the point of death. Followers of Jesus are called to follow his example.

> *For you have been called to live in freedom, my brothers and sisters. But don't use your freedom to satisfy your sinful nature. Instead, use your freedom to serve one another in love. For the whole law can be summed up in this one command: "Love your neighbor as yourself." – Galatians 5:13-14, page 1343*

The first call on our lives is to serve God Genesis 17:1, *page 20* • Deuteronomy 6:1-13, *page 208* • Joshua 24:14-24, *page 268* • Matthew 4:8-10, *page 1073* • Luke 16:13, *page 1182*

God's people are often described as his servants Genesis 26:23-24, *page 32* • Numbers 12:5-8, *page 168* • 1 Kings 8:22-30, *page 386* • 2 Corinthians 4:5, *page 1327* • 2 Peter 1:1, *page 1427* • Revelation 22:1-5, *page 1467*

God blesses those who serve well Genesis 39:1-6, *page 49* • Ruth 2:1-17, *page 300* • 1 Samuel 16:14-21, *page 324* • Matthew 25:14-30, *page 1109* • John 12:26, *page 1220*

Isaiah foresaw that the Messiah would come as God's ideal Servant Isaiah 42:1-4, *page 793* • Isaiah 49:1-6, *page 801* • Isaiah 50:4-9, *page 803* • Isaiah 52:13–53:12, *page 805*

Jesus came to serve Matthew 12:15-21, *page 1086* • Mark 10:35-45, *page 1137* • Luke 22:24-27, *page 1191* • John 13:1-17, *page 1221* • Philippians 2:3-11, *page 1356*

Christian leaders are especially called to serve Matthew 20:25-28, *page 1101* • 1 Peter 5:1-5, *page 1425*

In serving others, we are serving Jesus Matthew 25:31-46, *page 1109* • Mark 9:38-41, *page 1135*

We should not expect a reward for serving; we should simply recognize it as our duty Luke 17:7-10, *page 1182* • 1 Corinthians 9:13-19, *page 1312*

Serving is a spiritual gift Romans 12:6-9, *page 1296* • 1 Corinthians 12:27-31, *page 1316* • 1 Peter 4:10-11, *page 1424*

We are called to serve one another Galatians 5:13-15, *page 1343* • Hebrews 6:10, *page 1400* • 1 Peter 4:10, *page 1424*

We should always work as though we were serving God not people Ephesians 6:5-9, *page 1352* • Colossians 3:22-25, *page 1366*

▶ See ***Serving one another***, *page 461;* ***Serving God in our work***, *page 956;* ***Service***, *page 1424.*

Sex *see also Adultery; Homosexuality; Lust; Marriage*

The Bible tells us that sex is a wonderful gift from God; but it also warns that, not used properly, sex can have dangerous outcomes. The only proper place for sex, it insists, is in the faithful relationship of marriage between one man and one woman. Anything else both harms us and disappoints God. But if we fail in the area of sexual relationships, the Bible assures us that God can forgive in this area as much as in any other.

> *God created human beings in his own image. In the image of God he created them; male and female he created them. Then God blessed them and said, "Be fruitful and multiply. Fill the earth and govern it. Reign over the fish in the sea, the birds in the sky, and all the animals that scurry along the ground." – Genesis 1:27-28, page 5*

Sex and intimacy in marriage are God's gift to a husband and a wife Genesis 1:27-28, *page 5* • Genesis 2:22-25, *page 6* • Proverbs 5:15-21, *page 701* • Song of Songs 4:9-16, *page 743* • Hebrews 13:4, *page 1409*

Sexual intercourse joins a couple spiritually Genesis 2:24, *page 6* • Matthew 19:4-6, *page 1099* • 1 Corinthians 6:12-20, *page 1309*

God hates and forbids sexual abuse Genesis 19:1-29, *page 22* • Leviticus 18:1-30, *page 138* • Deuteronomy 22:13-30, *page 224*

Sexual relationships outside of marriage invariably lead to trouble Genesis 34:1-31, *page 42* • 2 Samuel 11:1-27, *page 352* • 2 Samuel 13:1-39, *page 355* • Proverbs 6:20-35, *page 702*

We should take all steps possible to avoid situations of sexual temptation Genesis 39:6-12, *page 49* • Matthew 5:27-30, *page 1076* • 1 Corinthians 6:18-20, *page 1310*

If we fail sexually, we can still find God's forgiveness 2 Samuel 12:1-25, *page 354* • Psalm 51:1-19, *page 633* • John 8:1-11, *page 1211* • 1 John 1:9-10, *page 1433*

Sex within marriage is meant to be a delight Song of Songs 3:1-5, *page 743* • Song of Songs 4:1-16, *page 743* • Song of Songs 7:1-13, *page 745*

Staying unmarried and sexually abstinent is a very real possibility for believers Matthew 19:1-12, *page 1098* • 1 Corinthians 7:25-38, *page 1310*

Sexual immorality has no place in the Christian life Romans 13:13, *page 1298* • 1 Corinthians 6:9-20, *page 1309* • 2 Corinthians 12:20-21, *page 1335* • Galatians 5:19-21, *page 1343* • Ephesians 5:1-14, *page 1351* • Colossians 3:1-10, *page 1365* • 1 Thessalonians 4:1-8, *page 1371*

A husband and wife should seek to satisfy each other's sexual desires 1 Corinthians 7:3-5, *page 1310*

▶ *See* ***Sexuality****, page 742.*

Shame *see Embarrassment*

Sharing our faith *see Witnessing*

Sickness *see Suffering*

Sin *see also Salvation*

The Bible describes sin in a number of ways: disobeying God, falling short of his standards, rebelling against him, acting independently. Sin spoils both our lives and our relationship with God. But God himself has made provision for dealing with our sin: the death of Jesus on the cross—foreshadowed by all the sacrifices of the Old Testament, which in themselves could achieve nothing—is God's way of paying for our sin. Through faith in Jesus, all sin can be forgiven, and we can be given a fresh start.

> *If we claim we have no sin, we are only fooling ourselves and not living in the truth. But if we confess our sins to him, he is faithful and just to forgive us our sins and to cleanse us from all wickedness. If we claim we have not sinned, we are calling God a liar and showing that his word has no place in our hearts. My dear children, I am writing this to you so that you will not sin. But if anyone does sin, we have an advocate who pleads our case before the Father. He is Jesus Christ, the one who is truly righteous. He himself is the sacrifice that atones for our sins—and not only our sins but the sins of all the world. – 1 John 1:8–2:2, page 1433*

Sin separates us from God and ultimately ends in death Genesis 2:15-17, *page 5* • Genesis 3:1-24, *page 6* • Deuteronomy 30:15-18, *page 233* • Romans 6:20-23, *page 1289* • Romans 8:12-13, *page 1291* • Galatians 6:7-8, *page 1344*

Sin offends God's holiness and makes him rightly angry Genesis 18:20–19:29, *page 22* • Deuteronomy 9:18-29, *page 212* • Jeremiah 4:3-4, *page 827* • Romans 1:18-27, *page 1283* • Romans 2:1-8, *page 1283* • Ephesians 2:1-3, *page 1347*

All sin is ultimately sin against God and not just other people Genesis 39:2-9, *page 49* • Numbers 16:1-11, *page 173* • 2 Samuel 12:1-10, *page 354* • Psalm 51:1-4, *page 633* • Luke 15:11-21, *page 1181* • Acts 5:1-4, *page 1242*

We should humbly confess our sins to God and repent of them Leviticus 5:5-6, *page 121* • Ezra 9:5-15, *page 532* • Psalm 51:1-10, *page 633* • Matthew 4:17, *page 1074* • Acts 2:37-39, *page 1239* • 1 John 1:8-9, *page 1433*

Blood has to be shed for sin to be forgiven Leviticus 17:11, *page 137* • Romans 3:23-26, *page 1286* • Hebrews 9:18-22, *page 1404* • Revelation 1:4-5, *page 1445*

Everyone has sinned in some way 1 Kings 8:46, *page 387* • Psalm 106:6, *page 669* • Romans 3:9, 23, *page 1285* • Romans 5:12-19, *page 1288*

God can wash away all our sin and cleanse our consciences Psalm 51:1-7, *page 633* • Isaiah 1:18, *page 749* • Zechariah 13:1, *page 1047* • Titus 2:11-14, *page 1390* • Hebrews 9:13-14, *page 1404* • Hebrews 10:19-22, *page 1406*

God himself provides atonement for our sin Isaiah 6:1-7, *page 755* • Isaiah 53:10-11, *page 806* • Acts 2:22-23, *page 1238* • Romans 3:23-26, *page 1286* • Ephesians 1:3-7, *page 1346*

Forgiving sin was foundational to Jesus' ministry Matthew 1:20-21, *page 1069* • Mark 2:1-12, *page 1120* • Luke 23:32-34, *page 1194* • John 8:1-11, *page 1211*

Jesus, God's sinless Son, paid the price for our sin on the cross and set us free Romans 3:21-26, *page 1286* • Romans 5:6-11, *page 1287* • Colossians 2:13-15, *page 1364* • 1 Peter 1:18-19, *page 1421* • 1 Peter 2:22-24, *page 1423* • Revelation 1:4-7, *page 1445* • Revelation 7:13-14, *page 1454*

Jesus' death frees us from sin's power Romans 6:1-23, *page 1289* • Romans 7:14-25, *page 1290* • Romans 8:1-2, *page 1290* • Galatians 5:1, *page 1343* • 1 John 3:9, *page 1436*

Becoming a Christian doesn't mean we won't still sin; but when we do sin, we should seek the cleansing of the Cross quickly Romans 7:21-25, *page 1290* • 1 John 2:1-2, *page 1433*

▸ *See* ***Sin****, page 387;* ***Is there anything God won't forgive?****, page 633;* ***Redemption****, page 1136;* ***Repentance****, page 1253;* ***Justification****, page 1288;* ***Does it matter if I sin?****, page 1289;* ***Reconciliation****, page 1328;* ***How can I be sure God has forgiven me?****, page 1433.*

Singing *see Music*

Singleness

People can be single for various reasons. They may have been married and lost their spouse through death or divorce, or they may have never been married through either choice or circumstances. Whatever the reason, singles need to know that God loves them no less than married couples, and the church needs to ensure that there is a key place for them in its life. After all, its founder was himself single.

> *I wish everyone were single, just as I am. Yet each person has a special gift from God, of one kind or another. – 1 Corinthians 7:7, page 1310*

In the Bible, singleness is not a higher calling; both marriage and singleness can equally be blessed Genesis 2:18-25, *page 6* • 1 Corinthians 7:25-28, *page 1310*

God cares for those who are alone Deuteronomy 10:17-18, *page 213* • Psalm 68:5-6, *page 642* • Jeremiah 49:11, *page 880*

God commands his people to show particular concern for those who are alone and unable to provide for themselves Deuteronomy 14:28-29, *page 217* • Deuteronomy 24:17-22, *page 227* • 1 Timothy 5:3-8, *page 1382* • James 1:27, *page 1413*

Singleness can be a challenging experience Ruth 1:1-14, *page 299* • 2 Kings 4:1-7, *page 415*

Jeremiah was called to be single because of his prophetic role and his circumstances Jeremiah 16:1-4, *page 843*

Some choose to remain single to work for God's Kingdom Matthew 19:10-12, *page 1099*

Singleness can be received as a gift from God 1 Corinthians 7:6-8, *page 1310*

Whether through choice or widowhood, Paul was single and used this to serve God 1 Corinthians 7:8

Single people can be more free to serve God 1 Corinthians 7:25-40, *page 1310*

▸ *See* ***Singleness****, page 642.*

Social justice *see Justice*

Society, Influence in *see Influence in society*

Sonship *see Adoption, Spiritual*

Sorrow *see Grief*

Soul *see also Heart; Mind; Spirit*

While many Christians today use the term "soul" of an "inner part"—the most important part—of us that is somehow separate from the rest, the Bible uses it in a much broader sense, the equivalent of what we today would call "our very self" or "our life." Unlike Greek philosophy, which saw a person as made up of separate parts, most often a spirit or soul trapped in a body, Jewish thinking saw a person as one single entity whose whole life should be used for God.

> *"Teacher, which is the most important commandment in the law of Moses?" Jesus replied, "'You must love the LORD your God with all your heart, all your soul, and all your mind.'" – Matthew 22:36-37, page 1104*

We should love God with our whole being—heart, soul, and mind Deuteronomy 6:1-5, *page 208* • Joshua 22:1-6, *page 265* • Matthew 22:36-40, *page 1104*

Our souls can despair or feel crushed at times Deuteronomy 28:63-65, *page 232* • Job 7:11, *page 570* • Psalm 13:1-2, *page 608* • Psalm 31:7, *page 619* • Matthew 26:36-39, *page 1111*

God's word can revive our souls Psalm 19:7-8, *page 613*

God's presence can bring rest to our souls Psalm 116:7, *page 676* • Jeremiah 6:16, *page 831* • Matthew 11:29, *page 1085*

People can destroy our bodies but not our souls Matthew 10:28, *page 1084*

Jesus promised rest for our weary souls Matthew 11:28-30, *page 1085*

Jesus said that our souls are the most valuable thing in life Mark 8:34-38, *page 1133*

Even Jesus experienced his soul feeling crushed Mark 14:32-34, *page 1143*

Although our bodies will decay, our souls will be saved 1 Corinthians 15:50-57, *page 1320* • Hebrews 10:39, *page 1407* • James 1:21, *page 1412* • 1 Peter 1:8-9, *page 1420*

Our souls are part of our whole being 1 Thessalonians 5:23, *page 1374*

The souls of those who have been martyred are safe with God Revelation 6:9-11, *page 1453*

▸ *See **Spirit, soul, and body**, page 1373.*

Speech *see also Complaining; Encouragement; Gossip*

The ability to speak to one another and to God through words is a precious gift. But it is a gift that can be used for good or for bad. The Bible is full of teaching on the power of the words we speak and the importance of being wise in our speech—and knowing when to say nothing at all.

> *If we could control our tongues, we would be perfect and could also control ourselves in every other way. We can make a large horse go wherever we want by means of a small bit in its mouth. And a small rudder makes a huge ship turn wherever the pilot chooses to go, even though the winds are strong. In the same way, the tongue is a small thing that makes grand speeches. But a tiny spark can set a great forest on fire. And among all the parts of the body, the tongue is a flame of fire. It is a whole world of wickedness, corrupting your entire body. It can set your whole life on fire, for it is set on fire by hell itself. – James 3:2-6, page 1415*

God himself shows us that words are powerful Genesis 1:1-3, *page 4* • Isaiah 55:8-11, *page 808* • Hebrews 4:12, *page 1400*

Sometimes it is better to say less or keep quiet Job 13:5, *page 575* • Proverbs 10:19-21, *page 706* • Proverbs 11:12-13, *page 708* • Ecclesiastes 3:1-8, *page 732*

We should remember that words can be destructive Job 19:1-3, *page 579* • Proverbs 11:9, *page 707* • Proverbs 16:27-28, *page 713* • James 3:1-12, *page 1415*

We need to control our speech Psalm 141:3-4, *page 690* • Proverbs 13:3, *page 709* • James 1:26, *page 1413* • James 3:1-12, *page 1415*

Profane words should not be part of our vocabulary Proverbs 4:24, *page 700* • Ephesians 4:29-31, *page 1351* • Ephesians 5:3-4, *page 1351* • Colossians 3:5-8, *page 1365*

Wise words bring benefits Proverbs 12:13-19, *page 708* • Proverbs 15:23, *page 712* • Proverbs 18:20, *page 715* • Proverbs 25:11, *page 722*

We should always speak the truth and do so simply Proverbs 12:17-19, *page 709* • Proverbs 24:24-26, *page 722* • Matthew 5:33-37, *page 1076* • James 5:12, *page 1417*

We should use words to encourage others Proverbs 12:25, *page 709* • Acts 15:30-32, *page 1260* • 1 Corinthians 14:1-4, *page 1317* • Ephesians 4:29, *page 1351* • Colossians 4:6, *page 1366*

Gentle and kind words can defuse difficult situations Proverbs 15:1, *page 711*

Gossip is condemned and forbidden Proverbs 16:28, *page 713* • Proverbs 20:19, *page 717* • Romans 1:28-32, *page 1283* • 2 Corinthians 12:19-20, *page 1334*

We should remember that our words express our inner character Matthew 12:33-37, *page 1087* • Matthew 15:16-20, *page 1093*

We will be judged for our words one day Matthew 12:36-37, *page 1087* • James 2:12-13, *page 1413*

▸ *See **Honesty**, page 707; **Speech**, page 1416.*

Spirit, Holy *see Holy Spirit*

Spirit, human *see also Heart; Mind; Soul*

In both Hebrew and Greek the word for "spirit" also means "breath" or "wind." It is therefore the intangible aspect of human life, often used in an overlapping way with "heart" and "mind" and ranging in meaning from our cognitive faculties and will to that aspect of us that relates to God through his Holy Spirit. While Greek philosophy (the root of much Western thinking) saw the human person as divisible into separate parts—body, mind, soul, spirit—the Bible sees us as a single entity, whose different aspects are considered only to highlight something about the whole.

> *You have not received a spirit that makes you fearful slaves. Instead, you received God's Spirit when he adopted you as his own children. Now we call him, "Abba, Father." For his Spirit joins with our spirit to affirm that we are God's children. – Romans 8:15-16, page 1291*

God is creator of the human spirit that gives us life Genesis 2:4-7, *page 5* • Job 34:14-15, *page 592* • Isaiah 42:5, *page 793* • Ezekiel 37:1-10, *page 939* • James 4:5, *page 1416*

Our spirit can be affected by our emotions and our circumstances, for good or for bad Genesis 45:21-27, *page 57* • Job 17:1-2, *page 578* • Proverbs 18:14, *page 715*

Trying to contact the spirits of the dead is both forbidden and futile Leviticus 19:31, *page 140* • Deuteronomy 18:9-14, *page 221* • Ecclesiastes 9:5-6, *page 737* • Isaiah 8:19-22, *page 757*

The spirit is that aspect of us that especially relates to God Psalm 51:7-11, *page 633* • Romans 8:12-16, *page 1291* • 1 Corinthians 2:10-16, *page 1305* • Philippians 4:23, *page 1360*

Our human spirit can be renewed by God's Spirit Psalm 51:9-11, *page 634* • Ezekiel 11:19-20, *page 909* • Ezekiel 36:25-27, *page 938* • John 3:1-8, *page 1202*

Our spirit is a distinct aspect of us, separate from body and soul Matthew 26:40-41, *page 1111* • 2 Corinthians 7:1, *page 1329* • 1 Thessalonians 5:23, *page 1374* • Hebrews 4:12, *page 1400*

Our spirit connects with God in worship and prayer Luke 1:46-47, *page 1153* • John 4:19-24, *page 1205* • 1 Corinthians 14:13-17, *page 1317*

Our spirit survives death Luke 23:44-46, *page 1194* • Acts 7:54-60, *page 1246* • Hebrews 12:22-23, *page 1409* • 1 Peter 3:18-20, *page 1424*

Our spirit will be united with our new resurrection body in God's new creation Romans 8:22-23, *page 1292* • 1 Corinthians 15:35-58, *page 1320* • 2 Corinthians 5:1-5, *page 1327*

What we do with our lives, including our body, affects our spirit 1 Corinthians 6:12-20, *page 1309* • 2 Corinthians 7:1, *page 1329*

▸ *See **Spirit, soul, and body**, page 1373.*

Spiritism *see Occult*

Spiritual adoption *see Adoption, Spiritual*

Spiritual gifts

Spiritual gifts are gifts of the Holy Spirit given to every follower of Jesus to help us build up the church and share the gospel effectively. There is a great diversity of spiritual gifts, and the Spirit decides which gifts he gives to which person. All the gifts should be used in an atmosphere of love and with a desire to serve others, not to draw attention to ourselves.

> *There are different kinds of spiritual gifts, but the same Spirit is the source of them all. There are different kinds of service, but we serve the same Lord. God works in different ways, but it is the same God who does the work in all of us. A spiritual gift is given to each of us so we can help each other. – 1 Corinthians 12:4-7, page 1315*

Jesus used various spiritual gifts, including teaching, healing, and prophecy Matthew 4:23-25, *page 1074* • Matthew 17:22-23, *page 1097* • John 4:16-19, *page 1204*

God expects us to use the gifts he gives us Romans 12:3-8, *page 1296*

There is a wide range of spiritual gifts Romans 12:4-8, *page 1296* • 1 Corinthians 12:7-11, 27-31, *page 1315* • Ephesians 4:7-16, *page 1350*

The Holy Spirit gives us our spiritual gifts 1 Corinthians 12:4-11, *page 1315*

The Holy Spirit distributes spiritual gifts according to his will 1 Corinthians 12:11, *page 1315* • Hebrews 2:4, *page 1397*

The variety of spiritual gifts is meant to show us our need of one another 1 Corinthians 12:12-31, *page 1315*

Love for others should guide all our use of gifts 1 Corinthians 13:1-13, *page 1316*

Spiritual gifts need to be used with clarity and purpose 1 Corinthians 14:1-25, *page 1317*

Spiritual gifts are meant to build up the body of Christ 1 Corinthians 14:1-12, *page 1317* • Ephesians 4:11-16, *page 1350*

Spiritual gifts can be used evangelistically 1 Corinthians 14:22-25, *page 1318*

Gifts of the Spirit can be used to encourage one another when we meet together 1 Corinthians 14:26-33, *page 1318*

Spiritual gifts should neither be denied nor overemphasized 1 Thessalonians 5:19-22, *page 1373*

Gifts should be used for the glory of God 1 Peter 4:10-11, *page 1424*

▸ *See **Gifts of the Holy Spirit**, page 1316.*

Spiritual growth *see Growth*

Spiritual warfare

As Christians, we are in a spiritual battle with the devil, the sinful world in which we live, and our own selfish human nature. But God provides us with spiritual armor to engage in this battle and to be victorious in it.

> *Put on all of God's armor so that you will be able to stand firm against all strategies of the devil. For we are not fighting against flesh-and-blood enemies, but against evil rulers and authorities of the unseen world, against mighty powers in this dark world, and against evil spirits in the heavenly places. Therefore, put on every piece of God's armor so you will be able to resist the enemy in the time of evil. Then after the battle you will still be standing firm. – Ephesians 6:11-13, page 1352*

Unseen spiritual battles go on around us 2 Kings 6:15-18, *page 419* • Daniel 10:1-14, *page 969* • Ephesians 6:11-13, *page 1352* • Revelation 12:7-9, *page 1457*

God gives us weapons for the battle Romans 13:12-14, *page 1298* • Ephesians 6:10-18, *page 1352*

We are urged to be strong and courageous in the battle 1 Corinthians 16:13, *page 1321*

God's weapons conquer Satan's strongholds 2 Corinthians 10:4-5, *page 1332*

The Spirit helps us to engage in battle against our selfish human nature Galatians 5:16-26, *page 1343*

Evil is already conquered through Jesus' victory on the cross Colossians 2:15, *page 1364* • Revelation 12:1-12, *page 1457*

We should always be alert to the devil's activity 1 Peter 5:8-9, *page 1425*

We are encouraged not to give in to the ways of the world because it will one day disappear 1 John 2:15-17, *page 1434*

The Holy Spirit, who lives within us, is greater than anything we have to face in the world 1 John 4:4-6, *page 1436*

Jesus will ultimately defeat Satan once and for all Revelation 20:7-10, *page 1464*

▶ *See **Spiritual warfare**, page 1353.*

Spiritualism *see Occult*

Stealing *see also Dishonesty*

The Bible says that stealing is, quite simply, wrong. Christians should not take what does not belong to them, whether from individuals or companies or stores, but should earn their money honestly and buy what they need. We should always be looking to give rather than to take.

If you are a thief, quit stealing. Instead, use your hands for good hard work, and then give generously to others in need. – Ephesians 4:28, page 1351

Stealing is forbidden in the Ten Commandments Exodus 20:15, *page 90* • Romans 13:8-10, *page 1298*

The Old Testament had laws governing stealing, including the requirement to pay compensation Exodus 22:1-15, *page 92* • Leviticus 19:11-13, *page 139*

We should not steal through dishonest business practices Deuteronomy 25:13-16, *page 227* • Proverbs 16:11, *page 713* • Amos 8:4-7, *page 1000* • Luke 19:8, *page 1185*

Stealing from God has consequences Joshua 7:1-26, *page 248* • Malachi 3:6-12, *page 1052* • Acts 5:1-11, *page 1242*

Stealing begins in the heart Mark 7:18-23, *page 1131*

If we are dishonest with money and possessions, God cannot trust us with spiritual treasures Luke 16:10-13, *page 1182*

Zacchaeus made restitution for what he had stolen Luke 19:1-10, *page 1185*

Judas's love of money led him to become a thief John 12:1-6, *page 1218*

Those who keep on stealing will not enter God's Kingdom 1 Corinthians 6:9-11, *page 1309*

We should not steal but rather should get our money honestly Ephesians 4:28, *page 1351*

We should not steal at our place of work Titus 2:9-10, *page 1390*

▶ *See **Cheating**, page 33; **Honesty**, page 707; **Lying**, page 1214.*

Stress *see also Worry*

The busy and demanding world in which we live often causes people to experience stress—mental and emotional pressure. The Bible encourages us not to overwork but to ensure we take a proper day of rest and bring God into all that we do, sharing our problems and challenges with him.

Jesus said, "Come to me, all of you who are weary and carry heavy burdens, and I will give you rest. Take my yoke upon you. Let me teach you, because I am humble and gentle at heart, and you will find rest for your souls. For my yoke is easy to bear, and the burden I give you is light." – Matthew 11:28-30, page 1085

Delegating work to others can help alleviate stress Exodus 18:13-26, *page 87*

A regular day of rest helps us deal with stress Exodus 20:8-11, *page 90* • Isaiah 58:13-14, *page 812*

BASIC TRUTHS • *page 1596*

We should always be ready to let others encourage us 1 Samuel 23:13-18, *page 332* • Job 2:11-13, *page 566* • Proverbs 12:25, *page 709* • 2 Corinthians 7:5-7, *page 1329*

We can find strength from God in times of stress 1 Samuel 30:1-6, *page 338* • 1 Kings 19:1-18, *page 404* • Psalm 18:1-36, *page 610* • Psalm 46:1-11, *page 630* • Psalm 62:1-8, *page 639*

We should take practical steps, like eating and resting properly, when we are stressed 1 Kings 19:3-8, *page 404* • Mark 6:30-31, *page 1129*

We can pray in times of stress 2 Kings 19:14-19, *page 437* • Psalm 69:1-36, *page 644* • Psalm 142:1-7, *page 691* • Philippians 4:6-9, *page 1359*

We can put our trust in God and know his peace Proverbs 3:5-6, *page 699* • Isaiah 26:1-4, *page 774* • Isaiah 40:28-31, *page 791* • Romans 15:13, *page 1299*

We should just take one day at a time Matthew 6:25-34, *page 1078*

Jesus said that learning to walk with him would help us handle the stresses of life Matthew 11:28-30, *page 1085*

Even Jesus experienced stress Mark 14:32-33, *page 1143* • John 12:27, *page 1220* • Hebrews 5:7-8, *page 1400*

We should remember that God is always with us, no matter what happens Romans 8:35-39, *page 1292*

When we face times of stress, God always brings us through them 2 Corinthians 4:8-14, *page 1327*

▸ *See* ***Depression****, page 404;* ***Resting in God****, page 676;* ***Trusting God when we cannot see the way ahead****, page 57;* ***Trusting God whatever happens****, page 959;* ***Worry****, page 1189.*

Stubbornness *see Heart*

Submission *see also Obedience*

In today's world, with its emphasis on human rights and equal rights, submission is not a concept that sits well with most people. Yet it is a thoroughly biblical concept, and one that Jesus himself modeled for us. Submission is not about seeing ourselves as less than someone else, but rather as adopting Jesus' loving attitude of service and wanting to put others' interests before our own.

> *You must have the same attitude that Christ Jesus had. Though he was God, he did not think of equality with God as something to cling to. Instead, he gave up his divine privileges; he took the humble position of a slave and was born as a human being. When he appeared in human form, he humbled himself in obedience to God and died a criminal's death on a cross. – Philippians 2:5-8, page 1356*

We should gladly submit to God's discipline, knowing it is for our good 1 Chronicles 21:1-13, *page 471* • Hebrews 12:5-13, *page 1408*

All of us are called to submit to God and to know the consequent blessing Job 22:21-28, *page 583* • Psalm 2:1-12, *page 602* • James 4:7-10, *page 1416* • 1 Peter 5:5-7, *page 1425*

Jesus is our example of submission to the Father's will Matthew 26:36-42, *page 1111* • John 5:19, *page 1206* • John 12:49-50, *page 1221* • Philippians 2:5-11, *page 1356* • Hebrews 5:5-10, *page 1400*

Discipleship is about learning how to submit to Jesus and walk in his ways Matthew 28:18-20, *page 1116* • Luke 9:23, *page 1169* • John 14:15, *page 1223*

We should submit to our government Romans 13:1-7, *page 1297* • 1 Peter 2:13-17, *page 1422*

God created lines of authority for harmonious relationships 1 Corinthians 11:2-16, *page 1314*

As a son, Jesus gladly continues to submit to his Father, even though they are equals 1 Corinthians 11:3, *page 1314* • 1 Corinthians 15:21-28, *page 1319*

Marriage calls for mutual submission Ephesians 5:21-33, *page 1351*

We should submit to our church leaders Hebrews 13:17, *page 1410* • 1 Peter 5:1-5, *page 1425*

▸ *See* ***Submission and relationships****, page 1352.*

Substitution *see Jesus Christ: his death*

Success

We live in a world where success is measured by things like money, popularity, and power. God does want us to succeed, but his measure of success will always be different from the world's measure. By any worldly measurement, Jesus' life and ministry was an absolute failure—at least until three days after his death. But his faithfulness to his Father's plan actually brought about the ultimate success. We should follow Jesus' example and measure the success of our lives and our churches by faithfulness to God, rather than by worldly values.

> *"Be strong and very courageous. Be careful to obey all the instructions Moses gave you. Do not deviate from them, turning either to the right or to the left. Then you will be successful in everything you do."* – *Joshua 1:7, page 242*

It is God's favor that gives us success
Genesis 24:12-27, *page 28* • Genesis 39:19-23, *page 49* • Deuteronomy 31:1-8, *page 234* • 1 Corinthians 3:1-9, *page 1305* • 1 Corinthians 15:10, *page 1319*

We should not forget God when we are successful Deuteronomy 8:6-18, *page 211* • Deuteronomy 32:1-18, *page 235* • Luke 12:13-21

Obedience is the best foundation for success Joshua 1:6-9, *page 242* • 1 Kings 2:1-4, *page 376* • Psalm 1:1-3, *page 602* • Matthew 7:24-27, *page 1079*

We should beware of pride after any success
1 Samuel 2:3-8, *page 306* • 1 Samuel 15:1-12, *page 321* • 2 Corinthians 12:1-10, *page 1333*

Listening to good advice can help produce success 2 Chronicles 20:1-30, *page 500* • Proverbs 11:14, *page 708* • Proverbs 15:22, *page 712*

We need to commit our plans to God if we hope to succeed Psalm 37:1-5, *page 623* • Proverbs 3:5-6, *page 699* • Proverbs 16:3, *page 712*

Success in itself does not bring fulfillment
Ecclesiastes 2:4-11, *page 731*

Success is linked to faithfulness Matthew 25:14-30, *page 1109* • Luke 16:10-12, *page 1182* • Luke 19:11-27, *page 1185* • 1 Corinthians 4:1-5, *page 1307*

Success in life is meaningless if we have not paid attention to our souls Mark 8:34-37, *page 1133*

Even when we are not successful but fail, Jesus remains faithful 2 Timothy 2:8-13, *page 1386*

Success can produce complacency Revelation 2:1-7, *page 1446* • Revelation 3:1-6, *page 1449*

▸ *See* ***Success and successors***, *page 189;* ***Handling failure***, *page 1232;* ***Faithfulness***, *page 1307.*

Suffering *see also Bad things: Why do they happen in life?; Comfort; Stress*

Sometimes suffering comes to us as the consequence of our foolish choices; but more often than not, it is simply "one of those things," the result of living in a fallen world that has become spoiled by human sin. When suffering comes, we should bring it to Jesus, who himself suffered and so knows what it is like, and who is therefore able to strengthen us to go through it. He has also given us one another to provide support through such times.

> *So to keep me from becoming proud, I was given a thorn in my flesh, a messenger from Satan to torment me and keep me from becoming proud. Three different times I begged the Lord to take it away. Each time he said, "My grace is all you need. My power works best in weakness." So now I am glad to boast about my weaknesses, so that the power of Christ can work through me. That's why I take pleasure in my weaknesses, and in the insults, hardships, persecutions, and troubles that I suffer for Christ. For when I am weak, then I am strong.* – *2 Corinthians 12:7-10, page 1334*

Suffering is a consequence of the Fall Genesis 3:16-19, *page 7* • Job 5:7, *page 569* • Job 14:1-12, *page 576* • Romans 8:19-22, *page 1291*

God cares for his people in their suffering
Exodus 2:23-25, *page 67* • Deuteronomy 33:26-29, *page 239* • Isaiah 40:1-11, *page 789*

We can ask for healing when we are suffering or sick 2 Kings 20:1-6, *page 438* • Matthew 8:1-17, *page 1079* • Acts 9:32-43, *page 1250* • James 5:13-18, *page 1417*

We can use natural or medical means to alleviate suffering 2 Kings 20:1-7, *page 438*

• Jeremiah 51:8, *page 884* • 1 Timothy 5:23, *page 1383*

We can trust God even in suffering Job 1:13-22, *page 565* • Psalm 55:1-23, *page 635* • Psalm 73:25-26, *page 647* • Habakkuk 3:17-18, *page 1027* • 2 Corinthians 12:7-10, *page 1334*

Those who suffer need encouragement Job 2:11-13, *page 566* • Job 16:1-6, *page 577* • 2 Corinthians 7:5-6, *page 1329* • 1 Thessalonians 4:13-18, *page 1372*

It was prophesied that the Messiah would suffer Isaiah 53:1-12, *page 805*

Suffering will sometimes come because we are Christians Luke 21:12-19, *page 1189* • Acts 5:17-42, *page 1243* • Acts 6:8–7:60, *page 1244* • Acts 14:1-22, *page 1258* • Acts 16:16-40, *page 1262* • 2 Timothy 1:8-12, *page 1384*

Suffering can refine our character Romans 5:3-5, *page 1287* • Hebrews 12:5-13, *page 1408* • James 1:2-4, *page 1412* • 1 Peter 1:6-7, *page 1420*

Our present suffering is nothing compared with our future glory Romans 8:18-25, *page 1291* • 2 Corinthians 4:16-18, *page 1327* • 1 Peter 4:12-13, *page 1425*

Jesus suffered, so he can help us through suffering Hebrews 2:11-18, *page 1398* • Hebrews 4:14-16, *page 1400* • 1 Peter 2:21-25, *page 1423*

There will be no suffering in God's new Kingdom Revelation 21:1-7, *page 1465*

▶ *See **Suffering: Why do bad things happen to good people?**, page 567; **Why do bad things happen in life?**, page 1025; **Miracles and healing**, page 1243.*

Sunday *see Day of rest*

Sure of my faith, How can I be? *see Assurance*

Sympathy *see Caring; Kindness; Love*

Teaching

The Bible emphasizes the need for all of us to be taught God's word and God's ways and to commit ourselves to being good disciples, constantly remaining teachable. Parents are called to teach their children; church leaders are called to teach church members. All of us need to be committed to receiving good teaching that will help us grow and become mature.

> *All the believers devoted themselves to the apostles' teaching, and to fellowship, and to sharing in meals (including the Lord's Supper), and to prayer. – Acts 2:42, page 1239*

Parents must teach their children about the Lord Deuteronomy 6:1-9, *page 208* • Ephesians 6:4, *page 1352*

We can only teach God's word if we are studying it ourselves Ezra 7:8-10, *page 529*

Teaching our children to follow God will pay off when they are older Proverbs 22:6, *page 719*

Teaching played a major role in Jesus' ministry Matthew 4:23-25, *page 1074* • Matthew 13:53-58, *page 1091* • Mark 4:1-34, *page 1124*

We need to not just listen to Jesus' teaching but also obey it Matthew 7:24-27, *page 1079* • James 1:22-25, *page 1412*

Jesus commissioned the apostles to make disciples by teaching them how to obey Matthew 28:19-20, *page 1116*

The Holy Spirit teaches truth John 14:16-17, *page 1223* • John 15:26-27, *page 1224* • John 16:13-15, *page 1225*

Believers should teach one another Colossians 3:15-17, *page 1365* • 2 Timothy 2:1-2, *page 1385*

Some qualities of a good teacher 2 Timothy 2:22-26, *page 1386*

The Bible is given to teach and train us 2 Timothy 3:16-17, *page 1387*

Some guidance to those who teach God's word Titus 2:1-15, *page 1390*

We shouldn't stop learning once we know the fundamentals of our faith Hebrews 5:11-14, *page 1400*

▶ *See **Bible teaching**, page 529; **From one generation to another**, page 651; **Teaching God's word**, page 1268.*

Temptation

All of us experience temptation—that strong urge to do something that we know isn't right. The deceitfulness of temptation lies in its convincing us that the pleasure gained will be worthwhile, even though we know we always feel bad after doing it. God wants to help us resist temptation, and Jesus showed us that with the help of God's Spirit, it really is possible.

God blesses those who patiently endure testing and temptation. Afterward they will receive the crown of life that God has promised to those who love him. And remember, when you are being tempted, do not say, "God is tempting me." God is never tempted to do wrong, and he never tempts anyone else. Temptation comes from our own desires, which entice us and drag us away. These desires give birth to sinful actions. And when sin is allowed to grow, it gives birth to death. – James 1:12-15, page 1412

Temptation is one of Satan's main weapons of attack against us Genesis 3:1-7, *page 6* • Matthew 4:1-11, *page 1073* • 2 Corinthians 11:3, *page 1332* • 1 Peter 5:8-9, *page 1425*

Temptation often comes from what we see Genesis 13:1-13, *page 16* • 2 Samuel 11:1-4, *page 352* • Matthew 5:27-30, *page 1076*

We should always flee from situations of temptation Genesis 39:6-12, *page 49* • Proverbs 6:20-29, *page 702* • 1 Corinthians 6:18-20, *page 1310* • 2 Timothy 2:22, *page 1386*

Meditating on Scripture can help us resist temptation Psalm 119:9-11, *page 678* • Proverbs 7:1-5, *page 703*

Jesus used the Scriptures to stand against Satan's temptations Matthew 4:1-11, *page 1073*

Learning to control our thinking is an important part of resisting temptation Matthew 5:27-30, *page 1076* • Philippians 4:8-9, *page 1360*

We should pray to avoid giving in to temptation Matthew 6:13, *page 1077* • Matthew 26:41, *page 1111*

We should take care not to become the source of temptation for others Luke 17:1-3, *page 1182*

God promises to provide a way of escape from every temptation for those who will take it 1 Corinthians 10:12-13, *page 1313*

We should help those who have been overcome by temptation, and not judge them Galatians 6:1, *page 1343*

Jesus can help us, for he, too, has faced temptation Hebrews 4:15-16, *page 1400*

Being accountable to someone else can help us overcome temptation James 5:16, *page 1417*

▶ *See **Temptation**, page 1313.*

Testing *see also Suffering*

God sometimes takes us through times of testing; but this isn't because he doesn't love us, but rather because he does. He wants to use these times to help us refine our faith and develop our character. Times of testing reveal what really matters to us in life.

So be truly glad. There is wonderful joy ahead, even though you must endure many trials for a little while. These trials will show that your faith is genuine. It is being tested as fire tests and purifies gold—though your faith is far more precious than mere gold. So when your faith remains strong through many trials, it will bring you much praise and glory and honor on the day when Jesus Christ is revealed to the whole world. – 1 Peter 1:6-7, page 1420

God tests his people's faith Genesis 22:1-18, *page 26* • Job 1:1–2:10, *page 565* • Matthew 4:1-11, *page 1073*

Times of testing develop our character Deuteronomy 8:1-5, *page 211* • Psalm 139:23-24, *page 690* • Romans 5:1-5, *page 1287* • 2 Corinthians 12:1-10, *page 1333*

Satan wants to use testing for our destruction, but he can never win Job 1:1-22, *page 565* • Luke 22:31-32, *page 1191*

Testing is always for our good Job 23:10, *page 583* • Psalm 119:71, *page 680* • James 1:2-4, *page 1412* • 1 Peter 1:3-9, *page 1420*

God's presence and peace will be with us in our trials and testing Psalm 23:1-6, *page 615* • John 16:32-33, *page 1225*

Jesus tested the faith of his disciples Mark 4:35-41, *page 1125* • John 6:1-6, *page 1207*

Any present times of testing are nothing compared to the joy of our relationship with Jesus and our hope in him Romans 8:18-25, *page 1291* • 2 Corinthians 4:16–5:10, *page 1327* • 1 Peter 4:12-13, *page 1425*

God works even the challenges of life into his good purpose for us Romans 8:28-39, *page 1292*

There will be a final testing of our lives and service when Jesus returns 1 Corinthians 3:10-15, *page 1306* • 2 Corinthians 5:9-10, *page 1327*

God never tests us beyond what he knows we can endure 1 Corinthians 10:12-13, *page 1313*

When we have come through a time of trouble and testing, we are in a better place to help others 2 Corinthians 1:3-11, *page 1324*

Jesus will protect his people at the end-time testing Revelation 3:10-13, *page 1450*

▶ *See **Trusting God when we cannot see the way ahead**, page 57; **Faith**, page 1286; **Pressing on**, page 1359.*

Thankfulness *see also Ungratefulness*

God wants us to develop a thankful attitude, both toward him and toward others, out of recognition of how blessed we are. Ingratitude is an inappropriate response for God's people, and thankfulness should be a hallmark of our lives. God wants us to have a constant attitude of gratitude.

> *Always be joyful. Never stop praying. Be thankful in all circumstances, for this is God's will for you who belong to Christ Jesus. – 1 Thessalonians 5:16-18, page 1373*

We should be thankful that God rescued us Exodus 15:1-21, *page 83* • Psalm 30:1-12, *page 619* • Psalm 35:9-10, *page 622* • Psalm 62:1-8, *page 639*

We should be thankful for answers to prayer 1 Samuel 1:27–2:10, *page 306* • Psalm 118:19-21, *page 677* • Psalm 138:1-3, *page 688* • John 11:39-42, *page 1218*

Our prayers should be interspersed with gratitude 1 Kings 8:22-26, *page 386* • Daniel 6:10, *page 963* • Philippians 4:4-7, *page 1359* • Colossians 4:2, *page 1366* • 1 Thessalonians 5:16-18, *page 1373*

We should be thankful for God's creation Psalm 8:1-9, *page 605* • Psalm 19:1-6, *page 612* • Psalm 104:1-35, *page 667* • Isaiah 40:25-28, *page 790*

Our whole lifestyle should be marked by gratitude Psalm 34:1-5, *page 621* • Ephesians 5:17-20, *page 1351* • Colossians 3:15-17, *page 1365* • Hebrews 13:15-16, *page 1410*

We should be thankful for God's care of us Psalm 95:6-7, *page 663* • Psalm 103:1-5, *page 666*

We should be thankful for God's goodness and faithfulness Psalm 100:1-5, *page 664* • Psalm 107:1-2, *page 671* • Psalm 136:1-26, *page 687*

We should be thankful for God's provision Psalm 147:7-9, *page 693* • Matthew 6:25-34, *page 1078* • Philippians 4:18-20, *page 1360*

Ingratitude makes us fools—worse than mere animals Isaiah 1:2-4, *page 748* • Romans 1:18-22, *page 1283*

We should be thankful for other people Romans 1:8-9, *page 1282* • Ephesians 1:15-18, *page 1346* • Colossians 1:3-10, *page 1362* • 2 Timothy 1:3-4, *page 1384* • Philemon 1:4-7, *page 1393*

We should be thankful for Jesus and what he has done for us 1 Corinthians 15:55-57, *page 1321* • Ephesians 2:4-10, *page 1347*

We should express our thankfulness to God through generosity to others 2 Corinthians 8:1–9:15, *page 1330*

▶ *See **Thanksgiving**, page 665; **Thankfulness**, page 1366.*

Theft *see Stealing*

Thinking *see Mind*

Threats *see Intimidation*

Time *see also Future; Past; Waiting*

In our busy lives, time is something that most of us claim we do not have enough of. Yet the Bible says that God, who created time and stands outside of it, has given us all the time we need to fulfill what he has planned for us. But we need to use that time wisely, learning from our past and inspired by our future, so that we may seize every moment in the present and make it count.

Lord, through all the generations you have been our home! Before the mountains were born, before you gave birth to the earth and the world, from beginning to end, you are God. You turn people back to dust, saying, "Return to dust, you mortals!" For you, a thousand years are as a passing day, as brief as a few night hours. You sweep people away like dreams that disappear. They are like grass that springs up in the morning. In the morning it blooms and flourishes, but by evening it is dry and withered. . . . Seventy years are given to us! Some even live to eighty. But even the best years are filled with pain and trouble; soon they disappear, and we fly away. Who can comprehend the power of your anger? Your wrath is as awesome as the fear you deserve. Teach us to realize the brevity of life, so that we may grow in wisdom. – Psalm 90:1-6, 10-12, page 659

God is outside of time and therefore eternal Genesis 1:1, *page 4* • Psalm 90:1-2, *page 659* • Psalm 93:1-2, *page 661* • Isaiah 43:13, *page 795* • John 1:1-2, *page 1199*

God created time Genesis 1:3-5, 14-18, *page 4*

The length of our lives and the timing of events in them are in God's hands Job 14:5, *page 576* • Psalm 31:14-15, *page 619* • Psalm 139:13-16, *page 689* • Acts 17:24-26, *page 1264*

We often have to wait on God's timing, but doing so brings blessing Psalm 37:1-7, *page 623* • Isaiah 64:4, *page 817* • James 5:7-8, *page 1417*

Human life is short and fragile Psalm 89:47-48, *page 659* • Psalm 90:1-12, *page 659* • James 4:13-15, *page 1416*

Our measurements of time are meaningless to the eternal God Psalm 90:1-4, *page 659* • 2 Peter 3:3-9, *page 1429*

There is a right time for everything Ecclesiastes 3:1-8, *page 732* • Ecclesiastes 8:2-6, *page 736*

God has put a sense of eternity into human hearts Ecclesiastes 3:11, *page 733*

Jesus said that God's Kingdom was breaking into our world right now, not just in the future Matthew 4:17, *page 1074* • Matthew 10:5-7, *page 1083* • Luke 10:8-9, *page 1171*

We should use time wisely in light of Jesus' return, which could happen at any moment Matthew 24:36–25:13, *page 1107* • 1 Thessalonians 5:1-11, *page 1372* • 2 Peter 3:8-14, *page 1429*

We should make the most of every opportunity and the time given us John 9:4-5, *page 1214* • Ephesians 5:15-20, *page 1351* • Colossians 4:5, *page 1366*

There will come a moment when time as we know it will end and we will live in eternity Revelation 21:1-5, *page 1465* • Revelation 22:1-5, *page 1467*

▸ *See **Waiting**, page 558; **The use of time**, page 732.*

Tiredness *see Rest*

Trials *see Testing*

Trinity *see God; Jesus Christ; Holy Spirit*

Trouble *see Stress; Suffering; Testing*

Trust *see Faith*

Truth *see also Integrity*

Truth is a key aspect of God's character. He himself is truth, and all his ways are true and just. As his people, we are called to reflect that character by being faithful and dependable in the words we speak and in the way we live. Satan hates the truth, but Jesus says that the truth always sets us free.

Jesus said to the people who believed in him, "You are truly my disciples if you remain faithful to my teachings. And you will know the truth, and the truth will set you free." – John 8:31-32, page 1213

BASIC TRUTHS • *page 1602*

Satan always tries to challenge God's truth, whether directly or indirectly Genesis 3:1-5, *page 6* • John 8:42-44, *page 1213* • 2 Timothy 3:10-17, *page 1386* • 2 John 1:7, *page 1438*

God is truth Numbers 23:19, *page 183* • Romans 3:3-4, *page 1285* • Hebrews 6:13-18, *page 1401*

God's people should always speak truth Psalm 15:1-5, *page 609* • Zechariah 8:16-17, *page 1043* • 2 Corinthians 4:1-2, *page 1327* • Ephesians 4:15, 17-25, *page 1350*

God's word is truth Psalm 119:160, *page 682* • John 17:17, *page 1226* • 2 Timothy 3:14-17, *page 1387*

Truth never changes, even in a changing world Proverbs 12:19, *page 709*

We must not only believe the truth but also live by it Matthew 7:24-27, *page 1079* • 1 John 1:5-7, *page 1433* • 2 John 1:4, *page 1438*

God always knows the truth about everything, and it will one day be revealed Luke 12:1-3, *page 1175*

We should worship God in spirit and truth John 4:19-24, *page 1205*

Truth always sets us free John 8:31-36, *page 1213* • 2 Corinthians 3:12-18, *page 1326*

Jesus is the truth and speaks the truth John 14:6, *page 1222* • John 18:37, *page 1228*

The Holy Spirit is the Spirit of truth John 14:15-17, *page 1223* • John 15:26-27, *page 1224* • John 16:12-15, *page 1225*

The gospel is the truth Ephesians 1:13-14, *page 1346* • Colossians 1:5, *page 1362* • 1 Timothy 2:3-7, *page 1380*

▶ *See* ***Honesty****, page 707;* ***Integrity****, page 1325;* ***Living according to the truth****, page 1439.*

Unbelief *see Doubt*

Unbelievers *see also Doubt*

Unbelievers are those who refuse to trust God or even to believe in him. The Bible urges us to share our faith with them, not just through words but also through the way we live, showing what a difference knowing God makes. But it also warns us to beware of becoming like them. We are called to influence them, not the other way around.

> *This is a trustworthy saying, and everyone should accept it: "Christ Jesus came into the world to save sinners"—and I am the worst of them all. But God had mercy on me so that Christ Jesus could use me as a prime example of his great patience with even the worst sinners. Then others will realize that they, too, can believe in him and receive eternal life.* – *1 Timothy 1:15-16, page 1379*

Unbelievers refuse to believe or trust in God Numbers 14:5-11, *page 170* • Psalm 78:17-22, *page 651* • John 5:36-40, *page 1207* • Hebrews 3:12-19, *page 1398*

We should not imitate the lifestyle of unbelievers 2 Kings 17:13-15, *page 432* • Psalm 1:1-6, *page 602* • Psalm 26:1-5, *page 616* • Ephesians 4:17-32, *page 1350*

We should set a godly example for unbelievers Matthew 5:13-16, *page 1075* • Colossians 4:5-6, *page 1366* • Titus 2:1-8, *page 1390* • 1 Peter 2:12, *page 1422* • 1 Peter 3:13-16, *page 1423*

God wants us to share the gospel with unbelievers Matthew 28:16-20, *page 1116* • Romans 10:13-15, *page 1294*

Remaining an unbeliever has serious consequences Mark 16:15-16, *page 1148* • John 3:18, *page 1203* • John 8:23-24, *page 1212* • Revelation 21:8, *page 1466*

God's grace can move us from unbelief to belief John 1:10-13, *page 1199* • Ephesians 2:1-8, *page 1347* • 1 Timothy 1:12-17, *page 1379*

The need to move from unbelief to belief in God is urgent Acts 17:30-31, *page 1264* • 2 Corinthians 6:1-2, *page 1328* • Hebrews 3:7-13, *page 1398*

Unbelievers cannot understand spiritual truths 1 Corinthians 2:6-14, *page 1305* • 2 Corinthians 4:3-4, *page 1327*

We should avoid relationships with unbelievers that may force us to compromise our beliefs 2 Corinthians 6:14-18, *page 1329*

God wants unbelievers to be saved 1 Timothy 2:1-6, *page 1380* • 2 Peter 3:9, *page 1429*

▶ *See* ***Backsliding****, page 841;* ***Can a Christian marry a non-Christian?****, page 1329;* ***The dangers of drifting****, page 1447;* ***Pressing on****, page 1359.*

Unemployment *see also Work*

A period of unemployment can feel soul-destroying, especially if it is long-term and we have been accustomed to working hard for our living. We should not lose hope at such times, but rather remember that God has promised to provide for us. We should be ready to accept any support that is offered to us, but equally we should not abuse it. Those of us who are in a position to help the unemployed should do so.

"There will always be some in the land who are poor. That is why I am commanding you to share freely with the poor and with other Israelites in need." – Deuteronomy 15:11, page 218

God wants his people to make provision for the unemployed and those in financial need Leviticus 19:9-10, *page 139* • Deuteronomy 15:1-11, *page 218* • Deuteronomy 24:19-22, *page 227* • Ruth 2:1-9, *page 300* • 2 Corinthians 8:10-15, *page 1330*

Even if we have lost everything we can still trust God Job 1:13-22, *page 565* • Psalm 37:22-28, *page 624* • Habakkuk 3:17-18, *page 1027*

God promises to be with us in the hard times of life Psalm 23:1-6, *page 615*

We should take care that laziness does not creep up on us while unemployed Proverbs 6:6-11, *page 701* • Proverbs 20:4, *page 716* • Proverbs 26:13-16, *page 724*

We do not need to be anxious, whatever our circumstances, for God promises to provide for our needs Matthew 6:25-34, *page 1078* • Philippians 4:6-9, *page 1359*

We should seek to provide work for the unemployed if we are able to Matthew 20:1-16, *page 1100*

If we are unemployed because of laziness, we shouldn't expect support but should seek employment quickly, remembering that work is God's good gift to us 1 Thessalonians 4:11-12, *page 1372* • 2 Thessalonians 3:6-13, *page 1375*

We should see unemployment as a time of testing that can do us good Hebrews 12:7-13, *page 1408* • James 1:2-4, *page 1412*

▸ *See **Work**, page 1376.*

Ungratefulness *see also Complaining; Thankfulness*

We can so easily let ungratefulness creep into our lives, as the history of Israel in the Old Testament shows us again and again. To guard against it we should develop a lifestyle of being thankful—both to God and to people—for everything.

You should know this, Timothy, that in the last days there will be very difficult times. For people will love only themselves and their money. They will be boastful and proud, scoffing at God, disobedient to their parents, and ungrateful. They will consider nothing sacred. They will be unloving and unforgiving; they will slander others and have no self-control. They will be cruel and hate what is good. They will betray their friends, be reckless, be puffed up with pride, and love pleasure rather than God. They will act religious, but they will reject the power that could make them godly. Stay away from people like that! – 2 Timothy 3:1-5, page 1386

Ingratitude is demonstrated in failing to trust or obey God Genesis 3:1-7, *page 6* • Psalm 78:9-32, *page 650*

People can often be ungrateful to us Genesis 40:5-23, *page 50* • 2 Chronicles 24:17-22, *page 506* • Jeremiah 18:18-20, *page 846* • Luke 17:11-19, *page 1183*

Israel was often ungrateful to God Exodus 16:1-3, *page 84* • Deuteronomy 32:6-18, *page 235* • Judges 8:33-34, *page 281* • Isaiah 1:2-4, *page 748*

Ungratefulness quickly leads to complaining Exodus 16:1-8, *page 84* • Numbers 14:1-38, *page 169* • Jonah 4:1-3, *page 1009*

We should beware of becoming ungrateful after we have been successful Deuteronomy 6:10-12, *page 209* • Deuteronomy 8:10-18, *page 211* • 1 Samuel 15:1-23, *page 321* • Psalm 106:6-7, *page 669*

Ingratitude can be expressed in repaying good with evil Psalm 35:11-12, *page 622* • Proverbs 17:13-14, *page 714* • Jeremiah 18:18-20, *page 846* • Romans 12:17-21, *page 1297*

Ungratefulness is an expression of ungodliness Romans 1:18-21, *page 1283* • 2 Timothy 3:1-2, *page 1386*

God wants us to be a grateful people Ephesians 5:15-20, *page 1351* • Philippians 4:4-6, *page 1359* • Colossians 3:16-17, *page 1365* • 1 Thessalonians 5:16-18, *page 1373* • Hebrews 12:28-29, *page 1409*

▸ *See **Thanksgiving**, page 665; **Thankfulness**, page 1366.*

Unity *see also Reconciliation*

Since unity is in the very nature of God—one God existing simultaneously in three equal persons—it shouldn't surprise us that he wants it to be reflected in his people. Unity—which can embrace variety—is therefore something that we must pursue and maintain, knowing that as we do, it brings God's blessing.

> *Make every effort to keep yourselves united in the Spirit, binding yourselves together with peace. For there is one body and one Spirit, just as you have been called to one glorious hope for the future. There is one Lord, one faith, one baptism, one God and Father of all, who is over all, in all, and living through all. – Ephesians 4:3-6, page 1350*

Unity can be used for bad as well as for good Genesis 11:1-9, *page 14* • Revelation 13:1-4, 11-15, *page 1458*

Unity lies within the very nature of God Deuteronomy 6:4 (see footnote), *page 208*

Unity among believers pleases God and brings his blessing Psalm 133:1-3, *page 686*

Unity requires agreement and commitment Amos 3:3, *page 995*

Unity in prayer is powerful Matthew 18:19-20, *page 1098* • Acts 4:23-31, *page 1241*

Jesus prayed for unity among his followers to reflect the unity within God himself John 17:21-26, *page 1226*

The first Christians were united in both spiritual and practical ways Acts 2:42-47, *page 1239* • Acts 4:32-37, *page 1242*

Christians should pursue unity and harmony among themselves Romans 15:5-7, *page 1299* • 1 Corinthians 1:10-17, *page 1303* • Philippians 1:27, *page 1356* • Philippians 4:2-3, *page 1359* • Colossians 3:12-15, *page 1365* • 1 Peter 3:8-12, *page 1423*

The Lord's Supper (also called Communion or the Eucharist) speaks of our unity and calls us back to it 1 Corinthians 10:16-18, *page 1314* • 1 Corinthians 11:17-34, *page 1314*

There can be unity even in great diversity in the church 1 Corinthians 12:12-30, *page 1315* • Ephesians 4:3-13, *page 1350*

God has destroyed the barriers between people that prevent unity Galatians 3:26-29, *page 1341* • Ephesians 2:11-22, *page 1347*

One day all God's people, no matter what their background, will be united around his throne Revelation 5:6-10, *page 1451* • Revelation 7:9-17, *page 1454*

▸ *See **Unity**, page 686.*

Vengeance *see Revenge*

Virgin Birth *see Jesus Christ: his life*

Waiting *see also Patience; Perseverance; Time*

Waiting is something that most of us find hard to do. Yet for God, who holds eternity in his hands, waiting is no big deal. He wants us as his children to learn to wait for him to act, for waiting demonstrates trust. The Bible promises that those who do wait for God will see him act on their behalf.

> *Since the world began, no ear has heard and no eye has seen a God like you, who works for those who wait for him! – Isaiah 64:4, page 817*

Because waiting isn't easy, we sometimes try—unwisely—to help God's plan along Genesis 16:1-16, *page 19* • 1 Samuel 13:1-14, *page 318*

Waiting can sometimes be very frustrating Job 24:1-12, *page 584* • Psalm 13:1-6, *page 608* • Psalm 69:1-3, *page 644* • Psalm 119:81-84, *page 680*

God sometimes has us wait to demonstrate our trust and obedience Psalm 27:1-14, *page 617* • Proverbs 20:22, *page 717* • Isaiah 8:16-18, *page 757*

We can wait patiently for God to act Psalm 37:1-7, *page 623* • Psalm 62:1-8, *page 639* • Lamentations 3:22-27, *page 895* • Isaiah 64:4, *page 817* • Hebrews 6:15, *page 1401*

When we wait upon God, he acts in response to our trust Psalm 40:1-3, *page 626* • Isaiah 40:28-31, *page 791* • Micah 7:7-10, *page 1016*

God patiently waits for people to turn back to him Isaiah 65:1-2, *page 818* • Luke 15:11-32, *page 1181* • Romans 10:16-21, *page 1294* • 1 Peter 3:18-20, *page 1424* • 2 Peter 3:8-9, *page 1429*

We need to wait upon God for his answers or direction Habakkuk 2:1-3, *page 1025*

We need to wait patiently and expectantly for Jesus' return and God's new creation Luke 12:35-48, *page 1176* • Romans 8:18-25, *page 1291* • Hebrews 9:27-28, *page 1405* • James 5:7-8, *page 1417*

Jesus told his disciples to wait for the Holy Spirit's empowering Luke 24:35-49, *page 1196* • Acts 1:1-8, *page 1236*

Waiting inevitably involves faith Hebrews 11:1-16, *page 1407*

▶ *See **Waiting for God's timing**, page 329; **Waiting**, page 558; **The use of time**, page 732; **Pressing on**, page 1359.*

Warfare, Spiritual *see Spiritual warfare*

Weakness *see Power; Rest*

Wealth *see Money*

Will of God *see God's will*

Wisdom *see also Discernment*

Wisdom is living a God-centered life by coming to know God better, allowing him to shape our thinking, and then working that out in every aspect of our lives. It is about taking God's wise words and applying them in God's wise ways. The book of Proverbs in particular is full of wisdom for daily living.

> *If you are wise and understand God's ways, prove it by living an honorable life, doing good works with the humility that comes from wisdom. But if you are bitterly jealous and there is selfish ambition in your heart, don't cover up the truth with boasting and lying. For jealousy and selfishness are not God's kind of wisdom. Such things are earthly, unspiritual, and demonic. For wherever there is jealousy and selfish ambition, there you will find disorder and evil of every kind. But the wisdom from above is first of all pure. It is also peace loving, gentle at all times, and willing to yield to others. It is full of mercy and the fruit of good deeds. It shows no favoritism and is always sincere. And those who are peacemakers will plant seeds of peace and reap a harvest of righteousness. – James 3:13-18, page 1415*

A right fear of God is the foundation of all true wisdom Job 28:20-28, *page 587* • Proverbs 1:7, *page 697*

Wisdom comes from God's word Psalm 19:7-14, *page 613* • Psalm 119:9-24, *page 678*

Wise people accept advice Proverbs 1:1-6, *page 697* • Proverbs 13:10, *page 709* • Proverbs 15:31-33, *page 712*

Gaining wisdom is one of the most important things in life Proverbs 4:1-13, *page 700*

Wisdom is a foundational aspect of who God is Proverbs 8:12-26, *page 704*

Wise people do not boast in their wisdom but rather boast in knowing God Jeremiah 9:23-24, *page 836*

Wise people build their lives on the solid foundation of Jesus' teaching Matthew 7:24-27, *page 1079*

Wisdom from the Spirit is needed even for practical things in life Acts 6:1-3, *page 1244* • Colossians 4:5, *page 1366*

God's wisdom can seem like foolishness from a human perspective 1 Corinthians 1:18–2:6, *page 1304*

We should pray for wisdom Ephesians 1:15-18, *page 1346* • James 1:5-8, *page 1412*

▶ *See **Wisdom**, page 701.*

Witchcraft *see Occult*

Witnessing

We may not all be called to be evangelists, but we are all called to be witnesses—that is, to tell what we know of what Jesus has done for us. We shouldn't look upon this as some kind of duty, as something that we "have to do"; rather, if we have grasped how much Jesus has done for us, then it will be natural for this to overflow in both our life and our conversation. Witnessing is not something we do; being a witness is something we are.

If someone asks about your hope as a believer, always be ready to explain it. But do this in a gentle and respectful way. Keep your conscience clear. Then if people speak against you, they will be ashamed when they see what a good life you live because you belong to Christ. – 1 Peter 3:15-16, page 1423

Bringing the Good News is a wonderful privilege Isaiah 52:7, *page 805*

Part of our witness is to be salt and light in the world Matthew 5:13-16, *page 1075*

We should pray for more people who are willing to share the Good News Matthew 9:35-38, *page 1083*

We should be unembarrassed in our witness Matthew 10:32-33, *page 1084* • Luke 12:8-9, *page 1175*

Jesus promised that the Holy Spirit would help us to witness Acts 1:8, *page 1236*

Being a witness is simply telling what we know and have experienced of Jesus Acts 2:32-36, *page 1239* • Acts 3:12-15, *page 1240* • Acts 5:29-32, *page 1243* • Acts 10:34-48, *page 1252*

Witnessing should be the natural overflow of our lives Acts 4:16-20, *page 1241*

Some people have the gift of being an evangelist Acts 21:8, *page 1270* • Ephesians 4:11-13, *page 1350*

We don't have to be ashamed about witnessing, for the Good News is God's power at work Romans 1:16-17, *page 1282*

People won't hear the Good News unless we tell them Romans 10:5-15, *page 1294*

We should always be ready to explain our faith 1 Peter 3:13-16, *page 1423*

▸ *See **Being a witness**, page 1456.*

Wives and husbands *see Marriage*

Women *see Humanity; Marriage*

Words *see Speech*

Work *see also Business*

Work is part of God's original good intention for us as people, although because of the Fall, work often becomes frustrating and burdensome. God wants us all to work hard and honestly, using the gifts he has given us, and he wants us to find fulfillment in it.

And now, dear brothers and sisters, we give you this command in the name of our Lord Jesus Christ: Stay away from all believers who live idle lives and don't follow the tradition they received from us. For you know that you ought to imitate us. We were not idle when we were with you. We never accepted food from anyone without paying for it. We worked hard day and night so we would not be a burden to any of you. We certainly had the right to ask you to feed us, but we wanted to give you an example to follow. Even while we were with you, we gave you this command: "Those unwilling to work will not get to eat." Yet we hear that some of you are living idle lives, refusing to work and meddling in other people's business. We command such people and urge them in the name of the Lord Jesus Christ to settle down and work to earn their own living. As for the rest of you, dear brothers and sisters, never get tired of doing good. – 2 Thessalonians 3:6-13, page 1375

God himself works Genesis 2:1-2, *page 5* • John 5:16-18, *page 1206*

Work was God's gift to humanity at Creation Genesis 2:15, *page 5*

The Fall made work burdensome, but it did not curse it Genesis 3:17-19, *page 7*

We should not overwork Exodus 18:13-26, *page 87* • Luke 12:15-21, *page 1175*

We need a day of rest from our work Exodus 20:8-11, *page 90* • Leviticus 23:3, *page 143* • Jeremiah 17:19-27, *page 845*

God gives us the ability to do our work Exodus 35:30-31, *page 108*

Hard work helps supply our basic needs Proverbs 28:19, *page 726* • Acts 20:32-35, *page 1269*

Work can be both frustrating and fulfilling Ecclesiastes 2:18-26, *page 732*

We should always do the best work we can Ecclesiastes 9:10, *page 737*

Even though he was God's Son, Jesus spent many years working in the family business Mark 6:3, *page 1127*

We should work honestly Ephesians 4:20-29, *page 1351*

We should work as though Jesus were our boss Ephesians 6:5-8, *page 1352* • Colossians 3:17, *page 1365* • Titus 2:9-10, *page 1390*

▶ *See **Serving God in our work**, page 956; **Working for the glory of God**, page 1265; **Work**, page 1376.*

World, The *see Earth*

Worry *see also Stress*

Worry or anxiety can be a natural human response to uncertainty; but Jesus said his followers do not need to worry, for we have a loving heavenly Father who knows all about us and is committed to caring for us. Instead of putting our energy into worrying, we should focus instead on God, seeking his Kingdom above all else and trusting him in everything.

Give all your worries and cares to God, for he cares about you. – 1 Peter 5:7, page 1425

We are encouraged to give all our worries and cares to God Psalm 55:22, *page 635* • Matthew 6:25-34, *page 1078* • 1 Peter 5:6-7, *page 1425*

Worry makes our hearts heavy Proverbs 12:25, *page 709* • Luke 21:34-36, *page 1190*

We are called to trust in God constantly Isaiah 26:3-4, *page 774*

We don't need to worry when we are put on the spot for our faith Matthew 10:16-20, *page 1083*

We are encouraged to bring all our burdens and worries to Jesus Matthew 11:28-30, *page 1085*

Worry can choke God's life within us Matthew 13:7, 22, *page 1088*

Worrying about getting our work done can distract us from what is important Luke 10:38-42, *page 1172*

Our worries are never bigger than God and his love Romans 8:38-39, *page 1292*

Prayer should take the place of worry Philippians 4:6-7, *page 1359*

▶ *See **Trusting God when we cannot see the way ahead**, page 57; **Trusting God whatever happens**, page 959.*

Worship

Worship should lie at the heart of the community of God's people, for in it we make him central to our lives, individually and corporately, and give him the adoration, esteem, and reverence that are rightly his, simply because of who he is. If people can so passionately express support of their favorite football or baseball team, proclaiming how great they are, how much more should God's people be eager to worship him.

Come, let us sing to the LORD! Let us shout joyfully to the Rock of our salvation. Let us come to him with thanksgiving. Let us sing psalms of praise to him. For the LORD is a great God, a great King above all gods. He holds in his hands the depths of the earth and the mightiest mountains. The sea belongs to him, for he made it. His hands formed the dry land, too. Come, let us worship and bow down. Let us kneel before the LORD our maker, for he is our God. We are the people he watches over, the flock under his care. If only you would listen to his voice today! – Psalm 95:1-7, page 663

Our attitudes must be right when we come to worship Genesis 4:1-7, *page 8* • 1 Samuel 15:12-23, *page 321* • Psalm 24:3-6, *page 615* • Matthew 5:21-24, *page 1075* • Matthew 15:1-9, *page 1092*

Worship is not a meeting, but an encounter with the living and holy God that should leave us in awe Exodus 3:1-6, *page 68* • 2 Chronicles 7:1-3, *page 488* • Isaiah 6:1-5, *page 755* • Hebrews 12:28-29, *page 1409* • Revelation 5:6-14, *page 1451*

God's people are meant to be a priestly, worshiping people Exodus 19:3-6, *page 88* • 1 Peter 2:4-9, *page 1422* • Revelation 1:4-6, *page 1445* • Revelation 5:6-10, *page 1451*

Worship is reserved for God alone, and to worship anyone or anything else is idolatry Exodus 20:3-6, *page 89* • Exodus 34:10-17, *page 106* • Deuteronomy 6:4-15, *page 208* • Matthew 4:10, *page 1073* • Acts 14:8-18, *page 1258*

We should worship God with our whole being Deuteronomy 6:4-5, *page 208* • Matthew 22:34-38, *page 1104*

God's word should have a key place in worship Nehemiah 8:1-12, *page 544* • Acts 2:42, *page 1239* • Acts 20:7-12, *page 1269* • 2 Timothy 4:1-2, *page 1387*

Some psalms of worship Psalm 8, *page 605* • Psalm 24, *page 615* • Psalm 34, *page 621* • Psalm 46, *page 630* • Psalm 48, *page 631* • Psalm 65, *page 640* • Psalm 66, *page 640* • Psalm 84, *page 655* • Psalm 95, *page 663* • Psalm 96, *page 663* • Psalm 100, *page 664* • Psalm 103, *page 666* • Psalm 111, *page 674* • Psalm 145, *page 692* • Psalm 148, *page 694* • Psalm 150, *page 695*

Worship must come from the heart, and not be mere ritual Isaiah 29:13, *page 778* • Isaiah 58:1-14, *page 810* • Micah 6:6-8, *page 1015* • Matthew 15:7-9, *page 1093* • Colossians 2:16-23, *page 1364*

Worship is a spiritual activity and is therefore not dependent on or restricted to special places John 4:19-24, *page 1205*

The Lord's Supper (also called Communion or the Eucharist) is an important part of Christian worship Acts 2:42, *page 1239* • Acts 20:7, *page 1269* • 1 Corinthians 11:17-34, *page 1314*

The early church's worship was participatory 1 Corinthians 12:4-11, *page 1315* • 1 Corinthians 14:26-33, *page 1318* • Colossians 3:16-17, *page 1365*

Heaven is a place of vibrant worship Revelation 5:1-14, *page 1451* • Revelation 7:9-12, *page 1454* • Revelation 15:1-8, *page 1460* • Revelation 19:1-8, *page 1463*

▶ *See **The power of praise**, page 501; **Worship**, page 662; **Preparing for worship**, page 683; **Hallelujah!**, page 693; **Forms of worship**, page 1205.*

Wrong, What do I do when I've done? *see Confession*

Youth *see also Children*

Youth—that period in life when a child begins to develop into an adult—is a time of both challenge and opportunity: challenge, because all kinds of emotions, feelings, and desires are combating with one another; opportunity, because the Bible shows that God often calls and uses people during their youth. God wants it to be a time when we learn how to make good and wise choices that will set us up well for life, and he wants older people to both mentor and make space for young people.

> *Don't let the excitement of youth cause you to forget your Creator. Honor him in your youth before you grow old and say, "Life is not pleasant anymore." – Ecclesiastes 12:1, page 739*

Young people are called to honor their parents Exodus 20:12, *page 90* • Luke 2:51-52, *page 1156* • Ephesians 6:1-3, *page 1352*

Young people should respect those who are older Leviticus 19:32, *page 140* • 1 Timothy 5:1-2, *page 1382* • 1 Peter 5:5-6, *page 1425*

Examples of young people who were called to serve God 1 Samuel 3:1-21, *page 308* • 1 Samuel 16:1-13, *page 323* • 2 Kings 22:1-2, *page 440* • Jeremiah 1:4-19, *page 822* • Luke 1:26-38, *page 1152*

Young people should learn from those who are older 1 Samuel 3:1-21, *page 308* • 1 Kings

12:1-19, *page 392* • Proverbs 1:8-9, *page 697* • Titus 2:3-8, *page 1390*

Young people need God's strength as much as any others Psalm 103:1-5, *page 666* • Isaiah 40:29-31, *page 791*

Young people should beware of the particular temptations of youth and pursue godliness instead Proverbs 7:1-27, *page 703* • Luke 15:11-32, *page 1181* • 1 Timothy 6:11-12, *page 1383* • 2 Timothy 2:20-22, *page 1386*

The excitement of youth should not distract us from God Ecclesiastes 11:9-10, *page 739* • Ecclesiastes 12:1-7, *page 739*

Young people can receive God's Spirit as much as any others Joel 2:28-29, *page 990* • Acts 2:1-18, *page 1237*

Young people can set an example for others 1 Timothy 4:11-12, *page 1382*

▶ *See **Timothy**, page 1380; **Young people**, page 1382; **Mentoring**, page 1385.*

Glossary

The concise explanations in this glossary are intended to supplement the outlines given in "Basic Truths of the Christian Faith" (page 1477) and the notes throughout the Bible, which expand on many of these topics. You can use this glossary to find concise definitions and then follow the cross-references for further discussion of the relevant topics.

Abba An Aramaic word meaning "daddy," used by Jesus of God (Mark 14:36) as a mark of his intimate relationship with him and subsequently adopted by the early church (Romans 8:15-16; Galatians 4:6).

See also ***Abba****, page 1144;* ***Living by the Spirit****, page 1342;* ***The Christian's relationship with the Holy Spirit****, page 1350.*

Accountability Being responsible to others for our thoughts and actions. As Christians we are primarily accountable to God, to whom we will one day have to give an account of our lives. But it is also good to be accountable to one another in a local church, just as the first Christians were (Acts 14:27-28; James 5:13-16).

See also ***Accountability****, page 1258;* ***Basic Truths: Accountability****, page 1478.*

Adoption, spiritual The privilege of becoming the children of God. When we turn to Jesus and put our faith in him, we are adopted into God's family and can know God as our Father, assured that he loves us and that all his resources are now at our disposal (John 1:10-13; Romans 8:14-17; Galatians 3:26; 4:4-7; Hebrews 12:5-11).

See also ***Now that you are a Christian****, page A13;* ***Basic Truths: Adoption, spiritual****, page 1478.*

Advent *see* ***Festivals, Major Christian***

Agape *see* ***Love***

Alpha and Omega The first and last letters of the Greek alphabet, used as a title of both God (Revelation 1:8; 21:6) and Jesus (Revelation 22:13) to signify their everlasting nature.

Altar A place where sacrifices were offered. Both Israel's Tabernacle and Temple had a large bronze altar in their courtyard for burnt offerings and a golden altar within the sanctuary itself for offering incense (Exodus 27:1-8; 30:1-10; 2 Chronicles 4:1, 19).

Amen A Hebrew word meaning "surely," used to affirm the truth of what has been said, especially in worship or prayer (1 Chronicles 16:36; 2 Corinthians 1:20).

Angels Spiritual beings, created to serve God as messengers (Psalm 103:20-21; Luke 1:26-38) and to bring his help or intervention (Genesis 22:9-12; Daniel 6:22). Despite their high status they are not to be worshiped, being significantly less glorious than Jesus (Hebrews 1:3-14).

See also ***Angels****, page 1397;* ***Basic Truths: Angels****, page 1482.*

Annunciation The angel Gabriel's announcement to Mary that she would give birth to the Messiah (Luke 1:26-38).

Anointing The act of pouring oil over somebody or something to indicate being set apart for God's service, symbolizing the outpouring of the Holy Spirit (Genesis 35:14-15; Exodus 28:40-41; 1 Samuel 10:1; Luke 4:16-19; James 5:14).

See also ***Anointing****, page 315.*

Antichrist A term used in the Bible, only by John (1 John 2:18, 22; 4:3; 2 John 1:7), not just of a single end-time opponent of Christ but of all who do not acknowledge him as God incarnate and Messiah. The Greek word "anti" means "instead of," so antichrist is anyone who seeks to take the place of Christ.

See also ***The man of lawlessness****, page 1375;* ***The Antichrist****, page 1434.*

Apocalyptic A type of literature that uses symbolic numbers and vivid, often fantastic or frightening images to communicate its message. Apocalyptic (meaning "revealed") reveals God's perspective on history, unfolding what is going on "behind the scenes" or at the end of the world.

See also ***Revelation (book introduction)****, page 1444.*

Apocrypha Jewish writings from the period between the Old and New Testaments that were not part of the original Hebrew Scriptures but were added later to its Greek translation (called the Septuagint). Some churches accept them as Scripture, but others do not, seeing them simply as providing helpful insights into Jewish beliefs at that time.

See also ***Between the two Testaments****, page 1054.*

Apologetics A reasoned defense of the good news of Jesus, such as Paul's speech before the city council in Athens (Acts 17:16-34). All Christians should be ready to explain their faith (1 Peter 3:15).

*See also **Being a witness**, page 1456; **Basic Truths: Witnessing**, page 1606.*

Apostle From a Greek word meaning "sent one," the term is used both of Jesus' twelve disciples, whom he sent out to preach the gospel (Mark 3:13-19), and of other key church leaders (Acts 14:1-4; Galatians 1:17-19; Ephesians 2:20) whose work included preaching the gospel and starting, equipping, and strengthening churches (Acts 14:1-3, 21-23; Ephesians 4:11-13).

*See also **Apostles of Jesus**, page 1122.*

Ark, Noah's The vessel Noah was commanded to build to save his family and the different kinds of animals in the great flood that God sent to wipe out human wickedness (Genesis 6:5-22).

*See also **The Flood and the ark**, page 11.*

Ark of the Covenant A gold-covered wooden box, measuring about 4 x 2 x 2 feet (1.2 x 0.7 x 0.7 meters) and containing the Ten Commandments, a jar of manna, and Aaron's staff that sprouted leaves (Hebrews 9:4). Symbolizing God's presence among his people, it was kept in the Most Holy Place in the Tabernacle and the Temple.

*See also **The Ark of the Covenant**, page 311.*

Armageddon The focal point of the gathering of God's enemies at the end of time, mentioned only in Revelation 16:16. Some interpret this battle literally and others symbolically.

*See also **Armageddon**, page 1461.*

Ascension, the The return of Jesus to his rightful place in heaven forty days after his resurrection (Acts 1:9-11).

*See also **Jesus' ascension**, page 1196.*

Assurance A firm conviction that we are accepted by God, not because of anything we have done but because of Jesus' sacrifice on the cross on our behalf (Romans 3:21-26; 5:1-2; 8:1). Through faith in him we have an unchanging status as children of God (Romans 8:14-17; Galatians 4:4-7).

*See also **Confidence**, page 1399; **Basic Truths: Assurance**, page 1484.*

Atonement The restoration of relationship with God through the "covering" (the root meaning of the Hebrew word) of sin through sacrifice. The New Testament sees Old Testament sacrifices as simply a foreshadowing of Jesus' sacrifice, which alone can remove sin (Hebrews 9:11–10:4). His death pays sin's price, brings forgiveness, and secures eternal relationship with God (Romans 3:23-26).

*See also **The Day of Atonement**, page 135; **The death of Jesus**, page 1114; **Justification**, page 1288; **Basic Truths: Jesus Christ: his death**, page 1546.*

Babel, tower of A temple-tower or *ziggurat* built as an expression of human pride whose construction led to God's judgment coming upon its builders (Genesis 11:1-9).

*See also **The tower of Babel**, page 14.*

Backsliding Turning or drifting away from God. If we see we are starting to backslide, we should take action quickly and renew our commitment to Jesus while there is still time (Jeremiah 3:22; Hebrews 3:12-15; Revelation 3:14-22).

*See also **Backsliding**, page 841; **Basic Truths: Backsliding**, page 1486.*

Baptism Originally a Jewish ritual that involved immersion in water as a sign of repentance (Matthew 3:1-10). It was adopted by the early church at Jesus' command (Matthew 28:18-20) as an expression of a person's commitment to Jesus in faith and repentance (Acts 2:38-41; 16:30-34).

*See also **Baptism**, page 1238; **Basic Truths: Baptism**, page 1488.*

Beatitudes The list of blessings (Matthew 5:1-12) at the beginning of Jesus' Sermon on the Mount. They express the values of God's Kingdom and are the opposite of what most people seek in life.

Bible The sacred text of Christianity, comprising the books of the Old and New Testaments. The word *Bible* comes from a Greek word meaning "the books." Though written by human authors, the Bible is the inspired and authoritative word of God (2 Timothy 3:16-17).

*See also **What is the Bible?**, page A15; **Meditation**, page 603; **Basic Truths: Bible**, page 1489.*

Birth, new *see **New birth***

Blasphemy Speech or actions that misuse or dishonor God's name, forbidden in the third commandment (Exodus 20:7). Jesus' claim to be equal with God was seen as blasphemy by the religious leaders (Matthew 26:62-65). Blasphemy against the Holy Spirit is unforgivable, for it involves determined, persistent rejection of the one who leads us to God (Matthew 12:24-32; Mark 3:20-30).

*See also **Basic Truths: Blasphemy**, page 1491.*

Blessing A prayer, declaration, or gift that reflects the kindness of the one who gives it. God loves to bless people (Genesis 1:28; 2 Corinthians 9:8; Ephesians 1:3) so that we can enjoy life to the full, and he calls his people to bless others also (Numbers 6:23-27; Luke 6:27-36).

*See also **The power of blessing**, page 160; **Basic Truths: Blessing**, page 1491.*

Blood In the Bible, a symbol of life (Leviticus 17:11); so shedding blood in a sacrifice signified life offered up in death as the price of sin. The expression "the blood of Christ" is used in the New Testament to speak of Christ's life offered on the cross to pay the price of our sin and inaugurate the new covenant (e.g., Romans 5:9; Hebrews 9:14; see also Romans 3:25; 1 Corinthians 11:25; Hebrews 9:22).

See also ***Old Testament sacrifices and offerings**, page 118; **Basic Truths: Blood**, page 1492.*

Body of Christ A term used both of Christ's physical body, offered on the cross for our salvation (1 Corinthians 11:23-29), and as an image of the church—the expression of Christ now on earth. Christ is the head of that body (Colossians 1:18), and Christians are its "members," called to serve one another (1 Corinthians 12:12-31).

See also ***The church**, page 1348; **Basic Truths: Body of Christ**, page 1492.*

Born again *see* ***New birth***

Bride of Christ A New Testament image of the church, reflecting the intimate union between Christ and his people (2 Corinthians 11:2; Ephesians 5:25-32). This image challenges the church to prepare for Christ's return so that, like any bride, it will be ready to welcome her groom (Revelation 19:7-9).
See also ***The church**, page 1348.*

Calvary *see* ***Golgotha***

Cherubim A high rank of heavenly beings that serve God. Unlike angels, cherubim (singular, cherub) have wings (Ezekiel 10:3-5), and gold representations of them were located above the Ark of the Covenant (Exodus 25:17-22).
See also ***The Ark of the Covenant**, page 311; **Angels**, page 1397.*

Chief/leading priests Senior priests in charge of the Temple in Jerusalem, seen as leading representatives of the Jews (Matthew 2:4). They rejected Jesus, whose teaching they saw as undermining their traditions, and conspired in his arrest and crucifixion (Matthew 26:3-5; John 11:45-53). They tried to prevent the apostles from preaching the gospel (Acts 4:1-22; 5:17-41).

Christ Not a name but a title—the Greek equivalent of the Hebrew "Messiah," meaning "Anointed One"—the King-Deliverer promised by the prophets and expected by Israel. See also *Messiah*.

Christian Found only three times in the New Testament (Acts 11:26; 26:28; 1 Peter 4:16), the term was first used as a nickname by outsiders but quickly became the most common term for "a follower of Christ."

See also ***Christian**, page 1254.*

Christmas *see* ***Festivals, Major Christian***

Church In New Testament terms, not a building or an institution, but Christians themselves—the gathered community of believers in Jesus, whatever their background. The New Testament emphasizes their unity through imagery such as the body of Christ (1 Corinthians 12:12-31; Ephesians 1:23), God's holy temple (1 Corinthians 3:16-17), and God's family and house (Ephesians 2:19-22). The church exists not to serve itself but to be God's people in the world (1 Peter 2:9).

See also ***The church**, page 1348; **Belonging to a church**, page 1406; **Basic Truths: Church**, page 1495.*

Circumcision The removal of the male foreskin when one week old, the Old Testament sign of being part of God's covenant people (Genesis 17:1-13). The New Testament, however, sees only the inward circumcision of the heart (a metaphor for obedience to Jesus) as having any value (Romans 2:25-29), and circumcision is unnecessary for Gentile converts to Jesus (Acts 15:1-21; Galatians 5:1-6).

Commitment Dedication to God, his work, and his Kingdom, whatever the cost and without drawing back. Jesus summed up commitment when he prayed, "I want your will to be done, not mine" (Matthew 26:39). Those who lack commitment are constantly challenged in the Bible (e.g., Joshua 24:14-28; Revelation 3:15-20).

See also ***Consecration**, page 267; **Discipleship and the cross**, page 1095; **Counting the cost**, page 1180; **Basic Truths: Commitment**, page 1497.*

Communion *see* ***Lord's Supper***

Confession Acknowledgment of our sin before God. God promises to forgive all who confess their sin, but he expects our words to be matched by our actions and that we will change how we live (Luke 3:1-18; John 8:10-11).

See also ***Is there anything God won't forgive?**, page 633; **Basic Truths: Confession**, page 1499.*

Conversion The experience by which someone turns to Jesus in repentance and faith (Acts 20:21) and is born again by God's Spirit, leading to a complete change of direction in their life.

See also ***The new birth**, page 1203; **Conversion**, page 1371.*

Covenant A binding contract, the Bible's main word for describing the relationship between God and his people. Out of love and grace God binds himself to his people, calling upon them in return to live grateful and godly lives. Although there were several covenants in the Old Testament, the prophets looked forward to "a new covenant" (Jeremiah 31:31-34; see also Ezekiel 36:25-27), which was fulfilled in Jesus (1 Corinthians 11:25).

See also ***Covenant**, page 19; **The new covenant**, page 861; **Basic Truths: Covenant**, page 1501.*

Creation God's act of bringing the universe into being out of nothing (Genesis 1–2; Hebrews 11:3), something that is assumed throughout the Bible and is seen as fundamental to God's nature. The Bible is not concerned with the specifics of how creation came into being, but rather constantly calls us to worship the One who created it in all its beauty.

See also ***Was the world really made in six days?**, page 5; **Basic Truths: Creation**, page 1502.*

Cross, crucifixion A brutal means of execution by torture that involved nailing criminals to a wooden stake.

Although Jews saw crucifixion as a curse (Deuteronomy 21:22-23), Jesus took that curse upon himself (Galatians 3:13), willingly embracing the cross as the only way our sins could be forgiven (1 Peter 2:24; 3:18). The cross is central to the New Testament's message (1 Corinthians 1:17-18).

See also ***The death of Jesus****, page 1114;* ***Jesus' seven sayings from the cross****, page 1229;* ***Basic Truths: Jesus Christ, his death****, page 1546.*

Curse Proclaiming trouble or misfortune over someone; the opposite of blessing. Both people and God pronounce curses in the Old Testament—people out of anger or disappointment, but God only out of righteous judgment. Jesus' death brings release from every curse upon us (Galatians 3:10-14).

Day of Atonement Israel's most holy day, held once a year, when all unconfessed sin was atoned for through special rituals performed by the high priest. The New Testament sees this as a picture of Jesus' work on the cross (Hebrews 9:6-14).

See also ***The Day of Atonement****, page 135.*

Day of the LORD The time of God's intervention in human history to judge his enemies and save his people (Isaiah 13:6-9; Joel 2:1-32; Amos 5:18-24). In the New Testament it is equated with the day of Jesus' return (1 Thessalonians 5:1-11; 2 Peter 3:10-14).

See also ***The day of the LORD****, page 988.*

Demons Evil spirit-beings that serve Satan and his purposes and oppose God's people, but that are shown in the Gospels to be subject to Jesus (Mark 1:21-28; 5:1-20). Jesus gave his followers his authority to free people from their influence (Luke 9:1-2).

See also ***Demons****, page 1126;* ***Angels****, page 1397;* ***Basic Truths: Demons****, page 1505.*

Disciple A New Testament term meaning "learner" or "pupil," used both of the twelve apostles (Matthew 10:1) and of Christian believers in general (Matthew 28:19; Acts 11:26, footnote). The term underlines the importance of being a lifelong learner with Jesus. See *Discipleship*.

Discipleship A term used to describe the way of life expected of those who follow Jesus. It is a common theme in the Gospels, where Jesus shows that discipleship involves committing your whole life to God and following Jesus, whatever the cost. Though this way of life may be costly, it is also richly rewarded (Matthew 6:25-34; Mark 10:28-31).

See also ***Discipleship and the cross****, page 1095;* ***Counting the cost****, page 1180;* ***Basic Truths: Discipleship****, page 1509.*

Doctrine The body of teachings of the Christian faith concerning its central beliefs, which serve to shape the life of God's people for service in the world and which are to be passed on faithfully from one generation to the next (Deuteronomy 6:1-9; 2 Timothy 2:2; 3:14-17).

See also ***Basic Truths: Doctrine****, page 1512.*

Doubt Uncertainty about our faith. The Bible encourages us to be honest about our doubts, to seek help from others, and to bring our doubts to God. In times of doubt or difficulty we should remember God's promises and trust in his power (Isaiah 40:27-31; Mark 9:14-29).

See also ***Trusting God when we cannot see the way ahead****, page 57;* ***Faith****, page 1286;* ***Doubt****, page 1414;* ***Basic Truths: Doubt****, page 1512.*

Easter *see* ***Festivals, Major Christian***

Elders In the Old Testament, men of recognized experience and wisdom who took charge of local affairs, offering wisdom, making decisions, and enforcing the Law (Exodus 3:16-18; Numbers 11:16-17; Deuteronomy 19:12; 1 Kings 12:6; Ezra 10:7-14). In the New Testament the term was adopted for those who led local churches (Acts 14:23; 20:17; 1 Timothy 5:17).

See also ***Leaders in the church****, page 1390.*

Election God's choice of his people. This privilege of being chosen by God brings great reassurance and calls for humility, gratitude, and a compulsion to go and find others God is calling. This calling does not diminish our human responsibility, however, either in terms of responding to God or in terms of obeying and serving him (Deuteronomy 7:7-11; John 15:15-16; Ephesians 1:3-10).

See also ***Repentance****, page 1253;* ***Election****, page 1257;* ***Faith****, page 1286;* ***Basic Truths: Election****, page 1513.*

End times A term not found in the Bible itself but often used by Christians to designate the period before Jesus' return and the events leading up to it.

See also ***The return of Jesus Christ****, page 1372;* ***Basic Truths: Jesus Christ: his return****, page 1549.*

Epiphany *see* ***Festivals, Major Christian***

Eschatology *see* ***Basic Truths: Jesus Christ: his return****, page 1549*

Eternal life Not just life that lasts forever, but life that has all the hallmarks of God's future Kingdom, which we can start to experience right now (John 3:16-17; 5:24; Romans 6:20-23; 1 Timothy 6:12).

See also ***Basic Truths: Eternal life****, page 1517.*

Eucharist *see* ***Lord's Supper***

Evangelism The proclamation of Jesus Christ as Lord and Savior to those who do not know him, not as a duty but as an overflow of his love in our hearts. While not all have the gift of being "an evangelist," all Christians are called to share their testimony of what Jesus has done for them (Matthew 28:19-20; Acts 1:8; 1 Peter 3:15).

See also ***Being a witness****, page 1456;* ***Basic Truths: Witnessing****, page 1606.*

Evil The expression of Satan's character and work, and the very opposite of all that God is. God hates evil (Habakkuk 1:13) and works to bring good out of it (Genesis 50:19-20; Romans 8:28-39); but evil will remain until Jesus returns, when it will finally be destroyed (Revelation 20:7-10; 21:1-8). In the meantime, Christians are called to expose and oppose evil, replacing it with good wherever they can (Ephesians 4:17-32; 5:10-17).

*See also **Satan**, page 566; **Demons**, page 1126; **Spiritual warfare**, page 1353; **Basic Truths: Evil**, page 1518.*

Exile, the The consequence of the collapse of the kingdoms of Israel (in 722 BC) and Judah (in 586 BC) when their inhabitants were taken as conquered people to Assyria and Babylonia respectively, seen in the Bible as God's judgment upon them (2 Kings 17:7-23; 2 Chronicles 36:15-20).

*See also **The Exile**, page 433.*

Exodus, the The name given to Israel's escape from slavery in Egypt. Through God's miraculous intervention (Exodus 7–14), the Israelites were freed to return to the Promised Land. On the way, God made them into a nation (Exodus 19:3-6), gave them his laws (Exodus 20–23), and confirmed his covenant (Exodus 24). The Exodus was constantly remembered as grounds for trusting God for future deliverance (e.g., Isaiah 43:16-21).

*See also **The ten plagues**, page 74; **The Passover**, page 80.*

Faith An attitude of complete trust in God, based on his revelation of himself and his promises. "Faith shows the reality of what we hope for; it is the evidence of things we cannot see" (Hebrews 11:1). It is not just a momentary decision (John 1:12), but a way of life (Galatians 2:20).

*See also **Trusting God when we cannot see the way ahead**, page 57; **Faith and works**, page 1415; **Basic Truths: Faith**, page 1519.*

Faithfulness A fundamental characteristic of God (Exodus 34:6-7), demonstrated in his unswerving commitment to his purposes and his people. God remains faithful even when others are not (Lamentations 3:22-23; 2 Timothy 2:11-13), and he calls us as his people to develop this quality too (Ruth 1:6-18; Matthew 25:14-30).

*See also **Faithfulness**, page 1307; **Basic Truths: Faithfulness**, page 1520.*

Fall, the A term used to describe Adam and Eve's disobedience to God (Genesis 3) and the consequences for the whole human race—separation from God (Romans 5:12-14).

*See also **The fall of humanity**, page 7.*

Fasting The practice of going without food, and sometimes drink, for a period of time in order to devote oneself to God, to pray, or to seek a breakthrough in a specific situation (2 Chronicles 20:1-4; Nehemiah 1:1-4; Daniel 9:1-3; Matthew 4:1-2; Acts 13:2-3; 14:23).

*See also **Does fasting have any value?**, page 1042; **Basic Truths: Fasting**, page 1521.*

Fellowship A New Testament term to express the strong relationships and sharing of life among Christians (Acts 2:42-47), based on the fellowship that we have with God as our Father and with his Son, Jesus (1 John 1:3).

*See also **Fellowship**, page 1357; **Basic Truths: Fellowship**, page 1522.*

Festivals, Major Christian Although not mentioned in the Bible as such, Christian festivals look back to key events in the life of God's people.

Advent This four-week season, which marks the start of the church year, prepares for the celebration of Jesus' first coming ("advent") at Christmas and anticipates his coming again at the end of the age.

Ascension Day Recalls the return of Jesus to his rightful place in heaven forty days after his resurrection (Acts 1:9-11).

*See also **Jesus' ascension**, page 1196.*

Christmas The celebration of the birth of Jesus (Matthew 1:18-25; Luke 2:1-20).

*See also **God's Kingdom**, page 1074; **The Virgin Birth**, page 1152; **Jesus: good news for all**, page 1164; **The Incarnation**, page 1199; **Basic Truths: Jesus Christ: his life**, page 1548.*

Easter The celebration of the resurrection of Jesus (Matthew 28:1-20; Mark 16:1-20; Luke 24:1-49; John 20:1-29; 1 Corinthians 15:1-8).

*See also **Christ's resurrection and ours**, page 1320; **Basic Truths: Resurrection**, page 1583.*

Epiphany The close of the Christmas season, marking the visit of the magi ("wise men") to Jesus (Matthew 2:1-12). Epiphany means "revelation," recalling how Jesus was revealed to the Gentile world as their Savior too.

Good Friday The day Christians remember the death of Jesus (Matthew 27:27-56; Mark 15:16-41; Luke 23:26-49; John 19:17-37).

*See also **Basic Truths: Jesus Christ: his death**, page 1546.*

Holy Week The week between Palm Sunday and Easter Sunday.

Lent The forty-day period leading up to Easter, recalling Jesus' time in the wilderness (Matthew 4:1-11) and seen as a time of preparation.

Palm Sunday The Sunday before Easter, remembering Jesus' triumphant entry into Jerusalem (Matthew 21:1-11; Mark 11:1-11; Luke 19:28-40; John 12:12-19).

Pentecost Remembers the coming of the Holy Spirit to Jesus' followers. See *Pentecost*.

Forgiveness Determining not to hold someone's actions against them. When God forgives us, he frees us from the guilt of our actions. The Christian life begins with receiving God's forgiveness through faith in Jesus and his death on the cross (Ephesians 1:7-8) and then living in that forgiveness (1 John 1:8-9). As Christians, we are called to forgive others because we understand how deeply God has forgiven us (Matthew 18:21-35).

*See also **Is there anything God won't forgive?**, page 633; **Forgiven and forgiving**, page 1098; **How can I be sure God has forgiven me?**, page 1433; **Basic Truths: Forgiveness**, page 1523.*

Freedom The liberty that Jesus brings. As Christians, we are free from the controlling power of sin. This does not mean that we are free to do whatever we please, but that we are free to be the people we were created to be and free to do what is right (Luke 4:14-21; John 8:34-36; Galatians 5:13-15).

*See also **Basic Truths: Freedom**, page 1524.*

Fruit of the Spirit The qualities of love, joy, peace, patience, kindness, goodness, faithfulness, gentleness, and self-control that the Holy Spirit produces in our lives as we allow him to fill us and lead us (Galatians 5:22-23).

*See also **Living by the Spirit**, page 1342; **Basic Truths: Fruitfulness**, page 1524.*

Gentiles A term used in the Bible to refer to all non-Jews. For Jews the word had a negative connotation, as they believed God had rejected the Gentiles; but Jesus came as "a light to reveal God to the nations" (Luke 2:32) and spoke of many Gentiles entering God's Kingdom (Matthew 8:11-12; 21:33-46). Jesus commanded his disciples to take his message to people of all nations (Matthew 28:19), and the book of Acts shows that many Gentiles responded. In Christ all ethnic barriers are now broken down (Ephesians 2:11-22).

*See also **The nations**, page 765.*

Gifts of the Spirit Spiritual gifts given by the Holy Spirit to every follower of Jesus to help them build up the church and share the Good News of Jesus effectively. There is great diversity in the range of spiritual gifts, and all are needed for the church to be effective (Romans 12:4-8; 1 Corinthians 12:4-11, 27-31; 14:1-25; Ephesians 4:7-16; 1 Peter 4:10-11).

*See also **Gifts of the Holy Spirit**, page 1316; **Basic Truths: Spiritual gifts**, page 1594.*

Giving The offering of our lives and all our resources to God. Since God gives generously to us, we are called to be generous givers too, both in our offerings to him and in our support of those in need (Matthew 6:1-4; Acts 2:44-45; 2 Corinthians 8:1-15; 9:6-15).

*See also **Should Christians still tithe?**, page 1052; **Giving**, page 1331; **Basic Truths: Giving**, page 1526.*

God The uncreated, eternal, personal creator of all things, who not only exists but makes himself known (Romans 1:20). In the New Testament the term "God" is frequently used to mean "God the Father," as distinct from the other two persons of the Trinity, God the Son and God the Holy Spirit (e.g., Romans 5:1-5).

*See also **Names and titles of God**, page 70; **The character of God**, page 104; **The one true God**, page 209; **Jesus' baptism**, page 1073; **Basic Truths: God**, page 1527.*

God's will His plan and purpose, and his ability to bring that about (Romans 8:28-39). The Bible urges us to seek God's will for our lives and to do all we can to pursue it, just as Jesus did (Psalm 40:6-8; Matthew 6:10; John 6:38).

*See also **Trusting God when we cannot see the way ahead**, page 57; **God's sovereignty**, page 584; **Why do bad things happen in life?**, page 1025; **Basic Truths: God's will**, page 1528.*

Golgotha The Aramaic name of the place of execution in Jerusalem where Jesus was crucified (Matthew 27:33; John 19:17). In the Latin Bible the word was translated as *Calvariae*, from which the word "Calvary" comes.

*See also **Golgotha**, page 1193.*

Good Friday *see **Festivals, Major Christian***

Gospel A Greek word meaning "good news," used in the New Testament to describe the message of who Jesus was, what he taught, and what he came to bring (Matthew 4:23; Mark 1:14-15; Romans 1:16-17; 1 Corinthians 15:1-8).

*See also **The gospel**, page 1120; **The power of the gospel**, page 1279; **Basic Truths: Gospel**, page 1529.*

Grace God's undeserved love and kindness toward sinners. Although seen supremely in his sending his Son, Jesus, to be our Savior (Ephesians 2:8-10), it is also a rich theme in the Old Testament, not least in God's revelation of himself at Mount Sinai (Exodus 34:5-7).

*See also **The character of God**, page 104; **Access to God**, page 1349; **Faith and works**, page 1415; **Basic Truths: Grace**, page 1531.*

Great commission Jesus' final command to his followers to go out to the whole world and preach his message (Matthew 28:18-20; Acts 1:8).

*See also **Being a witness**, page 1456.*

Growth Becoming mature as a Christian. As Christians, we have started a brand-new life that is designed to experience growth. God does not want us to stay as spiritual babies; he wants us to grow in both our knowledge and experience of him—and to never stop growing (John 15:1-8, 16; Galatians 5:22-23; Ephesians 4:14-16; 2 Peter 3:17-18).

*See also **Now that you are a Christian**, page A13; **Growing as a Christian**, page 1430; **Basic Truths: Growth**, page 1533.*

Guidance God's directing of our lives. We can look to God for guidance, expecting him to lead us, because we know he is our loving heavenly Father and always wants the best for us (Psalm 23; Acts 16:6-10).

*See also **Can God still speak through "fleeces"?**, page 277; **Guidance**, page 1261; **Basic Truths: Guidance**, page 1533.*

Guilt The sense of shame, disgrace, or despair that we feel when we have done wrong. Guilt is intended to drive us back to God and motivate us to confess our sins to him, for he longs to forgive and cleanse us (Psalm 32:1-5; 51:1-19; Hebrews 10:19-39; 1 John 1:8-9).

*See also **Guilt**, page 620; **Basic Truths: Guilt**, page 1534.*

Hallelujah A Hebrew expression meaning "praise" (*hallelu*) "the LORD" (*yah*), often used in biblical worship.

*See also **Hallelujah!**, page 693.*

Heaven Used in a variety of senses, but chiefly of the place where God lives (Deuteronomy 26:15; Matthew 6:9) and where believers go to be with him when they die (Luke 23:43; 2 Corinthians 5:1).

*See also **Heaven**, page 1451; **Basic Truths: Heaven**, page 1535.*

Hell A place of separation and punishment, the eternal destiny of all those who reject Jesus Christ.

*See also **Hell**, page 1108; **Basic Truths: Hell**, page 1536.*

High Council *see **Sanhedrin***

High priest Israel's leading priest, responsible for its spiritual welfare and for making atonement for their sins, especially on the Day of Atonement (Leviticus 16). The high priest Caiaphas and his fellow leading priests fiercely opposed Jesus (Matthew 26:3-5, 57-68), whom they felt threatened their position (John 11:45-53). The New Testament sees all believers as priests (1 Peter 2:9) and Jesus alone as our High Priest (Hebrews 8:1–9:15).

*See also **The Day of Atonement**, page 135; **Every Christian is a priest**, page 1422.*

Holiness The distinctive, perfect aspect of God that makes him different and separates him from everything else in his creation (1 Samuel 2:2; Isaiah 6:1-5). As his people, we too are called to be holy, leading lives that are clearly different from the lives of those around us, to reflect what God is like (Leviticus 11:44-45; Romans 6:19-22; 1 Peter 1:13-16; 2:9-12).

*See also **Holiness**, page 128; **Integrity**, page 1325; **Basic Truths: Holiness**, page 1537.*

Holy Spirit One of the three persons of the Trinity, fully equal with the Father and the Son, God's unseen presence and power in the world. Though the Holy Spirit was present in the Old Testament, he came to prominence at Pentecost (Acts 2). He assures people of their relationship with the Father (Romans 8:14-17), gives them his gifts (1 Corinthians 12:7-11), and empowers them for mission (Acts 1:8).

*See also **Jesus' baptism**, page 1073; **The Holy Spirit in Acts**, page 1236; **The Christian's relationship with the Holy Spirit**, page 1350; **Basic Truths: Holy Spirit**, page 1537.*

Holy Week *see **Festivals, Major Christian***

Hope Confident expectation that is based on God's faithfulness and his promises for the future, both for our life in this world and in the world to come (Colossians 1:4-5; 1 Thessalonians 4:13-18; Hebrews 6:13-20).

*See also **Hope**, page 895; **Christ's resurrection and ours**, page 1320; **Basic Truths: Hope**, page 1539.*

Hypocrisy Pretending to be one thing on the outside but in reality being something different underneath. Because God is a God of truth, he hates hypocrisy (Matthew 6:1-6; 15:3-9; 23:1-36).

*See also **Hypocrisy**, page 1106; **Basic Truths: Hypocrisy**, page 1541.*

I AM The personal name of Israel's God—in Hebrew, *Yahweh* (sometimes translated as "Jehovah" or "LORD")—which was revealed by God to Moses (Exodus 3:13-15). Jesus' use of this name was a clear indication of his claim to be God, and it led to accusations of blasphemy (John 8:58-59).

*See also **Names and titles of God**, page 70.*

Idols Representations of gods and goddesses, forbidden in the Ten Commandments (Exodus 20:3-6). Idolatry, the worship of such images, is constantly opposed in both Old and New Testaments (1 Kings 18:16-40; Isaiah 44:9-20; Acts 17:16-31; Romans 1:18-25). These days, idols are just as likely to be possessions or people.

*See also **Idols**, page 836; **Basic Truths: Idols**, page 1542.*

Incarnation, the The act of God becoming a human being in the person of Jesus Christ. Jesus was not merely a prophet or a holy man, but none other than God himself in human flesh. Jesus, the second person of the Trinity, humbled himself to take a real human nature, being both fully divine and fully human (John 1:1-4, 14-18; Philippians 2:5-8; Colossians 1:15-20).

*See also **The Virgin Birth**, page 1152; **The Incarnation**, page 1199.*

Intercession Praying for another person or situation. See *Prayer*.

Israel The name given to Jacob after he wrestled with God (Genesis 32:22-32). It means "God fights" or "he struggles with God." The twelve tribes descended from him became known as "the twelve tribes of Israel" (Genesis 49:28) or Israelites, and the land where they settled, as Israel. When the nation divided after Solomon's death, the northern part was known as Israel and the southern as Judah. By New Testament times, "Israel" was almost synonymous with "the Jews." See also *Judah*.

*See also **Jacob's family tree**, page 35; **What about Israel?**, page 1294.*

Jesus The name of the incarnate Son of God, the second person of the Trinity. His name, given to Mary by the angel Gabriel (Luke 1:26-33), is the equivalent of the Old Testament name Joshua (meaning "Yahweh saves") and sums up what he came to do.

*See also **God's Kingdom**, page 1074; **The Virgin Birth**, page 1152; **The Incarnation**, page 1199; **The deity of Jesus Christ**, page 1364; **Basic Truths: Jesus Christ: his death**, page 1546; **Basic Truths: Jesus Christ: his identity and character**, page 1547; **Basic Truths: Jesus Christ: his life**, page 1548; **Basic Truths: Jesus Christ: his return**, page 1549.*

Jews A term used from the Exile onward of the inhabitants of Judah, called Hebrews or Israelites in earlier history. While being a Jew is a great privilege (Romans 9:1-5), the New Testament stresses that all barriers between Jews and Gentiles are destroyed in Christ; through faith in him both can become true descendants of Abraham and partakers of God's promise to him (Galatians 3:28-29; Ephesians 2:11-22).

*See also **What about Israel?**, page 1294.*

Judah Jacob's fourth son, whose name means "Praise," and founder of the tribe of Judah. It became Israel's most important tribe and was the tribe from which Jesus was descended (Matthew 1:1-16). After the nation divided following Solomon's death, Judah became the name of the southern kingdom, which remained loyal to David's descendants (1 Kings 12:20). It was conquered by Babylon in 586 BC and by Rome in 63 BC, when it became known as Judea. See also *Israel*.

Judgment The expression of God's justice that calls everyone to account for their lives. God's judgment is always right, considering motives as well as actions, and he is slow to bring judgment (Psalm 103:8-18), giving us time to change (2 Peter 3:3-10). This judgment may come in some measure during our lifetime, but it is particularly associated with the Last Judgment when all will be judged (Acts 17:31). However, those who trust in Christ need not fear this judgment.

*See also **The Last Judgment**, page 1465; **Basic Truths: Judgment**, page 1550.*

Judgment day The time at the end of history when "we will all stand before the judgment seat of God" (Romans 14:10) and the righteous will be rewarded and the guilty punished (Revelation 20:11-15). Christians need not fear, however, for their judgment has already been taken by Christ, and they have already been made right with God (Romans 3:21-26; 8:1-4). Any future judgment for Christians does not concern their salvation but rather their stewardship of gifts and opportunities (1 Corinthians 3:12-15; 2 Corinthians 5:10).

*See also **The Last Judgment**, page 1465; **Basic Truths: Judgment**, page 1550.*

Justification The declaration of God, the righteous Judge, that we are now righteous before him, not because of anything we have done but only because of the substitutionary death and the resurrection of his Son, Jesus Christ, in whom we have put our trust (Romans 3:21-28; 4:1–5:11; 8:1-39; Galatians 2:15-21; 3:10-14).

*See also **Justification**, page 1288; **Basic Truths: Justification**, page 1551.*

Kingdom of God The central theme of Jesus' teaching (Mark 1:14-15), that God is King and is coming to rule. When we put ourselves under that rule, all of life is transformed, as Jesus demonstrated in his teaching (Matthew 5:1–7:29), miracles (Mark 1:21–2:12), and parables (Matthew 13:1-58). Out of respect for his Jewish-background readers, Matthew replaces the name of "God" with "Heaven" in this phrase, as was common in his day.

*See also **God's Kingdom**, page 1074; **Basic Truths: Kingdom of God/Kingdom of Heaven**, page 1553.*

Laity A term often used today of Christians who are not ordained priests or ministers. However, while the New Testament does speak of leadership roles in the church, it makes clear that all God's people are now his priests (1 Peter 2:5-9).

*See also **Every Christian is a priest**, page 1422.*

Lamb of God A title given to Jesus, underlining his sacrificial death for the sins of others (John 1:29; 1 Peter 1:19; Revelation 5:6-12). See also *Atonement*.

*See also **Names and titles of Jesus**, page 1070.*

Last days Although often used today to refer to the period immediately before Jesus' return, in the New Testament it refers to the whole period between Jesus' first coming and his second coming (Acts 2:16-18; see also Hebrews 1:1-2)—a time of both advancement of God's Kingdom (Matthew 13) and of a growth in wickedness and the persecution of Christians (2 Timothy 3:1-5).

*See also **Basic Truths: Jesus Christ: his return**, page 1549.*

Last Supper The final meal that Jesus shared with his disciples before he was betrayed, where he made clear both the sacrificial nature of his death that was about to follow and how it would inaugurate God's new covenant (Matthew 26:17-29). It became the basis of the church's celebration of Communion, or the Lord's Supper (1 Corinthians 11:23-34).

*See also **The Last Supper**, page 1110.*

Law The first five books of the Bible (called the Torah by Jews). As God's gift to Israel, the Law was a delight (Psalm 119), expressing the covenant between them and guiding every aspect of life. Jesus affirmed the Law (Matthew 5:17-18), yet rejected the religious leaders' additions and interpretations that made it burdensome (Matthew 23:1-4). Through his life and death, he fulfilled the Law for us, and his Spirit now helps us to live in a way that pleases God, guiding us from within rather than through external laws (Romans 8:1-17). See also *Pentateuch*.

*See also **Are the Ten Commandments still relevant today?**, page 89; **Legalism**, page 1339; **Basic Truths: Law**, page 1554.*

Laying on of hands Putting hands on someone's head or shoulders as a sign of commissioning, blessing, or healing. It symbolizes setting them apart for God (e.g., Numbers 27:18-23; Matthew 19:13; Luke 4:40; Acts 6:1-6; 13:1-3).

Legalism In the New Testament, an insistence on Christians keeping the Jewish Law, in addition to trusting Jesus, in order to be saved (Acts 15:1). Legalism was fiercely resisted by Paul (Galatians 3:1-29; 5:1-10). Today it often refers to insistence that others behave and believe in certain ways (beyond accepting Jesus as Savior) in order to be accepted as "real" Christians.

*See also **Legalism**, page 1339; **Basic Truths: Law**, page 1554.*

Lent *see **Festivals, Major Christian***

Leprosy Any of a number of chronic skin diseases common in Bible times, not just modern leprosy. Leprosy made sufferers ritually unclean (Leviticus 13–14), and as such they became social outcasts, which is why Jesus prioritized healing those who suffered from it (Matthew 8:1-4; 10:5-8; 11:4-5).

*See also **Leprosy**, page 508.*

Lord's Prayer, the A prayer, or model for praying, that Jesus taught his disciples (Matthew 6:9-13; Luke 11:2-4).

*See also **The Lord's Prayer**, page 1077.*

Lord's Supper The Bible's term for Holy Communion (also called Eucharist or Mass). It was inaugurated at Jesus' final meal with his disciples, when his words transformed what had been a Passover meal into a celebration of the new covenant (Luke 22:19-20; 1 Corinthians 11:23-26). Sharing bread and wine to recall his sacrificial death became a central feature of Christian worship (Acts 2:42, 46; 20:7, 11), often as part of a meal (1 Corinthians 11:33-34; Jude 1:12). Almost all churches today share bread and wine (or grape juice) together.

*See also **The Last Supper**, page 1110; **Basic Truths: Communion**, page 1497.*

Lordship Jesus Christ's position as Lord (master) over every aspect of our lives. Accepting Jesus' lordship involves a readiness to obey him completely, for he said we cannot call him Lord unless we are willing to do what he tells us (Luke 6:46-49).

*See also **Discipleship and the cross**, page 1095; **Counting the cost**, page 1180.*

Lots, casting of A common means of decision-making in the Old Testament (e.g., Joshua 18:3-10; Nehemiah 10:34; Jonah 1:7) that involved choosing marked stones or sticks from a container into which they had been "cast." It was believed that God, in his sovereignty, oversaw the choice of the lot, thus bringing his guidance. The practice is found only once in the New Testament (Acts 1:21-26), before the giving of the Holy Spirit. Christians soon realized that, with the Spirit's presence, they did not need such a means of guidance.

*See also **Guidance**, page 1261.*

Love Giving of yourself for the good of others. Love is one of God's greatest characteristics (Exodus 34:6-7; 1 John 4:16), expressed supremely in his sending Jesus to die for us (John 3:16-17; Romans 5:6-11), and his people are called to demonstrate such love too (Matthew 5:43-48; John 13:1-17; 1 Corinthians 13:1-8). The most common word for love in the New Testament is *agape*—commitment-love that never gives in or gives up.

*See also **Love your neighbor as yourself**, page 139; **Loving others**, page 1220; **The love of God**, page 1437; **Basic Truths: Love**, page 1559.*

Manna Food miraculously provided for the Israelites in the wilderness (Exodus 16). They called it manna (meaning "what is it?"), for it was unlike anything they had ever known. It continued to appear until they reached the Promised Land, and then it stopped (Joshua 5:12). Often called "bread from heaven" (Nehemiah 9:15; Psalm 78:24), manna was used by Jesus as a picture of himself—food from heaven, but this time food that would last forever (John 6:47-58).

*See also **Manna: What was it?**, page 85.*

Martyr Used of someone who suffers death for their beliefs. Stephen was the first martyr of the Christian church (Acts 7:54-60), though many others would follow (Acts 12:1-2; Revelation 6:9-11). The Old Testament also had martyrs who died because of their faith in the one true God (Genesis 4:1-8; 1 Kings 19:10; Luke 11:50-51; Hebrews 11:35-38).

Mass *see **Lord's Supper***

Mercy God's patient loving-kindness toward sinners, expressed in his readiness to forgive them (Exodus 34:5-7; Psalm 103:8-13; Ephesians 2:4-10). Jesus, as the Son of God, perfectly demonstrated God's mercy by responding to those in need, freeing those who were bound, and forgiving those who had done wrong—even when they did not deserve it (Matthew 9:9-13). As Christians, we are called to be merciful toward others, because we ourselves have received mercy from God (Matthew 18:21-35; Luke 6:35-36).

*See also **The character of God**, page 104; **Basic Truths: Mercy**, page 1561.*

Messiah From the Hebrew word *mashiaḥ*, meaning "Anointed One," translated into Greek as *christos*, from which the word "Christ" comes. It was used of Israel's long-awaited Deliverer-King, whom Israel believed would subdue their enemies and establish God's Kingdom—an expectation that was fervent in New Testament times (Matthew 21:1-11; Luke 3:15; Acts 1:6). This is why Jesus generally avoided the title, for he had come to bring God's Kingdom not with a sword but with a cross. See also *Christ*.

*See also **Anointing**, page 315; **Prophecies of the Messiah**, page 1044; **Names and titles of Jesus**, page 1070; **The mission of Jesus**, page 1159; **Basic Truths: Messiah**, page 1562.*

Millennium A period of one thousand years before the final overthrow of Satan (Revelation 20:1-10). There are three main interpretations of it: a literal one thousand years, marked by great success for the church, climaxing in Jesus' return (the postmillennial view); a literal one thousand years beginning when Jesus returns to bind Satan and reign on earth, though not finally overthrowing him until the End (the premillennial view); and a symbolic period signifying the time between Jesus' first and second comings (the amillennial or historic millennial view).

*See also **The return of Jesus Christ**, page 1372.*

Ministry Sometimes used to refer to "full-time Christian service," especially by becoming a minister or missionary. But in the New Testament, all Christians are called to ministry or service (Ephesians 4:11-16; 1 Peter 2:9), following the example of Jesus, who came as the promised Servant (Isaiah 42:1-9) and who constantly served others in their need, even to the point of death (Isaiah 52:13–53:12; Mark 10:35-45).

*See also **Serving one another**, page 461; **Serving God in our work**, page 956; **Service**, page 1424; **Basic Truths: Service**, page 1589.*

Miracles Powerful interventions of God that lie outside normal explanation. Never performed for their own sake, miracles are designed to reassure God's people, challenge their thinking, or highlight his purposes. Miracles never guarantee faith (Matthew 11:20; Luke 17:11-19); rather, they are gracious pointers to God's compassion and purposes, and invitations to trust in him again.

*See also **Jesus' miracles**, page 1128; **John's seven signs**, page 1201; **Miracles and healing**, page 1243.*

Mission The activity of sharing with God in his work of seeking and saving the lost (Luke 19:10).

*See also **Mission**, page 1082; **Basic Truths: Witnessing**, page 1606.*

Most Holy Place (Holy of Holies) The most sacred part of the Tabernacle and the Temple, containing the Ark of the Covenant, which symbolized God's presence among his people. Only the high priest could enter here, once a year, on the Day of Atonement (Leviticus 16).

*See also **The Tabernacle**, page 96; **The Temple**, page 382.*

Nations Often used as a symbol of those who do not trust in the living God. However, Jesus commanded his followers to make disciples of all nations (Matthew 28:18-20), and people from every nation will worship God in heaven (Revelation 7:9-10).

*See also **The nations**, page 765; **Basic Truths: Nations**, page 1566.*

New birth The fundamental inner spiritual change brought about by the Holy Spirit that is so radical that it is like starting life all over again, as Jesus explained to Nicodemus (John 3:1-21).

*See also **The new birth**, page 1203; **Basic Truths: Birth**, page 1490.*

New covenant God's commitment to his people and purposes expressed through the coming of Jesus, who shed his blood to forgive our sins and bring us into relationship with his Father (Matthew 26:27-28). This new covenant is the fulfillment of all the Old Testament covenants, as promised through Jeremiah (Jeremiah 31:31-34).

*See also **The new covenant**, page 861; **Basic Truths: Covenant**, page 1501.*

Occult Any practice that seeks to engage with the spirit world without reference to the living God. All types of occult practices are forbidden in the Bible (Deuteronomy 18:9-14).

*See also **The occult**, page 337; **Basic Truths: Occult**, page 1567.*

Pagan shrine (or "high place") A place of worship, often (though not always) on raised or higher ground, mainly used for idolatry and cultic prostitution (2 Kings 17:9-11; 23:13-15), both forbidden to God's people.

*See also **Pagan shrines**, page 427.*

Palm Sunday *see **Festivals, Major Christian***

Parable A short descriptive story from everyday life told to convey a message about God and his Kingdom. Parables were used in the Old Testament (Judges 9:7-20; 2 Samuel 12:1-10; Isaiah 5:1-7), but they were particularly important in Jesus' teaching about the Kingdom of God (e.g., Matthew 13:1-52; 25:1-46).

*See also **The parables of Jesus**, page 1088; **Jesus' parables**, page 1089.*

Paradise Based on a word borrowed from Persian meaning "a walled garden," "paradise" is used three times in the New Testament as a picture of the delights of heaven (Luke 23:43; 2 Corinthians 12:4; Revelation 2:7).

*See also **Paradise**, page 1194; **Heaven**, page 1451.*

Passion, the From a Greek word meaning "to suffer," "the Passion" refers to Jesus' sufferings during his final week on earth, climaxing in his betrayal (Matthew 26:21-25, 47-50), humiliation (Matthew 27:27-30), crucifixion (Matthew 27:27-56), and separation from his Father (Matthew 27:46).

*See also **Basic Truths: Jesus Christ: his death**, page 1546; **Basic Truths: Jesus Christ: his life**, page 1548.*

Passover One of three major annual festivals in Judaism when all Jewish men were required to go to the Temple in Jerusalem, Passover commemorated Israel's escape from slavery in Egypt.

*See also **The Passover**, page 80; **The Last Supper**, page 1110.*

Patriarchs A term for Israel's founding fathers: Abraham and his main descendants, Isaac, Jacob, and Joseph. Genesis 12–50 is often known as the patriarchal narratives.

*See also **Abraham**, page 16; **Isaac and Rebekah**, page 28; **Jacob and Esau**, page 40; **Joseph**, page 47.*

Pentateuch A term used by Christians, meaning "five scrolls," referring to the first five books of the Old Testament (called the Torah or Law by Jews). These five books contain a continuous story from the creation of the world to the point where Israel was about to enter the Promised Land. They show God's determination to fulfill his purposes and promises, despite human frailty and sin.

Pentecost One of three major annual festivals in Judaism when all Jewish men were required to go to the Temple in Jerusalem, Pentecost was a harvest festival (Exodus 23:16; Leviticus 23:15-22), originally called the Festival of Harvest (or Feast of Weeks). Because it was celebrated fifty days after Passover, it later became known as Pentecost (Greek for "fiftieth") and was seen as the anniversary of God giving the Law to Moses. In Christian usage it refers to the day when the Holy Spirit was first given to the church (Acts 2:1-4).

Persecution Suffering for our faith. We should not go looking for persecution, but Jesus said that being faithful to him would sometimes attract persecution from those who hate him and his message (Matthew 10:16-28; John 15:18-21; 2 Timothy 3:10-12; 1 Peter 3:8-18; Revelation 2:8-11).

*See also **Persecution**, page 1452; **Basic Truths: Persecution**, page 1572.*

Perseverance Pressing on as a Christian, especially when life gets tough or the devil seems to be opposing us. We should always remember that God is committed to bringing us into all the purposes he has for us (Philippians 1:6; 2:12-13; Jude 1:24-25), which should encourage us to keep going (Mark 13:9-13; Hebrews 10:19-25).

*See also **Now that you are a Christian**, page A13; **Trusting God when we cannot see the way ahead**, page 57; **Perseverance in prayer**, page 1184; **Pressing on**, page 1359; **Can a Christian lose their salvation?**, page 1401; **The dangers of drifting**, page 1447; **Basic Truths: Perseverance**, page 1572.*

Pharaoh The title of the kings of Egypt.

*See also **Pharaoh**, page 76.*

Praise Praise is about honoring God for who he is and what he has done—not because he needs it but because it is the right thing to do. It is the natural expression of being his people (1 Peter 2:9), and because it lifts him up, it can lead to the reversal of impossible situations (2 Chronicles 20:15-30; Acts 16:25-34). In the Bible praise is normally a noisy affair, often accompanied by music and dancing (Exodus 15:20-21; 2 Samuel 6:5; Psalm 150).

*See also **The power of praise**, page 501; **Worship**, page 662; **Thanksgiving**, page 665; **Hallelujah!**, page 693; **Basic Truths: Worship**, page 1607.*

Prayer In the Bible, prayer is not the recitation of religious phrases or formulas but, quite simply, conversation with our heavenly Father. While it may take several forms, its essence is utter honesty and openness before him as we bring our needs, concerns, thanksgiving, and confession. At its heart lies friendship with God, as Jesus demonstrated.

*See also **Praying in the moment**, page 537; **Does God mind if we are honest with him?**, page 848; **Prayer as intercession**, page 922; **The Lord's Prayer**, page 1077; **Basic Truths: Prayer**, page 1575.*

Prayer meeting A time when Christians gather to pray corporately. Notable prayer meetings in the early church include Acts 1:12-14; 4:23-31; 12:6-19; and 13:1-4.

*See also **The power of praise**, page 501; **Praying in the moment**, page 537; **Worship**, page 662; **Does God mind if we are honest with him?**, page 848; **The Lord's Prayer**, page 1077; **Basic Truths: Prayer**, page 1575; **Basic Truths: Worship**, page 1607.*

Promised Land A common term for the land of Canaan or Palestine, which God promised to Abraham and his descendants (Genesis 12:1-7).

*See also **Canaan**, page 21.*

Prophecy and prophets Prophecy is bringing a word directly from God under the inspiration of the Holy Spirit, and a prophet was someone, male or female, who brought that word. While prophecy was common in the Old Testament, it became available to all believers in the New Testament with the giving of the Holy Spirit (Acts 2:17-18)—at least in the sense of speaking a word from God to strengthen the church. Prophecy played an important role in the early church (Acts 11:27-28; 1 Corinthians 14).

*See also **Prophecy in the Old Testament**, page 903; **Prophecy in the New Testament**, page 1318; **Basic Truths: Prophecy**, page 1577.*

Quiet time A regular time set aside to pray, worship God, and read the Bible, usually on our own, as part of developing our relationship with him (Psalm 1:1-3; Daniel 6:10; Mark 1:35; Acts 17:11).

*See also **Meditation**, page 603; **Worship**, page 662; **Does God mind if we are honest with him?**, page 848;*

The Lord's Prayer, page 1077; ***Basic Truths: Bible,*** *page 1489;* ***Basic Truths: Prayer,*** *page 1575;* ***Basic Truths: Worship,*** *page 1607.*

Rabbi Jewish title for a teacher, used also as a mark of respect. Jesus was often called "Rabbi" (Mark 9:5; John 3:2).

Reconciliation The restoration of friendship with God through the atoning death of Jesus, and the consequent breaking down of all barriers between Christians (Romans 5:10-11; 2 Corinthians 5:17-21; Ephesians 2:14-22; Colossians 1:19-22).

See also ***Reconciliation,*** *page 1328;* ***Basic Truths: Reconciliation,*** *page 1578.*

Redemption Paying a price to buy back someone or something from some form of bondage or imprisonment. The idea is used of God's deliverance of the Israelites from slavery in Egypt (Exodus 6:6-8) and of Jesus' paying the ransom to free us from sin through his death on the cross (Mark 10:45; 1 Peter 1:18-19).

See also ***Redemption,*** *page 1136;* ***Basic Truths: Redemption,*** *page 1578.*

Regeneration *see* ***New birth***

Renewal God's restoring of us, individually and corporately, to a freshness of spiritual life by his Holy Spirit after we have recognized our need and asked him to revive us (2 Chronicles 7:13-14; Psalm 51:10-12; Ezekiel 37:1-14; Romans 12:1-2; Ephesians 4:21-23).

See also ***Renewal,*** *page 939;* ***Basic Truths: Renewal,*** *page 1579.*

Repentance Turning away from sin and turning toward God (Acts 3:19), leading to a changed way of living. Repentance means recognizing that how we have been thinking and living is wrong by God's standards, then confessing our sin to him, in order that we might receive his forgiveness and start living a new life with Jesus, eager to do things God's way from then on.

See also ***Repentance,*** *page 1253;* ***Basic Truths: Repentance,*** *page 1580.*

Resurrection The raising of Jesus from the dead by the Father after Jesus' death on the cross and burial, just as he prophesied (Matthew 16:21; 17:9; 20:17-19). The Resurrection proved Jesus' divinity and messiahship (Acts 2:29-36; Romans 1:4) and is the guarantee of the resurrection of all who believe in him (John 11:25-26; 1 Corinthians 15:12-28). The resurrection of Jesus lies at the heart of the Christian faith.

See also ***Christ's resurrection and ours,*** *page 1320;* ***Basic Truths: Resurrection,*** *page 1583.*

Return of Jesus *see* ***Second Coming***

Right with God, how do I get? *see* ***Justification***

Righteousness *see* ***Justification***

Sabbath The weekly day of rest (Saturday), given as God's gift to his people Israel (Exodus 20:8-11; 31:13). By New Testament times, keeping the Sabbath had become burdensome because of the many additional rules added by the religious leaders, a cause of frequent conflict between them and Jesus (e.g., Mark 2:23-28). The early church gathered to worship on Sunday instead of the Sabbath as a weekly commemoration of the Resurrection.

See also ***The Sabbath,*** *page 918;* ***Sunday,*** *page 1121;* ***Basic Truths: Day of rest,*** *page 1503.*

Sacrifice The offering up of life to God as an expression of gratitude or to make atonement for sin. Since "the wages of sin is death" (Romans 6:23), wherever there is sin, something has to die. In the Old Testament, God commanded his people to sacrifice animals as substitutes (Leviticus 1–4). But Old Testament sacrifices could not really deal with sin; they were simply "shadows" (Hebrews 10:1-4), pointing to the one true sacrifice that was coming—that of Jesus, God's Son, who made every other sacrifice obsolete (Hebrews 8:1–10:18).

See also ***Old Testament sacrifices and offerings,*** *page 118.*

Salvation God's rescue of humanity. This major theme is revealed in the form of a story, showing God's eternal plan to deal with sin. In the Old Testament the story's focal point is God's rescue of Israel from slavery in Egypt; in the New Testament its climax is the life, death, and resurrection of Jesus, which freed us from slavery to sin (Matthew 1:21; Luke 19:9-10). Salvation is God's gift that anyone can receive through faith in Jesus (Ephesians 2:8-9).

See also ***The death of Jesus,*** *page 1114;* ***Redemption,*** *page 1136;* ***The new birth,*** *page 1203;* ***Jesus: The only way to God,*** *page 1241;* ***Justification,*** *page 1288;* ***Christ's resurrection and ours,*** *page 1320;* ***Reconciliation,*** *page 1328;* ***Can a Christian lose their salvation?,*** *page 1401;* ***Basic Truths: Salvation,*** *page 1584.*

Sanctification The lifelong process of becoming more holy through the inner work of God's Holy Spirit (Romans 12:1-2; Ephesians 4:22-24; Philippians 3:12-16; 1 Thessalonians 4:3-8; 2 Peter 1:3-11).

See also ***Holiness,*** *page 128;* ***Growing as a Christian,*** *page 1430;* ***Becoming like Christ,*** *page 1435;* ***Basic Truths: Holiness,*** *page 1537.*

Sanhedrin (High Council) The ruling council of the Jews in New Testament times, comprising chief priests, elders, and scribes. It was Judaism's highest court and was granted political and religious powers by Rome, but they did not have the authority to impose the death penalty, which is why they needed to win over Pilate, the Roman governor, to have Jesus executed (Luke 20:20; John 18:31). Some early Christians were tried before them (Acts 4:1-22; 5:17-42; 22:30–23:11).

Satan One of the names of the devil, meaning "the accuser"—the personal evil spirit-being who opposes God and his people, but whose power was broken at the cross (John 12:31; Colossians 2:15; Hebrews 2:14) and who will be finally overthrown at the End (Revelation 20:7-10).

*See also **Satan**, page 566; **Basic Truths: Satan**, page 1585.*

Savior One who rescues people; used of God in the Old Testament as he came to rescue both individuals and the nation of Israel (e.g., 2 Samuel 22:3; Isaiah 43:3), and used in the New Testament of Jesus, who came to rescue us from the power of sin through his death on the cross (Matthew 1:21; Luke 19:9-10; Romans 3:23-28; 2 Timothy 1:10).

*See also **The death of Jesus**, page 1114; **Justification**, page 1288; **Reconciliation**, page 1328; **Basic Truths: Salvation**, page 1584.*

Scripture *see Bible*

Second Coming The personal and glorious return of Jesus Christ at the end of the age, just as he promised (Matthew 24), to raise the dead, judge sinners, destroy evil, and establish his new creation.

*See also **Hell**, page 1108; **The return of Jesus Christ**, page 1372; **Heaven**, page 1451; **The Last Judgment**, page 1465; **The new Jerusalem**, page 1466; **Basic Truths: Jesus Christ: his return**, page 1549.*

Septuagint The Greek translation of the Hebrew Scriptures. The name comes from the Greek word for "seventy" because, according to Jewish tradition, it was translated by seventy scholars. It was the version of the Old Testament used by most of the early church, which was largely Greek-speaking. This explains why some Old Testament quotations in the New Testament seem slightly different from the original text.

Service *see Ministry*

Sin Any thought, word, or action that is against God's will. Sin is the root of the fallen human condition, breaking relationship with God and ruining all our lives. While there are several different words for "sin" in Hebrew and Greek, the idea underlying them all is disobedience to God and his word (Psalm 51:1-6; Isaiah 59:1-2; Romans 3:23; 5:12-19; 1 John 3:4).

*See also **The fall of humanity**, page 7; **Sin**, page 387; **How can I be sure God has forgiven me?**, page 1433; **Basic Truths: Sin**, page 1590.*

Sonship *see Adoption, spiritual*

Spiritual warfare Fighting in a spiritual battle with the devil, the sinful world in which we live, and our own selfish human nature. God provides us with spiritual armor to engage in this battle and to be victorious in it (Ephesians 6:10-20; 1 Peter 5:8-9).

*See also **Spiritual warfare**, page 1353; **Basic Truths: Spiritual warfare**, page 1594.*

Submission Adopting Jesus' loving attitude of service and putting others' interests before our own. Jesus modeled this role and attitude for us (Matthew 26:36-42; Philippians 2:4-8), and submission is to characterize our relationships with others (Ephesians 5:21; 1 Peter 5:5-7).

*See also **Submission and relationships**, page 1352; **Basic Truths: Submission**, page 1596.*

Synagogue A local meeting place of the Jewish community. Synagogues developed during the Exile when the Jews were far from their Temple. They served as meeting places for reading the Law, hearing sermons, prayer, and community life. Each synagogue had a "leader" (Mark 5:22; Acts 18:8), and qualified laymen were allowed to teach there (Luke 4:16-21; Acts 13:14-15). The early Christians always began their evangelism at synagogues (Acts 9:20; 13:5, 14; 14:1; 17:1-2, 10, 16-17; 18:1-4, 19) but were eventually rejected, just as Jesus foresaw (Mark 13:9).

*See also **Synagogues**, page 1250.*

Tabernacle A special tent that served as the focal point of worship and sacrifice during Israel's wilderness wanderings and through the periods of the conquest of Canaan, the judges, and the early monarchy, until Solomon's building of the Temple. It was also called the Tent of Meeting or the Tent of the Testimony, and it was seen as God's dwelling place on earth (Exodus 25:8).

*See also **The Tabernacle**, page 96.*

Temple Israel's first permanent sanctuary, located in Jerusalem, which replaced the Tabernacle. Three successive temples were built: the first, by Solomon around 960 BC (1 Kings 6–9); the second, by the returning exiles, completed in 515 BC (Ezra 3:1–6:22); the third, by Herod the Great, completed in AD 64, just six years before it was destroyed by Rome, never to be rebuilt. Jesus predicted this destruction, saying the Temple had become "a den of thieves" rather than "a house of prayer" (Matthew 21:12-13; 24:1-2). For Christians, God's temple is now the church as the body of Christ (1 Corinthians 3:16).

*See also **The Temple**, page 382.*

Temptation The urge, whether from something within us or from some external provocation, to disobey God or to do something that we know is not right (e.g., Genesis 3:1-5; 39:6-12; 2 Samuel 11:1-4; Matthew 4:1-11). God wants to help us resist temptation (Matthew 6:13; 1 Corinthians 10:12-13; James 1:12-15), and Jesus showed us that with the help of God's Spirit, it really is possible (Romans 7:14-25; Hebrews 4:15-16; James 4:7).

*See also **Temptation**, page 1313; **Basic Truths: Temptation**, page 1599.*

Ten Commandments Called in Hebrew "the ten words," a series of commandments inscribed on two stone tablets at Mount Sinai (Exodus 20:1-17; Deuteronomy 5:1-22). The first four commandments deal with people's relationship with God, and the last six, with people's relationships with one another.

*See also **Are the Ten Commandments still relevant today?**, page 89.*

Testimony The personal story of our conversion and our experience of Jesus, shared with others. Giving our testimony can be a powerful witness to others and bring encouragement to them and ourselves (Acts 2:32-41; 4:16-20; Romans 10:9-15; 1 Peter 3:15-16).

*See also **Being a witness**, page 1456; **Basic Truths: Witnessing**, page 1606.*

Testing Difficult experiences that God sometimes takes us through, not because he doesn't love us, but because he does. God uses such times to refine our faith and develop our character (Genesis 22:1-18; Romans 5:1-5; James 1:2-18; 1 Peter 1:6-7).

*See also **Trusting God when we cannot see the way ahead**, page 57; **Faith**, page 1286; **Pressing on**, page 1359; **Basic Truths: Testing**, page 1599.*

Tithing The practice of giving one tenth of one's income to God, used in the Old Testament for support of the priests and Levites and for the upkeep of the sanctuary (Numbers 18:21-32). For Israel this was a commandment (Leviticus 27:30), and not to tithe was to cheat God (Malachi 3:8-9). Jesus stressed that tithing should be done with the right attitude (Matthew 23:23-24).

*See also **Should Christians still tithe?**, page 1052.*

Torah Jewish word for "the Law." See *Law*; *Pentateuch*.

Transfiguration The occasion when Jesus shone with the glory of God, and Moses and Elijah came to bear witness to him (Matthew 17:1-13; Mark 9:2-13; Luke 9:28-36).

*See also **The Transfiguration**, page 1169.*

Trials *see **Testing***

Trinity, the The doctrine of the Trinity affirms that the one God (see Deuteronomy 6:4, footnote) exists simultaneously in three persons as Father, Son, and Holy Spirit, each of whom is distinct from the others while yet being completely interrelated. All three persons are fully, equally, and eternally divine. While this doctrine is not explicitly set out in Scripture, it is evident from passages that ascribe the same titles, functions, privileges, and power to Jesus as to the Father (Mark 2:5-7; John 1:1-4; 8:54-58; Romans 9:5; Philippians 2:9-11), and to the Spirit as to the Son or the Father (Acts 5:3-4; 2 Corinthians 3:16-18; Galatians 4:6; Hebrews 3:7-12; 10:15-16). Additionally, the three are linked together in passages like Matthew 28:19 and 2 Corinthians 13:14.

*See also **Jesus' baptism**, page 1073; **The deity of Jesus Christ**, page 1364.*

Trust *see **Faith***

Unity Being together as one. Because God is one (Deuteronomy 6:4, footnote) and unity is his goal for his people and his creation (Ephesians 1:9-10), he wants unity to be reflected in his people right now (John 17:20-26; Acts 4:32-37; Galatians 3:26-29; Ephesians 2:11-22; 4:3-6). Such unity can embrace variety and is something we must pursue and maintain, knowing that as we do, it brings God's blessing (Psalm 133:1-3).

*See also **Unity**, page 686; **Basic Truths: Unity**, page 1604.*

Virgin Birth Mary's conception of Jesus while still a virgin, through the miraculous intervention of the Holy Spirit (Matthew 1:18-24; Luke 1:26-38). The Virgin Birth was essential for the Incarnation.

*See also **The Virgin Birth**, page 1152; **The Incarnation**, page 1199.*

Will of God *see **God's will***

Witness Being a witness for Jesus means being ready to give your testimony to what God has done through Jesus and the difference this has made in your life (Acts 2:32; 10:39). The rapid growth of the early church was due in large part to people being ready to speak about Jesus wherever they went (e.g., Acts 8:4-5).

*See also **Being a witness**, page 1456; **Basic Truths: Witnessing**, page 1606.*

Word of God *see **Bible; Jesus***

Works, good The natural consequence of being a follower of Jesus. Good works cannot save us (Ephesians 2:8-9), but they can show that we are saved (James 2:14-17).

*See also **Faith and works**, page 1415.*

Worship Passionately declaring the greatness of God and giving him the praise, adoration, and reverence that are rightly due to him. Worship is an encounter with the living and holy God (Exodus 3:1-6; Isaiah 6:1-5; Hebrews 12:28-29) that should leave us in awe. It involves making him central to our lives, individually and corporately (Psalms 95; 100; 103). Worship must always come from our hearts and not be a mere external ritual (Matthew 15:7-9; John 4:19-24; Hebrews 12:28-29).

*See also **Worship**, page 662; **Preparing for worship**, page 683; **Hallelujah!**, page 693; **Forms of worship**, page 1205; **Basic Truths: Worship**, page 1607.*

Yahweh The personal name of God, revealed to Moses at the burning bush (Exodus 3:1-15). Generally translated as "LORD" or "Jehovah," the name in Hebrew consists only of four consonants—YHWH—so we are unsure how it was pronounced, though "Yahweh" seems the most likely pronunciation. It emphasizes both God's eternal nature and that he is always with his people, the eternal "I AM" (Exodus 3:14).

*See also **Names and titles of God**, page 70.*

Zealot A Jewish nationalist who believed that Israel's true king was God and who therefore fought against Roman rule. Zealots were responsible for several revolts, one of which led to Jerusalem's destruction in AD 70. One of Jesus' disciples, Simon, had been a Zealot before he met Jesus (Mark 3:16-18).

Feature Index

C

D

E

F

G

H

I

J

K

L

Q

R

S

T

U

V

W

Y

Z

A NOTE TO READERS

The *Holy Bible,* New Living Translation, was first published in 1996. It quickly became one of the most popular Bible translations in the English-speaking world. While the NLT's influence was rapidly growing, the Bible Translation Committee determined that an additional investment in scholarly review and text refinement could make it even better. So shortly after its initial publication, the committee began an eight-year process with the purpose of increasing the level of the NLT's precision without sacrificing its easy-to-understand quality. This second-generation text was completed in 2004, with minor changes subsequently introduced in 2007, 2013, and 2015.

The goal of any Bible translation is to convey the meaning and content of the ancient Hebrew, Aramaic, and Greek texts as accurately as possible to contemporary readers. The challenge for our translators was to create a text that would communicate as clearly and powerfully to today's readers as the original texts did to readers and listeners in the ancient biblical world. The resulting translation is easy to read and understand, while also accurately communicating the meaning and content of the original biblical texts. The NLT is a general-purpose text especially good for study, devotional reading, and reading aloud in worship services.

We believe that the New Living Translation—which combines the latest biblical scholarship with a clear, dynamic writing style—will communicate God's word powerfully to all who read it. We publish it with the prayer that God will use it to speak his timeless truth to the church and the world in a fresh, new way.

THE PUBLISHERS

A full introduction to the NLT can be found at www.TheNLT.com/NLTintro.

A complete list of the translators can be found at www.TheNLT.com/scholars.

A Visual Overview of the Bible

Introduction

Sometimes we can understand something better by seeing it. That's what this section is all about. Here you will find maps, charts, and infographics that together summarize the "big picture" of the Bible's story. When we read the Bible, it can be easy to get lost in its individual stories and to forget that these individual stories—of people and kings and nations and churches—are all part of a much bigger story: the story of how God takes a broken world and broken people and works to fix them and the world they live in. It's a story that begins with God calling one man and giving him a family—a family that becomes a nation, from which the Messiah comes to save people of all nations.

All the key events of this big story are included here in visual form. Along with the Bible text and the notes that accompany it, these pages will help you see how all the separate pieces fit together. As you see the full picture, be amazed at God's exciting plan for rescuing people!

1 **WORLD OF THE PATRIARCHS:** A map of Abraham's journey to Canaan, the land God promised him

2 **THE PLAGUES OF EGYPT:** An infographic showing how the plagues demonstrated God's superiority to the gods of Egypt

3 **EXODUS FROM EGYPT:** A map showing the Israelites' route out of Egypt and through the wilderness to the Promised Land

4 **ISRAEL'S ANNUAL CALENDAR:** An infographic showing the agricultural and festival cycles that determined the rhythm of life for ancient Israel

5 **TWELVE TRIBES OF ISRAEL:** Maps showing Joshua's conquest of Canaan and how the land was divided among the tribes afterward

6 **KINGDOMS OF ISRAEL:** Maps showing the extent of Israel's territory at different points during the period of the monarchy

7 **THE BOOK OF PSALMS:** An infographic representing all 150 psalms according to size and topic

8 **THE PROPHETS:** An infographic representing the ministry of the prophets who wrote books of the Bible according to date and the size of their books

9 **THE EXILE:** A map showing the routes followed by those deported from Israel and Judah, and the eventual return of some of the exiles

10 **THE MINISTRY OF JESUS:** A map highlighting the significant locations in Jesus' ministry in Galilee, Samaria, and Judea

11 **PROPHECIES OF THE MESSIAH:** An infographic and a chart that trace the Old Testament prophecies fulfilled by Jesus in each of the four Gospels

12 **THE FIRST JOURNEYS OF CHRISTIAN LEADERS:** Maps of the travels of Peter, Paul (Saul), and Philip during the early days of the church

13 **PAUL'S MISSIONARY JOURNEYS:** A map of Paul's travels as he spread the Good News throughout the eastern Roman Empire, and a map of his journey to Rome

14 **THE OLD TESTAMENT IN THE NEW TESTAMENT LETTERS:** An infographic that shows the number of direct Old Testament quotations in the New Testament letters, and another that highlights some significant Old Testament allusions in Revelation

1 WORLD OF THE PATRIARCHS

God called Abraham to leave his homeland in Mesopotamia and travel to Canaan, which he promised to give to Abraham's descendants. Abraham and his son Isaac lived out their lives in Canaan, and then in a time of famine Isaac's son Jacob moved to Egypt with his entire family.

▶ *See* ***Abraham,*** *page 16;* ***Canaan,*** *page 21;* ***Isaac and Rebekah,*** *page 28;* ***Jacob and Esau,*** *page 40.*

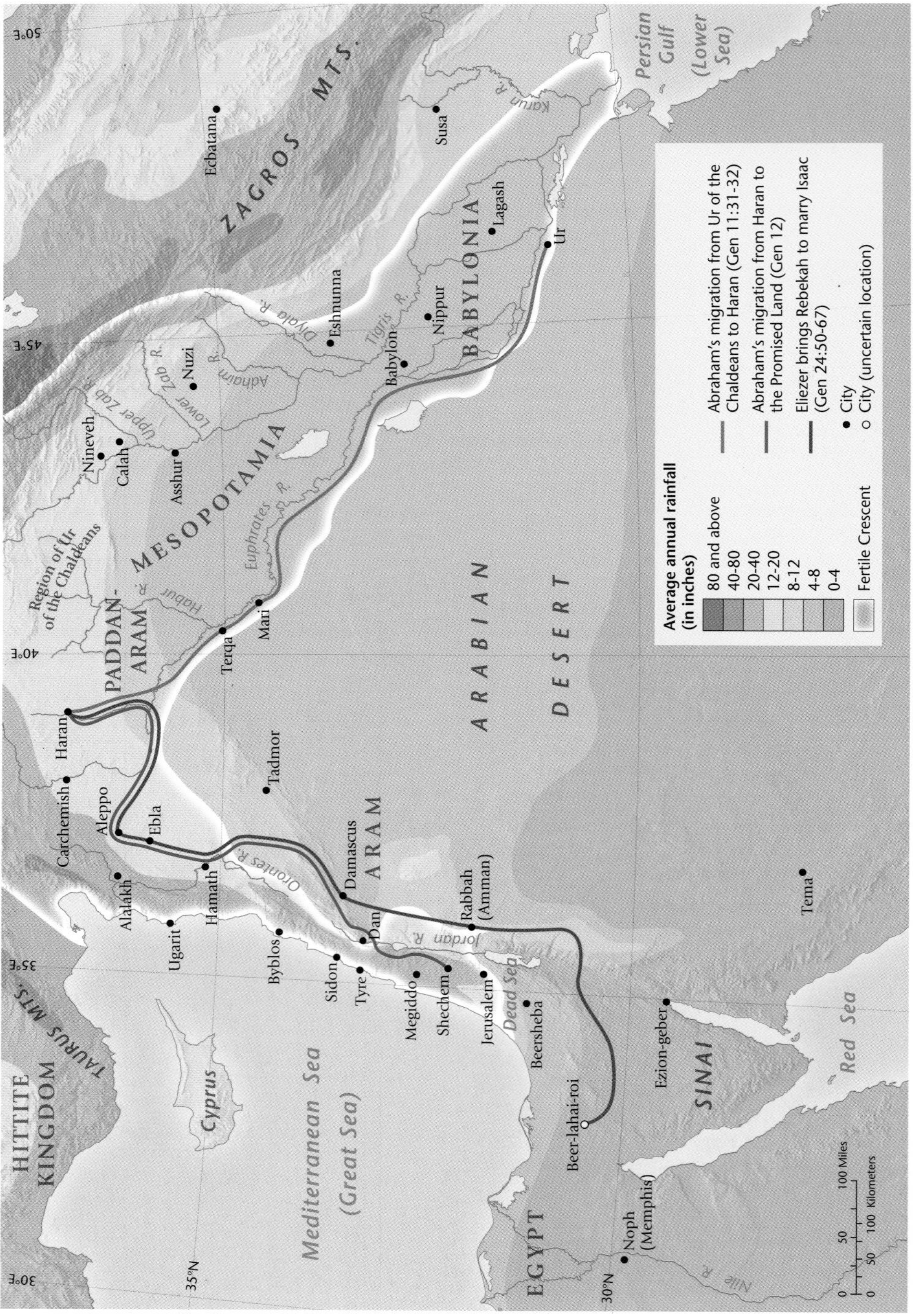

2 THE PLAGUES OF EGYPT

When God rescued his people from Egypt after many years of slavery there, he displayed his power over Egypt's gods through a series of plagues. Each plague can be seen as a direct challenge to a specific Egyptian deity.

▶ See ***The ten plagues,*** *page 74.*

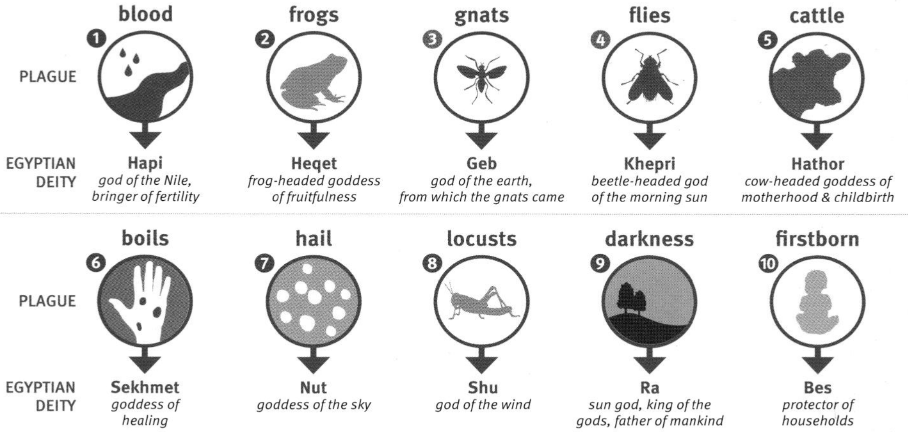

3 EXODUS FROM EGYPT

God led the Israelites out of Egypt and through the wilderness to Mount Sinai, where he gave them his Law. Because of their disobedience, the people spent forty years in the wilderness before they finally arrived at Acacia Grove (Shittim), across the Jordan River from the Promised Land of Canaan.

▶ See ***The Red Sea,*** *page 82;* ***Mount Sinai,*** *page 88;* ***Moses, the faithful servant,*** *page 239.*

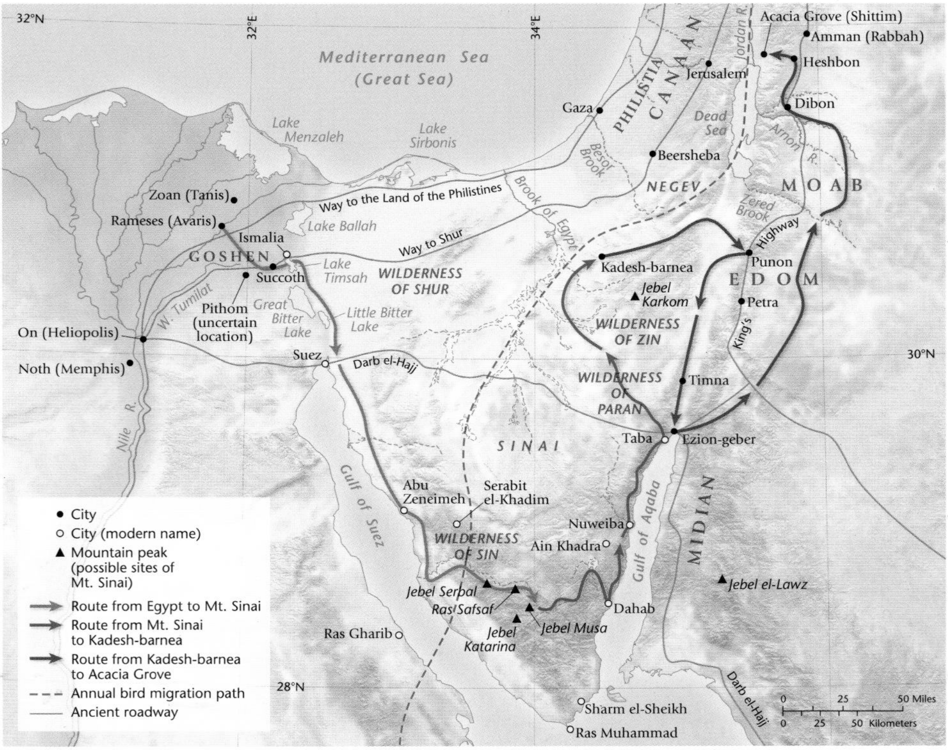

4 ISRAEL'S ANNUAL CALENDAR

Israel's annual cycle of festivals was an important part of God's Law, which was intended to govern every aspect of his people's lives. Three times each year, all Israelite men were to gather for worship and celebration: Passover, commemorating God's rescue of his people from Egypt; the Festival of Harvest (the Feast of Weeks, or Pentecost), celebrating God's provision at the harvest; and the Festival of Shelters (or the Feast of Tabernacles), remembering God's care for his people in the wilderness. Israel followed a lunar calendar, which explains why the months do not align with those of our modern solar calendar.

▶ *See* ***The Passover****, page 80;* ***Key Jewish religious festivals****, page 144;* ***The Festival of Purim****, page 561.*

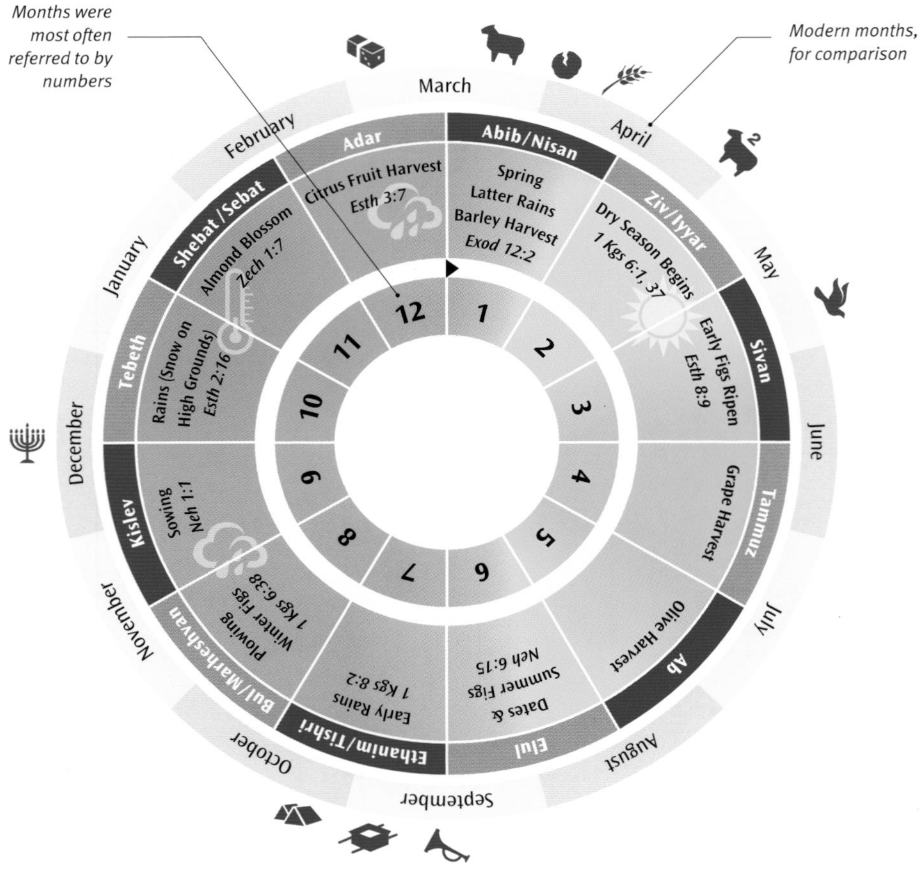

ANNUAL FESTIVALS

Passover (Lev 23:5)

Unleavened Bread (Lev 23:6-8)

First Harvest (Lev 23:9-14)

Later Passover (Num 9:4-12)

Harvest (Lev 23:15-22)

Trumpets (Lev 23:23-25)

Day of Atonement (Lev 23:26-32)

Shelters (Lev 23:33-43)

Dedication (John 10:22)

Purim (Esth 9:1-32)

TWELVE TRIBES OF ISRAEL

After the death of Moses, Joshua led the people of Israel across the Jordan River into the Promised Land of Canaan. God enabled his people to win a series of military victories against the Canaanites, sometimes through miraculous means, and they soon occupied the land, just as he had promised Abraham. At this point, Joshua oversaw the division of the land into portions for each of the twelve tribes descended from Jacob.

▶ *See **Jacob's family tree, showing the tribes of Israel**, page 35; **Joshua (book introduction)**, page 241.*

6 KINGDOMS OF ISRAEL

Joshua's death was followed by the turbulent period of the judges, after which the people of Israel asked the prophet Samuel for a king. At God's command, he anointed Saul, whose coronation marked the beginning of the united kingdom of Israel. The kingdom grew in size and influence under David and reached its height during the reign of his son Solomon. Solomon inherited a powerful kingdom, covering the entire area inhabited by the twelve tribes of Israel. Throughout Solomon's reign, his power and influence increased as he also gained control over many of the surrounding nations.

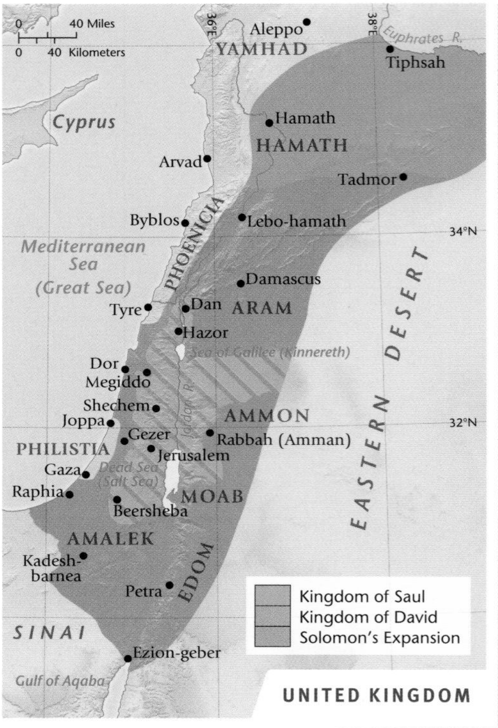

After the death of Solomon, the kingdom of Israel divided. Solomon's son Rehoboam remained king of the southern kingdom of Judah, with Jerusalem as its capital. Jeroboam became the king of the northern kingdom of Israel and rebuilt Shechem as his capital. He also built new worship centers in Bethel and Dan, influencing his people to stay away from Jerusalem and its annual religious festivals. The division of the kingdom of Israel began a downward spiral into idolatry and godless leadership for both nations, eventually leading to the exile of the northern kingdom to Assyria and the southern kingdom to Babylon.

▶ *See **King Saul**, page 318; **King David**, page 323; **King Solomon**, page 377; **Rulers of Israel and Judah**, page 393; **King Rehoboam**, page 394; **King Jeroboam I**, page 396.*

7 THE BOOK OF PSALMS

The psalms—the songs and prayers of Israel—express a wide range of emotions and originate from a variety of circumstances. This page represents all 150 psalms according to subject matter and length.

▶ *See* ***Psalms (book introduction)****, page 601;* ***The Psalms can help you when you are feeling*** *. . ., page 604;* ***Worship****, page 662.*

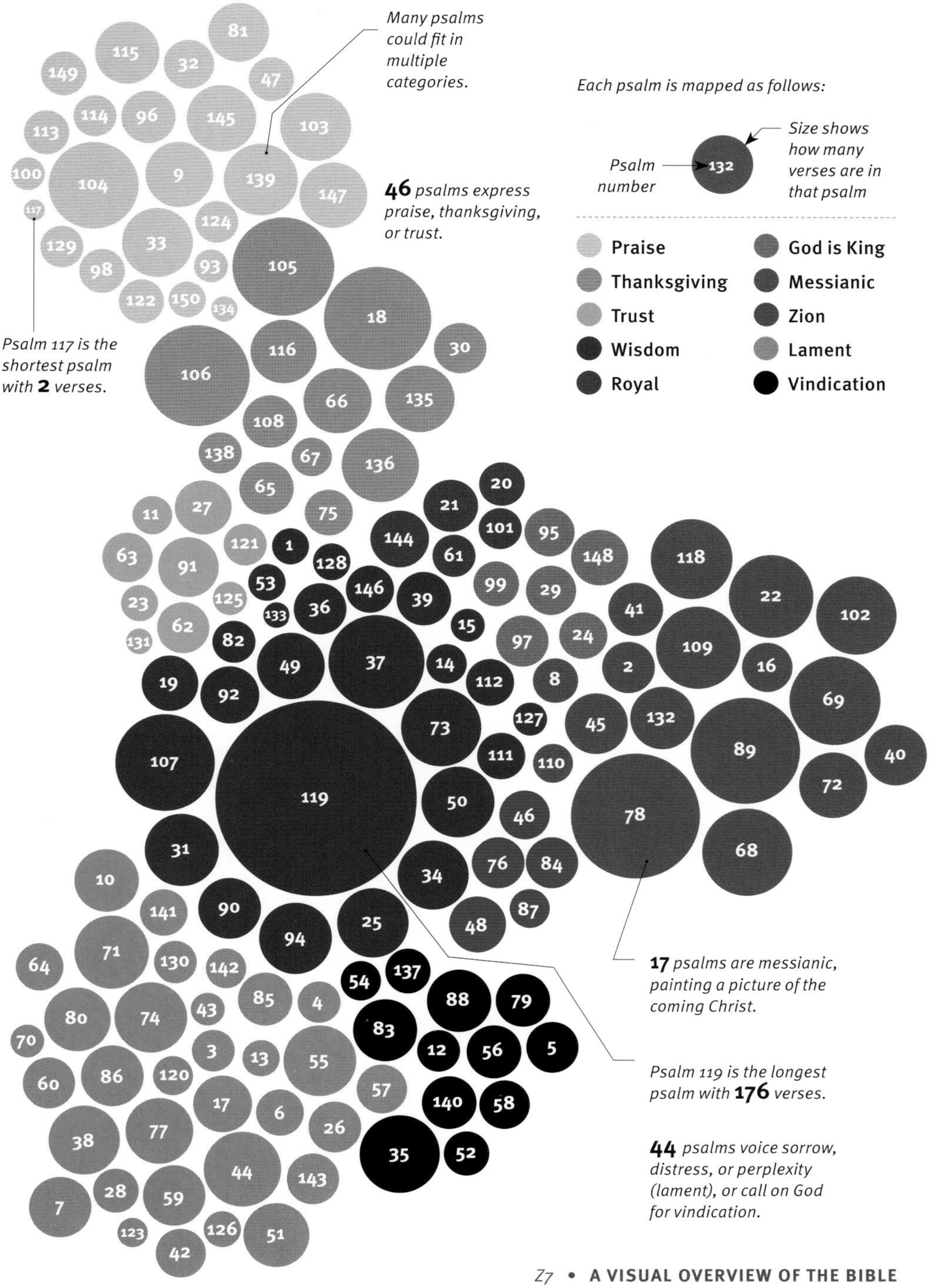
Many psalms could fit in multiple categories.
46 psalms express praise, thanksgiving, or trust.
Psalm 117 is the shortest psalm with 2 verses.
Each psalm is mapped as follows:
Psalm number
132
Size shows how many verses are in that psalm
Praise
Thanksgiving
Trust
Wisdom
Royal
God is King
Messianic
Zion
Lament
Vindication
17 psalms are messianic, painting a picture of the coming Christ.
Psalm 119 is the longest psalm with 176 verses.
44 psalms voice sorrow, distress, or perplexity (lament), or call on God for vindication.

8 THE PROPHETS

God's prophets brought his messages to his people, urging them to turn from sin, honor God, and deal justly with one another—or else face exile from their land. Though exile eventually came, the prophets also foresaw hope for the future. God's people would return to their land, and one day, God would send the Messiah to restore them. This page shows the books and ministries of the sixteen prophets who wrote books of the Bible.

▶ *See* ***Prophecy in the Old Testament,*** *page 903;* ***God's discipline,*** *page 1000;* ***Prophecies of the Messiah,*** *page 1004.*

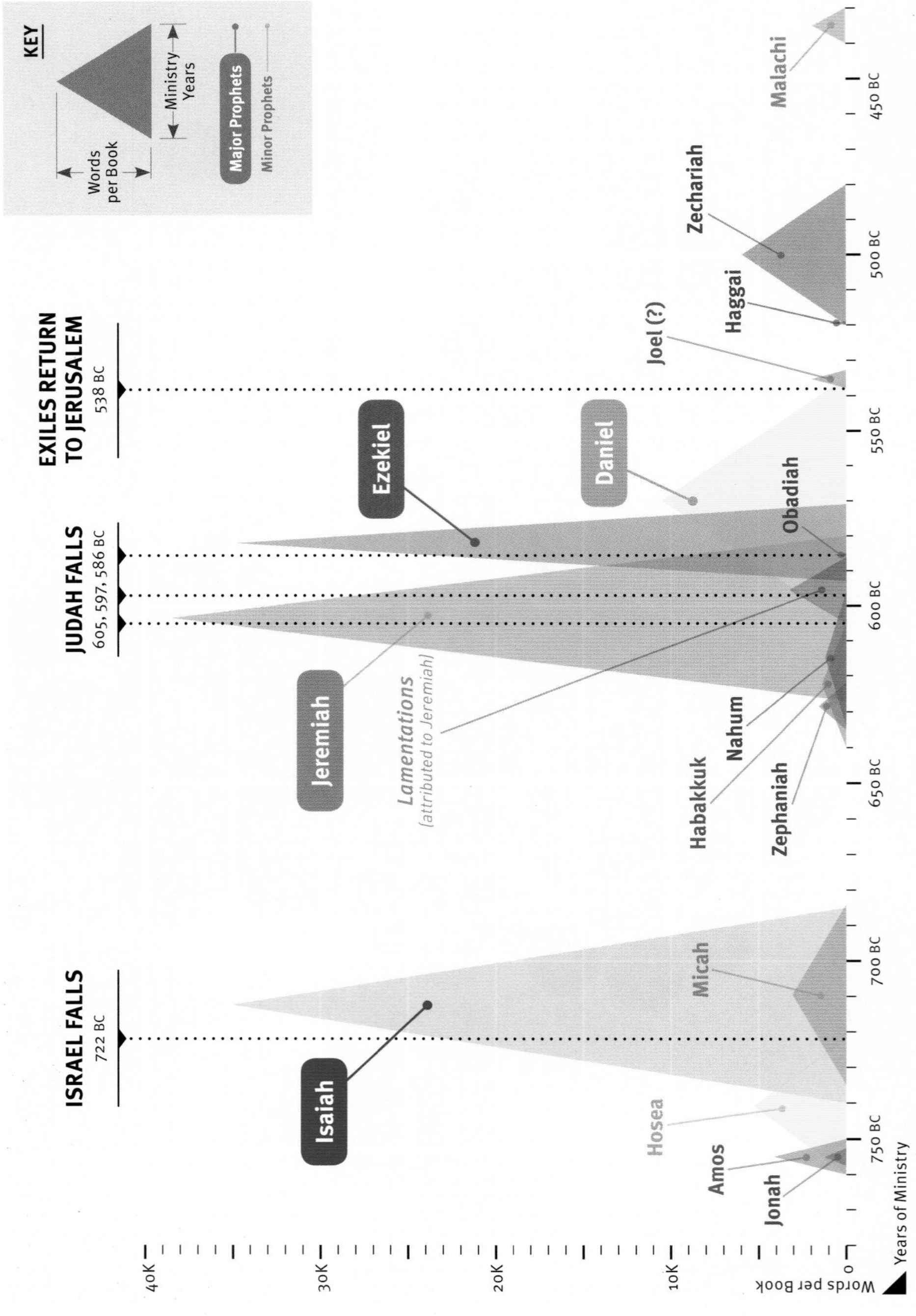

9 THE EXILE

As the prophets had warned, God's people were exiled as a result of their sin—Israel to Assyria in 722 BC and Judah to Babylon in three waves, culminating in 586 BC. But after Persia conquered Babylon in 539 BC, King Cyrus allowed the Jews to return and rebuild Jerusalem and the Temple.

▶ *See* ***Assyria,*** *page 431;* ***The Exile,*** *page 433;* ***Babylon,*** *page 445;* ***The fall of Jerusalem,*** *page 871.*

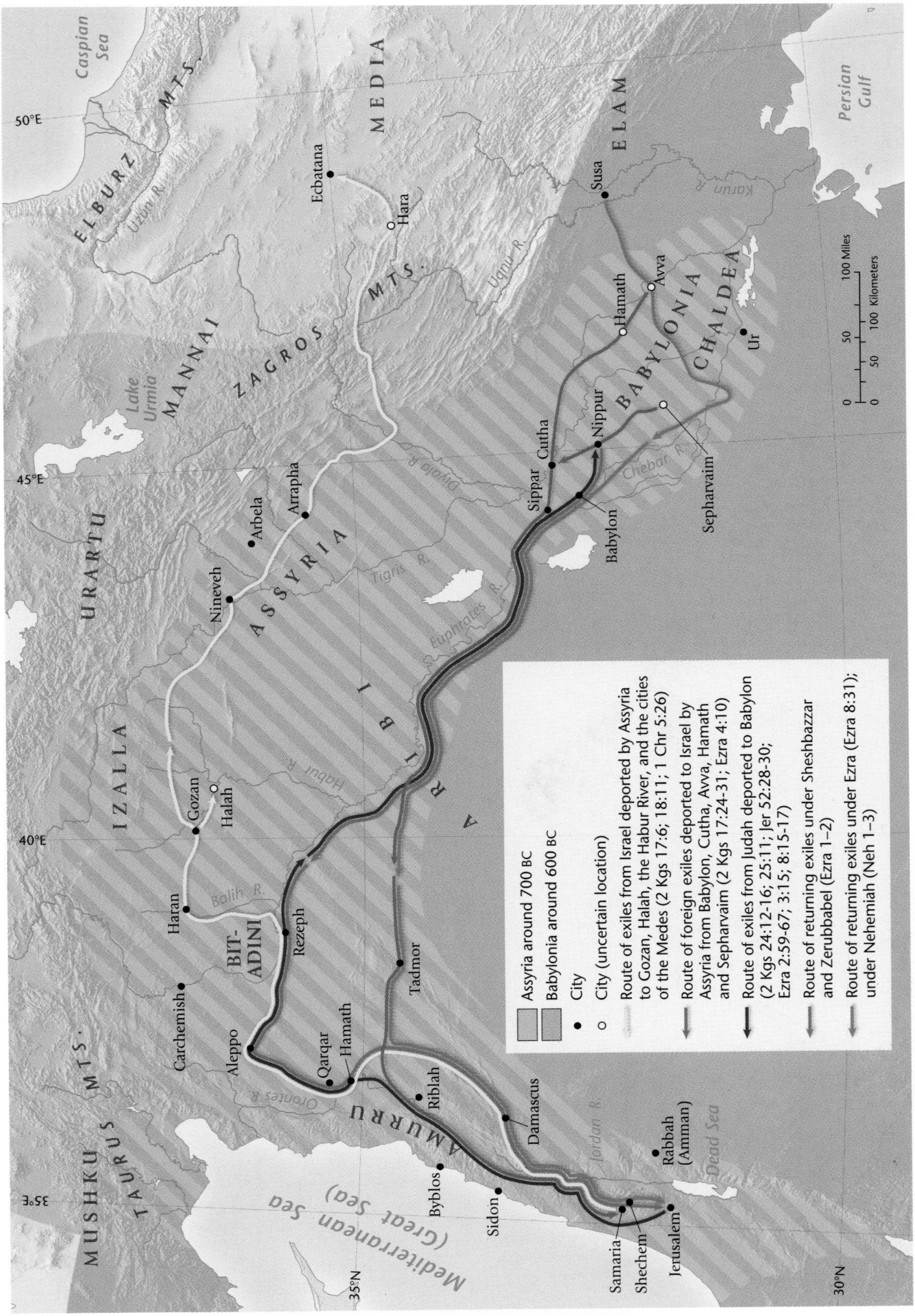

10 THE MINISTRY OF JESUS

Centuries after the prophets spoke of his coming, Jesus, the promised Messiah, was born to a virgin in Bethlehem. As an adult, he began announcing that God's Kingdom was near—and demonstrating what that Kingdom was all about through both his teaching and his miracles. The religious leaders thought his claim to be the Son of God was blasphemy, and they fiercely opposed him. Eventually, Jesus was betrayed, turned over to the Romans, and crucified. But on the third day, he rose from the dead, just as he had promised his disciples.

This map highlights the locations of key events in Jesus' life and ministry. These locations are listed roughly from north to south.

▸ *See* ***The parables of Jesus,*** *page 1088;* ***The death of Jesus,*** *page 1114;* ***Jesus' miracles,*** *page 1128;* ***The mission of Jesus,*** *page 1159;* ***John's seven signs,*** *page 1201.*

GALILEE *and regions to the north*

A **Region of Tyre:** Gentile woman's daughter healed (Matthew 15:21-28)

B **Caesarea Philippi:** Peter's great declaration (Matthew 16:13-20)

C **Mount Meron/Mount Tabor/Mount Hermon:** (1) possible locations of Transfiguration (Matthew 17:1-13); (2) demon-possessed boy healed nearby (Matthew 17:14-21)

D **Cana of Galilee:** (1) water changed to wine (John 2:1-11); (2) Capernaum official's son healed (John 4:46-54)

E **Gennesaret:** (1) possible location of feeding of multitudes (Matthew 14:13-21; 15:32-39); (2) many healings (Mark 6:53-56)

F **Korazin:** (1) judgment pronounced on the cities of Korazin, Bethsaida, and Capernaum (Matthew 11:20-24); (2) possible area of Sermon on the Mount (Matthew 5–7)

G **Capernaum:** (1) catch of fish (Luke 5:1-11); (2) evil spirit cast out (Mark 1:21-28); (3) possible area of Sermon on the Mount (Matthew 5–7); (4) Peter's mother-in-law healed (Matthew 8:14-15); (5) Roman officer's servant healed (Matthew 8:5-13); (6) paralyzed man healed (Mark 2:1-12); (7) woman with a hemorrhage healed (Mark 5:25-34); (8) Jairus's daughter raised (Luke 8:40-56); (9) two blind men healed (Matthew 9:27-31); (10) a mute, demon-possessed man healed (Matthew 9:32-34); (11) the twelve apostles sent out (Matthew 10:1-15); (12) man with deformed hand healed (Matthew 12:9-13); (13) another demon-possessed man healed (Matthew 12:22-37); (14) Temple tax provided (Matthew 17:24-27); (15) Bread of Life discourse (John 6:22-59)

H **Bethsaida:** (1) possible location of feeding of multitudes (Matthew 14:13-21; 15:32-39); (2) blind man healed (Mark 8:22-26)

I **Sea of Galilee near Bethsaida:** walking on water (Matthew 14:22-33)

J **Sea of Galilee:** storm quieted (Matthew 8:23-27)

K **Gergesa/Gadara:** possible location of casting out demons, which enter pigs; the pigs then rush down a steep bank and drown (Luke 8:26-39)

L **Nazareth:** (1) childhood home (Matthew 2:19-23); (2) rejected by townspeople (Luke 4:16-30)

M **Nain:** widow's son raised (Luke 7:11-17)

N **Region of Galilee:** (1) leper cleansed (Mark 1:40-45); (2) post-resurrection appearances to the disciples (Matthew 28:16-20)

SAMARIA *and regions between Galilee & Judea*

O **Decapolis (Region of Ten Towns):** many healings (Matthew 15:29-31; Mark 7:31-37)

P **Region between Galilee and Samaria:** (1) refused entry into village (Luke 9:51-56); (2) ten men with leprosy healed (Luke 17:11-19)

Q **Sychar:** talks with Samaritan woman at the well (John 4:1-42)

R **Ephraim:** enters into seclusion with the disciples (John 11:54)

S **Region of Perea:** (1) teaching on marriage (Matthew 19:1-12); (2) possible location of healing of woman with infirmity (Luke 13:10-13); (3) possible location of healing of man with swollen limbs (Luke 14:1-6); (4) possible location of the rich young ruler (Luke 18:18-30)

JUDEA

T **Jericho:** (1) Bartimaeus healed (Mark 10:46-52); (2) Zacchaeus converted (Luke 19:1-10)

U **Bethany:** (1) Lazarus raised (John 11:1-44); (2) anointing by Mary (John 12:1-11)

V **Jerusalem:** (1) taken to Temple (Luke 2:41-52); (2) discourse with Nicodemus (John 3:1-21); (3) Pool of Bethesda healing (John 5:2-9); (4) woman caught in adultery (John 8:2-11); (5) attempted stoning (John 8:12-59); (6) man blind from birth healed (John 9:1-12); (7) Triumphal Entry (Matthew 21:1-11); (8) Temple cleansed (John 2:13-22); (9) Last Supper (Luke 22:7-30); (10) trial and crucifixion (Matthew 26:57–27:50); (11) burial (Luke 23:50-56); (12) post-resurrection appearances to Mary and the disciples (John 20:1-31)

W **Emmaus:** post-resurrection appearance to two people (Luke 24:13-32)

X **Mount of Olives:** (1) Olivet discourse (Matthew 24:3–25:46); (2) agony and arrest at Gethsemane (Matthew 26:36-56); (3) Ascension (Acts 1:6-12)

Y **Bethlehem:** birthplace (Luke 2:1-20)

Mt. Hermon
Tyre
Caesarea Philippi
(Paneas)
TYRE
UPPER
GALILEE
Lake Hula
Gischala
33°N
Mt. Meron
(Jebel Jarmuk)
GAULANITIS
Ptolemais
(Acco)
LOWER
GALILEE
Korazin
Bethsaida
Capernaum
Gennesaret
Sea of Galilee
(Sea of Kinnereth)
Jotapata
Cana
Magdala
Gergesa
Hippus
Tiberias
Kishon R.
Sepphoris
Mediterranean Sea
(Great Sea)
Yarmuk R.
Nazareth
Mt. Tabor
ESDRAELON
VALLEY
Gadara
Nain
Bethany
beyond Jordan
(possible site)
Dora
Caesarea
Scythopolis
(Beth-shan)
Pella
SAMARIA
Aenon
Salim
DECAPOLIS
Jordan R.
Sebaste
(Samaria)
Gerasa
City
City (uncertain location)
Mountain peak
Mt. Ebal
Sychar
Mt. Gerizim
Jabbok R.
Yarkon R.
0
10
20 Miles
0
10
20 Kilometers
Antipatris
(Aphek)
Gadora
Alexandrium
Joppa
PEREA
32°N
Lydda
(Lod)
Ephraim
(Ophrah)
Philadelphia
(Amman)
Jamnia
Abila
Jericho
Emmaus
(Nicopolis)
Bethany
beyond Jordan
(traditional site)
Emmaus
Jerusalem
Bethany
Esbus
(Heshbon)
En-karim
Mt. of Olives
Qumran
Azotus
(Ashdod)
Bethlehem
JUDEA
WILDERNESS OF JUDEA
Ascalon
Machaerus
Marisa
Hebron
Dead
Sea
(Salt Sea)
Gaza
Arnon R.
Masada
Raphia
Besor Brook
NABATEA
Beersheba
IDUMEA
35°E
36°E
A
B
C
D
E
F
G
H
I
J
K
L
M
N
O
P
Q
R
S
T
U
V
W
X
Y

11 PROPHECIES OF THE MESSIAH

Jesus began his ministry by reading the words of Isaiah: "The Spirit of the LORD is upon me, for he has anointed me to bring Good News to the poor" (Luke 4:18; see Isaiah 61:1-2). And throughout his ministry, he regularly quoted and alluded to the words of Israel's prophets, which he was fulfilling. Following Jesus' example, the writers of the Gospels, especially Matthew, showed the many ways in which Jesus' life, death, and resurrection fulfilled God's Old Testament promises.

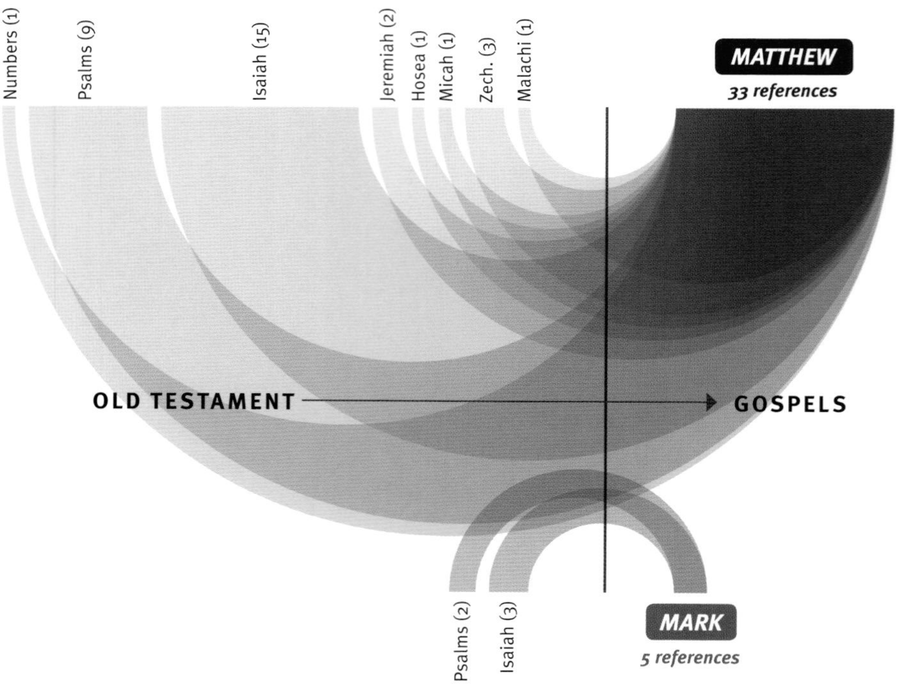

OLD TESTAMENT PROPHECY	*The Messiah is to be . . .*	NEW TESTAMENT FULFILLMENT
Isaiah 7:14	*born to a virgin and called Immanuel ("God is with us")*	Matthew 1:22-23; Luke 1:31-34
2 Samuel 7:11-12; Psalm 132:11; Isaiah 9:6-7; 16:5; Jeremiah 23:5	*heir to David's throne*	Luke 1:31-32
Psalm 72:10; Isaiah 60:3, 6	*visited by kings bearing gifts*	Matthew 2:1-12
Numbers 24:8; Hosea 11:1	*God's son called out of Egypt*	Matthew 2:13-15
Jeremiah 31:15	*attacked in a massacre of innocents*	Matthew 2:17-18
Micah 5:2	*born in Bethlehem*	Matthew 2:5-6; Luke 2:4-6
Isaiah 40:3-5, Malachi 3:1	*preceded by a messenger in the wilderness*	Matthew 3:1-3; Luke 1:76-78; 3:3-6
Isaiah 11:2; 61:1-2	*empowered by God's Spirit*	Luke 4:18-19
Isaiah 9:1-2; 42:1-3, 6-7; 49:6; 60:1-3	*a light for the Gentiles*	Matthew 4:13-17, 23-36
Deuteronomy 18:15, 18-19	*a prophet like Moses*	John 7:40
Isaiah 53:4	*a healer of sicknesses and diseases*	Matthew 8:16-17
Isaiah 6:9-10	*understood only by those who can hear and perceive him*	Matthew 13:10-15
Psalm 8:2	*praised by children*	Matthew 21:16
Psalm 118:22-23	*the cornerstone rejected by the builders*	Matthew 21:42
Zechariah 9:9	*the humble king who enters Jerusalem on a donkey*	Matthew 21:4-5; John 12:14-15
Psalms 69:9; 119:139	*passionate for God's house*	John 2:13-17
Isaiah 53:1, 3; Psalm 69:8	*rejected by his own people*	Matthew 26:3-4; John 1:11; 7:5; 12:37-38
Psalm 41:9	*betrayed by his friend*	Matthew 26:14-16, 47-50; Luke 22:21-23
Jeremiah 32:6-9; Zechariah 11:12-13	*valued at thirty pieces of silver*	Matthew 27:9-10

The infographic on these pages represents the connections between prophecies of the Messiah in the Old Testament, arranged by book, and their fulfillment in each of the four Gospels. The chart provides more specific information about each prophecy and fulfillment.

▶ *See **Jesus Christ in the Psalms,** page 614; **The Messianic King,** page 674; **Prophecies about Christ,** page 806; **Prophecies of the Messiah,** page 1044; **Jesus and the Old Testament,** page 1079.*

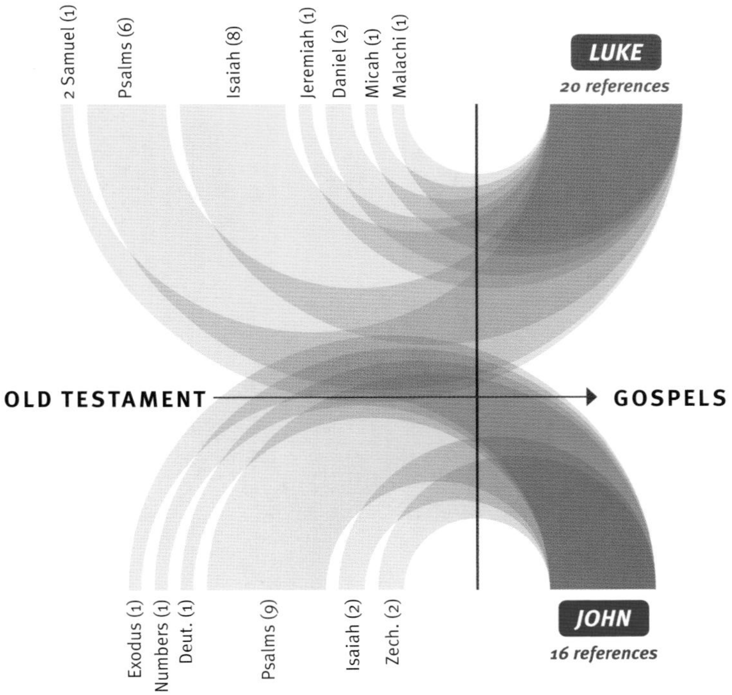

OLD TESTAMENT PROPHECY	*The Messiah is to be . . .*	NEW TESTAMENT FULFILLMENT
Zechariah 13:7	*deserted by his disciples*	Matthew 26:31, 56
Isaiah 53:3	*a man of sorrows*	Matthew 26:37-38
Isaiah 50:6	*slapped, beaten, mocked, and spit on*	Matthew 26:67; 27:26, 30; Mark 14:65
Isaiah 53:7	*silent in response to his accusers*	Matt. 27:12-14; Mark 15:3-5; Luke 23:8-10
Psalms 22:15; 69:21	*thirsty in his suffering*	John 19:28
Psalm 69:21	*given sour wine to drink*	Matthew 27:48; John 19:28-30
Psalm 22:18	*the one whose clothing they gambled for with dice*	Matthew 27:35; Luke 23:34; John 19:23-24
Isaiah 53:12	*suffering with criminals and praying for his enemies*	Matt. 27:38; Mark 15:27-28; Luke 23:32-34
Psalm 22:7-8	*mocked and insulted*	Matt. 27:39-44; Mk. 15:29-32; Luke 23:11, 35
Exodus 12:46; Numbers 9:12; Psalm 34:20	*without any broken bones*	John 19:33-36
Psalm 22:1-17; Zechariah 12:10	*stared at with pierced hands and feet*	John 19:34, 37
Psalm 31:5	*one who entrusts his spirit at death to God the Father*	Luke 23:46
Isaiah 53:5-6, 8, 10-12	*sacrificed to take away the sin of the world*	John 1:29; 11:49-52
Isaiah 53:9	*buried in a rich man's tomb*	Matthew 27:57-60
Psalm 16:10	*raised from the dead*	Matthew 28:2-7
Psalm 110:1	*seated at God's right hand*	Mark 16:19; Luke 24:50-51
Daniel 2:44; 7:14, 27	*king forever*	Luke 1:33

12 THE FIRST JOURNEYS OF CHRISTIAN LEADERS

After Jesus' resurrection and ascension into heaven, his followers—empowered by the Holy Spirit—began telling the Good News about him to everyone, and the young church grew rapidly. Even when persecution scattered the believers, the Good News spread out from Jerusalem into the surrounding areas as a result. Acts 8–11 describes several journeys of the apostles and their associates during these early days of the church.

▶ *See **The Holy Spirit in Acts**, page 1236; **Philip**, page 1247; **The apostle Paul**, page 1272; **Peter**, page 1421.*

PETER (Acts 9:32–11:18)

Sometime after meeting Saul in Jerusalem (Acts 9:26-28; see Galatians 1:18), Peter left Jerusalem and began traveling ❶. He first went to Lydda ❷ and then Joppa ❸, where he stayed "a long time" (Acts 9:39-43). He was there when the Lord sent messengers from Cornelius and prompted Peter to go to Caesarea ❹, where Cornelius and his household heard the Good News and believed (Acts 10). After staying a few days, Peter returned to Jerusalem ❺ and gave the church a report of what had happened (Acts 11:1-18).

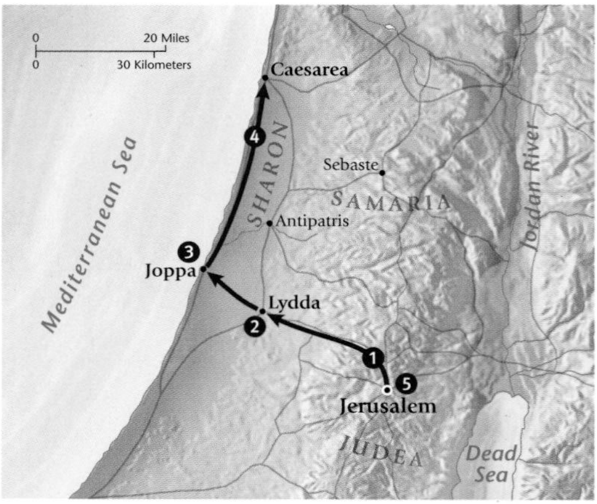

PAUL (SAUL) (Acts 9:1-31)

In his zeal to stamp out Christianity, Saul traveled north toward Damascus ❶, where he intended to arrest believers, but along the way Christ appeared to him. In Damascus, Saul was baptized and began preaching about Jesus (Acts 9:20-23). During this time, Saul evidently traveled to Arabia ❷ and back ❸ (see Galatians 1:17). After three years in Damascus, he escaped a plot against his life and went to Jerusalem ❹, where he finally met with the apostles (Acts 9:26-28; see Galatians 1:18). There, too, he faced death threats, so after a visit of about two weeks he was taken to Caesarea and sailed to Tarsus ❺, his hometown (Acts 9:29-30; 11:25-26).

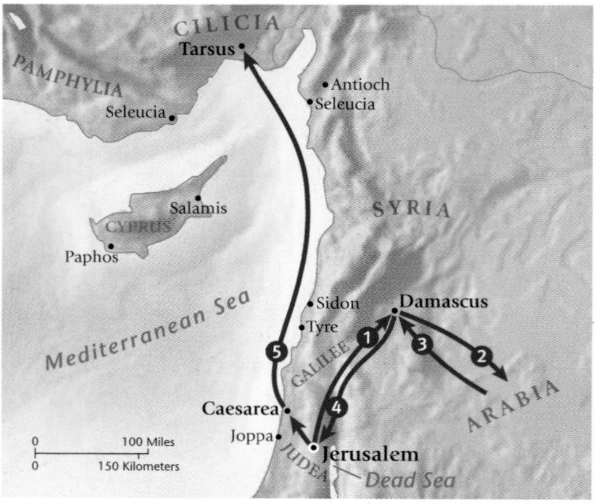

PHILIP (Acts 8:5-8, 23-40)

When persecution began sweeping over the church in Jerusalem (Acts 8:3-4), Philip traveled north to Samaria ❶, where he proclaimed the Good News and many people became believers. Later, God's Spirit directed Philip to go south toward Gaza. Along the way ❷, he evangelized an Ethiopian eunuch. After the eunuch was baptized, the Spirit "snatched Philip away" to Azotus ❸ (Acts 8:39-40). Philip kept preaching as he traveled north to Caesarea ❹, where he continued to live (Acts 21:8-9).

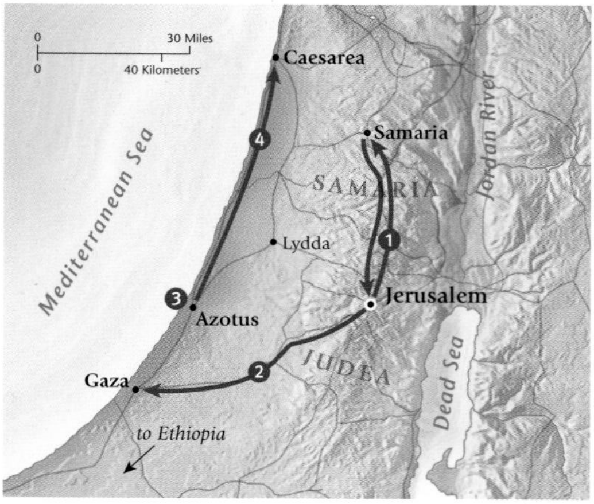

13 PAUL'S MISSIONARY JOURNEYS

The apostle Paul was committed to taking the Good News to places where it had not yet been heard. His travels took him across the eastern Roman Empire—through what is today Syria, Turkey, and Greece—and eventually to Rome itself, where he continued to preach boldly.

▶ *See **The apostle Paul**, page 1272.*

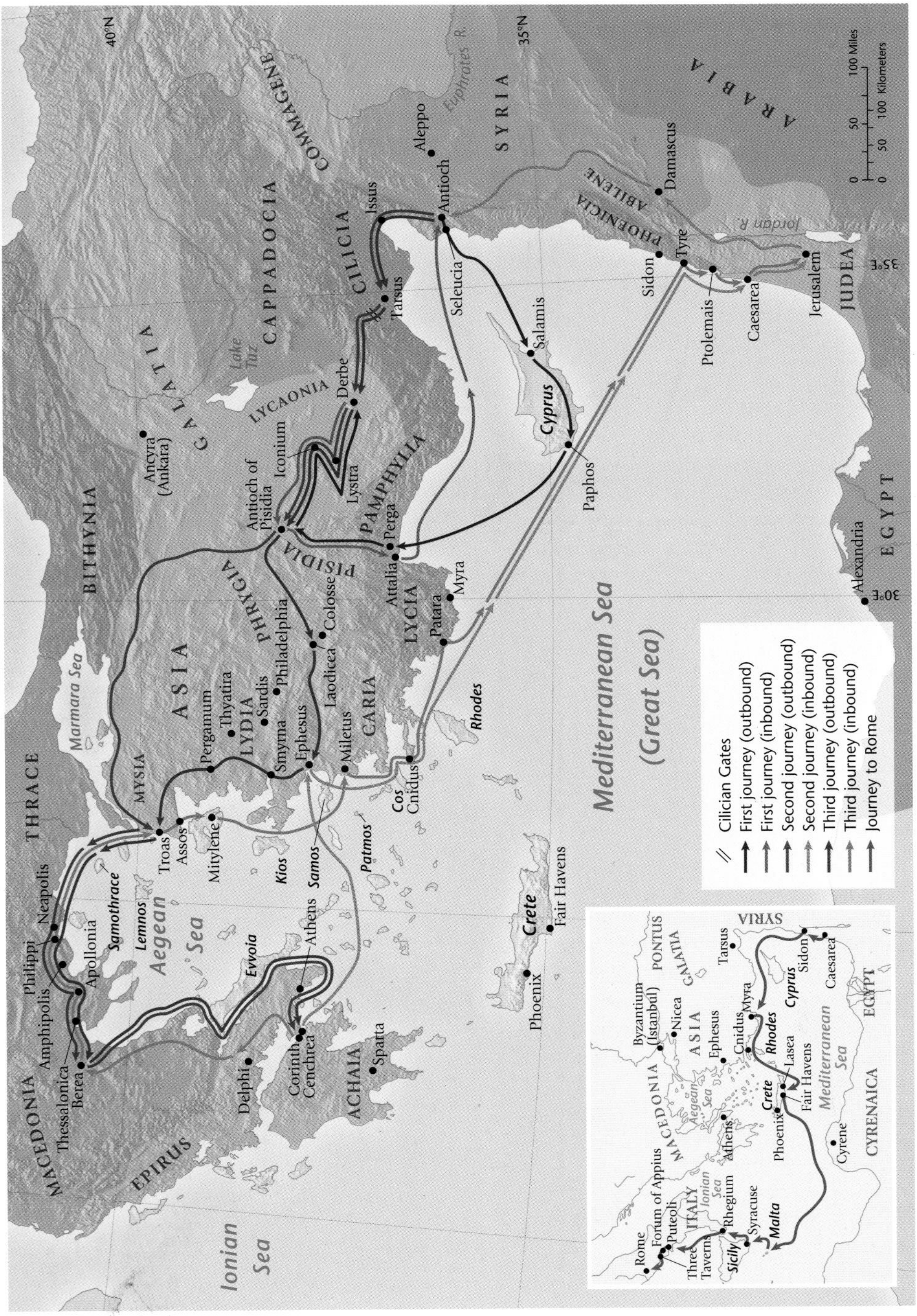

14 THE OLD TESTAMENT IN THE NEW TESTAMENT LETTERS

Just as Jesus himself and the writers of the Gospels often referred to the Old Testament, the writers of the New Testament letters also quoted it regularly as they taught and encouraged the young churches. By doing so, they demonstrated how Jesus fulfilled the plan of God revealed throughout the Old Testament's pages. The first infographic below represents these direct quotations. But in addition to direct quotations, the New Testament also has countless allusions to Old Testament themes or stories. Revelation, for example, has some five hundred allusions to the Old Testament. Seven of these are represented visually below.

▶ *See **Studying God's word**, page 1387; **The Old Testament in the New Testament**, page 1403.*

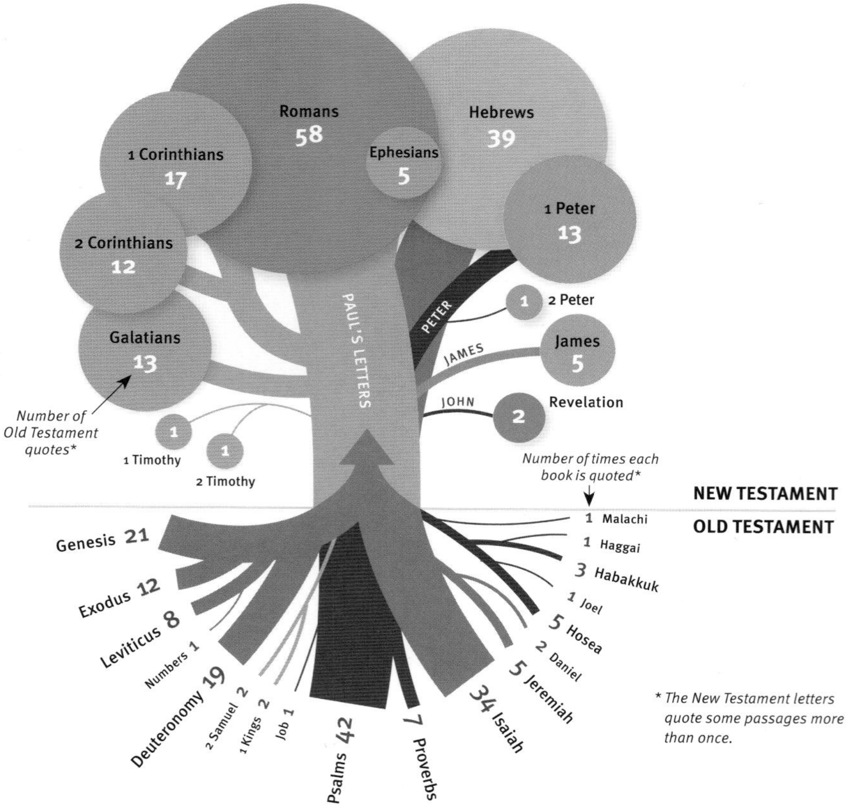

* *The New Testament letters quote some passages more than once.*

OLD TESTAMENT ALLUSIONS IN REVELATION